Peterson's Graduate Programs in the Humanities, Arts & Social Sciences

2009

PETERSON'S

A nelnet COMPANY

PETERSON'S

A nelnet COMPANY

About Peterson's

To succeed on your lifelong educational journey, you will need accurate, dependable, and practical tools and resources. That is why Peterson's is everywhere education happens. Because whenever and however you need education content delivered, you can rely on Peterson's to provide the information, know-how, and guidance to help you reach your goals. Tools to match the right students with the right school. It's here. Personalized resources and expert guidance. It's here. Comprehensive and dependable education content—delivered whenever and however you need it. It's all here.

For more information, contact Peterson's, 2000 Lenox Drive, Lawrenceville, NJ 08648; 800-338-3282; or find us on the World Wide Web at www.petersons.com/about.

Stephen Clemente, President; Fern A. Oram, Content Director; Bernadette Webster, Operations Director; Roger S. Williams, Sales and Marketing; Jill C. Schwartz, Production Editor; Bret Bollman, Michael Haines, Sally Ross, Pam Sullivan, Valerie Bolus Vaughan, Copy Editors; Ken Britschge, Research Project Manager; Courtney Foust, James Ranish, Amy L. Weber, Research Associates; Phyllis Johnson, Programmer; Ray Golaszewski, Manufacturing Manager; Linda M. Williams, Composition Manager; Janet Garwo, Mimi Kaufman, Karen Mount, Danielle Vreeland, Client Relations Representatives

ISSN 1097-1076
ISBN-13: 978-0-7689-2566-1
ISBN-10: 0-7689-2566-5

Printed in the United States of America

10 9 8 7 6 5 4 3 2 1 11 10 09

Forty-third Edition

CONTENTS

APPENDIXES

INDEXES

A Note from the Peterson's Editors

The six volumes of *Peterson's Graduate and Professional Programs*, the only annually updated reference work of its kind, provide wide-ranging information on the graduate and professional programs offered by accredited colleges and universities in the United States, U.S. territories, and Canada and by those institutions outside the United States that are accredited by U.S. accrediting bodies. More than 44,000 individual academic and professional programs at more than 2,200 institutions are listed. *Peterson's Graduate and Professional Programs* have been used for more than forty years by prospective graduate and professional students, placement counselors, faculty advisers, and all others interested in postbaccalaureate education.

Graduate & Professional Programs: An Overview contains information on institutions as a whole, while the other books in the series are devoted to specific academic and professional fields:

Graduate Programs in the Humanities, Arts & Social Sciences
Graduate Programs in the Biological Sciences
Graduate Programs in the Physical Sciences, Mathematics, Agricultural Sciences, the Environment & Natural Resources
Graduate Programs in Engineering & Applied Sciences
Graduate Programs in Business, Education, Health, Information Studies, Law & Social Work

The books may be used individually or as a set. For example, if you have chosen a field of study but do not know what institution you want to attend or if you have a college or university in mind but have not chosen an academic field of study, it is best to begin with the Overview guide.

Graduate & Professional Programs: An Overview presents several directories to help you identify programs of study that might interest you; you can then research those programs further in the other books in the series by using the Directory of Graduate and Professional Programs by Field, which lists 500 fields and gives the names of those institutions that offer graduate degree programs in each.

For geographical or financial reasons, you may be interested in attending a particular institution and will want to know what it has to offer. You should turn to the Directory of Institutions and Their Offerings, which lists the degree programs available at each institution. As in the Directory of Graduate and Professional Programs by Field, the level of degrees offered is also indicated.

All books in the series include advice on graduate education, including topics such as admissions tests, financial aid, and accreditation. **The Graduate Adviser** includes two essays and information about accreditation. The first essay, "The Admissions Process," discusses general admission requirements, admission tests, factors to consider when selecting a graduate school or program, when and how to apply, and how admission decisions are made. Special information for international students and tips for minority students are also included. The second essay, "Financial Support," is an overview of the broad range of support available at the graduate level. Fellowships, scholarships, and grants; assistantships and internships; federal and private loan programs, as well as Federal Work-Study; and the GI bill are detailed. This essay concludes with advice on applying for need-based financial aid. "Accreditation and Accrediting Agencies" gives information on accreditation and its purpose and lists institutional accrediting agencies first and then specialized accrediting agencies relevant to each volume's specific fields of study.

With information on more than 44,000 graduate programs in 500 disciplines, *Peterson's Graduate and Professional Programs* give you all the information you need about the programs that are of interest to you in three formats: **Profiles** (capsule summaries of basic information), **Announcements** (information that an institution or program wants to emphasize, written by administrators), and **Close-Ups** (also written by administrators, with more expansive information than the **Profiles**, emphasizing different aspects of the programs). By using these various formats of program information, coupled with **Appendixes** and **Indexes** covering directories and subject areas for all six books, you will find that these guides provide the most comprehensive, accurate, and up-to-date graduate study information available.

Peterson's publishes a full line of resources with information you need to guide you through the graduate admissions process. Peterson's publications can be found at your local bookstore or library—or visit us on the Web at www.petersons.com.

Colleges and universities will be pleased to know that Peterson's helped you in your selection. Admissions staff members are more than happy to answer questions, address specific problems, and help in any way they can. The editors at Peterson's wish you great success in your graduate program search!

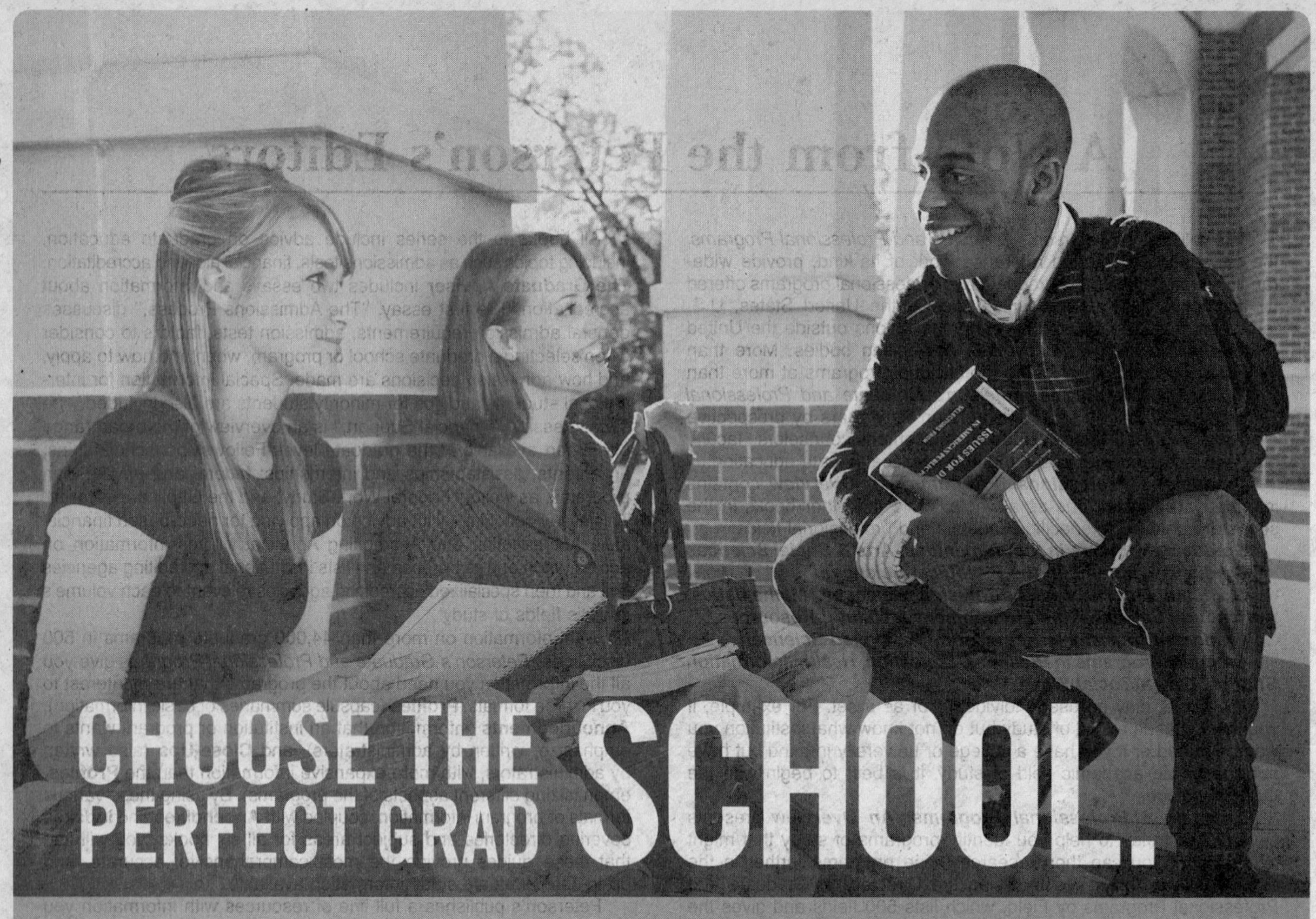

CHOOSE THE
PERFECT GRAD
SCHOOL.
Get help from our Grad Search at Petersons.com/grad.

Take your education and career to the next level with these helpful resources at Petersons.com:

- Grad school search by subject, location, or other criteria
- Detailed information about faculty, research, and admissions requirements
- Online courses and practice tests
- Free information from programs you contact
- Financial aid information
- Advice articles
- Monthly e-newsletters

VISIT PETERSONS.COM/GRAD TODAY.

PETERSON'S
A nelnet. COMPANY

THE GRADUATE ADVISER

The Admissions Process

Generalizations about graduate admissions practices are not always helpful because each institution has its own set of guidelines and procedures. Nevertheless, some broad statements can be made about the admissions process that may help you plan your strategy.

Factors Involved in Selecting a Graduate School or Program

Selecting a graduate school and a specific program of study is a complex matter. Quality of the faculty; program and course offerings; the nature, size, and location of the institution; admission requirements; cost; and the availability of financial assistance are among the many factors that affect one's choice of institution. Other considerations are job placement and achievements of the program's graduates and the institution's resources, such as libraries, laboratories, and computer facilities. If you are to make the best possible choice, you need to learn as much as you can about the schools and programs you are considering before you apply.

The following steps may help you narrow your choices.

- Talk to alumni of the programs or institutions you are considering to get their impressions of how well they were prepared for work in their fields of study.
- Remember that graduate school requirements change, so be sure to get the most up-to-date information possible.
- Talk to department faculty members and the graduate adviser at your undergraduate institution. They often have information about programs of study at other institutions.
- Visit the Web sites of the graduate schools in which you are interested to request a graduate catalog. Contact the department chair in your chosen field of study for additional information about the department and the field.
- Visit as many campuses as possible. Call ahead for an appointment with the graduate adviser in your field of interest and be sure to check out the facilities and talk to students.

General Requirements

Graduate schools and departments have requirements that applicants for admission must meet. Typically, these requirements include undergraduate transcripts (which provide information about undergraduate grade point average and course work applied toward a major), admission test scores, and letters of recommendation. Most graduate programs also ask for an essay or personal statement that describes your personal reasons for seeking graduate study. In some fields, such as art and music, portfolios or auditions may be required in addition to other evidence of talent. Some institutions require that the applicant have an undergraduate degree in the same subject as the intended graduate major.

Most institutions evaluate each applicant on the basis of the applicant's total record, and the weight accorded any given factor varies widely from institution to institution and from program to program.

The Application Process

You should begin the application process at least one year before you expect to begin your graduate study. Find out the application deadline for each institution (many are provided in the **Profile** section of this guide). Go to the institution's Web site and find out if you can apply online. If not, request a paper application form. Fill out this form thoroughly and neatly. Assume that the school needs all the information it is requesting and that the admissions officer will be sensitive to the neatness and overall quality of what you submit. Do not supply more information than the school requires.

The institution may ask at least one question that will require a three- or four-paragraph answer. Compose your response on the assumption that the admissions officer is interested in both what you think and how you express yourself. Keep your statement brief and to the point, but, at the same time, include all pertinent information about your past experiences and your educational goals. Individual statements vary greatly in style and content, which helps admissions officers differentiate among applicants. Many graduate departments give considerable weight to the statement in making their admissions decisions, so be sure to take the time to prepare a thoughtful and concise statement.

If recommendations are a part of the admissions requirements, carefully choose the individuals you ask to write them. It is generally best to ask current or former professors to write the recommendations, provided they are able to attest to your intellectual ability and motivation for doing the work required of a graduate student. It is advisable to provide stamped, preaddressed envelopes to people being asked to submit recommendations on your behalf.

Completed applications, including references, transcripts, and admission test scores, should be received at the institution by the specified date.

Be advised that institutions do not usually make admissions decisions until all materials have been received. Enclose a self-addressed postcard with your application, requesting confirmation of receipt. Allow at least 10 days for the return of the postcard before making further inquiries.

If you plan to apply for financial support, it is imperative that you file your application early.

ADMISSION TESTS

The major testing program used in graduate admissions is the Graduate Record Examinations (GRE) testing program, sponsored by the GRE Board and administered by Educational Testing Service, Princeton, New Jersey.

The Graduate Record Examinations testing program consists of a General Test and eight Subject Tests. The General Test measures critical thinking, verbal reasoning, quantitative reasoning, and analytical writing skills. It is offered as an Internet-based test (iBT) in the United States, Canada, and many other countries.

The typical computer-based General Test consists of one 30-minute verbal reasoning section, one 45-minute quantitative reasoning sections, one 45-minute issue analysis (writing) section, and one 30-minute argument analysis (writing) section. In addition, an unidentified verbal or quantitative section that doesn't count toward a score may be included and an identified research section that is not scored may also be included.

The Subject Tests measure achievement and assume undergraduate majors or extensive background in the following eight disciplines:

- Biochemistry, Cell and Molecular Biology
- Biology
- Chemistry
- Computer Science
- Literature in English
- Mathematics
- Physics
- Psychology

The Subject Tests are available three times per year as paper-based administrations around the world. Testing time is approximately 2 hours and 50 minutes. You can obtain more information about the GRE by visiting the ETS Web site at www.ets.org or consulting the *GRE Information and Registration Bulletin*. The *Bulletin* can be obtained at many undergraduate colleges. You can also download it from the ETS Web site or obtain it by contacting Graduate Record Examinations, Educational Testing Service, PO Box 6000, Princeton, NJ 08541-6000, telephone 1-609-771-7670.

If you expect to apply for admission to a program that requires any of the GRE tests, you should select a test date well in advance of the application deadline. Scores on the computer-based General Test are reported within ten to fifteen days; scores on the paper-based Subject Tests are reported within six weeks.

Another testing program, the Miller Analogies Test (MAT), is administered at more than 500 Controlled Testing Centers, licensed by Harcourt Assessment, Inc., in the United States, Canada, and other countries. The MAT computer-based test is now available. Testing time is 60 minutes. The test consists of 120 partial analogies. You can obtain the *Candidate Information Booklet,* which contains a list of test centers and instructions for taking the test, from http://www.milleranalogies.com or by calling 1-800-622-3231.

Check the specific requirements of the programs to which you are applying.

How Admission Decisions Are Made

The program you apply to is directly involved in the admissions process. Although the final decision is usually made by the graduate dean (or an associate) or the faculty admissions committee, recommendations from faculty members in your intended field are important. At some institutions, an interview is incorporated into the decision process.

A Special Note for International Students

In addition to the steps already described, there are some special considerations for international students who intend to apply for graduate study in the United States. All graduate schools require an indication of competence in English. The purpose of the Test of English as a Foreign Language (TOEFL) is to evaluate the English proficiency of people who are nonnative speakers of English and want to study at colleges and universities where English is the language of instruction. The TOEFL is administered by Educational Testing Service (ETS) under the general direction of a policy board established by the College Board and the Graduate Record Examinations Board.

The TOEFL iBT assesses the four basic language skills: listening, reading, writing, and speaking. It was administered for the first time in September 2005, and ETS continues to introduce the TOEFL iBT in selected cities. The Internet-based test is administered at secure, official test centers. The testing time is approximately 4 hours. Because the TOEFL iBT includes a speaking section, the Test of Spoken English (TSE) is no longer needed.

The TOEFL is also offered in the paper-based format in areas of the world where Internet-based testing is not available. The paper-based TOEFL consists of three sections—listening comprehension, structure and written expression, and reading comprehension. The testing time is approximately 3 hours. The Test of Written English (TWE) is also given. The TWE is a 30-minute essay that measures the examinee's ability to compose in English. Examinees receive a TWE score separate from their TOEFL score. The *Information Bulletin* contains information on local fees and registration procedures.

Additional information and registration materials are available from TOEFL Services, Educational Testing Service, P.O. Box 6151, Princeton, New Jersey 08541-6151. Telephone: 1-609-771-7100. Web site: www.toefl.org.

International students should apply especially early because of the number of steps required to complete the admissions process. Furthermore, many United States graduate schools have a limited number of spaces for international students, and many more students apply than the schools can accommodate.

International students may find financial assistance from institutions very limited. The U.S. government requires international applicants to submit a certification of support, which is a statement attesting to the applicant's financial resources. In addition, international students *must* have health insurance coverage.

Tips for Minority Students

Indicators of a university's values in terms of diversity are found both in its recruitment programs and its resources directed to student success. Important questions: Does the institution vigorously recruit minorities for its graduate programs? Is there funding available to help with the costs associated with visiting the school? Are minorities represented in the institution's brochures or Web site or on their faculty rolls? What campus-based resources or services (including assistance in locating housing or career counseling and placement) are available? Is funding available to members of underrepresented groups?

At the program level, it is particularly important for minority students to investigate the "climate" of a program under consideration. How many minority students are enrolled and how many have graduated? What opportunities are there to work with diverse faculty and mentors whose research interests match yours? How are conflicts resolved or concerns addressed? How interested are faculty in building strong and supportive relations with students? "Climate" concerns should be addressed by posing questions to various individuals, including faculty members, current students, and alumni.

Information is also available through various organizations, such as the Hispanic Association of Colleges & Universities (HACU), and publications such as *Diverse Issues in Higher Education* and *Hispanic Outlook* magazine. There are also books devoted to this topic, such as *The Multicultural Student's Guide to Colleges* by Robert Mitchell.

Financial Support

he range of financial support at the graduate level is very broad. The following descriptions will give you a general idea of what you might expect and what will be expected of you as a financial support recipient.

Fellowships, Scholarships, and Grants

These are usually outright awards of a few hundred to many thousands of dollars with no service to the institution required in return. Fellowships and scholarships are usually awarded on the basis of merit and are highly competitive. Grants are made on the basis of financial need or special talent in a field of study. Many fellowships, scholarships, and grants not only cover tuition, fees, and supplies but also include stipends for living expenses with allowances for dependents. However, the terms of each should be examined because some do not permit recipients to supplement their income with outside work. Fellowships, scholarships, and grants may vary in the number of years for which they are awarded.

In addition to the availability of these funds at the university or program level, many excellent fellowship programs are available at the national level and may be applied for before and during enrollment in a graduate program. A listing of many of these programs can be found at the Council of Graduate Schools' Web site: http://www.cgsnet.org. There is a wealth of information in the "Programs and Awards" section.

Assistantships and Internships

Many graduate students receive financial support through assistantships, particularly involving teaching or research duties. It is important to recognize that such appointments should not be viewed simply as employment relationships but rather should constitute an integral and important part of a student's graduate education. As such, the appointments should be accompanied by strong faculty mentoring and increasingly responsible apprenticeship experiences. The specific nature of these appointments in a given program should be considered in selecting that graduate program.

TEACHING ASSISTANTSHIPS

These usually provide a salary and full or partial tuition remission and may also provide health benefits. Unlike fellowships, scholarships, and grants, which require no service to the institution, teaching assistantships require recipients to provide the institution with a specific amount of undergraduate teaching, ideally related to the student's field of study. Some teaching assistants are limited to grading papers, compiling bibliographies, taking notes, or monitoring laboratories. At some graduate schools, teaching assistants must carry lighter course loads than regular full-time students.

RESEARCH ASSISTANTSHIPS

These are very similar to teaching assistantships in the manner in which financial assistance is provided. The difference is that recipients are given basic research assignments in their disciplines rather than teaching responsibilities. The work required is normally related to the student's field of study; in most instances, the assistantship supports the student's thesis or dissertation research.

ADMINISTRATIVE INTERNSHIPS

These are similar to assistantships in application of financial assistance funds, but the student is given an assignment on a part-time basis, usually as a special assistant with one of the university's administrative offices. The assignment may not necessarily be directly related to the recipient's discipline.

RESIDENCE HALL AND COUNSELING ASSISTANTSHIPS

These assistantships are frequently assigned to graduate students in psychology, counseling, and social work, but may be offered to students in other disciplines, especially if they have worked in this capacity during their undergraduate years. Duties can vary from being available in a dean's office for a specific number of hours for consultation with undergraduates to living in campus residences and being responsible for both counseling and administrative tasks or advising student activity groups. Residence hall assistantships often include a room and board allowance and, in some cases, tuition assistance and stipends. Contact the Housing and Student Life Office for more information.

Health Insurance

The availability and affordability of health insurance is an important issue and one that should be considered in an applicant's choice of institution and program. While often included with assistantships and fellowships, this is not always the case and, even if provided, the benefits may be limited. It is important to note that the U.S. government requires international students to have health insurance.

The GI Bill

This provides financial assistance for students who are veterans of the United States armed forces. If you are a veteran, contact your local Veterans Administration office to determine your eligibility and to get full details about benefits. There are a number of programs that offer educational benefits to current military enlistees. Some states have tuition assistance programs for members of the National Guard. Contact the VA office at the college for more information.

Federal Work-Study Program (FWS)

Employment is another way some students finance their graduate studies. The federally funded Federal Work-Study Program provides eligible students with employment opportunities, usually in public and private nonprofit organizations. Federal funds pay up to 75 percent of the wages, with the remainder paid by the employing agency. FWS is available to graduate students who demonstrate financial need. Not all schools have these funds, and some only award them to undergraduates. Each school sets its application deadline and work-study earnings limits. Wages vary and are related to the type of work done. You must file the Free Application for Federal Student Aid (FAFSA) to be eligible for this program.

Loans

Many graduate students borrow to finance their graduate programs when other sources of assistance (which do not have to be repaid) prove insufficient. You should always read and understand the terms of any loan program before submitting your application.

FEDERAL LOANS

Federal Stafford Loans. The Federal Stafford Loan Program offers government-sponsored, low-interest loans to students through a private lender such as a bank, credit union, or savings and loan association.

There are two components of the Federal Stafford Loan program. Under the *subsidized* component of the program, the federal government pays the interest on the loan while you are enrolled in graduate school on at least a half-time basis, as well as during any period of deferment. Under the *unsubsidized* component of the program, you pay the interest on the loan from the day proceeds are issued. Eligibility for the federal subsidy is based on demonstrated financial need as determined by the financial aid office from the information you provide on the FAFSA. A cosigner is not required, since the loan is not based on creditworthiness.

Although *unsubsidized* Federal Stafford Loans may not be as desirable as *subsidized* Federal Stafford Loans from the student's perspective, they are a useful source of support for those who may not qualify for the subsidized loans or who need additional financial assistance.

Graduate students may borrow up to $20,500 per year through the Stafford Loan Program, up to a cumulative maximum of $138,500, including undergraduate borrowing. This may include up to $8500 in *subsidized* Stafford Loans annually, depending on eligibility, up to a cumulative maximum of $65,500, including undergraduate borrowing. The amount of the loan borrowed through the *unsubsidized* Stafford Program equals the total amount of the loan (as much as $20,500) minus your eligibility for a *subsidized* Stafford Loan (as much as $8500). You may borrow up to the cost of attendance at the school in which you are enrolled or will attend, minus estimated financial assistance from other federal, state, and private sources, up to a maximum of $20,500.

Stafford Loans made on or after July 1, 2006, carry a fixed interest rate of 6.8% both for in-school and in-repayment borrowers.

Two fees may be deducted from the loan proceeds upon disbursement: a Federal Default Fee of 1 percent, which is deposited in an insurance pool to ensure repayment to the lender if the borrower defaults, and a federally mandated 1.5 percent origination fee, for loans made after July 1, 2007, which is used to offset the administrative cost of the Federal Stafford Loan Program. Many lenders do offer reduced-fee or "zero fee" loans. The origination fees are scheduled to be eliminated by July 1, 2010.

Under the *subsidized* Federal Stafford Loan Program, repayment begins six months after your last date of enrollment on at least a half-time basis. Under the *unsubsidized* program, repayment of interest begins within thirty days from disbursement of the loan proceeds, and repayment of the principal begins six months after your last enrollment on at least a half-time basis. Some borrowers may choose to defer interest payments while they are in school. The accrued interest is added to the loan balance when the borrower begins repayment. There are several repayment options.

Federal Direct Loans. Some schools participate in the Department of Education's William D. Ford Direct Loan Program instead of the Federal Stafford Loan Program. The two programs are essentially the same except that with the Direct Loans, schools themselves provide the loans with funds from the federal government. Terms and interest rates are virtually the same except that there are a few additional repayment options with Federal Direct Loans.

Federal Perkins Loans. The Federal Perkins Loan is available to students demonstrating financial need and is administered directly by the school. Not all schools have these funds, and some may award them to undergraduates only. Eligibility is determined from the information you provide on the FAFSA. The school will notify you of your eligibility.

Eligible graduate students may borrow up to $6000 per year, up to a maximum of $40,000, including undergraduate borrowing (even if your previous Perkins Loans have been repaid). The interest rate for Federal Perkins Loans is 5 percent, and no interest accrues while you remain in school at least half-time. There are no guarantee, loan, or disbursement fees. Repayment begins nine months after your last date of enrollment on at least a half-time basis and may extend over a maximum of ten years with no prepayment penalty.

Federal Graduate PLUS Loans. Effective July 1, 2006, graduate and professional students are eligible for Graduate PLUS loans. Graduate PLUS loans are identical to Parent PLUS loans, except that students borrow on their own behalf. This program allows students to borrow up to their cost of attendance, less any other aid received through this federal program. These loans have a fixed interest rate of 8.5% (7.9% for the Federal Direct PLUS), and interest begins to accrue at the time of disbursement. For more information, contact your FFELP lender or your college financial aid office.

Deferring Your Federal Loan Repayments. If you borrowed under the Federal Stafford Loan Program, Federal Direct Loan Program, or the Federal Perkins Loan Program for previous undergraduate or graduate study, your repayments may be deferred when you return to graduate school, depending on when you borrowed and under which program.

There are other deferment options available if you are temporarily unable to repay your loan. Information about these deferments is provided at your entrance and exit interviews. If you believe you are eligible for a deferment of your loan repayments, you must contact your lender to request a deferment form. The deferment must be filed prior to the time your repayment is due, and it must be refiled when it expires if you remain eligible for deferment at that time.

SUPPLEMENTAL (PRIVATE) LOANS

Many lending institutions offer supplemental loan programs and other financing plans, such as the ones described here, to students seeking additional assistance in meeting their educational expenses. Some loan programs target all types of graduate students; others are designed specifically for business, law, or medical students. In addition, you can use private loans not specifically designed for education to help finance your graduate degree.

If you are considering borrowing through a supplemental or private loan program, you should carefully consider the terms and be sure to "read the fine print." Check with the program sponsor for the most current terms that will be applicable to the amounts you intend to borrow for graduate study. Most supplemental loan programs for graduate study offer unsubsidized, credit-based loans. In general, a credit-ready borrower is one who has a satisfactory credit history or no credit history at all. A creditworthy borrower generally must pass a credit test to be eligible to borrow or act as a cosigner for the loan funds.

Many supplemental loan programs have minimum and maximum annual loan limits. Some offer amounts equal to the cost of attendance minus any other aid you will receive for graduate study. If you are planning to borrow for several years of graduate study, consider whether there is a cumulative or aggregate limit on the amount you may borrow. Often this cumulative or aggregate limit will include any amounts you borrowed and have not repaid for undergraduate or previous graduate study.

The combination of the annual interest rate, loan fees, and the repayment terms you choose will determine how much you will repay over time. Compare these features in combination before you decide which loan program to use. Some loans offer interest rates that are adjusted monthly, some quarterly, some annually. Some offer interest rates that are lower during the in-school, grace, and deferment periods and then increase when you begin repayment. Some programs include a loan "origination" fee, which is usually deducted from the principal amount you receive when the loan is disbursed and must be repaid along with the interest and other principal when you graduate, withdraw from school, or drop below half-time study. Sometimes the loan fees are reduced if you borrow with a qualified cosigner. Some programs allow you to defer interest and/or principal payments while you are enrolled in graduate school. Many programs allow you to capitalize your interest payments; the interest due on your loan is added to the outstanding balance of your loan, so you don't have to repay immediately, but this increases the amount you owe. Other programs allow you to pay the interest as you go, which reduces the amount you later have to repay.

Some examples of supplemental programs follow. The private loan market is very competitive, and your financial aid office can help you evaluate these and other programs.

CitiAssist Loans. Offered by Citibank, these no-fee loans help graduate students fill the gap between the financial aid they receive and the money they need for school. Visit www.studentloan.com for more loan information from Citibank.

EXCEL Loan. This program, sponsored by Nellie Mae, is designed for students who are not ready to borrow on their own and wish to borrow with a creditworthy cosigner. Visit www.nelliemae.com for more information.

Graduate Access Loan. Sponsored by the Access Group, this is for graduate students enrolled at least half-time. The Web site is www.accessgroup.com.

Signature Student Loan. A loan program for students who are enrolled at least half-time, this is sponsored by Sallie Mae. Visit www.salliemae.com for more information.

Nelnet Graduate and Professional Loans. These private loans are for graduate and professional students attending participating degree-granting institutions. For more information, go to www.nelnet.com.

Applying for Need-Based Financial Aid

Schools that award federal and institutional financial assistance based on need will require you to complete the FAFSA and, in some cases, an institutional financial aid application.

If you are applying for federal student assistance, you **must** complete the FAFSA. A service of the U.S. Department of Education, it is free to all applicants. Most applicants apply online at www.fafsa.ed.gov. Paper applications are available at the financial aid office of your local college.

After your FAFSA information has been processed, you will receive a Student Aid Report (SAR). If you provided an e-mail address on the FAFSA, this will be sent to you electronically; otherwise, it will be mailed to your home address.

Follow the instructions on the SAR if you need to correct information reported on your original application. If your situation changes after you file your FAFSA, contact your financial aid officer to discuss amending your information. You can also appeal your financial aid award if you have extenuating circumstances.

If you would like more information on federal student financial aid, visit the FAFSA Web site or download the most recent version of *Funding Education Beyond High School: The Guide to Federal Student Aid* at http://studentaid.ed.gov/students/publications/student_guide/index.html. This guide is also available in Spanish.

The U.S. Department of Education also has a toll-free number for questions concerning federal student aid programs. The number is 1-800-4-FED AID (1-800-433-3243). If you are hearing impaired, call toll-free, 1-800-730-8913.

Summary

Remember that these are generalized statements about financial assistance at the graduate level. Because each institution allots its aid differently, you should communicate directly with the school and the specific department of interest to you. It is not unusual, for example, to find that an endowment vested within a specific department supports one or more fellowships. You may fit its requirements and specifications precisely.

Accreditation and Accrediting Agencies

Colleges and universities in the United States, and their individual academic and professional programs, are accredited by nongovernmental agencies concerned with monitoring the quality of education in this country. Agencies with both regional and national jurisdictions grant accreditation to institutions as a whole, while specialized bodies acting on a nationwide basis—often national professional associations—grant accreditation to departments and programs in specific fields.

Institutional and specialized accrediting agencies share the same basic concerns: the purpose an academic unit—whether university or program—has set for itself and how well it fulfills that purpose, the adequacy of its financial and other resources, the quality of its academic offerings, and the level of services it provides. Agencies that grant institutional accreditation take a broader view, of course, and examine university-wide or college-wide services with which a specialized agency may not concern itself.

Both types of agencies follow the same general procedures when considering an application for accreditation. The academic unit prepares a self-evaluation, focusing on the concerns mentioned above and usually including an assessment of both its strengths and weaknesses; a team of representatives of the accrediting body reviews this evaluation, visits the campus, and makes its own report; and finally, the accrediting body makes a decision on the application. Often, even when accreditation is granted, the agency makes a recommendation regarding how the institution or program can improve. All institutions and programs are also reviewed every few years to determine whether they continue to meet established standards; if they do not, they may lose their accreditation.

Accrediting agencies themselves are reviewed and evaluated periodically by the U.S. Department of Education and the Council for Higher Education Accreditation (CHEA). Recognized agencies adhere to certain standards and practices, and their authority in matters of accreditation is widely accepted in the educational community.

This does not mean, however, that accreditation is a simple matter, either for schools wishing to become accredited or for students deciding where to apply. Indeed, in certain fields the very meaning and methods of accreditation are the subject of a good deal of debate. For their part, those applying to graduate school should be aware of the safeguards provided by regional accreditation, especially in terms of degree acceptance and institutional longevity. Beyond this, applicants should understand the role that specialized accreditation plays in their field, as this varies considerably from one discipline to another. In certain professional fields, it is necessary to have graduated from a program that is accredited in order to be eligible for a license to practice, and in some fields the federal government also makes this a hiring requirement. In other disciplines, however, accreditation is not as essential, and there can be excellent programs that are not accredited. In fact, some programs choose not to seek accreditation, although most do.

Institutions and programs that present themselves for accreditation are sometimes granted the status of candidate for accreditation, or what is known as "preaccreditation." This may happen, for example, when an academic unit is too new to have met all the requirements for accreditation. Such status signifies initial recognition and indicates that the school or program in question is working to fulfill all requirements; it does not, however, guarantee that accreditation will be granted.

Institutional Accrediting Agencies—Regional

MIDDLE STATES ASSOCIATION OF COLLEGES AND SCHOOLS
Accredits institutions in Delaware, District of Columbia, Maryland, New Jersey, New York, Pennsylvania, Puerto Rico, and the Virgin Islands.
Jean Avnet Morse, President
Middle States Commission on Higher Education
3624 Market Street
Philadelphia, Pennsylvania 19104
Phone: 267-284-5000
Fax: 215-662-5950
E-mail: info@msche.org
Web: www.msche.org

NEW ENGLAND ASSOCIATION OF SCHOOLS AND COLLEGES
Accredits institutions in Connecticut, Maine, Massachusetts, New Hampshire, Rhode Island, and Vermont.
Barbara E. Brittingham, Director
Commission on Institutions of Higher Education
209 Burlington Road
Bedford, Massachusetts 01730-1433
Phone: 781-271-0022
Fax: 781-271-0950
E-mail: bbrittingham@neasc.org
Web: www.neasc.org

NORTH CENTRAL ASSOCIATION OF COLLEGES AND SCHOOLS
Accredits institutions in Arizona, Arkansas, Colorado, Illinois, Indiana, Iowa, Kansas, Michigan, Minnesota, Missouri, Nebraska, New Mexico, North Dakota, Ohio, Oklahoma, South Dakota, West Virginia, Wisconsin, and Wyoming.
Sylvia Manning, President
The Higher Learning Commission
30 North LaSalle Street, Suite 2400
Chicago, Illinois 60602
Phone: 312-263-0456
Fax: 312-263-7462
E-mail: smanning@hlcommission.org
Web: www.ncahigherlearningcommission.org

NORTHWEST COMMISSION ON COLLEGES AND UNIVERSITIES
Accredits institutions in Alaska, Idaho, Montana, Nevada, Oregon, Utah, and Washington.
Sandra E. Elman, President
8060 165th Avenue, NE, Suite 100
Redmond, Washington 98052
Phone: 425-558-4224
Fax: 425-376-0596
E-mail: selman@nwccu.org
Web: www.nwccu.org

SOUTHERN ASSOCIATION OF COLLEGES AND SCHOOLS
Accredits institutions in Alabama, Florida, Georgia, Kentucky, Louisiana, Mississippi, North Carolina, South Carolina, Tennessee, Texas, and Virginia.
Belle S. Wheelan, President
Commission on Colleges
1866 Southern Lane
Decatur, Georgia 30033-4097
Phone: 404-679-4512
Fax: 404-679-4528
E-mail: bwheelan@sacscoc.org
Web: www.sacs.org

WESTERN ASSOCIATION OF SCHOOLS AND COLLEGES
Accredits institutions in California, Guam, and Hawaii.
Ralph Wolff, President and Executive Director
Accrediting Commission for Senior Colleges and Universities
985 Atlantic Avenue, Suite 100
Alameda, California 94501
Phone: 510-748-9001
Fax: 510-748-9797
E-mail: wascsr@wascsenior.org
Web: www.wascweb.org

Institutional Accrediting Agencies—Other

ACCREDITING COUNCIL FOR INDEPENDENT COLLEGES AND SCHOOLS
Sheryl L. Moody, Executive Director
750 First Street, NE, Suite 980
Washington, DC 20002-4242
Phone: 202-336-6780
Fax: 202-842-2593
E-mail: smoody@acics.org
Web: www.acics.org

DISTANCE EDUCATION AND TRAINING COUNCIL (DETC)
Accrediting Commission
Michael P. Lambert, Executive Director
1601 18th Street, NW
Washington, DC 20009
Phone: 202-234-5100
Fax: 202-332-1386
E-mail: detc@detc.org
Web: www.detc.org

Specialized Accrediting Agencies

[Only *Graduate & Professional Programs: An Overview* of *Peterson's Graduate and Professional Programs* Series includes the complete list of specialized accrediting groups recognized by the U.S. Department of Education and the Council on Higher Education Accreditation (CHEA). The lists in all other five books are abridged.]

ART AND DESIGN
Samuel Hope, Executive Director
National Association of Schools of Art and Design (NASAD)
Commission on Accreditation
11250 Roger Bacon Drive, Suite 21
Reston, Virginia 20190
Phone: 703-437-0700
Fax: 703-437-6312
E-mail: info@arts-accredit.org
Web: www.arts-accredit.org

CLINICAL PASTORAL EDUCATION
Teresa E. Snorton, Executive Director
Accreditation Commission
Association for Clinical Pastoral Education, Inc.
1549 Claremont Road, Suite 103
Decatur, Georgia 30033-4611
Phone: 404-320-1472
Fax: 404-320-0849
E-mail: acpe@acpe.edu
Web: www.acpe.edu

DANCE
Samuel Hope, Executive Director
National Association of Schools of Dance (NASD)
Commission on Accreditation
11250 Roger Bacon Drive, Suite 21
Reston, Virginia 20190
Phone: 703-437-0700
Fax: 703-437-6312
E-mail: info@arts-accredit.org
Web: www.arts-accredit.org

DIETETICS
Beverly E. Mitchell, Senior Director
American Dietetic Association
Commission on Accreditation for Dietetics Education (CADE-ADA)
120 South Riverside Plaza, Suite 2000
Chicago, Illinois 60606-6995
Phone: 312-899-4872
Fax: 312-899-4817
E-mail: bmitchell@eatright.org
Web: www.eatright.org/cade

INTERIOR DESIGN
Holly Mattson, Executive Director
Council for Interior Design Accreditation
146 Monroe Center, NW, Suite 1318
Grand Rapids, Michigan 49503
Phone: 616-458-0400
Fax: 616-458-0460
E-mail: info@accredit-id.org
Web: www.accredit-id.org

JOURNALISM AND MASS COMMUNICATIONS
Susanne Shaw, Executive Director
Accrediting Council on Education in Journalism and Mass Communications (ACEJMC)
School of Journalism
Stauffer-Flint Hall
University of Kansas
1435 Jayhawk Boulevard
Lawrence, Kansas 66047
Phone: 785-864-3986
Fax: 785-864-5225
E-mail: sshaw@ku.edu
Web: www2.ku.edu/~acejmc

LANDSCAPE ARCHITECTURE
Ronald C. Leighton, Executive Director
Landscape Architectural Accreditation Board
American Society of Landscape Architects
636 I. Street, NW
Washington, DC 20001
Phone: 202-898-2444
Fax: 202-898-1185
E-mail: rleighton@asla.org
Web: www.asla.org

MARRIAGE AND FAMILY THERAPY
Jeff S. Harmon, Director of Accreditation Services
Commission on Accreditation for Marriage and Family Therapy Education
American Association for Marriage and Family Therapy
112 South Alfred Street
Alexandria, Virginia 22314-3061
Phone: 703-253-0459
Fax: 703-253-0508
E-mail: jharmon@aamft.org
Web: www.aamft.org

MEDICAL ILLUSTRATION
Commission on Accreditation of Allied Health Education Programs (CAAHEP)
Kathleen Megivern, Executive Director
1361 Park Street
Clearwater, Florida 33756
Phone: 727-210-2350
Fax: 727-210-2354
E-mail: mail@caahep.org
Web: www.caahep.org

MUSIC
Samuel Hope, Executive Director
National Association of Schools of Music (NASM)
Commission on Accreditation
11250 Roger Bacon Drive, Suite 21
Reston, Virginia 20190
Phone: 703-437-0700
Fax: 703-437-6312
E-mail: info@arts-accredit.org
Web: www.arts-accredit.org

PLANNING
Shonagh Merits, Executive Director
American Institute of Certified Planners/Association of Collegiate Schools of Planning/American Planning Association

Planning Accreditation Board (PAB)
122 South Michigan Avenue, Suite 1600
Chicago, Illinois 60603
Phone: 312-334-1271
Fax: 312-334-1273
E-mail: pab@planning.org
Web: showcase.netins.net/web/pab_fi66/index.htm

PSYCHOLOGY AND COUNSELING
Susan Zlotlow, Director
Office of Program Consultation and Accreditation
American Psychological Association
750 First Street, NE
Washington, DC 20002-4242
Phone: 202-336-5979
Fax: 202-336-5978
E-mail: szlotlow@apa.org
Web: www.apa.org/ed/accreditation

Carol L. Bobby, Executive Director
Council for Accreditation of Counseling and Related Educational Programs
1001 North Fairfax Street, Suite 510
Alexandria, Virginia 22314
Phone: 703-535-5990
Fax: 703-739-6209
E-mail: cacrep@cacrep.org
Web: www.cacrep.org

PUBLIC AFFAIRS AND ADMINISTRATION
Crystal Calarusse, Executive Director
Commission on Peer Review and Accreditation
National Association of Schools of Public Affairs and Administration
1120 G Street, NW, Suite 730
Washington, DC 20005
Phone: 202-628-8965
Fax: 202-626-4978
E-mail: calarusse@naspaa.org
Web: www.naspaa.org

SPEECH-LANGUAGE PATHOLOGY AND AUDIOLOGY
Patrima L. Tice, Director of Credentialing
American Speech-Language-Hearing Association
2200 Research Boulevard
Rockville, Maryland 20850-3289
Phone: 301-897-5700
Fax: 301-571-0457
E-mail: ptice@asha.org
Web: www.asha.org

TECHNOLOGY
Elise Scanlon, Executive Director
Accrediting Commission of Career Schools and Colleges of Technology
2101 Wilson Boulevard, Suite 302
Arlington, Virginia 22201
Phone: 703-247-4212
Fax: 703-247-4533
E-mail: escanlon@accsct.org
Web: www.accsct.org

THEATER
Samuel Hope, Executive Director
National Association of Schools of Theatre
Commission on Accreditation
11250 Roger Bacon Drive, Suite 21
Reston, Virginia 20190
Phone: 703-437-0700
Fax: 703-437-6312
E-mail: info@arts-accredit.org
Web: www.arts-accredit.org

THEOLOGY
Bernard Fryshman, Executive Vice President
Association of Advanced Rabbinical and Talmudic Schools (AARTS)
Accreditation Commission
11 Broadway, Suite 405
New York, New York 10004
Phone: 212-363-1991
Fax: 212-533-5335

Daniel O. Aleshire, Executive Director
Association of Theological Schools in the United States and Canada (ATS)
Commission on Accrediting
10 Summit Park Drive
Pittsburgh, Pennsylvania 15275-1103
Phone: 412-788-6505
Fax: 412-788-6510
E-mail: ats@ats.edu
Web: www.ats.edu

Russell Guy Fitzgerald Jr., Executive Director
Transnational Association of Christian Colleges and Schools (TRACS)
Accreditation Commission
P.O. Box 328
Forest, Virginia 24551
Phone: 434-525-9539
Fax: 434-525-9538
E-mail: rfitzgerald@tracs.org
Web: www.tracs.org

How to Use These Guides

As you identify the particular programs and institutions that interest you, you can use both the ***Graduate & Professional Programs: An Overview*** volume and the specialized volumes in the series:

- ***Graduate Programs in the Physical Sciences, Mathematics, Agricultural Sciences, the Environment & Natural Resources***
- ***Graduate Programs in Engineering & Applied Sciences***
- ***Graduate Programs the Humanities, Arts & Social Sciences***
- ***Graduate Programs in the Biological Sciences***
- ***Graduate Programs in Business, Education, Health, Information Studies, Law & Social Work***

to obtain detailed information. Each of the specialized volumes in the series is divided into sections that contain one or more directories devoted to programs in a particular field. If you do not find a directory devoted to your field of interest in a specific volume, consult "Directories and Subject Areas" (located at the end of each volume). After you have identified the correct volume, consult the "Directories and Subject Areas in This Book" index, which shows (as does the more general directory) what directories cover subjects not specifically named in a directory or section title.

Each of the specialized volumes in the series has a number of general directories. These directories have entries for the largest unit at an institution granting graduate degrees in that field. For example, the general Engineering and Applied Sciences directory in the ***Graduate Programs in Engineering & Applied Sciences*** volume consists of **Profiles** for colleges, schools, and departments of engineering and applied sciences.

General directories are followed by other directories, or sections, that give more detailed information about programs in particular areas of the general field that has been covered. The general Engineering and Applied Sciences directory, in the previous example, is followed by nineteen sections with directories in specific areas of engineering, such as Chemical Engineering, Industrial/Management Engineering, and Mechanical Engineering.

Because of the broad nature of many fields, any system of organization is bound to involve a certain amount of overlap. Environmental studies, for example, is a field whose various aspects are studied in several types of departments and schools. Readers interested in such studies will find information on relevant programs in the ***Graduate Programs in the Biological Sciences*** volume under Ecology and Environmental Biology; in the ***Graduate Programs in the Physical Sciences, Mathematics, Agricultural Sciences, the Environment & Natural Resources*** volume under Environmental Management and Policy and Natural Resources; in the ***Graduate Programs in Engineering & Applied Sciences*** volume under Energy Management and Policy and Environmental Engineering; and in the ***Graduate Programs in Business, Education, Health, Information Studies, Law & Social Work*** volume under Environmental and Occupational Health. To help you find all of the programs of interest to you, the introduction to each section within the specialized volumes includes, if applicable, a paragraph suggesting other sections and directories with information on related areas of study.

Directory of Institutions with Programs in the Humanities, Arts & Social Sciences

This directory lists institutions in alphabetical order and includes beneath each name the academic fields in which each institution offers graduate programs. The degree level in each field is also indicated, provided that the institution has supplied that information in response to Peterson's Annual Survey of Graduate and Professional Institutions. An M indicates that a master's degree program is offered; a D indicates that a doctoral degree program is offered; a P indicates that the first professional degree is offered; an O signifies that other advanced degrees (e.g., certificates or specialist degrees) are offered; and an * (asterisk) indicates that a **Close-Up** and/or **Announcement** is located in this volume. See the index, "Close-Ups and Announcements," for the specific page number.

Profiles of Academic and Professional Programs in the Specialized Volumes

Each section of **Profiles** has a table of contents that lists the Program Directories, **Announcements**, and **Close-Ups.** Program Directories consist of the **Profiles** of programs in the relevant fields, with **Announcements** following if programs have chosen to include them. **Cross-Discipline Announcements**, if any programs have chosen to submit such entries, and **Close-Ups,** which are more individualized statements, again if programs have chosen to submit them, are also listed.

The **Profiles** found in the 500 directories in the specialized volumes provide basic data about the graduate units in capsule form for quick reference. To make these directories as useful as possible, **Profiles** are generally listed for an institution's smallest academic unit within a subject area. In other words, if an institution has a College of Liberal Arts that administers many related programs, the **Profile** for the individual program (e.g., Program in History), not the entire College, appears in the directory.

There are some programs that do not fit into any current directory and are not given individual **Profiles**. The directory structure is reviewed annually in order to keep this number to a minimum and to accommodate major trends in graduate education.

The following outline describes the **Profile** information found in the guides and explains how best to use that information. Any item that does not apply to or was not provided by a graduate unit is omitted from its listing. The format of the **Profiles** is constant, making it easy to compare one institution with another and one program with another.

Identifying Information. The institution's name, in boldface type, is followed by a complete listing of the administrative structure for that field of study. (For example, University of Akron, Buchtel College of Arts and Sciences, Department of Theoretical and Applied Mathematics, Program in Mathematics.) The last unit listed is the one to which all information in the **Profile** pertains. The institution's city, state, and zip code follow.

Offerings. Each field of study offered by the unit is listed with all postbaccalaureate degrees awarded. Degrees that are not preceded by a specific concentration are awarded in the general field listed in the unit name. Frequently, fields of study are broken down into subspecializations, and those appear following the degrees awarded; for example, "Offerings in secondary education (M.Ed.), including English education, mathematics education, science education." Students enrolled in the M.Ed. program would be able to specialize in any of the three fields mentioned.

Professional Accreditation. Some **Profiles** indicate whether a program is professionally accredited. Because it is possible for a program to receive or lose professional accreditation at any time, students entering fields in which accreditation is important to a career should verify the status of programs by contacting either the chairperson or the appropriate accrediting association.

Jointly Offered Degrees. Explanatory statements concerning programs that are offered in cooperation with other institutions are included in the list of degrees offered. This occurs most commonly on a regional basis (for example, two state universities offering a cooperative Ph.D. in special education) or where the specialized nature of the institutions encourages joint efforts (a J.D./M.B.A. offered by a law school at an institution with no formal business programs and an institution with a business school but lacking a law school). Only programs that are truly cooperative are listed; those involving only limited course work at another institution are not. Interested students should contact the heads of such units for further information.

Part-Time and Evening/Weekend Programs. When information regarding the availability of part-time or evening/weekend study appears in the **Profile**, it means that students are able to earn a degree exclusively through such study.

Postbaccalaureate Distance Learning Degrees. A postbaccalaureate distance learning degree program signifies that course requirements can be fulfilled with minimal or no on-campus study.

Faculty. Figures on the number of faculty members actively involved with graduate students through teaching or research are separated into full-and part-time as well as men and women whenever the information has been supplied.

Students. Figures for the number of students enrolled in graduate and professional programs pertain to the semester of highest enrollment from the 2007–08 academic year. These figures are broken down into full-and part-time and men and women whenever the data have been supplied. Information on the number of matriculated students enrolled in the unit who are members of a minority group or are international students appears here. The average age of the matriculated students is followed by the number of applicants, the percentage accepted, and the number enrolled for fall 2007.

Degrees Awarded. The number of degrees awarded in the calendar year is listed. Many doctoral programs offer a terminal master's degree if students leave the program after completing only part of the requirements for a doctoral degree; that is indicated here. All degrees are classified into one of four types: master's, doctoral, first professional, and other advanced degrees. A unit may award one or several degrees at a given level; however, the data are only collected by type and may therefore represent several different degree programs.

Degree Requirements. The information in this section is also broken down by type of degree, and all information for a degree level pertains to all degrees of that type unless otherwise specified. Degree requirements are collected in a simplified form to provide some very basic information on the nature of the program and on foreign language, thesis or dissertation, comprehensive exam, and registration requirements. Many units also provide a short list of additional requirements, such as fieldwork or an internship. For complete information on graduation requirements, contact the graduate school or program directly.

Entrance Requirements. Entrance requirements are broken down into the four degree levels of master's, doctoral, first professional, and other advanced degrees. Within each level, information may be provided in two basic categories: entrance exams and other requirements. The entrance exams are identified by the standard acronyms used by the testing agencies, unless they are not well known. Other entrance requirements are quite varied, but they often contain an undergraduate or graduate grade point average (GPA). Unless otherwise stated, the GPA is calculated on a 4.0 scale and is listed as a minimum required for admission. Additional exam requirements/recommendations for international students may be listed here. Application deadlines for domestic and international students, the application fee, and whether electronic applications are accepted may be listed here. Note that the deadline should be used for reference only; these dates are subject to change, and students interested in applying should always contact the graduate unit directly about application procedures and deadlines.

Expenses. The typical cost of study for the 2007–08 academic year is given in two basic categories: tuition and fees. Cost of study may be quite complex at a graduate institution. There are often sliding scales for part-time study, a different cost for first-year students, and other variables that make it impossible to completely cover the cost of study for each graduate program. To provide the most usable information, figures are given for full-time study for a full year where available and for part-time study in terms of a per-unit rate (per credit, per semester hour, etc.). Occasionally, variances may be noted in tuition and fees for reasons such as the type of program, whether courses are taken during the day or evening, whether courses are at the master's or doctoral level, or other institution-specific reasons. Expenses are usually subject to change; for exact costs at any given time, contact your chosen schools and programs directly. Keep in mind that the tuition of Canadian institutions is usually given in Canadian dollars.

Financial Support. This section contains data on the number of awards administered by the institution and given to graduate students during the 2007–08 academic year. The first figure given represents the total number of students receiving financial support enrolled in that unit. If the unit has provided information on graduate appointments, these are broken down into three major categories: fellowships give money to graduate students to cover the cost of study and living expenses and are not based on a work obligation or research commitment, research assistantships provide stipends to graduate students for assistance in a formal research project with a faculty member, and teaching assistantships provide stipends to graduate students for teaching or for assisting faculty members in teaching undergraduate classes. Within each category, figures are given for the total number of awards, the average yearly amount per award, and whether full or partial tuition reimbursements are awarded. In addition to graduate appointments, the availability of several other financial aid sources is covered in this section. Tuition waivers are routinely part of a graduate appointment, but units sometimes waive part or all of a student's tuition even if a graduate appointment is not available. Federal Work-Study is made available to students who demonstrate need and meet the federal guidelines; this form of aid normally includes 10 or more hours of work per week in an office of the institution. Institutionally sponsored loans are low-interest loans available to graduate students to cover both educational and living expenses. Career-related internships or fieldwork offer money to students who are participating in a formal off-campus research project or practicum. Grants, scholarships, traineeships, unspecified assistantships, and other awards may also be noted. The availability of financial support to part-time students is also indicated here.

Some programs list the financial aid application deadline and the forms that need to be completed for students to be eligible for financial awards. There are two forms: FAFSA, the Free Application for Federal Student Aid, which is required for federal aid, and the CSS PROFILE®.

Faculty Research. Each unit has the opportunity to list several keyword phrases describing the current research involving faculty members and graduate students. Space limitations prevent the unit from listing complete information on all research programs. The total expenditure for funded research from the previous academic year may also be included.

Unit Head and Application Contact. The head of the graduate program for each unit is listed with academic title and telephone and fax numbers and e-mail address if available. In addition to the unit head, many graduate programs list a separate contact for application and admission information, which follows the listing for the unit head. If no unit head or application contact is given, you should contact the overall institution for information on graduate admissions.

Announcements and Close-Ups

The **Announcements** and **Close-Ups** are supplementary insertions submitted by deans, chairs, and other administrators who wish to offer an additional, more individualized statement to readers. A number of graduate school and program administrators have attached **Announcements** to the end of their **Profile** listings. In them you will find information that an institution or program wants to emphasize. The **Close-Ups** are by their very nature more expansive and flexible than the **Profiles**, and the administrators who have written them may emphasize different aspects of their programs. All of the **Close-Ups** are organized in the same way (with the exception of a few that describe research and training opportunities instead of degree programs), and in each one you will find information on the same basic topics, such as programs of study, research facilities, tuition and fees, financial aid, and application procedures. If an institution or program has submitted a **Close-Up**, a boldface cross-reference appears below its **Profile**. As with the **Announcements**, all of the **Close-Ups** in the guides have been submitted by choice; the absence of an **Announcement** or **Close-Up** does not reflect any type of editorial judgment on the part of Peterson's and their presence in the guides should not be taken as an indication of status, quality, or approval. Statements regarding a university's objectives and accomplishments are a reflection of its own beliefs and are not the opinions of the Peterson's editors.

Cross-Discipline Announcements

In addition to the regular directories that present **Profiles** of programs in each field of study, many sections in the specialized volumes contain special notices under the heading **Cross-Discipline Announcements**. Appearing at the end of many **Profile** sections, these **Cross-Discipline Announcements** inform you about programs that you may find of interest described in a different section. A biochemistry department, for example, may place a notice under **Cross-Discipline Announcements** in the Chemistry section of the ***Graduate Programs in the Physical Sciences, Mathematics, Agricultural Sciences, the Environment & Natural Resources*** volume to alert chemistry students to that course of study. **Cross-Discipline Announcements**, also written by administrators to highlight their programs, will be helpful to you not only in finding out about programs in fields related to your own but also in locating departments that are actively recruiting students with a specific undergraduate major.

Appendixes

This section contains two appendixes. The first, "Institutional Changes Since the 2008 Edition," lists institutions that have closed, moved, merged, or changed their name or status since the last edition of the guides. The second, "Abbreviations Used in the Guides," gives abbreviations of degree names, along with what those abbreviations stand for. These appendixes are identical in all six volumes of ***Peterson's Graduate and Professional Programs***.

Indexes

There are three indexes presented here. The first index, "Close-Ups and Announcements," gives page references for all programs that have chosen to place **Close-Ups** and **Announcements** in this volume. It is arranged alphabetically by institution; within institutions, the arrangement is alphabetical by subject area. It is not an index to all programs in the book's directories of **Profiles**; readers must refer to the directories themselves for **Profile** information on programs that have not submitted the additional, more individualized statements. The second index, "Directories and Subject Areas in Other Books in This Series", gives book references for the directories in the specialized volumes and also includes cross-references for subject area names not used in the directory structure, for example, "Computing Technology (see Computer Science)." The third index, "Directories and Subject Areas in This Book," gives page references for the directories in this volume and cross-references for subject area names not used in this volume's directory structure.

Data Collection Procedures

The information published in the directories and **Profiles** of all the books is collected through Peterson's Annual Survey of Graduate and Professional Institutions. The survey is sent each spring to more than 2,200 institutions offering postbaccalaureate degree programs, including accredited institutions in the United States, U.S. territories, and Canada and those institutions outside the United States that are accredited by U.S. accrediting bodies. Deans and other administrators complete these surveys, providing information on programs in the 500 academic and professional fields covered in the guides as well as overall institutional information. While every effort has been made to ensure the accuracy and completeness of the data, information is sometimes unavailable or changes occur after publication deadlines. All usable information received in time for publication has been included. The omission of any particular item from a directory or **Profile** signifies either that the item is not applicable to the institution or program or that information was not available. **Profiles** of programs scheduled to begin during the 2008–09 academic year cannot, obviously, include statistics on enrollment or, in many cases, the number of faculty members. If no usable data were submitted by an institution, its name, address, and program name appear in order to indicate the availability of graduate work.

Criteria for Inclusion in This Guide

To be included in this guide, an institution must have full accreditation or be a candidate for accreditation (preaccreditation) status by an institutional or specialized accrediting body recognized by the U.S. Department of Education or the Council for Higher Education Accreditation (CHEA). Institutional accrediting bodies, which review each institution as a whole, include the six regional associations of schools and colleges (Middle States, New England, North Central, Northwest, Southern, and Western), each of which is responsible for a specified portion of the United States and its territories. Other institutional accrediting bodies are national in scope and accredit specific kinds of institutions (e.g., Bible colleges, independent colleges, and rabbinical and Talmudic schools). Program registration by the New York State Board of Regents is considered to be the equivalent of institutional accreditation, since the board requires that all programs offered by an institution meet its standards before recognition is granted. A Canadian institution must be chartered and authorized to grant degrees by the provincial government, affiliated with a chartered institution, or accredited by a recognized U.S. accrediting body. This guide also includes institutions outside the United States that are accredited by these U.S. accrediting bodies. There are recognized specialized or professional accrediting bodies in more than fifty different fields, each of which is authorized to accredit institutions or specific programs in its particular field. For specialized institutions that offer programs in one field only, we designate this to be the equivalent of institutional accreditation. A full explanation of the accrediting process and complete information on recognized institutional (regional and national) and specialized accrediting bodies can be found online at www.chea.org or at www.ed.gov/admins/finaid/accred/index.html.

DIRECTORY OF INSTITUTIONS WITH PROGRAMS IN HUMANITIES, ARTS & SOCIAL SCIENCES

ABILENE CHRISTIAN UNIVERSITY
- Clinical Psychology M
- Communication—General M
- Conflict Resolution and Mediation/Peace Studies M,O
- Counseling Psychology M
- English M
- Gerontology M,O
- Liberal Studies M
- Marriage and Family Therapy M
- Missions and Missiology M
- Pastoral Ministry and Counseling M,D
- Psychology—General M
- Rhetoric M
- School Psychology M
- Speech and Interpersonal Communication M
- Theology P,M
- Writing M

ACADEMY OF ART UNIVERSITY
- Applied Arts and Design—General M
- Architecture M
- Art/Fine Arts M
- Clothing and Textiles M
- Computer Art and Design M
- Film, Television, and Video Production M
- Graphic Design M
- Illustration M
- Industrial Design M
- Interior Design M
- Internet and Interactive Multimedia M
- Photography M
- Textile Design M

ACADIA UNIVERSITY
- Clinical Psychology M
- English M
- Political Science M
- Psychology—General M
- Sociology M
- Theology P,M,D

ADAMS STATE COLLEGE
- Art/Fine Arts M
- History M

ADELPHI UNIVERSITY
- Art/Fine Arts M*
- Clinical Psychology D,O
- Counseling Psychology M
- Emergency Management O
- Gerontology M,O
- Psychology—General M,D,O*
- Public Administration O
- School Psychology M
- Writing M*

ADLER GRADUATE SCHOOL
- Counseling Psychology M,O
- Industrial and Organizational Psychology M,O
- Marriage and Family Therapy M,O
- Psychoanalysis and Psychotherapy M,O

ADLER SCHOOL OF PROFESSIONAL PSYCHOLOGY
- Addictions/Substance Abuse Counseling M,D,O
- Art Therapy M,D,O
- Clinical Psychology M,D,O
- Counseling Psychology M,D,O
- Gerontology M,D,O
- Industrial and Organizational Psychology M,D,O
- Marriage and Family Therapy M,D,O
- Psychology—General M,D,O*

ALABAMA AGRICULTURAL AND MECHANICAL UNIVERSITY
- Agricultural Economics and Agribusiness M
- Clinical Psychology M,O
- Counseling Psychology M,O
- Economics M
- Family and Consumer Sciences-General M,D
- Music M
- Psychology—General M,O
- School Psychology M,O
- Urban and Regional Planning M

ALABAMA STATE UNIVERSITY
- Music M

ALASKA PACIFIC UNIVERSITY
- Counseling Psychology M
- Interdisciplinary Studies M
- Liberal Studies M

ALBANY STATE UNIVERSITY
- Criminal Justice and Criminology M
- Economics M
- Public Administration M
- Public Policy M

ALBERTUS MAGNUS COLLEGE
- Art Therapy M
- Liberal Studies M

ALCORN STATE UNIVERSITY
- Agricultural Economics and Agribusiness M

ALFRED UNIVERSITY
- Applied Arts and Design—General M
- Art/Fine Arts M,D
- Computer Art and Design M
- Internet and Interactive Multimedia M
- School Psychology M,D,O*

ALLIANCE THEOLOGICAL SEMINARY
- Missions and Missiology P,M
- Pastoral Ministry and Counseling P,M
- Theology P,M

ALLIANT INTERNATIONAL UNIVERSITY–FRESNO
- Clinical Psychology D*
- Forensic Psychology D*
- Industrial and Organizational Psychology M,D
- Psychology—General D

ALLIANT INTERNATIONAL UNIVERSITY–IRVINE
- Forensic Psychology D*
- Marriage and Family Therapy M,D*
- School Psychology M,D,O

ALLIANT INTERNATIONAL UNIVERSITY–LOS ANGELES
- Addictions/Substance Abuse Counseling M
- Clinical Psychology D*
- Forensic Psychology D*
- Gerontology M
- Industrial and Organizational Psychology M,D
- Marriage and Family Therapy M*
- Psychology—General M,D
- School Psychology M,D,O

ALLIANT INTERNATIONAL UNIVERSITY–MÉXICO CITY
- Counseling Psychology M
- International Affairs M

ALLIANT INTERNATIONAL UNIVERSITY–SACRAMENTO
- Clinical Psychology D*
- Industrial and Organizational Psychology D
- Marriage and Family Therapy M*
- Psychology—General M,D

ALLIANT INTERNATIONAL UNIVERSITY–SAN DIEGO
- Clinical Psychology M,D*
- Industrial and Organizational Psychology M,D
- International Affairs M
- Marriage and Family Therapy M,D*
- Psychology—General M,D
- School Psychology M,D,O

ALLIANT INTERNATIONAL UNIVERSITY–SAN FRANCISCO
- Clinical Psychology D,O*
- Industrial and Organizational Psychology M,D
- Psychology—General M,D,O
- School Psychology M,D,O

ALVERNIA COLLEGE
- Liberal Studies M
- Social Psychology M

AMBERTON UNIVERSITY
- Counseling Psychology M
- Interdisciplinary Studies M

AMBROSE UNIVERSITY COLLEGE
- Cultural Studies P,M,O
- Missions and Missiology P,M,O
- Pastoral Ministry and Counseling P,M,O
- Theology P,M,O

AMERICAN ACADEMY OF ART
- Art/Fine Arts M
- Computer Art and Design M
- Internet and Interactive Multimedia M

AMERICAN BAPTIST SEMINARY OF THE WEST
- Pastoral Ministry and Counseling P,M
- Theology P,M

AMERICAN CONSERVATORY THEATER
- Theater M,O

AMERICAN FILM INSTITUTE CONSERVATORY
- Film, Television, and Video Production M

AMERICAN GRADUATE SCHOOL OF INTERNATIONAL RELATIONS AND DIPLOMACY
- International Affairs M,D*

AMERICAN INTERCONTINENTAL UNIVERSITY ONLINE
- Industrial and Organizational Psychology M

AMERICAN INTERNATIONAL COLLEGE
- Child Development M,D,O
- Clinical Psychology M
- Forensic Psychology M
- Psychology—General M,D
- Public Administration M

AMERICAN JEWISH UNIVERSITY
- Jewish Studies M
- Theology M

AMERICAN PUBLIC UNIVERSITY SYSTEM
- Conflict Resolution and Mediation/Peace Studies M
- Criminal Justice and Criminology M
- Emergency Management M
- History M
- Homeland Security M
- Humanities M
- International Affairs M
- Military and Defense Studies M
- National Security M
- Political Science M
- Public Administration M

AMERICAN UNIVERSITY
- American Studies M,D,O
- Anthropology M,D,O
- Applied Economics M,D,O
- Applied Social Research M,O
- Art History M
- Art/Fine Arts M
- Arts Administration M,O
- Broadcast Journalism M
- Clinical Psychology D
- Communication—General M*
- Comparative Literature M
- Conflict Resolution and Mediation/Peace Studies M,D,O
- Criminal Justice and Criminology M,D
- Dance O
- Economics M,D,O
- Ethics M,D,O
- Experimental Psychology M
- Film, Television, and Video Production M
- French O
- History M,D
- Interdisciplinary Studies M
- International Affairs M,D,O*
- International Development M,D,O
- Journalism M
- Latin American Studies M,O
- Mass Communication M
- Media Studies M
- Philosophy M

- Political Science M,D,O
- Psychology—General M,D
- Public Administration M,D,O
- Public Affairs M
- Public Policy M
- Russian O
- Social Psychology M
- Sociology M,O
- Spanish M,O
- Translation and Interpretation M,O
- Writing M

THE AMERICAN UNIVERSITY IN CAIRO

- Anthropology M
- Broadcast Journalism M,O
- Communication—General M,O
- Comparative Literature M
- Economics M
- English M
- Journalism M,O
- Mass Communication M,O
- Near and Middle Eastern Languages M,O
- Near and Middle Eastern Studies M,O
- Political Science M
- Sociology M

THE AMERICAN UNIVERSITY OF ATHENS

- Corporate and Organizational Communication M
- Political Science M

AMERICAN UNIVERSITY OF BEIRUT

- Agricultural Economics and Agribusiness M
- Anthropology M
- Archaeology M
- Economics M
- English M
- Health Psychology M
- History M
- Near and Middle Eastern Languages M
- Near and Middle Eastern Studies M
- Philosophy M
- Political Science M
- Psychology—General M
- Public Administration M
- Sociology M
- Urban and Regional Planning M,D
- Urban Design M,D

THE AMERICAN UNIVERSITY OF PARIS

- Communication—General M
- Conflict Resolution and Mediation/Peace Studies M
- International Affairs M
- Near and Middle Eastern Studies M
- Public Administration M

AMERICAN UNIVERSITY OF PUERTO RICO

- Art History M
- Criminal Justice and Criminology M

AMRIDGE UNIVERSITY

- Counseling Psychology P,M,D
- Marriage and Family Therapy P,M,D
- Pastoral Ministry and Counseling P,M,D
- Religion P,M,D
- Theology P,M,D

ANDERSON UNIVERSITY

- Missions and Missiology P,M,D
- Theology P,M,D

ANDOVER NEWTON THEOLOGICAL SCHOOL

- Theology P,M,D

ANDREW JACKSON UNIVERSITY

- Criminal Justice and Criminology M
- Public Administration M

ANDREWS UNIVERSITY

- Architecture M
- Communication—General M
- Counseling Psychology D
- Developmental Psychology M,D
- Economics M
- English M
- History M
- International Development M
- Music M
- Pastoral Ministry and Counseling P,M,D,O
- Psychology—General M,D,O
- School Psychology M,O
- Social Psychology M
- Theology P,M,D,O

ANGELO STATE UNIVERSITY

- Communication—General M
- Counseling Psychology M
- English M
- History M
- Industrial and Organizational Psychology M
- Interdisciplinary Studies M
- Journalism M
- Psychology—General M
- Public Administration M

ANNA MARIA COLLEGE

- Art/Fine Arts M,O
- Counseling Psychology M
- Criminal Justice and Criminology M
- Emergency Management M,O
- Pastoral Ministry and Counseling M

ANTIOCH UNIVERSITY LOS ANGELES

- Clinical Psychology M
- Psychology—General M
- Writing M,O

ANTIOCH UNIVERSITY MCGREGOR

- Art/Fine Arts M
- Comparative Literature M
- Conflict Resolution and Mediation/Peace Studies M
- Counseling Psychology M
- Film, Television, and Video Production M
- Liberal Studies M*
- Psychology—General M
- Theater M
- Writing M

ANTIOCH UNIVERSITY NEW ENGLAND

- Clinical Psychology M,D
- Counseling Psychology M
- Interdisciplinary Studies M
- Marriage and Family Therapy M,D*
- Psychology—General M,D,O
- Therapies—Dance, Drama, and Music M

ANTIOCH UNIVERSITY SANTA BARBARA

- Clinical Psychology D
- Psychology—General M

ANTIOCH UNIVERSITY SEATTLE

- Corporate and Organizational Communication
- Industrial and Organizational Psychology M
- Psychology—General M,D

APEX SCHOOL OF THEOLOGY

- Theology P,M

APPALACHIAN STATE UNIVERSITY

- American Studies M
- Child Development M
- Clinical Psychology M,O
- Criminal Justice and Criminology M
- English M
- Experimental Psychology M,O
- Family and Consumer Sciences-General M
- Geography M
- Gerontology M
- Health Psychology M,O
- History M
- Industrial and Organizational Psychology M,O
- Marriage and Family Therapy M
- Music M
- Political Science M
- Psychology—General M,O
- Public Administration M
- Public History M
- Romance Languages M
- School Psychology M
- Social Psychology M
- Spanish M
- Therapies—Dance, Drama, and Music M

AQUINAS INSTITUTE OF THEOLOGY

- Pastoral Ministry and Counseling P,M,D,O
- Theology P,M,D,O

ARCADIA UNIVERSITY

- Child Development M,D,O
- Conflict Resolution and Mediation/Peace Studies M
- English M
- Forensic Sciences M
- Genetic Counseling M
- Humanities M
- International Affairs M
- Psychology—General M,D,O
- School Psychology M
- Social Psychology M
- Theater M,D,O

ARGOSY UNIVERSITY, ATLANTA

- Clinical Psychology M,D,O
- Health Psychology M,D,O
- Marriage and Family Therapy M,D,O
- Psychology—General M,D,O*
- Social Psychology M,D,O

ARGOSY UNIVERSITY, CHICAGO

- Clinical Psychology M*
- Counseling Psychology D
- Forensic Psychology D
- Forensic Sciences M,D
- Health Psychology D
- Human Development D
- Marriage and Family Therapy D
- Psychoanalysis and Psychotherapy D
- Psychology—General M,D
- Social Psychology M,D

ARGOSY UNIVERSITY, DALLAS

- Clinical Psychology M,D*
- Psychology—General M,D
- Social Psychology M

ARGOSY UNIVERSITY, DENVER

- Clinical Psychology M,D
- Counseling Psychology M,D
- Forensic Psychology M,D
- Marriage and Family Therapy M,D
- Psychology—General M,D
- Social Psychology M,D*

ARGOSY UNIVERSITY, HAWAI'I

- Addictions/Substance Abuse Counseling O
- Clinical Psychology M,D,O
- Counseling Psychology D
- Marriage and Family Therapy M
- Psychology—General M,D,O*
- School Psychology M

ARGOSY UNIVERSITY, INLAND EMPIRE

- Clinical Psychology M,D
- Counseling Psychology M,D*
- Forensic Psychology M,D
- Marriage and Family Therapy M,D
- Psychology—General M,D

ARGOSY UNIVERSITY, LOS ANGELES

- Clinical Psychology M,D*
- Counseling Psychology M,D
- Marriage and Family Therapy M,D
- Psychology—General M,D

ARGOSY UNIVERSITY, NASHVILLE

- Counseling Psychology M,D*
- Psychology—General M,D

ARGOSY UNIVERSITY, ORANGE COUNTY

- Clinical Psychology M,D
- Counseling Psychology M,D
- Forensic Psychology M
- Marriage and Family Therapy M,D
- Psychology—General M,D,O*
- Public Administration M,D,O
- Sport Psychology M

ARGOSY UNIVERSITY, PHOENIX

- Clinical Psychology M,D
- Counseling Psychology M
- Forensic Psychology M
- Psychology—General M,D*
- School Psychology M,D
- Sport Psychology M,D

ARGOSY UNIVERSITY, SALT LAKE CITY

- Counseling Psychology M,D

Marriage and Family Therapy M,D
Psychology—General M,D*

ARGOSY UNIVERSITY, SAN DIEGO
Clinical Psychology M,D
Counseling Psychology M,D*
Marriage and Family Therapy M,D
Psychology—General M,D

ARGOSY UNIVERSITY, SAN FRANCISCO BAY AREA
Clinical Psychology M,D
Counseling Psychology M,D
Forensic Psychology M
Psychology—General M,D*

ARGOSY UNIVERSITY, SARASOTA
Counseling Psychology M,D,O
Forensic Psychology M,D,O
Marriage and Family Therapy M,D,O
Pastoral Ministry and Counseling M,D,O
Psychology—General M,D,O*
School Psychology M,D,O
Social Psychology M,D,O

ARGOSY UNIVERSITY, SCHAUMBURG
Clinical Psychology M,D,O*
Counseling Psychology M,D,O
Forensic Psychology M,D,O
Health Psychology M,D,O
Marriage and Family Therapy M,D,O
Psychology—General M,D,O
Social Psychology M,D,O

ARGOSY UNIVERSITY, SEATTLE
Clinical Psychology M,D,O*
Counseling Psychology M,D
Psychology—General M,D,O

ARGOSY UNIVERSITY, TAMPA
Clinical Psychology M,D
Counseling Psychology M,D
Marriage and Family Therapy M,D
Psychology—General M,D*
Public Administration M,D

ARGOSY UNIVERSITY, TWIN CITIES
Clinical Psychology M,D,O
Forensic Psychology M,D,O
Health Psychology M,D,O
Marriage and Family Therapy M,D,O
Psychology—General M,D,O*

ARGOSY UNIVERSITY, WASHINGTON DC
Clinical Psychology M,D*
Counseling Psychology M,D
Forensic Psychology M,D
Health Psychology M,D
Marriage and Family Therapy M,D
Psychology—General M,D
Social Psychology M,D

ARIZONA STATE UNIVERSITY
Anthropology M,D
Applied Arts and Design—General M
Architectural History D
Architecture M
Art/Fine Arts M
Building Science M
Child and Family Studies M,D
Clinical Psychology D
Cognitive Sciences D
Communication—General M,D
Comparative Literature M,D
Counseling Psychology D
Dance M
Demography and Population Studies M,D
Developmental Psychology D
Economics M,D
English M,D
Environmental Design D
French M
Geography M,D
German M
History of Science and Technology M,D
History M,D
Human Development M,D
Humanities M
Journalism M*
Landscape Architecture M
Latin American Studies M,D
Linguistics M,D
Music M,D
Philosophy M,D
Political Science M,D
Psychology—General D
Public Affairs M,D
Public History M,D
Public Policy P,M
Religion M,D
Social Psychology D
Social Sciences M,D
Sociology M,D
Spanish M,D
Speech and Interpersonal Communication M,D
Theater M,D
Urban and Regional Planning M
Writing M

ARIZONA STATE UNIVERSITY AT THE POLYTECHNIC CAMPUS
Agricultural Economics and Agribusiness M
Psychology—General M

ARIZONA STATE UNIVERSITY AT THE WEST CAMPUS
Communication—General M
Criminal Justice and Criminology M,D
Gerontology M,O
Interdisciplinary Studies M

ARKANSAS STATE UNIVERSITY
Art/Fine Arts M
Communication—General M,O
Criminal Justice and Criminology M,O
English M,O
Gerontology M,O
Historic Preservation M,D
History M,O
Journalism M
Media Studies M
Music M,O
Political Science M,O
Public Administration M,O
Rehabilitation Counseling M,O
School Psychology M,O
Sociology M,O
Speech and Interpersonal Communication M,O
Theater M

ARKANSAS TECH UNIVERSITY
Art/Fine Arts M
Communication—General M
Emergency Management M
English M
History M
Homeland Security M
Journalism M
Social Sciences M
Spanish M

ARMSTRONG ATLANTIC STATE UNIVERSITY
Criminal Justice and Criminology M
History M
Liberal Studies M

ART CENTER COLLEGE OF DESIGN
Applied Arts and Design—General M*
Art/Fine Arts M
Computer Art and Design M
Environmental Design M
Film, Television, and Video Production M
Industrial Design M

THE ART INSTITUTE OF BOSTON AT LESLEY UNIVERSITY
Art/Fine Arts M*

ASBURY COLLEGE
English M,O
French M,O
Spanish M,O
Writing M,O

ASBURY THEOLOGICAL SEMINARY
Cultural Studies M
Missions and Missiology M
Pastoral Ministry and Counseling M,O
Theology M,D,O

ASHLAND THEOLOGICAL SEMINARY
History P,M,D,O
Pastoral Ministry and Counseling P,M,D,O
Theology P,M,D,O

ASHLAND UNIVERSITY
History M
Political Science M
Writing M

ASSEMBLIES OF GOD THEOLOGICAL SEMINARY
Missions and Missiology P,M,D
Pastoral Ministry and Counseling P,M,D
Theology P,M,D

ASSOCIATED MENNONITE BIBLICAL SEMINARY
Conflict Resolution and Mediation/Peace Studies P,M,O
Missions and Missiology P,M,O
Theology P,M,O

ASSUMPTION COLLEGE
Counseling Psychology M,O
Rehabilitation Counseling M,O
School Psychology M,O

ATHABASCA UNIVERSITY
Art Therapy M,O
Counseling Psychology M,O
Cultural Studies M
Interdisciplinary Studies M
International Development M
Psychology—General M,O

THE ATHENAEUM OF OHIO
Pastoral Ministry and Counseling P,M,O
Theology P,M,O

ATLANTIC COLLEGE
Graphic Design M

ATLANTIC SCHOOL OF THEOLOGY
Theology P,M,O

ATLANTIC UNIVERSITY
Art/Fine Arts M
Transpersonal and Humanistic Psychology M

A.T. STILL UNIVERSITY OF HEALTH SCIENCES
Gerontology M,D

AUBURN UNIVERSITY
Agricultural Economics and Agribusiness M,D
Applied Economics M,D
Architecture M
Building Science M
Child and Family Studies M,D
Clothing and Textiles M
Communication—General M
Counseling Psychology M,D,O
Economics M
English M,D*
Experimental Psychology M,D
History M,D
Human Development M,D
Industrial and Organizational Psychology M,D
Industrial Design M
Landscape Architecture M
Mass Communication M
Political Science M,D
Psychology—General M,D
Public Administration M,D*
Rehabilitation Counseling M,D
Rural Sociology M
School Psychology M,D,O
Social Psychology M,D,O
Sociology M
Spanish M
Urban and Regional Planning M

AUBURN UNIVERSITY MONTGOMERY
Criminal Justice and Criminology M
Liberal Studies M
Political Science M,D
Psychology—General M
Public Administration M,D

AUGUSTA STATE UNIVERSITY
Political Science M
Psychology—General M

AUSTIN GRADUATE SCHOOL OF THEOLOGY
Theology M

AUSTIN PEAY STATE UNIVERSITY
Communication—General M
English M
Military and Defense Studies M
Music M
Psychology—General M

AUSTIN PRESBYTERIAN THEOLOGICAL SEMINARY
Pastoral Ministry and Counseling P,M,D
Theology P,M,D

AVE MARIA UNIVERSITY
Pastoral Ministry and Counseling M,D
Theology M,D

AVILA UNIVERSITY
Art Therapy M
Counseling Psychology M
Psychology—General M

AZUSA PACIFIC UNIVERSITY
Art/Fine Arts M
Clinical Psychology M,D
Ethics M
Marriage and Family Therapy M,D
Music M
Pastoral Ministry and Counseling P,M
Psychology—General M,D
Religion M
School Psychology M
Theology M,D

BABEL UNIVERSITY SCHOOL OF TRANSLATION
Translation and Interpretation M

BAKER UNIVERSITY
Conflict Resolution and Mediation/Peace Studies M
Liberal Studies M

BAKKE GRADUATE UNIVERSITY
Pastoral Ministry and Counseling M,D

BALL STATE UNIVERSITY
Anthropology M
Architecture M
Art/Fine Arts M
Clinical Psychology M
Cognitive Sciences M
Communication—General M
Counseling Psychology M,D
English M,D
Family and Consumer Sciences-General M
Gerontology M
Historic Preservation M
History M
Journalism M
Landscape Architecture M
Linguistics D
Political Science M
Psychology—General M
Public Administration M
Rhetoric M
School Psychology M,D,O
Social Psychology M
Social Sciences M
Sociology M
Speech and Interpersonal Communication M
Urban and Regional Planning M*
Urban Design M
Writing M,D

BALTIMORE HEBREW UNIVERSITY
Jewish Studies M,D

BANGOR THEOLOGICAL SEMINARY
Theology P,M,D

BANK STREET COLLEGE OF EDUCATION
Child and Family Studies M
Museum Studies M

BAPTIST BIBLE COLLEGE
Cultural Studies P,M
Pastoral Ministry and Counseling P,M
Theology P,M

BAPTIST BIBLE COLLEGE OF PENNSYLVANIA
Missions and Missiology P,M,D
Pastoral Ministry and Counseling P,M,D
Religion P,M,D
Theology P,M,D

BAPTIST MISSIONARY ASSOCIATION THEOLOGICAL SEMINARY
Theology P,M

BAPTIST THEOLOGICAL SEMINARY AT RICHMOND
Music P,D
Pastoral Ministry and Counseling P,D
Theology P,D

BARD COLLEGE
Art History M,D
Art/Fine Arts M
Decorative Arts M,D
Museum Studies M
Music M
Photography M

BARD GRADUATE CENTER FOR STUDIES IN THE DECORATIVE ARTS, DESIGN, AND CULTURE
Art History M,D*
Decorative Arts M,D

BARRY UNIVERSITY
Art/Fine Arts M
Clinical Psychology M,O
Communication—General M,O
Corporate and Organizational Communication M,O
Liberal Studies M
Marriage and Family Therapy M,O
Pastoral Ministry and Counseling M,D
Photography M
Psychology—General M,O*
Public Administration M
Rehabilitation Counseling M,O
School Psychology M,O
Sport Psychology M
Theology M,D

BASTYR UNIVERSITY
Health Psychology M

BAYAMÓN CENTRAL UNIVERSITY
Criminal Justice and Criminology M
Pastoral Ministry and Counseling P,M
Psychology—General M
Theology P,M

BAYLOR UNIVERSITY
American Studies M
Clinical Psychology M,D
Communication—General M
Economics M
English M,D
History M
Interdisciplinary Studies M,D
International Affairs M,D
Journalism M
Museum Studies M
Music M
Philosophy M,D
Political Science M,D
Psychology—General M,D
Public Administration M,D
Public Policy M,D
Religion M,D
Sociology M,D
Spanish M
Theater M
Theology P,M,D

BEACON UNIVERSITY
Pastoral Ministry and Counseling P,M
Theology P,M

BELHAVEN COLLEGE (MS)
Public Administration M

BELLARMINE UNIVERSITY
Religion M

BELLEVUE UNIVERSITY
Communication—General M
Criminal Justice and Criminology M

BELMONT UNIVERSITY
English M
Music M
Writing M

BEMIDJI STATE UNIVERSITY
Counseling Psychology M
English M

BENEDICTINE UNIVERSITY
Clinical Psychology M
Emergency Management M

BENNINGTON COLLEGE
Dance M
English M
French M
Music M
Spanish M
Theater M
Writing M

BERNARD M. BARUCH COLLEGE OF THE CITY UNIVERSITY OF NEW YORK
Corporate and Organizational Communication M
Economics M
Industrial and Labor Relations M
Industrial and Organizational Psychology M,D,O
Public Administration M

BETHANY THEOLOGICAL SEMINARY
Conflict Resolution and Mediation/Peace Studies P,M,O
Pastoral Ministry and Counseling P,M,O
Religion P,M,O
Theology P,M,O

BETHANY UNIVERSITY
Clinical Psychology M

BETH BENJAMIN ACADEMY OF CONNECTICUT
Theology

BETHEL COLLEGE (IN)
Pastoral Ministry and Counseling M
Theology M

BETHEL SEMINARY
Marriage and Family Therapy P,M,D,O
Missions and Missiology P,M,D,O
Pastoral Ministry and Counseling P,M,D,O
Theology P,M,D,O

BETHEL UNIVERSITY
Communication—General M,O
Counseling Psychology M,O
Gerontology M

BETHESDA CHRISTIAN UNIVERSITY
Religion P,M
Theology P,M

BETH HAMEDRASH SHAAREI YOSHER INSTITUTE
Theology

BETH HATALMUD RABBINICAL COLLEGE
Theology

BETH MEDRASH GOVOHA
Theology

BETHUNE-COOKMAN UNIVERSITY
Theology M

BEULAH HEIGHTS UNIVERSITY
Religion M

BEXLEY HALL EPISCOPAL SEMINARY
Theology P,M

BIBLICAL THEOLOGICAL SEMINARY
Pastoral Ministry and Counseling P,M,D
Theology P,M,D

BIOLA UNIVERSITY
Cultural Studies M,D,O
Ethics P,M,D
Linguistics M,D,O

Missions and Missiology M,D,O
Psychology—General M,D
Religion P,M,D
Theology P,M,D

BIRMINGHAM-SOUTHERN COLLEGE

Music M
Public Administration M

BLESSED JOHN XXIII NATIONAL SEMINARY

Theology P

BOB JONES UNIVERSITY

Art/Fine Arts P,M,D,O
English P,M,D,O
Film, Television, and Video Production P,M,D,O
Graphic Design P,M,D,O
History P,M,D,O
Illustration P,M,D,O
Journalism P,M,D,O
Media Studies P,M,D,O
Music P,M,D,O
Pastoral Ministry and Counseling P,M,D,O
Religion P,M,D,O
Rhetoric P,M,D,O
Speech and Interpersonal Communication P,M,D,O
Theater P,M,D,O
Theology P,M,D,O

BOISE STATE UNIVERSITY

Art/Fine Arts M
Communication—General M
Criminal Justice and Criminology M
English M
History M
Interdisciplinary Studies M
Music M
Public Administration M
Public Policy M
Technical Communication M
Writing M

BORICUA COLLEGE

Latin American Studies M

BOSTON ARCHITECTURAL COLLEGE

Architecture M*
Interior Design M

BOSTON COLLEGE

Classics M
Counseling Psychology M,D
Developmental Psychology M,D
East European and Russian Studies M
Economics D
English M,D
French M,D*
History M,D
Italian M,D
Linguistics M
Pastoral Ministry and Counseling P,M,D,O
Philosophy M,D
Political Science M,D
Psychology—General M,D
Russian M
Slavic Languages M,D
Sociology M,D
Spanish M,D
Theology P,M,D,O*
Western European Studies M,D

THE BOSTON CONSERVATORY

Music M,O
Theater M

BOSTON GRADUATE SCHOOL OF PSYCHOANALYSIS

Counseling Psychology M
Psychoanalysis and Psychotherapy M,D,O
Psychology—General M*

BOSTON UNIVERSITY

African Studies M,O
African-American Studies M
American Studies D
Anthropology M,D
Archaeology M,D
Art History M,D,O
Art/Fine Arts M
Arts Administration M,O
Broadcast Journalism M
Classics M,D
Cognitive Sciences M,D
Communication—General M*
Counseling Psychology M,D*
Criminal Justice and Criminology M
Economics M,D
English M,D
Film, Television, and Video Production M
Film, Television, and Video Theory and Criticism M
Forensic Sciences M
French M,D
Geographic Information Systems M,D
Geography M,D
Graphic Design M
Historic Preservation M
History M,D
Human Development M,D,O
Interdisciplinary Studies M
International Affairs M,D,O
Journalism M
Liberal Studies M
Linguistics M,D
Mass Communication M
Media Studies M
Museum Studies M,D,O
Music M,D,O*
Philosophy M,D
Political Science M,D
Psychology—General M,D
Public Administration M,O
Religion M,D
Romance Languages M,D
Sociology M,D
Spanish M,D
Theater M,O
Theology P,M,D
Urban and Regional Planning M
Urban Studies M
Writing M,D

BOWIE STATE UNIVERSITY

Corporate and Organizational Communication M,O
Counseling Psychology M
English M
Public Administration M

BOWLING GREEN STATE UNIVERSITY

American Studies M,D
Applied Arts and Design—General M
Art History M
Art/Fine Arts M
Child and Family Studies M
Clinical Psychology M,D
Communication—General M,D
Computer Art and Design M
Counseling Psychology M
Criminal Justice and Criminology M
Demography and Population Studies M,D
Developmental Psychology M,D
Economics M
English M,D
Experimental Psychology M,D
Family and Consumer Sciences-General M
Film, Television, and Video Production M,D
French M
German M
Graphic Design M
History M,D
Human Development M
Industrial and Organizational Psychology M,D
Interdisciplinary Studies M,D
Music M,D
Philosophy M,D
Political Science M
Psychology—General M,D
Public Administration M
Rehabilitation Counseling M
Rhetoric M,D
School Psychology M,O
Social Psychology M,D
Sociology M,D
Spanish M
Speech and Interpersonal Communication M,D
Technical Communication M,D
Theater M,D
Writing M,D

BRADLEY UNIVERSITY

Applied Arts and Design—General M
Art/Fine Arts M
Comparative and Interdisciplinary Arts M
English M
Human Development M
Illustration M
Liberal Studies M
Photography M

BRANDEIS UNIVERSITY

American Studies M,D
Anthropology M,D
Art/Fine Arts O
Child and Family Studies M,D
Classics O
Cognitive Sciences M,D
Communication—General O
Conflict Resolution and Mediation/Peace Studies M
Cultural Studies M
Developmental Psychology M,D
Disability Studies M,D
Economics M,D*
English M,D
Genetic Counseling M
History M,D
International Affairs M,D
International Development M*
Jewish Studies M,D
Linguistics M
Music M,D
Near and Middle Eastern Languages M,D
Near and Middle Eastern Studies M,D
Political Science M,D
Psychology—General M,D
Public Policy M,D*
Social Psychology M,D
Sociology M,D
Sustainable Development M
Theater M
Women's Studies M

BRANDON UNIVERSITY

Music M
Rural Planning and Studies M,O

BRENAU UNIVERSITY

Psychology—General M

BRIDGEWATER STATE COLLEGE

Criminal Justice and Criminology M
English M
Psychology—General M
Public Administration M

BRIERCREST SEMINARY

Marriage and Family Therapy M
Missions and Missiology M
Pastoral Ministry and Counseling P,M
Religion P,M
Theology P,M

BRIGHAM YOUNG UNIVERSITY

Anthropology M
Art History M
Art/Fine Arts M
Child and Family Studies M,D
Clinical Psychology M,D
Communication—General M
Comparative and Interdisciplinary Arts M
Comparative Literature M
Counseling Psychology M,D,O
English M
Film, Television, and Video Production M
French M
Geography M
German M
Human Development M,D
Humanities M
Industrial Design M
Linguistics M,O
Marriage and Family Therapy M,D
Mass Communication M
Music M
Political Science M
Portuguese M
Psychology—General M,D
Public Administration M
Public Policy M
School Psychology M,D,O
Social Psychology M,D
Sociology M,D
Spanish M
Theater M

BRITISH AMERICAN COLLEGE LONDON

International Affairs M

BROCK UNIVERSITY

Child and Family Studies M
Classics M
Comparative Literature M
Cultural Studies M
Disability Studies M,O
Economics M
English M
Geography M
History M
Human Development M,D
International Affairs M
Philosophy M

- Political Science M
- Psychology—General M,D
- Public Administration M
- Social Psychology M,D

BROOKLYN COLLEGE OF THE CITY UNIVERSITY OF NEW YORK

- Art History M,D
- Art/Fine Arts M,D
- Counseling Psychology M,D,O
- Economics M
- English M,D
- Experimental Psychology M,D
- Film, Television, and Video Production M
- French M,D
- History M,D
- Industrial and Organizational Psychology M,D
- International Affairs M,D
- Internet and Interactive Multimedia M,O
- Jewish Studies M
- Liberal Studies M
- Music M,D,O
- Photography M,D
- Political Science M,D
- Psychology—General M,D
- Public Policy M,D
- School Psychology M,O
- Social Psychology M,D
- Sociology M,D
- Spanish M,D
- Speech and Interpersonal Communication M,D
- Thanatology M
- Theater M,D
- Urban Studies M,D
- Writing M

BROOKS INSTITUTE

- Photography M

BROWN UNIVERSITY

- American Studies M,D
- Anthropology M,D
- Archaeology M,D
- Art History M,D
- Classics M,D
- Cognitive Sciences M,D
- Comparative Literature M,D
- Demography and Population Studies D
- Economics M,D
- English M,D
- French M,D
- German M,D
- Hispanic Studies M,D
- History of Science and Technology M,D
- History M,D
- Italian M,D
- Jewish Studies M,D
- Latin American Studies M,D
- Linguistics M,D
- Music M,D
- Philosophy M,D
- Political Science M,D
- Psychology—General M,D
- Public Policy M
- Religion M,D
- Russian M,D
- Slavic Languages M,D
- Sociology M,D
- Theater M
- Western European Studies M,D
- Writing M

BRYN ATHYN COLLEGE OF THE NEW CHURCH

- Religion P,M
- Theology P,M

BRYN MAWR COLLEGE

- Archaeology M,D*
- Art History M,D*
- Classics M,D*
- Clinical Psychology D
- Developmental Psychology D
- French M,D
- Psychology—General D
- Russian M,D

BUCKNELL UNIVERSITY

- English M
- Psychology—General M
- School Psychology M

BUFFALO STATE COLLEGE, STATE UNIVERSITY OF NEW YORK

- Applied Economics M
- Criminal Justice and Criminology M
- Economics M
- English M
- Historic Preservation M,O
- History M
- Interdisciplinary Studies M

BUTLER UNIVERSITY

- English M
- History M
- Music M

CALDWELL COLLEGE

- Art Therapy M
- Counseling Psychology M
- Pastoral Ministry and Counseling M
- Psychology—General M

CALIFORNIA BAPTIST UNIVERSITY

- Counseling Psychology M
- English M
- Forensic Psychology M
- Marriage and Family Therapy M
- Music M
- Pastoral Ministry and Counseling M
- Public Administration M

CALIFORNIA COAST UNIVERSITY

- Psychology—General M

CALIFORNIA COLLEGE OF THE ARTS

- Applied Arts and Design—General M
- Architecture M
- Art/Fine Arts M*
- Film, Television, and Video Production M
- Film, Television, and Video Theory and Criticism M
- Museum Studies M
- Photography M
- Textile Design M
- Writing M

CALIFORNIA INSTITUTE OF INTEGRAL STUDIES

- Anthropology M,D
- Art Therapy M,D
- Asian Studies M,D
- Clinical Psychology M,D
- Counseling Psychology M,D
- Health Psychology M,D
- Humanities M,D*
- Philosophy M,D
- Psychology—General M,D*
- Religion M,D
- Social Psychology M,D
- Theology M,D
- Therapies—Dance, Drama, and Music M,D
- Women's Studies M,D

CALIFORNIA INSTITUTE OF TECHNOLOGY

- Economics M,D
- Political Science M,D
- Social Sciences M,D

CALIFORNIA INSTITUTE OF THE ARTS

- Applied Arts and Design—General M,O
- Art/Fine Arts M,O
- Dance M,O
- Film, Television, and Video Production M,O
- Graphic Design M,O
- Music M,O
- Photography M,O
- Theater M,O
- Writing M,O

CALIFORNIA LUTHERAN UNIVERSITY

- Clinical Psychology M
- Marriage and Family Therapy M
- Psychology—General M
- Public Administration M
- Public Policy M

CALIFORNIA POLYTECHNIC STATE UNIVERSITY, SAN LUIS OBISPO

- Agricultural Economics and Agribusiness M
- Architecture M
- English M
- History M
- Political Science M
- Psychology—General M
- Urban and Regional Planning M

CALIFORNIA STATE POLYTECHNIC UNIVERSITY, POMONA

- Architecture M
- Economics M
- English M
- History M
- Landscape Architecture M
- Psychology—General M
- Public Administration M
- Urban and Regional Planning M

CALIFORNIA STATE UNIVERSITY, BAKERSFIELD

- Anthropology M
- Counseling Psychology M
- English M
- History M
- Interdisciplinary Studies M
- Psychology—General M
- Public Administration M
- Sociology M
- Spanish M

CALIFORNIA STATE UNIVERSITY, CHICO

- Anthropology M
- Art History M
- Art/Fine Arts M
- Communication—General M
- English M
- Geography M
- History M
- Interdisciplinary Studies M
- Marriage and Family Therapy M
- Museum Studies M
- Music M
- Political Science M
- Psychology—General M
- Public Administration M
- Rural Planning and Studies M
- Social Sciences M
- Urban and Regional Planning M

CALIFORNIA STATE UNIVERSITY, DOMINGUEZ HILLS

- Applied Social Research M,O
- Clinical Psychology M
- Conflict Resolution and Mediation/Peace Studies M
- English M,O
- Humanities M
- Marriage and Family Therapy M
- Psychology—General M
- Public Administration M
- Rhetoric M,O
- Sociology M,O

CALIFORNIA STATE UNIVERSITY, EAST BAY

- Anthropology M
- Communication—General M
- Economics M
- English M
- Geography M
- History M
- Interdisciplinary Studies M,O
- Internet and Interactive Multimedia M
- Music M
- Public Administration M
- Sociology M

CALIFORNIA STATE UNIVERSITY, FRESNO

- Applied Arts and Design—General M
- Art/Fine Arts M
- Communication—General M
- Criminal Justice and Criminology M
- English M
- Family and Consumer Sciences-General M
- History M
- International Affairs M
- Journalism M
- Linguistics M
- Marriage and Family Therapy M
- Mass Communication M
- Music M
- Psychology—General M
- Public Administration M
- Rehabilitation Counseling M
- Spanish M
- Sport Psychology M
- Writing M

CALIFORNIA STATE UNIVERSITY, FULLERTON

- American Studies M
- Anthropology M
- Applied Arts and Design—General M
- Art History M
- Art/Fine Arts M
- Clinical Psychology M
- Communication—General M
- Comparative Literature M
- Dance M
- Economics M
- English M
- Film, Television, and Video Production M
- French M

Geography M
German M
Gerontology M
History M
Journalism M
Linguistics M
Media Studies M
Music M
Photography M
Political Science M
Psychology—General M
Public Administration M
Social Psychology M
Sociology M
Spanish M
Speech and Interpersonal Communication M
Theater M

CALIFORNIA STATE UNIVERSITY, LONG BEACH

Anthropology M
Art/Fine Arts M
Asian Studies M,O
Asian-American Studies M,O
Communication—General M
Consumer Economics M
Criminal Justice and Criminology M
Dance M
Economics M
Emergency Management M
English M
Family and Consumer Sciences-General M
French M
Geography M
German M
Gerontology M
History M
Interdisciplinary Studies M
Linguistics M
Music M
Philosophy M
Political Science M
Psychology—General M
Public Administration M
Public Policy M
Religion M
Spanish M
Theater M
Writing M

CALIFORNIA STATE UNIVERSITY, LOS ANGELES

Anthropology M
Applied Arts and Design—General M
Art History M
Art Therapy M
Art/Fine Arts M
Child Development M
Communication—General M
Criminal Justice and Criminology M
Economics M
English M
French M
Geography M
Graphic Design M
Hispanic Studies M
History M
Latin American Studies M
Music M
Philosophy M
Photography M
Political Science M
Psychology—General M
Public Administration M
Rehabilitation Counseling M
School Psychology M
Sociology M
Spanish M
Speech and Interpersonal Communication M

Textile Design M
Theater M

CALIFORNIA STATE UNIVERSITY, MONTEREY BAY

Public Policy M

CALIFORNIA STATE UNIVERSITY, NORTHRIDGE

Anthropology M
Archaeology M
Art History M
Art/Fine Arts M
Clinical Psychology M
Communication—General M
Comparative Literature M
English M
Experimental Psychology M
Family and Consumer Sciences-General M
Film, Television, and Video Production M
Geography M
Hispanic Studies M
History M
Interdisciplinary Studies M
Journalism M
Linguistics M
Marriage and Family Therapy M
Mass Communication M
Music M
Political Science M
Psychology—General M
Public Administration M
Rhetoric M
School Psychology M
Sociology M
Spanish M
Speech and Interpersonal Communication M
Theater M
Writing M

CALIFORNIA STATE UNIVERSITY, SACRAMENTO

Anthropology M
Art/Fine Arts M
Communication—General M
Counseling Psychology M
Criminal Justice and Criminology M
Dance M
English M
French M
German M
International Affairs M
Liberal Studies M
Music M
Political Science M
Psychology—General M
Public Administration M
Public History M
Public Policy M
School Psychology M
Sociology M
Spanish M
Theater M
Writing M

CALIFORNIA STATE UNIVERSITY, SAN BERNARDINO

Art/Fine Arts M
Child Development M
Clinical Psychology M
Communication—General M
Counseling Psychology M
Criminal Justice and Criminology M
English M
Experimental Psychology M
Human Development M

Industrial and Organizational Psychology M
Interdisciplinary Studies M
National Security M
Psychology—General M
Public Administration M
Rehabilitation Counseling M
Social Sciences M
Spanish M
Theater M

CALIFORNIA STATE UNIVERSITY, SAN MARCOS

English M
Psychology—General M
Sociology M
Spanish M
Writing M

CALIFORNIA STATE UNIVERSITY, STANISLAUS

Art/Fine Arts O
Child Development M,O
Criminal Justice and Criminology M
English M,O
Genetic Counseling M
Gerontology O
History M
Interdisciplinary Studies M
International Affairs M
Psychology—General M,O
Public Administration M
Rhetoric M,O
Sustainable Development M
Writing M,O

CALIFORNIA UNIVERSITY OF PENNSYLVANIA

Criminal Justice and Criminology M
School Psychology M
Social Sciences M
Sport Psychology M

CALVARY BIBLE COLLEGE AND THEOLOGICAL SEMINARY

Pastoral Ministry and Counseling P,M
Theology P,M

CALVIN THEOLOGICAL SEMINARY

Missions and Missiology P,M,D
Theology P,M,D

CAMBRIDGE COLLEGE

Counseling Psychology M,O

CAMERON UNIVERSITY

Psychology—General M

CAMPBELLSVILLE UNIVERSITY

Music M
Social Sciences M
Theology M

CAMPBELL UNIVERSITY

Interdisciplinary Studies M
Theology P,M,D

CANADIAN SOUTHERN BAPTIST SEMINARY

Theology P,M

CANISIUS COLLEGE

Corporate and Organizational Communication M
School Psychology M
Social Psychology M

CAPELLA UNIVERSITY

Addictions/Substance Abuse Counseling M,D,O
Child and Family Studies M,D,O
Clinical Psychology M,D,O
Counseling Psychology M,D,O
Criminal Justice and Criminology M,D,O
Industrial and Organizational Psychology M,D,O
Marriage and Family Therapy M,D,O
Psychology—General M,D,O
School Psychology M,D,O
Sport Psychology M,D,O

CAPITAL BIBLE SEMINARY

Pastoral Ministry and Counseling P,M,O
Theology P,M,O

CAPITAL UNIVERSITY

Music M

CARDINAL STRITCH UNIVERSITY

Applied Arts and Design—General M
Clinical Psychology M
Graphic Design M
History M
Liberal Studies M
Music M
Pastoral Ministry and Counseling M
Psychology—General M
Religion M

CAREY THEOLOGICAL COLLEGE

Theology M,D

CARIBBEAN UNIVERSITY

Art History M,D
Criminal Justice and Criminology M,D
Museum Studies M,D

CARLETON UNIVERSITY

Anthropology M
Architecture M
Art History M
Canadian Studies M,D
Cognitive Sciences D
Communication—General M,D
Comparative Literature D
Conflict Resolution and Mediation/Peace Studies M,O
East European and Russian Studies M,O
Economics M,D
English M,D
Film, Television, and Video Production M
French M
Geography M,D
History M,D
Industrial Design M
International Affairs M,D
Journalism M,D
Linguistics M
Music M
Philosophy M
Political Science M,D
Psychology—General M,D

Public Administration M,D
Public Policy M,D
Sociology M,D
Western European Studies M,O

CARLOS ALBIZU UNIVERSITY

Clinical Psychology M,D
Industrial and Organizational Psychology M,D
Psychology—General M,D

CARLOS ALBIZU UNIVERSITY, MIAMI CAMPUS

Clinical Psychology M,D
Counseling Psychology M,D
Industrial and Organizational Psychology M,D
Marriage and Family Therapy M,D
Psychology—General M,D
School Psychology M,D

CARLOW UNIVERSITY

Counseling Psychology M
Humanities M
Writing M

CARNEGIE MELLON UNIVERSITY

Applied Arts and Design—General D*
Architecture M,D
Art/Fine Arts M
Arts Administration M*
Building Science M,D
Cognitive Sciences D
Communication—General M,D
Comparative Literature M,D
Computer Art and Design M,D
Criminal Justice and Criminology M
Developmental Psychology D
Economics M,D
English M,D
Film, Television, and Video Production M
History M,D
Linguistics M,D
Media Studies M
Music M
Philosophy M,D
Psychology—General D
Public Administration M*
Public Policy M,D*
Rhetoric M
Social Psychology D
Social Sciences D
Sustainable Development M
Technical Writing M
Theater M
Urban Design M,D
Writing M*

CASE WESTERN RESERVE UNIVERSITY

Anthropology M,D
Art History M,D
Clinical Psychology D
Cognitive Sciences M
Comparative Literature M,D
Dance M
Economics M
English M,D
Experimental Psychology D
French M
Genetic Counseling M
Gerontology M,D,O
History M,D
Industrial and Labor Relations M
Linguistics M
Museum Studies M,D

Music M,D
Political Science M,D
Psychology—General D
Sociology D
Theater M

CASTLETON STATE COLLEGE

Forensic Psychology M
Psychology—General M

THE CATHOLIC DISTANCE UNIVERSITY

Theology M

CATHOLIC THEOLOGICAL UNION AT CHICAGO

Missions and Missiology P,M,D,O
Pastoral Ministry and Counseling P,M,D,O
Theology P,M,D,O

THE CATHOLIC UNIVERSITY OF AMERICA

Anthropology M,D
Architecture M
Classics M,D
Clinical Psychology D
Comparative Literature M,D
Economics M
English M,D
Experimental Psychology M,D
French M,D
History M,D
Human Development D
International Affairs M,D
Italian M,D
Medieval and Renaissance Studies M,D,O
Music M,D
Near and Middle Eastern Languages M,D
Philosophy M,D,O
Political Science M,D
Psychology—General M,D
Religion P,M,D,O
Rhetoric M,D
Romance Languages M,D
Sociology M,D
Spanish M,D
Theater M
Theology P,M,D,O
Urban and Regional Planning M
Western European Studies M

CEDAR CREST COLLEGE

Forensic Sciences M

CENTENARY COLLEGE

Counseling Psychology M

CENTRAL BAPTIST THEOLOGICAL SEMINARY

Missions and Missiology P,M,O
Theology P,M,O

CENTRAL BAPTIST THEOLOGICAL SEMINARY OF VIRGINIA BEACH

Theology P,M

CENTRAL CONNECTICUT STATE UNIVERSITY

Communication—General M
Corporate and Organizational Communication M
Criminal Justice and Criminology M
English M,O
French M,O

Geography M
Health Psychology M
History M,O
International Affairs M
Italian M,O
Marriage and Family Therapy M,O
Psychology—General M
Rehabilitation Counseling M,O
School Psychology M,O
Social Psychology M
Spanish M,O

CENTRAL EUROPEAN UNIVERSITY

Anthropology M,D
Economics M,D
Gender Studies M,D
History M,D
Humanities M,D*
International Affairs M,D
Medieval and Renaissance Studies M,D
Philosophy M,D
Political Science M,D
Public Policy M,D
Social Sciences M,D
Sociology M,D

CENTRAL MICHIGAN UNIVERSITY

Art/Fine Arts M
Child and Family Studies M
Clinical Psychology D
Communication—General M
Corporate and Organizational Communication M
Criminal Justice and Criminology M
Economics M
English M*
Experimental Psychology M,D
Family and Consumer Sciences-General M
Film, Television, and Video Production M
History M,D*
Human Development M
Humanities M*
Industrial and Organizational Psychology M,D
International Affairs M,O
Mass Communication M
Media Studies M
Music M
Political Science M
Psychology—General M,D,O
Public Administration M,O
School Psychology D,O
Sociology M
Spanish M
Speech and Interpersonal Communication M
Theater M
Writing M

CENTRAL WASHINGTON UNIVERSITY

Art/Fine Arts M
Child and Family Studies M
Counseling Psychology M
English M
Experimental Psychology M
Family and Consumer Sciences-General M
History M
Interdisciplinary Studies M
Music M
Psychology—General M
School Psychology M
Theater M

CENTRAL YESHIVA TOMCHEI TMIMIM-LUBAVITCH

Theology M

CENTRO DE ESTUDIOS AVANZADOS DE PUERTO RICO Y EL CARIBE

History M,D
Latin American Studies M,D

CHAMINADE UNIVERSITY OF HONOLULU

Conflict Resolution and Mediation/Peace Studies M
Counseling Psychology M
Criminal Justice and Criminology M,O
Forensic Sciences M
Homeland Security M,O
Pastoral Ministry and Counseling M
Theology M

CHAPMAN UNIVERSITY

Cultural Studies D
Disability Studies D
English M
Film, Television, and Video Production M
Marriage and Family Therapy M
School Psychology M,D,O
Writing M

CHARLESTON SOUTHERN UNIVERSITY

Criminal Justice and Criminology M

CHATHAM UNIVERSITY

Computer Art and Design M
Counseling Psychology M
Film, Television, and Video Production M
Interior Design M
Landscape Architecture M
Writing M

CHESTNUT HILL COLLEGE

Clinical Psychology M,D,O
Counseling Psychology M,O
Gerontology M,O
Psychology—General M,D,O
Religion M,O

CHEYNEY UNIVERSITY OF PENNSYLVANIA

Public Administration M
Spanish O

THE CHICAGO SCHOOL OF PROFESSIONAL PSYCHOLOGY

Clinical Psychology M,D,O*
Counseling Psychology M,D,O
Forensic Psychology M*
Industrial and Organizational Psychology M,D*
Psychology—General M,D,O
School Psychology O*

CHICAGO STATE UNIVERSITY

Criminal Justice and Criminology M
English M
Geography M
History M
Writing M

CHICAGO THEOLOGICAL SEMINARY

Jewish Studies P,M,D
Pastoral Ministry and Counseling P,M,D

Religion P,M,D
Theology P,M,D

CHRISTENDOM COLLEGE

Theology M

CHRISTIAN BROTHERS UNIVERSITY

Religion M

CHRISTIAN THEOLOGICAL SEMINARY

Marriage and Family Therapy P,M,D
Pastoral Ministry and Counseling P,M,D
Religion P,M,D
Theology P,M,D

CHRISTIE'S EDUCATION

Art History M
Museum Studies M

CHRISTOPHER NEWPORT UNIVERSITY

History M
Theater M

CHRIST THE KING SEMINARY

Pastoral Ministry and Counseling P,M,O
Theology P,M,O

CHURCH DIVINITY SCHOOL OF THE PACIFIC

Theology P,M,D,O

CHURCH OF GOD THEOLOGICAL SEMINARY

Missions and Missiology P,M
Pastoral Ministry and Counseling P,M
Theology P,M

CINCINNATI CHRISTIAN UNIVERSITY

Pastoral Ministry and Counseling M
Religion P,M
Theology P,M

THE CITADEL, THE MILITARY COLLEGE OF SOUTH CAROLINA

English M
History M
Psychology—General M
School Psychology M,O
Social Sciences M

CITY COLLEGE OF THE CITY UNIVERSITY OF NEW YORK

Architecture M
Art History M
Art/Fine Arts M
Clinical Psychology M,D
Counseling Psychology M
Economics M
English M
Experimental Psychology M,D
Graphic Design M
History M
International Affairs M
Landscape Architecture M,O
Media Studies M
Museum Studies M
Music M
Psychology—General M,D
Sociology M
Spanish M
Urban Design M
Writing M

CITY UNIVERSITY OF SEATTLE

Counseling Psychology M
School Psychology M,O

CLAREMONT GRADUATE UNIVERSITY

African Studies M,D,O
American Studies M,D,O
Art/Fine Arts M
Arts Administration M
Cognitive Sciences M,D,O
Comparative Literature M,D
Computer Art and Design M
Cultural Studies M,D,O
Developmental Psychology M,D,O
Economics M,D,O
English M,D
Ethics M,D
Film, Television, and Video Theory and Criticism M,D
Health Psychology M,D,O
History M,D,O
Human Development M,D,O
Humanities M,D,O
Industrial and Organizational Psychology M,D,O
International Affairs M,D
Media Studies M,D,O
Museum Studies M,D,O
Music M,D
Philosophy M,D
Photography M
Political Science M,D
Psychology—General M,D,O
Public Policy M,D,O
Religion M,D
Social Psychology M,D,O
Theology M,D
Western European Studies M,D,O
Women's Studies M,D
Writing M,D

CLAREMONT SCHOOL OF THEOLOGY

Pastoral Ministry and Counseling D
Religion M,D
Theology P,M,D

CLARION UNIVERSITY OF PENNSYLVANIA

Communication—General M
English M

CLARK ATLANTA UNIVERSITY

African-American Studies M,D
Criminal Justice and Criminology M
Economics M
English M,D
History M,D
Political Science M,D
Public Administration M
Romance Languages M,D
Sociology M
Women's Studies M,D

CLARK UNIVERSITY

Clinical Psychology D
Communication—General M
Developmental Psychology D
Economics D
English M
Geographic Information Systems M
Geography M,D
History M,D,O
Holocaust Studies D
International Development M
Liberal Studies M
Psychology—General D
Public Administration M,O
Social Psychology D
Sustainable Development M
Urban and Regional Planning M

CLAYTON STATE UNIVERSITY

Liberal Studies M

CLEMSON UNIVERSITY

Applied Economics M,D
Architecture M
Art/Fine Arts M
Child and Family Studies D
Communication—General M,D
Computer Art and Design M
Economics M
English M
Environmental Design D
Family and Consumer Sciences-General D
Historic Preservation M
History M
Human Development M
Industrial and Organizational Psychology D
Interdisciplinary Studies D,O
Landscape Architecture M
Psychology—General M,D
Public Administration M
Public Policy D,O
Rhetoric D
Sociology M
Urban and Regional Planning M
Writing M

CLEVELAND INSTITUTE OF MUSIC

Music M,D,O

CLEVELAND STATE UNIVERSITY

Art History M
Art/Fine Arts M
Clinical Psychology M,O
Communication—General M,O
Counseling Psychology D
Economics M,D,O
English M
Experimental Psychology M,O
Geographic Information Systems M,D,O
Health Communication M,O
History M
Industrial and Labor Relations M
Industrial and Organizational Psychology M,O
Museum Studies M
Music M
Philosophy M,O
Psychology—General M,O
Public Administration M,O
School Psychology M,O
Sociology M
Spanish M
Sport Psychology M
Urban and Regional Planning M,O
Urban Design M,O
Urban Studies M,D,O
Writing M

COLGATE ROCHESTER CROZER DIVINITY SCHOOL

Theology P,M,D,O

THE COLLEGE AT BROCKPORT, STATE UNIVERSITY OF NEW YORK

Art/Fine Arts M
Communication—General M
Counseling Psychology M,O
Dance M
English M
History M
Liberal Studies M
Psychology—General M
Public Administration M

COLLÈGE DOMINICAIN DE PHILOSOPHIE ET DE THÉOLOGIE

Pastoral Ministry and Counseling M
Philosophy M,D
Theology M,D,O

COLLEGE OF CHARLESTON

Arts Administration M,O
Communication—General M
Corporate and Organizational Communication O
English M
Historic Preservation M
History M
Public Administration M
Translation and Interpretation O

COLLEGE OF EMMANUEL AND ST. CHAD

Theology P,M

COLLEGE OF MOUNT ST. JOSEPH

Pastoral Ministry and Counseling M
Theology M

THE COLLEGE OF NEW JERSEY

Addictions/Substance Abuse Counseling M,O
English M
Marriage and Family Therapy O
Spanish M

THE COLLEGE OF NEW ROCHELLE

Art Therapy M
Art/Fine Arts M
Communication—General M,O
Counseling Psychology M,O
Gerontology M,O
Graphic Design M
School Psychology M
Social Psychology M

COLLEGE OF NOTRE DAME OF MARYLAND

Communication—General. M
Liberal Studies M

COLLEGE OF ST. CATHERINE

Theology M

COLLEGE OF SAINT ELIZABETH

Counseling Psychology M,O
Forensic Psychology M,O
Psychology—General M,O
Theology M

COLLEGE OF ST. JOSEPH

Program	Degrees
Addictions/Substance Abuse Counseling	M
Clinical Psychology	M
Counseling Psychology	M
Psychology—General	M
School Psychology	M
Social Psychology	M

THE COLLEGE OF SAINT ROSE

Program	Degrees
English	M
History	M
Mass Communication	M
Music	M
Political Science	M
School Psychology	M,O

COLLEGE OF STATEN ISLAND OF THE CITY UNIVERSITY OF NEW YORK

Program	Degrees
English	M
Film, Television, and Video Theory and Criticism	M
History	M
Liberal Studies	M
Media Studies	M

COLLEGE OF THE HUMANITIES AND SCIENCES, HARRISON MIDDLETON UNIVERSITY

Program	Degrees
Comparative Literature	M,D
Humanities	M,D
Philosophy	M,D
Religion	M,D
Social Sciences	M,D

THE COLLEGE OF WILLIAM AND MARY

Program	Degrees
Addictions/Substance Abuse Counseling	M,D
American Studies	M,D
Anthropology	M,D
Clinical Psychology	D
Experimental Psychology	M
History	M,D
Marriage and Family Therapy	M,D
Psychology—General	M,D
Public Policy	M
School Psychology	M,O

COLLÈGE UNIVERSITAIRE DE SAINT-BONIFACE

Program	Degrees
Canadian Studies	M

COLORADO CHRISTIAN UNIVERSITY

Program	Degrees
Counseling Psychology	M

COLORADO SCHOOL OF MINES

Program	Degrees
International Affairs	M,O
Mineral Economics	M,D

COLORADO STATE UNIVERSITY

Program	Degrees
Agricultural Economics and Agribusiness	M,D
Anthropology	M
Art/Fine Arts	M
Child and Family Studies	M
Consumer Economics	M
Economics	M,D
History	M
Human Development	M
Music	M
Philosophy	M
Political Science	M,D
Psychology—General	M,D
Sociology	M,D
Speech and Interpersonal Communication	M
Technical Communication	M
Technical Writing	M
Writing	M

COLORADO TECHNICAL UNIVERSITY COLORADO SPRINGS

Program	Degrees
Criminal Justice and Criminology	M

COLORADO TECHNICAL UNIVERSITY DENVER

Program	Degrees
Criminal Justice and Criminology	M

COLORADO TECHNICAL UNIVERSITY SIOUX FALLS

Program	Degrees
Criminal Justice and Criminology	M

COLUMBIA COLLEGE (MO)

Program	Degrees
Criminal Justice and Criminology	M

COLUMBIA COLLEGE (SC)

Program	Degrees
Conflict Resolution and Mediation/Peace Studies	M,O

COLUMBIA COLLEGE CHICAGO

Program	Degrees
Architecture	M
Arts Administration	M
Comparative and Interdisciplinary Arts	M
Film, Television, and Video Production	M
Interior Design	M
Journalism	M
Media Studies	M
Photography	M
Therapies—Dance, Drama, and Music	M,O
Writing	M

COLUMBIA INTERNATIONAL UNIVERSITY

Program	Degrees
Cultural Studies	P,M,D,O
Missions and Missiology	P,M,D,O
Pastoral Ministry and Counseling	P,M,D,O
Theology	P,M,D,O

COLUMBIA SOUTHERN UNIVERSITY

Program	Degrees
Criminal Justice and Criminology	M

COLUMBIA THEOLOGICAL SEMINARY

Program	Degrees
Theology	P,M,D

COLUMBIA UNIVERSITY

Program	Degrees
African Studies	O
African-American Studies	M
American Studies	M
Anthropology	M,D
Archaeology	M,D
Architecture	M,D
Art History	M,D
Art/Fine Arts	M
Asian Languages	M,D
Asian Studies	M,D,O
Classics	M,D
Communication—General	M,D
Comparative Literature	M,D
Conflict Resolution and Mediation/Peace Studies	M
Corporate and Organizational Communication	M
East European and Russian Studies	M,O
Economics	M,D
English	M,D
Environmental Design	M
Experimental Psychology	M,D
Film, Television, and Video Production	M
French	M,D
German	M,D
Historic Preservation	M
History	M,D
Interdisciplinary Studies	M
International Affairs	M*
Italian	M,D
Jewish Studies	M,D
Journalism	M,D*
Landscape Architecture	M
Latin American Studies	O
Liberal Studies	M
Medieval and Renaissance Studies	M
Music	M,D
Near and Middle Eastern Languages	M,D
Near and Middle Eastern Studies	M,D,O
Philosophy	M,D
Photography	M
Political Science	M,D
Psychology—General	M,D
Public Administration	M
Public Policy	M
Religion	M,D
Romance Languages	M,D
Russian	M,D
Slavic Languages	M,D
Social Psychology	M,D
Social Sciences	M
Sociology	M,D
Spanish	M,D
Sustainable Development	M,D
Theater	M,D*
Urban and Regional Planning	M,D
Urban Design	M
Western European Studies	M,O
Writing	M

COLUMBUS STATE UNIVERSITY

Program	Degrees
Counseling Psychology	M,O
Criminal Justice and Criminology	M
Public Administration	M

CONCORDIA LUTHERAN SEMINARY

Program	Degrees
Theology	P,M

CONCORDIA SEMINARY

Program	Degrees
Theology	P,M,D,O

CONCORDIA THEOLOGICAL SEMINARY

Program	Degrees
Theology	P,M,D

CONCORDIA UNIVERSITY (CA)

Program	Degrees
International Affairs	M
Theology	M

CONCORDIA UNIVERSITY (CANADA)

Program	Degrees
Anthropology	M
Applied Arts and Design—General	O
Art History	M,D
Art Therapy	M
Art/Fine Arts	M
Child and Family Studies	M
Clinical Psychology	M,D,O
Communication—General	M,D,O
Computer Art and Design	O
Economics	M,D,O
English	M
Film, Television, and Video Production	M
Film, Television, and Video Theory and Criticism	M
French	M,O
Geography	M,D,O
History	M,D
Humanities	D
Internet and Interactive Multimedia	M,O
Jewish Studies	M
Journalism	O
Linguistics	M,O
Media Studies	M,D,O
Music	O
Philosophy	M
Political Science	M,D
Psychology—General	M,D
Public Administration	M,D
Public Affairs	O
Public Policy	M,D
Religion	M,D
Rural Planning and Studies	M,D,O
Sociology	M
Theology	M
Translation and Interpretation	M,O
Urban and Regional Planning	O
Urban Studies	M,O
Writing	M

CONCORDIA UNIVERSITY CHICAGO

Program	Degrees
Counseling Psychology	M
Gerontology	M
Liberal Studies	M
Music	M
Psychology—General	M
Religion	M

CONCORDIA UNIVERSITY, NEBRASKA

Program	Degrees
Pastoral Ministry and Counseling	M

CONCORDIA UNIVERSITY, ST. PAUL

Program	Degrees
Child and Family Studies	M,O
Criminal Justice and Criminology	M
Pastoral Ministry and Counseling	M,O
Theology	M,O

CONCORDIA UNIVERSITY WISCONSIN

Program	Degrees
Child and Family Studies	M
Corporate and Organizational Communication	M
Counseling Psychology	M
Music	M
Psychology—General	M
Public Administration	M

CONNECTICUT COLLEGE

Program	Degrees
Psychology—General	M

CONSERVATORIO DE MUSICA

Program	Degrees
Music	O

CONVERSE COLLEGE

Program	Degrees
English	M
History	M
Liberal Studies	M
Marriage and Family Therapy	O
Music	M
Political Science	M

CONWAY SCHOOL OF LANDSCAPE DESIGN
Landscape Architecture M

COPPIN STATE UNIVERSITY
Addictions/Substance Abuse Counseling M
Criminal Justice and Criminology M
Rehabilitation Counseling M

CORCORAN COLLEGE OF ART AND DESIGN
Decorative Arts M
Interior Design M

CORNELL UNIVERSITY
African Studies M,D
African-American Studies M,D
Agricultural Economics and Agribusiness M,D
American Studies M,D
Anthropology D
Applied Economics D
Archaeology M,D
Architectural History M,D
Architecture M,D
Art History D
Art/Fine Arts M
Asian Languages M,D
Asian Studies M,D
Building Science M,D
Child and Family Studies D
Chinese M,D
Classics D
Clothing and Textiles M,D
Cognitive Sciences D
Communication—General M,D
Comparative Literature D
Computer Art and Design M,D
Conflict Resolution and Mediation/Peace Studies M,D
Consumer Economics M,D
Cultural Studies M,D
Demography and Population Studies M,D
Developmental Psychology D
East European and Russian Studies M,D
Economics M,D
English M,D
Environmental Design M
Ethnic Studies M,D
Experimental Psychology D
Family and Consumer Sciences-General M,D
French D
Gender Studies M,D
German M,D
Historic Preservation M,D
History of Science and Technology M,D
History M,D
Human Development D
Industrial and Labor Relations M,D*
Interior Design M
International Affairs D
International Development M
Italian D
Japanese M,D
Jewish Studies M,D
Landscape Architecture M
Latin American Studies M,D
Linguistics M,D
Medieval and Renaissance Studies M,D
Music M,D
Near and Middle Eastern Studies M,D
Philosophy D
Photography M
Political Science D
Psychology—General D
Public Affairs M*
Public Policy M,D
Religion D
Romance Languages M,D
Rural Planning and Studies M
Rural Sociology M,D
Scandinavian Languages M,D
Slavic Languages M,D
Social Psychology M,D
Sociology M,D
Spanish D
Textile Design M,D
Theater D
Urban and Regional Planning M,D
Urban Design M,D
Western European Studies M,D
Women's Studies M,D
Writing M,D

COVENANT THEOLOGICAL SEMINARY
Theology P,M,D,O

CRANBROOK ACADEMY OF ART
Applied Arts and Design—General M
Architecture M
Art/Fine Arts M*
Graphic Design M
Photography M
Textile Design M

CREIGHTON UNIVERSITY
Conflict Resolution and Mediation/Peace Studies M,O
English M
International Affairs M
Liberal Studies M
Theology M

THE CRISWELL COLLEGE
Pastoral Ministry and Counseling P,M
Theology P,M

CROWN COLLEGE
Theology M

CUMBERLAND UNIVERSITY
Public Administration M

CUNY GRADUATE SCHOOL OF JOURNALISM
Journalism M*

CURRY COLLEGE
Criminal Justice and Criminology M

THE CURTIS INSTITUTE OF MUSIC
Music M

DALHOUSIE UNIVERSITY
Anthropology M,D
Architecture M
Classics M,D
Clinical Psychology M,D
Economics M,D
English M,D
French M,D
German M
History M,D
Interdisciplinary Studies D
International Development M
Philosophy M,D
Political Science M,D
Psychology—General M,D
Public Administration M
Rural Planning and Studies M
Sociology M,D
Urban and Regional Planning M

DALLAS BAPTIST UNIVERSITY
Conflict Resolution and Mediation/Peace Studies M
Corporate and Organizational Communication M
Counseling Psychology M
Criminal Justice and Criminology M
Experimental Psychology M
Interdisciplinary Studies M
Liberal Studies M
Missions and Missiology M
Pastoral Ministry and Counseling M

DALLAS THEOLOGICAL SEMINARY
Media Studies M,D,O
Missions and Missiology M,D,O
Pastoral Ministry and Counseling M,D,O
Theology M,D,O

DARKEI NOAM RABBINICAL COLLEGE
Theology

DARTMOUTH COLLEGE
Cognitive Sciences D
Comparative Literature M
Liberal Studies M*
Music M
Psychology—General D

DELAWARE STATE UNIVERSITY
Historic Preservation M

DELAWARE VALLEY COLLEGE
Agricultural Economics and Agribusiness M

DELL'ARTE SCHOOL OF PHYSICAL THEATRE
Theater M

DELTA STATE UNIVERSITY
Criminal Justice and Criminology M
Urban and Regional Planning M

DENVER SEMINARY
Marriage and Family Therapy P,M,D,O
Pastoral Ministry and Counseling P,M,D,O
Religion P,M,D,O
Theology P,M,D,O

DEPAUL UNIVERSITY
Clinical Psychology M,D
Communication—General M
Computer Art and Design M,D
Corporate and Organizational Communication M
Economics M
English M
Experimental Psychology M,D
History M
Human Development M,D
Industrial and Organizational Psychology M,D
Interdisciplinary Studies M
Journalism M
Liberal Studies M
Media Studies M
Music M,O
Philosophy M,D
Psychology—General M,D
Public Administration M,O
Public Affairs M,O
Social Psychology M,D
Sociology M
Theater M,O
Urban and Regional Planning M,O
Writing M

DESALES UNIVERSITY
Criminal Justice and Criminology M

DEVRY UNIVERSITY
Communication—General M
Public Administration M

DIGITAL MEDIA ARTS COLLEGE
Computer Art and Design M
Graphic Design M
Media Studies M

DOMINICAN HOUSE OF STUDIES, PONTIFICAL FACULTY OF THE IMMACULATE CONCEPTION
Theology P,M,O

DOMINICAN SCHOOL OF PHILOSOPHY AND THEOLOGY
Philosophy M
Theology P,O

DOMINICAN UNIVERSITY OF CALIFORNIA
Counseling Psychology M
Gerontology M
Humanities M
Sustainable Development M

DOWLING COLLEGE
Human Development M,D,O
Liberal Studies M

DRAKE UNIVERSITY
American Studies M
Art/Fine Arts M
Communication—General M
History M
Journalism M
Public Administration M
Rehabilitation Counseling M
Sociology M
Speech and Interpersonal Communication M
Theater M

DREW UNIVERSITY
English M,D
Ethics M,D
History M,D
Holocaust Studies M,D,O
Humanities M,D,O
Interdisciplinary Studies M,D,O
Near and Middle Eastern Studies M,D
Religion M,D

Theology P,M,D,O
Women's Studies M

DREXEL UNIVERSITY
Applied Arts and Design—General M
Architecture M
Art Therapy M
Arts Administration M
Clinical Psychology M,D
Communication—General M
Economics M,D,O
Emergency Management M
Forensic Psychology M,D
Health Psychology M,D
History of Science and Technology M
Interior Design M
Journalism M
Marriage and Family Therapy M,D
Psychology—General M,D
Publishing M
Technical Writing M
Textile Design M
Therapies—Dance, Drama, and Music M

DRURY UNIVERSITY
Art/Fine Arts M
Communication—General M
Criminal Justice and Criminology M

DUKE UNIVERSITY
Anthropology D
Art History D
Art/Fine Arts D
Asian Studies M,O
Biological Anthropology D
Classics D
Clinical Psychology D
Cognitive Sciences D
Comparative Literature D
Developmental Psychology D
Economics M,D
English D
Experimental Psychology D
French D
German D
Health Psychology D
History of Medicine
History D
Human Development D
Humanities M
International Development M,O*
Latin American Studies M,D,O
Liberal Studies M
Medieval and Renaissance Studies O
Music M,D
Philosophy M,D
Political Science M,D
Psychology—General D
Public Policy M,D,O
Religion M,D
Slavic Languages M
Sociology M,D
Spanish D
Theology P,M,D
Women's Studies O

DUQUESNE UNIVERSITY
Clinical Psychology D
Communication—General M,D
Conflict Resolution and Mediation/Peace Studies M,O
English M,D
Ethics M
Forensic Sciences M
History M
Internet and Interactive Multimedia M,O
Liberal Studies M
Museum Studies M
Music M,O
Philosophy M,D
Psychology—General D
Public Administration M,O
Public Policy M,O
Rhetoric M,D
School Psychology M,D,O
Theology M,D

EARLHAM SCHOOL OF RELIGION
Religion P,M
Theology P,M

EAST CAROLINA UNIVERSITY
Addictions/Substance Abuse Counseling M
American Studies M
Anthropology M
Art/Fine Arts M
Child and Family Studies M
Child Development M
Clinical Psychology M
Criminal Justice and Criminology M
Economics M
English M
Geography M
Health Communication M
Health Psychology D
History M
International Affairs M
Marriage and Family Therapy M
Music M
Political Science M
Psychology—General M
Public Administration M
Rehabilitation Counseling M
School Psychology M
Sociology M
Therapies—Dance, Drama, and Music M
Western European Studies M

EAST CENTRAL UNIVERSITY
Criminal Justice and Criminology M
Psychology—General M
Rehabilitation Counseling M

EASTERN ILLINOIS UNIVERSITY
Art/Fine Arts M
Clinical Psychology M,O
Consumer Economics M
Economics M
English M
Family and Consumer Sciences-General M
Gerontology M
History M
Music M
Political Science M
Psychology—General M,O
Public History M
School Psychology M,O
Speech and Interpersonal Communication M

EASTERN KENTUCKY UNIVERSITY
Clinical Psychology M,O
Criminal Justice and Criminology M
English M
History M
Industrial and Organizational Psychology M,O
Music M
Political Science M
Psychology—General M,O
Public Administration M
School Psychology M,O
Urban and Regional Planning M
Writing M

EASTERN MENNONITE UNIVERSITY
Conflict Resolution and Mediation/Peace Studies M,O
Pastoral Ministry and Counseling P,M,O
Religion P,M,O
Theology P,M,O

EASTERN MICHIGAN UNIVERSITY
Addictions/Substance Abuse Counseling M,O
African-American Studies O
American Studies M,O
Applied Economics M
Art/Fine Arts M
Arts Administration M
Child and Family Studies M,O
Clinical Psychology M,D
Clothing and Textiles M
Communication—General M
Criminal Justice and Criminology M,O
Economics M
English M,O
French M,O
Gender Studies M
Geographic Information Systems M,O
Geography M,O
German M,O
Gerontology M,O
Hispanic Studies M,O
Historic Preservation M,O
History M,O
Interior Design M
Japanese M,O
Linguistics M
Music M
Political Science M
Psychology—General M,D
Public Administration M,O
Public Policy M,O
Social Psychology M,O
Social Sciences M,O
Sociology M
Spanish M,O
Technical Communication M,O
Theater M
Urban and Regional Planning M,O
Women's Studies M
Writing M,O

EASTERN NAZARENE COLLEGE
Counseling Psychology M
Marriage and Family Therapy M

EASTERN NEW MEXICO UNIVERSITY
Anthropology M
Communication—General M
English M

EASTERN UNIVERSITY
Counseling Psychology M
Economics M
Marriage and Family Therapy D
Missions and Missiology D
Pastoral Ministry and Counseling D
Theology P,M,D

EASTERN VIRGINIA MEDICAL SCHOOL
Art Therapy M
Clinical Psychology D

EASTERN WASHINGTON UNIVERSITY
Communication—General M
Counseling Psychology M
English M
History M
Interdisciplinary Studies M
Music M
Psychology—General M
Public Administration M
School Psychology M
Urban and Regional Planning M
Writing M

EAST STROUDSBURG UNIVERSITY OF PENNSYLVANIA
History M
Political Science M

EAST TENNESSEE STATE UNIVERSITY
Art History M
Art/Fine Arts M
Clinical Psychology M
Communication—General M
Computer Art and Design M
Criminal Justice and Criminology M
Economics M
English M
Gerontology M,O
History M
Human Development M
Liberal Studies M
Marriage and Family Therapy M
Psychology—General M
Sociology M
Urban and Regional Planning M
Urban Studies M

ECUMENICAL THEOLOGICAL SEMINARY
Pastoral Ministry and Counseling D
Theology P

EDEN THEOLOGICAL SEMINARY
Theology P,M,D

EDGEWOOD COLLEGE
Marriage and Family Therapy M
Religion M

EDINBORO UNIVERSITY OF PENNSYLVANIA
Art/Fine Arts M
Clinical Psychology M
Communication—General M
Media Studies M
Psychology—General M
Rehabilitation Counseling M
Social Sciences M

ELMHURST COLLEGE
English M
Industrial and Organizational Psychology M

ELMS COLLEGE
Religion M

EMERSON COLLEGE
Broadcast Journalism M
Communication—General M

Corporate and Organizational Communication M*
Film, Television, and Video Production M
Health Communication M
Journalism M*
Media Studies M*
Publishing M*
Theater M*
Writing M*

EMILY CARR INSTITUTE OF ART + DESIGN
Applied Arts and Design—General M
Art/Fine Arts M
Computer Art and Design M

EMMANUEL SCHOOL OF RELIGION
Religion P,M,D
Theology P,M,D

EMORY & HENRY COLLEGE
American Studies M
History M

EMORY UNIVERSITY
Anthropology D
Art History D
Clinical Psychology D
Cognitive Sciences D
Comparative Literature D,O
Developmental Psychology D
Economics D
English D,O
Film, Television, and Video Theory and Criticism M,D,O
French D,O
Gerontology M
History D
Interdisciplinary Studies D
Jewish Studies M
Music M
Near and Middle Eastern Studies D,O
Philosophy D,O
Political Science D
Portuguese D,O
Psychology—General D
Religion D,O
Sociology M,D*
Spanish D,O
Theology P,M,D
Women's Studies D,O

EMPORIA STATE UNIVERSITY
Art Therapy M
Clinical Psychology M
Counseling Psychology M
English M
History M
Industrial and Organizational Psychology M
Music M
Psychology—General M
Rehabilitation Counseling M
School Psychology M,O

EPISCOPAL DIVINITY SCHOOL
Theology P,M,D,O

EPISCOPAL THEOLOGICAL SEMINARY OF THE SOUTHWEST
Pastoral Ministry and Counseling P,M,O
Religion P,M,O
Theology P,M,O

ERIKSON INSTITUTE
Child Development M
Developmental Psychology M,O
Human Development M,O

ERSKINE THEOLOGICAL SEMINARY
Theology P,M,D

EVANGELICAL SEMINARY OF PUERTO RICO
Theology P,M,D

EVANGELICAL THEOLOGICAL SEMINARY
Marriage and Family Therapy P,M,O
Pastoral Ministry and Counseling P,M,O
Religion P,M,O
Theology P,M,O

EVANGEL UNIVERSITY
Clinical Psychology M
Counseling Psychology M
Psychology—General M
School Psychology M

EVEREST UNIVERSITY
Criminal Justice and Criminology M

EVEREST UNIVERSITY
Criminal Justice and Criminology M

EVEREST UNIVERSITY
Criminal Justice and Criminology M

EVEREST UNIVERSITY
Criminal Justice and Criminology M

THE EVERGREEN STATE COLLEGE
Public Administration M

EXCELSIOR COLLEGE
Liberal Studies M

FAIRFIELD UNIVERSITY
American Studies M
Communication—General M
Marriage and Family Therapy M
Psychology—General M,O
School Psychology M,O
Writing M

FAIRLEIGH DICKINSON UNIVERSITY, COLLEGE AT FLORHAM
Corporate and Organizational Communication M
Counseling Psychology M
Industrial and Organizational Psychology M
Psychology—General M,O
Public Administration M
Writing M

FAIRLEIGH DICKINSON UNIVERSITY, METROPOLITAN CAMPUS
Art/Fine Arts M
Clinical Psychology M,D*
Communication—General M
Comparative Literature M
English M
Experimental Psychology M,O
Forensic Psychology M
History M
Homeland Security M
International Affairs M
Media Studies M
Political Science M
Psychology—General M,D,O
Public Administration M,O
School Psychology M,D

FAIRMONT STATE UNIVERSITY
Criminal Justice and Criminology M

FAITH BAPTIST BIBLE COLLEGE AND THEOLOGICAL SEMINARY
Pastoral Ministry and Counseling P,M
Religion P,M
Theology P,M

FAITH EVANGELICAL LUTHERAN SEMINARY
Theology P,M,D

FASHION INSTITUTE OF TECHNOLOGY
Applied Arts and Design—General M*
Art History M
Arts Administration M
Clothing and Textiles M
Illustration M
Museum Studies M

FAYETTEVILLE STATE UNIVERSITY
Criminal Justice and Criminology M
English M
History M
Political Science M
Psychology—General M
Sociology M

FERRIS STATE UNIVERSITY
Applied Arts and Design—General M
Art/Fine Arts M
Criminal Justice and Criminology M

FIELDING GRADUATE UNIVERSITY
Clinical Psychology M,D,O
Human Development M,D,O
Psychology—General M,D,O*

FISK UNIVERSITY
Clinical Psychology M
Psychology—General M
Sociology M

FITCHBURG STATE COLLEGE
Communication—General M,O
Counseling Psychology M,O
Criminal Justice and Criminology M
English M,O
History M,O
Interdisciplinary Studies O
Marriage and Family Therapy M,O
Technical Writing M,O

FIVE TOWNS COLLEGE
Music M,D

FLORIDA AGRICULTURAL AND MECHANICAL UNIVERSITY
African-American Studies M
Agricultural Economics and Agribusiness M
Architecture M
Criminal Justice and Criminology M
Economics M
History M
International Affairs M
Journalism M
Landscape Architecture M
Political Science M
Psychology—General M
Public Administration M
School Psychology M
Social Psychology M
Social Sciences M
Sociology M

FLORIDA ATLANTIC UNIVERSITY
Anthropology M
Applied Arts and Design—General M
Art/Fine Arts M
Communication—General M
Comparative and Interdisciplinary Arts D
Comparative Literature M
Counseling Psychology M,O
Criminal Justice and Criminology M
Economics M
English M
French M
Geography M
German M
History M
Liberal Studies M
Marriage and Family Therapy M,O
Music M
Political Science M
Psychology—General M,D
Public Administration M,D
Rehabilitation Counseling M,O
Sociology M
Spanish M
Theater M
Urban and Regional Planning M
Women's Studies M,O
Writing M

FLORIDA GULF COAST UNIVERSITY
Criminal Justice and Criminology M
English M
Forensic Sciences M
Gerontology M
History M
Public Administration M

FLORIDA INSTITUTE OF TECHNOLOGY
Clinical Psychology M,D
Communication—General M

Industrial and Organizational Psychology M,D
Psychology—General M,D*
Public Administration M

FLORIDA INTERNATIONAL UNIVERSITY

African Studies M
Architecture M
Art/Fine Arts M
Asian Studies M
Conflict Resolution and Mediation/Peace Studies O
Counseling Psychology M
Criminal Justice and Criminology M
Developmental Psychology M,D
Economics M,D
English M
Forensic Sciences M,D
History M,D
Interior Design M
International Affairs M,D
Landscape Architecture M
Latin American Studies M
Liberal Studies M
Linguistics M
Mass Communication M
Music M
Political Science M,D
Psychology—General M,D
Public Administration M,D
Rehabilitation Counseling M
Religion M
School Psychology M,O
Sociology M,D
Spanish M,D
Writing M

FLORIDA STATE UNIVERSITY

American Studies M,O
Anthropology M,D
Applied Arts and Design—General M,D
Archaeology M,D
Art History M,D,O
Art/Fine Arts M
Arts Administration M,D
Asian Studies M
Child and Family Studies M,D
Child Development M,D
Classics M,D
Clinical Psychology D
Clothing and Textiles M,D
Cognitive Sciences D
Communication—General M,D
Consumer Economics M,D
Corporate and Organizational Communication M,D
Counseling Psychology M,D,O
Criminal Justice and Criminology M,D
Dance M
Demography and Population Studies M,O
Developmental Psychology D
East European and Russian Studies M
Economics M,D
English M,D
Family and Consumer Sciences-General M,D*
Film, Television, and Video Production M
French M,D
Geographic Information Systems M,D
Geography M,D
German M
History M,D
Humanities M,D,O
Interior Design M
International Affairs M
Italian M
Marriage and Family Therapy M,D
Mass Communication M,D
Media Studies M,D
Museum Studies M,D,O
Music M,D
Philosophy M,D
Political Science M,D
Psychology—General M,D
Public Administration M,D,O
Public History M,D
Public Policy M,D,O
Rehabilitation Counseling M,D,O
Religion M,D
Rhetoric M,D
School Psychology M,O
Slavic Languages M
Social Psychology D
Sociology M,D
Spanish M,D
Speech and Interpersonal Communication M,D
Sport Psychology M,D
Textile Design M,D
Theater M,D
Therapies—Dance, Drama, and Music M,D
Urban and Regional Planning M,D
Writing M,D

FONTBONNE UNIVERSITY

Art/Fine Arts M
Family and Consumer Sciences-General M
Theater M

FORDHAM UNIVERSITY

Classics M,D
Clinical Psychology D
Communication—General M
Corporate and Organizational Communication M
Counseling Psychology M,D,O
Developmental Psychology D
Economics M,D,O
English M,D
Ethics O
History M,D
International Affairs M,O
International Development M,O*
Latin American Studies M,O
Liberal Studies M
Mass Communication M
Media Studies M
Medieval and Renaissance Studies M,O
Pastoral Ministry and Counseling M,D,O
Philosophy M,D
Political Science M
Psychology—General D
Religion M,D,O
School Psychology M,D,O
Sociology M,D
Theology M,D

FORT HAYS STATE UNIVERSITY

Art/Fine Arts M
Communication—General M
English M
Geography M
History M
Liberal Studies M
Psychology—General M,O
School Psychology O

FORT VALLEY STATE UNIVERSITY

Counseling Psychology M
Rehabilitation Counseling M

FRAMINGHAM STATE COLLEGE

Art/Fine Arts M
Psychology—General M
Public Administration M
Spanish M

FRANCISCAN SCHOOL OF THEOLOGY

Theology P,M

FRANCISCAN UNIVERSITY OF STEUBENVILLE

Counseling Psychology M
Philosophy M
Theology M

FRANCIS MARION UNIVERSITY

Clinical Psychology M
Psychology—General M
School Psychology M
Social Psychology M

FRANKLIN UNIVERSITY

Corporate and Organizational Communication M

FRANK LLOYD WRIGHT SCHOOL OF ARCHITECTURE

Architecture M

FREDERICK S. PARDEE RAND GRADUATE SCHOOL

Public Policy D

FREED-HARDEMAN UNIVERSITY

Pastoral Ministry and Counseling M
Theology P,M

FRESNO PACIFIC UNIVERSITY

Conflict Resolution and Mediation/Peace Studies M
Interdisciplinary Studies M
School Psychology M

FRIENDS UNIVERSITY

Marriage and Family Therapy M
Theology M

FROSTBURG STATE UNIVERSITY

Counseling Psychology M
Interdisciplinary Studies M
Psychology—General M

FULLER THEOLOGICAL SEMINARY

Clinical Psychology M,D
Marriage and Family Therapy M
Missions and Missiology M,D
Psychology—General M,D
Theology P,M,D

FULL SAIL UNIVERSITY

Internet and Interactive Multimedia M

GALLAUDET UNIVERSITY

Clinical Psychology D
Counseling Psychology M
Developmental Psychology M,O
Linguistics M,D
Psychology—General M,D,O
School Psychology M,O

GANNON UNIVERSITY

Counseling Psychology D
English M
Gerontology O
Pastoral Ministry and Counseling M,O
Public Administration M,O

GARDNER-WEBB UNIVERSITY

Counseling Psychology M
English M
Missions and Missiology P,D
Pastoral Ministry and Counseling P,D
Psychology—General M
School Psychology M
Theology P,D

GARRETT-EVANGELICAL THEOLOGICAL SEMINARY

Music P,M,D
Pastoral Ministry and Counseling P,M,D
Theology P,M,D

GENERAL THEOLOGICAL SEMINARY

Theology P,M,D

GENEVA COLLEGE

Counseling Psychology M
Marriage and Family Therapy M
Psychology—General M

GEORGE FOX UNIVERSITY

Clinical Psychology M,D*
Counseling Psychology M,O
Marriage and Family Therapy M,O
Pastoral Ministry and Counseling P,M,D,O
Psychology—General M,D
Religion P,M,D,O
School Psychology M,O
Theology P,M,D,O

GEORGE MASON UNIVERSITY

Anthropology M
Art History M*
Arts Administration M,O
Clinical Psychology M,D
Communication—General M,D
Conflict Resolution and Mediation/Peace Studies M,D
Cultural Studies D*
Dance M
Developmental Psychology M,D
Economics M,D,O
English M,O
Film, Television, and Video Production M
Folklore M
Geographic Information Systems M,D,O
Geography M
Graphic Design M
History M,D,O
Homeland Security M,D
Industrial and Organizational Psychology M,D
Interdisciplinary Studies M
International Affairs M
Linguistics M,O
Music M,O
Political Science M,D
Psychology—General M,D
Public Affairs M,D
Public Policy M,D*
Religion M
School Psychology M

Social Sciences M,D,O
Sociology M
Women's Studies M
Writing M

GEORGETOWN UNIVERSITY
Communication—General M*
Conflict Resolution and Mediation/Peace Studies M
Demography and Population Studies M
East European and Russian Studies M
Economics D
English M
German M,D
History M,D
International Affairs M,D
Internet and Interactive Multimedia M
Latin American Studies M
Liberal Studies M
Linguistics M,D,O
National Security M
Near and Middle Eastern Languages M,D
Near and Middle Eastern Studies M,O
Philosophy M,D
Political Science M
Psychology—General D
Public Policy M*
Spanish M,D
Western European Studies M

THE GEORGE WASHINGTON UNIVERSITY
American Studies M,D
Anthropology M,D
Applied Arts and Design—General M,D
Art History M,D
Art Therapy M,O
Art/Fine Arts M,D
Asian Studies M
Clinical Psychology D
Cognitive Sciences D
Criminal Justice and Criminology M
East European and Russian Studies M
Economics M,D
Emergency Management M,D,O
English M,D
Folklore M
Forensic Sciences M
Geography M
Health Psychology D
Historic Preservation M
History M,D
Human Development M,D
Industrial and Organizational Psychology D
Interior Design M,D
International Affairs M
International Development M
International Trade Policy M
Latin American Studies M
Mass Communication M
Military and Defense Studies M
Museum Studies M,D,O
Philosophy M,D
Photography M,D
Political Science M,D
Psychology—General D
Public Administration M,D
Public Policy M,D
Publishing M
Rehabilitation Counseling M
Religion M
Social Psychology D
Sociology M
Theater M

Western European Studies M
Women's Studies M,D,O

GEORGIA COLLEGE & STATE UNIVERSITY
Criminal Justice and Criminology M
English M
History M
Public Administration M
Public Affairs M
Therapies—Dance, Drama, and Music M
Writing M

GEORGIA INSTITUTE OF TECHNOLOGY
Architecture M,D
Building Science M,D
Economics M
Geographic Information Systems M,D
History of Science and Technology M,D
International Affairs M*
Internet and Interactive Multimedia M
Psychology—General M,D
Public Policy M,D
Urban and Regional Planning M,D
Urban Design M,D

GEORGIAN COURT UNIVERSITY
Counseling Psychology M,O
Pastoral Ministry and Counseling M,O
Theology M,O

GEORGIA SOUTHERN UNIVERSITY
Applied Economics M
Art/Fine Arts M
English M
History M
Music M
Psychology—General M,D
Public Administration M
School Psychology M,O
Sociology M
Spanish M

GEORGIA STATE UNIVERSITY
Anthropology M
Art History M
Art/Fine Arts M
Communication—General M,D
Counseling Psychology M,D,O
Criminal Justice and Criminology M
Economics M,D,O
Emergency Management M,D,O
English M,D
Film, Television, and Video Production M,D
French M,O
Geographic Information Systems O
Geography M
German M
Gerontology M
Historic Preservation M,O
History M,D
Latin American Studies M,D,O
Linguistics M,D
Mass Communication M,D
Music M
Philosophy M
Photography M,D
Political Science M,D
Psychology—General M,D
Public Administration M
Public Policy D

Rehabilitation Counseling M
Religion M
Rhetoric M,D
School Psychology M,D,O
Sociology M,D
Spanish M,O
Speech and Interpersonal Communication M,D
Translation and Interpretation O
Urban and Regional Planning M,D,O
Urban Studies M
Women's Studies M
Writing M,D

GLOBAL UNIVERSITY
Missions and Missiology P,M
Theology P,M

GODDARD COLLEGE
Comparative and Interdisciplinary Arts M
Counseling Psychology M
Industrial and Organizational Psychology M
Interdisciplinary Studies M
Sustainable Development M
Writing M

GOLDEN GATE BAPTIST THEOLOGICAL SEMINARY
Pastoral Ministry and Counseling P,M,D,O
Theology P,M,D,O

GOLDEN GATE UNIVERSITY
Psychology—General M,D,O

GONZAGA UNIVERSITY
Communication—General M
Counseling Psychology M
Pastoral Ministry and Counseling M
Philosophy M
Religion M

GORDON-CONWELL THEOLOGICAL SEMINARY
Missions and Missiology P,M,D
Pastoral Ministry and Counseling P,M,D
Religion P,M,D
Theology P,M,D

GOUCHER COLLEGE
Arts Administration M
Historic Preservation M
Writing M

GOVERNORS STATE UNIVERSITY
Addictions/Substance Abuse Counseling M
Art/Fine Arts M
Communication—General M
Counseling Psychology M
English M
Media Studies M
Political Science M
Psychology—General M
Public Administration M

GRACE COLLEGE
Counseling Psychology M

GRACELAND UNIVERSITY
Pastoral Ministry and Counseling M
Religion M

GRACE THEOLOGICAL SEMINARY
Missions and Missiology P,M,D,O
Pastoral Ministry and Counseling P,M,D,O
Theology P,M,D,O

GRACE UNIVERSITY
Counseling Psychology M
Pastoral Ministry and Counseling M
Theology M

GRADUATE INSTITUTE OF APPLIED LINGUISTICS
Linguistics M,O

GRADUATE SCHOOL AND UNIVERSITY CENTER OF THE CITY UNIVERSITY OF NEW YORK
Anthropology D
Archaeology D
Architectural History D
Art History D
Classics M,D
Clinical Psychology D
Cognitive Sciences D
Comparative Literature M,D
Criminal Justice and Criminology D
Developmental Psychology D
Economics D
English D
Experimental Psychology D
French D
German M,D
History D
Industrial and Organizational Psychology D
Interdisciplinary Studies M,D
Italian M,D
Liberal Studies M
Linguistics M,D
Medieval and Renaissance Studies M,D
Music D
Philosophy M,D
Political Science M,D
Psychology—General D
Public Policy M,D
Social Psychology D
Sociology D
Spanish D
Theater D
Urban Studies M,D
Women's Studies M,D

GRADUATE THEOLOGICAL UNION
Art History M,D,O
Cultural Studies M,D,O
Ethics M,D,O
Jewish Studies M,D,O
Religion M,D,O
Social Sciences M,D,O
Theology M,D,O
Women's Studies M,D,O

GRAMBLING STATE UNIVERSITY
Criminal Justice and Criminology M
Mass Communication M
Public Administration M

GRAND CANYON UNIVERSITY
Addictions/Substance Abuse Counseling M
School Psychology M

GRAND RAPIDS THEOLOGICAL SEMINARY OF CORNERSTONE UNIVERSITY
Missions and Missiology P,M
Pastoral Ministry and Counseling P,M
Religion P,M
Theology P,M

GRAND VALLEY STATE UNIVERSITY
Communication—General M
Criminal Justice and Criminology M
English M
Public Administration M
School Psychology M

GRATZ COLLEGE
Jewish Studies M
Music M,O
Near and Middle Eastern Studies O

GREENVILLE COLLEGE
Pastoral Ministry and Counseling M

HAMLINE UNIVERSITY
Liberal Studies M,O
Public Administration M,D

HAMPTON UNIVERSITY
Museum Studies M

HARDING UNIVERSITY
Counseling Psychology M
Marriage and Family Therapy M
Pastoral Ministry and Counseling M

HARDING UNIVERSITY GRADUATE SCHOOL OF RELIGION
Pastoral Ministry and Counseling P,M,D
Religion P,M,D
Theology P,M,D

HARDIN-SIMMONS UNIVERSITY
English M
History M
Marriage and Family Therapy M
Music M
Pastoral Ministry and Counseling M
Psychology—General M
Religion M
Theology P,M

HARTFORD SEMINARY
Pastoral Ministry and Counseling M,D,O
Religion M,D,O
Theology M,D,O

HARVARD UNIVERSITY
African Studies D
African-American Studies D
American Studies D
Anthropology M,D
Archaeology M,D
Architectural History D
Architecture M,D
Art History D
Asian Languages M,D
Asian Studies M,D
Celtic Languages D
Chinese D
Classics D
Cognitive Sciences M,D
Communication—General M,O
Comparative Literature D
Demography and Population Studies M,D
Developmental Psychology D
East European and Russian Studies M
Economics D
English M,D,O
Experimental Psychology D
French M,D
German D
History of Science and Technology M,D
History D
Human Development M,D
International Affairs D
International Development M
Italian M,D
Japanese D
Jewish Studies M,D
Journalism M,O
Landscape Architecture M,D
Liberal Studies M,O
Linguistics D
Medieval and Renaissance Studies D
Museum Studies M,O
Music M,D
Near and Middle Eastern Languages M,D
Near and Middle Eastern Studies M,D
Philosophy M,D
Political Science M,D
Portuguese M,D
Psychology—General D
Public Administration M
Public Policy M,D
Religion D
Russian D
Scandinavian Languages D
Slavic Languages D
Social Psychology D
Sociology D
Spanish M,D
Technical Communication M
Theology P,M,D
Urban and Regional Planning M,D
Urban Design M

HAWAI'I PACIFIC UNIVERSITY
Communication—General M*
Corporate and Organizational Communication M
Economics M
Military and Defense Studies M*
Sustainable Development M

HAZELDEN GRADUATE SCHOOL OF ADDICTION STUDIES
Addictions/Substance Abuse Counseling M,O

HEBREW COLLEGE
Jewish Studies M,O
Music M,O
Theology M

HEBREW THEOLOGICAL COLLEGE
Theology O

HEBREW UNION COLLEGE–JEWISH INSTITUTE OF RELIGION (CA)
Jewish Studies M,D
Theology P

HEBREW UNION COLLEGE–JEWISH INSTITUTE OF RELIGION (NY)
Jewish Studies M
Music M
Near and Middle Eastern Languages D
Theology P,D

HEBREW UNION COLLEGE–JEWISH INSTITUTE OF RELIGION (OH)
Jewish Studies P,M,D
Near and Middle Eastern Studies M,D
Religion M,D
Theology P

HEC MONTREAL
Applied Economics M
Arts Administration O
Corporate and Organizational Communication O
Sustainable Development O

HEIDELBERG COLLEGE
Counseling Psychology M

HENDERSON STATE UNIVERSITY
Liberal Studies M
Social Psychology M

HERITAGE BAPTIST COLLEGE AND HERITAGE THEOLOGICAL SEMINARY
Theology M,O

HERITAGE CHRISTIAN UNIVERSITY
Classics M
Pastoral Ministry and Counseling M
Religion M

HERITAGE UNIVERSITY
English M

HIGH POINT UNIVERSITY
History M

HILLSDALE FREE WILL BAPTIST COLLEGE
Pastoral Ministry and Counseling M

HODGES UNIVERSITY
Criminal Justice and Criminology M
Interdisciplinary Studies M
Psychology—General M
Public Administration M

HOFSTRA UNIVERSITY
Addictions/Substance Abuse Counseling M,O
Art Therapy M
Art/Fine Arts M
Clinical Psychology M,D
Communication—General M
Comparative Literature M
Counseling Psychology M,O
English M
Film, Television, and Video Production M
French M
German M
Gerontology M,O
Humanities M
Industrial and Organizational Psychology M
Interdisciplinary Studies M
Journalism M
Linguistics M
Marriage and Family Therapy M,O
Music M
Psychology—General M,D,O
Rehabilitation Counseling M,O
Russian M
School Psychology M,D,O
Social Psychology M,D,O
Spanish M
Speech and Interpersonal Communication M
Writing M

HOLLINS UNIVERSITY
Art/Fine Arts M,O
Dance M
English M
Film, Television, and Video Production M
Film, Television, and Video Theory and Criticism M
Humanities M,O
Interdisciplinary Studies M,O
Liberal Studies M,O
Music M,O
Social Sciences M,O
Theater M
Writing M

HOLMES INSTITUTE
Pastoral Ministry and Counseling M

HOLY APOSTLES COLLEGE AND SEMINARY
Theology P,M,O

HOLY CROSS GREEK ORTHODOX SCHOOL OF THEOLOGY
Theology P,M

HOLY FAMILY UNIVERSITY
Counseling Psychology M

HOLY NAMES UNIVERSITY
Counseling Psychology M,O
Forensic Psychology M,O
Music M,O
Pastoral Ministry and Counseling M,O
Religion M,O

HOOD COLLEGE
Art/Fine Arts M,O
Human Development M,O
Humanities M
Psychology—General M,O
Thanatology M,O

HOOD THEOLOGICAL SEMINARY
Theology P,M,D

HOPE INTERNATIONAL UNIVERSITY
International Development M

Marriage and Family Therapy M
Missions and Missiology M
Music M
Religion M

HOUGHTON COLLEGE

Music M

HOUSTON BAPTIST UNIVERSITY

Counseling Psychology M
Liberal Studies M
Pastoral Ministry and Counseling M
Psychology—General M
Theology M

HOUSTON GRADUATE SCHOOL OF THEOLOGY

Pastoral Ministry and Counseling P,M,D
Theology P,M,D

HOWARD UNIVERSITY

African Studies M,D
Applied Arts and Design—General M
Art History M
Art/Fine Arts M
Clinical Psychology M,D
Communication—General M,D
Corporate and Organizational Communication M,D
Counseling Psychology M,D,O
Developmental Psychology M,D
Economics M,D
English M,D
Experimental Psychology M,D
Film, Television, and Video Production M
French M
History M,D
Human Development M
Mass Communication M,D
Media Studies M,D
Music M
Philosophy M
Photography M
Political Science M,D
Psychology—General M,D
Public Administration M
Public Affairs M
School Psychology M,D,O
Social Psychology M,D
Sociology M,D
Spanish M
Theology P,M,D

HUMBOLDT STATE UNIVERSITY

English M
Psychology—General M
Social Sciences M
Sociology M
Theater M

HUNTER COLLEGE OF THE CITY UNIVERSITY OF NEW YORK

Anthropology M
Applied Social Research M
Art History M
Art/Fine Arts M
Classics M
Cognitive Sciences M
Economics M
English M
French M
Geographic Information Systems M,O
Geography M,O
History M
Italian M
Media Studies M
Music M
Psychology—General M
Rehabilitation Counseling M
Romance Languages M
Social Psychology M
Sociology M
Spanish M
Theater M
Urban and Regional Planning M
Urban Studies M
Writing M

HUNTINGTON UNIVERSITY

Pastoral Ministry and Counseling M

HURON UNIVERSITY USA IN LONDON

Conflict Resolution and Mediation/Peace Studies M
International Affairs M
National Security M
Political Science M

IDAHO STATE UNIVERSITY

Anthropology M
Architecture M
Art/Fine Arts M
Clinical Psychology D
Counseling Psychology M,D,O
English M,D,O
Geographic Information Systems M,O
History M
Interdisciplinary Studies M
Marriage and Family Therapy M,D,O
Political Science M,D
Psychology—General M,D
Public Administration M
School Psychology M,D,O
Sociology M
Speech and Interpersonal Communication M
Theater M

ILIFF SCHOOL OF THEOLOGY

Pastoral Ministry and Counseling P,M,D
Religion P,M,D
Theology P,M,D

ILLINOIS INSTITUTE OF TECHNOLOGY

Applied Arts and Design—General M,D*
Architecture M,D
Clinical Psychology M,D
Communication—General M,D
Corporate and Organizational Communication M
Industrial and Organizational Psychology M,D
Landscape Architecture M,D
Psychology—General M,D
Public Administration M
Rehabilitation Counseling M,D
Sustainable Development M
Technical Writing M,D

ILLINOIS STATE UNIVERSITY

Agricultural Economics and Agribusiness M
Archaeology M
Art History M
Art/Fine Arts M
Clinical Psychology M,D,O
Communication—General M
Counseling Psychology M,D,O
Criminal Justice and Criminology M
Developmental Psychology M,D,O
Economics M
English M,D
Experimental Psychology M,D,O
Family and Consumer Sciences-General M
French M
German M
Graphic Design M
History M
Industrial and Organizational Psychology M,D,O
Music M
Photography M
Political Science M
Psychology—General M,D,O
School Psychology D,O
Sociology M
Spanish M
Textile Design M
Theater M
Writing M

IMMACULATA UNIVERSITY

Clinical Psychology M,D,O
Counseling Psychology M,D,O
Psychology—General M,D,O
School Psychology M,D,O
Therapies—Dance, Drama, and Music M

INDIANA STATE UNIVERSITY

Art/Fine Arts M
Clinical Psychology M,D
Communication—General M
Comparative Literature M
Consumer Economics M
Counseling Psychology M,D,O
Criminal Justice and Criminology M
English M
Family and Consumer Sciences-General M
Geography M,D
Graphic Design M
History M
Linguistics M,O
Media Studies M
Music M
Photography M
Political Science M
Psychology—General M,D
Public Administration M
School Psychology M,D,O
Writing M

INDIANA UNIVERSITY BLOOMINGTON

African Studies M
African-American Studies M
Anthropology M,D
Art History M,D
Art/Fine Arts M,D
Asian Languages M,D
Asian Studies M,D
Child and Family Studies M,D
Chinese M,D
Classics M,D
Cognitive Sciences M,D
Communication—General M,D*
Comparative Literature M,D
Computer Art and Design M,D
Counseling Psychology M,D,O
Criminal Justice and Criminology M,D*
Developmental Psychology M,D
East European and Russian Studies M,O
Economics M,D
English M,D
Folklore M,D
French M,D
Gender Studies D
Geography M,D
German M,D
History of Science and Technology M,D
History M,D
Human Development M,D
Italian M,D
Japanese M,D
Journalism M,D
Latin American Studies M
Linguistics M,D
Mass Communication M,D
Medieval and Renaissance Studies M,D
Music M,D,O
Near and Middle Eastern Languages M,D
Philosophy M,D
Political Science M,D
Portuguese M,D
Psychology—General M,D
Public Administration M,D,O
Public Affairs M,D,O*
Public Policy D
Religion M,D
School Psychology M,D,O
Slavic Languages M,D
Social Psychology M,D
Social Sciences P,M,D,O
Sociology M,D
Spanish M,D
Speech and Interpersonal Communication M,D
Theater M,D
Western European Studies M
Writing M,D

INDIANA UNIVERSITY KOKOMO

Liberal Studies M
Public Administration M

INDIANA UNIVERSITY NORTHWEST

Criminal Justice and Criminology M,O
Public Administration M,O
Public Affairs M,O

INDIANA UNIVERSITY OF PENNSYLVANIA

Art/Fine Arts M
Clinical Psychology D
Criminal Justice and Criminology M,D
English M,D
Geography M
History M
Industrial and Labor Relations M
Linguistics M,D
Music M
Political Science M
Psychology—General M,D
Public Affairs M
Rhetoric M,D
School Psychology D,O
Sociology M
Writing M,D

INDIANA UNIVERSITY–PURDUE UNIVERSITY FORT WAYNE

Communication—General M
English M,O
Liberal Studies M
Public Affairs M,O
Sociology M

INDIANA UNIVERSITY–PURDUE UNIVERSITY INDIANAPOLIS

Addictions/Substance Abuse Counseling M,D
Applied Arts and Design—General M
Art/Fine Arts M
Child and Family Studies M
Clinical Psychology M,D
Criminal Justice and Criminology M
Economics M
English M
Gender Studies M
Geographic Information Systems M,O
History M
Industrial and Organizational Psychology M
Internet and Interactive Multimedia M,D
Liberal Studies M,D,O
Museum Studies M,O
Music M
Philanthropic Studies M,D
Philosophy M,O
Political Science M,O
Psychology—General M,D
Public Administration M
Public Affairs M*
Public History M
Public Policy M
Rehabilitation Counseling M,D
Sociology M

INDIANA UNIVERSITY SOUTH BEND

English M
Liberal Studies M
Music M
Psychology—General M
Public Administration M,O
Public Affairs M,O

INDIANA UNIVERSITY SOUTHEAST

Liberal Studies M

INDIANA WESLEYAN UNIVERSITY

Counseling Psychology M
Marriage and Family Therapy M
Social Psychology M
Theology M

INSTITUTE FOR CHRISTIAN STUDIES

Philosophy M,D
Political Science M,D
Theology M,D

INSTITUTE OF PUBLIC ADMINISTRATION

Public Administration M,O

INSTITUTE OF TRANSPERSONAL PSYCHOLOGY

Clinical Psychology M,D
Counseling Psychology M,D
Psychology—General M,D,O
Transpersonal and Humanistic Psychology M,D,O*
Women's Studies M,D

THE INSTITUTE OF WORLD POLITICS

Military and Defense Studies M,O
National Security M,O
Political Science M,O*
Public Affairs M,O
Public Policy M,O

INSTITUTO CENTROAMERICANO DE ADMINISTRACIÓN DE EMPRESAS

Agricultural Economics and Agribusiness M
Economics M
Sustainable Development M

INSTITUTO TECNOLÓGICO DE SANTO DOMINGO

Linguistics M
Psychology—General M

INSTITUTO TECNOLÓGICO Y DE ESTUDIOS SUPERIORES DE MONTERREY, CAMPUS CENTRAL DE VERACRUZ

Humanities M

INSTITUTO TECNOLÓGICO Y DE ESTUDIOS SUPERIORES DE MONTERREY, CAMPUS CIUDAD DE MÉXICO

Economics M,D
Humanities M,D

INSTITUTO TECNOLÓGICO Y DE ESTUDIOS SUPERIORES DE MONTERREY, CAMPUS CIUDAD OBREGÓN

Communication—General M
International Affairs M

INSTITUTO TECNOLÓGICO Y DE ESTUDIOS SUPERIORES DE MONTERREY, CAMPUS ESTADO DE MÉXICO

Architecture M,D
Humanities M,D

INSTITUTO TECNOLÓGICO Y DE ESTUDIOS SUPERIORES DE MONTERREY, CAMPUS IRAPUATO

Architecture M,D
Humanities M,D

INSTITUTO TECNOLÓGICO Y DE ESTUDIOS SUPERIORES DE MONTERREY, CAMPUS MONTERREY

Communication—General M,D

INTER AMERICAN UNIVERSITY OF PUERTO RICO, AGUADILLA CAMPUS

Counseling Psychology M
Criminal Justice and Criminology M

INTER AMERICAN UNIVERSITY OF PUERTO RICO, METROPOLITAN CAMPUS

Criminal Justice and Criminology M
Economics M,D
History M
Industrial and Labor Relations M
Psychology—General M
Spanish M
Theology D

INTER AMERICAN UNIVERSITY OF PUERTO RICO, PONCE CAMPUS

Criminal Justice and Criminology M
Spanish M

INTER AMERICAN UNIVERSITY OF PUERTO RICO, SAN GERMÁN CAMPUS

Art/Fine Arts M
Counseling Psychology M,D
Industrial and Labor Relations M,D
Photography M
Psychology—General M,D
School Psychology M,D

INTERDENOMINATIONAL THEOLOGICAL CENTER

Theology P,M,D

INTERNATIONAL BAPTIST COLLEGE

Pastoral Ministry and Counseling M,D
Theology M

INTERNATIONAL UNIVERSITY IN GENEVA

Communication—General M
Media Studies M

IONA COLLEGE

Counseling Psychology M
Criminal Justice and Criminology M
English M
Experimental Psychology M
History M
Industrial and Organizational Psychology M
Italian M
Journalism M
Marriage and Family Therapy M,O
Mass Communication M
Pastoral Ministry and Counseling M,O
Psychology—General M
School Psychology M
Spanish M

IOWA STATE UNIVERSITY OF SCIENCE AND TECHNOLOGY

Agricultural Economics and Agribusiness M,D
Anthropology M
Applied Arts and Design—General M
Architecture M
Child and Family Studies M,D
Clothing and Textiles M,D
Cognitive Sciences D
Consumer Economics M,D
Corporate and Organizational Communication M,D
Counseling Psychology D
Economics M,D
English M,D
Family and Consumer Sciences-General M
Graphic Design M
History of Science and Technology M,D
History M,D
Human Development M,D
Interdisciplinary Studies M
Interior Design M
Journalism M
Landscape Architecture M
Marriage and Family Therapy M,D
Mass Communication M
Political Science M
Psychology—General D
Public Administration M
Rhetoric M,D
Rural Planning and Studies M,D
Rural Sociology M,D
Social Psychology D
Sociology M,D
Sustainable Development M,D
Urban and Regional Planning M

ITHACA COLLEGE

Communication—General M
Music M

JACKSON STATE UNIVERSITY

Clinical Psychology D
Criminal Justice and Criminology M
English M
History M
Mass Communication M
Political Science M
Psychology—General D
Public Administration M,D
Public Affairs M
Public Policy M,D
Rehabilitation Counseling M,O
Sociology M
Urban and Regional Planning M

JACKSONVILLE STATE UNIVERSITY

Criminal Justice and Criminology M
Emergency Management M
English M
History M
Liberal Studies M
Music M
Political Science M
Psychology—General M

JAMES MADISON UNIVERSITY

Art History M
Art/Fine Arts M
Clinical Psychology D
Counseling Psychology M,O
English M
History M
Music D
Photography M
Psychology—General M,D,O
Public Administration M
School Psychology M,D,O
Technical Writing M
Textile Design M

JESUIT SCHOOL OF THEOLOGY AT BERKELEY

Theology P,M,D,O

THE JEWISH THEOLOGICAL SEMINARY

Jewish Studies M,D
Music M
Religion M,D*
Theology M,D,O*

JEWISH UNIVERSITY OF AMERICA

Jewish Studies P,D
Pastoral Ministry and Counseling M,D

JOHN BROWN UNIVERSITY

Marriage and Family Therapy M
Pastoral Ministry and Counseling M

JOHN CARROLL UNIVERSITY

Program	Degree
Corporate and Organizational Communication	M
Counseling Psychology	M,O
English	M
History	M
Humanities	M
Religion	M

JOHN F. KENNEDY UNIVERSITY

Program	Degree
Art/Fine Arts	M
Comparative and Interdisciplinary Arts	M
Counseling Psychology	M
Health Psychology	M
Industrial and Organizational Psychology	M,O
Interdisciplinary Studies	M
Museum Studies	M,O
Psychology—General	M,D,O
Sport Psychology	M
Transpersonal and Humanistic Psychology	M

JOHN JAY COLLEGE OF CRIMINAL JUSTICE OF THE CITY UNIVERSITY OF NEW YORK

Program	Degree
Criminal Justice and Criminology	M,D
Forensic Psychology	M,D
Forensic Sciences	M,D
Public Administration	M
Public Policy	M,D

THE JOHNS HOPKINS UNIVERSITY

Program	Degree
Addictions/Substance Abuse Counseling	M,D,O
African Studies	M,D,O
Anthropology	D
Applied Economics	M*
Art History	M,D
Asian Studies	M,D,O
Canadian Studies	M,D,O
Classics	D
Clinical Psychology	M,D
Cognitive Sciences	D
Communication—General	M*
Comparative Literature	D
Conflict Resolution and Mediation/Peace Studies	M,D,O
Criminal Justice and Criminology	M
Demography and Population Studies	M,D
East European and Russian Studies	M,D,O
Economics	D
Emergency Management	M,O
English	D
French	D
Genetic Counseling	M,D
Geography	M,D
German	D
History of Science and Technology	M,D
History	D
Homeland Security	M,O
International Affairs	M,D,O
International Development	M,D,O
Italian	D
Latin American Studies	M,D,O
Liberal Studies	M,O*
Medical Illustration	M
Military and Defense Studies	M
Museum Studies	M*
Music	M,D,O
Near and Middle Eastern Studies	M,D,O
Pastoral Ministry and Counseling	M,O
Philosophy	M,D
Political Science	M,D,O*
Psychology—General	D
Public Policy	M*
Romance Languages	D
Social Sciences	M,D
Sociology	D
Spanish	D
Technical Writing	M
Western European Studies	M,D,O
Writing	M*

JOHNSON BIBLE COLLEGE

Program	Degree
Marriage and Family Therapy	M
Theology	M

JOHNSON STATE COLLEGE

Program	Degree
Art/Fine Arts	M

JOINT MILITARY INTELLIGENCE COLLEGE

Program	Degree
Military and Defense Studies	M,O

JONES INTERNATIONAL UNIVERSITY

Program	Degree
Conflict Resolution and Mediation/Peace Studies	M
Corporate and Organizational Communication	M

THE JUDGE ADVOCATE GENERAL'S SCHOOL, U.S. ARMY

Program	Degree
Military and Defense Studies	M

JUDSON UNIVERSITY

Program	Degree
Architecture	M

THE JUILLIARD SCHOOL

Program	Degree
Music	M,D,O

KANSAS STATE UNIVERSITY

Program	Degree
Agricultural Economics and Agribusiness	M,D
Architecture	M
Art/Fine Arts	M
Child and Family Studies	M,D
Clothing and Textiles	M,D
Economics	M,D
English	M
Family and Consumer Sciences-General	M,D
French	M
Geography	M,D
German	M
History	M,D
Human Development	D
International Affairs	M
Landscape Architecture	M
Marriage and Family Therapy	D
Mass Communication	M
Music	M
Political Science	M
Psychology—General	M,D
Public Administration	M
Rhetoric	M
Sociology	M,D
Spanish	M
Speech and Interpersonal Communication	M
Theater	M
Urban and Regional Planning	M

KAPLAN UNIVERSITY–DAVENPORT

Program	Degree
Criminal Justice and Criminology	M
Political Science	M,O

KEAN UNIVERSITY

Program	Degree
Addictions/Substance Abuse Counseling	M
Art/Fine Arts	M
Communication—General	M
Counseling Psychology	M
Criminal Justice and Criminology	M
Graphic Design	M
Holocaust Studies	M
Industrial and Organizational Psychology	M
Liberal Studies	M
Marriage and Family Therapy	O
Political Science	M
Public Administration	M
School Psychology	O
Spanish	M

KEHILATH YAKOV RABBINICAL SEMINARY

Program	Degree
Theology	

KEISER UNIVERSITY

Program	Degree
Criminal Justice and Criminology	M

KENNESAW STATE UNIVERSITY

Program	Degree
Conflict Resolution and Mediation/Peace Studies	M
Public Administration	M
Writing	M

KENRICK-GLENNON SEMINARY

Program	Degree
Theology	P,M,O

KENT STATE UNIVERSITY

Program	Degree
Anthropology	M
Architecture	M,O
Art History	M
Art/Fine Arts	M
Biological Anthropology	D
Classics	M,D
Clinical Psychology	M,D
Communication—General	M,D
Comparative Literature	M,D
Counseling Psychology	M
Criminal Justice and Criminology	M
Economics	M
English	M,D*
Experimental Psychology	M,D
Family and Consumer Sciences-General	M
French	M,D
Geography	M,D
German	M,D
Gerontology	M
Graphic Design	M
Historic Preservation	M,O
History	M,D
Human Development	M,D
Illustration	M
Japanese	M,D
Journalism	M
Liberal Studies	M
Mass Communication	M
Music	M,D
Philosophy	M
Political Science	M,D
Psychology—General	M,D
Public Administration	M
Public Policy	M,D
Rehabilitation Counseling	M,O
Rhetoric	M,D
Russian	M,D
School Psychology	M,D,O
Sociology	M,D
Spanish	M,D
Textile Design	M
Theater	M
Translation and Interpretation	M,D
Urban Design	M,O
Writing	M,D

KENTUCKY CHRISTIAN UNIVERSITY

Program	Degree
Religion	M
Theology	M

KENTUCKY STATE UNIVERSITY

Program	Degree
Public Administration	M

KEUKA COLLEGE

Program	Degree
Criminal Justice and Criminology	M

KNOX COLLEGE

Program	Degree
Theology	P,M,D

KNOX THEOLOGICAL SEMINARY

Program	Degree
Missions and Missiology	M
Pastoral Ministry and Counseling	D
Religion	M
Theology	P,M,O

KOL YAAKOV TORAH CENTER

Program	Degree
Theology	O

KUTZTOWN UNIVERSITY OF PENNSYLVANIA

Program	Degree
Counseling Psychology	M
English	M
Marriage and Family Therapy	M
Media Studies	M
Public Administration	M

LAKE FOREST COLLEGE

Program	Degree
Liberal Studies	M

LAKEHEAD UNIVERSITY

Program	Degree
Clinical Psychology	M,D
Economics	M
English	M
Experimental Psychology	M,D
Gerontology	M
History	M
Philosophy	M
Psychology—General	M,D
Sociology	M
Women's Studies	M

LAKELAND COLLEGE

Program	Degree
Theology	M

LAMAR UNIVERSITY

Program	Degree
Applied Arts and Design—General	M
Art History	M
Art/Fine Arts	M
Clinical Psychology	M
Criminal Justice and Criminology	M
English	M
Family and Consumer Sciences-General	M,O
History	M

Industrial and Organizational Psychology M
Music M
Photography M
Political Science M
Psychology—General M
Public Administration M
Social Psychology M
Theater M

LANCASTER BIBLE COLLEGE
Pastoral Ministry and Counseling M
Theology M

LANCASTER THEOLOGICAL SEMINARY
Theology P,M,D,O

LANGSTON UNIVERSITY
Rehabilitation Counseling M

LA SALLE UNIVERSITY
Clinical Psychology M,D
Corporate and Organizational Communication M
Counseling Psychology M
East European and Russian Studies M
Hispanic Studies M
History M
Latin American Studies M
Marriage and Family Therapy D
Pastoral Ministry and Counseling M
Psychology—General D
Rehabilitation Counseling D
Religion M
Theology M

LA SIERRA UNIVERSITY
English M
Religion M
School Psychology M,O

LAURA AND ALVIN SIEGAL COLLEGE OF JUDAIC STUDIES
Holocaust Studies M
Humanities M
Jewish Studies M

LAURENTIAN UNIVERSITY
History M
Human Development M
Humanities M
Sociology M

LAWRENCE TECHNOLOGICAL UNIVERSITY
Architecture M
Interior Design M
Technical Communication M

LEADERSHIP INSTITUTE OF SEATTLE
Counseling Psychology M
Psychology—General M

LEBANESE AMERICAN UNIVERSITY
International Affairs M

LEE UNIVERSITY
Counseling Psychology M
Music M
Religion M
Theology M

LEHIGH UNIVERSITY
American Studies M
Counseling Psychology M,D,O
Economics M,D
English M,D
History M,D
Human Development M,D
Political Science M
Psychology—General M,D
School Psychology D,O
Sociology M

LEHMAN COLLEGE OF THE CITY UNIVERSITY OF NEW YORK
Art/Fine Arts M
English M
History M
Spanish M

LENOIR-RHYNE COLLEGE
School Psychology M
Social Psychology M

LESLEY UNIVERSITY
Art Therapy M,D,O*
Art/Fine Arts M*
Clinical Psychology M,D,O
Counseling Psychology M*
Health Psychology M
Interdisciplinary Studies M
International Affairs M,O
Psychology—General M,D,O
School Psychology M
Social Psychology M,D,O
Therapies—Dance, Drama, and Music M,D,O
Women's Studies M
Writing M*

LEWIS & CLARK COLLEGE
Addictions/Substance Abuse Counseling M
Counseling Psychology M,O
Cultural Studies M,O
Marriage and Family Therapy M
School Psychology M,O

LEWIS UNIVERSITY
Counseling Psychology M
Criminal Justice and Criminology M
Public Administration M

LEXINGTON THEOLOGICAL SEMINARY
Theology P,M,D

LIBERTY UNIVERSITY
Communication—General M
Counseling Psychology M,D
Pastoral Ministry and Counseling M,D
Religion P,M,D
Theology P,M,D

LINCOLN CHRISTIAN SEMINARY
Pastoral Ministry and Counseling P,M,D
Theology P,M,D

LINCOLN UNIVERSITY (MO)
Criminal Justice and Criminology M
History M
Political Science M
Public Administration M
Public Policy M
Social Sciences M
Sociology M

LINDENWOOD UNIVERSITY
American Studies M
Art/Fine Arts M
Communication—General M,O
Counseling Psychology M,D,O
Criminal Justice and Criminology M,O
Gerontology M,O
Public Administration M
School Psychology M,D,O
Theater M
Writing M,O

LINDSEY WILSON COLLEGE
Counseling Psychology M
Human Development M

LIPSCOMB UNIVERSITY
Conflict Resolution and Mediation/Peace Studies M,O
Counseling Psychology M,O
Psychology—General M,O
Religion P,M
Sustainable Development M
Theology P,M

LOCK HAVEN UNIVERSITY OF PENNSYLVANIA
Liberal Studies M

LOGOS EVANGELICAL SEMINARY
Theology P,M,D

LOMA LINDA UNIVERSITY
Child and Family Studies M,D,O
Pastoral Ministry and Counseling M,O
Psychology—General D
Religion M

LONG ISLAND UNIVERSITY AT RIVERHEAD
Homeland Security M,O

LONG ISLAND UNIVERSITY, BRENTWOOD CAMPUS
Counseling Psychology M
Criminal Justice and Criminology M

LONG ISLAND UNIVERSITY, BROOKLYN CAMPUS
Clinical Psychology D
Comparative Literature M
Computer Art and Design M*
Economics M
English M*
History M,O
International Affairs M,O
Political Science M
Psychology—General M,D
Public Administration M
School Psychology M
Social Sciences M,O
Urban Studies M
Writing M

LONG ISLAND UNIVERSITY, C.W. POST CAMPUS
Art Therapy M
Art/Fine Arts M
Clinical Psychology D
Computer Art and Design M
Criminal Justice and Criminology M
English M
Gerontology M,O
History M
Interdisciplinary Studies M
International Affairs M
Internet and Interactive Multimedia M
Music M
Political Science M
Psychology—General M,D
Public Administration M,O
Social Sciences M
Spanish M
Theater M

LONG ISLAND UNIVERSITY, ROCKLAND GRADUATE CAMPUS
Counseling Psychology M*
Gerontology M,O
Public Administration M,O*

LONG ISLAND UNIVERSITY, WESTCHESTER GRADUATE CAMPUS
Counseling Psychology M
School Psychology M

LONGWOOD UNIVERSITY
Criminal Justice and Criminology M
English M
Writing M

LONGY SCHOOL OF MUSIC
Music M,O

LORAS COLLEGE
Pastoral Ministry and Counseling M
Psychology—General M
Theology M

LOUISIANA STATE UNIVERSITY AND AGRICULTURAL AND MECHANICAL COLLEGE
Agricultural Economics and Agribusiness M,D
Anthropology M,D
Applied Arts and Design—General M
Architecture M
Art History M
Art/Fine Arts M
Clinical Psychology M,D
Cognitive Sciences M,D
Communication—General M,D
Comparative Literature M,D
Developmental Psychology M,D
Economics M,D
English M,D
Family and Consumer Sciences-General M,D
French M,D
Geography M,D
Graphic Design M
Hispanic Studies M
History M,D
Industrial and Organizational Psychology M,D
Landscape Architecture M
Liberal Studies M
Linguistics M,D
Mass Communication M,D*
Media Studies M,D
Music M,D
Philosophy M
Photography M
Political Science M,D
Psychology—General M,D
Public Administration M,D
School Psychology M,D
Sociology M,D

Theater M,D
Writing M,D

LOUISIANA STATE UNIVERSITY HEALTH SCIENCES CENTER

Rehabilitation Counseling M

LOUISIANA STATE UNIVERSITY IN SHREVEPORT

Counseling Psychology M
Liberal Studies M
School Psychology O

LOUISIANA TECH UNIVERSITY

Applied Arts and Design—General M
Art/Fine Arts M
Counseling Psychology M,D
Economics M,D
English M
Family and Consumer Sciences-General M
Graphic Design M
History M
Industrial and Organizational Psychology M,D
Interior Design M
Photography M
Psychology—General M,D
Speech and Interpersonal Communication M

LOUISVILLE PRESBYTERIAN THEOLOGICAL SEMINARY

Religion P,M,D
Theology P,M,D

LOYOLA COLLEGE IN MARYLAND

Addictions/Substance Abuse Counseling M,O
Clinical Psychology M,D,O
Counseling Psychology M,O
Economics M
Liberal Studies M*
Pastoral Ministry and Counseling M,D,O*
Psychology—General M,D,O*

LOYOLA MARYMOUNT UNIVERSITY

English M
Film, Television, and Video Production M
Marriage and Family Therapy M
Pastoral Ministry and Counseling M
Philosophy M
School Psychology M
Theology M
Writing M

LOYOLA UNIVERSITY CHICAGO

Clinical Psychology D
Cognitive Sciences M
Corporate and Organizational Communication M
Counseling Psychology D
Criminal Justice and Criminology M
Developmental Psychology D
English M,D
History M,D
Industrial and Labor Relations M
International Affairs M,D
Pastoral Ministry and Counseling M,O
Philosophy M,D
Political Science M,D
Psychology—General M,D
Public History M,D
Public Policy M
Religion P,M,O
School Psychology M,D,O
Social Psychology M,D
Sociology M,D
Spanish M
Theology P,M,D,O

LOYOLA UNIVERSITY NEW ORLEANS

Criminal Justice and Criminology M
Music M
Theology M,O

LUBBOCK CHRISTIAN UNIVERSITY

Theology M

LUTHERAN SCHOOL OF THEOLOGY AT CHICAGO

Pastoral Ministry and Counseling P,M,D
Theology P,M,D

LUTHERAN THEOLOGICAL SEMINARY

Pastoral Ministry and Counseling P,M
Theology P,M

LUTHERAN THEOLOGICAL SEMINARY AT GETTYSBURG

Pastoral Ministry and Counseling P,M,D
Religion P,M,D
Theology P,M,D

THE LUTHERAN THEOLOGICAL SEMINARY AT PHILADELPHIA

Pastoral Ministry and Counseling P,M,D,O
Religion P,M,D,O
Theology P,M,D,O

LUTHERAN THEOLOGICAL SOUTHERN SEMINARY

Theology P,M,D

LUTHER RICE UNIVERSITY

Missions and Missiology P,M,D
Pastoral Ministry and Counseling P,M,D
Theology P,M,D

LUTHER SEMINARY

Theology P,M,D

LYNN UNIVERSITY

Criminal Justice and Criminology M,O
Emergency Management M,O
Mass Communication M,D
Media Studies M,D
Music M,O
Psychology—General M,O

MACHZIKEI HADATH RABBINICAL COLLEGE

Theology O

MADONNA UNIVERSITY

Clinical Psychology M
Criminal Justice and Criminology M
Liberal Studies M
Pastoral Ministry and Counseling M
Psychology—General M
Theology M

MAHARISHI UNIVERSITY OF MANAGEMENT

Asian Studies M,D
Sustainable Development M,D

MAINE COLLEGE OF ART

Art/Fine Arts M

MALONE COLLEGE

Pastoral Ministry and Counseling M
Theology M

MANHATTAN SCHOOL OF MUSIC

Music M,D,O

MANHATTANVILLE COLLEGE

Corporate and Organizational Communication M
Liberal Studies M
Writing M

MANSFIELD UNIVERSITY OF PENNSYLVANIA

Music M

MAPLE SPRINGS BAPTIST BIBLE COLLEGE AND SEMINARY

Pastoral Ministry and Counseling P,M,D,O
Theology P,M,D,O

MARANATHA BAPTIST BIBLE COLLEGE

Cultural Studies M
Pastoral Ministry and Counseling M
Theology M

MARIETTA COLLEGE

Corporate and Organizational Communication M
Psychology—General M

MARIST COLLEGE

Corporate and Organizational Communication M
Counseling Psychology M,O
Psychology—General M,O
Public Administration M
School Psychology M,O

MARLBORO COLLEGE

Internet and Interactive Multimedia M

MARQUETTE UNIVERSITY

Clinical Psychology M,D
Communication—General M
Economics M
English M,D
Ethics M,D
Health Communication M
History M,D
Interdisciplinary Studies D
International Affairs M
Journalism M
Mass Communication M
Media Studies M
Medieval and Renaissance Studies M,D
Philosophy M,D
Political Science M
Psychology—General M,D
Public Administration M
Spanish M
Speech and Interpersonal Communication M
Theology M,D

MARSHALL UNIVERSITY

Art/Fine Arts M
Classics M
Clinical Psychology M,D
Communication—General M
Criminal Justice and Criminology M
English M
Family and Consumer Sciences-General M
Geography M
History M
Humanities M
Industrial and Organizational Psychology M,D
Journalism M
Mass Communication M
Music M
Political Science M
Psychology—General M,D
School Psychology O
Sociology M

MARTIN UNIVERSITY

Pastoral Ministry and Counseling M
Psychology—General M
Social Psychology M

MARY BALDWIN COLLEGE

English M
Theater M

MARYGROVE COLLEGE

Pastoral Ministry and Counseling M
Translation and Interpretation M

MARYLAND INSTITUTE COLLEGE OF ART

Art/Fine Arts M,O
Computer Art and Design M
Graphic Design M
Photography M

MARYLHURST UNIVERSITY

Art Therapy M,O
Counseling Psychology M,O
Interdisciplinary Studies M
Theology P,M

MARYMOUNT UNIVERSITY

Counseling Psychology M,O
English M
Forensic Psychology M
Humanities M
Interior Design M
Pastoral Ministry and Counseling M,O
Social Psychology M

MARYVILLE UNIVERSITY OF SAINT LOUIS

Addictions/Substance Abuse Counseling M
Marriage and Family Therapy M
Rehabilitation Counseling M
Therapies—Dance, Drama, and Music M

MARYWOOD UNIVERSITY

Addictions/Substance Abuse Counseling M
Art Therapy M,O
Art/Fine Arts M
Clinical Psychology M,D
Communication—General M,O
Corporate and Organizational Communication M,O
Counseling Psychology M
Criminal Justice and Criminology M
Film, Television, and Video Production M,O
Gerontology M,O
Graphic Design M
Health Communication M,O
Human Development D
Illustration M
Interdisciplinary Studies M,O
Interior Design M
Media Studies M,O
Photography M
Psychology—General M
Public Administration M
School Psychology M,O
Textile Design M
Therapies—Dance, Drama, and Music M,O

MASSACHUSETTS COLLEGE OF ART AND DESIGN

Applied Arts and Design—General M
Art/Fine Arts M
Film, Television, and Video Production M
Photography M
Textile Design M
Theater M

MASSACHUSETTS INSTITUTE OF TECHNOLOGY

Archaeology M,D,O
Architectural History M,D
Architecture M,D*
Art History M,D
Cognitive Sciences D
Economics M,D
History of Science and Technology D
Humanities M
Linguistics D
Media Studies M,D
Philosophy D
Political Science M,D
Social Sciences D
Technical Writing M
Urban and Regional Planning M,D
Urban Studies M,D
Writing M

MASSACHUSETTS MARITIME ACADEMY

Emergency Management M

MASSACHUSETTS SCHOOL OF PROFESSIONAL PSYCHOLOGY

Clinical Psychology M,D,O
Counseling Psychology M,D,O
Forensic Psychology M,D,O
Industrial and Organizational Psychology M,D,O
Psychology—General M,D,O*
School Psychology M,D,O

THE MASTER'S COLLEGE AND SEMINARY

Pastoral Ministry and Counseling P,M,D
Theology P,M,D

MCCORMICK THEOLOGICAL SEMINARY

Pastoral Ministry and Counseling P,M,D,O
Theology P,M,D,O

MCDANIEL COLLEGE

Liberal Studies M

MCGILL UNIVERSITY

Agricultural Economics and Agribusiness M
Anthropology M,D
Architecture M,D,O
Art History M,D
Asian Studies M,D
Clinical Psychology M,D
Communication—General M,D
Counseling Psychology M,D,O
Developmental Psychology M,D,O
Economics M,D
English M,D
Experimental Psychology M,D
Forensic Sciences M,D,O
French M,D
Genetic Counseling M,D
Geography M,D
German M,D
Hispanic Studies M,D
History of Medicine M,D
History M,D
International Development M,D,O
Italian M,D
Jewish Studies M
Linguistics M,D
Music M,D
Near and Middle Eastern Studies M,D,O
Philosophy M,D
Political Science M,D
Psychology—General M,D
Religion M,D
Russian M,D
School Psychology M,D,O
Sociology M,D,O
Theology M,D
Urban and Regional Planning M,D

MCKENDREE UNIVERSITY

Counseling Psychology M

MCMASTER UNIVERSITY

Anthropology M,D
Classics M,D
Cultural Studies M,D
Economics M,D
English M,D
French M
Geography M,D
History M,D
Industrial and Labor Relations M
International Affairs M
Pastoral Ministry and Counseling P,M,D,O
Philosophy M,D
Political Science M,D
Psychology—General M,D
Public Administration M,D
Public Affairs M,D
Public Policy M,D
Religion M,D
Sociology M,D
Theology P,M,D,O

MCNEESE STATE UNIVERSITY

Counseling Psychology M
English M
Psychology—General M
School Psychology M
Writing M

MEADVILLE LOMBARD THEOLOGICAL SCHOOL

Pastoral Ministry and Counseling P,M,D
Theology P,M,D

MEDAILLE COLLEGE

Counseling Psychology M
Psychology—General M

MEDICAL COLLEGE OF GEORGIA

Medical Illustration M

MEMORIAL UNIVERSITY OF NEWFOUNDLAND

Anthropology M,D
Archaeology M,D
Classics M
Economics M
English M,D
Experimental Psychology M,D
Folklore M,D
French M
Gender Studies M,D
Geography M,D
German M
History M,D
Humanities M
Industrial and Labor Relations M
Linguistics M,D
Music M,D
Philosophy M
Political Science M
Psychology—General M,D
Religion M
Social Psychology M,D
Sociology M,D
Sport Psychology M
Women's Studies M

MEMPHIS COLLEGE OF ART

Applied Arts and Design—General M
Art/Fine Arts M*
Computer Art and Design M
Photography M
Textile Design M

MEMPHIS THEOLOGICAL SEMINARY

Theology P,M,D

MENNONITE BRETHREN BIBLICAL SEMINARY

Marriage and Family Therapy M,O
Missions and Missiology M
Pastoral Ministry and Counseling M
Theology P,M

MERCER UNIVERSITY

Music M
Theology P,D

MERCY COLLEGE

Addictions/Substance Abuse Counseling M,O
Counseling Psychology M,O
English M
Marriage and Family Therapy M,O
Psychology—General M
School Psychology M

MERCYHURST COLLEGE

Biological Anthropology M
Criminal Justice and Criminology M,O
Forensic Sciences M

MEREDITH COLLEGE

Music M

MESIVTA OF EASTERN PARKWAY RABBINICAL SEMINARY

Theology

MESIVTA TIFERETH JERUSALEM OF AMERICA

Theology

MESIVTA TORAH VODAATH RABBINICAL SEMINARY

Theology

METHODIST THEOLOGICAL SCHOOL IN OHIO

Theology P,M,D

METHODIST UNIVERSITY

Criminal Justice and Criminology M

METROPOLITAN COLLEGE OF NEW YORK

Corporate and Organizational Communication M
Media Studies M
Public Administration M

METROPOLITAN STATE UNIVERSITY

Liberal Studies M
Psychology—General M
Public Administration M,O
Technical Writing M

MIAMI INTERNATIONAL UNIVERSITY OF ART & DESIGN

Art/Fine Arts M
Computer Art and Design M
Film, Television, and Video Production M
Graphic Design M*
Interior Design M

MIAMI UNIVERSITY

Architecture M
Art/Fine Arts M*
Child and Family Studies M
Clinical Psychology D
Communication—General M
Economics M
English M,D
Experimental Psychology D
French M
Geography M
Gerontology M
History M,D
Mass Communication M
Music M

Program	Degrees
Philosophy	M
Political Science	M,D
Psychology—General	D
Religion	M
Rhetoric	M,D
School Psychology	M,O
Social Psychology	D
Spanish	M
Speech and Interpersonal Communication	M
Technical Writing	M
Theater	M
Writing	M,D

MICHIGAN SCHOOL OF PROFESSIONAL PSYCHOLOGY

Program	Degrees
Clinical Psychology	M,D
Psychology—General	M,D
Transpersonal and Humanistic Psychology	M,D

MICHIGAN STATE UNIVERSITY

Program	Degrees
African Studies	M,D
African-American Studies	M,D
Agricultural Economics and Agribusiness	M,D
American Studies	M,D
Anthropology	M,D
Art/Fine Arts	M
Child and Family Studies	M,D
Child Development	M,D
Communication—General	M,D
Criminal Justice and Criminology	M,D*
Economics	M,D
English	M,D
Environmental Design	M,D
Forensic Sciences	M,D
French	M,D
Geography	M,D
German	M,D
Health Communication	M
Hispanic Studies	M,D
History	M,D
Humanities	M
Industrial and Labor Relations	M,D
Interior Design	M,D
International Affairs	M
Journalism	M
Latin American Studies	D
Linguistics	M,D
Marriage and Family Therapy	M,D
Media Studies	M,D
Music	M,D
Philosophy	M,D
Political Science	M,D
Portuguese	M,D
Psychology—General	M,D
Rehabilitation Counseling	M,D,O
Rhetoric	M,D
Romance Languages	M,D
School Psychology	M,D,O
Social Sciences	M
Sociology	M,D
Spanish	M,D
Theater	M
Therapies—Dance, Drama, and Music	M,D
Urban and Regional Planning	M,D
Writing	M,D

MICHIGAN TECHNOLOGICAL UNIVERSITY

Program	Degrees
Archaeology	M,D
Historic Preservation	D
Mineral Economics	M
Rhetoric	M,D
Sustainable Development	O
Technical Communication	M,D

MICHIGAN THEOLOGICAL SEMINARY

Program	Degrees
Counseling Psychology	P,M,D
Theology	P,M,D

MID-AMERICA BAPTIST THEOLOGICAL SEMINARY

Program	Degrees
Theology	P,M,D

MID-AMERICA BAPTIST THEOLOGICAL SEMINARY NORTHEAST BRANCH

Program	Degrees
Theology	P

MIDAMERICA NAZARENE UNIVERSITY

Program	Degrees
Counseling Psychology	M

MID-AMERICA REFORMED SEMINARY

Program	Degrees
Theology	P,M

MIDDLEBURY COLLEGE

Program	Degrees
Chinese	M
English	M
French	M,D
German	M,D
Italian	M,D
Russian	M,D
Spanish	M,D

MIDDLE TENNESSEE STATE UNIVERSITY

Program	Degrees
Child and Family Studies	M
Child Development	M
Criminal Justice and Criminology	M
Economics	M,D*
English	M,D
Gerontology	O
History	M
Industrial and Organizational Psychology	M,O
Mass Communication	M
Music	M
Psychology—General	M
Public History	D
School Psychology	M,O
Sociology	M

MIDWESTERN BAPTIST THEOLOGICAL SEMINARY

Program	Degrees
Music	P,M,D
Pastoral Ministry and Counseling	P,M,D
Theology	P,M,D

MIDWESTERN STATE UNIVERSITY

Program	Degrees
Criminal Justice and Criminology	M
English	M
History	M
Political Science	M
Psychology—General	M
Public Administration	M

MIDWESTERN UNIVERSITY, DOWNERS GROVE CAMPUS

Program	Degrees
Clinical Psychology	M,D*

MIDWESTERN UNIVERSITY, GLENDALE CAMPUS

Program	Degrees
Clinical Psychology	D

MIDWEST UNIVERSITY

Program	Degrees
Theology	P,M,D

MILLERSVILLE UNIVERSITY OF PENNSYLVANIA

Program	Degrees
Clinical Psychology	M
Emergency Management	M
English	M
French	M
German	M
History	M
Psychology—General	M
School Psychology	M
Spanish	M

MILLS COLLEGE

Program	Degrees
Art/Fine Arts	M
Dance	M
English	M
Music	M
Photography	M
Public Policy	M
Writing	M

MINNEAPOLIS COLLEGE OF ART AND DESIGN

Program	Degrees
Applied Arts and Design—General	M
Art/Fine Arts	M,O
Computer Art and Design	O
Film, Television, and Video Production	M
Graphic Design	M
Illustration	M
Photography	M

MINNESOTA STATE UNIVERSITY MANKATO

Program	Degrees
Addictions/Substance Abuse Counseling	M
Anthropology	M
Art/Fine Arts	M
Clinical Psychology	M
English	M,O
Environmental Design	M,O
Ethnic Studies	M
French	M
Geography	M
Gerontology	M,O
History	M
Industrial and Organizational Psychology	M
Interdisciplinary Studies	M
Marriage and Family Therapy	M,D,O
Music	M
Political Science	M
Psychology—General	M
Public Administration	M
Rehabilitation Counseling	M
Social Psychology	M,D,O
Sociology	M
Spanish	M
Speech and Interpersonal Communication	M
Technical Communication	M,O
Theater	M
Urban and Regional Planning	M,O
Urban Studies	M,O
Women's Studies	M,O
Writing	M,O

MINNESOTA STATE UNIVERSITY MOORHEAD

Program	Degrees
Liberal Studies	M
Public Administration	M
School Psychology	M,O
Writing	M

MINOT STATE UNIVERSITY

Program	Degrees
Criminal Justice and Criminology	M
School Psychology	O

MIRRER YESHIVA

Program	Degrees
Theology	

MISSISSIPPI COLLEGE

Program	Degrees
Art/Fine Arts	M
Communication—General	M
Corporate and Organizational Communication	M
Counseling Psychology	M,O
Criminal Justice and Criminology	M,O
English	M
History	M,O
Liberal Studies	M
Marriage and Family Therapy	M,O
Music	M
Political Science	M,O
Social Sciences	M,O

MISSISSIPPI STATE UNIVERSITY

Program	Degrees
Agricultural Economics and Agribusiness	M,D
Anthropology	M,D
Applied Economics	M,D
Architecture	M
Art/Fine Arts	M
Clinical Psychology	M,D
Cognitive Sciences	M,D
Computer Art and Design	M
Economics	M,D
English	M
Experimental Psychology	M,D
French	M
German	M
History	M,D
Landscape Architecture	M
Political Science	M,D
Psychology—General	M,D
Public Administration	M,D
Public Policy	M,D
Sociology	M,D
Spanish	M

MISSISSIPPI VALLEY STATE UNIVERSITY

Program	Degrees
Criminal Justice and Criminology	M

MISSOURI BAPTIST UNIVERSITY

Program	Degrees
Pastoral Ministry and Counseling	M,O

MISSOURI STATE UNIVERSITY

Program	Degrees
Art/Fine Arts	M
Child and Family Studies	M
Communication—General	M
Criminal Justice and Criminology	M
English	M
Family and Consumer Sciences-General	M
French	M
Geography	M
German	M
History	M
Interior Design	M
International Affairs	M*
Military and Defense Studies	M
Music	M
Political Science	M
Psychology—General	M
Public Administration	M
Religion	M
Spanish	M
Textile Design	M
Theater	M
Urban and Regional Planning	M

MONMOUTH UNIVERSITY

Addictions/Substance Abuse Counseling	M,O
Communication—General	M,O
Corporate and Organizational Communication	M,O
Counseling Psychology	M,O
Criminal Justice and Criminology	M,O
English	M
History	M
Liberal Studies	M
Media Studies	M,O
Psychology—General	M,O
Public Policy	M

MONTANA STATE UNIVERSITY

Agricultural Economics and Agribusiness	M
American Indian/Native American Studies	M
Applied Economics	M
Architecture	M
Art/Fine Arts	M
English	M
Film, Television, and Video Production	M
History	M,D
Human Development	M
Psychology—General	M
Public Administration	M

MONTANA STATE UNIVERSITY–BILLINGS

Communication—General	M
Interdisciplinary Studies	M
Psychology—General	M
Public Administration	M
Rehabilitation Counseling	M

MONTANA TECH OF THE UNIVERSITY OF MONTANA

Technical Communication	M

MONTCLAIR STATE UNIVERSITY

Addictions/Substance Abuse Counseling	M,O
Art History	M,O
Art/Fine Arts	M,O
Arts Administration	M
Clinical Psychology	M,O
Communication—General	M
Conflict Resolution and Mediation/Peace Studies	M,O
Corporate and Organizational Communication	M
Counseling Psychology	M,O
Economics	M
English	M,O
French	M,O
Geographic Information Systems	M,D,O
History	M,O
Industrial and Organizational Psychology	M,O
Italian	M,O
Linguistics	M,O
Marriage and Family Therapy	M,O
Music	M,O
Philosophy	M,D,O
Psychology—General	M,O
School Psychology	M,O
Social Psychology	M,O
Social Sciences	M,O
Sociology	M
Spanish	M,O
Speech and Interpersonal Communication	M
Theater	M
Therapies—Dance, Drama, and Music	M,O
Translation and Interpretation	M,O

MONTEREY INSTITUTE OF INTERNATIONAL STUDIES

International Affairs	M*
International Trade Policy	M
Public Administration	M
Translation and Interpretation	M*

MOODY BIBLE INSTITUTE

Theology	P,M,O

MORAVIAN THEOLOGICAL SEMINARY

Theology	P,M

MOREHEAD STATE UNIVERSITY

Art/Fine Arts	M
Clinical Psychology	M
Communication—General	M
Counseling Psychology	M
Criminal Justice and Criminology	M
English	M
Experimental Psychology	M
Gerontology	M
Human Development	M
Music	M
Psychology—General	M
Public Administration	M
Sociology	M

MORGAN STATE UNIVERSITY

African-American Studies	M,D
Architecture	M
Economics	M
English	M,D
History	M,D
International Affairs	M
Landscape Architecture	M
Music	M
Psychology—General	M,D
Sociology	M
Urban and Regional Planning	M

MOUNTAIN STATE UNIVERSITY

Criminal Justice and Criminology	M
Interdisciplinary Studies	M*

MOUNT ALOYSIUS COLLEGE

Criminal Justice and Criminology	M
Psychology—General	M

MOUNT ANGEL SEMINARY

Theology	P,M

MOUNT HOLYOKE COLLEGE

Psychology—General	M

MOUNT MARTY COLLEGE

Pastoral Ministry and Counseling	M

MOUNT MARY COLLEGE

Art Therapy	M
English	M

MOUNT ST. MARY'S COLLEGE

Counseling Psychology	M
Humanities	M
Religion	M

MOUNT ST. MARY'S UNIVERSITY

Theology	P,M

MOUNT SAINT VINCENT UNIVERSITY

Child and Family Studies	M
Gerontology	M
School Psychology	M
Women's Studies	M

MOUNT SINAI SCHOOL OF MEDICINE OF NEW YORK UNIVERSITY

Genetic Counseling	M,D

MOUNT VERNON NAZARENE UNIVERSITY

Theology	M

MULTNOMAH BIBLE COLLEGE AND BIBLICAL SEMINARY

Pastoral Ministry and Counseling	M
Theology	P,M,O

MURRAY STATE UNIVERSITY

Clinical Psychology	M
Corporate and Organizational Communication	M
Economics	M
English	M
History	M
Mass Communication	M
Music	M
Psychology—General	M
Public Affairs	M
Writing	M

NAROPA UNIVERSITY

Art Therapy	M
Asian Languages	M
Clinical Psychology	M
Counseling Psychology	M
Psychoanalysis and Psychotherapy	M
Religion	M
Social Psychology	M
Theater	M
Theology	P
Therapies—Dance, Drama, and Music	M
Transpersonal and Humanistic Psychology	M*
Writing	M

NASHOTAH HOUSE

Theology	P,M,O

NATIONAL DEFENSE UNIVERSITY

Military and Defense Studies	M
National Security	M

NATIONAL-LOUIS UNIVERSITY

Addictions/Substance Abuse Counseling	M,O
Gerontology	M,O
Health Psychology	M,O
Human Development	M,D,O
Industrial and Organizational Psychology	M,O
Psychology—General	M,O
School Psychology	M,D,O
Social Psychology	M,O
Writing	M

NATIONAL THEATRE CONSERVATORY

Theater	M,O

NATIONAL UNIVERSITY

Art/Fine Arts	M
Communication—General	M
Computer Art and Design	M
Counseling Psychology	M
Economics	M
English	M
Forensic Sciences	M
Homeland Security	M
Humanities	M
Internet and Interactive Multimedia	M
Media Studies	M
Psychology—General	M
Public Administration	M
School Psychology	M
Writing	M

NATIONAL UNIVERSITY OF SINGAPORE

Public Administration	M,D
Public Affairs	M,D
Public Policy	M,D*

NAVAL POSTGRADUATE SCHOOL

International Affairs	M
Military and Defense Studies	M,D
National Security	M
Political Science	M

NAVAL WAR COLLEGE

National Security	M

NAZARENE THEOLOGICAL SEMINARY

Missions and Missiology	P,M,D
Theology	P,M,D

NAZARETH COLLEGE OF ROCHESTER

Art Therapy	M
Liberal Studies	M
Therapies—Dance, Drama, and Music	M

NEBRASKA WESLEYAN UNIVERSITY

Forensic Sciences	M
History	M

NER ISRAEL RABBINICAL COLLEGE

Theology	M,D,O

NER ISRAEL YESHIVA COLLEGE OF TORONTO

Theology	

NEUMANN COLLEGE

Pastoral Ministry and Counseling	M,O

NEW BRUNSWICK THEOLOGICAL SEMINARY

Pastoral Ministry and Counseling	D
Theology	P,M,D

NEW ENGLAND COLLEGE

Counseling Psychology	M
Public Policy	M
Writing	M

NEW ENGLAND CONSERVATORY OF MUSIC

Music M,D,O

NEW JERSEY CITY UNIVERSITY

Art/Fine Arts M
Counseling Psychology M
Criminal Justice and Criminology M
Music M
Psychology—General M,O
School Psychology M,O
Urban Studies M

NEW JERSEY INSTITUTE OF TECHNOLOGY

Architecture M
History M
Internet and Interactive Multimedia M
Technical Communication M
Urban Studies D

NEW LIFE THEOLOGICAL SEMINARY

Religion M

NEWMAN THEOLOGICAL COLLEGE

Theology P,M

NEW MEXICO HIGHLANDS UNIVERSITY

American Studies M
Anthropology M
Clinical Psychology M
English M
Internet and Interactive Multimedia M
Media Studies M
Psychology—General M
Public Affairs M
Rhetoric M
Sociology M
Writing M

NEW MEXICO STATE UNIVERSITY

Agricultural Economics and Agribusiness M
Anthropology M
Applied Arts and Design—General M
Art History M
Art/Fine Arts M
Communication—General M
Corporate and Organizational Communication M,D
Counseling Psychology M,D,O
Criminal Justice and Criminology M
Economics M
English M,D
Family and Consumer Sciences-General M
Geography M
History M
Interdisciplinary Studies M,D
Music M
Photography M
Political Science M
Psychology—General M,D
Rhetoric M,D
School Psychology M,D,O
Sociology M
Spanish M
Writing M,D

NEW ORLEANS BAPTIST THEOLOGICAL SEMINARY

Music M,D
Pastoral Ministry and Counseling P,M,D
Theology P,D

THE NEW SCHOOL: A UNIVERSITY

Anthropology M,D
Applied Arts and Design—General M
Applied Social Research M,D
Architecture M*
Art/Fine Arts M*
Clinical Psychology M,D
Communication—General M*
Computer Art and Design M*
Decorative Arts M*
Economics M,D
History M,D
Interior Design M
International Affairs M*
International Development M
Liberal Studies M
Lighting Design M*
Mass Communication M
Media Studies M
Music M,O
Philosophy M,D
Photography M*
Political Science M,D
Psychology—General M,D
Public Policy D*
Social Sciences M,D*
Sociology M,D
Theater M*
Urban Studies M*
Writing M*

NEWSCHOOL OF ARCHITECTURE & DESIGN

Architecture M

NEW YORK ACADEMY OF ART

Art/Fine Arts M

NEW YORK FILM ACADEMY

Film, Television, and Video Production M*

NEW YORK INSTITUTE OF TECHNOLOGY

Architecture M
Communication—General M
Counseling Psychology M
Human Development M
Industrial and Labor Relations M,O
Urban Design M

NEW YORK MEDICAL COLLEGE

Disability Studies M

NEW YORK SCHOOL OF INTERIOR DESIGN

Interior Design M*

NEW YORK THEOLOGICAL SEMINARY

Theology P,M,D

NEW YORK UNIVERSITY

African Studies M,D,O
American Studies M,D
Anthropology M,D
Applied Arts and Design—General M
Applied Economics M,D,O
Archaeology M,D
Art History M,D
Art Therapy M
Art/Fine Arts M,D
Arts Administration M
Asian Studies M,D
Classics M,D,O
Cognitive Sciences M,D,O
Communication—General M,D
Comparative Literature M,D
Computer Art and Design M*
Corporate and Organizational Communication M*
Counseling Psychology M,D,O
Cultural Studies M,D,O
Dance M,D
Developmental Psychology M,D
Economics M,D,O
English M,D
Film, Television, and Video Production M*
Film, Television, and Video Theory and Criticism M,D
French M,D,O
German M,D
Graphic Design M*
Historic Preservation
History M,D,O
Human Development M,D,O
Humanities M,O
Industrial and Organizational Psychology M,D,O
Interdisciplinary Studies M*
International Affairs M,D,O*
Internet and Interactive Multimedia M
Italian M,D
Jewish Studies M,D,O
Journalism M,D,O*
Latin American Studies M,O
Linguistics M,D
Media Studies M,D
Museum Studies M,D,O
Music M,D,O
Near and Middle Eastern Studies M,D,O
Philosophy M,D
Political Science M,D
Portuguese M,D
Psychoanalysis and Psychotherapy M,D,O
Psychology—General M,D,O
Public Administration M,D,O*
Public History M,D,O
Publishing M*
Religion M,O
Romance Languages M,D
Russian M
School Psychology M,D
Slavic Languages M
Social Psychology M,D,O
Social Sciences M,O
Sociology M,D
Spanish M,D
Speech and Interpersonal Communication M,D
Theater M,D,O
Therapies—Dance, Drama, and Music M,D
Urban and Regional Planning M,O
Western European Studies M
Writing M

NIAGARA UNIVERSITY

Criminal Justice and Criminology M
Interdisciplinary Studies M
School Psychology M,O

NICHOLLS STATE UNIVERSITY

Counseling Psychology M,O
School Psychology M,O

THE NIGERIAN BAPTIST THEOLOGICAL SEMINARY

Music P,M,O
Theology P,M,O

NORFOLK STATE UNIVERSITY

Art/Fine Arts M
Clinical Psychology M
Communication—General M
Criminal Justice and Criminology M
Media Studies M
Music M
Psychology—General M,D
Social Psychology M
Sociology M
Urban Studies M

NORTH CAROLINA AGRICULTURAL AND TECHNICAL STATE UNIVERSITY

African-American Studies M
Agricultural Economics and Agribusiness M
Applied Economics M
English M

NORTH CAROLINA CENTRAL UNIVERSITY

Criminal Justice and Criminology M
English M
Family and Consumer Sciences-General M
History M
Psychology—General M
Public Administration M
Sociology M

NORTH CAROLINA SCHOOL OF THE ARTS

Film, Television, and Video Production M
Music M
Theater M

NORTH CAROLINA STATE UNIVERSITY

Agricultural Economics and Agribusiness M
Anthropology M
Applied Arts and Design—General M,D
Architecture M
Clothing and Textiles D
Communication—General M
Corporate and Organizational Communication M
Developmental Psychology D
Economics M,D
English M
Experimental Psychology D
French M
Geographic Information Systems M,D
Graphic Design M
History M
Industrial and Organizational Psychology D
Industrial Design M
International Affairs M
Landscape Architecture M
Liberal Studies M
Psychology—General D
Public Administration M,D
Public History M
Rural Sociology M,D
School Psychology D
Social Psychology M
Sociology M,D

Spanish M
Technical Communication M
Writing M

NORTH CENTRAL COLLEGE
Liberal Studies M

NORTHCENTRAL UNIVERSITY
Psychology—General M,D,O

NORTH DAKOTA STATE UNIVERSITY
Agricultural Economics and Agribusiness M
Child and Family Studies M,D
Child Development M,D
Clinical Psychology M,D
Cognitive Sciences M,D
Communication—General M,D
Consumer Economics M,D
Criminal Justice and Criminology M,D
Emergency Management M,D
English M
Family and Consumer Sciences-General M
Gerontology M,D
Health Psychology M,D
History M,D
Human Development D
Marriage and Family Therapy M,D
Mass Communication M,D
Music M,D
Psychology—General M,D
Social Psychology M,D
Social Sciences M,D
Sociology M,D
Speech and Interpersonal Communication M,D

NORTHEASTERN ILLINOIS UNIVERSITY
English M
Geography M
Gerontology M
History M
Linguistics M
Music M
Political Science M
Speech and Interpersonal Communication M
Writing M

NORTHEASTERN SEMINARY AT ROBERTS WESLEYAN COLLEGE
Theology P,M,D

NORTHEASTERN STATE UNIVERSITY
American Studies M
Communication—General M
Counseling Psychology M
Criminal Justice and Criminology M
English M
Psychology—General M

NORTHEASTERN UNIVERSITY
Applied Economics M,D
Architecture M
Counseling Psychology M,D,O
Criminal Justice and Criminology M,D
Economics M,D*
English M,D,O
Experimental Psychology M,D
History M,D*
International Affairs M,D,O
Journalism M
Political Science M,D,O
Psychology—General M,D,O
Public Administration M,O
Public Affairs M,D,O
Public History M,D
Public Policy M,D
Rehabilitation Counseling M
School Psychology M,D,O
Sociology M,D
Speech and Interpersonal Communication D
Urban Studies M,O

NORTHERN ARIZONA UNIVERSITY
Anthropology M
Archaeology M
Communication—General M
Counseling Psychology D
Criminal Justice and Criminology M,O
English M
Geographic Information Systems M,O
Geography M,O
Health Psychology M
History M,D
Liberal Studies M
Linguistics M,D,O
Music M
Political Science M,D,O
Psychology—General M
Public Administration M,D,O
Public Policy M,D,O
Rhetoric M
School Psychology M,D
Sociology M
Writing M

NORTHERN BAPTIST THEOLOGICAL SEMINARY
Ethics P,M,D
Pastoral Ministry and Counseling P,M,D
Religion P,M,D
Theology P,M,D

NORTHERN ILLINOIS UNIVERSITY
Anthropology M
Art/Fine Arts M
Child and Family Studies M
Communication—General M
Dance M
Economics M,D
English M,D
French M
Geography M,D
History M,D
Music M,O
Philosophy M
Political Science M,D
Psychology—General M,D
Public Administration M
Romance Languages M
Sociology M
Spanish M
Theater M

NORTHERN KENTUCKY UNIVERSITY
Communication—General M
Counseling Psychology M,O
Health Psychology M,O
Industrial and Organizational Psychology M,O
Liberal Studies M
Public Administration M,O
Social Psychology M

NORTHERN MICHIGAN UNIVERSITY
Criminal Justice and Criminology M
English M
Psychology—General M
Public Administration M
Writing M

NORTH GEORGIA COLLEGE & STATE UNIVERSITY
Public Administration M
Social Psychology M

NORTH GREENVILLE UNIVERSITY
Pastoral Ministry and Counseling M

NORTH PARK THEOLOGICAL SEMINARY
Theology P,M,D,O

NORTH PARK UNIVERSITY
Urban and Regional Planning M

NORTHWEST BAPTIST SEMINARY
Theology P,M,D,O

NORTHWESTERN OKLAHOMA STATE UNIVERSITY
Counseling Psychology M

NORTHWESTERN STATE UNIVERSITY OF LOUISIANA
Archaeology M
Art/Fine Arts M
Clinical Psychology M
English M
Historic Preservation M
Music M
Psychology—General M

NORTHWESTERN UNIVERSITY
African Studies O
Anthropology D
Art History D
Art/Fine Arts M*
Broadcast Journalism M
Clinical Psychology D
Cognitive Sciences D
Communication—General M,D
Comparative Literature M,D,O
Corporate and Organizational Communication M
Counseling Psychology M*
Economics M,D
English M,D*
Film, Television, and Video Production M,D
French D,O
Gender Studies M
Genetic Counseling M
German D
History D
Human Development D
International Affairs P,M,O
Italian D,O
Journalism M
Liberal Studies M
Linguistics M,D
Marriage and Family Therapy M
Media Studies M,D
Music M,D,O
Philosophy D
Political Science M,D
Psychology—General D*
Public Policy D*
Publishing M
Slavic Languages D
Social Psychology D
Social Sciences M,O
Sociology D
Speech and Interpersonal Communication M,D
Theater M,D
Writing M

NORTHWEST MISSOURI STATE UNIVERSITY
Agricultural Economics and Agribusiness M
English M
Geographic Information Systems M,O
Geography M,O
History M
Psychology—General M

NORTHWEST NAZARENE UNIVERSITY
Marriage and Family Therapy M
Missions and Missiology P,M
Pastoral Ministry and Counseling P,M
Religion P,M
School Psychology M
Social Psychology M

NORTHWEST UNIVERSITY
Counseling Psychology M
Psychology—General M

NORWICH UNIVERSITY
Conflict Resolution and Mediation/Peace Studies M
Criminal Justice and Criminology M
International Affairs M
Military and Defense Studies M
Public Administration M

NOTRE DAME COLLEGE (OH)
Pastoral Ministry and Counseling M,O

NOTRE DAME DE NAMUR UNIVERSITY
Addictions/Substance Abuse Counseling M,O
Art Therapy M
Counseling Psychology M,O
English M,O
Gerontology M,O
Marriage and Family Therapy M
Music M
Psychology—General M,O
Public Administration M

NOTRE DAME SEMINARY
Theology P,M

NOVA SOUTHEASTERN UNIVERSITY
Child and Family Studies M,D
Clinical Psychology D,O*
Conflict Resolution and Mediation/Peace Studies M,D*
Counseling Psychology M*
Criminal Justice and Criminology M*
Humanities M,O
Interdisciplinary Studies M,O
Marriage and Family Therapy M,D,O
Psychology—General M,D,O
Public Administration M,D
School Psychology O*
Social Sciences M,O
Spanish M,O

NSCAD UNIVERSITY
Applied Arts and Design—General M
Art/Fine Arts M

NYACK COLLEGE
Social Sciences M

OAKLAND CITY UNIVERSITY
Theology P,D

OAKLAND UNIVERSITY
Counseling Psychology M,D,O
Economics O
English M
History M
Liberal Studies M
Linguistics M,O
Music M,D
Public Administration M

OBERLIN COLLEGE
Music M,O

OBLATE SCHOOL OF THEOLOGY
Pastoral Ministry and Counseling P,M,D,O
Religion P,M,D,O
Theology P,M,D,O

OCCIDENTAL COLLEGE
Liberal Studies M

OHIO DOMINICAN UNIVERSITY
Liberal Studies M
Theology M

THE OHIO STATE UNIVERSITY
African Studies M
African-American Studies M
Agricultural Economics and Agribusiness M,D
Anthropology M,D
Architecture M
Art History M,D
Art/Fine Arts M
Arts Administration M
Asian Languages M,D
Child and Family Studies M,D
Chinese M,D
Classics M,D
Clinical Psychology M,D
Clothing and Textiles M,D
Cognitive Sciences M,D
Communication—General M,D*
Consumer Economics M,D
Dance D
Developmental Psychology M,D
East European and Russian Studies M
Economics M,D
English M,D
Family and Consumer Sciences-General M
Film, Television, and Video Theory and Criticism M
French M,D
Geography M,D
German M,D
History M,D
Human Development M,D
Industrial and Labor Relations M,D
Industrial Design M
Interdisciplinary Studies M,D
Interior Design M
Italian M,D
Japanese M,D
Journalism M
Landscape Architecture M
Linguistics M,D
Music M,D
Near and Middle Eastern Languages M,D
Philosophy M,D
Photography M
Political Science M,D
Portuguese M,D
Psychology—General M,D
Public Affairs M,D*
Rural Sociology M,D
Slavic Languages M,D
Social Psychology M,D
Sociology M,D
Spanish M,D
Theater M,D
Urban and Regional Planning M,D
Women's Studies M,D

OHIO UNIVERSITY
African Studies M
Applied Economics M
Art History M
Art/Fine Arts M
Asian Studies M
Child and Family Studies M
Child Development M
Clinical Psychology D
Communication—General M,D
Comparative and Interdisciplinary Arts D
Economics M
English M,D
Experimental Psychology D
Family and Consumer Sciences-General M
Film, Television, and Video Production M
Film, Television, and Video Theory and Criticism M
French M
Geography M
Graphic Design M
History M,D
Industrial and Organizational Psychology D
International Affairs M
International Development M
Journalism M,D
Latin American Studies M
Linguistics M
Media Studies M,D
Music M,O
Philosophy M
Photography M
Political Science M
Psychology—General D
Public Administration M
Rehabilitation Counseling M,D
Social Sciences M
Sociology M
Spanish M
Speech and Interpersonal Communication D
Theater M
Therapies—Dance, Drama, and Music M,O

OHR HAMEIR THEOLOGICAL SEMINARY
Theology

OKLAHOMA CHRISTIAN UNIVERSITY
Pastoral Ministry and Counseling P,M
Theology P,M

OKLAHOMA CITY UNIVERSITY
Art/Fine Arts M
Comparative Literature M
Corporate and Organizational Communication M
Criminal Justice and Criminology M
Dance M
Liberal Studies M
Mass Communication M
Music M
Philosophy M
Religion M
Theater M
Writing M

OKLAHOMA STATE UNIVERSITY
Agricultural Economics and Agribusiness M,D
Applied Arts and Design—General M,D
Architecture M
Child and Family Studies M,D
Clinical Psychology M,D
Clothing and Textiles M,D
Criminal Justice and Criminology M,D
Economics M,D
Emergency Management M
English M,D
Experimental Psychology M,D
Family and Consumer Sciences-General M,D
Geography M,D
Gerontology M
History M,D
International Affairs M
Landscape Architecture M,D
Mass Communication M
Music M
Philosophy M
Political Science M
Psychology—General M,D
Sociology M,D
Technical Writing M,D
Theater M
Writing M,D

OKLAHOMA STATE UNIVERSITY CENTER FOR HEALTH SCIENCES
Forensic Psychology M,O
Forensic Sciences M,O

OLD DOMINION UNIVERSITY
Applied Economics M
Art/Fine Arts M
Clinical Psychology D
Criminal Justice and Criminology D
Economics M
English M,D*
Experimental Psychology D
History M
Humanities M
Industrial and Organizational Psychology D
International Affairs M,D
Linguistics M
Psychology—General M,D
Public Administration M,D
Sociology M
Urban and Regional Planning M
Urban Studies M,D
Writing M

OLIVET NAZARENE UNIVERSITY
Pastoral Ministry and Counseling M
Religion M
Theology M

ORAL ROBERTS UNIVERSITY
Marriage and Family Therapy P,M,D
Missions and Missiology P,M,D
Near and Middle Eastern Languages P,M,D
Pastoral Ministry and Counseling P,M,D
Theology P,M,D

OREGON HEALTH & SCIENCE UNIVERSITY
Gerontology M,O

OREGON STATE UNIVERSITY
Agricultural Economics and Agribusiness M,D
Anthropology M
Child and Family Studies M,D
Clothing and Textiles M,D
Economics M,D
English M
Family and Consumer Sciences-General M
Geography M,D
Gerontology M
History M,D
Human Development M,D
Interdisciplinary Studies M

OREGON STATE UNIVERSITY–CASCADES
School Psychology M
Social Psychology M

OTIS COLLEGE OF ART AND DESIGN
Art/Fine Arts M
Graphic Design M
Photography M
Writing M

OTTAWA UNIVERSITY
Art Therapy M
Counseling Psychology M
Marriage and Family Therapy M
Pastoral Ministry and Counseling M
School Psychology M

OUR LADY OF HOLY CROSS COLLEGE
Marriage and Family Therapy M

OUR LADY OF THE LAKE UNIVERSITY OF SAN ANTONIO
Counseling Psychology M,D
English M
Human Development M
Marriage and Family Therapy M,D
Psychology—General M,D
School Psychology M,D
Sociology M

OXFORD GRADUATE SCHOOL
Child and Family Studies M,D
Religion M,D

PACE UNIVERSITY
Addictions/Substance Abuse Counseling M*
Clinical Psychology D
Economics M
Forensic Sciences M*
Psychology—General M,D*
Public Administration M*
Publishing M*
School Psychology M
Theater M*

PACIFICA GRADUATE INSTITUTE
Clinical Psychology M,D
Counseling Psychology M,D
Psychology—General M,D

PACIFIC GRADUATE SCHOOL OF PSYCHOLOGY
Clinical Psychology D*
Psychology—General M,D*

PACIFIC LUTHERAN THEOLOGICAL SEMINARY
Theology P,M,D,O

PACIFIC LUTHERAN UNIVERSITY
Marriage and Family Therapy M
Writing M

PACIFIC OAKS COLLEGE
Human Development M
Marriage and Family Therapy M

PACIFIC SCHOOL OF RELIGION
Religion P,M,D,O
Theology P,M,D,O

PACIFIC UNIVERSITY
Psychology—General M,D

PALM BEACH ATLANTIC UNIVERSITY
Addictions/Substance Abuse Counseling M
Counseling Psychology M
Marriage and Family Therapy M

PARK UNIVERSITY
Emergency Management M
Public Administration M
Public Affairs M

PAYNE THEOLOGICAL SEMINARY
Theology P

PENN STATE HARRISBURG
American Studies M
Clinical Psychology M,D
Criminal Justice and Criminology M,D
Humanities M
Psychology—General M,D
Public Administration M,D
Social Psychology M,D

PENN STATE UNIVERSITY PARK
Agricultural Economics and Agribusiness M,D
Anthropology M,D
Architecture M
Art History M,D
Art/Fine Arts M,D
Child and Family Studies M,D
Clinical Psychology M,D
Cognitive Sciences M,D
Communication—General M,D
Comparative Literature M,D
Counseling Psychology M,D
Criminal Justice and Criminology M,D
Developmental Psychology M,D
Economics M,D
English M,D
French M,D
Geography M,D
German M,D
History M,D
Human Development M,D
Industrial and Labor Relations M
Industrial and Organizational Psychology M,D
Landscape Architecture M
Mass Communication M,D
Music M,D
Philosophy M,D
Photography M,D
Political Science M,D
Psychology—General M,D
Rural Sociology M,D
Russian M,D
School Psychology M,D
Social Psychology M,D
Sociology M,D
Spanish M,D
Theater M
Writing M,D

PENNSYLVANIA ACADEMY OF THE FINE ARTS
Art/Fine Arts M,O*

PEPPERDINE UNIVERSITY
Clinical Psychology M
Psychology—General M,D*

PEPPERDINE UNIVERSITY
American Studies M
Clinical Psychology M
Communication—General M
Conflict Resolution and Mediation/Peace Studies M
Economics M
History M
Humanities M
International Affairs M
Political Science M
Psychology—General M
Public Administration M
Public Policy M*
Religion P,M

PERU STATE COLLEGE
Economics M

PHILADELPHIA BIBLICAL UNIVERSITY
Pastoral Ministry and Counseling M
Theology P,M

PHILADELPHIA COLLEGE OF OSTEOPATHIC MEDICINE
Clinical Psychology M,D,O
Counseling Psychology M,D,O
Forensic Sciences M
Health Psychology M,D,O
Industrial and Organizational Psychology M,D,O
Psychology—General M,D,O*
School Psychology M,D,O

PHILADELPHIA UNIVERSITY
Clothing and Textiles M
Computer Art and Design M
Textile Design M

PHILLIPS GRADUATE INSTITUTE
Clinical Psychology D
Marriage and Family Therapy M,D

PHILLIPS THEOLOGICAL SEMINARY
Ethics P,M,D
Missions and Missiology P,M,D
Music P,M,D
Pastoral Ministry and Counseling D
Theology P,M,D

PIEDMONT BAPTIST COLLEGE AND GRADUATE SCHOOL
Theology M,D

PITTSBURGH THEOLOGICAL SEMINARY
Theology P,M,D

PITTSBURG STATE UNIVERSITY
Art/Fine Arts M
Communication—General M
English M
Graphic Design M,O
History M
Music M
Psychology—General M
School Psychology O
Social Psychology M
Theater M

POINT LOMA NAZARENE UNIVERSITY
Religion M

POINT PARK UNIVERSITY
Communication—General M*
Criminal Justice and Criminology M
Journalism M
Mass Communication M
Music M
Theater M

POLYTECHNIC INSTITUTE OF NYU
Communication—General O
Criminal Justice and Criminology M,D,O
Film, Television, and Video Production O
History of Science and Technology M
Humanities M,O
Internet and Interactive Multimedia M,O*
Journalism M
Psychology—General M
Technical Communication O
Technical Writing M

POLYTECHNIC UNIVERSITY OF PUERTO RICO
Landscape Architecture M

PONCE SCHOOL OF MEDICINE
Clinical Psychology D

PONTIFICAL CATHOLIC UNIVERSITY OF PUERTO RICO
Clinical Psychology M,D
Criminal Justice and Criminology M
Hispanic Studies M,O
History M
Industrial and Organizational Psychology M,D
Psychology—General M,D
Public Administration M
Rehabilitation Counseling M
Spanish M,O
Theology P

PONTIFICAL COLLEGE JOSEPHINUM
Theology P,M

PONTIFICIA UNIVERSIDAD CATOLICA MADRE Y MAESTRA
Architecture M
Criminal Justice and Criminology M
Industrial and Labor Relations M
Interior Design M
International Affairs M
Urban and Regional Planning M

PORTLAND STATE UNIVERSITY
Anthropology M,D,O
Applied Economics M,D
Applied Social Research M,D
Art/Fine Arts M
Conflict Resolution and Mediation/Peace Studies M
Criminal Justice and Criminology M,D
Economics M,D,O
English M
French M
Geography M,D
German M
Gerontology O
History M
Japanese M
Music M
Political Science M,D
Psychology—General M,D,O
Public Administration M,D
Sociology M,D,O
Spanish M
Speech and Interpersonal Communication M,O
Theater M
Urban and Regional Planning M
Urban Studies M,D

PRAIRIE VIEW A&M UNIVERSITY
Agricultural Economics and Agribusiness M
Architecture M
Clinical Psychology M,D
English M
Family and Consumer Sciences-General M
Forensic Psychology M,D
Sociology M
Urban Design M

PRATT INSTITUTE
Applied Arts and Design—General M,O
Architecture M*
Art History M
Art Therapy M
Art/Fine Arts M*
Arts Administration M
Graphic Design M
Historic Preservation M
Industrial Design M
Interior Design M
Internet and Interactive Multimedia M
Photography M
Therapies—Dance, Drama, and Music M
Urban and Regional Planning M
Urban Design M

PRESCOTT COLLEGE
Counseling Psychology M
History M
Humanities M

Social Psychology M
Sustainable Development M

PRINCETON THEOLOGICAL SEMINARY
Religion P,M,D
Theology P,M,D

PRINCETON UNIVERSITY
Anthropology D
Archaeology D
Architecture M,D
Asian Studies D
Classics D
Comparative Literature D
Demography and Population Studies D,O
Economics D,O
English D
French D
German D
History of Science and Technology D
History D
International Affairs M,D
Italian D
Music D
Near and Middle Eastern Studies M,D
Philosophy D
Political Science D
Portuguese D
Psychology—General D
Public Affairs M,D
Religion D
Slavic Languages D
Sociology D,O
Spanish D

THE PROTESTANT EPISCOPAL THEOLOGICAL SEMINARY IN VIRGINIA
Theology P,M,D

PROVIDENCE COLLEGE
History M
Pastoral Ministry and Counseling M
Religion M
Theology M

PROVIDENCE COLLEGE AND THEOLOGICAL SEMINARY
Counseling Psychology P,M,D,O
Missions and Missiology P,M,D,O
Pastoral Ministry and Counseling P,M,D,O
Theology P,M,D,O

PURCHASE COLLEGE, STATE UNIVERSITY OF NEW YORK
Art History M
Art/Fine Arts M
Dance M
Music M
Theater M

PURDUE UNIVERSITY
Agricultural Economics and Agribusiness M,D
American Studies M,D
Anthropology M,D
Applied Arts and Design—General M
Art/Fine Arts M
Child and Family Studies M,D
Child Development M,D
Clothing and Textiles M,D
Communication—General M,D
Comparative Literature M,D
Consumer Economics M,D
Economics D
English M,D
Family and Consumer Sciences-General M,D
French M,D
German M,D
History M,D
Human Development M,D
Linguistics M,D
Marriage and Family Therapy M,D
Philosophy M,D
Political Science M,D
Psychology—General D
Sociology M,D
Spanish M,D
Sport Psychology M,D
Theater M
Writing M,D

PURDUE UNIVERSITY CALUMET
Communication—General M
English M
History M
Marriage and Family Therapy M
Philosophy M
Political Science M

QUEENS COLLEGE OF THE CITY UNIVERSITY OF NEW YORK
Art History M
Art/Fine Arts M
Clinical Psychology M
English M
Family and Consumer Sciences-General M
French M
History M
Italian M
Liberal Studies M
Linguistics M
Music M
Psychology—General M
Romance Languages M
School Psychology M,O
Social Sciences M
Sociology M
Spanish M
Urban Studies M
Writing M

QUEEN'S UNIVERSITY AT KINGSTON
Classics M
Clinical Psychology M,D
Cognitive Sciences M,D
Developmental Psychology M,D
English M,D
French M,D
Geography M,D
German M,D
Industrial and Labor Relations M
Philosophy M,D
Political Science M,D
Psychology—General M,D
Public Policy M
Religion M
Social Psychology M,D
Sociology M,D
Spanish M
Sport Psychology M,D
Theology P,M
Urban and Regional Planning M

QUEENS UNIVERSITY OF CHARLOTTE
Corporate and Organizational Communication M
Writing M

QUINCY UNIVERSITY
Theology M

QUINNIPIAC UNIVERSITY
Communication—General M*
Economics M
Internet and Interactive Multimedia M
Journalism M

RABBI ISAAC ELCHANAN THEOLOGICAL SEMINARY
Theology O

RABBINICAL ACADEMY MESIVTA RABBI CHAIM BERLIN
Theology O

RABBINICAL COLLEGE BETH SHRAGA
Theology

RABBINICAL COLLEGE BOBOVER YESHIVA B'NEI ZION
Theology

RABBINICAL COLLEGE CH'SAN SOFER
Theology

RABBINICAL COLLEGE OF LONG ISLAND
Theology

RABBINICAL SEMINARY M'KOR CHAIM
Theology

RABBINICAL SEMINARY OF AMERICA
Theology

RADFORD UNIVERSITY
Art/Fine Arts M
Clinical Psychology M,D,O
Corporate and Organizational Communication M
Counseling Psychology M,D,O
Criminal Justice and Criminology M
English M
Experimental Psychology M,D,O
Industrial and Organizational Psychology M,D,O
Music M
Psychology—General M,D,O
School Psychology O
Therapies—Dance, Drama, and Music M

RAMAPO COLLEGE OF NEW JERSEY
Liberal Studies M

RECONSTRUCTIONIST RABBINICAL COLLEGE
Theology P,M,D,O

REED COLLEGE
Liberal Studies M

REFORMED PRESBYTERIAN THEOLOGICAL SEMINARY
Theology P,M,D

REFORMED THEOLOGICAL SEMINARY–CHARLOTTE CAMPUS
Pastoral Ministry and Counseling P,M,D
Religion P,M,D
Theology P,M,D

REFORMED THEOLOGICAL SEMINARY–JACKSON CAMPUS
Marriage and Family Therapy P,M,D,O
Missions and Missiology P,M,D,O
Pastoral Ministry and Counseling P,M,D,O
Theology P,M,D,O

REFORMED THEOLOGICAL SEMINARY–ORLANDO CAMPUS
Pastoral Ministry and Counseling P,M,D
Theology P,M,D

REFORMED THEOLOGICAL SEMINARY–WASHINGTON D.C.
Religion P,M
Theology P,M

REGENT COLLEGE
Theology P,M,O

REGENT UNIVERSITY
Art/Fine Arts M,D
Clinical Psychology M,D,O
Communication—General M,D
Counseling Psychology M,D,O
Economics M
Film, Television, and Video Production M,D
Homeland Security M
Journalism M,D
Missions and Missiology P,M,D
Pastoral Ministry and Counseling P,M,D
Political Science M
Public Administration M
Public Policy M
School Psychology M,D,O
Social Psychology M,D,O
Theater M,D
Theology P,M,D

REGIS COLLEGE (CANADA)
Pastoral Ministry and Counseling P,M,D,O
Theology P,M,D,O

REGIS COLLEGE (MA)
Corporate and Organizational Communication M
Public Administration M,O
Public Policy M,O

REGIS UNIVERSITY
Art/Fine Arts M,O
Arts Administration M,O
Communication—General M,O
Conflict Resolution and Mediation/Peace Studies M,O
Counseling Psychology M,O
Criminal Justice and Criminology M,O
Interdisciplinary Studies M,O
Marriage and Family Therapy M,O

Music M,O
Psychology—General M,O
Social Psychology M,O
Social Sciences M,O
Technical Writing M,O

RENSSELAER POLYTECHNIC INSTITUTE

Architecture M,D*
Art/Fine Arts M,D
Cognitive Sciences D*
Communication—General M,D*
Computer Art and Design M,D*
Economics M*
Historic Preservation M
History of Science and Technology M,D
Interdisciplinary Studies M,D
Lighting Design M
Rhetoric M,D
Speech and Interpersonal Communication M,D
Technical Communication M

RHODE ISLAND COLLEGE

Art/Fine Arts M
Arts Administration M
English M
History M
Psychology—General M
Public Administration M
Theater M
Writing M

RHODE ISLAND SCHOOL OF DESIGN

Applied Arts and Design—General M
Architecture M
Art/Fine Arts M
Computer Art and Design M
Graphic Design M
Industrial Design M
Interior Design M
Landscape Architecture M
Photography M
Textile Design M

RICE UNIVERSITY

Anthropology M,D
Architecture M,D
Cognitive Sciences M,D
Economics M,D
English M,D
French M,D
History M,D
Industrial and Organizational Psychology M,D
Linguistics M,D
Music M,D
Philosophy M,D
Political Science M,D
Psychology—General M,D
Religion D
Spanish M
Urban Design M,D

THE RICHARD STOCKTON COLLEGE OF NEW JERSEY

Criminal Justice and Criminology M
Holocaust Studies M

RICHMOND, THE AMERICAN INTERNATIONAL UNIVERSITY IN LONDON

Art History M

RIDER UNIVERSITY

French O
German O
School Psychology O
Spanish O

RIVIER COLLEGE

Counseling Psychology M,O
English M
Writing M

ROBERT MORRIS UNIVERSITY

Internet and Interactive Multimedia M,D

ROBERTS WESLEYAN COLLEGE

Child and Family Studies M
Pastoral Ministry and Counseling M
School Psychology M

ROCHESTER INSTITUTE OF TECHNOLOGY

Art/Fine Arts M
Communication—General M
Computer Art and Design M
Film, Television, and Video Production M
Gerontology O
Graphic Design M
Industrial Design M
Interdisciplinary Studies M
Internet and Interactive Multimedia M,O
Media Studies M
Medical Illustration M
Photography M
Psychology—General M
Public Policy M
School Psychology M,O
Technical Communication O

ROCKFORD COLLEGE

Music M

ROGER WILLIAMS UNIVERSITY

Architecture M
Criminal Justice and Criminology M*
Forensic Psychology M*
Public Administration M

ROLLINS COLLEGE

Liberal Studies M

ROOSEVELT UNIVERSITY

Anthropology M
Applied Economics M
Clinical Psychology M,D
Communication—General M
Corporate and Organizational Communication M
Economics M
English M
Gender Studies M,O
History M
Industrial and Organizational Psychology M
Journalism M
Music M,O
Political Science M
Psychology—General D
Public Administration M
Sociology M
Spanish M
Theater M
Women's Studies M,O
Writing M

ROSALIND FRANKLIN UNIVERSITY OF MEDICINE AND SCIENCE

Clinical Psychology M,D
Interdisciplinary Studies D
Psychology—General M,D

ROSEMONT COLLEGE

Counseling Psychology M
English M
Publishing M
Writing M

ROWAN UNIVERSITY

Counseling Psychology M,O
Criminal Justice and Criminology M
Music M
Psychology—General M,O
School Psychology M,O
Theater M
Writing M

ROYAL MILITARY COLLEGE OF CANADA

Military and Defense Studies M,D

ROYAL ROADS UNIVERSITY

Conflict Resolution and Mediation/Peace Studies M
Corporate and Organizational Communication M

RUTGERS, THE STATE UNIVERSITY OF NEW JERSEY, CAMDEN

Child Development M,D
Criminal Justice and Criminology M
English M
History M
International Affairs M
International Development M
Liberal Studies M
Psychology—General M
Public Administration M
Public History M
Public Policy M

RUTGERS, THE STATE UNIVERSITY OF NEW JERSEY, NEWARK

Cognitive Sciences D*
Criminal Justice and Criminology M,D
Economics M
English M
History M
International Affairs M,D*
Liberal Studies M
Music M
Political Science M
Psychology—General D
Public Administration M,D
Public Policy M,D
Social Psychology D
Urban Studies M,D

RUTGERS, THE STATE UNIVERSITY OF NEW JERSEY, NEW BRUNSWICK

African Studies D
African-American Studies D
Agricultural Economics and Agribusiness M
Anthropology M,D
Applied Arts and Design—General M
Art History M,D,O
Art/Fine Arts M
Asian Studies D
Classics M,D
Clinical Psychology M,D
Cognitive Sciences D
Communication—General D
Comparative Literature M,D
Counseling Psychology M
Economics M,D
English D
French M,D
Gender Studies M,D
Geography M,D
German M,D
Health Psychology D
Historic Preservation M,D,O
History of Medicine D
History of Science and Technology D
History D
Industrial and Labor Relations M,D*
Industrial and Organizational Psychology M,D
Interdisciplinary Studies D
International Affairs D
Italian M,D
Linguistics D
Medieval and Renaissance Studies D
Music M,D,O
Philosophy D
Political Science D
Psychology—General M,D
Public Policy M
School Psychology D
Social Psychology D
Sociology M,D
Spanish M,D
Theater M
Translation and Interpretation M,D
Urban and Regional Planning M,D
Women's Studies M,D
Writing M

RYERSON UNIVERSITY

Arts Administration M

SACRED HEART MAJOR SEMINARY

Pastoral Ministry and Counseling P,M
Theology P,M

SACRED HEART SCHOOL OF THEOLOGY

Theology P,M

SACRED HEART UNIVERSITY

Criminal Justice and Criminology M
Gerontology M
Internet and Interactive Multimedia M,O
Religion M

SAGE GRADUATE SCHOOL

Child and Family Studies M
Criminal Justice and Criminology M,O
Forensic Psychology M,O
Gerontology M
Psychology—General M,O
Public Administration M
Social Psychology M
Sociology M,O

SAGINAW VALLEY STATE UNIVERSITY

Communication—General M
Media Studies M
Public Administration M

ST. AMBROSE UNIVERSITY

Criminal Justice and Criminology M

Pastoral Ministry and Counseling	M

ST. ANDREW'S COLLEGE IN WINNIPEG

Theology	P

ST. AUGUSTINE'S SEMINARY OF TORONTO

Pastoral Ministry and Counseling	P,M,O
Theology	P,M,O

SAINT BERNARD'S SCHOOL OF THEOLOGY AND MINISTRY

Pastoral Ministry and Counseling	P,M,O
Theology	P,M,O

ST. BONAVENTURE UNIVERSITY

English	M
Theology	M,O

ST. CHARLES BORROMEO SEMINARY, OVERBROOK

Religion	M
Theology	P,M

ST. CLOUD STATE UNIVERSITY

Applied Economics	M
Archaeology	M
Child and Family Studies	M
Criminal Justice and Criminology	M
Economics	M
English	M
Geography	M
Gerontology	M
Historic Preservation	M
History	M
Industrial and Organizational Psychology	M
Marriage and Family Therapy	M
Mass Communication	M
Music	M
Psychology—General	M
Rehabilitation Counseling	M
Social Psychology	M

ST. EDWARD'S UNIVERSITY

Computer Art and Design	M
Conflict Resolution and Mediation/Peace Studies	M,O
Counseling Psychology	M
Ethics	M
Liberal Studies	M,O
Public Administration	M,O

SAINT FRANCIS SEMINARY

Pastoral Ministry and Counseling	P,M
Theology	P,M

ST. FRANCIS XAVIER UNIVERSITY

Cultural Studies	M

ST. JOHN FISHER COLLEGE

Counseling Psychology	M
International Affairs	M

ST. JOHN'S COLLEGE (MD)

Liberal Studies	M

ST. JOHN'S COLLEGE (NM)

Asian Languages	M
Asian Studies	M
Liberal Studies	M

ST. JOHN'S SEMINARY (CA)

Pastoral Ministry and Counseling	P,M
Theology	P,M

SAINT JOHN'S SEMINARY (MA)

Religion	P,M
Theology	P,M

SAINT JOHN'S UNIVERSITY (MN)

Music	P,M
Pastoral Ministry and Counseling	P,M
Theology	P,M

ST. JOHN'S UNIVERSITY (NY)

African Studies	M,O
Asian Studies	M,O
Clinical Psychology	D
Communication—General	M,D,O
Criminal Justice and Criminology	M
English	M,D
Experimental Psychology	M
History	M,D
Liberal Studies	M
Pastoral Ministry and Counseling	P,M,O
Philosophy	M
Political Science	M,O
Psychology—General	M,D
Rehabilitation Counseling	M,D,O
School Psychology	M,D
Sociology	M
Spanish	M,D
Theater	M,D,O
Theology	P,M,O

SAINT JOSEPH COLLEGE

Child and Family Studies	M,O
Counseling Psychology	M,O
Gerontology	O
Human Development	O
Marriage and Family Therapy	M,O
Pastoral Ministry and Counseling	M,O
Social Psychology	M,O

SAINT JOSEPH'S COLLEGE

Music	M,O

ST. JOSEPH'S SEMINARY

Theology	P,M

SAINT JOSEPH'S UNIVERSITY

Criminal Justice and Criminology	M,O
Gerontology	M,O
Homeland Security	M,O
Industrial and Organizational Psychology	M,O
Psychology—General	M,O
Writing	M

ST. LAWRENCE UNIVERSITY

Human Development	M,O

SAINT LEO UNIVERSITY

Criminal Justice and Criminology	M

Pastoral Ministry and Counseling	M

SAINT LOUIS UNIVERSITY

American Studies	M,D
Clinical Psychology	M,D
Communication—General	M
English	M,D
Experimental Psychology	M,D
French	M
Geographic Information Systems	M,D,O
History	M,D
Human Development	M,D,O
Industrial and Organizational Psychology	M,D
Marriage and Family Therapy	M,D,O
Philosophy	M,D
Political Science	M
Psychology—General	M,D
Public Administration	M,D,O
Public Policy	M,D,O
Spanish	M
Theology	M,D
Urban Studies	M,D,O

SAINT LOUIS UNIVERSITY, MADRID

English	M*
Spanish	M*

SAINT MARTIN'S UNIVERSITY

Counseling Psychology	M
Social Psychology	M

SAINT MARY-OF-THE-WOODS COLLEGE

Art Therapy	M,O
Pastoral Ministry and Counseling	M,O
Theology	M,O
Therapies—Dance, Drama, and Music	M

SAINT MARY'S COLLEGE OF CALIFORNIA

Liberal Studies	M
Marriage and Family Therapy	M
Writing	M

SAINT MARY SEMINARY AND GRADUATE SCHOOL OF THEOLOGY

Theology	P,M,D

ST. MARY'S SEMINARY AND UNIVERSITY

Theology	P,M,D,O*

SAINT MARY'S UNIVERSITY (CANADA)

Canadian Studies	M
Clinical Psychology	M
Criminal Justice and Criminology	M
History	M
Industrial and Organizational Psychology	M
International Development	M
Philosophy	M
Psychology—General	M
Women's Studies	M

ST. MARY'S UNIVERSITY (UNITED STATES)

Addictions/Substance Abuse Counseling	M,D,O
Clinical Psychology	M
Communication—General	M
Counseling Psychology	M
English	M
Industrial and Organizational Psychology	M
International Affairs	M
Marriage and Family Therapy	M,D
Pastoral Ministry and Counseling	M
Political Science	M
Psychology—General	M
Public Administration	M
School Psychology	M
Social Psychology	M
Theology	M

SAINT MARY'S UNIVERSITY OF MINNESOTA

Arts Administration	M
Counseling Psychology	M
Geographic Information Systems	M,O
Human Development	M
Marriage and Family Therapy	M,O
Pastoral Ministry and Counseling	M,O
Philanthropic Studies	M

SAINT MEINRAD SCHOOL OF THEOLOGY

Theology	P,M

SAINT MICHAEL'S COLLEGE

Clinical Psychology	M
Theology	M,O

ST. NORBERT COLLEGE

Theology	M

ST. PATRICK'S SEMINARY & UNIVERSITY

Theology	P,M

SAINT PAUL SCHOOL OF THEOLOGY

Theology	P,M,D

SAINT PAUL UNIVERSITY

Conflict Resolution and Mediation/Peace Studies	M
Counseling Psychology	M
Marriage and Family Therapy	M
Missions and Missiology	M
Pastoral Ministry and Counseling	M,D,O
Theology	M,D,O

ST. PETERSBURG THEOLOGICAL SEMINARY

Jewish Studies	P,M,D
Pastoral Ministry and Counseling	P,M,D
Theology	P,M,D

ST. PETER'S SEMINARY

Theology	P,M

SAINTS CYRIL AND METHODIUS SEMINARY
Pastoral Ministry and Counseling P,M
Theology P,M

ST. STEPHEN'S COLLEGE
Pastoral Ministry and Counseling M,D
Theology M,D

ST. THOMAS UNIVERSITY
Arts Administration M
Communication—General M,D,O
Counseling Psychology M
Criminal Justice and Criminology M,O
Film, Television, and Video Production M
Hispanic Studies M,O
Marriage and Family Therapy M,O
Pastoral Ministry and Counseling M,D,O
Public Administration M,O
Theology M,D,O

ST. TIKHON'S ORTHODOX THEOLOGICAL SEMINARY
Theology P

SAINT VINCENT DE PAUL REGIONAL SEMINARY
Theology P,M

SAINT VINCENT SEMINARY
Theology P,M

ST. VLADIMIR'S ORTHODOX THEOLOGICAL SEMINARY
Music P,M,D
Theology P,M,D

SAINT XAVIER UNIVERSITY
Counseling Psychology M,O
English M,O
Psychology—General M,O
Writing M,O

SALEM STATE COLLEGE
Counseling Psychology M
Criminal Justice and Criminology M
English M
Geography M
History M
Psychology—General M
Spanish M

SALISBURY UNIVERSITY
English M
Geographic Information Systems M
History M
Public Administration M
Writing M

SALVE REGINA UNIVERSITY
Art Therapy M,O
Counseling Psychology M,O
Criminal Justice and Criminology M
Homeland Security M,O
Humanities M,D
International Affairs M,O
Rehabilitation Counseling M,O

SAMFORD UNIVERSITY
Music M
Theology P,M,D

SAM HOUSTON STATE UNIVERSITY
Art/Fine Arts M
Clinical Psychology M,D
Criminal Justice and Criminology M,D
Dance M
English M
Family and Consumer Sciences-General M
Forensic Sciences M,D
History M
Humanities M,D
Music M
Political Science M
Psychology—General M,D
Public Administration M
School Psychology M,D
Sociology M

SAN DIEGO STATE UNIVERSITY
Anthropology M
Applied Arts and Design—General M
Art History M
Art/Fine Arts M
Asian Studies M
Child and Family Studies M
Child Development M
Clinical Psychology M,D
Communication—General M
Criminal Justice and Criminology M
Economics M
Emergency Management M,D
English M
Environmental Design M
Film, Television, and Video Production M
Geography M,D
Gerontology M
Graphic Design M
Health Psychology M,D
History M
Industrial and Organizational Psychology M,D
Interdisciplinary Studies M
Interior Design M
Internet and Interactive Multimedia M
Latin American Studies M
Liberal Studies M
Linguistics M,O
Media Studies M
Music M
Philosophy M
Political Science M
Psychology—General M,D
Public Administration M
Rehabilitation Counseling M
Rhetoric M
Romance Languages M
School Psychology M
Sociology M
Spanish M
Theater M
Urban and Regional Planning M
Western European Studies M
Women's Studies M
Writing M

SAN FRANCISCO ART INSTITUTE
Applied Arts and Design—General M,O
Art History M
Art/Fine Arts M,O*
Film, Television, and Video Production M,O
Museum Studies M
Photography M,O
Urban Studies M

SAN FRANCISCO CONSERVATORY OF MUSIC
Music M

SAN FRANCISCO STATE UNIVERSITY
Anthropology M
Art History M
Art/Fine Arts M
Asian-American Studies M
Chinese M
Classics M
Comparative Literature M
Counseling Psychology M
Cultural Studies M
Economics M
English M,O
Ethnic Studies M
Family and Consumer Sciences-General M
Film, Television, and Video Production M
Film, Television, and Video Theory and Criticism M
French M
Geography M
German M
Gerontology M
History M
Humanities M
Industrial Design M
International Affairs M
Italian M
Japanese M
Linguistics M
Marriage and Family Therapy M
Media Studies M
Museum Studies M
Music M
Philosophy M,O
Political Science M
Psychology—General M
Public Administration M
Public Policy M
Rehabilitation Counseling M
Spanish M
Speech and Interpersonal Communication M
Theater M
Women's Studies M
Writing M

SAN FRANCISCO THEOLOGICAL SEMINARY
Theology P,M,D

SAN JOSE STATE UNIVERSITY
Anthropology M
Applied Arts and Design—General M
Applied Economics M
Art History M
Art/Fine Arts M
Child and Family Studies M
Clinical Psychology M
Communication—General M
Comparative Literature M,O
Computer Art and Design M
Criminal Justice and Criminology M
Economics M
English M,O
Experimental Psychology M
Film, Television, and Video Production M
French M
Geographic Information Systems M,O
Geography M,O
Gerontology M,O
Hispanic Studies M
History M
Industrial and Organizational Psychology M
Interdisciplinary Studies M
Linguistics M,O
Mass Communication M
Music M
Philosophy M,O
Photography M
Psychology—General M
Public Administration M
Sociology M
Spanish M
Speech and Interpersonal Communication M
Theater M
Urban and Regional Planning M,O
Writing M,O

SANTA CLARA UNIVERSITY
Counseling Psychology M,O
Music M
Pastoral Ministry and Counseling M
Religion M

SARAH LAWRENCE COLLEGE
Child Development M
Dance M*
Genetic Counseling M
History M
Interdisciplinary Studies M
Theater M
Women's Studies M*
Writing M

SAVANNAH COLLEGE OF ART AND DESIGN
Applied Arts and Design—General M
Architectural History M
Architecture M
Art History M
Art/Fine Arts M*
Arts Administration M
Computer Art and Design M
Film, Television, and Video Production M
Film, Television, and Video Theory and Criticism M
Graphic Design M
Historic Preservation M
Illustration M
Industrial Design M
Interior Design M
Internet and Interactive Multimedia M
Media Studies M
Music M
Photography M
Textile Design M
Theater M
Urban Design M
Writing M

SAVANNAH STATE UNIVERSITY
Public Administration M
Urban Studies M

SAYBROOK GRADUATE SCHOOL AND RESEARCH CENTER
Clinical Psychology M,D
Health Psychology M,D
Marriage and Family Therapy M,D
Psychology—General M,D
Transpersonal and Humanistic Psychology M,D

SCHILLER INTERNATIONAL UNIVERSITY
- International Affairs M

SCHILLER INTERNATIONAL UNIVERSITY (UNITED KINGDOM)
- Corporate and Organizational Communication M
- International Affairs M

SCHOOL OF ADVANCED AIR AND SPACE STUDIES
- Military and Defense Studies M

THE SCHOOL OF PROFESSIONAL PSYCHOLOGY AT FOREST INSTITUTE
- Clinical Psychology M,D,O
- Psychology—General M,D,O

SCHOOL OF THE ART INSTITUTE OF CHICAGO
- Art History M,O
- Art Therapy M
- Art/Fine Arts M*
- Arts Administration M
- Film, Television, and Video Production M
- Graphic Design M
- Historic Preservation M
- Interior Design M
- Photography M
- Writing M

SCHOOL OF THE MUSEUM OF FINE ARTS, BOSTON
- Art/Fine Arts M

SCHOOL OF VISUAL ARTS
- Applied Arts and Design—General M
- Art Therapy M
- Art/Fine Arts M
- Computer Art and Design M
- Film, Television, and Video Production M
- Illustration M
- Internet and Interactive Multimedia M
- Photography M

SEABURY-WESTERN THEOLOGICAL SEMINARY
- Theology P,M,D,O

SEATTLE PACIFIC UNIVERSITY
- Clinical Psychology D
- Economics M
- Industrial and Organizational Psychology M,D
- Marriage and Family Therapy M
- Writing M

SEATTLE UNIVERSITY
- Criminal Justice and Criminology M
- Pastoral Ministry and Counseling M
- Psychology—General M
- Public Administration M
- School Psychology M,O
- Theology P,M,O
- Transpersonal and Humanistic Psychology M

SEMINARY OF THE IMMACULATE CONCEPTION
- Pastoral Ministry and Counseling P,M,D,O
- Theology P,M,D,O

SETON HALL UNIVERSITY
- Art/Fine Arts M
- Arts Administration M
- Asian Studies M*
- Communication—General M
- Corporate and Organizational Communication M*
- Counseling Psychology M,D
- English M*
- Experimental Psychology M*
- History M*
- International Affairs M*
- Jewish Studies M
- Marriage and Family Therapy M,D,O
- Mass Communication M
- Museum Studies M*
- Music M
- Pastoral Ministry and Counseling P,M,O
- Psychology—General M,D,O
- Public Administration M
- Public Policy M*
- Religion M*
- School Psychology O
- Speech and Interpersonal Communication M
- Theology P,M,O

SETON HILL UNIVERSITY
- Art Therapy M,O
- Holocaust Studies O
- Marriage and Family Therapy M
- Writing M

SEWANEE: THE UNIVERSITY OF THE SOUTH
- English M*
- Theology P,M,D
- Writing M

SHASTA BIBLE COLLEGE
- Pastoral Ministry and Counseling M

SHAW UNIVERSITY
- Theology P,M

SHENANDOAH UNIVERSITY
- Arts Administration M,D,O
- Dance M,D,O
- Music M,D,O*
- Public Administration M,D,O
- Therapies—Dance, Drama, and Music M,D,O
- Women's Studies M,D,O

SHIPPENSBURG UNIVERSITY OF PENNSYLVANIA
- Communication—General M
- Criminal Justice and Criminology M
- History M,O
- Marriage and Family Therapy M,O
- Psychology—General M
- Public Administration M
- Public History M,O
- Sociology M

SH'OR YOSHUV RABBINICAL COLLEGE
- Theology

SIMMONS COLLEGE
- Corporate and Organizational Communication M
- Cultural Studies M
- English M
- Gender Studies M
- Genetic Counseling O
- Public History
- Spanish M

SIMON FRASER UNIVERSITY
- Anthropology M,D
- Archaeology M,D
- Communication—General M,D
- Comparative and Interdisciplinary Arts M
- Criminal Justice and Criminology M,D
- Economics M,D
- English M,D
- French M
- Geography M,D
- Gerontology M,D
- History M,D
- Internet and Interactive Multimedia M,D
- Latin American Studies M
- Liberal Studies M
- Linguistics M,D
- Philosophy M,D
- Political Science M,D
- Psychology—General M,D
- Public Policy M
- Publishing M
- Sociology M,D
- Urban Studies M,O
- Women's Studies M,D

SIMPSON UNIVERSITY
- Cultural Studies P,M
- Missions and Missiology P,M
- Pastoral Ministry and Counseling P,M
- Religion P,M

SIOUX FALLS SEMINARY
- Marriage and Family Therapy M
- Pastoral Ministry and Counseling P,M
- Religion M
- Theology M,D,O

SIT GRADUATE INSTITUTE
- Conflict Resolution and Mediation/Peace Studies M
- International Affairs M
- Sustainable Development M

SKIDMORE COLLEGE
- Liberal Studies M

SLIPPERY ROCK UNIVERSITY OF PENNSYLVANIA
- English M
- History M
- Sustainable Development M

SMITH COLLEGE
- Dance M
- French M
- History M
- Theater M

SOJOURNER-DOUGLASS COLLEGE
- Public Administration M

SONOMA STATE UNIVERSITY
- Anthropology M
- Counseling Psychology M
- English M
- History M
- Interdisciplinary Studies M
- Marriage and Family Therapy M
- Political Science M
- Public Administration M
- Public History M
- Writing M

SOUTH CAROLINA STATE UNIVERSITY
- Agricultural Economics and Agribusiness M
- Child and Family Studies M
- Family and Consumer Sciences-General M
- Rehabilitation Counseling M

SOUTH DAKOTA STATE UNIVERSITY
- Clothing and Textiles M
- Communication—General M
- Economics M
- English M
- Family and Consumer Sciences-General M
- Geography M
- Human Development M
- Interior Design M
- Journalism M
- Rural Sociology M,D

SOUTHEASTERN BAPTIST THEOLOGICAL SEMINARY
- Ethics P,M,D
- Missions and Missiology P,M,D
- Music P,M,D
- Philosophy P,M,D
- Psychology—General P,M,D
- Theology P,M,D
- Women's Studies P,M,D

SOUTHEASTERN LOUISIANA UNIVERSITY
- Communication—General M
- English M
- History M
- Music M
- Psychology—General M
- Sociology M

SOUTHEASTERN UNIVERSITY
- Public Administration M

SOUTHEAST MISSOURI STATE UNIVERSITY
- Criminal Justice and Criminology M
- English M
- Family and Consumer Sciences-General M
- History M
- Public Administration M
- School Psychology M,O
- Social Psychology M,O

SOUTHERN ADVENTIST UNIVERSITY
- Counseling Psychology M
- Missions and Missiology M
- Psychology—General M

Program	Degrees
Religion	M
Theology	M

SOUTHERN ARKANSAS UNIVERSITY–MAGNOLIA

Program	Degrees
Counseling Psychology	M
Public Administration	M

SOUTHERN BAPTIST THEOLOGICAL SEMINARY

Program	Degrees
Missions and Missiology	P,M,D
Music	P,M,D
Pastoral Ministry and Counseling	P,M,D
Theology	P,M,D

SOUTHERN CALIFORNIA INSTITUTE OF ARCHITECTURE

Program	Degrees
Architecture	M*

SOUTHERN CALIFORNIA SEMINARY

Program	Degrees
Counseling Psychology	P,M,D
Psychology—General	P,M,D
Religion	P,M,D
Theology	P,M,D

SOUTHERN CONNECTICUT STATE UNIVERSITY

Program	Degrees
English	M
History	M
Marriage and Family Therapy	M
Political Science	M
Psychology—General	M
School Psychology	M,O
Sociology	M
Sport Psychology	M
Urban Studies	M
Women's Studies	M

SOUTHERN EVANGELICAL SEMINARY

Program	Degrees
Jewish Studies	M,D,O
Missions and Missiology	P,M,O
Near and Middle Eastern Studies	M,D,O
Pastoral Ministry and Counseling	P,M,O
Philosophy	M,D,O
Religion	P,M,D,O
Theology	P,M,D,O

SOUTHERN ILLINOIS UNIVERSITY CARBONDALE

Program	Degrees
Agricultural Economics and Agribusiness	M
Anthropology	M,D*
Applied Arts and Design—General	M*
Architecture	M
Art/Fine Arts	M
Clinical Psychology	M,D
Communication—General	M,D*
Counseling Psychology	M,D
Criminal Justice and Criminology	M
Cultural Studies	M
Economics	M,D*
English	M,D*
Experimental Psychology	M,D
Geography	M,D
History	M,D*
Human Development	M,D
Journalism	D
Linguistics	M
Mass Communication	M
Media Studies	M
Music	M
Philosophy	M,D*
Political Science	M,D*
Psychology—General	M,D*
Public Administration	M
Rehabilitation Counseling	M,D*
Rhetoric	M,D
Sociology	M,D*
Speech and Interpersonal Communication	M,D*
Theater	M,D*
Writing	M*

SOUTHERN ILLINOIS UNIVERSITY EDWARDSVILLE

Program	Degrees
Art Therapy	M,O
Art/Fine Arts	M
Clinical Psychology	M
Corporate and Organizational Communication	O
Economics	M
English	M,O
Geography	M
History	M
Industrial and Organizational Psychology	M
Mass Communication	M
Media Studies	O
Museum Studies	O
Music	M,O
Psychology—General	M,O
Public Administration	M
School Psychology	O
Sociology	M
Speech and Interpersonal Communication	M
Writing	M

SOUTHERN METHODIST UNIVERSITY

Program	Degrees
Anthropology	M,D
Applied Economics	M,D
Art History	M
Art/Fine Arts	M
Arts Administration	M
Clinical Psychology	D
Conflict Resolution and Mediation/Peace Studies	M
Dance	M
Economics	M,D
English	M,D
Film, Television, and Video Production	M
History	M,D
Interdisciplinary Studies	M
Medieval and Renaissance Studies	M
Music	M,O
Photography	M
Psychology—General	D
Religion	M,D
Theater	M
Theology	P,M,D

SOUTHERN NAZARENE UNIVERSITY

Program	Degrees
Counseling Psychology	M
Marriage and Family Therapy	M
Psychology—General	M
Religion	M
Theology	M

SOUTHERN NEW HAMPSHIRE UNIVERSITY

Program	Degrees
Addictions/Substance Abuse Counseling	M,O
Child Development	M,O
Clinical Psychology	M,O
Psychology—General	M,O
Public Policy	M,D
Writing	M,O

SOUTHERN OREGON UNIVERSITY

Program	Degrees
Music	M
Psychology—General	M
Social Sciences	M

SOUTHERN POLYTECHNIC STATE UNIVERSITY

Program	Degrees
Corporate and Organizational Communication	M,O
Internet and Interactive Multimedia	M,O
Technical Communication	M,O

SOUTHERN UNIVERSITY AND AGRICULTURAL AND MECHANICAL COLLEGE

Program	Degrees
Criminal Justice and Criminology	M
History	M
Mass Communication	M
Political Science	M
Psychology—General	M
Public Administration	M
Public Policy	D
Rehabilitation Counseling	M*
Social Sciences	M

SOUTHERN UTAH UNIVERSITY

Program	Degrees
Arts Administration	M
Communication—General	M
Forensic Sciences	M
Public Administration	M

SOUTHERN WESLEYAN UNIVERSITY

Program	Degrees
Pastoral Ministry and Counseling	M

SOUTH UNIVERSITY (AL)

Program	Degrees
Counseling Psychology	M*

SOUTH UNIVERSITY (FL)

Program	Degrees
Counseling Psychology	M*

SOUTH UNIVERSITY (GA)

Program	Degrees
Counseling Psychology	M*

SOUTH UNIVERSITY (SC)

Program	Degrees
Counseling Psychology	M*

SOUTHWESTERN ASSEMBLIES OF GOD UNIVERSITY

Program	Degrees
Counseling Psychology	M
Theology	M

SOUTHWESTERN BAPTIST THEOLOGICAL SEMINARY

Program	Degrees
Music	M,D,O
Theology	P,M,D,O

SOUTHWESTERN CHRISTIAN UNIVERSITY

Program	Degrees
Pastoral Ministry and Counseling	M

SOUTHWESTERN COLLEGE (KS)

Program	Degrees
Criminal Justice and Criminology	M
Pastoral Ministry and Counseling	M

SOUTHWESTERN COLLEGE (NM)

Program	Degrees
Art Therapy	M
Counseling Psychology	M,O*
Health Psychology	O
Psychology—General	O
Social Psychology	O
Thanatology	M,O

SOUTHWESTERN OKLAHOMA STATE UNIVERSITY

Program	Degrees
Music	M
School Psychology	M

SPALDING UNIVERSITY

Program	Degrees
Clinical Psychology	M,D
Communication—General	M
Corporate and Organizational Communication	M
Psychology—General	M,D
Writing	M

SPERTUS INSTITUTE OF JEWISH STUDIES

Program	Degrees
Jewish Studies	M,D

SPRING ARBOR UNIVERSITY

Program	Degrees
Child and Family Studies	M
Communication—General	M
Counseling Psychology	M
Pastoral Ministry and Counseling	M
Theology	M

SPRINGFIELD COLLEGE

Program	Degrees
Addictions/Substance Abuse Counseling	M,O
Art Therapy	M,O
Child and Family Studies	M,O
Counseling Psychology	M,O
Industrial and Organizational Psychology	M,O
Marriage and Family Therapy	M,O
Rehabilitation Counseling	M,O
Social Psychology	M
Sport Psychology	M,D,O

SPRING HILL COLLEGE

Program	Degrees
Liberal Studies	M
Theology	M

STANFORD UNIVERSITY

Program	Degrees
Anthropology	M,D
Art/Fine Arts	M,D
Asian Studies	M
Child and Family Studies	D
Chinese	M,D
Classics	M,D
Communication—General	M,D
Comparative Literature	D
Counseling Psychology	D
Developmental Psychology	D
East European and Russian Studies	M
Economics	D
English	M,D
French	M,D
German	M,D
History	M,D
Humanities	M
Interdisciplinary Studies	M,D
International Affairs	M
Italian	M,D
Japanese	M,D
Journalism	M,D
Linguistics	M,D
Music	M,D
Philosophy	M,D
Political Science	M,D
Psychology—General	D
Religion	M,D
Russian	M,D
Slavic Languages	M,D
Sociology	D
Spanish	M,D
Theater	D

STARR KING SCHOOL FOR THE MINISTRY

Theology P

STATE UNIVERSITY OF NEW YORK AT BINGHAMTON

Anthropology M,D
Art History M,D*
Clinical Psychology M,D
Cognitive Sciences M,D
Comparative Literature M,D
Cultural Studies M,D
Economics M,D
English M,D
French M
Geography M
History M,D
Italian M
Music M
Philosophy M,D
Political Science M,D
Psychology—General M,D
Public Administration M
Public Policy M,D
Sociology M,D
Spanish M,O
Theater M
Translation and Interpretation M,O

STATE UNIVERSITY OF NEW YORK AT FREDONIA

English M
Interdisciplinary Studies M
Music M

STATE UNIVERSITY OF NEW YORK AT NEW PALTZ

Art/Fine Arts M
Counseling Psychology M
English M
Interdisciplinary Studies M
Psychology—General M

STATE UNIVERSITY OF NEW YORK AT OSWEGO

Art/Fine Arts M
Child and Family Studies M
Consumer Economics M
Counseling Psychology M,O
English M
History M
School Psychology M,O

STATE UNIVERSITY OF NEW YORK AT PLATTSBURGH

Liberal Studies M
Psychology—General M,O
School Psychology M,O

STATE UNIVERSITY OF NEW YORK COLLEGE AT CORTLAND

American Studies O
English M
History M

STATE UNIVERSITY OF NEW YORK COLLEGE AT ONEONTA

Family and Consumer Sciences-General M
Museum Studies M

STATE UNIVERSITY OF NEW YORK COLLEGE AT POTSDAM

Communication—General M
English M
Music M

STATE UNIVERSITY OF NEW YORK COLLEGE OF ENVIRONMENTAL SCIENCE AND FORESTRY

Communication—General M,D
Landscape Architecture M
Urban and Regional Planning M,D
Urban Design M

STATE UNIVERSITY OF NEW YORK EMPIRE STATE COLLEGE

Industrial and Labor Relations M
Liberal Studies M
Public Policy M

STATE UNIVERSITY OF NEW YORK INSTITUTE OF TECHNOLOGY

Sociology M

STEPHEN F. AUSTIN STATE UNIVERSITY

Applied Arts and Design—General M
Art/Fine Arts M
Communication—General M
English M
Family and Consumer Sciences-General M
History M
Interdisciplinary Studies M
Mass Communication M
Music M
Psychology—General M
Public Administration M
School Psychology M

STETSON UNIVERSITY

English M
Marriage and Family Therapy M

STEVENS INSTITUTE OF TECHNOLOGY

Cognitive Sciences O
Communication—General M,D,O
Computer Art and Design M,D,O
Corporate and Organizational Communication O
Internet and Interactive Multimedia M,D,O

STEVENSON UNIVERSITY

Forensic Sciences M

STONY BROOK UNIVERSITY, STATE UNIVERSITY OF NEW YORK

Addictions/Substance Abuse Counseling M
African Studies M*
Anthropology M,D*
Art History M,D*
Art/Fine Arts M*
Clinical Psychology D*
Comparative Literature M,D*
Cultural Studies M,D
Economics M,D
English M,D,O*
Experimental Psychology D*
French M
Health Psychology D
Hispanic Studies M,D*
History M,D*
Italian M
Liberal Studies M,O
Linguistics M,D*
Music M,D*
Philosophy M,D*
Political Science M,D*
Psychology—General M,D
Public Policy M,D
Romance Languages M
Social Psychology D*
Social Sciences M,O
Sociology M,D*
Theater M*
Writing M*

STRAYER UNIVERSITY

Public Administration M

SUFFOLK UNIVERSITY

Applied Arts and Design—General M
Clinical Psychology D
Communication—General M
Criminal Justice and Criminology M
Developmental Psychology D
Disability Studies M,O
Economics M,D*
Graphic Design M
Interior Design M
Political Science M
Psychology—General D
Public Administration M,O
Women's Studies M

SULLIVAN UNIVERSITY

Conflict Resolution and Mediation/Peace Studies M

SUL ROSS STATE UNIVERSITY

Applied Arts and Design—General M
Art History M
Art/Fine Arts M
Criminal Justice and Criminology M
English M
History M
Political Science M
Psychology—General M
Public Administration M
Textile Design M

SYRACUSE UNIVERSITY

African Studies M
African-American Studies M
Anthropology M,D
Applied Arts and Design—General M
Architecture M
Art History M*
Art/Fine Arts M
Arts Journalism M
Broadcast Journalism M
Child and Family Studies M,D
Clinical Psychology D
Communication—General M,D*
Computer Art and Design M
Corporate and Organizational Communication M
Disability Studies O
Economics M,D
English M,D
Experimental Psychology D
Film, Television, and Video Production M
Film, Television, and Video Theory and Criticism M
French M
Geography M,D
Graphic Design M
History M,D
Illustration M
International Affairs
Internet and Interactive Multimedia M
Journalism M
Linguistics M
Marriage and Family Therapy M,D
Mass Communication M,D
Media Studies M
Museum Studies M
Music M
Philosophy M,D
Photography M
Political Science M,D
Psychology—General D
Public Administration M,D,O
Rehabilitation Counseling M
Religion M,D
Rhetoric M,D
School Psychology M,D,O
Social Psychology M,D
Social Sciences M,D
Sociology M,D
Spanish M
Textile Design M
Writing M,D

TALMUDIC COLLEGE OF FLORIDA

Theology M,D

TARLETON STATE UNIVERSITY

Counseling Psychology M,O
Criminal Justice and Criminology M
Economics M
English M
History M
Liberal Studies M
Political Science M
School Psychology M,O

TAYLOR UNIVERSITY COLLEGE AND SEMINARY

Cultural Studies P,M,O
Missions and Missiology P,M,O
Theology P,M,O

TEACHERS COLLEGE, COLUMBIA UNIVERSITY

Anthropology M,D*
Arts Administration M*
Clinical Psychology M,D
Communication—General M,D
Counseling Psychology M,D*
Developmental Psychology M,D*
Economics M,D
History M,D
Industrial and Organizational Psychology M,D
Interdisciplinary Studies M,D
Linguistics M,D
Political Science M,D
School Psychology M,D
Social Psychology M,D
Sociology M,D

TELSHE YESHIVA–CHICAGO

Jewish Studies O

TEMPLE BAPTIST SEMINARY

Theology P,M,D

TEMPLE UNIVERSITY

African-American Studies M,D
Anthropology D
Art History M,D*
Art/Fine Arts M
Arts Administration M,D
Clinical Psychology D
Cognitive Sciences D
Communication—General M,D

Corporate and Organizational Communication M,D
Counseling Psychology M,D
Criminal Justice and Criminology M,D
Dance M,D
Developmental Psychology D
Economics M,D
English M,D
Film, Television, and Video Production M
Geography M
Graphic Design M
History M,D
Industrial and Organizational Psychology M
Journalism M
Liberal Studies M
Linguistics M
Mass Communication D
Media Studies M,D
Music M,D
Philosophy M,D
Photography M
Political Science M,D
Psychology—General D
Religion M,D
School Psychology M,D
Social Psychology D
Sociology M,D
Spanish M,D
Textile Design M
Theater M
Therapies—Dance, Drama, and Music M,D
Urban and Regional Planning M
Urban Studies M
Writing M

TENNESSEE STATE UNIVERSITY

Counseling Psychology M,D
Criminal Justice and Criminology M
English M
Family and Consumer Sciences-General M
Psychology—General M,D
Public Administration M,D
School Psychology M,D

TENNESSEE TECHNOLOGICAL UNIVERSITY

English M

TEXAS A&M INTERNATIONAL UNIVERSITY

Counseling Psychology M
Criminal Justice and Criminology M
English M,D
Hispanic Studies M,D
History M
Political Science M
Psychology—General M
Public Administration M
Social Sciences M
Sociology M
Spanish M,D

TEXAS A&M UNIVERSITY

Agricultural Economics and Agribusiness M,D
Anthropology M,D
Architecture M,D
Clinical Psychology M,D
Cognitive Sciences M,D
Communication—General M,D
Counseling Psychology M,D
Developmental Psychology M,D
Economics M,D
English M,D
Geography M,D
History M,D
Homeland Security M,O
Human Development M,D
Industrial and Organizational Psychology M,D
Interdisciplinary Studies M,D
International Affairs M,O
International Development M,O
Landscape Architecture M,D
National Security M,O
Philosophy M,D
Political Science M,D
Psychology—General M,D
Public Administration M,O
Public Affairs M,O*
Public Policy M,O
School Psychology M,D
Social Psychology M,D
Sociology M,D*
Spanish M,D
Urban and Regional Planning M,D

TEXAS A&M UNIVERSITY–COMMERCE

Art History M
Art/Fine Arts M
Cognitive Sciences M,D
Counseling Psychology M,D
Economics M
English M,D
History M
Music M
Psychology—General M,D
Social Sciences M
Sociology M
Spanish M,D
Speech and Interpersonal Communication M
Theater M

TEXAS A&M UNIVERSITY–CORPUS CHRISTI

Art/Fine Arts M
English M
History M
Psychology—General M
Public Administration M

TEXAS A&M UNIVERSITY–KINGSVILLE

Agricultural Economics and Agribusiness M
Art/Fine Arts M
English M
Family and Consumer Sciences-General M
Gerontology M
History M
Political Science M
Psychology—General M
Sociology M
Spanish M

TEXAS A&M UNIVERSITY–TEXARKANA

Counseling Psychology M
English M
History M
Interdisciplinary Studies M
Psychology—General M

TEXAS CHRISTIAN UNIVERSITY

Art History M
Art/Fine Arts M
English M,D
History M,D
Journalism M
Liberal Studies M
Music M,O
Psychology—General M,D
Speech and Interpersonal Communication M

TEXAS SOUTHERN UNIVERSITY

Art/Fine Arts M
Communication—General M
Criminal Justice and Criminology M,D
English M
Family and Consumer Sciences-General M
History M
Music M
Psychology—General M
Public Administration M
Sociology M
Urban and Regional Planning M,D

TEXAS STATE UNIVERSITY–SAN MARCOS

Anthropology M
Child and Family Studies M
Communication—General M
Computer Art and Design M
Criminal Justice and Criminology M
English M
Geographic Information Systems M,D
Geography M,D
Graphic Design M
Health Psychology M
History M
Interdisciplinary Studies M
International Affairs M
Mass Communication M
Music M
Political Science M
Psychology—General M
Public Administration M
Rhetoric M
School Psychology M
Sociology M
Spanish M
Technical Communication M
Theater M
Writing M

TEXAS TECH UNIVERSITY

Agricultural Economics and Agribusiness M,D
Anthropology M
Applied Economics M,D
Architecture M
Art/Fine Arts M,D
Child and Family Studies M,D
Classics M
Clinical Psychology M,D
Communication—General M,D
Consumer Economics M,D
Counseling Psychology M,D
Dance M,D
Economics M,D
English M,D
Environmental Design M,D
Experimental Psychology M,D
Family and Consumer Sciences-General M,D
French M
German M
Gerontology M,D
Historic Preservation M
History M,D
Human Development M,D
Humanities M,D
Interdisciplinary Studies M
Landscape Architecture M
Linguistics M
Marriage and Family Therapy M,D
Mass Communication M,D
Museum Studies M
Music M,D
Philosophy M
Political Science M,D
Psychology—General M,D
Public Administration M,D
Rhetoric M,D
Romance Languages M,D
Sociology M
Spanish M,D
Technical Writing M,D
Theater M,D
Urban and Regional Planning M

TEXAS TECH UNIVERSITY HEALTH SCIENCES CENTER

Rehabilitation Counseling M

TEXAS WESLEYAN UNIVERSITY

Counseling Psychology M
Psychology—General M

TEXAS WOMAN'S UNIVERSITY

Art/Fine Arts M
Child and Family Studies M,D
Child Development M,D
Counseling Psychology M,D,O
Dance M,D
English M,D
History M
Marriage and Family Therapy M,D
Music M
Political Science M
Psychology—General M,D,O
Rhetoric M,D
School Psychology M,D,O
Sociology M,D
Theater M
Women's Studies M

THOMAS EDISON STATE COLLEGE

Homeland Security M,O
Liberal Studies M
Public Administration M,O

THOMAS JEFFERSON UNIVERSITY

Marriage and Family Therapy M

THOMAS UNIVERSITY

Rehabilitation Counseling M
Social Psychology M

TIFFIN UNIVERSITY

Criminal Justice and Criminology M
Forensic Psychology M
Homeland Security M
Humanities M

TORONTO SCHOOL OF THEOLOGY

Theology P,M,D

TOURO COLLEGE

Jewish Studies M

TOWSON UNIVERSITY

Art/Fine Arts M
Child and Family Studies O
Clinical Psychology M
Communication—General M,O
Corporate and Organizational Communication M
Counseling Psychology O
Forensic Sciences M
Geography M
Gerontology M,O
Homeland Security M,O
Humanities M
Internet and Interactive Multimedia D,O
Liberal Studies M
Music M

School Psychology O
Social Sciences M
Theater M
Women's Studies M,O
Writing M

TRENT UNIVERSITY

American Indian/Native American Studies M,D
Anthropology M
Canadian Studies M
Geography M,D
History M

TREVECCA NAZARENE UNIVERSITY

Counseling Psychology M
Marriage and Family Therapy M
Psychology—General M,D
Religion M
Theology M

TRINITY BAPTIST COLLEGE

Pastoral Ministry and Counseling M

TRINITY COLLEGE

American Studies M
Economics M
English M
Public Policy M

TRINITY EPISCOPAL SCHOOL FOR MINISTRY

Missions and Missiology P,M,D,O
Pastoral Ministry and Counseling P,M,D,O
Religion P,M,D,O
Theology P,M,D,O

TRINITY INTERNATIONAL UNIVERSITY

Archaeology P,M,D,O
Communication—General M
Counseling Psychology P,M,D,O
Missions and Missiology P,M,D,O
Pastoral Ministry and Counseling P,M,D,O
Theology P,M,D,O

TRINITY INTERNATIONAL UNIVERSITY, SOUTH FLORIDA CAMPUS

Counseling Psychology M
Religion M

TRINITY LUTHERAN SEMINARY

Music P,M
Theology P,M

TRINITY UNIVERSITY

School Psychology M

TRINITY (WASHINGTON) UNIVERSITY

Communication—General M

TRINITY WESTERN UNIVERSITY

Counseling Psychology M
English M
History M
Humanities M
Interdisciplinary Studies M
Linguistics M
Pastoral Ministry and Counseling P,M,D

Philosophy M
Theology P,M,D

TROPICAL AGRICULTURE RESEARCH AND HIGHER EDUCATION CENTER

Agricultural Economics and Agribusiness M,D

TROY UNIVERSITY

Art/Fine Arts M
Clinical Psychology M
Communication—General M
Criminal Justice and Criminology M
International Affairs M
Public Administration M
Rehabilitation Counseling M,O
School Psychology M

TRUMAN STATE UNIVERSITY

English M
Music M

TUFTS UNIVERSITY

Archaeology M
Art History M
Art/Fine Arts M
Child and Family Studies M,D,O
Child Development M,D,O*
Classics M
Conflict Resolution and Mediation/Peace Studies M,D
Dance M,D
Developmental Psychology M,D,O
Economics M
English M,D
Family and Consumer Sciences-General M,D,O
French M
German M
Health Communication M
History M,D
International Affairs M,D*
International Development M,D
Medieval and Renaissance Studies M,D
Museum Studies O
Music M
Philosophy M
Psychology—General M,D
Public Administration O
Public Policy M*
School Psychology M,O
Theater M,D*
Urban and Regional Planning M
Urban Studies M

TUI UNIVERSITY

Conflict Resolution and Mediation/Peace Studies M,D
Criminal Justice and Criminology M,D
Emergency Management M,D,O
Public Administration M,D

TULANE UNIVERSITY

Anthropology M,D
Architecture M
Art History M
Art/Fine Arts M
Classics M
Dance M
Economics M,D
English M,D
French M,D
Health Communication M
History M,D
International Development M,D
Latin American Studies M,D*

Liberal Studies M
Music M
Philosophy M,D
Political Science M,D
Portuguese M,D
Psychology—General M,D
Sociology M,D
Spanish M,D
Theater M

TUSKEGEE UNIVERSITY

Agricultural Economics and Agribusiness M

TYNDALE UNIVERSITY COLLEGE & SEMINARY

Missions and Missiology P,M,O
Pastoral Ministry and Counseling P,M,O
Theology P,M,O

UNIFICATION THEOLOGICAL SEMINARY

Theology P,M,D

UNIFORMED SERVICES UNIVERSITY OF THE HEALTH SCIENCES

Clinical Psychology D
History of Medicine M
History of Science and Technology M,D
Psychology—General D

UNION INSTITUTE & UNIVERSITY

Clinical Psychology D
Counseling Psychology M
Cultural Studies M
History M
Interdisciplinary Studies M,D
Psychology—General M
Writing M

UNION THEOLOGICAL SEMINARY AND PRESBYTERIAN SCHOOL OF CHRISTIAN EDUCATION

Theology P,M,D

UNION THEOLOGICAL SEMINARY IN THE CITY OF NEW YORK

Theology P,M,D

UNION UNIVERSITY

Cultural Studies M
Religion M

UNITED STATES ARMY COMMAND AND GENERAL STAFF COLLEGE

Military and Defense Studies M

UNITED STATES INTERNATIONAL UNIVERSITY

Counseling Psychology M
International Affairs M

UNITED TALMUDICAL SEMINARY

Theology

UNITED THEOLOGICAL SEMINARY

Theology P,M,D

UNITED THEOLOGICAL SEMINARY OF THE TWIN CITIES

Art/Fine Arts M

Pastoral Ministry and Counseling M,D
Religion M,O
Theology P,M,O
Women's Studies M

UNIVERSIDAD ADVENTISTA DE LAS ANTILLAS

History M
Spanish M

UNIVERSIDAD AUTONOMA DE GUADALAJARA

Architecture M,D
Corporate and Organizational Communication M,D
Criminal Justice and Criminology M,D
Philosophy M,D

UNIVERSIDAD CENTRAL DEL CARIBE

Addictions/Substance Abuse Counseling M

UNIVERSIDAD DE IBEROAMERICA

Clinical Psychology P,M
Forensic Psychology P,M

UNIVERSIDAD DE LAS AMERICAS, A.C.

International Affairs M
Marriage and Family Therapy M
Psychology—General M

UNIVERSIDAD DE LAS AMÉRICAS–PUEBLA

American Studies M
Anthropology M
Archaeology M
Computer Art and Design M
Economics M
English M
Linguistics M
Psychology—General M

UNIVERSIDAD DEL ESTE

Criminal Justice and Criminology M

UNIVERSIDAD DEL TURABO

Art/Fine Arts M
Arts Administration M
Counseling Psychology M
Criminal Justice and Criminology M
Forensic Sciences M
School Psychology M

UNIVERSIDAD NACIONAL PEDRO HENRIQUEZ URENA

Architecture P,M,D
Economics P,M,D
Historic Preservation P,M,D
Humanities P,M,D
International Affairs P,M,D
Public Administration P,M,D
Social Sciences P,M,D

UNIVERSITÉ DE MONCTON

Economics M
French M,D
History M
Public Administration M

UNIVERSITÉ DE MONTRÉAL

Program	Degrees
Addictions/Substance Abuse Counseling	M,D,O
Anthropology	M,D
Art History	M,D
Communication—General	M,D,O
Comparative Literature	M,D
Criminal Justice and Criminology	M,D
Demography and Population Studies	M,D
Developmental Psychology	M,D,O
Economics	M,D
English	M,D
Environmental Design	M,D,O
Film, Television, and Video Theory and Criticism	M,D
French	M,D
Geography	M,D,O
German	M
Hispanic Studies	M,D
History	M,D
Industrial and Labor Relations	M,D,O
Linguistics	M,D,O
Museum Studies	M
Music	M,D,O
Philosophy	M,D
Political Science	M,D
Psychology—General	M,D
Rehabilitation Counseling	O
Sociology	M,D
Spanish	M
Theology	M,D,O

UNIVERSITÉ DE SHERBROOKE

Program	Degrees
Canadian Studies	M,D
Comparative Literature	M,D
Conflict Resolution and Mediation/Peace Studies	P,M,D,O
Economics	M
Ethics	M,D,O
French	M,D
Geography	M,D
Gerontology	M
History	M
Linguistics	M,D
Philosophy	M,D,O
Psychology—General	M
Religion	M,D,O
Theater	M,D
Theology	M,D,O

UNIVERSITÉ DU QUÉBEC À CHICOUTIMI

Program	Degrees
Art/Fine Arts	M
Canadian Studies	M
Comparative Literature	M
Ethics	O
French	O
Linguistics	M
Theology	M,D

UNIVERSITÉ DU QUÉBEC À MONTRÉAL

Program	Degrees
Art History	M,D
Art/Fine Arts	M
Communication—General	M,D
Comparative Literature	M,D
Dance	M
Economics	M,D
Geographic Information Systems	O
Geography	M
History	M,D
Linguistics	M,D
Museum Studies	M
Philosophy	M,D
Political Science	M,D
Psychology—General	D
Public Administration	M
Religion	M,D
Sociology	M,D
Theater	M
Urban Studies	M,D

UNIVERSITÉ DU QUÉBEC À RIMOUSKI

Program	Degrees
Comparative Literature	M,D
Ethics	M,O
Social Psychology	M
Urban and Regional Planning	M,D,O

UNIVERSITÉ DU QUÉBEC À TROIS-RIVIÈRES

Program	Degrees
Canadian Studies	M,D
Comparative Literature	M
Industrial and Labor Relations	O
Philosophy	M,D
Psychology—General	M,D

UNIVERSITÉ DU QUÉBEC, ÉCOLE NATIONALE D'ADMINISTRATION PUBLIQUE

Program	Degrees
Public Administration	D,O
Urban Studies	M

UNIVERSITÉ DU QUÉBEC EN OUTAOUAIS

Program	Degrees
Industrial and Labor Relations	M,D,O
Urban and Regional Planning	M

UNIVERSITÉ DU QUÉBEC, INSTITUT NATIONAL DE LA RECHERCHE SCIENTIFIQUE

Program	Degrees
Demography and Population Studies	M,D
Urban Studies	M,D

UNIVERSITÉ LAVAL

Program	Degrees
Agricultural Economics and Agribusiness	M
Anthropology	M,D
Archaeology	M,D
Architecture	M
Art History	M,D
Art/Fine Arts	M
Clinical Psychology	D
Comparative Literature	M,D
Consumer Economics	O
Economics	M,D
English	M,D
Ethics	O
Ethnic Studies	M,D
Film, Television, and Video Theory and Criticism	M,D
French	M
Geography	M,D
Gerontology	O
Graphic Design	M
History	M,D
Industrial and Labor Relations	M
International Affairs	M
Journalism	O
Linguistics	M,D
Mass Communication	M
Museum Studies	O
Music	M,D
Philosophy	M,D
Political Science	M,D
Psychology—General	D
Religion	M,D
Rural Planning and Studies	O
Social Psychology	M,D
Sociology	M,D
Spanish	M,D
Theater	M,D
Theology	M,D
Translation and Interpretation	M,O
Urban and Regional Planning	M,D,
Women's Studies	O

UNIVERSITY AT ALBANY, STATE UNIVERSITY OF NEW YORK

Program	Degrees
African Studies	M
African-American Studies	M
Anthropology	M,D
Art/Fine Arts	M
Clinical Psychology	M,D,O
Communication—General	M,D
Counseling Psychology	M,D,O
Criminal Justice and Criminology	M,D
Demography and Population Studies	M,D,O
Economics	M,D,O
English	M,D
Experimental Psychology	M,D,O
Forensic Sciences	M
French	M,D
Geographic Information Systems	M,O
Geography	M,O
History	M,D,O
Industrial and Organizational Psychology	M,D,O
Italian	M
Latin American Studies	M,O
Liberal Studies	M
Philosophy	M,D
Political Science	M,D
Psychology—General	M,D,O
Public Administration	M,D,O
Public History	M,D,O
Public Policy	M,D,O
Rehabilitation Counseling	M
Russian	M,O
School Psychology	M,D,O
Social Psychology	M,D,O
Sociology	M,D,O
Spanish	M,D
Theater	M
Translation and Interpretation	M,O
Urban and Regional Planning	M
Urban Studies	M,D,O
Women's Studies	M,D

UNIVERSITY AT BUFFALO, THE STATE UNIVERSITY OF NEW YORK

Program	Degrees
American Studies	M,D
Anthropology	M,D
Architecture	M
Art History	M,O
Art/Fine Arts	M,O
Classics	M,D
Clinical Psychology	M,D
Cognitive Sciences	M,D
Communication—General	M,D
Comparative Literature	M,D
Counseling Psychology	M,D,O
Economics	M,D,O
English	M,D
French	M,D
Geographic Information Systems	M,D,O
Geography	M,D,O
History	M,D
Japanese	M,D,O
Linguistics	M,D
Media Studies	M,O
Museum Studies	M,O
Music	M,D
Philosophy	M,D
Political Science	M,D
Psychology—General	M,D
Rehabilitation Counseling	M,D,O
Romance Languages	M,D
School Psychology	M,D,O
Social Psychology	M,D
Sociology	M,D
Spanish	M,D
Urban and Regional Planning	M
Urban Design	M

UNIVERSITY COLLEGE OF THE FRASER VALLEY

Program	Degrees
Criminal Justice and Criminology	M

THE UNIVERSITY OF AKRON

Program	Degrees
Arts Administration	M
Child and Family Studies	M
Child Development	M
Clothing and Textiles	M
Cognitive Sciences	M,D
Communication—General	M
Counseling Psychology	M,D
Economics	M
English	M
Family and Consumer Sciences-General	M
Geographic Information Systems	M
Geography	M
History	M,D
Industrial and Organizational Psychology	M,D
Marriage and Family Therapy	M
Music	M
Political Science	M
Psychology—General	M,D
Public Administration	M
School Psychology	M
Sociology	M,D
Spanish	M
Theater	M
Urban and Regional Planning	M
Urban Studies	M,D
Writing	M

THE UNIVERSITY OF ALABAMA

Program	Degrees
American Studies	M
Anthropology	M,D
Art History	M
Art/Fine Arts	M
Child and Family Studies	M
Clinical Psychology	D
Clothing and Textiles	M
Communication—General	M,D
Consumer Economics	M
Criminal Justice and Criminology	M
Economics	M,D
English	M,D
Experimental Psychology	D
Family and Consumer Sciences-General	M,D
Film, Television, and Video Production	M
French	M,D
Geography	M
German	M,D
History	M,D
Human Development	M
Interior Design	M
Journalism	M
Mass Communication	D
Media Studies	M
Music	M,D
Photography	M
Political Science	M,D
Psychology—General	D
Public Administration	M,D
Rhetoric	M,D
Romance Languages	M,D
Spanish	M,D
Speech and Interpersonal Communication	M
Theater	M
Women's Studies	M
Writing	M,D

THE UNIVERSITY OF ALABAMA AT BIRMINGHAM

Anthropology M
Art History M
Communication—General M
Criminal Justice and Criminology M
English M
Forensic Sciences M
History M
Psychology—General M,D
Public Administration M
Sociology M,D

THE UNIVERSITY OF ALABAMA IN HUNTSVILLE

English M,O
History M
Psychology—General M
Public Affairs M
Technical Writing M,O

UNIVERSITY OF ALASKA ANCHORAGE

Anthropology M
Clinical Psychology M,D
English M
Interdisciplinary Studies M
Psychology—General M,D
Public Administration M
Social Psychology M,D
Writing M

UNIVERSITY OF ALASKA FAIRBANKS

Anthropology M,D
Art/Fine Arts M
Clinical Psychology D
Communication—General M
Corporate and Organizational Communication M
Criminal Justice and Criminology M
Cultural Studies M
Economics M
English M
Interdisciplinary Studies M,D
Linguistics M
Music M
Northern Studies M
Psychology—General D
Rural Planning and Studies M
Social Psychology D
Writing M

UNIVERSITY OF ALASKA SOUTHEAST

Public Administration M

UNIVERSITY OF ALBERTA

Agricultural Economics and Agribusiness M,D
Anthropology M,D
Applied Arts and Design—General M
Archaeology M,D
Art History M
Art/Fine Arts M
Asian Studies M
Chinese M
Classics M,D
Clothing and Textiles M,D
Communication—General M
Counseling Psychology M,D
Criminal Justice and Criminology M,D
Demography and Population Studies M,D
East European and Russian Studies M,D
Economics M,D
English M,D
Family and Consumer Sciences-General M,D
Folklore M,D
French M,D
German M,D
Hispanic Studies M,D
History M,D
Industrial and Labor Relations D
Italian M,D
Japanese M
Linguistics M,D
Music M,D
Philosophy M,D
Political Science M,D
Psychology—General M,D
Rural Sociology M,D
School Psychology M,D
Slavic Languages M,D
Sociology M,D
Theater M

THE UNIVERSITY OF ARIZONA

Agricultural Economics and Agribusiness M
American Indian/Native American Studies M,D
Anthropology M,D
Architecture M
Art History M,D
Art/Fine Arts M
Asian Studies M,D
Child and Family Studies M,D
Classics M
Communication—General M,D
Consumer Economics M,D
Economics M,D
English M,D
Family and Consumer Sciences-General M,D
French M,D
Geography M,D
German M,D
History M,D
Human Development M,D
Interdisciplinary Studies M,D
Landscape Architecture M
Latin American Studies M
Linguistics M,D
Media Studies M
Music M,D
Near and Middle Eastern Studies M,D
Philosophy M,D
Political Science M,D
Psychology—General D
Public Administration M,D
Public Policy M,D
Rehabilitation Counseling M,D,O
Rhetoric M,D
Russian M
Sociology M,D
Spanish M,D
Theater M
Women's Studies M,D
Writing M

UNIVERSITY OF ARKANSAS

Agricultural Economics and Agribusiness M
Anthropology M,D
Art/Fine Arts M
Communication—General M
Comparative Literature M,D
Economics M,D
English M,D
Family and Consumer Sciences-General M
French M
Geography M
German M
History M,D
Interdisciplinary Studies M,D
Journalism M
Music M
Philosophy M,D
Political Science M
Psychology—General M,D
Public Administration M
Public Policy D
Rehabilitation Counseling M,D
Sociology M
Spanish M
Theater M
Translation and Interpretation M
Writing M

UNIVERSITY OF ARKANSAS AT LITTLE ROCK

Art History M
Art/Fine Arts M
Conflict Resolution and Mediation/Peace Studies O
Criminal Justice and Criminology M
Gerontology O
Journalism M
Liberal Studies M
Marriage and Family Therapy O
Mass Communication M
Psychology—General M
Public Administration M
Public Affairs M,O
Public History M
Rehabilitation Counseling M,O
Rhetoric M
Speech and Interpersonal Communication M
Technical Writing M
Writing M

UNIVERSITY OF ARKANSAS FOR MEDICAL SCIENCES

Genetic Counseling M

UNIVERSITY OF BALTIMORE

Communication—General M,D*
Computer Art and Design M,D
Conflict Resolution and Mediation/Peace Studies M*
Counseling Psychology M
Criminal Justice and Criminology M*
Ethics M
Graphic Design M
Industrial and Organizational Psychology M
Psychology—General M*
Public Administration D
Public Affairs M,D*
Publishing M
Writing M

UNIVERSITY OF BRIDGEPORT

Conflict Resolution and Mediation/Peace Studies M
International Affairs M

THE UNIVERSITY OF BRITISH COLUMBIA

Agricultural Economics and Agribusiness M
Anthropology M,D
Archaeology M,D
Architecture M
Art History M,D,O
Art/Fine Arts M,D,O
Asian Studies M,D
Classics M,D
Clinical Psychology M,D
Cognitive Sciences M,D
Counseling Psychology M,D,O
Developmental Psychology M,D
East European and Russian Studies M,D
Economics M,D
English M,D
Film, Television, and Video Production M,O
Film, Television, and Video Theory and Criticism M,O
Forensic Psychology M,D
French M,D
Geography M,D
German M,D
Health Psychology M,D
Hispanic Studies M,D
History M,D
Human Development M,D,O
International Affairs M
Journalism M
Landscape Architecture M
Linguistics M,D
Museum Studies M,D,O
Music M,D
Philosophy M,D
Political Science M,D
Psychology—General M,D
Public History M,D
Religion M,D
School Psychology M,D,O
Social Psychology M,D
Sociology M,D
Theater M,D
Urban and Regional Planning M,D
Writing M,O

UNIVERSITY OF CALGARY

Anthropology M,D
Archaeology M,D
Architecture M,D
Art/Fine Arts M
Classics M,D
Clinical Psychology M,D
Communication—General M,D
Counseling Psychology M,D
Economics M,D
English M,D
Environmental Design M,D
Geography M,D
German M
History M,D
Human Development M,D
Linguistics M,D
Military and Defense Studies M,D
Music M,D
Philosophy M,D
Political Science M,D
Psychology—General M,D
Religion M,D
School Psychology M,D
Sociology M,D
Theater M

UNIVERSITY OF CALIFORNIA, BERKELEY

African-American Studies D
Agricultural Economics and Agribusiness D
Anthropology D
Applied Arts and Design—General M
Archaeology M,D
Architectural History M,D
Architecture M,D
Art History D
Art/Fine Arts M
Asian Languages M,D
Asian Studies M,D
Building Science M,D
Chinese D
Classics M,D
Comparative Literature D
Demography and Population Studies M,D
Economics D

English D
Environmental Design M
Ethnic Studies D
Folklore M
French D
Geography D
German D
Hispanic Studies D
History of Science and Technology D
History M,D
Human Development M,D
Industrial and Labor Relations D
International Affairs M
Italian D
Japanese D
Jewish Studies D
Journalism M
Landscape Architecture M
Latin American Studies M
Linguistics D
Music D
Near and Middle Eastern Studies M,D
Philosophy D
Political Science D
Psychology—General D
Public Policy M,D
Religion D
Rhetoric D
Romance Languages D
Russian D
Scandinavian Languages D
School Psychology
Slavic Languages D
Sociology M,D
Spanish D
Theater D
Urban and Regional Planning M,D
Urban Design M,D

UNIVERSITY OF CALIFORNIA, DAVIS

Agricultural Economics and Agribusiness M,D
American Indian/Native American Studies M,D
Anthropology M,D
Art History M*
Art/Fine Arts M
Child Development M
Clothing and Textiles M
Communication—General M
Comparative Literature D
Cultural Studies M,D
Economics M,D
English M,D
Forensic Sciences M
French D
Geography M,D
German M,D
History M,D
Human Development D
Linguistics M,D
Music M,D
Philosophy M,D
Political Science M,D
Psychology—General D
Sociology M,D
Spanish M,D
Textile Design M
Theater M,D
Urban and Regional Planning M
Writing M,D

UNIVERSITY OF CALIFORNIA, IRVINE

Anthropology M,D
Art History M,D
Art/Fine Arts M
Asian Languages M,D
Chinese M,D
Classics M,D
Comparative Literature M,D
Criminal Justice and Criminology M,D
Dance M
Demography and Population Studies M
Economics M,D
English M,D
French M,D
Genetic Counseling M
German M,D
History M,D
Japanese M,D
Music M
Philosophy M,D
Political Science D
Psychology—General D
Social Sciences M,D
Sociology M,D
Spanish M,D
Theater M,D
Urban and Regional Planning M,D*
Urban Studies M,D
Writing M

UNIVERSITY OF CALIFORNIA, LOS ANGELES

African Studies M
African-American Studies M
American Indian/Native American Studies M
Anthropology M,D
Applied Arts and Design—General M
Applied Social Research M,D
Archaeology M,D
Architecture M,D
Art History M,D
Art/Fine Arts M
Asian Languages M,D
Asian Studies M,D
Asian-American Studies M
Classics M,D
Comparative Literature M,D
Dance M,D
Economics M,D
English M,D
Film, Television, and Video Production M,D
French M,D
Geography M,D
German M,D
Hispanic Studies D
History M,D
Italian M,D
Latin American Studies M
Linguistics M,D
Music M,D
Near and Middle Eastern Languages M,D
Near and Middle Eastern Studies M,D
Philosophy M,D
Political Science M,D
Portuguese M
Psychology—General M,D
Public Policy M
Scandinavian Languages M
Slavic Languages M,D
Sociology M,D
Spanish M
Theater M,D
Urban and Regional Planning M,D
Urban Design M,D
Women's Studies M,D

UNIVERSITY OF CALIFORNIA, RIVERSIDE

Anthropology M,D
Art History M
Art/Fine Arts M
Asian Studies M
Classics D
Comparative Literature M,D
Dance M,D
Economics M,D*
English M,D
Ethnic Studies D
Hispanic Studies M,D
Historic Preservation M,D
History M,D
Museum Studies M,D
Music M
Philosophy M,D
Political Science M,D
Psychology—General M,D
Sociology M,D
Spanish M,D
Writing M

UNIVERSITY OF CALIFORNIA, SAN DIEGO

Anthropology D
Art/Fine Arts M,D
Clinical Psychology D
Cognitive Sciences D
Communication—General M,D
Comparative Literature M,D
Economics M,D
English M
Ethnic Studies M,D
French M
German M
History of Science and Technology M,D
History M,D
International Affairs M,D*
Jewish Studies M,D
Latin American Studies M
Linguistics D
Music M,D*
Philosophy D
Political Science M,D
Psychology—General D
Sociology D
Spanish M
Theater M,D

UNIVERSITY OF CALIFORNIA, SAN FRANCISCO

Anthropology D
History of Science and Technology M,D
Sociology D

UNIVERSITY OF CALIFORNIA, SANTA BARBARA

Agricultural Economics and Agribusiness M,D
Anthropology M,D
Archaeology M,D
Art History D
Art/Fine Arts M,D
Asian Languages M,D
Asian Studies M,D
Child and Family Studies M,D
Classics M,D
Clinical Psychology M,D
Cognitive Sciences M,D
Communication—General D
Comparative Literature D
Counseling Psychology M,D
Developmental Psychology M,D
Economics M,D
English D
Film, Television, and Video Production D
French M,D
Geography M,D
German M,D
Hispanic Studies M,D
History D
Human Development M,D
International Affairs M
Latin American Studies M,D
Linguistics M,D
Media Studies M,D
Medieval and Renaissance Studies D
Music M,D
Philosophy D
Political Science M,D
Portuguese M,D
Psychology—General D
Religion M,D
School Psychology M,D
Sociology D
Spanish M,D
Theater M,D
Women's Studies M,D

UNIVERSITY OF CALIFORNIA, SANTA CRUZ

Anthropology D
Applied Economics M
Archaeology D
Art/Fine Arts M
Communication—General O
Comparative Literature M,D
Computer Art and Design M
Economics D
English M,D
History M,D
Humanities D
Illustration O
International Affairs D
Linguistics M,D
Music M,D
Philosophy M,D
Political Science D
Psychology—General D
Social Sciences D
Sociology D
Technical Writing O
Theater O
Writing M

UNIVERSITY OF CENTRAL ARKANSAS

Computer Art and Design M
Counseling Psychology M
Economics M
English M
Family and Consumer Sciences-General M
Film, Television, and Video Production M
Geographic Information Systems M,O
Geography M,O
History M
Human Development M
Music M
Psychology—General M,D
School Psychology M,D
Social Psychology M

UNIVERSITY OF CENTRAL FLORIDA

Addictions/Substance Abuse Counseling M,O
Anthropology M
Art/Fine Arts M
Child and Family Studies M,O
Clinical Psychology M,D
Communication—General M
Computer Art and Design M
Criminal Justice and Criminology M,O
Economics M,D
Emergency Management M,O
English M
Experimental Psychology M,D
Film, Television, and Video Production M
Forensic Sciences M,D,O
Gerontology M,O
History M
Homeland Security M,O
Industrial and Organizational Psychology M,D
Interdisciplinary Studies M
International Affairs M
Internet and Interactive Multimedia M
Latin American Studies M,D,O
Marriage and Family Therapy M,O
Music M

Program	Degrees
Political Science	M
Psychology—General	M,D
Public Administration	M,O
Public Affairs	D
School Psychology	O
Sociology	M,D,O
Spanish	M
Technical Writing	M,D,O
Theater	M
Urban and Regional Planning	M,O
Writing	M

UNIVERSITY OF CENTRAL MISSOURI

Program	Degrees
Communication—General	M
Criminal Justice and Criminology	M,O
English	M
Gerontology	M
History	M
Mass Communication	M
Music	M
Psychology—General	M
Sociology	M
Speech and Interpersonal Communication	M
Theater	M

UNIVERSITY OF CENTRAL OKLAHOMA

Program	Degrees
Addictions/Substance Abuse Counseling	M
American Studies	M
Applied Arts and Design—General	M
Counseling Psychology	M
Criminal Justice and Criminology	M
English	M
Family and Consumer Sciences-General	M
Gerontology	M
History	M
Human Development	M
Interior Design	M
International Affairs	M
Museum Studies	M
Music	M
Political Science	M
Psychology—General	M
Urban Studies	M
Writing	M

UNIVERSITY OF CHICAGO

Program	Degrees
Anthropology	M,D
Archaeology	M,D
Art History	M,D
Art/Fine Arts	M
Asian Languages	M,D
Asian Studies	M,D
Classics	M,D
Comparative Literature	M,D
Economics	D
English	M,D
Film, Television, and Video Theory and Criticism	M,D
French	M,D
German	M,D
History	D
Human Development	D
Humanities	M
Interdisciplinary Studies	D
International Affairs	M
Italian	M,D
Latin American Studies	M
Linguistics	M,D
Media Studies	M,D
Music	M,D
Near and Middle Eastern Languages	M,D
Near and Middle Eastern Studies	M,D
Philosophy	M,D
Political Science	D
Psychology—General	D
Public Policy	M,D*
Religion	P,M,D
Romance Languages	M,D
Slavic Languages	M,D
Social Sciences	M,D*
Sociology	D
Spanish	M,D
Theology	P,M,D

UNIVERSITY OF CINCINNATI

Program	Degrees
Anthropology	M
Applied Arts and Design—General	M
Architecture	M
Art History	M
Art/Fine Arts	M
Arts Administration	M,D
Classics	M,D
Clinical Psychology	D
Communication—General	M
Criminal Justice and Criminology	M,D
Economics	M
English	M,D
Experimental Psychology	D
French	M,D
Genetic Counseling	M
Geography	M,D
German	M,D
Graphic Design	M
History	M,D
Industrial and Labor Relations	M
Industrial Design	M
Interdisciplinary Studies	D
Interior Design	M
Music	M,D,O
Philosophy	M,D
Political Science	M,D
Psychology—General	D
Romance Languages	M,D
School Psychology	D,O
Sociology	M,D
Spanish	M,D
Textile Design	M
Theater	M,D
Urban and Regional Planning	M
Women's Studies	M,O

UNIVERSITY OF COLORADO AT BOULDER

Program	Degrees
Anthropology	M,D
Art History	M
Art/Fine Arts	M
Asian Studies	M,D
Chinese	M,D
Classics	M,D
Communication—General	M,D
Comparative Literature	M,D
Dance	M,D
Economics	M,D
English	M,D
French	M,D
Geography	M,D
German	M
History	M,D
International Affairs	M,D
Japanese	M,D
Journalism	M,D
Linguistics	M,D
Mass Communication	M,D
Media Studies	D
Medieval and Renaissance Studies	M,D
Museum Studies	M
Music	M,D
Philosophy	M,D
Photography	M
Political Science	M,D
Psychology—General	M,D
Public Policy	M,D
Religion	M
Sociology	D
Spanish	M,D
Theater	M,D
Writing	M,D

UNIVERSITY OF COLORADO AT COLORADO SPRINGS

Program	Degrees
Cognitive Sciences	M,D
Communication—General	M
Criminal Justice and Criminology	M
Geography	M
History	M
Psychology—General	M,D
Public Administration	M
Public Affairs	M
Sociology	M

UNIVERSITY OF COLORADO DENVER

Program	Degrees
Anthropology	M
Architecture	M
Communication—General	M
Counseling Psychology	M,O
Criminal Justice and Criminology	M*
Economics	M
English	M,O
Genetic Counseling	M
Geographic Information Systems	M,D,O
History	M
Humanities	M
Landscape Architecture	M
Linguistics	M,O
Music	M
Political Science	M
Psychology—General	M
Public Administration	M*
Public Affairs	D
School Psychology	M,O
Social Sciences	M
Sociology	M
Spanish	M
Technical Communication	M
Urban and Regional Planning	M,D
Urban Design	M

UNIVERSITY OF CONNECTICUT

Program	Degrees
African Studies	M
Agricultural Economics and Agribusiness	M,D
Anthropology	M,D
Art History	M
Art/Fine Arts	M
Child and Family Studies	M,D,O
Clinical Psychology	M,D,O
Cognitive Sciences	M,D,O
Communication—General	M,D
Comparative Literature	M,D
Corporate and Organizational Communication	M,D
Counseling Psychology	M,D,O
Developmental Psychology	M,D,O
Economics	M,D
English	M,D*
Experimental Psychology	M,D,O
French	M,D
Geographic Information Systems	M,D,O
Geography	M,D,O
German	M,D
Health Psychology	M,D,O
History	M,D
Homeland Security	M
Human Development	M,D,O
Industrial and Organizational Psychology	M,D,O
International Affairs	M
Italian	M,D
Jewish Studies	M
Latin American Studies	M
Linguistics	M,D
Medieval and Renaissance Studies	M,D
Music	M,D,O
Philosophy	M,D
Political Science	M,D
Psychology—General	M,D,O
Public Administration	M,O
School Psychology	M,D,O
Social Psychology	M,D,O
Sociology	M,D
Spanish	M,D
Sustainable Development	M*
Theater	M
Western European Studies	M

UNIVERSITY OF DALLAS

Program	Degrees
American Studies	M
Art/Fine Arts	M
Comparative Literature	D
English	M
Humanities	M
Pastoral Ministry and Counseling	M
Philosophy	M,D
Political Science	M,D
Psychology—General	M
Theology	M

UNIVERSITY OF DAYTON

Program	Degrees
Clinical Psychology	M
Communication—General	M
English	M
Human Development	M,O
Pastoral Ministry and Counseling	M,D
Psychology—General	M
Public Administration	M
School Psychology	M,O
Social Psychology	M,O
Theology	M,D

UNIVERSITY OF DELAWARE

Program	Degrees
Agricultural Economics and Agribusiness	M
American Studies	M
Applied Arts and Design—General	M
Art History	M,D
Art/Fine Arts	M*
Child and Family Studies	M,D
Clinical Psychology	D
Cognitive Sciences	D
Communication—General	M
Criminal Justice and Criminology	M,D
Economics	M,D
English	M,D*
French	M
Geography	M,D
German	M
Historic Preservation	M,D
History of Science and Technology	M,D
History	M,D
Human Development	M,D
International Affairs	M,D
Liberal Studies	M
Linguistics	M,D
Music	M
Political Science	M,D
Psychology—General	D
Public Administration	M*
Public Policy	M,D
School Psychology	M,D,O
Social Psychology	D
Sociology	M,D
Spanish	M
Theater	M*
Urban Studies	M,D

UNIVERSITY OF DENVER

Program	Degrees
Anthropology	M

Art History M
Art/Fine Arts M
Child and Family Studies M,D,O
Clinical Psychology M,D
Communication—General M,D,O*
Computer Art and Design M
Conflict Resolution and Mediation/Peace Studies M
Counseling Psychology M,D,O
Criminal Justice and Criminology M,O
Economics M
English M,D
Film, Television, and Video Production M
Geographic Information Systems M,O
Geography M,D
International Affairs M,D
Liberal Studies M,O
Mass Communication M
Media Studies M
Museum Studies M
Music M,O
Psychology—General M,D
Public Policy M
Religion M,D
School Psychology M,D,O
Speech and Interpersonal Communication M,D
Theology D
Translation and Interpretation M,O

UNIVERSITY OF DETROIT MERCY

Addictions/Substance Abuse Counseling M,O
Clinical Psychology M,D
Criminal Justice and Criminology M
Industrial and Organizational Psychology M
Liberal Studies M
Psychology—General M,D,O
Religion M
School Psychology O

UNIVERSITY OF DUBUQUE

Communication—General M
Theology P,M,D

UNIVERSITY OF EVANSVILLE

Public Administration M

THE UNIVERSITY OF FINDLAY

Liberal Studies M
Public Administration M

UNIVERSITY OF FLORIDA

African Studies O
Agricultural Economics and Agribusiness M,D
Anthropology M,D
Architecture M,D
Art History M,D
Art/Fine Arts M,D
Arts Administration M
Building Science M,D
Classics M,D
Clinical Psychology D
Cognitive Sciences M,D
Communication—General M,D
Computer Art and Design M,D
Counseling Psychology M,D
Criminal Justice and Criminology M,D
Developmental Psychology M,D
Economics M,D
English M,D
Family and Consumer Sciences-General M
Forensic Sciences M,O
French M,D
Gender Studies M,O
Geography M,D
German M,D
Graphic Design M,D
Health Communication M,D,O
Health Psychology D
History M,D
Interior Design M,D
International Affairs M
International Development M,D,O
Internet and Interactive Multimedia M,D
Journalism M
Landscape Architecture M,D
Latin American Studies M,O
Linguistics M,D,O
Marriage and Family Therapy M,D,O
Mass Communication M,D
Media Studies M
Museum Studies M,D
Music M,D
Philosophy M,D
Photography M,D
Political Science M,D,O
Psychology—General M,D
Public Affairs M,D,O
Rehabilitation Counseling M
Religion M,D
School Psychology M,D,O
Social Psychology M,D
Social Sciences M
Sociology M,D
Spanish M,D
Sport Psychology M,D
Theater M
Urban and Regional Planning M,D
Women's Studies M,O
Writing M,D

UNIVERSITY OF GEORGIA

Agricultural Economics and Agribusiness M,D
Anthropology M,D
Applied Economics M,D
Archaeology M,D
Art History M
Art/Fine Arts M,D
Child and Family Studies M,D,O
Classics M
Clothing and Textiles M,D
Communication—General M,D
Comparative Literature M,D
Consumer Economics M,D
Economics M,D
English M,D
Family and Consumer Sciences-General M,D
French M
Geography M,D
German M
Gerontology O
Historic Preservation M
History M,D
Interior Design M,D
Internet and Interactive Multimedia M
Journalism M,D
Landscape Architecture M
Linguistics M,D
Mass Communication M,D
Music M,D
Philosophy M,D
Political Science M,D
Psychology—General M,D
Public Administration M,D
Public Policy M,D
Religion M
Romance Languages M,D
Sociology M,D
Spanish M
Speech and Interpersonal Communication M,D
Sustainable Development M,D
Theater M,D
Women's Studies O
Writing M,D

UNIVERSITY OF GREAT FALLS

Addictions/Substance Abuse Counseling O
Counseling Psychology M
Criminal Justice and Criminology M

UNIVERSITY OF GUAM

Art/Fine Arts M
English M
Graphic Design M
Public Administration M

UNIVERSITY OF GUELPH

Agricultural Economics and Agribusiness M,D
Anthropology M,D
Art/Fine Arts M
Child and Family Studies M,D
Clinical Psychology M,D
Cognitive Sciences M,D
Comparative Literature D
Consumer Economics M
Criminal Justice and Criminology M,D
Demography and Population Studies M,D
Economics M,D
English M
French M
Geography M,D
History M,D
Human Development M,D
Industrial and Organizational Psychology M,D
International Development M,D
Landscape Architecture M
Marriage and Family Therapy M,D
Medieval and Renaissance Studies D
Philosophy M,D
Political Science M
Psychology—General M,D
Public Administration M
Public Policy M
Rural Planning and Studies M,D
Social Psychology M,D
Sociology M,D
Theater M
Western European Studies M

UNIVERSITY OF HARTFORD

Architecture M
Art/Fine Arts M
Clinical Psychology M,D
Communication—General M
Experimental Psychology M
Music M,D,O
Psychology—General M,D
School Psychology M

UNIVERSITY OF HAWAII AT MANOA

American Studies M,D,O
Anthropology M,D
Architecture D
Art History M
Art/Fine Arts M
Asian Languages M,D
Asian Studies O
Chinese M,D,O
Clinical Psychology M,D,O
Communication—General M
Conflict Resolution and Mediation/Peace Studies O
Cultural Studies O
Dance M,D
Demography and Population Studies O
Disability Studies O
Economics M,D
English M,D
French M
Geography M,D,O
Historic Preservation O
History M,D
International Affairs O
Japanese M,D,O
Linguistics M,D
Museum Studies O
Music M,D
Philosophy M,D
Political Science M,D
Psychology—General M,D,O
Public Administration M,O
Public Policy O
Religion M
Social Psychology M,D,O
Sociology M,D,O
Spanish M
Speech and Interpersonal Communication M
Theater M,D*
Urban and Regional Planning M,D,O
Women's Studies O

UNIVERSITY OF HOUSTON

Anthropology M
Architecture M
Art/Fine Arts M
Clinical Psychology M,D
Communication—General M
Counseling Psychology M,D
Economics M,D
English M,D
Family and Consumer Sciences-General M
French M,D
History M,D
Human Development M
Industrial and Organizational Psychology M,D
Interior Design M
Linguistics M,D
Mass Communication M
Music M,D
Philosophy M
Photography M
Political Science M,D
Psychology—General M,D
Public History M,D
Social Psychology M,D
Sociology M
Spanish M,D
Speech and Interpersonal Communication M
Theater M
Writing M,D

UNIVERSITY OF HOUSTON–CLEAR LAKE

Clinical Psychology M
Criminal Justice and Criminology M
Cultural Studies M
English M
History M
Humanities M
Marriage and Family Therapy M
Psychology—General M
School Psychology M
Sociology M

UNIVERSITY OF HOUSTON–DOWNTOWN

Criminal Justice and Criminology M
English M
Technical Communication M
Writing M

UNIVERSITY OF HOUSTON–VICTORIA

Counseling Psychology M

Economics M
Interdisciplinary Studies M
Psychology—General M
School Psychology M

UNIVERSITY OF IDAHO

Agricultural Economics and Agribusiness M
Anthropology M
Applied Arts and Design—General M
Architecture M
Art/Fine Arts M
Consumer Economics M
English M
Geography M,D
History M,D
Interdisciplinary Studies M
Landscape Architecture M
Music M
Political Science M,D
Psychology—General M
Public Administration M
Public Affairs M,D
School Psychology O
Social Sciences M
Theater M
Writing M

UNIVERSITY OF ILLINOIS AT CHICAGO

Anthropology M,D
Architecture M
Art History M,D
Art/Fine Arts M
Communication—General M
Criminal Justice and Criminology M
Disability Studies M,D
East European and Russian Studies M,D
Economics M,D
English M,D
Forensic Sciences M
French M
Geography M
German M,D
Graphic Design M
Hispanic Studies M,D
History M,D
Human Development M,D
Industrial Design M
Linguistics M
Mass Communication M
Medical Illustration M
Philosophy M,D
Photography M
Political Science M,D
Psychology—General D
Public Administration M,D
Public Policy M,D
Rhetoric M,D
Slavic Languages M,D
Sociology M,D
Urban and Regional Planning M,D
Writing M,D

UNIVERSITY OF ILLINOIS AT SPRINGFIELD

Addictions/Substance Abuse Counseling M
Child and Family Studies M
Communication—General M
English M
Gerontology M
History M
Human Development M
Interdisciplinary Studies M
Journalism M
Political Science M
Public Administration M,D
Public History M
Social Sciences M

UNIVERSITY OF ILLINOIS AT URBANA–CHAMPAIGN

African Studies M
Agricultural Economics and Agribusiness M,D
Anthropology M,D
Applied Arts and Design—General M,D
Architecture M,D
Art History M,D
Art/Fine Arts M
Asian Languages M,D
Asian Studies M,D
Classics M,D
Communication—General D
Comparative Literature M,D
Consumer Economics M,D
Dance M
East European and Russian Studies M
Economics M,D*
English M,D
French M,D
Geography M,D
German M,D
Graphic Design M
History M,D
Human Development M,D
Industrial and Labor Relations M,D
Industrial Design M
Italian M,D
Journalism M
Landscape Architecture M,D
Latin American Studies M
Linguistics M,D
Music M,D,O
Philosophy M,D
Photography M
Political Science M,D
Portuguese M,D
Psychology—General M,D
Slavic Languages M,D
Sociology M,D
Spanish M,D
Speech and Interpersonal Communication M,D
Theater M,D
Urban and Regional Planning M,D
Writing M,D

UNIVERSITY OF INDIANAPOLIS

Art/Fine Arts M
Clinical Psychology M,D
Counseling Psychology M,D
English M
Gerontology M,O
History M
International Affairs M
Psychology—General M,D
Sociology M

THE UNIVERSITY OF IOWA

African-American Studies M
American Studies M,D
Anthropology M,D
Art History M,D
Art/Fine Arts M
Asian Studies M
Classics M,D
Communication—General M,D
Comparative Literature M,D
Counseling Psychology M,D,O
Dance M
Economics D
English M,D
Film, Television, and Video Production M
Film, Television, and Video Theory and Criticism M,D
French M,D
Geography M,D
German M,D
History M,D
Journalism M
Linguistics M,D
Mass Communication M,D
Media Studies M,D
Music M,D
Philosophy M,D
Political Science M,D
Psychology—General M,D,O
Rehabilitation Counseling M,D
Religion M,D
Rhetoric M,D
School Psychology M,D,O
Sociology M,D
Spanish M,D
Sport Psychology M,D
Theater M
Translation and Interpretation M
Urban and Regional Planning M
Women's Studies D
Writing M,D

UNIVERSITY OF KANSAS

American Indian/Native American Studies M
American Studies M,D
Anthropology M,D
Applied Arts and Design—General M
Architecture M
Art History M,D
Art/Fine Arts M
Asian Languages M
Asian Studies M
Classics M
Clinical Psychology M,D
Communication—General M,D
Computer Art and Design M
Counseling Psychology M,D
Developmental Psychology M,D
East European and Russian Studies M
Economics M,D
English M,D
Film, Television, and Video Theory and Criticism M,D
French M,D
Geography M,D
German M,D
Gerontology M,D
History M,D
Human Development M,D
Interdisciplinary Studies M,D
International Affairs M
Journalism M
Latin American Studies M,O
Linguistics M,D
Museum Studies M
Music M,D
Near and Middle Eastern Studies M
Philosophy M,D
Political Science M,D
Psychology—General M,D
Public Administration M,D
Religion M
School Psychology D,O
Slavic Languages M,D
Social Sciences M,D
Sociology M,D
Spanish M,D
Theater M,D
Therapies—Dance, Drama, and Music M
Urban and Regional Planning M
Writing M,D

UNIVERSITY OF KENTUCKY

Agricultural Economics and Agribusiness M,D
Anthropology M,D
Applied Arts and Design—General M
Architecture M
Art History M
Art/Fine Arts M
Child and Family Studies M,D
Classics M
Clinical Psychology M,D
Clothing and Textiles M
Communication—General M,D
Counseling Psychology M,D,O
Economics M,D
English M,D
Experimental Psychology M,D
French M
Geography M,D
German M
Gerontology D
Hispanic Studies M,D
Historic Preservation M
History M,D
Interior Design M
International Affairs M
Music M,D
Philosophy M,D
Political Science M,D
Psychology—General M,D
Public Administration M,D
Rehabilitation Counseling M,D
School Psychology M,D,O
Sociology M,D
Theater M

UNIVERSITY OF LA VERNE

Child and Family Studies M
Child Development M
Clinical Psychology D
Counseling Psychology M
Gerontology M,O
Marriage and Family Therapy M
Psychology—General M,D
Public Administration M,D,O
Social Psychology D

UNIVERSITY OF LETHBRIDGE

Addictions/Substance Abuse Counseling M,D
American Indian/Native American Studies M,D
Anthropology M,D
Archaeology M,D
Art/Fine Arts M,D
Canadian Studies M,D
Counseling Psychology M,D
Economics M,D
English M,D
French M,D
Geographic Information Systems M,D
Geography M,D
German M,D
History M,D
Media Studies M,D
Music M,D
Philosophy M,D
Political Science M,D
Psychology—General M,D
Religion M,D
Sociology M,D
Spanish M,D
Urban Studies M,D

UNIVERSITY OF LOUISIANA AT LAFAYETTE

American Studies D
Cognitive Sciences D
Communication—General M
English M,D
Family and Consumer Sciences-General M
Folklore M,D
French M,D
History M
Mass Communication M

Music M
Psychology—General M
Rehabilitation Counseling M
Rhetoric M,D
Writing M,D

UNIVERSITY OF LOUISIANA AT MONROE

Addictions/Substance Abuse Counseling M
Communication—General M
Criminal Justice and Criminology M
English M
Gerontology M,O
History M
Marriage and Family Therapy M,D
Music M
Psychology—General M,O
School Psychology O

UNIVERSITY OF LOUISVILLE

African Studies M
Art History M,D
Art Therapy M,D
Art/Fine Arts M
Clinical Psychology M,D
Counseling Psychology M,D
Criminal Justice and Criminology M
English M,D
Experimental Psychology D
French M
History M
Humanities M,D
Industrial and Labor Relations M
Interdisciplinary Studies M
Marriage and Family Therapy M,D,O
Music M,D
Philosophy M
Political Science M
Psychology—General M,D
Public Administration M
Public Affairs D
Public Policy M
Rhetoric D
Sociology M
Spanish M
Theater M
Urban and Regional Planning M
Urban Studies D
Women's Studies M,O

UNIVERSITY OF MAINE

Agricultural Economics and Agribusiness M
Clinical Psychology M,D
Communication—General M
Developmental Psychology M,D
Economics M
English M
Experimental Psychology M,D
French M
History M,D
Human Development M
Interdisciplinary Studies D
Liberal Studies M
Music M
Psychology—General M,D
Public Administration M,D*
Social Psychology M,D

UNIVERSITY OF MANAGEMENT AND TECHNOLOGY

Criminal Justice and Criminology M
Public Administration M,O

UNIVERSITY OF MANITOBA

Agricultural Economics and Agribusiness M,D
American Indian/Native American Studies M
Anthropology M,D
Architecture M
Canadian Studies M
Child and Family Studies M
Classics M
Clinical Psychology M,D
Clothing and Textiles M
Disability Studies M
Economics M,D
English M,D
Family and Consumer Sciences-General M
French M,D
Geography M,D
German M
History M,D
Interdisciplinary Studies M,D
Interior Design M
Italian M,D
Landscape Architecture M
Linguistics M,D
Music M
Northern Studies M
Philosophy M
Political Science M
Psychology—General M,D
Public Administration M
Religion M,D
Slavic Languages M
Sociology M,D
Spanish M,D
Urban and Regional Planning M

UNIVERSITY OF MARY HARDIN-BAYLOR

Counseling Psychology M
Marriage and Family Therapy M
Psychology—General M
School Psychology M
Social Psychology M

UNIVERSITY OF MARYLAND, BALTIMORE

Gerontology D

UNIVERSITY OF MARYLAND, BALTIMORE COUNTY

Art/Fine Arts M
Cognitive Sciences D
Communication—General M
Developmental Psychology D
Economics M
Gerontology M,D,O
History M
Industrial and Organizational Psychology D
Linguistics M
Music O
Psychology—General M,D
Public Policy M,D*
Social Sciences D
Sociology M,O
Women's Studies O

UNIVERSITY OF MARYLAND, COLLEGE PARK

Agricultural Economics and Agribusiness M,D
American Studies M,D
Anthropology M
Architecture M
Art History M,D
Art/Fine Arts M
Broadcast Journalism M,D
Child and Family Studies M,D*
Classics M
Clinical Psychology M,D
Cognitive Sciences D
Communication—General M,D
Comparative Literature M,D
Counseling Psychology M,D,O
Criminal Justice and Criminology M,D
Dance M
Developmental Psychology M,D
Economics M,D
English M,D
Experimental Psychology M,D
Family and Consumer Sciences-General M,D
French M,D
Geography M,D
German M,D
Historic Preservation M,O
History M,D
Human Development M,D
Industrial and Organizational Psychology M,D
Interdisciplinary Studies D
Japanese M,D
Jewish Studies M
Journalism M,D*
Linguistics M,D
Marriage and Family Therapy M,D
Media Studies M,D
Music M,D
Philosophy M,D
Political Science D
Portuguese M,D
Psychology—General M,D
Public Administration M
Public Policy M,D
Rehabilitation Counseling M,D,O
School Psychology M,D,O
Social Psychology M,D
Sociology M,D
Spanish M,D
Speech and Interpersonal Communication M,D
Survey Methodology M,D
Sustainable Development M
Theater M,D
Urban and Regional Planning M,D
Women's Studies M,D
Writing M,D

UNIVERSITY OF MARYLAND EASTERN SHORE

Criminal Justice and Criminology M
Rehabilitation Counseling M

UNIVERSITY OF MASSACHUSETTS AMHERST

African-American Studies M,D
Agricultural Economics and Agribusiness M,D
Anthropology M,D
Architecture M
Art History M
Art/Fine Arts M
Chinese M
Classics M
Clinical Psychology M,D
Communication—General M,D
Comparative Literature M,D
Economics M,D
English M,D
French M,D
Geography M
German M,D
History of Science and Technology M,D
History M,D
Industrial and Labor Relations M
Interior Design M
Italian M,D
Japanese M
Landscape Architecture M
Linguistics M,D
Music M,D
Philosophy M,D
Political Science M,D
Psychology—General M,D
Public Administration M
Public History M,D
Public Policy M
School Psychology D
Sociology M,D
Spanish M,D
Theater M
Urban and Regional Planning M,D
Writing M,D

UNIVERSITY OF MASSACHUSETTS BOSTON

American Studies M
Archaeology M
Clinical Psychology D
Conflict Resolution and Mediation/Peace Studies M,O
Counseling Psychology M,O
English M
Forensic Psychology M,O
Gerontology M,D,O
History M
Linguistics M
Marriage and Family Therapy M,O
Political Science M,D,O
Public Affairs M
Public History M
Public Policy D
Rehabilitation Counseling M,O
School Psychology M,O
Sociology M
Women's Studies M,D,O

UNIVERSITY OF MASSACHUSETTS DARTMOUTH

Applied Arts and Design—General M
Art/Fine Arts M,O
Clinical Psychology M
Computer Art and Design M
Graphic Design M
Illustration M
Latin American Studies M,D
Photography M
Portuguese M,D
Psychology—General M
Public Policy M
Textile Design M,O
Writing M,O

UNIVERSITY OF MASSACHUSETTS LOWELL

Criminal Justice and Criminology M
Economics M,O
Music M
Psychology—General M
Social Psychology M
Sociology M,O
Sustainable Development M,D,O

UNIVERSITY OF MEDICINE AND DENTISTRY OF NEW JERSEY

Counseling Psychology M,D,O
Interdisciplinary Studies M,D
Rehabilitation Counseling M,D

UNIVERSITY OF MEMPHIS

Anthropology M
Archaeology M
Architecture M
Art History M
Art/Fine Arts M
Clinical Psychology M,D
Communication—General M,D
Counseling Psychology M,D
Criminal Justice and Criminology M

Economics M,D
English M,D
Experimental Psychology M,D
Family and Consumer Sciences-General M
Film, Television, and Video Production M,D
French M
Gender Studies M
Graphic Design M
History M,D
Interior Design M
Journalism M
Liberal Studies M
Music M,D
Philosophy M,D
Photography M
Political Science M
Psychology—General M,D
Public Administration M
Public Policy M
Rehabilitation Counseling M,D
School Psychology M,D
Sociology M
Spanish M
Theater M
Urban and Regional Planning M
Women's Studies M
Writing M,D

UNIVERSITY OF MIAMI

Architecture M*
Art History M
Art/Fine Arts M
Broadcast Journalism M,D
Clinical Psychology M,D
Communication—General M,D*
Counseling Psychology D
Developmental Psychology M,D
Economics M,D
English M,D
Film, Television, and Video Production M,D
Film, Television, and Video Theory and Criticism M,D
French D
Geography M
Graphic Design M
History M,D
International Affairs M,D
Internet and Interactive Multimedia M
Journalism M,D
Latin American Studies M
Liberal Studies M
Marriage and Family Therapy M,O
Music M,D,O
Philosophy M,D
Photography M
Political Science M
Psychology—General M,D
Romance Languages D
Sociology M,D
Spanish M,D
Therapies—Dance, Drama, and Music M,D,O
Urban Design M
Writing M,D

UNIVERSITY OF MICHIGAN

American Studies M,D
Anthropology D
Applied Arts and Design—General M*
Applied Economics M
Archaeology D
Architecture M,D
Art History D
Art/Fine Arts M
Asian Languages M,D
Asian Studies M,D,O
Classics M,D,O
Clinical Psychology D
Communication—General D
Comparative Literature D
Dance M
Developmental Psychology D
East European and Russian Studies M,O
Economics M,D
English M,D,O
Experimental Psychology D
Film, Television, and Video Theory and Criticism D,O
French D
German M,D
History D,O
Jewish Studies M,O
Landscape Architecture M,D
Linguistics D
Mass Communication D
Media Studies M
Medieval and Renaissance Studies O
Music M,D,O
Near and Middle Eastern Languages M,D
Near and Middle Eastern Studies M,D
Philosophy M,D
Political Science M,D
Psychology—General D,O
Public Policy M,D
Romance Languages D
Russian M,D
Slavic Languages M,D
Social Psychology D
Social Sciences D
Sociology D,O
Spanish D
Survey Methodology M,D,O
Sustainable Development M,D
Theater M,D
Urban and Regional Planning M,D,O
Urban Design M
Women's Studies D,O
Writing M

UNIVERSITY OF MICHIGAN–DEARBORN

Clinical Psychology M
Health Psychology M
Liberal Studies M
Public Administration M,O
Public Policy M

UNIVERSITY OF MICHIGAN–FLINT

American Studies M
English M
Public Administration M*
Social Sciences M*

UNIVERSITY OF MINNESOTA, DULUTH

Anthropology M
Art/Fine Arts M
Criminal Justice and Criminology M
English M
Graphic Design M
Liberal Studies M
Music M
Sociology M

UNIVERSITY OF MINNESOTA, TWIN CITIES CAMPUS

American Studies D
Anthropology M,D
Applied Arts and Design—General M,D,O
Applied Economics M,D
Archaeology M,D
Architecture M
Art History M,D
Art/Fine Arts M
Asian Languages D
Asian Studies D
Child and Family Studies M,D
Child Development M,D
Classics M,D
Clinical Psychology D
Clothing and Textiles M,D,O
Cognitive Sciences D
Communication—General M,D,O
Comparative Literature D
Counseling Psychology D
Cultural Studies D
Dance M,D
Economics D
English M,D
French M,D
Genetic Counseling M,D
Geographic Information Systems M
Geography M,D
German M,D
History of Medicine M,D
History of Science and Technology M,D
History M,D
Industrial and Labor Relations M,D
Industrial and Organizational Psychology D
Interdisciplinary Studies D
Interior Design M,D,O
Landscape Architecture M
Linguistics M,D
Marriage and Family Therapy M,D
Mass Communication M,D
Medieval and Renaissance Studies M,D
Music M,D
Philosophy M,D
Political Science D
Portuguese M,D
Psychology—General D
Public Affairs M*
Public Policy M
Religion M,D
Scandinavian Languages M,D
School Psychology M,D,O
Social Psychology D
Sociology M,D
Spanish M,D
Textile Design M,D,O
Theater M,D
Urban and Regional Planning M
Women's Studies D

UNIVERSITY OF MISSISSIPPI

American Studies M
Anthropology M
Art History M
Art/Fine Arts M
Classics M
Clinical Psychology M,D
Economics M,D
English M,D
Experimental Psychology M,D
French M
German M
History M,D
Journalism M
Music M,D
Philosophy M
Political Science M,D
Psychology—General M,D
Sociology M
Spanish M

UNIVERSITY OF MISSOURI–COLUMBIA

Agricultural Economics and Agribusiness M,D
Anthropology M,D
Archaeology M,D
Architecture M
Art History M,D
Art/Fine Arts M
Child and Family Studies M,D
Classics M,D
Clothing and Textiles M
Communication—General M,D
Comparative Literature M,D
Computer Art and Design M
Conflict Resolution and Mediation/Peace Studies M
Consumer Economics M
Counseling Psychology M,D,O
Economics M,D
English M,D
Environmental Design M
Family and Consumer Sciences-General M,D
French M,D
Geography M
German M
History M,D
Human Development M,D
Journalism M,D
Music M
Philosophy M,D
Political Science M,D
Psychology—General M,D
Public Affairs M
Religion M
Romance Languages M,D
Rural Sociology M,D
School Psychology M,D,O
Sociology M,D
Spanish M,D
Theater M,D

UNIVERSITY OF MISSOURI–KANSAS CITY

Art History M,D
Art/Fine Arts M,D
Clinical Psychology M,D
Counseling Psychology M,D,O
Criminal Justice and Criminology M,D
Economics M,D
English M,D
History M,D
Interdisciplinary Studies D
Music M,D
Political Science M,D
Psychology—General M,D
Public Administration M,D
Public Affairs M,D
Romance Languages M,D
Social Psychology M,D
Sociology M,D
Theater M

UNIVERSITY OF MISSOURI–ST. LOUIS

Clinical Psychology M,D,O
Communication—General M
Conflict Resolution and Mediation/Peace Studies M
Criminal Justice and Criminology M,D
Economics M,O
English M,O
Gerontology M,O
Industrial and Organizational Psychology M,D,O
Linguistics M,O
Museum Studies M,O
Philosophy M
Political Science M,D
Psychology—General M,D,O
Public Administration M,D,O
Public Policy M,D,O
School Psychology D,O
Social Psychology M,D,O
Sociology M
Writing M,O

UNIVERSITY OF MOBILE

Marriage and Family Therapy M
Religion M
Theology M

THE UNIVERSITY OF MONTANA

Anthropology M,D
Art/Fine Arts M
Clinical Psychology M,D,O
Communication—General M
Counseling Psychology M,D,O
Criminal Justice and Criminology M
Developmental Psychology M,D,O
Economics M
English M
Experimental Psychology M,D,O
French M
Geographic Information Systems M
Geography M
German M
History M,D
Interdisciplinary Studies M,D
Jewish Studies M
Journalism M
Linguistics M,D
Music M
Philosophy M
Political Science M
Psychology—General M,D,O
Public Administration M
Rural Planning and Studies M
Rural Sociology M
School Psychology M,D,O
Sociology M
Spanish M
Theater M
Writing M

UNIVERSITY OF MONTEVALLO

English M
Marriage and Family Therapy M
Music M
Social Psychology M

UNIVERSITY OF NEBRASKA AT KEARNEY

English M
History M
School Psychology M,O
Writing M

UNIVERSITY OF NEBRASKA AT OMAHA

Communication—General M
Criminal Justice and Criminology M,D
Developmental Psychology M,D,O
Economics M
English M,O
Geography M,O
Gerontology M,O
History M
Industrial and Organizational Psychology M,D,O
Music M
Political Science M
Psychology—General M,D,O
Public Administration M,D,O
School Psychology M,D,O
Technical Communication M,O
Theater M
Writing M,O

UNIVERSITY OF NEBRASKA–LINCOLN

Agricultural Economics and Agribusiness M,D
Anthropology M
Architecture M
Art History M
Art/Fine Arts M
Child and Family Studies M,D
Classics M
Clothing and Textiles M
Communication—General M,D
Consumer Economics M,D
Economics M,D
English M,D
Family and Consumer Sciences-General M,D
French M,D
Geography M,D
German M,D
History M,D
Journalism M
Mass Communication M
Museum Studies M
Music M,D
Philosophy M,D
Political Science M,D
Psychology—General M,D
Sociology M,D
Spanish M,D
Survey Methodology M
Theater M,D
Urban and Regional Planning M

UNIVERSITY OF NEVADA, LAS VEGAS

Addictions/Substance Abuse Counseling M,O
Anthropology M,D
Architecture M
Art/Fine Arts M
Clinical Psychology M,D
Communication—General M
Criminal Justice and Criminology M
Economics M
Emergency Management M,D,O
English M,D
Ethics M
Experimental Psychology M,D
Film, Television, and Video Production M
History M,D
Journalism M
Marriage and Family Therapy M,O
Media Studies M
Music M,D
Political Science M
Psychology—General M,D
Public Administration M,D,O
Public Affairs M,D,O
Public Policy M,O
Rehabilitation Counseling M,O
School Psychology M,D,O
Sociology M,D
Spanish M
Theater M
Women's Studies O
Writing M,D

UNIVERSITY OF NEVADA, RENO

Agricultural Economics and Agribusiness M,D
Anthropology M,D
Applied Economics M,D
Art/Fine Arts M
Child and Family Studies M
Clinical Psychology D
Cognitive Sciences M,D
Criminal Justice and Criminology M
Economics M
English M,D
French M
Geography M,D
German M
History M,D
Human Development M
Journalism M
Music M
Philosophy M
Political Science M,D
Psychology—General M,D
Public Administration M
Social Psychology D
Sociology M
Spanish M
Speech and Interpersonal Communication M
Western European Studies D

UNIVERSITY OF NEW BRUNSWICK FREDERICTON

Anthropology M
Applied Economics M
Classics M
Clinical Psychology M,D
Conflict Resolution and Mediation/Peace Studies M
Economics M
English M,D
Experimental Psychology M,D
History M,D
Interdisciplinary Studies M,D
Philosophy M
Political Science M
Psychology—General M,D
Public Administration M
Public Policy M
Sociology M,D
Sustainable Development M

UNIVERSITY OF NEW BRUNSWICK SAINT JOHN

Clinical Psychology M,D
Experimental Psychology M,D
Psychology—General M,D

UNIVERSITY OF NEW ENGLAND

Addictions/Substance Abuse Counseling M,O
Gerontology M,O

UNIVERSITY OF NEW HAMPSHIRE

Art/Fine Arts M
Child and Family Studies M
Comparative Literature M,D
Economics M,D*
English M,D
History M,D
Liberal Studies M
Linguistics M,D
Marriage and Family Therapy M
Museum Studies M,D
Music M
Political Science M
Psychology—General D
Public Administration M,O
Sociology M,D
Spanish M
Writing M,D

UNIVERSITY OF NEW HAVEN

Criminal Justice and Criminology M*
Forensic Sciences M
Industrial and Labor Relations M
Industrial and Organizational Psychology M,O*
National Security M
Public Administration M
Social Psychology M,O

UNIVERSITY OF NEW MEXICO

American Studies M,D
Anthropology M,D
Architecture M
Art History M,D
Art/Fine Arts M
Child and Family Studies M,D
Clinical Psychology M,D
Communication—General M,D
Comparative Literature M,D
Criminal Justice and Criminology M
Dance M
Economics M,D
English M,D
French M,D
Geography M
German M,D
Historic Preservation O
History M,D
Landscape Architecture M
Latin American Studies M,D
Linguistics M,D
Music M
Philosophy M,D
Political Science M,D
Portuguese M,D
Psychology—General M,D
Public Administration M
Sociology M,D
Spanish M,D
Theater M
Urban and Regional Planning M
Urban Design O
Women's Studies O
Writing M,D

UNIVERSITY OF NEW ORLEANS

Art/Fine Arts M
Arts Administration M
Economics D
English M
Film, Television, and Video Production M
Geography M
History M
Music M
Political Science M,D
Psychology—General M,D
Public Administration M
Romance Languages M
Sociology M
Theater M
Urban and Regional Planning M
Urban Studies M,D

UNIVERSITY OF NORTH ALABAMA

Criminal Justice and Criminology M
English M
History M

THE UNIVERSITY OF NORTH CAROLINA AT ASHEVILLE

Liberal Studies M

THE UNIVERSITY OF NORTH CAROLINA AT CHAPEL HILL

Anthropology M,D
Archaeology M,D
Art History M,D
Art/Fine Arts M
Classics M,D
Clinical Psychology D
Cognitive Sciences D
Communication—General M,D
Comparative Literature M,D
Developmental Psychology D
East European and Russian Studies M
Economics M,D
English M,D
Experimental Psychology D
Folklore M
French M,D

Geography M,D
German M,D
History M,D
Italian M,D
Latin American Studies M,D,O
Linguistics M,D
Mass Communication M,D
Music M,D
Philosophy M,D
Political Science M,D
Portuguese M,D
Psychology—General D
Public Administration M
Public Policy D
Rehabilitation Counseling M,D
Religion M,D
Romance Languages M,D
Russian M,D
School Psychology M,D
Slavic Languages M,D
Social Psychology D
Sociology M,D
Spanish M,D
Theater M
Urban and Regional Planning M,D

THE UNIVERSITY OF NORTH CAROLINA AT CHARLOTTE

Architecture M
Child Development M,D
Clinical Psychology M
Communication—General M
Criminal Justice and Criminology M
Dance M
Economics M
English M
Geography M,D
Gerontology M
Health Psychology D
History M
Industrial and Organizational Psychology M,D
Liberal Studies M
Psychology—General M,D
Public Administration M,D
Public Policy D
Religion M
Social Psychology M
Sociology M
Spanish M
Theater M

THE UNIVERSITY OF NORTH CAROLINA AT GREENSBORO

Applied Economics M
Architecture M,O
Art/Fine Arts M
Child and Family Studies M,D
Classics M
Clinical Psychology M,D
Cognitive Sciences M,D
Communication—General M
Conflict Resolution and Mediation/Peace Studies M,O
Counseling Psychology M,D,O
Criminal Justice and Criminology M
Dance M
Developmental Psychology M,D
Economics D
English M,D
Family and Consumer Sciences-General M,D,O
Film, Television, and Video Production M
French M
Gender Studies M,O
Genetic Counseling M
Geographic Information Systems M,D,O
Geography M,D,O
Gerontology M,O
Hispanic Studies M,O
Historic Preservation M,O
History M,D,O
Human Development M,D
Interior Design M,O
Liberal Studies M
Marriage and Family Therapy M,D,O
Media Studies M
Museum Studies M,D,O
Music M,D
Political Science M,O
Psychology—General M,D
Public Affairs M,O
Rhetoric M,D
School Psychology M,D,O
Social Psychology M,D
Sociology M
Spanish M,O
Technical Writing M,D,O
Textile Design M,D
Theater M
Women's Studies M,D,O
Writing M

THE UNIVERSITY OF NORTH CAROLINA AT PEMBROKE

Public Administration M

THE UNIVERSITY OF NORTH CAROLINA WILMINGTON

Criminal Justice and Criminology M
English M
Hispanic Studies M,O
History M
Liberal Studies M
Psychology—General M
Public Administration M
Sociology M*
Writing M*

UNIVERSITY OF NORTH DAKOTA

Applied Economics M
Art/Fine Arts M
Clinical Psychology M,D
Communication—General M,D
Counseling Psychology M
Criminal Justice and Criminology D
English M,D
Experimental Psychology M,D
Forensic Psychology M,D
Geography M
History M,D
Linguistics M
Music M,D
Psychology—General M,D
Public Administration M
Sociology M
Theater M

UNIVERSITY OF NORTHERN BRITISH COLUMBIA

Disability Studies M,D,O
Gender Studies M,D,O
History M,D,O
Interdisciplinary Studies M,D,O
International Affairs M,D,O
Political Science M,D,O
Psychology—General M,D,O

UNIVERSITY OF NORTHERN COLORADO

Art/Fine Arts M
Communication—General M
Counseling Psychology D
English M
Gerontology M
History M
Interdisciplinary Studies M
Music M,D
Psychology—General M,D
Rehabilitation Counseling M,D
School Psychology D,O
Sociology M
Spanish M

UNIVERSITY OF NORTHERN IOWA

Art/Fine Arts M
Communication—General M
Criminal Justice and Criminology M
English M
French M
Gender Studies M
Geography M
German M
History M
Music M
Psychology—General M
Public Policy M
School Psychology M,O
Sociology M
Spanish M
Women's Studies M

UNIVERSITY OF NORTHERN VIRGINIA

Public Administration M,D

UNIVERSITY OF NORTH FLORIDA

Counseling Psychology M
Criminal Justice and Criminology M
English M
Ethics M,O
Gerontology M,O
History M
Philosophy M,O
Psychology—General M
Public Administration M
Rehabilitation Counseling M,O
Sociology M
Writing M

UNIVERSITY OF NORTH TEXAS

Anthropology M
Applied Arts and Design—General M
Applied Economics M
Art History M
Art/Fine Arts M
Child and Family Studies M
Clinical Psychology M,D
Clothing and Textiles M
Communication—General M
Counseling Psychology M,D
Criminal Justice and Criminology M
Economics M
English M,D
Experimental Psychology M,D
Film, Television, and Video Production M
French M
Geography M
Gerontology M,D,O
Health Psychology M,D
History M,D
Human Development M
Industrial and Labor Relations M
Interdisciplinary Studies M
Journalism M
Linguistics M,D
Music M,D
Philosophy M,D
Political Science M,D
Psychology—General M,D
Public Administration M,D
Rehabilitation Counseling M
Religion M,D
School Psychology M
Sociology M,D
Spanish M
Technical Writing M,D
Writing M,D

UNIVERSITY OF NORTH TEXAS HEALTH SCIENCE CENTER AT FORT WORTH

Forensic Sciences M,D

UNIVERSITY OF NOTRE DAME

Applied Arts and Design—General M
Architecture M
Art History M
Art/Fine Arts M
Cognitive Sciences D
Comparative Literature D
Conflict Resolution and Mediation/Peace Studies M
Counseling Psychology D
Developmental Psychology D
Economics M,D
English M,D
French M
Graphic Design M
History of Science and Technology M,D
History M,D
Industrial Design M
Italian M
Latin American Studies M
Medieval and Renaissance Studies M,D
Philosophy D
Photography M
Political Science D
Psychology—General D
Religion M
Romance Languages M
Sociology D
Spanish M
Theology P,M,D
Writing M

UNIVERSITY OF OKLAHOMA

American Indian/Native American Studies M
Anthropology M,D
Applied Arts and Design—General M
Architecture M
Art History M
Art/Fine Arts M
Communication—General M,D
Counseling Psychology D
Dance M
Economics M,D
English M,D
Film, Television, and Video Production M
French M,D
Geography M,D
German M
History of Science and Technology M,D
History M,D
Interdisciplinary Studies M,D
International Affairs M
Journalism M
Landscape Architecture M
Liberal Studies M
Mass Communication M
Museum Studies M
Music M,D
Philosophy M,D
Photography M
Political Science M,D
Psychology—General M,D
Public Administration M
School Psychology M,D
Social Psychology M
Sociology M,D
Spanish M,D
Theater M

Urban and Regional Planning	M
Writing	M

UNIVERSITY OF OKLAHOMA HEALTH SCIENCES CENTER

Genetic Counseling	M

UNIVERSITY OF OREGON

Anthropology	M,D
Architecture	M
Art History	M,D
Art/Fine Arts	M
Arts Administration	M*
Asian Languages	M,D
Asian Studies	M
Chinese	M,D
Classics	M
Clinical Psychology	D
Cognitive Sciences	M,D
Communication—General	M,D
Comparative Literature	M,D
Dance	M
Developmental Psychology	M,D
Economics	M,D
English	M,D
Folklore	M
French	M
Geography	M,D
German	M,D
Historic Preservation	M
History	M,D
Interdisciplinary Studies	M
Interior Design	M
International Affairs	M
Italian	M
Japanese	M,D
Journalism	M,D
Landscape Architecture	M
Linguistics	M,D
Music	M,D
Philosophy	M,D
Political Science	M,D
Psychology—General	M,D
Public Policy	M
Romance Languages	M,D
Russian	M
Social Psychology	M,D
Sociology	M,D
Spanish	M
Theater	M,D
Urban and Regional Planning	M
Writing	M

UNIVERSITY OF OTTAWA

Anthropology	M
Canadian Studies	D
Classics	M,D
Communication—General	M
Criminal Justice and Criminology	M,D
Economics	M,D
English	M,D
French	M,D
Geography	M,D
History	M,D
Interdisciplinary Studies	D,O
International Development	M
Linguistics	M,D
Music	M,O
Philosophy	M,D
Political Science	M,D
Psychology—General	D
Public Administration	D,O
Religion	M,D
Sociology	M
Spanish	M,D
Theater	M
Translation and Interpretation	M,D
Women's Studies	M

UNIVERSITY OF PENNSYLVANIA

American Studies	M,D
Anthropology	M,D
Archaeology	M,D
Architecture	M,D,O*
Art History	M,D
Art/Fine Arts	M
Asian Studies	M,D
Classics	M,D
Clinical Psychology	D
Communication—General	D
Comparative Literature	M,D
Computer Art and Design	M
Counseling Psychology	M
Criminal Justice and Criminology	M,D
Demography and Population Studies	M,D
Economics	M,D
English	M,D
Folklore	M,D
French	M,D
German	M,D
Historic Preservation	M,O
History of Science and Technology	M,D
History	M,D
Human Development	M,D
International Affairs	M
Italian	M,D
Landscape Architecture	M,O
Liberal Studies	M
Linguistics	M,D
Music	M,D
Near and Middle Eastern Studies	M,D
Philosophy	M,D
Political Science	M,D
Psychology—General	D
Public Administration	M*
Public Policy	M,D
Religion	D
Romance Languages	M,D
School Psychology	D
Social Psychology	D
Sociology	M,D
Spanish	M,D
Urban and Regional Planning	M,D,O
Urban Design	D
Writing	M,D

UNIVERSITY OF PHOENIX

Criminal Justice and Criminology	M
Psychology—General	M
Public Administration	M

UNIVERSITY OF PHOENIX–AUGUSTA CAMPUS

Criminal Justice and Criminology	M
Public Administration	M

UNIVERSITY OF PHOENIX–AUSTIN CAMPUS

Criminal Justice and Criminology	M
Psychology—General	M
Public Administration	M

UNIVERSITY OF PHOENIX–BAY AREA CAMPUS

Criminal Justice and Criminology	M
Marriage and Family Therapy	M
Public Administration	M

UNIVERSITY OF PHOENIX–CENTRAL VALLEY CAMPUS

Marriage and Family Therapy	M
Public Administration	M

UNIVERSITY OF PHOENIX–CHATTANOOGA CAMPUS

Criminal Justice and Criminology	M
Public Administration	M

UNIVERSITY OF PHOENIX–CHEYENNE CAMPUS

Criminal Justice and Criminology	M
Psychology—General	M
Public Administration	M

UNIVERSITY OF PHOENIX–CLEVELAND CAMPUS

Criminal Justice and Criminology	M
Psychology—General	M
Public Administration	M

UNIVERSITY OF PHOENIX–COLUMBUS GEORGIA CAMPUS

Public Administration	M

UNIVERSITY OF PHOENIX–DALLAS CAMPUS

Public Administration	M

UNIVERSITY OF PHOENIX–DENVER CAMPUS

Marriage and Family Therapy	M
Public Administration	M
School Psychology	M
Social Psychology	M

UNIVERSITY OF PHOENIX–DES MOINES CAMPUS

Criminal Justice and Criminology	M
Public Administration	M

UNIVERSITY OF PHOENIX–HARRISBURG CAMPUS

Criminal Justice and Criminology	M
Psychology—General	M
Public Administration	M

UNIVERSITY OF PHOENIX–HAWAII CAMPUS

Criminal Justice and Criminology	M
Marriage and Family Therapy	M
Psychology—General	M
Public Administration	M
Social Psychology	M

UNIVERSITY OF PHOENIX–HOUSTON CAMPUS

Public Administration	M

UNIVERSITY OF PHOENIX–IDAHO CAMPUS

Psychology—General	M

UNIVERSITY OF PHOENIX–INDIANAPOLIS CAMPUS

Criminal Justice and Criminology	M
Psychology—General	M

UNIVERSITY OF PHOENIX–JERSEY CITY CAMPUS

Criminal Justice and Criminology	M
Psychology—General	M
Public Administration	M

UNIVERSITY OF PHOENIX–KANSAS CITY CAMPUS

Criminal Justice and Criminology	M
Social Psychology	M

UNIVERSITY OF PHOENIX–LAS VEGAS CAMPUS

Counseling Psychology	M
Marriage and Family Therapy	M
School Psychology	M

UNIVERSITY OF PHOENIX–LOUISIANA CAMPUS

Criminal Justice and Criminology	M
Psychology—General	M
Public Administration	M

UNIVERSITY OF PHOENIX–MADISON CAMPUS

Public Administration	M

UNIVERSITY OF PHOENIX–MARYLAND CAMPUS

Criminal Justice and Criminology	M
Psychology—General	M
Public Administration	M

UNIVERSITY OF PHOENIX–MEMPHIS CAMPUS

Criminal Justice and Criminology	M
Public Administration	M

UNIVERSITY OF PHOENIX–NEW MEXICO CAMPUS

Marriage and Family Therapy	M

UNIVERSITY OF PHOENIX–NORTHERN NEVADA CAMPUS

Criminal Justice and Criminology	M
Marriage and Family Therapy	M
Psychology—General	M
Public Administration	M
School Psychology	M

UNIVERSITY OF PHOENIX–NORTHERN VIRGINIA CAMPUS

Criminal Justice and Criminology	M
Public Administration	M

UNIVERSITY OF PHOENIX–NORTH FLORIDA CAMPUS

Public Administration	M

UNIVERSITY OF PHOENIX–NORTHWEST ARKANSAS CAMPUS

Criminal Justice and Criminology	M
Public Administration	M

UNIVERSITY OF PHOENIX–OMAHA CAMPUS

Criminal Justice and Criminology	M
Public Administration	M

UNIVERSITY OF PHOENIX–OREGON CAMPUS
Criminal Justice and Criminology M
Psychology—General M

UNIVERSITY OF PHOENIX–PHOENIX CAMPUS
Social Psychology M,O

UNIVERSITY OF PHOENIX–PITTSBURGH CAMPUS
Criminal Justice and Criminology M
Psychology—General M
Public Administration M

UNIVERSITY OF PHOENIX–PUERTO RICO CAMPUS
Counseling Psychology M
Marriage and Family Therapy M
School Psychology M

UNIVERSITY OF PHOENIX–RENTON LEARNING CENTER
Criminal Justice and Criminology M
Public Administration M

UNIVERSITY OF PHOENIX–RICHMOND CAMPUS
Criminal Justice and Criminology M
Psychology—General M
Public Administration M

UNIVERSITY OF PHOENIX–SACRAMENTO VALLEY CAMPUS
Criminal Justice and Criminology M
Marriage and Family Therapy M
Public Administration M

UNIVERSITY OF PHOENIX–SAN ANTONIO CAMPUS
Criminal Justice and Criminology M
Psychology—General M
Public Administration M

UNIVERSITY OF PHOENIX–SAN DIEGO CAMPUS
Criminal Justice and Criminology M
Marriage and Family Therapy M

UNIVERSITY OF PHOENIX–SAVANNAH CAMPUS
Criminal Justice and Criminology M
Public Administration M

UNIVERSITY OF PHOENIX–SOUTHERN ARIZONA CAMPUS
Criminal Justice and Criminology M,O
Marriage and Family Therapy M,O

UNIVERSITY OF PHOENIX–SOUTHERN CALIFORNIA CAMPUS
Marriage and Family Therapy M,O

UNIVERSITY OF PHOENIX–SOUTHERN COLORADO CAMPUS
Marriage and Family Therapy M
School Psychology M,O
Social Psychology M

UNIVERSITY OF PHOENIX–SOUTH FLORIDA CAMPUS
Public Administration M

UNIVERSITY OF PHOENIX–SPRINGFIELD CAMPUS
Criminal Justice and Criminology M
Public Administration M

UNIVERSITY OF PHOENIX–UTAH CAMPUS
Counseling Psychology M
School Psychology M

UNIVERSITY OF PHOENIX–WEST FLORIDA CAMPUS
Public Administration M

UNIVERSITY OF PITTSBURGH
African Studies O
Anthropology M,D
Architectural History M,D
Art History M,D
Asian Studies M,O
Classics M,D
Cognitive Sciences D
Communication—General M,D
Conflict Resolution and Mediation/Peace Studies M
Criminal Justice and Criminology D
Cultural Studies M,D
Developmental Psychology M,D
Disability Studies O
East European and Russian Studies O
Economics M,D
Emergency Management M,D,O
English M,D*
French M,D
Genetic Counseling M
Geographic Information Systems M,D
German M,D
Gerontology M,D,O
Hispanic Studies M,D
History of Science and Technology M,D
History M,D
Interdisciplinary Studies D
International Affairs M,D,O
International Development M,D,O
Italian M
Latin American Studies O
Linguistics M,D
Military and Defense Studies M
Music M,D
National Security M
Philosophy M,D
Political Science M,D
Psychology—General M,D
Public Administration M,D,O*
Public Policy M,D,O
Rehabilitation Counseling M
Religion M,D
Slavic Languages M,D
Sociology M,D
Spanish M,D
Theater M,D
Urban and Regional Planning M,O
Western European Studies O
Women's Studies O
Writing M,D

UNIVERSITY OF PORTLAND
Communication—General M
Corporate and Organizational Communication M
Music M
Pastoral Ministry and Counseling M
Theater M

UNIVERSITY OF PRINCE EDWARD ISLAND
Geography M

UNIVERSITY OF PUERTO RICO, MAYAGÜEZ CAMPUS
Agricultural Economics and Agribusiness M
English M
Hispanic Studies M

UNIVERSITY OF PUERTO RICO, MEDICAL SCIENCES CAMPUS
Demography and Population Studies M
Gerontology M,O
Human Development M,O

UNIVERSITY OF PUERTO RICO, RÍO PIEDRAS
Architecture M
Clinical Psychology M,D
Comparative Literature M
Economics M
English M,D
Family and Consumer Sciences-General M
Hispanic Studies M,D
History M,D
Industrial and Organizational Psychology M
Linguistics M
Mass Communication M
Philosophy M
Psychology—General M,D
Public Administration M
Rehabilitation Counseling M
Sociology M
Translation and Interpretation M,O
Urban and Regional Planning M

UNIVERSITY OF PUGET SOUND
Pastoral Ministry and Counseling M
Social Psychology M

UNIVERSITY OF REDLANDS
Geographic Information Systems M
Music M

UNIVERSITY OF REGINA
American Indian/Native American Studies M
Anthropology M
Art/Fine Arts M
Canadian Studies M,D
Clinical Psychology M,D
Criminal Justice and Criminology M
Economics M,D,O
English M,D
Experimental Psychology M,D
French M
Geography M,D
Gerontology M
History M,D
Linguistics M
Music M,D
Philosophy M
Political Science M
Psychology—General M,D
Public Administration M,D,O
Public Policy M,D,O
Religion M,D
Social Sciences M,D
Sociology M,D
Women's Studies M

UNIVERSITY OF RHODE ISLAND
Child and Family Studies M
Clinical Psychology D
Clothing and Textiles M
Communication—General M
Counseling Psychology M
Economics M,D
English M,D
Forensic Sciences M,D,O
Gerontology M,D
History M
Industrial and Labor Relations M
International Affairs M,O
Music M
Political Science M,O
Psychology—General D
Public Administration M,O
Public Policy M,O
School Psychology M,D
Spanish M
Sport Psychology M,D

UNIVERSITY OF ROCHESTER
Art History M,D
Art/Fine Arts M,D*
Clinical Psychology M,D
Cognitive Sciences M,D
Developmental Psychology M,D
Economics M,D
English M,D
History M,D
Marriage and Family Therapy M
Music M,D
Philosophy M,D
Political Science M,D
Psychology—General M,D
Social Psychology M,D

UNIVERSITY OF SAINT FRANCIS (IN)
Art/Fine Arts M
Counseling Psychology M
Pastoral Ministry and Counseling M
Psychology—General M

UNIVERSITY OF SAINT MARY
Psychology—General M

UNIVERSITY OF SAINT MARY OF THE LAKE–MUNDELEIN SEMINARY
Theology P,M,D,O

UNIVERSITY OF ST. MICHAEL'S COLLEGE
Jewish Studies P,M,D,O
Pastoral Ministry and Counseling P,M,D,O
Theology P,M,D,O

UNIVERSITY OF ST. THOMAS (MN)
Art History M

Corporate and Organizational Communication	M
Counseling Psychology	M,D,O
English	M*
Human Development	M,D,O
Marriage and Family Therapy	M,D,O
Pastoral Ministry and Counseling	M
Psychology—General	M,D,O
Religion	M
Theology	P,M

UNIVERSITY OF ST. THOMAS (TX)

Liberal Studies	M
Philosophy	M,D
Theology	P,M

UNIVERSITY OF SAN DIEGO

Conflict Resolution and Mediation/Peace Studies	M
History	M
International Affairs	M
Marriage and Family Therapy	M
Pastoral Ministry and Counseling	M,O
Theater	M

UNIVERSITY OF SAN FRANCISCO

Asian Studies	M
Counseling Psychology	M,D
Economics	M
International Affairs	M
International Development	M
Internet and Interactive Multimedia	M
Marriage and Family Therapy	M,D
Public Administration	M
Theology	M
Writing	M

UNIVERSITY OF SASKATCHEWAN

Agricultural Economics and Agribusiness	M,D
Anthropology	M
Archaeology	M,D
Art/Fine Arts	M
Canadian Studies	M,D
East European and Russian Studies	M
Economics	M
English	M,D
French	M
Gender Studies	M,D
Geography	M,D
German	M
History	M,D
Industrial and Labor Relations	M
Music	M
Philosophy	M
Political Science	M
Psychology—General	M,D
Religion	M
Sociology	M,D
Theater	M
Women's Studies	M,D

THE UNIVERSITY OF SCRANTON

Counseling Psychology	M,O
History	M
Rehabilitation Counseling	M
Social Psychology	M
Theology	M

UNIVERSITY OF SOUTH AFRICA

Anthropology	M,D
Archaeology	M,D
Art History	M,D
Classics	M,D
Clinical Psychology	M,D
Communication—General	M,D
Counseling Psychology	M,D
Criminal Justice and Criminology	M,D
Economics	M,D
English	M,D
Ethics	M,D
Family and Consumer Sciences-General	M,D
French	M,D
Geography	M,D
German	M,D
History	M,D
Human Development	M,D
Industrial and Organizational Psychology	M,D
Italian	M,D
Linguistics	M,D
Missions and Missiology	M,D
Music	M,D
Near and Middle Eastern Languages	M,D
Near and Middle Eastern Studies	M,D
Pastoral Ministry and Counseling	M,D
Philosophy	M,D
Political Science	M,D
Portuguese	M,D
Psychology—General	M,D
Public Administration	M,D
Religion	M,D
Romance Languages	M,D
Russian	M,D
Sociology	M,D
Spanish	M,D
Theology	M,D

UNIVERSITY OF SOUTH ALABAMA

Communication—General	M
English	M
Gerontology	O
History	M
Psychology—General	M
Public Administration	M
Rehabilitation Counseling	M,D
School Psychology	M,D
Sociology	M

UNIVERSITY OF SOUTH CAROLINA

Anthropology	M,D
Art History	M
Art/Fine Arts	M
Clinical Psychology	M,D
Comparative Literature	M,D
Consumer Economics	M
Criminal Justice and Criminology	M,D
Economics	M,D
English	M,D
Experimental Psychology	M,D
French	M,D
Genetic Counseling	M
Geography	M,D
German	M,D
Gerontology	O
Historic Preservation	M,O
History	M,D,O
International Affairs	M,D
Journalism	M,D
Linguistics	M,D,O
Media Studies	M
Museum Studies	M
Music	M,D,O
Philosophy	M,D
Political Science	M,D
Psychology—General	M,D
Public Administration	M
Public History	M,O
Rehabilitation Counseling	M,O
Religion	M
School Psychology	D
Social Psychology	M,D
Sociology	M,D
Spanish	M,D
Speech and Interpersonal Communication	M,D
Theater	M,D
Women's Studies	O
Writing	M,D

UNIVERSITY OF SOUTH CAROLINA AIKEN

Clinical Psychology	M

THE UNIVERSITY OF SOUTH DAKOTA

Art/Fine Arts	M
Clinical Psychology	M,D
Communication—General	M
English	M,D
History	M
Interdisciplinary Studies	M
Music	M
Political Science	M,D
Psychology—General	M,D
Public Administration	M,D
Theater	M

UNIVERSITY OF SOUTHERN CALIFORNIA

American Studies	D
Architecture	M*
Art History	M,D,O
Art/Fine Arts	M,D,O
Arts Administration	M
Asian Languages	M,D
Asian Studies	M,D
Broadcast Journalism	M
Building Science	M
Classics	M,D
Communication—General	M,D*
Comparative Literature	M,D
Corporate and Organizational Communication	M,D
Counseling Psychology	M
Economics	M,D
English	M,D
Film, Television, and Video Production	M
Film, Television, and Video Theory and Criticism	M,D
French	M,D
Geographic Information Systems	M,D,O
Geography	M,D,O
Gerontology	M,D,O
Health Communication	M
Historic Preservation	M
History	D
International Affairs	M,D
Internet and Interactive Multimedia	M,D
Journalism	M
Landscape Architecture	M
Linguistics	D
Marriage and Family Therapy	M
Mass Communication	M,D
Media Studies	M,D
Music	M,D,O
Philosophy	M,D
Political Science	M,D
Psychology—General	
Public Administration	M,D,O
Public Policy	M
Religion	M,D
Slavic Languages	M,D
Sociology	D
Speech and Interpersonal Communication	M,D
Theater	M*
Urban and Regional Planning	M,D
Writing	M,D

UNIVERSITY OF SOUTHERN INDIANA

Liberal Studies	M
Public Administration	M

UNIVERSITY OF SOUTHERN MAINE

American Studies	M
Music	M
Public Policy	M,D,O
School Psychology	M,D,O
Urban and Regional Planning	M,O
Writing	M

UNIVERSITY OF SOUTHERN MISSISSIPPI

Anthropology	M
Child and Family Studies	M
Clinical Psychology	M,D
Counseling Psychology	M,D
Criminal Justice and Criminology	M,D
Economics	M,D
English	M,D
Experimental Psychology	M,D
Geography	M,D
History	M,D
International Affairs	M,D
International Development	M,D
Marriage and Family Therapy	M
Mass Communication	M,D
Music	M,D
Philosophy	M
Political Science	M,D
Psychology—General	M,D
School Psychology	M,D
Speech and Interpersonal Communication	M,D
Theater	M

UNIVERSITY OF SOUTH FLORIDA

African Studies	M
American Studies	M
Anthropology	M,D
Architecture	M
Art History	M
Art/Fine Arts	M
Clinical Psychology	M,D
Cognitive Sciences	M,D
Communication—General	M,D
Criminal Justice and Criminology	M,D
Economics	M,D
English	M,D
French	M
Geography	M
Gerontology	M,D
History	M
Industrial and Organizational Psychology	M,D
International Affairs	M
Latin American Studies	M,O
Liberal Studies	M
Linguistics	M
Mass Communication	M
Music	M
Philosophy	M,D
Political Science	M
Psychology—General	M,D
Public Administration	M
Rehabilitation Counseling	M
Religion	M
School Psychology	M,D,O
Sociology	M
Spanish	M
Women's Studies	M

THE UNIVERSITY OF TAMPA

Economics	M

THE UNIVERSITY OF TENNESSEE

Anthropology	M,D
Archaeology	M,D
Architecture	M
Art/Fine Arts	M
Child and Family Studies	M,D
Clinical Psychology	M,D
Clothing and Textiles	M,D
Communication—General	M,D
Consumer Economics	M,D
Counseling Psychology	M,D
Criminal Justice and Criminology	M,D
Economics	M,D
English	M,D
Experimental Psychology	M,D
Family and Consumer Sciences-General	D
French	M,D
Geography	M,D
German	M,D
Gerontology	M
Graphic Design	M
History	M,D
Industrial and Organizational Psychology	D
Italian	D
Journalism	M,D
Landscape Architecture	M
Linguistics	D
Media Studies	M,D
Music	M
Philosophy	M,D
Photography	M
Political Science	M,D
Portuguese	D
Psychology—General	M,D
Public Administration	M
Rehabilitation Counseling	M,D
Religion	M,D
Russian	D
School Psychology	M,D,O
Sociology	M,D
Spanish	M,D
Speech and Interpersonal Communication	M,D
Theater	M

THE UNIVERSITY OF TENNESSEE AT CHATTANOOGA

Criminal Justice and Criminology	M
English	M
Experimental Psychology	M
Industrial and Organizational Psychology	M
Music	M
Psychology—General	M
Public Administration	M,O
School Psychology	O

THE UNIVERSITY OF TENNESSEE AT MARTIN

Child and Family Studies	M
Child Development	M
Family and Consumer Sciences-General	M
Social Psychology	M

THE UNIVERSITY OF TEXAS AT ARLINGTON

Anthropology	M
Architecture	M
Art/Fine Arts	M
Communication—General	M
Criminal Justice and Criminology	M
Economics	M
English	M,D
Experimental Psychology	M,D
French	M
Health Psychology	M,D
History	M,D
Humanities	M
Interdisciplinary Studies	M
Landscape Architecture	M
Linguistics	M,D
Music	M
Political Science	M
Psychology—General	M,D
Public Administration	M
Public Affairs	D
Rhetoric	M,D
Sociology	M
Spanish	M
Urban and Regional Planning	M

THE UNIVERSITY OF TEXAS AT AUSTIN

American Studies	M,D
Anthropology	M,D
Applied Arts and Design—General	M
Archaeology	M,D
Architecture	M,D
Art History	M,D
Art/Fine Arts	M
Asian Languages	M,D
Asian Studies	M,D
Child and Family Studies	M,D
Child Development	M,D
Classics	M,D
Cognitive Sciences	M,D
Communication—General	M,D
Comparative Literature	M,D
Counseling Psychology	M,D
Dance	M,D
East European and Russian Studies	M
Economics	M,D
English	M,D
Family and Consumer Sciences-General	M,D
Film, Television, and Video Production	M,D
Folklore	M,D
French	M,D
Geography	M,D
German	M,D
History	M,D
Human Development	M,D
Journalism	M,D
Latin American Studies	M,D
Linguistics	M,D
Media Studies	M,D
Mineral Economics	M
Music	M,D
Near and Middle Eastern Languages	M,D
Near and Middle Eastern Studies	M,D
Philosophy	M,D
Political Science	M,D
Portuguese	M,D
Psychology—General	D
Public Affairs	M,D
Public History	M,D
Public Policy	M,D
Romance Languages	M,D
School Psychology	M,D
Slavic Languages	M,D
Sociology	M,D
Spanish	M,D
Theater	M,D
Urban and Regional Planning	M,D
Writing	M

THE UNIVERSITY OF TEXAS AT BROWNSVILLE

English	M
History	M
Interdisciplinary Studies	M
Political Science	M
Psychology—General	M
Public Administration	M
Public Policy	M
Spanish	M

THE UNIVERSITY OF TEXAS AT DALLAS

Child and Family Studies	M,D
Cognitive Sciences	M,D
Communication—General	D
Comparative Literature	M,D
Criminal Justice and Criminology	M,D
Economics	M,D*
Geographic Information Systems	M,D
Humanities	M,D
Interdisciplinary Studies	M
Political Science	D
Psychology—General	M,D
Public Affairs	M,D
Sociology	M

THE UNIVERSITY OF TEXAS AT EL PASO

Art/Fine Arts	M
Clinical Psychology	M,D
Communication—General	M
Economics	M
English	M
Experimental Psychology	M,D
History	M,D
Interdisciplinary Studies	M
Linguistics	M
Music	M
Political Science	M
Psychology—General	M,D
Rhetoric	M
Sociology	M
Spanish	M
Theater	M
Writing	M

THE UNIVERSITY OF TEXAS AT SAN ANTONIO

Anthropology	M,D
Architecture	M
Art History	M
Art/Fine Arts	M
Communication—General	M
Criminal Justice and Criminology	M
Cultural Studies	M,D
Demography and Population Studies	D
Economics	M
English	M,D
Hispanic Studies	M
History	M
Interdisciplinary Studies	M
Music	M
Political Science	M
Psychology—General	M
Public Administration	M
Sociology	M
Spanish	M

THE UNIVERSITY OF TEXAS AT TYLER

Art/Fine Arts	M
Clinical Psychology	M
Communication—General	M
Counseling Psychology	M
Criminal Justice and Criminology	M
English	M
History	M
Interdisciplinary Studies	M
Marriage and Family Therapy	M
Music	M
Political Science	M
Psychology—General	M
Public Administration	M
School Psychology	M
Social Sciences	M
Sociology	M

THE UNIVERSITY OF TEXAS HEALTH SCIENCE CENTER AT HOUSTON

Genetic Counseling	M

THE UNIVERSITY OF TEXAS MEDICAL BRANCH

Humanities	M,D

THE UNIVERSITY OF TEXAS OF THE PERMIAN BASIN

Clinical Psychology	M
Criminal Justice and Criminology	M
English	M
History	M
Psychology—General	M

THE UNIVERSITY OF TEXAS–PAN AMERICAN

Art/Fine Arts	M
Clinical Psychology	M
Communication—General	M
Criminal Justice and Criminology	M
Economics	D
English	M
Experimental Psychology	M
History	M
Interdisciplinary Studies	M
Music	M
Psychology—General	M
Public Administration	M
Rehabilitation Counseling	M
School Psychology	M
Sociology	M
Spanish	M
Theater	M

THE UNIVERSITY OF TEXAS SOUTHWESTERN MEDICAL CENTER AT DALLAS

Clinical Psychology	D
Medical Illustration	M
Rehabilitation Counseling	M

THE UNIVERSITY OF THE ARTS

Art/Fine Arts	M*
Industrial Design	M
Museum Studies	M
Music	M

UNIVERSITY OF THE DISTRICT OF COLUMBIA

Clinical Psychology	M
Counseling Psychology	M
English	M
Public Administration	M

UNIVERSITY OF THE INCARNATE WORD

Communication—General	M,O
Interdisciplinary Studies	M
Religion	M
Social Psychology	M

UNIVERSITY OF THE PACIFIC

Communication—General	M
International Affairs	P,M,D
Music	M
Psychology—General	M
Public Policy	P,M,D
School Psychology	M,D,O
Therapies—Dance, Drama, and Music	M

UNIVERSITY OF THE SACRED HEART

Program	Degrees
Communication—General	M
Conflict Resolution and Mediation/Peace Studies	M
Cultural Studies	M
Journalism	M
Mass Communication	M
Writing	M

UNIVERSITY OF THE SCIENCES IN PHILADELPHIA

Program	Degrees
Health Psychology	M
Technical Writing	M,O

UNIVERSITY OF THE VIRGIN ISLANDS

Program	Degrees
Public Administration	M

UNIVERSITY OF THE WEST

Program	Degrees
Religion	M,D

THE UNIVERSITY OF TOLEDO

Program	Degrees
Clinical Psychology	M,D
Cognitive Sciences	M,D
Communication—General	O
Criminal Justice and Criminology	M,O
Economics	M
English	M,O
Experimental Psychology	M,D
French	M
Geographic Information Systems	M,O
Geography	M,O*
German	M
Gerontology	O
History	M,D*
Homeland Security	M,O
Liberal Studies	M
Music	M
Philosophy	M
Political Science	M
Psychology—General	M,D*
Public Administration	M,O
School Psychology	M,D,O
Social Psychology	M,D,O
Sociology	M
Spanish	M
Urban and Regional Planning	M,O
Writing	M,O

UNIVERSITY OF TORONTO

Program	Degrees
Anthropology	M,D
Architecture	M
Art History	M,D
Art/Fine Arts	M,D
Asian Studies	M,D
Classics	M,D
Comparative Literature	M,D
Criminal Justice and Criminology	M,D
East European and Russian Studies	M
Economics	M,D
English	M,D
French	M,D
Genetic Counseling	M,D
Geography	M,D
German	M,D
History of Science and Technology	M,D
History	M,D
Industrial and Labor Relations	M,D
Italian	M,D
Linguistics	M,D
Medieval and Renaissance Studies	M,D
Museum Studies	M,D
Music	M,D
Near and Middle Eastern Studies	M,D
Philosophy	M,D
Political Science	M,D
Portuguese	M,D
Psychology—General	M,D
Religion	M,D
Slavic Languages	M,D
Sociology	M,D
Spanish	M,D
Theater	M,D
Urban and Regional Planning	M,D
Urban Design	M,D

UNIVERSITY OF TRINITY COLLEGE

Program	Degrees
Music	P,M,D,O
Pastoral Ministry and Counseling	P,M,D,O
Theology	P,M,D,O

UNIVERSITY OF TULSA

Program	Degrees
Anthropology	M
Art/Fine Arts	M
Clinical Psychology	M,D
English	M,D
History	M
Industrial and Organizational Psychology	M,D
Psychology—General	M,D

UNIVERSITY OF UTAH

Program	Degrees
American Studies	M,D
Anthropology	M,D
Architecture	M
Art History	M
Art/Fine Arts	M
Child and Family Studies	M
Clinical Psychology	D
Communication—General	M,D
Comparative Literature	M,D*
Consumer Economics	M
Counseling Psychology	M,D
Dance	M
Economics	M,D
English	M,D
Film, Television, and Video Production	M
French	M,D
Geography	M,D
German	M,D
Gerontology	M,O
Graphic Design	M
History	M,D
International Affairs	M
Linguistics	M,D
Music	M,D
Near and Middle Eastern Languages	M,D
Near and Middle Eastern Studies	M,D
Philosophy	M,D
Photography	M
Political Science	M,D
Psychology—General	D
Public Administration	M,O
Public Policy	M
Rhetoric	M,D
School Psychology	M,D
Sociology	M,D
Spanish	M,D
Urban and Regional Planning	M
Writing	M

UNIVERSITY OF VERMONT

Program	Degrees
Agricultural Economics and Agribusiness	M
Applied Economics	M
Classics	M
Clinical Psychology	D
Communication—General	M
Counseling Psychology	M
English	M
French	M
German	M
Historic Preservation	M
History	M
Psychology—General	D
Public Administration	M

UNIVERSITY OF VICTORIA

Program	Degrees
Anthropology	M
Art History	M,D
Art/Fine Arts	M
Asian Studies	M
Child and Family Studies	M,D
Classics	M,D
Clinical Psychology	M,D
Computer Art and Design	M
Conflict Resolution and Mediation/Peace Studies	M,D
Counseling Psychology	M,D
Developmental Psychology	M,D
Economics	M,D
English	M,D
Experimental Psychology	M,D
Film, Television, and Video Production	M
French	M
Geography	M,D
German	M
Hispanic Studies	M
History	M,D
Human Development	M,D
Italian	M
Linguistics	M,D
Music	M,D
Philosophy	M
Photography	M
Political Science	M,D
Psychology—General	M,D
Public Administration	M,D
Social Psychology	M,D
Sociology	M,D
Theater	M
Writing	M

UNIVERSITY OF VIRGINIA

Program	Degrees
Anthropology	M,D
Archaeology	M,D
Architectural History	M,D
Architecture	M
Art History	M,D
Asian Studies	M
Classics	M,D
Clinical Psychology	M,D,O
Economics	M,D
English	M,D
French	M,D
German	M,D
History	M,D
Interdisciplinary Studies	M,D
International Affairs	M,D
Italian	M
Landscape Architecture	M
Linguistics	M
Music	M,D
Philosophy	M,D
Political Science	M,D
Psychology—General	M,D
Public Policy	M
Religion	M,D
Romance Languages	M,D
School Psychology	M,D,O
Slavic Languages	M,D
Sociology	M,D
Spanish	M,D
Theater	M
Urban and Regional Planning	M
Writing	M

UNIVERSITY OF WASHINGTON

Program	Degrees
Anthropology	M,D
Architecture	M,D,O
Art History	M,D
Art/Fine Arts	M
Asian Languages	M,D
Asian Studies	M
Chinese	M,D
Classics	M,D
Clinical Psychology	D
Communication—General	M,D
Comparative Literature	M,D
Dance	M
East European and Russian Studies	M
Economics	M,D
English	M,D
French	M,D
Geography	M,D
German	M,D
Hispanic Studies	M
Historic Preservation	O
History	M,D
Human Development	M,D
International Affairs	M
Italian	M,D
Japanese	M,D
Landscape Architecture	M
Lighting Design	M,D,O
Linguistics	M,D
Museum Studies	M
Music	M,D
Near and Middle Eastern Studies	M,D
Philosophy	M,D
Political Science	M,D
Portuguese	M
Psychology—General	D
Public Affairs	M,D
Religion	M
Romance Languages	M,D
Russian	M,D
Scandinavian Languages	M,D
School Psychology	M,D
Slavic Languages	M,D
Sociology	M,D
Spanish	M
Sustainable Development	P,M,D
Technical Communication	M,D
Theater	M,D
Urban and Regional Planning	M,D
Urban Design	M,D,O
Women's Studies	M,D

UNIVERSITY OF WASHINGTON, BOTHELL

Program	Degrees
Public Policy	M

UNIVERSITY OF WASHINGTON, TACOMA

Program	Degrees
Interdisciplinary Studies	M

UNIVERSITY OF WATERLOO

Program	Degrees
Anthropology	M
Architecture	M
Art/Fine Arts	M
Economics	M,D
English	M,D
French	M,D
Geography	M,D
German	M,D
History	M,D
International Affairs	M,D
Near and Middle Eastern Studies	M
Philosophy	M,D
Political Science	M,D
Psychology—General	M,D
Public Affairs	M
Religion	D
Russian	M,D
Sociology	M,D
Technical Writing	M,D
Urban and Regional Planning	M,D

THE UNIVERSITY OF WESTERN ONTARIO

Program	Degrees
Anthropology	M,D
Classics	M
Comparative Literature	M,D
Counseling Psychology	M
Economics	M,D
English	M,D
French	M,D

Geography M,D
History M,D
Interdisciplinary Studies M,D
Journalism M
Media Studies M,D
Music M,D
Philosophy M,D
Political Science M,D
Psychology—General M,D
Sociology M,D
Spanish M,D
Sustainable Development M,D

UNIVERSITY OF WEST FLORIDA

Anthropology M
Archaeology M
Communication—General M
Counseling Psychology M
Criminal Justice and Criminology M
English M
Health Communication M
Historic Preservation M
History M
Humanities M
Industrial and Organizational Psychology M
Political Science M
Psychology—General M
Public Administration M
Public History M
Writing M

UNIVERSITY OF WEST GEORGIA

Criminal Justice and Criminology M
English M
Geographic Information Systems O
History M
Museum Studies O
Music M
Psychology—General M,D
Public Administration M,O
Rural Planning and Studies M
Sociology M

UNIVERSITY OF WINDSOR

Art/Fine Arts M
Clinical Psychology M,D
Communication—General M
Criminal Justice and Criminology M,D
Economics M
English M
History M
Philosophy M
Political Science M
Psychology—General M,D
Social Psychology M,D
Sociology M,D
Writing M

THE UNIVERSITY OF WINNIPEG

History M
Marriage and Family Therapy P,M,O
Public Administration M
Religion M
Theology P,M,O

UNIVERSITY OF WISCONSIN–EAU CLAIRE

English M
History M
Psychology—General M,O
School Psychology M,O

UNIVERSITY OF WISCONSIN–LA CROSSE

Psychology—General M,O
School Psychology M,O

UNIVERSITY OF WISCONSIN–MADISON

African Studies M,D
African-American Studies M
Agricultural Economics and Agribusiness M,D
Anthropology M,D
Applied Arts and Design—General M,D
Applied Economics M,D
Art History M,D
Art/Fine Arts M
Arts Administration M
Asian Languages M,D
Asian Studies M,D
Child and Family Studies M,D
Chinese M,D
Classics M,D
Clinical Psychology D
Cognitive Sciences D
Communication—General M,D
Comparative Literature M,D
Consumer Economics M,D
Counseling Psychology D
Developmental Psychology D
Economics D
English M,D
Family and Consumer Sciences-General M,D
French M,D,O
Geographic Information Systems M,D,O
Geography M,D,O
German M,D
History of Science and Technology M,D
History M,D
Human Development M,D
Industrial and Labor Relations M,D
Italian M,D
Japanese M,D
Jewish Studies M,D
Journalism M,D
Landscape Architecture M
Latin American Studies M
Linguistics M,D
Mass Communication M,D
Music M,D
Near and Middle Eastern Languages M,D
Philosophy M,D
Political Science M,D
Portuguese M,D
Psychology—General D
Public Affairs M
Rehabilitation Counseling M,D
Rural Sociology M,D
Scandinavian Languages M,D
Slavic Languages M,D
Social Psychology D
Social Sciences D
Sociology M,D
Spanish M,D
Sustainable Development M
Theater M,D
Urban and Regional Planning M,D

UNIVERSITY OF WISCONSIN–MILWAUKEE

Anthropology M,D,O
Architecture M,D,O
Art History M,O
Art/Fine Arts M
Classics M
Clinical Psychology M,D
Communication—General M,O
Comparative Literature M,D,O
Criminal Justice and Criminology M
Dance M
Economics M,D
English M,D,O
Film, Television, and Video Production M
French M
Geography M,D
German M
History M,D
Industrial and Labor Relations M,O
Interdisciplinary Studies D
Italian M
Jewish Studies M
Journalism M
Liberal Studies M
Mass Communication M
Museum Studies M,O
Music M,O
Philosophy M
Political Science M,D
Psychology—General M,D
Public Administration M
School Psychology O
Slavic Languages M
Sociology M
Spanish M
Theater M
Urban and Regional Planning M,O
Urban Studies M,D

UNIVERSITY OF WISCONSIN–OSHKOSH

English M
Experimental Psychology M
Industrial and Organizational Psychology M
Psychology—General M
Public Administration M

UNIVERSITY OF WISCONSIN–PLATTEVILLE

Criminal Justice and Criminology M

UNIVERSITY OF WISCONSIN–RIVER FALLS

Art/Fine Arts M
School Psychology M,O

UNIVERSITY OF WISCONSIN–STEVENS POINT

Communication—General M
Corporate and Organizational Communication M
English M
Family and Consumer Sciences-General M
History M
Human Development M
Mass Communication M
Speech and Interpersonal Communication M

UNIVERSITY OF WISCONSIN–STOUT

Child and Family Studies M
Counseling Psychology M
Human Development M
Marriage and Family Therapy M
Psychology—General M
Rehabilitation Counseling M
School Psychology M,O

UNIVERSITY OF WISCONSIN–SUPERIOR

Art History M
Art Therapy M
Art/Fine Arts M
Communication—General M
Mass Communication M
Social Psychology M
Speech and Interpersonal Communication M
Theater M

UNIVERSITY OF WISCONSIN–WHITEWATER

Communication—General M
Corporate and Organizational Communication M
Mass Communication M
Psychology—General M,O
School Psychology M,O
Social Psychology M

UNIVERSITY OF WYOMING

Agricultural Economics and Agribusiness M
American Studies M
Anthropology M,D
Applied Economics M
Child Development M
Communication—General M
Consumer Economics M
Economics M,D
English M
French M
Geography M
German M
History M
International Affairs M
Music M
Philosophy M
Political Science M
Psychology—General M,D
Public Administration M
Rural Planning and Studies M
Sociology M
Spanish M
Writing M

UPPER IOWA UNIVERSITY

Criminal Justice and Criminology M
Homeland Security M
Public Administration M

URSULINE COLLEGE

Art Therapy M
Historic Preservation M
Liberal Studies M
Theology M

UTAH STATE UNIVERSITY

American Studies M
Applied Economics M
Art/Fine Arts M
Child and Family Studies M,D
Clinical Psychology M,D
Communication—General M
Consumer Economics M
Counseling Psychology M,D
Disability Studies M,D,O
Economics M,D
English M
Family and Consumer Sciences-General M,D
Folklore M
Geography M,D
History M
Human Development M,D
Interior Design M
Landscape Architecture M

Marriage and Family Therapy M,D
Political Science M
Psychology—General M,D
Rehabilitation Counseling M
School Psychology M,D
Sociology M,D
Theater M
Urban and Regional Planning M,D
Writing M

UTICA COLLEGE

Criminal Justice and Criminology M
Liberal Studies M

VALDOSTA STATE UNIVERSITY

Clinical Psychology M,O
Counseling Psychology M,O
Criminal Justice and Criminology M
English M
History M
Industrial and Organizational Psychology M,O
Marriage and Family Therapy M
Music M
Psychology—General M,O
Public Administration M,D
School Psychology M,O
Sociology M

VALPARAISO UNIVERSITY

Asian Studies M
Clinical Psychology M,O
Counseling Psychology M,O
English M,O
Ethics M,O
Gerontology M,O
History M,O
Liberal Studies M,O
Psychology—General M,O
School Psychology
Theology M,O

VANCOUVER SCHOOL OF THEOLOGY

Theology P,M,O

VANDERBILT UNIVERSITY

Anthropology M,D
Child and Family Studies M
Classics M
Economics P,M,D
English M,D
French M,D
German M,D
History M,D
Human Development M
Latin American Studies M
Liberal Studies M
Philosophy M,D
Political Science M,D
Portuguese M,D
Psychology—General M,D
Public Policy M,D
Religion M,D
Sociology M,D
Spanish M,D
Theology P,M
Urban and Regional Planning M
Writing M

VANGUARD UNIVERSITY OF SOUTHERN CALIFORNIA

Clinical Psychology M
Religion M
Theology M

VICTORIA UNIVERSITY

Theology P,M,D,O

VILLANOVA UNIVERSITY

Classics M
Communication—General M
Criminal Justice and Criminology M
English M*
Hispanic Studies M
History M*
Liberal Studies M
Philosophy D
Political Science M*
Psychology—General M*
Public Administration M
Theater M*
Theology M

VIRGINIA COLLEGE AT BIRMINGHAM

Criminal Justice and Criminology M

VIRGINIA COMMONWEALTH UNIVERSITY

Applied Arts and Design—General M
Applied Social Research M,O
Architectural History M,D
Art History M,D
Art/Fine Arts M,D*
Clinical Psychology D
Communication—General D
Counseling Psychology M,D,O
Criminal Justice and Criminology M,O
Economics M
Emergency Management M,O
English M
Forensic Sciences M
Gender Studies O
Geographic Information Systems O
Gerontology M,D,O
Historic Preservation O
History M,D
Homeland Security M,O
Humanities M,D,O*
Interdisciplinary Studies M*
Interior Design M
Internet and Interactive Multimedia M
Journalism M
Mass Communication M
Media Studies D
Museum Studies M,D
Music M
Photography M
Political Science M,D,O
Psychology—General D
Public Administration M,D
Public Affairs M,D,O
Public Policy D
Rehabilitation Counseling M,O
Rhetoric M
Sociology M
Theater M
Urban and Regional Planning M,O
Writing M

VIRGINIA POLYTECHNIC INSTITUTE AND STATE UNIVERSITY

Agricultural Economics and Agribusiness M,D
Applied Arts and Design—General M
Applied Economics M,D
Architecture M
Arts Administration M
Child and Family Studies M,D
Child Development M,D
Clinical Psychology M,D
Clothing and Textiles M,D
Communication—General M
Consumer Economics M,D
Developmental Psychology M,D
Economics M,D
English M,D
Environmental Design D
Geography M,D
Gerontology M,D
History of Science and Technology M,D
History M
Human Development M,D
Industrial and Organizational Psychology M,D
Interdisciplinary Studies M,D
Interior Design M,D
International Affairs M,D
International Development M,D
Landscape Architecture M,D
Marriage and Family Therapy M,D
Philosophy M
Political Science M
Psychology—General M,D
Public Administration M,D,O
Public Affairs M,D
Public Policy M,D,O
Rural Planning and Studies M,D
Sociology M,D
Theater M
Urban and Regional Planning M,D
Urban Studies M,D

VIRGINIA STATE UNIVERSITY

Economics M
English M
History M
Interdisciplinary Studies M
Psychology—General M

VIRGINIA UNION UNIVERSITY

Theology P,D

VIRGINIA UNIVERSITY OF LYNCHBURG

Religion P

WAKE FOREST UNIVERSITY

Communication—General M
English M
Liberal Studies M
Psychology—General M
Religion M
Speech and Interpersonal Communication M

WALDEN UNIVERSITY

Child and Family Studies M,D
Clinical Psychology M,D,O
Counseling Psychology M,D,O
Criminal Justice and Criminology M,D
Developmental Psychology M,D,O
Health Psychology M,D,O
Homeland Security M,D
Industrial and Organizational Psychology M,D,O
International Affairs M,D
Psychology—General M,D,O
Public Administration M,D
Public Policy M,D
School Psychology M,D,O

WALLA WALLA UNIVERSITY

Counseling Psychology M

WALSH COLLEGE OF ACCOUNTANCY AND BUSINESS ADMINISTRATION

Economics M

WALSH UNIVERSITY

Counseling Psychology M
Theology M

WARNER PACIFIC COLLEGE

Ethics M
Pastoral Ministry and Counseling M
Religion M
Theology M

WARREN WILSON COLLEGE

Writing M

WARTBURG THEOLOGICAL SEMINARY

Theology P,M

WASHBURN UNIVERSITY

Clinical Psychology M
Criminal Justice and Criminology M
Liberal Studies M
Psychology—General M

WASHINGTON COLLEGE

English M
History M
Psychology—General M

WASHINGTON STATE UNIVERSITY

Agricultural Economics and Agribusiness M,D,O
American Studies M,D
Anthropology M,D
Applied Economics M,D,O
Archaeology M,D
Architecture M
Art/Fine Arts M
Asian Studies M,D
Clinical Psychology M,D
Clothing and Textiles M,D
Communication—General M,D
Computer Art and Design M
Corporate and Organizational Communication M,D
Counseling Psychology M,D,O
Criminal Justice and Criminology M,D
Cultural Studies M,D
Demography and Population Studies M,D
Economics M,D,O
English M,D
Ethnic Studies M,D
Experimental Psychology M,D
Health Communication M,D
History M,D
Human Development M
Interdisciplinary Studies D
Interior Design M,D
International Affairs M,D
Landscape Architecture M,D
Media Studies M,D
Music M
Philosophy M
Photography M
Political Science M,D
Psychology—General M,D
Public History M,D
Public Policy M,D
School Psychology M,D,O
Social Psychology M,D
Sociology M,D
Spanish M

Western European Studies	M,D
Women's Studies	M,D

WASHINGTON STATE UNIVERSITY SPOKANE

Architecture	M,D
Criminal Justice and Criminology	M,D
Interior Design	M,D
Landscape Architecture	M,D

WASHINGTON STATE UNIVERSITY VANCOUVER

History	M
Public Affairs	M

WASHINGTON THEOLOGICAL UNION

Theology	P,M,D

WASHINGTON UNIVERSITY IN ST. LOUIS

Anthropology	M,D
Archaeology	M,D
Architecture	M*
Art History	M,D
Art/Fine Arts	M
Asian Languages	M,D
Asian Studies	M,D*
Chinese	M,D
Classics	M
Clinical Psychology	M,D
Comparative Literature	M,D
Economics	M,D*
English	M,D
Experimental Psychology	M,D
French	M,D
German	M,D
History	M,D
Japanese	M,D
Jewish Studies	M
Music	M,D
Near and Middle Eastern Studies	M
Philosophy	M,D
Political Science	M,D
Psychology—General	M,D
Public Policy	M
Religion	M
Romance Languages	M,D
Social Psychology	M,D
Spanish	M,D
Speech and Interpersonal Communication	M,D
Theater	M
Urban Design	M
Writing	M

WAYLAND BAPTIST UNIVERSITY

Counseling Psychology	M
Criminal Justice and Criminology	M
Interdisciplinary Studies	M
Pastoral Ministry and Counseling	M
Public Administration	M
Religion	M

WAYNE STATE COLLEGE

Communication—General	M

WAYNE STATE UNIVERSITY

Addictions/Substance Abuse Counseling	O
Anthropology	M,D
Applied Arts and Design—General	M
Art History	M
Art/Fine Arts	M
Child and Family Studies	O
Classics	M
Clinical Psychology	M,D,O
Cognitive Sciences	M,D
Communication—General	M,D
Comparative Literature	M
Conflict Resolution and Mediation/Peace Studies	M,O
Corporate and Organizational Communication	M,D
Criminal Justice and Criminology	M
Developmental Psychology	M,D
Economics	M,D,O
English	M,D
French	M
Geography	M
German	M,D
Gerontology	O
History	M,D
Human Development	M
Industrial and Labor Relations	M
Industrial and Organizational Psychology	M,D
Italian	M
Linguistics	M
Media Studies	M,D
Music	M,O
Near and Middle Eastern Studies	M
Philosophy	M,D
Political Science	M,D
Psychology—General	M,D
Public Administration	M
Rehabilitation Counseling	M,D,O
Russian	M,D
School Psychology	M,D,O
Sociology	M,D
Spanish	M
Speech and Interpersonal Communication	M,D
Theater	M,D
Urban and Regional Planning	M
Writing	M,D

WEBER STATE UNIVERSITY

English	M

WEBSTER UNIVERSITY

Art/Fine Arts	M
Arts Administration	M
Communication—General	M
Corporate and Organizational Communication	M
Counseling Psychology	M
Criminal Justice and Criminology	M,D
Gerontology	M
International Affairs	M
Media Studies	M
Music	M
Public Administration	M,D

WESLEYAN UNIVERSITY

Liberal Studies	M,O
Music	M,D
Psychology—General	M

WESLEY BIBLICAL SEMINARY

Marriage and Family Therapy	P,M
Missions and Missiology	P,M
Pastoral Ministry and Counseling	P,M
Theology	P,M

WESLEY THEOLOGICAL SEMINARY

Theology	P,M,D

WEST CHESTER UNIVERSITY OF PENNSYLVANIA

Anthropology	M,O
Classics	M
Clinical Psychology	M,O
Communication—General	M
Criminal Justice and Criminology	M
Economics	M,O
Emergency Management	M,O
English	M
Ethics	M,O
French	M
Geographic Information Systems	M,O
Geography	M,O
German	M
Gerontology	M,O
Health Psychology	M,O
History	M,O
Holocaust Studies	M,O
Industrial and Organizational Psychology	M,O
Music	M,O
Philosophy	M,O
Psychology—General	M,O
Public Administration	M,O
Sociology	M,O
Spanish	M
Urban and Regional Planning	M,O
Women's Studies	M,O

WESTERN CAROLINA UNIVERSITY

Applied Arts and Design—General	M
Art/Fine Arts	M
English	M
History	M
Music	M
Psychology—General	M
Public Affairs	M
School Psychology	M
Social Psychology	M

WESTERN CONNECTICUT STATE UNIVERSITY

Art/Fine Arts	M
Criminal Justice and Criminology	M
English	M
History	M
Illustration	M
Social Psychology	M
Writing	M

WESTERN ILLINOIS UNIVERSITY

Clinical Psychology	M,O
Communication—General	M
Criminal Justice and Criminology	M,O
Economics	M
English	M
Geography	M,O
Graphic Design	M,O
History	M
Internet and Interactive Multimedia	M,O
Liberal Studies	M
Music	M
Political Science	M,O
Psychology—General	M,O
Public Administration	M,O
School Psychology	M,O
Social Psychology	M,O
Sociology	M
Sustainable Development	M,O
Theater	M
Writing	M

WESTERN INTERNATIONAL UNIVERSITY

Public Administration	M

WESTERN KENTUCKY UNIVERSITY

Anthropology	M
Communication—General	M
Comparative Literature	M
English	M
Geography	M
History	M
Interdisciplinary Studies	M
Political Science	M
Psychology—General	M,O
School Psychology	M,O
Sociology	M
Writing	M

WESTERN MICHIGAN UNIVERSITY

Anthropology	M
Applied Arts and Design—General	M
Applied Economics	M,D
Clinical Psychology	M,D,O
Communication—General	M
Corporate and Organizational Communication	M
Counseling Psychology	M,D
Economics	M,D
English	M,D
Experimental Psychology	M,D,O
Family and Consumer Sciences-General	M
Geography	M
Graphic Design	M
History	M,D
Industrial and Organizational Psychology	M,D,O
Marriage and Family Therapy	M,D
Medieval and Renaissance Studies	M
Music	M
Philosophy	M
Political Science	M,D
Psychology—General	M,D,O
Public Administration	M,D
Public Affairs	M,D
Rehabilitation Counseling	M
Religion	M,D
School Psychology	M,D,O
Sociology	M,D
Spanish	M
Textile Design	M
Writing	M,D

WESTERN NEW MEXICO UNIVERSITY

Interdisciplinary Studies	M
School Psychology	M

WESTERN OREGON UNIVERSITY

Criminal Justice and Criminology	M
Music	M
Rehabilitation Counseling	M

WESTERN SEMINARY

Marriage and Family Therapy	M
Pastoral Ministry and Counseling	P,M,D,O
Religion	M,O
Theology	M,O

WESTERN SEMINARY–SACRAMENTO CAMPUS

Marriage and Family Therapy	P,M

Pastoral Ministry and Counseling P,M
Theology P,M

WESTERN SEMINARY–SAN JOSE CAMPUS
Marriage and Family Therapy P,M
Pastoral Ministry and Counseling P,M
Theology P,M

WESTERN THEOLOGICAL SEMINARY
Theology P,M,D

WESTERN WASHINGTON UNIVERSITY
Anthropology M
Counseling Psychology M
English M
Experimental Psychology M
Geography M
History M
Music M
Political Science M
Psychology—General M
Rehabilitation Counseling M

WESTFIELD STATE COLLEGE
Counseling Psychology M
Criminal Justice and Criminology M
English M
History M
Psychology—General M

WESTMINSTER CHOIR COLLEGE OF RIDER UNIVERSITY
Music M

WESTMINSTER COLLEGE (UT)
Communication—General M
Counseling Psychology M
Writing M

WESTMINSTER SEMINARY CALIFORNIA
Religion P,M
Theology P,M

WESTMINSTER THEOLOGICAL SEMINARY
Missions and Missiology P,M,D,O
Pastoral Ministry and Counseling P,M,D,O
Religion P,M,D,O
Theology P,M,D,O

WEST TEXAS A&M UNIVERSITY
Agricultural Economics and Agribusiness M
Art/Fine Arts M
Communication—General M
Criminal Justice and Criminology M
Economics M
English M
History M
Interdisciplinary Studies M
Music M
Political Science M
Psychology—General M

WEST VIRGINIA STATE UNIVERSITY
Media Studies M

WEST VIRGINIA UNIVERSITY
African Studies M,D
African-American Studies M,D
Agricultural Economics and Agribusiness M
American Studies M,D
Applied Social Research M
Art History M
Art/Fine Arts M
Asian Studies M,D
Child and Family Studies M
Clinical Psychology M,D
Communication—General M,D
Corporate and Organizational Communication M,D
Counseling Psychology D
Developmental Psychology M,D
Economics M,D
English M,D
Forensic Sciences M,D
French M
Geographic Information Systems M,D
Geography M,D
Graphic Design M
History of Science and Technology M,D
History M,D
Human Development M,D
Industrial and Labor Relations M
International Affairs M
Journalism M
Latin American Studies M,D
Liberal Studies M
Linguistics M
Music M,D
Political Science M,D
Psychology—General M,D
Public Administration M,D
Public Policy M,D
Rehabilitation Counseling M
Sociology M
Spanish M
Sport Psychology M,D
Sustainable Development D
Theater M
Urban and Regional Planning M,D
Writing M

WHEATON COLLEGE
American Studies M
Archaeology M
Clinical Psychology M,D
Cultural Studies M,O
Missions and Missiology M,O
Pastoral Ministry and Counseling M,D
Psychology—General M,D
Religion M
Theology M,D

WHEELOCK COLLEGE
Child and Family Studies M
Human Development M

WHITTIER COLLEGE
Child Development M

WICHITA STATE UNIVERSITY
Anthropology M
Art/Fine Arts M
Clinical Psychology M,D
Communication—General M
Criminal Justice and Criminology M
Economics M
English M
Gerontology M
History M
Liberal Studies M
Music M

Political Science M
Psychology—General M,D
Public Administration M
School Psychology M,D,O
Social Psychology M,D
Sociology M
Spanish M
Writing M

WIDENER UNIVERSITY
Clinical Psychology D*
Criminal Justice and Criminology M
Liberal Studies M
Psychology—General
Public Administration M

WILFRID LAURIER UNIVERSITY
Archaeology M
Classics M
Cognitive Sciences M,D
Communication—General M
Cultural Studies M
Developmental Psychology M,D
Economics M
English M,D
Ethics P,M,D,O
Film, Television, and Video Theory and Criticism M,D
Geography M,D
History M,D
International Affairs M,D
Pastoral Ministry and Counseling P,M,D,O
Philosophy M
Political Science M
Psychology—General M,D
Public Policy M
Religion M,D
Social Psychology M,D
Sociology M
Theology P,M,D,O
Therapies—Dance, Drama, and Music M

WILKES UNIVERSITY
Writing M

WILLAMETTE UNIVERSITY
Public Administration M

WILLIAM CAREY UNIVERSITY
Counseling Psychology M
Psychology—General M

WILLIAM PATERSON UNIVERSITY OF NEW JERSEY
Art/Fine Arts M
Clinical Psychology M
Communication—General M
Counseling Psychology M
English M
History M
Media Studies M
Music M
Public Policy M
Sociology M

WILLIAMS COLLEGE
Art History M

WILLIAM WOODS UNIVERSITY
Agricultural Economics and Agribusiness M,O

WILMINGTON UNIVERSITY
Criminal Justice and Criminology M
Gerontology M

Homeland Security M
Internet and Interactive Multimedia M
Public Administration M
Social Psychology M

WINEBRENNER THEOLOGICAL SEMINARY
Theology P,M,D

WINONA STATE UNIVERSITY
English M

WINSTON-SALEM STATE UNIVERSITY
Rehabilitation Counseling M

WINTHROP UNIVERSITY
Art/Fine Arts M
Arts Administration M
English M
History M
Liberal Studies M
Music M
Psychology—General M,O
Spanish M

WISCONSIN SCHOOL OF PROFESSIONAL PSYCHOLOGY
Clinical Psychology M,D
Psychology—General M,D

WOODBURY UNIVERSITY
Architecture M

WORCESTER POLYTECHNIC INSTITUTE
Interdisciplinary Studies M,D
Social Sciences M,D

WORCESTER STATE COLLEGE
School Psychology M,O

WRIGHT INSTITUTE
Clinical Psychology D
Psychology—General D

WRIGHT STATE UNIVERSITY
Applied Economics M
Clinical Psychology D
Criminal Justice and Criminology M
Economics M
English M
History M
Humanities M
Industrial and Organizational Psychology M,D
Interdisciplinary Studies M
Music M
Psychology—General M,D
Public Administration M
Rehabilitation Counseling M
Rhetoric M
Urban Studies M
Writing M

WYCLIFFE COLLEGE
Religion P,M,D,O
Theology P,M,D,O

XAVIER UNIVERSITY
Clinical Psychology M,D
Criminal Justice and Criminology M
English M
Experimental Psychology M,D

Industrial and Organizational Psychology	M,D
Psychology—General	M,D
Theology	M

XAVIER UNIVERSITY OF LOUISIANA

Pastoral Ministry and Counseling	M
Theology	M

YALE UNIVERSITY

African Studies	M
African-American Studies	M,D
American Studies	M,D
Anthropology	M,D
Applied Arts and Design—General	M
Archaeology	M
Architecture	M
Art History	D
Art/Fine Arts	M
Asian Languages	D
Asian Studies	M
Classics	D
Comparative Literature	D
East European and Russian Studies	M
Economics	M,D
English	M,D
Environmental Design	M
French	M,D
German	M,D
Graphic Design	M
History of Medicine	M,D
History of Science and Technology	M,D
History	M,D
International Affairs	M
Italian	D
Linguistics	D
Medieval and Renaissance Studies	M,D
Music	M,D,O
Near and Middle Eastern Languages	M,D
Philosophy	D
Photography	M
Political Science	D
Portuguese	M,D
Psychology—General	D
Religion	D
Slavic Languages	D
Social Sciences	M,D
Sociology	D
Spanish	M,D
Theater	M,D,O
Theology	P,M

YESHIVA BETH MOSHE

Theology	O

YESHIVA KARLIN STOLIN RABBINICAL INSTITUTE

Theology	O

YESHIVA OF NITRA RABBINICAL COLLEGE

Theology	

YESHIVA SHAAR HATORAH TALMUDIC RESEARCH INSTITUTE

Theology	

YESHIVATH ZICHRON MOSHE

Theology	O

YESHIVA TORAS CHAIM TALMUDICAL SEMINARY

Theology	

YESHIVA UNIVERSITY

Clinical Psychology	D
Counseling Psychology	M
Health Psychology	D
Jewish Studies	M,D
Psychology—General	M,D
School Psychology	D

YORK UNIVERSITY

Anthropology	M,D
Applied Arts and Design—General	M
Art History	M,D
Art/Fine Arts	M,D
Communication—General	M,D
Dance	M
Disability Studies	M,D
Economics	M,D
Emergency Management	M
English	M,D
Film, Television, and Video Production	M,D
French	M
Geography	M,D
History	M,D
Humanities	M,D
Interdisciplinary Studies	M
International Affairs	M
Linguistics	M,D
Music	M,D
Philosophy	M,D
Political Science	M,D
Psychology—General	M,D
Public Administration	M
Public Affairs	M
Public Policy	M
Social Sciences	M
Sociology	M,D
Theater	M,D
Translation and Interpretation	M
Women's Studies	M,D

YOUNGSTOWN STATE UNIVERSITY

Criminal Justice and Criminology	M
Economics	M
English	M
History	M
Music	M

ACADEMIC AND PROFESSIONAL PROGRAMS IN ARTS AND ARCHITECTURE

Section 1
Applied Arts and Design

This section contains a directory of institutions offering graduate work in applied arts and design, followed by in-depth entries submitted by institutions that chose to prepare detailed program descriptions. Additional information about programs listed in the directory but not augmented by an in-depth entry may be obtained by writing directly to the dean of a graduate school or chair of a department at the address given in the directory.

For programs offering related work, see also in this book *Architecture* and *Art and Art History*. In another guide in this series: ***Graduate Programs in Business, Education, Health, Information Studies, Law & Social Work***
See *Advertising and Public Relations*

CONTENTS

Program Directories

Announcement

Close-Ups

See also:

Applied Arts and Design—General

Academy of Art University, Graduate Program, School of Advertising, San Francisco, CA 94105-3410. Offers MFA. Part-time programs available. Postbaccalaureate distance learning degree programs offered (no on-campus study). *Degree requirements:* For master's, thesis, final review. *Entrance requirements:* For master's, minimum GPA of 3.0, portfolio. Electronic applications accepted.

Alfred University, Graduate School, New York State College of Ceramics, School of Art and Design, Alfred, NY 14802-1205. Offers ceramic art (MFA); electronic integrated arts (MFA); glass art (MFA); sculpture (MFA). *Accreditation:* NASAD. *Students:* 34 full-time (19 women). Average age 26. 278 applicants, 6% accepted, 17 enrolled. In 2007, 17 degrees awarded. *Degree requirements:* For master's, exhibit. *Entrance requirements:* For master's, portfolio. Additional exam requirements/recommendations for international students: Required—TOEFL (minimum score 550 paper-based; 213 computer-based; 80 iBT), IELTS (minimum score 6). *Application deadline:* For fall admission, 1/15 for domestic students, 2/1 for international students. Application fee: $50. Electronic applications accepted. *Expenses:* Tuition: Full-time $32,016; part-time $680 per credit hour. Required fees: $850; $140 per year. *Financial support:* In 2007–08, 35 students received support; teaching assistantships with full tuition reimbursements available, tuition waivers (full) available. Financial award applicants required to submit FAFSA. *Faculty research:* Ceramic sculpture, functional ceramics, wood, mixed media, hot and cold glass. *Unit head:* Joseph Lewis, Dean, 607-871-2412, E-mail: lewis@alfred.edu. *Application contact:* Valerie Stephens, Coordinator of Graduate Admissions, 607-871-2141, Fax: 607-871-2198, E-mail: gradinquiry@alfred.edu.

Arizona State University, Graduate College, College of Architecture and Environmental Design, School of Design, Tempe, AZ 85287. Offers design (MSD). *Accreditation:* NASAD. *Degree requirements:* For master's, thesis optional. *Entrance requirements:* For master's, GRE General Test, design portfolio.

Art Center College of Design, Graduate Division, Pasadena, CA 91103-1999. Offers MFA, MS. *Accreditation:* NASAD. *Faculty:* 8 full-time (3 women), 32 part-time/adjunct (11 women). *Students:* 126 full-time (56 women), 18 part-time (9 women); includes 38 minority (3 African Americans, 2 American Indian/Alaska Native, 29 Asian Americans or Pacific Islanders, 4 Hispanic Americans), 42 international. Average age 28. 202 applicants, 43% accepted, 46 enrolled. In 2007, 32 degrees awarded. *Degree requirements:* For master's, thesis, studio project. *Entrance requirements:* For master's, portfolio. Additional exam requirements/recommendations for international students: Required—TOEFL (minimum score 100 iBT). *Application deadline:* For fall admission, 2/1 priority date for domestic and international students; for spring admission, 10/1 priority date for domestic and international students. Applications are processed on a rolling basis. Application fee: $50 ($70 for international students). *Expenses:* Tuition: Full-time $31,016. Required fees: $235. *Financial support:* In 2007–08, 63 students received support, including 26 teaching assistantships; career-related internships or fieldwork, Federal Work-Study, and scholarships/grants also available. Financial award application deadline: 3/1. *Faculty research:* Computer graphics, automobile aerodynamics. *Application contact:* Kit Baron, Vice President, Admissions, 626-396-2373, Fax: 626-795-0578, E-mail: admissions@artcenter.edu.

See Close-Up on page 109.

Bowling Green State University, Graduate College, College of Arts and Sciences, School of Art, Bowling Green, OH 43403. Offers 2-D studio art (MA, MFA); 3-D studio art (MA, MFA); art education (MA); art history (MA); computer art (MA); design (MFA); digital arts (MFA); graphics (MFA). *Accreditation:* NASAD. Part-time programs available. *Faculty:* 26 full-time (14 women), 7 part-time/adjunct (2 women). *Students:* 24 full-time (12 women), 3 part-time (all women); includes 1 minority (Asian American or Pacific Islander), 2 international. Average age 33. 59 applicants, 20% accepted, 8 enrolled. In 2007, 11 degrees awarded. *Degree requirements:* For master's, thesis or alternative, final exhibit (MFA). *Entrance requirements:* For master's, GRE General Test (MA), slide portfolio (15-20 slides). Additional exam requirements/recommendations for international students: Required—TOEFL. *Application deadline:* For fall admission, 2/15 for domestic students. Application fee: $30. Electronic applications accepted. *Financial support:* In 2007–08, 11 research assistantships with full and partial tuition reimbursements (averaging $8,404 per year), 8 teaching assistantships with full and partial tuition reimbursements (averaging $8,404 per year) were awarded; career-related internships or fieldwork, institutionally sponsored loans, and unspecified assistantships also available. Support available to part-time students. Financial award applicants required to submit FAFSA. *Faculty research:* Computer animation and virtual reality, Spanish still-life painting from 1600 to 1800, art and psychotherapy, Japanese wood-firing techniques in ceramics, non-toxic printmaking technologies. *Unit head:* Dr. Katerina Rüedi Ray, Director, 419-372-8575. *Application contact:* Shawn Morin, Graduate Coordinator, 419-372-7766.

Bradley University, Graduate School, Slane College of Communications and Fine Arts, Department of Art, Peoria, IL 61625-0002. Offers ceramics (MA, MFA); drawing/illustration (MA, MFA); interdisciplinary art (MA, MFA); painting (MA, MFA); photography (MA, MFA); printmaking (MA, MFA); sculpture (MA, MFA); visual communication and design (MA, MFA). *Accreditation:* NASAD. Part-time programs available. *Faculty:* 10. *Students:* 11 full-time (6 women), 1 international. 20 applicants, 40% accepted, 4 enrolled. In 2007, 2 degrees awarded. *Degree requirements:* For master's, comprehensive exam, thesis, final exhibit. *Entrance requirements:* For master's, portfolio, 2 letters of recommendation. Additional exam requirements/recommendations for international students: Required—TOEFL (minimum score 550 paper-based; 213 computer-based; 79 iBT). *Application deadline:* For fall admission, 4/1 priority date for domestic and international students; for spring admission, 11/1 priority date for domestic and international students. Applications are processed on a rolling basis. Application fee: $40 ($50 for international students). *Financial support:* Research assistantships with full and partial tuition reimbursements, scholarships/grants, tuition waivers (partial), and unspecified assistantships available. Financial award application deadline: 4/1. *Unit head:* Dr. Paul Krainak, Chairperson, 309-677-3330, E-mail: pkrainak@bradley.edu. *Application contact:* Fisher Stolz, Graduate Coordinator, 309-677-2969, E-mail: fisher@bradley.edu.

California College of the Arts, Graduate Programs, Program in Design, San Francisco, CA 94107. Offers MFA. *Faculty:* 2 full-time (0 women), 14 part-time/adjunct (5 women). *Students:* 19 full-time (12 women). Average age 30. 94 applicants, 67% accepted. In 2007, 8 degrees awarded. *Degree requirements:* For master's, thesis, exhibit. *Entrance requirements:* For master's, appropriate bachelor's degree, portfolio, resumé, letters of recommendation. Additional exam requirements/recommendations for international students: Required—TOEFL (minimum score 600 paper-based; 250 computer-based). *Application deadline:* For fall admission, 1/15 for domestic and international students. Application fee: $50. Electronic applications accepted. *Expenses:* Tuition: Part-time $1,017 per unit. *Financial support:* In 2007–08, 2 fellowships (averaging $10,000 per year), 1 teaching assistantship (averaging $2,000 per year) were awarded; career-related internships or fieldwork, Federal Work-Study, scholarships/grants, and health care benefits also available. Financial award application deadline: 3/2. *Unit head:* Brenda Laurel, Graduate Chair, 415-551-9283, Fax: 415-703-9539, E-mail: blaurel@cca.edu. *Application contact:* Kathryn Ward, Assistant Director of Graduate Admissions, 415-703-9523 Ext. 9593, Fax: 415-703-9539, E-mail: graduateprograms@cca.edu.

See Close-Up on page 233.

California College of the Arts, Graduate Programs, Program in Design Strategy, San Francisco, CA 94107. Offers MBA. *Students:* 77 applicants, 49% accepted. *Expenses:* Tuition: Part-time $1,017 per unit. *Unit head:* Nathan Shedroff, Program Chair, E-mail: nshedroff@cca.edu. *Application contact:* Kathryn Ward, Assistant Director of Graduate Admissions, 415-703-9523 Ext. 9593, Fax: 415-703-9539, E-mail: graduateprograms@cca.edu.

California Institute of the Arts, School of Art, Valencia, CA 91355-2340. Offers art (MFA, Adv C); graphic design (MFA, Adv C); photography (MFA, Adv C). *Accreditation:* NASAD (one or more programs are accredited). *Degree requirements:* For master's, final project. *Entrance requirements:* For master's, portfolio. Additional exam requirements/recommendations for international students: Required—TOEFL. Electronic applications accepted.

California State University, Fresno, Division of Graduate Studies, College of Arts and Humanities, Department of Art and Design, Fresno, CA 93740-8027. Offers art (MA). Part-time and evening/weekend programs available. *Faculty:* 10 full-time (5 women). *Students:* 51; includes 19 minority (3 African Americans, 3 Asian Americans or Pacific Islanders, 13 Hispanic Americans), 2 international. Average age 28. 4 applicants. In 2007, 3 degrees awarded. *Degree requirements:* For master's, thesis or alternative. *Entrance requirements:* For master's, GRE General Test, minimum GPA of 3.0, portfolio. Additional exam requirements/recommendations for international students: Required—TOEFL. *Application deadline:* For fall admission, 5/1 for domestic and international students; for spring admission, 10/1 for domestic and international students. Applications are processed on a rolling basis. Application fee: $55. Electronic applications accepted. *Financial support:* Career-related internships or fieldwork, Federal Work-Study, and scholarships/grants available. Support available to part-time students. Financial award application deadline: 3/1; financial award applicants required to submit FAFSA. *Faculty research:* Art history, graphic design, studio art. *Unit head:* Prof. Richard McQuone, Chair, 559-278-2516, Fax: 559-278-4706, E-mail: richard_mcquone@csufresno.edu. *Application contact:* Prof. Paula Durette, Graduate Program Coordinator, 559-278-2515, Fax: 559-278-4706, E-mail: pdurrette@csufresno.edu.

California State University, Fullerton, Graduate Studies, College of the Arts, Department of Art, Fullerton, CA 92834-9480. Offers art (MA, MFA), including ceramics (MFA), crafts, creative photography (MFA), design (MFA), drawing and painting, printmaking (MFA), sculpture; art history (MA); design (MA). *Accreditation:* NASAD (one or more programs are accredited). Part-time programs available. *Students:* 50 full-time (20 women), 28 part-time (20 women); includes 19 minority (2 African Americans, 2 American Indian/Alaska Native, 8 Asian Americans or Pacific Islanders, 7 Hispanic Americans), 2 international. Average age 36. 68 applicants, 47% accepted, 23 enrolled. In 2007, 29 degrees awarded. *Degree requirements:* For master's, project or thesis. *Entrance requirements:* For master's, minimum GPA of 2.5 in last 60 units of course work, portfolio. Application fee: $55. *Financial support:* Career-related internships or fieldwork, Federal Work-Study, institutionally sponsored loans, and scholarships/grants available. Support available to part-time students. Financial award application deadline: 3/1. *Unit head:* Larry Johnson, Chair, 714-278-3471. *Application contact:* Al Ching, Adviser, 714-278-3471.

California State University, Los Angeles, Graduate Studies, College of Arts and Letters, Department of Art, Los Angeles, CA 90032-8530. Offers art (MA), including art education, art history, art therapy, ceramics, metals, and textiles, design (MA, MFA), painting, sculpture, and graphic arts, photography; fine arts (MFA), including crafts, design (MA, MFA), studio arts. *Accreditation:* NASAD (one or more programs are accredited). Part-time and evening/weekend programs available. *Faculty:* 7 full-time (3 women). *Students:* 24 full-time (13 women), 59 part-time (42 women); includes 19 minority (2 African Americans, 1 American Indian/Alaska Native, 5 Asian Americans or Pacific Islanders, 11 Hispanic Americans), 16 international. Average age 39. In 2007, 28 degrees awarded. *Degree requirements:* For master's, comprehensive exam, project or thesis. *Entrance requirements:* For master's, portfolio. Additional exam requirements/recommendations for international students: Required—TOEFL. *Application deadline:* For fall admission, 6/30 for domestic students; for spring admission, 2/1 for domestic students. Applications are processed on a rolling basis. Application fee: $55. *Financial support:* Federal Work-Study available. Support available to part-time students. Financial award application deadline: 3/1. *Faculty research:* The artist and the book, conceptual art, ceramic processes, computer graphics, architectural graphics. *Unit head:* Dr. Robert Martin, Chair, 323-343-4010, Fax: 323-343-4045, E-mail: rjmartin@calstatela.edu.

Cardinal Stritch University, College of Arts and Sciences, Department of Art, Milwaukee, WI 53217-3985. Offers visual studies (MA). Part-time and evening/weekend programs available. *Degree requirements:* For master's, thesis, portfolio, exhibit. *Entrance requirements:* For master's, minimum GPA of 2.75; 3 letters of recommendation.

Carnegie Mellon University, College of Fine Arts, School of Design, Program in Design, Pittsburgh, PA 15213-3891. Offers PhD. *Accreditation:* NASAD. *Degree requirements:* For doctorate, one foreign language, comprehensive exam, thesis/dissertation. *Entrance requirements:* For doctorate, GRE, portfolio of relevant work. Additional exam requirements/recommendations for international students: Required—TOEFL (minimum score 600 paper-based; 250 computer-based). *Faculty research:* Design theory, typography and information design, new product development, organizational behavior, interaction design.

See Close-Up on page 111.

Concordia University, School of Graduate Studies, Faculty of Fine Arts, Department of Design and Computation Arts, Montréal, QC H3G 1M8, Canada. Offers digital technologies in design art practice (Certificate).

Cranbrook Academy of Art, Graduate School, Program in Fine Arts, Bloomfield Hills, MI 48303-0801. Offers ceramics (MFA); design (MFA), including graphic design; fiber arts (MFA); metal-smithing (MFA); painting (MFA); photography (MFA); printmaking (MFA); sculpture (MFA). *Accreditation:* NASAD. *Degree requirements:* For master's, thesis, exhibit. *Entrance requirements:* Additional exam requirements/recommendations for international students: Required—TOEFL (minimum score 550 paper-based; 213 computer-based).

See Close-Up on page 237.

Drexel University, College of Media Arts and Design, Philadelphia, PA 19104-2875. Offers architecture (M Arch); design (MS), including fashion design, interior design; media arts (MS); performing arts (MS), including arts administration. *Accreditation:* NASAD. Part-time and evening/weekend programs available. *Entrance requirements:* For master's, interview. Additional exam requirements/recommendations for international students: Required—TOEFL. Electronic applications accepted. Expenses: Contact institution.

Emily Carr Institute of Art + Design, Program in Applied Arts, Vancouver, BC V6H 3R9, Canada. Offers design (MAA); media arts (MAA); visual arts (MAA). *Degree requirements:* For master's, internship. *Entrance requirements:* For master's, minimum overall GPA of 3.0, visual portfolio, 3 letters of recommendation. Additional exam requirements/recommendations for international students: Required—TOEFL (minimum score 570 paper-based; 230 computer-based; 84 iBT), IELTS (minimum score 7), Michigan English language Assessment Battery (minimum score of 81). Electronic applications accepted.

Fashion Institute of Technology, School of Graduate Studies, New York, NY 10001-5992. Offers MA, MPS. *Accreditation:* NASAD. Part-time and evening/weekend programs available. *Faculty:* 8 full-time (6 women), 60 part-time/adjunct (34 women). *Students:* 123 full-time (97 women), 77 part-time (67 women); includes 15 minority (3 African Americans, 7 Asian Americans or Pacific Islanders, 5 Hispanic Americans), 45 international. Average age 30. 338 applicants, 37% accepted, 76 enrolled. In 2007, 66 master's awarded. *Degree requirements:* For master's, one foreign language, thesis, internship. *Entrance requirements:* For master's, GRE or GMAT, portfolio, letters of recommendation, resumé, transcripts. Additional exam requirements/recommendations for international students: Required—TOEFL (minimum score 550 paper-based; 213 computer-based). *Application deadline:* For fall admission, 2/15 priority date for domestic and international students. Applications are processed on a rolling basis. Application fee: $50. Electronic applications accepted. *Expenses:* Tuition, state resident: full-time $7,245; part-time $302 per credit. Tuition, nonresident: full-time $11,466; part-time $478 per credit.

Required fees: $440; $35 per term. *Financial support:* In 2007–08, 68 students received support. Federal Work-Study and scholarships/grants available. Financial award applicants required to submit FAFSA. *Faculty research:* Fashion history, material conservation, international marketing and global sourcing, sustainable economic development, luxury braiding in China. *Unit head:* Dr. Steven Zucker, Dean, 212-217-4300, Fax: 212-217-5156, E-mail: steven_zucker@fitnyc.edu. *Application contact:* Carole deSantis, Administrative Secretary, Graduate Admissions, 212-217-4314, Fax: 212-217-5156, E-mail: carole_desantis@fitnyc.edu.

See Close-Up on page 113.

Ferris State University, Kendall College of Art and Design, Big Rapids, MI 49307. Offers MFA. *Accreditation:* NASAD. Part-time programs available. *Faculty:* 14 full-time (10 women). *Students:* 30 full-time (16 women), 6 part-time (2 women); includes 3 minority (2 African Americans, 1 Asian American or Pacific Islander). Average age 32. 28 applicants, 86% accepted, 17 enrolled. In 2007, 11 degrees awarded. *Degree requirements:* For master's, thesis, seminars. *Entrance requirements:* For master's, portfolio, 3 letters of recommendation, curriculum vitae. Additional exam requirements/recommendations for international students: Required—TOEFL (minimum score 500 paper-based; 173 computer-based; 61 iBT). *Application deadline:* For fall admission, 2/15 for domestic and international students; for winter admission, 11/1 for domestic and international students. Applications are processed on a rolling basis. Application fee: $30. *Expenses:* Tuition, state resident: part-time $389 per credit. Tuition, nonresident: part-time $753 per credit. *Financial support:* In 2007–08, 32 students received support, including 2 fellowships (averaging $24,424 per year), 30 teaching assistantships (averaging $4,500 per year); research assistantships, scholarships/grants and unspecified assistantships also available. Financial award application deadline: 2/15. *Unit head:* Dr. Oliver H. Evans, President, 616-451-2787. *Application contact:* Sandra Britton, Director of Enrollment Management, 616-451-2787, Fax: 616-836-9689, E-mail: brittons@ferris.edu.

Florida Atlantic University, Dorothy F. Schmidt College of Arts and Letters, Department of Art, Boca Raton, FL 33431-0991. Offers art education (MAT); ceramics (MFA); painting (MFA). *Degree requirements:* For master's, one foreign language, project. *Entrance requirements:* For master's, GRE General Test, minimum GPA of 3.0 during last 60 hours of course work, slide portfolio. Electronic applications accepted. *Faculty research:* Painting, ceramics (traditional and non-traditional), installation, video and interactive sculpture.

Florida State University, Graduate Studies, College of Human Sciences, Department of Textiles and Consumer Sciences, Tallahassee, FL 32306. Offers apparel product development (MS); apparel/textile product development (PhD); creative design (MS); global product development (MS); professional merchandising (MS); retail merchandising (MS, PhD); textiles (MS). Part-time programs available. *Faculty:* 12 full-time (all women). *Students:* 28 full-time (26 women), 6 part-time (4 women); includes 14 minority (9 African Americans, 2 Asian Americans or Pacific Islanders, 3 Hispanic Americans), 2 international. 44 applicants, 25% accepted, 7 enrolled. In 2007, 13 master's, 5 doctorates awarded. *Degree requirements:* For master's, thesis optional; for doctorate, thesis/dissertation. *Entrance requirements:* For master's and doctorate, GRE General Test, minimum GPA of 3.0. Additional exam requirements/recommendations for international students: Required—TOEFL (minimum score 80 iBT). *Application deadline:* For fall admission, 7/1 priority date for domestic students, 5/1 for international students; for spring admission, 11/1 for domestic students, 12/1 for international students. Applications are processed on a rolling basis. Application fee: $30. Electronic applications accepted. *Expenses:* Tuition, state resident: part-time $248 per credit hour. Tuition, nonresident: part-time $880 per credit hour. Tuition and fees vary according to program. *Financial support:* In 2007–08, 20 students received support, including 1 fellowship with partial tuition reimbursement available (averaging $10,000 per year), research assistantships with partial tuition reimbursements available (averaging $8,000 per year), 15 teaching assistantships with partial tuition reimbursements available (averaging $8,000 per year); career-related internships or fieldwork, Federal Work-Study, institutionally sponsored loans, scholarships/grants, and unspecified assistantships also available. Financial award application deadline: 1/15; financial award applicants required to submit FAFSA. *Faculty research:* Soft goods retailing, small business strategies, textile product performance, consumer behavior, accessible housing. *Unit head:* Dr. Barbara Dyer, Chair, 850-644-2498, Fax: 850-645-4673, E-mail: bdyer@fsu.edu. *Application contact:* Sue Skornia, Academic Support Assistant, 850-644-2498, Fax: 850-645-4673, E-mail: sskornia@fsu.edu.

See Close-Up on page 1073.

The George Washington University, Columbian College of Arts and Sciences, Department of Fine Arts and Art History, Washington, DC 20052. Offers art history (MA, PhD), including art history (PhD), museum training (MA); ceramics (MFA); design (MFA); interior design (MFA); painting (MFA); photography (MFA); printmaking (MFA); sculpture (MFA). *Accreditation:* CIDA. Part-time and evening/weekend programs available. *Entrance requirements:* For master's, GRE General Test, bachelor's degree in field, minimum GPA of 3.0. Additional exam requirements/recommendations for international students: Required—TOEFL (minimum score 550 paper-based; 213 computer-based). Electronic applications accepted.

Howard University, Graduate School, Division of Fine Arts, Department of Art, Program in Fine Arts, Washington, DC 20059-0002. Offers 3D reality (sculpture and ceramics) (MFA); design (MFA); electronic studio (MFA); painting (MFA); photography (MFA). *Accreditation:* NASAD. *Degree requirements:* For master's, comprehensive exam, thesis, exhibit. *Entrance requirements:* For master's, minimum GPA of 3.0, portfolio. *Expenses:* Tuition: Full-time $16,175; part-time $899 per credit hour. Required fees: $805.

Illinois Institute of Technology, Graduate College, Institute of Design, Chicago, IL 60616-3793. Offers M Des, MSDM, PhD. *Faculty:* 9 full-time (1 woman), 23 part-time/adjunct (6 women). *Students:* 124 full-time (66 women), 28 part-time (11 women); includes 26 minority (2 African Americans, 20 Asian Americans or Pacific Islanders, 4 Hispanic Americans), 51 international. Average age 31. 145 applicants, 72% accepted, 62 enrolled. In 2007, 43 master's, 2 doctorates awarded. Terminal master's awarded for partial completion of doctoral program. *Degree requirements:* For master's, comprehensive exam; for doctorate, 2 foreign languages, comprehensive exam, thesis/dissertation. *Entrance requirements:* For master's, GRE General Test or GMAT; for doctorate, GRE General Test, master's degree in design, portfolio (MSDM degree). Additional exam requirements/recommendations for international students: Required—TOEFL (minimum score 600 paper-based; 250 computer-based; 100 iBT). *Application deadline:* For fall admission, 2/15 priority date for domestic students, 2/15 for international students; for spring admission, 10/15 priority date for domestic students, 10/15 for international students. Application fee: $50. *Expenses:* Tuition: Full-time $14,004; part-time $778 per credit. Required fees: $7 per credit. $235 per term. Tuition and fees vary according to class time, course level, course load, program and student level. *Financial support:* In 2007–08, fellowships (averaging $5,400 per year), research assistantships (averaging $10,000 per year), teaching assistantships (averaging $10,000 per year) were awarded; career-related internships or fieldwork, Federal Work-Study, institutionally sponsored loans, scholarships/grants, health care benefits, and unspecified assistantships also available. Support available to part-time students. Financial award applicants required to submit FAFSA. *Faculty research:* Design planning, human-centered design, new product definition, interactive systems, context-sensitive design. Total annual research expenditures: $238,113. *Unit head:* Rachel Williams Smothers, Director of Admissions and Retention, 312-808-4900, Fax: 312-808-4901, E-mail: rachels@iit.edu.

See Close-Up on page 115.

Indiana University–Purdue University Indianapolis, Herron School of Art and Design, Indianapolis, IN 46202-2896. Offers art education (MAE); furniture design (MFA); printmaking (MFA); sculpture (MFA); visual communication (MFA). *Accreditation:* NASAD. Part-time and evening/weekend programs available. *Faculty:* 2 full-time (both women). *Students:* 2 full-time (1 woman), 18 part-time (15 women); includes 1 minority (Hispanic American) Average age 37. In 2007, 1 degree awarded. *Entrance requirements:* For master's, portfolio, 44 hours of course work in art history and studio art. *Application deadline:* For fall admission, 6/1 priority date for domestic students, 3/15 priority date for international students; for spring admission, 11/1 priority date for domestic students, 10/15 priority date for international students. Applications are processed on a rolling basis. Application fee: $50 ($60 for international students). Electronic applications accepted. *Expenses:* Tuition, state resident: full-time $5,818; part-time $242 per credit hour. Tuition, nonresident: full-time $17,106; part-time $713 per credit hour. Required fees: $629. Tuition and fees vary according to course load, campus/location and program. *Financial support:* Career-related internships or fieldwork, Federal Work-Study, institutionally sponsored loans, scholarships/grants, and tuition waivers (partial) available. Support available to part-time students. Total annual research expenditures: $6,097. *Unit head:* Valerie Eickmeier, Dean, 317-278-9470, Fax: 317-278-9471, E-mail: herron@iupui.edu. *Application contact:* Herron Student Services Office, 317-378-9400, E-mail: herrart@iupui.edu.

Iowa State University of Science and Technology, Graduate College, College of Design, Department of Art and Design, Ames, IA 50011. Offers art and design (MA); art education (MA); graphic design (MFA); integrated visual arts (MFA); interior design (MFA). Part-time programs available. *Faculty:* 38 full-time (22 women). *Students:* 39 full-time (28 women), 4 part-time (1 woman); includes 3 minority (all Asian Americans or Pacific Islanders), 12 international. 35 applicants, 63% accepted, 12 enrolled. In 2007, 11 degrees awarded. *Degree requirements:* For master's, thesis (for some programs). *Entrance requirements:* For master's, portfolio, resumé. Additional exam requirements/recommendations for international students: Required—TOEFL (paper-based 550; computer-based 213) or IELTS (score 6.5). *Application deadline:* For fall admission, 5/1 priority date for domestic and international students. Applications are processed on a rolling basis. Application fee: $30 ($70 for international students). Electronic applications accepted. *Financial support:* In 2007–08, 5 research assistantships with full and partial tuition reimbursements (averaging $20,058 per year), 2 teaching assistantships with full and partial tuition reimbursements (averaging $18,288 per year) were awarded; career-related internships or fieldwork, Federal Work-Study, institutionally sponsored loans, and tuition waivers (partial) also available. Support available to part-time students. Financial award application deadline: 2/15; financial award applicants required to submit FAFSA. *Faculty research:* Computer applications, fire safety, human factors in design, art and design education, fine arts, craft design. *Unit head:* Roger Baer, Chair, 515-294-6724, Fax: 515-294-2725, E-mail: artdn@iastate.edu.

Lamar University, College of Graduate Studies, College of Fine Arts and Communication, Department of Art, Beaumont, TX 77710. Offers art history (MA); photography (MA); studio art (MA); visual design (MA). Part-time and evening/weekend programs available. *Faculty:* 6 full-time (3 women). *Students:* Average age 42. 2 applicants, 0% accepted. In 2007, 2 degrees awarded. *Degree requirements:* For master's, thesis. *Entrance requirements:* For master's, GRE General Test, minimum GPA of 2.5 in last 60 hours of undergraduate course work. Additional exam requirements/recommendations for international students: Required—TOEFL. *Application deadline:* For fall admission, 8/1 priority date for domestic students; for spring admission, 12/1 for domestic students. Applications are processed on a rolling basis. Application fee: $25 ($50 for international students). *Expenses:* Tuition, state resident: part-time $348 per semester hour. Tuition, nonresident: part-time $626 per semester hour. Tuition and fees vary according to course load. *Financial support:* Fellowships, career-related internships or fieldwork, Federal Work-Study, and scholarships/grants available. Financial award application deadline: 4/1. *Faculty research:* Nineteenth century academic paintings, metal casting, pigment color stability, computer modified photography, manipulated photography. *Unit head:* Donna M. Meeks, Chair, 409-880-8141, Fax: 409-880-1799, E-mail: meeksdm@lub002.lamar.edu.

Louisiana State University and Agricultural and Mechanical College, Graduate School, College of Art and Design, Baton Rouge, LA 70803. Offers M Arch, MA, MFA, MLA. *Accreditation:* ASLA (one or more programs are accredited); NASAD (one or more programs are accredited). Part-time programs available. *Faculty:* 56 full-time (14 women). *Students:* 112 full-time (57 women), 10 part-time (6 women); includes 8 minority (2 African Americans, 4 Asian Americans or Pacific Islanders, 2 Hispanic Americans), 17 international. Average age 31. 143 applicants, 40% accepted, 38 enrolled. In 2007, 35 master's awarded. *Degree requirements:* For master's, thesis. *Entrance requirements:* For master's, GRE General Test, minimum GPA of 3.0. Additional exam requirements/recommendations for international students: Required—TOEFL (minimum score 550 paper-based; 213 computer-based; 79 iBT). *Application deadline:* For fall admission, 1/25 priority date for domestic students, 5/15 for international students; for spring admission, 10/15 for international students. Applications are processed on a rolling basis. Application fee: $25. Electronic applications accepted. *Financial support:* In 2007–08, 100 students received support, including 26 research assistantships with partial tuition reimbursements available (averaging $7,154 per year), 40 teaching assistantships with partial tuition reimbursements available (averaging $6,771 per year); fellowships, career-related internships or fieldwork, Federal Work-Study, institutionally sponsored loans, scholarships/grants, health care benefits, tuition waivers (full and partial), and unspecified assistantships also available. Support available to part-time students. Financial award applicants required to submit FAFSA. *Faculty research:* Creative studio work, site design, computer applications, historic preservation, energy conservation. Total annual research expenditures: $87,171. *Unit head:* David Cronrath, Dean, 225-578-5400, Fax: 225-578-5040, E-mail: dc1@lsu.edu. *Application contact:* Theresa Mooney, Academic Counselor, 225-578-5400, Fax: 225-578-1445, E-mail: deacon1@lsu.edu.

Louisiana Tech University, Graduate School, College of Liberal Arts, School of Art, Ruston, LA 71272. Offers art and graphic design (MFA); photography (MFA); studio art (MFA). *Accreditation:* NASAD. Part-time programs available. *Degree requirements:* For master's, exhibit. *Entrance requirements:* For master's, GRE General Test, portfolio. *Application deadline:* For fall admission, 7/29 for domestic students; for spring admission, 2/3 for domestic students. Applications are processed on a rolling basis. Application fee: $20 ($30 for international students). *Financial support:* Fellowships, career-related internships or fieldwork, Federal Work-Study, institutionally sponsored loans, and unspecified assistantships available. Financial award application deadline: 2/1. *Unit head:* Jonathan Donchoo, Director, 318-257-3909, Fax: 318-257-4890.

Massachusetts College of Art and Design, Graduate Programs, Program in Fine Arts, Boston, MA 02115-5882. Offers ceramics (MFA); design (MFA); fibers (MFA); film (MFA); glass (MFA); media and performing arts (MFA); metals (MFA); painting (MFA); photography (MFA); printmaking (MFA); sculpture (MFA). *Accreditation:* NASAD. *Faculty:* 10 full-time (5 women), 8 part-time/adjunct (6 women). *Students:* 80 full-time (46 women), 11 part-time (9 women); includes 7 minority (1 African American, 4 Asian Americans or Pacific Islanders, 2 Hispanic Americans), 13 international. Average age 34. 310 applicants, 26% accepted, 50 enrolled. In 2007, 37 degrees awarded. *Degree requirements:* For master's, thesis, exhibit. *Entrance requirements:* For master's, 12 units of course work in art history, portfolio, resumé. *Application deadline:* For fall admission, 2/1 for domestic students. Application fee: $75. *Expenses:* Tuition, state resident: full-time $16,260; part-time $542 per credit. Tuition, nonresident: full-time $16,260; part-time $542 per credit. *Financial support:* In 2007–08, 50 research assistantships (averaging $2,000 per year), 30 teaching assistantships (averaging $2,000 per year) were awarded; career-related internships or fieldwork, Federal Work-Study, and clerical/technical assistantships also available. Support available to part-time students. Financial award application deadline: 5/1; financial award applicants required to submit FAFSA. *Application contact:* George Creamer, Director, 617-879-7163, Fax: 617-879-7171, E-mail: creamer@massart.edu.

Memphis College of Art, Graduate Programs, Memphis, TN 38104-2764. Offers art education (MA, MAT); computer arts (MFA); studio art (MFA), including fiber/surface design, painting, papermaking, photography, printmaking, sculpture. *Accreditation:* NASAD. Part-time programs available. *Faculty:* 16 full-time (7 women), 5 part-time/adjunct (3 women). *Students:* 18 full-time (8 women), 37 part-time (26 women); includes 7 minority (2 African Americans, 2 Asian Americans or Pacific Islanders, 3 Hispanic Americans). Average age 30. 80 applicants, 59% accepted, 33 enrolled. In 2007, 4 degrees awarded. *Degree requirements:* For master's, thesis. *Entrance requirements:* For master's, portfolio, interview, resumé. Additional exam requirements/recommendations for international students: Required—TOEFL (minimum score 525 paper-based; 195 computer-based). *Application deadline:* For fall admission, 3/1 priority date for domestic and international students; for spring admission, 11/1 priority date for

Applied Arts and Design—General

Memphis College of Art (continued)

domestic and international students. Application fee: $50. Electronic applications accepted. *Expenses:* Tuition: Full-time $22,000; part-time $435 per credit. Required fees: $560; $100 per course. Part-time tuition and fees vary according to course load and program. *Financial support:* In 2007–08, 5 teaching assistantships with partial tuition reimbursements (averaging $2,000 per year) were awarded; career-related internships or fieldwork, Federal Work-Study, institutionally sponsored loans, scholarships/grants, tuition waivers (partial), unspecified assistantships, and merit awards also available. Support available to part-time students. Financial award application deadline: 8/1; financial award applicants required to submit FAFSA. *Unit head:* Ken Strickland, Vice President Academic Affairs, 901-272-5100, Fax: 901-272-5104, E-mail: info@mca.edu. *Application contact:* Annette James Moore, Director of Admissions, 800-727-1088, Fax: 901-272-5158, E-mail: info@mca.edu.

See Close-Up on page 245.

Minneapolis College of Art and Design, Program in Visual Studies, Minneapolis, MN 55404-4347. Offers animation (MFA); comic art (MFA); drawing (MFA); filmmaking (MFA); fine arts (MFA); furniture design (MFA); graphic design (MFA); illustration (MFA); interactive media (MFA); painting (MFA); photography (MFA); printmaking (MFA); sculpture (MFA). *Accreditation:* NASAD. Part-time programs available. *Faculty:* 23 full-time (7 women), 9 part-time/adjunct (4 women). *Students:* 40 full-time (21 women), 1 (woman) part-time; includes 1 minority (American Indian/Alaska Native). Average age 27. 172 applicants, 24% accepted, 15 enrolled. In 2007, 7 degrees awarded. *Degree requirements:* For master's, thesis, thesis exhibit. *Entrance requirements:* For master's, portfolio, resumé, 3 letters of recommendation, statement . Additional exam requirements/recommendations for international students: Required—TOEFL (minimum score 550 paper-based; 213 computer-based; 79 iBT). *Application deadline:* For fall admission, 2/15 for domestic and international students. Application fee: $50. Electronic applications accepted. *Expenses:* Tuition: Full-time $27,000; part-time $900 per credit. Required fees: $100 per term. *Financial support:* In 2007–08, 23 students received support, including 15 teaching assistantships (averaging $6,000 per year); career-related internships or fieldwork, Federal Work-Study, scholarships/grants, and unspecified assistantships also available. Support available to part-time students. Financial award application deadline: 3/15; financial award applicants required to submit FAFSA. *Faculty research:* Visual arts. *Unit head:* Carole Fisher, Graduate Director, 612-874-3629, E-mail: carole_fisher@mcad.edu. *Application contact:* William Mullen, Vice President of Enrollment Management, 612-874-3762, Fax: 612-874-3701, E-mail: william_mullen@mcad.edu.

New Mexico State University, Graduate School, College of Arts and Sciences, Department of Art, Las Cruces, NM 88003-8001. Offers art history (MA); ceramics (MA, MFA); design (MA, MFA); drawing (MA, MFA); metals (MA, MFA); painting (MA, MFA); photography (MA, MFA); printmaking (MA, MFA); sculpture (MA, MFA). *Faculty:* 8 full-time (5 women), 1 (woman) part-time/adjunct. *Students:* 33 full-time (16 women), 3 part-time (1 woman); includes 6 minority (1 American Indian/Alaska Native, 5 Hispanic Americans), 1 international. Average age 35. 24 applicants, 58% accepted, 10 enrolled. In 2007, 7 degrees awarded. *Degree requirements:* For master's, comprehensive exam (for some programs), thesis, thesis exhibit. *Entrance requirements:* For master's, portfolio, 10-page paper (art history). *Application deadline:* For fall admission, 2/15 for domestic students; for winter admission, 10/15 for domestic students; for spring admission, 7/15 for domestic students. Application fee: $30 ($50 for international students). Electronic applications accepted. *Expenses:* Tuition, state resident: full-time $3,602; part-time $199 per credit. Tuition, nonresident: full-time $13,380; part-time $607 per credit. Required fees: $1,178. *Financial support:* In 2007–08, 1 fellowship, 29 teaching assistantships were awarded; research assistantships, Federal Work-Study and health care benefits also available. Support available to part-time students. Financial award application deadline: 3/1. *Faculty research:* Painting, graphic design, sculpture, printmaking, drawing. *Unit head:* Dr. Spencer Fidler, Head, 575-646-1705, Fax: 575-646-8036, E-mail: sfidler@nmsu.edu.

The New School: A University, Parsons The New School for Design, New York, NY 10011. Offers M Arch, MA, MFA. *Accreditation:* NASAD (one or more programs are accredited). *Faculty:* 30 full-time (13 women), 105 part-time/adjunct (41 women). *Students:* 339 full-time (219 women), 72 part-time (55 women); includes 56 minority (8 African Americans, 1 American Indian/Alaska Native, 34 Asian Americans or Pacific Islanders, 13 Hispanic Americans), 117 international. Average age 28. In 2007, 167 degrees awarded. *Entrance requirements:* Additional exam requirements/recommendations for international students: Required—TOEFL (minimum score 580 paper-based; 237 computer-based; 93 iBT). *Application deadline:* For fall admission, 3/1 priority date for domestic students. Applications are processed on a rolling basis. Application fee: $40. *Financial support:* Fellowships with partial tuition reimbursements, research assistantships with partial tuition reimbursements, teaching assistantships with partial tuition reimbursements, Federal Work-Study, scholarships/grants, and tuition waivers (partial) available. Financial award application deadline: 3/1; financial award applicants required to submit FAFSA. *Unit head:* Tim Marshall, Dean, 212-229-8950 Ext. 4201, E-mail: marshalt@newschool.edu. *Application contact:* Anthony Padilla, Director of Admissions, 212-229-8989 Ext. 4023, Fax: 212-229-8975, E-mail: padillaa@newschool.edu.

New York University, Tisch School of the Arts Asia, Singapore, NY 248923, Singapore. Offers animation and digital arts (MFA); dramatic writing (MFA); film production (MFA). *Faculty:* 6 full-time (3 women). *Students:* 33 full-time (16 women); includes 6 minority (1 African American, 5 Asian Americans or Pacific Islanders), 13 international. 55 applicants, 22% accepted. *Entrance requirements:* Additional exam requirements/recommendations for international students: Required—TOEFL (minimum score 610 paper-based; 250 computer-based; 105 iBT). *Application deadline:* For fall admission, 2/1 priority date for domestic and international students. Application fee: $60. Electronic applications accepted. *Financial support:* Fellowships with full and partial tuition reimbursements, research assistantships, teaching assistantships, Federal Work-Study, institutionally sponsored loans, and unspecified assistantships available. Financial award application deadline: 2/15; financial award applicants required to submit FAFSA.

See Close-Up on page 291.

New York University, Tisch School of the Arts, Department of Design for Stage and Film, New York, NY 10012-1019. Offers MFA. *Faculty:* 10 full-time, 11 part-time/adjunct. *Students:* 59 full-time (35 women); includes 8 minority (4 African Americans, 3 Asian Americans or Pacific Islanders, 1 Hispanic American), 11 international. Average age 28. 123 applicants, 27% accepted, 19 enrolled. In 2007, 20 degrees awarded. *Degree requirements:* For master's, thesis. *Entrance requirements:* For master's, interview, portfolio. Additional exam requirements/recommendations for international students: Required—TOEFL (minimum score 620 paper-based; 260 computer-based; 105 iBT), IELTS. *Application deadline:* For fall admission, 1/15 priority date for domestic and international students. Application fee: $60. Electronic applications accepted. *Financial support:* In 2007–08, 28 students received support, including 12 fellowships with full and partial tuition reimbursements available; Federal Work-Study, institutionally sponsored loans, tuition waivers (partial), and unspecified assistantships also available. Financial award application deadline: 2/15; financial award applicants required to submit FAFSA. *Unit head:* Susan Hilferty, Chair, 212-998-1950, Fax: 212-998-1953, E-mail: tisch.design@nyu.edu. *Application contact:* Dan Sandford, Director of Graduate Admissions, 212-998-1918, Fax: 212-995-4060, E-mail: tisch.gradadmissions@nyu.edu.

North Carolina State University, Graduate School, College of Design, Program in Art and Design, Raleigh, NC 27695. Offers MAD. *Degree requirements:* For master's, thesis optional. Electronic applications accepted.

North Carolina State University, Graduate School, College of Design, Program in Design, Raleigh, NC 27695. Offers PhD. *Degree requirements:* For doctorate, thesis/dissertation. *Entrance requirements:* For doctorate, GRE. Electronic applications accepted. *Faculty research:* Design and cognition, children's environments, community design, ecological design, sustainable communities and urban spatial development.

NSCAD University, Program in Fine Arts, Halifax, NS B3J 3J6, Canada. Offers craft (MFA); design (M Des); fine and media arts (MFA). *Faculty:* 42 full-time (18 women). *Students:* 25 full-time (12 women). Average age 33. 190 applicants, 5% accepted, 8 enrolled. In 2007, 10 degrees awarded. *Degree requirements:* For master's, thesis, exhibit. *Entrance requirements:* For master's, portfolio, at least 5 art history classes. Additional exam requirements/recommendations for international students: Required—Michigan English Language Assessment Battery (minimum score: 80), CanTEST (minimum score: 4.5), CAEL (minimum score: 70); Recommended—TOEFL (minimum score 575 paper-based; 233 computer-based; 90 iBT), IELTS (minimum score 7). *Application deadline:* For fall admission, 1/15 for domestic and international students. Application fee: $50. *Financial support:* In 2007–08, 10 students received support, including 10 teaching assistantships (averaging $5,000 per year); scholarships/grants also available. Financial award application deadline: 1/15. *Unit head:* Bruce Barber, Chair, 902-494-8155, Fax: 902-425-2420, E-mail: bbarber@nscad.ns.ca. *Application contact:* Dallas Ning, Administrative Assistant (Admissions), 902-494-8129, Fax: 902-425-2987, E-mail: dning@nscad.ns.ca.

Oklahoma State University, College of Human Environmental Sciences, Department of Design, Housing and Merchandising, Stillwater, OK 74078. Offers MS, PhD. *Faculty:* 17 full-time (11 women), 4 part-time/adjunct (3 women). *Students:* 14 full-time (11 women), 22 part-time (20 women); includes 3 minority (1 African American, 1 American Indian/Alaska Native, 1 Asian American or Pacific Islander), 15 international. Average age 31. 15 applicants, 60% accepted, 4 enrolled. In 2007, 4 degrees awarded. *Degree requirements:* For master's, thesis; for doctorate, thesis/dissertation. *Entrance requirements:* For master's and doctorate, GRE or GMAT. Additional exam requirements/recommendations for international students: Required—TOEFL. *Application deadline:* For fall admission, 3/1 priority date for international students; for spring admission, 8/1 priority date for international students. Applications are processed on a rolling basis. Application fee: $40 ($75 for international students). Electronic applications accepted. *Expenses:* Tuition, state resident: full-time $4,993; part-time $148 per credit hour. Tuition, nonresident: full-time $14,755; part-time $555 per credit hour. Tuition and fees vary according to program. *Financial support:* In 2007–08, 21 research assistantships (averaging $9,120 per year), 12 teaching assistantships (averaging $9,057 per year) were awarded; career-related internships or fieldwork, Federal Work-Study, scholarships/grants, health care benefits, tuition waivers (partial), and unspecified assistantships also available. Support available to part-time students. Financial award application deadline: 3/1. *Faculty research:* Environmental sciences design, housing & merchandising, creativity and physical environment; product development, production and evaluation; experimental learning and critical thinking, technology strategies and assessment, customer expectation and satisfaction. *Unit head:* Dr. Paulette Hebert, Head, 405-744-5049.

Pratt Institute, School of Art and Design, Brooklyn, NY 11205-3899. Offers MFA, MID, MPS, MS, Adv C, MS/MFA, MS/MS. *Accreditation:* NASAD (one or more programs are accredited). Part-time programs available. *Faculty:* 41 full-time (17 women), 200 part-time/adjunct (99 women). *Students:* 926 full-time (700 women), 63 part-time (50 women); includes 169 minority (55 African Americans, 3 American Indian/Alaska Native, 64 Asian Americans or Pacific Islanders, 47 Hispanic Americans), 311 international. Average age 29. 1,560 applicants, 40% accepted, 303 enrolled. In 2007, 332 degrees awarded. *Degree requirements:* For master's, thesis. *Entrance requirements:* Additional exam requirements/recommendations for international students: Required—TOEFL (minimum score 550 paper-based; 213 computer-based). *Application deadline:* For fall admission, 2/1 for domestic students; for spring admission, 10/1 for domestic students. Application fee: $50 ($90 for international students). Electronic applications accepted. *Expenses:* Tuition: Full-time $25,680. Required fees: $1,106. Tuition and fees vary according to program. *Financial support:* Career-related internships or fieldwork, Federal Work-Study, institutionally sponsored loans, scholarships/grants, health care benefits, and unspecified assistantships available. Support available to part-time students. Financial award application deadline: 2/1; financial award applicants required to submit FAFSA. *Faculty research:* Painting, sculpture, and printmaking; package, interior, and communications design; art therapy; graphic and industrial design; four-dimensional design. *Unit head:* Frank Lind, Chairperson, 718-636-3602, E-mail: flind@pratt.edu. *Application contact:* Young Hah, Director of Graduate Admissions, 718-636-3683, Fax: 718-399-4242, E-mail: yhah@pratt.edu.

See Close-Up on page 253.

Purdue University, Graduate School, College of Liberal Arts, Department of Visual and Performing Arts, West Lafayette, IN 47907. Offers art and design (MA); theatre (MA, MFA). *Accreditation:* NASAD; NAST. Part-time programs available. *Degree requirements:* For master's, terminal exhibit, project, or thesis. *Entrance requirements:* Additional exam requirements/recommendations for international students: Required—TOEFL. Electronic applications accepted. *Faculty research:* Design, fine arts, photography, acting, directing, theatre technology.

Rhode Island School of Design, Graduate Studies, Providence, RI 02903-2784. Offers M Arch, MA, MAT, MFA, MIA, MID, MLA. *Accreditation:* NASAD (one or more programs are accredited). *Degree requirements:* For master's, thesis, exhibit. *Entrance requirements:* For master's, portfolio, 3 letters of recommendation. Additional exam requirements/recommendations for international students: Required—TOEFL (minimum score 580 paper-based; 237 computer-based), IELTS (minimum score 7). Electronic applications accepted. *Faculty research:* Ceramics, glass, graphic design, sculpture, jewelry/metalsmithing, photography, painting, industrial design, architecture.

Rutgers, The State University of New Jersey, New Brunswick, Mason Gross School of the Arts, Department of Theater Arts, New Brunswick, NJ 08901-1281. Offers acting (MFA); design (MFA); directing (MFA); playwriting (MFA); stage management (MFA). *Degree requirements:* For master's, thesis (for some programs), performance project. *Entrance requirements:* For master's, audition, interview, portfolio. Electronic applications accepted. *Faculty research:* Faculty of working professional.

San Diego State University, Graduate and Research Affairs, College of Professional Studies and Fine Arts, School of Art, Design and Art History, San Diego, CA 92182. Offers art history (MA); studio arts (MA, MFA), including applied design, environmental design, graphic design, interior design, painting and printmaking, sculpture. *Accreditation:* NASAD (one or more programs are accredited). *Students:* 44 full-time (29 women), 18 part-time (11 women); includes 9 minority (4 Asian Americans or Pacific Islanders, 5 Hispanic Americans), 5 international. Average age 30. 83 applicants, 31% accepted, 31 enrolled. In 2007, 12 degrees awarded. *Degree requirements:* For master's, variable foreign language requirement, thesis. *Entrance requirements:* For master's, GRE General Test, bachelor's degree in related field, slide portfolio, typed slide information sheet, 2 letters of recommendation. Additional exam requirements/recommendations for international students: Required—TOEFL. *Application deadline:* For fall admission, 2/1 for domestic and international students. Applications are processed on a rolling basis. Application fee: $55. Electronic applications accepted. *Financial support:* In 2007–08, 21 teaching assistantships were awarded; career-related internships or fieldwork and unspecified assistantships also available. Financial award applicants required to submit FAFSA. *Unit head:* Arthur Ollman, Director, 619-594-1213, Fax: 619-594-1217. *Application contact:* JoAnne Berelowitz, Graduate Advisor, Art History, 619-594-4995, Fax: 619-594-1217, E-mail: jberelow@mail.sdsu.edu.

San Francisco Art Institute, Graduate Program, Department of Design and Technology, San Francisco, CA 94133. Offers MFA, Certificate. Part-time programs available. *Degree requirements:* For master's and Certificate, oral reviews. *Entrance requirements:* For master's and Certificate, portfolio. Additional exam requirements/recommendations for international students: Required—TOEFL (minimum score 580 paper-based; 237 computer-based). Electronic applications accepted.

San Jose State University, Graduate Studies and Research, College of Humanities and the Arts, School of Art and Design, San Jose, CA 95192-0001. Offers art education (MA); art history (MA); digital media (MFA); digital media in art history and education (MA); photography

(MFA); pictorial arts (MFA); spatial arts (MFA). *Accreditation:* NASAD (one or more programs are accredited). *Students:* 55 full-time (30 women), 15 part-time (12 women); includes 11 minority (1 African American, 7 Asian Americans or Pacific Islanders, 3 Hispanic Americans), 2 international. Average age 38. 78 applicants, 42% accepted, 24 enrolled. In 2007, 17 degrees awarded. *Entrance requirements:* For master's, GRE. *Application deadline:* For fall admission, 6/29 for domestic students; for spring admission, 11/30 for domestic students. Applications are processed on a rolling basis. Application fee: $59. Electronic applications accepted. *Financial support:* Applicants required to submit FAFSA. *Unit head:* Linda Walsh, Director, 408-924-4320, Fax: 408-924-4326.

Savannah College of Art and Design, Graduate School, Savannah, GA 31402-3146. Offers advertising design (MA, MFA); animation (MA, MFA); architectural history (MA, MFA); architecture (M Arch); art history (MA, MFA); arts administration (MA); broadcast design (MA, MFA); cinema studies (MA); commercial photography (MA); digital photography (MA); documentary photography (MA); fashion (MA, MFA); fibers (MA, MFA); film and television (MA, MFA); furniture design (MA, MFA); graphic design (MA, MFA); historic preservation (MA, MFA); illustration (MA, MFA); illustration design (MA); industrial design (MA, MFA); interactive design and game development (MA, MFA); interior design (MA, MFA); metals and jewelry (MA, MFA); painting (MA, MFA); performing arts (MA, MFA); photography (MA, MFA); printmaking (MA, MFA); production design (MA, MFA); professional education (MA); professional writing (MFA); sculpture (MA, MFA); sequential art (MA, MFA); sound design (MA, MFA); urban design and development (MA); visual effects (MA, MFA). Part-time programs available. Postbaccalaureate distance learning degree programs offered (no on-campus study). *Faculty:* 250 full-time (105 women), 53 part-time/adjunct (22 women). *Students:* 1,150 full-time (639 women), 297 part-time (154 women); includes 124 minority (69 African Americans, 6 American Indian/Alaska Native, 14 Asian Americans or Pacific Islanders, 35 Hispanic Americans), 326 international. Average age 25. 1,905 applicants, 48% accepted, 447 enrolled. In 2007, 374 degrees awarded. *Degree requirements:* For master's, thesis, internship. *Entrance requirements:* For master's, interview, 3 letters of recommendation. Additional exam requirements/recommendations for international students: Required—TOEFL (minimum score 500 paper-based; 133 computer-based). *Application deadline:* For fall admission, 4/1 priority date for domestic and international students. Applications are processed on a rolling basis. Application fee: $50. Electronic applications accepted. *Expenses:* Tuition: Full-time $24,840; part-time $552 per credit. One-time fee: $500 full-time. *Financial support:* Fellowships, career-related internships or fieldwork, Federal Work-Study, and scholarships/grants available. Financial award application deadline: 4/1; financial award applicants required to submit FAFSA. *Faculty research:* Urban planning for diverse communities, photovoltaics-powered environmental control, computer-aided design and virtual reality, multimedia design. *Application contact:* Darrell Tutchton, Director of Graduate and International Enrollment, 912-525-5961, Fax: 912-525-5985, E-mail: admission@scad.edu.

See Close-Up on page 257.

School of Visual Arts, Graduate Programs, Design Department, New York, NY 10010-3994. Offers MFA. *Accreditation:* NASAD. *Faculty:* 9 part-time/adjunct (1 woman). *Students:* 39 full-time (23 women); includes 6 minority (5 Asian Americans or Pacific Islanders, 1 Hispanic American), 12 international. Average age 27. 235 applicants, 22% accepted, 19 enrolled. In 2007, 18 degrees awarded. *Degree requirements:* For master's, final review, project or thesis. *Entrance requirements:* For master's, portfolio. Additional exam requirements/recommendations for international students: Required—TOEFL (minimum score 550 paper-based; 213 computer-based; 79 iBT). *Application deadline:* For fall admission, 2/1 for domestic students. Application fee: $80. Electronic applications accepted. *Expenses: Contact institution.* Tuition and fees vary according to program. *Financial support:* In 2007–08, 8 students received support. Career-related internships or fieldwork, Federal Work-Study, scholarships/grants, and unspecified assistantships available. Support available to part-time students. Financial award application deadline: 2/1; financial award applicants required to submit FAFSA. *Unit head:* Lita Talarico, Chair, 212-592-2600, Fax: 212-592-2627, E-mail: ltalarico@sva.edu.

School of Visual Arts, Graduate Programs, Program in Design Criticism, New York, NY 10010-3994. Offers MFA. *Expenses:* Tuition: Full-time $26,120; part-time $870 per credit. Tuition and fees vary according to program. *Unit head:* Alice Twemlow, Chair, 212-592-2561.

Southern Illinois University Carbondale, Graduate School, College of Liberal Arts, School of Art and Design, Carbondale, IL 62901-4701. Offers ceramics (MFA); drawing (MFA); fiber/weaving (MFA); glass (MFA); jewelry (MFA); metalsmithing/blacksmithing (MFA); painting (MFA); printmaking (MFA); sculpture (MFA). *Accreditation:* NASAD. *Faculty:* 23 full-time (7 women). *Students:* 36 full-time (15 women), 7 part-time (2 women); includes 2 minority (1 American Indian/Alaska Native, 1 Hispanic American), 12 international. Average age 29. 87 applicants, 16% accepted, 14 enrolled. In 2007, 26 degrees awarded. *Degree requirements:* For master's, thesis or alternative. *Entrance requirements:* For master's, minimum GPA of 2.7, portfolio, slides. Additional exam requirements/recommendations for international students: Required—TOEFL. *Application deadline:* For fall admission, 3/1 priority date for domestic students. Applications are processed on a rolling basis. Application fee: $20. *Financial support:* In 2007–08, 49 students received support, including 3 fellowships with full tuition reimbursements available, 5 research assistantships with full tuition reimbursements available, 40 teaching assistantships with full tuition reimbursements available; Federal Work-Study, institutionally sponsored loans, and tuition waivers (full) also available. Support available to part-time students. Financial award application deadline: 4/1. *Faculty research:* Prints/woodcuts, foundry, watercolor. *Unit head:* Harris Deller, Director, 618-453-4315, Fax: 618-453-7710, E-mail: ga4252@siu.edu. *Application contact:* Kathy Holt, Office Specialist, 618-453-4313, Fax: 618-453-7710, E-mail: kholt@siu.edu.

Announcement: The graduate program is perhaps best characterized as intense, individualized, and encompassing a diversity of students pursuing varied professional goals. Faculty members strive to select promising national and international candidates, providing a professional studio environment and encouraging high standards and productivity.

See Close-Up on page 133.

Stephen F. Austin State University, Graduate School, College of Fine Arts, School of Art, Nacogdoches, TX 75962. Offers art (MA); design (MFA); drawing (MFA); painting (MFA); sculpture (MFA). *Accreditation:* NASAD. Part-time programs available. *Degree requirements:* For master's, comprehensive exam, thesis, exhibit. *Entrance requirements:* For master's, GRE General Test, portfolio. Additional exam requirements/recommendations for international students: Required—TOEFL. *Faculty research:* Printmaking, jewelry, photography, ceramics, art history.

Suffolk University, College of Arts and Sciences, New England School of Art and Design, Boston, MA 02108-2770. Offers graphic design (MA); interior design (MA). *Accreditation:* CIDA; NASAD. Part-time and evening/weekend programs available. *Faculty:* 18 full-time (9 women), 14 part-time/adjunct (4 women). *Students:* 49 full-time (46 women), 69 part-time (63 women); includes 12 minority (2 African Americans, 1 American Indian/Alaska Native, 7 Asian Americans or Pacific Islanders, 2 Hispanic Americans), 15 international. Average age 29. 78 applicants, 87% accepted, 33 enrolled. In 2007, 26 degrees awarded. *Entrance requirements:* For master's, art portfolio, interview. Additional exam requirements/recommendations for international students: Required—TOEFL (minimum score 550 paper-based; 213 computer-based; 80 iBT). *Application deadline:* For fall admission, 6/15 priority date for domestic students, 6/15 for international students; for spring admission, 11/1 priority date for domestic students, 11/1 for international students. Applications are processed on a rolling basis. Application fee: $50. Electronic applications accepted. *Financial support:* In 2007–08, 65 students received support, including 10 fellowships with partial tuition reimbursements available (averaging $6,296 per year). Financial award application deadline: 4/1. *Faculty research:* Adaptive re-use of historical structures, universal design, American architecture history, interior design to reduce inefficiency, meditation SPA. *Unit head:* Dr. William Davis, Director, 617-994-4264, Fax: 617-536-0461, E-mail: wdavis@suffolk.edu. *Application contact:* Judith Reynolds, Director of Graduate Admissions, 617-573-8302, Fax: 617-523-0116, E-mail: grad.admission@suffolk.edu.

Sul Ross State University, School of Arts and Sciences, Department of Fine Arts and Communication, Alpine, TX 79832. Offers art education (M Ed); art history (M Ed); studio art (M Ed), including ceramics, design, drawing, jewelry, painting, printmaking, sculpture, weaving. Part-time programs available. *Degree requirements:* For master's, oral or written exam. *Entrance requirements:* For master's, GRE General Test, minimum GPA of 2.5 in last 60 hours of undergraduate work. *Faculty research:* Ceramic sculpture, watercolor, wood sculpture, rock art.

Syracuse University, Graduate School, College of Visual and Performing Arts, School of Art and Design, Syracuse, NY 13244. Offers art (MFA), including ceramics, fiber arts/materials studies, illustration, jewelry and metalsmithing, painting, printmaking, sculpture; art education (MS); museum studies (MA). *Accreditation:* NASAD (one or more programs are accredited). Part-time programs available. Postbaccalaureate distance learning degree programs offered (no on-campus study). *Students:* 58 full-time (43 women), 7 part-time (4 women); includes 6 minority (1 African American, 3 Asian Americans or Pacific Islanders, 2 Hispanic Americans), 7 international. 169 applicants, 29% accepted, 25 enrolled. In 2007, 34 degrees awarded. *Degree requirements:* For master's, thesis or alternative. *Entrance requirements:* For master's, portfolio. Additional exam requirements/recommendations for international students: Required—TOEFL. *Application deadline:* For fall admission, 1/1 priority date for domestic students; for spring admission, 3/1 priority date for domestic students. Applications are processed on a rolling basis. Application fee: $75. Electronic applications accepted. *Expenses:* Tuition: Full-time $18,216; part-time $1,012 per credit. Required fees: $980. Tuition and fees vary according to program. *Financial support:* Fellowships with full tuition reimbursements, research assistantships with full and partial tuition reimbursements, teaching assistantships with full and partial tuition reimbursements, Federal Work-Study and tuition waivers (partial) available. *Unit head:* Stephen Carlson, Associate Dean, 315-443-2507. *Application contact:* Harriett Conti, Associate Director, Graduate Student Services, 315-443-3089, E-mail: hmconti@syr.edu.

University of Alberta, Faculty of Graduate Studies and Research, Department of Art and Design, Edmonton, AB T6G 2E1, Canada. Offers drawing (MFA); history of art, design, and visual culture (MA); industrial design (M Des); painting (MFA); printmaking (MFA); sculpture (MFA); visual communication design (M Des). *Degree requirements:* For master's, thesis. *Entrance requirements:* For master's, portfolio (MFA and MDES). Additional exam requirements/recommendations for international students: Required—TOEFL (minimum score 550 paper-based; 213 computer-based).

University of California, Berkeley, Graduate Division, College of Environmental Design, Department of Architecture, Program in Design, Berkeley, CA 94720-1500. Offers MA. *Degree requirements:* For master's, thesis. *Entrance requirements:* For master's, GRE General Test, minimum GPA of 3.0, portfolio, 3 letters of recommendation. Additional exam requirements/recommendations for international students: Required—TOEFL. *Application deadline:* For fall admission, 2/1 for domestic students. Application fee: $70 ($90 for international students). *Financial support:* Unspecified assistantships available. *Application contact:* Lois H. Ito Koch, Student Affairs Officer, 510-642-5577, Fax: 510-643-5607, E-mail: archgrad@berkeley.edu.

University of California, Los Angeles, Graduate Division, School of the Arts and Architecture, Department of Design/Media Arts, Los Angeles, CA 90095. Offers MFA. *Degree requirements:* For master's, comprehensive exam. *Entrance requirements:* For master's, portfolio, 20 slides and/or videotape, minimum GPA of 3.0. Additional exam requirements/recommendations for international students: Required—TOEFL. Electronic applications accepted. *Expenses:* Tuition, nonresident: full-time $5,728. Required fees: $8,966. Full-time tuition and fees vary according to program and student level.

University of Central Oklahoma, College of Graduate Studies and Research, College of Arts, Media, and Design, Department of Design and Interior Design, Edmond, OK 73034-5209. Offers MFA. Part-time programs available. Postbaccalaureate distance learning degree programs offered (minimal on-campus study). *Faculty:* 8 full-time (5 women). *Students:* 7 full-time (1 woman), 1 (woman) part-time, 1 international. Average age 31. In 2007, 2 degrees awarded. *Entrance requirements:* Additional exam requirements/recommendations for international students: Required—TOEFL (minimum score 550 paper-based; 213 computer-based). *Application deadline:* For fall admission, 7/1 for international students; for spring admission, 11/1 for international students. Applications are processed on a rolling basis. Application fee: $25. Electronic applications accepted. *Expenses:* Tuition, state resident: full-time $3,516; part-time $147 per hour. Tuition, nonresident: full-time $9,054; part-time $377 per hour. Required fees: $433; $18 per hour. *Financial support:* Application deadline: 3/31; *Unit head:* Dr. Larry Hefner, Chair, 405-974-5211.

University of Cincinnati, Graduate School, College of Design, Architecture, Art, and Planning, School of Design, Cincinnati, OH 45221. Offers fashion design (M Des); graphic design (M Des); industrial design (M Des); interaction design (M Des); product development (M Des). *Accreditation:* NASAD. *Students:* 13 full-time (7 women), 6 part-time (5 women), 10 international. In 2007, 3 degrees awarded. *Degree requirements:* For master's, thesis. *Entrance requirements:* For master's, undergraduate degree in design or related field, 2 years of work experience in design or related field. Additional exam requirements/recommendations for international students: Required—TOEFL. *Application deadline:* For fall admission, 2/1 for domestic students. Application fee: $30. Electronic applications accepted. *Financial support:* Fellowships, career-related internships or fieldwork, Federal Work-Study, tuition waivers (partial), and unspecified assistantships available. *Faculty research:* Design theory, interdisciplinary design topics. *Unit head:* Prof. Dale Murray, Director, 513-556-1524, E-mail: dale.murray@uc.edu. *Application contact:* Dr. J. Chewning, Information Contact, 513-556-2996, Fax: 513-556-0240, E-mail: j.chewning@uc.edu.

University of Delaware, College of Arts and Sciences, Department of Art, Newark, DE 19716. Offers MA, MFA. *Faculty:* 7 full-time (2 women). *Students:* 17 full-time (9 women), 1 (woman) part-time; includes 2 minority (1 Asian American or Pacific Islander, 1 Hispanic American). Average age 27. 39 applicants, 36% accepted, 8 enrolled. In 2007, 11 degrees awarded. *Degree requirements:* For master's, exposition paper final exhibition. *Entrance requirements:* For master's, portfolio of creative work. *Application deadline:* For fall admission, 2/1 priority date for domestic students. Application fee: $60. Electronic applications accepted. *Financial support:* In 2007–08, 3 fellowships with tuition reimbursements (averaging $11,000 per year), 13 teaching assistantships with full and partial tuition reimbursements (averaging $4,908 per year) were awarded; career-related internships or fieldwork, Federal Work-Study, institutionally sponsored loans, scholarships/grants, and tuition waivers (full and partial) also available. Financial award application deadline: 2/1. *Faculty research:* Painting, printmaking, ceramics, photography, sculpture. *Unit head:* Prof. Virginia Bradley, Chair, 302-831-2244, Fax: 302-831-0505, E-mail: vbradley@udel.edu. *Application contact:* Gwen McCullough, Secretary, 302-831-2244, Fax: 302-831-0505, E-mail: kgm@udel.edu.

University of Idaho, College of Graduate Studies, College of Art and Architecture, Department of Art and Design, Moscow, ID 83844-2282. Offers art (MAT, MFA). *Accreditation:* NASAD. *Students:* 16. Average age 31. In 2007, 4 degrees awarded. *Degree requirements:* For master's, thesis (for some programs). *Entrance requirements:* For master's, minimum GPA of 2.8. *Application deadline:* For fall admission, 8/1 for domestic students; for spring admission, 12/15 for domestic students. Application fee: $55 ($60 for international students). *Financial support:* Research assistantships, teaching assistantships available. Financial award application deadline: 2/15. *Unit head:* William Woolston, Chair, 208-885-7837.

University of Illinois at Urbana–Champaign, Graduate College, College of Fine and Applied Arts, School of Art and Design, Champaign, IL 61820. Offers MA, MFA, PhD. *Accreditation:* NASAD. *Faculty:* 49 full-time (22 women), 3 part-time/adjunct (2 women). *Students:* 90

Applied Arts and Design—General

University of Illinois at Urbana–Champaign (continued)
full-time (60 women), 10 part-time (7 women); includes 8 minority (2 African Americans, 5 Asian Americans or Pacific Islanders, 1 Hispanic American), 20 international. 192 applicants, 22% accepted, 24 enrolled. In 2007, 26 master's, 3 doctorates awarded. *Degree requirements:* For doctorate, thesis/dissertation. *Entrance requirements:* For master's, minimum GPA of 3.0. *Application deadline:* For fall admission, 1/19 for domestic students; for spring admission, 12/1 for domestic students. Applications are processed on a rolling basis. Application fee: $60 ($75 for international students). *Financial support:* In 2007–08, 20 fellowships, 7 research assistantships, 61 teaching assistantships were awarded; tuition waivers (full and partial) also available. Financial award application deadline: 2/15. *Unit head:* David Weightman, Interim Director, 217-333-0855, Fax: 217-244-7688, E-mail: djw@uiuc.edu. *Application contact:* Marsha Biddle, Assistant to the Associate Director, 217-333-0642, Fax: 217-244-7688, E-mail: mbiddle@uiuc.edu.

University of Kansas, Research and Graduate Studies, School of Fine Arts, Department of Design, Program in Design, Lawrence, KS 66045. Offers MA, MFA. *Faculty:* 29. *Students:* 17 full-time (8 women), 1 (woman) part-time. Average age 31. 30 applicants, 40% accepted, 9 enrolled. In 2007, 7 degrees awarded. *Degree requirements:* For master's, thesis, gallery exhibition, oral exam. *Entrance requirements:* For master's, portfolio, 3 letters of recommendation, minimum GPA of 3.0, statement of design philosophy. Additional exam requirements/recommendations for international students: Required—TOEFL (minimum score 570 paper-based; 230 computer-based), IELTS. *Application deadline:* For fall admission, 2/1 for domestic and international students; for spring admission, 10/15 for domestic students. Application fee: $55 ($60 for international students). Electronic applications accepted. *Expenses:* Tuition, state resident: full-time $5,838. Tuition, nonresident: full-time $13,409. Tuition and fees vary according to program. *Financial support:* Fellowships, teaching assistantships with full tuition reimbursements, Federal Work-Study, scholarships/grants, and unspecified assistantships available. Financial award application deadline: 2/1; financial award applicants required to submit FAFSA. *Faculty research:* Ceramics, metalsmithing and jewelry, textiles, scenography. *Application contact:* Gina Westergard, Director, 785-864-4401, Fax: 785-864-4404, E-mail: ginaw@ku.edu.

University of Kentucky, Graduate School, College of Design, Lexington, KY 40506-0032. Offers M Arch, MAIDM, MHP, MSIDM. *Faculty:* 23 full-time (10 women), 2 part-time/adjunct (1 woman). *Students:* 46 full-time (31 women), 8 part-time (7 women); includes 3 minority (2 African Americans, 1 Hispanic American), 2 international. Average age 28. 70 applicants, 54% accepted, 28 enrolled. In 2007, 26 degrees awarded. *Entrance requirements:* For master's, GRE, minimum GPA of 2.75. Additional exam requirements/recommendations for international students: Required—TOEFL (minimum score 550 paper-based; 213 computer-based). *Application deadline:* For fall admission, 7/17 priority date for domestic students, 2/1 priority date for international students; for spring admission, 12/13 priority date for domestic students, 6/15 priority date for international students. Application fee: $50 ($65 for international students). Electronic applications accepted. *Expenses:* Tuition, state resident: part-time $437 per credit hour. Tuition, nonresident: part-time $931 per credit hour. *Financial support:* In 2007–08, 29 students received support, including 16 research assistantships with full tuition reimbursements available (averaging $4,000 per year), 13 teaching assistantships with full tuition reimbursements available (averaging $4,803 per year); fellowships with full tuition reimbursements available, Federal Work-Study, scholarships/grants, traineeships, health care benefits, tuition waivers (partial), and unspecified assistantships also available. Support available to part-time students. Financial award application deadline: 3/15; financial award applicants required to submit FAFSA. *Unit head:* Dr. David Mohney, Dean, 859-257-7619, Fax: 859-323-1990, E-mail: mohney@uky.edu. *Application contact:* Dr. Brian Jackson, Senior Associate Dean, 859-257-4667, Fax: 859-257-4676, E-mail: brian.jackson@uky.edu.

University of Massachusetts Dartmouth, Graduate School, College of Visual and Performing Arts, Program in Visual Design, North Dartmouth, MA 02747-2300. Offers digital multi-media (MFA); electronic imaging (MFA); graphic design (MFA); illustration (MFA); photography (MFA); typography (MFA). *Accreditation:* NASAD. *Faculty:* 17 full-time (7 women), 7 part-time/adjunct (3 women). *Students:* 8 full-time (6 women), 2 part-time (both women); includes 1 minority (Asian American or Pacific Islander), 2 international. Average age 35. 21 applicants, 24% accepted, 4 enrolled. In 2007, 3 degrees awarded. *Degree requirements:* For master's, visual thesis. *Entrance requirements:* For master's, portfolio, interview, minimum GPA of 3.0, 3 letters of recommendation. Additional exam requirements/recommendations for international students: Required—TOEFL (minimum score 500 paper-based). *Application deadline:* For fall admission, 3/1 priority date for domestic students, 1/1 priority date for international students. Applications are processed on a rolling basis. Application fee: $40 ($60 for international students). Electronic applications accepted. *Expenses:* Tuition, state resident: full-time $2,071; part-time $86 per credit. Tuition, nonresident: full-time $8,099; part-time $337 per credit. Part-time tuition and fees vary according to course load and program. *Financial support:* In 2007–08, 4 teaching assistantships (averaging $2,930 per year) were awarded; research assistantships, Federal Work-Study and unspecified assistantships also available. Support available to part-time students. Financial award application deadline: 3/1; financial award applicants required to submit FAFSA. Total annual research expenditures: $22,880. *Unit head:* Jarrad Nunes, Director, 508-999-8010, E-mail: jnunes@umassd.edu. *Application contact:* Carol Novo, Graduate Admissions Officer, 508-999-8604, Fax: 508-999-8183, E-mail: graduate@umassd.edu.

University of Michigan, Horace H. Rackham School of Graduate Studies, School of Art and Design, Ann Arbor, MI 48109. Offers art and design (MFA). *Accreditation:* NASAD. *Faculty:* 44 full-time, 20 part-time/adjunct. *Students:* 26 full-time (19 women); includes 4 minority (2 African Americans, 2 Hispanic Americans), 2 international. Average age 30. 93 applicants, 16% accepted, 8 enrolled. In 2007, 7 degrees awarded. *Degree requirements:* For master's, thesis, exhibit (MFA), slide lecture. *Entrance requirements:* For master's, portfolio. Additional exam requirements/recommendations for international students: Required—TOEFL, IELTS. *Application deadline:* For fall admission, 1/1 for domestic and international students. Application fee: $55. Electronic applications accepted. *Financial support:* In 2007–08, 26 students received support, including 30 fellowships with full and partial tuition reimbursements available, 50 teaching assistantships with full and partial tuition reimbursements available; research assistantships with full and partial tuition reimbursements available, Federal Work-Study, scholarships/grants, health care benefits, tuition waivers (partial), and unspecified assistantships also available. Support available to part-time students. Financial award application deadline: 3/15; financial award applicants required to submit FAFSA. *Faculty research:* Creative expression, commercial design, preparation for teaching. *Unit head:* Bryan Rogers, Dean, 734-764-0397, Fax: 734-936-0469, E-mail: blrogers@umich.edu. *Application contact:* Dr. Bradley R. Smith, Associate Dean for Graduate Studies, 734-647-0397, Fax: 734-936-0469, E-mail: brdsmith@umich.edu.

See Close-Up on page 135.

University of Minnesota, Twin Cities Campus, Graduate School, College of Design, Department of Design, Housing, and Apparel, Minneapolis, MN 55455-0213. Offers apparel (MA, MS, PhD); design communication (MA, MS, PhD); housing studies (MA, MS, PhD, Postbaccalaureate Certificate); interactive design (MFA); interior design (MA, MS, PhD). Part-time programs available. *Faculty:* 24 full-time (18 women), 5 part-time/adjunct (4 women). *Students:* 41 full-time (34 women), 28 part-time (21 women); includes 3 minority (1 African American, 1 Asian American or Pacific Islander, 1 Hispanic American), 20 international. 37 applicants, 54% accepted, 15 enrolled. In 2007, 3 master's, 8 doctorates awarded. *Median time to degree:* Of those who began their doctoral program in fall 1999, 100% received their degree in 8 years or less. *Degree requirements:* For master's and Postbaccalaureate Certificate, comprehensive exam, thesis (for some programs); for doctorate, comprehensive exam, thesis/dissertation. *Entrance requirements:* For master's, GRE General Test, minimum GPA of 3.0 (preferred), portfolio, 3 letters of recommendation; for doctorate, GRE General Test, minimum GPA of 3.0 (preferred), portfolio, 3 letters of recommendation, writing sample; for Postbaccalaureate Certificate, GRE General Test, minimum GPA of 3.0 (preferred). Additional exam requirements/recommendations for international students: Required—TOEFL (minimum score 550 paper-based; 213 computer-based; 79 iBT). *Application deadline:* For fall admission, 1/15 for domestic and international students. Application fee: $55 ($75 for international students). Electronic applications accepted. *Financial support:* In 2007–08, 34 students received support, including 13 research assistantships with partial tuition reimbursements available (averaging $12,652 per year), 24 teaching assistantships with partial tuition reimbursements available (averaging $12,652 per year); Federal Work-Study, institutionally sponsored loans, and unspecified assistantships also available. Financial award application deadline: 2/1; financial award applicants required to submit FAFSA. *Faculty research:* Housing policy and community development; consumer behavior; interactive design; design history; social, cultural, and behavioral issues related to designed environments. Total annual research expenditures: $320,058. *Unit head:* Becky Love Yust, Professor and Department Head, 612-624-7461, Fax: 612-624-2750, E-mail: byust@che.umn.edu. *Application contact:* Charleen Klarquist, Student Support Services Assistant, 612-626-1219, Fax: 612-624-2750, E-mail: dhagrad@umn.edu.

University of North Texas, Robert B. Toulouse School of Graduate Studies, College of Visual Arts and Design, Department of Design, Denton, TX 76203. Offers MFA. *Accreditation:* NASAD. *Faculty:* 17 full-time (8 women). *Students:* 8 full-time (all women), 6 part-time (5 women); includes 3 minority (1 African American, 2 Asian Americans or Pacific Islanders), 2 international. Average age 31. 19 applicants, 21% accepted, 2 enrolled. In 2007, 1 degree awarded. *Degree requirements:* For master's, problem or thesis. *Entrance requirements:* Additional exam requirements/recommendations for international students: Required—proof of English language proficiency; Recommended—TOEFL (minimum score 550 paper-based; 213 computer-based). *Application deadline:* For fall admission, 7/15 for domestic students; for spring admission, 11/15 for domestic students. Application fee: $50 ($75 for international students). *Financial support:* In 2007–08, 1 fellowship (averaging $8,250 per year), 2 teaching assistantships (averaging $7,350 per year) were awarded. *Faculty research:* Color, lighting, sustainable design, hand sewing techniques, ethics. *Unit head:* Cynthia Mohr, Chair, 940-565-3621, Fax: 940-565-4717, E-mail: mohr@unt.edu.

University of Notre Dame, Graduate School, College of Arts and Letters, Division of Humanities, Department of Art, Art History, and Design, Notre Dame, IN 46556. Offers art history (MA); design (MFA), including graphic design, industrial design; studio art (MFA), including ceramics, painting, photography, printmaking, sculpture. *Accreditation:* NASAD. *Faculty:* 19 full-time (6 women), 3 part-time/adjunct (1 woman). *Students:* 25 full-time (12 women), 1 (woman) part-time; includes 4 minority (1 African American, 1 Asian American or Pacific Islander, 2 Hispanic Americans), 1 international. 85 applicants, 14% accepted, 10 enrolled. In 2007, 7 degrees awarded. *Degree requirements:* For master's, comprehensive exam, thesis. *Entrance requirements:* For master's, GRE General Test, minimum GPA of 3.0. Additional exam requirements/recommendations for international students: Required—TOEFL (minimum score 600 paper-based; 250 computer-based; 80 iBT). *Application deadline:* For fall admission, 2/1 priority date for domestic and international students. Application fee: $50. Electronic applications accepted. *Financial support:* In 2007–08, 20 students received support, including fellowships with full tuition reimbursements available (averaging $12,000 per year), research assistantships with full tuition reimbursements available (averaging $12,000 per year), 15 teaching assistantships with full tuition reimbursements available (averaging $12,000 per year); scholarships/grants, tuition waivers (full), and unspecified assistantships also available. Financial award application deadline: 2/1. *Faculty research:* Studio art practice in ceramics, printing, photography, printmaking and sculpture, graphic design and industrial design, digital imaging in design and photography, Renaissance and American art history, contemporary art theory and criticism. *Unit head:* Prof. Jean Dibble, Director of Graduate Studies, 574-631-7602, E-mail: art.1@nd.edu. *Application contact:* Dr. Jarren Gonzales, Director of Graduate Admissions, 574-631-7706, Fax: 574-631-4183.

University of Oklahoma, Graduate College, College of Fine Arts, School of Drama, Norman, OK 73019-0390. Offers acting (MFA); design (MFA); directing (MFA); drama (MA). *Accreditation:* NAST. *Faculty:* 7 full-time (5 women), 1 (woman) part-time/adjunct. *Students:* 13 full-time (5 women), 1 part-time; includes 2 minority (1 African American, 1 Asian American or Pacific Islander), 3 international. 10 applicants, 60% accepted, 6 enrolled. In 2007, 5 degrees awarded. *Degree requirements:* For master's, comprehensive exam, thesis (MA), departmental qualifying exam. *Entrance requirements:* For master's, BA with 36 hours in drama, auditions. Additional exam requirements/recommendations for international students: Required—TOEFL (minimum score 550 paper-based; 213 computer-based). *Application deadline:* For fall admission, 6/1 for domestic students, 4/1 for international students; for spring admission, 11/1 for domestic students, 9/1 for international students. Applications are processed on a rolling basis. Application fee: $40 ($90 for international students). Electronic applications accepted. *Expenses:* Tuition, state resident: full-time $3,451; part-time $144 per credit hour. Tuition, nonresident: full-time $12,432; part-time $518 per credit hour. Required fees: $1,925; $70 per credit hour. $122 per semester. *Financial support:* In 2007–08, 5 students received support, including research assistantships with partial tuition reimbursements available (averaging $9,397 per year), teaching assistantships with partial tuition reimbursements available (averaging $9,397 per year); unspecified assistantships also available. Financial award application deadline: 4/7; financial award applicants required to submit FAFSA. *Faculty research:* Directing, scenic design, costume, lighting acting. *Unit head:* Dr. Tom Orr, Director, 405-325-4021, Fax: 405-325-0400, E-mail: thorr@ou.edu. *Application contact:* Dr. Judith Pender, Graduate Liaison, 405-325-5319, Fax: 405-325-0400, E-mail: jmpender@ou.edu.

The University of Texas at Austin, Graduate School, College of Fine Arts, Department of Art and Art History, Program in Design, Austin, TX 78712-1111. Offers MFA. *Accreditation:* NASAD. *Degree requirements:* For master's, thesis, oral exam, exhibition. *Entrance requirements:* For master's, minimum GPA of 3.0, portfolio. Electronic applications accepted.

University of Wisconsin–Madison, Graduate School, School of Human Ecology, Program in Design Studies, Madison, WI 53706-1380. Offers MFA, MS, PhD. *Degree requirements:* For master's, thesis (for some programs); for doctorate, comprehensive exam, thesis/dissertation. *Entrance requirements:* For master's, portfolio, scholarly paper, 3 letters of recommendation from faculty; for doctorate, letters of recommendation, scholarly paper. Additional exam requirements/recommendations for international students: Required—TOEFL (minimum score 580 paper-based; 237 computer-based). *Faculty research:* Feng shui, material culture, behavior and environment, use of pattern to enhance environment, design visualization.

Virginia Commonwealth University, Graduate School, School of the Arts, Department of Graphic Design, Richmond, VA 23284-9005. Offers design/visual communications (MFA); interior environment (MFA); photography and film (MFA). *Accreditation:* NASAD. *Faculty:* 15 full-time (3 women). *Students:* 42 full-time (31 women), 6 part-time (3 women); includes 6 minority (2 African Americans, 1 Asian American or Pacific Islander, 3 Hispanic Americans), 7 international. 80 applicants, 31% accepted, 20 enrolled. In 2007, 17 degrees awarded. *Degree requirements:* For master's, thesis, exhibition. *Entrance requirements:* For master's, portfolio. *Application deadline:* For fall admission, 3/1 for domestic students. Application fee: $50. *Expenses:* Tuition, state resident: full-time $7,224; part-time $401 per credit. Tuition, nonresident: full-time $16,072; part-time $891 per credit. Required fees: $1,679; $63 per credit. Tuition and fees vary according to campus/location. *Financial support:* Fellowships, teaching assistantships, career-related internships or fieldwork, Federal Work-Study, institutionally sponsored loans, and tuition waivers (full and partial) also available. Support available to part-time students. Financial award application deadline: 3/15. *Faculty research:* Film, photography, interior environments, visual communication. *Unit head:* John DeMao, Chair, 804-828-7329, E-mail: jdemao@vcu.edu.

See Close-Up on page 275.

Virginia Polytechnic Institute and State University, Graduate School, College of Architecture and Urban Studies, School of Architecture and Design, Blacksburg, VA 24061. Offers M Arch, MS. *Accreditation:* NASAD. *Entrance requirements:* For master's, GRE General Test. Additional exam requirements/recommendations for international students: Required—TOEFL (minimum score 550 paper-based; 213 computer-based). Electronic applications accepted. *Faculty* *research:* Computer applications in design, building technology, architectural design theory, solar/passive energy design, building assembly.

Wayne State University, College of Fine, Performing and Communication Arts, Department of Art and Art History, Program in Design and Merchandising, Detroit, MI 48202. Offers MA. *Students:* 2 full-time (both women), 2 part-time (both women); includes 1 minority (African American), 1 international. Average age 38. 8 applicants, 0% accepted. *Degree requirements:* For master's, one foreign language. *Entrance requirements:* Additional exam requirements/recommendations for international students: Required—TOEFL (minimum score 550 paper-based; 213 computer-based); Recommended—TWE (minimum score 6). *Application deadline:* For fall admission, 4/1 for domestic students, 6/1 for international students; for winter admission, 10/1 for international students; for spring admission, 2/1 for international students. Application fee: $30 ($50 for international students). Electronic applications accepted. *Expenses:* Tuition, state resident: part-time $403 per credit hour. Tuition, nonresident: part-time $890 per credit hour. *Application contact:* Brian Madigan, Associate Professor, 313-577-2685, E-mail: bmadigan@wayne.edu.

Western Carolina University, Graduate School, College of Fine and Performing Arts, School of Art and Design, Cullowhee, NC 28723. Offers MFA. Part-time programs available. *Faculty:* 18 full-time (12 women), 2 part-time/adjunct (both women). *Students:* 13 full-time (7 women), 3 part-time; includes 3 minority (all American Indian/Alaska Native). Average age 33. 21 applicants, 67% accepted, 10 enrolled. In 2007, 9 degrees awarded. *Degree requirements:* For master's, thesis. *Entrance requirements:* For master's, GRE, appropriate undergraduate, portfolio, letters of recommendation. Additional exam requirements/recommendations for international students: Required—TOEFL (minimum score 550 paper-based; 270 computer-based; 79 iBT). *Application deadline:* For fall admission, 3/1 for domestic students. Application fee: $40. *Expenses:* Tuition, state resident: full-time $2,314. Tuition, nonresident: full-time $11,899. Required fees: $2,033. Tuition and fees vary according to course load. *Financial support:* In 2007–08, 10 students received support, including 10 teaching assistantships with full and partial tuition reimbursements available (averaging $7,500 per year); fellowships, research assistantships with full and partial tuition reimbursements available, career-related internships or fieldwork, institutionally sponsored loans, scholarships/grants, and unspecified assistantships also available. Financial award application deadline: 3/31; financial award applicants required to submit FAFSA. *Faculty research:* Art and society, visual literacy, vernacular cultural studies and oral history, environments for aging, health and leisure. *Unit head:* Richard Tichich, Chair, 828-227-7210, Fax: 828-227-7505, E-mail: rtichich@email.wcu.edu.

Western Michigan University, Graduate College, College of Fine Arts, Department of Art, Kalamazoo, MI 49008-5202. Offers graphic design (MFA); performing arts administration (MFA); textile design (MA, MFA). *Accreditation:* NASAD (one or more programs are accredited). *Degree requirements:* For master's, thesis or alternative.

Yale University, School of Art, New Haven, CT 06520. Offers graphic design (MFA); painting/printmaking (MFA); photography (MFA); sculpture (MFA). *Faculty:* 11 full-time (3 women), 102 part-time/adjunct (48 women). *Students:* 119 full-time (57 women); includes 19 minority (5 African Americans, 6 Asian Americans or Pacific Islanders, 8 Hispanic Americans), 22 international. Average age 27. 1,218 applicants, 5% accepted, 57 enrolled. In 2007, 56 degrees awarded. *Degree requirements:* For master's, thesis (for some programs). *Entrance requirements:* Additional exam requirements/recommendations for international students: Required—TOEFL (minimum score 550 paper-based; 250 computer-based; 100 iBT). *Application deadline:* For fall admission, 1/7 for domestic and international students. Application fee: $90. *Expenses:* Contact institution. *Financial support:* In 2007–08, 90 students received support, including 56 teaching assistantships (averaging $1,600 per year); Federal Work-Study and scholarships/grants also available. Financial award application deadline: 3/1; financial award applicants required to submit FAFSA. *Unit head:* Robert Storr, Dean, 203-432-2606. *Application contact:* Patricia Ann DeChiara, Director of Academic Affairs, 203-432-2600, E-mail: artschool.info@yale.edu.

York University, Faculty of Graduate Studies, Faculty of Fine Arts, Program in Design, Toronto, ON M3J 1P3, Canada. Offers M Des. Electronic applications accepted.

Computer Art and Design

Academy of Art University, Graduate Program, School of Computer Arts/New Media, San Francisco, CA 94105-3410. Offers MFA. Part-time and evening/weekend programs available. *Degree requirements:* For master's, thesis, final review. *Entrance requirements:* For master's, portfolio. Electronic applications accepted.

Alfred University, Graduate School, New York State College of Ceramics, School of Art and Design, Alfred, NY 14802-1205. Offers ceramic art (MFA); electronic integrated arts (MFA); glass art (MFA); sculpture (MFA). *Accreditation:* NASAD. *Students:* 34 full-time (19 women). Average age 26. 278 applicants, 6% accepted, 17 enrolled. In 2007, 17 degrees awarded. *Degree requirements:* For master's, exhibit. *Entrance requirements:* For master's, portfolio. Additional exam requirements/recommendations for international students: Required—TOEFL (minimum score 550 paper-based; 213 computer-based; 80 iBT), IELTS (minimum score 6). *Application deadline:* For fall admission, 1/15 for domestic students, 2/1 for international students. Application fee: $50. Electronic applications accepted. *Expenses:* Tuition: Full-time $32,016; part-time $680 per credit hour. Required fees: $850; $140 per year. *Financial support:* In 2007–08, 35 students received support; teaching assistantships with full tuition reimbursements available, tuition waivers (full) available. Financial award applicants required to submit FAFSA. *Faculty research:* Ceramic sculpture, functional ceramics, wood, mixed media, hot and cold glass. *Unit head:* Joseph Lewis, Dean, 607-871-2412, E-mail: lewis@alfred.edu. *Application contact:* Valerie Stephens, Coordinator of Graduate Admissions, 607-871-2141, Fax: 607-871-2198, E-mail: gradinquiry@alfred.edu.

American Academy of Art, Graduate Programs, Program in Digital Media and Design, Chicago, IL 60604-4302. Offers MFA. *Degree requirements:* For master's, thesis, exhibition. *Entrance requirements:* For master's, interview, portfolio, 2 letters of recommendation. Additional exam requirements/recommendations for international students: Required—TOEFL (minimum score 500 paper-based; 173 computer-based). *Faculty research:* Animation, print design, digital film, communication theory.

Art Center College of Design, Graduate Division, Department of Media Design, Pasadena, CA 91103-1999. Offers MFA. *Accreditation:* NASAD. *Faculty:* 8 full-time (3 women). *Students:* 22 full-time (10 women), 5 part-time (2 women); includes 7 minority (all Asian Americans or Pacific Islanders), 10 international. Average age 29. 63 applicants, 41% accepted, 10 enrolled. In 2007, 13 degrees awarded. *Degree requirements:* For master's, thesis, studio project. *Entrance requirements:* For master's, portfolio. Additional exam requirements/recommendations for international students: Required—TOEFL (minimum score 600 paper-based; 250 computer-based; 100 iBT). *Application deadline:* For fall admission, 2/1 for domestic students, 2/1 priority date for international students. Application fee: $50 ($70 for international students). *Expenses:* Tuition: Full-time $31,016. Required fees: $235. *Financial support:* Teaching assistantships, career-related internships or fieldwork, Federal Work-Study, and scholarships/grants available. Support available to part-time students. Financial award application deadline: 2/1; financial award applicants required to submit FAFSA. *Unit head:* Anne Burdick, Chair, 626-396-2359, E-mail: anne.burdick@artcenter.edu. *Application contact:* Kit Baron, Vice President, Admissions, 626-396-2373, Fax: 626-795-0578, E-mail: admissions@artcenter.edu.

See Close-Up on page 109.

Bowling Green State University, Graduate College, College of Arts and Sciences, School of Art, Bowling Green, OH 43403. Offers 2-D studio art (MA, MFA); 3-D studio art (MA, MFA); art education (MA); art history (MA); computer art (MA); design (MFA); digital arts (MFA); graphics (MFA). *Accreditation:* NASAD. Part-time programs available. *Faculty:* 26 full-time (14 women), 7 part-time/adjunct (2 women). *Students:* 24 full-time (12 women), 3 part-time (all women); includes 1 minority (Asian American or Pacific Islander), 2 international. Average age 33. 59 applicants, 20% accepted, 8 enrolled. In 2007, 11 degrees awarded. *Degree requirements:* For master's, thesis or alternative, final exhibit (MFA). *Entrance requirements:* For master's, GRE General Test (MA), slide portfolio (15-20 slides). Additional exam requirements/recommendations for international students: Required—TOEFL. *Application deadline:* For fall admission, 2/15 for domestic students. Application fee: $30. Electronic applications accepted. *Financial support:* In 2007–08, 11 research assistantships with full and partial tuition reimbursements (averaging $8,404 per year), 8 teaching assistantships with full and partial tuition reimbursements (averaging $8,404 per year) were awarded; career-related internships or fieldwork, institutionally sponsored loans, and unspecified assistantships also available. Support available to part-time students. Financial award applicants required to submit FAFSA. *Faculty research:* Computer animation and virtual reality, Spanish still-life painting from 1600 to 1800, art and psychotherapy, Japanese wood-firing techniques in ceramics, non-toxic printmaking technologies. *Unit head:* Dr. Katerina Rüedi Ray, Director, 419-372-8575. *Application contact:* Shawn Morin, Graduate Coordinator, 419-372-7766.

Carnegie Mellon University, College of Fine Arts, School of Design, Program in Interaction Design, Pittsburgh, PA 15213-3891. Offers M Des, PhD. Part-time programs available. *Degree requirements:* For master's, thesis. *Entrance requirements:* For master's, GRE, portfolio of relevant work. Additional exam requirements/recommendations for international students: Required—TOEFL (minimum score 600 paper-based; 250 computer-based). *Faculty research:* Interaction and emotion, visual interface design, robotics, visualization and diagramming, design theory.

Chatham University, Program in Film and Digital Technology, Pittsburgh, PA 15232-2826. Offers MFA. *Students:* 6 full-time (5 women), 2 part-time. Average age 28. 9 applicants, 78% accepted, 7 enrolled. *Entrance requirements:* For master's, recommendation letters, portfolio of work. Additional exam requirements/recommendations for international students: Recommended—TOEFL (minimum score 600 paper-based; 250 computer-based; 100 iBT), IELTS (minimum score 7). *Application deadline:* For fall admission, 5/1 priority date for domestic students; for winter admission, 10/1 priority date for domestic students. Applications are processed on a rolling basis. Application fee: $45. Electronic applications accepted. *Unit head:* Dr. Prajna Parasher, Director, 412-365-1182, E-mail: parasher@chatham.edu. *Application contact:* Office of Graduate Admissions, 412-365-1825, Fax: 412-365-1609, E-mail: admissions@chatham.edu.

Claremont Graduate University, Graduate Programs, School of Arts and Humanities, Department of Art, Claremont, CA 91711-6160. Offers digital media (MA, MFA); drawing (MA, MFA); installation (MA, MFA); new genre (MA, MFA); painting (MA, MFA); performance (MA, MFA); photography (MA, MFA); sculpture (MA, MFA). Part-time programs available. *Faculty:* 3 full-time (0 women), 10 part-time/adjunct (5 women). *Students:* 61 full-time (36 women), 1 part-time; includes 11 minority (2 African Americans, 4 Asian Americans or Pacific Islanders, 5 Hispanic Americans), 4 international. Average age 33. In 2007, 34 degrees awarded. *Degree requirements:* For master's, final project show. *Entrance requirements:* For master's, BA in art or BFA, slide review. *Application deadline:* For fall admission, 2/15 priority date for domestic students. Applications are processed on a rolling basis. Electronic applications accepted. *Expenses:* Tuition: Full-time $31,640; part-time $1,376 per unit. Required fees: $145 per semester. Tuition and fees vary according to course load, degree level and program. *Financial support:* Fellowships, research assistantships, teaching assistantships, Federal Work-Study and institutionally sponsored loans available. Support available to part-time students. Financial award application deadline: 2/15; financial award applicants required to submit FAFSA. *Faculty research:* Acoustic sculpture, feminization of abstraction, installation sculpture. *Unit head:* David Pagel, Chair, 909-621-8071, Fax: 909-607-1276, E-mail: david.pagel@cgu.edu. *Application contact:* Marianne Elder, Assistant Coordinator, 909-607-2479, Fax: 909-607-1276, E-mail: marianne.elder@cgu.edu.

Clemson University, Graduate School, College of Architecture, Arts, and Humanities, Department of Art, Program in Digital Production Arts, Clemson, SC 29634. Offers MFA. *Students:* 13 full-time (1 woman), 9 part-time (1 woman); includes 5 minority (all African Americans), 3 international. 16 applicants, 63% accepted, 7 enrolled. In 2007, 5 degrees awarded. *Degree requirements:* For master's, thesis. *Entrance requirements:* For master's, GRE General Test, portfolio. Additional exam requirements/recommendations for international students: Required—TOEFL. *Application deadline:* For fall admission, 4/15 for domestic and international students; for spring admission, 9/15 for international students. Application fee: $55. *Financial support:* In 2007–08, 9 research assistantships were awarded; fellowships also available. *Unit head:* Dr. Timothy Davis, Coordinator, 864-656-0309.

Concordia University, School of Graduate Studies, Faculty of Fine Arts, Department of Design and Computation Arts, Montréal, QC H3G 1M8, Canada. Offers digital technologies in design art practice (Certificate).

Cornell University, Graduate School, Graduate Fields of Architecture, Art and Planning, Field of Architecture, Ithaca, NY 14853-0001. Offers architectural design (M Arch); architectural science (MS); building technology and environmental science (MS); computer graphics (MS); history of architecture (MA, PhD); history of urban development (MA, PhD); theory and criticism of architecture (M Arch); urban design (M Arch). *Faculty:* 33 full-time. *Students:* 101 full-time (33 women); includes 13 minority (1 African American, 7 Asian Americans or Pacific Islanders, 5 Hispanic Americans), 51 international. Average age 28. 305 applicants, 30% accepted, 39 enrolled. In 2007, 17 master's, 1 doctorate awarded. *Degree requirements:* For master's, one foreign language, thesis (MA, MS); for doctorate, 2 foreign languages, comprehensive exam, thesis/dissertation. *Entrance requirements:* For master's, GRE General Test, GRE Subject Test in computer science (computer graphics), 5-year bachelor's degree in architecture, portfolio (M Arch), 3 letters of recommendation; for doctorate, GRE General Test, 3 letters of recommendation. Additional exam requirements/recommendations for international students: Required—TOEFL (minimum score 600 paper-based; 250 computer-based; 77 iBT). *Application deadline:* For fall admission, 1/15 priority date for domestic students. Application fee: $70. Electronic applications accepted. *Financial support:* In 2007–08, 41 students received support, including 13 fellowships with full tuition reimbursements available, 1 research assistantship with full tuition reimbursement available, 27 teaching assistantships with full tuition reimbursements available; institutionally sponsored loans, scholarships/grants, health care benefits, tuition waivers (full and partial), and unspecified assistantships also available. Financial award applicants required to submit FAFSA. *Faculty research:* Architectural design

Computer Art and Design

Cornell University (continued)
and urban design, theory and criticism of architecture, computer graphics, building technology and environmental science, history of architecture and history of urban-development. *Unit head:* Director of Graduate Studies, 607-255-6701, Fax: 607-255-0291. *Application contact:* Graduate Field Assistant, 607-255-6701, Fax: 607-255-0291, E-mail: cuarch@cornell.edu.

DePaul University, School of Computer Science, Telecommunications, and Information Systems, Chicago, IL 60604-2287. Offers business information technology (MS); computational finance (MS); computer graphics and motion technology (MS); computer science (MS, PhD); computer, information and network security (MS), including applied technology; digital cinema (MFA, MS), including information technology project management (MS); e-commerce technology (MS); human-computer interaction (MS); information systems (MS); information technology (MA); instructional technology systems (MS); software engineering (MS); telecommunication systems (MS); MS/JD. Part-time and evening/weekend programs available. Postbaccalaureate distance learning degree programs offered (no on-campus study). *Faculty:* 53 full-time (8 women), 52 part-time/adjunct (5 women). *Students:* 1,029 full-time (267 women), 929 part-time (232 women); includes 431 minority (180 African Americans, 4 American Indian/Alaska Native, 172 Asian Americans or Pacific Islanders, 75 Hispanic Americans), 349 international. Average age 31. 928 applicants, 71% accepted, 360 enrolled. In 2007, 553 master's, 3 doctorates awarded. *Median time to degree:* Of those who began their doctoral program in fall 1999, 17% received their degree in 8 years or less. *Degree requirements:* For master's, comprehensive exam (for some programs); for doctorate, comprehensive exam, thesis/dissertation. *Entrance requirements:* For master's, GRE or GMAT (MS in computational finance), bachelor's degree; for doctorate, GRE, master's degree in computer science. Additional exam requirements/recommendations for international students: Required—TOEFL (minimum score 550 paper-based; 213 computer-based), IELTS (minimum score 7). *Application deadline:* For fall admission, 8/1 priority date for domestic students, 7/1 priority date for international students; for winter admission, 11/15 priority date for domestic students, 10/15 priority date for international students; for spring admission, 3/1 priority date for domestic students, 2/1 priority date for international students. Applications are processed on a rolling basis. Application fee: $25. Electronic applications accepted. *Expenses: Contact institution. Financial support:* In 2007–08, 81 students received support, including 2 fellowships with full tuition reimbursements available (averaging $18,000 per year), 75 teaching assistantships with full and partial tuition reimbursements available (averaging $5,780 per year); research assistantships, Federal Work-Study, scholarships/grants, tuition waivers (full and partial), and unspecified assistantships also available. Support available to part-time students. Financial award application deadline: 4/30; financial award applicants required to submit FAFSA. *Faculty research:* Computer graphics, computer vision, information systems technology, computer network, programming. Total annual research expenditures: $790,000. *Unit head:* Dr. David Miller, Dean, 312-362-8381, Fax: 312-362-5185. *Application contact:* Dr. Elizabeth Friedman, Assistant Dean of Student Services, 312-362-8714, Fax: 312-362-5327, E-mail: efriedm2@ctidepaul.edu.

Digital Media Arts College, Graduate Programs, Boca Raton, FL 33431. Offers graphic design (MFA); special FX animation (MFA).

East Tennessee State University, School of Graduate Studies, College of Business and Technology, Department of Technology and Geomatics, Johnson City, TN 37614. Offers digital media (MS); engineering technology (MS); industrial arts/technology education (MS). Part-time programs available. *Degree requirements:* For master's, thesis or alternative, final oral exam. *Entrance requirements:* For master's, bachelor's degree in technical or related area, minimum GPA of 3.0. Additional exam requirements/recommendations for international students: Required—TOEFL (minimum score 550 paper-based; 213 computer-based). *Faculty research:* Computer-integrated manufacturing, technology education, CAD/CAM, organizational change.

Emily Carr Institute of Art + Design, Program in Digital Media, Vancouver, BC V5T 1E1, Canada. Offers MDM. *Degree requirements:* For master's, internship. *Entrance requirements:* For master's, portfolio, minimum undergraduate B+ average, 3 reference letters. Additional exam requirements/recommendations for international students: Required—TOEFL (minimum score 86 iBT). Electronic applications accepted.

Indiana University Bloomington, School of Informatics, Bloomington, IN 47405-7000. Offers bioinformatics (MS); chemical informatics (MS); computer science (MS, PhD); health informatics (MS); human computer interaction (MS); informatics (PhD); laboratory informatics (MS); media arts and science (MS); music informatics (MS); MS/PhD. PhD offered through the University Graduate School. *Faculty:* 55 full-time (8 women). *Students:* 67 full-time (21 women), 71 part-time (40 women); includes 11 minority (4 African Americans, 4 Asian Americans or Pacific Islanders, 3 Hispanic Americans), 76 international. Average age 27. 181 applicants, 50% accepted, 57 enrolled. In 2007, 32 degrees awarded. *Entrance requirements:* For master's and doctorate, GRE, letters of reference. Additional exam requirements/recommendations for international students: Required—TOEFL. *Application deadline:* For fall admission, 1/17 for domestic students, 1/15 for international students; for spring admission, 4/15 for domestic students, 9/1 for international students. Application fee: $50 ($60 for international students). Electronic applications accepted. *Financial support:* Fellowships with full and partial tuition reimbursements, research assistantships, teaching assistantships, Federal Work-Study, institutionally sponsored loans, scholarships/grants, and tuition waivers (full and partial) available. Support available to part-time students. *Unit head:* Robert B. Schnabel, Dean, 812-856-1079, Fax: 812-856-4764, E-mail: informat@indiana.edu. *Application contact:* Martin Siegel, Associate Dean for Graduate Studies and Research, 812-856-1103, E-mail: msiegel@indiana.edu.

Long Island University, Brooklyn Campus, Richard L. Conolly College of Liberal Arts and Sciences, Department of Media Arts, Brooklyn, NY 11201-8423. Offers MA. Part-time and evening/weekend programs available. *Degree requirements:* For master's, integrated thesis project. *Entrance requirements:* For master's, 2 letters of recommendation. Additional exam requirements/recommendations for international students: Required—TOEFL (minimum score 500 paper-based; 173 computer-based). *Faculty research:* Film noir, art and photography, new media/new aesthetic.

See Close-Up on page 117.

Long Island University, C.W. Post Campus, School of Visual and Performing Arts, Department of Theatre, Film, Dance and Arts Management, Brookville, NY 11548-1300. Offers interactive multimedia (MA); theatre (MA). Part-time and evening/weekend programs available. *Faculty:* 2 full-time (both women), 23 part-time/adjunct (13 women). *Students:* 18 full-time (12 women), 18 part-time (9 women); includes 7 minority (1 African American, 5 Asian Americans or Pacific Islanders, 1 Hispanic American), 3 international. Average age 31. 26 applicants, 65% accepted, 11 enrolled. In 2007, 4 degrees awarded. *Degree requirements:* For master's, thesis. *Entrance requirements:* For master's, placement exam. *Application deadline:* Applications are processed on a rolling basis. Application fee: $30. Electronic applications accepted. *Expenses:* Tuition: Part-time $825 per credit. Tuition and fees vary according to course load. *Financial support:* Career-related internships or fieldwork, Federal Work-Study, institutionally sponsored loans, scholarships/grants, and production assistantships available. Support available to part-time students. Financial award application deadline: 5/15; financial award applicants required to submit CSS PROFILE or FAFSA. *Faculty research:* Playwriting, intercultural dance and theatre, translation, Suzuki, set and costume design. *Unit head:* Dr. Cara Gargano, Chair, 516-299-2353, E-mail: cgargano@liu.edu. *Application contact:* Beth Carson, Director of Graduate and International Admissions, 516-299-2900 Ext. 3952, Fax: 516-299-2137, E-mail: enroll@cwpost.liu.edu.

Maryland Institute College of Art, Graduate Studies, Program in Digital Arts, Baltimore, MD 21217. Offers MA. *Faculty:* 1 full-time (0 women), 1 (woman) part-time/adjunct. *Students:* 15 full-time (6 women); includes 3 minority (1 Asian American or Pacific Islander, 2 Hispanic Americans), 2 international. Average age 29. In 2007, 14 degrees awarded. *Degree requirements:* For master's, thesis, exhibit. *Entrance requirements:* For master's, portfolio, 40 studio credits, 6 credits in art history. Additional exam requirements/recommendations for international students: Required—TOEFL (minimum score 550 paper-based; 213 computer-based). *Application deadline:* For fall admission, 2/15 for domestic and international students. Application fee: $50. *Expenses:* Tuition: Full-time $29,700; part-time $1,238 per credit. Required fees: $980; $490 per term. *Financial support:* In 2007–08, 15 students received support, including 1 fellowship (averaging $15,685 per year), 9 teaching assistantships (averaging $1,500 per year); career-related internships or fieldwork and scholarships/grants also available. Financial award application deadline: 3/1; financial award applicants required to submit FAFSA. *Unit head:* Timothy Druckrey, Director, 410-462-7592, Fax: 410-669-1141. *Application contact:* Scott G. Kelly, Associate Dean of Graduate Admission, 410-225-2256, Fax: 410-225-2408, E-mail: graduate@mica.edu.

Memphis College of Art, Graduate Programs, Memphis, TN 38104-2764. Offers art education (MA, MAT); computer arts (MFA); studio art (MFA), including fiber/surface design, painting, papermaking, photography, printmaking, sculpture. *Accreditation:* NASAD. Part-time programs available. *Faculty:* 16 full-time (7 women), 5 part-time/adjunct (3 women). *Students:* 18 full-time (8 women), 37 part-time (26 women); includes 7 minority (2 African Americans, 2 Asian Americans or Pacific Islanders, 3 Hispanic Americans). Average age 30. 80 applicants, 59% accepted, 33 enrolled. In 2007, 4 degrees awarded. *Degree requirements:* For master's, thesis. *Entrance requirements:* For master's, portfolio, interview, resumé. Additional exam requirements/recommendations for international students: Required—TOEFL (minimum score 525 paper-based; 195 computer-based). *Application deadline:* For fall admission, 3/1 priority date for domestic and international students; for spring admission, 11/1 priority date for domestic and international students. Application fee: $50. Electronic applications accepted. *Expenses:* Tuition: Full-time $22,000; part-time $435 per credit. Required fees: $560; $100 per course. Part-time tuition and fees vary according to course load and program. *Financial support:* In 2007–08, 5 teaching assistantships with partial tuition reimbursements (averaging $2,000 per year) were awarded; career-related internships or fieldwork, Federal Work-Study, institutionally sponsored loans, scholarships/grants, tuition waivers (partial), unspecified assistantships, and merit awards also available. Support available to part-time students. Financial award application deadline: 8/1; financial award applicants required to submit FAFSA. *Unit head:* Ken Strickland, Vice President Academic Affairs, 901-272-5100, Fax: 901-272-5104, E-mail: info@mca.edu. *Application contact:* Annette James Moore, Director of Admissions, 800-727-1088, Fax: 901-272-5158, E-mail: info@mca.edu.

See Close-Up on page 245.

Miami International University of Art & Design, Program in Computer Animation, Miami, FL 33132-1418. Offers MFA. Postbaccalaureate distance learning degree programs offered.

See Close-Up on page 119.

Minneapolis College of Art and Design, Program in Arts, Minneapolis, MN 55404-4347. Offers design (Certificate); fine arts (Certificate); media (Certificate). Part-time programs available. *Faculty:* 23 full-time (7 women), 9 part-time/adjunct (4 women). *Students:* 3 full-time (2 women), 10 part-time (7 women). Average age 24. 18 applicants, 56% accepted, 4 enrolled. In 2007, 15 degrees awarded. *Degree requirements:* For Certificate, final project. *Entrance requirements:* For degree, resumé, portfolio, statement, letter of recommendation. Additional exam requirements/recommendations for international students: Required—TOEFL (minimum score 550 paper-based; 213 computer-based; 79 iBT). *Application deadline:* For fall admission, 2/15 for domestic and international students. Application fee: $50. Electronic applications accepted. *Expenses:* Tuition: Full-time $27,000; part-time $900 per credit. Required fees: $100 per term. *Financial support:* Career-related internships or fieldwork and scholarships/grants available. Financial award application deadline: 3/15; financial award applicants required to submit FAFSA. *Faculty research:* Visual arts. *Unit head:* Carole Fisher, Graduate Director, 612-874-3629, E-mail: carole_fisher@mcad.edu. *Application contact:* William Mullen, Vice President of Enrollment Management, 612-874-3762, Fax: 612-874-3701, E-mail: william_mullen@mcad.edu.

Mississippi State University, College of Architecture, Art and Design, Mississippi State, MS 39762. Offers MFA, MS. *Accreditation:* NASAD. *Faculty:* 42 full-time (14 women), 9 part-time/adjunct (1 woman). *Students:* 16 full-time (9 women), 5 part-time (2 women); includes 2 minority (1 African American, 1 Asian American or Pacific Islander), 7 international. Average age 31. 18 applicants, 83% accepted, 7 enrolled. In 2007, 9 degrees awarded. *Degree requirements:* For master's, comprehensive exam, thesis, final written and oral exam. *Entrance requirements:* For master's, GRE General Test, portfolio, minimum GPA of 3.0. Additional exam requirements/recommendations for international students: Required—TOEFL. *Application deadline:* For fall admission, 3/1 priority date for domestic students. Applications are processed on a rolling basis. Application fee: $30. Electronic applications accepted. *Expenses:* Tuition, state resident: full-time $4,978; part-time $274 per hour. Tuition, nonresident: full-time $11,469; part-time $635 per hour. *Financial support:* In 2007–08, 7 students received support; research assistantships with full tuition reimbursements available, career-related internships or fieldwork, Federal Work-Study, institutionally sponsored loans, and unspecified assistantships available. Financial award application deadline: 3/1; financial award applicants required to submit FAFSA. *Faculty research:* Digital art in architecture, process change and management, multi-media databases, 3-D modeling and animation, virtual archaeology. *Unit head:* James L. West, Dean, 662-325-2202, Fax: 662-325-8872, E-mail: jwest@coa.msstate.edu. *Application contact:* Dr. William A. Person, Interim Associate Vice President for Academic Affairs/Interim Dean of Graduate Studies, 662-325-7400, Fax: 662-325-1967, E-mail: grad@grad.msstate.edu.

National University, Academic Affairs, School of Media and Communication, Department of Media, La Jolla, CA 92037-1011. Offers digital cinema (MFA); educational and instructional technology (MS); video game production and design (MFA). Part-time and evening/weekend programs available. Postbaccalaureate distance learning degree programs offered (no on-campus study). *Faculty:* 7 full-time (2 women), 55 part-time/adjunct (22 women). *Students:* 69 full-time (35 women), 158 part-time (86 women); includes 54 minority (25 African Americans, 2 American Indian/Alaska Native, 7 Asian Americans or Pacific Islanders, 20 Hispanic Americans). Average age 39. 159 applicants, 143 enrolled. In 2007, 58 degrees awarded. *Degree requirements:* For master's, thesis. *Entrance requirements:* For master's, interview, minimum GPA of 2.5. Additional exam requirements/recommendations for international students: Required—TOEFL (minimum score 550 paper-based; 213 computer-based; 80 iBT), IELTS (minimum score 6). *Application deadline:* Applications are processed on a rolling basis. Application fee: $60 ($65 for international students). Electronic applications accepted. *Expenses:* Tuition: Full-time $8,262; part-time $306 per unit. One-time fee: $60. *Financial support:* Career-related internships or fieldwork, institutionally sponsored loans, scholarships/grants, and tuition waivers (partial) available. Support available to part-time students. Financial award application deadline: 6/30; financial award applicants required to submit FAFSA. *Unit head:* Dr. Timothy Langdell, Department Chair, 858-642-8466, Fax: 858-642-8743, E-mail: tlangdell@nu.edu. *Application contact:* Dominick Giovanniello, Associate Regional Dean—San Diego, 800-NAT-UNIV, Fax: 858-642-8709, E-mail: dgiovann@nu.edu.

The New School: A University, Parsons The New School for Design, Program in Design and Technology, New York, NY 10011. Offers MFA. *Accreditation:* NASAD. *Faculty:* 10 full-time (7 women), 40 part-time/adjunct (11 women). *Students:* 130 full-time (76 women), 8 part-time (3 women); includes 26 minority (3 African Americans, 18 Asian Americans or Pacific Islanders, 5 Hispanic Americans), 60 international. Average age 27. In 2007, 77 degrees awarded. *Entrance requirements:* For master's, portfolio. Additional exam requirements/recommendations for international students: Required—TOEFL (minimum score 580 paper-based; 237 computer-based; 93 iBT). *Application deadline:* For fall admission, 2/1 priority date for domestic students. Applications are processed on a rolling basis. Application fee: $50. *Financial support:* Fellowships with partial tuition reimbursements, research assistantships with partial tuition reimbursements, teaching assistantships with partial tuition reimbursements, Federal Work-Study and scholarships/grants available. Financial award application deadline: 3/1; financial award applicants required to submit FAFSA. *Unit head:* Colleen Macklin, Chair, 212-229-8908 Ext.

4097, E-mail: macklinc@newschool.edu. *Application contact:* Anthony Padilla, Director of Admissions, 212-229-8989 Ext. 4023, Fax: 212-229-8975, E-mail: padillaa@newschool.edu.

See Close-Up on page 121.

New York University, School of Continuing and Professional Studies, Center for Advanced Digital Applications, New York, NY 10012-1019. Offers digital imaging and design (MS). *Faculty:* 4 full-time (1 woman), 20 part-time/adjunct (2 women). *Students:* 53 full-time (15 women), 51 part-time (19 women); includes 24 minority (9 African Americans, 9 Asian Americans or Pacific Islanders, 6 Hispanic Americans), 10 international. Average age 30. 62 applicants, 71% accepted, 29 enrolled. In 2007, 12 degrees awarded. *Degree requirements:* For master's, comprehensive exam, thesis. *Entrance requirements:* For master's, GRE or GMAT (recommended), portfolio, 2 letters of recommendation, resumé, essay. Additional exam requirements/recommendations for international students: Required—TOEFL (minimum score 600 paper-based; 250 computer-based; 100 iBT), TWE. *Application deadline:* For fall admission, 3/15 priority date for domestic and international students; for spring admission, 10/15 priority date for domestic students, 8/15 priority date for international students. Applications are processed on a rolling basis. Application fee: $75. Electronic applications accepted. *Financial support:* In 2007–08, 67 students received support, including 67 fellowships with tuition reimbursements available (averaging $2,487 per year); career-related internships or fieldwork and scholarships/grants also available. Support available to part-time students. Financial award application deadline: 3/1; financial award applicants required to submit FAFSA. *Unit head:* Dr. Michael Hosenfeld, Director, 212-992-3370, Fax: 212-992-3377, E-mail: cada@nyu.edu. *Application contact:* Kathy Wang, Assistant Director, 212-992-3370, Fax: 212-992-3377, E-mail: cada@nyu.edu.

See Close-Up on page 127.

New York University, School of Continuing and Professional Studies, Division for Media Industry Studies and Design, Program in Graphic Communications Management and Technology, New York, NY 10012-1019. Offers MA. Part-time and evening/weekend programs available. *Faculty:* 20 part-time/adjunct (8 women). *Students:* 16 full-time (13 women), 58 part-time (31 women); includes 15 minority (3 African Americans, 11 Asian Americans or Pacific Islanders, 1 Hispanic American), 13 international. Average age 30. 35 applicants, 83% accepted, 23 enrolled. In 2007, 7 degrees awarded. *Degree requirements:* For master's, project. *Entrance requirements:* For master's, GRE General Test or GMAT (for recent graduates), resumé, 2 letters of recommendation, work experience, essay. Additional exam requirements/recommendations for international students: Required—TOEFL (minimum score 600 paper-based; 250 computer-based; 100 iBT), TWE. *Application deadline:* For fall admission, 3/15 priority date for domestic and international students; for spring admission, 10/15 priority date for domestic students, 8/15 priority date for international students. Applications are processed on a rolling basis. Application fee: $75. Electronic applications accepted. *Financial support:* In 2007–08, 36 students received support, including 36 fellowships (averaging $1,347 per year); scholarships/grants and tuition waivers (partial) also available. Support available to part-time students. Financial award application deadline: 3/1; financial award applicants required to submit FAFSA. *Faculty research:* Production operations management and marketing, human resources and quality management. *Unit head:* Bonnie Blake, Director, 212-992-3222, Fax: 212-992-3386. *Application contact:* 212-998-7100, Fax: 212-995-4674, E-mail: scps.gradadmissions@nyu.edu.

See Close-Up on page 129.

New York University, Tisch School of the Arts Asia, Singapore, NY 248923, Singapore. Offers animation and digital arts (MFA); dramatic writing (MFA); film production (MFA). *Faculty:* 6 full-time (3 women). *Students:* 33 full-time (16 women); includes 6 minority (1 African American, 5 Asian Americans or Pacific Islanders), 13 international. 55 applicants, 22% accepted. *Entrance requirements:* Additional exam requirements/recommendations for international students: Required—TOEFL (minimum score 610 paper-based; 250 computer-based; 105 iBT). *Application deadline:* For fall admission, 2/1 priority date for domestic and international students. Application fee: $60. Electronic applications accepted. *Financial support:* Fellowships with full and partial tuition reimbursements, research assistantships, teaching assistantships, Federal Work-Study, institutionally sponsored loans, and unspecified assistantships available. Financial award application deadline: 2/15; financial award applicants required to submit FAFSA.

See Close-Up on page 291.

Philadelphia University, School of Design and Media, Program in Digital Design, Philadelphia, PA 19144-5497. Offers MS. *Accreditation:* NASAD. *Entrance requirements:* For master's, portfolio. Additional exam requirements/recommendations for international students: Required—TOEFL (minimum score 550 paper-based; 213 computer-based; 79 iBT). Electronic applications accepted.

Rensselaer Polytechnic Institute, Graduate School, School of Humanities and Social Sciences, Department of the Arts, Program in Electronic Arts, Troy, NY 12180-3590. Offers MFA, PhD. *Faculty:* 13 full-time (7 women). *Students:* Average age 28. 47 applicants, 34% accepted, 8 enrolled. In 2007, 4 degrees awarded. *Degree requirements:* For master's, thesis, thesis in the form of a large-scale creative project; for doctorate, comprehensive exam, thesis/dissertation, dissertation or creative project and dissertation text. *Entrance requirements:* For master's, portfolio; for doctorate, portfolio, writing sample, evidence of research-based creative orientation. Additional exam requirements/recommendations for international students: Required—TOEFL (minimum score 570 paper-based; 230 computer-based; 88 iBT). *Application deadline:* For fall admission, 1/15 for domestic and international students. Applications are processed on a rolling basis. Application fee: $75. Electronic applications accepted. *Expenses:* Tuition: Full-time $34,900; part-time $1,454 per credit. Required fees: $1,802. *Financial support:* In 2007–08, 12 students received support, including 6 fellowships with full tuition reimbursements available (averaging $14,500 per year), 1 research assistantship with full tuition reimbursement available (averaging $14,500 per year), 5 teaching assistantships with full tuition reimbursements available (averaging $14,500 per year); career-related internships or fieldwork, institutionally sponsored loans, and unspecified assistantships also available. Financial award application deadline: 1/15. *Faculty research:* Computer music, video art, Net art, interactivity, bio art. *Application contact:* Jennifer Mumby, Assistant III, 518-276-4784, Fax: 518-276-4370, E-mail: mumbyj@rpi.edu.

See Close-Up on page 131.

Rhode Island School of Design, Graduate Studies, Program in Digital Media, Providence, RI 02903-2784. Offers MFA. *Entrance requirements:* Additional exam requirements/recommendations for international students: Required—TOEFL (minimum score 580 paper-based; 237 computer-based), IELTS (minimum score 7).

Rochester Institute of Technology, Graduate Enrollment Services, College of Imaging Arts and Sciences, School of Design, Program in Computer Graphics Design, Rochester, NY 14623-5603. Offers MFA. *Accreditation:* NASAD. *Students:* 38 full-time (16 women), 15 part-time (8 women); includes 2 minority (1 African American, 1 Asian American or Pacific Islander), 24 international. 69 applicants, 64% accepted, 19 enrolled. In 2007, 10 degrees awarded. *Degree requirements:* For master's, thesis. *Entrance requirements:* For master's, portfolio, minimum GPA of 3.0. Additional exam requirements/recommendations for international students: Required—TOEFL. *Application deadline:* For fall admission, 3/1 priority date for domestic students. Applications are processed on a rolling basis. Application fee: $50. *Expenses:* Tuition: Full-time $28,491; part-time $800 per credit hour. Required fees: $201; $67 per term. *Financial support:* Research assistantships with partial tuition reimbursements, teaching assistantships with partial tuition reimbursements, career-related internships or fieldwork, institutionally sponsored loans, scholarships/grants, and unspecified assistantships available. Support available to part-time students. Financial award applicants required to submit FAFSA. *Unit head:* Marianne O'Loughlin, Chairperson, 585-475-6125, E-mail: meofaa@rit.edu.

St. Edward's University, School of Management and Business, Area of Digital Media Management, Austin, TX 78704. Offers MBA. *Faculty:* 3 full-time (1 woman), 4 part-time/adjunct (1 woman). *Students:* 24 full-time (13 women); includes 4 minority (1 African American, 3 Hispanic Americans). Average age 26. 19 applicants, 63% accepted, 12 enrolled. In 2007, 10 degrees awarded. *Entrance requirements:* For master's, GRE or GMAT, interview, 2 letters of recommendation, minimum 3.0 GPA in last 60 hours of course work. Additional exam requirements/recommendations for international students: Required—TOEFL (minimum score 550 paper-based; 213 computer-based; 79 iBT). *Application deadline:* For fall admission, 2/15 priority date for domestic and international students. Applications are processed on a rolling basis. Application fee: $45 ($50 for international students). Electronic applications accepted. *Expenses: Contact institution.* Full-time tuition and fees vary according to program. Part-time tuition and fees vary according to course load. *Financial support:* Scholarships/grants available. *Unit head:* Russell Rains, Director, 512-428-1220, Fax: 512-448-8492, E-mail: russellr@stedwards.edu. *Application contact:* Bridget S. Davidson, Director, Center for Academic Progress, 512-428-1061, Fax: 512-428-1032, E-mail: bridgets@stedwards.edu.

San Jose State University, Graduate Studies and Research, College of Humanities and the Arts, School of Art and Design, San Jose, CA 95192-0001. Offers art education (MA); art history (MA); digital media (MFA); digital media in art history and education (MA); photography (MFA); pictorial arts (MFA); spatial arts (MFA). *Accreditation:* NASAD (one or more programs are accredited). *Students:* 55 full-time (30 women), 15 part-time (12 women); includes 11 minority (1 African American, 7 Asian Americans or Pacific Islanders, 3 Hispanic Americans), 2 international. Average age 38. 78 applicants, 42% accepted, 24 enrolled. In 2007, 17 degrees awarded. *Entrance requirements:* For master's, GRE. *Application deadline:* For fall admission, 6/29 for domestic students; for spring admission, 11/30 for domestic students. Applications are processed on a rolling basis. Application fee: $59. Electronic applications accepted. *Financial support:* Applicants required to submit FAFSA. *Unit head:* Linda Walsh, Director, 408-924-4320, Fax: 408-924-4326.

Savannah College of Art and Design, Graduate School, Program in Animation, Savannah, GA 31402-3146. Offers MA, MFA. Part-time programs available. *Faculty:* 9 full-time (3 women), 1 (woman) part-time/adjunct. *Students:* 94 full-time (33 women), 14 part-time (5 women); includes 8 minority (5 African Americans, 1 American Indian/Alaska Native, 1 Asian American or Pacific Islander, 1 Hispanic American), 39 international. 109 applicants, 48% accepted, 23 enrolled. In 2007, 36 degrees awarded. *Degree requirements:* For master's, thesis, internships. *Entrance requirements:* For master's, interview, portfolio. Additional exam requirements/recommendations for international students: Required—TOEFL (minimum score 450 paper-based; 133 computer-based). *Application deadline:* For fall admission, 4/1 priority date for domestic and international students. Applications are processed on a rolling basis. Application fee: $50. Electronic applications accepted. *Expenses:* Tuition: Full-time $24,840; part-time $552 per credit. One-time fee: $500 full-time. *Financial support:* Fellowships, career-related internships or fieldwork, Federal Work-Study, and scholarships/grants available. Financial award application deadline: 4/1; financial award applicants required to submit FAFSA. *Unit head:* Jeremy Moorshead, Chair, 912-525-8527, Fax: 912-525-8597, E-mail: jmoorshe@scad.edu. *Application contact:* Darrell Tutchton, Director of Graduate and International Enrollment, 912-525-5961, Fax: 912-525-5985, E-mail: admission@scad.edu.

Savannah College of Art and Design, Graduate School, Program in Broadcast Design, Savannah, GA 31402-3146. Offers MA, MFA. Part-time programs available. *Faculty:* 3 full-time (0 women), 1 part-time/adjunct (0 women). *Students:* 40 full-time (15 women), 16 part-time (4 women); includes 8 minority (6 African Americans, 1 Asian American or Pacific Islander, 1 Hispanic American), 21 international. 65 applicants, 51% accepted, 17 enrolled. In 2007, 16 degrees awarded. *Degree requirements:* For master's, thesis, internships. *Entrance requirements:* For master's, interview, portfolio. Additional exam requirements/recommendations for international students: Required—TOEFL (minimum score 450 paper-based; 133 computer-based). *Application deadline:* For fall admission, 4/1 priority date for domestic and international students. Applications are processed on a rolling basis. Application fee: $50. Electronic applications accepted. *Expenses:* Tuition: Full-time $24,840; part-time $552 per credit. One-time fee: $500 full-time. *Financial support:* Research assistantships, career-related internships or fieldwork, Federal Work-Study, and scholarships/grants available. Financial award application deadline: 4/1; financial award applicants required to submit FAFSA. *Unit head:* Jill Taffet, Chair, 912-525-8551, E-mail: jtaffet@scad.edu. *Application contact:* Darrell Tutchton, Director of Graduate and International Enrollment, 912-525-5961, Fax: 912-525-5985, E-mail: admission@scad.edu.

Savannah College of Art and Design, Graduate School, Program in Digital Photography, Savannah, GA 31402-3146. Offers MA. Part-time programs available. *Faculty:* 4 full-time (2 women). *Students:* 10 full-time (6 women), 13 part-time (3 women), 1 international. 54 applicants, 35% accepted, 10 enrolled. In 2007, 1 degree awarded. *Degree requirements:* For master's, thesis. *Entrance requirements:* For master's, interview, portfolio. Additional exam requirements/recommendations for international students: Required—TOEFL (minimum score 450 paper-based; 133 computer-based). *Application deadline:* For fall admission, 4/1 priority date for domestic and international students. Applications are processed on a rolling basis. Application fee: $50. Electronic applications accepted. *Expenses:* Tuition: Full-time $24,840; part-time $552 per credit. One-time fee: $500 full-time. *Financial support:* Fellowships, career-related internships or fieldwork, Federal Work-Study, and scholarships/grants available. Financial award application deadline: 4/1; financial award applicants required to submit FAFSA. *Unit head:* Thomas Fischer, Chair, 912-525-6570, Fax: 912-525-3507, E-mail: tfischer@scad.edu. *Application contact:* Darrell Tutchton, Director of Graduate and International Enrollment, 912-525-5961, Fax: 912-525-5985, E-mail: admission@scad.edu.

Savannah College of Art and Design, Graduate School, Program in Interactive Design and Game Development, Savannah, GA 31402-3146. Offers MA, MFA. Part-time programs available. *Faculty:* 8 full-time (1 woman), 1 part-time/adjunct (0 women). *Students:* 43 full-time (16 women), 16 part-time (5 women); includes 6 minority (3 African Americans, 1 Asian American or Pacific Islander, 2 Hispanic Americans), 14 international. Average age 26. 52 applicants, 46% accepted, 11 enrolled. In 2007, 13 degrees awarded. *Degree requirements:* For master's, thesis, internships. *Entrance requirements:* For master's, interview, portfolio. Additional exam requirements/recommendations for international students: Required—TOEFL (minimum score 450 paper-based; 133 computer-based). *Application deadline:* For fall admission, 4/1 priority date for domestic and international students. Applications are processed on a rolling basis. Application fee: $50. Electronic applications accepted. *Expenses:* Tuition: Full-time $24,840; part-time $552 per credit. One-time fee: $500 full-time. *Financial support:* Fellowships, career-related internships or fieldwork, Federal Work-Study, and scholarships/grants available. Financial award application deadline: 4/1; financial award applicants required to submit FAFSA. *Unit head:* Josephine Leong, Chair, 912-525-8523, E-mail: jleong@scad.edu. *Application contact:* Darrell Tutchton, Director of Graduate and International Enrollment, 912-525-5961, Fax: 912-525-5985, E-mail: admission@scad.edu.

School of Visual Arts, Graduate Programs, Computer Art Department, New York, NY 10010-3994. Offers MFA. *Accreditation:* NASAD. *Faculty:* 5 full-time (0 women), 33 part-time/adjunct (11 women). *Students:* 81 full-time (44 women), 15 part-time (10 women); includes 17 minority (6 African Americans, 8 Asian Americans or Pacific Islanders, 3 Hispanic Americans), 57 international. Average age 28. 175 applicants, 59% accepted, 39 enrolled. In 2007, 39 degrees awarded. *Degree requirements:* For master's, final review, project or thesis. *Entrance requirements:* For master's, portfolio. Additional exam requirements/recommendations for international students: Required—TOEFL (minimum score 550 paper-based; 213 computer-based; 79 iBT). *Application deadline:* For fall admission, 2/1 for domestic students. Application fee: $80. Electronic applications accepted. *Expenses:* Tuition: Full-time $26,120; part-time $870 per credit. Tuition and fees vary according to program. *Financial support:* In 2007–08, 44 students received support. Career-related internships or fieldwork, Federal Work-Study, scholarships/grants, and unspecified assistantships available. Support available to part-time students. Financial award application deadline: 2/1; financial award applicants required

Computer Art and Design

School of Visual Arts (continued)
to submit FAFSA. *Unit head:* Bruce Wands, Chair, 212-592-2530, Fax: 212-592-2509, E-mail: bwands@sva.edu.

Stevens Institute of Technology, Graduate School, Charles V. Schaefer Jr. School of Engineering, Department of Computer Science, Hoboken, NJ 07030. Offers computer graphics (Certificate); computer science (MS, PhD); computer systems (Certificate); database management systems (Certificate); distributed systems (Certificate); elements of computer science (Certificate); enterprise computing (Certificate); enterprise security and information assurance (Certificate); health informatics (Certificate); multimedia experience and management (Certificate); networks and systems administration (Certificate); security and privacy (Certificate); service oriented computing (Certificate); software design (Certificate); theoretical computer science (Certificate). Part-time and evening/weekend programs available. Terminal master's awarded for partial completion of doctoral program. *Degree requirements:* For master's, thesis optional; for doctorate, variable foreign language requirement, comprehensive exam, thesis/dissertation. *Entrance requirements:* For master's and doctorate, GRE, minimum GPA of 3.0. Additional exam requirements/recommendations for international students: Required—TOEFL. Electronic applications accepted. *Faculty research:* Semantics, reliability theory, programming language, cyber security.

Syracuse University, Graduate School, College of Visual and Performing Arts, Department of Transmedia, Syracuse, NY 13244. Offers art photography (MFA); art video (MFA); computer art (MFA); film (MFA). *Accreditation:* NASAD. Part-time programs available. *Students:* 32 full-time (17 women), 1 part-time; includes 6 minority (3 African Americans, 2 Asian Americans or Pacific Islanders, 1 Hispanic American), 8 international. 84 applicants, 38% accepted, 17 enrolled. In 2007, 9 degrees awarded. *Degree requirements:* For master's, thesis or alternative. *Entrance requirements:* For master's, portfolio. Additional exam requirements/recommendations for international students: Required—TOEFL. *Application deadline:* For fall admission, 1/1 priority date for domestic students. Applications are processed on a rolling basis. Application fee: $75. Electronic applications accepted. *Expenses:* Tuition: Full-time $18,216; part-time $1,012 per credit. Required fees: $980. Tuition and fees vary according to program. *Financial support:* Fellowships with full tuition reimbursements, research assistantships with full and partial tuition reimbursements, teaching assistantships with full and partial tuition reimbursements, tuition waivers (partial) available. *Unit head:* John Orentlicher, Chair, 315-443-1033, Fax: 315-443-1303, E-mail: jorentli@syr.edu. *Application contact:* Harriett Conti, Associate Director, Graduate Student Services, 315-443-3089, E-mail: hmconti@syr.edu.

Texas State University–San Marcos, Graduate School, College of Fine Arts and Communication, Department of Art and Design, Program in Communication Design, San Marcos, TX 78666. Offers MFA. *Entrance requirements:* For master's, 2.75 GPA on last 60 hours of undergrad work, 20 work portfolio. Additional exam requirements/recommendations for international students: Required—TOEFL (minimum score 550 paper-based; 213 computer-based). *Application deadline:* For fall admission, 3/15 for domestic and international students. Applications are processed on a rolling basis. Application fee: $40 ($90 for international students). Electronic applications accepted. *Expenses:* Tuition, state resident: full-time $3,780; part-time $210 per credit hour. Tuition, nonresident: full-time $8,784; part-time $488 per credit hour. Required fees: $493 per semester. Full-time tuition and fees vary according to course load. *Financial support:* Federal Work-Study and institutionally sponsored loans available. Support available to part-time students. Financial award application deadline: 4/1; financial award applicants required to submit FAFSA. *Unit head:* William Meek, Program Advisor, 512-245-0311, E-mail: w.meek@txstate.edu.

Universidad de las Américas–Puebla, Division of Graduate Studies, School of Humanities, Program in Information Design, Puebla, Mexico. Offers MA. Part-time and evening/weekend programs available. *Degree requirements:* For master's, one foreign language, thesis. *Entrance requirements:* Additional exam requirements/recommendations for international students: Required—TOEFL. *Faculty research:* Typography, project development, organizational image.

University of Baltimore, Graduate School, The Yale Gordon College of Liberal Arts, School of Information Arts and Technologies, Baltimore, MD 21201-5779. Offers communications design (DCD); human-computer interaction (MS); interaction design and information technology (MS). Part-time and evening/weekend programs available. *Faculty:* 6 full-time (3 women), 10 part-time/adjunct (6 women). *Students:* 11 full-time (6 women), 22 part-time (12 women); includes 5 minority (3 African Americans, 2 Asian Americans or Pacific Islanders), 2 international. Average age 34. 8 applicants, 100% accepted, 6 enrolled. In 2007, 5 degrees awarded. *Entrance requirements:* For master's, GRE or MAT, minimum undergraduate GPA of 3.0. Additional exam requirements/recommendations for international students: Required—TOEFL (minimum score 550 paper-based; 213 computer-based). *Application deadline:* For fall admission, 8/1 for domestic students, 6/1 for international students. Application fee: $45. *Expenses:* Tuition, state resident: part-time $518 per credit. Tuition, nonresident: part-time $751 per credit. Tuition and fees vary according to program. *Unit head:* Dr. Kathryn Summers, Director, MS in Interaction Design and Information Architecture, 410-837-6207, E-mail: ksummers@ubalt.edu. *Application contact:* Wendy Bolyard.

University of California, Santa Cruz, Division of Graduate Studies, Division of the Arts, Program in Digital Arts and New Media, Santa Cruz, CA 95064. Offers MFA. *Faculty:* 18 full-time (6 women), 16 part-time/adjunct (4 women). *Students:* 19 full-time (7 women); includes 5 minority (3 Asian Americans or Pacific Islanders, 2 Hispanic Americans). Average age 25. 52 applicants, 37% accepted, 14 enrolled. *Entrance requirements:* Additional exam requirements/recommendations for international students: Required—TOEFL; Recommended—IELTS. *Application deadline:* For fall admission, 2/15 for domestic and international students. Application fee: $60. Electronic applications accepted. *Expenses:* Tuition, nonresident: full-time $14,694. Required fees: $11,360. *Unit head:* Sharon Daniel, Program Chair, 831-459-3948, E-mail: sdaniel@ucsc.edu. *Application contact:* Felicia Rice, Program Manager, 831-459-1554, E-mail: fsrice@ucsc.edu.

University of Central Arkansas, Graduate School, College of Fine Arts and Communication, Program in Digital Filmmaking, Conway, AR 72035-0001. Offers MFA. *Accreditation:* NASAD. *Faculty:* 5 full-time (0 women). *Students:* 14 full-time (1 woman), 2 part-time; includes 1 minority (African American) 11 applicants, 82% accepted, 9 enrolled. *Degree requirements:* For master's, thesis. *Entrance requirements:* For master's, GRE General Test, minimum GPA of 2.7. Additional exam requirements/recommendations for international students: Required—TOEFL (minimum score 550 paper-based; 213 computer-based). *Application deadline:* For fall admission, 3/1 priority date for domestic and international students; for spring admission, 10/1 priority date for domestic and international students. Applications are processed on a rolling basis. Application fee: $25 ($50 for international students). *Expenses:* Tuition, state resident: full-time $4,513; part-time $240 per credit. Tuition, nonresident: full-time $8,805; part-time $440 per credit. International tuition: $9,700 full-time. Required fees: $100 per term. *Financial support:* Unspecified assistantships available. *Unit head:* Dr. Joseph Anderson, Chair, 501-450-3162, E-mail: josepha@uca.edu. *Application contact:* Brenda Herring, Admissions Assistant, 501-450-5065, Fax: 501-450-5678, E-mail: bherring@uca.edu.

University of Central Florida, College of Arts and Humanities, Department of Art, Orlando, FL 32816. Offers studio art and the computer (MFA). *Faculty:* 25 full-time (6 women), 4 part-time/adjunct (2 women). *Students:* 19 applicants, 68% accepted, 10 enrolled. *Expenses:* Tuition, state resident: full-time $6,484. Tuition, nonresident: full-time $23,938. Tuition and fees vary according to program. *Financial support:* Fellowships, research assistantships, teaching assistantships available. *Unit head:* Mark Price, Chair, 407-823-2676, Fax: 407-823-6470, E-mail: maprice@mail.ucf.edu.

University of Central Florida, College of Arts and Humanities, Division of Film and Digital Media, Orlando, FL 32816. Offers entrepreneurial digital cinema (MFA); interactive entertainment (MS); visual language and interactive media (MFA). *Faculty:* 28 full-time (11 women), 8 part-time/adjunct (2 women). *Expenses:* Tuition, state resident: full-time $6,484. Tuition, nonresident: full-time $23,938. Tuition and fees vary according to program. *Financial support:* Fellowships, research assistantships, teaching assistantships available. *Unit head:* Dr. David Vickers, Interim Head, 407-823-1736, E-mail: dvickers@mail.ucf.edu.

University of Denver, Faculty of Arts and Humanities/Social Sciences, School of Art and Art History, Denver, CO 80208. Offers art history (MA); art history/museum studies (MA); electronic media arts and design (MFA); studio art (MFA). *Accreditation:* NASAD. Part-time programs available. *Faculty:* 15 full-time (10 women). *Students:* 24 full-time (20 women), 2 part-time (1 woman); includes 2 minority (1 Asian American or Pacific Islander, 1 Hispanic American), 1 international. Average age 28. In 2007, 10 degrees awarded. *Degree requirements:* For master's, one foreign language, research paper. *Entrance requirements:* For master's, GRE. Additional exam requirements/recommendations for international students: Required—TOEFL. *Application deadline:* Applications are processed on a rolling basis. Application fee: $50. Electronic applications accepted. *Financial support:* In 2007–08, 5 teaching assistantships with full and partial tuition reimbursements (averaging $6,500 per year) were awarded; career-related internships or fieldwork, Federal Work-Study, institutionally sponsored loans, and scholarships/grants also available. Support available to part-time students. Financial award application deadline: 3/1; financial award applicants required to submit FAFSA. *Faculty research:* Images of women in alchemical manuscripts and books, Giovanni Benedetto, Salvatore Castiglione. *Unit head:* Dr. Annette Stott, Director, 303-871-2846. *Application contact:* Dr. M. Warlick, Graduate Advisor, 303-871-2846, E-mail: saah-interest@du.edu.

University of Florida, Graduate School, College of Engineering and College of Liberal Arts and Sciences, Department of Computer and Information Science and Engineering, Gainesville, FL 32611. Offers computer engineering (ME, MS, PhD); computer science (MS); digital arts and sciences (MS). Part-time programs available. *Faculty:* 31 full-time (4 women). *Students:* 421 (92 women); includes 20 minority (2 African Americans, 9 Asian Americans or Pacific Islanders, 9 Hispanic Americans) 357 international. In 2007, 79 master's, 15 doctorates awarded. *Degree requirements:* For master's, thesis (for some programs); for doctorate, thesis/dissertation. *Entrance requirements:* For master's and doctorate, GRE General Test, minimum GPA of 3.0. Additional exam requirements/recommendations for international students: Required—TOEFL (minimum score 550 paper-based; 213 computer-based). *Application deadline:* For fall admission, 6/1 priority date for domestic students; for spring admission, 11/1 for domestic students. Applications are processed on a rolling basis. Application fee: $30. Electronic applications accepted. *Expenses:* Tuition, state resident: full-time $7,478. Tuition, nonresident: full-time $22,603. *Financial support:* In 2007–08, 54 research assistantships (averaging $13,197 per year), 78 teaching assistantships (averaging $14,034 per year) were awarded; fellowships, unspecified assistantships also available. Financial award application deadline: 6/1. *Faculty research:* Artificial intelligence, networks security, distributed computing, parallel processing system, vision and visualization, database systems. *Unit head:* Dr. Sartaj Sahni, Chair, 352-392-1527, Fax: 352-392-1220, E-mail: sahni@cise.ufl.edu. *Application contact:* Dr. Jih-Kwon Peir, Graduate Coordinator, 352-392-1044, Fax: 352-392-1220, E-mail: peir@cise.ufl.edu.

University of Florida, Graduate School, College of Fine Arts, School of Art and Art History, Gainesville, FL 32611. Offers art (MFA), including ceramics, creative photography, drawing, electronic intermedia, graphic design, painting, printmaking, sculpture; art education (MA); art history (MA, PhD); digital arts and sciences (MA); museology (museum studies) (MA). *Accreditation:* NASAD. *Faculty:* 29 full-time (14 women), 2 part-time/adjunct (1 woman). *Students:* 82 (48 women); includes 4 minority (2 Asian Americans or Pacific Islanders, 2 Hispanic Americans) 4 international. In 2007, 20 degrees awarded. *Degree requirements:* For master's, variable foreign language requirement, project or thesis (MFA). *Entrance requirements:* For master's, portfolio (MFA), writing sample (MA), GRE General Test or minimum GPA of 3.0. Additional exam requirements/recommendations for international students: Required—TOEFL (minimum score 550 paper-based; 213 computer-based). *Application deadline:* For fall admission, 1/15 priority date for domestic students. Applications are processed on a rolling basis. Application fee: $30. Electronic applications accepted. *Expenses:* Tuition, state resident: full-time $7,478. Tuition, nonresident: full-time $22,603. *Financial support:* In 2007–08, 3 research assistantships with tuition reimbursements (averaging $9,515 per year), 67 teaching assistantships with tuition reimbursements (averaging $9,839 per year) were awarded; fellowships, Federal Work-Study, institutionally sponsored loans, and unspecified assistantships also available. Financial award applicants required to submit FAFSA. *Faculty research:* Studio production, art historical studies of style context. *Unit head:* Glenn Willumson, Program Director, 352-392-0201 Ext. 234. *Application contact:* Prof. Richard Heipp, Coordinator, 352-392-0201 Ext. 239, Fax: 352-392-8453, E-mail: heipp@ufl.edu.

University of Kansas, Research and Graduate Studies, School of Fine Arts, Department of Design, Lawrence, KS 66045. Offers design (MA, MFA); design management (MA); interaction design (MA); visual arts education (MA). *Accreditation:* NASAD (one or more programs are accredited). *Faculty:* 29. *Students:* 23 full-time (14 women), 5 part-time (all women), 1 international. Average age 30. 33 applicants, 39% accepted, 10 enrolled. In 2007, 10 degrees awarded. *Degree requirements:* For master's, thesis, oral exam. *Entrance requirements:* For master's, portfolio, 3 letters of recommendation, minimum GPA of 3.0. Additional exam requirements/recommendations for international students: Required—TOEFL, IELTS. *Application deadline:* For fall admission, 2/1 for domestic and international students; for spring admission, 10/15 for domestic students. Application fee: $55 ($60 for international students). Electronic applications accepted. *Expenses:* Tuition, state resident: full-time $5,838. Tuition, nonresident: full-time $13,409. Tuition and fees vary according to program. *Financial support:* Fellowships, teaching assistantships with full and partial tuition reimbursements, Federal Work-Study, scholarships/grants, and unspecified assistantships available. Financial award application deadline: 2/1; financial award applicants required to submit FAFSA. *Faculty research:* Crafts, interaction design, design management, scenography. *Unit head:* Prof. Gregory Thomas, Chairperson, 785-864-4401. *Application contact:* Gina Westergard, Director, 785-864-4401, Fax: 785-864-4404, E-mail: ginaw@ku.edu.

University of Massachusetts Dartmouth, Graduate School, College of Visual and Performing Arts, Program in Visual Design, North Dartmouth, MA 02747-2300. Offers digital multi-media (MFA); electronic imaging (MFA); graphic design (MFA); illustration (MFA); photography (MFA); typography (MFA). *Accreditation:* NASAD. *Faculty:* 17 full-time (7 women), 7 part-time/adjunct (3 women). *Students:* 8 full-time (6 women), 2 part-time (both women); includes 1 minority (Asian American or Pacific Islander), 2 international. Average age 35. 21 applicants, 24% accepted, 4 enrolled. In 2007, 3 degrees awarded. *Degree requirements:* For master's, visual thesis. *Entrance requirements:* For master's, portfolio, interview, minimum GPA of 3.0, 3 letters of recommendation. Additional exam requirements/recommendations for international students: Required—TOEFL (minimum score 500 paper-based). *Application deadline:* For fall admission, 3/1 priority date for domestic students, 1/1 priority date for international students. Applications are processed on a rolling basis. Application fee: $40 ($60 for international students). Electronic applications accepted. *Expenses:* Tuition, state resident: full-time $2,071; part-time $86 per credit. Tuition, nonresident: full-time $8,099; part-time $337 per credit. Part-time tuition and fees vary according to course load and program. *Financial support:* In 2007–08, 4 teaching assistantships (averaging $2,930 per year) were awarded; research assistantships, Federal Work-Study and unspecified assistantships also available. Support available to part-time students. Financial award application deadline: 3/1; financial award applicants required to submit FAFSA. Total annual research expenditures: $22,880. *Unit head:* Jarrad Nunes, Director, 508-999-8010, E-mail: jnunes@umassd.edu. *Application contact:* Carol Novo, Graduate Admissions Officer, 508-999-8604, Fax: 508-999-8183, E-mail: graduate@umassd.edu.

University of Missouri–Columbia, Graduate School, College of Human Environmental Science, Department of Architectural Studies, Columbia, MO 65211. Offers design with digital media (MA, MS); environmental design (MS). *Entrance requirements:* For master's, GRE General Test, minimum GPA of 3.0. Additional exam requirements/recommendations for international students: Required—TOEFL (minimum score 500 paper-based; 173 computer-based).

University of Pennsylvania, School of Engineering and Applied Science, Computer Graphics and Game Technology Program, Philadelphia, PA 19104. Offers MSE.

University of Victoria, Faculty of Graduate Studies, Faculty of Fine Arts, Department of Visual Arts, Victoria, BC V8W 2Y2, Canada. Offers digital multimedia (MFA); drawing (MFA); painting (MFA); photography (MFA); sculpture (MFA); video (MFA). *Faculty:* 8 full-time (4 women). *Students:* 10 full-time (7 women), 2 international. Average age 27. 72 applicants, 7% accepted. In 2007, 4 degrees awarded. *Degree requirements:* For master's, exhibit, oral exam. *Entrance requirements:* For master's, portfolio, BFA. Additional exam requirements/recommendations for international students: Required—TOEFL (minimum score 575 paper-based; 233 computer-based), IELTS (minimum score 7). *Application deadline:* For fall admission, 2/28 for domestic students, 12/15 priority date for international students. Applications are processed on a rolling basis. Application fee: $75 ($125 for international students). Electronic applications accepted. *Expenses:* Tuition, state resident: full-time $3,110. International tuition: $3,700 full-time. Tuition and fees vary according to program. *Financial support:* In 2007–08, 10 students received support, including 2 fellowships (averaging $13,400 per year), 7 teaching assistantships (averaging $6,000 per year); research assistantships, institutionally sponsored loans and scholarships/grants also available. Financial award application deadline: 2/15. *Unit head:* Allan Stichbury, Acting Chair, 250-721-8011, Fax: 250-721-6595, E-mail: astichbu@finearts.uvic.ca. *Application contact:* Nedra Tremblay, Graduate Secretary, 250-721-8011, Fax: 250-721-6595, E-mail: ntrembla@finearts.uvic.ca.

Washington State University, Graduate School, College of Liberal Arts, Department of Fine Arts, Pullman, WA 99164. Offers ceramics (MFA); digital media (MFA); drawing (MFA); painting (MFA); photography (MFA); print making (MFA); sculpture (MFA). *Faculty:* 16. *Students:* 16 full-time (6 women), 1 part-time; includes 1 minority (American Indian/Alaska Native), 2 international. Average age 29. 33 applicants, 30% accepted, 8 enrolled. In 2007, 8 degrees awarded. *Degree requirements:* For master's, comprehensive exam (for some programs), thesis, exhibit, oral exam. *Entrance requirements:* For master's, GRE, minimum GPA of 3.0, portfolio, 3 letters of recommendation. Additional exam requirements/recommendations for international students: Required—TOEFL (minimum score 550 paper-based; 213 computer-based). *Application deadline:* For fall admission, 1/15 for domestic and international students. Application fee: $50. Electronic applications accepted. *Financial support:* In 2007–08, fellowships with full and partial tuition reimbursements (averaging $3,114 per year), research assistantships with full and partial tuition reimbursements (averaging $13,917 per year), teaching assistantships with full and partial tuition reimbursements (averaging $13,056 per year) were awarded; career-related internships or fieldwork, Federal Work-Study, institutionally sponsored loans, tuition waivers (partial), and unspecified assistantships also available. Financial award application deadline: 4/1; financial award applicants required to submit FAFSA. *Faculty research:* Polynesian art, museum representation, number theory. *Unit head:* Dr. Carol Ivory, Chair, 509-335-7043, Fax: 509-335-7742, E-mail: ivorycs@wsu.edu. *Application contact:* Graduate School Admissions, 800-GRADWSU, Fax: 509-335-1949, E-mail: gradsch@wsu.edu.

Graphic Design

Academy of Art University, Graduate Program, School of Graphic Design, San Francisco, CA 94105-3410. Offers MFA. *Accreditation:* NASAD. Part-time programs available. Post-baccalaureate distance learning degree programs offered (no on-campus study). *Degree requirements:* For master's, final review. *Entrance requirements:* For master's, minimum GPA of 3.0, portfolio. Electronic applications accepted.

Atlantic College, Program in Graphic Arts, Guaynabo, PR 00970. Offers digital graphic design (MA, UA Undergraduate Associate). Part-time programs available. *Faculty:* 6 full-time (1 woman), 6 part-time/adjunct (3 women). *Students:* 47 full-time (43 women), 37 part-time (29 women); all Hispanic Americans 25 applicants, 100% accepted, 20 enrolled. In 2007, 29 degrees awarded. *Degree requirements:* For master's, thesis. *Entrance requirements:* For master's, minimum GPA of 3.0, 2 letters of recommendation, portfolio, interview. Application fee: $50. *Expenses:* Tuition: Full-time $6,240; part-time $170 per credit. Required fees: $170 per credit. $150 per term. *Financial support:* Federal Work-Study available. *Faculty research:* Digital design, technology. *Unit head:* Prof. Frances Grau Cesani, Dean of Graduate Program, 787-720-1022 Ext. 1003, Fax: 787-720-1092, E-mail: atlancol@coqui.net. *Application contact:* Zaida Perez, Information Contact, 787-720-0596, Fax: 787-720-1092, E-mail: admisiones@atlanticcollege.edu.

Bob Jones University, Graduate Programs, Greenville, SC 29614. Offers accountancy (MS); Bible (MA); Bible translation (MA); Biblical studies (Certificate); broadcast management (MS); business administration (MBA); church history (MA, PhD); church ministries (MA); church music (MM); cinema and video production (MA); counseling (MS); curriculum and instruction (Ed D); divinity (M Div); dramatic production (MA); educational leadership (MS, Ed D, Ed S); elementary education (M Ed, MAT); English (M Ed, MA, MAT); fine arts (MA); graphic design (MA); history (M Ed, MA); illustration (MA); interpretative speech (MA); mathematics (M Ed, MAT); medical missions (Certificate); ministry (MM, D Min); multi-categorical special education (M Ed, MAT); music (M Ed); New Testament interpretation (PhD); Old Testament interpretation (PhD); orchestral instrument performance (MM); organ performance (MM); pastoral studies (MA); personnel services (MS, Ed S); piano pedagogy (MM); piano performance (MM); platform arts (MA); radio and television broadcasting (MS); rhetoric and public address (MA); secondary education (M Ed); studio art (MA); teaching Bible (MA); theology (MA, PhD); voice performance (MM); youth ministries (MA); M Div/MM.

Boston University, College of Fine Arts, School of Visual Arts, Program in Graphic Design, Boston, MA 02215. Offers MFA. *Students:* 26 full-time (23 women), 3 part-time (all women), 13 international. Average age 27. 65 applicants, 42% accepted, 15 enrolled. In 2007, 15 degrees awarded. *Entrance requirements:* For master's, portfolio. Additional exam requirements/recommendations for international students: Required—TOEFL. *Application deadline:* For fall admission, 2/15 for domestic students, 2/15 priority date for international students. Applications are processed on a rolling basis. Application fee: $70. *Expenses:* Tuition: Full-time $34,930; part-time $1,092 per credit. Tuition and fees vary according to class time, course level and program. *Financial support:* Fellowships, teaching assistantships available. Financial award application deadline: 2/15. *Unit head:* Alston Purvis, Chairman, 617-353-3371, E-mail: apurvis@bu.edu. *Application contact:* Mark Krone, Manager, Graduate Admissions, 617-353-3350, E-mail: arts@bu.edu.

Bowling Green State University, Graduate College, College of Arts and Sciences, School of Art, Bowling Green, OH 43403. Offers 2-D studio art (MA, MFA); 3-D studio art (MA, MFA); art education (MA); art history (MA); computer art (MA); design (MFA); digital arts (MFA); graphics (MFA). *Accreditation:* NASAD. Part-time programs available. *Faculty:* 26 full-time (14 women), 7 part-time/adjunct (2 women). *Students:* 24 full-time (12 women), 3 part-time (all women); includes 1 minority (Asian American or Pacific Islander), 2 international. Average age 33. 59 applicants, 20% accepted, 8 enrolled. In 2007, 11 degrees awarded. *Degree requirements:* For master's, thesis or alternative, final exhibit (MFA). *Entrance requirements:* For master's, GRE General Test (MA), slide portfolio (15-20 slides). Additional exam requirements/recommendations for international students: Required—TOEFL. *Application deadline:* For fall admission, 2/15 for domestic students. Application fee: $30. Electronic applications accepted. *Financial support:* In 2007–08, 11 research assistantships with full and partial tuition reimbursements (averaging $8,404 per year), 8 teaching assistantships with full and partial tuition reimbursements (averaging $8,404 per year) were awarded; career-related internships or fieldwork, institutionally sponsored loans, and unspecified assistantships also available. Support available to part-time students. Financial award applicants required to submit FAFSA. *Faculty research:* Computer animation and virtual reality, Spanish still-life painting from 1600 to 1800, art and psychotherapy, Japanese wood-firing techniques in ceramics, non-toxic printmaking technologies. *Unit head:* Dr. Katerina Rüedi Ray, Director, 419-372-8575. *Application contact:* Shawn Morin, Graduate Coordinator, 419-372-7766.

California Institute of the Arts, School of Art, Valencia, CA 91355-2340. Offers art (MFA, Adv C); graphic design (MFA, Adv C); photography (MFA, Adv C). *Accreditation:* NASAD (one or more programs are accredited). *Degree requirements:* For master's, final project. *Entrance requirements:* For master's, portfolio. Additional exam requirements/recommendations for international students: Required—TOEFL. Electronic applications accepted.

California State University, Los Angeles, Graduate Studies, College of Arts and Letters, Department of Art, Los Angeles, CA 90032-8530. Offers art (MA), including art education, art history, art therapy, ceramics, metals, and textiles, design (MA, MFA), painting, sculpture, and graphic arts, photography; fine arts (MFA), including crafts, design (MA, MFA), studio arts. *Accreditation:* NASAD (one or more programs are accredited). Part-time and evening/weekend programs available. *Faculty:* 7 full-time (3 women). *Students:* 24 full-time (13 women), 59 part-time (42 women); includes 19 minority (2 African Americans, 1 American Indian/Alaska Native, 5 Asian Americans or Pacific Islanders, 11 Hispanic Americans), 16 international. Average age 39. In 2007, 28 degrees awarded. *Degree requirements:* For master's, comprehensive exam, project or thesis. *Entrance requirements:* For master's, portfolio. Additional exam requirements/recommendations for international students: Required—TOEFL. *Application deadline:* For fall admission, 6/30 for domestic students; for spring admission, 2/1 for domestic students. Applications are processed on a rolling basis. Application fee: $55. *Financial support:* Federal Work-Study available. Support available to part-time students. Financial award application deadline: 3/1. *Faculty research:* The artist and the book, conceptual art, ceramic processes, computer graphics, architectural graphics. *Unit head:* Dr. Robert Martin, Chair, 323-343-4010, Fax: 323-343-4045, E-mail: rjmartin@calstatela.edu.

Cardinal Stritch University, College of Arts and Sciences, Department of Art, Milwaukee, WI 53217-3985. Offers visual studies (MA). Part-time and evening/weekend programs available. *Degree requirements:* For master's, thesis, portfolio, exhibit. *Entrance requirements:* For master's, minimum GPA of 2.75; 3 letters of recommendation.

City College of the City University of New York, Graduate School, College of Liberal Arts and Science, Division of the Humanities and Arts, Department of Art, Program in Fine Arts, New York, NY 10031-9198. Offers advertising design (MFA); ceramic design (MFA); painting (MFA); printmaking (MFA); sculpture (MFA); wood and metal design (MFA). *Students:* 4. 19 applicants, 42% accepted, 4 enrolled. *Degree requirements:* For master's, thesis exhibit. *Entrance requirements:* For master's, 20 slide portfolio. Additional exam requirements/recommendations for international students: Required—TOEFL (minimum score 575 paper-based; 233 computer-based). *Application deadline:* For fall admission, 4/1 for domestic students; for spring admission, 11/1 for domestic students. Application fee: $125. *Financial support:* Fellowships, teaching assistantships, career-related internships or fieldwork, Federal Work-Study, institutionally sponsored loans, scholarships/grants, and tuition waivers (partial) available. Support available to part-time students. Financial award application deadline: 3/1. *Unit head:* Megan Foster, Head, 212-650-7425.

The College of New Rochelle, Graduate School, Division of Art and Communication Studies, Program in Studio Art, New Rochelle, NY 10805-2308. Offers MS. Part-time and evening/weekend programs available. *Faculty:* 1 full-time (0 women), 9 part-time/adjunct (7 women). *Students:* 2 full-time (both women), 10 part-time (9 women); includes 2 minority (1 African American, 1 Hispanic American). Average age 37. In 2007, 11 degrees awarded. *Degree requirements:* For master's, apprenticeship. *Entrance requirements:* For master's, portfolio, 36 credits of course work in studio art. *Application deadline:* For fall admission, 8/1 priority date for domestic students. Applications are processed on a rolling basis. Application fee: $35. *Expenses:* Tuition: Part-time $650 per credit. Required fees: $90 per term. *Financial support:* Career-related internships or fieldwork, scholarships/grants, tuition waivers (partial), and unspecified assistantships available. Support available to part-time students. *Faculty research:* Experimental computer graphics. *Unit head:* Dr. John Patton, Head, Division of Art and Communication Studies, 914-654-5208, Fax: 914-654-5593.

Cranbrook Academy of Art, Graduate School, Program in Fine Arts, Bloomfield Hills, MI 48303-0801. Offers ceramics (MFA); design (MFA), including graphic design; fiber arts (MFA); metalsmithing (MFA); painting (MFA); photography (MFA); printmaking (MFA); sculpture (MFA). *Accreditation:* NASAD. *Degree requirements:* For master's, thesis, exhibit. *Entrance requirements:* Additional exam requirements/recommendations for international students: Required—TOEFL (minimum score 550 paper-based; 213 computer-based).

See Close-Up on page 237.

Digital Media Arts College, Graduate Programs, Boca Raton, FL 33431. Offers graphic design (MFA); special FX animation (MFA).

George Mason University, College of Visual and Performing Arts, Program in Visual Technologies, Fairfax, VA 22030. Offers art and visual technology (MA, MFA); art education (MAT). *Faculty:* 21 full-time (11 women), 28 part-time/adjunct (14 women). *Students:* 11 full-time (8 women), 7 part-time (4 women); includes 4 minority (2 African Americans, 1 Asian American or Pacific Islander, 1 Hispanic American). Average age 33. 46 applicants, 26% accepted, 9 enrolled. In 2007, 7 degrees awarded. *Degree requirements:* For master's, thesis, apprenticeship in business. *Entrance requirements:* For master's, GRE General Test, minimum GPA of 3.0 in last 60 hours of course work, portfolio. *Application deadline:* For fall admission, 5/1 for domestic students; for spring admission, 11/1 for domestic students. Application fee: $60 ($75 for international students). Electronic applications accepted. *Financial support:* Teaching assistantships, career-related internships or fieldwork and Federal Work-Study available. Support available to part-time students. Financial award application deadline: 3/1; financial award applicants required to submit FAFSA. *Unit head:* Dr. Scott M. Martin, Director, 703-993-4574, Fax: 703-993-8798, E-mail: avt@gmu.edu.

Illinois State University, Graduate School, College of Fine Arts, School of Art, Normal, IL 61790-2200. Offers art history (MA, MS); ceramics (MFA, MS); drawing (MFA, MS); fibers (MFA, MS); glass (MFA, MS); graphic design (MFA, MS); metals (MFA, MS); painting (MFA, MS); photography (MFA, MS); printmaking (MFA, MS); sculpture (MFA, MS). *Accreditation:* NASAD (one or more programs are accredited). *Faculty:* 30 full-time (12 women). *Students:* 31 full-time (20 women), 5 part-time (4 women); includes 3 minority (1 African American, 2 Hispanic Americans), 3 international. 62 applicants, 29% accepted. In 2007, 17 degrees awarded. *Degree requirements:* For master's, thesis or alternative, internship. *Entrance requirements:* For master's, portfolio, sample of scholarly writing. *Application deadline:* Applications are processed on a rolling basis. Application fee: $40. *Expenses:* Tuition, state resident: full-time $3,492; part-time $194 per credit hour. Tuition, nonresident: full-time $7,272; part-time $404

Graphic Design

Illinois State University (continued)
per credit hour. Required fees: $1,024; $57 per credit hour. *Financial support:* In 2007–08, 23 teaching assistantships (averaging $6,661 per year) were awarded; career-related internships or fieldwork, Federal Work-Study, tuition waivers (full and partial), and unspecified assistantships also available. Support available to part-time students. Financial award application deadline: 4/1. *Faculty research:* General operations support: Normal Editions Workshop for FY2007. Total annual research expenditures: $4,160. *Unit head:* James Crowley, Chairperson, 309-438-5621.

Indiana State University, School of Graduate Studies, College of Arts and Sciences, Department of Art, Terre Haute, IN 47809-1401. Offers ceramics (MA, MFA); drawing (MA, MFA); graphic design (MA, MFA); painting (MA, MFA); photography (MA, MFA); printmaking (MA, MFA); sculpture (MA, MFA). *Accreditation:* NASAD (one or more programs are accredited). Part-time programs available. *Faculty:* 10 full-time (3 women), 1 part-time/adjunct (0 women). *Students:* 16 full-time (9 women), 9 part-time (1 woman); includes 1 minority (Hispanic American), 8 international. Average age 35. 17 applicants, 65% accepted, 6 enrolled. In 2007, 7 degrees awarded. *Degree requirements:* For master's, thesis or alternative, departmental qualifying exam. *Entrance requirements:* For master's, portfolio. Additional exam requirements/recommendations for international students: Required—TOEFL (minimum score 550 paper-based). *Application deadline:* For fall admission, 7/1 priority date for domestic students; for spring admission, 11/1 priority date for domestic students. Applications are processed on a rolling basis. Application fee: $35. *Expenses:* Tuition, state resident: full-time $7,056; part-time $294 per semester hour. Tuition, nonresident: full-time $14,016; part-time $584 per semester hour. Required fees: $175 per semester. *Financial support:* In 2007–08, 7 teaching assistantships with partial tuition reimbursements (averaging $7,200 per year) were awarded; career-related internships or fieldwork, Federal Work-Study, institutionally sponsored loans, scholarships/grants, and tuition waivers (partial) also available. Support available to part-time students. Financial award application deadline: 3/1; financial award applicants required to submit FAFSA. *Unit head:* Dr. Alden Cavanaugh, Chairperson, 812-237-3698.

Iowa State University of Science and Technology, Graduate College, College of Design, Department of Art and Design, Ames, IA 50011. Offers art and design (MA); art education (MA); graphic design (MFA); integrated visual arts (MFA); interior design (MFA). Part-time programs available. *Faculty:* 38 full-time (22 women). *Students:* 39 full-time (28 women), 4 part-time (1 woman); includes 3 minority (all Asian Americans or Pacific Islanders), 12 international. 35 applicants, 63% accepted, 12 enrolled. In 2007, 11 degrees awarded. *Degree requirements:* For master's, thesis (for some programs). *Entrance requirements:* For master's, portfolio, resumé. Additional exam requirements/recommendations for international students: Required—TOEFL (paper-based 550; computer-based 213) or IELTS (score 6.5). *Application deadline:* For fall admission, 5/1 priority date for domestic and international students. Applications are processed on a rolling basis. Application fee: $30 ($70 for international students). Electronic applications accepted. *Financial support:* In 2007–08, 5 research assistantships with full and partial tuition reimbursements (averaging $20,058 per year), 2 teaching assistantships with full and partial tuition reimbursements (averaging $18,288 per year) were awarded; career-related internships or fieldwork, Federal Work-Study, institutionally sponsored loans, and tuition waivers (partial) also available. Support available to part-time students. Financial award application deadline: 2/15; financial award applicants required to submit FAFSA. *Faculty research:* Computer applications, fire safety, human factors in design, art and design education, fine arts, craft design. *Unit head:* Roger Baer, Chair, 515-294-6724, Fax: 515-294-2725, E-mail: artdn@iastate.edu.

Kean University, School of Visual and Performing Arts, Program in Graphic Communication Technology Management, Union, NJ 07083. Offers MS. Part-time and evening/weekend programs available. *Faculty:* 13 full-time (4 women). *Students:* 17 full-time (11 women), 18 part-time (7 women); includes 4 African Americans, 2 Asian Americans or Pacific Islanders, 4 Hispanic Americans, 4 international. Average age 29. 10 applicants, 100% accepted, 7 enrolled. In 2007, 8 degrees awarded. *Degree requirements:* For master's, research. *Entrance requirements:* For master's, 2 letters of recommendation, minimum GPA of 3.0, departmental interview. *Application deadline:* For fall admission, 5/1 for domestic students; for spring admission, 11/1 for domestic students. Application fee: $60 ($150 for international students). Electronic applications accepted. *Expenses:* Tuition, state resident: full-time $9,384; part-time $391 per credit. Tuition, nonresident: full-time $12,720; part-time $530 per credit. Required fees: $2,382; $99 per credit. Part-time tuition and fees vary according to course load. *Financial support:* In 2007–08, 11 research assistantships with full tuition reimbursements (averaging $3,217 per year) were awarded; unspecified assistantships also available. *Unit head:* Dr. Cyril Nwako, Program Coordinator, 908-737-3538, E-mail: cnwako@kean.edu. *Application contact:* Joanne Morris, Director of Graduate Admissions, 908-737-3355, Fax: 908-737-3354, E-mail: grad-adm@kean.edu.

Kent State University, College of Communication and Information, School of Visual Communication Design, Kent, OH 44242-0001. Offers MA, MFA. *Accreditation:* NASAD. Part-time programs available. *Faculty:* 10 full-time (1 woman), 1 (woman) part-time/adjunct. *Students:* 11 full-time (2 women), 21 part-time (12 women); includes 3 minority (2 African Americans, 1 Hispanic American). Average age 25. 34 applicants, 44% accepted, 11 enrolled. In 2007, 7 degrees awarded. *Degree requirements:* For master's, thesis, portfolios. *Entrance requirements:* For master's, portfolio (studio majors), minimum GPA of 2.75, GPA of 3.0 in major. *Application deadline:* For fall admission, 7/12 for domestic students; for spring admission, 11/29 for domestic students. Applications are processed on a rolling basis. Application fee: $30. *Financial support:* In 2007–08, 1 research assistantship with full and partial tuition reimbursement (averaging $12,948 per year), 5 teaching assistantships with full and partial tuition reimbursements (averaging $12,948 per year) were awarded; career-related internships or fieldwork, Federal Work-Study, institutionally sponsored loans, health care benefits, tuition waivers (full and partial), and unspecified assistantships also available. Financial award application deadline: 2/1. *Faculty research:* Graphic design. Total annual research expenditures: $20,000. *Unit head:* Ann Marie LeBlanc, Director, 330-672-7856, Fax: 330-672-9714, E-mail: aleblanc@kent.edu. *Application contact:* Steven R. Timbrook, Graduate Coordinator, 330-672-7856, Fax: 330-672-9714, E-mail: stimbroo@kent.edu.

Louisiana State University and Agricultural and Mechanical College, Graduate School, College of Art and Design, School of Art, Program in Studio Art, Baton Rouge, LA 70803. Offers ceramics (MFA); graphic design (MFA); painting and drawing (MFA); photography (MFA); printmaking (MFA); sculpture (MFA). *Accreditation:* NASAD. *Students:* 47 full-time (29 women), 4 part-time (2 women); includes 1 African American, 1 Hispanic American, 6 international. 63 applicants, 25% accepted. In 2007, 16 degrees awarded. *Degree requirements:* For master's, thesis. *Entrance requirements:* For master's, minimum GPA of 3.0. Additional exam requirements/recommendations for international students: Required—TOEFL (minimum score 550 paper-based; 213 computer-based; 79 iBT). *Application deadline:* For fall admission, 1/25 priority date for domestic students, 5/15 for international students; for spring admission, 10/15 for international students. Applications are processed on a rolling basis. Electronic applications accepted. *Financial support:* In 2007–08, 25 students received support; research assistantships with partial tuition reimbursements available, teaching assistantships, career-related internships or fieldwork, Federal Work-Study, institutionally sponsored loans, scholarships/grants, and unspecified assistantships available. Support available to part-time students. Financial award application deadline: 3/15. *Unit head:* Chris Johns, Graduate Coordinator, 225-578-5411, Fax: 225-578-1445, E-mail: cjohns@lsu.edu.

Louisiana Tech University, Graduate School, College of Liberal Arts, School of Art, Ruston, LA 71272. Offers art and graphic design (MFA); photography (MFA); studio art (MFA). *Accreditation:* NASAD. Part-time programs available. *Degree requirements:* For master's, exhibit. *Entrance requirements:* For master's, GRE General Test, portfolio. *Application deadline:* For fall admission, 7/29 for domestic students; for spring admission, 2/3 for domestic students. Applications are processed on a rolling basis. Application fee: $20 ($30 for international students). *Financial support:* Fellowships, career-related internships or fieldwork, Federal Work-Study, institutionally sponsored loans, and unspecified assistantships available. Financial award application deadline: 2/1. *Unit head:* Jonathan Donchoo, Director, 318-257-3909, Fax: 318-257-4890.

Maryland Institute College of Art, Graduate Studies, Program in Graphic Design, Baltimore, MD 21217. Offers MFA. *Faculty:* 2 full-time (both women), 1 part-time/adjunct (0 women). *Students:* 16 full-time (10 women); includes 4 minority (3 Asian Americans or Pacific Islanders, 1 Hispanic American), 2 international. Average age 29. In 2007, 8 degrees awarded. *Degree requirements:* For master's, thesis, exhibit. *Entrance requirements:* For master's, 40 credits in studio art, 6 credits in art history, portfolio. Additional exam requirements/recommendations for international students: Required—TOEFL (minimum score 550 paper-based; 213 computer-based). *Application deadline:* For fall admission, 2/15 for domestic and international students. Application fee: $50. *Expenses:* Tuition: Full-time $29,700; part-time $1,238 per credit. Required fees: $980; $490 per term. *Financial support:* In 2007–08, 16 students received support, including 1 fellowship (averaging $15,680 per year), teaching assistantships (averaging $1,500 per year); career-related internships or fieldwork and scholarships/grants also available. Financial award application deadline: 3/1; financial award applicants required to submit FAFSA. *Unit head:* Ellen Lupton, Director, 410-225-2382, Fax: 410-669-1141. *Application contact:* Scott G. Kelly, Associate Dean of Graduate Admission, 410-225-2256, Fax: 410-225-2408, E-mail: graduate@mica.edu.

Marywood University, Academic Affairs, Insalaco College of Creative Arts and Management, Art Department, Program in Studio Art, Scranton, PA 18509-1598. Offers advertising design (MA); ceramics (MA); clay (MA); graphic design (MA); illustration (MA); interior architecture (MA); painting (MA); photography (MA); printmaking (MA); sculpture (MA); weaving (MA). *Accreditation:* NASAD. Part-time and evening/weekend programs available. *Students:* 5 full-time (3 women), 15 part-time (11 women), 1 international. Average age 41. 5 applicants, 80% accepted. In 2007, 7 degrees awarded. *Degree requirements:* For master's, comprehensive exam, thesis or alternative. *Entrance requirements:* For master's, portfolio. Additional exam requirements/recommendations for international students: Required—TOEFL (minimum score 550 paper-based; 213 computer-based). *Application deadline:* For fall admission, 4/15 priority date for domestic and international students; for spring admission, 11/15 priority date for domestic and international students. Applications are processed on a rolling basis. Application fee: $30. Electronic applications accepted. *Expenses:* Tuition: Full-time $15,290; part-time $695 per credit. Required fees: $990; $370 per term. Tuition and fees vary according to degree level. *Financial support:* Research assistantships with tuition reimbursements, scholarships/grants, tuition waivers (partial), and unspecified assistantships available. Support available to part-time students. Financial award application deadline: 2/15; financial award applicants required to submit FAFSA. *Faculty research:* Texture and line in clay, cast bronze sculpture, color theories, book art and illustration, sculptural form.

Marywood University, Academic Affairs, Insalaco College of Creative Arts and Management, Art Department, Program in Visual Arts, Scranton, PA 18509-1598. Offers advertising design (MFA); clay (MFA); fibers (MFA); graphic design (MFA); illustration (MFA); metals (MFA); painting (MFA); photography (MFA); printmaking (MFA). *Accreditation:* NASAD. Part-time and evening/weekend programs available. *Students:* 13 full-time (10 women), 25 part-time (13 women); includes 2 minority (1 American Indian/Alaska Native, 1 Asian American or Pacific Islander), 3 international. Average age 35. In 2007, 11 degrees awarded. *Degree requirements:* For master's, thesis or alternative, exhibit. *Entrance requirements:* For master's, portfolio. Additional exam requirements/recommendations for international students: Required—TOEFL (minimum score 550 paper-based; 213 computer-based). *Application deadline:* For fall admission, 4/15 priority date for domestic and international students; for spring admission, 11/15 priority date for domestic and international students. Applications are processed on a rolling basis. Application fee: $30. Electronic applications accepted. *Expenses: Contact institution.* Tuition and fees vary according to degree level. *Financial support:* Research assistantships with tuition reimbursements, scholarships/grants, tuition waivers (partial), and unspecified assistantships available. Support available to part-time students. Financial award application deadline: 2/15; financial award applicants required to submit FAFSA. *Faculty research:* Mariology, exploration of visual imagery, explorations involving drawing on the loom, clay as sculptural medium, oil paintings.

Miami International University of Art & Design, Program in Graphic Design, Miami, FL 33132-1418. Offers MFA. Postbaccalaureate distance learning degree programs offered.

See Close-Up on page 119.

Minneapolis College of Art and Design, Program in Visual Studies, Minneapolis, MN 55404-4347. Offers animation (MFA); comic art (MFA); drawing (MFA); filmmaking (MFA); fine arts (MFA); furniture design (MFA); graphic design (MFA); illustration (MFA); interactive media (MFA); painting (MFA); photography (MFA); printmaking (MFA); sculpture (MFA). *Accreditation:* NASAD. Part-time programs available. *Faculty:* 23 full-time (7 women), 9 part-time/adjunct (4 women). *Students:* 40 full-time (21 women), 1 (woman) part-time; includes 1 minority (American Indian/Alaska Native). Average age 27. 172 applicants, 24% accepted, 15 enrolled. In 2007, 7 degrees awarded. *Degree requirements:* For master's, thesis, thesis exhibit. *Entrance requirements:* For master's, portfolio, resumé, 3 letters of recommendation, statement . Additional exam requirements/recommendations for international students: Required—TOEFL (minimum score 550 paper-based; 213 computer-based; 79 iBT). *Application deadline:* For fall admission, 2/15 for domestic and international students. Application fee: $50. Electronic applications accepted. *Expenses:* Tuition: Full-time $27,000; part-time $900 per credit. Required fees: $100 per term. *Financial support:* In 2007–08, 23 students received support, including 15 teaching assistantships (averaging $6,000 per year); career-related internships or fieldwork, Federal Work-Study, scholarships/grants, and unspecified assistantships also available. Support available to part-time students. Financial award application deadline: 3/15; financial award applicants required to submit FAFSA. *Faculty research:* Visual arts. *Unit head:* Carole Fisher, Graduate Director, 612-874-3629, E-mail: carole_fisher@mcad.edu. *Application contact:* William Mullen, Vice President of Enrollment Management, 612-874-3762, Fax: 612-874-3701, E-mail: william_mullen@mcad.edu.

New York University, School of Continuing and Professional Studies, Division for Media Industry Studies and Design, Program in Graphic Communications Management and Technology, New York, NY 10012-1019. Offers MS. Part-time and evening/weekend programs available. *Faculty:* 20 part-time/adjunct (8 women). *Students:* 16 full-time (13 women), 58 part-time (31 women); includes 15 minority (3 African Americans, 11 Asian Americans or Pacific Islanders, 1 Hispanic American), 13 international. Average age 30. 35 applicants, 83% accepted, 23 enrolled. In 2007, 7 degrees awarded. *Degree requirements:* For master's, project. *Entrance requirements:* For master's, GRE General Test or GMAT (for recent graduates), resumé, 2 letters of recommendation, work experience, essay. Additional exam requirements/recommendations for international students: Required—TOEFL (minimum score 600 paper-based; 250 computer-based; 100 iBT), TWE. *Application deadline:* For fall admission, 3/15 priority date for domestic and international students; for spring admission, 10/15 priority date for domestic students, 8/15 priority date for international students. Applications are processed on a rolling basis. Application fee: $75. Electronic applications accepted. *Financial support:* In 2007–08, 36 students received support, including 36 fellowships (averaging $1,347 per year); scholarships/grants and tuition waivers (partial) also available. Support available to part-time students. Financial award application deadline: 3/1; financial award applicants required to submit FAFSA. *Faculty research:* Production operations management and marketing, human resources and quality management. *Unit head:* Bonnie Blake, Director, 212-992-3222, Fax: 212-992-3386. *Application contact:* 212-998-7100, Fax: 212-995-4674, E-mail: scps.gradadmissions@nyu.edu.

See Close-Up on page 129.

North Carolina State University, Graduate School, College of Design, Department of Graphic Design, Raleigh, NC 27695. Offers UA Undergraduate Associate. *Accreditation:* NASAD.

Degree requirements: For master's, thesis optional, oral exam. *Entrance requirements:* For master's, GRE General Test, portfolio. Electronic applications accepted. *Faculty research:* Typography, graphic design, interaction design, design and cognition, design and culture.

Ohio University, Graduate College, College of Fine Arts, School of Art, Athens, OH 45701-2979. Offers art history (MA); ceramics (MFA); graphic design (MFA); painting (MFA); photography (MFA); printmaking (MFA); sculpture (MFA). Part-time programs available. *Faculty:* 30 full-time (16 women), 7 part-time/adjunct (3 women). *Students:* 53 full-time (34 women), 11 part-time (7 women); includes 1 minority (Hispanic American), 7 international. Average age 27. 174 applicants, 22% accepted, 32 enrolled. In 2007, 18 degrees awarded. *Degree requirements:* For master's, thesis. *Entrance requirements:* For master's, portfolio. Additional exam requirements/recommendations for international students: Required—TOEFL. *Application deadline:* For fall admission, 2/1 for domestic students. Application fee: $50 ($55 for international students). *Financial support:* In 2007–08, 57 students received support, including 35 teaching assistantships with full and partial tuition reimbursements available (averaging $9,198 per year); career-related internships or fieldwork, Federal Work-Study, institutionally sponsored loans, scholarships/grants, tuition waivers (full), unspecified assistantships, and associateships also available. Financial award application deadline: 2/1. *Faculty research:* Vapor fired ceramics, video installation, art theory, digital photography, mixed and interdisciplinary media work. *Unit head:* David LaPalombara, Director, 740-593-4290, Fax: 740-593-0457, E-mail: lapalomb@ohio.edu. *Application contact:* Don Adleta, Associate Director and Chair, Graduate Programs, 740-593-9996, Fax: 740-593-0457, E-mail: adleta@ohio.edu.

Otis College of Art and Design, Program in Graphic Design, Los Angeles, CA 90045-9785. Offers MFA. *Entrance requirements:* Additional exam requirements/recommendations for international students: Required—TOEFL (minimum score 600 paper-based; 250 computer-based). *Application deadline:* For fall admission, 2/15 for domestic and international students. Electronic applications accepted. *Expenses:* Tuition: Full-time $30,764; part-time $1,026 per unit. Required fees: $700. *Unit head:* Kali Nikitas, Chair, Graduate Studies: Graphic Design, 310-665-6820, Fax: 310-665-6843, E-mail: jhayes@otis.edu. *Application contact:* Information Contact, 310-665-6820, Fax: 310-665-6821, E-mail: admissions@otis.edu.

Pittsburg State University, Graduate School, College of Technology, Departments of Graphics and Imaging Technologies and Technology Management, Pittsburg, KS 66762. Offers human resource development (MS); industrial education (Ed S); technology (MS), including printing management. *Degree requirements:* For master's, thesis or alternative.

Pratt Institute, School of Art and Design, Program in Communications Design, Brooklyn, NY 11205-3899. Offers MS. *Accreditation:* NASAD. Part-time programs available. *Faculty:* 5 full-time (2 women), 33 part-time/adjunct (9 women). *Students:* 188 full-time (140 women), 18 part-time (14 women); includes 40 minority (18 African Americans, 15 Asian Americans or Pacific Islanders, 7 Hispanic Americans), 116 international. Average age 28. 181 applicants, 56% accepted, 42 enrolled. In 2007, 78 degrees awarded. *Degree requirements:* For master's, thesis. *Entrance requirements:* For master's, portfolio, bachelor's degree, transcripts, letters of recommendation, statement. Additional exam requirements/recommendations for international students: Required—TOEFL (minimum score 550 paper-based; 213 computer-based). *Application deadline:* For fall admission, 2/1 for domestic students; for spring admission, 10/1 for domestic students. Application fee: $50 ($90 for international students). Electronic applications accepted. *Expenses:* Tuition: Full-time $25,680. Required fees: $1,106. Tuition and fees vary according to program. *Financial support:* Career-related internships or fieldwork, Federal Work-Study, institutionally sponsored loans, scholarships/grants, and unspecified assistantships available. Support available to part-time students. Financial award application deadline: 2/1; financial award applicants required to submit FAFSA. *Faculty research:* Graphics, film, photography, media presentations, computer graphics for community service organizations. *Unit head:* J. Guilfoyle, Chairperson, 212-647-7573, E-mail: jguilfoy@pratt.edu. *Application contact:* Young Hah, Director of Graduate Admissions, 718-636-3683, Fax: 718-399-4242, E-mail: yhah@pratt.edu.

See Close-Up on page 253.

Pratt Institute, School of Art and Design, Program in Digital Arts, Brooklyn, NY 11205-3899. Offers computer graphics (MFA). *Accreditation:* NASAD. Part-time programs available. *Faculty:* 6 full-time (1 woman), 17 part-time/adjunct (8 women). *Students:* 70 full-time (37 women), 1 part-time; includes 8 minority (3 African Americans, 3 Asian Americans or Pacific Islanders, 2 Hispanic Americans), 34 international. Average age 30. 173 applicants, 22% accepted, 12 enrolled. In 2007, 25 degrees awarded. *Degree requirements:* For master's, thesis, exhibit. *Entrance requirements:* For master's, portfolio or video tape, bachelor's degree, transcripts, letters of recommendation, statement. Additional exam requirements/recommendations for international students: Required—TOEFL (minimum score 550 paper-based; 213 computer-based). *Application deadline:* For fall admission, 2/1 for domestic students; for spring admission, 10/1 for domestic students. Applications are processed on a rolling basis. Application fee: $50 ($90 for international students). Electronic applications accepted. *Expenses:* Tuition: Full-time $25,680. Required fees: $1,106. Tuition and fees vary according to program. *Financial support:* Career-related internships or fieldwork, Federal Work-Study, institutionally sponsored loans, scholarships/grants, health care benefits, and unspecified assistantships available. Support available to part-time students. Financial award application deadline: 2/1; financial award applicants required to submit FAFSA. *Unit head:* Peter Patchen, Chair, 718-636-3693, E-mail: peter.patchen@pratt.edu. *Application contact:* Young Hah, Director of Graduate Admissions, 718-636-3683, Fax: 718-399-4242, E-mail: yhah@pratt.edu.

See Close-Up on page 253.

Rhode Island School of Design, Graduate Studies, Division of Architecture and Design, Department of Graphic Design, Providence, RI 02903-2784. Offers MFA. *Accreditation:* NASAD. *Degree requirements:* For master's, thesis, exhibit. *Entrance requirements:* For master's, portfolio, 3 letters of recommendation. Additional exam requirements/recommendations for international students: Required—TOEFL (minimum score 580 paper-based; 237 computer-based), IELTS (minimum score 7).

Rochester Institute of Technology, Graduate Enrollment Services, College of Imaging Arts and Sciences, School of Design, Program in Computer Graphics Design, Rochester, NY 14623-5603. Offers MFA. *Accreditation:* NASAD. *Students:* 38 full-time (16 women), 15 part-time (8 women); includes 2 minority (1 African American, 1 Asian American or Pacific Islander), 24 international. 69 applicants, 64% accepted, 19 enrolled. In 2007, 10 degrees awarded. *Degree requirements:* For master's, thesis. *Entrance requirements:* For master's, portfolio, minimum GPA of 3.0. Additional exam requirements/recommendations for international students: Required—TOEFL. *Application deadline:* For fall admission, 3/1 priority date for domestic students. Applications are processed on a rolling basis. Application fee: $50. *Expenses:* Tuition: Full-time $28,491; part-time $800 per credit hour. Required fees: $201; $67 per term. *Financial support:* Research assistantships with partial tuition reimbursements, teaching assistantships with partial tuition reimbursements, career-related internships or fieldwork, institutionally sponsored loans, scholarships/grants, and unspecified assistantships available. Support available to part-time students. Financial award applicants required to submit FAFSA. *Unit head:* Marianne O'Loughlin, Chairperson, 585-475-6125, E-mail: meofaa@rit.edu.

Rochester Institute of Technology, Graduate Enrollment Services, College of Imaging Arts and Sciences, School of Design, Program in Graphic Design, Rochester, NY 14623-5603. Offers MFA. *Accreditation:* NASAD. *Students:* 14 full-time (10 women); includes 1 minority (Hispanic American), 7 international. 72 applicants, 40% accepted, 9 enrolled. In 2007, 6 degrees awarded. *Degree requirements:* For master's, thesis (for some programs). *Entrance requirements:* For master's, portfolio, minimum GPA of 3.0. Additional exam requirements/recommendations for international students: Required—TOEFL. *Application deadline:* For fall admission, 3/1 priority date for domestic students. Applications are processed on a rolling basis. Application fee: $50. *Expenses:* Tuition: Full-time $28,491; part-time $800 per credit hour. Required fees: $201; $67 per term. *Financial support:* Teaching assistantships with partial tuition reimbursements, career-related internships or fieldwork, institutionally sponsored loans, scholarships/grants, and unspecified assistantships available. Support available to part-time students. Financial award applicants required to submit FAFSA. *Unit head:* Bruce Meader, Chairperson, 585-475-7826, E-mail: bimfaa@rit.edu.

Rochester Institute of Technology, Graduate Enrollment Services, College of Imaging Arts and Sciences, School of Print Media, Program in Print Media, Rochester, NY 14623-5603. Offers MS. *Students:* 23 full-time (10 women), 22 part-time (11 women); includes 3 minority (1 African American, 1 Asian American or Pacific Islander, 1 Hispanic American), 20 international. 24 applicants, 63% accepted, 14 enrolled. In 2007, 22 degrees awarded. *Entrance requirements:* For master's, minimum GPA of 3.0. Additional exam requirements/recommendations for international students: Required—TOEFL (minimum score 550 paper-based; 213 computer-based; 79 iBT). *Application deadline:* For fall admission, 3/1 priority date for domestic students. Applications are processed on a rolling basis. Application fee: $50. *Expenses:* Tuition: Full-time $28,491; part-time $800 per credit hour. Required fees: $201; $67 per term. *Financial support:* Research assistantships with partial tuition reimbursements, teaching assistantships with partial tuition reimbursements, career-related internships or fieldwork, institutionally sponsored loans, scholarships/grants, and unspecified assistantships available. Support available to part-time students. Financial award applicants required to submit FAFSA. *Unit head:* Twyla Cummings, Graduate Program Chair, 585-475-5567, E-mail: tjcppr@rit.edu.

San Diego State University, Graduate and Research Affairs, College of Professional Studies and Fine Arts, School of Art, Design and Art History, San Diego, CA 92182. Offers art history (MA); studio arts (MA, MFA), including applied design, environmental design, graphic design, interior design, painting and printmaking, sculpture. *Accreditation:* NASAD (one or more programs are accredited). *Students:* 44 full-time (29 women), 18 part-time (11 women); includes 9 minority (4 Asian Americans or Pacific Islanders, 5 Hispanic Americans), 5 international. Average age 30. 83 applicants, 31% accepted, 31 enrolled. In 2007, 12 degrees awarded. *Degree requirements:* For master's, variable foreign language requirement, thesis. *Entrance requirements:* For master's, GRE General Test, bachelor's degree in related field, slide portfolio, typed slide information sheet, 2 letters of recommendation. Additional exam requirements/recommendations for international students: Required—TOEFL. *Application deadline:* For fall admission, 2/1 for domestic and international students. Applications are processed on a rolling basis. Application fee: $55. Electronic applications accepted. *Financial support:* In 2007–08, 21 teaching assistantships were awarded; career-related internships or fieldwork and unspecified assistantships also available. Financial award applicants required to submit FAFSA. *Unit head:* Arthur Ollman, Director, 619-594-1213, Fax: 619-594-1217. *Application contact:* JoAnne Berelowitz, Graduate Advisor, Art History, 619-594-4995, Fax: 619-594-1217, E-mail: jberelow@mail.sdsu.edu.

Savannah College of Art and Design, Graduate School, Program in Advertising Design, Savannah, GA 31402-3146. Offers MA, MFA. Part-time programs available. *Faculty:* 4 full-time (0 women), 1 part-time/adjunct (0 women). *Students:* 34 full-time (21 women), 8 part-time (4 women); includes 7 minority (5 African Americans, 1 Asian American or Pacific Islander, 1 Hispanic American), 16 international. 55 applicants, 38% accepted, 10 enrolled. In 2007, 9 degrees awarded. *Degree requirements:* For master's, thesis, internships. *Entrance requirements:* For master's, interview, portfolio. Additional exam requirements/recommendations for international students: Required—TOEFL (minimum score 450 paper-based; 133 computer-based). *Application deadline:* For fall admission, 4/1 priority date for domestic and international students. Applications are processed on a rolling basis. Application fee: $50. Electronic applications accepted. *Expenses:* Tuition: Full-time $24,840; part-time $552 per credit. One-time fee: $500 full-time. *Financial support:* Fellowships, career-related internships or fieldwork, Federal Work-Study, and scholarships/grants available. Financial award application deadline: 4/1; financial award applicants required to submit FAFSA. *Unit head:* Stephen Hall, Chair, 912-525-5974. *Application contact:* Darrell Tutchton, Director of Graduate and International Enrollment, 912-525-5961, Fax: 912-525-5985, E-mail: admission@scad.edu.

Savannah College of Art and Design, Graduate School, Program in Graphic Design, Savannah, GA 31402-3146. Offers MA, MFA. Part-time programs available. *Faculty:* 18 full-time (4 women), 3 part-time/adjunct (2 women). *Students:* 180 full-time (114 women), 80 part-time (48 women); includes 24 minority (12 African Americans, 1 American Indian/Alaska Native, 1 Asian American or Pacific Islander, 10 Hispanic Americans), 50 international. Average age 26. 305 applicants, 47% accepted, 69 enrolled. In 2007, 43 degrees awarded. *Degree requirements:* For master's, thesis, exhibit, internships. *Entrance requirements:* For master's, interview, portfolio. Additional exam requirements/recommendations for international students: Required—TOEFL (minimum score 450 paper-based; 133 computer-based). *Application deadline:* For fall admission, 4/1 priority date for domestic and international students. Applications are processed on a rolling basis. Application fee: $50. Electronic applications accepted. *Expenses:* Tuition: Full-time $24,840; part-time $552 per credit. One-time fee: $500 full-time. *Financial support:* In 2007–08, 8 fellowships were awarded; career-related internships or fieldwork, Federal Work-Study, and scholarships/grants also available. Financial award application deadline: 4/1; financial award applicants required to submit FAFSA. *Unit head:* Quentin Currie, Chair, 912-525-5904, Fax: 912-525-5994, E-mail: qcurrie@scad.edu. *Application contact:* Darrell Tutchton, Director of Graduate and International Enrollment, 912-525-5961, Fax: 912-525-5985, E-mail: admission@scad.edu.

See Close-Up on page 257.

School of the Art Institute of Chicago, Graduate Division, Program in Visual Communication, Chicago, IL 60603-3103. Offers MFA. *Entrance requirements:* Additional exam requirements/recommendations for international students: Required—TOEFL.

See Close-Up on page 259.

Suffolk University, College of Arts and Sciences, New England School of Art and Design, Boston, MA 02108-2770. Offers graphic design (MA); interior design (MA). *Accreditation:* CIDA; NASAD. Part-time and evening/weekend programs available. *Faculty:* 18 full-time (9 women), 14 part-time/adjunct (4 women). *Students:* 49 full-time (46 women), 69 part-time (63 women); includes 12 minority (2 African Americans, 1 American Indian/Alaska Native, 7 Asian Americans or Pacific Islanders, 2 Hispanic Americans), 15 international. Average age 29. 78 applicants, 87% accepted, 33 enrolled. In 2007, 26 degrees awarded. *Entrance requirements:* For master's, art portfolio, interview. Additional exam requirements/recommendations for international students: Required—TOEFL (minimum score 550 paper-based; 213 computer-based; 80 iBT). *Application deadline:* For fall admission, 6/15 priority date for domestic students, 6/15 for international students; for spring admission, 11/1 priority date for domestic students, 11/1 for international students. Applications are processed on a rolling basis. Application fee: $50. Electronic applications accepted. *Financial support:* In 2007–08, 65 students received support, including 10 fellowships with partial tuition reimbursements available (averaging $6,296 per year). Financial award application deadline: 4/1. *Faculty research:* Adaptive re-use of historical structures, universal design, American architecture history, interior design to reduce inefficiency, meditation SPA. *Unit head:* Dr. William Davis, Director, 617-994-4264, Fax: 617-536-0461, E-mail: wdavis@suffolk.edu. *Application contact:* Judith Reynolds, Director of Graduate Admissions, 617-573-8302, Fax: 617-523-0116, E-mail: grad.admission@suffolk.edu.

Syracuse University, Graduate School, College of Visual and Performing Arts, School of Art and Design, Syracuse, NY 13244. Offers art (MFA), including ceramics, fiber arts/materials studies, illustration, jewelry and metalsmithing, painting, printmaking, sculpture; art education (MS); museum studies (MA). *Accreditation:* NASAD (one or more programs are accredited). Part-time programs available. Postbaccalaureate distance learning degree programs offered (no on-campus study). *Students:* 58 full-time (43 women), 7 part-time (4 women); includes 6 minority (1 African American, 3 Asian Americans or Pacific Islanders, 2 Hispanic Americans), 7 international. 169 applicants, 29% accepted, 25 enrolled. In 2007, 34 degrees awarded. *Degree requirements:* For master's, thesis or alternative. *Entrance requirements:* For master's,

Graphic Design

Syracuse University (continued)

portfolio. Additional exam requirements/recommendations for international students: Required—TOEFL. *Application deadline:* For fall admission, 1/1 priority date for domestic students; for spring admission, 3/1 priority date for domestic students. Applications are processed on a rolling basis. Application fee: $75. Electronic applications accepted. *Expenses:* Tuition: Full-time $18,216; part-time $1,012 per credit. Required fees: $980. Tuition and fees vary according to program. *Financial support:* Fellowships with full tuition reimbursements, research assistantships with full and partial tuition reimbursements, teaching assistantships with full and partial tuition reimbursements, Federal Work-Study and tuition waivers (partial) available. *Unit head:* Stephen Carlson, Associate Dean, 315-443-2507. *Application contact:* Harriett Conti, Associate Director, Graduate Student Services, 315-443-3089, E-mail: hmconti@syr.edu.

Temple University, Graduate School, Tyler School of Art, Department of Graphic Arts and Design, Philadelphia, PA 19122-6096. Offers graphic and interactive design (MFA); photography (MFA); printmaking (MFA). *Accreditation:* NASAD. *Degree requirements:* For master's, essay, exhibit. *Entrance requirements:* For master's, minimum GPA of 3.0; slide portfolio, 40 credits in studio art; 12 credits in art history. Additional exam requirements/recommendations for international students: Required—TOEFL (minimum score 550 paper-based; 213 computer-based; 79 iBT). Electronic applications accepted.

Texas State University–San Marcos, Graduate School, College of Fine Arts and Communication, Department of Art and Design, Program in Communication Design, San Marcos, TX 78666. Offers MFA. *Entrance requirements:* For master's, 2.75 GPA on last 60 hours of undergrad work, 20 work portfolio. Additional exam requirements/recommendations for international students: Required—TOEFL (minimum score 550 paper-based; 213 computer-based). *Application deadline:* For fall admission, 3/15 for domestic and international students. Applications are processed on a rolling basis. Application fee: $40 ($90 for international students). Electronic applications accepted. *Expenses:* Tuition, state resident: full-time $3,780; part-time $210 per credit hour. Tuition, nonresident: full-time $8,784; part-time $488 per credit hour. Required fees: $493 per semester. Full-time tuition and fees vary according to course load. *Financial support:* Federal Work-Study and institutionally sponsored loans available. Support available to part-time students. Financial award application deadline: 4/1; financial award applicants required to submit FAFSA. *Unit head:* William Meek, Program Advisor, 512-245-0311, E-mail: w.meek@txstate.edu.

Université Laval, Faculty of Architecture, Planning and Visual Arts, School of Visual Arts, Programs in Visual Arts, Québec, QC G1K 7P4, Canada. Offers graphic design and multimedia (MA); visual arts (MA). *Degree requirements:* For master's, thesis (for some programs). *Entrance requirements:* For master's, technical exam, interview, mastery of pertinent software, knowledge of French. Electronic applications accepted.

University of Baltimore, Graduate School, The Yale Gordon College of Liberal Arts, School of Communications Design, Program in Publications Design, Baltimore, MD 21201-5779. Offers MA. Part-time and evening/weekend programs available. *Faculty:* 6 full-time (3 women), 10 part-time/adjunct (6 women). *Students:* 42 full-time (35 women), 138 part-time (108 women); includes 41 minority (28 African Americans, 1 American Indian/Alaska Native, 5 Asian Americans or Pacific Islanders, 7 Hispanic Americans), 4 international. Average age 30. 102 applicants, 83% accepted, 78 enrolled. In 2007, 42 degrees awarded. *Degree requirements:* For master's, seminar project. *Entrance requirements:* For master's, minimum GPA of 3.0, portfolio, interview. Additional exam requirements/recommendations for international students: Required—TOEFL (minimum score 550 paper-based; 213 computer-based). *Application deadline:* For fall admission, 8/1 priority date for domestic students, 6/1 for international students; for spring admission, 12/15 for domestic students, 11/1 for international students. Applications are processed on a rolling basis. Application fee: $45. Electronic applications accepted. *Expenses:* Tuition, state resident: part-time $518 per credit. Tuition, nonresident: part-time $751 per credit. Tuition and fees vary according to program. *Financial support:* In 2007–08, 9 research assistantships were awarded; fellowships, career-related internships or fieldwork and Federal Work-Study also available. Support available to part-time students. Financial award application deadline: 4/1; financial award applicants required to submit FAFSA. *Faculty research:* Communication theory, graphic design, media technology. *Unit head:* Dr. Stephanie Gibson, Director, Main Publications Design, 410-837-6050, E-mail: sgibson@ubalt.edu. *Application contact:* Wendy Bolyard.

University of Cincinnati, Graduate School, College of Design, Architecture, Art, and Planning, School of Design, Cincinnati, OH 45221. Offers fashion design (M Des); graphic design (M Des); industrial design (M Des); interaction design (M Des); product development (M Des). *Accreditation:* NASAD. *Students:* 13 full-time (7 women), 6 part-time (5 women), 10 international. In 2007, 3 degrees awarded. *Degree requirements:* For master's, thesis. *Entrance requirements:* For master's, undergraduate degree in design or related field, 2 years of work experience in design or related field. Additional exam requirements/recommendations for international students: Required—TOEFL. *Application deadline:* For fall admission, 2/1 for domestic students. Application fee: $30. Electronic applications accepted. *Financial support:* Fellowships, career-related internships or fieldwork, Federal Work-Study, tuition waivers (partial), and unspecified assistantships available. *Faculty research:* Design theory, interdisciplinary design topics. *Unit head:* Prof. Dale Murray, Director, 513-556-1524, E-mail: dale.murray@uc.edu. *Application contact:* Dr. J. Chewning, Information Contact, 513-556-2996, Fax: 513-556-0240, E-mail: j.chewning@uc.edu.

University of Florida, Graduate School, College of Fine Arts, School of Art and Art History, Gainesville, FL 32611. Offers art (MFA), including ceramics, creative photography, drawing, electronic intermedia, graphic design, painting, printmaking, sculpture; art education (MA); art history (MA, PhD); digital arts and sciences (MA); museology (museum studies) (MA). *Accreditation:* NASAD. *Faculty:* 29 full-time (14 women), 2 part-time/adjunct (1 woman). *Students:* 82 (48 women); includes 4 minority (2 Asian Americans or Pacific Islanders, 2 Hispanic Americans) 4 international. In 2007, 20 degrees awarded. *Degree requirements:* For master's, variable foreign language requirement, project or thesis (MFA). *Entrance requirements:* For master's, portfolio (MFA), writing sample (MA), GRE General Test or minimum GPA of 3.0. Additional exam requirements/recommendations for international students: Required—TOEFL (minimum score 550 paper-based; 213 computer-based). *Application deadline:* For fall admission, 1/15 priority date for domestic students. Applications are processed on a rolling basis. Application fee: $30. Electronic applications accepted. *Expenses:* Tuition, state resident: full-time $7,478. Tuition, nonresident: full-time $22,603. *Financial support:* In 2007–08, 3 research assistantships with tuition reimbursements (averaging $9,515 per year), 67 teaching assistantships with tuition reimbursements (averaging $9,839 per year) were awarded; fellowships, Federal Work-Study, institutionally sponsored loans, and unspecified assistantships also available. Financial award applicants required to submit FAFSA. *Faculty research:* Studio production, art historical studies of style context. *Unit head:* Glenn Willumson, Program Director, 352-392-0201 Ext. 234. *Application contact:* Prof. Richard Heipp, Coordinator, 352-392-0201 Ext. 239, Fax: 352-392-8453, E-mail: heipp@ufl.edu.

University of Guam, Office of Graduate Studies, Liberal Arts and Social Sciences, Division of Fine Arts, Mangilao, GU 96923. Offers ceramics (MA); graphics (MA); painting (MA). *Faculty:* 3 full-time (0 women). *Students:* Average age 47. In 2007, 1 degree awarded. *Degree requirements:* For master's, thesis or alternative, exhibit, final oral exam. *Entrance requirements:* For master's, GRE General Test, portfolio. Additional exam requirements/recommendations for international students: Required—TOEFL. *Application deadline:* For fall admission, 6/11 priority date for domestic students, 3/24 priority date for international students; for spring admission, 11/16 priority date for domestic students, 9/8 priority date for international students. Applications are processed on a rolling basis. Application fee: $49 ($74 for international students). *Unit head:* Lewis Rifkowitz, Chair, 671-735-2716, Fax: 671-734-3575, E-mail: rifkowit@yahoo.com. *Application contact:* Charlie A. Alcantara, Program Coordinator, Graduate Studies Office, 671-735-2173, Fax: 671-734-3676, E-mail: charliea@uguam.uog.edu.

University of Illinois at Chicago, Graduate College, College of Architecture and Art, School of Art and Design, Chicago, IL 60607-7128. Offers electronic visualization (MFA); film animation (MFA); graphic design (MFA); industrial design (MFA); photography (MFA); studio arts (MFA). *Accreditation:* NASAD. *Degree requirements:* For master's, thesis, exhibit. *Entrance requirements:* For master's, MAT, portfolio. Additional exam requirements/recommendations for international students: Required—TOEFL. Electronic applications accepted.

University of Illinois at Urbana–Champaign, Graduate College, College of Fine and Applied Arts, School of Art and Design, Program in Design and Media, Champaign, IL 61820. Offers graphic design (MFA); industrial design (MFA). *Accreditation:* NASAD. *Students:* 7 full-time (5 women); includes 1 minority (Asian American or Pacific Islander), 5 international. 61 applicants, 11% accepted, 6 enrolled. In 2007, 6 master's awarded. *Entrance requirements:* For master's, minimum GPA of 3.0. *Application deadline:* Applications are processed on a rolling basis. Application fee: $60 ($75 for international students). Electronic applications accepted. *Financial support:* Fellowships, research assistantships, teaching assistantships available. Financial award application deadline: 2/15. *Unit head:* Dr. Nan Goggin, Program Chair, 217-333-9327, Fax: 217-244-7688, E-mail: goggin@uiuc.edu.

University of Massachusetts Dartmouth, Graduate School, College of Visual and Performing Arts, Program in Visual Design, North Dartmouth, MA 02747-2300. Offers digital multi-media (MFA); electronic imaging (MFA); graphic design (MFA); illustration (MFA); photography (MFA); typography (MFA). *Accreditation:* NASAD. *Faculty:* 17 full-time (7 women), 7 part-time/adjunct (3 women). *Students:* 8 full-time (6 women), 2 part-time (both women); includes 1 minority (Asian American or Pacific Islander), 2 international. Average age 35. 21 applicants, 24% accepted, 4 enrolled. In 2007, 3 degrees awarded. *Degree requirements:* For master's, visual thesis. *Entrance requirements:* For master's, portfolio, interview, minimum GPA of 3.0, 3 letters of recommendation. Additional exam requirements/recommendations for international students: Required—TOEFL (minimum score 500 paper-based). *Application deadline:* For fall admission, 3/1 priority date for domestic students, 1/1 priority date for international students. Applications are processed on a rolling basis. Application fee: $40 ($60 for international students). Electronic applications accepted. *Expenses:* Tuition, state resident: full-time $2,071; part-time $86 per credit. Tuition, nonresident: full-time $8,099; part-time $337 per credit. Part-time tuition and fees vary according to course load and program. *Financial support:* In 2007–08, 4 teaching assistantships (averaging $2,930 per year) were awarded; research assistantships, Federal Work-Study and unspecified assistantships also available. Support available to part-time students. Financial award application deadline: 3/1; financial award applicants required to submit FAFSA. Total annual research expenditures: $22,880. *Unit head:* Jarrad Nunes, Director, 508-999-8010, E-mail: jnunes@umassd.edu. *Application contact:* Carol Novo, Graduate Admissions Officer, 508-999-8604, Fax: 508-999-8183, E-mail: graduate@umassd.edu.

University of Memphis, Graduate School, College of Communication and Fine Arts, Department of Art, Memphis, TN 38152. Offers art history (MA), including Egyptian art and archaeology, general art history; ceramics (MFA); graphic design (MFA); interior design (MFA); painting (MFA); printmaking/photography (MFA); sculpture (MFA). *Accreditation:* NASAD (one or more programs are accredited). *Faculty:* 13 full-time (9 women). *Students:* 20 full-time (11 women), 2 part-time (1 woman); includes 1 Asian American or Pacific Islander, 1 international. Average age 27. 47 applicants, 55% accepted, 18 enrolled. In 2007, 14 degrees awarded. *Degree requirements:* For master's, 2 foreign languages, comprehensive exam, thesis. *Entrance requirements:* For master's, GRE General Test or MAT, portfolio (MFA). *Application deadline:* For fall admission, 8/1 for domestic students; for spring admission, 12/1 for domestic students. Applications are processed on a rolling basis. Application fee: $35 ($60 for international students). *Expenses:* Tuition, state resident: full-time $6,990; part-time $377 per hour. Tuition, nonresident: full-time $17,818; part-time $830 per hour. Tuition and fees vary according to course load and program. *Financial support:* In 2007–08, 23 research assistantships with full tuition reimbursements (averaging $4,200 per year), 10 teaching assistantships with full tuition reimbursements (averaging $5,250 per year) were awarded. *Faculty research:* Online collaborative learning, advanced art history studies, electronic publishing/design, studio arts, architectural studies. *Unit head:* Prof. Richard Lou, Chair, 901-678-2216, Fax: 901-678-2735, E-mail: gmyatt@memphis.edu. *Application contact:* Prof. Michael Hagge, Coordinator of Graduate Studies, 901-678-2677.

University of Miami, Graduate School, College of Arts and Sciences, Department of Art and Art History, Coral Gables, FL 33124. Offers art history (MA); ceramics/glass (MFA); graphic design/multimedia (MFA); painting (MFA); photography/digital imaging (MFA); printmaking (MFA); sculpture (MFA). Part-time programs available. *Faculty:* 14 full-time (6 women). *Students:* 23 full-time (15 women), 5 part-time (3 women); includes 5 minority (2 African Americans, 3 Hispanic Americans). Average age 29. 55 applicants, 18% accepted, 8 enrolled. In 2007, 8 degrees awarded. *Degree requirements:* For master's, variable foreign language requirement, thesis, exhibit (MFA), comprehensive exam (MA). *Entrance requirements:* For master's, GRE General Test (MA), research paper (MA), slide portfolio (MFA), artist statement (MFA). Additional exam requirements/recommendations for international students: Required—TOEFL. *Application deadline:* For fall admission, 2/15 for domestic students, 1/15 for international students; for winter admission, 9/15 for domestic students. Application fee: $50. Electronic applications accepted. *Financial support:* In 2007–08, 25 students received support, including 17 teaching assistantships with full tuition reimbursements available (averaging $10,000 per year); Federal Work-Study, institutionally sponsored loans, scholarships/grants, and tuition waivers (full) also available. Financial award application deadline: 3/1; financial award applicants required to submit FAFSA. *Faculty research:* Installation art, public art. *Unit head:* Prof. Lise Drost, Chair, 305-284-2542, Fax: 305-284-2115, E-mail: l.drost@miami.edu. *Application contact:* Prof. Brian Curtis, Graduate Secretary, 305-284-2542, Fax: 305-284-2115, E-mail: art-arh@miami.edu.

University of Minnesota, Duluth, Graduate School, School of Fine Arts, Department of Art and Design, Duluth, MN 55812-2496. Offers graphic design (MFA). Part-time programs available. *Faculty:* 15 full-time (10 women), 6 part-time/adjunct (5 women). *Students:* 8 full-time (4 women), 1 international. Average age 30. 11 applicants, 18% accepted, 2 enrolled. In 2007, 1 degree awarded. *Degree requirements:* For master's, final exhibit, project, supporting paper. *Entrance requirements:* For master's, minimum GPA of 3.0, writing sample, slide portfolio. Additional exam requirements/recommendations for international students: Required—TOEFL (minimum score 550 paper-based; 213 computer-based). *Application deadline:* For fall admission, 4/15 for domestic and international students; for spring admission, 11/1 for domestic and international students. Application fee: $55 ($75 for international students). *Expenses:* Tuition, state resident: part-time $812 per credit. Tuition, nonresident: part-time $1,403 per credit. Tuition and fees vary according to program. *Financial support:* In 2007–08, 8 students received support, including research assistantships with full and partial tuition reimbursements available (averaging $10,000 per year), teaching assistantships with full and partial tuition reimbursements available (averaging $6,000 per year); fellowships with partial tuition reimbursements available, career-related internships or fieldwork, institutionally sponsored loans, scholarships/grants, and health care benefits also available. Financial award application deadline: 3/15. *Faculty research:* Motion graphics, graphic design history, interactive design, typography, education. Total annual research expenditures: $50,000. *Unit head:* Prof. Janice Kmetz, Director of Graduate Studies, 218-726-8150, E-mail: jkmetz@d.umn.edu.

University of Notre Dame, Graduate School, College of Arts and Letters, Division of Humanities, Department of Art, Art History, and Design, Notre Dame, IN 46556. Offers art history (MA); design (MFA), including graphic design, industrial design; studio art (MFA), including ceramics, painting, photography, printmaking, sculpture. *Accreditation:* NASAD. *Faculty:* 19 full-time (6 women), 3 part-time/adjunct (1 woman). *Students:* 25 full-time (12 women), 1 (woman) part-time; includes 4 minority (1 African American, 1 Asian American or Pacific Islander, 2 Hispanic Americans), 1 international. 85 applicants, 14% accepted, 10 enrolled. In 2007, 7 degrees awarded. *Degree requirements:* For master's, comprehensive exam, thesis. *Entrance requirements:* For master's, GRE General Test, minimum GPA of 3.0. Additional exam requirements/recommendations for international students: Required—TOEFL (minimum score 600 paper-based; 250 computer-based; 80 iBT). *Application deadline:* For fall admission, 2/1 priority date for domestic and international students. Application fee: $50. Electronic applications accepted. *Financial support:* In 2007–08, 20 students received support, including fellowships with full tuition reimbursements available (averaging $12,000 per year), research assistantships with full tuition reimbursements available (averaging $12,000 per year), 15 teaching assistantships with full tuition reimbursements available (averaging $12,000 per year); scholarships/grants, tuition waivers (full), and unspecified assistantships also available. Financial award application deadline: 2/1. *Faculty research:* Studio art practice in ceramics, printing, photography, printmaking and sculpture, graphic design and industrial design, digital imaging in design and photography, Renaissance and American art history, contemporary art theory and criticism. *Unit head:* Prof. Jean Dibble, Director of Graduate Studies, 574-631-7602, E-mail: art.1@nd.edu. *Application contact:* Dr. Jarren Gonzales, Director of Graduate Admissions, 574-631-7706, Fax: 574-631-4183.

The University of Tennessee, Graduate School, College of Arts and Sciences, School of Art, Knoxville, TN 37996. Offers ceramics (MFA); drawing (MFA); graphic design (MFA); inter-area studies (MFA); media arts (MFA); painting (MFA); printmaking (MFA); sculpture (MFA); watercolor (MFA). *Accreditation:* NASAD. *Degree requirements:* For master's, thesis or alternative, exhibit. *Entrance requirements:* For master's, portfolio, minimum GPA of 2.7. Additional exam requirements/recommendations for international students: Required—TOEFL. Electronic applications accepted.

University of Utah, The Graduate School, College of Fine Arts, Department of Art and Art History, Salt Lake City, UT 84112-1107. Offers art history (MA); ceramics (MFA); community-based art education (MFA); drawing (MFA); graphic design (MFA); painting (MFA); photography/digital imaging (MFA); printmaking (MFA); sculpture/intermedia (MFA). *Faculty:* 21 full-time (10 women). *Students:* 12 full-time (5 women), 5 part-time (3 women). Average age 31. 36 applicants, 28% accepted, 3 enrolled. In 2007, 7 degrees awarded. *Degree requirements:* For master's, variable foreign language requirement, comprehensive exam (for some programs), thesis or alternative, exhibit (MFA), final project paper. *Entrance requirements:* For master's, CD portfolio (MFA), resumé, letters of recommendation. Additional exam requirements/recommendations for international students: Required—TOEFL (minimum score 575 paper-based; 183 computer-based; 75 iBT). *Application deadline:* For fall admission, 1/2 priority date for domestic and international students. Application fee: $45 ($65 for international students). Electronic applications accepted. *Financial support:* In 2007–08, 1 fellowship, 6 teaching assistantships with partial tuition reimbursements were awarded; research assistantships with tuition reimbursements, Federal Work-Study, institutionally sponsored loans, scholarships/grants, tuition waivers (partial), and unspecified assistantships also available. Financial award application deadline: 1/2; financial award applicants required to submit FAFSA. *Faculty research:* Intermedia, digital arts, installation, traditional media, Asian art, medieval arts. Total annual research expenditures: $21,844. *Unit head:* Dr. Elizabeth A. Peterson, Chair, 801-581-7012, Fax: 801-585-6171, E-mail: elizabeth.peterson@art.utah.edu.

Western Illinois University, School of Graduate Studies, College of Education and Human Services, Department of Instructional Design and Technology, Macomb, IL 61455-1390. Offers distance learning (Certificate); graphic applications (Certificate); instructional design and technology (MS); multimedia (Certificate); technology integration in education (Certificate); training development (Certificate). Part-time programs available. Postbaccalaureate distance learning degree programs offered (no on-campus study). *Students:* 19 full-time (5 women), 71 part-time (52 women); includes 8 minority (5 African Americans, 1 Asian American or Pacific Islander, 2 Hispanic Americans), 5 international. Average age 38. 20 applicants, 70% accepted. In 2007, 22 master's, 2 other advanced degrees awarded. *Degree requirements:* For master's, thesis or alternative. *Entrance requirements:* For master's, minimum GPA of 2.75. Additional exam requirements/recommendations for international students: Required—TOEFL (minimum score 550 paper-based; 213 computer-based; 80 iBT). *Application deadline:* Applications are processed on a rolling basis. Application fee: $30. Electronic applications accepted. *Expenses:* Tuition, state resident: part-time $217 per credit hour. Tuition, nonresident: part-time $433 per credit hour. Required fees: $54 per credit hour. *Financial support:* In 2007–08, 9 students received support, including 7 research assistantships with full tuition reimbursements available (averaging $6,800 per year), 2 teaching assistantships with full tuition reimbursements available (averaging $7,840 per year). Financial award applicants required to submit FAFSA. *Unit head:* Dr. Hoyet Hemphill, Chairperson, 309-298-1952. *Application contact:* Dr. Barbara Baily, Director of Graduate Studies/Associate Provost, 309-298-1806, Fax: 309-298-2345, E-mail: grad-office@wiu.edu.

Western Michigan University, Graduate College, College of Fine Arts, Department of Art, Kalamazoo, MI 49008-5202. Offers graphic design (MFA); performing arts administration (MFA); textile design (MA, MFA). *Accreditation:* NASAD (one or more programs are accredited). *Degree requirements:* For master's, thesis or alternative.

West Virginia University, College of Creative Arts, Division of Art and Design, Morgantown, WV 26506. Offers art education (MA); art history (MA); ceramics (MFA); graphic design (MFA); painting (MFA); printmaking (MFA); sculpture (MFA); studio art (MA). *Accreditation:* NASAD. *Faculty:* 17 full-time (7 women), 6 part-time/adjunct (0 women). *Students:* 21 full-time (11 women), 3 part-time (all women), 2 international. Average age 29. 49 applicants, 22% accepted, 7 enrolled. In 2007, 11 degrees awarded. *Degree requirements:* For master's, thesis, exhibit. *Entrance requirements:* For master's, minimum GPA of 2.75, portfolio. Additional exam requirements/recommendations for international students: Required—TOEFL. *Application deadline:* For fall admission, 3/1 for domestic students, 2/15 for international students; for spring admission, 10/15 for domestic and international students. Application fee: $45. *Expenses: Contact institution.* Tuition and fees vary according to program. *Financial support:* In 2007–08, 22 students received support, including 11 teaching assistantships with full tuition reimbursements available; research assistantships with full tuition reimbursements available, Federal Work-Study, institutionally sponsored loans, tuition waivers (full and partial), and graduate administrative assistantships also available. Financial award application deadline: 3/15; financial award applicants required to submit FAFSA. *Faculty research:* Medieval art history. Total annual research expenditures: $6,000. *Unit head:* Alison Helm, Interim Chair, 304-293-4841 Ext. 3140, Fax: 304-293-3136, E-mail: alison.helm@mail.wvu.edu.

Yale University, School of Art, New Haven, CT 06520. Offers graphic design (MFA); painting/printmaking (MFA); photography (MFA); sculpture (MFA). *Faculty:* 11 full-time (3 women), 102 part-time/adjunct (48 women). *Students:* 119 full-time (57 women); includes 19 minority (5 African Americans, 6 Asian Americans or Pacific Islanders, 8 Hispanic Americans), 22 international. Average age 27. 1,218 applicants, 5% accepted, 57 enrolled. In 2007, 56 degrees awarded. *Degree requirements:* For master's, thesis (for some programs). *Entrance requirements:* Additional exam requirements/recommendations for international students: Required—TOEFL (minimum score 550 paper-based; 250 computer-based; 100 iBT). *Application deadline:* For fall admission, 1/7 for domestic and international students. Application fee: $90. *Expenses: Contact institution. Financial support:* In 2007–08, 90 students received support, including 56 teaching assistantships (averaging $1,600 per year); Federal Work-Study and scholarships/grants also available. Financial award application deadline: 3/1; financial award applicants required to submit FAFSA. *Unit head:* Robert Storr, Dean, 203-432-2606. *Application contact:* Patricia Ann DeChiara, Director of Academic Affairs, 203-432-2600, E-mail: artschool.info@yale.edu.

Illustration

Academy of Art University, Graduate Program, School of Illustration, San Francisco, CA 94105-3410. Offers MFA. *Accreditation:* NASAD. Part-time programs available. Postbaccalaureate distance learning degree programs offered (no on-campus study). *Degree requirements:* For master's, final review. *Entrance requirements:* For master's, minimum GPA of 3.0, portfolio. Electronic applications accepted.

Bob Jones University, Graduate Programs, Greenville, SC 29614. Offers accountancy (MS); Bible (MA); Bible translation (MA); Biblical studies (Certificate); broadcast management (MS); business administration (MBA); church history (MA, PhD); church ministries (MA); church music (MM); cinema and video production (MA); counseling (MS); curriculum and instruction (Ed D); divinity (M Div); dramatic production (MA); educational leadership (MS, Ed D, Ed S); elementary education (M Ed, MAT); English (M Ed, MA, MAT); fine arts (MA); graphic design (MA); history (M Ed, MA); illustration (MA); interpretative speech (MA); mathematics (M Ed, MAT); medical missions (Certificate); ministry (MM, D Min); multi-categorical special education (M Ed, MAT); music (M Ed); New Testament interpretation (PhD); Old Testament interpretation (PhD); orchestral instrument performance (MM); organ performance (MM); pastoral studies (MA); personnel services (MS, Ed S); piano pedagogy (MM); piano performance (MM); platform arts (MA); radio and television broadcasting (MS); rhetoric and public address (MA); secondary education (M Ed); studio art (MA); teaching Bible (MA); theology (MA, PhD); voice performance (MM); youth ministries (MA); M Div/MM.

Bradley University, Graduate School, Slane College of Communications and Fine Arts, Department of Art, Peoria, IL 61625-0002. Offers ceramics (MA, MFA); drawing/illustration (MA, MFA); interdisciplinary art (MA, MFA); painting (MA, MFA); photography (MA, MFA); printmaking (MA, MFA); sculpture (MA, MFA); visual communication and design (MA, MFA). *Accreditation:* NASAD. Part-time programs available. *Faculty:* 10. *Students:* 11 full-time (6 women), 1 international. 20 applicants, 40% accepted, 4 enrolled. In 2007, 2 degrees awarded. *Degree requirements:* For master's, comprehensive exam, thesis, final exhibit. *Entrance requirements:* For master's, portfolio, 2 letters of recommendation. Additional exam requirements/recommendations for international students: Required—TOEFL (minimum score 550 paper-based; 213 computer-based; 79 iBT). *Application deadline:* For fall admission, 4/1 priority date for domestic and international students; for spring admission, 11/1 priority date for domestic and international students. Applications are processed on a rolling basis. Application fee: $40 ($50 for international students). *Financial support:* Research assistantships with full and partial tuition reimbursements, scholarships/grants, tuition waivers (partial), and unspecified assistantships available. Financial award application deadline: 4/1. *Unit head:* Dr. Paul Krainak, Chairperson, 309-677-3330, E-mail: pkrainak@bradley.edu. *Application contact:* Fisher Stolz, Graduate Coordinator, 309-677-2969, E-mail: fisher@bradley.edu.

Fashion Institute of Technology, School of Graduate Studies, Program in Illustration, New York, NY 10001-5992. Offers MA. *Entrance requirements:* Additional exam requirements/recommendations for international students: Required—TOEFL (minimum score 550 paper-based; 213 computer-based). *Application deadline:* For fall admission, 2/15 priority date for domestic and international students. Applications are processed on a rolling basis. Application fee: $50. Electronic applications accepted. *Expenses:* Tuition, state resident: full-time $7,245; part-time $302 per credit. Tuition, nonresident: full-time $11,466; part-time $478 per credit. Required fees: $440; $35 per term. *Unit head:* Vincent Di Fate, Acting Associate Chair, 212-217-8047.

Kent State University, College of Communication and Information, School of Visual Communication Design, Kent, OH 44242-0001. Offers MA, MFA. *Accreditation:* NASAD. Part-time programs available. *Faculty:* 10 full-time (1 woman), 1 (woman) part-time/adjunct. *Students:* 11 full-time (2 women), 21 part-time (12 women); includes 3 minority (2 African Americans, 1 Hispanic American). Average age 25. 34 applicants, 44% accepted, 11 enrolled. In 2007, 7 degrees awarded. *Degree requirements:* For master's, thesis, portfolios. *Entrance requirements:* For master's, portfolio (studio majors), minimum GPA of 2.75, GPA of 3.0 in major. *Application deadline:* For fall admission, 7/12 for domestic students; for spring admission, 11/29 for domestic students. Applications are processed on a rolling basis. Application fee: $30. *Financial support:* In 2007–08, 1 research assistantship with full and partial tuition reimbursement (averaging $12,948 per year), 5 teaching assistantships with full and partial tuition reimbursements (averaging $12,948 per year) were awarded; career-related internships or fieldwork, Federal Work-Study, institutionally sponsored loans, health care benefits, tuition waivers (full and partial), and unspecified assistantships also available. Financial award application deadline: 2/1. *Faculty research:* Graphic design. Total annual research expenditures: $20,000. *Unit head:* Ann Marie LeBlanc, Director, 330-672-7856, Fax: 330-672-9714, E-mail: aleblanc@kent.edu. *Application contact:* Steven R. Timbrook, Graduate Coordinator, 330-672-7856, Fax: 330-672-9714, E-mail: stimbroo@kent.edu.

Marywood University, Academic Affairs, Insalaco College of Creative Arts and Management, Art Department, Program in Studio Art, Scranton, PA 18509-1598. Offers advertising design (MA); ceramics (MA); clay (MA); graphic design (MA); illustration (MA); interior architecture (MA); painting (MA); photography (MA); printmaking (MA); sculpture (MA); weaving (MA). *Accreditation:* NASAD. Part-time and evening/weekend programs available. *Students:* 5 full-time (3 women), 15 part-time (11 women), 1 international. Average age 41. 5 applicants, 80% accepted. In 2007, 7 degrees awarded. *Degree requirements:* For master's, comprehensive exam, thesis or alternative. *Entrance requirements:* For master's, portfolio. Additional exam requirements/recommendations for international students: Required—TOEFL (minimum score 550 paper-based; 213 computer-based). *Application deadline:* For fall admission, 4/15 priority date for domestic and international students; for spring admission, 11/15 priority date for domestic and international students. Applications are processed on a rolling basis. Application fee: $30. Electronic applications accepted. *Expenses:* Tuition: Full-time $15,290; part-time $695 per credit. Required fees: $990; $370 per term. Tuition and fees vary according to degree level. *Financial support:* Research assistantships with tuition reimbursements, scholarships/grants, tuition waivers (partial), and unspecified assistantships available. Support available to part-time students. Financial award application deadline: 2/15; financial award applicants required to submit FAFSA. *Faculty research:* Texture and line in clay, cast bronze sculpture, color theories, book art and illustration, sculptural form.

Marywood University, Academic Affairs, Insalaco College of Creative Arts and Management, Art Department, Program in Visual Arts, Scranton, PA 18509-1598. Offers advertising design (MFA); clay (MFA); fibers (MFA); graphic design (MFA); illustration (MFA); metals (MFA); painting (MFA); photography (MFA); printmaking (MFA). *Accreditation:* NASAD. Part-time and evening/weekend programs available. *Students:* 13 full-time (10 women), 25 part-time (13 women); includes 2 minority (1 American Indian/Alaska Native, 1 Asian American or Pacific Islander), 3 international. Average age 35. In 2007, 11 degrees awarded. *Degree requirements:* For master's, thesis or alternative, exhibit. *Entrance requirements:* For master's, portfolio. Additional exam requirements/recommendations for international students: Required—TOEFL (minimum score 550 paper-based; 213 computer-based). *Application deadline:* For fall admission, 4/15 priority date for domestic and international students; for spring admission, 11/15 priority date for domestic and international students. Applications are processed on a rolling basis. Application fee: $30. Electronic applications accepted. *Expenses: Contact institution.* Tuition

Illustration

Marywood University (continued)

and fees vary according to degree level. *Financial support:* Research assistantships with tuition reimbursements, scholarships/grants, tuition waivers (partial), and unspecified assistantships available. Support available to part-time students. Financial award application deadline: 2/15; financial award applicants required to submit FAFSA. *Faculty research:* Mariology, exploration of visual imagery, explorations involving drawing on the loom, clay as sculptural medium, oil paintings.

Minneapolis College of Art and Design, Program in Visual Studies, Minneapolis, MN 55404-4347. Offers animation (MFA); comic art (MFA); drawing (MFA); filmmaking (MFA); fine arts (MFA); furniture design (MFA); graphic design (MFA); illustration (MFA); interactive media (MFA); painting (MFA); photography (MFA); printmaking (MFA); sculpture (MFA). *Accreditation:* NASAD. Part-time programs available. *Faculty:* 23 full-time (7 women), 9 part-time/adjunct (4 women). *Students:* 40 full-time (21 women), 1 (woman) part-time; includes 1 minority (American Indian/Alaska Native). Average age 27. 172 applicants, 24% accepted, 15 enrolled. In 2007, 7 degrees awarded. *Degree requirements:* For master's, thesis, thesis exhibit. *Entrance requirements:* For master's, portfolio, resumé, 3 letters of recommendation, statement . Additional exam requirements/recommendations for international students: Required—TOEFL (minimum score 550 paper-based; 213 computer-based; 79 iBT). *Application deadline:* For fall admission, 2/15 for domestic and international students. Application fee: $50. Electronic applications accepted. *Expenses:* Tuition: Full-time $27,000; part-time $900 per credit. Required fees: $100 per term. *Financial support:* In 2007–08, 23 students received support, including 15 teaching assistantships (averaging $6,000 per year); career-related internships or fieldwork, Federal Work-Study, scholarships/grants, and unspecified assistantships also available. Support available to part-time students. Financial award application deadline: 3/15; financial award applicants required to submit FAFSA. *Faculty research:* Visual arts. *Unit head:* Carole Fisher, Graduate Director, 612-874-3629, E-mail: carole_fisher@mcad.edu. *Application contact:* William Mullen, Vice President of Enrollment Management, 612-874-3762, Fax: 612-874-3701, E-mail: william_mullen@mcad.edu.

Savannah College of Art and Design, Graduate School, Program in Illustration, Savannah, GA 31402-3146. Offers MA, MFA. Part-time programs available. *Faculty:* 6 full-time (1 woman). *Students:* 54 full-time (31 women), 7 part-time (4 women); includes 10 minority (6 African Americans, 2 Asian Americans or Pacific Islanders, 2 Hispanic Americans), 11 international. Average age 25. 77 applicants, 43% accepted, 22 enrolled. In 2007, 14 degrees awarded. *Degree requirements:* For master's, thesis, exhibit, internships. *Entrance requirements:* For master's, interview, portfolio. Additional exam requirements/recommendations for international students: Required—TOEFL (minimum score 450 paper-based; 133 computer-based). *Application deadline:* For fall admission, 4/1 priority date for domestic and international students. Applications are processed on a rolling basis. Application fee: $50. Electronic applications accepted. *Expenses:* Tuition: Full-time $24,840; part-time $552 per credit. One-time fee: $500 full-time. *Financial support:* In 2007–08, 4 fellowships were awarded; career-related internships or fieldwork, Federal Work-Study, and scholarships/grants also available. Financial award application deadline: 4/1; financial award applicants required to submit FAFSA. *Unit head:* Allan Drummond, Chair, 912-525-5187, Fax: 912-525-5981, E-mail: adrummon@scad.edu. *Application contact:* Darrell Tutchton, Director of Graduate and International Enrollment, 912-525-5961, Fax: 912-525-5985, E-mail: admission@scad.edu.

See Close-Up on page 257.

Savannah College of Art and Design, Graduate School, Program in Illustration Design, Savannah, GA 31402-3146. Offers MA. Part-time programs available. *Faculty:* 2 full-time (0 women). *Students:* 10 full-time (6 women), 3 part-time (2 women), 4 international. 9 applicants, 44% accepted, 4 enrolled. In 2007, 2 degrees awarded. *Degree requirements:* For master's, thesis. *Entrance requirements:* For master's, interview, portfolio. Additional exam requirements/recommendations for international students: Required—TOEFL (minimum score 450 paper-based; 133 computer-based). *Application deadline:* For fall admission, 4/1 priority date for domestic and international students. Applications are processed on a rolling basis. Application fee: $50. Electronic applications accepted. *Expenses:* Tuition: Full-time $24,840; part-time $552 per credit. One-time fee: $500 full-time. *Financial support:* Fellowships, career-related internships or fieldwork, Federal Work-Study, and scholarships/grants available. Financial award application deadline: 4/1; financial award applicants required to submit FAFSA. *Unit head:* Allan Drummond, Chair, 912-525-5817, Fax: 912-525-5981, E-mail: adrummond@scad.edu. *Application contact:* Darrell Tutchton, Director of Graduate and International Enrollment, 912-525-5961, Fax: 912-525-5985, E-mail: admission@scad.edu.

Savannah College of Art and Design, Graduate School, Program in Sequential Art, Savannah, GA 31402-3146. Offers MA, MFA. Part-time programs available. *Faculty:* 8 full-time (1 woman), 2 part-time/adjunct (0 women). *Students:* 43 full-time (13 women), 6 part-time (1 woman); includes 6 minority (all African Americans), 1 international. Average age 24. 33 applicants, 58% accepted, 13 enrolled. In 2007, 10 degrees awarded. *Degree requirements:* For master's, thesis, exhibit, internships. *Entrance requirements:* For master's, interview, portfolio. Additional exam requirements/recommendations for international students: Required—TOEFL (minimum score 450 paper-based; 133 computer-based). *Application deadline:* For fall admission, 4/1 priority date for domestic and international students. Applications are processed on a rolling basis. Application fee: $50. Electronic applications accepted. *Expenses:* Tuition: Full-time $24,840; part-time $552 per credit. One-time fee: $500 full-time. *Financial support:* In 2007–08, 2 fellowships were awarded; career-related internships or fieldwork, Federal Work-Study, and scholarships/grants also available. Financial award application deadline: 4/1; financial award applicants required to submit FAFSA. *Unit head:* John Lowe, Chair, 912-525-4859, Fax: 912-525-5996, E-mail: jlowe@scad.edu. *Application contact:* Darrell Tutchton, Director of Graduate and International Enrollment, 912-525-5961, Fax: 912-525-5985, E-mail: admission@scad.edu.

See Close-Up on page 257.

School of Visual Arts, Graduate Programs, Illustration Department, New York, NY 10010-3994. Offers MFA. *Accreditation:* NASAD. *Faculty:* 1 full-time (0 women), 11 part-time/adjunct (5 women). *Students:* 40 full-time (18 women); includes 7 minority (2 African Americans, 2 Asian Americans or Pacific Islanders, 3 Hispanic Americans), 14 international. Average age 27. 102 applicants, 28% accepted, 25 enrolled. In 2007, 17 degrees awarded. *Degree requirements:* For master's, final review, project or thesis. *Entrance requirements:* For master's, portfolio. Additional exam requirements/recommendations for international students: Required—TOEFL (minimum score 550 paper-based; 213 computer-based; 79 iBT). *Application deadline:* For fall admission, 2/1 for domestic students. Application fee: $80. Electronic applications accepted. *Expenses:* Tuition: Full-time $26,120; part-time $870 per credit. Tuition and fees vary according to program. *Financial support:* In 2007–08, 21 students received support. Career-related internships or fieldwork, Federal Work-Study, scholarships/grants, and unspecified assistantships available. Support available to part-time students. Financial award application deadline: 2/1; financial award applicants required to submit FAFSA. *Unit head:* Marshall Arisman, Chair, 212-592-2210, Fax: 212-366-1675, E-mail: marisman@sva.edu.

Syracuse University, Graduate School, College of Visual and Performing Arts, School of Art and Design, Programs in Art, Syracuse, NY 13244. Offers ceramics (MFA); fiber arts/materials studies (MFA); illustration (MFA); jewelry and metalsmithing (MFA); painting (MFA); printmaking (MFA); sculpture (MFA). *Accreditation:* NASAD. Part-time programs available. *Students:* 40 full-time (27 women), 4 part-time (3 women); includes 4 minority (2 Asian Americans or Pacific Islanders, 2 Hispanic Americans), 6 international. 129 applicants, 15% accepted, 12 enrolled. In 2007, 26 master's awarded. *Degree requirements:* For master's, thesis or alternative. *Entrance requirements:* For master's, portfolio. Additional exam requirements/recommendations for international students: Required—TOEFL. *Application deadline:* For fall admission, 1/1 priority date for domestic students. Applications are processed on a rolling basis. Application fee: $75. Electronic applications accepted. *Expenses:* Tuition: Full-time $18,216; part-time $1,012 per credit. Required fees: $980. Tuition and fees vary according to program. *Financial support:* In 2007–08, 16 students received support; fellowships with full tuition reimbursements available, research assistantships with full and partial tuition reimbursements available, teaching assistantships with full and partial tuition reimbursements available, tuition waivers (partial) available. *Unit head:* Ann Clark, Chair, 315-443-4613, Fax: 315-443-1303. *Application contact:* Harriett Conti, Associate Director, Graduate Student Services, 315-443-3089, E-mail: hmconti@syr.edu.

University of California, Santa Cruz, Division of Graduate Studies, Division of Physical and Biological Sciences, Program in Science Communication, Santa Cruz, CA 95064. Offers science illustration (Certificate); science writing (Certificate). *Faculty:* 8 full-time (4 women). *Students:* 11 full-time (9 women); includes 3 minority (all Asian Americans or Pacific Islanders), 2 international. In 2007, 19 degrees awarded. *Entrance requirements:* For degree, GRE General Test, GRE Subject Test, bachelor's degree in science. Application fee: $60. Electronic applications accepted. *Expenses:* Tuition, nonresident: full-time $14,694. Required fees: $11,360. *Financial support:* Fellowships, research assistantships, teaching assistantships, career-related internships or fieldwork, Federal Work-Study, institutionally sponsored loans, and scholarships/grants available. Financial award application deadline: 2/1. *Unit head:* Robert Irion, Director, 831-459-4475. *Application contact:* Andrea Michels, Department Assistant, 831-459-4475, E-mail: scicom@ucsc.edu.

University of Massachusetts Dartmouth, Graduate School, College of Visual and Performing Arts, Program in Visual Design, North Dartmouth, MA 02747-2300. Offers digital multi-media (MFA); electronic imaging (MFA); graphic design (MFA); illustration (MFA); photography (MFA); typography (MFA). *Accreditation:* NASAD. *Faculty:* 17 full-time (7 women), 7 part-time/adjunct (3 women). *Students:* 8 full-time (6 women), 2 part-time (both women); includes 1 minority (Asian American or Pacific Islander), 2 international. Average age 35. 21 applicants, 24% accepted, 4 enrolled. In 2007, 3 degrees awarded. *Degree requirements:* For master's, visual thesis. *Entrance requirements:* For master's, portfolio, interview, minimum GPA of 3.0, 3 letters of recommendation. Additional exam requirements/recommendations for international students: Required—TOEFL (minimum score 500 paper-based). *Application deadline:* For fall admission, 3/1 priority date for domestic students, 1/1 priority date for international students. Applications are processed on a rolling basis. Application fee: $40 ($60 for international students). Electronic applications accepted. *Expenses:* Tuition, state resident: full-time $2,071; part-time $86 per credit. Tuition, nonresident: full-time $8,099; part-time $337 per credit. Part-time tuition and fees vary according to course load and program. *Financial support:* In 2007–08, 4 teaching assistantships (averaging $2,930 per year) were awarded; research assistantships, Federal Work-Study and unspecified assistantships also available. Support available to part-time students. Financial award application deadline: 3/1; financial award applicants required to submit FAFSA. Total annual research expenditures: $22,880. *Unit head:* Jarrad Nunes, Director, 508-999-8010, E-mail: jnunes@umassd.edu. *Application contact:* Carol Novo, Graduate Admissions Officer, 508-999-8604, Fax: 508-999-8183, E-mail: graduate@umassd.edu.

Western Connecticut State University, Division of Graduate Studies, School of Visual and Performing Arts, Department of Art, Danbury, CT 06810-6885. Offers illustration (MFA); painting (MFA). *Faculty:* 4 full-time (1 woman), 1 part-time/adjunct (0 women). *Students:* 17 full-time (11 women); includes 3 minority (1 African American, 1 Asian American or Pacific Islander, 1 Hispanic American). Average age 29. 12 applicants, 83% accepted, 9 enrolled. In 2007, 4 degrees awarded. *Degree requirements:* For master's, individual exhibition of artwork. *Entrance requirements:* For master's, portfolio review, minimum GPA of 2.5. *Application deadline:* For fall admission, 8/5 priority date for domestic students; for spring admission, 1/5 priority date for domestic students. Application fee: $50. *Expenses:* Tuition, state resident: full-time $4,169. Tuition, nonresident: full-time $11,614. Required fees: $3,278. *Financial support:* Career-related internships or fieldwork available. Support available to part-time students. Financial award application deadline: 5/1; financial award applicants required to submit FAFSA. *Unit head:* Margaret Grimes, Professor, 203-837-8402. *Application contact:* Chris Shankle, Associate Director of Graduate Admissions, 203-837-8244, Fax: 203-837-8338, E-mail: shanklec@wcsu.edu.

Industrial Design

Academy of Art University, Graduate Program, School of Industrial Design, San Francisco, CA 94105-3410. Offers MFA. Part-time programs available. Postbaccalaureate distance learning degree programs offered (no on-campus study). *Degree requirements:* For master's, final review. *Entrance requirements:* For master's, portfolio. Electronic applications accepted.

Art Center College of Design, Graduate Division, Industrial Design Department, Pasadena, CA 91103-1999. Offers environmental design (MS); product design (MS). *Accreditation:* NASAD. *Faculty:* 8 part-time/adjunct (1 woman). *Students:* 33 full-time (15 women), 5 part-time (4 women); includes 10 minority (all Asian Americans or Pacific Islanders), 16 international. Average age 29. 56 applicants, 36% accepted, 13 enrolled. In 2007, 2 degrees awarded. *Degree requirements:* For master's, thesis, studio project. *Entrance requirements:* For master's, portfolio. Additional exam requirements/recommendations for international students: Required—TOEFL (minimum score 600 paper-based; 250 computer-based; 100 iBT). *Application deadline:* For fall admission, 2/1 for domestic and international students. Application fee: $50 ($70 for international students). *Expenses:* Tuition: Full-time $31,016. Required fees: $235. *Financial support:* Teaching assistantships, career-related internships or fieldwork, Federal Work-Study, and scholarships/grants available. Financial award application deadline: 2/1. *Unit head:* Andrew Ogden, Chair, 626-396-2464. *Application contact:* Kit Baron, Vice President, Admissions, 626-396-2373, Fax: 626-795-0578, E-mail: admissions@artcenter.edu.

See Close-Up on page 109.

Auburn University, Graduate School, College of Architecture, Design, and Construction, Department of Industrial Design, Auburn University, AL 36849. Offers MID. *Accreditation:* NASAD. Part-time programs available. *Faculty:* 8 full-time (0 women). *Students:* 7 full-time (2 women), 8 part-time (2 women); includes 6 minority (4 African Americans, 1 Asian American or Pacific Islander, 1 Hispanic American). Average age 27. 16 applicants, 50% accepted, 6 enrolled. In 2007, 8 degrees awarded. *Entrance requirements:* For master's, GRE General Test. *Application deadline:* For fall admission, 9/1 for domestic students; for spring admission, 3/1 for domestic students. Applications are processed on a rolling basis. Application fee: $25 ($50 for international students). Electronic applications accepted. *Financial support:* Federal Work-Study available. Support available to part-time students. Financial award application deadline: 3/15. *Faculty research:* Design of space living facilities, color use in business communications.

Unit head: Clark E. Lundell, Head, 334-844-2364. *Application contact:* Dr. Joe Pittman, Interim Dean of the Graduate School, 334-844-4700.

Brigham Young University, Graduate Studies, Ira A. Fulton College of Engineering and Technology, School of Technology, Provo, UT 84602-1001. Offers construction management (MS); information technology (MS); manufacturing systems (MS); technology and engineering education (MS). *Faculty:* 27 full-time (0 women). *Students:* 33 full-time (3 women), 4 part-time; includes 1 minority (Asian American or Pacific Islander) Average age 25. 16 applicants, 56% accepted, 8 enrolled. In 2007, 12 degrees awarded. *Degree requirements:* For master's, thesis. *Entrance requirements:* For master's, GRE General Test, GMAT (construction management), minimum GPA of 3.0 in last 60 hours of course work. Additional exam requirements/recommendations for international students: Required—TOEFL (minimum score 580 paper-based; 237 computer-based; 85 iBT). *Application deadline:* For fall admission, 2/15 for domestic and international students; for winter admission, 9/15 for domestic and international students. Application fee: $50. Electronic applications accepted. *Financial support:* In 2007–08, 32 students received support, including 6 research assistantships (averaging $2,530 per year), 12 teaching assistantships (averaging $3,600 per year); fellowships, career-related internships or fieldwork also available. Financial award application deadline: 3/15. *Faculty research:* Real time process control in IT, electronic physical design, processing and non-linear systems, networking, computerized systems in CM. Total annual research expenditures: $52,110. *Unit head:* Val D. Hawks, Director, 801-422-6300, Fax: 801-422-0490, E-mail: hawksv@byu.edu. *Application contact:* Barry M. Lunt, Graduate Coordinator, 801-422-2264, Fax: 801-422-0490, E-mail: ralowe@byu.edu.

Carleton University, Faculty of Graduate Studies, Faculty of Engineering and Design, School of Industrial Design, Ottawa, ON K1S 5B6, Canada. Offers M Des. *Degree requirements:* For master's, thesis optional. *Entrance requirements:* For master's, honors degree. Additional exam requirements/recommendations for international students: Required—TOEFL. *Application deadline:* Applications are processed on a rolling basis. Application fee: $77. *Financial support:* Fellowships, research assistantships, teaching assistantships available. *Unit head:* James Budd, Chair, 613-520-2600 Ext. 3481, Fax: 613-562-5174. *Application contact:* Diane Smyth, Graduate Studies Administrator, 613-520-2600 Ext. 5591, Fax: 613-520-5682, E-mail: diane_smith@carleton.ca.

North Carolina State University, Graduate School, College of Design, Department of Industrial Design, Raleigh, NC 27695. Offers MID. *Accreditation:* NASAD. Part-time programs available. *Degree requirements:* For master's, thesis optional, oral exam, project. *Entrance requirements:* For master's, GRE General Test (recommended), portfolio. Electronic applications accepted. *Faculty research:* Computer graphics, ergonomics, product design.

The Ohio State University, Graduate School, College of the Arts, Department of Industrial, Interior, and Visual Communication Design, Columbus, OH 43210. Offers MA, MFA. *Accreditation:* NASAD. Part-time programs available. *Faculty:* 14. *Students:* 24 full-time (12 women), 7 part-time (5 women); includes 3 minority (1 African American, 2 Asian Americans or Pacific Islanders), 7 international. Average age 29. In 2007, 7 degrees awarded. *Degree requirements:* For master's, project or thesis. *Entrance requirements:* For master's, bachelor's degree in interior space, graphics, product design, or related field. Additional exam requirements/recommendations for international students: Recommended—TOEFL (minimum score 600 paper-based; 250 computer-based). *Application deadline:* For fall admission, 8/15 priority date for domestic students, 7/1 priority date for international students; for winter admission, 12/1 priority date for domestic students, 11/1 priority date for international students; for spring admission, 3/1 priority date for domestic students, 2/1 priority date for international students. Applications are processed on a rolling basis. Application fee: $40 ($50 for international students). Electronic applications accepted. *Financial support:* Fellowships, research assistantships, teaching assistantships, career-related internships or fieldwork, Federal Work-Study, institutionally sponsored loans, and unspecified assistantships available. Support available to part-time students. Financial award application deadline: 5/1. *Unit head:* R. Brian Stone, Graduate Studies Committee Chair, 614-688-6746, Fax: 614-292-0217, E-mail: stone.158@osu.edu. *Application contact:* 614-292-9444, Fax: 614-292-3895, E-mail: domestic.grad@osu.edu.

Pratt Institute, School of Art and Design, Program in Industrial Design, Brooklyn, NY 11205-3899. Offers MID. *Accreditation:* NASAD. Part-time programs available. *Faculty:* 6 full-time (1 woman), 26 part-time/adjunct (8 women). *Students:* 77 full-time (41 women), 7 part-time (6 women); includes 12 minority (1 African American, 1 American Indian/Alaska Native, 7 Asian Americans or Pacific Islanders, 3 Hispanic Americans), 16 international. Average age 29. 185 applicants, 23% accepted, 28 enrolled. In 2007, 36 degrees awarded. *Degree requirements:* For master's, thesis. *Entrance requirements:* For master's, portfolio, bachelor's degree, transcripts, letters of recommendation, statement. Additional exam requirements/recommendations for international students: Required—TOEFL (minimum score 550 paper-based; 213 computer-based). *Application deadline:* For fall admission, 2/1 for domestic students; for spring admission, 10/1 for domestic students. Application fee: $50 ($90 for international students). Electronic applications accepted. *Expenses:* Tuition: Full-time $25,680. Required fees: $1,106. Tuition and fees vary according to program. *Financial support:* Career-related internships or fieldwork, Federal Work-Study, institutionally sponsored loans, scholarships/grants, health care benefits, and unspecified assistantships available. Support available to part-time students. Financial award application deadline: 2/1; financial award applicants required to submit FAFSA. *Faculty research:* Universal design, design ethics, sustainability in design. Total annual research expenditures: $20,000. *Unit head:* Matthew Burger, Chairperson, 718-636-3520, Fax: 718-636-3553, E-mail: mburger@pratt.edu. *Application contact:* Young Hah, Director of Graduate Admissions, 718-636-3683, Fax: 718-399-4242, E-mail: yhah@pratt.edu.

See Close-Up on page 253.

Pratt Institute, School of Art and Design, Program in Package Design, Brooklyn, NY 11205-3899. Offers MS. *Accreditation:* NASAD. Part-time programs available. *Faculty:* 5 full-time (2 women), 33 part-time/adjunct (9 women). *Students:* 31 full-time (26 women), 1 (woman) part-time; includes 5 minority (3 Asian Americans or Pacific Islanders, 2 Hispanic Americans), 19 international. Average age 26. 37 applicants, 57% accepted, 12 enrolled. In 2007, 7 degrees awarded. *Degree requirements:* For master's, thesis. *Entrance requirements:* For master's, portfolio, bachelor's degree, transcripts, letters of recommendation, statement. Additional exam requirements/recommendations for international students: Required—TOEFL (minimum score 550 paper-based; 213 computer-based). *Application deadline:* For fall admission, 2/1 for domestic students; for spring admission, 10/1 for domestic students. Application fee: $50 ($90 for international students). Electronic applications accepted. *Expenses:* Tuition: Full-time $25,680. Required fees: $1,106. Tuition and fees vary according to program. *Financial support:* Career-related internships or fieldwork, Federal Work-Study, institutionally sponsored loans, scholarships/grants, health care benefits, and unspecified assistantships available. Support available to part-time students. Financial award application deadline: 2/1; financial award applicants required to submit FAFSA. *Unit head:* J. Guilfoyle, Chairperson, 212-647-7573, E-mail: jguilfoy@pratt.edu. *Application contact:* Young Hah, Director of Graduate Admissions, 718-636-3683, Fax: 718-399-4242, E-mail: yhah@pratt.edu.

See Close-Up on page 253.

Rhode Island School of Design, Graduate Studies, Division of Architecture and Design, Department of Industrial Design, Providence, RI 02903-2784. Offers MID. *Accreditation:* NASAD. *Degree requirements:* For master's, thesis, exhibit. *Entrance requirements:* For master's, portfolio, 3 letters of recommendation. Additional exam requirements/recommendations for international students: Required—TOEFL (minimum score 580 paper-based; 237 computer-based), IELTS (minimum score 7).

Rochester Institute of Technology, Graduate Enrollment Services, College of Imaging Arts and Sciences, School of Design, Program in Industrial Design, Rochester, NY 14623-5603. Offers MFA. *Accreditation:* NASAD. *Students:* 21 full-time (9 women), 6 part-time (2 women); includes 3 minority (2 African Americans, 1 Asian American or Pacific Islander), 15 international. 81 applicants, 43% accepted, 9 enrolled. In 2007, 4 degrees awarded. *Degree requirements:* For master's, thesis (for some programs). *Entrance requirements:* For master's, portfolio, minimum GPA of 3.0. Additional exam requirements/recommendations for international students: Required—TOEFL. *Application deadline:* For fall admission, 3/1 priority date for domestic students. Applications are processed on a rolling basis. Application fee: $50. *Expenses:* Tuition: Full-time $28,491; part-time $800 per credit hour. Required fees: $201; $67 per term. *Financial support:* Teaching assistantships with partial tuition reimbursements, career-related internships or fieldwork, institutionally sponsored loans, scholarships/grants, and unspecified assistantships available. Support available to part-time students. Financial award applicants required to submit FAFSA. *Unit head:* Charles Lewis, Chair, 585-475-6357, E-mail: cflfaa@rit.edu.

San Francisco State University, Division of Graduate Studies, College of Creative Arts, Department of Design and Industry, San Francisco, CA 94132-1722. Offers industrial arts (MA). *Unit head:* Ricardo Gomes, Chair, 415-338-2211. *Application contact:* Martin Linder, Graduate Coordinator, 415-338-2211, E-mail: mlinder@sfsu.edu.

Savannah College of Art and Design, Graduate School, Program in Industrial Design, Savannah, GA 31402-3146. Offers MA, MFA. Part-time programs available. *Faculty:* 5 full-time (0 women). *Students:* 32 full-time (10 women), 14 part-time (8 women); includes 2 minority (1 Asian American or Pacific Islander, 1 Hispanic American), 33 international. Average age 25. 74 applicants, 54% accepted, 18 enrolled. In 2007, 4 degrees awarded. *Degree requirements:* For master's, thesis, exhibit, internships. *Entrance requirements:* For master's, interview, portfolio. Additional exam requirements/recommendations for international students: Required—TOEFL (minimum score 450 paper-based; 133 computer-based). *Application deadline:* For fall admission, 4/1 priority date for domestic students, 4/1 for international students. Applications are processed on a rolling basis. Application fee: $50. Electronic applications accepted. *Expenses:* Tuition: Full-time $24,840; part-time $552 per credit. One-time fee: $500 full-time. *Financial support:* In 2007–08, 3 fellowships were awarded; career-related internships or fieldwork, Federal Work-Study, and scholarships/grants also available. Financial award application deadline: 4/1; financial award applicants required to submit FAFSA. *Unit head:* Tom Gattis, Chair, 912-525-6426, Fax: 912-525-6437, E-mail: tgattis@scad.edu. *Application contact:* Darrell Tutchton, Director of Graduate and International Enrollment, 912-525-5961, Fax: 912-525-5985, E-mail: admission@scad.edu.

See Close-Up on page 257.

University of Cincinnati, Graduate School, College of Design, Architecture, Art, and Planning, School of Design, Cincinnati, OH 45221. Offers fashion design (M Des); graphic design (M Des); industrial design (M Des); interaction design (M Des); product development (M Des). *Accreditation:* NASAD. *Students:* 13 full-time (7 women), 6 part-time (5 women), 10 international. In 2007, 3 degrees awarded. *Degree requirements:* For master's, thesis. *Entrance requirements:* For master's, undergraduate degree in design or related field, 2 years of work experience in design or related field. Additional exam requirements/recommendations for international students: Required—TOEFL. *Application deadline:* For fall admission, 2/1 for domestic students. Application fee: $30. Electronic applications accepted. *Financial support:* Fellowships, career-related internships or fieldwork, Federal Work-Study, tuition waivers (partial), and unspecified assistantships available. *Faculty research:* Design theory, interdisciplinary design topics. *Unit head:* Prof. Dale Murray, Director, 513-556-1524, E-mail: dale.murray@uc.edu. *Application contact:* Dr. J. Chewning, Information Contact, 513-556-2996, Fax: 513-556-0240, E-mail: j.chewning@uc.edu.

University of Illinois at Chicago, Graduate College, College of Architecture and Art, School of Art and Design, Chicago, IL 60607-7128. Offers electronic visualization (MFA); film animation (MFA); graphic design (MFA); industrial design (MFA); photography (MFA); studio arts (MFA). *Accreditation:* NASAD. *Degree requirements:* For master's, thesis, exhibit. *Entrance requirements:* For master's, MAT, portfolio. Additional exam requirements/recommendations for international students: Required—TOEFL. Electronic applications accepted.

University of Illinois at Urbana–Champaign, Graduate College, College of Fine and Applied Arts, School of Art and Design, Program in Design and Media, Champaign, IL 61820. Offers graphic design (MFA); industrial design (MFA). *Accreditation:* NASAD. *Students:* 7 full-time (5 women); includes 1 minority (Asian American or Pacific Islander), 5 international. 61 applicants, 11% accepted, 6 enrolled. In 2007, 6 master's awarded. *Entrance requirements:* For master's, minimum GPA of 3.0. *Application deadline:* Applications are processed on a rolling basis. Application fee: $60 ($75 for international students). Electronic applications accepted. *Financial support:* Fellowships, research assistantships, teaching assistantships available. Financial award application deadline: 2/15. *Unit head:* Dr. Nan Goggin, Program Chair, 217-333-9327, Fax: 217-244-7688, E-mail: goggin@uiuc.edu.

University of Notre Dame, Graduate School, College of Arts and Letters, Division of Humanities, Department of Art, Art History, and Design, Notre Dame, IN 46556. Offers art history (MA); design (MFA), including graphic design, industrial design; studio art (MFA), including ceramics, painting, photography, printmaking, sculpture. *Accreditation:* NASAD. *Faculty:* 19 full-time (6 women), 3 part-time/adjunct (1 woman). *Students:* 25 full-time (12 women), 1 (woman) part-time; includes 4 minority (1 African American, 1 Asian American or Pacific Islander, 2 Hispanic Americans), 1 international. 85 applicants, 14% accepted, 10 enrolled. In 2007, 7 degrees awarded. *Degree requirements:* For master's, comprehensive exam, thesis. *Entrance requirements:* For master's, GRE General Test, minimum GPA of 3.0. Additional exam requirements/recommendations for international students: Required—TOEFL (minimum score 600 paper-based; 250 computer-based; 80 iBT). *Application deadline:* For fall admission, 2/1 priority date for domestic and international students. Application fee: $50. Electronic applications accepted. *Financial support:* In 2007–08, 20 students received support, including fellowships with full tuition reimbursements available (averaging $12,000 per year), research assistantships with full tuition reimbursements available (averaging $12,000 per year), 15 teaching assistantships with full tuition reimbursements available (averaging $12,000 per year); scholarships/grants, tuition waivers (full), and unspecified assistantships also available. Financial award application deadline: 2/1. *Faculty research:* Studio art practice in ceramics, printing, photography, printmaking and sculpture, graphic design and industrial design, digital imaging in design and photography, Renaissance and American art history, contemporary art theory and criticism. *Unit head:* Prof. Jean Dibble, Director of Graduate Studies, 574-631-7602, E-mail: art.1@nd.edu. *Application contact:* Dr. Jarren Gonzales, Director of Graduate Admissions, 574-631-7706, Fax: 574-631-4183.

The University of the Arts, College of Art and Design, Department of Industrial Design, Philadelphia, PA 19102-4944. Offers MID. *Accreditation:* NASAD. *Degree requirements:* For master's, thesis. *Entrance requirements:* For master's, portfolio. Additional exam requirements/recommendations for international students: Required—TOEFL (minimum score 550 paper-based; 213 computer-based).

See Close-Up on page 273.

Interior Design

Academy of Art University, Graduate Program, School of Interior Architecture and Design, San Francisco, CA 94105-3410. Offers MFA. Part-time programs available. Postbaccalaureate distance learning degree programs offered (no on-campus study). *Degree requirements:* For master's, final review. *Entrance requirements:* For master's, portfolio. Electronic applications accepted.

Boston Architectural College, Graduate Programs, Boston, MA 02115-2795. Offers architecture (M Arch); interior design (MID). *Accreditation:* CIDA. *Degree requirements:* For master's, thesis. *Entrance requirements:* For master's, portfolio (recommended). Electronic applications accepted.

See Close-Up on page 159.

Chatham University, Program in Interior Architecture, Pittsburgh, PA 15232-2826. Offers MIA, MSIA. *Students:* 20 full-time (18 women), 16 part-time (14 women). Average age 35. 20 applicants, 85% accepted, 11 enrolled. In 2007, 6 degrees awarded. *Entrance requirements:* For master's, 2 letters of recommendation, resumé. Additional exam requirements/recommendations for international students: Recommended—TOEFL (minimum score 600 paper-based; 250 computer-based; 100 iBT), IELTS (minimum score 7). *Application deadline:* For fall admission, 5/1 priority date for domestic and international students; for winter admission, 10/1 priority date for domestic and international students. Applications are processed on a rolling basis. Application fee: $45. Electronic applications accepted. *Unit head:* Dr. John Martin-Rutherford, Director, 412-365-2978, E-mail: jmartinrutherford@chatham.edu. *Application contact:* Office of Graduate Admissions, 412-365-1825, Fax: 412-365-1609, E-mail: admissions@chatham.edu.

Columbia College Chicago, Graduate School, Program in Interior Design, Chicago, IL 60605-1996. Offers MFA. *Faculty:* 1 part-time/adjunct. *Students:* 11 full-time (all women), 8 part-time (6 women); includes 2 minority (both Hispanic Americans), 3 international. Average age 27. In 2007, 7 degrees awarded. *Degree requirements:* For master's, thesis. *Entrance requirements:* For master's, minimum GPA of 3.0, portfolio. Additional exam requirements/recommendations for international students: Required—TOEFL (minimum score 550 paper-based; 213 computer-based). *Application deadline:* For fall admission, 3/1 for domestic and international students. Application fee: $50. Electronic applications accepted. *Financial support:* Career-related internships or fieldwork, Federal Work-Study, and scholarships/grants available. Support available to part-time students. Financial award application deadline: 8/13; financial award applicants required to submit FAFSA. *Unit head:* Jay Wolke, Head, 312-344-7867, Fax: 312-344-8009, E-mail: jwolke@colum.edu. *Application contact:* Keith Cleveland, Acting Dean of the Graduate School, 312-344-7261, Fax: 312-344-8047, E-mail: kcleveland@colum.edu.

Corcoran College of Art and Design, Graduate Programs, Washington, DC 20006-4804. Offers art education (MAT); history of decorative arts (MA); interior design (MA). *Accreditation:* NASAD. Part-time programs available. *Entrance requirements:* Additional exam requirements/recommendations for international students: Required—TOEFL.

Cornell University, Graduate School, Graduate Fields of Human Ecology, Field of Design and Environmental Analysis, Ithaca, NY 14853-0001. Offers applied research in human-environment relations (MS); facilities planning and management (MS); housing and design (MS); human factors and ergonomics (MS); human-environment relations (MS); interior design (MA, MPS). *Faculty:* 14 full-time (6 women). *Students:* 24 full-time (19 women); includes 5 minority (2 Asian Americans or Pacific Islanders, 3 Hispanic Americans), 8 international. Average age 26. 33 applicants, 45% accepted, 12 enrolled. In 2007, 8 degrees awarded. *Degree requirements:* For master's, thesis. *Entrance requirements:* For master's, GRE General Test, portfolio or slides of recent work; bachelor's degree in interior design, architecture or related design discipline; 2 letters of recommendation. Additional exam requirements/recommendations for international students: Required—TOEFL (minimum score 600 paper-based; 250 computer-based; 105 iBT). *Application deadline:* For fall admission, 2/1 priority date for domestic students. Application fee: $70. Electronic applications accepted. *Financial support:* In 2007–08, 13 students received support, including 2 fellowships with full tuition reimbursements available, 11 teaching assistantships with full tuition reimbursements available; research assistantships with full tuition reimbursements available, institutionally sponsored loans, scholarships/grants, health care benefits, tuition waivers (full and partial), and unspecified assistantships also available. Financial award applicants required to submit FAFSA. *Faculty research:* Facility planning and management, environmental psychology, housing, interior design, ergonomics and human factors. *Unit head:* Director of Graduate Studies, 607-255-2168, Fax: 607-255-0305. *Application contact:* Graduate Field Assistant, 607-255-2168, Fax: 607-255-0305, E-mail: deagrad@cornell.edu.

Drexel University, College of Media Arts and Design, Philadelphia, PA 19104-2875. Offers architecture (M Arch); design (MS), including fashion design, interior design; media arts (MS); performing arts (MS), including arts administration. *Accreditation:* NASAD. Part-time and evening/weekend programs available. *Entrance requirements:* For master's, interview. Additional exam requirements/recommendations for international students: Required—TOEFL. Electronic applications accepted. Expenses: Contact institution.

Drexel University, College of Media Arts and Design, Department of Design, Program in Interior Design, Philadelphia, PA 19104-2875. Offers MS. *Accreditation:* NASAD. *Degree requirements:* For master's, thesis. *Entrance requirements:* For master's, interview. Additional exam requirements/recommendations for international students: Required—TOEFL. Electronic applications accepted. *Faculty research:* History of commercial interiors, hospice spaces, environmental sculpture, painting.

Eastern Michigan University, Graduate School, College of Technology, School of Engineering Technology, Program in Interior Design, Ypsilanti, MI 48197. Offers MS. Part-time and evening/weekend programs available. Postbaccalaureate distance learning degree programs offered (minimal on-campus study). *Students:* 5 full-time (all women), 19 part-time (17 women); includes 2 minority (1 African American, 1 Asian American or Pacific Islander), 2 international. Average age 36. In 2007, 3 degrees awarded. *Entrance requirements:* Additional exam requirements/recommendations for international students: Required—TOEFL. *Application deadline:* Applications are processed on a rolling basis. Application fee: $35. *Expenses:* Tuition, state resident: full-time $8,952; part-time $373 per credit hour. Tuition, nonresident: full-time $17,634; part-time $735 per credit hour. Required fees: $896; $34 per credit hour. Tuition and fees vary according to course level, degree level and program. *Financial support:* Fellowships, research assistantships with full tuition reimbursements, teaching assistantships with full tuition reimbursements, career-related internships or fieldwork, Federal Work-Study, institutionally sponsored loans, scholarships/grants, tuition waivers (partial), and unspecified assistantships available. Support available to part-time students. Financial award applicants required to submit FAFSA. *Unit head:* Dr. Louise Jones, Coordinator, 734-487-2040, Fax: 734-487-8755, E-mail: louise.jones@emich.edu.

Florida International University, College of Architecture and the Arts, School of Architecture, Interior Design Program, Miami, FL 33199. Offers MID. *Students:* 17 full-time (15 women), 3 part-time (2 women); includes 11 minority (2 African Americans, 2 Asian Americans or Pacific Islanders, 7 Hispanic Americans), 1 international. Average age 28. 23 applicants, 57% accepted, 8 enrolled. *Entrance requirements:* For master's, minimum GPA of 3.0 (upper level coursework). Additional exam requirements/recommendations for international students: Required—TOEFL (minimum score 550 paper-based; 213 computer-based). *Application deadline:* For fall admission, 2/1 for domestic and international students. Application fee: $30. Electronic applications accepted. *Expenses:* Tuition, state resident: full-time $6,106. Tuition, nonresident: full-time $15,528. Required fees: $284. *Financial support:* Research assistantships, teaching assistantships available. *Unit head:* Juan A. Bueno, Dean, 305-348-6101, Fax: 305-348-6716, E-mail: buenoj@fiu.edu.

Florida State University, Graduate Studies, College of Visual Arts, Theatre and Dance, Department of Interior Design, Tallahassee, FL 32306. Offers MA, MFA, MS. *Accreditation:* NASAD (one or more programs are accredited). *Faculty:* 8 full-time (3 women). *Students:* 37 full-time (34 women), 1 part-time; includes 2 minority (both African Americans), 2 international. Average age 30. 13 applicants, 92% accepted, 12 enrolled. In 2007, 14 degrees awarded. *Degree requirements:* For master's, thesis or alternative. *Entrance requirements:* For master's, GRE General Test, minimum GPA of 3.0 during previous 2 years. Additional exam requirements/recommendations for international students: Required—TOEFL (minimum score 550 paper-based). Application fee: $30. Electronic applications accepted. *Expenses:* Tuition, state resident: part-time $248 per credit hour. Tuition, nonresident: part-time $880 per credit hour. Tuition and fees vary according to program. *Financial support:* In 2007–08, 1 fellowship (averaging $18,000 per year), 10 research assistantships with tuition reimbursements (averaging $3,200 per year), 2 teaching assistantships with tuition reimbursements (averaging $3,200 per year) were awarded; career-related internships or fieldwork and unspecified assistantships also available. Financial award applicants required to submit FAFSA. *Faculty research:* Graphics techniques, history of interiors, technical proficiencies, computer-aided design and drafting, historic restoration. *Unit head:* Eric Wiedegreen, Chairman, 850-645-2504, Fax: 850-644-3112, E-mail: ewiedegr@fsu.edu. *Application contact:* Dr. Lisa Waxman, Director of Graduate Studies, 850-644-8326, Fax: 850-644-3112, E-mail: lwaxman@mailer.fsu.edu.

The George Washington University, Columbian College of Arts and Sciences, Department of Fine Arts and Art History, Washington, DC 20052. Offers art history (MA, PhD), including art history (PhD), museum training (MA); ceramics (MFA); design (MFA); interior design (MFA); painting (MFA); photography (MFA); printmaking (MFA); sculpture (MFA). *Accreditation:* CIDA. Part-time and evening/weekend programs available. *Entrance requirements:* For master's, GRE General Test, bachelor's degree in field, minimum GPA of 3.0. Additional exam requirements/recommendations for international students: Required—TOEFL (minimum score 550 paper-based; 213 computer-based). Electronic applications accepted.

Iowa State University of Science and Technology, Graduate College, College of Design, Department of Art and Design, Ames, IA 50011. Offers art and design (MA); art education (MA); graphic design (MFA); integrated visual arts (MFA); interior design (MFA). Part-time programs available. *Faculty:* 38 full-time (22 women). *Students:* 39 full-time (28 women), 4 part-time (1 woman); includes 3 minority (all Asian Americans or Pacific Islanders), 12 international. 35 applicants, 63% accepted, 12 enrolled. In 2007, 11 degrees awarded. *Degree requirements:* For master's, thesis (for some programs). *Entrance requirements:* For master's, portfolio, resumé. Additional exam requirements/recommendations for international students: Required—TOEFL (paper-based 550; computer-based 213) or IELTS (score 6.5). *Application deadline:* For fall admission, 5/1 priority date for domestic and international students. Applications are processed on a rolling basis. Application fee: $30 ($70 for international students). Electronic applications accepted. *Financial support:* In 2007–08, 5 research assistantships with full and partial tuition reimbursements (averaging $20,058 per year), 2 teaching assistantships with full and partial tuition reimbursements (averaging $18,288 per year) were awarded; career-related internships or fieldwork, Federal Work-Study, institutionally sponsored loans, and tuition waivers (partial) also available. Support available to part-time students. Financial award application deadline: 2/15; financial award applicants required to submit FAFSA. *Faculty research:* Computer applications, fire safety, human factors in design, art and design education, fine arts, craft design. *Unit head:* Roger Baer, Chair, 515-294-6724, Fax: 515-294-2725, E-mail: artdn@iastate.edu.

Lawrence Technological University, College of Architecture and Design, Southfield, MI 48075-1058. Offers architecture (M Arch); interior design (MID). *Accreditation:* NASAD. Part-time and evening/weekend programs available. *Faculty:* 9 full-time (2 women), 12 part-time/adjunct (3 women). *Students:* 25 full-time (16 women), 133 part-time (64 women); includes 21 minority (9 African Americans, 1 American Indian/Alaska Native, 6 Asian Americans or Pacific Islanders, 5 Hispanic Americans), 19 international. Average age 30. 95 applicants, 72% accepted, 42 enrolled. In 2007, 34 degrees awarded. *Degree requirements:* For master's, thesis. *Entrance requirements:* For master's, portfolio. Additional exam requirements/recommendations for international students: Required—TOEFL (minimum score 550 paper-based; 213 computer-based; 79 iBT). *Application deadline:* For fall admission, 2/1 priority date for domestic students, 2/1 for international students; for winter admission, 11/1 priority date for domestic students, 11/1 for international students; for spring admission, 2/1 priority date for domestic students, 2/1 for international students. Applications are processed on a rolling basis. Application fee: $50. Electronic applications accepted. *Expenses:* Tuition: Part-time $710 per credit hour. Tuition and fees vary according to campus/location and program. *Financial support:* In 2007–08, 105 students received support. Federal Work-Study available. Financial award application deadline: 4/1; financial award applicants required to submit FAFSA. *Unit head:* Glen LeRoy, Dean, 248-204-2800, Fax: 248-204-2900, E-mail: archdean@ltu.edu. *Application contact:* Jane Rohrback, Director of Admissions, 248-204-3160, Fax: 248-204-3188, E-mail: admissions@ltu.edu.

Louisiana Tech University, Graduate School, College of Liberal Arts, School of Architecture, Ruston, LA 71272. Offers interior design (MFA). *Entrance requirements:* For master's, GRE General Test. *Application deadline:* For fall admission, 7/29 for domestic students; for spring admission, 2/3 for domestic students. Applications are processed on a rolling basis. Application fee: $20 ($30 for international students). *Financial support:* Application deadline: 2/1. *Unit head:* Karl Puljak, Head, 318-257-2816, Fax: 318-257-4687.

Marymount University, School of Arts and Sciences, Program in Interior Design, Arlington, VA 22207-4299. Offers MA. *Accreditation:* CIDA. Part-time and evening/weekend programs available. *Faculty:* 6 full-time (5 women), 4 part-time/adjunct (3 women). *Students:* 27 full-time (all women), 33 part-time (32 women); includes 12 minority (7 African Americans, 3 Asian Americans or Pacific Islanders, 2 Hispanic Americans), 2 international. Average age 32. 31 applicants, 100% accepted, 12 enrolled. In 2007, 15 degrees awarded. *Degree requirements:* For master's, thesis or alternative. *Entrance requirements:* For master's, GRE, MAT, NCIDQ exam or NCARB Architectural Registration Exam, interview, portfolio, 2 letters of recommendation, resumé. Additional exam requirements/recommendations for international students: Required—TOEFL (minimum score 600 paper-based; 250 computer-based; 100 iBT). *Application deadline:* For fall admission, 4/1 priority date for domestic students. Applications are processed on a rolling basis. Application fee: $40. Electronic applications accepted. *Expenses:* Tuition: Full-time $11,790; part-time $655 per credit. Required fees: $121; $6.7 per credit. *Financial support:* Research assistantships with partial tuition reimbursements, career-related internships or fieldwork, scholarships/grants, and unspecified assistantships available. Support available to part-time students. Financial award applicants required to submit FAFSA. *Unit head:* Dr. Robert Meden, Chair, 703-284-1574, Fax: 703-284-3859, E-mail: robert.meden@marymount.edu.

Marywood University, Academic Affairs, Insalaco College of Creative Arts and Management, Art Department, Program in Studio Art, Scranton, PA 18509-1598. Offers advertising design (MA); ceramics (MA); clay (MA); graphic design (MA); illustration (MA); interior architecture (MA); painting (MA); photography (MA); printmaking (MA); sculpture (MA); weaving (MA). *Accreditation:* NASAD. Part-time and evening/weekend programs available. *Students:* 5 full-time (3 women), 15 part-time (11 women), 1 international. Average age 41. 5 applicants, 80% accepted. In 2007, 7 degrees awarded. *Degree requirements:* For master's, comprehensive exam, thesis or alternative. *Entrance requirements:* For master's, portfolio. Additional exam requirements/recommendations for international students: Required—TOEFL (minimum score 550 paper-based; 213 computer-based). *Application deadline:* For fall admission, 4/15 priority date for domestic and international students; for spring admission, 11/15 priority date for domestic and international students. Applications are processed on a rolling basis. Application fee: $30. Electronic applications accepted. *Expenses:* Tuition: Full-time $15,290; part-time $695 per credit. Required fees: $990; $370 per term. Tuition and fees vary according to degree level. *Financial support:* Research assistantships with tuition reimbursements, scholarships/grants, tuition waivers (partial), and unspecified assistantships available. Support available to part-time students. Financial award application deadline: 2/15; financial award applicants required to submit FAFSA. *Faculty research:* Texture and line in clay, cast bronze sculpture, color theories, book art and illustration, sculptural form.

Miami International University of Art & Design, Program in Interior Design, Miami, FL 33132-1418. Offers MFA.

See Close-Up on page 119.

Michigan State University, The Graduate School, College of Agriculture and Natural Resources and College of Social Science, School of Planning, Design and Construction, East Lansing, MI 48824. Offers construction management (MS, PhD); environmental design (MA); interior design and facilities management (MA); international planning studies (MIPS); urban and regional planning (MURP). Part-time and evening/weekend programs available. *Degree requirements:* For master's, thesis or alternative. *Entrance requirements:* Additional exam requirements/recommendations for international students: Required—TOEFL. Electronic applications accepted. *Expenses:* Tuition, state resident: part-time $379 per credit hour. Tuition, nonresident: part-time $800 per credit hour. Tuition and fees vary according to program.

Missouri State University, Graduate College, College of Natural and Applied Sciences, Department of Fashion and Interior Design, Springfield, MO 65804-0094. Offers secondary education (MS Ed), including consumer sciences. *Faculty:* 3 full-time (all women). *Degree requirements:* For master's, comprehensive exam, thesis or alternative. *Entrance requirements:* For master's, GRE (MNAS), 9–12 teaching certification (MS Ed), minimum GPA of 3.0 (MNAS). Additional exam requirements/recommendations for international students: Required—TOEFL (minimum score 550 paper-based; 213 computer-based; 79 iBT). *Application deadline:* For fall admission, 7/20 priority date for domestic students; for spring admission, 12/20 priority date for domestic students. Application fee: $35. *Expenses:* Tuition, state resident: full-time $3,708; part-time $206 per credit hour. Tuition, nonresident: full-time $7,236; part-time $206 per credit hour. Required fees: $622. Full-time tuition and fees vary according to course level, course load, program and reciprocity agreements. *Financial support:* Research assistantships, teaching assistantships with full tuition reimbursements, career-related internships or fieldwork, Federal Work-Study, scholarships/grants, and unspecified assistantships available. Financial award application deadline: 3/31; financial award applicants required to submit FAFSA. *Faculty research:* Clothing design, merchandising, hospitality and restaurant management, interior design. *Unit head:* Dr. Jeannie Ireland, Head, 417-836-5497, Fax: 417-836-4341, E-mail: jeannieireland@missouristate.edu.

The New School: A University, Parsons The New School for Design, Program in Interior Design, New York, NY 10011. Offers MFA. *Faculty:* 11. *Degree requirements:* For master's, thesis. *Application contact:* Anthony Padilla, Director of Admissions, 212-229-8989 Ext. 4023, Fax: 212-229-8975, E-mail: padillaa@newschool.edu.

The New School: A University, Parsons The New School for Design, Program in Lighting Design, New York, NY 10011. Offers MFA. *Accreditation:* NASAD. *Faculty:* 1 full-time (0 women), 13 part-time/adjunct (6 women). *Students:* 39 full-time (27 women); includes 1 minority (Asian American or Pacific Islander), 28 international. Average age 28. In 2007, 24 degrees awarded. *Entrance requirements:* For master's, portfolio. Additional exam requirements/recommendations for international students: Required—TOEFL (minimum score 580 paper-based; 237 computer-based; 93 iBT). *Application deadline:* For fall admission, 2/1 priority date for domestic students. Applications are processed on a rolling basis. Application fee: $50. *Financial support:* Federal Work-Study, scholarships/grants, and tuition waivers (partial) available. Financial award application deadline: 3/1; financial award applicants required to submit FAFSA. *Unit head:* Kent Kleinman, Chair, 212-229-8955 Ext. 2953, E-mail: kleinmak@newschool.edu. *Application contact:* Anthony Padilla, Director of Admissions, 212-229-8989 Ext. 4023, Fax: 212-229-8975, E-mail: padillaa@newschool.edu.

See Close-Up on page 165.

New York School of Interior Design, Program in Interior Design, New York, NY 10021-5110. Offers MFA. *Accreditation:* NASAD. *Faculty:* 9 part-time/adjunct (5 women). *Students:* 18 full-time (17 women), 15 international. Average age 25. 38 applicants, 50% accepted, 10 enrolled. In 2007, 6 degrees awarded. *Degree requirements:* For master's, thesis. *Entrance requirements:* For master's, portfolio, undergraduate degree in interior design or related field. Additional exam requirements/recommendations for international students: Required—TOEFL (minimum score 550 paper-based; 215 computer-based; 79 iBT). *Application deadline:* For fall admission, 3/1 priority date for domestic and international students. Applications are processed on a rolling basis. Application fee: $50 ($75 for international students). Electronic applications accepted. *Expenses:* Tuition: Full-time $20,500. *Financial support:* In 2007–08, 6 students received support, including 6 fellowships (averaging $10,000 per year); career-related internships or fieldwork, Federal Work-Study, institutionally sponsored loans, and scholarships/grants also available. Financial award application deadline: 5/1; financial award applicants required to submit FAFSA. *Faculty research:* History, theory, aesthetics, sociology, and green design; landscape, lighting, furniture, product, and set design. *Unit head:* Scott Ageloff, Dean, 212-472-1500 Ext. 301, Fax: 212-288-6577, E-mail: scott@nysid.edu. *Application contact:* David T. Sprouls, Director of Admissions, 212-472-1500 Ext. 202, Fax: 212-472-1867, E-mail: david@nysid.edu.

See Close-Up on page 125.

The Ohio State University, Graduate School, College of the Arts, Department of Industrial, Interior, and Visual Communication Design, Columbus, OH 43210. Offers MA, MFA. *Accreditation:* NASAD. Part-time programs available. *Faculty:* 14. *Students:* 24 full-time (12 women), 7 part-time (5 women); includes 3 minority (1 African American, 2 Asian Americans or Pacific Islanders), 7 international. Average age 29. In 2007, 7 degrees awarded. *Degree requirements:* For master's, project or thesis. *Entrance requirements:* For master's, bachelor's degree in interior space, graphics, product design, or related field. Additional exam requirements/recommendations for international students: Recommended—TOEFL (minimum score 600 paper-based; 250 computer-based). *Application deadline:* For fall admission, 8/15 priority date for domestic students, 7/1 priority date for international students; for winter admission, 12/1 priority date for domestic students, 11/1 priority date for international students; for spring admission, 3/1 priority date for domestic students, 2/1 priority date for international students. Applications are processed on a rolling basis. Application fee: $40 ($50 for international students). Electronic applications accepted. *Financial support:* Fellowships, research assistantships, teaching assistantships with full tuition reimbursements, career-related internships or fieldwork, Federal Work-Study, institutionally sponsored loans, and unspecified assistantships available. Support available to part-time students. Financial award application deadline: 5/1. *Unit head:* R. Brian Stone, Graduate Studies Committee Chair, 614-688-6746, Fax: 614-292-0217, E-mail: stone.158@osu.edu. *Application contact:* 614-292-9444, Fax: 614-292-3895, E-mail: domestic.grad@osu.edu.

Pontificia Universidad Catolica Madre y Maestra, Graduate School, Santiago, Dominican Republic. Offers administration (M Adm, M Ed); architecture of interiors (M Arch); architecture of tourist lodgings (M Arch); construction administration (ME); convergent networks (ME); corporate business law (LL M); criminal procedure law (LL M); earthquake-resistant engineering (ME); environmental engineering (MEE); finance (M Mgmt); human resources (EMBA); international business (M Mgmt); international relations (LL M); labor law and Social Security (M Mgmt); logistics management (ME); marketing (M Mgmt); urban planning (M Urb). *Entrance requirements:* For master's, curriculum vitae, interview.

Pratt Institute, School of Art and Design, Program in Interior Design, Brooklyn, NY 11205-3899. Offers MS. *Accreditation:* NASAD. Part-time programs available. *Faculty:* 4 full-time (1 woman), 27 part-time/adjunct (10 women). *Students:* 154 full-time (135 women), 9 part-time (7 women); includes 33 minority (11 African Americans, 1 American Indian/Alaska Native, 14 Asian Americans or Pacific Islanders, 7 Hispanic Americans), 50 international. Average age 29. 198 applicants, 58% accepted, 55 enrolled. In 2007, 48 degrees awarded. *Degree requirements:* For master's, thesis. *Entrance requirements:* For master's, portfolio, bachelor's degree, transcripts, letters of recommendation, statement. Additional exam requirements/recommendations for international students: Required—TOEFL (minimum score 575 paper-based; 232 computer-based). *Application deadline:* For fall admission, 2/1 for domestic students; for spring admission, 10/1 for domestic students. Application fee: $50 ($90 for international students). Electronic applications accepted. *Expenses:* Tuition: Full-time $25,680. Required fees: $1,106. Tuition and fees vary according to program. *Financial support:* Career-related internships or fieldwork, Federal Work-Study, institutionally sponsored loans, scholarships/grants, health care benefits, and unspecified assistantships available. Support available to part-time students. Financial award application deadline: 2/1; financial award applicants required to submit FAFSA. *Unit head:* Anita Cooney, Chairperson, 718-636-3630, Fax: 718-636-8553, E-mail: acooney@pratt.edu. *Application contact:* Young Hah, Director of Graduate Admissions, 718-636-3683, Fax: 718-399-4242, E-mail: yhah@pratt.edu.

See Close-Up on page 253.

Rhode Island School of Design, Graduate Studies, Division of Architecture and Design, Department of Interior Architecture, Providence, RI 02903-2784. Offers MIA. *Degree requirements:* For master's, thesis, exhibit. *Entrance requirements:* For master's, portfolio, 3 letters of recommendation. Additional exam requirements/recommendations for international students: Required—TOEFL (minimum score 580 paper-based; 237 computer-based), IELTS (minimum score 7).

San Diego State University, Graduate and Research Affairs, College of Professional Studies and Fine Arts, School of Art, Design and Art History, San Diego, CA 92182. Offers art history (MA); studio arts (MA, MFA), including applied design, environmental design, graphic design, interior design, painting and printmaking, sculpture. *Accreditation:* NASAD (one or more programs are accredited). *Students:* 44 full-time (29 women), 18 part-time (11 women); includes 9 minority (4 Asian Americans or Pacific Islanders, 5 Hispanic Americans), 5 international. Average age 30. 83 applicants, 31% accepted, 31 enrolled. In 2007, 12 degrees awarded. *Degree requirements:* For master's, variable foreign language requirement, thesis. *Entrance requirements:* For master's, GRE General Test, bachelor's degree in related field, slide portfolio, typed slide information sheet, 2 letters of recommendation. Additional exam requirements/recommendations for international students: Required—TOEFL. *Application deadline:* For fall admission, 2/1 for domestic and international students. Applications are processed on a rolling basis. Application fee: $55. Electronic applications accepted. *Financial support:* In 2007–08, 21 teaching assistantships were awarded; career-related internships or fieldwork and unspecified assistantships also available. Financial award applicants required to submit FAFSA. *Unit head:* Arthur Ollman, Director, 619-594-1213, Fax: 619-594-1217. *Application contact:* JoAnne Berelowitz, Graduate Advisor, Art History, 619-594-4995, Fax: 619-594-1217, E-mail: jberelow@mail.sdsu.edu.

Savannah College of Art and Design, Graduate School, Program in Interior Design, Savannah, GA 31402-3146. Offers MA, MFA. Part-time programs available. *Faculty:* 12 full-time (11 women), 2 part-time/adjunct (0 women). *Students:* 59 full-time (57 women), 22 part-time (19 women); includes 6 minority (4 African Americans, 1 Asian American or Pacific Islander, 1 Hispanic American), 27 international. Average age 25. 134 applicants, 50% accepted, 27 enrolled. In 2007, 28 degrees awarded. *Degree requirements:* For master's, thesis, internship. *Entrance requirements:* For master's, interview, portfolio. Additional exam requirements/recommendations for international students: Required—TOEFL (minimum score 450 paper-based; 133 computer-based). *Application deadline:* For fall admission, 4/1 priority date for domestic and international students. Applications are processed on a rolling basis. Application fee: $50. Electronic applications accepted. *Expenses:* Tuition: Full-time $24,840; part-time $552 per credit. One-time fee: $500 full-time. *Financial support:* In 2007–08, 4 fellowships were awarded; career-related internships or fieldwork, Federal Work-Study, and scholarships/grants also available. Financial award application deadline: 4/1; financial award applicants required to submit FAFSA. *Unit head:* Monica Letourneau, Acting Chair, 912-525-6910, Fax: 912-525-6904, E-mail: mletourn@scad.edu. *Application contact:* Darrell Tutchton, Director of Graduate and International Enrollment, 912-525-5961, Fax: 912-525-5985, E-mail: admission@scad.edu.

See Close-Up on page 257.

School of the Art Institute of Chicago, Graduate Division, Program in Interior Architecture, Chicago, IL 60603-3103. Offers MFA. *Entrance requirements:* Additional exam requirements/recommendations for international students: Required—TOEFL.

See Close-Up on page 259.

South Dakota State University, Graduate School, College of Family and Consumer Sciences, Department of Apparel Merchandising and Interior Design, Brookings, SD 57007. Offers MFCS. Part-time and evening/weekend programs available. Postbaccalaureate distance learning degree programs offered. *Entrance requirements:* Additional exam requirements/recommendations for international students: Required—TOEFL (minimum score 550 paper-based; 213 computer-based; 79 iBT). *Faculty research:* Rural internet shopping, professional development in apparel merchandising, gender, aesthetics.

Suffolk University, College of Arts and Sciences, New England School of Art and Design, Boston, MA 02108-2770. Offers graphic design (MA); interior design (MA). *Accreditation:* CIDA; NASAD. Part-time and evening/weekend programs available. *Faculty:* 18 full-time (9 women), 14 part-time/adjunct (4 women). *Students:* 49 full-time (46 women), 69 part-time (63 women); includes 12 minority (2 African Americans, 1 American Indian/Alaska Native, 7 Asian Americans or Pacific Islanders, 2 Hispanic Americans), 15 international. Average age 29. 78 applicants, 87% accepted, 33 enrolled. In 2007, 26 degrees awarded. *Entrance requirements:* For master's, art portfolio, interview. Additional exam requirements/recommendations for international students: Required—TOEFL (minimum score 550 paper-based; 213 computer-based; 80 iBT). *Application deadline:* For fall admission, 6/15 priority date for domestic students, 6/15 for international students; for spring admission, 11/1 priority date for domestic students, 11/1 for international students. Applications are processed on a rolling basis. Application fee: $50. Electronic applications accepted. *Financial support:* In 2007–08, 65 students received support, including 10 fellowships with partial tuition reimbursements available (averaging $6,296 per year). Financial award application deadline: 4/1. *Faculty research:* Adaptive re-use of historical structures, universal design, American architecture history, interior design to reduce inefficiency, meditation SPA. *Unit head:* Dr. William Davis, Director, 617-994-4264, Fax: 617-536-0461, E-mail: wdavis@suffolk.edu. *Application contact:* Judith Reynolds, Director of Graduate Admissions, 617-573-8302, Fax: 617-523-0116, E-mail: grad.admission@suffolk.edu.

The University of Alabama, Graduate School, College of Human Environmental Sciences, Department of Clothing, Textiles, and Interior Design, Tuscaloosa, AL 35487. Offers MSHES. *Faculty:* 3 full-time (all women). *Students:* 1 (woman) full-time. Average age 23. 1 applicant, 0% accepted. In 2007, 4 degrees awarded. *Degree requirements:* For master's, comprehensive exam, thesis optional. *Entrance requirements:* For master's, GRE General Test or MAT, minimum GPA of 3.0. *Application deadline:* For fall admission, 7/6 for domestic students. Applications are processed on a rolling basis. Application fee: $30. *Expenses:* Tuition, state resident: full-time $5,700. Tuition, nonresident: full-time $16,518. *Financial support:* In 2007–08, 1 research assistantship with full tuition reimbursement (averaging $8,100 per year), 2 teaching assistantships with full tuition reimbursements (averaging $8,100 per year) were awarded; fellowships, career-related internships or fieldwork, Federal Work-Study, and scholarships/grants also available. Financial award application deadline: 3/15. *Faculty research:* Archeological textiles, textile science, material culture, social psychology, international trade. *Unit head:* Dr. Carolyn Callis, Chair and Associate Professor, 205-348-6176, Fax: 205-348-0022, E-mail: ccallis@ches.ua.edu.

Interior Design

University of Central Oklahoma, College of Graduate Studies and Research, College of Arts, Media, and Design, Department of Design and Interior Design, Edmond, OK 73034-5209. Offers MFA. Part-time programs available. Postbaccalaureate distance learning degree programs offered (minimal on-campus study). *Faculty:* 8 full-time (5 women). *Students:* 7 full-time (1 woman), 1 (woman) part-time, 1 international. Average age 31. In 2007, 2 degrees awarded. *Entrance requirements:* Additional exam requirements/recommendations for international students: Required—TOEFL (minimum score 550 paper-based; 213 computer-based). *Application deadline:* For fall admission, 7/1 for international students; for spring admission, 11/1 for international students. Applications are processed on a rolling basis. Application fee: $25. Electronic applications accepted. *Expenses:* Tuition, state resident: full-time $3,516; part-time $147 per hour. Tuition, nonresident: full-time $9,054; part-time $377 per hour. Required fees: $433; $18 per hour. *Financial support:* Application deadline: 3/31; *Unit head:* Dr. Larry Hefner, Chair, 405-974-5211.

University of Central Oklahoma, College of Graduate Studies and Research, College of Education, Department of Human Environmental Sciences, Edmond, OK 73034-5209. Offers family and child studies (MS); family and consumer science education (MS); interior design (MS); nutrition-food management (MS). Part-time programs available. *Faculty:* 5 full-time (all women), 5 part-time/adjunct (3 women). *Students:* 38 full-time (32 women), 57 part-time (54 women); includes 24 minority (13 African Americans, 4 American Indian/Alaska Native, 3 Asian Americans or Pacific Islanders, 4 Hispanic Americans), 4 international. Average age 30. 21 applicants, 95% accepted. In 2007, 20 degrees awarded. *Entrance requirements:* Additional exam requirements/recommendations for international students: Required—TOEFL (minimum score 550 paper-based; 213 computer-based). *Application deadline:* For fall admission, 7/1 for international students; for spring admission, 11/1 for international students. Applications are processed on a rolling basis. Application fee: $25. Electronic applications accepted. *Expenses:* Tuition, state resident: full-time $3,516; part-time $147 per hour. Tuition, nonresident: full-time $9,054; part-time $377 per hour. Required fees: $433; $18 per hour. *Financial support:* Career-related internships or fieldwork and unspecified assistantships available. Financial award application deadline: 3/31; financial award applicants required to submit FAFSA. *Faculty research:* Dietetics and food science. *Unit head:* Dr. Kaye Sears, Chairperson, 405-974-5786.

University of Cincinnati, Graduate School, College of Design, Architecture, Art, and Planning, School of Architecture and Interior Design, Cincinnati, OH 45221. Offers architecture (M Arch). *Accreditation:* NASAD. *Faculty:* 24 full-time (4 women). *Students:* 187 full-time (73 women), 18 part-time (8 women); includes 15 minority (3 African Americans, 1 American Indian/Alaska Native, 7 Asian Americans or Pacific Islanders, 4 Hispanic Americans), 26 international. In 2007, 52 degrees awarded. *Degree requirements:* For master's, one foreign language, thesis. *Entrance requirements:* Additional exam requirements/recommendations for international students: Required—TOEFL. *Application deadline:* For fall admission, 2/1 for domestic students. Application fee: $30. *Financial support:* Fellowships, tuition waivers (full) and unspecified assistantships available. Support available to part-time students. Financial award application deadline: 5/1. *Faculty research:* Theory and history of architecture. Total annual research expenditures: $115,000. *Unit head:* Prof. Michaele Pride-Wells, Director, 513-556-6426, Fax: 513-556-1230, E-mail: m.pride-wells@uc.edu. *Application contact:* Prof. Patricia Kucker, Associate Director for Graduate Programs, 513-556-1614, E-mail: patricia.kucker@uc.edu.

University of Florida, Graduate School, College of Design, Construction and Planning, Department of Interior Design, Gainesville, FL 32611. Offers MID, PhD. *Faculty:* 8 full-time (6 women). *Students:* 14 (12 women); includes 4 minority (3 African Americans, 1 Asian American or Pacific Islander) 1 international. In 2007, 5 degrees awarded. *Entrance requirements:* For master's, GRE General Test, minimum GPA of 3.0. Additional exam requirements/recommendations for international students: Required—TOEFL. Application fee: $30. *Expenses:* Tuition, state resident: full-time $7,478. Tuition, nonresident: full-time $22,603. *Financial support:* In 2007–08, 3 research assistantships (averaging $8,990 per year), 3 teaching assistantships (averaging $8,321 per year) were awarded. *Unit head:* Dr. Margaret Portillo, Chair, 352-392-0252 Ext. 334, Fax: 352-392-7266, E-mail: mportill@ufl.edu. *Application contact:* Juanita Melchior, Coordinator, 352-392-0252 Ext. 303, Fax: 352-392-7266, E-mail: melchior@dcp.ufl.edu.

University of Georgia, Graduate School, College of Family and Consumer Sciences, Department of Textiles, Merchandising, and Interiors, Athens, GA 30602. Offers historic costume and textiles (MS); merchandising/international trade (MS); textile analysis (PhD); textile chemical processes (PhD); textile products and standards (PhD); textile science (MS). *Faculty:* 9 full-time (6 women). *Students:* 17 full-time (14 women), 1 part-time; includes 1 minority (African American), 10 international. 20 applicants, 50% accepted, 8 enrolled. In 2007, 5 master's, 4 doctorates awarded. *Degree requirements:* For master's, thesis; for doctorate, thesis/dissertation. *Entrance requirements:* For master's and doctorate, GRE General Test. *Application deadline:* For fall admission, 7/1 priority date for domestic students; for spring admission, 11/15 for domestic students. Application fee: $50. Electronic applications accepted. *Financial support:* Fellowships, research assistantships, teaching assistantships, unspecified assistantships available. *Unit head:* Dr. Patricia Hunt-Hurst, Department Head, 706-542-4891, Fax: 706-542-4862, E-mail: phunt@fcs.uga.edu.

University of Houston, College of Liberal Arts and Social Sciences, Department of Art, Houston, TX 77204. Offers interior design (MA); painting (MA); photography (MA); sculpture (MA); MFA/MA. *Faculty:* 16 full-time (7 women), 7 part-time/adjunct (5 women). *Students:* 37 full-time (23 women); includes 7 minority (1 Asian American or Pacific Islander, 6 Hispanic Americans), 4 international. Average age 33. 49 applicants, 31% accepted, 11 enrolled. In 2007, 10 degrees awarded. *Degree requirements:* For master's, comprehensive exam, visual thesis. *Entrance requirements:* For master's, GRE General Test, portfolio. *Application deadline:* For fall admission, 2/28 for domestic students; for spring admission, 10/30 for domestic students. Application fee: $25 ($100 for international students). *Expenses:* Tuition, state resident: full-time $6,297; part-time $262 per credit. Tuition, nonresident: full-time $12,969; part-time $540 per credit. Required fees: $2,696. *Financial support:* In 2007–08, 28 teaching assistantships with full tuition reimbursements (averaging $10,400 per year) were awarded; fellowships with full tuition reimbursements, research assistantships with full tuition reimbursements, career-related internships or fieldwork, Federal Work-Study, institutionally sponsored loans, scholarships/grants, health care benefits, and unspecified assistantships also available. Support available to part-time students. Financial award application deadline: 3/10. *Faculty research:* Alternative art projects. *Unit head:* Dr. John Reed, Chairperson, 713-743-3001, Fax: 713-743-2823, E-mail: jreed@uh.edu.

University of Kentucky, Graduate School, College of Design, Program in Interior Design, Merchandising, and Textiles, Lexington, KY 40506-0032. Offers MAIDM, MSIDM. *Faculty:* 8 full-time (7 women). *Students:* 13 full-time (11 women), 3 part-time (all women); includes 2 minority (1 African American, 1 Hispanic American), 2 international. Average age 25. 16 applicants, 38% accepted, 5 enrolled. In 2007, 5 degrees awarded. *Degree requirements:* For master's, comprehensive exam, thesis optional. *Entrance requirements:* For master's, GRE General Test, minimum undergraduate GPA of 2.75. Additional exam requirements/recommendations for international students: Required—TOEFL (minimum score 550 paper-based; 213 computer-based). *Application deadline:* For fall admission, 7/17 priority date for domestic students, 2/1 priority date for international students; for spring admission, 12/13 priority date for domestic students, 6/15 priority date for international students. Application fee: $50 ($65 for international students). Electronic applications accepted. *Expenses:* Tuition, state resident: part-time $437 per credit hour. Tuition, nonresident: part-time $931 per credit hour. *Financial support:* In 2007–08, 11 students received support, including 3 research assistantships with full tuition reimbursements available (averaging $4,803 per year), 8 teaching assistantships with full tuition reimbursements available (averaging $4,803 per year); fellowships with full tuition reimbursements available, Federal Work-Study, scholarships/grants, traineeships, health care benefits, tuition waivers (partial), and unspecified assistantships also available. Support available to part-time students. Financial award application deadline: 3/15; financial award applicants required to submit FAFSA. *Faculty research:* Interior design, apparel merchandising, textile evaluation, creativity in design, social-psychological aspects of dress and interiors. *Unit head:* Dr. Elizabeth Easter, Director of Graduate Studies, 859-257-7777, Fax: 859-257-1275, E-mail: hetliz@uky.edu. *Application contact:* Dr. Brian Jackson, Senior Associate Dean, 859-257-4667, Fax: 859-257-4676, E-mail: brian.jackson@uky.edu.

University of Manitoba, Faculty of Graduate Studies, Faculty of Architecture, Department of Interior Design, Winnipeg, MB R3T 2N2, Canada. Offers MID. *Accreditation:* CIDA.

University of Massachusetts Amherst, Graduate School, College of Humanities and Fine Arts, Department of Art, Programs in Architecture, Amherst, MA 01003. Offers architecture and design (M Arch); interior design (MS). *Students:* 23 full-time (9 women), 2 part-time (1 woman); includes 2 minority (1 African American, 1 Hispanic American), 5 international. Average age 29. 44 applicants, 82% accepted, 15 enrolled. In 2007, 1 degree awarded. *Degree requirements:* For master's, thesis or alternative. *Entrance requirements:* For master's, GRE General Test (MA), portfolio. Additional exam requirements/recommendations for international students: Required—TOEFL (minimum score 530 paper-based; 197 computer-based). *Application deadline:* For fall admission, 2/1 priority date for domestic and international students. Applications are processed on a rolling basis. Application fee: $50 ($65 for international students). Electronic applications accepted. *Expenses:* Tuition, state resident: full-time $2,640; part-time $110 per credit. Tuition, nonresident: full-time $9,936; part-time $414 per credit. Required fees: $7,455. One-time fee: $332. Tuition and fees vary according to course load, campus/location, program and reciprocity agreements. *Financial support:* Fellowships with full tuition reimbursements, research assistantships with full tuition reimbursements, teaching assistantships with full tuition reimbursements, career-related internships or fieldwork, Federal Work-Study, scholarships/grants, traineeships, and unspecified assistantships available. Support available to part-time students. Financial award application deadline: 2/1. *Unit head:* Dr. Jeanette Cole, Head, 413-545-6937, Fax: 413-545-3929.

University of Memphis, Graduate School, College of Communication and Fine Arts, Department of Art, Memphis, TN 38152. Offers art history (MA), including Egyptian art and archaeology, general art history; ceramics (MFA); graphic design (MFA); interior design (MFA); painting (MFA); printmaking/photography (MFA); sculpture (MFA). *Accreditation:* NASAD (one or more programs are accredited). *Faculty:* 13 full-time (9 women). *Students:* 20 full-time (11 women), 2 part-time (1 woman); includes 1 Asian American or Pacific Islander, 1 international. Average age 27. 47 applicants, 55% accepted, 18 enrolled. In 2007, 14 degrees awarded. *Degree requirements:* For master's, 2 foreign languages, comprehensive exam, thesis. *Entrance requirements:* For master's, GRE General Test or MAT, portfolio (MFA). *Application deadline:* For fall admission, 8/1 for domestic students; for spring admission, 12/1 for domestic students. Applications are processed on a rolling basis. Application fee: $35 ($60 for international students). *Expenses:* Tuition, state resident: full-time $6,990; part-time $377 per hour. Tuition, nonresident: full-time $17,818; part-time $830 per hour. Tuition and fees vary according to course load and program. *Financial support:* In 2007–08, 23 research assistantships with full tuition reimbursements (averaging $4,200 per year), 10 teaching assistantships with full tuition reimbursements (averaging $5,250 per year) were awarded. *Faculty research:* Online collaborative learning, advanced art history studies, electronic publishing/design, studio arts, architectural studies. *Unit head:* Prof. Richard Lou, Chair, 901-678-2216, Fax: 901-678-2735, E-mail: gmyatt@memphis.edu. *Application contact:* Prof. Michael Hagge, Coordinator of Graduate Studies, 901-678-2677.

University of Minnesota, Twin Cities Campus, Graduate School, College of Design, Department of Design, Housing, and Apparel, Minneapolis, MN 55455-0213. Offers apparel (MA, MS, PhD); design communication (MA, MS, PhD); housing studies (MA, MS, PhD, Postbaccalaureate Certificate); interactive design (MFA); interior design (MA, MS, PhD). Part-time programs available. *Faculty:* 24 full-time (18 women), 5 part-time/adjunct (4 women). *Students:* 41 full-time (34 women), 28 part-time (21 women); includes 3 minority (1 African American, 1 Asian American or Pacific Islander, 1 Hispanic American), 20 international. 37 applicants, 54% accepted, 15 enrolled. In 2007, 3 master's, 8 doctorates awarded. *Median time to degree:* Of those who began their doctoral program in fall 1999, 100% received their degree in 8 years or less. *Degree requirements:* For master's and Postbaccalaureate Certificate, comprehensive exam, thesis (for some programs); for doctorate, comprehensive exam, thesis/dissertation. *Entrance requirements:* For master's, GRE General Test, minimum GPA of 3.0 (preferred), portfolio, 3 letters of recommendation; for doctorate, GRE General Test, minimum GPA of 3.0 (preferred), portfolio, 3 letters of recommendation, writing sample; for Postbaccalaureate Certificate, GRE General Test, minimum GPA of 3.0 (preferred). Additional exam requirements/recommendations for international students: Required—TOEFL (minimum score 550 paper-based; 213 computer-based; 79 iBT). *Application deadline:* For fall admission, 1/15 for domestic and international students. Application fee: $55 ($75 for international students). Electronic applications accepted. *Financial support:* In 2007–08, 34 students received support, including 13 research assistantships with partial tuition reimbursements available (averaging $12,652 per year), 24 teaching assistantships with partial tuition reimbursements available (averaging $12,652 per year); Federal Work-Study, institutionally sponsored loans, and unspecified assistantships also available. Financial award application deadline: 2/1; financial award applicants required to submit FAFSA. *Faculty research:* Housing policy and community development; consumer behavior; interactive design; design history; social, cultural, and behavioral issues related to designed environments. Total annual research expenditures: $320,058. *Unit head:* Becky Love Yust, Professor and Department Head, 612-624-7461, Fax: 612-624-2750, E-mail: byust@che.umn.edu. *Application contact:* Charleen Klarquist, Student Support Services Assistant, 612-626-1219, Fax: 612-624-2750, E-mail: dhagrad@umn.edu.

The University of North Carolina at Greensboro, Graduate School, School of Human Environmental Sciences, Department of Interior Architecture, Greensboro, NC 27412-5001. Offers historic preservation (Certificate); interior architecture (MS); museum studies (Certificate). *Faculty:* 9 full-time (4 women), 1 part-time/adjunct (0 women). *Students:* 14 full-time (12 women), 1 (woman) part-time. 13 applicants, 38% accepted. *Degree requirements:* For master's, thesis. *Entrance requirements:* For master's, GRE General Test or MAT, bachelor's degree in interior design, interview, portfolio. Additional exam requirements/recommendations for international students: Required—TOEFL. *Application deadline:* For fall admission, 3/1 for domestic students. Application fee: $45. Electronic applications accepted. *Financial support:* Fellowships with full tuition reimbursements, research assistantships with full tuition reimbursements, teaching assistantships with full tuition reimbursements, career-related internships or fieldwork, Federal Work-Study, scholarships/grants, and traineeships available. Support available to part-time students. *Unit head:* Thomas Lambeth, Chairman, 336-334-5320, Fax: 336-334-5049, E-mail: ctlambeth@uncg.edu. *Application contact:* Michelle Harkleroad, Director of Graduate Admissions, 336-334-4884, Fax: 336-334-4424, E-mail: mbharkle@uncg.edu.

University of Oregon, Graduate School, School of Architecture and Allied Arts, Department of Architecture, Eugene, OR 97403. Offers architecture (M Arch); interior architecture (MI Arch). *Accreditation:* CIDA. *Faculty:* 23 full-time (9 women), 9 part-time/adjunct (4 women). *Students:* 199 full-time (86 women), 12 part-time (4 women); includes 7 Asian Americans or Pacific Islanders, 9 Hispanic Americans, 7 international. 156 applicants, 47% accepted. In 2007, 67 degrees awarded. *Degree requirements:* For master's, thesis (for some programs). *Entrance requirements:* For master's, GRE General Test. Additional exam requirements/recommendations for international students: Required—TOEFL. *Application deadline:* For fall admission, 1/1 for domestic students. Application fee: $50. *Financial support:* In 2007–08, 40 teaching assistantships were awarded; career-related internships or fieldwork, Federal Work-Study, and institutionally sponsored loans also available. Financial award application deadline: 3/1. *Faculty research:* Innovation in housing design and design production, climate responsive design, passive heating and cooling, computer software development for design applications, vernacular architecture. *Unit head:* Christine Theodoropoulos, Head, 541-346-3661. *Application contact:* Mike Clark, Admissions Contact, 541-346-1434, E-mail: mclark@uoregon.edu.

Utah State University, School of Graduate Studies, College of Humanities, Arts and Social Sciences, Program in Interior Design, Logan, UT 84322. Offers MS. Part-time programs available.

Postbaccalaureate distance learning degree programs offered. *Entrance requirements:* For master's, GRE General Test, MAT, minimum GPA of 3.0. Additional exam requirements/ recommendations for international students: Required—TOEFL.

Virginia Commonwealth University, Graduate School, School of the Arts, Department of Graphic Design, Richmond, VA 23284-9005. Offers design/visual communications (MFA); interior environment (MFA); photography and film (MFA). *Accreditation:* NASAD. *Faculty:* 15 full-time (3 women). *Students:* 42 full-time (31 women), 6 part-time (3 women); includes 6 minority (2 African Americans, 1 Asian American or Pacific Islander, 3 Hispanic Americans), 7 international. 80 applicants, 31% accepted, 20 enrolled. In 2007, 17 degrees awarded. *Degree requirements:* For master's, thesis, exhibition. *Entrance requirements:* For master's, portfolio. *Application deadline:* For fall admission, 3/1 for domestic students. Application fee: $50. *Expenses:* Tuition, state resident: full-time $7,224; part-time $401 per credit. Tuition, nonresident: full-time $16,072; part-time $891 per credit. Required fees: $1,679; $63 per credit. Tuition and fees vary according to campus/location. *Financial support:* Fellowships, teaching assistantships, career-related internships or fieldwork, Federal Work-Study, institutionally sponsored loans, and tuition waivers (full and partial) available. Support available to part-time students. Financial award application deadline: 3/15. *Faculty research:* Film, photography, interior environments, visual communication. *Unit head:* John DeMao, Chair, 804-828-7329, E-mail: jdemao@vcu.edu.

See Close-Up on page 275.

Virginia Polytechnic Institute and State University, Graduate School, College of Liberal Arts and Human Sciences, Department of Apparel, Housing, and Resource Management, Blacksburg, VA 24061. Offers apparel business and economics (MS, PhD); apparel product design and analysis (MS, PhD); apparel quality analysis (MS, PhD); consumer studies (MS, PhD); family financial management (MS, PhD); household equipment (MS, PhD); housing (MS, PhD); interior design (MS, PhD); resource management (MS, PhD). *Degree requirements:* For master's, thesis; for doctorate, thesis/dissertation. *Entrance requirements:* For master's and doctorate, GRE General Test. Additional exam requirements/recommendations for international students: Required—TOEFL (minimum score 550 paper-based; 213 computer-based). Electronic applications accepted. *Faculty research:* Housing for elderly, affordable housing, household time use, phosphate laundry study, economic well-living.

Washington State University, Graduate School, College of Agricultural, Human, and Natural Resource Sciences, Department of Apparel, Merchandising, Design, and Textiles, Pullman, WA 99164. Offers apparel, merchandising, design and textiles (MA); interdisciplinary (PhD); interior design (MA). *Faculty:* 8. *Students:* 7 full-time (all women), 2 part-time (both women); includes 1 minority (African American), 2 international. Average age 33. 7 applicants, 43% accepted, 2 enrolled. In 2007, 6 degrees awarded. *Degree requirements:* For master's, comprehensive exam (for some programs), thesis, oral exam; for doctorate, comprehensive exam, thesis/dissertation. *Entrance requirements:* For master's, GRE, minimum GPA of 3.0, 3 writing samples, 3 letters of recommendation, portfolio. Additional exam requirements/recommendations for international students: Required—TOEFL. *Application deadline:* For fall admission, 5/1 priority date for domestic students, 3/1 for international students; for spring admission, 11/1 for domestic students, 7/1 for international students. Applications are processed on a rolling basis. Application fee: $50. Electronic applications accepted. *Financial support:* In 2007–08, 9 students received support, including research assistantships with full and partial tuition reimbursements available (averaging $13,917 per year), 5 teaching assistantships with full and partial tuition reimbursements available (averaging $13,056 per year); career-related internships or fieldwork, Federal Work-Study, institutionally sponsored loans, and scholarships/grants also available. Financial award application deadline: 4/1; financial award applicants required to submit FAFSA. *Faculty research:* Product development, design theory, cultural diversity, computer design accessibility. *Unit head:* Dr. Karen K. Leonas, Department Chair, 509-335-6766, Fax: 509-355-7299, E-mail: amid@wsu.edu. *Application contact:* Graduate School Admissions, 800-GRADWSU, Fax: 509-335-1949, E-mail: gradsch@wsu.edu.

Washington State University Spokane, Graduate Programs, Interdisciplinary Design Institute, Spokane, WA 99210-1495. Offers architecture (M Arch, MS); design (Dr DES); interior design (MA); landscape architecture (MS). Part-time programs available. *Faculty:* 11 full-time (3 women), 3 part-time/adjunct (2 women). *Students:* 35 full-time (22 women), 5 part-time (3 women); includes 5 minority (2 American Indian/Alaska Native, 2 Asian Americans or Pacific Islanders, 1 Hispanic American), 2 international. Average age 35. 61 applicants, 67% accepted, 18 enrolled. *Degree requirements:* For master's, comprehensive exam (for some programs), thesis (for some programs); for doctorate, comprehensive exam, thesis/dissertation. *Entrance requirements:* For master's, minimum GPA of 3.0, portfolio of design work, 3 letters of recommendation (M Arch); for doctorate, minimum graduate GPA of 3.5. Additional exam requirements/recommendations for international students: Required—TOEFL (minimum score 550 paper-based; 213 computer-based). *Application deadline:* For fall admission, 4/1 priority date for domestic students, 3/1 for international students. Application fee: $50. *Financial support:* In 2007–08, 30 students received support, including 10 research assistantships with full and partial tuition reimbursements available (averaging $13,917 per year), teaching assistantships with full and partial tuition reimbursements available (averaging $13,056 per year). *Faculty research:* Environment-behavior relationships, land use and environmental planning, urban space as interior design, art and architectural aesthetics. Total annual research expenditures: $62,011. *Unit head:* Dr. Nancy H. Blossom, Director, 509-358-7515, E-mail: blossom@wsu.edu. *Application contact:* Graduate School Admissions, 800-GRADWSU, Fax: 509-335-1949, E-mail: gradsch@wsu.edu.

Medical Illustration

The Johns Hopkins University, School of Medicine, Graduate Programs in Medicine, Department of Art as Applied to Medicine, Baltimore, MD 21218-2699. Offers medical and biological illustration (MA). *Accreditation:* ARCMI. *Faculty:* 6 full-time (2 women), 17 part-time/adjunct (7 women). *Students:* 10 full-time (6 women); includes 5 minority (4 Asian Americans or Pacific Islanders, 1 Hispanic American). Average age 24. 37 applicants, 14% accepted, 5 enrolled. In 2007, 5 degrees awarded. *Degree requirements:* For master's, thesis. *Application deadline:* For fall admission, 1/15 for domestic and international students. Applications are processed on a rolling basis. Application fee: $75. Electronic applications accepted. *Financial support:* In 2007–08, 10 students received support, including 10 fellowships with partial tuition reimbursements available (averaging $17,000 per year), 6 teaching assistantships (averaging $500 per year); Federal Work-Study, institutionally sponsored loans, scholarships/grants, and tuition waivers also available. Financial award application deadline: 5/31; financial award applicants required to submit FAFSA. *Faculty research:* 3D modeling, instructional design, microreconstruction, visualization, digital media. *Unit head:* Gary Lees, Chairman and Director, 410-955-3213; Fax: 410-955-1085, E-mail: glees@jhmi.edu.

Medical College of Georgia, School of Graduate Studies, Program in Medical Illustration, Augusta, GA 30912-1500. Offers MS. *Accreditation:* ARCMI. *Faculty:* 2 full-time (0 women), 1 part-time/adjunct (0 women). *Students:* 17 full-time (8 women), 2 part-time (1 woman); includes 3 minority (1 African American, 1 Asian American or Pacific Islander, 1 Hispanic American). Average age 29. 14 applicants, 71% accepted, 9 enrolled. In 2007, 8 degrees awarded. *Degree requirements:* For master's, thesis or alternative, project. *Entrance requirements:* For master's, GRE General Test, portfolio. Additional exam requirements/recommendations for international students: Required—TOEFL (minimum score 550 paper-based; 213 computer-based; 79 iBT). *Application deadline:* For fall admission, 1/31 for domestic and international students. Application fee: $30. Electronic applications accepted. *Expenses:* Tuition, state resident: full-time $2,523; part-time $211 per credit hour. Tuition, nonresident: full-time $10,086; part-time $841 per credit hour. *Financial support:* In 2007–08, 15 students received support. Federal Work-Study and institutionally sponsored loans available. Support available to part-time students. Financial award application deadline: 5/31; financial award applicants required to submit FAFSA. *Faculty research:* Digital visual communication modalities, information science education, Southwestern Native American art pedagogy, medical illustration pedagogy, public health/visual education. *Unit head:* Dr. Shelley Mishoe, Dean and Professor, 706-721-2621, Fax: 706-721-7312, E-mail: smishoe@mail.mcg.edu. *Application contact:* Steven Harrison, Chair, Associate Professor and Graduate Program Director, 706-721-3266, E-mail: sharriso@mcg.edu.

Rochester Institute of Technology, Graduate Enrollment Services, College of Imaging Arts and Sciences, School of Art, Program in Medical Illustration, Rochester, NY 14623-5603. Offers MFA. *Students:* 5 full-time (4 women), 1 (woman) part-time; includes 1 minority (Asian American or Pacific Islander) 6 applicants, 67% accepted, 3 enrolled. In 2007, 1 degree awarded. *Degree requirements:* For master's, thesis. *Entrance requirements:* For master's, portfolio, 3.0 GPA. Additional exam requirements/recommendations for international students: Required—TOEFL (minimum score 550 paper-based; 213 computer-based; 79 iBT). *Application deadline:* For fall admission, 3/1 priority date for domestic and international students. Applications are processed on a rolling basis. Application fee: $50. *Expenses:* Tuition: Full-time $28,491; part-time $800 per credit hour. Required fees: $201; $67 per term. *Financial support:* Teaching assistantships with partial tuition reimbursements, career-related internships or fieldwork, institutionally sponsored loans, scholarships/grants, and unspecified assistantships available. Support available to part-time students. Financial award applicants required to submit FAFSA.

University of Illinois at Chicago, Graduate College, College of Applied Health Sciences, Program in Biomedical Visualization, Chicago, IL 60607-7128. Offers MAMS. *Accreditation:* ARCMI. *Degree requirements:* For master's, thesis. *Entrance requirements:* For master's, GRE General Test, minimum GPA of 2.75. Additional exam requirements/recommendations for international students: Required—TOEFL. Electronic applications accepted. Expenses: Contact institution. *Faculty research:* Medical illustration, graphics, reconstruction, anatomical modeling.

The University of Texas Southwestern Medical Center at Dallas, Southwestern Graduate School of Biomedical Sciences, Division of Applied Science, Biomedical Communications Program, Dallas, TX 75390. Offers MA. *Accreditation:* ARCMI. *Faculty:* 2 full-time (1 woman), 4 part-time/adjunct (2 women). *Students:* 17 full-time (10 women); includes 6 minority (2 Asian Americans or Pacific Islanders, 4 Hispanic Americans), 1 international. Average age 25. 24 applicants, 38% accepted, 6 enrolled. In 2007, 2 degrees awarded. *Degree requirements:* For master's, thesis. *Entrance requirements:* For master's, GRE General Test, minimum GPA of 3.0. *Application deadline:* For spring admission, 9/1 priority date for domestic students. Applications are processed on a rolling basis. Application fee: $0. Electronic applications accepted. *Financial support:* In 2007–08, 4 teaching assistantships were awarded; career-related internships or fieldwork and institutionally sponsored loans also available. Financial award application deadline: 3/1; financial award applicants required to submit FAFSA. *Faculty research:* Breast self-examination to indigent populations. *Unit head:* Lewis E. Calver, Chair, 214-648-4699, Fax: 214-648-5353, E-mail: lcalve@mednet.swmed.edu. *Application contact:* Marcie Hanson, Education Coordinator, 214-648-4634, Fax: 214-648-5353, E-mail: marcelle.hanson@utsouthwestern.edu.

Photography

Academy of Art University, Graduate Program, School of Photography, San Francisco, CA 94105-3410. Offers MFA. *Accreditation:* NASAD. Part-time programs available. Postbaccalaureate distance learning degree programs offered (no on-campus study). *Degree requirements:* For master's, final review. *Entrance requirements:* For master's, portfolio. Electronic applications accepted.

Bard College, International Center of Photography, Annandale-on-Hudson, NY 12504. Offers advanced photographic studies (MFA). *Faculty:* 1 full-time (0 women), 5 part-time/adjunct (3 women). *Students:* 24. *Unit head:* Nayland Blake, Chair, 212-857-0001, E-mail: icpbard@icp.edu. *Application contact:* Coco Lee Theuman, Degree and Certificate Programs Associate, 212-857-0063, E-mail: icpbard@icp.edu.

Barry University, School of Arts and Sciences, Department of Fine Arts, Miami Shores, FL 33161-6695. Offers photography (MA, MFA). *Degree requirements:* For master's, thesis (for some programs). *Entrance requirements:* For master's, GRE General Test, minimum GPA of 3.0. *Application deadline:* Applications are processed on a rolling basis. Application fee: $30. Electronic applications accepted. *Financial support:* Career-related internships or fieldwork available. Support available to part-time students. Financial award application deadline: 5/1; financial award applicants required to submit FAFSA. *Faculty research:* Inclusion education, exceptional education, art-based assessments. *Unit head:* Silvia Lizama, Interim Chair, 305-899-3421, Fax: 305-899-2972, E-mail: slizama@mail.barry.edu. *Application contact:* Dave Fletcher, Director of Graduate Admissions, 305-899-3113, Fax: 305-899-2971, E-mail: dfletcher@mail.barry.edu.

Bradley University, Graduate School, Slane College of Communications and Fine Arts, Department of Art, Peoria, IL 61625-0002. Offers ceramics (MA, MFA); drawing/illustration (MA, MFA); interdisciplinary art (MA, MFA); painting (MA, MFA); photography (MA, MFA); printmaking (MA, MFA); sculpture (MA, MFA); visual communication and design (MA, MFA). *Accreditation:* NASAD. Part-time programs available. *Faculty:* 10. *Students:* 11 full-time (6

Photography

Bradley University (continued)

women), 1 international. 20 applicants, 40% accepted, 4 enrolled. In 2007, 2 degrees awarded. *Degree requirements:* For master's, comprehensive exam, thesis, final exhibit. *Entrance requirements:* For master's, portfolio, 2 letters of recommendation. Additional exam requirements/recommendations for international students: Required—TOEFL (minimum score 550 paper-based; 213 computer-based; 79 iBT). *Application deadline:* For fall admission, 4/1 priority date for domestic and international students; for spring admission, 11/1 priority date for domestic and international students. Applications are processed on a rolling basis. Application fee: $40 ($50 for international students). *Financial support:* Research assistantships with full and partial tuition reimbursements, scholarships/grants, tuition waivers (partial), and unspecified assistantships available. Financial award application deadline: 4/1. *Unit head:* Dr. Paul Krainak, Chairperson, 309-677-3330, E-mail: pkrainak@bradley.edu. *Application contact:* Fisher Stolz, Graduate Coordinator, 309-677-2969, E-mail: fisher@bradley.edu.

Brooklyn College of the City University of New York, Division of Graduate Studies, Department of Art, Brooklyn, NY 11210-2889. Offers art history (MA, PhD); digital art (MFA); drawing and painting (MFA); photography (MFA); printmaking (MFA); sculpture (MFA). The department offers courses at Brooklyn College that are creditable toward the CUNY doctoral degree; MFA programs—Fall admissions only, application deadline 2/1. Part-time programs available. *Students:* 27 full-time (14 women), 18 part-time (14 women); includes 3 minority (2 African Americans, 1 Asian American or Pacific Islander), 1 international. 82 applicants, 48% accepted, 13 enrolled. In 2007, 21 degrees awarded. *Degree requirements:* For master's, thesis. *Entrance requirements:* For master's, bachelor's degree in art, portfolio, 2 letters of recommendation, portfolio, supplemental application. Additional exam requirements/recommendations for international students: Required—TOEFL. *Application deadline:* For fall admission, 2/1 for domestic and international students; for spring admission, 11/1 for domestic students. Application fee: $125. Electronic applications accepted. *Financial support:* Career-related internships or fieldwork, Federal Work-Study, institutionally sponsored loans, scholarships/grants, and painting awards available. Support available to part-time students. Financial award application deadline: 5/1; financial award applicants required to submit FAFSA. *Unit head:* Dr. Michael Mallory, Chairperson, 718-951-5181, E-mail: mmallory@brooklyn.cuny.edu. *Application contact:* Hernan Sierra, Graduate Admissions Coordinator, 718-951-4536, Fax: 718-951-4506, E-mail: grads@brooklyn.cuny.edu.

Brooks Institute, Graduate Program in Professional Photography, Santa Barbara, CA 93101. Offers MFA. Evening/weekend programs available. *Faculty:* 2 full-time (1 woman), 7 part-time/adjunct (0 women). *Students:* 14 full-time (5 women). Average age 36. 25 applicants, 80% accepted, 20 enrolled. In 2007, 17 degrees awarded. *Degree requirements:* For master's, thesis. *Entrance requirements:* For master's, portfolio review testing procedure (written exam), minimum GPA of 3.0, 3 letters of recommendation, official college transcripts. Additional exam requirements/recommendations for international students: Required—TOEFL (minimum score 580 paper-based; 237 computer-based). *Application deadline:* For fall admission, 9/7 for domestic students. Applications are processed on a rolling basis. Application fee: $200. Electronic applications accepted. *Expenses:* Tuition: Part-time $600 per credit. Required fees: $400 per year. One-time fee: $600 part-time. *Financial support:* Applicants required to submit FAFSA. *Unit head:* Glen Rand, Program Director, Graduate Program, 805-966-3888, E-mail: glenrand@aol.com. *Application contact:* Mike Smith, Admissions Representative-MFA, 805-966-3888, E-mail: mike.smith@brooks.edu.

California College of the Arts, Graduate Programs, Programs in Fine Art, San Francisco, CA 94107. Offers ceramics (MFA); film/video/performance (MFA); glass (MFA); jewelry/metal arts (MFA); painting/drawing (MFA); photography (MFA); printmaking (MFA); sculpture (MFA); textiles (MFA); wood/furniture (MFA). *Accreditation:* NASAD. *Faculty:* 17 full-time (9 women), 32 part-time/adjunct (12 women). *Students:* 101 full-time (73 women), 11 part-time (8 women). Average age 30. 437 applicants, 29% accepted, 51 enrolled. In 2007, 34 degrees awarded. *Degree requirements:* For master's, thesis, exhibit. *Entrance requirements:* For master's, appropriate bachelor's degree, portfolio. Additional exam requirements/recommendations for international students: Required—TOEFL (minimum score 600 paper-based; 250 computer-based). *Application deadline:* For fall admission, 1/15 for domestic and international students. Application fee: $50. Electronic applications accepted. *Expenses:* Tuition: Part-time $1,017 per unit. *Financial support:* In 2007–08, 5 fellowships (averaging $10,000 per year), 20 teaching assistantships (averaging $2,000 per year) were awarded; career-related internships or fieldwork, Federal Work-Study, scholarships/grants, and health care benefits also available. Financial award application deadline: 3/1; financial award applicants required to submit FAFSA. *Unit head:* Ted Purves, Chair, 415-551-9214, Fax: 415-703-9539, E-mail: tpurves@cca.edu. *Application contact:* Kathryn Ward, Assistant Director of Graduate Admissions, 415-703-9523 Ext. 9593, Fax: 415-703-9539, E-mail: graduateprograms@cca.edu.

California Institute of the Arts, School of Art, Valencia, CA 91355-2340. Offers art (MFA, Adv C); graphic design (MFA, Adv C); photography (MFA, Adv C). *Accreditation:* NASAD (one or more programs are accredited). *Degree requirements:* For master's, final project. *Entrance requirements:* For master's, portfolio. Additional exam requirements/recommendations for international students: Required—TOEFL. Electronic applications accepted.

California State University, Fullerton, Graduate Studies, College of the Arts, Department of Art, Fullerton, CA 92834-9480. Offers art (MA, MFA), including ceramics (MFA), crafts, creative photography (MFA), design (MFA), drawing and painting, printmaking (MFA), sculpture; art history (MA); design (MA). *Accreditation:* NASAD (one or more programs are accredited). Part-time programs available. *Students:* 50 full-time (20 women), 28 part-time (20 women); includes 19 minority (2 African Americans, 2 American Indian/Alaska Native, 8 Asian Americans or Pacific Islanders, 7 Hispanic Americans), 2 international. Average age 36. 68 applicants, 47% accepted, 23 enrolled. In 2007, 29 degrees awarded. *Degree requirements:* For master's, project or thesis. *Entrance requirements:* For master's, minimum GPA of 2.5 in last 60 units of course work, portfolio. Application fee: $55. *Financial support:* Career-related internships or fieldwork, Federal Work-Study, institutionally sponsored loans, and scholarships/grants available. Support available to part-time students. Financial award application deadline: 3/1. *Unit head:* Larry Johnson, Chair, 714-278-3471. *Application contact:* Al Ching, Adviser, 714-278-3471.

California State University, Los Angeles, Graduate Studies, College of Arts and Letters, Department of Art, Los Angeles, CA 90032-8530. Offers art (MA), including art education, art history, art therapy, ceramics, metals, and textiles, design (MA, MFA), painting, sculpture, and graphic arts, photography; fine arts (MFA), including crafts, design (MA, MFA), studio arts. *Accreditation:* NASAD (one or more programs are accredited). Part-time and evening/weekend programs available. *Faculty:* 7 full-time (3 women). *Students:* 24 full-time (13 women), 59 part-time (42 women); includes 19 minority (2 African Americans, 1 American Indian/Alaska Native, 5 Asian Americans or Pacific Islanders, 11 Hispanic Americans), 16 international. Average age 39. In 2007, 28 degrees awarded. *Degree requirements:* For master's, comprehensive exam, project or thesis. *Entrance requirements:* For master's, portfolio. Additional exam requirements/recommendations for international students: Required—TOEFL. *Application deadline:* For fall admission, 6/30 for domestic students; for spring admission, 2/1 for domestic students. Applications are processed on a rolling basis. Application fee: $55. *Financial support:* Federal Work-Study available. Support available to part-time students. Financial award application deadline: 3/1. *Faculty research:* The artist and the book, conceptual art, ceramic processes, computer graphics, architectural graphics. *Unit head:* Dr. Robert Martin, Chair, 323-343-4010, Fax: 323-343-4045, E-mail: rjmartin@calstatela.edu.

Claremont Graduate University, Graduate Programs, School of Arts and Humanities, Department of Art, Claremont, CA 91711-6160. Offers digital media (MA, MFA); drawing (MA, MFA); installation (MA, MFA); new genre (MA, MFA); painting (MA, MFA); performance (MA, MFA); photography (MA, MFA); sculpture (MA, MFA). Part-time programs available. *Faculty:* 3 full-time (0 women), 10 part-time/adjunct (5 women). *Students:* 61 full-time (36 women), 1 part-time; includes 11 minority (2 African Americans, 4 Asian Americans or Pacific Islanders, 5 Hispanic Americans), 4 international. Average age 33. In 2007, 34 degrees awarded. *Degree requirements:* For master's, final project show. *Entrance requirements:* For master's, BA in art or BFA, slide review. *Application deadline:* For fall admission, 2/15 priority date for domestic students. Applications are processed on a rolling basis. Electronic applications accepted. *Expenses:* Tuition: Full-time $31,640; part-time $1,376 per unit. Required fees: $145 per semester. Tuition and fees vary according to course load, degree level and program. *Financial support:* Fellowships, research assistantships, teaching assistantships, Federal Work-Study and institutionally sponsored loans available. Support available to part-time students. Financial award application deadline: 2/15; financial award applicants required to submit FAFSA. *Faculty research:* Acoustic sculpture, feminization of abstraction, installation sculpture. *Unit head:* David Pagel, Chair, 909-621-8071, Fax: 909-607-1276, E-mail: david.pagel@cgu.edu. *Application contact:* Marianne Elder, Assistant Coordinator, 909-607-2479, Fax: 909-607-1276, E-mail: marianne.elder@cgu.edu.

Columbia College Chicago, Graduate School, Department of Photography, Chicago, IL 60605-1996. Offers MA, MFA. *Students:* 1 (woman) full-time, 21 part-time (11 women); includes 1 minority (Asian American or Pacific Islander) Average age 26. In 2007, 11 degrees awarded. *Degree requirements:* For master's, thesis, project. *Entrance requirements:* For master's, minimum GPA of 3.0, portfolio. Additional exam requirements/recommendations for international students: Required—TOEFL (minimum score 550 paper-based; 213 computer-based). *Application deadline:* For fall admission, 2/1 for domestic and international students. Application fee: $50. Electronic applications accepted. *Financial support:* Fellowships, Federal Work-Study and scholarships/grants available. Support available to part-time students. Financial award application deadline: 8/13; financial award applicants required to submit FAFSA. *Unit head:* Bob Thall, Chairperson, 312-344-7328, Fax: 312-344-8068, E-mail: bthall@colum.edu. *Application contact:* Keith Cleveland, Acting Dean of the Graduate School, 312-344-7261, Fax: 312-344-8047, E-mail: kcleveland@colum.edu.

Columbia University, School of the Arts, Visual Arts Division, New York, NY 10027. Offers new genres (MFA); painting (MFA); photography (MFA); printmaking (MFA); sculpture (MFA). *Faculty:* 9 full-time (3 women), 53 part-time/adjunct (20 women). *Students:* 53 full-time (24 women); includes 3 minority (all Asian Americans or Pacific Islanders) Average age 27. 1,052 applicants, 2% accepted, 26 enrolled. In 2007, 24 degrees awarded. *Degree requirements:* For master's, thesis. *Entrance requirements:* For master's, 3 letters of recommendation, portfolio, personal statement, resumé, official transcript. Additional exam requirements/recommendations for international students: Required—TOEFL (minimum score 600 paper-based; 250 computer-based; 100 iBT). *Application deadline:* For fall admission, 1/15 for domestic and international students. Application fee: $120. Electronic applications accepted. *Expenses:* Tuition: Part-time $1,452 per credit. Required fees: $152 per term. One-time fee: $75 part-time. Full-time tuition and fees vary according to course level, course load, degree level and program. *Financial support:* In 2007–08, 26 fellowships (averaging $7,297 per year), 12 research assistantships (averaging $22,444 per year) were awarded; teaching assistantships, career-related internships or fieldwork, Federal Work-Study, scholarships/grants, health care benefits, and unspecified assistantships also available. Financial award applicants required to submit FAFSA. *Unit head:* Gregory Amenoff, Chair, 212-854-4065, E-mail: visualarts@columbia.edu. *Application contact:* Director of Admissions, 212-854-2134, E-mail: admissions-arts@columbia.edu.

See Close-Up on page 347.

Cornell University, Graduate School, Graduate Fields of Architecture, Art and Planning, Field of Art, Ithaca, NY 14853-0001. Offers creative visual arts (MFA), including painting, photography, printmaking, sculpture. *Faculty:* 12 full-time (3 women). *Students:* 12 full-time (4 women), 1 international. Average age 29. 102 applicants, 7% accepted, 6 enrolled. In 2007, 5 degrees awarded. *Degree requirements:* For master's, thesis, exhibit. *Entrance requirements:* For master's, slide portfolio of 10-20 slides, 3 letters of recommendation, resumé. Additional exam requirements/recommendations for international students: Required—TOEFL (minimum score 550 paper-based; 213 computer-based; 77 iBT). *Application deadline:* For fall admission, 2/15 for domestic students. Application fee: $70. Electronic applications accepted. *Financial support:* In 2007–08, 10 students received support, including 10 teaching assistantships with full tuition reimbursements available; fellowships with full tuition reimbursements available, research assistantships with full tuition reimbursements available, institutionally sponsored loans, scholarships/grants, health care benefits, tuition waivers (full and partial), and unspecified assistantships also available. Financial award applicants required to submit FAFSA. *Faculty research:* Painting, sculpture, photography, printmaking. *Unit head:* Director of Graduate Studies, 607-255-6730, Fax: 607-255-3462. *Application contact:* Graduate Field Assistant, 607-255-6730, Fax: 607-255-3462, E-mail: artinfo@cornell.edu.

Cranbrook Academy of Art, Graduate School, Program in Fine Arts, Bloomfield Hills, MI 48303-0801. Offers ceramics (MFA); design (MFA), including graphic design; fiber arts (MFA); metalsmithing (MFA); painting (MFA); photography (MFA); printmaking (MFA); sculpture (MFA). *Accreditation:* NASAD. *Degree requirements:* For master's, thesis, exhibit. *Entrance requirements:* Additional exam requirements/recommendations for international students: Required—TOEFL (minimum score 550 paper-based; 213 computer-based).

See Close-Up on page 237.

The George Washington University, Columbian College of Arts and Sciences, Department of Fine Arts and Art History, Washington, DC 20052. Offers art history (MA, PhD), including art history (PhD), museum training (MA); ceramics (MFA); design (MFA); interior design (MFA); painting (MFA); photography (MFA); printmaking (MFA); sculpture (MFA). *Accreditation:* CIDA. Part-time and evening/weekend programs available. *Entrance requirements:* For master's, GRE General Test, bachelor's degree in field, minimum GPA of 3.0. Additional exam requirements/recommendations for international students: Required—TOEFL (minimum score 550 paper-based; 213 computer-based). Electronic applications accepted.

Georgia State University, College of Arts and Sciences, Department of Communication, Atlanta, GA 30303-3083. Offers film/video/digital imaging (MA); human communication and social influence (MA); mass communication (MA); moving image studies (PhD); public communication (PhD). Part-time programs available. *Faculty:* 27 full-time (13 women). *Students:* 81 full-time (51 women), 61 part-time (41 women); includes 31 minority (26 African Americans, 2 Asian Americans or Pacific Islanders, 3 Hispanic Americans), 17 international. 179 applicants, 30% accepted, 29 enrolled. In 2007, 23 master's, 10 doctorates awarded. *Degree requirements:* For master's, one foreign language, thesis or alternative; for doctorate, comprehensive exam, thesis/dissertation. *Entrance requirements:* For master's and doctorate, GRE General Test. Additional exam requirements/recommendations for international students: Required—TOEFL (minimum score 80 computer-based). Application fee: $50. Electronic applications accepted. *Expenses:* Tuition, state resident: part-time $221 per credit hour. *Financial support:* In 2007–08, 1 fellowship with tuition reimbursement (averaging $15,000 per year) was awarded; research assistantships, teaching assistantships with tuition reimbursements, career-related internships or fieldwork, Federal Work-Study, institutionally sponsored loans, tuition waivers (partial), and unspecified assistantships also available. Support available to part-time students. Financial award applicants required to submit FAFSA. *Faculty research:* Critical/cultural studies, rhetoric studies, film/media studies, mass communications/journalism, audience studies. *Unit head:* Dr. David Cheshier, Chair, 404-413-5649, E-mail: dcheshier@gsu.edu. *Application contact:* Tawanna Tookes, Administrative Specialist, Managerial, 404-413-5652, E-mail: joutkt@langate.gsu.edu.

Howard University, Graduate School, Division of Fine Arts, Department of Art, Program in Fine Arts, Washington, DC 20059-0002. Offers 3D reality (sculpture and ceramics) (MFA); design (MFA); electronic studio (MFA); painting (MFA); photography (MFA). *Accreditation:* NASAD. *Degree requirements:* For master's, comprehensive exam, thesis, exhibit. *Entrance requirements:* For master's, minimum GPA of 3.0, portfolio. *Expenses:* Tuition: Full-time $16,175; part-time $899 per credit hour. Required fees: $805.

Illinois State University, Graduate School, College of Fine Arts, School of Art, Normal, IL 61790-2200. Offers art history (MA, MS); ceramics (MFA, MS); drawing (MFA, MS); fibers

(MFA, MS); glass (MFA, MS); graphic design (MFA, MS); metals (MFA, MS); painting (MFA, MS); photography (MFA, MS); printmaking (MFA, MS); sculpture (MFA, MS). *Accreditation:* NASAD (one or more programs are accredited). *Faculty:* 30 full-time (12 women). *Students:* 31 full-time (20 women); 5 part-time (4 women); includes 3 minority (1 African American, 2 Hispanic Americans), 3 international. 62 applicants, 29% accepted. In 2007, 17 degrees awarded. *Degree requirements:* For master's, thesis or alternative, internship. *Entrance requirements:* For master's, portfolio, sample of scholarly writing. *Application deadline:* Applications are processed on a rolling basis. Application fee: $40. *Expenses:* Tuition, state resident: full-time $3,492; part-time $194 per credit hour. Tuition, nonresident: full-time $7,272; part-time $404 per credit hour. Required fees: $1,024; $57 per credit hour. *Financial support:* In 2007–08, 23 teaching assistantships (averaging $6,661 per year) were awarded; career-related internships or fieldwork, Federal Work-Study, tuition waivers (full and partial), and unspecified assistantships also available. Support available to part-time students. Financial award application deadline: 4/1. *Faculty research:* General operations support: Normal Editions Workshop for FY2007. Total annual research expenditures: $4,160. *Unit head:* James Crowley, Chairperson, 309-438-5621.

Indiana State University, School of Graduate Studies, College of Arts and Sciences, Department of Art, Terre Haute, IN 47809-1401. Offers ceramics (MA, MFA); drawing (MA, MFA); graphic design (MA, MFA); painting (MA, MFA); photography (MA, MFA); printmaking (MA, MFA); sculpture (MA, MFA). *Accreditation:* NASAD (one or more programs are accredited). Part-time programs available. *Faculty:* 10 full-time (3 women), 1 part-time/adjunct (0 women). *Students:* 16 full-time (9 women), 9 part-time (1 woman); includes 1 minority (Hispanic American), 8 international. Average age 35. 17 applicants, 65% accepted, 6 enrolled. In 2007, 7 degrees awarded. *Degree requirements:* For master's, thesis or alternative, departmental qualifying exam. *Entrance requirements:* For master's, portfolio. Additional exam requirements/recommendations for international students: Required—TOEFL (minimum score 550 paper-based). *Application deadline:* For fall admission, 7/1 priority date for domestic students; for spring admission, 11/1 priority date for domestic students. Applications are processed on a rolling basis. Application fee: $35. *Expenses:* Tuition, state resident: full-time $7,056; part-time $294 per semester hour. Tuition, nonresident: full-time $14,016; part-time $584 per semester hour. Required fees: $175 per semester. *Financial support:* In 2007–08, 7 teaching assistantships with partial tuition reimbursements (averaging $7,200 per year) were awarded; career-related internships or fieldwork, Federal Work-Study, institutionally sponsored loans, scholarships/grants, and tuition waivers (partial) also available. Support available to part-time students. Financial award application deadline: 3/1; financial award applicants required to submit FAFSA. *Unit head:* Dr. Alden Cavanaugh, Chairperson, 812-237-3698.

Inter American University of Puerto Rico, San Germán Campus, Graduate Studies Center, Program in Fine Arts, San Germán, PR 00683-5008. Offers art (MFA); ceramics (MFA); drawing (MFA); engraving (MFA); painting (MFA); photography (MFA); sculpture (MFA). *Faculty:* 4 full-time, 2 part-time/adjunct. *Students:* 28. In 2007, 7 degrees awarded. *Degree requirements:* For master's, comprehensive exam, thesis. *Entrance requirements:* For master's, GRE General Test or EXADEP, minimum GPA of 3.0. *Application deadline:* For fall admission, 4/30 priority date for domestic students; for spring admission, 11/15 for domestic students. Applications are processed on a rolling basis. Application fee: $31. *Expenses:* Tuition: Full-time $3,258; part-time $181 per credit. Required fees: $258 per semester. Tuition and fees vary according to degree level. *Financial support:* Teaching assistantships, Federal Work-Study and unspecified assistantships available. *Application contact:* Prof. Maria Garcia, Graduate Coordinator, 787-264-1912 Ext. 7357, Fax: 787-892-6350, E-mail: hgarcia@sg.inter.edu.

James Madison University, The Graduate School, College of Visual and Performing Arts, School of Art and Art History, Harrisonburg, VA 22807. Offers art education (MA); art history (MA); ceramics (MFA); drawing/painting (MFA); metal/jewelry (MFA); photography (MFA); printmaking (MFA); sculpture (MFA); studio art (MA); weaving/fibers (MFA). *Accreditation:* NASAD. Part-time programs available. *Faculty:* 5 full-time (2 women), 1 part-time/adjunct (0 women). *Students:* 10 full-time (5 women), 2 part-time; includes 1 minority (Asian American or Pacific Islander) Average age 27. In 2007, 8 degrees awarded. *Degree requirements:* For master's, thesis (for some programs). *Entrance requirements:* For master's, GRE General Test, language exam in French or German, portfolio, 3 letters of recommendation, research paper. Additional exam requirements/recommendations for international students: Required—TOEFL. *Application deadline:* For fall admission, 2/15 priority date for domestic students, 2/15 for international students; for spring admission, 10/15 priority date for domestic students, 10/15 for international students. Applications are processed on a rolling basis. Application fee: $55. Electronic applications accepted. *Expenses:* Tuition, state resident: full-time $6,720; part-time $280 per credit hour. Tuition, nonresident: full-time $19,104; part-time $796 per credit hour. *Financial support:* In 2007–08, 8 students received support, including 3 teaching assistantships with full tuition reimbursements available (averaging $8,494 per year); Federal Work-Study, unspecified assistantships, and 5 graduate assistantships ($7,237) also available. Financial award application deadline: 3/1; financial award applicants required to submit FAFSA. *Unit head:* Leslie M. Bellavance, Academic Unit Head, 540-568-6216.

Lamar University, College of Graduate Studies, College of Fine Arts and Communication, Department of Art, Beaumont, TX 77710. Offers art history (MA); photography (MA); studio art (MA); visual design (MA). Part-time and evening/weekend programs available. *Faculty:* 6 full-time (3 women). *Students:* Average age 42. 2 applicants, 0% accepted. In 2007, 2 degrees awarded. *Degree requirements:* For master's, thesis. *Entrance requirements:* For master's, GRE General Test, minimum GPA of 2.5 in last 60 hours of undergraduate course work. Additional exam requirements/recommendations for international students: Required—TOEFL. *Application deadline:* For fall admission, 8/1 priority date for domestic students; for spring admission, 12/1 for domestic students. Applications are processed on a rolling basis. Application fee: $25 ($50 for international students). *Expenses:* Tuition, state resident: part-time $348 per semester hour. Tuition, nonresident: part-time $626 per semester hour. Tuition and fees vary according to course load. *Financial support:* Fellowships, career-related internships or fieldwork, Federal Work-Study, and scholarships/grants available. Financial award application deadline: 4/1. *Faculty research:* Nineteenth century academic paintings, metal casting, pigment color stability, computer modified photography, manipulated photography. *Unit head:* Donna M. Meeks, Chair, 409-880-8141, Fax: 409-880-1799, E-mail: meeksdm@lub002.lamar.edu.

Louisiana State University and Agricultural and Mechanical College, Graduate School, College of Art and Design, School of Art, Program in Studio Art, Baton Rouge, LA 70803. Offers ceramics (MFA); graphic design (MFA); painting and drawing (MFA); photography (MFA); printmaking (MFA); sculpture (MFA). *Accreditation:* NASAD. *Students:* 47 full-time (29 women), 4 part-time (2 women); includes 1 African American, 1 Hispanic American, 6 international. 63 applicants, 25% accepted. In 2007, 16 degrees awarded. *Degree requirements:* For master's, thesis. *Entrance requirements:* For master's, minimum GPA of 3.0. Additional exam requirements/recommendations for international students: Required—TOEFL (minimum score 550 paper-based; 213 computer-based; 79 iBT). *Application deadline:* For fall admission, 1/25 priority date for domestic students, 5/15 for international students; for spring admission, 10/15 for international students. Applications are processed on a rolling basis. Electronic applications accepted. *Financial support:* In 2007–08, 25 students received support; research assistantships with partial tuition reimbursements available, teaching assistantships, career-related internships or fieldwork, Federal Work-Study, institutionally sponsored loans, scholarships/grants, and unspecified assistantships available. Support available to part-time students. Financial award application deadline: 3/15. *Unit head:* Chris Johns, Graduate Coordinator, 225-578-5411, Fax: 225-578-1445, E-mail: cjohns@lsu.edu.

Louisiana Tech University, Graduate School, College of Liberal Arts, School of Art, Ruston, LA 71272. Offers art and graphic design (MFA); photography (MFA); studio art (MFA). *Accreditation:* NASAD. Part-time programs available. *Degree requirements:* For master's, exhibit. *Entrance requirements:* For master's, GRE General Test, portfolio. *Application deadline:* For fall admission, 7/29 for domestic students; for spring admission, 2/3 for domestic students. Applications are processed on a rolling basis. Application fee: $20 ($30 for international students). *Financial support:* Fellowships, career-related internships or fieldwork, Federal Work-Study, institutionally sponsored loans, and unspecified assistantships available. Financial award application deadline: 2/1. *Unit head:* Jonathan Donchoo, Director, 318-257-3909, Fax: 318-257-4890.

Maryland Institute College of Art, Graduate Studies, Program in Photography and Digital Imaging, Baltimore, MD 21217. Offers MFA. *Accreditation:* NASAD. *Faculty:* 1 full-time (0 women), 1 part-time/adjunct (0 women). *Students:* 16 full-time (9 women); includes 1 minority (Asian American or Pacific Islander) Average age 28. In 2007, 8 degrees awarded. *Degree requirements:* For master's, thesis, exhibit. *Entrance requirements:* For master's, portfolio, 40 studio credits, 6 credits in art history. Additional exam requirements/recommendations for international students: Required—TOEFL (minimum score 550 paper-based; 213 computer-based). *Application deadline:* For fall admission, 2/15 for domestic and international students. Application fee: $50. *Expenses:* Tuition: Full-time $29,700; part-time $1,238 per credit. Required fees: $980; $490 per term. *Financial support:* In 2007–08, 16 students received support, including 2 fellowships (averaging $15,680 per year), 13 teaching assistantships (averaging $1,500 per year); career-related internships or fieldwork and scholarships/grants also available. Financial award application deadline: 3/1; financial award applicants required to submit FAFSA. *Unit head:* Timothy Druckrey, Director, 410-225-2534, Fax: 410-669-1141. *Application contact:* Scott G. Kelly, Associate Dean of Graduate Admission, 410-225-2256, Fax: 410-225-2408, E-mail: graduate@mica.edu.

Marywood University, Academic Affairs, Insalaco College of Creative Arts and Management, Art Department, Program in Studio Art, Scranton, PA 18509-1598. Offers advertising design (MA); ceramics (MA); clay (MA); graphic design (MA); illustration (MA); interior architecture (MA); painting (MA); photography (MA); printmaking (MA); sculpture (MA); weaving (MA). *Accreditation:* NASAD. Part-time and evening/weekend programs available. *Students:* 5 full-time (3 women), 15 part-time (11 women), 1 international. Average age 41. 5 applicants, 80% accepted. In 2007, 7 degrees awarded. *Degree requirements:* For master's, comprehensive exam, thesis or alternative. *Entrance requirements:* For master's, portfolio. Additional exam requirements/recommendations for international students: Required—TOEFL (minimum score 550 paper-based; 213 computer-based). *Application deadline:* For fall admission, 4/15 priority date for domestic and international students; for spring admission, 11/15 priority date for domestic and international students. Applications are processed on a rolling basis. Application fee: $30. Electronic applications accepted. *Expenses:* Tuition: Full-time $15,290; part-time $695 per credit. Required fees: $990; $370 per term. Tuition and fees vary according to degree level. *Financial support:* Research assistantships with tuition reimbursements, scholarships/grants, tuition waivers (partial), and unspecified assistantships available. Support available to part-time students. Financial award application deadline: 2/15; financial award applicants required to submit FAFSA. *Faculty research:* Texture and line in clay, cast bronze sculpture, color theories, book art and illustration, sculptural form.

Marywood University, Academic Affairs, Insalaco College of Creative Arts and Management, Art Department, Program in Visual Arts, Scranton, PA 18509-1598. Offers advertising design (MFA); clay (MFA); fibers (MFA); graphic design (MFA); illustration (MFA); metals (MFA); painting (MFA); photography (MFA); printmaking (MFA). *Accreditation:* NASAD. Part-time and evening/weekend programs available. *Students:* 13 full-time (10 women), 25 part-time (13 women); includes 2 minority (1 American Indian/Alaska Native, 1 Asian American or Pacific Islander), 3 international. Average age 35. In 2007, 11 degrees awarded. *Degree requirements:* For master's, thesis or alternative, exhibit. *Entrance requirements:* For master's, portfolio. Additional exam requirements/recommendations for international students: Required—TOEFL (minimum score 550 paper-based; 213 computer-based). *Application deadline:* For fall admission, 4/15 priority date for domestic and international students; for spring admission, 11/15 priority date for domestic and international students. Applications are processed on a rolling basis. Application fee: $30. Electronic applications accepted. *Expenses: Contact institution.* Tuition and fees vary according to degree level. *Financial support:* Research assistantships with tuition reimbursements, scholarships/grants, tuition waivers (partial), and unspecified assistantships available. Support available to part-time students. Financial award application deadline: 2/15; financial award applicants required to submit FAFSA. *Faculty research:* Mariology, exploration of visual imagery, explorations involving drawing on the loom, clay as sculptural medium, oil paintings.

Massachusetts College of Art and Design, Graduate Programs, Program in Fine Arts, Boston, MA 02115-5882. Offers ceramics (MFA); design (MFA); fibers (MFA); film (MFA); glass (MFA); media and performing arts (MFA); metals (MFA); painting (MFA); photography (MFA); printmaking (MFA); sculpture (MFA). *Accreditation:* NASAD. *Faculty:* 10 full-time (5 women), 8 part-time/adjunct (6 women). *Students:* 80 full-time (46 women), 11 part-time (9 women); includes 7 minority (1 African American, 4 Asian Americans or Pacific Islanders, 2 Hispanic Americans), 13 international. Average age 34. 310 applicants, 26% accepted, 50 enrolled. In 2007, 37 degrees awarded. *Degree requirements:* For master's, thesis, exhibit. *Entrance requirements:* For master's, 12 units of course work in art history, portfolio, resumé. *Application deadline:* For fall admission, 2/1 for domestic students. Application fee: $75. *Expenses:* Tuition, state resident: full-time $16,260; part-time $542 per credit. Tuition, nonresident: full-time $16,260; part-time $542 per credit. *Financial support:* In 2007–08, 50 research assistantships (averaging $2,000 per year), 30 teaching assistantships (averaging $2,000 per year) were awarded; career-related internships or fieldwork, Federal Work-Study, and clerical/technical assistantships also available. Support available to part-time students. Financial award application deadline: 5/1; financial award applicants required to submit FAFSA. *Application contact:* George Creamer, Director, 617-879-7163, Fax: 617-879-7171, E-mail: creamer@massart.edu.

Memphis College of Art, Graduate Programs, Program in Studio Art, Memphis, TN 38104-2764. Offers fiber/surface design (MFA); painting (MFA); papermaking (MFA); photography (MFA); printmaking (MFA); sculpture (MFA). *Accreditation:* NASAD. Part-time programs available. *Faculty:* 11 full-time (5 women), 2 part-time/adjunct (1 woman). *Students:* 17 full-time (7 women); includes 2 minority (both Hispanic Americans) Average age 29. 45 applicants, 51% accepted, 8 enrolled. In 2007, 4 degrees awarded. *Degree requirements:* For master's, thesis, exhibit. *Entrance requirements:* For master's, portfolio, interview, resumé. Additional exam requirements/recommendations for international students: Required—TOEFL (minimum score 525 paper-based; 195 computer-based). *Application deadline:* For fall admission, 3/1 priority date for domestic and international students; for spring admission, 11/1 priority date for domestic and international students. Application fee: $50. Electronic applications accepted. *Expenses:* Tuition: Full-time $22,000; part-time $435 per credit. Required fees: $560; $100 per course. Part-time tuition and fees vary according to course load and program. *Financial support:* In 2007–08, 11 students received support, including 2 teaching assistantships (averaging $2,000 per year); career-related internships or fieldwork, Federal Work-Study, institutionally sponsored loans, scholarships/grants, tuition waivers (partial), unspecified assistantships, and merit awards also available. Support available to part-time students. Financial award application deadline: 8/1; financial award applicants required to submit FAFSA. *Unit head:* Howard Paine, Graduate Program Director, 901-272-5100, Fax: 901-272-5158, E-mail: hpaine@mca.edu. *Application contact:* Annette James Moore, Director of Admissions, 800-727-1088, Fax: 901-272-5158, E-mail: info@mca.edu.

See Close-Up on page 245.

Mills College, Graduate Studies, Department of Art, Oakland, CA 94613-1000. Offers ceramics (MFA); intermedia (MFA); painting (MFA); photography (MFA); sculpture (MFA). *Faculty:* 6 full-time (5 women), 11 part-time/adjunct (6 women). *Students:* 23 full-time (12 women); includes 4 minority (all Asian Americans or Pacific Islanders) Average age 33. 90 applicants, 30% accepted, 11 enrolled. In 2007, 12 degrees awarded. *Degree requirements:* For master's, thesis or alternative, exhibit. *Entrance requirements:* Additional exam requirements/recommendations for international students: Required—TOEFL. *Application deadline:* For fall admission, 2/1 for domestic students; for spring admission, 11/1 for domestic students. Application fee: $50. *Expenses: Contact institution.* Part-time tuition and fees vary according to course load and program. *Financial support:* In 2007–08, 10 fellowships with partial tuition

Photography

Mills College (continued)

reimbursements (averaging $2,125 per year), 12 teaching assistantships with partial tuition reimbursements (averaging $13,896 per year) were awarded; institutionally sponsored loans, scholarships/grants, tuition waivers (partial), and residence awards also available. Support available to part-time students. Financial award application deadline: 2/1; financial award applicants required to submit FAFSA. *Faculty research:* Contemporary Chinese/American art, Asian art, performance art, feminist theory, installation. *Unit head:* Ron Nagle, Chairperson, 510-430-3142, Fax: 510-430-3314. *Application contact:* Linda Guzman, Graduate Admission Specialist, 510-430-3309, Fax: 510-430-2159, E-mail: grad-studies@mills.edu.

Minneapolis College of Art and Design, Program in Visual Studies, Minneapolis, MN 55404-4347. Offers animation (MFA); comic art (MFA); drawing (MFA); filmmaking (MFA); fine arts (MFA); furniture design (MFA); graphic design (MFA); illustration (MFA); interactive media (MFA); painting (MFA); photography (MFA); printmaking (MFA); sculpture (MFA). *Accreditation:* NASAD. Part-time programs available. *Faculty:* 23 full-time (7 women), 9 part-time/adjunct (4 women). *Students:* 40 full-time (21 women), 1 (woman) part-time; includes 1 minority (American Indian/Alaska Native). Average age 27. 172 applicants, 24% accepted, 15 enrolled. In 2007, 7 degrees awarded. *Degree requirements:* For master's, thesis, thesis exhibit. *Entrance requirements:* For master's, portfolio, resumé, 3 letters of recommendation, statement . Additional exam requirements/recommendations for international students: Required—TOEFL (minimum score 550 paper-based; 213 computer-based; 79 iBT). *Application deadline:* For fall admission, 2/15 for domestic and international students. Application fee: $50. Electronic applications accepted. *Expenses:* Tuition: Full-time $27,000; part-time $900 per credit. Required fees: $100 per term. *Financial support:* In 2007–08, 23 students received support, including 15 teaching assistantships (averaging $6,000 per year); career-related internships or fieldwork, Federal Work-Study, scholarships/grants, and unspecified assistantships also available. Support available to part-time students. Financial award application deadline: 3/15; financial award applicants required to submit FAFSA. *Faculty research:* Visual arts. *Unit head:* Carole Fisher, Graduate Director, 612-874-3629, E-mail: carole_fisher@mcad.edu. *Application contact:* William Mullen, Vice President of Enrollment Management, 612-874-3762, Fax: 612-874-3701, E-mail: william_mullen@mcad.edu.

New Mexico State University, Graduate School, College of Arts and Sciences, Department of Art, Las Cruces, NM 88003-8001. Offers art history (MA); ceramics (MA, MFA); design (MA, MFA); drawing (MA, MFA); metals (MA, MFA); painting (MA, MFA); photography (MA, MFA); printmaking (MA, MFA); sculpture (MA, MFA). *Faculty:* 8 full-time (5 women), 1 (woman) part-time/adjunct. *Students:* 33 full-time (16 women), 3 part-time (1 woman); includes 6 minority (1 American Indian/Alaska Native, 5 Hispanic Americans), 1 international. Average age 35. 24 applicants, 58% accepted, 10 enrolled. In 2007, 7 degrees awarded. *Degree requirements:* For master's, comprehensive exam (for some programs), thesis, thesis exhibit. *Entrance requirements:* For master's, portfolio, 10-page paper (art history). *Application deadline:* For fall admission, 2/15 for domestic students; for winter admission, 10/15 for domestic students; for spring admission, 7/15 for domestic students. Application fee: $30 ($50 for international students). Electronic applications accepted. *Expenses:* Tuition, state resident: full-time $3,602; part-time $199 per credit. Tuition, nonresident: full-time $13,380; part-time $607 per credit. Required fees: $1,178. *Financial support:* In 2007–08, 1 fellowship, 29 teaching assistantships were awarded; research assistantships, Federal Work-Study and health care benefits also available. Support available to part-time students. Financial award application deadline: 3/1. *Faculty research:* Painting, graphic design, sculpture, printmaking, drawing. *Unit head:* Dr. Spencer Fidler, Head, 575-646-1705, Fax: 575-646-8036, E-mail: sfidler@nmsu.edu.

The New School: A University, Parsons The New School for Design, Program in Photography, New York, NY 10011. Offers MFA. *Faculty:* 6 full-time (2 women), 4 part-time/adjunct (0 women). *Students:* 9 full-time (7 women), 22 part-time (12 women); includes 2 minority (1 African American, 1 Asian American or Pacific Islander), 8 international. Average age 26. In 2007, 10 degrees awarded. *Entrance requirements:* Additional exam requirements/recommendations for international students: Required—TOEFL (minimum score 580 paper-based; 237 computer-based; 93 iBT). *Application deadline:* For fall admission, 2/1 priority date for domestic students. Applications are processed on a rolling basis. Application fee: $50. *Financial support:* Federal Work-Study, scholarships/grants, and tuition waivers (partial) available. Financial award application deadline: 3/1. *Unit head:* Michelle Bogre, Chair, 212-229-8923 Ext. 4239, E-mail: bogrem@newschool.edu. *Application contact:* Anthony Padilla, Director of Admissions, 212-229-8989 Ext. 4023, Fax: 212-229-8975, E-mail: padillaa@newschool.edu.

See Close-Up on page 123.

The Ohio State University, Graduate School, College of the Arts, Department of Photography and Cinema, Columbus, OH 43210. Offers MA. *Application deadline:* Applications are processed on a rolling basis. Application fee: $40 ($50 for international students). Electronic applications accepted. *Application contact:* Graduate Admissions, 614-292-6444, Fax: 614-292-3895, E-mail: domestic.grad@osu.edu.

Ohio University, Graduate College, College of Fine Arts, School of Art, Athens, OH 45701-2979. Offers art history (MA); ceramics (MFA); graphic design (MFA); painting (MFA); photography (MFA); printmaking (MFA); sculpture (MFA). Part-time programs available. *Faculty:* 30 full-time (16 women), 7 part-time/adjunct (3 women). *Students:* 53 full-time (34 women), 11 part-time (7 women); includes 1 minority (Hispanic American), 7 international. Average age 27. 174 applicants, 22% accepted, 32 enrolled. In 2007, 18 degrees awarded. *Degree requirements:* For master's, thesis. *Entrance requirements:* For master's, portfolio. Additional exam requirements/recommendations for international students: Required—TOEFL. *Application deadline:* For fall admission, 2/1 for domestic students. Application fee: $50 ($55 for international students). *Financial support:* In 2007–08, 57 students received support, including 35 teaching assistantships with full and partial tuition reimbursements available (averaging $9,198 per year); career-related internships or fieldwork, Federal Work-Study, institutionally sponsored loans, scholarships/grants, tuition waivers (full), unspecified assistantships, and associateships also available. Financial award application deadline: 2/1. *Faculty research:* Vapor fired ceramics, video installation, art theory, digital photography, mixed and interdisciplinary media work. *Unit head:* David LaPalombara, Director, 740-593-4290, Fax: 740-593-0457, E-mail: lapalomb@ohio.edu. *Application contact:* Don Adleta, Associate Director and Chair, Graduate Programs, 740-593-9996, Fax: 740-593-0457, E-mail: adleta@ohio.edu.

Ohio University, Graduate College, Scripps College of Communication, School of Visual Communication, Athens, OH 45701-2979. Offers MA. *Accreditation:* NASAD. *Faculty:* 11 full-time (2 women). *Students:* 26 full-time (15 women), 13 part-time (8 women); includes 5 minority (2 African Americans, 1 Asian American or Pacific Islander, 2 Hispanic Americans), 15 international. In 2007, 7 degrees awarded. *Entrance requirements:* For master's, minimum GPA of 2.5, portfolio. Additional exam requirements/recommendations for international students: Required—TOEFL (minimum score 600 paper-based; 250 computer-based). *Application deadline:* For fall admission, 2/1 for domestic students, 12/15 for international students. Application fee: $50 ($55 for international students). Electronic applications accepted. *Financial support:* In 2007–08, 30 students received support, including 1 fellowship, 2 research assistantships, 4 teaching assistantships with tuition reimbursements available; Federal Work-Study, institutionally sponsored loans, and tuition waivers (partial) also available. Financial award applicants required to submit FAFSA. *Faculty research:* Photographic communication (photojournalism, multimedia, and documentary), photographic illustration (product, editorial, architectural), multimedia (planning and design), media management. *Unit head:* Terry Eiler, Director, 740-595-4895, E-mail: eiler@ohio.edu. *Application contact:* Mike Williams, Associate Director, 740-597-1778, Fax: 740-593-0190, E-mail: william5@ohio.edu.

Otis College of Art and Design, Program in Fine Arts, Los Angeles, CA 90045-9785. Offers new genres (MFA); painting (MFA); photography (MFA); sculpture (MFA). *Accreditation:* NASAD. *Faculty:* 1 (woman) full-time, 8 part-time/adjunct (3 women). *Students:* 19 full-time (11 women), 2 part-time (both women); includes 1 Asian American or Pacific Islander, 2 international. Average age 32. 149 applicants, 20% accepted, 11 enrolled. In 2007, 15 degrees awarded. *Degree requirements:* For master's, thesis. *Entrance requirements:* For master's, portfolio. Additional exam requirements/recommendations for international students: Required—TOEFL (minimum score 600 paper-based; 250 computer-based). *Application deadline:* For fall admission, 2/15 for domestic and international students. Application fee: $50. Electronic applications accepted. *Expenses:* Tuition: Full-time $30,764; part-time $1,026 per unit. Required fees: $700. *Financial support:* Career-related internships or fieldwork, Federal Work-Study, scholarships/grants, and tuition waivers (partial) available. Financial award applicants required to submit FAFSA. *Unit head:* Roy Dowell, Chair, 310-665-6893, Fax: 310-665-6998, E-mail: grads@otis.edu. *Application contact:* Information Contact, 310-665-6820, Fax: 310-665-6821, E-mail: admissions@otis.edu.

Penn State University Park, Graduate School, College of Arts and Architecture, School of Visual Arts, State College, University Park, PA 16802-1503. Offers art (MFA), including ceramics, drawing/painting, photography, printmaking, sculpture; art education (M Ed, MS, PhD). *Accreditation:* NASAD. *Expenses:* Tuition, state resident: full-time $14,738; part-time $614 per credit. Tuition, nonresident: full-time $26,050; part-time $1,085 per credit. Tuition and fees vary according to course load, program and student level. *Unit head:* Dr. Charles R. Garoian, Director, 814-865-0444, Fax: 814-865-1158, E-mail: crg2@psu.edu.

Pratt Institute, School of Art and Design, Program in Fine Arts, Brooklyn, NY 11205-3899. Offers ceramics (MFA); metals (MFA); new forms (MFA); painting (MFA); photography (MFA); printmaking (MFA); sculpture (MFA); MS/MFA. *Accreditation:* NASAD. Part-time programs available. *Faculty:* 8 full-time (2 women), 30 part-time/adjunct (15 women). *Students:* 149 full-time (101 women), 6 part-time (3 women); includes 22 minority (4 African Americans, 1 American Indian/Alaska Native, 10 Asian Americans or Pacific Islanders, 7 Hispanic Americans), 34 international. Average age 29. 373 applicants, 35% accepted, 60 enrolled. In 2007, 49 degrees awarded. *Degree requirements:* For master's, thesis, exhibit. *Entrance requirements:* For master's, portfolio, bachelor's degree, transcripts, letters of recommendation, statement. Additional exam requirements/recommendations for international students: Required—TOEFL (minimum score 550 paper-based; 213 computer-based). *Application deadline:* For fall admission, 2/1 for domestic students; for spring admission, 10/1 for domestic students. Application fee: $50 ($90 for international students). Electronic applications accepted. *Expenses:* Tuition: Full-time $25,680. Required fees: $1,106. Tuition and fees vary according to program. *Financial support:* Career-related internships or fieldwork, Federal Work-Study, institutionally sponsored loans, scholarships/grants, health care benefits, and unspecified assistantships available. Support available to part-time students. Financial award application deadline: 2/1; financial award applicants required to submit FAFSA. *Unit head:* Donna Moran, Chairperson, 718-636-3602, E-mail: dmoran@pratt.edu. *Application contact:* Young Hah, Director of Graduate Admissions, 718-636-3683, Fax: 718-399-4242, E-mail: yhah@pratt.edu.

See Close-Up on page 253.

Rhode Island School of Design, Graduate Studies, Division of Fine Arts, Department of Photography, Providence, RI 02903-2784. Offers MFA. *Accreditation:* NASAD. *Degree requirements:* For master's, thesis, exhibit. *Entrance requirements:* For master's, portfolio, 3 letters of recommendation. Additional exam requirements/recommendations for international students: Required—TOEFL (minimum score 580 paper-based; 237 computer-based), IELTS (minimum score 7).

Rochester Institute of Technology, Graduate Enrollment Services, College of Imaging Arts and Sciences, School of Photographic Arts and Sciences, Program in Imaging Arts, Rochester, NY 14623-5603. Offers MFA. *Accreditation:* NASAD. *Students:* 76 full-time (34 women), 18 part-time (7 women); includes 9 minority (2 African Americans, 6 Asian Americans or Pacific Islanders, 1 Hispanic American), 28 international. 153 applicants, 40% accepted, 29 enrolled. In 2007, 28 degrees awarded. *Degree requirements:* For master's, thesis, exhibit. *Entrance requirements:* For master's, portfolio, minimum GPA of 3.0. Additional exam requirements/recommendations for international students: Required—TOEFL (minimum score 550 paper-based; 213 computer-based; 79 iBT). *Application deadline:* For fall admission, 3/1 priority date for domestic students. Applications are processed on a rolling basis. Application fee: $50. *Expenses:* Tuition: Full-time $28,491; part-time $800 per credit hour. Required fees: $201; $67 per term. *Financial support:* Fellowships with partial tuition reimbursements, research assistantships with partial tuition reimbursements, teaching assistantships with partial tuition reimbursements, career-related internships or fieldwork, institutionally sponsored loans, scholarships/grants, tuition waivers (partial), and unspecified assistantships available. Support available to part-time students. Financial award application deadline: 8/30; financial award applicants required to submit FAFSA. *Unit head:* Therese Mulligan, Head, 585-475-2616, E-mail: mtmpph@rit.edu.

San Francisco Art Institute, Graduate Program, Department of Photography, San Francisco, CA 94133. Offers MFA, Certificate. *Accreditation:* NASAD. Part-time programs available. *Degree requirements:* For master's and Certificate, oral reviews. *Entrance requirements:* For master's and Certificate, portfolio. Additional exam requirements/recommendations for international students: Required—TOEFL (minimum score 580 paper-based; 237 computer-based). Electronic applications accepted.

See Close-Up on page 255.

San Jose State University, Graduate Studies and Research, College of Humanities and the Arts, School of Art and Design, San Jose, CA 95192-0001. Offers art education (MA); art history (MA); digital media (MFA); digital media in art history and education (MA); photography (MFA); pictorial arts (MFA); spatial arts (MFA). *Accreditation:* NASAD (one or more programs are accredited). *Students:* 55 full-time (30 women), 15 part-time (12 women); includes 11 minority (1 African American, 7 Asian Americans or Pacific Islanders, 3 Hispanic Americans), 2 international. Average age 38. 78 applicants, 42% accepted, 24 enrolled. In 2007, 17 degrees awarded. *Entrance requirements:* For master's, GRE. *Application deadline:* For fall admission, 6/29 for domestic students; for spring admission, 11/30 for domestic students. Applications are processed on a rolling basis. Application fee: $59. Electronic applications accepted. *Financial support:* Applicants required to submit FAFSA. *Unit head:* Linda Walsh, Director, 408-924-4320, Fax: 408-924-4326.

Savannah College of Art and Design, Graduate School, Program in Commercial Photography, Savannah, GA 31402-3146. Offers MA. Part-time programs available. *Faculty:* 4 full-time (2 women). *Students:* 5 full-time (1 woman); includes 1 minority (African American), 2 international. 7 applicants, 57% accepted, 2 enrolled. *Degree requirements:* For master's, thesis. *Entrance requirements:* For master's, interview, portfolio. Additional exam requirements/recommendations for international students: Required—TOEFL (minimum score 450 paper-based; 133 computer-based). *Application deadline:* For fall admission, 4/1 priority date for domestic and international students. Applications are processed on a rolling basis. Application fee: $50. Electronic applications accepted. *Expenses:* Tuition: Full-time $24,840; part-time $552 per credit. One-time fee: $500 full-time. *Financial support:* Fellowships, career-related internships or fieldwork, Federal Work-Study, and scholarships/grants available. Financial award application deadline: 4/1; financial award applicants required to submit FAFSA. *Unit head:* Jenny Kuhla, Chair, 912-525-6502. *Application contact:* Darrell Tutchton, Director of Graduate and International Enrollment, 912-525-5961, Fax: 912-525-5985, E-mail: admission@scad.edu.

Savannah College of Art and Design, Graduate School, Program in Digital Photography, Savannah, GA 31402-3146. Offers MFA. Part-time programs available. *Faculty:* 4 full-time (2 women). *Students:* 10 full-time (6 women), 13 part-time (3 women), 1 international. 54 applicants, 35% accepted, 10 enrolled. In 2007, 1 degree awarded. *Degree requirements:* For master's, thesis. *Entrance requirements:* For master's, interview, portfolio. Additional exam requirements/recommendations for international students: Required—TOEFL (minimum score 450 paper-based; 133 computer-based). *Application deadline:* For fall admission, 4/1 priority date for domestic and international students. Applications are processed on a rolling basis.

Application fee: $50. Electronic applications accepted. *Expenses:* Tuition: Full-time $24,840; part-time $552 per credit. One-time fee: $500 full-time. *Financial support:* Fellowships, career-related internships or fieldwork, Federal Work-Study, and scholarships/grants available. Financial award application deadline: 4/1; financial award applicants required to submit FAFSA. *Unit head:* Thomas Fischer, Chair, 912-525-6570, Fax: 912-525-3507, E-mail: tfischer@scad.edu. *Application contact:* Darrell Tutchton, Director of Graduate and International Enrollment, 912-525-5961, Fax: 912-525-5985, E-mail: admission@scad.edu.

Savannah College of Art and Design, Graduate School, Program in Documentary Photography, Savannah, GA 31402-3146. Offers MA. Part-time programs available. *Faculty:* 1 full-time (0 women). *Students:* 8 applicants, 13% accepted, 1 enrolled. *Degree requirements:* For master's, thesis. *Entrance requirements:* For master's, interview, portfolio. Additional exam requirements/recommendations for international students: Required—TOEFL (minimum score 450 paper-based; 133 computer-based). *Application deadline:* For fall admission, 4/1 priority date for domestic and international students. Applications are processed on a rolling basis. Electronic applications accepted. *Expenses:* Tuition: Full-time $24,840; part-time $552 per credit. One-time fee: $500 full-time. *Financial support:* Fellowships, career-related internships or fieldwork, Federal Work-Study, and scholarships/grants available. Financial award application deadline: 4/1; financial award applicants required to submit FAFSA. *Unit head:* Jenny Kuhla, Chair, 912-525-6502. *Application contact:* Darrell Tutchton, Director of Graduate and International Enrollment, 912-525-5961, Fax: 912-525-5985, E-mail: admission@scad.edu.

Savannah College of Art and Design, Graduate School, Program in Photography, Savannah, GA 31402-3146. Offers MA, MFA. Part-time programs available. *Faculty:* 16 full-time (8 women), 1 (woman) part-time/adjunct. *Students:* 82 full-time (56 women), 9 part-time (5 women); includes 5 minority (3 African Americans, 2 Hispanic Americans), 9 international. Average age 25. 121 applicants, 42% accepted, 24 enrolled. In 2007, 13 degrees awarded. *Degree requirements:* For master's, thesis, exhibit, internships. *Entrance requirements:* For master's, interview, portfolio. Additional exam requirements/recommendations for international students: Required—TOEFL (minimum score 450 paper-based; 133 computer-based). *Application deadline:* For fall admission, 4/1 priority date for domestic and international students. Applications are processed on a rolling basis. Application fee: $50. Electronic applications accepted. *Expenses:* Tuition: Full-time $24,840; part-time $552 per credit. One-time fee: $500 full-time. *Financial support:* In 2007–08, 11 fellowships were awarded; career-related internships or fieldwork, Federal Work-Study, and scholarships/grants also available. Financial award application deadline: 4/1; financial award applicants required to submit FAFSA. *Unit head:* Jenny Kuhla, Chair, 912-525-6502. *Application contact:* Darrell Tutchton, Director of Graduate and International Enrollment, 912-525-5961, Fax: 912-525-5985, E-mail: admission@scad.edu.

See Close-Up on page 257.

School of the Art Institute of Chicago, Graduate Division, Department of Photography, Chicago, IL 60603-3103. Offers MFA. *Accreditation:* NASAD. *Entrance requirements:* Additional exam requirements/recommendations for international students: Required—TOEFL.

See Close-Up on page 259.

School of Visual Arts, Graduate Programs, Digital Photography Department, New York, NY 10010-3994. Offers MPS. *Students:* 14 full-time (5 women), 5 international. Average age 29. 39 applicants, 56% accepted, 14 enrolled. *Degree requirements:* For master's, thesis or project. *Entrance requirements:* For master's, portfolio. Additional exam requirements/recommendations for international students: Required—TOEFL (minimum score 550 paper-based; 213 computer-based; 79 iBT). *Application deadline:* For fall admission, 2/1 for domestic students. Application fee: $80. Electronic applications accepted. *Expenses:* Tuition: Full-time $26,120; part-time $870 per credit. Tuition and fees vary according to program. *Financial support:* Career-related internships or fieldwork, Federal Work-Study, scholarships/grants, and unspecified assistantships available. Support available to part-time students. *Unit head:* Katrin Eismann, Chair, 212-592-2000.

School of Visual Arts, Graduate Programs, Program in Photography, Video and Related Media, New York, NY 10010-3994. Offers MFA. *Accreditation:* NASAD. *Faculty:* 1 full-time (0 women), 29 part-time/adjunct (12 women). *Students:* 80 full-time (42 women), 8 part-time (4 women); includes 10 minority (2 African Americans, 1 Asian American or Pacific Islander, 7 Hispanic Americans), 22 international. Average age 29. 246 applicants, 35% accepted, 44 enrolled. In 2007, 28 degrees awarded. *Degree requirements:* For master's, final review, project or thesis. *Entrance requirements:* For master's, portfolio. Additional exam requirements/recommendations for international students: Required—TOEFL (minimum score 550 paper-based; 213 computer-based; 79 iBT). *Application deadline:* For fall admission, 2/1 for domestic students. Application fee: $80. Electronic applications accepted. *Expenses:* Tuition: Full-time $26,120; part-time $870 per credit. Tuition and fees vary according to program. *Financial support:* In 2007–08, 40 students received support. Career-related internships or fieldwork, Federal Work-Study, scholarships/grants, and unspecified assistantships available. Support available to part-time students. Financial award application deadline: 2/1; financial award applicants required to submit FAFSA. *Unit head:* Charles Traub, Chair, 212-592-2360, Fax: 212-592-2366, E-mail: ctraub@sva.edu.

Southern Methodist University, Meadows School of the Arts, Division of Art, Dallas, TX 75275. Offers studio art (MFA), including ceramics, drawing, painting, photography, printmaking, sculpture. *Accreditation:* NASAD. *Faculty:* 11 full-time (3 women), 6 part-time/adjunct (3 women). *Students:* 10 full-time (5 women); includes 1 minority (Hispanic American) Average age 35. 35 applicants, 20% accepted, 6 enrolled. In 2007, 6 degrees awarded. *Degree requirements:* For master's, thesis or alternative, exhibit. *Entrance requirements:* For master's, BFA or equivalent, letters of recommendation, portfolio. Additional exam requirements/recommendations for international students: Required—TOEFL (minimum score 550 paper-based; 213 computer-based; 80 iBT). *Application deadline:* For fall admission, 2/15 for domestic and international students. Application fee: $75. *Financial support:* In 2007–08, 5 fellowships (averaging $32,914 per year), 5 teaching assistantships (averaging $3,000 per year) were awarded; scholarships/grants and unspecified assistantships also available. Financial award application deadline: 3/1; financial award applicants required to submit FAFSA. *Faculty research:* American stoneware, Southwestern furniture traditions, photographic apparatus and techniques, American ceramists, architecture. Total annual research expenditures: $20,000. *Unit head:* James W. Sullivan, Chair, 214-768-2489, E-mail: jsulliva@smu.edu. *Application contact:* Jean Cherry, Director of Graduate Admissions and Records, 214-768-3765, Fax: 214-768-3272, E-mail: jcherry@smu.edu.

Syracuse University, Graduate School, College of Visual and Performing Arts, Department of Transmedia, Syracuse, NY 13244. Offers art photography (MFA); art video (MFA); computer art (MFA); film (MFA). *Accreditation:* NASAD. Part-time programs available. *Students:* 32 full-time (17 women), 1 part-time; includes 6 minority (3 African Americans, 2 Asian Americans or Pacific Islanders, 1 Hispanic American), 8 international. 84 applicants, 38% accepted, 17 enrolled. In 2007, 9 degrees awarded. *Degree requirements:* For master's, thesis or alternative. *Entrance requirements:* For master's, portfolio. Additional exam requirements/recommendations for international students: Required—TOEFL. *Application deadline:* For fall admission, 1/1 priority date for domestic students. Applications are processed on a rolling basis. Application fee: $75. Electronic applications accepted. *Expenses:* Tuition: Full-time $18,216; part-time $1,012 per credit. Required fees: $980. Tuition and fees vary according to program. *Financial support:* Fellowships with full tuition reimbursements, research assistantships with full and partial tuition reimbursements, teaching assistantships with full and partial tuition reimbursements, tuition waivers (partial) available. *Unit head:* John Orentlicher, Chair, 315-443-1033, Fax: 315-443-1303, E-mail: jorentli@syr.edu. *Application contact:* Harriett Conti, Associate Director, Graduate Student Services, 315-443-3089, E-mail: hmconti@syr.edu.

Syracuse University, Graduate School, S. I. Newhouse School of Public Communications, Department of Visual and Interactive Communications, Program in Photography, Syracuse, NY 13244. Offers MS. *Students:* 15 full-time (10 women), 4 part-time (3 women); includes 1 African American, 1 Hispanic American. 21 applicants, 86% accepted, 10 enrolled. In 2007, 3 degrees awarded. *Degree requirements:* For master's, thesis optional, special project. *Entrance requirements:* For master's, GRE General Test, portfolio. Additional exam requirements/recommendations for international students: Required—TOEFL (minimum score 600 paper-based; 250 computer-based). *Application deadline:* For fall admission, 2/1 for domestic and international students. Application fee: $75. Electronic applications accepted. *Expenses:* Tuition: Full-time $18,216; part-time $1,012 per credit. Required fees: $980. Tuition and fees vary according to program. *Financial support:* Federal Work-Study and tuition waivers (partial) available. *Application contact:* Graduate Admissions, 315-443-4039, Fax: 315-443-1834, E-mail: pcgrad@syr.edu.

See Close-Up on page 935.

Temple University, Graduate School, Tyler School of Art, Department of Graphic Arts and Design, Philadelphia, PA 19122-6096. Offers graphic and interactive design (MFA); photography (MFA); printmaking (MFA). *Accreditation:* NASAD. *Degree requirements:* For master's, essay, exhibit. *Entrance requirements:* For master's, minimum GPA of 3.0; slide portfolio, 40 credits in studio art; 12 credits in art history. Additional exam requirements/recommendations for international students: Required—TOEFL (minimum score 550 paper-based; 213 computer-based; 79 iBT). Electronic applications accepted.

The University of Alabama, Graduate School, College of Arts and Sciences, Department of Art, Tuscaloosa, AL 35487. Offers art history (MA); studio art (MA, MFA), including ceramics, painting, photography, printmaking, sculpture. *Accreditation:* NASAD. Part-time programs available. *Faculty:* 14 full-time (7 women). *Students:* 13 full-time (7 women), 1 (woman) part-time. Average age 30. 17 applicants, 41% accepted, 6 enrolled. In 2007, 9 degrees awarded. *Degree requirements:* For master's, one foreign language, comprehensive exam (for some programs), thesis (for some programs), oral exam, thesis statement, exhibit (studio art), thesis (art history). *Entrance requirements:* For master's, GRE General Test or MAT (art history), minimum GPA of 3.0, BFA or equivalent (studio art). Additional exam requirements/recommendations for international students: Required—TOEFL (minimum score 550 paper-based; 213 computer-based). *Application deadline:* For fall admission, 3/15 for domestic and international students; for spring admission, 10/15 for domestic and international students. Applications are processed on a rolling basis. Application fee: $30. Electronic applications accepted. *Expenses:* Tuition, state resident: full-time $5,700. Tuition, nonresident: full-time $16,518. *Financial support:* In 2007–08, 19 students received support, including 2 fellowships with full tuition reimbursements available (averaging $14,000 per year), 13 teaching assistantships with full and partial tuition reimbursements available (averaging $9,206 per year); career-related internships or fieldwork, institutionally sponsored loans, scholarships/grants, and unspecified assistantships also available. Financial award application deadline: 7/14. *Faculty research:* Nineteenth century American art history, Chinese art history, baroque art history, twentieth century art history, Asian art history. *Unit head:* William T. Dooley, Chairperson, 205-348-1890, Fax: 205-348-0287, E-mail: wtdooley@bama.ua.edu. *Application contact:* Craig R. Wedderspoon, Graduate Coordinator, 205-348-1898, Fax: 205-348-0287, E-mail: cwedders@bama.edu.

University of Colorado at Boulder, Graduate School, College of Arts and Sciences, Department of Art and Art History, Boulder, CO 80309. Offers art history (MA), including 19th century art, contemporary art criticism, early 20th century art, Russian and Soviet art; ceramics (MFA); drawing (MFA); painting (MFA); photography and media arts (MFA); printmaking (MFA); sculpture (MFA). *Faculty:* 27. *Students:* 42 full-time (22 women), 1 (woman) part-time; includes 4 minority (all Hispanic Americans), 1 international. Average age 32. 15 applicants, 73% accepted. In 2007, 16 degrees awarded. *Degree requirements:* For master's, variable foreign language requirement, comprehensive exam, thesis (for some programs). *Entrance requirements:* For master's, GRE General Test, minimum undergraduate GPA of 3.0, portfolio. *Application deadline:* For fall admission, 1/15 priority date for domestic students, 12/1 for international students. Application fee: $50 ($60 for international students). *Financial support:* In 2007–08, 32 fellowships (averaging $2,294 per year) were awarded; Federal Work-Study, scholarships/grants, and tuition waivers (full) also available. Financial award application deadline: 1/15. *Faculty research:* Drawing, painting, ceramics, sculpture, photography and media arts, printmaking (MFA); history-Russian and Soviet art, Early 20th Century art, contemporary art criticism, 19th Century art (MA). *Unit head:* James Johnson, Chair, 303-492-6504, Fax: 303-492-4886, E-mail: james.johnson@colorado.edu. *Application contact:* Graduate Program Assistant, 303-492-2419, Fax: 303-492-4886, E-mail: finearts@colorado.edu.

University of Florida, Graduate School, College of Fine Arts, School of Art and Art History, Gainesville, FL 32611. Offers art (MFA), including ceramics, creative photography, drawing, electronic intermedia, graphic design, painting, printmaking, sculpture; art education (MA); art history (MA, PhD); digital arts and sciences (MA); museology (museum studies) (MA). *Accreditation:* NASAD. *Faculty:* 29 full-time (14 women), 2 part-time/adjunct (1 woman). *Students:* 82 (48 women); includes 4 minority (2 Asian Americans or Pacific Islanders, 2 Hispanic Americans) 4 international. In 2007, 20 degrees awarded. *Degree requirements:* For master's, variable foreign language requirement, project or thesis (MFA). *Entrance requirements:* For master's, portfolio (MFA), writing sample (MA), GRE General Test or minimum GPA of 3.0. Additional exam requirements/recommendations for international students: Required—TOEFL (minimum score 550 paper-based; 213 computer-based). *Application deadline:* For fall admission, 1/15 priority date for domestic students. Applications are processed on a rolling basis. Application fee: $30. Electronic applications accepted. *Expenses:* Tuition, state resident: full-time $7,478. Tuition, nonresident: full-time $22,603. *Financial support:* In 2007–08, 3 research assistantships with tuition reimbursements (averaging $9,515 per year), 67 teaching assistantships with tuition reimbursements (averaging $9,839 per year) were awarded; fellowships, Federal Work-Study, institutionally sponsored loans, and unspecified assistantships also available. Financial award applicants required to submit FAFSA. *Faculty research:* Studio production, art historical studies of style context. *Unit head:* Glenn Willumson, Program Director, 352-392-0201 Ext. 234. *Application contact:* Prof. Richard Heipp, Coordinator, 352-392-0201 Ext. 239, Fax: 352-392-8453, E-mail: heipp@ufl.edu.

University of Houston, College of Liberal Arts and Social Sciences, Department of Art, Houston, TX 77204. Offers interior design (MA); painting (MA); photography (MA); sculpture (MA); MFA/MA. *Faculty:* 16 full-time (7 women), 7 part-time/adjunct (5 women). *Students:* 37 full-time (23 women); includes 7 minority (1 Asian American or Pacific Islander, 6 Hispanic Americans), 4 international. Average age 33. 49 applicants, 31% accepted, 11 enrolled. In 2007, 10 degrees awarded. *Degree requirements:* For master's, comprehensive exam, visual thesis. *Entrance requirements:* For master's, GRE General Test, portfolio. *Application deadline:* For fall admission, 2/28 for domestic students; for spring admission, 10/30 for domestic students. Application fee: $25 ($100 for international students). *Expenses:* Tuition, state resident: full-time $6,297; part-time $262 per credit. Tuition, nonresident: full-time $12,969; part-time $540 per credit. Required fees: $2,696. *Financial support:* In 2007–08, 28 teaching assistantships with full tuition reimbursements (averaging $10,400 per year) were awarded; fellowships with full tuition reimbursements, research assistantships with full tuition reimbursements, career-related internships or fieldwork, Federal Work-Study, institutionally sponsored loans, scholarships/grants, health care benefits, and unspecified assistantships also available. Support available to part-time students. Financial award application deadline: 3/10. *Faculty research:* Alternative art projects. *Unit head:* Dr. John Reed, Chairperson, 713-743-3001, Fax: 713-743-2823, E-mail: jreed@uh.edu.

University of Illinois at Chicago, Graduate College, College of Architecture and Art, School of Art and Design, Chicago, IL 60607-7128. Offers electronic visualization (MFA); film animation (MFA); graphic design (MFA); industrial design (MFA); photography (MFA); studio arts (MFA). *Accreditation:* NASAD. *Degree requirements:* For master's, thesis, exhibit. *Entrance requirements:* For master's, MAT, portfolio. Additional exam requirements/recommendations for international students: Required—TOEFL. Electronic applications accepted.

Photography

University of Illinois at Urbana–Champaign, Graduate College, College of Fine and Applied Arts, School of Art and Design, Program in Studio Arts, Champaign, IL 61820. Offers art and design (MFA); crafts (MFA); metals (MFA); painting (MFA); photography (MFA); sculpture (MFA). *Accreditation:* NASAD. *Students:* 31 full-time (14 women), 3 part-time (2 women); includes 5 minority (1 African American, 1 American Indian/Alaska Native, 2 Asian Americans or Pacific Islanders, 1 Hispanic American), 7 international. 75 applicants, 19% accepted, 12 enrolled. In 2007, 10 degrees awarded. *Entrance requirements:* For master's, minimum GPA of 3.0. *Application deadline:* Applications are processed on a rolling basis. Application fee: $60 ($75 for international students). Electronic applications accepted. *Financial support:* Application deadline: 2/15. *Unit head:* Alan Mette, Chair, 217-244-7496, Fax: 217-244-7688, E-mail: amette@uiuc.edu. *Application contact:* Marsha Biddle, Assistant to the Associate Director, 217-333-0642, Fax: 217-244-7688, E-mail: mbiddle@uiuc.edu.

University of Massachusetts Dartmouth, Graduate School, College of Visual and Performing Arts, Program in Visual Design, North Dartmouth, MA 02747-2300. Offers digital multi-media (MFA); electronic imaging (MFA); graphic design (MFA); illustration (MFA); photography (MFA); typography (MFA). *Accreditation:* NASAD. *Faculty:* 17 full-time (7 women), 7 part-time/adjunct (3 women). *Students:* 8 full-time (6 women), 2 part-time (both women); includes 1 minority (Asian American or Pacific Islander), 2 international. Average age 35. 21 applicants, 24% accepted, 4 enrolled. In 2007, 3 degrees awarded. *Degree requirements:* For master's, visual thesis. *Entrance requirements:* For master's, portfolio, interview, minimum GPA of 3.0, 3 letters of recommendation. Additional exam requirements/recommendations for international students: Required—TOEFL (minimum score 500 paper-based). *Application deadline:* For fall admission, 3/1 priority date for domestic students, 1/1 priority date for international students. Applications are processed on a rolling basis. Application fee: $40 ($60 for international students). Electronic applications accepted. *Expenses:* Tuition, state resident: full-time $2,071; part-time $86 per credit. Tuition, nonresident: full-time $8,099; part-time $337 per credit. Part-time tuition and fees vary according to course load and program. *Financial support:* In 2007–08, 4 teaching assistantships (averaging $2,930 per year) were awarded; research assistantships, Federal Work-Study and unspecified assistantships also available. Support available to part-time students. Financial award application deadline: 3/1; financial award applicants required to submit FAFSA. Total annual research expenditures: $22,880. *Unit head:* Jarrad Nunes, Director, 508-999-8010, E-mail: jnunes@umassd.edu. *Application contact:* Carol Novo, Graduate Admissions Officer, 508-999-8604, Fax: 508-999-8183, E-mail: graduate@umassd.edu.

University of Memphis, Graduate School, College of Communication and Fine Arts, Department of Art, Memphis, TN 38152. Offers art history (MA), including Egyptian art and archaeology, general art history; ceramics (MFA); graphic design (MFA); interior design (MFA); painting (MFA); printmaking/photography (MFA); sculpture (MFA). *Accreditation:* NASAD (one or more programs are accredited). *Faculty:* 13 full-time (9 women). *Students:* 20 full-time (11 women), 2 part-time (1 woman); includes 1 Asian American or Pacific Islander, 1 international. Average age 27. 47 applicants, 55% accepted, 18 enrolled. In 2007, 14 degrees awarded. *Degree requirements:* For master's, 2 foreign languages, comprehensive exam, thesis. *Entrance requirements:* For master's, GRE General Test or MAT, portfolio (MFA). *Application deadline:* For fall admission, 8/1 for domestic students; for spring admission, 12/1 for domestic students. Applications are processed on a rolling basis. Application fee: $35 ($60 for international students). *Expenses:* Tuition, state resident: full-time $6,990; part-time $377 per hour. Tuition, nonresident: full-time $17,818; part-time $830 per hour. Tuition and fees vary according to course load and program. *Financial support:* In 2007–08, 23 research assistantships with full tuition reimbursements (averaging $4,200 per year), 10 teaching assistantships with full tuition reimbursements (averaging $5,250 per year) were awarded. *Faculty research:* Online collaborative learning, advanced art history studies, electronic publishing/design, studio arts, architectural studies. *Unit head:* Prof. Richard Lou, Chair, 901-678-2216, Fax: 901-678-2735, E-mail: gmyatt@memphis.edu. *Application contact:* Prof. Michael Hagge, Coordinator of Graduate Studies, 901-678-2677.

University of Miami, Graduate School, College of Arts and Sciences, Department of Art and Art History, Coral Gables, FL 33124. Offers art history (MA); ceramics/glass (MFA); graphic design/multimedia (MFA); painting (MFA); photography/digital imaging (MFA); printmaking (MFA); sculpture (MFA). Part-time programs available. *Faculty:* 14 full-time (6 women). *Students:* 23 full-time (15 women), 5 part-time (3 women); includes 5 minority (2 African Americans, 3 Hispanic Americans). Average age 29. 55 applicants, 18% accepted, 8 enrolled. In 2007, 8 degrees awarded. *Degree requirements:* For master's, variable foreign language requirement, thesis, exhibit (MFA), comprehensive exam (MA). *Entrance requirements:* For master's, GRE General Test (MA), research paper (MA), slide portfolio (MFA), artist statement (MFA). Additional exam requirements/recommendations for international students: Required—TOEFL. *Application deadline:* For fall admission, 2/15 for domestic students, 1/15 for international students; for winter admission, 9/15 for domestic students. Application fee: $50. Electronic applications accepted. *Financial support:* In 2007–08, 25 students received support, including 17 teaching assistantships with full tuition reimbursements available (averaging $10,000 per year); Federal Work-Study, institutionally sponsored loans, scholarships/grants, and tuition waivers (full) also available. Financial award application deadline: 3/1; financial award applicants required to submit FAFSA. *Faculty research:* Installation art, public art. *Unit head:* Prof. Lise Drost, Chair, 305-284-2542, Fax: 305-284-2115, E-mail: l.drost@miami.edu. *Application contact:* Prof. Brian Curtis, Graduate Secretary, 305-284-2542, Fax: 305-284-2115, E-mail: art-arh@miami.edu.

University of Notre Dame, Graduate School, College of Arts and Letters, Division of Humanities, Department of Art, Art History, and Design, Notre Dame, IN 46556. Offers art history (MA); design (MFA), including graphic design, industrial design; studio art (MFA), including ceramics, painting, photography, printmaking, sculpture. *Accreditation:* NASAD. *Faculty:* 19 full-time (6 women), 3 part-time/adjunct (1 woman). *Students:* 25 full-time (12 women), 1 (woman) part-time; includes 4 minority (1 African American, 1 Asian American or Pacific Islander, 2 Hispanic Americans), 1 international. 85 applicants, 14% accepted, 10 enrolled. In 2007, 7 degrees awarded. *Degree requirements:* For master's, comprehensive exam, thesis. *Entrance requirements:* For master's, GRE General Test, minimum GPA of 3.0. Additional exam requirements/recommendations for international students: Required—TOEFL (minimum score 600 paper-based; 250 computer-based; 80 iBT). *Application deadline:* For fall admission, 2/1 priority date for domestic and international students. Application fee: $50. Electronic applications accepted. *Financial support:* In 2007–08, 20 students received support, including fellowships with full tuition reimbursements available (averaging $12,000 per year), research assistantships with full tuition reimbursements available (averaging $12,000 per year), 15 teaching assistantships with full tuition reimbursements available (averaging $12,000 per year); scholarships/grants, tuition waivers (full), and unspecified assistantships also available. Financial award application deadline: 2/1. *Faculty research:* Studio art practice in ceramics, printing, photography, printmaking and sculpture, graphic design and industrial design, digital imaging in design and photography, Renaissance and American art history, contemporary art theory and criticism. *Unit head:* Prof. Jean Dibble, Director of Graduate Studies, 574-631-7602, E-mail: art.1@nd.edu. *Application contact:* Dr. Jarren Gonzales, Director of Graduate Admissions, 574-631-7706, Fax: 574-631-4183.

University of Oklahoma, Graduate College, College of Fine Arts, School of Art and Art History, Norman, OK 73019-0390. Offers art (MA, MFA); art history (MA, MFA); ceramics (MFA); film and video (MFA); painting (MFA); photography (MFA); printmaking (MFA); visual communications (MFA). *Faculty:* 26 full-time (11 women), 1 part-time/adjunct (0 women). *Students:* 21 full-time (13 women), 10 part-time (9 women); includes 6 minority (1 African American, 5 American Indian/Alaska Native), 2 international. 24 applicants, 50% accepted, 7 enrolled. In 2007, 4 degrees awarded. *Degree requirements:* For master's, thesis (MA), exhibit (MFA), departmental qualifying exam. *Entrance requirements:* For master's, GRE General Test (MA), bachelor's degree in art (MFA) or art history (MA), minimum GPA of 3.0 in last 60 undergraduate hours, 3 letters of recommendation, written research paper. Additional exam requirements/recommendations for international students: Required—TOEFL (minimum score 550 paper-based; 213 computer-based). *Application deadline:* For fall admission, 2/1 priority date for domestic students, 2/1 for international students; for spring admission, 10/1 for domestic and international students. Applications are processed on a rolling basis. Application fee: $40 ($90 for international students). Electronic applications accepted. *Expenses:* Tuition, state resident: full-time $3,451; part-time $144 per credit hour. Tuition, nonresident: full-time $12,432; part-time $518 per credit hour. Required fees: $1,925; $70 per credit hour. $122 per semester. *Financial support:* In 2007–08, 20 students received support, including 8 research assistantships with partial tuition reimbursements available (averaging $9,370 per year), 7 teaching assistantships with partial tuition reimbursements available (averaging $9,450 per year); career-related internships or fieldwork, Federal Work-Study, institutionally sponsored loans, scholarships/grants, health care benefits, tuition waivers (full), and unspecified assistantships also available. Financial award application deadline: 4/7; financial award applicants required to submit FAFSA. Total annual research expenditures: $24,250. *Unit head:* Mary Jo Watson, Associate Dean, 405-325-2691, Fax: 405-325-1668, E-mail: mjwatson@ou.edu. *Application contact:* Heidi Mau, Graduate Liaison, 405-325-2691, Fax: 405-325-1668, E-mail: hmau@ou.edu.

The University of Tennessee, Graduate School, College of Arts and Sciences, School of Art, Knoxville, TN 37996. Offers ceramics (MFA); drawing (MFA); graphic design (MFA); inter-area studies (MFA); media arts (MFA); painting (MFA); printmaking (MFA); sculpture (MFA); watercolor (MFA). *Accreditation:* NASAD. *Degree requirements:* For master's, thesis or alternative, exhibit. *Entrance requirements:* For master's, portfolio, minimum GPA of 2.7. Additional exam requirements/recommendations for international students: Required—TOEFL. Electronic applications accepted.

University of Utah, The Graduate School, College of Fine Arts, Department of Art and Art History, Salt Lake City, UT 84112-1107. Offers art history (MA); ceramics (MFA); community-based art education (MFA); drawing (MFA); graphic design (MFA); painting (MFA); photography/digital imaging (MFA); printmaking (MFA); sculpture/intermedia (MFA). *Faculty:* 21 full-time (10 women). *Students:* 12 full-time (5 women), 5 part-time (3 women). Average age 31. 36 applicants, 28% accepted, 3 enrolled. In 2007, 7 degrees awarded. *Degree requirements:* For master's, variable foreign language requirement, comprehensive exam (for some programs), thesis or alternative, exhibit (MFA), final project paper. *Entrance requirements:* For master's, CD portfolio (MFA), resumé, letters of recommendation. Additional exam requirements/recommendations for international students: Required—TOEFL (minimum score 575 paper-based; 183 computer-based; 75 iBT). *Application deadline:* For fall admission, 1/2 priority date for domestic and international students. Application fee: $45 ($65 for international students). Electronic applications accepted. *Financial support:* In 2007–08, 1 fellowship, 6 teaching assistantships with partial tuition reimbursements were awarded; research assistantships with tuition reimbursements, Federal Work-Study, institutionally sponsored loans, scholarships/grants, tuition waivers (partial), and unspecified assistantships also available. Financial award application deadline: 1/2; financial award applicants required to submit FAFSA. *Faculty research:* Intermedia, digital arts, installation, traditional media, Asian art, medieval arts. Total annual research expenditures: $21,844. *Unit head:* Dr. Elizabeth A. Peterson, Chair, 801-581-7012, Fax: 801-585-6171, E-mail: elizabeth.peterson@art.utah.edu.

University of Victoria, Faculty of Graduate Studies, Faculty of Fine Arts, Department of Visual Arts, Victoria, BC V8W 2Y2, Canada. Offers digital multimedia (MFA); drawing (MFA); painting (MFA); photography (MFA); sculpture (MFA); video (MFA). *Faculty:* 8 full-time (4 women). *Students:* 10 full-time (7 women), 2 international. Average age 27. 72 applicants, 7% accepted. In 2007, 4 degrees awarded. *Degree requirements:* For master's, exhibit, oral exam. *Entrance requirements:* For master's, portfolio, BFA. Additional exam requirements/recommendations for international students: Required—TOEFL (minimum score 575 paper-based; 233 computer-based), IELTS (minimum score 7). *Application deadline:* For fall admission, 2/28 for domestic students, 12/15 priority date for international students. Applications are processed on a rolling basis. Application fee: $75 ($125 for international students). Electronic applications accepted. *Expenses:* Tuition, state resident: full-time $3,110. International tuition: $3,700 full-time. Tuition and fees vary according to program. *Financial support:* In 2007–08, 10 students received support, including 2 fellowships (averaging $13,400 per year), 7 teaching assistantships (averaging $6,000 per year); research assistantships, institutionally sponsored loans and scholarships/grants also available. Financial award application deadline: 2/15. *Unit head:* Allan Stichbury, Acting Chair, 250-721-8011, Fax: 250-721-6595, E-mail: astichbu@finearts.uvic.ca. *Application contact:* Nedra Tremblay, Graduate Secretary, 250-721-8011, Fax: 250-721-6595, E-mail: ntrembla@finearts.uvic.ca.

Virginia Commonwealth University, Graduate School, School of the Arts, Department of Graphic Design, Richmond, VA 23284-9005. Offers design/visual communications (MFA); interior environment (MFA); photography and film (MFA). *Accreditation:* NASAD. *Faculty:* 15 full-time (3 women). *Students:* 42 full-time (31 women), 6 part-time (3 women); includes 6 minority (2 African Americans, 1 Asian American or Pacific Islander, 3 Hispanic Americans), 7 international. 80 applicants, 31% accepted, 20 enrolled. In 2007, 17 degrees awarded. *Degree requirements:* For master's, thesis, exhibition. *Entrance requirements:* For master's, portfolio. *Application deadline:* For fall admission, 3/1 for domestic students. Application fee: $50. *Expenses:* Tuition, state resident: full-time $7,224; part-time $401 per credit. Tuition, nonresident: full-time $16,072; part-time $891 per credit. Required fees: $1,679; $63 per credit. Tuition and fees vary according to campus/location. *Financial support:* Fellowships, teaching assistantships, career-related internships or fieldwork, Federal Work-Study, institutionally sponsored loans, and tuition waivers (full and partial) available. Support available to part-time students. Financial award application deadline: 3/15. *Faculty research:* Film, photography, interior environments, visual communication. *Unit head:* John DeMao, Chair, 804-828-7329, E-mail: jdemao@vcu.edu.

See Close-Up on page 275.

Washington State University, Graduate School, College of Liberal Arts, Department of Fine Arts, Pullman, WA 99164. Offers ceramics (MFA); digital media (MFA); drawing (MFA); painting (MFA); photography (MFA); print making (MFA); sculpture (MFA). *Faculty:* 16. *Students:* 16 full-time (6 women), 1 part-time; includes 1 minority (American Indian/Alaska Native), 2 international. Average age 29. 33 applicants, 30% accepted, 8 enrolled. In 2007, 8 degrees awarded. *Degree requirements:* For master's, comprehensive exam (for some programs), thesis, exhibit, oral exam. *Entrance requirements:* For master's, GRE, minimum GPA of 3.0, portfolio, 3 letters of recommendation. Additional exam requirements/recommendations for international students: Required—TOEFL (minimum score 550 paper-based; 213 computer-based). *Application deadline:* For fall admission, 1/15 for domestic and international students. Application fee: $50. Electronic applications accepted. *Financial support:* In 2007–08, fellowships with full and partial tuition reimbursements (averaging $3,114 per year), research assistantships with full and partial tuition reimbursements (averaging $13,917 per year), teaching assistantships with full and partial tuition reimbursements (averaging $13,056 per year) were awarded; career-related internships or fieldwork, Federal Work-Study, institutionally sponsored loans, tuition waivers (partial), and unspecified assistantships also available. Financial award application deadline: 4/1; financial award applicants required to submit FAFSA. *Faculty research:* Polynesian art, museum representation, number theory. *Unit head:* Dr. Carol Ivory, Chair, 509-335-7043, Fax: 509-335-7742, E-mail: ivorycs@wsu.edu. *Application contact:* Graduate School Admissions, 800-GRADWSU, Fax: 509-335-1949, E-mail: gradsch@wsu.edu.

Yale University, School of Art, New Haven, CT 06520. Offers graphic design (MFA); painting/printmaking (MFA); photography (MFA); sculpture (MFA). *Faculty:* 11 full-time (3 women), 102 part-time/adjunct (48 women). *Students:* 119 full-time (57 women); includes 19 minority (5 African Americans, 6 Asian Americans or Pacific Islanders, 8 Hispanic Americans), 22 international. Average age 27. 1,218 applicants, 5% accepted, 57 enrolled. In 2007, 56 degrees awarded. *Degree requirements:* For master's, thesis (for some programs). *Entrance requirements:* Additional exam requirements/recommendations for international students: Required—TOEFL (minimum score 550 paper-based; 250 computer-based; 100 iBT). *Application* *deadline:* For fall admission, 1/7 for domestic and international students. Application fee: $90. *Expenses: Contact institution. Financial support:* In 2007–08, 90 students received support, including 56 teaching assistantships (averaging $1,600 per year); Federal Work-Study and scholarships/grants also available. Financial award application deadline: 3/1; financial award applicants required to submit FAFSA. *Unit head:* Robert Storr, Dean, 203-432-2606. *Application contact:* Patricia Ann DeChiara, Director of Academic Affairs, 203-432-2600, E-mail: artschool.info@yale.edu.

Textile Design

Academy of Art University, Graduate Program, School of Fashion, San Francisco, CA 94105-3410. Offers fashion design (MFA); fashion merchandising (MFA); fashion textiles (MFA); knitwear (MFA). Part-time programs available. Postbaccalaureate distance learning degree programs offered (no on-campus study). *Degree requirements:* For master's, thesis, final review. *Entrance requirements:* For master's, minimum GPA of 3.0, portfolio. Electronic applications accepted.

California College of the Arts, Graduate Programs, Programs in Fine Art, San Francisco, CA 94107. Offers ceramics (MFA); film/video/performance (MFA); glass (MFA); jewelry/metal arts (MFA); painting/drawing (MFA); photography (MFA); printmaking (MFA); sculpture (MFA); textiles (MFA); wood/furniture (MFA). *Accreditation:* NASAD. *Faculty:* 17 full-time (9 women), 32 part-time/adjunct (12 women). *Students:* 101 full-time (73 women), 11 part-time (8 women). Average age 30. 437 applicants, 29% accepted, 51 enrolled. In 2007, 34 degrees awarded. *Degree requirements:* For master's, thesis, exhibit. *Entrance requirements:* For master's, appropriate bachelor's degree, portfolio. Additional exam requirements/recommendations for international students: Required—TOEFL (minimum score 600 paper-based; 250 computer-based). *Application deadline:* For fall admission, 1/15 for domestic and international students. Application fee: $50. Electronic applications accepted. *Expenses:* Tuition: Part-time $1,017 per unit. *Financial support:* In 2007–08, 5 fellowships (averaging $10,000 per year), 20 teaching assistantships (averaging $2,000 per year) were awarded; career-related internships or fieldwork, Federal Work-Study, scholarships/grants, and health care benefits also available. Financial award application deadline: 3/1; financial award applicants required to submit FAFSA. *Unit head:* Ted Purves, Chair, 415-551-9214, Fax: 415-703-9539, E-mail: tpurves@cca.edu. *Application contact:* Kathryn Ward, Assistant Director of Graduate Admissions, 415-703-9523 Ext. 9593, Fax: 415-703-9539, E-mail: graduateprograms@cca.edu.

California State University, Los Angeles, Graduate Studies, College of Arts and Letters, Department of Art, Los Angeles, CA 90032-8530. Offers art (MA), including art education, art history, art therapy, ceramics, metals, and textiles, design (MA, MFA), painting, sculpture, and graphic arts, photography; fine arts (MFA), including crafts, design (MA, MFA), studio arts. *Accreditation:* NASAD (one or more programs are accredited). Part-time and evening/weekend programs available. *Faculty:* 7 full-time (3 women). *Students:* 24 full-time (13 women), 59 part-time (42 women); includes 19 minority (2 African Americans, 1 American Indian/Alaska Native, 5 Asian Americans or Pacific Islanders, 11 Hispanic Americans), 16 international. Average age 39. In 2007, 28 degrees awarded. *Degree requirements:* For master's, comprehensive exam, project or thesis. *Entrance requirements:* For master's, portfolio. Additional exam requirements/recommendations for international students: Required—TOEFL. *Application deadline:* For fall admission, 6/30 for domestic students; for spring admission, 2/1 for domestic students. Applications are processed on a rolling basis. Application fee: $55. *Financial support:* Federal Work-Study available. Support available to part-time students. Financial award application deadline: 3/1. *Faculty research:* The artist and the book, conceptual art, ceramic processes, computer graphics, architectural graphics. *Unit head:* Dr. Robert Martin, Chair, 323-343-4010, Fax: 323-343-4045, E-mail: rjmartin@calstatela.edu.

Cornell University, Graduate School, Graduate Fields of Human Ecology, Field of Textiles, Ithaca, NY 14853-0001. Offers apparel design (MA, MPS); fiber science (MS, PhD); polymer science (MS, PhD); textile science (MS, PhD). *Faculty:* 18 full-time (7 women). *Students:* 23 full-time (16 women); includes 2 minority (1 African American, 1 Hispanic American), 13 international. Average age 29. 36 applicants, 33% accepted, 8 enrolled. In 2007, 3 master's, 3 doctorates awarded. *Degree requirements:* For master's, thesis (MA, MS), project paper (MPS); for doctorate, comprehensive exam, thesis/dissertation. *Entrance requirements:* For master's, GRE General Test, 2 letters of recommendation, portfolio (functional apparel design); for doctorate, GRE General Test, 2 letters of recommendation. Additional exam requirements/recommendations for international students: Required—TOEFL (minimum score 600 paper-based; 250 computer-based; 77 iBT). *Application deadline:* For fall admission, 3/1 for domestic students; for spring admission, 10/1 for domestic students. Application fee: $70. Electronic applications accepted. *Financial support:* In 2007–08, 21 students received support, including 2 fellowships with full tuition reimbursements available, 12 research assistantships with full tuition reimbursements available, 7 teaching assistantships with full tuition reimbursements available; institutionally sponsored loans, scholarships/grants, health care benefits, tuition waivers (full and partial), and unspecified assistantships also available. Financial award applicants required to submit FAFSA. *Faculty research:* Apparel design, consumption, mass customization, 3-D body scanning. *Unit head:* Director of Graduate Studies, 607-255-3151, Fax: 607-255-1093. *Application contact:* Graduate Field Assistant, 607-255-3151, Fax: 607-255-1093, E-mail: textiles_grad@cornell.edu.

Cranbrook Academy of Art, Graduate School, Program in Fine Arts, Bloomfield Hills, MI 48303-0801. Offers ceramics (MFA); design (MFA), including graphic design; fiber arts (MFA); metalsmithing (MFA); painting (MFA); photography (MFA); printmaking (MFA); sculpture (MFA). *Accreditation:* NASAD. *Degree requirements:* For master's, thesis, exhibit. *Entrance requirements:* Additional exam requirements/recommendations for international students: Required—TOEFL (minimum score 550 paper-based; 213 computer-based).

See Close-Up on page 237.

Drexel University, College of Media Arts and Design, Philadelphia, PA 19104-2875. Offers architecture (M Arch); design (MS), including fashion design, interior design; media arts (MS); performing arts (MS), including arts administration. *Accreditation:* NASAD. Part-time and evening/weekend programs available. *Entrance requirements:* For master's, interview. Additional exam requirements/recommendations for international students: Required—TOEFL. Electronic applications accepted. Expenses: Contact institution.

Drexel University, College of Media Arts and Design, Department of Design, Program in Fashion Design, Philadelphia, PA 19104-2875. Offers MS. *Accreditation:* NASAD. *Degree requirements:* For master's, thesis, portfolio review. *Entrance requirements:* For master's, interview. Additional exam requirements/recommendations for international students: Required—TOEFL. Electronic applications accepted.

Florida State University, Graduate Studies, College of Human Sciences, Department of Textiles and Consumer Sciences, Tallahassee, FL 32306. Offers apparel product development (MS); apparel/textile product development (PhD); creative design (MS); global product development (MS); professional merchandising (MS); retail merchandising (MS, PhD); textiles (MS). Part-time programs available. *Faculty:* 12 full-time (all women). *Students:* 28 full-time (26 women), 6 part-time (4 women); includes 14 minority (9 African Americans, 2 Asian Americans or Pacific Islanders, 3 Hispanic Americans), 2 international. 44 applicants, 25% accepted, 7 enrolled. In 2007, 13 master's, 5 doctorates awarded. *Degree requirements:* For master's, thesis optional; for doctorate, thesis/dissertation. *Entrance requirements:* For master's and doctorate, GRE General Test, minimum GPA of 3.0. Additional exam requirements/recommendations for international students: Required—TOEFL (minimum score 80 iBT). *Application deadline:* For fall admission, 7/1 priority date for domestic students, 5/1 for international students; for spring admission, 11/1 for domestic students, 12/1 for international students. Applications are processed on a rolling basis. Application fee: $30. Electronic applications accepted. *Expenses:* Tuition, state resident: part-time $248 per credit hour. Tuition, nonresident: part-time $880 per credit hour. Tuition and fees vary according to program. *Financial support:* In 2007–08, 20 students received support, including 1 fellowship with partial tuition reimbursement available (averaging $10,000 per year), research assistantships with partial tuition reimbursements available (averaging $8,000 per year), 15 teaching assistantships with partial tuition reimbursements available (averaging $8,000 per year); career-related internships or fieldwork, Federal Work-Study, institutionally sponsored loans, scholarships/grants, and unspecified assistantships also available. Financial award application deadline: 1/15; financial award applicants required to submit FAFSA. *Faculty research:* Soft goods retailing, small business strategies, textile product performance, consumer behavior, accessible housing. *Unit head:* Dr. Barbara Dyer, Chair, 850-644-2498, Fax: 850-645-4673, E-mail: bdyer@fsu.edu. *Application contact:* Sue Skornia, Academic Support Assistant, 850-644-2498, Fax: 850-645-4673, E-mail: sskornia@fsu.edu.

See Close-Up on page 1073.

Illinois State University, Graduate School, College of Fine Arts, School of Art, Normal, IL 61790-2200. Offers art history (MA, MS); ceramics (MFA, MS); drawing (MFA, MS); fibers (MFA, MS); glass (MFA, MS); graphic design (MFA, MS); metals (MFA, MS); painting (MFA, MS); photography (MFA, MS); printmaking (MFA, MS); sculpture (MFA, MS). *Accreditation:* NASAD (one or more programs are accredited). *Faculty:* 30 full-time (12 women). *Students:* 31 full-time (20 women), 5 part-time (4 women); includes 3 minority (1 African American, 2 Hispanic Americans), 3 international. 62 applicants, 29% accepted. In 2007, 17 degrees awarded. *Degree requirements:* For master's, thesis or alternative, internship. *Entrance requirements:* For master's, portfolio, sample of scholarly writing. *Application deadline:* Applications are processed on a rolling basis. Application fee: $40. *Expenses:* Tuition, state resident: full-time $3,492; part-time $194 per credit hour. Tuition, nonresident: full-time $7,272; part-time $404 per credit hour. Required fees: $1,024; $57 per credit hour. *Financial support:* In 2007–08, 23 teaching assistantships (averaging $6,661 per year) were awarded; career-related internships or fieldwork, Federal Work-Study, tuition waivers (full and partial), and unspecified assistantships also available. Support available to part-time students. Financial award application deadline: 4/1. *Faculty research:* General operations support: Normal Editions Workshop for FY2007. Total annual research expenditures: $4,160. *Unit head:* James Crowley, Chairperson, 309-438-5621.

James Madison University, The Graduate School, College of Visual and Performing Arts, School of Art and Art History, Harrisonburg, VA 22807. Offers art education (MA); art history (MA); ceramics (MFA); drawing/painting (MFA); metal/jewelry (MFA); photography (MFA); printmaking (MFA); sculpture (MFA); studio art (MA); weaving/fibers (MFA). *Accreditation:* NASAD. Part-time programs available. *Faculty:* 5 full-time (2 women), 1 part-time/adjunct (0 women). *Students:* 10 full-time (5 women), 2 part-time; includes 1 minority (Asian American or Pacific Islander) Average age 27. In 2007, 8 degrees awarded. *Degree requirements:* For master's, thesis (for some programs). *Entrance requirements:* For master's, GRE General Test, language exam in French or German, portfolio, 3 letters of recommendation, research paper. Additional exam requirements/recommendations for international students: Required—TOEFL. *Application deadline:* For fall admission, 2/15 priority date for domestic students, 2/15 for international students; for spring admission, 10/15 priority date for domestic students, 10/15 for international students. Applications are processed on a rolling basis. Application fee: $55. Electronic applications accepted. *Expenses:* Tuition, state resident: full-time $6,720; part-time $280 per credit hour. Tuition, nonresident: full-time $19,104; part-time $796 per credit hour. *Financial support:* In 2007–08, 8 students received support, including 3 teaching assistantships with full tuition reimbursements available (averaging $8,494 per year); Federal Work-Study, unspecified assistantships, and 5 graduate assistantships ($7,237) also available. Financial award application deadline: 3/1; financial award applicants required to submit FAFSA. *Unit head:* Leslie M. Bellavance, Academic Unit Head, 540-568-6216.

Kent State University, College of the Arts, School of Art, Kent, OH 44242-0001. Offers art education (MA); art history (MA); crafts (MA, MFA), including ceramics (MA), glass, jewelry/metals, textiles/art; fine art (MA, MFA), including drawing/painting, printmaking, sculpture. *Accreditation:* NASAD (one or more programs are accredited). *Faculty:* 20 full-time (11 women), 4 part-time/adjunct (3 women). *Students:* 46 full-time (33 women), 41 part-time (27 women); includes 1 African American, 11 Asian Americans or Pacific Islanders. 81 applicants, 49% accepted, 24 enrolled. In 2007, 22 degrees awarded. *Degree requirements:* For master's, one foreign language, thesis. *Entrance requirements:* For master's, undergraduate degree in proposed area of study (for fine arts and crafts programs); minimum overall GPA of 2.75 (3.0 for art major); 3 letters of recommendation; portfolio (15-20 slides for MA, 20-25 for MFA), brief autobiographical statement (MFA). Additional exam requirements/recommendations for international students: Required—TOEFL. *Application deadline:* For fall admission, 2/15 for domestic students; for spring admission, 10/15 for domestic students. Applications are processed on a rolling basis. Application fee: $30. Electronic applications accepted. *Financial support:* In 2007–08, 21 teaching assistantships with full tuition reimbursements (averaging $6,700 per year) were awarded; career-related internships or fieldwork, Federal Work-Study, scholarships/grants, and tuition waivers (full) also available. Financial award application deadline: 2/15. *Unit head:* Dr. Christine Havice, Director, 330-672-2192, Fax: 330-672-4729, E-mail: chavice@kent.edu. *Application contact:* Janice Lessman-Moss, Coordinator of Graduate Studies, 330-672-1362, Fax: 330-672-2192, E-mail: jlessman@kent.edu.

Marywood University, Academic Affairs, Insalaco College of Creative Arts and Management, Art Department, Program in Studio Art, Scranton, PA 18509-1598. Offers advertising design (MA); ceramics (MA); clay (MA); graphic design (MA); illustration (MA); interior architecture (MA); painting (MA); photography (MA); printmaking (MA); sculpture (MA); weaving (MA). *Accreditation:* NASAD. Part-time and evening/weekend programs available. *Students:* 5 full-time (3 women), 15 part-time (11 women), 1 international. Average age 41. 5 applicants, 80% accepted. In 2007, 7 degrees awarded. *Degree requirements:* For master's, comprehensive exam, thesis or alternative. *Entrance requirements:* For master's, portfolio. Additional exam requirements/recommendations for international students: Required—TOEFL (minimum score 550 paper-based; 213 computer-based). *Application deadline:* For fall admission, 4/15 priority date for domestic and international students; for spring admission, 11/15 priority date for domestic and international students. Applications are processed on a rolling basis. Application fee: $30. Electronic applications accepted. *Expenses:* Tuition: Full-time $15,290; part-time $695 per credit. Required fees: $990; $370 per term. Tuition and fees vary according to degree level. *Financial support:* Research assistantships with tuition reimbursements, scholarships/grants, tuition waivers (partial), and unspecified assistantships available. Support available to part-time students. Financial award application deadline: 2/15; financial award applicants required to

Textile Design

Marywood University (continued)
submit FAFSA. *Faculty research:* Texture and line in clay, cast bronze sculpture, color theories, book art and illustration, sculptural form.

Marywood University, Academic Affairs, Insalaco College of Creative Arts and Management, Art Department, Program in Visual Arts, Scranton, PA 18509-1598. Offers advertising design (MFA); clay (MFA); fibers (MFA); graphic design (MFA); illustration (MFA); metals (MFA); painting (MFA); photography (MFA); printmaking (MFA). *Accreditation:* NASAD. Part-time and evening/weekend programs available. *Students:* 13 full-time (10 women), 25 part-time (13 women); includes 2 minority (1 American Indian/Alaska Native, 1 Asian American or Pacific Islander), 3 international. Average age 35. In 2007, 11 degrees awarded. *Degree requirements:* For master's, thesis or alternative, exhibit. *Entrance requirements:* For master's, portfolio. Additional exam requirements/recommendations for international students: Required—TOEFL (minimum score 550 paper-based; 213 computer-based). *Application deadline:* For fall admission, 4/15 priority date for domestic and international students; for spring admission, 11/15 priority date for domestic and international students. Applications are processed on a rolling basis. Application fee: $30. Electronic applications accepted. *Expenses:* Contact institution. Tuition and fees vary according to degree level. *Financial support:* Research assistantships with tuition reimbursements, scholarships/grants, tuition waivers (partial), and unspecified assistantships available. Support available to part-time students. Financial award application deadline: 2/15; financial award applicants required to submit FAFSA. *Faculty research:* Mariology, exploration of visual imagery, explorations involving drawing on the loom, clay as sculptural medium, oil paintings.

Massachusetts College of Art and Design, Graduate Programs, Program in Fine Arts, Boston, MA 02115-5882. Offers ceramics (MFA); design (MFA); fibers (MFA); film (MFA); glass (MFA); media and performing arts (MFA); metals (MFA); painting (MFA); photography (MFA); printmaking (MFA); sculpture (MFA). *Accreditation:* NASAD. *Faculty:* 10 full-time (5 women), 8 part-time/adjunct (6 women). *Students:* 80 full-time (46 women), 11 part-time (9 women); includes 7 minority (1 African American, 4 Asian Americans or Pacific Islanders, 2 Hispanic Americans), 13 international. Average age 34. 310 applicants, 26% accepted, 50 enrolled. In 2007, 37 degrees awarded. *Degree requirements:* For master's, thesis, exhibit. *Entrance requirements:* For master's, 12 units of course work in art history, portfolio, resumé. *Application deadline:* For fall admission, 2/1 for domestic students. Application fee: $75. *Expenses:* Tuition, state resident: full-time $16,260; part-time $542 per credit. Tuition, nonresident: full-time $16,260; part-time $542 per credit. *Financial support:* In 2007–08, 50 research assistantships (averaging $2,000 per year), 30 teaching assistantships (averaging $2,000 per year) were awarded; career-related internships or fieldwork, Federal Work-Study, and clerical/technical assistantships also available. Support available to part-time students. Financial award application deadline: 5/1; financial award applicants required to submit FAFSA. *Application contact:* George Creamer, Director, 617-879-7163, Fax: 617-879-7171, E-mail: creamer@massart.edu.

Memphis College of Art, Graduate Programs, Program in Studio Art, Memphis, TN 38104-2764. Offers fiber/surface design (MFA); painting (MFA); papermaking (MFA); photography (MFA); printmaking (MFA); sculpture (MFA). *Accreditation:* NASAD. Part-time programs available. *Faculty:* 11 full-time (5 women), 2 part-time/adjunct (1 woman). *Students:* 17 full-time (7 women); includes 2 minority (both Hispanic Americans) Average age 29. 45 applicants, 51% accepted, 8 enrolled. In 2007, 4 degrees awarded. *Degree requirements:* For master's, thesis, exhibit. *Entrance requirements:* For master's, portfolio, interview, resumé. Additional exam requirements/recommendations for international students: Required—TOEFL (minimum score 525 paper-based; 195 computer-based). *Application deadline:* For fall admission, 3/1 priority date for domestic and international students; for spring admission, 11/1 priority date for domestic and international students. Application fee: $50. Electronic applications accepted. *Expenses:* Tuition: Full-time $22,000; part-time $435 per credit. Required fees: $560; $100 per course. Part-time tuition and fees vary according to course load and program. *Financial support:* In 2007–08, 11 students received support, including 2 teaching assistantships (averaging $2,000 per year); career-related internships or fieldwork, Federal Work-Study, institutionally sponsored loans, scholarships/grants,.tuition waivers (partial), unspecified assistantships, and merit awards also available. Support available to part-time students. Financial award application deadline: 8/1; financial award applicants required to submit FAFSA. *Unit head:* Howard Paine, Graduate Program Director, 901-272-5100, Fax: 901-272-5158, E-mail: hpaine@mca.edu. *Application contact:* Annette James Moore, Director of Admissions, 800-727-1088, Fax: 901-272-5158, E-mail: info@mca.edu.

See Close-Up on page 245.

Missouri State University, Graduate College, College of Natural and Applied Sciences, Department of Fashion and Interior Design, Springfield, MO 65804-0094. Offers secondary education (MS Ed), including consumer sciences. *Faculty:* 3 full-time (all women). *Degree requirements:* For master's, comprehensive exam, thesis or alternative. *Entrance requirements:* For master's, GRE (MNAS), 9–12 teaching certification (MS Ed), minimum GPA of 3.0 (MNAS). Additional exam requirements/recommendations for international students: Required—TOEFL (minimum score 550 paper-based; 213 computer-based; 79 iBT). *Application deadline:* For fall admission, 7/20 priority date for domestic students; for spring admission, 12/20 priority date for domestic students. Application fee: $35. *Expenses:* Tuition, state resident: full-time $3,708; part-time $206 per credit hour. Tuition, nonresident: full-time $7,236; part-time $206 per credit hour. Required fees: $622. Full-time tuition and fees vary according to course level, course load, program and reciprocity agreements. *Financial support:* Research assistantships, teaching assistantships with full tuition reimbursements, career-related internships or fieldwork, Federal Work-Study, scholarships/grants, and unspecified assistantships available. Financial award application deadline: 3/31; financial award applicants required to submit FAFSA. *Faculty research:* Clothing design, merchandising, hospitality and restaurant management, interior design. *Unit head:* Dr. Jeannie Ireland, Head, 417-836-5497, Fax: 417-836-4341, E-mail: jeannieireland@missouristate.edu.

Philadelphia University, School of Engineering and Textiles, Program in Textile Design, Philadelphia, PA 19144-5497. Offers MS. *Accreditation:* NASAD. Part-time programs available. *Entrance requirements:* For master's, GRE or MAT, minimum GPA of 2.8. Additional exam requirements/recommendations for international students: Required—TOEFL (minimum score 550 paper-based; 213 computer-based; 79 iBT). Electronic applications accepted.

Rhode Island School of Design, Graduate Studies, Division of Fine Arts, Department of Textiles, Providence, RI 02903-2784. Offers MFA. *Accreditation:* NASAD. *Degree requirements:* For master's, thesis, exhibit. *Entrance requirements:* For master's, portfolio, 3 letters of recommendation. Additional exam requirements/recommendations for international students: Required—TOEFL (minimum score 580 paper-based; 237 computer-based), IELTS (minimum score 7).

Savannah College of Art and Design, Graduate School, Program in Fashion, Savannah, GA 31402-3146. Offers MA, MFA. Part-time programs available. *Faculty:* 5 full-time (all women), 3 part-time/adjunct (all women). *Students:* 26 full-time (25 women), 7 part-time (all women); includes 3 minority (1 African American, 1 Asian American or Pacific Islander, 1 Hispanic American), 7 international. Average age 27. 55 applicants, 49% accepted, 13 enrolled. In 2007, 10 degrees awarded. *Degree requirements:* For master's, thesis, internship. *Entrance requirements:* For master's, interview, portfolio. Additional exam requirements/recommendations for international students: Required—TOEFL (minimum score 450 paper-based; 133 computer-based). *Application deadline:* For fall admission, 4/1 priority date for domestic and international students. Applications are processed on a rolling basis. Application fee: $50. Electronic applications accepted. *Expenses:* Tuition: Full-time $24,840; part-time $552 per credit. One-time fee: $500 full-time. *Financial support:* In 2007–08, 2 fellowships were awarded; career-related internships or fieldwork, Federal Work-Study, and scholarships/grants also available. Financial award application deadline: 4/1; financial award applicants required to submit FAFSA. *Unit head:* Anthony Miller, Acting Chair, 912-525-6668, Fax: 912-525-6655, E-mail: asmiller@scad.edu. *Application contact:* Darrell Tutchton, Director of Graduate and International Enrollment, 912-525-5961, Fax: 912-525-5985, E-mail: admission@scad.edu.

See Close-Up on page 257.

Savannah College of Art and Design, Graduate School, Program in Fibers, Savannah, GA 31402-3146. Offers MA, MFA. Part-time programs available. *Faculty:* 6 full-time (5 women), 2 part-time/adjunct (both women). *Students:* 13 full-time (all women), 2 part-time (both women), 4 international. Average age 25. 25 applicants, 44% accepted, 5 enrolled. In 2007, 2 degrees awarded. *Degree requirements:* For master's, thesis, internship. *Entrance requirements:* For master's, interview, portfolio. Additional exam requirements/recommendations for international students: Required—TOEFL (minimum score 450 paper-based; 133 computer-based). *Application deadline:* For fall admission, 4/1 priority date for domestic and international students. Applications are processed on a rolling basis. Application fee: $50. Electronic applications accepted. *Expenses:* Tuition: Full-time $24,840; part-time $552 per credit. One-time fee: $500 full-time. *Financial support:* In 2007–08, 2 fellowships were awarded; career-related internships or fieldwork, Federal Work-Study, and scholarships/grants also available. Financial award application deadline: 4/1; financial award applicants required to submit FAFSA. *Unit head:* Cayoweh Easley, Chair, 912-525-4136. *Application contact:* Darrell Tutchton, Director of Graduate and International Enrollment, 912-525-5961, Fax: 912-525-5985, E-mail: admission@scad.edu.

See Close-Up on page 257.

Sul Ross State University, School of Arts and Sciences, Department of Fine Arts and Communication, Alpine, TX 79832. Offers art education (M Ed); art history (M Ed); studio art (M Ed), including ceramics, design, drawing, jewelry, painting, printmaking, sculpture, weaving. Part-time programs available. *Degree requirements:* For master's, oral or written exam. *Entrance requirements:* For master's, GRE General Test, minimum GPA of 2.5 in last 60 hours of undergraduate work. *Faculty research:* Ceramic sculpture, watercolor, wood sculpture, rock art.

Syracuse University, Graduate School, College of Visual and Performing Arts, School of Art and Design, Programs in Art, Syracuse, NY 13244. Offers ceramics (MFA); fiber arts/materials studies (MFA); illustration (MFA); jewelry and metalsmithing (MFA); painting (MFA); printmaking (MFA); sculpture (MFA). *Accreditation:* NASAD. Part-time programs available. *Students:* 40 full-time (27 women), 4 part-time (3 women); includes 4 minority (2 Asian Americans or Pacific Islanders, 2 Hispanic Americans), 6 international. 129 applicants, 15% accepted, 12 enrolled. In 2007, 26 master's awarded. *Degree requirements:* For master's, thesis or alternative. *Entrance requirements:* For master's, portfolio. Additional exam requirements/recommendations for international students: Required—TOEFL. *Application deadline:* For fall admission, 1/1 priority date for domestic students. Applications are processed on a rolling basis. Application fee: $75. Electronic applications accepted. *Expenses:* Tuition: Full-time $18,216; part-time $1,012 per credit. Required fees: $980. Tuition and fees vary according to program. *Financial support:* In 2007–08, 16 students received support; fellowships with full tuition reimbursements available, research assistantships with full and partial tuition reimbursements available, teaching assistantships with full and partial tuition reimbursements available, tuition waivers (partial) available. *Unit head:* Ann Clark, Chair, 315-443-4613, Fax: 315-443-1303. *Application contact:* Harriett Conti, Associate Director, Graduate Student Services, 315-443-3089, E-mail: hmconti@syr.edu.

Temple University, Graduate School, Tyler School of Art, Department of Crafts, Philadelphia, PA 19122-6096. Offers ceramics/glass (MFA); fibers and fabric design (MFA); metals/jewelry/CAD-CAM (MFA). *Accreditation:* NASAD. *Degree requirements:* For master's, essay, exhibit. *Entrance requirements:* For master's, minimum GPA of 3.0, slide portfolio, 40 credits in studio art, 12 credits in art history. Additional exam requirements/recommendations for international students: Required—TOEFL (minimum score 550 paper-based; 213 computer-based; 79 iBT). Electronic applications accepted.

University of California, Davis, Graduate Studies, Program in Textile Arts and Costume Design, Davis, CA 95616. Offers MFA. *Degree requirements:* For master's, presentation of an individual project/body of work. *Entrance requirements:* For master's, minimum GPA of 3.0, portfolio. Additional exam requirements/recommendations for international students: Required—TOEFL (minimum score 550 paper-based; 213 computer-based). Electronic applications accepted. *Faculty research:* Historic ethnographic and contemporary costume and textile design, computer-aided design.

University of Cincinnati, Graduate School, College of Design, Architecture, Art, and Planning, School of Design, Cincinnati, OH 45221. Offers fashion design (M Des); graphic design (M Des); industrial design (M Des); interaction design (M Des); product development (M Des). *Accreditation:* NASAD. *Students:* 13 full-time (7 women), 6 part-time (5 women), 10 international. In 2007, 3 degrees awarded. *Degree requirements:* For master's, thesis. *Entrance requirements:* For master's, undergraduate degree in design or related field, 2 years of work experience in design or related field. Additional exam requirements/recommendations for international students: Required—TOEFL. *Application deadline:* For fall admission, 2/1 for domestic students. Application fee: $30. Electronic applications accepted. *Financial support:* Fellowships, career-related internships or fieldwork, Federal Work-Study, tuition waivers (partial), and unspecified assistantships available. *Faculty research:* Design theory, interdisciplinary design topics. *Unit head:* Prof. Dale Murray, Director, 513-556-1524, E-mail: dale.murray@uc.edu. *Application contact:* Dr. J. Chewning, Information Contact, 513-556-2996, Fax: 513-556-0240, E-mail: j.chewning@uc.edu.

University of Massachusetts Dartmouth, Graduate School, College of Visual and Performing Arts, Program in Artisanry, North Dartmouth, MA 02747-2300. Offers ceramics (MFA, Postbaccalaureate Certificate); fibers (MFA); fibers/textiles (Postbaccalaureate Certificate); jewelry/metals (MFA, Postbaccalaureate Certificate); wood/furniture design (MFA, Postbaccalaureate Certificate). *Accreditation:* NASAD. *Faculty:* 6 full-time (3 women), 4 part-time/adjunct (all women). *Students:* 21 full-time (13 women), 14 part-time (9 women); includes 4 minority (3 Asian Americans or Pacific Islanders, 1 Hispanic American), 3 international. Average age 29. 47 applicants, 57% accepted, 17 enrolled. In 2007, 7 degrees awarded. *Degree requirements:* For master's, thesis, visual thesis. *Entrance requirements:* For master's, portfolio, interview, minimum GPA of 3.0, 3 letters of recommendation. Additional exam requirements/recommendations for international students: Required—TOEFL (minimum score 500 paper-based). *Application deadline:* For fall admission, 3/1 for domestic students, 1/1 for international students. Applications are processed on a rolling basis. Application fee: $40 ($60 for international students). Electronic applications accepted. *Expenses:* Tuition, state resident: full-time $2,071; part-time $86 per credit. Tuition, nonresident: full-time $8,099; part-time $337 per credit. Part-time tuition and fees vary according to course load and program. *Financial support:* In 2007–08, 16 teaching assistantships with full tuition reimbursements (averaging $2,930 per year) were awarded; Federal Work-Study and unspecified assistantships also available. Support available to part-time students. Financial award application deadline: 3/1; financial award applicants required to submit FAFSA. *Faculty research:* Processes of figurative sculpture: new materials and techniques. Total annual research expenditures: $9,880. *Unit head:* Jarrad Nunes, Director, 508-999-8010, E-mail: jnunes@umassd.edu. *Application contact:* Carol Novo, Graduate Admissions Officer, 508-999-8604, Fax: 508-999-8183, E-mail: graduate@umassd.edu.

University of Minnesota, Twin Cities Campus, Graduate School, College of Design, Department of Design, Housing, and Apparel, Minneapolis, MN 55455-0213. Offers apparel (MA, MS, PhD); design communication (MA, MS, PhD); housing studies (MA, MS, PhD, Postbaccalaureate Certificate); interactive design (MFA); interior design (MA, MS, PhD). Part-time programs available. *Faculty:* 24 full-time (18 women), 5 part-time/adjunct (4 women). *Students:* 41 full-time (34 women), 28 part-time (21 women); includes 3 minority (1 African American, 1 Asian American or Pacific Islander, 1 Hispanic American), 20 international. 37 applicants, 54% accepted, 15 enrolled. In 2007, 3 master's, 8 doctorates awarded. *Median time to degree:* Of those who began their doctoral program in fall 1999, 100% received their degree in 8 years or less. *Degree requirements:* For master's and Postbaccalaureate Certificate, comprehensive exam, thesis (for some programs); for doctorate, comprehensive exam, thesis/dissertation. *Entrance requirements:* For master's, GRE General Test, minimum GPA of 3.0 (preferred), portfolio, 3 letters of recommendation; for doctorate, GRE General Test, minimum GPA of 3.0 (preferred), portfolio, 3 letters of recommendation, writing sample; for Postbaccalaureate Certificate, GRE General Test, minimum GPA of 3.0 (preferred). Additional exam requirements/recommendations for international students: Required—TOEFL (minimum score 550 paper-based; 213 computer-based; 79 iBT). *Application deadline:* For fall admission, 1/15 for domestic and international students. Application fee: $55 ($75 for international students). Electronic applications accepted. *Financial support:* In 2007–08, 34 students received support, including 13 research assistantships with partial tuition reimbursements available (averaging $12,652 per year), 24 teaching assistantships with partial tuition reimbursements available (averaging $12,652 per year); Federal Work-Study, institutionally sponsored loans, and unspecified assistantships also available. Financial award application deadline: 2/1; financial award applicants required to submit FAFSA. *Faculty research:* Housing policy and community development; consumer behavior; interactive design; design history; social, cultural, and behavioral issues related to designed environments. Total annual research expenditures: $320,058. *Unit head:* Becky Love Yust, Professor and Department Head, 612-624-7461, Fax: 612-624-2750, E-mail: byust@che.umn.edu. *Application contact:* Charleen Klarquist, Student Support Services Assistant, 612-626-1219, Fax: 612-624-2750, E-mail: dhagrad@umn.edu.

The University of North Carolina at Greensboro, Graduate School, School of Human Environmental Sciences, Department of Consumer, Apparel, and Retail Studies, Greensboro, NC 27412-5001. Offers MS, PhD. *Faculty:* 6 full-time (4 women). *Students:* 18 full-time (16 women), 2 part-time (1 woman); includes 11 minority (3 African Americans, 7 Asian Americans or Pacific Islanders, 1 Hispanic American). 20 applicants, 35% accepted. *Degree requirements:* For master's, one foreign language; for doctorate, one foreign language, thesis/dissertation. *Entrance requirements:* For master's and doctorate, GRE General Test. Additional exam requirements/recommendations for international students: Required—TOEFL. *Application deadline:* For fall admission, 7/1 priority date for domestic students; for spring admission, 11/1 for domestic students. Applications are processed on a rolling basis. Application fee: $45. Electronic applications accepted. *Financial support:* Fellowships with full tuition reimbursements, research assistantships with full tuition reimbursements, teaching assistantships with full tuition reimbursements available. *Faculty research:* Impact of phosphate removal, protective clothing for pesticide workers, fabric hand: subjective and objective measurements. *Unit head:* Dr. Gwendolyn O'Neal, Chair, 336-334-5472, Fax: 336-334-5614, E-mail: gsoneal@uncg.edu. *Application contact:* Michelle Harkleroad, Director of Graduate Admissions, 336-334-4884, Fax: 336-334-4424, E-mail: mbharkle@uncg.edu.

Western Michigan University, Graduate College, College of Fine Arts, Department of Art, Kalamazoo, MI 49008-5202. Offers graphic design (MFA); performing arts administration (MFA); textile design (MA, MFA). *Accreditation:* NASAD (one or more programs are accredited). *Degree requirements:* For master's, thesis or alternative.

ArtCenter

ART CENTER COLLEGE OF DESIGN

Programs of Study

Art Center's graduate programs provide a framework in which students can pursue advanced studies in media design, broadcast cinema (film), art, and environmental and product design (industrial design). The graduate programs enable students to broaden their practical, conceptual, and analytical skills by requiring a balance between professional and theoretical approaches to art and design practice.

Every program has its own graduate seminar, which brings artists, designers, and critics to the campus regularly. In all cases, the curriculum is wide ranging so that students may follow their own interests and direction, yet it is designed to ensure that each student receives individual attention and regular critical feedback. In addition to regular meetings with graduate faculty members, students confer weekly with visiting advisers in one-on-one meetings.

Broadcast Cinema, the Art Center's M.F.A. program for filmmakers, is focused on the creation of works for existing, emerging, and future forms of broadcast and theatrical distribution. The traditional term "broadcast" represents the College's exploration of the vast potential of satellite distribution and "cinema", their respect for innovation in visual aesthetics and content. Early development of each student's individual creative identity is a priority. Students may choose to specialize in any creative leadership roles in filmmaking. The future is very bright for artists who prefer to embrace innovative content, forms, and methods of storytelling.

The M.F.A. program in media design is designed for students who are interested in exploring and extending the boundaries of graphic design, visual communication, and digital media. This interdisciplinary program encourages innovation and experimentation, theoretical research, the development of technological sophistication, and individual creativity. Students work in state-of-the-art facilities under the direction of a faculty of accomplished designers, technology specialists, and theorists and also have opportunities to meet visiting professionals.

The M.S. degree is also offered in industrial design. This graduate program in industrial design encourages students with a background in product or environmental design to expand their knowledge and expertise in an environment that encourages experimentation, innovation, and multidisciplinary research. Particular emphasis is placed on broadening students' intellectual grasp of design issues, using digital and written media for communication, and realizing the full potential of the creative process. The first year of the program is spent in a joint multidisciplinary project. Students work closely with a distinguished core faculty and with many visiting specialists.

The M.F.A. program in art brings together students and a varied faculty composed of internationally known artists. The size of the program—about 35 students and 7 graduate advisers—allows for intensive one-on-one dialogue while offering sufficient diversity to generate critical exchange and controversy. The program emphasizes both making and theorizing the art object and provides studios for independent work as well as classes in theory and technique.

Research Facilities

The James Lemont Fogg Memorial Library contains 69,000 volumes of books and periodicals, 110,000 slides, 8,000 videotapes, and DVDs of rare features, animation, documentaries, advertising, computer graphics, and instructional programs. A photo reference collection contains more than 90,000 pictures. The Rare Book Room houses limited and signed editions, portfolios, and other materials. Subscriptions are maintained for more than 400 magazines, and online subscriptions provide access to thousands of magazine articles and images. A CD-ROM workstation can be used to view a collection of more than 350 interactive CD-ROMs. Occidental College's library of more than 1 million volumes serves as another resource for Art Center students.

Art Center maintains state-of-the-art studios and shops, including a rapid-modeling machine that creates three-dimensional prototype models. Archetype Press, a 3,000-square-foot facility, houses fourteen presses and 2,400 drawers of rare type from American and European foundries. Students have access to a wide range of interactive multimedia and digital resources for exploring and refining their ideas, including sixty Silicon Graphics workstations, 140 Apple Macintosh computers, twelve Compaq Professional NT workstations, and the latest design software available.

Financial Aid

Grants and loans, including the California Graduate Fellowship and FFELP Loan Program, are available. A limited number of scholarships and teaching assistantships are also available. Candidates must demonstrate financial need and present an exceptional portfolio of work for scholarship consideration. Scholarships are awarded by a graduate scholarship committee.

Cost of Study

The cost of tuition for 2008 is $15,508 per fifteen-week semester.

Living and Housing Costs

The College does not currently maintain dormitories. A wide variety of housing is available in Pasadena and neighboring communities. The office of Student Life assists students in finding local rentals. The average cost of rent and food per semester is approximately $5000.

Student Group

Approximately 130 graduate students, of whom 60 percent are men and 40 percent are women, are enrolled in the College.

Student Outcomes

Most students pursue careers as practicing artists and designers within their professions.

Location

Art Center is located in Pasadena, California, a residential community near Los Angeles. With two campuses, one in a striking glass and steel facility on the hillsides of Pasadena and the other near old town Pasadena, the College is a short distance from greater Los Angeles. Students benefit from their proximity to art galleries, advertising and design agencies, and the entertainment industry.

The College

A private, nonprofit institution, Art Center College of Design was founded in 1930 with the purpose of educating students for careers of achievement in the visual arts professions. The total enrollment, including undergraduates, is 1,500. Eighteen percent of students are international and represent forty-seven different countries. The College is accredited by WASC and NASAD.

Applying

Applicants for the broadcast cinema and fine arts programs may apply for entry in any of the three scheduled terms each year: fall, spring, or summer. Applications are accepted on a rolling admissions basis, with consideration given as long as space is available in a class. Spaces in some graduate programs are extremely limited and may require application a number of semesters in advance. Media design and industrial design applicants may apply only for the fall semester, and the application deadline for these programs is February 1. Graduate programs are normally six semesters in length. However, the media design and broadcast cinema programs offer two- and three-year options. Applicants may consult the Admissions Office about the status of any entering class.

Correspondence and Information

Admissions Office
Art Center College of Design
1700 Lida Street
Pasadena, California 91103
Phone: 626-396-2373
Fax: 626-795-0578
E-mail: admissions@artcenter.edu
Web site: http://www.artcenter.edu

Art Center College of Design

THE FACULTY

The faculty members are core faculty advisers for graduate programs. Graduate students have access to a wide variety of classes and additional faculty members at Art Center.

Media Design Program

Anne Burdick, Chair; B.F.A., California Institute of the Arts. Designer, writer, editor; design editor, electronic book review; head, Alt-X Design Collective. Exhibitions include San Francisco Museum of Modern Art. Publications include *eye, I.D.,* and *Emigre* magazines. Projects include poetry installations for the Getty Research Institute, lexicography with the Austrian Academy of Sciences, experimental fiction at the Walker Art Center's Gallery 9, and books of literary/media criticism by authors such as Marshall McLuhan and N. Katherine Hayles. Burdick has been the design editor of *Electronic Book Review* since 1995.

Sean Donahue, M.A., Art Center College of Design. Principal of ResearchCenteredDesign, a Los Angeles–based design practice. His practice consists of professional commissions, self-initiated research, design advocacy, education and publishing. Donahue has lectured and published internationally at RISD, RCA, and North Carolina State University, where he was also the 2004 Designer-in-Residence. Published research: the University of Cambridge, Princeton Architectural Press, MIT Press, and *I.D.* magazine.

Ben Hooker, M.A., Royal College of Art (London). Collaborates with architects, industrial designers, and computer scientists working in the field of human-computer interaction, resulting in computer-generated data landscapes merging with real, physical spaces. Visiting Faculty at Intel's Research Lab in Berkeley. Clients include Shona Kitchen; San Jose International Airport, and projects for Vitra Design Museum and Art Center College of Design.

Philip Van Allen, B.A., California, Santa Cruz. Interaction designer/producer/technologist specializing in experimental, NOT-linear information and entertainment systems; principal, Commotion New Media; interactive art collaborations with Yoko Ono and Kim Abeles; exhibitions with SIGGRAPH Virtual Lounge. Other clients include Yahoo, U2, and George P. Johnson.

Industrial Design Program

Andrew Ogden, Chair; B.S., Art Center College of Design. Vice president and executive designer, Walt Disney Imagineering; designer, Honda R&D North America.

Mark Andersen, B.S., Art Center College of Design. Designer; founder/owner, ZoomOutDesign. Clients: Zaca Inc. and BioControl Inc. Exhibitions: *Brewery Art Walk 2005–06,* Los Angeles. Awards: IDSA silver for Zaca SpaceCab, IDSA bronze for Hycore Biomedical accuPINCH, and honorable mention, "Why Design?", Art Center faculty grant for 3-D digital modeling research.

Katherine Bennett, B.S.I.D., Philadelphia College of Art. Design research, product development, information architecture, strategic planning. Clients: Johnson Controls International, Avery Dennison. Formerly with Donald Chadwick Associates, Hauser, Saul Bass, Henry Dreyfuss Associates. Projects: contract and residential furniture, consumer products, equipment and instrumentation, communications. Publications (periodicals): *Los Angeles Times, Innovation, Modern Photography.*

Richard Keyes, B.F.A., Art Center College of Design. Owner, Keyes Design; former designer, Steven Jacobs, Fulton & Green, the Graphics Studio. Clients: Warner Brothers Records, Atlantic Richfield, Guess? Jeans, Convergent Technologies, His Holiness the Dalai Lama, Empire Berol (color consulting), Homebody, Los Angeles Housing Department, Parson's Engineering (design consultant). Former instructor: California State University, Los Angeles; Los Angeles Valley College; UCLA Extension.

Steven Montgomery, B.A., Michigan State. Industrial designer; principal, BioDesign, specializing in medical and consumer product design; former project manager for S. G. Hauser Associates, Inc.; designer, Huck & Studer Design, KMH Associates. Clients: Johnson & Johnson, Baxter Healthcare Corporation, Becton Dickinson, Omron Healthcare, Cepheid, Panasonic, Technicolor, Boeing/Teague, Bissell, Thomson Electronics, Reebok, Acer, Whirlpool, Hyundai, Honda R&D, Goldstar, Caterpillar, DaimlerChrysler, Nokia, Microsoft, Disney. Awards: IDSA.

Geoff Wardle, M.Des., Royal College of Art (London). Corporate design experience: British Leyland, Chrysler Europe, Saab, Ford Asia Pacific. Design consultant: Tatra, Czech Republic; TVS-Suzuki, India. Former chair of Transportation Design, Art Center Europe.

Broadcast Cinema Program

Robert W. Peterson, Chair; B.F.A., Art Center College of Design. Director/Director of Photography. Production design, visual effects design, commercials, music videos, documentary films, television, theater. Clients: 20th Century Fox, Paramount, Columbia, Universal, United Artists. Awards: Clio, Belding, Council for Advancement of Secondary Education, New York Film Festival.

Jean-Pierre Geuens, Ph.D., USC. Professor of Cinema, Los Angeles City College. Author: *Film Production Theory.* Publications: *Film Quarterly, Film Criticism, Spectator, LA/CA Journal.*

John Hartzog, Ph.D., USC. Director, Learning Resource Center, California State University, Northridge. Publications: *Film Quarterly, Magill Cinema Annual, Academe.*

Victoria Hochberg, B.A., Antioch College. Fulbright Fellowship. Writer/director: feature films, television, documentaries, music videos. Television: *Sex and the City, Ghost Whisperer, Kitchen Confidential, Reaper.* Feature writer: *The Love of Good Women,* performed with the San Francisco Mime Troupe, Pantomime Theatre of New York. Awards: two Emmy awards for writing and directing, four nominations and two Directors Guild of America awards, Writers Guild of America Award nomination. Member: National Board of the Directors Guild of America, including the Special Projects and Creative Rights Committees.

Elizabeth Moore, M.A., Minneapolis College of Art and Design. Painter/sculptor, designer for film and television. Exhibitions: White Gallery, New York; O.N.S., New York; Total Art Museum, Seoul; Site, LA County Contemporary Art; Washington Project for the Arts; Washington, D.C. Clients: Peter Gabriel, Bette Midler, Lenny Kravitz, Sheryl Crow, Stevie Nicks, Prince, B. B. King.

Ron Osborn, B.F.A., Art Center College of Design. Television producer/writer; feature writer television: executive producer/writer/director, *She Spies;* supervising producer/writer, *The West Wing;* executive producer/writer, *Cupid;* executive producer/writer/creator, *Duckman;* executive producer/writer, *Moonlighting;* executive story editor, *Night Court;* story editor, *Mork and Mindy;* features writer, *Meet Joe Black, Radioland Murders, Just My Luck* (rewrite), *The Flintstones* (rewrite), *The Hard Way* (rewrite). Awards: multiple Emmy nominations, Cable Ace Awards, Best Animated Show (Duckman), Banff International TV Festival.

Eric Sherman, B.A., Yale. Director, cinematographer, producer: *Pep Squad, Mystic Nights & Pirate Fights, After Freedom.* President, Film Transform. Author: *The Director's Event, Directing The Film, Frame by Frame, Selling Your Film, Home Entertainment–The Ultimate Movie Marketplace.* Publications: *Moviemaker.* Awards: Montreal Film Festival, Audience Award, Methodfest *(After Freedom),* New York, Bilbao, Columbus Film Festivals, Peabody Broadcasting Award. Member: Board of Trustees, American Cinematheque; Board of Directors, Film Forum.

Joan Tewkesbury. Director/writer/producer, playwright; Co-writer, *Thieves Like Us;* writer, *Nashville;* director, *Scattering Dad, Stagecoach Mary, Jammed, Sudie and Simpson, Cold Sassy Tree, Old Boyfriends, On Promised Land, Wild Texas Wind.* Features, documentaries, books.

Fine Art Program

Jeremy Gilbert-Rolfe, Chair; M.F.A., Florida State. Paintings exhibited nationally and internationally since 1971. Major publications include *Immanence and Contradiction: Recent Essays on the Artistic Device* and *Beyond Piety: Critical Essays on the Visual Arts, 1986–1993.* Recipient, John Simon Guggenheim Memorial Fellowship and the Frank Jewett Mather Award for distinction in art or architectural criticism.

Lita Albuquerque, B.A., UCLA. In the 1970s and 1980s, Albuquerque was a seminal part of the California Light and Space movement and a pioneer in Process Art, Environmental Art, and Earth Art. In recent years, she completed an installation on the pyramids in Egypt called Sol Star. She is currently preparing for a global project at the North and South Poles.

Richard Hawkins, M.F.A., California Institute of the Arts. Solo museum exhibition: Kunstverein Heilbronn, Germany (2003) and numerous national and international group exhibitions. Represented by Greene-Naftali, New York; Galerie Daniel Buchholz, Cologne; Corvi-Mora, London; and Richard Telles Fine Art, Los Angeles. Public collections: MoMA; MoCA; Sammlung Goetz, Munich; Sammlung Schurmann;, Aachen. Publication: Self-titled monograph (2004). Award: Japan Creative Artist Fellowship, Tokyo (2000).

Patricia E. Podesta, M.F.A., Claremont. Artist, production designer of feature films, *Bobby, Memento, Nowhere, Splendor, The Chumbscrubber.* Exhibitions: the Museum of Modern Art, the Rotterdame Film Festival, the American Film Institute, the Pacific Film Archives, LACMA, UCLA Hammer Museum. Awards: the National Endowment for the Arts 1985, 1987, 1989; Art Matters, Inc., 1987, 1989; the Western States Regional Media Award; the James Phelen Award in Film.

Diana Maria Thater, M.F.A., Art Center College of Design. Exhibitions: Dia Center for the Arts, the Museum of Modern Art, the Saint Louis Art Museum, the Renaissance Society at the University of Chicago, Walker Center for the Arts, Portland Art Museum, Vienna Secession, the Basel Kunsthalle, and the Salzburger Kunstverein, among many others. Grants: NEA and the Etants-Donnes Foundation, Guggenheim Fellowship, 2005–06.

Annette Weisser, M.A., Academy of Media Arts (Cologne). Solo exhibitions include *Annette Weisser/Ingo Vetter: Works 1996–2006,* Westphalian State Museum of Art and Culture, Munster (2006); *NameGame,* Hall for Art, Luneburg (2003); *NameGame,* platform ev, Berlin and Forum Citypark, , Graz (2002); *What counts is to absorb all the antitheses at once, rather than resolving them,* Bethany Arthouse, Berlin (1998); *Tableau,* Current Art Society, Munster (1998).

Carnegie Mellon

CARNEGIE MELLON UNIVERSITY

College of Fine Arts School of Design

Programs of Study

The School of Design at Carnegie Mellon University offers three distinct programs leading to a master's degree; in addition, Carnegie Mellon is one of very few institutions to offer a Ph.D. in design. The Master of Design (M.Des.) degree may be earned in communication planning and information design (CPID) or interaction design (IntD). The School of Design also jointly administers a program with the Department of Mechanical Engineering, leading to the Master of Product Development (M.P.D.) degree.

The Master of Design in communication planning and information design is a two-year professional program for students who want to explore the new arts of communication and the creative potential of the interplay between words and images in traditional and innovative media. This unique program is jointly offered by the School of Design and the English Department. The goal of the program is to prepare students for advanced levels of professional employment as communication planners and designers in the areas of print communication, design planning, systems design, dynamic information design, interactive multimedia, and Internet communication.

The CPID program provides a balanced mix of collaborative work and individual exploration. Some recent themes of exploration include new narrative structures in new media, visual voice and identity in print and digital formats, visualization of complex information spaces, and strategic planning for communication systems. Recent project sponsors include clients such as Microsoft, EliasArts, Samsung Electronics, the Carnegie Museum of Art, and the United States Postal Service.

The Master of Design in interaction design is a two-year professional program that trains students from diverse backgrounds to become practicing interaction designers. A combination of studio and seminar courses covers topics such as communication theory, user research and concept evaluation methods, advanced topics in interaction design, and client-based concept development. The program of study culminates in both a written thesis and a thesis project.

The interaction design program builds on the School's traditional areas of strength, including efficient, effective, and desirable human-computer communication; visualization and navigation through information spaces; time-based information design; and collaborative design practice among various disciplines and across distances. Situated in the midst of a renowned research university, students take classes across the campus in areas such as computer science, business, psychology, and entertainment technology to enrich their design education.

The Master of Product Development program is for engineers and designers who are seeking to play a more substantial role in product development. It is jointly offered by the Department of Mechanical Engineering and the School of Design, with support from the Tepper School of Business. The M.P.D. program is based on the interdisciplinary and team-working processes at the core of successful product development. In the first semester, in consultation with faculty advisers, students elect a curriculum tailored to their needs, allowing them to build a broadening complement to their current skill base, thereby enhancing their ability to contribute to a product development team. The capstone of the second semester is the Integrated Product Development class, in which interdisciplinary groups work with corporate sponsors to develop product solutions in response to real market opportunities.

The doctoral program is for students who want to investigate fundamental problems in the nature and practice of design. The program is grounded in the design disciplines but strongly encourages interdisciplinary study, drawing on the strengths of the School of Design and the resources of a leading research university with excellence in the arts and humanities, engineering, computer science, business, and the social and behavioral sciences. The goal of the program is to prepare researchers and educators who will consolidate what is known about design in its most sophisticated and well-grounded form and expand that knowledge through original inquiry. Students may concentrate in one of four closely related areas: design theory, interaction design, typography and information design, or new product development.

Research Facilities

All graduate students have dedicated workspaces within a group studio that they share with other students from their program. These spaces all offer amenities such as bottled water, couches, and larger tables for collaborative work or meetings, in addition to individual student spaces.

The School of Design's 2,400-square-foot 3-D lab comprises a machine room, an assembly room, a spray room, and a materials room. The 3-D lab is open 82 hours per week. Metal-, plastic-, and wood-forming equipment is available, and a wide variety of model-making materials are sold at cost.

The John Reese Memorial Electronic Studio is reserved for design students to do 3-D modeling, image processing, illustration, animation, and other creative digital work. It is open 110 hours per week, with support staff members always available.

The School of Design also has a shooting studio for photographing three-dimensional models and other subjects and a copy stand for photographing flat work. Darkrooms are available for developing, enlarging, and printing photographic images in black and white or color. These facilities are useful for documenting student projects as well as for producing original works.

The School of Design maintains five working flatbed proof presses and a collection of wood and cast type, representing all of the major type families. Students use these to explore uncommon aspects of type and print, including the activities of hand-setting type, preparing proof sheets and specimen sheets, and printing small-edition books and booklets.

Bookbinding facilities provide access to the necessary equipment for binding limited-edition books and booklets. During the academic year, design students often work with English students to produce limited-edition, hand-bound copies of student-authored literary works.

The Robert Smillie Digital Imaging Lab supports advanced teaching, research, and production with imaging technologies. The lab features eight Power Mac G5s, a 60-inch continuous-feed HP color printer, two smaller Epson printers, and assorted peripheral devices, including high-resolution scanners. The Robert Smillie Lab was made possible through a generous gift from Virginia Kaufman in honor of her friend, Pittsburgh designer Robert Smillie.

The Hunt Library houses the University's collections in humanities, fine arts, social sciences, and business. The University Libraries also house several unique collections, including the Posner Family Collection of rare books and artifacts, located in the Posner Center.

Financial Aid

All full-time graduate students are provided with $8000 per year as partial financial assistance in exchange for 6 hours of work per week as a teaching assistant, research assistant, or Web designer or in another position. Information about other potential sources of financial aid can be found on Carnegie Mellon's financial aid office Web site (http://www.cmu.edu/hub/fa/fa_grad.html).

Cost of Study

Tuition for the 2007–08 academic year was $31,500.

Living and Housing Costs

A wide range of affordable housing options are available close to the Carnegie Mellon campus. Housing costs in Pittsburgh are typically lower than those in other urban settings. Room and board for a single graduate student average around $5600 per semester. Carnegie Mellon does not provide housing for graduate students.

Student Group

There are currently 47 graduate students pursuing degree programs in the School of Design.

Student Outcomes

Recent graduates of the graduate programs of the Carnegie Mellon School of Design are shaping the future of interaction design around the world at companies large and small, such as Google, Microsoft, and Yahoo!; Intel, Motorola, Nokia, Philips Electronics, and Samsung; Meta Design, Method, and Smart Design; and the Mayo Clinic, as well as at universities around the world.

Location

Carnegie Mellon is located in Oakland, a cultural center of Pittsburgh, Pennsylvania, on a 90-acre campus adjacent to Schenley Park, the city's largest park. The campus is conveniently located for easy access to many cultural and sporting events and is only 4 miles from the downtown business and cultural district. Pittsburgh is the thirteenth-largest metropolitan area in the United States. The city has good public transportation, diverse cultural attractions, and three professional sports teams. New York City, Philadelphia, Toronto, and Washington, D.C., are all within driving distance. Many recreational facilities, including ski areas and state parks, are located nearby.

The University and The School

Carnegie Mellon was first established in 1900 as the Carnegie Technical School through a gift from Andrew Carnegie. In 1912, the name of the school was changed to Carnegie Institute of Technology. Mellon Institute, founded in 1913 by A. W. and R. B. Mellon, merged with Carnegie Institute of Technology in 1967 to become Carnegie Mellon University. The University has an enrollment of about 8,500, approximately 3,300 of whom are engaged in graduate study.

Applying

As part of the admissions process, all graduate applicants must submit a portfolio, representing the best of their academic and/or professional work. For information about the other materials required for applying to the graduate programs offered by the School of Design, as well as application deadlines, students should visit the School's Web site (http://www.design.cmu.edu/index.php).

Correspondence and Information

Anita Kulina Smith, Graduate Program Coordinator
School of Design, MMC 110
Carnegie Mellon University
5000 Forbes Avenue
Pittsburgh, Pennsylvania 15213

Phone: 412-268-6843
E-mail: grad-info@design.cmu.edu
Web site: http://www.design.cmu.edu/index.php

Carnegie Mellon University

THE FACULTY AND THEIR RESEARCH

Eric Anderson, Associate Professor; M.F.A., M.A. (design education), Ohio State. Eric Anderson teaches courses in industrial design, product design and development, and design drawing. His interests include interdisciplinary integrated product development, visualization within the context of design, and the emergence of "visual intelligence," the skill that allows designers to reason with complex information using varied tools and methods in order to shape environmental and behavioral conditions. Anderson's current research includes a grant to explore visualization across disciplines, with the goal of producing a digital tool that teaches novice designers and nondesigners ways to visualize effectively. In the community, he founded Design Camp, a weeklong summer experience for underserved African American boys. This experience introduces participants to design and new ways of thinking, understanding, creating, and communicating complex ideas. Anderson is also active in the Industrial Designers Society of America (IDSA), where he is the Executive Vice President. Prior to his teaching at Carnegie Mellon, Anderson founded To Envision, Inc., a design consultancy. (ea@andrew.cmu.edu; 412-268-3181)

Mark Baskinger, Assistant Professor, M.F.A. (industrial design), Illinois at Urbana-Champaign. Mark Baskinger teaches courses in design drawing and product design. His work spans graphic, product, interaction, and environmental design, with expertise in expressing information through product forms to make interaction understandable and intuitive. In addition, he has a deep interest in sculptural objects/functional art and centers much of his experimental work on issues of graphic impact and material permanence through physical form. Baskinger's research focuses on how products communicate through their form language, behavior, and context to inform interaction and shape user experience. His work has been featured in design publications and international magazines and has been exhibited in numerous galleries and museums, including the Museum of Modern Art (New York), I-Space Gallery (Chicago), the Krannert Museum (Champaign, Illinois), and the Regina Gouger Miller Gallery (Carnegie Mellon University). His work is also included in the permanent art collection of the University of Illinois. He has won numerous design awards from *International Design Magazine* (ID) and the Industrial Designers Society of America (IDEA) and holds multiple product patents. (baskinger@cmu.edu; 412-268-9843)

Dan Boyarski, Professor and Head, School of Design; M.F.A. (graphic design), Indiana; postgraduate studies (graphic design and film animation), Basel School of Design (Switzerland). Dan Boyarski teaches Graduate Studio I, Time Motion & Communication, and courses in typography. His interests lie in time-based communication, dynamic information design, interface design, and interaction design. Boyarski's long tenure at Carnegie Mellon has enabled him to collaborate in a wide variety of projects. He was recently a member of the Samsung Electronics Design Advisory Board, after working with Samsung as a project director in its Innovative Design Lab and on the New Interactions 2001 project, exploring modular television and 3G information devices. He explored possibilities for information design on the small screen in the DataViz Explorations project with Nortel Networks. Boyarski has served on several design juries and has given presentations around the world, including at the 2003 International Design Culture Conference at Seoul National University. He has curated and cocurated design exhibitions at the Hewlett and Miller Galleries at Carnegie Mellon. (boyarski@cmu.edu; 412-268-6842)

Charlee Brodsky, Professor of Photography; M.F.A., Yale. Charlee Brodsky is a fine arts and documentary photographer. Brodsky describes her work as dealing with human issues and beauty through everyday tales of life. One of Brodsky's current projects is on mental illness. Her work is being exhibited at mental health conferences and was published as a book entitled *Of Anguish, Compulsion, and the Blues* in spring 2008. Her book *Street*, with poet Jim Daniels, won the 2007 Tillie Olsen Award given by the Working Class Studies Association. In 2001, she and three others won an Emmy for their work on *Stephanie*, a video documentary about Stephanie Byram's life with breast cancer. Her photographs of Stephanie were also featured in the book *Knowing Stephanie*, which was one of the American Association of University Presses' outstanding illustrated books of 2004. With anthropologist Judith Modell Schacter, Brodsky explored Homestead, a former mill town. This work resulted in the book *A Town Without Steel, Envisioning Homestead*. (cb12@andrew.cmu.edu, 412-268-1232)

Richard Buchanan, Professor and Director of Doctoral Studies; Ph.D., Chicago. Richard Buchanan teaches design theory in the traditional areas of communication design and industrial design but also extends design thinking into new areas of application, such as interaction design and organization design. His work focuses on the rhetorical dimensions of design. He is an editor of *Design Issues*, an international journal of design history, theory, and criticism published by the MIT Press. He is also President of the Design Research Society, a multidisciplinary design research society based in the United Kingdom. Among his numerous publications are *Discovering Design: Explorations in Design Studies, The Idea of Design*, and *Pluralism in Theory and Practice*. (buchanan@andrew.cmu.edu; 412-268-1321)

Wayne Chung, Associate Professor; M.I.D., University of the Arts. Wayne Chung teaches ID Studio, Product and Systems, How Things are Made, and Applied Research Methods. Chung has been recognized by the *Design Intelligence Journal* as one of the "Most Admired Industrial Design Educators" in the U.S. He is interested in design research methods for collaboration and innovation, and his academic work investigates processes for managing design decisions through technology applications and applying people-centered research methods for appropriate solutions. Chung has worked and collaborated with a range of clients, industry sponsors, and partners, including Intel Digital Health, Apple Computer, Texas Instruments, Whirlpool Corporation, Rubbermaid, Evenflo Corporation, Procter & Gamble, and SonicRim. He also worked as a design information researcher for the Federal Highway Administration's Advanced Driver Interface Design and Assessment Project. (wcchung@andrew.cmu.edu; 412-268-3652)

Shelley Evenson, Associate Professor and Director of Graduate Studies; B.S. (industrial design/visual communications), Ohio State. Shelley Evenson teaches in the area of interaction and service design, including the courses Designing for Service, Introduction to Interaction & Visual Interface, and Graduate Design Studio. Evenson's work focuses on tapping into the needs of constituents, defining the best opportunities to respond to those needs, quickly prototyping the response, and iteratively reshaping it based on feedback. Her current interests include design languages and strategies, design prototyping, organizational interfaces, service design, and what lies beyond user-centered design. Prior to coming to Carnegie Mellon as a full-time faculty member, Evenson was cofounder of seeSpace and was Chief Experience Strategist for Scient. With more than twenty-five years' experience in multidisciplinary consulting practices, she has worked with clients such as Apple Computer, Bank of Montreal, CIBC, Kodak, Texas Instruments, Williamsburg Institute, and Xerox on a wide variety of design and development projects. (evenson@cmu.edu; 412-268-4638)

Jodi Forlizzi, Associate Professor, School of Design; Associate Professor, Human-Computer Interaction Institute; and A. Nico Habermann Chair in the School of Computer Science; M.Des. (interaction design), Ph.D. (design in human-computer interaction), Carnegie Mellon. Jodi Forlizzi teaches graduate-level courses in advanced interface and interaction design. She is interested in how people experience products, in order to develop a theory of experience as it relates to interaction design. She conducts research on how technology can bring people new kinds of experiences, beyond those traditionally associated with human-computer interaction. Forlizzi's research interests include assistive, social, and aesthetic technology products and systems and notification systems that range from ambient displays to avatars and embodied robots. Her current research projects include product ecology, designing for coexperience, What Is Design Research Within HCI?, The Project on People and Robots, The MOVE System: Maps Optimized for Vehicular Environments, ambient and peripheral displays, and When the Interface Is Your Face. (forlizzi@cs.cmu.edu; 412-268-4869)

Bruce Hanington, Associate Professor and Program Chair, Industrial Design; M.Env.Des. (industrial design), Calgary. Bruce Hanington teaches Design Studio I, How People Work, How People Work with Things, Research Methods for Human Centered Design, and The Meaning of Form, among other courses. His interests are in the personal, social, and cultural context of product design and interpretation. He is interested in human-centered product development, human factors, and research methods, with a focus on using ethnographic methods in design research. Hanington's recent projects include work with General Electric's appliance division designing human-centered appliances and research for Johnson & Johnson on design opportunities to enhance prescription skin-care compliance among teens. He has presented papers on human-centered design and design for human experience at the International Conference of the Design Research Society (DRS) and the International Conference on Design & Emotion. (hanington@cmu.edu; 412-268-1641)

Kristin Hughes, Associate Professor; M.F.A. (visual communication), Virginia Commonwealth. Kristin Hughes teaches a range of courses, including studios and typography. Recurring themes in her research and professional practice focus on utilizing design methods as a catalyst for community and civic engagement. She is currently looking at the design of products that allow participants agency over their own learning space. They are invited as cocreators in the design process, a process that they may eventually engage and sustain on their own. Most recently, this issue has led her to explore game design, examining learning processes and ways that play spaces provide a powerful platform for uninhibited learning. Hughes' most recent project, in collaboration with the University of Pittsburgh Medical Center, is Fitwits, a series of games designed to educate and encourage smart choices in nutrition, portion control, and physical activity. Other projects include Click! Urban Adventure, an interactive role-playing game designed to immerse middle school girls in discipline-specific science, technology, engineering, and mathematics activities. (kh@andrew.cmu.edu; 412-268-7098)

David S. Kaufer, Professor and Head of the English Department; Ph.D. (communication), Wisconsin. David Kaufer's interests are in qualitative and quantitative theories of rhetoric, writing, and written information. He is cochair of an interdisciplinary master's program between English and the School of Design in the College of Fine Arts, which dovetails with his interest in investigating rhetoric as an art of design. His research interests have led to theoretical (Kaufer & Butler, 1996) and more practical (Kaufer & Butler, 2000) books relating rhetoric and design. Kaufer's recent work has involved collaborating on software interfaces that allow researchers and students to analyze texts visually for their local patterns of rhetorical design. He is currently working on a book (with Suguru Ishizaki and Jeff Collins, along with Brian Butler) that associates multiword English patterns with rhetorical effects. This book explains the rhetorical/language theory behind the visualization software. He is developing new courses in rhetorical analysis and World Englishes. (kaufer+@andrew.cmu.edu; 412-268-2850)

Mark Mentzer, Professor and Associate Head of the School of Design; B.F.A. (art), Carnegie Mellon. Mark Mentzer teaches foundation design, including Design Drawing I, Design Drawing II, and Color and Communication. He also has a specialization in design drawing and design in public places. Mentzer is an active artist and has exhibited in some thirty-five group and one-person shows nationally, receiving numerous awards for his work. He has created at least one original drawing each day for more than sixteen years and has cataloged more than 6,000 of his drawings. (mentzer@andrew.cmu.edu; 412-268-6840)

Thomas Merriman, Teaching Professor; B.F.A. (sculpture), Carnegie Mellon. Thomas Merriman teaches courses in furniture design, form generation, and prototyping. His primary interest is in the process of reconciling design intent with the constraints of materials and process in the generation of form. As a Research Fellow in the STUDIO for Creative Inquiry, Merriman, in collaboration with his wife, Constance, studies the role of the natural world in urban environments and the role of humans in the natural world. Current projects with the STUDIO include Community Forest, an inquiry into the role of woodlands as community and cultural assets, and Save Hays Woods, a campaign to prevent the development of 635 acres of mature forest located in Pittsburgh, just 3 miles from the city center. Merriman also collaborates with faculty members from the School of Psychology at New York University to develop methods and instrumentation for studying motor skill development in infants. (merriman@andrew.cmu.edu; 412-268-2253)

Stacie Rohrbach, Assistant Professor; M.G.D., North Carolina State. Stacie Rohrbach teaches studio- and seminar-based design courses, including Design Studio I; Basic, Intermediate, and Graduate Typography; Senior Studio; Understanding Perception in Design; and Graduate Design Fundamentals. She is interested in the way people perceive and process information and how their ability to learn may be improved by using visuals, sound, and motion to translate complex, abstract information into concrete experiential forms. Rohrbach is also currently exploring the relationships that exist between print and dynamic mediums and the methodologies educators use to teach visual communication. Her areas of research interest include dynamic information design, the bearing of cognition on design, the correlation of print and dynamic media, and the methodologies used to teach visual communication. Rohrbach's current projects include two collaborative projects with English professor Suguru Ishizaki. Together, they are investigating and documenting the methodologies that educators use to teach visual communication. Rohrbach is also exploring how visuals, sound, and motion can enhance course syllabi to help students make connections within and among courses. (stacie@cmu.edu; 412-268-4281)

Stephen Stadelmeier, Associate Professor; M.S. (design and environmental analysis), Cornell. Stephen Stadelmeier teaches courses in product design. His interests include group problem formulation and working strategies and personal mobility, especially issues of autonomy related to disabled mobility. Stadelmeier is currently involved in a project on dynamic wheelchair seating in conjunction with Falcon Industries and the University of Pittsburgh and funded by a National Institutes of Health Small Business Innovative Research Award. He has consulted on group decisions and problem formulation with Boeing Commercial Aviation, Johnson & Johnson Consumer Products Worldwide, and Air Products & Chemical, Inc. He has more than thirty-five years of private and group consulting experience. (ss1u@andrew.cmu.edu; 412-268-6952)

Robert Swinehart, Professor; M.F.A., Northern Illinois. Robert Swinehart teaches courses in communication design, such as Type and the Package; Marks, Signs and Communications; and Branding and Identity. Swinehart's work has been exhibited in major shows in the United States, Eastern Europe, and Japan and is included in the permanent collection of the U.S. Library of Congress. He is Vice President of the International Institute of Information Design, a lifetime honorary member of the American Center for Design, a past President of the Graphic Design Education Association, and a past member of the national board of the American Institute of Graphic Arts. (ros@andrew.cmu.edu; 412-268-2825)

Dylan Vitone, Assistant Professor; M.F.A. (photography), Massachusetts College of Art. Dylan Vitone teaches Digital Photographic Imaging, Introduction to Photographic Design, Photo Documentation, special projects courses in communication design, and interdisciplinary courses within Carnegie Mellon's College of Fine Arts on topics in photography. With his interest in documentary photography, Vitone seeks out communities that are undergoing complex social changes, presenting wide-format panoramic photographic collages (http://www.dylanvitone.com/pittsburgh/index.html). His photographic works are in the permanent collections of the Smithsonian Institution, the George Eastman House, the Museum of Contemporary Photography, the Portland Art Museum, and other museums. His works have been on special exhibit at many institutions, including the Haas Gallery of Art, the Santa Fe Center for Photography, the Andy Warhol Museum, the Huntington Gallery, and the Photographic Resource Center. (dylanv@andrew.cmu.edu; 412-268-3220)

John Zimmerman, Assistant Professor, School of Design, and Assistant Professor, Human-Computer Interaction Institute; M.Des. (interaction design), Carnegie Mellon. John Zimmerman teaches interaction design, training students to translate the needs and desires of people into products and services, with a heavy focus on invention. In addition, he sometimes teaches human-computer interaction (HCI) methods, including formal methods for requirements gathering and usability testing. His research focuses on how people interact with intelligent systems, looking at both how families control smart homes and how workers engage with intelligent productivity software. He is also exploring how interaction design research can produce knowledge that has impact in the HCI research community. Before joining Carnegie Mellon University, Zimmerman was a senior researcher at Philips Research, where he designed interactive television products and intelligent devices for the home consumer market. (johnz@cs.cmu.edu; 412-268-1313)

FASHION INSTITUTE OF TECHNOLOGY

State University of New York

School of Graduate Studies

Programs of Study

The Fashion Institute of Technology (FIT), a State University of New York (SUNY) college of art and design, business, and technology, is home to a rich mix of innovative achievers, creative thinkers, and industry pioneers. FIT fosters interdisciplinary initiatives, advances study and research, and provides access to an international network of professionals. It offers six programs of graduate study leading to the Master of Arts (M.A.) and Master of Professional Studies (M.P.S.) degrees. The programs in Art Market: Principles and Practices; Exhibition Design; Fashion and Textile Studies: History, Theory, Museum Practice; and Illustration lead to the M.A. degree. The M.P.S. degree programs are Cosmetics and Fragrance Marketing and Management and Global Fashion Management. The School of Graduate Studies is also home to the Center for Executive Education, which offers advanced management programs for senior management in fashion retailing, marketing, or manufacturing.

Art Market: Principles and Practices is a 48-credit, full- or part-time M.A. program preparing students for careers in the business, collection, and exhibition of art. The curriculum includes art history, writing for the art market, gallery design and operation, business practices, computer technology for the art world, marketing, valuation and appraisal, exhibition theory, and art law and professional ethics. Students in the program are required to complete a relevant internship and to research and write a master's qualifying paper. Graduating students must also complete a practicum in which they assemble a group show from concept to execution at a New York City gallery. Their spring 2008 show, *Locus*, explored the way in which people personally, socially, and physically situate themselves and included painting, performance pieces, photography, sculpture, and video.

Cosmetics and Fragrance Marketing and Management is a 36-credit, part-time M.P.S. program providing industry professionals with high-level management skills and an interdisciplinary, global perspective. The curriculum is designed to encompass three skill sets that leaders in the cosmetics and fragrance industries have identified as crucial to managerial success: core business skills such as management, corporate finance, international business, and management communication; marketing skills such as advanced marketing theory, marketing communications, and market research and strategy; and technical and creative competencies such as cosmetics and fragrance product knowledge, retail and creative management, and an intellectual foundation in beauty and fashion culture. A global component sends students abroad for an intensive week of meetings with industry leaders in major overseas markets. The program culminates in a capstone seminar, in which student teams undertake marketing and management challenges reflecting current business trends and practices and present their solutions to a panel of faculty and industry experts.

The 36-credit, full-time Exhibition Design M.A. program prepares students for careers in the exhibition design and visual display production industry. The studio-driven, one-year course of study focuses on the designer's role within the exhibition team, with emphasis on the development of both design and fabrication skills. Studio projects—such as museum and gallery design, traveling exhibits, and corporate collections—are linked to graphic, lighting, and presentation courses. All graduating students complete an independent, theme-driven design project. Students are also required to complete a related internship.

The 48-credit, full- or part-time Fashion and Textile Studies: History, Theory, Museum Practice M.A. program prepares students for professional curatorial, conservation, education, and other scholarly careers that focus on historic clothing, accessories, textiles, and related materials. The curriculum incorporates conservation skills, current collections management methods, exhibition techniques, art historical methodologies, material culture studies, and gender studies and utilizes the resources of The Museum at FIT, one of the world's largest collections of clothing, textiles, and accessories. Students may elect either a conservation or curatorial emphasis; they may also select up to two independent study courses with an appropriate focus on their chosen specialization. All students are required to complete an internship in the field, write a master's qualifying paper based on original research, and take an active role in a yearlong course culminating in a professional exhibition. Their spring 2008 exhibition, *Sole Desire: The Shoes of Christian Louboutin*, examined the works of the celebrated shoe designer.

Global Fashion Management is a 36-credit, full-time M.P.S. program offered in collaboration with Hong Kong Polytechnic University in Hong Kong and the Institut Français de la Mode in Paris, preparing current fashion executives for senior managerial positions. The course of study is completed in a three-semester period and includes one intensive seminar course taught in each of the three participating institutions. The curriculum includes courses in production management and the supply chain, global marketing and fashion brand management, current technologies in the fashion industry, international team management, international culture and business, challenges to profitability, and politics and world trade.

The 37-credit, part-time, evening and weekend Illustration M.A. program is designed for working professionals seeking advanced study to further develop their skills as master illustrators. The program focuses on high-level techniques, new media applications, and illustration business practices. The curriculum encompasses digital and traditional studio methods, entrepreneurial research and writing, and opportunities in new and emerging markets. A faculty of noted, active professionals; assignments mirroring marketplace demands and specifications; and regular guest lecturers and off-campus visits maximize student exposure to New York City's art and design world. Students complete a capstone project and an independently researched and written master's thesis.

Research Facilities

The School of Graduate Studies is primarily located in the campus's Shirley Goodman Resource Center, which also houses the Gladys Marcus Library and The Museum at FIT. School of Graduate Studies facilities include conference rooms; a fully equipped conservation laboratory; a multipurpose laboratory for conservation projects and the dressing of mannequins; specialized storage facilities for costume and textile materials; a graduate student lounge with computer and printer access; a graduate student library reading room with computers, reference materials, and copies of past classes' qualifying and thesis papers; specialized wireless classrooms; and classrooms equipped with model stands, easels, and drafting tables.

The Gladys Marcus Library houses a collection of print, nonprint, multimedia, and digital resources comprising more than 300,000 volumes. Specialized holdings include industry reference materials, manufacturers' catalogues, original fashion sketches and scrapbooks, portfolios of plates, photographs, and sample books. The FIT Digital Library provides access to over 60 searchable online databases, including journals, images, books, and research reports.

The Museum at FIT houses one of the world's most important collections of clothing and textiles and is the only museum in New York City dedicated primarily to the art of fashion. The permanent collection encompasses more than 50,000 garments and accessories dating from the eighteenth century, with particular strength in twentieth-century fashion, as well as 30,000 textiles, 300,000 textile swatches, and 1,500 sample books. Award-winning exhibitions, lectures, and symposia inform and inspire nearly 100,000 visitors each year. Recent exhibitions include *Arbiters of Style: Women at the Forefront of Fashion, Exoticism,* and *Gothic: Dark Glamour.*

Financial Aid

FIT directly administers its institutional grants and scholarships. Federal funding administered by the college may include Federal Supplemental Educational Opportunity Grants, Federal Perkins Loans, federally subsidized and unsubsidized loans for students and parents, and the Federal Work-Study Program. New York State residents who meet state guidelines for eligibility may also receive Educational Opportunity Program funds. Priority for institutionally administered funds is given to students enrolled and designated as full-time.

Cost of Study

Tuition for New York State residents is $3623 per semester, or $302 per credit. Out-of-state residents' tuition is $5733 per semester, or $478 per credit. Tuition and fees are subject to change at the discretion of FIT's Board of Trustees. Additional expenses—for class materials, textbooks, and travel—may apply and vary per program.

Living and Housing Costs

Residence facilities are available to graduate students. Traditional residence hall accommodations (including meal plan) cost from $5220 to $5370 per semester. Apartment-style housing options (not including meal plan) cost from $4260 to $7935 per semester.

Student Group

Enrollment in the School of Graduate Studies is approximately 200 students per academic year, providing considerable individualized advisement. Students come to FIT from throughout the country and around the world.

Student Outcomes

Art Market: Principles and Practices graduates find employment as art gallery directors, public art program directors, art consultants for private and corporate collections, art foundation administrators, museum marketing and development directors, independent curators, auction house department heads, and artists' representatives. Students in the Cosmetics and Fragrance Marketing and Management and Global Fashion Management programs maintain full-time employment in the industry while working toward their degree, which provides the basis for advancement to positions of upper-level management responsibility. Graduates of the Exhibition Design program find employment with architectural and exhibition design firms, museums, historic trusts, and special-events companies. Graduates of the Fashion and Textile Studies: History, Theory, Museum Practice program find positions as museum curators, research specialists, collections managers and registrars, historic house directors, museum educators, independent exhibition curators, corporate curators, fashion and textile historians, costume and textile conservators, auction house department specialists and researchers, vintage clothing and textile dealers, and consultants. Students in the Illustration program graduate with the skills needed to succeed as freelance and in-house illustrators for advertising agencies, design firms, magazines, online media, and publishing houses.

Location

FIT is connected to New York City, to students, and to careers. Located in Manhattan's Chelsea neighborhood, it places students at the heart of the fashion, advertising, visual arts, design, business, and communications industries. Students gain unparalleled exposure to their field through guest lectures, field trips, internships, and sponsored competitions. Dining, entertainment, and shopping options are within walking distance, and the campus's location provides convenient access to major museums, galleries, and auction houses located throughout the city. Located near the hub of New York City's public transportation system, the college is easily accessible by subway, bus, and commuter rail lines.

Applying

Applicants to all School of Graduate Studies programs must hold a baccalaureate degree in an appropriate major from an accredited college or university, with a cumulative GPA of 3.0 or higher. International students from non-English-speaking countries are required to submit minimum TOEFL scores of 550 on the written test, 213 on the computer test, or 79 on the Internet test. Students applying to the Art Market: Principles and Practices; Fashion and Textile Studies: History, Theory, Museum Practice; and Global Fashion Management programs must submit GRE scores. Each major has additional, specialized prerequisites for admission; for detailed information, students should visit the School of Graduate Studies on FIT's Web site.

Domestic and international students use the same application when seeking admission. The deadline for completed applications with transcripts and supplemental materials is February 15 for Art Market: Principles and Practices; Exhibition Design; Fashion and Textile Studies: History, Theory, Museum Practice; Illustration; and Global Fashion Management. The deadline for Cosmetics and Fragrance Marketing and Management is March 15. After the deadline dates, applicants are considered on a rolling admissions basis. Interested candidates may apply online at http://www.fitnyc.edu/gradstudies.

Correspondence and Information

Dr. Steven Zucker, Dean
School of Graduate Studies
Room E315
Fashion Institute of Technology
Seventh Avenue at 27th Street
New York, New York 10001-5992

Phone: 212-217-4300
Fax: 212-217-4301
E-mail: gradinfo@fitnyc.edu
Web site: http://www.fitnyc.edu/gradstudies

Fashion Institute of Technology

THE FACULTY

Dean
Steven Zucker, Ph.D., CUNY Graduate Center.

Art Market: Principles and Practices
Katherine Jánszky Michaelsen, Associate Chairperson; Ph.D., Columbia.
Catherine Hannah Behrend, M.A., M.B.A., NYU; Certificate in Executive Education, INSEAD (France).
Ágnes Berecz, Ph.D., Paris (Sorbonne).
Eric Feinblatt, B.A., SUNY Empire State College.
Christine Helm, M.A., M.Ed., Columbia Teachers College.
John Lee, A.B., Vassar.
Sheri L. Pasquarella, Stony Brook, SUNY, and Columbia (Reid Hall).
Rose Polidoro, B.S., New Haven.
Lucille A. Roussin, Ph.D., Columbia; J.D., Yeshiva.
Martha Schwendener, M.A., Texas at Austin.
Beth Miller Servetar, M.F.A., Bennington.
Gayle M. Skluzacek, B.A., Barat.
Steven Zucker, Ph.D., CUNY Graduate Center.

Cosmetics and Fragrance Marketing and Management
Stephen Kanlian, Associate Chairperson; M.A., Durham (England); M.P.A., Pennsylvania.
Bruce Abramson, M.P.S., Fashion Institute of Technology; M.B.A., Fordham.
Jean Broom, M.S.W., Minnesota; M.M., Northwestern.
Dorothy C. Foster, J.D., Fordham.
Kenneth Freeman, M.B.A., Harvard.
Judy Galloway, A.B., Mary Baldwin.
Bradley Horowitz, M.B.A., Fordham.
Guillermo Jimenez, J.D., Berkeley.
Janice Levine, M.P.S., Fashion Institute of Technology.
Mary C. Manning, Institute of Marketing (England) and Kingston Upon Thames (England).
Mark Polson, M.P.S., Fashion Institute of Technology.
Cynthia Strite, Ph.D. candidate, Columbia Teachers College.
Mary Tumolo, former Vice President, Promotional Marketing, Lancôme, L'Oreal USA.
Pamela Vaile, M.B.A., Pace.
Karen Young, B.A., Denver.

Exhibition Design
Brenda Cowan, Associate Chairperson; M.S.Ed., Bank Street College of Education.
Norman Bleckner, B.I.D., Pratt.
Robin Drake, B.S., Pratt.
John Katimaris, M.F.A., Parsons; RA, AIA, IES, IIDA.
Lucian J. Leone, B.I.D., Pratt.
Ran Lerner, M.I.D., Domus Academy (Italy).
Scott Lundberg, M.I.D., Pratt.
Karl Matsuda, Certificate in Art, Cooper Union.
John Newman, M.A., Parsons; IES.
Michael Stiller, B.A., Bard.
Michele Y. T. Washington, M.S., Pratt.

Fashion and Textile Studies: History, Theory, Museum Practice
Denyse Montegut, Associate Chairperson; Ph.D. candidate, Delaware.
June Burns Bové, M.A., NYU.
Maria Ann Conelli, Ph.D., Columbia.
Nancy Deihl, M.A., NYU.
Marlene Eidelheit, M.A., Fashion Institute of Technology.
Judith Eisenberg, M.A., Wichita State.
Lourdes M. Font, Ph.D., NYU.
Joanne Dolan Ingersoll, M.A., Fashion Institute of Technology.
Désirée Koslin, M.F.A., CUNY, City College; Ph.D., NYU.
Diane Maglio, M.A., Fashion Institute of Technology.
Patricia E. Mears, M.A., Fashion Institute of Technology.
Maya Naunton, M.A. candidate, Conservation Certificate, NYU.
Denise Stone, M.A., Fashion Institute of Technology.

Global Fashion Management
Pamela Ellsworth, Associate Chairperson; M.P.S., Fashion Institute of Technology.
Praveen K. Chaudhry, Ph.D., Philadelphia University.
Thomas Claire, M.A., Brown; M.B.A., Columbia.
Virginia Cutchin, M.B.A., CUNY, Baruch.
Naomi Daremblum, Ph.D., NYU.
Kenneth Freeman, M.B.A., Harvard.
Guillermo Jimenez, J.D., Berkeley.
John Mincarelli, M.A., NYU.
Jeanette Nostra, B.S., Goddard.
Christine S. Pomeranz, M.B.A., NYU.

Illustration
Melanie Reim, Associate Chairperson; M.F.A., Syracuse.
Salvatore Catalano, B.A., SUNY Empire State College.
Vincent DiFate, M.A., Syracuse.
Dennis Dittrich, M.F.A., Syracuse.
Michael Hyde, M.F.A., Columbia; Ph.D., NYU.
Amy Lemmon, Ph.D., Cincinnati.
William Low, M.A., Syracuse.
Daniel Pelavin, M.F.A., Cranbrook Academy of Art.
Cheryl Phelps, B.F.A., Memphis College of Art.
Stanley Solomon, Ph.D., NYU.
Ed Soyka, B.F.A., Regents.
Nancy Stahl, Arizona.
Murray Tinkelman, Cooper Union.

The faculty members listed above constitute a partial listing. Guest lecturers are not included.

IIT Institute of Design

ILLINOIS INSTITUTE OF TECHNOLOGY

Institute of Design

Programs of Study

Founded in 1937 as the New Bauhaus, the Institute of Design (ID) at Illinois Institute of Technology (IIT) is distinguished by its insistence on user-centeredness; its development of rigorous, verifiable methods; and its emphasis on placing design at the center of the development process. ID is one of the few graduate programs in design that welcomes applicants with no prior design experience. Going beyond the traditional role of design as styling or execution of an existing idea, ID's mission is to develop, teach, and promote design methods that lead to more humane technology by helping innovation professionals better decide what to make. ID's methods are about understanding user needs as a platform for creating new offerings that bring meaningful value to people and businesses. They are about using design to reframe problems in unique ways, make sense of complex information, explore alternatives quickly and effectively, and visualize and communicate compelling solutions. As a result of their training, ID graduates are recognized worldwide as highly skilled leaders for creative teams of many kinds, with the tools to discover and solve a wide range of problems and deliver breakthrough innovations.

ID offers four programs of study. The Master of Design (M.Des.) degree is for those who wish to achieve mastery in the application of advanced design theories and processes. This two-year, full-time, 54-credit-hour program offers a variety of options for concentration in areas such as communication design, product and environment design, interaction, complex systems, strategic design planning, visualization, and user-centered research. In addition to experienced designers, students may enter this program with no formal design training by completing a one-year foundation program of introductory courses providing prerequisite skills and experience.

The Master of Design/Master of Business Administration (M.Des./M.B.A.) dual-degree program is offered jointly with the IIT Stuart School of Business. It provides a way to attain both degrees in a shortened period of time. Experienced designers can complete both degrees in two years plus one quarter of full-time study, including summer sessions. Students without design training who take the foundation sequence can complete both degrees in three years plus one quarter.

The Master of Design Methods (M.D.M.) is a two-semester (or a part-time four- or six-semester) professional master's degree for exceptional midcareer designers, managers, engineers, and other leaders of innovation, focusing exclusively on advanced methods and frameworks for leading innovation and strategy teams. It concentrates on the design theories and methods developed and taught at the Institute of Design, in areas such as user observation and research, prototyping, interaction design, visualization, and strategic design planning. The M.D.M. is open to both designers and nondesigners, provided they have demonstrated leadership experience.

The Doctor of Philosophy (Ph.D.) degree is for those who wish to conduct fundamental research to extend the body of knowledge about design theory and process. The Ph.D. program requires a minimum of 84 credit hours beyond the master's degree. A master's degree in design is prerequisite to enrollment in the Ph.D. program. For those without a design degree, the master's degree can be obtained at ID before admission to the Ph.D. program.

Research Facilities

Research at the Institute of Design is supported by a networked computing system that enables students to digitize and manipulate photographic images, analyze problems, model forms, create interactive multimedia and individualized publications, and develop new systems and tools. Equipment includes Silicon Graphics, Sun, and Apple computers and a wide range of peripherals.

Financial Aid

Limited graduate fellowships are available on a competitive basis. International students frequently obtain special scholarships from their governments or from international sources, e.g., Fulbright, LASPAU for South America, INLAKS Foundation UK for India, and others.

Cost of Study

The M.Des. and Ph.D. programs are full-time only. Graduate tuition in these programs for 2007–08 was $32,400 per academic year. The M.D.M. program may be completed on a part-time basis; the total tuition for the M.D.M. was $38,500 for the 30-credit-hour program or $1100 per credit. The thesis fee for the Ph.D. was $150. Books and studio materials cost approximately $800 per semester. Mandatory health insurance costs approximately $900 per year.

Living and Housing Costs

Rooms in Graduate Hall (based on double occupancy) range from $5566 to $6632 per year. There are also 356 apartments in four high-rise apartment buildings on the campus. Units range from efficiencies to three bedrooms, and rents, including all utilities except telephone and cable television, range from $579 to $1145 per month. Various meal plans are available at additional costs. Most students live off campus, as ID is located in downtown Chicago. Prospective students should contact Graduate Admissions by e-mail for more details.

Student Group

The Institute of Design is a focused community of very creative and highly motivated students. Graduate enrollment is about 150 students. Typically, half of the graduate students have been professional designers and half come from other disciplines. About 60 percent are from the United States, and the rest are from countries in the Americas, Europe, and Asia. Fifty percent are women.

Student Outcomes

Graduates typically work in design and planning consultancies such as Cheskin, Design Continuum, Doblin, IDEO, Smart Design, and Sapient or in corporations such as Hewlett-Packard, Microsoft, Motorola, Pitney Bowes, Philips, Sony, Steelcase, and Whirlpool.

Location

Chicago, one of the world's largest cities, has more than 7 million people in its metropolitan area. Located on the western shores of Lake Michigan, it is an international center of business, one of the world's largest inland ports, and an air and rail transportation hub. Chicago offers students an exceptional variety of educational, cultural, and recreational opportunities. The city is known for its architecture, sports teams, music and comedy clubs, museums, and symphony orchestra.

The Institute

Since its founding, the Institute of Design has attracted students and faculty members from around the world—people who have eagerly experimented with new media and have developed important new processes, concepts, and theories. Laszlo Moholy-Nagy, a master of the influential German Bauhaus school of design, brought Bauhaus principles to Chicago in 1937 and founded the New Bauhaus, which was later renamed the Institute of Design. In 1949, the school merged with Illinois Institute of Technology. IIT offers programs in engineering and science, architecture, business, technical communication, psychology, and law.

Applying

Students may be admitted to graduate study at the beginning of the regular semester, either fall or spring. Completed applications and supporting documents should be received by February 15 for fall enrollment or September 15 for spring enrollment. Under no circumstances are international applications considered after the stated deadlines. Applications for graduate fellowships should be submitted at the time of application for admission.

Applicants must hold a baccalaureate degree from an accredited educational institution. A portfolio is required of all applicants with a background in design or the visual arts. Regardless of previous degrees, students may be required to complete some prerequisite design courses before beginning their degree requirements. Applicants without design degrees are encouraged to apply. They are first required to complete a sequence of prerequisite courses and other appropriate background work, which normally takes two additional semesters.

Applicants with undergraduate degrees in disciplines other than design, all applicants to the Ph.D. program, and international applicants must submit GRE scores. Applicants from non-English-speaking countries must submit TOEFL scores, unless a college-level degree has been obtained from a U.S. institution prior to admission to ID.

Correspondence and Information

Graduate Admissions
Institute of Design
Illinois Institute of Technology
350 North LaSalle Street
Chicago, Illinois 60610-4726

Phone: 312-595-4900
Fax: 312-595-4901
E-mail: design@id.iit.edu
Web site: http://www.id.iit.edu

Illinois Institute of Technology

THE FACULTY

Jeremy Alexis, Assistant Professor; M.Des., IIT.
Chris Conley, Associate Professor and Head of Product Design; M.S.Des., IIT.
Dale Fahnstrom, Professor; M.F.A., Illinois.
Judith Gregory, Assistant Professor; Ph.D., California, San Diego.
John Grimes, Professor and Associate Director; M.S., IIT.
Vijay Kumar, Associate Professor; M.S., IIT.
Charles Owen, Distinguished Professor; M.S., IIT.
Greg Prygrocki, Associate Professor; M.V.A., Alberta.
Keiichi Sato, Professor; M.S., Osaka Institute of Technology (Japan); M.S., IIT.
Patrick Whitney, Steelcase/Robert C. Pew Professor and Director; M.F.A., Cranbrook Academy of Art.

Adjunct Faculty
Ken Douros, Program Manager, Human Interface Lab, Motorola, Schaumberg, Illinois.
Kim Erwin, Designer and Writer, Chicago.
Ronald Gordon, Ron Gordon Photographic Services, Chicago.
Tomoko Ichikawa, Information Designer, Doblin, Chicago.
Gitte Jansdatter, Designer, IDEO, Chicago.
Mark Jones, Designer, IDEO, Chicago.
JoEllen Kames, UI Manager, Motorola, Chicago.
Larry Keeley, President, Doblin, Chicago.
John Paul Kusz, IIT Stuart School of Business, Chicago.
Peter Laundy, Brand Strategist, Doblin, Chicago.
Tina Leto, Photographer, Chicago.
Aaron Marcus, President, Aaron Marcus and Associates, Berkeley.
Mathew Mayfield, Strategic Marketing, Motorola, Chicago.
Todd McCullough, Managing Director, Doblin, Chicago.
Tim McKeown, 3GSM Design Lead, Motorola, Chicago.
Brad Nemer, Asia Pacific 3G Portfolio Manager, Motorola, Chicago.
Peter Pfanner, Director, Global Design Integration, Motorola, Chicago.
Ryan Powell, Interaction Design Lead, Motorola, Chicago.
Russ Rosenzweig, CEO, Round Table Group, Chicago.
Scott Ternovits, B.S.Des., IIT; Principal, Gravity Tank, Chicago.
Bill Verplank, Ph.D., Stanford.
Denis Weil, Senior Director, Innovation Planning and Advanced Concepts, McDonald's Corporation, Chicago.

LONG ISLAND UNIVERSITY, BROOKLYN CAMPUS

Graduate Program in Media Arts

Program of Study

The Master of Arts in Media Arts Program blends traditional art theory, methods, and production with the technology of today's emerging new media. It is an interdisciplinary program whose goal is to build new bridges of understanding between media concepts and skills application and between media arts and other fields of study. The faculty of accomplished designers, producers, media experts, and award-winning artists offers students a high level of personalized academic instruction, guidance, and counseling. Students can choose a general program of study, or they can track in the following areas of concentration: business of media arts (independent producing, entrepreneurship, media management), computer graphics imaging (print, animation, interactive), digital audio (radio, music production, sound design), film and television studies (visual culture, history, aesthetics, theory), on-camera performance (acting, directing), photography (traditional, digital), screenwriting (television, cinema), and television and film production (digital video, directing, editing).

The degree requires that students complete 36 credits. After completing 6 credits of foundation theory courses, students can design their own course of study, according to their own interests and abilities. This includes an additional 3 credits of theory elective, 6 credits of general electives (in either production or theory), 15 credits of production courses, and 6 credits of an Integrated Thesis Project—a combination of production and theory.

At the advanced level, students may work individually but are encouraged to work within a creative, collaborative team, since this model is typical of most media workplaces today. Production is always informed by critical analysis of aesthetics as well as cultural and social issues.

Research Facilities

Facilities used by students in the program include a customized television studio, digital video and editing labs, advanced darkrooms, digital photography labs, digital audio studios, the Spike Lee Screening Room—a theater-sized video and film screening room, computer graphic labs, and a media library. The University's 2.3-million-volume library system includes extensive state-of-the-art academic and administrative computing facilities. The Brooklyn Campus Library is located on the third, fourth, and fifth floors of the Library Learning Center and houses 266,000 volumes, 2,000 journal titles, more than 6,000 videos, and other media, such as audiocassettes, compact discs, and computer software on diskette.

Financial Aid

Fellowships, assistantships, and scholarships are financed by the University, federal and state government agencies, and private corporations. Teaching fellowships consist of tuition remission and a stipend in exchange for 3 to 9 hours of teaching per week. Graduate assistants work for 10 to 20 hours per week in return for partial tuition remission. New York State residents are eligible for Tuition Assistance Program (TAP) awards of a maximum of $550 per year. Students may also be eligible for Guaranteed Student Loans of $8500 per year or up to $18,500 per year, totaling $138,500 in the aggregate when combined with their undergraduate Guaranteed Student Loans.

Cost of Study

Graduate student tuition for fall 2008 is $877 per credit, and fees range from $55 to $500.

Living and Housing Costs

The average cost of housing for graduate students is $4000 per semester.

Student Group

Students come from across the nation and around the world to participate in a program that prepares them to begin a career in broadcasting, communications, new media, and a host of other media-related fields. The student body reflects the diversity of its surrounding areas.

Student Outcomes

Graduates of the program go on to work in a variety of occupations within the entertainment and media industries, including photographer, animator, audio engineer, music producer, television technician, desktop publisher, film and video producer and director, and broadcast news personnel. They are prepared to bring their energy and talents to major companies and productions all over the country.

Location

The Brooklyn Campus, across from MetroTech, is within walking distance of the Brooklyn Bridge and includes the historic former Brooklyn Paramount Theatre. It is also part of the new Media Zone initiative surrounding the building of the largest sound studio complex east of Los Angeles (Steiner Studios) at the nearby Brooklyn Navy Yard. The campus is near most subway lines (2, 3, 4, 5, D, R, N, Q, A, B, C, M, F, and G) for convenient access to New York City.

The University

Long Island University was chartered in 1926 in Brooklyn and has evolved into one of the largest private universities in the nation, with nearly 29,000 students and more than 650 full-time faculty members. There are residential campuses in Brooklyn, Brookville, and Long Island's East End as well as regional campuses and centers worldwide. The Brooklyn Campus, which offers more than 600 undergraduate, graduate, certificate, and doctoral degree programs, is the home of a bookstore, the 320-seat Kumble Theater, and a $45-million athletics, recreation, and wellness center.

Applying

Applicants must file the application and supporting credentials no later than one month before the opening of the semester in which they expect to enroll. Applications should include the following: a completed and signed application; official transcripts from all undergraduate and graduate institutions attended; a nonrefundable check or money order for $30, made payable to Long Island University; and any additional requirements needed for the program of study.

Correspondence and Information

Media Arts Graduate Program Coordinator
Long Island University, Brooklyn Campus
1 University Plaza
Brooklyn, New York 11201-8423
Phone: 718-488-1052 or 1345
Fax: 718-780-4518
Web site: http://www.brooklyn.liunet.edu/cwis/bklyn/depts/mediarts/mediaarts.htm

Long Island University, Brooklyn Campus

THE FACULTY AND THEIR RESEARCH

In addition to the faculty members listed here, a large number of adjunct faculty members and visiting lecturers are drawn from professional media industries in New York.

Larry L. Banks, Assistant Professor and Department Chair. Cinematography and digital video production.
Audrey Bernstein, Associate Professor. Traditional and digital photography.
Dennis Broe, Assistant Professor. Film and television history studies, media theory.
Stuart Fishelson, Professor. Traditional and digital photography.
Claire Goodman, Associate Professor. Aesthetics, visual culture, screenwriting.
Ricardo Gutierrez, Assistant Professor. Web design and interactive.
Kevin Lauth, Professor. Multicamera studio production and digital video production.
Marjan Moghaddam, Associate Professor. Digital design and animation.
Maureen Nappi, Assistant Professor. Media theory, computer graphics.

Miami International University of Art & Design™

MIAMI INTERNATIONAL UNIVERSITY OF ART & DESIGN

Master's Programs

Programs of Study

Miami International University of Art & Design offers Master of Fine Arts degrees in computer animation, film, graphic design, interior design, and visual arts.

Many of the programs require students to take a course in teaching methodologies, enabling them to learn the language of the industry. In addition, students discover techniques that help them to communicate within an area of expertise. Aesthetics, planning, research, and writing are also important elements in rounding out the educational experience.

Most degrees require six quarters of study, for a total of 90 credits. Course work varies by program, and the detailed curriculum may be viewed online at http://www.artinstitutes.edu/miami.

Master of Fine Arts degrees may be obtained online through the school.

Research Facilities

Miami International University of Art & Design is located within a 60,000-square-foot academic and administration building. The facility includes industry-related equipment, a painting and sculpture studio, a production facility, and an editing facility. There are also interior design and fashion resource rooms.

Financial Aid

Financial aid is available to those who qualify. Students who require financial assistance to attend Miami International University of Art & Design must first submit a Free Application for Federal Student Aid (FAFSA) and then meet with a financial aid officer to determine the amount of aid needed and the types of aid available. Aid comes in the form of Federal Pell Grants, Federal Supplemental Educational Opportunity Grants (FSEOG), Florida Postsecondary Student Assistance Grants, and Florida Bright Futures Scholarships. Federal Perkins Loans, Federal PLUS Program awards, and Federal Stafford Student Loans may also be an option for students. Part-time employment is available, or students may apply for a number of scholarships, including those offered to international students. Scholarships award partial or full tuition, and deadlines and eligibility requirements vary.

Cost of Study

Tuition and other fees vary by graduate program and are due in full prior to matriculation for each quarter of study.

Living and Housing Costs

Students should contact the University for information on housing options and living expenses.

Student Group

Individuals enrolled in graduate programs at Miami International University of Art & Design come from a variety of backgrounds. Students (graduate and undergraduate) at the school are from out of state and across America; many also come from other countries.

Student Outcomes

The University works to foster the students' desire to maintain high levels of professionalism in their chosen careers. Special emphasis is placed on helping students to reach their personal, academic, and career goals. As part of this objective, the Office of Career Services works with students throughout their education and after graduation, offering career assessment and planning, job search assistance, and networking opportunities.

Location

Miami is a culturally rich region that celebrates year-round events, including the African-American Heritage Festival, Haitian Heritage Week, the Viva Mexico Celebration, the Israel Independence Celebration, and Asian Cultural Week. The city is home to professional sports teams, and residents enjoy the sandy beaches, international cuisine, local clubs, the historic Art Deco District, Coral Gables, and Key Biscayne. The Florida Keys, DisneyWorld, and the Bahamas are all just a short trip away.

The University

Students are creative, competitive, and open to new ideas. The University's faculty consists of full-time and part-time professors, many of whom have advanced degrees and professional experience in their respective fields.

Student clubs and organizations include the American Institute of Graphic Arts (AIGA), American Society of Interior Designers (ASID), International Student Club, and Student Council.

Miami International University of Art & Design is accredited by the Commission on Colleges of the Southern Association of Colleges and Schools (SACS; 1866 Southern Lane, Decatur, Georgia 30033-4097; phone: 404-679-4500; http://www.sacs.org) to award Associate of Arts, Bachelor of Arts, Bachelor of Fine Arts, and Master of Fine Arts degrees. Miami International University of Art & Design and its branch, The Art Institute of Tampa, hold a License by Means of Accreditation from the Florida Commission for Independent Education. Any questions regarding the License by Means of Accreditation should be directed to the Florida Department of Education, Commission for Independent Education, 325 West Gaines Street, Suite 1414, Tallahassee, Florida 32399-0400. The Bachelor of Fine Arts in Interior Design degree program is accredited by the Council for Interior Design Accreditation.

Applying

Applicants are interviewed, either in person or by telephone, to explore their background and interest in program offerings. Each applicant's transcript and essay are evaluated by the Admissions Acceptance Committee, which reserves the right to request additional records of accomplishment in core academic courses. There is a $50 application fee.

International students' transcripts must be prepared in English or include a complete and official English translation. Proof of English language proficiency or enrollment in the school's English as a second language (ESL) course is required for all prospective international students.

To obtain an application, make arrangements for an interview, or tour the school, prospective students should contact the University at the address listed in this description.

Correspondence and Information

Miami International University of Art & Design
1501 Biscayne Boulevard, Suite 100
Miami, Florida 33132-1418
Phone: 305-428-5700
800-225-9023 (toll-free)
Fax: 305-374-5933
Web site: http://www.artinstitutes.edu/miami

Miami International University of Art & Design

THE FACULTY AND THEIR RESEARCH

At Miami International University of Art & Design, students find an experienced faculty focused on providing students with the skills needed for the marketplace. Many faculty members are researchers and practitioners in their fields, who bring their experience into the classroom. These members are qualified to prepare students to face the challenges of the real world. The faculty members of the school are committed to the personal and professional development of their students.

The Art Institute of Atlanta®, GA; The Art Institute of California℠–Inland Empire; The Art Institute of California℠–Los Angeles; The Art Institute of California℠–Orange County; The Art Institute of California℠–San Diego; The Art Institute of California℠–San Francisco; The Art Institute of Charleston℠, SC, A branch of The Art Institute of Atlanta, GA; The Art Institute of Charlotte®, NC; The Art Institute of Colorado® (Denver); The Art Institute of Dallas®, TX; The Art Institute of Fort Lauderdale®, FL; The Art Institute of Houston®, TX; The Art Institute of Indianapolis℠, IN*; The Art Institute of Jacksonville℠, A branch of Miami International University of Art & Design, FL; The Art Institute of Las Vegas®, NV; The Art Institute of New York City®, NY; The Art Institute of Ohio℠–Cincinnati**; The Art Institute of Philadelphia®, PA; The Art Institute of Phoenix®, AZ; The Art Institute of Pittsburgh® PA; The Art Institute of Portland®, OR; The Art Institute of Seattle®, WA; The Art Institute of Tampa℠, FL, A branch of Miami International University of Art & Design; The Art Institute of Tennessee℠–Nashville, A branch of The Art Institute of Atlanta, GA; The Art Institute of Vancouver℠, BC (Burnaby location, Downtown location, Dubrulle Culinary Arts location); The Art Institute of Washington® (Arlington, VA), A branch of The Art Institute of Atlanta, GA; The Art Institute Online℠, A division of The Art Institute of Pittsburgh, PA; The Art Institutes International Minnesota℠ (Minneapolis); Bradley Academy for the Visual Arts℠ (York, PA); California Design College℠ (Wilshire Boulevard, Los Angeles); The Illinois Institute of Art®–Chicago; The Illinois Institute of Art®–Schaumburg; Miami International University of Art & Design℠, FL; The New England Institute of Art℠ (Boston, MA).

*The Art Institute of Indianapolis is licensed by the Indiana Commission on Proprietary Education, 302 West Washington Street, Room E201, Indianapolis, IN 46204, AC-0080.

**The Art Institute of Ohio–Cincinnati, 8845 Governors Hill Drive, Suite 100, Cincinnati, OH 45249-3317, Reg. #04-01-1698B.

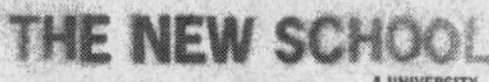

THE NEW SCHOOL: A UNIVERSITY

Parsons The New School for Design
Program in Design and Technology

Program of Study

Parsons' 64-credit M.F.A. in Design and Technology Program is an intense and rigorous program in which students explore the design implications of emerging technologies and the evolving connections between technology, design, and the human experience. The curriculum integrates critical discourse, theory, experimentation, and hands-on production, with an emphasis on critique in areas including multimedia, physical computing, animation, and broadcast design. Students complete individual and collaborative studio projects that demonstrate aesthetic and intellectual refinement as well as technical mastery. The program and its curriculum are closely linked to the real world, and students are actively engaged in effecting or responding to social change through their design projects.

Whether students are interested in the commercial world, academe, or fine arts, they graduate with far more than an expanded technology skill set; they bring the creative, intellectual, and philosophical ability to shape the future in meaningful ways. Students are expected to achieve advanced academic and professional levels in both design theory and practice, as demonstrated by the Thesis Project and Document. The thesis is the systematic study of a design question that requires students to identify an idea and area of study, research its major assumptions and precedents, explain the significance of the undertaking, set forth the process and method for proposing solutions, create prototypes, and offer a conclusion through the production of a body of work. The finished project demonstrates originality and experimentation, critical and independent thinking, appropriate organization and format, and thorough documentation.

Digital Boot Camp is a four-week summer course designed to enable students who may not be well versed in visual and interactive Web design and development to enter the fall semester with confidence, so they can focus on the conceptual and pragmatic concerns of the design process. Two primary areas are addressed in Boot Camp: Web development and interactive design. Some students are required to complete Boot Camp as a condition of their acceptance into the program. Students in Boot Camp earn 3 academic credits, applicable toward the 64 credits required for graduation.

Research Facilities

Collaboration Studios (or Collab Studios) team students with industry partners to undertake real-world projects. Many Collab Studios are dedicated to applied design research areas in the Parsons Design Lab, with cross-disciplinary teams formed from the various design disciplines at Parsons. Students have access to every lab on campus. Computing facilities are comprehensive and cutting edge. The Knowledge Union—the primary working environment of M.F.A. Design and Technology students—consists of state-of-the-art technology spread over four floors. Six hundred networked workstations include all relevant platforms. Servers support work ranging from traditional print output to online projects using webcasting and secure transaction technology.

Specialty work, whether audio/video production, MIDI, recording, or physical computing installation, takes place in the Design and Technology Lab. Portable production equipment, including digital still, video, and audio equipment, is readily available. Digital projectors, surround sound, and active white boards feed into equipment racks that enable presentation of all media types. M.F.A. Design and Technology students who wish to work from home have full access to the University network over the Internet and can take advantage of the University network and full Internet 2 connectivity while on campus.

Financial Aid

Graduate students are automatically considered for scholarship funds upon acceptance into the program. Scholarship recipients are notified of their award by either their program or a Student Financial Services award letter soon after being admitted. Graduate students should contact their academic department early in the admissions process for separate applications for institutional awards, such as assistantships. U.S. citizens and permanent residents applying for financial aid outside the University should file the Free Application for Federal Student Aid (FAFSA) by March 1. More information can be found at the Student Financial Services Web site at http://www.newschool.edu/studentservices/financialaid/.

Cost of Study

Full-time students pay $17,280 in tuition and $140 in fees per term. Additional fees may apply.

Living and Housing Costs

The University offers on-campus housing, University-run apartments, and assistance in finding housing off campus. The cost of housing, food, transportation, books, and living expenses in New York City averages $17,000 annually. For more information, interested students should visit http://www.newschool.edu/studentservices.html.

Student Group

There are 148 students in the program, 143 of whom are full-time. This includes 81 women, 30 students who are members of minority groups, and 64 international students.

Location

Parsons The New School for Design is located in Greenwich Village, at the heart of New York's vibrant architecture and design communities. In addition to using the neighborhoods, city streets, and wireless networks as laboratories for experimentation, students collaborate with an array of corporate, governmental, educational, nonprofit, and arts organizations to ensure a working environment that is both technically current and socially relevant.

The University and The School

Parsons is part of The New School, a leading university in New York City offering some of the nation's most distinguished programs in design, liberal arts, the performing arts, and social and political science, leading to seventy graduate and undergraduate degrees. To learn more, students should visit http://www.newschool.edu/degreeprograms. Parsons and The New School are fully accredited by the Commission on Higher Education of the Middle States Association of Colleges and Schools.

Applying

A Bachelor of Arts, a Bachelor of Fine Arts, or an equivalent international degree is required. Applicants are not required to have a degree in design or computer programming knowledge. Students must submit the completed application, the $50 application fee, a resume, a statement of interest, official copies of all college transcripts, two letters of recommendation, and a portfolio submitted in one of the following formats: CD-ROM, DVD, videotape, slides, or URLs for Web-based work. The portfolio must include an inventory list and clear run instructions. In addition, international students must submit TOEFL scores—a minimum of 580 on the written test or 237 on the computerized version. The application deadline is February 1.

Correspondence and Information

Master of Fine Arts in Design and Technology Program
Parsons The New School for Design
2 West 13th Street, 10th Floor
New York, New York 10011

Phone: 212-229-8908
Fax: 212-229-5941
E-mail: office@parsons.edu
Web site: http://www.newschool.edu/parsons
http://dt.parsons.edu

The New School: A University

THE FACULTY AND THEIR RESEARCH

Complete faculty biographies can be found at http://dt.parsons.edu/faculty.html.

Joao Amorim. Animation, including 3-D; design.
Cory Arcangel.
J. Z. Barrell. Commercial/industrial audio production (TV/radio/Internet), music production, narrative editing, teaching, composition.
John Blackford.
Mitchell Butler, Animation Director. Character and story, 3-D animation, 2-D Flash animation.
Louisa Campbell. Children's television, theater, and film.
David Carroll, Multimedia Director, Second Thought. Macromedia Flash MX design technology, inclusive of its commercial, academic, and artistic contexts, with a special interest in the possibilities of intersections and hybridized forms.
Adam Chapman, Award-winning artist. Writing, design.
James Dean Conklin. Animation, design.
Anthony Deen, Vice President of Design, CDI Group. Synchronization of design and technology.
Sharon Denning. Interactive media.
Andrea Dezso, Artist, award-winning graphic designer and typographer, illustrator, educator, and writer.
Nicole DiDio.
Nicholas Fortugno. Role playing, live action, game culture.
Morry Galonoy, Principal, Litchinut. Relative impact of technology on society and society on technology, with particular interest in global communications and culture.
Yury Gitman. New media art, broadcast design, wireless development.
Joshua Goldberg, Artist and programmer. Multimedia sampling and live video performance.
Rachel Johnson.
David Kanter. Web site and interactive development.
Christopher Kirwan, Principal, Urban Technologies.
Alison Lewis, Interactive digital design artist, engineer, and educator.
Colleen Macklin, Department Chair, Design and Technology. Digital art, interactive design emphasizing social interaction and collaboration.
Jonathan Marcus.
Nino Mendolia. Digitally manipulated 2-D and 3-D elements.
Robert Milazzo. Film directing, screenwriting, performance.
Katherine Moriwaki. How the disciplines of architecture, product design, and fashion converge with technological advances to form new modalities of expression.
Barbara Morris. Product design and development, writing.
Karen Nourse, Filmmaker.
Stephanie Owens, Cofounder and COO, Oddcast. Relationship between materiality and representation.
Nina Paley. Animation.
Igor Pusenjak. Experimental connections between the virtual and the physical using different materials and technologies.
Chris Romero, Design Partner, Oscillation Digital Design Studio. Interfaces between humans and computers.
Evan Roth. Artistic uses of technology in popular culture and the urban environment.
Katie Salen, Director, Design and Technology, Graduate Studies. Connections between game design, interactivity, and play.
Jun Sassa. 2-D and 3-D animation.
Anezka Sebek. Animation, all aspects of time-based work.
Sabine Seymour, Founder, Moondial, Inc. Next-generation wearables and the intertwining of aesthetics and function.
Mark Stafford, Coordinator, Critical Studies and Writing. Psychoanalysis, fiction and nonfiction.
Michael Sweet, Composer and sound designer.
Marko Tandefelt. Interface and concept design, 3-D/VR, physical computing art for public spaces, audiovisual interactive instrument design.
Tom Toth.
Sven Travis. Interactive media.
Michael Waldron, Creative Director, Nailgun. Broadcast design.
Loretta Wolozin. Multimedia for young children's literacy.
Marina Zurkow, Flash computer animator. Interactive design.

THE NEW SCHOOL
A UNIVERSITY

THE NEW SCHOOL: A UNIVERSITY

Parsons The New School for Design
Program in Photography

Program of Study

The M.F.A. in Photography Program at Parsons The New School for Design functions as a twenty-first-century atelier and think tank. Students are encouraged to develop individual vision in a collaborative environment and explore related technologies focusing on the relationship between concept and production. The goal of the program is to educate students about the expanding and evolving creative position of the photographer today, specifically in relation to emerging imaging technologies and new media. This program grounds students in both the evolving language of photography and the technology driving that evolution. Graduates are prepared to define the future of photography and its creative role within contemporary culture, either as scholars or as practicing artists.

Departing from the traditional semester format, the M.F.A. in Photography Program is a twenty-six-month, 64-credit program that blends practice and theory. The curriculum consists of technical and academic studies as well as significant studio work. Students earn credits through summer residencies and by utilizing the latest distributed-learning technologies. Participants complete requirements during three consecutive eight-week intensive summer sessions in residence at Parsons and engage in independent study and online learning during the fall/spring terms. The fall/spring semesters culminate in five-day intensive residencies in January and June.

Required courses are Graduate Studio, Graduate Seminars I–III, Independent Studio I–IV, Wired Studio, Think Tank, Thesis and Exhibition, and Cyber-Community Conference (CCC). In Graduate Studio, students explore a personal direction in their studio. In Graduate Seminars I–III, students utilize the artistic and intellectual wealth of the city to explore contemporary issues in art and photography. Independent Studio I–IV continues the personal studio work initiated in Graduate Studio. Wired Studio is a skills acquisition course designed to introduce participants to new photographic technologies and working methods. Think Tank brings into focus the impact of new technologies on working methods and production and how they are viewed. Thesis and Exhibition prepares students for their thesis exhibitions through close work with their advisory and graduate committees. Through asynchronous and live discussion groups and critique space, with guest lecturers and critics, CCC facilitates a free and creative exchange despite geographic boundaries.

Research Facilities

The Adam and Sophie Gimbel Library of Art and Design includes books on art and design, special collections, and several hundred rare books. The library also contains a collection of mounted plates, slides, and periodicals on the history and the latest developments in fine arts and design. The Gimbel Library has begun development of a digital image collection that will enable online access to images from Parsons' slide collection. The Angelo Donghia Materials Library and Study Center, funded by the Angelo Donghia Foundation, includes a library, a gallery, a computer lab, and a lecture hall. The library allows students and faculty members to review and check out state-of-the-art resources, putting the latest and most exclusive materials at their fingertips.

Financial Aid

Graduate students are automatically considered for scholarship funds upon acceptance into the program. Scholarship recipients are notified of their award by either their program or a Student Financial Services award letter soon after being admitted. Graduate students should contact their academic department early in the admissions process for separate applications for institutional awards, such as assistantships. U.S. citizens and permanent residents applying for financial aid outside the University should file the Free Application for Federal Student Aid (FAFSA) by March 1. More information can be found at the Student Financial Services Web site at http://www.newschool.edu/studentservices/financialaid/.

Cost of Study

Full-time students pay $1082 per credit in tuition and $140 in fees per term. Additional fees may apply.

Living and Housing Costs

The University offers on-campus housing, University-run apartments, and assistance in finding housing off campus. The cost of housing, food, transportation, books, and living expenses in New York City averages $17,000 annually. For more information, interested students should visit http://www.newschool.edu/studentservices.html.

Student Group

Of the 29 students in the program, 6 are full-time, 17 are women, and 6 are international. Students in the M.F.A. in Photography Program come from varied backgrounds, which adds to the diversity of visions and styles within the program.

Location

Parsons' main campus is located downtown in Greenwich Village, a historic neighborhood with a style and atmosphere found nowhere else in New York City. The Village is home to design and art studios, galleries, shops, and restaurants as well as avant-garde artists, musicians, and writers.

With rich cultural resources, international sophistication, and cutting-edge attitude, New York City is a vibrant environment that has inspired and challenged artists and designers throughout its history. New York is home to more than eighty museums, including the Metropolitan Museum of Art, the Museum of Modern Art, and Cooper-Hewitt, National Design Museum. To Parsons faculty members, the city is an extension of the classroom and is incorporated into the basic fabric of the curriculum.

The University and The School

Parsons is part of The New School, a leading university in New York City offering some of the nation's most distinguished programs in design, liberal arts, the performing arts, and social and political science, leading to seventy graduate and undergraduate degrees. To learn more, students should visit http://www.newschool.edu/degreeprograms. Parsons and The New School are fully accredited by the Commission on Higher Education of the Middle States Association of Colleges and Schools.

Applying

Applicants should have undergraduate or graduate degrees in photography, video, or other related media. Those whose bachelor's or graduate degrees are in an unrelated discipline should have considerable experience working in the field. Students must submit the completed application, the $50 application fee, a resume, a statement of interest, official copies of all college transcripts, two letters of recommendation, and a portfolio consisting of twenty examples of current work submitted as slides or on disk, CD, or videotape. An interview may be requested. International students must submit TOEFL scores—a minimum of 580 on the written test or 237 on the computerized version. The application deadline is February 1.

Correspondence and Information

Master of Fine Arts in Photography Program
Parsons The New School for Design
66 Fifth Avenue, 5th Floor
New York, New York 10011

Phone: 212-229-8923
Fax: 212-229-5619
E-mail: mfaphoto@newschool.edu
Web site: http://www.newschool.edu/parsons
http://www.parsons.newschool.edu/photography

The New School: A University

THE FACULTY AND THEIR RESEARCH

Complete faculty biographies are available at the Web site, http://www.parsons.newschool.edu/faculty_and_staff/directory.aspx.

Adam Ames, Photographer and Video Installation Artist; M.F.A., School of Visual Arts.
Anthony Aziz, Artist and Photographer; M.F.A., San Francisco Art Institute. Digital imaging.
Woody Batts. New media, relationship between technology and design.
Michelle Bogre, Photographer; B.J., Missouri.
Andrew Bordwin, B.A., NYU. Photography, video installation.
Martha H. Burgess, Photographer, Installation, and New Media Artist; M.F.A., Yale.
Sean Callahan, Photographer.
Sammy A. Cucher, Photographer; M.F.A., San Francisco Art Institute. Digitally based images.
Simone Douglas, Photographer and Designer.
Jenny Gage, Artist; M.F.A., Yale.
Thyrza Nichols Goodeve, Author.
Charles LaBelle.
Jonathan Lipkin, Photographer and Author. Relationship between art, culture, and technology.
Cay Sophie Rabinowitz, Senior Editor, *Parkett*.
James L. Ramer, Photographer and Installation Artist; M.F.A., Memphis College of Art.
Mark Stafford, Editor, Allworth Press, and Psychoanalyst; M.F.A., Edinburgh.
Jeff Weiss, Fine Artist and Photographer; B.S., Michigan.

Visiting Lecturers
Reverend Ethan Acres, Multidisciplinary Artist.
Shimon Attie, Photographer.
Ellen Birell, Multidisciplinary Artist.
Slater Bradley, Photographer.
Nathan Carter, Artist.
Daniel Conogar, Photographer.
Tim Davis, Photographer.
Stephanie Diamond, Photographer.
Ollivier Dyens, Artist, Essayist, and Poet.
Elliot Erwitt, Photographer.
Allan Frame, Writer, Photographer, and Director.
Anna Gaskell, Photographer.
Anthony Goicolea, Artist and Photographer.
Neil Goldberg, Photographer.
Dan Graham, Multidisciplinary Artist.
Sharon Harper, Photographer.
David Alan Harvey, Writer and Photographer.
Craig Kalpakjian, Photographer.
Eve Andre Larame, Installation Artist.
Glen Luchford, Photographer.
Joseph Maida, Fine Artist, Photographer, and Video Artist.
Joel Meyerowitz, Author and Photographer.
Antoni Muntadas, Media Artist.
Alix Pearlstein, Multidisciplinary Artist.
John Salvest, Artist.
Gary Scheider, Photographer.
Erik Schmidt, Multimedia Artist.
Carolee Schneemann, Photographer.
Collier Schorr, Photographer.
Laurie Simmons, Photographer.
Karina Aguilera Skvirsky, Photographer and Video Artist.
Larry Sulton, Photographer.
Javier Tellez, Photographer and Video Artist.
Catherine Wagner, Artist and Photographer.
Charlie White, Photographer.
Wendel White, Photographer.
Melanie Wiora, Photographer.

NEW YORK SCHOOL OF INTERIOR DESIGN

NEW YORK SCHOOL OF INTERIOR DESIGN

Master of Fine Arts in Interior Design

Program of Study

The Master of Fine Arts (M.F.A.) at the New York School of Interior Design is a postprofessional degree that is of particular interest to graduates of various design programs and to practitioners in interior design, architecture, and other related disciplines who wish to pursue advanced study. The M.F.A. in interior design program focuses on advanced studio and academic research in history, theory, and methods as they relate to an interdisciplinary approach to interiors and design. The M.F.A. curriculum is composed of 60 credits of study and is formulated to expand understanding of different design disciplines, with special emphasis on their interdependence.

There are four components of the program: a core design studio sequence, specialty studios, lectures and seminars, and electives. Students may earn up to 3 elective credits in a supervised internship arranged by the college. The core design studio sequence consists of a series of experiences of increasing complexity that culminate in the thesis studio. The thesis (11 credits) is required as a culminating project and consists of 3 credits of directed research followed by an 8-credit individually mentored studio project. Each student must demonstrate originality, research and design skill, and creative capacity to resolve advanced problems in design. The thesis is presented to a graduate faculty jury for evaluation.

Research Facilities

The library, with more than 10,000 books, periodicals, and indexes, covers every aspect of international art, design, decorative arts, architecture, professional practice, and related subjects and houses a materials collection of current trade catalogs and manufacturers' samples. There is access to the Internet and other electronic resources. New York School of Interior Design (NYSID) is part of a cooperative arrangement with prominent New York City universities that gives students and faculty members reciprocal access to over 2.6 million volumes. NYSID is also a member of the Metropolitan New York Library Council (METRO), a consortium of more than 300 regional libraries.

Financial Aid

NYSID offers a limited number of merit-based graduate fellowships. These fellowships are awarded in the amount of $5000 to $10,000 per academic year and are renewable in the second year on the basis of demonstrated continuing need and maintenance of good academic standing. Students may also qualify for financial assistance in the form of federal, state, private loan, and grant programs. For further information, applicants should contact the NYSID Financial Aid Administrator.

Cost of Study

Tuition for students in the graduating class of 2010 is $10,875 per semester for a total of 60 credits over four semesters.

Living and Housing Costs

For the nine-month academic year, transportation and living expenses for a single student are estimated at $15,000.

Student Group

The New York School of Interior Design enrolls up to 20 students in its master's degree program each year.

Student Outcomes

NYSID offers current students and graduates active career placement services, including individual counseling on writing a resume and preparing a portfolio. Recent placements have included such prominent residential and contract design firms as Clodagh Architectural Design, Aero Studios Ltd., John Saladino, Gensler & Associates, Skidmore Owings & Merrill, and The Rockwell Group.

Location

The New York School of Interior Design is located in Manhattan's Upper East Side Historic District. NYSID's campus is within easy walking distance of some of New York City's finest museums, showrooms, antiques shops, and auction houses.

The School

Founded in 1916, the New York School of Interior Design is the only private, nonprofit college in New York City that specializes solely in interior design. Chartered by the Board of Regents of the University of the State of New York in 1924, the New York School of Interior Design is authorized by the Board of Regents to confer the degrees of Associate in Applied Science (A.A.S.), Bachelor of Fine Arts (CIDA/FIDER accredited B.F.A.), and Master of Fine Arts (M.F.A.). NYSID is an accredited institutional member of the National Association of Schools of Art and Design (NASAD).

Applying

This postprofessional program is designed primarily for students who have earned professional-level degrees in interior design, architecture, environmental design, or a closely related field. Each applicant must submit a portfolio of a minimum of fifteen pieces of design work that demonstrate an ability to pursue advanced study in design. A personal interview is recommended for all applicants. Students are not required to take the Graduate Record Examinations, but a minimum score of 550 (paper-based), 213 (computer-based), or 79–80 (Internet-based) on the TOEFL is required of all international students whose language of education was not English. The preferred submission deadline is March 15. The application fee is $50 for U.S. applicants and $75 for international applicants.

Correspondence and Information

Office of Graduate Admissions
New York School of Interior Design
170 East 70th Street
New York, New York 10021
Phone: 212-472-1500 Ext. 204
E-mail: admissions@nysid.edu
Web site: http://www.nysid.edu

New York School of Interior Design

THE FACULTY

Scott Ageloff, Dean, NYSID; M.Arch., Yale; IDEC, ASID, AIA. Educator, interior designer, and architect. Certified by NCIDQ and the State of New York. Principal, Ageloff & Associates.
Peter Brandt, B.Arch., MIT. Architect, interior designer, and author. Certified by NCIDQ. Former Vice President and Managing Principal, Gensler and Associates. Principal, Brandt Design Associates.
Debra Bryant, M.F.A., Syracuse. Set designer. Production designer, CBS Evening News.
Renee Estacio, B.S.Arch., Santo Tomas (Philippines). Furniture and interior designer.
Donna Goodman, M.Arch., Columbia; AIA. Registered architect. Exhibitions and research funded by the Graham Foundation, the New York State Council of the Arts, and the J. M. Kaplan Fund.
Eileen Imber, M.U.P., CUNY Graduate Center; M.S., CUNY, Brooklyn; ASLA, President, 1 Land Design landscape architecture.
Barbara A. Lowenthal, M.Arch., Princeton. Registered architect. Principal, Barbara Lowenthal.
Kim Plaskon Nadel, M.S., Pratt; NCIDQ. LEED-Accredited Professional. President, NICHE Design.
John Otis, M.S., Massachusetts; IDSA. Interior, exhibit, furniture, and product designer. Director, Object Inc.
Matthew Postal, Ph.D., CUNY Graduate Center. Architectural historian.
Ann L. Schiffers, M.F.A., Parsons. Architectural lighting designer. Principal, Ann Schiffers Lighting Design.
Gregory Stanford, B.Arch., Syracuse. Interior designer and architect. Senior Designer, The Rockwell Group.
Edwin J. Zawadski, M. Arch., Yale. Principal, In Situ Design.

NEW YORK UNIVERSITY

School of Continuing and Professional Studies
Master of Science in Digital Imaging and Design

Program of Study

The M.S. in Digital Imaging and Design curriculum provides students with the theoretical and practical foundations of digital imaging with an intense focus on 2-D and 3-D production. Students learn both the artistic and technical aspects of production as they are applicable to a wide range of professions in the digital media industry, including commercials, broadcasting, and film. They are involved in the creative process and the management of digital content production beginning their first day of class.

Students earn this 42-credit degree on a part-time or full-time basis. Through full-time study, students can complete this program in two years; part-time study takes up to five years. After an introduction to general digital production techniques, students specialize in either 3-D or 2-D production. The curriculum for the M.S. in Digital Imaging and Design is continually reevaluated and updated in response to industry needs to provide the most up-to-date and relevant course of study.

Research Facilities

Seven digital studios at the Center for Advanced Digital Applications (CADA) provide students with a cutting-edge, high-end digital production experience in a rigorous academic setting. Facilities replicate the production process of a Hollywood studio with the best graphics capabilities, with IBM PCs and Apple G5 workstations operating at video and film resolution and using all the major professional software, including Maya, Softimage XSI, Renderman, Flint/Flame, After Effects, ProTools, and Final Cut Pro HD. In addition, each studio is equipped with advanced video recording devices, including digital decks, Betacam, and mini-DV as well as Sony and Canon digital video cameras, blue screens, and the DPS Velocity System.

Financial Aid

There are many financial aid options to consider, including fellowships and low-interest educational loans. New York University's (NYU) centralized Office of Financial Aid assists students with loan packages, scholarships, and the NYU monthly payment plan, which enables students to spread out their tuition payments. Department scholarships are also available. To learn more, interested students should visit http://www.nyu.edu/financial.aid.

Cost of Study

Tuition for part-time students for the 2008–09 academic year is $1326 per credit, plus fees. For full-time students (10–12 credits per semester), the cost of tuition is $13,260 per semester, plus fees. Fees vary somewhat by program. The Board of Trustees of New York University reserves the right to alter these costs without notice.

Living and Housing Costs

Graduate student housing is available on the University campus and is administered through the Office of Housing and Residence Life. However, students may choose to live off campus. NYU's Off-Campus Housing Office (OCHO) offers assistance to members of the NYU community in their search for non-University housing options. OCHO provides, exclusively to NYU students, listings of available locations for rent through private landlords, property managers, brokers, and real estate agents. Updated daily, these listings are accessible through OCHO's computer terminals or online for members of the NYU community.

Student Group

The student body encompasses graduate students of both full- and part-time status, with 101 students in the 2007–08 academic year. The student body consists of men and women between the ages of 22 and 40 from a variety of cultures and educational backgrounds, including computer science, film, television, Web design, and traditional arts.

Location

The School of Continuing and Professional Studies' Center for Advanced Digital Applications is located at NYU's Midtown Center at 11 West 42nd Street. Classrooms, academic advisers, career services, and faculty offices are located there as well. In film, TV production, music, advertising, publishing, architecture, new media, the medical industry, fine art, performance, and more, no other city comes close to New York City's ever-expanding spectrum of opportunities for artists.

The University, The School, and The Center

NYU is a private university composed of fourteen schools and colleges. The University was founded in 1831 and the School of Continuing and Professional Studies in 1934. The Center for Advanced Digital Applications, which offers the Master of Science degree, continuing education courses, and summer intensive programs, was founded in 1996.

Applying

Students may apply for fall or spring admission. Application packages must include official transcripts, results of the GRE or GMAT, TOEFL scores (for students whose native language is not English), the nature and extent of previous work as presented in a portfolio, professional and academic recommendations, and a statement of purpose.

Correspondence and Information

Office of Admissions
Master of Science in Digital Imaging and Design
New York University
145 Fourth Avenue, Room 219
New York, New York 10003
Phone: 212-998-7200 Ext. 411
Fax: 212-995-4675
E-mail: scps.gradadmissions@nyu.edu
Web site: http://www.scps.nyu.edu/411

New York University

THE ADMINISTRATION AND THE FACULTY

The Administration

Robert S. Lapiner, Ph.D., Dean, School of Continuing and Professional Studies.

Michael Hosenfeld, M.A., Academic Program Director and Clinical Associate Professor, Graduate Program in Digital Imaging and Design, Center for Advanced Digital Applications.

Kathy Wang, M.S., Assistant Director, Graduate Program in Digital Imaging and Design, Center for Advanced Digital Applications.

The Faculty

Michael Cushny, B.A., M.F.A., Clinical Associate Professor, Graduate Program in Digital Imaging and Design, Center for Advanced Digital Applications.

Patricia Heard-Greene, B.F.A., Clinical Assistant Professor, Graduate Program in Digital Imaging and Design, Center for Advanced Digital Applications.

Myles Tanaka, B.F.A., M.P.S., Clinical Assistant Professor, Graduate Program in Digital Imaging and Design, Center for Advanced Digital Applications.

NEW YORK UNIVERSITY

School of Continuing and Professional Studies
Master of Arts in Graphic Communications Management and Technology

Program of Study

The Master of Arts (M.A.) in Graphic Communications Management and Technology program, offered by New York University's (NYU) School of Continuing and Professional Studies (SCPS), is an innovative master's degree program that provides students with critical leadership skills specific to the field of graphic communications media. Students build expertise in management practices, learn to make the most of resources, and gain a thorough understanding of the capabilities of current and emerging technologies in a program designed to help students become leaders in the field.

Students are guided by a dedicated faculty of industry leaders, as well as a distinguished Advisory Board, who share their knowledge, experience, vision, and direction; offer generous academic scholarships; host networking events; and act as mentors to students. The program provides a dynamic forum for industry, academia, government, and students to explore and resolve issues in graphic communications.

The program offers a unique blend of classes in management practices and cross-media technology, as well as top-level internships at prestigious communications settings. Students form enduring connections with established professionals, attend major communications events and career fairs, and much more.

For the M.A. degree, students must complete 40 credits of graduate course work. The program consists of three phases: a required core of courses, specialization courses in management practices and cross-media technology, and the capstone project (thesis project). The M.A. is offered on a full-time or part-time basis. Through full-time study, students can complete the program in two years; part-time study can take up to five years. The curriculum for the M.A. in Graphic Communications Management and Technology is continually reevaluated and updated in response to industry needs to provide the most up-to-date and relevant course of study.

Research Facilities

The Elmer Holmes Bobst Library and Study Center, one of the largest open-stack research libraries in the world, houses more than 3 million of NYU's nearly 4.4 million volumes. In addition to books, journals, and other print materials, the library provides access to many nonprint resources. These include microforms, databases, and other electronic resources that students can connect to from their home or residence hall; extensive video and audio collections; and a variety of computer equipment and software programs.

NYU's central source for computing, information, network, and telecommunications services is Information Technology Services (ITS). ITS maintains four large, modern computer labs with high-end Macintosh and Windows computers, laser printers, multimedia equipment, and a wide variety of up-to-date software. The Client Services division of ITS provides comprehensive help on the materials and equipment available to students via telephone and e-mail, online, and in person.

Financial Aid

There are many financial aid options to consider, including low-interest educational loans. NYU's centralized Office of Financial Aid assists students with loan packages, scholarships, and the NYU monthly payment plan, which enables students to spread out their tuition payments. For more information, students should visit http://www.nyu.edu/financial.aid.

Cost of Study

Tuition for part-time students for the 2008–09 academic year is $1326 per credit plus fees. For full-time students (10–12 credits per semester), the cost of tuition and related fees is $13,260 per semester. Fees vary somewhat by program. The Board of Trustees of New York University reserves the right to alter these costs without notice.

Living and Housing Costs

Graduate student housing is available on the University campus and is administered through the Office of Housing and Residence Life. However, students may choose to live off campus. NYU's Off-Campus Housing Office (OCHO) offers assistance to members of the NYU community in their search for non-University housing options. OCHO provides, exclusively to NYU students, listings of available locations for rent through private landlords, property managers, brokers, and real estate agents. Updated daily, these listings are accessible through OCHO's computer terminals or online for members of the NYU community.

Student Group

In 2007–08, there were 90 students enrolled in the Master of Arts in Graphic Communications Management and Technology. The median age was 28, and 61 percent of the students were women. Part-time students accounted for 82 percent of those enrolled.

Location

The School of Continuing and Professional Studies' M.A. in Graphic Communications Management and Technology provides students with the unique opportunity to study in New York City, a global center of media and business.

The University and The School

NYU is a private university composed of fourteen schools and colleges. The University was founded in 1831 and the School of Continuing and Professional Studies in 1934. The School has been a leader for more than sixty years, offering an ever-expanding array of courses designed to develop senior-level professionals and leaders in the fields of print and electronic publishing, marketing, advertising, production, and design, among many others.

Applying

Students may apply for fall or spring admission. Matriculated students may take summer courses. Factors that are considered in evaluating an applicant include official transcripts of academic achievement in previous undergraduate and graduate course work, scores from the GRE or GMAT, TOEFL scores (for international students whose native language is not English), the nature and extent of previous work experience, professional recommendations, and a statement of purpose.

Correspondence and Information

Office of Admissions
Master of Arts in Graphic Communications Management and Technology
New York University
145 Fourth Avenue, Room 219
New York, New York 10003

Phone: 212-998-7200 Ext. 777
Fax: 212-995-4674
E-mail: scps.gradadmissions@nyu.edu
Web site: http://www.scps.nyu.edu/777

New York University

THE ADMINISTRATION

Robert S. Lapiner, Ph.D., Dean, School of Continuing and Professional Studies.

Bonnie Blake, M.A., Coordinating Chair, Division of Media Industry Studies and Design, and Academic Director and Clinical Instructor, Graduate Program in Graphic Communications Management and Technology.

RENSSELAER POLYTECHNIC INSTITUTE

Department of the Arts
Integrated Electronic Arts Programs

Programs of Study

The Department of the Arts at Rensselaer Polytechnic Institute features an integrated and multidisciplinary approach to the arts, with a focus on the use of electronic media in artistic creation and performance.

The Ph.D. in Electronic Arts is an interdisciplinary arts degree that integrates arts practice with theoretical and historical research. The core of the curriculum focuses on the student's personal creative practice, informed by course work and individual attention from advisers and culminating in a dissertation. One of the first Ph.D.'s of its kind, this program expands traditions of arts pedagogy through interdisciplinary research in contemporary media theory, practice, and production.

The Master of Fine Arts in Electronic Arts degree program (generally considered to be the first integrated electronic arts program within a research university in the U.S.) is designed for students pursuing artistic and academic careers emphasizing electronic media.

Arts department faculty members take varying approaches to the use of electronic media in artistic creation and performance. All are active artists/theoreticians whose works are represented internationally in museums, galleries, and performances. Arts students are required to become familiar with creative tools in a variety of electronic media and are encouraged to work with combinations of media.

Studio courses engage students in hands-on activities that stress creative and expressive development. They also encourage students to develop their perceptual sensitivity and build their confidence to apply creative exploration and problem-solving skills to a wide range of aesthetic challenges.

The center of such creative work is the Integrated Electronic Arts at Rensselaer (iEAR) Studios, which include professional-quality facilities in electronic and computer music, digital video production and postproduction, computer imaging and animation, interactive media, installation art, and performance art. In addition, qualified students in the Ph.D. and M.F.A. programs may use elective credits to explore Rensselaer's extensive interdisciplinary and technological resources. Numerous opportunities to engage in creative or research projects with students or faculty members from other departments or schools within the Institute are also available.

All students are expected to develop competency in using various media available at the iEAR Studios as well as in the theoretical and critical issues relevant to their fields of interest. Since the program is geared toward preparing students to participate actively in art and music communities, practical aspects of production and presentation of creative work are emphasized.

Research Facilities

Research is supported by state-of-the-art facilities and equipment, including the Rensselaer Libraries, whose electronic information system provides access to collections, databases, and the Internet from campus and remote terminals; the Rensselaer Computing System, which permeates the campus with a coherent array of more than 7,000 nodes of distributed laptops, desktops, advanced workstations, and servers; a shared toolkit of applications for interactive learning and research and high-speed Internet connectivity; one of the country's largest academically based, class 100 clean room facilities; high-performance campuswide computing facilities that allow for serial or parallel computation; and five core laboratories for molecular biology, proteomics, bioimaging, and tissue engineering.

Rensselaer's research capabilities have been enhanced with the addition of the Computational Center for Nanotechnology Innovations (CCNI). The result of a $100-million collaboration with IBM and New York State, the CCNI is the world's most powerful university-based supercomputing center and a top ten supercomputing center of any kind in the world. The CCNI is made up of massively parallel Blue Gene supercomputers, POWER-based Linux clusters, and Opteron-based clusters, providing more than 100 teraflops of computational muscle and approximately a petabyte of shared online storage.

Other facilities and research centers include the Center for Biotechnology and Interdisciplinary Studies; the George M. Low Center for Industrial Innovation; research centers for integrated electronics, terahertz science, nanotechnology, fuel cell and hydrogen research, lighting research, science and technology policy, and infrastructure and transportation studies; the Geotechnical Centrifuge Research Center; the Darrin Fresh Water Institute; and the Scientific Computation Research Center. In addition, academic departments and faculty laboratories have extensive discipline-specific research capabilities and equipment.

iEAR Studios comprise state-of-the-art facilities and studios spread out across the campus in three buildings. There are graduate studio spaces, undergraduate labs, multimedia classrooms and labs, traditional painting and drawing studios, and music practice rooms and rehearsal halls. For an overview of studio facilities, students should visit the arts department's Web site (http://www.arts.rpi.edu).

Financial Aid

Financial aid is available in the forms of teaching and research assistantships and fellowships, which include tuition scholarships and stipends. Rensselaer assistantships cover the academic year, with summer support available in many departments. University, corporate, or national fellowships fund many of Rensselaer's full-time graduate students. Outstanding students may qualify for university-sponsored Rensselaer Graduate Fellowship Awards, which carry a minimum stipend of $22,000 and a full tuition and fees scholarship. All fellowship awards are calendar-year awards for full-time graduate students. Low-interest, deferred-repayment graduate loans are available to U.S. citizens with demonstrated need.

Cost of Study

Full-time graduate tuition for the 2008–09 academic year is $36,950. Other costs (estimated living expenses, insurance, etc.) are projected to be about $13,680. Therefore, the cost of attendance for full-time graduate study is approximately $50,630. Part-time study and cohort programs are priced differently. Students should contact Rensselaer for specific cost information related to the programs they wish to study.

Living and Housing Costs

Graduate students at Rensselaer may choose from a variety of housing options. On campus, students can select one of the many residence halls and immerse themselves in campus life or choose from a select number of apartments designed for graduate students only. There are abundant, affordable options off campus as well, many within easy walking distance.

Student Group

Of the 1,176 graduate students, 29 percent are women and 92 percent are full-time, with 75 percent of full-time graduate students studying at the doctoral level.

Student Outcomes

Rensselaer's graduate students are hired in a variety of industries and sectors of the economy and by private and public organizations, the government, and institutions of higher education. Their starting salaries average $74,807 for master's degree recipients and $82,750 for Ph.D. recipients.

Location

Located just 10 miles northeast of Albany, New York State's capital city, Rensselaer's historic 275-acre campus sits on a hill overlooking the city of Troy, New York, and the Hudson River. The area offers a relaxed lifestyle with many cultural and recreational opportunities, with easy access to both the high-energy metropolitan centers of the Northeast—such as Boston, New York City, and Montreal, Canada—and the quiet beauty of the neighboring Adirondack Mountains.

The Institute

Recognized as a leader in interactive learning and interdisciplinary research, Rensselaer continues a tradition of excellence and technological innovation dating back to 1824. Rensselaer has five schools—Architecture, Engineering, Management, Science, and Humanities and Social Sciences—that offer more than 100 graduate programs in over forty-eight disciplines that attract top students, researchers, and professors. The discovery of new scientific concepts and technologies, especially in emerging interdisciplinary fields, is the lifeblood of Rensselaer's culture and a core goal for the faculty, staff, and students. Fueled by significant support from government, industry, and private donors, Rensselaer provides a world-class education in an environment tailored to the individual.

Applying

Admission is highly competitive. In addition to the standard transcripts, recommendations, and statement of background and goals, prospective M.F.A. and Ph.D. students must submit a portfolio of creative work. For the M.F.A. degree, applicants must have completed a bachelor's degree and display a high level of ability in any artistic medium. The primary consideration in the selection process is evidence of talent and commitment to personal development as a creative artist. For the Ph.D. degree, applicants must have an M.A., M.M., M.S., or M.F.A. Evaluation for admission to the program includes not only artistic merit, but also evidence of a creative orientation that is research based and appropriate for the type of in-depth interdisciplinary scholarly study the Ph.D. program provides. GRE scores are not required. Program entry is in the fall only. The admission deadline is January 1.

Correspondence and Information

Department of the Arts
West Hall, Room 107
Rensselaer Polytechnic Institute
110 8th Street
Troy, New York 12180

Phone: 518-276-4778
E-mail: ElectronicArts@rpi.edu
Web site: http://www.arts.rpi.edu/

Rensselaer Polytechnic Institute

THE FACULTY AND THEIR RESEARCH

Curtis Bahn, Ph.D. (music composition), Princeton. Curtis Bahn is a composer, improviser, and string bass player who specializes in live electronic performance using gestural controllers. Curtis is an active performer, playing in venues ranging from small alternative clubs and galleries to major international festivals. He has designed an electronic string bass outfitted with an array of sensors, the "SBass," that he uses when he performs with "interface," an electronic chamber ensemble with Dan Trueman, and also in performances with other musicians. Curtis' recent activities have involved him in the creation of a family of spherical speakers and "Sensor/Speaker Arrays" (SenSAs) with researchers Dan Trueman from Columbia University and Perry Cook from Princeton University, as well as the design of numerous gestural controllers for dance and live multimedia performance. This year, he and his colleagues have presented their research in live performances, demonstrations, and papers presented at the MIT Media Lab, the International Computer Music Conference, the national conference of the Acoustic Society of America, and the "New Interfaces for Musical Expression" symposium of the Computer/Human Interaction Conference. (crb@rpi.edu; http://www.arts.rpi.edu/crb)

Nao Bustamante, M.F.A., San Francisco Art Institute. Nao Bustamante is an internationally known performance art pioneer. Her work encompasses performance art, installation, video, pop music, and experimental rips in time. Bustamante's work has been presented at the Institute of Contemporary Arts in London, the San Francisco Museum of Modern Arts, and the Kiasma Museum of Helsinki, among other sites. She has performed at galleries, museums, universities, and underground sites throughout Asia, Africa, Europe, New Zealand, Australia, Canada, Mexico, and the United States. Her collaborations include working with such luminaries as Coco Fusco and Osseus Labrint. In 2001, she received the prestigious Anonymous Was a Woman fellowship. (bustan@rpi.edu; http://www.naobustamante.com)

Caren Canier, M.F.A., Boston University. Caren Canier has won numerous awards for her work, including the Pollack/Krasner Foundation Grant, the Ingram Merrill Foundation Grant, two Artist's Fellowships from the New York Foundation for the Arts, and the Rome Prize Fellowship from the American Academy in Rome. (caniec@rpi.edu; http://www.rpi.edu/~caniec)

Michael Century, M.A. (music history and theory), Berkeley. Michael Century has studied Javanese gamelan and West African drumming, piano performance, French at the Sorbonne, electronic music, sound engineering, orchestral conducting, and computer music. In his scholarly work, he studies the history and sociology of art-technology interactions in the twentieth century, highlighting the dynamics of innovation in creative software cultures. In progress is a monograph on the "emergence of the creative user" of computer animation software, based on the interactions among artists, engineers, and scientists from the 1960s to 1980s. Growing out of this interest is a research program concerned with the development of the "studio laboratory" as a distinctive site for techno-cultural innovation. A second research field is the new intellectual property conventions for the new kinds of distributed authorship arising in networked digital culture. Century is also a pianist and composer with a broad interest in solo and chamber classical repertoire, and he authors software for computer-improvisation systems. (century@rpi.edu; http://www.nextcentury.ca)

David Gibson, M.M., Yale. David Gibson's primary field of musical training was cello performance, and his most influential teachers were Luigi Silva, Claus Adam, and Dorthy DeLay. He studied conducting with Jorge Mester at Juilliard and composition with Jacob Druckman at Yale and had a close association with Morton Feldman while a member of the Center for the Creative and Performing Arts in Buffalo, New York. Mr. Gibson currently teaches cello at Mount Holyoke College and runs the theory and instrumental music program at Rensselaer. As a performer, David Gibson has been a pioneer in the field of electronic music. His repertoire includes music from the fourteenth century to the present, and he feels as much at home with Brahms as he does with David Behrman, with whom he has worked. (gibsod2@rpi.edu; http://www.arts.rpi.edu/people/gibsod2)

Tomie Hahn, Ph.D. (ethnomusicology), Wesleyan. Tomie Hahn is a performer and ethnologist whose activities span a wide range of topics, including Japanese traditional performing arts, Monster Truck rallies, issues of identity and creative expression of multiracial individuals, relationships of technology and culture, interactive dance/movement performance, and gestural control and extended human-computer interface in the performing arts. She is a teacher/performer of shakuhachi (Japanese bamboo flute) and of nihon buyo (Japanese traditional dance). Hahn has performed and lectured at venues such as the Metropolitan Museum of Art, American Museum of Natural History, Japan Society, Asia Society, Freer-Sackler Gallery of the Smithsonian Institute, MIT Media Lab, Franklin Furnace, ABC No Rio, Mobius, and Galapagos Art Space. She has collaborated with Curtis Bahn for several decades in the development of new experimental intermedia works and new performance technologies. Their work has been featured in the *New York Times, ArtByte,* and the Rensselaer magazine. (hahnt@rpi.edu; http://www.arts.rpi.edu/tomie)

Kathy High, M.A.H., SUNY at Buffalo. Kathy High is Associate Professor of Video and New Media in the Department of the Arts. She teaches digital video production, history, and theory and has been working in the area of documentary and experimental film, video, and photography for more than twenty years. She produces videos and installations posing queer and feminist inquiries into areas of medicine/bioscience, science fiction, and animal/interspecies collaborations. She has also recently started the BioArts Initiative at Rensselaer, a collaboration between the arts department and the Center for Biotechnology and Interdisciplinary Studies. Her video works have been shown in galleries and museums nationally and internationally, including the Guggenheim Museum and the Museum of Modern Art, NYC, as well as aired on PBS. She has received awards for her media works from the Rockefeller Foundation and the National Endowment for the Arts. Her most recent installation work, Embracing Animal, was exhibited in the Becoming Animal exhibition at MASS MoCA. Information on her video work may be found online at http://www.vdb.org. An upcoming publication entitled "TOOLS: Intersections Between Video Machines and Media Arts Histories" with coeditors Sherry Miller Hocking (ETC) and Mona Jimenez (NYU, Moving Image Arching and Preservation Program) looks at the history of tools used in creating media arts, the collaboration between artists and engineer designers, and the preservation of these tools. The basis of this project comes out of the archives of the Experimental Television Center. (high@rpi.edu; http://arts.rpi.edu/people/highk)

Larry Kagan, M.A. (studio arts), SUNY at Albany. Born in Germany, Larry Kagan has exhibited throughout the U.S. and Europe, and his works are included in the collections of the U.S. Embassy in St. Petersburg, Russia; the State University of New York at Albany; the Schenectady Museum and Planetarium; and the Jewish Museum in New York City. (kaganl@rpi.edu; http://www.arts.rpi.edu/~kagan)

Shawn Lawson, M.F.A. (art and technology), Art Institute of Chicago. Shawn Lawson is a media artist and programmer examining the experience of human-machine interaction. Lawson's installations perform real-time animation and video compositing based on tracking human presence and motion. Unique encounters are generated for each participant. His works have been exhibited at venues in Los Angeles, Pittsburgh, Milwaukee, Chicago, Tempe, Boston, Albany, Ann Arbor, and New York. His installations have been reviewed by the *Chicago Reader,* the *Arizona Republic,* the *Boston Herald,* and the *Boston Globe.* He is published in the ACM MultiMedia 2004 proceedings. In addition to his own work, Lawson's collaborative, Crudeoils, is represented by Flatfile Gallery, Chicago. Lawson studied fine arts at Carnegie Mellon University, Pittsburgh, and École Nationale Supèrieure des Beaux-Arts in Paris. He was a Visiting Assistant Professor at Carnegie Mellon University, an Artist in Residence in the virtual reality research group Stage3 at Carnegie Mellon University, and an intern at Walt Disney Imagineering with the DisneyQuest project. (lawsos2@rpi.edu; http://www.crudeoils.us/shawn)

Branda Miller, M.F.A., NYU. Branda Miller has been a cutting-edge videographer for more than twenty years. She has developed a portfolio of intriguing award-winning works, examining topics in areas such as environmentalism, consumerism, social behavior, and cyber culture. Branda Miller is an artist, educator, and activist who has been working with independent media since the 1970s. Her experimentation with media arts is integrally linked with community organizing. In her collaborative work with groups around the country, Miller involves participants in varied aspects of production so they take control of their own representation. The tapes produced in her youth-empowerment workshops focus on issues such as teenage pregnancy, dropping out, crime, prison, drugs, and AIDS, offering a realistic yet upbeat treatment of what growing up in America is like today. (milleb@rpi.edu; http://www.rpi.edu/~milleb)

Pauline Oliveros, D.M., Maryland. Pauline Oliveros is acclaimed internationally as a composer, performer, and humanitarian. Through Deep Listening Pieces and earlier Sonic Meditations, Oliveros introduced the concept of incorporating all environmental sounds into musical performance through listening. She can make the sound of a sweeping siren into another instrument of the ensemble. To make a pleasurable experience of this requires focus, concentrated musicianship, and strong improvisational skills, which are the hallmarks of Oliveros' form. In performance, Oliveros plays an accordion that has been retuned in two different systems of just intonation. In addition, she uses electronics to alter the sound of the accordion and to incorporate and transform room acoustics. (olivep@rpi.edu; http://arts.rpi.edu/people/olivep)

Neil Rolnick, Ph.D., Berkeley. Neil Rolnick's music has been receiving increasingly wide recognition and numerous performances, both in the U.S. and abroad. A pioneer in the use of computers in performance, beginning in the late 1970s, Rolnick has often included unexpected and unusual combinations of materials and media in his music. He has performed around the world, and his music has appeared on thirteen CDs. Though much of Rolnick's work has been in areas that connect music and technology and is therefore considered to be in the realm of "experimental" music, his music has always been highly melodic and accessible. Whether working with electronic sounds, improvisation, or multimedia, his music has been characterized by critics as "sophisticated" and "hummable and engaging" and as having "good senses of showmanship and humor." Since 2003, he has completed *The Shadow Quartet* for the NYC-based string quartet Ethel, *Fiddle Faddle* for violinist Todd Reynolds, *Body Work* for vocalist Joan La Barbara, *The Real Thief of Baghdad* for Tyrone Henderson, *Ambos Mundos* for the Quintet of the Americas, *Plays Well With Others* for Paul Dresher's Electro-Acoustic Band in San Francisco, *Making Light of It* for baritone Thomas Buckner, *Digits* for pianist Kathleen Supové, *Uptown Jump* for the MAYA Trio, *Segal's Billboard* for harpist Jacqueline Kerrod, *The Bridge* for the Albany Symphony's Dogs of Desire, and the *iFiddle Concerto* for the American Composers Orchestra with soloist Todd Reynolds. His thirteenth CD, *Digits,* was released in 2006 on the Innova label. He is founding director of the iEAR Studios at Rensselaer.

Kathleen Ruiz, M.A., NYU. Kathleen Ruiz is a media artist who creates simulations, games, sculpture, and photography. Her work explores issues about perception, behavior, interaction, and the confluence of the imaginary and the real, inviting inquiry into how conceptual constructs are built and how they serve to shape ethics and power. Kathleen develops and teaches courses in simulation, experimental game design, photography, and emerging genres. She is a founding member of the ErGoGenics Game Research Group designing games for health, fun, and education. She is a doctoral candidate in the Department of Media and Communications at the European Graduate School where she studied with French sociologist, cultural critic, and theorist Jean Baudrillard; political philosopher and media aesthetics theorist Jean Luc Nancy; media philosopher Wolfgang Schirmacher; French film maker Chantel Ackerman; British sculptor Antony Gormley; Palestinian/Israeli filmmaker Elia Suleiman; British artist, photographer, and culture and art critic Victor Burgin; performance artist, researcher in neurology, and anthropologist of the virtual world, Sandy Stone; and German philosopher of photography Hubertus von Amelunxen. Her research is centered on simulation and perspective. (ruiz@rpi.edu; http://www.rpi.edu/~ruiz)

Mary Anne Staniszewski, Ph.D. (art history), CUNY Graduate Center. Staniszewski is the Acting Head of the Department. She writes about art and culture in relation to social issues and as a means of promoting progressive aesthetic, cultural, and political perspectives. Her professional interests range from electronic, contemporary, and modern art and culture and their relation to concepts of self to "identity politics" such as women's, gender, and race studies, as well as activism and human rights. Staniszewski's major research and writing projects form a trilogy of books. The first, *Believing Is Seeing: Creating the Culture of Art* (Penguin), frames art as people know it, that is, art for art's sake, as an invention of the modern era and a manifestation of the age of the individual and the liberal, democratic, capitalist state. In the second, *The Power of Display: A History of Exhibition Installations at the Museum of Modern Art* (MIT Press), installations are analyzed not only as contexts for works of art, but also for those who view them. Museums are portrayed as sites for collective rituals that enhance particular notions of subjecthood. The third book, which is in the research and writing phase, is an analysis of historical and contemporary myths in the United States, featuring three key themes of race, sex, and life and death. Staniszewski is Director of a curatorial incubator, an initiative that invites young curators to present exhibitions, at the New York City cultural space Exit Art. (stanim@rpi.edu; http://arts.rpi.edu/people/stanim).

Igor Vamos, Associate Professor of Arts; M.F.A., California, San Diego. Igor Vamos is a media artist and culture jammer living and working in New York. Vamos is well known for his collaborative public art projects, such as the Barbie Liberation Organization, and the Center For Land Use Interpretation, a nonprofit organization dedicated to the increase and dissemination of knowledge about the nature of human interaction with the Earth. (vamosi@rpi.edu; http://www.arts.rpi.edu/people/vamosi)

SOUTHERN ILLINOIS UNIVERSITY CARBONDALE

School of Art and Design

Programs of Study

In its graduate studio programs, the School of Art and Design strives to maintain a vital, creative ambience in which developing artists with strong motivation develop a clear, mature, and professional focus. The core of the program involves frequent, sustained contact with professional faculty members and fellow students. Work is supported and extended through formal studio courses and studies in the history of art as well as through access to the many resources and possibilities available at a large, multipurpose university.

The School of Art and Design has a very robust graduate assistantship program. Assistantships are awarded on a competitive basis. These assistantships are allocated based on the students' abilities to carry out a specific position with a high degree of efficiency, effectiveness, and professionalism. Every attempt is made to provide all graduate students with an assistantship, but it is the students' responsibility to seek out those assistantships for which they are most qualified.

M.F.A. candidates, as well as other interested graduate students, are eligible to enroll in the certificate program in art history. A modest amount of additional course work in art history can significantly enhance graduates' academic knowledge, skills, and employment prospects.

The faculty members select promising national and international candidates, providing them with a professional studio environment and encouraging self-discipline, high standards, and productivity. High-quality creative activity is encouraged through peer exchange. A variety of career goals are addressed, ranging from preparation for an academic career to sustaining oneself as an independent artist. The School of Art and Design encourages diversity and dialogue and favors no single style or ideology. The School also recognizes the importance of addressing art issues from a global perspective, which Southern Illinois University Carbondale fosters in part through the multinational composition of its graduate student community. A solo thesis exhibition documents the graduate's experience.

Research Facilities

The School of Art and Design is housed mainly in five buildings spread about the campus. The most central building is the Allyn Building, which contains the administrative offices, art history and art education offices, printmaking facilities, and classrooms dedicated to painting, drawing, art history, and art education. The industrial wing of Pulliam Hall houses ceramics, metals, blacksmithing, and glass programs, areas that have all recently been renovated. The Glove Factory, named for what it once was, was thoroughly rehabbed in the early 1990s. Both buildings provide excellent individual studios for M.F.A. students and faculty members. The Glove Factory is also the location of a large, urban-style gallery space suitable for orthodox and unorthodox in-house exhibitions. Additional buildings around the campus house more studio facilities for glass, small metals, and sculpture.

Financial Aid

Quarter-time and half-time teaching and research assistantships and fellowships are a source of financial support for most students. Assistantships and fellowships come with full tuition waivers. Students who are accepted into the graduate program are automatically considered for assistantships and, whenever possible, are placed in positions that reflect their studio strengths. Assistantships are awarded on merit and programmatic needs. The School recommends that applicants with undergraduate GPAs of 3.5 and above include recent GRE scores with their applications so they may be considered for competitive campuswide fellowships. Special financial assistance, for first-year students only, is available through the Master's Fellowship, the Graduate Dean's Fellowship, and ICEOP and PROMPT Fellowships for members of minority groups and women. Applications are available on request.

Cost of Study

In-state graduate tuition is $313.90 per credit hour in 2008–09. Out-of-state tuition is 2.5 times the in-state tuition rate ($784.75 per credit hour). Graduate students with at least a 25 percent appointment as a graduate assistant receive a tuition scholarship. Fees vary from $511.26 (1 credit hour) to $1416.05 (12 credit hours). Students with a graduate assistantship receive a 25 percent reduction in the Primary Care Medical Fee.

Living and Housing Costs

For married couples, students with families, and single graduate students, the University has 690 efficiency and one-, two-, three-, and four-bedroom apartments that rent for $484 to $686 per month in 2008–09. Residence halls for single graduate students are also available, as are accessible residence hall rooms and apartments for students with disabilities.

Location

The School of Art and Design at Southern Illinois University Carbondale is located in Carbondale, a small city approximately 60 miles north of the southern tip of Illinois. Students from northern Illinois find Amtrak (train) and Interstate Route 57 the fastest and most direct routes. Students also have access to Williamson County Airport, on Route 13 east of Carbondale. Carbondale is about 110 miles (a 2-hour drive) southeast of Lambert–St. Louis International Airport, St. Louis, Missouri, and 330 miles (a 6-hour drive) south of Chicago, Illinois.

The University and The School

Founded in 1869, Southern Illinois University is currently home to more than 20,000 students, including 4,000 graduate and professional students. In keeping with the state's master plan, and with a commitment to enhance its Carnegie II Research status, the University's objective is to provide a comprehensive educational program meeting as many individual student needs as possible. The University comprises a faculty and the facilities to offer general and professional training ranging from two-year associate degree to doctoral programs. The School of Art and Design has sustained a strong national reputation for many years, with a stable graduate enrollment of about 50 students—one third of whom graduate each year with an M.F.A. degree.

Applying

Applicants are evaluated and selected by the faculty members of the specific studio discipline to which they apply. The portfolio should include a statement of intent, fifteen to twenty slides of recent work, transcripts, and three letters of recommendation. GRE scores are necessary only for students interested in applying for fellowships and are not necessary for all other forms of financial aid. The School affirmatively seeks to attract to its faculty, staff, and student body qualified individuals of diverse backgrounds.

Correspondence and Information

Chris Wildrick, Head of Graduate Studies
School of Art and Design
Southern Illinois University Carbondale
Carbondale, Illinois 62901-4301
Phone: 618-453-4313
Web site: http://www.artanddesign.siu.edu/home.html

Southern Illinois University Carbondale

THE FACULTY

Najjar Abdul-Musawwir, Assistant Professor; M.F.A., Southern Illinois Carbondale, 1997. Drawing, painting, core curriculum. (E-mail: mekka@siu.edu)
Steve Belletire, Associate Professor; B.F.A., Illinois at Urbana-Champaign, 1971. Industrial design. (E-mail: sbell@siu.edu)
Larry S. Briggs, Associate Professor; B.F.A., Oklahoma, 1956. Communication design. (E-mail: bbriggs@siu.edu)
Pattie Chalmers, Assistant Professor; M.F.A., Minnesota, 2001. Ceramics.
Peter Chametzky, Associate Professor and Head of Undergraduate Studies; Ph.D., CUNY, 1991. Art history. (E-mail: pchamet@siu.edu)
Harris Deller, Professor and Director; M.F.A., Cranbrook Academy of Art, 1973. Ceramics. (E-mail: ga4252@siu.edu)
Elina Gertsman, Assistant Professor; Ph.D., Boston University, 2004. Art history. (E-mail: gertsman@siu.edu)
Carma Gorman, Assistant Professor; Ph.D., Berkeley, 1998. Art history. (E-mail: cgorman@siu.edu)
Sally Gradle, Assistant Professor; Ed.D., Illinois at Urbana-Champaign, 2004. Art education. (E-mail: gradle@siu.edu)
Jason Howell, Assistant Professor; M.F.A., Oklahoma, 2001. Communication design. (E-mail: jason_w_howell@yahoo.com)
Jiyong Lee, Assistant Professor; M.F.A., RIT, 2000. Glass. (E-mail: jiyong@siu.edu)
Alex Lopez, Assistant Professor; M.F.A., Alfred, 1998. Foundations/sculpture. (E-mail: alxlpz@siu.edu)
Colleen Ludwig, Assistant Professor; M.F.A., Minnesota, 2005. Digital media.
Jerry Monteith, Associate Professor; M.F.A., Cranbrook Academy of Art, 1978. Sculpture. (E-mail: monteith@siu.edu)
Erin Palmer, Associate Professor; M.F.A., Yale, 1993. Drawing, painting. (Contact: Art Office, 618-453-4315)
Xuhong Shang, Associate Professor; M.F.A., Temple, 1992. Painting. (E-mail: xuhong@siu.edu)
Edward Shay, Professor; M.F.A., Illinois at Urbana-Champaign, 1971. Painting, printmaking, drawing. (E-mail: shay@siu.edu)
Stacey Sloboda, Assistant Professor; Ph.D., UCLA, 2004. Art history. (E-mail: sloboda@siu.edu)
Rick Smith, Assistant Professor; M.F.A., Southern Illinois Carbondale, 1992. Metalsmithing, blacksmithing. (E-mail: rsforge@aol.com)
Peter K. Storkerson, Assistant Professor; Ph.D., IIT, 2001. Communication design. (E-mail: pstork@siu.edu)
Jason Urban, Assistant Professor; M.F.A., Iowa, 2002. Printmaking. (E-mail: urban@siu.edu)
Chris Wildrick, Assistant Professor and Head of Graduate Studies; M.F.A., Wisconsin–Madison, 1999. Foundations. (E-mail: wildrick@siu.edu)
Kay Zivkovich, Associate Professor and Assistant Director; M.F.A., 1973, M.Ed., 1979, Southern Illinois Carbondale. Communication design. (E-mail: kmpzivko@siu.edu)

UNIVERSITY OF MICHIGAN

School of Art and Design

Programs of Study

The School of Art and Design, in association with the University of Michigan Horace H. Rackham School of Graduate Studies, offers a Master of Fine Arts in art and design degree program called Art and Design Plus (A&D+). This unique three-year M.F.A. program is structured to expand the intellectual reach of creative work, and to utilize a comprehensive process for bringing creative work into the world. In this program, all graduate students are required to reach beyond the cultures of art and design to develop robust engagement with one or more fields of knowledge and inquiry at the University of Michigan. Students are expected to carry out creative work informed by and interacting with the additional field of inquiry. The backgrounds and applications of successful applicants to the program will clearly reveal interests and abilities to carry out such work.

The program is conceptualized as a three-year progression from exploration to focus. Students complete 12 credits of course work during each of six semesters in residence: four 3-credit University electives in the first four semesters, six 3-credit A&D seminars, and 6 credits of studio practice in each semester. The four University electives form the "+" aspect of the A&D+ program. Knowledge and experience accrued in this component of the program are intended for integration into a student's creative work. The final two semesters together culminate in a thesis/exhibition/presentation project. Degree requirements include a public presentation of creative work; a written, illustrated thesis submitted as a hard-copy document, an electronic file (CD or DVD), and a Web site; and a final review with the student's committee. Degree requirements must be completed at the end of the third year.

Advising, student reviews, and presentations/exhibitions are integral to the program. Students select School faculty members as advisers for the first two years. For the final year, students develop a 4-person M.F.A. advisory committee that includes 2 faculty members from the School and 2 from other units at the University. Student reviews with ad hoc faculty committees occur at the end of each year to review students' work to date and to serve as the gateway to continuation in the program. Students utilize a variety of presentation modes, including Web-based technologies, for their reviews. All graduate students are required to participate in group presentations/exhibitions each year and are encouraged to seek out other exhibition opportunities. While there are no summer course requirements, summer collaborative projects are facilitated and encouraged, particularly with the School's international partners.

Research Facilities

The University of Michigan offers limitless creative research possibilities supported by world-class facilities. The Warren Robbins Gallery offers students opportunities to curate and manage exhibitions. Across the street from the School of Art and Design, the Duderstadt Center offers state-of-the-art research facilities and an art library. In addition, students have access to the University's libraries, museums, and electronic networks, and the programmatic resources of nineteen other schools and colleges. The School has restored a warehouse in Ann Arbor where all graduate students maintain individual private studios. This secure facility, equipped for a variety of work, is open around-the-clock. Convenient on-site parking is available.

Financial Aid

All students receive substantial and competitive financial support, which, for students who meet the standards for normal progress in the program, includes partial tuition, graduate assistantships, and discretionary funds for six semesters. Additional state-funded and federally funded loans are available through the University. Prospective students should contact the Office of Financial Aid (2001 Student Activities Building, Ann Arbor, Michigan 48109-1316; telephone: 734-763-6600) for a list of funding resources.

Cost of Study

Full-time tuition and fees for the 2006–07 academic year were $7546 per semester for Michigan residents and $15,276 per semester for non-Michigan residents.

Living and Housing Costs

Most graduate students live off campus, though limited on-campus housing is available. Housing options include a broad range of possibilities, from co-ops and studios to houses. Rent for a small, one-bedroom apartment averages about $550 per month; two-bedroom units range from $700 to $900 per month. For current listings, students may contact University Housing at 734-763-3164 or visit http://www.housing.umich.edu.

Student Group

Ten intellectually and creatively challenging students enroll in the School of Art and Design graduate program each year. Among students, there is gender balance with age, geographical, and cultural diversity. The School also enrolls 400 undergraduate students.

Student Outcomes

The traditional outcome for graduates from master's programs in art and design is lifelong commitment to creative practice. Graduates have established a variety of career paths, including independent art and design work, consulting, teaching, museum and curatorial practice, critical writing, and creative entrepreneurship.

Location

Ann Arbor has an intellectually rich, culturally diverse population of 120,000. Located in southeast Michigan on the Huron River, it is 50 miles from Detroit and Windsor, Ontario, 25 miles from a major airport, and 4 hours from Chicago by automobile. Additional information about Ann Arbor is available at http://www.annarbor.org.

The University and The School

The University of Michigan is one of the highest-ranking public institutions in the country. Approximately 35,500 students enroll in its nineteen schools and colleges on the Ann Arbor campus. As a major research institution, its libraries and research facilities rank among the best in the U.S. The University's museums, programs of study, visiting scholars and artists, lectures, and performances represent the full spectrum of intellectual and creative opportunity. Additional information about the University is available at http://www.umich.edu.

Seventy full- and part-time faculty members and 35 administrative and technical staff members support the School of Art and Design's academic programs. Additional information about the School is available on the Web site (http://www.art-design.umich.edu).

Applying

Applicants must have a bachelor's degree, demonstrate an ability to carry out creative work, must have a substantial interest in interdisciplinary work, a strong educational background, and sufficient life experience to draw upon in charting new directions for creative work. New full-time students are admitted for the fall semester. The application deadline is January 1; admission decisions are announced in late March; programs begin in early September. The portfolio, academic transcript, and written statement are all-important components of the application. Prospective students are encouraged to visit the campus and the School. The top 20 candidates interview in Ann Arbor during February.

Correspondence and Information

School of Art and Design
University of Michigan
2000 Bonisteel Boulevard
Ann Arbor, Michigan 48109-2069

Phone: 734-764-0397
E-mail: a&dgradinfo@umich.edu
Web site: http://www.art-design.umich.edu

University of Michigan

THE FACULTY

Jan-Henrik Andersen, Assistant Professor; Diploma (equivalent to M.F.A.), Oslo.
Vincent Castagnacci, Professor; M.F.A., Yale.
James Cogswell, Professor; M.F.A., New Mexico.
Daniel Herwitz, Professor; Ph.D., Chicago.
Holly Hughes, Associate Professor; B.A., Kalamazoo.
Sadashi Inuzuka, Associate Professor; M.F.A., Eastern Michigan.
Shaun Jackson, Associate Professor; President, Shaun Jackson Design.
Carol Jacobsen, Associate Professor; M.F.A., Eastern Michigan.
Andy Kirshner, Assistant Professor; D.M.A., Michigan.
Heidi Kumao, Assistant Professor; M.F.A., Art Institute of Chicago.
Joanne Leonard, Professor; B.A., Berkeley.
Lou Marinaro, Professor; M.F.A., Yale.
Rebakah Modrak, Visiting Associate Professor; M.F.A., Syracuse.
Anne Mondro, Visiting Assistant Professor; M.F.A., Kent State.
Dwayne Overmyer, Professor; M.F.A., Yale.
Cynthia Pachikara, Assistant Professor; M.F.A., Illinois at Urbana-Champaign.
Marianetta Porter, Associate Professor; M.F.A., Michigan.
Theodore K. Ramsay, Professor; M.F.A., Iowa; M.F.A., Cranbrook Academy of Art.
Michael Rodemer, Associate Professor; M.F.A., Ohio State.
Bryan Rogers, Professor and Dean; Ph.D., Berkeley.
Stephanie Rowden, Assistant Professor; M.A., Eastern Michigan.
Allen J. Samuels, Professor; B.F.A, Illinois.
Mary Schmidt, Lecturer and Associate Dean; M.A., Pittsburgh.
Bradley Smith, Associate Professor; Ph.D., Duke.
Sherri Smith, Professor; M.F.A., Cranbrook Academy of Art.
Satoru Takahashi, Assistant Professor; M.F.A., Yale.
Nicholas Tobier, Assistant Professor; M.F.A., Bard; M.A., Harvard.
Joseph Trumpey, Associate Professor; M.F.A., Michigan.
Alicyn Warren, Assistant Professor; Ph.D., Princeton.
Edward West, Professor; M.F.A., RIT.

Section 2
Architecture

This section contains a directory of institutions offering graduate work in architecture, followed by in-depth entries submitted by institutions that chose to prepare detailed program descriptions. Additional information about programs listed in the directory but not augmented by an in-depth entry may be obtained by writing directly to the dean of a graduate school or chair of a department at the address given in the directory.

For programs offering related work, see also in this book *Applied Arts and Design, Art and Art History,* and *Public, Regional, and Industrial Affairs. In another guide in this series:*

Graduate Programs in Engineering & Applied Sciences
See *Civil and Environmental Engineering*

CONTENTS

Program Directories

Close-Ups

See also:

Architectural History

Arizona State University, Graduate College, College of Architecture and Environmental Design, Program in Environmental Design and Planning, Tempe, AZ 85287. Offers design (PhD); history, theory, and criticism (PhD); planning (PhD). *Degree requirements:* For doctorate, thesis/dissertation.

Cornell University, Graduate School, Graduate Fields of Architecture, Art and Planning, Field of Architecture, Ithaca, NY 14853-0001. Offers architectural design (M Arch); architectural science (MS); building technology and environmental science (MS); computer graphics (MS); history of architecture (MA, PhD); history of urban development (MA, PhD); theory and criticism of architecture (M Arch); urban design (M Arch). *Faculty:* 33 full-time. *Students:* 101 full-time (33 women); includes 13 minority (1 African American, 7 Asian Americans or Pacific Islanders, 5 Hispanic Americans), 51 international. Average age 28. 305 applicants, 30% accepted, 39 enrolled. In 2007, 17 master's, 1 doctorate awarded. *Degree requirements:* For master's, one foreign language, thesis (MA, MS); for doctorate, 2 foreign languages, comprehensive exam, thesis/dissertation. *Entrance requirements:* For master's, GRE General Test, GRE Subject Test in computer science (computer graphics), 5-year bachelor's degree in architecture, portfolio (M Arch), 3 letters of recommendation; for doctorate, GRE General Test, 3 letters of recommendation. Additional exam requirements/recommendations for international students: Required—TOEFL (minimum score 600 paper-based; 250 computer-based; 77 iBT). *Application deadline:* For fall admission, 1/15 priority date for domestic students. Application fee: $70. Electronic applications accepted. *Financial support:* In 2007–08, 41 students received support, including 13 fellowships with full tuition reimbursements available, 1 research assistantship with full tuition reimbursement available, 27 teaching assistantships with full tuition reimbursements available; institutionally sponsored loans, scholarships/grants, health care benefits, tuition waivers (full and partial), and unspecified assistantships also available. Financial award applicants required to submit FAFSA. *Faculty research:* Architectural design and urban design, theory and criticism of architecture, computer graphics, building technology and environmental science, history of architecture and history of urban-development. *Unit head:* Director of Graduate Studies, 607-255-6701, Fax: 607-255-0291. *Application contact:* Graduate Field Assistant, 607-255-6701, Fax: 607-255-0291, E-mail: cuarch@cornell.edu.

Graduate School and University Center of the City University of New York, Graduate Studies, Program in Art History, New York, NY 10016-4039. Offers architecture (PhD); graphic arts (PhD); painting (PhD); photography (PhD); sculpture (PhD). *Faculty:* 16 full-time (11 women). *Students:* 159 full-time (121 women), 13 part-time (all women); includes 18 minority (5 African Americans, 2 Asian Americans or Pacific Islanders, 11 Hispanic Americans), 21 international. Average age 34. 89 applicants, 57% accepted, 30 enrolled. In 2007, 14 degrees awarded. *Degree requirements:* For doctorate, 2 foreign languages, thesis/dissertation. *Entrance requirements:* For doctorate, GRE General Test. Additional exam requirements/recommendations for international students: Required—TOEFL. *Application deadline:* For fall admission, 4/15 for domestic students; for spring admission, 11/15 for domestic students. Application fee: $125. Electronic applications accepted. *Financial support:* In 2007–08, 91 students received support, including 68 fellowships, 4 research assistantships, 12 teaching assistantships; career-related internships or fieldwork, Federal Work-Study, institutionally sponsored loans, and tuition waivers (full and partial) also available. Financial award application deadline: 2/1; financial award applicants required to submit FAFSA. *Unit head:* Dr. Kevin Murphy, Executive Officer, 212-817-8035, Fax: 212-817-1502, E-mail: kmurphy@gc.cuny.edu.

Harvard University, Graduate School of Arts and Sciences, Department of History of Art and Architecture, Cambridge, MA 02138. Offers ancient art (PhD); ancient Near Eastern art (PhD); baroque art (PhD); Byzantine art (PhD); classical art (PhD); Indian art (PhD); Islamic art (PhD); Japanese and Chinese art (PhD); medieval art (PhD); modern art (PhD); Renaissance and modern architecture (PhD); Renaissance art (PhD). *Degree requirements:* For doctorate, variable foreign language requirement, thesis/dissertation, general exams; reading exams in French, German, and Italian. *Entrance requirements:* For doctorate, GRE General Test. Additional exam requirements/recommendations for international students: Required—TOEFL. *Expenses:* Tuition: Full-time $31,456. Full-time tuition and fees vary according to program and student level.

Massachusetts Institute of Technology, School of Architecture and Planning, Department of Architecture, Cambridge, MA 02139-4307. Offers architecture (M Arch, PhD), including building technology (PhD), design and computation (PhD), history and theory of architecture (PhD), history and theory of art (PhD); architecture studies (SM Arch S); visual studies (SM Vis S, SMBT); M Arch/MCP; M Arch/SMRED; SM Arch S/MCP; SM Arch S/SMRED. *Faculty:* 31 full-time (8 women). *Students:* 223 full-time (103 women); includes 21 minority (3 African Americans, 13 Asian Americans or Pacific Islanders, 5 Hispanic Americans), 99 international. Average age 28. 665 applicants, 21% accepted, 67 enrolled. In 2007, 63 master's, 8 doctorates awarded. *Degree requirements:* For master's, thesis; for doctorate, comprehensive exam, thesis/dissertation. *Entrance requirements:* For master's, GRE General Test (for some programs), portfolio (for some programs); for doctorate, GRE General Test (for some programs). Additional exam requirements/recommendations for international students: Required—TOEFL. *Application deadline:* For fall admission, 12/15 for domestic and international students. Application fee: $70. Electronic applications accepted. *Expenses:* Tuition: Full-time $34,760; part-time $545 per unit. Required fees: $236. *Financial support:* In 2007–08, 178 students received support, including 117 fellowships with tuition reimbursements available (averaging $20,726 per year), 15 research assistantships with tuition reimbursements available (averaging $20,113 per year), 29 teaching assistantships with tuition reimbursements available (averaging $23,310 per year); career-related internships or fieldwork, Federal Work-Study, institutionally sponsored loans, scholarships/grants, health care benefits, and unspecified assistantships also available. Total annual research expenditures: $532,000. *Unit head:* Prof. Yung Ho Chang, Head, 617-253-7791, Fax: 617-253-8993. *Application contact:* Admissions Coordinator, 617-253-3613, Fax: 617-253-8993.

See Close-Up on page 161.

Savannah College of Art and Design, Graduate School, Program in Architectural History, Savannah, GA 31402-3146. Offers MA, MFA. Part-time programs available. *Faculty:* 6 full-time (1 woman). *Students:* 7 full-time (6 women), 1 (woman) part-time; includes 2 minority (1 American Indian/Alaska Native, 1 Hispanic American). Average age 25. 11 applicants, 91% accepted, 1 enrolled. In 2007, 4 degrees awarded. *Degree requirements:* For master's, one foreign language, thesis, internship. *Entrance requirements:* For master's, interview, research paper. Additional exam requirements/recommendations for international students: Required—TOEFL (minimum score 450 paper-based; 133 computer-based). *Application deadline:* For fall admission, 4/1 priority date for domestic and international students. Applications are processed on a rolling basis. Application fee: $50. Electronic applications accepted. *Expenses:* Tuition: Full-time $24,840; part-time $552 per credit. One-time fee: $500 full-time. *Financial support:* In 2007–08, 1 fellowship was awarded; career-related internships or fieldwork, Federal Work-Study, and scholarships/grants also available. Financial award application deadline: 4/1; financial award applicants required to submit FAFSA. *Unit head:* Dr. Robin Williams, Chair, 912-525-6058, Fax: 912-525-6050, E-mail: rwilliam@scad.edu. *Application contact:* Darrell Tutchton, Director of Graduate and International Enrollment, 912-525-5961, Fax: 912-525-5985, E-mail: admission@scad.edu.

See Close-Up on page 257.

University of California, Berkeley, Graduate Division, College of Environmental Design, Department of Architecture, Berkeley, CA 94720-1500. Offers architecture (M Arch); building science (MS, PhD); building structures, construction and materials (MS, PhD); design (MA); design theories, methods, and practices (MS, PhD); environmental design in developing countries (MS, PhD); history of architecture and urbanism (MS, PhD); social and cultural processes in architecture and urbanism (MS, PhD); M Arch/MCP; M Arch/MS; MLA/M Arch. *Degree requirements:* For master's, thesis; for doctorate, thesis/dissertation, qualifying exam. *Entrance requirements:* For master's and doctorate, GRE General Test, minimum GPA of 3.0, 3 letters of recommendation. Additional exam requirements/recommendations for international students: Required—TOEFL. Application fee: $70 ($90 for international students). Electronic applications accepted. *Financial support:* Unspecified assistantships available. *Unit head:* Mary Comerio, Chair, 510-642-4942, E-mail: mcomerio@berkeley.edu. *Application contact:* Lois H. Ito Koch, Student Affairs Officer, 510-642-5577, Fax: 510-643-5607, E-mail: archgrad@berkeley.edu.

University of Pittsburgh, School of Arts and Sciences, Department of History of Art and Architecture, Pittsburgh, PA 15260. Offers MA, PhD. Part-time programs available. *Faculty:* 13 full-time (7 women). *Students:* 33 full-time (28 women), 1 (woman) part-time; includes 6 minority (5 Asian Americans or Pacific Islanders, 1 Hispanic American). Average age 33. 38 applicants, 32% accepted, 7 enrolled. In 2007, 4 master's, 2 doctorates awarded. Terminal master's awarded for partial completion of doctoral program. *Median time to degree:* Of those who began their doctoral program in fall 1999, 50% received their degree in 8 years or less. *Degree requirements:* For master's, one foreign language, thesis; for doctorate, 2 foreign languages, comprehensive exam, thesis/dissertation. *Entrance requirements:* For doctorate, GRE General Test, 3 letters of recommendation, writing sample, personal statement, foreign language questionnaire. Additional exam requirements/recommendations for international students: Required—TOEFL. *Application deadline:* For fall admission, 1/15 for domestic and international students. Applications are processed on a rolling basis. Application fee: $50. Electronic applications accepted. *Financial support:* In 2007–08, 30 students received support, including 16 fellowships with full tuition reimbursements available (averaging $17,162 per year), 14 teaching assistantships with full tuition reimbursements available (averaging $14,485 per year); research assistantships with full tuition reimbursements available, career-related internships or fieldwork, Federal Work-Study, scholarships/grants, health care benefits, and tuition waivers (partial) also available. Financial award application deadline: 1/15. *Faculty research:* Asian, medieval, Renaissance/baroque, modern art and architecture, contemporary. Total annual research expenditures: $10,000. *Unit head:* Dr. Kirk Savage, Chair, 412-648-2405, Fax: 412-648-2792, E-mail: ksa@pitt.edu. *Application contact:* Dr. Anne Weis, Director, Graduate Studies, 412-648-2415, Fax: 412-648-2792, E-mail: weis@pitt.edu.

University of Virginia, College and Graduate School of Arts and Sciences, McIntire Department of Art, Charlottesville, VA 22904-4130. Offers classical art and archaeology (MA, PhD); history of art and architecture (MA, PhD). *Faculty:* 24 full-time (11 women), 2 part-time/adjunct (0 women). *Students:* 52 full-time (37 women); includes 1 minority (American Indian/Alaska Native), 4 international. Average age 29. 81 applicants, 35% accepted, 12 enrolled. In 2007, 11 master's awarded. *Median time to degree:* Of those who began their doctoral program in fall 1999, 50% received their degree in 8 years or less. *Degree requirements:* For master's, one foreign language, thesis, defense; for doctorate, 2 foreign languages, comprehensive exam, thesis/dissertation, defense. *Entrance requirements:* For master's and doctorate, GRE General Test, writing sample. Additional exam requirements/recommendations for international students: Recommended—TOEFL (minimum score 600 paper-based; 250 computer-based; 90 iBT), IELTS (minimum score 7). *Application deadline:* For fall admission, 12/7 for domestic students. Application fee: $60. Electronic applications accepted. *Financial support:* In 2007–08, 40 fellowships (averaging $7,950 per year), 1 research assistantship (averaging $2,000 per year), 12 teaching assistantships with full tuition reimbursements (averaging $8,800 per year) were awarded; career-related internships or fieldwork, Federal Work-Study, scholarships/grants, and unspecified assistantships also available. Financial award application deadline: 12/7; financial award applicants required to submit CSS PROFILE. *Faculty research:* Classical art, renaissance art and architecture, American material culture. Total annual research expenditures: $35,000. *Unit head:* Daniel Ehnbom, Director of Graduate Studies, 434-924-6130, Fax: 434-924-3647, E-mail: dje6r@virginia.edu. *Application contact:* Aaron Mills, Associate Dean of Graduate Academic Programs and Research, 434-924-6739, Fax: 434-924-6737, E-mail: grad-a-s@virginia.edu.

University of Virginia, School of Architecture, Department of Architectural History, Charlottesville, VA 22903. Offers M Arch H, PhD. *Faculty:* 5 full-time (3 women), 1 part-time/adjunct (0 women). *Students:* 23 full-time (18 women), 1 part-time; includes 1 minority (Asian American or Pacific Islander), 1 international. Average age 30. 25 applicants, 68% accepted, 6 enrolled. In 2007, 10 master's, 3 doctorates awarded. *Degree requirements:* For master's, one foreign language, thesis; for doctorate, one foreign language, comprehensive exam, thesis/dissertation. *Entrance requirements:* For master's and doctorate, GRE General Test. Additional exam requirements/recommendations for international students: Required—TOEFL (minimum score 600 paper-based; 250 computer-based). Application fee: $60. *Financial support:* Career-related internships or fieldwork, Federal Work-Study, and institutionally sponsored loans available. Financial award applicants required to submit FAFSA. *Faculty research:* Urban form, nineteenth and twentieth century American architecture. *Unit head:* Louis Nelson, Chair, 434-924-1428, Fax: 434-982-2678, E-mail: lnelson@virginia.edu. *Application contact:* Tracy Brookman, Admissions Officer, 434-924-6442, E-mail: arch-admissions@virginia.edu.

Virginia Commonwealth University, Graduate School, School of the Arts, Department of Art History, Richmond, VA 23284-9005. Offers architectural history (MA); art history (MA, PhD); historical studies (MA); museum studies (MA). *Accreditation:* NASAD. *Faculty:* 10 full-time (4 women). *Students:* 19 full-time (18 women), 24 part-time (20 women); includes 6 minority (2 African Americans, 2 Asian Americans or Pacific Islanders, 2 Hispanic Americans), 1 international. 54 applicants, 50% accepted, 13 enrolled. In 2007, 15 master's, 4 doctorates awarded. *Degree requirements:* For master's, thesis; for doctorate, comprehensive exam, thesis/dissertation. *Entrance requirements:* For master's and doctorate, GRE General Test. *Application deadline:* For fall admission, 1/15 for domestic students. Application fee: $50. *Expenses:* Tuition, state resident: full-time $7,224; part-time $401 per credit. Tuition, nonresident: full-time $16,072; part-time $891 per credit. Required fees: $1,679; $63 per credit. Tuition and fees vary according to campus/location. *Financial support:* Fellowships, teaching assistantships, career-related internships or fieldwork, Federal Work-Study, and institutionally sponsored loans available. Support available to part-time students. Financial award application deadline: 3/15. *Faculty research:* Modern, nineteenth century, Renaissance, American, and Medieval art. *Unit head:* Dr. James Farmer, Coordinator of Graduate Studies, 804-828-2784, Fax: 804-828-7468, E-mail: jfarmer@saturn.vcu.edu.

See Close-Up on page 275.

Architecture

Academy of Art University, Graduate Program, School of Architecture, San Francisco, CA 94105-3410. Offers M Arch, MFA. Part-time programs available. Postbaccalaureate distance learning degree programs offered (no on-campus study). *Degree requirements:* For master's, final review. *Entrance requirements:* For master's, portfolio, bachelor's degree in architecture or related field. Electronic applications accepted.

Andrews University, School of Graduate Studies, Division of Architecture, Berrien Springs, MI 49104. Offers M Arch.

Arizona State University, Graduate College, College of Architecture and Environmental Design, School of Architecture, Tempe, AZ 85287. Offers architecture (M Arch); building design (MS); MBA/M Arch. *Degree requirements:* For master's, thesis optional. *Entrance requirements:* For master's, GRE General Test, design portfolio.

Auburn University, Graduate School, College of Architecture, Design, and Construction, Auburn University, AL 36849. Offers MBS, MCP, MDB, MID, MLA, MPA/MCP. Part-time programs available. *Faculty:* 50 full-time (9 women). *Students:* 79 full-time (27 women), 23 part-time (12 women); includes 17 minority (11 African Americans, 4 Asian Americans or Pacific Islanders, 2 Hispanic Americans), 18 international. Average age 28. 111 applicants, 71% accepted, 45 enrolled. In 2007, 58 degrees awarded. *Entrance requirements:* For master's, GRE General Test. *Application deadline:* For fall admission, 7/7 for domestic students; for spring admission, 11/24 for domestic students. Applications are processed on a rolling basis. Application fee: $25 ($50 for international students). Electronic applications accepted. *Expenses:* Contact institution. *Financial support:* Fellowships, Federal Work-Study available. Support available to part-time students. Financial award application deadline: 3/15. *Unit head:* Dan D. Bennett, Dean, 334-844-4524. *Application contact:* Dr. Joe Pittman, Interim Dean of the Graduate School, 334-844-4700.

Ball State University, Graduate School, College of Architecture and Planning, Department of Architecture, Program in Architecture, Muncie, IN 47306-1099. Offers M Arch. *Faculty:* 25. *Students:* 54 full-time (18 women), 9 part-time (3 women); includes 6 minority (1 African American, 3 Asian Americans or Pacific Islanders, 2 Hispanic Americans), 4 international. Average age 27. 63 applicants, 83% accepted, 32 enrolled. In 2007, 10 degrees awarded. *Degree requirements:* For master's, thesis. *Entrance requirements:* For master's, minimum undergraduate B average, portfolio, writing sample. Application fee: $25 ($35 for international students). *Expenses:* Tuition, state resident: full-time $6,864. Tuition, nonresident: full-time $17,932. Required fees: $1,866. *Financial support:* Research assistantships with full tuition reimbursements, teaching assistantships with full tuition reimbursements available. Financial award application deadline: 3/1. *Unit head:* Dr. Stephen Kendall, Graduate Program Director, 765-285-1900, Fax: 765-285-1765.

Boston Architectural College, Graduate Programs, Boston, MA 02115-2795. Offers architecture (M Arch); interior design (MID). *Accreditation:* CIDA. *Degree requirements:* For master's, thesis. *Entrance requirements:* For master's, portfolio (recommended). Electronic applications accepted.

See Close-Up on page 159.

California College of the Arts, Graduate Programs, Program in Architecture, San Francisco, CA 94107. Offers M Arch. *Faculty:* 2 full-time (1 woman), 43 part-time/adjunct (13 women). *Students:* 77 full-time (33 women). Average age 30. 72 applicants, 86% accepted, 27 enrolled. In 2007, 7 degrees awarded. *Degree requirements:* For master's, thesis. *Entrance requirements:* For master's, appropriate bachelor's degree, portfolio, resumé, minimum 2 letters of recommendation. Additional exam requirements/recommendations for international students: Required—TOEFL (minimum score 600 paper-based; 250 computer-based). *Application deadline:* For fall admission, 1/15 for domestic and international students. Application fee: $50. *Expenses:* Tuition: Part-time $1,017 per unit. *Financial support:* In 2007–08, fellowships (averaging $10,000 per year), teaching assistantships (averaging $2,000 per year) were awarded; career-related internships or fieldwork, Federal Work-Study, scholarships/grants, and health care benefits also available. *Unit head:* Ila Berman, Chair, 415-703-9516, E-mail: iberman@cca.edu. *Application contact:* Kathryn Ward, Assistant Director of Graduate Admissions, 415-703-9523 Ext. 9593, Fax: 415-703-9539, E-mail: graduateprograms@cca.edu.

California Polytechnic State University, San Luis Obispo, College of Architecture and Environmental Design, Department of Architecture, San Luis Obispo, CA 93407. Offers MS. *Faculty:* 8 full-time (1 woman), 2 part-time/adjunct (both women). *Students:* 14 full-time (7 women), 7 part-time (5 women); includes 7 minority (1 African American, 4 Asian Americans or Pacific Islanders, 2 Hispanic Americans), 1 international. 22 applicants, 64% accepted, 13 enrolled. *Degree requirements:* For master's, thesis (for some programs). *Entrance requirements:* For master's, GRE, minimum GPA of 3.0, 2 letters of recommendation. Additional exam requirements/recommendations for international students: Required—TOEFL (minimum score 550 paper-based; 213 computer-based), TWE (minimum score 4.5). *Application deadline:* For fall admission, 7/1 for domestic students, 11/30 for international students; for winter admission, 11/1 for domestic students, 6/30 for international students. Applications are processed on a rolling basis. Application fee: $55. Electronic applications accepted. *Expenses:* Tuition, nonresident: part-time $226 per unit. Required fees: $1,777 per quarter. *Financial support:* Research assistantships, teaching assistantships, Federal Work-Study and institutionally sponsored loans available. Support available to part-time students. Financial award application deadline: 3/2; financial award applicants required to submit FAFSA. *Faculty research:* Computer assisted design, decision support systems, building science, facilities management. Total annual research expenditures: $2.4 million. *Unit head:* Dr. Jens Pohl, Graduate Coordinator, 805-756-2841, Fax: 805-756-1500, E-mail: jpohl@calpoly.edu.

California State Polytechnic University, Pomona, Academic Affairs, College of Environmental Design, Program in Architecture, Pomona, CA 91768-2557. Offers M Arch. Part-time programs available. *Students:* 52 full-time (33 women), 16 part-time (8 women); includes 20 minority (1 African American, 13 Asian Americans or Pacific Islanders, 6 Hispanic Americans), 4 international. Average age 30. 102 applicants, 23% accepted, 14 enrolled. In 2007, 8 degrees awarded. *Degree requirements:* For master's, thesis or alternative. *Application deadline:* For fall admission, 5/1 for domestic students; for winter admission, 10/15 priority date for domestic students; for spring admission, 1/20 priority date for domestic students. Applications are processed on a rolling basis. Application fee: $55. Electronic applications accepted. *Expenses:* Tuition, nonresident: full-time $7,232; part-time $226 per unit. Required fees:$3,920. One-time fee: $2,486 part-time. *Financial support:* Career-related internships or fieldwork, Federal Work-Study, and institutionally sponsored loans available. Support available to part-time students. Financial award application deadline: 3/2; financial award applicants required to submit FAFSA. *Unit head:* Kip Dickson, Graduate Coordinator, 909-869-2682, Fax: 909-869-4331.

Carleton University, Faculty of Graduate Studies, Faculty of Engineering and Design, School of Architecture, Ottawa, ON K1S 5B6, Canada. Offers design studies (M Arch). *Degree requirements:* For master's, thesis. *Entrance requirements:* For master's, honors degree. Additional exam requirements/recommendations for international students: Required—TOEFL. *Application deadline:* Applications are processed on a rolling basis. Application fee: $77 Canadian dollars. *Financial support:* Fellowships, research assistantships, teaching assistantships, institutionally sponsored loans, scholarships/grants, and unspecified assistantships available. *Faculty research:* Theoretical issues in architecture and culture, cultural diversity, architecture and technoscientific culture. *Unit head:* Marco Frascari, Director, 613-520-2600 Ext. 2855, Fax: 613-520-4849. *Application contact:* Stephen Fai, Supervisor of Graduate Studies, 613-520-2600 Ext. 2855, Fax: 613-520-4849.

Carnegie Mellon University, College of Fine Arts, School of Architecture, Pittsburgh, PA 15213-3891. Offers architecture (MSA); architecture, engineering, and construction management (M Sc, PhD); building performance and diagnostics (M Sc, PhD); computational design (M Sc, PhD); sustainable design (M Sc); urban design (M Sc). Terminal master's awarded for partial completion of doctoral program. *Degree requirements:* For doctorate, thesis/dissertation. *Entrance requirements:* For master's and doctorate, GRE General Test. Additional exam requirements/recommendations for international students: Required—TOEFL.

The Catholic University of America, School of Architecture and Planning, Washington, DC 20064. Offers M Arch, M Arch Studies. Part-time programs available. *Faculty:* 19 full-time (4 women), 28 part-time/adjunct (6 women). *Students:* 104 full-time (40 women), 15 part-time (12 women); includes 21 minority (8 African Americans, 8 Asian Americans or Pacific Islanders, 5 Hispanic Americans), 7 international. Average age 28. 126 applicants, 75% accepted, 50 enrolled. In 2007, 41 degrees awarded. *Degree requirements:* For master's, thesis. *Entrance requirements:* For master's, minimum GPA of 2.7, portfolio, 3 letters of recommendation. Additional exam requirements/recommendations for international students: Required—TOEFL (minimum score 500 paper-based; 173 computer-based). *Application deadline:* For fall admission, 2/1 priority date for domestic students; for spring admission, 11/15 priority date for domestic students. Applications are processed on a rolling basis. Application fee: $55. Electronic applications accepted. *Expenses:* Contact institution. *Financial support:* Teaching assistantships, Federal Work-Study, scholarships/grants, tuition waivers (partial), and unspecified assistantships available. Financial award application deadline: 2/1; financial award applicants required to submit FAFSA. *Faculty research:* Architectural history, sacred architecture, computers, technology, urban design, preservation. *Unit head:* Randall Ott, Dean, 202-319-5784, Fax: 202-319-5188, E-mail: ott@cua.edu. *Application contact:* Christine Mica, Director, University Admissions, 202-319-5305, Fax: 202-319-6533, E-mail: cua-admissions@cua.edu.

City College of the City University of New York, Graduate School, School of Architecture and Environmental Studies, Program in Architecture, New York, NY 10031-9198. Offers M Arch. *Students:* 28. 61 applicants, 66% accepted, 28 enrolled. *Entrance requirements:* For master's, GRE. Additional exam requirements/recommendations for international students: Required—TOEFL (minimum score 550 paper-based; 213 computer-based). *Application deadline:* For fall admission, 1/15 for domestic students. Application fee: $125. *Unit head:* Brad Horn, Head, 212-650-8319. *Application contact:* Sarah Morales, Information Contact, 212-650-8748, E-mail: archgrad@ccny.cuny.edu.

Clemson University, Graduate School, College of Architecture, Arts, and Humanities, Department of Architecture, Clemson, SC 29634. Offers M Arch, MS. *Faculty:* 19 full-time (4 women), 6 part-time/adjunct (2 women). *Students:* 44 full-time (20 women), 4 part-time (1 woman); includes 5 minority (3 African Americans, 1 American Indian/Alaska Native, 1 Asian American or Pacific Islander). Average age 27. 94 applicants, 31% accepted, 9 enrolled. In 2007, 27 degrees awarded. *Degree requirements:* For master's, thesis. *Entrance requirements:* For master's, GRE General Test, portfolio. Additional exam requirements/recommendations for international students: Required—TOEFL, IELTS. *Application deadline:* For fall admission, 2/1 for domestic students, 4/15 for international students; for spring admission, 9/15 for international students. Application fee: $55. Electronic applications accepted. *Financial support:* In 2007–08, 22 fellowships (averaging $5,900 per year), 31 research assistantships (averaging $3,300 per year), 9 teaching assistantships (averaging $2,800 per year) were awarded; unspecified assistantships also available. Financial award application deadline: 2/15; financial award applicants required to submit FAFSA. *Faculty research:* Color and computers, light energy, theory and philosophy, architecture for education, architecture for health. *Unit head:* Dr. Ted Cavinaugh, Chair, 864-656-3896, Fax: 864-656-0204. *Application contact:* Michelle McLane, Student Services, 864-656-3938, Fax: 864-656-1810, E-mail: wking@clemson.edu.

Columbia College Chicago, Graduate School, Program in Architectural Studies, Chicago, IL 60605-1996. Offers MFA. Part-time programs available. *Faculty:* 1 part-time/adjunct. *Students:* 1 (woman) full-time, 1 (woman) part-time. Average age 27. In 2007, 7 degrees awarded. *Degree requirements:* For master's, thesis. *Entrance requirements:* For master's, minimum GPA of 3.0, portfolio. Additional exam requirements/recommendations for international students: Required—TOEFL (minimum score 550 paper-based; 213 computer-based). *Application deadline:* For fall admission, 3/1 for domestic and international students. Application fee: $50. Electronic applications accepted. *Financial support:* Career-related internships or fieldwork, Federal Work-Study, and scholarships/grants available. Support available to part-time students. Financial award application deadline: 8/13; financial award applicants required to submit FAFSA. *Unit head:* Jay Wolke, Head, 312-344-7867, Fax: 312-344-8009, E-mail: jwolke@colum.edu. *Application contact:* Keith Cleveland, Acting Dean of the Graduate School, 312-344-7261, Fax: 312-344-8047, E-mail: kcleveland@colum.edu.

Columbia University, Graduate School of Architecture, Planning, and Preservation, Program in Advanced Architectural Design, New York, NY 10027. Offers MS. *Entrance requirements:* For master's, GRE General Test. *Expenses:* Tuition: Part-time $1,452 per credit. Required fees: $152 per term. One-time fee: $75 part-time. Full-time tuition and fees vary according to course level, course load, degree level and program.

Columbia University, Graduate School of Architecture, Planning, and Preservation, Program in Architecture, New York, NY 10027. Offers M Arch, PhD, M Arch/MS. PhD offered through the Graduate School of Arts and Science. *Degree requirements:* For master's, thesis optional. *Entrance requirements:* For master's, GRE General Test. *Expenses:* Tuition: Part-time $1,452 per credit. Required fees: $152 per term. One-time fee: $75 part-time. Full-time tuition and fees vary according to course level, course load, degree level and program.

Columbia University, Graduate School of Architecture, Planning, and Preservation, Program in Architecture and Urban Design, New York, NY 10027. Offers MS. *Entrance requirements:* For master's, GRE General Test. *Expenses:* Tuition: Part-time $1,452 per credit. Required fees: $152 per term. One-time fee: $75 part-time. Full-time tuition and fees vary according to course level, course load, degree level and program.

Cornell University, Graduate School, Graduate Fields of Architecture, Art and Planning, Field of Architecture, Ithaca, NY 14853-0001. Offers architectural design (M Arch); architectural science (MS); building technology and environmental science (MS); computer graphics (MS); history of architecture (MA, PhD); history of urban development (MA, PhD); theory and criticism of architecture (M Arch); urban design (M Arch). *Faculty:* 33 full-time. *Students:* 101 full-time (33 women); includes 13 minority (1 African American, 7 Asian Americans or Pacific Islanders, 5 Hispanic Americans), 51 international. Average age 28. 305 applicants, 30% accepted, 39 enrolled. In 2007, 17 master's, 1 doctorate awarded. *Degree requirements:* For master's, one foreign language, thesis (MA, MS); for doctorate, 2 foreign languages, comprehensive exam, thesis/dissertation. *Entrance requirements:* For master's, GRE General Test, GRE Subject Test in computer science (computer graphics), 5-year bachelor's degree in architecture, portfolio (M Arch), 3 letters of recommendation; for doctorate, GRE General Test, 3 letters of recommendation. Additional exam requirements/recommendations for international students: Required—TOEFL (minimum score 600 paper-based; 250 computer-based; 77 iBT). *Application deadline:* For fall admission, 1/15 priority date for domestic students. Application fee: $70. Electronic applications accepted. *Financial support:* In 2007–08, 41 students received support, including 13 fellowships with full tuition reimbursements available, 1 research assistantship with full tuition reimbursement available, 27 teaching assistantships with full tuition reimbursements available; institutionally sponsored loans, scholarships/grants, health care benefits, tuition waivers (full and partial), and unspecified assistantships also available. Financial award applicants required to submit FAFSA. *Faculty research:* Architectural design and urban design, theory and criticism of architecture, computer graphics, building technology and environmental science, history of architecture and history of urban-development. *Unit head:* Director of Graduate Studies, 607-255-6701, Fax: 607-255-0291. *Application contact:* Graduate Field Assistant, 607-255-6701, Fax: 607-255-0291, E-mail: cuarch@cornell.edu.

Architecture

Cranbrook Academy of Art, Graduate School, Program in Architecture, Bloomfield Hills, MI 48303-0801. Offers M Arch. *Degree requirements:* For master's, thesis, exhibit. *Entrance requirements:* Additional exam requirements/recommendations for international students: Required—TOEFL (minimum score 550 paper-based; 213 computer-based).

See Close-Up on page 237.

Dalhousie University, Faculty of Architecture and Planning, Halifax, NS B3H 4R2, Canada. Offers M Arch, M Pl, MEDS, MPS, M Eng/M Plan, MA Sc/M Plan. *Degree requirements:* For master's, thesis. *Entrance requirements:* Additional exam requirements/recommendations for international students: Required—TOEFL. *Application deadline:* For fall admission, 4/1 priority date for domestic students. Applications are processed on a rolling basis. Application fee: $60. *Financial support:* Career-related internships or fieldwork and scholarships/grants available. *Unit head:* Prof. Grant Wanzel, Dean, 902-494-3210, Fax: 902-423-6672, E-mail: arch.office@dal.ca. *Application contact:* Bev Nightingale, Graduate Secretary, 902-494-3973, Fax: 902-423-6672, E-mail: arch.office@dal.ca.

Drexel University, College of Media Arts and Design, Department of Architecture, Philadelphia, PA 19104-2875. Offers M Arch. Part-time and evening/weekend programs available. *Entrance requirements:* For master's, minimum GPA of 3.0, portfolio. Electronic applications accepted.

Florida Agricultural and Mechanical University, Division of Graduate Studies, Research, and Continuing Education, School of Architecture, Tallahassee, FL 32307-3200. Offers architectural studies (MS Arch); architecture (professional) (M Arch); landscape architecture (MLA). Part-time programs available. *Degree requirements:* For master's, thesis. *Entrance requirements:* For master's, GRE General Test, minimum GPA of 3.0, portfolio. Additional exam requirements/recommendations for international students: Required—TOEFL (minimum score 550 paper-based). *Faculty research:* Environmental technology, post-occupancy evaluation, building economics, design methods, computer-aided design.

Florida International University, College of Architecture and the Arts, Miami, FL 33199. Offers M Arch, MFA, MID, MLA, MM, MS. *Accreditation:* ASLA. Part-time and evening/weekend programs available. *Faculty:* 53 full-time (15 women). *Students:* 165 full-time (88 women), 44 part-time (24 women); includes 125 minority (14 African Americans, 8 Asian Americans or Pacific Islanders, 103 Hispanic Americans), 24 international. Average age 30. 201 applicants, 58% accepted, 77 enrolled. In 2007, 61 degrees awarded. *Degree requirements:* For master's, thesis. *Entrance requirements:* For master's, minimum GPA of 3.0 (upper level coursework). Additional exam requirements/recommendations for international students: Required—TOEFL (minimum score 550 paper-based; 213 computer-based). *Application deadline:* For fall admission, 6/1 for domestic students, 4/1 for international students; for spring admission, 10/1 for domestic students, 9/1 for international students. Applications are processed on a rolling basis. Application fee: $30. Electronic applications accepted. *Expenses:* Tuition, state resident: full-time $6,106. Tuition, nonresident: full-time $15,528. Required fees: $284. *Unit head:* Juan A. Bueno, Dean, 305-348-6101, Fax: 305-348-6716, E-mail: buenoj@fiu.edu.

Florida International University, College of Architecture and the Arts, School of Architecture, Architecture Program, Miami, FL 33199. Offers M Arch. Part-time and evening/weekend programs available. *Students:* 78 full-time (33 women), 10 part-time (4 women); includes 57 minority (7 African Americans, 4 Asian Americans or Pacific Islanders, 46 Hispanic Americans), 8 international. Average age 28. 92 applicants, 66% accepted, 39 enrolled. In 2007, 35 degrees awarded. *Entrance requirements:* For master's, minimum GPA of 3.0 (upper level coursework). Additional exam requirements/recommendations for international students: Required—TOEFL (minimum score 550 paper-based; 213 computer-based). *Application deadline:* For fall admission, 2/1 for domestic and international students. Application fee: $30. Electronic applications accepted. *Expenses:* Tuition, state resident: full-time $6,106. Tuition, nonresident: full-time $15,528. Required fees: $284. *Financial support:* Research assistantships, teaching assistantships available. *Unit head:* Juan A. Bueno, Dean, 305-348-6101, Fax: 305-348-6716, E-mail: buenoj@fiu.edu.

Frank Lloyd Wright School of Architecture, Graduate Program, Scottsdale, AZ 85261-4430. Offers M Arch. Summer session held in Spring Green, WI. *Degree requirements:* For master's, thesis or alternative. *Entrance requirements:* For master's, interviews, portfolio. Additional exam requirements/recommendations for international students: Required—TOEFL.

Georgia Institute of Technology, Graduate Studies and Research, College of Architecture, City and Regional Planning Program, Atlanta, GA 30332-0001. Offers architecture (PhD); economic development (MCRP); environmental planning and management (MCRP); geographic information systems (MCRP); land development (MCRP); land use planning (MCRP); transportation (MCRP); urban design (MCRP); MCP/MSCE. *Accreditation:* ACSP. *Degree requirements:* For master's, thesis, internship. *Entrance requirements:* For master's, GRE General Test, minimum GPA of 2.7. Additional exam requirements/recommendations for international students: Required—TOEFL. Electronic applications accepted.

Georgia Institute of Technology, Graduate Studies and Research, College of Architecture, Doctoral Program in Architecture, Atlanta, GA 30332-0001. Offers PhD. Part-time programs available. Postbaccalaureate distance learning degree programs offered. *Degree requirements:* For doctorate, comprehensive exam, thesis/dissertation. *Entrance requirements:* For doctorate, GRE General Test. Additional exam requirements/recommendations for international students: Required—TOEFL (minimum score 600 paper-based; 250 computer-based). Electronic applications accepted.

Georgia Institute of Technology, Graduate Studies and Research, College of Architecture, Master's Program in Architecture, Atlanta, GA 30332-0001. Offers M Arch, MS, M Arch/MCP. Part-time programs available. *Degree requirements:* For master's, thesis or alternative. *Entrance requirements:* For master's, GRE General Test. Additional exam requirements/recommendations for international students: Required—TOEFL (minimum score 600 paper-based; 250 computer-based). Electronic applications accepted.

Georgia Institute of Technology, Graduate Studies and Research, College of Architecture, Program in Building Construction, Atlanta, GA 30332-0001. Offers architecture (PhD); integrated facility management (MS); integrated project delivery systems (MS). Part-time and evening/weekend programs available. *Entrance requirements:* For master's and doctorate, GRE or GMAT. Additional exam requirements/recommendations for international students: Required—TOEFL (minimum score 550 paper-based; 213 computer-based). Electronic applications accepted. *Faculty research:* Design-build, mold, indoor air quality, real estate.

Harvard University, Graduate School of Arts and Sciences, Committee on Architecture, Landscape Architecture, and Urban Planning, Cambridge, MA 02138. Offers architecture (PhD); landscape architecture (PhD); urban planning (PhD). *Degree requirements:* For doctorate, one foreign language, thesis/dissertation, oral exam. *Entrance requirements:* For doctorate, GRE General Test. Additional exam requirements/recommendations for international students: Required—TOEFL. *Expenses:* Tuition: Full-time $31,456. Full-time tuition and fees vary according to program and student level.

Harvard University, Graduate School of Design, Department of Architecture, Cambridge, MA 02138. Offers M Arch. *Faculty:* 18 full-time (6 women), 47 part-time/adjunct (13 women). *Students:* 328 full-time (145 women); includes 74 minority (3 African Americans, 2 American Indian/Alaska Native, 57 Asian Americans or Pacific Islanders, 12 Hispanic Americans), 84 international. Average age 27. In 2007, 100 degrees awarded. *Degree requirements:* For master's, thesis (for some programs). *Entrance requirements:* For master's, GRE General Test. Additional exam requirements/recommendations for international students: Required—TOEFL (minimum score 600 paper-based; 250 computer-based; 100 iBT). *Application deadline:* For fall admission, 12/12 for domestic students. Application fee: $75. Electronic applications accepted. *Expenses:* Tuition: Full-time $31,456. Full-time tuition and fees vary according to program and student level. *Financial support:* Fellowships, teaching assistantships, Federal Work-Study available. Support available to part-time students. Financial award application deadline: 2/11; financial award applicants required to submit FAFSA. *Unit head:* Toshiko Mori, Chair, 617-495-2591. *Application contact:* Gail Gustafson, Director of Admissions, 617-495-5453, Fax: 617-495-8949, E-mail: ggustafson@gsd.harvard.edu.

Harvard University, Graduate School of Design, Program in Design, Cambridge, MA 02138. Offers Dr DES. *Students:* 31 full-time (15 women); includes 1 minority (Asian American or Pacific Islander), 21 international. Average age 33. In 2007, 9 degrees awarded. *Entrance requirements:* For doctorate, GRE General Test. Additional exam requirements/recommendations for international students: Required—TOEFL (minimum score 600 paper-based; 250 computer-based; 100 iBT). *Application deadline:* For fall admission, 1/16 for domestic students. Application fee: $75. Electronic applications accepted. *Expenses:* Tuition: Full-time $31,456. Full-time tuition and fees vary according to program and student level. *Financial support:* Fellowships, research assistantships, teaching assistantships, Federal Work-Study available. Support available to part-time students. Financial award application deadline: 2/11; financial award applicants required to submit FAFSA. *Unit head:* Antoine Picon, Director, 617-495-2337. *Application contact:* Gail Gustafson, Director of Admissions, 617-495-5453, Fax: 617-495-8949, E-mail: ggustafson@gsd.harvard.edu.

Harvard University, Graduate School of Design, Program in Design Studies, Cambridge, MA 02138. Offers M Des S. *Students:* 59 full-time (15 women); includes 11 minority (1 African American, 6 Asian Americans or Pacific Islanders, 4 Hispanic Americans), 30 international. Average age 32. In 2007, 9 degrees awarded. *Entrance requirements:* For master's, GRE General Test. Additional exam requirements/recommendations for international students: Required—TOEFL (minimum score 600 paper-based; 250 computer-based; 100 iBT). *Application deadline:* For fall admission, 1/16 for domestic students. Application fee: $75. Electronic applications accepted. *Expenses:* Tuition: Full-time $31,456. Full-time tuition and fees vary according to program and student level. *Financial support:* Fellowships, teaching assistantships, Federal Work-Study available. Support available to part-time students. Financial award application deadline: 2/11; financial award applicants required to submit FAFSA. *Unit head:* Daniel Schodek, Director, 617-495-2337. *Application contact:* Gail Gustafson, Director of Admissions, 617-495-5453, Fax: 617-495-8949, E-mail: ggustafson@gsd.harvard.edu.

Idaho State University, Office of Graduate Studies, College of Arts and Sciences, Department of Art and Pre-Architecture, Pocatello, ID 83209. Offers MFA. Part-time programs available. *Faculty:* 5 full-time (1 woman). *Students:* 7 full-time (3 women), 8 part-time (3 women); includes 1 minority (Hispanic American) Average age 38. In 2007, 3 degrees awarded. *Degree requirements:* For master's, comprehensive exam, thesis, exhibit. *Entrance requirements:* For master's, GRE General Test, GMAT or MAT, minimum GPA of 3.0 in all upper division classes, portfolio of work, 3 letters of recommendation. Additional exam requirements/recommendations for international students: Required—TOEFL (minimum score 550 paper-based; 213 computer-based; 80 iBT). *Application deadline:* For fall admission, 3/15 for domestic and international students; for spring admission, 10/15 for domestic and international students. Applications are processed on a rolling basis. Application fee: $55. Electronic applications accepted. *Expenses:* Tuition, state resident: full-time $2,882; part-time $259 per credit hour. Tuition, nonresident: full-time $11,566; part-time $379 per credit hour. Required fees: $2,278. Full-time tuition and fees vary according to program. Part-time tuition and fees vary according to course load. *Financial support:* In 2007–08, 3 teaching assistantships with full and partial tuition reimbursements (averaging $9,128 per year) were awarded; Federal Work-Study, institutionally sponsored loans, scholarships/grants, traineeships, health care benefits, and tuition waivers (full and partial) also available. Support available to part-time students. Financial award application deadline: 1/1; financial award applicants required to submit FAFSA. *Faculty research:* Computerized weaving, anodizing refractory metals, viscosity printing, neon, ceramic shell casting. *Unit head:* Rudy Kovacs, Chair, 208-282-2488, Fax: 208-282-4741, E-mail: kovarudo@isu.edu. *Application contact:* Ellen Combs, Graduate School Technical Records Specialist, 208-282-2150, Fax: 208-282-4847.

Illinois Institute of Technology, Graduate College, College of Architecture, Chicago, IL 60616-3793. Offers architecture (M Ar, PhD); landscape architecture (MLA). Part-time programs available. *Faculty:* 38 full-time (4 women), 59 part-time/adjunct (18 women). *Students:* 177 full-time (69 women), 30 part-time (13 women); includes 22 minority (4 African Americans, 8 Asian Americans or Pacific Islanders, 10 Hispanic Americans), 78 international. Average age 28. 347 applicants, 73% accepted, 76 enrolled. In 2007, 57 master's, 5 doctorates awarded. *Degree requirements:* For master's, comprehensive exam (for some programs), thesis (for some programs); for doctorate, comprehensive exam, thesis/dissertation. *Entrance requirements:* For master's, GRE General Test, minimum GPA of 3.0, portfolio, 3 letters of recommendation; for doctorate, GRE General Test, minimum GPA of 3.0, portfolio. Additional exam requirements/recommendations for international students: Required—TOEFL (minimum score 550 paper-based; 213 computer-based; 80 iBT). *Application deadline:* For fall admission, 1/15 for domestic and international students. Applications are processed on a rolling basis. Application fee: $40. Electronic applications accepted. *Expenses:* Tuition: Full-time $14,004; part-time $778 per credit. Required fees: $7 per credit. $235 per term. Tuition and fees vary according to class time, course level, course load, program and student level. *Financial support:* In 2007–08, 125 teaching assistantships (averaging $4,000 per year) were awarded; fellowships, career-related internships or fieldwork, Federal Work-Study, institutionally sponsored loans, scholarships/grants, and health care benefits also available. Support available to part-time students. Financial award applicants required to submit FAFSA. *Faculty research:* Sustainability and environmental design, comprehensive tall building design, innovative materials technology, advanced structural systems, digital design methods. Total annual research expenditures: $25,451. *Unit head:* Donna V. Robertson, John and Jeanne Rowe Chair, 312-567-3230, Fax: 312-567-5820, E-mail: robertson@iit.edu. *Application contact:* Sarah Pariseau, Coordinator for Academic Affairs, 312-567-3281, Fax: 312-567-5820.

Instituto Tecnológico y de Estudios Superiores de Monterrey, Campus Estado de México, Professional and Graduate Division, Estado de Mexico, Mexico. Offers administration of information technologies (MITA); architecture (M Arch); business administration (GMBA, MBA); computer sciences (MCS, PhD); education (M Ed); educational institution administration (MAD); educational technology and innovation (PhD); electronic commerce (MEC); environmental systems (MS); finance (MAF); humanistic studies (MHS); information sciences and knowledge management (MISKM); information systems (MS); manufacturing systems (MS); marketing (MEM); quality systems and productivity (MS); science and materials engineering (PhD); telecommunications management (MTM). Part-time programs available. Postbaccalaureate distance learning degree programs offered (minimal on-campus study). *Degree requirements:* For master's, one foreign language, thesis (for some programs); for doctorate, one foreign language, thesis/dissertation. *Entrance requirements:* For master's, E-PAEP 500, interview; for doctorate, E-PAEP 500, research proposal. Additional exam requirements/recommendations for international students: Required—TOEFL (minimum score 550 paper-based). *Faculty research:* Surface treatments by plasmas, mechanical properties, robotics, graphical computing, mechatronics security protocols.

Instituto Tecnológico y de Estudios Superiores de Monterrey, Campus Irapuato, Graduate Programs, Irapuato, Mexico. Offers administration (MBA); administration of information technology (MAIT); administration of telecommunications (MAT); architecture (M Arch); computer science (MCS); education (M Ed); educational administration (MEA); educational innovation and technology (DEIT); educational technology (MET); electronic commerce (MBA); environmental administration and planning (MEAP); environmental systems (MES); finances (MBA); humanistic studies (MHS); international management for Latin American executives (MIMLAE); library and information science (MLIS); manufacturing quality management (MMQM); marketing research (MBA).

Iowa State University of Science and Technology, Graduate College, College of Design, Department of Architecture, Ames, IA 50011. Offers architectural studies (MSAS); architecture (M Arch); M Arch/MBA; M Arch/MCRP; M Arch/MS. *Faculty:* 25 full-time (8 women), 1 part-time/adjunct (0 women). *Students:* 38 full-time (16 women), 6 part-time (2 women); includes 3 minority (1 Asian American or Pacific Islander, 2 Hispanic Americans), 4 international. 54 applicants, 41% accepted, 8 enrolled. In 2007, 14 degrees awarded. *Degree requirements:* For master's, thesis (for some programs). *Entrance requirements:* For master's, GRE General Test, portfolio, letters of reference. Additional exam requirements/recommendations for international students: Required—TOEFL (paper-based 600; computer-based 250; iBT 79) or IELTS (7.0). *Application deadline:* For fall admission, 1/1 priority date for domestic students. Applications are processed on a rolling basis. Application fee: $30 ($70 for international students). Electronic applications accepted. *Financial support:* In 2007–08, 30 students received support, including 2 research assistantships with full and partial tuition reimbursements available (averaging $19,530 per year), 20 teaching assistantships with partial tuition reimbursements available (averaging $19,530 per year); career-related internships or fieldwork, Federal Work-Study, institutionally sponsored loans, tuition waivers (partial), and unspecified assistantships also available. Support available to part-time students. Financial award application deadline: 2/1; financial award applicants required to submit FAFSA. *Faculty research:* Computer-aided architectural design, social dimensions of urban architecture, designing for the elderly, energy utilization in buildings, architectural theory. *Unit head:* Dr. Calvin F. Lewis, Chair, 515-294-2665, Fax: 515-294-1440, E-mail: calewis@iastate.edu. *Application contact:* Dr. Thomas Leslie, Director of Graduate Education, 515-294-2187, E-mail: jejonas@iastate.edu.

Judson University, Graduate Programs, Elgin, IL 60123-1498. Offers architecture (M Arch); literacy (M Ed); organizational leadership (MA); teaching (M Ed). Part-time and evening/weekend programs available. Postbaccalaureate distance learning degree programs offered (no on-campus study). *Faculty:* 21 part-time/adjunct (6 women). *Students:* 170 full-time (115 women); includes 24 minority (21 African Americans, 3 Hispanic Americans), 5 international. 94 applicants, 97% accepted, 91 enrolled. In 2007, 21 degrees awarded. *Degree requirements:* For master's, comprehensive exam (for some programs), thesis. *Entrance requirements:* For master's, essays, interviews. *Expenses:* Tuition: Full-time $1,700. *Unit head:* Dr. Jim Rohe, Vice President/Senior Dean, 847-628-1520, E-mail: jrohe@judsonu.edu.

Kansas State University, Graduate School, College of Architecture, Planning and Design, Department of Architecture, Manhattan, KS 66506. Offers M Arch. Part-time programs available. *Faculty:* 21 full-time (5 women), 1 (woman) part-time/adjunct. *Students:* 140 full-time (51 women), 2 part-time (1 woman); includes 5 minority (3 African Americans, 1 American Indian/Alaska Native, 1 Hispanic American), 2 international. Average age 25. 8 applicants, 63% accepted, 5 enrolled. In 2007, 6 degrees awarded. *Degree requirements:* For master's, thesis optional, residency. *Entrance requirements:* For master's, portfolio, minimum GPA of 3.0. Additional exam requirements/recommendations for international students: Required—TOEFL (minimum score 600 paper-based). *Application deadline:* For fall admission, 2/1 for domestic students; for spring admission, 10/1 for domestic students. Application fee: $70 ($80 for international students). *Financial support:* In 2007–08, 6 teaching assistantships with full tuition reimbursements (averaging $9,333 per year) were awarded; research assistantships, institutionally sponsored loans and scholarships/grants also available. Support available to part-time students. Financial award application deadline: 3/1; financial award applicants required to submit FAFSA. *Faculty research:* Design theory; environment behavior and place studies, ecological and sustainable design. Total annual research expenditures: $41,899. *Unit head:* Peter Magyar, Head, 785-532-5953, Fax: 785-532-6722, E-mail: pmagyar@ksu.edu. *Application contact:* Carol Martin Watts, Director, 785-532-1127, Fax: 785-532-6722, E-mail: cmwatts@ksu.edu.

Kent State University, College of Architecture and Environmental Design, Kent, OH 44242-0001. Offers architecture (M Arch); preservation architecture (Certificate); urban design (M Arch, MUD, Certificate). Part-time programs available. *Faculty:* 19 full-time (5 women), 21 part-time/adjunct (3 women). *Students:* 45 full-time (13 women), 6 part-time (5 women); includes 3 minority (1 African American, 2 Asian Americans or Pacific Islanders), 7 international. Average age 23. 77 applicants, 52% accepted, 37 enrolled. In 2007, 25 degrees awarded. *Degree requirements:* For master's, thesis optional. *Entrance requirements:* For master's, GRE, portfolio, minimum GPA of 2.75, 3 letters of reference, resumé, undergraduate architecture degree. Additional exam requirements/recommendations for international students: Required—TOEFL (minimum score 550 paper-based). *Application deadline:* For fall admission, 2/1 priority date for domestic and international students. Applications are processed on a rolling basis. Application fee: $30. Electronic applications accepted. *Financial support:* In 2007–08, 6 research assistantships with partial tuition reimbursements (averaging $6,800 per year), 2 teaching assistantships with partial tuition reimbursements (averaging $6,800 per year) were awarded; career-related internships or fieldwork, Federal Work-Study, and tuition waivers (partial) also available. Financial award application deadline: 2/1. *Faculty research:* History and theory, building technology, landscape architecture and urbanism, urbanism, sustainable development. *Unit head:* Dr. James Dalton, Interim Dean, 330-672-2917, Fax: 330-672-3809, E-mail: cmcwilli@kent.edu. *Application contact:* Dr. Maurizio R. Sabini, Graduate Studies Coordinator, 330-672-0927, Fax: 330-672-3809, E-mail: msabini@kent.edu.

Lawrence Technological University, College of Architecture and Design, Southfield, MI 48075-1058. Offers architecture (M Arch); interior design (MID). *Accreditation:* NASAD. Part-time and evening/weekend programs available. *Faculty:* 9 full-time (2 women), 12 part-time/adjunct (3 women). *Students:* 25 full-time (16 women), 133 part-time (64 women); includes 21 minority (9 African Americans, 1 American Indian/Alaska Native, 6 Asian Americans or Pacific Islanders, 5 Hispanic Americans), 19 international. Average age 30. 95 applicants, 72% accepted, 42 enrolled. In 2007, 34 degrees awarded. *Degree requirements:* For master's, thesis. *Entrance requirements:* For master's, portfolio. Additional exam requirements/recommendations for international students: Required—TOEFL (minimum score 550 paper-based; 213 computer-based; 79 iBT). *Application deadline:* For fall admission, 2/1 priority date for domestic students, 2/1 for international students; for winter admission, 11/1 priority date for domestic students, 11/1 for international students; for spring admission, 2/1 priority date for domestic students, 2/1 for international students. Applications are processed on a rolling basis. Application fee: $50. Electronic applications accepted. *Expenses:* Tuition: Part-time $710 per credit hour. Tuition and fees vary according to campus/location and program. *Financial support:* In 2007–08, 105 students received support. Federal Work-Study available. Financial award application deadline: 4/1; financial award applicants required to submit FAFSA. *Unit head:* Glen LeRoy, Dean, 248-204-2800, Fax: 248-204-2900, E-mail: archdean@ltu.edu. *Application contact:* Jane Rohrback, Director of Admissions, 248-204-3160, Fax: 248-204-3188, E-mail: admissions@ltu.edu.

Louisiana State University and Agricultural and Mechanical College, Graduate School, College of Art and Design, School of Architecture, Baton Rouge, LA 70803. Offers M Arch. Part-time programs available. *Faculty:* 13 full-time (2 women). *Students:* 28 full-time (9 women), 1 part-time; includes 3 minority (1 African American, 1 Asian American or Pacific Islander, 1 Hispanic American), 1 international. Average age 29. 29 applicants, 59% accepted, 8 enrolled. In 2007, 7 degrees awarded. *Degree requirements:* For master's, thesis. *Entrance requirements:* For master's, GRE General Test, minimum GPA of 3.0. Additional exam requirements/recommendations for international students: Required—TOEFL (minimum score 550 paper-based; 213 computer-based; 79 iBT). *Application deadline:* For fall admission, 1/25 priority date for domestic students, 5/15 for international students; for spring admission, 10/15 for international students. Applications are processed on a rolling basis. Application fee: $25. Electronic applications accepted. *Financial support:* In 2007–08, 22 students received support, including 7 research assistantships with full and partial tuition reimbursements available (averaging $6,600 per year), 1 teaching assistantship with full and partial tuition reimbursement available (averaging $7,429 per year); fellowships, career-related internships or fieldwork, Federal Work-Study, institutionally sponsored loans, scholarships/grants, health care benefits, tuition waivers (full and partial), and unspecified assistantships also available. Support available to part-time students. Financial award application deadline: 3/1; financial award applicants required to submit FAFSA. *Faculty research:* Architectural design, history of architecture, sustainable design, digital fabrication, community design. Total annual research expenditures: $52,788. *Unit head:* Thomas Sofranko, Director, 225-578-6885, Fax: 225-578-2168, E-mail: tsofranc@lsu.edu. *Application contact:* Chris Theis, Graduate Coordinator, 225-578-6885, Fax: 225-578-2168, E-mail: decod6@lsu.edu.

Massachusetts Institute of Technology, School of Architecture and Planning, Department of Architecture, Cambridge, MA 02139-4307. Offers architecture (M Arch, PhD), including building technology (PhD), design and computation (PhD), history and theory of architecture (PhD), history and theory of art (PhD); architecture studies (SM Arch S); visual studies (SM Vis S, SMBT); M Arch/MCP; M Arch/SMRED; SM Arch S/MCP; SM Arch S/SMRED. *Faculty:* 31 full-time (8 women). *Students:* 223 full-time (103 women); includes 21 minority (3 African Americans, 13 Asian Americans or Pacific Islanders, 5 Hispanic Americans), 99 international. Average age 28. 665 applicants, 21% accepted, 67 enrolled. In 2007, 63 master's, 8 doctorates awarded. *Degree requirements:* For master's, thesis; for doctorate, comprehensive exam, thesis/dissertation. *Entrance requirements:* For master's, GRE General Test (for some programs), portfolio (for some programs); for doctorate, GRE General Test (for some programs). Additional exam requirements/recommendations for international students: Required—TOEFL. *Application deadline:* For fall admission, 12/15 for domestic and international students. Application fee: $70. Electronic applications accepted. *Expenses:* Tuition: Full-time $34,760; part-time $545 per unit. Required fees: $236. *Financial support:* In 2007–08, 178 students received support, including 117 fellowships with tuition reimbursements available (averaging $20,726 per year), 15 research assistantships with tuition reimbursements available (averaging $20,113 per year), 29 teaching assistantships with tuition reimbursements available (averaging $23,310 per year); career-related internships or fieldwork, Federal Work-Study, institutionally sponsored loans, scholarships/grants, health care benefits, and unspecified assistantships also available. Total annual research expenditures: $532,000. *Unit head:* Prof. Yung Ho Chang, Head, 617-253-7791, Fax: 617-253-8993. *Application contact:* Admissions Coordinator, 617-253-3613, Fax: 617-253-8993.

See Close-Up on page 161.

McGill University, Faculty of Graduate and Postdoctoral Studies, Faculty of Engineering, School of Architecture, Montréal, QC H3A 2T5, Canada. Offers affordable homes (M Arch II, Diploma); architectural history and theory (M Arch II); architecture (PhD); domestic environment (M Arch II); domestic environments (Diploma); minimum cost housing in developing countries (M Arch II, Diploma); professional architecture (M Arch I). *Faculty:* 11 full-time (1 woman), 23 part-time/adjunct (8 women). *Students:* 98 full-time (55 women), 14 part-time (6 women). 225 applicants, 43% accepted, 53 enrolled. In 2007, 57 master's, 3 doctorates awarded.

Miami University, Graduate School, School of Fine Arts, Department of Architecture, Oxford, OH 45056. Offers M Arch. *Degree requirements:* For master's, thesis, final exam. *Entrance requirements:* For master's, portfolio, minimum undergraduate GPA of 3.0 during previous 2 years or 3.0 overall. Additional exam requirements/recommendations for international students: Required—TOEFL (minimum score 550 paper-based; 213 computer-based), TWE (minimum score 4).

Mississippi State University, College of Architecture, Art and Design, Mississippi State, MS 39762. Offers MFA, MS. *Accreditation:* NASAD. *Faculty:* 42 full-time (14 women), 9 part-time/adjunct (1 woman). *Students:* 16 full-time (9 women), 5 part-time (2 women); includes 2 minority (1 African American, 1 Asian American or Pacific Islander), 7 international. Average age 31. 18 applicants, 83% accepted, 7 enrolled. In 2007, 9 degrees awarded. *Degree requirements:* For master's, comprehensive exam, thesis, final written and oral exam. *Entrance requirements:* For master's, GRE General Test, portfolio, minimum GPA of 3.0. Additional exam requirements/recommendations for international students: Required—TOEFL. *Application deadline:* For fall admission, 3/1 priority date for domestic students. Applications are processed on a rolling basis. Application fee: $30. Electronic applications accepted. *Expenses:* Tuition, state resident: full-time $4,978; part-time $274 per hour. Tuition, nonresident: full-time $11,469; part-time $635 per hour. *Financial support:* In 2007–08, 7 students received support; research assistantships with full tuition reimbursements available, career-related internships or fieldwork, Federal Work-Study, institutionally sponsored loans, and unspecified assistantships available. Financial award application deadline: 3/1; financial award applicants required to submit FAFSA. *Faculty research:* Digital art in architecture, process change and management, multi-media databases, 3-D modeling and animation, virtual archaeology. *Unit head:* James L. West, Dean, 662-325-2202, Fax: 662-325-8872, E-mail: jwest@coa.msstate.edu. *Application contact:* Dr. William A. Person, Interim Associate Vice President for Academic Affairs/Interim Dean of Graduate Studies, 662-325-7400, Fax: 662-325-1967, E-mail: grad@grad.msstate.edu.

Montana State University, College of Graduate Studies, College of Arts and Architecture, Department of Architecture, Bozeman, MT 59717. Offers M Arch. Part-time programs available. *Faculty:* 18 full-time (4 women), 2 part-time/adjunct (1 woman). *Students:* 48 full-time (13 women), 12 part-time (3 women); includes 2 minority (both Asian Americans or Pacific Islanders) Average age 27. 55 applicants, 67% accepted, 39 enrolled. In 2007, 86 degrees awarded. *Degree requirements:* For master's, comprehensive exam. *Entrance requirements:* For master's, GRE General Test. Additional exam requirements/recommendations for international students: Required—TOEFL (minimum score 550 paper-based; 213 computer-based). *Application deadline:* For fall admission, 7/15 priority date for domestic students, 5/15 priority date for international students; for spring admission, 12/1 priority date for domestic students, 10/1 priority date for international students. Applications are processed on a rolling basis. Application fee: $30. Electronic applications accepted. *Expenses:* Tuition, state resident: full-time $5,176. Tuition, nonresident: full-time $13,070. *Financial support:* In 2007–08, 21 students received support; teaching assistantships with full and partial tuition reimbursements available, Federal Work-Study, scholarships/grants, and unspecified assistantships available. Financial award application deadline: 3/1; financial award applicants required to submit FAFSA. *Faculty research:* Sustainability, design. Total annual research expenditures: $77,243. *Unit head:* Steve Juroszek, Interim Head, 406-994-4256, Fax: 406-994-4257, E-mail: stevej@montana.edu.

Morgan State University, School of Graduate Studies, Institute of Architecture and Planning, Program in Architecture, Baltimore, MD 21251. Offers M Arch. *Faculty:* 4 full-time (1 woman). *Students:* 57. Average age 24. In 2007, 12 degrees awarded. *Degree requirements:* For master's, thesis. *Entrance requirements:* Additional exam requirements/recommendations for international students: Required—TOEFL (minimum score 550 paper-based; 213 computer-based). *Application deadline:* For fall admission, 2/1 priority date for domestic students; for spring admission, 10/1 priority date for domestic students. Applications are processed on a rolling basis. Application fee: $0. *Financial support:* Teaching assistantships, scholarships/grants available. Financial award application deadline: 2/1. *Unit head:* Dr. Ruth Connell, Graduate Coordinator, 443-885-1862, E-mail: ruth.connell@morgan.edu. *Application contact:* Dr. Mark Garrison, Associate Dean, 443-885-3185, Fax: 443-885-8226, E-mail: mark.garrison@morgan.edu.

New Jersey Institute of Technology, Office of Graduate Studies, School of Architecture, Program in Architecture, Newark, NJ 07102. Offers M Arch, MS, M Arch/MIP, M Arch/MS. Part-time and evening/weekend programs available. *Students:* 72 full-time (35 women), 12 part-time (6 women); includes 15 minority (5 African Americans, 5 Asian Americans or Pacific Islanders, 5 Hispanic Americans), 18 international. Average age 30. 102 applicants, 51% accepted, 29 enrolled. In 2007, 28 degrees awarded. *Degree requirements:* For master's, thesis (for some programs). *Entrance requirements:* For master's, GRE General Test, minimum GPA of 3.0. Additional exam requirements/recommendations for international students: Required—TOEFL (minimum score 550 paper-based; 213 computer-based). *Application deadline:* For fall admission, 6/5 priority date for domestic students; for spring admission, 10/15 for domestic students. Applications are processed on a rolling basis. Application fee: $60. Electronic applications accepted. *Expenses:* Tuition, state resident: full-time $12,730. Tuition, nonresident: full-time $18,090. Tuition and fees vary according to course load and campus/location. *Financial support:* Fellowships with full and partial tuition reimbursements, research assistantships with full and partial tuition reimbursements, teaching assistantships with full and partial tuition reimbursements, career-related internships or fieldwork, Federal

Architecture

New Jersey Institute of Technology (continued)
Work-Study, institutionally sponsored loans, and unspecified assistantships available. Financial award application deadline: 3/15. *Faculty research:* Management of new technologies, information systems management, operations management systems, marketing management, human resource management. *Unit head:* Anthony Schuman, Director, 973-596-6370, E-mail: anthony.w.schuman@njit.edu. *Application contact:* Kathryn Kelly, Director of Admissions, 973-596-3300, Fax: 973-596-3461, E-mail: admissions@njit.edu.

New Jersey Institute of Technology, Office of Graduate Studies, School of Architecture, Program in Infrastructure Planning, Newark, NJ 07102. Offers MIP. Part-time and evening/weekend programs available. *Students:* 4 full-time (3 women), 4 part-time (2 women); includes 2 minority (both Asian Americans or Pacific Islanders), 4 international. Average age 34. 19 applicants, 63% accepted, 5 enrolled. In 2007, 9 degrees awarded. *Degree requirements:* For master's, thesis (for some programs). *Entrance requirements:* For master's, GRE General Test, minimum GPA of 3.0. Additional exam requirements/recommendations for international students: Required—TOEFL (minimum score 550 paper-based; 213 computer-based). *Application deadline:* For fall admission, 6/5 priority date for domestic students; for spring admission, 10/15 for domestic students. Applications are processed on a rolling basis. Application fee: $60. Electronic applications accepted. *Expenses:* Tuition, state resident: full-time $12,730. Tuition, nonresident: full-time $18,090. Tuition and fees vary according to course load and campus/location. *Financial support:* Fellowships with full and partial tuition reimbursements, research assistantships with full and partial tuition reimbursements, teaching assistantships with full and partial tuition reimbursements, career-related internships or fieldwork, Federal Work-Study, institutionally sponsored loans, and unspecified assistantships available. Financial award application deadline: 3/15. *Unit head:* Antonio P. De Sousa Santos, Director, 973-596-3029, Fax: 973-596-3073, E-mail: antonio.de_sousa_santos@njit.edu. *Application contact:* Kathryn Kelly, Director of Admissions, 973-596-3300, Fax: 973-596-3461, E-mail: admissions@njit.edu.

The New School: A University, Parsons The New School for Design, Program in Architecture, New York, NY 10011. Offers M Arch. *Faculty:* 7 full-time (1 woman), 26 part-time/adjunct (10 women). *Students:* 59 full-time (29 women); includes 11 minority (3 African Americans, 5 Asian Americans or Pacific Islanders, 3 Hispanic Americans), 8 international. Average age 26. In 2007, 25 degrees awarded. *Degree requirements:* For master's, thesis or alternative. *Entrance requirements:* For master's, GRE General Test, portfolio. Additional exam requirements/recommendations for international students: Required—TOEFL (minimum score 580 paper-based; 237 computer-based; 93 iBT). *Application deadline:* For fall admission, 2/1 priority date for domestic students. Applications are processed on a rolling basis. Application fee: $50. *Financial support:* Federal Work-Study, scholarships/grants, and tuition waivers (partial) available. Financial award application deadline: 3/1; financial award applicants required to submit FAFSA. *Unit head:* David Lewis, Director, 212-229-8955 Ext. 2915, E-mail: lewisd@newschool.edu. *Application contact:* Anthony Padilla, Director of Admissions, 212-229-8989 Ext. 4023, Fax: 212-229-8975, E-mail: padillaa@newschool.edu.

See Close-Up on page 163.

Newschool of Architecture & Design, Program in Architecture, San Diego, CA 92101-6634. Offers M Arch, MS. Part-time and evening/weekend programs available. *Degree requirements:* For master's, thesis. *Entrance requirements:* For master's, portfolio, interview. *Faculty research:* Urban studies, regional studies, environmental design, structures, cross-cultural studies.

New York Institute of Technology, Graduate Division, School of Architecture, Old Westbury, NY 11568-8000. Offers urban and regional design (M Arch). Part-time programs available. *Students:* 11 full-time (6 women); includes 3 minority (1 African American, 1 Asian American or Pacific Islander, 1 Hispanic American), 7 international. Average age 33. 35 applicants, 49% accepted, 6 enrolled. In 2007, 7 degrees awarded. *Degree requirements:* For master's, thesis. *Entrance requirements:* For master's, minimum QPA of 2.85, portfolio. Additional exam requirements/recommendations for international students: Required—TOEFL (minimum score 550 paper-based; 213 computer-based). *Application deadline:* For fall admission, 7/1 priority date for domestic students; for spring admission, 12/1 priority date for domestic students. Applications are processed on a rolling basis. Application fee: $50. Electronic applications accepted. *Expenses:* Tuition: Part-time $739 per credit. Required fees: $75 per semester. *Financial support:* Research assistantships with partial tuition reimbursements, institutionally sponsored loans and tuition waivers (full and partial) available. Support available to part-time students. Financial award applicants required to submit FAFSA. *Faculty research:* Affordable housing, urban modeling and simulation, transport systems and infrastructure, relationships of policy and form. *Unit head:* Judith DiMaio, Dean, 516-686-7594, Fax: 516-686-7921, E-mail: jdimaio@nyit.edu. *Application contact:* Jacquelyn Nealon, Dean of Admissions and Financial Aid, 516-686-7925, Fax: 516-686-7613, E-mail: jnealon@nyit.edu.

North Carolina State University, Graduate School, College of Design, Department of Architecture, Raleigh, NC 27695. Offers M Arch. *Degree requirements:* For master's, thesis optional, oral exam, project. *Entrance requirements:* For master's, GRE General Test, portfolio. Electronic applications accepted. *Faculty research:* Architectural design, architectural history and theory, construction materials, sustainable design.

Northeastern University, School of Architecture, Boston, MA 02115-5096. Offers M Arch. *Faculty:* 8 full-time (3 women). *Students:* 51 full-time (20 women), 1 (woman) part-time. 81 applicants, 74% accepted. In 2007, 23 degrees awarded. *Entrance requirements:* Additional exam requirements/recommendations for international students: Required—TOEFL or IELTS. *Application deadline:* For fall admission, 8/1 for domestic students, 5/1 for international students. Applications are processed on a rolling basis. Application fee: $50. Electronic applications accepted. *Financial support:* Federal Work-Study and scholarships/grants available. Support available to part-time students. Financial award application deadline: 3/1; financial award applicants required to submit FAFSA. *Unit head:* George Thrush, Chair, 617-373-4637, Fax: 617-373-7080, E-mail: thrush@neu.edu. *Application contact:* Danielle Walquist, Administrative Assistant, 617-373-4637, Fax: 617-373-7080, E-mail: architecture@neu.edu.

The Ohio State University, Graduate School, College of Engineering, Austin E. Knowlton School of Architecture, Program in Architecture, Columbus, OH 43210. Offers M Arch, MAS. *Faculty:* 16. *Students:* 60 full-time (25 women); includes 4 minority (1 American Indian/Alaska Native, 3 Asian Americans or Pacific Islanders), 8 international. Average age 26. In 2007, 14 degrees awarded. *Degree requirements:* For master's, thesis optional. *Entrance requirements:* For master's, GRE General Test. Additional exam requirements/recommendations for international students: Required—TOEFL (minimum score 600 paper-based; 250 computer-based). *Application deadline:* For fall admission, 8/15 priority date for domestic students, 7/1 priority date for international students; for winter admission, 12/1 priority date for domestic students, 11/1 priority date for international students; for spring admission, 3/1 priority date for domestic students, 2/1 priority date for international students. Applications are processed on a rolling basis. Application fee: $40 ($50 for international students). Electronic applications accepted. *Financial support:* Fellowships, research assistantships, Federal Work-Study, institutionally sponsored loans, and unspecified assistantships available. Support available to part-time students. *Unit head:* Ashley E. Schafer, Graduate Studies Committee Chair, 614-688-4586, Fax: 614-282-7106, E-mail: schafer.111@osu.edu. *Application contact:* 614-292-9444, Fax: 614-292-3895, E-mail: domestic.grad@osu.edu.

Oklahoma State University, College of Engineering, Architecture and Technology, School of Architecture, Stillwater, OK 74078. Offers M Arch, M Arch E. *Faculty:* 17 full-time (3 women), 2 part-time/adjunct (0 women). *Students:* Average age 25. 4 applicants, 0% accepted. In 2007, 1 degree awarded. *Degree requirements:* For master's, thesis or alternative. *Entrance requirements:* For master's, GRE or GMAT. Additional exam requirements/recommendations for international students: Required—TOEFL. *Application deadline:* For fall admission, 3/1 priority date for international students; for spring admission, 8/1 priority date for international students. Applications are processed on a rolling basis. Application fee: $40 ($75 for international students). Electronic applications accepted. *Expenses:* Tuition, state resident: full-time $4,993; part-time $148 per credit hour. Tuition, nonresident: full-time $14,755; part-time $555 per credit hour. Tuition and fees vary according to program. *Financial support:* In 2007–08, 1 research assistantship (averaging $2,028 per year) was awarded; teaching assistantships, career-related internships or fieldwork, Federal Work-Study, scholarships/grants, health care benefits, tuition waivers (partial), and unspecified assistantships also available. Support available to part-time students. Financial award application deadline: 3/1. *Unit head:* Randy Seitsinger, Head, 405-744-6043.

Penn State University Park, Graduate School, College of Arts and Architecture, Department of Architecture, State College, University Park, PA 16802-1503. Offers M Arch. *Expenses:* Tuition, state resident: full-time $14,738; part-time $614 per credit. Tuition, nonresident: full-time $26,050; part-time $1,085 per credit. Tuition and fees vary according to course load, program and student level. *Unit head:* Dr. Daniel E. Willis, Head, 814-865-9535, Fax: 814-865-3289, E-mail: dew2@psu.edu.

Pontificia Universidad Catolica Madre y Maestra, Graduate School, Santiago, Dominican Republic. Offers administration (M Adm, M Ed); architecture of interiors (M Arch); architecture of tourist lodgings (M Arch); construction administration (ME); convergent networks (ME); corporate business law (LL M); criminal procedure law (LL M); earthquake-resistant engineering (ME); environmental engineering (MEE); finance (M Mgmt); human resources (EMBA); international business (M Mgmt); international relations (LL M); labor law and Social Security (M Mgmt); logistics management (ME); marketing (M Mgmt); urban planning (M Urb). *Entrance requirements:* For master's, curriculum vitae, interview.

Prairie View A&M University, School of Architecture, Prairie View, TX 77446-0519. Offers architecture (M Arch); community development (MCD). Part-time and evening/weekend programs available. *Faculty:* 8 full-time (1 woman), 8 part-time/adjunct (4 women). *Students:* 38 full-time (16 women), 24 part-time (7 women); includes 55 minority (50 African Americans, 5 Hispanic Americans), 3 international. Average age 30. 63 applicants, 100% accepted. In 2007, 39 degrees awarded. *Entrance requirements:* For master's, GRE General Test, portfolio (M Arch). Additional exam requirements/recommendations for international students: Required—TOEFL (minimum score 550 paper-based). *Application deadline:* For fall admission, 6/1 priority date for domestic and international students; for spring admission, 11/1 priority date for domestic students, 10/1 priority date for international students. Applications are processed on a rolling basis. Application fee: $50. Electronic applications accepted. *Financial support:* Fellowships with tuition reimbursements, research assistantships with tuition reimbursements, teaching assistantships, career-related internships or fieldwork, Federal Work-Study, institutionally sponsored loans, scholarships/grants, tuition waivers (full and partial), and unspecified assistantships available. Support available to part-time students. Financial award application deadline: 3/1; financial award applicants required to submit FAFSA. *Faculty research:* Community management, sustainable design. *Unit head:* Dr. Ikhlas Sabouni, Dean, 936-261-9810, Fax: 936-857-2350, E-mail: isabouni@pvamu.edu. *Application contact:* Kendrick Gibson, Assistant to the Dean for Operations and Recruitment, 936-857-9808, Fax: 936-857-9828, E-mail: klgibson@pvamu.edu.

Pratt Institute, School of Architecture, Program in Architecture, Brooklyn, NY 11205-3899. Offers M Arch, MS Arch. Part-time programs available. *Faculty:* 10 full-time (3 women), 47 part-time/adjunct (18 women). *Students:* 162 full-time (78 women), 1 (woman) part-time; includes 31 minority (2 African Americans, 15 Asian Americans or Pacific Islanders, 14 Hispanic Americans), 49 international. Average age 27. 470 applicants, 56% accepted, 58 enrolled. In 2007, 43 degrees awarded. *Degree requirements:* For master's, thesis. *Entrance requirements:* For master's, B Arch, portfolio, transcripts, letters of recommendation, statement. Additional exam requirements/recommendations for international students: Required—TOEFL (minimum score 550 paper-based; 213 computer-based). *Application deadline:* For fall admission, 2/1 for domestic students; for spring admission, 10/1 for domestic students. Application fee: $50 ($90 for international students). Electronic applications accepted. *Expenses:* Tuition: Full-time $25,680. Required fees: $1,106. Tuition and fees vary according to program. *Financial support:* Career-related internships or fieldwork, Federal Work-Study, institutionally sponsored loans, scholarships/grants, health care benefits, and unspecified assistantships available. Support available to part-time students. Financial award application deadline: 2/1; financial award applicants required to submit FAFSA. *Faculty research:* Design theory, advanced structural systems, urban investigations. *Unit head:* William J. Mac Donald, Chairperson, 718-636-4308, E-mail: wmacdona@pratt.edu. *Application contact:* Young Hah, Director of Graduate Admissions, 718-636-3683, Fax: 718-399-4242, E-mail: yhah@pratt.edu.

See Close-Up on page 167.

Princeton University, Graduate School, School of Architecture, Princeton, NJ 08544-1019. Offers M Arch, PhD. Terminal master's awarded for partial completion of doctoral program. *Degree requirements:* For master's, thesis; for doctorate, 2 foreign languages, comprehensive exam, thesis/dissertation. *Entrance requirements:* For master's, GRE General Test, design portfolio, math, 2 semesters of physics, and art/architecture survey; for doctorate, GRE General Test, samples of written work. Additional exam requirements/recommendations for international students: Required—TOEFL (minimum score 600 paper-based; 260 computer-based). Electronic applications accepted. *Faculty research:* Design, urban studies, landscape architecture, media and information technologies in architecture.

Rensselaer Polytechnic Institute, Graduate School, School of Architecture, Troy, NY 12180-3590. Offers architectural science (MS, PhD); architecture (M Arch); building conservation (MS); lighting (MS). Part-time programs available. *Faculty:* 16 full-time (4 women), 16 part-time/adjunct (5 women). *Students:* 64 full-time (25 women), 8 part-time (3 women); includes 9 minority (3 African Americans, 2 Asian Americans or Pacific Islanders, 4 Hispanic Americans), 17 international. Average age 29. 77 applicants, 73% accepted, 31 enrolled. In 2007, 27 degrees awarded. Terminal master's awarded for partial completion of doctoral program. *Degree requirements:* For master's, thesis (for some programs); for doctorate, comprehensive exam (for some programs), thesis/dissertation. *Entrance requirements:* For master's and doctorate, GRE, portfolio, letters of recommendation, resumé. Additional exam requirements/recommendations for international students: Required—TOEFL (minimum score 570 paper-based; 230 computer-based), IELTS (minimum score 7). *Application deadline:* For fall admission, 1/15 priority date for domestic and international students. Applications are processed on a rolling basis. Application fee: $75. Electronic applications accepted. *Expenses:* Tuition: Full-time $34,900; part-time $1,454 per credit. Required fees: $1,802. *Financial support:* In 2007–08, 37 students received support, including 6 fellowships with full tuition reimbursements available (averaging $20,000 per year), 15 research assistantships with full tuition reimbursements available (averaging $14,500 per year), 2 teaching assistantships with full tuition reimbursements available (averaging $14,500 per year); career-related internships or fieldwork, institutionally sponsored loans, scholarships/grants, tuition waivers (partial), and unspecified assistantships also available. Financial award application deadline: 1/15. *Faculty research:* Architectural design, architectural acoustics, lighting performance, built ecologies, materials. Total annual research expenditures: $4.2 million. *Unit head:* Prof. Ted Krueger, Chair, 518-276-2562, Fax: 518-276-3034, E-mail: krueger@rpi.edu. *Application contact:* James G. Nondorf, Vice President for Enrollment, 518-276-6216, Fax: 518-276-4072, E-mail: admissions@rpi.edu.

See Close-Up on page 169.

Rhode Island School of Design, Graduate Studies, Division of Architecture and Design, Department of Architecture, Providence, RI 02903-2784. Offers M Arch. *Degree requirements:* For master's, thesis, exhibit. *Entrance requirements:* For master's, portfolio, 3 letters of recommendation. Additional exam requirements/recommendations for international students: Required—TOEFL (minimum score 580 paper-based; 237 computer-based), IELTS (minimum score 7).

Rice University, Graduate Programs, School of Architecture, Houston, TX 77251-1892. Offers architecture (M Arch, D Arch); urban design (M Arch UD). *Degree requirements:* For master's, thesis; for doctorate, thesis/dissertation. *Entrance requirements:* For master's and doctorate, GRE General Test, minimum GPA of 3.0. Additional exam requirements/recommendations for international students: Required—TOEFL (minimum score 650 paper-based; 250 computer-based; 90 iBT).

Roger Williams University, School of Architecture, Art and Historic Preservation, Bristol, RI 02809. Offers architecture (M Arch). Students begin 5-6 year dual degree sequence as undergraduates. *Faculty:* 6 full-time (1 woman), 3 part-time/adjunct (0 women). *Students:* 34 full-time (11 women), 1 part-time; includes 2 minority (1 American Indian/Alaska Native, 1 Hispanic American), 3 international. Average age 24. 53 applicants, 53% accepted, 23 enrolled. In 2007, 11 degrees awarded. *Degree requirements:* For master's, thesis. *Entrance requirements:* For master's, portfolio. *Application deadline:* For fall admission, 3/15 priority date for domestic students. Applications are processed on a rolling basis. Application fee: $50. Electronic applications accepted. *Expenses: Contact institution. Financial support:* In 2007–08, 33 students received support; fellowships, career-related internships or fieldwork, scholarships/grants, health care benefits, and unspecified assistantships available. Financial award applicants required to submit FAFSA. *Unit head:* Stephen White, Dean, 401-254-3607, E-mail: swhite@rwu.edu. *Application contact:* Suzanne Faubl, Director of Graduate Admissions, 401-254-3809, Fax: 401-254-3557, E-mail: sfaubl@rwu.edu.

Savannah College of Art and Design, Graduate School, Program in Architecture, Savannah, GA 31402-3146. Offers M Arch. Part-time programs available. *Faculty:* 25 full-time (7 women), 3 part-time/adjunct (1 woman). *Students:* 117 full-time (50 women), 7 part-time (2 women); includes 13 minority (3 African Americans, 2 American Indian/Alaska Native, 1 Asian American or Pacific Islander, 7 Hispanic Americans), 18 international. Average age 27. 138 applicants, 75% accepted, 69 enrolled. In 2007, 72 degrees awarded. *Degree requirements:* For master's, thesis, internship. *Entrance requirements:* For master's, interview, portfolio. Additional exam requirements/recommendations for international students: Required—TOEFL (minimum score 450 paper-based; 133 computer-based). *Application deadline:* For fall admission, 4/1 priority date for domestic and international students. Applications are processed on a rolling basis. Application fee: $50. Electronic applications accepted. *Expenses:* Tuition: Full-time $24,840; part-time $552 per credit. One-time fee: $500 full-time. *Financial support:* In 2007–08, 3 fellowships were awarded; career-related internships or fieldwork, Federal Work-Study, and scholarships/grants also available. Financial award application deadline: 4/1; financial award applicants required to submit FAFSA. *Faculty research:* Computer-aided design, photovoltaics-powered environmental control. *Unit head:* Scott Singeisen, Chair, 912-525-6871. *Application contact:* Darrell Tutchton, Director of Graduate and International Enrollment, 912-525-5961, Fax: 912-525-5985, E-mail: admission@scad.edu.

See Close-Up on page 257.

Southern California Institute of Architecture, Graduate Program in Architecture, Los Angeles, CA 90013. Offers M Arch. *Degree requirements:* For master's, thesis, final project. *Entrance requirements:* For master's, GRE General Test, portfolio of architectural and creative work, letters of recommendation. *Faculty research:* Architectural theory.

See Close-Up on page 171.

Southern Illinois University Carbondale, Graduate School, College of Applied Science, School of Architecture, Carbondale, IL 62901-4701. Offers M Arch. *Students:* 11 full-time (2 women); includes 1 Hispanic American, 1 international. 1 applicant, 0% accepted. *Unit head:* Jack Kremers, Director of Graduate Studies, 618-453-3734, E-mail: jkremers@siu.edu.

Syracuse University, Graduate School, School of Architecture, Syracuse, NY 13244. Offers M Arch I, M Arch II. *Faculty:* 34 full-time (8 women), 12 part-time/adjunct (4 women). *Students:* 78 full-time (35 women); includes 11 minority (3 African Americans, 3 Asian Americans or Pacific Islanders, 5 Hispanic Americans), 8 international. 180 applicants, 51% accepted, 33 enrolled. In 2007, 28 degrees awarded. *Degree requirements:* For master's, thesis. *Entrance requirements:* For master's, GRE General Test, interview, portfolio. Additional exam requirements/recommendations for international students: Required—TOEFL. *Application deadline:* For fall admission, 2/1 priority date for domestic students. Applications are processed on a rolling basis. Application fee: $75. Electronic applications accepted. *Expenses:* Tuition: Full-time $18,216; part-time $1,012 per credit. Required fees: $980. Tuition and fees vary according to program. *Financial support:* Fellowships with full and partial tuition reimbursements, research assistantships with full and partial tuition reimbursements, teaching assistantships with full and partial tuition reimbursements, Federal Work-Study, institutionally sponsored loans, scholarships/grants, health care benefits, tuition waivers (full and partial), and unspecified assistantships available. *Faculty research:* Urban design, urban mapping, building systems, landscape, theory. *Unit head:* Mark Robbins, Dean, 315-443-1041, Fax: 315-443-5082. *Application contact:* Mark Linder, Graduate Director, 315-443-1041, Fax: 315-443-5082.

Texas A&M University, College of Architecture, Department of Architecture, College Station, TX 77843. Offers architecture (M Arch, MS Arch, PhD); visualization science (MS). *Faculty:* 44. *Students:* 174 full-time (70 women), 42 part-time (19 women); includes 33 minority (4 African Americans, 1 American Indian/Alaska Native, 13 Asian Americans or Pacific Islanders, 15 Hispanic Americans), 71 international. Average age 24. 189 applicants, 71% accepted, 71 enrolled. In 2007, 57 master's, 8 doctorates awarded. *Degree requirements:* For master's, comprehensive exam, thesis; for doctorate, comprehensive exam, thesis/dissertation. *Entrance requirements:* For master's, GRE General Test, portfolio, letters of recommendation; for doctorate, GRE General Test. Additional exam requirements/recommendations for international students: Required—TOEFL. *Application deadline:* For fall admission, 1/15 priority date for domestic and international students. Applications are processed on a rolling basis. Application fee: $50 ($75 for international students). Electronic applications accepted. *Expenses:* Tuition, state resident: full-time $6,129. Tuition, nonresident: full-time $11,689. Tuition and fees vary according to course load. *Financial support:* Fellowships, research assistantships, teaching assistantships, career-related internships or fieldwork, Federal Work-Study, institutionally sponsored loans, and scholarships/grants available. Financial award application deadline: 1/15; financial award applicants required to submit FAFSA. *Faculty research:* Energy optimization, architecture pedagogy, environment and behavior. *Unit head:* Phillip J. Tabb, Head, 979-845-1015, Fax: 979-862-1571, E-mail: ptabb@archone.tamu.edu. *Application contact:* 979-845-6582, Fax: 979-862-7119, E-mail: gradoff@archone.tamu.edu.

Texas Tech University, Graduate School, College of Architecture, Post-Professional Program in Architecture, Lubbock, TX 79409. Offers community design and development (MS); historical preservation (MS); visualization (MS). Part-time programs available. *Students:* 5 full-time (3 women), 7 part-time (2 women), 5 international. Average age 29. 12 applicants, 67% accepted, 3 enrolled. In 2007, 2 degrees awarded. *Degree requirements:* For master's, thesis. *Entrance requirements:* For master's, GRE General Test, portfolio. Additional exam requirements/recommendations for international students: Required—TOEFL (minimum score 550 paper-based; 213 computer-based). *Application deadline:* For fall admission, 3/1 priority date for domestic students; for spring admission, 11/1 priority date for domestic students. Applications are processed on a rolling basis. Application fee: $50 ($60 for international students). Electronic applications accepted. *Expenses:* Tuition, state resident: part-time $373 per credit hour. Tuition, nonresident: part-time $651 per credit hour. Tuition and fees vary according to program. *Financial support:* Research assistantships with partial tuition reimbursements, teaching assistantships with partial tuition reimbursements, career-related internships or fieldwork, Federal Work-Study, and institutionally sponsored loans available. Support available to part-time students. Financial award application deadline: 4/15; financial award applicants required to submit FAFSA. *Faculty research:* Historic preservation, visualization, community development and design, sustainable architecture, international architecture. *Unit head:* Glenn Eugene Hill, Associate Dean of Research and Post-Professional Graduate Studies, 806-742-3136, Fax: 806-742-2855, E-mail: glenn.hill@ttu.edu. *Application contact:* Jess Schwintz, Academic Program Assistant, 806-742-3136 Ext. 272, Fax: 806-742-2855, E-mail: jess.schwintz@ttu.edu.

Texas Tech University, Graduate School, College of Architecture, Professional Program in Architecture, Lubbock, TX 79409. Offers M Arch, M Arch/MBA. Part-time programs available. *Students:* 101 full-time (32 women), 6 part-time (4 women); includes 22 minority (1 African American, 1 American Indian/Alaska Native, 6 Asian Americans or Pacific Islanders, 14 Hispanic Americans). Average age 25. 40 applicants, 85% accepted, 12 enrolled. In 2007, 65 degrees awarded. *Degree requirements:* For master's, thesis. *Entrance requirements:* For master's, GRE General Test, portfolio. Additional exam requirements/recommendations for international students: Required—TOEFL (minimum score 550 paper-based; 213 computer-based). *Application deadline:* For fall admission, 3/1 priority date for international students; for spring admission, 11/1 priority date for international students. Applications are processed on a rolling basis. Application fee: $50 ($60 for international students). Electronic applications accepted. *Expenses:* Tuition, state resident: part-time $373 per credit hour. Tuition, nonresident: part-time $651 per credit hour. Tuition and fees vary according to program. *Financial support:* Research assistantships with partial tuition reimbursements, teaching assistantships with partial tuition reimbursements, career-related internships or fieldwork, Federal Work-Study, and institutionally sponsored loans available. Support available to part-time students. Financial award application deadline: 4/15; financial award applicants required to submit FAFSA. *Faculty research:* Historical preservation; visualization; community design; digital design and construction; healthcare facilities. *Unit head:* Michael Peters, Associate Dean for Academics, 806-742-3136, Fax: 806-742-2855, E-mail: architecture.programs@ttu.edu. *Application contact:* Lori Rodriguez, Academic Program Assistant, 806-742-3136 Ext. 247, Fax: 806-742-2855, E-mail: lori.rodriguez@ttu.edu.

Tulane University, School of Architecture, New Orleans, LA 70118-5669. Offers M Arch, MPS. Part-time programs available. *Degree requirements:* For master's, thesis. *Entrance requirements:* For master's, GRE, portfolio. Additional exam requirements/recommendations for international students: Required—TOEFL. Expenses: Contact institution. *Faculty research:* Design topics, preservation and environmental conservation, architecture and human health, computing.

Universidad Autonoma de Guadalajara, Graduate Programs, Guadalajara, Mexico. Offers advertising and corporate communications (MA); architecture (M Arch); business (MBA); computational science (MCC); education (Ed M, Ed D); international business (MIB); international corporate law (LL M); manufacturing systems (MMS); philosophy (MA, PhD); prosecution law (LL M); quality systems (MQS); renewable energy (MS); teaching mathematics (MA).

Universidad Nacional Pedro Henriquez Urena, Graduate School, Santo Domingo, Dominican Republic. Offers accounting and auditing (M Acct); animal production (M Agr); business administration (MBA, PhD); Caribbean tropical architecture (M Arch); conservation of monuments and cultural goods (M Arch); economics (M Econ); education (PhD); environmental engineering (MEE); horticulture (M Agr); hospital administration (PhD); humanities (PhD); international relations (MPS); management of natural resources (MNRM); project management (M Man, MPM); public administration (MPS); sanitary engineering (ME); social science (PhD); veterinary medicine (DVM).

Université Laval, Faculty of Architecture, Planning and Visual Arts, School of Architecture, Program in Architecture, Québec, QC G1K 7P4, Canada. Offers M Arch, M Sc. Part-time programs available. *Degree requirements:* For master's, thesis (for some programs). *Entrance requirements:* For master's, mastery of software (CAO), knowledge of French and English. Electronic applications accepted.

University at Buffalo, the State University of New York, Graduate School, School of Architecture and Planning, Department of Architecture, Buffalo, NY 14260. Offers M Arch, M Arch/MBA, M Arch/MFA, M Arch/MUP. Part-time programs available. *Degree requirements:* For master's, thesis or alternative, project. *Entrance requirements:* For master's, GRE, portfolio. Additional exam requirements/recommendations for international students: Required—TOEFL (minimum score 550 paper-based; 213 computer-based). Electronic applications accepted. *Faculty research:* Inclusive design, landscape and environment, theory and design, urban design, virtual architecture.

The University of Arizona, Graduate College, College of Architecture and Landscape Architecture, Tucson, AZ 85721. Offers architecture (M Arch); landscape architecture (ML Arch). Part-time programs available. *Faculty:* 43. *Students:* 65 full-time (37 women), 13 part-time (6 women); includes 2 minority (1 American Indian/Alaska Native, 1 Hispanic American), 14 international. Average age 33. 40 applicants, 48% accepted, 15 enrolled. In 2007, 26 degrees awarded. *Degree requirements:* For master's, comprehensive exam (for some programs), final project or thesis. *Entrance requirements:* For master's, portfolio, resumé, 3 references, statement of intent, transcripts. Additional exam requirements/recommendations for international students: Required—TOEFL (minimum score 550 paper-based; 213 computer-based; 80 iBT); Recommended—IELTS (minimum score 7). *Application deadline:* For fall admission, 3/1 for domestic students, 12/1 for international students; for spring admission, 3/1 priority date for domestic students, 3/1 for international students. Applications are processed on a rolling basis. Application fee: $50. *Expenses: Contact institution. Financial support:* In 2007–08, 25 students received support, including 4 fellowships with partial tuition reimbursements available, 3 research assistantships with partial tuition reimbursements available (averaging $4,916 per year), 15 teaching assistantships with partial tuition reimbursements available (averaging $4,916 per year); career-related internships or fieldwork, Federal Work-Study, scholarships/grants, health care benefits, tuition waivers (full), and unspecified assistantships also available. *Faculty research:* Design for arid climates, passive solar design, community design, historic preservation, emerging materials technology. Total annual research expenditures: $974,423. *Unit head:* Charles Albanese, Dean, 520-621-6751, Fax: 520-621-8700, E-mail: cala@u.arizona.edu. *Application contact:* Susan K.E. Moody, Assistant Dean, 520-621-6751, Fax: 520-621-8700, E-mail: skemoody@u.arizona.edu.

The University of British Columbia, Faculty of Graduate Studies, Faculty of Applied Science, School of Architecture and Landscape Architecture, Vancouver, BC V6T 1Z1, Canada. Offers architecture (M Arch, MASA); landscape architecture (MASLA, MLA). *Degree requirements:* For master's, thesis. *Entrance requirements:* For master's, portfolio, resumé, 3 reference letters. Additional exam requirements/recommendations for international students: Required—TOEFL (minimum score 600 paper-based; 250 computer-based; 100 iBT). Electronic applications accepted. Expenses: Contact institution. *Faculty research:* Energy and resource use of buildings, advanced design research, urban design and community activism, advanced research in computer applications, cultural studies.

University of Calgary, Faculty of Graduate Studies, Faculty of Environmental Design, Calgary, AB T2N 1N4, Canada. Offers architecture (M Arch); environmental design (M Env Des, PhD). *Faculty:* 30 full-time (8 women), 102 part-time/adjunct (18 women). *Students:* 246 full-time (135 women), 7 part-time (4 women). Average age 30. 299 applicants, 42% accepted, 79 enrolled. In 2007, 69 master's, 2 doctorates awarded. *Degree requirements:* For master's, thesis; for doctorate, thesis/dissertation. *Entrance requirements:* For master's, minimum GPA of 3.0; for doctorate, minimum GPA of 3.5. Additional exam requirements/recommendations for international students: Required—TOEFL (minimum score 550 paper-based; 213 computer-based). *Application deadline:* For fall admission, 2/1 for domestic and international students. Application fee: $100 ($130 for international students). *Financial support:* In 2007–08, 1 fellowship, 57 research assistantships, 9 teaching assistantships were awarded; career-related internships or fieldwork and scholarships/grants also available. *Faculty research:* Sustainable development in architecture, planning and product design, energy and environment, impact assessment, ecotourism. *Unit head:* Prof. L Fowlow, Dean, 403-220-6606, Fax: 403-284-4399. *Application contact:* L. Kallsen, Admissions Officer, 403-220-3630, Fax: 403-284-4399, E-mail: info@evds.ucalgary.ca.

Architecture

University of California, Berkeley, Graduate Division, College of Environmental Design, Department of Architecture, Berkeley, CA 94720-1500. Offers architecture (M Arch); building science (MS, PhD); building structures, construction and materials (MS, PhD); design (MA); design theories, methods, and practices (MS, PhD); environmental design in developing countries (MS, PhD); history of architecture and urbanism (MS, PhD); social and cultural processes in architecture and urbanism (MS, PhD); M Arch/MCP; M Arch/MS; MLA/M Arch. *Degree requirements:* For master's, thesis; for doctorate, thesis/dissertation, qualifying exam. *Entrance requirements:* For master's and doctorate, GRE General Test, minimum GPA of 3.0, 3 letters of recommendation. Additional exam requirements/recommendations for international students: Required—TOEFL. Application fee: $70 ($90 for international students). Electronic applications accepted. *Financial support:* Unspecified assistantships available. *Unit head:* Mary Comerio, Chair, 510-642-4942, E-mail: mcomerio@berkeley.edu. *Application contact:* Lois H. Ito Koch, Student Affairs Officer, 510-642-5577, Fax: 510-643-5607, E-mail: archgrad@berkeley.edu.

University of California, Los Angeles, Graduate Division, School of the Arts and Architecture, Department of Architecture and Urban Design, Los Angeles, CA 90095. Offers M Arch, MA, PhD. *Degree requirements:* For master's, thesis or alternative, comprehensive exam or design project; for doctorate, 2 foreign languages, thesis/dissertation, oral and written qualifying exams. *Entrance requirements:* For master's and doctorate, GRE General Test, portfolio. Additional exam requirements/recommendations for international students: Required—TOEFL. Electronic applications accepted. *Expenses:* Tuition, nonresident: full-time $5,728. Required fees:$8,966. Full-time tuition and fees vary according to program and student level. *Faculty research:* Urban poverty and low wage labor markets; environmental planning and politics; international political economy; physical planning, urban design, planning history; housing and land development; transportation and land use; critical urban and regional studies.

University of Cincinnati, Graduate School, College of Design, Architecture, Art, and Planning, School of Architecture and Interior Design, Cincinnati, OH 45221. Offers architecture (M Arch). *Accreditation:* NASAD. *Faculty:* 24 full-time (4 women). *Students:* 187 full-time (73 women), 18 part-time (8 women); includes 15 minority (3 African Americans, 1 American Indian/Alaska Native, 7 Asian Americans or Pacific Islanders, 4 Hispanic Americans), 26 international. In 2007, 52 degrees awarded. *Degree requirements:* For master's, one foreign language, thesis. *Entrance requirements:* Additional exam requirements/recommendations for international students: Required—TOEFL. *Application deadline:* For fall admission, 2/1 for domestic students. Application fee: $30. *Financial support:* Fellowships, tuition waivers (full) and unspecified assistantships available. Support available to part-time students. Financial award application deadline: 5/1. *Faculty research:* Theory and history of architecture. Total annual research expenditures: $115,000. *Unit head:* Prof. Michaele Pride-Wells, Director, 513-556-6426, Fax: 513-556-1230, E-mail: m.pride-wells@uc.edu. *Application contact:* Prof. Patricia Kucker, Associate Director for Graduate Programs, 513-556-1614, E-mail: patricia.kucker@uc.edu.

University of Colorado Denver, College of Architecture and Planning, Program in Architecture, Denver, CO 80217-3364. Offers M Arch. Part-time programs available. *Faculty:* 25 full-time (5 women). *Students:* 247 full-time (93 women), 30 part-time (16 women); includes 34 minority (3 African Americans, 12 Asian Americans or Pacific Islanders, 19 Hispanic Americans), 6 international. Average age 30. 194 applicants, 56% accepted, 75 enrolled. In 2007, 86 degrees awarded. *Degree requirements:* For master's, thesis optional. *Entrance requirements:* For master's, GRE or minimum GPA of 3.0, portfolio, course work in trigonometry and physics. Additional exam requirements/recommendations for international students: Required—TOEFL (minimum score 550 paper-based; 213 computer-based). *Application deadline:* For fall admission, 3/15 for domestic students; for spring admission, 10/1 for domestic students. Application fee: $50 ($75 for international students). *Financial support:* Teaching assistantships, career-related internships or fieldwork, Federal Work-Study, institutionally sponsored loans, and scholarships/grants available. Financial award application deadline: 4/1; financial award applicants required to submit FAFSA. *Faculty research:* Architectural design; history, theory, and criticism of architecture; regional and environmental issues; sustainability; intervention and transformation in the urban and rural landscape. *Unit head:* Hans Morgenthaler, Chair, 303-556-4227, Fax: 303-556-3687, E-mail: hans.morgenthaler@cudenver.edu. *Application contact:* Heather Zertuche, Administrative Assistant II, 303-556-3382, Fax: 303-556-3687, E-mail: anpdeansoffice@storm.cudenver.edu.

University of Florida, Graduate School, College of Design, Construction and Planning, Doctoral Program in Design, Construction and Planning, Gainesville, FL 32611. Offers PhD. *Faculty:* 24. *Degree requirements:* For doctorate, thesis/dissertation. *Entrance requirements:* For doctorate, GRE General Test, minimum GPA of 3.2. Additional exam requirements/recommendations for international students: Required—TOEFL. *Application deadline:* For fall admission, 4/1 for domestic students. Applications are processed on a rolling basis. Application fee: $30. Electronic applications accepted. *Expenses:* Tuition, state resident: full-time $7,478. Tuition, nonresident: full-time $22,603. *Financial support:* In 2007–08, 17 students received support; fellowships, research assistantships, teaching assistantships, unspecified assistantships available. *Faculty research:* Architecture, building construction, urban and regional planning. *Unit head:* Dr. Paul D. Zwick, Chair, 352-392-0997 Ext. 427, Fax: 352-392-3308, E-mail: paul@geoplan.ufl.edu. *Application contact:* Prof. Richard H. Schneider, Interim Director and Coordinator, 352-392-0997 Ext. 430, Fax: 352-392-3308, E-mail: rschnei@ufl.edu.

University of Florida, Graduate School, College of Design, Construction and Planning, School of Architecture, Gainesville, FL 32611. Offers M Arch, MSAS, PhD. *Faculty:* 27 full-time (7 women), 1 part-time/adjunct (0 women). *Students:* 140 (61 women); includes 41 minority (9 African Americans, 2 American Indian/Alaska Native, 15 Asian Americans or Pacific Islanders, 15 Hispanic Americans) 6 international. In 2007, 52 degrees awarded. *Expenses:* Tuition, state resident: full-time $7,478. Tuition, nonresident: full-time $22,603. *Financial support:* In 2007–08, 37 teaching assistantships (averaging $8,135 per year) were awarded. *Unit head:* Martha Kohen, Director, 352-392-0205, E-mail: mkohen@ufl.edu. *Application contact:* Rebecca Hudson, Coordinator, 352-392-0205 Ext. 202, E-mail: bhuds@ufl.edu.

University of Hartford, College of Engineering, Technology and Architecture, Program in Architecture, West Hartford, CT 06117-1599. Offers M Arch. *Faculty:* 2 full-time (0 women), 4 part-time/adjunct (1 woman). *Students:* 10 full-time (3 women); includes 4 minority (1 African American, 3 Hispanic Americans), 2 international. Average age 28. 12 applicants, 58% accepted, 2 enrolled. In 2007, 13 degrees awarded. *Entrance requirements:* For master's, 3 letters of recommendation, portfolio. Additional exam requirements/recommendations for international students: Required—TOEFL (minimum score 550 paper-based; 213 computer-based). *Application deadline:* For fall admission, 2/15 priority date for domestic students. Application fee: $45. *Expenses:* Tuition: Part-time $595 per credit. Required fees: $200 per term. *Financial support:* In 2007–08, 1 teaching assistantship (averaging $8,000 per year) was awarded. *Unit head:* Michael J. Crosbiu, Chair, 860-768-5136. *Application contact:* Reneé Murphy, Assistant Director of Graduate Admissions, 860-768-4371, Fax: 860-768-5160, E-mail: gettoknow@hartford.edu.

University of Hawaii at Manoa, School of Architecture, Honolulu, HI 96822. Offers D Arch. Application fee: $50. *Financial support:* Research assistantships, teaching assistantships, tuition waivers (full) available. *Faculty research:* Housing, future cities, environmental studies, preservation, professional practice. *Application contact:* Joyce Noe, Graduate Field Chairperson, 808-956-3506, Fax: 808-956-7778, E-mail: jmnoe@hawaii.edu.

University of Houston, College of Architecture, Houston, TX 77204-4431. Offers M Arch, MS. *Faculty:* 16 full-time (3 women), 18 part-time/adjunct (1 woman). *Students:* 56 full-time (29 women), 10 part-time (5 women); includes 15 minority (1 African American, 1 American Indian/Alaska Native, 5 Asian Americans or Pacific Islanders, 8 Hispanic Americans), 8 international. Average age 29. 66 applicants, 68% accepted, 15 enrolled. In 2007, 32 master's awarded. *Entrance requirements:* For master's, GRE General Test, portfolio. Additional exam requirements/recommendations for international students: Required—TOEFL. *Application deadline:* For fall admission, 2/1 priority date for domestic students; for spring admission, 10/1 for domestic students. Applications are processed on a rolling basis. Application fee: $10 ($75 for international students). *Expenses:* Tuition, state resident: full-time $6,297; part-time $262 per credit. Tuition, nonresident: full-time $12,969; part-time $540 per credit. Required fees: $2,696. *Financial support:* In 2007–08, 1 fellowship with full tuition reimbursement (averaging $9,700 per year), 1 research assistantship with full tuition reimbursement (averaging $9,700 per year), 7 teaching assistantships with full tuition reimbursements (averaging $9,200 per year) were awarded; career-related internships or fieldwork, Federal Work-Study, institutionally sponsored loans, scholarships/grants, health care benefits, and unspecified assistantships also available. Support available to part-time students. Financial award application deadline: 2/1. *Faculty research:* Extraterrestrial habitation, computer applications, methods and materials of construction, historic preservation, simulation, architectural design, urban design. Total annual research expenditures: $83,907. *Unit head:* Joseph Mashburn, Dean, 713-743-2400, Fax: 713-743-2358, E-mail: mashburn@uh.edu. *Application contact:* Thomas M. Colbert, Director of Graduate Studies, 713-743-2380, Fax: 713-743-2358, E-mail: colbert@bayou.uh.edu.

University of Idaho, College of Graduate Studies, College of Art and Architecture, Department of Architecture and Interior Design, Moscow, ID 83844-2282. Offers M Arch, MS. *Students:* 59. Average age 28. In 2007, 45 degrees awarded. *Entrance requirements:* For master's, minimum GPA of 2.8. *Application deadline:* For fall admission, 8/1 for domestic students; for spring admission, 12/15 for domestic students. Application fee: $55 ($60 for international students). *Financial support:* Research assistantships, teaching assistantships available. Financial award application deadline: 2/15. *Unit head:* Wendy McClure, Chair, 208-885-6473.

University of Illinois at Chicago, Graduate College, College of Architecture and Art, School of Architecture, Chicago, IL 60607-7128. Offers M Arch. *Entrance requirements:* For master's, GRE General Test, portfolio, minimum GPA of 3.0. Additional exam requirements/recommendations for international students: Required—TOEFL. Electronic applications accepted. *Faculty research:* Housing values, elderly housing, design theory, deconstructivism.

University of Illinois at Urbana–Champaign, Graduate College, College of Fine and Applied Arts, School of Architecture, Champaign, IL 61820. Offers architectural studies (MS); architecture (M Arch, PhD); M Arch/MBA; M Arch/MS; M Arch/MUP; MCS/M Arch; MRP/JD. *Faculty:* 28 full-time (5 women), 10 part-time/adjunct (0 women). *Students:* 205 full-time (81 women), 2 part-time (both women); includes 19 minority (5 African Americans, 10 Asian Americans or Pacific Islanders, 4 Hispanic Americans), 41 international. 368 applicants, 24% accepted, 76 enrolled. In 2007, 95 master's, 2 doctorates awarded. *Entrance requirements:* For master's, minimum GPA of 3.0. *Application deadline:* For fall admission, 2/2 for domestic students. Applications are processed on a rolling basis. Application fee: $60 ($75 for international students). Electronic applications accepted. *Financial support:* In 2007–08, 21 fellowships, 29 research assistantships, 49 teaching assistantships were awarded. Financial award application deadline: 2/15. *Unit head:* David Chasco, Director, 217-333-1331, Fax: 217-244-8866, E-mail: dchasco@uiuc.edu. *Application contact:* Gary Ambler, Admissions and Records Officer, II, 217-244-4723, Fax: 217-244-8866, E-mail: gambler1@uiuc.edu.

University of Kansas, Research and Graduate Studies, School of Architecture and Urban Planning, Program in Architecture, Lawrence, KS 66045. Offers academic track (M Arch); management track (M Arch); professional track (M Arch); M Arch/MUP. *Faculty:* 28. *Students:* 102 full-time (39 women), 20 part-time (8 women); includes 5 minority (2 African Americans, 2 Asian Americans or Pacific Islanders, 1 Hispanic American), 5 international. Average age 26. 57 applicants, 70% accepted, 25 enrolled. In 2007, 61 degrees awarded. Terminal master's awarded for partial completion of doctoral program. *Degree requirements:* For master's, thesis or alternative, 7 semesters of design studio, 1 summer abroad. *Entrance requirements:* For master's, portfolio, minimum GPA of 3.0. Additional exam requirements/recommendations for international students: Required—TOEFL. *Application deadline:* For fall admission, 3/1 priority date for domestic students, 2/1 priority date for international students; for spring admission, 11/1 priority date for domestic and international students. Applications are processed on a rolling basis. Application fee: $55 ($60 for international students). Electronic applications accepted. *Expenses:* Tuition, state resident: full-time $5,838. Tuition, nonresident: full-time $13,409. Tuition and fees vary according to program. *Financial support:* Fellowships, research assistantships with partial tuition reimbursements, teaching assistantships with full and partial tuition reimbursements, scholarships/grants, health care benefits, and unspecified assistantships available. Financial award application deadline: 2/1; financial award applicants required to submit FAFSA. *Faculty research:* Design build, sustainability, emergent technology, healthy places, urban design. *Unit head:* Prof. Keith Diazmoore, Chair, 785-864-5088, Fax: 785-864-5185, E-mail: archku@ku.edu.

University of Kentucky, Graduate School, College of Design, School of Architecture, Lexington, KY 40506-0032. Offers M Arch. *Faculty:* 14 full-time (3 women). *Students:* 12 full-time (2 women), 1 (woman) part-time; includes 1 minority (African American) Average age 28. 34 applicants, 53% accepted, 13 enrolled. In 2007, 9 degrees awarded. *Degree requirements:* For master's, comprehensive exam. *Entrance requirements:* For master's, GRE General Test, minimum undergraduate GPA of 2.75. Additional exam requirements/recommendations for international students: Required—TOEFL (minimum score 550 paper-based; 213 computer-based). *Application deadline:* For fall admission, 7/17 priority date for domestic students, 2/1 priority date for international students; for spring admission, 12/13 priority date for domestic students, 6/15 priority date for international students. Application fee: $50 ($65 for international students). Electronic applications accepted. *Expenses:* Tuition, state resident: part-time $437 per credit hour. Tuition, nonresident: part-time $931 per credit hour. *Financial support:* In 2007–08, 6 students received support, including 4 research assistantships with full tuition reimbursements available (averaging $6,200 per year), 2 teaching assistantships with full tuition reimbursements available (averaging $6,200 per year); fellowships with full tuition reimbursements available, Federal Work-Study, scholarships/grants, traineeships, health care benefits, tuition waivers (partial), and unspecified assistantships also available. Support available to part-time students. Financial award application deadline: 3/15; financial award applicants required to submit FAFSA. *Unit head:* Dr. David Biagi, Director, 859-257-2862, Fax: 859-288-4751, E-mail: dbiagi@uky.edu. *Application contact:* Dr. Brian Jackson, Senior Associate Dean, 859-257-4667, Fax: 859-257-4676, E-mail: brian.jackson@uky.edu.

University of Manitoba, Faculty of Graduate Studies, Faculty of Architecture, Department of Architecture, Winnipeg, MB R3T 2N2, Canada. Offers M Arch. *Degree requirements:* For master's, thesis or alternative.

University of Maryland, College Park, Graduate Studies, School of Architecture, Planning and Preservation, Program in Architecture, College Park, MD 20742. Offers M Arch, M Arch/MCP. Part-time and evening/weekend programs available. *Students:* 81 full-time (32 women), 25 part-time (8 women); includes 33 minority (10 African Americans, 1 American Indian/Alaska Native, 12 Asian Americans or Pacific Islanders, 10 Hispanic Americans), 4 international. 183 applicants, 32% accepted, 27 enrolled. In 2007, 18 degrees awarded. *Entrance requirements:* For master's, GRE General Test, portfolio, minimum GPA of 3.0, letters of recommendation. Additional exam requirements/recommendations for international students: Required—TOEFL. *Application deadline:* For fall admission, 1/1 for domestic and international students; for spring admission, 10/15 for domestic students, 6/1 for international students. Applications are processed on a rolling basis. Application fee: $60. Electronic applications accepted. *Financial support:* In 2007–08, 55 teaching assistantships with tuition reimbursements (averaging $13,858 per year) were awarded; fellowships with tuition reimbursements, research assistantships, career-related internships or fieldwork, Federal Work-Study, and scholarships/grants also available. Support available to part-time students. Financial award applicants required to submit FAFSA. *Faculty research:* Design, history, theory. *Unit head:* Brian Kelly, Director, 301-405-0325, Fax: 301-314-9583, E-mail: bkelly@umd.edu. *Application contact:* Dean of Graduate School, 301-405-0358, Fax: 301-314-9305.

University of Massachusetts Amherst, Graduate School, College of Humanities and Fine Arts, Department of Art, Programs in Architecture, Amherst, MA 01003. Offers architecture and design (M Arch); interior design (MS). *Students:* 23 full-time (9 women), 2 part-time (1 woman); includes 2 minority (1 African American, 1 Hispanic American), 5 international. Average age 29. 44 applicants, 82% accepted, 15 enrolled. In 2007, 1 degree awarded. *Degree requirements:* For master's, thesis or alternative. *Entrance requirements:* For master's, GRE General Test (MA), portfolio. Additional exam requirements/recommendations for international students: Required—TOEFL (minimum score 530 paper-based; 197 computer-based). *Application deadline:* For fall admission, 2/1 priority date for domestic and international students. Applications are processed on a rolling basis. Application fee: $50 ($65 for international students). Electronic applications accepted. *Expenses:* Tuition, state resident: full-time $2,640; part-time $110 per credit. Tuition, nonresident: full-time $9,936; part-time $414 per credit. Required fees: $7,455. One-time fee: $332. Tuition and fees vary according to course load, campus/location, program and reciprocity agreements. *Financial support:* Fellowships with full tuition reimbursements, research assistantships with full tuition reimbursements, teaching assistantships with full tuition reimbursements, career-related internships or fieldwork, Federal Work-Study, scholarships/grants, traineeships, and unspecified assistantships available. Support available to part-time students. Financial award application deadline: 2/1. *Unit head:* Dr. Jeanette Cole, Head, 413-545-6937, Fax: 413-545-3929.

University of Memphis, Graduate School, College of Communication and Fine Arts, Department of Architecture, Memphis, TN 38152. Offers M Arch. *Expenses:* Tuition, state resident: full-time $6,990; part-time $377 per hour. Tuition, nonresident: full-time $17,818; part-time $830 per hour. Tuition and fees vary according to course load and program. *Application contact:* Moira J. Logan, Associate Dean/Director of Research and Graduate Studies, 901-648-2350, Fax: 901-678-5118, E-mail: mlogan1@memphis.edu.

University of Miami, Graduate School, School of Architecture, Coral Gables, FL 33124. Offers architecture (M Arch); suburb and town design (M Arch). *Faculty:* 30 full-time (4 women), 22 part-time/adjunct (5 women). *Students:* 56 full-time (26 women), 6 part-time (2 women); includes 20 minority (2 African Americans, 18 Hispanic Americans), 5 international. Average age 29. 73 applicants, 51% accepted, 29 enrolled. In 2007, 31 master's awarded. *Entrance requirements:* For master's, GRE General Test, minimum GPA of 3.0, portfolio. Additional exam requirements/recommendations for international students: Required—TOEFL. *Application deadline:* For fall admission, 2/1 priority date for domestic students, 2/1 for international students. Applications are processed on a rolling basis. Application fee: $50. Electronic applications accepted. *Financial support:* In 2007–08, 56 students received support, including 25 research assistantships (averaging $2,000 per year), 25 teaching assistantships (averaging $2,000 per year); career-related internships or fieldwork, Federal Work-Study, institutionally sponsored loans, scholarships/grants, tuition waivers (partial), and unspecified assistantships also available. Support available to part-time students. Financial award application deadline: 2/1; financial award applicants required to submit FAFSA. *Faculty research:* Housing, town planning, retrofit. *Unit head:* Teofilo Victoria, Director of Graduate Studies, 305-284-3060, Fax: 305-284-6879, E-mail: tvictoria@miami.edu. *Application contact:* Jude Alexander, Coordinator, 305-284-3060, Fax: 305-284-6879, E-mail: jude@miami.edu.

See Close-Up on page 173.

University of Michigan, A. Alfred Taubman College of Architecture and Urban Planning, Doctoral Program in Architecture, Ann Arbor, MI 48109. Offers M Sc, PhD. Offered through the Horace H. Rackham School of Graduate Studies. *Faculty:* 18 full-time (6 women), 1 part-time/adjunct (0 women). *Students:* 34 full-time (17 women); includes 1 minority (Asian American or Pacific Islander), 21 international. 57 applicants, 26% accepted, 5 enrolled. In 2007, 1 doctorate awarded. Terminal master's awarded for partial completion of doctoral program. *Median time to degree:* Of those who began their doctoral program in fall 1999, 100% received their degree in 8 years or less. *Degree requirements:* For master's, thesis, research project; for doctorate, comprehensive exam, thesis/dissertation, oral defense of dissertation, preliminary exam, practicum. *Entrance requirements:* For master's and doctorate, GRE General Test. Additional exam requirements/recommendations for international students: Required—TOEFL (minimum score 560 paper-based; 220 computer-based; 84 iBT). *Application deadline:* For fall admission, 12/15 for domestic and international students. Application fee: $60 ($75 for international students). Electronic applications accepted. *Expenses: Contact institution. Financial support:* In 2007–08, 32 students received support, including 3 fellowships with partial tuition reimbursements available (averaging $15,600 per year), 1 research assistantship with full tuition reimbursement available (averaging $9,082 per year), 5 teaching assistantships with full tuition reimbursements available (averaging $9,120 per year); scholarships/grants, health care benefits, and unspecified assistantships also available. Financial award application deadline: 1/15; financial award applicants required to submit FAFSA. *Faculty research:* Environment and behavior, environmental technology, history-theory, design process and methods. Total annual research expenditures: $480,382. *Unit head:* Jean D. Wineman, Chair, 734-763-1497, Fax: 734-763-2322, E-mail: jwineman@umich.edu. *Application contact:* Lisa K. Hauser, Secretary, 734-763-1275, Fax: 734-763-2322, E-mail: weeze@umich.edu.

University of Michigan, A. Alfred Taubman College of Architecture and Urban Planning, Program in Architecture, Ann Arbor, MI 48109. Offers M Arch, M Sc, M Arch/M Eng, M Arch/MSE, M Arch/MUP, MBA/M Arch. *Students:* 220 full-time (87 women), 2 part-time; includes 24 minority (1 African American, 17 Asian Americans or Pacific Islanders, 6 Hispanic Americans), 64 international. 437 applicants, 62% accepted, 90 enrolled. In 2007, 78 degrees awarded. *Entrance requirements:* For master's, GRE. Additional exam requirements/recommendations for international students: Required—TOEFL (minimum score 600 paper-based; 250 computer-based; 100 iBT). *Application deadline:* For fall admission, 1/15 for domestic and international students. Application fee: $60 ($75 for international students). Electronic applications accepted. *Expenses: Contact institution. Financial support:* In 2007–08, 147 students received support, including 30 teaching assistantships with partial tuition reimbursements available (averaging $3,000 per year); Federal Work-Study, institutionally sponsored loans, scholarships/grants, and unspecified assistantships also available. Support available to part-time students. *Application contact:* Meghan Lee, Admissions Counselor, 734-764-1649, Fax: 734-763-2322, E-mail: meglee@umich.edu.

University of Minnesota, Twin Cities Campus, Graduate School, College of Design, School of Architecture, Minneapolis, MN 55455-0213. Offers architecture (M Arch); sustainable design (MS). First professional and post-professional tracks available in M Arch program. *Faculty:* 19 full-time (7 women), 28 part-time/adjunct (10 women). *Students:* 154 full-time (61 women), 20 part-time (10 women); includes 16 minority (1 African American, 11 Asian Americans or Pacific Islanders, 4 Hispanic Americans), 4 international. Average age 28. 225 applicants, 33% accepted, 55 enrolled. In 2007, 50 master's awarded. *Degree requirements:* For master's, thesis (for some programs). *Entrance requirements:* For master's, GRE General Test, suggested GPA of 3.0, portfolio. Additional exam requirements/recommendations for international students: Required—TOEFL (minimum score 550 paper-based; 213 computer-based; 79 iBT). *Application deadline:* For fall admission, 1/15 for domestic and international students. Application fee: $55. *Expenses: Contact institution. Financial support:* In 2007–08, 18 fellowships (averaging $2,800 per year), 7 research assistantships with partial tuition reimbursements (averaging $6,325 per year), 102 teaching assistantships with partial tuition reimbursements (averaging $6,325 per year) were awarded; career-related internships or fieldwork, Federal Work-Study, institutionally sponsored loans, and thesis awards also available. Financial award application deadline: 1/15; financial award applicants required to submit FAFSA. *Faculty research:* History, daylighting, computer-aided design, sustainable design, structures. Total annual research expenditures: $421,042. *Unit head:* Renee Cheng, Head of School and Professor, 612-624-5201, Fax: 612-624-5743. *Application contact:* Terence Rafferty, Director of Graduate Admissions and Recruitment, 612-624-8817, Fax: 612-624-5743, E-mail: raffe013@umn.edu.

University of Missouri–Columbia, Graduate School, College of Human Environmental Science, Department of Architectural Studies, Columbia, MO 65211. Offers design with digital media (MA, MS); environmental design (MS). *Entrance requirements:* For master's, GRE General Test, minimum GPA of 3.0. Additional exam requirements/recommendations for international students: Required—TOEFL (minimum score 500 paper-based; 173 computer-based).

University of Nebraska–Lincoln, Graduate College, College of Architecture, Department of Architecture, Graduate Program in Architecture, Lincoln, NE 68588. Offers MS. *Degree requirements:* For master's, comprehensive exam, thesis. *Entrance requirements:* For master's, GRE General Test. Additional exam requirements/recommendations for international students: Required—TOEFL (minimum score 550 paper-based; 213 computer-based). Electronic applications accepted. *Faculty research:* Housing, environmental design, architectural history, sustainable design, rural architecture.

University of Nebraska–Lincoln, Graduate College, College of Architecture, Department of Architecture, Professional Program in Architecture, Lincoln, NE 68588. Offers M Arch, M Arch/MBA, M Arch/MCRP. *Entrance requirements:* For master's, GRE General Test. Additional exam requirements/recommendations for international students: Required—TOEFL. *Faculty research:* Housing, environmental design, architectural history, sustainable design, rural architecture.

University of Nevada, Las Vegas, Graduate College, College of Fine Arts, School of Architecture, Las Vegas, NV 89154-9900. Offers M Arch. Part-time programs available. *Faculty:* 16 full-time (4 women), 5 part-time/adjunct (2 women). *Students:* 28 full-time (11 women), 5 part-time (2 women); includes 9 minority (3 Asian Americans or Pacific Islanders, 6 Hispanic Americans), 1 international. 53 applicants, 43% accepted, 12 enrolled. In 2007, 13 degrees awarded. *Degree requirements:* For master's, thesis (for some programs), comprehensive building design, comprehensive and oral exams. *Entrance requirements:* For master's, GRE, minimum GPA of 3.0. Additional exam requirements/recommendations for international students: Required—TOEFL (minimum score 550 paper-based; 213 computer-based; 80 iBT). *Application deadline:* For fall admission, 2/1 for domestic and international students. Application fee: $60 ($75 for international students). Electronic applications accepted. *Expenses:* Tuition, state resident: part-time $198 per credit. Tuition, nonresident: part-time $416 per credit. Required fees: $256 per semester. Tuition and fees vary according to course load and reciprocity agreements. *Financial support:* In 2007–08, 3 research assistantships with partial tuition reimbursements (averaging $10,000 per year), 8 teaching assistantships with partial tuition reimbursements (averaging $10,000 per year) were awarded; career-related internships or fieldwork, Federal Work-Study, institutionally sponsored loans, scholarships/grants, health care benefits, and unspecified assistantships also available. Support available to part-time students. Financial award application deadline: 3/1. *Unit head:* Dr. Michael Kroelihger, Director, 702-895-3031. *Application contact:* Graduate College Admissions Evaluator, 702-895-3320, Fax: 702-895-4180, E-mail: gradcollege@unlv.edu.

University of New Mexico, Graduate School, School of Architecture and Planning, Program in Architecture, Albuquerque, NM 87131-2039. Offers M Arch. *Students:* 76 full-time (28 women), 14 part-time (6 women); includes 27 minority (1 African American, 5 American Indian/Alaska Native, 1 Asian American or Pacific Islander, 20 Hispanic Americans), 9 international. Average age 34. 107 applicants, 43% accepted, 29 enrolled. In 2007, 31 degrees awarded. *Degree requirements:* For master's, thesis (for some programs), graduate review. *Entrance requirements:* For master's, experience in field. Additional exam requirements/recommendations for international students: Required—TOEFL (minimum score 550 paper-based; 213 computer-based). *Application deadline:* For fall admission, 2/15 priority date for domestic students. Application fee: $50. *Financial support:* In 2007–08, 56 students received support, including 6 fellowships, 14 research assistantships with partial tuition reimbursements available (averaging $6,000 per year); scholarships/grants, health care benefits, and unspecified assistantships also available. Financial award application deadline: 3/1; financial award applicants required to submit FAFSA. *Faculty research:* Professional practice, design theory, sustainable environments, architecture and children, environment and behavior. *Unit head:* Geraldine Forbes Isais, Director, 505-277-2053, Fax: 505-277-0076, E-mail: gforbes@unm.edu. *Application contact:* Mitzi Visil, Senior Academic Advisor, 505-277-1303, Fax: 505-277-0076, E-mail: mitziv@unm.edu.

The University of North Carolina at Charlotte, Graduate School, College of Architecture, Charlotte, NC 28223-0001. Offers M Arch. *Faculty:* 16 full-time (3 women), 5 part-time/adjunct (2 women). *Students:* 61 full-time (40 women), 9 part-time (5 women); includes 7 minority (4 African Americans, 2 Asian Americans or Pacific Islanders, 1 Hispanic American), 2 international. Average age 26. 68 applicants, 68% accepted, 31 enrolled. In 2007, 12 degrees awarded. *Degree requirements:* For master's, project or thesis. *Entrance requirements:* For master's, GRE General Test or MAT, resumé, portfolio. Additional exam requirements/recommendations for international students: Required—TOEFL (minimum score 557 paper-based; 220 computer-based). *Application deadline:* For fall admission, 2/15 for domestic students, 1/31 for international students. Application fee: $55. Electronic applications accepted. *Expenses:* Tuition, state resident: full-time $2,855. Tuition, nonresident: full-time $13,062. Required fees: $1,692. *Financial support:* In 2007–08, 2 research assistantships (averaging $2,050 per year), 7 teaching assistantships (averaging $6,018 per year) were awarded; fellowships, career-related internships or fieldwork, Federal Work-Study, institutionally sponsored loans, scholarships/grants, and unspecified assistantships also available. Support available to part-time students. Financial award application deadline: 4/1; financial award applicants required to submit FAFSA. *Faculty research:* Daylighting and energy control, urban design, history and theory, construction techniques. *Unit head:* Kenneth A. Lambla, Dean, 704-687-4841, Fax: 704-687-3353, E-mail: kalambla@email.uncc.edu. *Application contact:* Kathy B. Giddings, Director of Graduate Admissions, 704-687-3366, Fax: 704-687-3279, E-mail: agidding@uncc.edu.

The University of North Carolina at Greensboro, Graduate School, School of Human Environmental Sciences, Department of Interior Architecture, Greensboro, NC 27412-5001. Offers historic preservation (Certificate); interior architecture (MS); museum studies (Certificate). *Faculty:* 9 full-time (4 women), 1 part-time/adjunct (0 women). *Students:* 14 full-time (12 women), 1 (woman) part-time. 13 applicants, 38% accepted. *Degree requirements:* For master's, thesis. *Entrance requirements:* For master's, GRE General Test or MAT, bachelor's degree in interior design, interview, portfolio. Additional exam requirements/recommendations for international students: Required—TOEFL. *Application deadline:* For fall admission, 3/1 for domestic students. Application fee: $45. Electronic applications accepted. *Financial support:* Fellowships with full tuition reimbursements, research assistantships with full tuition reimbursements, teaching assistantships with full tuition reimbursements, career-related internships or fieldwork, Federal Work-Study, scholarships/grants, and traineeships available. Support available to part-time students. *Unit head:* Thomas Lambeth, Chairman, 336-334-5320, Fax: 336-334-5049, E-mail: ctlambeth@uncg.edu. *Application contact:* Michelle Harkleroad, Director of Graduate Admissions, 336-334-4884, Fax: 336-334-4424, E-mail: mbharkle@uncg.edu.

University of Notre Dame, Graduate School, School of Architecture, Notre Dame, IN 46556. Offers architectural design and urbanism (M ADU, M Arch); architecture (M Arch). *Faculty:* 20 full-time (2 women), 1 part-time/adjunct (0 women). *Students:* 39 full-time (14 women); includes 3 minority (2 Asian Americans or Pacific Islanders, 1 Hispanic American), 3 international. 68 applicants, 28% accepted, 16 enrolled. In 2007, 9 degrees awarded. *Degree requirements:* For master's, thesis or alternative. *Entrance requirements:* For master's, GRE General Test, portfolio. Additional exam requirements/recommendations for international students: Required—TOEFL (minimum score 600 paper-based; 250 computer-based; 80 iBT). *Application deadline:* For fall admission, 2/1 priority date for domestic and international students. Application fee: $50. Electronic applications accepted. *Financial support:* In 2007–08, fellowships with full tuition reimbursements (averaging $12,000 per year), 14 teaching assistantships (averaging $12,000 per year) were awarded; research assistantships, institutionally sponsored loans and tuition waivers (full) also available. Financial award application deadline: 2/1. *Faculty research:* Architectural theory, urban design, classical and traditional architecture and urbanism. *Unit head:* Prof. Philip Bess, Director of Graduate Studies, 574-631-3096, Fax: 574-631-8486.

Architecture

University of Notre Dame (continued)
Application contact: Dr. Jarren Gonzales, Director of Graduate Admissions, 574-631-7706, Fax: 574-631-4183.

University of Oklahoma, Graduate College, College of Architecture, Division of Architecture, Norman, OK 73019-0390. Offers M Arch. Part-time programs available. *Faculty:* 26 full-time (5 women), 1 (woman) part-time/adjunct. *Students:* 15 full-time (9 women), 11 part-time (1 woman); includes 2 minority (both American Indian/Alaska Native), 10 international. 19 applicants, 89% accepted, 11 enrolled. In 2007, 9 degrees awarded. *Degree requirements:* For master's, thesis or alternative, portfolio, project. *Entrance requirements:* For master's, GRE General Test, portfolio. Additional exam requirements/recommendations for international students: Required—TOEFL (minimum score 550 paper-based; 213 computer-based). *Application deadline:* For fall admission, 4/1 for domestic and international students; for spring admission, 11/1 for domestic students, 9/1 for international students. Applications are processed on a rolling basis. Application fee: $40 ($90 for international students). Electronic applications accepted. *Expenses:* Tuition, state resident: full-time $3,451; part-time $144 per credit hour. Tuition, nonresident: full-time $12,432; part-time $518 per credit hour. Required fees: $1,925; $70 per credit hour. $122 per semester. *Financial support:* In 2007–08, 7 students received support, including 4 teaching assistantships with partial tuition reimbursements available (averaging $11,813 per year); career-related internships or fieldwork, Federal Work-Study, scholarships/grants, tuition waivers (partial), and unspecified assistantships also available. Support available to part-time students. Financial award applicants required to submit FAFSA. *Faculty research:* Sustainability, regionalism, facilities management. Total annual research expenditures: $652,899. *Unit head:* Nickolas L. Harm, Interim Director, 405-325-2444, Fax: 405-325-0108, E-mail: nharm@ou.edu. *Application contact:* Terry Patterson, Professor/Graduate Liaison, 405-325-3869, Fax: 405-325-7558, E-mail: tpatterson@ou.edu.

University of Oklahoma, Graduate College, College of Architecture, Division of Construction Science, Norman, OK 73019-0390. Offers MS. Part-time and evening/weekend programs available. *Students:* 7 full-time (2 women), 17 part-time (4 women); includes 2 minority (1 American Indian/Alaska Native, 1 Hispanic American), 5 international. 12 applicants, 92% accepted, 7 enrolled. In 2007, 4 degrees awarded. *Degree requirements:* For master's, thesis or alternative, portfolio, project. *Entrance requirements:* For master's, GRE General Test, portfolio. Additional exam requirements/recommendations for international students: Required—TOEFL (minimum score 600 paper-based; 250 computer-based). *Application deadline:* For fall admission, 4/1 for domestic and international students; for spring admission, 11/1 for domestic students, 9/1 for international students. Applications are processed on a rolling basis. Application fee: $40 ($90 for international students). Electronic applications accepted. *Expenses:* Tuition, state resident: full-time $3,451; part-time $144 per credit hour. Tuition, nonresident: full-time $12,432; part-time $518 per credit hour. Required fees: $1,925; $70 per credit hour. $122 per semester. *Financial support:* In 2007–08, 6 students received support, including 1 research assistantship with partial tuition reimbursement available (averaging $12,510 per year), 1 teaching assistantship with partial tuition reimbursement available (averaging $9,450 per year); career-related internships or fieldwork, scholarships/grants, tuition waivers (partial), and unspecified assistantships also available. Support available to part-time students. Financial award applicants required to submit FAFSA. *Faculty research:* Online education, highway construction, lean construction, Hispanic construction worker design/safety, online instructional design. *Unit head:* Kenneth Robson, Director, 405-325-2444, Fax: 405-325-7558, E-mail: krobson@ou.edu. *Application contact:* Richard C. Ryan, Professor, 405-325-3976, Fax: 405-325-7558, E-mail: rryan@ou.edu.

University of Oregon, Graduate School, School of Architecture and Allied Arts, Department of Architecture, Eugene, OR 97403. Offers architecture (M Arch); interior architecture (MI Arch). *Accreditation:* CIDA. *Faculty:* 23 full-time (9 women), 9 part-time/adjunct (4 women). *Students:* 199 full-time (86 women), 12 part-time (4 women); includes 7 Asian Americans or Pacific Islanders, 9 Hispanic Americans, 7 international. 156 applicants, 47% accepted. In 2007, 67 degrees awarded. *Degree requirements:* For master's, thesis (for some programs). *Entrance requirements:* For master's, GRE General Test. Additional exam requirements/recommendations for international students: Required—TOEFL. *Application deadline:* For fall admission, 1/1 for domestic students. Application fee: $50. *Financial support:* In 2007–08, 40 teaching assistantships were awarded; career-related internships or fieldwork, Federal Work-Study, and institutionally sponsored loans also available. Financial award application deadline: 3/1. *Faculty research:* Innovation in housing design and design production, climate responsive design, passive heating and cooling, computer software development for design applications, vernacular architecture. *Unit head:* Christine Theodoropoulos, Head, 541-346-3661. *Application contact:* Mike Clark, Admissions Contact, 541-346-1434, E-mail: mclark@uoregon.edu.

University of Pennsylvania, School of Design, Graduate Group in Architecture, Philadelphia, PA 19104. Offers architecture (PhD); real estate design and development (PhD); urban design (PhD). Part-time programs available. *Degree requirements:* For doctorate, 2 foreign languages, comprehensive exam, thesis/dissertation, qualifying exam, final exam. *Entrance requirements:* For doctorate, GRE General Test, B Arch, M Arch, portfolio, writing sample. Additional exam requirements/recommendations for international students: Required—TOEFL. *Faculty research:* Theory, history, technology, representation, visualization, landscape, urban design, historic preservation.

See Close-Up on page 175.

University of Pennsylvania, School of Design, Master of Architecture Program, Philadelphia, PA 19104. Offers architecture (M Arch); real estate design and development (Certificate); urban design (Certificate). *Degree requirements:* For master's, thesis (for some programs). *Entrance requirements:* For master's and Certificate, GRE, portfolio. Additional exam requirements/recommendations for international students: Required—TOEFL. *Faculty research:* Computer modeling, metropolitan and regional urbanism, contemporary architectural theory structure and technology.

See Close-Up on page 175.

University of Puerto Rico, Río Piedras, School of Architecture, San Juan, PR 00931-3300. Offers M Arch. Part-time programs available. *Students:* 59 full-time (26 women), 18 part-time (4 women). Average age 25. 18 applicants, 100% accepted, 18 enrolled. In 2007, 27 degrees awarded. *Degree requirements:* For master's, comprehensive exam, thesis, design project. *Entrance requirements:* For master's, PAEG or GRE, bachelor's degree in architecture, interview, minimum GPA of 3.0, portfolio, 2 letters of recommendation. *Application deadline:* For fall admission, 2/1 for domestic and international students. Application fee: $45. *Expenses:* Tuition, state resident: full-time $1,808; part-time $113 per credit. Tuition, nonresident: full-time $5,248; part-time $328 per credit. Required fees: $72 per term. *Financial support:* Fellowships, research assistantships, teaching assistantships, Federal Work-Study, institutionally sponsored loans, and tuition waivers (partial) available. Financial award application deadline: 5/31. *Unit head:* Dr. Francisco Rodriguez-Suàrez, Dean, 809-763-2101 Ext. 2102. *Application contact:* Dr. Humberto Covollin, Graduate Program Coordinator, 787-764-000 Ext. 3449, Fax: 787-763-5377.

University of Southern California, Graduate School, School of Architecture, Program in Architecture, Los Angeles, CA 90089. Offers M Arch. *Faculty:* 50 full-time (25 women), 50 part-time/adjunct (25 women). *Students:* 41 full-time (19 women), 1 part-time; includes 7 minority (1 African American, 5 Asian Americans or Pacific Islanders, 1 Hispanic American), 15 international. 126 applicants, 59% accepted. In 2007, 12 master's awarded. *Entrance requirements:* For master's, GRE General Test. *Application deadline:* For fall admission, 1/15 priority date for domestic students. Applications are processed on a rolling basis. Application fee: $85. *Financial support:* Fellowships with tuition reimbursements, research assistantships with tuition reimbursements, teaching assistantships with tuition reimbursements, career-related internships or fieldwork, Federal Work-Study, and scholarships/grants available. Support available to part-time students. Financial award application deadline: 2/15; financial award applicants required to submit FAFSA.

See Close-Up on page 177.

University of Southern California, Graduate School, School of Architecture, Program in Historic Preservation, Los Angeles, CA 90089. Offers MHP. Part-time programs available. *Faculty:* 50 full-time (25 women), 50 part-time/adjunct (25 women). *Students:* 9 full-time (5 women), 6 part-time (5 women); includes 1 minority (Hispanic American), 1 international. 12 applicants, 92% accepted. In 2007, 5 master's awarded. *Entrance requirements:* For master's, GRE. *Application deadline:* For fall admission, 1/15 priority date for domestic students. Applications are processed on a rolling basis. Application fee: $85. *Financial support:* In 2007–08, fellowships with tuition reimbursements (averaging $15,000 per year); career-related internships or fieldwork, Federal Work-Study, and scholarships/grants also available. Support available to part-time students. Financial award applicants required to submit FAFSA. *Unit head:* Dr. Kenneth Breisch, Head, 213-740-2311.

University of South Florida, Graduate School, School of Architecture and Community Design, Tampa, FL 33620-9951. Offers M Arch. *Faculty:* 7 full-time (0 women), 8 part-time/adjunct (2 women). *Students:* 80 full-time (24 women), 38 part-time (14 women); includes 27 minority (3 African Americans, 1 American Indian/Alaska Native, 4 Asian Americans or Pacific Islanders, 19 Hispanic Americans), 5 international. Average age 30. 89 applicants, 38% accepted, 24 enrolled. In 2007, 44 degrees awarded. *Entrance requirements:* For master's, GRE General Test, minimum GPA of 3.0 in last 60 hours of coursework. *Application deadline:* For fall admission, 3/1 priority date for domestic students; for spring admission, 10/5 priority date for domestic students. Applications are processed on a rolling basis. Application fee: $30. Electronic applications accepted. *Financial support:* Career-related internships or fieldwork, scholarships/grants, and unspecified assistantships available. *Faculty research:* Community design, sustainability, portable classrooms. Total annual research expenditures: $104,899. *Unit head:* Stephen Schreiber, Director, 813-974-4031, Fax: 813-974-2557, E-mail: schreiber@arch.usf.edu. *Application contact:* Carol Trent, Admissions/Registrar Office, 813-974-4031, Fax: 813-974-2557, E-mail: trent@arch.usf.edu.

The University of Tennessee, Graduate School, College of Architecture and Design, Program in Architecture, Knoxville, TN 37996. Offers architecture (professional) (M Arch); architecture (research) (M Arch). *Degree requirements:* For master's, thesis. *Entrance requirements:* For master's, GRE General Test, completed application form, transcripts of undergraduate and/or graduate work, minimum GPA of 3.0, 3 letters of recommendation, samples of portfolio work (highly recommended for professional track). Additional exam requirements/recommendations for international students: Required—TOEFL (minimum score 550 paper-based).

The University of Texas at Arlington, Graduate School, School of Architecture, Program in Architecture, Arlington, TX 76019. Offers M Arch, M Arch/MCRP. *Students:* 82 full-time (27 women), 39 part-time (18 women); includes 23 minority (2 African Americans, 5 Asian Americans or Pacific Islanders, 16 Hispanic Americans), 9 international. In 2007, 29 degrees awarded. *Entrance requirements:* For master's, GRE General Test, minimum GPA of 3.0, portfolio. Additional exam requirements/recommendations for international students: Required—TOEFL (minimum score 550 paper-based; 213 computer-based). *Application deadline:* For fall admission, 6/16 for domestic students. Applications are processed on a rolling basis. Application fee: $35 ($50 for international students). *Expenses:* Tuition, state resident: full-time $5,934. Tuition, nonresident: full-time $10,938. *Financial support:* In 2007–08, fellowships (averaging $1,000 per year), research assistantships with partial tuition reimbursements (averaging $4,824 per year); teaching assistantships with partial tuition reimbursements (averaging $4,824 per year) were awarded; career-related internships or fieldwork also available. Financial award application deadline: 6/1; financial award applicants required to submit FAFSA. *Unit head:* Donald Gatzke, Director, 817-272-2801, Fax: 817-272-5098, E-mail: gatzke@uta.edu.

The University of Texas at Austin, Graduate School, School of Architecture, Austin, TX 78712-1111. Offers M Arch, MLA, MS Arch St, MSCRP, PhD, JD/MSCRP, MSCRP/MA, MSCRP/PhD. *Degree requirements:* For doctorate, thesis/dissertation. *Entrance requirements:* For master's and doctorate, GRE General Test. Additional exam requirements/recommendations for international students: Required—TOEFL (minimum score 550 paper-based; 213 computer-based). Electronic applications accepted.

The University of Texas at San Antonio, College of Architecture, San Antonio, TX 78249-0617. Offers M Arch. *Faculty:* 14 full-time (2 women), 1 part-time/adjunct (0 women). *Students:* 52 full-time (26 women), 21 part-time (8 women); includes 29 minority (2 African Americans, 2 Asian Americans or Pacific Islanders, 25 Hispanic Americans), 3 international. Average age 29. 44 applicants, 66% accepted, 29 enrolled. In 2007, 19 degrees awarded. *Degree requirements:* For master's, comprehensive exam, thesis. *Entrance requirements:* For master's, GRE General Test, minimum GPA of 3.0 in last 60 hours and in all architecture courses. Additional exam requirements/recommendations for international students: Required—TOEFL (minimum score 500 paper-based; 173 computer-based). *Application deadline:* For fall admission, 7/1 for domestic students, 4/1 for international students; for spring admission, 11/1 for domestic students, 9/1 for international students. Applications are processed on a rolling basis. Application fee: $45 ($80 for international students). Electronic applications accepted. *Financial support:* In 2007–08, 3 research assistantships (averaging $3,556 per year), 2 teaching assistantships (averaging $6,000 per year) were awarded; career-related internships or fieldwork, Federal Work-Study, scholarships/grants, and unspecified assistantships also available. Total annual research expenditures: $22,500. *Unit head:* Julius M. Gribou, Dean, 210-458-3090, Fax: 210-458-3016, E-mail: julius.gribou@utsa.edu. *Application contact:* Robert Baron, Graduate Advisor, 210-458-3010, E-mail: rbaron@utsa.edu.

University of Toronto, School of Graduate Studies, Social Sciences Division, Faculty of Architecture, Landscape and Design, Toronto, ON M5S 1A1, Canada. Offers M Arch, MLA, MUD. *Accreditation:* ASLA. *Faculty:* 3 full-time, 33 part-time/adjunct. *Students:* 337 full-time (150 women), 25 part-time, 27 international. 388 applicants, 64% accepted. In 2007, 1 degree awarded. *Entrance requirements:* For master's, minimum B average; 3 letters of reference; resumé; 3 writing samples; 5 samples of design work, drawing, or work in a related field. Additional exam requirements/recommendations for international students: Required—TOEFL (minimum score 580 paper-based; 237 computer-based), TWE (minimum score 5), MELAB (minimum score: 85), IELTS (minimum score: 7) or COPE (minimum score: 4). *Application deadline:* For fall admission, 1/28 for domestic students. Application fee: $100 Canadian dollars. *Expenses:* Contact institution. *Unit head:* Prof. George Baird, Dean, 416-978-5038, Fax: 416-971-2094. *Application contact:* Frederic Urban, Chair, Admissions and Recruitment Committee, 416-978-4323, Fax: 416-971-2094, E-mail: frederic.urban@utoronto.ca.

University of Utah, The Graduate School, College of Architecture and Planning, Salt Lake City, UT 84112-1107. Offers architectural studies (M Arch, MS); urban planning (MUP); M Arch/MBA. Part-time programs available. *Faculty:* 17 full-time (5 women), 9 part-time/adjunct (2 women). *Students:* 98 full-time (29 women), 12 part-time (5 women); includes 3 minority (1 Asian American or Pacific Islander, 2 Hispanic Americans), 11 international. Average age 30. 84 applicants, 65% accepted, 40 enrolled. In 2007, 45 degrees awarded. *Degree requirements:* For master's, thesis (for some programs), comprehensive project. *Entrance requirements:* For master's, minimum undergraduate GPA of 3.0. Additional exam requirements/recommendations for international students: Required—TOEFL (minimum score 500 paper-based; 173 computer-based). *Application deadline:* For fall admission, 4/1 for domestic and international students; for spring admission, 11/1 for domestic and international students. Applications are processed on a rolling basis. Application fee: $45 ($65 for international students). Electronic applications accepted. *Expenses:* Contact institution. *Financial support:* In 2007–08, 29 fellowships with full tuition reimbursements, 3 research assistantships with full tuition reimbursements, 29 teaching assistantships with partial tuition reimbursements were awarded; career-related internships or fieldwork, Federal Work-Study, and scholarships/grants also available. Financial award application deadline: 2/1; financial award applicants required to submit FAFSA. *Faculty* *research:* History, design, acoustics, photography, structures, architecture of American West, architectural communication and representation, impact of technology. Total annual research expenditures: $171,483. *Unit head:* Brenda Scheer, Dean, 801-581-8254, Fax: 801-581-8217, E-mail: scheer@arch.utah.edu. *Application contact:* Colleen Nielson, Admissions Advisor, 801-581-8254, Fax: 801-581-8217, E-mail: cnielson@arch.utah.edu.

University of Virginia, School of Architecture, Department of Architecture and Landscape Architecture, Charlottesville, VA 22903. Offers architecture (M Arch); landscape architecture (M Land Arch). *Faculty:* 25 full-time (10 women), 12 part-time/adjunct (4 women). *Students:* 118 full-time (74 women); includes 9 minority (1 African American, 8 Asian Americans or Pacific Islanders), 9 international. Average age 27. 512 applicants, 21% accepted, 40 enrolled. In 2007, 26 degrees awarded. *Entrance requirements:* For master's, GRE General Test. Additional exam requirements/recommendations for international students: Required—TOEFL (minimum score 600 paper-based; 250 computer-based). Application fee: $60. *Financial support:* Career-related internships or fieldwork, Federal Work-Study, and institutionally sponsored loans available. Financial award applicants required to submit FAFSA. *Unit head:* Craig Barton, Chair, 434-924-1493, Fax: 434-982-2678, E-mail: ceb8x@virginia.edu. *Application contact:* Tracy Brookman, Admissions Officer, 434-924-6442, E-mail: arch-admissions@virginia.edu.

University of Washington, Graduate School, College of Architecture and Urban Planning, Department of Architecture, Seattle, WA 98195. Offers architecture (M Arch, MS); built environment (PhD); design computing (Certificate); historic preservation (Certificate); lighting design (Certificate); urban design (Certificate). *Degree requirements:* For master's, thesis. *Entrance requirements:* For master's, GRE General Test, minimum GPA of 3.0, portfolio, 3 letters of recommendation. Additional exam requirements/recommendations for international students: Required—TOEFL. *Faculty research:* Lighting, materials, computing theory, media, culture, environment.

University of Waterloo, Graduate Studies, Faculty of Engineering, School of Architecture, Waterloo, ON N2L 3G1, Canada. Offers M Arch. Part-time programs available. *Faculty:* 19 full-time (7 women). *Students:* 92 full-time (47 women), 9 part-time (5 women). 54 applicants, 46% accepted, 21 enrolled. In 2007, 21 degrees awarded. *Degree requirements:* For master's, thesis. *Entrance requirements:* For master's, bachelor's degree in pre-professional architecture. *Application deadline:* For fall admission, 6/15 priority date for domestic students; for winter admission, 10/15 priority date for domestic students; for spring admission, 2/15 priority date for domestic students. Applications are processed on a rolling basis. Application fee: $75 Canadian dollars. Electronic applications accepted. *Financial support:* Fellowships, research assistantships, teaching assistantships available. *Unit head:* Eric Rick Haldenby, Director, 519-888-4544 Ext. 84544, Fax: 519-746-0072, E-mail: erhalden@uwaterloo.ca. *Application contact:* Lori A. McConnell, Graduate Student Advisor, 519-888-4567 Ext. 27603, Fax: 519-746-0512, E-mail: lmcconne@fes.waterloo.ca.

University of Wisconsin–Milwaukee, Graduate School, School of Architecture and Urban Planning, Department of Architecture, Milwaukee, WI 53201-0413. Offers M Arch, PhD, Certificate, M Arch/MUP. *Faculty:* 27 full-time (6 women). *Students:* 135 full-time (45 women), 15 part-time (7 women); includes 19 minority (5 African Americans, 1 American Indian/Alaska Native, 7 Asian Americans or Pacific Islanders, 6 Hispanic Americans), 12 international. 113 applicants, 72% accepted, 41 enrolled. In 2007, 22 master's, 4 doctorates awarded. *Degree requirements:* For master's, thesis; for doctorate, thesis/dissertation. *Entrance requirements:* For master's, GRE General Test, portfolio. *Application deadline:* For fall admission, 1/1 priority date for domestic students; for spring admission, 9/1 for domestic students. Applications are processed on a rolling basis. Application fee: $45 ($75 for international students). *Expenses:* Tuition, state resident: part-time $530 per credit. Tuition, nonresident: part-time $1,428 per credit. Required fees: $19 per credit. $229 per term. Tuition and fees vary according to course load and program. *Financial support:* In 2007–08, 18 teaching assistantships were awarded; fellowships, research assistantships, career-related internships or fieldwork and unspecified assistantships also available. Support available to part-time students. Financial award application deadline: 4/15. *Unit head:* Joan Simuncak, Representative, 414-229-4015, Fax: 414-229-6976, E-mail: joanarch@uwm.edu.

Virginia Polytechnic Institute and State University, Graduate School, College of Architecture and Urban Studies, School of Architecture and Design, Blacksburg, VA 24061. Offers M Arch, MS. *Accreditation:* NASAD. *Entrance requirements:* For master's, GRE General Test. Additional exam requirements/recommendations for international students: Required—TOEFL (minimum score 550 paper-based; 213 computer-based). Electronic applications accepted. *Faculty research:* Computer applications in design, building technology, architectural design theory, solar/passive energy design, building assembly.

Washington State University, Graduate School, College of Engineering and Architecture, School of Architecture and Construction Management, Pullman, WA 99164. Offers architecture (M Arch); architecture design theory (MS). *Faculty:* 22. *Students:* 25 full-time (7 women), 1 part-time; includes 2 minority (both Asian Americans or Pacific Islanders), 1 international. Average age 27. 87 applicants, 20% accepted, 13 enrolled. In 2007, 12 degrees awarded. *Degree requirements:* For master's, comprehensive exam (for some programs), thesis, oral exam. *Entrance requirements:* For master's, GRE General Test, minimum GPA of 3.0, 3 letters of recommendation. Additional exam requirements/recommendations for international students: Required—TOEFL. *Application deadline:* For fall admission, 1/15 priority date for domestic and international students. Applications are processed on a rolling basis. Application fee: $50. *Financial support:* In 2007–08, 25 students received support, including 2 fellowships (averaging $2,000 per year), research assistantships with full and partial tuition reimbursements available (averaging $13,917 per year), 12 teaching assistantships with full and partial tuition reimbursements available (averaging $13,056 per year); career-related internships or fieldwork, Federal Work-Study, institutionally sponsored loans, and tuition waivers (partial) also available. Financial award application deadline: 3/1; financial award applicants required to submit FAFSA. *Faculty research:* Cultural, technological, and environmental design. *Unit head:* Greg Kessler, Director, 509-335-5539, E-mail: gkessler@acm.wsu.edu. *Application contact:* Graduate School Admissions, 800-GRADWSU, Fax: 509-335-1949, E-mail: gradsch@wsu.edu.

Washington State University Spokane, Graduate Programs, Interdisciplinary Design Institute, Spokane, WA 99210-1495. Offers architecture (M Arch, MS); design (Dr DES); interior design (MA); landscape architecture (MS). Part-time programs available. *Faculty:* 11 full-time (3 women), 3 part-time/adjunct (2 women). *Students:* 35 full-time (22 women), 5 part-time (3 women); includes 5 minority (2 American Indian/Alaska Native, 2 Asian Americans or Pacific Islanders, 1 Hispanic American), 2 international. Average age 35. 61 applicants, 67% accepted, 18 enrolled. *Degree requirements:* For master's, comprehensive exam (for some programs), thesis (for some programs); for doctorate, comprehensive exam, thesis/dissertation. *Entrance requirements:* For master's, minimum GPA of 3.0, portfolio of design work, 3 letters of recommendation (M Arch); for doctorate, minimum graduate GPA of 3.5. Additional exam requirements/recommendations for international students: Required—TOEFL (minimum score 550 paper-based; 213 computer-based). *Application deadline:* For fall admission, 4/1 priority date for domestic students, 3/1 for international students. Application fee: $50. *Financial support:* In 2007–08, 30 students received support, including 10 research assistantships with full and partial tuition reimbursements available (averaging $13,917 per year), teaching assistantships with full and partial tuition reimbursements available (averaging $13,056 per year). *Faculty research:* Environment-behavior relationships, land use and environmental planning, urban space as interior design, art and architectural aesthetics. Total annual research expenditures: $62,011. *Unit head:* Dr. Nancy H. Blossom, Director, 509-358-7515, E-mail: blossom@wsu.edu. *Application contact:* Graduate School Admissions, 800-GRADWSU, Fax: 509-335-1949, E-mail: gradsch@wsu.edu.

Washington University in St. Louis, Sam Fox School of Design and Visual Arts, Graduate School of Architecture and Urban Design, Program in Architecture, St. Louis, MO 63130-4899. Offers M Arch, M Arch/MBA, M Arch/MCM, M Arch/MSW, M Arch/MUD. *Faculty:* 21 full-time (7 women), 40 part-time/adjunct (9 women). *Students:* 179 full-time (76 women); includes 8 minority (2 African Americans, 1 Asian American or Pacific Islander, 5 Hispanic Americans), 25 international. Average age 25. 248 applicants, 78% accepted, 61 enrolled. In 2007, 38 degrees awarded. *Degree requirements:* For master's, final project. *Entrance requirements:* For master's, GRE General Test, portfolio. Additional exam requirements/recommendations for international students: Required—TOEFL (minimum score 550 paper-based; 213 computer-based; 80 iBT), TWE. *Application deadline:* For fall admission, 2/1 priority date for domestic and international students; for spring admission, 10/1 for domestic and international students. Application fee: $50. *Financial support:* In 2007–08, 159 students received support, including 4 research assistantships (averaging $2,000 per year), 35 teaching assistantships (averaging $2,500 per year); Federal Work-Study and scholarships/grants also available. Support available to part-time students. Financial award application deadline: 2/15; financial award applicants required to submit FAFSA. *Faculty research:* Urban design development issues. *Unit head:* Prof. Adrian Luchini, Co-Director, Graduate Program, 314-935-6227. *Application contact:* Peter MacKeith, Director, Graduate Admissions, 314-935-6227, Fax: 314-935-7656, E-mail: mackeith@wustl.edu.

See Close-Up on page 179.

Woodbury University, School of Architecture, Burbank, CA 91504-1099. Offers real estate development (M Arch). *Faculty:* 6 part-time/adjunct (0 women). *Students:* 6 full-time (1 woman); includes 2 minority (both Hispanic Americans), 1 international. 23 applicants, 52% accepted. In 2007, 6 degrees awarded. *Degree requirements:* For master's, thesis. *Entrance requirements:* For master's, 3 letters of recommendation, portfolio. Additional exam requirements/recommendations for international students: Required—TOEFL (minimum score 550 paper-based; 213 computer-based), IELTS (minimum score 7). *Application deadline:* For fall admission, 3/1 priority date for domestic and international students. Application fee: $60. *Expenses:* Contact institution. *Unit head:* Norman Millar, Chair, 318-767-0888 Ext. 130, Fax: 318-504-9320, E-mail: norman.millar@woodbury.edu. *Application contact:* Debra Abel, Administrative Director, 619-235-2900, Fax: 619-235-2901, E-mail: debra.abel@woodbury.edu.

Yale University, School of Architecture, New Haven, CT 06520. Offers M Arch, M Env Des, MEM, M Arch/M Env Des, M Arch/MBA. *Faculty:* 18 full-time (6 women), 78 part-time/adjunct (20 women). *Students:* 207 full-time (87 women); includes 34 minority (1 African American, 24 Asian Americans or Pacific Islanders, 9 Hispanic Americans), 34 international. 702 applicants, 21% accepted, 81 enrolled. In 2007, 66 degrees awarded. *Entrance requirements:* For master's, GRE General Test, design portfolio. Additional exam requirements/recommendations for international students: Required—TOEFL. *Application deadline:* For fall admission, 1/3 for domestic students. Application fee: $85. *Expenses:* Contact institution. *Financial support:* In 2007–08, 164 students received support; fellowships, teaching assistantships, Federal Work-Study and institutionally sponsored loans available. Financial award application deadline: 2/1. *Unit head:* Robert A. M. Stern, Dean, 203-432-2279, Fax: 203-432-7175. *Application contact:* 203-432-2291, Fax: 203-432-6576.

Building Science

Arizona State University, Graduate College, College of Architecture and Environmental Design, School of Architecture, Tempe, AZ 85287. Offers architecture (M Arch); building design (MS); MBA/M Arch. *Degree requirements:* For master's, thesis optional. *Entrance requirements:* For master's, GRE General Test, design portfolio.

Auburn University, Graduate School, College of Architecture, Design, and Construction, Department of Building Science, Auburn University, AL 36849. Offers building science (MBS); construction management (MBS). *Faculty:* 17 full-time (2 women). *Students:* 20 full-time (3 women), 3 part-time (all women); includes 3 minority (1 African American, 2 Asian Americans or Pacific Islanders), 4 international. Average age 26. 47 applicants, 66% accepted, 15 enrolled. In 2007, 13 degrees awarded. *Entrance requirements:* For master's, GRE General Test. *Application deadline:* For fall admission, 7/17 for domestic students; for spring admission, 11/24 for domestic students. Applications are processed on a rolling basis. Application fee: $25 ($50 for international students). Electronic applications accepted. *Financial support:* Application deadline: 3/15. *Unit head:* John D. Murphy, Head, 334-844-4518. *Application contact:* Dr. Joe Pittman, Interim Dean of the Graduate School, 334-844-4700.

Auburn University, Graduate School, College of Architecture, Design, and Construction, Program in Design-Build, Auburn University, AL 36849. Offers MDB. *Application contact:* Dr. Joe Pittman, Interim Dean of the Graduate School, 334-844-4700.

Carnegie Mellon University, College of Fine Arts, School of Architecture, Pittsburgh, PA 15213-3891. Offers architecture (MSA); architecture, engineering, and construction management (M Sc, PhD); building performance and diagnostics (M Sc, PhD); computational design (M Sc, PhD); sustainable design (M Sc); urban design (M Sc). Terminal master's awarded for partial completion of doctoral program. *Degree requirements:* For doctorate, thesis/dissertation. *Entrance requirements:* For master's and doctorate, GRE General Test. Additional exam requirements/recommendations for international students: Required—TOEFL.

Cornell University, Graduate School, Graduate Fields of Architecture, Art and Planning, Field of Architecture, Ithaca, NY 14853-0001. Offers architectural design (M Arch); architectural science (MS); building technology and environmental science (MS); computer graphics (MS); history of architecture (MA, PhD); history of urban development (MA, PhD); theory and criticism of architecture (M Arch); urban design (M Arch). *Faculty:* 33 full-time. *Students:* 101 full-time (33 women); includes 13 minority (1 African American, 7 Asian Americans or Pacific Islanders, 5 Hispanic Americans), 51 international. Average age 28. 305 applicants, 30% accepted, 39 enrolled. In 2007, 17 master's, 1 doctorate awarded. *Degree requirements:* For master's, one foreign language, thesis (MA, MS); for doctorate, 2 foreign languages, comprehensive exam, thesis/dissertation. *Entrance requirements:* For master's, GRE General Test, GRE Subject Test in computer science (computer graphics), 5-year bachelor's degree in architecture, portfolio (M Arch), 3 letters of recommendation; for doctorate, GRE General Test, 3 letters of recommendation. Additional exam requirements/recommendations for international students: Required—TOEFL (minimum score 600 paper-based; 250 computer-based; 77 iBT). *Application deadline:* For fall admission, 1/15 priority date for domestic students. Application fee: $70. Electronic applications accepted. *Financial support:* In 2007–08, 41 students received support, including 13 fellowships with full tuition reimbursements available, 1 research assistantship with full tuition reimbursement available, 27 teaching assistantships with full tuition reimbursements available; institutionally sponsored loans, scholarships/grants, health care benefits, tuition waivers (full and partial), and unspecified assistantships also available.

Building Science

Cornell University (continued)
Financial award applicants required to submit FAFSA. *Faculty research:* Architectural design and urban design, theory and criticism of architecture, computer graphics, building technology and environmental science, history of architecture and history of urban-development. *Unit head:* Director of Graduate Studies, 607-255-6701, Fax: 607-255-0291. *Application contact:* Graduate Field Assistant, 607-255-6701, Fax: 607-255-0291, E-mail: cuarch@cornell.edu.

Georgia Institute of Technology, Graduate Studies and Research, College of Architecture, Program in Building Construction, Atlanta, GA 30332-0001. Offers architecture (PhD); integrated facility management (MS); integrated project delivery systems (MS). Part-time and evening/weekend programs available. *Entrance requirements:* For master's and doctorate, GRE or GMAT. Additional exam requirements/recommendations for international students: Required—TOEFL (minimum score 550 paper-based; 213 computer-based). Electronic applications accepted. *Faculty research:* Design-build, mold, indoor air quality, real estate.

University of California, Berkeley, Graduate Division, College of Environmental Design, Department of Architecture, Berkeley, CA 94720-1500. Offers architecture (M Arch); building science (MS, PhD); building structures, construction and materials (MS, PhD); design (MA); design theories, methods, and practices (MS, PhD); environmental design in developing countries (MS, PhD); history of architecture and urbanism (MS, PhD); social and cultural processes in architecture and urbanism (MS, PhD); M Arch/MCP; M Arch/MS; MLA/M Arch. *Degree requirements:* For master's, thesis; for doctorate, thesis/dissertation, qualifying exam. *Entrance requirements:* For master's and doctorate, GRE General Test, minimum GPA of 3.0, 3 letters of recommendation. Additional exam requirements/recommendations for international students: Required—TOEFL. Application fee: $70 ($90 for international students). Electronic applications accepted. *Financial support:* Unspecified assistantships available. *Unit head:* Mary Comerio, Chair, 510-642-4942, E-mail: mcomerio@berkeley.edu. *Application contact:* Lois H. Ito Koch, Student Affairs Officer, 510-642-5577, Fax: 510-643-5607, E-mail: archgrad@berkeley.edu.

University of Florida, Graduate School, College of Design, Construction and Planning, M. E. Rinker, Sr. School of Building Construction, Gainesville, FL 32611. Offers MBC, MICM, MSBC, PhD. Part-time programs available. *Faculty:* 18 full-time (3 women). *Students:* 111 (22 women); includes 14 minority (3 African Americans, 4 Asian Americans or Pacific Islanders, 7 Hispanic Americans) 15 international. In 2007, 47 degrees awarded. *Degree requirements:* For master's, thesis. *Entrance requirements:* For master's, GRE General Test, minimum GPA of 3.0. Additional exam requirements/recommendations for international students: Required—TOEFL. *Application deadline:* For fall admission, 3/16 priority date for domestic students; for spring admission, 10/15 for domestic students. Applications are processed on a rolling basis. Application fee: $30. Electronic applications accepted. *Expenses:* Tuition, state resident: full-time $7,478. Tuition, nonresident: full-time $22,603. *Financial support:* In 2007–08, 21 research assistantships with full tuition reimbursements (averaging $13,413 per year), 5 teaching assistantships with full tuition reimbursements (averaging $12,948 per year) were awarded; fellowships with full tuition reimbursements, career-related internships or fieldwork and unspecified assistantships also available. *Faculty research:* Safety, affordable housing, construction management, environmental issues, sustainable construction. *Unit head:* Dr. Abdol R. Chini, Director, 352-273-1150, Fax: 352-392-9606, E-mail: chini@ufl.edu. *Application contact:* Dr. Raymond Issa, Director of Graduate and Distance Education Programs, 352-273-1152, Fax: 352-392-7266, E-mail: raymond-issa@ufl.edu.

University of Southern California, Graduate School, School of Architecture, Program in Building Science, Los Angeles, CA 90089. Offers MBS. Part-time programs available. *Faculty:* 50 full-time (25 women), 50 part-time/adjunct (25 women). *Students:* 23 full-time (13 women), 4 part-time (2 women); includes 5 minority (3 Asian Americans or Pacific Islanders, 2 Hispanic Americans), 10 international. 25 applicants, 100% accepted. In 2007, 7 master's awarded. *Entrance requirements:* For master's, GRE General Test. *Application deadline:* For fall admission, 1/15 priority date for domestic students. Applications are processed on a rolling basis. Application fee: $85. *Financial support:* In 2007–08, fellowships (averaging $15,000 per year); career-related internships or fieldwork, Federal Work-Study, and scholarships/grants also available. Support available to part-time students. Financial award application deadline: 2/15; financial award applicants required to submit FAFSA. *Unit head:* Marc Schiler, Head, 213-740-2311.

See Close-Up on page 177.

University of Southern California, Graduate School, School of Architecture, Program in Historic Preservation, Los Angeles, CA 90089. Offers MHP. Part-time programs available. *Faculty:* 50 full-time (25 women), 50 part-time/adjunct (25 women). *Students:* 9 full-time (5 women), 6 part-time (5 women); includes 1 minority (Hispanic American), 1 international. 12 applicants, 92% accepted. In 2007, 5 master's awarded. *Entrance requirements:* For master's, GRE. *Application deadline:* For fall admission, 1/15 priority date for domestic students. Applications are processed on a rolling basis. Application fee: $85. *Financial support:* In 2007–08, fellowships with tuition reimbursements (averaging $15,000 per year); career-related internships or fieldwork, Federal Work-Study, and scholarships/grants also available. Support available to part-time students. Financial award applicants required to submit FAFSA. *Unit head:* Dr. Kenneth Breisch, Head, 213-740-2311.

Environmental Design

Arizona State University, Graduate College, College of Architecture and Environmental Design, Program in Environmental Design and Planning, Tempe, AZ 85287. Offers design (PhD); history, theory, and criticism (PhD); planning (PhD). *Degree requirements:* For doctorate, thesis/dissertation.

Art Center College of Design, Graduate Division, Industrial Design Department, Pasadena, CA 91103-1999. Offers environmental design (MS); product design (MS). *Accreditation:* NASAD. *Faculty:* 8 part-time/adjunct (1 woman). *Students:* 33 full-time (15 women), 5 part-time (4 women); includes 10 minority (all Asian Americans or Pacific Islanders), 16 international. Average age 29. 56 applicants, 36% accepted, 13 enrolled. In 2007, 2 degrees awarded. *Degree requirements:* For master's, thesis, studio project. *Entrance requirements:* For master's, portfolio. Additional exam requirements/recommendations for international students: Required—TOEFL (minimum score 600 paper-based; 250 computer-based; 100 iBT). *Application deadline:* For fall admission, 2/1 for domestic and international students. Application fee: $50 ($70 for international students). *Expenses:* Tuition: Full-time $31,016. Required fees: $235. *Financial support:* Teaching assistantships, career-related internships or fieldwork, Federal Work-Study, and scholarships/grants available. Financial award application deadline: 2/1. *Unit head:* Andrew Ogden, Chair, 626-396-2464. *Application contact:* Kit Baron, Vice President, Admissions, 626-396-2373, Fax: 626-795-0578, E-mail: admissions@artcenter.edu.

See Close-Up on page 109.

Clemson University, Graduate School, College of Architecture, Arts, and Humanities, Department of Planning and Landscape Architecture, Program in Environmental Design and Planning, Clemson, SC 29634. Offers PhD. *Students:* 10 full-time (1 woman), 4 part-time (1 woman); includes 1 minority (African American), 2 international. 18 applicants, 50% accepted, 5 enrolled. *Entrance requirements:* For doctorate, GRE. Additional exam requirements/recommendations for international students: Required—TOEFL. *Application deadline:* For fall admission, 4/15 for international students; for spring admission, 9/15 for international students. Applications are processed on a rolling basis. Application fee: $55. *Unit head:* Roger Liska, Coordinator, 864-656-0181, Fax: 864-656-0204, E-mail: riggor@clemson.edu. *Application contact:* Admissions, 864-656-3926, Fax: 864-656-7519.

Columbia University, School of Continuing Education, Program in Landscape Design, New York, NY 10027. Offers MS. Part-time programs available. *Faculty:* 9 part-time/adjunct (2 women). In 2007, 17 degrees awarded. *Degree requirements:* For master's, 36 credits. *Entrance requirements:* For master's, BA/BS with minimum GPA of 3.0. Additional exam requirements/recommendations for international students: Required—American Language Program (ALP) placement test. *Application deadline:* For fall admission, 6/16 for domestic students; for spring admission, 11/7 for domestic students. Application fee: $50. *Expenses:* Tuition: Part-time $1,452 per credit. Required fees: $152 per term. One-time fee: $75 part-time. Full-time tuition and fees vary according to course level, course load, degree level and program. *Financial support:* Institutionally sponsored loans available. Financial award applicants required to submit FAFSA. *Unit head:* Joseph Disponzio, Director, 212-854-9699, E-mail: jd52@columbia.edu. *Application contact:* 212-854-9666, E-mail: ce-advis@columbia.edu.

Cornell University, Graduate School, Graduate Fields of Human Ecology, Field of Design and Environmental Analysis, Ithaca, NY 14853-0001. Offers applied research in human-environment relations (MS); facilities planning and management (MS); housing and design (MS); human factors and ergonomics (MS); human-environment relations (MS); interior design (MA, MPS). *Faculty:* 14 full-time (6 women). *Students:* 24 full-time (19 women); includes 5 minority (2 Asian Americans or Pacific Islanders, 3 Hispanic Americans), 8 international. Average age 26. 33 applicants, 45% accepted, 12 enrolled. In 2007, 8 degrees awarded. *Degree requirements:* For master's, thesis. *Entrance requirements:* For master's, GRE General Test, portfolio or slides of recent work; bachelor's degree in interior design, architecture or related design discipline; 2 letters of recommendation. Additional exam requirements/recommendations for international students: Required—TOEFL (minimum score 600 paper-based; 250 computer-based; 105 iBT). *Application deadline:* For fall admission, 2/1 priority date for domestic students. Application fee: $70. Electronic applications accepted. *Financial support:* In 2007–08, 13 students received support, including 2 fellowships with full tuition reimbursements available, 11 teaching assistantships with full tuition reimbursements available; research assistantships with full tuition reimbursements available, institutionally sponsored loans, scholarships/grants, health care benefits, tuition waivers (full and partial), and unspecified assistantships also available. Financial award applicants required to submit FAFSA. *Faculty research:* Facility planning and management, environmental psychology, housing, interior design, ergonomics and human factors. *Unit head:* Director of Graduate Studies, 607-255-2168, Fax: 607-255-0305. *Application contact:* Graduate Field Assistant, 607-255-2168, Fax: 607-255-0305, E-mail: deagrad@cornell.edu.

Michigan State University, The Graduate School, College of Agriculture and Natural Resources and College of Social Science, School of Planning, Design and Construction, East Lansing, MI 48824. Offers construction management (MS, PhD); environmental design (MA); interior design and facilities management (MA); international planning studies (MIPS); urban and regional planning (MURP). Part-time and evening/weekend programs available. *Degree requirements:* For master's, thesis or alternative. *Entrance requirements:* Additional exam requirements/recommendations for international students: Required—TOEFL. Electronic applications accepted. *Expenses:* Tuition, state resident: part-time $379 per credit hour. Tuition, nonresident: part-time $800 per credit hour. Tuition and fees vary according to program.

Minnesota State University Mankato, College of Graduate Studies, College of Arts and Humanities, Department of English, Mankato, MN 56001. Offers creative writing (MFA); English (MA, MS); English literature (MA); teaching English (MS, MT); teaching English as a second language (MA); technical communication (Certificate). Part-time programs available. *Students:* 51 full-time (35 women), 78 part-time (54 women). Average age 32. In 2007, 29 degrees awarded. *Degree requirements:* For master's, one foreign language, comprehensive exam, thesis or alternative. *Entrance requirements:* For master's, minimum GPA of 3.0 during previous 2 years, writing sample (MFA). *Application deadline:* Applications are processed on a rolling basis. Application fee: $40. Electronic applications accepted. *Financial support:* Research assistantships with full tuition reimbursements, teaching assistantships with full tuition reimbursements, career-related internships or fieldwork, Federal Work-Study, and unspecified assistantships available. Financial award application deadline: 3/15; financial award applicants required to submit FAFSA. *Faculty research:* Keats and Christianity. *Unit head:* Dr. John Banschbach, Chairperson, 507-389-2117. *Application contact:* 507-389-2321, E-mail: grad@mnsu.edu.

San Diego State University, Graduate and Research Affairs, College of Professional Studies and Fine Arts, School of Art, Design and Art History, San Diego, CA 92182. Offers art history (MA); studio arts (MA, MFA), including applied design, environmental design, graphic design, interior design, painting and printmaking, sculpture. *Accreditation:* NASAD (one or more programs are accredited). *Students:* 44 full-time (29 women), 18 part-time (11 women); includes 9 minority (4 Asian Americans or Pacific Islanders, 5 Hispanic Americans), 5 international. Average age 30. 83 applicants, 31% accepted, 31 enrolled. In 2007, 12 degrees awarded. *Degree requirements:* For master's, variable foreign language requirement, thesis. *Entrance requirements:* For master's, GRE General Test, bachelor's degree in related field, slide portfolio, typed slide information sheet, 2 letters of recommendation. Additional exam requirements/recommendations for international students: Required—TOEFL. *Application deadline:* For fall admission, 2/1 for domestic and international students. Applications are processed on a rolling basis. Application fee: $55. Electronic applications accepted. *Financial support:* In 2007–08, 21 teaching assistantships were awarded; career-related internships or fieldwork and unspecified assistantships also available. Financial award applicants required to submit FAFSA. *Unit head:* Arthur Ollman, Director, 619-594-1213, Fax: 619-594-1217. *Application contact:* JoAnne Berelowitz, Graduate Advisor, Art History, 619-594-4995, Fax: 619-594-1217, E-mail: jberelow@mail.sdsu.edu.

Texas Tech University, Graduate School, College of Human Sciences, Department of Design, Lubbock, TX 79409. Offers environmental design (MS); environmental design and consumer economics (PhD); personal financial planning (PhD). *Faculty:* 4 full-time (2 women). *Students:* 20 full-time (8 women), 13 part-time (3 women); includes 7 minority (6 African Americans, 1 Asian American or Pacific Islander), 7 international. Average age 34. 26 applicants, 77% accepted, 6 enrolled. In 2007, 3 master's, 4 doctorates awarded. *Entrance requirements:* For master's and doctorate, GRE. Application fee: $50 ($60 for international students). *Expenses:* Tuition, state resident: part-time $373 per credit hour. Tuition, nonresident: part-time $651 per credit hour. Tuition and fees vary according to program. *Financial support:* In 2007–08, 19 students received support, including 2 teaching assistantships (averaging $12,580 per year); research assistantships. Financial award application deadline: 4/15. *Faculty research:* Meanings in the built environment, influence of technology on pedagogic environments, interior design components, computer usage in interior design, design and evaluation of physical environments for the elderly and physically and mentally challenged. Total annual research expenditures: $31,453. *Unit head:* Dr. Lynn Huffman, Interim Chair, 806-742-3068, Fax: 806-742-3042,

E-mail: lynn.huffman@ttu.edu. *Application contact:* Dr. Cherif Amor, Graduate Programs Director, 806-742-3050 Ext. 228, Fax: 806-742-1639, E-mail: cherif.amor@ttu.edu.

Université de Montréal, Faculty of Environmental Design and Planning, Montréal, QC H3C 3J7, Canada. Offers M Sc A, M Urb, PhD, DESS. *Accreditation:* ACSP. *Faculty:* 46 full-time (12 women), 27 part-time/adjunct (8 women). *Students:* 387 full-time (204 women), 45 part-time (25 women). 480 applicants, 36% accepted, 147 enrolled. In 2007, 110 master's, 7 doctorates, 16 other advanced degrees awarded. *Degree requirements:* For doctorate, thesis/dissertation, general exam. *Application deadline:* For fall admission, 2/1 priority date for domestic students; for winter admission, 11/1 priority date for domestic students; for spring admission, 2/1 priority date for domestic students. Application fee: $100. Electronic applications accepted. *Expenses: Contact institution. Faculty research:* Wayfinding, environmental evaluation, housing studies, urban design, urban and regional planning. *Unit head:* Giovanni de Paoli, Dean, 514-343-6001, Fax: 514-343-2183, E-mail: giovanni.de.paoli@umontreal.ca. *Application contact:* Tilu Poldma, Associate Dean Graduate Studies, 514-343-2125, E-mail: tilu.poldma@umontreal.ca.

University of Calgary, Faculty of Graduate Studies, Faculty of Environmental Design, Calgary, AB T2N 1N4, Canada. Offers architecture (M Arch); environmental design (M Env Des, PhD). *Faculty:* 30 full-time (8 women), 102 part-time/adjunct (18 women). *Students:* 246 full-time (135 women), 7 part-time (4 women). Average age 30. 299 applicants, 42% accepted, 79 enrolled. In 2007, 69 master's, 2 doctorates awarded. *Degree requirements:* For master's, thesis; for doctorate, thesis/dissertation. *Entrance requirements:* For master's, minimum GPA of 3.0; for doctorate, minimum GPA of 3.5. Additional exam requirements/recommendations for international students: Required—TOEFL (minimum score 550 paper-based; 213 computer-based). *Application deadline:* For fall admission, 2/1 for domestic and international students. Application fee: $100 ($130 for international students). *Financial support:* In 2007–08, 1 fellowship, 57 research assistantships, 9 teaching assistantships were awarded; career-related internships or fieldwork and scholarships/grants also available. *Faculty research:* Sustainable development in architecture, planning and product design, energy and environment, impact assessment, ecotourism. *Unit head:* Prof. L Fowlow, Dean, 403-220-6606, Fax: 403-284-4399. *Application contact:* L. Kallsen, Admissions Officer, 403-220-3630, Fax: 403-284-4399, E-mail: info@evds.ucalgary.ca.

University of California, Berkeley, Graduate Division, College of Environmental Design, Department of Architecture, Program in Design, Berkeley, CA 94720-1500. Offers MA. *Degree requirements:* For master's, thesis. *Entrance requirements:* For master's, GRE General Test, minimum GPA of 3.0, portfolio, 3 letters of recommendation. Additional exam requirements/recommendations for international students: Required—TOEFL. *Application deadline:* For fall admission, 2/1 for domestic students. Application fee: $70 ($90 for international students). *Financial support:* Unspecified assistantships available. *Application contact:* Lois H. Ito Koch, Student Affairs Officer, 510-642-5577, Fax: 510-643-5607, E-mail: archgrad@berkeley.edu.

University of California, Berkeley, Graduate Division, College of Environmental Design, Department of Landscape Architecture and Environmental Planning, Program in Landscape Architecture, Berkeley, CA 94720-1500. Offers environmental planning (MLA); landscape design and site planning (MLA); urban and community design (MLA); MLA/M Arch; MLA/MCP. *Accreditation:* ASLA. *Faculty:* 13 full-time, 6 part-time/adjunct. *Degree requirements:* For master's, professional project or thesis. *Entrance requirements:* For master's, GRE General Test, minimum GPA of 3.0, portfolio, 3 letters of recommendation. *Application deadline:* For fall admission, 1/5 for domestic students. Application fee: $70 ($90 for international students). *Financial support:* Fellowships, research assistantships, teaching assistantships, career-related internships or fieldwork, Federal Work-Study, institutionally sponsored loans, and unspecified assistantships available. *Application contact:* Yong No, Student Affairs Officer, 510-642-2965, Fax: 510-643-6166, E-mail: laepgrad@berkeley.edu.

University of Missouri–Columbia, Graduate School, College of Human Environmental Science, Department of Architectural Studies, Columbia, MO 65211. Offers design with digital media (MA, MS); environmental design (MS). *Entrance requirements:* For master's, GRE General Test, minimum GPA of 3.0. Additional exam requirements/recommendations for international students: Required—TOEFL (minimum score 500 paper-based; 173 computer-based).

Virginia Polytechnic Institute and State University, Graduate School, College of Architecture and Urban Studies, Program in Environmental Design and Planning, Blacksburg, VA 24061. Offers PhD. *Entrance requirements:* For doctorate, GRE General Test. Additional exam requirements/recommendations for international students: Required—TOEFL (minimum score 550 paper-based; 213 computer-based). Electronic applications accepted. *Faculty research:* Urban studies, architecture, landscape planning.

Yale University, School of Architecture, New Haven, CT 06520. Offers M Arch, M Env Des, MEM, M Arch/M Env Des, M Arch/MBA. *Faculty:* 18 full-time (6 women), 78 part-time/adjunct (20 women). *Students:* 207 full-time (87 women); includes 34 minority (1 African American, 24 Asian Americans or Pacific Islanders, 9 Hispanic Americans), 34 international. 702 applicants, 21% accepted, 81 enrolled. In 2007, 66 degrees awarded. *Entrance requirements:* For master's, GRE General Test, design portfolio. Additional exam requirements/recommendations for international students: Required—TOEFL. *Application deadline:* For fall admission, 1/3 for domestic students. Application fee: $85. *Expenses: Contact institution. Financial support:* In 2007–08, 164 students received support; fellowships, teaching assistantships, Federal Work-Study and institutionally sponsored loans available. Financial award application deadline: 2/1. *Unit head:* Robert A. M. Stern, Dean, 203-432-2279, Fax: 203-432-7175. *Application contact:* 203-432-2291, Fax: 203-432-6576.

Historic Preservation

Arkansas State University, Graduate School, College of Humanities and Social Sciences, Heritage Studies Program, Jonesboro, State University, AR 72467. Offers MA, PhD. Part-time programs available. *Faculty:* 2 full-time (1 woman), 2 part-time/adjunct (1 woman). *Students:* 12 full-time (9 women), 32 part-time (15 women); includes 8 minority (7 African Americans, 1 Asian American or Pacific Islander), 3 international. Average age 41. 13 applicants, 69% accepted, 4 enrolled. In 2007, 5 master's, 3 doctorates awarded. *Degree requirements:* For master's, comprehensive exam, thesis or alternative; for doctorate, comprehensive exam, thesis/dissertation or alternative. *Entrance requirements:* For master's, GRE, MAT or GMAT, appropriate bachelor's degree, letters of reference, official transcript; for doctorate, appropriate master's degree, interview, letters of reference, official transcript. Additional exam requirements/recommendations for international students: Required—TOEFL (minimum score 213 computer-based). Application fee: $30 ($40 for international students). *Expenses:* Tuition, state resident: full-time $3,528; part-time $196 per hour. Tuition, nonresident: full-time $8,928; part-time $496 per hour. Required fees: $842; $44 per hour. $25 per term. Tuition and fees vary according to course load and program. *Financial support:* Fellowships, teaching assistantships, scholarships/grants, tuition waivers (partial), and unspecified assistantships available. Financial award application deadline: 7/1; financial award applicants required to submit FAFSA. *Unit head:* Dr. Clyde Milner, Director, 870-972-3059, Fax: 870-972-3207, E-mail: cmilner@astate.edu.

Ball State University, Graduate School, College of Architecture and Planning, Department of Architecture, Program in Historic Preservation, Muncie, IN 47306-1099. Offers M Arch, MS. *Faculty:* 25. *Students:* 20 full-time (13 women). Average age 31. 26 applicants, 77% accepted, 14 enrolled. In 2007, 13 degrees awarded. *Degree requirements:* For master's, thesis. *Entrance requirements:* For master's, minimum undergraduate B average, portfolio, writing sample. Application fee: $25 ($35 for international students). *Expenses:* Tuition, state resident: full-time $6,864. Tuition, nonresident: full-time $17,932. Required fees: $1,866. *Financial support:* Research assistantships with full tuition reimbursements, teaching assistantships available. Financial award application deadline: 3/1. *Unit head:* Dr. Jonathan Spodek, Director, 765-285-1900, Fax: 765-285-1765, E-mail: jspodek@bsu.edu.

Boston University, Graduate School of Arts and Sciences, Program in Preservation Studies, Boston, MA 02215. Offers MA, JD/MA. *Students:* 4 full-time (all women), 6 part-time (5 women). Average age 31. 20 applicants, 70% accepted, 2 enrolled. In 2007, 3 degrees awarded. *Degree requirements:* For master's, one foreign language, thesis or alternative, internship. *Entrance requirements:* For master's, GRE General Test, scholarly writing sample, 3 letters of recommendation. Additional exam requirements/recommendations for international students: Required—TOEFL (minimum score 550 paper-based; 213 computer-based). *Application deadline:* For fall admission, 4/1 for domestic and international students. Application fee: $70. *Expenses:* Tuition: Full-time $34,930; part-time $1,092 per credit. Tuition and fees vary according to class time, course level and program. *Financial support:* In 2007–08, 2 research assistantships with partial tuition reimbursements were awarded; career-related internships or fieldwork, Federal Work-Study, and unspecified assistantships also available. Support available to part-time students. Financial award application deadline: 1/15; financial award applicants required to submit FAFSA. *Unit head:* Claire Dempsey, Interim Director, 617-353-9910, Fax: 617-353-2556, E-mail: dempseyc@bu.edu. *Application contact:* Jordan Hertzberg, Senior Program Coordinator, 617-353-2948, Fax: 617-353-2556, E-mail: jhertz@bu.edu.

Buffalo State College, State University of New York, Graduate Studies and Research, Faculty of Arts and Humanities, Department of Art Conservation, Buffalo, NY 14222-1095. Offers art conservation (CAS); conservation of historic works and art works (MA). *Degree requirements:* For master's, final oral exam; for CAS, internship. *Entrance requirements:* For master's, GRE General Test, minimum GPA of 2.8. Additional exam requirements/recommendations for international students: Required—TOEFL (minimum score 550 paper-based; 213 computer-based). *Faculty research:* Mechanics of deterioration of art, conservation of materials.

Clemson University, Graduate School, College of Architecture, Arts, and Humanities, Department of Planning and Landscape Architecture, Program in Historic Preservation, Clemson, SC 29634. Offers MS. *Students:* 21 full-time (14 women). 20 applicants, 60% accepted, 0 enrolled. In 2007, 7 degrees awarded. *Entrance requirements:* For master's, GRE General Test. *Application deadline:* For fall admission, 4/15 for international students; for spring admission, 9/15 for international students. Application fee: $55.

College of Charleston, Graduate School, School of the Arts, Program in Historic Preservation, Charleston, SC 29424-0001. Offers MS. *Faculty:* 6 full-time (4 women), 2 part-time/adjunct (0 women). Electronic applications accepted. *Expenses:* Tuition, state resident: full-time $7,778; part-time $324 per hour. Tuition, nonresident: full-time $18,732; part-time $781 per hour. *Unit head:* Jennifer McStotts, Co-Director, 843-953-5419, E-mail: mcstottsj@cofc.edu.

Columbia University, Graduate School of Architecture, Planning, and Preservation, Program in Historic Preservation, New York, NY 10027. Offers MS, M Arch/MS, MS/MS. *Degree requirements:* For master's, thesis. *Entrance requirements:* For master's, GRE General Test. *Expenses:* Tuition: Part-time $1,452 per credit. Required fees: $152 per term. One-time fee: $75 part-time. Full-time tuition and fees vary according to course level, course load, degree level and program.

Cornell University, Graduate School, Graduate Fields of Architecture, Art and Planning, Field of City and Regional Planning, Ithaca, NY 14853-0001. Offers city and regional planning (MRP, PhD); environmental planning and design (MRP, PhD); historic preservation planning (MA); international development planning (MRP, PhD); planning theory and systems analysis (MRP, PhD); regional economics and development planning (MRP, PhD); regional science (MRP, PhD); social and health systems planning (MRP, PhD); urban and regional theory (MRP, PhD); urban planning history (MRP, PhD). *Accreditation:* ACSP (one or more programs are accredited). *Faculty:* 30 full-time (8 women). *Students:* 103 full-time (67 women); includes 12 minority (4 African Americans, 5 Asian Americans or Pacific Islanders, 3 Hispanic Americans), 30 international. Average age 29. 210 applicants, 44% accepted, 36 enrolled. In 2007, 37 master's, 8 doctorates awarded. *Degree requirements:* For master's, thesis (MA); for doctorate, comprehensive exam, thesis/dissertation. *Entrance requirements:* For master's and doctorate, GRE General Test, 2 letters of recommendation. Additional exam requirements/recommendations for international students: Required—TOEFL (minimum score 600 paper-based; 250 computer-based; 77 iBT). *Application deadline:* For fall admission, 1/10 for domestic students. Application fee: $70. Electronic applications accepted. *Financial support:* In 2007–08, 89 students received support, including 14 fellowships with full tuition reimbursements available, 60 research assistantships with full tuition reimbursements available, 15 teaching assistantships with full tuition reimbursements available; institutionally sponsored loans, scholarships/grants, health care benefits, tuition waivers (full and partial), and unspecified assistantships also available. Financial award applicants required to submit FAFSA. *Faculty research:* Land use planning, economic development, international development, historic preservation, community development. *Unit head:* Director of Graduate Studies, 607-255-6848, Fax: 607-255-1971. *Application contact:* Graduate Field Assistant, 607-255-6848, Fax: 607-255-1971, E-mail: crp_admissions@cornell.edu.

Delaware State University, Graduate Programs, Department of History, Philosophy and Political Sciences, Dover, DE 19901-2277. Offers historic preservation (MA). *Students:* 1 applicant, 0% accepted. In 2007, 1 degree awarded. *Entrance requirements:* Additional exam requirements/recommendations for international students: Required—TOEFL (minimum score 550 paper-based). *Application deadline:* For fall admission, 6/30 for domestic and international students; for spring admission, 11/30 for domestic and international students. Applications are processed on a rolling basis. Application fee: $40. Electronic applications accepted. *Expenses:* Tuition, state resident: full-time $6,192; part-time $312 per credit hour. Tuition, nonresident: full-time $13,716; part-time $693 per credit hour. Required fees: $350; $290 per year. Tuition and fees vary according to degree level. *Financial support:* Application deadline: 3/8; *Unit head:* Dr. Samuel Hoff, Law Studies Director, 302-857-6633, Fax: 302-857-7898, E-mail: shoff@desu.edu.

Eastern Michigan University, Graduate School, College of Arts and Sciences, Department of Geography and Geology, Program in Historic Preservation, Ypsilanti, MI 48197. Offers heritage interpretation and tourism (MS); historic preservation (MS, Graduate Certificate). Part-time and evening/weekend programs available. Postbaccalaureate distance learning degree programs offered (minimal on-campus study). *Students:* 23 full-time (16 women), 44 part-time (30 women); includes 2 minority (1 African American, 1 Hispanic American). Average age 35. In 2007, 29 master's, 2 other advanced degrees awarded. *Entrance requirements:* Additional

Historic Preservation

Eastern Michigan University (continued)
exam requirements/recommendations for international students: Required—TOEFL. *Application deadline:* Applications are processed on a rolling basis. Application fee: $35. *Expenses:* Tuition, state resident: full-time $8,952; part-time $373 per credit hour. Tuition, nonresident: full-time $17,634; part-time $735 per credit hour. Required fees: $896; $34 per credit hour. Tuition and fees vary according to course level, degree level and program. *Financial support:* Fellowships, research assistantships with full tuition reimbursements, teaching assistantships with full tuition reimbursements, career-related internships or fieldwork, Federal Work-Study, institutionally sponsored loans, scholarships/grants, tuition waivers (partial), and unspecified assistantships available. Support available to part-time students. Financial award applicants required to submit FAFSA. *Application contact:* Dr. Ted Ligibel, Program Advisor, 734-487-0218, Fax: 734-487-6979, E-mail: tligibel@emich.edu.

The George Washington University, Columbian College of Arts and Sciences, Department of American Studies, Concentration in Historic Preservation, Washington, DC 20052. Offers MA. Evening/weekend programs available. *Degree requirements:* For master's, comprehensive exam, thesis. *Entrance requirements:* For master's, GRE General Test, minimum GPA of 3.0.

Georgia State University, College of Arts and Sciences, Department of History, Program in Heritage Preservation, Atlanta, GA 30303-3083. Offers MHP, Certificate. Part-time and evening/weekend programs available. *Faculty:* 7 full-time (2 women), 9 part-time/adjunct (5 women). *Students:* 16 full-time (12 women), 21 part-time (13 women); includes 5 minority (3 African Americans, 2 Hispanic Americans), 1 international. Average age 34. 15 applicants, 47% accepted, 6 enrolled. In 2007, 11 master's awarded. *Median time to degree:* Of those who began their doctoral program in fall 1999, 100% received their degree in 8 years or less. *Degree requirements:* For master's, exam, internship or thesis. *Entrance requirements:* For master's, GRE General Test, minimum GPA of 3.0. Additional exam requirements/recommendations for international students: Required—TOEFL. *Application deadline:* For fall admission, 4/15 for domestic and international students; for spring admission, 11/15 for domestic and international students. Applications are processed on a rolling basis. Application fee: $50. Electronic applications accepted. *Expenses:* Tuition, state resident: part-time $221 per credit hour. *Financial support:* In 2007–08, 9 research assistantships with full tuition reimbursements (averaging $5,000 per year) were awarded; career-related internships or fieldwork, Federal Work-Study, institutionally sponsored loans, scholarships/grants, tuition waivers (full), and unspecified assistantships also available. Support available to part-time students. Financial award application deadline: 7/15; financial award applicants required to submit FAFSA. *Faculty research:* Historic preservation, local history, public history, museum studies. *Unit head:* Richard Laub, Director of Graduate Studies, 404-463-9206, E-mail: hisrel@langate.gsu.edu.

Goucher College, Historic Preservation Program, Baltimore, MD 21204-2794. Offers MA. Part-time and evening/weekend programs available. Postbaccalaureate distance learning degree programs offered (minimal on-campus study). *Students:* 4 full-time (3 women), 32 part-time (21 women). Average age 42. In 2007, 11 degrees awarded. *Degree requirements:* For master's, thesis. *Entrance requirements:* For master's, 2 years of post-baccalaureate work or volunteer experience. *Application deadline:* For fall admission, 2/15 for domestic students. Application fee: $50. *Expenses: Contact institution. Financial support:* Career-related internships or fieldwork available. Support available to part-time students. Financial award application deadline: 1/31; financial award applicants required to submit FAFSA. *Unit head:* Richard Wagner, Director, 410-337-6200, Fax: 410-337-6085, E-mail: rwagner@goucher.edu.

Kent State University, College of Architecture and Environmental Design, Kent, OH 44242-0001. Offers architecture (M Arch); preservation architecture (Certificate); urban design (M Arch, MUD, Certificate). Part-time programs available. *Faculty:* 19 full-time (5 women), 21 part-time/adjunct (3 women). *Students:* 45 full-time (13 women), 6 part-time (5 women); includes 3 minority (1 African American, 2 Asian Americans or Pacific Islanders), 7 international. Average age 23. 77 applicants, 52% accepted, 37 enrolled. In 2007, 25 degrees awarded. *Degree requirements:* For master's, thesis optional. *Entrance requirements:* For master's, GRE, portfolio, minimum GPA of 2.75, 3 letters of reference, resumé, undergraduate architecture degree. Additional exam requirements/recommendations for international students: Required—TOEFL (minimum score 550 paper-based). *Application deadline:* For fall admission, 2/1 priority date for domestic and international students. Applications are processed on a rolling basis. Application fee: $30. Electronic applications accepted. *Financial support:* In 2007–08, 6 research assistantships with partial tuition reimbursements (averaging $6,800 per year), 2 teaching assistantships with partial tuition reimbursements (averaging $6,800 per year) were awarded; career-related internships or fieldwork, Federal Work-Study, and tuition waivers (partial) also available. Financial award application deadline: 2/1. *Faculty research:* History and theory, building technology, landscape architecture and urbanism, urbanism, sustainable development. *Unit head:* Dr. James Dalton, Interim Dean, 330-672-2917, Fax: 330-672-3809, E-mail: cmcwilli@kent.edu. *Application contact:* Dr. Maurizio R. Sabini, Graduate Studies Coordinator, 330-672-0927, Fax: 330-672-3809, E-mail: msabini@kent.edu.

Michigan Technological University, Graduate School, College of Sciences and Arts, Department of Social Sciences, Program in Industrial Heritage and Archeology, Houghton, MI 49931-1295. Offers PhD. Part-time programs available. *Faculty:* 15 full-time (5 women), 1 part-time/adjunct (0 women). *Students:* 2 full-time. Average age 35. 6 applicants, 50% accepted, 2 enrolled. *Degree requirements:* For doctorate, comprehensive exam, thesis/dissertation. *Entrance requirements:* Additional exam requirements/recommendations for international students: Required—TOEFL (minimum score 550 paper-based; 213 computer-based). *Application deadline:* For fall admission, 3/1 for domestic students, 3/15 priority date for international students. Applications are processed on a rolling basis. Electronic applications accepted. *Financial support:* In 2007–08, 2 students received support, including fellowships with full tuition reimbursements available (averaging $9,542 per year), 2 research assistantships with full tuition reimbursements available (averaging $9,542 per year), teaching assistantships with full tuition reimbursements available (averaging $9,542 per year); career-related internships or fieldwork, Federal Work-Study, scholarships/grants, health care benefits, tuition waivers (partial), and unspecified assistantships also available. Financial award applicants required to submit FAFSA. *Application contact:* Dr. Patrick E. Martin, Director, 906-487-2070, Fax: 906-487-2468, E-mail: pemartin@mtu.edu.

New York University, Graduate School of Arts and Science, Institute of Fine Arts, Program in Conservation Training, New York, NY 10012-1019. Offers MA/Diploma. *Application deadline:* For fall admission, 1/4 for domestic students. Application fee: $0. *Financial support:* Career-related internships or fieldwork, Federal Work-Study, and institutionally sponsored loans available. Financial award application deadline: 1/4; financial award applicants required to submit FAFSA. *Unit head:* Michele Marincola, Chair, Conservation Center, 212-992-5800, Fax: 212-992-5807, E-mail: ifa.program@nyu.edu. *Application contact:* Keith Kelly, Academic Administrator, 212-992-5868, Fax: 212-992-5807, E-mail: ifa.program@nyu.edu.

Northwestern State University of Louisiana, Graduate Studies and Research, Program in Heritage Resources, Natchitoches, LA 71497. Offers MA. *Faculty:* 4 full-time (3 women). *Students:* 16 full-time (11 women), 1 (woman) part-time. Average age 32. In 2007, 5 degrees awarded. *Degree requirements:* For master's, comprehensive exam, thesis or alternative. *Entrance requirements:* For master's, GRE General Test, minimum undergraduate GPA of 2.5. *Unit head:* Dr. Elizabeth Guin, Head, 318-357-4057, Fax: 318-357-6153, E-mail: guine@nsula.edu. *Application contact:* Dr. Steven G. Horton, Associate Provost/Dean, Graduate Studies, Research, and Information Systems, 318-357-5851, Fax: 318-357-5019, E-mail: grad_school@nsula.edu.

Pratt Institute, School of Architecture, Program in Historic Preservation, Brooklyn, NY 11205-3899. Offers MS. Part-time programs available. *Faculty:* 4 part-time/adjunct (1 woman). *Students:* 12 full-time (9 women), 3 part-time (2 women); includes 2 minority (1 African American, 1 Asian American or Pacific Islander), 2 international. Average age 33. 24 applicants, 96% accepted, 6 enrolled. In 2007, 10 degrees awarded. *Entrance requirements:* For master's, writing sample, bachelor's degree, transcripts, letters of recommendation, statement, portfolio. Additional exam requirements/recommendations for international students: Required—TOEFL (minimum score 550 paper-based; 213 computer-based). *Application deadline:* For fall admission, 2/1 for domestic students; for spring admission, 10/1 for domestic students. Application fee: $50 ($90 for international students). Electronic applications accepted. *Expenses:* Tuition: Full-time $25,680. Required fees: $1,106. Tuition and fees vary according to program. *Financial support:* Career-related internships or fieldwork, Federal Work-Study, institutionally sponsored loans, scholarships/grants, health care benefits, and unspecified assistantships available. Support available to part-time students. Financial award application deadline: 2/1; financial award applicants required to submit FAFSA. *Unit head:* Eric Allison, Coordinator, 212-647-7532, E-mail: eallison@pratt.edu. *Application contact:* Young Hah, Director of Graduate Admissions, 718-636-3683, Fax: 718-399-4242, E-mail: yhah@pratt.edu.

See Close-Up on page 167.

Rensselaer Polytechnic Institute, Graduate School, School of Architecture, Program in Building Conservation, Troy, NY 12180-3590. Offers MS. Part-time and evening/weekend programs available. *Faculty:* 1 full-time (0 women), 14 part-time/adjunct (4 women). *Students:* Average age 37. 4 applicants, 50% accepted, 2 enrolled. In 2007, 3 degrees awarded. *Degree requirements:* For master's, thesis (for some programs). *Entrance requirements:* For master's, resumé, letters of recommendation. Additional exam requirements/recommendations for international students: Required—TOEFL (minimum score 570 paper-based; 230 computer-based), IELTS (minimum score 7). *Application deadline:* For fall admission, 1/15 priority date for domestic and international students. Applications are processed on a rolling basis. Application fee: $75. Electronic applications accepted. *Expenses: Contact institution. Financial support:* Institutionally sponsored loans available. Financial award application deadline: 1/15. *Faculty research:* Building conservation, 20th century American architecture, historic structure and technology, preservation theory, historical archaeology. *Application contact:* Kathleen G. O'Connor, Senior Program Administrator, Graduate Programs, 518-276-3986, Fax: 518-276-3034, E-mail: oconnk2@rpi.edu.

See Close-Up on page 169.

Rutgers, The State University of New Jersey, New Brunswick, Graduate School, Program in Art History, New Brunswick, NJ 08901-1281. Offers art history (MA, PhD); curatorial studies (Certificate); historic preservation (Certificate). Part-time programs available. Terminal master's awarded for partial completion of doctoral program. *Degree requirements:* For master's, one foreign language, comprehensive exam; for doctorate, 2 foreign languages, comprehensive exam, thesis/dissertation. *Entrance requirements:* For master's and doctorate, GRE General Test, writing sample. Additional exam requirements/recommendations for international students: Required—TOEFL (minimum score 550 paper-based; 213 computer-based). Electronic applications accepted. *Faculty research:* Ancient and medieval art and architecture; Renaissance and Baroque art and architecture; modern and contemporary art and architecture; Italian studies; the arts of Asia, Africa, and the Americas.

St. Cloud State University, School of Graduate Studies, College of Social Sciences, Program in Cultural Resource Management Archeology, St. Cloud, MN 56301-4498. Offers MS. *Students:* 4 full-time (2 women); includes 1 minority (American Indian/Alaska Native). 4 applicants, 100% accepted, 3 enrolled. *Entrance requirements:* For master's, GRE General Test, minimum 2.75 GPA. Additional exam requirements/recommendations for international students: Required—MELAB; Recommended—TOEFL (minimum score 550 paper-based; 213 computer-based). *Application deadline:* For fall admission, 6/1 for domestic students, 4/1 for international students. Application fee: $35. *Expenses:* Tuition, state resident: part-time $267 per credit. Tuition, nonresident: part-time $418 per credit. Required fees: $28 per credit. *Unit head:* Dr. Mark Muniz, Coordinator, 320-308-4162, E-mail: mpmuniz@stcloudstate.edu. *Application contact:* Linda Lou Krueger, School of Graduate Studies, 320-308-2113, Fax: 320-308-5371, E-mail: lekrueger@stcloudstate.edu.

Savannah College of Art and Design, Graduate School, Program in Historic Preservation, Savannah, GA 31402-3146. Offers MA, MFA. Part-time programs available. *Faculty:* 4 full-time (1 woman), 1 part-time/adjunct (0 women). *Students:* 29 full-time (24 women), 16 part-time (6 women); includes 2 minority (1 African American, 1 Asian American or Pacific Islander). Average age 27. 75 applicants, 31% accepted, 17 enrolled. In 2007, 27 degrees awarded. *Degree requirements:* For master's, thesis, internship. *Entrance requirements:* For master's, interview, research paper. Additional exam requirements/recommendations for international students: Required—TOEFL (minimum score 450 paper-based; 133 computer-based). *Application deadline:* For fall admission, 4/1 priority date for domestic and international students. Applications are processed on a rolling basis. Application fee: $50. Electronic applications accepted. *Expenses:* Tuition: Full-time $24,840; part-time $552 per credit. One-time fee: $500 full-time. *Financial support:* In 2007–08, 5 fellowships were awarded; career-related internships or fieldwork, Federal Work-Study, and scholarships/grants also available. Financial award application deadline: 4/1; financial award applicants required to submit FAFSA. *Unit head:* Connie Pinkerton, Chair, 912-525-6989. *Application contact:* Darrell Tutchton, Director of Graduate and International Enrollment, 912-525-5961, Fax: 912-525-5985, E-mail: admission@scad.edu.

See Close-Up on page 257.

School of the Art Institute of Chicago, Graduate Division, Program in Historic Preservation, Chicago, IL 60603-3103. Offers MSHP. *Entrance requirements:* Additional exam requirements/recommendations for international students: Required—TOEFL.

See Close-Up on page 259.

Texas Tech University, Graduate School, College of Architecture, Post-Professional Program in Architecture, Lubbock, TX 79409. Offers community design and development (MS); historical preservation (MS); visualization (MS). Part-time programs available. *Students:* 5 full-time (3 women), 7 part-time (2 women), 5 international. Average age 29. 12 applicants, 67% accepted, 3 enrolled. In 2007, 2 degrees awarded. *Degree requirements:* For master's, thesis. *Entrance requirements:* For master's, GRE General Test, portfolio. Additional exam requirements/recommendations for international students: Required—TOEFL (minimum score 550 paper-based; 213 computer-based). *Application deadline:* For fall admission, 3/1 priority date for domestic students; for spring admission, 11/1 priority date for domestic students. Applications are processed on a rolling basis. Application fee: $50 ($60 for international students). Electronic applications accepted. *Expenses:* Tuition, state resident: part-time $373 per credit hour. Tuition, nonresident: part-time $651 per credit hour. Tuition and fees vary according to program. *Financial support:* Research assistantships with partial tuition reimbursements, teaching assistantships with partial tuition reimbursements, career-related internships or fieldwork, Federal Work-Study, and institutionally sponsored loans available. Support available to part-time students. Financial award application deadline: 4/15; financial award applicants required to submit FAFSA. *Faculty research:* Historic preservation, visualization, community development and design, sustainable architecture, international architecture. *Unit head:* Glenn Eugene Hill, Associate Dean of Research and Post-Professional Graduate Studies, 806-742-3136, Fax: 806-742-2855, E-mail: glenn.hill@ttu.edu. *Application contact:* Jess Schwintz, Academic Program Assistant, 806-742-3136 Ext. 272, Fax: 806-742-2855, E-mail: jess.schwintz@ttu.edu.

Texas Tech University, Graduate School, Program in Museum Science and Heritage Management, Lubbock, TX 79409. Offers heritage management (MS); museum science (MA). Part-time programs available. *Faculty:* 6 full-time (3 women). *Students:* 29 full-time (28 women), 10 part-time (7 women); includes 5 minority (1 African American, 4 Hispanic Americans). Average age 28. 31 applicants, 81% accepted, 14 enrolled. In 2007, 20 degrees awarded. *Degree requirements:* For master's, thesis. *Entrance requirements:* For master's, GRE General Test. Additional exam requirements/recommendations for international students: Required—TOEFL (minimum score 550 paper-based; 213 computer-based). *Application deadline:* For fall admission, 3/1 priority date for international students; for spring admission, 11/1 priority date for international students. Applications are processed on a rolling basis. Application fee: $50 ($60 for international students). Electronic applications accepted. *Expenses:* Tuition, state resident: part-time $373 per credit hour. Tuition, nonresident: part-time $651 per credit hour. Tuition and fees vary according to program. *Financial support:* In 2007–08, 36 students received support, including 5 research assistantships with partial tuition reimbursements available (averaging $9,289 per year); teaching assistantships with partial tuition reimbursements available, career-related internships or fieldwork, Federal Work-Study, and institutionally sponsored loans also available. Support available to part-time students. Financial award application deadline: 4/15; financial award applicants required to submit FAFSA. *Faculty research:* Lubbock lake landmark anthropology; regional American fine art, regional ethnology; anthropology of the southern plains, natural science research. Total annual research expenditures: $46,621. *Unit head:* Gary F. Edson, Chair, 806-742-2442, Fax: 806-742-1136, E-mail: gary.edson@ttu.edu. *Application contact:* Claudia Cory, Assistant to the Director, 806-742-2442 Ext. 222, Fax: 806-742-1136, E-mail: claudia.cory@ttu.edu.

Universidad Nacional Pedro Henriquez Urena, Graduate School, Santo Domingo, Dominican Republic. Offers accounting and auditing (M Acct); animal production (M Agr); business administration (MBA, PhD); Caribbean tropical architecture (M Arch); conservation of monuments and cultural goods (M Arch); economics (M Econ); education (PhD); environmental engineering (MEE); horticulture (M Agr); hospital administration (PhD); humanities (PhD); international relations (MPS); management of natural resources (MNRM); project management (M Man, MPM); public administration (MPS); sanitary engineering (ME); social science (PhD); veterinary medicine (DVM).

University of California, Riverside, Graduate Division, Department of History, Riverside, CA 92521-0102. Offers archival management (MA); historic preservation (MA); history (MA, PhD); museum curatorship (MA). Part-time programs available. *Faculty:* 28 full-time (12 women). *Students:* 76 full-time (36 women), 1 (woman) part-time; includes 12 minority (1 African American, 2 American Indian/Alaska Native, 5 Asian Americans or Pacific Islanders, 4 Hispanic Americans), 1 international. Average age 31. 63 applicants, 49% accepted, 21 enrolled. In 2007, 12 master's, 6 doctorates awarded. Terminal master's awarded for partial completion of doctoral program. *Median time to degree:* Of those who began their doctoral program in fall 1999, 50% received their degree in 8 years or less. *Degree requirements:* For master's, one foreign language, comprehensive exam, internship report and oral exams, or thesis; for doctorate, 2 foreign languages, thesis/dissertation, qualifying exams, teaching experience. *Entrance requirements:* For master's, GRE General Test, minimum GPA of 3.2; for doctorate, GRE General Test, MA in history, minimum GPA of 3.2. Additional exam requirements/recommendations for international students: Required—TOEFL (minimum score 550 paper-based; 213 computer-based; 80 iBT). *Application deadline:* For fall admission, 5/1 for domestic students, 2/1 for international students. Applications are processed on a rolling basis. Application fee: $60 ($75 for international students). Electronic applications accepted. *Financial support:* In 2007–08, 56 students received support, including fellowships with full tuition reimbursements available (averaging $13,000 per year), teaching assistantships with partial tuition reimbursements available (averaging $16,500 per year); career-related internships or fieldwork, Federal Work-Study, institutionally sponsored loans, health care benefits, and tuition waivers (full and partial) also available. Financial award application deadline: 1/5; financial award applicants required to submit FAFSA. *Faculty research:* Native American history, United States, public history, Russia, Europe. *Unit head:* Dr. Robert Patch, Chair, 951-827-5401 Ext. 11437, Fax: 951-827-5299, E-mail: history@ucr.edu.

University of Delaware, College of Arts and Sciences, Program in Art Conservation, Newark, DE 19716. Offers practicing art conservation (MS). *Faculty:* 3 full-time (2 women), 15 part-time/adjunct (8 women). *Students:* 30 full-time (28 women); includes 1 minority (Asian American or Pacific Islander) Average age 28. 52 applicants, 25% accepted, 9 enrolled. In 2007, 9 degrees awarded. *Degree requirements:* For master's, internship, portfolio, oral exam, oral presentation. *Entrance requirements:* For master's, GRE General Test, course work in chemistry, art history/anthropology and studio art; minimum of 400 hours of conservation experience. *Application deadline:* For fall admission, 1/15 for domestic students. Application fee: $60. Electronic applications accepted. *Financial support:* In 2007–08, 30 students received support, including 30 fellowships with full tuition reimbursements available (averaging $15,500 per year); career-related internships or fieldwork, Federal Work-Study, and institutionally sponsored loans also available. *Faculty research:* Emergency response cleaning techniques, degradation process, art history, artists, materials, techniques of preservation and treatment. Total annual research expenditures: $500,000. *Unit head:* Debra Hess Norris, Director, 302-831-3489, Fax: 302-831-4330, E-mail: dhnorris@udel.edu. *Application contact:* Information Contact, 302-831-3489, E-mail: dhnorris@udel.edu.

University of Delaware, College of Human Services, Education and Public Policy, Center for Energy and Environmental Policy, Program in Urban Affairs and Public Policy, Newark, DE 19716. Offers community development and nonprofit leadership (MA); energy and environmental policy (MA); governance, planning and management (PhD); historic preservation (MA); social and urban policy (PhD); technology, environment and society (PhD). Part-time programs available. Terminal master's awarded for partial completion of doctoral program. *Degree requirements:* For master's, analytical paper or thesis; for doctorate, thesis/dissertation. *Entrance requirements:* For master's, GRE General Test, minimum GPA of 3.0; for doctorate, GRE General Test, minimum GPA of 3.5. Additional exam requirements/recommendations for international students: Required—TOEFL. *Application deadline:* Applications are processed on a rolling basis. Application fee: $60. Electronic applications accepted. *Financial support:* Career-related internships or fieldwork, Federal Work-Study, and tuition waivers (full) available. *Faculty research:* Political economy; social policy analysis; technology and society; historic preservation; urban policy. Total annual research expenditures: $1 million.

See Close-Up on page 1635.

University of Georgia, Graduate School, College of Environment and Design, School of Environmental Design, Program in Historic Preservation, Athens, GA 30602. Offers MHP. *Students:* 27 full-time (15 women), 13 part-time (11 women); includes 1 minority (Asian American or Pacific Islander) 42 applicants, 71% accepted, 12 enrolled. In 2007, 8 degrees awarded. *Degree requirements:* For master's, thesis. *Entrance requirements:* For master's, GRE General Test. *Application deadline:* For fall admission, 7/1 priority date for domestic students; for spring admission, 11/15 for domestic students. Application fee: $50. Electronic applications accepted. *Financial support:* Fellowships, research assistantships, teaching assistantships, unspecified assistantships available. *Unit head:* Prof. John C. Waters, Graduate Coordinator, 706-542-4706, Fax: 706-542-4236, E-mail: jcwaters@uga.edu.

University of Hawaii at Manoa, Graduate Division, Colleges of Arts and Sciences, College of Arts and Humanities, Department of American Studies, Program in Historic Preservation, Honolulu, HI 96822. Offers Graduate Certificate. Part-time programs available. *Faculty:* 1 full-time (0 women). *Students:* 3 full-time (2 women), 7 part-time (4 women); includes 4 minority (3 Asian Americans or Pacific Islanders, 1 Hispanic American). 9 applicants, 78% accepted, 6 enrolled. *Entrance requirements:* Additional exam requirements/recommendations for international students: Required—TOEFL (minimum score 600 paper-based; 250 computer-based; 100 iBT), IELTS (minimum score 7). *Application deadline:* For fall admission, 3/1 for domestic and international students; for spring admission, 9/1 for domestic and international students. *Financial support:* In 2007–08, 1 research assistantship (averaging $15,552 per year), 1 teaching assistantship (averaging $13,296 per year) were awarded. *Application contact:* William Chapman, Director, 808-956-8826, Fax: 808-956-4733, E-mail: amstuh@hawaii.edu.

University of Kentucky, Graduate School, College of Design, Department of Historic Preservation, Lexington, KY 40506-0032. Offers MHP. *Faculty:* 1 full-time (0 women), 2 part-time/adjunct (1 woman). *Students:* 21 full-time (18 women), 4 part-time (3 women). Average age 30. 20 applicants, 70% accepted, 10 enrolled. In 2007, 12 degrees awarded. *Degree requirements:* For master's, comprehensive exam. *Entrance requirements:* For master's, GRE General Test, minimum undergraduate GPA of 2.75. Additional exam requirements/recommendations for international students: Required—TOEFL (minimum score 550 paper-based; 213 computer-based). *Application deadline:* For fall admission, 7/17 priority date for domestic students, 2/1 priority date for international students; for spring admission, 12/13 priority date for domestic students, 6/15 priority date for international students. Application fee: $50 ($65 for international students). Electronic applications accepted. *Expenses:* Tuition, state resident: part-time $437 per credit hour. Tuition, nonresident: part-time $931 per credit hour. *Financial support:* In 2007–08, 12 students received support, including 9 research assistantships with full tuition reimbursements available (averaging $4,000 per year), 3 teaching assistantships with full tuition reimbursements available (averaging $4,000 per year); fellowships with full tuition reimbursements available, Federal Work-Study, scholarships/grants, traineeships, health care benefits, tuition waivers (partial), and unspecified assistantships also available. Support available to part-time students. Financial award application deadline: 3/15; financial award applicants required to submit FAFSA. *Unit head:* Clyde R. Carpenter, Chair, 859-257-3651, Fax: 859-323-1990, E-mail: arc104@uky.edu. *Application contact:* Dr. Brian Jackson, Senior Associate Dean, 859-257-4667, Fax: 859-257-4676, E-mail: brian.jackson@uky.edu.

University of Maryland, College Park, Graduate Studies, School of Architecture, Planning and Preservation, Program in Historic Preservation, College Park, MD 20742. Offers MHP, Certificate. *Students:* 20 full-time (14 women), 5 part-time (4 women); includes 2 minority (both Hispanic Americans), 2 international. 46 applicants, 54% accepted, 12 enrolled. In 2007, 10 degrees awarded. *Degree requirements:* For Certificate, thesis. *Entrance requirements:* For master's, GRE, minimum GPA of 3.0, 3 letters of recommendation, writing sample. Additional exam requirements/recommendations for international students: Required—TOEFL. *Application deadline:* For fall admission, 1/1 for domestic and international students. Applications are processed on a rolling basis. Application fee: $60. Electronic applications accepted. *Financial support:* In 2007–08, 1 fellowship with full tuition reimbursement (averaging $7,178 per year), 12 teaching assistantships (averaging $13,470 per year) were awarded; career-related internships or fieldwork and tuition waivers also available. *Unit head:* Donald Linebaugh, Director, 301-405-6283, Fax: 301-314-9583, E-mail: dwline@umd.edu. *Application contact:* Dean of Graduate School, 301-405-0358, Fax: 301-314-9305.

University of New Mexico, Graduate School, School of Architecture and Planning, Program in Historic Preservation and Regionalism, Albuquerque, NM 87131-2039. Offers Graduate Certificate. Part-time and evening/weekend programs available. *Students:* 1 (woman) full-time, 6 part-time (3 women). Average age 42. 2 applicants, 100% accepted, 0 enrolled. *Application deadline:* For fall admission, 11/1 priority date for domestic students; for spring admission, 3/1 priority date for domestic students. Application fee: $50. *Financial support:* Career-related internships or fieldwork and scholarships/grants available. Support available to part-time students. *Unit head:* Chris Wilson, Director, 505-277-3303, Fax: 505-277-0897, E-mail: chwilson@unm.edu.

The University of North Carolina at Greensboro, Graduate School, School of Human Environmental Sciences, Department of Interior Architecture, Greensboro, NC 27412-5001. Offers historic preservation (Certificate); interior architecture (MS); museum studies (Certificate). *Faculty:* 9 full-time (4 women), 1 part-time/adjunct (0 women). *Students:* 14 full-time (12 women), 1 (woman) part-time. 13 applicants, 38% accepted. *Degree requirements:* For master's, thesis. *Entrance requirements:* For master's, GRE General Test or MAT, bachelor's degree in interior design, interview, portfolio. Additional exam requirements/recommendations for international students: Required—TOEFL. *Application deadline:* For fall admission, 3/1 for domestic students. Application fee: $45. Electronic applications accepted. *Financial support:* Fellowships with full tuition reimbursements, research assistantships with full tuition reimbursements, teaching assistantships with full tuition reimbursements, career-related internships or fieldwork, Federal Work-Study, scholarships/grants, and traineeships available. Support available to part-time students. *Unit head:* Thomas Lambeth, Chairman, 336-334-5320, Fax: 336-334-5049, E-mail: ctlambeth@uncg.edu. *Application contact:* Michelle Harkleroad, Director of Graduate Admissions, 336-334-4884, Fax: 336-334-4424, E-mail: mbharkle@uncg.edu.

University of Oregon, Graduate School, School of Architecture and Allied Arts, Program in Historic Preservation, Eugene, OR 97403. Offers MS. *Students:* 21 full-time (18 women), 4 part-time (3 women). 20 applicants, 70% accepted. In 2007, 4 degrees awarded. *Degree requirements:* For master's, thesis, internship. *Entrance requirements:* For master's, participation in Pacific Northwest Field School. Additional exam requirements/recommendations for international students: Required—TOEFL. *Application deadline:* For fall admission, 2/15 for domestic students. Application fee: $50. *Financial support:* In 2007–08, 3 teaching assistantships were awarded; career-related internships or fieldwork, Federal Work-Study, and institutionally sponsored loans also available. Support available to part-time students. *Faculty research:* Vernacular architecture, Native American architecture, masonry structure and details, wood construction systems, cultural landscapes. *Unit head:* Kingston Heath, Head, 541-346-3680, Fax: 541-346-3626. *Application contact:* Maia Howes, Admissions Contact, 541-346-2982, Fax: 541-346-3639, E-mail: mhowes@uoregon.edu.

University of Pennsylvania, School of Design, Graduate Group in Historic Preservation, Philadelphia, PA 19104. Offers conservation and heritage management (Certificate); historic conservation (Certificate); historic preservation (MS). Part-time programs available. *Degree requirements:* For master's, thesis. *Entrance requirements:* For master's, GRE. Additional exam requirements/recommendations for international students: Required—TOEFL. *Faculty research:* Historic building technology, architectural conservation, architectural theory, preservation in the Third World.

See Close-Up on page 175.

University of South Carolina, The Graduate School, College of Arts and Sciences, Department of History, Program in Public History, Columbia, SC 29208. Offers archives (MA); historic preservation (MA); museum (MA); museum management (Certificate); MLIS/MA. *Faculty:* 3 full-time (2 women). *Students:* 10 full-time (7 women), 3 part-time (2 women); includes 1 minority (Hispanic American) Average age 26. 34 applicants, 18% accepted. In 2007, 13 degrees awarded. *Degree requirements:* For master's, one foreign language, thesis, internship. *Entrance requirements:* For master's, GRE General Test, writing sample. Additional exam requirements/recommendations for international students: Required—TOEFL. *Application deadline:* For fall admission, 1/5 for domestic students. Application fee: $40. Electronic applications accepted. *Expenses:* Tuition, state resident: part-time $440 per hour. Tuition, nonresident: part-time $936 per hour. Required fees: $17 per hour. Tuition and fees vary according to program. *Financial support:* In 2007–08, 12 teaching assistantships with partial tuition reimbursements (averaging $11,000 per year) were awarded; fellowships with partial tuition reimbursements, research assistantships with partial tuition reimbursements, career-related internships or fieldwork, Federal Work-Study, and institutionally sponsored loans also available. Financial award application deadline: 1/5. *Faculty research:* Museum studies, historic preservation, archives administration. *Application contact:* Robert R. Weyeneth, Co-Director, 803-777-5195, Fax: 803-777-4494, E-mail: weyeneth@sc.edu.

University of Southern California, Graduate School, School of Architecture, Program in Historic Preservation, Los Angeles, CA 90089. Offers MHP. Part-time programs available. *Faculty:* 50 full-time (25 women), 50 part-time/adjunct (25 women). *Students:* 9 full-time (5 women), 6 part-time (5 women); includes 1 minority (Hispanic American), 1 international. 12 applicants, 92% accepted. In 2007, 5 master's awarded. *Entrance requirements:* For master's, GRE. *Application deadline:* For fall admission, 1/15 priority date for domestic students. Applications are processed on a rolling basis. Application fee: $85. *Financial support:* In 2007–08, fellowships with tuition reimbursements (averaging $15,000 per year); career-related internships or fieldwork, Federal Work-Study, and scholarships/grants also available. Support available to part-time students. Financial award applicants required to submit FAFSA. *Unit head:* Dr. Kenneth Breisch, Head, 213-740-2311.

Historic Preservation

University of Vermont, Graduate College, College of Arts and Sciences, Program in Historic Preservation, Burlington, VT 05405. Offers MS. *Students:* 28 (18 women). 31 applicants, 87% accepted, 9 enrolled. In 2007, 8 degrees awarded. *Entrance requirements:* For master's, GRE General Test, sample project or equivalent. Additional exam requirements/recommendations for international students: Required—TOEFL (minimum score 550 paper-based; 213 computer-based; 80 iBT). *Application deadline:* For fall admission, 3/1 for domestic students. Application fee: $40. Electronic applications accepted. *Financial support:* Fellowships, teaching assistantships available. Financial award application deadline: 3/1. *Faculty research:* Architectural environment. *Unit head:* T. Visser, Director, 802-656-3180.

University of Washington, Graduate School, Interdisciplinary Program in Preservation Planning and Design, Seattle, WA 98195. Offers Certificate. Offered in cooperation with the Departments of Architecture, Landscape Architecture, and Urban Design and Planning. Part-time programs available. Electronic applications accepted. *Faculty research:* History of the built environment, historic preservation planning, vernacular architecture, ethnic and gender issues in preservation, restoration.

University of West Florida, College of Arts and Sciences: Arts, Department of History, Pensacola, FL 32514-5750. Offers historic preservation (MA); history (MA); public history (MA). Part-time and evening/weekend programs available. *Faculty:* 6 full-time (2 women), 2 part-time/adjunct (both women). *Students:* 15 full-time (9 women), 27 part-time (14 women); includes 5 minority (2 African Americans, 2 American Indian/Alaska Native, 1 Hispanic American), 1 international. Average age 33. 22 applicants, 100% accepted, 15 enrolled. In 2007, 14 degrees awarded. *Degree requirements:* For master's, thesis or alternative. *Entrance requirements:* For master's, GRE General Test, minimum GPA of 3.0, minimum 15 hours of upper-level history courses. Additional exam requirements/recommendations for international students: Required—TOEFL (minimum score 550 paper-based; 213 computer-based). *Application deadline:* For fall admission, 6/1 for domestic students, 5/15 for international students; for spring admission, 11/1 for domestic students, 10/1 for international students. Applications are processed on a rolling basis. Application fee: $30. *Expenses:* Tuition, state resident: full-time $6,054; part-time $252 per credit. Tuition, nonresident: full-time $21,886; part-time $912 per credit. *Financial support:* In 2007–08, 3 research assistantships with partial tuition reimbursements (averaging $5,640 per year) were awarded; fellowships, teaching assistantships with partial tuition reimbursements, Federal Work-Study, institutionally sponsored loans, scholarships/grants, and unspecified assistantships also available. Financial award application deadline: 4/15; financial award applicants required to submit FAFSA. *Unit head:* Dr. John J. Clune, Chairperson, 850-474-2680.

Ursuline College, School of Graduate Studies, Program in Historic Preservation, Pepper Pike, OH 44124-4398. Offers MA. Part-time programs available. *Faculty:* 2 part-time/adjunct (1 woman). *Students:* Average age 34. 9 applicants, 100% accepted. *Degree requirements:* For master's, thesis. *Entrance requirements:* For master's, minimum undergraduate GPA of 3.0. Additional exam requirements/recommendations for international students: Required—TOEFL (minimum score 500 paper-based; 173 computer-based). *Application deadline:* For fall admission, 8/1 priority date for domestic students. Applications are processed on a rolling basis. Application fee: $25. *Expenses:* Tuition: Full-time $13,356; part-time $742 per credit hour. Required fees: $200; $60 per semester. Tuition and fees vary according to program. *Financial support:* In 2007–08, 4 students received support. Federal Work-Study available. Financial award application deadline: 3/1. *Unit head:* Dr. Tim Wagner, 440-646-8109. *Application contact:* Jo Mann, Secretary, 440-646-8119, Fax: 440-684-6088, E-mail: gradsch@ursuline.edu.

Virginia Commonwealth University, Graduate School, College of Humanities and Sciences, Wilder School of Government and Public Affairs, Department of Urban Studies and Planning, Program in Historic Preservation Planning, Richmond, VA 23284-9005. Offers Certificate. *Application deadline:* For fall admission, 4/15 for domestic students; for spring admission, 11/15 for domestic students. Applications are processed on a rolling basis. Application fee: $50. *Expenses:* Tuition, state resident: full-time $7,224; part-time $401 per credit. Tuition, nonresident: full-time $16,072; part-time $891 per credit. Required fees: $1,679; $63 per credit. Tuition and fees vary according to campus/location.

See Close-Up on page 457.

Landscape Architecture

Arizona State University, Graduate College, College of Architecture and Environmental Design, School of Planning and Landscape Architecture, Tempe, AZ 85287. Offers planning (MEP). *Accreditation:* ACSP. *Entrance requirements:* For master's, GRE General Test.

Auburn University, Graduate School, College of Architecture, Design, and Construction, Program in Landscape Architecture, Auburn University, AL 36849. Offers MLA. *Accreditation:* ASLA. *Faculty:* 10 full-time (3 women). *Students:* 36 full-time (14 women), 2 part-time; includes 2 minority (1 African American, 1 Hispanic American), 11 international. Average age 27. 23 applicants, 83% accepted, 11 enrolled. In 2007, 25 degrees awarded. *Entrance requirements:* For master's, 3 letters of recommendation. *Unit head:* Charlene Lebleu, Chair, 334-844-4516.

Ball State University, Graduate School, College of Architecture and Planning, Department of Landscape Architecture, Muncie, IN 47306-1099. Offers MLA. *Accreditation:* ASLA. *Faculty:* 13. *Students:* 21 full-time (9 women), 3 part-time (2 women), 1 international. Average age 29. 25 applicants, 80% accepted, 5 enrolled. In 2007, 5 degrees awarded. *Degree requirements:* For master's, thesis. *Entrance requirements:* For master's, writing sample. Application fee: $25 ($35 for international students). *Expenses:* Tuition, state resident: full-time $6,864. Tuition, nonresident: full-time $17,932. Required fees: $1,866. *Financial support:* In 2007–08, 4 teaching assistantships with full tuition reimbursements (averaging $6,956 per year) were awarded; research assistantships with full tuition reimbursements. Financial award application deadline: 3/1. *Unit head:* Malcolm O. Cairns, Chairperson, 765-285-1982, Fax: 765-285-1983, E-mail: mcairns@bsu.edu.

California State Polytechnic University, Pomona, Academic Affairs, College of Environmental Design, Program in Landscape Architecture, Pomona, CA 91768-2557. Offers M Land Arch. *Accreditation:* ASLA. Part-time programs available. *Students:* 39 full-time (17 women), 11 part-time (9 women); includes 11 minority (1 American Indian/Alaska Native, 10 Asian Americans or Pacific Islanders). Average age 31. 67 applicants, 0% accepted. In 2007, 19 degrees awarded. *Degree requirements:* For master's, thesis or alternative. *Application deadline:* For fall admission, 5/1 priority date for domestic students; for winter admission, 10/15 priority date for domestic students; for spring admission, 1/20 priority date for domestic students. Applications are processed on a rolling basis. Application fee: $55. Electronic applications accepted. *Expenses:* Tuition, nonresident: full-time $7,232; part-time $226 per unit. Required fees: $3,920. One-time fee: $2,486 part-time. *Financial support:* Career-related internships or fieldwork, Federal Work-Study, and institutionally sponsored loans available. Support available to part-time students. Financial award application deadline: 3/2; financial award applicants required to submit FAFSA. *Unit head:* Joan H. Woodward, Graduate Coordinator, 909-869-2715, Fax: 909-869-4460, E-mail: lagradprog@csupomona.edu.

Chatham University, Program in Landscape Architecture, Pittsburgh, PA 15232-2826. Offers landscape architecture (ML Arch); landscape studies (MA). Part-time and evening/weekend programs available. *Students:* 18 full-time (12 women), 13 part-time (7 women). Average age 35. 11 applicants, 91% accepted, 8 enrolled. In 2007, 6 degrees awarded. *Degree requirements:* For master's, thesis, capstone project. *Entrance requirements:* For master's, minimum undergraduate GPA of 3.0, 2 letters of recommendation, resumé. Additional exam requirements/recommendations for international students: Recommended—TOEFL (minimum score 600 paper-based; 250 computer-based; 100 iBT), IELTS (minimum score 7). *Application deadline:* Applications are processed on a rolling basis. Application fee: $45. Electronic applications accepted. *Financial support:* Career-related internships or fieldwork available. Financial award applicants required to submit FAFSA. *Unit head:* Lisa Kunst Vavaro, Director, 412-365-1882, E-mail: lvavro@chatham.edu. *Application contact:* 412-365-1825, Fax: 412-365-1609, E-mail: admissions@chatham.edu.

City College of the City University of New York, Graduate School, School of Architecture and Environmental Studies, New York, NY 10031-9198. Offers architecture (M Arch, PD); landscape architecture (PD); urban design (MUP). Part-time programs available. *Students:* 76 full-time (41 women), 1 (woman) part-time; includes 50 minority (18 African Americans, 11 Asian Americans or Pacific Islanders, 21 Hispanic Americans), 15 international. 123 applicants, 76% accepted, 46 enrolled. In 2007, 26 degrees awarded. *Degree requirements:* For master's, thesis. *Entrance requirements:* For master's, portfolio, professional degree in architecture or equivalent. Additional exam requirements/recommendations for international students: Required—TOEFL (minimum score 550 paper-based; 213 computer-based). Application fee: $125. *Financial support:* Fellowships, career-related internships or fieldwork and Federal Work-Study available. Support available to part-time students. *Unit head:* George Ranalli, Dean, 212-650-7284, Fax: 212-650-6566, E-mail: granalli@acis32.admin.ccny.cuny.edu. *Application contact:* Sarah Morales, Advisor, 212-650-8748, E-mail: archgrad@ccny.cuny.edu.

Clemson University, Graduate School, College of Architecture, Arts, and Humanities, Department of Planning and Landscape Architecture, Program in Landscape Architecture, Clemson, SC 29634. Offers MLA. *Students:* 32 full-time (19 women), 2 part-time (both women); includes 3 minority (1 African American, 1 Asian American or Pacific Islander, 1 Hispanic American), 4 international. 10 applicants, 60% accepted, 4 enrolled. In 2007, 1 degree awarded. *Entrance requirements:* Additional exam requirements/recommendations for international students: Required—TOEFL. *Application deadline:* For fall admission, 4/15 for international students; for spring admission, 9/15 for international students. Application fee: $55. *Unit head:* Umit Yilmaz, Coordinator, 864-656-7349, Fax: 864-656-7519, E-mail: uyilmaz@clemson.edu.

Columbia University, School of Continuing Education, Program in Landscape Design, New York, NY 10027. Offers MS. Part-time programs available. *Faculty:* 9 part-time/adjunct (2 women). In 2007, 17 degrees awarded. *Degree requirements:* For master's, 36 credits. *Entrance requirements:* For master's, BA/BS with minimum GPA of 3.0. Additional exam requirements/recommendations for international students: Required—American Language Program (ALP) placement test. *Application deadline:* For fall admission, 6/16 for domestic students; for spring admission, 11/7 for domestic students. Application fee: $50. *Expenses:* Tuition: Part-time $1,452 per credit. Required fees: $152 per term. One-time fee: $75 part-time. Full-time tuition and fees vary according to course level, course load, degree level and program. *Financial support:* Institutionally sponsored loans available. Financial award applicants required to submit FAFSA. *Unit head:* Joseph Disponzio, Director, 212-854-9699, E-mail: jd52@columbia.edu. *Application contact:* 212-854-9666, E-mail: ce-advis@columbia.edu.

Conway School of Landscape Design, Graduate Program in Landscape Design, Conway, MA 01341-0179. Offers landscape design/environmental planning (MA). *Degree requirements:* For master's, projects. *Faculty research:* Restoration of native plant communities; integration of humanities, environment, and design.

Cornell University, Graduate School, Graduate Fields of Agriculture and Life Sciences and Graduate Fields of Architecture, Art and Planning, Field of Landscape Architecture, Ithaca, NY 14853-0001. Offers MLA. *Accreditation:* ASLA. *Faculty:* 17 full-time (7 women). *Students:* 36 full-time (18 women); includes 3 minority (1 African American, 1 Asian American or Pacific Islander, 1 Hispanic American), 4 international. Average age 29. 85 applicants, 46% accepted, 13 enrolled. In 2007, 16 degrees awarded. *Degree requirements:* For master's, project or thesis. *Entrance requirements:* For master's, GRE General Test (recommended), portfolio, 2 letters of recommendation. Additional exam requirements/recommendations for international students: Required—TOEFL (minimum score 550 paper-based; 213 computer-based; 77 iBT). *Application deadline:* For fall admission, 2/15 priority date for domestic students. Applications are processed on a rolling basis. Application fee: $70. Electronic applications accepted. *Financial support:* In 2007–08, 12 students received support, including 3 fellowships with full tuition reimbursements available, 2 research assistantships with full tuition reimbursements available, 7 teaching assistantships with full tuition reimbursements available; institutionally sponsored loans, scholarships/grants, health care benefits, tuition waivers (full and partial), and unspecified assistantships also available. Financial award applicants required to submit FAFSA. *Faculty research:* Urban horticulture and landscape design, urban design research, cultural landscape history, women in landscape architecture, landscape design language, Japanese landscape architecture. *Unit head:* Director of Graduate Studies, 607-254-9552. *Application contact:* Graduate School Application Requests, Caldwell Hall, 607-254-9552, E-mail: lafield@cornell.edu.

Florida Agricultural and Mechanical University, Division of Graduate Studies, Research, and Continuing Education, School of Architecture, Tallahassee, FL 32307-3200. Offers architectural studies (MS Arch); architecture (professional) (M Arch); landscape architecture (MLA). Part-time programs available. *Degree requirements:* For master's, thesis. *Entrance requirements:* For master's, GRE General Test, minimum GPA of 3.0, portfolio. Additional exam requirements/recommendations for international students: Required—TOEFL (minimum score 550 paper-based). *Faculty research:* Environmental technology, post-occupancy evaluation, building economics, design methods, computer-aided design.

Florida International University, College of Architecture and the Arts, School of Architecture, Landscape Architecture Program, Miami, FL 33199. Offers MLA. *Students:* 30 full-time (19 women), 5 part-time (4 women); includes 4 minority (2 African Americans, 2 Hispanic Americans), 3 international. Average age 32. 32 applicants, 59% accepted, 12 enrolled. In 2007, 7 degrees awarded. *Entrance requirements:* For master's, minimum GPA of 3.0 (upper level coursework). Additional exam requirements/recommendations for international students: Required—TOEFL (minimum score 550 paper-based; 213 computer-based). *Application deadline:* For fall admission, 2/1 for domestic and international students. Application fee: $30. Electronic applications accepted. *Expenses:* Tuition, state resident: full-time $6,106. Tuition, nonresident: full-time $15,528. Required fees: $284. *Financial support:* Research assistantships, teaching assistantships available. *Unit head:* Juan A. Bueno, Dean, 305-348-6101, Fax: 305-348-6716, E-mail: buenoj@fiu.edu.

Harvard University, Graduate School of Arts and Sciences, Committee on Architecture, Landscape Architecture, and Urban Planning, Cambridge, MA 02138. Offers architecture (PhD); landscape architecture (PhD); urban planning (PhD). *Degree requirements:* For doctorate, one foreign language, thesis/dissertation, oral exam. *Entrance requirements:* For doctorate,

GRE General Test. Additional exam requirements/recommendations for international students: Required—TOEFL. *Expenses:* Tuition: Full-time $31,456. Full-time tuition and fees vary according to program and student level.

Harvard University, Graduate School of Design, Department of Landscape Architecture, Cambridge, MA 02138. Offers MLA. *Accreditation:* ASLA. *Faculty:* 6 full-time (3 women), 29 part-time/adjunct (14 women). *Students:* 83 full-time (59 women); includes 12 minority (8 Asian Americans or Pacific Islanders, 4 Hispanic Americans), 24 international. Average age 28. In 2007, 37 degrees awarded. *Entrance requirements:* For master's, GRE General Test. Additional exam requirements/recommendations for international students: Required—TOEFL (minimum score 600 paper-based; 250 computer-based; 100 iBT). *Application deadline:* For fall admission, 1/16 for domestic students. Application fee: $75. Electronic applications accepted. *Expenses:* Tuition: Full-time $31,456. Full-time tuition and fees vary according to program and student level. *Financial support:* Fellowships, teaching assistantships, Federal Work-Study available. Support available to part-time students. Financial award application deadline: 2/11; financial award applicants required to submit CSS PROFILE or FAFSA. *Unit head:* Niall Kirkwood, Chair, 617-495-2573. *Application contact:* Gail Gustafson, Director of Admissions, 617-495-5453, Fax: 617-495-8949, E-mail: ggustafson@gsd.harvard.edu.

Illinois Institute of Technology, Graduate College, College of Architecture, Chicago, IL 60616-3793. Offers architecture (M Ar, PhD); landscape architecture (MLA). Part-time programs available. *Faculty:* 38 full-time (4 women), 59 part-time/adjunct (18 women). *Students:* 177 full-time (69 women), 30 part-time (13 women); includes 22 minority (4 African Americans, 8 Asian Americans or Pacific Islanders, 10 Hispanic Americans), 78 international. Average age 28. 347 applicants, 73% accepted, 76 enrolled. In 2007, 57 master's, 5 doctorates awarded. *Degree requirements:* For master's, comprehensive exam (for some programs), thesis (for some programs); for doctorate, comprehensive exam, thesis/dissertation. *Entrance requirements:* For master's, GRE General Test, minimum GPA of 3.0, portfolio, 3 letters of recommendation; for doctorate, GRE General Test, minimum GPA of 3.0, portfolio. Additional exam requirements/recommendations for international students: Required—TOEFL (minimum score 550 paper-based; 213 computer-based; 80 iBT). *Application deadline:* For fall admission, 1/15 for domestic and international students. Applications are processed on a rolling basis. Application fee: $40. Electronic applications accepted. *Expenses:* Tuition: Full-time $14,004; part-time $778 per credit. Required fees: $7 per credit. $235 per term. Tuition and fees vary according to class time, course level, course load, program and student level. *Financial support:* In 2007–08, 125 teaching assistantships (averaging $4,000 per year) were awarded; fellowships, career-related internships or fieldwork, Federal Work-Study, institutionally sponsored loans, scholarships/grants, and health care benefits also available. Support available to part-time students. Financial award applicants required to submit FAFSA. *Faculty research:* Sustainability and environmental design, comprehensive tall building design, innovative materials technology, advanced structural systems, digital design methods. Total annual research expenditures: $25,451. *Unit head:* Donna V. Robertson, John and Jeanne Rowe Chair, 312-567-3230, Fax: 312-567-5820, E-mail: robertson@iit.edu. *Application contact:* Sarah Pariseau, Coordinator for Academic Affairs, 312-567-3281, Fax: 312-567-5820.

Iowa State University of Science and Technology, Graduate College, College of Design, Department of Landscape Architecture, Ames, IA 50011. Offers MLA, MCRP/MLA. Part-time programs available. *Faculty:* 13 full-time (4 women), 2 part-time/adjunct (0 women). *Students:* 6 full-time (2 women), 2 part-time (1 woman); includes 1 minority (African American) 13 applicants, 46% accepted, 3 enrolled. In 2007, 1 degree awarded. *Degree requirements:* For master's, thesis. *Entrance requirements:* For master's, GRE (highly recommended), portfolio. Additional exam requirements/recommendations for international students: Required—TOEFL (paper-based 600; computer-based 250; iBT 79) or IELTS (7.0). *Application deadline:* For fall admission, 1/1 priority date for domestic and international students. Applications are processed on a rolling basis. Application fee: $30 ($70 for international students). Electronic applications accepted. *Financial support:* In 2007–08, 4 research assistantships with full and partial tuition reimbursements (averaging $19,080 per year), 1 teaching assistantship with full and partial tuition reimbursement (averaging $19,080 per year) were awarded; career-related internships or fieldwork, Federal Work-Study, institutionally sponsored loans, tuition waivers (partial), and unspecified assistantships also available. Support available to part-time students. Financial award application deadline: 2/15; financial award applicants required to submit FAFSA. *Faculty research:* Landscape ecology, geographic information systems, landscape perception, historic preservation, resource management, design. Total annual research expenditures: $1.2 million. *Unit head:* Dr. Douglas Johnston, Chair, 515-294-6942, Fax: 515-294-2348, E-mail: landarch@iastate.edu. *Application contact:* Dr. Paul F. Anderson, Director of Graduate Education, 515-294-8958, E-mail: landarch@iastate.edu.

Kansas State University, Graduate School, College of Architecture, Planning and Design, Department of Landscape Architecture, Manhattan, KS 66506. Offers MLA. *Accreditation:* ASLA. Part-time programs available. *Faculty:* 15 full-time (4 women), 3 part-time/adjunct (0 women). *Students:* 49 full-time (19 women), 2 part-time (1 woman); includes 3 minority (1 American Indian/Alaska Native, 2 Asian Americans or Pacific Islanders), 2 international. Average age 30. 13 applicants, 100% accepted, 13 enrolled. In 2007, 5 degrees awarded. *Degree requirements:* For master's, thesis, residency, oral exam. *Entrance requirements:* For master's, portfolio. Additional exam requirements/recommendations for international students: Required—TOEFL (minimum score 600 paper-based). *Application deadline:* For fall admission, 2/1 priority date for domestic and international students; for spring admission, 10/1 priority date for domestic students, 8/1 priority date for international students. Applications are processed on a rolling basis. Application fee: $70 ($80 for international students). Electronic applications accepted. *Financial support:* In 2007–08, 2 research assistantships (averaging $5,969 per year), 7 teaching assistantships with full tuition reimbursements (averaging $7,000 per year) were awarded; fellowships, career-related internships or fieldwork, Federal Work-Study, institutionally sponsored loans, and scholarships/grants also available. Support available to part-time students. Financial award application deadline: 3/15; financial award applicants required to submit FAFSA. *Faculty research:* Community planning and design, design and planning theory, geospatial technology infrastructure, watershed restoration, landscape ecology. Total annual research expenditures: $47,942. *Unit head:* Dr. Dan Donelin, Head, 785-532-5961, Fax: 785-532-6722, E-mail: dandon@ksu.edu.

Louisiana State University and Agricultural and Mechanical College, Graduate School, College of Art and Design, School of Landscape Architecture, Baton Rouge, LA 70803. Offers MLA. *Accreditation:* ASLA. *Faculty:* 13 full-time (3 women). *Students:* 38 full-time (22 women), 1 (woman) part-time; includes 3 minority (1 African American, 2 Asian Americans or Pacific Islanders), 7 international. Average age 29. 43 applicants, 49% accepted, 14 enrolled. In 2007, 7 degrees awarded. *Degree requirements:* For master's, thesis. *Entrance requirements:* For master's, GRE General Test, minimum GPA of 3.0. Additional exam requirements/recommendations for international students: Required—TOEFL (minimum score 550 paper-based; 213 computer-based). *Application deadline:* For fall admission, 1/25 priority date for domestic students, 5/15 for international students; for spring admission, 10/15 for international students. Applications are processed on a rolling basis. Application fee: $25. Electronic applications accepted. *Financial support:* In 2007–08, 30 students received support, including 16 research assistantships with full and partial tuition reimbursements available (averaging $6,431 per year), 1 teaching assistantship with partial tuition reimbursement available (averaging $6,300 per year); fellowships, career-related internships or fieldwork, Federal Work-Study, institutionally sponsored loans, health care benefits, and unspecified assistantships also available. Financial award application deadline: 7/1; financial award applicants required to submit FAFSA. *Faculty research:* Digital representation, cultural landscapes, urban infrastructure, community design. Total annual research expenditures: $12,102. *Unit head:* Elizabeth Mossop, Director, 225-578-1434, Fax: 225-578-1445, E-mail: emossop@lsu.edu. *Application contact:* Dr. Lake Douglas, Graduate Coordinator, 225-578-9222, Fax: 225-578-1445, E-mail: wdougl1@lsu.edu.

Mississippi State University, College of Agriculture and Life Sciences, Department of Landscape Architecture, Mississippi State, MS 39762. Offers MLA. Part-time programs available. *Faculty:* 9 full-time (0 women), 1 part-time/adjunct (0 women). *Students:* 9 full-time (2 women), 7 part-time (2 women), 1 international. Average age 30. 9 applicants, 44% accepted, 3 enrolled. In 2007, 2 degrees awarded. *Degree requirements:* For master's, thesis. *Entrance requirements:* For master's, minimum GPA of 2.8. Additional exam requirements/recommendations for international students: Required—TOEFL (minimum score 600 paper-based). *Application deadline:* For fall admission, 8/15 priority date for domestic students; for winter admission, 12/15 priority date for domestic students. Applications are processed on a rolling basis. Application fee: $30. Electronic applications accepted. *Expenses:* Tuition, state resident: full-time $4,978; part-time $274 per hour. Tuition, nonresident: full-time $11,469; part-time $635 per hour. *Financial support:* In 2007–08, 4 teaching assistantships with full and partial tuition reimbursements (averaging $6,870 per year) were awarded; tuition waivers (partial) also available. *Faculty research:* Natchez Trace Fuel Buildup. *Unit head:* Sadik C. Artunc, Professor and Head, 662-325-3012, Fax: 662-325-7893, E-mail: sartunc@lalc.msstate.edu. *Application contact:* Dr. William A. Person, Interim Associate Vice President for Academic Affairs/Interim Dean of Graduate Studies, 662-325-7400, Fax: 662-325-1967, E-mail: grad@grad.msstate.edu.

Morgan State University, School of Graduate Studies, Institute of Architecture and Planning, Program in Landscape Architecture, Baltimore, MD 21251. Offers MLA, MSLA. *Accreditation:* ASLA. *Students:* 30. Average age 28. In 2007, 5 degrees awarded. *Degree requirements:* For master's, thesis. *Entrance requirements:* Additional exam requirements/recommendations for international students: Required—TOEFL (minimum score 550 paper-based; 213 computer-based). *Application deadline:* For fall admission, 2/1 priority date for domestic students; for spring admission, 10/1 priority date for domestic students. Applications are processed on a rolling basis. Application fee: $0. *Financial support:* Fellowships, research assistantships, Federal Work-Study and scholarships/grants available. Financial award application deadline: 2/1. *Faculty research:* Philosophy and design, urban design, design history and theory, computer-aided design and community design. Total annual research expenditures: $5,000. *Unit head:* Glenn Smith, Graduate Coordinator, 443-885-3225, E-mail: glenn.smith@morgan.edu. *Application contact:* Dr. Mark Garrison, Associate Dean, 443-885-3185, Fax: 443-885-8226, E-mail: mark.garrison@morgan.edu.

North Carolina State University, Graduate School, College of Design, Department of Landscape Architecture, Raleigh, NC 27695. Offers MLA. *Accreditation:* ASLA. *Degree requirements:* For master's, thesis optional, oral exam, project. *Entrance requirements:* For master's, GRE General Test (recommended), portfolio. Electronic applications accepted. *Faculty research:* Community development and co-operative engagement, landscape planning and design.

The Ohio State University, Graduate School, College of Engineering, Austin E. Knowlton School of Architecture, Program in Landscape Architecture, Columbus, OH 43210. Offers M Land Arch. *Accreditation:* ASLA. *Faculty:* 8. *Students:* 13 full-time (11 women), 4 part-time (3 women), 4 international. Average age 31. In 2007, 7 degrees awarded. *Degree requirements:* For master's, thesis or alternative. *Entrance requirements:* For master's, GRE General Test. Additional exam requirements/recommendations for international students: Required—TOEFL (minimum score 600 paper-based; 250 computer-based). *Application deadline:* For fall admission, 8/15 priority date for domestic students, 7/1 priority date for international students; for winter admission, 12/1 priority date for domestic students, 11/1 priority date for international students; for spring admission, 3/1 priority date for domestic students, 2/1 priority date for international students. Applications are processed on a rolling basis. Application fee: $40 ($50 for international students). Electronic applications accepted. *Financial support:* Fellowships, Federal Work-Study, institutionally sponsored loans, and unspecified assistantships available. Support available to part-time students. *Unit head:* John W. Simpson, Graduate Studies Committee Chair, 614-292-0081, Fax: 614-292-7106, E-mail: simpson.10@osu.edu. *Application contact:* 614-292-9444, Fax: 614-292-3895, E-mail: domestic.grad@osu.edu.

Oklahoma State University, College of Agricultural Science and Natural Resources, Department of Horticulture and Landscape Architecture, Stillwater, OK 74078. Offers crop science (PhD); environmental science (PhD); food science (PhD); horticulture (M Ag, MS); plant science (PhD). *Faculty:* 19 full-time (2 women), 4 part-time/adjunct (0 women). *Students:* Average age 30. 12 applicants, 33% accepted, 2 enrolled. *Degree requirements:* For master's, thesis or alternative. *Entrance requirements:* For master's and doctorate, GRE or GMAT. Additional exam requirements/recommendations for international students: Required—TOEFL. *Application deadline:* For fall admission, 3/1 priority date for international students; for spring admission, 8/1 priority date for international students. Applications are processed on a rolling basis. Application fee: $40 ($75 for international students). Electronic applications accepted. *Expenses:* Tuition, state resident: full-time $4,993; part-time $148 per credit hour. Tuition, nonresident: full-time $14,755; part-time $555 per credit hour. Tuition and fees vary according to program. *Financial support:* In 2007–08, 8 research assistantships (averaging $15,707 per year), 1 teaching assistantship (averaging $14,400 per year) were awarded; career-related internships or fieldwork, Federal Work-Study, scholarships/grants, health care benefits, tuition waivers (partial), and unspecified assistantships also available. Support available to part-time students. Financial award application deadline: 3/1. *Faculty research:* Stress and postharvest physiology; water utilization and runoff; IPM systems and nursery, turf, floriculture, vegetable, net and fruit produces and natural resources, food extraction, and processing; public garden management. *Unit head:* Dr. Dale Maronek, Head, 405-744-5414, Fax: 405-744-9709, E-mail: maronek@okstate.edu.

Penn State University Park, Graduate School, College of Arts and Architecture, Department of Landscape Architecture, State College, University Park, PA 16802-1503. Offers MLA. *Expenses:* Tuition, state resident: full-time $14,738; part-time $614 per credit. Tuition, nonresident: full-time $26,050; part-time $1,085 per credit. Tuition and fees vary according to course load, program and student level. *Unit head:* Brian A. Orland, Head, 814-865-9511, Fax: 814-863-8137, E-mail: boo1@psu.edu.

Polytechnic University of Puerto Rico, Graduate School, Hato Rey, PR 00919. Offers business administration (MBA), including general studies, management of information systems, management of international enterprises; civil engineering (ME, MS); competitiveness manufacturing (MCM, MMC, MS); computer engineering (ME, MS); electrical engineering (ME, MS); engineering management (MEM); environmental management (MEPM); landscape architecture (MLA); manufacturing engineering (ME, MS). Part-time and evening/weekend programs available. *Entrance requirements:* For master's, 3 letters of recommendation.

Rhode Island School of Design, Graduate Studies, Division of Architecture and Design, Department of Landscape Architecture, Providence, RI 02903-2784. Offers MLA. *Accreditation:* ASLA. *Degree requirements:* For master's, thesis, exhibit. *Entrance requirements:* For master's, portfolio, 3 letters of recommendation. Additional exam requirements/recommendations for international students: Required—TOEFL (minimum score 580 paper-based; 237 computer-based), IELTS (minimum score 7).

State University of New York College of Environmental Science and Forestry, Faculty of Landscape Architecture, Syracuse, NY 13210-2779. Offers community design and planning (MLA, MS); cultural landscape studies and conservation (MLA, MS); landscape and urban ecology (MLA, MS). *Accreditation:* ASLA (one or more programs are accredited). *Degree requirements:* For master's, comprehensive exam (for some programs), thesis (for some programs). *Entrance requirements:* For master's, GRE General Test, minimum GPA of 3.0. Additional exam requirements/recommendations for international students: Required—TOEFL (paper-based 550, computer-based 213, iBT 80) or IELTS (6) or STEP Aiken (Grade 1). *Faculty research:* Site analysis and design, city and regional planning, community environments.

Texas A&M University, College of Architecture, Department of Landscape Architecture and Urban Planning, College Station, TX 77843. Offers land development (MSLD); landscape architecture (MLA); urban and regional science (PhD); urban planning (MUP). *Accreditation:* ACSP (one or more programs are accredited); ASLA (one or more programs are accredited).

Landscape Architecture

Texas A&M University (continued)
Faculty: 25. *Students:* 136 full-time (46 women), 16 part-time (6 women); includes 12 minority (3 African Americans, 2 Asian Americans or Pacific Islanders, 7 Hispanic Americans), 68 international. Average age 31. 141 applicants, 84% accepted, 48 enrolled. In 2007, 35 master's, 6 doctorates awarded. Terminal master's awarded for partial completion of doctoral program. *Degree requirements:* For master's, thesis optional, professional internship; for doctorate, comprehensive exam, thesis/dissertation, methods statistics seminar. *Entrance requirements:* For master's, GMAT or GRE General Test, portfolio (MLA), minimum GPA of 3.0; for doctorate, GMAT or GRE General Test. Additional exam requirements/recommendations for international students: Required—TOEFL. *Application deadline:* For fall admission, 2/1 priority date for domestic students; for spring admission, 8/1 for domestic students. Applications are processed on a rolling basis. Application fee: $50 ($75 for international students). Electronic applications accepted. *Expenses:* Tuition, state resident: full-time $6,129. Tuition, nonresident: full-time $11,689. Tuition and fees vary according to course load. *Financial support:* In 2007–08, fellowships with tuition reimbursements (averaging $1,000 per year), research assistantships with partial tuition reimbursements (averaging $8,100 per year), teaching assistantships with partial tuition reimbursements (averaging $11,250 per year) were awarded; career-related internships or fieldwork, institutionally sponsored loans, and scholarships/grants also available. Financial award application deadline: 4/1; financial award applicants required to submit FAFSA. *Faculty research:* Erosion control/water quality, geographic information systems/spatial information technology, transport hazards, international sustainable development. *Unit head:* Dr. Walter Peacock, Head, 979-845-1019, Fax: 979-862-1784. *Application contact:* Marie Prihoda, Graduate Office, 979-845-6582, Fax: 979-845-4491, E-mail: mprihoda@archone.tamu.edu.

Texas Tech University, Graduate School, College of Agricultural Sciences and Natural Resources, Department of Landscape Architecture, Lubbock, TX 79409. Offers MLA. *Accreditation:* ASLA. Part-time programs available. *Faculty:* 6 full-time (1 woman). *Students:* 9 full-time (4 women), 5 part-time (1 woman), 3 international. Average age 29. 11 applicants, 45% accepted, 3 enrolled. In 2007, 2 degrees awarded. *Entrance requirements:* For master's, GRE General Test. Additional exam requirements/recommendations for international students: Required—TOEFL (minimum score 550 paper-based; 213 computer-based). *Application deadline:* For fall admission, 3/1 priority date for international students; for spring admission, 11/1 priority date for international students. Applications are processed on a rolling basis. Application fee: $50 ($60 for international students). Electronic applications accepted. *Expenses:* Tuition, state resident: part-time $373 per credit hour. Tuition, nonresident: part-time $651 per credit hour. Tuition and fees vary according to program. *Financial support:* In 2007–08, 9 students received support; research assistantships with partial tuition reimbursements available, teaching assistantships with partial tuition reimbursements available, Federal Work-Study and institutionally sponsored loans available. Support available to part-time students. Financial award application deadline: 4/15; financial award applicants required to submit FAFSA. *Faculty research:* Computer-aided design, environmental planning and design, therapeutic landscapes, geographic information systems in planning, creative problem solving; site planning. Total annual research expenditures: $15,206. *Unit head:* Alon Kvashny, Chair, 806-742-2894, Fax: 806-742-0770, E-mail: alon.kvashny@ttu.edu. *Application contact:* John C. Billing, Graduate Coordinator, 806-742-2858, Fax: 806-742-0770, E-mail: john.billing@ttu.edu.

The University of Arizona, Graduate College, College of Architecture and Landscape Architecture, School of Landscape Architecture, Tucson, AZ 85721. Offers ML Arch. *Accreditation:* ASLA. *Students:* 39 full-time (27 women), 3 part-time (2 women); includes 2 minority (both Hispanic Americans), 1 international. Average age 33. 38 applicants, 61% accepted, 13 enrolled. In 2007, 20 degrees awarded. *Degree requirements:* For master's, thesis. *Entrance requirements:* For master's, GRE General Test, minimum GPA of 3.2, 3 letters of reference, statement of intent, portfolio. Additional exam requirements/recommendations for international students: Required—TOEFL (minimum score 600 paper-based). *Application deadline:* For fall admission, 1/15 for domestic and international students. Applications are processed on a rolling basis. Application fee: $50. Electronic applications accepted. *Financial support:* In 2007–08, 14 students received support, including 7 fellowships (averaging $3,000 per year), 3 research assistantships with full tuition reimbursements available, 2 teaching assistantships with full tuition reimbursements available; career-related internships or fieldwork, scholarships/grants, health care benefits, tuition waivers (full), and unspecified assistantships also available. Financial award application deadline: 1/31. *Faculty research:* Children's environments, cultural landscapes, arid lands plant communities, geographic information systems and science (GS), computer-aided drafting and design (CAD). Total annual research expenditures: $737,892. *Unit head:* Prof. Ronald R. Stoltz, Director, 520-626-7730, Fax: 520-626-6448, E-mail: rstoltz@u.arizona.edu. *Application contact:* Debi A. Romero, Administrative Assistant, 520-621-1004, Fax: 520-626-6448, E-mail: landarch@u.arizona.edu.

The University of British Columbia, Faculty of Graduate Studies, Faculty of Applied Science, School of Architecture and Landscape Architecture, Programs in Landscape Architecture, Vancouver, BC V6T 1Z1, Canada. Offers MASLA, MLA. *Accreditation:* ASLA (one or more programs are accredited). *Degree requirements:* For master's, comprehensive exam or thesis. *Entrance requirements:* For master's, portfolio. Additional exam requirements/recommendations for international students: Required—TOEFL (minimum score 560 paper-based; 220 computer-based). Electronic applications accepted. *Faculty research:* Landscape design, urban-rural interface, urban ecology, sustainable development, collaborative planning and community forestry.

University of California, Berkeley, Graduate Division, College of Environmental Design, Department of Landscape Architecture and Environmental Planning, Program in Landscape Architecture, Berkeley, CA 94720-1500. Offers environmental planning (MLA); landscape design and site planning (MLA); urban and community design (MLA); MLA/M Arch; MLA/MCP. *Accreditation:* ASLA. *Faculty:* 13 full-time, 6 part-time/adjunct. *Degree requirements:* For master's, professional project or thesis. *Entrance requirements:* For master's, GRE General Test, minimum GPA of 3.0, portfolio, 3 letters of recommendation. *Application deadline:* For fall admission, 1/5 for domestic students. Application fee: $70 ($90 for international students). *Financial support:* Fellowships, research assistantships, teaching assistantships, career-related internships or fieldwork, Federal Work-Study, institutionally sponsored loans, and unspecified assistantships available. *Application contact:* Yong No, Student Affairs Officer, 510-642-2965, Fax: 510-643-6166, E-mail: laepgrad@berkeley.edu.

University of Colorado Denver, College of Architecture and Planning, Program in Landscape Architecture, Denver, CO 80217-3364. Offers MLA. *Accreditation:* ASLA. Part-time programs available. *Faculty:* 9 full-time (4 women). *Students:* 88 full-time (42 women), 9 part-time (7 women); includes 1 minority (Asian American or Pacific Islander), 6 international. Average age 30. 68 applicants, 59% accepted, 30 enrolled. In 2007, 23 degrees awarded. *Degree requirements:* For master's, thesis optional. *Entrance requirements:* For master's, GRE or minimum GPA of 3.0, portfolio. Additional exam requirements/recommendations for international students: Required—TOEFL (minimum score 550 paper-based; 213 computer-based). *Application deadline:* For fall admission, 3/15 for domestic students; for spring admission, 10/1 for domestic students. Application fee: $50 ($75 for international students). *Financial support:* Teaching assistantships, career-related internships or fieldwork, Federal Work-Study, institutionally sponsored loans, and scholarships/grants available. Financial award application deadline: 3/1; financial award applicants required to submit FAFSA. *Faculty research:* Landscape architectural design theory and process, urban design, advanced landscape technologies, landscape planning. *Unit head:* Austin Allen, Chair, 303-556-8564, Fax: 303-556-3687, E-mail: austin.allen@cudenver.edu. *Application contact:* Heather Zertuche, Administrative Assistant II, 303-556-3382, Fax: 303-556-3687, E-mail: anpdeansoffice@storm.cudenver.edu.

University of Florida, Graduate School, College of Design, Construction and Planning, Department of Landscape Architecture, Gainesville, FL 32611. Offers MLA, PhD. *Accreditation:* ASLA. Part-time programs available. *Faculty:* 5 full-time (2 women). *Students:* 15 (8 women); includes 2 minority (1 African American, 1 Asian American or Pacific Islander). In 2007, 11 degrees awarded. *Degree requirements:* For master's, thesis, internship. *Entrance requirements:* For master's, GRE General Test, minimum GPA of 3.0. *Application deadline:* For fall admission, 2/15 priority date for domestic students. Applications are processed on a rolling basis. Application fee: $30. Electronic applications accepted. *Expenses:* Tuition, state resident: full-time $7,478. Tuition, nonresident: full-time $22,603. *Financial support:* In 2007–08, 1 research assistantship (averaging $17,931 per year), 3 teaching assistantships (averaging $22,245 per year) were awarded; fellowships, career-related internships or fieldwork also available. *Faculty research:* Landscape reclamation, community development, landscape ethics, land-use planning, international conservation. *Unit head:* Prof. Robert R. Grist, Chair, 352-392-6098 Ext. 324, Fax: 352-392-7266, E-mail: grist@ufl.edu. *Application contact:* Juanita Melchior, Coordinator, 352-392-0252 Ext. 303, Fax: 352-392-7266, E-mail: melchior@dcp.ufl.edu.

University of Georgia, Graduate School, College of Environment and Design, School of Environmental Design, Program in Landscape Architecture, Athens, GA 30602. Offers MLA. *Accreditation:* ASLA. *Students:* 40 full-time (26 women), 11 part-time (4 women); includes 2 minority (both Hispanic Americans), 2 international. 61 applicants, 38% accepted, 13 enrolled. In 2007, 15 degrees awarded. *Degree requirements:* For master's, thesis. *Entrance requirements:* For master's, GRE General Test. Additional exam requirements/recommendations for international students: Required—TOEFL. *Application deadline:* For fall admission, 7/1 for domestic students; for spring admission, 11/15 priority date for domestic students. Application fee: $50. Electronic applications accepted. *Expenses:* Contact institution. *Financial support:* In 2007–08, 20 students received support; fellowships, research assistantships, teaching assistantships, tuition waivers (partial) and unspecified assistantships available. *Unit head:* Prof. Brian LaHale, Graduate Coordinator, 706-542-4704, Fax: 706-542-4236, E-mail: blahale@uga.edu.

University of Guelph, Graduate Program Services, Ontario Agricultural College, School of Environmental Design and Rural Development, Landscape Architecture Program, Guelph, ON N1G 2W1, Canada. Offers MLA. *Accreditation:* ASLA. *Faculty:* 11 full-time (4 women), 10 part-time/adjunct (6 women). *Students:* 49 full-time (31 women), 6 part-time (5 women). 42 applicants, 74% accepted, 16 enrolled. In 2007, 13 degrees awarded. *Degree requirements:* For master's, thesis. *Entrance requirements:* For master's, minimum B- average during previous 2 years of honors degree, portfolio and questionnaire. Additional exam requirements/recommendations for international students: Required—TOEFL (minimum score 600 paper-based; 250 computer-based; 89 iBT), IELTS (minimum score 7), Canadian Academic Language Assessment, Michigan English Language Assessment Battery. *Application deadline:* For winter admission, 2/1 for domestic and international students. Applications are processed on a rolling basis. Application fee: $85. Electronic applications accepted. *Financial support:* In 2007–08, 40 students received support, including 17 research assistantships (averaging $2,251 per year), 17 teaching assistantships (averaging $4,835 per year). *Faculty research:* Land planning, human factors in design, landscape assessment (biophysical and cultural), landscape ecology and restoration, community design. *Application contact:* Diana Foolen, Secretary, 519-824-4120 Ext. 56576, Fax: 519-767-1686, E-mail: dfoolen@uoguelph.ca.

University of Idaho, College of Graduate Studies, College of Art and Architecture, Department of Landscape Architecture, Moscow, ID 83844-2282. Offers MS. *Students:* 9. Average age 25. In 2007, 3 degrees awarded. Application fee: $55 ($60 for international students). *Unit head:* Stephen R. Drown, Chair, 208-885-7902, E-mail: larch@uidaho.edu.

University of Illinois at Urbana–Champaign, Graduate College, College of Fine and Applied Arts, Department of Landscape Architecture, Champaign, IL 61820. Offers MLA, PhD, MLA/MUP. *Accreditation:* ASLA. *Faculty:* 11 full-time (5 women). *Students:* 34 full-time (21 women), 2 part-time (both women); includes 2 minority (both African Americans), 8 international. 58 applicants, 40% accepted, 8 enrolled. In 2007, 3 master's awarded. *Entrance requirements:* For master's, GRE, minimum GPA of 3.0. *Application deadline:* For fall admission, 1/15 for domestic students. Applications are processed on a rolling basis. Application fee: $60 ($75 for international students). Electronic applications accepted. *Financial support:* In 2007–08, 3 fellowships, 10 research assistantships, 15 teaching assistantships were awarded; career-related internships or fieldwork and tuition waivers (full and partial) also available. Financial award application deadline: 2/15. *Unit head:* James L. Wescoat, Head, 217-333-0176, Fax: 217-244-4568, E-mail: wescoat@uiuc.edu. *Application contact:* Connie Coleman, Administrative Secretary, 214-244-1699, Fax: 214-244-4568, E-mail: cjcolema@uiuc.edu.

University of Manitoba, Faculty of Graduate Studies, Faculty of Architecture, Department of Landscape Architecture, Winnipeg, MB R3T 2N2, Canada. Offers M Land Arch. *Accreditation:* ASLA. *Degree requirements:* For master's, thesis or alternative.

University of Massachusetts Amherst, Graduate School, College of Natural Resources and the Environment, Department of Landscape Architecture and Regional Planning, Program in Landscape Architecture, Amherst, MA 01003. Offers MLA, MLA/MRP. *Accreditation:* ASLA. Part-time programs available. *Students:* 27 full-time (16 women), 2 part-time (1 woman), 3 international. Average age 32. 59 applicants, 71% accepted, 10 enrolled. In 2007, 8 degrees awarded. *Degree requirements:* For master's, thesis or alternative. *Entrance requirements:* For master's, GRE General Test, portfolio. Additional exam requirements/recommendations for international students: Required—TOEFL (minimum score 530 paper-based; 197 computer-based). *Application deadline:* For fall admission, 2/1 priority date for domestic and international students. Applications are processed on a rolling basis. Application fee: $50 ($65 for international students). Electronic applications accepted. *Expenses:* Tuition, state resident: full-time $2,640; part-time $110 per credit. Tuition, nonresident: full-time $9,936; part-time $414 per credit. Required fees: $7,455. One-time fee: $332. Tuition and fees vary according to course load, campus/location, program and reciprocity agreements. *Financial support:* Fellowships with full tuition reimbursements, research assistantships with full tuition reimbursements, teaching assistantships with full tuition reimbursements, career-related internships or fieldwork, Federal Work-Study, scholarships/grants, traineeships, and unspecified assistantships available. Support available to part-time students. Financial award application deadline: 2/1. *Unit head:* Dr. Mark Lindhult, Director, 413-545-2266, Fax: 413-545-1772, E-mail: lindhult@larp.umass.edu.

University of Massachusetts Amherst, Graduate School, College of Natural Resources and the Environment, Department of Landscape Architecture and Regional Planning, Program in Landscape Architecture and Regional Planning, Amherst, MA 01003. Offers MLA/MRP. *Accreditation:* ACSP; ASLA. Part-time programs available. *Students:* 6 full-time (3 women), 3 part-time (2 women), 2 international. Average age 31. 10 applicants, 50% accepted, 1 enrolled. *Entrance requirements:* Additional exam requirements/recommendations for international students: Required—TOEFL (minimum score 530 paper-based; 197 computer-based). *Application deadline:* For fall admission, 2/1 priority date for domestic and international students. Applications are processed on a rolling basis. Application fee: $50 ($65 for international students). Electronic applications accepted. *Expenses:* Tuition, state resident: full-time $2,640; part-time $110 per credit. Tuition, nonresident: full-time $9,936; part-time $414 per credit. Required fees: $7,455. One-time fee: $332. Tuition and fees vary according to course load, campus/location, program and reciprocity agreements. *Financial support:* Fellowships with full tuition reimbursements, research assistantships with full tuition reimbursements, teaching assistantships with full tuition reimbursements, career-related internships or fieldwork, Federal Work-Study, scholarships/grants, traineeships, and unspecified assistantships available. Support available to part-time students. Financial award application deadline: 2/1. *Unit head:* Dr. Robert Ryan, Director, 413-545-2266, Fax: 413-545-1772.

University of Michigan, School of Natural Resources and Environment, Program in Landscape Architecture, Ann Arbor, MI 48109. Offers MLA, PhD, MLA/M Arch, MLA/MBA, MLA/MUP. Offered through the Horace H. Rackham School of Graduate Studies. *Accreditation:* ASLA (one or more programs are accredited). *Faculty:* 4 full-time (3 women). *Students:* 40 full-time (29 women); includes 8 minority (all Asian Americans or Pacific Islanders), 5 international. Average age 27. 52 applicants, 77% accepted. In 2007, 11 degrees awarded. *Degree* *requirements:* For master's, thesis, practicum or group project; for doctorate, comprehensive exam, thesis/dissertation, oral defense of dissertation, preliminary exam. *Entrance requirements:* For master's, GRE General Test; for doctorate, GRE General Test, master's degree, portfolio. Additional exam requirements/recommendations for international students: Required—TOEFL (minimum score 560 paper-based; 220 computer-based; 84 iBT), TOEFL (paper-based 560, computer-based 220) or IELTS (6.5). *Application deadline:* For fall admission, 1/5 priority date for domestic and international students. Applications are processed on a rolling basis. Application fee: $60 ($75 for international students). *Financial support:* Fellowships with tuition reimbursements, research assistantships with tuition reimbursements, teaching assistantships with tuition reimbursements, career-related internships or fieldwork, Federal Work-Study, institutionally sponsored loans, scholarships/grants, health care benefits, and unspecified assistantships available. Support available to part-time students. Financial award application deadline: 1/5; financial award applicants required to submit FAFSA. *Faculty research:* Historic landscape documentation, ADA and landscape architecture, landscape perception, sustainable design, ecological design. Total annual research expenditures: $139,000. *Unit head:* Chris Ellis, Professor, 734-764-6453, Fax: 734-734-2195, E-mail: cdellis@umich.edu. *Application contact:* Graduate Admissions Team, 734-764-6453, Fax: 734-936-2195, E-mail: snre.gradteam@umich.edu.

University of Minnesota, Twin Cities Campus, Graduate School, College of Design, Department of Landscape Architecture, Minneapolis, MN 55455-0213. Offers MLA, MS. *Accreditation:* ASLA (one or more programs are accredited). *Faculty:* 8 full-time (3 women), 11 part-time/adjunct (2 women). *Students:* 75 full-time (37 women); includes 3 minority (2 Asian Americans or Pacific Islanders, 1 Hispanic American), 5 international. Average age 28. 70 applicants, 37% accepted, 25 enrolled. In 2007, 27 degrees awarded. *Degree requirements:* For master's, thesis (MS). *Entrance requirements:* For master's, GRE General Test (MS), suggested GPA of 3.0. Additional exam requirements/recommendations for international students: Required—TOEFL (minimum score 550 paper-based; 213 computer-based; 79 iBT). *Application deadline:* For fall admission, 1/15 for domestic and international students. Application fee: $55. Electronic applications accepted. *Expenses:* Contact institution. *Financial support:* In 2007–08, 20 fellowships (averaging $2,000 per year), 6 research assistantships with partial tuition reimbursements (averaging $6,000 per year), 30 teaching assistantships with partial tuition reimbursements (averaging $3,000 per year) were awarded; career-related internships or fieldwork, Federal Work-Study, institutionally sponsored loans, and tuition waivers (full and partial) also available. Financial award application deadline: 1/15. *Faculty research:* Landscape history, landscape ecology, urban design, sustainable design, public art/space. Total annual research expenditures: $1.1 million. *Unit head:* Lance Neckar, Department Head and Professor, 612-625-6596, Fax: 612-625-0710, E-mail: necka001@umn.edu. *Application contact:* Rebecca Krinke, Associate Professor and Director of Graduate Studies, 612-625-6860, Fax: 612-625-0710, E-mail: gsland@umn.edu.

University of New Mexico, Graduate School, School of Architecture and Planning, Program in Landscape Architecture, Albuquerque, NM 87131-2039. Offers MLA. *Accreditation:* ASLA. Part-time programs available. *Students:* 40 full-time (22 women), 10 part-time (7 women); includes 5 minority (1 American Indian/Alaska Native, 1 Asian American or Pacific Islander, 3 Hispanic Americans), 6 international. Average age 34. 41 applicants, 63% accepted, 18 enrolled. In 2007, 5 degrees awarded. *Degree requirements:* For master's, thesis optional, portfolio review, thesis studio. *Entrance requirements:* For master's, minimum GPA of 3.0. Additional exam requirements/recommendations for international students: Required—TOEFL. *Application deadline:* For fall admission, 2/15 priority date for domestic students; for spring admission, 11/1 for domestic students. Applications are processed on a rolling basis. Application fee: $50. *Expenses:* Contact institution. *Financial support:* In 2007–08, 25 students received support, including 10 fellowships (averaging $1,000 per year), 10 research assistantships with partial tuition reimbursements available (averaging $3,000 per year); scholarships/grants, health care benefits, tuition waivers (partial), and unspecified assistantships also available. Financial award application deadline: 3/1; financial award applicants required to submit FAFSA. *Faculty research:* Cultural landscape studies, arid landscape studies, urban design and sustainability, landscape and infrastructure. *Unit head:* Dr. Alfred Simon, Director, 505-277-4120, Fax: 505-277-0897, E-mail: asimon@unm.edu. *Application contact:* Patricia Walter, Senior Academic Advisor, 505-277-2910, Fax: 505-277-0076, E-mail: pwalter@unm.edu.

University of Oklahoma, Graduate College, College of Architecture, Division of Landscape Architecture, Norman, OK 73019-0390. Offers MLA, MRCP/MLA. *Accreditation:* ASLA.Part-time programs available. *Faculty:* 1 full-time (0 women). *Students:* 16 full-time (6 women), 3 part-time (2 women); includes 1 minority (Hispanic American), 1 international. 8 applicants, 100% accepted, 2 enrolled. In 2007, 5 degrees awarded. *Degree requirements:* For master's, comprehensive exam, portfolio, project. *Entrance requirements:* For master's, GRE General Test, portfolio. Additional exam requirements/recommendations for international students: Required—TOEFL (minimum score 550 paper-based; 213 computer-based). *Application deadline:* For fall admission, 4/1 for domestic and international students; for spring admission, 11/1 for domestic students, 9/1 for international students. Applications are processed on a rolling basis. Application fee: $40 ($90 for international students). Electronic applications accepted. *Expenses:* Tuition, state resident: full-time $3,451; part-time $144 per credit hour. Tuition, nonresident: full-time $12,432; part-time $518 per credit hour. Required fees: $1,925; $70 per credit hour. $122 per semester. *Financial support:* In 2007–08, 15 students received support, including 3 research assistantships with partial tuition reimbursements available (averaging $9,450 per year); teaching assistantships with tuition reimbursements available, career-related internships or fieldwork, Federal Work-Study, institutionally sponsored loans, scholarships/grants, and unspecified assistantships also available. Financial award applicants required to submit FAFSA. *Faculty research:* Sustainable urban design; greenways; community based design and planning; site design and site planning; meaning in built environments. *Unit head:* Thomas Schurch, Director, 405-325-2444, Fax: 405-325-5956, E-mail: schurch@ou.edu.

University of Oregon, Graduate School, School of Architecture and Allied Arts, Department of Landscape Architecture, Eugene, OR 97403. Offers MLA. *Accreditation:* ASLA. *Faculty:* 8 full-time (1 woman). *Students:* 36 full-time (24 women), 5 part-time (4 women); all minorities (1 Asian American or Pacific Islander, 2 Hispanic Americans), 1 international. 30 applicants, 43% accepted. In 2007, 7 degrees awarded. *Degree requirements:* For master's, thesis or alternative, project. *Entrance requirements:* For master's, portfolio. Additional exam requirements/recommendations for international students: Required—TOEFL. *Application deadline:* For fall admission, 2/15 for domestic students. Application fee: $50. *Financial support:* In 2007–08, 12 teaching assistantships were awarded; fellowships, research assistantships, career-related internships or fieldwork, Federal Work-Study, and institutionally sponsored loans also available. Support available to part-time students. *Faculty research:* Design, landscape planning analysis, history and theory, computer applications. Total annual research expenditures: $200,000. *Unit head:* Stan Jones, Head, 541-346-3634. *Application contact:* Chad Bush, Admissions Contact, 541-346-1433, E-mail: chad@uoregon.edu.

University of Pennsylvania, School of Design, Program in Landscape Architecture and Regional Planning, Philadelphia, PA 19104. Offers landscape architecture and regional planning (MLA); landscape studies (Certificate). *Accreditation:* ASLA (one or more programs are accredited). Part-time programs available. *Degree requirements:* For master's, thesis optional. *Entrance requirements:* For master's, GRE, portfolio. Additional exam requirements/recommendations for international students: Required—TOEFL. *Faculty research:* Early landscape architecture, natural distribution through landslides, urban gardens, landscape registration, watershed studies.

See Close-Up on page 175.

University of Southern California, Graduate School, School of Architecture, Program in Historic Preservation, Los Angeles, CA 90089. Offers MHP. Part-time programs available. *Faculty:* 50 full-time (25 women), 50 part-time/adjunct (25 women). *Students:* 9 full-time (5 women), 6 part-time (5 women); includes 1 minority (Hispanic American), 1 international. 12 applicants, 92% accepted. In 2007, 5 master's awarded. *Entrance requirements:* For master's, GRE. *Application deadline:* For fall admission, 1/15 priority date for domestic students. Applications are processed on a rolling basis. Application fee: $85. *Financial support:* In 2007–08, fellowships with tuition reimbursements (averaging $15,000 per year); career-related internships or fieldwork, Federal Work-Study, and scholarships/grants also available. Support available to part-time students. Financial award applicants required to submit FAFSA. *Unit head:* Dr. Kenneth Breisch, Head, 213-740-2311.

University of Southern California, Graduate School, School of Architecture, Program in Landscape Architecture, Los Angeles, CA 90089. Offers ML Arch. *Faculty:* 50 full-time (25 women), 50 part-time/adjunct (25 women). *Students:* 7 full-time (5 women); includes 1 minority (Asian American or Pacific Islander), 6 international. 25 applicants, 76% accepted. In 2007, 2 degrees awarded. *Entrance requirements:* For master's, GRE General Test. *Application deadline:* For fall admission, 1/15 priority date for domestic students. Applications are processed on a rolling basis. Application fee: $85. *Financial support:* In 2007–08, fellowships (averaging $18,300 per year); career-related internships or fieldwork, Federal Work-Study, and scholarships/grants also available. Support available to part-time students. `Financial award application deadline: 2/15; financial award applicants required to submit FAFSA. *Faculty research:* Urban landscapes, plant ecology, city and urban planning. *Unit head:* Robert Harris, Head, 213-740-2311.

See Close-Up on page 177.

The University of Tennessee, Graduate School, College of Architecture and Design, Program in Landscape Architecture, Knoxville, TN 37996. Offers landscape architecture (MLA); landscape architecture (research) (MA, MS). *Degree requirements:* For master's, oral exam, project and thesis optional (MLA); oral exam and thesis (MA, MS). *Entrance requirements:* For master's, GRE General Test, completed application form, transcripts of undergraduate and/or graduate work, minimum GPA of 3.0, 3 letters of recommendation, samples of portfolio work. Additional exam requirements/recommendations for international students: Required—TOEFL (minimum score 550 paper-based).

The University of Texas at Arlington, Graduate School, School of Architecture, Program in Landscape Architecture, Arlington, TX 76019. Offers MLA. *Accreditation:* ASLA. Part-time and evening/weekend programs available. *Students:* 27 full-time (15 women), 16 part-time (9 women); includes 3 minority (1 African American, 1 Asian American or Pacific Islander, 1 Hispanic American), 9 international. In 2007, 5 degrees awarded. *Degree requirements:* For master's, thesis. *Entrance requirements:* For master's, GRE General Test, minimum GPA of 3.0, portfolio. Additional exam requirements/recommendations for international students: Required—TOEFL (minimum score 550 paper-based; 213 computer-based). *Application deadline:* For fall admission, 6/16 for domestic students. Applications are processed on a rolling basis. Application fee: $35 ($50 for international students). *Expenses:* Tuition, state resident: full-time $5,934. Tuition, nonresident: full-time $10,938. *Financial support:* In 2007–08, 1 research assistantship with partial tuition reimbursement (averaging $4,824 per year), 2 teaching assistantships with partial tuition reimbursements (averaging $4,824 per year) were awarded; fellowships, career-related internships or fieldwork and tuition waivers (partial) also available. Financial award application deadline: 6/1; financial award applicants required to submit FAFSA. *Unit head:* Dr. Pat D. Taylor, Program Director, 817-272-2801, Fax: 817-272-5098, E-mail: pdt@uta.edu.

University of Virginia, School of Architecture, Department of Architecture and Landscape Architecture, Program in Landscape Architecture, Charlottesville, VA 22903. Offers M Land Arch. *Accreditation:* ASLA. *Students:* 41 full-time (30 women); includes 1 minority (Asian American or Pacific Islander), 4 international. Average age 29. 116 applicants, 34% accepted, 13 enrolled. In 2007, 7 degrees awarded. *Entrance requirements:* For master's, GRE General Test. Additional exam requirements/recommendations for international students: Required—TOEFL (minimum score 600 paper-based; 250 computer-based). Application fee: $60. *Financial support:* Applicants required to submit FAFSA. *Faculty research:* History of landscape architecture. *Application contact:* Tracy Brookman, Admissions Officer, 434-924-6442, E-mail: arch-admissions@virginia.edu.

University of Washington, Graduate School, College of Architecture and Urban Planning, Department of Landscape Architecture, Seattle, WA 98195. Offers MLA. *Accreditation:* ASLA. *Degree requirements:* For master's, thesis. *Entrance requirements:* For master's, GRE, minimum GPA of 3.0. Additional exam requirements/recommendations for international students: Required—TOEFL. *Faculty research:* Cultural landscape, history of gardens, urban stream restoration, campus master planning, urban ecology.

University of Wisconsin–Madison, Graduate School, College of Agricultural and Life Sciences, Department of Landscape Architecture, Madison, WI 53076. Offers MA, MS. Part-time programs available. *Degree requirements:* For master's, thesis. *Entrance requirements:* For master's, GRE (recommended), samples of creative work. Additional exam requirements/recommendations for international students: Required—TOEFL (minimum score 580 paper-based; 237 computer-based). Electronic applications accepted. *Faculty research:* Urban/landscape ecology, land restoration, cultural resource preservation, community design, conservation design.

Utah State University, School of Graduate Studies, College of Humanities, Arts and Social Sciences, Department of Landscape Architecture and Environmental Planning, Logan, UT 84322. Offers bioregional planning (MS); landscape architecture (MLA). *Accreditation:* ASLA (one or more programs are accredited). *Degree requirements:* For master's, thesis. *Entrance requirements:* For master's, GRE General Test, minimum GPA of 3.0. Additional exam requirements/recommendations for international students: Required—TOEFL. *Faculty research:* Visual resource management, planning for wildlife, agricultural land preservation, watershed planning, community planning and design.

Virginia Polytechnic Institute and State University, Graduate School, College of Architecture and Urban Studies, Department of Landscape Architecture, Blacksburg, VA 24061. Offers MLA. *Accreditation:* ASLA. *Entrance requirements:* For master's, GRE. Additional exam requirements/recommendations for international students: Required—TOEFL (minimum score 550 paper-based; 213 computer-based). Electronic applications accepted. *Faculty research:* Land planning issues in rural areas, landscape perception and visual management theory, universal design, accessibility, ecological and cultural processes.

Virginia Polytechnic Institute and State University, Graduate School, College of Architecture and Urban Studies, School of Public and International Affairs, Blacksburg, VA 24061. Offers environmental planning and policy (MURP); government and international affairs (MPIA); housing, community and economic development (MURP); international development planning (MURP); land use and physical planning (MURP); planning, governance and globalization (PhD), including environmental planning and landscape analysis, physical planning and urban design, public and international affairs, urban and environmental design and planning; urban and regional planning (MURP). *Accreditation:* ACSP. *Entrance requirements:* Additional exam requirements/recommendations for international students: Required—TOEFL (minimum score 550 paper-based; 213 computer-based). Electronic applications accepted. *Faculty research:* Design theory, environmental planning, town planning, transportation planning.

Washington State University, Graduate School, College of Agricultural, Human, and Natural Resource Sciences, Department of Horticulture and Landscape Architecture, Pullman, WA 99164. Offers horticulture (MS, PhD); landscape architecture (MSLA). Part-time programs available. *Faculty:* 24. *Students:* 19 full-time (9 women), 5 part-time (3 women); includes 1 minority (Hispanic American), 6 international. Average age 32. 31 applicants, 52% accepted, 8 enrolled. In 2007, 6 degrees awarded. *Degree requirements:* For master's, comprehensive exam (for some programs), thesis (for some programs), oral exam; for doctorate, comprehensive exam,

Landscape Architecture

Washington State University (continued)

thesis/dissertation, oral exam, written exam. *Entrance requirements:* For master's and doctorate, GRE General Test, GRE Subject Test, minimum GPA of 3.0, 3 letters of recommendation. Additional exam requirements/recommendations for international students: Required—TOEFL (minimum score 550 paper-based). *Application deadline:* For fall admission, 2/1 priority date for domestic students, 3/1 for international students; for spring admission, 9/1 for domestic students, 7/1 for international students. Applications are processed on a rolling basis. Application fee: $50. Electronic applications accepted. *Financial support:* In 2007–08, 16 students received support, including 4 fellowships (averaging $2,275 per year), 5 research assistantships with full and partial tuition reimbursements available (averaging $13,917 per year), 7 teaching assistantships with full and partial tuition reimbursements available (averaging $13,056 per year); career-related internships or fieldwork, Federal Work-Study, institutionally sponsored loans, and health care benefits also available. Financial award application deadline: 4/1; financial award applicants required to submit FAFSA. *Faculty research:* Post-harvest physiology, genetics/plant breeding, molecular biology. Total annual research expenditures: $2 million. *Unit head:* N. Richard Knowles, Chair, 509-335-9502, Fax: 509-335-8690, E-mail: rknowles@wsu.edu. *Application contact:* Graduate School Admissions, 800-GRADWSU, Fax: 509-335-1949, E-mail: gradsch@wsu.edu.

Washington State University Spokane, Graduate Programs, Interdisciplinary Design Institute, Spokane, WA 99210-1495. Offers architecture (M Arch, MS); design (Dr DES); interior design (MA); landscape architecture (MS). Part-time programs available. *Faculty:* 11 full-time (3 women), 3 part-time/adjunct (2 women). *Students:* 35 full-time (22 women), 5 part-time (3 women); includes 5 minority (2 American Indian/Alaska Native, 2 Asian Americans or Pacific Islanders, 1 Hispanic American), 2 international. Average age 35. 61 applicants, 67% accepted, 18 enrolled. *Degree requirements:* For master's, comprehensive exam (for some programs), thesis (for some programs); for doctorate, comprehensive exam, thesis/dissertation. *Entrance requirements:* For master's, minimum GPA of 3.0, portfolio of design work, 3 letters of recommendation (M Arch); for doctorate, minimum graduate GPA of 3.5. Additional exam requirements/recommendations for international students: Required—TOEFL (minimum score 550 paper-based; 213 computer-based). *Application deadline:* For fall admission, 4/1 priority date for domestic students, 3/1 for international students. Application fee: $50. *Financial support:* In 2007–08, 30 students received support, including 10 research assistantships with full and partial tuition reimbursements available (averaging $13,917 per year), teaching assistantships with full and partial tuition reimbursements available (averaging $13,056 per year). *Faculty research:* Environment-behavior relationships, land use and environmental planning, urban space as interior design, art and architectural aesthetics. Total annual research expenditures: $62,011. *Unit head:* Dr. Nancy H. Blossom, Director, 509-358-7515, E-mail: blossom@wsu.edu. *Application contact:* Graduate School Admissions, 800-GRADWSU, Fax: 509-335-1949, E-mail: gradsch@wsu.edu.

Lighting Design

The New School: A University, Parsons The New School for Design, Program in Lighting Design, New York, NY 10011. Offers MFA. *Accreditation:* NASAD. *Faculty:* 1 full-time (0 women), 13 part-time/adjunct (6 women). *Students:* 39 full-time (27 women); includes 1 minority (Asian American or Pacific Islander), 28 international. Average age 28. In 2007, 24 degrees awarded. *Entrance requirements:* For master's, portfolio. Additional exam requirements/recommendations for international students: Required—TOEFL (minimum score 580 paper-based; 237 computer-based; 93 iBT). *Application deadline:* For fall admission, 2/1 priority date for domestic students. Applications are processed on a rolling basis. Application fee: $50. *Financial support:* Federal Work-Study, scholarships/grants, and tuition waivers (partial) available. Financial award application deadline: 3/1; financial award applicants required to submit FAFSA. *Unit head:* Kent Kleinman, Chair, 212-229-8955 Ext. 2953, E-mail: kleinmak@newschool.edu. *Application contact:* Anthony Padilla, Director of Admissions, 212-229-8989 Ext. 4023, Fax: 212-229-8975, E-mail: padillaa@newschool.edu.

See Close-Up on page 165.

Rensselaer Polytechnic Institute, Graduate School, School of Architecture, Program in Lighting, Troy, NY 12180-3590. Offers MS. Part-time programs available. *Faculty:* 5 full-time (2 women), 5 part-time/adjunct (3 women). *Students:* Average age 26. 14 applicants, 86% accepted, 10 enrolled. In 2007, 12 degrees awarded. Terminal master's awarded for partial completion of doctoral program. *Degree requirements:* For master's, comprehensive exam (for some programs), thesis. *Entrance requirements:* For master's, GRE General Test, letters of recommendation, resumé, portfolio or sample of research writing. Additional exam requirements/recommendations for international students: Required—TOEFL (minimum score 570 paper-based; 230 computer-based), IELTS (minimum score 7). *Application deadline:* For fall admission, 1/15 priority date for domestic and international students. Applications are processed on a rolling basis. Application fee: $75. Electronic applications accepted. *Expenses:* Tuition: Full-time $34,900; part-time $1,454 per credit. Required fees: $1,802. *Financial support:* In 2007–08, 12 students received support, including 9 research assistantships with full tuition reimbursements available (averaging $14,500 per year); fellowships with full tuition reimbursements available, teaching assistantships, career-related internships or fieldwork, institutionally sponsored loans, scholarships/grants, and unspecified assistantships also available. Financial award application deadline: 1/15. *Faculty research:* Energy-efficient lighting, lighting product development, lighting design demonstration, daylighting, transportation lighting. Total annual research expenditures: $3.7 million. *Unit head:* Dr. Mark Rea, Director, Lighting Research Center, 518-687-7100. *Application contact:* Kathleen G. O'Connor, Senior Program Administrator, Graduate Programs, 518-276-6466, Fax: 518-276-3034, E-mail: oconnk2@rpi.edu.

University of Washington, Graduate School, College of Architecture and Urban Planning, Department of Architecture, Seattle, WA 98195. Offers architecture (M Arch, MS); built environment (PhD); design computing (Certificate); historic preservation (Certificate); lighting design (Certificate); urban design (Certificate). *Degree requirements:* For master's, thesis. *Entrance requirements:* For master's, GRE General Test, minimum GPA of 3.0, portfolio, 3 letters of recommendation. Additional exam requirements/recommendations for international students: Required—TOEFL. *Faculty research:* Lighting, materials, computing theory, media, culture, environment.

Urban Design

American University of Beirut, Graduate Programs, Faculty of Engineering and Architecture, Beirut, Lebanon. Offers civil engineering (ME, PhD); electrical and computer engineering (ME, PhD); engineering management (MEM); environmental and water resources (ME); environmental and water resources engineering (PhD); environmental technology (MSES); mechanical engineering (ME, PhD); urban design (MUD); urban planning and policy (MUP). Part-time programs available. *Faculty:* 50 full-time (5 women), 6 part-time/adjunct (0 women). *Students:* 149 full-time (59 women), 28 part-time (12 women). Average age 25. 211 applicants, 76% accepted, 51 enrolled. In 2007, 95 degrees awarded. *Degree requirements:* For master's, one foreign language, comprehensive exam, thesis (for some programs); for doctorate, one foreign language, comprehensive exam, thesis/dissertation, publications. *Entrance requirements:* For master's, letters of recommendation; for doctorate, letters of recommendation, master's degree, transcripts, curriculum vitae, interview. Additional exam requirements/recommendations for international students: Required—TOEFL (minimum score 600 paper-based; 250 computer-based; 100 iBT), IELTS (minimum score 8). *Application deadline:* For fall admission, 4/30 priority date for domestic and international students; for spring admission, 11/1 priority date for domestic students, 11/1 for international students. Applications are processed on a rolling basis. Application fee: $50. Electronic applications accepted. *Expenses:* Tuition: Full-time $9,954; part-time $553 per credit. Tuition and fees vary according to course load and program. *Financial support:* In 2007–08, 12 fellowships with full tuition reimbursements (averaging $10,800 per year), 24 research assistantships with full tuition reimbursements (averaging $6,000 per year), 56 teaching assistantships with full tuition reimbursements (averaging $3,000 per year) were awarded; career-related internships or fieldwork, institutionally sponsored loans, scholarships/grants, health care benefits, and unspecified assistantships also available. Total annual research expenditures: $855,886. *Unit head:* Ibrahim N. Hajj, Dean, 961-1350000 Ext. 3400, Fax: 961-1744462, E-mail: ihajj@aub.edu.lb. *Application contact:* Dr. Salim Kanaan, Director, Admissions Office, 961-1350000 Ext. 2594, Fax: 961-1750775, E-mail: sk00@aub.edu.lb.

Ball State University, Graduate School, College of Architecture and Planning, Department of Architecture, Program in Urban Design, Muncie, IN 47306-1099. Offers MUD. *Expenses:* Tuition, state resident: full-time $6,864. Tuition, nonresident: full-time $17,932. Required fees: $1,866. *Unit head:* Dr. Scott Truex, Head, 765-285-5188.

Carnegie Mellon University, College of Fine Arts, School of Architecture, Pittsburgh, PA 15213-3891. Offers architecture (MSA); architecture, engineering, and construction management (M Sc, PhD); building performance and diagnostics (M Sc, PhD); computational design (M Sc, PhD); sustainable design (M Sc); urban design (M Sc). Terminal master's awarded for partial completion of doctoral program. *Degree requirements:* For doctorate, thesis/dissertation. *Entrance requirements:* For master's and doctorate, GRE General Test. Additional exam requirements/recommendations for international students: Required—TOEFL.

City College of the City University of New York, Graduate School, School of Architecture and Environmental Studies, Program in Urban Design, New York, NY 10031-9198. Offers MUP. Part-time programs available. *Students:* 15. 31 applicants, 74% accepted, 15 enrolled. *Degree requirements:* For master's, thesis. *Entrance requirements:* For master's, portfolio, professional degree in architecture or equivalent. Additional exam requirements/recommendations for international students: Required—TOEFL (minimum score 550 paper-based; 213 computer-based). *Application deadline:* For fall admission, 1/1 for domestic students. Application fee: $125. *Financial support:* Fellowships, career-related internships or fieldwork available. *Faculty research:* Real estate, planning, law. *Unit head:* Michael Sorkin, Director, 212-650-6869, Fax: 212-650-6566, E-mail: msorkin@ccny.cuny.edu. *Application contact:* Sarah Morales, Advisor, 212-650-8748, E-mail: archgrad@ccny.cuny.edu.

Cleveland State University, College of Graduate Studies, Maxine Goodman Levin College of Urban Affairs, Program in Urban Planning, Design, and Development, Cleveland, OH 44115. Offers geographic information systems (Certificate); local and urban management (Certificate); urban economic development (Certificate); urban planning, design, and development (MUPDD); urban real estate development and finance (Certificate); JD/MUPDD. *Accreditation:* ACSP. Part-time and evening/weekend programs available. *Faculty:* 26 full-time (10 women), 12 part-time/adjunct (5 women). *Students:* 25 full-time (10 women), 46 part-time (23 women); includes 13 minority (12 African Americans, 1 Asian American or Pacific Islander), 7 international. Average age 30. 55 applicants, 82% accepted, 23 enrolled. In 2007, 7 degrees awarded. *Degree requirements:* For master's, project or thesis. *Entrance requirements:* For master's, GRE General Test (minimum score: verbal and quantitative 50th percentile, analytical writing 4.0), minimum GPA of 3.0. Additional exam requirements/recommendations for international students: Required—TOEFL (minimum score 525 paper-based; 197 computer-based). *Application deadline:* For fall admission, 7/15 priority date for domestic students, 5/15 for international students; for spring admission, 11/1 for international students. Applications are processed on a rolling basis. Application fee: $30. Electronic applications accepted. *Financial support:* In 2007–08, 21 students received support, including 13 research assistantships with full and partial tuition reimbursements available (averaging $6,960 per year); teaching assistantships with full and partial tuition reimbursements available, career-related internships or fieldwork, Federal Work-Study, tuition waivers (full and partial), and unspecified assistantships also available. Support available to part-time students. Financial award application deadline: 3/1. *Faculty research:* Housing and neighborhood development, urban housing policy, environmental sustainability, economic development. *Unit head:* Dr. W. Dennis Keating, Director, 216-687-2298, Fax: 216-687-2013, E-mail: w.keating@csuohio.edu. *Application contact:* Graduate Advisor, 216-523-7522, Fax: 216-687-5398, E-mail: urbanprograms@csuohio.edu.

Columbia University, Graduate School of Architecture, Planning, and Preservation, Program in Architecture and Urban Design, New York, NY 10027. Offers MS. *Entrance requirements:* For master's, GRE General Test. *Expenses:* Tuition: Part-time $1,452 per credit. Required fees: $152 per term. One-time fee: $75 part-time. Full-time tuition and fees vary according to course level, course load, degree level and program.

Cornell University, Graduate School, Graduate Fields of Architecture, Art and Planning, Field of Architecture, Ithaca, NY 14853-0001. Offers architectural design (M Arch); architectural science (MS); building technology and environmental science (MS); computer graphics (MS); history of architecture (MA, PhD); history of urban development (MA, PhD); theory and criticism of architecture (M Arch); urban design (M Arch). *Faculty:* 33 full-time. *Students:* 101 full-time (33 women); includes 13 minority (1 African American, 7 Asian Americans or Pacific Islanders, 5 Hispanic Americans), 51 international. Average age 28. 305 applicants, 30%

accepted, 39 enrolled. In 2007, 17 master's, 1 doctorate awarded. *Degree requirements:* For master's, one foreign language, thesis (MA, MS); for doctorate, 2 foreign languages, comprehensive exam, thesis/dissertation. *Entrance requirements:* For master's, GRE General Test, GRE Subject Test in computer science (computer graphics), 5-year bachelor's degree in architecture, portfolio (M Arch), 3 letters of recommendation; for doctorate, GRE General Test, 3 letters of recommendation. Additional exam requirements/recommendations for international students: Required—TOEFL (minimum score 600 paper-based; 250 computer-based; 77 iBT). *Application deadline:* For fall admission, 1/15 priority date for domestic students. Application fee: $70. Electronic applications accepted. *Financial support:* In 2007–08, 41 students received support, including 13 fellowships with full tuition reimbursements available, 1 research assistantship with full tuition reimbursement available, 27 teaching assistantships with full tuition reimbursements available; institutionally sponsored loans, scholarships/grants, health care benefits, tuition waivers (full and partial), and unspecified assistantships also available. Financial award applicants required to submit FAFSA. *Faculty research:* Architectural design and urban design, theory and criticism of architecture, computer graphics, building technology and environmental science, history of architecture and history of urban-development. *Unit head:* Director of Graduate Studies, 607-255-6701, Fax: 607-255-0291. *Application contact:* Graduate Field Assistant, 607-255-6701, Fax: 607-255-0291, E-mail: cuarch@cornell.edu.

Georgia Institute of Technology, Graduate Studies and Research, College of Architecture, City and Regional Planning Program, Atlanta, GA 30332-0001. Offers architecture (PhD); economic development (MCRP); environmental planning and management (MCRP); geographic information systems (MCRP); land development (MCRP); land use planning (MCRP); transportation (MCRP); urban design (MCRP); MCP/MSCE. *Accreditation:* ACSP. *Degree requirements:* For master's, thesis, internship. *Entrance requirements:* For master's, GRE General Test, minimum GPA of 2.7. Additional exam requirements/recommendations for international students: Required—TOEFL. Electronic applications accepted.

Harvard University, Graduate School of Design, Department of Urban Planning and Design, Cambridge, MA 02138. Offers urban planning (MUP); urban planning and design (MAUD, MLAUD). *Accreditation:* ACSP (one or more programs are accredited). *Faculty:* 10 full-time (2 women), 19 part-time/adjunct (3 women). *Students:* 90 full-time (50 women); includes 20 minority (5 African Americans, 9 Asian Americans or Pacific Islanders, 6 Hispanic Americans), 35 international. Average age 27. In 2007, 48 degrees awarded. *Entrance requirements:* For master's, GRE General Test. Additional exam requirements/recommendations for international students: Required—TOEFL (minimum score 600 paper-based; 250 computer-based; 100 iBT). *Application deadline:* For fall admission, 1/16 for domestic students. Application fee: $75. Electronic applications accepted. *Expenses:* Tuition: Full-time $31,456. Full-time tuition and fees vary according to program and student level. *Financial support:* Fellowships, teaching assistantships, Federal Work-Study available. Support available to part-time students. Financial award application deadline: 2/11; financial award applicants required to submit FAFSA. *Unit head:* Rodolfo Machado, Co-Chair, 617-495-2521. *Application contact:* Gail Gustafson, Director of Admissions, 617-495-5453, Fax: 617-495-8949, E-mail: ggustafson@gsd.harvard.edu.

Kent State University, College of Architecture and Environmental Design, Kent, OH 44242-0001. Offers architecture (M Arch); preservation architecture (Certificate); urban design (M Arch, MUD, Certificate). Part-time programs available. *Faculty:* 19 full-time (5 women), 21 part-time/adjunct (3 women). *Students:* 45 full-time (13 women), 6 part-time (5 women); includes 3 minority (1 African American, 2 Asian Americans or Pacific Islanders), 7 international. Average age 23. 77 applicants, 52% accepted, 37 enrolled. In 2007, 25 degrees awarded. *Degree requirements:* For master's, thesis optional. *Entrance requirements:* For master's, GRE, portfolio, minimum GPA of 2.75, 3 letters of reference, resumé, undergraduate architecture degree. Additional exam requirements/recommendations for international students: Required—TOEFL (minimum score 550 paper-based). *Application deadline:* For fall admission, 2/1 priority date for domestic and international students. Applications are processed on a rolling basis. Application fee: $30. Electronic applications accepted. *Financial support:* In 2007–08, 6 research assistantships with partial tuition reimbursements (averaging $6,800 per year), 2 teaching assistantships with partial tuition reimbursements (averaging $6,800 per year) were awarded; career-related internships or fieldwork, Federal Work-Study, and tuition waivers (partial) also available. Financial award application deadline: 2/1. *Faculty research:* History and theory, building technology, landscape architecture and urbanism, urbanism, sustainable development. *Unit head:* Dr. James Dalton, Interim Dean, 330-672-2917, Fax: 330-672-3809, E-mail: cmcwilli@kent.edu. *Application contact:* Dr. Maurizio R. Sabini, Graduate Studies Coordinator, 330-672-0927, Fax: 330-672-3809, E-mail: msabini@kent.edu.

New York Institute of Technology, Graduate Division, School of Architecture, Old Westbury, NY 11568-8000. Offers urban and regional design (M Arch). Part-time programs available. *Students:* 11 full-time (6 women); includes 3 minority (1 African American, 1 Asian American or Pacific Islander, 1 Hispanic American), 7 international. Average age 33. 35 applicants, 49% accepted, 6 enrolled. In 2007, 7 degrees awarded. *Degree requirements:* For master's, thesis. *Entrance requirements:* For master's, minimum QPA of 2.85, portfolio. Additional exam requirements/recommendations for international students: Required—TOEFL (minimum score 550 paper-based; 213 computer-based). *Application deadline:* For fall admission, 7/1 priority date for domestic students; for spring admission, 12/1 priority date for domestic students. Applications are processed on a rolling basis. Application fee: $50. Electronic applications accepted. *Expenses:* Tuition: Part-time $739 per credit. Required fees: $75 per semester. *Financial support:* Research assistantships with partial tuition reimbursements, institutionally sponsored loans and tuition waivers (full and partial) available. Support available to part-time students. Financial award applicants required to submit FAFSA. *Faculty research:* Affordable housing, urban modeling and simulation, transport systems and infrastructure, relationships of policy and form. *Unit head:* Judith DiMaio, Dean, 516-686-7594, Fax: 516-686-7921, E-mail: jdimaio@nyit.edu. *Application contact:* Jacquelyn Nealon, Dean of Admissions and Financial Aid, 516-686-7925, Fax: 516-686-7613, E-mail: jnealon@nyit.edu.

Prairie View A&M University, School of Architecture, Prairie View, TX 77446-0519. Offers architecture (M Arch); community development (MCD). Part-time and evening/weekend programs available. *Faculty:* 8 full-time (1 woman), 8 part-time/adjunct (4 women). *Students:* 38 full-time (16 women), 24 part-time (7 women); includes 55 minority (50 African Americans, 5 Hispanic Americans), 3 international. Average age 30. 63 applicants, 100% accepted. In 2007, 39 degrees awarded. *Entrance requirements:* For master's, GRE General Test, portfolio (M Arch). Additional exam requirements/recommendations for international students: Required—TOEFL (minimum score 550 paper-based). *Application deadline:* For fall admission, 6/1 priority date for domestic and international students; for spring admission, 11/1 priority date for domestic students, 10/1 priority date for international students. Applications are processed on a rolling basis. Application fee: $50. Electronic applications accepted. *Financial support:* Fellowships with tuition reimbursements, research assistantships with tuition reimbursements, teaching assistantships, career-related internships or fieldwork, Federal Work-Study, institutionally sponsored loans, scholarships/grants, tuition waivers (full and partial), and unspecified assistantships available. Support available to part-time students. Financial award application deadline: 3/1; financial award applicants required to submit FAFSA. *Faculty research:* Community management, sustainable design. *Unit head:* Dr. Ikhlas Sabouni, Dean, 936-261-9810, Fax: 936-857-2350, E-mail: isabouni@pvamu.edu. *Application contact:* Kendrick Gibson, Assistant to the Dean for Operations and Recruitment, 936-857-9808, Fax: 936-857-9828, E-mail: klgibson@pvamu.edu.

Pratt Institute, School of Architecture, Program in Architecture and Urban Design, Brooklyn, NY 11205-3899. Offers MS. Part-time programs available. *Faculty:* 4 part-time/adjunct (2 women). *Students:* 7 full-time (4 women), 6 international. Average age 25. 35 applicants, 66% accepted, 1 enrolled. In 2007, 2 degrees awarded. *Degree requirements:* For master's, thesis. *Entrance requirements:* For master's, portfolio, bachelor's degree, transcripts, letters of recommendation, statement. Additional exam requirements/recommendations for international students: Required—TOEFL (minimum score 550 paper-based; 213 computer-based). *Application deadline:* For fall admission, 2/1 for domestic students; for spring admission, 10/1 for domestic students. Applications are processed on a rolling basis. Application fee: $50 ($90 for international students). Electronic applications accepted. *Expenses:* Tuition: Full-time $25,680. Required fees: $1,106. Tuition and fees vary according to program. *Financial support:* Career-related internships or fieldwork, Federal Work-Study, institutionally sponsored loans, scholarships/grants, health care benefits, and unspecified assistantships available. Support available to part-time students. Financial award application deadline: 2/1; financial award applicants required to submit FAFSA. *Faculty research:* Urban development process; historical, social, and economic implications of planning. *Unit head:* William J. Mac Donald, Chairperson, 718-399-4357, E-mail: wmacdona@pratt.edu. *Application contact:* Young Hah, Director of Graduate Admissions, 718-636-3683, Fax: 718-399-4242, E-mail: yhah@pratt.edu.

See Close-Up on page 167.

Rice University, Graduate Programs, School of Architecture, Houston, TX 77251-1892. Offers architecture (M Arch, D Arch); urban design (M Arch UD). *Degree requirements:* For master's, thesis; for doctorate, thesis/dissertation. *Entrance requirements:* For master's and doctorate, GRE General Test, minimum GPA of 3.0. Additional exam requirements/recommendations for international students: Required—TOEFL (minimum score 650 paper-based; 250 computer-based; 90 iBT).

Savannah College of Art and Design, Graduate School, Program in Urban Design and Development, Savannah, GA 31402-3146. Offers MA. Part-time programs available. *Faculty:* 5 full-time (2 women), 1 part-time/adjunct (0 women). *Students:* 10 full-time (5 women), 6 part-time (1 woman), 10 international. 24 applicants, 63% accepted, 10 enrolled. In 2007, 1 degree awarded. *Degree requirements:* For master's, thesis. *Entrance requirements:* For master's, interview, portfolio. Additional exam requirements/recommendations for international students: Required—TOEFL (minimum score 450 paper-based; 133 computer-based). *Application deadline:* For fall admission, 4/1 priority date for domestic and international students. Application fee: $50. *Expenses:* Tuition: Full-time $24,840; part-time $552 per credit. One-time fee: $500 full-time. *Financial support:* Fellowships, career-related internships or fieldwork, Federal Work-Study, and scholarships/grants available. Financial award application deadline: 4/1; financial award applicants required to submit FAFSA. *Unit head:* Scott Singeisen, Chair, 912-525-6871. *Application contact:* Darrell Tutchton, Director of Graduate and International Enrollment, 912-525-5961, Fax: 912-525-5985, E-mail: admission@scad.edu.

State University of New York College of Environmental Science and Forestry, Faculty of Landscape Architecture, Syracuse, NY 13210-2779. Offers community design and planning (MLA, MS); cultural landscape studies and conservation (MLA, MS); landscape and urban ecology (MLA, MS). *Accreditation:* ASLA (one or more programs are accredited). *Degree requirements:* For master's, comprehensive exam (for some programs), thesis (for some programs). *Entrance requirements:* For master's, GRE General Test, minimum GPA of 3.0. Additional exam requirements/recommendations for international students: Required—TOEFL (paper-based 550, computer-based 213, iBT 80) or IELTS (6) or STEP Aiken (Grade 1). *Faculty research:* Site analysis and design, city and regional planning, community environments.

University at Buffalo, the State University of New York, Graduate School, School of Architecture and Planning, Department of Urban and Regional Planning, Buffalo, NY 14260. Offers planning (MUP); JD/MUP; M Arch/MUP. *Accreditation:* ACSP. Part-time programs available. *Degree requirements:* For master's, thesis or alternative, project. *Entrance requirements:* For master's, minimum GPA of 3.0. Additional exam requirements/recommendations for international students: Required—TOEFL (minimum score 550 paper-based; 213 computer-based; 79 iBT), IELTS (minimum score 7). Electronic applications accepted. *Faculty research:* International planning development, economic development, governance, information technology and geographic information systems in planning, environmental planning and policy.

University of California, Berkeley, Graduate Division, College of Environmental Design, Department of Architecture, Berkeley, CA 94720-1500. Offers architecture (M Arch); building science (MS, PhD); building structures, construction and materials (MS, PhD); design (MA); design theories, methods, and practices (MS, PhD); environmental design in developing countries (MS, PhD); history of architecture and urbanism (MS, PhD); social and cultural processes in architecture and urbanism (MS, PhD); M Arch/MCP; M Arch/MS; MLA/M Arch. *Degree requirements:* For master's, thesis; for doctorate, thesis/dissertation, qualifying exam. *Entrance requirements:* For master's and doctorate, GRE General Test, minimum GPA of 3.0, 3 letters of recommendation. Additional exam requirements/recommendations for international students: Required—TOEFL. Application fee: $70 ($90 for international students). Electronic applications accepted. *Financial support:* Unspecified assistantships available. *Unit head:* Mary Comerio, Chair, 510-642-4942, E-mail: mcomerio@berkeley.edu. *Application contact:* Lois H. Ito Koch, Student Affairs Officer, 510-642-5577, Fax: 510-643-5607, E-mail: archgrad@berkeley.edu.

University of California, Berkeley, Graduate Division, College of Environmental Design, Department of Landscape Architecture and Environmental Planning, Program in Landscape Architecture, Berkeley, CA 94720-1500. Offers environmental planning (MLA); landscape design and site planning (MLA); urban and community design (MLA); MLA/M Arch; MLA/MCP. *Accreditation:* ASLA. *Faculty:* 13 full-time, 6 part-time/adjunct. *Degree requirements:* For master's, professional project or thesis. *Entrance requirements:* For master's, GRE General Test, minimum GPA of 3.0, portfolio, 3 letters of recommendation. *Application deadline:* For fall admission, 1/5 for domestic students. Application fee: $70 ($90 for international students). *Financial support:* Fellowships, research assistantships, teaching assistantships, career-related internships or fieldwork, Federal Work-Study, institutionally sponsored loans, and unspecified assistantships available. *Application contact:* Yong No, Student Affairs Officer, 510-642-2965, Fax: 510-643-6166, E-mail: laepgrad@berkeley.edu.

University of California, Berkeley, Graduate Division, College of Environmental Design, Department of Landscape Architecture and Environmental Planning, Program in Urban Design, Berkeley, CA 94720-1500. Offers MUD. *Faculty:* 13 full-time, 6 part-time/adjunct. *Degree requirements:* For master's, professional project or thesis. *Entrance requirements:* For master's, GRE General Test, minimum GPA of 3.0, portfolio, 3 letters of recommendation. *Application deadline:* For fall admission, 1/5 for domestic students. Application fee: $70 ($90 for international students). *Financial support:* Unspecified assistantships available. *Unit head:* Louise Mozingo, Head, 510-643-9804, E-mail: lmozingo@berkeley.edu. *Application contact:* Yong No, Student Affairs Officer, 510-642-2965, Fax: 510-643-6166, E-mail: laepgrad@berkeley.edu.

University of California, Los Angeles, Graduate Division, School of the Arts and Architecture, Department of Architecture and Urban Design, Los Angeles, CA 90095. Offers M Arch, MA, PhD. *Degree requirements:* For master's, thesis or alternative, comprehensive exam or design project; for doctorate, 2 foreign languages, thesis/dissertation, oral and written qualifying exams. *Entrance requirements:* For master's and doctorate, GRE General Test, portfolio. Additional exam requirements/recommendations for international students: Required—TOEFL. Electronic applications accepted. *Expenses:* Tuition, nonresident: full-time $5,728. Required fees:$8,966. Full-time tuition and fees vary according to program and student level. *Faculty research:* Urban poverty and low wage labor markets; environmental planning and politics; international political economy; physical planning, urban design, planning history; housing and land development; transportation and land use; critical urban and regional studies.

University of Colorado Denver, College of Architecture and Planning, Program in Urban Design, Denver, CO 80217-3364. Offers MUD. Part-time programs available. *Students:* 4 full-time (3 women), 2 part-time (1 woman); includes 1 minority (Hispanic American), 3 international. Average age 33. 12 applicants, 67% accepted, 3 enrolled. In 2007, 11 degrees awarded. *Degree requirements:* For master's, thesis optional. *Entrance requirements:* For master's, BA in architecture, minimum GPA of 3.0, portfolio. Additional exam requirements/recommendations for international students: Required—TOEFL (minimum score 550 paper-based; 213 computer-based). *Application deadline:* For fall admission, 3/15 for domestic students; for spring admission, 10/1 for domestic students. Application fee: $50 ($75 for

Urban Design

University of Colorado Denver (continued)
international students). *Financial support:* Career-related internships or fieldwork, Federal Work-Study, institutionally sponsored loans, and scholarships/grants available. Financial award application deadline: 3/1; financial award applicants required to submit FAFSA. *Faculty research:* Architecture of the city, architectural experimentation and exploration, composition and decomposition, intervention and transformation in the urban and rural landscape. *Unit head:* Tom Clark, Chair, 303-556-3296, Fax: 303-492-6163, E-mail: tom.clark@cudenver.edu. *Application contact:* Heather Zertuche, Administrative Assistant II, 303-556-3382, Fax: 303-556-3687, E-mail: anpdeansoffice@storm.cudenver.edu.

University of Miami, Graduate School, School of Architecture, Program in Suburb and Town Design, Coral Gables, FL 33124. Offers M Arch. *Faculty:* 9 full-time (1 woman). *Students:* 15 full-time (6 women), 1 part-time; includes 2 minority (1 African American, 1 Hispanic American), 2 international. Average age 28. 22 applicants, 77% accepted, 11 enrolled. In 2007, 16 master's awarded. *Entrance requirements:* For master's, GRE General Test, minimum GPA of 3.0, portfolio. Additional exam requirements/recommendations for international students: Required—TOEFL. *Application deadline:* For fall admission, 2/1 priority date for domestic and international students. Applications are processed on a rolling basis. Application fee: $50. Electronic applications accepted. *Financial support:* In 2007–08, 8 research assistantships (averaging $2,000 per year), 8 teaching assistantships (averaging $2,000 per year) were awarded; Federal Work-Study, institutionally sponsored loans, and scholarships/grants also available. Support available to part-time students. Financial award applicants required to submit FAFSA. Total annual research expenditures: $400,000. *Unit head:* Jaime Correa, Faculty Director, 305-284-3060, Fax: 305-284-2999, E-mail: arch-grad@miami.edu. *Application contact:* Jude Alexander, Coordinator, 305-284-3060, Fax: 305-284-6879, E-mail: jude@miami.edu.

University of Michigan, A. Alfred Taubman College of Architecture and Urban Planning, Program in Urban Design, Ann Arbor, MI 48109. Offers MUD. *Faculty:* 6 full-time (1 woman). *Students:* 15 full-time (4 women); includes 1 minority (Asian American or Pacific Islander), 8 international. 56 applicants, 48% accepted, 15 enrolled. In 2007, 15 degrees awarded. *Entrance requirements:* For master's, GRE General Test, 5-year bachelor of architecture or M Arch or bachelor of landscape architecture or master of landscape architecture or MUP, portfolio. Additional exam requirements/recommendations for international students: Required—TOEFL (minimum score 560 paper-based; 220 computer-based; 84 iBT). *Application deadline:* For fall admission, 1/15 for domestic and international students. Application fee: $60 ($75 for international students). *Expenses:* Contact institution. *Financial support:* In 2007–08, 8 students received support, including 2 teaching assistantships with partial tuition reimbursements available (averaging $3,000 per year); Federal Work-Study, scholarships/grants, health care benefits, and unspecified assistantships also available. *Application contact:* Meghan Lee, Admissions Counselor, 734-764-1649, Fax: 734-763-2322, E-mail: meglee@umich.edu.

University of New Mexico, Graduate School, School of Architecture and Planning, Program in Town Design, Albuquerque, NM 87131-2039. Offers Graduate Certificate. Application fee: $50. *Unit head:* Chris Wilson.

University of Pennsylvania, School of Design, Graduate Group in Architecture, Philadelphia, PA 19104. Offers architecture (PhD); real estate design and development (PhD); urban design (PhD). Part-time programs available. *Degree requirements:* For doctorate, 2 foreign languages, comprehensive exam, thesis/dissertation, qualifying exam, final exam. *Entrance requirements:* For doctorate, GRE General Test, B Arch, M Arch, portfolio, writing sample. Additional exam requirements/recommendations for international students: Required—TOEFL. *Faculty research:* Theory, history, technology, representation, visualization, landscape, urban design, historic preservation.

See Close-Up on page 175.

University of Toronto, School of Graduate Studies, Social Sciences Division, Department of Geography, Toronto, ON M5S 1A1, Canada. Offers geography (M Sc, MA, PhD); planning (M Sc Pl); urban design studies (MUD). Part-time programs available. *Faculty:* 45 full-time, 19 part-time/adjunct. *Students:* 180 full-time (102 women), 13 part-time, 28 international. 201 applicants, 45% accepted. In 2007, 15 master's, 1 doctorate awarded. *Degree requirements:* For master's, thesis optional; for doctorate, thesis/dissertation. *Entrance requirements:* For master's, bachelor's degree or equivalent in geography or a closely related field, minimum B+ average in each of 2 final years of degree, 3 letters of reference; for doctorate, master of geography degree, minimum A–average. *Application deadline:* For fall admission, 2/2 priority date for domestic students. Application fee: $100 Canadian dollars. *Unit head:* Prof. Amrita Daniere, Graduate Chair, 416-978-3377, Fax: 416-946-3886, E-mail: daniere@geog.utoronto.ca. *Application contact:* Marianne Ishibashi, Graduate Counselor, 416-978-3377, Fax: 416-978-3886, E-mail: ishi@geog.utoronto.ca.

University of Washington, Graduate School, College of Architecture and Urban Planning, Department of Urban Design and Planning, Seattle, WA 98195. Offers urban design and planning (PhD); urban planning (MUP). *Accreditation:* ACSP (one or more programs are accredited). *Degree requirements:* For master's, thesis or alternative; for doctorate, thesis/dissertation. *Entrance requirements:* For master's and doctorate, GRE General Test, minimum GPA of 3.0. Additional exam requirements/recommendations for international students: Required—TOEFL. *Faculty research:* Land-use and growth management, urban form and travel behavior, geographic information systems/remote sensing, historic preservation, urban ecology and environmental planning.

University of Washington, Graduate School, Interdisciplinary Program in Urban Design, Seattle, WA 98195. Offers Certificate. Electronic applications accepted. *Faculty research:* Urban design process; urban form; place theory; place analysis; race, class, and gender in community design.

Washington University in St. Louis, Sam Fox School of Design and Visual Arts, Graduate School of Architecture and Urban Design, Program in Urban Design, St. Louis, MO 63130-4899. Offers MUD, M Arch/MUD, MUD/MSW. *Faculty:* 5 full-time (2 women), 3 part-time/adjunct (1 woman). *Students:* 8 full-time (6 women), (all international). Average age 25. 26 applicants, 54% accepted, 6 enrolled. In 2007, 4 degrees awarded. *Entrance requirements:* For master's, GRE General Test, portfolio. Additional exam requirements/recommendations for international students: Required—TOEFL (minimum score 600 paper-based; 250 computer-based; 100 iBT), TWE. *Application deadline:* For fall admission, 2/1 for domestic and international students. Application fee: $50. *Financial support:* In 2007–08, 6 students received support, including 1 research assistantship (averaging $2,000 per year), teaching assistantships (averaging $2,500 per year); Federal Work-Study, scholarships/grants, tuition waivers (partial), and unspecified assistantships also available. Support available to part-time students. Financial award application deadline: 2/15; financial award applicants required to submit FAFSA. *Faculty research:* Urban design development issues: city revitalization, sustainability and suburbanization; urban history and visualization of urban form. *Unit head:* Prof. John Hoal, Director, 314-935-6227, Fax: 314-935-7656, E-mail: hoal@wustl.edu. *Application contact:* Kathleen O'Donnell, Administrative Coordinator, 314-935-6227, Fax: 314-935-7656, E-mail: odonnell@architecture.wustl.edu.

See Close-Up on page 179.

BOSTON ARCHITECTURAL COLLEGE

School of Architecture
School of Interior Design

Programs of Study

The Boston Architectural College (BAC) is a private college that offers professionally accredited master's degrees in both architecture and interior design. Each degree program comprises two structured curricular components: academic and practice. To graduate, a Master of Architecture student must earn 105 academic credits and 54 practice credits; a Master of Interior Design student must earn 95 academic credits and 45 practice credits. The architecture program can be completed in 5½ years and the interior design program in five years. For students with advanced standing (i.e., bachelor's degree in architecture, interior design, or a related field), the program can be completed in less time. In addition, the BAC offers a Distance Master of Architecture program for practicing professionals, which may be completed from anywhere in the U.S. For more information about this program, students should visit the BAC Web site at http://www.the-bac.edu/x1100.xml.

To fulfill the practice component of the degree requirement, students are employed during the day in paid professional positions. BAC students enlist their supervisors as mentors and together they endorse a statement of professional goals and objectives. Practice skill levels range from entry-level clerical support to design and project management. Practice credits, which are earned through contract learning as approved by the American Council on Education, may be completed in approximately three years of full-time work. After completion of the practice curriculum degree requirement, work credit may be applied to the NCARB intern requirement and the NCIDQ intern requirement.

To fulfill academic requirements, students take courses during the evening (typically two or three nights a week) in history and theory, visual studies, technology and management, the arts and sciences, and design studios. Academic study is organized into three segments of approximately equal length. All students participate in similar Foundation courses during Segment I. In Segments II and III, architecture and interior design students focus on their respective disciplines. The BAC offers a one-year Academic-Only Program, with course work primarily in the day, for students with little academic and experiential background in design as preparation for subsequent enrollment in the concurrent program of theory and practice.

Research Facilities

The BAC Library houses a collection of 35,000 books and 120 periodicals that focus on architecture, interior design, urban planning, energy conservation, and architectural history. In addition, the BAC maintains a slide library that contains approximately 40,000 architecture and interior design images as well as an Interior Design Materials Library that houses reference materials pertaining to interior products and current samples of finishes, furniture, lighting equipment, and construction materials. Fully equipped computer facilities support several CAD applications for both two-dimensional and three-dimensional work, modeling and rendering applications, desktop publishing, multimedia production, and Web development software. Word processing and spreadsheet software as well as unrestricted high-speed Internet access are also available. Additional equipment includes large-format plotters, scanners, color and black-and-white laser printers, and a laser cutter. Media Services equipment, such as slide, overhead, and opaque projectors and videotape and DVD decks, is available. Students also have access to a videotape library, a photography studio, a copy stand, and extensive digital photography capabilities.

Financial Aid

The BAC provides both institutional and federal or state-funded assistance to qualified students who demonstrate financial need. Sources of aid include federally funded subsidized loans and federal, state, and institutional grants and scholarships. Tuition, fees, food, housing, books, supplies, transportation, and personal costs are taken into account to determine need. Institutional aid is available to qualified students who have completed one semester. Numerous design scholarships and awards are also available.

Cost of Study

BAC tuition for 2008–09 is approximately $7900 per semester for the concurrent evening program of study and $10,560 for the Academic Only Program (AOP). All students must pay a $10 student government fee. Massachusetts law requires that full-time students be covered by a qualifying health plan. For students without coverage, the BAC offers a health insurance package at an additional cost.

Living and Housing Costs

As the BAC does not maintain residence halls, students must locate and pay for housing on their own. The Admission Office provides advice on finding affordable housing and facilitates a roommate network for students interested in sharing housing costs. Finding housing in Boston can be time-consuming, so students are encouraged to begin the process well before beginning their program of study.

Student Group

BAC students represent a wide range of ages, ethnicities, and nationalities. The men-to-women ratio for the college as a whole is approximately 55:45. The average age of entering students is 26.

Student Outcomes

The fusion of academic and practice learning provides BAC graduates with a solid preparation for a career in design, a professional network, and the most direct route to a professional license. Students at the BAC graduate with several years of real-world experience on their resumes and are often already working in supervisory positions at the time of graduation. Prior to graduation, architecture students can complete the intern requirements for National Council of Architectural Registration Boards (NCARB) licensing. Interior design students can fulfill some of the intern requirements for National Council for Interior Design Qualification (NCIDQ) certification.

Location

Located in Boston's historic Back Bay, the BAC is close to many cultural and educational institutions and is easily accessible by public transportation. The College occupies four buildings on or near Newbury Street, which is known for its many fine restaurants and shops. Symphony Hall, Fenway Park, the Museum of Fine Arts, and Boston's Public Garden are within walking distance. The city of Boston itself, with its extensive and diverse history of architecture, allows students to benefit from immersion in an environment containing some of the most important and fascinating built design in the country.

The College

The BAC's origins can be traced to 1889, when the Boston Architectural Club established a formal school of architecture fashioned after the atelier teaching method. The atelier idea was practical: students would learn their profession by working for and being mentored by an architect. Today, the BAC's architecture and interior design programs integrate academic and practice-based learning for a unique education. The BAC is accredited by the New England Association of Schools and Colleges, the National Architectural Accreditation Board, and the Council for Interior Design Accreditation (formerly FIDER).

Applying

The BAC remains dedicated to its founders' goals of allowing an opportunity to all who are interested in pursuing a design education. Master's degree candidates must have completed a bachelor's degree from an accredited college. There is no requirement to have a background in design, though many students do. An official college transcript, a complete application, a 500-word essay, an updated resume, and an application fee are the only admission requirements. International students are encouraged to apply. Applications are reviewed on a rolling basis.

Correspondence and Information

Admission Office
Boston Architectural College
320 Newbury Street
Boston, Massachusetts 02115
Phone: 617-585-0123
Fax: 617-585-0121
E-mail: admissions@the-bac.edu
Web site: http://www.the-bac.edu

Boston Architectural College

THE FACULTY

Len Charney, Head of Practice.
Herb Childress, Ph.D., Director of Undergraduate Curriculum.
Chala Hadimi, M.Arch., S.M.Arch.S., Director of Foundation Program.
Dave Harrison, Head of the School of Interior Design.
Don Hunsicker, M.Arch., Head of the School of Design Studies.
Curt Lamb, M.Arch., M.Sc.Econ., Ph.D., Vice President for Education.
Pat Loheed, ASLA, Head of the School of Landscape Architecture.
Karen Nelson, M.Arch., Program Director, Advanced Architecture Studios.
Jeff Stein, AIA, Dean, Head of the School of Architecture.
Ian Taberner, AIA, Director of Master's Thesis.

MASSACHUSETTS INSTITUTE OF TECHNOLOGY

School of Architecture and Planning

Program of Study

The Massachusetts Institute of Technology (MIT) School of Architecture and Planning focuses on the study and design of the human environment—architectural, urban, and electronic. The School offers graduate degrees through the Departments of Architecture (M.Arch., S.M.Arch.S., S.M.B.T., S.M.Vis.S., and Ph.D.) and Urban Studies and Planning (M.C.P., S.M., and Ph.D.), the Program in Media Arts and Sciences (M.S. and Ph.D.), and the Center for Real Estate (M.S.R.E.D.).

The Department of Architecture offers a full range of professional and research degree programs. The M.Arch. is an accredited professional degree, requiring 3½ years of study for those without previous architectural training and usually 2½ years for those with a related preprofessional bachelor's degree. The master's degree in architecture studies (S.M.Arch.S.) requires two years of study and allows students to conduct original research in architecture and urbanism; design and computation; the history, theory, and criticism of architecture and art; and Islamic architecture, while the master's in building technology (S.M.B.T.) provides a focus for graduate students interested in the development and application of advanced technology for buildings. The master's program in visual studies (S.M.Vis.S.) is oriented toward projects in public art. The Ph.D. program trains future teachers and researchers in building technology, design and computation, and history, theory, and criticism.

A focus on practice and the development of practice-related skills is central to the Department of Urban Studies and Planning, particularly in the professional degree (M.C.P.) program. A practicum requirement integrates fieldwork with course work. The program offers specializations in city design and development; environmental policy and planning; housing, community, and economic development; and international development. There are three cross-cutting areas of study: regional planning, transportation, and urban information systems. It is also possible for students who have been admitted to the M.C.P. program to propose programs leading to joint degrees with the Departments of Architecture and of Civil and Environmental Engineering or the Center for Real Estate. The Ph.D. program emphasizes the development of fundamental research competence and flexibility in the exploration of questions no single academic discipline can answer, and students focus on subfields in which the faculty has expertise. A limited number of students are accepted each year to pursue the S.M. degree, working with a particular predetermined faculty member.

Master's and doctoral students in the Program in Media Arts and Sciences are engaged in research that focuses on the invention, study, and creative use of new technologies that change how people express themselves, how people communicate with each other, how people learn, and how people perceive and interact with the world. The field draws on a number of other disciplines, including computer science, cognitive sciences, communications, design, and the expressive arts. Its academic programs are intimately linked with the research programs of the Media Laboratory. Students enter the program from a wide variety of backgrounds, including electrical engineering, physics, computer science, cognitive science, mechanical engineering, art and design, and the learning sciences. Students in the four-semester master's program are expected to have advanced placement or an MIT experience with computer programming. The academic programs are intimately linked with the research programs of the Media Laboratory. Areas of research include software agents, machine understanding, how children learn, human and machine vision, audition, speech interfaces, wearable computers, affective computing (a branch of computing that relates to, arises from, or deliberately influences emotions), advanced interface design, tangible media, object-oriented video, interactive cinema, work in various forms of digital expression, and new approaches to spatial imaging, nanomedia, and nanoscale sensing.

The Master of Science in Real Estate Development (M.S.R.E.D.) is an interdisciplinary degree that combines education in design, planning, construction, management, finance, and real estate economics. The intensive twelve-month program prepares students to assume positions of responsibility in private real estate development, investment, and management companies; financial institutions; government agencies; nonprofit development organizations; and consulting firms. Faculty members associated with the Center for Real Estate are drawn from the Departments of Architecture, Civil and Environmental Engineering, Economics, and Urban Studies and Planning and from the Sloan School of Management.

Research Facilities

The core studio teaching spaces of the Departments of Architecture and Urban Studies and Planning provide flexible and sociable spaces equipped with state-of-the-art electronic capabilities. Ongoing collaborations with other universities, the engineering disciplines, and professionals in practice are an integral part of the curriculum. The Rotch Library and its visual collections house one of the country's leading research collections in architecture and planning.

The general Institute support for cross-registration gives professional students the opportunity to enrich their education at the Graduate School of Design, the Kennedy School of Government, and other divisions of Harvard University.

Financial Aid

MIT makes financial support to graduate students available from a variety of sources in several different forms—fellowships, scholarships, teaching and research assistantships, work-study, and loans. Approximately half of the graduate students in the School of Architecture and Planning are employed as teaching or research assistants as they progress toward their degrees.

Cost of Study

Tuition for graduate students in the School of Architecture and Planning for the 2007–08 academic year was $36,390, plus fees.

Living and Housing Costs

The majority of new single and married graduate students who apply for on-campus housing (dormitories and apartments for single students and apartments for student families) are assigned housing. Most residence assignments for new single students are given for one year only; there is a two-year option, however, for married students. Off-campus apartments are available within commuting distance of campus. Information about on-campus housing, including current rates, is found at http://web.mit.edu/housing/index.html. Housing estimates for off-campus accommodations range from $1100 per month for a one-bedroom apartment to as much as $4000 per month for a house.

Student Group

In 2007–08, the School of Architecture and Planning enrolled 442 graduate students. Percentages vary by program, but, overall, approximately 72 percent of the School's students are pursuing master's degrees and 28 percent doctorates. Women make up 38 percent of the School's population, while 7 percent are from historically underrepresented groups. Approximately 43 percent are international.

Student Outcomes

Graduates of the School pursue careers in architectural design and teaching; in planning for neighborhoods, cities, and remote rural areas; in real estate development for the public and private sectors; in politics as elected officials; in communications as researchers and producers developing the potential of electronic media; and in the arts with the latest computer tools at their command.

Location

MIT is located on the Cambridge banks of the Charles River, facing downtown Boston. The Boston metropolitan area has a population of more than 4 million and forms one of the great centers of contemporary intellectual and cultural life with a diverse array of universities and colleges, libraries and museums, research labs, and medical centers.

The Institute

MIT, a private, coeducational institution founded in 1861, is one of the world's great research universities. It enrolls more than 10,000 students in five schools—Engineering; Humanities, Arts, and Social Science; Management; Science; and Architecture and Planning—and is an international leader in the integration of the sciences and technology into issues of broad social, economic, and cultural interest.

Applying

Application deadlines for entry in September 2009 are December 15, 2008, for architecture and media arts and sciences; January 3, 2009, for urban studies and planning; and February 15, 2009, for real estate. Some programs require a portfolio of previous work in addition to the materials required of all applicants for graduate study at MIT.

Correspondence and Information

Graduate Admissions
Massachusetts Institute of Technology
77 Massachusetts Avenue, Room 3-103
Cambridge, Massachusetts 02139-4307

Phone: 617-253-2917
Fax: 617-258-8304
E-mail: admissions@mit.edu
Web site: http://sap.mit.edu/

Massachusetts Institute of Technology

DEPARTMENT AND PROGRAM HEADS

Adèle Naudé Santos, Dean of the School of Architecture and Planning.

Architecture
Yung Ho Chang, Head of the Department of Architecture. Additional information is available on the Web (http://architecture.mit.edu/). For information on programs and admissions, students should contact the Department of Architecture, MIT, Room 7-337, Cambridge, Massachusetts 02139 (phone: 617-253-7791; fax: 617-253-8993; e-mail: arch@mit.edu).

Media Arts and Sciences
Mitchel Resnick, Acting Academic Head of the Program in Media Arts and Sciences. Additional information is available on the Web (http://www.media.mit.edu/mas/). For information on programs and admissions, students should contact Ms. Gigi Shafer, Program in Media Arts and Sciences, MIT Room E15-401, Cambridge, Massachusetts 02139 (phone: 617-253-5114; fax: 617-253-8542; e-mail: mas-info@media.mit.edu).

Real Estate
David Geltner, Director of the Center for Real Estate. Additional information is available on the Web (http://web.mit.edu/cre/). For information on programs and admissions, students should contact the Center for Real Estate, MIT Room W31-310, Cambridge, Massachusetts 02139 (phone: 617-253-4373; fax: 617-258-6991; e-mail: mit-cre@mit.edu).

Urban Studies and Planning
Lawrence J. Vale, Head of the Department of Urban Studies and Planning. Additional information is available on the Web (http://dusp.mit.edu). For information on programs and admissions, students should contact the Department of Urban Studies and Planning, MIT Room 7-346, Cambridge, Massachusetts 02139 (phone: 617-253-4409; fax: 617-253-2654; e-mail: dusp-info@mit.edu).

THE NEW SCHOOL: A UNIVERSITY

Parsons The New School for Design
Program in Architecture

Program of Study

The Department of Architecture, Interior Design, and Lighting offers an NAAB-accredited professional Master of Architecture (M.Arch.) degree. The program emphasizes the study of architecture as a material and cultural practice. It places particular emphasis on the creative role of architects and fosters the task of translating the everyday into extraordinary works of architectural invention. Using the urban environment of New York as a laboratory, the department's rigorous curriculum integrates courses in studio, history, theory, and technology to investigate the capacity of architecture to shape social interaction in space; the relationship between space, the body, and sensory perception; the integration of material construction and speculative design; the impact of digital technologies and new media on design; and the ecology of technological and natural systems.

The Design Workshop focuses on materiality, detail, and form/space-making in their capacity to reflect and direct social practice. This unique "design-build" studio option is offered in the spring semester of the second year. Students explore the architectural design process from concept to actual construction over six months. The program's small size, atelier atmosphere, and urban environment create an intimate setting where students work closely with a faculty of distinguished professional architects, historians, and theorists drawn from New York's international design community. The department publishes a journal, *Scapes,* that focuses on global, metropolitan, and departmental perspectives on architecture. Students may enroll on a full-time basis only; classes are held Monday through Friday.

Students who already hold a B.Arch. First Professional Degree or an international equivalent typically enroll in the 1½-year postprofessional degree program (54 credits). This program offers a flexible course of study that allows students to custom-design course work to suit their academic interests.

Students with a four-year undergraduate degree in a nonarchitecture major pursue the three-year (106 credits) course of study leading to a First Professional Degree. Prior to entry into this program, students must take college-level courses in calculus, physics, and the history of architecture. It is also required that students without a design background prepare by taking the Parsons Summer Intensive Studio in Architectural Drawing and Modeling or an equivalent course elsewhere.

An M.Arch./M.F.A. dual degree in architecture and lighting design is also available.

Research Facilities

The heart of the architecture program is the large, open studio loft where students develop design projects in interaction with faculty members and peers. The 5,000-square-foot space is supported by wireless digital technology, which allows for direct printing and plotting from students' desks to the adjacent twenty-five-station computer laboratories. A curated material library and staffed model shop are also located next to the studio. Use of the fabrication shops in the Department of Fine Arts, located above the studio, is encouraged and promotes important exchanges with M.F.A. graduate students. The department's facilities are augmented by an extensive collection of books, periodicals, and slides housed at the Adam and Sophie Gimbel Library of Art and Design. In addition, a consortium membership gives Parsons students access to the libraries of The Cooper Union and New York University.

The Angelo Donghia Materials Library and Study Center, funded by the Angelo Donghia Foundation, includes a library, gallery, computer lab, and lecture hall. The library allows students and faculty members to review and check out state-of-the-art resources, putting the latest and most exclusive materials at their fingertips. Regular exhibitions at the gallery—run by a full-time curator—are open to the public, creating an open forum and dialogue with the larger interior design community.

Financial Aid

Graduate students are automatically considered for scholarship funds upon admission into the program. Scholarship recipients are notified of their award by either their program or a Student Financial Services award letter soon after being admitted. Graduate students should contact their academic department early in the admissions process for separate applications for institutional awards, such as assistantships. U.S. citizens and permanent residents applying for financial aid outside the University should file the Free Application for Federal Student Aid (FAFSA) by March 1. More information can be found at the Student Financial Services Web site at http://www.newschool.edu/studentservices/financialaid/.

Cost of Study

Full-time students pay $17,280 in tuition and $140 in fees per term. Additional fees may apply.

Living and Housing Costs

The University offers on-campus housing, University-run apartments, and assistance in finding housing off campus. The cost of housing, food, transportation, books, and living expenses in New York City averages $17,000 annually. For more information, interested students should visit http://www.newschool.edu/studentservices.html.

Student Group

There are 65 students, 31 of whom are women. Of the total, 13 students are members of minority groups and 7 are international.

Location

Parsons The New School for Design, located in Greenwich Village, is fortunate to be situated at the very crossroads of New York's vibrant architecture and design communities. Its location in the city provides students with some of their greatest resources. Students are encouraged to take advantage of the museums, performance venues, and other cultural institutions that are only a walk or subway ride away.

The University and The School

Parsons is part of The New School, a leading university in New York City offering some of the nation's most distinguished programs in design, liberal arts, the performing arts, and social and political science, leading to seventy graduate and undergraduate degrees. To learn more, students should visit http://www.newschool.edu/degreeprograms. Parsons and The New School are fully accredited by the Commission on Higher Education of the Middle States Association of Colleges and Schools.

Applying

Students must submit the completed application, the $50 application fee, a resume, GRE general test scores, a statement of interest, official copies of all college transcripts, two letters of recommendation, and a portfolio that does not exceed 9 inches by 12 inches. The portfolio may include drawings and photographs of architectural projects and should include examples of other artwork. Slides, films, and videos will not be viewed. International students must also submit TOEFL scores—a minimum of 580 on the written test or 237 on the computerized version. The .application deadline is February 1.

Correspondence and Information

Master of Architecture Program
Parsons The New School for Design
66 Fifth Avenue
New York, New York 10011
Phone: 212-229-8955
Fax: 212-229-8937
E-mail: aidl@newschool.edu
Web site: http://www.newschool.edu/parsons
http://www2.parsons.edu/architecture/aidl/march.html

The New School: A University

THE FACULTY AND THEIR RESEARCH

Complete faculty biographies can be found at http://www2.parsons.edu/architecture/aidl/march/marchfaculty.html

Kimberly Ackert, Architect and Principal, Ackert Architecture; B.Arch., Caltech.
Matthew Baird, Principal, Matthew Baird Design; M.Arch., Columbia.
Sunil Bald, Partner, studioSUMO; M.Arch., Columbia.
Stella Betts, Partner, Leven Betts Studio; M.Arch., Harvard.
Laura Briggs, Director, B.F.A., Architecture and Design; Partner, BriggsKnowles Architecture and Design; M.Arch., Columbia.
Eric Bunge, Principal, nARCHITECTS; M.Arch. II, Harvard.
Dilip da Cunha, Principal, Mathur/da Cunha; Ph.D., Berkeley.
Natalie Fizer, Principal, Fizer/Forley Design; M.Arch., Princeton.
Carlo Frugiuele, Partner, Urban Office Architecture; M.Des., Columbia.
Jean Gardner, Architecture and Landscape Historian; M.A., Columbia.
James Garrison, Principal, Garrison Siegel Architects; B.Arch., Syracuse.
Douglas Gauthier, Partner, SYSTEMarchitects; M.Arch., Columbia.
Ed Keller, Co-Founder, a/Um Studio; M.Arch., Columbia.
Silvia Kolbowski, Multimedia Artist; B.S., CUNY, Hunter.
James Koster, Principal, James Koster Architects; M.Arch., Princeton.
David J. Lewis, Director, M.Arch. Program; M.Arch., Princeton.
Harriet Markis, Structural Engineer and Partner, Dunne & Markis Consulting Structural Engineers; M.Eng., Cornell; PE.
Jonathan Marvel, Principal, Rogers/Marvel Architects; M.Arch., Harvard.
Michael McGough, Vice President, Laszlo Bodak Engineer; B.S.M.E., Columbia; PC.
Brian McGrath, Architect; M.Arch., Princeton.
Joanna Merwood-Salisbury, Associate Chair and Editor, *Scapes;* Ph.D., Princeton.
Luc Nadal, Architect and Scholar; Ph.D., Columbia.
Greg Otto, Senior Engineer, Buro Happold Consulting Engineers; MIT.
Mitchell B. Owen, Partner, Consolidated Design Studios, Ltd.; M.Arch., M.A., Princeton.
David Piscuskas, Partner, 1100 Architect; M.Arch., UCLA.
Derek Porter, Director, M.F.A., Lighting and Design; Principal, Derek Porter Studio; B.F.A., Kansas City Art Institute.
Gundula Proksch, Principal, TAAN Transatlantic Architectural Network; M.Arch., Cornell.
Mark Rakatansky, Principal, Mark Rakatansky Studio; M.Arch., Berkeley.
Juergen Riehm, Partner, 1100 Architect; Diploma in Architecture, Fachhochschule Rheinland-Pfalz (Germany).
Robert Rogers, Principal, Rogers/Marvel Architects; M.Des., Harvard.
Chris Sharples, Principal, Sharples Holden Pasquarelli; M.Arch., Columbia.
William Sharples, Principal, Sharples Holden Pasquarelli; M.Arch., Columbia.
Henry Smith-Miller, Partner, Smith-Miller+Hawkinson Architects; M.Arch., Pennsylvania.
Calvin Tsao, Partner, Tsao & McKowan; M.Arch., Harvard.
Timothy Ventimiglia, Associate/Project Director, Ralph Appelbaum Associates; M.Arch., Cornell.
Perry Winston, Senior Architect, Pratt Planning and Architectural Collaborative; M.Arch., Rice.

THE NEW SCHOOL
A UNIVERSITY

THE NEW SCHOOL: A UNIVERSITY

Parsons The New School for Design
Program in Lighting Design

Program of Study

Lighting design is integral to architecture, interior design, product design, theater, and many other disciplines. Offered by the Department of Architecture, Interior Design, and Lighting, the Parson's M.F.A. in Lighting Design Program provides a strong interdisciplinary education in the intellectual, aesthetic, and technical aspects of lighting design. This degree program has the distinction of being the first in the field of architectural lighting, as well as the only graduate lighting program focused primarily on design and social practice. The curriculum, which recognizes that human physiology and psychology are central to an understanding of light as a design medium, offers a broad and rigorous study in the design, history, practice, and theory of light and lighting. Students come into close contact with other graduate architecture and interior design students. Distinguished faculty members serve as mentors, and the large, supportive professional community in New York City supplements Parsons's formal studies with numerous programs and lectures in which students are always encouraged to participate.

The program is a two-year (four-semester) full-time course of study. A minimum of 64 credits of required courses are necessary to graduate. This total includes 52 credits of lighting-specific study, 3 credits in the history of architecture, and 9 credits of interdisciplinary departmental electives that include students from the programs in architecture and interior design. Six elective courses (up to a total of 19 credits per semester) are allowed and encouraged, but only three (one from each concentration) are required for the degree.

An M.Arch./M.F.A. dual degree in architecture and lighting design is also available.

Research Facilities

Lighting design students work in an open studio alongside graduate architecture and interior design students. A lighting resource library and a lighting laboratory are adjacent to the studio. All Department of Architecture, Interior Design, and Lighting resources are available to lighting students, including a large materials library and model shop located next to the second-floor architecture studio and the Donghia Materials Center on the third floor. Use of the fabrication shops in the Department of Fine Arts located above the studio is encouraged and promotes important exchanges with other M.F.A. students. The studio is equipped with wireless digital technology; students also have access to computer labs on both departmental floors and the University's computer centers nearby. Participation in the department's lecture series and exhibitions further the dialogue among lighting, architecture, and interior design.

Financial Aid

Graduate students are automatically considered for scholarship funds upon acceptance into the program. Scholarship recipients are notified of their award by either their program or a Student Financial Services award letter soon after being admitted. Graduate students should contact their academic department early in the admissions process for separate applications for institutional awards, such as assistantships. U.S. citizens and permanent residents applying for financial aid outside the University should file the Free Application for Federal Student Aid (FAFSA) by March 1. More information can be found at the Student Financial Services Web site at http://www.newschool.edu/studentservices/financialaid/.

Cost of Study

Full-time students pay $17,280 in tuition and $140 in fees per term. Additional fees may apply.

Living and Housing Costs

The University offers on-campus housing, University-run apartments, and assistance in finding housing off campus. The cost of housing, food, transportation, books, and living expenses in New York City averages $17,000 annually. For more information, interested students should visit http://www.newschool.edu/studentservices.html.

Student Group

There are 43 students, including 33 women, 4 students who are members of minority groups, and 26 international students. All of the students in the program attend full-time.

Student Outcomes

Graduates of the program have varied career choices and may fill an important role either as architectural lighting designers in private practice or as lighting specialists within architecture and interior design firms. Some graduates choose to concentrate in theatrical and/or exhibition lighting, while others become research professionals in companies designing lighting-related equipment.

Location

Parsons The New School for Design, located in Greenwich Village, is fortunate to be situated at the crossroads of New York's vibrant architecture and design communities. Its location in the city provides students with some of their greatest resources. Students are encouraged to take advantage of the museums, performance venues, and other cultural institutions that are only a walk or subway ride away.

The University and The School

Parsons is part of The New School, a leading university in New York City offering some of the nation's most distinguished programs in design, liberal arts, the performing arts, and social and political science, leading to seventy graduate and undergraduate degrees. To learn more, students should visit http://www.newschool.edu/degreeprograms. Parsons and The New School are fully accredited by the Commission on Higher Education of the Middle States Association of Colleges and Schools.

Applying

All applicants must have an undergraduate or graduate degree, preferably in architecture, environmental design, interior design, engineering, or theater arts. Applicants whose bachelor's degrees are in unrelated disciplines should have experience working in these fields. Students must submit the completed application, the $50 application fee, a resume, a statement of interest, official copies of all college transcripts, two letters of recommendation, GRE and general test scores, and a portfolio that does not exceed 9 inches by 12 inches. The portfolio may include drawings and photographs of projects and should include samples of other artwork. In addition, international students must submit TOEFL scores—a minimum of 580 on the written test or 237 on the computerized version. The application deadline is February 1.

Correspondence and Information

Master of Fine Arts in Lighting Design Program
Parsons The New School for Design
66 Fifth Avenue
New York, New York 10011
Phone: 212-229-8955
Fax: 212-229-8937
E-mail: aidl@newschool.edu
Web site: http://www.newschool.edu/parsons
http://www2.parsons.edu/architecture/aidl/lighting.html

The New School: A University

THE FACULTY

Complete faculty biographies can be found at http://www2.parsons.edu/architecture/aidl/mfaltd/lightingfaculty.html.

Kimberly Ackert, Architect and Principal, Ackert Architecture; B.Arch., Caltech.
James R. Brogan, Architect and Senior Associate Principal, Kohn Pedersen Fox, AIA; B.Arch., Pratt.
Jim Conti, Lighting Designer; M.F.A., Ohio State.
Jessica Corr, Product Designer and Founding Member, Collaborative; B.F.A., Parsons.
Jean Gardner, Art Historian, Author, and Co-founder, Environment '90; M.A., Columbia.
Stephen Horner, Senior Designer, Tillet Lighting Design, Inc.; M.F.A., Parsons.
Nelson Jenkins, Founder, Lumen Architecture; B.F.A., B.Arch., Rhode Island School of Design.
John Katimaris, Architect and Principal, Katimaris + Associates; M.F.A., Parsons.
Jungsoo Kim, Senior Associate, Brandston Partnership, Inc.; M.F.A., Ewha Women's (Korea); M.A., NYU; M.F.A., Parsons.
Pamela Z. Kladzyk, Art Historian and Artist; Ph.D., Catholic University (Lublin).
Kent Kleinman, Architect and Chair, Department of Architecture, Interior Design, and Lighting; M.Arch., Berkeley. Twentieth-century European modernism.
Chou Lien, Partner, Brandston Partnership, Inc.; M.F.A., SUNY at Buffalo; M.S., Pratt.
Mark Loeffler, Lighting and Sustainable Design Consultant, RETEC Group; M.F.A., Parsons.
Margaret Maile, Ph.D. candidate, Bard Graduate Center.
Paul Marantz, Principal, Fisher Marantz Stone.
Joanna Merwood-Salisbury, Director of Public Programs, Department of Architecture, Interior Design, and Lighting; Scholar of Architectural History and Theory; Ph.D., Princeton.
Enrique Peiniger, Co-founder, Office for Visual Interaction, Inc.; M.Arch., Berlin Technical.
Derek Porter, Director, M.F.A. Lighting Design Program and Principal, Derek Porter Studio; B.F.A., Kansas City Art Institute.
Robert Prouse, Partner, Brandston Partnership, Inc.; M.Arch., Colorado.
Caroline Razook, Designer, Rogers Marvel Architecture; M.Arch., Parsons.
Nathalie Rozot, Consultant, L'Observatoire International.
Leni Schwendinger, Leni Schwendinger Light Projects Ltd.
Christine Sciulli. Video installation, lighting consultant.
Amy Sharp.
Joel R. Siegel, Lighting Engineer and Vice President of Marketing and Sales, Edison Price Lighting; B.A., CUNY, City College.
David S. Singer, Principal, Arc Light Design; M.Arch., Washington (St. Louis).
Jean Sundin, Co-founder, Office for Visual Interaction, Inc.; B.F.A., Virginia Commonwealth.
Matthew Tanteri, Lighting Designer, Tanteri + Associates; M.F.A., Parsons.
Thomas Thompson, Principal, Thompson + Sears, LLC; B.A.E., Penn State.
Linnaea Tillett, Lighting Designer; Ph.D., CUNY.
Attila Uysal, Principal, Susan Brady Lighting Design; M.A., Pratt.
Alexa Griffith Winton, Design Historian; M.A., Bard Graduate Center.
James Yorgey, Technical Applications Manager, Lutron Electronics Company; B.S., Penn State.

PRATT INSTITUTE

School of Architecture

Programs of Study

The School of Architecture is dedicated to maintaining the connection between design theory and practice and to extending the range of knowledge necessary to an understanding of the built environment. The diversity of programs within the School and the accessibility of other programs within the Institute enable students to pursue a wide range of interests. Students can take electives in fine arts, film, computer graphics, industrial design, furniture design, interior design, and photography as well as electives in advanced architectural theory, design, technology, and management. The School has many internationally recognized faculty members who bring to the graduate programs a strong theoretical base and the high standards of their professional work. The programs are distinguished by strong studio cultures and creative approaches to architectural design. Many special courses are offered in contemporary theoretical and critical issues, advanced computing and media, building technology, architectural history, and experimental structures. The electronic laboratory is a fifty-station PC-based facility that offers instruction in a wide variety of two-dimensional and three-dimensional design programs. Students are exposed to the professional world through optional internship programs that place them in outstanding New York architectural offices, public agencies, and nonprofit design institutions, giving them first-hand work experience and credit towards their degree.

The School of Architecture offers at total of seven graduate programs. There are two graduate architecture programs: the first professional accredited Master of Architecture (M.Arch.) and the postprofessional Master of Architecture (M.S.Arch.). There are also five Master of Science programs: architecture and urban design, city and regional planning, environmental systems management, facilities management, and historic preservation.

The three-year M.Arch. is designed for students holding a four-year undergraduate program in any field, including architecture. Graduate courses and seminars are designed to familiarize students with all aspects of the discipline and practice of architecture. Design studios at Pratt find many of their coordinates within the rich territory of New York City. However, the program also reaches into areas worldwide and into other frames, such as global marketplaces, digital worlds, and historical, theoretical, and political networks. This program is fully accredited by NAAB. Students with a B.S. in architecture or other nonprofessional degree should apply for this M.Arch. program. The postprofessional M.S.Arch. program is for those who hold an accredited architecture degree or the equivalent. The program takes approximately three semesters to complete. Students with significant professional experience can also apply for work credit, which reduces total credit-hour requirements. The postprofessional M.S.Arch. allows intensive theoretical and technical engagement of architecture and the city and stresses research and experimentation concentrating on the relations between architecture and other urban forms, scales, and forces. Research is conducted primarily within the analytic and synthetic content of the design studio and culminates in a required thesis.

The Master of Science in architecture and urban design program is intended for students who are interested in careers that enhance the growth and development of the built urban environments, the context for an urban laboratory. The 33-credit program requires 17 hours of design studio and research, with the balance of the credits in required courses in urban history, theory, infrastructure, and implementation and electives in law, transportation, housing, and preservation. The program is open to those with professional undergraduate degrees in architecture.

The three programs offered by the Graduate Center for Planning and the Environment (GCPE)—the M.S. in city and regional planning (CRP), the M.S. in environmental systems management (ESM), and the M.S. in historic preservation—emphasize planning and preservation practice rooted in the principles of sustainability, equity, and public participation. The curricula are designed to build the professional skills and knowledge of students who desire to affect the built, natural, and social environments of the nation's cities and communities in positive ways. CRP and EMS courses are offered in the evenings, enabling students to work full-time. The city and regional planning program offers specializations in community development, environmental planning, physical planning, and preservation planning. The CRP program requires the completion of 60 credits, including the thesis or the Demonstration of Professional Competence course. The EMS program requires 40 credits of course work. Students with undergraduate degrees in architecture and engineering may have up to 9 credits waived in either the CRP or EMS program. GCPE's newest program is a two-year graduate program leading to the M.S. in historic preservation. The program, designed primarily for full-time students and based at the Manhattan campus, is a 44-credit sequence of courses that provides studies in community planning, history, interpretation, design, policy, and regulatory practice. Recognizing that today's field of preservation requires more than curatorial management, the program fosters the knowledge preservationists must have in order to participate in policy-making to revitalize urban areas, suburban communities, and rural landscapes. With its urban focus, the program emphasizes hands-on work and makes extensive use of New York City's rich resources. All three graduate programs in the GCPE maintain strong ties with Pratt's architecture and design programs and with the Pratt Center for Community Development, an innovative center for the practice of planning, design, and policy work that focuses on increasing quality of life and affecting social change in New York City's diverse communities.

The M.S. in facilities management program prepares individuals to assume leadership roles in corporations, institutions, and government. The degree requires the completion of 45 credits of course work and the 5-credit Demonstration of Professional Competence course, for a total of 50 credits. Students entering the program with prior professional experience or graduate work in related fields may be eligible for advanced standing; up to 12 credits may be waived. The facilities management program is offered at the Pratt Manhattan Center on an evening schedule, allowing maximum flexibility to combine full-time work with study and research.

Research Facilities

The Pratt Library has grown with the Institute to house one of the finest collections of reference material on art, design, and architecture. Recently remodeled and expanded to accommodate its growing collection, the library contains 186,589 bound volumes, serial backfiles, and other material, including government documents; 251,603 audiovisual materials; and 3,996 microforms and subscribes to 925 periodicals. Pratt maintains numerous studios, shops, and technical facilities for work in all media, as well as state-of-the-art computer facilities. Pratt also has extensive gallery space for the exhibition of works by the student body, alumni, faculty members, and well-known architects and designers.

Financial Aid

Financial aid is offered through a variety of programs funded by the institution and the federal and state governments. These include Federal Perkins Loan and Federal Work-Study programs, the Tuition Assistance Program of New York State, and Pratt loans and student help. Graduate scholarships are awarded to entering students on a competitive basis. Fellowships and assistantships are awarded on a competitive basis to continuing students in all departments. Special alumni-sponsored fellowships are also available.

Cost of Study

In 2007–08, tuition was $27,216 per year (24 credits, $1134 per credit). Student fees are $1190 per semester. The cost of books and supplies varies widely, depending on the program in which the student is enrolled.

Living and Housing Costs

Campus housing continues to be expanded to meet student needs and is available for single students on a first-come, first-served basis. Housing costs average $11,795 per academic year. There is a plentiful supply of moderately priced rentals in the immediate area and in adjacent neighborhoods for married students seeking housing as well as for those students choosing to reside off campus.

Student Group

There are more than 248 students enrolled in Pratt's School of Architecture graduate programs; 53 percent are women. They come from all parts of the United States and the world. The graduate programs are noted for an exceptional placement ratio, with more than 85 percent of the graduating students finding employment before graduation.

Location

Pratt Institute is located in the Clinton Hill section of Brooklyn, on a 25-acre park-like campus. Pratt's Manhattan campus houses the Institute's graduate arts and cultural management, communications design, design management, facilities management, historic preservation, and library and information science programs as well as offering courses in architecture, city and regional planning, creative arts therapy, and urban design.

The Institute

A private, nonsectarian institute of higher education, Pratt Institute was founded in 1887 by the industrialist and philanthropist Charles Pratt. Today, Pratt educates 3,066 undergraduates and 1,602 graduate students for careers in art and design, architecture, and library and information science.

Applying

The application deadline is January 5. Early submission of applications, together with all necessary credentials, is highly desirable. For the applicant who intends to file for merit-based scholarships, applications and all supporting documents need to be received no later than January 5 for the fall semester and October 1 for the spring semester. All application materials must be received by January 5, or the application may not be considered. Materials should be submitted in one package that includes the three letters of recommendation in sealed envelopes with the reference's signature across the flap.

Correspondence and Information

Graduate Admissions Office
Pratt Institute
200 Willoughby Avenue
Brooklyn, New York 11205

Phone: 718-636-3514
800-331-0834 (toll-free outside New York State)
Fax: 718-399-4242
E-mail: admissions@pratt.edu
Web site: http://www.pratt.edu

Pratt Institute

THE FACULTY

Tom Hanrahan, Dean; M.Arch., Harvard; AIA, NCARB.

Architecture/Urban Design

Alisa Andrasek, Visiting Assistant Professor; M.S., Columbia.
Phillip Anzalone, Visiting Assistant Professor; M.Arch., Columbia.
Anthony Arnold, Adjunct Associate Professor; B.Arch., Pratt.
Alexandra Barker, Adjunct Assistant Professor; M.Arch., Harvard.
Stephanie Bayard, Adjunct Assistant Professor; M.A., Columbia.
Sidney Blank, Visiting Instructor.
Ezio Blasetti, Visiting Instructor; M.S., Columbia.
Karen Brandt, Visiting Professor; M.Arch., Harvard.
Meta Brunzema, Adjunct Assistant Professor; M.Arch., Columbia.
Theodore Calvin, Visiting Professor; M.S., Columbia.
Amber Chapin, Visiting Assistant Professor.
Cory Clarke, Visiting Instructor; M.Arch., Columbia.
Theoharis David, Professor; M.Arch., Yale.
Manuel DeLanda, Adjunct Professor; B.F.A., School of Visual Arts.
Sarah Deyong, Visiting Assistant Professor; Ph.D. candidate, Princeton.
Jeremy Edmiston, Adjunct Assistant Professor; M.S., Columbia.
Alexander Eisenschmidt, Visiting Assistant Professor; Ph.D. candidate, Pennsylvania.
Giuiano Fiorenzoli, Professor; M.A.S., MIT; M.Arch., Florence.
Deborah Gans, Associate Professor; M.Arch., Princeton.
Jose Gonzalez, Visiting Assistant Professor.
Matthew Herman, Visiting Assistant Professor.
Kent Hikida, Adjunct Associate Professor; M.Arch., Columbia.
Alicia Imperiale, Visiting Assistant Professor; Ph.D. candidate, Princeton.
Catherine Ingraham, Professor.
Hina Jamelle, Visiting Assistant Professor.
Nico Kienzl, Visiting Instructor; D.Des., Harvard.
Karel Klein, Adjunct Associate Professor; M.Arch., Columbia.
Ferda Kolatan, Visiting Assistant Professor.
Franklin Lee, Visiting Instructor; M.S., Columbia.
John Lobell, Professor; M.Arch., Pennsylvania.
Peter Macapia, Adjunct Assistant Professor; Ph.D. candidate, Columbia.
Radhi Majmuder, Visiting Assistant Professor.
Elliot Maltby, Adjunct Associate Professor; M.L.A., Berkeley.
Harriet Markis, Adjunct Assistant Professor; M. Engr., Cornell.
Victoria Marshall, Adjunct Associate Professor; M.L.A., Pennsylvania.
Brian McGrath, Adjunct Associate Professor; M.Arch., Princeton.
Katherine Mearns, Visiting Assistant Professor.
Tali Mejicovsky, Visiting Instructor; B.S., B.A., Pennsylvania.
William Menking, Professor; Ph.D., CUNY.
Signe Nielsen, Adjunct Professor; B.S., Pratt.
Nilay Oza, Visiting Assistant Professor; M.S.Arch., MIT.
Phillip Parker, Adjunct Associate Professor; M.Arch., Yale.
Chris Perry, Adjunct Assistant Professor; M.Arch., Columbia.
Florencia Pita, Visiting Professor; M.A., Columbia.
Alessandra Ponte, Associate Professor; Ph.D., Instituto Universitario di Architettura (Venice).
Brent Porter, Adjunct Associate Professor; M.Arch., Penn State.
David Ruy, Adjunct Associate Professor; M.Arch., Columbia.
Anne Save de Beaurecueil, Visiting Instructor; B.Arch., Caltech.
Richard Scherr, Adjunct Professor; M.Arch., Columbia.
Erich Schoenberger, Visiting Instructor; M.S., Columbia.
Maria Sieira, Adjunct Instructor; M.Arch., Pennsylvania.
Henry Smith-Miller, Adjunct Professor; M.Arch., Pennsylvania.
Roland Snooks, Adjunct Assistant Professor; M.S., Columbia.
Jason Stoikoff, Visiting Assistant Professor; M.Arch., Columbia.
Michael Szivos, Visiting Assistant Professor.
Jeffrey Taras, Visiting Instructor; M.Arch., Columbia.
Meredith Tenhoor, Visiting Instructor; Ph.D. candidate, Princeton.
Oliver Touraine, Visiting Instructor; Dipl. Arch., Paris La Villette.
Ludovica Tramontin, Adjunct Assistant Professor; Ph.D., Cagliari.
Jason Vigneri-Beane, Adjunct Assistant Professor; M.Arch., Iowa State.
Aaron White, Visiting Instructor; M.Arch., Pratt.
Christopher Whitelaw, Visiting Instructor; M.Arch., Columbia.

Graduate Center for Planning and the Environment

Catherine Herman, Visiting Assistant Professor and Interim Chair.
Moshe Adler, Visiting Associate Professor; Ph.D., UCLA.
Robert Alpern, Visiting Associate Professor; I.L.B., Yale.
Jennifer Becker, Visiting Assistant Professor; M.S. CRP, Pratt.
Chris Benedict, Visiting Instructor; B.Arch., Cooper Union.
Carlton Brown, Visiting Instructor; B.A., Princeton.
Joan Byron, Visiting Assistant Professor; B. Arch., Pratt.
Darryl Cabbagestalk, Visiting Assistant Professor; B.A., Baruch; J.D., Pace.
Resa A. Dimino, Visiting Instructor; B.A., Dickinson.
Stefanie Feldman, Visiting Assistant Professor; M.S., NJIT.
Roland Gebhardt, Visiting Assistant Professor; M.A., Hamburg.
Henry Gifford, Visiting Instructor.
Lauren Gropper, Visiting Assistant Professor; M.S. CRP, Pratt.
Steven Hammer, Visiting Assistant Professor; Ph.D., London School of Economics and Political Science.
Eva Hanhardt, Adjunct Assistant Professor and Pratt Sustainability Coordinator; M.U.P., NYU.
Larissa Justine Heilner, Visiting Assistant Professor; M.L.A., Pennsylvania.
Catherine M. Herman, Visiting Assistant Professor; M.S. CRP, Pratt.
Jeanne Houck, Visiting Assistant Professor; Ph.D., NYU.
Rayna Huber, Visiting Instructor; B.Arch., Cornell.
Georges Jacquemart, Visiting Associate Professor; M.S., Stanford.
Brad Lander, Visting Assistant Professor; M.S. CRP, Pratt.
Floyd Lapp, Visiting Associate Professor; Ph.D., NYU.
Paul Mankiewicz, Visiting Associate Professor; Ph.D., CUNY.
Jonathan Martin, Visiting Assistant Professor; Ph.D., Cornell.
William Menking, Professor; M.S., London; M.S. CRP, Pratt.
Gita Nandan, Visiting Assistant Professor; M.Arch., Berkeley.
Marci Reaven, Visiting Assistant Professor; Ph.D. candidate, NYU.
Steven Romalewski, Visiting Assistant Professor; M.S., Columbia.
Ariella Rosenberg, Visiting Assistant Professor; M.S., MIT.
John Shapiro, Visiting Assistant Professor; M.S. CRP, Pratt.
Ron Shiffman, Professor and Director Emeritus; M.S. CRP, Pratt.
Anika Singh, Visiting Assistant Professor; J.D., NYU.
Mathy Stanislaus, Visiting Assistant Professor; J.D., IIT.
Ira Stern, Visiting Assistant Professor; M.S. CRP, Pratt.
Gelvin Stevenson, Visiting Associate Professor; Ph.D., Washington (St. Louis).
Samara Swanston, Visiting Assistant Professor; J.D., St. John's (New York).
Valerie Washington, Visiting Assistant Professor; J.D., Albany Law.
Joseph Weisbord, Visiting Assistant Professor; M.S. CRP, Pratt.
Perry Winston, Visiting Assistant Professor; M.Arch., Rice.
Laura Wolf-Powers, Assistant Professor; Ph.D., Rutgers.
Ayse Yonder, Associate Professor; Ph.D., Berkeley.
Kate Zidar, Visiting Assistant Professor; M.S. CRP, Pratt.

Historic Preservation

Eric Allison, Adjunct Associate Professor and Historic Preservation Coordinator; Ph.D., Columbia.
Erica Avrami, Visiting Assistant Professor; Ph.D. candidate, Rutgers.
Ned Kaufman, Adjunct Associate Professor; Ph.D., Yale.
Jane McNamara, Visiting Assistant Professor; M.A., NYU.
Marci Reaven, Visiting Assistant Professor; Ph.D. candidate, NYU.
Theodore Prudon, Visiting Associate Professor; Ph.D., Columbia.
Vicki Weiner, Visiting Assistant Professor; M.S., Columbia.
Kevin Wolfe, Visiting Assistant Professor; M.Arch., Columbia.

Facilities Management

Diane Kaufman Fredette; Professor and Chair; M.S., Columbia; M.Arch., Ohio State.
Jeffrey R. Cruz, Adjunct Associate Professor and Facilities Management Program Coordinator; J.D., Fordham.
William E. Henry, Visiting Assistant Professor; B.A., NYU.
James G. Howie, Adjunct Professor; B.Arch., Detroit.
Diane S. Kaese, Visiting Assistant Professor; M.S., Columbia.
Joseph LaRocca, Adjunct Associate Professor; B.C.E., Polytechnic of Brooklyn.
Michael F. Lynch, Visiting Assistant Professor; B.S., Clarkson.
Mary J. Matthews, Professor; M.S., Boston College.
Martin J. McManus, Visiting Assistant Professor; B.B.A., Pace.
Richard Nasereddin, Visiting Assistant Professor; M.S., Madrid.
Russell Olson, Visiting Assistant Professor; M.S., Pratt.
John E. Osborn, Visiting Associate Professor; J.D., South Carolina.
Edward D. Re Jr., Adjunct Associate Professor; M.S., Pratt.
Barrett Lynn Richards, Visiting Instructor; M.B.A., Hofstra.
William Stein, Visiting Assistant Professor; B.Arch., CUNY.

RENSSELAER POLYTECHNIC INSTITUTE

School of Architecture

Programs of Study

The School of Architecture at Rensselaer offers exceptional research degrees at an advanced level. The master's and doctoral degrees in architectural sciences are research-oriented programs with concentrations in architectural acoustics, built ecologies, and lighting. An additional degree is offered in lighting oriented toward practice. These advanced programs in architecture are founded on the understanding that the increasing demands for effective building performance, both perceptually and technically, can best be addressed through research.

The Master of Science in Architectural Sciences and the Master of Science in Lighting programs offer nonterminal research degrees in a variety of concentrations and culminate in a thesis or research project. There are two distinct arrangements. The one-year Master of Science in Architectural Sciences 30-credit-hour programs are tailored for students who are interested in pursuing the Ph.D. degree but who have not yet acquired the skills or knowledge to move directly into the program. They also serve those who are looking for qualifications in architectural research, university teaching, or specialized practices. Concentrations are offered in the fields of architectural acoustics, built ecologies, and lighting. The Master of Science in Lighting degree is a two-year program and shaped to specific objectives.

The School of Architecture offers the Doctor of Philosophy degree in architectural sciences to candidates who are prepared to undertake innovative and substantive research that adds to the body of knowledge drawn on by the design disciplines. The "sciences" in this context refer to those disciplines that support and shape mankind's understanding and production of the built environment, including its physical, biological, social, cognitive, and cultural contexts. The Ph.D. is an inherently interdisciplinary degree in which concentrations can be elected in architectural acoustics, built ecologies, and lighting. A distinguished faculty within the School and across the Institute provides support for research projects that are informed by both disciplinary depth and transdisciplinary integration. The degree is intended for those who desire a career in teaching, research, specialized professional practices, or consulting. The program is intended to build knowledge, skills, insight, and experiences that will enable these individuals to make an original and lasting contribution to their chosen field, beginning with their dissertation and continuing into their professional lives. The program is structured to foster a community of students and scholars, a collaborative environment in which lateral flows of ideas and influences enrich the research agenda of each member of the community.

Research Facilities

Research is supported by state-of-the-art facilities and equipment, including the Rensselaer Libraries, whose electronic information system provides access to collections, databases, and the Internet from campus and remote terminals; the Rensselaer Computing System, which permeates the campus with a coherent array of more than 7,000 nodes of distributed laptops, desktops, advanced workstations, and servers; a shared toolkit of applications for interactive learning and research and high-speed Internet connectivity; one of the country's largest, academically based, class 100 clean room facilities; high-performance campuswide computing facilities that allow for serial or parallel computation; and five core laboratories for molecular biology, proteomics, bioimaging, and tissue engineering.

Rensselaer's research capabilities have been enhanced with the addition of the Computational Center for Nanotechnology Innovations (CCNI). The result of a $100-million collaboration with IBM and New York State, the CCNI is one of the world's most powerful university-based supercomputing centers and a top 25 supercomputing center of any kind in the world. The CCNI is made up of massively parallel Blue Gene supercomputers, POWER-based Linux clusters, and Opteron-based clusters, providing more than 100 teraflops of computational muscle and approximately a petabyte of shared online storage.

Other facilities and research centers include the Center for Biotechnology and Interdisciplinary Studies; the George M. Low Center for Industrial Innovation; research centers for integrated electronics, terahertz science, nanotechnology, fuel-cell and hydrogen research, science and technology policy, and infrastructure and transportation studies; the Geotechnical Centrifuge Research Center; the Darrin Fresh Water Institute; and the Scientific Computation Research Center. In addition, academic departments and faculty laboratories have extensive discipline-specific research capabilities and equipment.

The Lighting Research Center contains 14,000 square feet of laboratory space for photometry, image processing, energy-efficiency measurement, and human factors research. It is the premier university-based research center for lighting and lighting technology in the United States.

The Jaffe Acoustics Laboratory contains a hemi-anechoic chamber and a large range of testing and recording equipment that is appropriate to both field and laboratory work in architectural acoustics.

The NYSTAR Virtual Classroom laboratory consists of two linked multimedia-equipped, high-quality variable acoustics spaces; a real-time multichannel auralization system; and large-format video projection. The facility is appropriate to research in multimedia telecollaborative environments and psychoacoustic research.

The Architecture Library supplements the School's instructional and research activities. It houses materials specific to, and related to, the discipline of architecture, including art and architecture electronic databases such as Avery Index to Architectural Periodicals, ARTBibliographies Modern, Bibliography of the History of Art, and the DAAI:Design and Applied Arts Index, among others.

The Human Interface Laboratory contains facilities for the fabrication of electronic devices, embedded computation, sensing, and actuation.

The fabrication facilities within the School of Architecture provide for a full range of material experimentation, from materials testing to the development of prototypes, models, mock-ups, and full-scale assemblies. Techniques, from traditional joinery, bending, and laminating to computer-controlled laser cutting, large-format three-axis milling, and rapid-prototyping are available. Additional machining and fabrication facilities can be found on the campus.

Financial Aid

Financial aid is available in the forms of teaching and research assistantships and fellowships, which include tuition scholarships and stipends. Rensselaer assistantships cover the academic year, with summer support available in many departments. University, corporate, or national fellowships fund many of Rensselaer's full-time graduate students. Outstanding students may qualify for university-sponsored Rensselaer Graduate Fellowship Awards, which carry a minimum stipend of $22,000 and a full tuition and fees scholarship. All fellowship awards are calendar-year awards for full-time graduate students. Low-interest, deferred-repayment graduate loans are available to U.S. citizens with demonstrated need.

Cost of Study

Full-time graduate tuition for the 2008–09 academic year is $36,950. Other costs (estimated living expenses, insurance, etc.) are projected to be about $13,680. Therefore, the cost of attendance for full-time graduate study is approximately $50,630. Part-time study and cohort programs are priced differently. Students should contact Rensselaer for specific cost information related to the programs they wish to study.

Living and Housing Costs

Graduate students at Rensselaer may choose from a variety of housing options. On campus, students can select one of the many residence halls and immerse themselves in campus life or choose from a select number of apartments designed for graduate students only. There are abundant, affordable options off campus as well, many within easy walking distance.

Student Group

Of the 1,176 graduate students, 29 percent are women and 92 percent are full-time, with 75 percent of full-time graduate students studying at the doctoral level.

Student Outcomes

Rensselaer's graduate students are hired in a variety of industries and sectors of the economy and by private and public organizations, the government, and institutions of higher education. Their starting salaries average $74,807 for master's degree recipients and $82,750 for Ph.D. recipients.

Location

Located just 10 miles northeast of Albany, New York State's capital city, Rensselaer's historic 275-acre campus sits on a hill overlooking the city of Troy, New York, and the Hudson River. The area offers a relaxed lifestyle with many cultural and recreational opportunities, with easy access to both the high-energy metropolitan centers of the Northeast—such as Boston, New York City, and Montreal, Canada—and the quiet beauty of the neighboring Adirondack Mountains.

The Institute

Recognized as a leader in interactive learning and interdisciplinary research, Rensselaer continues a tradition of excellence and technological innovation dating back to 1824. Rensselaer has five schools—Architecture, Engineering, Management, Science, and Humanities and Social Sciences—that offer more than 100 graduate programs in over forty-eight disciplines that attract top students, researchers, and professors. The discovery of new scientific concepts and technologies, especially in emerging interdisciplinary fields, is the lifeblood of Rensselaer's culture and a core goal for the faculty, staff, and students. Fueled by significant support from government, industry, and private donors, Rensselaer provides a world-class education in an environment tailored to the individual.

Applying

Applications and all supporting credentials should be submitted well in advance of the preferred semester of entry to allow sufficient time for departmental review and processing. Since the first departmental awards are made early in February for the next academic year, applicants are encouraged to submit all required credentials by January 1 to ensure full consideration for admission and assistance. Late applications are considered only with departmental approval.

Correspondence and Information

For written information about graduate studies:
Graduate Admissions Coordinator
School of Architecture
Rensselaer Polytechnic Institute
110 8th Street
Troy, New York 12180-3590
Phone: 518-276-6466
Web site: http://www.arch.rpi.edu

For application and admissions information:
Rensselaer Admissions
Rensselaer Polytechnic Institute
110 8th Street
Troy, New York 12180-3590
Phone: 518-276-6216
Fax: 518-276-4072
E-mail: admissions@rpi.edu
Web site: http://gradadmissions.rpi.edu

Rensselaer Polytechnic Institute

THE FACULTY AND THEIR RESEARCH

Professors
J. Goebel, M.A., M.Arch., Staaliche Hochschule. Music composition and performance.
R. Leslie, M.Arch., Rensselaer. Lighting, daylighting, environmental comfort technologies.
M. Rea, Ph.D., Ohio State. Vision science, lighting theory and applications.

Associate Professors
D. Bell, M.Arch., Virginia. Architectural design, theory, and history.
A. Dyson, M.Arch., Yale. Architectural design, structures technology, multidisciplinary design theory, ecology.
T. Krueger, M.Arch., Columbia. Human-environment interaction, design.
I. Markov, Ph.D., Cornell. Structural engineering, seismic vulnerability, masonry.
M. Mistur, M.S., Rensselaer. Architectural design, practice, technology.
N. Narendran, Ph.D., Rhode Island. Remote-source lighting, fiber-optic sensors, geometric and physical optics.
K. Warriner, B.Arch., Florida. Architectural and urban design and theory.
N. Xiang, Ph.D., Ruhr (Germany). Architectural acoustics, acoustic signal processing.

Assistant Professors
J. Braasch, Ph.D. (engineering and music), Ruhr-Bochum (Germany). Architectural acoustics, psychoacoustics.
P. Calamia, M.A., Princeton. Computational room acoustics, sound-field simulations.
J. Ellinger, M.Arch., Columbia. Design.
M. Figueiro, Ph.D., Rensselaer. Architectural design and construction management.
F. Garba, M.Arch., Pennsylvania. Architectural invention/design processes, cultural/technological productivity, socio-ecological structures/hierarchies and their effects on the built environment.
A. Saunders, M.Arch., Harvard; SOM Fellow, 2004. Architectural design, emerging technologies and surface logic.

Clinical Professors
C. Abbate-Gardner, M.Arch., Rome. Architectural and urban design, practice, and Italian studies.
E. Carver, M.Arch., Princeton. Design, visual culture, social change.
G. Crembil, M.Arch., Cranbrook Academy of Art. Architectural design, tactical technology.
T. Ngai, M.Arch., Harvard. Architectural design, emerging technologies, emerging practice.
M. Oatman, M.F.A., SUNY at Albany. Drawing, design. Painter and installation artist.
D. Riebe, M.S., Columbia. Architectural design, emerging technologies and practice. Practicing licensed architect.

Emeritus Faculty
P. Boyce, Ph.D., Reading (United Kingdom). Human factors.
D. Haviland, M.Arch., Rensselaer. Building industry, management, economics.
W. Kroner, M.Arch., Rensselaer. Resources and sustainable architecture, advanced building technologies, futurism, architectural design.
N. Pertuiset, Hons. Dipl.Arch. and Theory, Architectural Association. Architectural design and theory.
P. Quinn, M.Arch., Pennsylvania. Theory and architectural design, institutional and community facilities.

Adjunct and Visiting Faculty
A. Adibsoltani. Architectural design practice, art and architecture critic/essayist.
Y. Akashi, Ph.D., Musashi Institute of Technology. Human factors in lighting.
M. Barry, M.S., Arizona State. Community and regional planning, conservation planning, landscape interpretation.
S. Bedford, Ph.D., Columbia. Architectural history, regulatory compliance.
P. Bhiwapurkar, Ph.D., IIT. Energy-efficient buildings, urban climate change, social impacts of environmental change.
A. Bierman, M.S., Rensselaer. Mesopic vision, color vision, lighting controls, measurement of lighting efficiency.
J. Brons, M.S., Rensselaer. Lighting design, lighting technology, lighting energy-efficiency, human factors in lighting, light pollution.
J. Bullough, Ph.D., Rensselaer. Psychological and biological effects of light, lighting for transportation, technology transfer.
V. Byszewski, D.Sc., Ph.D., Warsaw; Ph.D., Polish Academy of Sciences. Lighting technology.
R. Campbell, B.S. in Arch., Arizona State. Architectural design, virtual/digital process, materials and construction, practice.
D. Comodromus, M.S., Columbia. Architectural design, practice and politics, materials and construction.
M. Coudert, B.S., Arizona State. Sustainable urban design.
C. Ebbing, M.S.E.E., SUNY at Buffalo. Industrial acoustics, research special noise control.
D. Hoffman, B.F.A., Carnegie Mellon. Theater, technical theater, stage design, stage lighting, theatrical engineering.
O. Holmes, B.S. (mathematics), SUNY College at Oneonta; B.S. (mechanical engineering), Syracuse. HVAC, building systems, energy management.
M. Kanonik, B.A.E., Penn State; PE. Structural design.
A. Keseru, Doctor of Foreign Languages and Literature, University Ca' Foscari (Italy). Italian language and culture.
V. Lam, M.Arch., Harvard. Architectural design.
R. Levin, Ph.D., Stanford. Lighting optics, lighting application, nonionizing radiation.
B. Miyagi, M.Arch., Princeton. Design of architecture, landscape and interior; integration of theoretical discourse and building practice.
P. Morante, B.S. (electrical engineering), Norwich. Marketing and electric power markets.
B. Nelson, B.Arch., Rensselaer. Professional practice, community planning, project management.
J. Nishimura, M.Arch., Columbia. Architectural design.
S. Reilly, B.Arch., B.S., Rensselaer. Architectural design, practice, preservation technology.
P. Rizzo, M.S., Rensselaer. Lighting design, with focus on energy-efficiency, sustainability, and universal design.
M. Szoska, M.Arch., Cranbrook Academy of Art. Art and architecture related practice.
R. Torres, Ph.D., Chalmers (Sweden). Architectural acoustics, auralization of sound fields, subjective effects of room acoustics.
J. Van Derlofske, Ph.D., Alabama in Huntsville. Illumination systems, optical design, optical computer modeling, prototype development.
A. Wadhwa, M.S. (lighting), Rensselaer. Architectural lighting design, systems integration and new technologies, sustainable systems, green practices, luminaire design.

S C I—ARC

SOUTHERN CALIFORNIA INSTITUTE OF ARCHITECTURE

Programs of Study

The Southern California Institute of Architecture (SCI-Arc) offers three levels of graduate study, all leading to the Master of Architecture (M.Arch.) degree. The Institute offers two professional degree programs, which are accredited by the National Architectural Accrediting Board (NAAB). The M.Arch 1 Program is a three-year, seven-semester program, open to students who have completed a degree in any discipline other than architecture. Students who have completed a four-year bachelor's degree in architecture are eligible to apply to the two-year, five-semester M.Arch 2 Program, which builds upon the student's previous education in architecture. Candidates for the M.Arch 2 Program must demonstrate achievement in design and must have completed the necessary undergraduate courses to meet the standards of SCI-Arc's graduate study.

SCI-Arc also offers two 1-year (three-term) postgraduate programs that offer nonprofessional M.Arch. degrees. The Southern California Institute for Future Initiatives (SCIFI) examines the conceptual territory between architecture and economic development. The studio-intensive program introduces students to contemporary urban design ideas and real estate economics to develop creative ways to realistically shape cities. MediaSCAPES has been established in response to the burgeoning influence of media production, and examines significant emerging relationships within the technology, software, media, film, and game spaces to produce new content and ideas in a think-tank R&D environment. Admission to the SCIFI and MediaSCAPES programs is open to applicants who hold a professional degree in architecture (B.Arch. or M.Arch. or equivalent) and have fulfilled the educational requirements for professional licensing in the country that the degree was granted; however, those holding a bachelor's degree in a field unrelated to architecture who wish to pursue a nontraditional career in urbanism or new media are also encouraged to apply. Exchange students and nondegree candidates are welcome on a case-by-case basis. Applicants enter in the fall term and must attend on a full-time basis for three consecutive terms. Admission to SCI-Arc's graduate programs is highly competitive.

Research Facilities

In SCI-Arc's renovation of the (1907) Freight Depot, a 1,250-foot-long industrial structure in Los Angeles' Artist District, lightweight steel structures were inserted inside a vast corridor of concrete and rebar to create a variety of work spaces. The on-campus community of 500 students and 90 faculty members work together, engaging this rich relationship between old and new and using the building as a laboratory for experimentation.

The Freight Depot, which houses all the school's facilities and is open to students 24 hours a day, includes individual studio spaces for each student; seminar and lecture rooms; the library; a media center; wood and metal shops; CNC facilities equipped with a laser cutter, milling machines, and 3-D printers; computer labs; and an exhibit gallery. The SCI-Arc Supply Store is located off campus, one block west of the depot. The computer labs are accessible 24 hours a day, seven days a week, and house both MACs and PCs equipped with the most up-to-date software.

Financial Aid

Financial assistance is available to qualified students who are citizens or permanent residents of the United States. International students do not qualify for federal financial assistance but may be eligible for private educational loans. A limited number of scholarships are available to entering students.

Cost of Study

Tuition and fees for the 2008–09 academic year are $22,690. Estimated living expenses are $13,856.

Living and Housing Costs

Housing costs for the academic year are estimated to be $13,856. On-campus housing is not available. Off-campus apartments and lofts are available in the downtown Artist District and in surrounding communities. Rents range from $650 to $900 or more per month.

Student Group

The SCI-Arc Student Union actively represents the students, who participate in all aspects of the operation of the school including the lecture series, student journals and other publications, and exhibitions. Student representatives sit on the board of directors, academic council, curriculum committee, and other academic committees. Students organize and produce the lecture series and the graduation ceremony and run the lottery for vertical studio placement.

Student Outcomes

SCI-Arc graduates are engaged in private practice or are employed by prominent architectural firms. Alumni practice on six continents and work in the field of architecture, related design fields, and in the areas of research and teaching, entertainment, and the arts.

Location

SCI-Arc's location in the heart of the Los Angeles Artist District, southeast of the downtown core, allows students and faculty members to participate fully in a vital urban environment. Adjacent to the toy and garment districts and just south of Little Tokyo, the school is close to museums, theaters, galleries, and many other cultural institutions. Neighbors include Gehry's Concert Hall, Mayne's Caltrans Headquarters, and Moneo's Cathedral.

The Institute

Southern California Institute of Architecture (SCI-Arc) is a creative voice for evolving paradigms of culture and building, using Los Angeles as an experimental field, with a constantly renewed community of faculty members and students who continue to "make it new." SCI-Arc's home in downtown Los Angeles allows students to experience firsthand the globalization of business, entertainment, media, and language, combined with the shifting boundaries of disciplines, cultures, and territories. The school stands at an urban pivot point on the east edge of downtown Los Angeles, at a confluence of races, politics, and urban tactics. The extreme social and natural conditions that make Los Angeles a focus of world attention serve as vantage points from which to debate the future of cities, the changing role of the architect, and the nature of architecture itself. As an independent degree-granting institution, the school tests the limits of architecture in order to transform existing conditions into the designs of the future. Its graduates meet the challenges of contemporary design practice by cultivating new visions that respond to the unfurling complexity of the contemporary urban environment. Using emerging technologies and tools, they develop new strategies for practice by uniting the conceptual and the technical. The curriculum tightly weaves the liberal arts and the disciplines of physical sciences, professional practice, and technology into architectural practice. This critical approach is manifested in building and object making, digital media, theoretical research, and creative design.

SCI-Arc began in 1972 when a small group of architects and students proposed a radical alternative to the conventional system of architectural education. United by their commitment to change, they established the school as a mechanism for invention, exploration, and criticism. The students and faculty members felt comfortable with uncertainty and risk and relished independent thinking. Coexistence of diverse approaches and purposeful action generated a community. A passion for developing ideas and constructing them into buildings and cities drove the curriculum. Society and architecture were seen as inseparable.

The Institute holds accreditation from the National Architecture Accrediting Board (NAAB) and the Western Association of Schools and Colleges (WASC).

Applying

Applicants to the graduate programs are required to submit a portfolio of creative work, statement of purpose, three letters of recommendation, academic records, and GRE scores. Applicants who hold a master's degree in another discipline are waived from submitting the GRE. In addition, applicants from non-English-speaking countries, for whom English is not the first language, are required to take the TOEFL or IELTS. Applications to the graduate and postgraduate programs are accepted for entrance in the fall term only. The application deadline is January 15.

Correspondence and Information

Admissions Office
Southern California Institute of Architecture
960 East 3rd Street
Los Angeles, California 90013-1822

Phone: 213-356-5320
Fax: 213-613-2260
E-mail: admissions@sciarc.edu
Web site: http://www.sciarc.edu

Southern California Institute of Architecture

THE FACULTY

Students and faculty members work together in a fluid, nonhierarchical manner, exploring and testing new ideas. The student-faculty ratio is 16:1. The overlap of teaching and practice encourages the sharing of skills and knowledge. The faculty, directed by Eric Owen Moss and the Academic Council, represent a wide range of contemporary approaches to design, history, and urban theory. Among the faculty members are some of the leading practitioners of the discipline of architecture as well as renowned theorists, critics, and historians. These Los Angeles–based practitioners have devoted their careers to investigating how broad aesthetic, social, and cultural concerns can be integrated into an overall understanding of the built and natural environments. Their work has been widely published both nationally and internationally. To complement the richness of local talent and the regional urban experience, SCI-Arc offers studios, workshops, lectures, and seminars by international visiting faculty members.

Faculty members have been awarded numerous Fulbright Fellowships, Graham Foundation Grants, Progressive Architecture awards, AIA awards, Rome prizes, and a MacArthur grant. In addition, books by faculty members have been published by Verso, the University of Michigan Press, Routledge, Princeton Architectural Press, Monacelli Press, MIT Press, Rockport Editions, Rizzoli, Academy Editions, Rotovision, the University of California Press, and Artemis.

The Southern California Institute of Architecture.

UNIVERSITY OF MIAMI

School of Architecture

Programs of Study The School of Architecture offers both professional and postprofessional graduate programs. The Professional Master of Architecture degree has two tracks, one for students with preprofessional degrees in architecture and one for students with degrees outside of architecture. Candidates with a preprofessional architecture degree typically pursue the two-year track of concentrated study. Students with degrees in other disciplines follow a program of 3½ years' duration.

The postprofessional Master of Architecture in Suburb and Town Design program has attracted international recognition for its efforts to develop guiding principles for the building of communities. Designed for students already holding a professional degree, the one-calendar-year curriculum includes special opportunities to work directly with municipalities, civic and neighborhood groups, and other governmental agencies and prepares students to be effective designers and advocates for both private and public development and public-sector redevelopment enterprises.

The Master of Real Estate Development and Urbanism (MRED+U) is an interdisciplinary one-year graduate program that blends the fundamentals of real estate development with livable community planning and design. The Master of Real Estate Development and Urbanism draws on the combined interdisciplinary strengths of the School of Architecture, an international leader in urbanism and livable community design; the School of Business Administration, named the number 1 business school in Florida by the *Wall Street Journal* and the number 5 business school in the nation by *Hispanic Business;* the School of Law, which offers an LL.M. degree in real property; the College of Engineering, with strong civil, architectural, and environmental engineering programs; and the Urban Studies Program, directed by faculty members from the College of Arts and Science.

The MRED+U program is administered by the School of Architecture, which is led by Dean Elizabeth Plater-Zyberk. The University of Miami's School of Architecture was ranked number 1 in the nation for the study of New Urbanism in a survey conducted by *New Urban News* and was awarded the John Nolen Medal for Contributions to Urbanism in Florida in 2007. The MRED+U program is designed to provide students with the tools and practical experiences needed to compete in the fast-paced and changing world of urban real estate development. Students benefit from the program's location in the heart of one of the world's most exciting and dynamic real estate markets and from leading experts, entrepreneurs, and business leaders in the real estate industry. Course topics include cutting-edge practice in real estate finance, market analysis, real estate law, land-use policies and codes, project management, public-private partnerships, the development process, sustainable development, and entrepreneurship. The MRED+U prepares real estate industry professionals who are capable of tapping the power of the market to deliver compact, walkable, mixed-use development that offers a high quality of life for diverse populations to live, work, and carry out their daily activities in attractive, sustainable neighborhoods and communities.

Research Facilities The architecture library includes books, journals, magazines, and an archive of maps and drawings. Computer terminals provide access to the catalogs of the University's main library and other research libraries in South Florida. The University's Richter Library has specialized collections in government publications and Floridiana and a growing archive of New Urbanism. CD-ROM databases and other extensive databases are available. In addition to the conventional software, the School's computer laboratory has advanced programs in computer-aided design, imaging, animation, and geographical information systems. Opportunities for research are available through the School's Center for Urban and Community Design, which offers the opportunity for graduate students to work with faculty members on issues critical to the region.

Financial Aid The University of Miami provides financial assistance in the form of fellowships, tuition scholarships, assistantships in research or instruction, loans, and student employment for full-time graduate students.

To be considered for these sources of financial aid, applicants must have all academic credentials, letters of recommendation, and examination scores in prior to February 1. Decisions on applications are announced in March and April. The normal workload of the assistantship is 10–12 hours per week during the academic year. Assistantship stipends vary depending upon the field of work.

Cost of Study The cost per credit hour for the 2008–09 academic year is $1424, with additional fees of $328.

Living and Housing Costs The Department of Residence Halls provides limited accommodations for full-time graduate students. Graduate students live in single or up to four-bedroom units in the University's newest residential community, University Village. For 2008–09, monthly rental rates range from $1522 to $6955. Annual rates range from $10,080 to $16,692. Housing is not available for married students or families. The University maintains off-campus listings.

Student Group Students in the graduate degree program come from various humanities, art, and science backgrounds. Approximately half of the students are women, and there are numerous international students. Overall, the majority of graduate students receive financial aid in the form of tuition scholarships, graduate assistantships, or both.

Student Outcomes Miami alumni are sought after by employers. Recent graduates can be found working in renowned architecture and planning firms across the country and internationally as well as with real estate development companies and municipal government. Many open their own professional practice.

Location The main campus of the University of Miami is situated in Coral Gables, one of America's notable garden cities. There are links by Metrorail to downtown Miami. The campus is less than 3 miles from Biscayne Bay and Miami Beach.

The University and The School George Merrick, the visionary founder of Coral Gables, inspired the founding of the architecture program in the early 1920s when he encouraged the association of the planners and designers of the new community with the newly formed University of Miami. That initial association of architects, planners, landscape architects, and artists—working within the context of an emerging region—remains a hallmark of the School.

Today, the School of Architecture reaches beyond the region to a worldwide network of professional contacts, affiliations, and alumni. These associations generate numerous opportunities for collaborative studies, exchange programs, summer internships, and career placement upon graduation.

Applying Applications submitted to the School of Architecture Office of Graduate Admissions by March 1 receive the highest consideration. Requests for assistantships or scholarships should be submitted at the same time. To be admitted to the graduate programs, an applicant is required to hold a baccalaureate degree from an accredited institution. The academic record should be outstanding. Prior to admission, an applicant is required to present scores from the verbal and quantitative sections of the Graduate Record Examinations (GRE). The application fee is $65 for mailed-in forms and $55 for online submissions.

Correspondence and Information

Teofilo Victoria
Director of Graduate Studies
School of Architecture
University of Miami
P.O. Box 249178
Coral Gables, Florida 33124
Phone: 305-284-3731
Fax: 305-284-6879

University of Miami

THE FACULTY AND THEIR RESEARCH

Roberto M. Behar, Associate Professor in Practice; Diploma in Architecture, National University of Rosario (Argentina). Design, theory.
Charles C. Bohl, Associate Professor; Ph.D., North Carolina at Chapel Hill. Real estate development, community building.
Jacob Brillhart, Lecturer; M.S.A.A.D., Columbia; M.Arch., Tulane. Design, graphics.
Rocco Ceo, Professor; M.Arch., Harvard. Design, graphics.
Sonia Chao, Research Associate Professor; M.Arch., Columbia. Design, community building.
Jaime Correa, Associate Professor in Practice; M.A.U.D., M.C.P., Pennsylvania. Urban design, town planning, theory.
Adib Cure, Lecturer; M.Arch., Harvard. Design, building systems.
David Fix, Research Assistant Professor; M.Arch., Yale. Design, technology.
Jose Gelabert-Navia, Professor; M.F.A., Cornell. Design, graphics, history of architecture.
Gary C. Greenan, Professor; M.C.R.P., Catholic University. Design, landscape architecture.
Carmen Guerrero, Research Associate Professor; M.Arch., Cornell. Design, history of architecture.
Denis Hector, Associate Professor and Associate Dean; M.S., Pennsylvania. Design, structures, technology.
Jorge L. Hernandez, Professor; M.Arch., Virginia. Historic preservation, design, theory, graphics.
Jan Hochstim, Professor; M.A., Miami (Florida). Design, history of architecture.
Richard John, Assistant Professor; M.Phil., Warburg. History of architecture and urbanism.
Jean-François Lejeune, Professor; Diploma in Engineering and Architecture, Liege (Belgium). Design, theory, history of cities.
Joanna Lee Lombard, Professor; M.Arch., Harvard. Design, environmental studies, history of landscape.
Tomas L. Lopez-Gottardi, Professor and Director of Undergraduate Studies; M.A.U.D., M.C.P., Pennsylvania. Design, theory.
Catherine Lynn, Visiting Assistant Professor; Ph.D., Yale. Historic preservation.
Frank Martinez, Associate Professor; M.Arch., Princeton. Design, methods, graphics.
Joseph Middlebrooks, Professor; M.Arch., M.C.P., Yale. Design, professional practice.
Aristides J. Millas, Associate Professor; M.Arch., Harvard. Design, history of architecture.
Nicholas N. Patricios, Professor; Ph.D., University College, London. Urban planning, behavioral studies.
Carie Ann Penabad, Assistant Professor; M.Arch., Harvard. Design, graphics.
Elizabeth Plater-Zyberk, Distinguished Professor and Dean; M.Arch., Yale. Design, urban design.
Allan Schulman, Research Assistant Professor; M.Arch., Miami (Florida). Design, historic preservation, housing.
Vincent Scully, Distinguished Visiting Professor; Ph.D., Yale. History of architecture.
Thomas Alton Spain, Professor; M.Des., Harvard. Design, visual studies.
Jorge Trelles, Lecturer; M.Arch., Cornell. Design.
Luis Trelles, Assistant Professor; M.Arch., Cornell. Design, technology.
Teofilo Victoria, Associate Professor and Director of Graduate Studies; M.Arch., Columbia. Design, theory.
Katherine Wheeler, Assistant Professor, Ph.D., MIT. History of architecture, graphics.

UNIVERSITY OF PENNSYLVANIA

School of Design

Programs of Study

For men and women who wish to study design and planning within a rich, cross-disciplinary context, the University of Pennsylvania's School of Design offers exceptional opportunities. Founded more than 100 years ago, the School is known throughout the world for its exceptional mix of programs and for fostering seminal thought about the way we shape and are shaped by the natural and man-made environment.

The School offers professional master's degrees in fine arts, architecture, landscape architecture, city planning, and historic preservation. Great emphasis is placed on interdisciplinary study, and a series of both dual-degree options and certificates is offered to enable students to take their creative and intellectual study and research in-depth across conventional departmental or program boundaries. Collaborative studios and cooperative programming with Penn's Wharton School and the School of Arts and Sciences provide students with opportunities to interact with the multiple disciplines they are likely to encounter later on in professional practice. To Ph.D. candidates, the graduate groups in architecture and city and regional planning offer advanced training for teaching and research.

Research Facilities

The Architectural Archives of the University of Pennsylvania preserve the works of more than 200 designers from the eighteenth century to the present and include the Louis I. Kahn Collection. The Architectural Conservation Laboratory of the graduate program in historic preservation is devoted to advanced training and research in the conservation of the built environment. The PennDesign Computing Center supports a variety of computing activities, including CAD, GIS, and urban simulation modeling, as well as database, spreadsheet, and word processing applications. The Fabrication Center includes both conventional and computer-driven equipment. The University of Pennsylvania library is a composite of fourteen campus libraries of which the Jerome and Anne Fisher Fine Arts Library is one, as well as the Perkins Rare Architectural Book Collection and the Slide Collection.

Financial Aid

The School of Design provides its students with assistance in planning for and securing adequate financing for graduate school. New students apply for fellowships and scholarships at the time of application to their chosen department. Diversity scholarships are available.

Cost of Study

The tuition and general fee for full-time graduate students in the School of Design was $35,640 for the 2007–08 academic year. This included a general fee of $2010. The 2007–08 nine-month budget was estimated at $56,850, which included tuition and fees, room, board, and all other expenses.

Living and Housing Costs

There are several residential options offering both apartment and suite living arrangements for single and married students as well as students with families. Many graduate students live off campus, where housing is available at varying costs that begin at approximately $400 per month.

Student Group

The student body is drawn from all over the United States, from many other countries, and from a variety of undergraduate disciplines. There is an enrollment of approximately 575 full-time students. An active PennDesign Student Council and a University Graduate and Professional Student Association provide the opportunity for interaction among the departments and the twelve schools of the University.

Location

Philadelphia was founded more than 300 years ago and is famous for its historic significance. It is today the nation's sixth-largest city, the home to major cultural institutions, and a vibrant mosaic of many cultures. Philadelphia and the surrounding region act as a laboratory for PennDesign students and faculty members.

The University and The School

Founded in 1740 by Benjamin Franklin, the University of Pennsylvania is composed of twelve graduate, professional, and undergraduate schools. The guiding philosophy of "one university" connotes the spirit of cooperation unifying the diverse intellectual and social activities of the University. PennDesign students are encouraged to take advantage of courses offered by the other graduate and professional schools through electives and audits.

Applying

Applicants to each degree program in the School of Design must submit an online application form, application fee, three letters of recommendation, official transcripts, and GRE scores. In addition, there are specific requirements for portfolios, slides, or written statements by individual departments. The application fee is $75. The application deadline is January 2 for the Ph.D. and M.S. programs, January 15 for the Master of Architecture program, and February 1 for all other programs.

Correspondence and Information

Office of Admissions
School of Design
110 Meyerson Hall
University of Pennsylvania
Philadelphia, Pennsylvania 19104-6311
Phone: 215-898-6520
Fax: 215-573-3927
E-mail: admissions@design.upenn.edu
Web site: http://www.design.upenn.edu

University of Pennsylvania

THE FACULTY AND THEIR RESEARCH

Architecture
Tony Atkin, M.Arch., Adjunct Associate Professor. Cultural and architectural design.
Cecil Balmond, M.Sc., Paul Philippe Cret Practice Professor of Architecture. Structural engineering, design.
William Braham, Ph.D., Associate Professor. Design and building systems, lighting, color.
Winka Dubbeldam, M.Arch., Practice Associate Professor. Design practice.
Homa Farjadi, M.Arch., Practice Professor. Design practice.
Richard Farley, M.Arch., Adjunct Associate Professor. Structures, architecture practice.
Annette Fierro, M.Arch., Associate Professor. Construction technology, design.
Helene Furján, Ph.D., Assistant Professor. History and theory.
Gary A. Hack, Ph.D., Dean and Paley Professor. Urban design and physical planning.
Stephen Kieran, M.Arch., Adjunct Professor. Building systems, design.
David Leatherbarrow, Ph.D., Professor. History and theory of architecture.
Ali Malkawi, Ph.D., Associate Professor. Energy systems and design.
Peter McCleary, D.I.C., Emeritus Professor. Philosophy and history of architectural technology.
Detlef Mertins, Ph.D., Professor and Chair. History and theory.
Enrique Norten, M.Arch., Miller Practice Professor. Design.
Ali Rahim, M.Arch., Associate Professor. Design theory and digital media.
Witold Rybczynski, M.Arch., Meyerson Professor of Urbanism. Design history and theory.
James Timberlake, M.Arch., Adjunct Professor. Building systems, design.
Cathrine Veikos, M.Arch., Assistant Professor. Digital methods and design.
Marion Weiss, M.Arch., Professor. Design, drawing, urbanism.
Richard Wesley, M.Arch., Adjunct Associate Professor and Undergraduate Chair. Design, theory.

City and Regional Planning
Jonathan Barnett, M.Arch., Practice Professor of City and Regional Planning. Physical planning and urban design.
Eugenie L. Birch, Ph.D., Professor and Chair. History of planning, inner-city revitalization, international planning.
Thomas L. Daniels, Ph.D., Professor. Growth management, watershed protection, farmland preservation.
Gary A. Hack, Ph.D., Dean and Paley Professor. Urban design and physical planning.
Amy Hillier, Ph.D., Assistant Professor. Geographic information systems.
John Landis, Ph.D., Professor. Growth management, transportation and land use, planning history.
Michael Larice, Ph.D., Associate Professor. Community and regional planning.
Lynne B. Sagalyn, Ph.D., Professor. Real estate finance and development.
Harris Steinberg, M.Arch., Adjunct Assistant Professor. Professional practice.
Domenic Vitiello, Ph.D., Assistant Professor. Urban studies.
Rachel Weinberger, Ph.D., Assistant Professor. Transportation and land use.
Robert Yaro, M.C.P., Practice Professor. Regional planning and growth strategies.

Fine Arts
Terry Adkins, M.F.A., M.S., Associate Professor. Sculpture.
Laurie Churchman, M.F.A., Assistant Professor. Graphic design.
Sharka Brod Hyland, M.F.A., Adjunct Assistant Professor. Graphic design, digital imaging.
Susana Jacobson, M.F.A., Adjunct Associate Professor. Painting.
John Moore, M.F.A., Monroe and Edna Gutman Professor of Fine Arts and Chair. Painting.
Joshua Mosley, M.F.A., Associate Professor. Digital animation.
Julie Schneider, M.F.A., Adjunct Associate Professor. Drawing and painting.
Jackie Tileston, M.F.A., Associate Professor. Painting.

Historic Preservation
David De Long, Ph.D., Emeritus Professor. Historic preservation, history and theory of architecture.
Randall Mason, Ph.D., Associate Professor. Preservation planning, cultural policy, site management.
Frank Matero, M.S., Professor and Chairman and Director, Architecture Conservation Laboratory. Building and conservation technology.
John Milner, B.Arch., Adjunct Professor. Restoration and adaptive reuse of historic buildings, design of new buildings.

Landscape Architecture and Regional Planning
Anita Berrizbeitia, M.L.A., Associate Professor. Design theory.
Paolo Bûrgi, Adjunct Professor. Design practice.
James Corner, M.L.A., Professor and Chair. Landscape urbanism.
John Dixon Hunt, Ph.D., Professor. Landscape history and theory.
Peter Latz, M.A., Adjunct Professor. Landscape remediation.
Anuradha Mathur, M.L.A., Associate Professor. Landscape design and theory.
Karen M'Closkey, M.L.A., Assistant Professor.
Cora Olgyay, M.L.A., Adjunct Assistant Professor. Landscape materials.
Laurie Olin, B.Arch., Practice Professor. Design practice.
Margie Ruddick, M.L.A., Adjunct Associate Professor. Design practice.
Lucinda Sanders, M.L.A., Adjunct Associate Professor. Design practice.
C. Dana Tomlin, Ph.D., Professor. Geographic information systems.

UNIVERSITY OF SOUTHERN CALIFORNIA

School of Architecture
Graduate Programs in Architecture, Landscape Architecture, Historic Preservation, and Building Science

Programs of Study

The School of Architecture at the University of Southern California (USC) offers interrelated graduate programs in architecture, building science, landscape architecture, and historic preservation and dual-degree options with the School of Policy, Planning, and Development's Master of Urban Planning program. The School has recently added graduate certificates in urbanism and the built environment, building science, and landscape architecture, in addition to the existing certificate in historic preservation. Students enjoy a student-faculty ratio of 10:1.

The Master of Architecture postprofessional and Master of Landscape Architecture degrees are intended for students holding a first professional degree in the appropriate field. The Master of Building Science (M.B.S.) degree program considers applicants with a professional degree or a nonprofessional degree with an emphasis in an area of science. Advanced standing in these programs provides an opportunity to reduce the length of residency by one semester.

A two-year NAAB-accredited Master of Architecture professional degree program is available for those with a bachelor's degree in a preprofessional architecture program.

Research Facilities

The University of Southern California is among the top twenty research institutions in the country. A state-of-the-art model and workshop support a strong tradition of model building as a method for design exploration. Recently, construction was completed on a 22,000-square-foot addition to the School, providing new studio space for the graduate programs, faculty offices, research suites, "sky gardens," and review spaces. Three computer labs are open to students daily, along with a computer center in every studio. The labs contain computer-aided design (CAD); structural, thermal, lighting, and site analysis software; and access to the rest of the campus computer network.

The Helen Topping Architecture and Fine Arts Library, the oldest and best in southern California, houses more than 80,000 volumes in the areas of architecture, landscape architecture, urban design, art history, graphics, and photography. The periodical collection is extensive in both English and foreign language journals. The slide library contains more than a quarter million slides in all areas of architecture and fine arts. The USC central library system holds more than 2.75 million volumes, all accessible through a computerized index.

The School owns two historic homes, available for instruction and research of architectural styles and historic preservation and restoration. The Gamble House is a well-known example of the Craftsman style of Charles and Henry Greene. Frank Lloyd Wright's Freeman House is being restored for use as a residence for distinguished visiting scholars. A strong foundation in architectural history is enhanced through yearly opportunities to study abroad.

Financial Aid

The School of Architecture awards substantial merit-based scholarships as well as research assistantships. The School and professional community provide internship scholarships that give valuable and paid work experience with southern California's most prestigious architectural professionals. The University provides guaranteed student loans and grants.

Cost of Study

Tuition for the 2007–08 academic year was approximately $35,000 for students attending a University of Southern California School of Architecture program.

Living and Housing Costs

The University estimated the cost of room, board, and fees for the 2007–08 academic year to be approximately $19,000.

Student Group

The diversity of the student body, from a wide variety of backgrounds in the United States and abroad, greatly enriches the educational experience for all students. All graduate students possess an undergraduate degree in architecture or engineering, and many have had several years of professional experience. There is a graduate student association; student chapters of the AIAS, CLEA, the National Organization of Minority Architects, Alpha Rho Chi, the Association of Women Architects, Asian American Architects and Engineers Student Chapter; and a student council.

Location

USC is located in the heart of Los Angeles, the second-largest city in the United States and a world leader in design. Los Angeles is a city with 200 years of architectural heritage. The city offers one of the best laboratories in which to understand twentieth-century urban conditions and their architectural implications. The campus is a beautiful, landscaped site only minutes from the downtown central business district. The natural and man-made geography of the dense urban centers, the suburbs, the beaches, deserts, mountains, and coastal plains offers a vast and unequaled environmental context in which to study architecture and the urban fabric. The strong USC tradition of outstanding design education provides extensive and diverse employment opportunities in the growing southern California, West, and Pacific Rim areas.

The School

The School of Architecture has a continuing commitment to explore issues at the heart of the contemporary urban experience. The faculty includes prominent architects, many of whom are internationally renowned. The fundamental premises of the School include recognition of the interdependence of theory and practice, understanding the basis of architecture as a response to the human condition, respect for the disciplines of visual form, and acknowledgment of the necessity for technology to be an extension of human capacity in order to sustain the environment.

Applying

All students applying to the graduate programs should demonstrate an exceptional command of design inquiry and resolution. Applicants to the Graduate Programs in Architecture and Landscape Architecture must submit a portfolio that shows work appropriate to the graduate level. Basic requirements for admission include the appropriate first degree from an accredited university, intellectual promise and indication of the ability to complete satisfactory graduate work, satisfactory scores on the Graduate Record Examinations, and strong personal qualifications. International students must also submit the results of the TOEFL. Priority for admission and financial aid is given to students who apply by February 1.

Correspondence and Information

Graduate Admissions
School of Architecture
University of Southern California
Los Angeles, California 90089-0291

Phone: 213-821-2168
Fax: 213-740-8884
E-mail: archgrad@usc.edu
Web site: http://arch.usc.edu

University of Southern California

THE FACULTY

Qingyun Ma, Dean; M.Arch., Pennsylvania.
Kenneth Breisch, Associate Professor of the Practice of Architecture and Director, Historic Preservation Program; Ph.D., Michigan.
Sara Loe, Assistant Professor of the Practice of Architecture and Assistant Director, Master of Architecture Programs; M.Arch., UCLA.
Robert Harris, Professor and Director, Master of Architecture Program; M.F.A. (architecture), Princeton.
Marc Schiler, Professor and Director, Master of Building Science Program; M.Arch., Cornell; FASES, LC.
Brian Andrews, Assistant Professor; M.Arch., Princeton.
Michael Arden, Lecturer; M.A., Santa Monica.
Valery Augustin, Lecturer; M.Arch., UCLA.
Tigran Ayrapetyan, Lecturer.
Kara Bartelt, Assistant Professor; M.Arch., Yale.
Sharon Ben-Joseph, Lecturer.
Rachel Berney, Lecturer; Ph.D., Berkeley.
Vinayak Bharne, Lecturer; M.Arch., USC.
Nathan Bishop, Lecturer.
Mark Bittoni, Lecturer; M.Arch., UCLA.
Gail Peter Borden, Assistant Professor; M.Arch., Harvard; AIA.
Kenneth Breisch, Associate Professor of the Practice of Architecture; Ph.D., Michigan.
Douglas A. Campbell, Lecturer; ASLA.
Regula F. Campbell Associate Professor; AIA.
Mina Chow, Lecturer; M.Arch., Harvard; AIA.
Michael Chung, Lecturer; M.Arch., Yale.
Mario Cipresso, Lecturer; M.Arch., UCLA; AIA.
Christopher Coe, Lecturer; M.Arch., Yale; AIA.
Kim Coleman, Professor; M.Arch., Virginia.
Arminda Diaz, Lecturer; B.Arch., Cornell.
Frank Dimster, Professor; M.Arch., Washington (St. Louis); FAIA.
Janek Dombrowa, Assistant Professor of the Practice of Architecture; M.Arch., Princeton; AIA.
Liz Falletta, Lecturer; M.Arch., M.R.E.D., USC.
Hunter Fleetwood, Lecturer.
Miller Fong, Lecturer; B.A.Arch., USC.
Mark Gangi, Lecturer.
Diane Ghirardo, Professor; Ph.D., Stanford.
Arthur Golding, Associate Professor of the Practice of Architecture; M.Arch., Yale; AIA.
Arianne Groth, Lecturer; AIA.
Jeff Guh, Adjunct Associate Professor; Ph.D., Berkeley; ASCE.
Yo-ichiro Hakomori, Adjunct Associate Professor; Ph.D., Tokyo; AIA.
Peyton Hall, Lecturer; M.E.D., Yale; FAIA.
Robert S. Harris, Lecturer; M.F.A. (architecture), Princeton; FAIA.
Michael Hricak, Lecturer; M.Arch., Harvard; FAIA.
Ying-Yu Hung, Lecturer; M.L.Arch., Harvard; ASLA.
Christoph Kapeller, Lecturer; M.Arch., USC; AIA, ZT.
Karen Kensek, Lecturer; M.Arch., Berkeley.
Gerald Knowles, Lecturer; M.Arch, Houston.
Ralph Knowles, Distinguished Professor Emeritus; M.Arch., MIT; ACSA.
Bung Ko, Lecturer; M.Arch., Harvard.
Charles Lagreco, Lecturer; M.F.A. (architecture), Princeton; AIA.
Steffen Leisner, Lecturer; M.Arch., Southern California Institute of Architecture.
Ken Lewis, Lecturer.
Andrew Liang, Lecturer; M.Arch., Columbia.
Sara Loe, Lecturer; M.Arch., UCLA.
Rebecca Lowry, Lecturer; M.Arch., Harvard.
Qingyun Ma, Lecturer; M.Arch., Pennsylvania.
Anna Maria Mann, Lecturer; M.F.A.
Erik Mar, Lecturer; M.Arch., MIT.
Leonard Marvin, Lecturer; M.B.A., Illinois at Urbana-Champaign; AIA, CSI, CCCA.
Michael McGowan, Lecturer; M.L.Arch., California Polytechnic, Pomona.
Murray Milne, Lecturer; M.S., Michigan.
Melanie Moossaian, Lecturer; M.L.Arch., Harvard.
Graeme M. Morland, Lecturer; Diploma in Architecture, Glasgow; AIA, RIBA, RIAS.
Amy Murphy, Lecturer; M.F.A., USC.
John V. Mutlow, Lecturer; M.Arch., UCLA; FAIA, RIBA.
Marc Neveu, Lecturer; Ph.D., McGill.
Douglas Noble, Lecturer; Ph.D., Berkeley; FAIA.
Lee Olvera, Lecturer; M.Arch., Texas at Austin
Victor Regnier, Lecturer; M.Arch., USC; FAIA.
Trudi Sandmeier, Lecturer.
Jade Satterthwaite, Lecturer; M.L.Arch., USC.
G. Goetz Schierle, Lecturer; Ph.D., Berkeley; FAIA.
Goetz Schierle, Lecturer; Ph.D., Berkeley; FAIA.
Marc Schiler, Lecturer; M.S. Arch. Sci., Cornell; FASES, LC.
Susanna Seierup, Lecturer; M.Arch., Harvard.
Roger Sherwood, Lecturer; M.S.Arch., Columbia; M.R.P., Cornell.
Janice Shimizu, Lecturer; M.Arch.
Niloofar Shokoohy, Lecturer; B.Arch., USC.
Thomas Spiegelhalter, Lecturer; Dipl.Arch., University of the Arts (Berlin, and Bremen, Germany).
James Steele, Lecturer; Ph.D., USC.
Joe Sturges, Lecturer; B.F.A.
Doris Sung, Lecturer; M.Arch., Columbia.
Paul R. Tang, Lecturer; M.Arch., Harvard; AIA.
Selwyn Ting, Lecturer; M.Arch., Colorado; AIA.
James Tyler, Lecturer; B.Arch., Utah; FAIA.
Dimitry Vergun, Lecturer; M.S. (structural engineering), Stanford.
Roland Wahlroos-Ritter, Lecturer.
Christopher Warren, Lecturer; M.Arch., Pennsylvania.
Emily White, Lecturer.
Ed Woll, Lecturer; Ph.D., Carnegie Mellon; AIA.
Eui-SungYi, Lecturer; M.Arch., Harvard.

Future architectural leaders enjoy one-on-one faculty-student interaction in studios that promote inquiry, refine principles and values, and teach disciplines required to work with other professionals.

Pritzker Prize–winning architect and USC alumnus Frank Gehry informally meets with students and faculty members.

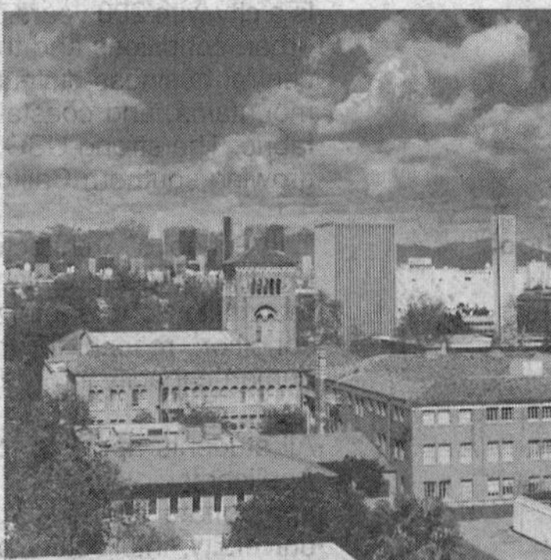

USC derives much of its vitality and diversity from the University's strategic location in the heart of the Los Angeles urban complex.

WASHINGTON UNIVERSITY IN ST. LOUIS

Sam Fox School of Design & Visual Arts
Graduate School of Architecture & Urban Design

Programs of Study Washington University's graduate programs in architecture and urban design provide students with rigorous design skills, challenging intellectual inquiry, and thorough professional development. Within an environment known for academic excellence and innovation, Master of Architecture (M.Arch.) and Master of Urban Design (M.U.D.) degrees are offered along with opportunities for international study and interdisciplinary work with other divisions of the University. Dual graduate degrees are also available with the John M. Olin School of Business, the George Warren Brown School of Social Work, and the School of Engineering and Applied Science.

The Master of Architecture program leads to an NAAB–accredited first professional degree and is open to those who already hold baccalaureate degrees in architecture as well as in other fields. The program focuses on the synthetic activity of design and on the critical role of architects in society and culture. The aim is to educate expressive, skillful designers prepared to act as thoughtful, effective members of the profession and practice of architecture. Depending on an applicant's prior experiences and academic qualifications, this course of study may be completed in 2 to 3½ years.

The Master of Urban Design (M.U.D.) program focuses on contemporary urban issues through a unique blend of architectural, landscape, and planning perspectives. The one-year postprofessional program combines course work with research design studios and a summer practicum. The program provides training for professional architects and landscape architects who wish to further their knowledge base and become conversant in the contemporary metropolitan issues faced in practice.

The postprofessional Master of Architecture program is open to those who already hold NAAB–accredited professional degrees. This highly independent and self-directed program offers opportunities for advanced design work and research to qualified and motivated individuals.

The Graduate School's faculty members offer expertise in history and theory, building technology, landscape and environmental design, digital media, urban design, and professional practice. The skills of the resident faculty members are augmented by the School's long-distinguished Visiting Faculty Program that attracts designers, lecturers, and critics from around the world. Graduate-level international semesters are offered in Barcelona, Buenos Aires, and Helsinki.

Research Facilities The Kenneth and Nancy Kranzberg Art and Architecture Library contains a collection of more than 105,000 volumes in all formats and is part of the larger campus library system with holdings of more than 3 million volumes and facilities for research in the humanities, social sciences, engineering, and mathematics. Other resources available to architecture students include diverse and distributed computer and media technologies as well as fully equipped metal and woodworking shops.

Financial Aid Financial aid for the 2007–08 academic year was offered to 100 percent of the financial aid applicants and to 93 percent of the total graduate enrollment. Awards are based on academic excellence and financial need. Aid is available in the form of scholarships and loans (federally, state, and/or locally financed). Highly qualified students are considered for a full-tuition scholarship and the partial-tuition Danforth Scholarship that is offered by the school, as well as for teaching and research assistantships. An Asian Student Scholarship Fund is also available.

Cost of Study Tuition for the 2007–08 academic year was $34,500.

Living and Housing Costs St. Louis is considered among the ten most livable areas in the United States, and its residents enjoy a pleasant environment and an extremely modest cost of living. Most graduate students live off campus in large and affordable apartments that are plentiful and convenient to the School of Architecture. The University's estimate of living expenses for the nine-month academic year, including room and board, books and supplies, clothing, recreation, incidentals, and medical insurance, is $17,833.

Student Group The School currently has an enrollment of 178 graduate and 204 undergraduate students. These students come from all over the world, with 15 percent from countries other than the United States. Approximately 47 percent of the entering students have a baccalaureate degree with a major in architecture; the remaining 53 percent of graduate students come with varied backgrounds, including math, history, art, music, business, and psychology. Women make up 45 percent of the graduate class. The student-faculty ratio is approximately 10:1.

Student Outcomes Most graduates pursue design careers in architecture, while others choose to concentrate in teaching, development, construction, business, social work, development, and government work related to architecture. Students receive career planning and placement support from a career specialist on the School's staff. Graduates are employed in all geographic areas of the U.S. and in many international markets.

Location Washington University is located in metropolitan St. Louis, which lies in the heart of the American Midwest at the confluence of the Mississippi and Missouri Rivers. The location provides a unique design laboratory in both urban issues and the regional landscape. St. Louis and the surrounding region possess a rich and varied architectural heritage, from the Cahokia Mounds to Louis Sullivan's Wainwright Building to Eero Saarinen's Gateway Arch to Tadao Ando's Pulitzer Foundation for the Arts. Culturally, the city offers a world-renowned symphony, diverse visual arts institutions, a range of theater companies, and successful professional sports teams.

The University and The School Established in 1853, Washington University is an independent major university characterized by academic excellence in many fields at the undergraduate and graduate levels. Graduate and professional programs in architecture, law, business, medicine, and social work are nationally recognized. The Graduate School of Architecture & Urban Design, part of the Sam Fox School of Design & Visual Arts, is housed in Givens and Steinberg Halls, which sit on the eastern edge of a historic, tree-lined campus plan that is adjacent to remarkable residential areas and one of the country's largest urban parks. The nearby Mildred Lane Kemper Museum, designed by Fumihiko Maki for the Sam Fox School, was dedicated in October 2006, greatly expanding the resources available to students in architecture and art.

Applying Applicants to all graduate programs must submit a completed application form, transcript(s) of undergraduate work, three letters of evaluation, and GRE scores by February 1. All applicants must also submit a portfolio showing examples of visual material. M.Arch 3 candidates are advised to include in their portfolio creative design efforts such as drawing, sculpture, or other efforts in the visual arts to demonstrate a potential for further creative accomplishment. Applicants to all other graduate programs must include architectural design work; however, other types of artistic endeavors are also welcome. For nonnative English speakers, a minimum TOEFL score of 550 on the paper-based test, 213 on the computer-based test, or 80 on the Internet-based test is required for admission.

Correspondence and Information
Office of Graduate Admissions
Graduate School of Architecture & Urban Design
Campus Box 1079
Washington University in St. Louis
One Brookings Drive
St. Louis, Missouri 63130
Phone: 314-935-6227
800-295-6227 (toll-free in the continental U.S.)
Fax: 314-935-7656
E-mail: wuarch@architecture.wustl.edu
Web site: http://www.arch.wustl.edu

Washington University in St. Louis

THE FACULTY AND THEIR RESEARCH

Carmon Colangelo, Dean of the Sam Fox School of Design & Visual Arts; M.F.A., Louisiana State. Administration. Collaboration within community of architects and artists.
Peter MacKeith, Associate Dean of the Sam Fox School of Design & Visual Arts and Associate Professor of Architecture; M.Arch., Yale. Design. Design studio, Scandinavian architecture, concepts and principles of architecture.
Bruce Lindsey, Dean of the College of Architecture and Graduate School of Architecture & Urban Design; M.Arch., Yale. Design, sustainable architecture, collaboration of architecture and the arts.

Jeffrey Berk, Affiliate Associate Professor (Buenos Aires); M.Arch., Buenos Aires. Design studio.
Randy Burkett, Lecturer; B.Arch.Eng., Penn State. Architectural lighting.
Gerardo Caballaro, Affiliate Associate Professor (Buenos Aires); M.Arch., Washington (St. Louis). Design studio.
Gustavo Cardon, Affiliate Associate Professor (Buenos Aires); M.Arch., Miami (Florida). Design studio.
Gia Daskalakis, Associate Professor; B.Arch., B.F.A., Rhode Island School of Design. Design studio and theory courses. Intersection of architecture, urbanism, and landscape architecture; study of early twentieth-century avant-garde phenomenon.
Paul Donnelly, Professor and Co-Director, Graduate Program; M.S., Columbia. Design studio. Building systems, structures and construction technology, technology transfer.
Iain Fraser, Professor and Director, Undergraduate Studies; M.Arch., Washington (St. Louis). Design studio. Design methods, architecture and urban typology.
Gay Goldman-Lorberbaum, Affiliate Associate Professor; M.Arch, Washington (St. Louis). Fundamental design.
Esley Hamilton, Affiliate Assistant Professor; M.S., Wisconsin. Historic preservation/urban design.
Robert Hansman, Associate Professor; B.F.A., Kansas. Graphics, drawing and painting.
John Hoal, Associate Professor; Ph.D., Washington (St. Louis). Design studio and theories of urban design and urban planning. City and land use revitalization, master planning for parks and communities.
Philip Holden, Affiliate Associate Professor; M.Arch., Washington (St. Louis). Design studio.
Richard Janis, Affiliate Associate Professor; M.Arch, M.S., Washington (St. Louis). Mechanical systems.
George Johannes, Affiliate Assistant Professor; M.Arch., Washington (St. Louis). Professional practice.
Sung Ho Kim, Assistant Professor; S.M.Arch.S., MIT. Design studio, digital technology. Research using newly emerging digital media and mechanical/material procedures.
Stephen Leet, Associate Professor; B.Arch., Kentucky. Design studio. Exhibit design and curation, modern American and Italian architecture and industrial design, photography.
Zeuler Lima, Assistant Professor; M.S., São Paolo (Brazil). Design studio and history-theory, Modernism and post-World War II architecture and urbanism.
Adrian Luchini, Professor and Co-Director, Graduate Program; M.Arch., Harvard. Design and theory. Relationship between architectural theory and practice, international architecture.
Paula Lupkin, Assistant Professor; Ph.D., Pennsylvania. Architectural history. Modern American architecture and urbanism, social reform and modernism as it relates to architecture.
Roy Manttari, Affiliate Assistant Professor (Helsinki); M.S.Arch., Helsinki. Design studio.
Igor Marjanovic, Assistant Professor; M.Arch., Illinois at Chicago. Design studio and architectural theory. History of design pedagogy.
Robert McCarter, Professor; M.Arch., Columbia. Design studio, history and theory.
Eric Mumford, Associate Professor and Director, Master of Urban Design Program; Ph.D., Princeton. Architectural history and urbanism. American urban design education, global considerations of urban design practice.
Jana Pereau, Affiliate Associate Professor; Dr.D.E.S., Harvard. Design studio.
Michael Repovich, Affiliate Assistant Professor; B.Arch., Kansas State. Construction technology, sustainable architecture.
Carl B. Safe, Professor; M.E.D., Yale. Design studio. Principles of humane design, design/build studios, furniture design.
James J. Scott, Lecturer; J.D., St. Louis. Professional practice.
Phillip Shinn, Affiliate Assistant Professor; B.S., Princeton. Structures.
William Wischmeyer, Affiliate Associate Professor; M.Arch., Washington (St. Louis). Design studio.
Jane Wolff, Assistant Professor; M.L.A., Harvard. Landscape, site planning, urban issues. Hybrid landscapes produced by natural process and cultural intervention.
Heather Woofter, Assistant Professor; M.Arch., Harvard. Design studio. Investigation of measured drawing and spatial procedures that question perception through emerging technologies.

Visiting Faculty
Donald Koster, Weese Fellow Visiting Assistant Professor; M.Arch., Washington (St. Louis). Design studio and representation.
Mitchell Joachim, Visiting Assistant Professor; Ph.D., MIT. Design studio.
Jen Maigret, Weese, Fellow Visiting Assistant Professor; M.Arch., Michigan. Design studio and representation. Architecture as a component within broader environmental and social ecologies.
Jodi Polzin, Visiting Assistant Professor; M.Arch., Columbia. Design studio and representation. Explorations of cities and representations of place.

Section 3
Art and Art History

This section contains a directory of institutions offering graduate work in art and art history, followed by in-depth entries submitted by institutions that chose to prepare detailed program descriptions. Additional information about programs listed in the directory but not augmented by an in-depth entry may be obtained by writing directly to the dean of a graduate school or chair of a department at the address given in the directory.

For programs offering related work, see also in this book *Applied Arts and Design; Architecture; Area and Cultural Studies; Film, Television, and Video; Performing Arts;* and *Sociology, Anthropology, and Archaeology.* In another guide in this series:

Graduate Programs in Business, Education, Health, Information Studies, Law & Social Work

See *Subject Areas (Art Education)*

CONTENTS

Art/Fine Arts

Academy of Art University, Graduate Program, School of Fine Art, San Francisco, CA 94105-3410. Offers figurative painting (MFA); non-figurative painting (MFA); printmaking (MFA); sculpture (MFA). *Accreditation:* NASAD. Part-time programs available. Postbaccalaureate distance learning degree programs offered (no on-campus study). *Degree requirements:* For master's, final review. *Entrance requirements:* For master's, minimum GPA of 3.0, portfolio. Electronic applications accepted.

Adams State College, The Graduate School, Department of Art, Alamosa, CO 81102. Offers MA. Part-time programs available. *Degree requirements:* For master's, thesis, departmental qualifying exam. *Entrance requirements:* For master's, GRE General Test or MAT, minimum undergraduate GPA of 2.75. *Application deadline:* For fall admission, 5/1 for domestic students; for spring admission, 12/1 for domestic students. Application fee: $30. *Financial support:* In 2007–08, fellowships with partial tuition reimbursements (averaging $4,000 per year), teaching assistantships with partial tuition reimbursements (averaging $4,000 per year) were awarded; career-related internships or fieldwork, Federal Work-Study, institutionally sponsored loans, and unspecified assistantships also available. Support available to part-time students. Financial award application deadline: 4/15; financial award applicants required to submit FAFSA. *Unit head:* Margaret Doell, Chair, 719-587-7823, Fax: 719-587-7330, E-mail: ascart@adams.edu.

Adelphi University, Graduate School of Arts and Sciences, Department of Art and Art History, Garden City, NY 11530-0701. Offers MA. Part-time programs available. *Students:* 4 full-time (3 women), 21 part-time (15 women); includes 4 minority (all Hispanic Americans) Average age 30. In 2007, 8 degrees awarded. *Degree requirements:* For master's, art exhibit. *Entrance requirements:* For master's, portfolio, 2 letters of recommendation. Additional exam requirements/recommendations for international students: Required—TOEFL (minimum score 550 paper-based; 213 computer-based). *Application deadline:* For fall admission, 5/1 for international students; for spring admission, 12/1 for international students. Applications are processed on a rolling basis. Application fee: $50. Electronic applications accepted. *Financial support:* Research assistantships with full and partial tuition reimbursements, career-related internships or fieldwork, Federal Work-Study, institutionally sponsored loans, and unspecified assistantships available. Financial award application deadline: 2/15; financial award applicants required to submit FAFSA. *Unit head:* David Hornung, Chairperson, 516-877-4458, E-mail: hornung@adelphi.edu. *Application contact:* Christine Murphy, Director of Admissions, 516-877-3050, Fax: 516-877-3039, E-mail: graduateadmissions@adelphi.edu.

See Close-Up on page 225.

Alfred University, Graduate School, New York State College of Ceramics, School of Art and Design, Alfred, NY 14802-1205. Offers ceramic art (MFA); electronic integrated arts (MFA); glass art (MFA); sculpture (MFA). *Accreditation:* NASAD. *Students:* 34 full-time (19 women). Average age 26. 278 applicants, 6% accepted, 17 enrolled. In 2007, 17 degrees awarded. *Degree requirements:* For master's, exhibit. *Entrance requirements:* For master's, portfolio. Additional exam requirements/recommendations for international students: Required—TOEFL (minimum score 550 paper-based; 213 computer-based; 80 iBT), IELTS (minimum score 6). *Application deadline:* For fall admission, 1/15 for domestic students, 2/1 for international students. Application fee: $50. Electronic applications accepted. *Expenses:* Tuition: Full-time $32,016; part-time $680 per credit hour. Required fees: $850; $140 per year. *Financial support:* In 2007–08, 35 students received support; teaching assistantships with full tuition reimbursements available, tuition waivers (full) available. Financial award applicants required to submit FAFSA. *Faculty research:* Ceramic sculpture, functional ceramics, wood, mixed media, hot and cold glass. *Unit head:* Joseph Lewis, Dean, 607-871-2412, E-mail: lewis@alfred.edu. *Application contact:* Valerie Stephens, Coordinator of Graduate Admissions, 607-871-2141, Fax: 607-871-2198, E-mail: gradinquiry@alfred.edu.

Alfred University, Graduate School, New York State College of Ceramics, School of Engineering, Alfred, NY 14802-1205. Offers biomedical materials engineering science (MS); ceramic engineering (MS); ceramics (PhD); electrical engineering (MS); glass science (MS, PhD); materials science and engineering (MS, PhD); mechanical engineering (MS). *Faculty:* 21 full-time (3 women), 4 part-time/adjunct (0 women). *Students:* 40 full-time (8 women), 7 part-time (1 woman). Average age 24. 71 applicants, 46% accepted, 21 enrolled. In 2007, 13 master's, 5 doctorates awarded. *Median time to degree:* Of those who began their doctoral program in fall 1999, 100% received their degree in 8 years or less. *Degree requirements:* For master's, thesis; for doctorate, thesis/dissertation. *Entrance requirements:* Additional exam requirements/recommendations for international students: Required—TOEFL (minimum score 590 paper-based; 243 computer-based). *Application deadline:* For fall admission, 5/1 priority date for international students; for spring admission, 11/1 priority date for international students. Applications are processed on a rolling basis. Application fee: $50. Electronic applications accepted. *Expenses: Contact institution. Financial support:* In 2007–08, 40 students received support; fellowships with tuition reimbursements available, research assistantships with tuition reimbursements available, teaching assistantships with tuition reimbursements available, tuition waivers (full and partial) available. Financial award applicants required to submit FAFSA. *Faculty research:* Fine-particle technology, x-ray diffraction, superconductivity, electronic materials. *Unit head:* Dr. Doreen Edwards, Graduate Program Director, School of Engineering, 607-871-2284, E-mail: dedwards@alfred.edu. *Application contact:* Valerie Stephens, Coordinator of Graduate Admissions, 607-871-2141, Fax: 607-871-2198, E-mail: gradinquiry@alfred.edu.

American Academy of Art, Graduate Programs, Program in Painting and Drawing, Chicago, IL 60604-4302. Offers MFA. Part-time and evening/weekend programs available. *Degree requirements:* For master's, thesis, exhibition. *Entrance requirements:* For master's, interview, portfolio, 2 letters of recommendation. Additional exam requirements/recommendations for international students: Required—TOEFL (minimum score 500 paper-based; 173 computer-based). *Faculty research:* Painting, drawing, sculpture, representational art.

American University, College of Arts and Sciences, Department of Art, Programs in Painting, Sculpture and Printmaking, Washington, DC 20016-8001. Offers MFA. *Students:* 24 full-time (12 women); includes 2 minority (both Hispanic Americans) Average age 27. In 2007, 8 degrees awarded. *Degree requirements:* For master's, comprehensive exam, thesis. *Entrance requirements:* For master's, GRE, portfolio. *Application deadline:* For fall admission, 1/15 priority date for domestic students. Application fee: $50. *Expenses:* Tuition: Full-time $19,998; part-time $1,111 per credit hour. Required fees: $380. Tuition and fees vary according to program. *Financial support:* Teaching assistantships with partial tuition reimbursements, career-related internships or fieldwork, Federal Work-Study, and institutionally sponsored loans available. Support available to part-time students. Financial award application deadline: 1/15. *Faculty research:* Drawing. *Application contact:* Glenna K. Haynie, Administrative Coordinator, 202-885-1671.

Anna Maria College, Graduate Division, Program in Education, Paxton, MA 01612. Offers early childhood development (M Ed); education (CAGS); elementary education (M Ed); reading (M Ed); visual art (M Ed). Part-time and evening/weekend programs available. *Faculty:* 4 full-time (all women), 8 part-time/adjunct (6 women). *Students:* 1 (woman) full-time, 85 part-time (84 women); includes 2 minority (1 Asian American or Pacific Islander, 1 Hispanic American). Average age 33. In 2007, 30 master's, 2 CAGSs awarded. *Entrance requirements:* For master's, bachelor's degree in liberal arts or sciences, minimum GPA of 3.0. Additional exam requirements/recommendations for international students: Required—TOEFL (minimum score 500 paper-based). *Application deadline:* For fall admission, 3/1 priority date for domestic and international students; for spring admission, 11/1 priority date for domestic and international students. Applications are processed on a rolling basis. Application fee: $40. Electronic applications accepted. *Expenses:* Tuition: Part-time $1,272 per course. *Financial support:* Applicants required to submit FAFSA. *Unit head:* Christine Holmes, Director, 508-849-3418, Fax: 508-849-3343, E-mail: cholmes@annamaria.edu. *Application contact:* Dennis Braun, Director, Graduate and Continuing Education Recruitment, 508-849-3293, Fax: 508-819-3362, E-mail: dbraun@annamaria.edu.

Anna Maria College, Graduate Division, Program in Visual Art, Paxton, MA 01612. Offers M Ed, MA. Part-time and evening/weekend programs available. *Faculty:* 1 (woman) full-time, 1 (woman) part-time/adjunct. *Students:* Average age 45. In 2007, 1 degree awarded. *Degree requirements:* For master's, thesis. *Entrance requirements:* For master's, minimum GPA of 2.7, undergraduate major in art, portfolio. Additional exam requirements/recommendations for international students: Required—TOEFL (minimum score 500 paper-based). *Application deadline:* For fall admission, 3/1 priority date for domestic and international students; for spring admission, 11/1 priority date for domestic and international students. Applications are processed on a rolling basis. Application fee: $40. Electronic applications accepted. *Expenses:* Tuition: Part-time $1,272 per course. *Unit head:* Dennis Braun, Director, Graduate and Continuing Education Recruitment, 508-849-3293, Fax: 508-819-3362, E-mail: dbraun@annamaria.edu. *Application contact:* Janet LaPointe, Admissions Coordinator, Graduate and Continuing Education, 508-849-3234, Fax: 508-819-3362, E-mail: jlapointe@annamaria.edu.

Antioch University McGregor, Graduate Programs, Individualized Liberal and Professional Studies Program, Yellow Springs, OH 45387-1609. Offers liberal and professional studies (MA), including counseling, creative writing, education, film studies, liberal studies, management, modern literature, psychology, theatre, visual arts. Part-time and evening/weekend programs available. Postbaccalaureate distance learning degree programs offered (minimal on-campus study). *Faculty:* 2 full-time (1 woman), 3 part-time/adjunct (2 women). *Students:* Average age 40. 35 applicants, 63% accepted, 17 enrolled. In 2007, 31 degrees awarded. *Degree requirements:* For master's, thesis or alternative. *Entrance requirements:* For master's, resumé, 2 letters of reference. *Application deadline:* For fall admission, 8/25 for domestic students; for winter admission, 12/5 for domestic students; for spring admission, 3/8 for domestic students. Applications are processed on a rolling basis. Application fee: $50. Electronic applications accepted. *Expenses: Contact institution. Financial support:* Federal Work-Study available. Financial award applicants required to submit FAFSA. *Unit head:* Suzanne Fest, Chair, 937-769-1876, Fax: 937-769-1807, E-mail: sfest@mcgregor.edu. *Application contact:* Seth Gordon, Assistant Director of Admissions, 937-769-1800 Ext. 1825, Fax: 937-769-1804, E-mail: sgordon@mcgregor.edu.

See Close-Up on page 443.

Arizona State University, Graduate College, College of Fine Arts, School of Art, Tempe, AZ 85287. Offers MA, MFA.

Arkansas State University, Graduate School, College of Fine Arts, Department of Art, Jonesboro, State University, AR 72467. Offers MA. *Accreditation:* NASAD. Part-time programs available. *Faculty:* 9 full-time (4 women). *Students:* 4 full-time (2 women), 2 part-time (both women). Average age 37. 3 applicants, 67% accepted, 2 enrolled. *Degree requirements:* For master's, comprehensive exam, thesis. *Entrance requirements:* For master's, GRE General Test or MAT, portfolio, appropriate bachelor's degree, letters of reference, official transcript. Additional exam requirements/recommendations for international students: Required—TOEFL (minimum score 213 computer-based). *Application deadline:* Applications are processed on a rolling basis. Application fee: $30 ($40 for international students). Electronic applications accepted. *Expenses:* Tuition, state resident: full-time $3,528; part-time $196 per hour. Tuition, nonresident: full-time $8,928; part-time $496 per hour. Required fees: $842; $44 per hour. $25 per term. Tuition and fees vary according to course load and program. *Financial support:* Teaching assistantships, scholarships/grants and unspecified assistantships available. Financial award application deadline: 7/1; financial award applicants required to submit FAFSA. *Faculty research:* Art and visual psychology, digital photography, graphic design, modern art, painting-reverse on plexiglass. *Unit head:* Curtis Steele, Chair, 870-972-3050, Fax: 870-972-3932, E-mail: csteele@astate.edu.

Arkansas Tech University, Graduate School, School of Liberal and Fine Arts, Russellville, AR 72801. Offers communication (MLA); English (M Ed, MA); fine arts (MLA); history (MA); multi-media journalism (MA); social science (MLA); social studies (M Ed); Spanish (MA, MLA); teaching English as a second language (MA, MLA). Part-time programs available. *Students:* 54 full-time (43 women), 79 part-time (54 women); includes 11 minority (3 African Americans, 1 American Indian/Alaska Native, 1 Asian American or Pacific Islander, 6 Hispanic Americans), 29 international. Average age 33. In 2007, 71 degrees awarded. *Degree requirements:* For master's, project. *Entrance requirements:* For master's, GRE General Test or MAT. Additional exam requirements/recommendations for international students: Required—TOEFL (minimum score 500 paper-based; 173 computer-based; 61 iBT). *Application deadline:* For fall admission, 3/1 priority date for domestic students, 5/1 priority date for international students; for winter admission, 10/1 priority date for international students; for spring admission, 10/1 priority date for domestic and international students. Applications are processed on a rolling basis. Application fee: $0 ($30 for international students). Electronic applications accepted. *Expenses:* Tuition, state resident: full-time $3,150; part-time $175 per hour. Tuition, nonresident: full-time $6,300; part-time $350 per hour. Required fees: $384; $8 per hour. $120 per term. Tuition and fees vary according to course load. *Financial support:* In 2007–08, teaching assistantships with full tuition reimbursements (averaging $4,000 per year); career-related internships or fieldwork, Federal Work-Study, scholarships/grants, health care benefits, and unspecified assistantships also available. Support available to part-time students. Financial award application deadline: 4/15; financial award applicants required to submit FAFSA. *Unit head:* Dr. Georgena Duncan, Dean, 479-968-0266, Fax: 479-968-0275, E-mail: georgena.duncan@atu.edu. *Application contact:* Dr. Eldon G. Clary, Dean of Graduate School, 479-968-0398, Fax: 479-964-0542, E-mail: graduate.school@atu.edu.

Art Center College of Design, Graduate Division, Fine Arts Department, Pasadena, CA 91103-1999. Offers MFA. *Accreditation:* NASAD. *Faculty:* 19 part-time/adjunct (9 women). *Students:* 33 full-time (17 women), 2 part-time (1 woman); includes 6 minority (3 American Indian/Alaska Native, 3 Asian Americans or Pacific Islanders), 5 international. Average age 27. 58 applicants, 48% accepted, 10 enrolled. In 2007, 12 degrees awarded. *Degree requirements:* For master's, thesis, studio project. *Entrance requirements:* For master's, portfolio. Additional exam requirements/recommendations for international students: Required—TOEFL (minimum score 600 paper-based; 250 computer-based; 100 iBT). *Application deadline:* For fall admission, 3/1 priority date for domestic students; for winter admission, 9/15 priority date for domestic students. Applications are processed on a rolling basis. Application fee: $50 ($70 for international students). *Expenses:* Tuition: Full-time $31,016. Required fees: $235. *Financial support:* Teaching assistantships, career-related internships or fieldwork, Federal Work-Study, and scholarships/grants available. Financial award application deadline: 3/1. *Unit head:* Dr. Jeremy Gilbert-Rolfe, Chair, 626-584-8424. *Application contact:* Kit Baron, Vice President, Admissions, 626-396-2373, Fax: 626-795-0578, E-mail: admissions@artcenter.edu.

See Close-Up on page 109.

The Art Institute of Boston at Lesley University, Program in Visual Arts, Boston, MA 02215-2598. Offers MFA. *Accreditation:* NASAD.

See Close-Up on page 227.

Atlantic University, Program in Visionary Art and Consciousness, Virginia Beach, VA 23451-2061. Offers MFA. Part-time and evening/weekend programs available. Postbaccalaureate distance learning degree programs offered (no on-campus study). *Faculty:* 2 part-time/adjunct (1 woman). *Degree requirements:* For master's, thesis. *Entrance requirements:* For master's, BFA or BA or BS in Studio Art with 40 studio credits or more. Additional exam requirements/recommendations for international students: Required—TOEFL (minimum score 550 paper-based; 213 computer-based). *Application deadline:* For fall admission, 3/31 for domestic and international students. Application fee: $50. *Expenses:* Contact institution. *Unit head:* Kevin J. Todeschi, Chief Executive Officer, 757-631-8101, Fax: 757-631-8096, E-mail: info@atlanticuniv.edu. *Application contact:* R. Gregory Deming, Director of Admissions, 757-631-8101, Fax: 757-631-8096, E-mail: admissions@atlanticuniv.edu.

Azusa Pacific University, College of Liberal Arts and Sciences, Program in Fine Arts in Visual Art, Azusa, CA 91702-7000. Offers MFA.

Ball State University, Graduate School, College of Fine Arts, Department of Art, Muncie, IN 47306-1099. Offers art (MA); art education (MA, MAE). *Accreditation:* NASAD. *Faculty:* 18. *Students:* 7 full-time (5 women), 8 part-time (5 women), 1 international. Average age 27. 11 applicants, 64% accepted, 6 enrolled. In 2007, 7 degrees awarded. Application fee: $25 ($35 for international students). *Expenses:* Tuition, state resident: full-time $6,864. Tuition, nonresident: full-time $17,932. Required fees: $1,866. *Financial support:* In 2007–08, 5 teaching assistantships with full tuition reimbursements (averaging $7,000 per year) were awarded; research assistantships with full tuition reimbursements. Financial award application deadline: 3/1. *Unit head:* David Jackson, Head, 765-285-5838, Fax: 765-285-5275. *Application contact:* Kenton Hall, Director, 765-285-5838, Fax: 765-285-5275, E-mail: khall@bsu.edu.

Bard College, Milton Avery Graduate School of the Arts, Annandale-on-Hudson, NY 12504. Offers MFA. *Faculty:* 3 full-time (1 woman), 53 part-time/adjunct (24 women). *Students:* 75 full-time. Average age 34. 416 applicants, 7% accepted, 29 enrolled. In 2007, 33 degrees awarded. *Degree requirements:* For master's, thesis, project, 8-week summer residency, independent study. *Entrance requirements:* For master's, interview, portfolio, 2 letters of recommendation, personal statement, history of work in the arts. Additional exam requirements/recommendations for international students: Required—TOEFL (minimum score 550 paper-based; 213 computer-based). *Application deadline:* For fall admission, 1/15 for international students. Application fee: $60. Electronic applications accepted. *Financial support:* Fellowships, scholarships/grants available. Financial award application deadline: 3/15; financial award applicants required to submit FAFSA. *Faculty research:* Original work in painting, writing, sculpture, photography, video/film, sound/music. *Unit head:* Arthur Gibbons, Director, 845-758-7481, Fax: 845-758-7507, E-mail: mfa@bard.edu. *Application contact:* Susan Treekrem, Managing Director, 845-758-7481, Fax: 845-758-7507, E-mail: mfa@bard.edu.

Barry University, School of Arts and Sciences, Department of Fine Arts, Miami Shores, FL 33161-6695. Offers photography (MA, MFA). *Degree requirements:* For master's, thesis (for some programs). *Entrance requirements:* For master's, GRE General Test, minimum GPA of 3.0. *Application deadline:* Applications are processed on a rolling basis. Application fee: $30. Electronic applications accepted. *Financial support:* Career-related internships or fieldwork available. Support available to part-time students. Financial award application deadline: 5/1; financial award applicants required to submit FAFSA. *Faculty research:* Inclusion education, exceptional education, art-based assessments. *Unit head:* Silvia Lizama, Interim Chair, 305-899-3421, Fax: 305-899-2972, E-mail: slizama@mail.barry.edu. *Application contact:* Dave Fletcher, Director of Graduate Admissions, 305-899-3113, Fax: 305-899-2971, E-mail: dfletcher@mail.barry.edu.

Bob Jones University, Graduate Programs, Greenville, SC 29614. Offers accountancy (MS); Bible (MA); Bible translation (MA); Biblical studies (Certificate); broadcast management (MS); business administration (MBA); church history (MA, PhD); church ministries (MA); church music (MM); cinema and video production (MA); counseling (MS); curriculum and instruction (Ed D); divinity (M Div); dramatic production (MA); educational leadership (MS, Ed D, Ed S); elementary education (M Ed, MAT); English (M Ed, MA, MAT); fine arts (MA); graphic design (MA); history (M Ed, MA); illustration (MA); interpretative speech (MA); mathematics (M Ed, MAT); medical missions (Certificate); ministry (MM, D Min); multi-categorical special education (M Ed, MAT); music (M Ed); New Testament interpretation (PhD); Old Testament interpretation (PhD); orchestral instrument performance (MM); organ performance (MM); pastoral studies (MA); personnel services (MS, Ed S); piano pedagogy (MM); piano performance (MM); platform arts (MA); radio and television broadcasting (MS); rhetoric and public address (MA); secondary education (M Ed); studio art (MA); teaching Bible (MA); theology (MA, PhD); voice performance (MM); youth ministries (MA); M Div/MM.

Boise State University, Graduate College, College of Arts and Sciences, Department of Art, Program in Visual Arts, Boise, ID 83725-0399. Offers MFA. *Accreditation:* NASAD. Part-time programs available. *Degree requirements:* For master's, thesis. *Entrance requirements:* For master's, minimum GPA of 3.0, portfolio. Additional exam requirements/recommendations for international students: Required—TOEFL (minimum score 587 paper-based; 240 computer-based). Electronic applications accepted.

Boston University, College of Fine Arts, School of Visual Arts, Boston, MA 02215. Offers art education (MFA); graphic design (MFA); painting (MFA); sculpture (MFA); studio teaching (MFA). *Faculty:* 17 full-time, 4 part-time/adjunct. *Students:* 31 full-time (22 women); includes 5 minority (1 Asian American or Pacific Islander, 4 Hispanic Americans), 1 international. Average age 28. 281 applicants, 28% accepted. In 2007, 38 degrees awarded. *Entrance requirements:* For master's, portfolio. Additional exam requirements/recommendations for international students: Required—TOEFL. *Application deadline:* For fall admission, 2/15 for domestic and international students. Applications are processed on a rolling basis. Application fee: $70. *Expenses:* Tuition: Full-time $34,930; part-time $1,092 per credit. Tuition and fees vary according to class time, course level and program. *Financial support:* Fellowships, teaching assistantships available. Financial award application deadline: 2/15. *Unit head:* Lynne Allen, Director, 617-353-3371. *Application contact:* Mark Krone, Manager, Graduate Admissions, 617-353-3350, E-mail: arts@bu.edu.

See Close-Up on page 345.

Bowling Green State University, Graduate College, College of Arts and Sciences, School of Art, Bowling Green, OH 43403. Offers 2-D studio art (MA, MFA); 3-D studio art (MA, MFA); art education (MA); art history (MA); computer art (MA, MFA); design (MFA); digital arts (MFA); graphics (MFA). *Accreditation:* NASAD. Part-time programs available. *Faculty:* 26 full-time (14 women), 7 part-time/adjunct (2 women). *Students:* 24 full-time (12 women), 3 part-time (all women); includes 1 minority (Asian American or Pacific Islander), 2 international. Average age 33. 59 applicants, 20% accepted, 8 enrolled. In 2007, 11 degrees awarded. *Degree requirements:* For master's, thesis or alternative, final exhibit (MFA). *Entrance requirements:* For master's, GRE General Test (MA), slide portfolio (15-20 slides). Additional exam requirements/recommendations for international students: Required—TOEFL. *Application deadline:* For fall admission, 2/15 for domestic students. Application fee: $30. Electronic applications accepted. *Financial support:* In 2007–08, 11 research assistantships with full and partial tuition reimbursements (averaging $8,404 per year), 8 teaching assistantships with full and partial tuition reimbursements (averaging $8,404 per year) were awarded; career-related internships or fieldwork, institutionally sponsored loans, and unspecified assistantships also available. Support available to part-time students. Financial award applicants required to submit FAFSA. *Faculty research:* Computer animation and virtual reality, Spanish still-life painting from 1600 to 1800, art and psychotherapy, Japanese wood-firing techniques in ceramics, non-toxic printmaking technologies. *Unit head:* Dr. Katerina Rüedi Ray, Director, 419-372-8575. *Application contact:* Shawn Morin, Graduate Coordinator, 419-372-7766.

Bradley University, Graduate School, Slane College of Communications and Fine Arts, Department of Art, Peoria, IL 61625-0002. Offers ceramics (MA, MFA); drawing/illustration (MA, MFA); interdisciplinary art (MA, MFA); painting (MA, MFA); photography (MA, MFA); printmaking (MA, MFA); sculpture (MA, MFA); visual communication and design (MA, MFA). *Accreditation:* NASAD. Part-time programs available. *Faculty:* 10. *Students:* 11 full-time (6 women), 1 international. 20 applicants, 40% accepted, 4 enrolled. In 2007, 2 degrees awarded. *Degree requirements:* For master's, comprehensive exam, thesis, final exhibit. *Entrance requirements:* For master's, portfolio, 2 letters of recommendation. Additional exam requirements/recommendations for international students: Required—TOEFL (minimum score 550 paper-based; 213 computer-based; 79 iBT). *Application deadline:* For fall admission, 4/1 priority date for domestic and international students; for spring admission, 11/1 priority date for domestic and international students. Applications are processed on a rolling basis. Application fee: $40 ($50 for international students). *Financial support:* Research assistantships with full and partial tuition reimbursements, scholarships/grants, tuition waivers (partial), and unspecified assistantships available. Financial award application deadline: 4/1. *Unit head:* Dr. Paul Krainak, Chairperson, 309-677-3330, E-mail: pkrainak@bradley.edu. *Application contact:* Fisher Stolz, Graduate Coordinator, 309-677-2969, E-mail: fisher@bradley.edu.

Brandeis University, Graduate School of Arts and Sciences, Program in Studio Art, Waltham, MA 02454-9110. Offers Certificate. *Faculty:* 7 full-time (2 women), 3 part-time/adjunct (2 women). *Students:* 13 full-time (8 women); includes 3 minority (1 African American, 1 Asian American or Pacific Islander, 1 Hispanic American), 1 international. 23 applicants, 91% accepted, 12 enrolled. In 2007, 16 Certificates awarded. *Degree requirements:* For Certificate, thesis, exhibit of work. *Entrance requirements:* For degree, resumé, sample of work, studio work; letters of recommendation. Additional exam requirements/recommendations for international students: Required—TOEFL (minimum score 600 paper-based; 250 computer-based; 100 iBT), IELTS (minimum score 7). *Application deadline:* Applications are processed on a rolling basis. Application fee: $55. Electronic applications accepted. *Expenses:* Contact institution. *Financial support:* In 2007–08, 18 students received support, including 18 teaching assistantships with partial tuition reimbursements available (averaging $2,000 per year); scholarships/grants and tuition waivers (partial) also available. Financial award application deadline: 4/15; financial award applicants required to submit CSS PROFILE. *Faculty research:* Painting, sculpture, three-dimensional design, printmaking, drawing. *Unit head:* Sean Downey, Faculty Coordinator, 781-736-2660, Fax: 781-736-2672, E-mail: sdowney@brandeis.edu.

Brigham Young University, Graduate Studies, College of Fine Arts and Communications, Department of Visual Arts, Provo, UT 84602-1001. Offers art education (MA); art history (MA); studio art (MFA). Art education applications accepted biennially. *Accreditation:* NASAD. *Faculty:* 28 full-time (7 women), 2 part-time/adjunct (1 woman). *Students:* 43 full-time (28 women); includes 5 minority (all Asian Americans or Pacific Islanders) Average age 26. 25 applicants, 28% accepted, 7 enrolled. In 2007, 18 degrees awarded. *Degree requirements:* For master's, 2 foreign languages, thesis (art history), selected project (MFA), curriculum project (art education). *Entrance requirements:* For master's, GRE (art history), minimum GPA of 3.0 (MFA, MA in art education), 3.3 (MA in art history), portfolio in slide form (MFA), writing samples (MA in art education, art history). Additional exam requirements/recommendations for international students: Required—TOEFL (minimum score 500 paper-based). *Application deadline:* For fall admission, 2/1 for domestic and international students. Application fee: $50. Electronic applications accepted. *Financial support:* In 2007–08, 31 students received support; research assistantships, teaching assistantships with partial tuition reimbursements available, scholarships/grants and tuition waivers (partial) available. Financial award application deadline: 2/1. *Faculty research:* Methodology-standards-assessment, Medieval architecture, classical/Islamic eighteenth- and nineteenth-century art, Netherlandish art, contemporary art. Total annual research expenditures: $83,932. *Unit head:* Linda A. Sullivan, Chair, 801-422-4429, Fax: 801-422-0695, E-mail: sullivan@byu.edu. *Application contact:* Sharon Lyn Heelis, Secretary, 801-422-4429, Fax: 801-422-0695, E-mail: sharon_heelis@byu.edu.

Brooklyn College of the City University of New York, Division of Graduate Studies, Department of Art, Brooklyn, NY 11210-2889. Offers art history (MA, PhD); digital art (MFA); drawing and painting (MFA); photography (MFA); printmaking (MFA); sculpture (MFA). The department offers courses at Brooklyn College that are creditable toward the CUNY doctoral degree; MFA programs—Fall admissions only, application deadline 2/1. Part-time programs available. *Students:* 27 full-time (14 women), 18 part-time (14 women); includes 3 minority (2 African Americans, 1 Asian American or Pacific Islander), 1 international. 82 applicants, 48% accepted, 13 enrolled. In 2007, 21 degrees awarded. *Degree requirements:* For master's, thesis. *Entrance requirements:* For master's, bachelor's degree in art, portfolio, 2 letters of recommendation, portfolio, supplemental application. Additional exam requirements/recommendations for international students: Required—TOEFL. *Application deadline:* For fall admission, 2/1 for domestic and international students; for spring admission, 11/1 for domestic students. Application fee: $125. Electronic applications accepted. *Financial support:* Career-related internships or fieldwork, Federal Work-Study, institutionally sponsored loans, scholarships/grants, and painting awards available. Support available to part-time students. Financial award application deadline: 5/1; financial award applicants required to submit FAFSA. *Unit head:* Dr. Michael Mallory, Chairperson, 718-951-5181, E-mail: mmallory@brooklyn.cuny.edu. *Application contact:* Hernan Sierra, Graduate Admissions Coordinator, 718-951-4536, Fax: 718-951-4506, E-mail: grads@brooklyn.cuny.edu.

California College of the Arts, Graduate Programs, Program in Visual and Critical Studies, San Francisco, CA 94107. Offers MA. *Faculty:* 5 full-time (4 women), 6 part-time/adjunct (3 women). *Students:* 15 full-time (12 women). Average age 30. 31 applicants, 68% accepted, 13 enrolled. In 2007, 7 degrees awarded. *Degree requirements:* For master's, thesis, exhibit. *Entrance requirements:* For master's, appropriate bachelor's degree, portfolio. Additional exam requirements/recommendations for international students: Required—TOEFL (minimum score 600 paper-based; 250 computer-based). *Application deadline:* For fall admission, 1/15 for domestic and international students. Application fee: $50. Electronic applications accepted. *Expenses:* Tuition: Part-time $1,017 per unit. *Financial support:* In 2007–08, 1 fellowship (averaging $7,000 per year), 1 teaching assistantship (averaging $2,000 per year) were awarded; career-related internships or fieldwork, Federal Work-Study, scholarships/grants, and health care benefits also available. Financial award application deadline: 3/2; financial award applicants required to submit FAFSA. *Unit head:* Tirza Latimer, Chair, 415-551-9250, E-mail: tlatimer@cca.edu. *Application contact:* Kathryn Ward, Assistant Director of Graduate Admissions, 415-703-9523 Ext. 9593, Fax: 415-703-9539, E-mail: graduateprograms@cca.edu.

See Close-Up on page 233.

California College of the Arts, Graduate Programs, Programs in Fine Art, San Francisco, CA 94107. Offers ceramics (MFA); film/video/performance (MFA); glass (MFA); jewelry/metal arts (MFA); painting/drawing (MFA); photography (MFA); printmaking (MFA); sculpture (MFA); textiles (MFA); wood/furniture (MFA). *Accreditation:* NASAD. *Faculty:* 17 full-time (9 women), 32 part-time/adjunct (12 women). *Students:* 101 full-time (73 women), 11 part-time (8 women). Average age 30. 437 applicants, 29% accepted, 51 enrolled. In 2007, 34 degrees awarded. *Degree requirements:* For master's, thesis, exhibit. *Entrance requirements:* For master's, appropriate bachelor's degree, portfolio. Additional exam requirements/recommendations for international students: Required—TOEFL (minimum score 600 paper-based; 250 computer-based). *Application deadline:* For fall admission, 1/15 for domestic and international students. Application fee: $50. Electronic applications accepted. *Expenses:* Tuition: Part-time $1,017 per unit. *Financial support:* In 2007–08, 5 fellowships (averaging $10,000 per year), 20 teaching assistantships (averaging $2,000 per year) were awarded; career-related internships or fieldwork, Federal Work-Study, scholarships/grants, and health care benefits also available. Financial award application deadline: 3/1; financial award applicants required to submit FAFSA. *Unit head:* Ted Purves, Chair, 415-551-9214, Fax: 415-703-9539, E-mail: tpurves@cca.edu. *Application contact:* Kathryn Ward, Assistant Director of Graduate Admissions, 415-703-9523 Ext. 9593, Fax: 415-703-9539, E-mail: graduateprograms@cca.edu.

California Institute of the Arts, School of Art, Valencia, CA 91355-2340. Offers art (MFA, Adv C); graphic design (MFA, Adv C); photography (MFA, Adv C). *Accreditation:* NASAD (one or more programs are accredited). *Degree requirements:* For master's, final project. *Entrance requirements:* For master's, portfolio. Additional exam requirements/recommendations for international students: Required—TOEFL. Electronic applications accepted.

California State University, Chico, Graduate School, College of Humanities and Fine Arts, Department of Art and Art History, Program in Fine Arts, Chico, CA 95929-0722. Offers MFA. *Accreditation:* NASAD. *Students:* 9 full-time (7 women), 1 (woman) part-time; includes 1

Art/Fine Arts

California State University, Chico (continued)
minority (Hispanic American) Average age 33. 18 applicants, 39% accepted, 6 enrolled. In 2007, 4 degrees awarded. *Degree requirements:* For master's, thesis or alternative. *Entrance requirements:* For master's, Two letters of recommendation, statement of purpose, department application. Additional exam requirements/recommendations for international students: Required—TOEFL (minimum score 550 paper-based; 213 computer-based; 80 iBT), IELTS (minimum score 7). *Application deadline:* For fall admission, 3/1 priority date for domestic students, 3/1 for international students; for spring admission, 9/15 priority date for domestic students, 9/15 for international students. Applications are processed on a rolling basis. Application fee: $55. Electronic applications accepted. *Unit head:* Dr. Cameron Crawford, Graduate Coordinator, 530-898-6860.

California State University, Fresno, Division of Graduate Studies, College of Arts and Humanities, Department of Art and Design, Fresno, CA 93740-8027. Offers art (MA). Part-time and evening/weekend programs available. *Faculty:* 10 full-time (5 women). *Students:* 51; includes 19 minority (3 African Americans, 3 Asian Americans or Pacific Islanders, 13 Hispanic Americans), 2 international. Average age 28. 4 applicants. In 2007, 3 degrees awarded. *Degree requirements:* For master's, thesis or alternative. *Entrance requirements:* For master's, GRE General Test, minimum GPA of 3.0, portfolio. Additional exam requirements/recommendations for international students: Required—TOEFL. *Application deadline:* For fall admission, 5/1 for domestic and international students; for spring admission, 10/1 for domestic and international students. Applications are processed on a rolling basis. Application fee: $55. Electronic applications accepted. *Financial support:* Career-related internships or fieldwork, Federal Work-Study, and scholarships/grants available. Support available to part-time students. Financial award application deadline: 3/1; financial award applicants required to submit FAFSA. *Faculty research:* Art history, graphic design, studio art. *Unit head:* Prof. Richard McQuone, Chair, 559-278-2516, Fax: 559-278-4706, E-mail: richard_mcquone@csufresno.edu. *Application contact:* Prof. Paula Durette, Graduate Program Coordinator, 559-278-2515, Fax: 559-278-4706, E-mail: pdurrette@csufresno.edu.

California State University, Fullerton, Graduate Studies, College of the Arts, Department of Art, Fullerton, CA 92834-9480. Offers art (MA, MFA), including ceramics (MFA), crafts, creative photography (MFA), design (MFA), drawing and painting, printmaking (MFA), sculpture; art history (MA); design (MA). *Accreditation:* NASAD (one or more programs are accredited). Part-time programs available. *Students:* 50 full-time (20 women), 28 part-time (20 women); includes 19 minority (2 African Americans, 2 American Indian/Alaska Native, 8 Asian Americans or Pacific Islanders, 7 Hispanic Americans), 2 international. Average age 36. 68 applicants, 47% accepted, 23 enrolled. In 2007, 29 degrees awarded. *Degree requirements:* For master's, project or thesis. *Entrance requirements:* For master's, minimum GPA of 2.5 in last 60 units of course work, portfolio. Application fee: $55. *Financial support:* Career-related internships or fieldwork, Federal Work-Study, institutionally sponsored loans, and scholarships/grants available. Support available to part-time students. Financial award application deadline: 3/1. *Unit head:* Larry Johnson, Chair, 714-278-3471. *Application contact:* Al Ching, Adviser, 714-278-3471.

California State University, Long Beach, Graduate Studies, College of the Arts, Department of Art, Long Beach, CA 90840. Offers MA, MFA. *Accreditation:* NASAD. Part-time programs available. *Faculty:* 40 full-time (18 women), 74 part-time/adjunct (40 women). *Students:* 60 full-time (39 women), 41 part-time (29 women); includes 25 minority (1 African American, 2 American Indian/Alaska Native, 8 Asian Americans or Pacific Islanders, 14 Hispanic Americans). Average age 37. *Degree requirements:* For master's, thesis (for some programs). *Entrance requirements:* For master's, minimum GPA of 3.0 in last 60 hours. *Application deadline:* For fall admission, 7/1 for domestic students; for spring admission, 12/1 for domestic students. Applications are processed on a rolling basis. Application fee: $55. Electronic applications accepted. *Financial support:* Federal Work-Study, institutionally sponsored loans, and scholarships/grants available. Financial award application deadline: 3/2. *Unit head:* David A Hadlock, Chair, 562-985-7819, Fax: 562-985-1650, E-mail: dhadlock@csulb.edu. *Application contact:* Jay Kvapil, Graduate Advisor, 562-985-7910, Fax: 562-985-1650, E-mail: kvapil@csulb.edu.

California State University, Los Angeles, Graduate Studies, College of Arts and Letters, Department of Art, Los Angeles, CA 90032-8530. Offers art (MA), including art education, art history, art therapy, ceramics, metals, and textiles, design (MA, MFA), painting, sculpture, and graphic arts, photography; fine arts (MFA), including crafts, design (MA, MFA), studio arts. *Accreditation:* NASAD (one or more programs are accredited). Part-time and evening/weekend programs available. *Faculty:* 7 full-time (3 women). *Students:* 24 full-time (13 women), 59 part-time (42 women); includes 19 minority (2 African Americans, 1 American Indian/Alaska Native, 5 Asian Americans or Pacific Islanders, 11 Hispanic Americans), 16 international. Average age 39. In 2007, 28 degrees awarded. *Degree requirements:* For master's, comprehensive exam, project or thesis. *Entrance requirements:* For master's, portfolio. Additional exam requirements/recommendations for international students: Required—TOEFL. *Application deadline:* For fall admission, 6/30 for domestic students; for spring admission, 2/1 for domestic students. Applications are processed on a rolling basis. Application fee: $55. *Financial support:* Federal Work-Study available. Support available to part-time students. Financial award application deadline: 3/1. *Faculty research:* The artist and the book, conceptual art, ceramic processes, computer graphics, architectural graphics. *Unit head:* Dr. Robert Martin, Chair, 323-343-4010, Fax: 323-343-4045, E-mail: rjmartin@calstatela.edu.

California State University, Northridge, Graduate Studies, College of Arts, Media, and Communication, Department of Art, Northridge, CA 91330. Offers art education (MA); art history (MA); studio art (MA, MFA); visual communications (MA, MFA). *Accreditation:* NASAD. *Faculty:* 23 full-time (11 women), 58 part-time/adjunct (29 women). *Students:* 26 full-time (19 women), 35 part-time (28 women); includes 10 minority (1 American Indian/Alaska Native, 3 Asian Americans or Pacific Islanders, 6 Hispanic Americans), 4 international. Average age 39. 55 applicants, 45% accepted, 16 enrolled. In 2007, 18 degrees awarded. *Application deadline:* For fall admission, 11/30 for domestic students. Application fee: $55. *Financial support:* Application deadline: 3/1. *Unit head:* Prof. Edward Alfano, Chair, 818-677-2242, E-mail: art.dept@csun.edu.

California State University, Sacramento, Graduate Studies, College of Arts and Letters, Department of Art, Sacramento, CA 95819-6048. Offers studio art (MA). *Accreditation:* NASAD. Part-time programs available. *Students:* 13 full-time (6 women), 5 part-time (4 women); includes 8 minority (2 Asian Americans or Pacific Islanders, 6 Hispanic Americans), 1 international. Average age 36. 37 applicants, 59% accepted. *Degree requirements:* For master's, thesis or alternative, departmental qualifying exam, writing proficiency exam. *Entrance requirements:* For master's, minimum GPA of 3.0 during previous 2 years. Additional exam requirements/recommendations for international students: Required—TOEFL. *Application deadline:* Applications are processed on a rolling basis. Application fee: $55. Electronic applications accepted. *Expenses:* Tuition, state resident: full-time $3,414. Tuition, nonresident: full-time $13,584; part-time $339 per unit. Required fees: $786; $393 per semester. *Financial support:* Career-related internships or fieldwork and Federal Work-Study available. Support available to part-time students. Financial award application deadline: 3/1. *Unit head:* Dr. Daniel Frye, Chair, 916-278-6166, Fax: 916-278-4588.

California State University, San Bernardino, Graduate Studies, College of Arts and Letters, Department of Art, San Bernardino, CA 92407-2397. Offers MA. *Accreditation:* NASAD. *Faculty:* 7 full-time, 26 part-time/adjunct. *Students:* 2 full-time (0 women), 8 part-time (4 women); includes 3 minority (1 Asian American or Pacific Islander, 2 Hispanic Americans). Average age 34. 18 applicants, 22% accepted. *Application deadline:* For fall admission, 8/31 priority date for domestic students. Application fee: $55. *Unit head:* Dr. Thomas McGovern, Chair, 909-537-7267, Fax: 909-537-7068.

California State University, Stanislaus, College of the Arts, Department of Art, Turlock, CA 95382. Offers printmaking (Certificate). *Accreditation:* NASAD. Part-time programs available. *Degree requirements:* For Certificate, portfolio submission, exhibition participation. *Entrance requirements:* For degree, BA—Arts, 2.50 GPA, portfolio evaluation, 3 letters of reference, personal statement. *Application deadline:* For fall admission, 11/30 priority date for domestic and international students. Application fee: $55. Electronic applications accepted. *Expenses:* Tuition, nonresident: full-time $10,170; part-time $339 per unit. Required fees: $3,972; $2,538 per term. $1,165 per semester. *Application contact:* Gordon Senior, Chair, 209-667-3431, Fax: 209-664-3782, E-mail: coa@csustan.edu.

Carnegie Mellon University, College of Fine Arts, School of Art, Pittsburgh, PA 15213-3891. Offers MFA. *Accreditation:* NASAD. *Degree requirements:* For master's, thesis, exhibit. *Entrance requirements:* For master's, portfolio. Additional exam requirements/recommendations for international students: Required—TOEFL.

Central Michigan University, College of Graduate Studies, College of Communication and Fine Arts, Department of Art, Mount Pleasant, MI 48859. Offers MA, MFA. *Accreditation:* NASAD. *Degree requirements:* For master's, thesis or alternative. *Entrance requirements:* For master's, 20 hours of course work in art, 12 undergraduate hours of course work in art history, minimum GPA of 2.5, slide portfolio. *Faculty research:* Laser holography, computer graphics, postmodern sculptural events, twentieth century architecture, contemporary titanium metal forming.

Central Washington University, Graduate Studies, Research and Continuing Education, College of Arts and Humanities, Department of Art, Ellensburg, WA 98926. Offers MA, MFA. *Faculty:* 8 full-time (3 women). *Students:* 6 full-time (4 women). 14 applicants, 7% accepted, 1 enrolled. In 2007, 2 degrees awarded. *Degree requirements:* For master's, thesis or alternative. *Entrance requirements:* For master's, minimum GPA of 3.0, portfolio. Additional exam requirements/recommendations for international students: Required—TOEFL (minimum score 550 paper-based; 213 computer-based; 79 iBT). *Application deadline:* For fall admission, 3/1 for domestic students; for winter admission, 10/1 for domestic students; for spring admission, 1/1 for domestic students. Applications are processed on a rolling basis. Application fee: $50. Electronic applications accepted. *Expenses:* Tuition, state resident: full-time $2,209; part-time $221 per credit. Tuition, nonresident: full-time $4,939; part-time $442 per credit. Required fees: $207 per quarter. Tuition and fees vary according to degree level. *Financial support:* In 2007–08, 5 teaching assistantships with partial tuition reimbursements (averaging $8,100 per year) were awarded; research assistantships with partial tuition reimbursements, Federal Work-Study, health care benefits, and unspecified assistantships also available. Financial award application deadline: 3/1; financial award applicants required to submit FAFSA. *Unit head:* Dr. William Folkestad, Chair, 509-963-2665, Fax: 209-963-1918, E-mail: folkesta@cwu.edu. *Application contact:* Justine Eason, Admissions Program Coordinator, 509-963-3103, Fax: 509-963-1799, E-mail: masters@cwu.edu.

City College of the City University of New York, Graduate School, College of Liberal Arts and Science, Division of the Humanities and Arts, Department of Art, Program in Fine Arts, New York, NY 10031-9198. Offers advertising design (MFA); ceramic design (MFA); painting (MFA); printmaking (MFA); sculpture (MFA); wood and metal design (MFA). *Students:* 4. 19 applicants, 42% accepted, 4 enrolled. *Degree requirements:* For master's, thesis exhibit. *Entrance requirements:* For master's, 20 slide portfolio. Additional exam requirements/recommendations for international students: Required—TOEFL (minimum score 575 paper-based; 233 computer-based). *Application deadline:* For fall admission, 4/1 for domestic students; for spring admission, 11/1 for domestic students. Application fee: $125. *Financial support:* Fellowships, teaching assistantships, career-related internships or fieldwork, Federal Work-Study, institutionally sponsored loans, scholarships/grants, and tuition waivers (partial) available. Support available to part-time students. Financial award application deadline: 3/1. *Unit head:* Megan Foster, Head, 212-650-7425.

Claremont Graduate University, Graduate Programs, School of Arts and Humanities, Department of Art, Claremont, CA 91711-6160. Offers digital media (MA, MFA); drawing (MA, MFA); installation (MA, MFA); new genre (MA, MFA); painting (MA, MFA); performance (MA, MFA); photography (MA, MFA); sculpture (MA, MFA). Part-time programs available. *Faculty:* 3 full-time (0 women), 10 part-time/adjunct (5 women). *Students:* 61 full-time (36 women), 1 part-time; includes 11 minority (2 African Americans, 4 Asian Americans or Pacific Islanders, 5 Hispanic Americans), 4 international. Average age 33. In 2007, 34 degrees awarded. *Degree requirements:* For master's, final project show. *Entrance requirements:* For master's, BA in art or BFA, slide review. *Application deadline:* For fall admission, 2/15 priority date for domestic students. Applications are processed on a rolling basis. Electronic applications accepted. *Expenses:* Tuition: Full-time $31,640; part-time $1,376 per unit. Required fees: $145 per semester. Tuition and fees vary according to course load, degree level and program. *Financial support:* Fellowships, research assistantships, teaching assistantships, Federal Work-Study and institutionally sponsored loans available. Support available to part-time students. Financial award application deadline: 2/15; financial award applicants required to submit FAFSA. *Faculty research:* Acoustic sculpture, feminization of abstraction, installation sculpture. *Unit head:* David Pagel, Chair, 909-621-8071, Fax: 909-607-1276, E-mail: david.pagel@cgu.edu. *Application contact:* Marianne Elder, Assistant Coordinator, 909-607-2479, Fax: 909-607-1276, E-mail: marianne.elder@cgu.edu.

Clemson University, Graduate School, College of Architecture, Arts, and Humanities, Department of Art, Program in Visual Arts, Clemson, SC 29634. Offers MFA. *Accreditation:* NASAD. *Students:* 19 full-time (13 women). 31 applicants, 32% accepted, 6 enrolled. In 2007, 6 degrees awarded. *Entrance requirements:* For master's, GRE General Test. Additional exam requirements/recommendations for international students: Required—TOEFL. *Application deadline:* For fall admission, 4/15 for international students; for spring admission, 9/15 for international students. Application fee: $50. *Unit head:* Dave Detrick, Coordinator, 864-656-3890, Fax: 864-656-0204, E-mail: ddavid@clemson.edu.

Cleveland State University, College of Graduate Studies, College of Liberal Arts and Social Sciences, Department of Art, Cleveland, OH 44115. Offers art education (M Ed); art history (MA). *Students:* 1 (woman) full-time, 4 part-time (all women). In 2007, 2 degrees awarded. *Unit head:* Howie Smith, Chair, 212-523-7546, E-mail: art.chair@csuohio.edu.

The College at Brockport, State University of New York, School of Arts and Performance, Visual Studies Workshop, Brockport, NY 14420-2997. Offers visual studies (MFA). *Students:* 16 full-time (9 women), 11 part-time (7 women); includes 2 minority (1 Asian American or Pacific Islander, 1 Hispanic American), 4 international. 18 applicants, 78% accepted, 11 enrolled. In 2007, 8 degrees awarded. *Degree requirements:* For master's, thesis or alternative, internship, final project. *Entrance requirements:* For master's, portfolio, letters of recommendation, minimum GPA of 3.0. Additional exam requirements/recommendations for international students: Required—TOEFL (minimum score 550 paper-based; 213 computer-based; 79 iBT). *Application deadline:* For fall admission, 2/15 for domestic and international students. Application fee: $50. *Expenses:* Tuition, state resident: full-time $6,900; part-time $288 per credit. Tuition, nonresident: full-time $10,920; part-time $455 per credit. Required fees: $738; $31 per credit. *Financial support:* Federal Work-Study and scholarships/grants available. Support available to part-time students. Financial award application deadline: 3/15; financial award applicants required to submit FAFSA. *Faculty research:* Photography, film, video, digital media, artists' books. *Unit head:* James B. Wyman, Director, 585-442-8676, Fax: 585-442-1992, E-mail: jwyman@brockport.edu or wyman@vsw.org. *Application contact:* Director, Visual Studies Workshop, 585-442-8676, Fax: 585-442-1992, E-mail: info@vsw.org.

The College of New Rochelle, Graduate School, Division of Art and Communication Studies, Program in Studio Art, New Rochelle, NY 10805-2308. Offers MS. Part-time and evening/weekend programs available. *Faculty:* 1 full-time (0 women), 9 part-time/adjunct (7 women). *Students:* 2 full-time (both women), 10 part-time (9 women); includes 2 minority (1 African American, 1 Hispanic American). Average age 37. In 2007, 11 degrees awarded. *Degree requirements:* For master's, apprenticeship. *Entrance requirements:* For master's, portfolio, 36 credits of course work in studio art. *Application deadline:* For fall admission, 8/1 priority date for domestic students. Applications are processed on a rolling basis. Application fee: $35. *Expenses:* Tuition: Part-time $650 per credit. Required fees: $90 per term. *Financial support:*

Career-related internships or fieldwork, scholarships/grants, tuition waivers (partial), and unspecified assistantships available. Support available to part-time students. *Faculty research:* Experimental computer graphics. *Unit head:* Dr. John Patton, Head, Division of Art and Communication Studies, 914-654-5208, Fax: 914-654-5593.

Colorado State University, Graduate School, College of Liberal Arts, Department of Art, Fort Collins, CO 80523-0015. Offers MFA. *Faculty:* 22 full-time (9 women), 2 part-time/adjunct (0 women). *Students:* 16 full-time (12 women), 6 part-time (3 women); includes 1 minority (Asian American or Pacific Islander) Average age 30. 69 applicants, 16% accepted, 8 enrolled. In 2007, 9 degrees awarded. *Degree requirements:* For master's, thesis, exhibition. *Entrance requirements:* For master's, portfolio. Additional exam requirements/recommendations for international students: Required—TOEFL. *Application deadline:* For fall admission, 2/15 priority date for domestic students; for spring admission, 7/15 priority date for domestic students. Applications are processed on a rolling basis. Application fee: $50. Electronic applications accepted. *Expenses:* Contact institution. *Financial support:* In 2007–08, 10 students received support, including 9 teaching assistantships with tuition reimbursements available (averaging $8,483 per year); fellowships, research assistantships, Federal Work-Study, institutionally sponsored loans, scholarships/grants, health care benefits, and unspecified assistantships also available. Support available to part-time students. Financial award application deadline: 3/1; financial award applicants required to submit FAFSA. *Faculty research:* African art history, bronze castings, etching/lithography, pre-Columbian art history, contemporary crafts. Total annual research expenditures: $6,830. *Unit head:* Patrick Fahey, Chair, 970-491-5895, E-mail: patrick.fahey@colostate.edu. *Application contact:* Tom Lundberg, Graduate Coordinator, 970-491-5734, E-mail: thomas.lundberg@colostate.edu.

Columbia University, School of the Arts, Visual Arts Division, New York, NY 10027. Offers new genres (MFA); painting (MFA); photography (MFA); printmaking (MFA); sculpture (MFA). *Faculty:* 9 full-time (3 women), 53 part-time/adjunct (20 women). *Students:* 53 full-time (24 women); includes 3 minority (all Asian Americans or Pacific Islanders) Average age 27. 1,052 applicants, 2% accepted, 26 enrolled. In 2007, 24 degrees awarded. *Degree requirements:* For master's, thesis. *Entrance requirements:* For master's, 3 letters of recommendation, portfolio, personal statement, resumé, official transcript. Additional exam requirements/recommendations for international students: Required—TOEFL (minimum score 600 paper-based; 250 computer-based; 100 iBT). *Application deadline:* For fall admission, 1/15 for domestic and international students. Application fee: $120. Electronic applications accepted. *Expenses:* Tuition: Part-time $1,452 per credit. Required fees: $152 per term. One-time fee: $75 part-time. Full-time tuition and fees vary according to course level, course load, degree level and program. *Financial support:* In 2007–08, 26 fellowships (averaging $7,297 per year), 12 research assistantships (averaging $22,444 per year) were awarded; teaching assistantships, career-related internships or fieldwork, Federal Work-Study, scholarships/grants, health care benefits, and unspecified assistantships also available. Financial award applicants required to submit FAFSA. *Unit head:* Gregory Amenoff, Chair, 212-854-4065, E-mail: visualarts@columbia.edu. *Application contact:* Director of Admissions, 212-854-2134, E-mail: admissions-arts@columbia.edu.

See Close-Up on page 347.

Concordia University, School of Graduate Studies, Faculty of Fine Arts, Department of Studio Arts, Montréal, QC H3G 1M8, Canada. Offers studio arts (MFA), including film production, open media, painting, photography, print media, sculpture, ceramics and fibers. *Degree requirements:* For master's, thesis or alternative. *Entrance requirements:* For master's, portfolio.

Cornell University, Graduate School, Graduate Fields of Architecture, Art and Planning, Field of Art, Ithaca, NY 14853-0001. Offers creative visual arts (MFA), including painting, photography, printmaking, sculpture. *Faculty:* 12 full-time (3 women). *Students:* 12 full-time (4 women), 1 international. Average age 29. 102 applicants, 7% accepted, 6 enrolled. In 2007, 5 degrees awarded. *Degree requirements:* For master's, thesis, exhibit. *Entrance requirements:* For master's, slide portfolio of 10-20 slides, 3 letters of recommendation, resumé. Additional exam requirements/recommendations for international students: Required—TOEFL (minimum score 550 paper-based; 213 computer-based; 77 iBT). *Application deadline:* For fall admission, 2/15 for domestic students. Application fee: $70. Electronic applications accepted. *Financial support:* In 2007–08, 10 students received support, including 10 teaching assistantships with full tuition reimbursements available; fellowships with full tuition reimbursements available, research assistantships with full tuition reimbursements available, institutionally sponsored loans, scholarships/grants, health care benefits, tuition waivers (full and partial), and unspecified assistantships also available. Financial award applicants required to submit FAFSA. *Faculty research:* Painting, sculpture, photography, printmaking. *Unit head:* Director of Graduate Studies, 607-255-6730, Fax: 607-255-3462. *Application contact:* Graduate Field Assistant, 607-255-6730, Fax: 607-255-3462, E-mail: artinfo@cornell.edu.

Cranbrook Academy of Art, Graduate School, Program in Fine Arts, Bloomfield Hills, MI 48303-0801. Offers ceramics (MFA); design (MFA), including graphic design; fiber arts (MFA); metalsmithing (MFA); painting (MFA); photography (MFA); printmaking (MFA); sculpture (MFA). *Accreditation:* NASAD. *Degree requirements:* For master's, thesis, exhibit. *Entrance requirements:* Additional exam requirements/recommendations for international students: Required—TOEFL (minimum score 550 paper-based; 213 computer-based).

See Close-Up on page 237.

Drake University, School of Education, Department of Teaching and Learning, Program in Secondary Education, Des Moines, IA 50311-4516. Offers art (MAT); biology (MAT); business (MAT); chemistry (MAT); English (MAT); general science (MAT); history-American (MAT); history-world (MAT); journalism (MAT); mathematics (MAT); physical science (MAT); physics (MAT); sociology (MAT); speech (MAT); speech communication (MAT); theatre (MAT). Part-time programs available. *Faculty:* 10 full-time (3 women), 28 part-time/adjunct (16 women). *Students:* 13 full-time (7 women), 33 part-time (20 women). 41 applicants, 56% accepted. In 2007, 12 degrees awarded. *Degree requirements:* For master's, comprehensive exam, thesis (for some programs), internships (for some programs). *Entrance requirements:* For master's, GRE General Test, MAT, or Drake Writing Assessment, resumé, 2 letters of recommendation. Additional exam requirements/recommendations for international students: Required—TOEFL (minimum score 550 paper-based; 213 computer-based). *Application deadline:* For fall admission, 7/1 priority date for domestic students, 6/1 priority date for international students; for spring admission, 11/1 priority date for domestic students, 10/1 priority date for international students. Applications are processed on a rolling basis. Application fee: $25. Electronic applications accepted. *Expenses:* Tuition: Full-time $26,030; part-time $370 per credit hour. Required fees: $406; $40 per semester. Tuition and fees vary according to program. *Financial support:* Career-related internships or fieldwork and unspecified assistantships available. Support available to part-time students. *Faculty research:* Counseling and rehabilitation, behavioral supports, inquiry-based science methods, teacher quality enhancement. Total annual research expenditures: $1.5 million. *Application contact:* Ann J. Martin, Graduate Coordinator, 515-271-2034, Fax: 515-271-2831, E-mail: ann.martin@drake.edu.

Drury University, Program in Studio Art and Theory, Springfield, MO 65802. Offers MA. *Entrance requirements:* For master's, GRE or MAT. Additional exam requirements/recommendations for international students: Required—TOEFL. *Application deadline:* Applications are processed on a rolling basis. Application fee: $25. Electronic applications accepted. *Unit head:* Tom Parker, Chair and Professor of Art and History, 417-873-7239, E-mail: tparker@drury.edu. *Application contact:* Kay Lowder, Graduate Programs Office Coordinator, 417-873-6948, Fax: 417-873-6681, E-mail: grad@drury.edu.

Duke University, Graduate School, Department of Art, Art History and Visual Studies, Durham, NC 27708-0764. Offers PhD. *Faculty:* 15 full-time. *Students:* 33 full-time (27 women); includes 6 minority (3 African Americans, 1 Asian American or Pacific Islander, 2 Hispanic Americans), 10 international. 67 applicants, 19% accepted, 8 enrolled. In 2007, 2 doctorates awarded. *Degree requirements:* For doctorate, thesis/dissertation. *Entrance requirements:* For doctorate, GRE General Test. Additional exam requirements/recommendations for international students: Required—TOEFL (minimum score 550 paper-based; 213 computer-based; 83 iBT), IELTS (minimum score 7). *Application deadline:* For fall admission, 12/15 priority date for domestic and international students. Application fee: $75. Electronic applications accepted. *Financial support:* Fellowships, teaching assistantships available. Financial award application deadline: 12/15. *Unit head:* Gennifer Weisenfeld, Director of Graduate Studies, 919-684-2224, Fax: 919-684-4398, E-mail: lbst@duke.edu.

East Carolina University, Graduate School, College of Fine Arts and Communication, School of Art and Design, Greenville, NC 27858-4353. Offers MA, MA Ed, MFA. *Accreditation:* NASAD (one or more programs are accredited). Part-time and evening/weekend programs available. *Faculty:* 34 full-time (12 women). *Students:* 39 full-time (20 women), 22 part-time (15 women); includes 5 minority (1 African American, 3 Asian Americans or Pacific Islanders, 1 Hispanic American). Average age 31. 23 applicants, 4% accepted, 1 enrolled. In 2007, 14 degrees awarded. *Degree requirements:* For master's, comprehensive exam, thesis (for some programs). *Entrance requirements:* For master's, GRE General Test or MAT, portfolio. Additional exam requirements/recommendations for international students: Required—TOEFL. *Application deadline:* For fall admission, 2/1 for domestic students; for spring admission, 10/1 for domestic students. Applications are processed on a rolling basis. Application fee: $50. *Financial support:* Research assistantships with partial tuition reimbursements, teaching assistantships with partial tuition reimbursements, Federal Work-Study available. Support available to part-time students. Financial award application deadline: 6/1. *Unit head:* Carl Billingsley, Interim Co-Director of Graduate Studies, 252-328-6270, Fax: 252-328-6441, E-mail: billingsleyc@ecu.edu. *Application contact:* Dr. Linda H. Nelson, Information Contact, 252-328-1886, Fax: 252-328-6441, E-mail: nelsonlh@ecu.edu.

Eastern Illinois University, Graduate School, College of Arts and Humanities, Department of Art, Charleston, IL 61920-3099. Offers art (MA); art education (MA). *Accreditation:* NASAD. *Faculty:* 18 full-time (7 women). *Students:* 11 applicants, 64% accepted. In 2007, 7 degrees awarded. *Degree requirements:* For master's, thesis or alternative, portfolio. *Application deadline:* For fall admission, 7/31 priority date for domestic students. Applications are processed on a rolling basis. Application fee: $30. *Expenses:* Tuition, state resident: part-time $218 per hour. Tuition, nonresident: part-time $654 per hour. *Financial support:* In 2007–08, research assistantships with tuition reimbursements (averaging $7,200 per year), 6 teaching assistantships with tuition reimbursements (averaging $7,200 per year) were awarded. *Unit head:* Glenn Hild, Chairperson, 217-581-3410. *Application contact:* Chris Kahler, Coordinator, 217-581-6259, E-mail: cbkahler@eiu.edu.

Eastern Michigan University, Graduate School, College of Arts and Sciences, Department of Art, Ypsilanti, MI 48197. Offers art (MA); art education (MA); studio art (MA, MFA). Part-time and evening/weekend programs available. Postbaccalaureate distance learning degree programs offered (minimal on-campus study). *Faculty:* 28 full-time (14 women). *Students:* 14 full-time (12 women), 21 part-time (17 women); includes 6 minority (2 African Americans, 2 Asian Americans or Pacific Islanders, 2 Hispanic Americans), 1 international. Average age 39. In 2007, 18 degrees awarded. *Entrance requirements:* Additional exam requirements/recommendations for international students: Required—TOEFL. *Application deadline:* Applications are processed on a rolling basis. Application fee: $35. *Expenses:* Tuition, state resident: full-time $8,952; part-time $373 per credit hour. Tuition, nonresident: full-time $17,634; part-time $735 per credit hour. Required fees: $896; $34 per credit hour. Tuition and fees vary according to course level, degree level and program. *Financial support:* Fellowships, research assistantships with full tuition reimbursements, teaching assistantships with full tuition reimbursements, career-related internships or fieldwork, Federal Work-Study, institutionally sponsored loans, scholarships/grants, tuition waivers (partial), and unspecified assistantships available. Support available to part-time students. Financial award applicants required to submit FAFSA. *Unit head:* Dr. Thomas Venner, Head, 734-487-1268, Fax: 734-487-2324, E-mail: tom.venner@emich.edu. *Application contact:* Prof. Christopher Bocklage, Graduate Coordinator, 734-487-1268, Fax: 734-487-2324, E-mail: christopher.bocklage@emich.edu.

East Tennessee State University, School of Graduate Studies, College of Arts and Sciences, Department of Art and Design, Johnson City, TN 37614. Offers art education (MA); art history (MA); studio art (MA, MFA). *Accreditation:* NASAD. *Degree requirements:* For master's, thesis, exhibit, oral exam (MFA). *Entrance requirements:* For master's, GRE General Test, portfolio (MFA), bachelor's degree in art, minimum GPA of 3.0. Additional exam requirements/recommendations for international students: Required—TOEFL (minimum score 550 paper-based; 213 computer-based). *Faculty research:* History of sculpture, art and senior citizens, encaustic paintings, digital media in art history.

Edinboro University of Pennsylvania, Graduate Studies and Research, School of Liberal Arts, Department of Art, Program in Art, Edinboro, PA 16444. Offers MA. *Accreditation:* NASAD. Evening/weekend programs available. *Students:* 2 full-time (0 women), 3 part-time (all women). Average age 33. *Degree requirements:* For master's, thesis or alternative, competency exam, exhibit, portfolio, final. *Entrance requirements:* For master's, GRE or MAT, interview, minimum QPA of 2.5, portfolio. *Application deadline:* Applications are processed on a rolling basis. Application fee: $30. Electronic applications accepted. *Expenses:* Tuition, state resident: full-time $6,214; part-time $345 per credit. Tuition, nonresident: full-time $9,944; part-time $552 per credit. Required fees: $46 per credit. *Financial support:* Research assistantships, Federal Work-Study, scholarships/grants, and unspecified assistantships available. Financial award application deadline: 2/15. *Unit head:* John Lysak, Head, 814-732-2271, E-mail: jlysak@edinboro.edu. *Application contact:* Dr. R. Scott Baldwin, Dean, 814-732-2752, Fax: 814-732-2268, E-mail: sbaldwin@edinboro.edu.

Edinboro University of Pennsylvania, Graduate Studies and Research, School of Liberal Arts, Department of Art, Program in Fine Arts, Edinboro, PA 16444. Offers ceramics (MFA); jewelry/metalsmithing (MFA); painting (MFA); printmaking (MFA); sculpture (MFA). *Accreditation:* NASAD. Evening/weekend programs available. *Students:* 18 full-time (7 women), 1 part-time, 1 international. Average age 28. In 2007, 4 degrees awarded. *Degree requirements:* For master's, comprehensive exam, thesis or alternative, competency exam, exhibit, portfolio. *Entrance requirements:* For master's, GRE or MAT, interview, minimum QPA of 2.5, portfolio. *Application deadline:* Applications are processed on a rolling basis. Application fee: $30. Electronic applications accepted. *Expenses:* Tuition, state resident: full-time $6,214; part-time $345 per credit. Tuition, nonresident: full-time $9,944; part-time $552 per credit. Required fees: $46 per credit. *Financial support:* In 2007–08, 13 research assistantships with full and partial tuition reimbursements (averaging $3,850 per year) were awarded; Federal Work-Study, scholarships/grants, and unspecified assistantships also available. Financial award application deadline: 2/15. *Application contact:* Dr. R. Scott Baldwin, Dean, 814-732-2752, Fax: 814-732-2268, E-mail: sbaldwin@edinboro.edu.

Emily Carr Institute of Art + Design, Program in Applied Arts, Vancouver, BC V6H 3R9, Canada. Offers design (MAA); media arts (MAA); visual arts (MAA). *Degree requirements:* For master's, internship. *Entrance requirements:* For master's, minimum overall GPA of 3.0, visual portfolio, 3 letters of recommendation. Additional exam requirements/recommendations for international students: Required—TOEFL (minimum score 570 paper-based; 230 computer-based; 84 iBT), IELTS (minimum score 7), Michigan English language Assessment Battery (minimum score of 81). Electronic applications accepted.

Fairleigh Dickinson University, Metropolitan Campus, University College: Arts, Sciences, and Professional Studies, School of Art and Media Studies, Teaneck, NJ 07666-1914. Offers MA. *Students:* 8 full-time (3 women), 5 part-time (3 women). Average age 31. 5 applicants, 80% accepted, 1 enrolled. In 2007, 10 degrees awarded. *Application deadline:* Applications are processed on a rolling basis. Application fee: $40. *Expenses:* Tuition: Part-time $869 per credit. Tuition and fees vary according to degree level, campus/location and program. *Unit head:* Jason Scorza, Director, 201-692-2000.

Art/Fine Arts

Ferris State University, Kendall College of Art and Design, Big Rapids, MI 49307. Offers MFA. *Accreditation:* NASAD. Part-time programs available. *Faculty:* 14 full-time (10 women). *Students:* 30 full-time (16 women), 6 part-time (2 women); includes 3 minority (2 African Americans, 1 Asian American or Pacific Islander). Average age 32. 28 applicants, 86% accepted, 17 enrolled. In 2007, 11 degrees awarded. *Degree requirements:* For master's, thesis, seminars. *Entrance requirements:* For master's, portfolio, 3 letters of recommendation, curriculum vitae. Additional exam requirements/recommendations for international students: Required—TOEFL (minimum score 500 paper-based; 173 computer-based; 61 iBT). *Application deadline:* For fall admission, 2/15 for domestic and international students; for winter admission, 11/1 for domestic and international students. Applications are processed on a rolling basis. Application fee: $30. *Expenses:* Tuition, state resident: part-time $389 per credit. Tuition, nonresident: part-time $753 per credit. *Financial support:* In 2007–08, 32 students received support, including 2 fellowships (averaging $24,424 per year), 30 teaching assistantships (averaging $4,500 per year); research assistantships, scholarships/grants and unspecified assistantships also available. Financial award application deadline: 2/15. *Unit head:* Dr. Oliver H. Evans, President, 616-451-2787. *Application contact:* Sandra Britton, Director of Enrollment Management, 616-451-2787, Fax: 616-836-9689, E-mail: brittons@ferris.edu.

Florida Atlantic University, Dorothy F. Schmidt College of Arts and Letters, Department of Art, Boca Raton, FL 33431-0991. Offers art education (MAT); ceramics (MFA); painting (MFA). *Degree requirements:* For master's, one foreign language, project. *Entrance requirements:* For master's, GRE General Test, minimum GPA of 3.0 during last 60 hours of course work, slide portfolio. Electronic applications accepted. *Faculty research:* Painting, ceramics (traditional and non-traditional), installation, video and interactive sculpture.

Florida International University, College of Architecture and the Arts, School of Art and Art History, Miami, FL 33199. Offers visual arts (MFA). *Accreditation:* NASAD. *Faculty:* 15 full-time (6 women). *Students:* 10 full-time (7 women), 4 part-time (1 woman); includes 6 minority (1 Asian American or Pacific Islander, 5 Hispanic Americans). Average age 40. 19 applicants, 26% accepted, 4 enrolled. In 2007, 8 degrees awarded. *Entrance requirements:* For master's, minimum GPA of 3.0 (upper level coursework), 3 letters of recommendation, 20 slides of creative work. Additional exam requirements/recommendations for international students: Required—TOEFL (minimum score 550 paper-based; 213 computer-based). *Application deadline:* For fall admission, 2/15 for domestic and international students. Application fee: $30. Electronic applications accepted. *Expenses:* Tuition, state resident: full-time $6,106. Tuition, nonresident: full-time $15,528. Required fees: $284. *Financial support:* Teaching assistantships available. *Unit head:* Dr. Juan Martinez, Director, 305-348-2897, Fax: 305-348-0513, E-mail: juan.martinez@fiu.edu.

Florida State University, Graduate Studies, College of Visual Arts, Theatre and Dance, Department of Art, Tallahassee, FL 32306. Offers studio art (MFA). *Accreditation:* NASAD. *Faculty:* 21 full-time (10 women). *Students:* 31 full-time (18 women); includes 2 minority (1 African American, 1 Asian American or Pacific Islander). Average age 26. 43 applicants, 33% accepted, 12 enrolled. In 2007, 4 degrees awarded. *Degree requirements:* For master's, thesis, exhibit. *Entrance requirements:* For master's, portfolio, minimum GPA of 3.0. Additional exam requirements/recommendations for international students: Required—TOEFL (minimum score 550 paper-based). *Application deadline:* For fall admission, 2/27 priority date for domestic students, 2/27 for international students. Application fee: $30. Electronic applications accepted. *Expenses:* Tuition, state resident: part-time $248 per credit hour. Tuition, nonresident: part-time $880 per credit hour. Tuition and fees vary according to program. *Financial support:* In 2007–08, 30 students received support, including 1 fellowship with partial tuition reimbursement available (averaging $18,000 per year), 15 research assistantships with partial tuition reimbursements available (averaging $5,000 per year), 7 teaching assistantships with partial tuition reimbursements available (averaging $5,000 per year); Federal Work-Study, institutionally sponsored loans, and unspecified assistantships also available. Financial award application deadline: 2/27; financial award applicants required to submit FAFSA. *Faculty research:* Photography, painting, sculpture, printmaking, ceramics. *Unit head:* Joe E. Sanders, Professor and Chairperson, 850-644-6474, Fax: 850-644-8977, E-mail: jesanders@fsu.edu. *Application contact:* George Blakely, Graduate Director, 850-644-6474, Fax: 850-644-8977, E-mail: gblakely@fsu.edu.

Fontbonne University, Graduate Programs, Department of Fine Arts, St. Louis, MO 63105-3098. Offers art (MA); fine arts (MFA); theater education (MA). Part-time and evening/weekend programs available. *Degree requirements:* For master's, thesis exhibit (MFA). *Entrance requirements:* For master's, minimum GPA of 3.0, portfolio.

Fort Hays State University, Graduate School, College of Arts and Sciences, Department of Art, Hays, KS 67601-4099. Offers studio art (MFA). Part-time programs available. *Faculty:* 10 full-time (4 women). *Students:* 11 full-time (5 women), 1 part-time; includes 1 minority (American Indian/Alaska Native). Average age 41. 10 applicants, 70% accepted. In 2007, 7 degrees awarded. *Degree requirements:* For master's, comprehensive exam, thesis. *Entrance requirements:* For master's, slides. Additional exam requirements/recommendations for international students: Required—TOEFL (minimum score 550 paper-based; 213 computer-based; 79 iBT). *Application deadline:* For fall admission, 3/1 priority date for domestic students. Applications are processed on a rolling basis. Application fee: $35. Electronic applications accepted. *Expenses:* Tuition, state resident: part-time $155 per credit hour. Tuition, nonresident: part-time $409 per credit hour. Tuition and fees vary according to class time, course level, course load, degree level, campus/location and program. *Financial support:* Research assistantships, teaching assistantships, institutionally sponsored loans and tuition waivers (full and partial) available. Support available to part-time students. *Faculty research:* Migration art of Germanic tribes, iconographic and stylistic development, graphic design, photography, lithography. *Unit head:* Leland Powers, Chair, 785-628-4247, E-mail: lpowers@fhsu.edu.

Framingham State College, Division of Graduate and Continuing Education, Program in Art, Framingham, MA 01701-9101. Offers M Ed. *Students:* 16. In 2007, 7 degrees awarded. *Unit head:* Prof. Barbara Milot, Coordinator, 508-626-4550, Fax: 508-626-4030, E-mail: bmilot@frc.mass.edu. *Application contact:* Graduate Officer, 508-626-4550, Fax: 508-626-4030, E-mail: dgce@frc.mass.edu.

The George Washington University, Columbian College of Arts and Sciences, Department of Fine Arts and Art History, Washington, DC 20052. Offers art history (MA, PhD), including art history (PhD), museum training (MA); ceramics (MFA); design (MFA); interior design (MFA); painting (MFA); photography (MFA); printmaking (MFA); sculpture (MFA). *Accreditation:* CIDA. Part-time and evening/weekend programs available. *Entrance requirements:* For master's, GRE General Test, bachelor's degree in field, minimum GPA of 3.0. Additional exam requirements/recommendations for international students: Required—TOEFL (minimum score 550 paper-based; 213 computer-based). Electronic applications accepted.

Georgia Southern University, Jack N. Averitt College of Graduate Studies, College of Liberal Arts and Social Sciences, Department of Art, Statesboro, GA 30460. Offers fine arts (MFA). *Accreditation:* NASAD. Part-time programs available. *Students:* 9 full-time (7 women), 3 part-time (1 woman); includes 2 minority (both African Americans), 1 international. Average age 32. 11 applicants, 64% accepted, 6 enrolled. In 2007, 3 degrees awarded. *Degree requirements:* For master's, thesis. *Entrance requirements:* For master's, minimum GPA of 2.5, 18 semester hours of course work in studio art, 9 semester hours of course work in art history, portfolio, letters of reference. Additional exam requirements/recommendations for international students: Required—TOEFL (minimum score 550 paper-based; 213 computer-based). *Application deadline:* For fall admission, 3/1 priority date for domestic and international students; for spring admission, 10/1 priority date for domestic students, 10/1 for international students. Applications are processed on a rolling basis. Application fee: $50. Electronic applications accepted. *Expenses:* Tuition, state resident: full-time $3,516; part-time $147 per semester hour. Tuition, nonresident: full-time $14,060; part-time $586 per semester hour. Required fees: $562 per term. *Financial support:* In 2007–08, 1 student received support, including research assistantships with partial tuition reimbursements available (averaging $6,850 per year), teaching assistantships with partial tuition reimbursements available (averaging $6,850 per year); career-related internships or fieldwork, Federal Work-Study, scholarships/grants, tuition waivers (partial), and unspecified assistantships also available. Support available to part-time students. Financial award application deadline: 4/15; financial award applicants required to submit FAFSA. *Faculty research:* International design trends, folk art, cultural diversity in art education and art appreciation, public sculpture, studio arts. *Unit head:* Patricia Carter, Chair, 912-478-5358, Fax: 912-478-5104, E-mail: pwcarter@georgiasouthern.edu. *Application contact:* 912-478-5384, Fax: 912-478-0740, E-mail: gradadmissions@georgiasouthern.edu.

Georgia State University, College of Arts and Sciences, Ernest G. Welch School of Art and Design, Program in Studio Art, Atlanta, GA 30303-3083. Offers MFA. *Accreditation:* NASAD. *Faculty:* 18 full-time (9 women). *Students:* 41 full-time (26 women); includes 9 minority (4 African Americans, 4 Asian Americans or Pacific Islanders, 1 Hispanic American). Average age 25. 56 applicants, 38% accepted, 17 enrolled. In 2007, 11 degrees awarded. *Degree requirements:* For master's, thesis, exhibit, presentations, screening. *Entrance requirements:* For master's, portfolio. Additional exam requirements/recommendations for international students: Required—TOEFL (minimum score 550 paper-based; 213 computer-based). *Application deadline:* For fall admission, 1/6 for domestic and international students. Application fee: $50. Electronic applications accepted. *Expenses:* Tuition, state resident: part-time $221 per credit hour. *Financial support:* In 2007–08, 13 fellowships (averaging $1,250 per year), 22 research assistantships with full tuition reimbursements (averaging $5,000 per year), 16 teaching assistantships with full tuition reimbursements (averaging $5,000 per year) were awarded; career-related internships or fieldwork, Federal Work-Study, institutionally sponsored loans, scholarships/grants, health care benefits, and unspecified assistantships also available. Financial award application deadline: 1/6; financial award applicants required to submit FAFSA. *Faculty research:* Photography, drawing/painting, printmaking, sculpture, ceramics. *Application contact:* Prof. Joe Peragine, Director of Graduate Studies, 404-413-5229, Fax: 404-413-5261, E-mail: artgrad@gsu.edu.

Governors State University, College of Arts and Sciences, Program in Art, University Park, IL 60466-0975. Offers MA. Part-time and evening/weekend programs available. *Faculty:* 4 full-time (2 women), 2 part-time/adjunct (1 woman). *Students:* 3 full-time, 28 part-time. Average age 39. *Degree requirements:* For master's, thesis or alternative. *Entrance requirements:* For master's, portfolio, bachelor's degree in humanities. *Application deadline:* For fall admission, 7/15 priority date for domestic students; for spring admission, 11/10 for domestic students. Applications are processed on a rolling basis. Application fee: $25. *Financial support:* Research assistantships, Federal Work-Study, institutionally sponsored loans, and scholarships/grants available. Support available to part-time students. Financial award application deadline: 5/1. *Faculty research:* Historical study of art of selected ethnic groups of southwestern Zaire. *Unit head:* Dr. Eric V. Martin, Dean, College of Arts and Sciences, 708-534-4101.

Hofstra University, School of Education and Allied Human Services, Department of Curriculum and Teaching, Program in Fine Arts Education, Hempstead, NY 11549. Offers MA, MS Ed. Part-time and evening/weekend programs available. *Students:* 28 full-time (24 women), 10 part-time (9 women); includes 2 minority (1 African American, 1 Hispanic American). Average age 28. 29 applicants, 86% accepted, 17 enrolled. In 2007, 23 degrees awarded. *Degree requirements:* For master's, one foreign language, thesis or alternative, teaching portfolio. *Entrance requirements:* For master's, 2 letters of recommendation, portfolio, teacher certification (MA), essay. Additional exam requirements/recommendations for international students: Required—TOEFL (minimum score 550 paper-based; 213 computer-based). *Application deadline:* Applications are processed on a rolling basis. Application fee: $60. Electronic applications accepted. *Expenses:* Tuition: Full-time $14,220; part-time $820 per credit. Required fees: $970; $165 per term. Tuition and fees vary according to program. *Financial support:* In 2007–08, 31 students received support, including 1 fellowship with tuition reimbursement available (averaging $3,000 per year); research assistantships with full and partial tuition reimbursements available, career-related internships or fieldwork, Federal Work-Study, institutionally sponsored loans, scholarships/grants, tuition waivers (full and partial), and unspecified assistantships also available. Support available to part-time students. Financial award applicants required to submit FAFSA. *Faculty research:* Art education and interdisciplinary curricula, teacher/artist role in identity issues, early childhood art education, marginalization of the arts in education, gender issues. *Unit head:* Dr. Susan G. Zwirn, Director, 516-463-4976, Fax: 516-463-6196, E-mail: catsgz@hofstra.edu. *Application contact:* Carol Drummer, Dean of Graduate Admissions, 516-463-4876, Fax: 516-463-4664, E-mail: gradstudent@hofstra.edu.

Hollins University, Graduate Programs, Program in Liberal Studies, Roanoke, VA 24020-1603. Offers humanities (MALS); interdisciplinary studies (MALS); justice and legal studies (MALS); liberal studies (CAS); social science (MALS); visual and performing arts (MALS). Part-time and evening/weekend programs available. *Faculty:* 9 full-time (2 women), 12 part-time/adjunct (5 women). *Students:* 20 full-time (17 women), 89 part-time (74 women); includes 15 minority (11 African Americans, 1 American Indian/Alaska Native, 2 Asian Americans or Pacific Islanders, 1 Hispanic American). Average age 39. 30 applicants, 93% accepted, 20 enrolled. In 2007, 48 degrees awarded. *Degree requirements:* For master's, thesis. *Entrance requirements:* For master's, letters of recommendation, interview. Additional exam requirements/recommendations for international students: Required—TOEFL (minimum score 550 paper-based; 213 computer-based). *Application deadline:* For fall admission, 7/1 priority date for domestic and international students; for spring admission, 12/10 priority date for domestic and international students. Applications are processed on a rolling basis. Application fee: $40. Electronic applications accepted. *Expenses:* Tuition: Part-time $265 per credit hour. Tuition and fees vary according to course load and program. *Financial support:* In 2007–08, 53 students received support, including 4 fellowships (averaging $1,060 per year); Federal Work-Study and scholarships/grants also available. Support available to part-time students. Financial award application deadline: 7/15; financial award applicants required to submit FAFSA. *Faculty research:* Elderly blacks, film, feminist economics, U.S. voting patterns, Wagner, diversity. *Unit head:* Dr. Edward A. Lynch, Director, 540-362-6475, Fax: 540-362-6288, E-mail: elynch@hollins.edu. *Application contact:* Cathy S. Koon, Manager of Graduate Services, 540-362-6326, Fax: 540-362-6288, E-mail: ckoon@hollins.edu.

Hood College, Graduate School, Program in Ceramic Arts, Frederick, MD 21701-8575. Offers MFA, Certificate. *Entrance requirements:* For degree, portfolio.

Howard University, Graduate School, Division of Fine Arts, Department of Art, Program in Fine Arts, Washington, DC 20059-0002. Offers 3D reality (sculpture and ceramics) (MFA); design (MFA); electronic studio (MFA); painting (MFA); photography (MFA). *Accreditation:* NASAD. *Degree requirements:* For master's, comprehensive exam, thesis, exhibit. *Entrance requirements:* For master's, minimum GPA of 3.0, portfolio. *Expenses:* Tuition: Full-time $16,175; part-time $899 per credit hour. Required fees: $805.

Hunter College of the City University of New York, Graduate School, School of Arts and Sciences, Department of Art, Program in Studio Art, New York, NY 10021-5085. Offers fine arts (MFA). Part-time and evening/weekend programs available. *Faculty:* 18 full-time (12 women), 2 part-time/adjunct (1 woman). *Students:* Average age 30. 672 applicants, 4% accepted, 22 enrolled. In 2007, 35 degrees awarded. *Degree requirements:* For master's, exhibit, project. *Entrance requirements:* For master's, minimum of 24 credits of course work in studio art and 9 credits of course work in art history, portfolio. Additional exam requirements/recommendations for international students: Required—TOEFL. *Application deadline:* For fall admission, 2/1 for domestic students; for spring admission, 10/1 for domestic students. Application fee: $125. *Expenses:* Tuition, state resident: full-time $6,400; part-time $270 per credit. Tuition, nonresident: part-time $500 per credit. One-time fee: $125 full-time. Tuition and fees vary according to program. *Financial support:* Career-related internships or fieldwork, Federal Work-Study, scholarships/grants, and tuition waivers (partial) available. Support available to part-time students. Financial award application deadline: 4/15. *Faculty research:* Color theory, public printmaking and environmental commissions in painting and sculpture, graphics, ceramics, contemporary film and video. *Unit head:* Joel Carreiro, Graduate Adviser, 212-650-3398, E-mail: grad.arthistoryadvisor@hunter.cuny.edu.

Idaho State University, Office of Graduate Studies, College of Arts and Sciences, Department of Art and Pre-Architecture, Pocatello, ID 83209. Offers MFA. Part-time programs available. *Faculty:* 5 full-time (1 woman). *Students:* 7 full-time (3 women), 8 part-time (3 women); includes 1 minority (Hispanic American) Average age 38. In 2007, 3 degrees awarded. *Degree requirements:* For master's, comprehensive exam, thesis, exhibit. *Entrance requirements:* For master's, GRE General Test, GMAT or MAT, minimum GPA of 3.0 in all upper division classes, portfolio of work, 3 letters of recommendation. Additional exam requirements/recommendations for international students: Required—TOEFL (minimum score 550 paper-based; 213 computer-based; 80 iBT). *Application deadline:* For fall admission, 3/15 for domestic and international students; for spring admission, 10/15 for domestic and international students. Applications are processed on a rolling basis. Application fee: $55. Electronic applications accepted. *Expenses:* Tuition, state resident: full-time $2,882; part-time $259 per credit hour. Tuition, nonresident: full-time $11,566; part-time $379 per credit hour. Required fees: $2,278. Full-time tuition and fees vary according to program. Part-time tuition and fees vary according to course load. *Financial support:* In 2007–08, 3 teaching assistantships with full and partial tuition reimbursements (averaging $9,128 per year) were awarded; Federal Work-Study, institutionally sponsored loans, scholarships/grants, traineeships, health care benefits, and tuition waivers (full and partial) also available. Support available to part-time students. Financial award application deadline: 1/1; financial award applicants required to submit FAFSA. *Faculty research:* Computerized weaving, anodizing refractory metals, viscosity printing, neon, ceramic shell casting. *Unit head:* Rudy Kovacs, Chair, 208-282-2488, Fax: 208-282-4741, E-mail: kovarudo@isu.edu. *Application contact:* Ellen Combs, Graduate School Technical Records Specialist, 208-282-2150, Fax: 208-282-4847.

Illinois State University, Graduate School, College of Fine Arts, Program in Arts Technology, Normal, IL 61790-2200. Offers MS. *Accreditation:* NASAD. *Degree requirements:* For master's, thesis or alternative. Application fee: $40. *Expenses:* Tuition, state resident: full-time $3,492; part-time $194 per credit hour. Tuition, nonresident: full-time $7,272; part-time $404 per credit hour. Required fees: $1,024; $57 per credit hour. *Unit head:* Dr. James Major, Interim Dean, College of Fine Arts, 309-438-8321.

Illinois State University, Graduate School, College of Fine Arts, School of Art, Normal, IL 61790-2200. Offers art history (MA, MS); ceramics (MFA, MS); drawing (MFA, MS); fibers (MFA, MS); glass (MFA, MS); graphic design (MFA, MS); metals (MFA, MS); painting (MFA, MS); photography (MFA, MS); printmaking (MFA, MS); sculpture (MFA, MS). *Accreditation:* NASAD (one or more programs are accredited). *Faculty:* 30 full-time (12 women). *Students:* 31 full-time (20 women), 5 part-time (4 women); includes 3 minority (1 African American, 2 Hispanic Americans), 3 international. 62 applicants, 29% accepted. In 2007, 17 degrees awarded. *Degree requirements:* For master's, thesis or alternative, internship. *Entrance requirements:* For master's, portfolio, sample of scholarly writing. *Application deadline:* Applications are processed on a rolling basis. Application fee: $40. *Expenses:* Tuition, state resident: full-time $3,492; part-time $194 per credit hour. Tuition, nonresident: full-time $7,272; part-time $404 per credit hour. Required fees: $1,024; $57 per credit hour. *Financial support:* In 2007–08, 23 teaching assistantships (averaging $6,661 per year) were awarded; career-related internships or fieldwork, Federal Work-Study, tuition waivers (full and partial), and unspecified assistantships also available. Support available to part-time students. Financial award application deadline: 4/1. *Faculty research:* General operations support: Normal Editions Workshop for FY2007. Total annual research expenditures: $4,160. *Unit head:* James Crowley, Chairperson, 309-438-5621.

Indiana State University, School of Graduate Studies, College of Arts and Sciences, Department of Art, Terre Haute, IN 47809-1401. Offers ceramics (MA, MFA); drawing (MA, MFA); graphic design (MA, MFA); painting (MA, MFA); photography (MA, MFA); printmaking (MA, MFA); sculpture (MA, MFA). *Accreditation:* NASAD (one or more programs are accredited). Part-time programs available. *Faculty:* 10 full-time (3 women), 1 part-time/adjunct (0 women). *Students:* 16 full-time (9 women), 9 part-time (1 woman); includes 1 minority (Hispanic American), 8 international. Average age 35. 17 applicants, 65% accepted, 6 enrolled. In 2007, 7 degrees awarded. *Degree requirements:* For master's, thesis or alternative, departmental qualifying exam. *Entrance requirements:* For master's, portfolio. Additional exam requirements/recommendations for international students: Required—TOEFL (minimum score 550 paper-based). *Application deadline:* For fall admission, 7/1 priority date for domestic students; for spring admission, 11/1 priority date for domestic students. Applications are processed on a rolling basis. Application fee: $35. *Expenses:* Tuition, state resident: full-time $7,056; part-time $294 per semester hour. Tuition, nonresident: full-time $14,016; part-time $584 per semester hour. Required fees: $175 per semester. *Financial support:* In 2007–08, 7 teaching assistantships with partial tuition reimbursements (averaging $7,200 per year) were awarded; career-related internships or fieldwork, Federal Work-Study, institutionally sponsored loans, scholarships/grants, and tuition waivers (partial) also available. Support available to part-time students. Financial award application deadline: 3/1; financial award applicants required to submit FAFSA. *Unit head:* Dr. Alden Cavanaugh, Chairperson, 812-237-3698.

Indiana University Bloomington, University Graduate School, College of Arts and Sciences, Henry Radford Hope School of Fine Arts, Bloomington, IN 47405-7000. Offers MA, MFA, PhD. *Accreditation:* NASAD (one or more programs are accredited). *Faculty:* 17 full-time (10 women). *Students:* 89 full-time (49 women), 41 part-time (30 women); includes 7 minority (2 African Americans, 4 Asian Americans or Pacific Islanders, 1 Hispanic American), 10 international. Average age 30. In 2007, 7 degrees awarded. *Degree requirements:* For doctorate, 2 foreign languages, thesis/dissertation. *Entrance requirements:* For master's, portfolio (MFA); for doctorate, minimum GPA of 3.0. Additional exam requirements/recommendations for international students: Required—TOEFL. *Application deadline:* For fall admission, 1/15 priority date for domestic students, 12/15 for international students; for spring admission, 9/1 for domestic and international students. Applications are processed on a rolling basis. Application fee: $50 ($60 for international students). *Financial support:* Fellowships with tuition reimbursements, research assistantships with tuition reimbursements, teaching assistantships with tuition reimbursements, career-related internships or fieldwork, Federal Work-Study, scholarships/grants, tuition waivers (full and partial), and stipends available. Financial award application deadline: 2/15. *Faculty research:* Infrared reflectography, Italian Renaissance painters, hand papermaking, British Romantic landscape painting, late nineteenth century American art. *Unit head:* Paul Brown, Director, 812-855-7498. *Application contact:* Brad Wicklund, Graduate Services Coordinator, 812-855-7766, E-mail: bwicklun@indiana.edu.

Indiana University of Pennsylvania, School of Graduate Studies and Research, College of Fine Arts, Department of Art, Program in Art, Indiana, PA 15705-1087. Offers MA, MFA. *Accreditation:* NASAD. Part-time programs available. *Faculty:* 8 full-time (4 women), 1 (woman) part-time/adjunct. *Students:* 15 full-time (8 women), 4 part-time (2 women), 3 international. Average age 32. 26 applicants, 42% accepted, 9 enrolled. In 2007, 8 degrees awarded. *Degree requirements:* For master's, thesis optional. *Entrance requirements:* For master's, 3 letters of recommendation, portfolio. Additional exam requirements/recommendations for international students: Required—TOEFL. *Application deadline:* For fall admission, 7/1 priority date for domestic students; for spring admission, 11/1 for domestic students. Applications are processed on a rolling basis. Application fee: $30. *Expenses:* Tuition, state resident: full-time $6,214; part-time $345 per credit. Tuition, nonresident: full-time $9,944; part-time $552 per credit. Required fees: $43 per credit. One-time fee: $140 part-time. Tuition and fees vary according to course load. *Financial support:* In 2007–08, fellowships (averaging $250 per year), 17 research assistantships with full and partial tuition reimbursements (averaging $1,250 per year) were awarded; career-related internships or fieldwork and Federal Work-Study also available. Support available to part-time students. Financial award application deadline: 3/15; financial award applicants required to submit FAFSA.

Indiana University–Purdue University Indianapolis, Herron School of Art and Design, Indianapolis, IN 46202-2896. Offers art education (MAE); furniture design (MFA); printmaking (MFA); sculpture (MFA); visual communication (MFA). *Accreditation:* NASAD. Part-time and evening/weekend programs available. *Faculty:* 2 full-time (both women). *Students:* 2 full-time (1 woman), 18 part-time (15 women); includes 1 minority (Hispanic American) Average age 37. In 2007, 1 degree awarded. *Entrance requirements:* For master's, portfolio, 44 hours of course work in art history and studio art. *Application deadline:* For fall admission, 6/1 priority date for domestic students, 3/15 priority date for international students; for spring admission, 11/1 priority date for domestic students, 10/15 priority date for international students. Applications are processed on a rolling basis. Application fee: $50 ($60 for international students). Electronic applications accepted. *Expenses:* Tuition, state resident: full-time $5,818; part-time $242 per credit hour. Tuition, nonresident: full-time $17,106; part-time $713 per credit hour. Required fees: $629. Tuition and fees vary according to course load, campus/location and program. *Financial support:* Career-related internships or fieldwork, Federal Work-Study, institutionally sponsored loans, scholarships/grants, and tuition waivers (partial) available. Support available to part-time students. Total annual research expenditures: $6,097. *Unit head:* Valerie Eickmeier, Dean, 317-278-9470, Fax: 317-278-9471, E-mail: herron@iupui.edu. *Application contact:* Herron Student Services Office, 317-378-9400, E-mail: herrart@iupui.edu.

Inter American University of Puerto Rico, San Germán Campus, Graduate Studies Center, Program in Fine Arts, San Germán, PR 00683-5008. Offers art (MFA); ceramics (MFA); drawing (MFA); engraving (MFA); painting (MFA); photography (MFA); sculpture (MFA). *Faculty:* 4 full-time, 2 part-time/adjunct. *Students:* 28. In 2007, 7 degrees awarded. *Degree requirements:* For master's, comprehensive exam, thesis. *Entrance requirements:* For master's, GRE General Test or EXADEP, minimum GPA of 3.0. *Application deadline:* For fall admission, 4/30 priority date for domestic students; for spring admission, 11/15 for domestic students. Applications are processed on a rolling basis. Application fee: $31. *Expenses:* Tuition: Full-time $3,258; part-time $181 per credit. Required fees: $258 per semester. Tuition and fees vary according to degree level. *Financial support:* Teaching assistantships, Federal Work-Study and unspecified assistantships available. *Application contact:* Prof. Maria Garcia, Graduate Coordinator, 787-264-1912 Ext. 7357, Fax: 787-892-6350, E-mail: hgarcia@sg.inter.edu.

James Madison University, The Graduate School, College of Visual and Performing Arts, School of Art and Art History, Harrisonburg, VA 22807. Offers art education (MA); art history (MA); ceramics (MFA); drawing/painting (MFA); metal/jewelry (MFA); photography (MFA); printmaking (MFA); sculpture (MFA); studio art (MA); weaving/fibers (MFA). *Accreditation:* NASAD. Part-time programs available. *Faculty:* 5 full-time (2 women), 1 part-time/adjunct (0 women). *Students:* 10 full-time (5 women), 2 part-time; includes 1 minority (Asian American or Pacific Islander) Average age 27. In 2007, 8 degrees awarded. *Degree requirements:* For master's, thesis (for some programs). *Entrance requirements:* For master's, GRE General Test, language exam in French or German, portfolio, 3 letters of recommendation, research paper. Additional exam requirements/recommendations for international students: Required—TOEFL. *Application deadline:* For fall admission, 2/15 priority date for domestic students, 2/15 for international students; for spring admission, 10/15 priority date for domestic students, 10/15 for international students. Applications are processed on a rolling basis. Application fee: $55. Electronic applications accepted. *Expenses:* Tuition, state resident: full-time $6,720; part-time $280 per credit hour. Tuition, nonresident: full-time $19,104; part-time $796 per credit hour. *Financial support:* In 2007–08, 8 students received support, including 3 teaching assistantships with full tuition reimbursements available (averaging $8,494 per year); Federal Work-Study, unspecified assistantships, and 5 graduate assistantships ($7,237) also available. Financial award application deadline: 3/1; financial award applicants required to submit FAFSA. *Unit head:* Leslie M. Bellavance, Academic Unit Head, 540-568-6216.

John F. Kennedy University, Graduate School of Holistic Studies, Department of Arts and Consciousness, Program in Studio Arts, Pleasant Hill, CA 94523-4817. Offers MFA. Part-time and evening/weekend programs available. *Degree requirements:* For master's, thesis or alternative. *Entrance requirements:* For master's, interview, portfolio. Additional exam requirements/recommendations for international students: Required—TOEFL. Expenses: Contact institution.

Johnson State College, Program in Studio Arts, Johnson, VT 05656-9405. Offers drawing (MFA); mixed media (MFA); painting (MFA); sculpture (MFA). Part-time programs available. Postbaccalaureate distance learning degree programs offered (minimal on-campus study). *Faculty:* 3 full-time (2 women). *Students:* 1 (woman) full-time, 24 part-time (19 women). *Entrance requirements:* For master's, portfolio. Additional exam requirements/recommendations for international students: Required—TOEFL. *Application deadline:* For fall admission, 2/15 for domestic and international students. Application fee: $35. *Expenses: Contact institution. Financial support:* Federal Work-Study and unspecified assistantships available. Support available to part-time students. Financial award application deadline: 3/1; financial award applicants required to submit FAFSA. *Application contact:* Catherine H. Higley, Program Coordinator, 800-635-2356 Ext. 1244, Fax: 802-635-1248, E-mail: catherine.higley@jsc.edu.

Kansas State University, Graduate School, College of Arts and Sciences, Department of Art, Manhattan, KS 66506. Offers MFA. *Accreditation:* NASAD. Part-time programs available. *Faculty:* 9 full-time (3 women), 1 part-time/adjunct (0 women). *Students:* 30 full-time (12 women), 1 part-time; includes 1 minority (Asian American or Pacific Islander), 4 international. 27 applicants, 26% accepted, 6 enrolled. In 2007, 16 degrees awarded. *Degree requirements:* For master's, thesis, gallery exhibit. *Entrance requirements:* For master's, slides of artistic work, portfolio. Additional exam requirements/recommendations for international students: Required—TOEFL (minimum score 550 paper-based; 213 computer-based). *Application deadline:* For fall admission, 2/15 for domestic students, 2/1 for international students; for winter admission, 12/1 for international students; for spring admission, 10/15 for domestic students, 8/1 for international students. Application fee: $30 ($55 for international students). *Financial support:* In 2007–08, 19 teaching assistantships with full tuition reimbursements (averaging $6,578 per year) were awarded; research assistantships, career-related internships or fieldwork, Federal Work-Study, institutionally sponsored loans, and scholarships/grants also available. Support available to part-time students. Financial award application deadline: 3/1; financial award applicants required to submit FAFSA. *Faculty research:* Drawing, painting, sculpture, metalsmithing, visual communication. *Unit head:* Gerry Craig, Head, 785-532-6605, Fax: 785-532-0334, E-mail: gkcraig@ksu.edu. *Application contact:* Elliot Pujol, Director, 785-532-6605, Fax: 785-532-0334, E-mail: hepujol@ksu.edu.

Kean University, School of Visual and Performing Arts, Union, NJ 07083. Offers MA, MS. Part-time and evening/weekend programs available. *Faculty:* 27 full-time (9 women). *Students:* 42 full-time (30 women), 74 part-time (44 women); includes 23 minority (10 African Americans, 3 Asian Americans or Pacific Islanders, 10 Hispanic Americans), 4 international. Average age 33. 33 applicants, 97% accepted, 24 enrolled. In 2007, 32 degrees awarded. *Degree requirements:* For master's, comprehensive exam (for some programs), thesis (for some programs). *Entrance requirements:* For master's, minimum GPA of 3.0, 3 letters of recommendation, portfolio. *Application deadline:* For fall admission, 5/1 for domestic students; for spring admission, 11/1 for domestic students. Application fee: $60 ($150 for international students). *Expenses:* Tuition, state resident: full-time $9,384; part-time $391 per credit. Tuition, nonresident: full-time $12,720; part-time $530 per credit. Required fees: $2,382; $99 per credit. Part-time tuition and fees vary according to course load. *Financial support:* In 2007–08, 1 research assistantship with full tuition reimbursement (averaging $3,217 per year) was awarded; unspecified assistantships also available. *Unit head:* Dr. Carole Shaffer-Koros, Dean, 908-737-4376, Fax: 908-737-4377, E-mail: ckoros@kean.edu. *Application contact:* Joanne Morris, Director of Graduate Admissions, 908-737-3355, Fax: 908-737-3354, E-mail: grad-adm@kean.edu.

Kent State University, College of the Arts, School of Art, Kent, OH 44242-0001. Offers art education (MA); art history (MA); crafts (MA, MFA), including ceramics (MA), glass, jewelry/metals, textiles/art; fine art (MA, MFA), including drawing/painting, printmaking, sculpture. *Accreditation:* NASAD (one or more programs are accredited). *Faculty:* 20 full-time (11 women), 4 part-time/adjunct (3 women). *Students:* 46 full-time (33 women), 41 part-time (27 women); includes 1 African American, 11 Asian Americans or Pacific Islanders. 81 applicants, 49%

Art/Fine Arts

Kent State University (continued)
accepted, 24 enrolled. In 2007, 22 degrees awarded. *Degree requirements:* For master's, one foreign language, thesis. *Entrance requirements:* For master's, undergraduate degree in proposed area of study (for fine arts and crafts programs); minimum overall GPA of 2.75 (3.0 for art major); 3 letters of recommendation; portfolio (15-20 slides for MA, 20-25 for MFA), brief autobiographical statement (MFA). Additional exam requirements/recommendations for international students: Required—TOEFL. *Application deadline:* For fall admission, 2/15 for domestic students; for spring admission, 10/15 for domestic students. Applications are processed on a rolling basis. Application fee: $30. Electronic applications accepted. *Financial support:* In 2007–08, 21 teaching assistantships with full tuition reimbursements (averaging $6,700 per year) were awarded; career-related internships or fieldwork, Federal Work-Study, scholarships/grants, and tuition waivers (full) also available. Financial award application deadline: 2/15. *Unit head:* Dr. Christine Havice, Director, 330-672-2192, Fax: 330-672-4729, E-mail: chavice@kent.edu. *Application contact:* Janice Lessman-Moss, Coordinator of Graduate Studies, 330-672-1362, Fax: 330-672-2192, E-mail: jlessman@kent.edu.

Lamar University, College of Graduate Studies, College of Fine Arts and Communication, Department of Art, Beaumont, TX 77710. Offers art history (MA); photography (MA); studio art (MA); visual design (MA). Part-time and evening/weekend programs available. *Faculty:* 6 full-time (3 women). *Students:* Average age 42. 2 applicants, 0% accepted. In 2007, 2 degrees awarded. *Degree requirements:* For master's, thesis. *Entrance requirements:* For master's, GRE General Test, minimum GPA of 2.5 in last 60 hours of undergraduate course work. Additional exam requirements/recommendations for international students: Required—TOEFL. *Application deadline:* For fall admission, 8/1 priority date for domestic students; for spring admission, 12/1 for domestic students. Applications are processed on a rolling basis. Application fee: $25 ($50 for international students). *Expenses:* Tuition, state resident: part-time $348 per semester hour. Tuition, nonresident: part-time $626 per semester hour. Tuition and fees vary according to course load. *Financial support:* Fellowships, career-related internships or fieldwork, Federal Work-Study, and scholarships/grants available. Financial award application deadline: 4/1. *Faculty research:* Nineteenth century academic paintings, metal casting, pigment color stability, computer modified photography, manipulated photography. *Unit head:* Donna M. Meeks, Chair, 409-880-8141, Fax: 409-880-1799, E-mail: meeksdm@lub002.lamar.edu.

Lehman College of the City University of New York, Division of Arts and Humanities, Department of Art, Bronx, NY 10468-1589. Offers MA, MFA. Part-time and evening/weekend programs available. *Entrance requirements:* For master's, 33 undergraduate credits in art, interview, portfolio. *Faculty research:* Graphic art, modern and contemporary art, sculpture, primitive and pre-Columbian art, medieval art.

Lesley University, Graduate School of Arts and Social Sciences, Program in Visual Arts, Cambridge, MA 02138-2790. Offers MFA. Postbaccalaureate distance learning degree programs offered. *Faculty:* 1 (woman) full-time. *Students:* 67 full-time (41 women), 21 part-time (13 women); includes 2 minority (1 African American, 1 American Indian/Alaska Native), 1 international. Average age 39. 52 applicants, 54% accepted, 19 enrolled. In 2007, 35 degrees awarded. *Entrance requirements:* For master's, portfolio. Additional exam requirements/recommendations for international students: Required—TOEFL (minimum score 550 paper-based; 213 computer-based; 80 iBT). Application fee: $50. *Expenses:* Contact institution. *Financial support:* In 2007–08, 1 student received support. Federal Work-Study and scholarships/grants available. Support available to part-time students. Financial award application deadline: 4/15; financial award applicants required to submit FAFSA. *Unit head:* Judith Barry, Director, 617-585-6712, Fax: 617-585-6721, E-mail: jbarry2@lesley.edu. *Application contact:* Louise Goldenberg, Administrative Director, 617-585-6770, E-mail: lgoldenb@lesley.edu.

See Close-Up on page 227.

Lindenwood University, Graduate Programs, Division of Fine and Performing Arts, St. Charles, MO 63301-1695. Offers arts management (MA); communication arts (MA); studio art (MA, MFA); theatre (MA, MFA). Part-time programs available. *Faculty:* 19 full-time (9 women). *Students:* 17 full-time (11 women), 21 part-time (12 women); includes 3 minority (all African Americans), 3 international. Average age 34. In 2007, 23 degrees awarded. *Degree requirements:* For master's, thesis (for some programs). *Entrance requirements:* For master's, audition or interview, minimum GPA of 3.0. Additional exam requirements/recommendations for international students: Required—TOEFL (minimum score 550 paper-based; 213 computer-based; 80 iBT). *Application deadline:* For fall admission, 8/30 priority date for domestic and international students; for spring admission, 12/30 priority date for domestic and international students. Applications are processed on a rolling basis. Application fee: $30 ($100 for international students). Electronic applications accepted. *Expenses:* Tuition: Full-time $12,400; part-time $350 per hour. Full-time tuition and fees vary according to degree level and program. *Financial support:* Career-related internships or fieldwork, institutionally sponsored loans, tuition waivers (partial), and unspecified assistantships available. Financial award application deadline: 6/30; financial award applicants required to submit FAFSA. *Unit head:* Marsha Parker, Dean of Fine Arts, 636-949-4906, Fax: 636-949-4910, E-mail: mparker@lindenwood.edu. *Application contact:* Brett Barger, Dean of Evening Admissions and Extension Campuses, 636-949-4934, Fax: 636-949-4109, E-mail: adultadmissions@lindenwood.edu.

Long Island University, C.W. Post Campus, School of Visual and Performing Arts, Department of Art, Brookville, NY 11548-1300. Offers art (MA); art education (MS); clinical art therapy (MA); fine art and design (MFA). Part-time and evening/weekend programs available. *Faculty:* 9 full-time (4 women), 14 part-time/adjunct (6 women). *Students:* 52 full-time (44 women), 29 part-time (25 women); includes 14 minority (2 African Americans, 12 Asian Americans or Pacific Islanders), 7 international. Average age 32. 68 applicants, 69% accepted, 22 enrolled. In 2007, 44 degrees awarded. *Degree requirements:* For master's, thesis. *Application deadline:* Applications are processed on a rolling basis. Application fee: $30. Electronic applications accepted. *Expenses:* Tuition: Part-time $825 per credit. Tuition and fees vary according to course load. *Financial support:* Teaching assistantships, career-related internships or fieldwork, Federal Work-Study, institutionally sponsored loans, and unspecified assistantships available. Support available to part-time students. Financial award application deadline: 5/15; financial award applicants required to submit CSS PROFILE or FAFSA. *Faculty research:* Painting, sculpture, installation, computers, video. Total annual research expenditures: $17,346. *Unit head:* Prof. Donna Tuman, Chair, 516-299-2464, E-mail: donna.tuman@liu.edu. *Application contact:* Cathy Morante, Graduate Advisor, 516-299-2405 Ext. 2465, E-mail: cathy.morante@liu.edu.

Louisiana State University and Agricultural and Mechanical College, Graduate School, College of Art and Design, School of Art, Program in Studio Art, Baton Rouge, LA 70803. Offers ceramics (MFA); graphic design (MFA); painting and drawing (MFA); photography (MFA); printmaking (MFA); sculpture (MFA). *Accreditation:* NASAD. *Students:* 47 full-time (29 women), 4 part-time (2 women); includes 1 African American, 1 Hispanic American, 6 international. 63 applicants, 25% accepted. In 2007, 16 degrees awarded. *Degree requirements:* For master's, thesis. *Entrance requirements:* For master's, minimum GPA of 3.0. Additional exam requirements/recommendations for international students: Required—TOEFL (minimum score 550 paper-based; 213 computer-based; 79 iBT). *Application deadline:* For fall admission, 1/25 priority date for domestic students, 5/15 for international students; for spring admission, 10/15 for international students. Applications are processed on a rolling basis. Electronic applications accepted. *Financial support:* In 2007–08, 25 students received support; research assistantships with partial tuition reimbursements available, teaching assistantships, career-related internships or fieldwork, Federal Work-Study, institutionally sponsored loans, scholarships/grants, and unspecified assistantships available. Support available to part-time students. Financial award application deadline: 3/15. *Unit head:* Chris Johns, Graduate Coordinator, 225-578-5411, Fax: 225-578-1445, E-mail: cjohns@lsu.edu.

Louisiana Tech University, Graduate School, College of Liberal Arts, School of Art, Ruston, LA 71272. Offers art and graphic design (MFA); photography (MFA); studio art (MFA). *Accreditation:* NASAD. Part-time programs available. *Degree requirements:* For master's, exhibit. *Entrance requirements:* For master's, GRE General Test, portfolio. *Application deadline:* For fall admission, 7/29 for domestic students; for spring admission, 2/3 for domestic students. Applications are processed on a rolling basis. Application fee: $20 ($30 for international students). *Financial support:* Fellowships, career-related internships or fieldwork, Federal Work-Study, institutionally sponsored loans, and unspecified assistantships available. Financial award application deadline: 2/1. *Unit head:* Jonathan Donchoo, Director, 318-257-3909, Fax: 318-257-4890.

Maine College of Art, Program in Studio Arts, Portland, ME 04101. Offers MFA. *Accreditation:* NASAD. *Degree requirements:* For master's, thesis. *Entrance requirements:* Additional exam requirements/recommendations for international students: Required—TOEFL (minimum score 550 paper-based; 213 computer-based). Electronic applications accepted.

Marshall University, Academic Affairs Division, College of Fine Arts, Department of Art, Huntington, WV 25755. Offers MA. Evening/weekend programs available. *Faculty:* 11 full-time (5 women), 11 part-time/adjunct (10 women). *Students:* 7 full-time (all women), 2 part-time (both women). Average age 30. In 2007, 6 degrees awarded. *Degree requirements:* For master's, thesis optional. *Entrance requirements:* For master's, GRE General Test, portfolio. Application fee: $40. *Unit head:* Prof. Byron Clercx, Chair, 304-696-5451, Fax: 304-696-6505, E-mail: clercx@marshall.edu. *Application contact:* Information Contact, 304-746-1900, Fax: 304-746-1902, E-mail: services@marshall.edu.

Maryland Institute College of Art, Graduate Studies, Fine Arts Post Baccalaureate Certificate Program, Baltimore, MD 21217. Offers Certificate. Part-time programs available. *Faculty:* 1 full-time (0 women), 2 part-time/adjunct (1 woman). *Students:* 23 full-time (16 women); includes 3 minority (1 African American, 2 Hispanic Americans), 2 international. Average age 31. In 2007, 15 degrees awarded. *Degree requirements:* For Certificate, thesis. *Entrance requirements:* For degree, portfolio, 40 studio credits, 6 credits in art history. Additional exam requirements/recommendations for international students: Required—TOEFL (minimum score 550 paper-based; 213 computer-based). *Application deadline:* For fall admission, 2/15 for domestic and international students; for spring admission, 10/1 for domestic and international students. Application fee: $50. *Expenses:* Tuition: Full-time $29,700; part-time $1,238 per credit. Required fees: $980; $490 per term. *Financial support:* In 2007–08, 22 students received support. Scholarships/grants available. Financial award application deadline: 3/1; financial award applicants required to submit FAFSA. *Unit head:* William Schmidt, Director, 410-230-0568, Fax: 410-225-2408. *Application contact:* Scott G. Kelly, Associate Dean of Graduate Admission, 410-225-2256, Fax: 410-225-2408, E-mail: graduate@mica.edu.

Maryland Institute College of Art, Graduate Studies, Hoffberger School of Painting, Baltimore, MD 21217. Offers MFA. *Accreditation:* NASAD. *Faculty:* 1 (woman) full-time, 1 part-time/adjunct (0 women). *Students:* 14 full-time (9 women); includes 1 minority (Hispanic American), 1 international. Average age 29. In 2007, 8 degrees awarded. *Degree requirements:* For master's, thesis, exhibit. *Entrance requirements:* For master's, portfolio, 40 studio credits, 6 credits in art history. Additional exam requirements/recommendations for international students: Required—TOEFL (minimum score 550 paper-based; 213 computer-based). *Application deadline:* For fall admission, 2/15 for domestic and international students. Application fee: $50. *Expenses:* Tuition: Full-time $29,700; part-time $1,238 per credit. Required fees: $980; $490 per term. *Financial support:* In 2007–08, 14 students received support, including fellowships (averaging $15,680 per year), teaching assistantships (averaging $1,500 per year); career-related internships or fieldwork and scholarships/grants also available. Financial award application deadline: 3/1; financial award applicants required to submit FAFSA. *Unit head:* Grace Hartigan, Director, 410-225-2534, Fax: 410-225-2408, E-mail: graduate@mica.edu. *Application contact:* Scott G. Kelly, Associate Dean of Graduate Admission, 410-225-2256, Fax: 410-225-2408, E-mail: graduate@mica.edu.

Maryland Institute College of Art, Graduate Studies, Mount Royal School of Art, Baltimore, MD 21217. Offers painting (MFA). *Faculty:* 1 (woman) full-time, 3 part-time/adjunct (1 woman). *Students:* 24 full-time (11 women); includes 5 minority (2 African Americans, 1 Asian American or Pacific Islander, 2 Hispanic Americans), 1 international. Average age 27. In 2007, 15 degrees awarded. *Degree requirements:* For master's, thesis, exhibit. *Entrance requirements:* For master's, 40 credits in studio art, 6 credits in art history, portfolio. Additional exam requirements/recommendations for international students: Required—TOEFL (minimum score 550 paper-based; 213 computer-based). *Application deadline:* For fall admission, 2/15 for domestic and international students. Application fee: $50. *Expenses:* Tuition: Full-time $29,700; part-time $1,238 per credit. Required fees: $980; $490 per term. *Financial support:* In 2007–08, 24 students received support, including fellowships (averaging $15,680 per year), teaching assistantships (averaging $1,500 per year); career-related internships or fieldwork and scholarships/grants also available. Financial award application deadline: 3/1; financial award applicants required to submit FAFSA. *Unit head:* Frances Barth, Director, 410-225-2534, Fax: 410-225-2408, E-mail: graduate@mica.edu. *Application contact:* Scott G. Kelly, Associate Dean of Graduate Admission, 410-225-2256, Fax: 410-225-2408, E-mail: graduate@mica.edu.

Maryland Institute College of Art, Graduate Studies, Program in Community Arts, Baltimore, MD 21217. Offers MA. Part-time programs available. *Faculty:* 2 full-time (1 woman), 3 part-time/adjunct (all women). *Students:* Average age 28. In 2007, 9 degrees awarded. *Degree requirements:* For master's, thesis. *Entrance requirements:* For master's, portfolio, professional certification (BFA), 40 studio credits, 6 credits in art history. Additional exam requirements/recommendations for international students: Required—TOEFL (minimum score 550 paper-based; 213 computer-based). *Application deadline:* For fall admission, 2/15 for domestic and international students. Application fee: $50. *Expenses:* Tuition: Full-time $29,700; part-time $1,238 per credit. Required fees: $980; $490 per term. *Financial support:* In 2007–08, 22 students received support, including fellowships (averaging $15,680 per year); career-related internships or fieldwork and scholarships/grants also available. Financial award application deadline: 3/1; financial award applicants required to submit FAFSA. *Unit head:* Ken Krafchek, Director, 410-225-2587, Fax: 410-225-2574. *Application contact:* Scott G. Kelly, Associate Dean of Graduate Admission, 410-225-2256, Fax: 410-225-2408, E-mail: graduate@mica.edu.

Maryland Institute College of Art, Graduate Studies, Program in Studio Art, Baltimore, MD 21217. Offers MFA. Offered during summer only. Part-time programs available. *Faculty:* 2 full-time (1 woman), 1 (woman) part-time/adjunct. *Students:* 9 full-time (all women), 27 part-time (19 women); includes 3 minority (1 African American, 1 American Indian/Alaska Native, 1 Asian American or Pacific Islander). Average age 36. In 2007, 9 degrees awarded. *Degree requirements:* For master's, thesis. *Entrance requirements:* For master's, portfolio, professional certification (BFA), 40 studio credits, 6 credits in art history. Additional exam requirements/recommendations for international students: Required—TOEFL (minimum score 550 paper-based; 213 computer-based). *Application deadline:* For fall admission, 2/15 for domestic and international students. Application fee: $50. *Expenses:* Tuition: Full-time $29,700; part-time $1,238 per credit. Required fees: $980; $490 per term. *Financial support:* In 2007–08, 33 students received support, including 1 fellowship (averaging $7,840 per year); career-related internships or fieldwork and scholarships/grants also available. Financial award application deadline: 3/1; financial award applicants required to submit FAFSA. *Unit head:* Zlata Baum, Director, 410-225-2297, Fax: 410-225-2257. *Application contact:* Scott G. Kelly, Associate Dean of Graduate Admission, 410-225-2256, Fax: 410-225-2408, E-mail: graduate@mica.edu.

Maryland Institute College of Art, Graduate Studies, Rinehart School of Sculpture, Baltimore, MD 21217. Offers MFA. *Accreditation:* NASAD. *Faculty:* 1 (woman) full-time. *Students:* 11 full-time (7 women); includes 2 minority (1 Asian American or Pacific Islander, 1 Hispanic American). Average age 31. In 2007, 3 degrees awarded. *Degree requirements:* For master's, thesis, exhibit. *Entrance requirements:* For master's, portfolio, 40 studio credits, 6 credits in art history. Additional exam requirements/recommendations for international students: Required—TOEFL (minimum score 550 paper-based; 213 computer-based). *Application deadline:* For fall admission, 2/15 for domestic and international students. Application fee: $50. *Expenses:* Tuition: Full-time $29,700; part-time $1,238 per credit. Required fees: $980; $490 per term. *Financial support:* In 2007–08, 11 students received support, including 2 fellowships (averaging $15,680 per year), 8 teaching assistantships (averaging $1,500 per year); career-related internships or fieldwork and scholarships/grants also available. Financial award application deadline: 3/1; financial award applicants required to submit FAFSA. *Unit head:* Maren Hassinger, Director, 410-225-2534, Fax: 410-225-2408. *Application contact:* Scott G. Kelly, Associate Dean of Graduate Admission, 410-225-2256, Fax: 410-225-2408, E-mail: graduate@mica.edu.

Marywood University, Academic Affairs, Insalaco College of Creative Arts and Management, Art Department, Program in Studio Art, Scranton, PA 18509-1598. Offers advertising design (MA); ceramics (MA); clay (MA); graphic design (MA); illustration (MA); interior architecture (MA); painting (MA); photography (MA); printmaking (MA); sculpture (MA); weaving (MA). *Accreditation:* NASAD. Part-time and evening/weekend programs available. *Students:* 5 full-time (3 women), 15 part-time (11 women), 1 international. Average age 41. 5 applicants, 80% accepted. In 2007, 7 degrees awarded. *Degree requirements:* For master's, comprehensive exam, thesis or alternative. *Entrance requirements:* For master's, portfolio. Additional exam requirements/recommendations for international students: Required—TOEFL (minimum score 550 paper-based; 213 computer-based). *Application deadline:* For fall admission, 4/15 priority date for domestic and international students; for spring admission, 11/15 priority date for domestic and international students. Applications are processed on a rolling basis. Application fee: $30. Electronic applications accepted. *Expenses:* Tuition: Full-time $15,290; part-time $695 per credit. Required fees: $990; $370 per term. Tuition and fees vary according to degree level. *Financial support:* Research assistantships with tuition reimbursements, scholarships/grants, tuition waivers (partial), and unspecified assistantships available. Support available to part-time students. Financial award application deadline: 2/15; financial award applicants required to submit FAFSA. *Faculty research:* Texture and line in clay, cast bronze sculpture, color theories, book art and illustration, sculptural form.

Marywood University, Academic Affairs, Insalaco College of Creative Arts and Management, Art Department, Program in Visual Arts, Scranton, PA 18509-1598. Offers advertising design (MFA); clay (MFA); fibers (MFA); graphic design (MFA); illustration (MFA); metals (MFA); painting (MFA); photography (MFA); printmaking (MFA). *Accreditation:* NASAD. Part-time and evening/weekend programs available. *Students:* 13 full-time (10 women), 25 part-time (13 women); includes 2 minority (1 American Indian/Alaska Native, 1 Asian American or Pacific Islander), 3 international. Average age 35. In 2007, 11 degrees awarded. *Degree requirements:* For master's, thesis or alternative, exhibit. *Entrance requirements:* For master's, portfolio. Additional exam requirements/recommendations for international students: Required—TOEFL (minimum score 550 paper-based; 213 computer-based). *Application deadline:* For fall admission, 4/15 priority date for domestic and international students; for spring admission, 11/15 priority date for domestic and international students. Applications are processed on a rolling basis. Application fee: $30. Electronic applications accepted. *Expenses: Contact institution.* Tuition and fees vary according to degree level. *Financial support:* Research assistantships with tuition reimbursements, scholarships/grants, tuition waivers (partial), and unspecified assistantships available. Support available to part-time students. Financial award application deadline: 2/15; financial award applicants required to submit FAFSA. *Faculty research:* Mariology, exploration of visual imagery, explorations involving drawing on the loom, clay as sculptural medium, oil paintings.

Massachusetts College of Art and Design, Graduate Programs, Program in Fine Arts, Boston, MA 02115-5882. Offers ceramics (MFA); design (MFA); fibers (MFA); film (MFA); glass (MFA); media and performing arts (MFA); metals (MFA); painting (MFA); photography (MFA); printmaking (MFA); sculpture (MFA). *Accreditation:* NASAD. *Faculty:* 10 full-time (5 women), 8 part-time/adjunct (6 women). *Students:* 80 full-time (46 women), 11 part-time (9 women); includes 7 minority (1 African American, 4 Asian Americans or Pacific Islanders, 2 Hispanic Americans), 13 international. Average age 34. 310 applicants, 26% accepted, 50 enrolled. In 2007, 37 degrees awarded. *Degree requirements:* For master's, thesis, exhibit. *Entrance requirements:* For master's, 12 units of course work in art history, portfolio, resumé. *Application deadline:* For fall admission, 2/1 for domestic students. Application fee: $75. *Expenses:* Tuition, state resident: full-time $16,260; part-time $542 per credit. Tuition, nonresident: full-time $16,260; part-time $542 per credit. *Financial support:* In 2007–08, 50 research assistantships (averaging $2,000 per year), 30 teaching assistantships (averaging $2,000 per year) were awarded; career-related internships or fieldwork, Federal Work-Study, and clerical/technical assistantships also available. Support available to part-time students. Financial award application deadline: 5/1; financial award applicants required to submit FAFSA. *Application contact:* George Creamer, Director, 617-879-7163, Fax: 617-879-7171, E-mail: creamer@massart.edu.

Memphis College of Art, Graduate Programs, Program in Studio Art, Memphis, TN 38104-2764. Offers fiber/surface design (MFA); painting (MFA); papermaking (MFA); photography (MFA); printmaking (MFA); sculpture (MFA). *Accreditation:* NASAD. Part-time programs available. *Faculty:* 11 full-time (5 women), 2 part-time/adjunct (1 woman). *Students:* 17 full-time (7 women); includes 2 minority (both Hispanic Americans) Average age 29. 45 applicants, 51% accepted, 8 enrolled. In 2007, 4 degrees awarded. *Degree requirements:* For master's, thesis, exhibit. *Entrance requirements:* For master's, portfolio, interview, resumé. Additional exam requirements/recommendations for international students: Required—TOEFL (minimum score 525 paper-based; 195 computer-based). *Application deadline:* For fall admission, 3/1 priority date for domestic and international students; for spring admission, 11/1 priority date for domestic and international students. Application fee: $50. Electronic applications accepted. *Expenses:* Tuition: Full-time $22,000; part-time $435 per credit. Required fees: $560; $100 per course. Part-time tuition and fees vary according to course load and program. *Financial support:* In 2007–08, 11 students received support, including 2 teaching assistantships (averaging $2,000 per year); career-related internships or fieldwork, Federal Work-Study, institutionally sponsored loans, scholarships/grants, tuition waivers (partial), unspecified assistantships, and merit awards also available. Support available to part-time students. Financial award application deadline: 8/1; financial award applicants required to submit FAFSA. *Unit head:* Howard Paine, Graduate Program Director, 901-272-5100, Fax: 901-272-5158, E-mail: hpaine@mca.edu. *Application contact:* Annette James Moore, Director of Admissions, 800-727-1088, Fax: 901-272-5158, E-mail: info@mca.edu.

See Close-Up on page 245.

Miami International University of Art & Design, Program in Visual Arts, Miami, FL 33132-1418. Offers MFA. Postbaccalaureate distance learning degree programs offered.

See Close-Up on page 119.

Miami University, Graduate School, School of Fine Arts, Department of Art, Program in Studio Art, Oxford, OH 45056. Offers MFA. *Accreditation:* NASAD. *Degree requirements:* For master's, thesis, final project. *Entrance requirements:* For master's, portfolio, minimum undergraduate GPA of 3.0 during previous 2 years or 2.75 overall.

Announcement: The MFA degree is offered in studio areas of painting, printmaking, sculpture, ceramics, and metals/jewelry. The master's degree is offered in art education. The MFA requires 60 semester credits in studio and related art courses; MA requires 30 semester hours. Assistantships are available, including tuition waiver, stipend, and studio space. For more information, phone: 513-529-2900, fax: 513-529-1532, e-mail: art@muohio.edu, Web site: www.muohio.edu/art/.

Michigan State University, The Graduate School, College of Arts and Letters, Department of Art and Art History, East Lansing, MI 48824. Offers studio art (MFA). *Entrance requirements:* For master's, minimum GPA of 3.0, portfolio, resumé. Additional exam requirements/recommendations for international students: Required—TOEFL, Michigan State University ELT (85), Michigan ELAB (83). Electronic applications accepted. *Expenses:* Tuition, state resident: part-time $379 per credit hour. Tuition, nonresident: part-time $800 per credit hour. Tuition and fees vary according to program.

Mills College, Graduate Studies, Department of Art, Oakland, CA 94613-1000. Offers ceramics (MFA); intermedia (MFA); painting (MFA); photography (MFA); sculpture (MFA). *Faculty:* 6 full-time (5 women), 11 part-time/adjunct (6 women). *Students:* 23 full-time (12 women); includes 4 minority (all Asian Americans or Pacific Islanders) Average age 33. 90 applicants, 30% accepted, 11 enrolled. In 2007, 12 degrees awarded. *Degree requirements:* For master's, thesis or alternative, exhibit. *Entrance requirements:* Additional exam requirements/recommendations for international students: Required—TOEFL. *Application deadline:* For fall admission, 2/1 for domestic students; for spring admission, 11/1 for domestic students. Application fee: $50. *Expenses: Contact institution.* Part-time tuition and fees vary according to course load and program. *Financial support:* In 2007–08, 10 fellowships with partial tuition reimbursements (averaging $2,125 per year), 12 teaching assistantships with partial tuition reimbursements (averaging $13,896 per year) were awarded; institutionally sponsored loans, scholarships/grants, tuition waivers (partial), and residence awards also available. Support available to part-time students. Financial award application deadline: 2/1; financial award applicants required to submit FAFSA. *Faculty research:* Contemporary Chinese/American art, Asian art, performance art, feminist theory, installation. *Unit head:* Ron Nagle, Chairperson, 510-430-3142, Fax: 510-430-3314. *Application contact:* Linda Guzman, Graduate Admission Specialist, 510-430-3309, Fax: 510-430-2159, E-mail: grad-studies@mills.edu.

Minneapolis College of Art and Design, Program in Arts, Minneapolis, MN 55404-4347. Offers design (Certificate); fine arts (Certificate); media (Certificate). Part-time programs available. *Faculty:* 23 full-time (7 women), 9 part-time/adjunct (4 women). *Students:* 3 full-time (2 women), 10 part-time (7 women). Average age 24. 18 applicants, 56% accepted, 4 enrolled. In 2007, 15 degrees awarded. *Degree requirements:* For Certificate, final project. *Entrance requirements:* For degree, resumé, portfolio, statement, letter of recommendation. Additional exam requirements/recommendations for international students: Required—TOEFL (minimum score 550 paper-based; 213 computer-based; 79 iBT). *Application deadline:* For fall admission, 2/15 for domestic and international students. Application fee: $50. Electronic applications accepted. *Expenses:* Tuition: Full-time $27,000; part-time $900 per credit. Required fees: $100 per term. *Financial support:* Career-related internships or fieldwork and scholarships/grants available. Financial award application deadline: 3/15; financial award applicants required to submit FAFSA. *Faculty research:* Visual arts. *Unit head:* Carole Fisher, Graduate Director, 612-874-3629, E-mail: carole_fisher@mcad.edu. *Application contact:* William Mullen, Vice President of Enrollment Management, 612-874-3762, Fax: 612-874-3701, E-mail: william_mullen@mcad.edu.

Minneapolis College of Art and Design, Program in Visual Studies, Minneapolis, MN 55404-4347. Offers animation (MFA); comic art (MFA); drawing (MFA); filmmaking (MFA); fine arts (MFA); furniture design (MFA); graphic design (MFA); illustration (MFA); interactive media (MFA); painting (MFA); photography (MFA); printmaking (MFA); sculpture (MFA). *Accreditation:* NASAD. Part-time programs available. *Faculty:* 23 full-time (7 women), 9 part-time/adjunct (4 women). *Students:* 40 full-time (21 women), 1 (woman) part-time; includes 1 minority (American Indian/Alaska Native). Average age 27. 172 applicants, 24% accepted, 15 enrolled. In 2007, 7 degrees awarded. *Degree requirements:* For master's, thesis, thesis exhibit. *Entrance requirements:* For master's, portfolio, resumé, 3 letters of recommendation, statement . Additional exam requirements/recommendations for international students: Required—TOEFL (minimum score 550 paper-based; 213 computer-based; 79 iBT). *Application deadline:* For fall admission, 2/15 for domestic and international students. Application fee: $50. Electronic applications accepted. *Expenses:* Tuition: Full-time $27,000; part-time $900 per credit. Required fees: $100 per term. *Financial support:* In 2007–08, 23 students received support, including 15 teaching assistantships (averaging $6,000 per year); career-related internships or fieldwork, Federal Work-Study, scholarships/grants, and unspecified assistantships also available. Support available to part-time students. Financial award application deadline: 3/15; financial award applicants required to submit FAFSA. *Faculty research:* Visual arts. *Unit head:* Carole Fisher, Graduate Director, 612-874-3629, E-mail: carole_fisher@mcad.edu. *Application contact:* William Mullen, Vice President of Enrollment Management, 612-874-3762, Fax: 612-874-3701, E-mail: william_mullen@mcad.edu.

Minnesota State University Mankato, College of Graduate Studies, College of Arts and Humanities, Department of Art, Mankato, MN 56001. Offers art education (MS); studio art (MA); teaching art (MAT, MT). *Accreditation:* NASAD (one or more programs are accredited). Part-time programs available. *Students:* 9 full-time (5 women), 4 part-time (3 women). Average age 31. In 2007, 4 degrees awarded. *Degree requirements:* For master's, one foreign language, comprehensive exam, thesis or alternative. *Entrance requirements:* For master's, minimum GPA of 3.0 during previous 2 years, portfolio (MA). Additional exam requirements/recommendations for international students: Required—TOEFL. *Application deadline:* For fall admission, 7/1 priority date for domestic students; for spring admission, 11/1 for domestic students. Applications are processed on a rolling basis. Application fee: $40. Electronic applications accepted. *Financial support:* Research assistantships, teaching assistantships with full tuition reimbursements, unspecified assistantships available. Financial award application deadline: 3/15; financial award applicants required to submit FAFSA. *Faculty research:* Photographic documentation. *Unit head:* James Johnson, Chairperson, 507-389-6412. *Application contact:* 507-389-2321, E-mail: grad@mnsu.edu.

Mississippi College, Graduate School, College of Arts and Sciences, School of Christian Studies and the Arts, Department of Art, Clinton, MS 39058. Offers M Ed, MA, MFA. Part-time and evening/weekend programs available. *Faculty:* 6 full-time (1 woman), 2 part-time/adjunct (1 woman). *Students:* 13 full-time (7 women), 8 part-time (4 women); includes 3 minority (all African Americans), 5 international. Average age 36. In 2007, 7 degrees awarded. *Degree requirements:* For master's, one foreign language, comprehensive exam, thesis (for some programs). *Entrance requirements:* For master's, GRE or NTE, minimum GPA of 2.5. Additional exam requirements/recommendations for international students: Recommended—IELTS. *Application deadline:* For fall admission, 8/15 priority date for domestic students. Applications are processed on a rolling basis. Application fee: $25. Electronic applications accepted. *Expenses:* Tuition: Full-time $7,470; part-time $415 per hour. Required fees: $1,160 per term. Part-time tuition and fees vary according to course load and degree level. *Financial support:* Teaching assistantships, career-related internships or fieldwork, Federal Work-Study, scholarships/grants, and unspecified assistantships available. Support available to part-time students. Financial award application deadline: 4/1; financial award applicants required to submit FAFSA. *Unit head:* Dr. Randolph B. Miley, Chair, 601-925-3912, Fax: 601-925-3926, E-mail: rmiley@mc.edu.

Mississippi State University, College of Architecture, Art and Design, Department of Art, Mississippi State, MS 39762. Offers electronic visualization (MFA). *Accreditation:* NASAD. *Faculty:* 22 full-time (9 women), 3 part-time/adjunct (1 woman). *Students:* Average age 40. 20 applicants, 30% accepted. *Degree requirements:* For master's, thesis, comprehensive oral or written exam. *Entrance requirements:* For master's, minimum GPA of 3.0, bachelor's degree in visual arts. Additional exam requirements/recommendations for international students: Required—TOEFL. *Application deadline:* For fall admission, 2/15 for domestic students; for spring admission, 11/1 for domestic students. Applications are processed on a rolling basis. Application fee: $30. *Expenses:* Tuition, state resident: full-time $4,978; part-time $274 per hour. Tuition, nonresident: full-time $11,469; part-time $635 per hour. *Financial support:* Teaching assistantships with full tuition reimbursements, Federal Work-Study, institutionally sponsored loans, and unspecified assistantships available. Financial award applicants required to submit FAFSA. *Faculty research:* Multimedia/CD-ROM design, computer animation. *Unit head:* Katherine U. DeMarsche, Head, 662-325-2970, Fax: 662-325-3850, E-mail: kud2@ra.msstate.edu. *Application contact:* Dr. William A. Person, Interim Associate Vice President for Academic Affairs/Interim Dean of Graduate Studies, 662-325-7400, Fax: 662-325-1967, E-mail: grad@grad.msstate.edu.

Missouri State University, Graduate College, College of Arts and Letters, Department of Art and Design, Springfield, MO 65804-0094. Offers secondary education (MS Ed), including art. *Faculty:* 8 full-time (3 women). *Students:* Average age 28. 2 applicants, 100% accepted, 0

Art/Fine Arts

Missouri State University (continued)
enrolled. In 2007, 1 degree awarded. *Entrance requirements:* For master's, minimum GPA of 3.0, 9-12 certification. Additional exam requirements/recommendations for international students: Required—TOEFL (minimum score 550 paper-based; 213 computer-based; 79 iBT). *Application deadline:* For fall admission, 7/20 priority date for domestic students; for spring admission, 12/20 priority date for domestic students. Application fee: $35. *Expenses:* Tuition, state resident: full-time $3,708; part-time $206 per credit hour. Tuition, nonresident: full-time $7,236; part-time $206 per credit hour. Required fees: $622. Full-time tuition and fees vary according to course level, course load, program and reciprocity agreements. *Financial support:* Applicants required to submit FAFSA. *Unit head:* Wade S. Thompson, Acting Head, 417-836-6055, E-mail: artanddesign@missouristate.edu. *Application contact:* Judith Fowler, Graduate Program Director, E-mail: judyfowler@missouristate.edu.

Montana State University, College of Graduate Studies, College of Arts and Architecture, Department of Art, Bozeman, MT 59717. Offers MFA. *Accreditation:* NASAD. Part-time programs available. *Faculty:* 17 full-time (6 women), 11 part-time/adjunct (8 women). *Students:* 9 full-time (5 women), 1 (woman) part-time, 1 international. Average age 31. 25 applicants, 16% accepted, 1 enrolled. In 2007, 5 degrees awarded. *Degree requirements:* For master's, comprehensive exam. *Entrance requirements:* For master's, GRE General Test. Additional exam requirements/recommendations for international students: Required—TOEFL (minimum score 550 paper-based; 213 computer-based). *Application deadline:* For fall admission, 7/15 priority date for domestic students, 5/15 priority date for international students; for spring admission, 12/1 priority date for domestic students, 10/1 priority date for international students. Applications are processed on a rolling basis. Application fee: $30. Electronic applications accepted. *Expenses:* Tuition, state resident: full-time $5,176. Tuition, nonresident: full-time $13,070. *Financial support:* In 2007–08, 11 students received support, including 2 research assistantships with partial tuition reimbursements available (averaging $2,000 per year), 9 teaching assistantships with partial tuition reimbursements available (averaging $7,500 per year); Federal Work-Study, health care benefits, tuition waivers (partial), and unspecified assistantships also available. Financial award application deadline: 3/1; financial award applicants required to submit FAFSA. *Faculty research:* Digital animation, printmaking, ceramics, metalsmithing, sculpture. *Unit head:* Richard Helzer, Head, 406-994-4501, Fax: 406-994-3680, E-mail: helzer@montana.edu.

Montclair State University, The Office of Graduate Admissions and Support Services, School of the Arts, Department of Art and Design, Montclair, NJ 07043-1624. Offers art education (MA, Certificate); art history (MA); studio arts (MA, MFA). *Accreditation:* NASAD (one or more programs are accredited). Part-time and evening/weekend programs available. *Faculty:* 24 full-time (10 women), 46 part-time/adjunct (30 women). *Students:* 31 full-time (21 women), 42 part-time (37 women); includes 6 minority (1 African American, 3 Asian Americans or Pacific Islanders, 2 Hispanic Americans), 2 international. 70 applicants, 39% accepted, 20 enrolled. In 2007, 17 master's, 8 other advanced degrees awarded. *Degree requirements:* For master's, project. *Entrance requirements:* For master's, GRE General Test or MAT (MA), portfolio, undergraduate degree in fine arts or equivalent, 2 letters of recommendation, teaching certificate (art education). Additional exam requirements/recommendations for international students: Required—TOEFL (minimum score 83 computer-based). *Application deadline:* For fall admission, 2/1 for domestic and international students. Applications are processed on a rolling basis. Application fee: $60. Electronic applications accepted. *Financial support:* In 2007–08, 4 research assistantships with full tuition reimbursements (averaging $7,000 per year) were awarded; Federal Work-Study, scholarships/grants, and unspecified assistantships also available. Support available to part-time students. Financial award application deadline: 3/1; financial award applicants required to submit FAFSA. *Unit head:* John Luttropp, Chairperson, 973-655-7295. *Application contact:* Dr. Dorothy Heard, Adviser, 973-655-7295, E-mail: heardd@mail.montclair.edu.

Morehead State University, Graduate Programs, Caudill College of Humanities, Department of Art, Morehead, KY 40351. Offers art education (MA); studio art (MA). Part-time and evening/weekend programs available. *Faculty:* 11 full-time (3 women). *Students:* 11 full-time (5 women), 5 part-time (all women); includes 1 minority (African American) Average age 30. In 2007, 5 degrees awarded. *Degree requirements:* For master's, comprehensive exam, thesis (for some programs), oral exam. *Entrance requirements:* For master's, GRE General Test, minimum GPA of 3.0 in major, 2.5 overall; portfolio; bachelor's degree in art. Additional exam requirements/recommendations for international students: Required—TOEFL (minimum score 500 paper-based; 173 computer-based). *Application deadline:* For fall admission, 8/1 priority date for domestic and international students; for spring admission, 12/1 priority date for domestic and international students. Applications are processed on a rolling basis. Application fee: $0 ($55 for international students). Electronic applications accepted. *Financial support:* In 2007–08, 6 teaching assistantships (averaging $6,000 per year) were awarded; career-related internships or fieldwork, Federal Work-Study, and unspecified assistantships also available. Financial award application deadline: 4/1; financial award applicants required to submit FAFSA. *Faculty research:* Computer art, painting, drawing, ceramics, photography. *Unit head:* Robert Franzini, Chair, 606-783-2193, Fax: 606-783-5048, E-mail: r.franzi@moreheadstate.edu. *Application contact:* Michelle Barber, Graduate Admissions Counselor, 606-783-2039, Fax: 606-783-5061, E-mail: m.barber@moreheadstate.edu.

National University, Academic Affairs, College of Letters and Sciences, Department of Art and Humanities, La Jolla, CA 92037-1011. Offers creative writing (MFA); English (MA). Part-time and evening/weekend programs available. Postbaccalaureate distance learning degree programs offered (no on-campus study). *Faculty:* 18 full-time (6 women), 219 part-time/adjunct (120 women). *Students:* 139 full-time (101 women), 353 part-time (250 women); includes 91 minority (41 African Americans, 4 American Indian/Alaska Native, 15 Asian Americans or Pacific Islanders, 31 Hispanic Americans). Average age 37. 371 applicants, 330 enrolled. In 2007, 100 degrees awarded. *Degree requirements:* For master's, thesis (for some programs). *Entrance requirements:* For master's, interview, minimum GPA of 2.5. Additional exam requirements/recommendations for international students: Required—TOEFL (minimum score 550 paper-based; 213 computer-based; 80 iBT), IELTS (minimum score 6). *Application deadline:* Applications are processed on a rolling basis. Application fee: $60 ($65 for international students). Electronic applications accepted. *Expenses:* Tuition: Full-time $8,262; part-time $306 per unit. One-time fee: $60. *Financial support:* Career-related internships or fieldwork, institutionally sponsored loans, scholarships/grants, and tuition waivers (partial) available. Support available to part-time students. Financial award application deadline: 6/30; financial award applicants required to submit FAFSA. *Unit head:* Dr. Janet Baker, Chair, 858-642-8472, Fax: 858-642-8715, E-mail: jbaker@nu.edu. *Application contact:* Dominick Giovanniello, Associate Regional Dean—San Diego, 800-NAT-UNIV, Fax: 858-642-8709, E-mail: dgiovann@nu.edu.

New Jersey City University, Graduate Studies and Continuing Education, College of Arts and Sciences, Department of Art, Jersey City, NJ 07305-1597. Offers art (MFA); art education (MA); studio art (MFA). *Accreditation:* NASAD. Evening/weekend programs available. *Faculty:* 6. *Students:* 2 full-time (1 woman), 5 part-time (4 women); includes 1 minority (Hispanic American) Average age 33. In 2007, 1 degree awarded. *Degree requirements:* For master's, thesis or alternative, exhibit. *Entrance requirements:* For master's, GRE General Test or MAT, portfolio. Additional exam requirements/recommendations for international students: Required—TOEFL. *Application deadline:* For fall admission, 8/1 priority date for domestic students; for spring admission, 12/1 for domestic students. Applications are processed on a rolling basis. Application fee: $0. *Expenses:* Tuition, state resident: full-time $7,462. Tuition, nonresident: full-time $13,762. Required fees: $1,296. *Financial support:* Unspecified assistantships available. *Unit head:* Dr. Herbert Rosenberg, Chairperson, 201-200-2367.

New Mexico State University, Graduate School, College of Arts and Sciences, Department of Art, Las Cruces, NM 88003-8001. Offers art history (MA); ceramics (MA, MFA); design (MA, MFA); drawing (MA, MFA); metals (MA, MFA); painting (MA, MFA); photography (MA, MFA); printmaking (MA, MFA); sculpture (MA, MFA). *Faculty:* 8 full-time (5 women), 1 (woman) part-time/adjunct. *Students:* 33 full-time (16 women), 3 part-time (1 woman); includes 6 minority (1 American Indian/Alaska Native, 5 Hispanic Americans), 1 international. Average age 35. 24 applicants, 58% accepted, 10 enrolled. In 2007, 7 degrees awarded. *Degree requirements:* For master's, comprehensive exam (for some programs), thesis, thesis exhibit. *Entrance requirements:* For master's, portfolio, 10-page paper (art history). *Application deadline:* For fall admission, 2/15 for domestic students; for winter admission, 10/15 for domestic students; for spring admission, 7/15 for domestic students. Application fee: $30 ($50 for international students). Electronic applications accepted. *Expenses:* Tuition, state resident: full-time $3,602; part-time $199 per credit. Tuition, nonresident: full-time $13,380; part-time $607 per credit. Required fees: $1,178. *Financial support:* In 2007–08, 1 fellowship, 29 teaching assistantships were awarded; research assistantships, Federal Work-Study and health care benefits also available. Support available to part-time students. Financial award application deadline: 3/1. *Faculty research:* Painting, graphic design, sculpture, printmaking, drawing. *Unit head:* Dr. Spencer Fidler, Head, 575-646-1705, Fax: 575-646-8036, E-mail: sfidler@nmsu.edu.

The New School: A University, Parsons The New School for Design, Program in Fine Arts, New York, NY 10011. Offers MFA. *Faculty:* 2 full-time (0 women), 9 part-time/adjunct (4 women). *Students:* 44 full-time (23 women); includes 7 minority (1 African American, 1 American Indian/Alaska Native, 3 Asian Americans or Pacific Islanders, 2 Hispanic Americans), 9 international. Average age 29. In 2007, 18 degrees awarded. *Entrance requirements:* Additional exam requirements/recommendations for international students: Required—TOEFL (minimum score 580 paper-based; 237 computer-based; 93 iBT). *Application deadline:* For fall admission, 2/1 priority date for domestic students. Applications are processed on a rolling basis. Application fee: $50. *Financial support:* Fellowships, Federal Work-Study and scholarships/grants available. Financial award application deadline: 3/1. *Unit head:* Donald Porcaro, Chair, 212-229-8942 Ext. 2960, E-mail: porcarod@newschool.edu. *Application contact:* Anthony Padilla, Director of Admissions, 212-229-8989 Ext. 4023, Fax: 212-229-8975, E-mail: padillaa@newschool.edu.

See Close-Up on page 247.

New York Academy of Art, Program in Figurative Art, New York, NY 10013-2911. Offers MFA. *Faculty:* 5 full-time (1 woman), 29 part-time/adjunct (7 women). *Students:* 110 full-time (44 women), 1 (woman) part-time; includes 29 minority (4 African Americans, 1 American Indian/Alaska Native, 17 Asian Americans or Pacific Islanders, 7 Hispanic Americans), 20 international. Average age 30. 98 applicants, 71% accepted, 58 enrolled. In 2007, 53 degrees awarded. *Degree requirements:* For master's, project. *Entrance requirements:* For master's, slide portfolio. Additional exam requirements/recommendations for international students: Required—TOEFL. *Application deadline:* For fall admission, 4/15 priority date for domestic and international students. Applications are processed on a rolling basis. Application fee: $80. *Expenses:* Tuition: Full-time $22,000. Required fees: $700. *Financial support:* In 2007–08, 3 fellowships (averaging $30,000 per year) were awarded; career-related internships or fieldwork and scholarships/grants also available. Financial award application deadline: 9/1; financial award applicants required to submit FAFSA. *Unit head:* Wayne A. Linker, Executive Director, 212-966-0300, Fax: 212-966-3217, E-mail: info@nyaa.edu. *Application contact:* Andrew Mueller, Director of Admissions/Registration, 212-966-0300, Fax: 212-966-3217, E-mail: andrew@nyaa.edu.

New York University, Graduate School of Arts and Science, Institute of Fine Arts, New York, NY 10012-1019. Offers art history and archaeology (MA, PhD), including architectural studies (PhD), art history and archaeology, classical art and archaeology (PhD), curatorial studies (PhD), East and South Asian art (PhD), Near Eastern art and archaeology (PhD); MA/Diploma; PhD/Certificate. Part-time programs available. *Faculty:* 19 full-time (5 women). *Students:* 200 full-time (157 women), 88 part-time (70 women); includes 28 minority (19 Asian Americans or Pacific Islanders, 9 Hispanic Americans), 34 international. Average age 32. 295 applicants, 33% accepted, 41 enrolled. In 2007, 26 master's, 26 doctorates awarded. Terminal master's awarded for partial completion of doctoral program. *Degree requirements:* For master's, 2 foreign languages, thesis or alternative, 2 qualifying papers; for doctorate, 2 foreign languages, thesis/dissertation. *Entrance requirements:* For master's, GRE General Test; for doctorate, GRE General Test, MA. Additional exam requirements/recommendations for international students: Required—TOEFL. *Application deadline:* For fall admission, 12/18 for domestic students. Application fee: $85. *Financial support:* Fellowships with tuition reimbursements, research assistantships with tuition reimbursements, teaching assistantships with tuition reimbursements, career-related internships or fieldwork, Federal Work-Study, institutionally sponsored loans, and tuition waivers (partial) available. Financial award application deadline: 12/18; financial award applicants required to submit FAFSA. *Unit head:* Mariet Westermann, Chair, 212-992-5800, E-mail: ifa.program@nyu.edu. *Application contact:* Priscilla Saucek, Director of Graduate Studies, 212-992-5800, Fax: 212-992-5807, E-mail: ifa.program@nyu.edu.

New York University, Steinhardt School of Culture, Education and Human Development, Department of Art and Art Professions, Program in Studio Art, New York, NY 10012-1019. Offers MA, MFA. Part-time and evening/weekend programs available. *Faculty:* 11 full-time (5 women). *Students:* 26 full-time (10 women), 11 part-time (10 women); includes 6 minority (3 Asian Americans or Pacific Islanders, 3 Hispanic Americans), 9 international. 274 applicants, 14% accepted, 26 enrolled. In 2007, 28 degrees awarded. *Degree requirements:* For master's, thesis (for some programs). *Entrance requirements:* For master's, portfolio, interview, presentation. Additional exam requirements/recommendations for international students: Required—TOEFL. *Application deadline:* For fall admission, 12/15 priority date for domestic and international students; for spring admission, 11/1 for domestic and international students. Applications are processed on a rolling basis. Application fee: $50. *Financial support:* Career-related internships or fieldwork, Federal Work-Study, institutionally sponsored loans, scholarships/grants, tuition waivers (partial), and unspecified assistantships available. Support available to part-time students. Financial award application deadline: 2/1; financial award applicants required to submit FAFSA. *Faculty research:* Media and culture, video art and digital media, multimedia works, multiculturalism, critical theory. *Unit head:* John Torreano, Co-Director, 212-998-5700, Fax: 212-995-4320, E-mail: jt2@nyu.edu. *Application contact:* 212-998-5030, Fax: 212-995-4328, E-mail: stein.hardt.gradadmissions@nyu.edu.

New York University, Steinhardt School of Culture, Education and Human Development, Department of Art and Art Professions, Program in Visual Culture, New York, NY 10012-1019. Offers visual culture: costume studies (MA); visual culture: theory (MA, PhD). Part-time and evening/weekend programs available. *Faculty:* 2 full-time (1 woman). *Students:* 19 full-time (17 women), 19 part-time (18 women); includes 3 minority (all Asian Americans or Pacific Islanders), 6 international. 62 applicants, 74% accepted, 16 enrolled. In 2007, 8 degrees awarded. *Degree requirements:* For master's, thesis (for some programs). *Entrance requirements:* For doctorate, GRE General Test, interview. Additional exam requirements/recommendations for international students: Required—TOEFL. *Application deadline:* For fall admission, 12/15 priority date for domestic and international students; for spring admission, 11/1 for domestic and international students. Applications are processed on a rolling basis. Application fee: $50. *Financial support:* Career-related internships or fieldwork, Federal Work-Study, institutionally sponsored loans, and scholarships/grants available. Support available to part-time students. Financial award application deadline: 2/1; financial award applicants required to submit FAFSA. *Faculty research:* Textiles as material culture, contemporary visual culture and globalization, cultural theory. *Unit head:* Dr. Nicholas Mirzoeff, Director, 212-998-5700, E-mail: nm45@nyu.edu. *Application contact:* 212-998-5030, Fax: 212-995-4328, E-mail: steinhardt.gradadmissions@nyu.edu.

New York University, Tisch School of the Arts Asia, Singapore, NY 248923, Singapore. Offers animation and digital arts (MFA); dramatic writing (MFA); film production (MFA). *Faculty:* 6 full-time (3 women). *Students:* 33 full-time (16 women); includes 6 minority (1 African American, 5 Asian Americans or Pacific Islanders), 13 international. 55 applicants, 22% accepted. *Entrance requirements:* Additional exam requirements/recommendations for international students:

Required—TOEFL (minimum score 610 paper-based; 250 computer-based; 105 iBT). *Application deadline:* For fall admission, 2/1 priority date for domestic and international students. Application fee: $60. Electronic applications accepted. *Financial support:* Fellowships with full and partial tuition reimbursements, research assistantships, teaching assistantships, Federal Work-Study, institutionally sponsored loans, and unspecified assistantships available. Financial award application deadline: 2/15; financial award applicants required to submit FAFSA.

See Close-Up on page 291.

New York University, Tisch School of the Arts, Program in Arts Politics, New York, NY 10012-1019. Offers MA. *Faculty:* 3 full-time (2 women), 4 part-time/adjunct (3 women). *Students:* 5 full-time (all women), 1 (woman) part-time; includes 2 minority (both Asian Americans or Pacific Islanders), 2 international. Average age 25. 22 applicants, 64% accepted, 6 enrolled. *Degree requirements:* For master's, thesis. *Entrance requirements:* For master's, professional resumé, writing sample, statement of purpose. Additional exam requirements/recommendations for international students: Required—TOEFL, IELTS. *Application deadline:* For fall admission, 1/8 for domestic and international students. Application fee: $60. *Financial support:* In 2007–08, 2 students received support. Federal Work-Study and scholarships/grants available. Financial award application deadline: 2/15; financial award applicants required to submit FAFSA. *Application contact:* Dan Sandford, Director of Graduate Admissions, 212-998-1918, Fax: 212-995-4060, E-mail: tisch.gradadmissions@nyu.edu.

Norfolk State University, School of Graduate Studies, School of Liberal Arts, Department of Fine Arts, Norfolk, VA 23504. Offers visual studies (MA, MFA). Part-time programs available. *Degree requirements:* For master's, thesis or alternative. *Entrance requirements:* For master's, portfolio, interview, letters of recommendation. Additional exam requirements/recommendations for international students: Required—TOEFL (minimum score 500 paper-based).

Northern Illinois University, Graduate School, College of Visual and Performing Arts, School of Art, De Kalb, IL 60115-2854. Offers MA, MFA, MS. *Accreditation:* NASAD (one or more programs are accredited). Part-time and evening/weekend programs available. *Faculty:* 36 full-time (15 women), 1 (woman) part-time/adjunct. *Students:* 61 full-time (42 women), 36 part-time (28 women); includes 6 minority (2 African Americans, 1 Asian American or Pacific Islander, 3 Hispanic Americans), 3 international. Average age 32. 83 applicants, 45% accepted, 22 enrolled. In 2007, 32 degrees awarded. *Degree requirements:* For master's, variable foreign language requirement, comprehensive exam, thesis (for some programs), show or project. *Entrance requirements:* For master's, GRE General Test, minimum GPA of 2.75, portfolio. Additional exam requirements/recommendations for international students: Required—TOEFL (minimum score 550 paper-based; 213 computer-based). *Application deadline:* For fall and spring admission, 3/1 for domestic and international students. Applications are processed on a rolling basis. Application fee: $30. Electronic applications accepted. *Expenses:* Tuition, area resident: Part-time $226 per credit hour. Tuition, state resident: full-time $5,424; part-time $225 per credit hour. Tuition, nonresident: full-time $10,848. Required fees: $2,416; $64 per credit hour. *Financial support:* In 2007–08, 1 research assistantship with full tuition reimbursement, 26 teaching assistantships with full tuition reimbursements were awarded; fellowships with full tuition reimbursements, career-related internships or fieldwork, Federal Work-Study, scholarships/grants, tuition waivers (full), and unspecified assistantships also available. Support available to part-time students. Financial award applicants required to submit FAFSA. *Faculty research:* Art education, portfolio assessment, central European design history, relationship between modern art and industrialism. *Unit head:* Adrian Tio, Director, 815-753-7856, Fax: 815-753-7701, E-mail: artio@niu.edu. *Application contact:* Yale Factor, Graduate Coordinator, 815-753-3801, E-mail: yfactor@niu.edu.

Northwestern State University of Louisiana, Graduate Studies and Research, School of Creative and Performing Arts, Program in Art, Natchitoches, LA 71497. Offers fine and graphic arts (MA). *Accreditation:* NASAD. *Faculty:* 5 full-time (2 women), 5 part-time/adjunct (4 women). *Students:* 4 full-time (2 women), 10 part-time (6 women); includes 5 minority (4 African Americans, 1 American Indian/Alaska Native). Average age 36. In 2007, 10 degrees awarded. *Degree requirements:* For master's, comprehensive exam, thesis or alternative. *Entrance requirements:* For master's, GRE General Test, minimum undergraduate GPA of 2.5. *Application deadline:* For fall admission, 8/1 priority date for domestic students; for spring admission, 1/10 for domestic students. Applications are processed on a rolling basis. Application fee: $20 ($30 for international students). *Financial support:* Career-related internships or fieldwork and Federal Work-Study available. Support available to part-time students. Financial award application deadline: 7/15. *Unit head:* Dr. Roger Chandler, Head, 318-357-4476, Fax: 318-357-5906, E-mail: chandlerr@nsula.edu. *Application contact:* Dr. Steven G. Horton, Associate Provost/Dean, Graduate Studies, Research, and Information Systems, 318-357-5851, Fax: 318-357-5019, E-mail: grad_school@nsula.edu.

Northwestern University, The Graduate School, Judd A. and Marjorie Weinberg College of Arts and Sciences, Department of Art Theory and Practice, Evanston, IL 60208. Offers visual arts (MFA). Admissions and degrees offered through The Graduate School. *Degree requirements:* For master's, essay, exhibit. *Entrance requirements:* For master's, 20 slides of recent work. Additional exam requirements/recommendations for international students: Required—TOEFL. Electronic applications accepted.

Announcement: Intensive program leading to the Master of Fine Arts. Faculty members include Pamela Bannos, Jeanne Dunning, Kelly Kaczynski, Judy Ledgerwood, Michael Rakowitz, Steve Reinke, and Lane Relyea. Fellowships, assistantships available. Autumn quarter admission is based on outstanding academic record (BA or other), 20 slides of recent work, statement, recommendations. Call 847-491-7346 for application. Visit www.art.northwestern.edu.

NSCAD University, Program in Fine Arts, Halifax, NS B3J 3J6, Canada. Offers craft (MFA); design (M Des); fine and media arts (MFA). *Faculty:* 42 full-time (18 women). *Students:* 25 full-time (12 women). Average age 33. 190 applicants, 5% accepted, 8 enrolled. In 2007, 10 degrees awarded. *Degree requirements:* For master's, thesis, exhibit. *Entrance requirements:* For master's, portfolio, at least 5 art history classes. Additional exam requirements/recommendations for international students: Required—Michigan English Language Assessment Battery (minimum score: 80), CanTEST (minimum score: 4.5), CAEL (minimum score: 70); Recommended—TOEFL (minimum score 575 paper-based; 233 computer-based; 90 iBT), IELTS (minimum score 7). *Application deadline:* For fall admission, 1/15 for domestic and international students. Application fee: $50. *Financial support:* In 2007–08, 10 students received support, including 10 teaching assistantships (averaging $5,000 per year); scholarships/grants also available. Financial award application deadline: 1/15. *Unit head:* Bruce Barber, Chair, 902-494-8155, Fax: 902-425-2420, E-mail: bbarber@nscad.ns.ca. *Application contact:* Dallas Ning, Administrative Assistant (Admissions), 902-494-8129, Fax: 902-425-2987, E-mail: dning@nscad.ns.ca.

The Ohio State University, Graduate School, College of the Arts, Department of Art, Columbus, OH 43210. Offers MFA. *Accreditation:* NASAD. *Faculty:* 27. *Students:* 50 full-time (25 women), 2 part-time (1 woman); includes 4 minority (1 African American, 3 Hispanic Americans). Average age 28. In 2007, 24 degrees awarded. *Degree requirements:* For master's, thesis, exhibit, oral exams. *Entrance requirements:* For master's, portfolio. Additional exam requirements/recommendations for international students: Recommended—TOEFL (minimum score 600 paper-based; 250 computer-based). *Application deadline:* For fall admission, 8/15 priority date for domestic students, 7/1 priority date for international students; for winter admission, 12/1 priority date for domestic students, 11/1 priority date for international students; for spring admission, 3/1 priority date for domestic students, 2/1 priority date for international students. Applications are processed on a rolling basis. Application fee: $40 ($50 for international students). Electronic applications accepted. *Financial support:* Fellowships, teaching assistantships, Federal Work-Study, institutionally sponsored loans, and unspecified assistantships available. Support available to part-time students. *Unit head:* Michael Mercil, Graduate Studies Committee Chair, 614-292-5072, Fax: 614-292-1674, E-mail: mercil.1@osu.edu. *Application contact:* 614-292-9444, Fax: 614-292-3895, E-mail: domestic.grad@osu.edu.

Ohio University, Graduate College, College of Fine Arts, School of Art, Athens, OH 45701-2979. Offers art history (MA); ceramics (MFA); graphic design (MFA); painting (MFA); photography (MFA); printmaking (MFA); sculpture (MFA). Part-time programs available. *Faculty:* 30 full-time (16 women), 7 part-time/adjunct (3 women). *Students:* 53 full-time (34 women), 11 part-time (7 women); includes 1 minority (Hispanic American), 7 international. Average age 27. 174 applicants, 22% accepted, 32 enrolled. In 2007, 18 degrees awarded. *Degree requirements:* For master's, thesis. *Entrance requirements:* For master's, portfolio. Additional exam requirements/recommendations for international students: Required—TOEFL. *Application deadline:* For fall admission, 2/1 for domestic students. Application fee: $50 ($55 for international students). *Financial support:* In 2007–08, 57 students received support, including 35 teaching assistantships with full and partial tuition reimbursements available (averaging $9,198 per year); career-related internships or fieldwork, Federal Work-Study, institutionally sponsored loans, scholarships/grants, tuition waivers (full), unspecified assistantships, and associateships also available. Financial award application deadline: 2/1. *Faculty research:* Vapor fired ceramics, video installation, art theory, digital photography, mixed and interdisciplinary media work. *Unit head:* David LaPalombara, Director, 740-593-4290, Fax: 740-593-0457, E-mail: lapalomb@ohio.edu. *Application contact:* Don Adleta, Associate Director and Chair, Graduate Programs, 740-593-9996, Fax: 740-593-0457, E-mail: adleta@ohio.edu.

Oklahoma City University, Petree College of Arts and Sciences, Program in Liberal Arts, Oklahoma City, OK 73106-1402. Offers art (MLA); general studies (MLA); leadership/management (MLA); literature (MLA); mass communications (MLA); philosophy (MLA); writing (MLA). Part-time and evening/weekend programs available. *Faculty:* 18 full-time (7 women), 14 part-time/adjunct (4 women). *Students:* 24 full-time (18 women), 23 part-time (17 women); includes 6 minority (3 African Americans, 1 American Indian/Alaska Native, 1 Asian American or Pacific Islander, 1 Hispanic American), 14 international. Average age 31. 20 applicants, 95% accepted. In 2007, 13 degrees awarded. *Degree requirements:* For master's, comprehensive exam, thesis optional. *Entrance requirements:* Additional exam requirements/recommendations for international students: Required—TOEFL. *Application deadline:* For fall admission, 8/22 for domestic students; for spring admission, 1/15 for domestic students. Applications are processed on a rolling basis. Application fee: $30 ($70 for international students). *Expenses:* Tuition: Full-time $14,040; part-time $780 per hour. Required fees: $881; $32 per hour. *Financial support:* Fellowships with partial tuition reimbursements, career-related internships or fieldwork, Federal Work-Study, institutionally sponsored loans, and tuition waivers (partial) available. Support available to part-time students. Financial award application deadline: 8/1; financial award applicants required to submit FAFSA. *Unit head:* Dr. Regina Benuett, Director, 405-208-5178, Fax: 405-208-5451, E-mail: rebeunett@okcu.edu. *Application contact:* Leslie McKenzie, Director, Graduate Admissions, 800-633-7242, Fax: 405-208-5356, E-mail: gadmissions@okcu.edu.

Old Dominion University, College of Arts and Letters, Program in Visual Studies, Norfolk, VA 23529. Offers MA, MFA. *Accreditation:* NASAD. Part-time programs available. *Faculty:* 17 full-time (3 women), 3 part-time/adjunct (all women). *Students:* Average age 45. 15 applicants, 20% accepted, 1 enrolled. *Degree requirements:* For master's, thesis, exhibition. *Entrance requirements:* For master's, sample of work. Additional exam requirements/recommendations for international students: Required—TOEFL (minimum score 500 paper-based). *Application deadline:* For fall admission, 3/1 for domestic and international students. Application fee: $35. *Expenses:* Tuition, state resident: part-time $304 per credit hour. Tuition, nonresident: part-time $761 per credit hour. *Financial support:* In 2007–08, 4 students received support, including 2 teaching assistantships with partial tuition reimbursements available (averaging $8,000 per year); career-related internships or fieldwork and scholarships/grants also available. Support available to part-time students. Financial award application deadline: 2/15; financial award applicants required to submit FAFSA. *Faculty research:* Sculpture, painting, photography, printmaking, graphic design. *Unit head:* Prof. Elliott C. Jones, Graduate Program Director, 757-683-4047, Fax: 757-683-5923, E-mail: artgpd@odu.edu.

Otis College of Art and Design, Program in Fine Arts, Los Angeles, CA 90045-9785. Offers new genres (MFA); painting (MFA); photography (MFA); sculpture (MFA). *Accreditation:* NASAD. *Faculty:* 1 (woman) full-time, 8 part-time/adjunct (3 women). *Students:* 19 full-time (11 women), 2 part-time (both women); includes 1 Asian American or Pacific Islander, 2 international. Average age 32. 149 applicants, 20% accepted, 11 enrolled. In 2007, 15 degrees awarded. *Degree requirements:* For master's, thesis. *Entrance requirements:* For master's, portfolio. Additional exam requirements/recommendations for international students: Required—TOEFL (minimum score 600 paper-based; 250 computer-based). *Application deadline:* For fall admission, 2/15 for domestic and international students. Application fee: $50. Electronic applications accepted. *Expenses:* Tuition: Full-time $30,764; part-time $1,026 per unit. Required fees: $700. *Financial support:* Career-related internships or fieldwork, Federal Work-Study, scholarships/grants, and tuition waivers (partial) available. Financial award applicants required to submit FAFSA. *Unit head:* Roy Dowell, Chair, 310-665-6893, Fax: 310-665-6998, E-mail: grads@otis.edu. *Application contact:* Information Contact, 310-665-6820, Fax: 310-665-6821, E-mail: admissions@otis.edu.

Otis College of Art and Design, Program in Public Practice, Los Angeles, CA 90045-9785. Offers MFA. *Faculty:* 7 part-time/adjunct (5 women). *Students:* 8 full-time (6 women); includes 3 minority (2 African Americans, 1 Hispanic American). 19 applicants, 63% accepted. *Entrance requirements:* Additional exam requirements/recommendations for international students: Required—TOEFL (minimum score 600 paper-based; 250 computer-based). *Application deadline:* For fall admission, 2/15 for domestic and international students. Application fee: $50. Electronic applications accepted. *Expenses:* Tuition: Full-time $30,764; part-time $1,026 per unit. Required fees: $700. *Unit head:* Suzanne Lacy, Chair, Graduate Studies: Public Practice, 310-665-6820, Fax: 310-846-2612, E-mail: cvelasco@otis.edu. *Application contact:* Information Contact, 310-665-6820, Fax: 310-665-6821, E-mail: admissions@otis.edu.

Penn State University Park, Graduate School, College of Arts and Architecture, School of Visual Arts, State College, University Park, PA 16802-1503. Offers art (MFA), including ceramics, drawing/painting, photography, printmaking, sculpture; art education (M Ed, MS, PhD). *Accreditation:* NASAD. *Expenses:* Tuition, state resident: full-time $14,738; part-time $614 per credit. Tuition, nonresident: full-time $26,050; part-time $1,085 per credit. Tuition and fees vary according to course load, program and student level. *Unit head:* Dr. Charles R. Garoian, Director, 814-865-0444, Fax: 814-865-1158, E-mail: crg2@psu.edu.

Pennsylvania Academy of the Fine Arts, Graduate School, Philadelphia, PA 19102. Offers drawing (MFA, Postbaccalaureate Certificate); painting (MFA, Postbaccalaureate Certificate); printmaking (MFA, Postbaccalaureate Certificate); sculpture (MFA, Postbaccalaureate Certificate). *Accreditation:* NASAD (one or more programs are accredited). *Faculty:* 15 full-time (4 women), 13 part-time/adjunct (8 women). *Students:* 87 full-time (47 women); includes 9 minority (8 Asian Americans or Pacific Islanders, 1 Hispanic American). Average age 26. 115 applicants, 52% accepted, 34 enrolled. In 2007, 33 master's, 12 other advanced degrees awarded. *Degree requirements:* For master's, thesis, thesis exhibit. *Entrance requirements:* For master's, 10-20 slides of work and slide list, 3 letters of recommendation. Additional exam requirements/recommendations for international students: Required—TOEFL (minimum score 500 paper-based). *Application deadline:* For fall admission, 2/1 for domestic and international students. Application fee: $40. Electronic applications accepted. *Expenses:* Tuition: Full-time $26,870. *Financial support:* Federal Work-Study, institutionally sponsored loans, and scholarships/grants available. Financial award application deadline: 3/1; financial award applicants required to submit FAFSA. *Unit head:* Sarah Squire, Graduate Program Coordinator, 215-972-2027, Fax: 215-569-0153, E-mail: ssquire@pafa.edu. *Application contact:* Stan Greidus, Vice President of Admissions and Financial Aid, 215-972-2047, Fax: 215-569-0153, E-mail: sgreidus@pafa.edu.

See Close-Up on page 251.

Pittsburg State University, Graduate School, College of Arts and Sciences, Department of Art, Pittsburg, KS 66762-7512. Offers art education (MA); studio art (MA). *Degree requirements:* For master's, thesis or alternative.

Art/Fine Arts

Portland State University, Graduate Studies, School of Fine and Performing Arts, Department of Art, Portland, OR 97207-0751. Offers drawing (MFA); mixed media (MFA); painting (MFA); printmaking (MFA); sculpture (MFA). *Accreditation:* NASAD. *Faculty:* 24 full-time (14 women), 38 part-time/adjunct (24 women). *Students:* 19 full-time (11 women), 3 part-time (2 women); includes 2 minority (1 Asian American or Pacific Islander, 1 Hispanic American). Average age 29. 39 applicants, 36% accepted, 12 enrolled. In 2007, 6 degrees awarded. *Degree requirements:* For master's, variable foreign language requirement, thesis, exhibit. *Entrance requirements:* For master's, minimum GPA of 3.0 in upper-division course work or 2.75 overall, portfolio, 3 letters of recommendation. Additional exam requirements/recommendations for international students: Required—TOEFL (minimum score 550 paper-based; 213 computer-based). *Application deadline:* For fall admission, 3/1 for domestic and international students. Application fee: $50. *Expenses:* Tuition, state resident: full-time $7,047. Tuition, nonresident: full-time $11,178. *Financial support:* Research assistantships with full tuition reimbursements, teaching assistantships with full tuition reimbursements, Federal Work-Study, scholarships/grants, and unspecified assistantships available. Support available to part-time students. Financial award application deadline: 3/1; financial award applicants required to submit FAFSA. *Unit head:* William LePore, Chair, 503-725-3515, Fax: 503-725-4541. *Application contact:* Ellen Wack, Administrative Coordinator, 503-725-8450, Fax: 503-725-4541, E-mail: wacke@pdx.edu.

Pratt Institute, School of Art and Design, Program in Fine Arts, Brooklyn, NY 11205-3899. Offers ceramics (MFA); metals (MFA); new forms (MFA); painting (MFA); photography (MFA); printmaking (MFA); sculpture (MFA); MS/MFA. *Accreditation:* NASAD. Part-time programs available. *Faculty:* 8 full-time (2 women), 30 part-time/adjunct (15 women). *Students:* 149 full-time (101 women), 6 part-time (3 women); includes 22 minority (4 African Americans, 1 American Indian/Alaska Native, 10 Asian Americans or Pacific Islanders, 7 Hispanic Americans), 34 international. Average age 29. 373 applicants, 35% accepted, 60 enrolled. In 2007, 49 degrees awarded. *Degree requirements:* For master's, thesis, exhibit. *Entrance requirements:* For master's, portfolio, bachelor's degree, transcripts, letters of recommendation, statement. Additional exam requirements/recommendations for international students: Required—TOEFL (minimum score 550 paper-based; 213 computer-based). *Application deadline:* For fall admission, 2/1 for domestic students; for spring admission, 10/1 for domestic students. Application fee: $50 ($90 for international students). Electronic applications accepted. *Expenses:* Tuition: Full-time $25,680. Required fees: $1,106. Tuition and fees vary according to program. *Financial support:* Career-related internships or fieldwork, Federal Work-Study, institutionally sponsored loans, scholarships/grants, health care benefits, and unspecified assistantships available. Support available to part-time students. Financial award application deadline: 2/1; financial award applicants required to submit FAFSA. *Unit head:* Donna Moran, Chairperson, 718-636-3602, E-mail: dmoran@pratt.edu. *Application contact:* Young Hah, Director of Graduate Admissions, 718-636-3683, Fax: 718-399-4242, E-mail: yhah@pratt.edu.

See Close-Up on page 253.

Purchase College, State University of New York, School of Art and Design, Purchase, NY 10577-1400. Offers MFA. *Accreditation:* NASAD. *Faculty:* 12 full-time (6 women), 3 part-time/adjunct (2 women). *Students:* 11 full-time (6 women), 2 part-time (1 woman); includes 1 minority (Hispanic American), 2 international. Average age 33. 102 applicants, 10% accepted, 6 enrolled. In 2007, 4 degrees awarded. *Degree requirements:* For master's, thesis, exhibit. *Entrance requirements:* For master's, portfolio. *Application deadline:* For fall admission, 3/1 for domestic students. Applications are processed on a rolling basis. Application fee: $50. Electronic applications accepted. *Expenses:* Tuition, state resident: full-time $6,900; part-time $288 per credit. Tuition, nonresident: full-time $10,920; part-time $455 per credit. Required fees: $1,506; $125 per credit. Tuition and fees vary according to program. *Financial support:* In 2007–08, 8 students received support; fellowships, teaching assistantships, Federal Work-Study, scholarships/grants, and tuition waivers (partial) available. Support available to part-time students. Financial award application deadline: 3/15; financial award applicants required to submit FAFSA. *Unit head:* Denise Mullen, Dean, 914-251-6750, Fax: 914-251-6793. *Application contact:* Sabrina Johnston, Counselor, 914-251-6479, Fax: 914-251-6314, E-mail: admissn@purchase.edu.

Purdue University, Graduate School, College of Liberal Arts, Department of Visual and Performing Arts, West Lafayette, IN 47907. Offers art and design (MA); theatre (MA, MFA). *Accreditation:* NASAD; NAST. Part-time programs available. *Degree requirements:* For master's, terminal exhibit, project, or thesis. *Entrance requirements:* Additional exam requirements/recommendations for international students: Required—TOEFL. Electronic applications accepted. *Faculty research:* Design, fine arts, photography, acting, directing, theatre technology.

Queens College of the City University of New York, Division of Graduate Studies, Arts and Humanities Division, Department of Art, Program in Fine Arts, Flushing, NY 11367-1597. Offers MFA. *Faculty:* 12 full-time (6 women). *Students:* 16 full-time (7 women), 3 part-time (2 women). 37 applicants, 16% accepted, 6 enrolled. In 2007, 7 degrees awarded. *Degree requirements:* For master's, art show. *Entrance requirements:* For master's, minimum GPA of 3.0, portfolio. Additional exam requirements/recommendations for international students: Required—TOEFL. *Application deadline:* For fall admission, 3/15 for domestic students; for spring admission, 10/15 for domestic students. Application fee: $125. *Financial support:* Career-related internships or fieldwork, Federal Work-Study, institutionally sponsored loans, and tuition waivers (partial) available. Support available to part-time students. Financial award application deadline: 4/1; financial award applicants required to submit FAFSA. *Unit head:* Dr. Arthur Cohen, Graduate Advisor, 718-997-4770. *Application contact:* Mario Caruso, Director of Graduate Admissions, 718-997-5200, Fax: 718-997-5193, E-mail: graduate_admissions@qc.edu.

Radford University, Graduate College, College of Visual and Performing Arts, Department of Art, Radford, VA 24142. Offers MFA. Part-time programs available. *Faculty:* 14 full-time (5 women), 4 part-time/adjunct (3 women). *Students:* 9 full-time (5 women), 13 part-time (8 women); includes 3 minority (1 African American, 1 Asian American or Pacific Islander, 1 Hispanic American), 2 international. Average age 34. 16 applicants, 81% accepted, 6 enrolled. In 2007, 9 degrees awarded. *Degree requirements:* For master's, comprehensive exam, thesis. *Entrance requirements:* Additional exam requirements/recommendations for international students: Required—TOEFL. *Application deadline:* For fall admission, 3/15 priority date for domestic students, 12/1 for international students; for spring admission, 10/1 for domestic students, 7/1 for international students. Applications are processed on a rolling basis. Application fee: $40. Electronic applications accepted. *Financial support:* In 2007–08, 16 students received support, including 11 research assistantships with partial tuition reimbursements available (averaging $8,000 per year), 3 teaching assistantships with partial tuition reimbursements available (averaging $8,700 per year); fellowships with tuition reimbursements available, career-related internships or fieldwork, Federal Work-Study, institutionally sponsored loans, scholarships/grants, and unspecified assistantships also available. Financial award application deadline: 3/1; financial award applicants required to submit FAFSA. *Unit head:* Dr. Steve S. Arbury, Chair, 540-831-5475, Fax: 540-831-6799, E-mail: sarbury@radford.edu.

Regent University, Graduate School, School of Communication and the Arts, Virginia Beach, VA 23464-9800. Offers acting and directing (MFA); cinema arts (MA); communication (MA, PhD); fine arts (MFA); journalism (MA); script and screenwriting (MFA); television arts (MA); theatre arts (MA). Part-time programs available. Postbaccalaureate distance learning degree programs offered (minimal on-campus study). *Faculty:* 23 full-time (3 women), 12 part-time/adjunct (3 women). *Students:* 123 full-time (66 women), 145 part-time (83 women); includes 71 minority (54 African Americans, 2 American Indian/Alaska Native, 3 Asian Americans or Pacific Islanders, 12 Hispanic Americans), 14 international. Average age 33. 176 applicants, 66% accepted, 64 enrolled. In 2007, 60 master's, 15 doctorates awarded. *Degree requirements:* For master's, thesis or alternative; for doctorate, thesis/dissertation. *Entrance requirements:* For master's, GRE General Test or MAT, minimum undergraduate GPA of 3.0, writing sample, computer literacy survey, recommendation, resumé, interview, audition (MFA programs); for doctorate, GRE General Test, minimum graduate GPA of 3.0, writing sample, computer literacy survey, recommendation, interview, transcripts. Additional exam requirements/recommendations for international students: Required—TOEFL (minimum score 577 paper-based; 233 computer-based). *Application deadline:* For fall admission, 3/1 priority date for domestic students; for spring admission, 10/1 priority date for domestic students. Applications are processed on a rolling basis. Application fee: $50. Electronic applications accepted. *Expenses: Contact institution.* *Financial support:* In 2007–08, 247 students received support, including 5 fellowships with full and partial tuition reimbursements available (averaging $7,245 per year); scholarships/grants, tuition waivers (full and partial), and unspecified assistantships also available. Support available to part-time students. Financial award application deadline: 9/1; financial award applicants required to submit FAFSA. *Faculty research:* Southern gospel music, education and entertainment, celebrities and the media, journalism and ethics, C. S. Lewis. *Unit head:* Michael Patrick, Dean, 757-226-4970, Fax: 757-226-4279, E-mail: michpat@regent.edu. *Application contact:* Althea Bishard, Registrar and Executive Director of Enrollment and Academic Services, 800-373-5504, Fax: 757-226-4381, E-mail: admissions@regent.edu.

Regis University, College for Professional Studies, Program in Teacher Education, Denver, CO 80221-1099. Offers adult learning, training, and development (M Ed); curriculum, instruction, and assessment (M Ed); early childhood (M Ed); educational technology (Certificate); elementary (M Ed); ESL (M Ed); fine arts (M Ed), including arts, music; instructional technology (M Ed); professional leadership (M Ed); reading (M Ed); secondary (M Ed); self-designed (M Ed); space studies (M Ed); special education (M Ed); teacher licensure (M Ed). Program also offered in Henderson and Las Vegas (Summerlin), NV. Part-time and evening/weekend programs available. Postbaccalaureate distance learning degree programs offered (no on-campus study). *Faculty:* 107. *Students:* 728 (574 women). Average age 36. In 2007, 209 degrees awarded. *Degree requirements:* For master's, thesis. *Entrance requirements:* For master's, essays, resumé, minimum GPA of 2.75, criminal background check. Additional exam requirements/recommendations for international students: Required—TOEFL (minimum score 213 computer-based), TWE (minimum score 5). *Application deadline:* For fall admission, 7/23 priority date for domestic students; for winter admission, 9/17 priority date for domestic students; for spring admission, 12/3 priority date for domestic students. Applications are processed on a rolling basis. Application fee: $75. Electronic applications accepted. *Financial support:* Federal Work-Study and scholarships/grants available. *Faculty research:* Issues of equity in the middle school classroom, professional learning communities, school reform, socialinguistic and discursive obstacles to student integration, inclusive language arts curriculum. *Unit head:* Dr. Suzie Perry, Dean, 303-458-4302.

Rensselaer Polytechnic Institute, Graduate School, School of Humanities and Social Sciences, Department of the Arts, Program in Electronic Arts, Troy, NY 12180-3590. Offers MFA, PhD. *Faculty:* 13 full-time (7 women). *Students:* Average age 28. 47 applicants, 34% accepted, 8 enrolled. In 2007, 4 degrees awarded. *Degree requirements:* For master's, thesis, thesis in the form of a large-scale creative project; for doctorate, comprehensive exam, thesis/dissertation, dissertation or creative project and dissertation text. *Entrance requirements:* For master's, portfolio; for doctorate, portfolio, writing sample, evidence of research-based creative orientation. Additional exam requirements/recommendations for international students: Required—TOEFL (minimum score 570 paper-based; 230 computer-based; 88 iBT). *Application deadline:* For fall admission, 1/15 for domestic and international students. Applications are processed on a rolling basis. Application fee: $75. Electronic applications accepted. *Expenses:* Tuition: Full-time $34,900; part-time $1,454 per credit. Required fees: $1,802. *Financial support:* In 2007–08, 12 students received support, including 6 fellowships with full tuition reimbursements available (averaging $14,500 per year), 1 research assistantship with full tuition reimbursement available (averaging $14,500 per year), 5 teaching assistantships with full tuition reimbursements available (averaging $14,500 per year); career-related internships or fieldwork, institutionally sponsored loans, and unspecified assistantships also available. Financial award application deadline: 1/15. *Faculty research:* Computer music, video art, Net art, interactivity, bio art. *Application contact:* Jennifer Mumby, Assistant III, 518-276-4784, Fax: 518-276-4370, E-mail: mumbyj@rpi.edu.

See Close-Up on page 131.

Rhode Island College, School of Graduate Studies, Faculty of Arts and Sciences, Department of Art, Providence, RI 02908-1991. Offers art (MA); art education (MAT); media studies (MA). *Accreditation:* NASAD (one or more programs are accredited). Part-time and evening/weekend programs available. *Faculty:* 7 full-time (4 women), 1 (woman) part-time/adjunct. *Students:* 6 full-time (3 women), 9 part-time (5 women); includes 1 minority (Asian American or Pacific Islander), 2 international. Average age 32. In 2007, 10 degrees awarded. *Degree requirements:* For master's, thesis. *Entrance requirements:* For master's, GRE General Test or MAT, portfolio (MA), 3 letters of recommendation, interview. *Application deadline:* For fall admission, 4/1 for domestic students; for spring admission, 11/1 for domestic students. Applications are processed on a rolling basis. Application fee: $50. *Expenses:* Tuition, state resident: full-time $6,240; part-time $260 per credit hour. Tuition, nonresident: full-time $13,104; part-time $546 per credit hour. Required fees: $332; $14 per credit hour. One-time fee: $66 part-time. *Financial support:* Teaching assistantships with full tuition reimbursements, career-related internships or fieldwork, Federal Work-Study, scholarships/grants, health care benefits, and unspecified assistantships available. Support available to part-time students. Financial award application deadline: 5/15; financial award applicants required to submit FAFSA. *Unit head:* Heemong Kim, Chair, 401-456-8054.

Rhode Island School of Design, Graduate Studies, Division of Fine Arts, Department of Ceramics, Providence, RI 02903-2784. Offers MFA. *Accreditation:* NASAD. *Degree requirements:* For master's, thesis, exhibit. *Entrance requirements:* For master's, portfolio. Additional exam requirements/recommendations for international students: Required—TOEFL (minimum score 580 paper-based; 237 computer-based), IELTS (minimum score 7).

Rhode Island School of Design, Graduate Studies, Division of Fine Arts, Department of Glass, Providence, RI 02903-2784. Offers MFA. *Accreditation:* NASAD. *Degree requirements:* For master's, thesis, exhibit. *Entrance requirements:* For master's, portfolio, 3 letters of recommendation. Additional exam requirements/recommendations for international students: Required—TOEFL (minimum score 580 paper-based; 237 computer-based), IELTS (minimum score 7).

Rhode Island School of Design, Graduate Studies, Division of Fine Arts, Department of Jewelry and Light Metals, Providence, RI 02903-2784. Offers MFA. *Accreditation:* NASAD. *Degree requirements:* For master's, thesis, exhibit. *Entrance requirements:* For master's, portfolio, 3 letters of recommendation. Additional exam requirements/recommendations for international students: Required—TOEFL (minimum score 580 paper-based; 237 computer-based), IELTS (minimum score 7).

Rhode Island School of Design, Graduate Studies, Division of Fine Arts, Department of Painting, Providence, RI 02903-2784. Offers MFA. *Accreditation:* NASAD. *Degree requirements:* For master's, thesis, exhibit. *Entrance requirements:* For master's, portfolio, 3 letters of recommendation. Additional exam requirements/recommendations for international students: Required—TOEFL (minimum score 580 paper-based; 237 computer-based), IELTS (minimum score 7).

Rhode Island School of Design, Graduate Studies, Division of Fine Arts, Department of Printmaking, Providence, RI 02903-2784. Offers MFA. *Entrance requirements:* For master's, portfolio, 3 letters of recommendation. Additional exam requirements/recommendations for international students: Required—TOEFL (minimum score 580 paper-based; 237 computer-based), IELTS (minimum score 7).

Rhode Island School of Design, Graduate Studies, Division of Fine Arts, Department of Sculpture, Providence, RI 02903-2784. Offers MFA. *Accreditation:* NASAD. *Degree requirements:* For master's, thesis, exhibit. *Entrance requirements:* For master's, portfolio, 3 letters of recommendation. Additional exam requirements/recommendations for international students: Required—TOEFL (minimum score 580 paper-based; 237 computer-based), IELTS (minimum score 7).

Rochester Institute of Technology, Graduate Enrollment Services, College of Imaging Arts and Sciences, School for American Crafts, Program in Ceramics, Rochester, NY 14623-5603. Offers MFA. *Accreditation:* NASAD. *Students:* 13 full-time (8 women), 2 international. 22 applicants, 36% accepted, 6 enrolled. In 2007, 7 degrees awarded. *Entrance requirements:* For master's, portfolio, 3.0 GPA. Additional exam requirements/recommendations for international students: Required—TOEFL (minimum score 550 paper-based; 230 computer-based; 79 iBT). *Application deadline:* For fall admission, 3/1 priority date for domestic students. Application fee: $50. *Expenses:* Tuition: Full-time $28,491; part-time $800 per credit hour. Required fees: $201; $67 per term. *Financial support:* Teaching assistantships with partial tuition reimbursements, career-related internships or fieldwork, institutionally sponsored loans, scholarships/grants, and unspecified assistantships available. Support available to part-time students. Financial award applicants required to submit FAFSA. *Unit head:* Julia Galloway, Chairperson, School for American Crafts, 585-475-5778, E-mail: jmgsac@rit.edu.

Rochester Institute of Technology, Graduate Enrollment Services, College of Imaging Arts and Sciences, School for American Crafts, Program in Glass, Rochester, NY 14623-5603. Offers MFA. *Accreditation:* NASAD. *Students:* 4 full-time (1 woman), 1 (woman) part-time, 1 international. 18 applicants, 33% accepted, 1 enrolled. In 2007, 1 degree awarded. *Entrance requirements:* For master's, portfolio, 3.0 GPA. Additional exam requirements/recommendations for international students: Required—TOEFL (minimum score 550 paper-based; 230 computer-based; 79 iBT). *Expenses:* Tuition: Full-time $28,491; part-time $800 per credit hour. Required fees: $201; $67 per term. *Financial support:* Teaching assistantships with partial tuition reimbursements, career-related internships or fieldwork, institutionally sponsored loans, scholarships/grants, and unspecified assistantships available. Support available to part-time students. Financial award applicants required to submit FAFSA. *Unit head:* Julia Galloway, Chairperson, School for American Crafts, 585-475-5778, E-mail: jmgsac@rit.edu.

Rochester Institute of Technology, Graduate Enrollment Services, College of Imaging Arts and Sciences, School for American Crafts, Program in Metal Crafts and Jewelry, Rochester, NY 14623-5603. Offers MFA. *Accreditation:* NASAD. *Students:* 5 full-time (3 women), 4 part-time (2 women), 6 international. 12 applicants, 58% accepted, 2 enrolled. In 2007, 3 degrees awarded. *Entrance requirements:* For master's, portfolio, 3.0 GPA. Additional exam requirements/recommendations for international students: Required—TOEFL (minimum score 550 paper-based; 230 computer-based; 79 iBT). *Expenses:* Tuition: Full-time $28,491; part-time $800 per credit hour. Required fees: $201; $67 per term. *Financial support:* Teaching assistantships with partial tuition reimbursements, career-related internships or fieldwork, institutionally sponsored loans, scholarships/grants, and unspecified assistantships available. Support available to part-time students. Financial award applicants required to submit FAFSA. *Unit head:* Julia Galloway, Chairperson, School for American Crafts, 585-475-5778, E-mail: jmgsac@rit.edu.

Rochester Institute of Technology, Graduate Enrollment Services, College of Imaging Arts and Sciences, School for American Crafts, Program in Woodworking and Furniture Design, Rochester, NY 14623-5603. Offers MFA. *Students:* 11 full-time (2 women), 1 part-time; includes 1 minority (Asian American or Pacific Islander), 1 international. 9 applicants, 78% accepted, 3 enrolled. *Entrance requirements:* For master's, portfolio, 3.0 GPA. Additional exam requirements/recommendations for international students: Required—TOEFL (minimum score 550 paper-based; 213 computer-based; 79 iBT). *Expenses:* Tuition: Full-time $28,491; part-time $800 per credit hour. Required fees: $201; $67 per term. *Financial support:* Teaching assistantships with partial tuition reimbursements, career-related internships or fieldwork, institutionally sponsored loans, scholarships/grants, and unspecified assistantships available. Support available to part-time students. Financial award applicants required to submit FAFSA. *Unit head:* Julia Galloway, Chairperson, School for American Crafts, 585-475-5778, E-mail: jmgsac@rit.edu.

Rochester Institute of Technology, Graduate Enrollment Services, College of Imaging Arts and Sciences, School of Art, Program in Fine Arts, Rochester, NY 14623-5603. Offers fine arts studio (MST); painting (MFA); printmaking (MFA). *Accreditation:* NASAD. *Students:* 15 full-time (7 women), 7 part-time (4 women); includes 3 minority (1 African American, 2 Hispanic Americans), 2 international. 36 applicants, 72% accepted, 12 enrolled. In 2007, 10 degrees awarded. *Degree requirements:* For master's, thesis (for some programs). *Entrance requirements:* For master's, portfolio, minimum GPA of 3.0. Additional exam requirements/recommendations for international students: Required—TOEFL (minimum score 550 paper-based; 213 computer-based; 79 iBT). *Application deadline:* For fall admission, 3/1 priority date for domestic students. Applications are processed on a rolling basis. Application fee: $50. *Expenses:* Tuition: Full-time $28,491; part-time $800 per credit hour. Required fees: $201; $67 per term. *Financial support:* Teaching assistantships, career-related internships or fieldwork, institutionally sponsored loans, scholarships/grants, and unspecified assistantships available. Support available to part-time students. Financial award applicants required to submit FAFSA.

Rutgers, The State University of New Jersey, New Brunswick, Mason Gross School of the Arts, Program in Visual Arts, New Brunswick, NJ 08901-1281. Offers drawing (MFA); painting (MFA); sculpture (MFA). *Degree requirements:* For master's, thesis, exhibit. *Entrance requirements:* For master's, portfolio. Additional exam requirements/recommendations for international students: Required—TOEFL (minimum score 550 paper-based; 213 computer-based). Electronic applications accepted. *Faculty research:* Media, painting, sculpture, photography, film.

Sam Houston State University, College of Arts and Sciences, Department of Art, Huntsville, TX 77341. Offers MA, MFA. Part-time programs available. *Degree requirements:* For master's, thesis (for some programs), exhibit. *Entrance requirements:* For master's, GRE General Test, minimum GPA of 3.0 in last 60 hours, portfolio. Additional exam requirements/recommendations for international students: Required—TOEFL (minimum score 550 paper-based; 213 computer-based). *Application deadline:* For fall admission, 8/1 for domestic students; for spring admission, 2/1 for domestic students. Application fee: $20. *Expenses:* Tuition, state resident: full-time $5,026; part-time $184 per semester hour. Tuition, nonresident: full-time $10,586; part-time $462 per semester hour. Required fees: $494 per semester. *Financial support:* Research assistantships, teaching assistantships, Federal Work-Study available. Financial award application deadline: 5/31; financial award applicants required to submit FAFSA. *Unit head:* Tony Shipp, Chair, 936-294-1314, E-mail: art_trs@shsu.edu. *Application contact:* Anita Shipman, Advisor, 936-294-3962.

San Diego State University, Graduate and Research Affairs, College of Professional Studies and Fine Arts, School of Art, Design and Art History, San Diego, CA 92182. Offers art history (MA); studio arts (MA, MFA), including applied design, environmental design, graphic design, interior design, painting and printmaking, sculpture. *Accreditation:* NASAD (one or more programs are accredited). *Students:* 44 full-time (29 women), 18 part-time (11 women); includes 9 minority (4 Asian Americans or Pacific Islanders, 5 Hispanic Americans), 5 international. Average age 30. 83 applicants, 31% accepted, 31 enrolled. In 2007, 12 degrees awarded. *Degree requirements:* For master's, variable foreign language requirement, thesis. *Entrance requirements:* For master's, GRE General Test, bachelor's degree in related field, slide portfolio, typed slide information sheet, 2 letters of recommendation. Additional exam requirements/recommendations for international students: Required—TOEFL. *Application deadline:* For fall admission, 2/1 for domestic and international students. Applications are processed on a rolling basis. Application fee: $55. Electronic applications accepted. *Financial support:* In 2007–08, 21 teaching assistantships were awarded; career-related internships or fieldwork and unspecified assistantships also available. Financial award applicants required to submit FAFSA. *Unit head:* Arthur Ollman, Director, 619-594-1213, Fax: 619-594-1217. *Application contact:* JoAnne Berelowitz, Graduate Advisor, Art History, 619-594-4995, Fax: 619-594-1217, E-mail: jberelow@mail.sdsu.edu.

San Francisco Art Institute, Graduate Program, Department of Painting, San Francisco, CA 94133. Offers MFA, Certificate. *Accreditation:* NASAD. Part-time programs available. *Degree requirements:* For master's and Certificate, oral reviews. *Entrance requirements:* For master's and Certificate, portfolio. Additional exam requirements/recommendations for international students: Required—TOEFL (minimum score 580 paper-based; 237 computer-based). Electronic applications accepted.

See Close-Up on page 255.

San Francisco Art Institute, Graduate Program, Department of Printmaking, San Francisco, CA 94133. Offers MFA, Certificate. *Accreditation:* NASAD. Part-time programs available. *Degree requirements:* For master's and Certificate, oral reviews. *Entrance requirements:* For master's and Certificate, portfolio. Additional exam requirements/recommendations for international students: Required—TOEFL (minimum score 580 paper-based; 237 computer-based). Electronic applications accepted.

See Close-Up on page 255.

San Francisco Art Institute, Graduate Program, Department of Sculpture, San Francisco, CA 94133. Offers MFA, Certificate. *Accreditation:* NASAD. Part-time programs available. *Degree requirements:* For master's and Certificate, oral reviews. *Entrance requirements:* For master's and Certificate, portfolio. Additional exam requirements/recommendations for international students: Required—TOEFL (minimum score 580 paper-based; 237 computer-based).

See Close-Up on page 255.

San Francisco State University, Division of Graduate Studies, College of Creative Arts, Department of Art, San Francisco, CA 94132-1722. Offers art (MFA); art history (MA). *Accreditation:* NASAD (one or more programs are accredited). *Unit head:* Dr. Barbara Foster, Chair, 415-338-2176. *Application contact:* Dr. Gail Dawson, Graduate Coordinator, 415-338-2176, E-mail: artgrad@sfsu.edu.

San Jose State University, Graduate Studies and Research, College of Humanities and the Arts, School of Art and Design, San Jose, CA 95192-0001. Offers art education (MA); art history (MA); digital media (MFA); digital media in art history and education (MA); photography (MFA); pictorial arts (MFA); spatial arts (MFA). *Accreditation:* NASAD (one or more programs are accredited). *Students:* 55 full-time (30 women), 15 part-time (12 women); includes 11 minority (1 African American, 7 Asian Americans or Pacific Islanders, 3 Hispanic Americans), 2 international. Average age 38. 78 applicants, 42% accepted, 24 enrolled. In 2007, 17 degrees awarded. *Entrance requirements:* For master's, GRE. *Application deadline:* For fall admission, 6/29 for domestic students; for spring admission, 11/30 for domestic students. Applications are processed on a rolling basis. Application fee: $59. Electronic applications accepted. *Financial support:* Applicants required to submit FAFSA. *Unit head:* Linda Walsh, Director, 408-924-4320, Fax: 408-924-4326.

Savannah College of Art and Design, Graduate School, Program in Metals and Jewelry, Savannah, GA 31402-3146. Offers MFA. Part-time programs available. *Faculty:* 5 full-time (all women). *Students:* 5 full-time (all women), 4 part-time (all women), 7 international. Average age 25. 16 applicants, 44% accepted, 1 enrolled. In 2007, 2 degrees awarded. *Degree requirements:* For master's, thesis, internship. *Entrance requirements:* For master's, interview, portfolio. Additional exam requirements/recommendations for international students: Required—TOEFL (minimum score 450 paper-based; 133 computer-based). *Application deadline:* For fall admission, 4/1 priority date for domestic and international students. Applications are processed on a rolling basis. Application fee: $50. Electronic applications accepted. *Expenses:* Tuition: Full-time $24,840; part-time $552 per credit. One-time fee: $500 full-time. *Financial support:* In 2007–08, 1 fellowship was awarded; career-related internships or fieldwork, Federal Work-Study, and scholarships/grants also available. Financial award application deadline: 4/1; financial award applicants required to submit FAFSA. *Unit head:* Kimberlie Tataliek, Chair, 912-525-8451, Fax: 912-525-8453, E-mail: ktatalie@scad.edu. *Application contact:* Darrell Tutchton, Director of Graduate and International Enrollment, 912-525-5961, Fax: 912-525-5985, E-mail: admission@scad.edu.

Savannah College of Art and Design, Graduate School, Program in Painting, Savannah, GA 31402-3146. Offers MA, MFA. Part-time programs available. *Faculty:* 10 full-time (6 women), 3 part-time/adjunct (2 women). *Students:* 60 full-time (35 women), 10 part-time (7 women); includes 4 minority (1 African American, 1 American Indian/Alaska Native, 2 Hispanic Americans), 9 international. Average age 25. 137 applicants, 38% accepted, 19 enrolled. In 2007, 17 degrees awarded. *Degree requirements:* For master's, thesis, exhibit, internships. *Entrance requirements:* For master's, interview, portfolio. Additional exam requirements/recommendations for international students: Required—TOEFL (minimum score 450 paper-based; 133 computer-based). *Application deadline:* For fall admission, 4/1 priority date for domestic and international students. Applications are processed on a rolling basis. Application fee: $50. Electronic applications accepted. *Expenses:* Tuition: Full-time $24,840; part-time $552 per credit. One-time fee: $500 full-time. *Financial support:* In 2007–08, 9 fellowships were awarded; career-related internships or fieldwork, Federal Work-Study, and scholarships/grants also available. Financial award application deadline: 4/1; financial award applicants required to submit FAFSA. *Unit head:* Greg Eltringham, Chair, 912-525-6610. *Application contact:* Darrell Tutchton, Director of Graduate and International Enrollment, 912-525-5961, Fax: 912-525-5985, E-mail: admission@scad.edu.

Announcement: SCAD emphasizes individual attention and career preparation, cultivating the unique qualities of each student through an interesting curriculum, in inspiring environments, and under the leadership of involved professors. SCAD offers MA, MArch, and MFA degrees, as well as a Master of Arts in Teaching and a Master of Urban Design. More than thirty programs are available, including a variety of online offerings via SCAD-eLearning.

Savannah College of Art and Design, Graduate School, Program in Printmaking, Savannah, GA 31402-3146. Offers MA, MFA. Part-time programs available. *Faculty:* 2 full-time (1 woman). *Students:* 2 full-time (1 woman), (both international). 9 applicants, 33% accepted, 0 enrolled. *Degree requirements:* For master's, thesis. *Entrance requirements:* For master's, interview, portfolio. Additional exam requirements/recommendations for international students: Required—TOEFL (minimum score 450 paper-based; 133 computer-based). *Application deadline:* For fall admission, 4/1 priority date for domestic and international students. Applications are processed on a rolling basis. Application fee: $50. Electronic applications accepted. *Expenses:* Tuition: Full-time $24,840; part-time $552 per credit. One-time fee: $500 full-time. *Financial support:* Fellowships, career-related internships or fieldwork, Federal Work-Study, and scholarships/grants available. Financial award application deadline: 4/1; financial award applicants required to submit FAFSA. *Unit head:* Richard Gere, Chair, 912-523-3309, Fax: 912-525-6409, E-mail: rgere@scad.edu. *Application contact:* Darrell Tutchton, Director of Graduate and International Enrollment, 912-525-5961, Fax: 912-525-5985, E-mail: admission@scad.edu.

Savannah College of Art and Design, Graduate School, Program in Sculpture, Savannah, GA 31402-3146. Offers MA, MFA. Part-time programs available. *Faculty:* 1 full-time (0 women), 1 part-time/adjunct (0 women). *Students:* 2 full-time (1 woman), 1 (woman) part-time, 2 international. 12 applicants, 58% accepted, 2 enrolled. *Degree requirements:* For master's, thesis. *Entrance requirements:* For master's, interview, portfolio. Additional exam requirements/recommendations for international students: Required—TOEFL (minimum score 450 paper-based; 133 computer-based). *Application deadline:* For fall admission, 4/1 priority date for domestic and international students. Applications are processed on a rolling basis. Application fee: $50. Electronic applications accepted. *Expenses:* Tuition: Full-time $24,840; part-time $552 per credit. One-time fee: $500 full-time. *Financial support:* Fellowships, career-related internships or fieldwork, Federal Work-Study, and scholarships/grants available. Financial award application deadline: 4/1; financial award applicants required to submit FAFSA. *Unit head:* Susan Krause, Chair, 404-253-2700, Fax: 404-253-3466, E-mail: skrause@scad.edu. *Application contact:*

Art/Fine Arts

Savannah College of Art and Design (continued)
Darrell Tutchton, Director of Graduate and International Enrollment, 912-525-5961, Fax: 912-525-5985, E-mail: admission@scad.edu.

School of the Art Institute of Chicago, Graduate Division, Art and Technology Department, Chicago, IL 60603-3103. Offers MFA. *Entrance requirements:* Additional exam requirements/recommendations for international students: Required—TOEFL.

See Close-Up on page 259.

School of the Art Institute of Chicago, Graduate Division, Department of Ceramics, Chicago, IL 60603-3103. Offers MFA. *Accreditation:* NASAD. *Entrance requirements:* Additional exam requirements/recommendations for international students: Required—TOEFL.

See Close-Up on page 259.

School of the Art Institute of Chicago, Graduate Division, Department of Fiber, Chicago, IL 60603-3103. Offers MFA. *Accreditation:* NASAD. *Entrance requirements:* Additional exam requirements/recommendations for international students: Required—TOEFL.

See Close-Up on page 259.

School of the Art Institute of Chicago, Graduate Division, Department of Painting and Drawing, Chicago, IL 60603-3103. Offers MFA. *Accreditation:* NASAD. *Entrance requirements:* Additional exam requirements/recommendations for international students: Required—TOEFL.

See Close-Up on page 259.

School of the Art Institute of Chicago, Graduate Division, Department of Performance Art, Chicago, IL 60603-3103. Offers MFA. *Entrance requirements:* Additional exam requirements/recommendations for international students: Required—TOEFL.

School of the Art Institute of Chicago, Graduate Division, Department of Printmaking, Chicago, IL 60603-3103. Offers MFA. *Accreditation:* NASAD. *Entrance requirements:* Additional exam requirements/recommendations for international students: Required—TOEFL.

See Close-Up on page 259.

School of the Art Institute of Chicago, Graduate Division, Department of Sculpture, Chicago, IL 60603-3103. Offers MFA. *Accreditation:* NASAD. *Entrance requirements:* Additional exam requirements/recommendations for international students: Required—TOEFL.

See Close-Up on page 259.

School of the Museum of Fine Arts, Boston, Graduate Program, Boston, MA 02115. Offers MAT, MFA. *Accreditation:* NASAD (one or more programs are accredited). *Faculty:* 49 full-time (25 women), 34 part-time/adjunct (19 women). *Students:* 87 full-time (61 women); includes 11 minority (2 African Americans, 4 Asian Americans or Pacific Islanders, 5 Hispanic Americans), 9 international. Average age 30. 250 applicants, 31% accepted, 34 enrolled. In 2007, 45 master's awarded. *Median time to degree:* Of those who began their doctoral program in fall 1999, 92% received their degree in 8 years or less. *Degree requirements:* For master's, thesis, exhibition thesis. *Entrance requirements:* For master's, BFA or bachelor's degree in related area, portfolio. Additional exam requirements/recommendations for international students: Required—TOEFL. *Application deadline:* For fall admission, 1/15 for domestic and international students. Application fee: $60. *Financial support:* In 2007–08, 9 fellowships (averaging $2,400 per year), 20 teaching assistantships (averaging $2,000 per year) were awarded; career-related internships or fieldwork, Federal Work-Study, scholarships/grants, tuition waivers (partial), and unspecified assistantships also available. Support available to part-time students. Financial award application deadline: 3/15; financial award applicants required to submit FAFSA. *Faculty research:* Public art commissions, National Endowment for the Arts grant recipients, international exhibitions. *Unit head:* David L. Brown, Associate Dean of Academic Affairs, Graduate Programs, 617-369-3870, E-mail: dbrown@smfa.edu. *Application contact:* Jesse Tarantino, Assistant Director of Admissions, 617-369-3626, Fax: 617-369-4264, E-mail: admissions@smfa.edu.

School of Visual Arts, Graduate Programs, Computer Art Department, New York, NY 10010-3994. Offers MFA. *Accreditation:* NASAD. *Faculty:* 5 full-time (0 women), 33 part-time/adjunct (11 women). *Students:* 81 full-time (44 women), 15 part-time (10 women); includes 17 minority (6 African Americans, 8 Asian Americans or Pacific Islanders, 3 Hispanic Americans), 57 international. Average age 28. 175 applicants, 59% accepted, 39 enrolled. In 2007, 39 degrees awarded. *Degree requirements:* For master's, final review, project or thesis. *Entrance requirements:* For master's, portfolio. Additional exam requirements/recommendations for international students: Required—TOEFL (minimum score 550 paper-based; 213 computer-based; 79 iBT). *Application deadline:* For fall admission, 2/1 for domestic students. Application fee: $80. Electronic applications accepted. *Expenses:* Tuition: Full-time $26,120; part-time $870 per credit. Tuition and fees vary according to program. *Financial support:* In 2007–08, 44 students received support. Career-related internships or fieldwork, Federal Work-Study, scholarships/grants, and unspecified assistantships available. Support available to part-time students. Financial award application deadline: 2/1; financial award applicants required to submit FAFSA. *Unit head:* Bruce Wands, Chair, 212-592-2530, Fax: 212-592-2509, E-mail: bwands@sva.edu.

School of Visual Arts, Graduate Programs, Design Department, New York, NY 10010-3994. Offers MFA. *Accreditation:* NASAD. *Faculty:* 9 part-time/adjunct (1 woman). *Students:* 39 full-time (23 women); includes 6 minority (5 Asian Americans or Pacific Islanders, 1 Hispanic American), 12 international. Average age 27. 235 applicants, 22% accepted, 19 enrolled. In 2007, 18 degrees awarded. *Degree requirements:* For master's, final review, project or thesis. *Entrance requirements:* For master's, portfolio. Additional exam requirements/recommendations for international students: Required—TOEFL (minimum score 550 paper-based; 213 computer-based; 79 iBT). *Application deadline:* For fall admission, 2/1 for domestic students. Application fee: $80. Electronic applications accepted. *Expenses: Contact institution.* Tuition and fees vary according to program. *Financial support:* In 2007–08, 8 students received support. Career-related internships or fieldwork, Federal Work-Study, scholarships/grants, and unspecified assistantships available. Support available to part-time students. Financial award application deadline: 2/1; financial award applicants required to submit FAFSA. *Unit head:* Lita Talarico, Chair, 212-592-2600, Fax: 212-592-2627, E-mail: ltalarico@sva.edu.

School of Visual Arts, Graduate Programs, Fine Arts Department, New York, NY 10010-3994. Offers painting (MFA); printmaking (MFA); sculpture (MFA). *Accreditation:* NASAD. *Faculty:* 1 (woman) full-time, 24 part-time/adjunct (9 women). *Students:* 63 full-time (33 women); includes 10 minority (2 African Americans, 5 Asian Americans or Pacific Islanders, 3 Hispanic Americans), 16 international. Average age 29. 408 applicants, 27% accepted, 32 enrolled. In 2007, 29 degrees awarded. *Degree requirements:* For master's, final review, project or thesis. *Entrance requirements:* For master's, portfolio. Additional exam requirements/recommendations for international students: Required—TOEFL (minimum score 550 paper-based; 213 computer-based; 79 iBT). *Application deadline:* For fall admission, 2/1 for domestic students. Application fee: $80. Electronic applications accepted. *Expenses:* Tuition: Full-time $26,120; part-time $870 per credit. Tuition and fees vary according to program. *Financial support:* In 2007–08, 48 students received support. Career-related internships or fieldwork, Federal Work-Study, scholarships/grants, and unspecified assistantships available. Support available to part-time students. Financial award application deadline: 2/1; financial award applicants required to submit FAFSA. *Unit head:* David Shirey, Chair, 212-592-2500, Fax: 212-592-2503, E-mail: dshirey@sva.edu.

School of Visual Arts, Graduate Programs, Illustration Department, New York, NY 10010-3994. Offers MFA. *Accreditation:* NASAD. *Faculty:* 1 full-time (0 women), 11 part-time/adjunct (5 women). *Students:* 40 full-time (18 women); includes 7 minority (2 African Americans, 2 Asian Americans or Pacific Islanders, 3 Hispanic Americans), 14 international. Average age 27. 102 applicants, 28% accepted, 25 enrolled. In 2007, 17 degrees awarded. *Degree requirements:* For master's, final review, project or thesis. *Entrance requirements:* For master's, portfolio. Additional exam requirements/recommendations for international students: Required—TOEFL (minimum score 550 paper-based; 213 computer-based; 79 iBT). *Application deadline:* For fall admission, 2/1 for domestic students. Application fee: $80. Electronic applications accepted. *Expenses:* Tuition: Full-time $26,120; part-time $870 per credit. Tuition and fees vary according to program. *Financial support:* In 2007–08, 21 students received support. Career-related internships or fieldwork, Federal Work-Study, scholarships/grants, and unspecified assistantships available. Support available to part-time students. Financial award application deadline: 2/1; financial award applicants required to submit FAFSA. *Unit head:* Marshall Arisman, Chair, 212-592-2210, Fax: 212-366-1675, E-mail: marisman@sva.edu.

School of Visual Arts, Graduate Programs, Program in Photography, Video and Related Media, New York, NY 10010-3994. Offers MFA. *Accreditation:* NASAD. *Faculty:* 1 full-time (0 women), 29 part-time/adjunct (12 women). *Students:* 80 full-time (42 women), 8 part-time (4 women); includes 10 minority (2 African Americans, 1 Asian American or Pacific Islander, 7 Hispanic Americans), 22 international. Average age 29. 246 applicants, 35% accepted, 44 enrolled. In 2007, 28 degrees awarded. *Degree requirements:* For master's, final review, project or thesis. *Entrance requirements:* For master's, portfolio. Additional exam requirements/recommendations for international students: Required—TOEFL (minimum score 550 paper-based; 213 computer-based; 79 iBT). *Application deadline:* For fall admission, 2/1 for domestic students. Application fee: $80. Electronic applications accepted. *Expenses:* Tuition: Full-time $26,120; part-time $870 per credit. Tuition and fees vary according to program. *Financial support:* In 2007–08, 40 students received support. Career-related internships or fieldwork, Federal Work-Study, scholarships/grants, and unspecified assistantships available. Support available to part-time students. Financial award application deadline: 2/1; financial award applicants required to submit FAFSA. *Unit head:* Charles Traub, Chair, 212-592-2360, Fax: 212-592-2366, E-mail: ctraub@sva.edu.

Seton Hall University, College of Arts and Sciences, Department of Art and Music, South Orange, NJ 07079-2697. Offers museum professions (MA). *Accreditation:* NASM. Part-time and evening/weekend programs available. *Degree requirements:* For master's, thesis or alternative. *Entrance requirements:* For master's, GRE General Test, previous course work in art history. Electronic applications accepted. *Faculty research:* History of museums, museum education, theory of museums, nineteenth century art, African-American art, Renaissance art history, museum registration.

See Close-Up on page 261.

Southern Illinois University Carbondale, Graduate School, College of Liberal Arts, School of Art and Design, Carbondale, IL 62901-4701. Offers ceramics (MFA); drawing (MFA); fiber/weaving (MFA); glass (MFA); jewelry (MFA); metalsmithing/blacksmithing (MFA); painting (MFA); printmaking (MFA); sculpture (MFA). *Accreditation:* NASAD. *Faculty:* 23 full-time (7 women). *Students:* 36 full-time (15 women), 7 part-time (2 women); includes 2 minority (1 American Indian/Alaska Native, 1 Hispanic American), 12 international. Average age 29. 87 applicants, 16% accepted, 14 enrolled. In 2007, 26 degrees awarded. *Degree requirements:* For master's, thesis or alternative. *Entrance requirements:* For master's, minimum GPA of 2.7, portfolio, slides. Additional exam requirements/recommendations for international students: Required—TOEFL. *Application deadline:* For fall admission, 3/1 priority date for domestic students. Applications are processed on a rolling basis. Application fee: $20. *Financial support:* In 2007–08, 49 students received support, including 3 fellowships with full tuition reimbursements available, 5 research assistantships with full tuition reimbursements available, 40 teaching assistantships with full tuition reimbursements available; Federal Work-Study, institutionally sponsored loans, and tuition waivers (full) also available. Support available to part-time students. Financial award application deadline: 4/1. *Faculty research:* Prints/woodcuts, foundry, watercolor. *Unit head:* Harris Deller, Director, 618-453-4315, Fax: 618-453-7710, E-mail: ga4252@siu.edu. *Application contact:* Kathy Holt, Office Specialist, 618-453-4313, Fax: 618-453-7710, E-mail: kholt@siu.edu.

See Close-Up on page 133.

Southern Illinois University Edwardsville, Graduate Studies and Research, College of Arts and Sciences, Department of Art and Design, Program in Studio Art, Edwardsville, IL 62026-0001. Offers MFA. Part-time programs available. *Students:* 22 full-time (14 women), 2 part-time (both women), 1 international. 46 applicants, 22% accepted. In 2007, 9 degrees awarded. *Degree requirements:* For master's, thesis, exhibition. *Entrance requirements:* For master's, portfolio. *Application deadline:* For fall admission, 2/1 for domestic and international students. Application fee: $30. Electronic applications accepted. *Financial support:* In 2007–08, 12 teaching assistantships with full tuition reimbursements were awarded; fellowships with full tuition reimbursements, research assistantships with full tuition reimbursements, Federal Work-Study, institutionally sponsored loans, and unspecified assistantships also available. Support available to part-time students. Financial award application deadline: 3/1. *Unit head:* Dr. Thad Duhigg, Chair, Department of Art and Design, 618-650-3074.

Southern Methodist University, Meadows School of the Arts, Division of Art, Dallas, TX 75275. Offers studio art (MFA), including ceramics, drawing, painting, photography, printmaking, sculpture. *Accreditation:* NASAD. *Faculty:* 11 full-time (3 women), 6 part-time/adjunct (3 women). *Students:* 10 full-time (5 women); includes 1 minority (Hispanic American) Average age 35. 35 applicants, 20% accepted, 6 enrolled. In 2007, 6 degrees awarded. *Degree requirements:* For master's, thesis or alternative, exhibit. *Entrance requirements:* For master's, BFA or equivalent, letters of recommendation, portfolio. Additional exam requirements/recommendations for international students: Required—TOEFL (minimum score 550 paper-based; 213 computer-based; 80 iBT). *Application deadline:* For fall admission, 2/15 for domestic and international students. Application fee: $75. *Financial support:* In 2007–08, 5 fellowships (averaging $32,914 per year), 5 teaching assistantships (averaging $3,000 per year) were awarded; scholarships/grants and unspecified assistantships also available. Financial award application deadline: 3/1; financial award applicants required to submit FAFSA. *Faculty research:* American stoneware, Southwestern furniture traditions, photographic apparatus and techniques, American ceramists, architecture. Total annual research expenditures: $20,000. *Unit head:* James W. Sullivan, Chair, 214-768-2489, E-mail: jsulliva@smu.edu. *Application contact:* Jean Cherry, Director of Graduate Admissions and Records, 214-768-3765, Fax: 214-768-3272, E-mail: jcherry@smu.edu.

Stanford University, School of Humanities and Sciences, Department of Art and Art History, Stanford, CA 94305-9991. Offers art history (PhD); art practice (MFA); MS/MFA. *Degree requirements:* For master's, thesis (for some programs), faculty reviews; for doctorate, 2 foreign languages, thesis/dissertation. *Entrance requirements:* For master's and doctorate, GRE General Test. Additional exam requirements/recommendations for international students: Required—TOEFL. Electronic applications accepted.

State University of New York at New Paltz, Graduate School, Faculty of Fine and Performing Arts, Department of Fine Arts, New Paltz, NY 12561. Offers ceramics (MA, MFA); interdisciplinary (MA); metal (MA, MFA); painting (MA, MFA); printmaking (MA, MFA); sculpture (MA, MFA). *Accreditation:* NASAD (one or more programs are accredited). Part-time and evening/weekend programs available. *Faculty:* 29 full-time (20 women), 37 part-time/adjunct (18 women). *Students:* 61 full-time (44 women), 23 part-time (11 women); includes 6 minority (2 Asian Americans or Pacific Islanders, 4 Hispanic Americans), 10 international. Average age 29. 107 applicants. In 2007, 27 degrees awarded. *Degree requirements:* For master's, thesis, portfolio. *Entrance requirements:* For master's, minimum GPA of 3.0, portfolio. Additional exam requirements/recommendations for international students: Required—TOEFL (minimum score 550 paper-based; 213 computer-based; 80 iBT). *Application deadline:* For fall admission, 2/15 for domestic and international students. Application fee: $50. Electronic applications accepted. *Expenses:* Tuition, state resident: full-time $6,900; part-time $288 per credit hour. Tuition, nonresident: full-time $10,920; part-time $455 per credit hour. Required fees: $1,040; $30 per credit hour. $153 per credit hour. Tuition and fees vary according to program. *Financial support:* In 2007–08, 13 students received support, including 2 research assistantships with partial tuition reimbursements available (averaging $5,000 per year), 8 teaching assistantships with partial tuition reimbursements available (averaging $5,000 per year); Federal Work-Study and institutionally sponsored loans also available. *Unit head:* Prof. Francois Deschamps, Chair, 845-257-2787, E-mail: deschamf@newpaltz.edu. *Application contact:* Dr. Anat Shiftan, Coordinator, 845-257-3834, E-mail: shiftana@newpaltz.edu.

State University of New York at Oswego, Graduate Studies, College of Arts and Sciences, Department of Art, Oswego, NY 13126. Offers MA. *Accreditation:* NASAD. Part-time programs available. *Faculty:* 7 full-time, 2 part-time/adjunct. *Students:* 5 full-time (2 women), 1 (woman) part-time. Average age 25. 11 applicants, 82% accepted. In 2007, 4 degrees awarded. *Degree requirements:* For master's, exhibit, final presentation. *Entrance requirements:* For master's, slides of previous work. Additional exam requirements/recommendations for international students: Required—TOEFL (minimum score 560 paper-based; 220 computer-based). *Application deadline:* For fall admission, 4/1 for domestic students; for spring admission, 10/1 for domestic students. Applications are processed on a rolling basis. Application fee: $50. *Expenses:* Tuition, state resident: full-time $6,900; part-time $288 per credit. Tuition, nonresident: full-time $10,920; part-time $455 per credit. Required fees: $607; $32 per credit. $225 per term. Tuition and fees vary according to degree level. *Financial support:* In 2007–08, 4 students received support, including 4 teaching assistantships with full and partial tuition reimbursements available (averaging $3,800 per year); career-related internships or fieldwork, Federal Work-Study, institutionally sponsored loans, scholarships/grants, health care benefits, tuition waivers (partial), and unspecified assistantships also available. Support available to part-time students. Financial award application deadline: 4/1; financial award applicants required to submit FAFSA. *Faculty research:* Ancient and primitive art, nineteenth century art, medieval art, Renaissance art. *Unit head:* Cynthia Clabough, Chair, 315-312-2111. *Application contact:* Juan Perdiguero, Program Coordinator, 315-312-2111.

Stephen F. Austin State University, Graduate School, College of Fine Arts, School of Art, Nacogdoches, TX 75962. Offers art (MA); design (MFA); drawing (MFA); painting (MFA); sculpture (MFA). *Accreditation:* NASAD. Part-time programs available. *Degree requirements:* For master's, comprehensive exam, thesis, exhibit. *Entrance requirements:* For master's, GRE General Test, portfolio. Additional exam requirements/recommendations for international students: Required—TOEFL. *Faculty research:* Printmaking, jewelry, photography, ceramics, art history.

Stony Brook University, State University of New York, Graduate School, College of Arts and Sciences, Department of Art, Program in Studio Art, Stony Brook, NY 11794. Offers MFA. *Students:* 17 full-time (11 women), 1 part-time; includes 2 minority (1 American Indian/Alaska Native, 1 Hispanic American), 7 international. Average age 32. 22 applicants, 41% accepted. In 2007, 2 degrees awarded. *Degree requirements:* For master's, comprehensive exam, thesis, reading knowledge of German, French, or Italian; exhibition. *Entrance requirements:* For master's, GRE General Test, minimum undergraduate GPA of 3.0. Additional exam requirements/recommendations for international students: Required—TOEFL. *Application deadline:* For fall admission, 1/15 priority date for domestic students. Application fee: $60. *Unit head:* Stephanie Dinkins, Director, 631-632-7254, E-mail: sdinkins@ms.cc.sunysb.edu. *Application contact:* Dr. Michele Bogart, Director, 631-632-7270.

See Close-Up on page 265.

Sul Ross State University, School of Arts and Sciences, Department of Fine Arts and Communication, Alpine, TX 79832. Offers art education (M Ed); art history (M Ed); studio art (M Ed), including ceramics, design, drawing, jewelry, painting, printmaking, sculpture, weaving. Part-time programs available. *Degree requirements:* For master's, oral or written exam. *Entrance requirements:* For master's, GRE General Test, minimum GPA of 2.5 in last 60 hours of undergraduate work. *Faculty research:* Ceramic sculpture, watercolor, wood sculpture, rock art.

Syracuse University, Graduate School, College of Arts and Sciences, Department of Fine Arts, Syracuse, NY 13244. Offers art history (MA). *Students:* 29 full-time (19 women), 1 (woman) part-time; includes 3 minority (1 American Indian/Alaska Native, 1 Asian American or Pacific Islander, 1 Hispanic American). 46 applicants, 85% accepted, 25 enrolled. In 2007, 10 degrees awarded. *Entrance requirements:* For master's, GRE General Test, research writing sample, knowledge of a second language. Additional exam requirements/recommendations for international students: Required—TOEFL. *Application deadline:* For fall admission, 1/1 priority date for domestic students. Applications are processed on a rolling basis. Application fee: $75. Electronic applications accepted. *Expenses:* Tuition: Full-time $18,216; part-time $1,012 per credit. Required fees: $980. Tuition and fees vary according to program. *Financial support:* Fellowships with full tuition reimbursements, teaching assistantships with full tuition reimbursements available. *Unit head:* Dr. Wayne Frantis, Chair, 315-443-5068. *Application contact:* Linda Straub, Information Contact, 315-443-4185, E-mail: ljstraub@syr.edu.

Syracuse University, Graduate School, College of Visual and Performing Arts, School of Art and Design, Programs in Art, Syracuse, NY 13244. Offers ceramics (MFA); fiber arts/materials studies (MFA); illustration (MFA); jewelry and metalsmithing (MFA); painting (MFA); printmaking (MFA); sculpture (MFA). *Accreditation:* NASAD. Part-time programs available. *Students:* 40 full-time (27 women), 4 part-time (3 women); includes 4 minority (2 Asian Americans or Pacific Islanders, 2 Hispanic Americans), 6 international. 129 applicants, 15% accepted, 12 enrolled. In 2007, 26 master's awarded. *Degree requirements:* For master's, thesis or alternative. *Entrance requirements:* For master's, portfolio. Additional exam requirements/recommendations for international students: Required—TOEFL. *Application deadline:* For fall admission, 1/1 priority date for domestic students. Applications are processed on a rolling basis. Application fee: $75. Electronic applications accepted. *Expenses:* Tuition: Full-time $18,216; part-time $1,012 per credit. Required fees: $980. Tuition and fees vary according to program. *Financial support:* In 2007–08, 16 students received support; fellowships with full tuition reimbursements available, research assistantships with full and partial tuition reimbursements available, teaching assistantships with full and partial tuition reimbursements available, tuition waivers (partial) available. *Unit head:* Ann Clark, Chair, 315-443-4613, Fax: 315-443-1303. *Application contact:* Harriett Conti, Associate Director, Graduate Student Services, 315-443-3089, E-mail: hmconti@syr.edu.

Temple University, Graduate School, Tyler School of Art, Department of Crafts, Philadelphia, PA 19122-6096. Offers ceramics/glass (MFA); fibers and fabric design (MFA); metals/jewelry/CAD-CAM (MFA). *Accreditation:* NASAD. *Degree requirements:* For master's, essay, exhibit. *Entrance requirements:* For master's, minimum GPA of 3.0, slide portfolio, 40 credits in studio art, 12 credits in art history. Additional exam requirements/recommendations for international students: Required—TOEFL (minimum score 550 paper-based; 213 computer-based; 79 iBT). Electronic applications accepted.

Temple University, Graduate School, Tyler School of Art, Department of Graphic Arts and Design, Philadelphia, PA 19122-6096. Offers graphic and interactive design (MFA); photography (MFA); printmaking (MFA). *Accreditation:* NASAD. *Degree requirements:* For master's, essay, exhibit. *Entrance requirements:* For master's, minimum GPA of 3.0; slide portfolio, 40 credits in studio art; 12 credits in art history. Additional exam requirements/recommendations for international students: Required—TOEFL (minimum score 550 paper-based; 213 computer-based; 79 iBT). Electronic applications accepted.

Temple University, Graduate School, Tyler School of Art, Department of Painting, Drawing, and Sculpture, Philadelphia, PA 19122-6096. Offers painting (MFA); sculpture (MFA). *Accreditation:* NASAD. *Degree requirements:* For master's, essay, exhibit. *Entrance requirements:* For master's, minimum GPA of 3.0, slide portfolio, 40 credits in studio art, 12 credits in art history. Additional exam requirements/recommendations for international students: Required—TOEFL (minimum score 550 paper-based; 213 computer-based; 79 iBT). Electronic applications accepted.

Texas A&M University–Commerce, Graduate School, College of Arts and Sciences, Department of Art, Commerce, TX 75429-3011. Offers art (MA, MS); art history (MA); fine arts (MFA); studio art (MA). Part-time programs available. *Faculty:* 6 full-time (2 women). *Students:* 8 full-time (4 women), 11 part-time (3 women); includes 2 minority (both Hispanic Americans), 1 international. Average age 36. In 2007, 1 master's awarded. *Degree requirements:* For master's, comprehensive exam, thesis (for some programs). *Entrance requirements:* For master's, GRE General Test. *Application deadline:* For fall admission, 6/1 priority date for domestic students; for spring admission, 11/1 priority date for domestic students. Applications are processed on a rolling basis. Application fee: $0 ($25 for international students). Electronic applications accepted. *Financial support:* In 2007–08, research assistantships (averaging $7,875 per year), teaching assistantships (averaging $7,875 per year) were awarded; Federal Work-Study, institutionally sponsored loans, and scholarships/grants also available. Financial award application deadline: 5/1; financial award applicants required to submit FAFSA. *Faculty research:* Use of different art media. *Unit head:* Dr. Kay Coughenour, Head, 903-886-5208. *Application contact:* Tammi Thompson, Graduate Admissions Adviser, 843-886-5167, Fax: 843-886-5165, E-mail: tammi_thompson@tamu-commerce.edu.

Texas A&M University–Corpus Christi, Graduate Studies and Research, College of Liberal Arts, Program in Studio Arts, Corpus Christi, TX 78412-5503. Offers MA, MFA. Part-time and evening/weekend programs available. *Students:* 10 full-time (2 women), 16 part-time (12 women); includes 8 minority (all Hispanic Americans), 1 international. 13 applicants, 100% accepted, 13 enrolled. In 2007, 10 degrees awarded. *Degree requirements:* For master's, comprehensive exam, thesis (for some programs). *Entrance requirements:* For master's, GRE General Test. Additional exam requirements/recommendations for international students: Required—TOEFL. *Application deadline:* For fall admission, 7/15 priority date for domestic students, 5/1 priority date for international students; for spring admission, 11/15 priority date for domestic students, 9/1 priority date for international students. Applications are processed on a rolling basis. Application fee: $30 ($50 for international students). Electronic applications accepted. *Expenses:* Tuition, state resident: part-time $63 per credit hour. Tuition, nonresident: part-time $341 per credit hour. Tuition and fees vary according to course load. *Financial support:* Research assistantships, teaching assistantships, career-related internships or fieldwork, Federal Work-Study, institutionally sponsored loans, scholarships/grants, health care benefits, and unspecified assistantships available. Support available to part-time students. Financial award application deadline: 3/15; financial award applicants required to submit FAFSA. *Unit head:* Jack Gron, Head, 361-825-3473, E-mail: jack.gron@tamucc.edu. *Application contact:* Maria Martinez, Graduate Admissions Coordinator, 361-825-2177, Fax: 361-825-2755, E-mail: gradweb@tamucc.edu.

Texas A&M University–Kingsville, College of Graduate Studies, College of Arts and Sciences, Department of Art, Kingsville, TX 78363. Offers MA, MS. Part-time programs available. *Degree requirements:* For master's, comprehensive exam, thesis or alternative. *Entrance requirements:* For master's, GRE General Test, minimum GPA of 3.0. Additional exam requirements/recommendations for international students: Required—TOEFL.

Texas Christian University, College of Fine Arts, Department of Art and Art History, Fort Worth, TX 76129. Offers art history (MA); studio art (MFA). Part-time programs available. *Degree requirements:* For master's, thesis, internship, foreign language exam. *Entrance requirements:* For master's, GRE General Test, writing sample. Additional exam requirements/recommendations for international students: Required—TOEFL. *Application deadline:* For fall admission, 3/15 for domestic students. Applications are processed on a rolling basis. Application fee: $0. *Expenses:* Tuition: Part-time $865 per credit hour. Required fees: $48 per year. *Financial support:* Unspecified assistantships available. Financial award application deadline: 3/1. *Unit head:* Ron Watson, Chairperson, 817-257-7643, E-mail: r.watson@tcu.edu. *Application contact:* Dr. Joseph Butler, Associate Dean, College of Fine Arts, E-mail: j.butler@tcu.edu.

Texas Southern University, Graduate School, College of Liberal Arts and Behavioral Sciences, Department of Fine Arts, Houston, TX 77004-4584. Offers fine arts (MA); music (MA). Part-time programs available. *Faculty:* 2 full-time (1 woman). *Students:* Average age 37. 1 applicant, 100% accepted, 0 enrolled. In 2007, 1 degree awarded. *Degree requirements:* For master's, one foreign language, comprehensive exam, recital. *Entrance requirements:* For master's, GRE General Test, minimum GPA of 2.5. Additional exam requirements/recommendations for international students: Required—TOEFL. *Application deadline:* For fall admission, 7/15 priority date for domestic students. Application fee: $50 ($75 for international students). Electronic applications accepted. *Financial support:* Fellowships, teaching assistantships with partial tuition reimbursements, Federal Work-Study, institutionally sponsored loans, scholarships/grants, and unspecified assistantships available. Financial award application deadline: 5/1. *Faculty research:* Music theory, choral music, composition, percussion composition, ethnic musicology. *Unit head:* Dianne F. Jemison–Pollard, Chair, 713-313-7337, Fax: 713-313-1869, E-mail: jemison_dp@tsu.edu.

Texas Tech University, Graduate School, College of Visual and Performing Arts, Fine Arts Doctoral Program, Lubbock, TX 79409. Offers arts (PhD); music (PhD); theatre arts (PhD). *Accreditation:* NAST. *Students:* 40 full-time (16 women), 33 part-time (16 women); includes 8 minority (4 African Americans, 1 American Indian/Alaska Native, 1 Asian American or Pacific Islander, 2 Hispanic Americans), 9 international. Average age 37. 26 applicants, 62% accepted, 9 enrolled. In 2007, 10 degrees awarded. *Degree requirements:* For doctorate, thesis/dissertation. *Entrance requirements:* For doctorate, GRE General Test. Additional exam requirements/recommendations for international students: Required—TOEFL (minimum score 550 paper-based; 213 computer-based). *Application deadline:* For fall admission, 3/1 priority date for international students; for spring admission, 11/1 priority date for international students. Applications are processed on a rolling basis. Application fee: $50 ($60 for international students). Electronic applications accepted. *Expenses:* Tuition, state resident: part-time $373 per credit hour. Tuition, nonresident: part-time $651 per credit hour. Tuition and fees vary according to program. *Financial support:* Research assistantships with partial tuition reimbursements, teaching assistantships with partial tuition reimbursements available. Financial award application deadline: 4/15. *Faculty research:* Art criticism and theory, music, aesthetics, theatre arts. *Unit head:* Dr. Brian Steele, Director, 806-742-0700, Fax: 806-742-0695, E-mail: brian.steele@ttu.edu.

Texas Tech University, Graduate School, College of Visual and Performing Arts, School of Art, Lubbock, TX 79409. Offers art education (MAE); fine arts (PhD); visual studies (MFA). *Accreditation:* NASAD (one or more programs are accredited). Part-time programs available. *Faculty:* 19 full-time (8 women), 1 (woman) part-time/adjunct. *Students:* 40 full-time (23 women), 23 part-time (17 women); includes 6 minority (1 American Indian/Alaska Native, 5 Hispanic Americans), 5 international. Average age 34. 82 applicants, 68% accepted, 20 enrolled. In 2007, 13 master's, 1 doctorate awarded. *Degree requirements:* For master's, thesis (for some programs); for doctorate, thesis/dissertation. *Entrance requirements:* For master's and doctorate, GRE General Test. Additional exam requirements/recommendations for international students: Required—TOEFL (minimum score 550 paper-based; 213 computer-based). *Application deadline:* For fall admission, 3/1 priority date for international students; for spring admission, 11/1 priority date for international students. Applications are processed on a rolling basis. Application fee: $50 ($60 for international students). Electronic applications accepted. *Expenses:* Tuition, state resident: part-time $373 per credit hour. Tuition, nonresident: part-time $651 per credit hour. Tuition and fees vary according to program. *Financial support:* In 2007–08, 44 students received support, including 41 teaching assistantships with partial tuition reimbursements available (averaging $7,565 per year); research assistantships with partial tuition reimbursements available, career-related internships or fieldwork, Federal Work-Study, and institutionally sponsored loans also available. Support available to part-time students. Financial award application deadline: 4/15; financial award applicants required to submit FAFSA. *Faculty research:* Studio, art history, art education. *Unit*

Art/Fine Arts

Texas Tech University (continued)

head: Dr. Todd DeVriese, Director, 806-742-3825 Ext. 255, Fax: 806-742-1971, E-mail: todd.devriese@ttu.edu. *Application contact:* Andrew Martin, Graduate Advisor, 806-742-3825 Ext. 228, Fax: 806-742-1971, E-mail: andrew.martin@ttu.edu.

Texas Tech University, Graduate School, College of Visual and Performing Arts, School of Music, Lubbock, TX 79409. Offers composition (MM, DMA); conducting (DMA); fine arts-music (PhD); music theory (MM); musicology (MM); pedagogy (MM); performance (MM, DMA); piano pedagogy (DMA). *Accreditation:* NASM. Part-time programs available. *Faculty:* 35 full-time (11 women), 1 part-time/adjunct (0 women). *Students:* 98 full-time (38 women), 24 part-time (13 women); includes 10 minority (1 African American, 1 American Indian/Alaska Native, 2 Asian Americans or Pacific Islanders, 6 Hispanic Americans), 26 international. Average age 38. 101 applicants, 75% accepted, 36 enrolled. In 2007, 19 master's, 16 doctorates awarded. *Degree requirements:* For master's, thesis (for some programs); for doctorate, thesis/dissertation. *Entrance requirements:* For master's and doctorate, GRE General Test. Additional exam requirements/recommendations for international students: Required—TOEFL (minimum score 550 paper-based; 213 computer-based). *Application deadline:* For fall admission, 3/1 priority date for international students; for spring admission, 11/1 priority date for international students. Applications are processed on a rolling basis. Application fee: $50 ($60 for international students). Electronic applications accepted. *Expenses:* Tuition, state resident: part-time $373 per credit hour. Tuition, nonresident: part-time $651 per credit hour. Tuition and fees vary according to program. *Financial support:* In 2007–08, 77 students received support, including 68 teaching assistantships with partial tuition reimbursements available (averaging $7,497 per year); research assistantships with partial tuition reimbursements available, Federal Work-Study and institutionally sponsored loans also available. Support available to part-time students. Financial award application deadline: 4/15; financial award applicants required to submit FAFSA. *Faculty research:* Strategies for music pedagogy in grades K-12, performance practice of traditional music, role of the woman piano virtuoso, vernacular music center; voice health and culture. *Unit head:* Prof. William Ballenger, School of Music Director, 806-742-2270, Fax: 806-742-2294, E-mail: william.ballenger@ttu.edu. *Application contact:* Janeen Gilliam, Admissions and Scholarship Coordinator, 806-742-2270 Ext. 225, Fax: 806-742-2294, E-mail: janeen.gilliam@ttu.edu.

Texas Woman's University, Graduate School, College of Arts and Sciences, School of the Arts, Department of Visual Arts, Denton, TX 76201. Offers art (MA, MFA). *Students:* 16 full-time (15 women), 27 part-time (24 women); includes 8 minority (1 African American, 3 American Indian/Alaska Native, 1 Asian American or Pacific Islander, 3 Hispanic Americans), 1 international. Average age 37. In 2007, 7 master's awarded. *Degree requirements:* For master's, thesis (for some programs), exhibit (MFA), oral exam, thesis or professional paper (MA). *Entrance requirements:* For master's, GRE General Test (MFA), portfolio, interview, curriculum vitae, letter of intent. Additional exam requirements/recommendations for international students: Required—TOEFL (minimum score 550 paper-based; 213 computer-based; 79 iBT). *Application deadline:* For fall admission, 5/31 priority date for domestic students, 4/1 for international students; for spring admission, 10/16 priority date for domestic students, 8/1 for international students. Applications are processed on a rolling basis. Application fee: $30 ($50 for international students). Electronic applications accepted. *Expenses:* Tuition, state resident: full-time $3,294; part-time $183 per credit. Tuition, nonresident: full-time $8,298; part-time $461 per credit. Required fees: $985; $55 per credit. Tuition and fees vary according to degree level. *Financial support:* In 2007–08, 20 teaching assistantships (averaging $9,684 per year) were awarded; career-related internships or fieldwork, Federal Work-Study, institutionally sponsored loans, scholarships/grants, traineeships, health care benefits, and unspecified assistantships also available. Support available to part-time students. Financial award application deadline: 3/1; financial award applicants required to submit FAFSA. *Faculty research:* Art education and electronic technology, film noir, handmade paper, one-of-a-kind art books, women in film. *Unit head:* John Weinkein, Chair, 940-898-2530, Fax: 940-898-2496, E-mail: jweinkein@mail.twu.edu. *Application contact:* Samuel Wheeler, Assistant Director of Admissions, 940-898-3188, Fax: 940-898-3081, E-mail: wheelersr@twu.edu.

Towson University, College of Graduate Studies and Research, Program in Studio Arts, Towson, MD 21252-0001. Offers MFA. *Faculty:* 10 full-time (2 women). *Students:* 18 full-time (13 women), 4 part-time (2 women); includes 1 minority (Asian American or Pacific Islander), 1 international. Average age 30. 11 applicants, 100% accepted, 6 enrolled. In 2007, 12 degrees awarded. *Degree requirements:* For master's, exam. *Entrance requirements:* For master's, portfolio, minimum GPA of 3.0. Additional exam requirements/recommendations for international students: Required—TOEFL (minimum score 550 paper-based). *Application deadline:* For fall admission, 2/1 for domestic students; for spring admission, 11/1 for domestic students. Application fee: $50. Electronic applications accepted. *Expenses:* Tuition, state resident: part-time $286 per credit. Tuition, nonresident: part-time $600 per credit. Required fees: $75 per credit. *Financial support:* Federal Work-Study and unspecified assistantships available. Financial award application deadline: 4/1; financial award applicants required to submit FAFSA. *Unit head:* Tonia Matthews, Graduate Program Director, 410-704-2803, E-mail: tmatthews@towson.edu. *Application contact:* 410-704-2501, Fax: 410-704-4675, E-mail: grads@towson.edu.

Troy University, Graduate School, College of Communication and Fine Arts, Troy, AL 36082. Offers MS. *Degree requirements:* For master's, comprehensive exam, thesis optional. *Entrance requirements:* For master's, GRE, MAT, or GMAT. Additional exam requirements/recommendations for international students: Required—TOEFL (minimum score 523 paper-based; 200 computer-based). *Application deadline:* For fall admission, 6/1 for international students; for spring admission, 10/15 for international students. Application fee: $50. *Unit head:* Dr. Maryjo Cochran, Dean, 334-670-3869, Fax: 334-670-3547, E-mail: macochran@troy.edu. *Application contact:* Brenda K. Campbell, Director of Graduate Admissions, 334-670-3178, Fax: 334-670-3733, E-mail: bcamp@troy.edu.

Tufts University, Graduate School of Arts and Sciences, Department of Art and Art History, Program in Studio Art, Medford, MA 02155. Offers MFA, MA/MFA, MFA/Certificate. *Faculty:* 11 full-time, 5 part-time/adjunct. *Students:* 72 (48 women); includes 12 minority (2 African Americans, 1 American Indian/Alaska Native, 4 Asian Americans or Pacific Islanders, 5 Hispanic Americans) 10 international. 233 applicants, 23% accepted, 21 enrolled. In 2007, 32 degrees awarded. *Degree requirements:* For master's, exhibit. *Entrance requirements:* For master's, portfolio. Additional exam requirements/recommendations for international students: Required—TOEFL (minimum score 550 paper-based; 213 computer-based; 80 iBT). *Application deadline:* For fall admission, 1/15 for domestic students, 12/30 for international students. Applications are processed on a rolling basis. Electronic applications accepted. *Expenses:* Tuition: Full-time $35,052. *Financial support:* Federal Work-Study, scholarships/grants, and tuition waivers (partial) available. Financial award application deadline: 1/15; financial award applicants required to submit FAFSA. *Unit head:* Deborah Dluhy, Dean, School of the Museum of Fine Arts, 617-267-6100, Fax: 617-424-6271.

Tulane University, School of Liberal Arts, Department of Art, New Orleans, LA 70118-5669. Offers art (MFA); art history (MA). *Degree requirements:* For master's, one foreign language, thesis. *Entrance requirements:* For master's, GRE General Test, minimum B average in undergraduate course work. Additional exam requirements/recommendations for international students: Required—TOEFL. Electronic applications accepted.

United Theological Seminary of the Twin Cities, Graduate and Professional Programs, Program in Theology, New Brighton, MN 55112-2598. Offers religion and theology (MA); theology and the arts (MA); women's studies (MA). Part-time programs available. *Faculty:* 12 full-time (7 women), 22 part-time/adjunct (10 women). *Students:* 9 full-time (4 women), 16 part-time (12 women). Average age 43. 13 applicants, 100% accepted, 12 enrolled. In 2007, 1 degree awarded. *Degree requirements:* For master's, thesis. *Entrance requirements:* For master's, minimum GPA of 2.75. *Application deadline:* For fall admission, 8/1 priority date for domestic students; for winter admission, 12/1 priority date for domestic students; for spring admission, 1/1 priority date for domestic students. Application fee: $40. *Expenses:* Tuition: Part-time $373 per credit hour. *Financial support:* Career-related internships or fieldwork, institutionally sponsored loans, and scholarships/grants available. Support available to part-time students. *Application contact:* Rev. Glen Herrington-Hall, Director of Admissions, 651-255-6107, Fax: 651-633-4315, E-mail: gherrington-hall@unitedseminary.edu.

Universidad del Turabo, Graduate Programs, Programs in Education, Program in Teaching of Fine Arts, Gurabo, PR 00778-3030. Offers MFA. *Students:* 47 full-time (32 women), 62 part-time (46 women); all Hispanic Americans Average age 35. In 2007, 63 degrees awarded. *Expenses:* Tuition: Full-time $5,560. *Application contact:* Virginia González, Admissions Officer, 787-746-3009.

Université du Québec à Chicoutimi, Graduate Programs, Program in Fine Arts, Chicoutimi, QC G7H 2B1, Canada. Offers MA. Part-time programs available. *Degree requirements:* For master's, thesis optional. *Entrance requirements:* For master's, appropriate bachelor's degree, proficiency in French.

Université du Québec à Montréal, Graduate Programs, Program in Fine Arts, Montréal, QC H3C 3P8, Canada. Offers MA. Part-time programs available. *Degree requirements:* For master's, thesis optional. *Entrance requirements:* For master's, appropriate bachelor's degree or equivalent, proficiency in French.

Université Laval, Faculty of Architecture, Planning and Visual Arts, School of Visual Arts, Programs in Visual Arts, Québec, QC G1K 7P4, Canada. Offers graphic design and multimedia (MA); visual arts (MA). *Degree requirements:* For master's, thesis (for some programs). *Entrance requirements:* For master's, technical exam, interview, mastery of pertinent software, knowledge of French. Electronic applications accepted.

University at Albany, State University of New York, College of Arts and Sciences, Department of Art, Albany, NY 12222-0001. Offers MA, MFA. *Students:* 37 full-time (20 women). Average age 31. 50 applicants, 52% accepted, 17 enrolled. In 2007, 8 degrees awarded. *Degree requirements:* For master's, exhibit. *Entrance requirements:* For master's, portfolio. Additional exam requirements/recommendations for international students: Required—TOEFL (minimum score 550 paper-based; 213 computer-based). *Application deadline:* For fall admission, 4/15 for domestic and international students; for spring admission, 11/1 for domestic and international students. Application fee: $75. *Expenses:* Tuition, state resident: part-time $576 per credit. Tuition, nonresident: part-time $910 per credit. Tuition and fees vary according to program. *Financial support:* Federal Work-Study available. Financial award application deadline: 4/1. *Faculty research:* Art history, sculpture, painting and drawing, photography, digital media. *Unit head:* Daniel S. Goodwin, Chair, 518-442-4020.

University at Buffalo, the State University of New York, Graduate School, College of Arts and Sciences, Department of Visual Studies, Buffalo, NY 14260. Offers art (MFA), including fine arts; art history (MA, Certificate), including art history (MA), critical museum studies (Certificate). *Degree requirements:* For master's, thesis.

The University of Alabama, Graduate School, College of Arts and Sciences, Department of Art, Tuscaloosa, AL 35487. Offers art history (MA); studio art (MA, MFA), including ceramics, painting, photography, printmaking, sculpture. *Accreditation:* NASAD. Part-time programs available. *Faculty:* 14 full-time (7 women). *Students:* 13 full-time (7 women), 1 (woman) part-time. Average age 30. 17 applicants, 41% accepted, 6 enrolled. In 2007, 9 degrees awarded. *Degree requirements:* For master's, one foreign language, comprehensive exam (for some programs), thesis (for some programs), oral exam, thesis statement, exhibit (studio art), thesis (art history). *Entrance requirements:* For master's, GRE General Test or MAT (art history), minimum GPA of 3.0, BFA or equivalent (studio art). Additional exam requirements/recommendations for international students: Required—TOEFL (minimum score 550 paper-based; 213 computer-based). *Application deadline:* For fall admission, 3/15 for domestic and international students; for spring admission, 10/15 for domestic and international students. Applications are processed on a rolling basis. Application fee: $30. Electronic applications accepted. *Expenses:* Tuition, state resident: full-time $5,700. Tuition, nonresident: full-time $16,518. *Financial support:* In 2007–08, 19 students received support, including 2 fellowships with full tuition reimbursements available (averaging $14,000 per year), 13 teaching assistantships with full and partial tuition reimbursements available (averaging $9,206 per year); career-related internships or fieldwork, institutionally sponsored loans, scholarships/grants, and unspecified assistantships also available. Financial award application deadline: 7/14. *Faculty research:* Nineteenth century American art history, Chinese art history, baroque art history, twentieth century art history, Asian art history. *Unit head:* William T. Dooley, Chairperson, 205-348-1890, Fax: 205-348-0287, E-mail: wtdooley@bama.ua.edu. *Application contact:* Craig R. Wedderspoon, Graduate Coordinator, 205-348-1898, Fax: 205-348-0287, E-mail: cwedders@bama.edu.

University of Alaska Fairbanks, College of Liberal Arts, Department of Art, Fairbanks, AK 99775-7520. Offers MFA. Part-time programs available. *Degree requirements:* For master's, thesis or alternative, oral exam. *Entrance requirements:* For master's, GRE General Test, portfolio. Additional exam requirements/recommendations for international students: Required—TOEFL (minimum score 550 paper-based; 213 computer-based). Electronic applications accepted. *Faculty research:* Computer art, survey of arts in Alaska, found object art, visualization and animation, painting from the wilderness.

University of Alberta, Faculty of Graduate Studies and Research, Department of Art and Design, Edmonton, AB T6G 2E1, Canada. Offers drawing (MFA); history of art, design, and visual culture (MA); industrial design (M Des); painting (MFA); printmaking (MFA); sculpture (MFA); visual communication design (M Des). *Degree requirements:* For master's, thesis. *Entrance requirements:* For master's, portfolio (MFA and MDES). Additional exam requirements/recommendations for international students: Required—TOEFL (minimum score 550 paper-based; 213 computer-based).

The University of Arizona, Graduate College, College of Fine Arts, School of Art, Program in Studio Art, Tucson, AZ 85721. Offers MFA. *Accreditation:* NASAD. Part-time programs available. *Faculty:* 26 full-time, 14 part-time/adjunct. *Students:* 49 full-time (23 women), 1 (woman) part-time; includes 5 minority (1 American Indian/Alaska Native, 1 Asian American or Pacific Islander, 3 Hispanic Americans), 2 international. Average age 34. 110 applicants, 25% accepted, 20 enrolled. In 2007, 8 degrees awarded. *Degree requirements:* For master's, thesis or alternative. *Entrance requirements:* For master's, portfolio, minimum GPA of 3.0 for last 60 units, 3 letters of recommendation, resumé or curriculum vitae. Additional exam requirements/recommendations for international students: Required—TOEFL (minimum score 550 paper-based). *Application deadline:* For fall admission, 2/1 for domestic students, 12/1 for international students. Application fee: $50. *Financial support:* In 2007–08, 2 fellowships with full and partial tuition reimbursements (averaging $10,000 per year), 15 teaching assistantships with full tuition reimbursements (averaging $5,000 per year) were awarded; career-related internships or fieldwork, Federal Work-Study, institutionally sponsored loans, scholarships/grants, and tuition waivers (full) also available. Support available to part-time students. Financial award application deadline: 4/1; financial award applicants required to submit FAFSA. *Faculty research:* Painting, photography and intermedia, sculpture, printmaking, ceramics. *Unit head:* Dr. Julie Plax, Associate Director, Academic Affairs, 621-7000, E-mail: jplax@email.arizona.edu. *Application contact:* Kimberly Mast, Graduate Coordinator, 520-621-8518, E-mail: kmast@email.arizona.edu.

University of Arkansas, Graduate School, J. William Fulbright College of Arts and Sciences, Department of Art, Fayetteville, AR 72701-1201. Offers MFA. *Students:* 10 full-time (5 women), 2 part-time (1 woman), 2 international. In 2007, 3 degrees awarded. *Degree requirements:* For master's, exhibit or thesis. Application fee: $40 ($50 for international students). *Financial support:* In 2007–08, 1 fellowship was awarded; research assistantships, teaching assistantships, career-related internships or fieldwork and Federal Work-Study also available. Support available to part-time students. Financial award application deadline: 4/1; financial award applicants required to submit FAFSA. *Unit head:* Lynn Jacobs, Departmental Chairperson, 479-575-5202, Fax: 479-575-2062, E-mail: ljacobs@uark.edu. *Application contact:* Michael Peven, Graduate Coordinator, 479-575-6714, Fax: 479-575-2062, E-mail: mpeven@uark.edu.

University of Arkansas at Little Rock, Graduate School, College of Arts, Humanities, and Social Science, Department of Art, Little Rock, AR 72204-1099. Offers art education (MA); art history (MA); studio art (MA). *Accreditation:* NASAD. Part-time programs available. *Students:* Average age 38. *Degree requirements:* For master's, 4 foreign languages, oral exam, oral defense of thesis or exhibit. *Entrance requirements:* For master's, portfolio review or term paper evaluation, minimum GPA of 2.7. *Application deadline:* Applications are processed on a rolling basis. Application fee: $25 ($30 for international students). *Financial support:* Research assistantships with tuition reimbursements, teaching assistantships with tuition reimbursements, Federal Work-Study, institutionally sponsored loans, and unspecified assistantships available. Support available to part-time students. *Unit head:* Dr. Winefurd Bruhl, Chairperson, 501-569-3182, E-mail: wgbruhl@ualr.edu. *Application contact:* Marjorie Williams-Smith, Coordinator, 501-569-3182, E-mail: mwsmith@ualr.edu.

The University of British Columbia, Faculty of Arts and Faculty of Graduate Studies, Department of Art History, Visual Art, and Theory, Vancouver, BC V6T 1Z1, Canada. Offers art history (MA, PhD, Diploma); critical and curatorial studies (MA); visual art (MFA). Part-time programs available. *Faculty:* 19 full-time (11 women), 1 part-time/adjunct (0 women). *Students:* 74 full-time (53 women), 1 part-time. 178 applicants, 26% accepted, 17 enrolled. In 2007, 16 master's, 5 doctorates awarded. *Degree requirements:* For master's, one foreign language, thesis, final exhibition (MFA, MA, CCST); for doctorate, 2 foreign languages, comprehensive exam, thesis/dissertation. *Entrance requirements:* For master's, bachelor's degree with minimum B+ average for MFA; for doctorate, master's degree with minimum A- average. Additional exam requirements/recommendations for international students: Required—TOEFL (minimum score 600 paper-based; 250 computer-based). *Application deadline:* For fall admission, 2/1 for domestic and international students. Application fee: $90 Canadian dollars ($150 Canadian dollars for international students). Electronic applications accepted. *Financial support:* In 2007–08, 22 fellowships (averaging $16,000 per year), 20 research assistantships (averaging $4,600 per year), 21 teaching assistantships (averaging $10,490 per year) were awarded; Federal Work-Study, scholarships/grants, health care benefits, and unspecified assistantships also available. *Faculty research:* Conceptual art, Asian art, indigenous North American art, post-second war art, eighteenth and nineteenth century art. *Unit head:* Dr. Rhodri Windsor-Liscombe, Head, 604-822-5650, Fax: 604-822-9003, E-mail: rhodri@interchange.ubc.ca. *Application contact:* Audrey Van Slyck, Graduate Secretary, 604-822-4340, Fax: 604-822-9003, E-mail: ahvagrad@interchange.ubc.ca.

University of Calgary, Faculty of Graduate Studies, Faculty of Fine Arts, Department of Art, Calgary, AB T2N 1N4, Canada. Offers MA, MFA. *Degree requirements:* For master's, thesis. *Entrance requirements:* Additional exam requirements/recommendations for international students: Required—TOEFL. *Faculty research:* Painting, sculpture, drawing, photography, printmaking, new media.

University of California, Berkeley, Graduate Division, College of Letters and Science, Department of Art Practice, Berkeley, CA 94720-1500. Offers MFA. *Faculty:* 7 full-time, 12 part-time/adjunct. *Entrance requirements:* For master's, GRE General Test, minimum GPA of 3.0, sample of work, 3 letters of recommendation. Additional exam requirements/recommendations for international students: Required—TOEFL (minimum score 570 paper-based; 230 computer-based). *Application deadline:* For fall admission, 12/15 for domestic students. Application fee: $70 ($90 for international students). Electronic applications accepted. *Financial support:* Fellowships, teaching assistantships, unspecified assistantships available. Financial award applicants required to submit FAFSA. *Unit head:* Loren Partridge, Chair, 501-642-2582, E-mail: lpart@berkeley.edu. *Application contact:* Dee Levister, Graduate Assistant, 510-643-2582, Fax: 510-643-0884, E-mail: artgrad@berkeley.edu.

University of California, Davis, Graduate Studies, Program in Art, Davis, CA 95616. Offers MFA. *Degree requirements:* For master's, final exhibit. *Entrance requirements:* For master's, minimum GPA of 3.0, portfolio. Additional exam requirements/recommendations for international students: Required—TOEFL (minimum score 550 paper-based; 213 computer-based). Electronic applications accepted. *Faculty research:* Drawing, painting, photography, video, interactive art.

University of California, Irvine, Office of Graduate Studies, Claire Trevor School of the Arts, Department of Studio Art, Irvine, CA 92697. Offers MFA. *Students:* 32 full-time (18 women); includes 5 minority (1 African American, 4 Asian Americans or Pacific Islanders), 1 international. In 2007, 12 degrees awarded. *Degree requirements:* For master's, thesis. *Entrance requirements:* For master's, minimum GPA of 3.0. *Application deadline:* For fall admission, 1/15 for domestic students; for winter admission, 10/15 for domestic students. Applications are processed on a rolling basis. Application fee: $60. Electronic applications accepted. *Financial support:* Fellowships with tuition reimbursements, research assistantships with tuition reimbursements, teaching assistantships with tuition reimbursements, institutionally sponsored loans, traineeships, health care benefits, and unspecified assistantships available. Financial award application deadline: 3/1; financial award applicants required to submit FAFSA. *Faculty research:* Experimental concepts, processes relevant to contemporary issues. *Unit head:* Yong Soon Min, Chair, 949-824-5779, E-mail: ysmin@uci.edu. *Application contact:* Colleen Grigg, Administrative Assistant, 949-824-6648, Fax: 949-824-5297, E-mail: cgrigg@uci.edu.

University of California, Los Angeles, Graduate Division, School of the Arts and Architecture, Department of Art, Los Angeles, CA 90095-1615. Offers MA, MFA. *Degree requirements:* For master's, comprehensive exam. *Entrance requirements:* For master's, 20 slides and/or videotape, minimum GPA of 3.0. Electronic applications accepted. *Expenses:* Tuition, nonresident: full-time $5,728. Required fees: $8,966. Full-time tuition and fees vary according to program and student level.

University of California, Riverside, Graduate Division, Program in Visual Arts, Riverside, CA 92521-0102. Offers MFA. *Faculty:* 7 full-time (3 women). *Students:* 11 full-time (6 women); includes 2 minority (1 Asian American or Pacific Islander, 1 Hispanic American). Average age 30. In 2007, 4 degrees awarded. *Degree requirements:* For master's, thesis. *Entrance requirements:* For master's, portfolio, minimum GPA of 3.2. Additional exam requirements/recommendations for international students: Required—TOEFL (minimum score 550 paper-based; 213 computer-based; 80 iBT). *Application deadline:* For fall admission, 1/15 for domestic and international students. Application fee: $60 ($75 for international students). Electronic applications accepted. *Financial support:* In 2007–08, fellowships with partial tuition reimbursements (averaging $12,000 per year), teaching assistantships with tuition reimbursements (averaging $16,500 per year) were awarded; career-related internships or fieldwork, institutionally sponsored loans, scholarships/grants, health care benefits, tuition waivers (partial), and unspecified assistantships also available. Financial award application deadline: 1/5; financial award applicants required to submit FAFSA. *Faculty research:* Painting, photography, sculpture, digital art, video. *Application contact:* Charles Long, Graduate Advisor, 951-827-7756, Fax: 951-827-2385, E-mail: charles.long@ucr.edu.

University of California, San Diego, Office of Graduate Studies, Department of Visual Arts, La Jolla, CA 92093. Offers MFA, PhD. *Degree requirements:* For master's, thesis, exhibit, oral exam. Electronic applications accepted. *Faculty research:* Developments within art and art theory.

University of California, Santa Barbara, Graduate Division, College of Letters and Sciences, Division of Humanities and Fine Arts, Department of Art, Santa Barbara, CA 93106. Offers art (MFA). *Faculty:* 6 full-time (3 women), 6 part-time/adjunct (1 woman). *Students:* 12 full-time (7 women); includes 1 minority (Hispanic American), 1 international. Average age 27. 49 applicants, 24% accepted, 5 enrolled. In 2007, 9 degrees awarded. *Degree requirements:* For master's, thesis, thesis exhibition. *Entrance requirements:* For master's, 20 slide portfolio, minimum GPA of 3.0, 3 letters of recommendation. Additional exam requirements/recommendations for international students: Required—TOEFL (minimum score 550 paper-based; 213 computer-based; 80 iBT). *Application deadline:* For fall admission, 1/7 for domestic and international students. Application fee: $60. Electronic applications accepted. *Expenses:* Tuition, nonresident: full-time $14,888. Required fees: $10,108. *Financial support:* In 2007–08, 12 students received support, including 11 fellowships with full tuition reimbursements available (averaging $6,100 per year), teaching assistantships with full tuition reimbursements available (averaging $15,579 per year); research assistantships, career-related internships or fieldwork, Federal Work-Study, institutionally sponsored loans, scholarships/grants, and health care benefits also available. Financial award application deadline: 1/7; financial award applicants required to submit FAFSA. *Faculty research:* Digital media, drawing and painting, printing, photo, sculpture, evolving roles of images in culture, race/ethnicity classification and pop culture analysis. *Unit head:* Prof. Jane Callister, Chair, 805-893-3138, E-mail: jane@arts.ucsb.edu. *Application contact:* Yumi Kinoshita, Graduate Advisor, 805-893-5962, Fax: 805-893-7206, E-mail: ykinoshita@arts.ucsb.edu.

University of California, Santa Barbara, Graduate Division, College of Letters and Sciences, Division of Humanities and Fine Arts, Department of Media Arts and Technology, Santa Barbara, CA 93106. Offers electronic music and sound design (MA, PhD); multimedia engineering (MS, PhD); visual and spatial arts (MA, PhD). *Faculty:* 1 full-time (0 women), 12 part-time/adjunct (3 women). *Students:* 32 full-time (4 women); includes 3 minority (all Hispanic Americans), 9 international. Average age 30. 66 applicants, 36% accepted, 10 enrolled. In 2007, 11 master's, 1 doctorate awarded. Terminal master's awarded for partial completion of doctoral program. *Degree requirements:* For master's, thesis, 1 project; for doctorate, comprehensive exam, thesis/dissertation. *Entrance requirements:* For master's and doctorate, GRE, portfolios, programming language, calculus-based math, expertise in 1 discipline and experience in another. Additional exam requirements/recommendations for international students: Required—TOEFL (minimum score 550 paper-based; 213 computer-based; 80 iBT). *Application deadline:* For fall admission, 1/15 for domestic students, 3/1 for international students. Application fee: $60. Electronic applications accepted. *Expenses:* Tuition, nonresident: full-time $14,888. Required fees: $10,108. *Financial support:* In 2007–08, 28 students received support, including 11 fellowships with full and partial tuition reimbursements available (averaging $17,400 per year), 16 teaching assistantships; career-related internships or fieldwork, Federal Work-Study, scholarships/grants, health care benefits, and unspecified assistantships also available. Financial award application deadline: 12/15; financial award applicants required to submit FAFSA. *Faculty research:* Networking requirements for multimedia-capable systems, ceration of development of multimedia theatre, graphical user interfaces, distributed programming, speech image and video compression, audio signal processing, wireless communications. *Unit head:* Prof. Matthew Turk, Chair, 805-893-4236, E-mail: mturk@cs.ucsb.edu. *Application contact:* Diane Harden, Graduate Program Assistant, 805-893-2887, Fax: 805-893-2930, E-mail: harden@mat.ucsb.edu.

University of California, Santa Cruz, Division of Graduate Studies, Division of the Arts, Program in Digital Arts and New Media, Santa Cruz, CA 95064. Offers MFA. *Faculty:* 18 full-time (6 women), 16 part-time/adjunct (4 women). *Students:* 19 full-time (7 women); includes 5 minority (3 Asian Americans or Pacific Islanders, 2 Hispanic Americans). Average age 25. 52 applicants, 37% accepted, 14 enrolled. *Entrance requirements:* Additional exam requirements/recommendations for international students: Required—TOEFL; Recommended—IELTS. *Application deadline:* For fall admission, 2/15 for domestic and international students. Application fee: $60. Electronic applications accepted. *Expenses:* Tuition, nonresident: full-time $14,694. Required fees: $11,360. *Unit head:* Sharon Daniel, Program Chair, 831-459-3948, E-mail: sdaniel@ucsc.edu. *Application contact:* Felicia Rice, Program Manager, 831-459-1554, E-mail: fsrice@ucsc.edu.

University of Central Florida, College of Arts and Humanities, Department of Art, Orlando, FL 32816. Offers studio art and the computer (MFA). *Faculty:* 25 full-time (6 women), 4 part-time/adjunct (2 women). *Students:* 19 applicants, 68% accepted, 10 enrolled. *Expenses:* Tuition, state resident: full-time $6,484. Tuition, nonresident: full-time $23,938. Tuition and fees vary according to program. *Financial support:* Fellowships, research assistantships, teaching assistantships available. *Unit head:* Mark Price, Chair, 407-823-2676, Fax: 407-823-6470, E-mail: maprice@mail.ucf.edu.

University of Chicago, Division of the Humanities, Committee on the Visual Arts, Chicago, IL 60637-1513. Offers MFA. *Students:* 19. 42 applicants, 36% accepted, 10 enrolled. *Entrance requirements:* For master's, GRE General Test. *Application deadline:* For fall admission, 12/15 for domestic students. Application fee: $55. *Financial support:* Fellowships, tuition waivers (full and partial) available. Financial award application deadline: 12/15; financial award applicants required to submit FAFSA. *Unit head:* Dr. Laura Letinsky, Chair, 773-753-4821.

University of Cincinnati, Graduate School, College of Design, Architecture, Art, and Planning, School of Art, Program in Fine Arts, Cincinnati, OH 45221. Offers MFA. *Accreditation:* NASAD. Part-time programs available. *Students:* 36 full-time (16 women), 5 part-time (4 women); includes 2 minority (both African Americans), 5 international. Average age 23. In 2007, 19 degrees awarded. *Degree requirements:* For master's, thesis, oral exam. *Entrance requirements:* Additional exam requirements/recommendations for international students: Required—TOEFL. *Application deadline:* For fall admission, 2/1 for domestic students. Application fee: $30. Electronic applications accepted. *Financial support:* In 2007–08, 10 fellowships (averaging $7,000 per year) were awarded; Federal Work-Study, tuition waivers (partial), and unspecified assistantships also available. Financial award application deadline: 3/1. *Faculty research:* Painting, drawing, ceramics, printmaking, sculpture. *Application contact:* Prof. Kimberly Burleigh, Director, 513-556-2075, Fax: 513-556-2887, E-mail: kimberly.burleigh@uc.edu.

University of Colorado at Boulder, Graduate School, College of Arts and Sciences, Department of Art and Art History, Boulder, CO 80309. Offers art history (MA), including 19th century art, contemporary art criticism, early 20th century art, Russian and Soviet art; ceramics (MFA); drawing (MFA); painting (MFA); photography and media arts (MFA); printmaking (MFA); sculpture (MFA). *Faculty:* 27. *Students:* 42 full-time (22 women), 1 (woman) part-time; includes 4 minority (all Hispanic Americans), 1 international. Average age 32. 15 applicants, 73% accepted. In 2007, 16 degrees awarded. *Degree requirements:* For master's, variable foreign language requirement, comprehensive exam, thesis (for some programs). *Entrance requirements:* For master's, GRE General Test, minimum undergraduate GPA of 3.0, portfolio. *Application deadline:* For fall admission, 1/15 priority date for domestic students, 12/1 for international students. Application fee: $50 ($60 for international students). *Financial support:* In 2007–08, 32 fellowships (averaging $2,294 per year) were awarded; Federal Work-Study, scholarships/grants, and tuition waivers (full) also available. Financial award application deadline: 1/15. *Faculty research:* Drawing, painting, ceramics, sculpture, photography and media arts, printmaking (MFA); history-Russian and Soviet art, Early 20th Century art, contemporary art criticism, 19th Century art (MA). *Unit head:* James Johnson, Chair, 303-492-6504, Fax: 303-492-4886, E-mail: james.johnson@colorado.edu. *Application contact:* Graduate Program Assistant, 303-492-2419, Fax: 303-492-4886, E-mail: finearts@colorado.edu.

University of Connecticut, Graduate School, School of Fine Arts, Department of Art and Art History, Field of Studio Art, Storrs, CT 06269. Offers MFA. *Accreditation:* NASAD. *Faculty:* 18 full-time (11 women). *Students:* 10 full-time (5 women); includes 1 minority (African American) Average age 27. 46 applicants, 11% accepted, 5 enrolled. In 2007, 5 degrees awarded. *Entrance requirements:* Additional exam requirements/recommendations for international students: Required—TOEFL (minimum score 550 paper-based; 213 computer-based). *Application deadline:* For fall admission, 2/1 priority date for domestic and international students; for spring admission, 11/1 for domestic students, 10/1 for international students. Applications are processed on a rolling basis. Application fee: $55. Electronic applications accepted. *Expenses:* Tuition, state resident: part-time $469 per credit hour. Tuition, nonresident: part-time $1,218 per credit hour. *Financial support:* In 2007–08, 10 research assistantships were awarded; teaching assistantships with full tuition reimbursements, Federal Work-Study, health care

Art/Fine Arts

University of Connecticut (continued)
benefits, and unspecified assistantships also available. Financial award application deadline: 2/1; financial award applicants required to submit FAFSA. *Unit head:* Charles Hagen, Chairperson, 860-486-2659, E-mail: chagen@finearts.sfa.uconn.edu. *Application contact:* Kelly Gillett, Administrative Assistant, 860-486-3930.

University of Dallas, Braniff Graduate School of Liberal Arts, Program in Art, Irving, TX 75062-4736. Offers MA, MFA. Part-time programs available. *Faculty:* 2 full-time (0 women), 6 part-time/adjunct (3 women). *Students:* 15 full-time (8 women); includes 2 minority (1 African American, 1 Hispanic American). Average age 32. 26 applicants, 35% accepted, 6 enrolled. In 2007, 10 degrees awarded. *Degree requirements:* For master's, exhibit, oral exam. *Entrance requirements:* For master's, GRE General Test, portfolio. Additional exam requirements/recommendations for international students: Required—TOEFL (minimum score 550 paper-based; 213 computer-based). *Application deadline:* For fall admission, 2/15 for domestic students. Applications are processed on a rolling basis. Application fee: $50. *Expenses:* Tuition: Part-time $600 per credit. Required fees: $15 per credit. *Financial support:* In 2007–08, 5 students received support; research assistantships, scholarships/grants available. Financial award application deadline: 2/15; financial award applicants required to submit FAFSA. *Faculty research:* Ceramics, printmaking, sculpture, art history, religious imagery and architecture. *Unit head:* Dan Hammett, Chairman, 972-721-5318, Fax: 972-721-5017, E-mail: hammett@udallas.edu. *Application contact:* Graduate Coordinator, 972-721-5106, Fax: 972-721-5280, E-mail: graduate@acad.udallas.edu.

University of Delaware, College of Arts and Sciences, Department of Art, Newark, DE 19716. Offers MA, MFA. *Faculty:* 7 full-time (2 women). *Students:* 17 full-time (9 women), 1 (woman) part-time; includes 2 minority (1 Asian American or Pacific Islander, 1 Hispanic American). Average age 27. 39 applicants, 36% accepted, 8 enrolled. In 2007, 11 degrees awarded. *Degree requirements:* For master's, exposition paper final exhibition. *Entrance requirements:* For master's, portfolio of creative work. *Application deadline:* For fall admission, 2/1 priority date for domestic students. Application fee: $60. Electronic applications accepted. *Financial support:* In 2007–08, 3 fellowships with tuition reimbursements (averaging $11,000 per year), 13 teaching assistantships with full and partial tuition reimbursements (averaging $4,908 per year) were awarded; career-related internships or fieldwork, Federal Work-Study, institutionally sponsored loans, scholarships/grants, and tuition waivers (full and partial) also available. Financial award application deadline: 2/1. *Faculty research:* Painting, printmaking, ceramics, photography, sculpture. *Unit head:* Prof. Virginia Bradley, Chair, 302-831-2244, Fax: 302-831-0505, E-mail: vbradley@udel.edu. *Application contact:* Gwen McCullough, Secretary, 302-831-2244, Fax: 302-831-0505, E-mail: kgm@udel.edu.

Announcement: *Newark, Delaware, is located midway between New York City and Washington, DC. The department has 17 faculty members, all exhibiting artists, and 9 graduate teaching assistantships. Studio and darkroom space provided. Graduate programs include the following disciplines: ceramics, painting, photography, printmaking, and sculpture. Web site: http://udel.edu/art.*

University of Denver, Faculty of Arts and Humanities/Social Sciences, School of Art and Art History, Denver, CO 80208. Offers art history (MA); art history/museum studies (MA); electronic media arts and design (MFA); studio art (MFA). *Accreditation:* NASAD. Part-time programs available. *Faculty:* 15 full-time (10 women). *Students:* 24 full-time (20 women), 2 part-time (1 woman); includes 2 minority (1 Asian American or Pacific Islander, 1 Hispanic American), 1 international. Average age 28. In 2007, 10 degrees awarded. *Degree requirements:* For master's, one foreign language, research paper. *Entrance requirements:* For master's, GRE. Additional exam requirements/recommendations for international students: Required—TOEFL. *Application deadline:* Applications are processed on a rolling basis. Application fee: $50. Electronic applications accepted. *Financial support:* In 2007–08, 5 teaching assistantships with full and partial tuition reimbursements (averaging $6,500 per year) were awarded; career-related internships or fieldwork, Federal Work-Study, institutionally sponsored loans, and scholarships/grants also available. Support available to part-time students. Financial award application deadline: 3/1; financial award applicants required to submit FAFSA. *Faculty research:* Images of women in alchemical manuscripts and books, Giovanni Benedetto, Salvatore Castiglione. *Unit head:* Dr. Annette Stott, Director, 303-871-2846. *Application contact:* Dr. M. Warlick, Graduate Advisor, 303-871-2846, E-mail: saah-interest@du.edu.

University of Florida, Graduate School, College of Fine Arts, School of Art and Art History, Gainesville, FL 32611. Offers art (MFA), including ceramics, creative photography, drawing, electronic intermedia, graphic design, painting, printmaking, sculpture; art education (MA); art history (MA, PhD); digital arts and sciences (MA); museology (museum studies) (MA). *Accreditation:* NASAD. *Faculty:* 29 full-time (14 women), 2 part-time/adjunct (1 woman). *Students:* 82 (48 women); includes 4 minority (2 Asian Americans or Pacific Islanders, 2 Hispanic Americans) 4 international. In 2007, 20 degrees awarded. *Degree requirements:* For master's, variable foreign language requirement, project or thesis (MFA). *Entrance requirements:* For master's, portfolio (MFA), writing sample (MA), GRE General Test or minimum GPA of 3.0. Additional exam requirements/recommendations for international students: Required—TOEFL (minimum score 550 paper-based; 213 computer-based). *Application deadline:* For fall admission, 1/15 priority date for domestic students. Applications are processed on a rolling basis. Application fee: $30. Electronic applications accepted. *Expenses:* Tuition, state resident: full-time $7,478. Tuition, nonresident: full-time $22,603. *Financial support:* In 2007–08, 3 research assistantships with tuition reimbursements (averaging $9,515 per year), 67 teaching assistantships with tuition reimbursements (averaging $9,839 per year) were awarded; fellowships, Federal Work-Study, institutionally sponsored loans, and unspecified assistantships also available. Financial award applicants required to submit FAFSA. *Faculty research:* Studio production, art historical studies of style context. *Unit head:* Glenn Willumson, Program Director, 352-392-0201 Ext. 234. *Application contact:* Prof. Richard Heipp, Coordinator, 352-392-0201 Ext. 239, Fax: 352-392-8453, E-mail: heipp@ufl.edu.

University of Georgia, Graduate School, College of Arts and Sciences, Lamar Dodd School of Art, Program in Art, Athens, GA 30602. Offers MFA, PhD. *Accreditation:* NASAD. *Students:* 59 full-time (37 women), 7 part-time (5 women); includes 5 minority (1 African American, 2 Asian Americans or Pacific Islanders, 2 Hispanic Americans), 3 international. 220 applicants, 11% accepted, 15 enrolled. In 2007, 24 degrees awarded. *Degree requirements:* For doctorate, one foreign language, thesis/dissertation. *Entrance requirements:* For master's and doctorate, GRE General Test. *Application deadline:* For fall admission, 7/1 priority date for domestic students; for spring admission, 11/15 for domestic students. Application fee: $50. Electronic applications accepted. *Financial support:* Fellowships, research assistantships, teaching assistantships, unspecified assistantships available. *Application contact:* Larry Millard, Graduate Coordinator, 706-542-1665, Fax: 706-542-0226, E-mail: millard@uga.edu.

University of Guam, Office of Graduate Studies, Liberal Arts and Social Sciences, Division of Fine Arts, Mangilao, GU 96923. Offers ceramics (MA); graphics (MA); painting (MA). *Faculty:* 3 full-time (0 women). *Students:* Average age 47. In 2007, 1 degree awarded. *Degree requirements:* For master's, thesis or alternative, exhibit, final oral exam. *Entrance requirements:* For master's, GRE General Test, portfolio. Additional exam requirements/recommendations for international students: Required—TOEFL. *Application deadline:* For fall admission, 6/11 priority date for domestic students, 3/24 priority date for international students; for spring admission, 11/16 priority date for domestic students, 9/8 priority date for international students. Applications are processed on a rolling basis. Application fee: $49 ($74 for international students). *Unit head:* Lewis Rifkowitz, Chair, 671-735-2716, Fax: 671-734-3575, E-mail: rifkowit@yahoo.com. *Application contact:* Charlie A. Alcantara, Program Coordinator, Graduate Studies Office, 671-735-2173, Fax: 671-734-3676, E-mail: charliea@uguam.uog.edu.

University of Guelph, Graduate Program Services, College of Arts, School of Fine Art and Music, Guelph, ON N1G 2W1, Canada. Offers studio art (MFA). *Faculty:* 14 full-time (7 women), 8 part-time/adjunct (3 women). *Students:* 16 full-time (9 women). Average age 30. 79 applicants, 10% accepted, 8 enrolled. In 2007, 6 degrees awarded. *Degree requirements:* For master's, exhibition, support paper, oral defense. *Entrance requirements:* For master's, minimum B- average during previous 2 years of course work. Additional exam requirements/recommendations for international students: Required—TOEFL. *Application deadline:* For fall admission, 1/15 for domestic and international students. Application fee: $75. Electronic applications accepted. *Financial support:* In 2007–08, 7 students received support, including research assistantships (averaging $11,268 per year), teaching assistantships (averaging $11,268 per year); Federal Work-Study, scholarships/grants, and unspecified assistantships also available. *Faculty research:* Studio practice in painting, sculpture, print, photo, drawing, video. *Unit head:* Dr. John D. Kissick, Director, 519-824-4120 Ext. 56930, Fax: 519-821-5482, E-mail: jkissick@uoguelph.ca. *Application contact:* Robin McGinnis, Graduate Secretary, 519-824-4120, Fax: 519-821-5482 Ext. 54671, E-mail: rmcginni@uoguelph.ca.

University of Hartford, Hartford Art School, West Hartford, CT 06117-1599. Offers MFA. *Accreditation:* NASAD. Part-time programs available. *Faculty:* 3 full-time (1 woman), 2 part-time/adjunct (0 women). *Students:* 9 full-time (5 women), 18 part-time (7 women); includes 4 minority (2 Asian Americans or Pacific Islanders, 2 Hispanic Americans). Average age 44. 22 applicants, 18% accepted, 2 enrolled. In 2007, 21 degrees awarded. *Degree requirements:* For master's, thesis. *Entrance requirements:* For master's, portfolio, 3 letters of recommendation. Additional exam requirements/recommendations for international students: Required—TOEFL (minimum score 550 paper-based; 213 computer-based). *Application deadline:* For fall admission, 3/1 priority date for domestic students. Applications are processed on a rolling basis. Application fee: $45. Electronic applications accepted. *Expenses:* Contact institution. *Financial support:* In 2007–08, 10 fellowships with partial tuition reimbursements (averaging $6,000 per year) were awarded; teaching assistantships, Federal Work-Study also available. Support available to part-time students. Financial award application deadline: 6/1; financial award applicants required to submit FAFSA. *Unit head:* Power Boothe, Dean, 860-768-4391. *Application contact:* Ellen Carey, Director, 860-768-4616, Fax: 860-768-5160, E-mail: ecarey@mail.hartford.edu.

University of Hawaii at Manoa, Graduate Division, Colleges of Arts and Sciences, College of Arts and Humanities, Department of Art and Art History, Honolulu, HI 96822. Offers art (MA); art history (MA); visual arts (MFA). Part-time programs available. *Faculty:* 23 full-time (12 women), 1 part-time/adjunct (0 women). *Students:* 30 full-time (12 women), 6 part-time (1 woman); includes 6 minority (all Asian Americans or Pacific Islanders), 3 international. Average age 36. 71 applicants, 30% accepted, 12 enrolled. *Degree requirements:* For master's, thesis optional. *Entrance requirements:* For master's, GRE General Test, BFA, 18 hours of course work in art history. Additional exam requirements/recommendations for international students: Required—TOEFL (minimum score 600 paper-based; 250 computer-based; 100 iBT), IELTS (minimum score 7). *Application deadline:* For fall admission, 1/15 for domestic students, 12/15 for international students; for spring admission, 9/1 for domestic students, 8/1 for international students. Application fee: $50. *Financial support:* In 2007–08, 3 teaching assistantships (averaging $13,296 per year) were awarded; fellowships, research assistantships, Federal Work-Study, scholarships/grants, and tuition waivers (full and partial) also available. Financial award application deadline: 3/1; financial award applicants required to submit FAFSA. *Faculty research:* Painting, sculpture, glass, design, printmaking. Total annual research expenditures: $9,805. *Application contact:* Richard Mills, Graduate Field Chairperson, 808-956-8251, Fax: 808-956-9043, E-mail: rlmills@hawaii.edu.

University of Houston, College of Liberal Arts and Social Sciences, Department of Art, Houston, TX 77204. Offers interior design (MA); painting (MA); photography (MA); sculpture (MA); MFA/MA. *Faculty:* 16 full-time (7 women), 7 part-time/adjunct (5 women). *Students:* 37 full-time (23 women); includes 7 minority (1 Asian American or Pacific Islander, 6 Hispanic Americans), 4 international. Average age 33. 49 applicants, 31% accepted, 11 enrolled. In 2007, 10 degrees awarded. *Degree requirements:* For master's, comprehensive exam, visual thesis. *Entrance requirements:* For master's, GRE General Test, portfolio. *Application deadline:* For fall admission, 2/28 for domestic students; for spring admission, 10/30 for domestic students. Application fee: $25 ($100 for international students). *Expenses:* Tuition, state resident: full-time $6,297; part-time $262 per credit. Tuition, nonresident: full-time $12,969; part-time $540 per credit. Required fees: $2,696. *Financial support:* In 2007–08, 3 teaching assistantships with full tuition reimbursements (averaging $10,400 per year) were awarded; fellowships with full tuition reimbursements, research assistantships with full tuition reimbursements, career-related internships or fieldwork, Federal Work-Study, institutionally sponsored loans, scholarships/grants, health care benefits, and unspecified assistantships also available. Support available to part-time students. Financial award application deadline: 3/10. *Faculty research:* Alternative art projects. *Unit head:* Dr. John Reed, Chairperson, 713-743-3001, Fax: 713-743-2823, E-mail: jreed@uh.edu.

University of Idaho, College of Graduate Studies, College of Art and Architecture, Department of Art and Design, Moscow, ID 83844-2282. Offers art (MAT, MFA). *Accreditation:* NASAD. *Students:* 16. Average age 31. In 2007, 4 degrees awarded. *Degree requirements:* For master's, thesis (for some programs). *Entrance requirements:* For master's, minimum GPA of 2.8. *Application deadline:* For fall admission, 8/1 for domestic students; for spring admission, 12/15 for domestic students. Application fee: $55 ($60 for international students). *Financial support:* Research assistantships, teaching assistantships available. Financial award application deadline: 2/15. *Unit head:* William Woolston, Chair, 208-885-7837.

University of Illinois at Chicago, Graduate College, College of Architecture and Art, School of Art and Design, Chicago, IL 60607-7128. Offers electronic visualization (MFA); film animation (MFA); graphic design (MFA); industrial design (MFA); photography (MFA); studio arts (MFA). *Accreditation:* NASAD. *Degree requirements:* For master's, thesis, exhibit. *Entrance requirements:* For master's, MAT, portfolio. Additional exam requirements/recommendations for international students: Required—TOEFL. Electronic applications accepted.

University of Illinois at Urbana–Champaign, Graduate College, College of Fine and Applied Arts, School of Art and Design, Program in Studio Arts, Champaign, IL 61820. Offers art and design (MFA); crafts (MFA); metals (MFA); painting (MFA); photography (MFA); sculpture (MFA). *Accreditation:* NASAD. *Students:* 31 full-time (14 women), 3 part-time (2 women); includes 5 minority (1 African American, 1 American Indian/Alaska Native, 2 Asian Americans or Pacific Islanders, 1 Hispanic American), 7 international. 75 applicants, 19% accepted, 12 enrolled. In 2007, 10 degrees awarded. *Entrance requirements:* For master's, minimum GPA of 3.0. *Application deadline:* Applications are processed on a rolling basis. Application fee: $60 ($75 for international students). Electronic applications accepted. *Financial support:* Application deadline: 2/15. *Unit head:* Alan Mette, Chair, 217-244-7496, Fax: 217-244-7688, E-mail: amette@uiuc.edu. *Application contact:* Marsha Biddle, Assistant to the Associate Director, 217-333-0642, Fax: 217-244-7688, E-mail: mbiddle@uiuc.edu.

University of Indianapolis, Graduate Programs, College of Arts and Sciences, Department of Art, Indianapolis, IN 46227-3697. Offers MA. *Accreditation:* NASAD. Part-time and evening/weekend programs available. *Faculty:* 2 full-time (0 women). *Students:* Average age 37. *Entrance requirements:* For master's, GRE Subject Test. *Application deadline:* Applications are processed on a rolling basis. Application fee: $50. *Financial support:* Federal Work-Study available. Financial award application deadline: 5/1; financial award applicants required to submit FAFSA. *Unit head:* Dee Schaad, Chair, 317-788-3253, E-mail: dschaad@uindy.edu. *Application contact:* Dr. Daniel Briere, Dean, 317-788-3395, Fax: 317-788-3480, E-mail: dbriere@uindy.edu.

The University of Iowa, Graduate College, College of Liberal Arts and Sciences, School of Art and Art History, Programs in Art, Iowa City, IA 52242-1316. Offers MA, MFA. *Degree requirements:* For master's, thesis, final exam. *Entrance requirements:* For master's, GRE General Test, portfolio. Additional exam requirements/recommendations for international students: Required—TOEFL (minimum score 550 paper-based; 213 computer-based). Electronic applications accepted. *Expenses:* Tuition, state resident: part-time $349 per hour. Tuition, nonresident: part-time $349 per hour. Tuition and fees vary according to course load and program. *Faculty research:* Ceramics, painting and drawing, design, printmaking, photography.

University of Kansas, Research and Graduate Studies, School of Fine Arts, Department of Art, Lawrence, KS 66045. Offers MFA. *Accreditation:* NASAD. *Faculty:* 18. *Students:* 15 full-time (9 women); includes 1 minority (Hispanic American) Average age 27. 58 applicants, 19% accepted, 8 enrolled. In 2007, 7 degrees awarded. *Degree requirements:* For master's, thesis, gallery exhibition, oral defense. *Entrance requirements:* For master's, slide or dvd portfolio, minimum GPA of 3.0, 3 letters of recommendation, statement of purpose. Additional exam requirements/recommendations for international students: Required—TOEFL, IELTS. *Application deadline:* For fall admission, 2/1 for domestic and international students. Application fee: $55 ($60 for international students). Electronic applications accepted. *Expenses:* Tuition, state resident: full-time $5,838. Tuition, nonresident: full-time $13,409. Tuition and fees vary according to program. *Financial support:* In 2007–08, fellowships (averaging $12,000 per year); teaching assistantships with full and partial tuition reimbursements, Federal Work-Study, scholarships/grants, and unspecified assistantships also available. Financial award application deadline: 2/1; financial award applicants required to submit FAFSA. *Faculty research:* Painting, sculpture, printmaking, mixed media, installation and performance, drawing. *Unit head:* Dawn Marie Guernsey, Chair, 785-864-4401, Fax: 785-864-4404, E-mail: guernsey@ku.edu. *Application contact:* Gina Westergard, Director, 785-864-4401, Fax: 785-864-4404, E-mail: ginaw@ku.edu.

University of Kansas, Research and Graduate Studies, School of Fine Arts, Department of Design, Program in Visual Arts Education, Lawrence, KS 66045. Offers MA. Part-time programs available. *Faculty:* 29. *Students:* 5 full-time (all women), 3 part-time (all women). Average age 29. 3 applicants, 33% accepted, 1 enrolled. In 2007, 3 degrees awarded. *Degree requirements:* For master's, thesis or alternative. *Entrance requirements:* For master's, portfolio, 3 letters of recommendation, minimum GPA of 3.0. Additional exam requirements/recommendations for international students: Required—TOEFL (paper-based 570; computer-based 230) or IELTS (6.5). *Application deadline:* For fall admission, 5/1 for domestic and international students; for spring admission, 10/15 for domestic and international students. Application fee: $55 ($60 for international students). Electronic applications accepted. *Expenses:* Tuition, state resident: full-time $5,838. Tuition, nonresident: full-time $13,409. Tuition and fees vary according to program. *Financial support:* Teaching assistantships with full tuition reimbursements, Federal Work-Study, scholarships/grants, and unspecified assistantships available. Financial award application deadline: 5/1. *Faculty research:* Museum education, art educator education. *Application contact:* Gina Westergard, Director, 785-864-4401, Fax: 785-864-4404, E-mail: ginaw@ku.edu.

University of Kentucky, Graduate School, College of Fine Arts, Program in Art Studio, Lexington, KY 40506-0032. Offers MFA. *Faculty:* 19 full-time (7 women). *Students:* 11 full-time (8 women), 2 part-time (both women); includes 1 minority (African American) Average age 31. 27 applicants, 22% accepted, 2 enrolled. In 2007, 2 degrees awarded. *Degree requirements:* For master's, comprehensive exam. *Entrance requirements:* For master's, GRE General Test, minimum undergraduate GPA of 2.75. Additional exam requirements/recommendations for international students: Required—TOEFL (minimum score 550 paper-based; 213 computer-based). *Application deadline:* For fall admission, 7/17 for domestic students, 2/1 priority date for international students; for spring admission, 12/13 for domestic students, 6/15 priority date for international students. Application fee: $50 ($65 for international students). Electronic applications accepted. *Expenses:* Tuition, state resident: part-time $437 per credit hour. Tuition, nonresident: part-time $931 per credit hour. *Financial support:* In 2007–08, 7 students received support, including 3 research assistantships with full tuition reimbursements available (averaging $9,480 per year), 4 teaching assistantships with full tuition reimbursements available (averaging $9,548 per year); fellowships with full tuition reimbursements available, Federal Work-Study, scholarships/grants, traineeships, health care benefits, tuition waivers (partial), and unspecified assistantships also available. Support available to part-time students. Financial award application deadline: 3/15. *Unit head:* Dr. Dennis Carpenter, Director of Graduate Studies, 859-257-6041, Fax: 859-257-3042. *Application contact:* Dr. Brian Jackson, Senior Associate Dean, 859-257-4667, Fax: 859-257-4676, E-mail: brian.jackson@uky.edu.

University of Lethbridge, School of Graduate Studies, Lethbridge, AB T1K 3M4, Canada. Offers accounting (MScM); addictions counseling (M Sc); agricultural biotechnology (M Sc); agricultural studies (M Sc, MA); anthropology (MA); archaeology (MA); art (MA); biochemistry (M Sc); biological sciences (M Sc); biomolecular science (PhD); biosystems and biodiversity (PhD); Canadian studies (MA); chemistry (M Sc); computer science (M Sc); computer science and geographical information science (M Sc); counseling psychology (M Ed); dramatic arts (MA); earth, space, and physical science (PhD); economics (MA); educational leadership (M Ed); English (MA); environmental science (M Sc); evolution and behavior (PhD); exercise science (M Sc); finance (MScM); French (MA); French/German (MA); French/Spanish (MA); general education (M Ed); general management (MScM); geography (M Sc, MA); German (MA); health sciences (M Sc, MA); history (MA); human resource management and labour relations (MScM); individualized multidisciplinary (M Sc, MA); information systems (MScM); international management (MScM); kinesiology (M Sc, MA); management (M Sc, MA); marketing (MScM); mathematics (M Sc); music (MA); Native American studies (MA); neuroscience (M Sc, PhD); new media (MA); nursing (M Sc); philosophy (MA); physics (M Sc); policy and strategy (MScM); political science (MA); psychology (M Sc, MA); religious studies (MA); sociology (MA); theoretical and computational science (PhD); urban and regional studies (MA). Part-time and evening/weekend programs available. *Students:* 215 full-time, 98 part-time. In 2007, 87 master's, 1 doctorate awarded. *Degree requirements:* For doctorate, comprehensive exam, thesis/dissertation. *Entrance requirements:* For master's, GMAT (M Sc in management), bachelor's degree in related field, minimum GPA of 3.0 during previous 20 graded semester courses, 2 years teaching or related experience (M Ed); for doctorate, master's degree, minimum graduate GPA of 3.5. Additional exam requirements/recommendations for international students: Required—TOEFL. Application fee: $60 Canadian dollars. *Financial support:* Fellowships, research assistantships, teaching assistantships, scholarships/grants, health care benefits, and unspecified assistantships available. *Faculty research:* Movement and brain plasticity, gibberellin physiology, photosynthesis, carbon cycling, molecular properties of main-group ring components. *Unit head:* Dr. Jo-Anne Fiske, Interim Dean, 403-329-2121, Fax: 403-329-2097. *Application contact:* Jennifer Geddes, Graduate Liaison Officer, 403-329-2762, Fax: 403-329-5159, E-mail: jennifer.geddes@uleth.ca.

University of Louisville, Graduate School, College of Arts and Sciences, Department of Fine Arts, Program in Creative Art, Louisville, KY 40292-0001. Offers MA. *Students:* 14 full-time (8 women), 18 part-time (13 women), 1 international. Average age 38. In 2007, 7 degrees awarded. Application fee: $50. *Unit head:* Dr. James T. Grubola, Chair, Department of Fine Arts, 502-852-0759, Fax: 502-852-6791, E-mail: grubola@louisville.edu.

University of Maryland, Baltimore County, Graduate School, College of Arts, Humanities and Social Sciences, Department of Visual Arts, Baltimore, MD 21250. Offers imaging and digital arts (MFA). *Faculty:* 21 full-time (10 women), 1 part-time/adjunct (0 women). *Students:* 16 full-time (7 women), 2 part-time (both women); includes 1 Asian American or Pacific Islander, 2 Hispanic Americans. Average age 32. 20 applicants, 45% accepted, 7 enrolled. In 2007, 5 degrees awarded. *Degree requirements:* For master's, thesis, oral defense, thesis exhibition. *Entrance requirements:* For master's, minimum GPA of 3.0. Additional exam requirements/recommendations for international students: Required—TOEFL. *Application deadline:* For fall admission, 2/1 for domestic and international students. Application fee: $45. Electronic applications accepted. *Financial support:* In 2007–08, 14 students received support, including 12 research assistantships with full and partial tuition reimbursements available (averaging $13,800 per year); scholarships/grants and health care benefits also available. Financial award application deadline: 2/1. *Faculty research:* Advanced visual studies, digital imaging and interactive art, studio and computer art, video art. Total annual research expenditures: $22,500. *Unit head:* Prof. Franc Nunoo-Quarcoo, Chair, 410-455-2150, Fax: 410-455-1053, E-mail: franc@umbc.edu. *Application contact:* Prof. Steve Bradley, Graduate Program Director, 410-455-2721, Fax: 410-455-1053, E-mail: sbradley@umbc.edu.

University of Maryland, College Park, Graduate Studies, College of Arts and Humanities, Department of Art, College Park, MD 20742. Offers MFA. *Faculty:* 18 full-time (6 women), 11 part-time/adjunct (6 women). *Students:* 13 full-time (6 women); includes 1 minority (African American), 3 international. 49 applicants, 16% accepted, 5 enrolled. In 2007, 4 degrees awarded. *Degree requirements:* For master's, thesis, oral defense. *Entrance requirements:* For master's, minimum GPA of 3.0, portfolio, 15 slides, 3 letters of recommendation. *Application deadline:* For fall admission, 1/16 for domestic students, 2/1 for international students. Applications are processed on a rolling basis. Application fee: $60. Electronic applications accepted. *Financial support:* In 2007–08, 3 fellowships with full tuition reimbursements (averaging $6,660 per year), 11 teaching assistantships with tuition reimbursements (averaging $14,478 per year) were awarded; research assistantships with tuition reimbursements, Federal Work-Study and scholarships/grants also available. Support available to part-time students. Financial award applicants required to submit FAFSA. *Faculty research:* Studio art. *Unit head:* Dr. John Ruppert, Chair, 301-405-7790, Fax: 301-314-9740, E-mail: ruppertj@umd.edu. *Application contact:* Dean of Graduate School, 301-405-4190, Fax: 301-314-9305.

University of Massachusetts Amherst, Graduate School, College of Humanities and Fine Arts, Department of Art, Program in Art, Amherst, MA 01003. Offers MA, MFA. Part-time programs available. *Students:* 28 full-time (18 women), 15 part-time (11 women); includes 1 Asian American or Pacific Islander, 2 Hispanic Americans, 4 international. Average age 30. 79 applicants, 25% accepted, 11 enrolled. In 2007, 14 degrees awarded. *Degree requirements:* For master's, thesis (for some programs). *Entrance requirements:* For master's, portfolio. Additional exam requirements/recommendations for international students: Required—TOEFL (minimum score 530 paper-based; 197 computer-based). *Application deadline:* For fall admission, 2/1 for domestic and international students. Applications are processed on a rolling basis. Application fee: $50 ($65 for international students). Electronic applications accepted. *Expenses:* Tuition, state resident: full-time $2,640; part-time $110 per credit. Tuition, nonresident: full-time $9,936; part-time $414 per credit. Required fees: $7,455. One-time fee: $332. Tuition and fees vary according to course load, campus/location, program and reciprocity agreements. *Financial support:* In 2007–08, 1 fellowship (averaging $3,344 per year), 30 teaching assistantships (averaging $6,317 per year) were awarded; research assistantships, career-related internships or fieldwork, Federal Work-Study, scholarships/grants, traineeships, and unspecified assistantships also available. Support available to part-time students. Financial award application deadline: 2/1. *Unit head:* Dr. Max Page, Head, 413-545-6937, Fax: 413-545-3929, E-mail: mpage@art.umass.edu.

University of Massachusetts Dartmouth, Graduate School, College of Visual and Performing Arts, Program in Artisanry, North Dartmouth, MA 02747-2300. Offers ceramics (MFA, Postbaccalaureate Certificate); fibers (MFA); fibers/textiles (Postbaccalaureate Certificate); jewelry/metals (MFA, Postbaccalaureate Certificate); wood/furniture design (MFA, Postbaccalaureate Certificate). *Accreditation:* NASAD. *Faculty:* 6 full-time (3 women), 4 part-time/adjunct (all women). *Students:* 21 full-time (13 women), 14 part-time (9 women); includes 4 minority (3 Asian Americans or Pacific Islanders, 1 Hispanic American), 3 international. Average age 29. 47 applicants, 57% accepted, 17 enrolled. In 2007, 7 degrees awarded. *Degree requirements:* For master's, thesis, visual thesis. *Entrance requirements:* For master's, portfolio, interview, minimum GPA of 3.0, 3 letters of recommendation. Additional exam requirements/recommendations for international students: Required—TOEFL (minimum score 500 paper-based). *Application deadline:* For fall admission, 3/1 for domestic students, 1/1 for international students. Applications are processed on a rolling basis. Application fee: $40 ($60 for international students). Electronic applications accepted. *Expenses:* Tuition, state resident: full-time $2,071; part-time $86 per credit. Tuition, nonresident: full-time $8,099; part-time $337 per credit. Part-time tuition and fees vary according to course load and program. *Financial support:* In 2007–08, 16 teaching assistantships with full tuition reimbursements (averaging $2,930 per year) were awarded; Federal Work-Study and unspecified assistantships also available. Support available to part-time students. Financial award application deadline: 3/1; financial award applicants required to submit FAFSA. *Faculty research:* Processes of figurative sculpture: new materials and techniques. Total annual research expenditures: $9,880. *Unit head:* Jarrad Nunes, Director, 508-999-8010, E-mail: jnunes@umassd.edu. *Application contact:* Carol Novo, Graduate Admissions Officer, 508-999-8604, Fax: 508-999-8183, E-mail: graduate@umassd.edu.

University of Massachusetts Dartmouth, Graduate School, College of Visual and Performing Arts, Program in Fine Arts, North Dartmouth, MA 02747-2300. Offers drawing (MFA); painting (MFA); printmaking (MFA); sculpture (MFA). *Faculty:* 12 full-time (4 women), 8 part-time/adjunct (3 women). *Students:* 14 full-time (10 women), 3 part-time (1 woman); includes 1 minority (Hispanic American), 2 international. Average age 30. 28 applicants, 57% accepted, 8 enrolled. In 2007, 5 degrees awarded. *Degree requirements:* For master's, visual thesis. *Entrance requirements:* For master's, minimum GPA of 3.0, portfolio, 3 letters of recommendation. Additional exam requirements/recommendations for international students: Required—TOEFL (minimum score 500 paper-based). *Application deadline:* For fall admission, 3/1 priority date for domestic students, 1/1 priority date for international students. Applications are processed on a rolling basis. Application fee: $40 ($60 for international students). Electronic applications accepted. *Expenses:* Tuition, state resident: full-time $2,071; part-time $86 per credit. Tuition, nonresident: full-time $8,099; part-time $337 per credit. Part-time tuition and fees vary according to course load and program. *Financial support:* In 2007–08, 8 teaching assistantships (averaging $2,930 per year) were awarded; Federal Work-Study and unspecified assistantships also available. Support available to part-time students. Financial award application deadline: 3/1. Total annual research expenditures: $19,240. *Unit head:* Jarrad Nunes, Director, 508-999-8010, E-mail: jnunes@umassd.edu. *Application contact:* Carol Novo, Graduate Admissions Officer, 508-999-8604, Fax: 508-999-8183, E-mail: graduate@umassd.edu.

University of Memphis, Graduate School, College of Communication and Fine Arts, Department of Art, Memphis, TN 38152. Offers art history (MA), including Egyptian art and archaeology, general art history; ceramics (MFA); graphic design (MFA); interior design (MFA); painting (MFA); printmaking/photography (MFA); sculpture (MFA). *Accreditation:* NASAD (one or more programs are accredited). *Faculty:* 13 full-time (9 women). *Students:* 20 full-time (11 women), 2 part-time (1 woman); includes 1 Asian American or Pacific Islander, 1 international. Average age 27. 47 applicants, 55% accepted, 18 enrolled. In 2007, 14 degrees awarded. *Degree requirements:* For master's, 2 foreign languages, comprehensive exam, thesis. *Entrance requirements:* For master's, GRE General Test or MAT, portfolio (MFA). *Application deadline:* For fall admission, 8/1 for domestic students; for spring admission, 12/1 for domestic students. Applications are processed on a rolling basis. Application fee: $35 ($60 for international students). *Expenses:* Tuition, state resident: full-time $6,990; part-time $377 per hour. Tuition, nonresident: full-time $17,818; part-time $830 per hour. Tuition and fees vary according to course load and program. *Financial support:* In 2007–08, 23 research assistantships with full tuition reimbursements (averaging $4,200 per year), 10 teaching assistantships with full tuition reimbursements (averaging $5,250 per year) were awarded. *Faculty research:* Online collaborative learning, advanced art history studies, electronic publishing/design, studio arts, architectural studies. *Unit head:* Prof. Richard Lou, Chair, 901-678-2216, Fax: 901-678-2735, E-mail: gmyatt@memphis.edu. *Application contact:* Prof. Michael Hagge, Coordinator of Graduate Studies, 901-678-2677.

University of Miami, Graduate School, College of Arts and Sciences, Department of Art and Art History, Coral Gables, FL 33124. Offers art history (MA); ceramics/glass (MFA); graphic design/multimedia (MFA); painting (MFA); photography/digital imaging (MFA); printmaking (MFA); sculpture (MFA). Part-time programs available. *Faculty:* 14 full-time (6 women). *Students:* 23 full-time (15 women), 5 part-time (3 women); includes 5 minority (2 African Americans, 3 Hispanic Americans). Average age 29. 55 applicants, 18% accepted, 8 enrolled. In 2007, 8 degrees awarded. *Degree requirements:* For master's, variable foreign language requirement, thesis, exhibit (MFA), comprehensive exam (MA). *Entrance requirements:* For master's, GRE General Test (MA), research paper (MA), slide portfolio (MFA), artist statement (MFA). Additional

Art/Fine Arts

University of Miami (continued)

exam requirements/recommendations for international students: Required—TOEFL. *Application deadline:* For fall admission, 2/15 for domestic students, 1/15 for international students; for winter admission, 9/15 for domestic students. Application fee: $50. Electronic applications accepted. *Financial support:* In 2007–08, 25 students received support, including 17 teaching assistantships with full tuition reimbursements available (averaging $10,000 per year); Federal Work-Study, institutionally sponsored loans, scholarships/grants, and tuition waivers (full) also available. Financial award application deadline: 3/1; financial award applicants required to submit FAFSA. *Faculty research:* Installation art, public art. *Unit head:* Prof. Lise Drost, Chair, 305-284-2542, Fax: 305-284-2115, E-mail: l.drost@miami.edu. *Application contact:* Prof. Brian Curtis, Graduate Secretary, 305-284-2542, Fax: 305-284-2115, E-mail: art-arh@miami.edu.

University of Michigan, Horace H. Rackham School of Graduate Studies, School of Art and Design, Ann Arbor, MI 48109. Offers art and design (MFA). *Accreditation:* NASAD. *Faculty:* 44 full-time, 20 part-time/adjunct. *Students:* 26 full-time (19 women); includes 4 minority (2 African Americans, 2 Hispanic Americans), 2 international. Average age 30. 93 applicants, 16% accepted, 8 enrolled. In 2007, 7 degrees awarded. *Degree requirements:* For master's, thesis, exhibit (MFA), slide lecture. *Entrance requirements:* For master's, portfolio. Additional exam requirements/recommendations for international students: Required—TOEFL, IELTS. *Application deadline:* For fall admission, 1/1 for domestic and international students. Application fee: $55. Electronic applications accepted. *Financial support:* In 2007–08, 26 students received support, including 30 fellowships with full and partial tuition reimbursements available, 50 teaching assistantships with full and partial tuition reimbursements available; research assistantships with full and partial tuition reimbursements available, Federal Work-Study, scholarships/grants, health care benefits, tuition waivers (partial), and unspecified assistantships also available. Support available to part-time students. Financial award application deadline: 3/15; financial award applicants required to submit FAFSA. *Faculty research:* Creative expression, commercial design, preparation for teaching. *Unit head:* Bryan Rogers, Dean, 734-764-0397, Fax: 734-936-0469, E-mail: blrogers@umich.edu. *Application contact:* Dr. Bradley R. Smith, Associate Dean for Graduate Studies, 734-647-0397, Fax: 734-936-0469, E-mail: brdsmith@umich.edu.

See Close-Up on page 135.

University of Minnesota, Duluth, Graduate School, School of Fine Arts, Department of Art and Design, Duluth, MN 55812-2496. Offers graphic design (MFA). Part-time programs available. *Faculty:* 15 full-time (10 women), 6 part-time/adjunct (5 women). *Students:* 8 full-time (4 women), 1 international. Average age 30. 11 applicants, 18% accepted, 2 enrolled. In 2007, 1 degree awarded. *Degree requirements:* For master's, final exhibit, project, supporting paper. *Entrance requirements:* For master's, minimum GPA of 3.0, writing sample, slide portfolio. Additional exam requirements/recommendations for international students: Required—TOEFL (minimum score 550 paper-based; 213 computer-based). *Application deadline:* For fall admission, 4/15 for domestic and international students; for spring admission, 11/1 for domestic and international students. Application fee: $55 ($75 for international students). *Expenses:* Tuition, state resident: part-time $812 per credit. Tuition, nonresident: part-time $1,403 per credit. Tuition and fees vary according to program. *Financial support:* In 2007–08, 8 students received support, including research assistantships with full and partial tuition reimbursements available (averaging $10,000 per year), teaching assistantships with full and partial tuition reimbursements available (averaging $6,000 per year); fellowships with partial tuition reimbursements available, career-related internships or fieldwork, institutionally sponsored loans, scholarships/grants, and health care benefits also available. Financial award application deadline: 3/15. *Faculty research:* Motion graphics, graphic design history, interactive design, typography, education. Total annual research expenditures: $50,000. *Unit head:* Prof. Janice Kmetz, Director of Graduate Studies, 218-726-8150, E-mail: jkmetz@d.umn.edu.

University of Minnesota, Twin Cities Campus, Graduate School, College of Liberal Arts, Department of Art, Minneapolis, MN 55455-0213. Offers MFA. *Faculty:* 20 full-time (11 women), 20 part-time/adjunct (11 women). *Students:* 38 full-time (20 women), 1 (woman) part-time; includes 8 minority (3 African Americans, 1 Asian American or Pacific Islander, 4 Hispanic Americans), 4 international. Average age 26. 142 applicants, 13% accepted, 13 enrolled. In 2007, 15 degrees awarded. *Degree requirements:* For master's, oral exam, supporting paper, thesis exhibit. *Entrance requirements:* For master's, portfolio, letters of recommendation, 3.0 GPA. Additional exam requirements/recommendations for international students: Required—TOEFL (minimum score 550 paper-based; 213 computer-based). *Application deadline:* For fall admission, 1/5 for domestic and international students. Application fee: $55 ($75 for international students). Electronic applications accepted. *Financial support:* In 2007–08, 39 students received support, including 13 fellowships (averaging $6,000 per year), 13 teaching assistantships with partial tuition reimbursements available (averaging $6,100 per year); Federal Work-Study, scholarships/grants, health care benefits, tuition waivers (partial), and unspecified assistantships also available. Financial award application deadline: 1/5; financial award applicants required to submit FAFSA. *Faculty research:* Photography as code and symbol, sculpture with an emphasis on multimedia, high-fired salt glazed and utilitarian ceramic earthenware, performance and installations contemporary theory, electronic technology and the human body. Total annual research expenditures: $11,855. *Unit head:* Clarence Morgan, Chair, 612-625-8096, Fax: 612-625-7881, E-mail: morga005@umn.edu. *Application contact:* Alexis Kuhr, Director of Graduate Studies, 612-625-8096, Fax: 612-625-7881.

University of Mississippi, Graduate School, College of Liberal Arts, Department of Art, Oxford, University, MS 38677. Offers art education (MA); art history (MA); fine arts (MFA). *Accreditation:* NASAD (one or more programs are accredited). Part-time programs available. *Faculty:* 12 full-time (8 women), 6 part-time/adjunct (4 women). *Students:* 13 full-time (8 women); includes 3 minority (all African Americans), 2 international. In 2007, 3 degrees awarded. *Degree requirements:* For master's, thesis (for some programs). *Entrance requirements:* For master's, GRE General Test, minimum GPA of 3.0. Additional exam requirements/recommendations for international students: Required—TOEFL. *Application deadline:* For fall admission, 3/1 for domestic students; for spring admission, 10/1 for domestic students. Applications are processed on a rolling basis. Application fee: $25. Electronic applications accepted. *Expenses:* Tuition, state resident: full-time $4,932. Tuition, nonresident: full-time $11,436. *Financial support:* Fellowships, scholarships/grants and unspecified assistantships available. Financial award application deadline: 3/1; financial award applicants required to submit FAFSA. *Unit head:* Dr. Nancy Wicker, Chair, 662-915-7193, Fax: 662-915-5013, E-mail: nwicker@olemiss.edu.

University of Missouri–Columbia, Graduate School, College of Arts and Sciences, Department of Art, Columbia, MO 65211. Offers MFA. *Degree requirements:* For master's, thesis. *Entrance requirements:* For master's, GRE General Test, minimum GPA of 3.0. Additional exam requirements/recommendations for international students: Required—TOEFL (minimum score 530 paper-based; 197 computer-based; 71 iBT), IELTS (minimum score 6).

University of Missouri–Kansas City, College of Arts and Sciences, Department of Art and Art History, Kansas City, MO 64110-2499. Offers art history (MA, PhD); studio art (MA). Part-time programs available. *Faculty:* 11 full-time (5 women), 11 part-time/adjunct (6 women). *Students:* 9 full-time (6 women), 34 part-time (32 women); includes 3 minority (2 African Americans, 1 Asian American or Pacific Islander), 4 international. Average age 32. 23 applicants, 61% accepted, 8 enrolled. In 2007, 8 degrees awarded. Terminal master's awarded for partial completion of doctoral program. *Degree requirements:* For master's, thesis, qualifying exam; for doctorate, thesis/dissertation, exams. *Entrance requirements:* For master's, good general education in the humanities. Additional exam requirements/recommendations for international students: Required—TOEFL. *Application deadline:* For fall admission, 3/1 priority date for domestic and international students; for spring admission, 10/15 for domestic and international students. Applications are processed on a rolling basis. Application fee: $35 ($50 for international students). Electronic applications accepted. *Expenses:* Tuition, state resident: part-time $287 per hour. Tuition, nonresident: part-time $741 per hour. Required fees: $31 per hour. Tuition and fees vary according to program. *Financial support:* In 2007–08, 5 teaching assistantships with partial tuition reimbursements (averaging $12,168 per year) were awarded; fellowships, research assistantships with partial tuition reimbursements, career-related internships or fieldwork, Federal Work-Study, institutionally sponsored loans, and tuition waivers (full and partial) also available. Support available to part-time students. Financial award application deadline: 3/1; financial award applicants required to submit FAFSA. *Faculty research:* Painting, electronic media, Western and non-Western art history, photography. *Unit head:* Dr. Burton Dunbar, Acting Chair, 816-235-2531, Fax: 816-235-5507, E-mail: dunbarb@umkc.edu. *Application contact:* Dr. Rochelle Ziskin, Associate Professor, 816-235-2991, Fax: 816-235-5507, E-mail: ziskinr@umkc.edu.

The University of Montana, Graduate School, School of Fine Arts, Department of Art, Missoula, MT 59812-0002. Offers fine arts (MA, MFA), including art (MA), art history (MA), ceramics (MFA), integrated arts and education (MA), media arts (MFA), painting and drawing (MFA), photography (MFA), printmaking (MFA), sculpture (MFA). *Accreditation:* NASAD (one or more programs are accredited). *Degree requirements:* For master's, thesis exhibit. *Entrance requirements:* For master's, GRE General Test, portfolio.

The University of Montana, Graduate School, School of Fine Arts, Department of Drama/Dance, Missoula, MT 59812-0002. Offers fine arts (MA, MFA), including acting (MFA), design/technology (MFA), directing (MFA), drama (MA), integrated arts and education (MA), media arts (MFA). *Accreditation:* NAST (one or more programs are accredited). *Degree requirements:* For master's, thesis or alternative. *Entrance requirements:* For master's, GRE General Test, audition, portfolio, production notebook.

University of Nebraska–Lincoln, Graduate College, College of Fine and Performing Arts, Department of Art and Art History, Lincoln, NE 68588. Offers MFA. *Accreditation:* NASAD. *Degree requirements:* For master's, thesis. *Entrance requirements:* For master's, slide portfolio. Additional exam requirements/recommendations for international students: Required—TOEFL (minimum score 550 paper-based; 213 computer-based). Electronic applications accepted. *Faculty research:* Classical archaeology, contemporary art, printmaking, photography.

University of Nevada, Las Vegas, Graduate College, College of Fine Arts, Department of Art, Las Vegas, NV 89154-9900. Offers MFA. *Accreditation:* NASAD. Part-time programs available. *Faculty:* 14 full-time (5 women), 4 part-time/adjunct (3 women). *Students:* 13 full-time (6 women); includes 1 minority (Hispanic American), 1 international. 46 applicants, 13% accepted, 5 enrolled. In 2007, 7 degrees awarded. *Degree requirements:* For master's, comprehensive exam, thesis. *Entrance requirements:* For master's, minimum GPA of 3.0, portfolio. Additional exam requirements/recommendations for international students: Required—TOEFL (minimum score 550 paper-based; 213 computer-based; 80 iBT). *Application deadline:* For fall admission, 2/1 for domestic and international students. Application fee: $60 ($75 for international students). Electronic applications accepted. *Expenses:* Tuition, state resident: part-time $198 per credit. Tuition, nonresident: part-time $416 per credit. Required fees: $256 per semester. Tuition and fees vary according to course load and reciprocity agreements. *Financial support:* In 2007–08, 11 research assistantships with partial tuition reimbursements (averaging $10,000 per year), 2 teaching assistantships with partial tuition reimbursements (averaging $10,000 per year) were awarded; career-related internships or fieldwork, Federal Work-Study, institutionally sponsored loans, scholarships/grants, health care benefits, and unspecified assistantships also available. Support available to part-time students. Financial award application deadline: 3/1. *Unit head:* Dr. Thomas Holder, Interim Chair, 702-895-3237. *Application contact:* Graduate College Admissions Evaluator, 702-895-3320, Fax: 702-895-4180, E-mail: gradcollege@unlv.edu.

University of Nevada, Reno, Graduate School, College of Liberal Arts, Department of Fine Arts, Reno, NV 89557. Offers MFA. *Faculty:* 9. *Students:* 5 full-time (2 women); includes 1 minority (Hispanic American) Average age 31. 20 applicants, 15% accepted, 3 enrolled. *Expenses:* Tuition, state resident: full-time $2,774; part-time $154 per credit. Tuition, nonresident: full-time $13,578; part-time $330 per credit. Required fees: $49 per semester. *Unit head:* Tamera Scronce, Head, 775-784-6682.

University of New Hampshire, Graduate School, College of Liberal Arts, Program in Painting, Durham, NH 03824. Offers MFA. Part-time programs available. *Faculty:* 11 full-time (4 women). *Students:* 8 full-time (4 women). Average age 29. 21 applicants, 76% accepted, 4 enrolled. In 2007, 4 degrees awarded. *Degree requirements:* For master's, thesis or alternative. *Entrance requirements:* For master's, slide portfolio. Additional exam requirements/recommendations for international students: Required—TOEFL (minimum score 550 paper-based; 213 computer-based; 80 iBT). *Application deadline:* For fall admission, 4/1 priority date for domestic students, 4/1 for international students. Applications are processed on a rolling basis. Application fee: $60. Electronic applications accepted. *Financial support:* In 2007–08, 2 teaching assistantships were awarded; fellowships, research assistantships, career-related internships or fieldwork, Federal Work-Study, and scholarships/grants also available. Support available to part-time students. Financial award application deadline: 2/15. *Unit head:* Michael McConnell, Chair, 603-862-2190. *Application contact:* Eileen Wang, Information Contact, 603-862-3820, E-mail: mfa.painting@unh.edu.

University of New Mexico, Graduate School, College of Fine Arts, Department of Art and Art History, Program in Studio Arts, Albuquerque, NM 87131-2039. Offers MFA. Part-time programs available. *Faculty:* 19 full-time (12 women), 30 part-time/adjunct (29 women). *Students:* 42 full-time (22 women), 7 part-time (5 women); includes 10 minority (1 African American, 3 American Indian/Alaska Native, 4 Asian Americans or Pacific Islanders, 2 Hispanic Americans), 1 international. Average age 33. 132 applicants, 16% accepted, 14 enrolled. *Degree requirements:* For master's, comprehensive exam, thesis or alternative, studio reviews, qualifying exams. *Entrance requirements:* Additional exam requirements/recommendations for international students: Required—TOEFL (minimum score 550 paper-based; 213 computer-based). *Application deadline:* For fall admission, 1/15 for domestic students. Application fee: $50. Electronic applications accepted. *Financial support:* In 2007–08, 5 research assistantships with tuition reimbursements (averaging $6,700 per year), 40 teaching assistantships with partial tuition reimbursements (averaging $6,700 per year) were awarded; Federal Work-Study, scholarships/grants, health care benefits, and unspecified assistantships also available. Support available to part-time students. Financial award application deadline: 3/1; financial award applicants required to submit FAFSA. *Faculty research:* Photography, painting, drawing, printmaking, sculpture & ceramics, electronic arts, land arts. *Unit head:* Dr. Joyce Szabo, Graduate Director, 505-277-5861, Fax: 505-277-5955, E-mail: szabo@unm.edu. *Application contact:* Kat Heatherington, Graduate Advisor, 505-277-6672, Fax: 505-277-5955, E-mail: art255@unm.edu.

University of New Orleans, Graduate School, College of Liberal Arts, Department of Fine Arts, New Orleans, LA 70148. Offers MFA. *Accreditation:* NASAD. *Students:* 15 (11 women). Average age 35. In 2007, 1 degree awarded. *Degree requirements:* For master's, thesis. *Entrance requirements:* For master's, GRE General Test, slide review. Additional exam requirements/recommendations for international students: Required—TOEFL (minimum score 550 paper-based; 213 computer-based; 79 iBT). *Application deadline:* For fall admission, 7/1 priority date for domestic students, 6/1 for international students; for spring admission, 11/15 priority date for domestic students, 10/1 for international students. Applications are processed on a rolling basis. Application fee: $40. Electronic applications accepted. *Financial support:* Research assistantships, teaching assistantships, Federal Work-Study and institutionally sponsored loans available. Financial award application deadline: 5/15; financial award applicants required to submit FAFSA. *Faculty research:* Large-scale painting and sculpture, black-and-white and color photography, computer graphics. *Unit head:* Dr. A. Lawrence Jenkens, Chairperson, 504-280-6411, Fax: 504-280-7346. *Application contact:* Jim Richard, Graduate Coordinator, 504-280-7367, E-mail: finearts@uno.edu.

The University of North Carolina at Chapel Hill, Graduate School, College of Arts and Sciences, Department of Art, Studio Art Program, Chapel Hill, NC 27599. Offers MFA. *Degree requirements:* For master's, variable foreign language requirement. *Entrance requirements:*

For master's, minimum GPA of 3.0, portfolio. Electronic applications accepted. *Faculty research:* Environmental installation, painting, photography, mixed media, printmaking.

The University of North Carolina at Greensboro, Graduate School, College of Arts and Sciences, Department of Art, Greensboro, NC 27412-5001. Offers studio arts (MFA). *Faculty:* 19 full-time (10 women), 5 part-time/adjunct (3 women). *Students:* 16 full-time (8 women); includes 5 minority (1 African American, 2 Asian Americans or Pacific Islanders, 2 Hispanic Americans). 44 applicants, 18% accepted. *Degree requirements:* For master's, thesis (for some programs). *Entrance requirements:* For master's, GRE General Test, 39 hours of course work in studio art, 15 hours of course work in art history, portfolio. Additional exam requirements/recommendations for international students: Required—TOEFL. *Application deadline:* For fall admission, 2/16 for domestic students. Electronic applications accepted. *Financial support:* Fellowships with full tuition reimbursements, research assistantships with full tuition reimbursements, teaching assistantships with full tuition reimbursements available. Financial award applicants required to submit FAFSA. *Unit head:* Patricia Wasserboehr, Head, 336-334-5248, Fax: 336-334-5270, E-mail: p_wasser@uncg.edu. *Application contact:* Michelle Harkleroad, Director of Graduate Admissions, 336-334-4884, Fax: 336-334-4424, E-mail: mbharkle@uncg.edu.

University of North Dakota, Graduate School, College of Arts and Sciences, Department of Visual Arts, Grand Forks, ND 58202. Offers MFA. *Accreditation:* NASAD. *Faculty:* 9 full-time (3 women). *Students:* 3 full-time (0 women), 10 part-time (2 women); includes 1 minority (African American), 3 international. 9 applicants, 11% accepted, 1 enrolled. In 2007, 2 degrees awarded. *Degree requirements:* For master's, thesis or alternative, comprehensive evaluation, professional exhibition. *Entrance requirements:* For master's, minimum GPA of 3.0. Additional exam requirements/recommendations for international students: Required—TOEFL (minimum score 550 paper-based; 213 computer-based; 79 iBT), IELTS (minimum score 7). *Application deadline:* For fall admission, 2/15 priority date for domestic and international students; for spring admission, 10/15 priority date for domestic and international students. Applications are processed on a rolling basis. Application fee: $35. Electronic applications accepted. *Expenses:* Tuition, state resident: full-time $4,050; part-time $225 per credit. Tuition, nonresident: full-time $10,818; part-time $601 per credit. Required fees: $110 per semester. Tuition and fees vary according to class time, campus/location, program and reciprocity agreements. *Financial support:* In 2007–08, 1 research assistantship (averaging $10,413 per year), 5 teaching assistantships with full tuition reimbursements (averaging $10,413 per year) were awarded; fellowships with full and partial tuition reimbursements, Federal Work-Study, institutionally sponsored loans, scholarships/grants, health care benefits, tuition waivers (full and partial), and unspecified assistantships also available. Support available to part-time students. Financial award application deadline: 3/15; financial award applicants required to submit FAFSA. *Faculty research:* Ceramics, drawing, metalsmithing, printmaking, painting. *Unit head:* Dr. Anita Monsebroten, Graduate Director, 701-777-2257, Fax: 701-777-2903, E-mail: anita_monsebroten@und.nodak.edu.

University of Northern Colorado, Graduate School, College of Performing and Visual Arts, School of Visual Arts, Greeley, CO 80639. Offers visual arts (MA). Part-time programs available. *Faculty:* 5 full-time (3 women). *Students:* 3 full-time (all women), 8 part-time (6 women); includes 1 minority (American Indian/Alaska Native), 1 international. Average age 38. 3 applicants, 33% accepted, 1 enrolled. In 2007, 4 degrees awarded. *Degree requirements:* For master's, comprehensive exam, thesis. *Entrance requirements:* For master's, GRE General Test, portfolio, 3 letters of recommendation, minimum undergraduate GPA of 3.0. *Application deadline:* Applications are processed on a rolling basis. Application fee: $50 ($60 for international students). Electronic applications accepted. *Expenses:* Tuition, state resident: part-time $222 per credit. Tuition, nonresident: part-time $627 per credit. Required fees: $36 per credit. *Financial support:* In 2007–08, 3 research assistantships (averaging $2,458 per year) were awarded; fellowships, teaching assistantships, unspecified assistantships also available. Financial award application deadline: 3/1; financial award applicants required to submit FAFSA. *Unit head:* Dr. Dennis Morimoto, Director, 970-351-2143, Fax: 970-351-2299.

University of Northern Iowa, Graduate College, College of Humanities and Fine Arts, Department of Art, Cedar Falls, IA 50614. Offers art (MA); art education (MA). *Accreditation:* NASAD. Part-time and evening/weekend programs available. *Students:* 5 full-time (3 women), 3 part-time (2 women). 6 applicants, 33% accepted, 1 enrolled. In 2007, 1 degree awarded. *Degree requirements:* For master's, comprehensive exam (for some programs), thesis or alternative. *Entrance requirements:* For master's, minimum GPA of 3.0, portfolio. Additional exam requirements/recommendations for international students: Required—TOEFL (minimum score 500 paper-based; 180 computer-based; 61 iBT). *Application deadline:* For fall admission, 8/1 priority date for domestic students. Applications are processed on a rolling basis. Application fee: $30 ($50 for international students). Electronic applications accepted. *Expenses:* Tuition, state resident: full-time $6,246; part-time $694 per credit hour. Tuition, nonresident: full-time $14,554; part-time $694 per credit hour. Required fees: $838; $119 per semester. *Financial support:* Career-related internships or fieldwork, Federal Work-Study, scholarships/grants, and tuition waivers (full and partial) available. Support available to part-time students. Financial award application deadline: 2/1. *Unit head:* Dr. Jeffery Byrd, Acting Head, 319-273-2077, Fax: 319-273-7333, E-mail: jeffery.byrd@uni.edu.

University of North Texas, Robert B. Toulouse School of Graduate Studies, College of Visual Arts and Design, Department of Studio Art, Denton, TX 76203. Offers MFA. *Faculty:* 25 full-time (10 women). *Students:* 40 full-time (25 women), 11 part-time (7 women); includes 8 minority (3 African Americans, 5 Hispanic Americans), 3 international. 51 applicants, 35% accepted, 11 enrolled. In 2007, 14 degrees awarded. *Degree requirements:* For master's, MFA exhibition, extended artists statement disk of 20 images from MFA show, MFA committee approval. *Entrance requirements:* For master's, GRE, 2 letters of recommendation, statement of intent, portfolio of 20 works, transcripts. Additional exam requirements/recommendations for international students: Recommended—TOEFL (minimum score 550 paper-based; 213 computer-based). *Application deadline:* For fall admission, 7/15 for domestic students; for spring admission, 11/15 for domestic students. Application fee: $50 ($75 for international students). *Financial support:* In 2007–08, 6 students received support, including 8 fellowships with tuition reimbursements available (averaging $4,800 per year), 60 teaching assistantships with tuition reimbursements available (averaging $4,600 per year); unspecified assistantships also available. Financial award application deadline: 1/15. *Faculty research:* Altered terrain, enameling on metal, electrical and mechanical interactivity, interactive animation. *Unit head:* Jerry Austin, Head, 940-369-7671, E-mail: jaustin@unt.edu.

University of Notre Dame, Graduate School, College of Arts and Letters, Division of Humanities, Department of Art, Art History, and Design, Notre Dame, IN 46556. Offers art history (MA); design (MFA), including graphic design, industrial design; studio art (MFA), including ceramics, painting, photography, printmaking, sculpture. *Accreditation:* NASAD. *Faculty:* 19 full-time (6 women), 3 part-time/adjunct (1 woman). *Students:* 25 full-time (12 women), 1 (woman) part-time; includes 4 minority (1 African American, 1 Asian American or Pacific Islander, 2 Hispanic Americans), 1 international. 85 applicants, 14% accepted, 10 enrolled. In 2007, 7 degrees awarded. *Degree requirements:* For master's, comprehensive exam, thesis. *Entrance requirements:* For master's, GRE General Test, minimum GPA of 3.0. Additional exam requirements/recommendations for international students: Required—TOEFL (minimum score 600 paper-based; 250 computer-based; 80 iBT). *Application deadline:* For fall admission, 2/1 priority date for domestic and international students. Application fee: $50. Electronic applications accepted. *Financial support:* In 2007–08, 20 students received support, including fellowships with full tuition reimbursements available (averaging $12,000 per year), research assistantships with full tuition reimbursements available (averaging $12,000 per year), 15 teaching assistantships with full tuition reimbursements available (averaging $12,000 per year); scholarships/grants, tuition waivers (full), and unspecified assistantships also available. Financial award application deadline: 2/1. *Faculty research:* Studio art practice in ceramics, printing, photography, printmaking and sculpture, graphic design and industrial design, digital imaging in design and photography, Renaissance and American art history, contemporary art theory and criticism. *Unit head:* Prof. Jean Dibble, Director of Graduate Studies, 574-631-7602, E-mail: art.1@nd.edu. *Application contact:* Dr. Jarren Gonzales, Director of Graduate Admissions, 574-631-7706, Fax: 574-631-4183.

University of Oklahoma, Graduate College, College of Fine Arts, School of Art and Art History, Norman, OK 73019-0390. Offers art (MA, MFA); art history (MA, MFA); ceramics (MFA); film and video (MFA); painting (MFA); photography (MFA); printmaking (MFA); visual communications (MFA). *Faculty:* 26 full-time (11 women), 1 part-time/adjunct (0 women). *Students:* 21 full-time (13 women), 10 part-time (9 women); includes 6 minority (1 African American, 5 American Indian/Alaska Native), 2 international. 24 applicants, 50% accepted, 7 enrolled. In 2007, 4 degrees awarded. *Degree requirements:* For master's, thesis (MA), exhibit (MFA), departmental qualifying exam. *Entrance requirements:* For master's, GRE General Test (MA), bachelor's degree in art (MFA) or art history (MA), minimum GPA of 3.0 in last 60 undergraduate hours, 3 letters of recommendation, written research paper. Additional exam requirements/recommendations for international students: Required—TOEFL (minimum score 550 paper-based; 213 computer-based). *Application deadline:* For fall admission, 2/1 priority date for domestic students, 2/1 for international students; for spring admission, 10/1 for domestic and international students. Applications are processed on a rolling basis. Application fee: $40 ($90 for international students). Electronic applications accepted. *Expenses:* Tuition, state resident: full-time $3,451; part-time $144 per credit hour. Tuition, nonresident: full-time $12,432; part-time $518 per credit hour. Required fees: $1,925; $70 per credit hour. $122 per semester. *Financial support:* In 2007–08, 20 students received support, including 8 research assistantships with partial tuition reimbursements available (averaging $9,370 per year), 7 teaching assistantships with partial tuition reimbursements available (averaging $9,450 per year); career-related internships or fieldwork, Federal Work-Study, institutionally sponsored loans, scholarships/grants, health care benefits, tuition waivers (full), and unspecified assistantships also available. Financial award application deadline: 4/7; financial award applicants required to submit FAFSA. Total annual research expenditures: $24,250. *Unit head:* Mary Jo Watson, Associate Dean, 405-325-2691, Fax: 405-325-1668, E-mail: mjwatson@ou.edu. *Application contact:* Heidi Mau, Graduate Liaison, 405-325-2691, Fax: 405-325-1668, E-mail: hmau@ou.edu.

University of Oregon, Graduate School, School of Architecture and Allied Arts, Department of Art, Eugene, OR 97403. Offers MFA. *Accreditation:* NASAD. *Faculty:* 16 full-time (10 women). *Students:* 35 full-time (18 women); includes 3 minority (2 Asian Americans or Pacific Islanders, 1 Hispanic American), 3 international. 114 applicants, 16% accepted. In 2007, 9 degrees awarded. *Degree requirements:* For master's, thesis or alternative. *Entrance requirements:* For master's, BFA or equivalent. Additional exam requirements/recommendations for international students: Required—TOEFL. *Application deadline:* For fall admission, 2/1 for domestic students. Application fee: $50. *Financial support:* In 2007–08, 22 teaching assistantships were awarded; Federal Work-Study also available. *Unit head:* Kathleen Wagle, Head, 541-346-3610. *Application contact:* Bonnie Lawrence, Admissions Contact, 541-346-3618, E-mail: blawrence@uoregon.edu.

University of Pennsylvania, School of Design, Department of Fine Arts, Philadelphia, PA 19104. Offers MFA. *Entrance requirements:* For master's, slide portfolio. Additional exam requirements/recommendations for international students: Required—TOEFL. *Faculty research:* Painting, sculpture, printmaking, combined media.

See Close-Up on page 175.

University of Regina, Faculty of Graduate Studies and Research, Faculty of Fine Arts, Department of Visual Arts, Regina, SK S4S 0A2, Canada. Offers MA, MFA. *Faculty:* 11 full-time (6 women). *Students:* 5 full-time (2 women), 2 part-time (both women). Average age 30. 10 applicants, 40% accepted, 4 enrolled. *Degree requirements:* For master's, exhibition, support paper, oral defense. *Entrance requirements:* For master's, 20 slides of recent work, slide list, BFA or the equivalent. Additional exam requirements/recommendations for international students: Required—TOEFL (minimum score 580 paper-based; 237 computer-based; 88 iBT). *Application deadline:* For fall admission, 2/15 for domestic students. Application fee: $85 ($100 for international students). *Financial support:* In 2007–08, 7 students received support, including 4 fellowships (averaging $15,750 per year), 1 research assistantship (averaging $13,875 per year), 1 teaching assistantship (averaging $13,060 per year); scholarships/grants also available. Financial award application deadline: 6/15. *Faculty research:* Painting, sculpture, ceramics, printmaking, intermedia. *Unit head:* Dr. Alison Hayford, Graduate Program Coordinator, 306-585-5552, Fax: 306-585-5526, E-mail: alison.hayford@uregina.ca.

University of Rochester, The College, Arts and Sciences, Department of Art and Art History, Rochester, NY 14627-0250. Offers visual and cultural studies (MA, PhD). Terminal master's awarded for partial completion of doctoral program. *Degree requirements:* For master's, thesis optional; for doctorate, one foreign language, thesis/dissertation, qualifying exam. *Entrance requirements:* For master's and doctorate, GRE General Test. Additional exam requirements/recommendations for international students: Required—TOEFL.

See Close-Up on page 271.

University of Saint Francis, Graduate School, Department of Art and Visual Communication, Fort Wayne, IN 46808-3994. Offers fine art (MA). *Accreditation:* NASAD. Part-time and evening/weekend programs available. *Faculty:* 9 full-time (6 women), 2 part-time/adjunct (1 woman). *Students:* Average age 38. 8 applicants, 100% accepted. In 2007, 6 degrees awarded. *Degree requirements:* For master's, thesis, exhibit. *Entrance requirements:* For master's, minimum GPA of 3.0 in art, portfolio. *Application deadline:* For fall admission, 7/1 priority date for domestic students; for spring admission, 11/1 priority date for domestic students. Applications are processed on a rolling basis. Application fee: $20. *Financial support:* In 2007–08, 5 students received support. Federal Work-Study, scholarships/grants, and unspecified assistantships available. Financial award applicants required to submit FAFSA. *Unit head:* Rick Cartwright, Dean, 260-434-3235, Fax: 260-434-4604, E-mail: rcartwright@sf.edu. *Application contact:* Michelle Kuhlhorst, Admissions Counselor, 260-434-7748, Fax: 260-434-7590, E-mail: mkuhlhorst@sf.edu.

University of Saskatchewan, College of Graduate Studies and Research, College of Arts and Sciences, Department of Art and Art History, Saskatoon, SK S7N 5A2, Canada. Offers MFA. Part-time programs available. *Degree requirements:* For master's, thesis. *Entrance requirements:* Additional exam requirements/recommendations for international students: Required—TOEFL.

University of South Carolina, The Graduate School, College of Arts and Sciences, Department of Art, Columbia, SC 29208. Offers art education (IMA, MA, MAT); art history (MA); art studio (MA); media arts (MMA); studio art (MFA). *Accreditation:* NASAD. *Faculty:* 38 full-time (16 women), 17 part-time/adjunct (6 women). *Students:* 64 full-time (53 women), 15 part-time (10 women); includes 15 minority (10 African Americans, 4 Asian Americans or Pacific Islanders, 1 Hispanic American). Average age 24. 54 applicants, 50% accepted. In 2007, 28 degrees awarded. *Degree requirements:* For master's, comprehensive exam (for some programs), thesis (for some programs). *Entrance requirements:* For master's, GRE General Test or MAT, portfolio. Additional exam requirements/recommendations for international students: Required—TOEFL. *Application deadline:* For fall admission, 3/1 for domestic students; for spring admission, 11/1 for domestic students. Application fee: $40. Electronic applications accepted. *Expenses:* Tuition, state resident: part-time $440 per hour. Tuition, nonresident: part-time $936 per hour. Required fees: $17 per hour. Tuition and fees vary according to program. *Financial support:* In 2007–08, 10 research assistantships with partial tuition reimbursements (averaging $3,000 per year), 18 teaching assistantships with partial tuition reimbursements (averaging $6,000 per year) were awarded; fellowships, career-related internships or fieldwork, Federal Work-Study, and unspecified assistantships also available. *Faculty research:* Script writing, teaching art at the elementary and secondary levels of education, history of art and architecture. *Unit head:* Dr. Cynthia B. Colbert, Chair, Department of Art, 803-777-4237, Fax: 803-777-0535, E-mail: colbert@sc.edu. *Application contact:* Ben Truesdale, Graduate Studies Admissions Specialist, 803-777-6438, Fax: 803-777-0535, E-mail: ben.t@sc.edu.

Art/Fine Arts

The University of South Dakota, Graduate School, College of Fine Arts, Department of Art, Vermillion, SD 57069-2390. Offers MFA. *Accreditation:* NASAD. *Faculty:* 7 full-time (1 woman), 2 part-time/adjunct (1 woman). *Students:* 12 (7 women). In 2007, 5 degrees awarded. *Degree requirements:* For master's, thesis or alternative. *Entrance requirements:* For master's, portfolio, minimum GPA of 2.7. Additional exam requirements/recommendations for international students: Required—TOEFL (minimum score 550 paper-based; 213 computer-based; 79 iBT). *Application deadline:* Applications are processed on a rolling basis. Application fee: $35. Electronic applications accepted. *Financial support:* In 2007–08, research assistantships with partial tuition reimbursements (averaging $4,626 per year), teaching assistantships with partial tuition reimbursements (averaging $4,626 per year) were awarded; Federal Work-Study and unspecified assistantships also available. Support available to part-time students. Financial award applicants required to submit FAFSA. *Unit head:* Cory Knedler, Chair, 605-677-5636, Fax: 605-677-5988, E-mail: cknedler@usd.edu.

University of Southern California, Graduate School, College of Letters, Arts and Sciences, Department of Art History, Los Angeles, CA 90089. Offers art history (MA, PhD); visual studies (Certificate). *Faculty:* 12 full-time (9 women), 7 part-time/adjunct (5 women). *Students:* 36 full-time (31 women); includes 11 minority (6 Asian Americans or Pacific Islanders, 5 Hispanic Americans), 4 international. 56 applicants, 16% accepted. In 2007, 6 master's, 2 doctorates awarded. *Degree requirements:* For doctorate, 2 foreign languages, thesis/dissertation. *Entrance requirements:* For doctorate, GRE General Test. *Application deadline:* For fall admission, 12/1 for domestic students. Application fee: $85. *Financial support:* In 2007–08, 43 students received support, including fellowships (averaging $18,800 per year), teaching assistantships (averaging $18,800 per year); research assistantships, institutionally sponsored loans, scholarships/grants, and tuition waivers (full) also available. Financial award application deadline: 2/1. *Faculty research:* Art and ideology in the early Roman Empire, gender in Renaissance paintings, religious and scientific images in Northern Renaissance paintings. *Unit head:* Dr. Eunice Howe, Head, 213-740-2311.

University of Southern California, Graduate School, School of Fine Arts, Program in Fine Arts, Los Angeles, CA 90089. Offers MFA. *Faculty:* 5 full-time (3 women), 1 part-time/adjunct (0 women). *Students:* 16 full-time (7 women); includes 4 minority (1 African American, 1 American Indian/Alaska Native, 2 Hispanic Americans). Average age 27. 252 applicants, 3% accepted. In 2007, 7 degrees awarded. *Degree requirements:* For master's, thesis. *Application deadline:* For fall admission, 2/1 for domestic students. Application fee: $85. *Financial support:* In 2007–08, 8 students received support; fellowships, research assistantships, teaching assistantships with full and partial tuition reimbursements available available. Financial award application deadline: 2/1. *Unit head:* Charlie White, Head, 213-740-2311. *Application contact:* Audrey Jones, Information Contact, 213-740-2311, Fax: 213-740-8938.

University of South Florida, Graduate School, College of Visual and Performing Arts, School of Art and Art History, Tampa, FL 33620-9951. Offers art history (MA); studio art (MFA). *Accreditation:* NASAD. *Faculty:* 16 full-time (7 women), 1 part-time/adjunct (0 women). *Students:* 40 full-time (22 women), 7 part-time (6 women); includes 8 minority (1 African American, 3 Asian Americans or Pacific Islanders, 4 Hispanic Americans), 2 international. 59 applicants, 41% accepted, 18 enrolled. In 2007, 14 degrees awarded. *Degree requirements:* For master's, thesis, 1 foreign language (MA). *Entrance requirements:* For master's, GRE General Test (MA), minimum GPA of 3.0 in last 60 hours of coursework. *Application deadline:* For fall admission, 1/15 for domestic and international students. Application fee: $30. *Financial support:* In 2007–08, 8 fellowships with full tuition reimbursements (averaging $7,640 per year), 34 teaching assistantships with full and partial tuition reimbursements (averaging $4,486 per year) were awarded; career-related internships or fieldwork, Federal Work-Study, scholarships/grants, health care benefits, and unspecified assistantships also available. Financial award application deadline: 2/15. *Faculty research:* Contemporary art and role of the artist, identity strategies, political iconography, art practice and technology, construction of race in art. Total annual research expenditures: $33,916. *Unit head:* Prof. Wallace Wilson, Director, 813-974-2360, Fax: 813-974-9226, E-mail: wilson@arts.usf.edu. *Application contact:* Richard Olinger, Academic Advisor, 813-974-3160, Fax: 813-974-4165, E-mail: olinger@arts.usf.edu.

The University of Tennessee, Graduate School, College of Arts and Sciences, School of Art, Knoxville, TN 37996. Offers ceramics (MFA); drawing (MFA); graphic design (MFA); inter-area studies (MFA); media arts (MFA); painting (MFA); printmaking (MFA); sculpture (MFA); watercolor (MFA). *Accreditation:* NASAD. *Degree requirements:* For master's, thesis or alternative, exhibit. *Entrance requirements:* For master's, portfolio, minimum GPA of 2.7. Additional exam requirements/recommendations for international students: Required—TOEFL. Electronic applications accepted.

The University of Texas at Arlington, Graduate School, College of Liberal Arts, Department of Fine Arts, Arlington, TX 76019. Offers MFA. Part-time and evening/weekend programs available. *Students:* 4 full-time (1 woman), 1 (woman) part-time; includes 3 minority (1 American Indian/Alaska Native, 2 Hispanic Americans). 11 applicants, 55% accepted, 6 enrolled. *Degree requirements:* For master's, thesis or alternative. *Entrance requirements:* Additional exam requirements/recommendations for international students: Required—TOEFL (minimum score 550 paper-based; 213 computer-based). *Expenses:* Tuition, state resident: full-time $5,934. Tuition, nonresident: full-time $10,938. *Financial support:* In 2007–08, 1 fellowship (averaging $1,000 per year), 2 research assistantships (averaging $9,000 per year) were awarded. *Unit head:* Dr. Robert Hower, Professor, 817-272-2891, E-mail: hower@uta.edu. *Application contact:* Dr. Nancy Palmieri, Associate Professor, 817-272-2891, E-mail: palmieri@uta.edu.

The University of Texas at Austin, Graduate School, College of Fine Arts, Department of Art and Art History, Program in Studio Art, Austin, TX 78712-1111. Offers MFA. *Accreditation:* NASAD. *Degree requirements:* For master's, thesis, oral exam. *Entrance requirements:* For master's, minimum GPA of 3.0, portfolio of 15 slides. Electronic applications accepted. *Faculty research:* Painting, sculpture, transmedia, photography, printmaking.

The University of Texas at El Paso, Graduate School, College of Liberal Arts, Department of Art, El Paso, TX 79968-0001. Offers MA. Part-time and evening/weekend programs available. *Degree requirements:* For master's, thesis optional. *Entrance requirements:* For master's, minimum GPA of 3.0. Additional exam requirements/recommendations for international students: Required—TOEFL. Electronic applications accepted.

The University of Texas at San Antonio, College of Liberal and Fine Arts, Department of Art and Art History, San Antonio, TX 78249-0617. Offers art history (MA); studio art (MFA). *Accreditation:* NASAD (one or more programs are accredited). *Faculty:* 9 full-time (2 women), 2 part-time/adjunct (0 women). *Students:* 29 full-time (15 women), 10 part-time (7 women); includes 17 minority (all Hispanic Americans), 2 international. Average age 32. 33 applicants, 55% accepted, 17 enrolled. In 2007, 9 degrees awarded. *Degree requirements:* For master's, comprehensive exam, thesis. *Entrance requirements:* For master's, GRE General Test, portfolio, minimum GPA of 3.0 in last 60 hours, 3 letters of recommendation. Additional exam requirements/recommendations for international students: Required—TOEFL (minimum score 500 paper-based; 173 computer-based). *Application deadline:* For fall admission, 7/1 for domestic students, 4/1 for international students; for spring admission, 11/1 for domestic students, 9/1 for international students. Applications are processed on a rolling basis. Application fee: $45 ($80 for international students). Electronic applications accepted. *Financial support:* In 2007–08, 7 research assistantships (averaging $2,977 per year), 1 teaching assistantship (averaging $5,350 per year) were awarded; career-related internships or fieldwork, Federal Work-Study, institutionally sponsored loans, scholarships/grants, tuition waivers (partial), and unspecified assistantships also available. Support available to part-time students. *Faculty research:* Wide variety of artistic production in all media, art history and criticism, focusing on American and Hispanic art. Total annual research expenditures: $7,031. *Unit head:* Kent T. Rush, Chair, 210-458-4362, Fax: 210-458-4356, E-mail: kent.rush@utsa.edu. *Application contact:* Ken Little, Graduate Advisor, 210-458-4352, Fax: 210-458-4356, E-mail: klittle@utsa.edu.

The University of Texas at Tyler, College of Arts and Sciences, Department of Art, Tyler, TX 75799-0001. Offers MA, MAIS, MFA. *Faculty:* 6 full-time (2 women), 2 part-time/adjunct (1 woman). *Students:* 2 full-time (0 women), 4 part-time (1 woman); includes 1 minority (Asian American or Pacific Islander) Average age 37. 3 applicants, 1 enrolled. *Degree requirements:* For master's, thesis, graduate committee review. *Entrance requirements:* For master's, GRE General Test, minimum GPA of 3.0. *Application deadline:* Applications are processed on a rolling basis. Application fee: $0. *Expenses:* Tuition, state resident: part-time $627 per semester hour. Tuition, nonresident: part-time $908 per semester hour. Required fees: $107 per semester hour. Tuition and fees vary according to course load. *Financial support:* Application deadline: 7/1; *Faculty research:* Classical myths in contemporary art, social issues in contemporary art, casting methods, Renaissance art. *Unit head:* Gary Hatcher, Chair, 903-566-7486, Fax: 903-566-7062, E-mail: ghatcher@mail.uttyl.edu. *Application contact:* Pam Morrow, Assistant to Dean for Enrollment Management, 903-566-7205, Fax: 903-566-7068, E-mail: pmorrow@uttyler.edu.

The University of Texas–Pan American, College of Arts and Humanities, Department of Art, Edinburg, TX 78541-2999. Offers MFA. Part-time programs available. *Degree requirements:* For master's, thesis, thesis show of artwork. *Entrance requirements:* For master's, bachelor's degree in fine arts, portfolio, 3 letters of reference. *Faculty research:* Creative art, ceramics, painting, sculpture, computer art.

The University of the Arts, College of Art and Design, Department of Book Arts/Printmaking, Philadelphia, PA 19102-4944. Offers MFA. *Accreditation:* NASAD. Part-time programs available. *Degree requirements:* For master's, thesis. *Entrance requirements:* For master's, portfolio. Additional exam requirements/recommendations for international students: Required—TOEFL (minimum score 550 paper-based; 213 computer-based).

See Close-Up on page 273.

The University of the Arts, College of Art and Design, Program in Ceramics, Philadelphia, PA 19102-4944. Offers MFA. Offered during summer only. *Accreditation:* NASAD. Part-time programs available. *Degree requirements:* For master's, thesis, summer residency. *Entrance requirements:* For master's, portfolio. Additional exam requirements/recommendations for international students: Required—TOEFL (minimum score 550 paper-based; 213 computer-based). Electronic applications accepted.

See Close-Up on page 273.

The University of the Arts, College of Art and Design, Program in Painting, Philadelphia, PA 19102-4944. Offers MFA. Offered during summer only. *Accreditation:* NASAD. Part-time programs available. *Degree requirements:* For master's, thesis, summer residency. *Entrance requirements:* For master's, portfolio. Additional exam requirements/recommendations for international students: Required—TOEFL (minimum score 550 paper-based; 213 computer-based).

See Close-Up on page 273.

The University of the Arts, College of Art and Design, Program in Sculpture, Philadelphia, PA 19102-4944. Offers MFA. Offered during summer only. *Accreditation:* NASAD. Part-time programs available. *Degree requirements:* For master's, thesis, summer residency. *Entrance requirements:* For master's, portfolio. Additional exam requirements/recommendations for international students: Required—TOEFL (minimum score 550 paper-based; 213 computer-based).

See Close-Up on page 273.

University of Toronto, School of Graduate Studies, Humanities Division, Department of Art, Toronto, ON M5S 1A1, Canada. Offers art history (MA, PhD); visual studies (MVS). Part-time programs available. *Faculty:* 22 full-time, 8 part-time/adjunct. *Students:* 74 full-time (62 women), 5 part-time, 20 international. 197 applicants, 41% accepted. In 2007, 20 master's, 2 doctorates awarded. *Degree requirements:* For master's, 2 foreign languages, language proficiency exams; for doctorate, 2 foreign languages, comprehensive exam, thesis/dissertation. *Entrance requirements:* For master's, coursework in a foreign language, 3 letters of reference, sample research paper, minimum B+ average in senior art history and/or humanities courses; for doctorate, minimum A– average in senior art history and/or humanities courses, 2 letters of reference, sample research paper. *Application deadline:* For fall admission, 1/15 for domestic students. Application fee: $100 Canadian dollars. *Financial support:* Teaching assistantships available. *Unit head:* Prof. Mark A. Cheetham, Chair, 416-978-7891, Fax: 416-978-1491. *Application contact:* Gaby Binette, Secretary, 416-978-7892, Fax: 416-978-1491, E-mail: gaby.binette@utoronto.ca.

University of Tulsa, Graduate School, College of Arts and Sciences, Department of Art, Tulsa, OK 74104-3189. Offers MA, MFA, MTA. Part-time programs available. *Faculty:* 10 full-time (5 women), 5 part-time/adjunct (3 women). *Students:* 11 full-time (6 women), 1 part-time; includes 1 minority (American Indian/Alaska Native). Average age 39. 7 applicants, 43% accepted, 2 enrolled. In 2007, 2 degrees awarded. *Degree requirements:* For master's, comprehensive exam (for some programs), thesis (for some programs). *Entrance requirements:* For master's, portfolio. Additional exam requirements/recommendations for international students: Required—TOEFL (minimum score 575 paper-based; 231 computer-based; 91 iBT), IELTS (minimum score 7). *Application deadline:* Applications are processed on a rolling basis. Application fee: $40. Electronic applications accepted. *Expenses:* Tuition: Full-time $14,004; part-time $778 per credit hour. Required fees: $60; $30 per term. Tuition and fees vary according to course load. *Financial support:* In 2007–08, 7 students received support, including 7 teaching assistantships with full and partial tuition reimbursements available (averaging $10,734 per year); fellowships with full tuition reimbursements available, research assistantships with full tuition reimbursements available, career-related internships or fieldwork, Federal Work-Study, scholarships/grants, traineeships, tuition waivers (full and partial), and unspecified assistantships also available. Support available to part-time students. Financial award application deadline: 2/1; financial award applicants required to submit FAFSA. *Faculty research:* Drawing, painting, photography, printmaking, ceramics, graphic design. Total annual research expenditures: $5,500. *Unit head:* Dr. Susan Dixon, Chairperson, 918-631-2740, E-mail: susan-dixon@utulsa.edu. *Application contact:* Dr. Whitney Forsyth, Adviser, 918-631-3700, Fax: 918-631-3423, E-mail: whitney-forsyth@utulsa.edu.

University of Utah, The Graduate School, College of Fine Arts, Department of Art and Art History, Salt Lake City, UT 84112-1107. Offers art history (MA); ceramics (MFA); community-based art education (MFA); drawing (MFA); graphic design (MFA); painting (MFA); photography/digital imaging (MFA); printmaking (MFA); sculpture/intermedia (MFA). *Faculty:* 21 full-time (10 women). *Students:* 12 full-time (5 women), 5 part-time (3 women). Average age 31. 36 applicants, 28% accepted, 3 enrolled. In 2007, 7 degrees awarded. *Degree requirements:* For master's, variable foreign language requirement, comprehensive exam (for some programs), thesis or alternative, exhibit (MFA), final project paper. *Entrance requirements:* For master's, CD portfolio (MFA), resumé, letters of recommendation. Additional exam requirements/recommendations for international students: Required—TOEFL (minimum score 575 paper-based; 183 computer-based; 75 iBT). *Application deadline:* For fall admission, 1/2 priority date for domestic and international students. Application fee: $45 ($65 for international students). Electronic applications accepted. *Financial support:* In 2007–08, 1 fellowship, 6 teaching assistantships with partial tuition reimbursements were awarded; research assistantships with tuition reimbursements, Federal Work-Study, institutionally sponsored loans, scholarships/grants, tuition waivers (partial), and unspecified assistantships also available. Financial award application deadline: 1/2; financial award applicants required to submit FAFSA. *Faculty research:* Intermedia, digital arts, installation, traditional media, Asian art, medieval arts. Total annual research expenditures: $21,844. *Unit head:* Dr. Elizabeth A. Peterson, Chair, 801-581-7012, Fax: 801-585-6171, E-mail: elizabeth.peterson@art.utah.edu.

University of Victoria, Faculty of Graduate Studies, Faculty of Fine Arts, Department of Visual Arts, Victoria, BC V8W 2Y2, Canada. Offers digital multimedia (MFA); drawing (MFA); painting (MFA); photography (MFA); sculpture (MFA); video (MFA). *Faculty:* 8 full-time (4 women). *Students:* 10 full-time (7 women), 2 international. Average age 27. 72 applicants, 7% accepted. In 2007, 4 degrees awarded. *Degree requirements:* For master's, exhibit, oral exam. *Entrance requirements:* For master's, portfolio, BFA. Additional exam requirements/recommendations for international students: Required—TOEFL (minimum score 575 paper-based; 233 computer-based), IELTS (minimum score 7). *Application deadline:* For fall admission, 2/28 for domestic students, 12/15 priority date for international students. Applications are processed on a rolling basis. Application fee: $75 ($125 for international students). Electronic applications accepted. *Expenses:* Tuition, state resident: full-time $3,110. International tuition: $3,700 full-time. Tuition and fees vary according to program. *Financial support:* In 2007–08, 10 students received support, including 2 fellowships (averaging $13,400 per year), 7 teaching assistantships (averaging $6,000 per year); research assistantships, institutionally sponsored loans and scholarships/grants also available. Financial award application deadline: 2/15. *Unit head:* Allan Stichbury, Acting Chair, 250-721-8011, Fax: 250-721-6595, E-mail: astichbu@finearts.uvic.ca. *Application contact:* Nedra Tremblay, Graduate Secretary, 250-721-8011, Fax: 250-721-6595, E-mail: ntrembla@finearts.uvic.ca.

University of Washington, Graduate School, College of Arts and Sciences, School of Art, Division of Art and Design, Seattle, WA 98195. Offers art (MFA). *Degree requirements:* For master's, thesis, exhibit. *Entrance requirements:* For master's, BFA or equivalent academic work in art, 20 slide portfolio. Additional exam requirements/recommendations for international students: Required—TOEFL. Electronic applications accepted.

University of Waterloo, Graduate Studies, Faculty of Arts, Department of Fine Arts, Waterloo, ON N2L 3G1, Canada. Offers studio art (MFA). *Faculty:* 7 full-time (2 women), 4 part-time/adjunct (3 women). *Students:* 9. 33 applicants, 27% accepted, 8 enrolled. In 2007, 3 degrees awarded. *Degree requirements:* For master's, thesis exhibit. *Entrance requirements:* For master's, honors degree, minimum A- average, sample of work. Additional exam requirements/recommendations for international students: Required—TOEFL, TWE. *Application deadline:* For fall admission, 3/31 for domestic students. Application fee: $75 Canadian dollars. Electronic applications accepted. *Financial support:* In 2007–08, 4 teaching assistantships (averaging $4,000 per year) were awarded; career-related internships or fieldwork and scholarships/grants also available. Financial award application deadline: 3/31. *Faculty research:* Ceramic sculpture, computer imaging, painting, drawing, contemporary art theory. *Unit head:* Jane G. Buyers, Chair, 519-888-4567 Ext. 32614, Fax: 519-746-4982. *Application contact:* Doug Kirton, Graduate Officer, 519-888-4567 Ext. 33763, Fax: 519-746-4982, E-mail: dkirton@uwaterloo.ca.

University of Windsor, Faculty of Graduate Studies, Faculty of Arts and Social Sciences, School of Visual Arts, Windsor, ON N9B 3P4, Canada. Offers MFA. *Faculty:* 7 full-time (4 women), 1 part-time/adjunct (0 women). *Students:* 9 full-time (4 women). 26 applicants, 27% accepted. In 2007, 4 degrees awarded. *Degree requirements:* For master's, thesis. *Entrance requirements:* For master's, minimum B average, portfolio. Additional exam requirements/recommendations for international students: Required—TOEFL (minimum score 560 paper-based; 220 computer-based). *Application deadline:* For fall admission, 7/1 for domestic students; for winter admission, 11/1 for domestic students; for spring admission, 3/1 for domestic students. Applications are processed on a rolling basis. Application fee: $55. Electronic applications accepted. *Financial support:* In 2007–08, 7 teaching assistantships (averaging $8,901 per year) were awarded; scholarships/grants, tuition waivers (full and partial), and unspecified assistantships also available. Financial award application deadline: 2/15. *Unit head:* Prof. Brenda Francis Pelkey, Head, 519-253-3000 Ext. 2828, Fax: 519-971-3647, E-mail: bjfp@uwindsor.ca. *Application contact:* Applicant Services, 519-253-3000 Ext. 6459, Fax: 519-971-3653, E-mail: gradadmit@uwindsor.ca.

University of Wisconsin–Madison, Graduate School, School of Education, Department of Art, Madison, WI 53706-1380. Offers art (MA, MFA); art education (MA). *Accreditation:* NASAD. *Application deadline:* For fall admission, 1/10 for domestic students. Application fee: $45. Electronic applications accepted. *Financial support:* Fellowships with full tuition reimbursements, research assistantships with full tuition reimbursements, teaching assistantships with full tuition reimbursements, project assistantships available. *Unit head:* Elaine Scheer, Chair, 608-262-1662.

University of Wisconsin–Milwaukee, Graduate School, Peck School of the Arts, Department of Art, Milwaukee, WI 53201-0413. Offers art (MA, MFA); art education (MA, MFA, MS). Part-time programs available. *Faculty:* 19 full-time (10 women). *Students:* 17 full-time (8 women), 6 part-time (4 women), 2 international. 58 applicants, 31% accepted, 7 enrolled. In 2007, 20 degrees awarded. *Degree requirements:* For master's, thesis or alternative. *Application deadline:* For fall admission, 1/1 priority date for domestic students; for spring admission, 9/1 for domestic students. Applications are processed on a rolling basis. Application fee: $45 ($75 for international students). *Expenses:* Tuition, state resident: part-time $530 per credit. Tuition, nonresident: part-time $1,428 per credit. Required fees: $19 per credit. $229 per term. Tuition and fees vary according to course load and program. *Financial support:* In 2007–08, 9 teaching assistantships were awarded; fellowships, research assistantships, career-related internships or fieldwork and unspecified assistantships also available. Support available to part-time students. Financial award application deadline: 4/15. *Unit head:* Marna Brauner, Representative, 414-229-4762, E-mail: marnab@uwm.edu.

University of Wisconsin–River Falls, Outreach and Graduate Studies, College of Arts and Science, Program in Fine Arts, River Falls, WI 54022-5001. Offers MSE. *Unit head:* Lynn Jermal, Coordinator, 715-425-3374.

University of Wisconsin–Superior, Graduate Division, Department of Visual Arts, Superior, WI 54880-4500. Offers art education (MA); art history (MA); art therapy (MA); studio arts (MA). Part-time programs available. *Degree requirements:* For master's, comprehensive exam, exhibit. *Entrance requirements:* For master's, minimum GPA of 2.75, portfolio.

Utah State University, School of Graduate Studies, College of Humanities, Arts and Social Sciences, Department of Art, Logan, UT 84322. Offers MA, MFA. *Degree requirements:* For master's, thesis, exhibit. *Entrance requirements:* For master's, GRE General Test or MAT, minimum GPA of 3.0, slide portfolio of art. Additional exam requirements/recommendations for international students: Required—TOEFL. *Faculty research:* Painting, drawing, sculpture, ceramics, photography.

Virginia Commonwealth University, Graduate School, College of Humanities and Sciences, School of Mass Communications, Program in Media, Art, and Text, Richmond, VA 23284-9005. Offers PhD. *Students:* 18 full-time (12 women), 5 part-time (2 women); includes 4 minority (2 African Americans, 2 Hispanic Americans), 1 international. 33 applicants, 52% accepted, 12 enrolled. *Entrance requirements:* For doctorate, GRE, MA, MAE, or MFA in appropriate field of study (English, art history, studio art, poetry, mass communications); 3 letters of recommendation. *Application deadline:* For fall admission, 3/15 for domestic students. *Expenses:* Tuition, state resident: full-time $7,224; part-time $401 per credit. Tuition, nonresident: full-time $16,072; part-time $891 per credit. Required fees: $1,679; $63 per credit. Tuition and fees vary according to campus/location. *Unit head:* Thom Didato, Director, 804-828-1329, E-mail: tndidato@vcu.edu.

See Close-Up on page 457.

Virginia Commonwealth University, Graduate School, School of the Arts, Richmond, VA 23284-9005. Offers art education (MAE); art history (MA, PhD), including architectural history (MA), art history, historical studies (MA), museum studies (MA); ceramics (MFA); fibers (MFA); furniture design (MFA); glassworking (MFA); graphic design (MFA), including design/visual communications, interior environment, photography and film; jewelry/metalworking (MFA); kinetic imaging (MFA); music (MM), including education; painting (MFA); photography and film (MFA); printmaking (MFA); sculpture (MFA); theatre (MFA), including acting, costume design, directing, pedagogy, scene design/technical theater. Part-time programs available. *Faculty:* 91 full-time (22 women). *Students:* 171 full-time (114 women), 65 part-time (44 women); includes 10 African Americans, 4 Asian Americans or Pacific Islanders, 10 Hispanic Americans, 18 international. 745 applicants, 19% accepted, 93 enrolled. In 2007, 103 master's, 4 doctorates awarded. *Entrance requirements:* For doctorate, GRE General Test. Application fee: $50. *Expenses:* Tuition, state resident: full-time $7,224; part-time $401 per credit. Tuition, nonresident: full-time $16,072; part-time $891 per credit. Required fees: $1,679; $63 per credit. Tuition and fees vary according to campus/location. *Financial support:* Fellowships, teaching assistantships, career-related internships or fieldwork, Federal Work-Study, institutionally sponsored loans, and tuition waivers (full and partial) available. Support available to part-time students. *Unit head:* Dr. Richard E. Toscan, Dean, 804-828-2787, Fax: 804-828-6469, E-mail: rtoscan@vcu.edu.

See Close-Up on page 275.

Washington State University, Graduate School, College of Liberal Arts, Department of Fine Arts, Pullman, WA 99164. Offers ceramics (MFA); digital media (MFA); drawing (MFA); painting (MFA); photography (MFA); print making (MFA); sculpture (MFA). *Faculty:* 16. *Students:* 16 full-time (6 women), 1 part-time; includes 1 minority (American Indian/Alaska Native), 2 international. Average age 29. 33 applicants, 30% accepted, 8 enrolled. In 2007, 8 degrees awarded. *Degree requirements:* For master's, comprehensive exam (for some programs), thesis, exhibit, oral exam. *Entrance requirements:* For master's, GRE, minimum GPA of 3.0, portfolio, 3 letters of recommendation. Additional exam requirements/recommendations for international students: Required—TOEFL (minimum score 550 paper-based; 213 computer-based). *Application deadline:* For fall admission, 1/15 for domestic and international students. Application fee: $50. Electronic applications accepted. *Financial support:* In 2007–08, fellowships with full and partial tuition reimbursements (averaging $3,114 per year), research assistantships with full and partial tuition reimbursements (averaging $13,917 per year), teaching assistantships with full and partial tuition reimbursements (averaging $13,056 per year) were awarded; career-related internships or fieldwork, Federal Work-Study, institutionally sponsored loans, tuition waivers (partial), and unspecified assistantships also available. Financial award application deadline: 4/1; financial award applicants required to submit FAFSA. *Faculty research:* Polynesian art, museum representation, number theory. *Unit head:* Dr. Carol Ivory, Chair, 509-335-7043, Fax: 509-335-7742, E-mail: ivorycs@wsu.edu. *Application contact:* Graduate School Admissions, 800-GRADWSU, Fax: 509-335-1949, E-mail: gradsch@wsu.edu.

Washington University in St. Louis, Sam Fox School of Design and Visual Arts, Graduate School of Art, St. Louis, MO 63130-4899. Offers MFA. *Accreditation:* NASAD. *Faculty:* 20 full-time (8 women), 1 part-time/adjunct (0 women). *Students:* 40 full-time (28 women); includes 3 minority (2 African Americans, 1 Hispanic American), 2 international. Average age 30. In 2007, 14 master's awarded. *Degree requirements:* For master's, thesis. *Entrance requirements:* For master's, portfolio. Additional exam requirements/recommendations for international students: Required—TOEFL (minimum score 550 paper-based; 213 computer-based). *Application deadline:* For fall admission, 1/15 for domestic and international students. Application fee: $75. *Expenses:* Contact institution. *Financial support:* In 2007–08, 39 students received support, including research assistantships with partial tuition reimbursements available (averaging $4,000 per year), teaching assistantships with partial tuition reimbursements available (averaging $4,000 per year); fellowships with partial tuition reimbursements available, Federal Work-Study, institutionally sponsored loans, scholarships/grants, health care benefits, tuition waivers (partial), and unspecified assistantships also available. Financial award application deadline: 2/1; financial award applicants required to submit FAFSA. *Faculty research:* New media, design, fine arts. *Unit head:* Ronald Leax, Dean, 314-935-6500, Fax: 914-935-4862, E-mail: leax@samfox.wustl.edu. *Application contact:* Patricia Olynyk, Director of Graduate Studies, 314-935-5884, Fax: 314-935-8413, E-mail: olynyk@samfox.wustl.edu.

Wayne State University, College of Fine, Performing and Communication Arts, Department of Art and Art History, Program in Art, Detroit, MI 48202. Offers MA, MFA. *Students:* 16 full-time (11 women), 9 part-time (5 women); includes 3 minority (2 Asian Americans or Pacific Islanders, 1 Hispanic American), 5 international. Average age 40. 21 applicants, 24% accepted, 3 enrolled. In 2007, 11 degrees awarded. *Degree requirements:* For master's, thesis (MFA). *Entrance requirements:* Additional exam requirements/recommendations for international students: Required—TOEFL (minimum score 550 paper-based; 213 computer-based); Recommended—TWE (minimum score 6). *Application deadline:* For fall admission, 4/1 for domestic students, 6/1 for international students; for winter admission, 10/1 for international students; for spring admission, 2/1 for international students. Application fee: $30 ($50 for international students). Electronic applications accepted. *Expenses:* Tuition, state resident: part-time $403 per credit hour. Tuition, nonresident: part-time $890 per credit hour. *Faculty research:* Painting, drawing, computer art. *Application contact:* Brian Madigan, Associate Professor, 313-577-2685, E-mail: bmadigan@wayne.edu.

Webster University, Leigh Gerdine College of Fine Arts, Department of Art, St. Louis, MO 63119-3194. Offers art (MA); arts management and leadership (MFA). *Students:* 4 full-time (all women), 7 part-time (3 women); includes 1 minority (African American) Average age 34. In 2007, 4 degrees awarded. *Degree requirements:* For master's, thesis. *Entrance requirements:* For master's, BA or BFA in related field, interview, portfolio. *Application deadline:* Applications are processed on a rolling basis. Application fee: $35 ($50 for international students). *Expenses:* Tuition: Full-time $9,360; part-time $520 per credit. *Financial support:* Federal Work-Study available. Support available to part-time students. Financial award application deadline: 4/1; financial award applicants required to submit FAFSA. *Unit head:* Tom K. Lang, Chairperson, 314-968-7158, Fax: 314-968-7139, E-mail: langrk@webster.edu. *Application contact:* Director of Graduate and Evening Student Admissions, Fax: 314-968-7116, E-mail: gadmit@webster.edu.

Western Carolina University, Graduate School, College of Fine and Performing Arts, Cullowhee, NC 28723. Offers MFA, MM. Part-time programs available. *Faculty:* 23 full-time (13 women), 2 part-time/adjunct (both women). *Students:* 17 full-time (9 women), 4 part-time; includes 3 minority (all American Indian/Alaska Native). Average age 31. 23 applicants, 70% accepted, 12 enrolled. In 2007, 13 degrees awarded. *Degree requirements:* For master's, comprehensive exam, thesis optional. *Entrance requirements:* For master's, GRE, appropriate undergraduate, portfolio, letters of recommendation, letter of intent, live audition and/or interview. Additional exam requirements/recommendations for international students: Required—TOEFL (minimum score 550 paper-based; 270 computer-based; 79 iBT). *Application deadline:* For fall admission, 3/1 for domestic students. Applications are processed on a rolling basis. Application fee: $40. *Expenses:* Tuition, state resident: full-time $2,314. Tuition, nonresident: full-time $11,899. Required fees: $2,033. Tuition and fees vary according to course load. *Financial support:* In 2007–08, 15 students received support, including 3 research assistantships with full and partial tuition reimbursements available (averaging $7,000 per year), 12 teaching assistantships with full and partial tuition reimbursements available (averaging $7,417 per year); fellowships, career-related internships or fieldwork, institutionally sponsored loans, scholarships/grants, and unspecified assistantships also available. Financial award application deadline: 3/31; financial award applicants required to submit FAFSA. *Faculty research:* Vernacular cultural studies and oral history, sound mixing for television, music technology. *Unit head:* Dr. Robert Kehrberg, Dean, 828-227-7028, Fax: 828-227-7707, E-mail: rkehrberg@email.wcu.edu. *Application contact:* Admissions Specialist for Fine and Performing Arts, 828-227-7398, Fax: 828-227-7480, E-mail: gradsch@email.wcu.edu.

Western Connecticut State University, Division of Graduate Studies, School of Visual and Performing Arts, Department of Art, Danbury, CT 06810-6885. Offers illustration (MFA); painting (MFA). *Faculty:* 4 full-time (1 woman), 1 part-time/adjunct (0 women). *Students:* 17 full-time (11 women); includes 3 minority (1 African American, 1 Asian American or Pacific Islander, 1 Hispanic American). Average age 29. 12 applicants, 83% accepted, 9 enrolled. In 2007, 4 degrees awarded. *Degree requirements:* For master's, individual exhibition of artwork.

Art/Fine Arts

Western Connecticut State University (continued)

Entrance requirements: For master's, portfolio review, minimum GPA of 2.5. *Application deadline:* For fall admission, 8/5 priority date for domestic students; for spring admission, 1/5 priority date for domestic students. Application fee: $50. *Expenses:* Tuition, state resident: full-time $4,169. Tuition, nonresident: full-time $11,614. Required fees: $3,278. *Financial support:* Career-related internships or fieldwork available. Support available to part-time students. Financial award application deadline: 5/1; financial award applicants required to submit FAFSA. *Unit head:* Margaret Grimes, Professor, 203-837-8402. *Application contact:* Chris Shankle, Associate Director of Graduate Admissions, 203-837-8244, Fax: 203-837-8338, E-mail: shanklec@wcsu.edu.

West Texas A&M University, College of Fine Arts and Humanities, Department of Art, Communication, and Theater, Program in Art, Canyon, TX 79016-0001. Offers MA. Part-time programs available. *Degree requirements:* For master's, comprehensive exam, thesis optional, exhibit, portfolio review. *Entrance requirements:* For master's, GRE General Test, interview, portfolio. Additional exam requirements/recommendations for international students: Required—TOEFL (minimum score 550 paper-based). Electronic applications accepted. *Faculty research:* Ceramics, graphic design, woodblock prints, art history, aesthetics, glassblowing.

West Texas A&M University, College of Fine Arts and Humanities, Department of Art, Communication, and Theater, Program in Studio Art, Canyon, TX 79016-0001. Offers MFA. Part-time programs available. *Degree requirements:* For master's, comprehensive exam, thesis optional, exhibit, portfolio review, professional paper. *Entrance requirements:* For master's, GRE General Test, interview, portfolio. Additional exam requirements/recommendations for international students: Required—TOEFL (minimum score 550 paper-based). *Faculty research:* Ceramics, printmaking, graphic design, art history, aesthetics, glass blowing.

West Virginia University, College of Creative Arts, Division of Art and Design, Morgantown, WV 26506. Offers art education (MA); art history (MA); ceramics (MFA); graphic design (MFA); painting (MFA); printmaking (MFA); sculpture (MFA); studio art (MA). *Accreditation:* NASAD. *Faculty:* 17 full-time (7 women), 6 part-time/adjunct (0 women). *Students:* 21 full-time (11 women), 3 part-time (all women), 2 international. Average age 29. 49 applicants, 22% accepted, 7 enrolled. In 2007, 11 degrees awarded. *Degree requirements:* For master's, thesis, exhibit. *Entrance requirements:* For master's, minimum GPA of 2.75, portfolio. Additional exam requirements/recommendations for international students: Required—TOEFL. *Application deadline:* For fall admission, 3/1 for domestic students, 2/15 for international students; for spring admission, 10/15 for domestic and international students. Application fee: $45. *Expenses:* Contact institution. Tuition and fees vary according to program. *Financial support:* In 2007–08, 22 students received support, including 11 teaching assistantships with full tuition reimbursements available; research assistantships with full tuition reimbursements available, Federal Work-Study, institutionally sponsored loans, tuition waivers (full and partial), and graduate administrative assistantships also available. Financial award application deadline: 3/15; financial award applicants required to submit FAFSA. *Faculty research:* Medieval art history. Total annual research expenditures: $6,000. *Unit head:* Alison Helm, Interim Chair, 304-293-4841 Ext. 3140, Fax: 304-293-3136, E-mail: alison.helm@mail.wvu.edu.

Wichita State University, Graduate School, College of Fine Arts, School of Art and Design, Wichita, KS 67260. Offers art education (MA); studio arts (MFA). *Degree requirements:* For master's, project. *Entrance requirements:* For master's, GRE, BAE or BFA, portfolio. Additional exam requirements/recommendations for international students: Required—TOEFL. Electronic applications accepted.

William Paterson University of New Jersey, College of the Arts and Communication, Department of Art, Wayne, NJ 07470-8420. Offers art (MFA); visual arts (MA). *Accreditation:* NASAD. Part-time and evening/weekend programs available. *Students:* 10 full-time (8 women), 14 part-time (5 women); includes 5 minority (2 African Americans, 1 Asian American or Pacific Islander, 2 Hispanic Americans), 1 international. In 2007, 3 degrees awarded. *Degree requirements:* For master's, oral exam, portfolio review, thesis exhibit. *Entrance requirements:* For master's, minimum GPA of 2.75, portfolio, writing sample. *Application deadline:* Applications are processed on a rolling basis. Application fee: $50. Electronic applications accepted. *Financial support:* Research assistantships with tuition reimbursements, career-related internships or fieldwork, Federal Work-Study, and unspecified assistantships available. Support available to part-time students. Financial award application deadline: 4/1; financial award applicants required to submit FAFSA. *Unit head:* Dr. James Brown, Program Director, 973-720-3278. *Application contact:* Danielle Liautaud, Director, 973-720-3579, Fax: 973-720-2035, E-mail: liautaudd@wpunj.edu.

Winthrop University, College of Visual and Performing Arts, Department of Art, Rock Hill, SC 29733. Offers art (MFA); art administration (MA); art education (MA). *Accreditation:* NASAD. Part-time programs available. *Faculty:* 17 full-time (7 women), 7 part-time/adjunct (4 women). *Students:* 7 full-time (5 women), 26 part-time (21 women); includes 1 minority (American Indian/Alaska Native). Average age 29. In 2007, 4 degrees awarded. *Degree requirements:* For master's, thesis, documented exhibit, oral exam. *Entrance requirements:* For master's, GRE General Test or MAT, PRAXIS (MA), minimum GPA of 3.0, resumé, slide portfolio, teaching certificate (MA). *Application deadline:* For fall admission, 3/1 priority date for domestic students; for spring admission, 9/1 for domestic students. Applications are processed on a rolling basis. Application fee: $50. Electronic applications accepted. *Expenses:* Tuition, state resident: full-time $9,834; part-time $412 per credit hour. Tuition, nonresident: full-time $18,280; part-time $763 per credit hour. *Financial support:* In 2007–08, 5 research assistantships with full tuition reimbursements (averaging $3,600 per year) were awarded; Federal Work-Study, scholarships/grants, and unspecified assistantships also available. Support available to part-time students. Financial award application deadline: 2/1; financial award applicants required to submit FAFSA. *Unit head:* Dr. Tom Stanley, Chair, 803-323-2653, E-mail: stanleyt@winthrop.edu. *Application contact:* 800-411-7041, Fax: 803-323-2292, E-mail: graduatestu@winthrop.edu.

Yale University, School of Art, New Haven, CT 06520. Offers graphic design (MFA); painting/printmaking (MFA); photography (MFA); sculpture (MFA). *Faculty:* 11 full-time (3 women), 102 part-time/adjunct (48 women). *Students:* 119 full-time (57 women); includes 19 minority (5 African Americans, 6 Asian Americans or Pacific Islanders, 8 Hispanic Americans), 22 international. Average age 27. 1,218 applicants, 5% accepted, 57 enrolled. In 2007, 56 degrees awarded. *Degree requirements:* For master's, thesis (for some programs). *Entrance requirements:* Additional exam requirements/recommendations for international students: Required—TOEFL (minimum score 550 paper-based; 250 computer-based; 100 iBT). *Application deadline:* For fall admission, 1/7 for domestic and international students. Application fee: $90. *Expenses:* Contact institution. *Financial support:* In 2007–08, 90 students received support, including 56 teaching assistantships (averaging $1,600 per year); Federal Work-Study and scholarships/grants also available. Financial award application deadline: 3/1; financial award applicants required to submit FAFSA. *Unit head:* Robert Storr, Dean, 203-432-2606. *Application contact:* Patricia Ann DeChiara, Director of Academic Affairs, 203-432-2600, E-mail: artschool.info@yale.edu.

York University, Faculty of Graduate Studies, Faculty of Fine Arts, Program in Visual Arts, Toronto, ON M3J 1P3, Canada. Offers MFA, PhD. *Degree requirements:* For master's, thesis. *Entrance requirements:* For master's, portfolio. Electronic applications accepted.

Art History

American University, College of Arts and Sciences, Department of Art, Program in Art History, Washington, DC 20016-8001. Offers MA. Part-time programs available. *Students:* 7 full-time (all women), 24 part-time (all women); includes 1 minority (Hispanic American) Average age 28. In 2007, 8 degrees awarded. *Degree requirements:* For master's, one foreign language, comprehensive exam, thesis or alternative. *Entrance requirements:* For master's, GRE, 24 hours of undergraduate course work in art history, portfolio. *Application deadline:* For fall admission, 2/1 priority date for domestic students; for spring admission, 10/1 for domestic students. Application fee: $50. *Expenses:* Tuition: Full-time $19,998; part-time $1,111 per credit hour. Required fees: $380. Tuition and fees vary according to program. *Financial support:* Fellowships, research assistantships with partial tuition reimbursements, teaching assistantships with partial tuition reimbursements, career-related internships or fieldwork, Federal Work-Study, and institutionally sponsored loans available. Support available to part-time students. Financial award application deadline: 1/15. *Faculty research:* Renaissance, twentieth century, American, baroque, rococo. *Application contact:* Glenna K. Haynie, Administrative Coordinator, 202-885-1671.

American University of Puerto Rico, Program in Education, Bayamón, PR 00960-2037. Offers art history (M Ed); elementary education (4-6) (M Ed); elementary education (k-3) (M Ed); general science education (M Ed); physical education (k-12) (M Ed); special education at secondary level (transition) (M Ed). *Entrance requirements:* For master's, EXADEP or GRE or MAT, 2 letters of recommendation, minimum GPA of 2.5.

Bard College, Program in History of the Decorative Arts, Design and Culture, Annandale-on-Hudson, NY 12504. Offers MA, PhD. Part-time programs available. *Faculty:* 13 full-time (6 women), 17 part-time/adjunct (8 women). *Students:* 73 full-time (67 women), 23 part-time (19 women). Average age 25. 99 applicants, 37% accepted, 27 enrolled. In 2007, 35 master's, 1 doctorate awarded. *Degree requirements:* For master's, one foreign language, thesis, internship; for doctorate, 2 foreign languages, thesis/dissertation, exams. *Entrance requirements:* For master's, GRE General Test, writing sample, 3 letters of recommendation; for doctorate, GRE General Test, master's thesis or equivalent, 3 letters of recommendation. Additional exam requirements/recommendations for international students: Required—TOEFL. *Application deadline:* For fall admission, 1/15 for domestic and international students. Application fee: $60. *Expenses:* Contact institution. *Financial support:* In 2007–08, 53 students received support, including 20 fellowships with tuition reimbursements available, 3 research assistantships, 2 teaching assistantships; career-related internships or fieldwork, Federal Work-Study, scholarships/grants, health care benefits, and unspecified assistantships also available. Financial award application deadline: 1/15; financial award applicants required to submit FAFSA. *Unit head:* Susan Weber Soros, Director, 212-501-3000, Fax: 212-501-3079. *Application contact:* Elena Pinto Simon, Dean, Academic Administration and Student Affairs, 212-501-3057, Fax: 212-501-3065, E-mail: simon@bgc.bard.edu.

Bard Graduate Center for Studies in the Decorative Arts, Design, and Culture, Program in History of the Decorative Arts, Design and Culture, New York, NY 10024-3602. Offers MA, PhD. Bard Graduate Center for Studies in the Decorative Arts is a unit of Bard College. Part-time programs available. *Faculty:* 13 full-time (6 women), 17 part-time/adjunct (8 women). *Students:* 73 full-time (67 women), 23 part-time (19 women). Average age 25. 99 applicants, 37% accepted, 27 enrolled. In 2007, 35 master's, 1 doctorate awarded. *Degree requirements:* For master's, one foreign language, thesis, internship; for doctorate, 2 foreign languages, thesis/dissertation, exams. *Entrance requirements:* For master's, GRE General Test, writing sample, 3 letters of recommendation; for doctorate, GRE General Test, master's thesis or equivalent, 3 letters of recommendation. Additional exam requirements/recommendations for international students: Required—TOEFL. *Application deadline:* For fall admission, 1/15 for domestic and international students. Application fee: $60. *Expenses:* Tuition: Full-time $24,570; part-time $910 per credit. Required fees: $150 per semester. Tuition and fees vary according to degree level. *Financial support:* In 2007–08, 53 students received support, including 20 fellowships with tuition reimbursements available, 3 research assistantships, 2 teaching assistantships; career-related internships or fieldwork, Federal Work-Study, scholarships/grants, health care benefits, and unspecified assistantships also available. Financial award application deadline: 1/15; financial award applicants required to submit FAFSA. *Faculty research:* English craftsmen, ancient furniture, aesthetics and politics, Art Nouveau jewelry, European sculpture. *Unit head:* Susan Weber Soros, Director, 212-501-3000, Fax: 212-501-3079. *Application contact:* Elena Pinto Simon, Dean, Academic Administration and Student Affairs, 212-501-3057, Fax: 212-501-3065, E-mail: simon@bgc.bard.edu.

See Close-Up on page 229.

Boston University, Graduate School of Arts and Sciences, Department of Art History, Boston, MA 02215. Offers art history (MA, PhD); museum studies (Certificate). *Students:* 49 full-time (43 women), 14 part-time (all women); includes 2 minority (both African Americans), 3 international. Average age 33. 160 applicants, 30% accepted, 13 enrolled. In 2007, 18 degrees awarded. Terminal master's awarded for partial completion of doctoral program. *Degree requirements:* For master's, one foreign language, comprehensive exam, thesis; for doctorate, 2 foreign languages, comprehensive exam, thesis/dissertation. *Entrance requirements:* For master's and doctorate, GRE General Test, 3 letters of recommendation; for Certificate, GRE General Test. Additional exam requirements/recommendations for international students: Required—TOEFL (minimum score 600 paper-based; 250 computer-based). *Application deadline:* For fall admission, 1/15 for domestic and international students; for spring admission, 10/15 for domestic and international students. Application fee: $70. *Expenses:* Tuition: Full-time $34,930; part-time $1,092 per credit. Tuition and fees vary according to class time, course level and program. *Financial support:* In 2007–08, 23 students received support, including 2 fellowships (averaging $18,000 per year), 1 research assistantship (averaging $16,500 per year), 6 teaching assistantships with full tuition reimbursements available (averaging $16,500 per year); career-related internships or fieldwork, Federal Work-Study, and unspecified assistantships also available. Support available to part-time students. Financial award application deadline: 1/15; financial award applicants required to submit FAFSA. *Unit head:* Fred S. Kleiner, Chairman, 617-353-2520, Fax: 617-353-3243, E-mail: fsk@bu.edu. *Application contact:* Cheryl Crombie, Administrative Assistant, 617-353-2522, Fax: 617-353-3243, E-mail: ccrombie@bu.edu.

Bowling Green State University, Graduate College, College of Arts and Sciences, School of Art, Bowling Green, OH 43403. Offers 2-D studio art (MA, MFA); 3-D studio art (MA, MFA); art education (MA); art history (MA); computer art (MA); design (MFA); digital arts (MFA); graphics (MFA). *Accreditation:* NASAD. Part-time programs available. *Faculty:* 26 full-time (14 women), 7 part-time/adjunct (2 women). *Students:* 24 full-time (12 women), 3 part-time (all women); includes 1 minority (Asian American or Pacific Islander), 2 international. Average age 33. 59 applicants, 20% accepted, 8 enrolled. In 2007, 11 degrees awarded. *Degree requirements:* For master's, thesis or alternative, final exhibit (MFA). *Entrance requirements:* For master's, GRE General Test (MA), slide portfolio (15-20 slides). Additional exam requirements/recommendations for international students: Required—TOEFL. *Application deadline:* For fall admission, 2/15 for domestic students. Application fee: $30. Electronic applications accepted.

Financial support: In 2007–08, 11 research assistantships with full and partial tuition reimbursements (averaging $8,404 per year), 8 teaching assistantships with full and partial tuition reimbursements (averaging $8,404 per year) were awarded; career-related internships or fieldwork, institutionally sponsored loans, and unspecified assistantships also available. Support available to part-time students. Financial award applicants required to submit FAFSA. *Faculty research:* Computer animation and virtual reality, Spanish still-life painting from 1600 to 1800, art and psychotherapy, Japanese wood-firing techniques in ceramics, non-toxic printmaking technologies. *Unit head:* Dr. Katerina Rüedi Ray, Director, 419-372-8575. *Application contact:* Shawn Morin, Graduate Coordinator, 419-372-7766.

Brigham Young University, Graduate Studies, College of Fine Arts and Communications, Department of Visual Arts, Provo, UT 84602-1001. Offers art education (MA); art history (MA); studio art (MFA). Art education applications accepted biennially. *Accreditation:* NASAD. *Faculty:* 28 full-time (7 women), 2 part-time/adjunct (1 woman). *Students:* 43 full-time (28 women); includes 5 minority (all Asian Americans or Pacific Islanders) Average age 26. 25 applicants, 28% accepted, 7 enrolled. In 2007, 18 degrees awarded. *Degree requirements:* For master's, 2 foreign languages, thesis (art history), selected project (MFA), curriculum project (art education). *Entrance requirements:* For master's, GRE (art history), minimum GPA of 3.0 (MFA, MA in art education), 3.3 (MA in art history), portfolio in slide form (MFA), writing samples (MA in art education, art history). Additional exam requirements/recommendations for international students: Required—TOEFL (minimum score 500 paper-based). *Application deadline:* For fall admission, 2/1 for domestic and international students. Application fee: $50. Electronic applications accepted. *Financial support:* In 2007–08, 31 students received support; research assistantships, teaching assistantships with partial tuition reimbursements available, scholarships/grants and tuition waivers (partial) available. Financial award application deadline: 2/1. *Faculty research:* Methodology-standards-assessment, Medieval architecture, classical/Islamic eighteenth- and nineteenth-century art, Netherlandish art, contemporary art. Total annual research expenditures: $83,932. *Unit head:* Linda A. Sullivan, Chair, 801-422-4429, Fax: 801-422-0695, E-mail: sullivan@byu.edu. *Application contact:* Sharon Lyn Heelis, Secretary, 801-422-4429, Fax: 801-422-0695, E-mail: sharon_heelis@byu.edu.

Brooklyn College of the City University of New York, Division of Graduate Studies, Department of Art, Program in Art History, Brooklyn, NY 11210-2889. Offers MA, PhD. The department offers courses at Brooklyn College that are creditable toward the CUNY doctoral degree (with permission of the executive officer of the doctoral program). Part-time programs available. *Students:* 2 full-time (both women), 16 part-time (13 women); includes 2 minority (both African Americans), 1 international. 18 applicants, 89% accepted, 3 enrolled. In 2007, 2 degrees awarded. *Degree requirements:* For master's, one foreign language, thesis or alternative, 2 publishable papers or thesis. *Entrance requirements:* For master's, bachelor's degree in art, minimum GPA of 3.0, portfolio, interview. Additional exam requirements/recommendations for international students: Required—TOEFL. *Application deadline:* For fall admission, 3/1 priority date for domestic students, 2/1 for international students; for spring admission, 11/1 for domestic students, 10/1 for international students. Applications are processed on a rolling basis. Application fee: $125. Electronic applications accepted. *Financial support:* Career-related internships or fieldwork, Federal Work-Study, institutionally sponsored loans, and scholarships/grants available. Support available to part-time students. Financial award application deadline: 5/1; financial award applicants required to submit FAFSA. *Faculty research:* Contemporary art, ancient Near East art, northern baroque art, nineteenth-century French art, Italian Renaissance art. *Unit head:* Dr. Mona Hadler, Deputy Chairperson, 718-951-5181, E-mail: mhadler@brooklyn.cuny.edu. *Application contact:* Hernan Sierra, Graduate Admissions Coordinator, 718-951-4536, Fax: 718-951-4506, E-mail: grads@brooklyn.cuny.edu.

Brown University, Graduate School, Department of History of Art and Architecture, Providence, RI 02912. Offers AM, PhD. *Degree requirements:* For master's, 2 foreign languages, thesis; for doctorate, 2 foreign languages, thesis/dissertation, oral exam. *Entrance requirements:* For master's, GRE General Test; for doctorate, GRE General Test, MA with distinction.

Brown University, Graduate School, Joukowsky Institute for Archaeology and the Ancient World, Providence, RI 02912. Offers PhD. *Degree requirements:* For doctorate, thesis/dissertation.

Bryn Mawr College, Graduate School of Arts and Sciences, Department of History of Art, Bryn Mawr, PA 19010-2899. Offers MA, PhD. Part-time programs available. *Faculty:* 8. *Students:* 15 full-time (12 women), 19 part-time (18 women); includes 5 minority (4 Asian Americans or Pacific Islanders, 1 Hispanic American), 3 international. 45 applicants, 22% accepted, 4 enrolled. In 2007, 4 master's, 1 doctorate awarded. *Degree requirements:* For master's, 2 foreign languages, thesis; for doctorate, 2 foreign languages, comprehensive exam, thesis/dissertation. *Entrance requirements:* For master's and doctorate, GRE General Test. Additional exam requirements/recommendations for international students: Required—TOEFL (minimum score 600 paper-based; 250 computer-based). *Application deadline:* For fall admission, 1/3 for domestic and international students. Application fee: $30. *Financial support:* Fellowships with full tuition reimbursements, teaching assistantships with partial tuition reimbursements, Federal Work-Study, scholarships/grants, tuition waivers (full and partial), and unspecified assistantships available. Support available to part-time students. Financial award application deadline: 1/3. *Unit head:* Dr. David Cast, Chairman, 610-526-5053, E-mail: dcast@brynmawr.edu. *Application contact:* Lea R. Miller, Secretary, 610-526-5072, Fax: 610-526-5076, E-mail: lrmiller@brynmawr.edu.

See Close-Up on page 231.

California State University, Chico, Graduate School, College of Humanities and Fine Arts, Department of Art and Art History, Program in Art History, Chico, CA 95929-0722. Offers MA. *Accreditation:* NASAD. *Students:* 1 full-time (0 women), 1 (woman) part-time. Average age 45. 3 applicants, 33% accepted, 1 enrolled. *Degree requirements:* For master's, thesis or alternative. *Entrance requirements:* For master's, Two letters of recommendation, Statement of Purpose, Department Application. Additional exam requirements/recommendations for international students: Required—TOEFL (minimum score 550 paper-based; 213 computer-based; 80 iBT), IELTS (minimum score 7). *Application deadline:* For fall admission, 3/1 priority date for domestic students, 3/1 for international students; for spring admission, 9/15 priority date for domestic students, 9/15 for international students. Application fee: $55. *Unit head:* Dr. Cameron Crawford, Graduate Coordinator, 530-898-6860.

California State University, Fullerton, Graduate Studies, College of the Arts, Department of Art, Fullerton, CA 92834-9480. Offers art (MA, MFA), including ceramics (MFA), crafts, creative photography (MFA), design (MFA), drawing and painting, printmaking (MFA), sculpture; art history (MA); design (MA). *Accreditation:* NASAD (one or more programs are accredited). Part-time programs available. *Students:* 50 full-time (20 women), 28 part-time (20 women); includes 19 minority (2 African Americans, 2 American Indian/Alaska Native, 8 Asian Americans or Pacific Islanders, 7 Hispanic Americans), 2 international. Average age 36. 68 applicants, 47% accepted, 23 enrolled. In 2007, 29 degrees awarded. *Degree requirements:* For master's, project or thesis. *Entrance requirements:* For master's, minimum GPA of 2.5 in last 60 units of course work, portfolio. Application fee: $55. *Financial support:* Career-related internships or fieldwork, Federal Work-Study, institutionally sponsored loans, and scholarships/grants available. Support available to part-time students. Financial award application deadline: 3/1. *Unit head:* Larry Johnson, Chair, 714-278-3471. *Application contact:* Al Ching, Adviser, 714-278-3471.

California State University, Los Angeles, Graduate Studies, College of Arts and Letters, Department of Art, Los Angeles, CA 90032-8530. Offers art (MA), including art education, art history, art therapy, ceramics, metals, and textiles, design (MA, MFA), painting, sculpture, and graphic arts, photography; fine arts (MFA), including crafts, design (MA, MFA), studio arts. *Accreditation:* NASAD (one or more programs are accredited). Part-time and evening/weekend programs available. *Faculty:* 7 full-time (3 women). *Students:* 24 full-time (13 women), 59 part-time (42 women); includes 19 minority (2 African Americans, 1 American Indian/Alaska Native, 5 Asian Americans or Pacific Islanders, 11 Hispanic Americans), 16 international. Average age 39. In 2007, 28 degrees awarded. *Degree requirements:* For master's, comprehensive exam, project or thesis. *Entrance requirements:* For master's, portfolio. Additional exam requirements/recommendations for international students: Required—TOEFL. *Application deadline:* For fall admission, 6/30 for domestic students; for spring admission, 2/1 for domestic students. Applications are processed on a rolling basis. Application fee: $55. *Financial support:* Federal Work-Study available. Support available to part-time students. Financial award application deadline: 3/1. *Faculty research:* The artist and the book, conceptual art, ceramic processes, computer graphics, architectural graphics. *Unit head:* Dr. Robert Martin, Chair, 323-343-4010, Fax: 323-343-4045, E-mail: rjmartin@calstatela.edu.

California State University, Northridge, Graduate Studies, College of Arts, Media, and Communication, Department of Art, Northridge, CA 91330. Offers art education (MA); art history (MA); studio art (MA, MFA); visual communications (MA, MFA). *Accreditation:* NASAD. *Faculty:* 23 full-time (11 women), 58 part-time/adjunct (29 women). *Students:* 26 full-time (19 women), 35 part-time (28 women); includes 10 minority (1 American Indian/Alaska Native, 3 Asian Americans or Pacific Islanders, 6 Hispanic Americans), 4 international. Average age 39. 55 applicants, 45% accepted, 16 enrolled. In 2007, 18 degrees awarded. *Application deadline:* For fall admission, 11/30 for domestic students. Application fee: $55. *Financial support:* Application deadline: 3/1. *Unit head:* Prof. Edward Alfano, Chair, 818-677-2242, E-mail: art.dept@csun.edu.

Caribbean University, Graduate School, Bayamón, PR 00960-0493. Offers accounting (MBA); administration and supervision (MA Ed); criminal justice (MA); curriculum and instruction (MA Ed); education (PhD); gerontology (MSN); human resources (MBA); museology, archiving and art history (MA Ed); neonatal pediatrics (MSN); physical education (MA Ed); special education (MA Ed). *Entrance requirements:* For master's, interview, minimum GPA of 2.5.

Carleton University, Faculty of Graduate Studies, Faculty of Arts and Social Sciences, School for Studies in Art and Culture, Program in Art History: Art and its Institutions, Ottawa, ON K1S 5B6, Canada. Offers MA. *Degree requirements:* For master's, thesis. *Entrance requirements:* For master's, honors degree. Application fee: $77. *Unit head:* Ming Tiampo, Graduate Supervisor, 613-520-2600 Ext. 2342, Fax: 613-520-3575, E-mail: ssac@carleton.ca. *Application contact:* Barbara Shannon, Graduate Secretary, 613-520-2600 Ext. 2342, Fax: 613-520-3575, E-mail: ssac@carleton.ca.

Case Western Reserve University, School of Graduate Studies, Department of Art History and Art, Program in Art History, Cleveland, OH 44106. Offers MA, PhD. MA, PhD (art history) offered jointly with the Cleveland Museum of Art. Part-time programs available. *Faculty:* 8 full-time (4 women), 10 part-time/adjunct (5 women). *Students:* 6 full-time (5 women), 23 part-time (19 women), 1 international. Average age 31. 33 applicants, 79% accepted, 10 enrolled. In 2007, 6 master's, 3 doctorates awarded. *Degree requirements:* For master's, one foreign language, thesis or alternative; for doctorate, 2 foreign languages, thesis/dissertation. *Entrance requirements:* For master's, GRE General Test, 2 samples of written work; for doctorate, GRE General Test, 3 samples of written work or MA thesis. Additional exam requirements/recommendations for international students: Required—TOEFL. *Application deadline:* For fall admission, 3/1 priority date for domestic students. Applications are processed on a rolling basis. Application fee: $50. Electronic applications accepted. *Financial support:* Fellowships, research assistantships, teaching assistantships, career-related internships or fieldwork available. Financial award application deadline: 3/1. *Faculty research:* Greek art and architecture, Northern baroque art, Italian baroque sculpture, abstract expressionism, Indian art, nineteenth-century French art, American and Contemporary art. *Application contact:* Debby Tenenbaum, Assistant, 216-368-4118, Fax: 216-368-4681, E-mail: deborah.tenenbaum@case.edu.

Christie's Education, Program in Modern Art, Connoisseurship, and the History of the Art Market, New York, NY 10036. Offers MA. *Faculty:* 5 full-time (4 women), 1 (woman) part-time/adjunct. *Students:* 45 full-time (41 women). In 2007, 45 master's awarded. *Degree requirements:* For master's, one foreign language, thesis. *Entrance requirements:* For master's, GRE, writing sample, 3 letters of recommendation, transcripts from all secondary schools and essay statement. Additional exam requirements/recommendations for international students: Required—TOEFL. *Application deadline:* For fall admission, 1/15 priority date for domestic and international students. Applications are processed on a rolling basis. Application fee: $75. *Financial support:* In 2007–08, 3 research assistantships (averaging $7,000 per year) were awarded. *Unit head:* Dr. Véronique Chagnon-Burke, Director of Studies, 212-355-2545, Fax: 212-355-7370, E-mail: vchagnonburke@christies.edu. *Application contact:* Margaret Conklin, Registrar/Bursar, 212-355-1501 Ext. 302, Fax: 212-355-7370, E-mail: mconklin@christies.edu.

City College of the City University of New York, Graduate School, College of Liberal Arts and Science, Division of the Humanities and Arts, Department of Art, Concentrations in Art History and Museum Studies, New York, NY 10031-9198. Offers art history (MA); museum studies (MA). Part-time programs available. *Students:* 22 applicants, 50% accepted, 8 enrolled. *Degree requirements:* For master's, one foreign language, thesis. *Entrance requirements:* For master's, GRE, minimum GPA of 3.0, portfolio, art history paper. Additional exam requirements/recommendations for international students: Required—TOEFL (minimum score 575 paper-based; 233 computer-based). *Application deadline:* For fall admission, 5/1 for domestic students; for spring admission, 11/1 for domestic students. Application fee: $125. *Financial support:* Fellowships, teaching assistantships, career-related internships or fieldwork, Federal Work-Study, institutionally sponsored loans, and tuition waivers (partial) available. Support available to part-time students. Financial award application deadline: 3/1. *Faculty research:* Egyptian, Greek, medieval, Romanesque, and Ottoman art. *Unit head:* Harriet Senie, Head, 212-650-7430, E-mail: hsenie@ccny.cuny.edu.

Cleveland State University, College of Graduate Studies, College of Liberal Arts and Social Sciences, Department of Art, Cleveland, OH 44115. Offers art education (M Ed); art history (MA). *Students:* 1 (woman) full-time, 4 part-time (all women). In 2007, 2 degrees awarded. *Unit head:* Howie Smith, Chair, 212-523-7546, E-mail: art.chair@csuohio.edu.

Columbia University, Graduate School of Arts and Sciences, Division of Humanities, Department of Art History and Archaeology, New York, NY 10027. Offers archaeology (M Phil, MA, PhD); art history and archaeology (M Phil, MA, PhD); modern art (MA). *Faculty:* 24 full-time, 12 part-time/adjunct. *Students:* 217 full-time (160 women), 24 part-time (21 women); includes 21 minority (3 African Americans, 15 Asian Americans or Pacific Islanders, 3 Hispanic Americans), 24 international. Average age 35. 329 applicants, 33% accepted. In 2007, 22 master's, 20 doctorates awarded. *Degree requirements:* For master's, 2 foreign languages, thesis; for doctorate, 3 foreign languages, thesis/dissertation. *Entrance requirements:* For master's and doctorate, GRE General Test. Additional exam requirements/recommendations for international students: Required—TOEFL. Application fee: $90. *Expenses:* Tuition: Part-time $1,452 per credit. Required fees: $152 per term. One-time fee: $75 part-time. Full-time tuition and fees vary according to course level, course load, degree level and program. *Financial support:* Fellowships, teaching assistantships, Federal Work-Study and institutionally sponsored loans available. Support available to part-time students. Financial award application deadline: 1/5; financial award applicants required to submit FAFSA. *Unit head:* Bob Harrist, Chair, 212-854-4505, Fax: 212-854-7329, E-mail: reh23@columbia.edu.

Concordia University, School of Graduate Studies, Faculty of Fine Arts, Department of Art History, Montréal, QC H3G 1M8, Canada. Offers MA, PhD. *Degree requirements:* For master's, one foreign language, thesis. *Entrance requirements:* For master's, BFA or equivalent, minimum B average in major. *Faculty research:* Ancient and modern Canadian art and architecture, Canadian decorative arts, museum studies.

Cornell University, Graduate School, Graduate Fields of Arts and Sciences, Field of History of Art and Archaeology, Ithaca, NY 14853. Offers American art (PhD); ancient art and archaeology (PhD); Asian art (PhD); baroque art (PhD); medieval art (PhD); modern art (PhD); Renaissance art (PhD); Southeast Asian art (PhD); theory and criticism (PhD). *Faculty:* 21 full-

Art History

Cornell University (continued)

time (14 women). *Students:* 22 full-time (17 women); includes 6 minority (2 African Americans, 2 Asian Americans or Pacific Islanders, 2 Hispanic Americans), 6 international. Average age 32. 61 applicants, 15% accepted, 4 enrolled. In 2007, 2 doctorates awarded. *Degree requirements:* For doctorate, one foreign language, comprehensive exam, thesis/dissertation, general exams in 3 areas. *Entrance requirements:* For doctorate, GRE General Test, sample of written work, 3 letters of recommendation. Additional exam requirements/recommendations for international students: Required—TOEFL (minimum score 550 paper-based; 213 computer-based; 77 iBT). *Application deadline:* For fall admission, 1/15 for domestic students. Application fee: $70. Electronic applications accepted. *Financial support:* In 2007–08, 17 students received support, including 10 fellowships with full tuition reimbursements available, 7 teaching assistantships with full tuition reimbursements available; research assistantships with full tuition reimbursements available, institutionally sponsored loans, scholarships/grants, health care benefits, tuition waivers (full and partial), and unspecified assistantships also available. Financial award applicants required to submit FAFSA. *Unit head:* Director of Graduate Studies, 607-255-4905, Fax: 607-255-0566, E-mail: art_history@cornell.edu. *Application contact:* Director of Graduate Studies, 607-255-4905, Fax: 607-255-0566, E-mail: art_history@cornell.edu.

Duke University, Graduate School, Department of Art, Art History and Visual Studies, Durham, NC 27708-0764. Offers PhD. *Faculty:* 15 full-time. *Students:* 33 full-time (27 women); includes 6 minority (3 African Americans, 1 Asian American or Pacific Islander, 2 Hispanic Americans), 10 international. 67 applicants, 19% accepted, 8 enrolled. In 2007, 2 doctorates awarded. *Degree requirements:* For doctorate, thesis/dissertation. *Entrance requirements:* For doctorate, GRE General Test. Additional exam requirements/recommendations for international students: Required—TOEFL (minimum score 550 paper-based; 213 computer-based; 83 iBT), IELTS (minimum score 7). *Application deadline:* For fall admission, 12/15 priority date for domestic and international students. Application fee: $75. Electronic applications accepted. *Financial support:* Fellowships, teaching assistantships available. Financial award application deadline: 12/15. *Unit head:* Gennifer Weisenfeld, Director of Graduate Studies, 919-684-2224, Fax: 919-684-4398, E-mail: lbst@duke.edu.

East Tennessee State University, School of Graduate Studies, College of Arts and Sciences, Department of Art and Design, Johnson City, TN 37614. Offers art education (MA); art history (MA); studio art (MA, MFA). *Accreditation:* NASAD. *Degree requirements:* For master's, thesis, exhibit, oral exam (MFA). *Entrance requirements:* For master's, GRE General Test, portfolio (MFA), bachelor's degree in art, minimum GPA of 3.0. Additional exam requirements/recommendations for international students: Required—TOEFL (minimum score 550 paper-based; 213 computer-based). *Faculty research:* History of sculpture, art and senior citizens, encaustic paintings, digital media in art history.

Emory University, Graduate School of Arts and Sciences, Department of Art History, Atlanta, GA 30322-1100. Offers PhD. *Degree requirements:* For doctorate, 2 foreign languages, comprehensive exam, thesis/dissertation, oral exam. *Entrance requirements:* For doctorate, GRE General Test. Electronic applications accepted.

Fashion Institute of Technology, School of Graduate Studies, Program in Art Market: Principles and Practices, New York, NY 10001-5992. Offers MA. *Accreditation:* NASAD. *Degree requirements:* For master's, one foreign language, thesis, internship. *Entrance requirements:* For master's, GRE General Test, previous course work in art history, 4 semesters of a foreign language. Additional exam requirements/recommendations for international students: Required—TOEFL (minimum score 550 paper-based; 213 computer-based). *Application deadline:* For fall admission, 2/15 priority date for domestic and international students. Applications are processed on a rolling basis. Application fee: $50. Electronic applications accepted. *Expenses:* Tuition, state resident: full-time $7,245; part-time $302 per credit. Tuition, nonresident: full-time $11,466; part-time $478 per credit. Required fees: $440; $35 per term. *Financial support:* Federal Work-Study and scholarships/grants available. Financial award applicants required to submit FAFSA. *Unit head:* Dr. Katherine Michaelsen, Associate Chair, 212-217-4661, Fax: 212-217-5156, E-mail: katherin_michaelsen@fitnyc.edu. *Application contact:* Carole deSantis, Administrative Secretary, Graduate Admissions, 212-217-4314, Fax: 212-217-5156, E-mail: carole_desantis@fitnyc.edu.

See Close-Up on page 113.

Florida State University, Graduate Studies, College of Visual Arts, Theatre and Dance, Department of Art History, Tallahassee, FL 32306. Offers art history (MA, PhD); museum studies (Certificate). *Accreditation:* NASAD. Part-time programs available. *Faculty:* 13 full-time (7 women), 1 (woman) part-time/adjunct. *Students:* 27 full-time (24 women), 22 part-time (18 women); includes 4 minority (1 African American, 2 Asian Americans or Pacific Islanders, 1 Hispanic American). Average age 32. 33 applicants, 70% accepted, 15 enrolled. In 2007, 7 master's, 2 doctorates awarded. Terminal master's awarded for partial completion of doctoral program. *Median time to degree:* Of those who began their doctoral program in fall 1999, 0% received their degree in 8 years or less. *Degree requirements:* For master's, one foreign language, thesis (for some programs), review; for doctorate, 2 foreign languages, comprehensive exam, thesis/dissertation, review. *Entrance requirements:* For master's, GRE General Test, minimum GPA of 3.0; for doctorate, GRE General Test, minimum GPA of 3.5. Additional exam requirements/recommendations for international students: Required—TOEFL. *Application deadline:* For fall admission, 1/5 priority date for domestic and international students. Application fee: $30. Electronic applications accepted. *Expenses:* Tuition, state resident: part-time $248 per credit hour. Tuition, nonresident: part-time $880 per credit hour. Tuition and fees vary according to program. *Financial support:* In 2007–08, 24 students received support, including 2 fellowships with full tuition reimbursements available (averaging $18,000 per year), 21 research assistantships with full tuition reimbursements available (averaging $5,000 per year), 1 teaching assistantship with full tuition reimbursement available (averaging $14,000 per year); career-related internships or fieldwork, Federal Work-Study, institutionally sponsored loans, scholarships/grants, and unspecified assistantships also available. Financial award application deadline: 1/12; financial award applicants required to submit FAFSA. *Faculty research:* Asian art; modern art and critical theory; non-Western art; medieval, renaissance and baroque art; Pre-Colombian. *Unit head:* Dr. Richard K. Emmerson, Professor of Art History/Department Chair, 850-644-7066, Fax: 850-644-3259, E-mail: remmerson@fsu.edu. *Application contact:* Kathy Braun, Graduate Student Advisor, 850-644-8207, Fax: 850-644-7065, E-mail: kbraun@fsu.edu.

George Mason University, College of Humanities and Social Sciences, Department of History and Art History, Program in Art History, Fairfax, VA 22030. Offers MA. *Degree requirements:* For master's, comprehensive exam. *Entrance requirements:* For master's, GRE, resumé, 2 letters of recommendation.

See Close-Up on page 239.

The George Washington University, Columbian College of Arts and Sciences, Department of Fine Arts and Art History, Program in Art History, Washington, DC 20052. Offers art history (PhD); museum training (MA). Part-time and evening/weekend programs available. *Degree requirements:* For master's, one foreign language, comprehensive exam, thesis or alternative. *Entrance requirements:* For master's, GRE General Test, bachelor's degree in field, minimum GPA of 3.0. Additional exam requirements/recommendations for international students: Required—TOEFL (minimum score 550 paper-based; 213 computer-based). Electronic applications accepted.

Georgia State University, College of Arts and Sciences, Ernest G. Welch School of Art and Design, Program in Art History, Atlanta, GA 30303-3083. Offers MA. *Accreditation:* NASAD. *Faculty:* 5 full-time (3 women). *Students:* 15 full-time (13 women); includes 3 minority (all African Americans) 9 applicants, 56% accepted, 4 enrolled. *Degree requirements:* For master's, one foreign language, comprehensive exam, thesis. *Entrance requirements:* For master's, GRE General Test, writing sample. Additional exam requirements/recommendations for international students: Required—TOEFL (minimum score 550 paper-based; 213 computer-based). *Application deadline:* For fall admission, 1/6 for domestic and international students. Application fee: $50. Electronic applications accepted. *Expenses:* Tuition, state resident: part-time $221 per credit hour. *Financial support:* In 2007–08, 13 fellowships (averaging $1,250 per year), 4 research assistantships with full tuition reimbursements (averaging $4,800 per year) were awarded; career-related internships or fieldwork, Federal Work-Study, institutionally sponsored loans, scholarships/grants, health care benefits, and unspecified assistantships also available. Financial award application deadline: 1/6. *Faculty research:* Latin American art, contemporary art, Egypt/Near East art, African American art, 19th/20th century art. *Application contact:* Prof. Joe Peragine, Director of Graduate Studies, 404-413-5229, Fax: 404-413-5261, E-mail: artgrad@gsu.edu.

Graduate School and University Center of the City University of New York, Graduate Studies, Program in Art History, New York, NY 10016-4039. Offers architecture (PhD); graphic arts (PhD); painting (PhD); photography (PhD); sculpture (PhD). *Faculty:* 16 full-time (11 women). *Students:* 159 full-time (121 women), 13 part-time (all women); includes 18 minority (5 African Americans, 2 Asian Americans or Pacific Islanders, 11 Hispanic Americans), 21 international. Average age 34. 89 applicants, 57% accepted, 30 enrolled. In 2007, 14 degrees awarded. *Degree requirements:* For doctorate, 2 foreign languages, thesis/dissertation. *Entrance requirements:* For doctorate, GRE General Test. Additional exam requirements/recommendations for international students: Required—TOEFL. *Application deadline:* For fall admission, 4/15 for domestic students; for spring admission, 11/15 for domestic students. Application fee: $125. Electronic applications accepted. *Financial support:* In 2007–08, 91 students received support, including 68 fellowships, 4 research assistantships, 12 teaching assistantships; career-related internships or fieldwork, Federal Work-Study, institutionally sponsored loans, and tuition waivers (full and partial) also available. Financial award application deadline: 2/1; financial award applicants required to submit FAFSA. *Unit head:* Dr. Kevin Murphy, Executive Officer, 212-817-8035, Fax: 212-817-1502, E-mail: kmurphy@gc.cuny.edu.

Graduate Theological Union, Graduate Programs, Berkeley, CA 94709-1212. Offers art and religion (MA, PhD); biblical languages (MA); biblical studies (Old and New Testament) (MA, PhD, Th D); Buddhist studies (MA); Christian spirituality (MA, PhD); cultural and historical studies of religions (MA, PhD); ethics and social theory (PhD); history (MA, PhD, Th D); homiletics (MA, PhD, Th D); interdisciplinary studies (PhD, Th D); Jewish studies (MA, PhD, Certificate); liturgical studies (MA, PhD, Th D); Near Eastern religions (PhD); Orthodox Christian studies (MA); Orthodox studies (Certificate); religion and psychology (MA, PhD); religion and society/ethics and social theory (MA); systematic and philosophical theology (MA, PhD, Th D); women's studies in religion (Certificate); MA/M Div. *Accreditation:* ATS. *Faculty:* 119 full-time (44 women), 34 part-time/adjunct (9 women). *Students:* 317 full-time (152 women), 35 part-time (19 women); includes 49 minority (15 African Americans, 2 American Indian/Alaska Native, 21 Asian Americans or Pacific Islanders, 11 Hispanic Americans), 74 international. Average age 38. 257 applicants, 59% accepted, 79 enrolled. In 2007, 45 master's, 22 doctorates awarded. Terminal master's awarded for partial completion of doctoral program. *Median time to degree:* Of those who began their doctoral program in fall 1999, 52% received their degree in 8 years or less. *Degree requirements:* For master's, one foreign language, thesis; for doctorate, one foreign language, comprehensive exam, thesis/dissertation. *Entrance requirements:* For master's, GRE General Test; for doctorate, GRE General Test, MA or M Div. Additional exam requirements/recommendations for international students: Required—TOEFL. *Application deadline:* For fall admission, 12/15 for domestic and international students; for winter admission, 2/15 for domestic and international students; for spring admission, 9/30 for domestic and international students. Application fee: $40. Electronic applications accepted. *Expenses:* Tuition: Full-time $13,310. Tuition and fees vary according to degree level and program. *Financial support:* In 2007–08, 122 students received support, including 109 fellowships (averaging $11,581 per year), 1 research assistantship (averaging $3,000 per year), 22 teaching assistantships (averaging $3,500 per year); Federal Work-Study, scholarships/grants, and tuition waivers (partial) also available. Support available to part-time students. Financial award application deadline: 2/1; financial award applicants required to submit FAFSA. *Unit head:* Dr. Arthur G. Holder, Dean, 510-649-2440, Fax: 510-649-1417, E-mail: aholder@gtu.edu. *Application contact:* Dr. Kathleen Kook, Assistant Dean for Admissions, 800-826-4488, Fax: 510-649-1730, E-mail: gtuadm@gtu.edu.

Harvard University, Graduate School of Arts and Sciences, Department of History of Art and Architecture, Cambridge, MA 02138. Offers ancient art (PhD); ancient Near Eastern art (PhD); baroque art (PhD); Byzantine art (PhD); classical art (PhD); Indian art (PhD); Islamic art (PhD); Japanese and Chinese art (PhD); medieval art (PhD); modern art (PhD); Renaissance and modern architecture (PhD); Renaissance art (PhD). *Degree requirements:* For doctorate, variable foreign language requirement, thesis/dissertation, general exams; reading exams in French, German, and Italian. *Entrance requirements:* For doctorate, GRE General Test. Additional exam requirements/recommendations for international students: Required—TOEFL. *Expenses:* Tuition: Full-time $31,456. Full-time tuition and fees vary according to program and student level.

Howard University, Graduate School, Division of Fine Arts, Department of Art, Program in Art History, Washington, DC 20059-0002. Offers art history (MA); history of art and visual culture (MA). *Accreditation:* NASAD. Part-time programs available. *Degree requirements:* For master's, comprehensive exam, thesis. *Entrance requirements:* For master's, GRE General Test, minimum GPA of 3.0, BA in art history or related field, portfolio. *Expenses:* Tuition: Full-time $16,175; part-time $899 per credit hour. Required fees: $805.

Hunter College of the City University of New York, Graduate School, School of Arts and Sciences, Department of Art, Program in Art History, New York, NY 10021-5085. Offers MA. Part-time and evening/weekend programs available. *Faculty:* 10 full-time (7 women), 3 part-time/adjunct (1 woman). *Students:* 4 full-time (all women), 100 part-time (91 women); includes 5 minority (4 Asian Americans or Pacific Islanders, 1 Hispanic American). Average age 31. 70 applicants, 46% accepted, 11 enrolled. In 2007, 24 degrees awarded. *Degree requirements:* For master's, one foreign language, comprehensive exam, thesis. *Entrance requirements:* For master's, GRE General Test, minimum 12 credits of course work in art history, reading knowledge of a foreign language (Italian, French or German), 2 letters of recommendation. Additional exam requirements/recommendations for international students: Required—TOEFL. *Application deadline:* For fall admission, 3/1 for domestic students; for spring admission, 10/1 for domestic students. Application fee: $125. *Expenses:* Tuition, state resident: full-time $6,400; part-time $270 per credit. Tuition, nonresident: part-time $500 per credit. One-time fee: $125 full-time. Tuition and fees vary according to program. *Financial support:* Teaching assistantships, career-related internships or fieldwork, Federal Work-Study, scholarships/grants, and tuition waivers (partial) available. Support available to part-time students. Financial award application deadline: 4/15. *Faculty research:* Islamic art, Renaissance and Baroque, Impressionism, critical theory, Modernism. *Unit head:* Dr. Richard Stapleford, Graduate Adviser, 212-650-5052, E-mail: grad.arthisotryadvisor@hunter.cuny.edu.

Illinois State University, Graduate School, College of Fine Arts, School of Art, Normal, IL 61790-2200. Offers art history (MA, MS); ceramics (MFA, MS); drawing (MFA, MS); fibers (MFA, MS); glass (MFA, MS); graphic design (MFA, MS); metals (MFA, MS); painting (MFA, MS); photography (MFA, MS); printmaking (MFA, MS); sculpture (MFA, MS). *Accreditation:* NASAD (one or more programs are accredited). *Faculty:* 30 full-time (12 women). *Students:* 31 full-time (20 women), 5 part-time (4 women); includes 3 minority (1 African American, 2 Hispanic Americans), 3 international. 62 applicants, 29% accepted. In 2007, 17 degrees awarded. *Degree requirements:* For master's, thesis or alternative, internship. *Entrance requirements:* For master's, portfolio, sample of scholarly writing. *Application deadline:* Applications are processed on a rolling basis. Application fee: $40. *Expenses:* Tuition, state resident: full-time $3,492; part-time $194 per credit hour. Tuition, nonresident: full-time $7,272; part-time $404 per credit hour. Required fees: $1,024; $57 per credit hour. *Financial support:* In 2007–08, 23 teaching assistantships (averaging $6,661 per year) were awarded; career-related internships or fieldwork, Federal Work-Study, tuition waivers (full and partial), and unspecified assistantships also available. Support available to part-time students. Financial award application deadline: 4/1. *Faculty research:* General operations support: Normal Editions Workshop for FY2007. Total annual research expenditures: $4,160. *Unit head:* James Crowley, Chairperson, 309-438-5621.

Indiana University Bloomington, University Graduate School, College of Arts and Sciences, Henry Radford Hope School of Fine Arts, Department of the History of Art, Bloomington, IN 47405-7000. Offers MA, PhD. *Accreditation:* NASAD. *Faculty:* 11 full-time (7 women), 1 (woman) part-time/adjunct. *Students:* 41 full-time (32 women), 11 part-time (10 women); includes 2 minority (1 African American, 1 Asian American or Pacific Islander), 2 international. Average age 31. 48 applicants, 50% accepted, 10 enrolled. In 2007, 11 master's, 1 doctorate awarded. Terminal master's awarded for partial completion of doctoral program. *Degree requirements:* For master's, one foreign language, thesis; for doctorate, 2 foreign languages, comprehensive exam, thesis/dissertation. *Entrance requirements:* For master's, GRE, transcript, writing sample, 3 letters of recommendation; for doctorate, GRE, transcript, writing samples, 3 letters of recommendation. Additional exam requirements/recommendations for international students: Required—TOEFL (minimum score 550 paper-based; 213 computer-based). *Application deadline:* For fall admission, 10/15 for domestic students; for winter admission, 12/1 for international students; for spring admission, 1/15 for domestic students. Application fee: $50 ($60 for international students). Electronic applications accepted. *Financial support:* Fellowships with full tuition reimbursements, research assistantships with full tuition reimbursements, teaching assistantships with tuition reimbursements, career-related internships or fieldwork and Federal Work-Study available. Financial award application deadline: 2/15. *Faculty research:* Art and social history, consumer culture, feminist art and theory, classical revivals. *Unit head:* Patrick McNaughton, Chair, 812-855-4924, Fax: 812-855-7498, E-mail: mcnaught@indiana.edu. *Application contact:* Fenella Jean Alice Flinn, Administrative Assistant, 812-855-9556, Fax: 812-855-7498, E-mail: fflinn@indiana.edu.

James Madison University, The Graduate School, College of Visual and Performing Arts, School of Art and Art History, Harrisonburg, VA 22807. Offers art education (MA); art history (MA); ceramics (MFA); drawing/painting (MFA); metal/jewelry (MFA); photography (MFA); printmaking (MFA); sculpture (MFA); studio art (MA); weaving/fibers (MFA). *Accreditation:* NASAD. Part-time programs available. *Faculty:* 5 full-time (2 women), 1 part-time/adjunct (0 women). *Students:* 10 full-time (5 women), 2 part-time; includes 1 minority (Asian American or Pacific Islander) Average age 27. In 2007, 8 degrees awarded. *Degree requirements:* For master's, thesis (for some programs). *Entrance requirements:* For master's, GRE General Test, language exam in French or German, portfolio, 3 letters of recommendation, research paper. Additional exam requirements/recommendations for international students: Required—TOEFL. *Application deadline:* For fall admission, 2/15 priority date for domestic students, 2/15 for international students; for spring admission, 10/15 priority date for domestic students, 10/15 for international students. Applications are processed on a rolling basis. Application fee: $55. Electronic applications accepted. *Expenses:* Tuition, state resident: full-time $6,720; part-time $280 per credit hour. Tuition, nonresident: full-time $19,104; part-time $796 per credit hour. *Financial support:* In 2007–08, 8 students received support, including 3 teaching assistantships with full tuition reimbursements available (averaging $8,494 per year); Federal Work-Study, unspecified assistantships, and 5 graduate assistantships ($7,237) also available. Financial award application deadline: 3/1; financial award applicants required to submit FAFSA. *Unit head:* Leslie M. Bellavance, Academic Unit Head, 540-568-6216.

The Johns Hopkins University, Zanvyl Krieger School of Arts and Sciences, Department of History of Art, Baltimore, MD 21218-2699. Offers MA, PhD. *Faculty:* 5 full-time (1 woman), 3 part-time/adjunct (2 women). *Students:* 15 full-time (9 women); includes 1 minority (Asian American or Pacific Islander), 5 international. Average age 29. 46 applicants, 9% accepted, 4 enrolled. In 2007, 16 degrees awarded. Terminal master's awarded for partial completion of doctoral program. *Median time to degree:* Of those who began their doctoral program in fall 1999, 35% received their degree in 8 years or less. *Degree requirements:* For master's, 2 foreign languages; for doctorate, 2 foreign languages, thesis/dissertation. *Entrance requirements:* For master's and doctorate, GRE General Test. Additional exam requirements/recommendations for international students: Required—TOEFL (minimum score 600 paper-based; 250 computer-based). *Application deadline:* For fall admission, 1/15 for domestic students. Application fee: $60. Electronic applications accepted. *Financial support:* In 2007–08, 3 fellowships (averaging $16,000 per year) were awarded; research assistantships, teaching assistantships, Federal Work-Study and institutionally sponsored loans also available. Financial award application deadline: 4/15; financial award applicants required to submit FAFSA. *Faculty research:* Modern art, Renaissance art, Medieval art, Roman art. *Unit head:* Dr. Stephen Campbell, Chair, 410-516-4928, Fax: 410-516-5188, E-mail: stephen.campbell@jhu.edu. *Application contact:* Nikki Andrews, Graduate Administrative Coordinator, 410-516-7117, Fax: 410-516-5188, E-mail: arthist@jhu.edu.

Kent State University, College of the Arts, School of Art, Kent, OH 44242-0001. Offers art education (MA); art history (MA); crafts (MA, MFA), including ceramics (MA), glass, jewelry/metals, textiles/art; fine art (MA, MFA), including drawing/painting, printmaking, sculpture. *Accreditation:* NASAD (one or more programs are accredited). *Faculty:* 20 full-time (11 women), 4 part-time/adjunct (3 women). *Students:* 46 full-time (33 women), 41 part-time (27 women); includes 1 African American, 11 Asian Americans or Pacific Islanders. 81 applicants, 49% accepted, 24 enrolled. In 2007, 22 degrees awarded. *Degree requirements:* For master's, one foreign language, thesis. *Entrance requirements:* For master's, undergraduate degree in proposed area of study (for fine arts and crafts programs); minimum overall GPA of 2.75 (3.0 for art major); 3 letters of recommendation; portfolio (15-20 slides for MA, 20-25 for MFA), brief autobiographical statement (MFA). Additional exam requirements/recommendations for international students: Required—TOEFL. *Application deadline:* For fall admission, 2/15 for domestic students; for spring admission, 10/15 for domestic students. Applications are processed on a rolling basis. Application fee: $30. Electronic applications accepted. *Financial support:* In 2007–08, 21 teaching assistantships with full tuition reimbursements (averaging $6,700 per year) were awarded; career-related internships or fieldwork, Federal Work-Study, scholarships/grants, and tuition waivers (full) also available. Financial award application deadline: 2/15. *Unit head:* Dr. Christine Havice, Director, 330-672-2192, Fax: 330-672-4729, E-mail: chavice@kent.edu. *Application contact:* Janice Lessman-Moss, Coordinator of Graduate Studies, 330-672-1362, Fax: 330-672-2192, E-mail: jlessman@kent.edu.

Lamar University, College of Graduate Studies, College of Fine Arts and Communication, Department of Art, Beaumont, TX 77710. Offers art history (MA); photography (MA); studio art (MA); visual design (MA). Part-time and evening/weekend programs available. *Faculty:* 6 full-time (3 women). *Students:* Average age 42. 2 applicants, 0% accepted. In 2007, 2 degrees awarded. *Degree requirements:* For master's, thesis. *Entrance requirements:* For master's, GRE General Test, minimum GPA of 2.5 in last 60 hours of undergraduate course work. Additional exam requirements/recommendations for international students: Required—TOEFL. *Application deadline:* For fall admission, 8/1 priority date for domestic students; for spring admission, 12/1 for domestic students. Applications are processed on a rolling basis. Application fee: $25 ($50 for international students). *Expenses:* Tuition, state resident: part-time $348 per semester hour. Tuition, nonresident: part-time $626 per semester hour. Tuition and fees vary according to course load. *Financial support:* Fellowships, career-related internships or fieldwork, Federal Work-Study, and scholarships/grants available. Financial award application deadline: 4/1. *Faculty research:* Nineteenth century academic paintings, metal casting, pigment color stability, computer modified photography, manipulated photography. *Unit head:* Donna M. Meeks, Chair, 409-880-8141, Fax: 409-880-1799, E-mail: meeksdm@lub002.lamar.edu.

Louisiana State University and Agricultural and Mechanical College, Graduate School, College of Art and Design, School of Art, Program in Art History, Baton Rouge, LA 70803. Offers MA. *Accreditation:* NASAD. *Students:* 7 full-time (all women), 4 part-time (2 women). 8 applicants, 38% accepted. In 2007, 5 degrees awarded. *Degree requirements:* For master's, one foreign language, thesis. *Entrance requirements:* For master's, GRE General Test, minimum GPA of 3.0. Additional exam requirements/recommendations for international students: Required—TOEFL (minimum score 550 paper-based; 213 computer-based; 79 iBT). *Application deadline:* For fall admission, 1/25 priority date for domestic students, 5/15 for international students; for spring admission, 10/15 for international students. Applications are processed on a rolling basis. Application fee: $25. Electronic applications accepted. *Financial support:* In 2007–08, 2 students received support; research assistantships with partial tuition reimbursements available, teaching assistantships with partial tuition reimbursements available, career-related internships or fieldwork, Federal Work-Study, institutionally sponsored loans, scholarships/grants, traineeships, health care benefits, and unspecified assistantships available. Support available to part-time students. Financial award application deadline: 3/15. *Faculty research:* Liturgical art, Greco-Roman art, Renaissance prints, American twentieth century art, performance art. *Unit head:* Dr. Mark Zucker, Coordinator, 225-578-5460, E-mail: mzucker@lsu.edu.

Massachusetts Institute of Technology, School of Architecture and Planning, Department of Architecture, Cambridge, MA 02139-4307. Offers architecture (M Arch, PhD), including building technology (PhD), design and computation (PhD), history and theory of architecture (PhD), history and theory of art (PhD); architecture studies (SM Arch S); visual studies (SM Vis S, SMBT); M Arch/MCP; M Arch/SMRED; SM Arch S/MCP; SM Arch S/SMRED. *Faculty:* 31 full-time (8 women). *Students:* 223 full-time (103 women); includes 21 minority (3 African Americans, 13 Asian Americans or Pacific Islanders, 5 Hispanic Americans), 99 international. Average age 28. 665 applicants, 21% accepted, 67 enrolled. In 2007, 63 master's, 8 doctorates awarded. *Degree requirements:* For master's, thesis; for doctorate, comprehensive exam, thesis/dissertation. *Entrance requirements:* For master's, GRE General Test (for some programs), portfolio (for some programs); for doctorate, GRE General Test (for some programs). Additional exam requirements/recommendations for international students: Required—TOEFL. *Application deadline:* For fall admission, 12/15 for domestic and international students. Application fee: $70. Electronic applications accepted. *Expenses:* Tuition: Full-time $34,760; part-time $545 per unit. Required fees: $236. *Financial support:* In 2007–08, 178 students received support, including 117 fellowships with tuition reimbursements available (averaging $20,726 per year), 15 research assistantships with tuition reimbursements available (averaging $20,113 per year), 29 teaching assistantships with tuition reimbursements available (averaging $23,310 per year); career-related internships or fieldwork, Federal Work-Study, institutionally sponsored loans, scholarships/grants, health care benefits, and unspecified assistantships also available. Total annual research expenditures: $532,000. *Unit head:* Prof. Yung Ho Chang, Head, 617-253-7791, Fax: 617-253-8993. *Application contact:* Admissions Coordinator, 617-253-3613, Fax: 617-253-8993.

See Close-Up on page 161.

McGill University, Faculty of Graduate and Postdoctoral Studies, Faculty of Arts, Department of Art History and Communication Studies, Montréal, QC H3A 2T5, Canada. Offers MA, PhD. *Faculty:* 14 full-time (8 women), 8 part-time/adjunct (4 women). *Students:* 96 full-time (66 women), 10 part-time (7 women). 215 applicants, 18% accepted, 13 enrolled. In 2007, 7 master's, 11 doctorates awarded.

Montclair State University, The Office of Graduate Admissions and Support Services, School of the Arts, Department of Art and Design, Montclair, NJ 07043-1624. Offers art education (MA, Certificate); art history (MA); studio arts (MA, MFA). *Accreditation:* NASAD (one or more programs are accredited). Part-time and evening/weekend programs available. *Faculty:* 24 full-time (10 women), 46 part-time/adjunct (30 women). *Students:* 31 full-time (21 women), 42 part-time (37 women); includes 6 minority (1 African American, 3 Asian Americans or Pacific Islanders, 2 Hispanic Americans), 2 international. 70 applicants, 39% accepted, 20 enrolled. In 2007, 17 master's, 8 other advanced degrees awarded. *Degree requirements:* For master's, project. *Entrance requirements:* For master's, GRE General Test or MAT (MA), portfolio, undergraduate degree in fine arts or equivalent, 2 letters of recommendation, teaching certificate (art education). Additional exam requirements/recommendations for international students: Required—TOEFL (minimum score 83 computer-based). *Application deadline:* For fall admission, 2/1 for domestic and international students. Applications are processed on a rolling basis. Application fee: $60. Electronic applications accepted. *Financial support:* In 2007–08, 4 research assistantships with full tuition reimbursements (averaging $7,000 per year) were awarded; Federal Work-Study, scholarships/grants, and unspecified assistantships also available. Support available to part-time students. Financial award application deadline: 3/1; financial award applicants required to submit FAFSA. *Unit head:* John Luttropp, Chairperson, 973-655-7295. *Application contact:* Dr. Dorothy Heard, Adviser, 973-655-7295, E-mail: heardd@mail.montclair.edu.

New Mexico State University, Graduate School, College of Arts and Sciences, Department of Art, Las Cruces, NM 88003-8001. Offers art history (MA); ceramics (MA, MFA); design (MA, MFA); drawing (MA, MFA); metals (MA, MFA); painting (MA, MFA); photography (MA, MFA); printmaking (MA, MFA); sculpture (MA, MFA). *Faculty:* 8 full-time (5 women), 1 (woman) part-time/adjunct. *Students:* 33 full-time (16 women), 3 part-time (1 woman); includes 6 minority (1 American Indian/Alaska Native, 5 Hispanic Americans), 1 international. Average age 35. 24 applicants, 58% accepted, 10 enrolled. In 2007, 7 degrees awarded. *Degree requirements:* For master's, comprehensive exam (for some programs), thesis, thesis exhibit. *Entrance requirements:* For master's, portfolio, 10-page paper (art history). *Application deadline:* For fall admission, 2/15 for domestic students; for winter admission, 10/15 for domestic students; for spring admission, 7/15 for domestic students. Application fee: $30 ($50 for international students). Electronic applications accepted. *Expenses:* Tuition, state resident: full-time $3,602; part-time $199 per credit. Tuition, nonresident: full-time $13,380; part-time $607 per credit. Required fees: $1,178. *Financial support:* In 2007–08, 1 fellowship, 29 teaching assistantships were awarded; research assistantships, Federal Work-Study and health care benefits also available. Support available to part-time students. Financial award application deadline: 3/1. *Faculty research:* Painting, graphic design, sculpture, printmaking, drawing. *Unit head:* Dr. Spencer Fidler, Head, 575-646-1705, Fax: 575-646-8036, E-mail: sfidler@nmsu.edu.

New York University, Graduate School of Arts and Science, Institute of Fine Arts, Program in Art History and Archaeology, New York, NY 10012-1019. Offers architectural studies (PhD); art history and archaeology (MA, PhD); classical art and archaeology (PhD); curatorial studies (PhD); East and South Asian art (PhD); Near Eastern art and archaeology (PhD); MA/Diploma; PhD/Certificate. Part-time programs available. *Students:* 199 full-time (156 women), 88 part-time (70 women); includes 28 minority (19 Asian Americans or Pacific Islanders, 9 Hispanic Americans), 34 international. Average age 32. 295 applicants, 33% accepted, 41 enrolled. In 2007, 26 master's, 26 doctorates awarded. Terminal master's awarded for partial completion of doctoral program. *Degree requirements:* For master's, 2 foreign languages, thesis or alternative, 2 qualifying papers; for doctorate, 2 foreign languages, thesis/dissertation. *Entrance requirements:* For master's, GRE General Test; for doctorate, GRE General Test, MA. Additional exam requirements/recommendations for international students: Required—TOEFL. *Application deadline:* For fall admission, 12/18 for domestic students. Application fee: $85. *Financial support:* Fellowships with tuition reimbursements, research assistantships with tuition reimbursements, teaching assistantships with tuition reimbursements, career-related internships or fieldwork, Federal Work-Study, and institutionally sponsored loans available. Financial award application deadline: 12/18; financial award applicants required to submit FAFSA. *Application contact:* Priscilla Saucek, Director of Graduate Studies, 212-992-5800, Fax: 212-992-5807, E-mail: ifa.program@nyu.edu.

Northwestern University, The Graduate School, Judd A. and Marjorie Weinberg College of Arts and Sciences, Department of Art History, Evanston, IL 60208. Offers PhD. Admissions and degrees offered through The Graduate School. *Degree requirements:* For doctorate, 2 foreign languages, comprehensive exam, thesis/dissertation, major and minor field exercises. *Entrance requirements:* For doctorate, GRE General Test. Additional exam requirements/recommendations for international students: Required—TOEFL. Electronic applications accepted. *Faculty research:* Modern American and European art and architecture, prehistoric and ancient

Art History

Northwestern University (continued)
art, central Asian art, medieval manuscripts and early printed books, history of museums, art of Western Africa, theory of culture.

The Ohio State University, Graduate School, College of the Arts, Department of History of Art, Columbus, OH 43210. Offers MA, PhD. *Accreditation:* NASAD. *Faculty:* 20. *Students:* 44 full-time (34 women), 7 part-time (6 women); includes 3 minority (1 African American, 2 Asian Americans or Pacific Islanders), 6 international. Average age 31. In 2007, 15 master's, 3 doctorates awarded. *Degree requirements:* For master's, one foreign language, thesis optional; for doctorate, 2 foreign languages, thesis/dissertation. *Entrance requirements:* For master's and doctorate, GRE General Test. Additional exam requirements/recommendations for international students: Recommended—TOEFL (minimum score 600 paper-based; 250 computer-based). *Application deadline:* For fall admission, 8/15 priority date for domestic students, 7/1 priority date for international students; for winter admission, 12/1 priority date for domestic students, 11/1 priority date for international students; for spring admission, 3/1 priority date for domestic students, 2/1 priority date for international students. Applications are processed on a rolling basis. Application fee: $40 ($50 for international students). Electronic applications accepted. *Financial support:* Fellowships, teaching assistantships, Federal Work-Study and institutionally sponsored loans available. Support available to part-time students. *Faculty research:* Western and Oriental art, African art and archaeology. *Unit head:* Lisa C. Florman, Graduate Studies Committee Chair, 614-292-7481, Fax: 614-292-4401, E-mail: florman.4@osu.edu. *Application contact:* 614-688-9444, Fax: 614-292-3895, E-mail: domestic.grad@osu.edu.

Ohio University, Graduate College, College of Fine Arts, School of Art, Athens, OH 45701-2979. Offers art history (MA); ceramics (MFA); graphic design (MFA); painting (MFA); photography (MFA); printmaking (MFA); sculpture (MFA). Part-time programs available. *Faculty:* 30 full-time (16 women), 7 part-time/adjunct (3 women). *Students:* 53 full-time (34 women), 11 part-time (7 women); includes 1 minority (Hispanic American), 7 international. Average age 27. 174 applicants, 22% accepted, 32 enrolled. In 2007, 18 degrees awarded. *Degree requirements:* For master's, thesis. *Entrance requirements:* For master's, portfolio. Additional exam requirements/recommendations for international students: Required—TOEFL. *Application deadline:* For fall admission, 2/1 for domestic students. Application fee: $50 ($55 for international students). *Financial support:* In 2007–08, 57 students received support, including 35 teaching assistantships with full and partial tuition reimbursements available (averaging $9,198 per year); career-related internships or fieldwork, Federal Work-Study, institutionally sponsored loans, scholarships/grants, tuition waivers (full), unspecified assistantships, and associateships also available. Financial award application deadline: 2/1. *Faculty research:* Vapor fired ceramics, video installation, art theory, digital photography, mixed and interdisciplinary media work. *Unit head:* David LaPalombara, Director, 740-593-4290, Fax: 740-593-0457, E-mail: lapalomb@ohio.edu. *Application contact:* Don Adleta, Associate Director and Chair, Graduate Programs, 740-593-9996, Fax: 740-593-0457, E-mail: adleta@ohio.edu.

Penn State University Park, Graduate School, College of Arts and Architecture, Department of Art History, State College, University Park, PA 16802-1503. Offers MA, PhD. *Expenses:* Tuition, state resident: full-time $14,738; part-time $614 per credit. Tuition, nonresident: full-time $26,050; part-time $1,085 per credit. Tuition and fees vary according to course load, program and student level. *Unit head:* Dr. Craig R. Zabel, Head, 814-865-4874, Fax: 814-865-1242, E-mail: cxz3@psu.edu. *Application contact:* Dr. Brian Curran, Graduate Officer, 814-865-4886, E-mail: bac18@psu.edu.

Pratt Institute, School of Art and Design, Program in Art History, Brooklyn, NY 11205-3899. Offers art history (MS); theory and criticism (MS); MS/MFA; MS/MS. *Accreditation:* NASAD. Part-time programs available. *Faculty:* 5 full-time (3 women), 12 part-time/adjunct (7 women). *Students:* 39 full-time (28 women), 7 part-time (all women); includes 7 minority (3 African Americans, 1 Asian American or Pacific Islander, 3 Hispanic Americans), 1 international. Average age 29. 52 applicants, 44% accepted, 8 enrolled. In 2007, 10 degrees awarded. *Degree requirements:* For master's, one foreign language, thesis. *Entrance requirements:* For master's, GRE General Test, bachelor's degree, transcripts, letters of recommendation, statement, portfolio. Additional exam requirements/recommendations for international students: Required—TOEFL (minimum score 600 paper-based; 250 computer-based). *Application deadline:* For fall admission, 2/1 for domestic students; for spring admission, 10/1 for domestic students. Application fee: $50 ($90 for international students). Electronic applications accepted. *Expenses:* Tuition: Full-time $25,680. Required fees: $1,106. Tuition and fees vary according to program. *Financial support:* Career-related internships or fieldwork, Federal Work-Study, institutionally sponsored loans, scholarships/grants, health care benefits, and unspecified assistantships available. Support available to part-time students. Financial award application deadline: 2/1; financial award applicants required to submit CSS PROFILE or FAFSA. *Faculty research:* Conservation techniques, women artists from previous centuries, art of 16th century Veneto, design history, 19th century Germany. *Unit head:* Frima Fox Hofrichter, Chairperson, 718-636-3598, E-mail: ffhofric@pratt.edu. *Application contact:* Young Hah, Director of Graduate Admissions, 718-636-3683, Fax: 718-399-4242, E-mail: yhah@pratt.edu.

See Close-Up on page 253.

Purchase College, State University of New York, Division of Humanities, Purchase, NY 10577-1400. Offers art history (MA). *Accreditation:* NASAD. *Faculty:* 3 full-time (all women), 2 part-time/adjunct (1 woman). *Students:* 13 full-time (11 women), 5 part-time (4 women); includes 1 minority (African American), 1 international. Average age 31. 17 applicants, 59% accepted, 6 enrolled. In 2007, 5 degrees awarded. *Degree requirements:* For master's, one foreign language, thesis. *Entrance requirements:* For master's, BA or BFA, previous course work in art history. *Application deadline:* For fall admission, 3/15 for domestic students. Application fee: $50. *Expenses:* Tuition, state resident: full-time $6,900; part-time $288 per credit. Tuition, nonresident: full-time $10,920; part-time $455 per credit. Required fees: $1,506; $125 per credit. Tuition and fees vary according to program. *Financial support:* In 2007–08, 1 student received support, including 1 fellowship (averaging $5,000 per year); Federal Work-Study, scholarships/grants, and tuition waivers (partial) also available. Support available to part-time students. Financial award application deadline: 3/15; financial award applicants required to submit FAFSA. *Unit head:* Jonathan Levin, Dean, Division of Humanities, 914-251-6000. *Application contact:* Sabrina Johnston, Counselor, 914-251-6479, Fax: 914-251-6314, E-mail: admissn@purchase.edu.

Queens College of the City University of New York, Division of Graduate Studies, Arts and Humanities Division, Department of Art, Program in Art History, Flushing, NY 11367-1597. Offers MA. Part-time and evening/weekend programs available. *Faculty:* 6 full-time (3 women). *Students:* 17 (all women) 20 applicants, 75% accepted, 11 enrolled. In 2007, 4 degrees awarded. *Degree requirements:* For master's, 2 foreign languages, thesis, qualifying exam. *Entrance requirements:* For master's, minimum GPA of 3.0. Additional exam requirements/recommendations for international students: Required—TOEFL. *Application deadline:* For fall admission, 4/1 for domestic students; for spring admission, 11/1 for domestic students. Applications are processed on a rolling basis. Application fee: $125. *Financial support:* Career-related internships or fieldwork, Federal Work-Study, institutionally sponsored loans, and tuition waivers (partial) available. Support available to part-time students. Financial award application deadline: 4/1; financial award applicants required to submit FAFSA. *Unit head:* Dr. James Saslow, Head, 718-997-4820. *Application contact:* Mario Caruso, Director of Graduate Admissions, 718-997-5200, Fax: 718-997-5193, E-mail: graduate_admissions@qc.edu.

Richmond, The American International University in London, Program in Art History, Richmond, United Kingdom. Offers MA. Part-time programs available. *Degree requirements:* For master's, thesis. *Entrance requirements:* For master's, minimum GPA of 3.0. Additional exam requirements/recommendations for international students: Required—TOEFL, IELTS. Electronic applications accepted. Expenses: Contact institution. *Faculty research:* Archaeology of art and representation, contemporary paganisms, nineteenthn century modernisms, American twentieth century art, sound media.

Rutgers, The State University of New Jersey, New Brunswick, Graduate School, Program in Art History, New Brunswick, NJ 08901-1281. Offers art history (MA, PhD); curatorial studies (Certificate); historic preservation (Certificate). Part-time programs available. Terminal master's awarded for partial completion of doctoral program. *Degree requirements:* For master's, one foreign language, comprehensive exam; for doctorate, 2 foreign languages, comprehensive exam, thesis/dissertation. *Entrance requirements:* For master's and doctorate, GRE General Test, writing sample. Additional exam requirements/recommendations for international students: Required—TOEFL (minimum score 550 paper-based; 213 computer-based). Electronic applications accepted. *Faculty research:* Ancient and medieval art and architecture; Renaissance and Baroque art and architecture; modern and contemporary art and architecture; Italian studies; the arts of Asia, Africa, and the Americas.

San Diego State University, Graduate and Research Affairs, College of Professional Studies and Fine Arts, School of Art, Design and Art History, San Diego, CA 92182. Offers art history (MA); studio arts (MA, MFA), including applied design, environmental design, graphic design, interior design, painting and printmaking, sculpture. *Accreditation:* NASAD (one or more programs are accredited). *Students:* 44 full-time (29 women), 18 part-time (11 women); includes 9 minority (4 Asian Americans or Pacific Islanders, 5 Hispanic Americans), 5 international. Average age 30. 83 applicants, 31% accepted, 31 enrolled. In 2007, 12 degrees awarded. *Degree requirements:* For master's, variable foreign language requirement, thesis. *Entrance requirements:* For master's, GRE General Test, bachelor's degree in related field, slide portfolio, typed slide information sheet, 2 letters of recommendation. Additional exam requirements/recommendations for international students: Required—TOEFL. *Application deadline:* For fall admission, 2/1 for domestic and international students. Applications are processed on a rolling basis. Application fee: $55. Electronic applications accepted. *Financial support:* In 2007–08, 21 teaching assistantships were awarded; career-related internships or fieldwork and unspecified assistantships also available. Financial award applicants required to submit FAFSA. *Unit head:* Arthur Ollman, Director, 619-594-1213, Fax: 619-594-1217. *Application contact:* JoAnne Berelowitz, Graduate Advisor, Art History, 619-594-4995, Fax: 619-594-1217, E-mail: jberelow@mail.sdsu.edu.

San Francisco Art Institute, Graduate Program, Department of History and Theory of Contemporary Art, San Francisco, CA 94133. Offers MA. *Entrance requirements:* Additional exam requirements/recommendations for international students: Required—TOEFL (minimum score 580 paper-based; 237 computer-based).

San Francisco State University, Division of Graduate Studies, College of Creative Arts, Department of Art, San Francisco, CA 94132-1722. Offers art (MFA); art history (MA). *Accreditation:* NASAD (one or more programs are accredited). *Unit head:* Dr. Barbara Foster, Chair, 415-338-2176. *Application contact:* Dr. Gail Dawson, Graduate Coordinator, 415-338-2176, E-mail: artgrad@sfsu.edu.

San Jose State University, Graduate Studies and Research, College of Humanities and the Arts, School of Art and Design, San Jose, CA 95192-0001. Offers art education (MA); art history (MA); digital media (MFA); digital media in art history and education (MA); photography (MFA); pictorial arts (MFA); spatial arts (MFA). *Accreditation:* NASAD (one or more programs are accredited). *Students:* 55 full-time (30 women), 15 part-time (12 women); includes 11 minority (1 African American, 7 Asian Americans or Pacific Islanders, 3 Hispanic Americans), 2 international. Average age 38. 78 applicants, 42% accepted, 24 enrolled. In 2007, 17 degrees awarded. *Entrance requirements:* For master's, GRE. *Application deadline:* For fall admission, 6/29 for domestic students; for spring admission, 11/30 for domestic students. Applications are processed on a rolling basis. Application fee: $59. Electronic applications accepted. *Financial support:* Applicants required to submit FAFSA. *Unit head:* Linda Walsh, Director, 408-924-4320, Fax: 408-924-4326.

Savannah College of Art and Design, Graduate School, Program in Art History, Savannah, GA 31402-3146. Offers MA, MFA. Part-time programs available. *Faculty:* 27 full-time (17 women). *Students:* 8 full-time (all women); includes 1 minority (African American) Average age 28. 26 applicants, 38% accepted, 3 enrolled. In 2007, 5 degrees awarded. *Degree requirements:* For master's, one foreign language, comprehensive exam, thesis, internship. *Entrance requirements:* For master's, art history paper, interview. Additional exam requirements/recommendations for international students: Required—TOEFL (minimum score 550 paper-based; 213 computer-based). *Application deadline:* For fall admission, 4/1 priority date for domestic and international students. Applications are processed on a rolling basis. Application fee: $50. Electronic applications accepted. *Expenses:* Tuition: Full-time $24,840; part-time $552 per credit. One-time fee: $500 full-time. *Financial support:* In 2007–08, 2 fellowships were awarded; career-related internships or fieldwork, Federal Work-Study, and scholarships/grants also available. Financial award application deadline: 4/1; financial award applicants required to submit FAFSA. *Faculty research:* Contemporary art. *Unit head:* Dr. Desire Houngues, Acting Chair, 912-525-5816, Fax: 912-525-5886, E-mail: dhoungue@scad.edu. *Application contact:* Darrell Tutchton, Director of Graduate and International Enrollment, 912-525-5961, Fax: 912-525-5985, E-mail: admission@scad.edu.

See Close-Up on page 257.

School of the Art Institute of Chicago, Graduate Division, Department of Art History, Theory, and Criticism, Chicago, IL 60603-3103. Offers MA, Certificate. *Accreditation:* NASAD. *Entrance requirements:* For master's, GRE. Additional exam requirements/recommendations for international students: Required—TOEFL.

See Close-Up on page 259.

Southern Methodist University, Meadows School of the Arts, Division of Art History, Dallas, TX 75275. Offers MA. Part-time and evening/weekend programs available. *Faculty:* 7 full-time (4 women), 2 part-time/adjunct (1 woman). *Students:* 10 full-time (8 women), 10 part-time (all women); includes 1 minority (Hispanic American), 2 international. Average age 30. 22 applicants, 59% accepted, 7 enrolled. In 2007, 11 degrees awarded. *Degree requirements:* For master's, one foreign language, thesis, translation exam. *Entrance requirements:* For master's, GRE, 12 upper-level hours in art history, sample research paper. Additional exam requirements/recommendations for international students: Required—TOEFL (minimum score 550 paper-based; 213 computer-based; 80 iBT). *Application deadline:* For fall admission, 2/15 priority date for domestic and international students; for spring admission, 11/1 for domestic and international students. Application fee: $75. *Financial support:* In 2007–08, 13 students received support, including 13 teaching assistantships (averaging $3,500 per year); scholarships/grants and unspecified assistantships also available. Financial award application deadline: 3/1; financial award applicants required to submit FAFSA. *Faculty research:* American art, nineteenth- and twentieth-century art, classical and Byzantine art, Hispanic art, Mesoamerican art, Renaissance-Baroque. *Unit head:* Randall Griffin, Chair, 214-768-2615, E-mail: randallg@smu.edu. *Application contact:* Jean Cherry, Director of Graduate Admissions and Records, 214-768-3765, Fax: 214-768-3272, E-mail: jcherry@smu.edu.

State University of New York at Binghamton, Graduate School, School of Arts and Sciences, Department of Art History, Binghamton, NY 13902-6000. Offers MA, PhD. *Faculty:* 8 full-time (4 women), 2 part-time/adjunct (0 women). *Students:* 20 full-time (16 women), 16 part-time (12 women); includes 5 minority (1 African American, 1 Asian American or Pacific Islander, 3 Hispanic Americans), 18 international. Average age 34. 26 applicants, 65% accepted, 8 enrolled. In 2007, 3 doctorates awarded. *Degree requirements:* For master's, one foreign language, comprehensive exam, thesis; for doctorate, 2 foreign languages, comprehensive exam, thesis/dissertation, oral exam. *Entrance requirements:* For master's and doctorate, GRE General Test, writing sample. Additional exam requirements/recommendations for international students: Required—TOEFL. *Application deadline:* For fall admission, 1/15 priority date for domestic and international students; for spring admission, 10/1 priority date for domestic and international students. Applications are processed on a rolling basis. Application fee: $60. Electronic applications accepted. *Financial support:* In 2007–08, 4 fellowships with full tuition reimbursements (averaging $8,000 per year), 9 teaching assistantships with full tuition reimbursements (averaging $14,000 per year) were awarded; research assistantships with full tuition reimbursements, Federal Work-Study, scholarships/grants, and unspecified assistantships also available. Financial award application deadline: 1/15. *Faculty research:* History of art and architecture. *Unit head:* Dr. John Tagg, Professor and Chair, 607-777-2112, Fax: 607-777-4466, E-mail: jtagg@binghamton.edu. *Application contact:* 607-777-2112, Fax: 607-777-4466.

Announcement: Advanced studies and research in history and theory of art and architecture, with distinctive commitment to new theoretical, cross-disciplinary, global, and comparative cultural analyses. Drawing on University interdisciplinary strengths, this very international program develops analytical, theoretical, and professional skills for scholars, curators, educators, and urban and planning professionals.

Stony Brook University, State University of New York, Graduate School, College of Arts and Sciences, Department of Art, Program in Art History and Criticism, Stony Brook, NY 11794. Offers MA, PhD. Part-time programs available. *Students:* 33 full-time (23 women), 4 part-time (2 women); includes 2 minority (1 Asian American or Pacific Islander, 1 Hispanic American), 5 international. Average age 30. 57 applicants, 44% accepted. In 2007, 2 degrees awarded. *Degree requirements:* For master's, comprehensive exam, thesis, reading knowledge of German or French; for doctorate, comprehensive exam, thesis/dissertation, qualifying paper, reading knowledge of German and French, qualifying examination. *Entrance requirements:* For master's, GRE General Test, minimum undergraduate GPA of 3.0; for doctorate, GRE General Test, minimum graduate GPA of 3.0. Additional exam requirements/recommendations for international students: Required—TOEFL (minimum score 550 paper-based; 213 computer-based), IELTS (minimum score 7). *Application deadline:* For fall admission, 1/15 for domestic students. Application fee: $60. *Unit head:* Barbara E. Frank, Director, 631-632-7264, E-mail: bfrank@notas.cc.sunysb.edu. *Application contact:* Dr. Michele Bogart, Director, 631-632-7270.

See Close-Up on page 263.

Sul Ross State University, School of Arts and Sciences, Department of Fine Arts and Communication, Alpine, TX 79832. Offers art education (M Ed); art history (M Ed); studio art (M Ed), including ceramics, design, drawing, jewelry, painting, printmaking, sculpture, weaving. Part-time programs available. *Degree requirements:* For master's, oral or written exam. *Entrance requirements:* For master's, GRE General Test, minimum GPA of 2.5 in last 60 hours of undergraduate work. *Faculty research:* Ceramic sculpture, watercolor, wood sculpture, rock art.

Syracuse University, Graduate School, College of Arts and Sciences, Department of Fine Arts, Program in Art History, Syracuse, NY 13244. Offers MA. *Students:* 27 full-time (19 women), 1 (woman) part-time; includes 2 minority (1 Asian American or Pacific Islander, 1 Hispanic American). 46 applicants, 85% accepted, 25 enrolled. In 2007, 10 degrees awarded. *Degree requirements:* For master's, one foreign language, symposium presentation. *Entrance requirements:* For master's, GRE, research writing sample; second language. Additional exam requirements/recommendations for international students: Required—TOEFL. *Application deadline:* For fall admission, 1/1 priority date for domestic students. Applications are processed on a rolling basis. Application fee: $75. *Expenses:* Tuition: Full-time $18,216; part-time $1,012 per credit. Required fees: $980. Tuition and fees vary according to program. *Financial support:* In 2007–08, 4 fellowships were awarded; teaching assistantships. *Unit head:* Mary Warner Marien, Director of Graduate Studies, 315-443-4156. *Application contact:* Linda Straub, Information Contact, 315-443-4185, E-mail: ljstraub@syr.edu.

Announcement: The MA is offered in art history in two distinct programs. The General Studies Program offers two to four teaching assistantships annually. The more specialized Florence Program offers four fellowships, including remitted tuition and a stipend of $18,000 for the study of Italian Renaissance art in Syracuse and Florence.

Temple University, Graduate School, Tyler School of Art, Department of Art History, Philadelphia, PA 19122-6096. Offers MA, PhD. *Accreditation:* NASAD. Part-time programs available. Terminal master's awarded for partial completion of doctoral program. *Degree requirements:* For master's, 2 foreign languages, thesis, comprehensive slide exam; for doctorate, thesis/dissertation, qualifying exam. *Entrance requirements:* For master's, GRE General Test, minimum GPA of 3.0; for doctorate, MA in art history. Additional exam requirements/recommendations for international students: Required—TOEFL. Electronic applications accepted. *Faculty research:* Aegean, Greek, and Roman art; early Christian art; Medieval art and architecture; Renaissance and baroque painting, sculpture, and architecture; nineteenth and twentieth century painting and sculpture.

See Close-Up on page 269.

Texas A&M University–Commerce, Graduate School, College of Arts and Sciences, Department of Art, Commerce, TX 75429-3011. Offers art (MA, MS); art history (MA); fine arts (MFA); studio art (MA). Part-time programs available. *Faculty:* 6 full-time (2 women). *Students:* 8 full-time (4 women), 11 part-time (3 women); includes 2 minority (both Hispanic Americans), 1 international. Average age 36. In 2007, 1 master's awarded. *Degree requirements:* For master's, comprehensive exam, thesis (for some programs). *Entrance requirements:* For master's, GRE General Test. *Application deadline:* For fall admission, 6/1 priority date for domestic students; for spring admission, 11/1 priority date for domestic students. Applications are processed on a rolling basis. Application fee: $0 ($25 for international students). Electronic applications accepted. *Financial support:* In 2007–08, research assistantships (averaging $7,875 per year), teaching assistantships (averaging $7,875 per year) were awarded; Federal Work-Study, institutionally sponsored loans, and scholarships/grants also available. Financial award application deadline: 5/1; financial award applicants required to submit FAFSA. *Faculty research:* Use of different art media. *Unit head:* Dr. Kay Coughenour, Head, 903-886-5208. *Application contact:* Tammi Thompson, Graduate Admissions Adviser, 843-886-5167, Fax: 843-886-5165, E-mail: tammi_thompson@tamu-commerce.edu.

Texas Christian University, College of Fine Arts, Department of Art and Art History, Fort Worth, TX 76129. Offers art history (MA); studio art (MFA). Part-time programs available. *Degree requirements:* For master's, thesis, internship, foreign language exam. *Entrance requirements:* For master's, GRE General Test, writing sample. Additional exam requirements/recommendations for international students: Required—TOEFL. *Application deadline:* For fall admission, 3/15 for domestic students. Applications are processed on a rolling basis. Application fee: $0. *Expenses:* Tuition: Part-time $865 per credit hour. Required fees: $48 per year. *Financial support:* Unspecified assistantships available. Financial award application deadline: 3/1. *Unit head:* Ron Watson, Chairperson, 817-257-7643, E-mail: r.watson@tcu.edu. *Application contact:* Dr. Joseph Butler, Associate Dean, College of Fine Arts, E-mail: j.butler@tcu.edu.

Tufts University, Graduate School of Arts and Sciences, Department of Art and Art History, Program in Art History, Medford, MA 02155. Offers MA. Part-time programs available. *Faculty:* 12 full-time, 1 part-time/adjunct. *Students:* 27 (24 women); includes 1 minority (Hispanic American) 1 international. 111 applicants, 20% accepted, 12 enrolled. In 2007, 11 degrees awarded. *Degree requirements:* For master's, one foreign language, thesis (for some programs). *Entrance requirements:* For master's, GRE General Test, previous course work in art history, writing sample. Additional exam requirements/recommendations for international students: Required—TOEFL (minimum score 550 paper-based; 213 computer-based; 80 iBT). *Application deadline:* For fall admission, 1/15 for domestic students, 12/30 for international students. Applications are processed on a rolling basis. Application fee: $70. Electronic applications accepted. *Expenses:* Tuition: Full-time $35,052. *Financial support:* Teaching assistantships, career-related internships or fieldwork, Federal Work-Study, scholarships/grants, and tuition waivers (partial) available. Financial award application deadline: 1/15; financial award applicants required to submit FAFSA.

Tulane University, School of Liberal Arts, Department of Art, Program in Art History, New Orleans, LA 70118-5669. Offers MA. *Degree requirements:* For master's, one foreign language, thesis. *Entrance requirements:* For master's, GRE General Test, minimum B average in undergraduate course work. Additional exam requirements/recommendations for international students: Required—TOEFL. Electronic applications accepted.

Université de Montréal, Faculty of Arts and Sciences, Department of Art History, Montréal, QC H3C 3J7, Canada. Offers art history (MA, PhD); film studies (MA). *Faculty:* 24 full-time (12 women), 3 part-time/adjunct (1 woman). *Students:* 108 full-time (63 women), 2 part-time (1 woman). 98 applicants, 45% accepted, 39 enrolled. In 2007, 24 master's, 2 doctorates awarded. *Degree requirements:* For master's, thesis. *Application deadline:* For fall admission, 2/1 priority date for domestic students; for winter admission, 11/1 priority date for domestic students; for spring admission, 2/1 priority date for domestic students. Application fee: $100. Electronic applications accepted. *Financial support:* Research assistantships, teaching assistantships available. *Faculty research:* Western art from the Middle Ages, classic and modern theory, modern and contemporary art, Canadian art. *Unit head:* Christine Bernier, Director, 514-343-6184, Fax: 514-343-2393, E-mail: christine_bernier@umontreal.ca. *Application contact:* Carmita Joachim Dorce, Information Contact, 514-343-6111 Ext. 3678, E-mail: c.joachim.dorce@umontreal.ca.

Université du Québec à Montréal, Graduate Programs, Program in Art Studies, Montréal, QC H3C 3P8, Canada. Offers art history (PhD); art studies (MA); study and practices of the arts (PhD). Part-time programs available. *Degree requirements:* For master's, thesis; for doctorate, thesis/dissertation. *Entrance requirements:* For master's, appropriate bachelor's degree or equivalent, proficiency in French; for doctorate, appropriate master's degree or equivalent, proficiency in French.

Université Laval, Faculty of Letters, Department of History, Programs in Art History, Québec, QC G1K 7P4, Canada. Offers MA, PhD. Terminal master's awarded for partial completion of doctoral program. *Degree requirements:* For master's, thesis; for doctorate, comprehensive exam, thesis/dissertation. *Entrance requirements:* For master's, English test (comprehension of written English), knowledge of French; for doctorate, English test (comprehension of written English), knowledge of French and English, knowledge of a third language. Electronic applications accepted.

University at Buffalo, the State University of New York, Graduate School, College of Arts and Sciences, Department of Visual Studies, Program in Art History, Buffalo, NY 14260. Offers art history (MA); critical museum studies (Certificate). Part-time programs available. *Degree requirements:* For master's, one foreign language, thesis, field exam. *Entrance requirements:* Additional exam requirements/recommendations for international students: Required—TOEFL. Electronic applications accepted. *Faculty research:* Frank Lloyd Wright, non-Western art, Renaissance, Bronze Age Crete, American art.

The University of Alabama, Graduate School, College of Arts and Sciences, Department of Art, Tuscaloosa, AL 35487. Offers art history (MA); studio art (MA, MFA), including ceramics, painting, photography, printmaking, sculpture. *Accreditation:* NASAD. Part-time programs available. *Faculty:* 14 full-time (7 women). *Students:* 13 full-time (7 women), 1 (woman) part-time. Average age 30. 17 applicants, 41% accepted, 6 enrolled. In 2007, 9 degrees awarded. *Degree requirements:* For master's, one foreign language, comprehensive exam (for some programs), thesis (for some programs), oral exam, thesis statement, exhibit (studio art), thesis (art history). *Entrance requirements:* For master's, GRE General Test or MAT (art history), minimum GPA of 3.0, BFA or equivalent (studio art). Additional exam requirements/recommendations for international students: Required—TOEFL (minimum score 550 paper-based; 213 computer-based). *Application deadline:* For fall admission, 3/15 for domestic and international students; for spring admission, 10/15 for domestic and international students. Applications are processed on a rolling basis. Application fee: $30. Electronic applications accepted. *Expenses:* Tuition, state resident: full-time $5,700. Tuition, nonresident: full-time $16,518. *Financial support:* In 2007–08, 19 students received support, including 2 fellowships with full tuition reimbursements available (averaging $14,000 per year), 13 teaching assistantships with full and partial tuition reimbursements available (averaging $9,206 per year); career-related internships or fieldwork, institutionally sponsored loans, scholarships/grants, and unspecified assistantships also available. Financial award application deadline: 7/14. *Faculty research:* Nineteenth century American art history, Chinese art history, baroque art history, twentieth century art history, Asian art history. *Unit head:* William T. Dooley, Chairperson, 205-348-1890, Fax: 205-348-0287, E-mail: wtdooley@bama.ua.edu. *Application contact:* Craig R. Wedderspoon, Graduate Coordinator, 205-348-1898, Fax: 205-348-0287, E-mail: cwedders@bama.edu.

The University of Alabama at Birmingham, School of Arts and Humanities, Department of Art and Art History, Birmingham, AL 35294. Offers art history (MA). *Accreditation:* NASAD. *Students:* 8 full-time (7 women), 9 part-time (8 women); includes 1 minority (Hispanic American), 1 international. Average age 29. 5 applicants, 80% accepted. In 2007, 3 degrees awarded. *Degree requirements:* For master's, one foreign language, comprehensive exam, thesis optional. *Entrance requirements:* For master's, GRE General Test or MAT, minimum GPA of 2.75. *Application deadline:* Applications are processed on a rolling basis. Application fee: $35 ($60 for international students). Electronic applications accepted. *Financial support:* Research assistantships, Federal Work-Study and tuition waivers (partial) available. Financial award application deadline: 5/1. *Unit head:* Erin Wright, Chair, 205-934-4941. *Application contact:* Heather McPherson, Graduate Director, 205-934-4941.

University of Alberta, Faculty of Graduate Studies and Research, Department of Art and Design, Edmonton, AB T6G 2E1, Canada. Offers drawing (MFA); history of art, design, and visual culture (MA); industrial design (M Des); painting (MFA); printmaking (MFA); sculpture (MFA); visual communication design (M Des). *Degree requirements:* For master's, thesis. *Entrance requirements:* For master's, portfolio (MFA and MDES). Additional exam requirements/recommendations for international students: Required—TOEFL (minimum score 550 paper-based; 213 computer-based).

The University of Arizona, Graduate College, College of Fine Arts, School of Art, Program in Art History, Tucson, AZ 85721. Offers art history (MA); history and theory of art (PhD). *Accreditation:* NASAD. Part-time programs available. *Students:* 9 applicants, 44% accepted. In 2007, 3 degrees awarded. Terminal master's awarded for partial completion of doctoral program. *Degree requirements:* For master's, one foreign language, thesis; for doctorate, 2 foreign languages, comprehensive exam, thesis/dissertation. *Entrance requirements:* For master's, GRE General Test, minimum GPA of 3.0, writing sample, 3 letters of recommendation, statement of purpose, resumè. Additional exam requirements/recommendations for international students: Required—TOEFL (minimum score 550 paper-based; 213 computer-based). *Application deadline:* For fall admission, 1/15 for domestic students, 12/1 for international students. Application fee: $50. *Financial support:* In 2007–08, 2 fellowships with full and partial tuition reimbursements (averaging $10,000 per year), 2 research assistantships with full and partial tuition reimbursements (averaging $10,000 per year), 10 teaching assistantships with full and partial tuition reimbursements (averaging $5,000 per year) were awarded; career-related internships or fieldwork, Federal Work-Study, institutionally sponsored loans, scholarships/grants, tuition waivers (full and partial), and unspecified assistantships also available. Support available to part-time students. Financial award application deadline: 4/1; financial award applicants required to submit FAFSA. *Faculty research:* American art, history of photography, Mexican art, contemporary African art. *Application contact:* Brooke Grucella, Graduate Program Coordinator, 520-621-8518, Fax: 520-621-2955, E-mail: brookeg@email.arizona.edu.

Art History

University of Arkansas at Little Rock, Graduate School, College of Arts, Humanities, and Social Science, Department of Art, Little Rock, AR 72204-1099. Offers art education (MA); art history (MA); studio art (MA). *Accreditation:* NASAD. Part-time programs available. *Students:* Average age 38. *Degree requirements:* For master's, 4 foreign languages, oral exam, oral defense of thesis or exhibit. *Entrance requirements:* For master's, portfolio review or term paper evaluation, minimum GPA of 2.7. *Application deadline:* Applications are processed on a rolling basis. Application fee: $25 ($30 for international students). *Financial support:* Research assistantships with tuition reimbursements, teaching assistantships with tuition reimbursements, Federal Work-Study, institutionally sponsored loans, and unspecified assistantships available. Support available to part-time students. *Unit head:* Dr. Winefurd Bruhl, Chairperson, 501-569-3182, E-mail: wgbruhl@ualr.edu. *Application contact:* Marjorie Williams-Smith, Coordinator, 501-569-3182, E-mail: mwsmith@ualr.edu.

The University of British Columbia, Faculty of Arts and Faculty of Graduate Studies, Department of Art History, Visual Art, and Theory, Vancouver, BC V6T 1Z1, Canada. Offers art history (MA, PhD, Diploma); critical and curatorial studies (MA); visual art (MFA). Part-time programs available. *Faculty:* 19 full-time (11 women), 1 part-time/adjunct (0 women). *Students:* 74 full-time (53 women), 1 part-time. 178 applicants, 26% accepted, 17 enrolled. In 2007, 16 master's, 5 doctorates awarded. *Degree requirements:* For master's, one foreign language, thesis, final exhibition (MFA, MA, CCST); for doctorate, 2 foreign languages, comprehensive exam, thesis/dissertation. *Entrance requirements:* For master's, bachelor's degree with minimum B+ average for MFA; for doctorate, master's degree with minimum A- average. Additional exam requirements/recommendations for international students: Required—TOEFL (minimum score 600 paper-based; 250 computer-based). *Application deadline:* For fall admission, 2/1 for domestic and international students. Application fee: $90 Canadian dollars ($150 Canadian dollars for international students). Electronic applications accepted. *Financial support:* In 2007–08, 22 fellowships (averaging $16,000 per year), 20 research assistantships (averaging $4,600 per year), 21 teaching assistantships (averaging $10,490 per year) were awarded; Federal Work-Study, scholarships/grants, health care benefits, and unspecified assistantships also available. *Faculty research:* Conceptual art, Asian art, indigenous North American art, post-second war art, eighteenth and nineteenth century art. *Unit head:* Dr. Rhodri Windsor-Liscombe, Head, 604-822-5650, Fax: 604-822-9003, E-mail: rhodri@interchange.ubc.ca. *Application contact:* Audrey Van Slyck, Graduate Secretary, 604-822-4340, Fax: 604-822-9003, E-mail: ahvagrad@interchange.ubc.ca.

University of California, Berkeley, Graduate Division, College of Letters and Science, Department of History of Art, Berkeley, CA 94720-1500. Offers PhD. *Degree requirements:* For doctorate, 2 foreign languages, thesis/dissertation, qualifying exam. *Entrance requirements:* For doctorate, GRE General Test, minimum GPA of 3.0, 3 letters of recommendation. Additional exam requirements/recommendations for international students: Required—TOEFL. *Application deadline:* For fall admission, 12/15 for domestic students. Application fee: $70 ($90 for international students). *Financial support:* Fellowships, research assistantships, teaching assistantships, career-related internships or fieldwork, Federal Work-Study, institutionally sponsored loans, tuition waivers (full and partial), and unspecified assistantships available. Financial award applicants required to submit FAFSA. *Faculty research:* Modernism, Italian Renaissance art and architecture, Gothic art and architecture, women artists' representations of the body, the body in ancient Greece. *Unit head:* Patricia Berger, Chair, 510-642-4523, E-mail: pberger@berkeley.edu. *Application contact:* Anna Kathleen Gazdowicz, Graduate Student Affairs Officer, 510-642-5510, Fax: 540-643-2185, E-mail: arthist_grad@berkeley.edu.

University of California, Davis, Graduate Studies, Program in Art History, Davis, CA 95616. Offers MA. *Degree requirements:* For master's, thesis. *Entrance requirements:* For master's, GRE, minimum GPA of 3.0, writing sample. Additional exam requirements/recommendations for international students: Required—TOEFL (minimum score 550 paper-based; 213 computer-based). Electronic applications accepted.

Announcement: Master of Arts in the history of art. Special emphasis on the art and architecture of the ancient Mediterranean world, early and modern China, early and modern Islamic world, early and modern Italy, and Europe and America from 1750 to present; critical theory; histories of photography, architecture and urban design, collecting, and museums. Excellent library, nearby museums. Interdisciplinary work encouraged. Applicants from other fields with a strong interest in art history welcome. Gateway degree for museum careers, community college teaching, and top PhD programs.

University of California, Irvine, Office of Graduate Studies, School of Humanities, Department of Art History, Irvine, CA 92697. Offers visual studies (MA, PhD). *Students:* 45 full-time (26 women); includes 8 minority (2 African Americans, 3 Asian Americans or Pacific Islanders, 3 Hispanic Americans), 3 international. In 2007, 6 master's, 3 doctorates awarded. *Degree requirements:* For doctorate, thesis/dissertation. *Entrance requirements:* For master's, GRE, minimum GPA of 3.0; for doctorate, GRE General Test, writing sample. Additional exam requirements/recommendations for international students: Required—TOEFL (minimum score 550 paper-based; 213 computer-based). *Application deadline:* For fall admission, 1/15 for domestic students; for winter admission, 10/15 for domestic students. Application fee: $60. Electronic applications accepted. *Financial support:* Fellowships, teaching assistantships, institutionally sponsored loans, traineeships, health care benefits, and unspecified assistantships available. Financial award application deadline: 3/1; financial award applicants required to submit FAFSA. *Faculty research:* Interdisciplinary study and research in art history, critical theory, women's studies, cultural studies, film studies. *Unit head:* James D. Herbert, Chair, 949-824-4014, E-mail: jdherb@uci.edu. *Application contact:* Jewel Wilson, Manager, 949-824-6635, Fax: 949-824-2509, E-mail: jtwilson@uci.edu.

University of California, Los Angeles, Graduate Division, College of Letters and Science, Department of Art History, Los Angeles, CA 90095. Offers MA, PhD. *Students:* 63 full-time (49 women); includes 13 minority (2 African Americans, 6 Asian Americans or Pacific Islanders, 5 Hispanic Americans), 7 international. Average age 33. 103 applicants, 19% accepted, 7 enrolled. In 2007, 6 master's, 7 doctorates awarded. Terminal master's awarded for partial completion of doctoral program. *Median time to degree:* Of those who began their doctoral program in fall 1999, 22% received their degree in 8 years or less. *Degree requirements:* For master's, one foreign language, thesis; for doctorate, one foreign language, thesis/dissertation, oral and written qualifying exams. *Entrance requirements:* For master's, Degree objective must be Ph.D; for doctorate, GRE General Test, 2 samples of research writing or thesis, minimum undergraduate GPA of 3.0, 3 letters of recommendation. *Application deadline:* For fall admission, 11/30 for domestic students. Application fee: $60 ($80 for international students). Electronic applications accepted. *Expenses:* Tuition, nonresident: full-time $5,728. Required fees: $8,966. Full-time tuition and fees vary according to program and student level. *Financial support:* In 2007–08, 63 students received support, including 49 fellowships with full and partial tuition reimbursements available, 16 research assistantships with full and partial tuition reimbursements available, 31 teaching assistantships with full and partial tuition reimbursements available; scholarships/grants also available. Financial award application deadline: 3/1; financial award applicants required to submit FAFSA. *Unit head:* Dr. Irene Bierman-McKinnof, Chair, 310-825-1181. *Application contact:* Departmental Office, 310-825-3480, E-mail: mvazquez@humnet.ucla.edu.

University of California, Riverside, Graduate Division, Department of Art History, Riverside, CA 92521-0102. Offers MA. Part-time programs available. *Faculty:* 9 full-time (5 women), 2 part-time/adjunct (0 women). *Students:* 13 full-time (9 women), 1 (woman) part-time; includes 2 minority (1 Asian American or Pacific Islander, 1 Hispanic American), 2 international. Average age 32. In 2007, 10 degrees awarded. *Degree requirements:* For master's, one foreign language, thesis. *Entrance requirements:* For master's, GRE General Test, sample of written work, minimum GPA of 3.2. Additional exam requirements/recommendations for international students: Required—TOEFL (minimum score 550 paper-based; 213 computer-based; 80 iBT). *Application deadline:* For fall admission, 5/1 for domestic students, 2/1 for international students; for winter admission, 9/1 for domestic students, 7/1 for international students; for spring admission, 12/1 for domestic students, 10/1 for international students. Applications are processed on a rolling basis. Application fee: $60 ($75 for international students). Electronic applications accepted. *Financial support:* In 2007–08, fellowships with full and partial tuition reimbursements (averaging $12,000 per year), teaching assistantships with partial tuition reimbursements (averaging $16,500 per year) were awarded; research assistantships with partial tuition reimbursements, career-related internships or fieldwork, institutionally sponsored loans, scholarships/grants, tuition waivers (full and partial), and readerships also available. Financial award application deadline: 1/5; financial award applicants required to submit FAFSA. *Faculty research:* Ancient, medieval, Renaissance, seventeenth and eighteenth century art; modern European art; contemporary art and theory; modern architecture and urbanism; history of photography. *Unit head:* Dr. Patricia Morton, Chair, 951-827-2674, Fax: 951-827-2331, E-mail: arthist@ucr.edu. *Application contact:* Graduate Advisor, 951-827-2676, Fax: 951-827-2331, E-mail: arthist@ucr.edu.

University of California, Santa Barbara, Graduate Division, College of Letters and Sciences, Division of Humanities and Fine Arts, Department of History of Art and Architecture, Santa Barbara, CA 93106. Offers PhD, MA/PhD. *Faculty:* 17 full-time (7 women), 3 part-time/adjunct (1 woman). *Students:* 39 full-time (34 women); includes 7 minority (3 Asian Americans or Pacific Islanders, 4 Hispanic Americans), 3 international. Average age 32. 76 applicants, 29% accepted, 5 enrolled. In 2007, 6 doctorates awarded. Terminal master's awarded for partial completion of doctoral program. *Median time to degree:* Of those who began their doctoral program in fall 1999, 9% received their degree in 8 years or less. *Degree requirements:* For doctorate, 2 foreign languages, comprehensive exam, thesis/dissertation. *Entrance requirements:* For doctorate, GRE, sample of written work. Additional exam requirements/recommendations for international students: Required—TOEFL (minimum score 550 paper-based; 213 computer-based; 80 iBT). *Application deadline:* For fall admission, 12/15 for domestic and international students. Application fee: $60. Electronic applications accepted. *Expenses:* Tuition, nonresident: full-time $14,888. Required fees: $10,108. *Financial support:* In 2007–08, 34 students received support, including 24 fellowships with full and partial tuition reimbursements available (averaging $7,500 per year), 2 research assistantships with full and partial tuition reimbursements available (averaging $6,300 per year), 55 teaching assistantships with partial tuition reimbursements available (averaging $16,391 per year); career-related internships or fieldwork, Federal Work-Study, institutionally sponsored loans, scholarships/grants, health care benefits, and unspecified assistantships also available. Financial award application deadline: 12/15; financial award applicants required to submit FAFSA. *Faculty research:* Renaissance/Baroque, theory, architectural history, Medieval, Northern Renaissance. *Unit head:* Prof. Peter C. Sturman, Chair, 805-893-8710. *Application contact:* L. Fredrickson, Graduate Program Administrator, 805-893-2454, Fax: 805-893-7117, E-mail: gdahist@arthistory.ucsb.edu.

University of Chicago, Division of the Humanities, Department of Art History, Chicago, IL 60637-1513. Offers AM, PhD. *Students:* 80. 144 applicants, 12% accepted, 9 enrolled. *Degree requirements:* For master's, variable foreign language requirement, thesis; for doctorate, variable foreign language requirement, thesis/dissertation. *Entrance requirements:* For master's and doctorate, GRE General Test. *Application deadline:* For fall admission, 12/15 for domestic students. Application fee: $55. *Financial support:* Fellowships, Federal Work-Study and institutionally sponsored loans available. Financial award application deadline: 12/15; financial award applicants required to submit FAFSA. *Unit head:* Dr. Martha Ward, Chair, 773-702-0278.

University of Cincinnati, Graduate School, College of Design, Architecture, Art, and Planning, School of Art, Program in Art History, Cincinnati, OH 45221. Offers MA. *Accreditation:* NASAD. Part-time programs available. *Students:* 20 full-time (13 women), 11 part-time (9 women), 2 international. In 2007, 11 degrees awarded. *Degree requirements:* For master's, one foreign language, comprehensive exam, thesis. *Application deadline:* For fall admission, 2/1 for domestic students. Application fee: $30. Electronic applications accepted. *Financial support:* In 2007–08, 4 fellowships (averaging $7,000 per year) were awarded; tuition waivers (partial) and unspecified assistantships also available. Financial award application deadline: 3/1. *Application contact:* Dr. Theresa Leninger-Miller, Information Contact, 513-556-0273, Fax: 513-556-2887, E-mail: theresa.leininger@uc.edu.

University of Colorado at Boulder, Graduate School, College of Arts and Sciences, Department of Art and Art History, Boulder, CO 80309. Offers art history (MA), including 19th century art, contemporary art criticism, early 20th century art, Russian and Soviet art; ceramics (MFA); drawing (MFA); painting (MFA); photography and media arts (MFA); printmaking (MFA); sculpture (MFA). *Faculty:* 27. *Students:* 42 full-time (22 women), 1 (woman) part-time; includes 4 minority (all Hispanic Americans), 1 international. Average age 32. 15 applicants, 73% accepted. In 2007, 16 degrees awarded. *Degree requirements:* For master's, variable foreign language requirement, comprehensive exam, thesis (for some programs). *Entrance requirements:* For master's, GRE General Test, minimum undergraduate GPA of 3.0, portfolio. *Application deadline:* For fall admission, 1/15 priority date for domestic students, 12/1 for international students. Application fee: $50 ($60 for international students). *Financial support:* In 2007–08, 32 fellowships (averaging $2,294 per year) were awarded; Federal Work-Study, scholarships/grants, and tuition waivers (full) also available. Financial award application deadline: 1/15. *Faculty research:* Drawing, painting, ceramics, sculpture, photography and media arts, printmaking (MFA); history-Russian and Soviet art, Early 20th Century art, contemporary art criticism, 19th Century art (MA). *Unit head:* James Johnson, Chair, 303-492-6504, Fax: 303-492-4886, E-mail: james.johnson@colorado.edu. *Application contact:* Graduate Program Assistant, 303-492-2419, Fax: 303-492-4886, E-mail: finearts@colorado.edu.

University of Connecticut, Graduate School, School of Fine Arts, Department of Art and Art History, Field of Art History, Storrs, CT 06269. Offers MA. *Accreditation:* NASAD. *Faculty:* 18 full-time (11 women). *Students:* 10 full-time (all women); includes 2 minority (1 African American, 1 Asian American or Pacific Islander), 1 international. Average age 26. 10 applicants, 40% accepted, 4 enrolled. In 2007, 3 degrees awarded. *Degree requirements:* For master's, comprehensive exam. *Entrance requirements:* Additional exam requirements/recommendations for international students: Required—TOEFL (minimum score 550 paper-based; 213 computer-based). *Application deadline:* For fall admission, 2/1 priority date for domestic and international students; for spring admission, 11/1 for domestic students, 10/1 for international students. Applications are processed on a rolling basis. Application fee: $55. Electronic applications accepted. *Expenses:* Tuition, state resident: part-time $469 per credit hour. Tuition, nonresident: part-time $1,218 per credit hour. *Financial support:* In 2007–08, 8 research assistantships, 2 teaching assistantships with full tuition reimbursements were awarded; Federal Work-Study, health care benefits, and unspecified assistantships also available. Financial award application deadline: 2/1; financial award applicants required to submit FAFSA. *Unit head:* Robin Greeley, Chairperson, 860-486-3365, E-mail: robin.greeley@uconn.edu. *Application contact:* Lorraine McConnell, Administrative Assistant, 860-486-8919, E-mail: lorraine.mcconnell@uconn.edu.

University of Delaware, College of Arts and Sciences, Department of Art History, Newark, DE 19716. Offers MA, PhD. Part-time programs available. *Faculty:* 13 full-time (9 women). *Students:* 64 full-time (55 women); includes 7 minority (3 African Americans, 2 Asian Americans or Pacific Islanders, 2 Hispanic Americans), 1 international. Average age 33. 76 applicants, 17% accepted, 9 enrolled. In 2007, 6 master's, 2 doctorates awarded. *Median time to degree:* Of those who began their doctoral program in fall 1999, 50% received their degree in 8 years or less. *Degree requirements:* For master's, one foreign language, thesis; for doctorate, 2 foreign languages, comprehensive exam, thesis/dissertation. *Entrance requirements:* For master's and doctorate, GRE General Test, writing sample. Additional exam requirements/recommendations for international students: Required—TOEFL. *Application deadline:* For fall admission, 1/1 for domestic students. Application fee: $60. Electronic applications accepted. *Financial support:* In 2007–08, 32 students received support, including 9 fellowships with tuition reimbursements available (averaging $14,000 per year), 10 research assistantships with tuition reimbursements available (averaging $14,000 per year), 13 teaching assistantships with tuition reimbursements available (averaging $14,000 per year); career-related internships or fieldwork, Federal Work-Study, health care benefits, and tuition waivers (full) also available. Financial award application deadline: 1/1. *Faculty research:* Art of Europe and the United States, art theory, vernacular architecture, medieval manuscripts, African art and architecture. Total annual research expenditures: $26,800. *Unit head:* Bernard L. Herman, Chair, 302-831-8415, Fax: 302-831-8243. *Application contact:* Dr. David Stone, Director of Graduate Studies, 302-831-6789, Fax: 302-831-8243.

University of Denver, Faculty of Arts and Humanities/Social Sciences, School of Art and Art History, Denver, CO 80208. Offers art history (MA); art history/museum studies (MA); electronic media arts and design (MFA); studio art (MFA). *Accreditation:* NASAD. Part-time programs available. *Faculty:* 15 full-time (10 women). *Students:* 24 full-time (20 women), 2 part-time (1 woman); includes 2 minority (1 Asian American or Pacific Islander, 1 Hispanic American), 1 international. Average age 28. In 2007, 10 degrees awarded. *Degree requirements:* For master's, one foreign language, research paper. *Entrance requirements:* For master's, GRE. Additional exam requirements/recommendations for international students: Required—TOEFL. *Application deadline:* Applications are processed on a rolling basis. Application fee: $50. Electronic applications accepted. *Financial support:* In 2007–08, 5 teaching assistantships with full and partial tuition reimbursements (averaging $6,500 per year) were awarded; career-related internships or fieldwork, Federal Work-Study, institutionally sponsored loans, and scholarships/grants also available. Support available to part-time students. Financial award application deadline: 3/1; financial award applicants required to submit FAFSA. *Faculty research:* Images of women in alchemical manuscripts and books, Giovanni Benedetto, Salvatore Castiglione. *Unit head:* Dr. Annette Stott, Director, 303-871-2846. *Application contact:* Dr. M. Warlick, Graduate Advisor, 303-871-2846, E-mail: saah-interest@du.edu.

University of Florida, Graduate School, College of Fine Arts, School of Art and Art History, Gainesville, FL 32611. Offers art (MFA), including ceramics, creative photography, drawing, electronic intermedia, graphic design, painting, printmaking, sculpture; art education (MA); art history (MA, PhD); digital arts and sciences (MA); museology (museum studies) (MA). *Accreditation:* NASAD. *Faculty:* 29 full-time (14 women), 2 part-time/adjunct (1 woman). *Students:* 82 (48 women); includes 4 minority (2 Asian Americans or Pacific Islanders, 2 Hispanic Americans) 4 international. In 2007, 20 degrees awarded. *Degree requirements:* For master's, variable foreign language requirement, project or thesis (MFA). *Entrance requirements:* For master's, portfolio (MFA), writing sample (MA), GRE General Test or minimum GPA of 3.0. Additional exam requirements/recommendations for international students: Required—TOEFL (minimum score 550 paper-based; 213 computer-based). *Application deadline:* For fall admission, 1/15 priority date for domestic students. Applications are processed on a rolling basis. Application fee: $30. Electronic applications accepted. *Expenses:* Tuition, state resident: full-time $7,478. Tuition, nonresident: full-time $22,603. *Financial support:* In 2007–08, 3 research assistantships with tuition reimbursements (averaging $9,515 per year), 67 teaching assistantships with tuition reimbursements (averaging $9,839 per year) were awarded; fellowships, Federal Work-Study, institutionally sponsored loans, and unspecified assistantships also available. Financial award applicants required to submit FAFSA. *Faculty research:* Studio production, art historical studies of style context. *Unit head:* Glenn Willumson, Program Director, 352-392-0201 Ext. 234. *Application contact:* Prof. Richard Heipp, Coordinator, 352-392-0201 Ext. 239, Fax: 352-392-8453, E-mail: heipp@ufl.edu.

University of Georgia, Graduate School, College of Arts and Sciences, Lamar Dodd School of Art, Program in Art History, Athens, GA 30602. Offers MA. *Accreditation:* NASAD. *Students:* 12 full-time (10 women), 6 part-time (4 women). 27 applicants, 37% accepted, 3 enrolled. In 2007, 3 degrees awarded. *Degree requirements:* For master's, one foreign language, thesis. *Entrance requirements:* For master's, GRE General Test. *Application deadline:* For fall admission, 7/1 priority date for domestic students; for spring admission, 11/15 for domestic students. Application fee: $50. Electronic applications accepted. *Financial support:* Fellowships, research assistantships, teaching assistantships, unspecified assistantships available. *Application contact:* Larry Millard, Graduate Coordinator, 706-542-1665, Fax: 706-542-0226, E-mail: millard@uga.edu.

University of Hawaii at Manoa, Graduate Division, Colleges of Arts and Sciences, College of Arts and Humanities, Department of Art and Art History, Honolulu, HI 96822. Offers art (MA); art history (MA); visual arts (MFA). Part-time programs available. *Faculty:* 23 full-time (12 women), 1 part-time/adjunct (0 women). *Students:* 30 full-time (12 women), 6 part-time (1 woman); includes 6 minority (all Asian Americans or Pacific Islanders), 3 international. Average age 36. 71 applicants, 30% accepted, 12 enrolled. *Degree requirements:* For master's, thesis optional. *Entrance requirements:* For master's, GRE General Test, BFA, 18 hours of course work in art history. Additional exam requirements/recommendations for international students: Required—TOEFL (minimum score 600 paper-based; 250 computer-based; 100 iBT), IELTS (minimum score 7). *Application deadline:* For fall admission, 1/15 for domestic students, 12/15 for international students; for spring admission, 9/1 for domestic students, 8/1 for international students. Application fee: $50. *Financial support:* In 2007–08, 3 teaching assistantships (averaging $13,296 per year) were awarded; fellowships, research assistantships, Federal Work-Study, scholarships/grants, and tuition waivers (full and partial) also available. Financial award application deadline: 3/1; financial award applicants required to submit FAFSA. *Faculty research:* Painting, sculpture, glass, design, printmaking. Total annual research expenditures: $9,805. *Application contact:* Richard Mills, Graduate Field Chairperson, 808-956-8251, Fax: 808-956-9043, E-mail: rlmills@hawaii.edu.

University of Illinois at Chicago, Graduate College, College of Architecture and Art, Program in Art History, Chicago, IL 60607-7128. Offers MA, PhD. Part-time and evening/weekend programs available. Terminal master's awarded for partial completion of doctoral program. *Degree requirements:* For master's, one foreign language, thesis or alternative; for doctorate, thesis/dissertation. *Entrance requirements:* For master's, GRE General Test, minimum GPA of 2.75, 3 letters of recommendation; for doctorate, GRE General Test, M.A. in art history or equivalent, minimum GPA of 3.0. Additional exam requirements/recommendations for international students: Required—TOEFL. Electronic applications accepted. *Faculty research:* Modern painting and sculpture, history of architecture, city planning and design, history of photography.

University of Illinois at Urbana–Champaign, Graduate College, College of Fine and Applied Arts, School of Art and Design, Program in Art History, Champaign, IL 61820. Offers MA, PhD. *Accreditation:* NASAD. *Students:* 26 full-time (22 women), 12 part-time (9 women); includes 3 minority (1 African American, 1 Asian American or Pacific Islander, 1 Hispanic American), 8 international. 40 applicants, 23% accepted, 9 enrolled. In 2007, 5 master's, 3 doctorates awarded. *Degree requirements:* For doctorate, thesis/dissertation. *Entrance requirements:* For master's, minimum GPA of 3.0. *Application deadline:* Applications are processed on a rolling basis. Application fee: $60 ($75 for international students). Electronic applications accepted. *Financial support:* Application deadline: 2/15. *Unit head:* David O'Brien, Chair, 217-333-7102, Fax: 217-244-7688, E-mail: obrien1@uiuc.edu.

The University of Iowa, Graduate College, College of Liberal Arts and Sciences, School of Art and Art History, Program in Art History, Iowa City, IA 52242-1316. Offers MA, PhD. *Degree requirements:* For master's, one foreign language, thesis, exam; for doctorate, 2 foreign languages, comprehensive exam, thesis/dissertation, final exams. *Entrance requirements:* For master's, GRE General Test; for doctorate, GRE General Test, MA in art history. Additional exam requirements/recommendations for international students: Required—TOEFL (minimum score 550 paper-based; 213 computer-based). Electronic applications accepted. *Expenses:* Tuition, state resident: part-time $349 per hour. Tuition, nonresident: part-time $349 per hour. Tuition and fees vary according to course load and program. *Faculty research:* African, American, ancient, baroque, Medieval, and Renaissance art.

University of Kansas, Research and Graduate Studies, College of Liberal Arts and Sciences, History of Art Department, Lawrence, KS 66045. Offers MA, PhD. Part-time programs available. *Faculty:* 13. *Students:* 54 full-time (45 women), 13 part-time (10 women); includes 6 minority (1 African American, 1 American Indian/Alaska Native, 4 Asian Americans or Pacific Islanders), 13 international. Average age 35. 37 applicants, 54% accepted, 9 enrolled. In 2007, 6 master's, 2 doctorates awarded. Terminal master's awarded for partial completion of doctoral program. *Degree requirements:* For master's, one foreign language, comprehensive exam, thesis optional, 30 credit hours of coursework; for doctorate, 2 foreign languages, comprehensive exam, thesis/dissertation, 1 year full-time enrollment. *Entrance requirements:* For master's, GRE, minimum undergraduate GPA of 3.3, 18 credit hours of art history; for doctorate, GRE, MA in art history or related field. Additional exam requirements/recommendations for international students: Required—TOEFL, TWE (minimum score 4.5). *Application deadline:* For fall admission, 1/1 for domestic and international students; for spring admission, 10/15 for domestic and international students. Application fee: $55 ($60 for international students). Electronic applications accepted. *Expenses:* Tuition, state resident: full-time $5,838. Tuition, nonresident: full-time $13,409. Tuition and fees vary according to program. *Financial support:* Fellowships with full tuition reimbursements, research assistantships with partial tuition reimbursements, teaching assistantships with full tuition reimbursements, scholarships/grants and unspecified assistantships available. Financial award application deadline: 1/1. *Faculty research:* American art, history of photography, African art, Asian art, European art, modern art. *Unit head:* Linda Stone-Ferrier, Chair, 785-864-4713, Fax: 785-864-5091, E-mail: lsf@ku.edu. *Application contact:* Karen Brichoux, Graduate Admissions, 785-864-4713, Fax: 785-864-5091, E-mail: arthist@ku.edu.

University of Kentucky, Graduate School, College of Fine Arts, Program in Art History, Lexington, KY 40506-0032. Offers MA. *Faculty:* 19 full-time (7 women). *Students:* 10 full-time (8 women), 3 part-time (2 women), 1 international. Average age 33. 13 applicants, 54% accepted, 1 enrolled. In 2007, 3 degrees awarded. *Degree requirements:* For master's, 2 foreign languages, comprehensive exam, thesis. *Entrance requirements:* For master's, GRE General Test, minimum undergraduate GPA of 2.75. Additional exam requirements/recommendations for international students: Required—TOEFL (minimum score 550 paper-based; 213 computer-based). *Application deadline:* For fall admission, 7/17 priority date for domestic students, 2/1 priority date for international students; for spring admission, 12/18 priority date for domestic students, 6/15 priority date for international students. Application fee: $50 ($65 for international students). Electronic applications accepted. *Expenses:* Tuition, state resident: part-time $437 per credit hour. Tuition, nonresident: part-time $931 per credit hour. *Financial support:* In 2007–08, 4 students received support, including fellowships with full tuition reimbursements available (averaging $2,077 per year), 1 research assistantship with full tuition reimbursement available (averaging $9,616 per year), 3 teaching assistantships with full tuition reimbursements available (averaging $9,480 per year); Federal Work-Study, institutionally sponsored loans, scholarships/grants, traineeships, tuition waivers (partial), and unspecified assistantships also available. Support available to part-time students. Financial award application deadline: 3/15. *Faculty research:* Northern European prints and drawings, nineteenth century French painting and drawing, Roman sarcophagus sculpture, manuscript illumination, history and theory of photography. *Unit head:* Dr. Dennis Carpenter, Director of Graduate Studies, 859-257-6041, Fax: 859-257-3042. *Application contact:* Dr. Brian Jackson, Senior Associate Dean, 859-257-4667, Fax: 859-257-4676, E-mail: brian.jackson@uky.edu.

University of Louisville, Graduate School, College of Arts and Sciences, Department of Fine Arts, Program in Art History, Louisville, KY 40292-0001. Offers MA, PhD. *Students:* 11 full-time (9 women), 7 part-time (5 women); includes 2 minority (both African Americans), 1 international. Average age 42. In 2007, 1 degree awarded. *Degree requirements:* For master's, thesis; for doctorate, thesis/dissertation. *Entrance requirements:* For master's and doctorate, GRE General Test. *Application deadline:* Applications are processed on a rolling basis. Application fee: $50. *Financial support:* Teaching assistantships available. *Unit head:* Dr. James T. Grubola, Chair, Department of Fine Arts, 502-852-0759, Fax: 502-852-6791, E-mail: grubola@louisville.edu.

University of Maryland, College Park, Graduate Studies, College of Arts and Humanities, Department of Art History and Archaeology, College Park, MD 20742. Offers art history (MA, PhD). *Faculty:* 11 full-time (5 women), 8 part-time/adjunct (6 women). *Students:* 42 full-time (33 women), 3 part-time (all women); includes 8 minority (1 African American, 1 American Indian/Alaska Native, 6 Asian Americans or Pacific Islanders), 7 international. 111 applicants, 22% accepted, 9 enrolled. In 2007, 3 master's, 9 doctorates awarded. *Median time to degree:* Of those who began their doctoral program in fall 1999, 33% received their degree in 8 years or less. *Degree requirements:* For master's, one foreign language, thesis, oral exam; for doctorate, 2 foreign languages, thesis/dissertation, oral exam. *Entrance requirements:* For master's, GRE General Test, minimum GPA of 3.0, writing sample, 3 letters of recommendation. Additional exam requirements/recommendations for international students: Required—TOEFL. *Application deadline:* For fall admission, 12/10 for domestic students, 2/1 for international students. Applications are processed on a rolling basis. Application fee: $60. Electronic applications accepted. *Financial support:* In 2007–08, 8 fellowships with full tuition reimbursements (averaging $14,552 per year), 23 teaching assistantships with tuition reimbursements (averaging $14,829 per year) were awarded; research assistantships, Federal Work-Study and scholarships/grants also available. Support available to part-time students. Financial award applicants required to submit FAFSA. *Faculty research:* Western, African, pre-Columbian, American, and East Asian art. Total annual research expenditures: $29,318. *Unit head:* Dr. William Pressley, Chair, 301-405-1479, Fax: 301-314-9305. *Application contact:* Dean of Graduate School, 301-405-4190, Fax: 301-314-9305.

University of Massachusetts Amherst, Graduate School, College of Humanities and Fine Arts, Department of Art, Program in Art History, Amherst, MA 01003. Offers MA. Part-time programs available. *Students:* 13 full-time (11 women), 4 part-time (all women), 1 international. Average age 26. 33 applicants, 64% accepted, 7 enrolled. In 2007, 7 degrees awarded. *Degree requirements:* For master's, thesis or alternative. *Entrance requirements:* For master's, GRE General Test. Additional exam requirements/recommendations for international students: Required—TOEFL (minimum score 530 paper-based; 197 computer-based). *Application deadline:* For fall admission, 1/15 for domestic and international students; for spring admission, 10/1 for domestic and international students. Applications are processed on a rolling basis. Application fee: $50 ($65 for international students). Electronic applications accepted. *Expenses:* Tuition, state resident: full-time $2,640; part-time $110 per credit. Tuition, nonresident: full-time $9,936; part-time $414 per credit. Required fees: $7,455. One-time fee: $332. Tuition and fees vary according to course load, campus/location, program and reciprocity agreements. *Financial support:* In 2007–08, 1 fellowship with full tuition reimbursement (averaging $3,344 per year), 15 teaching assistantships with tuition reimbursements (averaging $5,930 per year) were awarded; research assistantships with full tuition reimbursements, career-related internships or fieldwork, Federal Work-Study, scholarships/grants, traineeships, and unspecified assistantships also available. Support available to part-time students. Financial award application deadline: 2/1. *Unit head:* Dr. Monika Schmitter, Director, 413-545-3595, Fax: 413-545-3929.

University of Memphis, Graduate School, College of Communication and Fine Arts, Department of Art, Program in Art History, Memphis, TN 38152. Offers Egyptian art and archaeology (MA); general art history (MA). *Accreditation:* NASAD. *Students:* 20 full-time (17 women), 3 part-time (all women); includes 2 minority (both African Americans) Average age 27. 23 applicants, 57% accepted, 9 enrolled. In 2007, 5 degrees awarded. *Degree requirements:* For master's, comprehensive exam. *Entrance requirements:* For master's, GRE General Test or MAT, sample of written work. *Application deadline:* For fall admission, 8/1 for domestic students. Application fee: $35 ($60 for international students). *Expenses:* Tuition, state resident: full-time $6,990; part-time $377 per hour. Tuition, nonresident: full-time $17,818; part-time $830 per hour. Tuition and fees vary according to course load and program. *Financial support:* Research assistantships, teaching assistantships available. *Faculty research:* Egyptology, intersection of art and religion, arts of African Diaspora, native American art, early Netherlandish painting. *Application contact:* Prof. William McKeown, Coordinator of Graduate Studies, 901-678-2842, Fax: 901-678-2735, E-mail: mwcarlsl@memphis.edu.

University of Miami, Graduate School, College of Arts and Sciences, Department of Art and Art History, Coral Gables, FL 33124. Offers art history (MA); ceramics/glass (MFA); graphic

Art History

University of Miami (continued)
design/multimedia (MFA); painting (MFA); photography/digital imaging (MFA); printmaking (MFA); sculpture (MFA). Part-time programs available. *Faculty:* 14 full-time (6 women). *Students:* 23 full-time (15 women), 5 part-time (3 women); includes 5 minority (2 African Americans, 3 Hispanic Americans). Average age 29. 55 applicants, 18% accepted, 8 enrolled. In 2007, 8 degrees awarded. *Degree requirements:* For master's, variable foreign language requirement, thesis, exhibit (MFA), comprehensive exam (MA). *Entrance requirements:* For master's, GRE General Test (MA), research paper (MA), slide portfolio (MFA), artist statement (MFA). Additional exam requirements/recommendations for international students: Required—TOEFL. *Application deadline:* For fall admission, 2/15 for domestic students, 1/15 for international students; for winter admission, 9/15 for domestic students. Application fee: $50. Electronic applications accepted. *Financial support:* In 2007–08, 25 students received support, including 17 teaching assistantships with full tuition reimbursements available (averaging $10,000 per year); Federal Work-Study, institutionally sponsored loans, scholarships/grants, and tuition waivers (full) also available. Financial award application deadline: 3/1; financial award applicants required to submit FAFSA. *Faculty research:* Installation art, public art. *Unit head:* Prof. Lise Drost, Chair, 305-284-2542, Fax: 305-284-2115, E-mail: l.drost@miami.edu. *Application contact:* Prof. Brian Curtis, Graduate Secretary, 305-284-2542, Fax: 305-284-2115, E-mail: art-arh@miami.edu.

University of Michigan, Horace H. Rackham School of Graduate Studies, College of Literature, Science, and the Arts, Department of History of Art, Ann Arbor, MI 48109. Offers PhD. *Faculty:* 19 full-time (11 women), 4 part-time/adjunct (1 woman). *Students:* 32 full-time (29 women); includes 4 minority (2 Asian Americans or Pacific Islanders, 2 Hispanic Americans), 5 international. Average age 26. 120 applicants, 11% accepted, 6 enrolled. In 2007, 4 degrees awarded. *Degree requirements:* For doctorate, 2 foreign languages, thesis/dissertation, oral defense of dissertation, preliminary exam. *Entrance requirements:* For doctorate, GRE General Test. *Application deadline:* For fall admission, 12/12 for domestic and international students. Application fee: $60 ($75 for international students). Electronic applications accepted. *Financial support:* In 2007–08, 17 fellowships with full tuition reimbursements (averaging $15,199 per year), 1 research assistantship with full tuition reimbursement (averaging $15,199 per year), 13 teaching assistantships with full tuition reimbursements (averaging $15,199 per year) were awarded; career-related internships or fieldwork also available. Financial award application deadline: 1/1. *Faculty research:* Asian, African and African-American, ancient, medieval and Byzantine, early modern, and modern art. Total annual research expenditures: $25,000. *Unit head:* Celeste Brusati, Chair, 734-764-5400, Fax: 734-647-4121, E-mail: cbrusati@umich.edu. *Application contact:* Debbie L. Fitch, Student Services Coordinator, 734-764-5401, Fax: 734-647-4121, E-mail: dlfitch@umich.edu.

University of Michigan, Horace H. Rackham School of Graduate Studies, College of Literature, Science, and the Arts, Interdepartmental Program in Classical Art and Archaeology, Ann Arbor, MI 48109. Offers PhD. *Faculty:* 10 full-time. *Students:* 26 full-time (17 women); includes 5 minority (3 Asian Americans or Pacific Islanders, 2 Hispanic Americans), 3 international. Average age 28. 53 applicants, 8% accepted, 4 enrolled. In 2007, 4 degrees awarded. *Degree requirements:* For doctorate, 4 foreign languages, thesis/dissertation, oral defense of dissertation, preliminary exam. *Entrance requirements:* For doctorate, GRE General Test. Additional exam requirements/recommendations for international students: Required—TOEFL (minimum score 560 paper-based; 220 computer-based). *Application deadline:* For fall admission, 1/1 for domestic and international students. Applications are processed on a rolling basis. Application fee: $55. Electronic applications accepted. *Financial support:* In 2007–08, 21 students received support, including 8 fellowships with full tuition reimbursements available (averaging $14,000 per year), 2 research assistantships with full tuition reimbursements available (averaging $74,000 per year), 9 teaching assistantships with full tuition reimbursements available (averaging $14,000 per year); career-related internships or fieldwork also available. Financial award application deadline: 3/15. *Unit head:* Elaine K Gazda, Director, 734-764-6323, Fax: 734-763-8976, E-mail: gazda@umich.edu. *Application contact:* Alex Zwinak, Student Administrative Assistant Senior, 734-764-6323, Fax: 734-763-8976, E-mail: ipcaa.office@umich.edu.

University of Minnesota, Twin Cities Campus, Graduate School, College of Liberal Arts, Department of Art History, Minneapolis, MN 55455-0213. Offers MA, PhD. *Faculty:* 13 full-time (5 women), 3 part-time/adjunct (all women). *Students:* 26 full-time (20 women), 8 part-time (all women); includes 2 minority (both Asian Americans or Pacific Islanders), 10 international. Average age 26. 47 applicants, 15% accepted, 5 enrolled. In 2007, 4 master's, 4 doctorates awarded. *Median time to degree:* Of those who began their doctoral program in fall 1999, 30% received their degree in 8 years or less. *Degree requirements:* For master's, one foreign language, comprehensive exam, thesis; for doctorate, 2 foreign languages, comprehensive exam, thesis/dissertation. *Entrance requirements:* For master's and doctorate, GRE, transcripts, 3 letters of recommendation, writing sample. Additional exam requirements/recommendations for international students: Required—TOEFL. *Application deadline:* For fall admission, 12/1 for domestic and international students. Application fee: $55 ($75 for international students). Electronic applications accepted. *Financial support:* In 2007–08, 28 students received support, including 10 fellowships with tuition reimbursements available, 3 research assistantships with tuition reimbursements available (averaging $13,455 per year), 15 teaching assistantships with tuition reimbursements available (averaging $13,455 per year); career-related internships or fieldwork, Federal Work-Study, institutionally sponsored loans, scholarships/grants, and unspecified assistantships also available. Support available to part-time students. Financial award application deadline: 1/2. *Faculty research:* Asian art, ancient art, modern art, contemporary art, early modern. *Unit head:* Steven F. Ostrow, Chair, 612-624-4500, Fax: 612-626-8679, E-mail: ostro133@tc.umn.edu. *Application contact:* John McEwen, Information Contact, 612-624-4500, Fax: 612-626-8679, E-mail: arthist@umn.edu.

University of Minnesota, Twin Cities Campus, Graduate School, College of Liberal Arts, Department of Classical and Near Eastern Studies, Minneapolis, MN 55455-0213. Offers ancient and medieval art and archaeology (MA, PhD); classics (MA, PhD); Greek (MA, PhD); Latin (MA, PhD); religions in antiquity (MA). Part-time programs available. *Faculty:* 12 full-time (2 women), 3 part-time/adjunct (2 women). *Students:* 24 full-time (10 women), 8 part-time (2 women); includes 1 minority (African American), 1 international. Average age 29. 37 applicants, 32% accepted, 9 enrolled. In 2007, 4 master's, 1 doctorate awarded. Terminal master's awarded for partial completion of doctoral program. *Degree requirements:* For master's, 2 foreign languages, comprehensive exam, thesis or alternative; for doctorate, variable foreign language requirement, comprehensive exam, thesis/dissertation. *Entrance requirements:* For master's and doctorate, GRE, 3 letters of recommendation, department application, writing sample, copies of transcripts, personal statement. Additional exam requirements/recommendations for international students: Required—TOEFL. *Application deadline:* For fall admission, 1/4 for domestic students. Application fee: $55 ($75 for international students). Electronic applications accepted. *Financial support:* In 2007–08, 10 fellowships with full and partial tuition reimbursements (averaging $11,165 per year), 4 research assistantships (averaging $23,166 per year), 20 teaching assistantships (averaging $23,357 per year) were awarded; career-related internships or fieldwork, Federal Work-Study, institutionally sponsored loans, and tuition waivers (full and partial) also available. Support available to part-time students. Financial award application deadline: 1/4. *Faculty research:* Greek and Latin literature, archaeology, religions in antiquity, ancient Near East. Total annual research expenditures: $14,849. *Unit head:* George A. Sheets, Chair, 612-625-3326, Fax: 612-624-4894, E-mail: gasheets@umn.edu. *Application contact:* Victoria Keller, Administrative Assistant, Fax: 612-624-4894, E-mail: kell0801@umn.edu.

University of Mississippi, Graduate School, College of Liberal Arts, Department of Art, Oxford, University, MS 38677. Offers art education (MA); art history (MA); fine arts (MFA). *Accreditation:* NASAD (one or more programs are accredited). Part-time programs available. *Faculty:* 12 full-time (8 women), 6 part-time/adjunct (4 women). *Students:* 13 full-time (8 women); includes 3 minority (all African Americans), 2 international. In 2007, 3 degrees awarded. *Degree requirements:* For master's, thesis (for some programs). *Entrance requirements:* For master's, GRE General Test, minimum GPA of 3.0. Additional exam requirements/recommendations for international students: Required—TOEFL. *Application deadline:* For fall admission, 3/1 for domestic students; for spring admission, 10/1 for domestic students. Applications are processed on a rolling basis. Application fee: $25. Electronic applications accepted. *Expenses:* Tuition, state resident: full-time $4,932. Tuition, nonresident: full-time $11,436. *Financial support:* Fellowships, scholarships/grants and unspecified assistantships available. Financial award application deadline: 3/1; financial award applicants required to submit FAFSA. *Unit head:* Dr. Nancy Wicker, Chair, 662-915-7193, Fax: 662-915-5013, E-mail: nwicker@olemiss.edu.

University of Missouri–Columbia, Graduate School, College of Arts and Sciences, Department of Art History and Archaeology, Columbia, MO 65211. Offers MA, PhD. Terminal master's awarded for partial completion of doctoral program. *Degree requirements:* For master's, 2 foreign languages, thesis; for doctorate, 2 foreign languages, thesis/dissertation. *Entrance requirements:* For master's and doctorate, GRE General Test, minimum GPA of 3.0. Additional exam requirements/recommendations for international students: Required—TOEFL (minimum score 500 paper-based; 173 computer-based; 61 iBT), IELTS (minimum score 6).

University of Missouri–Kansas City, College of Arts and Sciences, Department of Art and Art History, Kansas City, MO 64110-2499. Offers art history (MA, PhD); studio art (MA). Part-time programs available. *Faculty:* 11 full-time (5 women), 11 part-time/adjunct (6 women). *Students:* 9 full-time (6 women), 34 part-time (32 women); includes 3 minority (2 African Americans, 1 Asian American or Pacific Islander), 4 international. Average age 32. 23 applicants, 61% accepted, 8 enrolled. In 2007, 8 degrees awarded. Terminal master's awarded for partial completion of doctoral program. *Degree requirements:* For master's, thesis, qualifying exam; for doctorate, thesis/dissertation, exams. *Entrance requirements:* For master's, good general education in the humanities. Additional exam requirements/recommendations for international students: Required—TOEFL. *Application deadline:* For fall admission, 3/1 priority date for domestic and international students; for spring admission, 10/15 for domestic and international students. Applications are processed on a rolling basis. Application fee: $35 ($50 for international students). Electronic applications accepted. *Expenses:* Tuition, state resident: part-time $287 per hour. Tuition, nonresident: part-time $741 per hour. Required fees: $31 per hour. Tuition and fees vary according to program. *Financial support:* In 2007–08, 5 teaching assistantships with partial tuition reimbursements (averaging $12,168 per year) were awarded; fellowships, research assistantships with partial tuition reimbursements, career-related internships or fieldwork, Federal Work-Study, institutionally sponsored loans, and tuition waivers (full and partial) also available. Support available to part-time students. Financial award application deadline: 3/1; financial award applicants required to submit FAFSA. *Faculty research:* Painting, electronic media, Western and non-Western art history, photography. *Unit head:* Dr. Burton Dunbar, Acting Chair, 816-235-2531, Fax: 816-235-5507, E-mail: dunbarb@umkc.edu. *Application contact:* Dr. Rochelle Ziskin, Associate Professor, 816-235-2991, Fax: 816-235-5507, E-mail: ziskinr@umkc.edu.

University of Nebraska–Lincoln, Graduate College, College of Fine and Performing Arts, Department of Art and Art History, Lincoln, NE 68588. Offers MFA. *Accreditation:* NASAD. *Degree requirements:* For master's, thesis. *Entrance requirements:* For master's, slide portfolio. Additional exam requirements/recommendations for international students: Required—TOEFL (minimum score 550 paper-based; 213 computer-based). Electronic applications accepted. *Faculty research:* Classical archaeology, contemporary art, printmaking, photography.

University of New Mexico, Graduate School, College of Fine Arts, Department of Art and Art History, Program in Art History, Albuquerque, NM 87131-2039. Offers MA, PhD. Part-time programs available. *Faculty:* 19 full-time (12 women), 30 part-time/adjunct (29 women). *Students:* 21 full-time (13 women), 9 part-time (4 women); includes 10 minority (1 American Indian/Alaska Native, 2 Asian Americans or Pacific Islanders, 7 Hispanic Americans), 5 international. Average age 40. 47 applicants, 36% accepted, 8 enrolled. In 2007, 9 master's, 1 doctorate awarded. *Degree requirements:* For master's, one foreign language, comprehensive exam, thesis, symposium; for doctorate, 2 foreign languages, comprehensive exam, thesis/dissertation, symposium. *Entrance requirements:* Additional exam requirements/recommendations for international students: Required—TOEFL (minimum score 550 paper-based; 213 computer-based). *Application deadline:* For fall admission, 1/15 for domestic students; for spring admission, 11/15 for domestic students. Application fee: $50. Electronic applications accepted. *Financial support:* In 2007–08, 15 students received support, including research assistantships with tuition reimbursements available (averaging $6,700 per year), teaching assistantships with partial tuition reimbursements available (averaging $6,700 per year); Federal Work-Study, scholarships/grants, health care benefits, and unspecified assistantships also available. Support available to part-time students. Financial award application deadline: 3/1; financial award applicants required to submit FAFSA. *Faculty research:* Native American art, modern Latin American art, photographic art, pre-Columbian art, architectural art, American art, Medieval art. *Unit head:* Dr. Joyce Szabo, Graduate Director, 505-277-5861, Fax: 505-277-5955, E-mail: szabo@unm.edu. *Application contact:* Kat Heatherington, Graduate Advisor, 505-277-6672, Fax: 505-277-5955, E-mail: art255@unm.edu.

The University of North Carolina at Chapel Hill, Graduate School, College of Arts and Sciences, Department of Art, Program in Art History, Chapel Hill, NC 27599. Offers MA, PhD. *Degree requirements:* For master's, one foreign language, comprehensive exam, thesis; for doctorate, one foreign language, comprehensive exam, thesis/dissertation. *Entrance requirements:* For master's and doctorate, GRE General Test, minimum GPA of 3.0.

University of North Texas, Robert B. Toulouse School of Graduate Studies, College of Visual Arts and Design, Department of Art Education and Art History, Denton, TX 76203. Offers art education (MA, MS); art history (MA). *Faculty:* 13 full-time (11 women). *Students:* 38 full-time (34 women), 31 part-time (22 women); includes 13 minority (1 African American, 1 American Indian/Alaska Native, 1 Asian American or Pacific Islander, 10 Hispanic Americans), 5 international. Average age 31. 44 applicants, 68% accepted, 19 enrolled. In 2007, 15 master's awarded. *Degree requirements:* For master's, one foreign language, comprehensive exam (for some programs), thesis (for some programs). *Entrance requirements:* For master's, GRE, writing sample, statement of purpose. Additional exam requirements/recommendations for international students: Required—proof of English language proficiency required for non-native English speakers; Recommended—TOEFL (minimum score 550 paper-based; 213 computer-based). *Application deadline:* For fall admission, 7/15 for domestic students; for spring admission, 11/15 for domestic students. Application fee: $50 ($75 for international students). *Financial support:* In 2007–08, 6 fellowships with partial tuition reimbursements (averaging $18,500 per year), 6 research assistantships with partial tuition reimbursements (averaging $4,500 per year), 45 teaching assistantships with partial tuition reimbursements (averaging $4,900 per year) were awarded; career-related internships or fieldwork, Federal Work-Study, scholarships/grants, health care benefits, and unspecified assistantships also available. Support available to part-time students. *Faculty research:* Aesthetics, visual culture arts leadership, British art, Latin American art, French art, Indian art. Total annual research expenditures: $15,000. *Unit head:* Dr. Kelly Donahue-Wallace, Chair, 940-565-4777, Fax: 940-565-4717, E-mail: kwallace@unt.edu.

University of Notre Dame, Graduate School, College of Arts and Letters, Division of Humanities, Department of Art, Art History, and Design, Notre Dame, IN 46556. Offers art history (MA); design (MFA), including graphic design, industrial design; studio art (MFA), including ceramics, painting, photography, printmaking, sculpture. *Accreditation:* NASAD. *Faculty:* 19 full-time (6 women), 3 part-time/adjunct (1 woman). *Students:* 25 full-time (12 women), 1 (woman) part-time; includes 4 minority (1 African American, 1 Asian American or Pacific Islander, 2 Hispanic Americans), 1 international. 85 applicants, 14% accepted, 10 enrolled. In 2007, 7 degrees awarded. *Degree requirements:* For master's, comprehensive exam, thesis. *Entrance requirements:* For master's, GRE General Test, minimum GPA of 3.0. Additional exam requirements/recommendations for international students: Required—TOEFL (minimum score 600 paper-based; 250 computer-based; 80 iBT). *Application deadline:* For fall admission, 2/1 priority date for domestic and international students. Application fee: $50. Electronic applications accepted. *Financial support:* In 2007–08, 20 students received support, including fellowships with full tuition reimbursements available (averaging $12,000 per year), research assistantships with full tuition reimbursements available (averaging $12,000 per year), 15 teaching assistantships with full tuition reimbursements available (averaging $12,000 per year); scholarships/grants, tuition waivers (full), and unspecified assistantships also available. Financial award application deadline: 2/1. *Faculty research:* Studio art practice in ceramics, printing, photography, printmaking and sculpture, graphic design and industrial design, digital imaging in design and photography, Renaissance and American art history, contemporary art theory and criticism. *Unit head:* Prof. Jean Dibble, Director of Graduate Studies, 574-631-7602, E-mail: art.1@nd.edu. *Application contact:* Dr. Jarren Gonzales, Director of Graduate Admissions, 574-631-7706, Fax: 574-631-4183.

University of Oklahoma, Graduate College, College of Fine Arts, School of Art and Art History, Program in Art History, Norman, OK 73019-0390. Offers MA. *Students:* 9 full-time (7 women), 9 part-time (8 women); includes 3 minority (all American Indian/Alaska Native), 1 international. 4 applicants, 75% accepted, 3 enrolled. In 2007, 1 degree awarded. *Degree requirements:* For master's, one foreign language, thesis, departmental qualifying exam, reading proficiency in French/German. *Entrance requirements:* For master's, GRE General Test, minimum GPA of 3.0, 18 undergraduate hours in art history, writing sample, 3 letters of recommendation. Additional exam requirements/recommendations for international students: Required—TOEFL (minimum score 550 paper-based; 213 computer-based). *Application deadline:* For fall admission, 2/1 priority date for domestic students, 2/1 for international students; for spring admission, 10/1 for domestic and international students. Applications are processed on a rolling basis. Application fee: $40 ($90 for international students). Electronic applications accepted. *Expenses:* Tuition, state resident: full-time $3,451; part-time $144 per credit hour. Tuition, nonresident: full-time $12,432; part-time $518 per credit hour. Required fees: $1,925; $70 per credit hour. $122 per semester. *Financial support:* In 2007–08, 11 students received support. Career-related internships or fieldwork, scholarships/grants, tuition waivers (full and partial), and unspecified assistantships available. Support available to part-time students. Financial award application deadline: 4/7; financial award applicants required to submit FAFSA. *Faculty research:* Art of the American West, Native American art, Medieval; Renaissance and Baroque; ancient and Byzantine; contemporary. *Application contact:* Susan Caldwell, Assistant Director, MA Program, 405-325-3252, Fax: 405-325-1668, E-mail: shcaldwell@ou.edu.

University of Oregon, Graduate School, School of Architecture and Allied Arts, Department of Art History, Eugene, OR 97403. Offers MA, PhD. *Faculty:* 8 full-time (4 women), 2 part-time/adjunct (0 women). *Students:* 24 full-time (18 women), 2 part-time (both women). 30 applicants, 43% accepted. In 2007, 5 master's, 1 doctorate awarded. *Degree requirements:* For master's, one foreign language, thesis or alternative; for doctorate, 2 foreign languages, thesis/dissertation. *Entrance requirements:* For master's, GRE General Test, minimum GPA of 3.0; for doctorate, minimum GPA of 3.0. Additional exam requirements/recommendations for international students: Required—TOEFL. *Application deadline:* For fall admission, 1/15 for domestic students. Application fee: $50. *Financial support:* In 2007–08, 8 teaching assistantships were awarded; career-related internships or fieldwork and Federal Work-Study also available. Financial award application deadline: 2/28. *Faculty research:* Scytho-Siberian art, modern Chinese painting, European landscape painting, American architecture, German expressionist graphics. *Unit head:* Sherwin Simmons, Head, 541-346-1418. *Application contact:* Laurel Dunn, Graduate Secretary, 541-346-3675, E-mail: ldunn@uoregon.edu.

University of Pennsylvania, School of Arts and Sciences, Graduate Group in the History of Art, Philadelphia, PA 19104. Offers AM, PhD. Terminal master's awarded for partial completion of doctoral program. *Degree requirements:* For master's, 2 foreign languages, thesis; for doctorate, 2 foreign languages, thesis/dissertation. *Entrance requirements:* For master's and doctorate, GRE, language background according to subfield of interest. Additional exam requirements/recommendations for international students: Required—TOEFL. Electronic applications accepted.

University of Pittsburgh, School of Arts and Sciences, Department of History of Art and Architecture, Pittsburgh, PA 15260. Offers MA, PhD. Part-time programs available. *Faculty:* 13 full-time (7 women). *Students:* 33 full-time (28 women), 1 (woman) part-time; includes 6 minority (5 Asian Americans or Pacific Islanders, 1 Hispanic American). Average age 33. 38 applicants, 32% accepted, 7 enrolled. In 2007, 4 master's, 2 doctorates awarded. Terminal master's awarded for partial completion of doctoral program. *Median time to degree:* Of those who began their doctoral program in fall 1999, 50% received their degree in 8 years or less. *Degree requirements:* For master's, one foreign language, thesis; for doctorate, 2 foreign languages, comprehensive exam, thesis/dissertation. *Entrance requirements:* For doctorate, GRE General Test, 3 letters of recommendation, writing sample, personal statement, foreign language questionnaire. Additional exam requirements/recommendations for international students: Required—TOEFL. *Application deadline:* For fall admission, 1/15 for domestic and international students. Applications are processed on a rolling basis. Application fee: $50. Electronic applications accepted. *Financial support:* In 2007–08, 30 students received support, including 16 fellowships with full tuition reimbursements available (averaging $17,162 per year), 14 teaching assistantships with full tuition reimbursements available (averaging $14,485 per year); research assistantships with full tuition reimbursements available, career-related internships or fieldwork, Federal Work-Study, scholarships/grants, health care benefits, and tuition waivers (partial) also available. Financial award application deadline: 1/15. *Faculty research:* Asian, medieval, Renaissance/baroque, modern art and architecture, contemporary. Total annual research expenditures: $10,000. *Unit head:* Dr. Kirk Savage, Chair, 412-648-2405, Fax: 412-648-2792, E-mail: ksa@pitt.edu. *Application contact:* Dr. Anne Weis, Director, Graduate Studies, 412-648-2415, Fax: 412-648-2792, E-mail: weis@pitt.edu.

University of Rochester, The College, Arts and Sciences, Department of Art and Art History, Rochester, NY 14627-0250. Offers visual and cultural studies (MA, PhD). Terminal master's awarded for partial completion of doctoral program. *Degree requirements:* For master's, thesis optional; for doctorate, one foreign language, thesis/dissertation, qualifying exam. *Entrance requirements:* For master's and doctorate, GRE General Test. Additional exam requirements/recommendations for international students: Required—TOEFL.

See Close-Up on page 271.

University of St. Thomas, Graduate Studies, College of Arts and Sciences, Department of Art History, St. Paul, MN 55105-1096. Offers MA. Part-time and evening/weekend programs available. *Degree requirements:* For master's, one foreign language, thesis, oral exam, reading proficiency in one foreign language. *Entrance requirements:* For master's, bachelor's degree in art history or related field; letters of recommendation (3); writing sample. Additional exam requirements/recommendations for international students: Required—TOEFL. *Faculty research:* Pictorial narrative and theory; feminist theory and women's artistic practice; art, ritual, and popular culture; architectural history; modernism.

University of South Africa, College of Human Sciences, Pretoria, South Africa. Offers adult education (M Ed); African languages (MA, PhD); African politics (MA, PhD); Afrikaans (MA, PhD); ancient history (MA, PhD); ancient Near Eastern studies (MA, PhD); anthropology (MA, PhD); applied linguistics (MA); Arabic (MA, PhD); archaeology (MA); art history (MA); Biblical archaeology (MA); Biblical studies (M Th, D Th, PhD); Christian spirituality (M Th, D Th); church history (M Th, D Th); classical studies (MA, PhD); clinical psychology (MA); communication (MA, PhD); comparative education (M Ed, Ed D); consulting psychology (D Admin, D Com, PhD); curriculum studies (M Ed, Ed D); development studies (M Admin, MA, D Admin, PhD); didactics (M Ed, Ed D); education (M Tech); education management (M Ed, Ed D); educational psychology (M Ed); English (MA); environmental education (M Ed); French (MA, PhD); German (MA, PhD); Greek (MA); guidance and counseling (M Ed); health studies (MA, PhD), including health sciences education (MA), health services management (MA), medical and surgical nursing science (critical care general) (MA), midwifery and neonatal nursing science (MA), trauma and emergency care (MA); history (MA, PhD); history of education (Ed D); inclusive education (M Ed, Ed D); information and communications technology policy and regulation (MA); information science (MA, MIS, PhD); international politics (MA, PhD); Islamic studies (MA, PhD); Italian (MA, PhD); Judaica (MA, PhD); linguistics (MA, PhD); mathematical education (M Ed); mathematics education (MA); missiology (M Th, D Th); modern Hebrew (MA, PhD); musicology (MA, MMus, D Mus, PhD); natural science education (M Ed); New Testament (M Th, D Th); Old Testament (D Th); pastoral therapy (M Th, D Th); philosophy (MA); philosophy of education (M Ed, Ed D); politics (MA, PhD); Portuguese (MA, PhD); practical theology (M Th, D Th); psychology (MA, MS, PhD); psychology of education (M Ed, Ed D); public health (MA); religious studies (MA, D Th, PhD); Romance languages (MA); Russian (MA, PhD); Semitic languages (MA, PhD); social behavior studies in HIV/AIDS (MA); social science (mental health) (MA); social science in development studies (MA); social science in psychology (MA); social science in social work (MA); social science in sociology (MA); social work (MSW, DSW, PhD); socio-education (M Ed, Ed D); sociolinguistics (MA); sociology (MA, PhD); Spanish (MA, PhD); systematic theology (M Th, D Th); TESOL (teaching English to speakers of other languages) (MA); theological ethics (M Th, D Th); theory of literature (MA, PhD); urban ministries (D Th); urban ministry (M Th).

University of South Carolina, The Graduate School, College of Arts and Sciences, Department of Art, Program in Art History, Columbia, SC 29208. Offers MA. *Accreditation:* NASAD. Part-time programs available. *Faculty:* 3 full-time (0 women), 1 part-time/adjunct (0 women). *Students:* 15 full-time (14 women), 1 part-time; includes 1 minority (Asian American or Pacific Islander) Average age 30. 10 applicants, 50% accepted. In 2007, 5 degrees awarded. *Degree requirements:* For master's, one foreign language, comprehensive exam, thesis. *Entrance requirements:* For master's, GRE General Test or MAT, writing sample. Additional exam requirements/recommendations for international students: Required—TOEFL. *Application deadline:* For fall admission, 3/1 for domestic students; for spring admission, 11/1 for domestic students. Application fee: $40. Electronic applications accepted. *Expenses:* Tuition, state resident: part-time $440 per hour. Tuition, nonresident: part-time $936 per hour. Required fees: $17 per hour. Tuition and fees vary according to program. *Financial support:* In 2007–08, 4 research assistantships with partial tuition reimbursements (averaging $3,000 per year) were awarded; fellowships, teaching assistantships with partial tuition reimbursements, unspecified assistantships also available. *Faculty research:* History of art and architecture. *Unit head:* Brad Collins, Associate Professor, 803-777-9158, Fax: 803-777-0535, E-mail: collinsb@gwm.sc.edu. *Application contact:* Ben Truesdale, Graduate Studies Admissions Specialist, 803-777-6438, Fax: 803-777-0535, E-mail: ben.t@sc.edu.

University of Southern California, Graduate School, College of Letters, Arts and Sciences, Department of Art History, Los Angeles, CA 90089. Offers art history (MA, PhD); visual studies (Certificate). *Faculty:* 12 full-time (9 women), 7 part-time/adjunct (5 women). *Students:* 36 full-time (31 women); includes 11 minority (6 Asian Americans or Pacific Islanders, 5 Hispanic Americans), 4 international. 56 applicants, 16% accepted. In 2007, 6 master's, 2 doctorates awarded. *Degree requirements:* For doctorate, 2 foreign languages, thesis/dissertation. *Entrance requirements:* For doctorate, GRE General Test. *Application deadline:* For fall admission, 12/1 for domestic students. Application fee: $85. *Financial support:* In 2007–08, 43 students received support, including fellowships (averaging $18,800 per year), teaching assistantships (averaging $18,800 per year); research assistantships, institutionally sponsored loans, scholarships/grants, and tuition waivers (full) also available. Financial award application deadline: 2/1. *Faculty research:* Art and ideology in the early Roman Empire, gender in Renaissance paintings, religious and scientific images in Northern Renaissance paintings. *Unit head:* Dr. Eunice Howe, Head, 213-740-2311.

University of South Florida, Graduate School, College of Visual and Performing Arts, School of Art and Art History, Tampa, FL 33620-9951. Offers art history (MA); studio art (MFA). *Accreditation:* NASAD. *Faculty:* 16 full-time (7 women), 1 part-time/adjunct (0 women). *Students:* 40 full-time (22 women), 7 part-time (6 women); includes 8 minority (1 African American, 3 Asian Americans or Pacific Islanders, 4 Hispanic Americans), 2 international. 59 applicants, 41% accepted, 18 enrolled. In 2007, 14 degrees awarded. *Degree requirements:* For master's, thesis, 1 foreign language (MA). *Entrance requirements:* For master's, GRE General Test (MA), minimum GPA of 3.0 in last 60 hours of coursework. *Application deadline:* For fall admission, 1/15 for domestic and international students. Application fee: $30. *Financial support:* In 2007–08, 8 fellowships with full tuition reimbursements (averaging $7,640 per year), 34 teaching assistantships with full and partial tuition reimbursements (averaging $4,486 per year) were awarded; career-related internships or fieldwork, Federal Work-Study, scholarships/grants, health care benefits, and unspecified assistantships also available. Financial award application deadline: 2/15. *Faculty research:* Contemporary art and role of the artist, identity strategies, political iconography, art practice and technology, construction of race in art. Total annual research expenditures: $33,916. *Unit head:* Prof. Wallace Wilson, Director, 813-974-2360, Fax: 813-974-9226, E-mail: wilson@arts.usf.edu. *Application contact:* Richard Olinger, Academic Advisor, 813-974-3160, Fax: 813-974-4165, E-mail: olinger@arts.usf.edu.

The University of Texas at Austin, Graduate School, College of Fine Arts, Department of Art and Art History, Program in Art History, Austin, TX 78712-1111. Offers MA, PhD. *Accreditation:* NASAD. Part-time programs available. *Degree requirements:* For master's, one foreign language, thesis; for doctorate, 2 foreign languages, thesis/dissertation, oral and written qualifying exam. *Entrance requirements:* For master's, GRE General Test, 2 samples of written work; for doctorate, GRE General Test, minimum GPA of 3.0, 2 samples of written work. Electronic applications accepted.

The University of Texas at San Antonio, College of Liberal and Fine Arts, Department of Art and Art History, San Antonio, TX 78249-0617. Offers art history (MA); studio art (MFA). *Accreditation:* NASAD (one or more programs are accredited). *Faculty:* 9 full-time (2 women), 2 part-time/adjunct (0 women). *Students:* 29 full-time (15 women), 10 part-time (7 women); includes 17 minority (all Hispanic Americans), 2 international. Average age 32. 33 applicants, 55% accepted, 17 enrolled. In 2007, 9 degrees awarded. *Degree requirements:* For master's, comprehensive exam, thesis. *Entrance requirements:* For master's, GRE General Test, portfolio, minimum GPA of 3.0 in last 60 hours, 3 letters of recommendation. Additional exam requirements/recommendations for international students: Required—TOEFL (minimum score 500 paper-based; 173 computer-based). *Application deadline:* For fall admission, 7/1 for domestic students, 4/1 for international students; for spring admission, 11/1 for domestic students, 9/1 for international students. Applications are processed on a rolling basis. Application fee: $45 ($80 for international students). Electronic applications accepted. *Financial support:* In 2007–08, 7 research assistantships (averaging $2,977 per year), 1 teaching assistantship (averaging $5,350 per year) were awarded; career-related internships or fieldwork, Federal Work-Study, institutionally sponsored loans, scholarships/grants, tuition waivers (partial), and unspecified assistantships also available. Support available to part-time students. *Faculty research:* Wide variety of artistic production in all media, art history and criticism, focusing on American and Hispanic art. Total annual research expenditures: $7,031. *Unit head:* Kent T. Rush, Chair, 210-458-4362, Fax: 210-458-4356, E-mail: kent.rush@utsa.edu. *Application contact:* Ken Little, Graduate Advisor, 210-458-4352, Fax: 210-458-4356, E-mail: klittle@utsa.edu.

University of Toronto, School of Graduate Studies, Humanities Division, Department of Art, Toronto, ON M5S 1A1, Canada. Offers art history (MA, PhD); visual studies (MVS). Part-time programs available. *Faculty:* 22 full-time, 8 part-time/adjunct. *Students:* 74 full-time (62 women), 5 part-time, 20 international. 197 applicants, 41% accepted. In 2007, 20 master's, 2 doctorates awarded. *Degree requirements:* For master's, 2 foreign languages, language proficiency exams; for doctorate, 2 foreign languages, comprehensive exam, thesis/dissertation. *Entrance requirements:* For master's, coursework in a foreign language, 3 letters of reference, sample research paper, minimum B+ average in senior art history and/or humanities courses; for doctorate, minimum A– average in senior art history and/or humanities courses, 2 letters of reference, sample research paper. *Application deadline:* For fall admission, 1/15 for domestic students. Application fee: $100 Canadian dollars. *Financial support:* Teaching assistantships available. *Unit head:* Prof. Mark A. Cheetham, Chair, 416-978-7891, Fax: 416-978-1491.

Art History

University of Toronto (continued)

Application contact: Gaby Binette, Secretary, 416-978-7892, Fax: 416-978-1491, E-mail: gaby.binette@utoronto.ca.

University of Utah, The Graduate School, College of Fine Arts, Department of Art and Art History, Program in Art History, Salt Lake City, UT 84112-1107. Offers MA. Part-time programs available. *Faculty:* 4 full-time (2 women). *Students:* 3 full-time (2 women), 2 part-time (both women). Average age 27. 9 applicants, 33% accepted, 2 enrolled. In 2007, 2 degrees awarded. *Degree requirements:* For master's, one foreign language, comprehensive exam, thesis, thesis defense. *Entrance requirements:* For master's, curriculum vitae, writing sample, letters of recommendation. Additional exam requirements/recommendations for international students: Required—TOEFL (minimum score 600 paper-based; 173 computer-based). *Application deadline:* For fall admission, 1/2 priority date for domestic and international students. Application fee: $45 ($65 for international students). Electronic applications accepted. *Financial support:* In 2007–08, 1 fellowship, 6 teaching assistantships with tuition reimbursements were awarded; research assistantships with tuition reimbursements, Federal Work-Study, institutionally sponsored loans, scholarships/grants, tuition waivers (partial), and unspecified assistantships also available. Financial award application deadline: 1/2; financial award applicants required to submit FAFSA. *Faculty research:* Asian art, medieval art, Baroque art, American art, 20th century art. *Unit head:* Dr. Sheila Muller, Director of the Art History Program, 801-581-8677, Fax: 801-585-6171, E-mail: sheila.muller@art.utah.edu. *Application contact:* Dr. Monty Paret, Director of Graduate Studies, 801-581-8677, Fax: 801-585-6171, E-mail: paul.paret@utah.edu.

University of Victoria, Faculty of Graduate Studies, Faculty of Fine Arts, Department of History in Art, Victoria, BC V8W 2Y2, Canada. Offers MA, PhD. *Faculty:* 8 full-time (5 women). *Students:* 26 full-time, 2 international. Average age 35. 24 applicants, 17% accepted, 4 enrolled. In 2007, 4 degrees awarded. *Degree requirements:* For master's, one foreign language, thesis (for some programs), oral defense; for doctorate, 2 foreign languages, comprehensive exam, thesis/dissertation, oral defense. *Entrance requirements:* For master's, minimum B+ average in undergraduate course work; for doctorate, minimum B+ average in graduate course work. Additional exam requirements/recommendations for international students: Required—TOEFL (minimum score 575 paper-based; 233 computer-based), IELTS (minimum score 7). *Application deadline:* For fall admission, 1/15 for domestic students, 12/15 priority date for international students. Applications are processed on a rolling basis. Application fee: $75 ($125 for international students). Electronic applications accepted. *Expenses:* Tuition, state resident: full-time $3,110. International tuition: $3,700 full-time. Tuition and fees vary according to program. *Financial support:* In 2007–08, 4 fellowships (averaging $14,250 per year), 12 research assistantships, 14 teaching assistantships with partial tuition reimbursements (averaging $5,202 per year) were awarded; career-related internships or fieldwork, institutionally sponsored loans, and scholarships/grants also available. Financial award application deadline: 1/15. *Faculty research:* Europe, Southeast Asia, China and Islamic world, architecture of North America and the Islamic World, film. *Unit head:* Dr. Catherine Harding, Chair, 250-721-7940, E-mail: charding@finearts.uvic.ca. *Application contact:* Dr. Astri Wright, Graduate Adviser, 250-721-7949, Fax: 250-721-7941, E-mail: astri@finearts.uvic.ca.

University of Virginia, College and Graduate School of Arts and Sciences, McIntire Department of Art, Charlottesville, VA 22904-4130. Offers classical art and archaeology (MA, PhD); history of art and architecture (MA, PhD). *Faculty:* 24 full-time (11 women), 2 part-time/adjunct (0 women). *Students:* 52 full-time (37 women); includes 1 minority (American Indian/Alaska Native), 4 international. Average age 29. 81 applicants, 35% accepted, 12 enrolled. In 2007, 11 master's awarded. *Median time to degree:* Of those who began their doctoral program in fall 1999, 50% received their degree in 8 years or less. *Degree requirements:* For master's, one foreign language, thesis, defense; for doctorate, 2 foreign languages, comprehensive exam, thesis/dissertation, defense. *Entrance requirements:* For master's and doctorate, GRE General Test, writing sample. Additional exam requirements/recommendations for international students: Recommended—TOEFL (minimum score 600 paper-based; 250 computer-based; 90 iBT), IELTS (minimum score 7). *Application deadline:* For fall admission, 12/7 for domestic students. Application fee: $60. Electronic applications accepted. *Financial support:* In 2007–08, 40 fellowships (averaging $7,950 per year), 1 research assistantship (averaging $2,000 per year), 12 teaching assistantships with full tuition reimbursements (averaging $8,800 per year) were awarded; career-related internships or fieldwork, Federal Work-Study, scholarships/grants, and unspecified assistantships also available. Financial award application deadline: 12/7; financial award applicants required to submit CSS PROFILE. *Faculty research:* Classical art, renaissance art and architecture, American material culture. Total annual research expenditures: $35,000. *Unit head:* Daniel Ehnbom, Director of Graduate Studies, 434-924-6130, Fax: 434-924-3647, E-mail: dje6r@virginia.edu. *Application contact:* Aaron Mills, Associate Dean of Graduate Academic Programs and Research, 434-924-6739, Fax: 434-924-6737, E-mail: grad-a-s@virginia.edu.

University of Virginia, College and Graduate School of Arts and Sciences, Program in Art and Architectural History, Charlottesville, VA 22903. Offers MA, PhD. *Students:* 50 full-time (35 women), 3 international. Average age 33. 83 applicants, 31% accepted, 13 enrolled. In 2007, 11 degrees awarded. *Degree requirements:* For master's, 2 foreign languages, comprehensive exam, thesis; for doctorate, 2 foreign languages, thesis/dissertation, oral exam. *Unit head:* Lawrence O. Goedde, Chair, 434-924-6123, Fax: 434-924-3647, E-mail: artdept@virginia.edu.

University of Washington, Graduate School, College of Arts and Sciences, School of Art, Division of Art History, Seattle, WA 98195. Offers MA, PhD. *Faculty:* 11 full-time (8 women), 2 part-time/adjunct (both women). *Students:* 27 full-time (22 women), 9 part-time (7 women); includes 8 minority (2 American Indian/Alaska Native, 6 Asian Americans or Pacific Islanders). Average age 36. 74 applicants, 16% accepted, 3 enrolled. In 2007, 9 master's, 1 doctorate awarded. Terminal master's awarded for partial completion of doctoral program. *Degree requirements:* For master's, 2 foreign languages, practicum or thesis; for doctorate, 2 foreign languages, thesis/dissertation. *Entrance requirements:* For master's, GRE General Test, minimum undergraduate GPA of 3.0, undergraduate major in art history or equivalent; for doctorate, GRE General Test, MA in art history, minimum graduate GPA of 3.0. Additional exam requirements/recommendations for international students: Required—TOEFL (minimum score 580 paper-based; 237 computer-based). *Application deadline:* For fall admission, 1/15 for domestic students, 11/1 priority date for international students; for winter admission, 1/15 for international students. Application fee: $50. Electronic applications accepted. *Financial support:* In 2007–08, 2 research assistantships with full tuition reimbursements (averaging $13,059 per year), 33 teaching assistantships with full tuition reimbursements (averaging $13,059 per year) were awarded; career-related internships or fieldwork, Federal Work-Study, institutionally sponsored loans, scholarships/grants, health care benefits, unspecified assistantships, and readerships also available. Financial award application deadline: 2/28; financial award applicants required to submit FAFSA. *Faculty research:* European-American (all periods), Japanese, Chinese, African, and Native American art. *Unit head:* Prof. Christine Göttler, Chair, 206-616-6583, Fax: 206-616-3515. *Application contact:* Prof. Patricia A. Failing, Graduate Program Coordinator, 206-543-4876, Fax: 206-616-3515, E-mail: failing@u.washington.edu.

University of Wisconsin–Madison, Graduate School, College of Letters and Science, Department of Art History, Madison, WI 53706-1380. Offers MA, PhD. Part-time programs available. Terminal master's awarded for partial completion of doctoral program. *Degree requirements:* For master's, one foreign language; for doctorate, 2 foreign languages, thesis/dissertation. *Entrance requirements:* For master's and doctorate, GRE. Additional exam requirements/recommendations for international students: Required—TOEFL. Electronic applications accepted. *Faculty research:* Twentieth-century, African art, Italian Renaissance, Dutch, material culture.

University of Wisconsin–Milwaukee, Graduate School, College of Letters and Sciences, Department of Art History, Milwaukee, WI 53201-0413. Offers art history (MA); art museum studies (Certificate). Part-time programs available. *Faculty:* 8 full-time (3 women). *Students:* 21 full-time (18 women), 14 part-time (11 women); includes 2 minority (1 African American, 1 American Indian/Alaska Native), 1 international. 27 applicants, 59% accepted, 11 enrolled. In 2007, 5 degrees awarded. *Degree requirements:* For master's, one foreign language, thesis or alternative. *Application deadline:* For fall admission, 1/1 priority date for domestic students; for spring admission, 9/1 for domestic students. Applications are processed on a rolling basis. Application fee: $45 ($75 for international students). *Expenses:* Tuition, state resident: part-time $530 per credit. Tuition, nonresident: part-time $1,428 per credit. Required fees: $19 per credit. $229 per term. Tuition and fees vary according to course load and program. *Financial support:* In 2007–08, 5 teaching assistantships were awarded; fellowships, research assistantships, career-related internships or fieldwork and unspecified assistantships also available. Support available to part-time students. Financial award application deadline: 4/15. *Unit head:* Kenneth Bendiner, Representative, 414-229-5015, Fax: 414-229-2935, E-mail: bendiner@uwm.edu.

University of Wisconsin–Superior, Graduate Division, Department of Visual Arts, Superior, WI 54880-4500. Offers art education (MA); art history (MA); art therapy (MA); studio arts (MA). Part-time programs available. *Degree requirements:* For master's, comprehensive exam, exhibit. *Entrance requirements:* For master's, minimum GPA of 2.75, portfolio.

Virginia Commonwealth University, Graduate School, School of the Arts, Department of Art History, Richmond, VA 23284-9005. Offers architectural history (MA); art history (MA, PhD); historical studies (MA); museum studies (MA). *Accreditation:* NASAD. *Faculty:* 10 full-time (4 women). *Students:* 19 full-time (18 women), 24 part-time (20 women); includes 6 minority (2 African Americans, 2 Asian Americans or Pacific Islanders, 2 Hispanic Americans), 1 international. 54 applicants, 50% accepted, 13 enrolled. In 2007, 15 master's, 4 doctorates awarded. *Degree requirements:* For master's, thesis; for doctorate, comprehensive exam, thesis/dissertation. *Entrance requirements:* For master's and doctorate, GRE General Test. *Application deadline:* For fall admission, 1/15 for domestic students. Application fee: $50. *Expenses:* Tuition, state resident: full-time $7,224; part-time $401 per credit. Tuition, nonresident: full-time $16,072; part-time $891 per credit. Required fees: $1,679; $63 per credit. Tuition and fees vary according to campus/location. *Financial support:* Fellowships, teaching assistantships, career-related internships or fieldwork, Federal Work-Study, and institutionally sponsored loans available. Support available to part-time students. Financial award application deadline: 3/15. *Faculty research:* Modern, nineteenth century, Renaissance, American, and Medieval art. *Unit head:* Dr. James Farmer, Coordinator of Graduate Studies, 804-828-2784, Fax: 804-828-7468, E-mail: jfarmer@saturn.vcu.edu.

See Close-Up on page 275.

Washington University in St. Louis, Graduate School of Arts and Sciences, Department of Art History and Archaeology, St. Louis, MO 63130-4899. Offers art history (MA, PhD); classical archaeology (MA, PhD). *Degree requirements:* For doctorate, 2 foreign languages, comprehensive exam, thesis/dissertation. *Entrance requirements:* For master's and doctorate, GRE General Test, sample of written work. Electronic applications accepted.

Washington University in St. Louis, Graduate School of Arts and Sciences, Program in East Asian Studies, St. Louis, MO 63130-4899. Offers art history (PhD); Chinese (MA); Chinese and comparative literature (PhD); East Asian studies (MA); history (PhD); Japanese (MA); Japanese and comparative literature (PhD); JD/MA; MBA/MA. PhD offered through specific departments. *Entrance requirements:* For master's and doctorate, GRE General Test. Electronic applications accepted.

See Close-Up on page 815.

Wayne State University, College of Fine, Performing and Communication Arts, Department of Art and Art History, Program in Art History, Detroit, MI 48202. Offers MA. *Students:* 1 (woman) full-time, 3 part-time (all women); includes 3 minority (all Hispanic Americans), 1 international. Average age 36. 3 applicants, 0% accepted. In 2007, 1 degree awarded. *Degree requirements:* For master's, one foreign language. *Entrance requirements:* Additional exam requirements/recommendations for international students: Required—TOEFL (minimum score 550 paper-based; 213 computer-based); Recommended—TWE (minimum score 6). *Application deadline:* For fall admission, 4/1 for domestic students, 6/1 for international students; for winter admission, 10/1 for international students; for spring admission, 2/1 for international students. Application fee: $30 ($50 for international students). Electronic applications accepted. *Expenses:* Tuition, state resident: part-time $403 per credit hour. Tuition, nonresident: part-time $890 per credit hour. *Faculty research:* Ancient, medieval, and nineteenth and twentieth century art history; theory and criticism. *Application contact:* Brian Madigan, Associate Professor, 313-577-2685, E-mail: bmadigan@wayne.edu.

West Virginia University, College of Creative Arts, Division of Art and Design, Morgantown, WV 26506. Offers art education (MA); art history (MA); ceramics (MFA); graphic design (MFA); painting (MFA); printmaking (MFA); sculpture (MFA); studio art (MA). *Accreditation:* NASAD. *Faculty:* 17 full-time (7 women), 6 part-time/adjunct (0 women). *Students:* 21 full-time (11 women), 3 part-time (all women), 2 international. Average age 29. 49 applicants, 22% accepted, 7 enrolled. In 2007, 11 degrees awarded. *Degree requirements:* For master's, thesis, exhibit. *Entrance requirements:* For master's, minimum GPA of 2.75, portfolio. Additional exam requirements/recommendations for international students: Required—TOEFL. *Application deadline:* For fall admission, 3/1 for domestic students, 2/15 for international students; for spring admission, 10/15 for domestic and international students. Application fee: $45. *Expenses:* Contact institution. Tuition and fees vary according to program. *Financial support:* In 2007–08, 22 students received support, including 11 teaching assistantships with full tuition reimbursements available; research assistantships with full tuition reimbursements available, Federal Work-Study, institutionally sponsored loans, tuition waivers (full and partial), and graduate administrative assistantships also available. Financial award application deadline: 3/15; financial award applicants required to submit FAFSA. *Faculty research:* Medieval art history. Total annual research expenditures: $6,000. *Unit head:* Alison Helm, Interim Chair, 304-293-4841 Ext. 3140, Fax: 304-293-3136, E-mail: alison.helm@mail.wvu.edu.

Williams College, Program in the History of Art, Williamstown, MA 01267. Offers MA. Offered jointly with Sterling and Francine Clark Art Institute. Part-time programs available. *Faculty:* 24. *Students:* 25 full-time (22 women); includes 1 minority (Asian American or Pacific Islander), 2 international. Average age 26. 85 applicants, 22% accepted, 12 enrolled. In 2007, 11 degrees awarded. *Degree requirements:* For master's, 2 foreign languages, symposium paper and lecture. *Entrance requirements:* For master's, GRE General Test. Additional exam requirements/recommendations for international students: Required—TOEFL. *Application deadline:* For fall admission, 1/1 for domestic students. Application fee: $50. Electronic applications accepted. *Financial support:* In 2007–08, 18 students received support, including 4 fellowships with full and partial tuition reimbursements available (averaging $14,000 per year); tuition waivers (full and partial) also available. Support available to part-time students. Financial award application deadline: 4/1; financial award applicants required to submit FAFSA. *Unit head:* Dr. Marc Gotlieb, Director of Graduate Art History, 413-458-0598, Fax: 413-458-2317, E-mail: marc.gotlieb@williams.edu. *Application contact:* Karen E. Kowitz, Program Administrator, 413-458-0596, Fax: 413-458-2317, E-mail: karen.kowitz@williams.edu.

Yale University, Graduate School of Arts and Sciences, Department of History of Art, New Haven, CT 06520. Offers PhD. *Degree requirements:* For doctorate, 2 foreign languages, thesis/dissertation. *Entrance requirements:* For doctorate, GRE General Test.

York University, Faculty of Graduate Studies, Faculty of Fine Arts, Program in Art History, Toronto, ON M3J 1P3, Canada. Offers MA, PhD. Part-time programs available. *Degree requirements:* For master's, one foreign language, thesis or alternative. Electronic applications accepted.

Arts Administration

American University, College of Arts and Sciences, Department of Performing Arts, Program in Arts Management, Washington, DC 20016-8001. Offers MA, Certificate. Part-time and evening/weekend programs available. *Students:* 30 full-time (26 women), 13 part-time (11 women); includes 4 minority (3 African Americans, 1 Asian American or Pacific Islander), 6 international. Average age 27. In 2007, 21 master's, 1 other advanced degree awarded. *Degree requirements:* For master's, comprehensive exam, thesis or alternative. *Entrance requirements:* For master's, GRE, previous course work in theater, dance, music, or related field; minimum GPA of 3.0; for Certificate, Bachelor's Degree. *Application deadline:* For fall admission, 1/15 priority date for domestic students. Application fee: $50. *Expenses:* Tuition: Full-time $19,998; part-time $1,111 per credit hour. Required fees: $380. Tuition and fees vary according to program. *Financial support:* Fellowships, teaching assistantships, career-related internships or fieldwork, Federal Work-Study, and institutionally sponsored loans available. Support available to part-time students. Financial award application deadline: 2/1. *Faculty research:* Arts policy, arts education.

Boston University, Metropolitan College (Continuing Education), Program in Arts Administration, Boston, MA 02215. Offers arts administration (MS, Graduate Certificate); fundraising management (Graduate Certificate). Part-time and evening/weekend programs available. *Faculty:* 2 full-time (0 women), 17 part-time/adjunct (7 women). *Students:* 11 full-time (10 women), 65 part-time (54 women); includes 6 minority (2 African Americans, 2 Asian Americans or Pacific Islanders, 2 Hispanic Americans), 11 international. Average age 29. 89 applicants, 47% accepted, 33 enrolled. In 2007, 43 degrees awarded. *Degree requirements:* For master's, internship. *Entrance requirements:* Additional exam requirements/recommendations for international students: Required—TOEFL (minimum score 590 paper-based; 213 computer-based; 84 iBT), IELTS, TWE, GRE or GMAT. *Application deadline:* For fall admission, 3/31 priority date for domestic students; for winter admission, 11/15 priority date for domestic students. Applications are processed on a rolling basis. Application fee: $70. Electronic applications accepted. *Expenses:* Tuition: Full-time $34,930; part-time $1,092 per credit. Tuition and fees vary according to class time, course level and program. *Financial support:* Career-related internships or fieldwork and office assistantships available. *Faculty research:* Cultural policy, artists' rights, museum practices, audience development. *Unit head:* Daniel Ranalli, Associate Professor/Director, 617-353-4064, Fax: 617-353-1230, E-mail: artsad@bu.edu. *Application contact:* Jeannie Motherwell, Program Assistant, 617-353-4064, Fax: 617-358-1230, E-mail: jmoth@bu.edu.

Carnegie Mellon University, H. John Heinz III School of Public Policy and Management, Institute for the Management of Creative Enterprises and College of Fine Arts, Program in Arts Management, Pittsburgh, PA 15213-3891. Offers MAM. *Degree requirements:* For master's, internship. *Entrance requirements:* For master's, GMAT or GRE, previous course work in pre-calculus and statistics. Electronic applications accepted.

See Close-Up on page 235.

Claremont Graduate University, Graduate Programs, Program in Arts and Cultural Management, Claremont, CA 91711-6160. Offers MA. *Faculty:* 1 (woman) part-time/adjunct. *Students:* 6 full-time (3 women), 2 part-time (both women); includes 1 minority (African American) Average age 34. In 2007, 4 degrees awarded. *Entrance requirements:* For master's, GRE General Test. *Application deadline:* For fall admission, 2/15 priority date for domestic students. Applications are processed on a rolling basis. Electronic applications accepted. *Expenses:* Tuition: Full-time $31,640; part-time $1,376 per unit. Required fees: $145 per semester. Tuition and fees vary according to course load, degree level and program. *Financial support:* Fellowships, research assistantships, teaching assistantships, Federal Work-Study and institutionally sponsored loans available. Support available to part-time students. Financial award application deadline: 2/15; financial award applicants required to submit FAFSA. *Unit head:* Patricia Easton, Co-Director, 909-607-9440, Fax: 909-607-1221, E-mail: patricia.easton@cgu.edu. *Application contact:* Justin Evans, Admissions Coordinator, 909-607-1278, Fax: 909-607-1221, E-mail: humanities@cgu.edu.

College of Charleston, Graduate School, School of the Arts, Program in Arts Management, Charleston, SC 29424-0001. Offers MPA, Certificate. Evening/weekend programs available. *Faculty:* 2 full-time (both women), 2 part-time/adjunct (1 woman). *Entrance requirements:* For degree, minimum GPA of 3.0, writing sample. *Expenses:* Tuition, state resident: full-time $7,778; part-time $324 per hour. Tuition, nonresident: full-time $18,732; part-time $781 per hour. *Unit head:* Scott Peterson, Director, 843-953-8421, E-mail: petersons@cofc.edu.

Columbia College Chicago, Graduate School, Department of Arts, Entertainment and Media Management, Chicago, IL 60605-1996. Offers arts, entertainment and media management (MA), including media management, music business, performing arts management, visual arts management. Evening/weekend programs available. *Students:* 117 full-time (84 women), 83 part-time (51 women); includes 50 minority (35 African Americans, 1 American Indian/Alaska Native, 3 Asian Americans or Pacific Islanders, 11 Hispanic Americans), 15 international. Average age 27. In 2007, 50 degrees awarded. *Degree requirements:* For master's, thesis, internship. *Entrance requirements:* For master's, interview, minimum GPA of 3.0. Additional exam requirements/recommendations for international students: Required—TOEFL (minimum score 550 paper-based; 213 computer-based). *Application deadline:* For fall admission, 6/1 for domestic students, 3/1 for international students; for spring admission, 10/3 for domestic students. Applications are processed on a rolling basis. Application fee: $50. Electronic applications accepted. *Financial support:* Fellowships, career-related internships or fieldwork, Federal Work-Study, and scholarships/grants available. Support available to part-time students. Financial award application deadline: 8/13; financial award applicants required to submit FAFSA. *Unit head:* Dr. J. Dennis Rich, Chairperson, 312-344-7659 Ext. 5260, Fax: 312-344-8063, E-mail: drich@colum.edu. *Application contact:* Keith Cleveland, Acting Dean of the Graduate School, 312-344-7261, Fax: 312-344-8047, E-mail: kcleveland@colum.edu.

Drexel University, College of Media Arts and Design, Department of Performing Arts, Philadelphia, PA 19104-2875. Offers arts administration (MS). *Accreditation:* NASAD. Part-time and evening/weekend programs available. *Degree requirements:* For master's, thesis, internship. *Entrance requirements:* For master's, GRE, interview, minimum GPA of 3.0, previous course work in arts and business. Additional exam requirements/recommendations for international students: Required—TOEFL. Electronic applications accepted. *Faculty research:* Evaluation of art administration structures, funding for the arts, impact of politics in the arts, computer applications.

Eastern Michigan University, Graduate School, College of Arts and Sciences, Department of Communication and Theatre Arts, Program in Arts Administration, Ypsilanti, MI 48197. Offers theatre arts-arts administration (MA). Part-time and evening/weekend programs available. Postbaccalaureate distance learning degree programs offered (minimal on-campus study). *Students:* 3 full-time (2 women), 10 part-time (9 women); includes 4 minority (3 African Americans, 1 Asian American or Pacific Islander), 2 international. Average age 33. In 2007, 1 degree awarded. *Entrance requirements:* Additional exam requirements/recommendations for international students: Required—TOEFL. *Application deadline:* Applications are processed on a rolling basis. Application fee: $35. *Expenses:* Tuition, state resident: full-time $8,952; part-time $373 per credit hour. Tuition, nonresident: full-time $17,634; part-time $735 per credit hour. Required fees: $896; $34 per credit hour. Tuition and fees vary according to course level, degree level and program. *Financial support:* Fellowships, research assistantships with full tuition reimbursements, teaching assistantships with full tuition reimbursements, career-related internships or fieldwork, Federal Work-Study, institutionally sponsored loans, scholarships/grants, tuition waivers (partial), and unspecified assistantships available. Support available to part-time students. Financial award applicants required to submit FAFSA. *Unit head:* Kenneth Stevens, Coordinator, 734-487-3130, Fax: 734-487-3443, E-mail: ken.stevens@emich.edu. *Application contact:* Dr. Lee Stille, Graduate Coordinator, 734-487-3131, Fax: 734-487-3443, E-mail: lee.stille@emich.edu.

Fashion Institute of Technology, School of Graduate Studies, Program in Art Market: Principles and Practices, New York, NY 10001-5992. Offers MA. *Accreditation:* NASAD. *Degree requirements:* For master's, one foreign language, thesis, internship. *Entrance requirements:* For master's, GRE General Test, previous course work in art history, 4 semesters of a foreign language. Additional exam requirements/recommendations for international students: Required—TOEFL (minimum score 550 paper-based; 213 computer-based). *Application deadline:* For fall admission, 2/15 priority date for domestic and international students. Applications are processed on a rolling basis. Application fee: $50. Electronic applications accepted. *Expenses:* Tuition, state resident: full-time $7,245; part-time $302 per credit. Tuition, nonresident: full-time $11,466; part-time $478 per credit. Required fees: $440; $35 per term. *Financial support:* Federal Work-Study and scholarships/grants available. Financial award applicants required to submit FAFSA. *Unit head:* Dr. Katherine Michaelsen, Associate Chair, 212-217-4661, Fax: 212-217-5156, E-mail: katherin_michaelsen@fitnyc.edu. *Application contact:* Carole deSantis, Administrative Secretary, Graduate Admissions, 212-217-4314, Fax: 212-217-5156, E-mail: carole_desantis@fitnyc.edu.

See Close-Up on page 113.

Florida State University, Graduate Studies, College of Music, Tallahassee, FL 32306. Offers accompanying (MM); arts administration (MA); choral conducting (MM); composition (MM, DM); ethnomusicology (MM); general music (MA); instrumental accompanying (MM); instrumental conducting (MM); jazz studies (MM); music education (MM Ed, PhD); music theory (MM, PhD); music therapy (MM); musicology (MM, PhD), including ethnomusicology (PhD), historical musicology; opera (MM); performance (MM, DM); piano pedagogy (MM); piano technology (MA); vocal accompanying (MM). *Accreditation:* NASM. *Faculty:* 88 full-time, 13 part-time/adjunct. *Students:* 406 full-time (211 women); includes 98 minority (28 African Americans, 38 Asian Americans or Pacific Islanders, 32 Hispanic Americans). Average age 26. 525 applicants, 38% accepted, 145 enrolled. In 2007, 102 master's, 41 doctorates awarded. *Degree requirements:* For master's, comprehensive exam (for some programs), thesis (for some programs), departmental qualifying exam; for doctorate, comprehensive exam (for some programs), thesis/dissertation, departmental qualifying exam. *Entrance requirements:* For master's and doctorate, audition, GRE General Test or minimum GPA of 3.0. Additional exam requirements/recommendations for international students: Required—TOEFL (minimum score 550 paper-based; 213 computer-based). *Application deadline:* For fall admission, 7/1 for domestic students, 5/2 for international students; for spring admission, 11/3 for domestic students, 9/1 for international students. Applications are processed on a rolling basis. Application fee: $30. Electronic applications accepted. *Expenses:* Tuition, state resident: part-time $248 per credit hour. Tuition, nonresident: part-time $880 per credit hour. Tuition and fees vary according to program. *Financial support:* In 2007–08, 225 students received support, including 3 fellowships with full tuition reimbursements available (averaging $15,000 per year), 9 research assistantships with full tuition reimbursements available (averaging $4,000 per year), 173 teaching assistantships with full tuition reimbursements available (averaging $4,000 per year); career-related internships or fieldwork, Federal Work-Study, and tuition waivers (partial) also available. Support available to part-time students. Financial award application deadline: 2/28; financial award applicants required to submit FAFSA. *Unit head:* Don Gibson, Dean, 850-644-4361, Fax: 850-644-2033. *Application contact:* Dr. Seth Beckman, Assistant Dean for Academic Affairs/Director of Graduate Studies, 850-644-5848, Fax: 850-644-2033, E-mail: sbeckman@admin.fsu.edu.

George Mason University, College of Visual and Performing Arts, Fairfax, VA 22030. Offers arts entrepreneurship (Certificate); arts management (MA); dance (MFA); music (MA, MM, Certificate), including artist certificate (Certificate), composition (MA), conducting (MA), music (MM), music education (MA, Certificate), pedagogy and performance (MA), performance (MA); visual technologies (MA, MAT, MFA), including art and visual technology (MA, MFA), art education (MAT). Part-time and evening/weekend programs available. *Faculty:* 47 full-time (25 women), 63 part-time/adjunct (37 women). *Students:* 63 full-time (48 women), 93 part-time (66 women); includes 30 minority (16 African Americans, 9 Asian Americans or Pacific Islanders, 5 Hispanic Americans), 9 international. Average age 31. 173 applicants, 53% accepted, 75 enrolled. In 2007, 65 degrees awarded. *Degree requirements:* For master's, 3 foreign languages, music-vocal performance MM. *Entrance requirements:* For master's, interviews, portfolios, auditions. Additional exam requirements/recommendations for international students: Required—TOEFL (minimum score 570 paper-based; 88 computer-based). *Application deadline:* For fall admission, 5/1 for domestic students; for spring admission, 11/1 for domestic students. Application fee: $60 ($75 for international students). Electronic applications accepted. *Financial support:* In 2007–08, 14 students received support; fellowships with partial tuition reimbursements available, research assistantships with partial tuition reimbursements available, teaching assistantships with partial tuition reimbursements available, career-related internships or fieldwork, Federal Work-Study, institutionally sponsored loans, and tuition waivers (partial) available. Support available to part-time students. Financial award application deadline: 3/1; financial award applicants required to submit FAFSA. *Unit head:* William Reeder, Dean, 703-993-8624, Fax: 703-993-8883. *Application contact:* Dr. Scott M. Martin, Director, 703-993-4574, Fax: 703-993-8798, E-mail: avt@gmu.edu.

Goucher College, Program in Arts Administration, Baltimore, MD 21204-2794. Offers MA. Part-time programs available. Postbaccalaureate distance learning degree programs offered (minimal on-campus study). *Students:* 17 full-time (14 women), 24 part-time (18 women). Average age 36. In 2007, 10 degrees awarded. *Degree requirements:* For master's, internship, major paper. *Entrance requirements:* For master's, 2 years of post-baccalaureate work experience. *Application deadline:* For fall admission, 3/15 for domestic students. Application fee: $50. *Expenses:* Contact institution. *Financial support:* Institutionally sponsored loans available. Financial award application deadline: 3/15. *Unit head:* Dr. Jean Brody, Director, 410-337-6200, Fax: 410-337-6085, E-mail: jbrody@goucher.edu.

HEC Montreal, School of Business Administration, Diploma Programs in Administration, Program in Management of Cultural Organizations, Montréal, QC H3T 2A7, Canada. Offers Diploma. All courses are given in French. Part-time programs available. *Students:* 30 full-time (24 women), 123 part-time (104 women). 88 applicants, 80% accepted, 52 enrolled. In 2007, 25 degrees awarded. *Degree requirements:* For Diploma, one foreign language. *Entrance requirements:* For degree, 2 years of relevant work experience, 2 letters of recommendation. *Application deadline:* For fall admission, 4/15 for domestic and international students; for winter admission, 10/1 for domestic and international students. Application fee: $75 Canadian dollars. Electronic applications accepted. Tuition charges are reported in Canadian dollars. *Expenses:* Tuition, state resident: full-time $5,800 Canadian dollars. Tuition, nonresident: full-time $12,200 Canadian dollars. International tuition: $23,300 Canadian dollars full-time. *Financial support:* Scholarships/grants available. *Application contact:* Francine Blais, Administrative Director, 514-340-6112, Fax: 514-340-6411, E-mail: francine.blais@hec.ca.

Montclair State University, The Office of Graduate Admissions and Support Services, School of the Arts, Department of Theatre and Dance, Montclair, NJ 07043-1624. Offers theatre (MA), including arts management, production/stage management, theatre studies. *Accreditation:* NAST. Part-time and evening/weekend programs available. *Faculty:* 7 full-time (3 women), 4 part-time/adjunct (2 women). *Students:* 9 full-time (8 women), 19 part-time (11 women); includes 4 minority (3 African Americans, 1 Hispanic American), 2 international. 16 applicants, 56% accepted, 6 enrolled. In 2007, 3 degrees awarded. *Degree requirements:* For master's, comprehensive exam, thesis or alternative. *Entrance requirements:* For master's, GRE General Test, minimum GPA of 3.0, undergraduate degree or work in theatre, oral interpretation, broadcasting, speech communication or media; 2 letters of recommendation. Additional exam requirements/recommendations for international students: Required—TOEFL (minimum score 83 computer-based). *Application deadline:* For fall admission, 6/1 for international students; for spring admission, 10/1 for international students. Applications are processed on a rolling basis.

Arts Administration

Montclair State University (continued)

Application fee: $60. Electronic applications accepted. *Financial support:* In 2007–08, 1 research assistantship with full tuition reimbursement (averaging $7,000 per year) was awarded; Federal Work-Study, scholarships/grants, and unspecified assistantships also available. Support available to part-time students. Financial award application deadline: 3/1; financial award applicants required to submit FAFSA. *Unit head:* Dr. Jane Peterson, Chairperson, 973-655-4217, E-mail: peterson@mail.montclair.edu. *Application contact:* Dr. Jane Peterson, Adviser, 973-655-4109, E-mail: petersonj@mail.montclair.edu.

New York University, Steinhardt School of Culture, Education and Human Development, Department of Art and Art Professions, Program in Visual Arts Administration, New York, NY 10012-1019. Offers for-profit sector (MA); not-for-profit sector (MA). Part-time and evening/weekend programs available. *Faculty:* 2 full-time (1 woman). *Students:* 58 full-time (54 women), 28 part-time (26 women); includes 13 minority (4 African Americans, 7 Asian Americans or Pacific Islanders, 2 Hispanic Americans), 17 international. 113 applicants, 53% accepted, 40 enrolled. In 2007, 27 degrees awarded. *Degree requirements:* For master's, thesis (for some programs). *Entrance requirements:* For master's, interview. Additional exam requirements/recommendations for international students: Required—TOEFL. *Application deadline:* For fall admission, 12/15 priority date for domestic and international students; for spring admission, 11/1 for domestic and international students. Applications are processed on a rolling basis. Application fee: $50. *Financial support:* Career-related internships or fieldwork, Federal Work-Study, institutionally sponsored loans, scholarships/grants, and tuition waivers (partial) available. Support available to part-time students. Financial award application deadline: 2/1; financial award applicants required to submit FAFSA. *Faculty research:* Corporate philanthropy, contemporary art and culture, public art and urban development, cultural policy, arts advocacy. *Unit head:* Sandra Lang, Head, 212-998-5700, Fax: 212-995-4320, E-mail: sandra.lang@nyu.edu. *Application contact:* 212-998-5030, Fax: 212-995-4328, E-mail: steinhardt.gradadmissions@nyu.edu.

New York University, Steinhardt School of Culture, Education and Human Development, Department of Music and Performing Arts Professions, Program in Performing Arts Administration, New York, NY 10012-1019. Offers MA. Part-time and evening/weekend programs available. *Faculty:* 1 full-time (0 women). *Students:* 35 full-time (30 women), 19 part-time (all women); includes 8 minority (3 African Americans, 4 Asian Americans or Pacific Islanders, 1 Hispanic American), 16 international. 133 applicants, 39% accepted, 30 enrolled. In 2007, 25 degrees awarded. *Degree requirements:* For master's, thesis (for some programs). *Entrance requirements:* For master's, interview. Additional exam requirements/recommendations for international students: Required—TOEFL. *Application deadline:* For fall admission, 12/15 priority date for domestic students, 1/15 for international students; for spring admission, 11/1 for domestic and international students. Applications are processed on a rolling basis. Application fee: $50. *Financial support:* Career-related internships or fieldwork, Federal Work-Study, scholarships/grants, and tuition waivers (partial) available. Support available to part-time students. Financial award application deadline: 2/1; financial award applicants required to submit FAFSA. *Faculty research:* Legal dimensions of arts management, global arts management, cultural policy. *Unit head:* Brann J. Wry, Director, 212-998-5424, Fax: 212-995-4560. *Application contact:* 212-998-5030, Fax: 212-995-4328, E-mail: steinhardt.gradadmissions@nyu.edu.

New York University, Tisch School of the Arts, Program in Arts Politics, New York, NY 10012-1019. Offers MA. *Faculty:* 3 full-time (2 women), 4 part-time/adjunct (3 women). *Students:* 5 full-time (all women), 1 (woman) part-time; includes 2 minority (both Asian Americans or Pacific Islanders), 2 international. Average age 25. 22 applicants, 64% accepted, 6 enrolled. *Degree requirements:* For master's, thesis. *Entrance requirements:* For master's, professional resumé, writing sample, statement of purpose. Additional exam requirements/recommendations for international students: Required—TOEFL, IELTS. *Application deadline:* For fall admission, 1/8 for domestic and international students. Application fee: $60. *Financial support:* In 2007–08, 2 students received support. Federal Work-Study and scholarships/grants available. Financial award application deadline: 2/15; financial award applicants required to submit FAFSA. *Application contact:* Dan Sandford, Director of Graduate Admissions, 212-998-1918, Fax: 212-995-4060, E-mail: tisch.gradadmissions@nyu.edu.

The Ohio State University, Graduate School, College of the Arts, Department of Art Education, Program in Arts Policy and Administration, Columbus, OH 43210. Offers MA. *Faculty:* 14. *Students:* 17 full-time (15 women), 3 part-time (all women); includes 2 minority (1 African American, 1 Asian American or Pacific Islander), 4 international. Average age 25. In 2007, 3 degrees awarded. *Degree requirements:* For master's, thesis. *Entrance requirements:* For master's, GRE General Test. Additional exam requirements/recommendations for international students: Required—TOEFL (minimum score 600 paper-based; 250 computer-based). *Application deadline:* For fall admission, 8/15 priority date for domestic students, 7/1 priority date for international students; for winter admission, 12/1 priority date for domestic students, 11/1 priority date for international students; for spring admission, 3/1 priority date for domestic students, 2/1 priority date for international students. Applications are processed on a rolling basis. Application fee: $40 ($50 for international students). Electronic applications accepted. *Financial support:* Fellowships, career-related internships or fieldwork and unspecified assistantships available. Support available to part-time students. Financial award application deadline: 4/5; financial award applicants required to submit FAFSA. *Faculty research:* Public policy and advocacy. *Application contact:* 614-292-9444, Fax: 614-292-3895, E-mail: domestic.grad@osu.edu.

Pratt Institute, School of Art and Design, Program in Arts and Cultural Management, Brooklyn, NY 11205-3899. Offers MPS. Part-time programs available. *Faculty:* 1 (woman) full-time, 13 part-time/adjunct (9 women). *Students:* 46 full-time (40 women), 6 part-time (5 women); includes 12 minority (3 African Americans, 2 Asian Americans or Pacific Islanders, 7 Hispanic Americans), 20 international. Average age 27. 67 applicants, 60% accepted, 24 enrolled. In 2007, 13 degrees awarded. *Degree requirements:* For master's, thesis. *Entrance requirements:* For master's, bachelor's degree, transcripts, letters of recommendation, statement, portfolio. Additional exam requirements/recommendations for international students: Required—TOEFL (minimum score 600 paper-based; 250 computer-based). *Application deadline:* For fall admission, 2/1 for domestic students; for spring admission, 10/1 for domestic students. Application fee: $50 ($90 for international students). Electronic applications accepted. *Expenses:* Tuition: Full-time $25,680. Required fees: $1,106. Tuition and fees vary according to program. *Financial support:* Career-related internships or fieldwork, Federal Work-Study, institutionally sponsored loans, scholarships/grants, health care benefits, and unspecified assistantships available. Support available to part-time students. Financial award application deadline: 2/1; financial award applicants required to submit FAFSA. *Unit head:* Monica Shay, Director, 718-647-7560, E-mail: mshay@pratt.edu. *Application contact:* Young Hah, Director of Graduate Admissions, 718-636-3683, Fax: 718-399-4242, E-mail: yhah@pratt.edu.

Pratt Institute, School of Art and Design, Program in Design Management, Brooklyn, NY 11205-3899. Offers MPS. Part-time programs available. *Faculty:* 2 full-time (both women), 8 part-time/adjunct (4 women). *Students:* 52 full-time (39 women); includes 10 minority (7 African Americans, 2 Asian Americans or Pacific Islanders, 1 Hispanic American), 16 international. Average age 30. 89 applicants, 34% accepted, 25 enrolled. In 2007, 23 degrees awarded. *Degree requirements:* For master's, thesis. *Entrance requirements:* For master's, bachelor's degree, transcripts, letters of recommendation, statement, portfolio. Additional exam requirements/recommendations for international students: Required—TOEFL (minimum score 600 paper-based; 250 computer-based). *Application deadline:* For fall admission, 2/1 for domestic students; for spring admission, 10/1 for domestic students. Application fee: $50 ($90 for international students). Electronic applications accepted. *Expenses:* Tuition: Full-time $25,680. Required fees: $1,106. Tuition and fees vary according to program. *Financial support:* Career-related internships or fieldwork, Federal Work-Study, institutionally sponsored loans, scholarships/grants, health care benefits, and unspecified assistantships available. Support available to part-time students. Financial award application deadline: 2/1; financial award applicants required to submit FAFSA. *Unit head:* Mary McBride, Chairperson, 212-647-7538, E-mail: mmcb1033@pratt.edu. *Application contact:* Young Hah, Director of Graduate Admissions, 718-636-3683, Fax: 718-399-4242, E-mail: yhah@pratt.edu.

See Close-Up on page 253.

Regis University, College for Professional Studies, MA Program, Denver, CO 80221-1099. Offers criminology (MA); fine arts administration (Certificate); language and communication (MA); mediation (Certificate); psychology (MA); self-designed major (MA); social justice, peace, and reconciliation (Certificate); social science (MA); technical communication (Certificate). Program also offered in Henderson and Las Vegas (Summerlin), NV. Part-time and evening/weekend programs available. Postbaccalaureate distance learning degree programs offered (minimal on-campus study). *Faculty:* 84. *Students:* 218 (167 women). Average age 41. In 2007, 52 degrees awarded. *Degree requirements:* For master's, thesis, research project. *Entrance requirements:* For master's, resumé, recommendations, essays. Additional exam requirements/recommendations for international students: Required—TOEFL (minimum score 213 computer-based), TWE (minimum score 5). *Application deadline:* For fall admission, 8/13 priority date for domestic students, 7/13 priority date for international students; for winter admission, 10/8 priority date for domestic students, 9/8 priority date for international students; for spring admission, 12/17 priority date for domestic students, 11/17 for international students. Applications are processed on a rolling basis. Application fee: $75. Electronic applications accepted. *Expenses:* Contact institution. *Financial support:* Federal Work-Study available. Support available to part-time students. Financial award application deadline: 3/15; financial award applicants required to submit FAFSA. *Faculty research:* Independent/nonresidential graduate study: new methods and models, adult learning and the capstone experience, Goal Setting, behavior of Adult students, Innovative Studies for Community Colleges. *Unit head:* Dr. Robert Collins, Chair, 303-458-4302, Fax: 303-964-5538. *Application contact:* Graduate Admissions, 800-677-9270 Ext. 4080, Fax: 303-964-5538, E-mail: masters@regis.edu.

Rhode Island College, School of Graduate Studies, Faculty of Arts and Sciences, Department of Art, Providence, RI 02908-1991. Offers art (MA); art education (MAT); media studies (MA). *Accreditation:* NASAD (one or more programs are accredited). Part-time and evening/weekend programs available. *Faculty:* 7 full-time (4 women), 1 (woman) part-time/adjunct. *Students:* 6 full-time (3 women), 9 part-time (5 women); includes 1 minority (Asian American or Pacific Islander), 2 international. Average age 32. In 2007, 10 degrees awarded. *Degree requirements:* For master's, thesis. *Entrance requirements:* For master's, GRE General Test or MAT, portfolio (MA), 3 letters of recommendation, interview. *Application deadline:* For fall admission, 4/1 for domestic students; for spring admission, 11/1 for domestic students. Applications are processed on a rolling basis. Application fee: $50. *Expenses:* Tuition, state resident: full-time $6,240; part-time $260 per credit hour. Tuition, nonresident: full-time $13,104; part-time $546 per credit hour. Required fees: $332; $14 per credit hour. One-time fee: $66 part-time. *Financial support:* Teaching assistantships with full tuition reimbursements, career-related internships or fieldwork, Federal Work-Study, scholarships/grants, health care benefits, and unspecified assistantships available. Support available to part-time students. Financial award application deadline: 5/15; financial award applicants required to submit FAFSA. *Unit head:* Heemong Kim, Chair, 401-456-8054.

Ryerson University, School of Graduate Studies, Program in Photographic Preservation and Collections Management, Toronto, ON M5B 2K3, Canada. Offers MA.

Saint Mary's University of Minnesota, Schools of Graduate and Professional Programs, Graduate School of Business and Technology, Arts and Cultural Management Program, Winona, MN 55987-1399. Offers MA. *Unit head:* Paula Justich, Director, 612-728-5165, Fax: 612-728-5121, E-mail: pjustich@smumn.edu.

St. Thomas University, School of Leadership Studies, Program in Art Management, Miami Gardens, FL 33054-6459. Offers MA. *Application contact:* Marilyn Carballosa, Assistant Director of Admissions, 305-628-6546, Fax: 305-628-6591, E-mail: graduate@stu.edu.

Savannah College of Art and Design, Graduate School, Program in Arts Administration, Savannah, GA 31402-3146. Offers MA. Part-time programs available. *Faculty:* 2 full-time (both women). *Students:* 16 full-time (15 women), 6 part-time (all women); includes 1 Hispanic American, 2 international. 52 applicants, 48% accepted, 18 enrolled. *Degree requirements:* For master's, thesis. *Entrance requirements:* For master's, interview. Additional exam requirements/recommendations for international students: Required—TOEFL (minimum score 450 paper-based; 133 computer-based). *Application deadline:* For fall admission, 4/1 priority date for domestic and international students. *Expenses:* Tuition: Full-time $24,840; part-time $552 per credit. One-time fee: $500 full-time. *Financial support:* Fellowships, career-related internships or fieldwork, Federal Work-Study, and scholarships/grants available. Financial award application deadline: 4/1; financial award applicants required to submit FAFSA. *Unit head:* Dr. Desirè Houngues, Acting Chair, 912-525-5816, Fax: 912-525-5886, E-mail: dhoungue@scad.edu. *Application contact:* Darrell Tutchton, Director of Graduate and International Enrollment, 912-525-5961, Fax: 912-525-5985, E-mail: admission@scad.edu.

School of the Art Institute of Chicago, Graduate Division, Program in Arts Administration, Chicago, IL 60603-3103. Offers MAAA. *Accreditation:* NASAD. *Degree requirements:* For master's, thesis, telephone interview. *Entrance requirements:* Additional exam requirements/recommendations for international students: Required—TOEFL. *Faculty research:* Latin American artists, activist art, community-based art.

See Close-Up on page 259.

Seton Hall University, College of Arts and Sciences, Department of Public and Healthcare Administration, South Orange, NJ 07079-2697. Offers arts administration (MPA); health policy and management (MPA); healthcare administration (MHA); nonprofit organization management (MPA); public service: leadership, governance, and policy (MPA). *Accreditation:* NASPAA. Part-time and evening/weekend programs available. Postbaccalaureate distance learning degree programs offered (minimal on-campus study). *Degree requirements:* For master's, research project. Electronic applications accepted.

Shenandoah University, Shenandoah Conservatory, Winchester, VA 22601-5195. Offers arts administration (MS); church music (MM, Certificate); composition (MM); conducting (MM); dance (MA, MFA, MS); dance accompanying (MM); music (MS); music education (MME, DMA); music therapy (MMT, Certificate); pedagogy (MM); performance (MM, DMA, Artist Diploma); piano accompanying (MM). *Accreditation:* NASM. Part-time and evening/weekend programs available. *Faculty:* 35 full-time (17 women), 12 part-time/adjunct (6 women). *Students:* 69 full-time (39 women), 126 part-time (72 women); includes 5 minority (3 African Americans, 2 Hispanic Americans), 27 international. Average age 40. 90 applicants, 92% accepted, 59 enrolled. In 2007, 28 master's, 12 doctorates, 6 other advanced degrees awarded. *Degree requirements:* For master's, comprehensive exam (for some programs), thesis (for some programs), internship (MS), recital (MM), research teaching project or thesis (MME), project (MA); for doctorate, comprehensive exam, thesis/dissertation (for some programs), dissertation or teaching project, recital. *Entrance requirements:* For master's, audition, minimum GPA of 2.5, writing sample, resumé; for doctorate, audition, minimum GPA of 3.25, 2 letters of recommendation, writing sample, resumé. Additional exam requirements/recommendations for international students: Required—TOEFL (minimum score 527 paper-based; 197 computer-based; 71 iBT). *Application deadline:* Applications are processed on a rolling basis. Application fee: $30. Electronic applications accepted. *Expenses:* Tuition: Part-time $640 per credit. Part-time tuition and fees vary according to degree level and program. *Financial support:* In 2007–08, 154 students received support, including 23 teaching assistantships with partial tuition reimbursements available (averaging $5,440 per year); fellowships with partial tuition reimbursements available, career-related internships or fieldwork, institutionally sponsored loans, scholarships/grants, and unspecified assistantships also available. Support available to part-time students. Financial award application deadline: 3/15; financial award applicants required to submit FAFSA. *Faculty research:* Creative activity, performance practice, music therapy aging, composition, Motown music. Total annual research expenditures: $4,272. *Unit head:* Dr. Laurence A. Kaptain, Dean, 540-665-4600, Fax: 540-665-5402, E-mail: lkaptain@su.edu. *Application contact:* David Anthony, Dean of Admissions, 540-665-4581, Fax: 540-665-4627, E-mail: admit@su.edu.

See Close-Up on page 357.

Southern Methodist University, Meadows School of the Arts, Division of Arts Administration, Dallas, TX 75275. Offers MA/MBA. *Faculty:* 1 (woman) full-time, 1 (woman) part-time/adjunct. *Students:* 18 full-time (16 women); includes 3 minority (1 Asian American or Pacific Islander, 2 Hispanic Americans). Average age 26. 18 applicants, 72% accepted, 7 enrolled. *Entrance requirements:* Additional exam requirements/recommendations for international students: Required—TOEFL (minimum score 600 paper-based; 250 computer-based; 100 iBT). *Application deadline:* For fall admission, 1/15 priority date for domestic and international students. Applications are processed on a rolling basis. Application fee: $75. Electronic applications accepted. *Unit head:* Dr. P. Gregory Warden, Interim Chair, 214-768-3425, E-mail: lhilliar@smu.edu. *Application contact:* Lynette Hilliard, Assistant Director, 214-768-3425, E-mail: ihilliar@smu.edu.

Southern Utah University, College of Performing and Visual Arts, Program in Arts Administration, Cedar City, UT 84720-2498. Offers MFA. *Faculty:* 1 full-time (0 women). *Students:* 11 full-time (6 women). Average age 26. 26 applicants, 23% accepted, 6 enrolled. In 2007, 4 degrees awarded. *Entrance requirements:* For master's, GRE General Test, interview, 3 letters of recommendation, resumé, minimum GPA of 3.0. *Application deadline:* For fall admission, 3/31 for domestic students. Applications are processed on a rolling basis. Application fee: $50 ($65 for international students). Electronic applications accepted. *Financial support:* In 2007–08, 10 fellowships with full tuition reimbursements (averaging $7,700 per year) were awarded. *Application contact:* Matt Neves, Director, 435-586-7873, Fax: 435-865-8657, E-mail: neves@suu.edu.

Teachers College, Columbia University, Graduate Faculty of Education, Department of Arts and Humanities, Program in Arts Administration, New York, NY 10027-6696. Offers MA. *Faculty:* 1 (woman) full-time, 2 part-time/adjunct. *Students:* 52 full-time (46 women), 15 part-time (12 women); includes 19 minority (7 African Americans, 1 American Indian/Alaska Native, 8 Asian Americans or Pacific Islanders, 3 Hispanic Americans), 13 international. Average age 28. 151 applicants, 26% accepted, 27 enrolled. In 2007, 20 degrees awarded. *Degree requirements:* For master's, thesis, internship. *Entrance requirements:* For master's, GRE, approximately 3 years of related experience. Additional exam requirements/recommendations for international students: Required—TOEFL. *Application deadline:* For fall admission, 1/15 priority date for domestic students. Application fee: $70. *Financial support:* Career-related internships or fieldwork, Federal Work-Study, institutionally sponsored loans, tuition waivers (partial), and unspecified assistantships available. Financial award application deadline: 2/1. *Faculty research:* Artists' career development, arts law, American culture, strategic management, international training.

See Close-Up on page 267.

Temple University, Graduate School, Tyler School of Art, Department of Art History, Philadelphia, PA 19122-6096. Offers MA, PhD. *Accreditation:* NASAD. Part-time programs available. Terminal master's awarded for partial completion of doctoral program. *Degree requirements:* For master's, 2 foreign languages, thesis, comprehensive slide exam; for doctorate, thesis/dissertation, qualifying exam. *Entrance requirements:* For master's, GRE General Test, minimum GPA of 3.0; for doctorate, MA in art history. Additional exam requirements/recommendations for international students: Required—TOEFL. Electronic applications accepted. *Faculty research:* Aegean, Greek, and Roman art; early Christian art; Medieval art and architecture; Renaissance and baroque painting, sculpture, and architecture; nineteenth and twentieth century painting and sculpture.

See Close-Up on page 269.

Universidad del Turabo, Graduate Programs, School of Social Sciences and Humanities, Programs in Public Affairs, Program in Arts Administration, Gurabo, PR 00778-3030. Offers MA. *Students:* 3 full-time (2 women), 5 part-time (all women); all minorities (all Hispanic Americans) Average age 34. In 2007, 3 degrees awarded. *Expenses:* Tuition: Full-time $5,560. *Application contact:* Virginia González, Admissions Officer, 787-746-3009.

The University of Akron, Graduate School, College of Fine and Applied Arts, School of Dance, Theatre, and Arts Administration, Program in Arts Administration, Akron, OH 44325. Offers MA. *Accreditation:* NASAD. *Students:* 24 full-time (17 women), 4 part-time (2 women); includes 1 minority (African American), 2 international. Average age 30. 19 applicants, 95% accepted, 8 enrolled. In 2007, 3 degrees awarded. *Degree requirements:* For master's, thesis optional. *Entrance requirements:* For master's, minimum GPA of 2.75, interview, personal statement. Additional exam requirements/recommendations for international students: Required—TOEFL (minimum score 550 paper-based; 213 computer-based; 79 iBT). *Application deadline:* For fall admission, 3/15 for domestic and international students. Applications are processed on a rolling basis. Application fee: $30 ($40 for international students). Electronic applications accepted. *Expenses:* Tuition, state resident: full-time $6,164; part-time $342 per credit. Tuition, nonresident: full-time $10,575; part-time $588 per credit. Required fees: $806; $43 per credit. $12 per term. Tuition and fees vary according to course load, degree level and program. *Unit head:* Durand Pope, Coordinator, 330-972-5380, E-mail: dpope@uakron.edu.

University of Cincinnati, Graduate School, College-Conservatory of Music, Divisions of Opera, Musical Theater, Drama, and Arts Administration, Cincinnati, OH 45221. Offers arts administration (MA); directing (MFA); theater design and production (MFA); voice and opera (MM, DMA); MBA/MA. *Accreditation:* NAST (one or more programs are accredited). *Faculty:* 25 full-time (6 women). *Students:* 53 full-time (35 women), 10 part-time (7 women); includes 22 minority (7 African Americans, 1 American Indian/Alaska Native, 9 Asian Americans or Pacific Islanders, 5 Hispanic Americans), 15 international. Average age 28. 71 applicants, 49% accepted. In 2007, 19 degrees awarded. *Degree requirements:* For master's, final project. *Entrance requirements:* For master's, GMAT (MA), audition/interview. Additional exam requirements/recommendations for international students: Required—TOEFL (minimum score 520 paper-based; 190 computer-based). *Application deadline:* For fall admission, 2/1 for domestic students. Applications are processed on a rolling basis. Application fee: $85. Electronic applications accepted. *Financial support:* In 2007–08, 31 teaching assistantships with full tuition reimbursements (averaging $4,897 per year) were awarded; fellowships, research assistantships, career-related internships or fieldwork, Federal Work-Study, scholarships/grants, tuition waivers (full), and unspecified assistantships also available. Financial award application deadline: 3/1. *Unit head:* R. Terrell Finney, Chair, 513-556-5803, Fax: 513-556-3399, E-mail: terrell.finney@uc.edu. *Application contact:* Paul R. Hillner, Assistant Dean for Admissions and Student Services, 513-556-5462, Fax: 513-556-1028, E-mail: paul.hillner@uc.edu.

University of Florida, Graduate School, Warrington College of Business Administration, Hough Graduate School of Business, Programs in Business Administration, Gainesville, FL 32611. Offers accounting (MBA); arts administration (MBA); business strategy and public policy (MBA); competitive strategy (MBA); decision and information sciences (MBA); electronic commerce (MBA); finance (MBA); general business (MBA); global management (MBA); Graham-Buffett security analysis (MBA); health administration (MBA); human resources management (MBA); international studies (MBA); Latin American business (MBA); management (MBA); marketing (MBA); sports administration (MBA); JD/MBA; MBA/MS; MBA/PhD; MBA/Pharm D; MD/MBA. *Accreditation:* AACSB. Part-time and evening/weekend programs available. Postbaccalaureate distance learning degree programs offered. *Faculty:* 14. *Students:* 942 (255 women); includes 219 minority (34 African Americans, 3 American Indian/Alaska Native, 92 Asian Americans or Pacific Islanders, 90 Hispanic Americans) 32 international. In 2007, 485 degrees awarded. *Entrance requirements:* For master's, GMAT, minimum GPA of 3.0, interview. Additional exam requirements/recommendations for international students: Required—TOEFL (minimum score 550 paper-based; 213 computer-based). *Application deadline:* For fall admission, 4/15 for domestic students; for winter admission, 10/15 priority date for domestic students; for spring admission, 2/15 for domestic students. Applications are processed on a rolling basis. Application fee: $30. Electronic applications accepted. *Expenses:* Tuition, state resident: full-time $7,478. Tuition, nonresident: full-time $22,603. *Financial support:* Fellowships, research assistantships, teaching assistantships, career-related internships or fieldwork, scholarships/grants, and unspecified assistantships available. Support available to part-time students. Financial award application deadline: 2/15; financial award applicants required to submit FAFSA. *Faculty research:* Accounting, finance, insurance, management, real estate and urban analysis marketing. *Unit head:* Alex Sevilla, Director, 352-392-7992 Ext. 1206. *Application contact:* Patrick Foran, Associate Director of Admissions, 352-392-7992 Ext. 282, Fax: 352-392-8791, E-mail: patrick.foran@cba.ufl.edu.

University of New Orleans, Graduate School, College of Liberal Arts, Program in Arts Administration, New Orleans, LA 70148. Offers MA. Part-time programs available. *Students:* 26 (23 women). Average age 29. In 2007, 14 degrees awarded. *Degree requirements:* For master's, internship. *Entrance requirements:* For master's, GMAT, GRE General Test. Additional exam requirements/recommendations for international students: Required—TOEFL (minimum score 550 paper-based; 213 computer-based; 79 iBT). *Application deadline:* For fall admission, 7/1 priority date for domestic students, 6/1 for international students; for spring admission, 11/15 priority date for domestic students, 10/1 for international students. Applications are processed on a rolling basis. Application fee: $40. Electronic applications accepted. *Financial support:* Research assistantships, career-related internships or fieldwork available. Financial award application deadline: 3/15; financial award applicants required to submit FAFSA. *Unit head:* Dr. Harmon Greenblatt, Director, 504-280-6158, Fax: 504-280-7339, E-mail: artsadm@uno.edu.

University of Oregon, Graduate School, School of Architecture and Allied Arts, Program in Arts and Administration, Eugene, OR 97403-5230. Offers arts management (MA, MS). *Faculty:* 4 full-time (3 women), 1 (woman) part-time/adjunct. *Students:* 30 full-time (27 women), 5 part-time (4 women); includes 5 minority (1 African American, 1 American Indian/Alaska Native, 3 Hispanic Americans), 5 international. 45 applicants, 62% accepted. In 2007, 17 degrees awarded. *Degree requirements:* For master's, summer internship, thesis/project. *Entrance requirements:* For master's, minimum GPA of 3.0; bachelor's degree in history, practice of visual, performing arts or other related degree. Additional exam requirements/recommendations for international students: Required—TOEFL. *Application deadline:* For fall admission, 2/1 for domestic students. Application fee: $50. *Financial support:* In 2007–08, 11 teaching assistantships were awarded; career-related internships or fieldwork, Federal Work-Study, and institutionally sponsored loans also available. Support available to part-time students. Financial award application deadline: 3/1. *Faculty research:* Museum education, arts program evaluation, community arts, information management, arts marketing. *Unit head:* Doug Blandy, Director, 541-346-5600, Fax: 541-346-3639. *Application contact:* Maia Howes, Admissions Contact, 541-346-2982, Fax: 541-346-3639, E-mail: mhowes@uoregon.edu.

Announcement: The Arts and Administration Program offers a Master of Arts Management, with concentrations in museum studies, community arts, and performing arts. Full-time faculty members address cultural policy, community arts, museum education, events management, administration, evaluation, and aesthetics. Participating faculty members offer courses in information design, artistic administration, and nonprofit management.

University of Southern California, Graduate School, School of Fine Arts, Program in Public Art Studies, Los Angeles, CA 90089. Offers MPAS. *Faculty:* 1 full-time (0 women), 6 part-time/adjunct (4 women). *Students:* 36 full-time (32 women), 1 (woman) part-time; includes 14 minority (3 African Americans, 2 Asian Americans or Pacific Islanders, 9 Hispanic Americans), 1 international. 49 applicants, 69% accepted. In 2007, 10 degrees awarded. *Degree requirements:* For master's, thesis, final project. *Entrance requirements:* For master's, GRE General Test. *Application deadline:* For fall admission, 2/1 priority date for domestic students. Applications are processed on a rolling basis. Application fee: $85. *Financial support:* In 2007–08, 15 students received support; fellowships, research assistantships, teaching assistantships with full tuition reimbursements available, career-related internships or fieldwork, Federal Work-Study, institutionally sponsored loans, and scholarships/grants available. Financial award application deadline: 2/1. *Unit head:* Joshua Decter, Head, 213-740-2311. *Application contact:* Elizabeth Lovins, Information Contact, 213-740-2311.

University of Wisconsin–Madison, Graduate School, Wisconsin School of Business, Wisconsin Full-Time MBA Program, Madison, WI 53706-1380. Offers applied corporate finance (MBA); applied security analysis (MBA); arts administration (MBA); brand and product management (MBA); entrepreneurial management (MBA); marketing research (MBA); operations and technology management (MBA); real estate (MBA); risk management and insurance (MBA); strategic human resource management (MBA); strategic management in the life and engineering sciences (MBA); supply chain management (MBA). *Faculty:* 66 full-time (13 women), 13 part-time/adjunct (3 women). *Students:* 224 full-time (65 women); includes 27 minority (12 African Americans, 1 American Indian/Alaska Native, 6 Asian Americans or Pacific Islanders, 8 Hispanic Americans), 57 international. Average age 29. 447 applicants, 33% accepted, 106 enrolled. In 2007, 111 degrees awarded. *Degree requirements:* For master's, minimum GPA of 3.0. *Entrance requirements:* For master's, GMAT, bachelors or equivalent degree, 2 years of work experience. Additional exam requirements/recommendations for international students: Required—TOEFL (minimum score 600 paper-based; 250 computer-based; 90 iBT). *Application deadline:* For fall admission, 11/1 for domestic and international students; for winter admission, 1/23 for domestic and international students; for spring admission, 5/15 for domestic and international students. Applications are processed on a rolling basis. Application fee: $45. Electronic applications accepted. *Financial support:* In 2007–08, 163 students received support, including 24 fellowships with full and partial tuition reimbursements available (averaging $13,498 per year), 88 research assistantships with full tuition reimbursements available (averaging $8,196 per year), 36 teaching assistantships with full tuition reimbursements available (averaging $10,201 per year); scholarships/grants, health care benefits, and unspecified assistantships also available. Financial award application deadline: 3/26. *Unit head:* Ken Kawajecz, Associate Dean of Master's Programs, 608-265-3494, E-mail: kkavajecz@bus.wisc.edu. *Application contact:* Seann Sweeney, Assistant Director of MBA Marketing and Recruiting, 608-262-4000, Fax: 608-265-4192, E-mail: ssweeney@bus.wisc.edu.

Virginia Polytechnic Institute and State University, Graduate School, College of Liberal Arts and Human Sciences, Department of Theatre Arts, Blacksburg, VA 24061. Offers arts administration (MFA); costume design (MFA); lighting design (MFA); property management (MFA); scenic design (MFA); stage management (MFA); technical theatre (MFA). *Accreditation:* NAST. *Entrance requirements:* Additional exam requirements/recommendations for international students: Required—TOEFL (minimum score 550 paper-based; 213 computer-based). Electronic applications accepted.

Webster University, Leigh Gerdine College of Fine Arts, Department of Art, Program in Arts Management and Leadership, St. Louis, MO 63119-3194. Offers MFA. Part-time and evening/weekend programs available. *Students:* 3 full-time (all women), 3 part-time (2 women); includes 1 minority (African American) Average age 33. In 2007, 1 degree awarded. *Degree requirements:* For master's, thesis. *Entrance requirements:* For master's, GRE, BA or BFA in related field, interview. *Application deadline:* Applications are processed on a rolling basis. Application fee: $35 ($50 for international students). *Expenses:* Tuition: Full-time $9,360; part-time $520 per credit. *Financial support:* In 2007–08, 1 fellowship (averaging $6,000 per year) was awarded; Federal Work-Study also available. Support available to part-time students. Financial award application deadline: 4/1. *Unit head:* Joanne Kohn, Director, 314-968-7171, Fax: 314-968-7139. *Application contact:* Denise Harrell, Associate Director of Graduate and Evening Student Admissions, 314-968-6983, Fax: 314-968-7116, E-mail: gadmit@webster.edu.

Arts Administration

Winthrop University, College of Visual and Performing Arts, Department of Art, Rock Hill, SC 29733. Offers art (MFA); art administration (MA); art education (MA). *Accreditation:* NASAD. Part-time programs available. *Faculty:* 17 full-time (7 women), 7 part-time/adjunct (4 women). *Students:* 7 full-time (5 women), 26 part-time (21 women); includes 1 minority (American Indian/Alaska Native). Average age 29. In 2007, 4 degrees awarded. *Degree requirements:* For master's, thesis, documented exhibit, oral exam. *Entrance requirements:* For master's, GRE General Test or MAT, PRAXIS (MA), minimum GPA of 3.0, resumé, slide portfolio, teaching certificate (MA). *Application deadline:* For fall admission, 3/1 priority date for domestic students; for spring admission, 9/1 for domestic students. Applications are processed on a rolling basis. Application fee: $50. Electronic applications accepted. *Expenses:* Tuition, state resident: full-time $9,834; part-time $412 per credit hour. Tuition, nonresident: full-time $18,280; part-time $763 per credit hour. *Financial support:* In 2007–08, 5 research assistantships with full tuition reimbursements (averaging $3,600 per year) were awarded; Federal Work-Study, scholarships/grants, and unspecified assistantships also available. Support available to part-time students. Financial award application deadline: 2/1; financial award applicants required to submit FAFSA. *Unit head:* Dr. Tom Stanley, Chair, 803-323-2653, E-mail: stanleyt@winthrop.edu. *Application contact:* 800-411-7041, Fax: 803-323-2292, E-mail: graduatestu@winthrop.edu.

Art Therapy

Adler School of Professional Psychology, Programs in Psychology, Chicago, IL 60601-7203. Offers art therapy (Certificate); clinical hypnosis (Certificate); clinical psychology (Psy D); counseling psychology (MACP); counseling psychology/art therapy (MACAT); gerontology (MAGP); marriage and family counseling (MAMFC); marriage and family therapy (Certificate); organizational psychology (MAO); substance abuse counseling (MASAC, Certificate); Psy D/Certificate; Psy D/MACAT; Psy D/MACP; Psy D/MAMFC; Psy D/MASAC. *Accreditation:* APA. Part-time and evening/weekend programs available. Terminal master's awarded for partial completion of doctoral program. *Degree requirements:* For master's, thesis or alternative, oral exam, practicum; for doctorate, thesis/dissertation, clinical exam, internship, oral exam, practicum, written qualifying exam. *Entrance requirements:* For master's, 12 semester hours in psychology, minimum GPA of 3.0; for doctorate, 18 semester hours in psychology, minimum GPA of 3.25; for Certificate, appropriate master's or doctoral degree.

See Close-Up on page 1363.

Albertus Magnus College, Program in Art Therapy, New Haven, CT 06511-1189. Offers MAAT. Part-time and evening/weekend programs available. *Faculty:* 7 full-time (6 women), 6 part-time/adjunct (4 women). *Students:* 15 full-time (all women), 31 part-time (30 women); includes 14 minority (5 African Americans, 9 Hispanic Americans). Average age 35. 12 applicants, 67% accepted, 8 enrolled. In 2007, 5 degrees awarded. *Degree requirements:* For master's, thesis. *Entrance requirements:* For master's, interview, writing sample. *Application deadline:* For fall admission, 8/30 for domestic students; for spring admission, 12/30 for domestic students. Application fee: $35. *Financial support:* Available to part-time students. Application deadline: 8/17. *Unit head:* Donna Kaiser, Director, 203-773-8903, Fax: 203-773-3117.

Athabasca University, Graduate Centre for Applied Psychology, Athabasca, AB T9S 3A3, Canada. Offers art therapy (MC); career counseling (MC); counseling (Advanced Certificate); counseling psychology (MC); school counseling (MC). *Faculty:* 3 full-time (2 women), 2 part-time/adjunct (0 women). Tuition and fees charges are reported in Canadian dollars. *Expenses:* Tuition, state resident: part-time $1,795 Canadian dollars per credit. Required fees: $70 Canadian dollars per year. One-time fee: $360 Canadian dollars part-time. Part-time tuition and fees vary according to program. *Unit head:* Dr. Sandra Collins, Program Director, 888-611-7121, E-mail: sandrac@athabascau.ca.

Avila University, Department of Psychology, Kansas City, MO 64145-1698. Offers counseling and art therapy (MS); counseling psychology (MS); general psychology (MS). Part-time and evening/weekend programs available. *Faculty:* 7 full-time (5 women), 12 part-time/adjunct (9 women). *Students:* 109 full-time (94 women), 19 part-time (15 women); includes 24 minority (19 African Americans, 1 Asian American or Pacific Islander, 4 Hispanic Americans), 4 international. Average age 35. In 2007, 30 degrees awarded. *Entrance requirements:* For master's, minimum GPA of 3.0 in last 60 hours, 2 letters of recommendation, transcripts, application with letter of intent. Additional exam requirements/recommendations for international students: Required—TOEFL. *Application deadline:* Applications are processed on a rolling basis. Application fee: $0. *Expenses:* Tuition: Part-time $435 per credit hour. Required fees: $19 per credit hour. Tuition and fees vary according to program. *Financial support:* Career-related internships or fieldwork and scholarships/grants available. Support available to part-time students. Financial award applicants required to submit FAFSA. *Faculty research:* Preparation for working in mental health services. *Unit head:* Dr. Regina Staves, Director of Graduate Psychology, 816-501-3665, Fax: 816-501-2455, E-mail: gradpsych@avila.edu.

Caldwell College, Graduate Studies, Program in Counseling Psychology, Caldwell, NJ 07006-6195. Offers art therapy (MA); counseling psychology (MA); school counseling (MA). Part-time and evening/weekend programs available. *Degree requirements:* For master's, comprehensive exam, practicum. *Entrance requirements:* For master's, GRE General Test, minimum GPA of 3.0. Additional exam requirements/recommendations for international students: Required—TOEFL (minimum score 580 paper-based; 237 computer-based). Electronic applications accepted.

California Institute of Integral Studies, Graduate Programs, School of Professional Psychology, San Francisco, CA 94103. Offers clinical psychology (Psy D); community mental health (MA); drama therapy (MA); expressive arts therapy (MA); integral counseling psychology (MA); integral counseling, psychology-weekend (MA); psychology (Psy D), including clinical psychology; somatic psychology (MA). *Accreditation:* APA. Part-time programs available. *Faculty:* 28 full-time, 54 part-time/adjunct. *Students:* 591; includes 113 minority (19 African Americans, 3 American Indian/Alaska Native, 48 Asian Americans or Pacific Islanders, 43 Hispanic Americans). Average age 37. 383 applicants, 75% accepted, 155 enrolled. In 2007, 109 master's, 20 doctorates awarded. *Degree requirements:* For master's, comprehensive exam; for doctorate, comprehensive exam, thesis/dissertation. *Entrance requirements:* For master's, minimum GPA of 3.0, letters of recommendation, writing sample; for doctorate, GRE, MA in psychology or social work with appropriate practical experience for advanced standing, or BA with a minimum GPA of 3.1; letters of recommendation; writing sample. Additional exam requirements/recommendations for international students: Required—TOEFL. *Application deadline:* For fall admission, 2/1 priority date for domestic and international students; for spring admission, 10/15 priority date for domestic and international students. Applications are processed on a rolling basis. Application fee: $65. Electronic applications accepted. *Expenses:* Tuition: Full-time $16,930; part-time $780 per unit. Tuition and fees vary according to course load and program. *Financial support:* In 2007–08, 393 students received support; research assistantships with tuition reimbursements available, teaching assistantships with tuition reimbursements available, career-related internships or fieldwork, Federal Work-Study, institutionally sponsored loans, scholarships/grants, and tuition waivers (partial) available. Support available to part-time students. Financial award application deadline: 3/15; financial award applicants required to submit FAFSA. *Faculty research:* Somatic psychology, comparative psychology, art therapy, transpersonal psychology, eco-psychology. *Application contact:* David Townes, Senior Admissions Counselor, 415-575-6152, Fax: 415-575-1268, E-mail: dtownes@ciis.edu.

See Close-Up on page 1421.

California State University, Los Angeles, Graduate Studies, College of Arts and Letters, Department of Art, Los Angeles, CA 90032-8530. Offers art (MA), including art education, art history, art therapy, ceramics, metals, and textiles, design (MA, MFA), painting, sculpture, and graphic arts, photography; fine arts (MFA), including crafts, design (MA, MFA), studio arts. *Accreditation:* NASAD (one or more programs are accredited). Part-time and evening/weekend programs available. *Faculty:* 7 full-time (3 women). *Students:* 24 full-time (13 women), 59 part-time (42 women); includes 19 minority (2 African Americans, 1 American Indian/Alaska Native, 5 Asian Americans or Pacific Islanders, 11 Hispanic Americans), 16 international. Average age 39. In 2007, 28 degrees awarded. *Degree requirements:* For master's, comprehensive exam, project or thesis. *Entrance requirements:* For master's, portfolio. Additional exam requirements/recommendations for international students: Required—TOEFL. *Application deadline:* For fall admission, 6/30 for domestic students; for spring admission, 2/1 for domestic students. Applications are processed on a rolling basis. Application fee: $55. *Financial support:* Federal Work-Study available. Support available to part-time students. Financial award application deadline: 3/1. *Faculty research:* The artist and the book, conceptual art, ceramic processes, computer graphics, architectural graphics. *Unit head:* Dr. Robert Martin, Chair, 323-343-4010, Fax: 323-343-4045, E-mail: rjmartin@calstatela.edu.

The College of New Rochelle, Graduate School, Division of Art and Communication Studies, Program in Art Therapy, New Rochelle, NY 10805-2308. Offers art therapy (MS); art therapy/counseling (MS). Part-time and evening/weekend programs available. *Faculty:* 2 full-time (1 woman), 5 part-time/adjunct (all women). *Students:* 19 full-time (all women), 18 part-time (16 women); includes 3 minority (1 African American, 1 American Indian/Alaska Native, 1 Asian American or Pacific Islander), 1 international. Average age 30. In 2007, 13 degrees awarded. *Degree requirements:* For master's, thesis, practicum, fieldwork. *Entrance requirements:* For master's, 12 credits in psychology, 15 credits in studio art, portfolio. *Application deadline:* For fall admission, 8/1 priority date for domestic students. Applications are processed on a rolling basis. Application fee: $35. *Expenses:* Tuition: Part-time $650 per credit. Required fees: $90 per term. *Financial support:* In 2007–08, 2 research assistantships with tuition reimbursements were awarded; career-related internships or fieldwork, scholarships/grants, tuition waivers (partial), and unspecified assistantships also available. Support available to part-time students. *Faculty research:* Phototherapy, assessment and evaluation, developmental stages in art, creativity and mental illness. *Unit head:* Dr. John Patton, Head, Division of Art and Communication Studies, 914-654-5208, Fax: 914-654-5593.

Concordia University, School of Graduate Studies, Faculty of Fine Arts, Department of Creative Arts Therapies, Montréal, QC H3G 1M8, Canada. Offers MA.

Drexel University, College of Nursing and Health Professions, Program in Creative Arts in Therapy, Specialization in Art Therapy, Philadelphia, PA 19104-2875. Offers MA. *Accreditation:* NASAD. *Degree requirements:* For master's, comprehensive exam, thesis. *Entrance requirements:* For master's, GRE General Test or MAT, interview, minimum GPA of 2.75, portfolio. Electronic applications accepted.

Eastern Virginia Medical School, Art Therapy Program, Norfolk, VA 23501-1980. Offers MS. *Faculty:* 4 full-time (3 women), 1 part-time/adjunct (0 women). *Students:* 20 full-time (19 women); includes 2 minority (1 African American, 1 Asian American or Pacific Islander). Average age 20. 32 applicants, 72% accepted, 12 enrolled. In 2007, 10 degrees awarded. *Degree requirements:* For master's, comprehensive exam, thesis, practicum. *Entrance requirements:* For master's, GRE General Test, MAT, 12 credit hours in psychology, 18 credit hours in studio art, interview, portfolio. *Application deadline:* For fall admission, 2/15 priority date for domestic and international students. Applications are processed on a rolling basis. Application fee: $60. *Expenses:* *Contact institution.* *Financial support:* In 2007–08, 10 students received support. Federal Work-Study, institutionally sponsored loans, and scholarships/grants available. Financial award application deadline: 5/15; financial award applicants required to submit CSS PROFILE or FAFSA. *Faculty research:* Art therapy projective imagery assessment: a collection of children's drawings. *Unit head:* Abby Calisch, Director, 757-446-5895, Fax: 757-446-6179, E-mail: artthrpy@evms.edu. *Application contact:* Kiera Dorsey, Administrative Support Coordinator, 757-446-5895, Fax: 757-446-6179, E-mail: dorseyks@evms.edu.

Emporia State University, School of Graduate Studies, The Teachers College, Department of Psychology and Special Education, Program in Art Therapy, Emporia, KS 66801-5087. Offers MS. *Accreditation:* NASAD. Part-time programs available. *Students:* 8 applicants, 38% accepted, 3 enrolled. In 2007, 4 degrees awarded. *Degree requirements:* For master's, comprehensive exam or thesis, internship. *Entrance requirements:* For master's, GRE General Test or MAT, graduate essay exam, appropriate bachelor's degree. Additional exam requirements/recommendations for international students: Required—TOEFL. *Application deadline:* For fall admission, 6/1 for domestic students; for spring admission, 10/1 for domestic students. Applications are processed on a rolling basis. Application fee: $30 ($75 for international students). Electronic applications accepted. *Expenses:* Tuition, state resident: part-time $157 per credit hour. Tuition, nonresident: part-time $475 per credit hour. Required fees: $47 per credit hour. Tuition and fees vary according to campus/location. *Financial support:* Career-related internships or fieldwork, Federal Work-Study, institutionally sponsored loans, health care benefits, and unspecified assistantships available. Financial award application deadline: 3/15; financial award applicants required to submit FAFSA. *Unit head:* Dr. Kenneth A. Weaver, Chair, Department of Psychology and Special Education, 620-341-5317, E-mail: kweaver@emporia.edu.

The George Washington University, Columbian College of Arts and Sciences, Department of Art Therapy, Washington, DC 20052. Offers MA, Certificate. *Degree requirements:* For master's, internship, practicum paper. *Entrance requirements:* For master's, GRE General Test, interview, minimum GPA of 3.0; for Certificate, interview, minimum GPA of 3.0. Additional exam requirements/recommendations for international students: Required—TOEFL (minimum score 550 paper-based; 213 computer-based).

Hofstra University, School of Education and Allied Human Services, Department of Counseling, Research, Special Education and Rehabilitation, Program in Creative Arts Therapy, Hempstead, NY 11549. Offers creative arts therapy (MA); creative arts therapy and special education (birth-grade 2) (MS Ed); creative arts therapy and special education (grades 1-12) (MS Ed). Part-time programs available. *Students:* 51 full-time (49 women), 19 part-time (all women); includes 8 minority (2 African Americans, 4 Asian Americans or Pacific Islanders, 2 Hispanic Americans), 8 international. Average age 30. 74 applicants, 72% accepted, 26 enrolled. In 2007, 16 degrees awarded. *Degree requirements:* For master's, thesis optional. *Entrance requirements:* For master's, interview, portfolio, 3 letters of recommendation, 12 hours of course work in psychology, 18 hours of course work in studio art, essay. Additional exam requirements/recommendations for international students: Required—TOEFL (minimum score 550 paper-based; 213 computer-based). *Application deadline:* Applications are processed on a rolling basis. Application fee: $60. Electronic applications accepted. *Expenses:* Tuition: Full-time $14,220; part-time $820 per credit. Required fees: $970; $165 per term. Tuition and fees vary according to program. *Financial support:* In 2007–08, 23 students received support, including 1 fellowship with tuition reimbursement available (averaging $3,000 per year), 3 research assistantships with full and partial tuition reimbursements available (averaging $11,100 per year); career-related internships or fieldwork, Federal Work-Study, institutionally sponsored loans, scholarships/grants, and tuition waivers (full and partial) also available. Support available to part-time students. Financial award applicants required to submit FAFSA. *Faculty research:* Creativity for non-artists, medical art therapy, play and sand tray therapy, cultural centex. *Unit head:* Dr. Joan S. Bloomgarden, Director, 516-463-5300, Fax: 516-463-6184, E-mail: cprjsb@hofstra.edu. *Application contact:* Carol Drummer, Dean of Graduate Admissions, 516-463-4876, Fax: 516-463-4664, E-mail: gradstudent@hofstra.edu.

Lesley University, Graduate School of Arts and Social Sciences, Division of Expressive Therapies, Cambridge, MA 02138-2790. Offers art (MA); dance (MA); expressive therapies (MA, PhD, CAGS); music (MA). *Faculty:* 9 full-time (8 women), 32 part-time/adjunct (27 women). *Students:* 174 full-time (161 women), 227 part-time (215 women); includes 4 minority (1 American Indian/Alaska Native, 1 Asian American or Pacific Islander, 2 Hispanic Americans), 22 international. Average age 32. 244 applicants, 88% accepted, 157 enrolled. In 2007, 138 master's, 1 doctorate awarded. Terminal master's awarded for partial completion of doctoral program. *Degree requirements:* For master's, internship, practicum; for doctorate, thesis/dissertation. *Entrance requirements:* For master's, art portfolio, performance DVD; for doctorate, GRE or MAT. Additional exam requirements/recommendations for international students: Required—TOEFL (minimum score 550 paper-based; 213 computer-based; 80 iBT). *Application deadline:* Applications are processed on a rolling basis. Application fee: $50. *Financial support:* In 2007–08, 24 students received support, including 1 teaching assistantship (averaging $7,298 per year); Federal Work-Study, scholarships/grants, and unspecified assistantships also available. Support available to part-time students. Financial award application deadline: 4/15; financial award applicants required to submit FAFSA. *Unit head:* Julia Byers, Director, 617-349-8121, E-mail: jbyers@lesley.edu. *Application contact:* Gilda Resmini-Walsh, Assistant Director, Advising and Student Services, 617-349-8444, E-mail: gresmini@lesley.edu.

See Close-Up on page 243.

Long Island University, C.W. Post Campus, School of Visual and Performing Arts, Department of Art, Brookville, NY 11548-1300. Offers art (MA); art education (MS); clinical art therapy (MA); fine art and design (MFA). Part-time and evening/weekend programs available. *Faculty:* 9 full-time (4 women), 14 part-time/adjunct (6 women). *Students:* 52 full-time (44 women), 29 part-time (25 women); includes 14 minority (2 African Americans, 12 Asian Americans or Pacific Islanders), 7 international. Average age 32. 68 applicants, 69% accepted, 22 enrolled. In 2007, 44 degrees awarded. *Degree requirements:* For master's, thesis. *Application deadline:* Applications are processed on a rolling basis. Application fee: $30. Electronic applications accepted. *Expenses:* Tuition: Part-time $825 per credit. Tuition and fees vary according to course load. *Financial support:* Teaching assistantships, career-related internships or fieldwork, Federal Work-Study, institutionally sponsored loans, and unspecified assistantships available. Support available to part-time students. Financial award application deadline: 5/15; financial award applicants required to submit CSS PROFILE or FAFSA. *Faculty research:* Painting, sculpture, installation, computers, video. Total annual research expenditures: $17,346. *Unit head:* Prof. Donna Tuman, Chair, 516-299-2464, E-mail: donna.tuman@liu.edu. *Application contact:* Cathy Morante, Graduate Advisor, 516-299-2405 Ext. 2465, E-mail: cathy.morante@liu.edu.

Marylhurst University, Department of Art Therapy Counseling, Marylhurst, OR 97036-0261. Offers art therapy (PGC); art therapy counseling (MA); counseling (PGC). Part-time and evening/weekend programs available. *Faculty:* 2 full-time (both women), 6 part-time/adjunct (all women). *Students:* 50 full-time (47 women), 7 part-time (all women); includes 1 minority (African American) Average age 32. In 2007, 11 degrees awarded. *Degree requirements:* For master's, comprehensive exam. *Entrance requirements:* For master's, MAT, minimum GPA of 3.0, course work in psychology and art, slide portfolio, letters of reference, resumé, autobiography, personal statement. Additional exam requirements/recommendations for international students: Required—TOEFL. *Application deadline:* For fall admission, 2/15 priority date for domestic and international students. Applications are processed on a rolling basis. Application fee: $40 ($50 for international students). *Expenses:* Contact institution. One-time fee: $85 part-time. Tuition and fees vary according to course load and program. *Financial support:* Federal Work-Study and scholarships/grants available. Support available to part-time students. Financial award applicants required to submit FAFSA. *Faculty research:* Scientific approaches to art therapy research, child and adolescent psychotherapy, multicultural counseling. *Unit head:* Christine Turner, Chair, 503-636-8141, Fax: 503-636-9526, E-mail: cturner@marylhurst.edu. *Application contact:* Kathleen Schneff, Admissions Specialist, 800-634-9982 Ext. 3322, Fax: 503-635-6585, E-mail: admissions@marylhurst.edu.

Marywood University, Academic Affairs, Insalaco College of Creative Arts and Management, Art Department, Program in Art Therapy, Scranton, PA 18509-1598. Offers MA, Certificate. *Accreditation:* NASAD. Part-time and evening/weekend programs available. *Students:* 18 full-time (all women), 6 part-time (5 women); includes 1 minority (African American), 2 international. Average age 31. In 2007, 7 degrees awarded. *Degree requirements:* For master's, comprehensive exam, thesis or alternative, internship, practicum. *Entrance requirements:* For master's, portfolio. Additional exam requirements/recommendations for international students: Required—TOEFL (minimum score 550 paper-based; 213 computer-based). *Application deadline:* For fall admission, 4/15 priority date for domestic and international students; for spring admission, 11/15 priority date for domestic and international students. Applications are processed on a rolling basis. Application fee: $30. Electronic applications accepted. *Expenses:* Tuition: Full-time $15,290; part-time $695 per credit. Required fees: $990; $370 per term. Tuition and fees vary according to degree level. *Financial support:* Research assistantships with tuition reimbursements, career-related internships or fieldwork, scholarships/grants, tuition waivers (partial), and unspecified assistantships available. Support available to part-time students. Financial award application deadline: 2/15; financial award applicants required to submit FAFSA. *Faculty research:* Perspectives of leading educators in art therapy, current trends in art education. *Unit head:* Barbara Parker-Bell, Director, 570-348-6211 Ext. 2525, E-mail: parkerbell@marywood.edu.

Mount Mary College, Graduate Programs, Program in Art Therapy, Milwaukee, WI 53222-4597. Offers MS. Evening/weekend programs available. *Faculty:* 3 full-time (2 women), 11 part-time/adjunct (9 women). *Students:* 40 full-time (38 women), 2 part-time (both women); includes 3 minority (1 African American, 2 Hispanic Americans). Average age 28. 32 applicants, 75% accepted, 25 enrolled. In 2007, 14 degrees awarded. *Degree requirements:* For master's, thesis or alternative, internship. *Entrance requirements:* For master's, minimum GPA of 2.75, portfolio. Additional exam requirements/recommendations for international students: Required—TOEFL (minimum score 500 paper-based; 173 computer-based). *Application deadline:* For fall admission, 3/15 for domestic and international students. Application fee: $35 ($75 for international students). Electronic applications accepted. *Expenses:* Tuition: Part-time $545 per credit. Required fees: $60 per semester. Part-time tuition and fees vary according to program. *Financial support:* In 2007–08, 2 students received support. Career-related internships or fieldwork and Federal Work-Study available. Support available to part-time students. Financial award application deadline: 5/1; financial award applicants required to submit FAFSA. *Faculty research:* Art-based research in art therapy, consensus-group supervision, art therapy in public school programs. *Unit head:* Dr. Bruce Moon, Director, 414-256-1215, E-mail: moonb@mtmary.edu.

Naropa University, Graduate Programs, Program in Transpersonal Counseling Psychology, Concentration in Art Therapy, Boulder, CO 80302-6697. Offers MA. *Faculty:* 5 full-time, 7 part-time/adjunct. *Students:* 31 full-time (25 women), 15 part-time (14 women); includes 5 minority (1 African American, 2 Asian Americans or Pacific Islanders, 2 Hispanic Americans), 1 international. Average age 31. 61 applicants, 34% accepted, 15 enrolled. In 2007, 9 degrees awarded. *Degree requirements:* For master's, internship. *Entrance requirements:* For master's, portfolio (21 slides), in-person interview, course work in psychology and art. Additional exam requirements/recommendations for international students: Required—TOEFL (minimum score 600 paper-based; 250 computer-based). *Application deadline:* For fall admission, 1/15 priority date for domestic and international students; for spring admission, 10/15 priority date for domestic students. Applications are processed on a rolling basis. Application fee: $60. Electronic applications accepted. *Expenses:* Tuition: Full-time $15,070; part-time $685 per credit. Required fees: $250 per semester. Tuition and fees vary according to course load. *Financial support:* In 2007–08, 30 students received support, including 1 research assistantship with partial tuition reimbursement available (averaging $3,000 per year), 1 teaching assistantship with partial tuition reimbursement available (averaging $3,000 per year); career-related internships or fieldwork, Federal Work-Study, scholarships/grants, tuition waivers (partial), and unspecified assistantships also available. Support available to part-time students. Financial award application deadline: 3/1; financial award applicants required to submit FAFSA. *Unit head:* Michael Franklin, Director, 303-546-3545. *Application contact:* Alice Di Tullio, Admissions Counselor, 303-546-3598, Fax: 303-546-3583, E-mail: aliced@naropa.edu.

See Close-Up on page 1449.

Nazareth College of Rochester, Graduate Studies, Department of Creative Arts Therapy, Program in Art Therapy, Rochester, NY 14618-3790. Offers MS. Part-time programs available. *Faculty:* 1 (woman) full-time, 6 part-time/adjunct (5 women). *Students:* 30 full-time (25 women), 2 part-time (both women), 1 international. Average age 30. 37 applicants, 68% accepted, 16 enrolled. In 2007, 9 degrees awarded. *Entrance requirements:* For master's, minimum GPA of 3.0, portfolio review. *Application deadline:* For fall admission, 1/15 for domestic students. Application fee: $40. *Financial support:* Research assistantships with partial tuition reimbursements available. Financial award application deadline: 3/1; financial award applicants required to submit FAFSA. *Application contact:* Judith G. Baker, Director, Graduate Admissions, 585-389-2050, Fax: 585-389-2817, E-mail: gradstudies@naz.edu.

New York University, Steinhardt School of Culture, Education and Human Development, Department of Art and Art Professions, Program in Art Therapy, New York, NY 10012-1019. Offers MA. Part-time and evening/weekend programs available. *Faculty:* 1 (woman) full-time. *Students:* 37 full-time (35 women), 8 part-time (7 women); includes 12 minority (8 Asian Americans or Pacific Islanders, 4 Hispanic Americans), 5 international. 108 applicants, 28% accepted, 18 enrolled. In 2007, 24 degrees awarded. *Degree requirements:* For master's, thesis (for some programs). *Entrance requirements:* For master's, interview, portfolio. Additional exam requirements/recommendations for international students: Required—TOEFL. *Application deadline:* For fall admission, 12/15 priority date for domestic and international students; for spring admission, 11/1 for domestic and international students. Applications are processed on a rolling basis. Application fee: $50. *Financial support:* Career-related internships or fieldwork, Federal Work-Study, institutionally sponsored loans, scholarships/grants, and tuition waivers (partial) available. Support available to part-time students. Financial award application deadline: 2/1; financial award applicants required to submit FAFSA. *Faculty research:* Art therapy in non-clinical settings, international art therapy. *Unit head:* Ikuko Acosta, Director, 212-998-5700, Fax: 212-995-4320. *Application contact:* 212-998-5030, Fax: 212-995-4328, E-mail: steinhardt.gradadmissions@nyu.edu.

Notre Dame de Namur University, Division of Academic Affairs, School of Sciences, Department of Art Therapy Psychology, Belmont, CA 94002-1908. Offers MAAT, MAMFT. Part-time and evening/weekend programs available. *Faculty:* 2 full-time (1 woman), 8 part-time/adjunct (7 women). *Students:* 38 full-time (all women), 56 part-time (54 women); includes 17 minority (1 African American, 11 Asian Americans or Pacific Islanders, 5 Hispanic Americans), 4 international. Average age 30. 33 applicants, 94% accepted, 22 enrolled. In 2007, 15 degrees awarded. *Degree requirements:* For master's, oral presentation, portfolio. *Entrance requirements:* For master's, interview, minimum GPA of 2.5. Additional exam requirements/recommendations for international students: Required—TOEFL. *Application deadline:* For fall admission, 8/1 priority date for domestic students; for spring admission, 12/1 priority date for domestic students. Applications are processed on a rolling basis. Application fee: $50. Electronic applications accepted. *Financial support:* Career-related internships or fieldwork available. Support available to part-time students. Financial award applicants required to submit FAFSA. *Unit head:* Dr. Richard Carolan, Chair, 650-508-3556, Fax: 650-508-3736. *Application contact:* Helen Valine, Director of Graduate Admissions, 650-508-3534, Fax: 650-508-3426, E-mail: grad.admit@ndnu.edu.

Ottawa University, Graduate Studies-Arizona, Program in Professional Counseling, Ottawa, KS 66067-3399. Offers Christian counseling (MA); expressive arts therapy (MA); marriage and family therapy (MA); treatment of trauma, abuse and deprivation (MA). Programs offered in Mesa, Phoenix, Tempe and West Valley, AZ. Part-time and evening/weekend programs available. Postbaccalaureate distance learning degree programs offered. *Degree requirements:* For master's, comprehensive exam, thesis or alternative, field experience, practicum. *Entrance requirements:* For master's, minimum undergraduate GPA of 3.0; course work in theories of personality, abnormal psychology, and human growth and development. Additional exam requirements/recommendations for international students: Required—TOEFL (minimum score 550 paper-based; 213 computer-based).

Pratt Institute, School of Art and Design, Programs in Creative Arts Therapy, Brooklyn, NY 11205-3899. Offers art therapy and creativity development (MPS); art therapy-special education (MPS); dance/movement therapy (MS). *Accreditation:* NASAD (one or more programs are accredited). Part-time programs available. *Faculty:* 3 full-time (all women), 19 part-time/adjunct (16 women). *Students:* 100 full-time (96 women), 2 part-time (both women); includes 18 minority (5 African Americans, 5 Asian Americans or Pacific Islanders, 8 Hispanic Americans), 4 international. Average age 31. 173 applicants, 35% accepted, 30 enrolled. In 2007, 31 degrees awarded. *Degree requirements:* For master's, thesis. *Entrance requirements:* For master's, bachelor's degree, transcripts, letters of recommendation, statement, portfolio. Additional exam requirements/recommendations for international students: Required—TOEFL (minimum score 600 paper-based; 250 computer-based). *Application deadline:* For fall admission, 2/1 for domestic students; for spring admission, 10/1 for domestic students. Applications are processed on a rolling basis. Application fee: $50 ($90 for international students). Electronic applications accepted. *Expenses:* Tuition: Full-time $25,680. Required fees: $1,106. Tuition and fees vary according to program. *Financial support:* Career-related internships or fieldwork, Federal Work-Study, institutionally sponsored loans, scholarships/grants, health care benefits, tuition waivers (full), and unspecified assistantships available. Support available to part-time students. Financial award application deadline: 2/1; financial award applicants required to submit FAFSA. *Faculty research:* Psychology and aesthetic interaction, art therapy and AIDS, art therapy and autism, art diagnosis. *Unit head:* Laurel Thompson, Chairperson, 718-636-4532, Fax: 718-636-3597, E-mail: lthompso@pratt.edu. *Application contact:* Young Hah, Director of Graduate Admissions, 718-636-3683, Fax: 718-399-4242, E-mail: yhah@pratt.edu.

See Close-Up on page 253.

Saint Mary-of-the-Woods College, Program in Art Therapy, Saint Mary-of-the-Woods, IN 47876. Offers MA, Post-Master's Certificate. Part-time and evening/weekend programs available. Postbaccalaureate distance learning degree programs offered (minimal on-campus study). *Degree requirements:* For master's, thesis or project. *Entrance requirements:* For master's, minimum GPA of 2.5; for Post-Master's Certificate, 12 credit hours in abnormal and developmental psychology, 15 credit hours in studio art skills, art portfolio, interview, minimum GPA of 2.5. Electronic applications accepted.

Salve Regina University, Graduate Studies, Program in Holistic Counseling, Newport, RI 02840-4192. Offers expressive and creative arts (CAGS); holistic counseling (MA); mental health (CAGS). Part-time and evening/weekend programs available. *Degree requirements:* For master's, internship, project. *Entrance requirements:* For master's, GMAT, GRE General Test, or MAT. Additional exam requirements/recommendations for international students: Required—TOEFL or IELTS. Electronic applications accepted.

Art Therapy

School of the Art Institute of Chicago, Graduate Division, Program in Art Therapy, Chicago, IL 60603-3103. Offers MAAT. *Accreditation:* NASAD. *Degree requirements:* For master's, thesis, personal interview. *Entrance requirements:* Additional exam requirements/recommendations for international students: Required—TOEFL. *Faculty research:* Migraine, ousider art, community-based practice.

See Close-Up on page 259.

School of Visual Arts, Graduate Programs, Art Therapy Department, New York, NY 10010-3994. Offers MPS. *Faculty:* 1 (woman) full-time, 12 part-time/adjunct (11 women). *Students:* 48 full-time (46 women), 1 (woman) part-time; includes 12 minority (1 African American, 6 Asian Americans or Pacific Islanders, 5 Hispanic Americans), 2 international. Average age 29. 74 applicants, 74% accepted, 24 enrolled. In 2007, 15 degrees awarded. *Degree requirements:* For master's, thesis or 750 internship hours. *Entrance requirements:* For master's, portfolio, bachelor's degree with 12 credits in undergraduate psychology including child and abnormal psychology, 18 credits of studio art. Additional exam requirements/recommendations for international students: Required—TOEFL (minimum score 550 paper-based; 213 computer-based; 79 iBT). *Application deadline:* For fall admission, 2/1 for domestic students. Application fee: $80. Electronic applications accepted. *Expenses:* Tuition: Full-time $26,120; part-time $870 per credit. Tuition and fees vary according to program. *Financial support:* In 2007–08, 7 students received support. Career-related internships or fieldwork, Federal Work-Study, scholarships/grants, and unspecified assistantships available. Support available to part-time students. Financial award application deadline: 2/1. *Unit head:* Deborah Farber, Chairperson, 212-592-2610, Fax: 212-592-2633, E-mail: dfarber@sva.edu.

Seton Hill University, Program in Art Therapy, Greensburg, PA 15601. Offers MA, Certificate. Part-time programs available. *Faculty:* 1 (woman) full-time, 2 part-time/adjunct (both women). *Students:* 24 full-time (all women), 12 part-time (11 women); includes 2 minority (1 Asian American or Pacific Islander, 1 Hispanic American). Average age 30. 38 applicants, 76% accepted, 15 enrolled. In 2007, 14 degrees awarded. *Degree requirements:* For master's, thesis or alternative. *Entrance requirements:* For master's, portfolio, 12 undergraduate credits in psychology, 15 undergraduate credits in art, minimum GPA of 3.0. Additional exam requirements/recommendations for international students: Required—TOEFL (minimum score 600 paper-based; 250 computer-based). *Application deadline:* For fall admission, 8/15 priority date for domestic students; for spring admission, 12/15 for domestic students. Applications are processed on a rolling basis. Application fee: $35. Electronic applications accepted. *Expenses:* Tuition: Full-time $17,955; part-time $665 per credit. Tuition and fees vary according to program. *Financial support:* In 2007–08, 32 students received support. Federal Work-Study, scholarships/grants, tuition waivers (partial), and unspecified assistantships available. Support available to part-time students. Financial award application deadline: 8/15; financial award applicants required to submit FAFSA. *Faculty research:* Art therapy with the deaf, art therapy with children. *Unit head:* Nina Denninger, Director, 724-830-1047, Fax: 724-830-1294, E-mail: denninger@setonhill.edu. *Application contact:* Dane Zimmer, Advisor, 724-838-4209, Fax: 724-830-1891, E-mail: zimmer@setonhill.edu.

Southern Illinois University Edwardsville, Graduate Studies and Research, College of Arts and Sciences, Department of Art and Design, Program in Art Therapy Counseling, Edwardsville, IL 62026-0001. Offers MA, Postbaccalaureate Certificate. *Students:* 18 full-time (all women), 7 part-time (all women); includes 1 minority (African American), 1 international. 33 applicants, 30% accepted. In 2007, 8 degrees awarded. *Degree requirements:* For master's, thesis or alternative, project. *Entrance requirements:* For master's, MAT. *Application deadline:* For fall admission, 2/1 for domestic and international students. Application fee: $30. Electronic applications accepted. *Financial support:* In 2007–08, 1 fellowship was awarded; research assistantships, teaching assistantships with full tuition reimbursements. *Unit head:* Dr. Patricia Klorer, Program Director, 618-650-3183, E-mail: pklorer@siue.edu.

Southwestern College, Program in Art Therapy/Counseling, Santa Fe, NM 87502-4788. Offers MA. Part-time and evening/weekend programs available. *Faculty:* 2 full-time (both women), 8 part-time/adjunct (all women). *Students:* 53 full-time (50 women), 17 part-time (all women); includes 2 African Americans, 1 American Indian/Alaska Native, 4 Hispanic Americans. Average age 31. 48 applicants, 44% accepted, 21 enrolled. In 2007, 16 degrees awarded. *Degree requirements:* For master's, internship. *Entrance requirements:* For master's, resumé, slide portfolio, interview, 3 letters of reference, personal statement of 3 pages. *Application deadline:* For fall admission, 6/1 priority date for domestic students; for winter admission, 10/15 priority date for domestic students; for spring admission, 1/30 priority date for domestic students. Applications are processed on a rolling basis. Application fee: $50. *Expenses:* Tuition: Full-time $16,416. *Financial support:* In 2007–08, 25 students received support. Career-related internships or fieldwork, institutionally sponsored loans, and scholarships/grants available. Support available to part-time students. Financial award application deadline: 6/1; financial award applicants required to submit FAFSA. *Unit head:* Debbie Schroder, Chair, 505-471-5756. *Application contact:* Dru Phoenix, Director of Admissions, 505-471-5756 Ext. 26, Fax: 505-471-4071, E-mail: admissions@swc.edu.

Springfield College, Graduate Programs, Program in Art Therapy, Springfield, MA 01109-3797. Offers M Ed, MS, CAGS. Part-time programs available. *Faculty:* 2 full-time (1 woman), 9 part-time/adjunct (8 women). *Students:* 23 full-time, 7 part-time. Average age 30. 32 applicants, 94% accepted, 17 enrolled. In 2007, 15 master's, 1 other advanced degree awarded. *Degree requirements:* For master's, research project, final art exhibition. *Entrance requirements:* For master's, portfolio, prerequisite courses required for accreditation. Additional exam requirements/recommendations for international students: Required—TOEFL (minimum score 550 paper-based; 213 computer-based). *Application deadline:* For fall admission, 1/15 for domestic students; for winter admission, 11/1 for domestic students; for spring admission, 12/1 for domestic students. Applications are processed on a rolling basis. Application fee: $50. Electronic applications accepted. *Expenses:* Tuition: Full-time $12,942; part-time $719 per semester hour. Required fees: $25. Tuition and fees vary according to program. *Financial support:* In 2007–08, 1 teaching assistantship with partial tuition reimbursement was awarded; fellowships with partial tuition reimbursements, career-related internships or fieldwork, Federal Work-Study, institutionally sponsored loans, and tuition waivers (partial) also available. Financial award application deadline: 3/1. *Faculty research:* Stage development in art, psychopathology of expression, art history and art therapy. *Unit head:* Dr. Simone Alter-Muri, Director, 413-748-3752, E-mail: saltermuri@spfldcol.edu. *Application contact:* Donald James Shaw, Director of Graduate Admissions, 413-748-3060, Fax: 413-748-3069, E-mail: donald_shaw_jr@spfldcol.edu.

University of Louisville, Graduate School, College of Education and Human Development, Department of Educational and Counseling Psychology, Programs in Counseling and Personnel Services, Louisville, KY 40292-0001. Offers expressive therapies (M Ed); school counseling and guidance (M Ed, PhD). *Students:* 142 full-time (110 women), 96 part-time (80 women); includes 46 minority (42 African Americans, 1 American Indian/Alaska Native, 3 Asian Americans or Pacific Islanders), 7 international. Average age 33. In 2007, 66 master's, 4 doctorates awarded.

University of Wisconsin–Superior, Graduate Division, Department of Visual Arts, Superior, WI 54880-4500. Offers art education (MA); art history (MA); art therapy (MA); studio arts (MA). Part-time programs available. *Degree requirements:* For master's, comprehensive exam, exhibit. *Entrance requirements:* For master's, minimum GPA of 2.75, portfolio.

Ursuline College, School of Graduate Studies, Program in Art Therapy Counseling, Pepper Pike, OH 44124-4398. Offers MA. Part-time programs available. *Faculty:* 4 full-time (all women), 4 part-time/adjunct (3 women). *Students:* 20 full-time (all women), 50 part-time (49 women); includes 5 minority (3 African Americans, 1 Asian American or Pacific Islander, 1 Hispanic American), 1 international. Average age 33. 18 applicants, 100% accepted, 18 enrolled. In 2007, 15 degrees awarded. *Degree requirements:* For master's, thesis, 700 hour internship. *Entrance requirements:* For master's, BA in psychology, social sciences, or related field; minimum undergraduate GPA of 3.0; portfolio; work experience with human service agency. Additional exam requirements/recommendations for international students: Required—TOEFL (minimum score 500 paper-based; 173 computer-based). *Application deadline:* For fall admission, 8/1 priority date for domestic students. Applications are processed on a rolling basis. Application fee: $25. *Expenses:* Tuition: Full-time $13,356; part-time $742 per credit hour. Required fees: $200; $60 per semester. Tuition and fees vary according to program. *Financial support:* In 2007–08, 57 students received support. Federal Work-Study available. Financial award application deadline: 3/1; financial award applicants required to submit FAFSA. *Faculty research:* Art therapy used with psychiatric and geriatric populations, art therapy used in treatment of chemical dependency, family therapy, child art therapy. *Unit head:* Gale Rule-Hoffman, Director, 440-646-8138, Fax: 440-684-6088. *Application contact:* Jo Mann, Secretary, 440-646-8119, Fax: 440-684-6088, E-mail: gradsch@ursuline.edu.

Decorative Arts

Bard College, Program in History of the Decorative Arts, Design and Culture, Annandale-on-Hudson, NY 12504. Offers MA, PhD. Part-time programs available. *Faculty:* 13 full-time (6 women), 17 part-time/adjunct (8 women). *Students:* 73 full-time (67 women), 23 part-time (19 women). Average age 25. 99 applicants, 37% accepted, 27 enrolled. In 2007, 35 master's, 1 doctorate awarded. *Degree requirements:* For master's, one foreign language, thesis, internship; for doctorate, 2 foreign languages, thesis/dissertation, exams. *Entrance requirements:* For master's, GRE General Test, writing sample, 3 letters of recommendation; for doctorate, GRE General Test, master's thesis or equivalent, 3 letters of recommendation. Additional exam requirements/recommendations for international students: Required—TOEFL. *Application deadline:* For fall admission, 1/15 for domestic and international students. Application fee: $60. *Expenses:* Contact institution. *Financial support:* In 2007–08, 53 students received support, including 20 fellowships with tuition reimbursements available, 3 research assistantships, 2 teaching assistantships; career-related internships or fieldwork, Federal Work-Study, scholarships/grants, health care benefits, and unspecified assistantships also available. Financial award application deadline: 1/15; financial award applicants required to submit FAFSA. *Unit head:* Susan Weber Soros, Director, 212-501-3000, Fax: 212-501-3079. *Application contact:* Elena Pinto Simon, Dean, Academic Administration and Student Affairs, 212-501-3057, Fax: 212-501-3065, E-mail: simon@bgc.bard.edu.

Bard Graduate Center for Studies in the Decorative Arts, Design, and Culture, Program in History of the Decorative Arts, Design and Culture, New York, NY 10024-3602. Offers MA, PhD. Bard Graduate Center for Studies in the Decorative Arts is a unit of Bard College. Part-time programs available. *Faculty:* 13 full-time (6 women), 17 part-time/adjunct (8 women). *Students:* 73 full-time (67 women), 23 part-time (19 women). Average age 25. 99 applicants, 37% accepted, 27 enrolled. In 2007, 35 master's, 1 doctorate awarded. *Degree requirements:* For master's, one foreign language, thesis, internship; for doctorate, 2 foreign languages, thesis/dissertation, exams. *Entrance requirements:* For master's, GRE General Test, writing sample, 3 letters of recommendation; for doctorate, GRE General Test, master's thesis or equivalent, 3 letters of recommendation. Additional exam requirements/recommendations for international students: Required—TOEFL. *Application deadline:* For fall admission, 1/15 for domestic and international students. Application fee: $60. *Expenses:* Tuition: Full-time $24,570; part-time $910 per credit. Required fees: $150 per semester. Tuition and fees vary according to degree level. *Financial support:* In 2007–08, 53 students received support, including 20 fellowships with tuition reimbursements available, 3 research assistantships, 2 teaching assistantships; career-related internships or fieldwork, Federal Work-Study, scholarships/grants, health care benefits, and unspecified assistantships also available. Financial award application deadline: 1/15; financial award applicants required to submit FAFSA. *Faculty research:* English craftsmen, ancient furniture, aesthetics and politics, Art Nouveau jewelry, European sculpture. *Unit head:* Susan Weber Soros, Director, 212-501-3000, Fax: 212-501-3079. *Application contact:* Elena Pinto Simon, Dean, Academic Administration and Student Affairs, 212-501-3057, Fax: 212-501-3065, E-mail: simon@bgc.bard.edu.

See Close-Up on page 229.

Corcoran College of Art and Design, Graduate Programs, Washington, DC 20006-4804. Offers art education (MAT); history of decorative arts (MA); interior design (MA). *Accreditation:* NASAD. Part-time programs available. *Entrance requirements:* Additional exam requirements/recommendations for international students: Required—TOEFL.

The New School: A University, Parsons The New School for Design, Program in the History of Decorative Arts, New York, NY 10011. Offers MA. Offered jointly with the Cooper-Hewitt Museum and the Smithsonian Institution. *Accreditation:* NASAD. *Faculty:* 4 full-time (3 women), 13 part-time/adjunct (10 women). *Students:* 58 full-time (54 women), 42 part-time (40 women); includes 9 minority (6 Asian Americans or Pacific Islanders, 3 Hispanic Americans), 4 international. Average age 33. In 2007, 13 degrees awarded. *Degree requirements:* For master's, one foreign language. *Entrance requirements:* For master's, GRE General Test (recommended), sample of written work. Additional exam requirements/recommendations for international students: Required—TOEFL (minimum score 580 paper-based; 237 computer-based; 93 iBT). *Application deadline:* For fall admission, 2/1 priority date for domestic students. Applications are processed on a rolling basis. Application fee: $50. *Financial support:* Fellowships with partial tuition reimbursements, research assistantships with partial tuition reimbursements, teaching assistantships with partial tuition reimbursements, Federal Work-Study, scholarships/grants, tuition waivers (partial), and unspecified assistantships available. Financial award application deadline: 3/1; financial award applicants required to submit FAFSA. *Unit head:* Dr. Sarah E. Lawrence, Director, 212-849-8345, E-mail: lawrences@si.edu. *Application contact:* Anthony Padilla, Director of Admissions, 212-229-8989 Ext. 4023, Fax: 212-229-8975, E-mail: padillaa@newschool.edu.

See Close-Up on page 249.

Museum Studies

Bank Street College of Education, Graduate School, Department of Curriculum and Instruction, Program in Museum Education, New York, NY 10025. Offers museum education (MS Ed); museum education: elementary education certification (MS Ed); museum education: middle school certification (MS Ed); museum studies (MS Ed). *Students:* 25 full-time (23 women), 33 part-time (32 women); includes 6 minority (2 African Americans, 2 Asian Americans or Pacific Islanders, 2 Hispanic Americans). Average age 28. 47 applicants, 79% accepted, 26 enrolled. In 2007, 24 degrees awarded. *Degree requirements:* For master's, thesis. *Entrance requirements:* For master's, interview. Additional exam requirements/recommendations for international students: Required—TOEFL (minimum score 600 paper-based; 250 computer-based; 100 iBT). *Application deadline:* For fall admission, 3/1 priority date for domestic and international students; for spring admission, 11/1 priority date for domestic and international students. Applications are processed on a rolling basis. Application fee: $50. *Expenses:* Tuition: Part-time $1,010 per credit. *Financial support:* Federal Work-Study and scholarships/grants available. Support available to part-time students. Financial award application deadline: 4/15; financial award applicants required to submit FAFSA. *Faculty research:* Equitable access and openness to diversity in museum settings, exhibition display and development, museum/school partnerships. *Unit head:* Nina Jensen, Director, 212-875-4491, Fax: 212-875-4753, E-mail: ninajensen@bankstreet.edu. *Application contact:* Ann Morgan, Director of Graduate Admissions, 212-875-4403, Fax: 212-875-4678, E-mail: amorgan@bankstreet.edu.

Bard College, Center for Curatorial Studies, Annandale-on-Hudson, NY 12504. Offers MA. *Faculty:* 1 (woman) full-time, 12 part-time/adjunct (7 women). *Students:* 24. Average age 28. 98 applicants, 19% accepted, 14 enrolled. In 2007, 12 degrees awarded. *Degree requirements:* For master's, thesis, exhibition. *Entrance requirements:* For master's, statement of interest, exhibition review, 3 letters of recommendation. Additional exam requirements/recommendations for international students: Required—TOEFL (minimum score 550 paper-based). *Application deadline:* For fall admission, 2/1 for domestic and international students. Application fee: $50. Electronic applications accepted. *Expenses: Contact institution. Financial support:* In 2007–08, 18 students received support; fellowships, research assistantships, career-related internships or fieldwork, scholarships/grants, and unspecified assistantships available. Financial award application deadline: 3/15; financial award applicants required to submit FAFSA. *Faculty research:* Contemporary art, history of exhibition, curatorial practice. *Unit head:* Maria Lind, Director, 845-758-7598, Fax: 845-758-2442, E-mail: ccs@bard.edu. *Application contact:* Letitia Smith, Assistant to the Director, 845-758-7598, Fax: 845-758-2442, E-mail: lsmith@bard.edu.

Baylor University, Graduate School, College of Arts and Sciences, Department of Museum Studies, Waco, TX 76798. Offers MA. *Faculty:* 6 part-time/adjunct (3 women). *Students:* 14 full-time (12 women), 1 part-time; includes 1 minority (American Indian/Alaska Native). 13 applicants, 85% accepted. In 2007, 8 degrees awarded. *Degree requirements:* For master's, thesis or alternative. *Entrance requirements:* For master's, GRE General Test. *Application deadline:* For fall admission, 4/30 priority date for domestic students. Applications are processed on a rolling basis. Application fee: $25. Electronic applications accepted. *Financial support:* In 2007–08, 3 research assistantships with partial tuition reimbursements (averaging $7,200 per year) were awarded; career-related internships or fieldwork, Federal Work-Study, institutionally sponsored loans, tuition waivers (full and partial), and unspecified assistantships also available. Support available to part-time students. Financial award application deadline: 6/1; financial award applicants required to submit FAFSA. *Faculty research:* Paleontology/archaeology, preservation. *Unit head:* Dr. Kenneth Hafertepe, Graduate Program Director, 254-710-1233, Fax: 254-710-1173, E-mail: kenneth_hafertepe@baylor.edu. *Application contact:* Suzanne Keener, Administrative Assistant, 254-710-3588, Fax: 254-710-3870.

Boston University, Graduate School of Arts and Sciences, Department of Art History, Boston, MA 02215. Offers art history (MA, PhD); museum studies (Certificate). *Students:* 49 full-time (43 women), 14 part-time (all women); includes 2 minority (both African Americans), 3 international. Average age 33. 160 applicants, 30% accepted, 13 enrolled. In 2007, 18 degrees awarded. Terminal master's awarded for partial completion of doctoral program. *Degree requirements:* For master's, one foreign language, comprehensive exam, thesis; for doctorate, 2 foreign languages, comprehensive exam, thesis/dissertation. *Entrance requirements:* For master's and doctorate, GRE General Test, 3 letters of recommendation; for Certificate, GRE General Test. Additional exam requirements/recommendations for international students: Required—TOEFL (minimum score 600 paper-based; 250 computer-based). *Application deadline:* For fall admission, 1/15 for domestic and international students; for spring admission, 10/15 for domestic and international students. Application fee: $70. *Expenses:* Tuition: Full-time $34,930; part-time $1,092 per credit. Tuition and fees vary according to class time, course level and program. *Financial support:* In 2007–08, 23 students received support, including 2 fellowships (averaging $18,000 per year), 1 research assistantship (averaging $16,500 per year), 6 teaching assistantships with full tuition reimbursements available (averaging $16,500 per year); career-related internships or fieldwork, Federal Work-Study, and unspecified assistantships also available. Support available to part-time students. Financial award application deadline: 1/15; financial award applicants required to submit FAFSA. *Unit head:* Fred S. Kleiner, Chairman, 617-353-2520, Fax: 617-353-3243, E-mail: fsk@bu.edu. *Application contact:* Cheryl Crombie, Administrative Assistant, 617-353-2522, Fax: 617-353-3243, E-mail: ccrombie@bu.edu.

California College of the Arts, Graduate Programs, Program in Curatorial Practice, San Francisco, CA 94107. Offers MA. *Faculty:* 2 full-time (1 woman), 8 part-time/adjunct (2 women). *Students:* 22 full-time (18 women). 20 applicants, 85% accepted, 10 enrolled. *Entrance requirements:* For master's, appropriate bachelor's degree, portfolio, resumé, letters of recommendation. Additional exam requirements/recommendations for international students: Required—TOEFL (minimum score 600 paper-based; 250 computer-based). *Application deadline:* For fall admission, 1/15 for domestic and international students. Application fee: $50. Electronic applications accepted. *Expenses:* Tuition: Part-time $1,017 per unit. *Financial support:* In 2007–08, 1 fellowship (averaging $10,000 per year), teaching assistantships (averaging $2,000 per year) were awarded; career-related internships or fieldwork, Federal Work-Study, scholarships/grants, and health care benefits also available. *Unit head:* Leagh Markopolous, Chair, 415-551-9249, E-mail: lmarkopolous@cca.edu. *Application contact:* Kathryn Ward, Assistant Director of Graduate Admissions, 415-703-9523 Ext. 9593, Fax: 415-703-9539, E-mail: graduateprograms@cca.edu.

California State University, Chico, Graduate School, College of Behavioral and Social Sciences, Department of Anthropology, Chico, CA 95929-0400. Offers museum studies (MA). *Students:* 24 full-time (20 women), 2 part-time (1 woman); includes 4 minority (all Hispanic Americans) Average age 27. 42 applicants, 43% accepted, 9 enrolled. In 2007, 9 degrees awarded. *Degree requirements:* For master's, thesis. *Entrance requirements:* For master's, GRE General Test, statement of purpose, 2 letters of recommendation. Additional exam requirements/recommendations for international students: Required—TOEFL (minimum score 550 paper-based; 213 computer-based; 80 iBT), IELTS (minimum score 7). *Application deadline:* For fall admission, 1/15 for domestic students, 3/1 for international students. Application fee: $55. Electronic applications accepted. *Financial support:* Fellowships, career-related internships or fieldwork available. *Unit head:* Dr. William Collins, Graduate Coordinator, 530-898-4953.

Caribbean University, Graduate School, Bayamón, PR 00960-0493. Offers accounting (MBA); administration and supervision (MA Ed); criminal justice (MA); curriculum and instruction (MA Ed); education (PhD); gerontology (MSN); human resources (MBA); museology, archiving and art history (MA Ed); neonatal pediatrics (MSN); physical education (MA Ed); special education (MA Ed). *Entrance requirements:* For master's, interview, minimum GPA of 2.5.

Case Western Reserve University, School of Graduate Studies, Department of Art History and Art, Program in Art History and Museum Studies, Cleveland, OH 44106. Offers MA, PhD. Part-time programs available. *Faculty:* 8 full-time (4 women), 10 part-time/adjunct (5 women). *Students:* 10 full-time (8 women), 15 part-time (13 women); includes 2 minority (1 African American, 1 Hispanic American). Average age 26. 31 applicants, 55% accepted, 7 enrolled. In 2007, 4 master's awarded. *Degree requirements:* For master's, one foreign language, thesis or alternative; for doctorate, 2 foreign languages, thesis/dissertation. *Entrance requirements:* For master's, GRE General Test, 2 samples of written work; for doctorate, GRE General Test, 3 samples of written work or MA thesis. Additional exam requirements/recommendations for international students: Required—TOEFL. *Application deadline:* For fall admission, 3/1 priority date for domestic students. Applications are processed on a rolling basis. Application fee: $50. Electronic applications accepted. *Financial support:* Fellowships, research assistantships, teaching assistantships, career-related internships or fieldwork available. Financial award application deadline: 3/1. *Faculty research:* Greek art and architecture, northern baroque, Italian Renaissance and baroque, abstract expressionism, Indian art, nineteenth-century French art, American and Contemporary art. *Application contact:* Debby Tenenbaum, Assistant, 216-368-4118, Fax: 216-368-4681, E-mail: deborah.tenenbaum@case.edu.

Christie's Education, Program in Modern Art, Connoisseurship, and the History of the Art Market, New York, NY 10036. Offers MA. *Faculty:* 5 full-time (4 women), 1 (woman) part-time/adjunct. *Students:* 45 full-time (41 women). In 2007, 45 master's awarded. *Degree requirements:* For master's, one foreign language, thesis. *Entrance requirements:* For master's, GRE, writing sample, 3 letters of recommendation, transcripts from all secondary schools and essay statement. Additional exam requirements/recommendations for international students: Required—TOEFL. *Application deadline:* For fall admission, 1/15 priority date for domestic and international students. Applications are processed on a rolling basis. Application fee: $75. *Financial support:* In 2007–08, 3 research assistantships (averaging $7,000 per year) were awarded. *Unit head:* Dr. Véronique Chagnon-Burke, Director of Studies, 212-355-2545, Fax: 212-355-7370, E-mail: vchagnonburke@christies.edu. *Application contact:* Margaret Conklin, Registrar/Bursar, 212-355-1501 Ext. 302, Fax: 212-355-7370, E-mail: mconklin@christies.edu.

City College of the City University of New York, Graduate School, College of Liberal Arts and Science, Division of the Humanities and Arts, Department of Art, Concentrations in Art History and Museum Studies, New York, NY 10031-9198. Offers art history (MA); museum studies (MA). Part-time programs available. *Students:* 22 applicants, 50% accepted, 8 enrolled. *Degree requirements:* For master's, one foreign language, thesis. *Entrance requirements:* For master's, GRE, minimum GPA of 3.0, portfolio, art history paper. Additional exam requirements/recommendations for international students: Required—TOEFL (minimum score 575 paper-based; 233 computer-based). *Application deadline:* For fall admission, 5/1 for domestic students; for spring admission, 11/1 for domestic students. Application fee: $125. *Financial support:* Fellowships, teaching assistantships, career-related internships or fieldwork, Federal Work-Study, institutionally sponsored loans, and tuition waivers (partial) available. Support available to part-time students. Financial award application deadline: 3/1. *Faculty research:* Egyptian, Greek, medieval, Romanesque, and Ottoman art. *Unit head:* Harriet Senie, Head, 212-650-7430, E-mail: hsenie@ccny.cuny.edu.

Claremont Graduate University, Graduate Programs, School of Arts and Humanities, Department of Cultural Studies, Claremont, CA 91711-6160. Offers Africana studies (Certificate); cultural studies (MA, PhD); media studies (MA, PhD); museum studies (MA). Part-time programs available. *Faculty:* 2 full-time (1 woman), 2 part-time/adjunct (0 women). *Students:* 48 full-time (33 women), 10 part-time (4 women); includes 19 minority (10 African Americans, 5 Asian Americans or Pacific Islanders, 4 Hispanic Americans), 5 international. Average age 35. In 2007, 7 master's, 4 doctorates awarded. *Degree requirements:* For master's, one foreign language, thesis; for doctorate, 2 foreign languages, comprehensive exam, thesis/dissertation. *Entrance requirements:* For master's and doctorate, GRE General Test. *Application deadline:* For fall admission, 2/15 priority date for domestic students. Applications are processed on a rolling basis. Electronic applications accepted. *Expenses:* Tuition: Full-time $31,640; part-time $1,376 per unit. Required fees: $145 per semester. Tuition and fees vary according to course load, degree level and program. *Financial support:* Fellowships, research assistantships, career-related internships or fieldwork, Federal Work-Study, and institutionally sponsored loans available. Support available to part-time students. Financial award application deadline: 2/15; financial award applicants required to submit FAFSA. *Unit head:* Henry Krips, Chair, 909-607-7803, Fax: 909-621-8609, E-mail: henry.krips@cgu.edu.

Cleveland State University, College of Graduate Studies, College of Liberal Arts and Social Sciences, Department of History, Cleveland, OH 44115. Offers history (MA); museum studies (MA). Part-time and evening/weekend programs available. *Faculty:* 21 full-time (8 women), 2 part-time/adjunct (0 women). *Students:* 8 full-time (3 women), 20 part-time (12 women); includes 2 minority (both African Americans) Average age 34. 23 applicants, 61% accepted, 9 enrolled. In 2007, 14 degrees awarded. *Degree requirements:* For master's, thesis optional. *Entrance requirements:* For master's, minimum GPA of 3.0, bachelor's degree in history. Additional exam requirements/recommendations for international students: Required—TOEFL (minimum score 525 paper-based; 197 computer-based). *Application deadline:* For fall admission, 7/15 priority date for domestic students. Applications are processed on a rolling basis. Application fee: $30. Electronic applications accepted. *Financial support:* In 2007–08, 7 students received support, including research assistantships with full tuition reimbursements available (averaging $8,600 per year); career-related internships or fieldwork and unspecified assistantships also available. *Faculty research:* African diaspora, social history and the city, early modern Europe, local history. *Unit head:* Dr. Joyce M. Mastboom, Chairperson, 216-687-3920, Fax: 216-687-5592, E-mail: j.mastboom@csuohio.edu. *Application contact:* Dr. Robert S. Shelton, Graduate Director, 216-687-3927, E-mail: r.s.shelton@csuohio.edu.

Duquesne University, Graduate School of Liberal Arts, Department of History, Pittsburgh, PA 15282-0001. Offers archival, museum, and editing studies (MA); history (MA). Part-time and evening/weekend programs available. *Faculty:* 6 full-time (1 woman), 3 part-time/adjunct (1 woman). *Students:* 35 full-time (18 women), 10 part-time (5 women). Average age 26. In 2007, 15 degrees awarded. *Degree requirements:* For master's, comprehensive exam (for some programs), thesis optional. *Entrance requirements:* For master's, GRE General Test, writing sample. Additional exam requirements/recommendations for international students: Required—TOEFL. *Application deadline:* For fall admission, 8/15 for domestic students, 5/1 for international students; for spring admission, 11/1 priority date for domestic students. Applications are processed on a rolling basis. Application fee: $50. *Expenses:* Tuition: Part-time $774 per credit. Required fees: $74 per credit. Tuition and fees vary according to program. *Financial support:* In 2007–08, 4 research assistantships with full tuition reimbursements (averaging $4,800 per year) were awarded; career-related internships or fieldwork, Federal Work-Study, scholarships/grants, tuition waivers (full and partial), and unspecified assistantships also available. Support available to part-time students. Financial award application deadline: 5/1. *Faculty research:* American studies, immigration history, local social history, applied history, Eastern European history. *Unit head:* Dr. Holly Mayer, Chair, 412-396-6470.

Fashion Institute of Technology, School of Graduate Studies, Programs in Fashion and Textile Studies: History, Theory, and Museum Practice, New York, NY 10001-5992. Offers MA. *Accreditation:* NASAD. *Degree requirements:* For master's, one foreign language, thesis, internship. *Entrance requirements:* For master's, GRE General Test or GRE Subject Test, previous course work in art history and chemistry, 4 semesters of a foreign language. Additional exam requirements/recommendations for international students: Required—TOEFL (minimum score 550 paper-based; 213 computer-based). *Application deadline:* For fall admission, 2/15 priority date for domestic and international students. Applications are processed on a rolling basis. Application fee: $50. Electronic applications accepted. *Expenses:* Tuition, state resident: full-time $7,245; part-time $302 per credit. Tuition, nonresident: full-time $11,466; part-time $478 per credit. Required fees: $440; $35 per term. *Financial support:* Federal Work-Study and scholarships/grants available. Financial award applicants required to submit FAFSA. *Unit*

Museum Studies

Fashion Institute of Technology (continued)

head: Denyse Montegut, Associate Chair, 212-217-4308, Fax: 212-217-5156, E-mail: denyse_montegut@fitnyc.edu. *Application contact:* Carole deSantis, Administrative Secretary, Graduate Admissions, 212-217-4314, Fax: 212-217-5156, E-mail: carole_desantis@fitnyc.edu.

See Close-Up on page 113.

Florida State University, Graduate Studies, College of Visual Arts, Theatre and Dance, Department of Art History, Tallahassee, FL 32306. Offers art history (MA, PhD); museum studies (Certificate). *Accreditation:* NASAD. Part-time programs available. *Faculty:* 13 full-time (7 women), 1 (woman) part-time/adjunct. *Students:* 27 full-time (24 women), 22 part-time (18 women); includes 4 minority (1 African American, 2 Asian Americans or Pacific Islanders, 1 Hispanic American). Average age 32. 33 applicants, 70% accepted, 15 enrolled. In 2007, 7 master's, 2 doctorates awarded. Terminal master's awarded for partial completion of doctoral program. *Median time to degree:* Of those who began their doctoral program in fall 1999, 0% received their degree in 8 years or less. *Degree requirements:* For master's, one foreign language, thesis (for some programs), review; for doctorate, 2 foreign languages, comprehensive exam, thesis/dissertation, review. *Entrance requirements:* For master's, GRE General Test, minimum GPA of 3.0; for doctorate, GRE General Test, minimum GPA of 3.5. Additional exam requirements/recommendations for international students: Required—TOEFL. *Application deadline:* For fall admission, 1/5 priority date for domestic and international students. Application fee: $30. Electronic applications accepted. *Expenses:* Tuition, state resident: part-time $248 per credit hour. Tuition, nonresident: part-time $880 per credit hour. Tuition and fees vary according to program. *Financial support:* In 2007–08, 24 students received support, including 2 fellowships with full tuition reimbursements available (averaging $18,000 per year), 21 research assistantships with full tuition reimbursements available (averaging $5,000 per year), 1 teaching assistantship with full tuition reimbursement available (averaging $14,000 per year); career-related internships or fieldwork, Federal Work-Study, institutionally sponsored loans, scholarships/grants, and unspecified assistantships also available. Financial award application deadline: 1/12; financial award applicants required to submit FAFSA. *Faculty research:* Asian art; modern art and critical theory; non-Western art; medieval, renaissance and baroque art; Pre-Colombian. *Unit head:* Dr. Richard K. Emmerson, Professor of Art History/Department Chair, 850-644-7066, Fax: 850-644-3259, E-mail: remmerson@fsu.edu. *Application contact:* Kathy Braun, Graduate Student Advisor, 850-644-8207, Fax: 850-644-7065, E-mail: kbraun@fsu.edu.

Florida State University, Graduate Studies, College of Visual Arts, Theatre and Dance, Program in Museum Studies, Tallahassee, FL 32306. Offers Certificate. Part-time programs available. *Students:* Average age 24. 10 applicants, 100% accepted, 10 enrolled. In 2007, 14 degrees awarded. *Degree requirements:* For Certificate, internship. *Entrance requirements:* For degree, GRE, graduate degree or current study towards a graduate degree. *Application deadline:* For fall admission, 8/1 priority date for domestic and international students. Applications are processed on a rolling basis. Application fee: $30. *Expenses:* Tuition, state resident: part-time $248 per credit hour. Tuition, nonresident: part-time $880 per credit hour. Tuition and fees vary according to program. *Financial support:* Career-related internships or fieldwork available. *Unit head:* Lana A. Burgess, Academic Coordinator, 850-644-0819, Fax: 850-644-7229, E-mail: lab0077@fsu.edu. *Application contact:* Lana A. Burgess, Academic Coordinator, 850-644-0819, Fax: 850-644-7229, E-mail: lab0077@fsu.edu.

The George Washington University, Columbian College of Arts and Sciences, Department of American Studies, Concentration in Material Culture, Washington, DC 20052. Offers MA. *Degree requirements:* For master's, comprehensive exam, thesis or alternative. *Entrance requirements:* For master's, GRE General Test, minimum GPA of 3.0. Additional exam requirements/recommendations for international students: Required—TOEFL (minimum score 550 paper-based; 213 computer-based).

The George Washington University, Columbian College of Arts and Sciences, Department of Fine Arts and Art History, Washington, DC 20052. Offers art history (MA, PhD), including art history (PhD), museum training (MA); ceramics (MFA); design (MFA); interior design (MFA); painting (MFA); photography (MFA); printmaking (MFA); sculpture (MFA). *Accreditation:* CIDA. Part-time and evening/weekend programs available. *Entrance requirements:* For master's, GRE General Test, bachelor's degree in field, minimum GPA of 3.0. Additional exam requirements/recommendations for international students: Required—TOEFL (minimum score 550 paper-based; 213 computer-based). Electronic applications accepted.

The George Washington University, Columbian College of Arts and Sciences, Department of Fine Arts and Art History, Program in Art History, Concentration in Museum Training, Washington, DC 20052. Offers MA. *Degree requirements:* For master's, one foreign language, comprehensive exam, thesis or alternative. *Entrance requirements:* For master's, GRE General Test, bachelor's degree in field, minimum GPA of 3.0. Additional exam requirements/recommendations for international students: Required—TOEFL (minimum score 550 paper-based; 213 computer-based). Electronic applications accepted.

The George Washington University, Columbian College of Arts and Sciences, Program in Museum Studies, Washington, DC 20052. Offers MA, Certificate. Part-time and evening/weekend programs available. *Degree requirements:* For master's, comprehensive exam, internship. *Entrance requirements:* For master's, GRE General Test, minimum GPA of 3.0. Additional exam requirements/recommendations for international students: Required—TOEFL (minimum score 550 paper-based; 213 computer-based). Electronic applications accepted.

Hampton University, Graduate College, Program in Museum Studies, Hampton, VA 23668. Offers MA. Part-time and evening/weekend programs available. *Degree requirements:* For master's, thesis optional. *Entrance requirements:* For master's, GRE General Test. *Faculty research:* Preservation studies, historical site research.

Harvard University, Extension School, Cambridge, MA 02138-3722. Offers applied sciences (CAS); biotechnology (ALM); educational technologies (ALM); educational technology (CET); English for graduate and professional studies (DGP); environmental management (ALM, CEM); information technology (ALM); journalism (ALM); liberal arts (ALM); management (ALM, CM); mathematics for teaching (ALM); museum studies (ALM); premedical studies (Diploma); publication and communication (CPC). Part-time and evening/weekend programs available. *Faculty:* 242 part-time/adjunct. *Students:* Average age 35. In 2007, 190 master's, 78 other advanced degrees awarded. *Degree requirements:* For master's, thesis. *Entrance requirements:* For master's, 3 completed graduate courses with grade of B or higher. Additional exam requirements/recommendations for international students: Required—TOEFL (minimum score 600 paper-based; 250 computer-based), TWE (minimum score 5). *Application deadline:* Applications are processed on a rolling basis. Application fee: $75. *Expenses: Contact institution.* Full-time tuition and fees vary according to program and student level. *Financial support:* In 2007–08, 198 students received support. Scholarships/grants available. Support available to part-time students. Financial award application deadline: 8/6; financial award applicants required to submit FAFSA. *Unit head:* Michael Shinagel, Dean, 617-495-1000. *Application contact:* Program Director, 617-495-4024, Fax: 617-495-9176.

Indiana University–Purdue University Indianapolis, School of Liberal Arts, Department of Museum Studies, Indianapolis, IN 46202. Offers MS, Certificate. *Entrance requirements:* For master's, GRE. *Application deadline:* For fall admission, 2/1 for domestic students; for spring admission, 10/1 for domestic students. Application fee: $50 ($60 for international students). *Expenses:* Tuition, state resident: full-time $5,818; part-time $242 per credit hour. Tuition, nonresident: full-time $17,106; part-time $713 per credit hour. Required fees: $629. Tuition and fees vary according to course load, campus/location and program. *Financial support:* In 2007–08, 1 fellowship with partial tuition reimbursement (averaging $9,000 per year), 3 teaching assistantships (averaging $9,667 per year) were awarded. Financial award application deadline: 2/1; financial award applicants required to submit FAFSA. *Application contact:* Becky Ellis, Information Contact, 317-274-1490, E-mail: museum@iupui.edu.

John F. Kennedy University, School of Education and Liberal Arts, Department of Museum Studies, Berkeley, CA 94702. Offers museum studies (MA, Certificate), including administration, collections management, public programming. Part-time programs available. *Degree requirements:* For master's, project. *Entrance requirements:* For master's, interview. Additional exam requirements/recommendations for international students: Required—TOEFL, TWE. *Faculty research:* Emerging museum philosophies, multicultural diversity issues in museums, trends in collections management and preventive conservation, effective programming techniques and application for diverse audiences.

The Johns Hopkins University, Zanvyl Krieger School of Arts and Sciences, Advanced Academic Programs, Program in Museum Studies, Baltimore, MD 21218-2699. Offers MA. Postbaccalaureate distance learning degree programs offered (minimal on-campus study). *Faculty:* 28. Application fee: $70. *Financial support:* Scholarships/grants available. *Unit head:* Robert Kargon, Program Chair, 202-452-1968. *Application contact:* Phyllis Hecht, Associate Program Chair, 202-452-1968, E-mail: phecht@jhu.edu.

See Close-Up on page 241.

New York University, Graduate School of Arts and Science, Department of History, New York, NY 10012-1019. Offers African diaspora (PhD); African history (PhD); archival management and historical editing (Advanced Certificate); Atlantic history (PhD); French studies/history (PhD); Hebrew and Judaic studies/history (PhD); history (MA, PhD), including Europe (PhD), Latin American and the Caribbean (PhD), United States (PhD), women's history (MA); Middle Eastern history (MA); Middle Eastern studies/history (PhD); public history (Advanced Certificate); world history (MA); JD/MA; MA/Advanced Certificate. Part-time programs available. *Faculty:* 43 full-time (19 women), 18 part-time/adjunct. *Students:* 106 full-time (68 women), 48 part-time (34 women); includes 29 minority (18 African Americans, 4 Asian Americans or Pacific Islanders, 7 Hispanic Americans), 26 international. Average age 31. 413 applicants, 19% accepted, 40 enrolled. In 2007, 17 master's, 7 doctorates awarded. Terminal master's awarded for partial completion of doctoral program. *Degree requirements:* For master's, seminar paper; for doctorate, one foreign language, thesis/dissertation, oral and written exams; for Advanced Certificate, internship. *Entrance requirements:* For master's, GRE General Test, minimum GPA of 3.0, writing sample; for doctorate, GRE. Additional exam requirements/recommendations for international students: Required—TOEFL. *Application deadline:* For fall admission, 12/12 for domestic students. Application fee: $85. *Financial support:* Fellowships with tuition reimbursements, research assistantships, teaching assistantships with tuition reimbursements, career-related internships or fieldwork, Federal Work-Study, institutionally sponsored loans, scholarships/grants, health care benefits, and unspecified assistantships available. Financial award application deadline: 12/12; financial award applicants required to submit FAFSA. *Faculty research:* African, East Asian, Medieval, early modern, and modern European history; U.S. history; African and African diaspora; Latin American history; Atlantic World. *Unit head:* Michael Gomez, Chair, 212-998-8600, Fax: 212-995-4017, E-mail: history.dept@nyu.edu. *Application contact:* Gregory Grandin, Director of Graduate Studies, 212-998-8600, Fax: 212-995-4017, E-mail: history.dept@nyu.edu.

New York University, Graduate School of Arts and Science, Program in Museum Studies, New York, NY 10012-1019. Offers museum studies (MA, Advanced Certificate), including Africana studies (MA), Hebrew and Judaic studies (MA), Latin American and Caribbean studies (MA), Near Eastern studies (MA). Part-time and evening/weekend programs available. *Faculty:* 4 full-time (1 woman), 6 part-time/adjunct. *Students:* 55 full-time (46 women), 26 part-time (23 women); includes 11 minority (1 American Indian/Alaska Native, 5 Asian Americans or Pacific Islanders, 5 Hispanic Americans), 19 international. Average age 28. 141 applicants, 66% accepted, 35 enrolled. In 2007, 25 master's awarded. *Entrance requirements:* For degree, master's or PhD. *Application deadline:* For fall admission, 2/1 for domestic students; for spring admission, 11/1 for domestic students. Application fee: $85. *Financial support:* Application deadline: 2/1. *Faculty research:* Modern and contemporary art, history of museums and exhibitions, conservation of cultural materials, museum anthropology, ethnography. *Unit head:* Bruce Altshuler, Director, 212-998-8080, Fax: 212-995-4185, E-mail: museum.studies@nyu.edu. *Application contact:* Tatiana Kamorina, Information Contact, 212-998-8080, Fax: 212-995-4185, E-mail: museum.studies@nyu.edu.

San Francisco Art Institute, Graduate Program, Department of Exhibition and Museum Studies, San Francisco, CA 94133. Offers MA. *Entrance requirements:* Additional exam requirements/recommendations for international students: Required—TOEFL (minimum score 580 paper-based; 237 computer-based). Electronic applications accepted.

San Francisco State University, Division of Graduate Studies, College of Humanities, Museum Studies Program, San Francisco, CA 94132-1722. Offers MA. Part-time programs available. *Financial support:* Career-related internships or fieldwork and Federal Work-Study available. *Unit head:* Dr. Linda Ellis, Director, 415-338-1612, E-mail: ellisl@sfsu.edu.

Seton Hall University, College of Arts and Sciences, Department of Art and Music, South Orange, NJ 07079-2697. Offers museum professions (MA). *Accreditation:* NASM. Part-time and evening/weekend programs available. *Degree requirements:* For master's, thesis or alternative. *Entrance requirements:* For master's, GRE General Test, previous course work in art history. Electronic applications accepted. *Faculty research:* History of museums, museum education, theory of museums, nineteenth century art, African-American art, Renaissance art history, museum registration.

See Close-Up on page 261.

Southern Illinois University Edwardsville, Graduate Studies and Research, College of Arts and Sciences, Department of Historical Studies, Program in Museum Studies, Edwardsville, IL 62026-0001. Offers Postbaccalaureate Certificate. *Students:* 5 applicants, 60% accepted. In 2007, 3 degrees awarded. *Entrance requirements:* Additional exam requirements/recommendations for international students: Required—TOEFL. *Application deadline:* For fall admission, 7/20 for domestic students, 6/1 for international students; for spring admission, 12/14 for domestic students, 10/1 for international students. Application fee: $30. Electronic applications accepted. *Financial support:* Fellowships with full tuition reimbursements, research assistantships with full tuition reimbursements, teaching assistantships with full tuition reimbursements available. *Unit head:* Dr. Laura Fowler Milsk, Director, 618-650-2145, E-mail: lmilsk@siue.edu.

State University of New York College at Oneonta, Graduate Education, Cooperstown Graduate Program in History Museum Studies, Oneonta, NY 13820-4015. Offers MA. *Students:* 31 full-time (24 women). 16 applicants, 100% accepted, 16 enrolled. In 2007, 21 degrees awarded. *Degree requirements:* For master's, research paper or thesis. *Entrance requirements:* For master's, GRE General Test. *Application deadline:* For fall admission, 1/10 for domestic students. Application fee: $50. *Expenses: Contact institution.* *Unit head:* Gretchen Sorin, Director, 607-547-2586, Fax: 607-547-8926, E-mail: sorings@oneonta.edu.

Syracuse University, Graduate School, College of Visual and Performing Arts, School of Art and Design, Program in Museum Studies, Syracuse, NY 13244. Offers MA. *Accreditation:* NASAD. Part-time programs available. *Students:* 18 full-time (16 women), 3 part-time (1 woman); includes 2 minority (1 African American, 1 Asian American or Pacific Islander), 1 international. 40 applicants, 75% accepted, 13 enrolled. In 2007, 8 degrees awarded. *Degree requirements:* For master's, thesis or alternative. *Entrance requirements:* Additional exam requirements/recommendations for international students: Required—TOEFL. *Application deadline:* For fall admission, 1/1 priority date for domestic students. Applications are processed on a rolling basis. Application fee: $75. *Expenses:* Tuition: Full-time $18,216; part-time $1,012 per credit. Required fees: $980. Tuition and fees vary according to program. *Financial support:* Fellowships with full tuition reimbursements, research assistantships with full and partial tuition reimbursements, teaching assistantships with full and partial tuition reimbursements, Federal Work-Study and tuition waivers (partial) available. *Unit head:* Dr. Edward Aiken, Chair, 315-

443-4098, Fax: 315-443-1303, E-mail: eaaiken@syr.edu. *Application contact:* Harriett Conti, Associate Director, Graduate Student Services, 315-443-3089, E-mail: hmconti@syr.edu.

Texas Tech University, Graduate School, Program in Museum Science and Heritage Management, Lubbock, TX 79409. Offers heritage management (MS); museum science (MA). Part-time programs available. *Faculty:* 6 full-time (3 women). *Students:* 29 full-time (28 women), 10 part-time (7 women); includes 5 minority (1 African American, 4 Hispanic Americans). Average age 28. 31 applicants, 81% accepted, 14 enrolled. In 2007, 20 degrees awarded. *Degree requirements:* For master's, thesis. *Entrance requirements:* For master's, GRE General Test. Additional exam requirements/recommendations for international students: Required—TOEFL (minimum score 550 paper-based; 213 computer-based). *Application deadline:* For fall admission, 3/1 priority date for international students; for spring admission, 11/1 priority date for international students. Applications are processed on a rolling basis. Application fee: $50 ($60 for international students). Electronic applications accepted. *Expenses:* Tuition, state resident: part-time $373 per credit hour. Tuition, nonresident: part-time $651 per credit hour. Tuition and fees vary according to program. *Financial support:* In 2007–08, 36 students received support, including 5 research assistantships with partial tuition reimbursements available (averaging $9,289 per year); teaching assistantships with partial tuition reimbursements available, career-related internships or fieldwork, Federal Work-Study, and institutionally sponsored loans also available. Support available to part-time students. Financial award application deadline: 4/15; financial award applicants required to submit FAFSA. *Faculty research:* Lubbock lake landmark anthropology; regional American fine art, regional ethnology; anthropology of the southern plains, natural science research. Total annual research expenditures: $46,621. *Unit head:* Gary F. Edson, Chair, 806-742-2442, Fax: 806-742-1136, E-mail: gary.edson@ttu.edu. *Application contact:* Claudia Cory, Assistant to the Director, 806-742-2442 Ext. 222, Fax: 806-742-1136, E-mail: claudia.cory@ttu.edu.

Tufts University, Graduate School of Arts and Sciences, Graduate Certificate Programs, Museum Studies Program, Medford, MA 02155. Offers Certificate. Part-time and evening/weekend programs available. *Students:* Average age 35. 47 applicants, 72% accepted, 25 enrolled. In 2007, 16 degrees awarded. *Application deadline:* For fall admission, 4/1 for domestic students. Application fee: $70. *Expenses: Contact institution. Financial support:* Career-related internships or fieldwork available. Support available to part-time students. Financial award application deadline: 5/1; financial award applicants required to submit FAFSA. *Application contact:* Angela Foss, Program Administrator, 617-627-3395, Fax: 617-627-3016, E-mail: gradschool@ase.tufts.edu.

Université de Montréal, Faculty of Arts and Sciences, Program in Museology, Montréal, QC H3C 3J7, Canada. Offers MA. *Students:* 40 full-time (37 women), 12 part-time (10 women). Average age 25. 25 applicants, 64% accepted, 18 enrolled. In 2007, 18 degrees awarded. *Application deadline:* For fall admission, 2/1 priority date for domestic students; for winter admission, 11/1 priority date for domestic students; for spring admission, 2/1 priority date for domestic students. Application fee: $100. Electronic applications accepted. *Faculty research:* Museum exhibits, museum education, natural science and museums, new technologies and museums. Total annual research expenditures: $500,000. *Unit head:* Colette Dufresne-Tassé, Director, 514-343-7351, Fax: 514-343-2314, E-mail: colette.dufresne.tasse@umontreal.ca.

Université du Québec à Montréal, Graduate Programs, Program in Museology, Montréal, QC H3C 3P8, Canada. Offers MA. Part-time programs available. *Entrance requirements:* For master's, appropriate bachelor's degree or equivalent and proficiency in French.

Université Laval, Faculty of Letters, Department of History, Program in Museology, Québec, QC G1K 7P4, Canada. Offers Diploma. Part-time programs available. *Entrance requirements:* For degree, English exam (comprehension of English), knowledge of French. Electronic applications accepted.

University at Buffalo, the State University of New York, Graduate School, College of Arts and Sciences, Department of Visual Studies, Program in Art History, Buffalo, NY 14260. Offers art history (MA); critical museum studies (Certificate). Part-time programs available. *Degree requirements:* For master's, one foreign language, thesis, field exam. *Entrance requirements:* Additional exam requirements/recommendations for international students: Required—TOEFL. Electronic applications accepted. *Faculty research:* Frank Lloyd Wright, non-Western art, Renaissance, Bronze Age Crete, American art.

The University of British Columbia, Faculty of Arts and Faculty of Graduate Studies, Department of Art History, Visual Art, and Theory, Vancouver, BC V6T 1Z1, Canada. Offers art history (MA, PhD, Diploma); critical and curatorial studies (MA); visual art (MFA). Part-time programs available. *Faculty:* 19 full-time (11 women), 1 part-time/adjunct (0 women). *Students:* 74 full-time (53 women), 1 part-time. 178 applicants, 26% accepted, 17 enrolled. In 2007, 16 master's, 5 doctorates awarded. *Degree requirements:* For master's, one foreign language, thesis, final exhibition (MFA, MA, CCST); for doctorate, 2 foreign languages, comprehensive exam, thesis/dissertation. *Entrance requirements:* For master's, bachelor's degree with minimum B+ average for MFA; for doctorate, master's degree with minimum A- average. Additional exam requirements/recommendations for international students: Required—TOEFL (minimum score 600 paper-based; 250 computer-based). *Application deadline:* For fall admission, 2/1 for domestic and international students. Application fee: $90 Canadian dollars ($150 Canadian dollars for international students). Electronic applications accepted. *Financial support:* In 2007–08, 22 fellowships (averaging $16,000 per year), 20 research assistantships (averaging $4,600 per year), 21 teaching assistantships (averaging $10,490 per year) were awarded; Federal Work-Study, scholarships/grants, health care benefits, and unspecified assistantships also available. *Faculty research:* Conceptual art, Asian art, indigenous North American art, post-second war art, eighteenth and nineteenth century art. *Unit head:* Dr. Rhodri Windsor-Liscombe, Head, 604-822-5650, Fax: 604-822-9003, E-mail: rhodri@interchange.ubc.ca. *Application contact:* Audrey Van Slyck, Graduate Secretary, 604-822-4340, Fax: 604-822-9003, E-mail: ahvagrad@interchange.ubc.ca.

University of California, Riverside, Graduate Division, Department of History, Riverside, CA 92521-0102. Offers archival management (MA); historic preservation (MA); history (MA, PhD); museum curatorship (MA). Part-time programs available. *Faculty:* 28 full-time (12 women). *Students:* 76 full-time (36 women), 1 (woman) part-time; includes 12 minority (1 African American, 2 American Indian/Alaska Native, 5 Asian Americans or Pacific Islanders, 4 Hispanic Americans), 1 international. Average age 31. 63 applicants, 49% accepted, 21 enrolled. In 2007, 12 master's, 6 doctorates awarded. Terminal master's awarded for partial completion of doctoral program. *Median time to degree:* Of those who began their doctoral program in fall 1999, 50% received their degree in 8 years or less. *Degree requirements:* For master's, one foreign language, comprehensive exam, internship report and oral exams, or thesis; for doctorate, 2 foreign languages, thesis/dissertation, qualifying exams, teaching experience. *Entrance requirements:* For master's, GRE General Test, minimum GPA of 3.2; for doctorate, GRE General Test, MA in history, minimum GPA of 3.2. Additional exam requirements/recommendations for international students: Required—TOEFL (minimum score 550 paper-based; 213 computer-based; 80 iBT). *Application deadline:* For fall admission, 5/1 for domestic students, 2/1 for international students. Applications are processed on a rolling basis. Application fee: $60 ($75 for international students). Electronic applications accepted. *Financial support:* In 2007–08, 56 students received support, including fellowships with full tuition reimbursements available (averaging $13,000 per year), teaching assistantships with partial tuition reimbursements available (averaging $16,500 per year); career-related internships or fieldwork, Federal Work-Study, institutionally sponsored loans, health care benefits, and tuition waivers (full and partial) also available. Financial award application deadline: 1/5; financial award applicants required to submit FAFSA. *Faculty research:* Native American history, United States, public history, Russia, Europe. *Unit head:* Dr. Robert Patch, Chair, 951-827-5401 Ext. 11437, Fax: 951-827-5299, E-mail: history@ucr.edu.

University of Central Oklahoma, College of Graduate Studies and Research, College of Liberal Arts, Department of History, Edmond, OK 73034-5209. Offers history (MA); museum studies (MA); social studies teaching (MA); Southwestern studies (MA). Part-time programs available. *Faculty:* 12 full-time (3 women). *Students:* 12 full-time (6 women), 15 part-time (9 women); includes 1 minority (Hispanic American) Average age 32. 10 applicants, 100% accepted. In 2007, 8 degrees awarded. *Degree requirements:* For master's, thesis optional. *Entrance requirements:* Additional exam requirements/recommendations for international students: Required—TOEFL (minimum score 550 paper-based; 213 computer-based). *Application deadline:* For fall admission, 7/1 for international students; for spring admission, 11/1 for international students. Applications are processed on a rolling basis. Application fee: $25. Electronic applications accepted. *Expenses:* Tuition, state resident: full-time $3,516; part-time $147 per hour. Tuition, nonresident: full-time $9,054; part-time $377 per hour. Required fees: $433; $18 per hour. *Financial support:* Career-related internships or fieldwork, Federal Work-Study, and unspecified assistantships available. Financial award application deadline: 3/31; financial award applicants required to submit FAFSA. *Faculty research:* China, Russia, civil war, American naval logistics. *Unit head:* Dr. Stanley Adamial, Chairman, 405-974-5451, Fax: 405-974-3823. *Application contact:* Dr. Carolyn Pool, Director, 405-974-5671, Fax: 405-974-3823, E-mail: cpool@ucok.edu.

University of Colorado at Boulder, Graduate School, College of Arts and Sciences, Museum and Field Studies Program, Boulder, CO 80309. Offers MS. *Students:* 19 full-time (15 women), 1 (woman) part-time; includes 4 minority (2 American Indian/Alaska Native, 1 Asian American or Pacific Islander, 1 Hispanic American). Average age 31. 13 applicants, 92% accepted. In 2007, 5 degrees awarded. *Degree requirements:* For master's, comprehensive exam, thesis or alternative. *Entrance requirements:* For master's, GRE General Test, GRE Subject Test, minimum undergraduate GPA of 3.0. *Application deadline:* For fall admission, 1/15 for domestic students, 12/1 for international students. Application fee: $50 ($60 for international students). *Financial support:* In 2007–08, 4 fellowships (averaging $5,750 per year), 1 research assistantship (averaging $16,767 per year) were awarded; career-related internships or fieldwork, Federal Work-Study, institutionally sponsored loans, and tuition waivers (partial) also available. Financial award application deadline: 2/1; financial award applicants required to submit FAFSA. Total annual research expenditures: $118,592. *Unit head:* Linda Cordell, Director, 303-492-0666, Fax: 303-492-4195, E-mail: linda.cordell@colorado.edu. *Application contact:* Graduate Coordinator, 303-492-5437, Fax: 303-735-0218, E-mail: mfsinfo@colorado.edu.

University of Denver, Faculty of Arts and Humanities/Social Sciences, School of Art and Art History, Denver, CO 80208. Offers art history (MA); art history/museum studies (MA); electronic media arts and design (MFA); studio art (MFA). *Accreditation:* NASAD. Part-time programs available. *Faculty:* 15 full-time (10 women). *Students:* 24 full-time (20 women), 2 part-time (1 woman); includes 2 minority (1 Asian American or Pacific Islander, 1 Hispanic American), 1 international. Average age 28. In 2007, 10 degrees awarded. *Degree requirements:* For master's, one foreign language, research paper. *Entrance requirements:* For master's, GRE. Additional exam requirements/recommendations for international students: Required—TOEFL. *Application deadline:* Applications are processed on a rolling basis. Application fee: $50. Electronic applications accepted. *Financial support:* In 2007–08, 5 teaching assistantships with full and partial tuition reimbursements (averaging $6,500 per year) were awarded; career-related internships or fieldwork, Federal Work-Study, institutionally sponsored loans, and scholarships/grants also available. Support available to part-time students. Financial award application deadline: 3/1; financial award applicants required to submit FAFSA. *Faculty research:* Images of women in alchemical manuscripts and books, Giovanni Benedetto, Salvatore Castiglione. *Unit head:* Dr. Annette Stott, Director, 303-871-2846. *Application contact:* Dr. M. Warlick, Graduate Advisor, 303-871-2846, E-mail: saah-interest@du.edu.

University of Florida, Graduate School, College of Fine Arts, School of Art and Art History, Gainesville, FL 32611. Offers art (MFA), including ceramics, creative photography, drawing, electronic intermedia, graphic design, painting, printmaking, sculpture; art education (MA); art history (MA, PhD); digital arts and sciences (MA); museology (museum studies) (MA). *Accreditation:* NASAD. *Faculty:* 29 full-time (14 women), 2 part-time/adjunct (1 woman). *Students:* 82 (48 women); includes 4 minority (2 Asian Americans or Pacific Islanders, 2 Hispanic Americans) 4 international. In 2007, 20 degrees awarded. *Degree requirements:* For master's, variable foreign language requirement, project or thesis (MFA). *Entrance requirements:* For master's, portfolio (MFA), writing sample (MA), GRE General Test or minimum GPA of 3.0. Additional exam requirements/recommendations for international students: Required—TOEFL (minimum score 550 paper-based; 213 computer-based). *Application deadline:* For fall admission, 1/15 priority date for domestic students. Applications are processed on a rolling basis. Application fee: $30. Electronic applications accepted. *Expenses:* Tuition, state resident: full-time $7,478. Tuition, nonresident: full-time $22,603. *Financial support:* In 2007–08, 3 research assistantships with tuition reimbursements (averaging $9,515 per year), 67 teaching assistantships with tuition reimbursements (averaging $9,839 per year) were awarded; fellowships, Federal Work-Study, institutionally sponsored loans, and unspecified assistantships also available. Financial award applicants required to submit FAFSA. *Faculty research:* Studio production, art historical studies of style context. *Unit head:* Glenn Willumson, Program Director, 352-392-0201 Ext. 234. *Application contact:* Prof. Richard Heipp, Coordinator, 352-392-0201 Ext. 239, Fax: 352-392-8453, E-mail: heipp@ufl.edu.

University of Hawaii at Manoa, Graduate Division, Colleges of Arts and Sciences, College of Arts and Humanities, Department of American Studies, Program in Museum Studies, Honolulu, HI 96822. Offers Graduate Certificate. Part-time programs available. *Faculty:* 7 full-time (3 women). *Students:* 12 full-time (8 women), 7 part-time (3 women); includes 7 minority (6 Asian Americans or Pacific Islanders, 1 Hispanic American), 2 international. 13 applicants, 54% accepted, 4 enrolled. In 2007, 5 degrees awarded. *Entrance requirements:* Additional exam requirements/recommendations for international students: Required—TOEFL (minimum score 600 paper-based; 250 computer-based; 100 iBT), IELTS (minimum score 7). *Application deadline:* For fall admission, 3/1 for domestic and international students; for spring admission, 9/1 for domestic and international students. Application fee: $50. *Financial support:* In 2007–08, 3 teaching assistantships (averaging $14,014 per year) were awarded. *Application contact:* Karen Kosasa, Director, 808-956-8676, Fax: 808-956-4733, E-mail: kosasa@hawaii.edu.

University of Kansas, Research and Graduate Studies, College of Liberal Arts and Sciences, Museum Studies Program, Lawrence, KS 66045. Offers MA. Part-time programs available. *Faculty:* 7. *Students:* 22 full-time (19 women), 10 part-time (6 women); includes 1 minority (Asian American or Pacific Islander), 1 international. Average age 29. 33 applicants, 70% accepted. In 2007, 10 degrees awarded. *Degree requirements:* For master's, comprehensive exam. *Entrance requirements:* For master's, GRE. Additional exam requirements/recommendations for international students: Required—TOEFL. *Application deadline:* For fall admission, 1/15 priority date for domestic and international students; for spring admission, 10/1 for domestic and international students. Applications are processed on a rolling basis. Application fee: $55 ($60 for international students). Electronic applications accepted. *Expenses:* Tuition, state resident: full-time $5,838. Tuition, nonresident: full-time $13,409. Tuition and fees vary according to program. *Financial support:* In 2007–08, 2 students received support; research assistantships with partial tuition reimbursements available available. *Faculty research:* Museum history, collection studies, indigenous nations, natural history, collections management. *Unit head:* Dr. Marjorie Swann, Director, 785-864-2306, E-mail: msswann@ku.edu. *Application contact:* Sherlyn Kay Isbell, Administrative Associate, 785-864-2306, Fax: 785-864-5772, E-mail: kisbell@ku.edu.

University of Missouri–St. Louis, College of Arts and Sciences, Department of History, St. Louis, MO 63121. Offers museum studies (MA, Certificate). Part-time and evening/weekend programs available. *Faculty:* 25 full-time (8 women), 1 part-time/adjunct (0 women). *Students:* 24 full-time (15 women), 57 part-time (31 women); includes 4 minority (2 African Americans, 1 American Indian/Alaska Native, 1 Hispanic American), 1 international. Average age 33. In 2007, 22 degrees awarded. *Degree requirements:* For master's, thesis (for some programs). *Entrance requirements:* For master's, minimum GPA of 2.75, writing sample, supplemental

Museum Studies

University of Missouri–St. Louis (continued)
application (museum studies). Additional exam requirements/recommendations for international students: Required—TOEFL (minimum score 550 paper-based; 213 computer-based). *Application deadline:* For fall admission, 7/1 priority date for domestic students. Applications are processed on a rolling basis. Application fee: $35 ($40 for international students). Electronic applications accepted. *Financial support:* In 2007–08, 3 research assistantships (averaging $5,500 per year), 5 teaching assistantships with full and partial tuition reimbursements (averaging $5,500 per year) were awarded; career-related internships or fieldwork also available. *Faculty research:* U.S., European, East Asian, Latin American, and African history. *Unit head:* Dr. Winston Hsieh, Director of Graduate Studies, 314-516-5681, Fax: 314-516-5415, E-mail: hsiehw@umsl.edu. *Application contact:* 314-516-5458, Fax: 314-516-6996, E-mail: gradadm@umsl.edu.

University of Nebraska–Lincoln, Graduate College, Department of Museum Studies, Lincoln, NE 68588. Offers MA, MS. *Degree requirements:* For master's, thesis optional. *Entrance requirements:* For master's, GRE General Test. Additional exam requirements/recommendations for international students: Required—TOEFL (minimum score 550 paper-based; 213 computer-based). Electronic applications accepted.

University of New Hampshire, Graduate School, College of Liberal Arts, Department of History, Durham, NH 03824. Offers history (MA, PhD); museum studies (MA). Part-time programs available. *Faculty:* 26 full-time. *Students:* 29 full-time (22 women), 24 part-time (14 women); includes 3 minority (2 American Indian/Alaska Native, 1 Asian American or Pacific Islander), 2 international. Average age 35. 75 applicants, 43% accepted, 12 enrolled. In 2007, 8 master's, 3 doctorates awarded. *Degree requirements:* For master's, thesis or alternative; for doctorate, 2 foreign languages, thesis/dissertation. *Entrance requirements:* For master's and doctorate, GRE General Test. Additional exam requirements/recommendations for international students: Required—TOEFL (minimum score 550 paper-based; 213 computer-based; 80 iBT). *Application deadline:* For fall admission, 2/15 priority date for domestic students, 2/15 for international students. Applications are processed on a rolling basis. Application fee: $60. Electronic applications accepted. *Financial support:* In 2007–08, 1 research assistantship, 15 teaching assistantships were awarded; fellowships, career-related internships or fieldwork, Federal Work-Study, scholarships/grants, and tuition waivers (full and partial) also available. Support available to part-time students. Financial award application deadline: 2/15. *Unit head:* Dr. Janet Polasky, Chairperson, 603-862-3789. *Application contact:* Susan Kilday, Administrative Assistant, 603-862-1764, E-mail: history.grad@unh.edu.

The University of North Carolina at Greensboro, Graduate School, College of Arts and Sciences, Department of History, Greensboro, NC 27412-5001. Offers historic preservation (Certificate); history (MA); museum studies (Certificate); U.S. history (PhD). Part-time programs available. *Faculty:* 23 full-time (8 women). *Students:* 62 full-time (38 women), 11 part-time (4 women); includes 8 minority (5 African Americans, 1 Asian American or Pacific Islander, 2 Hispanic Americans). 136 applicants, 31% accepted. In 2007, 15 degrees awarded. *Entrance requirements:* For master's, GRE General Test. Additional exam requirements/recommendations for international students: Required—TOEFL. *Application deadline:* For fall admission, 3/1 for domestic students; for spring admission, 11/1 for domestic students. Electronic applications accepted. *Financial support:* Fellowships with full tuition reimbursements, research assistantships with full tuition reimbursements, teaching assistantships with full tuition reimbursements, career-related internships or fieldwork, Federal Work-Study, scholarships/grants, traineeships, and unspecified assistantships available. Support available to part-time students. *Faculty research:* Simultaneous discovery in science, progressive social reform, Robert Mayer. *Unit head:* Dr. Chuck Bolton, Head, 336-334-5910, Fax: 336-334-5910, E-mail: ccbolton@uncg.edu. *Application contact:* Michelle Harkleroad, Director of Graduate Admissions, 336-334-4884, Fax: 336-334-4424, E-mail: mbharkle@uncg.edu.

The University of North Carolina at Greensboro, Graduate School, School of Human Environmental Sciences, Department of Interior Architecture, Greensboro, NC 27412-5001. Offers historic preservation (Certificate); interior architecture (MS); museum studies (Certificate). *Faculty:* 9 full-time (4 women), 1 part-time/adjunct (0 women). *Students:* 14 full-time (12 women), 1 (woman) part-time. 13 applicants, 38% accepted. *Degree requirements:* For master's, thesis. *Entrance requirements:* For master's, GRE General Test or MAT, bachelor's degree in interior design, interview, portfolio. Additional exam requirements/recommendations for international students: Required—TOEFL. *Application deadline:* For fall admission, 3/1 for domestic students. Application fee: $45. Electronic applications accepted. *Financial support:* Fellowships with full tuition reimbursements, research assistantships with full tuition reimbursements, teaching assistantships with full tuition reimbursements, career-related internships or fieldwork, Federal Work-Study, scholarships/grants, and traineeships available. Support available to part-time students. *Unit head:* Thomas Lambeth, Chairman, 336-334-5320, Fax: 336-334-5049, E-mail: ctlambeth@uncg.edu. *Application contact:* Michelle Harkleroad, Director of Graduate Admissions, 336-334-4884, Fax: 336-334-4424, E-mail: mbharkle@uncg.edu.

University of Oklahoma, Graduate College, College of Liberal Studies, Norman, OK 73019-0390. Offers administrative leadership (MLS); integrated studies (MLS); interprofessional human and health services (MLS); museum studies (MLS). Part-time programs available. Postbaccalaureate distance learning degree programs offered (no on-campus study). *Faculty:* 11 full-time (6 women), 13 part-time/adjunct (3 women). *Students:* 16 full-time (8 women), 264 part-time (153 women); includes 59 minority (32 African Americans, 12 American Indian/Alaska Native, 6 Asian Americans or Pacific Islanders, 9 Hispanic Americans). 117 applicants, 96% accepted, 71 enrolled. In 2007, 52 degrees awarded. *Degree requirements:* For master's, thesis, research project, internship. *Entrance requirements:* For master's, minimum GPA of 3.0 in last 60 hours, writing sample. Additional exam requirements/recommendations for international students: Required—TOEFL (minimum score 550 paper-based; 213 computer-based). *Application deadline:* For fall admission, 7/15 priority date for domestic students, 4/1 for international students; for spring admission, 12/1 for domestic students, 9/1 for international students. Applications are processed on a rolling basis. Application fee: $40 ($90 for international students). Electronic applications accepted. *Expenses:* Tuition, state resident: full-time $3,451; part-time $144 per credit hour. Tuition, nonresident: full-time $12,432; part-time $518 per credit hour. Required fees: $1,925; $70 per credit hour. $122 per semester. *Financial support:* In 2007–08, 112 students received support. Career-related internships or fieldwork, scholarships/grants, and tuition waivers (partial) available. Support available to part-time students. Financial award applicants required to submit FAFSA. *Faculty research:* Distance education, adult learning processes, student satisfaction, administrative leadership, organizations, museum studies. *Unit head:* Dr. James Pappas, Dean and Vice President, 405-325-1061, Fax: 405-325-7132, E-mail: jpappas@ou.edu. *Application contact:* Dr. Julie Raadschelders, MA Program Coordinator, 405-325-1061, Fax: 405-325-9632, E-mail: jraadschelders@ou.edu.

University of South Carolina, The Graduate School, College of Arts and Sciences, Department of History, Program in Public History, Columbia, SC 29208. Offers archives (MA); historic preservation (MA); museum (MA); museum management (Certificate); MLIS/MA. *Faculty:* 3 full-time (2 women). *Students:* 10 full-time (7 women), 3 part-time (2 women); includes 1 minority (Hispanic American) Average age 26. 34 applicants, 18% accepted. In 2007, 13 degrees awarded. *Degree requirements:* For master's, one foreign language, thesis, internship. *Entrance requirements:* For master's, GRE General Test, writing sample. Additional exam requirements/recommendations for international students: Required—TOEFL. *Application deadline:* For fall admission, 1/5 for domestic students. Application fee: $40. Electronic applications accepted. *Expenses:* Tuition, state resident: part-time $440 per hour. Tuition, nonresident: part-time $936 per hour. Required fees: $17 per hour. Tuition and fees vary according to program. *Financial support:* In 2007–08, 12 teaching assistantships with partial tuition reimbursements (averaging $11,000 per year) were awarded; fellowships with partial tuition reimbursements, research assistantships with partial tuition reimbursements, career-related internships or fieldwork, Federal Work-Study, and institutionally sponsored loans also available. Financial award application deadline: 1/5. *Faculty research:* Museum studies, historic preservation, archives administration. *Application contact:* Robert R. Weyeneth, Co-Director, 803-777-5195, Fax: 803-777-4494, E-mail: weyeneth@sc.edu.

The University of the Arts, College of Art and Design, Department of Museum Studies, Philadelphia, PA 19102-4944. Offers museum communication (MA); museum education (MA); museum exhibition planning and design (MFA). *Accreditation:* NASAD. Part-time programs available. *Degree requirements:* For master's, thesis, internship. *Entrance requirements:* For master's, portfolio. Additional exam requirements/recommendations for international students: Required—TOEFL (minimum score 550 paper-based; 213 computer-based).

See Close-Up on page 273.

University of Toronto, School of Graduate Studies, Humanities Division, Department of Art, Toronto, ON M5S 1A1, Canada. Offers art history (MA, PhD); visual studies (MVS). Part-time programs available. *Faculty:* 22 full-time, 8 part-time/adjunct. *Students:* 74 full-time (62 women), 5 part-time, 20 international. 197 applicants, 41% accepted. In 2007, 20 master's, 2 doctorates awarded. *Degree requirements:* For master's, 2 foreign languages, language proficiency exams; for doctorate, 2 foreign languages, comprehensive exam, thesis/dissertation. *Entrance requirements:* For master's, coursework in a foreign language, 3 letters of reference, sample research paper, minimum B+ average in senior art history and/or humanities courses; for doctorate, minimum A– average in senior art history and/or humanities courses, 2 letters of reference, sample research paper. *Application deadline:* For fall admission, 1/15 for domestic students. Application fee: $100 Canadian dollars. *Financial support:* Teaching assistantships available. *Unit head:* Prof. Mark A. Cheetham, Chair, 416-978-7891, Fax: 416-978-1491. *Application contact:* Gaby Binette, Secretary, 416-978-7892, Fax: 416-978-1491, E-mail: gaby.binette@utoronto.ca.

University of Toronto, School of Graduate Studies, Humanities Division, Program in Museum Studies, Toronto, ON M5S 1A1, Canada. Offers MM St. *Faculty:* 3 full-time, 9 part-time/adjunct. *Students:* 48 full-time (42 women), 8 international. 89 applicants, 60% accepted. In 2007, 11 degrees awarded. Application fee: $100 Canadian dollars. *Expenses:* Contact institution. *Financial support:* Career-related internships or fieldwork available. *Unit head:* Prof. Wendy Duff, Interim Director, 416-978-4211, Fax: 416-978-8821. *Application contact:* Robin Breon, Secretary, 416-978-4211, Fax: 416-978-8821, E-mail: robin.breon@utoronto.ca.

University of Washington, Graduate School, Museology Graduate Program, Seattle, WA 98195. Offers MA. *Faculty:* 2 full-time (1 woman), 12 part-time/adjunct (8 women). *Students:* 52 full-time (44 women); includes 7 minority (1 American Indian/Alaska Native, 2 Asian Americans or Pacific Islanders, 4 Hispanic Americans), 2 international. Average age 26. 139 applicants, 40% accepted, 25 enrolled. In 2007, 11 degrees awarded. *Degree requirements:* For master's, thesis or alternative. *Entrance requirements:* For master's, GRE General Test, minimum GPA of 3.0. Additional exam requirements/recommendations for international students: Required—TOEFL. *Application deadline:* For fall admission, 2/1 for domestic students, 11/1 priority date for international students. Application fee: $45. Electronic applications accepted. *Expenses:* Contact institution. *Financial support:* Career-related internships or fieldwork, Federal Work-Study, institutionally sponsored loans, and scholarships/grants available. Financial award application deadline: 2/15; financial award applicants required to submit FAFSA. *Faculty research:* Collection management, conservation, art history, anthropology, administration. *Unit head:* Dr. Kris Morrissey, Director, 206-685-8207, Fax: 206-543-3552, E-mail: morriss8@u.washington.edu. *Application contact:* Maya Procel, Program Administrator, 206-616-8280, Fax: 206-543-3552, E-mail: acad-programs@extn.washington.edu.

University of West Georgia, Graduate School, College of Arts and Sciences, Department of History, Program in Museum Studies, Carrollton, GA 30118. Offers Certificate. *Expenses:* Tuition, state resident: full-time $2,448; part-time $136 per semester hour. Tuition, nonresident: full-time $9,774; part-time $543 per semester hour. Required fees: $26 per semester hour. $173 per semester. *Application contact:* Dr. Charles W. Clark, Interim Dean, 678-839-6508, E-mail: cclark@westga.edu.

University of Wisconsin–Milwaukee, Graduate School, College of Letters and Sciences, Department of Art History, Milwaukee, WI 53201-0413. Offers art history (MA); art museum studies (Certificate). Part-time programs available. *Faculty:* 8 full-time (3 women). *Students:* 21 full-time (18 women), 14 part-time (11 women); includes 2 minority (1 African American, 1 American Indian/Alaska Native), 1 international. 27 applicants, 59% accepted, 11 enrolled. In 2007, 5 degrees awarded. *Degree requirements:* For master's, one foreign language, thesis or alternative. *Application deadline:* For fall admission, 1/1 priority date for domestic students; for spring admission, 9/1 for domestic students. Applications are processed on a rolling basis. Application fee: $45 ($75 for international students). *Expenses:* Tuition, state resident: part-time $530 per credit. Tuition, nonresident: part-time $1,428 per credit. Required fees: $19 per credit. $229 per term. Tuition and fees vary according to course load and program. *Financial support:* In 2007–08, 5 teaching assistantships were awarded; fellowships, research assistantships, career-related internships or fieldwork and unspecified assistantships also available. Support available to part-time students. Financial award application deadline: 4/15. *Unit head:* Kenneth Bendiner, Representative, 414-229-5015, Fax: 414-229-2935, E-mail: bendiner@uwm.edu.

Virginia Commonwealth University, Graduate School, School of the Arts, Department of Art History, Richmond, VA 23284-9005. Offers architectural history (MA); art history (MA, PhD); historical studies (MA); museum studies (MA). *Accreditation:* NASAD. *Faculty:* 10 full-time (4 women). *Students:* 19 full-time (18 women), 24 part-time (20 women); includes 6 minority (2 African Americans, 2 Asian Americans or Pacific Islanders, 2 Hispanic Americans), 1 international. 54 applicants, 50% accepted, 13 enrolled. In 2007, 15 master's, 4 doctorates awarded. *Degree requirements:* For master's, thesis; for doctorate, comprehensive exam, thesis/dissertation. *Entrance requirements:* For master's and doctorate, GRE General Test. *Application deadline:* For fall admission, 1/15 for domestic students. Application fee: $50. *Expenses:* Tuition, state resident: full-time $7,224; part-time $401 per credit. Tuition, nonresident: full-time $16,072; part-time $891 per credit. Required fees: $1,679; $63 per credit. Tuition and fees vary according to campus/location. *Financial support:* Fellowships, teaching assistantships, career-related internships or fieldwork, Federal Work-Study, and institutionally sponsored loans available. Support available to part-time students. Financial award application deadline: 3/15. *Faculty research:* Modern, nineteenth century, Renaissance, American, and Medieval art. *Unit head:* Dr. James Farmer, Coordinator of Graduate Studies, 804-828-2784, Fax: 804-828-7468, E-mail: jfarmer@saturn.vcu.edu.

See Close-Up on page 275.

ADELPHI UNIVERSITY

College of Arts and Sciences
Program in Fine Arts

Programs of Study

The study of art is the study of making. To make is to create, to interpret, and, finally, to understand one's own vision of the world. To study art and the history of art is to study the very essence of the self and of civilization. The Department of Art and Art History offers a program of study that leads to the Master of Arts degree in studio art. Course requirements total 36 credits. Students generally concentrate in a primary area of studio work (up to 15 credits), supplemented by one or more secondary areas of studio concentration. Concentration areas include ceramics, painting, photography, printmaking, and sculpture. Completion of degree requirements may be undertaken on a part-time basis or by attending summer sessions. Information on these options may be obtained from the department.

The department also offers course options for the Master of Arts degree in art education for those seeking New York State certification for teaching primary and secondary level. Students who successfully complete the program graduate with a Master of Arts degree from the School of Education. Students should consult with the department chair or their graduate faculty adviser to determine the necessary courses to fulfill the degree requirements.

Research Facilities

The University's primary research holdings are at Swirbul Library and include 667,383 volumes (including bound periodicals and government publications), 805,179 items in microformats, 23,230 audiovisual items, 1,635 periodical subscriptions, and access to over 27,000 electronic journal titles. Online access is provided to 233 research databases.

Opened in fall 2005, the 18,000-square-foot Fine Arts and Facilities Building greatly expands Adelphi's art studio and classroom space. The one-story building takes advantages of natural light to illuminate two painting studios, a sculpture and ceramics studio, and a printmaking studio. An outdoor courtyard contains kilns and display boxes for student artwork. The department retained its space on the third floor of Blodgett Hall, including its state-of-the-art digital graphics design studio and faculty offices.

Financial Aid

Adelphi University offers a wide variety of federal aid programs, state grants, scholarship and fellowship programs, on- and off-campus employment, and teaching and research assistantships.

Cost of Study

For the 2007–08 academic year, the tuition rate was $755 per credit. University fees ranged from $300 to $500 per semester.

Living and Housing Costs

The University assists single and married students in finding suitable accommodations whenever possible. The cost of living is dependent upon location and the number of rooms rented.

Location

Located in historic Garden City, New York, 45 minutes from Manhattan and 20 minutes from Queens, Adelphi's 75-acre suburban campus is known for the beauty of its landscape and architecture. The campus is a short walk from the Long Island Rail Road and is convenient to New York's major airports and several major highways. Off-campus centers are located in Manhattan, Hauppauge, and Poughkeepsie.

The University and The College

Founded in 1896, Adelphi is a fully accredited, private university with 8,300 undergraduate, graduate, and returning-adult students in the arts and sciences, business, clinical psychology, education, nursing, and social work. Students come from thirty-seven states and from forty-five countries. *The Princeton Review* named Adelphi University a Best College in the Northeastern Region, and *Fiske Guide to Colleges* recognized Adelphi as a "Best Buy" in higher education for two years in a row. The University is the only private institution on Long Island and one of only twenty-six in the nation to earn this recognition.

Mindful of the cultural inheritance of the past, the College of Arts and Sciences encompasses those realms of inquiry that have characterized the modern pursuit of knowledge. The faculty members of the College place a high priority on their students' intellectual development in and out of the classroom and structure programs and opportunities to foster that growth. Students analyze original research or other creative work, develop firsthand facility with creative or research methodologies, undertake collaborative work with peers and mentors, engage in serious internships, and hone communicative skills.

Applying

An applicant must have earned a baccalaureate degree from an accredited four-year college and have developed a portfolio of art work in a representative range of media. A student must submit the completed application form, the $50 application fee, official college transcripts, and two letters of recommendation. A formal portfolio presentation is required of all applicants. All portfolios are reviewed by a faculty committee, and selected applicants are invited to campus for a tour and interview. Portfolios should contain twelve to fifteen examples of recent work.

Correspondence and Information

David Hornung, Department Chair
Blodgett Hall, Room 301
College of Arts and Sciences
Adelphi University
Garden City, New York 11530
Phone: 516-877-4460
Fax: 516-877-4459
E-mail: hornung@adelphi.edu
Web site: http://academics.adelphi.edu/artsci/art/graduate/

Adelphi University

THE FACULTY

Hugh Crean, Professor; Ph.D., Yale, 2001.
Dale Flashner, Graphic Design Studio Art Director and Senior Adjunct Professor.
Carson Fox, Assistant Professor; M.F.A., Rutgers, 1999.
Geoffrey Grogan, Associate Professor; M.F.A., M.S., Pratt, 1996.
David Hornung, Associate Professor; M.F.A., Wisconsin, 1976.
Jennifer Maloney, Visiting Assistant Professor; M.F.A., CUNY, Brooklyn.
Thomas McAnulty, Professor; M.F.A., Indiana, 1976.
Kellyann Monaghan, Assistant Professor; M.F.A., CUNY, Brooklyn, 2001.
Jean Sorabella, Assistant Professor; Ph.D., Columbia, 2000.

THE ART INSTITUTE OF BOSTON AT LESLEY UNIVERSITY

M.F.A. in Visual Arts

Programs of Study Lesley University offers a low-residency Master of Fine Arts (M.F.A.) in Visual Arts program. The M.F.A. in Visual Arts program, offered by The Art Institute of Boston (AIB) at Lesley University, provides the ideal solution for artists, teachers, and professionals in related fields who are seeking professional advancement in the field of visual arts. The M.F.A. in Visual Arts program allows students, with the guidance of a faculty adviser and a local studio mentor, to design their own studio and academic plans for each semester. This M.F.A. in Visual Arts program builds on the traditions of collaboration, innovation, and strength in the arts that characterize existing AIB and Lesley programs. It also benefits from the success of Lesley's low-residency model, a longstanding feature of several Lesley programs that meet the diverse needs of adult learners. The M.F.A. in visual arts is a degree that can advance the careers of artists, teachers, or professionals in other art-related fields.

The interdisciplinary focus of the M.F.A. program encourages students to explore the integration of a variety of visual arts media. The M.F.A. in visual arts focuses on developing the tools and expertise to create an individual vision. Students advance their study of art history, culture, and critical thinking through the rigorous academic components of the program while discovering how to situate their own work within a broadly defined contemporary art context. The M.F.A. program broadens the students' knowledge of visual arts as a profession, including relationships with galleries, grant and proposal preparation, public and private commission, and the ongoing development of media and art-making tools.

Over the course of four semesters and five residencies, students learn to devise their own methodology for producing a focused plan of ongoing studio work and research, earning 15 credits per semester. During these intensive residencies, studio work, as outlined in each semester's study-plan contract, is evaluated for credit through critiques with faculty members, visiting artists, and peers. Academic studies are addressed through seminars, lectures, and planning sessions with academic advisers. During the semester, students' work, both academic and studio, is supervised by both a local studio mentor and an M.F.A. faculty adviser. Studio components are 48 credits and academic components are 12 credits, for a total of 60 credits.

The M.F.A. in Visual Arts program is fully accredited by both the New England Association of Schools and Colleges (NEASC) and the National Association of Schools of Art and Design (NASAD) and is the only low-residency program based on the two 10-day residencies to be approved by NASAD. Lesley University is licensed by many states' Commission on Higher Education to offer programs in those states.

Research Facilities During each residency, students have access to The Art Institute of Boston at Lesley University's state-of-the-art facilities and technology to ensure that they achieve their artistic goals. Regardless of their field of interest in the visual arts, students always find the tools they need at Lesley to realize their vision. In addition, Ludcke Library at Lesley University maintains a working collection of books, periodicals, microfilm, microfiche, nonprint materials, and software resources. The library provides Internet resources and database access to general and subject-specific resources that are appropriate to the subject focuses of the University. Through the Fenway Consortium, students can access thirteen other libraries in the Boston-Cambridge area.

Financial Aid The Lesley University Financial Aid Office assists students as needed in obtaining various types of educational assistance, including Federal Pell Grants, Federal Stafford Student Loans, and Federal Perkins Loans.

Cost of Study In 2008–09, the tuition for the M.F.A. in Visual Arts Program is $7665 per semester. Additional program fees may apply.

Living and Housing Costs Information on local housing is available upon request.

Student Group The graduate on-campus and off-campus enrollment at Lesley University consists of approximately 10,000 students—men and women ranging in age from their early 20s to their early 70s in all stages of professional development. Students come from fifty states and thirty-two countries.

Location Lesley University occupies a campus between Harvard and Porter Squares in Cambridge. The Art Institute of Boston at Lesley University occupies a campus in Kenmore Square in Boston. The University is conveniently connected to downtown Boston by public transportation. Numerous historical sites and cultural attractions are easily accessed by train or bus or on foot, including theaters, museums, and concerts.

The University Lesley University, founded in 1909 as a women's teaching college, continues its commitment to educating undergraduate men and women while also offering undergraduate and graduate programs for men and women in the fields of education, human services, management, the environment, and the arts. Lesley University has successfully pioneered a wide variety of flexible programs for adult learners that share a commitment to quality, innovation, and the integration of theory with practice. Lesley offers degree programs through four schools: Lesley College, The Art Institute of Boston, the Graduate School of Arts and Social Sciences, and the School of Education. The University also supports several centers and hosts a variety of academic and professional conferences and institutes. Lesley programs operate throughout Massachusetts and in twenty-two other states as well as at affiliated international sites.

Applying Applications for the M.F.A. program should be completed by March 15 for the summer residency and September 15 for the winter residency. Applications completed after those dates are considered on a space-available basis. Requirements for admission to the M.F.A. program are a bachelor's degree from a regionally accredited college or university as well as a satisfactory grade average, official transcripts of undergraduate work, three letters of recommendation, a written personal statement that describes the applicant's work in relation to contemporary art issues and interests, a portfolio review in the form of twenty slides submitted with the application, and a nonrefundable $50 application fee. Applicants seeking a B.A. Waiver should contact the Office of Graduate Admissions. Application materials for the M.F.A. program should be requested from the Office of Graduate Admissions.

Correspondence and Information

Office of Graduate Admissions
Lesley University
29 Everett Street
Cambridge, Massachusetts 02138-2790

Phone: 617-349-8300
888-LESLEY-U (toll-free)
Fax: 617-349-8313
E-mail: info@lesley.edu/mfa
Web site: http://www.aiboston.edu/mfa

The Art Institute of Boston at Lesley University

THE FACULTY AND THEIR RESEARCH

Anthony Apesos received his M.F.A. from Pennsylvania Academy of the Fine Arts and also attended Milton Avery Graduate School of the Fine Arts at Bard College. Selected exhibitions include F.A.N. Gallery, More Gallery, Pine Manor College, St. Joseph's University, Villanova University Art Gallery, Levy Gallery, Michael Dunev Gallery, University of Pennsylvania, Group-Sketch Club, Andrea Marquit Fine Arts, Baum School of Art, Allentown Art Museum, Amos Eno Gallery, Butler Institute of American Art, and Tiajin Fine Arts College, People's Republic of China. He is also a critic for *New Art Examiner.*

Jan Avgikos is an art critic and historian based in New York City and a contributing editor with *Artforum* international magazine. Her writings appear internationally in magazines, museum catalogs, and anthologies of critical writing. Recent texts include a monograph on Katy Grannan (Aperture Books) and an essay on Roni Horn for Dia's ongoing series of collected lectures from the Robert Lehman series. Catalog essays include Lili Dujourie (for the Palais des Beaux Arts in Brussels) and Matts Leiderstam (for the Magasin in Stockholm). Ms. Avgikos is an adjunct member of the faculty for the Graduate Visual Arts Programs at Columbia and NYU and a professor at the School for the Visual Arts in Manhattan. She lectures regularly for the Dia Foundation for contemporary arts and at Sotheby's in their graduate American art program.

Hannah Barrett draws on the techniques of collage and oil painting to fuse and invent, creating a detailed world of androgynous characters that are familiar yet unreal. She has exhibited at the Museum of Fine Arts, Boston in Traveling Scholars in 2006 and has had solo shows at Howard Yezerski Gallery in 2006 and 2007 and Clifford Smith Gallery in 2003. She received her M.F.A. from Boston University and has taught at The Art Institute of Boston since 1999, the School of the Museum of Fine Arts, Boston College, and the College of Fine Art at Boston University.

Judith Barry, Director of the M.F.A. program, is an artist and writer whose work crosses a number of disciplines: performance, installation, sculpture, architecture, photography, and new media. She has exhibited internationally at such venues as the Berlin Biennale, Venice Biennale of Art/Architecture, Sao Paolo Biennale, Nagoya Biennale, Carnegie International, Whitney Biennale, and Australian Biennale. Recent publications include *Projections: mise en abyme* (1997) and the catalog for the *Study for the Mirror and Garden*, in Granada, Spain (2003). Recent full-time teaching positions include the Visual and Performing Arts Department at MIT (2002–03) and the Merz Akademie in Stuttgart, Germany (2003–04). Currently she is Senior Fellow at CAVS at MIT and Honorary Chair of the Arts Council at UCLA.

Dike Blair is a painter and sculptor who lives in New York City. He has shown his work in museums and galleries in the U.S. and abroad for many years, including more than thirty solo exhibitions. His work was included in the 2004 Whitney Biennial and Vanishing Point at the Wexner Art Center in 2005. Blair was an associate editor of the Paris-based magazine, *Purple*, and has contributed articles to a number of magazines, including *Art Forum, ArtNews, Bomb, Paper, Art Presse, Parkett,* and *Harper's*. He is an adjunct painting professor at the Rhode Island School of Design. For more information, students should visit http://www.thing.net/~lilyvac or http://featureinc.com.

Deborah Davidson received her M.F.A. from the School of the Museum of Fine Arts/Tufts University. She has taught at Massachusetts College of Art, The Art Institute of Boston, and the School of the Museum School of Fine Arts. Ms. Davidson has worked as an independent curator and was the director and curator of the Starr Gallery, Newton, for three years. She currently is the curator for the New Center for Arts and Culture and oversaw the seven exhibitions for the New Center's inaugural program, Words on Fire, in 2003. She also exhibits her own work widely, most recently at Montserrat College of Art, Jane Deering Gallery, William Scott Gallery, Tufts Art Gallery, New Art Center, Art Complex Museum, and Plum Gallery. Her work is in many private and public collections, including Yale; Wellesley College; the Boston Public Library; the Museum of Fine Arts, Boston; and the Houghton Library, Harvard University.

Jesseca Ferguson works in a variety of nineteenth-century photographic processes and in collage. She received an M.F.A. from Tufts University. Her work is included in solo and group exhibitions in the U.S., Poland, France, Italy, Belgium, Denmark, the Czech Republic, and England. Public collections include Bibliothèque Nationale de France; Museet fur Fotokunst; Muzeum Historii Fotografii; Fogg Art Museum; Museum of Fine Arts, Boston; and Polaroid Collection. Ferguson cocurated the exhibition, Made in Poland: Contemporary Pinhole Photography, which was held in 2007 in the main AIB gallery.

John Kramer is an artist and graphic designer. His first solo show (digital photography) was recently exhibited at HallSpace Gallery and DNA Gallery. He has shown monotypes, video, and a post-it note installation. He currently runs his own design business, John Kramer Design, and has worked extensively in corporate and academic environments as an electronic prepress specialist and trainer. He has done sets, props, and costumes and taught conventional black-and-white photography and graphic design. He is a member of the adjunct faculty in graphic design in the B.F.A. program at The Art Institute of Boston.

Jack Lueders-Booth is a documentary photographer who taught photography at Harvard University from 1970 to 1998; Rhode Island School of Design; the School of the Museum of Fine Arts, Boston; Massachusetts College of Art; The Art Institute of Boston; and Tufts University. He has produced many documentary, and his photographs are included in the collections of the Addison Gallery of American Art; Center for Documentary Studies at Duke University; David Rockefeller Center for Latin American Studies at Harvard University; DeCordova Museum; Fogg Art Museum; the Hood Museum of Art at Dartmouth College; the Museum of Contemporary Photography at Columbia College; MoMA, NYC; the San Diego Museum of Photographic Arts; and San Francisco Museum of Modern Art. He has been Artist-in-Residence at Dartmouth College and Visiting Artist at Yale University.

Adam McEwen received his B.F.A. from Oxford University (1984–87) and continued his studies at the California Institute of the Arts (1989-91). Through a broad range of media, the artist explores society's perception of human progress and its realities, as demonstrated in his obituaries of living luminaries and his recent chewing gum–dotted paintings, which refer to desecrated postwar German landscapes. McEwen has had solo exhibitions at Nicole Klagsbrun Gallery, Galerie Art Concept, and Jack Hanley Gallery. His work was included in the 2006 Whitney Biennial and is held in the permanent collections of the Solomon M. Guggenheim Museum, the Whitney Museum of American Art, the Aberdeen Art Gallery and Museum, and the Arts Council of Great Britain. McEwen has also curated the recent exhibitions at Gagosian Gallery, Nicole Klagsbrun Gallery, and Roth Horowitz.

Carrie Moyer is a New York–based painter. Her work has been widely exhibited both nationally and internationally, including PS1/Institute on Contemporary Art, the Palm Beach ICA, Yerba Buena Center for the Arts, the Weatherspoon, Cooper-Hewitt Museum, Tang Museum, Shedhalle, Le Magasin, and the Project Centre. Moyer is also one half of the public art project, Dyke Action Machine! (DAM!). Moyer's work has been reviewed in such publications as *Art in America, Art Forum, Flash Art, Contemporary,* and the *New York Times.* Moyer received an M.F.A. from Bard. She currently teaches at Tyler School of Art and the Cooper Union.

Michael Newman is Associate Professor in Art History, Theory, and Criticism at the School of the Art Institute of Chicago. He holds degrees in literature and art history and a doctorate in philosophy from the Katholeike Universiteit Leuven, Belgium. He has written extensively on contemporary art and has curated several exhibitions, including the Art Gallery of York University and Musée d'Art Moderne de la Ville de Paris. His book *Richard Prince: Untitled (couple)* (Afterall and MIT) was published in 2006, and his monograph *Jeff Wall: Works and Writings* (Poligrafia) was published in June 2007. He is coeditor of *Re-Writing Conceptual Art* (London, Reaktion Books, 1999). He is currently writing a book on the trace.

Tim Norris is a lecturer, writer, theorist, and multimedia performance artist. A Ph.D. candidate at Birmingham University, England, Norris received an M.A. in aesthetics and art theory from Middlesex University, England, and an M.S.M. in arts administration from Lesley University. Norris recently recorded the sound work, Falling Ships. He has presented at the Northeast Popular Culture/American Culture Association and at the Philosophy/Interpretation/Culture Conference. His recent projects include Strangers on a Train, Hegel and Hitchcock, presented at the eleventh Performance Studies International Conference, at Brown University, 2005.

Oscar Palacio is a Columbian-born, Boston-based photographer. He received his M.F.A. in photography from the Massachusetts College of Art + Design in 1998. His work is included in the permanent collections of the Fogg Art Museum at Harvard University, the Center for Creative Photography at the University of Arizona, and the Addison Gallery of American Art at Phillips Academy in Andover. His work has been exhibited at Smith College Museum of Art, Julie Saul Gallery, Bonni Benrubi Gallery, Howard Yezerski Gallery, and Elias Fine Art. His work has been reviewed in many publications. In 2004 and 2005, he was the Edward E. Elson Artist-in-Residence at the Addison Gallery of American Art, where he had his first solo museum exhibition. He is an adjunct professor in studio foundations at the Massachusetts College of Art + Design. In August 2008, he is scheduled to be artist-in-residence at Light Work, Syracuse University. For more information, students should visit http://www.oscarpalacio.net.

Constanze Ruhm is an artist and filmmaker based in Vienna and Berlin. Her films and installations have been exhibited internationally at the Busan Biennale, Korea, 3rd Berlin Biennale, and the Venice Biennale, among many other venues. In 2004, she had a solo exhibition at Kunsthalle. Exhibitions include Museo de Arte Reina Sofia, Engholm Gallery and Generali Foundation, and 57 Berlinale. She has also curated a number of exhibitions and film-screening programs. She has been a Professor for Film and Video at Merz Academy Stuttgart and currently is Professor for Art and Media at the Academy of Fine Arts in Vienna. To see her work, students should visit http://www.constanzeruhm.net.

Sunanda K. Sanyal is an art historian with a Ph.D. in art history from Emory. He has been teaching at The Art Institute of Boston since 1999 and has chaired panels on contemporary artists of color at various conferences. Sanyal's recent publications include *Kabiito Richard's Paintings: A Local Reinvention in a Global Perspective* (*African Arts*, 2004); *The Local and Beyond: Francis Nnaggenda's Sculptural Innovations (NKA* spring/summer, 2003); *Transgressing Borders, Shaping an Art History: Rose Kirumira and Makerere's Legacy* (In *African Art, Visual Culture and the Museum: Sights/Sites of Creativity and Conflict*, ed. Tobias Doering); *Art Training in Kenya and Tanzania* (In *An Anthology of African Art: The Twentieth Century*, eds. Jean Loup Pivin and N'Gone Fall); and *Modernism and Cultural Politics in East Africa: Cecil Todd's Drawings of the Uganda Martyr (African Arts* UCLA, 39(1), 2006, pp. 50–9).

Julia Scher is a video, photo, and installation artist who often works with Surveillance. Scher reminds us of the fact that we are often unaware of the dangers constituted by the increasingly omnipresent surveillance systems, constantly monitoring us in the public space and in our private rooms. Security By Julia combines interactive surveillance apparatuses with fake guards, where ordinary people play the role of artist-on-alert. Her work has been widely exhibited in Europe, Asia, and North America. Her books include *Tell Me When You're Ready* (PFM Publishers, 2002) and *Julia Scher: Always There* (Lukas and Sternberg Publishers, 2002). More information can be found at http://web.mit.edu/vap/workandresearch/pub/publications_scher_books.html.

Laurel Sparks is a Boston-based painter who received her M.F.A. from the Milton Avery Graduate School of Art at Bard College '04. She is represented by the Howard Yezerski Gallery. Exhibitions include the DeCordova Museum, Hessel Museum at Bard College, and the Museum of Fine Arts, Boston. She has taught at the School of the Museum of Fine Arts, Boston; Massachusetts College of Art; Montserrat College of Art; and The Art Institute of Boston's M.F.A. in Visual Arts Program.

Stuart Steck has worked as both a curator and an academic. His current interests focus on postwar art and critical theory. He has taught at The Art Institute of Boston since 1998. In addition to serving on the faculty at AIB, he has held teaching positions at MIT, Brown, Boston University, and Suffolk University. Most recently, Steck published essays on Ellsworth Kelly and Sung Ho Kim (forthcoming), with whom he recently collaborated on an architectural project. Steck received his M.A. in art history from Boston University, where he is currently a doctoral candidate. His dissertation is entitled *Veiling the Subject: Ellsworth Kelly and the Discourses of Modernism.* Steck has taught critical theory in the M.F.A. program at AIB for the last three residencies.

James Stroud, after receiving a master's degree in painting and printmaking from the Yale School of Art in 1984, established Center Street Studio, a professional printmaking workshop where he publishes prints with established and emerging artists. He has collaborated on hundreds of images with artists, employing a wide range of techniques, including intaglio, woodcut, and monotype projects. An active painter and printmaker himself, he is currently represented by the Barbara Krakow Gallery. His work is in a number of public collections, including the Museum of Fine Arts, Boston; the Fogg Art Museum at Harvard University; the Yale University Art Gallery; the Pushkin Museum in Moscow; the New York Public Library; and the Boston Public Library.

Oliver Wasow, photographer, is currently represented by the Kathleen Cullen Gallery in New York City. He has had a number of one-person exhibitions, including shows at the Janet Borden Gallery, Tom Solomon Gallery, the South Eastern Center for Contemporary Art, and Galerie De Poche. His work has also been included in numerous national and international group shows, including Image World at the Whitney Museum of Art in New York City and The Photography of Invention at the National Gallery of Art in Washington, D.C. His photographs are included in a number of private collections and various prominent public collections, including the Whitney Museum of Art and the Museum of Modern Art in New York City. Reviews of his work have been featured in most major art publications, including *Art Forum, ArtNews,* and the *New York Times.*

Deb Todd Wheeler is a Boston-area artist whose recent work is inspired by the idiosyncratic collections of the Kunstkammerns of nineteenth-century Europe as well as a timeless fascination with collecting, cataloging, and examining. Folding modern technology (such as microcontrollers, sensors, and motors) into the vernacular of eighteenth-century scientific instruments results in elaborate brass, glass, and steel viewing devices.

Visiting Artists, Curators, and Critics

Bill Arning, Nayland Blake, Holly Block, Barbara Bloom, Laura Donaldson, Maureen Gallace, Dan Graham, Gamaliel Herrera, Dana Hoey, Jacqueline Humphries, Wendy Jacob, Byron Kim, Steve Locke, Barbara London, Tony Matelli, Annu Matthew, Adam McEwen, Marilyn Minter, Gean Moreno, Rebecca Morris, Tom Patti, Alexis Rockman, Constanze Ruhm, Shelburne Thurber.

THE BARD GRADUATE CENTER FOR STUDIES IN THE DECORATIVE ARTS, DESIGN, AND CULTURE

Programs of Study

The Bard Graduate Center (BGC) for Studies in the Decorative Arts, Design, and Culture is a graduate institute affiliated with Bard College committed to the encyclopedic study of things in their historical context, drawing on methodologies and approaches from art and design history, economic history, history of technology, philosophy, anthropology, and archaeology. The project of the school is to study the cultural history of the material world.

Founded in 1993, the BGC offers M.A. and Ph.D. degrees. It is an international study and exhibition center in New York City devoted to the interdisciplinary study of the decorative arts, design, cultural history, history and theory of museums, Renaissance and early modern studies, cultural geography, American art and culture, Asian Art, the Arts of Antiquity, eighteenth through twentieth century design and European Studies, and the material culture of New York City. Programs are designed to prepare students for careers or career advancement in museums; galleries; auction houses; government agencies; art-related education, research, publishing, and communications; landscape architecture; historic preservation; and public garden administration.

There is hands-on examination of materials and objects and an extensive connection to special programs and exhibition projects with the Metropolitan Museum of Art, the New York Historical Society, the Brooklyn Museum of Art, and other major cultural institutions. As part of their studies, all students undertake an internship at one of more than 250 institutions.

A semiannual interdisciplinary journal, *Studies in the Decorative Arts*, is published by the BGC and features scholarly articles about the decorative arts and their interpretation as well as book reviews. Advanced graduate students are invited to submit articles for possible publication.

Research Facilities

The Bard Graduate Center occupies a six-story town house at 18 West 86th Street, a second town house at 38 West 86th Street, and a residence hall at 410 West 58th Street in Manhattan. Its facilities include a 40,000-volume research library with an extensive collection of periodicals, slides, and videotapes on the decorative arts and related disciplines; exhibition galleries; classrooms; a student lounge; and offices.

Financial Aid

The BGC offers fellowships, scholarships, and a student campus employment program. Aid is awarded on the basis of need and merit. Financial aid applications are due by January 15. About 85 percent of students receive aid.

Cost of Study

The average annual tuition for incoming full-time students in the 2007–08 academic year was $24,570 for M.A. students, based on a cost of $910 per credit; new M.A. students also paid fees totaling $500. Tuition and fees for Ph.D. students averaged $30,776 for incoming full-time students in the 2007–08 academic year; they vary for subsequent years of doctoral work. Students may contact the Office of Admissions for more detailed and updated fee schedules.

Living and Housing Costs

Bard Hall, located at 410 West 58th Street, provides housing for students, faculty members, and visiting scholars. Nine residential floors offer a variety of furnished studios and one- and two-bedroom suites with kitchens and baths. Apartments are offered for an 11½-month residency beginning July 1 and continuing through June 15. For the 2007–08 academic year, the cost for an 11½-month term was $12,075 for a studio unit, $14,490 for a one-bedroom unit, and $11,960 per student for a two-bedroom unit.

Student Group

The Bard Graduate Center accepts approximately 20–25 full-time and a limited number of part-time students into the program annually. Applications are received from many countries and from across the United States. The BGC welcomes students of all ages and backgrounds as well as working professionals.

Location

The Bard Graduate Center is located on the Upper West Side of Manhattan, near Central Park. It is situated in a landmark neighborhood conveniently served by public transportation, with easy access to the innumerable museums, libraries, auction houses, and galleries of metropolitan New York.

The College and The Center

Established by Bard College in 1993, the Bard Graduate Center is one of the many "satellite" institutions that surround the 133-year-old undergraduate liberal arts college. Others include the Jerome Levy Economics Institute of Bard College, the Milton Avery Graduate School of the Arts, and the Center for Curatorial Studies in Art and Contemporary Culture. Other graduate divisions are located in Annandale, New York.

Applying

Students are admitted to the graduate programs annually for fall admission. The application deadline for admission and financial aid is January 15. Applicants to the M.A. program must have a bachelor's degree or the equivalent; applicants to the Ph.D. program are expected to have completed a master's degree in either the decorative arts or a related field. Because of the interdisciplinary nature of the program, there are no limitations on the applicant's prior field of study. Successful applicants, however, will have had some previous study, training, or work experience in the history of art, architecture, the decorative arts, cultural history, or material culture studies.

Applications should include scores on the General Test of the Graduate Record Examinations (GRE), three letters of recommendation, a short resume, a sample of scholarly writing, and a statement of intent describing academic and professional objectives. International candidates must submit TOEFL scores and a Certification of Finances. An interview is required. The application fee for 2008–09 is $50.

Correspondence and Information

Office of Admissions
The Bard Graduate Center for Studies in the Decorative Arts, Design, and Culture
18 West 86th Street
New York, New York 10024

Phone: 212-501-3019
Fax: 212-501-3065
E-mail: admissions@bgc.bard.edu
Web site: http://www.bgc.bard.edu

The Bard Graduate Center for Studies in the Decorative Arts, Design, and Culture

THE FACULTY AND THEIR RESEARCH

The BGC maintains a distinguished core of full-time faculty members, supplemented by eminent decorative arts scholars visiting from a broad range of national and international museums and institutions of higher learning.

The Bard Graduate Center Faculty

Susan Weber Soros, Iris Horowitz Professor in the History of the Decorative Arts and Director; Ph.D., Royal College of Art. Furniture studies.
Peter N. Miller, Professor and Chair of Academic Programs; Ph.D., Cambridge. European cultural history.
Kenneth Ames, Professor; Ph.D., Pennsylvania. Nineteenth century.
Stefano Carboni, Professor; Ph.D., London. Islamic art.
Jeffrey Collins, Professor; Ph.D., Yale. Eighteenth-century European art and culture.
David Jaffee, Professor; Ph.D., Harvard. Landscape history and cultural geography.
Pat Kirkham, Professor; Ph.D., London. Eighteenth-, nineteenth-, and twentieth-century design history and gender studies.
Deborah L. Krohn, Associate Professor; Ph.D., Harvard. Early Modern material culture in southern Europe and museum studies.
François Louis, Associate Professor; Ph.D., Zurich. Art history of Tang and Song China, Chinese goldsmithing.
Michele Majer, Assistant Professor; M.A., NYU. Costume historian.
Andrew Morrall, Professor; Ph.D., Courtauld Institute of Art (England). Fourteenth- to eighteenth-century European arts.
Amy Ogata, Associate Professor; Ph.D., Princeton. Nineteenth- and twentieth-century design history.
Elizabeth Simpson, Professor; Ph.D., Pennsylvania. The arts of the ancient world.
Catherine Whalen, Assistant Professor; Ph.D., Yale. American material culture and twentieth-century design.

Visiting Faculty

Timothy Benton, M.A., Courtauld Institute of Art (England). Twentieth-century art and architecture.
Thomas Campbell, Ph.D., Courtauld Institute of Art (England). Textile historian.
Ellen Paul Denker, M.A., Delaware. American ceramics.
Timothy Husband, M.A., Institute of Fine Arts, New York. Medieval decorative arts.
Juliet Kinchin, M.A., Courtauld Institute of Art (England). Twentieth-century architecture and design.
Pamela Long, Ph.D., Maryland. Medieval and Renaissance technology.
Caroline Maniaque, Ph.D., Paris VIII. Architecture and urbanism.
Robert J. Moes, M.A., Michigan. The arts of Japan and Korea.
Kevin L. Stayton, M.Phil., Yale. American decorative arts.
Paul Stirton, M.A., Edinburgh. Design history.

BRYN MAWR COLLEGE

Graduate School of Arts and Sciences
Department of History of Art

Programs of Study

Bryn Mawr's Department of History of Art offers M.A. and Ph.D. degrees in all areas of Western art history from late antiquity through the present, including film. It is one of three independent departments that comprise the Graduate Group in Archaeology, Classics, and History of Art.

The program of study is flexible and can be tailored to the goals and interests of individual students. Faculty members offer seminars on topics related to their current research, including late Gothic painting, Mannerism, seventeenth-century Spain and its colonies, German art criticism and aesthetics, self-portraiture, assemblage, video art, visual art and the Holocaust, and theories of authorship in cinema. Faculty members and students regularly participate in interdisciplinary seminars (GSems) offered by the Graduate Group, which also sponsors internships in Philadelphia-area museums. Recent GSems include Public Space, History and Memory, Rome and Its Representation, and Vienna 1900.

All course work and the M.A. thesis should be completed within two or three years. Ph.D. preliminary examinations should be taken in the fourth or fifth year, followed by the dissertation. For the Ph.D., the average time-to-degree for recent graduates is 8.5 years; over half graduated in 7.5 years or less.

Faculty members work closely with students to identify dissertation projects well suited to their strengths and interests. Recent topics include anatomical investigation and the gendered imagination in sixteenth-century Florentine art; Bronzino and the style(s) of Mannerism; Rembrandt's spaces; art and evangelization at Santiago Apóstol at Cuilapan; gesture, costume, and identity in Goya; intersections in the careers of Mary Cassatt and Edgar Degas; Byzantium in Bavaria; Kirchner's "Berlin Style" and its affinities with Bohumil Kubišta; the painting and writing of Giorgio de Chirico; the nature of representation in the art of Bruce Nauman; Andy Warhol, Robert Gober, Matthew Barney, and the contemporary object of art; modern primitive body art; and art, AIDS, and collective identity.

Graduates are prepared principally for academic and curatorial careers, but recent Ph.D.s are also employed or self-employed in business and not-for-profit corporations.

Research Facilities

The award-winning Rhys Carpenter Library, inaugurated in 1997, is a specialized library for history of art, archaeology, and classics. Fully wired carrels are reserved there for all graduate students in these fields. In addition to the more than 135,000 volumes in Carpenter Library, the tri-college library consortium of Bryn Mawr, Haverford, and Swarthmore Colleges contains more than 2 million volumes. Bryn Mawr currently subscribes to more than fifty art history journals. Online reference sources include the Bibliography of the History of Art, Art Index, ARTbibliographies Modern, Avery Index, ARTstor, and JSTOR.

Bryn Mawr's art collection numbers more than 25,000 items and is especially strong in works on paper. The College also owns more than 45,000 rare books, including one of the largest collections of incunables in the United States, and more than 13,000 photographs illustrating the development of photography since the mid-nineteenth century.

Financial Aid

Bryn Mawr offers a number of fellowships for full-time study, as well as grants, tuition awards, and summer stipends. Fellowship stipends begin at $17,500, including a summer stipend, and can be guaranteed for multiple years. Special awards include Areté (Excellence) Fellowships with a package of $18,500 plus health insurance. Each year, the Department offers four teaching assistantships and one collections assistantship, with stipends ranging from $14,000 to $19,150 including health insurance. Opportunities reserved for students in the Graduate Group in Archaeology, Classics, and History of Art are fellowships for multidisciplinary study, with twelve-month stipends of $19,000, and curatorial internships. Currently, 80 percent of the students enrolled in the program in history of art receive some form of financial aid.

Cost of Study

Full-time tuition, consisting of six courses per year, is $30,140; part-time tuition is $5090 per course. Units of supervised work cost $815, and the fee for maintaining matriculation (continuing enrollment) is $415 per semester.

Living and Housing Costs

Students live locally or in Philadelphia. Shared apartments can be rented for $600 to $900 per month, studio apartments begin at $700 per month, and food costs are about $200 per month. Other expenses include transportation (about $150 per month if commuting from Philadelphia) and health insurance ($1590 to $5150 per year, depending on age, for domestic students; $1432 for international students).

Student Group

In 2008–09, there are 30 students enrolled in history of art, 26 women and 4 men. One is international. Seventeen students have progressed to Ph.D. candidacy, 4 are candidates for the M.A., and the remainder are in course work

Student Outcomes

About half (51 percent) of Ph.D. graduates of the past ten years hold teaching positions at colleges and universities, including Aurora University; Colorado State University; Harvard University; Illinois State University; Maryland Institute College of Art; Rice University; Rochester Institute of Technology; Villanova University; University of Georgia; University of London; University of Minnesota, Duluth; University of Nebraska at Kearney; University of Pittsburgh; University of the South; University of Tennessee, Knoxville; University of Wisconsin–Madison; Touro College; and Ursinus College. Fourteen percent are employed in museums such as the Art Institute of Chicago, Carnegie Museum of Art, Dallas Museum of Art, Figge Art Museum, and the Whitney Museum. Others work in the private sector and for nonprofit organizations.

Location

Bryn Mawr is a suburb of Philadelphia, the fifth-largest city in the U.S. It is well served by rail lines and by bus. Philadelphia is renowned for music, museums, and sports, and it is also a culinary mecca, with restaurants serving many cuisines. The metropolitan area has more than 100 museums and fifty colleges and universities, with a total population of 220,000 students.

The College and The Department

Bryn Mawr is a liberal arts college for women, founded in 1885. It was the first women's college to offer graduate education through the Ph.D. and the first U.S. institution to offer fellowships to women for graduate study. Throughout its history, the College has been committed first and foremost to providing the most rigorous and challenging education to women and, in the Graduate School of Arts and Sciences, also to men. The current enrollment is 1,405 undergraduate students, 164 graduate students in the Graduate School of Arts and Sciences, and about 250 students in the Graduate School of Social Work and Social Research.

The Department of History of Art was founded in 1913 by Georgiana Goddard King, whose courses in Spanish art were the first graduate instruction in that field in the U.S. The graduate program was significantly enlarged by Charles Mitchell (1961–1980). Mitchell established an enduring strength in the Italian Renaissance and the classical tradition that was enhanced by Phyllis Pray Bober (1973–1991), while James Snyder (1964–1989) offered a complementary emphasis on Northern Europe. Collaboration with the program in Growth and Structure of Cities founded by Barbara Miller Lane (1962–1999), created a significant strength in the history of European and American architecture. The diversity of the current Department is due to the maintenance of these traditional specialties in combination with new areas of concentration (contemporary art, film) and rigorous attention to poststructural theory. The weekly colloquiums of the Center for Visual Culture enrich the mix with research presentations by scientists and social scientists as well by specialists in art, literature, and film.

Applying

Application for admission and financial aid should be made on the form available from the Graduate School of Arts and Sciences. Applicants can also download this form from the Graduate School's Web site at http://www.brynmawr.edu/gsas/. The deadline for admission with financial aid is January 2, 2009. Applications for admission without financial aid are accepted until June 30, 2009.

Students admitted to graduate work in history of art typically have reading knowledge of German or French (preferably both) and undergraduate training in art history and/or cognate disciplines in the humanities. Applicants must submit GRE scores; TOEFL scores, if not native speakers of English; a statement of interest, and a recent research paper or critical essay.

Students are encouraged to contact the Department and to visit. The Department's Web site is http://www.brynmawr.edu/hart/.

Correspondence and Information

Lea Miller, Secretary
Graduate School of Arts and Sciences
Bryn Mawr College
101 North Merion Avenue
Bryn Mawr, Pennsylvania 19010
Phone: 610-526-5072
Fax: 610-526-5076
E-mail: gsas@brynmawr.edu
Web site: http://www.brynmawr.edu/gsas/

Bryn Mawr College

THE FACULTY AND THEIR RESEARCH

David J. Cast, Professor; Ph.D., Columbia, 1970. Renaissance art and criticism, architecture post-1400, twentieth-century British art.

Christiane Hertel, Professor; Ph.D., Tübingen, 1985. German, Austrian, and Netherlandish art and architecture; German intellectual history; aesthetics and art theory.

Homay King, Associate Professor; Ph.D., Berkeley, 2003. American film history; film, feminist, psychoanalytic, and rhetorical theory.

Dale Kinney, Eugenia Chase Guild Professor in the Humanities; Ph.D., NYU, 1975. Late antique and medieval Italian art, medieval architecture, spolia.

Steven Z. Levine, Leslie Clark Professor in the Humanities; Ph.D., Harvard, 1974. Sixteenth- to twentieth-century French painting, psychoanalysis, self-portraiture, visual theory.

Gridley McKim-Smith, Andrew W. Mellon Professor in the Humanities; Ph.D., Harvard, 1974. Seventeenth-century Spanish painting and sculpture, scientific analysis of works of art, costume.

Lisa Saltzman, Professor and Director of the Center for Visual Culture; Ph.D., Harvard, 1994. Post–World War II art and theory, gender and identity, memory and trauma.

Affiliated Faculty

A. A. Donohue, Professor, Department of Classical and Near Eastern Archaeology; Ph.D., NYU, 1984. History and historiography of classical art.

Martha Easton, Lecturer, Department of History of Art; Ph.D., NYU, 2001. Medieval illuminated manuscripts, hagiography, feminist and gender theory.

Timothy Harte, Associate Professor, Department of Russian; Ph.D., Harvard, 2001. Russian avant-garde literature and painting, Russian and Soviet film, contemporary Russian culture.

Carola Hein, Associate Professor, Program in Growth and Structure of Cities; Dr.-Ing., Hochschule für bildende Künste (Hamburg), 1995. City planning and design, post–World War II Japan, architecture and planning education.

Madhavi Kale, Professor, Department of History; Ph.D., Pennsylvania, 1992. Postcolonial theory, labor history, Indian cinema.

Imke Meyer, Associate Professor, Department of German; Ph.D., Washington (Seattle), 1993. Modern German and Austrian literature and film, gender and sexuality.

Roberta Ricci, Assistant Professor, Department of Italian; Ph.D., Johns Hopkins, 1998. Medieval and Renaissance literature, philology, Jewish-Italian literature, comparative literature.

CALIFORNIA COLLEGE OF THE ARTS

Programs of Study

California College of the Arts (CCA) offers graduate programs in architecture, curatorial practice, design, design strategy, fine arts, visual and critical studies, and writing. All are two-year programs except architecture, which is a three-year program.

The Master of Architecture (M.Arch.) Program is accredited by the National Architectural Accrediting Board (NAAB). It integrates material, artistic, and critical approaches with the study and practice of architecture, focusing on design and fabrication. This three-year first professional master's degree program is designed for those who have earned a bachelor's degree in another discipline. Advanced standing may be granted to students who have previous education in the field or a B.Arch. degree.

The M.A. Graduate Program in Curatorial Practice offers an expanded perspective on curating contemporary art and culture, exploring the impact of artist-led initiatives and other efforts that take place outside conventional venues. Core faculty members include curators from Bay Area museums and galleries. The program prepares students for careers in museums and galleries, public art, project management, and publishing.

The M.F.A. Graduate Program in Design offers concentrations in communication design, industrial design, and interaction design. It is distinguished by its interdisciplinary nature and its emphasis on research, strategy, entrepreneurship, and futurism. Graduates are prepared to enter the professional design world at the highest levels. In a 2007 issue, *BusinessWeek* magazine named CCA one of the world's best design schools.

The M.B.A. in Design Strategy program, one of the very first of its kind, unites the fields of design, finance, and management. It combines lectures and seminars in organizational development, business strategy, leadership, entrepreneurship, and sustainability with practical studios and sponsored projects. Its unique residency structure—five once-a-month, four-day weekends on campus—accommodates working professionals.

The M.F.A. Graduate Program in Fine Arts is rooted in critically engaged studio practice. Interdisciplinary seminars, critiques, and visiting-artist programs ground students in critical theory and practice while they explore the potential of diverse media. The program explores both the specifics of particular disciplines and the points of interaction and overlap among disciplines. Students may choose to emphasize either studio practice or social practice.

The M.A. Graduate Program in Visual and Critical Studies is intended for students who aspire to write professionally about art, culture, architecture, and design. It emphasizes interdisciplinary and cross-cultural study, historical grounding, and the aesthetic aspects of written communication. Students explore and develop three crucial skills: attentive viewing, the development of analytical perspective, and creative and critical writing. The dual-degree option—an M.A. in visual and critical studies and an M.F.A. in fine arts, writing, or design—is for artists who wish to merge their studio practices with a deep critical understanding of visual culture.

The M.F.A. Program in Writing is for writers in every genre who wish to study in the creative environment of an art college. The program offers traditional workshops but also allows those interested in the large, evolving field of text and image to take courses in performance art, book art, video, film, and multimedia.

Research Facilities

CCA has two main libraries serving the fields of contemporary art, design, and architecture. Their combined collections include some 73,000 volumes, more than 2,000 videos, and 300 current periodical subscriptions. Students have free online access to more than 2,500 electronic journals and reference resources. More than 500,000 digital images are contained in the online ARTstor database. Students in the Visual and Critical Studies and Writing programs also have borrowing privileges at the libraries of the University of California, Berkeley.

CCA offers a wireless network and a wide range of digital technologies on campus. Studios and technological resources are usually accessible 16–24 hours daily. Campus media centers have a wide variety of equipment available for checkout. Thirteen dedicated labs offer a diverse and complete range of software and hardware for print and Web graphics, audio/video editing, animation, 3-D modeling, rapid prototyping, large-format color printing, and laser cutting.

The Graduate Studies Lecture Series features some of the world's most influential and innovative artists, architects, writers, scholars, designers, and curators. Each speaker typically also makes class visits or meets one-on-one with students. The fall 2008 lecturers are Monica Majoli, Eve Fowler, Wendy Ju, Rajkamal Kahlon, Anne Wagner, Kris Martin, Philip Kuberski, Vik Muniz, Maria Lind, Mami Kataoka, Paul Muldoon, Joel Sanders, Caroline Bergvall, Simon Leung, Rochelle Steiner, Blake Rayne, and Howard Rheingold.

The CCA Wattis Institute, located on campus, presents international contemporary art exhibitions and sponsors an impressive array of public artist talks, symposia, and performances.

Financial Aid

Financial assistance is available in the form of merit-based, need-based, and diversity scholarships; grants; teaching assistantships; federal loans; and work-study. Merit and diversity scholarships are awarded by the admissions committee; there is no separate scholarship application. Those who wish to apply for financial aid should complete the Free Application for Federal Student Aid (http://www.fafsa.ed.gov) and visit http://www.cca.edu/financialaid for more information.

Cost of Study

Tuition and fees for full-time study for the 2008–09 school year are $19,754 for the Graduate Program in Visual and Critical Studies and $32,690 for all other graduate programs.

Living and Housing Costs

Graduate students live off campus. Limited housing is available to CCA graduate students at the University of California's Mission Bay campus.

Student Group

In 2008–09, approximately 325 of CCA's 1,600 enrolled students are in the graduate division.

Location

CCA is located in the San Francisco Bay Area, a region known for creative and technological innovation and a thriving art and design community. The San Francisco campus is in the Potrero Hill neighborhood, near the city's design district and the growing Mission Bay neighborhood. It houses all seven graduate programs, a newly completed graduate center, and a graduate writing studio. CCA's 4-acre Oakland campus houses state-of-the-art facilities for ceramics, glass, jewelry, metal arts, photography, printmaking, and textiles.

The College

Founded in 1907, CCA is noted for the interdisciplinarity and breadth of its programs. In addition to its seven graduate programs, it offers twenty undergraduate majors in the areas of fine arts, architecture, design, and writing. Noted faculty members and alumni include the painters Nathan Oliveira and Raymond Saunders; ceramicists Robert Arneson, Viola Frey, and Peter Voulkos; filmmaker Wayne Wang; conceptual artists David Ireland and Dennis Oppenheim; and designers Lucille Tenazas and Michael Vanderbyl.

Applying

Applications for CCA's graduate programs must be received by January 15 for fall admission. Students may apply online or download an application at http://www.cca.edu.

Correspondence and Information

Enrollment Services Office–Graduate Admissions
California College of the Arts
1111 Eighth Street
San Francisco, California 94107-2247
Phone: 415-703-9523
800-447-1ART (toll-free)
Fax: 415-703-9539
E-mail: graduateprograms@cca.edu
Web site: http://www.cca.edu

California College of the Arts

THE FACULTY

Information about individual faculty members may be found at the College's Web site, http://www.cca.edu.

Juvenal Acosta (Writing)
Cassandra Adams (Architecture)
Opal Palmer Adisa (Writing)
Stephen Ajay (Writing)
Peter Anderson (Architecture)
T. Jason Anderson (Architecture)
Kim Anno (Fine Arts)
Craig Baldwin (Fine Arts)
Tom Barbash (Writing)
John Barone (Architecture)
Mara Baum (Architecture)
Brendan Beazley (Architecture)
Leslie Becker (Visual and Critical Studies)
Hugh Behm-Steinberg (Writing)
Dodie Bellamy (Writing)
Jeffrey Benningfield (Architecture)
Ila Berman (Architecture)
Michael Bernard (Architecture)
Kory Bieg (Architecture)
Rebekah Bloyd (Writing)
Keith Boadwee (Fine Arts)
Vivian Bobka (Fine Arts)
Michael Bogan (Architecture)
Rebeca Bollinger (Fine Arts)
Carol Buhrmann (Architecture)
Douglas Burnham (Architecture)
Raul Cabra (Design)
Gabrielle Calvocoressi (Writing)
Andre Caradec (Architecture)
Tammy Rae Carland (Fine Arts)
Sydney Carson (Writing)
Julian Carter (Visual and Critical Studies)
Valerie Casey (Design)
Kami Chisholm (Fine Arts, Visual and Critical Studies)
Alan Christ (Architecture)
Susan Ciriclio (Fine Arts)
Brian Conley (Fine Arts)
Lia Cook (Fine Arts)
Sekou Cooke (Architecture)
Benjamin Corotis (Architecture)
Betsy Davids (Writing)
Donna de la Perrière (Writing)
Sergio de la Torre (Fine Arts)
Gregory Di Paolo (Architecture)
Steve Diller (M.B.A. in Design Strategy)
Anthony Discenza (Fine Arts)
Mark Donohue (Architecture)
Susanna Douglas (Architecture)
Beth Dungan (Fine Arts)
Sally Elesby (Fine Arts)
Mona El-Khafif (Architecture)
Carol Elkovich (Fine Arts)
Kota Ezawa (Fine Arts)
Christopher Falliers (Architecture)
Thom Faulders (Architecture)
Maria Fedorchenko (Architecture)
Lisa Findley (Architecture)
Chris Finley (Fine Arts)
Jeanne Finley (Fine Arts)
Karen Fiss (Visual and Critical Studies)
Linda Fleming (Fine Arts)
James Forcier (M.B.A. in Design Strategy)
John Foster (M.B.A. in Design Strategy)
Amy Franceschini (Fine Arts)
Jacqueline Francis (Visual and Critical Studies)
Kathleen Fraser (Writing)
Gloria Frym (Writing)
Linda Geary (Fine Arts)
Jordan Geiger (Architecture)
David Gissen (Architecture)
James Gobel (Fine Arts)
Jim Goldberg (Fine Arts)
Caroline Goodwin (Writing)
Sharon Green (M.B.A. in Design Strategy)
Josh Greene (Fine Arts)
Anthony Grudin (Curatorial Practice, Fine Arts)
Doris Guerrero (Architecture)
Stephen Hartzog (Design)
Glen Helfand (Fine Arts)
Jens Hoffmann (Curatorial Practice)
Steven Skov Holt (Design)
David Huffman (Fine Arts)
Hugh Hynes (Architecture)
Margaret Ikeda (Architecture)
Matthew Iribarne (Writing)
Christian Jankowski (Fine Arts)
Oblio Jenkins (Architecture)
Evan Jones (Architecture)
Jordan Kantor (Fine Arts)
Geoff Kaplan (Design)
David Karam (Design)
Barry Katz (Design)
Lara Kaufman (Architecture)
Kevin Killian (Writing)
Lynn Kirby (Fine Arts)
Andrew Kudless (Architecture)
Genevieve L'Heureux (Architecture)
Amy Larimer (Architecture)
John Laskey (Writing)
Tirza True Latimer (Visual and Critical Studies)
Brenda Laurel (Design)
John Jota Leaños (Fine Arts)
Joseph Lease (Writing)
Steven Leiber (Curatorial Practice, Fine Arts)
Ines Lejarraga (Architecture)
Bruce Levin (Design)
Brendon Levitt (Architecture)
Kenneth Lum (Fine Arts)
Nathan Lynch (Fine Arts)
Sean Madden (Design)
Raimundas Malasauskas (Curatorial Practice, Fine Arts)
Elizabeth Mangini (Fine Arts, Visual and Critical Studies)
Robert Marcial (Architecture)
Ari Marcopoulos (Fine Arts)
Anne N. Marino (Writing)
Leigh Markopoulos (Curatorial Practice)
Christina Marsh (Architecture)
Daria Martin (Fine Arts)
Marina McDougall (Curatorial Practice)
Emily McVarish (Design)
Maria McVarish (Design)
Susannah Meek (Architecture)
Miranda F. Mellis (Writing)
Jeremy Mende (Design)
E. B. Min (Architecture)
Raffi Minasian (M.B.A. in Design Strategy)
Paul Montgomery (Design)
Carol Moukheiber (Architecture)
Ranu Mukherjee (Fine Arts)
Julian Myers (Curatorial Practice)
Scott Nazarian (Design)
Denise Newman (Writing)
James Nisbet (Design)
Margeigh Novotny (Design)
Shaun O'Dell (Fine Arts)
David Ogorzalek (Architecture)
Eric Olsen (Architecture)
Colin Owen (Design)
Miriam Paeslack (Visual and Critical Studies)
Holly Payne (Writing)
Sandra Percival (Curatorial Practice)
Peter Pfau (Architecture)
Aimee Phan (Writing)
Keith Plymale (Architecture)
Maria Porges (Fine Arts)
Renny Pritikin (Curatorial Practice)
Ted Purves (Fine Arts)
Michelle Richmond (Writing)
Katherine Rinne (Architecture)
Lacy Jane Roberts (Fine Arts)
Leslie Carol Roberts (Design, Writing)
Lisa Robertson (Architecture, Fine Arts, Writing)
Clare Robinson (Architecture)
Zack Rogow (Writing)
Rachel Schreiber (Visual and Critical Studies)
Neal Schwartz (Architecture)
Mitchell Schwarzer (Visual and Critical Studies)
Craig Scott (Architecture)
Judith Serin (Writing)
Sanjit Sethi (Fine Arts)
Matthew Shears (Writing)
Nathan Shedroff (M.B.A. in Design Strategy)
Linda Sheldon (M.B.A. in Design Strategy)
Kristen Sidell (Architecture)
Brad Simon (M.B.A. in Design Strategy)
Kathrina Simonen (Architecture)
Kristian Simsarian (Design)
Mara Holt Skov (Design)
Mary Snowden (Fine Arts)
Andrew Sparks (Architecture)
Raphael Sperry (Architecture)
Naomi Stanford (M.B.A. in Design Strategy)
Antje Steinmuller (Architecture)
Ryan Stroupe (Architecture)
Larry Sultan (Fine Arts)
Tina Takemoto (Fine Arts, Visual and Critical Studies)
Michael Tauber (Architecture)
Brian Teare (Writing)
Mark Thompson (Fine Arts)
Bruce Tomb (Architecture)
Ignacio Valero (Design, Visual and Critical Studies)
Deborah Valoma (Fine Arts)
Martin Venesky (Design)
Sandra Vivanco (Architecture)
Asher Waldfogel (M.B.A. in Design Strategy)
Ethan Watters (Design)
Megan Werner (Design)
Amanda Williams (Architecture)
Sarah Willmer (Architecture)
Federico Windhausen (Visual and Critical Studies)
Cooley Windsor (Writing)
Bill Wurz (M.B.A. in Design Strategy)
Ben Yalom (Writing)
Linda "L" Yaven (M.B.A. in Design Strategy)
Mario Ybarra Jr. (Fine Arts)
John Zurier (Fine Arts)
Leonardo Zylberberg (Architecture)

2008 MFA Exhibition (photo by Matthew Hughes Boyko).

The new Materials Resource Center contains more than 1,100 samples, from tufts of synthetic fur to futuristic aluminum foam.

All seven graduate programs are housed on CCA's San Francisco campus.

Carnegie Mellon

CARNEGIE MELLON UNIVERSITY

H. John Heinz III School of Public Policy and Management
Institute for the Management of Creative Enterprises
Master of Arts Management

Program of Study

The Institute for the Management of Creative Enterprises (IMCE) is a joint unit of the H. John Heinz III School of Public Policy and Management and the College of Fine Arts at Carnegie Mellon. The IMCE offers two distinct graduate degrees, the Master of Arts Management and the Master of Entertainment Industry Management.

The Master of Arts Management (M.A.M.) degree provides advantages and opportunities that cannot be found in an undergraduate education, in an M.B.A. program, or even in on-the-job learning. A business school is focused on managing in the corporate world, whereas an arts school focuses on the arts. But the M.A.M. program combines skills from both areas, providing aspiring arts managers with the tools and techniques they need to improve the efficiency and effectiveness in arts organizations.

The program's comprehensive curriculum blends the theoretical and the practical aspects of arts management. Core courses cover management, technology, financial, quantitative, and communication skills within the context of creative enterprises, both nonprofit and for-profit. Elective courses delve more deeply into specific management, technical, or arts areas. The Systems Synthesis, a group capstone project, allows students to apply new skills in problem-solving settings and gain experience in a team environment. The summer internship provides the opportunity to apply management skills and the beginning of a strong network of professional contacts.

The program is offered in a two-year track or a one-year track for those with substantial relevant professional experience. Students in the one-year track enroll in the summer and attend for three semesters, earning 168 units. All students must earn a GPA of 3.0 or higher. Students in the two-year track begin in the fall and must complete 198 units. In addition to the core curriculum and Systems Synthesis, these students must also undertake a summer internship between the first and second years. During the second year, students may also elect to undertake an apprenticeship with a local arts organization.

The M.A.M. program is host to a unique opportunity for graduate students in the Future Tenant exhibition and performance venue located in downtown Pittsburgh. Student directors at Future Tenant find a direct application for the theory they are learning in the classroom by administering every aspect of management for the space. Over the past six years, Future Tenant has allowed students to create, invent, and maintain imaginative, entertaining, and sometimes controversial forms of expression while keeping them connected to their artistic roots.

Research Facilities

The Center for Arts Management and Technology was created to investigate existing and emerging information and communication technology and stimulate thinking about the practical application of this technology for arts managers. Staff members work with researchers and practitioners interested in information systems technology, explore its viability and applicability in the management of visual and performing arts, and provide opportunities for managers to test the technology in their own organizations. The Hunt Library houses the University's collections in humanities, fine arts, social sciences, and business. The University Libraries also house several unique collections, including the Posner Family Collection of rare books and artifacts, located in the Posner Center.

Financial Aid

The Heinz School offers merit-based scholarships to eligible students entering the M.A.M. program. No additional application is required. Merit-based scholarships are awarded at the time of admission. Fulbright Scholars are eligible for half-tuition scholarships. Alumni scholarships are awarded based on public-interest work experience. Scholarships of at least $6000 per semester are awarded to Coro Fellows, returned Peace Corps volunteers, and Teach for America alumni. A limited number of Regional Leaders Scholarships are awarded to incoming full-time students who have demonstrated a commitment to the Pittsburgh community. Other merit scholarships are available, and eligible students may borrow up to $18,500 under the Federal Stafford Student Loan Program. Federal Perkins Loans are also available.

Cost of Study

In the 2008–09 academic year, full-time tuition is $18,000 per semester. Other expenses include $1000 annually for health insurance and $200 per semester in miscellaneous fees. Students can also expect to spend approximately $460 per semester on books and supplies.

Living and Housing Costs

A wide range of affordable housing options are available close to the Carnegie Mellon campus. Housing costs in Pittsburgh are typically lower than those in other urban settings. Room and board for a single graduate student average around $5600 per semester. Carnegie Mellon does not provide housing for graduate students.

Student Group

The M.A.M. program welcomes 45 new students each year, two thirds of whom are women and 25 percent of whom are international. Most students have a fine arts background, but many have backgrounds in business, liberal arts, and other fields. Nearly 75 percent of the students have been in the workplace for three years or less, while 15 percent have been working for five years or longer.

Student Outcomes

Graduates of the program are employed in a variety of professional and management positions that often support the mission and needs of artists or in arts, cultural, and other organizations that shape and influence the arts community. They are often promoted within one to two years of starting their first job.

Location

Carnegie Mellon is located in Oakland, a cultural center of Pittsburgh, Pennsylvania, on a 90-acre campus adjacent to Schenley Park, the city's largest park. The campus is conveniently located for easy access to many cultural and sporting events and is only 4 miles from the downtown business and cultural district. Pittsburgh is the thirteenth-largest metropolitan area in the United States. The city has good public transportation, diverse cultural attractions, and three professional sports teams. New York City, Philadelphia, Toronto, and Washington, D.C., are all within driving distance. Many recreational facilities, including ski areas and state parks, are located nearby.

The University and The School

Carnegie Mellon was first established in 1900 as the Carnegie Technical School through a gift from Andrew Carnegie. In 1912, the name of the school was changed to Carnegie Institute of Technology. Mellon Institute, founded in 1913 by A. W. and R. B. Mellon, merged with Carnegie Institute of Technology in 1967 to become Carnegie Mellon University. The University has an enrollment of about 8,500, approximately 3,300 of whom are engaged in graduate study. Rated one of the country's top public policy schools by *U.S. News & World Report,* the Heinz School advances public interest through research and education. By strategically integrating expertise in policy, management, and information technology, the faculty focuses on critical public issues, including arts management, crime and violence, health care, information systems and technology, and public policy.

Applying

Admission requires an undergraduate degree from an accredited university; a college-level quantitative course or completion of the Heinz School's Quantitative Skills Summer Program; and, for applicants to the one-year-track program, at least three years of relevant work experience or time in the Peace Corps, AmeriCorps, or the Coro Fellows program. Applicants must submit an online application form, official transcripts from all colleges attended, official GMAT or GRE scores, a current resume, a 1,000-word essay describing professional goals, and three academic or professional recommendations. Students whose native language is not English must submit TOEFL or IELTS scores. The deadline to apply is February 1.

Correspondence and Information

Jerry Coltin, M.A.M. Program Director
H. John Heinz III School of Public Policy and Management
Carnegie Mellon University
5000 Forbes Avenue
Pittsburgh, Pennsylvania 15213-3890

Phone: 412-268-2164
E-mail: hnzadmit@andrew.cmu.edu
Web site: http://www.heinz.cmu.edu/mam/

Carnegie Mellon University

THE FACULTY AND THEIR RESEARCH

Linda C. Babcock, James M. Walton Professor of Economics; Ph.D. (economics), Wisconsin–Madison. Negotiations and dispute resolution, gender differences in the propensity to initiate negotiations and how people react to women when they negotiate.

Jerry A. Coltin, Adjunct Faculty and Program Director; M.F.A. (visual arts), Kent State.

Pamela Lewis, Teaching Professor; D.A. (voice and speech), Carnegie Mellon. The Alexander Technique and its effectiveness in improving psychophysical efficiency in daily activity.

Donald Marinelli, Professor of Drama and Arts Management; Ph.D. (theater, history, literature, and criticism), Pittsburgh.

Dan Martin, Associate Professor of Drama and Program Chair; M.F.A. (arts administration), CUNY, Brooklyn. Use of information and computer technology in the arts management process, organizational and board structures.

Daniel Nagin, Teresa and H. John Heinz III Professor of Public Policy; Ph.D., Carnegie Mellon. Evolution of criminal and antisocial behaviors, deterrent effect of criminal and noncriminal penalties on illegal behaviors, development of statistical methods for analyzing longitudinal data.

Lowell J. Taylor, Assistant Professor of Economics and Public Policy; Ph.D. (economics), Michigan. Labor and demographic economics: effects of undocumented immigration for U.S. labor markets, minimum wage legislation on wages in low-wage industries, and food stamp use among low-income households.

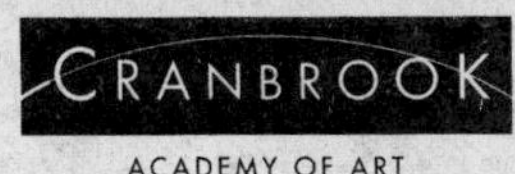

CRANBROOK ACADEMY OF ART

Programs in Fine Arts and Architecture

Programs of Study

Cranbrook Academy of Art, the only independent U.S. art school dedicated solely to graduate study, offers a two-year program for the Master of Fine Arts and Master of Architecture degrees. The Academy provides an intensely challenging and questioning environment for its community of artists. Departments of study are Architecture, Ceramics, Design (both two- and three-dimensional), Fiber, Metalsmithing, Painting, Photography, Print Media, and Sculpture. One artist-in-residence directs each department. There are no formal courses of instruction at the Academy. Students are provided with a studio and the responsibility to define and resolve their own creative projects. The context of work in the studios and academic progress is shaped by reading groups and seminars, regular departmental critiques, research and presentation projects, visiting artists, yearly full reviews by faculty members, and discussions of work on a one-to-one basis with the director and the student's department head. Lectures, symposia on current topics, gallery and museum visits, and field trips also contribute to the ongoing critical dialogue. Described as "a working place for creative art," the Academy is small, which provides an intimate social setting that fosters creative growth and expansive community experiences. Graduate students from around the world choose to study and work at Cranbrook because of its renowned faculty and its superb environment, which was designed in total by Eliel Saarinen. Graduation requirements are the completion of 60 credit hours (four semesters), a degree show mounted in the Cranbrook Art Museum, and the presentation of a written thesis.

All students attend full-time; part-time enrollment is not permitted.

Research Facilities

The Academy Library, which is oriented to the study of fine art, has an extensive rare book collection. The library is linked to six other libraries within the Cranbrook Educational Community to allow simple computer searches for all material within the Cranbrook archives. The library is also linked with other public and private libraries to facilitate interlibrary loans and research without students leaving the campus. The Academy supports a staffed media lab and a fully equipped woodshop and modelshop for fabrication of projects. The Cranbrook Art Museum features exhibits exploring new forms and ideas in the arts, crafts, architecture, and design. The museum conducts educational outreach programs and is the setting for lectures, degree shows, and the student-run Forum Gallery.

Financial Aid

Cranbrook offers competitive need-based aid for U.S. citizens and permanent resident aliens, maximized at one third of tuition. Merit scholarships and department assistantships, ranging from $1000 to $6000, are possible for second-year students. If funds are available, some first-year students may receive merit aid. The Academy participates in the Federal Stafford Student Loan Program and Federal Work-Study Program. Need-based aid is not available for international students. Cranbrook does not offer teaching assistantships or fellowships.

Cost of Study

Fixed costs for 2008–09 are as follows: tuition, $24,960; lab and activity fees, $600; accident and sickness insurance, $705 matriculation fee, $100; dormitory (double), $2250; and dormitory (single), $3950. Estimated additional costs for 2008–09 include the following: supplies, $3500; meals, $3500; transportation, $1900; and personal expenses, $2100. Costs are for a nine-month session and are subject to change.

Living and Housing Costs

Single students may need $15,000 for food, housing, and basic expenses. This budget assumes very minimal accommodations and does not reflect an allowance for spouses or dependents. The campus accommodates about 85 dormitory students at a very reasonable cost; there is no housing on campus for couples.

Student Group

The Academy of Art enrolls a maximum of 150 students, averaging 15 per department. Students from minority groups comprise about 6 percent of enrollment and international students up to 20 percent. The median age is 28.

Student Outcomes

The Cranbrook program is one of enrichment, and the Academy does not provide placement or keep statistics on placement. The primary goals for students are enhancing personal expression and expertise in their fields; teaching art, design, and architecture at the college level; and using the advanced credential in business and industry to enhance employment opportunities.

Location

The Academy is located in Bloomfield Hills, an affluent suburb about 25 miles north of Detroit, Michigan. The nearby city of Birmingham offers numerous galleries, restaurants and coffee shops, theaters, and shopping opportunities. Cranbrook is within easy reach of freeways to all areas of Detroit and its environs. A variety of theater, dance, opera, and musical productions, as well as arenas for professional sports, are readily available. Students actively participate in alternative art activities in the Detroit vicinity.

The Academy

The Academy is part of the Cranbrook Educational Community, which also includes an elementary school, middle school, and two high schools, along with the Cranbrook Institute of Science and the Cranbrook Art Museum. The Academy is a privately endowed institution devoted to superlative graduate education in the visual and applied arts. The Academy is accredited by the North Central Association and by the National Association of Schools of Art and Design. Cranbrook Educational Community is an Equal Opportunity/Affirmative Action educator and employer.

Applying

Admissions and financial aid applications, including the required Free Application for Federal Student Aid (FAFSA), must be submitted by February 15 for the following fall and November 1 for the following January. International applicants for whom English is a second language must have a minimum TOEFL score of 213 on the computer-based test or 80 on the Internet-based test. The Academy does not require the GRE. Admission is based primarily and competitively upon the student's portfolio. Interviews are not necessarily required as part of the application process but are encouraged for finalists.

Correspondence and Information

Dean of Admissions
Cranbrook Academy of Art
39221 Woodward Avenue
P.O. Box 801
Bloomfield Hills, Michigan 48303-0801

Phone: 248-645-3300
Fax: 248-646-0046
E-mail: caaadmissions@cranbrook.edu
Web site: http://www.cranbrookart.edu

Cranbrook Academy of Art

THE FACULTY

Director: Reed Kroloff, M.Arch., Texas at Austin, 1986.
Architecture: William Massie, M.Arch., Columbia, 1991.
Ceramics: *Appointment pending.*
Graphic Design/New Media: Elliott Earls, M.F.A., Cranbrook Academy of Art, 1993.
Three-Dimensional Design: T. Scott Klinker, M.F.A., Cranbrook Academy of Art, 1996.
Fiber: Mark Newport, M.F.A., Art Institute of Chicago, 1986.
Metalsmithing: Iris Eichenberg, Gerrit Reitveld Academy (Amsterdam), 1994.
Painting: Beverly Fishman, M.F.A., Yale, 1980.
Photography: *Appointment pending.*
Print Media: Randy Bolton, M.F.A., Ohio State, 1982.
Sculpture: Heather McGill, M.F.A., San Francisco Art Institute, 1984.

Renowned for its architectural beauty, the Cranbrook campus is enhanced by sculptures and fountains by Swedish sculptor Carl Milles.

Students' individual working studios, residences, and resource facilities form a harmonious small community.

GEORGE MASON UNIVERSITY

Department of History and Art History
Master of Arts in Art History

Program of Study

The general M.A. in Art History Program at George Mason University (GMU) offers a curriculum designed to prepare students for a variety of arts-related careers in museum or administrative positions and secondary teaching and for graduate studies at the Ph.D. level. Because it places special emphasis on new media skills, museology, and preprofessional internships, the program is unique in the region.

The Art History Program's 30-credit curriculum features required courses in art historiography and methods, history and new media, and the museum; a research seminar; and directed readings in preparation for the comprehensive exams. Students may elect courses from diverse graduate offerings, related fields, and internship opportunities. The University's joint Department of History and Art History affords students possibilities for related historical studies and training through the Center for History and New Media. Since the program began in 2006, students have gained experience from graduate internships at Dumbarton Oaks, the Textile Museum, and Christie's Auction House and through study abroad in London through the Sotheby's program.

The Department of Art and Art History's widely published faculty members teach and conduct research in many areas. Their interests and expertise range from ancient to contemporary in time periods; they span the globe to cover Europe, North and South America, Asia, and the Middle East; and they consider a full spectrum of art and artifacts. Students can expect small classes with personal attention to individual interests and career goals and the opportunity to get to know and study with one another in a small and collegial environment.

Highlights of the Master of Arts in Art History Program include training in new media as well as traditional research skills, seminar-size classes, late afternoon and evening classes, an individual tutorial class for each student, internships, and, of course, the unparalleled museum and library resources of Washington, D.C. An undergraduate art history degree is not required for admission.

Students in the program select a variety of elective courses in art history. Several specific courses in history, sociology, anthropology, and cultural studies may be included in the program. All students are required to complete a minimum of 30 semester hours of graduate-level work with a GPA of no less than 3.0. This includes 3 hours of Art History (ARTH) 600 Methods and Research in Art History; 15 hours of general elective 500- and 600-level course work in art history and related courses; 3 hours of applied learning: ARTH 593 Art History Internships or ARTH 594 The Museum; 3 hours technology/new media: HIST 696 Clio Wired: An Introduction to History and New Media or HIST 697 Creating (Art) History in New Media; 3 hours graduate research seminar: ARTH 699 Topics in Art History; 3 hours ARTH 696 Independent Directed Readings (an individualized tutorial that prepares students for the comprehensive exam); and a comprehensive exam. Students must also demonstrate reading ability in one relevant research language, to be approved by graduate coordinator. Students who did not major in art history as undergraduates are welcome to apply. They may be required to take up to four foundation courses (12 hours) at the undergraduate level beyond the credits required for the M.A. in art history. Full-time students generally complete the program in two years. Part-time students may take up to six years to complete the degree requirements.

Research Facilities

Students have access to the Department of Art and Art History's slide/digital image collection of 80,000 images as well as access to the University's subscription to Artstor, a digital library of approximately 550,000 images in the areas of art, architecture, the humanities, and social sciences with a set of tools to view, present, and manage images for research and pedagogical purposes.

George Mason is part of the D.C. Consortium of Universities, which also includes American University, Catholic University, Corcoran College of Art and Design, George Washington, Georgetown, and the University of Maryland. Students may enroll in courses at these universities as well as use their library facilities.

Students in the Art History Program also take full advantage of George Mason University's Center for History and New Media (CHNM). Since 1994, the Center for History and New Media has used digital media and computer technology to democratize history—to incorporate multiple voices, reach diverse audiences, and encourage popular participation in presenting and preserving the past. CHNM combines cutting-edge digital media with the latest and best historical scholarship to promote an inclusive and democratic understanding of the past as well as a broad historical literacy.

Financial Aid

At this time, student loans are the only available form of financial aid. However, Department staff members are working on securing a merit-based fellowship and 1–2 teaching assistant positions for the program.

Cost of Study

In-state tuition is $337 per credit hour, and out-of-state tuition is $845 per credit hour. There is a $60 graduate student fee.

Living and Housing Costs

Since GMU borders a major metropolitan area and resides in a nationally expensive county, the cost of living is relatively high. There are a variety of services available to students to locate affordable housing; the University provides no student housing for graduate students.

Student Group

The M.A. in Art History is a new program; there are currently 8 students enrolled in course work. Some anticipate going on for the Ph.D. in art history. Several others are looking to gallery or museum work, and 1 student will move into secondary school teaching combining history and art history.

In evaluating applicants to the program, faculty members examine both the liberal arts and humanities as well as the art history background of students, with the expectation that there is some prior experience in art history. They also look for evidence of writing, speaking, and research ability.

Location

Located in Fairfax, Virginia, just 15 miles from Washington, D.C., George Mason has emerged in the past decade as a major university in the state and the nation. Its development has been shaped in response to the educational needs of the northern Virginia cosmopolitan constituency. Near the D.C. metro, the University is within close reach of two major airports and the Northeast corridor via Amtrak.

Students benefit from proximity to the Library of Congress and the region's rich variety of museums, including the National Gallery of Art, the Corcoran, the Hirshhorn, the Freer-Sackler Galleries of Asian Art, the National Museum of African Art, the Phillips Collection, Dumbarton Oaks, the Textile Museum, the Renwick Gallery, the Smithsonian American Art Museum, the National Portrait Gallery, the National Museum of Women in the Arts, the Art Museum of the Americas, and the National Museum of the American Indian, among others. The D.C. area boasts major professional teams in football, basketball, baseball, and hockey and offers scores of musical and theatrical entertainments at the Kennedy Center for the Performing Arts, the Shakespeare Theater, and the Arena Stage.

The University and The Department

George Mason University's Department of History and Art History features a distinguished faculty. Five members of the Department have won Guggenheim awards; 1 was granted a MacArthur Fellowship. In addition, faculty members have received fellowships from a variety of institutions, including the National Endowment for the Humanities, the American Council of Learned Societies, the Getty Museum, the Clark Institute, DAAD, the Center for Advanced Study in the Visual Arts at the National Gallery of Art, the Fulbright Program, and the Andrew W. Mellon Foundation, and several teaching awards. George Mason art historians also have been recognized with book awards, such as the James R. Wiseman Book Award from the Archaeological Institute of America. The Art History Program offers a curriculum in ancient, medieval, early modern, and modern European, American, Asian, Islamic, and Latin American art history. Affiliated with the Center for History and New Media, the program benefits from the center's international reputation for innovatively applying new technology to the study, preservation, and teaching of history and art history. Various foundations and agencies support the center's work, including the National Endowment for the Humanities and the Sloan, Kellogg, and Gould foundations.

As a relatively new institution, George Mason University is distinguished by the diversity of its campus population and programs. The residential population of undergraduates now provides a substantial collegiate feeling as do the University's Johnson Center and Fine and Performing Arts institutions.

The undergraduate and graduate degree programs in art history are located within the larger Department of History and Art History, which is part of the College of Humanities and Social Sciences within the University. The studio art programs are located in the College of Visual and Performing Arts.

Applying

For admission to the program, the applicant's undergraduate record, broadly with attention to art historical preparation, is considered. It is expected that students hold the equivalent of a minor in art history at the time of admission, although provisional admission may be granted without it. Students must also submit a resume and goals statement, two letters of academic recommendation, GRE scores, and an academic writing sample. GRE scores are waived if the student completed a bachelor's degree ten or more years ago or holds another graduate degree.

While applications are reviewed on a year-round, rolling, space-available basis, the date for spring admission is November 1 and for fall, April 15. Those interested in assistantships should apply by April 15. For further information, students should contact Ellen Wiley Todd, Graduate Director, at etodd@gmu.edu or 703-993-4374 or Sharon Bloomquist, Graduate Administrative Assistant, at 703-993-1248 or sbloomqu@gmu.edu.

Correspondence and Information

Ellen Wiley Todd, Associate Professor, Art History
M.A. Graduate Coordinator
Department of History and Art History
George Mason University
4400 University Drive, MS 3G1
Fairfax, Virginia 22030
Phone: 703-993-4374
Fax: 703-993-1251
E-mail: etodd@gmu.edu
Web site: http://historyarthistory.gmu.edu/art-history/masters/

Applicants should send materials to:
Graduate Admissions Office
MSN 3A4
George Mason University
4400 University Drive
Fairfax, Virginia 22030-4444

George Mason University

THE FACULTY AND THEIR RESEARCH

Lawrence Butler, Associate Professor; Ph.D., Pennsylvania, 1989. Medieval, Byzantine, and Islamic art history and architecture.
Robert DeCaroli, Associate Professor; Ph.D., UCLA, 1999. Asia, Southeast and South Asian art history.
Marion Deshmukh, Associate Professor; Ph.D., Columbia, 1975. Modern European and German art history, intersection between painting and politics in nineteenth- and twentieth-century Germany.
Michele Greet, Assistant Professor; Ph.D., NYU, 2004. Latin American and Modern European art.
Christopher Gregg, Term Assistant Professor; Ph.D., North Carolina at Chapel Hill, 2000. Greek and Roman art.
Carol C. Mattusch, Full Professor; Ph.D., North Carolina at Chapel Hill, 1975. Greek and Roman art and archaeology.
Margaret Richardson, Term Assistant Professor; Ph.D., Virginia Commonwealth, 2005. Modern and contemporary art of Asia.
Ellen Wiley Todd, Associate Professor; Ph.D., Stanford, 1987. Art of the United States.

THE JOHNS HOPKINS UNIVERSITY

Zanvyl Krieger School of Arts and Sciences Advanced Academic Programs Master of Arts in Museum Studies

Program of Study

Museums of the twenty-first century are in the midst of a tremendous period of growth and change. New demands and challenges are emerging in every aspect of the museum landscape. Innovations in information and communication technologies are being integrated into the core strategies of the museum. The Johns Hopkins museum studies graduate program, an almost fully online degree program, aims to provide a perspective on the theory and practice of museums in a changing technological, social, and political environment for current and future museum professionals. The program emphasizes the role of technology as a pervasive aspect in today's museum; examines new models of education, exhibition, and business strategies; and explores the role of the museum as an agent of social change.

Students take nine online courses and one 2-week on-site seminar in Washington, D.C., to complete the degree. All online classes are offered as asynchronous learning experiences, allowing maximum flexibility in a student's schedule. As this is an online program, it is able to offer the expertise of highly regarded professors and museum professionals from around the world, innovative virtual field trips, and global resources from a wide array of museums. An international student body provides diverse perspectives and experiences in a dynamic online learning environment.

Students interested in all types of museums, including history, technology, science, art, special-topic, or themed museums; historic sites; national parks; and zoos, are welcome to apply.

Research Facilities

The Sheridan Libraries encompass the Milton S. Eisenhower Library and its collections at the Albert D. Hutzler Reading Room, the John Work Garrett Library at Evergreen House, and the George Peabody Library at Mt. Vernon Place. Together, these collections provide the major research library resources for the University. The Milton S. Eisenhower Library, the University's principal research library, includes specialized facilities and collections in medicine, public health, engineering, international affairs, and music. The Sheridan Libraries collections contain more than 2.6 million books, over 30,000 print and electronic journal subscriptions, more than 600,000 e-books, over 7,000 videos and DVDs, 215,000 maps, and 4.1 million microforms. University students have access to the libraries at five academic centers in the Baltimore-Washington metropolitan area. In addition, the interlibrary loan department makes the research collection of the nation available to faculty members and students. The library also provides easy access to a wide selection of electronic information resources, including the library's online catalog, and numerous electronic abstracting and indexing tools. Many of the databases are accessible remotely. The library offers a variety of instructional services, including orientation tours, and electronic classrooms designed to explain the library resources available for research and scholarship. Librarians help students on-site and electronically, and the library maintains an extensive Web site to take visitors through all of its services and material. Course material is available as electronic reserves for student use.

Financial Aid

Federal financial aid in the form of student loans is available on a limited basis to degree candidates who are enrolled in two or more courses per semester or term. More information is available from the Office of Student Financial Services (http://advanced.jhu.edu/admissions/financial-aid/).

Cost of Study

Tuition is $2560 per course in 2008–09. A $100 technology fee applies to online courses. Ten courses are required to complete the degree.

Living and Housing Costs

Students enrolled in the museum studies program are able to remain in their local home area while they take nine of the ten courses. A list of housing options in Washington, D.C., is made available for the required two-week on-site seminar.

Student Group

The Master of Arts in Museum Studies at Johns Hopkins attracts current and future museum professionals. Students with a wide range of undergraduate degrees (e.g., anthropology, art, art history, science, history, technology, philosophy, religion) are accepted into the program.

Location

The museum studies program is taught online within a course management tool, where students access course content and participate in discussion forums. A one-week orientation course, offered by the University, introduces students to the online learning tools and is required before taking the first online class. The on-site seminar takes place at the Johns Hopkins Washington Center near Dupont Circle in Washington, D.C.

The University

Privately endowed, the Johns Hopkins University was founded in 1876 as the first true American university based on the European model—a graduate institution with an associated preparatory college, a place where knowledge would be created and assembled as well as taught. The Zanvyl Krieger School of Arts and Sciences is at the heart of a small but unusually diverse coeducational university. The core institution of the Johns Hopkins complex of schools, centers, and institutes, the School recognizes the intellectual strength and education requirements of working adults. Through the Advanced Academic Programs, the School offers a Hopkins education to those wishing to attend graduate school part-time.

Applying

Students must submit the completed application form, the nonrefundable application fee, official transcripts of all previous college work, a resume, a statement of purpose, and two letters of recommendation.

Students may apply throughout the year and begin study during any of the three terms. When an application is received, every effort is made to render a decision and notify an applicant in time for the upcoming term. For more information, students should visit http://advanced.jhu.edu/admissions.

Correspondence and Information

Advanced Academic Programs
Zanvyl Krieger School of Arts and Sciences
The Johns Hopkins University
1717 Massachusetts Avenue, NW, Suite 104
Washington, D.C. 20036-1717

Phone: 800-847-3330 (toll-free)
E-mail: advanced@jhu.edu
Web site: http://museum-studies.jhu.edu

The Johns Hopkins University

THE FACULTY

Aaron Bryant, Ph.D. candidate, Exhibition Curator, James E. Lewis Museum of Art, Morgan State University.
Susan Chun, Cultural Heritage Consultant.
Laura Coyle, Ph.D., Proprietor, Curator-at-Large.
Herminia Wei-Hsin Din, Ph.D., Assistant Professor of Art Education, Department of Art, University of Alaska Anchorage.
Elizabeth Eder, Ph.D., Lecturer.
Bruce Falk, J.D., Contracting Officer, United States Holocaust Memorial Museum.
Kate Haley Goldman, Senior Research Associate, Institute for Learning Innovation.
David Greenfield, M.A., Instructional Technology Analyst, Loyola Marymount University.
Phyllis Hecht, M.A., Associate Program Chair.
Nik Honeysett, M.Sc., Head of Administration, J. Paul Getty Museum.
Deborah Seid Howes, M.A., Museum Educator in Charge of Educational Media, Metropolitan Museum of Art.
Robert Kargon, Ph.D., Willis K. Shepard Professor of the History of Science; Program Chair, Master of Arts in Museum Studies; and Program Chair, Master of Arts in Communication in Contemporary Society Program, Johns Hopkins University.
Susan Higman Larsen, M.A., Director of Publications, Detroit Institute of Arts.
Miriam R. Levin, Ph.D., Associate Professor of History and Art History, Case Western Reserve University.
Matthew D. MacArthur, M.A., Director, New Media Program, National Museum of American History, Smithsonian Institution.
Shelley Mannion, M.A., Freelance Designer and Developer of Cultural Media.
Sarah S. Marcotte, Education Programs Manager, Kidspace Children's Museum.
Carolyn Margolis, Special Assistant, National Museum of Natural History, Smithsonian Institution.
Marla A. Misunas, M.A., Collections Information Manager, San Francisco Museum of Modern Art.
Arthur P. Molella, Ph.D., Senior Lecturer, History of Science Department, Zanvyl Krieger School of Arts and Sciences, Johns Hopkins University.
Charles Patch, M.S., Museum Information Management Consultant.
Douglas Robertson, Ph.D., Financial Economist, Office of the Comptroller of the Currency.
Peter Samis, M.A., Associate Curator, Interpretation, San Francisco Museum of Modern Art.
Scott Sayre, Ed.D., Principal, Sandbox Studios/Museum411.
Angela T. Spinazze, M.A., Principal, ATSPIN Consulting.
Leonard Steinbach, Principal, Cultural Technology Strategies.
Robert Sullivan, Ph.D. candidate, Vice President, Chora.
J. D. Talasek, M.A., M.F.A., Director, Cultural Programs, National Academy of Sciences.
Selma Thomas, M.A., Independent Producer and President, Watertown Productions, Inc.
Kris Wetterlund, Principal, Sandbox Studios/Museum-Ed.
Holly R. Witchey, Ph.D., Director of New Media Initiatives, Cleveland Museum of Art.
Carole R. Zawatsky, M.A., Associate Director for Arts, Ideas, and Jewish Life, Jewish Community Center of San Francisco.
Deborah Ziska, Chief of Press and Public Information, National Gallery of Art.

LESLEY UNIVERSITY Let's wake up the world.™

LESLEY UNIVERSITY

Programs in Expressive Therapies

Programs of Study

Expressive therapists integrate the modalities of dance, drama, literature, music, poetry, and the visual arts with the practice of psychotherapy. For more than thirty years, Lesley University's expressive therapies programs have been at the forefront of expressive therapies training, offering degree and certificate programs that enable students to engage in the healing process through the therapeutic use of the arts. Its programs are accredited by the American Art Therapy Association, the American Dance Therapy Association, and the American Music Therapy Association.

The Master of Arts program is designed for individuals pursuing licensure who wish to practice expressive therapies interventions with a variety of clinical populations. The degree requires 60 credits of course work, a 150-hour practicum, a 300-hour internship during the first year, and a 600-hour internship in a clinical setting. The program can be completed in twenty-four months (including two summer terms) or in three academic years of full-time study. The nonlicensure option, which requires 48 credits of course work and 600 hours of field work, can be completed in two years of full-time study. Specializations in art therapy, dance therapy, and music therapy are available.

The Ph.D. program prepares students to become skilled educators, practitioners, and supervisors who contribute to scholarly research and practice in the field. During the first phase of study, students complete 24 credits of advanced graduate course work and write a plan identifying an area of doctoral study they wish to pursue. During the second phase, students take 15 credits of electives in their professional concentration, write qualifying papers, and fulfill their professional field service and socio-cultural perspective requirements. During the third phase, students construct dissertation proposals for their doctoral research and write their doctoral dissertations under the supervision of a dissertation committee.

Research Facilities

The Eleanor DeWolfe Ludcke Library houses more than 100,000 titles and 700 print journal subscriptions and offers a growing list of electronic resources. The collections are strong in all curricular areas, with an emphasis on education, psychology, human services, management, and expressive arts therapies. The library is a member of the Fenway Library Consortium and participates in Fenway Libraries Online, which allows library patrons to utilize the resources of all other area libraries.

The Institute for Body, Mind, and Spirituality was established for the purpose of promoting inquiry, training professionals, conducting research, developing new programs, and providing leadership in the area of mind-body health and education. The Institute draws upon the University's expertise in counseling psychology, expressive therapies, arts, education, and environmental studies to integrate holistic principles and methods into professional practice within a diverse society. The Institute adheres to a transformational approach to education and to the application of the principles of reflective practice.

Financial Aid

The Graduate Assistantship Program offers students the opportunity to assist faculty and staff members in academic activities. Merit-based institutional grants are awarded to students in on-campus programs. Graduate students who are enrolled at least half-time may also be eligible for as much as $18,500 in unsubsidized Stafford loans. Repayment begins six months after the student is no longer enrolled at least half-time. The Federal Work-Study Program offers students the opportunity to earn money through part-time employment. Awards traditionally do not do not exceed $2000 per year. Students who do not apply for work-study may still find part-time work through various University offices.

Cost of Study

In the 2008–09 academic year, graduate tuition is $765 per credit. Other fees include a $30 registration fee per semester and a $295 field experience fee.

Living and Housing Costs

Housing is not available for graduate students on campus. Information about local housing and housing assistance is available upon request from the Residence Life Office of Student Affairs.

Student Group

Students in the program represent a stimulating mix of personal, academic, and career experiences. Students typically range in age from 21 to 65, and several come from other countries. Many have had professional careers as artists and hold advanced degrees in art and other related fields. Others have less background in art but are committed to helping people through creativity. Students who enroll directly from undergraduate programs usually have prior clinical experience.

Student Outcomes

Graduates are prepared to work in a variety of clinical settings, including psychiatric hospitals, community mental health centers, adult day treatment programs, geriatric centers, schools, and clinics. They may work alone or in multidisciplinary teams with other mental health professionals, such as psychiatrists, psychologists, social workers, and mental health counselors.

Location

Lesley University occupies a campus near Harvard Square in Cambridge, an area that benefits from the many advantages of the cities of Boston and Cambridge. The University is connected to downtown Boston by public transportation. Within a 6-mile radius are numerous historical sites and cultural attractions, including theaters, museums, and concerts.

The University

Lesley University, founded in 1909 as a women's teaching college, continues its commitment to educating undergraduates while also offering graduate and Ph.D. programs in the fields of education, environmental studies, human services, counseling and psychology, expressive therapies, and the arts. With today's student in mind, Lesley University has successfully pioneered a wide variety of flexible programs for adult learners that share a commitment to quality, innovation, and the integration of theory with practice.

Lesley offers degree programs for learners at all levels. The University also supports several centers and hosts a variety of academic and professional conferences and institutes. Lesley programs operate throughout Massachusetts and in twenty-three other states as well as at an affiliated site in Israel.

Applying

Prospective students are required to submit a completed application form, official transcripts from all colleges previously attended, three letters of recommendation, a 3–5 page personal statement describing professional goals, a current resume, and a $50 application fee. Each specialization may have additional application requirements. All applicants are also required to schedule an in-person or telephone interview. An admissions decision is made as soon as all application materials are received.

Correspondence and Information

Office of Graduate and Adult Bachelor's Admissions
Lesley University
29 Everett Street
Cambridge, Massachusetts 02138-2790

Phone: 617-349-8300
888-LESLEY.U (toll-free)
E-mail: info@lesley.edu
Web site: http://www.lesley.edu/oncampus/

Lesley University

THE FACULTY AND THEIR RESEARCH

Nancy Beardall, Professor and Dance Therapy Coordinator; Ph.D.
Julia Byers, Professor; Ed.D., Toronto.
Mariagnese Cattaneo, Professor and Director of Field Training; Ph.D., Union (Ohio).
Robyn Flaum Cruz, Associate Professor; Ph.D., Arizona.
Karen Estrella, Assistant Professor and Expressive Therapies Coordinator; M.A., Fielding Institute.
Michele Forinash, Associate Professor, Music Therapy Coordinator, and Ph.D. Program Director; D.A., NYU.
Julia Halevy, Professor and Dean; Dott. Ped., Florence (Italy).
Michaela Kirby, Assistant Professor and Art Therapy Coordinator; Psy.D., Massachusetts School of Professional Psychology.
Mitchell Kossak, Division Director, Instructor, and Academic Coordinator of International Expressive Therapies; M.A., Lesley.
Vivien Marcow-Speiser, Professor; Ph.D., Union Institute.
Martha B. McKenna, Professor and Provost; Ed.D., Columbia.
Shaun McNiff, University Professor; Ph.D., Union (Ohio).

MEMPHIS COLLEGE OF ART

Graduate Programs in Studio Practice and Art Education

Programs of Study

Memphis College of Art is a professional center of art and design education, dedicated to preparing individuals for lives of creating, problem solving, and critical thinking. Small by choice and purpose, MCA is a cultural wellspring of creativity, nurturing and educating artists of all levels since 1936. Located within 340-acre Overton Park, MCA offers state-of-the-art facilities, excellent faculty members, interdisciplinary programs, and cutting-edge exhibitions to the public and those pursuing B.F.A., M.F.A., M.A. in art education, and M.A.T. degrees.

As a studio-intensive program, the M.F.A. at Memphis College of Art offers a catalytic environment with the goal of developing artistic practices that contribute significantly to contemporary culture. The program offers the opportunity to focus on traditional studio practice, digital technologies, or an interdisciplinary course of study. Areas of study include, but are not limited to, painting, drawing, photography, printmaking, papermaking/book arts, sculpture, digital media, or an individually tailored program of interdisciplinary study. Studio practice is enhanced with course work in issues of history, theory, and criticism. The program consists of structured course work and independent studio practice, with the second year culminating in the M.F.A. thesis exhibition and written thesis document.

The M.A. in Art Education program is designed for experienced, licensed educators who are ready to further develop their artistic, scholarly, and leadership capabilities in art education. The program explores new approaches to creating, teaching, and researching visual art processes. The M.A.T. in Art Education program is designed for artists committed to the growth and development of others through the exchange of knowledge, but who are not yet certified as teachers. It is a full-time, two-year program that integrates hands-on experience in teaching with in-depth studio preparation; ensuring students are informed by practice, current theory, and research. Upon completion of this program and obtaining passing scores on the required Praxis exams, graduates are eligible for K–12 certification in art in Tennessee and, by reciprocal agreement, most other states.

Research Facilities

Graduate students have full 24-hour access to the Graduate Center, a separate building that supports most of their activities. It includes a conference and seminar room, three dedicated computer labs, individual semiprivate studio spaces, three gallery spaces used throughout the year to exhibit graduate student work, and a separate space that accommodates installation work. Full-time graduate students have studio access during the summer between their two years of study. Available undergraduate facilities in Rust Hall include a 4,400-square-foot shop for woodworking, metalworking, mat cutting, glass cutting, and stretcher and frame construction; large metal, clay, and sculpture studios as well as a separate foundry and welding area for castings and metalwork; printmaking, papermaking, and book arts facilities for lithography, etching, serigraphy, and other print processes; and letterpresses and a bindery, wet room equipped with beaters, a 36-square foot vacuum table, hydraulic press, and pulper. The photo lab includes large- and medium-format work stations, a digital imaging area with digital cameras, slide and transparency scanners, flatbed scanners, high-resolution film printers; a lighting studio with electronic strobe equipment, and facilities for non-silver and alternative photo processes. A large-format digital printing lab for oversized imaging is also available.

Financial Aid

Aid is available for the M.F.A. and M.A.T. programs through renewable scholarships for incoming students, teaching assistantships (in the third semester only), work-study, and Federal Stafford Student Loans and PLUS loans, and merit-based scholarship opportunities are available for second-year students. Students interested in government-based aid are required to complete the Free Application for Federal Student Aid (FAFSA). Applicants should contact the Financial Aid Office or the Admissions Office for forms and information.

Cost of Study

Tuition and fees for the M.F.A. and M.A.T. programs for the 2008–09 academic year are $22,560. This does not include the cost of materials, supplies, books, and fees, which is estimated at $2500. The M.A. in Art Education and Alternative Licensure programs are $435 per credit hour.

Living and Housing Costs

The estimated average cost of food and housing and miscellaneous expenses for the 2008–09 school year is $12,000. There is a large variety of affordable housing available. Student residences conveniently located within walking distance of the campus provide living space for more than 150 students. Suite-style living (single rooms with shared common areas), shared apartments for two, and several single, efficiency apartments are available. The Office of Admissions assists students in locating a place to live and in obtaining roommate referrals.

Student Group

The student body is composed of students who have demonstrated achievement in their field. Many have pursued careers as fine artists, graphic designers, photographers, professional weavers, surface designers, interior designers, and teachers. There are nearly equal numbers of men and women. The students in the graduate program come from all regions of the United States and from several other countries.

Location

Memphis is a great place for an aspiring artist to study. Known for blues, barbecue, and Elvis, Memphis is also home to Fortune 500 companies, an NBA team, a symphony, an opera company, a theater, a number of colleges and universities, museums, art galleries, and almost 1 million residents. Annual festivals and celebrations are popular with students. The College itself is located in a 342-acre wooded park in midtown Memphis, adjacent to the Memphis Brooks Museum of Art, the Memphis Zoo, and a nine-hole golf course.

The College and The Programs

The College, founded in 1936, is accredited by the National Association of Schools of Art and Design and the Southern Association of Colleges and Schools. All of the College's graduate programs stress independent work toward self-defined career goals relative to the program chosen.

Applying

M.F.A. applications must be submitted by March 1 for the fall semester and November 1 for the spring semester. Graduate Education applications are accepted on a rolling basis. Application requirements include college transcripts, a portfolio with a minimum of fifteen slides (or other appropriate format), a resume, and one letter of recommendation each from a collegiate adviser or instructor and a contemporary. The applicant must also prepare a written statement of not less than 250 words describing his or her reasons for wishing to join the graduate program, life goals, and creative dreams. A personal interview or conference call may be required—a date and time is arranged by the Director of Admissions after all application requirements have been met. Students are accepted for admissions in either the fall or spring semester (or summer for the graduate programs in education), based on space availability. In addition, international students must submit a minimum TOEFL score of 525 (195 on the computer-based test), certified translations of academic records, and an affidavit of support verifying ability to meet projected annual costs.

Correspondence and Information

Office of Admissions, MFA
Memphis College of Art
1930 Poplar Avenue
Overton Park
Memphis, Tennessee 38104-2764

Phone: 901-272-5151
800-727-1088 (toll-free)
Fax: 901-272-5158
E-mail: info@mca.edu
Web site: http://www.mca.edu

Memphis College of Art

THE FACULTY

In addition to the regular faculty members listed below, there are guest faculty members and advisers each semester.

Nona Bolin, Professor; M.A., Memphis; M.A., Vanderbilt. Liberal studies.
Fred Burton, Professor; M.F.A., Wichita State; M.A., Kent State. Painting/drawing.
Haley Morris Cafiero, Assistant Professor; M.F.A., Arizona. Photography.
Rob Canfield, Associate Professor; Ph.D., Arizona. Liberal studies.
David Chioffi, Assistant Professor; M.A., Wesleyan. Graphic design.
Ellen Daugherty, Assistant Professor; Ph.D., Virginia. Art history.
Maritza Davila, Professor; M.F.A., Pratt. Printmaking.
Adrian Duran, Assistant Professor; Ph.D., Delaware. Art history.
Tom Lee, Associate Professor; M.F.A., Mississippi. Sculpture.
Susan Maakestad, Associate Professor; M.A., Central Washington; M.F.A., Iowa. Painting.
Remy Miller, Professor; M.F.A., Bowling Green State. Drawing.
Howard Paine, Director of M.F.A. Programs; M.F.A., Washington (St. Louis). Computer arts/design.
Joel Priddy, Assistant Professor; M.F.A., School of Visual Arts. Illustration.
Bill Price, Instructor; M.F.A., Southern Illinois. Sculpture/metals.
James Ramsey, Assistant Professor; Ph.D., Tulane. Art history.
Robert Riseling, Professor; M.A., Northern Iowa; M.F.A., Wisconsin. Painting/drawing.
Meredith Root, Assistant Professor; M.F.A., Wisconsin. Digital media.
Jennifer Sargent, Associate Professor; M.F.A., Arizona State. Surface design.
Cynthia Thompson, Associate Professor; M.F.A., Rutgers. Papermaking/book arts.
Leandra Urrutia, Assistant Professor; M.F.A., Mississippi. Sculpture.
Cathy Wilson, Director of Graduate Programs in Education; M.A.T., Ed.D., Memphis.
Jill Wissmiller, Assistant Professor; M.F.A., Northwestern. Digital media.

Memphis College of Art offers its students modern computer facilities.

A student at work at Memphis College of Art.

THE NEW SCHOOL: A UNIVERSITY

Parsons The New School for Design
Program in Fine Arts

Program of Study

Students committed to traditional studio practices in painting and sculpture often develop their work in an atmosphere of rigorous formal and intellectual involvement while being exposed to relevant theories and histories. For students interested in pursuing more groundbreaking territories in new media, Parsons' curriculum, faculty, and facilities provide opportunities for further exploration. The Master of Fine Arts is a two-year, 64-credit program for advanced students, offering a comprehensive experience in studio practice, critical studies, and the ever-expanding role of the artist in the contemporary art world. Students benefit from contact with members of the unparalleled artistic community of New York City and the larger university environment. Students have their own studios, work independently, and meet with faculty members for weekly one-on-one tutorials. These extensive individual meetings are augmented by interactions with visiting artists.

All students complete 52 studio credits, which are broken down into two components—graduate fine arts and graduate seminar—and 12 critical studies credits. Students work with each of the 5 core faculty members in a series of rotations. First-year students cycle through all 5 faculty members; second-year students choose 2 faculty members and return to each of them for two 5-week periods. Open sign-up periods and group critiques occur between the rotations. There are approximately 1 to 1½ hours of group discussion each week within the rotations. The balance of the time is spent working in studios with faculty members making one-on-one rounds.

The first-year graduate seminar is meant to expose students to a variety of significant discourses in twentieth- and twenty-first-century art, including the discourses of modernism, postmodernism, feminism, colonialism, and issues of racial representation; commodity culture, including ideas about collecting; and technology and the digital revolution. This is done through selected readings, video and film viewing, and art exhibitions. All of these are discussed in written assignments and in class. The seminar work is interspersed with studio visits. Each student is responsible for one major research paper, written in consultation with an instructor, in addition to small writing assignments that accompany each set of readings.

The second-year graduate seminar is thesis driven. Weekly and bimonthly writing assignments break down the required thesis subjects into smaller elements. Drawing assignments, individual studio visits, and slide lectures on the student's work augment the writing assignments and promote class discussion. At the end of the second year, students present a body of work completed in the program and a written thesis for the final master's review.

Research Facilities

The Adam and Sophie Gimbel Library of Art and Design includes books on art and design, special collections, and several hundred rare books. The library also contains a collection of mounted plates, slides, and periodicals on the history and the latest developments in fine arts and design. The Gimbel Library is developing a digital image collection that enables online access to images from Parsons' slide collection. The Angelo Donghia Materials Library and Study Center, funded by the Angelo Donghia Foundation, includes a library, a gallery, a computer lab, and a lecture hall. The library allows students and faculty members to review and check out state-of-the-art resources, putting the latest and most exclusive materials at their fingertips. A consortium links the libraries of The New School, New York University, and The Cooper Union.

Financial Aid

Graduate students are automatically considered for scholarship funds upon acceptance into the program. Scholarship recipients are notified of their award by either their program or a Student Financial Services award letter soon after being admitted. Graduate students should contact their academic department early in the admissions process for separate applications for institutional awards, such as assistantships. U.S. citizens and permanent residents applying for financial aid outside the University should file the Free Application for Federal Student Aid (FAFSA) by March 1. More information can be found at the Student Financial Services Web site at http://www.newschool.edu/studentservices/financialaid/.

Cost of Study

Full-time students pay $17,280 in tuition and $140 in fees per term. Additional fees may apply.

Living and Housing Costs

The University offers on-campus housing, University-run apartments, and assistance in finding housing off campus. The cost of housing, food, transportation, books, and living expenses in New York City averages $17,000 annually. For more information, interested students should visit http://www.newschool.edu/studentservices.html.

Student Group

There are 44 full-time students, 24 of whom are women. Of the total, 4 students are members of minority groups, and 8 are international students.

Location

Parsons The New School for Design, located in Greenwich Village, is at the heart of New York's vibrant architecture and design communities. Students are encouraged to take advantage of the museums, performance venues, and other cultural institutions that are only a walk or subway ride away.

The University and The School

Parsons is part of The New School, a leading university in New York City offering some of the nation's most distinguished programs in design, liberal arts, the performing arts, and social and political science, leading to seventy graduate and undergraduate degrees. To learn more, students should visit http://www.newschool.edu/degreeprograms. Parsons and The New School are fully accredited by the Commission on Higher Education of the Middle States Association of Colleges and Schools.

Applying

Students must submit the completed application, the $50 application fee, a resume, a statement of interest, official copies of all college transcripts, two letters of recommendation, and a portfolio consisting of twenty images of recent artwork as slides or in CD-ROM format, including an inventory list. DVDs and videotapes are also accepted for installations and performances. An interview may be requested. International students must also submit TOEFL scores—a minimum of 580 on the written test or 237 on the computerized version. The admissions application deadline is February 1.

Correspondence and Information

Donald Porcaro, Chair
Tom Butter, Director of Fine Arts M.F.A. Program
Master of Fine Arts Program
Parsons The New School for Design
25 East 13th Street, 5th Floor
New York, New York 10003

Phone: 212-229-8942
Fax: 212-741-3485
E-mail: porcarod@newschool.edu
butter@newschool.edu
Web site: http://www.newschool.edu/parsons
http://www.parsons.newschool.edu/finearts/

The New School: A University

THE FACULTY AND THEIR RESEARCH

Jackie Brookner, Environmental Artist and Writer; Ph.D. candidate, Harvard. Collaborates with ecologists and earth scientists on bioremediation/public art projects in the United States and abroad, including commissions near Dresden, Cincinnati, West Palm Beach, and St. Louis. Awards from the New York Foundation for the Arts, the National Endowment for the Arts, the Nancy Gray Foundation for Art in the Environment, and the Trust for Mutual Understanding. Exhibited at the Miro Foundation, Barcelona; the National Civil Rights Museum, Memphis; McKissick Museum, Columbia; Pamela Auchincloss Gallery and Oscarsson-Hood Gallery, New York City. Guest editor of the *ArtJournal* issue, "Art and Ecology."

Tom Butter, M.F.A. Program Director and Artist; Curator, "Delving and Tinkering," E. S. Vandam Gallery, New York; M.F.A., Washington (St. Louis). Taught at Yale, RISD, Tyler School of Art, and Brandeis University. Awards from the New York Foundation for the Arts and the National Endowment for the Arts. Exhibits in New York City since 1981. Published in *Artforum, Art in America, ArtNews,* and the *New York Times.* Selected collections in the Albright Knox Gallery, Buffalo; the Walker Art Center, Minneapolis; the Metropolitan Museum of Art, New York City; and the Pennsylvania Academy of Fine Arts, Philadelphia.

Peter Drake, Artist; B.F.A., Pratt. Solo exhibitions at the Lisa Sette Gallery, Scottsdale, Arizona; Elizabeth Leach Gallery, Portland, Oregon; and the Loew Gallery, Atlanta. Group exhibitions at Surface, Terence Rogers Gallery, Los Angeles; 3M and Fish Tank Gallery, New York City. Taught at New York Academy of Art and Maryland Institute, Baltimore.

Glenn Goldberg, Painter; M.F.A., CUNY, Queens. Awards from the Edward Albee Foundation, the National Endowment for the Arts, and the Guggenheim Fellowship. Selected shows at the Hill Gallery and Charles Cowles Gallery, New York City. Exhibited in the United States and Europe. Selected collections at the Brooklyn Museum; the Museum of Contemporary Art, Los Angeles; the Metropolitan Museum of Art; and the National Gallery of Art, Washington, D.C.

Sharon Loudon, Artist; M.F.A., Yale. Solo exhibitions at the Neuberger Museum of Art; Numark Gallery; Anthony Grant, Inc.; Kemper Museum of Contemporary Art; Urban Institute of Contemporary Arts; Rhona Hoffman Gallery; Dee/Glasoe Gallery; Haines Gallery; and Carnegie Mellon University. Group exhibitions at Berkshire Museum, Wave Hill, Williams Proctor Institute, the Hempel–London, Metaphor Gallery, Krannert Art Museum, and Museum of Art–Athens. Taught at NYU, Massachusetts College of Art, and College of St. Rose, Albany.

Lenore Malen, Artist and Writer; M.A., Pennsylvania. Solo exhibitions at Art in General, Rutgers University, University of Vermont, and Rhode Island School of Design. Group exhibitions at Fischer-Landau Center, Long Island City; and O'Hara Gallery, Bard College. Member of the Art Critics Association. Former executive editor of *Art Journal.* Senior fellow at Terra Foundation. Featured in *Sculpture, Village Voice, Art in America,* and the *New York Times.* Collections at Princeton, the Museum of Modern Art, Brown, Yale, and the New York Public Library.

Alix Pearlstein, Artist; M.F.A., SUNY College at Purchase. Exhibited at Artemis and Greenberg Van Doren Gallery, New York City; Lugar Commum, Lisbon; the Grossman Gallery, School of the Museum of Fine Arts, Boston; the Museum of Contemporary Art, Chicago; and Postmasters Gallery, New York City. Group exhibitions at the Solomon R. Guggenheim Museum, New York City; SMAK, Ghent; Whitney Museum of American Art, New York City; Hirshhorn Museum and Sculpture Garden, Washington, D.C.; Haus der Kunst, Munich; and Museum of Modern Art, New York City.

Bruce Pearson, Artist; B.F.A., San Francisco Art Institute. Solo exhibitions at Ronald Feldman Fine Arts, Gallery of Art Carlsen Center, and the Pierogi Gallery. Group exhibitions at the Galerie Les Filles Du Calvaire (Paris), Rotunda Gallery, Marlborough Gallery, DC Moore Gallery, White Box, Times Square Gallery, Miami Art Museum, Galerie Bernard Jordan (Paris), Robert V. Fullerton Art Museum, Cheryl Pelavin Fine Arts, Colby College Museum of Art, Apex Art, Dee/Glasoe, and the Rose Art Museum at Brandeis University. Public collections at the Karl Ernst Haus Museum (Germany), MoMA, Rose Art Museum, and the Whitney Museum of American Art.

Donald Porcaro, Chair and Artist; M.F.A., Columbia. Distinguished Teaching Award from Parsons The New School for Design. Solo exhibitions at the Kouros Gallery, New York City; Lowe Gallery, Atlanta; Lowe Gallery, Los Angeles; Grounds for Sculpture, Trenton; Nancy Solomon Gallery, Atlanta; and Byron Cohen Gallery, Kansas City. Collections at the Radford University Art Museum, Virginia; CUNY Staten Island; South Bay Center, California; and Rhone-Poulenc Rorer, Inc., Collegeville, Pennsylvania. Large-scale outdoor installations at Socrates Sculpture Park, Long Island City; Ward's Island, New York; and South Beach Sculpture Garden, Staten Island.

Mira Schor, Painter and Writer; M.F.A., California College of the Arts. Participant in Womanhouse Project of the Feminist Art Program, CalArts (1972). Taught at Nova Scotia College of Art and Design; SUNY Purchase, UC Berkeley, RISD, Sarah Lawrence, and the Skowhegan School. Previous co-publisher/co-editor, *M/E/A/N/I/N/G,* a journal of contemporary art issues. Published works include *M/E/A/N/I/N/G: An Anthology of Artists' Writings, Theory, and Criticism; Wet: On Painting, Feminism, and Art Culture,* a collection of essays; *Art Issues;* and *Art Journal.* Solo exhibition at Horodner Romley Gallery. Group exhibitions at the Marianne Boesky Gallery, P.S. 1 Museum, Santa Monica Museum, Neuberger Museum, and the Aldrich Museum. Awards from the NEA, Guggenheim, Pollock-Krasner, Rockefeller Foundation, College Art Association's Frank Jewett Mather Award, and Art Criticism.

Brian Tolle, Artist; M.F.A., Yale. Solo exhibitions at the Shoshana Wayne Gallery, Santa Monica; Schmidt Contemporary Art, St. Louis; and Basilico Fine Arts, New York City. Commissioned piece at the Irish Hunger Memorial, Battery Park City, New York. Group exhibitions at the Whitney Museum of American Art, New York City (2002); and in the Netherlands, Belgium, Italy, Germany, Switzerland, Great Britain, and Korea.

Visiting Critics and Lecturers

Almost 700 adjunct faculty members give Parsons students the unique opportunity to learn from New York's successful working artists and designers. Faculty members and visiting critics are principals in their own design firms, hold key positions in the art and design community, and frequently have their work exhibited and published. Parsons' strong ties to industry bring numerous guest lecturers and critics into forums and classrooms.

THE NEW SCHOOL: A UNIVERSITY

Parsons The New School for Design
Program in History of Decorative Arts and Design

Program of Study

Parsons The New School for Design offers a two-year Master of Arts (M.A.) in the History of Decorative Arts and Design Program jointly with Cooper-Hewitt, National Design Museum. The degree leads graduates to careers at museums, historic houses, appraisal firms, auction houses, galleries, publishing houses, and universities for decorative arts. The program focuses on the history of European and American decorative arts and design since the Renaissance, offering courses that address issues such as stylistics, techniques, social history, and critical theory. Its unique character is defined by its location within the Cooper-Hewitt—the only museum in the United States devoted exclusively to historical and contemporary design.

The curriculum offers courses in the media of ceramics, costume, furniture, glass, graphic design, metalwork, textiles, and works on paper. These courses go beyond connoisseurship to address a wide range of issues in decorative arts and design, emphasizing object-based teaching using museum collections. Students have the opportunity to work in the Cooper-Hewitt's four curatorial departments—Drawings, Prints, and Graphic Design; Product Design and Decorative Arts; Textiles; and Wall Coverings. Teaching experience is gained through assistantships in the undergraduate program at Parsons. The experience of graduate school in a professional setting facilitates the transition from academic training to career.

The degree is awarded upon completion of 48 credits with a minimum grade point average of 3.0 and the successful completion of the M.A. examination or thesis. Required courses are Proseminar, Survey of Decorative Arts I and II, and either Museology or Theory of Decorative Arts. The student declares a major and minor area of concentration at the completion of 24 credits or, with a 3.5 minimum grade point average, may petition to write an M.A. thesis. An M.A. examination is taken in the student's final semester; students writing a thesis are not required to take the exam. The program is two to three years of full-time study or four years of part-time study.

Research Facilities

Located in the landmark Andrew Carnegie Mansion on Museum Mile, the Cooper-Hewitt has encyclopedic collections of European and American furniture, glass, ceramics, metalwork, architectural and ornamental drawings and prints, textiles, wall coverings, and graphic and industrial design. In addition, the museum has the premier design library in the United States, with a collection of more than 55,000 books and periodicals related to the history of design, as well as extensive holdings of trade catalogs and archives of African American, Latino-Hispanic, and American designers.

The Adam & Sophie Gimbel Library of Art and Design includes books on art and design, special collections, and several hundred rare books. The library also contains a collection of mounted plates, slides, and periodicals, providing information on the history and the latest developments in fine arts and design. The Gimbel Library has begun development of a digital image collection that will enable online access to images from Parsons's slide collection. The Angelo Donghia Materials Library and Study Center, funded by the Angelo Donghia Foundation, includes a library, a gallery, a computer lab, and a lecture hall. The library allows students and faculty members to review and check out state-of-the-art resources, putting the latest and most exclusive materials at their fingertips. A consortium links the libraries of The New School, New York University, and The Cooper Union.

Financial Aid

Graduate students are automatically considered for scholarship funds upon acceptance into the program. Scholarship recipients are notified of their award by either their program or a Student Financial Services award letter soon after being admitted. Graduate students should contact their academic department early in the admissions process for separate applications for institutional awards, such as assistantships. U.S. citizens and permanent residents applying for financial aid outside the University should file the Free Application for Federal Student Aid (FAFSA) by March 1. More information can be found at the Student Financial Services Web site at http://www.newschool.edu/studentservices/financialaid/.

Cost of Study

Full-time students pay $17,280 in tuition and $140 in fees per term. Additional fees may apply.

Living and Housing Costs

The University offers on-campus housing, University-run apartments, and assistance finding housing off campus. The cost of housing, food, transportation, books, and living expenses in New York City averages $17,000 annually. For more information, students should visit http://www.newschool.edu/studentservices.

Student Group

There are 88 students in the program, 51 of whom are full-time, and 82 are women. This includes 13 students who are members of minority groups.

Location

Parsons' main campus is located downtown in Greenwich Village, a historic neighborhood with a style and atmosphere found nowhere else in New York City. The Village is home to design and art studios, galleries, shops, and restaurants as well as avant-garde artists, musicians, and writers.

With rich cultural resources, international sophistication, and cutting-edge attitude, New York City is a vibrant environment that has inspired and challenged artists and designers throughout its history. To Parsons' faculty, the city is an extension of the classroom and is incorporated into the basic fabric of the curriculum. New York is home to more than eighty museums, such as the Metropolitan Museum of Art; Cooper-Hewitt, National Design Museum; and the Museum of Modern Art. Parsons faculty members teach the architecture of the city, the fabric of its populations, and the language of its commercial and private communication.

The University and The School

Parsons is part of The New School, a leading university in New York City offering some of the nation's most distinguished programs in design, liberal arts, the performing arts, and social and political science, leading to seventy graduate and undergraduate degrees. To learn more, students should visit http://www.newschool.edu/degreeprograms. Parsons and The New School are fully accredited by the Commission on Higher Education of the Middle States Association of Colleges and Schools.

Applying

A minimum of 6 credits in American and/or European art history or equivalent experience are required. Students must submit the completed application, the $50 application fee, a resume, a statement of interest, official copies of all college transcripts, and two letters of recommendation—at least one from a faculty member. Applicants who live within 200 miles of New York City are required to be interviewed; those who live farther away are strongly encouraged to make arrangements to be interviewed. In addition, international students must submit TOEFL scores—a minimum of 650 on the written test or 280 on the computerized version. The application deadline is February 1.

Correspondence and Information

Master of History of Decorative Arts and Design Program
Cooper-Hewitt, National Design Museum
2 East 91st Street
New York, New York 10128

Phone: 212-849-8344
Fax: 212-849-8347
E-mail: historyofdecarts@si.edu
Web site: http://www.newschool.edu/parsons
http://www.cooperhewitt.org

The New School: A University

THE FACULTY AND THEIR RESEARCH

Complete faculty biographies can be found at: http://www.parsons.edu/faculty_and_staff/directory.aspx.

Donald Albrecht, Independent Curator; B.Arch., IIT. American architecture.
Eric Anderson, Ph.D. candidate, Columbia. Nineteenth-century German architecture and theory of design.
Laura E. Auricchio, Ph.D., Columbia. Eighteenth-century French women artists and contemporary visual culture.
David Brody, Ph.D., Boston University. Material culture, visual culture, and design studies.
Hazel Clark, Chair of Art and Design Studies; Ph.D., Brighton (England). Material artifacts and their relationships to social and cultural contexts; design theory and cultural studies.
Marilyn Cohen, Ph.D., NYU (Institute of Fine Arts). Popular culture.
Elyssa S. da Cruz, Research Associate, Costume Institute at the Metropolitan Museum of Art; M.A., Fashion Institute of Technology. Twentieth-century fashion and accessory design.
Elizabeth De Rosa, Administrator, American Friends of the Attingham Summer School; Ph.D., Columbia. Art nouveau and American and European art glass.
Clive Dilnot, Full-Time Faculty. Fine art, history of art, social philosophy.
Tracy Ehrlich, Ph.D., Columbia. Architecture and landscape design of early modern Italy.
Barry R. Harwood, Curator, Decorative Arts at the Brooklyn Museum; Ph.D., Princeton.
Kristin Herron, Director, Museum Program for the New York State Council on the Arts; M.A., Wintertur Program. Historic house museums.
Sarah E. Lawrence, Director, Master of Arts in the History of Decorative Arts and Design Program; Ph.D., Columbia. Art theory and Renaissance art.
Ulrich Leben, Associate Curator, Furniture of the Rothschild Collection at Waddesdon Manor, Buckinghamshire, Great Britain; Ph.D., Bonn. French and German decorative arts.
Sarah A. Lichtman, Graduate Teaching Fellow and Instructor; Ph.D. candidate, Bard Graduate Center. Interiors, feminist design history, twentieth-century design.
Mary M. Cheek Mills, Manager of School and Docent Programs, Corning Museum of Glass; M.A., Appalachian State. Western glassmaking methods.
Christopher Mount, Director of Exhibitions and Public Programs at Parsons.
Jeffrey Munger, Associate Curator, European Sculpture and Decorative Arts, Metropolitan Museum of Art; M.A., Harvard. European ceramics.
Tessa Murdoch, Deputy Keeper, Victoria and Albert Museum; Ph.D., London. Metalwork, eighteenth- and nineteenth-century English silver.
Anne-Marie Quette, Conférencière at the Musées Nationaux de France and Musée des Arts Decoratifs in Paris. Development of French furniture and interiors.
Ethan Robey, Assistant Director, Master of Arts in the History of Decorative Arts and Design Program; Ph.D., Columbia. American and European nineteenth- and twentieth-century visual culture.
Maria Ruvoldt, Specialist; Ph.D., Columbia. Renaissance art and feminist theory.
Denny Stone, Collections Manager, European Sculpture and Decorative Arts at the Metropolitan Museum of Art; M.A., Fashion Institute of Technology. Jewelry and costume.
Ioanna Theocharopoulou, M.Phil., Columbia. History of modern design.
Deborah Dependahl Waters, Deputy Director, Collections and Exhibitions at the Museum of the City of New York; Ph.D., Delaware. Nineteenth-century British and American silver.
John Wilton-Ely, Professor Emeritus, Hull. Grand Tour's widespread influence on the arts of England; eighteenth-century art, architecture, and decorative arts.

Pennsylvania Academy of the Fine Arts
Celebrating 200 Years

PENNSYLVANIA ACADEMY OF THE FINE ARTS

Graduate Program

Program of Study

The Master of Fine Arts (M.F.A.) program at the Pennsylvania Academy of the Fine Arts is a two-year (60 credit) course of study in studio art that involves daily interaction with an outstanding faculty of resident and visiting artists, regular private and group critiques, seminars in critical readings, a written thesis component, exposure to an outstanding visiting artist program, and participation in graduate drawing and painting courses that reflect the Pennsylvania Academy's emphasis on achieving a high degree of skill in drawing and studio art-making practice.

The master's degree program is centered in the traditional studio arts of painting, drawing, printmaking, and sculpture but within these disciplines displays a considerable diversity in approach. During both years of study, students enroll in drawing and seminar classes. Students may also elect to take classes within the Academy's Certificate program, with its emphasis on working from life and the acquisition of traditional art-making skills. The Studio Critique system allows the student to choose 3 faculty critics from a faculty of more than 25 visiting and resident artist/critics representing a wide range of studio practice.

All students are provided a private studio in the Samuel M.V. Hamilton Building and have access to the galleries of the Academy's renowned collection of historic and contemporary American art. The program of study culminates in the Annual Student Exhibit (ASE) in the museum galleries of the Samuel M.V. Hamilton Building.

The Post-Baccalaureate Certificate in Graduate Studies is a one-year, 30-credit nondegree course of study involving independent studio work, graduate-level class work and critiques from graduate faculty members. It is intended for new and developing artists with an undergraduate degree and a minimum of 30 semester credits in studio arts who may need an additional year of studio work in a rigorous, supportive community environment in order to develop a strong and competitive body of work, to prepare for application to an M.F.A. program, or to change artistic direction or media. Each student in the post-baccalaureate program has access to a private studio for the entire academic year. The program has an assigned faculty of artist-critics, and students may enroll in graduate-level studio classes or seminars in critical readings. Students may also elect to take classes within the Academy's Certificate program, with its emphasis on working from life and the acquisition of traditional art-making skills.

Research Facilities

With a collection of 16,000 volumes, the Academy Library supports the informational needs of the entire Academy community. The library provides research tools in print and electronic formats and more than 300,000 digital images, 150 journal subscriptions, 20,000 slides, and 250 videos (VHS and DVD). There are computer stations for research and writing papers, and wireless Internet access. A new Digital Lab is scheduled to open in September 2006.

The Pennsylvania Academy's High Victorian Gothic building was built in 1876 and designed by Frank Furness and George W. Hewitt. Identified as a National Historic Landmark, this building is one of the internationally known examples of historic, American architecture. It houses the Historic Studios and Cast Halls and has its outstanding collection of American art on permanent display. The six historic studios are designed in the tradition of the beaux-arts schools of Europe, with 20-foot vaulted ceilings and skylights with northern exposure. These majestic spaces contain the Academy's famous cast collections of antique and Renaissance sculpture, which have been part of the Academy's curriculum for nearly 200 years. Students study cast and figure drawing, modeling, and painting in the same studios used by Thomas Eakins and his students.

The Samuel M.V. Hamilton Building houses private studios for the students and faculty members of the B.F.A., Certificate, Post-Baccalaureate, and Master of Fine Arts programs. It contains large sky-lit painting studios, additional painting and drawing classrooms, a critique/lecture room, a student lounge with a panoramic view of the city, a rooftop painting terrace, and the offices of the painting and graduate programs. The first and second floors house the Fisher Brooks exhibition galleries, the Sculpture Study Center, and the School Gallery.

Financial Aid

The Academy's goal is to make it financially possible for any student accepted into the program to attend. Need- and merit-based scholarships, federal work-study opportunities, federal and private loans, and a ten-month tuition management plan are available. Aid is awarded on the basis of demonstrated financial need. Students applying for financial aid must file the Free Application for Federal Student Aid (FAFSA) by the March 1 deadline for fall semester. International students are eligible for partial, merit-based scholarship support and should complete the simple financial aid form that is available on the Academy's Web site, from the Director of Financial Aid's office at dcoulter@pafa.edu, or by calling 215-972-2019.

Cost of Study

Tuition for the M.F.A. program for the 2008–09 school year is $28,480, plus fees. There are additional costs associated with certain courses. Tuition for the post-baccalaureate program for the year is $22,770, plus fees.

Living and Housing Costs

Newly admitted students are eligible for Academy-sponsored, single-room housing at the International House–Philadelphia (I-House). Located adjacent to the campus of the University of Pennsylvania, just a 15-minute trolley ride from the Academy's buildings, I-House offers extraordinary student-oriented housing and programming opportunities. Other students choose to live off campus in a broad variety of housing options throughout the Philadelphia area. The Student Affairs Office offers assistance to new students seeking accommodations. The cost of living varies with the type of housing desired and the student's budget requirements.

Student Group

The Graduate Program enrolls approximately 40 new M.F.A. students each fall. There are about the same number of men and women, and 10–15 percent are international students from Europe and many other countries, including Japan, Korea, France, and Canada. The Post-Baccalaureate Certificate Program usually enrolls 10 to 15 new students each fall.

Location

The Academy's location in Center City Philadelphia is one of its greatest assets. Recently called "the next great American city" by *National Geographic Traveler* magazine, Philadelphia has a very active artistic and cultural scene and was recently rated one of the country's most livable cities, most affordable cities, and one of the safest among the larger urban centers. It has all of the advantages of a major (fifth-largest) historic city but its friendly, small-town character allows for easy navigation and quick mastering of resources. The Academy is located at the intersection of the Avenue of the Arts and the Museum District.

The arts are a major part of life in Philadelphia—theater, readings, concerts, exhibitions, cooperative galleries, and free access to many of the major museums with an Academy student identification card. Among the cultural institutions within walking distance of the Academy are the Franklin Institute, the Philadelphia Museum of Art, the Rodin Museum, the Philadelphia Free Library, the Kimmel Center for the Performing Arts (home of the world-famous Philadelphia Orchestra), and the Academy of Music. Only seven blocks away is Independence National Historical Park, which encompasses twenty-six historic sites, including Independence Hall, the Liberty Bell, and the Betsy Ross House. New York, Baltimore, and Washington, D.C., are all within 2 hours of Philadelphia by car, bus, or train.

The Academy

The Pennsylvania Academy of the Fine Arts has been attracting the finest faculty members and students for more than two centuries. One of the Nation's major cultural institutions, it is the union of an international contemporary school of fine arts and an outstanding museum collection of historic and contemporary American art. Founded in 1805, the Academy is the nation's oldest art school and museum of fine arts. An education at the Academy fuses the rich traditions of classical academic training with the most contemporary ideas and techniques. The faculty members of the Academy respect each student's individuality and strive to assist each student to fulfill his or her unique artistic needs and goals. The School of Fine Arts is dedicated to educating aspiring artists in the aesthetics, methodology, and history of the fine arts, specifically in drawing, painting, printmaking, and sculpture. The Academy accomplishes this by being a community of working artists dedicated to maintaining an inspired environment that fosters a commitment to engaging art and the creative act as a lifelong pursuit of the highest order.

Applying

Applications may be obtained online at http://www.pafa.edu. The deadline for admission to the M.F.A. program is February 1. The deadline for admission to the post-baccalaureate program is April 1. Applications are considered after the deadline on a space-available basis. A nonrefundable application fee of $40, payable by check, money order, or credit card, must accompany the application.

A portfolio of original artwork is required for admission. Portfolios should include examples of the applicant's most recent work and demonstrate both skill and the ability to work in a sustained manner. Fifteen to twenty separate pieces are required for the post-baccalaureate program and twenty for the Master of Fine Arts program. Slides containing three-dimensional works may include multiple views of single pieces. If using slides, portfolios must be presented in a standard 35mm slide format and placed in plastic slide sleeves. All slides and disks must be properly labeled, and the applicant must also supply an accompanying slide or disk inventory sheet listing pertinent information. Slides and disks are returned if the applicant provides a self-addressed stamped envelope.

Correspondence and Information

Stan Greidus, Vice President of Admissions and Financial Aid
Donovan Entrekin or Jena Campbell, Admissions Associates
Office of Admissions
Pennsylvania Academy of the Fine Arts
128 North Broad Street
Philadelphia, Pennsylvania 19102

Phone: 215-972-7625
Fax: 215-569-0153
E-mail: admissions@pafa.edu
financialaid@pafa.edu
Web site: http://www.pafa.edu

Pennsylvania Academy of the Fine Arts

THE FACULTY

Martha Armstrong: Painting.
Jan Baltzell: Drawing and painting.
Mark Blavat: Drawing and painting.
Katherine Bradford: Painting.
Tom Csaszar: Painting/writing/criticism.
Vincent Desiderio: Painting.
Murray Dessner: Painting.
Joel Fisher: Drawing, painting, printmaking, sculpture, and writing.
Sidney Goodman: Drawing, painting, and sculpture.
Neysa Grassi: Painting.
Denise Greene: Drawing, painting, and writing.
Gillian Jagger: Drawing and sculpture.
Daniel Miller, Acting Chair of Graduate Programs; Drawing, painting, and printmaking.
Kate Moran: Drawing and sculpture.
Michael Moore: Chair, Post-Baccalaureate Certificate Program; Drawing and printmaking.
Eileen Neff: Photography/writing/criticism.
William Scott Noel: Painting/drawing.
Irving Petlin: Drawing, painting, and printmaking.
Jody Pinto: Drawing and sculpture.
Kevin Richards, Art history/writing/criticism.
Osvaldo Romberg: Drawing, painting, and sculpture.
James Rosen: Painting and writing.
Bruce Samuelson: Drawing and painting.
Richard Torchia: Installation and writing.

PRATT INSTITUTE

School of Art and Design

Programs of Study Pratt has been educating professionals for productive careers in the fields of art and design since its founding in 1887. Pratt's School of Art and Design, one of the largest of its kind, offers an outstanding professional art and design education taught by a faculty of working professionals who bring high standards and current practices to the classroom. Faculty members have received more than eighteen Tiffany, Fulbright, and Guggenheim awards as well as other prestigious professional awards. Pratt's industrial design program was ranked third nationally by *DesignIntelligence,* as was Pratt's interior design program.

Pratt offers master's degrees in a variety of programs, including Master of Fine Arts in digital arts (computer graphics), history of art and design, or studio arts (new forms–nontraditional investigations, painting and drawing, photography, printmaking, sculpture); Master of Science in art and design education, communication and package design, dance/movement therapy, history of art and design, or interior design; Master of Industrial Design; and Master of Professional Studies in art therapy, art therapy–special education, arts and cultural management, or design management. A postbaccalaureate New York State certification program for the teaching of art in grades pre-K–12 is available for fine arts graduate students. Art therapy majors electing a special education concentration are eligible for provisional New York State teaching certification. Pratt also offers a dual degree in fine arts and library and information science as well as a certificate in museum studies.

Graduates of Pratt's design programs have the competitive edge needed to obtain top administrative and creative positions in design studios, businesses, various industries, and arts organizations; graduates of the computer graphics program may also work in interactive media or computer animation. Art and design education graduates are prepared to pursue careers in pre-K–12 schools, museums and cultural institutions, or colleges. Graduates of the creative arts therapy program work in psychiatric, medical rehabilitation, geriatric, and family therapy, school, substance abuse, and child-life settings. They also learn to work with a variety of patient populations, including patients with eating disorders and the homeless.

All graduate art and design curricula include supportive course work in the humanities. Students can choose from a wide array of course offerings, including art and design history, comparative literature, philosophy, foreign languages, and social sciences. The graduate programs require the completion of 34 to 68 credits (75 credits for the M.S./M.F.A. dual-degree program) and last from 2 to 3 years, depending on the curriculum and the number of prerequisites that have not been met at the time of admission. For the granting of degrees, all of the graduate programs require the submission of a thesis or a comparable effort. For the M.F.A., an exhibition and supporting corollary statement are required. Candidates for the M.S. and the M.I.D. degrees must present a thesis project that demonstrates a meaningful contribution to design and documents the supportive research that informs all phases of design and construction. For the M.P.S. in art therapy and the M.S. in dance/movement therapy, the thesis project may involve research, an extended case study, the development of a project implementing innovative techniques in therapy, or the opportunity to publish an article. For the M.P.S. in design management, the thesis project is the preparation of a business case study.

Research Facilities The Pratt Library contains 186,589 bound volumes, serial backfiles, and other material (including government documents); 251,603 audiovisual materials; and 3,996 microforms and subscribes to 925 periodicals. Pratt maintains numerous studios, shops, and technical facilities for work in all media as well as state-of-the-art computer facilities. Computer graphics labs include state-of-the-art Macintosh, PC/NT, and UNIX operating systems as well as digital video and audio systems. Pratt also has extensive gallery space for exhibitions.

Financial Aid Financial aid awards are offered through a variety of institutional, state, and federally funded programs. These include the Graduate Scholarships awarded by departments on the basis of merit, Federal Perkins Loan and Federal Work-Study Programs, the Tuition Assistance Program of New York State, and Pratt loans and student help. Assistantships are awarded on a competitive basis to continuing students in all departments. Special alumni-sponsored fellowships are also available.

Cost of Study Tuition for 2007–08 was $27,216 per year (24 credits, $1134 per credit), and student fees were $1190 per year. The cost of books and supplies varies widely, depending on the program in which the student is enrolled. Updated cost information is available at http://www.pratt.edu/financial_aid#.

Living and Housing Costs Campus housing continues to be expanded to meet students' needs and is available for single students on a first-come, first-served basis. Housing costs average $11,794 per academic year. Pratt offers limited graduate student housing two blocks away from the campus. There is a plentiful supply of moderately priced rentals in the immediate area and in adjacent neighborhoods for married students seeking housing and for those students choosing to reside off campus.

Student Group In educating more than four generations of students to be creative, technically skilled, and adaptable professionals, Pratt has gained an international reputation that attracts more than 4,600 undergraduate and graduate students annually from forty-seven states and more than fifty countries.

Location Pratt Institute's 25-acre, parklike main campus is situated among the turn-of-the-century mansions, Victorian brownstones, and wide, tree-lined boulevards of Clinton Hill, one of Brooklyn's landmark-designated historic neighborhoods. Midtown Manhattan, the heart of New York City, is only 25 minutes away by subway and offers students a vast array of professional, cultural, and recreational opportunities. Pratt also maintains a satellite facility in Manhattan's Chelsea district. Pratt Manhattan houses the Institute's graduate arts and cultural management, communications/packaging design, design management, facilities management, historic preservation, library and information science, and urban design; it also offers Associate of Occupational Studies (A.O.S.) and Associate of Applied Science (A.A.S.) degree programs.

The Institute A private, nonsectarian institute of higher education, Pratt Institute was founded by the industrialist and philanthropist Charles Pratt. Changing with the needs and requirements of the professional world for which it prepares its graduates, Pratt today educates 3,066 undergraduate and1,602 graduate students for careers in art and design, architecture, and library and information science.

Applying The deadline for applications and all supporting materials, including portfolio, is January 5. Applicants should include everything in one package, including recommendations in sealed envelopes with the reference's signature across the flap. Early submission of applications with all necessary credentials is highly desirable. For applicants who intend to file for financial aid, applications and all supporting documents should be received no later than January 5 for the fall semester and October 1 for the spring semester. Applications received after these dates are considered if openings exist in a particular program.

Correspondence and Information

Graduate Admissions Office
Pratt Institute
200 Willoughby Avenue
Brooklyn, New York 11205
Phone: 718-636-3514
800-331-0834 (toll-free)
Fax: 718-399-4242
E-mail: admissions@pratt.edu
Web site: http://www.pratt.edu
http://www.pratt.edu/admiss/request (to request information)

Pratt Institute

THE FACULTY

Art and Design Education
Amy Brook Snider, Professor and Chair; Ph.D., NYU.
Lisa Capone, Adjunct Instructor; M.F.A., Pratt.
Barbara Danish, Adjunct Associate Professor; Ph.D., NYU.
Mary Elmer-Dewit, Visiting Instructor; M.S., Pratt.
Sandra Edmonds, Adjunct Assistant Professor; Ed.D., Columbia Teachers College.
Theodora Skipitares, Adjunct Assistant Professor; M.F.A., NYU.
Aileen Wilson, Assistant Professor and Director, Saturday Art School; Ed.M., Columbia Teachers College.

Arts and Cultural Management
Monica Shay, Assistant Professor and Director; M.A., Regis.
James Clark, Visiting Assistant Professor; M.A., NYU.
Laurie Cumbo, Visiting Assistant Professor; M.A., NYU.
Larry DeGaetano, Adjunct Assistant Professor; M.B.A., NYU.
Bonita Kolb, Visiting Assistant Professor; Ph.D., Golden Gate.
Brad McCallum, Visiting Assistant Professor; M.F.A., Yale.
Elissa Moorehead, Visiting Assistant Professor.
Mario Moorehead, Visiting Assistant Professor.
Dorothy Ryan, Visiting Assistant Professor; B.A., Brown.
Susan Schear, Visiting Assistant Professor.
Denise Tahara, Visiting Assistant Professor; Ph.D., NYU.
Yolanda Trincere, Visiting Assistant Professor; Ph.D., NYU.

Communications/Packaging Design
Roger Guilfoyle, Professor and Acting Chair.
Chava Ben-Amos, Professor.
James Anderson, Visiting Assistant Professor; M.S., Pratt.
Warren Bernard, Visiting Instructor; M.S., Pratt.
Meri Bourgard, Adjunct Professor; M.A., Pratt.
Andrew Brenits, Visiting Instructor; M.S., Pratt.
Jean Brennan, Adjunct Assistant Professor; M.S., Pratt.
Steven Burnett, Visiting Associate Professor; M.S., Pratt.
Antonio DiSpigna, Professor; B.F.A., Pratt.
Tom Dolle, Adjunct Associate Professor; B.F.A., Rhode Island School of Design.
Kevin Gatta, Professor; M.S. Pratt.
Bob Gill, Visiting Associate Professor.
Graham Hanson, Adjunct Assistant Professor; B.F.A., Iowa State.
Bill Hilson, Adjunct Associate Professor; M.S., NYIT.
Milt Kass, Visiting Assistant Professor; B.I.D., Pratt.
Alvin Katz, Visiting Associate Professor; B.F.A., Ohio State.
Saima Kazmi, Visiting Instructor; M.S., Pratt.
Kim Kiser, Visiting Instructor; M.S., Pratt.
Tom Klinkowstein, Adjunct Professor; M.S., Syracuse.
Pinar LaCroix, Visiting Instructor; M.S., Pratt.
Gusty Lange, Adjunct Associate Professor; M.P.S., M.S., Pratt.
EunSun Lee, Visiting Instructor; M.S., Pratt.
Alex Liebergesell, Visiting Associate Professor; M.F.A., Yale.
Marilyn Lyons, Adjunct Associate Professor.
Scott Menchin, Visiting Associate Professor.
Ann Morris, Visiting Assistant Professor; M.A., CUNY, Hunter.
Eric O'Toole, Adjunct Assistant Professor; B.I.D., Pratt.
Peter Jay Pultorak, Visiting Instructor; B.A., Notre Dame.
Linda Root, Visiting Assistant Professor; M.S., Pratt.
Marc Rosen, Visiting Associate Professor; M.S., Pratt.
Bill Schiffmiller, Visiting Assistant Professor; B.F.A., RIT.
Marc Schneider, Visiting Instructor; M.S., NYU.
Christine Shin, Visiting Instructor; M.S., Pratt.
Cheryl Stockton, Adjunct Associate Professor; B.A., Point Park.
Alisa Zamir, Professor; M.S., Pratt.

Creative Arts Therapy
Laurel Thompson, Adjunct Professor and Chair; Ph.D. candidate, Union (Ohio).
Josie Abbenante, Adjunct Assistant Professor; M.A., Louisville.
Claudia Bader, Visiting Instructor; M.P.S., Pratt.
Donna Bassin, Visiting Associate Professor; Ph.D., Union (Ohio).
Beate Becker, Adjunct Associate Professor; M.A., Columbia Teachers College; M.S., CUNY, Hunter.
Pierre Boenig-Scherel, Adjunct Assistant Professor; M.P.S., Pratt.
Kim Bush, Visiting Instructor; M.F.A., Parsons.
Angela Cooper, Visiting Instructor; M.P.S., Pratt.
Barbara Cooper, Adjunct Associate Professor; M.P.S., Pratt.
Jean Davis, Adjunct Assistant Professor; M.P.S., Pratt.
Christina Devereaux, Visiting Assistant Professor; Ph.D. candidate, Santa Barbara Graduate Institute.
Ted Ehrhardt, Visiting Assistant Professor; M.A., CUNY, Hunter.
Judi Evans, Visiting Instructor; M.P.S., Pratt.
Alison Gigl George, Adjunct Assistant Professor; M.P.S., Pratt.
Corinna Hiller, Visiting Instructor; M.A., SUNY Albany.
Melissa Klay, Visiting Instructor; Ph.D. candidate, Pacifica Graduate.
Judith Luongo, Adjunct Associate Professor.
Julie Miller, Assistant Instructor; M.A., M.S.W., CUNY, Hunter.
Virginia Reed, Visiting Assistant Professor; M.A., New School.
Arthur Robbins, Professor; Ed.D., Columbia Teachers College.
Dina Schapiro, Adjunct Assistant Professor and Practicum Coordinator; M.P.S., Pratt.
Linda Siegel, Assistant Professor and Art Therapy Director; M.P.S., Pratt; M.S.C., New Seminary.
Suzi Tortora, Visiting Assistant Professor; Ed.D., Columbia Teachers College.
Elissa White, Visiting Assistant Professor; B.A., Goucher.
Joan Wittig, Assistant Professor; M.S., CUNY, Hunter.
Robert Irwin Wolf, Visiting Assistant Professor; M.P.S., Pratt.
Eva Young, Visiting Instructor; M.F.A., Art Institute of Chicago.

Design Management
Mary McBride, Chair; Ph.D., NYU.
Christopher Collette, Visiting Assistant Professor; M.A., Denison.
Lawrence De Gaetano, Adjunct Assistant Professor; M.B.A., NYU.
Michele Ferenz, Visiting Assistant Professor; M.A., Harvard.
Richard Green, Professor; M.S., Temple.
Jacqueline McCormack, Adjunct Associate Professor; M.S., Pratt.
James Murray, Visiting Assistant Professor; M.P.S., Pratt.
JoAnn Stonier, Visiting Assistant Professor; J.D., Saint John's (Minnesota).
Denise Tahara, Visiting Assistant Professor; M.B.A., NYU.
Marvin Waldman, Visiting Associate Professor; M.A., New School.

Digital Arts
Peter Patchen, Chair; M.F.A., Oregon.
Jamie Allen, Visiting Assistant Professor; M.F.A., NYU.
Melissa Barrett-Lundquist, Assistant Chair; M.F.A., Yale.
Rick Barry, Professor; M.F.A., Pratt.
Thomas Boné, Visiting Assistant Professor; B.A., Pratt.
Sjvetlana Bukvich-Nichols, Visiting Associate Professor; M.F.A., Rensselaer.
Edward Darino, Adjunct Associate Professor; M.F.A., NYU.
Carla Gannis, Visiting Instructor; M.F.A., Boston University.
Matt Guzzardo, Visiting Instructor; B.F.A, Pratt.
Claudia Hart, Adjunct Associate Professor; M.S., Columbia.
Claudia Herbst, Associate Professor; M.F.A., Maryland, Baltimore.
Kay Hines, Visiting Assistant Professor; B.A., Barnard.
Cesar Kuriyama, Visiting Instructor; B.F.A., Pratt.
Linda Lauro-Lazin, Adjunct Associate Professor; M.A., NYIT.
Peter Mackey, Professor; M.F.A., USC.
Natalie Moore, Adjunct Assistant Professor; M.A., NYU.
Rob O'Neill, Assistant Professor; M.F.A., Parsons.
Michael O'Rourke, Professor; Ed.M., Harvard.
Jo Ann Patel, Visiting Assistant Professor; M.F.A., Florida Atlantic.
Gap-Yeul Seo, Visiting Instructor; B.F.A., Pratt.
Sean Sullivan, Adjunct Assistant Professor; M.F.A., Pratt.
Beth Warshafsky, Adjunct Assistant Professor; M.F.A., Columbia.

Fine Arts
Donna Moran, Adjunct Associate Professor and Chair; M.F.A., Pratt.
Michael Brennan, Adjunct Assistant Professor; M.F.A., Pratt.
Jim Costanzo, Adjunct Associate Professor.
Kelly Driscoll, Assistant Professor; M.F.A., CUNY.
Aleksandar Duravcevic, Visiting Instructor; M.F.A., Pratt.
Allen Frame, Visiting Associate Professor.
Linda Francis, Adjunct Associate Professor; M.A., CUNY, Hunter.
Arthur Freed, Professor; B.F.A., San Francisco Art Institute.
Daniel Gerzog, Associate Professor; M.A., NYU.
Rupert Goldsworthy, Visiting Assistant Professor; Ph.D. candidate, NYU.
Jonathan Goodman, Visiting Assistant Professor; M.A., Pennsylvania.
Gillian Jagger, Professor; M.A., NYU.
Shirley Kaneda, Associate Professor; B.F.A., Parsons.
Vivian Knussi, Adjunct Instructor; Ph.D. candidate, Columbia.
Ted Kurahara, Professor; M.A., Bradley.
Catherine LeCliere, Visiting Assistant Professor; M.F.A., USC.
Frank Lind, Professor and Dean, School of Art and Design; M.F.A., Pratt.
Patricia Madeja, Adjunct Associate Professor; B.F.A., Pratt.
Ann Mandelbaum, Adjunct Associate Professor; M.F.A., Pratt.
Dennis McNett, Visiting Instructor.
Anne Messner, Adjunct Professor; B.F.A., Pratt.
Robert Morgan, Adjunct Professor; Ed.M., Northeastern; Ph.D., NYU.
James Moroney, Professor; M.F.A., Pratt.
Cyrilla Mozenter, Adjunct Professor; M.F.A., Pratt.
Mario Naves, Visiting Instructor; M.F.A., Pratt.
Ross Neher, Adjunct Associate Professor.
Thirwell Nolen, Adjunct Assistant Professor; M.A., Georgia Tech.
Doug Parry, Visiting Instructor; M.F.A., Pratt.
Sheila Pepe, Visiting Associate Professor and Assistant Chair; M.F.A., Tufts.
Philip Perkis, Professor Emeritus; B.F.A., San Francisco Art Institute.
Ernesto Pujol, Adjunct Assistant Professor; B.A., San Juan.
Catherine Redmond, Adjunct Assistant Professor.
Howard Rosenthal, Visiting Assistant Professor; M.F.A., Pratt.
Linda Schrank, Adjunct Professor; M.A., NYU.
Carla Shapiro, Visiting Assistant Professor; B.F.A., Syracuse.
Lori Sikorski, Visiting Instructor; M.F.A., Pratt.
Joseph Smith, Professor; B.F.A., Pratt.
Debbi Sutton, Adjunct Professor; M.F.A., CUNY, Hunter.
Irv Tepper, Adjunct Professor; M.F.A., Wisconsin.
Marjorie Welish, Adjunct Associate Professor; B.S., Columbia.
Christopher White, Adjunct Assistant Professor; A.B., Harvard.
Chris Wright, Adjunct Assistant Professor; M.F.A., Pratt.
Robert Zakarian, Professor; M.F.A., Pratt.

History of Art and Design
Frima Fox Hofrichter, Professor and Chair; Ph.D., Rutgers.
Sam Bryan, Adjunct Associate Professor; D.A., Carnegie Mellon.
Edward DeCarbo, Adjunct Associate Professor; Ph.D., Indiana.
Mary Edwards, Adjunct Professor; Ph.D., Columbia.
Rico Franses, Adjunct Assistant Professor; Ph.D., London.
Diana Gisolfi, Professor; Ph.D., Chicago.
Judith Gura, Visiting Associate Professor; M.A., Bard.
Dimitri Hazzikostas, Assistant Professor; Ph.D., Columbia.
Daniel Huppatz, Assistant Professor; Ph.D., Monash (Australia).
Evie Joselow, Visiting Associate Professor; Ph.D., CUNY.
Janet Kardon, Visiting Associate Professor; M.A., Pennsylvania.
Vivien Knussi, Adjunct Instructor; Ph.D. candidate, Columbia.
Gayle Rodda Kurtz, Adjunct Assistant Professor; Ph.D., CUNY Graduate Center.
William Lorenzo, Visiting Instructor; B.A., CUNY, Brooklyn.
Barbara Mayer, Visiting Assistant Professor; M.A., Bard.
Marsha Morton, Professor; Ph.D., NYU.
Kenneth S. Moser, Visiting Professor; B.A., Colgate.
Antoinette Owen, Visiting Associate Professor; M.A., SUNY College at Oneonta.
John F. Pile, Professor Emeritus; B.Arch., Pennsylvania.
Joyce Polistena, Adjunct Associate Professor; Ph.D., CUNY Graduate Center.
Katarina V. Posch, Assistant Associate Professor; Ph.D., Tokyo.
Edward Powers, Visiting Assistant Professor; J.D., Columbia; Ph.D., NYU.
Ann Schoenfeld, Adjunct Assistant Professor; Ph.D., CUNY Graduate Center.
Dorothy Shepard, Adjunct Associate Professor; Ph.D., Bryn Mawr.
Bor-Hua Wang, Adjunct Assistant Professor; Ph.D., Columbia.

Industrial Design
Matthew Burger, Chair; B.I.D., Pratt.
Jose Alcala, Visiting Instructor; M.I.D., Pratt.
Jamie Allen, Visiting Assistant Professor; M.I.T.P., NYU.
Leonard Bacich, Professor; M.I.D., Pratt.
Peter Barna, Associate Professor and Provost; M.I.D., Pratt.
Harvey Bernstein, Adjunct Assistant Professor; B.I.D., Pratt.
Frederick Blumlein, Adjunct Professor; B.I.D., Pratt.
Meri Bourgard, Adjunct Professor; M.A., Pratt.
Gina Caspi, Visiting Professor; M.I.D., Pratt.
Linda Celentano, Adjunct Assistant Professor; B.I.D., Pratt Institute.
Gihyun Cho, Visiting Assistant Professor; M.I.D., Syracuse.
Allan Chochinov, Adjunct Assistant Professor; M.I.D., Pratt.
David Conroy, Visiting Instructor; B.I.D., Pratt.
Lucia DeRespinis, Adjunct Professor; M.S., St. Lawrence.
Erika Doering, Visiting Instructor; M.I.D., Pratt.
Lisa Dillin, Visiting Assistant Professor; M.F.A., Cranbrook Academy of Art.
Peter Erickson, Visiting Instructor; M.I.D., Pratt.
Patrick Fenton, Visiting Instructor; M.F.A., Stanford.
Katheryn Filla, Associate Professor; M.I.D., Pratt.
Colin Gentle, Visiting Instructor.
Mark W. Goetz, Adjunct Professor; B.I.D., Pratt.
Richard Goodwin, Assistant Chair; M.I.D., Pratt.
Bruce Hannah, Professor; B.I.D., Pratt.
Kate Hixon, Visiting Assistant Professor; B.I.D., Pratt.
Debera Johnson, Associate Professor; B.I.D., Pratt.
Jeffrey Kapec, Visiting Associate Professor; B.I.D., Pratt.
John Kraljevich, Visiting Instructor; B.F.A., Michigan.
Robert Langhorn, Visiting Assistant Professor; M.A., Royal College of Art (London).
Jay Levy, Visiting Associate Professor; M.Arch., Columbia.
Mark J. S. Lim, Adjunct Professor; M.F.A., Pratt.
Scott Lundberg, Visiting Instructor; M.I.D., Pratt.
Marilyn Lyons, Adjunct Associate Professor; Pratt.
Marit Meisler, Visiting Instructor; B.I.D., Bezalel (Jerusalem).
Steven Mercurio, Visiting Assistant Professor; M.S., SUNY at Stony Brook.
Frank Millero, Visiting Instructor.
Katrin Mueller-Russo, Adjunct Associate Professor; Diplom.Des., Hamburg Visual Arts (Germany).
Gary Natsume, Visiting Associate Professor; M.I.D., Cranbrook Academy of Art.
Daniel November, Professor; B.F.A., Pratt.
Judy Nylen, Assistant Professor; M.F.A., M.I.L.S., Pratt.
Rebecca Pailes-Friedman, Adjunct Assistant Professor.
Jeanne Pfordresher, Adjunct Instructor; B.F.A., Cleveland Institute of Art.
Tim Richartz, Adjunct Assistant Professor; B.I.D., Pratt.
Andrew Roberto, Visiting Instructor; B.F.A., B.I.D., Pratt.
Molly Roberts, Visiting Associate Professor; M.I.D., Pratt.
Andrew Schloss, Visiting Assistant Professor; M.I.D., Pratt.
Arthur (Tip) Sempliner, Adjunct Associate Professor; M.B.A., Michigan.
Martin Skalski, Professor; M.I.D, Pratt.
Kimberly Snyder, Adjunct Associate Professor; M.F.A., Rhode Island School of Design.
Jordan Steckel, Adjunct Associate Professor; B.F.A., Yale.
Karen Stone, Adjunct Associate Professor; M.I.D., Pratt.
Cordy Swope, Visiting Professor; M.I.D, Pratt.
Irvin Tepper, Adjunct Professor; M.F.A., Washington (Seattle).
Jonathan Thayer, Assistant Professor; B.I.D., Pratt.
William Tolbert, Visiting Associate Professor; M.F.A., Yale.
Brett Tom, Visiting Instructor; B.I.D., Pratt.
Stephen Turbek, Visiting Instructor; B.I.D., Pratt.
Scott Vandervoort, Adjunct Instructor; B.I.D., Pratt.
Kim Walter, Adjunct Instructor; M.I.D., Pratt.
Rebecca Welz, Adjunct Associate Professor; B.F.A., School of the Museum of Fine Arts.
Joel Wennerstrom, Adjunct Assistant Professor; M.I.D., Pratt.
Robert Woertendyke, M.I.D., Pratt.
Henry Yoo, Visiting Assistant Professor; M.I.D., Pratt.

Interior Design
Anita Cooney, Adjunct Assistant Professor and Chair; B.Arch., Pratt.
Tarek Ashkar, Visiting Assistant Professor.
Jonathan Baker, Visiting Assistant Professor; M.Arch., Columbia.
Harvey Bernstein, Adjunct Professor; B.I.D., Pratt.
Meri Bourgard-Rohrs, Adjunct Professor; M.F.A., Pratt.
Edward Brant, Visiting Assistant Professor.
Christian Bunce, Visiting Instructor; M.F.A., Washington (Seattle).
Mary Burke, Visiting Assistant Professor.
Maneswar Cheemalapati, Visiting Assistant Professor; M.S., Southern California Institute of Architecture.
Ike Cheung, Visiting Assistant Professor.
James Conti, Adjunct Associate Professor; M.F.A., Ohio State.
Carol Crawford, Adjunct Assistant Professor; M.S., Pratt.
Lucia DeRespinis, Adjunct Professor; M.S., St. Lawrence.
William Du Bose, Visiting Assistant Professor; M.Arch., Michigan.
Philip Farrell, Adjunct Professor; M.S., Pratt.
Alan Feltoon, Visiting Assistant Professor; M.Arch., Pennsylvania.
Asdrubal Franco, Visiting Assistant Professor; B.S.A., NJIT.
Christopher Hall, Visiting Assistant Professor; M.Arch., Yale.
Jennifer Hanlin, Visiting Assistant Professor; M.Arch., Harvard.
Kelly Hanson, Visiting Assistant Professor; M.F.A., California, San Diego.
Mark Karlen, Professor; Ph.D., Union (Ohio).
Poonam Khanna, Visiting Assistant Professor; M.S., Columbia.
Margaret Kirk, Visiting Assistant Professor; M.Arch., Pratt.
Eunju Lee, Adjunct Assistant Professor; M.S., Pratt.
Marilyn Lyons, Adjunct Associate Professor.
Carmen Malvar, Adjunct Assistant Professor.
Gregory Marinic, Visiting Assistant Professor; M.Arch., Maryland.
Anthony Mekel, Adjunct Assistant Professor.
Christopher Metz, Visiting Assistant Professor.
Jon Otis, Associate Professor; M.S., Massachusetts.
John Pfeiffer, Visiting Assistant Professor.
Salvatore Raffone, Visiting Assistant Professor; M.Arch., Harvard.
Christian Rietzke, Visiting Assistant Professor.
Gustav Rohrs, Professor; B.Arch., MIT.
Hazel Siegel, Visiting Assistant Professor.
Steve Smith, Adjunct Associate Professor; B.S., Pratt.
Lee Stout, Adjunct Professor; B.F.A., Pratt.
Keena Suh, Adjunct Assistant Professor; M.Arch., Columbia.
Myonggi Sul, Professor; M.S., Pratt.
Karen Tehve, Visiting Assistant Professor; M.Arch., Harvard.
Jack Travis, Adjunct Assistant Professor; M.S., Illinois.
Michael Zuckerman, Adjunct Associate Professor; B.Arch., CUNY.

sfai
san francisco. art. institute.
since 1871.

SAN FRANCISCO ART INSTITUTE

Program in Fine Arts and Liberal Arts

Programs of Study

San Francisco Art Institute (SFAI) consists of two schools: the School of Studio Practice and the School of Interdisciplinary Studies. The School of Studio Practice offers M.F.A. and low-residency summer M.F.A. degree programs and postbaccalaureate certificates in design and technology, film, new genres, painting, photography, printmaking, and sculpture. The School of Interdisciplinary Studies offers M.A. degree programs in the history and theory of contemporary art, urban studies, and exhibition and museum studies. All of SFAI's graduate programs are committed to creative research that investigates the relationship between inquiry and practice and how this dynamic manifests itself in contemporary and historical approaches to cultural production in times of accelerated paradigm shifts. In the graduate programs, students are trained to be inquisitive thinkers within an environment of rigorous studio practice and interdisciplinary study. Spheres of Interest, the graduate lecture series, engages students with the thoughts and productions of a wide array of international guest participants. The presentations, seminars, and one-on-one discussions are opportunities to grapple with productions, conditions, and perspectives that can stimulate other kinds of responses.

The Master of Fine Arts program develops the artist's vision through studio-based experiments and the understanding that the work of the artist is an essential part of society. In the two-year M.F.A. program, students explore studio production and theoretical work in a flexible structure that encourages individual development within an interdisciplinary context. Students are exposed to methodologies of inquiry that foster innovative, analytic, and speculative thinking skills necessary for artistic development and creative production. The low-residency summer M.F.A. program (three or four years) has the same rigor and faculty as the two-year M.F.A. program, except that it is designed for artists, teachers, and other art professionals who currently have an active studio practice and for whom a low-residency program accommodates their employment or academic schedule. The combination of intensive summer sessions and guided independent study gives students a strong sense of artistic community while allowing them to continue to develop work over a longer period of time. Participation in the M.F.A. Exhibition is the final requirement for the M.F.A. degree. In their final year, students prepare for this important event, which is the largest of its kind in the San Francisco Bay Area. A great deal of discussion ensues about the nature of work being produced as well as issues surrounding its presentation and exhibition. Noted for diverse, provocative, and innovative work, the M.F.A. Exhibition attracts significant critical attention from the public and draws curators, gallery directors, and collectors from the West Coast and beyond.

SFAI's Master of Arts in History and Theory of Contemporary Art provides an in-depth and critical understanding of the history of the ideas, conditions, institutions, and discourses surrounding contemporary art and culture and how these inform the study, interpretation, analysis, and exhibition of art today. The program's curriculum addresses complex issues such as the dismantling of the hierarchies of artistic mediums initiated by the historical avant-gardes, the globalization of culture, the intersection of Western and non-Western modernity, the role of technology in art making, and the question of authorship in the practice of contemporary art.

The Master of Arts in Urban Studies integrates courses and resources from the School of Studio Practice and School of Interdisciplinary Studies to create a unique platform for learning and social engagement. The program offers a studio- and research-based curriculum developed specifically to address the contributions of art, artists, and researchers to the understanding and shaping of the subjectivity of the city.

The Master of Arts in Exhibition and Museum Studies is founded on the understanding that museums and exhibitions are both historical objects and subjects. Through this program, students develop a thorough understanding of the history and roles of institutions of modernity (museums, historical societies, archives, libraries, architectural commissions) in contemporary culture, the economy of the art world, and the politics that affect it. The curriculum comprises curatorial models, exhibition systems, institutional mediation, and education and addresses such topics as historical preservation, heritage management, the ethics of trade in antiquities, and the complex issue of cross-cultural and cross-disciplinary curating involving works understood primarily as ethnographic, anthropologic, and archaeological.

SFAI's Postbaccalaureate Certificate program is ideal for students who want to prepare themselves and their portfolios for entrance into an M.F.A. program and for those who simply want to enhance their skills and knowledge without having specific plans to enter a graduate program. Students spend a year of intensive work in their studio workspace at SFAI's Graduate Center, either focusing on a specific area of inquiry or experimenting with a variety of media and ideas. The curriculum combines the tutorial aspects of the graduate program with the upper-division course work of the undergraduate program.

Research Facilities

Graduate Center facilities include a digital lab, film and sound studios, darkrooms, a wood shop, seminar classrooms, a gallery, and installation critique rooms where students can present finished works or works in progress.

Graduate students also use the resources at SFAI's main campus in San Francisco's Russian Hill neighborhood, which houses painting, drawing, and sculpture studios; photography studios and darkrooms; black-box studios for shooting film and video; and printmaking areas for lithography, intaglio, silkscreen, and digital printmaking. Postproduction facilities include darkrooms, mural printing, and large-scale digital photo output; Super-8 and 16 mm editing; digital video and Final Cut Pro editing; an HDCAM- and DVCAM-equipped video-finishing suite; black-and-white and color film processing for photography and film; and sound studios. Film and video production equipment includes sync and nonsync Super-8 and 16-mm cameras, standard NTSC and 24p digital video cameras, and a CineAlta HDCAM package. The lecture hall is equipped for 16-mm and digital projection and is available to students for screenings and performances. The Digital Media Studio is an interdisciplinary campus resource available to all students for both static and time-based digital work. Equipment includes G5 Dual Processor Power Macs, scanners, and digital video editing stations. In addition, the Digital Imaging Studio provides an array of large-format, archival, photo-quality Epson printers.

SFAI's Anne Bremer Memorial Library is a valuable resource for books and primary source material on artists. The library holds more than 29,000 volumes, including an outstanding collection of exhibition catalogues, artists' books, rare books, historic archives of original material documenting art in California since 1871, and subscriptions to more than 200 periodicals as well as collections of slides, audio- and videotapes, films, and DVDs.

Financial Aid

Graduate students are considered for Graduate Fellowships, loans, grants, and Federal Work-Study opportunities. The Graduate Fellowship program provides scholarship support for incoming graduate students who have demonstrated a particular suitability for SFAI through their art work and personal accomplishments. Application for all types of need-based financial aid administered by SFAI requires a completed application for admission and a valid FAFSA, which should include SFAI's federal school code of 003948. Students should visit the SFAI Web site for application deadlines to receive priority consideration for available financial aid funds.

Cost of Study

Tuition for full-time graduate study for the 2007–08 academic year was $30,210.

Living and Housing Costs

SFAI's Office of Student Affairs provides a range of services for students, including a roommate-referral service and housing bulletin boards. The Housing Coordinator advises students on housing options in the area. Although the cost of living in the Bay Area varies widely according to individual lifestyle, housing and food for a single student is estimated to average about $10,800 per academic year.

Student Group

The Legion of Graduate Students (LOGS) includes all graduate students and encourages participation of graduate alumni. LOGS oversees the Swell Gallery and the Alternative Lecture Series and serves as a forum for graduate students.

Location

SFAI's main campus was completed in 1926 in the residential neighborhood of Russian Hill. The architecture combines a historic Mediterranean-style building with a distinctive Modernist addition from 1970. The two buildings offer traditional studios, with natural light from windows and skylights; black-box performance, production, and editing studios; galleries and exhibition spaces for student work; and seminar, screening, and lecture spaces. The campus features spectacular views of San Francisco Bay, including the Golden Gate, Bay Bridge, and Richmond Bridge, as well as Alcatraz and Angel Island. Many of San Francisco's historic and diverse neighborhoods are also nearby, including North Beach, Chinatown, and the South of Market area, or SoMa, home to many of the city's major museums, including the San Francisco Museum of Modern Art and Yerba Buena Center for the Arts.

The Graduate Center occupies the second floor of a large converted industrial building along the San Francisco Bay, an area of artist lofts and art-related services. The 62,000-square-foot facility provides individual and group studios, many with natural light; 24-hour access; and convenience to public transportation. Potrero Hill, SoMa, and the Mission district are nearby.

The San Francisco Bay area is the country's sixth-largest metropolitan area and is home to an exciting art scene that includes museums, galleries, and alternative spaces. The area also offers a wealth of cultural and educational resources—opera, dance, traditional and experimental theater, a wide range of music, cinema, and libraries. Favored by a climate that is mild year-round, San Francisco is among the world's most livable cities.

The Institute

Founded in 1871 by artists, writers, and community leaders who possessed a cultural vision for the West, the San Francisco Art Association (SFAA) became a locus for artists and thinkers. The California School of Design (renamed California School of Fine Arts in 1916 and San Francisco Art Institute in 1961) was launched by SFAA two years later and has been central to the development of many of this country's most notable art movements.

Applying

All aspects of applications are reviewed by the faculty and the admissions staff. Admission decisions are made on an individual basis, taking into account artistic and/or scholastic achievement and personal maturity and dedication as well as academic background.

Deadlines vary according to semester and program—details and an online application form are available on the SFAI Web site at http://www.sfai.edu. Required are the artist's statement or statement of purpose; portfolio (M.F.A. only); transcripts of all undergraduate and graduate work, both completed and in progress; two letters of recommendation; and a personal interview. Additional requirements apply for international applicants.

Correspondence and Information

Office of Admissions
San Francisco Art Institute
800 Chestnut Street
San Francisco, California 94133

Phone: 415-749-4500
800-345-SFAI (7324)(toll-free)
E-mail: admissions@sfai.edu
Web site: http://www.sfai.edu

San Francisco Art Institute

THE FACULTY

With a faculty of more than 130, SFAI enjoys an extraordinary student-faculty ratio of 5:1. Students work closely with faculty members and develop important and lasting relationships that continue beyond graduation.

Faculty members include artists, curators, writers, historians, theorists, activists, critics, urbanists, designers, performers, philosophers, musicians, and scientists. Okwui Enwezor, Dean of Academic Affairs, is a curator and writer and was the artistic director of the 2006 Bienal Internacional de Arte Contemporaneo in Seville, Spain. Renée Green is Dean of Graduate Studies at SFAI, and her work has been seen throughout the world in museums, galleries, biennials, and festivals. Hou Hanru, Chair of SFAI's Exhibitions and Museum Studies program, is the curator of the Chinese pavilion at the 2007 Venice Biennale and director of the 2007 Istanbul Biennial. Trisha Donnelly's work was included in the 2004 and 2006 Whitney biennials. Martin Schmidt (of Matmos) has toured with Bjork and has a new CD, *The Rose Has Teeth in the Mouth of the Beast.* Caitlin Mitchell-Dayton's paintings were used in the film *Art School Confidential.* Henry Wessel's photographs were recently published as a five-volume boxed set by Steidl. Jon Phillips is an open-source programmer for Creative Commons. Mark Van Proyen is one of the editors of *AfterBurn: Reflections on Burning Man.* Amy Franceschini is the founder of Futurefarmers and has been involved in numerous projects aimed at raising public awareness of critical ecological issues. Thomas Humphrey is a nuclear physicist and director of exhibitions at the Exploratorium.

In addition to working with SFAI's esteemed full- and part-time faculty, students are introduced to a spectrum of visiting artists and scholars. SFAI provides students direct access to an exhibition program showcasing the work of regional and international artists as well as SFAI students; an extensive roster of lectures that brings more than 60 artists, designers, curators, and writers to campus every year; and film screenings, symposia, and panel discussions that engage in contemporary issues and ideas.

Key elements of SFAI's approach to the intersection of academic and public inquiries are the new fellowships sponsored by the Centers of Interdisciplinary Study. Internationally recognized artists work in residence for a minimum of five weeks. Fellowships provide artists with an environment to engage in the ongoing development of new ideas in their work, test those ideas, and teach and collaborate with SFAI students and faculty members. Recent Fellows include Raqs Media Collective, from New Delhi; Alfredo Jaar, an artist, architect, and filmmaker known for his public interventions; and Hilton Als, a staff writer for *The New Yorker* and recent coeditor of *White Noise: An Eminem Reader.*

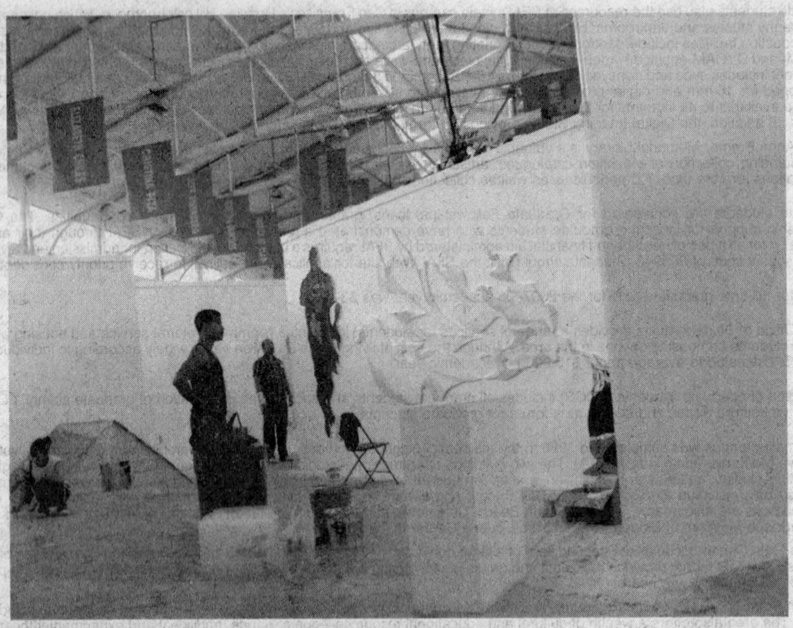

M.F.A. students installing work for the Graduate Exhibition.

Savannah College of Art and Design®

SAVANNAH COLLEGE OF ART AND DESIGN

Graduate School

Programs of Study

Savannah College of Art and Design (SCAD) offers Master of Architecture (M.Arch.), Master of Arts (M.A.), Master of Arts in Teaching (M.A.T.), Master of Fine Arts (M.F.A.), and Master of Urban Design (M.U.D.) degrees as well as graduate certificates.

The M.A. program is a one-year course of study requiring 45 credit hours. The M.F.A. and M.U.D. programs are two-year courses of study requiring 90 credit hours. The M.A. and M.F.A. are offered in advertising design, animation, architectural history, broadcast design and motion graphics, design management, fashion, fibers, film and television, furniture design, graphic design, historic preservation, illustration, industrial design, interactive design and game development, interior design, metals and jewelry, painting, performing arts, photography, printmaking, production design, sculpture, sequential art, sound design, and visual effects. In addition, M.A. degrees are offered in art history, arts administration, cinema studies, commercial photography, digital photography, documentary photography, and illustration design. An M.F.A. degree in professional writing is also available. The M.A.T. program requires 60 credit hours completed in one full year of intensive study and field experience.

The professional Master of Architecture program requires 225 quarter hours: 180 undergraduate and 45 graduate. The postprofessional M.Arch. degree—for students with an accredited professional architecture degree who wish to pursue computer-aided design—requires 45 graduate quarter hours. The five-year professional M.Arch. degree is accredited by the National Architectural Accrediting Board.

Online programs (M.A., M.F.A., and graduate certificates) are offered via SCAD-eLearning.

Research Facilities

Architecture, interior design, and historic preservation facilities include an intranet of PCs configured with electronic-design software, including AutoCAD, Bentley Microstation V8, Adobe Photoshop, 3D Studio VIZ, SURFCAM, Autodesk Maya, and Revit. A video microscope, as well as architectural conservation, metals conservation, and paint-analysis labs also are available in the School of Building Arts.

Animation, broadcast design, interactive design and game development, and visual effects facilities offer ready access to high-end industry-standard equipment and software, including an intranet of Macintosh G4, Pentium IV, and SGI workstations configured with a diverse range of graphics software; high-end 2-D, 3-D, interactive, and compositing tools, including the Adobe product line; Flipbook; Autodesk Maya; Anime Studio; Side Effects' Houdini products; Pixar's Renderman; Discreet's 3ds max; Unreal's game engine; Z-Brush; and Shake. Other tools include Lightwave and Macromedia products. SCAD's cutting-edge computer systems are combined with two green-screen stages, HD cameras, and a Vicon motion-capture studio to provide visual effects students with a complete digital production facility.

Fashion and fibers students use computer-aided design workstations and scanners; Juki industrial sewing machines and sergers; a heat transfer press; customized dress forms; weaving facilities, including a variety of four- and eight-shaft floor looms, two AVL CompuDobby looms, and an AVL electronic Jacquard loom; a digital fabric printer; a dye lab; and a screenprinting studio. Fibers students use NedGraphics, an industry-standard software program.

The Gulfstream Center for Furniture and Industrial Design in Savannah is a 43,000-square-foot facility with a woodworking and metals and plastics fabrication lab; bench rooms and design studios; a plastics working area; a welding facility; a three-axis, computer numeric controlled (CNC), vertical milling machine; spray booths and a finishing room; and state-of-the-art electronic design studios configured with the latest versions of design and visualization software, such as Auto CAD, Autodesk Studio, Rhino 3-D, SolidWorks, and Maya. The computer lab has two 3-D printers with capabilities to print polycarbonate or ABS 3-D models of computer-generated designs.

Advertising design, graphic design, and illustration facilities include Macintosh computers with CD and DVD burners, scanners, black and white laser printers, light tables, and digital cameras. The Adobe product line (Macromedia Director, Dreamweaver, Flash, and FreeHand), Quark Xpress, and other graphics packages are available.

Photography students have access to Macintosh digital imaging labs with extensive peripherals, wide-format inkjet printers, a Durst Theta printer, Imacon scanners, professional RA-4 color print processing machines for both negative and reversal papers, E-6 and C-41 color film processing machines, an alternative processes lab, studios, lighting equipment, view-camera systems, medium-format-camera systems, and digital SLR systems. Some labs are graduate use only.

Metals and jewelry studios include an FDM Prodigy Plus rapid prototyping 3-D printer with capabilities for ABS or wax models of CAD prototypes and four-axis CNC milling machines.

Film and television facilities include the Steadicam EFP and Super Panther Dolly, a chroma key/green screen studio, and a sound stage. The department houses Avid Adrenaline, Symphony, and Xpress DV workstations; MiniDV and DVC Pro cameras; Sony digital high-definition television cameras; 16mm, Super-16mm, and 35mm cameras; and an all-digital studio. Sound design equipment and software includes ten DH Pro Tools labs, two dedicated surround sound mix/mastering rooms, a MIDI lab, a recording studio for music production and Foley, two suites for dialog recording and editing, and a professionally equipped location sound cart for film production.

Located next to the High Museum of Art in midtown Atlanta, the sculpture facility is one of the finest in the Southeast. Designed by architect Renzo Piano, the facility contains a comprehensive wood and metal shop, a foundry for bronze and stainless steel, studios and support equipment, as well as exhibition space.

Performing Arts facilites include the 1,200-seat historic Lucas Theatre for the Arts, the 1,100-seat Trustees Theater, the ninety-seat Afifi Amphitheater at the Pei Ling Chan Garden for the Arts, and the 150-seat black-box Mondanaro Theater.

Financial Aid

Scholarships and fellowships may be offered to entering students based on academic and/or artistic achievement and financial need. For more information, students should visit http://www.scad.edu/scholarships.

Cost of Study

Graduate tuition for 2008–09 is $26,415.

Living and Housing Costs

Housing fees for the 2008–09 academic year range from $6555 for dormitory style to $7900 for an apartment-style unit with a separate bedroom. The basic meal plan rate per quarter is $1260.

Student Group

The total enrollment is more than 8,000 students, of whom 16 percent are graduate students. Approximately 20 percent of the graduate students are international.

Location

The College has locations in Savannah and Atlanta, Georgia, and in Lacoste, France. The Savannah location offers a full university experience in one of the largest National Historic Landmark districts in the United States. The Atlanta facility is strictly state-of-the-art, situated in the fast-paced professional marketplace of a major metropolitan hub for business, the arts, and transportation. Students take classes at any time of day or night, from anywhere in the world, through SCAD-eLearning.

The College

The Savannah College of Art and Design exists to prepare talented students for professional careers, emphasizing learning through individual attention in a positively oriented university environment. The goal of the College is to nurture and cultivate the unique qualities of each student through an interesting curriculum, in an inspiring environment, under the leadership of involved professors.

The Savannah College of Art and Design is a private, nonprofit institution accredited by the Commission on Colleges of the Southern Association of Colleges and Schools (1866 Southern Lane, Decatur, Georgia 30033-4097; telephone: 404-679-4501) to award bachelor's and master's degrees. The five-year professional M.Arch. degree program is accredited by the National Architectural Accrediting Board.

Applying

Applicants must submit a completed application for admission, either a $25 application fee for online applications or a $50 application fee for applications submitted in paper form, an official transcript from each college attended, three letters of recommendation, a statement of purpose, a portfolio or audition, and a resume. An interview is recommended but not required. GRE scores are recommended. Portfolio requirements vary; applicants should consult the Web site for information. International applicants whose first language is not English must have a minimum TOEFL score of 450 or other proof of English proficiency. An English as a second language program is offered.

As a general rule, applications for the fall quarter should be completed no later than March 1 for admission decisions to be rendered by April 1. Scholarships for the fall quarter are awarded by May 1, and students are requested to indicate their acceptance of admission and of institutional scholarship offers by June 1 through payment of a one-time matriculation fee. Applications received less than one month prior to the intended entry date are considered only on a space-available basis.

Correspondence and Information

Savannah College of Art and Design
P.O. Box 2072
Savannah, Georgia 31402-2072
Phone: 912-525-5100
800-869-7223 (toll-free)
Fax: 912-525-5986
E-mail: admission@scad.edu
Web site: http://www.scad.edu

Savannah College of Art and Design

THE FACULTY

Full-Time Faculty
James Abraham, M.A., Ball State.
Jesus Rojas Ache, M.A., SCAD.
Rebekah Adkins, M.F.A., SCAD.
Emad Afifi, D.Arch., Michigan.
Steven Aishman, M.F.A., Tufts.
Manuel Aja-Herrera, M.A., Central Saint Martins (London).
Marie Aja-Herrera, M.A., Central Saint Martins (London).
Judith Ott Allen, Ph.D., Ohio State.
Robert Allen, J.D., M.L.T., Alabama.
Margo Ames, M.Mus., Florida State.
Larry Anderson, M.V.A., Georgia State.
Emeka Anonyuo, Ph.D., Ohio State.
Rhonda Arntsen, M.F.A., Minnesota.
Christopher Auer, M.A., Regent (Virginia).
Carolyn Babcock, Ph.D., Utah.
Ryan Bacha, M.Arch., Virginia Tech.
Louis Baker, M.F.A., SCAD.
Fathi Bakkoush, M.F.A., East Tennessee State.
Laurence Ballard.
Nancy Bandiera, M.F.A., Ph.D., Texas at Austin.
Edward Barbier, M.F.A., Illinois.
Beth Baronian, M.F.A., Academy of Art College.
Curtis Bartone, M.F.A., Northwestern.
Stephanie Batcos, Ph.D., Delaware.
George Bauer, Ph.D., Texas Tech.
John Bauernfeind, M.A., Central Saint Martins (London).
Avantika Bawa, M.F.A., Art Institute of Chicago.
Mark Bazil, B.F.A., College for Creative Studies.
Robin Beauchamp, Ed.S., Georgia Southern.
Zoran Belic, M.F.A., Rutgers.
Cynda Benson, Ph.D., Kansas.
Ronald Bernard, M.F.A., SCAD.
Anne Bessac, M.F.A., North Carolina.
Margaret Betz, Ph.D., CUNY.
Richard Bjornseth, M.F.A., Florida State.
Scott Boylston, M.S., Pratt.
Kenneth Brandt, Ph.D., Florida State.
Brenda Brathwaite, B.S., Clarkson.
Deborah Brooks, M.S., North Carolina.
Vincent Brosseau, M.F.A., Ohio State.
Paul Brown, M.F.A., SCAD.
Robert Brown, M.F.A., Texas.
Kristie Bruzenak, M.F.A., Pennsylvania Academy of the Fine Arts.
Matthew Burge, M.F.A., Art Institute of Chicago.
Adriana Burgos, M.F.A., SCAD.
Sandra Burke, M.F.A., New Mexico.
Patricia Butz, Ph.D., USC.
Cheryl Cabrera, M.F.A., SCAD.
Catherine Cardarelli, M.F.A., Georgia.
Mary Ann Casem, M.A., SCAD.
Greg Ceo, M.F.A., SCAD.
Michael Chaney, M.F.A., Tufts.
Pei-Jung Chen, M.F.A., SCAD.
Pete Christman, M.F.A., Syracuse.
Dale Clifford, M.F.A., Clemson.
Marcia Cohen, M.A., New Mexico.
Julie Collins, M.F.A., SCAD.
Sarah Collins, M.F.A., SCAD.
Aram Cookson, M.F.A., SCAD.
Jaclyn Cori Norman, M.F.A., SCAD.
Pamela Corkey, M.F.A., American Film Institute.
Tracy Cox-Stanton, Ph.D., Florida.
Shirley Cribbs, M.F.A., SCAD.
Shawn Crystal, M.F.A., SCAD.
Catherine Cupps, Ph.D., Ohio State.
Quentin Currie, Ph.D. candidate, Capella.
Charles da Costa, Ph.D., University College for the Creative Arts (UK).
Mohamed Danawi, M.F.A., SCAD.
Kenneth Daniel, M.A., Central Michigan.
Liz Darlington, M.F.A., SCAD.
Adam Davies, M.F.A., Syracuse.
Mary Lou Davis, Ph.D., Michigan.
Henry Dean, M.F.A., SCAD.
Sherran Deems, M.F.A., Virginia Commonwealth.
Kate Deeny, M.F.A., SCAD.
Gustavo Delao, M.F.A., Pratt.
Harvey Deneroff, Ph.D., USC.
Esma Burçin Dengiz, M.F.A., Bilkent (Turkey).
Gauri Deshpande, M.F.A., Massachusetts College of Art.
Jeffrey DeVincent, M.F.A., Pittsburgh.
Heather Deyling, M.F.A., Tyler School of Art.
Scott Dietz, M.Arch., Florida.
Joseph DiGioia, M.F.A., RIT.
Larry Dixon, M.F.A., Florida.
Mary Aswell Doll, Ph.D., Syracuse.
Nancy Doolan, M.F.A., Radford.
Craig Drennen, M.F.A., Ohio.
John Drop, M.A., Ohio State.
Allan Drummond, M.A., Royal College of Art.
David Duncan, M.F.A., Arizona.
Cayewah Easley, M.F.A., Cranbrook Academy of Art.
Jeffrey Eley, M.Arch.Hist., Virginia.
Dennis Elkins, Ph.D., Colorado.
Dominique Elliott, M.F.A., Southeastern Massachusetts.
Beverly Elson, Ph.D., Maryland.
Gregory Eltringham, M.F.A., SCAD.
Nancy Emmeluth, D.A., SUNY at Albany.
Rosemary Erpf, Ph.D., CUNY.
Denise Falk, M.F.A., Art Institute of Chicago.
Robert Fee, B.F.A., Kansas City Art Institute and School of Design.
Gayle Fichtinger, M.F.A., Arizona State.
Jonathan Field, Ph.D., Lancaster (England).
Deborah First, M.F.A., Cranbrook Academy of Art.
Thomas Fischer, M.F.A., Stanford.
Joy L. Flynn, M.F.A., North Dakota.
John Foerster, M.F.A., Michigan.
David Foote, M.F.A., SCAD.
Larry Forrest, Ph.D., Indiana.
Peter Fossick, M.S., Strathclyde (UK).
Jason Fox, M.F.A., SCAD.
Thomas Francis, M.F.A., Wisconsin.
Kathleen Fritz, M.A., Boston Architectural Center.
SuAnne Fu, M.S., Cornell.
Matthew Gamber, M.F.A., Tufts.
Rebecca Klein Ganz, M.F.A., Rhode Island School of Design.
Stephen Gardner, M.F.A., Parsons.
Michael Gargiulo, M.F.A., School of Visual Arts.
Thomas Gattis, M.S., Bemidji State.
Bridget Gaynor, M.A., William Paterson.
Stephen Geller, M.F.A., Yale.
Thomas Gensheimer, Ph.D., Berkeley.
Richard Gere, M.F.A., Tennessee.
Sari Gilbert, M.A., Columbia.
David Gildersleeve, M.F.A., SCAD.
Neil Gilks, M.A., Central Saint Martins (London).
R. Mark Giuliano, D.Min., Vanderbilt.
James Gladman, M.F.A., San Francisco Art Institute.
Michael Glaser, M.F.A, Ohio State.
David Gobel, Ph.D., Princeton.
Valerie Gonzales, Ph.D., Aix-Marsielle.
Ray Goto, M.F.A., SCAD.
Teresa Griffis, Ph.D., Southern Mississippi.
Frederick Gross, Ph.D., CUNY.
Samuel Gross, M.S., Penn State.
Lois Gruberger, M.F.A., Art Institute of Chicago.
Celeste Lovette Guichard, Ph.D. candidate, Columbia.
Troy Gustafson, B.F.A., Kansas City Art Institute.
Lindsay Hadley, B.A., Franklin College; M.F.A., SCAD.
Afshin Hafizi, Ph.D., Florida State.
Gregory Hall, Ph.D., Hong Kong.
Shana Hall, M.A.T., University of the Arts.
Stephen Hall, M.A., Syracuse.
Jeffrey Hamilton, Ph.D., Delaware.
Krista Harberson, M.F.A., Florida State.
Colin Hariskov, Ph.D., South Carolina.
John Harkins, M.F.A., Wayne State.
David Harmon, M.F.A., Penn State.
Elizabeth Hart, M.F.A., UCLA.
Annette Haywood-Carter, B.A.J., Georgia.
Joshua Hecht, Ed.D., San Francisco.
Merrick Henry, M.F.A., Kansas State.
Laura A. D. Hernandez, M.F.A., Alfred.
Jeffrey Scot Hicks, M.F.A., Winthrop.
Andrew Hieronymi, M.F.A., UCLA.
Yuki Hirao, M.F.A., Rhode Island School of Design.
Renee Hodge, M.F.A., SCAD.
Wynne Hodges, M.F.A., Radford.
Jason Hoelscher, M.F.A., Pratt Institute.
Thomas Hoffman, B.S., Villanova.
Michael Hofstein, B.A., Texas at Austin.
Patrick Hogan, M.Des., Carnegie Mellon.
Sachiko Honda, M.Ed., North Carolina.
Lucilla Hoshor, M.A., NYIT.
Hsu-Jen Huang, Ph.D., Glasgow (Scotland).
Paul Hudson, M.F.A., SCAD.
Cynthia Huff, M.F.A., Notre Dame.
Chin-Cheng Hung, M.F.A., SCAD.
Gene Hutchinson, M.Arch., Morgan State.
Alessandro Imperato, Ph.D., Keele (England).
Suzanne Jackson, M.F.A., Yale.
Timothy Allen Jackson, Ph.D., Penn State.
Zig Jackson, M.F.A., San Francisco Art Institute
Cherylnn Jacobs, Ph.D., Maryland.
Jared Jaffe, M.F.A., Nevada.
James Janson, Ph.D., Case Western Reserve.
Gabriela Jasin, Ph.D., Rutgers.
David Jeffreys, Ph.D., Essex (England).
Gregory Johnson, M.F.A., SCAD.
Pernell Johnson, M.F.A., SCAD.
Margo Jones, B.V.A., Georgia State.
Stefani Joseph, M.F.A., SCAD.
David Kaul, M.F.A., Ohio State.
Timothy Keating, M.F.A., UCLA.
Malcolm Kesson, M.A., Middlesex Polytechnic.
Jacqueline Keuler, M.A., Syracuse.
Joseph Keuler, Ph.D., Syracuse.
Lanelle Keyes, M.F.A., Washington (Seattle).
Jacques Khouri, M.F.A., SCAD.
Chris Kienke, M.F.A., Southern Illinois.
Henry Hongmin Kim, M.F.A., Art Institute of Chicago.
Edward Kinney, M.F.A., RIT.
Joseph Kline, Ph.D., Texas Tech.
Mark Kneece, M.A., South Carolina.
Stephen Knudsen, M.F.A., SCAD.
Lubomir Kocka, M.A., University of Music and Dramatic Arts.
Craig Kovacs, M.A., William Patterson.
Susan Krause, M.F.A., Yale.
Richard Krepel, M.F.A., SCAD.
Bonnie Kubasta, M.F.A., Oregon.
Jenny Kuhla, M.F.A., Tufts.
Karim Ladha, M.A., Berkeley.
James Langley, M.F.A., New York Academy of Art.
John Larison, M.F.A., SCAD.
Larry Lauria, B.F.A., Art Center College of Design.
Thelma Lazo-Flores, Ph.D., Chiba (Japan).
Fiona Le Brun, Ph.D., Keele (England).
Tad Leckman, B.A., California, Santa Cruz.
Eun Sook Lee, M.F.A., Notre Dame.
Josephine Leong, M.S., Essex (England).
Amy Lerner-Maddox, M.F.A., NYU.
Monica Letourneau, M.F.A., SCAD.
Daniel Levine, Ph.D., Indiana.
Julie Lieberman, M.F.A., School of Visual Arts.
John Longworth, M.Ed., Auburn.
Chercy Ione Lott, M.F.A., SCAD.
Doris Louie, M.F.A., Cranbrook Academy of Art.
Richard Lovell, B.F.A., Auburn.
John Paul Lowe, M.F.A., SCAD.
Tom Lyle, B.A., Florida.
Vivian Majkowski, M.F.A., Moscow Art Theater School.
Debra Malschick, M.F.A., California State.
Anne-Marie Manker, M.F.A., Georgia State.
Jeff Markowsky, M.F.A., School of Visual Arts.
Carl Marxer, M.F.A., SCAD.
Lesa Mason, Ph.D., Indiana.
Sheila Matyjasik, M.F.A., SCAD.
Jason Maurer, B.F.A., SCAD.
Stephen May, M.F.A., SCAD.
Kevin McCarey, M.A., Oregon.
Christopher McDonnell, Des.R.C.A., Royal College of Art.
Shawn McKinney, M.F.A., California Institute of the Arts.
Patrick McKinnon, M.F.A., SCAD.
Sharon McNeil, M.F.A., California State.
Aaron Memmott, M.F.A., Academy of Art College.
Angela Merta, M.F.A., Minnesota.
Andrew Meyer, B.A., Bucknell.
David Meyers, M.F.A., Syracuse.
Natalija Mijatovic, M.F.A., Pennsylvania Academy of the Fine Arts.
Harold Miles.
Anthony Scott Miller, B.F.A., Parsons (Otis).
Robert Miller, M.F.A., California Institute of the Arts.
Bonnie Million, Ph.D., Utah.
Terry Moeller, M.F.A., Stephen F. Austin.
Randy Moffett, Ph.D., West Virginia.
Patrick Mohr, M.F.A., Maryland Institute College of Art.
Robert Mond, M.F.A., Wisconsin–Madison.
Jorge Montero, M.F.A., Iowa.
Laraine Montgomery, M.Arch., North Carolina State.
Debra Moorshead, M.A., Royal College of Art.
Jeremy Moorshead, M.F.A., SCAD.
Michael Morford, Ph.D. candidate, Case Western Reserve.
John Morris, M.I.D., Auburn.
Deborah Mosch, M.F.A., SCAD.
Steven Mosch, M.F.A., RIT.
Laura Mosquera, M.F.A., Art Institute of Chicago.
Helena Moussatché, Ph.D., Rio de Janeiro.
Julie Mueller-Brown, M.F.A., Missouri.
Fernando Munilla, M.Arch., Virginia Tech.
Christine Neal, Ph.D., Missouri.
Marcia Neblett, M.F.A., SUNY at Stony Brook.
Andrew Nedd, Ph.D. candidate, USC.
Kathleen Newell, Ph.D., Delaware.
Robert Newman, B.F.A., Pratt.
Huy Sinh Ngo, M.Arch., Texas Tech.
Christopher Nitsche, M.F.A., New Mexico.
Rebecca Nolan, M.F.A., Oregon.
Michael Nolin, M.A., USC.
Sam Norgard, M.F.A., Cincinnati.
Art Novak, M.A., Michigan State.
Tina O'Hailey, M.S., Regis.
Debra Oden, M.F.A., Nebraska–Lincoln.
Samuel Olin, M.Arch., North Carolina State.
Brett Osborn, M.F.A., California State.
Sharon Ott, B.A., Bennington.
Gokhan Ozaysin, Ph.D., Anadolu (Turkey).
Carole Pacheco, M.F.A., Colorado.
Marlborough Packard, M.F.A., SCAD.
Verena Paepcke, M.F.A., Ohio State.
Periklis Pagratis, M.F.A., George Washington.
Evelyn Pappas, M.A., Syracuse.
Yves Paquette, M.F.A., Ohio.
Melanie Parker, M.S. candidate, Georgia Tech.
Suellen Parker, M.F.A., School of Visual Arts.
Carl Parrish, M.A., Emory.
Joe Pasquale, M.F.A., SCAD.
Jesse Payne, M.F.A., Northern Illinois.
Robert Pendarvis, M.F.A., SCAD.
George Perez, M.F.A., Massachusetts.
Patricia Perrone, M.F.A., Carnegie Mellon.
Allen Peterson, M.F.A., Minnesota.
Dawn Peterson, M.F.A., SCAD.
George Peterson, B.A., San Francisco State.
Alexandria Pierce, Ph.D., McGill.
John Pierson, M.A., San Diego State.
Connie Pinkerton, M.A., SCAD.
Daniel Powers, M.F.A., Marywood.
Richard Prisco, M.F.A., RIT.
Tricia Quakenbush, M.A., Ball State.
Pat Quinn, M.F.A., SCAD.
Nan Rainey, M.F.A., Pratt.
Catherine Ramsdell, Ph.D., Auburn.
Steven A. Ramsey, M.F.A., Illinois State.
Dennis Randall, Ph.D., Georgia.
Conrad Rathmann, M.Arch., Clemson.
John Rauh, M.F.A., California Institute of the Arts.
Roger Rawlings, Ph.D., CUNY.
Sandra Reed, M.F.A., George Washington.
Jane Rehl, Ph.D., Emory.
Joyce Reifsteck, B.S., Tennessee.
Judith Reno, M.Arch., UCLA.
John Rise, M.F.A., New Mexico.
Liset Robinson, M.Arch., Georgia Tech.
Don Rogers, M.F.A., SCAD.
Julie Rogers-Varland, M.Arch., CUNY; Columbia.
Mark Rokfalusi, M.F.A., Syracuse.
Frederique Rolland-Mills, Ph.D., Kentucky.
Arpad Daniel Ronaszegi, M.Arch., Illinois.
Barry Roseman, M.F.A., Yale.
E. G. Daves Rossell, Ph.D., Berkeley.
Andrea Rountree, M.F.A., Northern Illinois.
Andre Ruschkowski, Ph.D., Humboldt (Germany).
Joyce Ryan, M.F.A., Washington (St. Louis).
Ruben Salinas, M.F.A., Stephen F. Austin State.
Judy Salzinger, B.F.A., Moore College of Art.
Morgan Santander, M.F.A., Chicago.
Mary Elizabeth Sargent, M.F.A., Cranbrook Academy of Art.
Todd Schroeder, M.F.A., Kent State.
Peter Schroth, M.F.A., Colorado.
Karl Schuler, Ph.D., NYU.
Andrew Scott, M.F.A., Ohio State.
K. Michelle Scott, Ph.D., Nova Southeastern.
Burton Sears, M.F.A., USC.
Charles Shami, M.F.A., SCAD.
William Shanahan, Ph.D., Thunderbird.
Rachel Shane, Ph.D., Ohio State.
Nisha Shanghavi, M.A., Texas at Austin.
John Sharp, Ph.D. candidate, Indiana.
Jose Luis Silva, M.F.A., SCAD.
Christoph Simon, M.A., Royal College of Art.
Scott R. Singeisen, M.Arch., SCAD.
John Sisti.
Denise Smith, Ph.D., New Mexico.
Hyun Jong Song, M.F.A., SCAD.
Yafong Song, Ph.D., Washington State.
David Spencer, B.F.A., Atlanta College of Art.
Clark Stallworthe, M.F.A., Ohio State.
Craig Stevens, M.F.A., Ohio.
Robert Stewart, M.A., New Mexico.
David Demare Stivers, Ph.D., Delaware.
Matthew Stromberg, M.F.A., North Texas.
Catalina Strother, M.Arch., Ion Mincu (Bucharest).
Anne Swartz, Ph.D., Case Western Reserve.
Heather Szatmary, M.F.A., SCAD.
Jill Taffet, B.F.A., Cooper Union.
Durwin Talon, M.A., Syracuse.
Ming Tang, M.Arch., Tsinghua (China).
Christina Tarbell, M.A., SCAD.
Tan Tascioglu, M.F.A., SCAD.
Kimberlie Tatalick, M.F.A., Temple.
Lewis Tate, M.S., Nova Southeastern.
Dawn Testa, M.S., Emerson.
Scott Thorp, M.F.A., Maryland Institute College of Art.
Marie Timberlake, Ph.D., UCLA.
Hal Tine, B.F.A., Carnegie Tech.
Matthew Toole, M.F.A., Southern Illinois.
Sean Trapani, B.A., Florida State.
Doris Treptow, M.F.A, SCAD.
Rebecca Trittel, Ph.D., Essex.
Peter Tsaykel, B.F.A., San Francisco State.
Tony Tseng, M.P.S., NYU.
Richard Tunney, M.F.A., Texas at Austin.
V. Elizabeth Turk, M.V.A., Georgia State.
Rebecca Turner, Ph.D., Yale.
Mark Tymchyshyn, M.F.A., Wayne State.
Mark Uzmann, M.F.A., SCAD.
John Valentine, Ph.D., Vanderbilt.
Larry Valentine, M.F.A., SUNY at New Paltz.
Kurt Vargo, School of Visual Arts.
Joel Varland, M.F.A., SUNY at Buffalo.
Christine Wacta, M.Arch., Minnesota.
Stephen Wagner, Ph.D., Delaware.
Steven J. Wagner, Ph.D., Clemson.
Michael Wainstein, M.F.A., Cincinnati.
Ashley C. Waldvogel, M.F.A., Pratt.
Roger Walton, M.F.A., CUNY, Brooklyn.
Peili Wang, M.F.A., SCAD.
Linda Warner, M.A., Syracuse.
John Waters, B.F.A., Virginia Commonwealth.
Pamela Wiley, M.F.A., Cranbrook Academy of Art.
Christopher Williams, M.F.A., Maryland Institute College of Art.
Emily Allen Williams, D.A., Clark Atlanta.
George Williams, Ph.D., Houston.
Robin Williams, Ph.D., Pennsylvania.
Kirt Witte, M.F.A., SCAD.
Joel Wittkamp, M.Des., Royal College of Art.
Peter Wong, M.F.A., Cranbrook Academy of Art.
Timothy Woods, M.Arch., Virginia Tech.
Lynn Wright, M.F.A., SCAD.
Maher Yacoub, M.F.A., Syracuse.
Dihua Yang, M.Arch., Maryland.
Weisheng Yang, Ph.D., SUNY at Albany.
Woon Kee Yong, M.F.A., SCAD.
Josh Yu, M.F.A., SCAD.
Filis Hagi Zaid, M. Des., Cincinnati.
Weihua Zhang, D.A., SUNY at Albany.
Jason Zimmer, M.F.A., New York Academy of Art.

SCHOOL OF THE ART INSTITUTE OF CHICAGO

Graduate Division

Programs of Study

Graduate programs at the School of the Art Institute of Chicago (SAIC) leading to the M.F.A. in Studio degree are offered in the following studio areas: art and technology studies; ceramics; designed objects; design for emerging technologies; fiber and material studies; film, video, and new media; interior architecture; painting and drawing; performance; photography; printmedia; sculpture; sound; visual communication; and writing. Other advanced degree programs offered are an M.A. in Arts Administration and Policy; an M.A. in Art Education; an M.A. in Art Therapy; an M.A. in Modern Art History, Theory, and Criticism; an M.A. in Teaching; an M.A. in Visual and Critical Studies; an M.S. in Historic Preservation; a dual-degree M.A. in Modern Art History, Theory, and Criticism/M.A. in Arts Administration and Policy; and a Graduate Certificate in Art History, Theory, and Criticism. Since 2006 SAIC has offered the Master of Architecture; the Master of Architecture, with an emphasis in interior design; and the Master of Design in Designed Objects degrees.

Postbaccalaureate certificates in fashion (new for fall 2008), studio, and writing are also offered.

New programs offered by SAIC as of fall 2008 include a Master of Design in Fashion, Body, and Garment and a Master of Arts in New Arts Journalism.

Research Facilities

Among the facilities for research and study, in addition to the studio areas provided by individual departments, are the school library, with more than 85,000 books, periodicals, films, videos, records, CDs, and picture files; the 4,500-volume Joan Flasch Artists' Book Collection; and the Film Study Collections of 800 short and experimental films for class study. The Ryerson and Burnham libraries, the second-largest art and architecture reference libraries in the country, are housed in the Art Institute of Chicago and have approximately 220,000 volumes. Other resources include the Video Data Bank, with more than 600 artists' videotapes; the Gene Siskel Film Center; the Poetry Center; the Fashion Resource Center; and the Roger Brown Study Collection.

Financial Aid

Financial assistance for graduate students is available in the form of fellowships, merit and need-based scholarships, assistantships, grants, institutionally sponsored loans, Federal Perkins Loans, and Federal Work-Study Program awards. All students who wish to apply for financial assistance must file the Free Application for Federal Student Aid (FAFSA) form. All financial aid forms and instructions may be obtained through the School's Financial Aid office. Of the full-time graduate students, 83 percent are partially or completely funded.

Cost of Study

Tuition and fees for full-time M.F.A. graduate study (15 credit hours per term) for 2007–08 were $34,200 ($1140 per credit hour).

Living and Housing Costs

Estimated academic-year expenses for an independent, single student, exclusive of tuition, range from $8000 to $12,000, depending upon the housing choice a student makes. (This estimate includes room and board, transportation, supplies, and personal expenses.)

Student Group

Of a total enrollment of 2,463, there are 599 students registered in the Graduate Division. Approximately 65 percent are women, and about 18 percent are international students.

Location

The School of the Art Institute of Chicago offers the advantages of a central location in a large, culturally rich, metropolitan center. The Chicago area has a population of about 7 million and, as an urban center, offers a broad range of cultural activities, along with an efficient public transportation system and well-established, diversified neighborhoods.

The School

The Art Institute of Chicago, comprising the School and the museum, was founded under another name by a small group of artists in 1866. Their purpose was to provide an exceptional education in the studio arts in conjunction with exhibition opportunities. The small art school expanded from a rented facility to its present location in the heart of Chicago's downtown area. The School has become one of the largest independent schools of art and design in the country. Its modern facility adjoins the Art Institute of Chicago Museum, which was built for the World's Columbian Exhibition in 1893. The museum's extensive collection of masterpieces constitutes one of the finest in the world. The partnership between the museum and the School offers unlimited resources for research and study; students have unlimited access to the permanent collection, the traveling exhibitions, the Prints and Drawings Room, and the Photography Study Center.

Applying

The School of the Art Institute of Chicago invites applications for admission from students of exceptional promise who have graduated from liberal arts colleges, fine arts schools, and state universities and colleges, as well as those who have completed partial M.F.A. degree programs at other schools. The Admissions Review Committee carefully reviews the portfolios and academic credentials of all applicants. Students are required to submit a portfolio of up to twenty examples of recent work, transcripts from each college previously attended, a statement of purpose, and two letters of recommendation. The M.F.A. (in studio areas) application deadline is January 10 for fall admission. Students interested in applying to other degree programs should visit http://www.saic.edu for application guidelines.

Correspondence and Information

Graduate Admissions
Admissions Office
School of the Art Institute of Chicago
36 South Wabash Avenue, Suite 1201
Chicago, Illinois 60603

Phone: 312-629-6100
800-232-7242 (toll-free)
E-mail: admiss@saic.edu
Web site: http://www.saic.edu

School of the Art Institute of Chicago

THE FACULTY

ARCHITECTURE, INTERIOR ARCHITECTURE, AND DESIGNED OBJECTS
Hennie Reynders, Chair. Cynthia Coleman, Rebecca Dalvesco, Garret Eakin, May Hawfield, Jaak Jurisson, Don Kalec, Linda Keane, Thomas Kong, Carl Ray Miller, Anders Nereim, Ben Nicholson, Helen Marie Nugent, Douglas Pancoast.

ART AND TECHNOLOGY STUDIES
Tiffany Holmes, Chair. Benjamin Chang, Coordinator. Wafaa Bilal, Shawn Decker, Peter Gena, William Harper, Jason Hopkins, Eduardo Kac, John Manning, Dan Miller, Judd Morrissey, Greg Mowery, Joan Truckenbrod, Steve Waldek.

ART EDUCATION
John Ploof, Chair and Director, Master of Arts in Teaching (MAT). Andres Hernandez, Director, Master of Arts in Art Education (MAAE). Jerome Hausman, Drea Howenstein, Rebecca Keller, Giselle Mercier, Angela Paterakis, Patricia Pelletier, Therese Quinn, David Rodriguez.

ART THERAPY
Catherine Moon, Chair. Danniel Anthon, Deborah Benke, Barbara Fish, William Miles, Joanne Ramseyer, Suellen Semekowski, Terri Sweig, Randy Vick.

ARTS ADMINISTRATION AND POLICY
Nicholas Lowe, Chair. Bob Brodsky, John Corbett, Michael Dorf, Julia Marsh, Adelheid Mers, Maureen Pskowski, Amy Reichert, Michael Ryan, Rachel Weiss.

CERAMICS
Xavier Toubes, Chair. Patricia Rieger, Katherine Ross.

DESIGN FOR EMERGING TECHNOLOGIES
Anders Nereim, Coordinator. Benjamin Chang, Shawn Decker, Peter Gena, Linda Keane, John Manning, Carl Ray Miller, Dan Miller, Douglas Pancoast.

DESIGNED OBJECTS
Helen Maria Nugent, Coordinator. Linda Keane, Carl Ray Miller, Anders Nereim, Lisa Norton, Douglas Pancoast, Bruce Tharp.

FASHION
Nick Cave, Chair. Katrin Schnabl, Interim Program Director. Sandra Michel Adams, Bambi Breakstone, Gillion Carrara, Conrad Hamather, Anke Loh, Andrea Reynders, Liat Smestad.

FIBER AND MATERIALS STUDIES
Christine Tarkowski, Chair. Amy Honchel, Graduate Coordinator. Marianne Fairbanks, Diana Guerrero-Macia, Kathryn Hixson, Joan Livingstone, Darrel Morris, Ellen Rothenberg, Fraser Taylor, Anne Wilson.

FILM, VIDEO, AND NEW MEDIA
Christopher Sullivan, Chair. Tatsuyuki Aoki, Lisa Barcy, Greg Bordowitz, Jon Cates, Thomas Comerford, Sharon Couzin, Daniel Eisenberg, Shellie Fleming, Michele Mahoney, Mary Patten, John Petrakis, Anne Quirynen, Jim Trainor, Danielle Wilmouth, Scott Wolniak.

HISTORIC PRESERVATION
Vincent L. Michael, Chair. Rolf Achilles, Craig Deller, Carol Dyson, Richard Friedman, Martha Frish, Yunxia Gao, Jean Guarino, Elaine Harrington, Donald Kalec, Charles Pipal, Anthony Rubano, Anne Sullivan, Terry Tatum, Neal Vogel, Tim Wittman, Carol Yetken.

LIBERAL ARTS
Raja Halwani, Chair. Paul Ashley, Romi Crawford, Calvin Forbes, Peter Gena, Barbara Guenther, Marilyn Houlberg, James McManus, Karen Morris, Michael Nagelbach, Patrick Rivers, Elizabeth Wright, Andrew Yang.

MODERN ART HISTORY, THEORY, AND CRITICISM
Kym Pinder, Chair. David Raskin, Director, Master of Arts in Modern Art History, Theory, and Criticism (MAAH). Rolf Achilles, Simon Anderson, Shane Campbell, Gillion Carrara, Alan Cohen, Audrey Colby, Christopher Cutrone, Jim Elkins, Patricia Erens, David Getsy, Joseph Grigely, Marilyn Houlberg, James Hugunin, Rebecca Keller, Maud Lavin, Deborah Mancoff, Stanley Murashige, Michael Newman, Margaret Olin, Michael Rabe, Jerry Saltz, Shawn Michelle Smith, Robin Stern, Charles Stuckey, Lisa Wainwright, Tim Wittman, James Yood.

NEW ARTS JOURNALISM
James Yood, Program Director. Stanford Carpenter, Cynthia Coleman, Margaret Hawkins, Tiffany Holmes, Dunkan MacKenzie, Michel Miner. Additional faculty members in Criticism and Cultural Commentary: James Elkins, Maud Lavin, Terry Meyers, Michal Newman.

PAINTING AND DRAWING
Susanne Doremus, Chair. Candida Alvarez, Susanna Coffey, Dan Devening, Judith Geichman, Gaylen Gerber, Michelle Grabner, Sheridan Gustin, Philip Hanson, Richard Hull, Michiko Itatani, Susan Kraut, Marion Kryczka, Jim Lutes, Terry Myers, Jim Nutt, Elizabeth Ockwell, John Phillips, Frank Piatek, Scott Reeder, Richard Rezec, Kay Rosen, Barbara Rossi, John Rozelle, Elizabeth Rupprecht, Jerry Saltz, Joanne Scott, Hazma Walker, Kevin Wolff.

PERFORMANCE
Faith Wilding, Chair. Werner Herterich, Lin Hixson, Mark Jeffery, Ginger Krebs, Trevor Martin, Blair Thomas.

PHOTOGRAPHY
Barbara DeGenevieve, Chair. Aimee Beaubien, Lynne Brown, Patty Carroll, Robert Clarke-Davis, Ken Fandell, Alan Labb, Mayumi Lake, Claire Pentecost, Marco Poloni, Karen Savage, Lewis Toby.

PRINTMEDIA
Peter Power, Chair. Sally Alatalo, Jeanine Coupe-Ryding, Doug Huston, Myungah Hyon, Michael Miller, Mark Pascale, Karen Savage, Christopher Sperandio.

SCULPTURE
Mary Jane Jacob, Chair. Jose Ferreira, Graduate Coordinator. Joe Cavalier, Preston Jackson, Jin Soo Kim, Paul Martin, Adelheid Mers, Fred Nagelbach, Lisa Norton, Carolyn Ottmers, Laurie Palmer, Stephen Reber, Richard Rezac, James Zanzi.

SOUND
Shawn Decker, Chair. Nicholas Collins, John Corbett, Rob Drinkwater, Douglas Ewart, Peter Gena, Eric Leonarson, Lou Mallozzi, Robert Snyder, Lori Talley.

VISUAL AND CRITICAL STUDIES
Maud Lavin, Chair. Joseph Grigely, Graduate Director. Gregg Bordowitz, Stanford Carpenter, James Elkins, Terri Kapsalis, Peg Olin, Patrick Rivers, Shawn Michelle Smith.

VISUAL COMMUNICATION
Stephen Farrell, Chair. Frank DeBose, John Bowers, Gokhan Ersan, Alysia Kaplan, B. J. Krivanek, Maud Lavin, Mouli Marur, Michael Miner, Jennifer Moody, Daniel Morgenthaler, Olivia Petrides, Catherine Ruggie-Saunders, Ann Tyler, Connie White.

WRITING
Calvin Forbes, Chair. Carol Anshaw, Rosellen Brown, Anne Calcagno, Elizabeth Cross, Mary Cross, Janet Desaulniers, Amy England, Thea Goodman, Matthew Goulish, Joseph Grigley, Sara Levine, James McManus, Michael Meyers, Beth Nugent, Beau O'Reilly, Elise Paschen, Bin Ramke, Jill Riddell, David Robbins, Ellen Rothenberg, Margaret Sloane, Leila Wilson.

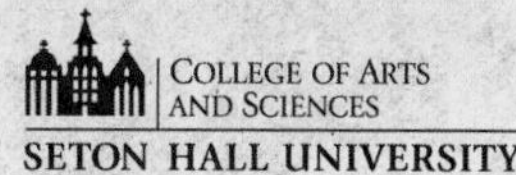

SETON HALL UNIVERSITY

Department of Art and Music
Master of Arts in Museum Professions

Program of Study

The Department of Art and Music offers a Master of Arts (M.A.) in Museum Professions degree program to those interested in pursuing careers in museums and related cultural institutions. Balancing structure and flexibility, this cutting-edge program comprises a small number of core courses (including a mandatory internship), a choice of concentrations or tracks (in museum education, museum management, museum registration, or exhibition development), and four elective courses (for example, yearly seminars abroad in Amsterdam, Berlin, Paris, or Rome). Courses such as Exhibitions A–Z, Museums and Community, Museum Fundraising Fundamentals, Museum Technologies, and Object Care are offered on a rolling schedule.

The program takes advantage of Seton Hall's own rich resources as well as the University's proximity to New York City, which boasts some of the finest museums in the world. Courses are taught by museum professionals from New York and New Jersey, and classes feature regular fieldtrips to museums as diverse as the Museum of Modern Art in midtown Manhattan, the Studio Museum in Harlem, the Newark Museum, and museums in Philadelphia, which are only an hour's drive away. Visiting lecturers from such institutions further enrich the curriculum. Museums have become complex, multipurpose organizations in the modern world; this program has been designed to meet the need for professionally trained employees.

The 39-credit program (thirteen courses) may be followed on a full-time (three courses per semester) or part-time basis. The program can be completed in twenty months; however, many students take longer, depending on family and employment obligations. Courses are offered in the evenings and sometimes on weekends to accommodate those with full- or part-time jobs.

Further details are available at http://www.shu.edu/academics/artsci/ma-museum-professions/index.cfm.

Research Facilities

The 155,000-square-foot Walsh Library has an excellent collection of the latest books and journals in museum studies, and it offers a variety of facilities, including carrels, group-study rooms, computer labs, and scholars' studies. Students have access to libraries and museums of the greater metropolitan area and their state-of-the-art resources. Library services include research support, bibliographic instruction, and interlibrary borrowing. Available technology includes CD-ROM databases, multimedia PC and Macintosh labs, electronic visual aids, and the Setoncat, an online catalog of the Walsh Library holdings that is accessible both on site and via the campus network.

The Walsh Library Gallery offers a year-round program of art and history exhibitions. Students in the M.A. in Museum Professions program frequently are involved in the planning, implementation, and educational aspects of these exhibitions, especially when they enroll in the course entitled Producing an Exhibition.

Financial Aid

Graduate assistantships, which provide tuition benefits and a stipend, are offered on a competitive basis. Resident assistant positions, which offer housing only, are available as well. Students can apply for two types of federal student loans.

To qualify for financial aid, students must take at least 6 credits per term. Additional information on financial aid and graduate assistantships is available at http://www.shu.edu/applying/graduate/grad-finaid.cfm.

Cost of Study

In 2008–09, tuition is $875 per credit. Full-time students pay $305 per semester in University and technology fees; part-time students pay $185.

Living and Housing Costs

Housing and living costs in South Orange and surrounding towns are comparable to most suburban cities, with studio and one-bedroom apartments renting for $750 to $1000 per month.

Student Group

Each year, about 20 students enter the program. The student body is diverse in age, race, and geographic origins, as students come from many states and countries. Some recently completed their undergraduate education; others are career changers who wish to prepare for new positions in museum environments. This diversity helps the program, as museums of today seek employees of diverse backgrounds. The students have strong collegial ties and are in close touch with faculty members. Indeed, the program fosters a sense of community.

Student Outcomes

Graduates and current students have held and are holding positions in such institutions as Children's Museum of Manhattan, New York City; Christie's Auction House, New York City; Citibank Art Advisory Service; Dallas Museum of Art, Texas; Edison National Historic Site, West Orange, New Jersey; El Museo del Barrio, New York City; Frick Collection, New York City; Guggenheim Museum, New York City; Hermitage Historic House, Ho-Ho-Kus, New Jersey; Historical Society of Princeton, New Jersey; International Center for Photography, New York City; JP Morgan Chase, Philanthropic Division, New York City; Jersey City Museum, New Jersey; Maritime Museum of San Diego, California; Metropolitan Museum of Art, New York City; Montclair Art Museum, New Jersey; Morris County Historical Society, Morristown, New Jersey; Museum of Arts and Design, New York City; Museum of Early Trades and Crafts, Madison, New Jersey; Museum of Jewish Heritage, New York City; Museum of Modern Art, New York City; Museum of the City of New York, New York City; National Air & Space Museum, Washington, D.C.; National Canal Museum, Easton, Pennsylvania; Newark Museum, Newark, New Jersey; Olana State Historic Site, Hudson, New York; Princeton Art Museum, Princeton, New Jersey; Ringling Museum of Art, Sarasota, Florida; Riverfront Center for the Arts, Millville, New Jersey; Ross Gallery of the University of Pennsylvania, Philadelphia, Pennsylvania; Rubin Museum of Art, New York City; Studio Museum in Harlem, New York City; Taft Museum, Cincinnati, Ohio; The Pew Charitable Trusts, Philadelphia, Pennsylvania; Vietnam Era Educational Center, Holmdel, New Jersey; Waterloo Village, New Jersey; and the Whitney Museum of American Art, New York City.

Location

Set in a suburban village, Seton Hall is a 5-minute drive from a 2,000-acre recreational reservation and a 30-minute bus or train ride to New York City with its wealth of museums and other cultural institutions. The campus buildings range from a nineteenth-century Victorian carriage house to a world-class fitness center. SOPAC, the South Orange Performing Arts Center, opened in November 2006 and features a five-screen Cineplex and a 415-seat theater center.

The University and The Program

Seton Hall University, founded in 1856, is the largest and oldest diocesan university in the country. It welcomes and educates men and women of all races, creeds, and ethnic origins. The Graduate Program in Museum Professions was founded in 1994 in order to prepare students for the challenges facing museums of the next century, which are to make museums relevant to a public of diverse backgrounds and traditions. At the graduate level, Seton Hall has more than sixty degree programs. The University is large enough to provide adequate facilities and resources, yet small enough to give individual attention to students.

Applying

Admission to the program is open to those with a baccalaureate degree in archaeology, anthropology, art history, or history or a degree in another field with a minimum of 12 undergraduate credits in one of those disciplines (these credits may be completed after conditional admission to the program). The program seeks students with a good academic record (preferable 3.0 or higher) and a strong desire to become a part of the museum world. An interview is necessary, as are two letters of recommendation, GRE scores (waived for applicants who have graduated more than five years ago), and a personal essay. Application forms are sent upon request or can be found online at http://www.shu.edu/academics/artsci/apply.cfm.

Correspondence and Information

Dr. Petra Chu, Director of Graduate Studies
M.A. in Museum Professions
Department of Art and Music
Art Center
Seton Hall University
400 South Orange Avenue
South Orange, New Jersey 07079
Phone: 973-761-9430 or 9459
Fax: 973-275-2368
E-mail: museumgrad@shu.edu
Web site: http://www.shu.edu/academics/artsci/ma-museum-professions/index.cfm

Seton Hall University

THE FACULTY

Director
Petra ten-Doesschate Chu, Ph.D., Columbia.

Full-Time Faculty
Petra ten-Doesschate Chu, Ph.D., Columbia.
Jürgen Heinrichs, Ph.D., Yale.
Susan Leshnoff, Ed.D., Columbia.
Janet Marstine, Ph.D., Pittsburgh.
Charlotte Nichols, Ph.D., NYU.

Adjunct Faculty
Jeanne Brasile, M.A., Seton Hall; Director, Walsh Library Gallery, Seton Hall.
Lori Beth Finkelstein, Ph.D., NYU; Director of Public Programs and Education, Baltimore Museum of Industry.
Nicholas Holmes, LL.D., Michigan; In-House Legal Counsel, Whitney Museum of American Art
Lisa Mantone, M.A., William Patterson; Director of Development, The Museum of Modern Art.
Antonia Moser, M.A., Seton Hall; Associate Registrar, Newark Museum.
Steven Miller, B.A., Bard; Director, The Morris Museum.
Claudia Ocello, M.S., Bank Street College of Education; Associate Director, Education and Public Programs, Save Ellis Island.
John Warren, M.S., Bank Street College of Education; Educational Specialist, National Parks of New York Harbor Education Center.
Margaret Wastie, M.A. (two degrees), Seton Hall and Kean; Education Coordinator, Museum of Early Trades and Crafts.
Katherine Witzig, M.A., Seton Hall; Collections Manager, Vietnam Era Educational Center.

Graduate faculty members of the Center for Public Service and the School of Education also participate in this program.

President's Hall.

The Arts Center.

STONY BROOK UNIVERSITY, STATE UNIVERSITY OF NEW YORK

Department of Art
Art History and Criticism

Programs of Study

The Department of Art at Stony Brook University offers Master of Arts (M.A.) and Doctor of Philosophy (Ph.D.) degrees in art history and criticism, as well as a Master of Fine Arts (M.F.A.) degree in studio art.

The Master of Arts degree in art history and criticism is a two-year, 36-credit program with an integrated curriculum of art history, criticism, and theory designed to prepare students to continue their studies at the doctoral level or to enter the professional art world. While the focus of the program is on modern and contemporary art, criticism, and visual culture, students take courses from across the broad spectrum of art history and in related fields of the humanities and social sciences. Requirements include a comprehensive exam on the history of art, a one-semester teaching practicum, and a written thesis.

The Doctor of Philosophy degree in art history and criticism is a 60-credit program that allows students to pursue their interests more intensively beyond the master's level. The goals of the program include the development of the curator-critic-historian, who can combine the various fields of traditional art historical study with a critical consciousness of broader intellectual issues involved in such study. The program is designed to ensure that students have sufficient depth of knowledge in their chosen fields to produce an original work of scholarship and the breadth to compete successfully for positions as members of college or university faculties, museum staffs, or other professional positions in the field. Requirements include qualifying exams taken at the end of the third year, two semesters of teaching practicum, and public defense of their dissertations.

Students in both programs are encouraged to enhance their intellectual development through completion of one of a number of graduate certificate programs offered at Stony Brook, especially those in art and philosophy, cultural studies, and women's studies.

Research Facilities

The Department of Art is housed in the Staller Center for the Arts, a vibrant hub of lectures, concerts, performances, classes, and other cultural activities. The Visual Resources Library offers an extensive slide collection to support the teaching and research needs of the Department, videos and print journals, and computer equipment for the ongoing development of a database and digital imaging capacity. The spacious University Art Gallery offers curatorial opportunities for exhibitions specializing in contemporary art. The main library on campus maintains extensive holdings of major reference materials, monographs, and exhibition catalogs for student research. The Pollock-Krasner House in East Hampton and the Pollock-Krasner Study Center—soon to be located at the Stony Brook Southampton campus—are other important resources. The Pollock-Krasner Study Center hosts a yearlong series of lectures, seminars, exhibitions, and other activities and houses reference materials and archives, including books, photographs, oral histories, and journals available for research. Classes, lectures, and conferences are now offered at Stony Brook Manhattan, the University's facility located at 28th Street and Park Avenue South. These are designed with the Big Apple in mind and include trips to museums, artists' studios, literary sites, film festivals, and music venues.

Financial Aid

The Department provides full tuition scholarships to Ph.D. students for the duration of their course work, presuming timely completion of requirements. Full graduate teaching assistantships with a stipend of $15,145 are offered to Ph.D. students on a competitive basis for up to four years of study. Two Presidential Fellowships of $4000 per year may be awarded each year to outstanding incoming students. Since 2004, the Pollock-Krasner Graduate Assistantship has been awarded annually to an advanced Ph.D. student based on academic merit and relevance of the field of study. In addition, the Department regularly nominates applicants for several University-wide academically based fellowships, including Graduate Council Fellowships and Dorothy Pieper Merit Awards, as well as W. Burghardt Turner Fellowships for underrepresented minorities. Unfunded students may find graduate or research assistantships elsewhere on campus, such as in the main library. Included in most of these assistantships is a health insurance plan.

Cost of Study

In 2008–09, full-time tuition at 12 credits for entering in-state residents is $3450 per semester, while out-of-state residents and international students pay $5460. Additional fees for each semester, including (but not limited to) the infirmary, activity, technology, and transportation fees, total about $875. International students also pay a service fee of approximately $35 per semester and an orientation fee of $50. Fees for the mandatory Student Health Insurance Plan vary depending on citizenship and employment status.

Living and Housing Costs

For 2008–09, Stony Brook calculates the cost of education excluding tuition, fees, and insurance at $14,228 per year. On-campus apartments range in cost from approximately $336 per month to approximately $1456 per month, depending on the size of the unit and the number of students sharing the space. Off-campus housing options include rooms, houses, and apartments that can be rented from approximately $350 to $2500 per month. Costs including books, food, and transportation may vary depending on academic program and/or personal circumstances.

Student Group

Of the 42 students currently in the program, 12 have completed everything but their dissertation, 13 are completing Ph.D. course work, and 17 are at the M.A. level. The gender balance reflects the field, in that there are more women (31) than men (10). All Ph.D. students are full-time. Students come from institutions across the country and abroad, including, at present, 6 international students.

Student Outcomes

Since the inception of the M.A. program in art history and criticism in 1985, Stony Brook has been very successful in placing graduates into competitive doctoral programs, including those at Columbia, City University of New York, New York University, Harvard, Rochester, Case Western Reserve, Rutgers, and Northwestern, among others. The Ph.D. program in art history and criticism was established in 1996. To date, the program has awarded thirteen Ph.D. degrees. Many alumni have moved directly into the professional art world of galleries, museums, and publishing houses, while others have gone on to academic careers.

Location

Ideally located halfway between the art centers of New York City and the Hamptons, Stony Brook offers a unique opportunity to study in a serene and spacious setting, while maintaining close contact with the pulse of the art world. The emphasis on modern and contemporary art requires students to take advantage of the full range of exhibitions, performances, screenings, and lectures in New York City. The new Stony Brook Manhattan site and the Pollock-Krasner House and Study Center in East Hampton are important resources for research, lectures, and other activities.

The University and The Department

The Department of Art at Stony Brook University offers a dynamic and interdisciplinary program of art history and criticism within the context of a major research institution. The particular orientation of the M.A. and Ph.D. programs toward theory and criticism of modern and contemporary art and visual culture is enhanced by the strength of the Department's M.F.A. program in studio art and by a new multidisciplinary initiative centering upon digital media. The university setting not only provides students access to the distinguished faculty of artists and art historians within the Department but also to faculty members and students in music, theater arts, philosophy, history, and comparative studies, among others.

Applying

The most successful applications reflect an awareness of the Department's emphasis on modern and contemporary art, theory, and criticism and interdisciplinary opportunities at Stony Brook. Applicants need to provide two official transcripts of undergraduate and graduate course work, official Graduate Record Examinations (GRE) scores, an acceptable score on the TOEFL or its equivalent for international students, three letters of recommendation, and a nonrefundable $60 fee. In addition, applicants should submit a sample of written work along with their application. The deadline for receipt of applications and supporting materials for fall admission is January 15. Students are admitted for the spring semester only under special circumstances. Admission is subject to final approval by the Graduate School.

Correspondence and Information

Lisa Perez, Graduate Coordinator
Department of Art
Staller Center 2225
Stony Brook University, State University of New York
Stony Brook, New York 11794-5400

Phone: 631-632-7270
Fax: 631-632-7261
E-mail: liperez@notes.cc.sunysb.edu
Web site: http://www.stonybrook.edu/art

Stony Brook University, State University of New York

THE FACULTY AND THEIR RESEARCH

The expertise of the art history and criticism faculty of the Department of Art ranges broadly from contemporary art and architecture to the arts of the ancient world, from the politics of art and public sculpture to post-structuralist theory and psychoanalysis, and from the Italian Renaissance to the arts of Africa. They are actively engaged in lecturing, publishing, and curating in a wide range of regional, national, and international venues. Their high profile is reflected in the fellowships and grants they have received from the Getty, Guggenheim, Fulbright, Ford, and MacArthur Foundations; the Social Science Research Council; the National Endowments for the Arts and for the Humanities, and the Smithsonian Institution, among others.

Michele H. Bogart, Professor; Ph.D., Chicago, 1979. American art and material culture, especially, public art and urban design; commercial art and animation. Author, *The Politics of Urban Beauty: New York and Its Art Commission* (University of Chicago Press, 2006), *Artists, Advertising, and the Borders of Art* (University of Chicago Press, 1995), and *Public Sculpture and the Civic Ideal in New York City, 1890–1930* (University of Chicago Press, 1989; paperback: Smithsonian Institution Press, 1997), which received the Charles C. Eldredge Prize in 1991. Author of articles in *Art History, American Art, Winterthur Portfolio, Prospects,* and *Journal of Urban History*. Recipient of fellowships from the Smithsonian Institution, Winterthur Museum, National Endowment for the Humanities, and the John Simon Guggenheim Memorial Foundation. Appearance in the PBS documentary on movie poster artist Reynold Brown. Scholarly consultant for Save Outdoor Sculpture! and Vice President of the Fine Arts Federation of New York. Former Vice President of the Art Commission of the City of New York and presently a member of its Conservation Advisory Group.

Barbara E. Frank, Associate Professor; Ph.D., Indiana, 1988. African art historian, primarily, Mali, West Africa; issues of artist identity, style, technology, and craft production; travel, teaching, and research in Sierra Leone, Senegal, Gambia, Benin, Madagascar, Côte d'Ivoire, Mexico, China, and Europe. Dr. Frank has held several major fellowships, including an NEH Fellowship for College Teachers, a Social Science Research Council Grant, and two Fulbright-Hays Research Abroad Fellowships. Most recently, she was the recipient of a Senior Fellowship at the Smithsonian Institution's Museum of African Art. Major publications include *Mande Potters and Leatherworkers; Art and Heritage in West Africa* (Smithsonian, 1998), selected as a Choice Outstanding Academic Book; and an edited volume, *Status and Identity in West Africa: Nyamakalaw of Mande* (Indiana, 1995).

Shoki Goodarzi, Lecturer; Ph.D., Berkeley, 1999. The art of ancient Iran and Turkey. Dr. Goodarzi comes to SUNY Stony Book from the Metropolitan Museum of Art where she served as an assistant curator in the Department of Ancient Near East, having worked on a number of projects, including two major exhibitions: the Golden Deer of Eurasia and the Art of the First Cities. Dr. Goodarzi has also worked on numerous archaeological excavations around the globe, most recently in Uzbekistan where she served as the field director of Sangyr Tepe, a fourth-century B.C. period site. Her publications stem from her wide interest in the Ancient world—from worked bone tools to female figurines from second-millennium B.C. sites in Iran. Currently she is working on publishing the volume of bone tools from the Neolithic period site of Hallan Çemi Tepesi in southeast Turkey.

Helen A. Harrison, Adjunct Lecturer and Director, Pollock-Krasner House and Study Center; M.A., Case Western Reserve, 1975. Art historian, museum director, and journalist; former curator of the Parrish Art Museum in Southampton, the Queens Museum of Art in Flushing, and Guild Hall Museum in East Hampton; and former director of the Public Art Preservation Committee in Manhattan. Ms. Harrison is the visual arts commentator for WLIU 88.3 FM Radio. She has written reviews and articles for the Long Island section of the *New York Times* (1978–2006) and essays in the *Journal of American Studies* (U.K.), *Prospects, Archives of American Art Journal, American Art, Provincetown Arts,* and *Winterthur Portfolio*. She is the author of *Dawn of a New Day: The New York World's Fair 1939/40* (New York University Press, 1980) and a monograph on the artist Larry Rivers (Harper & Row, 1984). Her anthology, *Such Desperate Joy: Imagining Jackson Pollock*, was published by Thunder's Mouth Press in 2000. Her most recent book (with C. A. Denne) is *Hamptons Bohemia: Two Centuries of Artists and Writers on the Beach*, published by Chronicle Books in 2002.

Donald B. Kuspit, Professor; D.Phil., Frankfurt, 1960; Ph.D., Michigan, 1971; honorary doctorates, Davidson College, San Francisco Art Institute, Illinois at Urbana-Champaign, and Cornell (the A. D. White Professorship). Received Frank Jewett Mather Award for Distinction in Art Criticism (1983), the Citation for Distinguished Service to the Visual Arts (1997) from the National Association of the Schools of Art and Design, and was Robertson Fellow at the University of Glasgow. Delivered the Getty lectures in 2000 and has also received Ford, Fulbright, and Guggenheim fellowships, as well as support from the National Endowments for the Humanities and for the Arts. Among his numerous publications are *The Rebirth of Painting in the Late Twentieth Century, Psychostrategies of Avant-Garde Art, The Dialectic of Decadence, Redeeming Art: Critical Reveries, The End of Art* (in Chinese, Polish, Spanish, and Turkish as well as English), and "A Critical History of Twentieth-Century Art," which is being published serially on artnet.com and will be completely online by September 2006. Contributing editor, *Artforum, New Art Examiner, Sculpture,* and *artnet.com* and on the board of the *Centennial Review* and the Lucy Daniels Foundation for the Psychoanalytic Study of Creativity.

Richard Leslie, Visiting Assistant Professor; Ph.D., City University of New York. Richard Leslie's current research and writing concentrate on the intersections of art criticism with cultural studies and sociology. As a founding board member of Arts & Sciences Collaboration, Inc. (ASCI), he studies and facilitates the effects of technology and science on contemporary art and theory. As the instructor of the Department's undergraduate introductory survey courses he presents a global history of art within the context of larger cultural traditions and social and religious institutions and provides basic teacher training for graduate students. He has degrees in philosophy, art theory, criticism, and art history and taught at the School of the Art Institute of Chicago, Rutgers, City College, and the School of Visual Arts in Manhattan as well as at Stony Brook. His publications include books on Picasso, Surrealism, and Pop art. He is a foreign correspondent for Art Nexus, an international bilingual magazine specializing in the arts of Latin America, and has published dozens of reviews and essays on contemporary art in print and digital formats.

John Lutterbie. Affiliated Associate Professor; Ph.D. Washington (Seattle). Performance theory, theory of theater, performance art. Dr. Lutterbie teaches theory, history, and criticism and directs. In addition to being a member of the Theater Arts Faculty, he is an affiliate member of the Department of Art. His primary research area is in performance theory, where he examines the intersection of phenomenology and the neuroscience of emotion and consciousness and of culture and inter-subjectivity. The University of Michigan Press publishes his book, *Hearing Voices: Modern Drama and the Problem of Subjectivity*. In addition, he has published in numerous journals including *Theatre Journal*, the *Journal of Dramatic Theory and Criticism, Performance Research*, the *Journal of Psychiatry and the Humanities*, and *Modern Drama*. His recent directing credits include *A Macbeth, Happy Days, Angels in American: Perestrioka,* and *Blood Wedding*. He is a member of the Association for Theatre in Higher Education, the Literary Managers and Dramaturgs of the Americas, the Modern Language Association, the American Society of Theatre Research, and Performance International.

Joseph Monteyne, Assistant Professor; Ph.D., British Columbia, 2000. Interests range from early modern art and print culture and the historiography and methodology of art history to twentieth-century art and theory. Dr. Monteyne has been the recipient of numerous awards and fellowships, including a Governor General of Canada's medal for his master's thesis, postdoctoral fellowships from the Paul Mellon Center for Studies in British Art and the Social Sciences and Humanities Research Council of Canada, the latter of which he undertook at the Courtauld Institute in London. He has also been a summer researcher at the Huntington Library with support from an Andrew Mellon fellowship and a William Keck Fellowship for Junior Faculty, as well as the recipient of a Residential Fellowship from the Yale Center for British Art. He has published on seventeenth-century art, twentieth-century art, contemporary independent magazine culture, and American popular imagery in such international journals as *Art History, Oxford Art Journal,* and *Collapse*, as well as in edited volumes published by Bis/Gingko/Thames and Hudson and Nouveau Monde Editions. His book *The Printed Image in Early Modern London: Urban Space, Visual Representation, and Social Exchange* is scheduled to be published by Ashgate in 2007.

Anita Moskowitz, Professor; Ph.D., NYU, 1978. Specialist in Italian Gothic and Renaissance sculpture and nineteenth-century neo-Renaissance sculpture. Grants and awards include a fellowship at I Tatti (Harvard University's Center for Renaissance Studies in Florence), three NEH fellowships, several ACLS grants, and a CASVA Senior Visiting Fellowship at the National Gallery of Art, Washington, D.C. Author of numerous articles and essays, ranging from a ceramic vessel of the Amazon to painting and sculpture from the Italian Gothic through the High Renaissance and nineteenth-century. Major publications include *Nicola and Giovanni Pisano Pulpits: Pious Devotion Pious Diversion* (Harvey Miller Press, 2005), *Italian Gothic Sculpture ca. 1250–1400* (Cambridge University Press, 2001), *Nicola Pisano's Arca di San Domenico and its Legacy* (College Art Association Monograph, 1994), and *The Sculpture of Andrea and Nino Pisano* (Cambridge University Press, 1986). Speaker and/or Chair of numerous scholarly conferences. Distinguished Kreitman Fellow lecture at Ben Gurion University in the Negev.

Zabet Patterson, Assistant Professor; Ph.D., Berkeley, 2007. Specializes in the history and theory of digital media, with a particular emphasis on the intersection of computational media and art in the postwar period. She received her Ph.D. in rhetoric from UC Berkeley in 2007. Her dissertation, entitled "Visionary Machines: A Genealogy of the Digital Image," was supported by fellowships from the Townsend Humanities Center, the Rhetoric Department, and the Josephine de Karman Foundation. Zabet spent 2005–06 as Visiting Assistant Professor in the Departments of Art History and Art at Northwestern University. Her publications include "Consuming Fantasy in the Digital Era" in *PornographyOn/Scene*, a collection edited by Linda Williams, as well as forthcoming articles on Jim Campbell and John and James Whitney. She is a member of the Consortium for Digital Arts, Culture, and Technology (cDACT).

James H. Rubin, Professor; Ph.D., Harvard, 1972; education includes the Institut d'Art et d'Archéologie of the Sorbonne (Paris). Specializes in the history, theory, and criticism of nineteenth-century European art, especially that of France; interdisciplinary areas, with special attention to cultural history and art and politics. He has taught at Harvard, Boston University, and Princeton and continues to teach at Cooper Union. He has published widely on subjects ranging from the eighteenth century to the present, including *Impressionist Cats and Dogs* (2003), *Nadar* (2001), *Impressionism* (1999), *Courbet* (1997), *Manet's Silence and the Poetics of Bouquets* (1994); *Eugène Delacroix's "Dantebarke"* (1987), *Realism and Social Vision in Courbet and Proudhon* (1981), and *Eighteenth Century French Life-Drawing* (1977).

Andrew V. Uroskie, Assistant Professor; Ph.D., Berkeley, 2005. Specializes in the history and criticism of late modernism, with an emphasis on the use of film and photography in the art of the 1960s and 1970s. His interdisciplinary work is broadly informed by an interest in psychoanalysis, phenomenology, and post-structuralist critical theory. He has held research fellowships at the Townsend Center for the Humanities and the Stanford Humanities Laboratory and has presented conference papers and public lectures in Venice, Edinburgh, London, Vancouver, and across the United States. His book *Between the Black Box and the White Cube: The Emergence of the Moving Image in Contemporary Art* (forthcoming, University of Chicago Press) locates the origins of contemporary video installation within the historically and conceptually neglected terrain of "Expanded Cinema" in the early 1960s. Other publications include "La Jetée en Spirale: Robert Smithson's Stratigraphic Cinema" (*Grey Room*). His recent work on the conjunction of cinema and site-specificity in contemporary art is being anthologized in *Art and the Moving Image: A Critical Reader* (Tate, 2008), *The Place of the Moving Image* (Minnesota), *Screen/Space: The Projected Image in Contemporary Art* (Manchester), and *Impossible Cinema*, volume two of the Spanish artist Olga Adelantado's project Six Impossible Things Before Breakfast (Centro Montehermoso).

STONY BROOK UNIVERSITY, STATE UNIVERSITY OF NEW YORK

Department of Art
Studio Art

Programs of Study The Department of Art at Stony Brook University offers a Master of Fine Arts (M.F.A.) degree in studio art and M.A. and Ph.D. degrees in art history and criticism. The M.F.A. degree in studio art is a flexible, three-year, 60-credit terminal-degree program combining studio practice and critical inquiry. The degree is especially suitable for students who plan professional involvement in either the making or teaching of art, but may also be useful for those interested in arts administration or museum and gallery work. The program provides ample studio space to develop a body of work within or across disciplines. Students benefit from interactions with the entire studio faculty during midterm and final critiques. First-year students have a group exhibition through the summer following their first year in residence, and all students have solo exhibitions in the Library Gallery in their second and third years. In addition, third-year candidates for the degree contribute work to a group exhibition in the University Art Gallery's large professional exhibition space in Staller Center for the Arts. Proximity to New York City's many galleries also provides exhibition and internship opportunities. Although the degree requirements concentrate on the development of their work, M.F.A. candidates are encouraged to enrich their studies by taking advantage of the strengths of the art history and criticism faculty members as well as others from the larger campus community. They are required to take at least three liberal arts courses in art history and criticism, philosophy, cultural studies, or others. A minimum of one semester observing and one semester teaching a free-standing, undergraduate studio course are also required as part of graduate training. A written thesis is required for completion of the degree.

Research Facilities The Department of Art is housed in the Staller Center for the Arts, which is a vibrant hub of lectures, concerts, performances, classes, and other cultural activities. Studio facilities include full foundry, metals, and wood shops; a ceramics and ceramic-sculpture studio; spacious painting, drawing, and design classrooms; printmaking studios with etching, plate, and stone lithography and screen printing facilities; digital facilities, including a state-of-the-art eMedia SINC site and advanced media studios; and a photo studio with newly renovated darkrooms. The heart of the M.F.A. program is a dedicated facility at Nassau Hall, in which each M.F.A. student is provided individual studio space. There are large common spaces used regularly for discussion, temporary exhibitions or installations, and documentation of work, as well as a woodshop and several networked computers for imaging, audio, and DV video editing.

Financial Aid The Department has available a number of half-tuition teaching assistantships ($7572.50), which are awarded on a competitive basis for the three years of the studio program. These students receive tuition scholarships equivalent to half of the in-state tuition rate for the duration of their course work, presuming timely completion of requirements. In addition, the Department regularly nominates applicants for several University-wide academically based fellowships, including Graduate Council Fellowships and the Dorothy Pieper Memorial Purchase Award, as well as W. Burghardt Turner Fellowships for underrepresented minorities. Unfunded students may find graduate or research assistantships elsewhere on campus, such as in the Main Library. Included in most of these assistantships is a health insurance plan.

Cost of Study In 2008–09, full-time tuition at 12 credits for entering in-state residents is $3450 per semester, while out-of-state residents and international students pay $5460. Additional fees for each semester, including (but not limited to) the infirmary, activity, technology, and transportation fees, total about $875. International students also pay a service fee of approximately $35 per semester and an orientation fee of $50. Fees for the mandatory Student Health Insurance Plan vary depending on citizenship and employment status.

Living and Housing Costs For 2008–09, Stony Brook calculates the cost of education excluding tuition, fees, and insurance at $14,228 per year. On-campus apartments range in cost from approximately $336 per month to approximately $1456 per month, depending on the size of the unit and the number of students sharing the space. Off-campus housing options include rooms, houses, and apartments that can be rented from approximately $350 to $2500 per month. Costs including books, food, and transportation may vary depending on academic program and/or personal circumstances.

Student Group There are currently 15 students in the program; 4 have just completed their third and final year. All are full-time (part-time study is not allowed). Students come from across the country and abroad, including, at present, 4 international students. For admission to the program, faculty members look for students with a promising portfolio of work, strong recommendations, and demonstrated commitment to the making of art. GRE scores are just one of a number of criteria used for admission.

Student Outcomes Since the inception of the M.F.A. program in studio art in 1985, Stony Brook has awarded seventy-four M.F.A. degrees. The program has been very successful in placing graduates in a variety of teaching and professional institutions, and most are continuing to produce art, exhibiting widely in national and international venues.

Location Ideally located halfway between the art centers of New York City and the Hamptons, Stony Brook offers a unique opportunity to study in a serene and spacious setting while maintaining close contact with the pulse of the art world. Faculty members encourage students to take advantage of the full range of exhibitions, performances, screenings, and lectures in New York City. The Pollock-Krasner House and Study Center in East Hampton and the new Stony Brook Manhattan site are important resources for research, lectures, and other activities.

The University and The Program The Department of Art at Stony Brook University offers a dynamic and interdisciplinary degree in studio art within the context of a major research institution. The M.F.A. program is enhanced by the orientation of the M.A. and Ph.D. degree programs toward theory and criticism of modern and contemporary art and visual culture and by a new multidisciplinary initiative centered upon digital media. The university setting not only provides students access to the distinguished faculty of artists and art historians, but also to faculty members and fellow students in music, theater arts, philosophy, history, and comparative studies, among others.

Applying Applicants need to provide two official transcripts of undergraduate and graduate course work, official Graduate Record Examinations (GRE) scores, an acceptable score on the TOEFL for international students, three letters of recommendation, and a nonrefundable $60 fee. Applicants must submit twenty slides or other appropriate media, including a slide/video script, CDs, and tapes; a statement of purpose; a resume; and an outline of any technical abilities that would assist in the assignment of a teaching position. Students should include a self-addressed stamped envelope if they wish materials to be returned. Applications and all supporting materials must be submitted by January 15 to be considered for Graduate Council, Turner, or other fellowships. All other applications must be received no later than March 1. Admission is for the fall semester only. Part-time study is not allowed in the M.F.A. program. Admission is subject to final approval by the Graduate School.

Correspondence and Information

Lisa Perez, Graduate Coordinator
Department of Art
Staller Center 2225
State University of New York at Stony Brook
Stony Brook, New York 11794-5400
Phone: 631-632-7270
Fax: 631-632-7261
E-mail: liperezlili@notes.cc.sunysb.edu
Web site: http://www.stonybrook.edu/art

Stony Brook University, State University of New York

THE FACULTY AND THEIR RESEARCH

The studio faculty members of the Department of Art are accomplished artists as well as dedicated teachers and mentors. They work not only in the traditional media of painting, sculpture, and printmaking, but also in photography, electronic media, installation, and public sculpture. They are actively engaged in lecturing, publishing, curating, jurying, and exhibiting in a wide range of regional, national, and international venues. Their high profile is reflected in the fellowships and grants they have received from the Guggenheim and Warhol Foundations, as well as the National Endowments for the Arts, among others.

Toby Buonagurio, Professor and Studio Coordinator; M.A., CUNY, City College, 1971. Toby Buonagurio is a lifetime resident of New York City, best known for her colorful, offbeat, tongue-in-cheek, ceramic sculpture. She has exhibited her work in twenty-seven solo exhibitions in museums and art galleries in the United States and Japan. Her ceramic sculpture has been included in more than 200 international group shows. In 1997, she was the recipient of a fellowship from the Shigaraki Ceramic Cultural Park in Japan and, as an "Invited Guest Artist," created her art work, lectured, and traveled throughout the country for two months. Her work has been written about extensively in national periodicals and professional publications and has been featured in television documentaries on the arts. Her work is represented in numerous private and public collections internationally. Her artwork was commissioned by the New York Metropolitan Transportation Authority for its Arts for Transit program for the Times Square–42 Street Subway Station, in the heart of New York City. The work, titled "Times Square Times: 35 Times," comprises thirty-five one-of-a-kind glazed, sculptural ceramic reliefs installed in glass-covered lighted boxes. The entire permanent installation wraps through 800 feet of glass-block clad walls in the Times Square–42 Street subway station and is viewed by more than a half million subway riders daily.

Stephanie Dinkins, Associate Professor; M.F.A., Maryland Institute, College of Art, 1997. Stephanie Dinkins is an interdisciplinary artist whose work explores issues of value and visibility through an image-based art practice. Her installations, sculptures, and images are shown internationally. Recently she has completed publicity situated works for Jamaica Flux 2007 and The Laundromat Project, both in New York. Her work has also been featured at the Bridge Art Fair, Miami, Florida; Arlington Art Center; The Soap Factory, Minneapolis, Minnesota; and the Studio Museum in Harlem, New York. Her M.F.A. degree is in photography, and she is an alumna of the Independent Studies Program of the Whitney Museum of American Art. Her awards and honors include a Puffin Foundation Grant, a Philip Morris Artist of Color Fellowship, two American Photography Institute National Graduate Seminar Fellowships, and an LEF Foundation Grant.

Christa Erickson, Associate Professor; M.F.A., California, San Diego, 1995. Christa Erickson's research interests include electronic installation, video art, net.art, gender and technology, queer studies, and art and politics. She is an interdisciplinary artist who investigates the politics, pleasures, and pains of spaces mediated by electronic technologies. Her works experiment with combinations of media, sculpture, performance, and the Internet and often take the form of installations. Her individual and collaborative works have been exhibited widely, including galleries in New York City, the binational InSITE 1994, the Walker Art Center in Minneapolis, the California Museum of Photography, the Institute for Studies in the Arts in Arizona, and the Banff Center for the Arts in Canada. Her recent installation, "Mnemonic Devices," stages a playground of actual (a seesaw memory editor) and virtual (multiuser Web game) interfaces to consider questions of memory and connection in the digital age. She is director of the Digital Arts Studio and codirector of the Laboratory for Technology Arts. She previously founded the digital media area at Indiana University and taught computing in the arts at the University of California, San Diego.

Grady Gerbracht, Assistant Professor; S.M.Vis.S., MIT, 1999. Grady Gerbracht is a graduate of the Cooper Union for Science and Art and an alumnus of the Whitney Museum of American Art Independent Study Program in Architecture and Urbanism. He is a multidisciplinary artist whose work focuses on the ordering systems of everyday life. Inspired by personal observations and life experiences, Gerbracht's projects employ art, architecture, sound, and social dynamics to render these systems temporarily visible. His projects have been published and exhibited in the U.S., Brazil, Japan, Korea, and Europe. He has organized numerous exhibitions, including Back and Forth, a series of exhibitions involving notions of commutes and itineraries, and Global Priority, an exhibition that explores how artists are responding to the accelerating hybridization of identities in relation to dispersed flows of economic and cultural values. He is currently working on an exhibition entitled Civic Performance. Recent artworks focus on the interrelationships of sound, bodies, and space. These include the ongoing series Site&Sound and Sonic Architectures. The artist records sonic portraits, which capture the unique acoustic characteristics of each site as he performs the architectural spaces with his body. Sound compositions derived from the performances are later reinserted into the original context.

Martin Levine, Associate Professor and Director of Undergraduate Studies; M.F.A., California College of Arts and Crafts, 1972. Artist/printmaker Martin Levine was born in New York City. He works mainly in etching and lithography, depicting realistically rendered cityscapes. His work has been included extensively in both international and American invitational and juried exhibitions. His prints and drawings are in many important collections, including the Brooklyn Museum, the Museum of Fine Arts in Boston, the Art Institute of Chicago, and the Victoria and Albert Museum in London. He is the recipient of more than 120 awards, including a National Endowment for the Arts grant in printmaking. He has been on the jury for numerous international exhibitions, including Biennials in Varna, Bulgaria; Lodz, Poland; Belgrade, Serbia; and Bristol, England. He is the former president of the Society of American Graphic Artists and was elected to the National Academy of Design in 1997.

Nobuho Nagasawa, Associate Professor; M.F.A., Hochschule der Kunste Berlin (Germany), 1985. Nagasawa was born in Tokyo and raised in Europe and Japan. Based in New York City since 2001, she came to the United States as a visiting scholar through the invitation of California Institute of the Arts in 1986, where she studied visual art, critical theory, and music. She is an interdisciplinary artist whose site-specific work explores the places, politics, ecology, and psychological dimensions of space and people. Her work involves in-depth research into cultural history, memory, and extensive community participation. Her exhibition records include: the Royal Garden of the Prague Castle in the Czech Republic, Ludwig Museums in Germany and Hungary, Rufino Tamayo Museum in Mexico, the Getty Center for the History of Art and Humanities in the United States, Alexandria Library in Egypt, as well as exhibitions in Denmark, Italy, and Japan. She has been a representative of international venues such as Asian Art Biennial (Bangladesh, 2002), International Biennial (Egypt, 2002), Sharjah Biennial (United Arab Emirates, 2003), Echigo-Tsumari Triennial (Japan, 2003), and Sinop Biennial (Turkey, 2006). She has received numerous grants from DAAD in Germany, the Berlin State Grant, Rockefeller Grant, California Arts Council Fellowships Award, Brody Arts Fund, and Japan Foundation Grants, among others. In New York, she was a recipient of The Space Program of the Marie Walsh Sharpe Foundation and of the Established Artist Studio Fellowship from Urban Glass. Her work has been reviewed in the *Los Angeles Times, Art in America, Art Asia Pacific,* and *Sculpture* magazine and most recently in *The New York Times* by Holland Cotter. Her work has been published in the following books: *Japanese Art After 1945: Scream Against the Sky* (Alexandra Munroe, Abrams, Inc., 1994), *Lure of the Local: Senses of Place in Multicentered Society* (Lucy Lippard, New Press, 1997), and *Epicenter: San Francisco Bay Area Art Now* (Mark Johnstone, Leslie Aboud Holzman, Chronicle Books, 2002). She has been commissioned for more than twenty public art projects in California, Washington, Texas, New York, Berlin, and Japan. She received the Design Excellence Award for Architecture and Public Art in 1997 through the Office of Cultural Affairs in Los Angeles. In 2000, she designed a 42,000-square-foot plaza for the Urban Government Center, commissioned by the Ministry of Construction of the Metropolitan Government in Japan. Her public art project for the Austin City Hall and Public Plaza with Antoine Predock was featured as one of the best projects nationwide in *Art in America 05–06 Annual Review*. In 2005 she created a suspended light and sound tapestry sculpture of woven fiber optic for the Seattle City Hall by using some of the leading-edge development in science and technology. The pulsations of shifting hues of blue light, cascading up and down the length of the fiber tapestry, are synchronized through real-time acoustic analysis with the ebb and flow of the waves of the Puget Sound. Her current projects include work in San Francisco and Los Angeles. In 2006, her work was included in *artnet*'s artist catalog and at the Sotheby's Contemporary Art Auction. In New York, she has been working on a Greenway project along the river on Columbia Street commissioned by the Office of the Cultural Affairs Percent for Art Program in 2004. This year, she was awarded a commission for the main entrance of the UCLA hospital designed by I.M. Pei in Los Angeles.

Melvin H. Pekarsky, Professor and Chair; M.A., Northwestern, 1956. Mel Pekarsky studied painting, art history, and theory at the School of the Art Institute of Chicago and Northwestern University. He taught at Northwestern, Kendall College, the School of Visual Arts, and New York University before coming to Stony Brook. He was a founding member of City Walls, Inc., an artist-run public art corporation that evolved into New York's Public Art Fund. He has shown his work widely in this country and abroad, where his paintings, drawings, prints, and artist's books, which range from wall to pocket-size, can be found in public, private, and corporate collections. For three decades, his work has focused on images of the desert as icons of the earth's fragility and on the tenuous balance between abstraction and representation. He teaches painting, drawing, theory, and public art. A book of his drawings of the desert was recently included in the Fogg Museum of Art's *Under Cover: Artist's Sketchbooks*.

Howardena Pindell, Professor and M.F.A. Director; M.F.A., Yale, 1967. Howardena Pindell is a painter whose work is in the collections of numerous museums, including the Metropolitan Museum, the Museum of Modern Art, the Whitney Museum of American Art, the Fogg Museum at Harvard University, the Philadelphia Museum of Art, and in a number of corporate collections. She has received numerous awards and fellowships, including a U.S.-Japan Friendship Commission Exchange Artist Fellowship, a Guggenheim Fellowship, two National Endowment for the Arts grants, a Joan Mitchell painting award, the Studio Museum in Harlem Award, as well as the 1990 College Art Association Award for the Most Distinguished Body of Work. Before coming to Stony Brook, she was an associate curator of prints and illustrated books at the Museum of Modern Art in New York.

TEACHERS COLLEGE, COLUMBIA UNIVERSITY

Department of Arts and Humanities

Programs of Study

The Department of Arts and Humanities at Teachers College, Columbia University, is committed to the education of reflective practitioners, the integration of theory, the improvement of learning, and research and practice in students' chosen fields of study. Intellectual and creative ideas and practices within the Department extend beyond the traditional concerns of schooling. Each program shares a concern with the learner's construction of knowledge, the art and methods of teaching, the realities of the contemporary classroom, the relationship of schools to their communities, and the underlying philosophies of school reform.

The Department offers the following ten programs: applied linguistics, art and art education, arts administration, history and education, music and music education, philosophy and education, teaching of social studies, teaching of English, teaching of English to speakers of other languages (TESOL), and TESOL, TOKYO. Further information about these programs and their requirements can be found in the *Academic Catalog*, which is available online at http://www.tc.columbia.edu/admissions/catalog-archives/0809/.

Research Facilities

The Gottesman Libraries, with more than a million books and materials, is one of the nation's largest and most comprehensive research libraries in education, psychology, and health services. Students also have access to the 9.5 million volumes in the Columbia University library system. Organized research and service activities at Teachers College, in addition to being carried out by individual professors, are conducted through special projects and major institutes.

Financial Aid

Each year, Teachers College awards approximately $5 million of its own funds in scholarship and stipend aid and $2 million of endowed funds to new and continuing students. Most scholarship awards are made on the basis of academic merit. Scholarships are applied to tuition only, and students should expect to provide additional funds for the tuition balance, fees, medical insurance, academic, and living expenses.

Cost of Study

For the 2008–09 academic year, tuition is $1085 per point, with 12 or more points considered full-time. Fees include the Teachers College, $358; Teachers College research, $358; health service, $387; continuous doctoral advisement registration, $3255; and Ph.D. oral defense, $4581. The tuition deposit is $300. Medical insurance ranges from about $591 to $1303.

Living and Housing Costs

Teachers College offers a variety of on-campus housing options that are unique to the area and convenient to the campus. Housing for a single student ranges from $3600 to $8750 per semester, depending on the type of setting selected. Family housing ranges from $7200 to $8600 per semester. Teachers College has approximately 705 spaces available for single students and 150 apartments for students with families. The buildings are located in the vibrant and historic urban neighborhood of Morningside Heights. Current residence halls are historic buildings similar to other apartment-style buildings that were in New York City in the early 1900s.

Student Group

There are approximately 5,000 students enrolled at Teachers College. About 77 percent are women, 10 percent are African American, 13 percent are Asian American, and 7 percent are Latino/a. The student body is composed of 15 percent international students from eighty different countries and 87 percent domestic students from all fifty states. While about one third of TC students are working toward or developing their teaching career, the balance of the TC student community are pursuing careers in a wide range of fields, including educational policy, educational administration and leadership, arts administration, technology, psychology, social and behavioral sciences, health, communication, and international and comparative education.

Location

The College is located in the Morningside Heights section of Manhattan's Upper West Side, home to such venerable New York landmarks as Lincoln Center, the Cathedral of St. John the Divine, Grant's Tomb, Morningside Park, and the Manhattan School of Music. The Upper West Side is bounded by Central Park on the east and the Hudson River on the west. Because the College is located in New York City, students have access to an outstanding array of learning organizations, including museums, libraries, galleries, corporate learning centers, and K–12 schools.

The College and The University

Teachers College was founded in 1887 to provide a new form of schooling for the teachers of children from low-income families of New York, one that combined a humanitarian concern to help others with a scientific approach to human development. For more than 100 years, Teachers College has conducted research on the central issues facing education, prepared generations of education leaders, and shaped debate and public policy in education. The College provides programs of study in administration, counseling, curriculum development, and school health care and continues its efforts to strengthen teaching skills, prepare leaders to develop and administer psychological and health-care programs, and develop new teaching software. In 1898, Teachers College became affiliated with Columbia University.

Columbia University was founded in 1754 as King's College by royal charter of King George II of England. It is the oldest institution of higher learning in the state of New York and the fifth-oldest in the United States. From its beginnings in a schoolhouse in lower Manhattan, the University has grown to encompass two principal campuses: the historic, neoclassical campus in Morningside Heights and the modern Medical Center in Washington Heights. Today, Columbia is one of the top academic and research institutions in the world, conducting research in medicine, science, the arts, and the humanities. It includes three undergraduate schools, thirteen graduate and professional schools, and a school of continuing education. Sixty-four Nobel laureates have taught or studied at Columbia. Each year, the faculty of approximately 4,000 teaches more than 24,000 students from more than 150 countries.

Applying

Teachers College welcomes applicants who wish to pursue graduate study associated with the education, psychology, and health-related professions. All applicants receive consideration for admission without regard to race, color, creed, religion, sex, national origin, age, or disability. In order to be considered for scholarships, students must meet the early deadline. Admissions applications received after the early deadline may be considered on a space-available basis. Certain programs have special application deadlines. The 2007–08 early deadline for Ph.D. and all psychology doctoral programs is December 15. The early deadline for Ed.D. programs is January 2, with a final deadline of April 1. The early deadline for master's programs is January 15, with a final deadline of April 15. For applicants wishing to start in the spring semester, the early deadline is November 1.

Teachers College requests that applicants collect the required documents for the application process and submit the complete application to the Office of Admission at one time. Admission application deadlines always refer to the date by which the Teachers College Office of Admissions must have received the application components and any other supporting material required by the Department. For more information on applying to Teachers College and for an online application, prospective students may visit the College's Web site at http://www.tc.columbia.edu/admissions.

Correspondence and Information

Teachers College, Columbia University
525 West 120th Street, Box 302
New York, New York 10027

Phone: 212-678-3710
Web site: http://www.tc.columbia.edu/discover
http://www.tc.columbia.edu/a&h

Teachers College Columbia University

THE FACULTY AND THEIR RESEARCH

The following is a brief listing of current Teachers College faculty members. For a complete listing and more detailed information, including profiles selected publications, news, and photos, students should visit the Web site at http://www.tc.columbia.edu/faculty.

Professors
Harold F. Abeles (Music).
Leslie M. Beebe (Applied Linguistics/TESOL).
Judith M. Burton (Art).
Margaret Smith Crocco (Social Studies).
Steven Dubin (Arts Administration).
Maxine Greene, Emerita (Philosophy and Aesthetics).
David T. Hansen (Philosophy).
Janet L. Miller (English).
Ruth Vinz (English).

Adjunct Professors.
Dino Anagnost (Voice, Conducting).
Mary C. Boys (Union Theological Seminary).
Gay Brookes (TESOL).
Joan Jeffri (Arts Administration).
Ronald Knapp (Social Studies).
Bert Konowitz (Jazz).

Associate Professors
John Baldacchino (Art).
John M. Broughton (Cultural Studies).
Lori Custodero (Music).
William Gaudelli (Social Studies).
ZhaoHong Han (TESOL).
Megan Laverty (Philosophy).
Lenore M. Pogonowski (Music).
James E. Purpura (Applied Linguistics/TESOL).
Graeme Sullivan (Art).
Cally L. Waite (History).

Adjunct Associate Professors
Evelyn Chen (Piano).
Alvin Fossner (Oboe, Saxophone).
Franklin E. Horowitz (Applied Linguistics).
Robert Horowitz (Music).
Joy Moser (Painting).
Jean-Marc Oppenheim (Social Studies).
Geraldo Piña Rosales (Spanish).
Terry Royce (TESOL, Tokyo).

Assistant Professors
Randall Allsup (Music).
Reneé Cherow-O'Leary (English).
Olga Hubard (Art).
Anand R. Marri (Social Studies).
Mikki Shaw (English).
Patricia Zumhagen (English).

Assistant Professor of Practice
Barbara Hruska (TESOL).

Adjunct Assistant Professors
Philip Aarons (Arts Administration).
Lorraine Cella (English).
Jasmin Cowin (Harp).
Herman Jie Sam Foek (Art).
James Frankel (Music).
Benjamin Fryman (Cultural Studies).
John Gavalichin (Piano).
Andrew Henderson (Organ).
Kate Hickey (English).
Richard Jacobowski (Guitar).
Ami Kantawala (Art Education).
I. Fred Koenigsberg (Arts Administration).
Ada Kopetz-Korf (Piano).
John D. Kuentzel (Religion).
Margaret Leibowitz (Arts Administration).
Roberta Martin (Social Studies).
Lori McCann (Voice).
Angelo Miranda (Percussion).
Patricia Rohrer (Philosophy).
Patricia St. John (Music).
Barbara Tischler (Social Studies).
Jerry Weiner (Social Studies).

Lecturers
Caroline Fuchs (TESOL).
Jeanne Goffi-Fynn (Music and Music Education).
Hansun Zhang Waring (TESOL).
Bette Weneck (History).
Howard A. Williams (Applied Linguistics).

Instructors
Brooke Anderson (Art Education, Museum Education).
Sheyda Ardalan (Art).
John Balbi (TESOL).
Mary Barto (Flute).
John Beaumont (TESOL).
Sergio Bessa (Museum Education).
Iris Bildstein (Art).
Harrigan Bouman (Photography).
Wendy Bowcher (TESOL, Tokyo).
John Browne (English).
Rika Burnham (Art).
Ingrid Butterer (Art).
Christine Casanave (TESOL, Tokyo).
Alexander K. Cates (TESOL, Tokyo).
Phil Choong (TESOL).
Carolyn Clark (Arts Administration).
Charles Combs (TESOL).
Jennifer Cutsforth (Social Studies).
Renee Darvin (Art Education, Museum Education).
Judith Davidoff (Renaissance/Baroque Instruments).
Kristen DiGennaro (TESOL).
Mariah Doren (Photography).
Monika Ekiert (TESOL).
Bayard Faithfull (Social Studies).
Mah Bobe Ghods (Printmaking).
Erick Gordon (English).
Carolyn Graham (TESOL).
Nanci Graves (TESOL, Tokyo).
Mark Helgeson (TESOL, Tokyo).
Sang Bin Im (Art Technology).
Rebekah Johnson (TESOL).
Cathleen Kiebert-Gruen (Art).
Hyunjoo Kim (Applied Linguistics).
Tatsuya Komatsu (TESOL, Tokyo).
Karen LaBonté (English).
Naomi Lifschitz (Art).
Thomas Lollar (Ceramics).
Jane McIntosh (Arts Administration).
Maurizio Pellegrin (Art).
Diane Pinkley (TESOL).
Greg Pitts (Ceramics).
Raymond S. Pultinas (English).
John D. Purdy (Applied Linguistics).
Ted Quock (TESOL, Tokyo).
Shyla Rao (Art).
Yasayo Sakawi (Applied Linguistics).
Sophia Sarigianides (English).
Yasushi Sekiya (TESOL, Tokyo).
David Shea (TESOL, Tokyo).
Natalie Shifano (Art Education).
Susan Stempleski (TESOL).
Jason Swift (Sculpture).
Peter Swords (Arts Administration).
Richard Pearson Thomas (Music Composition).
Tak Uemura (TESOL, Tokyo).
Sharon Vatsky (Museum Education).
Gerard Vezzuso (Photography).
Martin Vinik (Arts Administration).
June Wai (TESOL).
Linda Wine (Applied Linguistics).

Visiting Professors
Sheridan Blau (English).
Mordechai Gordon (Philosophy).
Yolanda Sealey-Ruiz (English).

TEMPLE UNIVERSITY

of the Commonwealth System of Higher Education

Tyler School of Art
Department of Art History

Programs of Study

The Department of Art History offers a course of study that leads to the M.A. and Ph.D. degrees. A special option combining art history courses with those given in the Graduate School of Business and Management is available to students studying for a master's degree who are interested in the administration of art collections and related cultural institutions. The graduate curriculum covers all areas of Western and Mediterranean art history, from ancient art to modern; it also introduces the student to a wide variety of critical methods and approaches. For Ph.D. students, the faculty concentrates on ancient/medieval, Renaissance/Baroque, and modern/contemporary art.

The objective of the master's degree program is to provide students with a thorough preparation for further graduate work or, for those for whom it is a terminal degree, specialized training as the foundation of a career. Requirements include 30 graduate credits; reading examinations in German and in French, Italian, or Spanish; a thesis; and a comprehensive examination. The fine arts administration option requires 36 graduate credits (15–18 in art history, 12–15 in business administration), a semester-long internship (6 credits, 20 hours per week), and the language and comprehensive examinations. The Ph.D. program is intended to prepare students for college teaching or for other research-oriented positions requiring advanced specialized study. The degree requires 60 graduate-level (5000-level or above) credits in art history beyond the B.A.; up to 9 of these credits may be taken in graduate-level courses, relevant to the student's field, outside the Department (but at Temple). Candidacy is granted upon acceptance of the dissertation proposal.

Research Facilities

Temple's library system contains nearly 2 million volumes and rich online resources; more than 60,000 books and periodicals are concerned with art and architecture. These holdings are supplemented by those of area libraries, including those at the University of Pennsylvania and Bryn Mawr College and at the Philadelphia Free Library. The research facilities of Washington, D.C.; Princeton University; and New York are only an hour or so away.

Financial Aid

The Department recommends full-time students for assistantships each term, with priority given to Ph.D. students. Funding is not normally available for M.A. candidates. Each assistantship carries a waiver of all tuition fees plus a stipend of $14,000 per academic year. Assistants are required to work 20 hours per week. Prestigious University-wide fellowships are awarded by the Graduate School upon recommendation by the Department; these provide full tuition and a stipend ($20,000). The Graduate School also awards Future Faculty Fellowships to students who intend to seek a terminal degree leading to a career in an area of academia underrepresented by their ethnic group. These fellowships are reserved for full-time students and provide funding of up to $14,000 per year plus full tuition remission. Loans, which are available only to American citizens, can be arranged through the Office of Financial Aid. The Department has a fellowship for predissertation study in Rome, which is awarded to a qualified student whose research will benefit by residence in Rome.

Cost of Study

In-state graduate tuition was $559 per credit in 2007–08; out-of-state graduate tuition was $823.

Living and Housing Costs

Minimum living expenses for the academic year are estimated at $15,000 for single students ($8600 for those commuting from home). Dormitory housing adjacent to the main campus of Temple and to Tyler campus is available.

Student Group

The Department accepts about 15 students each year. While most are recent college graduates, others are returning students. The majority of students attend full-time; however, serious, qualified applicants are also admitted on a part-time basis. Graduate courses are held on weekdays, usually in the late afternoon.

Student Outcomes

Alumni from the master's program have pursued various options. Some attend Ph.D. programs at Temple and other institutions, while others teach at colleges and high schools. Several graduates are working in galleries or museums. The University's fine arts administration graduates tend to acquire positions in financial or developmental areas at art institutions, galleries, or museums.

Location

Philadelphia, the nation's fifth-largest city, is famous for its historic buildings and monuments and its outstanding museums—the Philadelphia Museum of Art, the University of Pennsylvania Museum, the Pennsylvania Academy of the Fine Arts, the Barnes Foundation, and the Rodin Museum. Among its cultural assets are the city's world-renowned orchestra, lively dance offerings, experimental and pre-Broadway theater, and film societies. The Jersey Shore and the Pocono Mountains are within an hour's drive.

The University and The Department

With more than 34,000 students and 1,700 faculty members, Temple University (a member institution of Pennsylvania's Commonwealth System of Higher Education) operates on four campuses in the Philadelphia area and on the Temple Abroad campuses in Rome and Tokyo; the Rome program is housed in the Villa Caproni, a nineteenth-century palazzo with classrooms and studios overlooking the Tiber. The Department of Art History is located on the main campus in Ritter Hall Annex; this facility has faculty offices, a study lounge and computer facilities for graduate students, an auxiliary slide and digital image center, and a seminar room.

Applying

Although the Department makes admission decisions (on the basis of completed files) throughout the academic year, application deadlines for those applying for fellowships or assistantships are January 15 (for the following September) and October 15 (for the following January). Late applications are considered, but late applicants for assistantships or fellowships are at a disadvantage. In addition to an application form (available at http://www.temple.edu/grad) and a $50 fee (payable by credit card or bank account), two sets of the following credentials are required: a statement of goals (indicating the intended terminal degree), official transcripts of all undergraduate and graduate study, an original GRE score report form, a writing sample, and at least two letters of reference. International students must also send TOEFL scores. For the master's programs, applicants must hold a baccalaureate degree (any major). Students with an art history background are given preference. Because it is the objective of the program to give students training across the range of Western and Mediterranean art, students may be required to make up deficiencies in distribution at the discretion of the Director of Graduate Studies. Students seeking admission to the doctoral program must hold a master's degree in art history or in a related discipline, as determined at the discretion of the Director of Graduate Studies. Students admitted without a degree in art history are expected to take courses in areas where they are deficient. For both degrees, German is required, as is a second foreign language, usually French or Italian. When it is appropriate for a student's course of study, another relevant language may be substituted with the approval of the Director of Graduate Studies.

Correspondence and Information

For more information about the program:

Department of Art History
Temple University
1301 Cecil B. Moore Avenue
Ritter Annex 857
Philadelphia, Pennsylvania 19122
Phone: 215-204-7837
Fax: 215-204-6951
E-mail: ahgrad@temple.edu

To request or return application forms:

Admissions Department
Tyler School of Art
Temple University
7725 Penrose Avenue
Elkins Park, Pennsylvania 19027
Phone: 215-782-2828

Temple University

THE FACULTY

Philip P. Betancourt, Laura H. Carnell Professor; Ph.D., Pennsylvania, 1970. Aegean Bronze Age and Greek art.
Elizabeth Bolman, Associate Professor; Ph.D., Bryn Mawr, 1997. Early medieval and Byzantine art.
Alan Braddock, Assistant Professor; Ph.D., Delaware, 2002. Nineteenth-century American art.
Tracy Cooper, Associate Professor; Ph.D., Princeton, 1990. Italian Renaissance and Baroque art and architecture.
Therese Dolan, Professor; Ph.D., Bryn Mawr, 1979. Nineteenth-century French art and criticism.
Jane DeRose Evans, Associate Professor and Chair; Ph.D., Pennsylvania, 1985. Roman art.
Susanna W. Gold, Lecturer; Ph.D., Pennsylvania, 2004. Nineteenth-century American art.
Marcia B. Hall, Professor; Ph.D., Harvard, 1967. Italian Renaissance art.
Gerald Silk, Professor; Ph.D., Virginia, 1976. Modern art.

A graduate assistant teaching at the Philadelphia Museum of Art.

Villa Caproni, Temple Abroad's headquarters in Rome.

Ritter Hall Annex on Temple's main campus in Philadelphia.

UNIVERSITY OF ROCHESTER

Department of Art and Art History
Visual and Cultural Studies Program

Program of Study

The Visual and Cultural Studies Program, housed in the Department of Art and Art History, offers students the chance to earn a master's or doctoral degree by doing intensive work simultaneously in several of Rochester's humanities departments. Primary faculty members for the Visual and Cultural Studies Program teach in the Departments of Art and Art History, English, and Modern Languages and Cultures, all in the College of Arts and Sciences. Students take courses in those departments and may also take courses in such departments as anthropology, history, music, and philosophy. About 20 faculty members participate in the program each year, including the Visual and Cultural Studies Steering Committee, which guides the program.

An innovative graduate program with a unique emphasis on visual and cultural representation, Rochester's Visual and Cultural Studies Program provides students with an opportunity to study critically and analyze culture from a social-historical perspective. The program stresses interpretation of art, film, and media within historical and ideological frameworks. Because the main contributing faculty members work in art and art history, film and media studies, and comparative literature, students are able to relate recent developments in literary and cultural theory to visual works and investigate the interrelationships between visual texts and critical theory.

All doctoral students take eight core courses: four in visual studies and four in critical theory. In addition, they take six electives, chosen from an extensive list of courses offered by the three primary departments; when appropriate, they may substitute courses from other disciplines. All students participate in the Visual and Cultural Studies Colloquium in the fall semester of their first year of study.

Most Ph.D. students spend 3½ years completing 60 credits of course work and 30 credits of research. After this, they take a qualifying exam, based on their reading and preliminary work on their dissertation. Students serve as teaching assistants for a number of introductory courses or as research assistants.

Research Facilities

The University's libraries contain holdings of 2.5 million volumes and 16,000 periodicals. Housed within the Rush Rhees Library, the Art and Music Library includes 40,000 books and bound journals, 300 journal subscriptions and standing orders for monograph series, and a growing collection of videotapes. The Visual Resource Collection at the University consists of more than 140,000 slides and mounted pictures. The University's Memorial Art Gallery also maintains its own library of 17,000 books and bound periodicals. The Film and Media Studies Center has several thousand films and videotapes available for viewing. Students can use the film and photograph collections at the world-renowned International Museum of Photography in the George Eastman House in Rochester.

Financial Aid

The Visual and Cultural Studies Steering Committee awards graduate teaching and research assistantships to students in the program. Tuition scholarships are also offered to qualified doctoral candidates. Assistantships currently carry an annual award of up to $15,000 beyond tuition. The University also awards Sproull Fellowships and Provost's Fellowships on a competitive basis, which carry a maximum stipend of $20,000 annually for up to two years. Students can receive extra funding by assisting in studio art courses or by teaching summer school.

Cost of Study

Tuition for full-time graduate study for 2008–09 is $1138 per credit hour.

Living and Housing Costs

Accommodations for graduate students are available in four University-owned projects and in off-campus housing; for a brochure, a rate sheet, an application, and off-campus housing listings, applicants should write the Housing Coordinator at the Community Living Program, 020 Gates Wing, Susan B. Anthony Halls, P.O. Box 270468, Rochester, New York 14627-0468.

Student Group

The Department accepts 5 to 7 students each year, generally all of whom are full-time. Currently, there are 27 students in residence. The diverse graduate group is equally divided between men and women, and most students are receiving some form of financial aid.

Location

Located on the south shore of Lake Ontario, Rochester is the cultural and technological center of upstate New York. More than 800,000 residents of the metropolitan area can enjoy the Memorial Art Gallery, the George Eastman House (the world's leading museum and archive of photography and motion pictures), and the University's Eastman Theatre, where concerts are given by the Rochester Philharmonic Orchestra.

The University

The University, established in 1850, is private and coeducational. Four of the University's seven schools and colleges, including the College of Arts and Science, are located on the River Campus. The School of Medicine and Dentistry and the School of Nursing are within a 5-minute walk, and the Eastman School of Music is 2 miles away in the downtown area. Graduate work is carried on in each of the University's units. There are 1,000 full-time faculty members.

Applying

The deadline for applications is February 1 for the following September; offers of admission are sent to applicants on or about March 15. The application is available online only. Along with the online application, students should submit a personal statement, three letters of recommendation, official undergraduate and graduate transcripts, a writing sample, and GRE scores. International students must also supply TOEFL scores.

Correspondence and Information

Visual and Cultural Studies Program
Department of Art and Art History
424 Morey Hall, RC Box 270456
University of Rochester
Rochester, New York 14627

Phone: 585-275-9249
E-mail: art_arthist@cc.rochester.edu
Web site: http://www.rochester.edu/college/AAH/

University of Rochester

THE FACULTY AND THEIR RESEARCH

Visual and Cultural Studies Core Faculty and Associated Faculty

Janet Berlo, Professor of Art History/Visual and Cultural Studies; Ph.D., Yale. Native American art history and museum representation of Native peoples, Plains Indians drawings, Native American women and art, textiles and American visual culture.

Douglas Crimp, Fanny Knapp Allen Professor of Art History/Visual and Cultural Studies; Ph.D., CUNY. Contemporary art and criticism, race and representation, gay studies.

Thomas DiPiero, Professor of French/Visual and Cultural Studies; Ph.D., Cornell. French prose fiction of the seventeenth and eighteenth centuries.

Paul Duro, Professor of Art History/Visual and Cultural Studies and Chair, Department of Art and Art History; Ph.D., Essex (England). Theories of imitation in European painting, institutions of art.

Robert Foster, Professor of Anthropology; Ph.D., Chicago. Social theory, nationalism, globalization, mass consumption.

Susan Gustafson, Professor of German; Ph.D., Stanford. Eighteenth-century German literature, psychoanalysis, and feminism.

Rachel Haidu, Assistant Professor of Art History; Ph.D., Columbia. Postwar American and European art, history of photography.

Rosemary Kegl, Associate Professor of English; Ph.D., Cornell. Sixteenth- and seventeenth-century English literature, contemporary Marxist and feminist theory.

John Michael, Professor of English/Visual and Cultural Studies; Ph.D., Johns Hopkins. American literature, cultural studies, and critical theory.

Greta Niu, Assistant Professor of English; Ph.D., Duke. Film studies, Asian literature.

Joan Saab, Associate Professor of Art History/Visual and Cultural Studies and Director of the Program in Visual and Cultural Studies; Ph.D., NYU. Twentieth-century American history, media and culture, urban and community studies, popular culture, cultural studies.

Jeffrey Tucker, Associate Professor of English; Ph.D., Princeton. African American literature, twentieth-century American literature, science fiction.

Sharon Willis, Professor of French/Visual and Cultural Studies; Ph.D., Cornell. Modern French literature and literary theory, critical and feminist theory, film theory and visual analysis.

UArts
THE UNIVERSITY OF THE ARTS

UNIVERSITY OF THE ARTS

Graduate Programs

Programs of Study

The University of the Arts (UArts), located on the Avenue of the Arts in Center City Philadelphia, offers graduate programs in art education; art education with a concentration in educational media; book arts/printmaking; ceramics, painting, and sculpture; industrial design; jazz studies; museum communication; museum education; museum exhibition, planning, and design; music education; teaching visual arts; postbaccalaureate certificate in crafts; postbaccalaureate teaching program (nondegree); and postbaccalaureate teaching program professional semester. The graduate programs offer an impressive combination of strengths: exceptionally accomplished faculty members, a remarkably individualized and interactive learning environment, access to outstanding facilities and resources, specialized studios, and programs of study that are both highly focused and highly flexible.

In the visual arts, programs include the Master of Arts in art education, which is designed to develop the studio, intellectual, and professional education background for educators; the Master of Arts in Teaching visual arts, which incorporates preparation for certification to teach art in grades K–12; the Master of Fine Arts in book arts/printmaking, which builds on the University's thirty-year tradition of involvement with the book and the printed image; and the Master of Fine Arts in ceramics, painting, or sculpture. These programs are designed to be completed in three years through part-time study. Also offered are the Master of Fine Arts in museum exhibition planning and design, which was developed with the support of the National Association of Museum Exhibition (NAME); the Master of Art in museum communication; the Master of Art in museum education; and the Master of Industrial Design.

In performance, the Master of Arts in Teaching in music education is a one-year-plus-summer program designed for students who have a bachelor's degree in music theory/composition, music history/literature, or other noneducation courses of study. The Master of Music in jazz studies is a one-year, 32-credit program. Designed as a finishing program in jazz performance, components of the program include advanced private instruction, hands-on internships and pedagogy study, and ensemble performances.

Research Facilities

Students use state-of-the-art digital-technology facilities, which include computer labs that support professional-level creative work, collaboration, and research. There is a dedicated Mac lab for graduate students and a wireless network throughout UArts buildings. In addition to multiple high-end graphics labs using enhanced Power Macintosh G4s and G5s, the University hosts a New Media Center comprising two dual-platform digital laboratories that enable the integration of animation and 3-D modeling. Also available on campus are the Borowsky Center for Publication Arts; photography, film, and animation facilities with studios and darkrooms, video editing suites, and two Master Series Oxberry Animation stands; recording studios, state-of-the-art music technology MIDI studios and editing suites, and practice rooms; a bronze foundry and plaster workshop; and crafts studios and workshops for ceramics, metals, wood, glassblowing, papermaking, and fibers. Other important facilities include the digital forge 3-D printer, a bookbindery, and stone and metal welding shops.

Financial Aid

The Free Application for Federal Student Aid (FAFSA) must be filed by applicants for financial aid. Graduate teaching assistantships are available for qualified applicants. Some teaching and technical assistantships are awarded by the University of the Arts; the amounts of these awards vary.

Cost of Study

Tuition for 2008–09 is $29,500 plus applicable technology, book supplies, and activity fees.

Living and Housing Costs

There is limited University housing for graduate students.

Student Group

Students come from forty states and territories and thirty countries; about 5 percent of the total enrollment of 2,500 are international students. The graduate programs enrolled 84 students in 2007–08.

Location

The University of the Arts campus is located in the heart of Philadelphia's Avenue of the Arts, in the heart of the cultural community. The area has theaters, museums, galleries, music and dance facilities, restaurants, and shopping. Philadelphia offers a broad mix of strong cultural and educational experiences. In addition to being of historic importance, the city is also a supporter of the arts. Urban and sophisticated, it is also a series of small, close-knit neighborhoods. Fairmount Park, the largest city park in the world, provides facilities for boating, fishing, hiking, biking, picnicking, and relaxing.

The University

The University of the Arts is composed of the College of Art and Design, the College of Performing Arts, and the College of Media and Communication. The largest comprehensive educational institution of its kind in the United States, UArts prepares students for more than a hundred professional career paths in the visual, performing, and communication arts. The College of Art and Design is a professional community dedicated to the visual arts, where art is the primary and central concern. Founded in 1870 to train artists to translate the technological advances of the Industrial Revolution, it is today one of the nation's leading art colleges. The College of Performing Arts focuses on the areas of music, dance, acting, and musical theater. Founded in 1870 to educate musicians, it has expanded to offer demanding undergraduate programs of ballet, modern dance, and jazz dance as well as a program in theater arts. In 1996, the College of Media and Communication (CMAC) was founded and dedicated to the integration of art, technology, and communication. The College of Media and Communication offers undergraduate programs in writing, multimedia, and communication.

UArts sponsors a variety of activities that include social events, lectures, performances, and regular gallery and museum trips to New York City and Washington, D.C.

Applying

Required application materials include the University's Application for Graduate Study, a personal statement of intent, a nonrefundable fee of $60, official college transcripts, and at least three letters of recommendation. Portfolios must be submitted by applicants to the visual arts programs. An audition is required for applicants to the music program. International students must submit a Certification of Finance and TOEFL scores in the event the student's first language is other than English.

Applications for admission in September should be submitted by January 15 for priority consideration. Applications submitted after January 15 are considered on a space-available basis. Applications for January admission (art education, museum communications, museum education, and music only) should be submitted by the preceding November 15. Applications for the part-time M.F.A. (summer residence) should be submitted by January 1.

Correspondence and Information

Director of Admission
University of the Arts
320 South Broad Street
Philadelphia, Pennsylvania 19102
Phone: 215-717-6030
800-616-ARTS (toll-free)
Fax: 215-717-6045
E-mail: admissions@uarts.edu
Web site: http://www.uarts.edu

University of the Arts

THE FACULTY

College of Art and Design
Paul Adorno, Adjunct Assistant Professor; M.S.Ed., Pennsylvania.
Jane Bedno, Professor Emeritus; J.D., William and Mary.
Rande Blank, Senior Lecturer; M.Ed., Beaver.
Gerard Brown, Senior Lecturer; M.F.A., Art Institute of Chicago.
Allegra Burnette, Senior Lecturer; M.F.A., University of the Arts.
Karen Clark-Schock, Adjunct Assistant Professor; Psy.D., Immaculata.
Raye Cohen, Adjunct Assistant Professor; M.F.A., M.A., University of the Arts.
David Comberg, Adjunct Associate Professor; M.F.A., Yale.
Richard Cress, Senior Lecturer; B.F.A., Virginia Commonwealth.
Tom Csaszar, Master Lecturer; B.F.A., Pennsylvania.
Alice Dommert, Senior Lecturer; M.F.A., University of the Arts.
Paul Flazone, Senior Lecturer; Ph.D. candidate, Pennsylvania.
Marita Fitzpatrick, Senior Lecturer; M.A.T., University of the Arts.
Virginia Fitzpatrick, Adjunct Associate Professor; Ph.D., Indiana.
Laura H. Foster, Adjunct Associate Professor; J.D., Baltimore.
Diane Foxman, Senior Lecturer; M.A., Goddard.
Nancy Gerber, Senior Lecturer; Psy.D., Immaculata.
Aaron Goldblatt, Adjunct Assistant Professor; M.F.A., Tyler.
Arlene Gostin, Associate Professor; M.A., Philadelphia College of Art.
Randy Granger, Adjunct Assistant Professor; B.F.A., Philadelphia College of Art.
James Green, Master Lecturer; M.L.S., Columbia, M.Ph., Yale.
Anthony Guido, Associate Professor; B.S.I.D., Ohio State.
Diane Hricko, Adjunct Assistant Professor; B.S., SUNY.
Jamer Hunt, Associate Professor; Ph.D., Rice.
Jeanne Jaffe, Professor; M.F.A., Alfred, College of Ceramics.
Lois M. Johnson, Professor; M.F.A., Wisconsin–Madison.
June Julian, Associate Professor; Ed.D., NYU.
Susan Kaye-Huntington, Adjunct Assistant Professor; Psy.D., Immaculata.
Nathan Knobler, Professor Emeritus; M.F.A., Florida State.
Peter Kruty, Master Lecturer; M.L.S., M.A., Alabama.
Hedi Kyle, Adjunct Professor; Dipl., Werk-Kunst Schule, Wiesbaden (Germany).
Sumi Maeshima, Senior Lecturer; M.F.A., University of the Arts.
Polly McKenna-Cress, Associate Professor; M.F.A., University of the Arts.
Jonas Milder, Associate Professor; M.I.D., Hochschule der Kuenste Berlin (Germany).
Slavko Milekic, Associate Professor; M.Sc., M.D., Belgrade (Yugoslavia); Ph.D., Connecticut.
Carol Moore, Associate Professor; M.F.A., Temple.
Eileen Neff, Adjunct Associate Professor; M.F.A., Temple.
Gerald Nichols, Professor; M.F.A., Pennsylvania.
Mary Phelan, Associate Professor; M.A., Wisconsin–Madison.
Amy Phillips-Iverson, Lecturer; M.A., University of the Arts.
Tom Porett, Professor; M.S., IIT.
Robin Rice, Adjunct Associate Professor; M.A., Missouri.
Susan Rodriguez, Adjunct Professor; M.Ed., Temple.
James Rosenthal, Senior Lecturer.
Barent Roth, Junior Lecturer; M.I.D., University of the Arts.
Pearl B. Schaeffer, Adjunct Associate Professor; M.F.A., University of the Arts.
Irene Sfakianos, Senior Lecturer; M.F.A., MIT.
Jennie Shanker, Adjunct Assistant Professor; M.F.A., Yale.
Patricia Smith, Associate Professor; M.A., Philadelphia College of Art.
Lori Spencer, Adjunct Associate Professor; M.F.A., University of the Arts.
Portia Hamilton Sperr, Adjunct Associate Professor; B.A., Barnard.
Patricia Stewart, Adjunct Associate Professor; B.A., Pennsylvania.
Barbara Suplee, Associate Professor; Ph.D., Penn State.
Jane Swanson, Lecturer; B.S., Iowa State.
Susan T. Viguers, Professor; Ph.D., Bryn Mawr.
Susan White, Senior Lecturer; M.F.A., University of the Arts.
Jo Ann Wright, Adjunct Assistant Professor; B.A., Rowan.
Mira Zergani, Senior Lecturer; B.A., Temple.

College of Performing Arts
Robert Brosh, Adjunct Associate Professor; D.A.., NYU.
Marc Dicciani, Professor; B.M., Philadelphia Musical Academy.
Annette DiMedio, Professor; Ph.D., Bryn Mawr.
William Garton, Senior Lecturer; M.A., Glassboro State.
Richard Genovese, Adjunct Assistant Professor; Certificate, Curtis.
Don Glanden, Professor; M.M., Rutgers.
Marjorie Goldberg, Senior Lecturer; B.M.E., Hartford (Hartt).
Patrick Jones, Head of M.A.T. Program; Ph.D., Penn State.
Michael Kennedy, Senior Lecturer; M.M., University of the Arts.
Ronald Kerber, Professor; B.M., Philadelphia College of the Performing Arts.
Jeffrey Kern, Associate Professor; M.M., Michigan.
Christopher Maute, Lecturer; B.M., University of the Arts.
Joseph Nero, Adjunct Associate Professor; Diploma, Curtis.
James Paxson, Adjunct Associate Professor.
Robert Quaile Jr., Senior Lecturer; B.M.E., Philadelphia Musical Academy.
Thomas Rudolph, Adjunct Assistant Professor; M.M., West Chester.
Gerald Veasley, Master Lecturer, B.A., Pennsylvania.
Gia Walton, Senior Lecturer; M.M., Temple.
Dennis Wasko, Adjunct Assistant Professor; B.M., Philadelphia College of the Performing Arts.

VIRGINIA COMMONWEALTH UNIVERSITY

School of the Arts

Programs of Study

The School of the Arts at Virginia Commonwealth University (VCUarts) is one of the nation's largest arts and design schools. It has an exceptional faculty whose work is recognized by major museums, art and design publications, PBS television, National Public Radio, the Kennedy Center, regional theatres across the country, and the National Endowment for the Arts. VCUarts graduates have made an impact on nearly every area of the arts and design in America. They have been awarded Guggenheim Fellowships, MacArthur "Genius" Awards, Academy Awards, Joan Mitchell Awards in the Visual Arts, Pollock-Krasner Awards, television's Emmys, and advertising's Clios. Their work is published in *Newsweek, Psychology Today, Metropolitan Home, Sports Illustrated, Fortune, Vogue, Communication Arts, Graphis, House Beautiful, Harper's Bazaar, Architectural Digest,* and *The New York Times.* The work of VCUarts graduates has appeared in the Chicago International Film Festival, Cooper-Hewitt Museum of Design, New York City Opera, Metropolitan Opera, Guggenheim Museum, Joffrey Ballet, Metropolitan Museum of Art, Corcoran Gallery, Hirshhorn Museum, Museum of Modern Art, Tate Modern, Carnegie Hall, Nike advertising, MTV, the Library of Congress, Sundance Film Festival, Whitney Museum, the collections of Bill Blass and Oscar de la Renta, Disney Studios, Spike Lee Productions, Tokyo Museum, and San Francisco MOMA.

VCUarts is widely recognized as one of the nation's great schools of the arts and design. With more than 3,000 students from seven countries and thirty-four states, the VCU School of the Arts offers programs in Art Education, Art History, Interior Environments, Design/Visual Communications, Kinetic Imaging, Ceramics, Fiber, Furniture Design, Glass, Jewelry/Metal, Painting/Printmaking, Sculpture, Theatre, Music, and Media, Art, & Text. The VCUarts Master of Fine Arts program is ranked as the number 1 public university visual arts and design program in America by *U.S. News & World Report* (2005). Specialty rankings are as follows: number 1 graduate sculpture program among all universities, public and private; number 1 graphic design program among all public universities in the country; number 4 among all universities, public and private; number 6 painting program among all public universities in the country; and number 10 among all universities, public and private.

Research Facilities

VCU libraries provide a combined capacity of more than 1.7 million volumes and 10,200 periodical titles and an online bibliographic search service accessing hundreds of databases. In addition, the Virginia State and Richmond Public Libraries are within walking distance of both VCU campuses. Academic Computing provides a variety of microcomputer, minicomputer, and mainframe computing services to support the research and instructional endeavors of the faculty and students, including consultation, instruction, and computer acquisition.

Well known for presenting the work of nationally and internationally renowned artists, emerging figures, and regional names, the Anderson Gallery mounts exhibitions that explore currents in contemporary art and design. The Anderson Gallery publishes new writing on contemporary art every year, featuring essays by guest authorities, curators, and gallery faculty members. Catalogs, which combine new scholarship with innovative design, are produced for each major exhibition. The gallery's publications have received awards from the American Association of Museums (AAM), the Southeastern Museum Conference & Association (SEMC), and design industries, including the Print Industries of Virginia (PIVA). In addition to presenting important exhibitions, publications, and lecture series, the Anderson Gallery is known for its extensive permanent collection.

Financial Aid

In addition to need-based financial aid awarded through the Office of Financial Aid, graduate students at VCU are eligible for a number of University-sponsored financing options, including scholarships, employment opportunities, and fellowships and teaching assistantships. All forms of graduate student support are reported to the Office of Financial Aid and are considered when determining need-based support.

A number of assistantships, fellowships, and scholarships are awarded each year to new and continuing graduate students on the basis of a variety of criteria. Awards vary by program, and selection is made at the department level; therefore, inquiry about such awards should be made directly to the director of the program.

Students may contact the Office of Financial Aid at 804-828-6669 (Monroe Park Campus) or 804-828-2702 (MCV Campus) or visit http://www.vcu.edu/enroll/finaid/ for current information on financial aid programs, policies, and procedures.

Cost of Study

For full-time graduate study (9–15 credits) in 2008–09, Virginia residents pay tuition and fees of $4739 per semester; nonresidents, $9106 per semester. For part-time graduate study, Virginia residents pay tuition and fees of $495 per hour; nonresidents, $978 per hour.

For full-time doctoral study (9–15 credits) in 2008–09, Virginia residents pay tuition and fees of $4523 per semester; nonresidents, $8947 per semester. For part-time graduate study, Virginia residents pay tuition and fees of $471 per hour; nonresidents, $960 per hour.

Some programs require additional fees. On the Medical College of Virginia (MCV) campus, tuition, fees, and other expenses vary in the Medicine, Pharmacy, Nurse Anesthesia, Dentistry, and School of Allied Health programs

Living and Housing Costs

Graduate student housing is available on both the MCV campus and the academic campus of Virginia Commonwealth University. Many graduate students live in off-campus housing, which is reasonably priced and readily available in a variety of styles and settings in nearby residential areas or within easy commuting distance. On-campus housing information is available on the Web at http://www.housing.vcu.edu/. Off-campus housing information is available at http://www.usca.vcu.edu/offcampus/.

Student Group

VCU enrolls nearly 32,000 students, 8,149 of whom are graduate students. More than 200 clubs and organizations reflect the diverse social, recreational, educational, political, and religious interests of the student body.

Location

Richmond is Virginia's capital and a major East Coast financial and manufacturing center that offers students a wide range of cultural, educational, and recreational activities. Richmond is located in central Virginia at the intersection of Interstates 95 and 64, 2 hours south of Washington, D.C., and nestled between the Blue Ridge Mountains and the Atlantic coast. The Richmond region is easily accessible by plane, car, and train. With nearly 1 million residents, the historic city of Richmond combines big-city offerings with small-town hospitality. Applicants are encouraged to explore http://www.visit.richmond.com/ for more information on the city.

The University and The School

Virginia Commonwealth University is a state-supported coeducational university with a graduate school, a major teaching hospital, and twelve academic and professional units that offer sixty-two undergraduate, sixty-nine master's, forty postbaccalaureate and post-master's certificate programs, and thirty-one Ph.D. programs. VCU also offers M.D., D.D.S., D.P.T., and Pharm.D. programs as well as cooperative degree programs with other major Virginia colleges and universities. The academic campus is located in Richmond's historic Fan District. The health sciences campus and hospital are located 2 miles east in the downtown business district. A University bus service provides free intercampus transportation for faculty members and students.

With more than $211 million in annual research funding, VCU is classified as one of the nation's top research universities by the Carnegie Foundation for the Advancement of Teaching. More than 32,000 undergraduate, certificate, graduate, post-master's, professional, and doctoral students are enrolled in 205 academic programs, sixty-five of which are unique in the commonwealth of Virginia. The faculty members represent the finest American and international graduate institutions and enhance the University's position among the important institutions of higher learning in the United States and the world via their work in the classroom, laboratory, studio, and clinic and in their scholarly publications.

Applying

Admission procedures and program requirements are detailed in the *Graduate Bulletin.* Application deadlines and materials, including the application and the *Graduate Bulletin,* are available online at the Graduate School Web site at http://www.graduate.vcu.edu. Virginia Commonwealth University is an equal opportunity/affirmative action institution providing access to education and employment without regard to age, race, color, national origin, gender, religion, sexual orientation, veteran's status, political affiliation, or disability.

Correspondence and Information

School of the Arts
Virginia Commonwealth University
325 North Harrison Street
Richmond, Virginia 23284

Phone: 804-828-2787
E-mail: arts@vcu.edu
Web site: http://www.vcu.edu/arts/prospective_students/graduate_studies

Virginia Commonwealth University

THE FACULTY

For information about the faculty committees and members in the School of the Arts at Virginia Commonwealth University, prospective students should visit the Web site at http://www.vcu.edu/arts/inside_vcu_arts/faculty_committees.html.

Section 4
Comparative and Interdisciplinary Arts

This section contains a directory of institutions offering graduate work in comparative and interdisciplinary arts. Additional information about programs listed in the directory but not augmented by an in-depth entry may be obtained by writing directly to the dean of a graduate school or chair of a department at the address given in the directory.

For programs offering related work, see also in this book *Applied Arts and Design, Architecture, Art and Art History,* and *Performing Arts*. In another guide in this series:

Graduate Programs in Business, Education, Health, Information Studies, Law & Social Work

See *Subject Areas (Art Education)*

CONTENTS

Program Directory

Comparative and Interdisciplinary Arts

Bradley University, Graduate School, Slane College of Communications and Fine Arts, Department of Art, Peoria, IL 61625-0002. Offers ceramics (MA, MFA); drawing/illustration (MA, MFA); interdisciplinary art (MA, MFA); painting (MA, MFA); photography (MA, MFA); printmaking (MA, MFA); sculpture (MA, MFA); visual communication and design (MA, MFA). *Accreditation:* NASAD. Part-time programs available. *Faculty:* 10. *Students:* 11 full-time (6 women), 1 international. 20 applicants, 40% accepted, 4 enrolled. In 2007, 2 degrees awarded. *Degree requirements:* For master's, comprehensive exam, thesis, final exhibit. *Entrance requirements:* For master's, portfolio, 2 letters of recommendation. Additional exam requirements/recommendations for international students: Required—TOEFL (minimum score 550 paper-based; 213 computer-based; 79 iBT). *Application deadline:* For fall admission, 4/1 priority date for domestic and international students; for spring admission, 11/1 priority date for domestic and international students. Applications are processed on a rolling basis. Application fee: $40 ($50 for international students). *Financial support:* Research assistantships with full and partial tuition reimbursements, scholarships/grants, tuition waivers (partial), and unspecified assistantships available. Financial award application deadline: 4/1. *Unit head:* Dr. Paul Krainak, Chairperson, 309-677-3330, E-mail: pkrainak@bradley.edu. *Application contact:* Fisher Stolz, Graduate Coordinator, 309-677-2969, E-mail: fisher@bradley.edu.

Brigham Young University, Graduate Studies, College of Humanities, Department of Humanities, Classics, and Comparative Literature, Provo, UT 84602-1001. Offers comparative literature (MA); comparative studies (MA); humanities (MA). *Faculty:* 26 full-time (4 women). *Students:* 27 full-time (14 women). Average age 27. 15 applicants, 80% accepted, 6 enrolled. In 2007, 5 degrees awarded. *Degree requirements:* For master's, 2 foreign languages, thesis. *Entrance requirements:* For master's, GRE, minimum GPA of 3.0 in last 60 hours. *Application deadline:* For fall admission, 3/1 for domestic and international students. Application fee: $50. Electronic applications accepted. *Financial support:* In 2007–08, 27 students received support, including 7 research assistantships (averaging $4,680 per year), 29 teaching assistantships (averaging $65,678 per year); fellowships, career-related internships or fieldwork, institutionally sponsored loans, scholarships/grants, tuition waivers (full and partial), and student instructorships also available. Support available to part-time students. *Unit head:* Dr. Michael J. Call, Chair, 801-422-2550, Fax: 801-422-0305, E-mail: michael_call@byu.edu. *Application contact:* Carolyn Hone, Graduate Secretary for Humanities and Comparative Literature, 801-422-4430, Fax: 801-422-0305, E-mail: carolyn_hone@byu.edu.

Columbia College Chicago, Graduate School, Program in Interdisciplinary Arts, Chicago, IL 60605-1996. Offers interdisciplinary arts (MA); interdisciplinary book and paper arts (MFA). Part-time and evening/weekend programs available. *Faculty:* 4 full-time, 12 part-time/adjunct. *Students:* 30 full-time (20 women), 39 part-time (31 women); includes 6 minority (2 African Americans, 3 Asian Americans or Pacific Islanders, 1 Hispanic American), 1 international. Average age 33. In 2007, 29 degrees awarded. *Degree requirements:* For master's, thesis. *Entrance requirements:* For master's, interview, minimum GPA of 3.0, portfolio. Additional exam requirements/recommendations for international students: Required—TOEFL (minimum score 550 paper-based; 213 computer-based). *Application deadline:* For fall admission, 2/14 for domestic and international students. Application fee: $50. Electronic applications accepted. *Financial support:* Fellowships, career-related internships or fieldwork, Federal Work-Study, and scholarships/grants available. Support available to part-time students. Financial award application deadline: 8/13; financial award applicants required to submit FAFSA. *Unit head:* Suzanne Cohan-Lange, Director, 312-344-7670, Fax: 312-344-8054, E-mail: scohan-lange@colum.edu. *Application contact:* Keith Cleveland, Acting Dean of the Graduate School, 312-344-7261, Fax: 312-344-8047, E-mail: kcleveland@colum.edu.

Florida Atlantic University, Dorothy F. Schmidt College of Arts and Letters, Program in Comparative Studies, Boca Raton, FL 33431-0991. Offers PhD. Part-time programs available. *Degree requirements:* For doctorate, one foreign language, comprehensive exam, thesis/dissertation. *Entrance requirements:* For doctorate, GRE, minimum GPA of 3.5, 3 references. Additional exam requirements/recommendations for international students: Required—TOEFL. *Faculty research:* Arts, humanities, social sciences.

Goddard College, Graduate Program, Program in Interdisciplinary Arts, Plainfield, VT 05667-9432. Offers MFA. Postbaccalaureate distance learning degree programs offered (minimal on-campus study). *Faculty:* 18 full-time (12 women). *Students:* 96 full-time. Average age 44. 39 applicants, 82% accepted, 32 enrolled. *Degree requirements:* For master's, thesis. *Entrance requirements:* For master's, professional work experience. *Application deadline:* Applications are processed on a rolling basis. Application fee: $40. Electronic applications accepted. *Expenses:* Tuition: Full-time $14,038. *Financial support:* In 2007–08, 89 students received support. Applicants required to submit FAFSA. *Unit head:* Danielle Boutet, Director, 802-454-8311, Fax: 802-454-8017, E-mail: dboutet@compuserve.com. *Application contact:* David DeLucca, Admissions Counselor, 800-906-8312 Ext. 248, Fax: 802-454-1029, E-mail: david.delucca@goddard.edu.

John F. Kennedy University, Graduate School of Holistic Studies, Department of Arts and Consciousness, Program in Transformative Arts, Pleasant Hill, CA 94523-4817. Offers MA. Part-time and evening/weekend programs available. *Degree requirements:* For master's, thesis or alternative. *Entrance requirements:* For master's, interview. Additional exam requirements/recommendations for international students: Required—TOEFL. Expenses: Contact institution.

Ohio University, Graduate College, College of Fine Arts, School of Interdisciplinary Arts, Athens, OH 45701-2979. Offers PhD. *Faculty:* 7 full-time (3 women). *Students:* 15 full-time (6 women); includes 1 minority (Hispanic American), 3 international. 14 applicants, 36% accepted, 5 enrolled. In 2007, 5 degrees awarded. *Degree requirements:* For doctorate, 2 foreign languages, comprehensive exam, thesis/dissertation. *Entrance requirements:* For doctorate, GRE, MAT, master's degree. Additional exam requirements/recommendations for international students: Required—TOEFL. *Application deadline:* For fall admission, 1/31 priority date for domestic students. Applications are processed on a rolling basis. Application fee: $50 ($55 for international students). Electronic applications accepted. *Financial support:* Teaching assistantships with tuition reimbursements, Federal Work-Study and institutionally sponsored loans available. Financial award application deadline: 1/31. *Faculty research:* Comparative studies of theater, music, and the visual arts. *Unit head:* Dr. Dora J. Wilson, Director, 740-593-9413, Fax: 740-593-0578, E-mail: wilsond@ohio.edu.

Simon Fraser University, Graduate Studies, Faculty of Arts and Social Sciences, School for the Contemporary Arts, Burnaby, BC V5A 1S6, Canada. Offers MFA. *Degree requirements:* For master's, thesis or alternative. *Entrance requirements:* For master's, minimum GPA of 3.0. Additional exam requirements/recommendations for international students: Required—TOEFL or IELTS. *Faculty research:* Dance theory, screenplays, drawing and painting, acting, electroacoustic music.

Section 5
Film, Television, and Video

This section contains a directory of institutions offering graduate work in film, television, and video, followed by in-depth entries submitted by institutions that chose to prepare detailed program descriptions. Additional information about programs listed in the directory but not augmented by an in-depth entry may be obtained by writing directly to the dean of a graduate school or chair of a department at the address given in the directory.

For programs offering related work, see also in this book *Art and Art History* and *Communication and Media*. In the other guides in this series:

Graduate Programs in Engineering & Applied Sciences
See *Telecommunications*

Graduate Programs in Business, Education, Health, Information Studies, Law & Social Work
See *Advertising and Public Relations*

CONTENTS

Program Directories

Close-Ups

See also:

Film, Television, and Video Production

Academy of Art University, Graduate Program, School of Animation and Visual Effects, San Francisco, CA 94105-3410. Offers 2D animation (MFA); 3D animation (MFA); 3D modeling (MFA); games (MFA); visual effects (MFA). Part-time programs available. Postbaccalaureate distance learning degree programs offered (no on-campus study). *Degree requirements:* For master's, final review. *Entrance requirements:* For master's, portfolio. Electronic applications accepted.

Academy of Art University, Graduate Program, School of Motion Pictures and Television, San Francisco, CA 94105-3410. Offers MFA. Part-time programs available. Postbaccalaureate distance learning degree programs offered (no on-campus study). *Degree requirements:* For master's, final review. *Entrance requirements:* For master's, portfolio. Electronic applications accepted.

American Film Institute Conservatory, Graduate Program, Los Angeles, CA 90027-1657. Offers cinematography (MFA); directing (MFA); editing (MFA); producing (MFA); production design (MFA); screenwriting (MFA). *Faculty:* 11 full-time (1 woman), 57 part-time/adjunct (14 women). *Students:* 347 full-time (115 women); includes 60 minority (23 African Americans, 2 American Indian/Alaska Native, 20 Asian Americans or Pacific Islanders, 15 Hispanic Americans), 90 international. Average age 27. 607 applicants, 33% accepted, 140 enrolled. In 2007, 118 degrees awarded. *Degree requirements:* For master's, thesis, production of film or screenplay, portfolio piece. *Entrance requirements:* For master's, portfolio, resumé, letters of recommendation, interview. Additional exam requirements/recommendations for international students: Required—TOEFL (minimum score 600 paper-based; 250 computer-based; 100 iBT). *Application deadline:* For fall admission, 12/1 for domestic and international students. Application fee: $75. *Expenses:* Tuition: Full-time $32,523. Required fees: $2,200. *Financial support:* In 2007–08, 89 students received support, including 14 teaching assistantships with partial tuition reimbursements available (averaging $3,000 per year); career-related internships or fieldwork, scholarships/grants, and unspecified assistantships also available. Financial award application deadline: 4/15; financial award applicants required to submit FAFSA. *Faculty research:* Film production, TV production. *Unit head:* Robert Mandel, Dean, 323-856-7600, Fax: 323-467-4578. *Application contact:* Angela Wheaton, Admissions Counselor, 323-856-7842, Fax: 323-856-7720, E-mail: awheaton@afi.com.

American University, School of Communication, Film and Electronic Media Program, Washington, DC 20016-8001. Offers MFA. *Faculty:* 14 full-time (6 women). *Students:* 33 full-time (19 women), 42 part-time (22 women). 51 applicants, 73% accepted, 22 enrolled. In 2007, 141 degrees awarded. *Degree requirements:* For master's, comprehensive exam, thesis or alternative. *Entrance requirements:* For master's, GRE General Test. Additional exam requirements/recommendations for international students: Required—TOEFL (minimum score 600 paper-based; 250 computer-based). *Application deadline:* For fall admission, 2/1 priority date for domestic and international students; for spring admission, 11/15 for domestic and international students. Applications are processed on a rolling basis. Application fee: $50. Electronic applications accepted. *Expenses:* Tuition: Full-time $19,998; part-time $1,111 per credit hour. Required fees: $380. Tuition and fees vary according to program. *Financial support:* In 2007–08, 10 students received support, including 2 fellowships with partial tuition reimbursements available (averaging $13,000 per year), 2 research assistantships with partial tuition reimbursements available (averaging $11,000 per year), 4 teaching assistantships with partial tuition reimbursements available (averaging $11,000 per year); career-related internships or fieldwork, Federal Work-Study, institutionally sponsored loans, scholarships/grants, tuition waivers (partial), and unspecified assistantships also available. Financial award application deadline: 2/1. *Faculty research:* Documentary film production, social media, media and public policy, visual literacy, new technology. *Unit head:* Prof. John Douglass, Director, Film and Media Arts Division, 202-885-2045, Fax: 202-885-2019, E-mail: jdougla@american.edu. *Application contact:* Sharmeen Ahsan-Bracciale, Graduate Admissions Office, 202-885-2040, Fax: 202-885-2019, E-mail: sharmeen@american.edu.

American University, School of Communication, Film and Video Program, Washington, DC 20016-8001. Offers film and video (MA); producing film and video (MA). Part-time and evening/weekend programs available. *Faculty:* 14 full-time (6 women). *Students:* 11 full-time (6 women), 63 part-time (37 women). 95 applicants, 56% accepted, 32 enrolled. In 2007, 29 degrees awarded. *Degree requirements:* For master's, comprehensive exam, thesis or alternative. *Entrance requirements:* For master's, GRE General Test. Additional exam requirements/recommendations for international students: Required—TOEFL (minimum score 660 paper-based; 250 computer-based). *Application deadline:* For fall admission, 2/1 priority date for domestic and international students; for spring admission, 11/15 for domestic and international students. Applications are processed on a rolling basis. Application fee: $50. Electronic applications accepted. *Expenses:* Tuition: Full-time $19,998; part-time $1,111 per credit hour. Required fees: $380. Tuition and fees vary according to program. *Financial support:* In 2007–08, 2 research assistantships with partial tuition reimbursements (averaging $11,000 per year), 4 teaching assistantships with partial tuition reimbursements (averaging $11,000 per year) were awarded; career-related internships or fieldwork, Federal Work-Study, institutionally sponsored loans, scholarships/grants, tuition waivers (partial), and unspecified assistantships also available. Financial award application deadline: 2/1. *Faculty research:* Documentary film and video production, visual literacy, Eastern European cinema, media and public policy, social media. *Unit head:* Prof. John Douglass, Director, Film and Media Arts Division, 202-885-2045, Fax: 202-885-2019, E-mail: jdougla@american.edu. *Application contact:* Sharmeen Ahsan-Bracciale, Graduate Admissions Office, 202-885-2040, Fax: 202-885-2019, E-mail: sharmeen@american.edu.

See Close-Up on page 881.

American University, School of Communication, Weekend Programs in Communication, Washington, DC 20016-8001. Offers interactive journalism (MA); news media studies (MA); producing for film and video (MA); public communication (MA). *Accreditation:* ACEJMC. Part-time and evening/weekend programs available. *Faculty:* 5 part-time/adjunct (2 women). *Students:* 137 applicants, 61% accepted, 61 enrolled. In 2007, 15 degrees awarded. *Degree requirements:* For master's, comprehensive exam, thesis or alternative. *Entrance requirements:* Additional exam requirements/recommendations for international students: Required—TOEFL (minimum score 600 paper-based; 250 computer-based). *Application deadline:* For fall admission, 8/1 for domestic students. Applications are processed on a rolling basis. Application fee: $50. Electronic applications accepted. *Expenses:* Tuition: Full-time $19,998; part-time $1,111 per credit hour. Required fees: $380. Tuition and fees vary according to program. *Financial support:* In 2007–08, 3 fellowships (averaging $3,500 per year) were awarded; institutionally sponsored loans also available. *Unit head:* Wendell Cochran, Journalism Weekend Program Director, 202-885-2075, E-mail: cochran@american.edu. *Application contact:* Sharmeen Ahsan-Bracciale, Graduate Admissions Office, 202-885-2040, Fax: 202-885-2019, E-mail: sharmeen@american.edu.

See Close-Up on page 881.

Antioch University McGregor, Graduate Programs, Individualized Liberal and Professional Studies Program, Yellow Springs, OH 45387-1609. Offers liberal and professional studies (MA), including counseling, creative writing, education, film studies, liberal studies, management, modern literature, psychology, theatre, visual arts. Part-time and evening/weekend programs available. Postbaccalaureate distance learning degree programs offered (minimal on-campus study). *Faculty:* 2 full-time (1 woman), 3 part-time/adjunct (2 women). *Students:* Average age 40. 35 applicants, 63% accepted, 17 enrolled. In 2007, 31 degrees awarded. *Degree requirements:* For master's, thesis or alternative. *Entrance requirements:* For master's, resumé, 2 letters of reference. *Application deadline:* For fall admission, 8/25 for domestic students; for winter admission, 12/5 for domestic students; for spring admission, 3/8 for domestic students. Applications are processed on a rolling basis. Application fee: $50. Electronic applications accepted. *Expenses:* Contact institution. *Financial support:* Federal Work-Study available. Financial award applicants required to submit FAFSA. *Unit head:* Suzanne Fest, Chair, 937-769-1876, Fax: 937-769-1807, E-mail: sfest@mcgregor.edu. *Application contact:* Seth Gordon, Assistant Director of Admissions, 937-769-1800 Ext. 1825, Fax: 937-769-1804, E-mail: sgordon@mcgregor.edu.

See Close-Up on page 443.

Art Center College of Design, Graduate Division, Broadcast Cinema Department, Pasadena, CA 91103-1999. Offers MFA. *Accreditation:* NASAD. *Faculty:* 3 part-time/adjunct (0 women). *Students:* 32 full-time (9 women), 5 part-time (2 women); includes 11 minority (2 African Americans, 7 Asian Americans or Pacific Islanders, 2 Hispanic Americans), 11 international. Average age 29. 24 applicants, 88% accepted, 13 enrolled. In 2007, 2 degrees awarded. *Degree requirements:* For master's, thesis, studio project. *Entrance requirements:* For master's, portfolio. Additional exam requirements/recommendations for international students: Required—TOEFL (minimum score 100 iBT). *Application deadline:* For fall admission, 3/1 priority date for domestic and international students; for spring admission, 10/1 priority date for domestic and international students. Applications are processed on a rolling basis. Application fee: $50 ($70 for international students). *Expenses:* Tuition: Full-time $31,016. Required fees: $235. *Financial support:* Teaching assistantships, career-related internships or fieldwork, Federal Work-Study, and scholarships/grants available. Financial award application deadline: 3/1. *Unit head:* Robert Peterson, Chair, 626-396-2274. *Application contact:* Kit Baron, Vice President, Admissions, 626-396-2373, Fax: 626-795-0578, E-mail: admissions@artcenter.edu.

See Close-Up on page 109.

Bob Jones University, Graduate Programs, Greenville, SC 29614. Offers accountancy (MS); Bible (MA); Bible translation (MA); Biblical studies (Certificate); broadcast management (MS); business administration (MBA); church history (MA, PhD); church ministries (MA); church music (MM); cinema and video production (MA); counseling (MS); curriculum and instruction (Ed D); divinity (M Div); dramatic production (MA); educational leadership (MS, Ed D, Ed S); elementary education (M Ed, MAT); English (M Ed, MA, MAT); fine arts (MA); graphic design (MA); history (M Ed, MA); illustration (MA); interpretative speech (MA); mathematics (M Ed, MAT); medical missions (Certificate); ministry (MM, D Min); multi-categorical special education (M Ed, MAT); music (M Ed); New Testament interpretation (PhD); Old Testament interpretation (PhD); orchestral instrument performance (MM); organ performance (MM); pastoral studies (MA); personnel services (MS, Ed S); piano pedagogy (MM); piano performance (MM); platform arts (MA); radio and television broadcasting (MS); rhetoric and public address (MA); secondary education (M Ed); studio art (MA); teaching Bible (MA); theology (MA, PhD); voice performance (MM); youth ministries (MA); M Div/MM.

Boston University, College of Communication, Department of Film and Television, Boston, MA 02215. Offers film production (MFA); film studies (MFA); screenwriting (MFA); television (MS); television management (MS); MBA/MS. *Faculty:* 13 full-time, 27 part-time/adjunct. *Students:* 115 full-time (63 women), 17 part-time (12 women); includes 13 minority (4 African Americans, 1 American Indian/Alaska Native, 4 Asian Americans or Pacific Islanders, 4 Hispanic Americans), 14 international. Average age 26. In 2007, 10 degrees awarded. *Degree requirements:* For master's, thesis. *Entrance requirements:* For master's, GMAT (MS in television management), GRE General Test, sample of written or creative work. Additional exam requirements/recommendations for international students: Required—TOEFL. *Application deadline:* For fall admission, 2/1 for domestic students. Electronic applications accepted. *Expenses:* Tuition: Full-time $34,930; part-time $1,092 per credit. Tuition and fees vary according to class time, course level and program. *Financial support:* Teaching assistantships with partial tuition reimbursements, career-related internships or fieldwork, Federal Work-Study, institutionally sponsored loans, scholarships/grants, and unspecified assistantships available. Support available to part-time students. Financial award application deadline: 2/1; financial award applicants required to submit FAFSA. *Unit head:* Charles Merzbacher, Chairman, 617-353-3483, Fax: 617-353-1084, E-mail: ftvchair@bu.edu. *Application contact:* William A. Taylor, Assistant Director, Graduate Services and Financial Aid, 617-353-3481, Fax: 617-358-0399, E-mail: comgrad@bu.edu.

See Close-Up on page 885.

Bowling Green State University, Graduate College, College of Arts and Sciences, Department of Theatre and Film, Bowling Green, OH 43403. Offers MA, PhD. *Accreditation:* NAST. Part-time programs available. *Faculty:* 13 full-time (4 women), 2 part-time/adjunct (both women). *Students:* 27 full-time (14 women), 6 part-time (5 women); includes 2 minority (1 African American, 1 American Indian/Alaska Native), 1 international. Average age 30. 24 applicants, 46% accepted, 4 enrolled. In 2007, 7 master's awarded. Terminal master's awarded for partial completion of doctoral program. *Degree requirements:* For master's, thesis or alternative; for doctorate, comprehensive exam, thesis/dissertation, 9 hour research tool. *Entrance requirements:* For master's and doctorate, GRE General Test. Additional exam requirements/recommendations for international students: Required—TOEFL. *Application deadline:* For fall admission, 1/15 for domestic students. Application fee: $30. Electronic applications accepted. *Financial support:* In 2007–08, 1 fellowship with full tuition reimbursement (averaging $14,707 per year), 4 research assistantships with full tuition reimbursements (averaging $10,925 per year), 20 teaching assistantships with full tuition reimbursements (averaging $10,421 per year) were awarded; Federal Work-Study and unspecified assistantships also available. Financial award applicants required to submit FAFSA. *Faculty research:* Theatre history, dramatic theory, cultural studies, performance studies, American theatre history. *Unit head:* Dr. Ronald Shields, Chair, 419-372-6812. *Application contact:* Dr. Jonathan Chambers, Graduate Coordinator, 419-372-9618.

Brigham Young University, Graduate Studies, College of Fine Arts and Communications, Department of Theatre and Media Arts, Provo, UT 84602-1001. Offers production design (MFA); theatre and media arts (MA). MFA program accepts applications in odd-numbered years only. *Accreditation:* NAST (one or more programs are accredited). *Faculty:* 14 full-time (5 women). *Students:* 20 full-time (16 women), 4 part-time (2 women). Average age 33. 23 applicants, 61% accepted, 12 enrolled. In 2007, 5 degrees awarded. *Degree requirements:* For master's, comprehensive exam, thesis, oral defense, MA, 32 hours, MFA 60 hours. *Entrance requirements:* For master's, GRE General Test, writing samples, MFA—portfolio, interview. Additional exam requirements/recommendations for international students: Required—TOEFL (minimum score 580 paper-based; 237 computer-based; 85 iBT). *Application deadline:* For fall admission, 2/1 priority date for domestic and international students. Application fee: $50. Electronic applications accepted. *Financial support:* In 2007–08, 24 students received support, including 3 research assistantships with partial tuition reimbursements available (averaging $3,500 per year), 12 teaching assistantships with partial tuition reimbursements available (averaging $3,500 per year); career-related internships or fieldwork, institutionally sponsored loans, scholarships/grants, health care benefits, tuition waivers (partial), unspecified assistantships, and administrative aides also available. Support available to part-time students. *Faculty research:* Media library, children's media, theatre studies, costume and scenic design. *Unit head:* Dr. Rodger D. Sorensen, Department Chair, 801-422-8132, Fax: 801-422-0654, E-mail: rodger_sorensen@byu.edu. *Application contact:* Kim Poole, Secretary, 801-422-3750, Fax: 801-422-0654, E-mail: kim_poole@byu.edu.

Brooklyn College of the City University of New York, Division of Graduate Studies, Department of Television and Radio, Brooklyn, NY 11210-2889. Offers television and radio (MS); television production (MFA). MFA applicants admitted in fall of even-numbered years. Part-time and evening/weekend programs available. *Students:* 19 full-time (8 women), 26 part-time (16 women); includes 14 minority (11 African Americans, 1 Asian American or Pacific Islander, 2 Hispanic Americans), 18 international. 31 applicants, 94% accepted, 25 enrolled. In 2007, 17 degrees awarded. *Degree requirements:* For master's, comprehensive exam. *Entrance* *requirements:* For master's, GRE General Test or MAT, 12 credits in television/radio with a minimum B average, 2 letters of recommendation. *Application deadline:* For fall admission, 3/1 priority date for domestic students, 2/1 priority date for international students; for spring admission, 11/1 priority date for domestic students, 10/1 priority date for international students. Applications are processed on a rolling basis. Application fee: $125. Electronic applications accepted. *Financial support:* Career-related internships or fieldwork, Federal Work-Study, and institutionally sponsored loans available. Support available to part-time students. Financial award application deadline: 5/1; financial award applicants required to submit FAFSA. *Faculty research:* Criticism, research methods, audience behavior, policy and regulation, program history, international television and radio. *Unit head:* Dr. George Rodman, Chairperson, 718-951-5555, E-mail: grodman@brooklyn.cuny.edu. *Application contact:* Hernan Sierra, Graduate Admissions Coordinator, 718-951-4536, Fax: 718-951-4506, E-mail: grads@brooklyn.cuny.edu.

California College of the Arts, Graduate Programs, Programs in Fine Art, San Francisco, CA 94107. Offers ceramics (MFA); film/video/performance (MFA); glass (MFA); jewelry/metal arts (MFA); painting/drawing (MFA); photography (MFA); printmaking (MFA); sculpture (MFA); textiles (MFA); wood/furniture (MFA). *Accreditation:* NASAD. *Faculty:* 17 full-time (9 women), 32 part-time/adjunct (12 women). *Students:* 101 full-time (73 women), 11 part-time (8 women). Average age 30. 437 applicants, 29% accepted, 51 enrolled. In 2007, 34 degrees awarded. *Degree requirements:* For master's, thesis, exhibit. *Entrance requirements:* For master's, appropriate bachelor's degree, portfolio. Additional exam requirements/recommendations for international students: Required—TOEFL (minimum score 600 paper-based; 250 computer-based). *Application deadline:* For fall admission, 1/15 for domestic and international students. Application fee: $50. Electronic applications accepted. *Expenses:* Tuition: Part-time $1,017 per unit. *Financial support:* In 2007–08, 5 fellowships (averaging $10,000 per year), 20 teaching assistantships (averaging $2,000 per year) were awarded; career-related internships or fieldwork, Federal Work-Study, scholarships/grants, and health care benefits also available. Financial award application deadline: 3/1; financial award applicants required to submit FAFSA. *Unit head:* Ted Purves, Chair, 415-551-9214, Fax: 415-703-9539, E-mail: tpurves@cca.edu. *Application contact:* Kathryn Ward, Assistant Director of Graduate Admissions, 415-703-9523 Ext. 9593, Fax: 415-703-9539, E-mail: graduateprograms@cca.edu.

California Institute of the Arts, School of Film/Video, Valencia, CA 91355-2340. Offers experimental animation (MFA); film directing (MFA, Adv C); film/video (Adv C). *Entrance requirements:* For master's, portfolio. Additional exam requirements/recommendations for international students: Required—TOEFL. Electronic applications accepted. *Faculty research:* Experimental and character animation, experimental film/video, video graphics.

California State University, Fullerton, Graduate Studies, College of the Arts, Department of Theatre and Dance, Fullerton, CA 92834-9480. Offers acting (MFA); acting and directing (MA); dance (MA); directing (MFA); dramatic literature/criticism (MA); oral interpretation (MA); playwriting (MA); technical theater (MA); technical theater and design (MFA); television (MA); theatre for children (MA); theatre history (MA). *Accreditation:* NASD; NAST (one or more programs are accredited). Part-time programs available. *Students:* 14 full-time (9 women), 2 part-time; includes 3 minority (1 African American, 1 Asian American or Pacific Islander, 1 Hispanic American), 1 international. Average age 27. 3 applicants, 0% accepted. In 2007, 8 degrees awarded. *Degree requirements:* For master's, oral and written exam, project or thesis. *Entrance requirements:* For master's, major in theatre or related field, audition or interview, minimum GPA of 2.5 in last 60 units of course work. Application fee: $55. *Financial support:* Teaching assistantships, career-related internships or fieldwork, Federal Work-Study, institutionally sponsored loans, and scholarships/grants available. Support available to part-time students. Financial award application deadline: 3/1. *Unit head:* Dr. Susan Hallman, Chair, 714-278-3628. *Application contact:* Gretchen Kanne, Adviser, 714-278-3628.

California State University, Northridge, Graduate Studies, College of Arts, Media, and Communication, Department of Cinema and Television Arts, Northridge, CA 91330. Offers screenwriting (MA). *Faculty:* 15 full-time (5 women), 25 part-time/adjunct (11 women). *Students:* 19 full-time (1 woman), 19 part-time (7 women); includes 6 minority (2 African Americans, 2 American Indian/Alaska Native, 1 Asian American or Pacific Islander, 1 Hispanic American), 3 international. Average age 34. 45 applicants, 62% accepted, 12 enrolled. In 2007, 12 degrees awarded. *Entrance requirements:* For master's, GRE if cumulative undergraduate GPA below 3.0. *Unit head:* John E. Schultheiss, Chair, 818-677-3192.

Carleton University, Faculty of Graduate Studies, Faculty of Arts and Social Sciences, School for Studies in Art and Culture, Program in Film Studies, Ottawa, ON K1S 5B6, Canada. Offers MA. *Degree requirements:* For master's, thesis. *Entrance requirements:* For master's, honors degree. Additional exam requirements/recommendations for international students: Required—TOEFL. *Application deadline:* Applications are processed on a rolling basis. Application fee: $77. *Unit head:* Mark Langer, Supervisor of Graduate Studies, 613-520-2600 Ext. 2342, Fax: 613-520-3575, E-mail: ssac@carleton.ca. *Application contact:* Barbara Shannon, Graduate Secretary, 613-520-2600 Ext. 2342, Fax: 613-520-3575, E-mail: barbara_shannon@carleton.ca.

Carnegie Mellon University, School of Computer Science and College of Fine Arts, Program in Entertainment Technology, Pittsburgh, PA 15213-3891. Offers MET.

Central Michigan University, College of Graduate Studies, College of Communication and Fine Arts, Department of Broadcast and Cinematic Arts, Mount Pleasant, MI 48859. Offers MA. *Degree requirements:* For master's, thesis or alternative. *Entrance requirements:* For master's, GRE, 30 semester hours in broadcasting or related course work, minimum undergraduate GPA of 2.7. *Faculty research:* TV, film history and criticism, writing for the media, international broadcasting and media systems, history of American broadcasting.

Chapman University, Graduate Studies, Dodge College of Film and Media Arts, Conservatory of Motion Pictures, Orange, CA 92866. Offers film and television producing (MFA); film production (MFA); film studies (MA); screenwriting (MFA). Part-time and evening/weekend programs available. *Faculty:* 34 full-time (7 women), 52 part-time/adjunct (16 women). *Students:* 230 full-time (86 women), 11 part-time (3 women); includes 31 minority (8 African Americans, 2 American Indian/Alaska Native, 7 Asian Americans or Pacific Islanders, 14 Hispanic Americans), 40 international. Average age 27. 342 applicants, 44% accepted, 85 enrolled. In 2007, 76 degrees awarded. *Degree requirements:* For master's, thesis. *Entrance requirements:* For master's, GRE General Test, minimum undergraduate GPA of 2.5, portfolio. Additional exam requirements/recommendations for international students: Required—TOEFL (minimum score 550 paper-based). *Application deadline:* For fall admission, 3/1 priority date for domestic students. Application fee: $55. Electronic applications accepted. *Expenses:* Contact institution. *Financial support:* Fellowships, Federal Work-Study and scholarships/grants available. Financial award application deadline: 6/30; financial award applicants required to submit FAFSA. *Unit head:* Joseph Slowensky, Director, 714-744-7882, E-mail: jslowens@chapman.edu. *Application contact:* Jojo Delfin, Information Contact, 714-997-6786, Fax: 714-997-6713, E-mail: delfin@chapman.edu.

Chatham University, Program in Film and Digital Technology, Pittsburgh, PA 15232-2826. Offers MFA. *Students:* 6 full-time (5 women), 2 part-time. Average age 28. 9 applicants, 78% accepted, 7 enrolled. *Entrance requirements:* For master's, recommendation letters, portfolio of work. Additional exam requirements/recommendations for international students: Recommended—TOEFL (minimum score 600 paper-based; 250 computer-based; 100 iBT), IELTS (minimum score 7). *Application deadline:* For fall admission, 5/1 priority date for domestic students; for winter admission, 10/1 priority date for domestic students. Applications are processed on a rolling basis. Application fee: $45. Electronic applications accepted. *Unit head:* Dr. Prajna Parasher, Director, 412-365-1182, E-mail: parasher@chatham.edu. *Application contact:* Office of Graduate Admissions, 412-365-1825, Fax: 412-365-1609, E-mail: admissions@chatham.edu.

Columbia College Chicago, Graduate School, Department of Film and Video, Chicago, IL 60605-1996. Offers MFA. Part-time programs available. *Students:* 14 full-time (9 women), 45 part-time (26 women); includes 17 minority (9 African Americans, 1 American Indian/Alaska Native, 3 Asian Americans or Pacific Islanders, 4 Hispanic Americans), 5 international. Average age 31. In 2007, 5 degrees awarded. *Degree requirements:* For master's, thesis, film project. *Entrance requirements:* For master's, interview, minimum GPA of 3.0, portfolio or script. Additional exam requirements/recommendations for international students: Required—TOEFL (minimum score 550 paper-based; 213 computer-based). *Application deadline:* For fall admission, 1/3 for domestic and international students. Application fee: $50. Electronic applications accepted. *Financial support:* Fellowships, career-related internships or fieldwork, Federal Work-Study, and scholarships/grants available. Support available to part-time students. Financial award application deadline: 8/13; financial award applicants required to submit FAFSA. *Unit head:* Dr. Bruce Sheridan, Chairperson, 312-344-6710, Fax: 312-344-8044, E-mail: bsheridan@colum.edu. *Application contact:* Keith Cleveland, Acting Dean of the Graduate School, 312-344-7261, Fax: 312-344-8047, E-mail: kcleveland@colum.edu.

Columbia University, School of the Arts, Film Division, New York, NY 10027. Offers directing (MFA); film studies (MA); producing (MFA); screen writing (MFA). *Faculty:* 15 full-time (4 women), 46 part-time/adjunct (16 women). *Students:* 336 full-time (129 women); includes 87 minority (21 African Americans, 2 American Indian/Alaska Native, 40 Asian Americans or Pacific Islanders, 24 Hispanic Americans). Average age 29. 577 applicants, 22% accepted, 78 enrolled. In 2007, 45 degrees awarded. *Degree requirements:* For master's, thesis. *Entrance requirements:* For master's, 3 letters of recommendation, writing sample, complete a scene, feature film treatment (optional visual submission). Additional exam requirements/recommendations for international students: Required—TOEFL (minimum score 600 paper-based; 250 computer-based; 100 iBT). *Application deadline:* For fall admission, 12/1 for domestic and international students. Application fee: $120. Electronic applications accepted. *Expenses:* Tuition: Part-time $1,452 per credit. Required fees: $152 per term. One-time fee: $75 part-time. Full-time tuition and fees vary according to course level, course load, degree level and program. *Financial support:* In 2007–08, 119 fellowships (averaging $4,596 per year), 8 research assistantships (averaging $11,235 per year), 26 teaching assistantships with partial tuition reimbursements (averaging $6,540 per year) were awarded; career-related internships or fieldwork, Federal Work-Study, and scholarships/grants also available. Financial award applicants required to submit FAFSA. *Unit head:* Jamal Joseph, Chair, 212-854-2815, E-mail: film@columbia.edu. *Application contact:* Director of Admissions, 212-854-2134, E-mail: admissions-arts@columbia.edu.

See Close-Up on page 347.

Concordia University, School of Graduate Studies, Faculty of Fine Arts, Department of Studio Arts, Montréal, QC H3G 1M8, Canada. Offers studio arts (MFA), including film production, open media, painting, photography, print media, sculpture, ceramics and fibers. *Degree requirements:* For master's, thesis or alternative. *Entrance requirements:* For master's, portfolio.

Concordia University, School of Graduate Studies, Faculty of Fine Arts, Mel Hoppenheim School of Cinema, Montréal, QC H3G 1M8, Canada. Offers film studies (MA).

Emerson College, Graduate Studies, School of the Arts, Department of Visual and Media Arts, Programs in Audio, Television/Video, and New Media Production, Boston, MA 02116-4624. Offers audio production (MA); new media production (MA); television/video production (MA). Part-time programs available. *Faculty:* 37 full-time (12 women). *Students:* 104 full-time (46 women), 37 part-time (20 women); includes 3 African Americans, 2 Hispanic Americans, 1 international. Average age 25. 148 applicants, 73% accepted, 55 enrolled. In 2007, 41 degrees awarded. *Degree requirements:* For master's, thesis or alternative. *Entrance requirements:* For master's, GRE General Test. Additional exam requirements/recommendations for international students: Required—TOEFL (minimum score 550 paper-based; 213 computer-based; 80 iBT), IELTS (minimum score 7). *Application deadline:* For fall admission, 3/1 priority date for domestic students; for spring admission, 11/1 priority date for domestic students. Applications are processed on a rolling basis. Application fee: $60 ($75 for international students). *Expenses:* Tuition: Full-time $16,800; part-time $840 per credit. Required fees: $60 per semester. One-time fee: $160. *Financial support:* In 2007–08, 1 fellowship with partial tuition reimbursement (averaging $14,000 per year), 14 research assistantships with partial tuition reimbursements (averaging $10,000 per year) were awarded; teaching assistantships with partial tuition reimbursements, career-related internships or fieldwork, scholarships/grants, and unspecified assistantships also available. Support available to part-time students. Financial award application deadline: 3/1; financial award applicants required to submit FAFSA. *Faculty research:* Media studies. *Unit head:* Prof. Jan Roberts Breslin, Director, 617-824-8800. *Application contact:* 617-824-8610, Fax: 617-824-8614, E-mail: gradapp@emerson.edu.

See Close-Up on page 895.

Florida State University, Graduate Studies, College of Motion Picture, Television, and Recording Arts, Tallahassee, FL 32306. Offers production (MFA); screen and play writing (MFA). *Faculty:* 11 full-time (3 women). *Students:* 58 full-time (20 women); includes 21 minority (6 African Americans, 12 Asian Americans or Pacific Islanders, 3 Hispanic Americans), 9 international. Average age 27. 207 applicants, 14% accepted, 30 enrolled. In 2007, 28 degrees awarded. *Degree requirements:* For master's, thesis, thesis project. *Entrance requirements:* For master's, GRE General Test, minimum GPA of 3.0, film/video experience. Additional exam requirements/recommendations for international students: Required—TOEFL (minimum score 550 paper-based; 253 computer-based; 80 iBT). *Application deadline:* For fall admission, 12/15 for domestic and international students. Application fee: $30. *Expenses:* Tuition, state resident: part-time $248 per credit hour. Tuition, nonresident: part-time $880 per credit hour. Tuition and fees vary according to program. *Financial support:* In 2007–08, 1 fellowship with partial tuition reimbursement (averaging $6,300 per year), 20 teaching assistantships with partial tuition reimbursements (averaging $4,100 per year) were awarded; Federal Work-Study and unspecified assistantships also available. Financial award application deadline: 1/1; financial award applicants required to submit FAFSA. *Faculty research:* Producing, screenwriting, directing, cinematography, editing. *Unit head:* Frank Patterson, Dean, 850-644-0453, Fax: 850-644-2626. *Application contact:* Cynthia Lugo, Assistant to Associate Dean, 850-644-8524, Fax: 850-644-2626, E-mail: clugo@film.fsu.edu.

George Mason University, College of Humanities and Social Sciences, Interdisciplinary Studies Program, Fairfax, VA 22030. Offers anthropology (MAIS); community college teaching (MAIS); folklore (MAIS); higher education (MAIS); individualized studies (MAIS); religion, cultures, and values (MAIS); video-based production (MAIS); women's studies (MAIS); zoo and aquarium leadership (MAIS). Part-time and evening/weekend programs available. *Faculty:* 6 full-time (4 women), 6 part-time/adjunct (5 women). *Students:* 25 full-time (17 women), 90 part-time (76 women); includes 24 minority (5 African Americans, 1 American Indian/Alaska Native, 7 Asian Americans or Pacific Islanders, 11 Hispanic Americans), 3 international. Average age 33. 68 applicants, 72% accepted, 35 enrolled. In 2007, 19 degrees awarded. *Degree requirements:* For master's, thesis optional. *Entrance requirements:* For master's, GRE, GMAT, or MAT, interview, minimum GPA of 3.0 in last 60 hours of course work. *Application deadline:* For fall admission, 5/1 priority date for domestic students; for spring admission, 11/1 for domestic students. Applications are processed on a rolling basis. Application fee: $60 ($75 for international students). Electronic applications accepted. *Financial support:* Fellowships, teaching assistantships, career-related internships or fieldwork, Federal Work-Study, and institutionally sponsored loans available. Support available to part-time students. Financial award application deadline: 3/1; financial award applicants required to submit FAFSA. *Unit head:* John Burns, Chair, 703-993-1291, Fax: 703-993-1297, E-mail: mais@gmu.edu. *Application contact:* Dr. Johannes D. Bergmann, Information Contact, 703-993-8762, E-mail: mais@gmu.edu.

Georgia State University, College of Arts and Sciences, Department of Communication, Atlanta, GA 30303-3083. Offers film/video/digital imaging (MA); human communication and

Film, Television, and Video Production

Georgia State University (continued)
social influence (MA); mass communication (MA); moving image studies (PhD); public communication (PhD). Part-time programs available. *Faculty:* 27 full-time (13 women). *Students:* 81 full-time (51 women), 61 part-time (41 women); includes 31 minority (26 African Americans, 2 Asian Americans or Pacific Islanders, 3 Hispanic Americans), 17 international. 179 applicants, 30% accepted, 29 enrolled. In 2007, 23 master's, 10 doctorates awarded. *Degree requirements:* For master's, one foreign language, thesis or alternative; for doctorate, comprehensive exam, thesis/dissertation. *Entrance requirements:* For master's and doctorate, GRE General Test. Additional exam requirements/recommendations for international students: Required—TOEFL (minimum score 80 computer-based). Application fee: $50. Electronic applications accepted. *Expenses:* Tuition, state resident: part-time $221 per credit hour. *Financial support:* In 2007–08, 1 fellowship with tuition reimbursement (averaging $15,000 per year) was awarded; research assistantships, teaching assistantships with tuition reimbursements, career-related internships or fieldwork, Federal Work-Study, institutionally sponsored loans, tuition waivers (partial), and unspecified assistantships also available. Support available to part-time students. Financial award applicants required to submit FAFSA. *Faculty research:* Critical/cultural studies, rhetoric studies, film/media studies, mass communications/journalism, audience studies. *Unit head:* Dr. David Cheshier, Chair, 404-413-5649, E-mail: dcheshier@gsu.edu. *Application contact:* Tawanna Tookes, Administrative Specialist, Managerial, 404-413-5652, E-mail: joutkt@langate.gsu.edu.

Hofstra University, School of Communication, Department of Audio/Video/Film, Hempstead, NY 11549. Offers documentary studies and production (MFA). Part-time and evening/weekend programs available. *Faculty:* 2 full-time (1 woman), 1 (woman) part-time/adjunct. *Students:* 3 full-time (all women), 2 part-time (both women); includes 3 minority (1 African American, 1 Asian American or Pacific Islander, 1 Hispanic American). Average age 43. 7 applicants, 100% accepted, 5 enrolled. *Degree requirements:* For master's, thesis, Thesis. *Entrance requirements:* For master's, 2 letters of recommendation, essay, portfolio, interview. Additional exam requirements/recommendations for international students: Required—TOEFL (minimum score 550 paper-based; 213 computer-based). *Application deadline:* Applications are processed on a rolling basis. Application fee: $60. Electronic applications accepted. *Expenses:* Tuition: Full-time $14,220; part-time $820 per credit. Required fees: $970; $165 per term. Tuition and fees vary according to program. *Financial support:* In 2007–08, 3 students received support; fellowships with tuition reimbursements available, research assistantships with full and partial tuition reimbursements available, Federal Work-Study, institutionally sponsored loans, scholarships/grants, tuition waivers (full and partial), and unspecified assistantships available. Support available to part-time students. Financial award applicants required to submit FAFSA. *Faculty research:* Community radio; animation; feminism and documentary; working class women; film aesthetics and theory. *Unit head:* Dr. Matthew Sobnosky, Director, 516-463-7141, E-mail: sphmjs@hofstra.edu. *Application contact:* Carol Drummer, Dean of Graduate Admissions, 516-463-4876, Fax: 516-463-4664, E-mail: gradstudent@hofstra.edu.

Hollins University, Graduate Programs, Program in Screenwriting and Film Studies, Roanoke, VA 24020-1603. Offers MA, MFA. Offered during summer only. Part-time programs available. *Faculty:* 1 full-time (0 women), 5 part-time/adjunct (2 women). *Students:* 34 full-time (18 women), 1 (woman) part-time; includes 6 minority (4 African Americans, 2 Hispanic Americans). Average age 33. 28 applicants, 96% accepted, 14 enrolled. In 2007, 7 degrees awarded. *Degree requirements:* For master's, one foreign language, comprehensive exam, thesis. *Entrance requirements:* For master's, letters of recommendation, portfolio. Additional exam requirements/recommendations for international students: Required—TOEFL (minimum score 550 paper-based; 213 computer-based). *Application deadline:* For fall admission, 2/15 for domestic and international students. Application fee: $40. Electronic applications accepted. *Expenses:* Tuition: Part-time $265 per credit hour. Tuition and fees vary according to course load and program. *Financial support:* In 2007–08, 24 students received support, including 14 fellowships (averaging $857 per year); Federal Work-Study and scholarships/grants also available. Support available to part-time students. Financial award application deadline: 2/15; financial award applicants required to submit FAFSA. *Faculty research:* German film, women in film, censorship, minorities in film. *Unit head:* Dr. Klaus Phillips, Director, 540-362-6308, E-mail: kphillips@hollins.edu. *Application contact:* Cathy S. Koon, Manager of Graduate Services, 540-362-6326, Fax: 540-362-6288, E-mail: ckoon@hollins.edu.

Howard University, School of Communications, Department of Radio, Television and Film, Washington, DC 20059-0002. Offers film (MFA). Part-time programs available. *Degree requirements:* For master's, thesis optional. *Entrance requirements:* For master's, GRE General Test, minimum GPA of 3.0. *Expenses:* Tuition: Full-time $16,175; part-time $899 per credit hour. Required fees: $805.

Loyola Marymount University, Graduate Division, School of Film and Television, Program in Production (Film and Television), Los Angeles, CA 90045-2659. Offers MFA. *Faculty:* 10 full-time (2 women). *Students:* 51 full-time (18 women), 4 part-time (2 women); includes 17 minority (8 African Americans, 2 Asian Americans or Pacific Islanders, 7 Hispanic Americans), 9 international. Average age 26. 83 applicants, 22% accepted, 9 enrolled. In 2007, 14 degrees awarded. *Degree requirements:* For master's, thesis, film. *Entrance requirements:* For master's, GRE General Test. *Application deadline:* For fall admission, 3/15 for domestic students. Application fee: $50. Electronic applications accepted. *Financial support:* In 2007–08, 23 students received support, including 4 research assistantships (averaging $12,370 per year); career-related internships or fieldwork and scholarships/grants also available. Support available to part-time students. Financial award application deadline: 6/1; financial award applicants required to submit FAFSA. *Unit head:* Dr. Eric Xavier, Graduate Director, 310-338-2779, Fax: 310-338-3030, E-mail: exavier@lmu.edu. *Application contact:* Dr. Eric Xavier, Graduate Director, 310-338-2779, Fax: 310-338-3030, E-mail: exavier@lmu.edu.

Marywood University, Academic Affairs, Insalaco College of Creative Arts and Management, Department of Communication Arts, Program in Communication Arts, Scranton, PA 18509-1598. Offers corporate communication (Certificate); e-business (Certificate); health communication (Certificate); instructional technology (Certificate); interdisciplinary (MA); library science/information specialist (Certificate); media management (MA); production (MA). *Students:* 10 full-time (6 women), 22 part-time (15 women); includes 4 minority (1 African American, 3 Hispanic Americans). Average age 28. In 2007, 8 degrees awarded. Application fee: $30. *Expenses:* Tuition: Full-time $15,290; part-time $695 per credit. Required fees: $990; $370 per term. Tuition and fees vary according to degree level.

Massachusetts College of Art and Design, Graduate Programs, Program in Fine Arts, Boston, MA 02115-5882. Offers ceramics (MFA); design (MFA); fibers (MFA); film (MFA); glass (MFA); media and performing arts (MFA); metals (MFA); painting (MFA); photography (MFA); printmaking (MFA); sculpture (MFA). *Accreditation:* NASAD. *Faculty:* 10 full-time (5 women), 8 part-time/adjunct (6 women). *Students:* 80 full-time (46 women), 11 part-time (9 women); includes 7 minority (1 African American, 4 Asian Americans or Pacific Islanders, 2 Hispanic Americans), 13 international. Average age 34. 310 applicants, 26% accepted, 50 enrolled. In 2007, 37 degrees awarded. *Degree requirements:* For master's, thesis, exhibit. *Entrance requirements:* For master's, 12 units of course work in art history, portfolio, resumé. *Application deadline:* For fall admission, 2/1 for domestic students. Application fee: $75. *Expenses:* Tuition, state resident: full-time $16,260; part-time $542 per credit. Tuition, nonresident: full-time $16,260; part-time $542 per credit. *Financial support:* In 2007–08, 50 research assistantships (averaging $2,000 per year), 30 teaching assistantships (averaging $2,000 per year) were awarded; career-related internships or fieldwork, Federal Work-Study, and clerical/technical assistantships also available. Support available to part-time students. Financial award application deadline: 5/1; financial award applicants required to submit FAFSA. *Application contact:* George Creamer, Director, 617-879-7163, Fax: 617-879-7171, E-mail: creamer@massart.edu.

Miami International University of Art & Design, Program in Film, Miami, FL 33132-1418. Offers MFA. Postbaccalaureate distance learning degree programs offered.

See Close-Up on page 119.

Minneapolis College of Art and Design, Program in Visual Studies, Minneapolis, MN 55404-4347. Offers animation (MFA); comic art (MFA); drawing (MFA); filmmaking (MFA); fine arts (MFA); furniture design (MFA); graphic design (MFA); illustration (MFA); interactive media (MFA); painting (MFA); photography (MFA); printmaking (MFA); sculpture (MFA). *Accreditation:* NASAD. Part-time programs available. *Faculty:* 23 full-time (7 women), 9 part-time/adjunct (4 women). *Students:* 40 full-time (21 women), 1 (woman) part-time; includes 1 minority (American Indian/Alaska Native). Average age 27. 172 applicants, 24% accepted, 15 enrolled. In 2007, 7 degrees awarded. *Degree requirements:* For master's, thesis, thesis exhibit. *Entrance requirements:* For master's, portfolio, resumé, 3 letters of recommendation, statement . Additional exam requirements/recommendations for international students: Required—TOEFL (minimum score 550 paper-based; 213 computer-based; 79 iBT). *Application deadline:* For fall admission, 2/15 for domestic and international students. Application fee: $50. Electronic applications accepted. *Expenses:* Tuition: Full-time $27,000; part-time $900 per credit. Required fees: $100 per term. *Financial support:* In 2007–08, 23 students received support, including 15 teaching assistantships (averaging $6,000 per year); career-related internships or fieldwork, Federal Work-Study, scholarships/grants, and unspecified assistantships also available. Support available to part-time students. Financial award application deadline: 3/15; financial award applicants required to submit FAFSA. *Faculty research:* Visual arts. *Unit head:* Carole Fisher, Graduate Director, 612-874-3629, E-mail: carole_fisher@mcad.edu. *Application contact:* William Mullen, Vice President of Enrollment Management, 612-874-3762, Fax: 612-874-3701, E-mail: william_mullen@mcad.edu.

Montana State University, College of Graduate Studies, College of Arts and Architecture, Department of Media and Theatre Arts, Program in Science and Natural History Filmmaking, Bozeman, MT 59717. Offers MFA. *Degree requirements:* For master's, comprehensive exam. *Entrance requirements:* For master's, GRE General Test. Additional exam requirements/recommendations for international students: Required—TOEFL (minimum score 550 paper-based; 213 computer-based). *Expenses:* Tuition, state resident: full-time $5,176. Tuition, nonresident: full-time $13,070. *Faculty research:* Documentary, experimental video.

New York Film Academy, Program in Filmmaking–Hollywood, Los Angeles, CA 90068. Offers acting for film (MFA); filmmaking (MFA); producing (MFA); screenwriting (MFA).

See Close-Up on page 289.

New York Film Academy, Program in Filmmaking–New York, New York, NY 10003. Offers acting for film (MFA); filmmaking (MFA); producing (MFA); screenwriting (MFA).

See Close-Up on page 289.

New York Film Academy, Program in Filmmaking–United Arab Emirates, Abu Dhabi, CA 90068, United Arab Emirates. Offers acting for film (MFA); filmmaking (MFA); producing (MFA); screenwriting (MFA).

See Close-Up on page 289.

New York University, Tisch School of the Arts Asia, Singapore, NY 248923, Singapore. Offers animation and digital arts (MFA); dramatic writing (MFA); film production (MFA). *Faculty:* 6 full-time (3 women). *Students:* 33 full-time (16 women); includes 6 minority (1 African American, 5 Asian Americans or Pacific Islanders), 13 international. 55 applicants, 22% accepted. *Entrance requirements:* Additional exam requirements/recommendations for international students: Required—TOEFL (minimum score 610 paper-based; 250 computer-based; 105 iBT). *Application deadline:* For fall admission, 2/1 priority date for domestic and international students. Application fee: $60. Electronic applications accepted. *Financial support:* Fellowships with full and partial tuition reimbursements, research assistantships, teaching assistantships, Federal Work-Study, institutionally sponsored loans, and unspecified assistantships available. Financial award application deadline: 2/15; financial award applicants required to submit FAFSA.

See Close-Up on page 291.

New York University, Tisch School of the Arts and Graduate School of Arts and Science, Department of Cinema Studies, Program in Moving Image Archiving and Preservation, New York, NY 10012-1019. Offers MA. *Faculty:* 2 full-time, 4 part-time/adjunct. *Students:* 15 full-time (8 women), 2 part-time (1 woman); includes 3 minority (1 Asian American or Pacific Islander, 2 Hispanic Americans), 2 international. Average age 28. 32 applicants, 25% accepted, 7 enrolled. In 2007, 6 degrees awarded. *Degree requirements:* For master's, internship. *Entrance requirements:* For master's, GRE. Additional exam requirements/recommendations for international students: Required—TOEFL or IELTS. *Application deadline:* For fall admission, 12/15 for domestic and international students. Application fee: $60. Electronic applications accepted. *Financial support:* In 2007–08, 11 students received support, including 5 fellowships with full and partial tuition reimbursements available; tuition waivers (partial) also available. Financial award application deadline: 2/15. *Unit head:* Howard Besser, Head, 212-998-1618. *Application contact:* Dan Sandford, Director of Graduate Admissions, 212-998-1918, Fax: 212-995-4060, E-mail: tisch.gradadmissions@nyu.edu.

New York University, Tisch School of the Arts, Kanbar Institute of Film and Television, New York, NY 10012-1019. Offers MFA. *Faculty:* 19 full-time, 20 part-time/adjunct. *Students:* 149 full-time (72 women), 68 part-time (26 women); includes 66 minority (22 African Americans, 3 American Indian/Alaska Native, 36 Asian Americans or Pacific Islanders, 5 Hispanic Americans), 43 international. Average age 25. 707 applicants, 8% accepted, 36 enrolled. In 2007, 30 degrees awarded. *Degree requirements:* For master's, 4 films. *Entrance requirements:* For master's, portfolio. Additional exam requirements/recommendations for international students: Required—TOEFL or IELTS. *Application deadline:* For fall admission, 12/1 for domestic and international students. Application fee: $60. Electronic applications accepted. *Financial support:* In 2007–08, 60 students received support, including 16 fellowships with full and partial tuition reimbursements available, 6 teaching assistantships with tuition reimbursements available; Federal Work-Study, institutionally sponsored loans, scholarships/grants, tuition waivers (full and partial), and unspecified assistantships also available. Financial award application deadline: 2/15; financial award applicants required to submit FAFSA. *Unit head:* John Tintori, Chair, 212-998-1780, E-mail: jt42@nyu.edu. *Application contact:* Dan Sandford, Director of Graduate Admissions, 212-998-1918, Fax: 212-995-4060, E-mail: tisch.gradadmissions@nyu.edu.

North Carolina School of the Arts, School of Filmmaking, Winston-Salem, NC 27127-2188. Offers film music composition (MFA). *Faculty:* 2 full-time (0 women). *Students:* 19 full-time (4 women); includes 2 minority (both Asian Americans or Pacific Islanders) Average age 25. 3 applicants, 100% accepted, 3 enrolled. In 2007, 2 degrees awarded. *Entrance requirements:* For master's, audition, performance, portfolio, interview. *Application deadline:* For fall admission, 4/1 priority date for domestic students. Applications are processed on a rolling basis. Application fee: $60 ($100 for international students). *Expenses:* Tuition, state resident: full-time $3,636. Tuition, nonresident: full-time $15,220. Required fees: $1,688. *Financial support:* In 2007–08, fellowships (averaging $2,000 per year); career-related internships or fieldwork and Federal Work-Study also available. Support available to part-time students. Financial award application deadline: 3/15; financial award applicants required to submit FAFSA. *Unit head:* Jordan Kerner, Dean, 336-770-1330, Fax: 336-770-1339, E-mail: kernerj@ncarts.edu. *Application contact:* Sheeler Lawson, Director of Admissions, 336-770-3290, Fax: 336-770-3370, E-mail: admissions@ncarts.edu.

Northwestern University, The Graduate School, School of Communication, Department of Radio/Television/Film, Evanston, IL 60208. Offers MA, MFA, PhD. Admissions and degrees offered through The Graduate School. Part-time programs available. Terminal master's awarded for partial completion of doctoral program. *Degree requirements:* For master's, comprehensive exam or thesis; for doctorate, thesis/dissertation, qualifying exam. *Entrance requirements:* For master's and doctorate, GRE General Test. Additional exam requirements/recommendations for international students: Required—TOEFL. Electronic applications accepted. *Faculty research:* Art and new media, media theory and criticism, gender, media history, documentary.

Film, Television, and Video Production

Ohio University, Graduate College, College of Fine Arts, School of Film, Athens, OH 45701-2979. Offers film (MFA); film studies (MA). *Faculty:* 8 full-time (2 women), 2 part-time/adjunct (1 woman). *Students:* 45 full-time (22 women); includes 10 minority (3 African Americans, 4 Asian Americans or Pacific Islanders, 3 Hispanic Americans), 9 international. Average age 25. 125 applicants, 12% accepted, 12 enrolled. In 2007, 7 degrees awarded. *Degree requirements:* For master's, one foreign language, thesis. *Entrance requirements:* Additional exam requirements/recommendations for international students: Required—TOEFL (minimum score 550 paper-based; 239 computer-based). *Application deadline:* For fall admission, 1/30 for domestic and international students. Application fee: $50 ($55 for international students). Electronic applications accepted. *Financial support:* In 2007–08, 34 students received support, including 2 research assistantships with full tuition reimbursements available, 19 teaching assistantships with full tuition reimbursements available; institutionally sponsored loans, scholarships/grants, tuition waivers (full and partial), and unspecified assistantships also available. Financial award application deadline: 1/30. *Faculty research:* Scriptwriting, sound, editing, cinematography, film theory, digital pest production. *Unit head:* Jody Lamb, Director, 740-593-1323, Fax: 740-593-1328, E-mail: lambj@ohio.edu. *Application contact:* Tamra LaGraff, Administrative Assistant, 740-593-1323, Fax: 740-593-1328, E-mail: lagraff@ohio.edu.

Polytechnic Institute of NYU, Department of Electrical and Computer Engineering, Major in Image Processing, Brooklyn, NY 11201-2990. Offers Certificate. *Entrance requirements:* Additional exam requirements/recommendations for international students: Required—TOEFL (minimum score 550 paper-based; 213 computer-based); Recommended—IELTS (minimum score 7). *Application deadline:* For fall admission, 7/15 priority date for domestic students, 4/1 priority date for international students; for spring admission, 12/15 priority date for domestic students, 10/1 priority date for international students. Applications are processed on a rolling basis. Application fee: $55. Electronic applications accepted. *Expenses:* Tuition: Full-time $18,486; part-time $1,027 per credit. Required fees: $352 per semester. *Application contact:* Anthea Jeffrey, Graduate Admissions, 718-260-3200, Fax: 718-260-3624, E-mail: gradinfo@poly.edu.

Regent University, Graduate School, School of Communication and the Arts, Virginia Beach, VA 23464-9800. Offers acting and directing (MFA); cinema arts (MA); communication (MA, PhD); fine arts (MFA); journalism (MA); script and screenwriting (MFA); television arts (MA); theatre arts (MA). Part-time programs available. Postbaccalaureate distance learning degree programs offered (minimal on-campus study). *Faculty:* 23 full-time (3 women), 12 part-time/adjunct (3 women). *Students:* 123 full-time (66 women), 145 part-time (83 women); includes 71 minority (54 African Americans, 2 American Indian/Alaska Native, 3 Asian Americans or Pacific Islanders, 12 Hispanic Americans), 14 international. Average age 33. 176 applicants, 66% accepted, 64 enrolled. In 2007, 60 master's, 15 doctorates awarded. *Degree requirements:* For master's, thesis or alternative; for doctorate, thesis/dissertation. *Entrance requirements:* For master's, GRE General Test or MAT, minimum undergraduate GPA of 3.0, writing sample, computer literacy survey, recommendation, resumé, interview, audition (MFA programs); for doctorate, GRE General Test, minimum graduate GPA of 3.0, writing sample, computer literacy survey, recommendation, interview, transcripts. Additional exam requirements/recommendations for international students: Required—TOEFL (minimum score 577 paper-based; 233 computer-based). *Application deadline:* For fall admission, 3/1 priority date for domestic students; for spring admission, 10/1 priority date for domestic students. Applications are processed on a rolling basis. Application fee: $50. Electronic applications accepted. *Expenses:* Contact institution. *Financial support:* In 2007–08, 247 students received support, including 5 fellowships with full and partial tuition reimbursements available (averaging $7,245 per year); scholarships/grants, tuition waivers (full and partial), and unspecified assistantships also available. Support available to part-time students. Financial award application deadline: 9/1; financial award applicants required to submit FAFSA. *Faculty research:* Southern gospel music, education and entertainment, celebrities and the media, journalism and ethics, C. S. Lewis. *Unit head:* Michael Patrick, Dean, 757-226-4970, Fax: 757-226-4279, E-mail: michpat@regent.edu. *Application contact:* Althea Bishard, Registrar and Executive Director of Enrollment and Academic Services, 800-373-5504, Fax: 757-226-4381, E-mail: admissions@regent.edu.

Rochester Institute of Technology, Graduate Enrollment Services, College of Imaging Arts and Sciences, School of Photographic Arts and Sciences, Program in Imaging Arts, Rochester, NY 14623-5603. Offers MFA. *Accreditation:* NASAD. *Students:* 76 full-time (34 women), 18 part-time (7 women); includes 9 minority (2 African Americans, 6 Asian Americans or Pacific Islanders, 1 Hispanic American), 28 international. 153 applicants, 40% accepted, 29 enrolled. In 2007, 28 degrees awarded. *Degree requirements:* For master's, thesis, exhibit. *Entrance requirements:* For master's, portfolio, minimum GPA of 3.0. Additional exam requirements/recommendations for international students: Required—TOEFL (minimum score 550 paper-based; 213 computer-based; 79 iBT). *Application deadline:* For fall admission, 3/1 priority date for domestic students. Applications are processed on a rolling basis. Application fee: $50. *Expenses:* Tuition: Full-time $28,491; part-time $800 per credit hour. Required fees: $201; $67 per term. *Financial support:* Fellowships with partial tuition reimbursements, research assistantships with partial tuition reimbursements, teaching assistantships with partial tuition reimbursements, career-related internships or fieldwork, institutionally sponsored loans, scholarships/grants, tuition waivers (partial), and unspecified assistantships available. Support available to part-time students. Financial award application deadline: 8/30; financial award applicants required to submit FAFSA. *Unit head:* Therese Mulligan, Head, 585-475-2616, E-mail: mtmpph@rit.edu.

St. Thomas University, School of Leadership Studies, Program in Electronic Media, Miami Gardens, FL 33054-6459. Offers MA. *Application contact:* Marilyn Carballosa, Assistant Director of Admissions, 305-628-6546, Fax: 305-628-6591, E-mail: graduate@stu.edu.

San Diego State University, Graduate and Research Affairs, College of Professional Studies and Fine Arts, School of Theater, Television and Film, Program in Television, Film, and New Media Production, San Diego, CA 92182. Offers MA. *Students:* 9 full-time (3 women), 19 part-time (10 women); includes 4 minority (1 African American, 1 Asian American or Pacific Islander, 2 Hispanic Americans), 6 international. 26 applicants, 42% accepted, 8 enrolled. In 2007, 12 degrees awarded. *Entrance requirements:* For master's, GRE General Test, 3 letters of recommendation, resumé, sample reel, influential book list, influential films list, hobby list. Additional exam requirements/recommendations for international students: Required—TOEFL. *Application deadline:* For fall admission, 3/1 for domestic students, 3/1 priority date for international students; for spring admission, 10/1 for domestic students, 10/1 priority date for international students. Applications are processed on a rolling basis. Application fee: $55. Electronic applications accepted. *Financial support:* Career-related internships or fieldwork available. Financial award applicants required to submit FAFSA. *Faculty research:* Experimental film and television programs, documentary film, television research and production. Total annual research expenditures: $25,000. *Unit head:* Greg Durbin, Graduate Advisor, 619-594-6856, E-mail: gdurbin@sciences.sdsu.edu. *Application contact:* Greg Durbin, Graduate Advisor, 619-594-6856, E-mail: gdurbin@sciences.sdsu.edu.

San Francisco Art Institute, Graduate Program, Department of Film, San Francisco, CA 94133. Offers MFA, Certificate. *Accreditation:* NASAD. Part-time programs available. *Degree requirements:* For master's and Certificate, oral reviews. *Entrance requirements:* For master's and Certificate, portfolio. Additional exam requirements/recommendations for international students: Required—TOEFL (minimum score 580 paper-based; 237 computer-based). Electronic applications accepted.

See Close-Up on page 255.

San Francisco Art Institute, Graduate Program, Department of New Genres, San Francisco, CA 94133. Offers new genres (Certificate); performance/video (MFA). *Accreditation:* NASAD. Part-time programs available. *Degree requirements:* For master's and Certificate, oral reviews. *Entrance requirements:* For master's and Certificate, portfolio. Additional exam requirements/recommendations for international students: Required—TOEFL (minimum score 580 paper-based; 237 computer-based). Electronic applications accepted.

See Close-Up on page 255.

San Francisco State University, Division of Graduate Studies, College of Creative Arts, Department of Broadcast and Electronic Communication Arts, San Francisco, CA 94132-1722. Offers radio and television (MA). *Unit head:* Dr. Scott Patterson, Chair, 415-338-1788, Fax: 415-338-1688. *Application contact:* Dr. Nancy Reist, Graduate Coordinator, 415-338-1788, E-mail: becagrad@sfsu.edu.

San Francisco State University, Division of Graduate Studies, College of Creative Arts, Department of Cinema, San Francisco, CA 94132-1722. Offers cinema (MFA); cinema studies (MA). *Unit head:* Stephen Ujlaki, Chair, 415-338-1724.

San Jose State University, Graduate Studies and Research, College of Humanities and the Arts, Department of Television, Radio, Film and Theatre, San Jose, CA 95192-0001. Offers theatre arts (MA). *Accreditation:* NAST. *Students:* 10 full-time (5 women), 25 part-time (16 women); includes 10 minority (6 African Americans, 1 Asian American or Pacific Islander, 3 Hispanic Americans), 3 international. Average age 36. 19 applicants, 74% accepted, 7 enrolled. In 2007, 4 degrees awarded. *Degree requirements:* For master's, written exam. *Entrance requirements:* Additional exam requirements/recommendations for international students: Required—TOEFL (minimum score 570 paper-based). *Application deadline:* For fall admission, 6/29 for domestic students; for spring admission, 11/30 for domestic students. Applications are processed on a rolling basis. Application fee: $59. Electronic applications accepted. *Financial support:* Scholarships/grants available. Financial award applicants required to submit FAFSA. *Unit head:* Dr. Mike Adams, Chair, 408-924-4545, Fax: 408-924-4574. *Application contact:* Dr. David Kahn, Graduate Coordinator, 408-924-4530, E-mail: dkahn@email.sjsu.edu.

Savannah College of Art and Design, Graduate School, Program in Animation, Savannah, GA 31402-3146. Offers MA, MFA. Part-time programs available. *Faculty:* 9 full-time (3 women), 1 (woman) part-time/adjunct. *Students:* 94 full-time (33 women), 14 part-time (5 women); includes 8 minority (5 African Americans, 1 American Indian/Alaska Native, 1 Asian American or Pacific Islander, 1 Hispanic American), 39 international. 109 applicants, 48% accepted, 23 enrolled. In 2007, 36 degrees awarded. *Degree requirements:* For master's, thesis, internships. *Entrance requirements:* For master's, interview, portfolio. Additional exam requirements/recommendations for international students: Required—TOEFL (minimum score 450 paper-based; 133 computer-based). *Application deadline:* For fall admission, 4/1 priority date for domestic and international students. Applications are processed on a rolling basis. Application fee: $50. Electronic applications accepted. *Expenses:* Tuition: Full-time $24,840; part-time $552 per credit. One-time fee: $500 full-time. *Financial support:* Fellowships, career-related internships or fieldwork, Federal Work-Study, and scholarships/grants available. Financial award application deadline: 4/1; financial award applicants required to submit FAFSA. *Unit head:* Jeremy Moorshead, Chair, 912-525-8527, Fax: 912-525-8597, E-mail: jmoorshe@scad.edu. *Application contact:* Darrell Tutchton, Director of Graduate and International Enrollment, 912-525-5961, Fax: 912-525-5985, E-mail: admission@scad.edu.

Savannah College of Art and Design, Graduate School, Program in Film and Television, Savannah, GA 31402-3146. Offers MA, MFA. Part-time programs available. *Faculty:* 9 full-time (3 women), 2 part-time/adjunct (1 woman). *Students:* 66 full-time (26 women), 9 part-time (2 women); includes 8 minority (5 African Americans, 1 Asian American or Pacific Islander, 2 Hispanic Americans), 14 international. Average age 25. 92 applicants, 45% accepted, 19 enrolled. In 2007, 13 degrees awarded. *Degree requirements:* For master's, thesis, internship. *Entrance requirements:* For master's, interview, videotape. Additional exam requirements/recommendations for international students: Required—TOEFL (minimum score 450 paper-based; 133 computer-based). *Application deadline:* For fall admission, 4/1 priority date for domestic and international students. Applications are processed on a rolling basis. Application fee: $50. Electronic applications accepted. *Expenses:* Tuition: Full-time $24,840; part-time $552 per credit. One-time fee: $500 full-time. *Financial support:* In 2007–08, 4 fellowships were awarded; career-related internships or fieldwork, Federal Work-Study, and scholarships/grants also available. Financial award application deadline: 4/1; financial award applicants required to submit FAFSA. *Unit head:* Christopher Auer, Chair, 912-525-6418, Fax: 912-525-6488, E-mail: cjaver@scad.edu. *Application contact:* Darrell Tutchton, Director of Graduate and International Enrollment, 912-525-5961, Fax: 912-525-5985, E-mail: admission@scad.edu.

See Close-Up on page 257.

Savannah College of Art and Design, Graduate School, Program in Sound Design, Savannah, GA 31402-3146. Offers MA, MFA. Part-time programs available. *Faculty:* 2 full-time (0 women), 1 part-time/adjunct (0 women). *Students:* 18 full-time (5 women), 3 part-time; includes 1 minority (African American), 2 international. 19 applicants, 58% accepted, 6 enrolled. In 2007, 1 degree awarded. *Degree requirements:* For master's, thesis, internships. *Entrance requirements:* For master's, interview, portfolio. Additional exam requirements/recommendations for international students: Required—TOEFL (minimum score 450 paper-based; 133 computer-based). *Application deadline:* For fall admission, 4/1 priority date for domestic and international students. Application fee: $50. *Expenses:* Tuition: Full-time $24,840; part-time $552 per credit. One-time fee: $500 full-time. *Financial support:* Fellowships, career-related internships or fieldwork, Federal Work-Study, and scholarships/grants available. Financial award application deadline: 4/1; financial award applicants required to submit FAFSA. *Unit head:* Robin Beauchamp, Chair, 912-525-6463, Fax: 912-525-6459, E-mail: rbeaucha@scad.edu. *Application contact:* Darrell Tutchton, Director of Graduate and International Enrollment, 912-525-5961, Fax: 912-525-5985, E-mail: admission@scad.edu.

School of the Art Institute of Chicago, Graduate Division, Department of Filmmaking, Chicago, IL 60603-3103. Offers MFA. *Accreditation:* NASAD. *Degree requirements:* For master's, thesis exhibit. *Entrance requirements:* Additional exam requirements/recommendations for international students: Required—TOEFL.

See Close-Up on page 259.

School of the Art Institute of Chicago, Graduate Division, Department of Video, Chicago, IL 60603-3103. Offers MFA. *Accreditation:* NASAD. *Entrance requirements:* Additional exam requirements/recommendations for international students: Required—TOEFL.

See Close-Up on page 259.

School of Visual Arts, Graduate Programs, Program in Photography, Video and Related Media, New York, NY 10010-3994. Offers MFA. *Accreditation:* NASAD. *Faculty:* 1 full-time (0 women), 29 part-time/adjunct (12 women). *Students:* 80 full-time (42 women), 8 part-time (4 women); includes 10 minority (2 African Americans, 1 Asian American or Pacific Islander, 7 Hispanic Americans), 22 international. Average age 29. 246 applicants, 35% accepted, 44 enrolled. In 2007, 28 degrees awarded. *Degree requirements:* For master's, final review, project or thesis. *Entrance requirements:* For master's, portfolio. Additional exam requirements/recommendations for international students: Required—TOEFL (minimum score 550 paper-based; 213 computer-based; 79 iBT). *Application deadline:* For fall admission, 2/1 for domestic students. Application fee: $80. Electronic applications accepted. *Expenses:* Tuition: Full-time $26,120; part-time $870 per credit. Tuition and fees vary according to program. *Financial support:* In 2007–08, 40 students received support. Career-related internships or fieldwork, Federal Work-Study, scholarships/grants, and unspecified assistantships available. Support available to part-time students. Financial award application deadline: 2/1; financial award applicants required to submit FAFSA. *Unit head:* Charles Traub, Chair, 212-592-2360, Fax: 212-592-2366, E-mail: ctraub@sva.edu.

Southern Methodist University, Meadows School of the Arts, Division of Cinema—Television, Dallas, TX 75275. Offers MA. Part-time and evening/weekend programs available. *Faculty:* 9 full-time (3 women), 6 part-time/adjunct (1 woman). *Students:* 13 full-time (5 women), 1 (woman) part-time; includes 2 minority (1 African American, 1 American Indian/Alaska Native), 8 international. Average age 27. 9 applicants, 78% accepted, 4 enrolled. In 2007, 2 degrees awarded. *Degree requirements:* For master's, thesis or alternative. *Entrance requirements:* For master's, GRE General Test, minimum undergraduate GPA of 3.0 in major

Film, Television, and Video Production

Southern Methodist University (continued)

field during last 2 years. Additional exam requirements/recommendations for international students: Required—TOEFL (minimum score 550 paper-based; 213 computer-based; 80 iBT). *Application deadline:* For fall admission, 3/1 priority date for domestic and international students. Application fee: $75. *Financial support:* In 2007–08, 7 students received support, including 7 teaching assistantships (averaging $6,500 per year); research assistantships, scholarships/grants, tuition waivers (full), and unspecified assistantships also available. Financial award application deadline: 3/15. *Faculty research:* Digital sound; new technology; film and gender study; popular film and TV genres; Asian cinema. Total annual research expenditures:$10,000. *Unit head:* Rick Worland, Chair, 214-768-3708, Fax: 214-768-2784, E-mail: rworland@smu.edu. *Application contact:* Jean Cherry, Director of Graduate Admissions and Records, 214-768-3765, Fax: 214-768-3272, E-mail: jcherry@smu.edu.

Syracuse University, Graduate School, College of Visual and Performing Arts, Department of Transmedia, Syracuse, NY 13244. Offers art photography (MFA); art video (MFA); computer art (MFA); film (MFA). *Accreditation:* NASAD. Part-time programs available. *Students:* 32 full-time (17 women), 1 part-time; includes 6 minority (3 African Americans, 2 Asian Americans or Pacific Islanders, 1 Hispanic American), 8 international. 84 applicants, 38% accepted, 17 enrolled. In 2007, 9 degrees awarded. *Degree requirements:* For master's, thesis or alternative. *Entrance requirements:* For master's, portfolio. Additional exam requirements/recommendations for international students: Required—TOEFL. *Application deadline:* For fall admission, 1/1 priority date for domestic students. Applications are processed on a rolling basis. Application fee: $75. Electronic applications accepted. *Expenses:* Tuition: Full-time $18,216; part-time $1,012 per credit. Required fees: $980. Tuition and fees vary according to program. *Financial support:* Fellowships with full tuition reimbursements, research assistantships with full and partial tuition reimbursements, teaching assistantships with full and partial tuition reimbursements, tuition waivers (partial) available. *Unit head:* John Orentlicher, Chair, 315-443-1033, Fax: 315-443-1303, E-mail: jorentli@syr.edu. *Application contact:* Harriett Conti, Associate Director, Graduate Student Services, 315-443-3089, E-mail: hmconti@syr.edu.

Syracuse University, Graduate School, S. I. Newhouse School of Public Communications, Department of Television, Radio, and Film, Program in Documentary Film and History, Syracuse, NY 13244. Offers MA. *Students:* 5 full-time (3 women); includes 1 minority (African American) 14 applicants, 71% accepted. *Entrance requirements:* For master's, GRE General Test. *Application deadline:* For fall admission, 2/1 for domestic students. Application fee: $75. *Expenses:* Tuition: Full-time $18,216; part-time $1,012 per credit. Required fees: $980. Tuition and fees vary according to program. *Unit head:* Richard Breyer, Director, 315-443-4004. *Application contact:* Graduate Records Office, 315-443-4039, Fax: 315-443-1834, E-mail: pcgrad@syr.edu.

Temple University, Graduate School, School of Communications and Theater, Department of Film and Media Arts, Philadelphia, PA 19122-6096. Offers MFA. Part-time programs available. *Degree requirements:* For master's, comprehensive exam, project. *Entrance requirements:* For master's, GRE General Test, minimum GPA of 3.0; exhibit. Additional exam requirements/recommendations for international students: Required—TOEFL (minimum score 550 paper-based; 213 computer-based; 79 iBT). Electronic applications accepted. *Faculty research:* Filmmaking and videography, documentary theory and practice, screenwriting, media culture studies, film studies.

The University of Alabama, Graduate School, College of Communication and Information Sciences, Department of Telecommunication and Film, Tuscaloosa, AL 35487. Offers MA. *Faculty:* 7 full-time (2 women). *Students:* 9 full-time (6 women), 1 (woman) part-time; includes 1 minority (Hispanic American), 2 international. Average age 24. 9 applicants, 44% accepted, 4 enrolled. In 2007, 6 degrees awarded. *Degree requirements:* For master's, comprehensive exam, thesis or alternative. *Entrance requirements:* For master's, GRE, minimum GPA of 3.0. Additional exam requirements/recommendations for international students: Required—TOEFL. *Application deadline:* For fall admission, 2/15 priority date for domestic students; for spring admission, 11/1 for domestic students. Applications are processed on a rolling basis. Application fee: $30. Electronic applications accepted. *Expenses:* Tuition, state resident: full-time $5,700. Tuition, nonresident: full-time $16,518. *Financial support:* In 2007–08, 2 research assistantships with tuition reimbursements (averaging $9,825 per year), 2 teaching assistantships with tuition reimbursements (averaging $9,825 per year) were awarded; institutionally sponsored loans also available. Financial award application deadline: 2/15. *Faculty research:* Entertainment theory, news and public affairs, effects of telecommunications, management. Total annual research expenditures: $18,719. *Unit head:* Dr. Loy A. Singleton, Chair, 205-348-6350, Fax: 205-348-5162, E-mail: loy.singleton@ua.edu. *Application contact:* Dr. Gary Copeland, Graduate Coordinator, 205-348-6350, Fax: 205-348-5162, E-mail: copeland@ua.edu.

The University of British Columbia, Faculty of Arts, Creative Writing Program, Vancouver, BC V6T 1Z1, Canada. Offers creative writing (MFA); creative writing and film (MFA); creative writing and theatre (MFA). Part-time programs available. Postbaccalaureate distance learning degree programs offered (minimal on-campus study). *Faculty:* 7 full-time (4 women), 14 part-time/adjunct (7 women). *Students:* 57 full-time (41 women), 90 part-time (67 women). 308 applicants, 22% accepted, 62 enrolled. In 2007, 24 degrees awarded. *Degree requirements:* For master's, thesis. *Entrance requirements:* For master's, sample of written work. Additional exam requirements/recommendations for international students: Required—TOEFL (minimum score 550 paper-based; 213 computer-based). *Application deadline:* For fall admission, 11/7 for domestic and international students; for winter admission, 9/12 for domestic and international students. Application fee: $90 Canadian dollars ($150 Canadian dollars for international students). Electronic applications accepted. *Expenses: Contact institution. Financial support:* In 2007–08, 13 students received support, including 5 fellowships (averaging $16,000 per year), research assistantships (averaging $1,500 per year), 2 teaching assistantships (averaging $3,000 per year); Federal Work-Study, institutionally sponsored loans, and unspecified assistantships also available. *Faculty research:* Writing of fiction; poetry, creative nonfiction, plays for stage, screen, television, radio, writing for children and translation, song lyrics and libretto. *Unit head:* Keith Maillard, Chair, 604-822-3058, Fax: 604-822-3616. *Application contact:* Bryan Wade, Residential Graduate Adviser, 604-822-3023, Fax: 604-822-3616, E-mail: bwade@interchange.ubc.ca.

The University of British Columbia, Faculty of Arts and Faculty of Graduate Studies, Department of Theatre and Film, Film Program, Vancouver, BC V6T 1Z1, Canada. Offers creative writing and film production (MFA); film production (MFA, Diploma); film studies (MA). *Faculty:* 5 full-time (2 women). *Students:* 12 full-time (8 women). Average age 25. 22 applicants, 14% accepted, 2 enrolled. In 2007, 4 degrees awarded. *Degree requirements:* For master's, thesis (MA), thesis or project (MFA). *Entrance requirements:* For master's, bachelor's degree in film production or equivalent, BA in film studies. Additional exam requirements/recommendations for international students: Required—TOEFL (minimum score 600 paper-based). *Application deadline:* For fall admission, 2/1 for domestic and international students. Application fee: $90 Canadian dollars ($150 Canadian dollars for international students). Electronic applications accepted. *Financial support:* In 2007–08, 4 fellowships (averaging $18,000 per year), 2 research assistantships (averaging $4,000 per year), 9 teaching assistantships (averaging $9,933 per year) were awarded. Financial award application deadline: 1/1. *Faculty research:* Film history, theory, criticism; producing; experimental film. *Unit head:* Prof. Sharon McGowan, Chair, 604-822-9201, Fax: 604-822-0508, E-mail: sharonmcgowan@ubc.ca. *Application contact:* Zanna Downes, Secretary, 604-822-6037, Fax: 604-822-0508, E-mail: film@interchange.ubc.ca.

University of California, Los Angeles, Graduate Division, School of Theater, Film and Television, Department of Film, Television, and Digital Media, Los Angeles, CA 90095. Offers film and television (MA, MFA, PhD); MFA/MA. *Students:* 278 full-time (139 women); includes 75 minority (18 African Americans, 6 American Indian/Alaska Native, 23 Asian Americans or Pacific Islanders, 28 Hispanic Americans), 21 international. Average age 30. 960 applicants, 14% accepted, 83 enrolled. In 2007, 81 master's, 5 doctorates awarded. *Degree requirements:* For master's, comprehensive exam; for doctorate, one foreign language, thesis/dissertation, oral and written qualifying exams. *Entrance requirements:* For master's, film or TV project, animation, or script (MFA), 3.0 minimum GPA; for doctorate, GRE General Test, minimum undergraduate GPA of 3.0. *Application deadline:* For fall admission, 11/1 for domestic students. Application fee: $60. Electronic applications accepted. *Financial support:* In 2007–08, 296 fellowships with full and partial tuition reimbursements, 16 research assistantships with full and partial tuition reimbursements, 134 teaching assistantships with full and partial tuition reimbursements were awarded; Federal Work-Study, institutionally sponsored loans, scholarships/grants, and tuition waivers (full and partial) also available. Financial award application deadline: 3/1; financial award applicants required to submit FAFSA. *Unit head:* Barbara Boyle, Chair, 310-825-8787. *Application contact:* Departmental Office, 310-825-8787, E-mail: info@tft.ucla.edu.

University of California, Santa Barbara, Graduate Division, College of Letters and Sciences, Division of Humanities and Fine Arts, Department of Film and Media Studies, Santa Barbara, CA 93106. Offers PhD, MA/PhD. *Faculty:* 12 full-time (6 women), 9 part-time/adjunct (5 women). *Students:* 16 full-time (9 women); includes 1 minority (Hispanic American), 2 international. Average age 27. 118 applicants, 18% accepted, 7 enrolled.Terminal master's awarded for partial completion of doctoral program. *Degree requirements:* For doctorate, one foreign language, comprehensive exam, thesis/dissertation. *Entrance requirements:* For doctorate, GRE. Additional exam requirements/recommendations for international students: Required—TOEFL (minimum score 600 paper-based; 250 computer-based; 100 iBT). *Application deadline:* For fall admission, 12/1 for domestic and international students. Application fee: $60. Electronic applications accepted. *Expenses:* Tuition, nonresident: full-time $14,888. Required fees: $10,108. *Financial support:* In 2007–08, 14 students received support, including 10 fellowships with full and partial tuition reimbursements available (averaging $13,100 per year), 35 teaching assistantships with full and partial tuition reimbursements available (averaging $27,000 per year); career-related internships or fieldwork, Federal Work-Study, institutionally sponsored loans, scholarships/grants, health care benefits, and unspecified assistantships also available. Financial award application deadline: 12/1; financial award applicants required to submit FAFSA. *Faculty research:* Media history and theory, cultural studies and criticism, film history, history and memory, new media. *Unit head:* Dr. Anna Everett, Chair, 805-893-5549, E-mail: everett@filmandmedia.ucsb.edu. *Application contact:* Edward Branigan, Director of Graduate Studies, 805-893-2320, Fax: 805-893-8630, E-mail: grad@filmandmedia.ucsb.edu.

University of Central Arkansas, Graduate School, College of Fine Arts and Communication, Program in Digital Filmmaking, Conway, AR 72035-0001. Offers MFA. *Accreditation:* NASAD. *Faculty:* 5 full-time (0 women). *Students:* 14 full-time (1 woman), 2 part-time; includes 1 minority (African American) 11 applicants, 82% accepted, 9 enrolled. *Degree requirements:* For master's, thesis. *Entrance requirements:* For master's, GRE General Test, minimum GPA of 2.7. Additional exam requirements/recommendations for international students: Required—TOEFL (minimum score 550 paper-based; 213 computer-based). *Application deadline:* For fall admission, 3/1 priority date for domestic and international students; for spring admission, 10/1 priority date for domestic and international students. Applications are processed on a rolling basis. Application fee: $25 ($50 for international students). *Expenses:* Tuition, state resident: full-time $4,513; part-time $240 per credit. Tuition, nonresident: full-time $8,805; part-time $440 per credit. International tuition: $9,700 full-time. Required fees: $100 per term. *Financial support:* Unspecified assistantships available. *Unit head:* Dr. Joseph Anderson, Chair, 501-450-3162, E-mail: josepha@uca.edu. *Application contact:* Brenda Herring, Admissions Assistant, 501-450-5065, Fax: 501-450-5678, E-mail: bherring@uca.edu.

University of Central Florida, College of Arts and Humanities, Division of Film and Digital Media, Orlando, FL 32816. Offers entrepreneurial digital cinema (MFA); interactive entertainment (MS); visual language and interactive media (MFA). *Faculty:* 28 full-time (11 women), 8 part-time/adjunct (2 women). *Expenses:* Tuition, state resident: full-time $6,484. Tuition, nonresident: full-time $23,938. Tuition and fees vary according to program. *Financial support:* Fellowships, research assistantships, teaching assistantships available. *Unit head:* Dr. David Vickers, Interim Head, 407-823-1736, E-mail: dvickers@mail.ucf.edu.

University of Denver, Faculty of Arts and Humanities/Social Sciences, School of Communication, Department of Mass Communications, Denver, CO 80208. Offers advertising management (MS); digital media studies (MA); mass communications (MA); public relations (MS); video production (MA). Part-time programs available. *Faculty:* 14 full-time (9 women). *Students:* 7 full-time (5 women), 30 part-time (23 women); includes 5 minority (1 African American, 4 Hispanic Americans), 1 international. Average age 26. In 2007, 19 degrees awarded. *Degree requirements:* For master's, thesis (for some programs). *Entrance requirements:* For master's, GRE General Test. Additional exam requirements/recommendations for international students: Required—TOEFL, TWE. *Application deadline:* Applications are processed on a rolling basis. Application fee: $50. Electronic applications accepted. *Financial support:* In 2007–08, 3 research assistantships with full and partial tuition reimbursements (averaging $8,400 per year), 5 teaching assistantships with full and partial tuition reimbursements (averaging $10,000 per year) were awarded; career-related internships or fieldwork, Federal Work-Study, institutionally sponsored loans, and scholarships/grants also available. Support available to part-time students. Financial award application deadline: 3/1; financial award applicants required to submit FAFSA. *Faculty research:* Youth and civic engagement. Total annual research expenditures: $117,000. *Unit head:* Dr. Diane Waldman, Chair, 303-871-2166. *Application contact:* Information Contact, 303-871-2166, E-mail: mcomadm@du.edu.

See Close-Up on page 939.

The University of Iowa, Graduate College, College of Liberal Arts and Sciences, Department of Cinema and Comparative Literature, Program in Film and Video Production, Iowa City, IA 52242-1316. Offers MA, MFA. *Students:* 7 full-time (3 women), 5 part-time (3 women). 22 applicants, 32% accepted, 3 enrolled. In 2007, 3 degrees awarded. *Degree requirements:* For master's, thesis (for some programs), exam. *Entrance requirements:* For master's, GRE General Test, minimum GPA of 3.0. Additional exam requirements/recommendations for international students: Required—TOEFL (minimum score 550 paper-based; 213 computer-based; 81 iBT). *Application deadline:* For fall admission, 1/11 priority date for domestic and international students. Application fee: $60 ($85 for international students). Electronic applications accepted. *Expenses:* Tuition, state resident: part-time $349 per hour. Tuition, nonresident: part-time $349 per hour. Tuition and fees vary according to course load and program. *Financial support:* In 2007–08, 2 fellowships, 1 research assistantship with partial tuition reimbursement, 6 teaching assistantships with partial tuition reimbursements were awarded. Financial award applicants required to submit FAFSA. *Unit head:* Sasha Waters Freyer, Director, 319-353-2922, Fax: 319-335-3446. *Application contact:* Information Contact, 319-335-0330.

University of Memphis, Graduate School, College of Communication and Fine Arts, Department of Communication, Memphis, TN 38152. Offers communication (MA); communication arts (PhD); film and video production (MA). Part-time programs available. *Faculty:* 16 full-time (6 women). *Students:* 29 full-time (14 women), 20 part-time (8 women); includes 9 minority (8 African Americans, 1 Asian American or Pacific Islander). Average age 37. 33 applicants, 55% accepted, 9 enrolled. In 2007, 9 master's, 5 doctorates awarded. *Degree requirements:* For master's, comprehensive exam, thesis or alternative; for doctorate, comprehensive exam, thesis/dissertation. *Entrance requirements:* For master's and doctorate, GRE General Test. Additional exam requirements/recommendations for international students: Required—TOEFL (minimum score 550 paper-based; 210 computer-based). *Application deadline:* For fall admission, 8/1 for domestic students. Application fee: $35 ($60 for international students). *Expenses:* Tuition, state resident: full-time $6,990; part-time $377 per hour. Tuition, nonresident: full-time $17,818; part-time $830 per hour. Tuition and fees vary according to course load and program. *Financial support:* In 2007–08, 8 research assistantships with full tuition reimbursements (averaging $5,700 per year), 16 teaching assistantships with full tuition reimbursements (averaging $7,350 per year) were awarded; unspecified assistantships also available. *Faculty* *research:* Rhetoric, media studies, applied communication (health communication). *Unit head:* Dr. Mike Leff, Chair, 901-678-2565, Fax: 901-678-4331, E-mail: m_leff@bellsouth.net. *Application contact:* Dr. Sandra Sarkela, Coordinator of Graduate Studies, 901-678-3173, Fax: 901-678-4331, E-mail: ssarkela@memphis.edu.

University of Miami, Graduate School, School of Communication, Coral Gables, FL 33124. Offers communication (PhD); communication studies (MA); film studies (MA, PhD); motion pictures (MFA), including production, producing, and screenwriting; print journalism (MA); public relations (MA); Spanish language journalism (MA); television broadcast journalism (MA). *Accreditation:* ACEJMC. Part-time programs available. *Faculty:* 39 full-time (12 women). *Students:* 113 full-time (61 women), 16 part-time (5 women); includes 28 minority (8 African Americans, 1 Asian American or Pacific Islander, 19 Hispanic Americans), 14 international. Average age 27. 374 applicants, 56% accepted, 64 enrolled. In 2007, 48 master's, 2 doctorates awarded. *Degree requirements:* For master's, comprehensive exam (for some programs), thesis (for some programs); for doctorate, comprehensive exam, thesis/dissertation. *Entrance requirements:* For master's, GRE General Test; for doctorate, GRE General Test, master's thesis or scholarly research. Additional exam requirements/recommendations for international students: Required—TOEFL (minimum score 600 paper-based; 250 computer-based; 100 iBT). *Application deadline:* For fall admission, 12/15 priority date for domestic and international students. Applications are processed on a rolling basis. Application fee: $50. Electronic applications accepted. *Financial support:* In 2007–08, 68 students received support, including 10 teaching assistantships with full tuition reimbursements available; fellowships with full tuition reimbursements available, Federal Work-Study, institutionally sponsored loans, scholarships/grants, tuition waivers (partial), and unspecified assistantships also available. Financial award application deadline: 3/1; financial award applicants required to submit FAFSA. *Faculty research:* Communication studies, mass communication, international/interpersonal communication, film studies, journalism. *Unit head:* Dr. Sam L. Grogg, Dean, 305-284-3420, Fax: 305-284-2454, E-mail: sgrogg@miami.edu. *Application contact:* Dr. Leonardo C. Ferreira, Director of Graduate Studies, 305-284-3180, Fax: 305-284-8701, E-mail: lferreira@miami.edu.

See Close-Up on page 943.

University of Nevada, Las Vegas, Graduate College, College of Fine Arts, Department of Film, Las Vegas, NV 89154-9900. Offers screenwriting (MFA). Part-time programs available. *Faculty:* 5 full-time (0 women), 2 part-time/adjunct (0 women). *Students:* 6 full-time (3 women); includes 1 minority (Asian American or Pacific Islander) 8 applicants, 13% accepted, 1 enrolled. *Degree requirements:* For master's, comprehensive exam, creative project. *Entrance requirements:* Additional exam requirements/recommendations for international students: Required—TOEFL (minimum score 550 paper-based; 213 computer-based). *Application deadline:* For fall admission, 1/15 for domestic and international students. Application fee: $60 ($75 for international students). Electronic applications accepted. *Expenses:* Tuition, state resident: part-time $198 per credit. Tuition, nonresident: part-time $416 per credit. Required fees: $256 per semester. Tuition and fees vary according to course load and reciprocity agreements. *Financial support:* In 2007–08, 5 teaching assistantships with partial tuition reimbursements (averaging $10,000 per year) were awarded; career-related internships or fieldwork, Federal Work-Study, institutionally sponsored loans, scholarships/grants, health care benefits, and unspecified assistantships also available. Support available to part-time students. *Unit head:* Francisco Menendez, Chair, 702-895-3547, Fax: 702-895-4395. *Application contact:* Graduate College Admissions Evaluator, 702-895-3320, Fax: 702-895-4180, E-mail: gradcollege@unlv.edu.

University of New Orleans, Graduate School, College of Liberal Arts, Department of Film, Theatre and Communication Arts, New Orleans, LA 70148. Offers film production (MFA); theatre directing (MFA); theatre performance (MFA). *Accreditation:* NAST. *Students:* 110 (60 women). Average age 34. In 2007, 22 degrees awarded. *Degree requirements:* For master's, comprehensive exam, thesis. *Entrance requirements:* Additional exam requirements/recommendations for international students: Required—TOEFL (minimum score 550 paper-based; 213 computer-based; 79 iBT). *Application deadline:* For fall admission, 7/1 priority date for domestic students, 6/1 for international students; for spring admission, 11/15 priority date for domestic students, 10/1 for international students. Applications are processed on a rolling basis. Application fee: $40. Electronic applications accepted. *Financial support:* Teaching assistantships, career-related internships or fieldwork available. Financial award application deadline: 5/15; financial award applicants required to submit FAFSA. *Faculty research:* Mass communication theory, nineteenth- and twentieth-century theater history, film criticism and history. *Unit head:* Dr. Phillip Karnell, Chairperson, 504-280-6317, Fax: 504-280-6318, E-mail: pkarnell@uno.edu. *Application contact:* Dr. John McGowan-Hartmann, Graduate Coordinator, 504-280-6803, Fax: 504-280-6318, E-mail: jmcgowan@uno.edu.

The University of North Carolina at Greensboro, Graduate School, College of Arts and Sciences, Department of Broadcasting and Cinema, Greensboro, NC 27412-5001. Offers film and video production (MFA). *Application contact:* Michelle Harkleroad, Director of Graduate Admissions, 336-334-4884, Fax: 336-334-4424, E-mail: mbharkle@uncg.edu.

University of North Texas, Robert B. Toulouse School of Graduate Studies, College of Arts and Sciences, Department of Radio, Television and Film, Denton, TX 76203. Offers MA, MFA, MS. Part-time programs available. *Faculty:* 15 full-time (6 women). *Students:* 34 full-time (15 women), 14 part-time (8 women); includes 9 minority (2 African Americans, 3 Asian Americans or Pacific Islanders, 4 Hispanic Americans), 3 international. Average age 30. 34 applicants, 56% accepted, 13 enrolled. In 2007, 8 degrees awarded. *Degree requirements:* For master's, thesis, thesis production (MFA). *Entrance requirements:* For master's, GRE General Test, 2 letters of recommendation, writing sample, goal statement (MA/MS), portfolio, 3 letters of recommendation, writing sample, goal statement (MFA). Additional exam requirements/recommendations for international students: Required—proof of English language proficiency required for non-native English speakers; Recommended—TOEFL (minimum score 550 paper-based; 213 computer-based). *Application deadline:* For fall admission, 7/15 for domestic students; for spring admission, 11/15 for domestic students. Application fee: $50 ($75 for international students). *Financial support:* In 2007–08, fellowships (averaging $10,000 per year), teaching assistantships (averaging $7,800 per year) were awarded; research assistantships, career-related internships or fieldwork, Federal Work-Study, and institutionally sponsored loans also available. Financial award application deadline: 4/1. *Faculty research:* Media law and regulation, audio/video/film production, film and broadcasting history. *Unit head:* Dr. Melinda Levin, Chair, 940-565-2537, Fax: 940-369-7383, E-mail: melinda@unt.edu. *Application contact:* Dr. Samuel J. Sauls, Director of Graduate Studies, 940-565-2537, Fax: 940-369-7838, E-mail: sauls@unt.edu.

University of Oklahoma, Graduate College, College of Fine Arts, School of Art and Art History, Norman, OK 73019-0390. Offers art (MA, MFA); art history (MA, MFA); ceramics (MFA); film and video (MFA); painting (MFA); photography (MFA); printmaking (MFA); visual communications (MFA). *Faculty:* 26 full-time (11 women), 1 part-time/adjunct (0 women). *Students:* 21 full-time (13 women), 10 part-time (9 women); includes 6 minority (1 African American, 5 American Indian/Alaska Native), 2 international. 24 applicants, 50% accepted, 7 enrolled. In 2007, 4 degrees awarded. *Degree requirements:* For master's, thesis (MA), exhibit (MFA), departmental qualifying exam. *Entrance requirements:* For master's, GRE General Test (MA), bachelor's degree in art (MFA) or art history (MA), minimum GPA of 3.0 in last 60 undergraduate hours, 3 letters of recommendation, written research paper. Additional exam requirements/recommendations for international students: Required—TOEFL (minimum score 550 paper-based; 213 computer-based). *Application deadline:* For fall admission, 2/1 priority date for domestic students, 2/1 for international students; for spring admission, 10/1 for domestic and international students. Applications are processed on a rolling basis. Application fee: $40 ($90 for international students). Electronic applications accepted. *Expenses:* Tuition, state resident: full-time $3,451; part-time $144 per credit hour. Tuition, nonresident: full-time $12,432; part-time $518 per credit hour. Required fees: $1,925; $70 per credit hour. $122 per semester. *Financial support:* In 2007–08, 20 students received support, including 8 research assistantships with partial tuition reimbursements available (averaging $9,370 per year), 7 teaching assistantships with partial tuition reimbursements available (averaging $9,450 per year); career-related internships or fieldwork, Federal Work-Study, institutionally sponsored loans, scholarships/grants, health care benefits, tuition waivers (full), and unspecified assistantships also available. Financial award application deadline: 4/7; financial award applicants required to submit FAFSA. Total annual research expenditures: $24,250. *Unit head:* Mary Jo Watson, Associate Dean, 405-325-2691, Fax: 405-325-1668, E-mail: mjwatson@ou.edu. *Application contact:* Heidi Mau, Graduate Liaison, 405-325-2691, Fax: 405-325-1668, E-mail: hmau@ou.edu.

University of Southern California, Graduate School, School of Cinematic Arts, Division of Animation and Digital Arts, Program in Film, Video, and Computer Animation, Los Angeles, CA 90089. Offers MFA. *Students:* 60 full-time (25 women); includes 6 minority (1 African American, 3 Asian Americans or Pacific Islanders, 2 Hispanic Americans), 19 international. 59 applicants, 39% accepted. In 2007, 10 degrees awarded. *Entrance requirements:* For master's, GRE General Test. Application fee: $85.

University of Southern California, Graduate School, School of Cinematic Arts, Division of Film and Television Production, Program in Film and Video Production, Los Angeles, CA 90089. Offers MFA. *Students:* 317 full-time (115 women), 29 part-time (9 women); includes 107 minority (25 African Americans, 3 American Indian/Alaska Native, 49 Asian Americans or Pacific Islanders, 30 Hispanic Americans), 40 international. 312 applicants, 25% accepted. In 2007, 83 degrees awarded. Application fee: $85.

University of Southern California, Graduate School, School of Cinematic Arts, Master's Program in Screen and Television Writing, Los Angeles, CA 90089. Offers MFA. *Faculty:* 16 full-time (3 women), 42 part-time/adjunct (16 women). *Students:* 64 full-time (28 women), 4 part-time (3 women); includes 19 minority (5 African Americans, 7 Asian Americans or Pacific Islanders, 7 Hispanic Americans), 2 international. 168 applicants, 23% accepted. In 2007, 27 degrees awarded. *Entrance requirements:* For master's, GRE General Test. Application fee: $85. *Financial support:* Career-related internships or fieldwork, scholarships/grants, and unspecified assistantships available. Financial award application deadline: 2/15; financial award applicants required to submit FAFSA. *Faculty research:* Filmmaking. *Unit head:* Jack Epps, Head, 213-740-3303.

University of Southern California, Graduate School, School of Cinematic Arts, Program in Producing, Los Angeles, CA 90089. Offers MFA. *Faculty:* 1 full-time (0 women), 20 part-time/adjunct (3 women). *Students:* 48 full-time (21 women); includes 11 minority (3 African Americans, 5 Asian Americans or Pacific Islanders, 3 Hispanic Americans), 9 international. 182 applicants, 15% accepted. In 2007, 26 degrees awarded. *Degree requirements:* For master's, thesis, internship. *Entrance requirements:* For master's, GRE General Test. *Application deadline:* For fall admission, 12/10 for domestic students. Application fee: $85. *Financial support:* In 2007–08, 20 students received support, including teaching assistantships with partial tuition reimbursements available (averaging $10,000 per year); career-related internships or fieldwork, Federal Work-Study, institutionally sponsored loans, and scholarships/grants also available. Financial award application deadline: 2/15; financial award applicants required to submit FAFSA. *Faculty research:* Motion pictures and television. *Unit head:* Lawrence Turman, Head, 213-740-2311.

The University of Texas at Austin, Graduate School, College of Communication, Department of Radio-Television-Film, Austin, TX 78712-1111. Offers film/video production (MFA); radio-television-film (MA, PhD). *Degree requirements:* For master's, thesis (for some programs); for doctorate, thesis/dissertation. *Entrance requirements:* For master's and doctorate, GRE General Test. Electronic applications accepted. *Faculty research:* International communication, film studies, media and culture, telecommunication and new media, gender and sexuality.

University of Utah, The Graduate School, College of Fine Arts, Division of Film Studies, Salt Lake City, UT 84112-1107. Offers MFA. *Faculty:* 6 full-time (2 women), 5 part-time/adjunct (2 women). *Students:* 8 full-time (5 women), 1 (woman) part-time; includes 1 minority (Asian American or Pacific Islander), 1 international. Average age 32. 43 applicants, 5% accepted, 2 enrolled. In 2007, 3 degrees awarded. *Degree requirements:* For master's, comprehensive exam, film or video portfolio. *Entrance requirements:* For master's, minimum GPA of 3.0. Additional exam requirements/recommendations for international students: Required—TOEFL (minimum score 500 paper-based; 173 computer-based). *Application deadline:* For fall admission, 12/31 for domestic and international students. Application fee: $45 ($65 for international students). *Financial support:* In 2007–08, 10 students received support, including teaching assistantships with full and partial tuition reimbursements available (averaging $8,500 per year); career-related internships or fieldwork, Federal Work-Study, institutionally sponsored loans, and health care benefits also available. Financial award application deadline: 3/1; financial award applicants required to submit FAFSA. *Faculty research:* Film history, criticism, cultural studies, production of narrative and documentary films . Total annual research expenditures: $29,596. *Unit head:* Prof. Kevin D. Hauson, Chair, 801-581-7428, Fax: 801-585-3192, E-mail: kevin.hauson@utah.edu. *Application contact:* Prof. Chris Lippard, PhD, Director of Graduate Studies, 801-585-9358, Fax: 801-585-3192, E-mail: c.lippard@utah.edu.

University of Victoria, Faculty of Graduate Studies, Faculty of Fine Arts, Department of Visual Arts, Victoria, BC V8W 2Y2, Canada. Offers digital multimedia (MFA); drawing (MFA); painting (MFA); photography (MFA); sculpture (MFA); video (MFA). *Faculty:* 8 full-time (4 women). *Students:* 10 full-time (7 women), 2 international. Average age 27. 72 applicants, 7% accepted. In 2007, 4 degrees awarded. *Degree requirements:* For master's, exhibit, oral exam. *Entrance requirements:* For master's, portfolio, BFA. Additional exam requirements/recommendations for international students: Required—TOEFL (minimum score 575 paper-based; 233 computer-based), IELTS (minimum score 7). *Application deadline:* For fall admission, 2/28 for domestic students, 12/15 priority date for international students. Applications are processed on a rolling basis. Application fee: $75 ($125 for international students). Electronic applications accepted. *Expenses:* Tuition, state resident: full-time $3,110. International tuition: $3,700 full-time. Tuition and fees vary according to program. *Financial support:* In 2007–08, 10 students received support, including 2 fellowships (averaging $13,400 per year), 7 teaching assistantships (averaging $6,000 per year); research assistantships, institutionally sponsored loans and scholarships/grants also available. Financial award application deadline: 2/15. *Unit head:* Allan Stichbury, Acting Chair, 250-721-8011, Fax: 250-721-6595, E-mail: astichbu@finearts.uvic.ca. *Application contact:* Nedra Tremblay, Graduate Secretary, 250-721-8011, Fax: 250-721-6595, E-mail: ntrembla@finearts.uvic.ca.

University of Wisconsin–Milwaukee, Graduate School, Peck School of the Arts, Program in Performing Arts, Milwaukee, WI 53201-0413. Offers dance (MFA); film (MFA); theatre (MFA). Part-time programs available. *Faculty:* 29 full-time (14 women). *Students:* 15 full-time (10 women), 3 part-time (all women); includes 1 minority (Hispanic American), 2 international. 32 applicants, 25% accepted, 6 enrolled. In 2007, 16 degrees awarded. *Degree requirements:* For master's, variable foreign language requirement, thesis or alternative. *Entrance requirements:* For master's, audition, interview. *Application deadline:* For fall admission, 1/1 priority date for domestic students; for spring admission, 9/1 for domestic students. Applications are processed on a rolling basis. Application fee: $45 ($75 for international students). *Expenses:* Tuition, state resident: part-time $530 per credit. Tuition, nonresident: part-time $1,428 per credit. Required fees: $19 per credit. $229 per term. Tuition and fees vary according to course load and program. *Financial support:* In 2007–08, 9 teaching assistantships were awarded; fellowships, research assistantships, career-related internships or fieldwork and unspecified assistantships also available. Support available to part-time students. Financial award application deadline: 4/15. *Unit head:* Simone Ferro, Representative, 414-229-4178, E-mail: sferro@uwm.edu.

York University, Faculty of Graduate Studies, Faculty of Fine Arts, Program in Film, Toronto, ON M3J 1P3, Canada. Offers MA, MFA, PhD. *Degree requirements:* For master's, thesis. *Entrance requirements:* For master's, portfolio. Electronic applications accepted.

Film, Television, and Video Theory and Criticism

Boston University, College of Communication, Department of Film and Television, Boston, MA 02215. Offers film production (MFA); film studies (MFA); screenwriting (MFA); television (MS); television management (MS); MBA/MS. *Faculty:* 13 full-time, 27 part-time/adjunct. *Students:* 115 full-time (63 women), 17 part-time (12 women); includes 13 minority (4 African Americans, 1 American Indian/Alaska Native, 4 Asian Americans or Pacific Islanders, 4 Hispanic Americans), 14 international. Average age 26. In 2007, 10 degrees awarded. *Degree requirements:* For master's, thesis. *Entrance requirements:* For master's, GMAT (MS in television management), GRE General Test, sample of written or creative work. Additional exam requirements/recommendations for international students: Required—TOEFL. *Application deadline:* For fall admission, 2/1 for domestic students. Electronic applications accepted. *Expenses:* Tuition: Full-time $34,930; part-time $1,092 per credit. Tuition and fees vary according to class time, course level and program. *Financial support:* Teaching assistantships with partial tuition reimbursements, career-related internships or fieldwork, Federal Work-Study, institutionally sponsored loans, scholarships/grants, and unspecified assistantships available. Support available to part-time students. Financial award application deadline: 2/1; financial award applicants required to submit FAFSA. *Unit head:* Charles Merzbacher, Chairman, 617-353-3483, Fax: 617-353-1084, E-mail: ftvchair@bu.edu. *Application contact:* William A. Taylor, Assistant Director, Graduate Services and Financial Aid, 617-353-3481, Fax: 617-358-0399, E-mail: comgrad@bu.edu.

See Close-Up on page 885.

California College of the Arts, Graduate Programs, Program in Visual and Critical Studies, San Francisco, CA 94107. Offers MA. *Faculty:* 5 full-time (4 women), 6 part-time/adjunct (3 women). *Students:* 15 full-time (12 women). Average age 30. 31 applicants, 68% accepted, 13 enrolled. In 2007, 7 degrees awarded. *Degree requirements:* For master's, thesis, exhibit. *Entrance requirements:* For master's, appropriate bachelor's degree, portfolio. Additional exam requirements/recommendations for international students: Required—TOEFL (minimum score 600 paper-based; 250 computer-based). *Application deadline:* For fall admission, 1/15 for domestic and international students. Application fee: $50. Electronic applications accepted. *Expenses:* Tuition: Part-time $1,017 per unit. *Financial support:* In 2007–08, 1 fellowship (averaging $7,000 per year), 1 teaching assistantship (averaging $2,000 per year) were awarded; career-related internships or fieldwork, Federal Work-Study, scholarships/grants, and health care benefits also available. Financial award application deadline: 3/2; financial award applicants required to submit FAFSA. *Unit head:* Tirza Latimer, Chair, 415-551-9250, E-mail: tlatimer@cca.edu. *Application contact:* Kathryn Ward, Assistant Director of Graduate Admissions, 415-703-9523 Ext. 9593, Fax: 415-703-9539, E-mail: graduateprograms@cca.edu.

See Close-Up on page 233.

Claremont Graduate University, Graduate Programs, School of Arts and Humanities, Department of English, Claremont, CA 91711-6160. Offers American studies (MA, PhD); critical theory (MA, PhD); early modern studies (MA, PhD); English (M Phil, MA, PhD); literary theory (PhD); literature (MA, PhD); literature and creative writing (MA); literature and film (MA); MBA/MA; MBA/PhD. Part-time programs available. *Faculty:* 2 full-time (1 woman), 2 part-time/adjunct (0 women). *Students:* 81 full-time (49 women), 14 part-time (10 women); includes 18 minority (3 American Indian/Alaska Native, 10 Asian Americans or Pacific Islanders, 5 Hispanic Americans), 3 international. Average age 35. In 2007, 14 master's, 5 doctorates awarded. *Degree requirements:* For master's, one foreign language, comprehensive exam; for doctorate, 2 foreign languages, comprehensive exam, thesis/dissertation. *Entrance requirements:* For master's, GRE General Test; for doctorate, GRE General Test, MA in literature. *Application deadline:* For fall admission, 2/15 priority date for domestic students; for spring admission, 11/15 for domestic students. Applications are processed on a rolling basis. Electronic applications accepted. *Expenses:* Tuition: Full-time $31,640; part-time $1,376 per unit. Required fees: $145 per semester. Tuition and fees vary according to course load, degree level and program. *Financial support:* Fellowships, Federal Work-Study and institutionally sponsored loans available. Support available to part-time students. Financial award application deadline: 2/15; financial award applicants required to submit FAFSA. *Faculty research:* American, comparative, and English Renaissance literature; modernism; feminist literature and theory. *Unit head:* Wendy Martin, Chair, 909-621-8612, Fax: 909-607-1221, E-mail: wendy.martin@cgu.edu.

College of Staten Island of the City University of New York, Graduate Programs, Program in Cinema and Media Studies, Staten Island, NY 10314-6600. Offers MA. Part-time and evening/weekend programs available. *Faculty:* 6 full-time (3 women). *Students:* 1 full-time (0 women), 13 part-time (6 women); includes 1 minority (African American); 4 international. Average age 30. 12 applicants, 83% accepted, 6 enrolled. In 2007, 7 degrees awarded. *Degree requirements:* For master's, comprehensive exam, thesis optional, written thesis, original film or media or production thesis or written examination. *Entrance requirements:* For master's, 10-12 page critical writing sample on film or media topic, minimum GPA of 3.0 in cinema studies or communications, 3 letters of recommendation, personal statement. Additional exam requirements/recommendations for international students: Required—TOEFL (minimum score 550 paper-based; 213 computer-based; 79 iBT). *Application deadline:* For fall admission, 4/15 priority date for domestic and international students. Applications are processed on a rolling basis. Application fee: $125. Electronic applications accepted. *Expenses:* Tuition, state resident: part-time $270 per credit. Tuition, nonresident: part-time $500 per credit. Required fees: $38 per semester. One-time fee: $15 part-time. Tuition and fees vary according to course load. *Financial support:* In 2007–08, 1 student received support, including 7 fellowships (averaging $1,200 per year), 4 teaching assistantships (averaging $1,250 per year). Financial award application deadline: 4/1; financial award applicants required to submit CSS PROFILE or FAFSA. *Faculty research:* The historical, culture, and pedagogical legacy of Dun Mingjins documentary film practice; Australian Chinatowns in comparative perspectives; nickelodeons in Newark, from puppets to pictures; real costs: bringing environmental impact to e-commerce; culture of complaint: media decency book proposal. *Unit head:* Dr. Matthew Solomon, Coordinator, 718-982-2548, E-mail: cinemamasters@mail.csi.cuny.edu. *Application contact:* Sasha Spence, Assistant Director of Graduate Recruitment Admissions, 718-982-2699, Fax: 718-982-2500, E-mail: spence@mail.csi.cuny.edu.

Concordia University, School of Graduate Studies, Faculty of Fine Arts, Mel Hoppenheim School of Cinema, Montréal, QC H3G 1M8, Canada. Offers film studies (MA).

Emory University, Graduate School of Arts and Sciences, Department of Film Studies, Atlanta, GA 30322-1100. Offers MA, PhD/Certificate. *Degree requirements:* For master's, comprehensive exam, thesis or alternative. *Entrance requirements:* For master's, GRE General Test, 3 letters of reference, 2 writing samples. Additional exam requirements/recommendations for international students: Required—TOEFL. Electronic applications accepted. *Faculty research:* International film history, film theory, film style, feminism and film, reception.

Emory University, Graduate School of Arts and Sciences, Department of Spanish and Portuguese, Atlanta, GA 30322-1100. Offers comparative literature (Certificate); film studies (Certificate); Spanish (PhD); women's studies (Certificate). *Degree requirements:* For doctorate, 2 foreign languages, comprehensive exam, thesis/dissertation. *Entrance requirements:* For doctorate, GRE General Test. Additional exam requirements/recommendations for international students: Required—TOEFL. Electronic applications accepted. *Faculty research:* Spanish literature, Spanish-American literature, literary theory, criticism, cultural studies.

Hollins University, Graduate Programs, Program in Screenwriting and Film Studies, Roanoke, VA 24020-1603. Offers MA, MFA. Offered during summer only. Part-time programs available. *Faculty:* 1 full-time (0 women), 5 part-time/adjunct (2 women). *Students:* 34 full-time (18 women), 1 (woman) part-time; includes 6 minority (4 African Americans, 2 Hispanic Americans). Average age 33. 28 applicants, 96% accepted, 14 enrolled. In 2007, 7 degrees awarded. *Degree requirements:* For master's, one foreign language, comprehensive exam, thesis. *Entrance requirements:* For master's, letters of recommendation, portfolio. Additional exam requirements/recommendations for international students: Required—TOEFL (minimum score 550 paper-based; 213 computer-based). *Application deadline:* For fall admission, 2/15 for domestic and international students. Application fee: $40. Electronic applications accepted. *Expenses:* Tuition: Part-time $265 per credit hour. Tuition and fees vary according to course load and program. *Financial support:* In 2007–08, 24 students received support, including 14 fellowships (averaging $857 per year); Federal Work-Study and scholarships/grants also available. Support available to part-time students. Financial award application deadline: 2/15; financial award applicants required to submit FAFSA. *Faculty research:* German film, women in film, censorship, minorities in film. *Unit head:* Dr. Klaus Phillips, Director, 540-362-6308, E-mail: kphillips@hollins.edu. *Application contact:* Cathy S. Koon, Manager of Graduate Services, 540-362-6326, Fax: 540-362-6288, E-mail: ckoon@hollins.edu.

New York University, Tisch School of the Arts and Graduate School of Arts and Science, Department of Cinema Studies, New York, NY 10012-1019. Offers cinema studies (MA, PhD); moving image archiving and preservation (MA). *Faculty:* 15 full-time, 9 part-time/adjunct. *Students:* 102 full-time (53 women), 22 part-time (12 women); includes 15 minority (3 African Americans, 10 Asian Americans or Pacific Islanders, 2 Hispanic Americans), 81 international. Average age 31. 269 applicants, 32% accepted, 44 enrolled. In 2007, 26 master's, 8 doctorates awarded. *Degree requirements:* For master's, comprehensive exam; for doctorate, one foreign language, thesis/dissertation, 3 comprehensive exams. *Entrance requirements:* For master's, GRE, sample of written work; for doctorate, GRE, master's degree, writing sample. Additional exam requirements/recommendations for international students: Required—TOEFL or IELTS. *Application deadline:* For fall admission, 12/15 for domestic and international students. Application fee: $60. Electronic applications accepted. *Expenses:* Contact institution. *Financial support:* In 2007–08, 59 students received support, including 45 fellowships with full and partial tuition reimbursements available, 10 research assistantships, 4 teaching assistantships; Federal Work-Study, institutionally sponsored loans, tuition waivers (full and partial), and unspecified assistantships also available. Support available to part-time students. Financial award application deadline: 2/15; financial award applicants required to submit FAFSA. *Faculty research:* History and aesthetics of American, European, and Third World cinemas; theory of film and the moving image; cultural studies; gay and lesbian media. *Unit head:* Dr. Richard Allen, Chair, 212-998-1600. *Application contact:* Dan Sandford, Director of Graduate Admissions, 212-998-1918, Fax: 212-995-4060, E-mail: tisch.gradadmissions@nyu.edu.

The Ohio State University, Graduate School, College of the Arts, Department of Photography and Cinema, Columbus, OH 43210. Offers MA. *Application deadline:* Applications are processed on a rolling basis. Application fee: $40 ($50 for international students). Electronic applications accepted. *Application contact:* Graduate Admissions, 614-292-6444, Fax: 614-292-3895, E-mail: domestic.grad@osu.edu.

Ohio University, Graduate College, College of Fine Arts, School of Film, Athens, OH 45701-2979. Offers film (MFA); film studies (MA). *Faculty:* 8 full-time (2 women), 2 part-time/adjunct (1 woman). *Students:* 45 full-time (22 women); includes 10 minority (3 African Americans, 4 Asian Americans or Pacific Islanders, 3 Hispanic Americans), 9 international. Average age 25. 125 applicants, 12% accepted, 12 enrolled. In 2007, 7 degrees awarded. *Degree requirements:* For master's, one foreign language, thesis. *Entrance requirements:* Additional exam requirements/recommendations for international students: Required—TOEFL (minimum score 550 paper-based; 239 computer-based). *Application deadline:* For fall admission, 1/30 for domestic and international students. Application fee: $50 ($55 for international students). Electronic applications accepted. *Financial support:* In 2007–08, 34 students received support, including 2 research assistantships with full tuition reimbursements available, 19 teaching assistantships with full tuition reimbursements available; institutionally sponsored loans, scholarships/grants, tuition waivers (full and partial), and unspecified assistantships also available. Financial award application deadline: 1/30. *Faculty research:* Scriptwriting, sound, editing, cinematography, film theory, digital pest production. *Unit head:* Jody Lamb, Director, 740-593-1323, Fax: 740-593-1328, E-mail: lambj@ohio.edu. *Application contact:* Tamra LaGraff, Administrative Assistant, 740-593-1323, Fax: 740-593-1328, E-mail: lagraff@ohio.edu.

San Francisco State University, Division of Graduate Studies, College of Creative Arts, Department of Cinema, San Francisco, CA 94132-1722. Offers cinema (MFA); cinema studies (MA). *Unit head:* Stephen Ujlaki, Chair, 415-338-1724.

Savannah College of Art and Design, Graduate School, Program in Cinema Studies, Savannah, GA 31402-3146. Offers MA. Part-time programs available. *Faculty:* 2 full-time (1 woman). *Students:* 7 full-time (5 women), 3 part-time (2 women). 7 applicants, 71% accepted, 4 enrolled. *Degree requirements:* For master's, thesis. *Entrance requirements:* For master's, interview. Additional exam requirements/recommendations for international students: Required—TOEFL (minimum score 450 paper-based; 133 computer-based). *Application deadline:* For fall admission, 4/1 priority date for domestic and international students. Applications are processed on a rolling basis. Application fee: $50. Electronic applications accepted. *Expenses:* Tuition: Full-time $24,840; part-time $552 per credit. One-time fee: $500 full-time. *Financial support:* Fellowships, career-related internships or fieldwork, Federal Work-Study, and scholarships/grants available. Financial award application deadline: 4/1; financial award applicants required to submit FAFSA. *Unit head:* Dr. Desirè Houngues, Acting Chair, 912-525-5816, Fax: 912-525-5886, E-mail: dhoungue@scad.edu. *Application contact:* Darrell Tutchton, Director of Graduate and International Enrollment, 912-525-5961, Fax: 912-525-5985, E-mail: admission@scad.edu.

Syracuse University, Graduate School, S. I. Newhouse School of Public Communications, Department of Television, Radio, and Film, Program in Documentary Film and History, Syracuse, NY 13244. Offers MA. *Students:* 5 full-time (3 women); includes 1 minority (African American) 14 applicants, 71% accepted. *Entrance requirements:* For master's, GRE General Test. *Application deadline:* For fall admission, 2/1 for domestic students. Application fee: $75. *Expenses:* Tuition: Full-time $18,216; part-time $1,012 per credit. Required fees: $980. Tuition and fees vary according to program. *Unit head:* Richard Breyer, Director, 315-443-4004. *Application contact:* Graduate Records Office, 315-443-4039, Fax: 315-443-1834, E-mail: pcgrad@syr.edu.

Université de Montréal, Faculty of Arts and Sciences, Department of Art History, Montréal, QC H3C 3J7, Canada. Offers art history (MA, PhD); film studies (MA). *Faculty:* 24 full-time (12 women), 3 part-time/adjunct (1 woman). *Students:* 108 full-time (63 women), 2 part-time (1 woman). 98 applicants, 45% accepted, 39 enrolled. In 2007, 24 master's, 2 doctorates awarded. *Degree requirements:* For master's, thesis. *Application deadline:* For fall admission, 2/1 priority date for domestic students; for winter admission, 11/1 priority date for domestic students; for spring admission, 2/1 priority date for domestic students. Application fee: $100. Electronic applications accepted. *Financial support:* Research assistantships, teaching assistantships available. *Faculty research:* Western art from the Middle Ages, classic and modern theory, modern and contemporary art, Canadian art. *Unit head:* Christine Bernier, Director, 514-343-6184, Fax: 514-343-2393, E-mail: christine_bernier@umontreal.ca. *Application contact:* Carmita Joachim Dorce, Information Contact, 514-343-6111 Ext. 3678, E-mail: c.joachim.dorce@umontreal.ca.

Université de Montréal, Faculty of Arts and Sciences, Department of Literatures and Modern Languages, Montréal, QC H3C 3J7, Canada. Offers German literature (PhD); German studies (MA); Hispanic literature (PhD); Hispanic studies (MA); literature and cinema (PhD). *Faculty:* 13 full-time (5 women), 1 (woman) part-time/adjunct. *Students:* 44 full-time (30 women), 5 part-time (4 women). 28 applicants, 79% accepted, 19 enrolled. In 2007, 7 degrees awarded. Terminal master's awarded for partial completion of doctoral program. *Degree requirements:* For master's, 2 foreign languages, thesis; for doctorate, 2 foreign languages, thesis/dissertation, general exam. *Application deadline:* For fall admission, 2/1 priority date for domestic students; for winter admission, 11/1 priority date for domestic students; for spring admission, 2/1 priority date for domestic students. Application fee: $100. Electronic applications accepted. *Financial support:* Teaching assistantships available. *Unit head:* Monique Moser, Director, 514-343-7050, Fax: 514-343-2255, E-mail: monique.moser@umontreal.ca. *Application contact:* Nikola von Merveldt, Responsible for German Studies Program, 514-343-5905, Fax: 514-343-2255, E-mail: n.von.merveldt@umontreal.ca.

Université Laval, Faculty of Letters, Department of Literature, Programs in Literature and the Screen and Stage, Québec, QC G1K 7P4, Canada. Offers MA, PhD. Part-time programs available. Terminal master's awarded for partial completion of doctoral program. *Degree requirements:* For master's, thesis; for doctorate, comprehensive exam, thesis/dissertation. *Entrance requirements:* For master's and doctorate, linguistics exams, knowledge of French, knowledge of a second language. Electronic applications accepted.

The University of British Columbia, Faculty of Arts and Faculty of Graduate Studies, Department of Theatre and Film, Film Program, Vancouver, BC V6T 1Z1, Canada. Offers creative writing and film production (MFA); film production (MFA, Diploma); film studies (MA). *Faculty:* 5 full-time (2 women). *Students:* 12 full-time (8 women). Average age 25. 22 applicants, 14% accepted, 2 enrolled. In 2007, 4 degrees awarded. *Degree requirements:* For master's, thesis (MA), thesis or project (MFA). *Entrance requirements:* For master's, bachelor's degree in film production or equivalent, BA in film studies. Additional exam requirements/recommendations for international students: Required—TOEFL (minimum score 600 paper-based). *Application deadline:* For fall admission, 2/1 for domestic and international students. Application fee: $90 Canadian dollars ($150 Canadian dollars for international students). Electronic applications accepted. *Financial support:* In 2007–08, 4 fellowships (averaging $18,000 per year), 2 research assistantships (averaging $4,000 per year), 9 teaching assistantships (averaging $9,933 per year) were awarded. Financial award application deadline: 1/1. *Faculty research:* Film history, theory, criticism; producing; experimental film. *Unit head:* Prof. Sharon McGowan, Chair, 604-822-9201, Fax: 604-822-0508, E-mail: sharonmcgowan@ubc.ca. *Application contact:* Zanna Downes, Secretary, 604-822-6037, Fax: 604-822-0508, E-mail: film@interchange.ubc.ca.

University of Chicago, Division of the Humanities, Committee on Cinema and Media Studies, Chicago, IL 60637-1513. Offers AM, PhD. *Students:* 39. 136 applicants, 4% accepted, 3 enrolled. *Degree requirements:* For master's, one foreign language, thesis; for doctorate, 2 foreign languages, thesis/dissertation. *Application deadline:* For fall admission, 12/15 for domestic students. *Financial support:* Fellowships available. Financial award application deadline: 12/15; financial award applicants required to submit FAFSA. *Unit head:* Dr. Thomas Gunning, Chair, 773-702-0264.

The University of Iowa, Graduate College, College of Liberal Arts and Sciences, Department of Cinema and Comparative Literature, Program in Film Studies, Iowa City, IA 52242-1316. Offers MA, PhD. *Students:* 18 full-time (7 women), 12 part-time (5 women); includes 2 minority (both Hispanic Americans), 7 international. 137 applicants, 12% accepted, 7 enrolled. In 2007, 5 master's, 2 doctorates awarded. *Degree requirements:* For master's, thesis optional, exam; for doctorate, comprehensive exam, thesis/dissertation. *Entrance requirements:* For master's and doctorate, GRE General Test, minimum GPA of 3.0. Additional exam requirements/recommendations for international students: Required—TOEFL (minimum score 550 paper-based; 213 computer-based; 81 iBT). *Application deadline:* For fall admission, 1/11 priority date for domestic and international students. Application fee: $60 ($85 for international students). Electronic applications accepted. *Expenses:* Tuition, state resident: part-time $349 per hour. Tuition, nonresident: part-time $349 per hour. Tuition and fees vary according to course load and program. *Financial support:* In 2007–08, 1 fellowship, 6 research assistantships with partial tuition reimbursements, 19 teaching assistantships with partial tuition reimbursements were awarded. Financial award applicants required to submit FAFSA. *Unit head:* Rick Altman, Director, 319-353-2262, Fax: 319-335-3446.

University of Kansas, Research and Graduate Studies, College of Liberal Arts and Sciences, Department of Theatre and Film, Lawrence, KS 66045. Offers theatre and film (MA, PhD); theatre-international theatre studies (MA). *Faculty:* 23. *Students:* 35 full-time (13 women), 3 part-time (1 woman); includes 2 minority (both Asian Americans or Pacific Islanders), 11 international. Average age 34. 30 applicants, 80% accepted, 8 enrolled. In 2007, 3 master's, 4 doctorates awarded. *Degree requirements:* For master's, thesis; for doctorate, one foreign language, comprehensive exam, thesis/dissertation. *Entrance requirements:* For master's, GRE General Test, minimum GPA of 3.2; for doctorate, GRE General Test, minimum GPA of 3.5, MA or MFA in Theatre, Film, or Related Field. Additional exam requirements/recommendations for international students: Required—TOEFL. *Application deadline:* For fall admission, 1/1 priority date for domestic students, 1/1 for international students. Application fee: $55 ($60 for international students). Electronic applications accepted. *Expenses:* Tuition, state resident: full-time $5,838. Tuition, nonresident: full-time $13,409. Tuition and fees vary according to program. *Financial support:* Fellowships with tuition reimbursements, teaching assistantships with full and partial tuition reimbursements, Federal Work-Study, scholarships/grants, and unspecified assistantships available. Financial award application deadline: 1/1. *Faculty research:* Film history, theatre history, film theory, cultural studies, performance studies. *Unit head:* John Staniunas, Chair, 785-864-3511, Fax: 785-864-5251. *Application contact:* Henry Bial, Director of Graduate Studies, 785-864-3511, Fax: 785-331-5251, E-mail: tfdgs@ku.edu.

University of Miami, Graduate School, School of Communication, Coral Gables, FL 33124. Offers communication (PhD); communication studies (MA); film studies (MA, PhD); motion pictures (MFA), including production, producing, and screenwriting; print journalism (MA); public relations (MA); Spanish language journalism (MA); television broadcast journalism (MA). *Accreditation:* ACEJMC. Part-time programs available. *Faculty:* 39 full-time (12 women). *Students:* 113 full-time (61 women), 16 part-time (5 women); includes 28 minority (8 African Americans, 1 Asian American or Pacific Islander, 19 Hispanic Americans), 14 international. Average age 27. 374 applicants, 56% accepted, 64 enrolled. In 2007, 48 master's, 2 doctorates awarded. *Degree requirements:* For master's, comprehensive exam (for some programs), thesis (for some programs); for doctorate, comprehensive exam, thesis/dissertation. *Entrance requirements:* For master's, GRE General Test; for doctorate, GRE General Test, master's thesis or scholarly research. Additional exam requirements/recommendations for international students: Required—TOEFL (minimum score 600 paper-based; 250 computer-based; 100 iBT). *Application deadline:* For fall admission, 12/15 priority date for domestic and international students. Applications are processed on a rolling basis. Application fee: $50. Electronic applications accepted. *Financial support:* In 2007–08, 68 students received support, including 10 teaching assistantships with full tuition reimbursements available; fellowships with full tuition reimbursements available, Federal Work-Study, institutionally sponsored loans, scholarships/grants, tuition waivers (partial), and unspecified assistantships also available. Financial award application deadline: 3/1; financial award applicants required to submit FAFSA. *Faculty research:* Communication studies, mass communication, international/interpersonal communication, film studies, journalism. *Unit head:* Dr. Sam L. Grogg, Dean, 305-284-3420, Fax: 305-284-2454, E-mail: sgrogg@miami.edu. *Application contact:* Dr. Leonardo C. Ferreira, Director of Graduate Studies, 305-284-3180, Fax: 305-284-8701, E-mail: lferreira@miami.edu.

See Close-Up on page 943.

University of Michigan, Horace H. Rackham School of Graduate Studies, College of Literature, Science, and the Arts, Department of Screen Arts and Cultures, Ann Arbor, MI 48109. Offers PhD, Certificate. Part-time programs available. *Faculty:* 9 full-time (5 women). *Students:* 20 (13 women); includes 1 African American, 1 Asian American or Pacific Islander, 2 Hispanic Americans. 32 applicants, 19% accepted, 4 enrolled. In 2007, 5 degrees awarded. *Degree requirements:* For doctorate, one foreign language, comprehensive exam, thesis/dissertation; for Certificate, 15 credit hours (3 directed study). *Application deadline:* For fall admission, 12/15 for domestic and international students. Applications are processed on a rolling basis. Application fee: $60 ($75 for international students). Electronic applications accepted. *Financial support:* In 2007–08, 8 students received support, including 2 fellowships with full tuition reimbursements available (averaging $15,000 per year), 3 teaching assistantships with full tuition reimbursements available (averaging $15,000 per year); health care benefits and summer research funds also available. *Faculty research:* Transnational cinema, classical Hollywood cinema, silent cinema, film theory, television. *Unit head:* Richard Abel, Chair, 734-763-1314, Fax: 734-936-1846, E-mail: richardabel@umich.edu. *Application contact:* Carrin Moore, Secretary Intermediate, 734-764-0147, Fax: 734-936-1846, E-mail: ctave@umich.edu.

University of Southern California, Graduate School, School of Cinematic Arts, Programs in Critical Studies, Los Angeles, CA 90089. Offers MA, PhD. *Faculty:* 15 full-time (8 women), 5 part-time/adjunct (1 woman). *Students:* 96 full-time (56 women), 4 part-time; includes 27 minority (8 African Americans, 9 Asian Americans or Pacific Islanders, 10 Hispanic Americans), 16 international. 176 applicants, 22% accepted. In 2007, 16 master's, 9 doctorates awarded. *Degree requirements:* For doctorate, thesis/dissertation. *Entrance requirements:* For master's and doctorate, GRE General Test. *Application deadline:* For fall admission, 12/1 for domestic students. Application fee: $85. *Financial support:* In 2007–08, 68 students received support, including research assistantships (averaging $18,500 per year), teaching assistantships (averaging $18,500 per year); fellowships, Federal Work-Study and scholarships/grants also available. Financial award application deadline: 2/15; financial award applicants required to submit FAFSA. *Faculty research:* Transnational cinema, global media, television studies, American film history. *Unit head:* Dr. Anne Friedberg, Chair, 213-740-2311.

Wilfrid Laurier University, Faculty of Graduate Studies, Faculty of Arts, Department of English and Film Studies, Waterloo, ON N2L 3C5, Canada. Offers MA, PhD. *Faculty:* 25 full-time. *Students:* 29 full-time, 1 part-time. 73 applicants, 42% accepted, 19 enrolled. In 2007, 12 degrees awarded. *Degree requirements:* For master's, thesis optional; for doctorate, thesis/dissertation. *Entrance requirements:* For master's, honours BA or the equivalent in English, minimum B+ in English courses above first year level; for doctorate, MA in English, minimum A- average in graduate work. Additional exam requirements/recommendations for international students: Recommended—TOEFL (minimum score 230 computer-based; 89 iBT). *Application deadline:* For fall admission, 2/1 priority date for domestic students. Application fee: $75. Electronic applications accepted. *Financial support:* Fellowships, research assistantships, teaching assistantships available. *Faculty research:* Gender and genre, Canadian studies, early modern studies, postcolonial studies, nineteenth century studies. *Unit head:* Eleanor Ty, Chairperson, 519-884-0710 Ext. 3581, E-mail: ety@wlu.ca. *Application contact:* Jennifer Poppe, Student Contact, 519-884-0710 Ext. 3536, Fax: 519-884-1020, E-mail: gradstudies@wlu.ca.

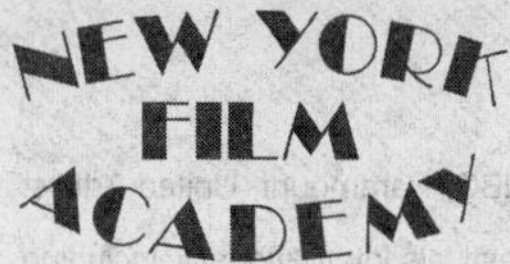

NEW YORK FILM ACADEMY

M.F.A. in Acting For Film, Filmmaking, Producing, and Screenwriting

Program of Study

The New York Film Academy is proud to offer Master of Fine Arts (M.F.A.) in Filmmaking, Acting For Film, Producing, and Screenwriting programs at locations in New York City; Los Angeles (Universal Studios); Abu Dhabi, United Arab Emirates; and its newest campus in Madrid, Spain.

The two-year, conservatory-based M.F.A. in Filmmaking program is designed to educate talented and committed prospective filmmakers in a hands-on, total immersion, professional, and supportive environment. The intensive curriculum challenges, inspires, and prepares candidates for professional work in the motion picture industry. The program offers qualified students a full course of production and study, including the opportunity to direct a feature-length film in the second year of film school. Students in the program are instructed in a multidisciplinary environment. Because filmmaking is a highly integrated art form, students explore and study the major artistic and intellectual influences on leading filmmakers, on themselves, and on the works they create. The program emphasizes visual storytelling and production. It offers students approximately 4,000 hours of instruction and production experience. All students write, shoot, direct, and edit nine of their own film projects. They shoot in 16mm film, 24p and HD video, and 35mm film and edit digitally.

The M.F.A. in Acting for Film is an accelerated, four-semester (16-weeks per semester) conservatory-based, full-time program. The program is intended for students who are passionate, imaginative, and versatile in their craft but who also have a strong desire to further develop these attributes as they apply to the discipline of acting for film. Students are immersed in class work and community, an environment created for professional development and creative freedom. They follow an intense curriculum and achieve multiple learning and production goals. In a combination of hands-on classroom education and intense acting seminars, students acquire a sound understanding and appreciation of performing as visual artists in the motion picture arts and learn to integrate knowledge and professional experience.

The M.F.A. in Producing is a four- or five-semester, conservatory-based, full-time program. The Academy provides a creative setting with which to challenge, inspire, and perfect the talents of dedicated prospective producers in a total immersion, professional environment. Students follow an intensive curriculum and achieve multiple learning and production goals. By combining seminars and lectures with intense hands-on film shoots, students acquire a sound understanding and appreciation of motion picture arts and learn to integrate knowledge and professional experience.

The M.F.A. in Screenwriting is a four-semester, conservatory-based, full-time program. Designed to immerse gifted and energetic prospective screenwriters in all aspects of the discipline, it provides a creative setting with which to challenge, inspire, and perfect its students' talents. Students follow an intensive curriculum and achieve multiple learning goals. The strength of the program is its high concentration of intense writing workshops designed to challenge the individual writer beyond the status quo and into a new realm, further enhanced by a sampling of hands-on production experience not usually associated with advanced writing programs.

Research Facilities

The Academy's film school has two facilities in Manhattan: headquarters overlooking Union Square Park in the historic Tammany Hall building on Park Avenue and its new facility in the heart of SoHo at Prince Street and Broadway. Students shoot films in virtually every neighborhood in the city. The support system—production offices, supply houses, actors, theaters, and labs—is enormous. The Academy offers more than 250 Arriflex 16 mm, Panasonic 24p DV cameras and 200 Final Cut Pro editing stations. Students can check out camera and lighting packages for three to ten days, depending on the project, and editing rooms are open 24 hours a day.

The Universal Studios location sprawls over 390 acres. In-class production exercises are shot on Universal's prestigious and widely used backlot. For weekend films, students shoot in the Los Angeles area, where a wide variety of locations can be found. Students have unparalleled access to the film equipment they need.

The emirate of Abu Dhabi has made a massive commitment to developing the film and television industry in the region as well as promoting international culture and art. Filmmaking students shoot on 16mm, 35mm, HD, and 24p digital video. Acting For Film students work with digital cameras. Students edit on Apple computers using Final Cut Pro. All equipment is comparable to that of leading film programs in the U.S.

The New York Film Academy in Madrid is located in the headquarters of Mundo Ficcion, the film and television production unit of the media giant "El Mundo." Students will benefit from the Academy's collaboration with El Mundo as they learn and shoot in state-of-the-art film and television studios at Torrejon de Ardoz.

Financial Aid

Through the generosity of Brett Ratner, the New York Film Academy is able to offer a limited number (fifty) of $10,000 Brett Ratner Tuition Grants based on financial need. Only applicants to the one- and two-year filmmaking programs are eligible to apply.

Cost of Study

In 2008–09, tuition for these M.F.A. programs is $17,000 per semester.

Living and Housing Costs

In New York City, Academy students can expect to pay $850–$1500 a month for a shared furnished apartment. Furnished studio apartments may cost at least $1800 per month. Private rooms in a residential housing facility are approximately $900–$1500 per month. Less expensive options can be found if one lives farther away and arrives a week or two early to visit places. Food expenses vary. For questions regarding housing in the New York City area, students should call 212-674-4300 or e-mail housingny@nyfa.com.

Students at the Universal Studios location with cars can find a variety of apartments starting at $700, depending on the location and size of the apartment. Oakwood Apartments, across the street from Universal Studios, offers one- and two-bedroom apartments with kitchenettes. Prices range from $1400 to $3200 and up, depending on the number of rooms and amenities. Students should expect to spend at least $700 per month on food expenses. For housing assistance, students should contact the Academy at 818-733-2600 or e-mail LAHousing@nyfa.com.

Students studying in Abu Dhabi may choose to reside in Abu Dhabi or nearby Dubai. The Academy runs daily shuttle buses between these two locations.

Student Group

An extraordinarily eclectic group of students attend the New York Film Academy from all over the world. Students develop an invaluable network of classmates who often provide opportunities for future work in the film industry.

Location

The Academy's New York City film and acting schools are easily accessible to the rest of the city. Union Square Park, which lies over the 14th Street/Union Square subway complex served by the 4, 5, 6, L, N, Q, R, and W trains, was recently listed as one of the top areas to shoot in New York City. Neighborhoods around the park are the Flatiron District to the north, Chelsea to the west, Greenwich Village and NYU to the south, and Gramercy to the east.

Universal Studios is the West Coast headquarters for the Academy's film schools. The Los Angeles area boasts a myriad of cultural and recreational activities—from film openings to fine restaurants to beach volleyball. Proximity to the rest of the city makes it a perfect starting point to explore the city. Many of the country's most beautiful beaches are located within driving distance. Making films on the back lot of a major Hollywood studio can represent the culmination of a lifetime of struggle. The Academy opens the studio's doors to the filmmakers-to-be of the world. Students live and breathe filmmaking within the very heart of the action.

Abu Dhabi is the name of both the capital city of the United Arab Emirates (UAE) and the largest of the seven individual emirates that make up the country. Abu Dhabi brings together old world charm and cosmopolitan sophistication in a clean and safe environment offering a distinctive blend of East and West. Abu Dhabi is proud of its ancient Bedouin culture and heritage and carries on the traditions of desert hospitality, welcoming newcomers with genuine warmth and friendliness. Much of the Abu Dhabi Emirate is made up of the Rub Al Khali (or Empty Quarter) a vast arid desert famous for its spectacular sand dunes. In addition, Al Ain, the garden city on the emirate's border with Oman, the Liwa oasis set amidst towering red dunes, and much more inspire filmmakers.

Madrid is not only Spain's capital, it is also the most cosmopolitan and vibrant city in the country, combining a grand classical heritage with a cutting-edge sense of fashion and design. It is a wonderfully walkable city, linked by charming squares that define the character of its many neighborhoods. Often compared to New York, the energy of Madrid continues to draw the most creative and passionate people to its streets. Whether visiting the museums; learning from the master works of Goya, El Grecco, Dali, and Picasso; or filming in the local streets, markets, or countryside, the Madrid campus promises to provide students an unforgettable experience.

The Academy

The New York Film Academy offers intensive, hands-on programs. Every course and workshop curriculum at this film school stems from its philosophy of learning by doing. Some of Hollywood's greatest filmmakers and stars, including Steven Spielberg, Susan Sarandon, and Kevin Kline, have chosen to send their sons and daughters to the film schools and acting schools of the New York Film Academy. Yet, some of the best projects to come out of the Academy are from students with no connections to the industry.

Applying

An ideal applicant for the New York Film Academy M.F.A. programs must demonstrate a sincere passion for the aspect of filmmaking they wish to pursue and the ability and desire to collaborate with other artists in a creative environment and must submit a creative portfolio that illustrates the applicant's ability to undertake graduate-level study, possession of an accelerated level of talent, and potential for success within the profession.

Candidates for admission to the M.F.A. program must possess a bachelor's degree from a postsecondary institution recognized by the United States Department of Education. Candidates who possess a bachelor's degree from a New York or California state approved school are also considered for admission. No particular major or minor is required as a prerequisite for admission, but applicants with a strong background in storytelling and/or the visual arts are preferred. While GPA is taken into consideration and is an important component of the admissions process, the strength of the candidate's creative portfolio is the primary determining factor for admission. Special attention is given to grades assigned in areas of study related to any aspects of filmmaking, such as the visual arts, design, theater arts, fine arts, performing arts, and the humanities. A grade of B- or better is required in these areas for M.F.A. applicants.

Applicants who have received a bachelor's or equivalent degree from a foreign institution must submit a credentials comparison evaluation of all undergraduate work in order to verify their bachelor's degree equivalency. All transcripts and portfolio materials documenting prior college-level work (including credentials comparison evaluation, if applicable) are evaluated by the Academy faculty members and Admissions Committee. Faculty members and the Admissions Committee are also responsible for reviewing all applications and ensuring, via direct interviews and other pre-enrollment portfolio assessment sessions with prospective students, that the Academy does not admit students who are obviously unqualified or do not have a reasonable prospect of successfully completing the program of instruction.

In addition to the current application booklet, applicants must submit a narrative statement, resume, TOEFL scores or other means of verifying proficiency in English (if first language is not English), supporting materials (see Web site for examples; will not be returned), sealed official academic transcripts from prior institution(s) sent directly from the issuing institution to the New York Film Academy Registrar's Office, two letters of recommendation verifying the applicant's ability to undertake graduate study in the field successfully, and a $50 nonrefundable application fee (check or money order only in U.S. dollars made payable to NYFA).

Correspondence and Information

New York Film Academy
100 East 17th Street
New York, New York 10003

Phone: 212-674-4300
Fax: 212-477-1414
E-mail: mfa@nyfa.com
studios@nyfa.com
film@nyfa.com
Web site: http://www.nyfa.com

New York Film Academy

THE FACULTY

Jerry Sherlock, President and Founder. Executive Producer, *Hunt for Red October;* independent producer: Universal, EMI, Disney, Tristar, NBC, Paramount, United Artists; produced *Lolita* on Broadway with Donald Sutherland.
Michael J. Young, Provost and Director of Education; M.F.A., NYU. Student Academy Award finalist; award-winning film *McJew* screened at festivals internationally, including Oberhausen, Cinema Du Reel, Clermont-Ferrand, Tel-Aviv, and Ann Arbor; NEA grant; Scorsese postproduction award; founding faculty of NYFA.
David Klein, Senior Director; M.F.A., NYU. Awarded Tisch Excellence in Producing Award; winner of Warner Bros. Production Award for *To Dye For;* wrote and directed numerous other projects including the award-winning short film *Gone With the Moon.*
Elli Ventouras, Academic Dean; M.F.A., Parsons; M.A., NYIT. Award-winning film *Voices* screened internationally at Golden Gate Documentary Film Festival in San Francisco, Miami Short Film Festival, Barcelona Short Film Festival, and Festival Du Cinema de Bruxelles; *Voices* was also semifinalist at Boston Motion Picture Awards.
Dan Mackler, Director, NYFA Universal Studios; M.F.A., NYU. Russian film scholar; consulted on Spike Lee's *25th Hour;* director, feature film *The Karaoke King.*
Robert Appleton, Animation. Art Director Bloomberg Europe 3-D; animator, Watchit.com et al.
Matt Arnold, Directing; M.F.A., USC. Writer/director of award-winning short *Resurrection Mary* starring Wilford Brimley.
Melanie Ashley, Scene Study, Monologues; M.F.A., North Carolina.
Geoffray Barbier, Producer. Segment Line Producer, HBO's *Addiction;* director, music videos for Shivaree and Elliot Murphy; producer "Behind the Scenes" for Def Jam, NIKE, V2, and Universal.
Pablo Berger, Directing; M.F.A., NYU. Feature film, *Torremolinos 73%.*
Lea Brandenburg, Acting for Film; B.A., Illinois. Actor in films and theater including *Julie Johnson* with Lili Taylor and *Earthy Possessions* for HBO with Susan Sarandon.
Anna M. Cianciulli, Acting for Film. Editor, Sanford Meisner's *On Acting,* Italian edition; nominated Best Actress, International Festival of Cinema and Technology; Artistic Director of BdA the Arts [enter] Theater; numerous leading roles on New York stage and film.
Seamus Dever, Acting for Film; M.F.A., Moscow Art Theatre and Carnegie-Mellon. Veteran of over fifty plays; lead in the LA premiere of *A Clockwork Orange* and won a Backstage West Garland Award; nominated for LA's Ovation Award and a Los Angeles Drama Critics Circle Award; recent television work includes *Charmed* (WB), *JAG* (CBS), and *Cold Case* (CBS); lifetime member of The Actors Studio.
Seth Michael Donsky, Writing, Directing; M.F.A., Columbia. Award-winning feature film, *Twisted* (1997); recipient of the 2002 Hallmark Development Grant for the short film *Loopy.*
Liz Foley, Producing; M.F.A., Columbia. Director, writer, and producer of numerous film and television productions including *Funny Peculiar, Ode to Joy,* and *The It Factor.*
Lonnie Dean Halouska, Producing. An entertainment, media, and telecommunications transactional lawyer and business consultant; producer of numerous television commercials; has worked for CBS, ABC, Warner Bros., and Republic Pictures and Telecommunications, Inc.
Matthew Harrison, Acting for Film, Directing; B.F.A., Cooper Union; Certificate of Cinema, NYU. Writer and director for feature films, *Kicked in the Head,* whose Executive Producer was Martin Scorsese, and *Rhythm Thief;* Jury Prize winner at Sundance Film Festival; directed episodes for *Sex and the City.*
Ben Hopkin, Coordinator of Acting Program at Universal; M.F.A., Globe Theater of San Diego.
Mike Jacobs Jr., Producing. Executive producer, *The Thirteenth Year;* co-producer, *Their Second Chance,* starring Lindsay Wagner, for ABC Pictures; feature credits include *Driven.*
Claude Kerven, Director; M.F.A., NYU. Directed more than twenty-five shorts for *Saturday Night Live;* director for *Afterschool Specials, Birthday Boy, Candy Store,* and the *David Brenner Show;* cowrote *Mortal Thoughts,* starring Bruce Willis, Demi Moore, and Harvey Keitel.
Matthew Kohnen, Cinematography; M.F.A., USC. Award-winning cinematographer of feature films, documentaries, and television.
Zenon Kruszelnicki, Acting/Directing; M.F.A. (acting), National Academy of Drama (Poland); M.F.A. (directing), New School. Member of SSDC, The Actors Studio, FIA, ZASP, and SAG; in 2004, professionally coached Willem Dafoe; received an artistic grant from the Liberace Foundation for the Performing and Creative Arts in 1998–2000.
Michael Laibson, Acting for Film; B.A., UCLA. Executive producer of soaps including *Guiding Light, Another World,* and *As the World Turns.*
Larry Leahy, Directing; M.F.A., NYU. Wrote and directed the feature film, *Confessions of a Hitman;* has worked with directors such as Sam Mendes, Robert Zemeckis, and James L. Brooks.
Rusty Lemorande, Producing. Executive producer, *Caddyshack;* producer, the Academy-Award-winning musical, *Yentl;* writer and producer for various projects at Universal, Paramount, Warner Bros, Turner, and MGM for stars including Madonna, Michael Jackson, and Barbra Streisand and Francis Coppola and George Lucas.
Heng-Tatt Lim, Directing, Cinematography; M.F.A., NYU. Awarded Excellence in Filmmaking at NYU's First Run Festival, 1991; Wien Scholar, Brandeis University; worked on over fifty films.
Dana Lustig, Producing; Graduate, AFI. Directed and produced sixteen feature films, including *Confessions of a Sociopathic Social Climber,* Oxygen Network, which stars Jennifer Love Hewitt; co-produced *Brick* and *Dancing at the Blue Iguana.*
Ben Maraniss, Screenwriting; M.F.A., USC.
Carol Mayes, Directing; M.F.A.; AFI. Writer/director of award-winning films, including *Commitments, Rituals,* and *Tendrils;* Student Oscar Finalist; CINE Golden Eagle Winner; Black Filmmakers Hall of Fame Award for Best Short Film.
Alan Metter, Directing; B.A., Arizona. Student Academy Award finalist; directed *Girls Just Want to Have Fun, Back To School,* and *Police Academy 5: Mission To Moscow;* wrote, produced, and directed music videos for George Harrison, Donna Summer, and Chicago.
Benjamin Morgan, Ninth Year Director, High School Program at Universal Studios; M.F.A. Thesis film has appeared in festivals worldwide and on cable television.
Tim Naylor, Camera, Lighting. Cinematographer of music videos, including Busta Rhymes; Last Call from Westchester—Spike Lee Award; Transeltown, San Francisco's Gay and Lesbian Festival; Marvin Feldheim Award, Cine Eagle Prize, Merit Award, Chicago Film Festival.
Sol Negrin, Advanced Camera and Lighting; ASC. Instructor, NYU; President, New York Cinematography Union; credits include *Robocop, Superman, Coming to America,* and the *Kojak* TV series.
Adam Nimoy, Directing. Director, *NYPD Blue, The Practice,* and *Gilmore Girls;* cowrote, directed, and performed in *Art of the Brain.*
Bryan Norton, Directing; M.F.A., NYU.
Melanie Williams Oram, Directing, Writing; M.F.A., Columbia. Peabody Award, HBO 90-minute documentary, *Dare To Compete;* Emmy Award, HBO series *Real Sports.*
Rebecca Peters, Directing and Camera; B.A., Westminster. Camera credits on feature films such as *Goldeneye, The Saint, Entrapment,* and *Eyes Wide Shut.*
Robert Pietri, Directing, Editing; B.F.A., NYU. Carnegie-Mellon Fox Searchlab New Directors program.
James Price, Meisner Technique. Former protégé of Sanford Meisner; Founding Artistic Director of The Acting Studio, Inc., and Chelsea Repertory Company; graduate and teacher at The Neighborhood Playhouse under the tutelage of Sandord Meisner.
Nicole Ricciardi, Acting for Film; M.F.A. (acting), Carnegie Mellon. Directed at Royal Academy of Dramatic Arts and Syracuse and Drew Universities; winner Barnes Scholarship for Excellence in the Performing Arts; Member Circle East Theater Company, Actor's Equity.
John Henry Richardson, Acting for Film; B.A., Los Angeles. Has starred in dozens of television shows and feature films.
Tassos Rigopoulos, Directing; M.F.A., Texas at Austin. Writer/director/editor of features, shorts, documentaries, TV series, commercials, and corporate videos; Student Emmy Award Winner.
Crickett Rumley, Writing; M.F.A., Columbia. Studied under screenwriting legend William Goldman.
Michael Sandoval, Director of NYFA for the Dalton Program; M.F.A., NYU and Michigan; Ang Lee Fellowship, NYU. Writer and director of short film, *The Good Son,* screened in competition at Berlin.
Shira-Lee Shalit, Acting for Film, Directing Actors; M.F.A. (film), Columbia. Student Academy Award finalist for short film, *Full Cycle;* winner, Presidential Scholar of the Arts for Acting; winner, Acting Award, National Foundation of the Arts.
Richard Shore, Director's Vision, Cinematography; M.A. (cinema), USC; ASC. Winner of three Emmies; credits include *Bang the Drum Slowly, In the American Grain Night of the Dark Shadows, The Responsive Eye,* and *Three Women Alone;* director of photography on hundreds of commercials, documentaries, and educational and scientific films.
Nick Sivakumaran, Directing; M.F.A., USC. Director, *Diwali;* Director's Guild of America Student Film Award; Kodak's Emerging Filmmaker Showcase at the 2002 Cannes International Film Festival.
Nora Stone, Scene Study, Directing Actors; B.A., California, Santa Barbara. Acted for numerous film, television, and theater projects, including several recurring roles on *Days of Our Lives.*
Ron Stacker Thompson, Screenwriting. Producer, *A Rage In Harlem, Deep Cover, The Cemetery Club, Sister Act 2,* and *Hoodlum;* has worked with Whoopi Goldberg, Maggie Smith, Laurence Fishburne, Ellen Burstyn, Danny Glover, Christina Ricci, Jeff Goldblum, and Andy Garcia.
John Terry, Producing; M.F.A., American Film Institute. Produced Panavision New Filmmaker Grant independent feature *Five Spices.*
Sam Turich, Acting for Film; B.A., Columbia. Wrote and stared in *The Box;* TV appearances include *Law and Order* and *Blind Spot* on NBC.
Anita Tovich, Producing; B.F.A., Carnegie Mellon. Producer, Emmy Award–Winning *Nick News;* segment director for *Dr. Phil* show.
Michael Urban, Screenwriting; M.F.A., American Film Institute. Wrote the screenplay for *Saved!* starring Mandy Moore and Macaulay Culkin.
Michael Unger, Directing, Chair Filmmaking Program; M.F.A., Columbia. Short films screened internationally; feature film, Gravity.
Paul Warner, Directing; M.F.A., American Film Institute. Princess Grace Award; Ashley Amulis Fellowship for directing; feature film, *Fall Time,* winner of the Cine Golden Eagle.
Paul Wheeler, Cinematography; BSC. Member of the BBC film department; author of three books on film, digital, and HD cinematography.

All workshops are solely owned and operated by the New York Film Academy, and such workshops are not affiliated with Harvard University, Universal Studios, or Disney-MGM Studios.

NEW YORK UNIVERSITY

Tisch School of the Arts Asia

Programs of Study

At New York University Tisch School of the Arts Asia, students have the opportunity to earn a Master of Fine Arts (M.F.A) degree in one of three areas: animation and digital arts, dramatic writing, or film production.

The Master of Fine Arts program in animation and digital arts is a two-year program that teaches the traditional forms of the art of animation and explores a sandbox of advanced techniques and digital technologies. From capturing the motion of a dancer to animating facial expressions following a human voice, students explore ways to re-create motion and to create relationships through storytelling. Students also learn to master digital animation and video techniques for observation, capture, analysis, and visualization of motion from real life. Students complete a short animated film project each semester.

The Master of Fine Arts program in dramatic writing is a two-year sequence of full-time study with concentrations in playwriting, screenwriting, or television writing. At the beginning of the program, students enroll in the Division of Playwriting and also in the Division of Film and Television Writing. As their studies advance, students select one medium for concentration.

The Master of Fine Arts program in film and television is a concentrated three-year course of study integrating theory and practice in an effort to develop individual creative filmmaking potential. It provides detailed instruction and practical experience in the various aspects of film production, including writing, directing, acting, cinematography, editing, sound recording, and applied aesthetics.

Research Facilities

The media library consists of audition/rehearsal rooms, screening rooms, and an extensive collection of screenplays.

The Production Center consists of five areas, which include the Advanced and Fundamental Equipment Areas, Repair Shop, Equipment Reservations Office, and the Production Office, which provides the students with the supplies and resources needed to produce a film or video.

Film, video, and sound editing; audio mixing; film-to-tape transfers; and interformat duplication are provided in the Post Production Area. Students receiving training are given access to Steenbeck flatbed editing, Betacam SP cuts-only, a state-of-the-art sound-mixing studio, Pro Tools, Final Cut Pro and Avid Media Composer, Xpress, Xpress-DV, and Symphony.

The Teaching Soundstage provides students with a place to be trained in lighting and shooting scenes for film and video in a professional setting. It is equipped with cameras and film stock, grip and lighting equipment, props, and a house set.

Financial Aid

For U.S. students, financial aid can be obtained from a variety of sources, including federal, state, New York University, and private sources of funding. Although some financial aid is based on merit, most is based on a combination of merit and financial need. For U.S. citizens, the Free Application for Federal Student Aid (FAFSA) is the form required to determine financial need. Additional Information about financial aid and eligibility can be found on the NYU financial aid Web site at http://www.nyu.edu/financial.aid/.

For international students, the government of Singapore offers a number of financial aid options, including tuition-free grants, bursaries, study loans, and other financial aid. To learn more, students should visit the Singapore education financial aid Web site at http://www.singaporeedu.gov.sg/htm/stu/stu0304.htm.

Cost of Study

Tuition rates for the Asia and New York campus are the same. Fees for registration, services, and laboratory and equipment insurance are different. Estimated 2007–08 tuition in U.S currency was $38,260, which included nonrefundable registration and services fees and laboratory equipment insurance fees. Estimated 2007–08 tuition in Singapore currency was $56,360,260, which included nonrefundable registration and services fees and laboratory equipment insurance fees.

Living and Housing Costs

Students at NYU Tisch School of the Arts Asia are responsible for securing their own housing in Singapore. Options are available for both short-term and long-term accommodations, and students accepted into the program are given detailed information about housing agencies and roommate-matching forums.

Student Group

Students at New York University Tisch School of the Arts Asia come from a wide variety of undergraduate and professional backgrounds, including designers, journalists, musicians, teachers, and software engineers. They are diligent artists who are passionate about storytelling. They are courageous adventurers, seeking exciting locales for their projects, cultivating new styles influenced by the world around them, and using the latest technologies in order to take their audiences on dazzling new artistic journeys

Student Outcomes

Tisch alumni are award-winning artists, many of whom have received Oscars, Tony Awards, and Pulitzer Prizes. Their work is also showcased at major festivals around the world, including the Sundance Film Festival, receiving top honors. Famous Tisch alumni include Christopher Columbus, *Harry Potter;* Amy Heckerling, *Clueless;* Karyn Kusama, *Aeon Flux;* Ang Lee, *Brokeback Mountain;* Spike Lee, *Inside Man;* Brett Ratner, *Rush Hour;* Martin Scorsese, *The Departed;* Susan Seidelman, *Desperately Seeking Susan;* and Oliver Stone, *World Trade Center.*

Location

The location, diversity, and entrepreneurial spirit of Singapore are enticing. Students find it easy to immerse themselves in Singapore's vibrant arts districts, ethnic neighborhoods, and annual festivities, including the Singapore Arts Festival and the Singapore International Film Festival.

A significant portion of the island has been set aside for recreation and nature conservation. Singapore is a small tropical island geographically situated in such a way that locations in China, India, Indonesia, Japan, Malaysia, the Philippines, South Korea, Thailand, and Vietnam become an extension of the campus.

The University and The School

New York University is a private, metropolitan university. Founded in 1831, the University now comprises fourteen schools, colleges, and divisions at four centers in Manhattan, seven international campuses, and a 500-acre site at Sterling Forest near Tuxedo, New York, where certain of the University's facilities—notably the Institute of Environmental Medicine—are located. In September 2007, New York University Tisch School of the Arts opened its first-ever branch campus in Singapore. New York University Tisch School of the Arts Asia is the first American art school to set up residence in Singapore.

Applying

NYU Tisch School of the Arts Asia offers advanced course work to qualified men and women who have an accredited baccalaureate degree. An artistic review is required for most programs. Each department has its own specifications for review. A portfolio of work is required for all programs. Prospective students may apply for admission to a maximum of two programs in any given year. Applicants to two programs must submit separate applications for both programs. The application deadline for fall 2008 is January 8, 2008.

Correspondence and Information

Virginia Gonzalez
Associate Director of Admissions
Tisch School of the Arts Asia
New York University
721 Broadway, 12th Floor
New York, New York 10003

Phone: 212-998-1575
E-mail: virginia.gonzalez@nyu.edu
Web site: http://www.tischasia.nyu.edu.sg

New York University

THE ADMINISTRATION

John Tintori, Chairman, Graduate Division of Film and Television, Kanbar Institute of Film and Television, Tisch School of the Arts, and Chairman, Graduate Department of Film and Television, NYU Tisch School of the Arts Asia.

Richard Wesley, Chairman, Goldberg Department of Dramatic Writing, Tisch School of the Arts, and Chairman, Graduate Department of Dramatic Writing, NYU Tisch School of the Arts Asia.

Jean-Marc Gauthier, Director, Department of Animation and Digital Arts, NYU Tisch School of the Arts Asia.

Section 6
Performing Arts

This section contains a directory of institutions offering graduate work in performing arts, followed by in-depth entries submitted by institutions that chose to prepare detailed program descriptions. Additional information about programs listed in the directory but not augmented by an in-depth entry may be obtained by writing directly to the dean of a graduate school or chair of a department at the address given in the directory.

For programs offering related work, see also in this book *Area and Cultural Studies, Art and Art History, Communication and Media,* and *Film, Television, and Video.* In another guide in this series:

Graduate Programs in Business, Education, Health, Information Studies, Law & Social Work

See *Leisure Studies and Recreation, Subject Areas (Music Education),* and *Physical Education and Kinesiology*

CONTENTS

Program Directories

Announcements

Close-Ups

See also:

Dance

American University, College of Arts and Sciences, Department of Performing Arts, Program in Dance, Washington, DC 20016-8001. Offers Certificate. Part-time and evening/weekend programs available. *Degree requirements:* For Certificate, minimum 15 credit hours related course work. *Entrance requirements:* For degree, Bachelor's Degree. *Application deadline:* For fall admission, 4/15 priority date for domestic students; for spring admission, 10/1 priority date for domestic students. Application fee: $50. *Expenses:* Tuition: Full-time $19,998; part-time $1,111 per credit hour. Required fees: $380. Tuition and fees vary according to program. *Financial support:* Teaching assistantships, career-related internships or fieldwork, Federal Work-Study, and institutionally sponsored loans available. Support available to part-time students. Financial award application deadline: 2/1. *Faculty research:* Pageantry, festivals, popular culture.

Arizona State University, Graduate College, College of Fine Arts, Department of Dance, Tempe, AZ 85287. Offers MFA. *Degree requirements:* For master's, thesis optional.

Bennington College, Graduate Programs, Program in Dance, Bennington, VT 05201. Offers MFA. Part-time programs available. *Faculty:* 3 full-time (2 women), 2 part-time/adjunct (both women). *Students:* 1 (woman) full-time. Average age 43. 8 applicants, 25% accepted, 1 enrolled. In 2007, 1 degree awarded. *Degree requirements:* For master's, performances. *Application deadline:* For fall admission, 2/1 for domestic students. Application fee: $60. *Expenses:* Tuition: Full-time $20,640; part-time $2,890 per course. One-time fee: $75 full-time. Tuition and fees vary according to program. *Financial support:* In 2007–08, 1 student received support, including 1 teaching assistantship; unspecified assistantships also available. Financial award application deadline: 4/1; financial award applicants required to submit FAFSA. *Faculty research:* Exploration of relationship between emergent improvisational complex systems. *Unit head:* Terry Creach, Associate Dean for Academic Affairs, 802-440-4406, Fax: 802-440-4876, E-mail: tcreach@bennington.edu. *Application contact:* Ken Himmelman, Dean of Admissions and Financial Aid, 802-440-4312, Fax: 802-440-4320, E-mail: admissions@bennington.edu.

California Institute of the Arts, School of Dance, Valencia, CA 91355-2340. Offers MFA, Adv C. *Accreditation:* NASD. *Degree requirements:* For master's, thesis presentation. *Entrance requirements:* For master's, audition, video of choreography. Additional exam requirements/recommendations for international students: Required—TOEFL.

California State University, Fullerton, Graduate Studies, College of the Arts, Department of Theatre and Dance, Fullerton, CA 92834-9480. Offers acting (MFA); acting and directing (MA); dance (MA); directing (MFA); dramatic literature/criticism (MA); oral interpretation (MA); playwriting (MA); technical theater (MA); technical theater and design (MFA); television (MA); theatre for children (MA); theatre history (MA). *Accreditation:* NASD; NAST (one or more programs are accredited). Part-time programs available. *Students:* 14 full-time (9 women), 2 part-time; includes 3 minority (1 African American, 1 Asian American or Pacific Islander, 1 Hispanic American), 1 international. Average age 27. 3 applicants, 0% accepted. In 2007, 8 degrees awarded. *Degree requirements:* For master's, oral and written exam, project or thesis. *Entrance requirements:* For master's, major in theatre or related field, audition or interview, minimum GPA of 2.5 in last 60 units of course work. Application fee: $55. *Financial support:* Teaching assistantships, career-related internships or fieldwork, Federal Work-Study, institutionally sponsored loans, and scholarships/grants available. Support available to part-time students. Financial award application deadline: 3/1. *Unit head:* Dr. Susan Hallman, Chair, 714-278-3628. *Application contact:* Gretchen Kanne, Adviser, 714-278-3628.

California State University, Long Beach, Graduate Studies, College of the Arts, Department of Dance, Long Beach, CA 90840. Offers dance (performance) (MFA). *Accreditation:* NASD. Part-time programs available. *Faculty:* 7 full-time (4 women), 27 part-time/adjunct (19 women). *Students:* 6 full-time (4 women). Average age 36. *Degree requirements:* For master's, thesis. *Application deadline:* For fall admission, 7/1 for domestic students; for spring admission, 12/1 for domestic students. Applications are processed on a rolling basis. Application fee: $5. Electronic applications accepted. *Financial support:* Federal Work-Study, institutionally sponsored loans, scholarships/grants, and traineeships available. Financial award application deadline:3/2. *Unit head:* Dr. Judy Allen, Chair, 562-985-4747, Fax: 562-985-7896, E-mail: judyalle@csulb.edu. *Application contact:* Doug Nielsen, Graduate Advisor, 562-985-7039, Fax: 562-985-7896.

California State University, Sacramento, Graduate Studies, College of Arts and Letters, Department of Theatre and Dance, Sacramento, CA 95819-6048. Offers MA. *Accreditation:* NAST. Part-time programs available. *Students:* 7 full-time (6 women), 7 part-time (5 women); includes 2 minority (both African Americans) Average age 33. 20 applicants, 50% accepted, 5 enrolled. *Degree requirements:* For master's, thesis or alternative, writing proficiency exam. *Entrance requirements:* For master's, GRE General Test, BA in drama or equivalent, minimum GPA of 2.5 during previous 2 years of course work. Additional exam requirements/recommendations for international students: Required—TOEFL. *Application deadline:* Applications are processed on a rolling basis. Application fee: $55. Electronic applications accepted. *Expenses:* Tuition, state resident: full-time $3,414. Tuition, nonresident: full-time $13,584; part-time $339 per unit. Required fees: $786; $393 per semester. *Financial support:* Research assistantships, teaching assistantships, career-related internships or fieldwork and Federal Work-Study available. Support available to part-time students. Financial award application deadline: 3/1. *Unit head:* Dr. Linda Goodrich, Chair, 916-278-6368 Ext. 4784, Fax: 916-278-5681.

Case Western Reserve University, School of Graduate Studies, Department of Theater and Dance, Cleveland, OH 44106. Offers acting (MFA); contemporary dance (MFA); dance (MA); theater (MFA). *Faculty:* 8 full-time (3 women), 3 part-time/adjunct (0 women). *Students:* 20 full-time (10 women), 4 part-time (2 women); includes 1 minority (African American), 4 international. Average age 26. 17 applicants, 76% accepted, 10 enrolled. In 2007, 3 master's awarded. *Degree requirements:* For master's, thesis, oral presentation and defense, portfolio. *Entrance requirements:* For master's, audition, interview. Additional exam requirements/recommendations for international students: Required—TOEFL. *Application deadline:* For fall admission, 8/25 for domestic students. Applications are processed on a rolling basis. Application fee: $50. Electronic applications accepted. *Financial support:* Fellowships, career-related internships or fieldwork and tuition waivers (full and partial) available. Financial award application deadline: 3/1. *Faculty research:* Playwriting; history of theater; participation in professional area theaters in performing, design, acting, coaching. *Unit head:* Ron Wilson, Chairman, 216-368-6142, Fax: 216-368-5184, E-mail: ron.wilson@case.edu. *Application contact:* Scarlett Grala, Department Assistant II, 216-368-4868, Fax: 216-368-5184, E-mail: ksg@po.cwru.edu.

The College at Brockport, State University of New York, School of Arts and Performance, Department of Dance, Brockport, NY 14420-2997. Offers MA, MFA. *Accreditation:* NASD.Part-time programs available. *Students:* 18 full-time (16 women), 4 part-time (all women); includes 3 minority (all African Americans), 1 international. 29 applicants, 45% accepted, 9 enrolled. In 2007, 9 degrees awarded. *Degree requirements:* For master's, thesis or alternative. *Entrance requirements:* For master's, local writing assessment assignment, audition/interview, minimum GPA of 3.0, letters of recommendation. Additional exam requirements/recommendations for international students: Required—TOEFL (minimum score 550 paper-based; 213 computer-based; 79 iBT). *Application deadline:* For fall admission, 2/1 for domestic and international students. Application fee: $50. *Expenses:* Tuition, state resident: full-time $6,900; part-time $288 per credit. Tuition, nonresident: full-time $10,920; part-time $455 per credit. Required fees: $738; $31 per credit. *Financial support:* In 2007–08, 1 fellowship with tuition reimbursement (averaging $7,500 per year), 3 teaching assistantships with tuition reimbursements (averaging $6,000 per year) were awarded; Federal Work-Study, scholarships/grants, and unspecified assistantships also available. Support available to part-time students. Financial award application deadline: 3/15; financial award applicants required to submit FAFSA. *Faculty research:* Choreography and performance, world dance and culture, dance process and theory, dance education, dance science and somatics. *Unit head:* Dr. Darwin Prioleau, Chairperson, 585-395-2153, E-mail: dpriolea@brockport.edu.

Florida State University, Graduate Studies, College of Visual Arts, Theatre and Dance, Department of Dance, Tallahassee, FL 32306. Offers American dance studies (MA); dance (MFA); studio and related studies (MA). *Accreditation:* NASD. *Faculty:* 18 full-time (10 women), 8 part-time/adjunct (7 women). *Students:* 38 full-time (35 women); includes 10 minority (7 African Americans, 2 Asian Americans or Pacific Islanders, 1 Hispanic American). Average age 28. 30 applicants, 67% accepted, 17 enrolled. In 2007, 10 degrees awarded. *Degree requirements:* For master's, comprehensive exam (for some programs), thesis (for some programs), technical proficiency (MFA), 1 foreign language (MA). *Entrance requirements:* For master's, GRE General Test (MA in American Dance Studies), audition, writing sample (MFA) Dance and MA Studio and related studies. Additional exam requirements/recommendations for international students: Required—TOEFL (minimum score 550 paper-based; 213 computer-based). *Application deadline:* For fall admission, 7/1 priority date for domestic students, 3/1 priority date for international students; for spring admission, 11/1 priority date for domestic students, 7/1 priority date for international students. Applications are processed on a rolling basis. Application fee: $30. Electronic applications accepted. *Expenses:* Tuition, state resident: part-time $248 per credit hour. Tuition, nonresident: part-time $880 per credit hour. Tuition and fees vary according to program. *Financial support:* In 2007–08, 38 students received support, including research assistantships with full tuition reimbursements available (averaging $5,000 per year), teaching assistantships with full tuition reimbursements available (averaging $5,000 per year); fellowships with full tuition reimbursements available, scholarships/grants, health care benefits, and unspecified assistantships also available. Financial award application deadline: 6/30; financial award applicants required to submit FAFSA. *Faculty research:* Choreography, performance, dance and cultural significance, American dance history, dance technology. Total annual research expenditures: $131,959. *Unit head:* Russell Sandifer, Assistant Professor and Co-Chair, 850-644-1024, Fax: 850-644-1277, E-mail: sandifer@dance.fsu.edu. *Application contact:* Prof. Patricia Phillips, Co-Chair, 850-644-1023, Fax: 850-644-1277, E-mail: pphillip@mailer.fsu.edu.

George Mason University, College of Visual and Performing Arts, Program in Dance, Fairfax, VA 22030. Offers MFA. *Faculty:* 8 full-time (6 women), 8 part-time/adjunct (7 women). *Students:* 4 full-time (all women); includes 2 minority (1 African American, 1 Asian American or Pacific Islander). Average age 36. 5 applicants, 40% accepted, 2 enrolled. *Degree requirements:* For master's, choreographed performance. *Entrance requirements:* For master's, video of choreography or performance. *Application deadline:* For fall admission, 5/1 for domestic students; for spring admission, 11/1 for domestic students. Application fee: $60 ($75 for international students). Electronic applications accepted. *Financial support:* Fellowships, career-related internships or fieldwork and institutionally sponsored loans available. Support available to part-time students. Financial award application deadline: 3/1; financial award applicants required to submit FAFSA. *Faculty research:* Choreography, performance. *Unit head:* Elizabeth Price, Chair, 703-993-2137. *Application contact:* Karen Studd, Associate Professor, 703-993-1114, Fax: 703-993-2191, E-mail: dance@gmu.edu.

Hollins University, Graduate Programs, Program in Dance, Roanoke, VA 24020-1603. Offers MFA. *Faculty:* 2 full-time (1 woman), 3 part-time/adjunct (2 women). *Students:* 15 full-time (13 women), 5 part-time (2 women); includes 1 minority (African American) Average age 34. 66 applicants, 32% accepted, 17 enrolled. In 2007, 16 degrees awarded. *Degree requirements:* For master's, thesis. *Entrance requirements:* For master's, videotape of selected works, 3 letters of recommendation, resumé. Additional exam requirements/recommendations for international students: Required—TOEFL. *Application deadline:* For fall admission, 12/1 for domestic and international students. Application fee: $40. Electronic applications accepted. *Expenses:* Tuition: Part-time $265 per credit hour. Tuition and fees vary according to course load and program. *Financial support:* In 2007–08, 30 students received support, including 25 fellowships (averaging $5,550 per year), 7 teaching assistantships (averaging $7,680 per year). Support available to part-time students. Financial award application deadline: 2/2. *Unit head:* Donna Faye Burchfield, Artistic Director, 540-362-6596, E-mail: dburchfield@hollins.edu. *Application contact:* Cathy S. Koon, Manager of Graduate Services, 540-362-6326, Fax: 540-362-6288, E-mail: ckoon@hollins.edu.

Mills College, Graduate Studies, Department of Dance, Oakland, CA 94613-1000. Offers MA, MFA. Part-time programs available. *Faculty:* 5 full-time (all women), 5 part-time/adjunct (4 women). *Students:* 20 full-time (19 women); includes 2 minority (both Hispanic Americans) Average age 27. 26 applicants, 81% accepted, 10 enrolled. In 2007, 8 degrees awarded. *Degree requirements:* For master's, comprehensive exam, thesis, performance. *Entrance requirements:* For master's, audition or tape. Additional exam requirements/recommendations for international students: Required—TOEFL. *Application deadline:* For fall admission, 2/1 priority date for domestic students. Applications are processed on a rolling basis. Application fee: $50. *Expenses:* Tuition: Full-time $22,792; part-time $5,702 per credit. Required fees: $828. Part-time tuition and fees vary according to course load and program. *Financial support:* In 2007–08, 17 fellowships with partial tuition reimbursements (averaging $4,976 per year), 9 teaching assistantships with partial tuition reimbursements (averaging $3,799 per year) were awarded; institutionally sponsored loans, scholarships/grants, tuition waivers (partial), and residence awards also available. Support available to part-time students. Financial award application deadline: 2/1; financial award applicants required to submit CSS PROFILE or FAFSA. *Faculty research:* Video and dance, modern dance technique, performance art, rhythmic analysis. *Unit head:* Sonya Delwaide, Head, 510-430-3258, E-mail: sdelwaid@mills.edu. *Application contact:* Linda Guzman, Graduate Admission Specialist, 510-430-3309, Fax: 510-430-2159, E-mail: grad-studies@mills.edu.

New York University, Steinhardt School of Culture, Education and Human Development, Department of Music and Performing Arts Professions, Program in Dance Education, New York, NY 10012-1019. Offers MA, Ed D, PhD. Part-time and evening/weekend programs available. *Faculty:* 2 full-time (both women). *Students:* 32 full-time (31 women), 24 part-time (23 women); includes 14 minority (10 African Americans, 1 Asian American or Pacific Islander, 3 Hispanic Americans), 14 international. 41 applicants, 73% accepted, 24 enrolled. In 2007, 33 master's awarded. Terminal master's awarded for partial completion of doctoral program. *Degree requirements:* For master's, thesis (for some programs); for doctorate, thesis/dissertation. *Entrance requirements:* For master's, audition, interview; for doctorate, GRE General Test, audition, interview. Additional exam requirements/recommendations for international students: Required—TOEFL. *Application deadline:* For fall admission, 12/15 priority date for domestic and international students; for spring admission, 11/1 for domestic and international students. Applications are processed on a rolling basis. Application fee: $50. *Financial support:* Career-related internships or fieldwork, Federal Work-Study, institutionally sponsored loans, and scholarships/grants available. Support available to part-time students. Financial award application deadline: 2/1; financial award applicants required to submit FAFSA. *Faculty research:* Dance cognition and creativity, technology in dance, development of teacher expertise. *Unit head:* Dr. Susan Koff, Acting Director, 212-998-5424, Fax: 212-995-4043, E-mail: sk120@nyu.edu. *Application contact:* 212-998-5030, Fax: 212-995-4328, E-mail: steinhardt.gradadmissions@nyu.edu.

New York University, Tisch School of the Arts, Department of Dance, New York, NY 10012-1019. Offers MFA. *Faculty:* 11 full-time, 16 part-time/adjunct. *Students:* 32 full-time (24 women); includes 3 minority (2 African Americans, 1 Asian American or Pacific Islander), 7 international. Average age 27. 79 applicants, 39% accepted, 15 enrolled. In 2007, 13 degrees awarded. *Entrance requirements:* For master's, audition. Additional exam requirements/recommendations for international students: Required—TOEFL or IELTS. *Application deadline:* For fall admission, 1/8 priority date for domestic students, 1/8 for international students. Application fee: $60. Electronic applications accepted. *Financial support:* In 2007–08, 19 fellowships with full and partial tuition reimbursements were awarded; Federal Work-Study, institutionally sponsored loans, tuition waivers (partial), and unspecified assistantships also available. Financial award application deadline: 2/15; financial award applicants required to submit FAFSA. *Unit head:* Linda Tarnay, Chair, 212-998-1980, Fax: 212-995-4644. *Application contact:* Dan Sandford, Director of Graduate Admissions, 212-998-1918, Fax: 212-995-4060, E-mail: tisch.gradadmissions@nyu.edu.

New York University, Tisch School of the Arts and Graduate School of Arts and Science, Department of Performance Studies, New York, NY 10012-1019. Offers MA, PhD. *Faculty:* 12 full-time (7 women), 4 part-time/adjunct (3 women). *Students:* 93 full-time (71 women), 11 part-time (6 women); includes 19 minority (6 African Americans, 1 American Indian/Alaska Native, 6 Asian Americans or Pacific Islanders, 6 Hispanic Americans), 26 international. Average age 31. 203 applicants, 50% accepted, 60 enrolled. In 2007, 36 master's, 7 doctorates awarded. *Degree requirements:* For doctorate, one foreign language, comprehensive exam, thesis/dissertation, dissertation defense, qualifying exam. *Entrance requirements:* For master's, sample of written work; for doctorate, master's degree, writing sample. Additional exam requirements/recommendations for international students: Required—TOEFL or IELTS. *Application deadline:* For fall admission, 12/15 for domestic and international students. Application fee: $60. Electronic applications accepted. *Expenses:* Contact institution. *Financial support:* In 2007–08, 32 students received support, including 24 fellowships with full and partial tuition reimbursements available, 4 research assistantships, 4 teaching assistantships; Federal Work-Study, institutionally sponsored loans, tuition waivers (partial), and unspecified assistantships also available. Financial award application deadline: 2/15; financial award applicants required to submit CSS PROFILE or FAFSA. *Faculty research:* Performance theory, dance, folklore and festivals, postcolonial theory, anthropology and gender studies. *Unit head:* Jose Munoz, Chair, 212-998-1620, Fax: 212-995-4571, E-mail: performance.studies@nyu.edu. *Application contact:* Dan Sandford, Director of Graduate Admissions, 212-998-1918, Fax: 212-995-4060, E-mail: tisch.gradadmissions@nyu.edu.

Northern Illinois University, Graduate School, College of Visual and Performing Arts, School of Theatre and Dance, De Kalb, IL 60115-2854. Offers MFA. *Accreditation:* NAST. Part-time programs available. *Faculty:* 16 full-time (9 women). *Students:* 26 full-time (8 women); includes 2 minority (both African Americans), 3 international. Average age 28. 43 applicants, 49% accepted, 19 enrolled. In 2007, 17 degrees awarded. *Degree requirements:* For master's, comprehensive exam, final project and defense. *Entrance requirements:* For master's, minimum GPA of 2.75, audition or portfolio. Additional exam requirements/recommendations for international students: Required—TOEFL (minimum score 550 paper-based; 213 computer-based). *Application deadline:* For fall admission, 4/1 priority date for domestic students, 5/1 for international students; for spring admission, 10/15 priority date for domestic students, 10/1 for international students. Applications are processed on a rolling basis. Application fee: $30. Electronic applications accepted. *Expenses:* Tuition, area resident: Part-time $226 per credit hour. Tuition, state resident: full-time $5,424; part-time $225 per credit hour. Tuition, nonresident: full-time $10,848. Required fees: $2,416; $64 per credit hour. *Financial support:* In 2007–08, 2 research assistantships with full tuition reimbursements, 9 teaching assistantships with full tuition reimbursements were awarded; fellowships with full tuition reimbursements, career-related internships or fieldwork, Federal Work-Study, scholarships/grants, tuition waivers (full), and unspecified assistantships also available. Support available to part-time students. Financial award applicants required to submit FAFSA. *Faculty research:* Theatre history, choreography, performance art spectacles, storytelling, computer visualization of the ethical space. *Unit head:* Alexander Gelman, Director, 815-753-8253, Fax: 815-753-8415, E-mail: agelman@niu.edu. *Application contact:* Terrence McClellan, Information Contact, 815-753-8257, E-mail: tmcclell@niu.edu.

The Ohio State University, Graduate School, College of the Arts, Department of Dance, Program in Dance Studies, Columbus, OH 43210. Offers PhD. *Students:* 2 full-time (both women), 1 (woman) part-time. Average age 35. *Application deadline:* Applications are processed on a rolling basis. Application fee: $40 ($50 for international students). Electronic applications accepted. *Application contact:* 614-292-9444, Fax: 614-292-3895, E-mail: domestic.grad@osu.edu.

Oklahoma City University, Margaret E. Petree College of Performing Arts, Ann Lacy School of American Dance and Arts Management, Oklahoma City, OK 73106-1402. Offers dance (MFA). *Students:* 1 (woman) full-time, 1 (woman) part-time. Average age 25. *Expenses:* Tuition: Full-time $14,040; part-time $780 per hour. Required fees: $881; $32 per hour. *Unit head:* John Bedford, Dean, E-mail: jbedford@okcu.edu. *Application contact:* Leslie McKenzie, Director, Graduate Admissions, 800-633-7242, Fax: 405-208-5356, E-mail: gadmissions@okcu.edu.

Purchase College, State University of New York, Conservatory of Dance, Purchase, NY 10577-1400. Offers MFA. *Faculty:* 5 part-time/adjunct. *Students:* 9 full-time (8 women); includes 2 minority (1 Asian American or Pacific Islander, 1 Hispanic American), 3 international. Average age 29. 20 applicants, 40% accepted, 6 enrolled. In 2007, 5 degrees awarded. *Degree requirements:* For master's, performance. *Entrance requirements:* For master's, audition. *Application deadline:* For fall admission, 3/15 priority date for domestic students. Applications are processed on a rolling basis. Application fee: $50. Electronic applications accepted. *Expenses:* Tuition, state resident: full-time $6,900; part-time $288 per credit. Tuition, nonresident: full-time $10,920; part-time $455 per credit. Required fees: $1,506; $125 per credit. Tuition and fees vary according to program. *Financial support:* Fellowships, teaching assistantships, Federal Work-Study, scholarships/grants, and tuition waivers (partial) available. Support available to part-time students. Financial award application deadline: 3/15; financial award applicants required to submit FAFSA. *Faculty research:* Choreography and performance. *Unit head:* Carol Shiffman, Dean, 914-251-6800, Fax: 914-251-6806. *Application contact:* Sabrina Johnston, Counselor, 914-251-6479, Fax: 914-251-6314, E-mail: admissn@purchase.edu.

Sam Houston State University, College of Arts and Sciences, Department of Theatre and Dance, Huntsville, TX 77341. Offers dance (MFA). *Faculty:* 6 full-time (5 women). *Students:* 5 full-time (all women), 6 part-time (all women); includes 2 minority (1 African American, 1 Hispanic American). Average age 25. In 2007, 4 degrees awarded. *Degree requirements:* For master's, thesis, project. *Entrance requirements:* For master's, GRE General Test. Additional exam requirements/recommendations for international students: Required—TOEFL (minimum score 550 paper-based; 213 computer-based). *Application deadline:* For fall admission, 8/1 for domestic students; for spring admission, 12/1 for domestic students. Applications are processed on a rolling basis. Application fee: $20. *Expenses:* Tuition, state resident: full-time $5,026; part-time $184 per semester hour. Tuition, nonresident: full-time $10,586; part-time $462 per semester hour. Required fees: $494 per semester. *Financial support:* Teaching assistantships, career-related internships or fieldwork, Federal Work-Study, and institutionally sponsored loans available. Financial award application deadline: 5/31; financial award applicants required to submit FAFSA. *Unit head:* Penelope Hasekoester, Chair, 936-294-1330, Fax: 936-294-3898, E-mail: drm_pah@shsu.edu.

Sarah Lawrence College, Graduate Studies, Program in Dance, Bronxville, NY 10708-5999. Offers MFA. *Faculty:* 25 part-time/adjunct (16 women). *Students:* 8 full-time (all women), 1 part-time, 2 international. Average age 29. 28 applicants, 43% accepted, 4 enrolled. In 2007, 4 degrees awarded. *Degree requirements:* For master's, performance. *Entrance requirements:* For master's, audition, minimum B average in undergraduate course work. *Application deadline:* For fall admission, 1/15 for domestic and international students. Application fee: $60. *Expenses:* Tuition: Part-time $1,034 per credit. Required fees: $430 per year. Tuition and fees vary according to program. *Financial support:* In 2007–08, 8 fellowships (averaging $3,813 per year) were awarded; career-related internships or fieldwork, scholarships/grants, and health care benefits also available. Support available to part-time students. Financial award application deadline: 3/1; financial award applicants required to submit FAFSA. *Unit head:* Sara Rudner, Director, 914-395-2433. *Application contact:* Susan Guma, Dean of Graduate Studies, 914-395-2373, E-mail: sguma@mail.slc.edu.

See Close-Up on page 355.

Shenandoah University, Shenandoah Conservatory, Winchester, VA 22601-5195. Offers arts administration (MS); church music (MM, Certificate); composition (MM); conducting (MM); dance (MA, MFA, MS); dance accompanying (MM); music (MS); music education (MME, DMA); music therapy (MMT, Certificate); pedagogy (MM); performance (MM, DMA, Artist Diploma); piano accompanying (MM). *Accreditation:* NASM. Part-time and evening/weekend programs available. *Faculty:* 35 full-time (17 women), 12 part-time/adjunct (6 women). *Students:* 69 full-time (39 women), 126 part-time (72 women); includes 5 minority (3 African Americans, 2 Hispanic Americans), 27 international. Average age 40. 90 applicants, 92% accepted, 59 enrolled. In 2007, 28 master's, 12 doctorates, 6 other advanced degrees awarded. *Degree requirements:* For master's, comprehensive exam (for some programs), thesis (for some programs), internship (MS), recital (MM), research teaching project or thesis (MME), project (MA); for doctorate, comprehensive exam, thesis/dissertation (for some programs), dissertation or teaching project, recital. *Entrance requirements:* For master's, audition, minimum GPA of 2.5, writing sample, resumé; for doctorate, audition, minimum GPA of 3.25, 2 letters of recommendation, writing sample, resumé. Additional exam requirements/recommendations for international students: Required—TOEFL (minimum score 527 paper-based; 197 computer-based; 71 iBT). *Application deadline:* Applications are processed on a rolling basis. Application fee: $30. Electronic applications accepted. *Expenses:* Tuition: Part-time $640 per credit. Part-time tuition and fees vary according to degree level and program. *Financial support:* In 2007–08, 154 students received support, including 23 teaching assistantships with partial tuition reimbursements available (averaging $5,440 per year); fellowships with partial tuition reimbursements available, career-related internships or fieldwork, institutionally sponsored loans, scholarships/grants, and unspecified assistantships also available. Support available to part-time students. Financial award application deadline: 3/15; financial award applicants required to submit FAFSA. *Faculty research:* Creative activity, performance practice, music therapy aging, composition, Motown music. Total annual research expenditures: $4,272. *Unit head:* Dr. Laurence A. Kaptain, Dean, 540-665-4600, Fax: 540-665-5402, E-mail: lkaptain@su.edu. *Application contact:* David Anthony, Dean of Admissions, 540-665-4581, Fax: 540-665-4627, E-mail: admit@su.edu.

See Close-Up on page 357.

Smith College, Graduate Programs, Department of Dance, Northampton, MA 01063. Offers MFA. Part-time programs available. *Faculty:* 2 full-time (1 woman), 1 (woman) part-time/adjunct. *Students:* Average age 30. 16 applicants, 31% accepted, 4 enrolled. In 2007, 4 degrees awarded. *Degree requirements:* For master's, thesis performance. *Entrance requirements:* For master's, audition. Additional exam requirements/recommendations for international students: Required—TOEFL. *Application deadline:* For fall admission, 1/15 for domestic and international students. Application fee: $60. *Expenses:* Tuition: Full-time $33,940; part-time $1,060 per credit. Tuition and fees vary according to course load. *Financial support:* In 2007–08, 8 students received support, including 8 teaching assistantships with full tuition reimbursements available (averaging $5,720 per year); institutionally sponsored loans and scholarships/grants also available. Support available to part-time students. Financial award application deadline: 1/15; financial award applicants required to submit CSS PROFILE or FAFSA. *Unit head:* Rodger Blum, Chair, 413-585-3234, E-mail: rblum@smith.edu. *Application contact:* Susan Waltner, Graduate Student Adviser, 413-585-3236, E-mail: swaltner@smith.edu.

Southern Methodist University, Meadows School of the Arts, Division of Dance, Dallas, TX 75275. Offers MFA. *Accreditation:* NASD. *Faculty:* 9 full-time (6 women), 2 part-time/adjunct (both women). In 2007, 4 degrees awarded. *Degree requirements:* For master's, thesis or alternative, written qualifying exam. *Entrance requirements:* For master's, BA or BFA in dance, interview, professional-level experience. Additional exam requirements/recommendations for international students: Required—TOEFL (minimum score 550 paper-based; 213 computer-based; 80 iBT). *Application deadline:* For fall admission, 3/1 priority date for domestic and international students. Applications are processed on a rolling basis. Application fee: $75. *Financial support:* In 2007–08, 4 students received support, including 4 teaching assistantships (averaging $3,000 per year); scholarships/grants and unspecified assistantships also available. Financial award application deadline: 3/1; financial award applicants required to submit FAFSA. *Faculty research:* Labanotation, dance preservation and documentation, dance history. *Unit head:* Myra Woodruff, Chair, 214-768-2718, Fax: 214-768-4540, E-mail: woodruff@smu.edu. *Application contact:* Jean Cherry, Director of Graduate Admissions and Records, 214-768-3765, Fax: 214-768-3272, E-mail: jcherry@smu.edu.

Temple University, Graduate School, Esther Boyer College of Music and Dance, Department of Dance, Philadelphia, PA 19122-6096. Offers Ed M, MFA, PhD. *Accreditation:* NASD.Part-time programs available. *Degree requirements:* For master's, thesis optional, professional project; for doctorate, thesis/dissertation. *Entrance requirements:* For master's and doctorate, minimum GPA of 3.0, audition/interview. Additional exam requirements/recommendations for international students: Required—TOEFL. Electronic applications accepted. *Faculty research:* Cultural studies, dance education, dance technology, aesthetics.

Texas Tech University, Graduate School, College of Visual and Performing Arts, Department of Theatre and Dance, Lubbock, TX 79409. Offers fine arts (PhD); theatre arts (MA, MFA), including arts administration (MFA), design (MFA), performance/pedagogy (MFA), playwriting (MFA). *Accreditation:* NAST. Part-time programs available. *Faculty:* 9 full-time (5 women). *Students:* 35 full-time (18 women), 25 part-time (12 women); includes 5 minority (3 African Americans, 1 Asian American or Pacific Islander, 1 Hispanic American), 4 international. Average age 35. 32 applicants, 69% accepted, 16 enrolled. In 2007, 10 master's, 5 doctorates awarded. *Degree requirements:* For master's, variable foreign language requirement, thesis; for doctorate, thesis/dissertation. *Entrance requirements:* For master's and doctorate, GRE General Test. Additional exam requirements/recommendations for international students: Required—TOEFL (minimum score 550 paper-based; 213 computer-based). *Application deadline:* For fall admission, 3/1 priority date for international students; for spring admission, 11/1 priority date for international students. Applications are processed on a rolling basis. Application fee: $50 ($60 for international students). Electronic applications accepted. *Expenses:* Tuition, state resident: part-time $373 per credit hour. Tuition, nonresident: part-time $651 per credit hour. Tuition and fees vary according to program. *Financial support:* In 2007–08, 42 students received support, including 27 teaching assistantships with partial tuition reimbursements available (averaging $10,239 per year); research assistantships with partial tuition reimbursements available, Federal Work-Study and institutionally sponsored loans also available. Support available to part-time students. Financial award application deadline: 4/15; financial award applicants required to submit FAFSA. *Faculty research:* New student plays program, theatre planning, dramaturgy; feminist theatre; arts administration. *Unit head:* Prof. Frederick B. Christoffel, Chair, 806-742-3601 Ext. 228, Fax: 806-742-1338, E-mail: fred.christoffel@ttu.edu. *Application contact:* Dr. Linda Donahue, Graduate Adviser, 806-742-3601 Ext. 225, Fax: 806-742-1338, E-mail: linda.donahue@ttu.edu.

Texas Tech University, Graduate School, College of Visual and Performing Arts, Fine Arts Doctoral Program, Lubbock, TX 79409. Offers arts (PhD); music (PhD); theatre arts (PhD). *Accreditation:* NAST. *Students:* 40 full-time (16 women), 33 part-time (11 women); includes 8 minority (4 African Americans, 1 American Indian/Alaska Native, 1 Asian American or Pacific Islander, 2 Hispanic Americans), 9 international. Average age 37. 26 applicants, 62% accepted, 9 enrolled. In 2007, 10 degrees awarded. *Degree requirements:* For doctorate, thesis/dissertation. *Entrance requirements:* For doctorate, GRE General Test. Additional exam requirements/recommendations for international students: Required—TOEFL (minimum score 550 paper-based; 213 computer-based). *Application deadline:* For fall admission, 3/1 priority date for international students; for spring admission, 11/1 priority date for international students. Applications are processed on a rolling basis. Application fee: $50 ($60 for international students). Electronic applications accepted. *Expenses:* Tuition, state resident: part-time $373 per credit hour. Tuition, nonresident: part-time $651 per credit hour. Tuition and fees vary according to program. *Financial support:* Research assistantships with partial tuition reimbursements, teaching assistantships with partial tuition reimbursements available. Financial award application deadline:

Dance

Texas Tech University (continued)

4/15. *Faculty research:* Art criticism and theory, music, aesthetics, theatre arts. *Unit head:* Dr. Brian Steele, Director, 806-742-0700, Fax: 806-742-0695, E-mail: brian.steele@ttu.edu.

Texas Woman's University, Graduate School, College of Arts and Sciences, School of the Arts, Department of Dance, Denton, TX 76201. Offers MA, MFA, PhD. *Accreditation:* NASD. *Students:* 32 full-time (30 women), 6 part-time (all women); includes 3 minority (2 African Americans, 1 Hispanic American), 5 international. Average age 34. In 2007, 6 master's, 4 doctorates awarded. *Degree requirements:* For master's, thesis (for some programs), choreography portfolio, professional paper; for doctorate, comprehensive exam, thesis/dissertation. *Entrance requirements:* For master's, audition, 3 letters of recommendation, interview, writing sample, solo performance, resumé, personal essay; for doctorate, audition, portfolio, interview, 3 letters of reference, writing sample, resumé, personal essay, curriculum vitae. Additional exam requirements/recommendations for international students: Required—TOEFL (minimum score 550 paper-based; 213 computer-based; 79 iBT). *Application deadline:* For fall admission, 2/1 priority date for domestic and international students. Applications are processed on a rolling basis. Application fee: $30 ($50 for international students). Electronic applications accepted. *Expenses:* Tuition, state resident: full-time $3,294; part-time $183 per credit. Tuition, nonresident: full-time $8,298; part-time $461 per credit. Required fees: $985; $55 per credit. Tuition and fees vary according to degree level. *Financial support:* In 2007–08, 1 research assistantship (averaging $11,862 per year), 1 teaching assistantship (averaging $11,862 per year) were awarded; career-related internships or fieldwork, Federal Work-Study, institutionally sponsored loans, scholarships/grants, traineeships, health care benefits, tuition waivers (partial), and unspecified assistantships also available. Support available to part-time students. Financial award application deadline: 3/1; financial award applicants required to submit FAFSA. *Faculty research:* Performance, choreography, pedagogy, somatic practices, theorizing artistic practice. *Application contact:* Samuel Wheeler, Assistant Director of Admissions, 940-898-3188, Fax: 940-898-3081, E-mail: wheelersr@twu.edu.

Tufts University, Graduate School of Arts and Sciences, Department of Drama and Dance, Medford, MA 02155. Offers dance (MA, PhD); drama (MA); dramatic literature and criticism (PhD); theater history (PhD). Part-time programs available. *Faculty:* 11 full-time, 8 part-time/adjunct. *Students:* 27 (18 women); includes 4 minority (1 African American, 3 Asian Americans or Pacific Islanders) 2 international. 37 applicants, 32% accepted, 4 enrolled. In 2007, 1 master's, 4 doctorates awarded. Terminal master's awarded for partial completion of doctoral program. *Degree requirements:* For master's, one foreign language, thesis; for doctorate, 2 foreign languages, thesis/dissertation, oral exam, written general exam. *Entrance requirements:* For master's and doctorate, GRE General Test, writing sample. Additional exam requirements/recommendations for international students: Required—TOEFL (minimum score 600 paper-based; 250 computer-based; 80 iBT). *Application deadline:* For fall admission, 1/15 for domestic students, 12/30 for international students. Applications are processed on a rolling basis. Application fee: $70. Electronic applications accepted. *Expenses:* Tuition: Full-time $35,052. *Financial support:* Fellowships with full and partial tuition reimbursements, teaching assistantships with full and partial tuition reimbursements, Federal Work-Study, scholarships/grants, and tuition waivers (partial) available. Support available to part-time students. Financial award application deadline: 1/15; financial award applicants required to submit FAFSA. *Unit head:* Dr. Barbara Grossman, Chair, 617-627-3524. *Application contact:* Dr. Laurence Senelick, Head, 617-627-3524.

Tulane University, School of Liberal Arts, Department of Theatre and Dance, New Orleans, LA 70118-5669. Offers design and technical production (MFA). *Entrance requirements:* For master's, GRE General Test, minimum B average in undergraduate course work. Additional exam requirements/recommendations for international students: Required—TOEFL. Electronic applications accepted. *Faculty research:* Scene design, stage management, costume design, technical direction, lighting design.

Université du Québec à Montréal, Graduate Programs, Program in Dance, Montréal, QC H3C 3P8, Canada. Offers MA. Part-time programs available. *Degree requirements:* For master's, thesis optional. *Entrance requirements:* For master's, appropriate bachelor's degree or equivalent and proficiency in French.

University of California, Irvine, Office of Graduate Studies, Claire Trevor School of the Arts, Department of Dance, Irvine, CA 92697. Offers MFA. *Students:* 22 full-time (19 women); includes 6 minority (1 African American, 1 Asian American or Pacific Islander, 4 Hispanic Americans). In 2007, 10 degrees awarded. *Degree requirements:* For master's, thesis. *Entrance requirements:* For master's, minimum GPA of 3.0. *Application deadline:* For fall admission, 1/15 priority date for domestic students; for winter admission, 10/15 priority date for domestic students. Applications are processed on a rolling basis. Application fee: $60. Electronic applications accepted. *Financial support:* Fellowships, teaching assistantships, institutionally sponsored loans, traineeships, health care benefits, and unspecified assistantships available. Financial award application deadline: 3/1; financial award applicants required to submit FAFSA. *Faculty research:* Dance science, digital technology, history and theory, choreography. *Unit head:* Alan Terricciano, Chair, 949-824-5744, Fax: 949-824-4563, E-mail: aterricc@uci.edu. *Application contact:* Karen Ricketts, Departmental Manager, 949-824-6929, Fax: 949-824-4563, E-mail: kbricket@uci.edu.

University of California, Los Angeles, Graduate Division, School of the Arts and Architecture, Department of World Arts and Cultures, Los Angeles, CA 90095. Offers culture and performance (MA, PhD); dance (MA, MFA). *Degree requirements:* For master's, comprehensive exam or thesis; for doctorate, one foreign language, thesis/dissertation, oral and written qualifying exams. *Entrance requirements:* For master's, minimum GPA of 3.0; for doctorate, GRE General Test, writing sample. Electronic applications accepted. *Expenses:* Tuition, nonresident: full-time $5,728. Required fees: $8,966. Full-time tuition and fees vary according to program and student level.

University of California, Riverside, Graduate Division, Department of Dance, Riverside, CA 92521-0102. Offers dance (MFA); dance history and theory (MA, PhD). *Faculty:* 9 full-time (7 women). *Students:* 33 full-time (29 women); includes 5 minority (1 African American, 3 Asian Americans or Pacific Islanders, 1 Hispanic American), 8 international. Average age 31. In 2007, 3 master's, 5 doctorates awarded. *Degree requirements:* For doctorate, 2 foreign languages, thesis/dissertation, qualifying exams. *Entrance requirements:* For master's, choreographed piece (MFA); for doctorate, GRE General Test, minimum GPA of 3.2, writing sample. Additional exam requirements/recommendations for international students: Required—TOEFL (minimum score 550 paper-based; 213 computer-based; 80 iBT). *Application deadline:* For fall admission, 5/1 for domestic students, 2/1 for international students; for winter admission, 9/1 for domestic students, 7/1 for international students; for spring admission, 12/1 for domestic students, 10/1 for international students. Applications are processed on a rolling basis. Application fee: $60 ($75 for international students). Electronic applications accepted. *Financial support:* In 2007–08, fellowships with full tuition reimbursements (averaging $12,000 per year), teaching assistantships with full tuition reimbursements (averaging $15,600 per year) were awarded; research assistantships with tuition reimbursements, career-related internships or fieldwork, Federal Work-Study, institutionally sponsored loans, and tuition waivers (full and partial) also available. Financial award application deadline: 1/5; financial award applicants required to submit FAFSA. *Faculty research:* Movement analysis, cultural postcolonial gender studies of performance, theories of dance, anthropology of dance, history and reconstruction of dance. *Unit head:* Jacqueline Shea-Murphy, Chair, 951-827-3988, E-mail: jacqueline.sheamurphy@ucr.edu. *Application contact:* Anthea Kraut, Graduate Adviser, 951-827-7108, Fax: 951-827-4651, E-mail: performingarts@ucr.edu.

University of Colorado at Boulder, Graduate School, College of Arts and Sciences, Department of Theatre and Dance, Boulder, CO 80309. Offers dance (MFA); theatre (MA, PhD). *Faculty:* 14. *Students:* 33 full-time (24 women), 8 part-time (6 women); includes 5 minority (3 African Americans, 2 Hispanic Americans), 1 international. Average age 36. 15 applicants, 80% accepted. In 2007, 8 master's, 5 doctorates awarded. Terminal master's awarded for partial completion of doctoral program. *Degree requirements:* For master's, comprehensive exam, thesis; for doctorate, one foreign language, thesis/dissertation. *Entrance requirements:* For master's, GRE General Test (MA), audition (MFA), minimum undergraduate GPA of 2.75. *Application deadline:* For fall admission, 1/15 priority date for domestic students, 12/1 for international students. Application fee: $50 ($60 for international students). *Financial support:* In 2007–08, 27 fellowships (averaging $4,240 per year) were awarded; tuition waivers (full) also available. Financial award application deadline: 1/15. *Faculty research:* Performance choreography; pedagogy administration; body therapies; multi-media forms; film, video, and cultural studies, non-concert forms, music, poetry writing, literature, kinesiology (dance); theater history, theory and literature . Total annual research expenditures: $22,500. *Unit head:* Bud Coleman, Chair, 303-492-5809, Fax: 303-492-7722, E-mail: bud.coleman@colorado.edu. *Application contact:* Graduate Program Assistant, 303-492-7356, Fax: 303-492-7722, E-mail: thtrdnce@colorado.edu.

University of Hawaii at Manoa, Graduate Division, Colleges of Arts and Sciences, College of Arts and Humanities, Department of Theatre and Dance, Honolulu, HI 96822. Offers dance (MA, MFA); theatre (MA, MFA, PhD). *Faculty:* 17 full-time (10 women), 4 part-time/adjunct (all women). *Students:* 53 full-time (38 women), 4 part-time (3 women); includes 8 minority (1 American Indian/Alaska Native, 7 Asian Americans or Pacific Islanders), 8 international. 55 applicants, 58% accepted, 26 enrolled. *Entrance requirements:* Additional exam requirements/recommendations for international students: Required—TOEFL. *Application deadline:* For fall admission, 2/1 for domestic students, 1/15 for international students; for spring admission, 9/1 for domestic students, 8/1 for international students. Application fee: $50. *Financial support:* In 2007–08, 1 research assistantship (averaging $16,824 per year), 15 teaching assistantships (averaging $13,609 per year) were awarded; fellowships, Federal Work-Study, institutionally sponsored loans, tuition waivers (full), and unspecified assistantships also available. Financial award application deadline: 2/1. *Faculty research:* Asian theatre, feminist theatre and dance, Russian theatre, Australian theatre.

University of Illinois at Urbana–Champaign, Graduate College, College of Fine and Applied Arts, Department of Dance, Champaign, IL 61820. Offers MFA. *Accreditation:* NASD. *Faculty:* 9 full-time (7 women), 1 (woman) part-time/adjunct. *Students:* 11 full-time (9 women), 1 (woman) part-time, 3 international. 21 applicants, 24% accepted, 5 enrolled. In 2007, 8 master's awarded. *Entrance requirements:* For master's, audition, minimum GPA of 3.0. *Application deadline:* Applications are processed on a rolling basis. Application fee: $60 ($75 for international students). Electronic applications accepted. *Financial support:* In 2007–08, 6 fellowships, 11 teaching assistantships were awarded; research assistantships, tuition waivers (full and partial) also available. Financial award application deadline: 2/15. *Unit head:* Jan Erkert, Interim Head, 217-333-1010, Fax: 217-333-3000, E-mail: erkert@uiuc.edu. *Application contact:* Cynthia C. Howard, Program Coordinator, 217-333-1011, Fax: 217-333-3000, E-mail: choward1@uiuc.edu.

The University of Iowa, Graduate College, College of Liberal Arts and Sciences, Department of Dance, Iowa City, IA 52242-1316. Offers MFA. *Faculty:* 8 full-time, 4 part-time/adjunct. *Students:* 11 full-time (8 women), 1 part-time; includes 2 minority (1 African American, 1 Hispanic American), 1 international. 17 applicants, 47% accepted, 6 enrolled. In 2007, 5 degrees awarded. *Degree requirements:* For master's, thesis, exam. *Entrance requirements:* For master's, minimum GPA of 3.0. Additional exam requirements/recommendations for international students: Required—TOEFL (minimum score 550 paper-based; 213 computer-based; 81 iBT). *Application deadline:* For fall admission, 12/15 priority date for domestic and international students; for spring admission, 10/15 priority date for domestic and international students. Application fee: $60 ($85 for international students). Electronic applications accepted. *Expenses:* Tuition, state resident: part-time $349 per hour. Tuition, nonresident: part-time $349 per hour. Tuition and fees vary according to course load and program. *Financial support:* In 2007–08, 3 fellowships, 1 research assistantship with partial tuition reimbursement, 4 teaching assistantships with partial tuition reimbursements were awarded. Financial award applicants required to submit FAFSA. *Unit head:* Alan Sener, Chair, 319-335-2184, Fax: 319-335-3246.

University of Maryland, College Park, Graduate Studies, College of Arts and Humanities, Department of Dance, College Park, MD 20742. Offers MFA. *Faculty:* 8 full-time (4 women), 5 part-time/adjunct (4 women). *Students:* 10 full-time (all women); includes 2 minority (1 African American, 1 Hispanic American), 1 international. 16 applicants, 31% accepted, 5 enrolled. In 2007, 2 degrees awarded. *Degree requirements:* For master's, final project. *Entrance requirements:* For master's, audition/interview, video tapes/writing sample. Additional exam requirements/recommendations for international students: Required—TOEFL. *Application deadline:* For fall admission, 2/1 for domestic and international students. Applications are processed on a rolling basis. Application fee: $60. Electronic applications accepted. *Financial support:* In 2007–08, 2 research assistantships (averaging $13,200 per year), 6 teaching assistantships (averaging $14,534 per year) were awarded; fellowships, Federal Work-Study and scholarships/grants also available. *Faculty research:* Performance and choreography. Total annual research expenditures: $8,000. *Unit head:* Daniel M. Wagner, Acting Chair, 301-405-1411, E-mail: dmwagner@umd.edu. *Application contact:* Dean of Graduate School, 301-405-4190, Fax: 301-314-9305.

University of Michigan, Horace H. Rackham School of Graduate Studies, The School of Music, Theatre, and Dance, Department of Dance, Ann Arbor, MI 48109. Offers modern dance performance and choreography (MFA). Offered through the Horace H. Rackham School of Graduate Studies. *Accreditation:* NASD. *Degree requirements:* For master's, thesis. *Entrance requirements:* For master's, audition. Additional exam requirements/recommendations for international students: Required—TOEFL (minimum score 600 paper-based; 250 computer-based). Electronic applications accepted. *Faculty research:* Life forms software, Donald McKayles 'Rainbow Suite", Carlos Orta of Jose Limon, World Wide Rhythms concert.

University of Minnesota, Twin Cities Campus, Graduate School, College of Liberal Arts, Department of Theatre Arts and Dance, Minneapolis, MN 55455-0213. Offers design technology (MFA); theatre arts and dance (MA, PhD). *Accreditation:* NASD; NAST (one or more programs are accredited). *Faculty:* 15 full-time (6 women), 3 part-time/adjunct (2 women). *Students:* 26 full-time (17 women), 13 part-time (7 women); includes 9 minority (2 African Americans, 3 Asian Americans or Pacific Islanders, 4 Hispanic Americans), 2 international. Average age 31. 43 applicants, 23% accepted, 9 enrolled. In 2007, 4 master's, 3 doctorates awarded. Terminal master's awarded for partial completion of doctoral program. *Median time to degree:* Of those who began their doctoral program in fall 1999, 50% received their degree in 8 years or less. *Degree requirements:* For master's, thesis (for some programs), final creative project (MFA), foreign language (MA); for doctorate, one foreign language, thesis/dissertation, oral defense, written exams. *Entrance requirements:* For master's, GRE General Test, minimum GPA of 3.0, audition or portfolio; for doctorate, GRE General Test, minimum GPA of 3.0, writing sample, 1 foreign language. Additional exam requirements/recommendations for international students: Required—TOEFL (minimum score 550 paper-based; 213 computer-based; 79 iBT). *Application deadline:* For fall admission, 1/15 priority date for domestic and international students. Applications are processed on a rolling basis. Application fee: $55 ($75 for international students). Electronic applications accepted. *Financial support:* In 2007–08, 30 students received support, including 3 fellowships with full tuition reimbursements available (averaging $14,000 per year), 27 teaching assistantships with full tuition reimbursements available (averaging $12,253 per year); career-related internships or fieldwork, Federal Work-Study, scholarships/grants, health care benefits, tuition waivers (partial), and unspecified assistantships also available. Financial award application deadline: 4/15; financial award applicants required to submit FAFSA. *Faculty research:* Theatre history; Eastern European theatre; performance studies; medieval studies. Total annual research expenditures: $42,506. *Unit head:* Michal Kobialka, Chair, 612-625-0048, Fax: 612-625-6334, E-mail: kobia001@tc.umn.edu. *Application contact:* Ginni Arons, Graduate Studies Assistant, 612-625-5029, Fax: 612-625-6334, E-mail: theatre@tc.umn.edu.

University of New Mexico, Graduate School, College of Fine Arts, Department of Theatre and Dance, Albuquerque, NM 87131-2039. Offers dramatic writing (MFA); theater and dance

(MA). *Accreditation:* NASD; NAST. *Faculty:* 12 full-time (7 women), 28 part-time/adjunct (18 women). *Students:* 16 full-time (11 women), 5 part-time (3 women); includes 7 minority (2 American Indian/Alaska Native, 1 Asian American or Pacific Islander, 4 Hispanic Americans), 1 international. Average age 35. 22 applicants, 200% accepted, 6 enrolled. In 2007, 1 master's awarded. *Degree requirements:* For master's, comprehensive exam (for some programs), thesis (for some programs). *Entrance requirements:* For master's, minimum GPA of 3.0, undergraduate major in theatre, dance or closely related field, 3 letters of recommendation, letter of intent. *Application deadline:* For fall admission, 4/15 for domestic students; for spring admission, 11/10 for domestic students. Application fee: $50. Electronic applications accepted. *Financial support:* In 2007–08, 14 students received support, including 5 research assistantships with partial tuition reimbursements available (averaging $8,000 per year), 6 teaching assistantships with partial tuition reimbursements available (averaging $8,000 per year); Federal Work-Study, health care benefits, tuition waivers (partial), and unspecified assistantships also available. Financial award application deadline: 3/1; financial award applicants required to submit FAFSA. *Faculty research:* Theater education and outreach, choreography, dramatic writing, dance history/criticism. *Unit head:* Susan Pearson, Chair, 505-277-4332, Fax: 505-277-8921, E-mail: speardav@unm.edu. *Application contact:* Christina Squire, Graduate Coordinator, 505-277-7362, Fax: 505-277-8921, E-mail: csquire@unm.edu.

The University of North Carolina at Charlotte, Graduate School, College of Education, Program in Teacher Education, Charlotte, NC 28223-0001. Offers art education (K-12) (MAT); dance education (K-12) (MAT); elementary education (K-6) (MAT); English as a second language (K-12) (MAT); foreign language education (K-12) (MAT); general teacher education (MAT); middle grades education (6-9) (MAT); music education (K-12) (MAT); secondary education (9-12) (MAT); special education (K-12) (MAT); theatre education (K-12) (MAT). *Students:* 19 full-time (15 women), 166 part-time (138 women); includes 24 minority (22 African Americans, 1 American Indian/Alaska Native, 1 Asian American or Pacific Islander), 2 international. Average age 32. 94 applicants, 89% accepted, 66 enrolled. In 2007, 90 degrees awarded. *Entrance requirements:* For master's, GRE or MAT. Additional exam requirements/recommendations for international students: Required—TOEFL (minimum score 557 paper-based; 220 computer-based). *Application deadline:* For fall admission, 7/1 for domestic students, 5/1 for international students; for spring admission, 11/1 for domestic students, 10/1 for international students. Applications are processed on a rolling basis. Application fee: $55. Electronic applications accepted. *Expenses:* Tuition, state resident: full-time $2,855. Tuition, nonresident: full-time $13,062. Required fees: $1,692. *Financial support:* Fellowships, research assistantships, teaching assistantships, career-related internships or fieldwork, Federal Work-Study, institutionally sponsored loans, scholarships/grants, and unspecified assistantships available. Support available to part-time students. Financial award application deadline: 4/1; financial award applicants required to submit FAFSA. *Unit head:* Dr. Kimberly J. Hartman, Coordinator, 704-687-8883, Fax: 704-687-6430, E-mail: khartman@email.uncc.edu. *Application contact:* Kathy B. Giddings, Director of Graduate Admissions, 704-687-3366, Fax: 704-687-3279, E-mail: agidding@uncc.edu.

The University of North Carolina at Greensboro, Graduate School, School of Health and Human Performance, Department of Dance, Greensboro, NC 27412-5001. Offers MA, MFA. *Accreditation:* NASD. *Faculty:* 10 full-time (7 women), 2 part-time/adjunct (0 women). *Students:* 18 full-time (17 women), 8 part-time (all women); includes 1 minority (African American) 22 applicants, 41% accepted. *Degree requirements:* For master's, thesis. *Entrance requirements:* For master's, GRE General Test or MAT, audition or video (MFA). Additional exam requirements/recommendations for international students: Required—TOEFL. *Application deadline:* For fall admission, 2/12 priority date for domestic students. Application fee: $45. Electronic applications accepted. *Financial support:* Fellowships with full tuition reimbursements, research assistantships with full tuition reimbursements, teaching assistantships with full tuition reimbursements, career-related internships or fieldwork, Federal Work-Study, scholarships/grants, traineeships, and unspecified assistantships available. Support available to part-time students. *Faculty research:* Consciousness-raising images, perspectives on ballet. *Unit head:* Dr. Jan Van Dyke, Head, 336-334-5570, Fax: 336-334-3238, E-mail: jevandyk@uncg.edu. *Application contact:* Michelle Harkleroad, Director of Graduate Admissions, 336-334-4884, Fax: 336-334-4424, E-mail: mbharkle@uncg.edu.

University of Oklahoma, Graduate College, College of Fine Arts, School of Dance, Norman, OK 73019-0390. Offers MFA. *Faculty:* 5 full-time (2 women). *Students:* 6 full-time (all women); includes 2 minority (both Hispanic Americans), 2 international. 4 applicants, 75% accepted, 2 enrolled. In 2007, 2 degrees awarded. *Degree requirements:* For master's, comprehensive exam, departmental qualifying exams, solo performance or choreography of a work. *Entrance requirements:* For master's, minimum GPA of 3.0 or equivalent experience, resumé, audition, interview, 3 letters of reference, video, and personal choreography. Additional exam requirements/recommendations for international students: Required—TOEFL (minimum score 550 paper-based; 213 computer-based). *Application deadline:* For fall admission, 6/1 for domestic students, 4/1 for international students; for spring admission, 11/1 for domestic students, 9/1 for international students. Applications are processed on a rolling basis. Application fee: $40 ($90 for international students). Electronic applications accepted. *Expenses:* Tuition, state resident: full-time $3,451; part-time $144 per credit hour. Tuition, nonresident: full-time $12,432; part-time $518 per credit hour. Required fees: $1,925; $70 per credit hour. $122 per semester. *Financial support:* In 2007–08, 3 students received support, including 2 fellowships with full tuition reimbursements available (averaging $8,000 per year), 6 teaching assistantships with partial tuition reimbursements available (averaging $11,715 per year); scholarships/grants, health care benefits, and unspecified assistantships also available. Financial award application deadline: 3/15; financial award applicants required to submit FAFSA. *Unit head:* Mary Margaret Holt, Director, 405-325-4051, Fax: 405-325-7024, E-mail: mmholt@ou.edu. *Application contact:* Jeremy Lindberg, Associate Professor/Graduate Liaison, 405-325-5312, Fax: 405-325-7024, E-mail: jlindberg@ou.edu.

University of Oregon, Graduate School, School of Music, Department of Dance, Eugene, OR 97403. Offers MA, MS. *Faculty:* 4 full-time (2 women), 1 (woman) part-time/adjunct. *Students:* 7 full-time (6 women); includes 1 minority (American Indian/Alaska Native). Average age 23. 14 applicants, 21% accepted. In 2007, 1 degree awarded. *Degree requirements:* For master's, thesis or alternative. *Entrance requirements:* For master's, minimum GPA of 3.0. Additional exam requirements/recommendations for international students: Required—TOEFL. *Application deadline:* For fall admission, 6/1 for domestic students. Application fee: $50. *Financial support:* In 2007–08, 6 teaching assistantships were awarded; Federal Work-Study and institutionally sponsored loans also available. Financial award application deadline: 2/1. *Faculty research:* Choreography, dance history, dance pedagogy, scientific aspects of dance. *Unit head:* Jennifer Craig, Department Chair, 541-346-3386. *Application contact:* Marian Moser, Admissions Contact, 541-346-3386, E-mail: mmoser@uoregon.edu.

The University of Texas at Austin, Graduate School, College of Fine Arts, Department of Theatre and Dance, Austin, TX 78712-1111. Offers dance (MFA); theatre (MA, MFA, PhD). *Accreditation:* NASD. *Degree requirements:* For master's, thesis; for doctorate, variable foreign language requirement, thesis/dissertation. *Entrance requirements:* For master's and doctorate, GRE General Test.

University of Utah, The Graduate School, College of Fine Arts, Department of Ballet, Salt Lake City, UT 84112-1107. Offers MFA. *Faculty:* 6 full-time (3 women), 1 part-time/adjunct (0 women). *Students:* 8 full-time (all women), 1 (woman) part-time; includes 1 minority (Asian American or Pacific Islander), 2 international. Average age 26. 26 applicants, 19% accepted, 5 enrolled. In 2007, 2 degrees awarded. *Degree requirements:* For master's, one foreign language, choreography projects, performance, teaching experience with written support. *Entrance requirements:* For master's, audition, videos/DVDs of teaching and choreography. Additional exam requirements/recommendations for international students: Required—TOEFL (minimum score 500 paper-based; 173 computer-based). *Application deadline:* For fall admission, 4/1 for domestic and international students; for spring admission, 10/1 for domestic and international students. Applications are processed on a rolling basis. Application fee: $45 ($65 for international students). *Financial support:* In 2007–08, 1 teaching assistantship with full and partial tuition reimbursement (averaging $5,700 per year) was awarded; Federal Work-Study, institutionally sponsored loans, and scholarships/grants also available. Financial award application deadline: 3/1; financial award applicants required to submit FAFSA. *Faculty research:* Choreography, jazz, technique, fitness and dance injuries. *Unit head:* Carol N. Iwasaki, Department Chair, 801-581-8231, Fax: 801-581-5442, E-mail: cni1@utah.edu. *Application contact:* Richard Wacko, Associate Professor, 801-587-3742, E-mail: richard.wacko@utah.edu.

University of Utah, The Graduate School, College of Fine Arts, Department of Modern Dance, Salt Lake City, UT 84112-1107. Offers MA, MFA. *Faculty:* 10 full-time (6 women), 2 part-time/adjunct (both women). *Students:* 18 full-time (17 women), 7 part-time (6 women); includes 3 minority (2 Asian Americans or Pacific Islanders, 1 Hispanic American), 2 international. Average age 30. 30 applicants, 67% accepted, 7 enrolled. In 2007, 3 degrees awarded. *Degree requirements:* For master's, thesis, project, oral examination. *Entrance requirements:* For master's, audition, interview, minimum GPA of 3.0. Additional exam requirements/recommendations for international students: Required—TOEFL (minimum score 500 paper-based; 173 computer-based). *Application deadline:* For fall admission, 3/1 for domestic and international students. Applications are processed on a rolling basis. Application fee: $45 ($65 for international students). Electronic applications accepted. *Financial support:* In 2007–08, 14 students received support; fellowships with tuition reimbursements available, teaching assistantships with tuition reimbursements available, Federal Work-Study, institutionally sponsored loans, scholarships/grants, health care benefits, and unspecified assistantships available. Financial award application deadline: 3/1; financial award applicants required to submit FAFSA. *Faculty research:* Choreography, teaching methods, performance, cultural studies, dance technology. Total annual research expenditures: $3,716. *Unit head:* Donna White, Chair, 801-581-7327, Fax: 801-581-5442, E-mail: d.m.white@utah.edu. *Application contact:* Steve Koester, Director of Graduate Studies, 801-581-9808, Fax: 801-581-5442, E-mail: stephen.koester@utah.edu.

University of Washington, Graduate School, College of Arts and Sciences, Program in Dance, Seattle, WA 98195. Offers MFA. *Faculty:* 5 full-time (4 women), 1 (woman) part-time/adjunct. *Students:* 6 full-time (4 women). Average age 32. 12 applicants, 25% accepted. In 2007, 3 degrees awarded. *Degree requirements:* For master's, performance, project. *Entrance requirements:* For master's, 8 years of professional dance experience, resumé, performance DVD or VHS tape, 3 letters of reference. *Application deadline:* For fall admission, 11/15 for domestic and international students. Application fee: $50. Electronic applications accepted. *Financial support:* In 2007–08, 6 students received support; teaching assistantships with full tuition reimbursements available, health care benefits available. Financial award application deadline: 11/15. *Faculty research:* Choreography, history, anatomy. *Unit head:* Elizabeth Cooper, Director, 206-543-4178, Fax: 206-543-8610, E-mail: bcoop@u.washington.edu. *Application contact:* Jennifer Sack, Associate Professor, 206-543-55*94, Fax: 206-543-8610, E-mail: jsack@u.washington.edu.

University of Wisconsin–Milwaukee, Graduate School, Peck School of the Arts, Program in Performing Arts, Milwaukee, WI 53201-0413. Offers dance (MFA); film (MFA); theatre (MFA). Part-time programs available. *Faculty:* 29 full-time (14 women). *Students:* 15 full-time (10 women), 3 part-time (all women); includes 1 minority (Hispanic American), 2 international. 32 applicants, 25% accepted, 6 enrolled. In 2007, 16 degrees awarded. *Degree requirements:* For master's, variable foreign language requirement, thesis or alternative. *Entrance requirements:* For master's, audition, interview. *Application deadline:* For fall admission, 1/1 priority date for domestic students; for spring admission, 9/1 for domestic students. Applications are processed on a rolling basis. Application fee: $45 ($75 for international students). *Expenses:* Tuition, state resident: part-time $530 per credit. Tuition, nonresident: part-time $1,428 per credit. Required fees: $19 per credit. $229 per term. Tuition and fees vary according to course load and program. *Financial support:* In 2007–08, 9 teaching assistantships were awarded; fellowships, research assistantships, career-related internships or fieldwork and unspecified assistantships also available. Support available to part-time students. Financial award application deadline: 4/15. *Unit head:* Simone Ferro, Representative, 414-229-4178, E-mail: sferro@uwm.edu.

York University, Faculty of Graduate Studies, Faculty of Fine Arts, Program in Dance, Toronto, ON M3J 1P3, Canada. Offers MA, MFA. *Degree requirements:* For master's, thesis or alternative. Electronic applications accepted.

Music

Alabama Agricultural and Mechanical University, School of Graduate Studies, School of Education, Department of Curriculum and Instruction, Area in Music Education, Huntsville, AL 35811. Offers music (MS); music education (M Ed). *Accreditation:* NCATE. Part-time and evening/weekend programs available. *Faculty:* 9 full-time (3 women), 7 part-time/adjunct (5 women). *Degree requirements:* For master's, comprehensive exam. *Entrance requirements:* For master's, GRE General Test. *Application deadline:* For fall admission, 5/1 for domestic students. Applications are processed on a rolling basis. Application fee: $25. Electronic applications accepted. *Financial support:* Career-related internships or fieldwork and traineeships available. Financial award application deadline: 4/1. *Faculty research:* Jazz and black music, Alabama folk music. *Unit head:* Dr. Horace Carney, Chairperson, 256-372-5512.

Alabama State University, School of Graduate Studies, Department of Music, Montgomery, AL 36101-0271. Offers instrumental music (M Ed); vocal/choral music (M Ed). *Accreditation:* NASM. Part-time programs available. *Degree requirements:* For master's, comprehensive exam. *Entrance requirements:* For master's, GRE General Test or MAT, graduate writing competency test. Additional exam requirements/recommendations for international students: Required—TOEFL (minimum score 500 paper-based; 173 computer-based). *Faculty research:* Computer applications.

Andrews University, School of Graduate Studies, College of Arts and Sciences, Department of Music, Berrien Springs, MI 49104. Offers M Mus, MA. *Accreditation:* NASM. *Degree requirements:* For master's, variable foreign language requirement. *Entrance requirements:* For master's, GRE Subject Test, minimum undergraduate GPA of 2.6.

Appalachian State University, Cratis D. Williams Graduate School, School of Music, Boone, NC 28608. Offers music education (MM); music performance (MM); music therapy (MMT). *Accreditation:* NASM. *Faculty:* 26 full-time (7 women). *Students:* 18 full-time (10 women), 9 part-time (4 women); includes 2 minority (1 African American, 1 Asian American or Pacific Islander), 2 international. 24 applicants, 75% accepted, 12 enrolled. In 2007, 6 master's awarded. *Degree requirements:* For master's, comprehensive exam, thesis or alternative. *Entrance*

Music

Appalachian State University (continued)
requirements: For master's, GRE General Test, 3 letters of ref + audition. Additional exam requirements/recommendations for international students: Required—TOEFL (minimum score 550 paper-based; 230 computer-based). *Application deadline:* For fall admission, 7/1 for domestic students, 1/1 for international students; for spring admission, 11/1 for domestic students, 6/1 for international students. Application fee: $50. *Expenses:* Tuition, state resident: part-time $127 per semester hour. Tuition, nonresident: part-time $597 per semester hour. Required fees: $18 per semester. *Financial support:* In 2007–08, 8 research assistantships (averaging $7,000 per year) were awarded; fellowships, teaching assistantships, career-related internships or fieldwork, Federal Work-Study, scholarships/grants, tuition waivers (partial), and unspecified assistantships also available. Financial award application deadline: 4/1. *Faculty research:* Music of the holocaust, Celtic folk music, early 19th century performance practice, hypermeter and phase rhythm, world music, music and psychoneuroimmunology. Total annual research expenditures: $45,853. *Unit head:* Dr. William Harbinson, Graduate Director and Associate Dean, 828-262-6446, E-mail: harbinsonwg@appstate.edu. *Application contact:* Dr. Nancy Schneeloch-Bingham, Graduate Program Director, 828-262-6463, E-mail: schneelochna@appstate.edu.

Arizona State University, Graduate College, College of Fine Arts, School of Music, Tempe, AZ 85287. Offers MA, MM, DMA. *Accreditation:* NASM. *Degree requirements:* For doctorate, thesis/dissertation. *Entrance requirements:* For master's, GRE or MAT; for doctorate, GRE.

Arkansas State University, Graduate School, College of Fine Arts, Department of Music, Jonesboro, State University, AR 72467. Offers music education (MME, SCCT); performance (MM). *Accreditation:* NASM (one or more programs are accredited). Part-time programs available. *Faculty:* 14 full-time (3 women), 2 part-time/adjunct (both women). *Students:* 5 full-time (3 women), 8 part-time (2 women), 2 international. Average age 27. 9 applicants, 78% accepted, 3 enrolled. In 2007, 5 master's, 1 other advanced degree awarded. *Degree requirements:* For master's, 2 foreign languages, comprehensive exam, thesis or alternative; for SCCT, comprehensive exam. *Entrance requirements:* For master's, GRE General Test or MAT (MME), university entrance exam, appropriate bachelor's degree, audition, official transcript; for SCCT, GRE General Test or MAT, interview, master's degree, official transcript. Additional exam requirements/recommendations for international students: Required—TOEFL (minimum score 213 computer-based). *Application deadline:* Applications are processed on a rolling basis. Application fee: $30 ($40 for international students). Electronic applications accepted. *Expenses:* Tuition, state resident: full-time $3,528; part-time $196 per hour. Tuition, nonresident: full-time $8,928; part-time $496 per hour. Required fees: $842; $44 per hour. $25 per term. Tuition and fees vary according to course load and program. *Financial support:* Teaching assistantships, scholarships/grants and unspecified assistantships available. Financial award application deadline: 7/1; financial award applicants required to submit FAFSA. *Faculty research:* Classical period sacred choral music, film music, music theory, musical theatre, music business. *Unit head:* Dr. Tom O'Connor, Chair, 870-972-2094, Fax: 870-972-3932, E-mail: toconnor@astate.edu.

Austin Peay State University, College of Graduate Studies, College of Arts and Letters, Department of Music, Clarksville, TN 37044. Offers music education (M Mu); performance (M Mu). *Accreditation:* NASM. Part-time programs available. *Faculty:* 11 full-time (5 women), 1 (woman) part-time/adjunct. *Students:* 10 full-time (6 women), 9 part-time (4 women); includes 4 minority (3 African Americans, 1 Asian American or Pacific Islander), 1 international. Average age 28. In 2007, 9 degrees awarded. *Degree requirements:* For master's, comprehensive exam, thesis optional. *Entrance requirements:* For master's, GRE General Test, diagnostic exams, audition. Additional exam requirements/recommendations for international students: Required—TOEFL (minimum score 500 paper-based; 173 computer-based). *Application deadline:* For fall admission, 7/31 priority date for domestic students; for spring admission, 12/17 priority date for domestic students. Applications are processed on a rolling basis. Application fee: $25. Electronic applications accepted. *Expenses:* Tuition, state resident: full-time $5,446; part-time $288 per credit hour. Tuition, nonresident: full-time $15,722; part-time $734 per credit hour. Required fees: $1,180. Part-time tuition and fees vary according to course load. *Financial support:* In 2007–08, research assistantships (averaging $10,368 per year); career-related internships or fieldwork, Federal Work-Study, institutionally sponsored loans, scholarships/grants, and unspecified assistantships also available. Support available to part-time students. Financial award application deadline: 3/1; financial award applicants required to submit FAFSA. *Faculty research:* American sacred music, Cecilian music, hypermedia instructional systems, Chinese music, baroque guitar. *Unit head:* Dr. Gail M. Robinson-Oturu, Chair, 931-221-7818, Fax: 931-221-7529, E-mail: oturug@apsu.edu.

Azusa Pacific University, School of Music, Azusa, CA 91702-7000. Offers education (M Mus); performance (M Mus). *Accreditation:* NASM. Part-time and evening/weekend programs available. *Degree requirements:* For master's, recital. *Entrance requirements:* For master's, interview, audition. Additional exam requirements/recommendations for international students: Required—TOEFL (minimum score 550 paper-based). *Faculty research:* Tribal music of northeast India, rare Motown recordings in England.

Baptist Theological Seminary at Richmond, Graduate and Professional Program, Richmond, VA 23227. Offers children and family ministry (M Div); Christian education (M Div); church music (M Div); theology (D Min); youth and student ministry (M Div); M Div/MS; M Div/MSW. *Accreditation:* ATS. Part-time programs available. Postbaccalaureate distance learning degree programs offered (minimal on-campus study). *Faculty:* 14 full-time (6 women), 8 part-time/adjunct (1 woman). *Students:* 117 full-time (64 women), 17 part-time (7 women); includes 10 minority (6 African Americans, 1 Asian American or Pacific Islander, 3 Hispanic Americans), 1 international. Average age 46. In 2007, 37 first professional degrees, 6 doctorates awarded. *Median time to degree:* Of those who began their doctoral program in fall 1999, 92% received their degree in 8 years or less. *Degree requirements:* For doctorate, one foreign language, comprehensive exam, thesis/dissertation, field study, independent study; for M Div, one foreign language, comprehensive exam (for some programs), thesis/dissertation optional, mission immersion experience, internship. *Entrance requirements:* For doctorate, MAT, M Div, 3 years of full-time ministry experience. Additional exam requirements/recommendations for international students: Required—TOEFL (minimum score 481 paper-based; 213 computer-based). *Application deadline:* For fall admission, 8/1 priority date for domestic students, 5/1 priority date for international students; for winter admission, 12/1 priority date for domestic students, 9/1 priority date for international students; for spring admission, 1/1 priority date for domestic students, 10/1 priority date for international students. Applications are processed on a rolling basis. Application fee: $35. *Expenses:* Tuition: Full-time $7,500; part-time $750 per credit. Required fees: $45 per term. Full-time tuition and fees vary according to degree level. *Financial support:* In 2007–08, 98 students received support, including 16 teaching assistantships (averaging $1,300 per year); scholarships/grants and tuition waivers (partial) also available. Financial award application deadline: 2/1. *Faculty research:* New Testament studies, Old Testament studies, pastoral care, church history, theology. *Unit head:* Dr. Ronald W. Crawford, President, 804-355-8135, Fax: 804-355-8182. *Application contact:* Director of Admissions, 804-355-8135, Fax: 804-355-8182.

Bard College, Conservatory of Music, The Conductors Institute, Annandale-on-Hudson, NY 12504. Offers MFA. *Faculty:* 1 full-time (0 women), 5 part-time/adjunct (0 women). *Students:* 6 full-time (1 woman). 10 applicants, 70% accepted, 6 enrolled. In 2007, 2 degrees awarded. *Entrance requirements:* For master's, resumé, 3 letters of recommendation. Application fee: $30. *Unit head:* Harold Farberman, Artistic Director, 845-758-7425, E-mail: ci@bard.edu. *Application contact:* Huie McEvoy, Manager of Music Programs/Administrative Director, 845-758-7425, E-mail: ci@bard.edu.

Bard College, Conservatory of Music, Graduate Program in Vocal Arts, Annandale-on-Hudson, NY 12504. Offers MM. *Faculty:* 1 (woman) full-time, 6 part-time/adjunct (4 women). *Students:* 14 full-time (10 women). *Entrance requirements:* For master's, statement of interest, portfolio, 3 letters of recommendation, headshot, repertoire list. *Application deadline:* For fall admission, 2/1 for domestic and international students. Application fee: $50. *Financial support:* Application deadline: 3/14. *Unit head:* Dawn Upshaw, Artistic Director, 845-758-7131, E-mail: vap@bard.edu. *Application contact:* Nathan Madson, Coordinator of Conservatory Admissions, 845-758-7131, E-mail: vap@bard.edu.

Baylor University, Graduate School, School of Music, Waco, TX 76798. Offers church music (MM); collaborative piano (MM); composition (MM); conducting (MM); music history and literature (MM); music theory (MM); performance (MM); piano pedagogy and performance (MM); M Div/MM. *Accreditation:* NASM. *Students:* 12 full-time (7 women), 41 part-time (16 women); includes 4 minority (1 American Indian/Alaska Native, 3 Hispanic Americans), 8 international. In 2007, 20 degrees awarded. *Degree requirements:* For master's, variable foreign language requirement, thesis (for some programs). *Entrance requirements:* For master's, GRE General Test. *Application deadline:* For fall admission, 8/1 for domestic students; for spring admission, 12/1 for domestic students. Applications are processed on a rolling basis. Application fee: $25. *Financial support:* In 2007–08, 43 teaching assistantships with full tuition reimbursements (averaging $5,990 per year) were awarded; Federal Work-Study and institutionally sponsored loans also available. *Unit head:* Dr. Harry Elzinga, Graduate Program Director, 254-710-1161, Fax: 254-710-1191, E-mail: harry_elzinga@baylor.edu. *Application contact:* Suzanne Keener, Administrative Assistant, 254-710-3588, Fax: 254-710-3870.

Belmont University, College of Visual and Performing Arts, School of Music, Nashville, TN 37212-3757. Offers church music (MM); composition (MM); music education (MM); pedagogy (MM); performance (MM). *Accreditation:* NASM. Part-time programs available. *Faculty:* 24 full-time (7 women), 16 part-time/adjunct (8 women). *Students:* 14 full-time (9 women), 38 part-time (20 women); includes 5 minority (2 African Americans, 1 Asian American or Pacific Islander, 2 Hispanic Americans). Average age 28. 19 applicants, 89% accepted, 13 enrolled. In 2007, 17 degrees awarded. *Degree requirements:* For master's, comprehensive exam, thesis (for some programs). *Entrance requirements:* For master's, placement exam, GRE or MAT, audition, interview, minimum GPA of 2.75. Additional exam requirements/recommendations for international students: Required—TOEFL (minimum score 500 paper-based; 173 computer-based). *Application deadline:* For fall admission, 5/1 priority date for domestic students, 5/1 for international students; for spring admission, 11/1 priority date for domestic students, 11/1 for international students. Applications are processed on a rolling basis. Application fee: $50. Electronic applications accepted. *Expenses:* Tuition: Part-time $775 per credit hour. Required fees: $135 per semester. *Financial support:* In 2007–08, 33 fellowships (averaging $1,000 per year), 5 teaching assistantships (averaging $2,000 per year) were awarded; career-related internships or fieldwork, scholarships/grants, and unspecified assistantships also available. Financial award application deadline: 3/1; financial award applicants required to submit FAFSA. *Unit head:* Dr. Robert Gregg, Director, 615-460-8111, Fax: 615-386-0239, E-mail: greggr@mail.belmont.edu. *Application contact:* Russ Cornwall, Graduate Secretary, 615-460-8117, Fax: 615-386-0239, E-mail: cornwallr@mail.belmont.edu.

Bennington College, Graduate Programs, Program in Music, Bennington, VT 05201. Offers MFA. Part-time programs available. *Faculty:* 5 full-time (1 woman), 5 part-time/adjunct (2 women). *Students:* 1 (woman) full-time, 1 part-time, 1 international. Average age 32. 6 applicants, 17% accepted, 1 enrolled. In 2007, 1 degree awarded. *Degree requirements:* For master's, thesis, concert performances. *Application deadline:* For fall admission, 2/1 for domestic students. Application fee: $60. *Expenses:* Tuition: Full-time $20,640; part-time $2,890 per course. One-time fee: $75 full-time. Tuition and fees vary according to program. *Financial support:* In 2007–08, 2 students received support, including 2 teaching assistantships. Financial award application deadline: 4/1; financial award applicants required to submit FAFSA. *Unit head:* Allen Shawn, Director, 802-440-4525, E-mail: ashawn@bennington.edu. *Application contact:* Ken Himmelman, Dean of Admissions and Financial Aid, 802-440-4312, Fax: 802-440-4320, E-mail: admissions@bennington.edu.

Birmingham-Southern College, Program in Music, Birmingham, AL 35254. Offers MM. *Accreditation:* NASM.

Bob Jones University, Graduate Programs, Greenville, SC 29614. Offers accountancy (MS); Bible (MA); Bible translation (MA); Biblical studies (Certificate); broadcast management (MS); business administration (MBA); church history (MA, PhD); church ministries (MA); church music (MM); cinema and video production (MA); counseling (MS); curriculum and instruction (Ed D); divinity (M Div); dramatic production (MA); educational leadership (MS, Ed D, Ed S); elementary education (M Ed, MAT); English (M Ed, MA, MAT); fine arts (MA); graphic design (MA); history (M Ed, MA); illustration (MA); interpretative speech (MA); mathematics (M Ed, MAT); medical missions (Certificate); ministry (MM, D Min); multi-categorical special education (M Ed, MAT); music (M Ed); New Testament interpretation (PhD); Old Testament interpretation (PhD); orchestral instrument performance (MM); organ performance (MM); pastoral studies (MA); personnel services (MS, Ed S); piano pedagogy (MM); piano performance (MM); platform arts (MA); radio and television broadcasting (MS); rhetoric and public address (MA); secondary education (M Ed); studio art (MA); teaching Bible (MA); theology (MA, PhD); voice performance (MM); youth ministries (MA); M Div/MM.

Boise State University, Graduate College, College of Arts and Sciences, Department of Music, Boise, ID 83725-0399. Offers music (MM); music education (MM); pedagogy (MM); performance (MM). *Accreditation:* NASM. Part-time programs available. *Degree requirements:* For master's, thesis optional. *Entrance requirements:* For master's, minimum GPA of 3.0, performance demonstration. Electronic applications accepted.

The Boston Conservatory, Graduate Division, Music Division, Boston, MA 02215. Offers music (MM, ADP, Certificate); music education (MM). Part-time programs available. *Faculty:* 19 full-time (8 women), 39 part-time/adjunct (16 women). *Students:* 128 full-time (82 women), 9 part-time (6 women); includes 22 Asian Americans or Pacific Islanders, 3 Hispanic Americans. Average age 27. 268 applicants, 57% accepted, 53 enrolled. In 2007, 62 master's, 8 ADPs awarded. *Degree requirements:* For master's, thesis (for some programs), recital; for other advanced degree, recital. *Entrance requirements:* For master's and other advanced degree, audition. *Application deadline:* For fall admission, 12/1 for domestic and international students; for spring admission, 11/1 for domestic and international students. Application fee: $100. Electronic applications accepted. *Expenses:* Tuition: Full-time $26,700; part-time $1,170 per credit hour. Required fees: $110; $60 per year. *Financial support:* In 2007–08, 88 students received support. Federal Work-Study, institutionally sponsored loans, scholarships/grants, and work assistantships available. Financial award application deadline: 12/1; financial award applicants required to submit FAFSA. *Unit head:* Dr. Karl Paulnack, Division Director, 617-912-9124, E-mail: kpaulnack@bostonconservatory.edu. *Application contact:* Director of Admissions, 617-912-9153, Fax: 617-912-9101, E-mail: admissions@bostonconservatory.edu.

Boston University, College of Fine Arts, School of Music, Boston, MA 02215. Offers collaborative piano (MM, DMA); composition (MM, DMA); conducting (MM, Artist Diploma, Performance Diploma); historical performance (MM, DMA, Artist Diploma, Performance Diploma); music education (MM, DMA); music theory (MM); musicology (MM); opera performance (Certificate); performance (MM, DMA, Artist Diploma, Performance Diploma). *Accreditation:* NASM. Part-time programs available. *Faculty:* 36 full-time, 21 part-time/adjunct. *Students:* 275 full-time (178 women), 6 part-time (4 women); includes 25 minority (7 African Americans, 2 American Indian/Alaska Native, 12 Asian Americans or Pacific Islanders, 4 Hispanic Americans), 105 international. Average age 29. 632 applicants, 48% accepted, 110 enrolled. In 2007, 61 master's, 11 doctorates, 14 Artist Diplomas awarded. *Degree requirements:* For master's, thesis; for doctorate, 2 foreign languages, thesis/dissertation. *Entrance requirements:* Additional exam requirements/recommendations for international students: Required—TOEFL. *Application deadline:* For fall admission, 1/15 priority date for domestic and international students. Application fee: $60. Electronic applications accepted. *Expenses:* Tuition: Full-time $34,930; part-time $1,092 per credit. Tuition and fees vary according to class time, course level and program. *Financial support:* Fellowships, teaching assistantships available. Financial award application deadline: 1/15. *Unit head:* Andre de Quadros, Director, 617-353-8789, Fax:

617-353-7455, E-mail: jfilippi@bu.edu. *Application contact:* Mark Krone, Manager, Graduate Admissions, E-mail: arts@bu.edu.

See Close-Up on page 345.

Boston University, Graduate School of Arts and Sciences, Department of Music, Boston, MA 02215. Offers composition (MA); music education (MA); music history/theory (PhD); musicology (MA, PhD). *Accreditation:* NASM. *Students:* 2 full-time (1 woman). Average age 31. 13 applicants, 38% accepted, 0 enrolled. In 2007, 1 degree awarded. *Degree requirements:* For master's, 2 foreign languages, comprehensive exam, thesis; for doctorate, 2 foreign languages, comprehensive exam, thesis/dissertation. *Entrance requirements:* For master's and doctorate, GRE General Test, musical composition or research paper, 3 letters of recommendation. Additional exam requirements/recommendations for international students: Required—TOEFL (minimum score 550 paper-based; 213 computer-based). *Application deadline:* For fall admission, 3/15 for domestic and international students; for spring admission, 10/15 for domestic and international students. Application fee: $70. *Expenses:* Tuition: Full-time $34,930; part-time $1,092 per credit. Tuition and fees vary according to class time, course level and program. *Financial support:* Federal Work-Study, scholarships/grants, and unspecified assistantships available. Support available to part-time students. Financial award application deadline: 1/15; financial award applicants required to submit FAFSA. *Unit head:* Victor Coelho, Director, 617-358-4412, Fax: 617-353-7455, E-mail: blues@bu.edu. *Application contact:* Student Contact, 617-353-8789, Fax: 617-353-7455.

Bowling Green State University, Graduate College, College of Musical Arts, Bowling Green, OH 43403. Offers composition (MM); contemporary music (DMA), including composition, performance; ethnomusicology (MM); music education (MM), including choral, comprehensive, instrumental; music history (MM); music theory (MM); performance (MM). *Accreditation:* NASM. Part-time programs available. *Faculty:* 54 full-time (21 women), 20 part-time/adjunct (8 women). *Students:* 100 full-time (56 women), 12 part-time (5 women); includes 7 minority (3 African Americans, 1 American Indian/Alaska Native, 1 Asian American or Pacific Islander, 2 Hispanic Americans), 29 international. Average age 26. 184 applicants, 39% accepted, 46 enrolled. In 2007, 62 degrees awarded. *Degree requirements:* For master's, thesis or alternative, recitals; for doctorate, comprehensive exam, thesis/dissertation. *Entrance requirements:* For master's, GRE General Test, diagnostic placement exams in music history and theory, audition, interview. Additional exam requirements/recommendations for international students: Required—TOEFL. *Application deadline:* For fall admission, 3/1 priority date for domestic students. Application fee: $30. Electronic applications accepted. *Financial support:* In 2007–08, 16 research assistantships with full tuition reimbursements (averaging $5,614 per year), 70 teaching assistantships with full tuition reimbursements (averaging $5,771 per year) were awarded; career-related internships or fieldwork, Federal Work-Study, and unspecified assistantships also available. Financial award applicants required to submit FAFSA. *Faculty research:* Ethnomusicology. *Unit head:* Dr. Richard Kennell, Dean, 419-372-2188. *Application contact:* Dr. Robert Satterlee, Graduate Coordinator, 419-372-2360.

Brandeis University, Graduate School of Arts and Sciences, Department of Music, Waltham, MA 02454-9110. Offers composition and theory (MA, MFA, PhD); music and women's studies (MA); musicology (MA, MFA, PhD). Part-time programs available. *Faculty:* 9 full-time (1 woman), 7 part-time/adjunct (3 women). *Students:* 41 full-time (18 women); includes 2 minority (both Hispanic Americans), 4 international. Average age 28. 66 applicants, 23% accepted, 9 enrolled. In 2007, 8 master's, 2 doctorates awarded. Terminal master's awarded for partial completion of doctoral program. *Degree requirements:* For master's, one foreign language, thesis or alternative; for doctorate, 2 foreign languages, comprehensive exam, thesis/dissertation. *Entrance requirements:* For master's, GRE General Test (musicology), resumé, sample of work (music composition), letters of recommendation; for doctorate, GRE General Test (musicology), resumé, writing sample (musicology), letters of recommendation, sample of work—recording (composition). Additional exam requirements/recommendations for international students: Required—TOEFL (minimum score 600 paper-based; 250 computer-based; 100 iBT), IELTS (minimum score 7). *Application deadline:* For fall admission, 1/31 for domestic and international students. Application fee: $55. Electronic applications accepted. *Financial support:* In 2007–08, 25 students received support, including 23 fellowships with full tuition reimbursements available (averaging $17,000 per year), 2 teaching assistantships with tuition reimbursements available (averaging $3,000 per year); research assistantships, scholarships/grants, health care benefits, and tuition waivers (full and partial) also available. Support available to part-time students. Financial award application deadline: 4/15; financial award applicants required to submit CSS PROFILE or FAFSA. *Faculty research:* History of theory; music of Monteverdi, Bach, Mozart, Lizst, and Wagner; compositional process; computer music. *Unit head:* Mary Ruth Ray, Chair, 781-736-3314. *Application contact:* Mark Kagan, Senior Academic Administrator, 781-736-3311, E-mail: kagan@brandeis.edu.

Brandon University, School of Music, Brandon, MB R7A 6A9, Canada. Offers composition (M Mus); music education (M Mus); performance and literature (M Mus), including piano, strings. Part-time programs available. *Faculty:* 8 full-time (4 women). *Students:* 8 full-time (4 women), 1 part-time, 2 international. Average age 25. 7 applicants, 100% accepted. In 2007, 2 degrees awarded. *Degree requirements:* For master's, comprehensive exam (for some programs), thesis (for some programs). *Entrance requirements:* For master's, B Mus. Additional exam requirements/recommendations for international students: Required—TOEFL (580 paper-based; 237 computer-based) or IELTS. *Application deadline:* For spring admission, 5/1 priority date for domestic students. Applications are processed on a rolling basis. Application fee: $60 ($125 for international students). Electronic applications accepted. *Financial support:* In 2007–08, 4 students received support, including 1 research assistantship, 3 teaching assistantships (averaging $3,250 per year). Financial award application deadline: 5/1. *Faculty research:* Philosophy of music. *Unit head:* Dr. Michael Kim, Dean, 204-727-9633, Fax: 204-728-6839, E-mail: kimm@brandonu.ca. *Application contact:* Dr. Sheila Scott, Joint Chair of Graduate Music Department, 204-727-7435, Fax: 204-728-6839.

Brigham Young University, Graduate Studies, College of Fine Arts and Communications, School of Music, Provo, UT 84602-1001. Offers composition (MM); conducting (MM); music education (MA, MM); musicology (MA); performance (MM). *Accreditation:* NASM. *Faculty:* 47 full-time (9 women), 3 part-time/adjunct (1 woman). *Students:* 57 full-time (31 women), 13 part-time (5 women); includes 4 minority (all Asian Americans or Pacific Islanders) Average age 30. 65 applicants, 48% accepted, 26 enrolled. In 2007, 22 degrees awarded. *Degree requirements:* For master's, comprehensive exam (for some programs), thesis (for some programs), recital, project or composition (for some programs). *Entrance requirements:* For master's, graduate placement exam, minimum GPA of 3.0 in last 60 hours, bachelor of music degree. Additional exam requirements/recommendations for international students: Required—TOEFL (minimum score 580 paper-based; 237 computer-based), IELTS. *Application deadline:* For fall admission, 2/1 priority date for domestic students, 1/1 priority date for international students. Application fee: $50. Electronic applications accepted. *Financial support:* In 2007–08, 60 students received support, including 37 teaching assistantships (averaging $5,000 per year); research assistantships, career-related internships or fieldwork, institutionally sponsored loans, scholarships/grants, tuition waivers (partial), and unspecified assistantships also available. Support available to part-time students. Financial award application deadline: 2/1; financial award applicants required to submit FAFSA. *Faculty research:* Pergolesi, Louis Armstrong, NY Art School, rock and roll, beauty and the voice. *Unit head:* Dr. Dale E. Monson, Director, 801-422-6304, Fax: 801-422-0533, E-mail: dale_monson@byu.edu. *Application contact:* Dr. Thomas L. Durham, Graduate Coordinator, 801-422-3226, Fax: 801-422-0533, E-mail: thomas_durham@byu.edu.

Brooklyn College of the City University of New York, Division of Graduate Studies, Conservatory of Music, Brooklyn, NY 11210-2889. Offers composition (MM); music (DMA, PhD); music education (MA); musicology (MA); performance (MM); performance practice (MA). The department offers courses at Brooklyn College that are creditable toward the CUNY doctoral degree (with permission of the executive officer of the doctoral program). Part-time programs available. *Students:* 1 full-time (0 women), 66 part-time (38 women); includes 10 minority (4 African Americans, 1 Asian American or Pacific Islander, 5 Hispanic Americans), 26 international. 65 applicants, 78% accepted, 29 enrolled. In 2007, 24 degrees awarded. *Degree requirements:* For master's, one foreign language, comprehensive exam, thesis. *Entrance requirements:* For master's, 36 credits in music, audition, completed composition, writing sample, placement exam. Additional exam requirements/recommendations for international students: Required—TOEFL. *Application deadline:* For fall admission, 3/1 priority date for domestic students, 2/1 priority date for international students; for spring admission, 11/1 priority date for domestic students, 10/1 priority date for international students. Applications are processed on a rolling basis. Application fee: $125. Electronic applications accepted. *Financial support:* Career-related internships or fieldwork, Federal Work-Study, institutionally sponsored loans, and scholarships/grants available. Support available to part-time students. Financial award application deadline: 5/1; financial award applicants required to submit FAFSA. *Faculty research:* American music, computer music. *Unit head:* Dr. Bruce MacIntyre, Chairperson, 718-951-5286, E-mail: brucem@brooklyn.cuny.edu. *Application contact:* Hernan Sierra, Graduate Admissions Coordinator, 718-951-4536, Fax: 718-951-4506, E-mail: grads@brooklyn.cuny.edu.

Brooklyn College of the City University of New York, Division of Graduate Studies, Program in Performance and Interactive Media Arts, Brooklyn, NY 11210-2889. Offers MFA, CAS. *Students:* 9 full-time (6 women), 8 part-time (2 women); includes 7 minority (3 African Americans, 1 Asian American or Pacific Islander, 3 Hispanic Americans). 25 applicants, 76% accepted, 10 enrolled. In 2007, 3 degrees awarded. *Entrance requirements:* For master's, 2 letters of recommendation, resumé, portfolio, interview; for CAS, 2 letters of recommendation. *Application deadline:* For fall admission, 3/1 priority date for domestic students, 2/1 priority date for international students; for spring admission, 11/1 priority date for domestic students, 10/1 priority date for international students. Applications are processed on a rolling basis. Application fee: $125. Electronic applications accepted. *Financial support:* Application deadline: 5/1. *Unit head:* Dr. John Jannone, Director, E-mail: jannone brooklyn.cuny.edu. *Application contact:* Hernan Sierra, Graduate Admissions Coordinator, 718-951-4536, Fax: 718-951-4506, E-mail: grads@brooklyn.cuny.edu.

Brown University, Graduate School, Department of Music, Providence, RI 02912. Offers AM, PhD. *Degree requirements:* For master's, one foreign language, thesis or alternative, departmental qualifying exam; for doctorate, 2 foreign languages, comprehensive exam, thesis/dissertation, departmental qualifying exam. *Entrance requirements:* For master's and doctorate, GRE General Test. *Faculty research:* Ethnomusicology.

Butler University, Jordan College of Fine Arts, Department of Music, Indianapolis, IN 46208-3485. Offers composition (MM); conducting (MM); music (MM); music education (MM); music history (MM); organ (MM); performance (MM). *Accreditation:* NASM. Part-time and evening/weekend programs available. *Faculty:* 21 full-time (6 women), 11 part-time/adjunct (4 women). *Students:* 8 full-time (3 women), 28 part-time (11 women); includes 3 minority (1 Asian American or Pacific Islander, 2 Hispanic Americans), 3 international. Average age 28. 21 applicants, 95% accepted, 11 enrolled. In 2007, 14 degrees awarded. *Degree requirements:* For master's, thesis (for some programs). *Entrance requirements:* For master's, GRE General Test, GRE Subject Test, audition, interview. *Application deadline:* For fall admission, 8/15 priority date for domestic students. Applications are processed on a rolling basis. Application fee: $35. Electronic applications accepted. *Expenses:* Tuition: Full-time $6,300; part-time $350 per credit. Tuition and fees vary according to program. *Financial support:* In 2007–08, 15 teaching assistantships with full tuition reimbursements (averaging $2,500 per year) were awarded; fellowships, career-related internships or fieldwork, institutionally sponsored loans, and scholarships/grants also available. Support available to part-time students. Financial award application deadline: 7/15; financial award applicants required to submit FAFSA. *Unit head:* Dr. Andrea Gullickson, Head, 317-940-9988, Fax: 317-940-9658, E-mail: agullick@butler.edu. *Application contact:* Kathy Lang, Admission Representative, 317-940-9646, Fax: 317-940-9658, E-mail: klang@butler.edu.

California Baptist University, Program in Music, Riverside, CA 92504-3206. Offers MM. *Accreditation:* NASM. Part-time programs available. *Faculty:* 3. *Students:* 12 full-time (9 women); includes 2 minority (1 Asian American or Pacific Islander, 1 Hispanic American), 3 international. 8 applicants, 63% accepted, 5 enrolled. In 2007, 1 degree awarded. *Degree requirements:* For master's, thesis or alternative. *Entrance requirements:* For master's, minimum undergraduate GPA of 2.75. Additional exam requirements/recommendations for international students: Required—TOEFL (minimum score 575 paper-based; 230 computer-based), IELTS (minimum score 7). *Application deadline:* For fall admission, 9/1 for domestic students, 7/1 for international students; for spring admission, 1/3 for domestic students, 10/15 for international students. Applications are processed on a rolling basis. Application fee: $45. Electronic applications accepted. *Expenses:* Tuition: Full-time $7,992; part-time $444 per semester hour. Required fees: $510; $125 per semester. *Financial support:* Federal Work-Study available. Support available to part-time students. *Unit head:* Dr. Gary Bonner, Dean, School of Music, 951-343-4251, Fax: 951-343-4570, E-mail: gbonner@calbaptist.edu. *Application contact:* Gail Ronveaux, Dean of Graduate Enrollment, 951-343-5045, Fax: 951-343-5095, E-mail: graduateadmissions@calbaptist.edu.

California Institute of the Arts, School of Music, Valencia, CA 91355-2340. Offers African music (MFA, Adv C); composition (MFA, Adv C); composition/new media (MFA, Adv C); Indonesian music (MFA, Adv C); jazz (MFA, Adv C); North Indian music (MFA, Adv C); performance (MFA, Adv C); performer/composer (MFA, Adv C); voice (MFA, Adv C); world music performance (MFA). *Accreditation:* NASM. Part-time programs available. *Degree requirements:* For master's, composition or recital. *Entrance requirements:* For master's, audition or portfolio. Additional exam requirements/recommendations for international students: Required—TOEFL. Electronic applications accepted. *Faculty research:* Music composition and twentieth century performance practice, interactive multimedia and computer music, music cognition.

California State University, Chico, Graduate School, College of Humanities and Fine Arts, Department of Music, Chico, CA 95929-0805. Offers MA. *Accreditation:* NASM. *Students:* 16 full-time (7 women), 2 part-time (1 woman); includes 3 minority (1 American Indian/Alaska Native, 1 Asian American or Pacific Islander, 1 Hispanic American), 1 international. Average age 33. 10 applicants, 70% accepted, 7 enrolled. In 2007, 7 degrees awarded. *Degree requirements:* For master's, thesis or alternative, recital. *Entrance requirements:* For master's, GRE General Test, departmental exam, audition tape (off-campus applicants), music scores (for composers), 2 letters of recommendation, statement of purpose. Additional exam requirements/recommendations for international students: Required—TOEFL (minimum score 550 paper-based; 213 computer-based; 80 iBT), IELTS (minimum score 7). *Application deadline:* For fall admission, 3/1 priority date for domestic students, 3/1 for international students; for spring admission, 9/15 priority date for domestic students, 9/15 for international students. Applications are processed on a rolling basis. Application fee: $55. Electronic applications accepted. *Financial support:* Teaching assistantships available. *Unit head:* Dr. Warren Pinckney, Graduate Coordinator, 530-898-4795.

California State University, East Bay, Academic Programs and Graduate Studies, College of Letters, Arts, and Social Sciences, Department of Music, Hayward, CA 94542-3000. Offers MA. *Accreditation:* NASM. Part-time programs available. *Faculty:* 5 full-time (1 woman), 2 part-time/adjunct (0 women). *Students:* 5 full-time (3 women), 9 part-time (4 women); includes 4 minority (2 African Americans, 1 Asian American or Pacific Islander, 1 Hispanic American), 2 international. Average age 37. 17 applicants, 82% accepted, 8 enrolled. In 2007, 5 degrees awarded. *Degree requirements:* For master's, variable foreign language requirement, comprehensive exam, project, recital, or thesis. *Entrance requirements:* For master's, minimum GPA of 3.0 in field. Additional exam requirements/recommendations for international students: Required—TOEFL (minimum score 550 paper-based; 213 computer-based). *Application deadline:* For fall admission, 5/31 for domestic students, 4/30 for international students; for winter admission, 9/30 for domestic and international students; for spring admission, 12/31 for domestic students,

Music

California State University, East Bay (continued)
11/30 for international students. Applications are processed on a rolling basis. Application fee: $55. Electronic applications accepted. *Expenses:* Required fees: $3,987; $851 per quarter. *Financial support:* Federal Work-Study and institutionally sponsored loans available. Support available to part-time students. Financial award application deadline: 3/2. *Unit head:* Dr. Frank La Rocca, Chair, 510-885-3135, E-mail: frank.larocca@csueastbay.edu. *Application contact:* My Huynh, Graduate Prospect Specialist, 510-885-2989, Fax: 510-885-4059, E-mail: my.huynh@csueastbay.edu.

California State University, Fresno, Division of Graduate Studies, College of Arts and Humanities, Department of Music, Fresno, CA 93740-8027. Offers music (MA); music education (MA); performance (MA). *Accreditation:* NASM. Part-time programs available. *Faculty:* 14 full-time (4 women). *Students:* 44; includes 11 minority (5 Asian Americans or Pacific Islanders, 6 Hispanic Americans), 2 international. Average age 28. In 2007, 5 degrees awarded. *Degree requirements:* For master's, thesis or alternative. *Entrance requirements:* For master's, GRE General Test, BA in music, minimum GPA of 3.0. Additional exam requirements/recommendations for international students: Required—TOEFL. *Application deadline:* For fall admission, 5/1 for domestic and international students; for spring admission, 10/1 for domestic and international students. Applications are processed on a rolling basis. Application fee: $55. Electronic applications accepted. *Financial support:* Teaching assistantships, career-related internships or fieldwork, Federal Work-Study, and scholarships/grants available. Support available to part-time students. Financial award application deadline: 3/1; financial award applicants required to submit FAFSA. *Faculty research:* Technology transfer, folk art. *Unit head:* Dr. Thomas Hiebert, Chair, 559-278-2654, Fax: 559-278-6800, E-mail: tomh@csufresno.edu. *Application contact:* Dr. Teresa Beaman, Graduate Program Coordinator, 559-278-2654, Fax: 559-278-6800, E-mail: teresa_beaman@csufresno.edu.

California State University, Fullerton, Graduate Studies, College of the Arts, Department of Music, Fullerton, CA 92834-9480. Offers music education (MA); music history and literature (MA); performance (MM); piano pedagogy (MA); theory-composition (MM). *Accreditation:* NASM. Part-time programs available. *Students:* 27 full-time (19 women), 35 part-time (21 women); includes 18 minority (2 African Americans, 12 Asian Americans or Pacific Islanders, 4 Hispanic Americans), 14 international. Average age 29. 74 applicants, 55% accepted, 28 enrolled. In 2007, 19 degrees awarded. *Degree requirements:* For master's, comprehensive exam, project or thesis. *Entrance requirements:* For master's, audition, major in music or related field, minimum GPA of 2.5 in last 60 units of course work. Application fee: $55. *Financial support:* Teaching assistantships, Federal Work-Study, institutionally sponsored loans, and scholarships/grants available. Support available to part-time students. Financial award application deadline: 3/1. *Unit head:* Dr. Marc Dickey, Chair, 714-278-3511. *Application contact:* Dr. Mitch Fennell, Adviser, 714-278-3511.

California State University, Long Beach, Graduate Studies, College of the Arts, Department of Dance, Long Beach, CA 90840. Offers dance (performance) (MFA). *Accreditation:* NASD. Part-time programs available. *Faculty:* 7 full-time (4 women), 27 part-time/adjunct (19 women). *Students:* 6 full-time (4 women). Average age 36. *Degree requirements:* For master's, thesis. *Application deadline:* For fall admission, 7/1 for domestic students; for spring admission, 12/1 for domestic students. Applications are processed on a rolling basis. Application fee: $5. Electronic applications accepted. *Financial support:* Federal Work-Study, institutionally sponsored loans, scholarships/grants, and traineeships available. Financial award application deadline:3/2. *Unit head:* Dr. Judy Allen, Chair, 562-985-4747, Fax: 562-985-7896, E-mail: judyalle@csulb.edu. *Application contact:* Doug Nielsen, Graduate Advisor, 562-985-7039, Fax: 562-985-7896.

California State University, Long Beach, Graduate Studies, College of the Arts, Department of Music, Long Beach, CA 90840. Offers music (MA); music (performing) (MM). *Accreditation:* NASM. Part-time programs available. *Faculty:* 19 full-time (4 women), 88 part-time/adjunct (30 women). *Students:* 29 full-time (17 women), 23 part-time (13 women); includes 17 minority (2 African Americans, 11 Asian Americans or Pacific Islanders, 4 Hispanic Americans). Average age 36. *Degree requirements:* For master's, thesis or alternative, departmental qualifying exam. *Application deadline:* For fall admission, 7/1 for domestic students; for spring admission, 12/1 for domestic students. Applications are processed on a rolling basis. Application fee: $55. Electronic applications accepted. *Financial support:* Federal Work-Study, institutionally sponsored loans, and scholarships/grants available. Financial award application deadline: 3/2. *Unit head:* John A Carnahan, Chair, 562-985-4781, Fax: 562-985-2490, E-mail: jcarnaha@csulb.edu. *Application contact:* Dr. Kristine Forney, Graduate Coordinator, 562-985-4788, Fax: 562-985-2490, E-mail: kforney@csulb.edu.

California State University, Long Beach, Graduate Studies, College of the Arts, Department of Theatre Arts, Long Beach, CA 90840. Offers theatre arts (professional performance/design) (MFA); theatre arts/drama (MA). *Accreditation:* NAST. Part-time programs available. *Faculty:* 11 full-time (5 women), 24 part-time/adjunct (12 women). *Students:* 41 full-time (25 women), 16 part-time (9 women); includes 10 minority (1 African American, 7 Asian Americans or Pacific Islanders, 2 Hispanic Americans). Average age 32. *Degree requirements:* For master's, thesis or alternative. *Application deadline:* For fall admission, 7/1 for domestic students; for spring admission, 12/1 for domestic students. Applications are processed on a rolling basis. Application fee: $55. Electronic applications accepted. *Financial support:* Research assistantships, teaching assistantships, Federal Work-Study, institutionally sponsored loans, scholarships/grants, and traineeships available. Financial award application deadline: 3/2. *Unit head:* Dr. Joanne L. Gordon, Chair, 562-985-7891, Fax: 562-985-2263, E-mail: jgordon@csulb.edu. *Application contact:* Barbara Matthews, Graduate Adviser, 562-985-4042, Fax: 562-985-2263, E-mail: jmatthew@csulb.edu.

California State University, Los Angeles, Graduate Studies, College of Arts and Letters, Department of Music, Los Angeles, CA 90032-8530. Offers music composition (MM); music education (MA); musicology (MA); performance (MM). *Accreditation:* NASM. Part-time and evening/weekend programs available. *Faculty:* 14 full-time (3 women), 3 part-time/adjunct (2 women). *Students:* 53 full-time (26 women), 44 part-time (16 women); includes 35 minority (2 African Americans, 12 Asian Americans or Pacific Islanders, 21 Hispanic Americans), 20 international. Average age 34. 16 applicants. In 2007, 20 degrees awarded. *Degree requirements:* For master's, comprehensive exam, project or thesis. *Entrance requirements:* For master's, audition. Additional exam requirements/recommendations for international students: Required—TOEFL. *Application deadline:* For fall admission, 6/30 for domestic students; for spring admission, 2/1 for domestic students. Applications are processed on a rolling basis. Application fee: $55. *Financial support:* Career-related internships or fieldwork and Federal Work-Study available. Support available to part-time students. Financial award application deadline: 3/1. *Faculty research:* Gregorian semiology, baroque opera. *Unit head:* Dr. David Connors, Chair, 323-343-4060, Fax: 323-343-4063, E-mail: david.connors@calstatela.edu.

California State University, Northridge, Graduate Studies, College of Arts, Media, and Communication, Department of Music, Northridge, CA 91330. Offers composition (MM); conducting (MM); music education (MA); performance (MM). *Accreditation:* NASM. *Faculty:* 19 full-time (5 women), 56 part-time/adjunct (17 women). *Students:* 22 full-time (10 women), 25 part-time (16 women); includes 8 minority (5 Asian Americans or Pacific Islanders, 3 Hispanic Americans), 6 international. Average age 31. 78 applicants, 47% accepted, 20 enrolled. In 2007, 14 degrees awarded. *Degree requirements:* For master's, thesis. *Entrance requirements:* For master's, audition, GRE General Test or minimum GPA of 3.0. Additional exam requirements/recommendations for international students: Required—TOEFL. *Application deadline:* For fall admission, 11/30 for domestic students. Application fee: $55. *Financial support:* Application deadline: 3/1. *Faculty research:* Touring program. *Unit head:* Dr. Ric Alviso, Chair, 816-677-2155, E-mail: ric.alviso@csun.edu. *Application contact:* John Roscigno, Graduate Advisor, 818-677-6834, E-mail: john.roscigno@csun.edu.

California State University, Sacramento, Graduate Studies, College of Arts and Letters, Department of Music, Sacramento, CA 95819-6048. Offers MM. *Accreditation:* NASM.Part-time programs available. *Students:* 22 full-time (13 women), 20 part-time (9 women); includes 8 minority (3 African Americans, 1 American Indian/Alaska Native, 3 Asian Americans or Pacific Islanders, 1 Hispanic American), 2 international. Average age 30. 39 applicants, 79% accepted, 24 enrolled. *Degree requirements:* For master's, thesis or alternative, writing proficiency exam. *Entrance requirements:* For master's, BA in music or equivalent, minimum GPA of 2.5 during previous 2 years of course work. Additional exam requirements/recommendations for international students: Required—TOEFL. *Application deadline:* Applications are processed on a rolling basis. Application fee: $55. Electronic applications accepted. *Expenses:* Tuition, state resident: full-time $3,414. Tuition, nonresident: full-time $13,584; part-time $339 per unit. Required fees: $786; $393 per semester. *Financial support:* Research assistantships, teaching assistantships, career-related internships or fieldwork and Federal Work-Study available. Support available to part-time students. Financial award application deadline: 3/1. *Unit head:* Dr. Ernie Hills, Chair, 916-278-7488, Fax: 916-278-4588.

Campbellsville University, School of Music, Campbellsville, KY 42718-2799. Offers church music (MM); music (MA); music education (MM). *Accreditation:* NASM. Part-time programs available. *Degree requirements:* For master's, thesis (for some programs), paper or recital. *Entrance requirements:* For master's, GRE General Test or PRAXIS, minimum GPA of 2.75. Additional exam requirements/recommendations for international students: Required—TOEFL (minimum score 550 paper-based). Electronic applications accepted.

Capital University, Conservatory of Music, Columbus, OH 43209-2394. Offers music education (MM), including instrumental emphasis, Kodály emphasis. Program offered only in summer. *Accreditation:* NASM. Part-time programs available. *Degree requirements:* For master's, comprehensive exam, thesis or alternative, chamber performance exam. *Entrance requirements:* For master's, music theory exam, minimum undergraduate GPA of 3.0. Additional exam requirements/recommendations for international students: Required—TOEFL (minimum score 550 paper-based; 213 computer-based; 80 iBT). Electronic applications accepted. Expenses: Contact institution. *Faculty research:* Folk song research, Kodály method, performance, composition.

Cardinal Stritch University, College of Arts and Sciences, Music Department, Milwaukee, WI 53217-3985. Offers piano (MM). Part-time programs available. *Degree requirements:* For master's, comprehensive exam, recital permission audition. *Entrance requirements:* For master's, placement test in music theory and music history, 3 letters of recommendation, audition. Electronic applications accepted.

Carleton University, Faculty of Graduate Studies, Faculty of Arts and Social Sciences, School for Studies in Art and Culture, Program in Music and Culture, Ottawa, ON K1S 5B6, Canada. Offers MA. Application fee: $77. *Unit head:* James Deaville, Graduate Supervisor, 613-520-2600, Fax: 613-520-3575, E-mail: ssac@carleton.ca.

Carnegie Mellon University, College of Fine Arts, School of Music, Pittsburgh, PA 15213-3891. Offers composition (MM); conducting (MM); music education (MM); performance (MM). *Accreditation:* NASM. Part-time programs available. *Degree requirements:* For master's, comprehensive exam, recital. *Entrance requirements:* For master's, audition. *Faculty research:* Computer music, music history.

Case Western Reserve University, School of Graduate Studies, Department of Music, Cleveland, OH 44106. Offers early music (MA, D Mus A); music education (MA, PhD); music history (MA); musicology (PhD). *Accreditation:* NASM (one or more programs are accredited). *Faculty:* 12 full-time (4 women), 13 part-time/adjunct (4 women). *Students:* 21 full-time (9 women), 7 part-time (2 women); includes 1 minority (Asian American or Pacific Islander) Average age 29. 23 applicants, 61% accepted, 9 enrolled. In 2007, 5 master's, 3 doctorates awarded. *Degree requirements:* For doctorate, thesis/dissertation. *Entrance requirements:* For master's, audition. Additional exam requirements/recommendations for international students: Required—TOEFL. *Application deadline:* For fall admission, 1/15 for domestic students. Application fee: $50. Electronic applications accepted. *Financial support:* Fellowships, research assistantships, teaching assistantships, career-related internships or fieldwork and tuition waivers (full) available. Financial award application deadline: 1/15; financial award applicants required to submit FAFSA. *Faculty research:* Early music performance practices; sixteenth-, seventeenth-, and twentieth-centuries; Mahler; wind ensemble direction; measurement/evaluation in music education. *Unit head:* Ross Duffin, Acting Chair, 216-368-2412, Fax: 216-368-6557, E-mail: ross.duffin@case.edu. *Application contact:* Laura Stauffer, Admissions, 216-368-2400, Fax: 216-368-6557, E-mail: laura.stauffer@case.edu.

The Catholic University of America, The Benjamin T. Rome School of Music, Program in Composition, Washington, DC 20064. Offers MM, DMA. *Accreditation:* NASM. Part-time programs available. *Students:* 5 full-time (0 women), 3 part-time (1 woman); includes 3 minority (1 African American, 1 Asian American or Pacific Islander, 1 Hispanic American). Average age 31. 10 applicants, 50% accepted, 2 enrolled. In 2007, 1 degree awarded. *Degree requirements:* For master's, composition; for doctorate, compositions, lecture-recital. *Entrance requirements:* For master's, theory placement test, 2 letters of recommendation, original compositions; for doctorate, school qualifying exams, 2 letters of recommendation, original compositions. Additional exam requirements/recommendations for international students: Required—TOEFL (minimum score 580 paper-based; 237 computer-based). *Application deadline:* For fall admission, 2/1 priority date for domestic students; for spring admission, 11/15 priority date for domestic students. Applications are processed on a rolling basis. Application fee: $55. Electronic applications accepted. *Financial support:* Career-related internships or fieldwork, Federal Work-Study, scholarships/grants, tuition waivers (full and partial), and unspecified assistantships available. Support available to part-time students. Financial award application deadline: 2/1; financial award applicants required to submit FAFSA. *Application contact:* Christine Mica, Director, University Admissions, 202-319-5305, Fax: 202-319-6533, E-mail: cua-admissions@cua.edu.

The Catholic University of America, The Benjamin T. Rome School of Music, Program in Conducting, Washington, DC 20064. Offers instrumental conducting (MM, DMA). *Accreditation:* NASM. Part-time programs available. *Students:* 1 full-time (0 women), 1 international. Average age 32. *Degree requirements:* For master's, recital; for doctorate, one foreign language, lecture-recital, recitals. *Entrance requirements:* For master's, theory placement test, audition, recital, interview, 2 letters of recommendation; for doctorate, school qualifying exams, recital, 2 letters of recommendation, experience record, critical reviews. Additional exam requirements/recommendations for international students: Required—TOEFL (minimum score 580 paper-based; 237 computer-based). *Application deadline:* For fall admission, 2/1 priority date for domestic students; for spring admission, 11/15 priority date for domestic students. Applications are processed on a rolling basis. Application fee: $55. Electronic applications accepted. *Financial support:* Career-related internships or fieldwork, Federal Work-Study, scholarships/grants, tuition waivers (full and partial), and unspecified assistantships available. Support available to part-time students. Financial award application deadline: 2/1; financial award applicants required to submit FAFSA. *Application contact:* Christine Mica, Director, University Admissions, 202-319-5305, Fax: 202-319-6533, E-mail: cua-admissions@cua.edu.

The Catholic University of America, The Benjamin T. Rome School of Music, Program in Musicology, Washington, DC 20064. Offers MA, PhD, MSLS/MA. *Accreditation:* NASM.Part-time programs available. *Students:* 6 full-time (5 women), 13 part-time (8 women); includes 2 minority (both African Americans), 1 international. Average age 34. 8 applicants, 75% accepted, 4 enrolled. *Degree requirements:* For master's, one foreign language, comprehensive exam, thesis; for doctorate, 2 foreign languages, comprehensive exam, thesis/dissertation. *Entrance requirements:* For master's and doctorate, theory placement test, research paper, 2 letters of recommendation. Additional exam requirements/recommendations for international students: Required—TOEFL (minimum score 580 paper-based; 237 computer-based). *Application deadline:* For fall admission, 2/1 priority date for domestic students; for spring admission,

11/15 priority date for domestic students. Applications are processed on a rolling basis. Application fee: $55. Electronic applications accepted. *Financial support:* Career-related internships or fieldwork, Federal Work-Study, scholarships/grants, tuition waivers (full and partial), and unspecified assistantships available. Support available to part-time students. Financial award application deadline: 2/1; financial award applicants required to submit FAFSA. *Application contact:* Christine Mica, Director, University Admissions, 202-319-5305, Fax: 202-319-6533, E-mail: cua-admissions@cua.edu.

The Catholic University of America, The Benjamin T. Rome School of Music, Program in Orchestral Instruments, Washington, DC 20064. Offers MM, DMA. *Accreditation:* NASM.Part-time programs available. *Students:* 15 full-time (13 women), 14 part-time (5 women); includes 3 minority (2 Asian Americans or Pacific Islanders, 1 Hispanic American), 8 international. Average age 31. 20 applicants, 65% accepted, 7 enrolled. In 2007, 3 master's, 6 doctorates awarded. *Degree requirements:* For master's, recital; for doctorate, lecture-recital, recitals. *Entrance requirements:* For master's, theory placement test, audition, recital, 2 letters of recommendation; for doctorate, school qualifying exams, recital, 2 letters of recommendation, experience record, critical reviews. Additional exam requirements/recommendations for international students: Required—TOEFL (minimum score 580 paper-based; 237 computer-based). *Application deadline:* For fall admission, 2/1 priority date for domestic students; for spring admission, 11/15 priority date for domestic students. Applications are processed on a rolling basis. Application fee: $55. Electronic applications accepted. *Financial support:* Career-related internships or fieldwork, Federal Work-Study, scholarships/grants, tuition waivers (full and partial), and unspecified assistantships available. Support available to part-time students. Financial award application deadline: 2/1; financial award applicants required to submit FAFSA. *Application contact:* Christine Mica, Director, University Admissions, 202-319-5305, Fax: 202-319-6533, E-mail: cua-admissions@cua.edu.

The Catholic University of America, The Benjamin T. Rome School of Music, Program in Piano, Washington, DC 20064. Offers accompanying and chamber music (MM); chamber music (DMA); performance (MM, DMA); piano pedagogy (MM, DMA); vocal accompanying (DMA). *Accreditation:* NASM. Part-time programs available. *Students:* 5 full-time (all women), 19 part-time (17 women); includes 7 minority (2 African Americans, 5 Asian Americans or Pacific Islanders), 12 international. Average age 34. 18 applicants, 56% accepted, 3 enrolled. In 2007, 1 master's, 1 doctorate awarded. *Degree requirements:* For master's, variable foreign language requirement, thesis (for some programs), recital; for doctorate, variable foreign language requirement, lecture-recital, recitals. *Entrance requirements:* For master's, theory placement test, audition or recital, 2 letters of recommendation, experience record; for doctorate, school qualifying exams, recital, 2 letters of recommendation, experience record. Additional exam requirements/recommendations for international students: Required—TOEFL (minimum score 580 paper-based; 237 computer-based). *Application deadline:* For fall admission, 2/1 priority date for domestic students; for spring admission, 11/15 priority date for domestic students. Applications are processed on a rolling basis. Application fee: $55. Electronic applications accepted. *Financial support:* Career-related internships or fieldwork, Federal Work-Study, scholarships/grants, tuition waivers (full and partial), and unspecified assistantships available. Support available to part-time students. Financial award application deadline: 2/1; financial award applicants required to submit FAFSA. *Application contact:* Christine Mica, Director, University Admissions, 202-319-5305, Fax: 202-319-6533, E-mail: cua-admissions@cua.edu.

The Catholic University of America, The Benjamin T. Rome School of Music, Program in Sacred Music, Washington, DC 20064. Offers MMSM, DMA. *Accreditation:* NASM. Part-time programs available. *Students:* 8 full-time (2 women), 3 part-time (2 women); includes 1 minority (Hispanic American), 1 international. Average age 28. 7 applicants, 43% accepted, 3 enrolled. *Degree requirements:* For master's, comprehensive exam, recital; for doctorate, comprehensive exam, thesis/dissertation, recital, oral exam. *Entrance requirements:* For master's, theory placement test, audition or composition, 2 letters of recommendation; for doctorate, school qualifying exams, compositions or recital, experience record, 2 letters of recommendation. Additional exam requirements/recommendations for international students: Required—TOEFL (minimum score 580 paper-based; 237 computer-based). *Application deadline:* For fall admission, 2/1 priority date for domestic students; for spring admission, 11/15 priority date for domestic students. Applications are processed on a rolling basis. Application fee: $55. Electronic applications accepted. *Financial support:* Career-related internships or fieldwork, Federal Work-Study, scholarships/grants, tuition waivers (full and partial), and unspecified assistantships available. Support available to part-time students. Financial award application deadline: 2/1; financial award applicants required to submit FAFSA. *Application contact:* Christine Mica, Director, University Admissions, 202-319-5305, Fax: 202-319-6533, E-mail: cua-admissions@cua.edu.

The Catholic University of America, The Benjamin T. Rome School of Music, Program in Voice, Washington, DC 20064. Offers vocal pedagogy (MM); vocal performance (MM); voice pedagogy and performance (DMA). *Accreditation:* NASM. Part-time programs available. *Students:* 10 full-time (all women), 17 part-time (11 women); includes 9 minority (3 African Americans, 3 Asian Americans or Pacific Islanders, 3 Hispanic Americans), 4 international. Average age 34. 18 applicants, 83% accepted, 5 enrolled. In 2007, 3 master's, 1 doctorate awarded. *Degree requirements:* For master's, 3 foreign languages, thesis (for some programs), recital; for doctorate, 3 foreign languages, comprehensive exam, thesis/dissertation, recitals. *Entrance requirements:* For master's, theory placement test, audition or recital; 2 letters of recommendation; proficiency in French, German and Italian; for doctorate, school qualifying exams, recital; 2 letters of recommendation; proficiency in French, German and Italian. Additional exam requirements/recommendations for international students: Required—TOEFL (minimum score 580 paper-based; 237 computer-based). *Application deadline:* For fall admission, 2/1 priority date for domestic students; for spring admission, 11/15 priority date for domestic students. Applications are processed on a rolling basis. Application fee: $55. Electronic applications accepted. *Financial support:* Career-related internships or fieldwork, Federal Work-Study, scholarships/grants, tuition waivers (full and partial), and unspecified assistantships available. Support available to part-time students. Financial award application deadline: 2/1; financial award applicants required to submit FAFSA. *Application contact:* Christine Mica, Director, University Admissions, 202-319-5305, Fax: 202-319-6533, E-mail: cua-admissions@cua.edu.

Central Michigan University, College of Graduate Studies, College of Communication and Fine Arts, School of Music, Mount Pleasant, MI 48859. Offers music education and supervision (MM); music performance (MM). *Accreditation:* NASM. *Degree requirements:* For master's, thesis or alternative. *Entrance requirements:* For master's, GRE Revised Music Test, audition, interview, minimum undergraduate GPA of 3.0 in music, minimum GPA of 2.7 overall.

Central Washington University, Graduate Studies, Research and Continuing Education, College of Arts and Humanities, Department of Music, Ellensburg, WA 98926. Offers MM. *Accreditation:* NASM. *Faculty:* 21 full-time (3 women). *Students:* 6 full-time (5 women); all minorities (all Hispanic Americans) 14 applicants, 50% accepted, 7 enrolled. In 2007, 6 degrees awarded. *Degree requirements:* For master's, thesis or alternative. *Entrance requirements:* For master's, minimum GPA of 3.0. Additional exam requirements/recommendations for international students: Required—TOEFL (minimum score 550 paper-based; 213 computer-based; 79 iBT). *Application deadline:* For fall admission, 4/1 priority date for domestic students; for winter admission, 10/1 for domestic students; for spring admission, 1/1 for domestic students. Applications are processed on a rolling basis. Application fee: $50. Electronic applications accepted. *Expenses:* Tuition, state resident: full-time $2,209; part-time $221 per credit. Tuition, nonresident: full-time $4,939; part-time $442 per credit. Required fees: $207 per quarter. Tuition and fees vary according to degree level. *Financial support:* In 2007–08, 11 teaching assistantships with partial tuition reimbursements (averaging $8,100 per year) were awarded; research assistantships with partial tuition reimbursements, Federal Work-Study, health care benefits, and unspecified assistantships also available. Financial award application deadline: 3/1; financial award applicants required to submit FAFSA. *Unit head:* Dr. Peter Gries, Chair, 509-963-1216, Fax: 509-963-1239, E-mail: griesp@cwu.edu. *Application contact:* Justine Eason, Admissions Program Coordinator, 509-963-3103, Fax: 509-963-1799, E-mail: masters@cwu.edu.

City College of the City University of New York, Graduate School, College of Liberal Arts and Science, Division of the Humanities and Arts, Department of Music, New York, NY 10031-9198. Offers MA. Part-time programs available. *Students:* 25. 17 applicants, 100% accepted, 9 enrolled. *Degree requirements:* For master's, one foreign language, thesis. *Entrance requirements:* For master's, minimum GPA of 3.0, portfolio (composition), writing samples (history and theory), audition (performance). Additional exam requirements/recommendations for international students: Required—TOEFL (minimum score 575 paper-based; 233 computer-based). *Application deadline:* For fall admission, 4/1 for domestic students; for spring admission, 11/1 for domestic students. Application fee: $125. *Financial support:* Fellowships, teaching assistantships, Federal Work-Study and tuition waivers (partial) available. Support available to part-time students. Financial award application deadline: 5/1. *Faculty research:* Tonal theory, American music, musicology, atonal theory, performance. *Unit head:* Stephen Jablonsky, Chair, 212-650-5411, Fax: 212-650-5428, E-mail: sjablonsky@ccny.cuny.edu. *Application contact:* Chad Jenkins, Adviser, 212-650-7666, Fax: 212-650-5428.

Claremont Graduate University, Graduate Programs, School of Arts and Humanities, Department of Music, Claremont, CA 91711-6160. Offers church music (MA, DCM); composition (MA, DMA); historical performance practices (MA, DMA); musicology (MA, PhD); performance (MA, DMA); MBA/PhD. Part-time programs available. *Faculty:* 3 full-time (1 woman), 13 part-time/adjunct (6 women). *Students:* 53 full-time (30 women), 9 part-time (3 women); includes 12 minority (6 Asian Americans or Pacific Islanders, 6 Hispanic Americans), 14 international. Average age 37. In 2007, 4 master's, 5 doctorates awarded. Terminal master's awarded for partial completion of doctoral program. *Degree requirements:* For master's, one foreign language, comprehensive exam, thesis (for some programs), oral and written qualifying exams, recitals; for doctorate, 2 foreign languages, comprehensive exam, thesis/dissertation (for some programs), oral and written qualifying exams, oral defense of dissertation, recitals. *Entrance requirements:* For master's and doctorate, GRE General Test, auditions, compositions, or papers. *Application deadline:* For fall admission, 2/15 priority date for domestic students. Applications are processed on a rolling basis. Electronic applications accepted. *Expenses:* Tuition: Full-time $31,640; part-time $1,376 per unit. Required fees: $145 per semester. Tuition and fees vary according to course load, degree level and program. *Financial support:* Fellowships, research assistantships, teaching assistantships, Federal Work-Study and institutionally sponsored loans available. Support available to part-time students. Financial award application deadline: 2/15; financial award applicants required to submit FAFSA. *Unit head:* Robert Zappulla, Chair, 909-607-9664, Fax: 909-607-3694, E-mail: robert.zappulla@cgu.edu.

Cleveland Institute of Music, Graduate Programs, Cleveland, OH 44106-1776. Offers MM, DMA, AD, CPS. *Accreditation:* NASM (one or more programs are accredited). *Degree requirements:* For master's, comprehensive exam, recital; for doctorate, comprehensive exam, thesis/dissertation (for some programs), final projects; for other advanced degree, recital. *Entrance requirements:* For master's, theory placement tests, audition; for doctorate, diagnostic exams, theory placement test, audition; for other advanced degree, audition. Additional exam requirements/recommendations for international students: Required—TOEFL (minimum score 550 paper-based; 213 computer-based). Electronic applications accepted.

Cleveland State University, College of Graduate Studies, College of Liberal Arts and Social Sciences, Department of Music, Cleveland, OH 44115. Offers composition (MM); music education (MM); performance (MM). *Accreditation:* NASM. Part-time and evening/weekend programs available. *Faculty:* 12 full-time (5 women). *Students:* 9 full-time (2 women), 35 part-time (17 women); includes 8 minority (3 African Americans, 3 Asian Americans or Pacific Islanders, 2 Hispanic Americans). Average age 29. 36 applicants, 75% accepted, 15 enrolled. *Degree requirements:* For master's, comprehensive exam, thesis or recital. *Entrance requirements:* For master's, departmental assessment in music history, minimum undergraduate GPA of 2.75. Additional exam requirements/recommendations for international students: Required—TOEFL (minimum score 525 paper-based; 197 computer-based). *Application deadline:* For fall admission, 7/15 priority date for domestic students. Applications are processed on a rolling basis. Application fee: $30. *Financial support:* In 2007–08, 15 students received support, including 11 research assistantships with full tuition reimbursements available (averaging $3,612 per year); tuition waivers (partial) and unspecified assistantships also available. Financial award application deadline: 3/1. *Faculty research:* Ethnomusicology, classical-romantic music, new performance practices, electronic music, interdisciplinary studies. Total annual research expenditures: $121,000. *Unit head:* Dr. Eric E. Ziolek, Chairperson, 216-687-2301, Fax: 216-687-9279, E-mail: e.ziolek@csuohio.edu. *Application contact:* Dr. Birch Browning, Coordinator of Graduate Studies and Admission, 216-687-3768, Fax: 216-687-9279, E-mail: b.browning@csuohio.edu.

The College of Saint Rose, Graduate Studies, School of Arts and Humanities, Music Department, Program in Music, Albany, NY 12203-1419. Offers MA. *Accreditation:* NASM. *Faculty:* 9 full-time (3 women), 24 part-time/adjunct (11 women). *Students:* 1 full-time (0 women), 2 part-time (1 woman). Average age 36. 2 applicants, 0% accepted. In 2007, 6 degrees awarded. *Degree requirements:* For master's, final project. *Entrance requirements:* For master's, audition, minimum undergraduate GPA of 3.0. Additional exam requirements/recommendations for international students: Required—TOEFL (minimum score 550 paper-based; 213 computer-based). *Application deadline:* For fall admission, 7/15 priority date for domestic and international students; for spring admission, 11/15 priority date for domestic and international students. Applications are processed on a rolling basis. Application fee: $35. Electronic applications accepted. *Financial support:* Scholarships/grants, tuition waivers (partial), and unspecified assistantships available. Support available to part-time students. Financial award application deadline: 3/1; financial award applicants required to submit FAFSA. *Application contact:* Susan Patterson, Assistant Vice President for Graduate Admission, 518-454-5136, Fax: 518-458-5479, E-mail: ace@strose.edu.

Colorado State University, Graduate School, College of Liberal Arts, Department of Music, Theater, and Dance, Fort Collins, CO 80523-0015. Offers music (MM). *Accreditation:* NASM. Part-time programs available. *Faculty:* 25 full-time (6 women). *Students:* 32 full-time (22 women), 27 part-time (23 women); includes 6 minority (1 American Indian/Alaska Native, 4 Asian Americans or Pacific Islanders, 1 Hispanic American), 6 international. Average age 29. 51 applicants, 63% accepted, 22 enrolled. In 2007, 22 degrees awarded. *Degree requirements:* For master's, comprehensive exam, thesis (for some programs), 2 recitals, project. *Entrance requirements:* For master's, minimum GPA of 3.0, audition. Additional exam requirements/recommendations for international students: Required—TOEFL (minimum score 550 paper-based; 213 computer-based). *Application deadline:* For fall admission, 3/1 priority date for domestic and international students. Applications are processed on a rolling basis. Application fee: $50. Electronic applications accepted. *Expenses:* Tuition, state resident: full-time $4,887; part-time $272 per credit. Tuition, nonresident: full-time $16,425; part-time $913 per credit. Required fees: $1,379; $75 per credit. *Financial support:* In 2007–08, 15 teaching assistantships with full and partial tuition reimbursements (averaging $6,408 per year) were awarded; fellowships, research assistantships with partial tuition reimbursements, career-related internships or fieldwork, Federal Work-Study, scholarships/grants, traineeships, and unspecified assistantships also available. Financial award application deadline: 3/1; financial award applicants required to submit FAFSA. *Faculty research:* Neurobiology, musicology, music literacy, music learning. *Unit head:* Dr. Michael H. Thaut, Chair, 970-491-5533, Fax: 970-491-7541. *Application contact:* Heather Brooks, Administrative Assistant, 970-491-5533, Fax: 970-491-7541, E-mail: heather.brooks@colostate.edu.

Columbia University, Graduate School of Arts and Sciences, Division of Humanities, Department of Music, New York, NY 10027. Offers M Phil, MA, DMA, PhD. *Faculty:* 18 full-time, 4 part-time/adjunct. *Students:* 87 full-time (34 women), 10 part-time (2 women); includes 14 minority (2 African Americans, 8 Asian Americans or Pacific Islanders, 4 Hispanic

Music

Columbia University (continued)

Americans), 23 international. Average age 33. 149 applicants, 40% accepted. In 2007, 8 master's, 7 doctorates awarded. *Degree requirements:* For master's, 2 foreign languages, thesis or alternative; for doctorate, variable foreign language requirement, thesis/dissertation. *Entrance requirements:* For master's and doctorate, GRE General Test, GRE Subject Test, sample of written work. Additional exam requirements/recommendations for international students: Required—TOEFL. Application fee: $90. *Expenses:* Tuition: Part-time $1,452 per credit. Required fees: $152 per term. One-time fee: $75 part-time. Full-time tuition and fees vary according to course level, course load, degree level and program. *Financial support:* Fellowships, teaching assistantships, Federal Work-Study and institutionally sponsored loans available. Support available to part-time students. Financial award application deadline: 1/5; financial award applicants required to submit FAFSA. *Faculty research:* Historical musicology, ethnomusicology, composition and theory. *Unit head:* Joseph Dubiel, Chair, 212-854-6697, Fax: 212-854-8191, E-mail: jpd5@columbia.edu.

See Close-Up on page 347.

Concordia University, School of Graduate Studies, Faculty of Fine Arts, Department of Music, Montréal, QC H3G 1M8, Canada. Offers advanced music performance studies (Diploma). *Degree requirements:* For Diploma, performance, 2 recitals.

Concordia University Chicago, College of Arts and Sciences, Program in Church Music, River Forest, IL 60305-1499. Offers MCM. *Accreditation:* NASM. Part-time programs available. *Degree requirements:* For master's, composition, recital, or thesis. *Entrance requirements:* For master's, minimum GPA of 2.9, audition. Additional exam requirements/recommendations for international students: Required—TOEFL (minimum score 550 paper-based; 195 computer-based). Electronic applications accepted. *Faculty research:* Twentieth-century sacred choral music, liturgical context of sacred music after the Council of Trent, dance and music of J.S. Bach.

Concordia University Chicago, College of Arts and Sciences, Program in Music, River Forest, IL 60305-1499. Offers MA. Part-time programs available. *Degree requirements:* For master's, composition, recital, or thesis. *Entrance requirements:* For master's, minimum GPA of 2.9, audition. Additional exam requirements/recommendations for international students: Required—TOEFL (minimum score 550 paper-based; 195 computer-based). Electronic applications accepted.

Concordia University Wisconsin, Graduate Programs, School of Arts and Sciences, Program in Church Music, Mequon, WI 53097-2402. Offers MCM. *Degree requirements:* For master's, comprehensive exam, thesis or alternative. *Entrance requirements:* For master's, minimum GPA of 3.0. Additional exam requirements/recommendations for international students: Required—TOEFL.

Conservatorio de Musica, Program in Musical Performance, San Juan, PR 00918-2199. Offers instrumental performance (Diploma); vocal performance (Diploma). *Entrance requirements:* For degree, 3 letters of recommendation, audition, degree in music, minimum GPA of 2.5.

Converse College, Carroll McDaniel Petrie School of Music, Spartanburg, SC 29302-0006. Offers instrumental performance (M Mus); music education (M Mus); piano pedagogy (M Mus); vocal performance (M Mus). *Accreditation:* NASM. Part-time and evening/weekend programs available. *Degree requirements:* For master's, variable foreign language requirement, comprehensive exam, thesis (for some programs), recitals. *Entrance requirements:* For master's, NTE (music education), audition, 3 letters of recommendation. Additional exam requirements/recommendations for international students: Required—TOEFL. Electronic applications accepted. *Faculty research:* Chamber music, opera, performance, composition, recording.

Cornell University, Graduate School, Graduate Fields of Arts and Sciences, Field of Music, Ithaca, NY 14853-0001. Offers composition (DMA); musicology (PhD); performance practice (DMA); theory of music (MA). *Faculty:* 20 full-time (7 women). *Students:* 33 full-time (14 women), 16 international. Average age 28. 134 applicants, 10% accepted, 7 enrolled. In 2007, 6 master's, 4 doctorates awarded. *Degree requirements:* For doctorate, comprehensive exam, thesis/dissertation, 1 foreign language (DMA), 2 foreign languages (PhD). *Entrance requirements:* For doctorate, GRE General Test, 2 music papers; 2 recent scores (with recording) and 1 music paper (DMA composition); 1 music paper, recording and audition (DMA performance practice). Additional exam requirements/recommendations for international students: Required—TOEFL (minimum score 600 paper-based; 250 computer-based; 77 iBT). *Application deadline:* For fall admission, 1/15 for domestic students. Application fee: $70. Electronic applications accepted. *Financial support:* In 2007–08, 29 students received support, including 13 fellowships with full tuition reimbursements available, 16 teaching assistantships with full tuition reimbursements available; research assistantships with full tuition reimbursements available, institutionally sponsored loans, scholarships/grants, health care benefits, tuition waivers (full and partial), and unspecified assistantships also available. Financial award applicants required to submit FAFSA. *Faculty research:* Music history, music theory, performance practice, ethnomusicology, composition. *Unit head:* Director of Graduate Studies, 607-255-9078. *Application contact:* Graduate Field Assistant, 607-255-9078, E-mail: grad_music@cornell.edu.

The Curtis Institute of Music, Graduate Studies, Philadelphia, PA 19103-6107. Offers opera (MM). *Accreditation:* NASM. *Entrance requirements:* For master's, audition or performance in 2 or more principal roles or 6 major scenes.

Dartmouth College, Arts and Sciences Graduate Programs, Department of Music, Hanover, NH 03755. Offers electro-acoustic music (AM). *Faculty:* 7 full-time (1 woman), 20 part-time/adjunct (6 women). *Students:* 6 full-time (3 women); includes 1 minority (Hispanic American), 1 international. Average age 26. 20 applicants, 20% accepted, 3 enrolled. In 2007, 2 degrees awarded. *Degree requirements:* For master's, thesis or alternative. *Entrance requirements:* Additional exam requirements/recommendations for international students: Required—TOEFL. *Application deadline:* For fall admission, 2/1 priority date for domestic students. Application fee: $35. *Financial support:* In 2007–08, 6 students received support, including fellowships with full tuition reimbursements available (averaging $13,547 per year), research assistantships with full tuition reimbursements available (averaging $13,547 per year); career-related internships or fieldwork, institutionally sponsored loans, and tuition waivers (full) also available. *Faculty research:* Composition and design of computer music software and related topics. Total annual research expenditures: $7,215. *Unit head:* Larry Polansky, Director, Graduate Program in Electro-Acoustic Music, 603-646-2139, Fax: 603-646-0258. *Application contact:* Theresa Ciamba, Administrative Assistant, 603-646-3974, Fax: 603-646-0258, E-mail: theresa.ciamba@dartmouth.edu.

DePaul University, School of Music, Chicago, IL 60604-2287. Offers applied music (performance) (MM, Certificate); jazz studies (MM), including composition, performance; music composition (MM); music education (MM). *Accreditation:* NASM (one or more programs are accredited). Part-time and evening/weekend programs available. *Faculty:* 11 full-time (2 women), 50 part-time/adjunct (14 women). *Students:* 66 full-time (25 women), 51 part-time (27 women); includes 16 minority (4 African Americans, 4 Asian Americans or Pacific Islanders, 8 Hispanic Americans), 29 international. Average age 27. 175 applicants, 46% accepted. In 2007, 40 master's, 5 Certificates awarded. *Degree requirements:* For master's, comprehensive exam, terminal project. *Entrance requirements:* For master's, bachelor's degree in music or related field, audition, minimum GPA of 3.0; for Certificate, master's degree in performance or related field. Additional exam requirements/recommendations for international students: Required—TOEFL (minimum score 550 paper-based; 213 computer-based; 80 iBT). *Application deadline:* For fall admission, 1/15 priority date for domestic and international students. Applications are processed on a rolling basis. Electronic applications accepted. *Expenses:* Contact institution. *Financial support:* In 2007–08, 4 fellowships with partial tuition reimbursements were awarded; teaching assistantships, career-related internships or fieldwork, Federal Work-Study, scholarships/grants, and tuition waivers also available. Support available to part-time students. Financial award application deadline: 1/15. *Unit head:* Dr. Donald E. Casey, Dean, 773-325-7256. *Application contact:* Ross Beacraft, Director of Admissions, 773-325-7444, Fax: 773-325-7429, E-mail: rbeacraft@depaul.edu.

Duke University, Graduate School, Department of Music, Durham, NC 27708. Offers music composition (AM, PhD); musicology (AM, PhD); performance practice (AM, PhD). Part-time programs available. *Faculty:* 10 full-time. *Students:* 33 full-time (18 women); includes 2 minority (both Asian Americans or Pacific Islanders), 6 international. 62 applicants, 18% accepted, 4 enrolled. In 2007, 4 doctorates awarded. Terminal master's awarded for partial completion of doctoral program. *Degree requirements:* For master's, 2 foreign languages; for doctorate, 3 foreign languages, thesis/dissertation. *Entrance requirements:* For master's and doctorate, GRE General Test. Additional exam requirements/recommendations for international students: Required—TOEFL (minimum score 550 paper-based; 213 computer-based; 83 iBT), IELTS (minimum score 7). *Application deadline:* For fall admission, 12/15 priority date for domestic and international students; for spring admission, 11/1 for domestic students. Application fee: $75. Electronic applications accepted. *Financial support:* Fellowships, research assistantships, teaching assistantships, Federal Work-Study available. Financial award application deadline: 12/31. *Unit head:* Thomas Brothers, Director of Graduate Studies, 919-660-3301, Fax: 919-660-3308.

Duquesne University, Mary Pappert School of Music, Pittsburgh, PA 15282-0001. Offers music composition (MM); music education (MM); music performance (MM, AD); music technology (MM); music theory (MM); sacred music (MM). *Accreditation:* NASM. Part-time programs available. Postbaccalaureate distance learning degree programs offered (minimal on-campus study). *Faculty:* 26 full-time (9 women), 73 part-time/adjunct (14 women). *Students:* 66 full-time (32 women), 28 part-time (13 women); includes 3 minority (2 African Americans, 1 Hispanic American), 24 international. Average age 23. 83 applicants, 86% accepted, 34 enrolled. In 2007, 43 master's, 5 ADs awarded. *Degree requirements:* For master's, comprehensive exam, thesis (for some programs), recital (music performance); for AD, recital. *Entrance requirements:* For master's, audition, minimum undergraduate QPA of 3.0 in music, portfolio of original compositions, theoretical papers, or music education experience; for AD, audition. Additional exam requirements/recommendations for international students: Required—TOEFL (minimum score 550 paper-based; 213 computer-based; 79 iBT). *Application deadline:* For fall admission, 9/1 priority date for domestic students; for spring admission, 12/1 for domestic students. Applications are processed on a rolling basis. Application fee: $50. *Expenses:* Contact institution. Tuition and fees vary according to program. *Financial support:* In 2007–08, 48 fellowships with full and partial tuition reimbursements were awarded; career-related internships or fieldwork, Federal Work-Study, institutionally sponsored loans, and tuition waivers (full and partial) also available. Support available to part-time students. Financial award application deadline: 4/1. *Faculty research:* Performance; computer-assisted instruction in music at elementary and secondary levels; electronic music; contemporary music, theory, and analysis; development of on-line graduate music courses. Total annual research expenditures: $6,000. *Unit head:* Dr. Edward W. Kocher, Dean, 412-396-6082, Fax: 412-396-1524, E-mail: kocher@duq.edu. *Application contact:* Peggy Eiseman, Administrative Assistant of Admissions, 412-396-5064, Fax: 412-396-5479, E-mail: eiseman@duq.edu.

East Carolina University, Graduate School, College of Fine Arts and Communication, School of Music, Greenville, NC 27858-4353. Offers music education (MM); music therapy (MM); performance (MM); theory and composition (MM). *Accreditation:* NASM. Part-time programs available. *Faculty:* 37 full-time (10 women). *Students:* 37 full-time (20 women), 20 part-time (12 women); includes 6 minority (4 African Americans, 1 Asian American or Pacific Islander, 1 Hispanic American), 4 international. Average age 28. 24 applicants, 13% accepted, 3 enrolled. In 2007, 22 degrees awarded. *Degree requirements:* For master's, comprehensive exam, thesis optional. *Entrance requirements:* For master's, GRE General Test or MAT. Additional exam requirements/recommendations for international students: Required—TOEFL. *Application deadline:* For fall admission, 6/1 priority date for domestic students. Applications are processed on a rolling basis. Application fee: $50. *Financial support:* Fellowships, research assistantships, teaching assistantships, Federal Work-Study available. Support available to part-time students. Financial award application deadline: 6/1. *Unit head:* Dr. J. Christopher Buddo, Director, 252-328-6131. *Application contact:* Dean of Graduate School, 252-328-6012, Fax: 252-328-6071, E-mail: gradschool@ecu.edu.

Eastern Illinois University, Graduate School, College of Arts and Humanities, Department of Music, Charleston, IL 61920-3099. Offers MA. *Accreditation:* NASM. *Faculty:* 21 full-time (3 women). In 2007, 4 degrees awarded. *Degree requirements:* For master's, thesis or alternative, recital. *Application deadline:* For fall admission, 7/31 priority date for domestic students. Applications are processed on a rolling basis. Application fee: $30. *Expenses:* Tuition, state resident: part-time $218 per hour. Tuition, nonresident: part-time $654 per hour. *Financial support:* In 2007–08, research assistantships with tuition reimbursements (averaging $7,200 per year), 8 teaching assistantships with tuition reimbursements (averaging $7,200 per year) were awarded. *Unit head:* Dr. Parker Melvin, Chairperson, 217-581-3010, Fax: 217-581-2722, E-mail: wpmelvin@eiu.edu. *Application contact:* Paul Johnston, Coordinator, 217-581-6656, E-mail: prjohnston@eiu.edu.

Eastern Kentucky University, The Graduate School, College of Arts and Sciences, Department of Music, Richmond, KY 40475-3102. Offers choral conducting (MM); performance (MM); theory/composition (MM). *Accreditation:* NASM. Part-time programs available. *Faculty:* 9 full-time (2 women), 3 part-time/adjunct (2 women). *Students:* 10 full-time (2 women), 13 part-time (9 women); includes 1 minority (African American) Average age 29. 15 applicants, 40% accepted, 5 enrolled. In 2007, 9 degrees awarded. *Degree requirements:* For master's, thesis optional. *Entrance requirements:* For master's, GRE General Test, minimum GPA of 2.5. Application fee: $35. *Financial support:* In 2007–08, research assistantships (averaging $10,000 per year), teaching assistantships (averaging $10,000 per year) were awarded; Federal Work-Study also available. Support available to part-time students. *Faculty research:* Technology. *Unit head:* Dr. Robert James, Chair, 859-622-3266, Fax: 859-622-1333, E-mail: rob.james@eku.edu. *Application contact:* Dr. Karin Schmann, Director of Graduate Studies, 859-622-3266, Fax: 859-622-1333, E-mail: karin.schmann@eku.edu.

Eastern Michigan University, Graduate School, College of Arts and Sciences, Department of Communication and Theatre Arts, Program in Theatre, Ypsilanti, MI 48197. Offers interpretation/performance studies (MA); theatre arts (MA). Part-time and evening/weekend programs available. Postbaccalaureate distance learning degree programs offered (minimal on-campus study). *Students:* 4 full-time (2 women), 10 part-time (5 women); includes 1 minority (African American), 2 international. Average age 30. In 2007, 4 degrees awarded. *Degree requirements:* For master's, thesis or alternative. *Entrance requirements:* Additional exam requirements/recommendations for international students: Required—TOEFL. *Application deadline:* Applications are processed on a rolling basis. Application fee: $35. *Expenses:* Tuition, state resident: full-time $8,952; part-time $373 per credit hour. Tuition, nonresident: full-time $17,634; part-time $735 per credit hour. Required fees: $896; $34 per credit hour. Tuition and fees vary according to course level, degree level and program. *Financial support:* Fellowships, research assistantships with full tuition reimbursements, teaching assistantships with full tuition reimbursements, career-related internships or fieldwork, Federal Work-Study, institutionally sponsored loans, scholarships/grants, tuition waivers (partial), and unspecified assistantships available. Support available to part-time students. Financial award applicants required to submit FAFSA. *Unit head:* Kenneth Stevens, Coordinator, 734-487-3130, Fax: 734-487-3443, E-mail: ken.stevens@emich.edu. *Application contact:* Dr. Lee Stille, Graduate Coordinator, 734-487-3131, Fax: 734-487-3443, E-mail: lee.stille@emich.edu.

Eastern Michigan University, Graduate School, College of Arts and Sciences, Department of Music and Dance, Ypsilanti, MI 48197. Offers music composition (MM); music education (MM); music pedagogy (MM); music performance (MM). *Accreditation:* NASM. Part-time and evening/weekend programs available. Postbaccalaureate distance learning degree programs offered (minimal on-campus study). *Faculty:* 29 full-time (12 women). *Students:* 8 full-time (3 women), 28 part-time (16 women); includes 2 minority (both African Americans), 8 international. Average age 31. In 2007, 4 degrees awarded. *Entrance requirements:* Additional exam requirements/recommendations for international students: Required—TOEFL. *Application deadline:* Applications are processed on a rolling basis. Application fee: $35. *Expenses:* Tuition, state resident: full-time $8,952; part-time $373 per credit hour. Tuition, nonresident: full-time $17,634; part-time $735 per credit hour. Required fees: $896; $34 per credit hour. Tuition and fees vary according to course level, degree level and program. *Financial support:* Fellowships, research assistantships with full tuition reimbursements, teaching assistantships with full tuition reimbursements, career-related internships or fieldwork, Federal Work-Study, institutionally sponsored loans, scholarships/grants, tuition waivers (partial), and unspecified assistantships available. Support available to part-time students. Financial award applicants required to submit FAFSA. *Unit head:* Dr. David Woike, Head, 734-487-4380, Fax: 734-487-6939, E-mail: dave.woike@emich.edu. *Application contact:* Dr. David Pierce, Coordinator of Music Advising, 734-487-4114, Fax: 734-487-6939, E-mail: david.pierce@emich.edu.

Eastern Washington University, Graduate Studies, College of Arts and Letters, Department of Music, Cheney, WA 99004-2431. Offers composition (MA); instrumental/vocal performance (MA); music education (MA); music history and literature (MA). *Accreditation:* NASM. Part-time programs available. *Degree requirements:* For master's, comprehensive exam, thesis or alternative. *Entrance requirements:* For master's, GRE General Test, minimum GPA of 3.0.

Emory University, Graduate School of Arts and Sciences, Department of Music, Atlanta, GA 30322-1100. Offers choral conducting (MM, MSM); organ performance (MM, MSM). *Accreditation:* NASM. *Degree requirements:* For master's, comprehensive exam, recital or worship service/recital. *Entrance requirements:* For master's, GRE General Test, audition, interview. Additional exam requirements/recommendations for international students: Required—TOEFL. Electronic applications accepted. *Faculty research:* 19th century criticism, Schenker, Bach Aria styles, contemporary passion music, Andriesson, cross-cultural research, organ performance.

Emporia State University, School of Graduate Studies, College of Liberal Arts and Sciences, Department of Music, Emporia, KS 66801-5087. Offers music education (MM), including instrumental, vocal; performance (MM). *Accreditation:* NASM. Part-time programs available. *Faculty:* 12 full-time (2 women), 5 part-time/adjunct (4 women). *Students:* 2 full-time (0 women), 14 part-time (9 women), 2 international. 4 applicants, 50% accepted, 2 enrolled. In 2007, 3 degrees awarded. *Degree requirements:* For master's, comprehensive exam or thesis. *Entrance requirements:* For master's, music qualifying exam, appropriate undergraduate degree. Additional exam requirements/recommendations for international students: Required—TOEFL (minimum score 450 paper-based; 133 computer-based). *Application deadline:* For fall admission, 8/15 priority date for domestic students. Applications are processed on a rolling basis. Application fee: $30 ($75 for international students). Electronic applications accepted. *Expenses:* Tuition, state resident: part-time $157 per credit hour. Tuition, nonresident: part-time $475 per credit hour. Required fees: $47 per credit hour. Tuition and fees vary according to campus/location. *Financial support:* In 2007–08, 2 research assistantships with full tuition reimbursements (averaging $6,887 per year), 4 teaching assistantships with full tuition reimbursements (averaging $6,887 per year) were awarded; Federal Work-Study, institutionally sponsored loans, health care benefits, and unspecified assistantships also available. Financial award application deadline: 3/15; financial award applicants required to submit FAFSA. *Unit head:* Dr. Marie C. Miller, Chair, 620-341-5431, E-mail: mmiller@emporia.edu. *Application contact:* Dr. Andrew Houchins, Graduate Coordinator, 620-341-6089, E-mail: ahouchin@emporia.edu.

Five Towns College, Department of Music, Dix Hills, NY 11746-6055. Offers jazz/commercial music (MM); music (DMA); music education (MM). Part-time programs available. *Faculty:* 13 full-time (all women), 12 part-time/adjunct (2 women). *Students:* 13 full-time (7 women), 41 part-time (23 women); includes 3 minority (2 African Americans, 1 Hispanic American), 11 international. Average age 35. 82 applicants, 100% accepted. In 2007, 27 degrees awarded. *Degree requirements:* For master's, exams, major composition or capstone project, recital; for doctorate, comprehensive exam, thesis/dissertation, final oral exam. *Entrance requirements:* For master's, audition, bachelor's degree in music or music education, minimum GPA of 2.75, 36 hours of course work in performance; for doctorate, master's degree in music, minimum GPA of 3.0, 3 letters of recommendation. Additional exam requirements/recommendations for international students: Required—TOEFL (minimum score 550 paper-based; 213 computer-based; 80 iBT). *Application deadline:* Applications are processed on a rolling basis. Application fee: $50. *Financial support:* Fellowships with tuition reimbursements, tuition waivers (partial) available. Financial award applicants required to submit FAFSA. *Faculty research:* Teaching methods, teaching strategies and techniques, analysis of modern music, jazz. *Unit head:* Dr. Jill Miller-Thorn, Dean of Graduate Studies, 631-656-2100, Fax: 631-656-2172, E-mail: jmillerthorn@ftc.edu. *Application contact:* Jerry Cohen, Dean of Enrollment, 631-656-2121, Fax: 631-656-2172, E-mail: jcohen@ftc.edu.

Florida Atlantic University, Dorothy F. Schmidt College of Arts and Letters, Department of Music, Boca Raton, FL 33431-0991. Offers MA. *Accreditation:* NASM. Part-time programs available. *Degree requirements:* For master's, lecture/recital or thesis. *Entrance requirements:* For master's, audition, minimum GPA of 3.0 in last 60 hours of course work, placement evaluations in music history and theory. *Faculty research:* Classical guitar history and literature, women composers, Mozart opera, composition, performance.

Florida International University, College of Architecture and the Arts, School of Music, Miami, FL 33199. Offers music (MM); music education (MS). Part-time and evening/weekend programs available. *Faculty:* 25 full-time (5 women). *Students:* 30 full-time (14 women), 22 part-time (13 women); includes 29 minority (3 African Americans, 1 Asian American or Pacific Islander, 25 Hispanic Americans), 12 international. Average age 32. 30 applicants, 57% accepted, 12 enrolled. In 2007, 8 degrees awarded. *Degree requirements:* For master's, thesis. *Entrance requirements:* For master's, minimum GPA of 3.0, audition or interview, depending area. Additional exam requirements/recommendations for international students: Required—TOEFL (minimum score 550 paper-based; 213 computer-based). *Application deadline:* For fall admission, 6/1 for domestic students, 4/1 for international students; for spring admission, 10/1 for domestic students, 9/1 for international students. Applications are processed on a rolling basis. Application fee: $30. *Expenses:* Tuition, state resident: full-time $6,106. Tuition, nonresident: full-time $15,528. Required fees: $284. *Financial support:* Teaching assistantships available. *Unit head:* Kathleen Wilson, Director, 305-348-2896, Fax: 305-348-4073, E-mail: kathleen.wilson@fiu.edu.

Florida State University, Graduate Studies, College of Arts and Sciences, Department of English, Tallahassee, FL 32306. Offers creative writing (MFA, PhD); literature (MA, PhD); rhetoric and composition (MA, PhD). Part-time programs available. *Faculty:* 57 full-time (25 women), 14 part-time/adjunct (9 women). *Students:* 148 full-time (105 women), 20 part-time (10 women); includes 30 minority (13 African Americans, 1 American Indian/Alaska Native, 8 Asian Americans or Pacific Islanders, 8 Hispanic Americans). Average age 30. 427 applicants, 17% accepted, 57 enrolled. In 2007, 25 master's, 18 doctorates awarded. *Median time to degree:* Of those who began their doctoral program in fall 1999, 80% received their degree in 8 years or less. *Degree requirements:* For master's, one foreign language, thesis or alternative; for doctorate, 2 foreign languages, thesis/dissertation. *Entrance requirements:* For master's, GRE General Test, GRE Subject Test (literature), sample of written work, 3 letters of recommendation; for doctorate, GRE General Test, sample of written work, 3 letters of recommendation. *Application deadline:* For fall admission, 2/1 priority date for domestic students. Application fee: $30. Electronic applications accepted. *Expenses:* Tuition, state resident: part-time $248 per credit hour. Tuition, nonresident: part-time $880 per credit hour. Tuition and fees vary according to program. *Financial support:* In 2007–08, 155 students received support, including 5 fellowships, 150 teaching assistantships (averaging $11,375 per year); career-related internships or fieldwork, Federal Work-Study, and institutionally sponsored loans also available. Financial award application deadline: 2/1; financial award applicants required to submit FAFSA. *Faculty research:* British literature, American literature, creative writing, rhetoric, multiethnic literature. *Unit head:* Dr. Ralph Berry, Chairman, 850-644-5158, Fax: 850-644-0811, E-mail: rberry@fsu.edu. *Application contact:* Dr. Stan Gontarski, Director, 850-644-6038, Fax: 850-644-0811, E-mail: sgontarski@fsu.edu.

Florida State University, Graduate Studies, College of Music, Tallahassee, FL 32306. Offers accompanying (MM); arts administration (MA); choral conducting (MM); composition (MM, DM); ethnomusicology (MM); general music (MA); instrumental accompanying (MM); instrumental conducting (MM); jazz studies (MM); music education (MM Ed, PhD); music theory (MM, PhD); music therapy (MM); musicology (MM, PhD), including ethnomusicology (PhD), historical musicology; opera (MM); performance (MM, DM); piano pedagogy (MM); piano technology (MA); vocal accompanying (MM). *Accreditation:* NASM. *Faculty:* 88 full-time, 13 part-time/adjunct. *Students:* 406 full-time (211 women); includes 98 minority (28 African Americans, 38 Asian Americans or Pacific Islanders, 32 Hispanic Americans). Average age 26. 525 applicants, 38% accepted, 145 enrolled. In 2007, 102 master's, 41 doctorates awarded. *Degree requirements:* For master's, comprehensive exam (for some programs), thesis (for some programs), departmental qualifying exam; for doctorate, comprehensive exam (for some programs), thesis/dissertation, departmental qualifying exam. *Entrance requirements:* For master's and doctorate, audition, GRE General Test or minimum GPA of 3.0. Additional exam requirements/recommendations for international students: Required—TOEFL (minimum score 550 paper-based; 213 computer-based). *Application deadline:* For fall admission, 7/1 for domestic students, 5/2 for international students; for spring admission, 11/3 for domestic students, 9/1 for international students. Applications are processed on a rolling basis. Application fee: $30. Electronic applications accepted. *Expenses:* Tuition, state resident: part-time $248 per credit hour. Tuition, nonresident: part-time $880 per credit hour. Tuition and fees vary according to program. *Financial support:* In 2007–08, 225 students received support, including 3 fellowships with full tuition reimbursements available (averaging $15,000 per year), 9 research assistantships with full tuition reimbursements available (averaging $4,000 per year), 173 teaching assistantships with full tuition reimbursements available (averaging $4,000 per year); career-related internships or fieldwork, Federal Work-Study, and tuition waivers (partial) also available. Support available to part-time students. Financial award application deadline: 2/28; financial award applicants required to submit FAFSA. *Unit head:* Don Gibson, Dean, 850-644-4361, Fax: 850-644-2033. *Application contact:* Dr. Seth Beckman, Assistant Dean for Academic Affairs/Director of Graduate Studies, 850-644-5848, Fax: 850-644-2033, E-mail: sbeckman@admin.fsu.edu.

Garrett-Evangelical Theological Seminary, Graduate and Professional Programs, Evanston, IL 60201-3298. Offers Bible and culture (PhD); Christian education (MA); Christian education and congregational studies (PhD); contemporary theology and culture (PhD); divinity (M Div); ethics, church, and society (MA); liturgical studies (PhD); ministry (D Min); music ministry (MA); pastoral care and counseling (MA); pastoral theology, personality, and culture (PhD); spiritual formation and evangelism (MA); theological studies (MTS); M Div/MSW. *Accreditation:* ACIPE; ATS (one or more programs are accredited). Part-time programs available. *Degree requirements:* For master's, thesis (for some programs); for doctorate, thesis/dissertation. *Entrance requirements:* For doctorate, GRE (PhD). Additional exam requirements/recommendations for international students: Required—TOEFL (minimum score 560 paper-based; 230 computer-based). Electronic applications accepted.

George Mason University, College of Visual and Performing Arts, Department of Music, Fairfax, VA 22030. Offers artist certificate (Certificate); composition (MA); conducting (MA); music (MM); music education (MA, Certificate); pedagogy and performance (MA); performance (MA). *Accreditation:* NASM. Part-time and evening/weekend programs available. *Faculty:* 15 full-time (6 women), 24 part-time/adjunct (13 women). *Students:* 19 full-time (14 women), 43 part-time (32 women); includes 9 minority (7 African Americans, 2 Asian Americans or Pacific Islanders), 2 international. Average age 30. 60 applicants, 58% accepted, 25 enrolled. In 2007, 20 degrees awarded. *Degree requirements:* For master's, comprehensive exam, thesis (for some programs), recital for all but MM music education. *Entrance requirements:* For master's, BA or BM as appropriate for the desired master's program of study. *Application deadline:* For fall admission, 5/1 priority date for domestic students; for spring admission, 11/1 priority date for domestic students. Applications are processed on a rolling basis. Application fee: $60 ($75 for international students). Electronic applications accepted. *Expenses:* Contact institution. *Financial support:* In 2007–08, 16 students received support, including 2 teaching assistantships with partial tuition reimbursements available (averaging $9,000 per year); fellowships with partial tuition reimbursements available, tuition waivers (partial) also available. Support available to part-time students. Financial award application deadline: 3/1; financial award applicants required to submit FAFSA. *Unit head:* James Gardner, Chairman, 703-993-1380, Fax: 703-993-1394, E-mail: jgardne2@gmu.edu. *Application contact:* Dr. Tom Owens, Information Contact, 703-993-1236, E-mail: music@gmu.edu.

Georgia Southern University, Jack N. Averitt College of Graduate Studies, College of Liberal Arts and Social Sciences, Department of Music, Statesboro, GA 30460. Offers MM. *Accreditation:* NASM. Part-time and evening/weekend programs available. *Students:* 7 full-time (1 woman), 6 part-time (2 women); includes 2 minority (1 African American, 1 Asian American or Pacific Islander). Average age 28. 7 applicants, 86% accepted, 6 enrolled. In 2007, 7 degrees awarded. *Degree requirements:* For master's, comprehensive exam. *Entrance requirements:* For master's, GRE General Test, music theory and music history proficiency test, minimum GPA of 2.5, audition, letters of recommendation. Additional exam requirements/recommendations for international students: Required—TOEFL (minimum score 550 paper-based; 213 computer-based; 80 iBT). *Application deadline:* For fall admission, 3/1 priority date for domestic and international students; for spring admission, 10/1 priority date for domestic students, 10/1 for international students. Applications are processed on a rolling basis. Application fee: $50. Electronic applications accepted. *Expenses:* Tuition, state resident: full-time $3,516; part-time $147 per semester hour. Tuition, nonresident: full-time $14,060; part-time $586 per semester hour. Required fees: $562 per term. *Financial support:* In 2007–08, 12 students received support, including research assistantships with partial tuition reimbursements available (averaging $6,850 per year), teaching assistantships with partial tuition reimbursements available (averaging $6,850 per year); Federal Work-Study, scholarships/grants, tuition waivers (partial), and unspecified assistantships also available. Support available to part-time students. Financial award application deadline: 4/15; financial award applicants required to submit FAFSA. *Faculty research:* Music history and literature, technology in music, music composition, music performance, music/education. *Unit head:* Dr. Curtis Ricker, Acting Chair, 912-478-3396, Fax: 912-478-1295, E-mail: cricker@georgiasouthern.edu. *Application contact:* Office of Graduate Admissions, 912-478-5384, Fax: 912-478-0740, E-mail: gradadmissions@georgiasouthern.edu.

Georgia State University, College of Arts and Sciences, School of Music, Atlanta, GA 30303-3083. Offers M Mu. *Accreditation:* NASM. Part-time and evening/weekend programs available. *Faculty:* 23 full-time (3 women). *Students:* 56 full-time (31 women), 13 part-time (12 women); includes 18 minority (12 African Americans, 2 Asian Americans or Pacific Islanders, 4 Hispanic Americans), 5 international. 60 applicants, 38% accepted, 17 enrolled. In 2007, 24 degrees awarded. *Degree requirements:* For master's, comprehensive exam, thesis (for some programs), recital, exam. *Entrance requirements:* For master's, GRE General Test or MAT (music education), GRE (composition), departmental supplemental form, audition. Additional exam requirements/recommendations for international students: Required—TOEFL. *Application deadline:* For fall admission, 4/15 for domestic students, 3/15 for international students; for spring admission, 10/15 for domestic students, 9/15 for international students. Applications are processed on a rolling basis. Application fee: $50. Electronic applications accepted. *Expenses:* Tuition, state resident: part-time $221 per credit hour. *Financial support:* In 2007–08, 37 students received support, including 1 fellowship with full tuition reimbursement available (averaging $5,000 per year), 30 research assistantships with full tuition reimbursements available (averaging $6,000 per year), 3 teaching assistantships with full tuition reimbursements available (averaging $12,000 per year); career-related internships or fieldwork, Federal Work-Study, institutionally sponsored loans, tuition waivers (full), and unspecified assistant-

Music

Georgia State University (continued)
ships also available. Support available to part-time students. Financial award application deadline: 4/15; financial award applicants required to submit FAFSA. *Faculty research:* Teaching effectiveness assessment, computer music applications, arts/arts education policy, community music, psychology of music learning. Total annual research expenditures: $350,000. *Unit head:* W. Dwight Coleman, Director, 404-413-5919, Fax: 404-413-5910, E-mail: wcoleman@gsu.edu. *Application contact:* Dr. Steven Andrew Harper, Director of Graduate Studies, 404-413-5943, Fax: 404-413-5910, E-mail: sharper@gsu.edu.

Graduate School and University Center of the City University of New York, Graduate Studies, Program in Music, New York, NY 10016-4039. Offers DMA, PhD. *Faculty:* 62 full-time (9 women). *Students:* 192 full-time (98 women), 6 part-time (2 women); includes 19 minority (3 African Americans, 1 American Indian/Alaska Native, 8 Asian Americans or Pacific Islanders, 7 Hispanic Americans), 47 international. Average age 36. 167 applicants, 28% accepted, 21 enrolled. In 2007, 5 degrees awarded. *Degree requirements:* For doctorate, 2 foreign languages, thesis/dissertation. *Entrance requirements:* For doctorate, GRE General Test. Additional exam requirements/recommendations for international students: Required—TOEFL. *Application deadline:* For fall admission, 1/1 for domestic students. Application fee: $125. Electronic applications accepted. *Financial support:* In 2007–08, 92 students received support, including 76 fellowships, 3 research assistantships, 6 teaching assistantships; career-related internships or fieldwork, Federal Work-Study, institutionally sponsored loans, and tuition waivers (full and partial) also available. Financial award application deadline: 2/1; financial award applicants required to submit FAFSA. *Unit head:* Dr. David W. Olan, Executive Officer, 212-817-8591, Fax: 212-817-1529, E-mail: dolan@gc.cuny.edu.

Gratz College, Graduate Programs, Program in Jewish Music, Melrose Park, PA 19027. Offers MA, Certificate, MA/MA. Part-time programs available. *Degree requirements:* For master's, one foreign language, comprehensive exam, recital or thesis. *Entrance requirements:* For master's, audition, interview.

Hardin-Simmons University, Graduate School, School of Music, Abilene, TX 79698-0001. Offers church music (MM); music education (MM); music performance (MM); theory-composition (MM). *Accreditation:* NASM. Part-time programs available. *Faculty:* 13 full-time (6 women), 2 part-time/adjunct (1 woman). *Students:* 6 full-time (3 women), 2 part-time (1 woman). Average age 30. 11 applicants, 55% accepted, 4 enrolled. In 2007, 7 degrees awarded. *Degree requirements:* For master's, one foreign language, comprehensive exam, thesis (for some programs). *Entrance requirements:* For master's, minimum undergraduate GPA of 3.0 in major, 2.7 overall; performance; writing sample; demonstrated knowledge in chosen area. Additional exam requirements/recommendations for international students: Required—TOEFL (minimum score 550 paper-based; 213 computer-based). *Application deadline:* For fall admission, 8/15 priority date for domestic students; for spring admission, 1/5 priority date for domestic students. Applications are processed on a rolling basis. Application fee: $50 ($100 for international students). *Expenses:* Tuition: Full-time $9,810; part-time $545 per hour. Required fees: $590; $75 per semester. One-time fee: $50 part-time. *Financial support:* In 2007–08, 10 students received support, including 8 fellowships (averaging $1,050 per year); career-related internships or fieldwork and scholarships/grants also available. Support available to part-time students. Financial award application deadline: 6/30; financial award applicants required to submit FAFSA. *Unit head:* Dr. Leigh Anne Hunsaker, Director, 325-670-1391, Fax: 325-670-5873, E-mail: hunsaker@hsutx.edu. *Application contact:* Dr. Gary Stanlake, Dean of Graduate Studies, 325-670-1298, Fax: 325-670-1564, E-mail: gradoff@hsutx.edu.

Harvard University, Graduate School of Arts and Sciences, Department of Music, Cambridge, MA 02138. Offers composition (AM, PhD); musicology (AM); musicology and ethnomusicology (PhD); theory (AM, PhD). *Degree requirements:* For doctorate, 3 foreign languages, thesis/dissertation, composition, analytical paper. *Entrance requirements:* For master's and doctorate, GRE General Test. Additional exam requirements/recommendations for international students: Required—TOEFL. *Expenses:* Tuition: Full-time $31,456. Full-time tuition and fees vary according to program and student level.

Hebrew College, Program in Jewish Studies, Newton Centre, MA 02459. Offers Jewish liturgical music (Certificate); Jewish music education (Certificate); Jewish studies (MA). Part-time and evening/weekend programs available. Postbaccalaureate distance learning degree programs offered (minimal on-campus study). *Degree requirements:* For master's, one foreign language. *Entrance requirements:* For master's, GRE, interview. Additional exam requirements/recommendations for international students: Required—TOEFL.

Hebrew Union College–Jewish Institute of Religion, School of Sacred Music, New York, NY 10012-1186. Offers MSM. *Degree requirements:* For master's, one foreign language, thesis, recital. *Entrance requirements:* For master's, GRE, minimum 2 years of college-level Hebrew, bachelor's degree in music or related area, trained singing voice. Additional exam requirements/recommendations for international students: Required—TOEFL. Expenses: Contact institution.

Hofstra University, School of Education and Allied Human Services, Department of Curriculum and Teaching, Program in Music Education, Hempstead, NY 11549. Offers music education (MA, MS Ed); wind conducting (MA). Part-time programs available. *Students:* 15 full-time (5 women), 35 part-time (17 women); includes 3 minority (2 African Americans, 1 Asian American or Pacific Islander). Average age 26. 24 applicants, 88% accepted, 8 enrolled. In 2007, 20 degrees awarded. *Degree requirements:* For master's, one foreign language, thesis (for some programs). *Entrance requirements:* For master's, 2 letters of recommendation, teacher certification (MA), essay. Additional exam requirements/recommendations for international students: Required—TOEFL (minimum score 550 paper-based; 213 computer-based). *Application deadline:* Applications are processed on a rolling basis. Application fee: $60. Electronic applications accepted. *Expenses:* Tuition: Full-time $14,220; part-time $820 per credit. Required fees: $970; $165 per term. Tuition and fees vary according to program. *Financial support:* In 2007–08, 21 students received support, including 4 fellowships with tuition reimbursements available (averaging $2,250 per year); research assistantships with full and partial tuition reimbursements available, Federal Work-Study, institutionally sponsored loans, scholarships/grants, tuition waivers (full and partial), and unspecified assistantships also available. Support available to part-time students. Financial award applicants required to submit FAFSA. *Faculty research:* Creative thinking, musical thinking, curriculum design, teacher preparation. *Unit head:* Dr. Nathalie G. Robinson, Program Director, 516-463-4514, Fax: 516-463-6393, E-mail: musngr@hofstra.edu. *Application contact:* Carol Drummer, Dean of Graduate Admissions, 516-463-4876, Fax: 516-463-4664, E-mail: gradstudent@hofstra.edu.

Hollins University, Graduate Programs, Program in Liberal Studies, Roanoke, VA 24020-1603. Offers humanities (MALS); interdisciplinary studies (MALS); justice and legal studies (MALS); liberal studies (CAS); social science (MALS); visual and performing arts (MALS). Part-time and evening/weekend programs available. *Faculty:* 9 full-time (2 women), 12 part-time/adjunct (5 women). *Students:* 20 full-time (17 women), 89 part-time (74 women); includes 15 minority (11 African Americans, 1 American Indian/Alaska Native, 2 Asian Americans or Pacific Islanders, 1 Hispanic American). Average age 39. 30 applicants, 93% accepted, 20 enrolled. In 2007, 48 degrees awarded. *Degree requirements:* For master's, thesis. *Entrance requirements:* For master's, letters of recommendation, interview. Additional exam requirements/recommendations for international students: Required—TOEFL (minimum score 550 paper-based; 213 computer-based). *Application deadline:* For fall admission, 7/1 priority date for domestic and international students; for spring admission, 12/10 priority date for domestic and international students. Applications are processed on a rolling basis. Application fee: $40. Electronic applications accepted. *Expenses:* Tuition: Part-time $265 per credit hour. Tuition and fees vary according to course load and program. *Financial support:* In 2007–08, 53 students received support, including 4 fellowships (averaging $1,060 per year); Federal Work-Study and scholarships/grants also available. Support available to part-time students. Financial award application deadline: 7/15; financial award applicants required to submit FAFSA. *Faculty research:* Elderly blacks, film, feminist economics, U.S. voting patterns, Wagner, diversity. *Unit head:* Dr. Edward A. Lynch, Director, 540-362-6475, Fax: 540-362-6288, E-mail: elynch@hollins.edu. *Application contact:* Cathy S. Koon, Manager of Graduate Services, 540-362-6326, Fax: 540-362-6288, E-mail: ckoon@hollins.edu.

Holy Names University, Graduate Division, Department of Music, Oakland, CA 94619-1699. Offers Kodály music education (Certificate); music education with a Kodály emphasis (MM); performance (MM); piano pedagogy (MM); piano pedagogy with Suzuki emphasis (Certificate). *Faculty:* 2 full-time (1 woman), 6 part-time/adjunct (4 women). *Students:* 3 full-time (2 women), 12 part-time (10 women); includes 4 minority (3 Asian Americans or Pacific Islanders, 1 Hispanic American), 2 international. Average age 38. 9 applicants, 44% accepted, 2 enrolled. In 2007, 5 degrees awarded. *Degree requirements:* For master's, comprehensive exam, recital. *Entrance requirements:* For master's, audition, minimum undergraduate GPA of 2.6 overall, 3.0 in major. Additional exam requirements/recommendations for international students: Required—TOEFL. *Application deadline:* For fall admission, 8/1 priority date for domestic students; for spring admission, 12/1 priority date for domestic students. Applications are processed on a rolling basis. Application fee: $65. *Expenses:* Tuition: Part-time $635 per unit. One-time fee: $340 part-time. Tuition and fees vary according to program. *Financial support:* In 2007–08, 4 students received support. Scholarships/grants available. Support available to part-time students. Financial award application deadline: 3/2; financial award applicants required to submit FAFSA. *Faculty research:* Performance practice with special interest in baroque, Romantic, and twentieth-century instrumental and vocal music; choral pedagogy; Hungarian music education. *Unit head:* Anne Laskey, Director, 510-436-1234. *Application contact:* 800-430-1351, Fax: 510-436-1325, E-mail: admissions@hnu.edu.

Hope International University, School of Graduate Studies, Programs in Ministry, Fullerton, CA 92831-3138. Offers Christian leadership (MCM); church music (MA); church music (Korean track) (MCM); church planting (MCM); intercultural studies (MCM); worship (MCM). Part-time and evening/weekend programs available. Postbaccalaureate distance learning degree programs offered (minimal on-campus study). *Faculty:* 25. *Students:* 12 full-time (2 women), 42 part-time (15 women); includes 11 minority (2 African Americans, 7 Asian Americans or Pacific Islanders, 2 Hispanic Americans), 9 international. Average age 38. 16 applicants, 94% accepted, 14 enrolled. In 2007, 28 degrees awarded. *Degree requirements:* For master's, thesis (for some programs), project. *Entrance requirements:* For master's, minimum GPA of 3.0, MCM program requires an undergraduate degree in music, application, official transcripts, 2 references, statement of purpose. Additional exam requirements/recommendations for international students: Required—TOEFL (minimum score 550 paper-based; 213 computer-based; 86 iBT); Recommended—IELTS (minimum score 7). *Application deadline:* For fall admission, 8/3 priority date for domestic and international students; for winter admission, 12/14 priority date for domestic and international students; for spring admission, 1/4 priority date for domestic and international students. Applications are processed on a rolling basis. Application fee: $75. Electronic applications accepted. *Expenses:* Contact institution. *Financial support:* Scholarships/grants, health care benefits, and tuition waivers (partial) available. Support available to part-time students. Financial award applicants required to submit FAFSA. *Faculty research:* Church dynamics, growth methodologies. *Unit head:* Dr. David Timms, Chair, 714-879-3401 Ext. 2720, Fax: 714-681-7450, E-mail: djtimms@hiu.edu. *Application contact:* Ed Bort, Assistant Director of Admissions, 800-762-1294 Ext. 2322, Fax: 714-681-7450, E-mail: ebort@hiu.edu.

Houghton College, Greatbatch School of Music, Houghton, NY 14744. Offers collaborative studies (MMus); composition (MMus); conducting (MMus); music (MA); performance (MMus). *Accreditation:* NASM. *Faculty:* 13 full-time (4 women), 6 part-time/adjunct (3 women). *Students:* 13 full-time (8 women), 1 (woman) part-time; includes 1 minority (Asian American or Pacific Islander) Average age 24. 16 applicants, 88% accepted, 9 enrolled. In 2007, 9 degrees awarded. *Degree requirements:* For master's, comprehensive exam (for some programs), thesis (for some programs), recitals (for some programs). *Entrance requirements:* For master's, bachelor of music or equivalent. Additional exam requirements/recommendations for international students: Required—TOEFL (minimum score 600 paper-based; 250 computer-based). *Application deadline:* For fall admission, 3/15 priority date for domestic and international students. Applications are processed on a rolling basis. Application fee: $40. Electronic applications accepted. *Expenses:* Tuition: Part-time $697 per credit hour. *Financial support:* In 2007–08, 13 students received support, including 15 fellowships with full tuition reimbursements available (averaging $7,200 per year); unspecified assistantships also available. Financial award application deadline: 3/15. *Faculty research:* Bach Studies; original compositions; professional performance; contemporary women composers; music in Christian worship. *Unit head:* Dr. Ben R. King, Director and Associate Dean for Music, 585-567-9400, Fax: 585-567-9517, E-mail: ben.king@houghton.edu. *Application contact:* Mindy Airhart, Graduate Music Program Coordinator.

Howard University, Graduate School, Division of Fine Arts, Department of Music, Washington, DC 20059-0002. Offers applied music (MM); instrument (MM Ed); jazz studies (MM); organ (MM Ed); piano (MM Ed); voice (MM Ed). *Accreditation:* NASM. Part-time programs available. *Degree requirements:* For master's, comprehensive exam, thesis or alternative, departmental qualifying exam, recital. *Entrance requirements:* For master's, minimum GPA of 3.0, bachelor's degree in music or music education. Additional exam requirements/recommendations for international students: Required—TOEFL. *Expenses:* Tuition: Full-time $16,175; part-time $899 per credit hour. Required fees: $805.

Hunter College of the City University of New York, Graduate School, School of Arts and Sciences, Department of Music, New York, NY 10021-5085. Offers music (MA); music education (MA). Part-time and evening/weekend programs available. *Faculty:* 9 full-time (3 women), 6 part-time/adjunct (3 women). *Students:* 2 full-time (1 woman), 45 part-time (24 women); includes 9 minority (1 African American, 6 Asian Americans or Pacific Islanders, 2 Hispanic Americans). Average age 34. 38 applicants, 53% accepted, 13 enrolled. In 2007, 15 degrees awarded. *Degree requirements:* For master's, one foreign language, thesis, composition, essay, or recital; proficiency exam. *Entrance requirements:* For master's, undergraduate major in music (minimum 24 credits) or equivalent, sample of work, research paper. Additional exam requirements/recommendations for international students: Required—TOEFL. *Application deadline:* For fall admission, 4/1 for domestic students, 2/1 for international students; for spring admission, 11/1 for domestic students, 9/1 for international students. Applications are processed on a rolling basis. Application fee: $125. *Expenses:* Tuition, state resident: full-time $6,400; part-time $270 per credit. Tuition, nonresident: part-time $500 per credit. One-time fee: $125 full-time. Tuition and fees vary according to program. *Financial support:* In 2007–08, 4 fellowships (averaging $1,000 per year) were awarded; Federal Work-Study, tuition waivers (partial), and lesson stipends also available. Support available to part-time students. Financial award application deadline: 4/15. *Faculty research:* African and African-American music, Bach, Renaissance music, early romantic music, theory of tonal music. *Unit head:* Dr. Paul F. Mueller, Chair, 212-772-5020, Fax: 212-772-5022, E-mail: music@hunter.cuny.edu. *Application contact:* Dr. L. Poundie Burstein, Graduate Adviser, 212-650-5152, E-mail: huntermus@aol.com.

Illinois State University, Graduate School, College of Fine Arts, School of Music, Normal, IL 61790-2200. Offers MM, MM Ed. *Accreditation:* NASM. *Faculty:* 27 full-time (10 women). *Students:* 48 full-time (34 women), 25 part-time (18 women); includes 9 minority (2 African Americans, 5 Asian Americans or Pacific Islanders, 2 Hispanic Americans), 18 international. 39 applicants, 82% accepted. In 2007, 34 master's awarded. *Degree requirements:* For master's, thesis or alternative, performance. *Entrance requirements:* For master's, minimum GPA of 3.0 in music, 2.6 overall; auditions. *Application deadline:* Applications are processed on a rolling basis. Application fee: $40. *Expenses:* Tuition, state resident: full-time $3,492; part-time $194 per credit hour. Tuition, nonresident: full-time $7,272; part-time $404 per credit hour. Required fees: $1,024; $57 per credit hour. *Financial support:* In 2007–08, 1 research assistantship (averaging $7,650 per year), 40 teaching assistantships (averaging $5,906 per year) were awarded; tuition waivers (full) and unspecified assistantships also available. Financial award application deadline: 4/1. *Faculty research:* Concerts on the Quad summer concert series. Total annual research expenditures: $2,300. *Unit head:* Dr. Stephen Parsons, Acting Chairperson, 309-438-7631.

Indiana State University, School of Graduate Studies, College of Arts and Sciences, Department of Music, Terre Haute, IN 47809-1401. Offers music performance (MM). *Accreditation:* NASM. *Faculty:* 7 full-time (3 women), 1 part-time/adjunct (0 women). *Students:* 13 full-time (8 women), 8 part-time (5 women); includes 1 minority (African American), 5 international. Average age 27. 14 applicants, 100% accepted, 7 enrolled. In 2007, 2 degrees awarded. *Degree requirements:* For master's, comprehensive exam, thesis (for some programs), departmental qualifying exam. *Application deadline:* For fall admission, 7/1 priority date for domestic students; for spring admission, 11/1 priority date for domestic students. Applications are processed on a rolling basis. Application fee: $35. Electronic applications accepted. *Expenses:* Tuition, state resident: full-time $7,056; part-time $294 per semester hour. Tuition, nonresident: full-time $14,016; part-time $584 per semester hour. Required fees: $175 per semester. *Financial support:* In 2007–08, 6 teaching assistantships with partial tuition reimbursements (averaging $7,000 per year) were awarded; research assistantships with partial tuition reimbursements, tuition waivers (partial) also available. Financial award application deadline: 3/1; financial award applicants required to submit FAFSA.

Indiana University Bloomington, Jacobs School of Music, Bloomington, IN 47405-7000. Offers MA, MM, MM/MLS, MME, MS, DM, DME, PhD, AD, Performance Diploma, Spec, MA/MLS. PhD offered through University Graduate School. *Accreditation:* NASM (one or more programs are accredited). *Faculty:* 139 full-time (35 women), 11 part-time/adjunct (3 women). *Students:* 507 full-time (269 women), 305 part-time (139 women); includes 81 minority (20 African Americans, 2 American Indian/Alaska Native, 45 Asian Americans or Pacific Islanders, 14 Hispanic Americans), 214 international. Average age 29. 1,745 applicants, 33% accepted, 339 enrolled. In 2007, 131 master's, 34 doctorates, 45 other advanced degrees awarded. Terminal master's awarded for partial completion of doctoral program. *Degree requirements:* For master's, comprehensive exam (for some programs); for doctorate, comprehensive exam, thesis/dissertation. *Entrance requirements:* For master's and doctorate, GRE, audition, 3 letters of recommendation. Additional exam requirements/recommendations for international students: Required—TOEFL (minimum score 560 paper-based; 223 computer-based; 84 iBT). *Application deadline:* For fall admission, 12/1 for domestic and international students; for spring admission, 9/1 for domestic and international students. Applications are processed on a rolling basis. Application fee: $100 ($110 for international students). Electronic applications accepted. *Expenses: Contact institution. Financial support:* In 2007–08, 225 students received support, including 6 fellowships with full and partial tuition reimbursements available (averaging $17,000 per year), 85 teaching assistantships with full tuition reimbursements available (averaging $6,000 per year); research assistantships with tuition reimbursements available, Federal Work-Study, institutionally sponsored loans, scholarships/grants, tuition waivers (full and partial), and unspecified assistantships also available. Support available to part-time students. Financial award application deadline: 3/1; financial award applicants required to submit FAFSA. Total annual research expenditures: $8,300. *Unit head:* Gwyn Richards, Dean, 812-855-2435, E-mail: jln@indiana.edu. *Application contact:* Music Admissions, 812-855-7998, Fax: 812-856-6086, E-mail: musicadm@indiana.edu.

Indiana University Bloomington, University Graduate School, College of Arts and Sciences, Department of Folklore and Ethnomusicology, Bloomington, IN 47408-3890. Offers folklore (MA, PhD), including ethnomusicology. Part-time programs available. *Faculty:* 12 full-time (5 women), 11 part-time/adjunct (6 women). *Students:* 97 full-time (67 women), 21 part-time (12 women); includes 25 minority (11 African Americans, 1 American Indian/Alaska Native, 6 Asian Americans or Pacific Islanders, 7 Hispanic Americans), 23 international. Average age 34. 81 applicants, 53% accepted, 18 enrolled. In 2007, 11 master's, 7 doctorates awarded. *Median time to degree:* Of those who began their doctoral program in fall 1999, 33% received their degree in 8 years or less. *Degree requirements:* For master's, one foreign language, comprehensive exam, thesis or alternative, project or thesis; for doctorate, 2 foreign languages, comprehensive exam, thesis/dissertation, registration is required for candidacy. *Entrance requirements:* For master's and doctorate, GRE General Test, minimum GPA of 3.0. Additional exam requirements/recommendations for international students: Required—TOEFL (minimum score 550 paper-based; 213 computer-based; 79 iBT). *Application deadline:* For fall admission, 1/15 for domestic students, 12/1 for international students. Application fee: $50 ($60 for international students). Electronic applications accepted. *Financial support:* In 2007–08, 27 students received support; fellowships with full tuition reimbursements available, research assistantships with full tuition reimbursements available, teaching assistantships with full tuition reimbursements available, Federal Work-Study and unspecified assistantships available. Financial award application deadline: 3/1; financial award applicants required to submit FAFSA. *Faculty research:* Narrative, performance studies, material culture, popular culture, music. *Unit head:* Dr. Portia Maultsby, Chair, 812-855-0395, Fax: 812-855-4008, E-mail: maultsby@indiana.edu. *Application contact:* Christopher Roush, Graduate Secretary, 812-855-0389, Fax: 812-855-4008, E-mail: croush@indiana.edu.

Indiana University of Pennsylvania, School of Graduate Studies and Research, College of Fine Arts, Department of Music and Music Education, Program in Music, Indiana, PA 15705-1087. Offers music education (MA); music history and literature (MA); music theory and composition (MA); performance (MA). *Accreditation:* NASM. Part-time programs available. *Faculty:* 11 full-time (4 women). *Students:* 7 full-time (2 women), 2 part-time, 1 international. Average age 28. 17 applicants, 47% accepted, 7 enrolled. In 2007, 10 degrees awarded. *Degree requirements:* For master's, thesis optional. *Entrance requirements:* For master's, 2 letters of recommendation, audition. Additional exam requirements/recommendations for international students: Required—TOEFL. *Application deadline:* For fall admission, 7/1 priority date for domestic students; for spring admission, 11/1 for domestic students. Applications are processed on a rolling basis. Application fee: $30. *Expenses:* Tuition, state resident: full-time $6,214; part-time $345 per credit. Tuition, nonresident: full-time $9,944; part-time $552 per credit. Required fees: $43 per credit. One-time fee: $140 part-time. Tuition and fees vary according to course load. *Financial support:* In 2007–08, fellowships (averaging $500 per year), 5 research assistantships with full and partial tuition reimbursements (averaging $2,495 per year) were awarded; Federal Work-Study also available. Support available to part-time students. Financial award application deadline: 3/15; financial award applicants required to submit FAFSA. *Unit head:* Dr. Keith Young, Head, 724-357-4408.

Indiana University–Purdue University Indianapolis, School of Music, Indianapolis, IN 46202-2896. Offers music technology (MS). Part-time and evening/weekend programs available. Postbaccalaureate distance learning degree programs offered. *Students:* 9 full-time (3 women), 39 part-time (13 women); includes 4 minority (3 African Americans, 1 Asian American or Pacific Islander), 4 international. In 2007, 13 master's awarded. *Degree requirements:* For master's, internship or final project. *Entrance requirements:* For master's, audition, minimum GPA of 3.0. Additional exam requirements/recommendations for international students: Required—TOEFL. *Application deadline:* For fall admission, 4/15 priority date for domestic students, 3/15 for international students; for spring admission, 11/15 priority date for domestic students, 11/15 for international students. Applications are processed on a rolling basis. Application fee: $50 ($60 for international students). *Expenses:* Tuition, state resident: full-time $5,818; part-time $242 per credit hour. Tuition, nonresident: full-time $17,106; part-time $713 per credit hour. Required fees: $629. Tuition and fees vary according to course load, campus/location and program. *Financial support:* Teaching assistantships with full tuition reimbursements, Federal Work-Study, institutionally sponsored loans, and scholarships/grants available. Support available to part-time students. Financial award application deadline: 11/15. *Unit head:* G. David Peters, Director, 317-278-2594.

Indiana University South Bend, School of the Arts, South Bend, IN 46634-7111. Offers music (MM); studio teaching (MM). Part-time programs available. *Faculty:* 1 full-time (0 women). *Students:* 7 full-time (5 women), 1 (woman) part-time, 6 international. Average age 31. In 2007, 7 master's awarded. *Entrance requirements:* For master's, performance audition. *Application deadline:* For fall admission, 7/1 priority date for domestic students; for spring admission, 11/1 for domestic students. Applications are processed on a rolling basis. Application fee: $46 ($58 for international students). *Expenses:* Tuition, state resident: full-time $4,762; part-time $198 per credit hour. Tuition, nonresident: full-time $11,720; part-time $488 per credit hour. Required fees: $422; $422 per year. Full-time tuition and fees vary according to course load, campus/location and program. *Financial support:* In 2007–08, 4 fellowships (averaging $2,855 per year), 1 teaching assistantship (averaging $1,320 per year) were awarded; Federal Work-Study also available. Support available to part-time students. Financial award application deadline: 3/1; financial award applicants required to submit FAFSA. *Faculty research:* Orchestral conducting. *Unit head:* Dr. Thomas Miller, Dean, 574-520-4301, Fax: 574-520-4317, E-mail: messelst@iusb.edu.

Ithaca College, Graduate Studies, School of Music, Program in Music and Music Education, Ithaca, NY 14850-7020. Offers composition (MM); conducting (MM); music education (MM, MS); performance (MM); Suzuki pedagogy (MM). *Accreditation:* NASM. Part-time programs available. *Faculty:* 59 full-time (20 women), 2 part-time/adjunct (1 woman). *Students:* 38 full-time (18 women), 9 part-time (5 women); includes 2 minority (1 Asian American or Pacific Islander, 1 Hispanic American), 3 international. Average age 25. 124 applicants, 40% accepted, 19 enrolled. In 2007, 33 degrees awarded. *Degree requirements:* For master's, comprehensive exam, thesis (for some programs). *Entrance requirements:* For master's, audition, minimum GPA of 3.0. Additional exam requirements/recommendations for international students: Required—TOEFL (minimum score 550 paper-based; 213 computer-based; 80 iBT). *Application deadline:* For fall admission, 3/1 for domestic students; for spring admission, 12/1 for domestic students. Applications are processed on a rolling basis. Application fee: $40. *Expenses: Contact institution. Financial support:* In 2007–08, 39 students received support, including 31 teaching assistantships (averaging $9,217 per year); career-related internships or fieldwork, Federal Work-Study, scholarships/grants, and unspecified assistantships also available. Support available to part-time students. Financial award application deadline: 4/1; financial award applicants required to submit FAFSA. *Faculty research:* Musical performance and performance studies; musical composition, music theory and analysis; music history and musicology; musical direction and conducting. *Unit head:* Dr. Timothy Johnson, Chairperson, 607-274-3527, Fax: 607-274-1263, E-mail: gps@ithaca.edu.

Jacksonville State University, College of Graduate Studies and Continuing Education, College of Arts and Sciences, Department of Music, Jacksonville, AL 36265-1602. Offers MA. *Accreditation:* NASM. *Faculty:* 10 full-time (6 women), 2 part-time/adjunct (0 women). *Students:* 3 full-time (2 women), 9 part-time (5 women); includes 4 minority (3 African Americans, 1 American Indian/Alaska Native). In 2007, 1 degree awarded. *Degree requirements:* For master's, thesis optional. *Entrance requirements:* For master's, GRE General Test or MAT. *Application deadline:* Applications are processed on a rolling basis. Application fee: $20. *Financial support:* In 2007–08, 4 teaching assistantships were awarded. Support available to part-time students. Financial award application deadline: 4/1. *Unit head:* Dr. Legare McIntosh, Head, 256-782-5560. *Application contact:* 256-782-5329, Fax: 256-782-5321, E-mail: graduate@jsu.edu.

James Madison University, The Graduate School, College of Visual and Performing Arts, School of Music, Musical Arts Program, Harrisonburg, VA 22807. Offers DMA. Part-time programs available. *Faculty:* 16 full-time (3 women), 2 part-time/adjunct (1 woman). *Students:* 7 full-time (1 woman), 1 part-time; includes 1 minority (Hispanic American), 2 international. Average age 27. *Degree requirements:* For doctorate, comprehensive exam, written and oral exams. *Entrance requirements:* For doctorate, GRE General Test, written statement of future goals (professional and educational). 3 letters of recommendation Audition. Additional exam requirements/recommendations for international students: Required—TOEFL. *Application deadline:* For fall admission, 4/1 priority date for domestic students, 4/1 for international students; for spring admission, 4/1 priority date for domestic students, 4/1 for international students. Applications are processed on a rolling basis. Application fee: $55. Electronic applications accepted. *Expenses:* Tuition, state resident: full-time $6,720; part-time $280 per credit hour. Tuition, nonresident: full-time $19,104; part-time $796 per credit hour. *Financial support:* In 2007–08, 6 students received support. 6 doctoral assistantships ($14,216) available. Financial award application deadline: 3/1; financial award applicants required to submit FAFSA. *Application contact:* Dr. Mary Jane Speare, Graduate Coordinator, 540-568-6197.

The Jewish Theological Seminary, H. L. Miller Cantorial School and College of Jewish Music, New York, NY 10027-4649. Offers MSM. *Faculty:* 62 full-time (21 women), 69 part-time/adjunct (33 women). *Students:* 43 full-time (21 women). Average age 31. 13 applicants, 69% accepted, 7 enrolled. In 2007, 9 master's awarded. *Degree requirements:* For master's, one foreign language, comprehensive exam, departmental qualifying exam, recitals. *Entrance requirements:* For master's, music aptitude test, audition, interview, 3 letters of recommendation. Additional exam requirements/recommendations for international students: Required—TOEFL. *Application deadline:* For fall admission, 1/1 priority date for domestic students. Applications are processed on a rolling basis. Application fee: $50. *Expenses: Contact institution.* Full-time tuition and fees vary according to degree level, program and student level. *Financial support:* In 2007–08, 3 fellowships (averaging $667 per year) were awarded; career-related internships or fieldwork also available. Support available to part-time students. Financial award application deadline: 3/1; financial award applicants required to submit FAFSA. *Unit head:* Hazzan Henry Rosenblum, Dean, 212-678-8036, Fax: 212-678-8947, E-mail: herosenblum@jtsa.edu. *Application contact:* Cheryl Goldwasser, Admissions Coordinator, 212-678-8037, Fax: 212-662-8989, E-mail: shgoldwasser@jtsa.edu.

The Johns Hopkins University, Peabody Conservatory of Music, Baltimore, MD 21218-2699. Offers MA, MM, DMA, AD, GPD. *Faculty:* 72 full-time (19 women), 55 part-time/adjunct (16 women). *Students:* 336 full-time (186 women), 30 part-time (17 women); includes 45 minority (10 African Americans, 1 American Indian/Alaska Native, 24 Asian Americans or Pacific Islanders, 10 Hispanic Americans), 171 international. Average age 24. 734 applicants, 49% accepted, 167 enrolled. In 2007, 100 master's, 5 doctorates, 23 other advanced degrees awarded. *Degree requirements:* For master's, thesis (for some programs), departmental qualifying exam, recital; for doctorate, 2 foreign languages, thesis/dissertation (for some programs), departmental qualifying exam, recitals; for other advanced degree, recitals. *Entrance requirements:* For master's and other advanced degree, audition; for doctorate, audition, interview. Additional exam requirements/recommendations for international students: Required—TOEFL (minimum score 550 paper-based; 213 computer-based; 79 iBT). *Application deadline:* For fall admission, 12/1 for domestic students. Application fee: $100. *Expenses: Contact institution. Financial support:* In 2007–08, 277 students received support, including 56 teaching assistantships (averaging $24,082 per year); Federal Work-Study, scholarships/grants, and unspecified assistantships also available. Financial award application deadline: 2/1; financial award applicants required to submit FAFSA. *Unit head:* Jeffrey Sharkey, Director, 410-659-8100 Ext. 3060, Fax: 410-659-8131. *Application contact:* David Lane, Director of Admissions, 800-368-2521, Fax: 410-659-8102, E-mail: admissions@peabody.jhu.edu.

The Juilliard School, Program in Music, New York, NY 10023-6588. Offers MM, DMA, Artist Diploma, Diploma. *Faculty:* 298 full-time (145 women), 29 part-time/adjunct (11 women). *Students:* 306 full-time (148 women), 35 part-time (15 women); includes 132 minority (15 African Americans, 1 American Indian/Alaska Native, 105 Asian Americans or Pacific Islanders, 11 Hispanic Americans), 124 international. Average age 25. 1,567 applicants, 12% accepted, 158 enrolled. In 2007, 97 master's, 7 doctorates, 39 Artist Diplomas awarded. *Degree requirements:* For master's and other advanced degree, performance jury, recital; for doctorate, one foreign language, thesis/dissertation, performance jury, 3 recitals. *Entrance requirements:* For master's and other advanced degree, audition; for doctorate, audition, interview, dossier. Additional exam requirements/recommendations for international students: Required—TOEFL (minimum score 570 paper-based; 230 computer-based; 89 iBT). *Application deadline:* For fall admission, 12/1 for domestic and international students. Application fee: $100. Electronic applications accepted. *Expenses:* Tuition: Full-time $27,150. One-time fee: $200 full-time. *Financial support:* In 2007–08, 308 students received support; fellowships, research assistantships, teaching assistantships, Federal Work-Study, institutionally sponsored loans, scholarships/grants, and unspecified assistantships available. Support available to part-time students. Financial award application deadline: 3/1; financial award applicants required to submit FAFSA. *Unit head:* Ara Guzelimian, Provost and Dean, 212-799-5000 Ext. 204, Fax: 212-724-0263.

Music

The Juilliard School (continued)

Application contact: Lee Cioppa, Associate Dean for Admissions, 212-799-5000 Ext. 223, Fax: 212-724-6420, E-mail: admissions@juilliard.edu.

Kansas State University, Graduate School, College of Arts and Sciences, Department of Music, Manhattan, KS 66506. Offers music education (MM); music education/band conducting (MM); music history and literature (MM); performance (MM); performance with pedagogy emphasis (MM); theory and composition (MM). *Accreditation:* NASM. Part-time programs available. *Faculty:* 17 full-time (4 women). *Students:* 24 full-time (13 women), 4 part-time (1 woman); includes 1 minority (Hispanic American), 1 international. Average age 25. 6 applicants, 100% accepted, 6 enrolled. In 2007, 6 degrees awarded. *Degree requirements:* For master's, thesis optional. *Entrance requirements:* For master's, GRE, audition (in person or recording), interview (music education). Additional exam requirements/recommendations for international students: Required—TOEFL (minimum score 600 paper-based). *Application deadline:* For fall admission, 2/1 priority date for domestic and international students; for spring admission, 10/1 priority date for domestic students, 8/1 priority date for international students. Applications are processed on a rolling basis. Application fee: $30 ($55 for international students). Electronic applications accepted. *Financial support:* In 2007–08, 11 teaching assistantships with full tuition reimbursements (averaging $7,091 per year) were awarded; institutionally sponsored loans, scholarships/grants, and tuition waivers (full and partial) also available. Support available to part-time students. Financial award application deadline: 3/1; financial award applicants required to submit FAFSA. *Faculty research:* Music since 1945, music by women composers, American music, opera, current performance practices. Total annual research expenditures: $30,256. *Unit head:* Dr. Gary Mortenson, Head, 785-532-3828, Fax: 785-532-7732, E-mail: garym@ksu.edu. *Application contact:* Fred Burrack, Director, 785-532-5764, Fax: 785-532-7732, E-mail: fburrack@ksu.edu.

Kent State University, College of the Arts, Hugh A. Glauser School of Music, Kent, OH 44242-0001. Offers composition (MA); conducting (MM); ethnomusicology (MA); music education (MM, PhD); musicology (MA); musicology-ethnomusicology (PhD); performance (MM); theory (MA); theory and composition (PhD). *Accreditation:* NASM. *Faculty:* 29 full-time, 13 part-time/adjunct. *Students:* Average age 27. 48 applicants, 83% accepted, 30 enrolled. In 2007, 15 master's, 4 doctorates awarded. *Median time to degree:* Of those who began their doctoral program in fall 1999, 75% received their degree in 8 years or less. *Degree requirements:* For master's, variable foreign language requirement, comprehensive exam, 2 recitals, essay and recital, or thesis; for doctorate, variable foreign language requirement, comprehensive exam, thesis/dissertation. *Entrance requirements:* For master's, diagnostic exams in music history and theory, audition, minimum GPA of 2.75; for doctorate, diagnostic exams in music history and theory, master's thesis or scholarly paper, minimum GPA of 3.0. Additional exam requirements/recommendations for international students: Required—TOEFL. *Application deadline:* For fall admission, 7/12 for domestic students; for spring admission, 11/29 for domestic students. Applications are processed on a rolling basis. Application fee: $30. Electronic applications accepted. *Financial support:* In 2007–08, 43 students received support, including 43 teaching assistantships with full tuition reimbursements available (averaging $6,134 per year); fellowships with full tuition reimbursements available, research assistantships with full tuition reimbursements available, Federal Work-Study and unspecified assistantships also available. Financial award application deadline: 2/1; financial award applicants required to submit FAFSA. *Faculty research:* Music composition, performance, teaching and history. *Unit head:* Josef Knott, Director, 330-672-2172, E-mail: jknott1@kent.edu. *Application contact:* Ralph Lorenz, Graduate Coordinator, 330-672-2937, E-mail: rlorenz@kent.edu.

Lamar University, College of Graduate Studies, College of Fine Arts and Communication, Department of Music, Theatre, and Dance, Beaumont, TX 77710. Offers music education (MM Ed); music performance (MM); theatre (MS). *Accreditation:* NASM (one or more programs are accredited). *Faculty:* 11 full-time (4 women), 3 part-time/adjunct (1 woman). *Students:* 3 full-time (2 women), 4 part-time (all women). Average age 29. 5 applicants, 80% accepted, 2 enrolled. In 2007, 4 degrees awarded. *Degree requirements:* For master's, comprehensive exam, thesis optional. *Entrance requirements:* For master's, GRE General Test, theory placement exams, audition. Additional exam requirements/recommendations for international students: Required—TOEFL. *Application deadline:* For fall admission, 8/1 for domestic students; for spring admission, 12/1 for domestic students. Applications are processed on a rolling basis. Application fee: $25 ($50 for international students). *Expenses:* Tuition, state resident: part-time $348 per semester hour. Tuition, nonresident: part-time $626 per semester hour. Tuition and fees vary according to course load. *Financial support:* In 2007–08, 4 fellowships with tuition reimbursements (averaging $2,000 per year), 2 teaching assistantships were awarded; institutionally sponsored loans and tuition waivers (partial) also available. Support available to part-time students. Financial award application deadline: 4/1. *Faculty research:* Performance: ensembles and personal. *Unit head:* Dr. L. Randolph Babin, Chair, 409-880-8144, Fax: 409-880-8143, E-mail: babinlr@hal.lamar.edu. *Application contact:* Dr. Robert M. Culbertson, Adviser, 409-880-8073, Fax: 409-880-8143, E-mail: culbertsrm@hal.lamar.edu.

Lee University, Program in Music, Cleveland, TN 37320-3450. Offers church music (MCM); music education (MME); performance (MMMP). *Accreditation:* NASM. Part-time programs available. *Faculty:* 15 full-time (4 women), 3 part-time/adjunct (1 woman). *Students:* 18 full-time (9 women), 17 part-time (8 women); includes 3 minority (1 African American, 2 Hispanic Americans), 3 international. Average age 30. 24 applicants, 71% accepted, 9 enrolled. In 2007, 12 degrees awarded. *Degree requirements:* For master's, variable foreign language requirement, comprehensive exam, thesis, internship. *Entrance requirements:* For master's, audition, resumé, interview, minimum GPA of 2.75. Additional exam requirements/recommendations for international students: Required—TOEFL. *Application deadline:* For fall admission, 4/1 for domestic students; for spring admission, 10/1 for domestic students. Applications are processed on a rolling basis. Application fee: $25. *Expenses:* Tuition: Full-time $10,392; part-time $433 per credit. Required fees: $65 per term. Tuition and fees vary according to course load. *Financial support:* In 2007–08, 13 teaching assistantships (averaging $2,275 per year) were awarded; career-related internships or fieldwork, Federal Work-Study, institutionally sponsored loans, and scholarships/grants also available. Financial award application deadline: 3/1; financial award applicants required to submit FAFSA. *Unit head:* Dr. Jim W. Burns, Director, 423-614-8240, Fax: 423-614-8242, E-mail: gradmusic@leeuniversity.edu. *Application contact:* Vicki Glasscock, Graduate Admissions Director, 423-614-8059, E-mail: vglasscock@leeuniversity.edu.

Long Island University, C.W. Post Campus, School of Visual and Performing Arts, Department of Music, Brookville, NY 11548-1300. Offers music (MA); music education (MS). Part-time programs available. *Faculty:* 4 full-time (3 women), 61 part-time/adjunct (24 women). *Students:* 11 full-time (3 women), 13 part-time (6 women); includes 3 minority (2 African Americans, 1 Asian American or Pacific Islander). Average age 31. 19 applicants, 63% accepted, 6 enrolled. In 2007, 20 degrees awarded. *Degree requirements:* For master's, thesis. *Entrance requirements:* For master's, GRE General Test (MA), GRE Subject Test in music, minimum undergraduate GPA of 3.0, 2 professional and/or academic letters of recommendation, current resumé. *Application deadline:* Applications are processed on a rolling basis. Application fee: $30. Electronic applications accepted. *Expenses:* Tuition: Part-time $825 per credit. Tuition and fees vary according to course load. *Financial support:* Federal Work-Study and unspecified assistantships available. Support available to part-time students. Financial award application deadline: 5/15; financial award applicants required to submit CSS PROFILE or FAFSA. *Faculty research:* Performance, composing, musicology, conducting, computer-based music technology. Total annual research expenditures: $4,956. *Unit head:* Stephanie Watt, Chair, 516-299-2474, E-mail: stephanie.watt@liu.edu. *Application contact:* John Meschi, Advisor, 516-299-2105, E-mail: jmeschi@liu.edu.

Longy School of Music, Conservatory at Longy, Cambridge, MA 02138. Offers chamber ensemble (Artist Diploma); collaborative piano (MM, Artist Diploma, GPD); composition (MM); Dalcroze eurhythmics (MM); early music (MM, Artist Diploma, GPD); instrumental performance (MM, Artist Diploma, GPD); modern American music (MM, GPD); opera performance (MM, GPD); organ performance (MM, Artist Diploma, GPD); piano performance (MM, Artist Diploma, GPD); vocal performance (MM, Artist Diploma, GPD). *Accreditation:* NASM. Part-time programs available. *Faculty:* 98 part-time/adjunct (52 women). *Students:* 130 full-time (91 women), 41 part-time (22 women); includes 16 minority (6 African Americans, 9 Asian Americans or Pacific Islanders, 1 Hispanic American), 46 international. Average age 28. 196 applicants, 70% accepted, 70 enrolled. In 2007, 39 master's, 21 Artist Diplomas awarded. *Degree requirements:* For master's, thesis (for some programs), recital; for other advanced degree, recital. *Entrance requirements:* For master's and other advanced degree, audition. Additional exam requirements/recommendations for international students: Required—TOEFL (minimum score 500 paper-based; 173 computer-based; 61 iBT). *Application deadline:* For fall admission, 1/15 priority date for domestic and international students; for spring admission, 12/1 for domestic and international students. Applications are processed on a rolling basis. Application fee: $90. *Expenses:* Tuition: Full-time $24,350; part-time $1,380 per credit. Required fees: $450; $450 per year. Tuition and fees vary according to program. *Financial support:* In 2007–08, 145 students received support, including 8 teaching assistantships (averaging $1,890 per year); scholarships/grants and unspecified assistantships also available. Financial award application deadline: 3/1; financial award applicants required to submit FAFSA. *Unit head:* Karen Zorn, President, 617-876-0956, Fax: 617-876-9326, E-mail: music@longy.edu. *Application contact:* Heather McCowen, Director of Admissions, 617-876-0956 Ext. 521, Fax: 617-876-9326, E-mail: music@longy.edu.

Louisiana State University and Agricultural and Mechanical College, Graduate School, College of Music and Dramatic Arts, School of Music, Baton Rouge, LA 70803. Offers music (MM, DMA, PhD); music education (PhD). *Accreditation:* NASM. Part-time programs available. *Faculty:* 50 full-time (16 women), 2 part-time/adjunct (both women). *Students:* 143 full-time (82 women), 33 part-time (23 women); includes 21 minority (9 African Americans, 7 Asian Americans or Pacific Islanders, 5 Hispanic Americans), 30 international. Average age 30. 139 applicants, 61% accepted, 57 enrolled. In 2007, 30 master's, 21 doctorates awarded. Terminal master's awarded for partial completion of doctoral program. *Degree requirements:* For doctorate, thesis/dissertation (for some programs). *Entrance requirements:* For master's, minimum GPA of 3.0, audition/interview; for doctorate, GRE General Test, minimum GPA of 3.0, audition/interview. Additional exam requirements/recommendations for international students: Required—TOEFL (minimum score 550 paper-based; 213 computer-based; 79 iBT). *Application deadline:* For fall admission, 3/15 priority date for domestic students, 5/15 for international students; for spring admission, 10/15 for international students. Applications are processed on a rolling basis. Application fee: $25. Electronic applications accepted. *Financial support:* In 2007–08, 130 students received support, including 5 fellowships (averaging $26,248 per year), 1 research assistantship with full and partial tuition reimbursement available (averaging $7,000 per year), 82 teaching assistantships with full and partial tuition reimbursements available (averaging $10,491 per year); Federal Work-Study, institutionally sponsored loans, scholarships/grants, health care benefits, tuition waivers (full and partial), and unspecified assistantships also available. Support available to part-time students. Financial award applicants required to submit FAFSA. *Faculty research:* Music education, music literature, formal and harmonic analysis, pedagogy, performance. Total annual research expenditures: $79,779. *Application contact:* Dr. Lori Bade, Director of Graduate Studies, 225-578-3261, Fax: 225-578-2562, E-mail: lbade1@lsu.edu.

Loyola University New Orleans, College of Music and Fine Arts, New Orleans, LA 70118-6195. Offers MMP, MMT. *Accreditation:* NASM. Part-time programs available. *Students:* 8 full-time (5 women), 2 part-time; includes 4 minority (2 African Americans, 1 Asian American or Pacific Islander, 1 Hispanic American). Average age 27. 12 applicants, 100% accepted. In 2007, 5 degrees awarded. *Degree requirements:* For master's, comprehensive exam, thesis, comprehensive written and oral exams. *Entrance requirements:* For master's, performance audition, appropriate bachelor's degree, minimum GPA of 3.0, transcript, letters of recommendation, resumé, essay. Additional exam requirements/recommendations for international students: Required—TOEFL (minimum score 550 paper-based; 213 computer-based). *Application deadline:* For fall admission, 8/15 priority date for domestic and international students; for spring admission, 1/1 priority date for domestic and international students. Applications are processed on a rolling basis. Application fee: $20. Electronic applications accepted. *Expenses:* Contact institution. *Financial support:* Career-related internships or fieldwork, Federal Work-Study, institutionally sponsored loans, scholarships/grants, and unspecified assistantships available. Support available to part-time students. Financial award application deadline: 5/1; financial award applicants required to submit FAFSA. *Faculty research:* Music business, music therapy, musicology, music theory, music education. *Unit head:* Dr. Edward J. Kvet, Dean, 504-865-3039, Fax: 504-865-2852, E-mail: ekvet@loyno.edu. *Application contact:* Dr. Anthony A. Decuir, Associate Dean, 504-865-3037, Fax: 504-865-2852, E-mail: decuir@loyno.edu.

Lynn University, Conservatory of Music, Boca Raton, FL 33431-5598. Offers music performance (MM); professional performance (Certificate). *Accreditation:* NASM. Part-time and evening/weekend programs available. *Degree requirements:* For Certificate, performance, recitals, orchestra, chamber music. *Entrance requirements:* For master's, resumé, 2 letters of recommendation, minimum undergraduate GPA of 3.0; for Certificate, bachelor's degree in music performance or equivalent, audition. Additional exam requirements/recommendations for international students: Required—TOEFL (minimum score 550 paper-based; 213 computer-based).

Manhattan School of Music, Graduate Programs, New York, NY 10027-4698. Offers composition (MM, DMA); jazz (MM, DMA); music performance (MM, DMA); orchestral performance (MM). *Faculty:* 50 full-time (0 women), 162 part-time/adjunct (74 women). *Students:* 392 full-time (211 women), 10 part-time (8 women); includes 75 minority (19 African Americans, 2 American Indian/Alaska Native, 39 Asian Americans or Pacific Islanders, 15 Hispanic Americans), 148 international. Average age 22. 1,309 applicants, 34% accepted, 204 enrolled. In 2007, 160 master's, 14 doctorates awarded. *Median time to degree:* Of those who began their doctoral program in fall 1999, 90% received their degree in 8 years or less. *Degree requirements:* For master's, recital; for doctorate, variable foreign language requirement, thesis/dissertation, departmental qualifying exam, recitals. *Entrance requirements:* For master's, audition; for doctorate, departmental exam, audition, interview. Additional exam requirements/recommendations for international students: Required—TOEFL (minimum score 550 paper-based; 213 computer-based). *Application deadline:* For fall admission, 12/1 for domestic and international students. Application fee: $100. Electronic applications accepted. *Expenses:* Tuition: Full-time $28,750. Required fees: $475. *Financial support:* In 2007–08, 306 students received support, including 14 teaching assistantships with partial tuition reimbursements available (averaging $4,700 per year); Federal Work-Study, scholarships/grants, and tuition waivers (full and partial) also available. Support available to part-time students. Financial award application deadline: 3/1; financial award applicants required to submit FAFSA. *Unit head:* Dr. Marjorie Merryman, Dean of Academic Affair, 212-749-2802 Ext. 4584, Fax: 212-749-5471, E-mail: mmerryman@msmnyc.edu. *Application contact:* Amy A. Anderson, Associate Dean for Enrollment Management, 917-493-4501, Fax: 212-749-3025, E-mail: aanderson@msmnyc.edu.

Manhattan School of Music, Professional Studies Certificate Program, New York, NY 10027-4698. Offers instrumental music (CPS), including accompanying, brass, composition, guitar, orchestral performance, organ, piano, strings, voice, woodwinds; vocal music (CPS), including accompanying, brass, composition, guitar, orchestral performance, organ, piano, strings, voice, woodwinds. *Faculty:* 50 full-time (0 women), 162 part-time/adjunct (74 women). *Students:* 34 full-time (22 women); includes 2 minority (1 African American, 1 Asian American or Pacific Islander), 22 international. Average age 24. 146 applicants, 64% accepted, 35 enrolled. In 2007, 35 degrees awarded. *Degree requirements:* For CPS, graduation recital. *Entrance requirements:* For degree, audition. Additional exam requirements/recommendations for international students: Required—TOEFL (minimum score 550 paper-based; 213 computer-based). *Application deadline:* For fall admission, 12/1 for domestic and international students. Application fee: $100. Electronic applications accepted. *Expenses:* Tuition: Full-time $28,750.

Required fees: $475. *Financial support:* In 2007–08, 40 students received support. Federal Work-Study, scholarships/grants, and tuition waivers (full and partial) available. Support available to part-time students. Financial award application deadline: 3/1; financial award applicants required to submit FAFSA. *Unit head:* Dr. Marjorie Merryman, Dean of Academic Affair, 212-749-2802 Ext. 4584, Fax: 212-749-5471, E-mail: mmerryman@msmnyc.edu. *Application contact:* Amy A. Anderson, Associate Dean for Enrollment Management, 917-493-4501, Fax: 212-749-3025, E-mail: aanderson@msmnyc.edu.

Mansfield University of Pennsylvania, Graduate Studies, Department of Music, Mansfield, PA 16933. Offers band conducting (MA); choral conducting (MA); performance (MA). *Accreditation:* NASM. Part-time and evening/weekend programs available. *Faculty:* 25 full-time (10 women), 7 part-time/adjunct (1 woman). *Students:* 8 full-time (5 women), 13 part-time (10 women); includes 1 minority (African American) Average age 27. 12 applicants, 100% accepted, 4 enrolled. In 2007, 14 degrees awarded. *Degree requirements:* For master's, comprehensive exam, thesis optional. *Entrance requirements:* For master's, GRE, NTE, minimum GPA of 3.0, audition. Additional exam requirements/recommendations for international students: Required—TOEFL (minimum score 550 paper-based; 220 computer-based). *Application deadline:* For fall admission, 8/1 priority date for domestic students, 6/1 for international students; for spring admission, 11/1 priority date for domestic students, 9/1 for international students. Applications are processed on a rolling basis. Application fee: $25. Electronic applications accepted. *Expenses:* Tuition, state resident: part-time $345 per credit. Tuition, nonresident: part-time $552 per credit. Required fees: $114 per credit. *Financial support:* Career-related internships or fieldwork and unspecified assistantships available. Financial award application deadline: 5/1; financial award applicants required to submit FAFSA. *Unit head:* Dr. Adam Brennan, Chairperson, 570-662-4710, E-mail: abrennan@mansfield.edu. *Application contact:* Judi Brayer, Assistant Director of Enrollment Management/Graduate Admissions, 570-662-4818, Fax: 570-662-4121, E-mail: jbrayer@mansfield.edu.

Marshall University, Academic Affairs Division, College of Fine Arts, Department of Music, Huntington, WV 25755. Offers MA. *Accreditation:* NASM. Evening/weekend programs available. *Faculty:* 14 full-time (4 women), 25 part-time/adjunct (13 women). *Students:* 16 full-time (9 women), 7 part-time (2 women), 5 international. Average age 29. In 2007, 2 degrees awarded. *Degree requirements:* For master's, thesis optional. Application fee: $40. *Unit head:* Dr. Jeffrey Pappas, Chairperson, 304-696-3117, E-mail: pappas@marshall.edu. *Application contact:* Information Contact, 304-746-1900, Fax: 304-746-1902, E-mail: services@marshall.edu.

McGill University, Faculty of Graduate and Postdoctoral Studies, Schulich School of Music, Montréal, QC H3A 2T5, Canada. Offers composition (M Mus, D Mus, PhD); music education (MA, PhD); music technology (MA, PhD); musicology (MA, PhD); performance (M Mus); performance studies (D Mus); sound recording (M Mus, PhD); theory (MA, PhD). *Faculty:* 60 full-time (10 women), 50 part-time/adjunct (14 women). *Students:* 261 full-time (117 women), 5 part-time (3 women). 463 applicants, 39% accepted, 112 enrolled. In 2007, 71 master's, 7 doctorates awarded. *Financial support:* Application deadline: 1/1.

Memorial University of Newfoundland, School of Graduate Studies, Interdisciplinary Program in Ethnomusicology, St. John's, NL A1C 5S7, Canada. Offers MA, PhD. *Degree requirements:* For master's, thesis optional, research paper (non-thesis option); for doctorate, one foreign language, comprehensive exam, thesis/dissertation, oral defense of thesis. *Entrance requirements:* For master's, minimum B+ average with a B Mus or humanities/social sciences degree; for doctorate, MA in ethnomusicology or a related field.

Memorial University of Newfoundland, School of Graduate Studies, School of Music, St. John's, NL A1C 5S7, Canada. Offers conducting (MMus); performance pedagogy (MMus); performing (MMus). *Entrance requirements:* For master's, diagnostic exams measuring skills and knowledge in musical literacy, B Mus with first-class standing, audition (ca. 60 min. performance). Electronic applications accepted.

Mercer University, Graduate Studies, Macon Campus, School of Music, Macon, GA 31207-0003. Offers choral conducting (MM); church music (MM); performance (MM). *Faculty:* 1 full-time (0 women). *Students:* 14 full-time (8 women), 3 part-time (2 women); includes 2 minority (both African Americans), 3 international. Average age 30. In 2007, 3 degrees awarded. *Degree requirements:* For master's, comprehensive exam, recitals. *Entrance requirements:* For master's, GRE, audition. Application fee: $50. *Unit head:* John E. Simons, Director of Graduate Studies, 478-301-4012, E-mail: simons_je@mercer.edu. *Application contact:* Gina Cook Nelson, Director of Admissions, 478-301-2307, E-mail: nelson_gc@mercer.edu.

Meredith College, John E. Weems Graduate School, Department of Music, Raleigh, NC 27607-5298. Offers MM. *Accreditation:* NASM. Part-time and evening/weekend programs available. *Faculty:* 1 full-time (0 women), 2 part-time/adjunct (1 woman). *Students:* Average age 40. 7 applicants, 71% accepted, 4 enrolled. In 2007, 1 degree awarded. *Degree requirements:* For master's, thesis optional. *Entrance requirements:* For master's, audition, interview, letters of recommendation. *Application deadline:* For fall admission, 7/1 priority date for domestic and international students; for spring admission, 11/1 priority date for domestic and international students. Applications are processed on a rolling basis. Application fee: $50. Electronic applications accepted. *Expenses:* Contact institution. *Financial support:* Institutionally sponsored loans, scholarships/grants, and tuition waivers (partial) available. Support available to part-time students. Financial award application deadline: 2/15; financial award applicants required to submit FAFSA. *Unit head:* Dr. David Lynch, Head, 919-760-8536, Fax: 919-760-2359, E-mail: lynchd@meredith.edu. *Application contact:* Dr. James Fogle, Coordinator, 919-760-8576, Fax: 919-760-2359, E-mail: foglej@meredith.edu.

Miami University, Graduate School, School of Fine Arts, Department of Music, Program in Music Performance, Oxford, OH 45056. Offers MM. *Entrance requirements:* For master's, audition, minimum undergraduate GPA of 3.0 during previous 2 years or 3.0 overall. Additional exam requirements/recommendations for international students: Required—TOEFL, TWE.

Michigan State University, The Graduate School, College of Music, East Lansing, MI 48824. Offers music (PhD); music composition (M Mus, DMA); music conducting (M Mus, DMA); music education (M Mus); music performance (M Mus, DMA); music theory (M Mus); music therapy (M Mus); musicology (MA); piano pedagogy (M Mus). *Accreditation:* NASM. *Entrance requirements:* Additional exam requirements/recommendations for international students: Required—TOEFL. Electronic applications accepted. *Expenses:* Tuition, state resident: part-time $379 per credit hour. Tuition, nonresident: part-time $800 per credit hour. Tuition and fees vary according to program.

Middle Tennessee State University, College of Graduate Studies, College of Liberal Arts, School of Music, Murfreesboro, TN 37132. Offers MA. *Accreditation:* NASM. Part-time and evening/weekend programs available. Postbaccalaureate distance learning degree programs offered. *Faculty:* 15 full-time (5 women), 2 part-time/adjunct (1 woman). *Students:* 2 full-time (0 women), 22 part-time (8 women); includes 4 minority (1 African American, 1 Asian American or Pacific Islander, 2 Hispanic Americans). Average age 28. 26 applicants, 73% accepted. In 2007, 9 degrees awarded. *Degree requirements:* For master's, one foreign language, comprehensive exam, thesis optional. *Entrance requirements:* For master's, GRE or MAT. Additional exam requirements/recommendations for international students: Required—TOEFL (paper-based 525; computer-based 195; IBT 71) or IELTS (6.0). *Application deadline:* For fall admission, 8/1 priority date for domestic students. Applications are processed on a rolling basis. Application fee: $25. Electronic applications accepted. *Financial support:* In 2007–08, 12 students received support. Institutionally sponsored loans available. Support available to part-time students. Financial award application deadline: 5/1; financial award applicants required to submit FAFSA. *Unit head:* Dr. George Riordan, Director, 615-898-2469, Fax: 615-898-5037.

Middle Tennessee State University, College of Graduate Studies, College of Mass Communication, Department of Recording Industry, Murfreesboro, TN 37132. Offers recording arts and technologies (MFA). Part-time and evening/weekend programs available. Postbaccalaureate distance learning degree programs offered. *Faculty:* 15 full-time (1 woman). *Students:* 12 full-time (4 women), 15 part-time (1 woman); includes 6 minority (all African Americans) Average age 28. 42 applicants, 26% accepted. *Degree requirements:* For master's, comprehensive exam, thesis optional. *Entrance requirements:* For master's, GRE. Additional exam requirements/recommendations for international students: Required—TOEFL (paper-based 525; computer-based 195; IBT 71) or IELTS (6.0). *Financial support:* In 2007–08, 4 students received support. Institutionally sponsored loans available. Support available to part-time students. Financial award application deadline: 5/1. *Faculty research:* Digital audio, music production. *Unit head:* Dr. John Omachionu, Interim Dean, College of Mass Communication, 615-898-2813, Fax: 615-898-5682.

Midwestern Baptist Theological Seminary, Graduate and Professional Programs, Kansas City, MO 64118-4697. Offers Biblical studies (MA); Christian education (MACE); divinity/ministry (M Div); ministry (D Min); sacred music (MCM). *Accreditation:* ATS. Part-time programs available. Postbaccalaureate distance learning degree programs offered (minimal on-campus study). *Degree requirements:* For doctorate, thesis/dissertation; for M Div, 2 foreign languages. *Entrance requirements:* For doctorate, MAT. Electronic applications accepted. *Faculty research:* Ministerial studies, Biblical and theological studies, missions, counseling.

Mills College, Graduate Studies, Department of Music, Oakland, CA 94613-1000. Offers composition (MA); electronic music and recording media (MFA); music performance and literature (MFA). Part-time programs available. *Faculty:* 6 full-time (1 woman), 3 part-time/adjunct (all women). *Students:* 45 full-time (16 women); includes 2 Asian Americans or Pacific Islanders, 4 Hispanic Americans, 5 international. Average age 28. 50 applicants, 64% accepted, 17 enrolled. In 2007, 20 degrees awarded. *Degree requirements:* For master's, variable foreign language requirement, thesis, performance or recital. *Entrance requirements:* For master's, tape. Additional exam requirements/recommendations for international students: Required—TOEFL. *Application deadline:* For fall admission, 2/1 priority date for domestic students; for spring admission, 11/1 for domestic students. Applications are processed on a rolling basis. Application fee: $50. Electronic applications accepted. *Expenses:* Tuition: Full-time $22,792; part-time $5,702 per credit. Required fees: $828. Part-time tuition and fees vary according to course load and program. *Financial support:* In 2007–08, 19 fellowships with partial tuition reimbursements (averaging $9,001 per year), 25 teaching assistantships with partial tuition reimbursements (averaging $7,977 per year) were awarded; institutionally sponsored loans, scholarships/grants, and residence awards also available. Support available to part-time students. Financial award application deadline: 2/1; financial award applicants required to submit CSS PROFILE or FAFSA. *Faculty research:* Electronic and computer music, twentieth century theory and performance practice, Mozart, music theory. *Unit head:* David Bernstein, Chairperson, 510-430-2171, Fax: 510-430-3314, E-mail: grad-studies@mills.edu. *Application contact:* Linda Guzman, Graduate Admission Specialist, 510-430-3309, Fax: 510-430-2159, E-mail: grad-studies@mills.edu.

Minnesota State University Mankato, College of Graduate Studies, College of Arts and Humanities, Department of Music, Mankato, MN 56001. Offers MM, MT. *Accreditation:* NASM. *Students:* 3 full-time (0 women), 12 part-time (5 women). Average age 32. In 2007, 3 degrees awarded. *Degree requirements:* For master's, comprehensive exam, thesis or alternative. *Entrance requirements:* For master's, minimum GPA of 3.0 during previous 2 years, audition or test. Additional exam requirements/recommendations for international students: Required—TOEFL. *Application deadline:* For fall admission, 7/1 priority date for domestic students; for spring admission, 11/1 for domestic students. Applications are processed on a rolling basis. Application fee: $40. Electronic applications accepted. *Financial support:* Research assistantships with full tuition reimbursements, teaching assistantships with full tuition reimbursements, career-related internships or fieldwork, Federal Work-Study, and institutionally sponsored loans available. Support available to part-time students. Financial award application deadline: 3/15. *Unit head:* Dr. John Lindberg, Chairperson, 507-389-2118. *Application contact:* 507-389-2321, E-mail: grad@mnsu.edu.

Mississippi College, Graduate School, College of Arts and Sciences, School of Christian Studies and the Arts, Department of Music, Clinton, MS 39058. Offers applied music performance (MM); conducting (MM); music education (MM); music performance: organ (MM); vocal pedagogy (MM). *Accreditation:* NASM. Part-time and evening/weekend programs available. *Faculty:* 9 full-time (5 women), 4 part-time/adjunct (2 women). *Students:* 3 full-time (all women), 20 part-time (13 women); includes 1 minority (African American), 14 international. Average age 26. In 2007, 5 degrees awarded. *Degree requirements:* For master's, comprehensive exam, recital. *Entrance requirements:* For master's, GRE, minimum GPA of 2.5. Additional exam requirements/recommendations for international students: Recommended—IELTS. *Application deadline:* For fall admission, 8/15 priority date for domestic students. Applications are processed on a rolling basis. Application fee: $25. Electronic applications accepted. *Expenses:* Tuition: Full-time $7,470; part-time $415 per hour. Required fees: $1,160 per term. Part-time tuition and fees vary according to course load and degree level. *Financial support:* Teaching assistantships, Federal Work-Study, scholarships/grants, and unspecified assistantships available. Support available to part-time students. Financial award application deadline: 4/1; financial award applicants required to submit FAFSA. *Unit head:* Dr. James Meaders, Chair, 601-925-3441, Fax: 601-925-3945, E-mail: meaders@mc.edu.

Missouri State University, Graduate College, College of Arts and Letters, Department of Music, Springfield, MO 65804-0094. Offers music (MM); secondary education (MS Ed), including music. *Accreditation:* NASM. Part-time and evening/weekend programs available. *Faculty:* 23 full-time (8 women). *Students:* 9 full-time (5 women), 25 part-time (11 women); includes 1 minority (Asian American or Pacific Islander) Average age 28. 16 applicants, 100% accepted, 11 enrolled. In 2007, 15 degrees awarded. *Degree requirements:* For master's, comprehensive exam, thesis or alternative. *Entrance requirements:* For master's, GRE, 9-12 teaching certification (MS Ed). Additional exam requirements/recommendations for international students: Required—TOEFL (minimum score 550 paper-based; 213 computer-based; 79 iBT). *Application deadline:* For fall admission, 7/20 for domestic students; for spring admission, 12/20 for domestic students. Applications are processed on a rolling basis. Application fee: $35. Electronic applications accepted. *Expenses:* Tuition, state resident: full-time $3,708; part-time $206 per credit hour. Tuition, nonresident: full-time $7,236; part-time $206 per credit hour. Required fees: $622. Full-time tuition and fees vary according to course level, course load, program and reciprocity agreements. *Financial support:* In 2007–08, 13 teaching assistantships with full tuition reimbursements (averaging $7,050 per year) were awarded; research assistantships with full tuition reimbursements, Federal Work-Study, institutionally sponsored loans, scholarships/grants, tuition waivers (partial), and unspecified assistantships also available. Financial award application deadline: 3/31; financial award applicants required to submit FAFSA. *Unit head:* Dr. Roger Stoner, Head, 417-836-4122, Fax: 417-836-7665, E-mail: music@missouristate.edu.

Montclair State University, The Office of Graduate Admissions and Support Services, School of the Arts, Department of Music, Montclair, NJ 07043-1624. Offers music (AD); music education (MA); music therapy (MA); performance (MA, Certificate); theory/composition (MA). *Accreditation:* NASM. Part-time and evening/weekend programs available. *Faculty:* 19 full-time (7 women), 57 part-time/adjunct (26 women). *Students:* 19 full-time (17 women), 33 part-time (19 women); includes 3 minority (2 African Americans, 1 Hispanic American), 9 international. 57 applicants, 39% accepted, 22 enrolled. In 2007, 12 master's, 2 other advanced degrees awarded. *Degree requirements:* For master's, comprehensive exam, compositions, recitals, or thesis. *Entrance requirements:* For master's, GRE General Test, audition; undergraduate degree in music or at least 40 semester hours of work in theory, music history, performance; 2 letters of recommendation; teaching certificate (MA in music education). Additional exam requirements/recommendations for international students: Required—TOEFL (minimum score 83 computer-based). *Application deadline:* For fall admission, 6/1 for international students; for spring admission, 10/1 for international students. Applications are processed on a rolling basis. Application fee: $60. Electronic applications accepted. *Financial support:* In 2007–08, 2 research assistantships with full tuition reimbursements (averaging $7,000 per year) were awarded;

Music

Montclair State University (continued)

Federal Work-Study, scholarships/grants, and unspecified assistantships also available. Support available to part-time students. Financial award application deadline: 3/1; financial award applicants required to submit FAFSA. *Unit head:* Prof. Robert Aldridge, Chairperson, 973-655-7212.

Morehead State University, Graduate Programs, Caudill College of Humanities, Department of Music, Morehead, KY 40351. Offers music education (MM); music performance (MM). *Accreditation:* NASM. Part-time and evening/weekend programs available. *Faculty:* 27 full-time (8 women), 1 (woman) part-time/adjunct. *Students:* 13 full-time (6 women), 10 part-time (5 women); includes 3 minority (2 African Americans, 1 Asian American or Pacific Islander), 1 international. Average age 25. In 2007, 10 degrees awarded. *Degree requirements:* For master's, oral and written exams. *Entrance requirements:* For master's, minimum GPA of 3.0 in music, 2.5 overall; audition. Additional exam requirements/recommendations for international students: Required—TOEFL (minimum score 550 paper-based; 173 computer-based). *Application deadline:* For fall admission, 8/1 priority date for domestic and international students; for spring admission, 12/1 priority date for domestic and international students. Applications are processed on a rolling basis. Application fee: $0 ($55 for international students). Electronic applications accepted. *Financial support:* In 2007–08, 1 teaching assistantship (averaging $6,000 per year) was awarded; career-related internships or fieldwork, Federal Work-Study, and unspecified assistantships also available. Financial award application deadline: 4/1; financial award applicants required to submit FAFSA. *Faculty research:* Musical instrument digital interface (MIDI) applications, tonal concepts of euphonium and baritone horn, digital synthesis, computer-assisted instruction in music, musical composition. *Unit head:* Dr. Scott McBride, Chair, 606-783-2473, Fax: 606-783-5004, E-mail: s.mcbride@moreheadstate.edu. *Application contact:* Michelle Barber, Graduate Admissions Counselor, 606-783-2039, Fax: 606-783-5061, E-mail: m.barber@moreheadstate.edu.

Morgan State University, School of Graduate Studies, College of Liberal Arts, Department of Music, Baltimore, MD 21251. Offers MA. *Accreditation:* NASM. Part-time and evening/weekend programs available. *Faculty:* 4 full-time (0 women). *Students:* 8; all minorities (all African Americans) *Degree requirements:* For master's, comprehensive exam, thesis. *Entrance requirements:* Additional exam requirements/recommendations for international students: Required—TOEFL (minimum score 550 paper-based; 213 computer-based). *Application deadline:* For fall admission, 2/1 priority date for domestic students; for spring admission, 10/1 priority date for domestic students. Applications are processed on a rolling basis. Application fee: $0. *Financial support:* Fellowships with tuition reimbursements, research assistantships with tuition reimbursements, career-related internships or fieldwork, Federal Work-Study, institutionally sponsored loans, scholarships/grants, health care benefits, tuition waivers (full and partial), and unspecified assistantships available. Support available to part-time students. Financial award application deadline: 2/1. *Unit head:* Dr. Eric Conway, Chairperson, 443-885-3286, E-mail: eric.conway@morgan.edu. *Application contact:* Dr. Mark Garrison, Associate Dean, 443-885-3185, Fax: 443-885-8226, E-mail: mark.garrison@morgan.edu.

Murray State University, College of Humanities and Fine Arts, Program in Music, Murray, KY 42071. Offers music education (MME). *Accreditation:* NASM. Part-time programs available. *Entrance requirements:* For master's, GRE General Test or MAT. Additional exam requirements/recommendations for international students: Required—TOEFL.

New England Conservatory of Music, Graduate Program in Music, Boston, MA 02115-5000. Offers MM, DMA, Diploma. *Accreditation:* NASM (one or more programs are accredited). *Faculty:* 89 full-time (32 women), 133 part-time/adjunct (40 women). *Students:* 382 full-time (212 women), 12 part-time (9 women); includes 52 minority (12 African Americans, 1 American Indian/Alaska Native, 31 Asian Americans or Pacific Islanders, 8 Hispanic Americans), 142 international. Average age 25. 1,391 applicants, 30% accepted, 179 enrolled. In 2007, 148 master's, 6 doctorates, 28 other advanced degrees awarded. *Degree requirements:* For master's, thesis (for some programs), recital, 3 foreign languages (vocal majors); for doctorate, one foreign language, comprehensive exam, thesis/dissertation, qualifying exams, recital. *Entrance requirements:* For master's and Diploma, audition; for doctorate, music theory and musicology exam, audition. Additional exam requirements/recommendations for international students: Required—TOEFL (minimum score 550 paper-based; 213 computer-based). *Application deadline:* For fall admission, 12/1 priority date for domestic and international students; for spring admission, 11/1 for domestic and international students. Applications are processed on a rolling basis. Application fee: $100. *Expenses:* Tuition: Full-time $30,650; part-time $2,000 per credit hour. Required fees: $325 per year. *Financial support:* In 2007–08, 364 students received support, including 341 fellowships with partial tuition reimbursements available (averaging $12,992 per year); teaching assistantships, Federal Work-Study, scholarships/grants, and tuition waivers (partial) also available. Support available to part-time students. Financial award application deadline: 12/1; financial award applicants required to submit FAFSA. *Unit head:* Tom Novak, Dean of the College, 617-585-1304, Fax: 617-585-1303, E-mail: tnovak@newenglandconservatory.edu. *Application contact:* Christina Daly, Director of Admissions, 617-585-1101, Fax: 617-585-1115, E-mail: christina.daly@newenglandconservatory.edu.

New Jersey City University, Graduate Studies and Continuing Education, College of Arts and Sciences, Department of Music, Dance and Theatre, Jersey City, NJ 07305-1597. Offers music education (MA); performance (MM). *Accreditation:* NASM. Evening/weekend programs available. *Faculty:* 5. *Students:* 1 full-time (0 women), 15 part-time (9 women); includes 4 minority (1 African American, 3 Asian Americans or Pacific Islanders), 1 international. Average age 33. In 2007, 4 degrees awarded. *Degree requirements:* For master's, thesis optional, recital. *Entrance requirements:* For master's, GRE General Test or MAT. Additional exam requirements/recommendations for international students: Required—TOEFL. *Application deadline:* For fall admission, 8/1 priority date for domestic students; for spring admission, 12/1 for domestic students. Applications are processed on a rolling basis. Application fee: $0. *Expenses:* Tuition, state resident: full-time $7,462. Tuition, nonresident: full-time $13,762. Required fees: $1,296. *Financial support:* Unspecified assistantships available. *Unit head:* Dr. Edward Raditz, Chairperson, 201-200-3157, E-mail: eraditz@njcu.edu.

New Mexico State University, Graduate School, College of Arts and Sciences, Department of Music, Las Cruces, NM 88003-8001. Offers conducting (MM); music education (MM); performance (MM). *Accreditation:* NASM. Part-time programs available. *Faculty:* 4 full-time (1 woman). *Students:* 10 full-time (2 women), 8 part-time (5 women); includes 6 minority (1 African American, 1 Asian American or Pacific Islander, 4 Hispanic Americans), 3 international. Average age 31. 16 applicants, 94% accepted, 7 enrolled. In 2007, 6 degrees awarded. *Degree requirements:* For master's, comprehensive exam (for some programs), thesis (for some programs), recital. *Entrance requirements:* For master's, diagnostic exam, audition, bachelor's degree or equivalent from an accredited institution. Additional exam requirements/recommendations for international students: Required—TOEFL. *Application deadline:* For fall admission, 7/1 priority date for domestic students; for spring admission, 11/1 for domestic students. Applications are processed on a rolling basis. Application fee: $30 ($50 for international students). Electronic applications accepted. *Expenses: Contact institution. Financial support:* In 2007–08, 6 students received support, including 5 teaching assistantships; fellowships, Federal Work-Study and health care benefits also available. Support available to part-time students. Financial award application deadline: 3/1. *Faculty research:* Music education, contemporary wind band literature, performance. *Unit head:* Dr. Ken Van Winkle, Head, 575-646-2421, Fax: 575-646-8199, E-mail: kvanwink@nmsu.edu. *Application contact:* Dr. Lisa Van Winkle, Assistant Professor, 575-646-2523, Fax: 575-646-2472, E-mail: lvanwink@nmsu.edu.

New Orleans Baptist Theological Seminary, Graduate and Professional Programs, Division of Church Music Ministries, New Orleans, LA 70126-4858. Offers MMCM, DMA. *Accreditation:* NASM. *Degree requirements:* For doctorate, one foreign language, thesis/dissertation. *Entrance requirements:* For doctorate, GRE General Test.

The New School: A University, Mannes College The New School for Music, New York, NY 10011. Offers music performance (MM, PD). *Faculty:* 5 full-time (1 woman), 27 part-time/adjunct (8 women). *Students:* 181 full-time (113 women), 1 part-time; includes 16 minority (1 African American, 9 Asian Americans or Pacific Islanders, 6 Hispanic Americans), 107 international. Average age 25. In 2007, 59 master's, 22 other advanced degrees awarded. *Degree requirements:* For master's, recital and professional performance obligation. *Entrance requirements:* For master's, audition. Additional exam requirements/recommendations for international students: Required—TOEFL (minimum score 550 paper-based; 213 computer-based). *Application deadline:* For fall admission, 11/15 for domestic students. Application fee: $100. *Financial support:* Fellowships with partial tuition reimbursements, research assistantships with partial tuition reimbursements, teaching assistantships with partial tuition reimbursements, career-related internships or fieldwork, Federal Work-Study, scholarships/grants, and tuition waivers (partial) available. Support available to part-time students. Financial award application deadline: 3/1; financial award applicants required to submit FAFSA. *Unit head:* Joel Lester, Dean, 212-580-0210 Ext. 4848. *Application contact:* Director of Admissions, 212-580-0210 Ext. 263.

New York University, Graduate School of Arts and Science, Department of Music, New York, NY 10012-1019. Offers composition and theory (MA, PhD); early music performance (Advanced Certificate); ethnomusicology (MA, PhD). *Faculty:* 10 full-time (2 women), 12 part-time/adjunct. *Students:* 54 full-time (29 women), 7 part-time (3 women); includes 10 minority (3 African Americans, 6 Asian Americans or Pacific Islanders, 1 Hispanic American), 8 international. Average age 35. 183 applicants, 5% accepted, 8 enrolled. In 2007, 4 master's, 3 doctorates awarded. Terminal master's awarded for partial completion of doctoral program. *Degree requirements:* For master's, one foreign language, thesis (for some programs), general exam; for doctorate, 2 foreign languages, thesis/dissertation, general and special exams. *Entrance requirements:* For master's, GRE General Test, bachelor's degree in liberal arts or music; for doctorate, GRE General Test, master's degree in music; for Advanced Certificate, bachelor's degree in music. Additional exam requirements/recommendations for international students: Required—TOEFL. *Application deadline:* For fall admission, 1/4 for domestic students. Application fee: $85. *Financial support:* Fellowships with tuition reimbursements, teaching assistantships with tuition reimbursements, Federal Work-Study, institutionally sponsored loans, scholarships/grants, health care benefits, and unspecified assistantships available. Financial award application deadline: 1/4; financial award applicants required to submit FAFSA. *Faculty research:* Early music (nineteenth century), Wagner, Verdi, performance practice. *Unit head:* Michael Beckerman, Chair, 212-998-8300, Fax: 212-995-4147, E-mail: fas.music.gradadmissions@nyu.edu. *Application contact:* Ana Maria Ochoa, Director of Graduate Studies, 212-998-8300, Fax: 212-995-4147, E-mail: fas.music.gradadmissions@nuy.edu.

New York University, Steinhardt School of Culture, Education and Human Development, Department of Music and Performing Arts Professions, Program in Music Business, New York, NY 10012-1019. Offers MA. Part-time and evening/weekend programs available. *Faculty:* 2 full-time (both women). *Students:* 49 full-time (30 women), 20 part-time (12 women); includes 16 minority (13 African Americans, 2 Asian Americans or Pacific Islanders, 1 Hispanic American), 15 international. 139 applicants, 27% accepted, 30 enrolled. In 2007, 24 degrees awarded. *Degree requirements:* For master's, thesis (for some programs). *Entrance requirements:* For master's, interview, supplementary essay. Additional exam requirements/recommendations for international students: Required—TOEFL. *Application deadline:* For fall admission, 12/15 priority date for domestic and international students; for spring admission, 11/1 for domestic and international students. Applications are processed on a rolling basis. Application fee: $50. *Financial support:* Career-related internships or fieldwork, Federal Work-Study, scholarships/grants, and tuition waivers (partial) available. Support available to part-time students. Financial award application deadline: 2/1; financial award applicants required to submit FAFSA. *Faculty research:* Strategic marketing, new technologies, intellectual property, entrepreneurship. *Unit head:* Dr. Catherine Moore, Director, 212-998-5424, Fax: 212-998-4560. *Application contact:* 212-998-5030, Fax: 212-995-4328, E-mail: steinhardt.gradadmissions@nyu.edu.

New York University, Steinhardt School of Culture, Education and Human Development, Department of Music and Performing Arts Professions, Program in Music Performance and Composition, New York, NY 10012-1019. Offers MA, PhD. Part-time and evening/weekend programs available. *Faculty:* 10 full-time (3 women). *Students:* 149 full-time (79 women), 89 part-time (38 women); includes 32 minority (6 African Americans, 16 Asian Americans or Pacific Islanders, 10 Hispanic Americans), 86 international. 280 applicants, 61% accepted, 86 enrolled. In 2007, 92 master's awarded. Terminal master's awarded for partial completion of doctoral program. *Degree requirements:* For master's, thesis (for some programs); for doctorate, thesis/dissertation. *Entrance requirements:* For master's, audition; for doctorate, GRE General Test, audition, interview. Additional exam requirements/recommendations for international students: Required—TOEFL. *Application deadline:* For fall admission, 12/15 priority date for domestic and international students; for spring admission, 11/1 for domestic and international students. Applications are processed on a rolling basis. Application fee: $50. *Financial support:* Fellowships with full and partial tuition reimbursements, Federal Work-Study, scholarships/grants, and tuition waivers (partial) available. Support available to part-time students. Financial award application deadline: 2/1; financial award applicants required to submit FAFSA. *Faculty research:* Aesthetics, performance analysis, twentieth century music, music methodologies for arts criticism and analysis. *Unit head:* Dr. Dinu D. Ghezzo, Director, 212-998-5438, Fax: 212-995-4043, E-mail: dino.ghezzo@nyu.edu. *Application contact:* 212-998-5030, Fax: 212-995-4328, E-mail: steinhardt.gradadmissions@nyu.edu.

New York University, Steinhardt School of Culture, Education and Human Development, Department of Music and Performing Arts Professions, Program in Music Technology, New York, NY 10012-1019. Offers MM. Part-time and evening/weekend programs available. *Faculty:* 4 full-time (1 woman). *Students:* 61 full-time (21 women), 35 part-time (8 women); includes 15 minority (4 African Americans, 1 American Indian/Alaska Native, 6 Asian Americans or Pacific Islanders, 4 Hispanic Americans), 30 international. 79 applicants, 77% accepted, 37 enrolled. In 2007, 20 degrees awarded. *Degree requirements:* For master's, thesis (for some programs). *Entrance requirements:* For master's, portfolio. Additional exam requirements/recommendations for international students: Required—TOEFL. *Application deadline:* For fall admission, 12/15 priority date for domestic and international students; for spring admission, 11/1 for domestic and international students. Applications are processed on a rolling basis. Application fee: $50. *Financial support:* Career-related internships or fieldwork, Federal Work-Study, scholarships/grants, and tuition waivers (partial) available. Support available to part-time students. Financial award application deadline: 2/1; financial award applicants required to submit FAFSA. *Faculty research:* Pattern processing in music, computer music, acoustics, music perception, interactive music systems. *Unit head:* Dr. Kenneth J. Peacock, Director, 212-998-5424, Fax: 212-995-4043. *Application contact:* 212-998-5030, Fax: 212-995-4328, E-mail: steinhardt.gradadmissions@nyu.edu.

New York University, Tisch School of the Arts, Graduate Musical Theatre Writing Program, New York, NY 10012-1019. Offers MFA. *Faculty:* 6 full-time, 14 part-time/adjunct. *Students:* 52 full-time (24 women); includes 3 minority (1 African American, 1 Asian American or Pacific Islander, 1 Hispanic American), 14 international. Average age 28. 57 applicants, 63% accepted, 24 enrolled. In 2007, 21 master's awarded. *Degree requirements:* For master's, full-length musical theatre work. *Entrance requirements:* For master's, interview, portfolio. Additional exam requirements/recommendations for international students: Required—TOEFL or IELTS. *Application deadline:* For fall admission, 2/1 priority date for domestic and international students. Application fee: $60. Electronic applications accepted. *Financial support:* In 2007–08, 18 students received support; fellowships with tuition reimbursements available, career-related internships or fieldwork, Federal Work-Study, tuition waivers (partial), and unspecified assistantships available. Financial award application deadline: 2/15; financial award applicants required to submit FAFSA. *Unit head:* Sarah Schlesinger, Chair, 212-998-1830, Fax: 212-995-4873, E-mail: musical.theatre@nyu.edu. *Application contact:* Dan Sandford, Director of Graduate Admissions, 212-998-1918, Fax: 212-995-4060, E-mail: tisch.gradadmissions@nyu.edu.

The Nigerian Baptist Theological Seminary, Graduate Studies, Ogbomoso, Nigeria. Offers church music (Diploma); divinity (M Div); theological studies (MATS); theology (M Th). Part-time programs available. *Degree requirements:* For master's, thesis, 2 Nigerian languages; for M Div, thesis/dissertation (for some programs), 2 biblical languages; for Diploma, thesis or alternative.

Norfolk State University, School of Graduate Studies, School of Liberal Arts, Department of Music, Norfolk, VA 23504. Offers music (MM); music education (MM); performance (MM); theory and composition (MM). *Accreditation:* NASM. Part-time programs available. *Degree requirements:* For master's, thesis or alternative. *Entrance requirements:* For master's, minimum GPA of 2.7, letters of recommendation. Additional exam requirements/recommendations for international students: Required—TOEFL.

North Carolina School of the Arts, School of Filmmaking, Winston-Salem, NC 27127-2188. Offers film music composition (MFA). *Faculty:* 2 full-time (0 women). *Students:* 19 full-time (4 women); includes 2 minority (both Asian Americans or Pacific Islanders) Average age 25. 3 applicants, 100% accepted, 3 enrolled. In 2007, 2 degrees awarded. *Entrance requirements:* For master's, audition, performance, portfolio, interview. *Application deadline:* For fall admission, 4/1 priority date for domestic students. Applications are processed on a rolling basis. Application fee: $60 ($100 for international students). *Expenses:* Tuition, state resident: full-time $3,636. Tuition, nonresident: full-time $15,220. Required fees: $1,688. *Financial support:* In 2007–08, fellowships (averaging $2,000 per year); career-related internships or fieldwork and Federal Work-Study also available. Support available to part-time students. Financial award application deadline: 3/15; financial award applicants required to submit FAFSA. *Unit head:* Jordan Kerner, Dean, 336-770-1330, Fax: 336-770-1339, E-mail: kernerj@ncarts.edu. *Application contact:* Sheeler Lawson, Director of Admissions, 336-770-3290, Fax: 336-770-3370, E-mail: admissions@ncarts.edu.

North Carolina School of the Arts, School of Music, Winston-Salem, NC 27127-2188. Offers music performance (MM), including chamber music performance, guitar performance, opera performance, organ performance, percussion performance, piano performance, strings performance, wind and brass performance; orchestral conducting (MM). *Faculty:* 30 full-time (9 women), 11 part-time/adjunct (3 women). *Students:* 60 full-time (19 women); includes 5 minority (3 African Americans, 1 American Indian/Alaska Native, 1 Hispanic American), 26 international. Average age 25. In 2007, 14 degrees awarded. *Degree requirements:* For master's, recital/film score. *Entrance requirements:* For master's, audition (music performance), interview, original score. *Application deadline:* For fall admission, 4/1 priority date for domestic students. Applications are processed on a rolling basis. Application fee: $60 ($100 for international students). *Expenses:* Tuition, state resident: full-time $3,636. Tuition, nonresident: full-time $15,220. Required fees: $1,688. *Financial support:* In 2007–08, 8 fellowships with partial tuition reimbursements (averaging $2,000 per year), 10 teaching assistantships with partial tuition reimbursements (averaging $3,000 per year) were awarded; career-related internships or fieldwork and Federal Work-Study also available. Support available to part-time students. Financial award application deadline: 3/15; financial award applicants required to submit FAFSA. *Unit head:* Dr. Thomas Clark, Dean, 336-770-3251, Fax: 336-770-3248, E-mail: clarkt@ncarts.edu. *Application contact:* Sheeler Lawson, Director of Admissions, 336-770-3290, Fax: 336-770-3370, E-mail: admissions@ncarts.edu.

North Dakota State University, College of Graduate and Interdisciplinary Studies, College of Arts, Humanities and Social Sciences, Department of Music, Fargo, ND 58105. Offers M Ed, MM, DMA. *Accreditation:* NASM. *Students:* 14 full-time (5 women), 6 part-time (5 women), 1 international. *Degree requirements:* For master's, 2 foreign languages, comprehensive exam, thesis or alternative, recitals; for doctorate, 2 foreign languages, comprehensive exam, thesis/dissertation or alternative, recitals. *Entrance requirements:* For master's and doctorate, music history, music theory, performance audition. Additional exam requirements/recommendations for international students: Required—TOEFL (minimum score 525 paper-based; 197 computer-based; 71 iBT). *Application deadline:* Applications are processed on a rolling basis. Application fee: $45 ($60 for international students). Electronic applications accepted. *Expenses:* Tuition, state resident: full-time $5,376; part-time $224 per credit. Tuition, nonresident: full-time $14,354; part-time $598 per credit. Required fees: $962; $40 per credit. Part-time tuition and fees vary according to course load and reciprocity agreements. *Financial support:* In 2007–08, 16 students received support; fellowships with full tuition reimbursements available, teaching assistantships with full tuition reimbursements available, tuition waivers (partial) and unspecified assistantships available. Support available to part-time students. Financial award applicants required to submit FAFSA. *Faculty research:* Performance, conducting. *Unit head:* Dr. John Miller, Director, Division of Fine Arts, 701-231-7932, E-mail: ej.miller@ndsu.edu. *Application contact:* Dr. Jo Ann Miller, Director, Graduate Studies, 701-231-7822, E-mail: jo.miller@ndsu.edu.

Northeastern Illinois University, Graduate College, College of Arts and Sciences, Department of Music, Program in Music, Chicago, IL 60625-4699. Offers MA. Part-time and evening/weekend programs available. *Faculty:* 16 full-time (6 women), 18 part-time/adjunct (4 women). *Students:* 7 full-time (2 women), 11 part-time (10 women); includes 2 minority (1 Asian American or Pacific Islander, 1 Hispanic American), 5 international. Average age 38. 10 applicants, 80% accepted. In 2007, 11 degrees awarded. *Degree requirements:* For master's, comprehensive exam, thesis optional, minimum GPA of 3.0. *Entrance requirements:* For master's, departmental exam, audition, minimum GPA of 2.75. Additional exam requirements/recommendations for international students: Required—TOEFL (minimum score 550 paper-based; 213 computer-based; 80 iBT). *Application deadline:* Applications are processed on a rolling basis. Application fee: $25. Electronic applications accepted. *Expenses:* Tuition, state resident: part-time $243 per credit hour. Tuition, nonresident: part-time $443 per credit hour. *Financial support:* In 2007–08, 15 students received support, including 1 research assistantship with full tuition reimbursement available (averaging $6,600 per year); career-related internships or fieldwork, Federal Work-Study, institutionally sponsored loans, scholarships/grants, tuition waivers (full and partial), and unspecified assistantships also available. Support available to part-time students. Financial award applicants required to submit FAFSA. *Faculty research:* World music, computers as applied instruments, vocal pedagogy, vocal interpretation, jazz repertory.

Northern Arizona University, Graduate College, College of Arts and Letters, School of Music, Flagstaff, AZ 86011. Offers choral conducting (MM); instrumental conducting (MM); instrumental performance (MM); music education (MM); music history (MM); theory and composition (MM); vocal performance (MM). *Accreditation:* NASM.

Northern Illinois University, Graduate School, College of Visual and Performing Arts, School of Music, De Kalb, IL 60115-2854. Offers MM, Performer's Certificate. *Accreditation:* NASM. Part-time programs available. *Faculty:* 33 full-time (3 women), 14 part-time/adjunct (3 women). *Students:* 72 full-time (43 women), 34 part-time (19 women); includes 18 minority (10 African Americans, 6 Asian Americans or Pacific Islanders, 2 Hispanic Americans), 20 international. Average age 31. 74 applicants, 61% accepted, 27 enrolled. In 2007, 36 master's, 8 other advanced degrees awarded. *Degree requirements:* For master's, comprehensive exam, thesis optional, recital or project; for Performer's Certificate, recitals. *Entrance requirements:* For master's, minimum GPA of 2.75, appropriate bachelor's degree, audition, interview; for Performer's Certificate, minimum GPA of 2.75 (undergraduate), 3.2 (graduate); audition. Additional exam requirements/recommendations for international students: Required—TOEFL (minimum score 550 paper-based; 213 computer-based). *Application deadline:* For fall admission, 4/1 for domestic students, 5/1 for international students; for spring admission, 11/1 for domestic students, 10/1 for international students. Applications are processed on a rolling basis. Application fee: $30. Electronic applications accepted. *Expenses:* Tuition, area resident: Part-time $226 per credit hour. Tuition, state resident: full-time $5,424; part-time $225 per credit hour. Tuition, nonresident: full-time $10,848. Required fees: $2,416; $64 per credit hour. *Financial support:* In 2007–08, 10 teaching assistantships with full tuition reimbursements were awarded; fellowships with full tuition reimbursements, research assistantships with full tuition reimbursements, Federal Work-Study, scholarships/grants, tuition waivers (full), and unspecified assistantships also available. Support available to part-time students. Financial award applicants required to submit FAFSA. *Faculty research:* Impact of music on urban children and acquisition of language skills, music in 17th century Madrid, Finnish music and culture, jazz studies. *Unit head:* Dr. Paul Bauer, Director, 815-753-1551, Fax: 815-753-1759, E-mail: paulbauer@niu.edu. *Application contact:* Dr. Charles T. Blickhan, Graduate Coordinator, 815-753-0394, E-mail: blickhan@niu.edu.

Northwestern State University of Louisiana, Graduate Studies and Research, School of Creative and Performing Arts, Program in Music, Natchitoches, LA 71497. Offers MM. *Accreditation:* NASM. *Faculty:* 7 full-time (2 women), 3 part-time/adjunct (1 woman). *Students:* 15 full-time (6 women), 4 part-time; includes 1 minority (African American), 5 international. Average age 27. In 2007, 6 degrees awarded. *Degree requirements:* For master's, comprehensive exam, thesis or alternative. *Entrance requirements:* For master's, GRE General Test, minimum undergraduate GPA of 2.5. *Application deadline:* For fall admission, 8/1 priority date for domestic students; for spring admission, 1/10 for domestic students. Applications are processed on a rolling basis. Application fee: $20 ($30 for international students). *Financial support:* Application deadline: 7/15. *Application contact:* Dr. Steven G. Horton, Associate Provost/Dean, Graduate Studies, Research, and Information Systems, 318-357-5851, Fax: 318-357-5019, E-mail: grad_school@nsula.edu.

Northwestern University, The Graduate School, School of Communication, Department of Performance Studies, Evanston, IL 60208. Offers MA, PhD. Admissions and degrees offered through The Graduate School. Part-time programs available. Terminal master's awarded for partial completion of doctoral program. *Degree requirements:* For master's, recital; for doctorate, one foreign language, thesis/dissertation, recital. *Entrance requirements:* For master's and doctorate, GRE General Test. Additional exam requirements/recommendations for international students: Required—TOEFL. *Faculty research:* Adaptation/performance of literature, ethnography of performance, critical cultural studies, performance theory, intercultural performance, gender studies.

Northwestern University, Henry and Leigh Bienen School of Music, Department of Music Performance, Evanston, IL 60208. Offers collaborative arts (DM); conducting (MM, DM); jazz (MM); performance (MM), including string chamber music and orchestral literature; piano performance (MM, DM, CP); piano performance and collaborative arts (MM); piano performance and pedagogy (MM); string performance and pedagogy (MM); strings (MM, DM); strings, winds and percussion (CP); voice (MM, DM, CP); winds and percussion (MM, DM). *Accreditation:* NASM. *Students:* 151 full-time (57 women). 759 applicants, 22% accepted, 85 enrolled. In 2007, 61 master's, 16 doctorates, 6 CPs awarded. *Degree requirements:* For master's, recital; for doctorate, comprehensive exam, thesis/dissertation, 3 recitals; for CP, 2 recitals. *Entrance requirements:* For master's, audition, preliminary tapes in voice, flute, percussion; for doctorate, written essay exam (theory and music history), audition, preliminary tapes; for CP, audition, preliminary tapes. Additional exam requirements/recommendations for international students: Required—TOEFL (minimum score 600 paper-based; 250 computer-based; 100 iBT). *Application deadline:* For fall admission, 12/15 for domestic and international students. Application fee: $55. *Financial support:* In 2007–08, 100 students received support; teaching assistantships with partial tuition reimbursements available, career-related internships or fieldwork, Federal Work-Study, institutionally sponsored loans, scholarships/grants, tuition waivers (full and partial), and unspecified assistantships available. Financial award application deadline: 5/1; financial award applicants required to submit FAFSA. *Unit head:* Karen Brunssen, Co-chair, 847-491-7228, Fax: 847-467-2363. *Application contact:* Linda A. Garton, Assistant Dean, Music Admission and Student Affairs, 847-491-3141, Fax: 847-467-7440, E-mail: lgarton@northwestern.edu.

Northwestern University, Henry and Leigh Bienen School of Music, Department of Music Studies, Evanston, IL 60208. Offers music cognition (PhD); music composition (DM); music education (MM, PhD); music technology (MM); music technology/new media (DM); music theory (MM, PhD); musicology (MM, PhD). PhD admissions and degree offered through The Graduate School. *Accreditation:* NASM. *Faculty:* 20 full-time (5 women). *Students:* 34 full-time (20 women). 176 applicants, 20% accepted, 18 enrolled. In 2007, 28 master's, 7 doctorates awarded. *Degree requirements:* For doctorate, comprehensive exam, thesis/dissertation. *Entrance requirements:* For master's, portfolio or research papers; for doctorate, GRE General Test (PhD), portfolio, research papers. Additional exam requirements/recommendations for international students: Required—TOEFL (minimum score 600 paper-based; 250 computer-based; 100 iBT), TOEFL (paper-based 560; computer-based 220) or IELTS (paper-based 6). *Application deadline:* For fall admission, 12/15 for domestic and international students. Application fee: $55. *Financial support:* In 2007–08, 30 students received support, including 10 fellowships with full tuition reimbursements available (averaging $20,000 per year); research assistantships, teaching assistantships, Federal Work-Study, institutionally sponsored loans, scholarships/grants, tuition waivers (partial), and unspecified assistantships also available. Financial award application deadline: 5/1; financial award applicants required to submit FAFSA. *Faculty research:* Music cognition, cognitive learning, aesthetic education, computer music, technology in education. *Unit head:* Maud Hickey, Chair, 847-491-5740. *Application contact:* Linda A. Garton, Assistant Dean, Music Admission and Student Affairs, 847-491-3141, Fax: 847-467-7440, E-mail: lgarton@northwestern.edu.

Notre Dame de Namur University, Division of Academic Affairs, School of Arts and Humanities, Department of Music, Belmont, CA 94002-1908. Offers music (MM); pedagogy (MM); performance (MM). Part-time and evening/weekend programs available. *Faculty:* 3 full-time (2 women), 8 part-time/adjunct (4 women). *Students:* 8 full-time (6 women), 5 part-time (3 women); includes 2 minority (1 Asian American or Pacific Islander, 1 Hispanic American), 1 international. Average age 32. 6 applicants, 100% accepted, 5 enrolled. In 2007, 3 degrees awarded. *Degree requirements:* For master's, exams. *Entrance requirements:* For master's, audition, appropriate bachelor's degree, minimum GPA of 2.5. Additional exam requirements/recommendations for international students: Required—TOEFL. *Application deadline:* For fall admission, 8/1 priority date for domestic students; for spring admission, 12/1 priority date for domestic students. Applications are processed on a rolling basis. Application fee: $50. Electronic applications accepted. *Financial support:* Available to part-time students. Applicants required to submit FAFSA. *Unit head:* Debra Lambert, Chair, 650-580-3694. *Application contact:* Helen Valine, Director of Graduate Admissions, 650-508-3534, Fax: 650-508-3426, E-mail: grad.admit@ndnu.edu.

Oakland University, Graduate Study and Lifelong Learning, College of Arts and Sciences, Department of Music, Rochester, MI 48309-4401. Offers music (MM); music education (PhD). *Accreditation:* NASM. *Faculty:* 12 full-time (4 women), 4 part-time/adjunct (3 women). *Students:* 6 full-time (5 women), 45 part-time (31 women); includes 1 minority (Hispanic American), 3 international. Average age 34. 14 applicants, 64% accepted, 6 enrolled. In 2007, 11 master's awarded. *Entrance requirements:* For master's, minimum GPA of 3.0 for unconditional admission. Additional exam requirements/recommendations for international students: Required—TOEFL (minimum score 550 paper-based; 213 computer-based). *Application deadline:* For fall admission, 7/15 priority date for domestic students, 5/1 priority date for international students; for winter admission, 12/1 priority date for domestic students, 9/1 priority date for international students; for spring admission, 3/15 priority date for domestic students. Applications are processed on a rolling basis. Application fee: $35. Electronic applications accepted. *Expenses: Contact institution. Financial support:* Federal Work-Study, institutionally sponsored loans, and tuition waivers (full) available. Financial award application deadline: 3/1; financial award applicants required to submit FAFSA. *Unit head:* Dr. Jacqueline H. Wiggins, Acting Chair, 248-370-2030, Fax: 248-370-2041, E-mail: jwiggins@oakland.edu.

Oberlin College, Conservatory of Music, Oberlin, OH 44074. Offers MM, MMT, AD. *Accreditation:* NASM. *Students:* 12 full-time (8 women). 4 applicants, 50% accepted, 2 enrolled. In 2007, 2 degrees awarded. *Degree requirements:* For master's, 2 recitals. *Entrance requirements:* For master's, audition. Additional exam requirements/recommendations for international students: Required—TOEFL (minimum score 550 paper-based; 213 computer-

Music

Oberlin College (continued)
based; 79 iBT). *Application deadline:* For fall admission, 12/1 for domestic and international students. Application fee: $100. Electronic applications accepted. *Financial support:* Career-related internships or fieldwork, Federal Work-Study, and scholarships/grants available. Financial award application deadline: 2/15; financial award applicants required to submit CSS PROFILE or FAFSA. *Unit head:* David Stull, Dean, 440-775-8200. *Application contact:* Michael Manderen, Director of Conservatory Admissions, 440-775-8413, Fax: 440-775-6972, E-mail: conservatory.admissions@oberlin.edu.

The Ohio State University, Graduate School, College of the Arts, Department of Dance, Columbus, OH 43210. Offers choreography (MFA); dance (MA, MFA, PhD); dance and technology (MFA); dance studies (PhD); Labanotation (MFA); lighting (MFA); performance (MFA). *Accreditation:* NASD. *Faculty:* 17. *Students:* 26 full-time (23 women), 1 (woman) part-time; includes 4 minority (1 African American, 1 Asian American or Pacific Islander, 2 Hispanic Americans), 3 international. Average age 29. In 2007, 14 degrees awarded. *Degree requirements:* For master's, thesis optional. *Entrance requirements:* For master's, GRE General Test (MA); for doctorate, GRE General Test. Additional exam requirements/recommendations for international students: Recommended—TOEFL (minimum score 600 paper-based; 250 computer-based). *Application deadline:* For fall admission, 8/15 priority date for domestic students, 7/1 priority date for international students; for winter admission, 12/1 priority date for domestic students, 11/1 priority date for international students; for spring admission, 3/1 priority date for domestic students, 2/1 priority date for international students. Applications are processed on a rolling basis. Application fee: $40 ($50 for international students). Electronic applications accepted. *Financial support:* Fellowships, teaching assistantships, Federal Work-Study and institutionally sponsored loans available. Support available to part-time students. *Unit head:* Victoria E. Uris, Graduate Studies Committee Chair, 614-292-0984, Fax: 614-292-0939, E-mail: uris.1@osu.edu. *Application contact:* 614-292-9444, Fax: 614-292-3895, E-mail: domestic.grad@osu.edu.

The Ohio State University, Graduate School, College of the Arts, School of Music, Columbus, OH 43210. Offers M Mus, MA, DMA, PhD. *Accreditation:* NASM. Part-time programs available. *Faculty:* 59. *Students:* 122 full-time (73 women), 51 part-time (26 women); includes 19 minority (12 African Americans, 1 American Indian/Alaska Native, 2 Asian Americans or Pacific Islanders, 4 Hispanic Americans), 34 international. Average age 30. In 2007, 44 master's, 11 doctorates awarded. *Degree requirements:* For master's, thesis optional; for doctorate, 2 foreign languages, thesis/dissertation. *Entrance requirements:* For master's and doctorate, GRE General Test. Additional exam requirements/recommendations for international students: Recommended—TOEFL (minimum score 600 paper-based; 250 computer-based). *Application deadline:* For fall admission, 8/15 priority date for domestic students, 7/1 priority date for international students; for winter admission, 12/1 priority date for domestic students, 11/1 priority date for international students; for spring admission, 3/1 priority date for domestic students, 2/1 priority date for international students. Applications are processed on a rolling basis. Application fee: $40 ($50 for international students). Electronic applications accepted. *Financial support:* Fellowships, research assistantships, teaching assistantships, Federal Work-Study, institutionally sponsored loans, and unspecified assistantships available. Support available to part-time students. *Unit head:* Patrick Woliver, Graduate Studies Committee Chair, 614-292-7664, Fax: 614-292-1102, E-mail: woliver.1@osu.edu. *Application contact:* 614-292-9444, Fax: 614-292-3895, E-mail: domestic.grad@osu.edu.

Ohio University, Graduate College, College of Fine Arts, School of Music, Athens, OH 45701-2979. Offers accompanying (MM); composition (MM); conducting (MM); history/literature (MM); music education (MM); music therapy (MM); performance (MM, Certificate); performance/pedagogy (MM); theory (MM). *Accreditation:* NASM. Postbaccalaureate distance learning degree programs offered (minimal on-campus study). *Faculty:* 35 full-time (10 women), 1 part-time/adjunct (0 women). *Students:* 31 full-time (15 women), 13 part-time (7 women); includes 2 minority (both African Americans), 12 international. 49 applicants, 55% accepted, 16 enrolled. In 2007, 22 degrees awarded. *Degree requirements:* For master's, thesis (for some programs), oral exam. *Entrance requirements:* For master's, audition, interview, and/or portfolio. Additional exam requirements/recommendations for international students: Required—TOEFL. *Application deadline:* For fall admission, 8/15 priority date for domestic students. Application fee: $50 ($55 for international students). *Financial support:* In 2007–08, 35 students received support, including 35 teaching assistantships with full and partial tuition reimbursements available (averaging $4,500 per year); career-related internships or fieldwork, Federal Work-Study, institutionally sponsored loans, and tuition waivers (full and partial) also available. Financial award application deadline: 3/15. *Unit head:* Dr. Michael Parkinson, Director, 740-593-4244, Fax: 740-593-1429, E-mail: parkinsw@ohio.edu. *Application contact:* Dr. Richard Wetzel, Graduate Chair, 740-593-1652, Fax: 740-593-1429, E-mail: wetzel@ohio.edu.

Oklahoma City University, Margaret E. Petree College of Performing Arts, Wanda L. Bass School of Music, Oklahoma City, OK 73106-1402. Offers composition (MM); conducting (MM); musical theatre (MM); opera performance (MM); performance (MM). *Accreditation:* NASM. Part-time programs available. *Faculty:* 19 full-time (6 women), 25 part-time/adjunct (12 women). *Students:* 64 full-time (42 women), 3 part-time (2 women); includes 2 minority (1 American Indian/Alaska Native, 1 Asian American or Pacific Islander), 24 international. Average age 25. 45 applicants, 91% accepted. In 2007, 6 degrees awarded. *Degree requirements:* For master's, thesis, departmental qualifying exam, recital. *Entrance requirements:* For master's, audition, bachelor's degree in music, minimum GPA of 3.0. Additional exam requirements/recommendations for international students: Required—TOEFL. *Application deadline:* For fall admission, 8/22 for domestic students; for spring admission, 1/15 for domestic students. Applications are processed on a rolling basis. Application fee: $30 ($70 for international students). *Expenses:* Tuition: Full-time $14,040; part-time $780 per hour. Required fees: $881; $32 per hour. *Financial support:* Fellowships with partial tuition reimbursements, career-related internships or fieldwork, Federal Work-Study, and institutionally sponsored loans available. Financial award application deadline: 4/1; financial award applicants required to submit FAFSA. *Unit head:* Mark Parker, Dean, 405-208-5474, Fax: 405-208-5971, E-mail: mparker@okcu.edu. *Application contact:* Leslie Mckenzie, Director Graduate Admissions, 800-633-7242, Fax: 405-208-5356, E-mail: gadmissions@okcu.edu.

Oklahoma State University, College of Arts and Sciences, Department of Music, Stillwater, OK 74078. Offers pedagogy and performance (MM). *Accreditation:* NASM. *Faculty:* 29 full-time (12 women), 5 part-time/adjunct (2 women). *Students:* 9 full-time (3 women), 7 part-time (2 women); includes 1 minority (African American), 1 international. Average age 28. 20 applicants, 45% accepted, 7 enrolled. In 2007, 3 degrees awarded. *Degree requirements:* For master's, final project and oral exam. *Entrance requirements:* For master's, GRE or GMAT, audition. Additional exam requirements/recommendations for international students: Required—TOEFL. *Application deadline:* For fall admission, 3/1 priority date for international students; for spring admission, 8/1 priority date for international students. Applications are processed on a rolling basis. Application fee: $40 ($75 for international students). Electronic applications accepted. *Expenses:* Tuition, state resident: full-time $4,993; part-time $148 per credit hour. Tuition, nonresident: full-time $14,755; part-time $555 per credit hour. Tuition and fees vary according to program. *Financial support:* In 2007–08, 10 teaching assistantships (averaging $8,305 per year) were awarded; scholarships/grants, health care benefits, and unspecified assistantships also available. Financial award application deadline: 3/1. *Faculty research:* Discovery and presentation of music literature of other countries, transportation of ancient music literature to modern notation. *Unit head:* Dr. Julia Combs, Head, 405-744-6133, Fax: 405-744-9324, E-mail: julie.combs@okstate.edu.

Penn State University Park, Graduate School, College of Arts and Architecture, School of Music, State College, University Park, PA 16802-1503. Offers composition/theory (M Mus); conducting (M Mus); music education (MME, PhD); music theory (MA); music theory and history (MA); musicology (MA); performance (M Mus); piano, pedagogy and performance (M Mus); voice performance and pedagogy (M Mus). *Accreditation:* NASM. *Expenses:* Tuition, state resident: full-time $14,738; part-time $614 per credit. Tuition, nonresident: full-time $26,050; part-time $1,085 per credit. Tuition and fees vary according to course load, program and student level. *Unit head:* Sue E. Haug, Director, 814-863-4421, Fax: 814-865-6785, E-mail: seh22@psu.edu.

Phillips Theological Seminary, Programs in Theology, Tulsa, OK 74116. Offers administration of church agencies (M Div); campus ministry (M Div); church-related social work (M Div); college and seminary teaching (M Div); global mission work (M Div); institutional chaplaincy (M Div); ministerial vocations in Christian education (M Div); ministry (D Min), including parish ministry, pastoral counseling, practices of ministry; ministry and culture (MAMC), including Christian education, congregational leadership, history and practice of Christian spirituality, theology, ethics, and culture; ministry of music (M Div); pastoral care and counseling (M Div); pastoral ministry (M Div); theological studies (MTS). *Accreditation:* ATS. Part-time programs available. Postbaccalaureate distance learning degree programs offered (minimal on-campus study). *Degree requirements:* For master's, thesis (for some programs); for doctorate, thesis/dissertation. *Entrance requirements:* For master's, minimum GPA of 2.5; for doctorate, M Div, minimum GPA of 3.0. *Faculty research:* Biblical studies, historical studies, theology and culture, practical theology, theology and film.

Pittsburg State University, Graduate School, College of Arts and Sciences, Department of Music, Pittsburg, KS 66762. Offers instrumental music education (MM); music history/music literature (MM); performance (MM), including orchestral performance, organ, piano, voice; theory and composition (MM); vocal music education (MM). *Accreditation:* NASM. *Degree requirements:* For master's, thesis or alternative.

Point Park University, Conservatory of Performing Arts, Pittsburgh, PA 15222-1984. Offers theatre arts-acting (MFA). *Faculty:* 4 full-time, 3 part-time/adjunct. *Students:* 5 full-time (3 women), 1 part-time. Average age 39. 1 applicant, 0% accepted. *Entrance requirements:* For master's, interview. *Application deadline:* Applications are processed on a rolling basis. Application fee: $30. Electronic applications accepted. *Expenses:* Tuition: Full-time $10,566; part-time $587 per credit. Required fees: $360; $20 per credit. *Financial support:* Teaching assistantships with full tuition reimbursements, scholarships/grants available. Financial award application deadline: 5/1; financial award applicants required to submit FAFSA. *Unit head:* Ronald Allan-Lindblom, Dean/Artistic Producing Director, 412-392-3454, Fax: 412-392-2424, E-mail: rlindblom@pointpark.edu. *Application contact:* Debbie P. Bateman, Director, Adult Academic Services, 412-392-3433, Fax: 412-392-6164, E-mail: dbateman@pointpark.edu.

Portland State University, Graduate Studies, School of Fine and Performing Arts, Department of Music, Portland, OR 97207-0751. Offers conducting (MMC); music education (MAT, MST); performance (MMP). *Accreditation:* NASM. Part-time programs available. *Faculty:* 23 full-time (8 women), 24 part-time/adjunct (8 women). *Students:* 19 full-time (9 women), 13 part-time (8 women); includes 4 minority (1 African American, 2 Asian Americans or Pacific Islanders, 1 Hispanic American), 4 international. Average age 30. 19 applicants, 89% accepted, 11 enrolled. In 2007, 9 degrees awarded. *Degree requirements:* For master's, variable foreign language requirement, exit exam. *Entrance requirements:* For master's, departmental exam, GRE General Test, minimum GPA of 3.0 in upper-division course work or 2.75 overall. Additional exam requirements/recommendations for international students: Required—TOEFL (minimum score 550 paper-based; 213 computer-based). *Application deadline:* For fall admission, 8/1 priority date for domestic students, 8/1 for international students; for winter admission, 10/1 for domestic and international students; for spring admission, 2/1 for domestic and international students. Applications are processed on a rolling basis. Application fee: $50. *Expenses:* Tuition, state resident: full-time $7,047. Tuition, nonresident: full-time $11,178. *Financial support:* Research assistantships with full tuition reimbursements, teaching assistantships with full tuition reimbursements, Federal Work-Study, scholarships/grants, and unspecified assistantships available. Support available to part-time students. Financial award application deadline: 3/1; financial award applicants required to submit FAFSA. *Faculty research:* Composition, music analysis, music history, jazz. *Unit head:* Bryan Johanson, Chair, 503-725-3003, Fax: 503-725-8215.

Princeton University, Graduate School, Department of Music, Princeton, NJ 08544-1019. Offers composition (PhD); musicology (PhD). *Degree requirements:* For doctorate, variable foreign language requirement, thesis/dissertation. *Entrance requirements:* For doctorate, GRE General Test, sample of written work. Additional exam requirements/recommendations for international students: Required—TOEFL (minimum score 600 paper-based; 250 computer-based). Electronic applications accepted. *Faculty research:* Computer synthesis, history of Western music, comparative musicology, theory.

Purchase College, State University of New York, Conservatory of Music, Purchase, NY 10577-1400. Offers composition (MM); instrumental performance (MM); jazz studies (MM); studio composition (MM); voice and opera studies (MM). *Faculty:* 11 full-time (5 women), 39 part-time/adjunct (17 women). *Students:* 106 full-time (41 women), 5 part-time (4 women); includes 6 minority (2 African Americans, 4 Asian Americans or Pacific Islanders), 19 international. Average age 30. 161 applicants, 40% accepted, 56 enrolled. In 2007, 43 degrees awarded. *Degree requirements:* For master's, thesis or alternative, composition, performance. *Entrance requirements:* For master's, audition. *Application deadline:* For fall admission, 3/1 for domestic students. Application fee: $50. Electronic applications accepted. *Expenses:* Tuition, state resident: full-time $6,900; part-time $288 per credit. Tuition, nonresident: full-time $10,920; part-time $455 per credit. Required fees: $1,506; $125 per credit. Tuition and fees vary according to program. *Financial support:* In 2007–08, 32 students received support; fellowships, teaching assistantships, career-related internships or fieldwork, Federal Work-Study, scholarships/grants, and tuition waivers (partial) available. Support available to part-time students. Financial award application deadline: 3/15; financial award applicants required to submit FAFSA. *Faculty research:* Performance practice, jazz history, popular music history, composition. *Unit head:* Laura Kaminsky, Dean, 914-251-6700, Fax: 914-251-6739, E-mail: laura.kaminsky@purchase.edu. *Application contact:* Sabrina Johnston, Counselor, 914-251-6479, Fax: 914-251-6314, E-mail: admissn@purchase.edu.

Queens College of the City University of New York, Division of Graduate Studies, Arts and Humanities Division, Aaron Copland School of Music, Flushing, NY 11367-1597. Offers MA. Part-time programs available. *Faculty:* 25 full-time (5 women). *Students:* 17 full-time (8 women), 91 part-time (38 women). 139 applicants, 52% accepted, 59 enrolled. In 2007, 31 degrees awarded. *Degree requirements:* For master's, one foreign language, qualifying exams, recital. *Entrance requirements:* For master's, audition, bachelor's degree in music, minimum GPA of 3.0. Additional exam requirements/recommendations for international students: Required—TOEFL. *Application deadline:* For fall admission, 4/1 for domestic students; for spring admission, 11/1 for domestic students. Applications are processed on a rolling basis. Application fee: $125. *Financial support:* Career-related internships or fieldwork, Federal Work-Study, institutionally sponsored loans, tuition waivers (partial), and adjunct lectureships available. Support available to part-time students. Financial award application deadline: 4/1; financial award applicants required to submit FAFSA. *Unit head:* Dr. Edward Smaldone, Chair/Director, 718-997-3800, E-mail: edward_smaldone@qc.edu.

Radford University, Graduate College, College of Visual and Performing Arts, Department of Music, Radford, VA 24142. Offers music (MA); music therapy (MS). *Accreditation:* NASM. Part-time programs available. *Faculty:* 12 full-time (4 women). *Students:* 7 full-time (6 women), 6 part-time (3 women); includes 1 minority (African American), 1 international. Average age 27. 13 applicants, 85% accepted, 5 enrolled. In 2007, 8 degrees awarded. *Degree requirements:* For master's, comprehensive exam, thesis or alternative. *Entrance requirements:* For master's, GRE General Test, GRE Subject Test (music), or PRAXIS II. Additional exam requirements/recommendations for international students: Required—TOEFL. *Application deadline:* For fall admission, 3/1 priority date for domestic students, 12/1 for international students; for spring admission, 10/1 for domestic students, 7/1 for international students. Applications are processed on a rolling basis. Application fee: $40. Electronic applications accepted. *Financial support:* In 2007–08, 11 students received support, including 5 research assistantships with partial tuition reimbursements available (averaging $8,000 per year), 6 teaching assistantships with partial tuition reimbursements available (averaging $8,700 per year); career-related internships or fieldwork, Federal Work-Study, institutionally sponsored loans, scholarships/grants, and unspecified assistantships also available. Financial award application deadline: 3/1; financial award applicants required to submit FAFSA. *Unit head:* Dr. Eugene C. Fellin, Chair, 540-831-5177, Fax: 540-831-6133, E-mail: efellin@radford.edu.

Regis University, College for Professional Studies, Program in Teacher Education, Denver, CO 80221-1099. Offers adult learning, training, and development (M Ed); curriculum, instruction, and assessment (M Ed); early childhood (M Ed); educational technology (Certificate); elementary (M Ed); ESL (M Ed); fine arts (M Ed), including arts, music; instructional technology (M Ed); professional leadership (M Ed); reading (M Ed); secondary (M Ed); self-designed (M Ed); space studies (M Ed); special education (M Ed); teacher licensure (M Ed). Program also offered in Henderson and Las Vegas (Summerlin), NV. Part-time and evening/weekend programs available. Postbaccalaureate distance learning degree programs offered (no on-campus study). *Faculty:* 107. *Students:* 728 (574 women). Average age 36. In 2007, 209 degrees awarded. *Degree requirements:* For master's, thesis. *Entrance requirements:* For master's, essays, resumé, minimum GPA of 2.75, criminal background check. Additional exam requirements/recommendations for international students: Required—TOEFL (minimum score 213 computer-based), TWE (minimum score 5). *Application deadline:* For fall admission, 7/23 priority date for domestic students; for winter admission, 9/17 priority date for domestic students; for spring admission, 12/3 priority date for domestic students. Applications are processed on a rolling basis. Application fee: $75. Electronic applications accepted. *Financial support:* Federal Work-Study and scholarships/grants available. *Faculty research:* Issues of equity in the middle school classroom, professional learning communities, school reform, socialinguistic and discursive obstacles to student integration, inclusive language arts curriculum. *Unit head:* Dr. Suzie Perry, Dean, 303-458-4302.

Rice University, Graduate Programs, Shepherd School of Music, Houston, TX 77251-1892. Offers composition (MM, DMA); conducting (MM); history (MM); performance (MM, DMA); theory (MM). *Degree requirements:* For master's, thesis (for some programs), 2 recitals; for doctorate, one foreign language, comprehensive exam, thesis/dissertation, 4 recitals. *Entrance requirements:* For master's, minimum GPA of 3.0; for doctorate, GRE General Test, minimum GPA of 3.0. Additional exam requirements/recommendations for international students: Required—TOEFL (minimum score 600 paper-based; 250 computer-based; 90 iBT). Electronic applications accepted. *Faculty research:* Musicology, performance, theory, composition.

Rockford College, Graduate Studies, Department of Education, Program in Secondary Education, Rockford, IL 61108-2393. Offers art education (MAT); education (MAT); English (MAT); history (MAT); math (MAT); physical education (MAT); political science (MAT); secondary education (MAT); social sciences (MAT); theatre arts (MAT). Part-time and evening/weekend programs available. *Faculty:* 15 full-time (2 women), 8 part-time/adjunct (6 women). *Students:* Average age 31. In 2007, 14 degrees awarded. *Degree requirements:* For master's, thesis optional. *Entrance requirements:* For master's, GRE General Test, application fee, official transcripts, basic skills. *Application deadline:* Applications are processed on a rolling basis. Application fee: $50. *Expenses:* Tuition: Part-time $610 per credit. Required fees: $30 per term. *Unit head:* Jo Ellen Vause, Director of MAT Program, 815-226-4013, Fax: 815-226-4119.

Roosevelt University, Graduate Division, Chicago College of Performing Arts, The Music Conservatory, Chicago, IL 60605-1394. Offers music (MM); piano pedagogy (Diploma). *Accreditation:* NASM. Part-time and evening/weekend programs available. *Students:* 124 full-time (67 women), 15 part-time (9 women); includes 17 minority (6 African Americans, 7 Asian Americans or Pacific Islanders, 4 Hispanic Americans), 41 international. Average age 25. 281 applicants, 25% accepted, 67 enrolled. In 2007, 38 degrees awarded. *Application deadline:* For fall admission, 6/1 priority date for domestic students. Applications are processed on a rolling basis. Application fee: $25 ($35 for international students). *Financial support:* Federal Work-Study available. Support available to part-time students. Financial award application deadline: 2/15. *Unit head:* Linda Berna, Director, 312-341-3785. *Application contact:* Joanne Canyon-Heller, Coordinator of Graduate Admission, 877-APPLY RU, Fax: 312-281-3356, E-mail: applyru@roosevelt.edu.

Rowan University, Graduate School, College of Fine and Performing Arts, Program in Music, Glassboro, NJ 08028-1701. Offers MM. *Accreditation:* NASM. Part-time and evening/weekend programs available. *Faculty:* 13 full-time (3 women), 9 part-time/adjunct (3 women). *Students:* 4 full-time (1 woman), 6 part-time (2 women); includes 1 minority (Asian American or Pacific Islander) Average age 32. 8 applicants, 50% accepted, 2 enrolled. In 2007, 3 degrees awarded. *Entrance requirements:* Additional exam requirements/recommendations for international students: Required—TOEFL. *Application deadline:* Applications are processed on a rolling basis. Application fee: $50. Electronic applications accepted. *Expenses:* Tuition, nonresident: full-time $9,882; part-time $549 per credit. Required fees: $104,385 per credit. *Financial support:* Career-related internships or fieldwork, Federal Work-Study, and unspecified assistantships available. Support available to part-time students. *Unit head:* Prof. Brian Appleby-Wineberg, Adviser, 856-256-4500 Ext. 3526.

Rutgers, The State University of New Jersey, Newark, Graduate School, Program in Jazz History and Research, Newark, NJ 07102. Offers MA. *Entrance requirements:* For master's, GRE, minimum B average. Electronic applications accepted.

Rutgers, The State University of New Jersey, New Brunswick, Mason Gross School of the Arts, Program in Music, New Brunswick, NJ 08901-1281. Offers collaborative piano (MM, DMA); conducting: choral (MM, DMA); conducting: instrumental (MM, DMA); conducting: orchestral (MM, DMA); jazz studies (MM); music (DMA, AD); music education (MM, DMA); music performance (MM). *Accreditation:* NASM. *Degree requirements:* For doctorate, one foreign language. *Entrance requirements:* For doctorate, audition. Additional exam requirements/recommendations for international students: Required—TOEFL (minimum score 550 paper-based; 213 computer-based). Electronic applications accepted. *Faculty research:* Performance, twentieth century music, jazz.

St. Cloud State University, School of Graduate Studies, College of Fine Arts and Humanities, Department of Music, St. Cloud, MN 56301-4498. Offers conducting and literature (MM); music education (MM); piano pedagogy (MM). *Accreditation:* NASM. *Faculty:* 16 full-time (7 women), 1 part-time/adjunct (0 women). *Students:* 5 full-time (4 women), 14 part-time (7 women), 3 international. 6 applicants, 100% accepted. In 2007, 4 degrees awarded. *Degree requirements:* For master's, comprehensive exam (for some programs), thesis or alternative. *Entrance requirements:* For master's, GRE General Test, minimum GPA of 2.75. Additional exam requirements/recommendations for international students: Required—MELAB; Recommended—TOEFL (minimum score 550 paper-based; 213 computer-based), IELTS (minimum score 7). *Application deadline:* For fall admission, 6/1 priority date for domestic students, 4/1 for international students; for spring admission, 10/1 priority date for domestic students, 8/1 for international students. Applications are processed on a rolling basis. Application fee: $35. Electronic applications accepted. *Expenses:* Tuition, state resident: part-time $267 per credit. Tuition, nonresident: part-time $418 per credit. Required fees: $28 per credit. *Financial support:* Federal Work-Study, scholarships/grants, and unspecified assistantships available. Financial award application deadline: 3/1. *Unit head:* Dr. Mark Springer, Chairperson, 320-308-3223, Fax: 320-308-2902. *Application contact:* Linda Lou Krueger, School of Graduate Studies, 320-308-2113, Fax: 320-308-5371, E-mail: lekrueger@stcloudstate.edu.

Saint John's University, Saint John's School of Theology and Seminary, Collegeville, MN 56321. Offers divinity (M Div); liturgical music (MA); liturgical studies (MA); pastoral ministry (MA); theology (MA), including church history, liturgy, monastic studies, scripture, spirituality, systematics; M Div/MA. *Accreditation:* ATS. Part-time programs available. Postbaccalaureate distance learning degree programs offered (no on-campus study). *Degree requirements:* For master's, one foreign language, comprehensive exam (for some programs), thesis (for some programs). *Entrance requirements:* For master's, GRE General Test or MAT. Electronic applications accepted. *Faculty research:* Religious education, biblical literature.

Saint Joseph's College, Rensselaer Program of Church Music and Liturgy, Rensselaer, IN 47978. Offers music (MA); pastoral liturgy (Diploma). Offered during summer only. Part-time programs available. *Degree requirements:* For master's, thesis, research paper, service recital. *Entrance requirements:* For master's, entrance exams in music theory, conducting, keyboard, voice, and history.

St. Vladimir's Orthodox Theological Seminary, Graduate School of Theology, Crestwood, NY 10707-1699. Offers general theological studies (MA); liturgical music (MA); religious education (MA); theology (M Div, M Th, D Min); M Div/MA. MA in general theological studies, M Div offered jointly with St. Nersess Seminary. *Accreditation:* ATS. Part-time programs available. *Degree requirements:* For master's, one foreign language, thesis, fieldwork; for doctorate, thesis/dissertation, fieldwork; for M Div, one foreign language, thesis/dissertation, fieldwork. *Entrance requirements:* For doctorate, M Div, minimum GPA of 3.0. Additional exam requirements/recommendations for international students: Required—TOEFL (minimum score 250 computer-based).

Samford University, School of the Arts, Birmingham, AL 35229. Offers church music (MM); music education (MME); piano pedagogy (MM). *Accreditation:* NASM. Part-time programs available. *Faculty:* 11 full-time (2 women), 7 part-time/adjunct (2 women). *Students:* 10 full-time (6 women), 4 part-time (2 women). Average age 24. 12 applicants, 67% accepted, 8 enrolled. In 2007, 2 degrees awarded. *Degree requirements:* For master's, oral exams. *Entrance requirements:* For master's, GRE General Test or MAT, minimum 3.0 GPA, institutional graduate exam. Additional exam requirements/recommendations for international students: Required—TOEFL (minimum score 550 paper-based; 213 computer-based). *Application deadline:* For fall admission, 9/1 for domestic students; for spring admission, 1/20 for domestic students. Application fee: $25. *Financial support:* In 2007–08, 1 student received support, including research assistantships (averaging $2,000 per year); Federal Work-Study, scholarships/grants, and tuition waivers (partial) also available. Financial award application deadline: 9/1. *Faculty research:* Hymnology, choral techniques, assessment of music learning at elementary and secondary levels, piano pedagogy. *Unit head:* Dr. Joseph H. Hopkins, Dean, 205-726-2165, E-mail: jhhopkin@samford.edu. *Application contact:* Dr. Moya Nordlund, Director, Graduate Studies, 205-726-2651, Fax: 205-726-2165.

Sam Houston State University, College of Arts and Sciences, School of Music, Huntsville, TX 77341. Offers conducting (MM); music (MM); music education (M Ed, MM). *Accreditation:* NASM. Part-time programs available. *Faculty:* 15 full-time (4 women). *Students:* 10 full-time (2 women), 9 part-time (3 women); includes 3 minority (1 African American, 2 Hispanic Americans), 2 international. Average age 27. In 2007, 9 degrees awarded. *Degree requirements:* For master's, thesis (for some programs), departmental qualifying exam. *Entrance requirements:* For master's, GRE General Test. Additional exam requirements/recommendations for international students: Required—TOEFL (minimum score 550 paper-based; 213 computer-based). *Application deadline:* For fall admission, 8/1 for domestic students; for spring admission, 12/1 for domestic students. Applications are processed on a rolling basis. Application fee: $20. *Expenses:* Tuition, state resident: full-time $5,026; part-time $184 per semester hour. Tuition, nonresident: full-time $10,586; part-time $462 per semester hour. Required fees: $494 per semester. *Financial support:* Teaching assistantships, Federal Work-Study and scholarships/grants available. Financial award application deadline: 5/31; financial award applicants required to submit FAFSA. *Unit head:* Dr. James Bankhead, Chair, 936-294-3808, Fax: 936-294-3765, E-mail: bankhead@shsu.edu. *Application contact:* Scott Plugge, Advisor, 936-294-1393, E-mail: plugge@shsu.edu.

San Diego State University, Graduate and Research Affairs, College of Professional Studies and Fine Arts, School of Music and Dance, San Diego, CA 92182. Offers composition (acoustic and electronic) (MM); conducting (MM); ethnomusicology (MA); jazz studies (MM); musicology (MA); performance (MM); piano pedagogy (MA); theory (MA). *Students:* 24 full-time (13 women), 28 part-time (15 women); includes 17 minority (5 African Americans, 5 Asian Americans or Pacific Islanders, 7 Hispanic Americans), 7 international. Average age 29. 34 applicants, 68% accepted, 20 enrolled. In 2007, 19 degrees awarded. *Degree requirements:* For master's, comprehensive exam (for some programs), thesis (for some programs). *Entrance requirements:* For master's, GRE General Test, bachelor's degree in related field, 2 letters of reference. Additional exam requirements/recommendations for international students: Required—TOEFL. *Application deadline:* For fall admission, 5/1 for domestic and international students; for spring admission, 11/1 for domestic students, 10/1 for international students. Applications are processed on a rolling basis. Application fee: $55. Electronic applications accepted. *Financial support:* Fellowships, teaching assistantships, career-related internships or fieldwork and unspecified assistantships available. Financial award applicants required to submit FAFSA. Total annual research expenditures: $14,000. *Unit head:* Donna Conaty, Director, 619-594-1692, Fax: 619-594-1692. *Application contact:* Martin Chambers, Director, 619-594-1691, Fax: 619-594-1692, E-mail: mchambers@mail.sdsu.edu.

San Francisco Conservatory of Music, Graduate Division, San Francisco, CA 94122-4411. Offers chamber music (MM); classical guitar (MM); composition (MM); conducting (MM); keyboards (MM); orchestral instruments (MM); voice (MM). *Accreditation:* NASM. Part-time programs available. *Faculty:* 25 full-time (9 women), 74 part-time/adjunct (24 women). *Students:* 187 full-time (115 women), 2 part-time (both women); includes 25 minority (1 African American, 17 Asian Americans or Pacific Islanders, 7 Hispanic Americans), 62 international. Average age 24. 446 applicants, 43% accepted, 107 enrolled. In 2007, 49 degrees awarded. *Degree requirements:* For master's, variable foreign language requirement, 2 recitals, departmental qualifying exam. *Entrance requirements:* For master's, audition, recommendations. Additional exam requirements/recommendations for international students: Required—TOEFL (minimum score 500 paper-based; 173 computer-based; 61 iBT). *Application deadline:* For fall admission, 12/1 for domestic and international students; for spring admission, 10/1 for domestic and international students. Application fee: $100. Electronic applications accepted. *Expenses:* Tuition: Full-time $29,700. *Financial support:* In 2007–08, 177 students received support, including 177 fellowships (averaging $14,300 per year); Federal Work-Study, scholarships/grants, and unspecified assistantships also available. Support available to part-time students. Financial award application deadline: 2/15; financial award applicants required to submit FAFSA. *Unit head:* Mary Ellen Poole, Dean, 415-503-6212, Fax: 415-503-6299, E-mail: mep@sfcm.edu. *Application contact:* Alexander Brose, Director of Admissions, 415-503-6231, Fax: 415-503-6299, E-mail: admit@sfcm.edu.

San Francisco State University, Division of Graduate Studies, College of Creative Arts, School of Music and Dance, San Francisco, CA 94132-1722. Offers chamber music (MM); classical performance (MM); composition (MA); conducting (MM); music education (MA); music history (MA). *Accreditation:* NASM. *Unit head:* Dr. George DeGraffenreid, Director, 415-338-1432. *Application contact:* Dr. Cyrus Ginwala, Graduate Coordinator, 415-338-1432, E-mail: cginwala@sfsu.edu.

San Jose State University, Graduate Studies and Research, College of Humanities and the Arts, School of Music and Dance, San Jose, CA 95192-0001. Offers music (MA). *Accreditation:* NASM. *Students:* 20 full-time (11 women), 17 part-time (8 women); includes 7 minority (5 Asian Americans or Pacific Islanders, 2 Hispanic Americans), 6 international. Average age 31. 30 applicants, 67% accepted, 17 enrolled. In 2007, 3 degrees awarded. *Degree requirements:* For master's, thesis or alternative. *Entrance requirements:* For master's, GRE. Additional exam requirements/recommendations for international students: Required—TOEFL (minimum score 590 paper-based). *Application deadline:* For fall admission, 6/29 for domestic students; for spring admission, 11/30 for domestic students. Applications are processed on a rolling basis. Application fee: $59. Electronic applications accepted. *Financial support:* Applicants required to submit FAFSA. *Unit head:* Dr. Edward C. Harris, Director, 408-924-4677, Fax: 408-924-4773.

Music

Santa Clara University, School of Education, Counseling Psychology, and Pastoral Ministries, Program in Pastoral Ministries, Program in Liturgical Music, Santa Clara, CA 95053. Offers MA. Part-time and evening/weekend programs available. *Students:* Average age 32. In 2007, 1 degree awarded. *Degree requirements:* For master's, comprehensive exam, thesis. *Entrance requirements:* Additional exam requirements/recommendations for international students: Required—TOEFL. *Application deadline:* Applications are processed on a rolling basis. *Financial support:* Application deadline: 3/1; *Unit head:* Fr. Tom Powers, S.J., Director, Program in Pastoral Ministries, 408-554-4322.

Savannah College of Art and Design, Graduate School, Savannah, GA 31402-3146. Offers advertising design (MA, MFA); animation (MA, MFA); architectural history (MA, MFA); architecture (M Arch); art history (MA, MFA); arts administration (MA); broadcast design (MA, MFA); cinema studies (MA); commercial photography (MA); digital photography (MA); documentary photography (MA); fashion (MA, MFA); fibers (MA, MFA); film and television (MA, MFA); furniture design (MA, MFA); graphic design (MA, MFA); historic preservation (MA, MFA); illustration (MA, MFA); illustration design (MA); industrial design (MA, MFA); interactive design and game development (MA, MFA); interior design (MA, MFA); metals and jewelry (MA, MFA); painting (MA, MFA); performing arts (MA, MFA); photography (MA, MFA); printmaking (MA, MFA); production design (MA, MFA); professional education (MA); professional writing (MFA); sculpture (MA, MFA); sequential art (MA, MFA); sound design (MA, MFA); urban design and development (MA); visual effects (MA, MFA). Part-time programs available. Postbaccalaureate distance learning degree programs offered (no on-campus study). *Faculty:* 250 full-time (105 women), 53 part-time/adjunct (22 women). *Students:* 1,150 full-time (639 women), 297 part-time (154 women); includes 124 minority (69 African Americans, 6 American Indian/Alaska Native, 14 Asian Americans or Pacific Islanders, 35 Hispanic Americans), 326 international. Average age 25. 1,905 applicants, 48% accepted, 447 enrolled. In 2007, 374 degrees awarded. *Degree requirements:* For master's, thesis, internship. *Entrance requirements:* For master's, interview, 3 letters of recommendation. Additional exam requirements/recommendations for international students: Required—TOEFL (minimum score 500 paper-based; 133 computer-based). *Application deadline:* For fall admission, 4/1 priority date for domestic and international students. Applications are processed on a rolling basis. Application fee: $50. Electronic applications accepted. *Expenses:* Tuition: Full-time $24,840; part-time $552 per credit. One-time fee: $500 full-time. *Financial support:* Fellowships, career-related internships or fieldwork, Federal Work-Study, and scholarships/grants available. Financial award application deadline: 4/1; financial award applicants required to submit FAFSA. *Faculty research:* Urban planning for diverse communities, photovoltaics-powered environmental control, computer-aided design and virtual reality, multimedia design. *Application contact:* Darrell Tutchton, Director of Graduate and International Enrollment, 912-525-5961, Fax: 912-525-5985, E-mail: admission@scad.edu.

See Close-Up on page 257.

Seton Hall University, College of Arts and Sciences, Department of Art and Music, South Orange, NJ 07079-2697. Offers museum professions (MA). *Accreditation:* NASM. Part-time and evening/weekend programs available. *Degree requirements:* For master's, thesis or alternative. *Entrance requirements:* For master's, GRE General Test, previous course work in art history. Electronic applications accepted. *Faculty research:* History of museums, museum education, theory of museums, nineteenth century art, African-American art, Renaissance art history, museum registration.

See Close-Up on page 261.

Shenandoah University, Shenandoah Conservatory, Winchester, VA 22601-5195. Offers arts administration (MS); church music (MM, Certificate); composition (MM); conducting (MM); dance (MA, MFA, MS); dance accompanying (MM); music (MS); music education (MME, DMA); music therapy (MMT, Certificate); pedagogy (MM); performance (MM, DMA, Artist Diploma); piano accompanying (MM). *Accreditation:* NASM. Part-time and evening/weekend programs available. *Faculty:* 35 full-time (17 women), 12 part-time/adjunct (6 women). *Students:* 69 full-time (39 women), 126 part-time (72 women); includes 5 minority (3 African Americans, 2 Hispanic Americans), 27 international. Average age 40. 90 applicants, 92% accepted, 59 enrolled. In 2007, 28 master's, 12 doctorates, 6 other advanced degrees awarded. *Degree requirements:* For master's, comprehensive exam (for some programs), thesis (for some programs), internship (MS), recital (MM), research teaching project or thesis (MME), project (MA); for doctorate, comprehensive exam, thesis/dissertation (for some programs), dissertation or teaching project, recital. *Entrance requirements:* For master's, audition, minimum GPA of 2.5, writing sample, resumé; for doctorate, audition, minimum GPA of 3.25, 2 letters of recommendation, writing sample, resumé. Additional exam requirements/recommendations for international students: Required—TOEFL (minimum score 527 paper-based; 197 computer-based; 71 iBT). *Application deadline:* Applications are processed on a rolling basis. Application fee: $30. Electronic applications accepted. *Expenses:* Tuition: Part-time $640 per credit. Part-time tuition and fees vary according to degree level and program. *Financial support:* In 2007–08, 154 students received support, including 23 teaching assistantships with partial tuition reimbursements available (averaging $5,440 per year); fellowships with partial tuition reimbursements available, career-related internships or fieldwork, institutionally sponsored loans, scholarships/grants, and unspecified assistantships also available. Support available to part-time students. Financial award application deadline: 3/15; financial award applicants required to submit FAFSA. *Faculty research:* Creative activity, performance practice, music therapy aging, composition, Motown music. Total annual research expenditures: $4,272. *Unit head:* Dr. Laurence A. Kaptain, Dean, 540-665-4600, Fax: 540-665-5402, E-mail: lkaptain@su.edu. *Application contact:* David Anthony, Dean of Admissions, 540-665-4581, Fax: 540-665-4627, E-mail: admit@su.edu.

See Close-Up on page 357.

Southeastern Baptist Theological Seminary, Graduate and Professional Programs, Wake Forest, NC 27588-1889. Offers advanced biblical studies (M Div); Christian education (M Div, MACE); Christian ethics (PhD); Christian ministry (M Div); Christian planting (M Div); church music (MACM); counseling (MACO); evangelism (PhD); language (M Div); ministry (D Min); New Testament (PhD); Old Testament (PhD); philosophy (PhD); theology (Th M, PhD); women's studies (M Div). *Accreditation:* ACIPE; ATS (one or more programs are accredited). *Degree requirements:* For master's, thesis (for some programs), oral exam; for doctorate, thesis/dissertation, fieldwork; for M Div, supervised ministry. *Entrance requirements:* For master's, Cooperative English Test, minimum GPA of 2.0, M Div or equivalent (Th M); for doctorate, GRE General Test or MAT, Cooperative English Test, M Div or equivalent, 3 years of professional experience.

Southeastern Louisiana University, College of Arts, Humanities and Social Sciences, Department of Music and Dramatic Arts, Hammond, LA 70402. Offers music (M Mus). *Accreditation:* NASM. Part-time programs available. *Faculty:* 9 full-time (1 woman). *Students:* 15 full-time (5 women), 5 part-time (3 women); includes 5 minority (all African Americans), 8 international. Average age 26. 8 applicants, 88% accepted, 7 enrolled. In 2007, 3 degrees awarded. *Degree requirements:* For master's, comprehensive exam, thesis (for some programs), senior recital. *Entrance requirements:* For master's, bachelor's degree in music, senior recital. Additional exam requirements/recommendations for international students: Required—TOEFL (minimum score 500 paper-based; 173 computer-based). *Application deadline:* For fall admission, 7/15 priority date for domestic students, 6/1 priority date for international students; for spring admission, 12/1 priority date for domestic students, 10/1 priority date for international students. Applications are processed on a rolling basis. Application fee: $20 ($30 for international students). Electronic applications accepted. *Expenses:* Tuition, state resident: full-time $2,216; part-time $123 per credit. Tuition, nonresident: full-time $6,716; part-time $373 per credit. Required fees: $1,105; $61 per credit. *Financial support:* Career-related internships or fieldwork, Federal Work-Study, institutionally sponsored loans, scholarships/grants, unspecified assistantships, and administrative assistantships available. Support available to part-time students. Financial award application deadline: 5/1; financial award applicants required to submit FAFSA. *Faculty research:* Music composition, pedagogical clinics, music and column editing, music theory, music performance. Total annual research expenditures: $49,835. *Unit head:* Dr. David Evenson, Department Head, 985-549-2184, Fax: 985-549-2892, E-mail: devenson@selu.edu. *Application contact:* Sandra Meyers, Graduate Admissions Analyst, 985-549-2066, Fax: 985-549-5632, E-mail: admissions@selu.edu.

Southern Baptist Theological Seminary, School of Church Music and Worship, Louisville, KY 40280-0004. Offers M Div, MCM, DMA, DMM. *Accreditation:* NASM. *Degree requirements:* For master's, comprehensive exam; for doctorate, one foreign language, thesis/dissertation. *Entrance requirements:* For doctorate, GRE General Test, MAT, auditions. Additional exam requirements/recommendations for international students: Required—TOEFL, TWE. *Faculty research:* Baptist hymnody, church music drama, keyboard literature, impact of contemporary pop culture on church music.

Southern Illinois University Carbondale, Graduate School, College of Liberal Arts, School of Music, Carbondale, IL 62901-4701. Offers composition and theory (MM); history and literature (MM); music education (MM); opera/music theater (MM); performance (MM); piano pedagogy (MM). *Accreditation:* NASM. Part-time programs available. *Faculty:* 22 full-time (6 women). *Students:* 13 full-time (8 women), 20 part-time (11 women); includes 2 minority (both African Americans), 9 international. Average age 24. 42 applicants, 52% accepted, 8 enrolled. In 2007, 8 degrees awarded. *Degree requirements:* For master's, one foreign language, thesis or alternative. *Entrance requirements:* For master's, audition, minimum GPA of 2.7. Additional exam requirements/recommendations for international students: Required—TOEFL. *Application deadline:* Applications are processed on a rolling basis. Application fee: $0. *Financial support:* In 2007–08, 16 students received support, including 2 fellowships with full tuition reimbursements available, 12 teaching assistantships with full tuition reimbursements available; research assistantships with full tuition reimbursements available, Federal Work-Study, institutionally sponsored loans, and tuition waivers (full) also available. Support available to part-time students. Financial award application deadline: 4/1. *Faculty research:* Performance practices, historical research, operatic development. *Unit head:* Jeanine Wagner, Interim Director, 618-453-2541. *Application contact:* Dr. Frank Stemper, Graduate Coordinator, 618-536-7505, E-mail: gradmus@siu.edu.

Southern Illinois University Edwardsville, Graduate Studies and Research, College of Arts and Sciences, Department of Music, Edwardsville, IL 62026-0001. Offers music education (MM); music performance (MM); piano pedagogy (Postbaccalaureate Certificate); vocal pedagogy (Postbaccalaureate Certificate). *Accreditation:* NASM. Part-time programs available. *Faculty:* 16 full-time (5 women). *Students:* 13 full-time (6 women), 14 part-time (9 women); includes 2 minority (1 African American, 1 Asian American or Pacific Islander), 1 international. Average age 33. 24 applicants, 79% accepted. In 2007, 12 degrees awarded. *Degree requirements:* For master's, one foreign language, thesis or alternative, departmental qualifying exam, final exam, recital. *Entrance requirements:* For master's, audition (music performance). Additional exam requirements/recommendations for international students: Required—TOEFL. *Application deadline:* For fall admission, 7/20 for domestic students, 6/1 for international students; for spring admission, 12/14 for domestic students, 10/1 for international students. Application fee: $30. Electronic applications accepted. *Financial support:* Fellowships with full tuition reimbursements, research assistantships with full tuition reimbursements, teaching assistantships with full tuition reimbursements, Federal Work-Study, institutionally sponsored loans, and unspecified assistantships available. Support available to part-time students. Financial award application deadline: 3/1. *Unit head:* Dr. Prince Wells, Chair, 618-650-3900, E-mail: pwells@siue.edu. *Application contact:* Dr. Darryl Coan, Director, 618-650-2012, E-mail: dcoan@siue.edu.

Southern Methodist University, Meadows School of the Arts, Division of Music, Dallas, TX 75275. Offers conducting (MM); music composition (MM); music education (MM); music history (MM); music theory (MM); performance (MM, Certificate); piano performance and pedagogy (MM); sacred music (MSM). *Accreditation:* NASM. Part-time programs available. *Faculty:* 32 full-time (11 women), 44 part-time/adjunct (16 women). *Students:* 34 full-time (18 women), 67 part-time (36 women); includes 15 minority (4 African Americans, 2 Asian Americans or Pacific Islanders, 9 Hispanic Americans), 31 international. Average age 26. 125 applicants, 70% accepted, 56 enrolled. In 2007, 43 master's, 10 Certificates awarded. *Degree requirements:* For master's, variable foreign language requirement, comprehensive exam, thesis (for some programs), project, recital, or thesis. *Entrance requirements:* For master's, placement exams in music history and theory, audition, bachelor's degree in music or equivalent, minimum GPA of 3.0 (research paper in history; theory; education). Additional exam requirements/recommendations for international students: Required—TOEFL (minimum score 550 paper-based; 213 computer-based; 80 iBT). *Application deadline:* For fall admission, 3/1 priority date for domestic and international students; for spring admission, 11/1 for domestic and international students. Applications are processed on a rolling basis. Application fee: $75. *Financial support:* In 2007–08, 77 students received support, including 70 teaching assistantships with full and partial tuition reimbursements available (averaging $4,000 per year); career-related internships or fieldwork, Federal Work-Study, scholarships/grants, tuition waivers (full and partial), and unspecified assistantships also available. Financial award application deadline: 3/1; financial award applicants required to submit FAFSA. *Faculty research:* Music perception and cognition, computer-based instruction, music medicine and therapy, theoretical and historical analysis–medieval to contemporary. *Unit head:* Nancy Cochran, Director, 214-768-1951, Fax: 214-768-4669, E-mail: ncochran@smu.edu. *Application contact:* Jean Cherry, Director of Graduate Admissions and Records, 214-768-3765, Fax: 214-768-3272, E-mail: jcherry@smu.edu.

Southern Oregon University, Graduate Studies, School of Arts and Letters, Department of Music, Ashland, OR 97520. Offers MA, MS. Offered jointly with the American Band College. *Accreditation:* NASM. *Degree requirements:* For master's, comprehensive exam, thesis. *Entrance requirements:* For master's, GRE General Test, minimum GPA of 3.0.

Southwestern Baptist Theological Seminary, School of Church Music, Fort Worth, TX 76122-0000. Offers MACM, MAWSHP, MM, DMA, PhD, SPCM. *Accreditation:* NASM. Part-time programs available. Terminal master's awarded for partial completion of doctoral program. *Degree requirements:* For master's, comprehensive exam, thesis; for doctorate, comprehensive exam, thesis/dissertation. *Entrance requirements:* For master's, audition; for doctorate, MM or equivalent. Additional exam requirements/recommendations for international students: Required—TOEFL (minimum score 550 paper-based; 213 computer-based). Electronic applications accepted. *Faculty research:* Musicology, conducting, composition, pedagogy.

Southwestern Oklahoma State University, College of Arts and Sciences, Department of Music, Weatherford, OK 73096-3098. Offers music education (MM); performance (MM). *Accreditation:* NASM. Part-time programs available. *Degree requirements:* For master's, comprehensive exam, recital (music performance). *Entrance requirements:* For master's, minimum GPA of 2.5. Additional exam requirements/recommendations for international students: Required—TOEFL.

Stanford University, School of Humanities and Sciences, Department of Music, Stanford, CA 94305-9991. Offers computer-based music theory and acoustics (MA, PhD); music composition (MA, DMA); music history (MA); music, science, and technology (MA); musicology (PhD). Terminal master's awarded for partial completion of doctoral program. *Degree requirements:* For master's, variable foreign language requirement, thesis or alternative, project; for doctorate, variable foreign language requirement, thesis/dissertation (for some programs), qualifying, special area, and oral exams (PhD); composition project, lecture-demonstration exams (DMA). *Entrance requirements:* For master's and doctorate, GRE General Test, departmental theory/analysis test, samples of work. Additional exam requirements/recommendations for international students: Required—TOEFL. Electronic applications accepted.

State University of New York at Binghamton, Graduate School, School of Arts and Sciences, Department of Music, Binghamton, NY 13902-6000. Offers MA, MM. *Accreditation:* NASM. *Faculty:* 9 full-time (3 women), 27 part-time/adjunct (10 women). *Students:* 18 full-time

(14 women), 2 part-time (both women); includes 2 minority (both African Americans), 4 international. Average age 25. 32 applicants, 69% accepted, 13 enrolled. In 2007, 15 master's awarded. *Degree requirements:* For master's, one foreign language, thesis. *Entrance requirements:* For master's, GRE General Test, GRE Subject Test. Additional exam requirements/recommendations for international students: Required—TOEFL. *Application deadline:* For fall admission, 4/15 priority date for domestic students, 1/15 priority date for international students; for spring admission, 11/1 for domestic students, 10/1 priority date for international students. Applications are processed on a rolling basis. Application fee: $60. Electronic applications accepted. *Financial support:* In 2007–08, 14 students received support, including 2 fellowships with full tuition reimbursements available (averaging $8,500 per year), 8 teaching assistantships with full tuition reimbursements available (averaging $9,000 per year); research assistantships with full tuition reimbursements available, career-related internships or fieldwork, Federal Work-Study, institutionally sponsored loans, tuition waivers (full and partial), and unspecified assistantships also available. Support available to part-time students. Financial award application deadline: 2/15. *Unit head:* Dr. Timothy Perry, Chairperson, 607-777-2591, E-mail: tperry@binghamton.edu.

State University of New York at Fredonia, Graduate Studies, School of Music, Program in Music, Fredonia, NY 14063-1136. Offers MM. *Accreditation:* NASM. Part-time and evening/weekend programs available. *Degree requirements:* For master's, thesis optional.

State University of New York College at Potsdam, Crane School of Music, Potsdam, NY 13676. Offers composition (MM); history and literature (MM); music education (MM); music theory (MM); performance (MM). Part-time programs available. *Faculty:* 12 full-time (4 women), 1 part-time/adjunct (0 women). *Students:* 6 full-time (3 women), 4 part-time (3 women); includes 1 minority (Asian American or Pacific Islander), 1 international. In 2007, 14 degrees awarded. *Degree requirements:* For master's, variable foreign language requirement, thesis. *Entrance requirements:* For master's, audition, minimum GPA of 3.0. Additional exam requirements/recommendations for international students: Required—TOEFL (minimum score 550 paper-based; 213 computer-based; 80 iBT), IELTS (minimum score 6). *Application deadline:* For fall admission, 3/1 for domestic students. Applications are processed on a rolling basis. Application fee: $50. *Financial support:* In 2007–08, 2 students received support; teaching assistantships with full tuition reimbursements available, career-related internships or fieldwork, Federal Work-Study, scholarships/grants, and unspecified assistantships available. Support available to part-time students. Financial award applicants required to submit FAFSA. *Unit head:* Dr. Alan Solomon, Dean, 315-267-2415, Fax: 315-267-2413, E-mail: solomon@potsdam.edu. *Application contact:* Peter Cutler, Graduate Admissions Counselor, 315-267-3154, Fax: 315-267-4802, E-mail: cutlerpj@potsdam.edu.

Stephen F. Austin State University, Graduate School, College of Fine Arts, School of Music, Nacogdoches, TX 75962. Offers MA, MM. *Accreditation:* NASM (one or more programs are accredited). Part-time programs available. *Degree requirements:* For master's, comprehensive exam, thesis optional. *Entrance requirements:* For master's, GRE General Test, audition. Additional exam requirements/recommendations for international students: Required—TOEFL. *Faculty research:* Music classroom methodology, serial music, seventeenth century sacred music, vocal pedagogy, organ duet literature.

Stony Brook University, State University of New York, Graduate School, College of Arts and Sciences, Department of Music, Program in Ethnomusicology, Stony Brook, NY 11794. Offers MA, PhD. *Entrance requirements:* For master's and doctorate, GRE, 3 letters of recommendation. Additional exam requirements/recommendations for international students: Required—TOEFL. *Application deadline:* For fall admission, 1/15 for domestic students. Application fee: $60. *Financial support:* Teaching assistantships, scholarships/grants available. *Unit head:* Judith Lochhead, Graduate Director, 631-632-7330, Fax: 631-632-7404, E-mail: judith.lochhead@stonybrook.edu.

See Close-Up on page 363.

Stony Brook University, State University of New York, Graduate School, College of Arts and Sciences, Department of Music, Program in Music History/Theory, Stony Brook, NY 11794. Offers MA, PhD. *Students:* 38 full-time (17 women), 3 part-time (1 woman); includes 3 minority (1 African American, 2 Hispanic Americans), 11 international. 107 applicants, 26% accepted. In 2007, 4 master's, 1 doctorate awarded. *Degree requirements:* For doctorate, thesis/dissertation. *Entrance requirements:* For master's and doctorate, GRE General Test. Additional exam requirements/recommendations for international students: Required—TOEFL. *Application deadline:* For fall admission, 1/15 for domestic students. Application fee: $60. Electronic applications accepted. *Application contact:* Dr. Peter Winkler, Director, 631-632-7330, Fax: 631-632-7404, E-mail: pwinkler@notes.cc.sunysb.edu.

See Close-Up on page 365.

Stony Brook University, State University of New York, Graduate School, College of Arts and Sciences, Department of Music, Program in Music Performance, Stony Brook, NY 11794. Offers MM, DMA. *Students:* 164 full-time (99 women), 19 part-time (9 women); includes 30 minority (3 African Americans, 21 Asian Americans or Pacific Islanders, 6 Hispanic Americans), 63 international. 358 applicants, 21% accepted. In 2007, 7 master's, 23 doctorates awarded. *Degree requirements:* For doctorate, thesis/dissertation. *Entrance requirements:* For master's and doctorate, GRE General Test. Additional exam requirements/recommendations for international students: Required—TOEFL. *Application deadline:* For fall admission, 1/15 for domestic students. Application fee: $60. *Application contact:* Dr. Peter Winkler, Director, 631-632-7330, Fax: 631-632-7404, E-mail: peter.winkler@storybrook.edu.

See Close-Up on page 367.

Syracuse University, Graduate School, College of Visual and Performing Arts, Setnor School of Music, Syracuse, NY 13244. Offers conducting (M Mu); music composition (M Mus); organ (M Mus); percussion (M Mus); piano (M Mus); strings (M Mus); voice (M Mus); wind instruments (M Mus). *Accreditation:* NASM. Part-time programs available. *Students:* 19 full-time (11 women); includes 1 minority (Hispanic American), 7 international. 32 applicants, 59% accepted, 12 enrolled. In 2007, 10 degrees awarded. *Entrance requirements:* For master's, audition, interview. Additional exam requirements/recommendations for international students: Required—TOEFL. *Application deadline:* For fall admission, 1/1 priority date for domestic students; for spring admission, 3/1 priority date for domestic students. Applications are processed on a rolling basis. Application fee: $75. Electronic applications accepted. *Expenses:* Tuition: Full-time $18,216; part-time $1,012 per credit. Required fees: $980. Tuition and fees vary according to program. *Financial support:* Fellowships with full tuition reimbursements, research assistantships with full and partial tuition reimbursements, teaching assistantships with full and partial tuition reimbursements, Federal Work-Study and tuition waivers (partial) available. *Unit head:* Dr. Bradley Ethington, Director, 315-443-5892, E-mail: bpething@syr.edu. *Application contact:* Harriett Conti, Associate Director, Graduate Student Services, 315-443-3089, E-mail: hmconti@syr.edu.

Temple University, Graduate School, Esther Boyer College of Music and Dance, Department of Choral Activities, Philadelphia, PA 19122-6096. Offers MM. Part-time and evening/weekend programs available. *Entrance requirements:* Additional exam requirements/recommendations for international students: Required—TOEFL. Electronic applications accepted.

Temple University, Graduate School, Esther Boyer College of Music and Dance, Department of Instrumental Studies, Philadelphia, PA 19122-6096. Offers MM, DMA. Part-time programs available. *Entrance requirements:* Additional exam requirements/recommendations for international students: Required—TOEFL. Electronic applications accepted.

Temple University, Graduate School, Esther Boyer College of Music and Dance, Department of Music Studies, Philadelphia, PA 19122-6096. Offers composition (MM, DMA); music history (MM); music theory (MM). *Accreditation:* NASM. Part-time and evening/weekend programs available. *Degree requirements:* For master's, one foreign language, thesis (for some programs), compositions, recitals; for doctorate, one foreign language, thesis/dissertation, compositions, recitals. *Entrance requirements:* For doctorate, GRE or MAT. Additional exam requirements/recommendations for international students: Required—TOEFL. Electronic applications accepted. *Faculty research:* Computer composition, computer music synthesis, musical instrument digital interface (MIDI) applications.

Temple University, Graduate School, Esther Boyer College of Music and Dance, Department of Voice and Opera, Philadelphia, PA 19122-6096. Offers MM, DMA. *Accreditation:* NASM. Part-time and evening/weekend programs available. *Degree requirements:* For master's, compositions, recitals; for doctorate, compositions, 6 recitals. *Entrance requirements:* Additional exam requirements/recommendations for international students: Required—TOEFL. Electronic applications accepted.

Texas A&M University–Commerce, Graduate School, College of Arts and Sciences, Department of Music, Commerce, TX 75429-3011. Offers music (MA, MS); music composition (MA, MM); music education (MA, MM, MS); music literature (MA); music performance (MA, MM); music theory (MA, MM). *Accreditation:* NASM. Part-time programs available. *Faculty:* 6 full-time (2 women). *Students:* 4 full-time (2 women), 6 part-time (2 women); includes 3 minority (1 African American, 2 Hispanic Americans), 1 international. Average age 36. In 2007, 3 degrees awarded. *Degree requirements:* For master's, comprehensive exam, thesis (for some programs). *Entrance requirements:* For master's, GRE General Test. *Application deadline:* For fall admission, 6/1 priority date for domestic students; for spring admission, 11/1 priority date for domestic students. Applications are processed on a rolling basis. Application fee: $0 ($25 for international students). Electronic applications accepted. *Financial support:* In 2007–08, research assistantships (averaging $7,875 per year), teaching assistantships (averaging $7,875 per year) were awarded; Federal Work-Study, institutionally sponsored loans, and scholarships/grants also available. Financial award application deadline: 5/1; financial award applicants required to submit FAFSA. *Unit head:* Gene Lockhart, Head, 903-886-5303, Fax: 903-468-6010, E-mail: gene_lockhart@tamu-commerce.edu. *Application contact:* Tammi Thompson, Graduate Admissions Adviser, 843-886-5167, Fax: 843-886-5165, E-mail: tammi_thompson@tamu-commerce.edu.

Texas Christian University, College of Fine Arts, School of Music, Fort Worth, TX 76129-0002. Offers conducting (M Mus); music education (MM Ed); musicology (M Mus); organ performance (M Mus); piano (Artist Diploma); piano pedagogy (M Mus); piano performance (M Mus); string performance (M Mus); theory/composition (M Mus); vocal performance (M Mus); voice pedagogy (M Mus); wind and percussion performance (M Mus). *Accreditation:* NASM. Part-time and evening/weekend programs available. *Degree requirements:* For master's, one foreign language, thesis (for some programs). *Entrance requirements:* For master's, GRE General Test, audition or composition/theory, letters of recommendation. Additional exam requirements/recommendations for international students: Required—TOEFL. *Application deadline:* For fall admission, 3/1 for domestic students; for spring admission, 12/1 for domestic students. Applications are processed on a rolling basis. Application fee: $0. *Expenses:* Tuition: Part-time $865 per credit hour. Required fees: $48 per year. *Financial support:* Unspecified assistantships available. Financial award application deadline: 3/1. *Unit head:* Dr. Richard Gipson, Director, 817-257-7602. *Application contact:* Dr. Joseph Butler, Associate Dean, College of Fine Arts, E-mail: j.butler@tcu.edu.

Texas Southern University, Graduate School, College of Liberal Arts and Behavioral Sciences, Department of Fine Arts, Houston, TX 77004-4584. Offers fine arts (MA); music (MA). Part-time programs available. *Faculty:* 2 full-time (1 woman). *Students:* Average age 37. 1 applicant, 100% accepted, 0 enrolled. In 2007, 1 degree awarded. *Degree requirements:* For master's, one foreign language, comprehensive exam, recital. *Entrance requirements:* For master's, GRE General Test, minimum GPA of 2.5. Additional exam requirements/recommendations for international students: Required—TOEFL. *Application deadline:* For fall admission, 7/15 priority date for domestic students. Application fee: $50 ($75 for international students). Electronic applications accepted. *Financial support:* Fellowships, teaching assistantships with partial tuition reimbursements, Federal Work-Study, institutionally sponsored loans, scholarships/grants, and unspecified assistantships available. Financial award application deadline: 5/1. *Faculty research:* Music theory, choral music, composition, percussion composition, ethnic musicology. *Unit head:* Dianne F. Jemison-Pollard, Chair, 713-313-7337, Fax: 713-313-1869, E-mail: jemison_dp@tsu.edu.

Texas State University–San Marcos, Graduate School, College of Fine Arts and Communication, School of Music, Program in Music Performance, San Marcos, TX 78666. Offers MM. *Accreditation:* NASM. Part-time programs available. *Faculty:* 6 full-time (0 women). *Students:* 34 full-time (22 women), 20 part-time (10 women); includes 9 minority (2 African Americans, 1 Asian American or Pacific Islander, 6 Hispanic Americans), 9 international. Average age 30. 29 applicants, 97% accepted, 15 enrolled. In 2007, 18 degrees awarded. *Degree requirements:* For master's, comprehensive exam. *Entrance requirements:* For master's, minimum GPA of 2.75 in last 60 hours of course work. Additional exam requirements/recommendations for international students: Required—TOEFL (minimum score 550 paper-based; 213 computer-based). *Application deadline:* For fall admission, 6/15 priority date for domestic students; for spring admission, 10/15 priority date for domestic students. Applications are processed on a rolling basis. Application fee: $40 ($90 for international students). Electronic applications accepted. *Expenses:* Tuition, state resident: full-time $3,780; part-time $210 per credit hour. Tuition, nonresident: full-time $8,784; part-time $488 per credit hour. Required fees: $493 per semester. Full-time tuition and fees vary according to course load. *Financial support:* In 2007–08, 46 students received support, including 14 teaching assistantships (averaging $1,182 per year); career-related internships or fieldwork, Federal Work-Study, and institutionally sponsored loans also available. Support available to part-time students. Financial award application deadline: 4/1; financial award applicants required to submit FAFSA. *Unit head:* Dr. Nico Schuler, Graduate Advisor, 512-245-2651, Fax: 512-245-8181, E-mail: ns13@txstate.edu. *Application contact:* Dr. J. Michael Willoughby, Dean of Graduate School, 512-245-2581, Fax: 512-245-8365, E-mail: gradcollege@txstate.edu.

Texas State University–San Marcos, Graduate School, College of Liberal Arts, Department of English, Program in Rhetoric and Composition, San Marcos, TX 78666. Offers MA. Part-time programs available. *Faculty:* 4 full-time (2 women). *Students:* 6 full-time (5 women), 3 part-time (2 women); includes 1 Hispanic American. Average age 33. 2 applicants, 100% accepted, 2 enrolled. *Entrance requirements:* For master's, 3.25 in a minimum of 24 hours of undergrad English, 6 hours foreign language. Additional exam requirements/recommendations for international students: Required—TOEFL (minimum score 550 paper-based; 213 computer-based). *Application deadline:* For fall admission, 6/15 for domestic students, 6/1 for international students; for spring admission, 10/15 for domestic students, 10/1 for international students. Applications are processed on a rolling basis. Application fee: $40 ($90 for international students). Electronic applications accepted. *Expenses:* Tuition, state resident: full-time $3,780; part-time $210 per credit hour. Tuition, nonresident: full-time $8,784; part-time $488 per credit hour. Required fees: $493 per semester. Full-time tuition and fees vary according to course load. *Financial support:* In 2007–08, 7 students received support, including 4 teaching assistantships (averaging $5,076 per year); Federal Work-Study and institutionally sponsored loans also available. Support available to part-time students. Financial award application deadline: 4/1; financial award applicants required to submit FAFSA. *Unit head:* Dr. Rebecca Jackson, Graduate Advisor, 512-245-2163, E-mail: rj10@txstate.edu.

Texas Tech University, Graduate School, College of Visual and Performing Arts, Department of Theatre and Dance, Lubbock, TX 79409. Offers fine arts (PhD); theatre arts (MA, MFA), including arts administration (MFA), design (MFA), performance/pedagogy (MFA), playwriting (MFA). *Accreditation:* NAST. Part-time programs available. *Faculty:* 9 full-time (5 women). *Students:* 35 full-time (18 women), 25 part-time (12 women); includes 5 minority (3 African Americans, 1 Asian American or Pacific Islander, 1 Hispanic American), 4 international. Average age 35. 32 applicants, 69% accepted, 16 enrolled. In 2007, 10 master's, 5 doctorates awarded. *Degree requirements:* For master's, variable foreign language requirement, thesis; for doctorate,

Music

Texas Tech University (continued)

thesis/dissertation. *Entrance requirements:* For master's and doctorate, GRE General Test. Additional exam requirements/recommendations for international students: Required—TOEFL (minimum score 550 paper-based; 213 computer-based). *Application deadline:* For fall admission, 3/1 priority date for international students; for spring admission, 11/1 priority date for international students. Applications are processed on a rolling basis. Application fee: $50 ($60 for international students). Electronic applications accepted. *Expenses:* Tuition, state resident: part-time $373 per credit hour. Tuition, nonresident: part-time $651 per credit hour. Tuition and fees vary according to program. *Financial support:* In 2007–08, 42 students received support, including 27 teaching assistantships with partial tuition reimbursements available (averaging $10,239 per year); research assistantships with partial tuition reimbursements available, Federal Work-Study and institutionally sponsored loans also available. Support available to part-time students. Financial award application deadline: 4/15; financial award applicants required to submit FAFSA. *Faculty research:* New student plays program, theatre planning, dramaturgy; feminist theatre; arts administration. *Unit head:* Prof. Frederick B. Christoffel, Chair, 806-742-3601 Ext. 228, Fax: 806-742-1338, E-mail: fred.christoffel@ttu.edu. *Application contact:* Dr. Linda Donahue, Graduate Adviser, 806-742-3601 Ext. 225, Fax: 806-742-1338, E-mail: linda.donahue@ttu.edu.

Texas Tech University, Graduate School, College of Visual and Performing Arts, Fine Arts Doctoral Program, Lubbock, TX 79409. Offers arts (PhD); music (PhD); theatre arts (PhD). *Accreditation:* NAST. *Students:* 40 full-time (16 women), 33 part-time (16 women); includes 8 minority (4 African Americans, 1 American Indian/Alaska Native, 1 Asian American or Pacific Islander, 2 Hispanic Americans), 9 international. Average age 37. 26 applicants, 62% accepted, 9 enrolled. In 2007, 10 degrees awarded. *Degree requirements:* For doctorate, thesis/dissertation. *Entrance requirements:* For doctorate, GRE General Test. Additional exam requirements/recommendations for international students: Required—TOEFL (minimum score 550 paper-based; 213 computer-based). *Application deadline:* For fall admission, 3/1 priority date for international students; for spring admission, 11/1 priority date for international students. Applications are processed on a rolling basis. Application fee: $50 ($60 for international students). Electronic applications accepted. *Expenses:* Tuition, state resident: part-time $373 per credit hour. Tuition, nonresident: part-time $651 per credit hour. Tuition and fees vary according to program. *Financial support:* Research assistantships with partial tuition reimbursements, teaching assistantships with partial tuition reimbursements available. Financial award application deadline: 4/15. *Faculty research:* Art criticism and theory, music, aesthetics, theatre arts. *Unit head:* Dr. Brian Steele, Director, 806-742-0700, Fax: 806-742-0695, E-mail: brian.steele@ttu.edu.

Texas Tech University, Graduate School, College of Visual and Performing Arts, School of Music, Lubbock, TX 79409. Offers composition (MM, DMA); conducting (DMA); fine arts-music (PhD); music theory (MM); musicology (MM); pedagogy (MM); performance (MM, DMA); piano pedagogy (DMA). *Accreditation:* NASM. Part-time programs available. *Faculty:* 35 full-time (11 women), 1 part-time/adjunct (0 women). *Students:* 98 full-time (38 women), 24 part-time (13 women); includes 10 minority (1 African American, 1 American Indian/Alaska Native, 2 Asian Americans or Pacific Islanders, 6 Hispanic Americans), 26 international. Average age 38. 101 applicants, 75% accepted, 36 enrolled. In 2007, 19 master's, 16 doctorates awarded. *Degree requirements:* For master's, thesis (for some programs); for doctorate, thesis/dissertation. *Entrance requirements:* For master's and doctorate, GRE General Test. Additional exam requirements/recommendations for international students: Required—TOEFL (minimum score 550 paper-based; 213 computer-based). *Application deadline:* For fall admission, 3/1 priority date for international students; for spring admission, 11/1 priority date for international students. Applications are processed on a rolling basis. Application fee: $50 ($60 for international students). Electronic applications accepted. *Expenses:* Tuition, state resident: part-time $373 per credit hour. Tuition, nonresident: part-time $651 per credit hour. Tuition and fees vary according to program. *Financial support:* In 2007–08, 77 students received support, including 68 teaching assistantships with partial tuition reimbursements available (averaging $7,497 per year); research assistantships with partial tuition reimbursements available, Federal Work-Study and institutionally sponsored loans also available. Support available to part-time students. Financial award application deadline: 4/15; financial award applicants required to submit FAFSA. *Faculty research:* Strategies for music pedagogy in grades K-12, performance practice of traditional music, role of the woman piano virtuoso, vernacular music center; voice health and culture. *Unit head:* Prof. William Ballenger, School of Music Director, 806-742-2270, Fax: 806-742-2294, E-mail: william.ballenger@ttu.edu. *Application contact:* Janeen Gilliam, Admissions and Scholarship Coordinator, 806-742-2270 Ext. 225, Fax: 806-742-2294, E-mail: janeen.gilliam@ttu.edu.

Texas Woman's University, Graduate School, College of Arts and Sciences, School of the Arts, Department of Music and Drama, Denton, TX 76201. Offers drama (MA); music (MA). *Accreditation:* NASM. Part-time programs available. *Students:* 45 full-time (35 women), 22 part-time (19 women); includes 10 minority (1 African American, 1 American Indian/Alaska Native, 1 Asian American or Pacific Islander, 7 Hispanic Americans), 9 international. Average age 32. In 2007, 14 master's awarded. *Degree requirements:* For master's, thesis optional, project recital. *Entrance requirements:* For master's, music history/theory placement exam, audition, interview, sample of professional work, licensure as a music therapist, piano and aural skills. Additional exam requirements/recommendations for international students: Required—TOEFL (minimum score 550 paper-based; 213 computer-based; 79 iBT). *Application deadline:* For fall admission, 4/1 for international students; for spring admission, 8/1 for international students. Applications are processed on a rolling basis. Application fee: $30 ($50 for international students). Electronic applications accepted. *Expenses:* Tuition, state resident: full-time $3,294; part-time $183 per credit. Tuition, nonresident: full-time $8,298; part-time $461 per credit. Required fees: $985; $55 per credit. Tuition and fees vary according to degree level. *Financial support:* In 2007–08, 9 teaching assistantships (averaging $9,684 per year) were awarded; career-related internships or fieldwork, Federal Work-Study, institutionally sponsored loans, scholarships/grants, traineeships, health care benefits, tuition waivers (partial), and unspecified assistantships also available. Support available to part-time students. Financial award application deadline: 3/1; financial award applicants required to submit FAFSA. *Faculty research:* Musical development in early childhood, little known or neglected compositions for flute (especially by women composers), relationship of visual art to piano music, pedagogical development of the singing voice, guided imagery and music. *Unit head:* Dr. James Chenevert, Chair, 940-898-2500, Fax: 940-898-2494, E-mail: jchenevert@mail.twu.edu. *Application contact:* Samuel Wheeler, Assistant Director of Admissions, 940-898-3188, Fax: 940-898-3081, E-mail: wheelersr@twu.edu.

Towson University, College of Graduate Studies and Research, Program in Music Performance and Composition, Towson, MD 21252-0001. Offers MM. *Accreditation:* NASM. Part-time and evening/weekend programs available. *Faculty:* 20 full-time (5 women), 16 part-time/adjunct (6 women). *Students:* 4 full-time (3 women), 12 part-time (6 women); includes 2 minority (1 African American, 1 Asian American or Pacific Islander), 2 international. Average age 30. 4 applicants, 100% accepted, 3 enrolled. In 2007, 4 degrees awarded. *Degree requirements:* For master's, exam. *Entrance requirements:* For master's, audition, bachelor's degree in music or music education, minimum GPA of 3.0. *Application deadline:* Applications are processed on a rolling basis. Application fee: $50. Electronic applications accepted. *Expenses:* Tuition, state resident: part-time $286 per credit. Tuition, nonresident: part-time $600 per credit. Required fees: $75 per credit. *Financial support:* Teaching assistantships, Federal Work-Study and unspecified assistantships available. Financial award application deadline: 4/1; financial award applicants required to submit FAFSA. *Unit head:* Dr. Donald Watts, Graduate Program Director, 410-704-2819, E-mail: dwatts@towson.edu. *Application contact:* 410-704-2501, Fax: 410-704-4675, E-mail: grads@towson.edu.

Trinity Lutheran Seminary, Graduate and Professional Programs, Columbus, OH 43209-2334. Offers church music (MA); divinity (M Div); lay ministry (MA); sacred theology (STM); theological studies (MTS); MSN/MTS; MTS/JD. *Accreditation:* ACIPE; ATS. Part-time programs available. *Faculty:* 20 full-time (9 women), 15 part-time/adjunct (5 women). *Students:* 114 full-time (51 women), 46 part-time (18 women); includes 13 minority (9 African Americans, 3 Asian Americans or Pacific Islanders, 1 Hispanic American), 3 international. Average age 36. 95 applicants, 64% accepted, 53 enrolled. In 2007, 28 first professional degrees, 13 master's awarded. *Degree requirements:* For master's, thesis (for some programs); for M Div, 2 foreign languages, internship. *Entrance requirements:* For master's, M Div or equivalent (STM). Additional exam requirements/recommendations for international students: Required—TOEFL (minimum score 500 paper-based). *Application deadline:* For fall admission, 7/15 priority date for domestic students. Applications are processed on a rolling basis. Application fee: $25. *Expenses:* Tuition: Full-time $10,560. One-time fee: $100 full-time. Tuition and fees vary according to course load. *Financial support:* In 2007–08, 115 students received support. Career-related internships or fieldwork, Federal Work-Study, institutionally sponsored loans, and scholarships/grants available. Support available to part-time students. Financial award application deadline: 5/1; financial award applicants required to submit FAFSA. *Unit head:* Dr. Donald L. Huber, Dean, 614-235-4136, Fax: 614-236-3129, E-mail: dhuber@trinitylutheranseminary.edu. *Application contact:* Rev. Sheri L. Ayers, Director of Admissions, 614-235-4136 Ext. 4614, Fax: 866-610-8572, E-mail: sayers@trinitylutheranseminary.edu.

Truman State University, Graduate School, College of Arts and Sciences, Program in Music, Kirksville, MO 63501-4221. Offers MA. *Accreditation:* NASM. *Students:* 10 full-time (3 women), 1 (woman) part-time. 3 applicants, 100% accepted. In 2007, 4 degrees awarded. *Degree requirements:* For master's, comprehensive exam, thesis or alternative. *Entrance requirements:* For master's, GRE General Test, minimum GPA of 3.0. Additional exam requirements/recommendations for international students: Required—TOEFL (minimum score 550 paper-based; 213 computer-based). *Application deadline:* For fall admission, 6/15 priority date for domestic students, 6/15 for international students; for spring admission, 11/1 priority date for domestic students, 11/1 for international students. Applications are processed on a rolling basis. Application fee: $0. Electronic applications accepted. *Expenses:* Tuition, state resident: part-time $280 per credit hour. Tuition, nonresident: part-time $478 per credit hour. *Financial support:* In 2007–08, research assistantships with tuition reimbursements (averaging $8,000 per year), teaching assistantships with tuition reimbursements (averaging $8,000 per year) were awarded; career-related internships or fieldwork and Federal Work-Study also available. Financial award application deadline: 5/1; financial award applicants required to submit FAFSA. *Unit head:* Dr. Warren Gooch, Program Director, 660-785-4429, Fax: 660-785-7463, E-mail: wgooch@truman.edu. *Application contact:* Doris Snyder, Graduate Office Secretary, E-mail: dsnyder@truman.edu.

Tufts University, Graduate School of Arts and Sciences, Department of Music, Medford, MA 02155. Offers ethnomusicology (MA); music history and literature (MA); music theory and composition (MA). Part-time programs available. *Faculty:* 12 full-time, 16 part-time/adjunct. *Students:* 19 (10 women) 3 international. 30 applicants, 60% accepted, 11 enrolled. In 2007, 8 degrees awarded. *Degree requirements:* For master's, one foreign language, thesis. *Entrance requirements:* For master's, writing sample or musical score. Additional exam requirements/recommendations for international students: Required—TOEFL (minimum score 550 paper-based; 213 computer-based; 80 iBT). *Application deadline:* For fall admission, 2/1 for domestic students, 12/30 for international students. Applications are processed on a rolling basis. Application fee: $70. Electronic applications accepted. *Expenses:* Tuition: Full-time $35,052. *Financial support:* Teaching assistantships with full and partial tuition reimbursements, Federal Work-Study, scholarships/grants, and tuition waivers (partial) available. Financial award application deadline: 2/1; financial award applicants required to submit FAFSA. *Unit head:* Joseph Auner, Chair, 617-627-3564, Fax: 617-627-3967.

Tulane University, School of Liberal Arts, Department of Music, New Orleans, LA 70118-5669. Offers MA, MFA. *Degree requirements:* For master's, one foreign language, thesis (for some programs), recital or composition (MA). *Entrance requirements:* For master's, GRE General Test, minimum B average in undergraduate course work. Additional exam requirements/recommendations for international students: Required—TOEFL. Electronic applications accepted. *Faculty research:* New Orleans music, composition, piano, voice, music theatre, classical guitar.

Université de Montréal, Faculty of Music, Montréal, QC H3C 3J7, Canada. Offers composition (M Mus, D Mus); musicology and ethnomusicology (MA, PhD); orchestra conducting (M Mus, D Mus); orchestral repertoire (DESS); performance interpretation (DESS); voice and instruments interpretation (M Mus, D Mus). *Faculty:* 50 full-time (18 women), 45 part-time/adjunct (17 women). *Students:* 287 full-time (129 women), 7 part-time (1 woman). 247 applicants, 45% accepted, 104 enrolled. In 2007, 52 master's, 19 doctorates, 15 other advanced degrees awarded. *Degree requirements:* For doctorate, thesis/dissertation, general exam. *Application deadline:* For fall admission, 2/1 priority date for domestic students; for winter admission, 11/1 priority date for domestic students; for spring admission, 2/1 priority date for domestic students. Application fee: $100. Electronic applications accepted. *Faculty research:* Semiology, music in Creole areas, computer-assisted composition, Argentinean tango. *Unit head:* Jacques Boucher, Dean, 514-343-6429, Fax: 514-343-5727, E-mail: jacques.boucher@umontreal.ca. *Application contact:* Sylvain Caron, Vice Dean Graduate Studies, 514-343-5897, Fax: 514-343-5727, E-mail: sylvain.caron@umontreal.ca.

Université Laval, Faculty of Music, Programs in Music, Québec, QC G1K 7P4, Canada. Offers composition (M Mus); instrumental didactics (M Mus); interpretation (M Mus); music (PhD); music education (M Mus); musicology (M Mus). Terminal master's awarded for partial completion of doctoral program. *Degree requirements:* For master's, thesis (for some programs); for doctorate, comprehensive exam, thesis/dissertation. *Entrance requirements:* For master's, English exam, audition, knowledge of French; for doctorate, English exam, knowledge of French, third language. Electronic applications accepted.

University at Buffalo, the State University of New York, Graduate School, College of Arts and Sciences, Department of Music, Buffalo, NY 14260. Offers historical musicology and music theory (PhD); music composition (MA, PhD); music history (MA); music performance (MM); music theory (MA). Terminal master's awarded for partial completion of doctoral program. *Degree requirements:* For master's, variable foreign language requirement, comprehensive exam (for some programs), thesis optional, recitals (MM); for doctorate, variable foreign language requirement, comprehensive exam, thesis/dissertation. *Entrance requirements:* For master's, GRE General Test, audition (MM), compositions, writing sample; for doctorate, GRE General Test, compositions, writing sample. Additional exam requirements/recommendations for international students: Required—TOEFL (minimum score 550 paper-based; 213 computer-based). Electronic applications accepted. *Faculty research:* Concert performance, analytical theory, musicology/history, computer composition.

The University of Akron, Graduate School, College of Fine and Applied Arts, School of Music, Program in Composition, Akron, OH 44325. Offers MM. *Students:* 1 (woman) full-time. Average age 29. 2 applicants, 100% accepted, 0 enrolled. In 2007, 1 degree awarded. *Degree requirements:* For master's, comprehensive exam, thesis or project. *Entrance requirements:* For master's, minimum GPA of 2.75, interview, audition. Additional exam requirements/recommendations for international students: Required—TOEFL (minimum score 550 paper-based; 213 computer-based; 79 iBT). *Application deadline:* Applications are processed on a rolling basis. Application fee: $30 ($40 for international students). Electronic applications accepted. *Expenses:* Tuition, state resident: full-time $6,164; part-time $342 per credit. Tuition, nonresident: full-time $10,575; part-time $588 per credit. Required fees: $806; $43 per credit. $12 per term. Tuition and fees vary according to course load, degree level and program. *Unit head:* Dr. Daniel W. McCarthy, Head, 330-972-2199, E-mail: dmccarthy@uakron.edu.

The University of Akron, Graduate School, College of Fine and Applied Arts, School of Music, Program in Music History and Literature, Akron, OH 44325. Offers MM. *Students:* 1 full-time (0 women). Average age 26. 4 applicants, 100% accepted. In 2007, 1 degree awarded. *Degree requirements:* For master's, comprehensive exam, thesis or project. *Entrance requirements:* For master's, minimum GPA of 2.75, interview, audition. Additional exam requirements/recommendations for international students: Required—TOEFL (minimum score

550 paper-based; 213 computer-based; 79 iBT). *Application deadline:* Applications are processed on a rolling basis. Application fee: $30 ($40 for international students). Electronic applications accepted. *Expenses:* Tuition, state resident: full-time $6,164; part-time $342 per credit. Tuition, nonresident: full-time $10,575; part-time $588 per credit. Required fees: $806; $43 per credit. $12 per term. Tuition and fees vary according to course load, degree level and program. *Unit head:* Dr. Brooks Toliver, Head, 330-972-5207, E-mail: brooks@uakron.edu.

The University of Akron, Graduate School, College of Fine and Applied Arts, School of Music, Program in Music Technology, Akron, OH 44325. Offers MM. *Students:* 1 full-time (0 women); minority (African American) Average age 36. 2 applicants, 50% accepted, 0 enrolled. In 2007, 1 degree awarded. *Degree requirements:* For master's, comprehensive exam, thesis or project. *Entrance requirements:* For master's, minimum GPA of 2.75, interview, audition. Additional exam requirements/recommendations for international students: Required—TOEFL (minimum score 550 paper-based; 213 computer-based; 79 iBT). *Application deadline:* Applications are processed on a rolling basis. Application fee: $30 ($40 for international students). Electronic applications accepted. *Expenses:* Tuition, state resident: full-time $6,164; part-time $342 per credit. Tuition, nonresident: full-time $10,575; part-time $588 per credit. Required fees: $806; $43 per credit. $12 per term. Tuition and fees vary according to course load, degree level and program. *Unit head:* V. Douglas Hicks, Head, 330-972-6356, E-mail: vhicks@uakron.edu.

The University of Akron, Graduate School, College of Fine and Applied Arts, School of Music, Program in Performance, Akron, OH 44325. Offers MM. *Students:* 47 full-time (26 women), 8 part-time (6 women); includes 5 minority (all Hispanic Americans), 10 international. Average age 27. 53 applicants, 91% accepted, 22 enrolled. In 2007, 15 degrees awarded. *Degree requirements:* For master's, comprehensive exam. *Entrance requirements:* For master's, minimum GPA of 2.75, interview, audition. Additional exam requirements/recommendations for international students: Required—TOEFL (minimum score 550 paper-based; 213 computer-based; 79 iBT). *Application deadline:* Applications are processed on a rolling basis. Application fee: $30 ($40 for international students). Electronic applications accepted. *Expenses:* Tuition, state resident: full-time $6,164; part-time $342 per credit. Tuition, nonresident: full-time $10,575; part-time $588 per credit. Required fees: $806; $43 per credit. $12 per term. Tuition and fees vary according to course load, degree level and program.

The University of Akron, Graduate School, College of Fine and Applied Arts, School of Music, Program in Theory, Akron, OH 44325. Offers MM. *Students:* 3 full-time (0 women). Average age 31. 2 applicants, 100% accepted, 1 enrolled. *Degree requirements:* For master's, comprehensive exam, thesis optional, thesis or project. *Entrance requirements:* For master's, minimum GPA of 2.75, interview, audition. Additional exam requirements/recommendations for international students: Required—TOEFL (minimum score 550 paper-based; 213 computer-based; 79 iBT). *Application deadline:* Applications are processed on a rolling basis. Application fee: $30 ($40 for international students). Electronic applications accepted. *Expenses:* Tuition, state resident: full-time $6,164; part-time $342 per credit. Tuition, nonresident: full-time $10,575; part-time $588 per credit. Required fees: $806; $43 per credit. $12 per term. Tuition and fees vary according to course load, degree level and program. *Unit head:* Dr. Daniel W. McCarthy, Head, 330-972-2199, E-mail: dmccarthy@uakron.edu.

The University of Alabama, Graduate School, College of Arts and Sciences, Department of English, Tuscaloosa, AL 35487. Offers composition and rhetoric (PhD); creative writing (MFA), including fiction, poetry; literature (MA, PhD); rhetoric and composition (MA); teaching English as a second language (MATESOL). *Faculty:* 30 full-time (12 women). *Students:* 119 full-time (66 women), 16 part-time (12 women); includes 18 minority (11 African Americans, 2 American Indian/Alaska Native, 3 Asian Americans or Pacific Islanders, 2 Hispanic Americans), 7 international. Average age 28. 252 applicants, 20% accepted, 31 enrolled. In 2007, 28 master's, 7 doctorates awarded. *Median time to degree:* Of those who began their doctoral program in fall 1999, 100% received their degree in 8 years or less. *Degree requirements:* For master's, one foreign language, comprehensive exam, thesis (for some programs); for doctorate, 2 foreign languages, comprehensive exam, thesis/dissertation. *Entrance requirements:* For master's and doctorate, GRE, minimum GPA of 3.0, critical writing sample. Additional exam requirements/recommendations for international students: Required—TOEFL. *Application deadline:* For fall admission, 1/15 priority date for domestic students, 1/15 for international students. Application fee: $30. Electronic applications accepted. *Expenses:* Tuition, state resident: full-time $5,700. Tuition, nonresident: full-time $16,518. *Financial support:* In 2007–08, 7 fellowships with full tuition reimbursements (averaging $15,000 per year), 1 research assistantship (averaging $11,708 per year), 106 teaching assistantships with full tuition reimbursements (averaging $11,708 per year) were awarded; career-related internships or fieldwork, scholarships/grants, health care benefits, and unspecified assistantships also available. Financial award application deadline: 1/15. *Faculty research:* Critical theory; modern, Renaissance, and African-American literature. *Unit head:* Dr. Catherine E. Davies, Director of Graduate Studies, 205-348-8499, E-mail: cdavies@bama.ua.edu. *Application contact:* Vernita W. James, Office Assistant II, 205-348-0766, Fax: 205-348-1388, E-mail: vwjames@bama.ua.edu.

The University of Alabama, Graduate School, College of Arts and Sciences, School of Music, Tuscaloosa, AL 35487. Offers arranging (MM); choral conducting (MM, DMA); composition (MM, DMA); music education (MA, PhD); music history (MM); performance (MM, DMA); theory (MM); wind conducting (MM, DMA). *Accreditation:* NASM. *Faculty:* 23 full-time (9 women). *Students:* 61 full-time (27 women), 20 part-time (9 women); includes 15 minority (6 African Americans, 5 Asian Americans or Pacific Islanders, 4 Hispanic Americans), 14 international. Average age 30. 49 applicants, 76% accepted, 28 enrolled. In 2007, 16 master's, 5 doctorates awarded. *Median time to degree:* Of those who began their doctoral program in fall 1999, 50% received their degree in 8 years or less. *Degree requirements:* For master's, comprehensive exam, thesis, oral and written exams, recital; for doctorate, comprehensive exam, thesis/dissertation, oral and written exams, recital. *Entrance requirements:* For master's and doctorate, Audition. Additional exam requirements/recommendations for international students: Required—TOEFL, TOEFL or IELTS. *Application deadline:* For fall admission, 2/1 priority date for domestic and international students; for winter admission, 2/1 for domestic students, 2/1 priority date for international students; for spring admission, 2/1 priority date for domestic and international students. Applications are processed on a rolling basis. Application fee: $30. Electronic applications accepted. *Expenses:* Tuition, state resident: full-time $5,700. Tuition, nonresident: full-time $16,518. *Financial support:* In 2007–08, 22 students received support, including 1 fellowship with tuition reimbursement available (averaging $30,000 per year), 40 teaching assistantships with full and partial tuition reimbursements available (averaging $8,181 per year); Federal Work-Study, institutionally sponsored loans, and unspecified assistantships also available. Financial award application deadline: 7/14. *Faculty research:* Performance practice, musicology, theory, composition. *Unit head:* Charles G. Snead, Director, 205-348-7110, Fax: 205-348-1473, E-mail: ssnead@music.ua.edu. *Application contact:* Dr. Marvin Johnson, Director of Graduate Studies, 205-348-6604, Fax: 205-348-1473, E-mail: mjohnson@music.ua.edu.

University of Alaska Fairbanks, College of Liberal Arts, Department of Music, Fairbanks, AK 99775-7520. Offers Alaskan ethnomusicology (MA); music education (MA); music history (MA); music theory (MA); performance (MA). *Accreditation:* NASM. Part-time programs available. *Degree requirements:* For master's, comprehensive exam, thesis or alternative, oral exam. *Entrance requirements:* For master's, GRE General Test, BA in music. Additional exam requirements/recommendations for international students: Required—TOEFL (minimum score 550 paper-based; 213 computer-based). Electronic applications accepted. *Faculty research:* Symphony, opera, jazz, chamber and solo performance.

University of Alberta, Faculty of Graduate Studies and Research, Department of Music, Edmonton, AB T6G 2E1, Canada. Offers applied music (M Mus); choral conducting (M Mus); composition (M Mus); music (PhD); organ and choral conductors (D Mus); piano (D Mus). *Degree requirements:* For master's, one foreign language, thesis; for doctorate, one foreign language, thesis/dissertation. *Entrance requirements:* Additional exam requirements/recommendations for international students: Required—TOEFL (minimum score 550 paper-based; 213 computer-based). Electronic applications accepted. *Faculty research:* Classical/Indian and West African music, popular music, choral conducting, theory and composition, musicology, applied music.

The University of Arizona, Graduate College, College of Fine Arts, School of Music, Tucson, AZ 85721. Offers composition (MM, A Mus D); conducting (MM, A Mus D); music education (MM, PhD); music theory (MM, PhD); musicology (MM); performance (MM, A Mus D). *Accreditation:* NASD (one or more programs are accredited); NASM (one or more programs are accredited). Part-time programs available. *Faculty:* 30. *Students:* 154 full-time (69 women), 36 part-time (16 women); includes 29 minority (2 African Americans, 1 American Indian/Alaska Native, 8 Asian Americans or Pacific Islanders, 18 Hispanic Americans), 35 international. Average age 32. 166 applicants, 42% accepted, 46 enrolled. In 2007, 24 master's, 12 doctorates awarded. *Degree requirements:* For master's, thesis or alternative, orals; for doctorate, comprehensive exam, thesis/dissertation or alternative. *Entrance requirements:* For master's and doctorate, minimum GPA of 3.0, audition, 3 letters of recommendation, state of purpose. Additional exam requirements/recommendations for international students: Required—TOEFL (minimum score 550 paper-based). *Application deadline:* For fall admission, 6/1 for domestic students, 12/1 for international students; for spring admission, 10/1 for domestic students, 6/1 for international students. Applications are processed on a rolling basis. Application fee: $50. Electronic applications accepted. *Financial support:* In 2007–08, 151 students received support, including 2 fellowships with partial tuition reimbursements available (averaging $10,000 per year), 82 teaching assistantships with partial tuition reimbursements available (averaging $5,225 per year); career-related internships or fieldwork, institutionally sponsored loans, scholarships/grants, health care benefits, and tuition waivers (full) also available. Support available to part-time students. Financial award application deadline: 2/1. *Faculty research:* Music in general education, psychology of music learning, innovation in string music education, Zarzuela, Franz Liszt's work. Total annual research expenditures: $52,880. *Unit head:* Dr. Peter A. McAllister, Director, 520-621-7023, Fax: 520-621-1351, E-mail: pmcallis@email.arizona.edu. *Application contact:* Lyneen Elmore, 520-621-5929, Fax: 520-621-8118, E-mail: lyneen@u.arizona.edu.

The University of Arizona, Graduate College, College of Humanities, Department of English, Rhetoric, Composition and the Teaching of English Program, Tucson, AZ 85721. Offers MA, PhD. *Students:* 32 applicants, 28% accepted. In 2007, 3 master's, 1 doctorate awarded. *Degree requirements:* For master's, one foreign language, comprehensive exam; for doctorate, one foreign language, comprehensive exam, thesis/dissertation. *Entrance requirements:* For master's, GRE, 3 letters of recommendation, minimum GPA of 3.0, statement of purpose, writing sample. Additional exam requirements/recommendations for international students: Required—TOEFL (minimum score 550 paper-based). *Application deadline:* For fall admission, 1/1 for domestic students, 12/1 for international students. Applications are processed on a rolling basis. Application fee: $50. Electronic applications accepted. *Unit head:* John Warnock, Director, 520-621-3255, Fax: 520-621-7397, E-mail: johnw@u.arizona.edu. *Application contact:* Alison Miller, Program Assistant, 520-621-7213, Fax: 520-621-7397, E-mail: admiller@u.arizona.edu.

University of Arkansas, Graduate School, J. William Fulbright College of Arts and Sciences, Department of Music, Fayetteville, AR 72701-1201. Offers MM. *Accreditation:* NASM. *Students:* 23 full-time (8 women), 11 part-time (5 women); includes 4 minority (1 African American, 2 Asian Americans or Pacific Islanders, 1 Hispanic American), 4 international. In 2007, 13 degrees awarded. *Entrance requirements:* For master's, GRE General Test. Application fee: $40 ($50 for international students). *Financial support:* In 2007–08, 20 teaching assistantships were awarded; fellowships, research assistantships, career-related internships or fieldwork and Federal Work-Study also available. Support available to part-time students. Financial award application deadline: 4/1; financial award applicants required to submit FAFSA. *Unit head:* Stephen Gates, Chair, 479-575-4701. *Application contact:* Dr. Rhonda Mains, Graduate Coordinator, 479-575-4701, E-mail: rmains@uark.edu.

The University of British Columbia, Faculty of Arts and Faculty of Graduate Studies, School of Music, Vancouver, BC V6T 1Z1, Canada. Offers M Mus, MA, DMA, PhD. Part-time programs available. *Faculty:* 28 full-time (7 women), 62 part-time/adjunct (22 women). *Students:* 117 full-time (60 women); includes 24 minority (2 American Indian/Alaska Native, 18 Asian Americans or Pacific Islanders, 4 Hispanic Americans), 15 international. Average age 24. 234 applicants, 25% accepted, 51 enrolled. In 2007, 31 master's, 11 doctorates awarded. *Median time to degree:* Of those who began their doctoral program in fall 1999, 100% received their degree in 8 years or less. *Degree requirements:* For master's, recital (M Mus), thesis (MA); for doctorate, one foreign language, comprehensive exam, thesis/dissertation (for some programs), public performance or composition (DMA), dissertation (PhD). *Entrance requirements:* For master's, audition/performance (M Mus); for doctorate, audition/performance (DMA). Additional exam requirements/recommendations for international students: Required—TOEFL (minimum score 580 paper-based; 237 computer-based; 93 iBT). *Application deadline:* For fall admission, 1/30 priority date for domestic and international students. Applications are processed on a rolling basis. Application fee: $90 Canadian dollars ($150 Canadian dollars for international students). Electronic applications accepted. *Financial support:* In 2007–08, 72 students received support, including 9 fellowships with tuition reimbursements available (averaging $16,000 Canadian dollars per year), 7 research assistantships (averaging $3,000 Canadian dollars per year), 39 teaching assistantships (averaging $5,100 Canadian dollars per year); institutionally sponsored loans, scholarships/grants, tuition waivers (partial), and unspecified assistantships also available. Financial award application deadline: 1/30. *Faculty research:* Performance, composition, opera, musicology, ethnomusicology, theory. Total annual research expenditures: $121,492. *Unit head:* Dr. Richard B. Kurth, Director, 604-822-2079, Fax: 604-822-4884, E-mail: richard.kurth@ubc.ca. *Application contact:* Miriam Nechemia, Graduate Admissions Secretary, 604-822-5750, Fax: 604-822-4884, E-mail: miriamn@interchange.ubc.ca.

University of Calgary, Faculty of Graduate Studies, Faculty of Fine Arts, Department of Music, Calgary, AB T2N 1N4, Canada. Offers M Mus, MA, PhD. *Degree requirements:* For master's, one foreign language, thesis; for doctorate, 2 foreign languages, thesis/dissertation. *Entrance requirements:* For master's, audition (performance), 3 compositions. Additional exam requirements/recommendations for international students: Required—TOEFL. Electronic applications accepted. *Faculty research:* Musicology, theory and composition, performance and performance practice, teaching methodology, folk music collection and analyses.

University of California, Berkeley, Graduate Division, College of Letters and Science, Department of Music, Berkeley, CA 94720-1500. Offers composition (PhD); ethnomusicology (PhD); musicology (PhD). *Faculty:* 21 full-time, 53 part-time/adjunct. *Degree requirements:* For doctorate, 2 foreign languages, thesis/dissertation, qualifying exam. *Entrance requirements:* For doctorate, GRE General Test, minimum GPA of 3.0, examples of work, 3 letters of recommendation. Additional exam requirements/recommendations for international students: Required—TOEFL (minimum score 570 paper-based; 230 computer-based). *Application deadline:* For fall admission, 12/15 for domestic students. Application fee: $70 ($90 for international students). *Financial support:* Fellowships with full tuition reimbursements, research assistantships, teaching assistantships with full tuition reimbursements, Federal Work-Study, institutionally sponsored loans, scholarships/grants, health care benefits, and unspecified assistantships available. Financial award applicants required to submit FAFSA. *Faculty research:* Historical musicology, music criticism, computer music. *Unit head:* Bonnie Wade, Chair, 510-642-1460, E-mail: bcwade@berkeley.edu. *Application contact:* Melissa Hacker, Student Affairs Officer, 510-642-2678, Fax: 510-642-8482, E-mail: melhacker@berkeley.edu.

University of California, Davis, Graduate Studies, Program in Music, Davis, CA 95616. Offers composition (MA, PhD); conducting (MA, PhD); musicology (MA, PhD). Terminal master's awarded for partial completion of doctoral program. *Degree requirements:* For master's, one foreign language, thesis; for doctorate, 2 foreign languages, thesis/dissertation. *Entrance*

Music

University of California, Davis (continued)

requirements: For master's, minimum GPA of 3.0; for doctorate, GRE, minimum GPA of 3.0. Additional exam requirements/recommendations for international students: Required—TOEFL (minimum score 550 paper-based; 213 computer-based). Electronic applications accepted.

University of California, Davis, Graduate Studies, Program in Performance Studies, Davis, CA 95616. Offers dramatic art (PhD). *Degree requirements:* For doctorate, 2 foreign languages, thesis/dissertation. *Entrance requirements:* For doctorate, GRE, minimum GPA of 3.25. Additional exam requirements/recommendations for international students: Required—TOEFL (minimum score 550 paper-based; 213 computer-based). Electronic applications accepted.

University of California, Irvine, Office of Graduate Studies, Claire Trevor School of the Arts, Department of Music, Irvine, CA 92697. Offers accompanying (MFA); choral conducting (MFA); composition and technology (MFA); guitar/lute performance (MFA); instrumental performance (MFA); jazz instrumental/composition (MFA); piano performance (MFA); vocal performance (MFA). *Students:* 15 full-time (7 women); includes 3 minority (2 Asian Americans or Pacific Islanders, 1 Hispanic American), 2 international. In 2007, 7 degrees awarded. *Degree requirements:* For master's, one foreign language, thesis. *Entrance requirements:* For master's, minimum GPA of 3.0. *Application deadline:* For fall admission, 3/1 priority date for domestic students; for winter admission, 10/15 priority date for domestic students; for spring admission, 3/1 priority date for domestic students. Applications are processed on a rolling basis. Application fee: $60. Electronic applications accepted. *Financial support:* Fellowships, teaching assistantships, institutionally sponsored loans, traineeships, health care benefits, and unspecified assistantships available. Financial award application deadline: 3/1; financial award applicants required to submit FAFSA. *Faculty research:* Composition, instrumental and choral performance, African-American music, Italian baroque music and performance practice. *Unit head:* Dr. George C. Harvey, Chair, 949-824-6614, Fax: 949-824-4914, E-mail: gcharvey@uci.edu. *Application contact:* Sally L. Avila, Administrative Assistant, 949-824-6615, Fax: 949-824-4914, E-mail: slavila@uci.edu.

University of California, Los Angeles, Graduate Division, College of Letters and Science, Department of Musicology, Los Angeles, CA 90095. Offers MA, PhD. *Students:* 31 full-time (18 women); includes 4 minority (1 American Indian/Alaska Native, 2 Asian Americans or Pacific Islanders, 1 Hispanic American), 2 international. Average age 29. 54 applicants, 13% accepted, 4 enrolled. In 2007, 3 master's, 3 doctorates awarded. Terminal master's awarded for partial completion of doctoral program. *Degree requirements:* For master's, one foreign language, thesis; for doctorate, 2 foreign languages, thesis/dissertation, oral and written qualifying exams. *Entrance requirements:* For master's, minimum GPA of 3.0, sample of written work, degree objective of Ph.D; for doctorate, minimum undergraduate GPA of 3.0, MA or equivalent in music, sample of written work. *Application deadline:* For fall admission, 12/1 for domestic students. Application fee: $60. Electronic applications accepted. *Expenses:* Tuition, nonresident: full-time $5,728. Required fees: $8,966. Full-time tuition and fees vary according to program and student level. *Financial support:* In 2007–08, 50 fellowships with full and partial tuition reimbursements, 6 research assistantships with full and partial tuition reimbursements, 18 teaching assistantships with full and partial tuition reimbursements were awarded. Financial award application deadline: 3/1; financial award applicants required to submit FAFSA. *Unit head:* Dr. Raymond Knapp, Chair, 310-206-5187. *Application contact:* Departmental Office, 310-206-5187, E-mail: buannost@humnet.ucla.edu.

University of California, Los Angeles, Graduate Division, School of the Arts and Architecture, Department of Ethnomusicology, Los Angeles, CA 90095. Offers MA, PhD. *Degree requirements:* For master's, one foreign language; for doctorate, 2 foreign languages, thesis/dissertation, oral and written qualifying exams. *Entrance requirements:* For master's, minimum GPA of 3.0, sample research paper, musical performance ability. Electronic applications accepted. *Expenses:* Tuition, nonresident: full-time $5,728. Required fees: $8,966. Full-time tuition and fees vary according to program and student level.

University of California, Los Angeles, Graduate Division, School of the Arts and Architecture, Department of Music, Los Angeles, CA 90095. Offers composition (MA, PhD); performance (MM, DMA). *Degree requirements:* For master's, one foreign language, thesis, final recital (MM), oral and written qualifying exams (MA); for doctorate, one foreign language, thesis/dissertation, oral/written qualifying exams; lecture recital (DMA); 2 foreign languages (PhD). *Entrance requirements:* For master's, departmental assessment exams, minimum GPA of 3.0, audition (MM); sample of work (MA); for doctorate, departmental assessment exams, minimum GPA of 3.0, audition (DMA); sample of work (PhD). Electronic applications accepted. *Expenses:* Tuition, nonresident: full-time $5,728. Required fees: $8,966. Full-time tuition and fees vary according to program and student level.

University of California, Riverside, Graduate Division, Department of Music, Riverside, CA 92521-0102. Offers MA. *Faculty:* 9 full-time (3 women). *Students:* 18 full-time (5 women); includes 4 minority (1 African American, 2 Asian Americans or Pacific Islanders, 1 Hispanic American). Average age 31. In 2007, 7 degrees awarded. *Degree requirements:* For master's, one foreign language, comprehensive exam, thesis (for some programs), oral exams. *Entrance requirements:* For master's, GRE General Test, minimum GPA of 3.2. Additional exam requirements/recommendations for international students: Required—TOEFL (minimum score 550 paper-based; 213 computer-based; 80 iBT). *Application deadline:* For fall admission, 5/1 for domestic students, 2/1 for international students; for winter admission, 9/1 for domestic students, 7/1 for international students; for spring admission, 12/1 for domestic students, 10/1 for international students. Applications are processed on a rolling basis. Application fee: $60 ($75 for international students). Electronic applications accepted. *Financial support:* In 2007–08, fellowships with full and partial tuition reimbursements (averaging $12,000 per year), teaching assistantships with partial tuition reimbursements (averaging $16,500 per year) were awarded; research assistantships, career-related internships or fieldwork, Federal Work-Study, institutionally sponsored loans, health care benefits, and tuition waivers (full and partial) also available. Financial award applicants required to submit FAFSA. *Faculty research:* Composition, ethnomusicology (especially Southeast Asian and Asian-American music), cultural musicology, gender studies, performance practice. Total annual research expenditures: $60,695. *Unit head:* Dr. Walter Clark, Chair, 951-827-2114, Fax: 951-827-4651, E-mail: walter.clark@ucr.edu. *Application contact:* Dr. Leonora Saavedva, Graduate Adviser, 951-827-4351, Fax: 951-827-4651, E-mail: music@ucr.edu.

University of California, San Diego, Office of Graduate Studies, Department of Music, La Jolla, CA 92093. Offers MA, DMA, PhD. *Degree requirements:* For master's, thesis; for doctorate, thesis/dissertation. Electronic applications accepted. *Faculty research:* Computer music, extended instrumental techniques, comparison of brain wave resonances with musical resonances, composition, performance.

Announcement: UCSD offers degree emphases in composition (MA, PhD), performance (MA, DMA), computer music (MA, PhD), and critical studies/experimental practices (MA, PhD). The department is dedicated to contemporary music-making and encourages collaboration among composers, performers, and researchers. Numerous ensemble and performance opportunities, symphony orchestra, colloquia, distinguished visitors, and state-of-the-art electronic and computer facilities.

University of California, Santa Barbara, Graduate Division, College of Letters and Sciences, Division of Humanities and Fine Arts, Department of Music, Santa Barbara, CA 93106. Offers brass (MM); composition (MA, PhD); conducting (MM, DMA); ethnomusicology (MA, PhD); keyboard (MM, DMA); musicology (MA, PhD); piano accompanying (MM); strings (MM, DMA); theory (MA, PhD); voice (MM, DMA); woodwinds (MM); MA/PhD; MM/DMA. *Faculty:* 23 full-time (6 women), 13 part-time/adjunct (1 woman). *Students:* 66 full-time (29 women); includes 3 minority (all Asian Americans or Pacific Islanders), 3 international. Average age 31. 93 applicants, 23% accepted, 14 enrolled. In 2007, 12 master's, 11 doctorates awarded. Terminal master's awarded for partial completion of doctoral program. *Median time to degree:* Of those who began their doctoral program in fall 1999, 46% received their degree in 8 years or less. *Degree requirements:* For master's, variable foreign language requirement, comprehensive exam, thesis (for some programs), recitals, lecture, and compositions (for some programs); for doctorate, variable foreign language requirement, comprehensive exam, thesis/dissertation, recitals, lecture, and compositions (for some programs). *Entrance requirements:* For master's, GRE, 3 letters of recommendation, tape/audition, media (performance), portfolio (composition), writing sample; for doctorate, 3 letters of recommendation, tape/audition (DMA), media (performance), portfolio (composition), writing sample. Additional exam requirements/recommendations for international students: Required—TOEFL (minimum score 550 paper-based; 213 computer-based; 80 iBT). *Application deadline:* For fall admission, 1/15 for domestic and international students. Applications are processed on a rolling basis. Application fee: $60. Electronic applications accepted. *Expenses:* Tuition, nonresident: full-time $14,888. Required fees: $10,108. *Financial support:* In 2007–08, 60 students received support, including 42 fellowships with full and partial tuition reimbursements available (averaging $5,300 per year), 38 teaching assistantships with full and partial tuition reimbursements available (averaging $10,344 per year); Federal Work-Study, institutionally sponsored loans, scholarships/grants, health care benefits, and unspecified assistantships also available. Financial award application deadline: 1/15; financial award applicants required to submit FAFSA. *Faculty research:* Music theory, ethnomusicology, musicology, music performance, music composition. *Unit head:* Dr. Paul Berkowitz, Chair, 805-893-2066, Fax: 805-893-7194, E-mail: berkowit@music.ucsb.edu. *Application contact:* David Holmes, Student Affairs Officer, 805-893-4603, Fax: 805-893-7194, E-mail: dholmes@music.ucsb.edu.

University of California, Santa Cruz, Division of Graduate Studies, Division of the Arts, Department of Music, Santa Cruz, CA 95064. Offers music (MA, PhD); music composition (DMA). *Faculty:* 13 full-time (5 women). *Students:* 14 full-time (4 women), 3 part-time (2 women); includes 1 minority (Hispanic American), 1 international. Average age 31. 13 applicants, 85% accepted, 7 enrolled. In 2007, 5 degrees awarded. *Degree requirements:* For master's, one foreign language, thesis. *Entrance requirements:* For master's, GRE General Test. *Application deadline:* For fall admission, 1/15 for domestic students. Application fee: $60. Electronic applications accepted. *Expenses:* Tuition, nonresident: full-time $14,694. Required fees: $11,360. *Financial support:* Teaching assistantships, Federal Work-Study and institutionally sponsored loans available. Financial award application deadline: 2/1. *Faculty research:* Western music history, new music, composition, ethnomusicology, musicology. *Unit head:* Dr. Paul Nauert, Chairperson, 831-459-2292. *Application contact:* Yalenda Listmann, Department Assistant, 831-459-3199, E-mail: yalenda@ucsc.edu.

University of Central Arkansas, Graduate School, College of Fine Arts and Communication, Department of Music, Conway, AR 72035-0001. Offers choral conducting (MM); instrumental conducting (MM); music education (MM); music theory (MM); performance (MM). *Accreditation:* NASM. Part-time programs available. *Faculty:* 12 full-time (4 women), 1 part-time/adjunct (0 women). *Students:* 12 full-time (7 women), 4 part-time (1 woman); includes 1 minority (African American) 9 applicants, 67% accepted, 6 enrolled. In 2007, 5 degrees awarded. *Degree requirements:* For master's, comprehensive exam, thesis optional. *Entrance requirements:* For master's, GRE General Test, minimum GPA of 2.7. Additional exam requirements/recommendations for international students: Required—TOEFL (minimum score 550 paper-based; 213 computer-based). *Application deadline:* For fall admission, 3/1 priority date for domestic students; for spring admission, 10/1 priority date for domestic students. Applications are processed on a rolling basis. Application fee: $25 ($50 for international students). *Expenses:* Tuition, state resident: full-time $4,513; part-time $240 per credit. Tuition, nonresident: full-time $8,805; part-time $440 per credit. International tuition: $9,700 full-time. Required fees: $100 per term. *Financial support:* Federal Work-Study, scholarships/grants, tuition waivers (partial), and unspecified assistantships available. Financial award application deadline: 2/15; financial award applicants required to submit FAFSA. *Unit head:* Jeffrey Jarvis, Unit Head, 501-450-3163. *Application contact:* Brenda Herring, Admissions Assistant, 501-450-5065, Fax: 501-450-5678, E-mail: bherring@uca.edu.

University of Central Florida, College of Arts and Humanities, Department of Music, Orlando, FL 32816. Offers MA. *Accreditation:* NASM; NCATE. Part-time and evening/weekend programs available. *Faculty:* 25 full-time (3 women), 14 part-time/adjunct (8 women). *Entrance requirements:* For master's, GRE General Test. Additional exam requirements/recommendations for international students: Required—TOEFL. *Application deadline:* For fall admission, 7/15 for domestic students; for spring admission, 12/1 for domestic students. Application fee: $30. Electronic applications accepted. *Expenses:* Tuition, state resident: full-time $6,484. Tuition, nonresident: full-time $23,938. Tuition and fees vary according to program. *Financial support:* Fellowships with partial tuition reimbursements, research assistantships with partial tuition reimbursements, teaching assistantships with partial tuition reimbursements, career-related internships or fieldwork, Federal Work-Study, institutionally sponsored loans, tuition waivers (partial), and unspecified assistantships available. Financial award application deadline: 3/1; financial award applicants required to submit FAFSA. *Unit head:* Dr. Johnny Pherigo, Chair, 407-823-2879, Fax: 407-823-3378, E-mail: jpherigo@mail.ucf.edu.

University of Central Missouri, The Graduate School, College of Arts, Humanities and Social Sciences, Department of Music, Warrensburg, MO 64093. Offers MA. *Accreditation:* NASM. Part-time programs available. *Faculty:* 19 full-time (3 women). *Students:* 10 full-time (7 women), 5 part-time (2 women), 1 international. Average age 32. 10 applicants, 90% accepted, 3 enrolled. In 2007, 2 degrees awarded. *Degree requirements:* For master's, thesis (for some programs), comprehensive review, evaluation. *Entrance requirements:* For master's, minimum GPA of 2.5 in music, 30 hours of course work in music. Additional exam requirements/recommendations for international students: Required—TOEFL (minimum score 500 paper-based; 173 computer-based). *Application deadline:* For fall admission, 6/1 priority date for domestic students, 5/1 priority date for international students; for spring admission, 10/1 priority date for domestic students, 10/1 for international students. Applications are processed on a rolling basis. Application fee: $30 ($50 for international students). *Expenses:* Tuition, state resident: full-time $6,259; part-time $256 per credit hour. Tuition, nonresident: full-time $11,915; part-time $491 per credit hour. Required fees: $604; $20 per credit hour. *Financial support:* In 2007–08, 4 students received support; teaching assistantships with full tuition reimbursements available, Federal Work-Study, scholarships/grants, unspecified assistantships, and administrative and laboratory assistantships available. Support available to part-time students. Financial award application deadline: 3/1; financial award applicants required to submit FAFSA. *Unit head:* Dr. Lester Brothers, Chair, 660-543-4530, Fax: 660-543-8271, E-mail: brothers@ucmo.edu.

University of Central Oklahoma, College of Graduate Studies and Research, College of Arts, Media, and Design, Department of Music, Edmond, OK 73034-5209. Offers music education (MM); performance (MM). *Accreditation:* NASM. Part-time programs available. *Students:* 14 full-time (4 women), 4 part-time (3 women); includes 5 minority (2 African Americans, 1 American Indian/Alaska Native, 1 Asian American or Pacific Islander, 1 Hispanic American). Average age 32. 10 applicants, 100% accepted. In 2007, 7 degrees awarded. *Entrance requirements:* Additional exam requirements/recommendations for international students: Required—TOEFL (minimum score 550 paper-based; 213 computer-based). *Application deadline:* For fall admission, 7/1 for international students; for spring admission, 11/1 for international students. Applications are processed on a rolling basis. Application fee: $25. Electronic applications accepted. *Expenses:* Tuition, state resident: full-time $3,516; part-time $147 per hour. Tuition, nonresident: full-time $9,054; part-time $377 per hour. Required fees: $433; $18 per hour. *Financial support:* Federal Work-Study and unspecified assistantships available. Financial award application deadline: 3/31; financial award applicants required to submit FAFSA. *Faculty research:* Opera/orchestral composition, western/world music, ethnomusicology, literature for librettos. *Unit head:* Dr. Kent Kidwell, Chair, 405-974-5175.

University of Chicago, Division of the Humanities, Department of Music, Chicago, IL 60637-1513. Offers AM, PhD. *Students:* 87. 115 applicants, 22% accepted, 11 enrolled. *Degree requirements:* For master's, 2 foreign languages, thesis; for doctorate, 3 foreign languages, thesis/dissertation. *Entrance requirements:* For master's and doctorate, GRE General Test.

Additional exam requirements/recommendations for international students: Required—TOEFL. *Application deadline:* For fall admission, 12/15 for domestic students. Application fee: $55. *Financial support:* Fellowships, Federal Work-Study available. Financial award application deadline: 12/15; financial award applicants required to submit FAFSA. *Unit head:* Dr. Martha Feldman, Chair, 773-702-8484.

University of Cincinnati, Graduate School, College-Conservatory of Music, Division of Composition, Musicology and Theory, Cincinnati, OH 45221. Offers composition (MM, DMA); music history (MM); music theory (MM, PhD); musicology (PhD). *Accreditation:* NASM. *Faculty:* 13 full-time (5 women), 2 part-time/adjunct (0 women). *Students:* 31 full-time (11 women), 43 part-time (20 women); includes 2 minority (both Hispanic Americans), 15 international. 63 applicants, 40% accepted. In 2007, 5 master's, 1 doctorate awarded. *Degree requirements:* For master's, variable foreign language requirement, comprehensive exam, thesis; for doctorate, variable foreign language requirement, comprehensive exam, thesis/dissertation. *Entrance requirements:* For master's and doctorate, GRE General Test, interview. Additional exam requirements/recommendations for international students: Required—TOEFL (minimum score 520 paper-based; 190 computer-based). *Application deadline:* For fall admission, 2/1 for domestic students. Applications are processed on a rolling basis. Application fee: $85. Electronic applications accepted. *Financial support:* In 2007–08, 21 teaching assistantships with full tuition reimbursements (averaging $7,020 per year) were awarded; fellowships, research assistantships, Federal Work-Study, scholarships/grants, tuition waivers (full and partial), and unspecified assistantships also available. Financial award application deadline: 3/1. *Unit head:* Dr. Robert Zierolf, Chair, 513-556-6046, E-mail: robert.zierolf@uc.edu. *Application contact:* Paul R. Hillner, Assistant Dean for Admissions and Student Services, 513-556-5462, Fax: 513-556-1028, E-mail: paul.hillner@uc.edu.

University of Cincinnati, Graduate School, College-Conservatory of Music, Division of Ensembles and Conducting, Cincinnati, OH 45221. Offers choral conducting (MM, DMA); orchestral conducting (MM, DMA); wind conducting (MM, DMA). *Accreditation:* NASM. *Faculty:* 6 full-time (1 woman). *Students:* 27 full-time (4 women), 17 part-time (2 women); includes 1 minority (Hispanic American), 13 international. 68 applicants, 24% accepted. In 2007, 8 master's, 3 doctorates awarded. *Degree requirements:* For master's, comprehensive exam, conducting performances; for doctorate, one foreign language, comprehensive exam, thesis/dissertation, conducting performances, lecture recital. *Entrance requirements:* For master's and doctorate, GRE General Test, audition, interview. Additional exam requirements/recommendations for international students: Required—TOEFL (minimum score 520 paper-based; 190 computer-based). *Application deadline:* For fall admission, 2/1 for domestic students. Applications are processed on a rolling basis. Application fee: $85. Electronic applications accepted. *Financial support:* In 2007–08, 17 teaching assistantships with full tuition reimbursements (averaging $6,496 per year) were awarded; fellowships, research assistantships, Federal Work-Study, scholarships/grants, tuition waivers (full and partial), and unspecified assistantships also available. Financial award application deadline: 3/1. *Unit head:* Dr. Earl Rivers, Chair, 513-556-2696, E-mail: earl.rivers@uc.edu. *Application contact:* Paul R. Hillner, Assistant Dean for Admissions and Student Services, 513-556-5462, Fax: 513-556-1028, E-mail: paul.hillner@uc.edu.

University of Cincinnati, Graduate School, College-Conservatory of Music, Division of Keyboard Studies, Cincinnati, OH 45221. Offers MM, DMA, AD. *Faculty:* 10 full-time (3 women), 2 part-time/adjunct (both women). *Students:* 112; includes 9 minority (1 African American, 7 Asian Americans or Pacific Islanders, 1 Hispanic American), 65 international. 183 applicants, 22% accepted. In 2007, 8 master's, 15 doctorates awarded. *Degree requirements:* For master's, comprehensive exam; for doctorate, one foreign language, comprehensive exam, thesis/dissertation. *Entrance requirements:* For master's and doctorate, GRE General Test, audition; for AD, audition. Additional exam requirements/recommendations for international students: Required—TOEFL (minimum score 520 paper-based; 190 computer-based). *Application deadline:* For fall admission, 2/1 for domestic students. Applications are processed on a rolling basis. Application fee: $85. Electronic applications accepted. *Financial support:* In 2007–08, 28 teaching assistantships with full tuition reimbursements (averaging $6,184 per year) were awarded; Federal Work-Study, scholarships/grants, and unspecified assistantships also available. *Unit head:* Roberta Gary, Head, 513-556-4041, E-mail: roberta.gary@uc.edu.

University of Cincinnati, Graduate School, College-Conservatory of Music, Division of Performance Studies, Cincinnati, OH 45221. Offers performance (MM, DMA, AD). MM, DMA, and AD are available for every instrument. *Accreditation:* NASM. *Degree requirements:* For master's, comprehensive exam, recitals; for doctorate, one foreign language, comprehensive exam, thesis/dissertation, recitals; for AD, recitals. *Entrance requirements:* For master's and doctorate, GRE General Test, audition. Additional exam requirements/recommendations for international students: Required—TOEFL (minimum score 520 paper-based; 190 computer-based). Electronic applications accepted. *Faculty research:* Performance, guest teaching.

University of Cincinnati, Graduate School, College-Conservatory of Music, Divisions of Opera, Musical Theater, Drama, and Arts Administration, Cincinnati, OH 45221. Offers arts administration (MA); directing (MFA); theater design and production (MFA); voice and opera (MM, DMA); MBA/MA. *Accreditation:* NAST (one or more programs are accredited). *Faculty:* 25 full-time (6 women). *Students:* 53 full-time (35 women), 10 part-time (7 women); includes 22 minority (7 African Americans, 1 American Indian/Alaska Native, 9 Asian Americans or Pacific Islanders, 5 Hispanic Americans), 15 international. Average age 28. 71 applicants, 49% accepted. In 2007, 19 degrees awarded. *Degree requirements:* For master's, final project. *Entrance requirements:* For master's, GMAT (MA), audition/interview. Additional exam requirements/recommendations for international students: Required—TOEFL (minimum score 520 paper-based; 190 computer-based). *Application deadline:* For fall admission, 2/1 for domestic students. Applications are processed on a rolling basis. Application fee: $85. Electronic applications accepted. *Financial support:* In 2007–08, 31 teaching assistantships with full tuition reimbursements (averaging $4,897 per year) were awarded; fellowships, research assistantships, career-related internships or fieldwork, Federal Work-Study, scholarships/grants, tuition waivers (full), and unspecified assistantships also available. Financial award application deadline: 3/1. *Unit head:* R. Terrell Finney, Chair, 513-556-5803, Fax: 513-556-3399, E-mail: terrell.finney@uc.edu. *Application contact:* Paul R. Hillner, Assistant Dean for Admissions and Student Services, 513-556-5462, Fax: 513-556-1028, E-mail: paul.hillner@uc.edu.

University of Colorado at Boulder, Graduate School, College of Music, Boulder, CO 80309. Offers church music (M Mus); composition (M Mus, D Mus A); conducting (M Mus, D Mus A); music education (M Mus Ed, PhD); music literature (M Mus); musicology (PhD); pedagogy (M Mus, D Mus A); performance (M Mus, D Mus A). *Accreditation:* NASM. *Faculty:* 52. *Students:* 186 full-time (99 women), 60 part-time (29 women); includes 25 minority (4 African Americans, 2 American Indian/Alaska Native, 9 Asian Americans or Pacific Islanders, 10 Hispanic Americans), 31 international. Average age 30. 185 applicants, 74% accepted. In 2007, 28 master's, 19 doctorates awarded. Terminal master's awarded for partial completion of doctoral program. *Degree requirements:* For master's, variable foreign language requirement, comprehensive exam, thesis or alternative, recital; for doctorate, variable foreign language requirement, thesis/dissertation. *Entrance requirements:* For master's, GRE General Test, GRE Subject Test (music literature), minimum undergraduate GPA of 2.75; for doctorate, GRE General Test, GRE Subject Test, audition, sample of research. *Application deadline:* For fall admission, 3/1 priority date for domestic students, 12/1 for international students. Applications are processed on a rolling basis. Application fee: $50 ($60 for international students). *Financial support:* In 2007–08, 141 fellowships (averaging $2,588 per year) were awarded; tuition waivers (full) also available. Financial award application deadline: 3/1. *Unit head:* Daniel P. Sher, Dean, 303-492-7505, Fax: 303-492-5619, E-mail: daniel.sher@colorado.edu. *Application contact:* Associate Dean for Graduate Studies, 303-492-2207, Fax: 303-492-5619, E-mail: gradmusc@colorado.edu.

University of Colorado Denver, College of Arts and Media, Program in Recording Arts, Denver, CO 80217-3364. Offers MS. *Accreditation:* NASM. Part-time and evening/weekend programs available. *Faculty:* 3 full-time (1 woman). *Students:* 11 full-time (2 women), 5 part-time; includes 1 minority (African American), 1 international. Average age 29. 12 applicants, 92% accepted, 8 enrolled. In 2007, 3 degrees awarded. *Degree requirements:* For master's, thesis or alternative. *Entrance requirements:* For master's, GRE General Test, minimum GPA of 2.75, portfolio, resumé, interview, 3 letters of recommendation. Additional exam requirements/recommendations for international students: Required—TOEFL (minimum score 500 paper-based; 173 computer-based). *Application deadline:* For fall admission, 6/1 for domestic students; for spring admission, 11/1 for domestic students. Applications are processed on a rolling basis. Application fee: $50 ($75 for international students). Electronic applications accepted. *Financial support:* Federal Work-Study, institutionally sponsored loans, and scholarships/grants available. Support available to part-time students. Financial award application deadline: 4/1; financial award applicants required to submit FAFSA. *Unit head:* Richard Sanders, Chair, 303-556-2796, Fax: 303-556-2335, E-mail: rich@saltproductions.com. *Application contact:* Dr. Roy Pritts, Program Director, 303-556-2795, Fax: 303-556-2335, E-mail: rpritts@carbon.cudenver.edu.

University of Connecticut, Graduate School, School of Fine Arts, Department of Music, Field of Music, Storrs, CT 06269. Offers conducting (M Mus, DMA); historical musicology (MA); music (Performer's Certificate); music education (M Mus, PhD); music theory (MA); music theory and history (PhD); performance (M Mus, DMA). *Accreditation:* NASM. *Faculty:* 19 full-time (5 women). *Students:* 38 full-time (22 women), 25 part-time (13 women); includes 6 minority (1 American Indian/Alaska Native, 3 Asian Americans or Pacific Islanders, 2 Hispanic Americans), 8 international. Average age 32. 65 applicants, 29% accepted, 19 enrolled. In 2007, 16 master's, 3 doctorates, 4 other advanced degrees awarded. Terminal master's awarded for partial completion of doctoral program. *Degree requirements:* For master's, comprehensive exam; for doctorate, thesis/dissertation. *Entrance requirements:* For master's, GRE General Test, GRE Subject Test, audition; for doctorate, GRE Subject Test, MAT, audition. Additional exam requirements/recommendations for international students: Required—TOEFL (minimum score 550 paper-based; 213 computer-based). *Application deadline:* For fall admission, 2/1 priority date for domestic and international students; for spring admission, 11/1 for domestic students, 10/1 for international students. Applications are processed on a rolling basis. Application fee: $55. Electronic applications accepted. *Expenses:* Tuition, state resident: part-time $469 per credit hour. Tuition, nonresident: part-time $1,218 per credit hour. *Financial support:* In 2007–08, 3 research assistantships, 28 teaching assistantships with full tuition reimbursements were awarded; fellowships, Federal Work-Study, health care benefits, and unspecified assistantships also available. Financial award application deadline: 2/1; financial award applicants required to submit FAFSA. *Application contact:* Debbie Trahan, Administrative Assistant, 860-486-3731, E-mail: dtrahan@finearts.sfa.uconn.edu.

University of Delaware, College of Arts and Sciences, Department of Music, Newark, DE 19716. Offers composition (MM); music education (MM); performance (MM). *Accreditation:* NASM. Part-time programs available. *Faculty:* 25 full-time (10 women), 11 part-time/adjunct (2 women). *Students:* 19 full-time (9 women), 6 part-time (5 women); includes 2 minority (both Hispanic Americans), 3 international. Average age 29. 32 applicants, 53% accepted, 12 enrolled. In 2007, 6 degrees awarded. *Entrance requirements:* For master's, audition. Additional exam requirements/recommendations for international students: Required—TOEFL. *Application deadline:* For fall admission, 7/1 for domestic students. Application fee: $60. Electronic applications accepted. *Financial support:* In 2007–08, 6 students received support, including 3 teaching assistantships with full tuition reimbursements available (averaging $11,000 per year); tuition waivers (full) also available. Financial award application deadline: 3/1. *Faculty research:* Teaching of music. *Unit head:* Dr. Paul D. Head, Interim Chair, 302-831-2577, Fax: 302-831-3589. *Application contact:* Information Contact, 302-831-2578.

University of Denver, Faculty of Arts and Humanities/Social Sciences, Lamont School of Music, Denver, CO 80208. Offers composition (MA); conducting (MA); jazz and commercial music (Certificate); music (MM); music education (MA); music history and literature (MA); Orff-Schulwerk (MA); performance (MA); piano pedagogy (MA); Suzuki pedagogy (MA); Suzuki teaching (Certificate); theory (MA). *Accreditation:* NASM. Part-time programs available. *Faculty:* 24 full-time (6 women). *Students:* 23 full-time (8 women), 33 part-time (19 women); includes 3 minority (1 African American, 2 Hispanic Americans), 9 international. Average age 29. In 2007, 24 degrees awarded. *Degree requirements:* For master's, thesis (for some programs), recital or project, 2 years language (performance, music history and literature). *Entrance requirements:* For master's, GRE General Test, music history and theory qualifying exams. Additional exam requirements/recommendations for international students: Required—TOEFL. *Application deadline:* Applications are processed on a rolling basis. Application fee: $50. Electronic applications accepted. *Financial support:* In 2007–08, 35 teaching assistantships with full and partial tuition reimbursements (averaging $4,400 per year) were awarded; career-related internships or fieldwork, Federal Work-Study, institutionally sponsored loans, and scholarships/grants also available. Support available to part-time students. Financial award application deadline: 4/15; financial award applicants required to submit FAFSA. *Unit head:* Joseph Docksey, Director, 303-871-6973. *Application contact:* Graduate Adviser, 303-871-6973, E-mail: marhuels@du.edu.

University of Florida, Graduate School, College of Fine Arts, School of Music, Gainesville, FL 32611. Offers choral conducting (MM, PhD); composition/theory (MM, PhD); ethnomusicology (PhD); instrumental conducting (MM, PhD); music (MM, PhD); music education (MM, PhD); music history and literature (MM); musicology (PhD); performance (MM); sacred music (MM). *Accreditation:* NASM. *Faculty:* 38 full-time (9 women). *Students:* 109 (55 women); includes 9 minority (3 African Americans, 1 American Indian/Alaska Native, 1 Asian American or Pacific Islander, 4 Hispanic Americans) 20 international. In 2007, 27 master's, 6 doctorates awarded. *Degree requirements:* For master's, variable foreign language requirement, thesis; for doctorate, thesis/dissertation. *Entrance requirements:* For master's and doctorate, audition, GRE General Test or minimum GPA of 3.0. Additional exam requirements/recommendations for international students: Required—TOEFL (minimum score 550 paper-based; 213 computer-based). *Application deadline:* For fall admission, 6/1 priority date for domestic students. Applications are processed on a rolling basis. Application fee: $30. Electronic applications accepted. *Expenses:* Tuition, state resident: full-time $7,478. Tuition, nonresident: full-time $22,603. *Financial support:* In 2007–08, 2 research assistantships with tuition reimbursements (averaging $9,514 per year), 38 teaching assistantships with tuition reimbursements (averaging $10,335 per year) were awarded; fellowships with full tuition reimbursements, unspecified assistantships also available. *Unit head:* Will Kesling, Program Director, 352-392-0223 Ext. 207. *Application contact:* Dr. Leslie Odom, Coordinator, 352-392-0223 Ext. 231, Fax: 352-352-0461, E-mail: lodom@ufl.edu.

University of Georgia, Graduate School, College of Arts and Sciences, School of Music, Athens, GA 30602. Offers MA, MM, DMA, PhD. *Accreditation:* NASM. *Faculty:* 43 full-time (10 women). *Students:* 89 full-time (40 women), 26 part-time (14 women); includes 3 African Americans, 5 Asian Americans or Pacific Islanders, 20 international. 124 applicants, 60% accepted, 40 enrolled. In 2007, 20 master's, 11 doctorates awarded. *Degree requirements:* For master's, variable foreign language requirement, thesis (MA); for doctorate, variable foreign language requirement, thesis/dissertation. *Entrance requirements:* For master's and doctorate, GRE General Test. *Application deadline:* For fall admission, 7/1 priority date for domestic students; for spring admission, 11/15 for domestic students. Application fee: $50. Electronic applications accepted. *Financial support:* Fellowships, research assistantships, teaching assistantships, unspecified assistantships available. *Unit head:* Dr. Donald R. Lowe, Director, 706-542-2276, Fax: 706-542-2773, E-mail: dlowe@uga.edu. *Application contact:* Dr. Kenneth M. Fischer, Graduate Coordinator, 206-542-2784, E-mail: kfischer@uga.edu.

University of Hartford, The Hartt School, West Hartford, CT 06117-1599. Offers choral conducting (MM Ed); composition (MM, DMA, Artist Diploma, Diploma); conducting (MM, DMA, Artist Diploma, Diploma), including choral (MM, Diploma), instrumental (MM, Diploma); early childhood education (MM Ed); instrumental conducting (MM Ed); Kodály (MM Ed); music (CAGS); music education (DMA, PhD); music history (MM); music theory (MM); pedagogy

Music

University of Hartford (continued)
(MM Ed); performance (MM, MM Ed, DMA, Artist Diploma, Diploma); research (MM Ed); technology (MM Ed). Part-time programs available. *Faculty:* 36 full-time (5 women), 31 part-time/adjunct (13 women). *Students:* 95 full-time (52 women), 39 part-time (22 women); includes 10 minority (4 African Americans, 3 Asian Americans or Pacific Islanders, 3 Hispanic Americans), 32 international. Average age 29. 186 applicants, 58% accepted, 49 enrolled. In 2007, 46 master's, 7 doctorates, 10 other advanced degrees awarded. *Degree requirements:* For master's, variable foreign language requirement, thesis (for some programs), recital; for doctorate, variable foreign language requirement, thesis/dissertation (for some programs), recital; for other advanced degree, recital. *Entrance requirements:* For master's, audition, letters of recommendation; for doctorate, proficiency exam, audition, interview, research paper; for other advanced degree, audition. Additional exam requirements/recommendations for international students: Required—TOEFL. *Application deadline:* For fall admission, 4/1 priority date for domestic students. Applications are processed on a rolling basis. Application fee: $45. Electronic applications accepted. *Expenses:* Contact institution. *Financial support:* Fellowships, teaching assistantships, Federal Work-Study available. Support available to part-time students. Financial award application deadline: 6/1; financial award applicants required to submit FAFSA. *Unit head:* Dr. Malcolm Morrison, Dean, 860-768-4468, E-mail: morrison@mail.hartford.edu. *Application contact:* Lynne Johnson, Director of Admissions, 860-768-4115, Fax: 860-768-4441, E-mail: johnson@hartford.edu.

University of Hawaii at Manoa, Graduate Division, Colleges of Arts and Sciences, College of Arts and Humanities, Department of Music, Honolulu, HI 96822. Offers M Mus, MA, PhD. *Accreditation:* NASM. Part-time programs available. *Faculty:* 24 full-time (9 women). *Students:* 35 full-time (19 women), 32 part-time (13 women); includes 15 minority (1 American Indian/Alaska Native, 14 Asian Americans or Pacific Islanders), 9 international. Average age 33. 74 applicants, 30% accepted, 16 enrolled. *Degree requirements:* For master's, variable foreign language requirement, thesis optional; for doctorate, variable foreign language requirement, comprehensive exam, thesis/dissertation. *Entrance requirements:* For master's, diagnostic exams in acoustics theory, GRE General Test; for doctorate, diagnostic exams in music history and theory, GRE General Test. Additional exam requirements/recommendations for international students: Required—TOEFL (minimum score 540 paper-based; 207 computer-based; 76 iBT), IELTS (minimum score 5). *Application deadline:* For fall admission, 2/1 for domestic students, 1/15 for international students; for spring admission, 9/1 for domestic students, 8/1 for international students. Application fee: $50. *Financial support:* In 2007–08, 14 students received support, including 11 teaching assistantships (averaging $13,841 per year); fellowships, research assistantships, Federal Work-Study and tuition waivers (full) also available. *Faculty research:* Original compositions, nineteenth century German music, Korean and Indonesian music, piano/voice performance, Pacific music. *Application contact:* Thomas Yee, Graduate Field Chairperson, 808-956-7756, Fax: 808-956-9657, E-mail: tyeet@hawaii.edu.

University of Houston, College of Liberal Arts and Social Sciences, Moores School of Music, Houston, TX 77204. Offers accompanying (MM); applied music (MM); composition (MM, DMA); conducting (DMA); music education (MM, DMA); music literature (MM); music performance and pedagogy (DMA); music theory (MM); performance (DMA). *Accreditation:* NASM. Part-time programs available. *Faculty:* 29 full-time (6 women), 22 part-time/adjunct (8 women). *Students:* 90 full-time (46 women), 43 part-time (17 women); includes 18 minority (7 African Americans, 5 Asian Americans or Pacific Islanders, 6 Hispanic Americans), 25 international. Average age 29. 121 applicants, 54% accepted, 42 enrolled. In 2007, 34 master's, 4 doctorates awarded. *Degree requirements:* For master's, variable foreign language requirement, thesis (for some programs), departmental comprehensive exam, recital; for doctorate, one foreign language, thesis/dissertation, departmental qualifying exam, recitals. *Entrance requirements:* For master's, GRE General Test, audition; for doctorate, GRE General Test, GRE Subject Test, audition. *Application deadline:* For fall admission, 7/1 priority date for domestic students. Applications are processed on a rolling basis. Application fee: $0 ($75 for international students). *Expenses:* Tuition, state resident: full-time $6,297; part-time $262 per credit. Tuition, nonresident: full-time $12,969; part-time $540 per credit. Required fees: $2,696. *Financial support:* In 2007–08, 42 teaching assistantships with full tuition reimbursements (averaging $9,800 per year) were awarded; fellowships with full tuition reimbursements, research assistantships with full tuition reimbursements, career-related internships or fieldwork, Federal Work-Study, institutionally sponsored loans, scholarships/grants, health care benefits, and unspecified assistantships also available. Support available to part-time students. Financial award application deadline: 2/1. *Faculty research:* Twentieth century music, baroque music, history of music theory, music analysis. *Unit head:* David Ashley White, Chairperson, 713-743-3009, Fax: 713-743-3166, E-mail: daw@orpheus.music.uh.edu. *Application contact:* Howard Pollack, Director of Graduate Studies, 713-743-3314, Fax: 713-743-3166.

University of Idaho, College of Graduate Studies, College of Letters, Arts and Social Sciences, Lionel Hampton School of Music, Moscow, ID 83844-2282. Offers M Mus, MA. *Accreditation:* NASM. *Students:* 17 (9 women). Average age 36. In 2007, 9 degrees awarded. *Degree requirements:* For master's, one foreign language, thesis or alternative. *Entrance requirements:* For master's, minimum GPA of 2.8. *Application deadline:* For fall admission, 8/1 for domestic students; for spring admission, 12/15 for domestic students. Application fee: $55 ($60 for international students). *Financial support:* Research assistantships, teaching assistantships available. Financial award application deadline: 2/15. *Unit head:* Dr. Kevin B. Woelfel, Director, 208-885-6231.

University of Illinois at Urbana–Champaign, Graduate College, College of Fine and Applied Arts, School of Music, Champaign, IL 61820. Offers music (M Mus, DMA, AD); music education (MME, MS, Ed D, PhD, CAS); musicology (PhD). *Accreditation:* NASM. *Faculty:* 72 full-time (12 women), 5 part-time/adjunct (2 women). *Students:* 287 full-time (140 women), 78 part-time (49 women); includes 26 minority (5 African Americans, 1 American Indian/Alaska Native, 17 Asian Americans or Pacific Islanders, 3 Hispanic Americans), 131 international. 590 applicants, 43% accepted, 99 enrolled. In 2007, 53 master's, 29 doctorates awarded. *Degree requirements:* For doctorate, one foreign language, thesis/dissertation. *Entrance requirements:* For master's, minimum GPA of 3.0. *Application deadline:* For fall admission, 1/16 priority date for domestic students; for spring admission, 1/3 for domestic students. Applications are processed on a rolling basis. Application fee: $60 ($75 for international students). Electronic applications accepted. *Financial support:* In 2007–08, 32 fellowships, 9 research assistantships, 137 teaching assistantships were awarded; tuition waivers (full and partial) also available. Financial award application deadline: 2/15. *Unit head:* Karl Kramer, Director, 217-244-2676, Fax: 217-244-4585, E-mail: kramerk@uiuc.edu. *Application contact:* Jennifer Todd, Secretary III, 217-333-2620, Fax: 217-244-4585, E-mail: jtodd@uiuc.edu.

The University of Iowa, Graduate College, College of Liberal Arts and Sciences, School of Music, Iowa City, IA 52242-1316. Offers MA, MFA, DMA, PhD. *Accreditation:* NASM. *Faculty:* 44 full-time, 15 part-time/adjunct. *Students:* 132 full-time (66 women), 79 part-time (39 women); includes 8 minority (2 African Americans, 2 Asian Americans or Pacific Islanders, 4 Hispanic Americans), 39 international. 181 applicants, 60% accepted, 57 enrolled. In 2007, 25 master's, 11 doctorates awarded. *Degree requirements:* For master's, thesis (for some programs), exam; for doctorate, comprehensive exam, thesis/dissertation. *Entrance requirements:* For master's and doctorate, minimum GPA of 3.0. Additional exam requirements/recommendations for international students: Required—TOEFL (minimum score 550 paper-based; 213 computer-based; 81 iBT). *Application deadline:* For fall admission, 2/1 priority date for international students. Applications are processed on a rolling basis. Application fee: $60 ($85 for international students). Electronic applications accepted. *Expenses:* Tuition, state resident: part-time $349 per hour. Tuition, nonresident: part-time $349 per hour. Tuition and fees vary according to course load and program. *Financial support:* In 2007–08, 6 fellowships, 16 research assistantships with partial tuition reimbursements, 63 teaching assistantships with partial tuition reimbursements were awarded. Financial award applicants required to submit FAFSA. *Unit head:* Kristin Thelander, Director, 319-335-1601.

University of Kansas, Research and Graduate Studies, School of Fine Arts, Department of Music and Dance, Program in Music, Lawrence, KS 66045. Offers MM, DMA, PhD. *Faculty:* 56. *Students:* 110 full-time (49 women), 29 part-time (16 women); includes 15 minority (1 African American, 1 American Indian/Alaska Native, 5 Asian Americans or Pacific Islanders, 8 Hispanic Americans), 23 international. Average age 29. 125 applicants, 64% accepted, 46 enrolled. In 2007, 14 master's, 19 doctorates awarded. *Degree requirements:* For master's, comprehensive exam (for some programs), thesis (for some programs), recitals (MM); for doctorate, comprehensive exam, thesis/dissertation, recitals (DMA). *Entrance requirements:* For master's, minimum GPA of 3.0, audition (performance), MM-KU Musicology and Music Theory diagnostic exam; for doctorate, GRE (PhD), minimum GPA of 3.0, audition (DMA), DMA/PhD music theory-KU Musicology and Music Theory diagnostic exam. Additional exam requirements/recommendations for international students: Required—TOEFL or IELTS (6.0). *Application deadline:* For fall admission, 12/15 priority date for domestic and international students; for spring admission, 5/15 priority date for domestic and international students. Applications are processed on a rolling basis. Application fee: $55 ($60 for international students). Electronic applications accepted. *Expenses:* Tuition, state resident: full-time $5,838. Tuition, nonresident: full-time $13,409. Tuition and fees vary according to program. *Financial support:* Fellowships with full tuition reimbursements, research assistantships with partial tuition reimbursements, teaching assistantships with full and partial tuition reimbursements, institutionally sponsored loans, scholarships/grants, and unspecified assistantships available. Financial award application deadline: 12/15; financial award applicants required to submit FAFSA. *Faculty research:* Musicology, music theory, church music, music composition, performance. *Application contact:* Director of Graduate Studies, 785-864-9699, Fax: 785-864-5866, E-mail: choir@ku.edu.

University of Kentucky, Graduate School, College of Fine Arts, Program in Music, Lexington, KY 40506-0032. Offers music (PhD); music composition (MM); music education (MM); music performance (MM); music theory (MA); musical arts (DMA); musicology (MA). *Accreditation:* NASM. Part-time and evening/weekend programs available. *Faculty:* 32 full-time (9 women). *Students:* 131 full-time (68 women), 30 part-time (16 women); includes 18 minority (11 African Americans, 1 American Indian/Alaska Native, 6 Hispanic Americans), 15 international. Average age 33. 124 applicants, 37% accepted, 28 enrolled. In 2007, 14 master's, 4 doctorates awarded. *Median time to degree:* Of those who began their doctoral program in fall 1999, 58% received their degree in 8 years or less. *Degree requirements:* For master's, variable foreign language requirement, comprehensive exam, thesis (for some programs); for doctorate, variable foreign language requirement, comprehensive exam, thesis/dissertation. *Entrance requirements:* For master's, GRE General Test, minimum undergraduate GPA of 2.75; for doctorate, GRE General Test, minimum undergraduate GPA of 2.75, graduate work GPA of 3.0. Additional exam requirements/recommendations for international students: Required—TOEFL (minimum score 550 paper-based; 213 computer-based). *Application deadline:* For fall admission, 7/17 priority date for domestic students, 2/1 priority date for international students; for spring admission, 12/13 priority date for domestic students, 6/15 priority date for international students. Application fee: $50 ($65 for international students). Electronic applications accepted. *Expenses:* Tuition, state resident: part-time $437 per credit hour. Tuition, nonresident: part-time $931 per credit hour. *Financial support:* In 2007–08, 78 students received support, including 16 fellowships with full tuition reimbursements available (averaging $2,987 per year), 22 research assistantships with full tuition reimbursements available (averaging $5,350 per year), 46 teaching assistantships with full tuition reimbursements available (averaging $10,362 per year); Federal Work-Study, institutionally sponsored loans, scholarships/grants, traineeships, health care benefits, tuition waivers (partial), and unspecified assistantships also available. Support available to part-time students. Financial award application deadline: 3/15; financial award applicants required to submit FAFSA. *Faculty research:* Musicology, music theory, jazz, music education, performance and conducting. Total annual research expenditures: $23,000. *Unit head:* Dr. Cecilia Wang, Director of Graduate Studies, 859-230-2306, Fax: 859-257-9576. *Application contact:* Dr. Brian Jackson, Senior Associate Dean, 859-257-4667, Fax: 859-257-4676, E-mail: brian.jackson@uky.edu.

University of Lethbridge, School of Graduate Studies, Lethbridge, AB T1K 3M4, Canada. Offers accounting (MScM); addictions counseling (M Sc); agricultural biotechnology (M Sc); agricultural studies (M Sc, MA); anthropology (MA); archaeology (MA); art (MA); biochemistry (M Sc); biological sciences (M Sc); biomolecular science (PhD); biosystems and biodiversity (PhD); Canadian studies (MA); chemistry (M Sc); computer science (M Sc); computer science and geographical information science (M Sc); counseling psychology (M Ed); dramatic arts (MA); earth, space, and physical science (PhD); economics (MA); educational leadership (M Ed); English (MA); environmental science (M Sc); evolution and behavior (PhD); exercise science (M Sc); finance (MScM); French (MA); French/German (MA); French/Spanish (MA); general education (M Ed); general management (MScM); geography (M Sc, MA); German (MA); health sciences (M Sc, MA); history (MA); human resource management and labour relations (MScM); individualized multidisciplinary (M Sc, MA); information systems (MScM); international management (MScM); kinesiology (M Sc, MA); management (M Sc, MA); marketing (MScM); mathematics (M Sc); music (MA); Native American studies (MA); neuroscience (M Sc, PhD); new media (MA); nursing (M Sc); philosophy (MA); physics (M Sc); policy and strategy (MScM); political science (MA); psychology (M Sc, MA); religious studies (MA); sociology (MA); theoretical and computational science (PhD); urban and regional studies (MA). Part-time and evening/weekend programs available. *Students:* 215 full-time, 98 part-time. In 2007, 87 master's, 1 doctorate awarded. *Degree requirements:* For doctorate, comprehensive exam, thesis/dissertation. *Entrance requirements:* For master's, GMAT (M Sc in management), bachelor's degree in related field, minimum GPA of 3.0 during previous 20 graded semester courses, 2 years teaching or related experience (M Ed); for doctorate, master's degree, minimum graduate GPA of 3.5. Additional exam requirements/recommendations for international students: Required—TOEFL. Application fee: $60 Canadian dollars. *Financial support:* Fellowships, research assistantships, teaching assistantships, scholarships/grants, health care benefits, and unspecified assistantships available. *Faculty research:* Movement and brain plasticity, gibberellin physiology, photosynthesis, carbon cycling, molecular properties of main-group ring components. *Unit head:* Dr. Jo-Anne Fiske, Interim Dean, 403-329-2121, Fax: 403-329-2097. *Application contact:* Jennifer Geddes, Graduate Liaison Officer, 403-329-2762, Fax: 403-329-5159, E-mail: jennifer.geddes@uleth.ca.

University of Louisiana at Lafayette, Graduate School, College of the Arts, School of Music, Lafayette, LA 70504. Offers conducting (MM); pedagogy (MM); vocal and instrumental performance (MM). *Accreditation:* NASM. *Degree requirements:* For master's, thesis or alternative. *Entrance requirements:* For master's, GRE General Test, minimum GPA of 2.75. Additional exam requirements/recommendations for international students: Required—TOEFL (minimum score 550 paper-based; 213 computer-based). Electronic applications accepted. *Faculty research:* Nineteenth century American music, trumpet pedagogy, fifteenth century Renaissance polyphony, Charles Ives.

University of Louisiana at Monroe, Graduate Studies and Research, College of Arts and Sciences, School of Visual and Performing Arts, Program in Music, Monroe, LA 71209-0001. Offers MM. *Accreditation:* NASM. Part-time programs available. *Faculty:* 9 full-time (3 women). *Students:* 8 full-time (3 women), 5 part-time (2 women); includes 3 minority (all African Americans) Average age 32. In 2007, 4 degrees awarded. *Entrance requirements:* For master's, GRE. Additional exam requirements/recommendations for international students: Required—TOEFL (minimum score 500 paper-based; 173 computer-based; 61 iBT). *Application deadline:* For fall admission, 8/22 priority date for domestic students, 7/1 for international students; for winter admission, 12/12 priority date for domestic students; for spring admission, 1/17 for domestic students, 11/1 for international students. Application fee: $20 ($30 for international students). *Expenses:* Tuition, state resident: full-time $2,220. Tuition, nonresident: full-time $8,172. *Financial support:* In 2007–08, 5 teaching assistantships with full tuition reimbursements (averaging $2,500 per year) were awarded; research assistantships with full tuition reimbursements, career-related internships or fieldwork, Federal Work-Study, and unspecified assistantships also available. Financial award application deadline: 4/1; financial award applicants required to submit FAFSA. *Unit head:* Dr. Mark R. Clark, Dean, 318-342-1569, Fax: 318-342-1599, E-mail: mclark@ulm.edu.

University of Louisville, Graduate School, School of Music, Program in Music History, Louisville, KY 40292-0001. Offers music history and literature (MM); musicology (PhD). *Accreditation:* NASM (one or more programs are accredited). Part-time programs available. *Degree requirements:* For master's, one foreign language, thesis; for doctorate, 2 foreign languages, thesis/dissertation. *Entrance requirements:* For master's, GRE General Test, music history and theory exam; for doctorate, GRE General Test. *Application deadline:* For fall admission, 3/15 priority date for domestic students; for winter admission, 10/1 priority date for domestic students. Applications are processed on a rolling basis. Application fee: $50. *Financial support:* Unspecified assistantships available. *Unit head:* Dr. Jean M. Christensen, Division Head, 502-852-0540, Fax: 502-852-0520, E-mail: jmchri01@gwise.louisville.edu.

University of Louisville, Graduate School, School of Music, Program in Music Performance, Louisville, KY 40292-0001. Offers performance (MM); theory and composition (MM). *Accreditation:* NASM. Part-time programs available. *Students:* 56 full-time (20 women), 5 part-time (1 woman); includes 6 minority (2 African Americans, 2 Asian Americans or Pacific Islanders, 2 Hispanic Americans), 11 international. Average age 27. In 2007, 31 degrees awarded. *Degree requirements:* For master's, 3 foreign languages, thesis (for some programs), recital. *Entrance requirements:* For master's, GRE General Test, music history and theory exam, jazz entrance exams (for jazz students), performance audition. *Application deadline:* For fall admission, 3/15 priority date for domestic students. Applications are processed on a rolling basis. Application fee: $50. *Financial support:* Teaching assistantships with tuition reimbursements, scholarships/grants and unspecified assistantships available. *Unit head:* John R. Jones, Division Head, 502-852-4342, Fax: 502-852-0520, E-mail: jrjone02@louisville.edu.

University of Maine, Graduate School, College of Liberal Arts and Sciences, School of Performing Arts, Department of Music, Orono, ME 04469. Offers MM. *Accreditation:* NASM. Part-time programs available. *Faculty:* 14 full-time (4 women), 6 part-time/adjunct (3 women). *Students:* 5 full-time (all women), 2 part-time, 1 international. Average age 32. 7 applicants, 57% accepted, 4 enrolled. In 2007, 1 master's awarded. *Degree requirements:* For master's, rehearsal demonstration, recital. *Entrance requirements:* For master's, GRE General Test, audition. Additional exam requirements/recommendations for international students: Required—TOEFL. *Application deadline:* For fall admission, 2/1 priority date for domestic students. Applications are processed on a rolling basis. Application fee: $60. Electronic applications accepted. *Financial support:* In 2007–08, 3 teaching assistantships with tuition reimbursements (averaging $9,010 per year) were awarded; fellowships, research assistantships, career-related internships or fieldwork, Federal Work-Study, institutionally sponsored loans, scholarships/grants, and tuition waivers (full and partial) also available. Financial award application deadline: 3/1. *Faculty research:* Curriculum development, rehearsal techniques, faculty development, pedagogical technology. *Unit head:* Dr. Dennis Cox, Coordinator, 207-581-1245. *Application contact:* Scott G. Delcourt, Associate Dean of the Graduate School, 207-581-3219, Fax: 207-581-3232, E-mail: graduate@maine.edu.

University of Manitoba, Faculty of Graduate Studies, Faculty of Music, Winnipeg, MB R3T 2N2, Canada. Offers M Mus.

University of Maryland, Baltimore County, Graduate School, College of Arts, Humanities and Social Sciences, Department of Music, Baltimore, MD 21250. Offers American contemporary music (Postbaccalaureate Certificate). Part-time programs available. *Faculty:* 9 full-time (4 women). *Students:* 5 full-time (all women), 2 part-time (1 woman), 5 international. Average age 23. 8 applicants, 88% accepted, 7 enrolled. In 2007, 7 degrees awarded. *Entrance requirements:* For degree, minimum GPA of 3.0, resumé, reference letters, VHS tape of performance. *Application deadline:* For fall admission, 12/1 priority date for domestic and international students; for winter admission, 1/30 priority date for domestic and international students; for spring admission, 5/15 for domestic students, 3/1 for international students. Applications are processed on a rolling basis. Application fee: $50. *Faculty research:* Music, composition, performance, music technology, contemporary music. *Unit head:* Dr. Linda Dusman, Chair, 410-455-2026, E-mail: dusman@umbc.edu. *Application contact:* Dr. Kazuko Tanosaki, Director, 410-455-2814, Fax: 410-455-1181, E-mail: tanosaki@umbc.edu.

University of Maryland, College Park, Graduate Studies, College of Arts and Humanities, School of Music, Program in Ethnomusicology, College Park, MD 20742. Offers MA. *Students:* 25 full-time (18 women), 4 part-time (3 women); includes 6 minority (3 African Americans, 1 American Indian/Alaska Native, 1 Asian American or Pacific Islander, 1 Hispanic American), 10 international. 13 applicants, 46% accepted, 4 enrolled. In 2007, 1 master's awarded. *Degree requirements:* For master's, comprehensive exam, thesis optional, oral defense. *Entrance requirements:* Additional exam requirements/recommendations for international students: Required—TOEFL. *Application deadline:* For fall admission, 12/1 for domestic students, 2/1 for international students; for spring admission, 11/1 for domestic students, 6/1 for international students. Application fee: $60. *Financial support:* In 2007–08, 1 fellowship (averaging $10,800 per year), 13 teaching assistantships (averaging $15,323 per year) were awarded. *Application contact:* Dean of Graduate School, 301-405-0358, Fax: 301-314-9305.

University of Maryland, College Park, Graduate Studies, College of Arts and Humanities, School of Music, Program in Music, College Park, MD 20742. Offers M Ed, MA, MM, DMA, Ed D, PhD. *Students:* 193 full-time (115 women), 79 part-time (40 women); includes 35 minority (7 African Americans, 26 Asian Americans or Pacific Islanders, 2 Hispanic Americans), 68 international. 573 applicants, 23% accepted, 72 enrolled. In 2007, 47 master's, 30 doctorates awarded. *Median time to degree:* Of those who began their doctoral program in fall 1999, 53% received their degree in 8 years or less. *Entrance requirements:* Additional exam requirements/recommendations for international students: Required—TOEFL. *Application deadline:* For fall admission, 12/1 for domestic students, 2/1 for international students; for spring admission, 11/1 for domestic students, 6/1 for international students. Application fee: $60. *Financial support:* In 2007–08, 1 fellowship (averaging $13,926 per year) was awarded. *Application contact:* Dean of Graduate School, 301-405-0358, Fax: 301-314-9305.

University of Massachusetts Amherst, Graduate School, College of Humanities and Fine Arts, Department of Music and Dance, Amherst, MA 01003. Offers music (MM, PhD). *Accreditation:* NASM. Part-time programs available. Postbaccalaureate distance learning degree programs offered. *Faculty:* 16 full-time (3 women). *Students:* 48 full-time (22 women), 25 part-time (15 women); includes 5 minority (2 African Americans, 2 Asian Americans or Pacific Islanders, 1 Hispanic American), 14 international. Average age 29. 62 applicants, 69% accepted, 23 enrolled. In 2007, 29 degrees awarded. *Degree requirements:* For master's, one foreign language, thesis or alternative; for doctorate, 2 foreign languages, thesis/dissertation. *Entrance requirements:* For master's, GRE General Test, placement tests, original scores, research papers, or audition tape and placement tests; for doctorate, GRE General Test. Additional exam requirements/recommendations for international students: Required—TOEFL (minimum score 530 paper-based; 197 computer-based). *Application deadline:* For fall admission, 2/1 priority date for domestic and international students; for spring admission, 10/1 for domestic and international students. Applications are processed on a rolling basis. Application fee: $50 ($65 for international students). Electronic applications accepted. *Expenses:* Tuition, state resident: full-time $2,640; part-time $110 per credit. Tuition, nonresident: full-time $9,936; part-time $414 per credit. Required fees: $7,455. One-time fee: $332. Tuition and fees vary according to course load, campus/location, program and reciprocity agreements. *Financial support:* In 2007–08, 15 fellowships with full tuition reimbursements (averaging $3,455 per year), 47 teaching assistantships with full tuition reimbursements (averaging $5,795 per year) were awarded; research assistantships with full tuition reimbursements, career-related internships or fieldwork, Federal Work-Study, scholarships/grants, traineeships, and unspecified assistantships also available. Support available to part-time students. Financial award application deadline: 2/1. *Unit head:* Dr. Jeff Cox, Chair, 413-545-0311, Fax: 413-545-2092, E-mail: jcox@music.umass.edu.

University of Massachusetts Lowell, College of Arts and Sciences, Department of Music, Lowell, MA 01854-2881. Offers music education (MM); sound recording technology (MM). *Accreditation:* NASM. Part-time programs available. *Faculty:* 14. *Degree requirements:* For master's, one foreign language, thesis. *Entrance requirements:* For master's, MAT, audition. *Application deadline:* For fall admission, 4/1 priority date for domestic students; for spring admission, 10/1 for domestic students. Applications are processed on a rolling basis. Application fee: $20 ($35 for international students). Electronic applications accepted. *Financial support:* Fellowships, teaching assistantships, career-related internships or fieldwork, Federal Work-Study, and scholarships/grants available. Support available to part-time students. Financial award application deadline: 4/1. *Unit head:* Paula Telesco, Chairperson, 978-934-3870, E-mail: paula_telesco@uml.edu. *Application contact:* Anthony Mele, Coordinator, 978-934-3896, E-mail: anthony_mele@uml.edu.

University of Memphis, Graduate School, College of Communication and Fine Arts, Rudi E. Scheidt School of Music, Memphis, TN 38152. Offers applied music (M Mu, DMA); composition (M Mu, DMA); conducting (M Mu, DMA); historical musicology (PhD); jazz and studio performance (M Mu); music education (M Mu, DMA); musicology (M Mu). *Accreditation:* NASM. Part-time programs available. *Faculty:* 38 full-time (9 women), 6 part-time/adjunct (3 women). *Students:* 84 full-time (35 women), 51 part-time (18 women); includes 21 minority (17 African Americans, 1 American Indian/Alaska Native, 2 Asian Americans or Pacific Islanders, 1 Hispanic American), 34 international. Average age 32. 101 applicants, 50% accepted, 28 enrolled. In 2007, 13 master's, 4 doctorates awarded. Terminal master's awarded for partial completion of doctoral program. *Degree requirements:* For master's, comprehensive exam, thesis or alternative; for doctorate, one foreign language, comprehensive exam, thesis/dissertation, exam. *Entrance requirements:* For master's, GRE General Test or MAT, proficiency exam, audition; for doctorate, GRE General Test or MAT, proficiency exam, audition, master's degree. Additional exam requirements/recommendations for international students: Required—TOEFL. *Application deadline:* For fall admission, 8/1 for domestic students; for spring admission, 12/1 for domestic students. Applications are processed on a rolling basis. Application fee: $35 ($60 for international students). *Expenses:* Tuition, state resident: full-time $6,990; part-time $377 per hour. Tuition, nonresident: full-time $17,818; part-time $830 per hour. Tuition and fees vary according to course load and program. *Financial support:* In 2007–08, 32 research assistantships with full and partial tuition reimbursements (averaging $6,050 per year), 35 teaching assistantships with full and partial tuition reimbursements (averaging $6,200 per year) were awarded. *Faculty research:* Spanish Renaissance, twentieth century music, Project OPTIMUS, composition, musical performance, regional music, performance, performance practice, composition. *Unit head:* Dr. Patricia J. Hoy, Director, 901-678-3764, Fax: 901-678-0708, E-mail: phoy@memphis.edu. *Application contact:* Dr. John Baur, Assistant Director for Graduate Admissions, 901-678-3764, Fax: 901-678-0708, E-mail: jbaur@memphis.edu.

University of Miami, Graduate School, Frost School of Music, Department of Instrumental Performance, Coral Gables, FL 33124. Offers instrumental conducting (MM, DMA); instrumental performance (MM, DMA, AD); multiple woodwinds (MM, DMA). *Accreditation:* NASM. *Faculty:* 13 full-time (2 women), 9 part-time/adjunct (3 women). *Students:* 45 full-time (19 women), 2 part-time (1 woman); includes 3 minority (1 African American, 1 Asian American or Pacific Islander, 1 Hispanic American), 13 international. Average age 28. 58 applicants, 47% accepted, 15 enrolled. In 2007, 10 master's, 4 doctorates awarded. *Median time to degree:* Of those who began their doctoral program in fall 1999, 100% received their degree in 8 years or less. *Degree requirements:* For master's, thesis, recital paper, recital; for doctorate, thesis/dissertation, essay, 2 research tools, 3 recitals. *Entrance requirements:* For master's and doctorate, GRE General Test, audition. Additional exam requirements/recommendations for international students: Required—TOEFL (minimum score 550 paper-based; 213 computer-based; 59 iBT). *Application deadline:* For fall admission, 2/1 priority date for domestic and international students; for spring admission, 11/1 priority date for domestic and international students. Applications are processed on a rolling basis. Application fee: $65. Electronic applications accepted. *Financial support:* In 2007–08, 32 students received support, including 1 fellowship with tuition reimbursement available (averaging $22,000 per year), 21 teaching assistantships with full tuition reimbursements available (averaging $10,000 per year); career-related internships or fieldwork, Federal Work-Study, and tuition waivers (full and partial) also available. Financial award application deadline: 2/1. *Unit head:* Gary Green, Chair and Director, 305-284-7926, E-mail: gdgreen@miami.edu.

University of Miami, Graduate School, Frost School of Music, Department of Keyboard Performance, Coral Gables, FL 33124. Offers accompanying and chamber music (MM, DMA); keyboard performance and pedagogy (MM, DMA); piano performance (MM, DMA, AD). *Accreditation:* NASM. *Faculty:* 7 full-time (2 women), 1 part-time/adjunct (0 women). *Students:* 34 full-time (26 women); includes 3 minority (1 Asian American or Pacific Islander, 2 Hispanic Americans), 23 international. Average age 28. 35 applicants, 37% accepted, 8 enrolled. In 2007, 3 master's, 7 doctorates awarded. *Degree requirements:* For master's, thesis, recital paper, recital; for doctorate, thesis/dissertation, essay, 2 research tools, 3 recitals. *Entrance requirements:* For master's and doctorate, GRE General Test, audition. Additional exam requirements/recommendations for international students: Required—TOEFL (minimum score 555 paper-based; 213 computer-based; 59 iBT). *Application deadline:* For fall admission, 2/1 priority date for domestic and international students; for spring admission, 11/1 priority date for domestic and international students. Applications are processed on a rolling basis. Application fee: $65. Electronic applications accepted. *Financial support:* In 2007–08, 20 students received support, including fellowships with full tuition reimbursements available (averaging $22,000 per year), 12 teaching assistantships with full and partial tuition reimbursements available (averaging $10,000 per year); career-related internships or fieldwork, Federal Work-Study, and tuition waivers (full and partial) also available. Financial award application deadline: 2/1. *Unit head:* Dr. Robert J. Floyd, Chair, 305-284-4886, E-mail: jbfloyd@miami.edu. *Application contact:* Dr. Edward Paul Asmus, Associate Dean for Graduate Studies, 305-284-2241, Fax: 305-284-6475, E-mail: ed.asmus@miami.edu.

University of Miami, Graduate School, Frost School of Music, Department of Music Media and Industry, Coral Gables, FL 33124. Offers music business and entertainment industries (MM); music engineering (MS). *Accreditation:* NASM. *Faculty:* 6 full-time (1 woman), 1 part-time/adjunct (0 women). *Students:* 26 full-time (9 women); includes 6 minority (3 African Americans, 1 American Indian/Alaska Native, 2 Hispanic Americans), 5 international. 43 applicants, 49% accepted, 14 enrolled. In 2007, 24 master's awarded. *Median time to degree:* Of those who began their doctoral program in fall 1999, 100% received their degree in 8 years or less. *Degree requirements:* For master's, thesis, internship (MM, music business and entertainment industries), research project (MS). *Entrance requirements:* For master's, GRE General Test. Additional exam requirements/recommendations for international students: Required—TOEFL (minimum score 550 paper-based; 213 computer-based; 59 iBT). *Application deadline:* For fall admission, 2/1 priority date for domestic and international students; for spring admission, 11/1 priority date for domestic and international students. Applications are processed on a rolling basis. Application fee: $65. Electronic applications accepted. *Financial support:* In 2007–08, 24 students received support, including 7 teaching assistantships with full tuition reimbursements available (averaging $10,000 per year); tuition waivers (partial) also available. Financial award application deadline: 2/1. *Unit head:* Prof. James Progris, Chair and Director, 305-284-6252, E-mail: jp@miami.edu. *Application contact:* Dr. Edward Paul Asmus, Associate Dean for Graduate Studies, 305-284-2241, Fax: 305-284-6475, E-mail: ed.asmus@miami.edu.

University of Miami, Graduate School, Frost School of Music, Department of Musicology, Coral Gables, FL 33124. Offers MM. *Accreditation:* NASM. *Faculty:* 3 full-time (2 women), 1 part-time/adjunct (0 women). *Students:* 5 full-time (4 women); includes 1 minority (Asian American or Pacific Islander), 1 international. Average age 34. 3 applicants, 100% accepted, 3 enrolled. In 2007, 1 degree awarded. *Degree requirements:* For master's, thesis. *Entrance requirements:* For master's, GRE General Test. Additional exam requirements/recommendations for international students: Required—TOEFL (minimum score 550 paper-based; 213 computer-based; 59 iBT). *Application deadline:* For fall admission, 2/1 priority date for domestic and international students; for spring admission, 11/1 priority date for domestic and international

Music

University of Miami (continued)
students. Applications are processed on a rolling basis. Application fee: $65. Electronic applications accepted. *Financial support:* In 2007–08, 4 students received support, including 2 teaching assistantships with full tuition reimbursements available (averaging $10,000 per year); tuition waivers (partial) also available. Financial award application deadline: 2/1. *Unit head:* Dr. Deborah Schwartz-Kates, Chair, 305-284-2241, E-mail: dkates@miami.edu. *Application contact:* Dr. Edward Paul Asmus, Associate Dean for Graduate Studies, 305-284-2241, Fax: 305-284-6475, E-mail: ed.asmus@miami.edu.

University of Miami, Graduate School, Frost School of Music, Department of Music Theory-Composition, Coral Gables, FL 33124. Offers composition (MM, DMA); electronic music (MM); media writing and production (MM); music theory (MM). *Accreditation:* NASM. *Faculty:* 7 full-time (0 women), 1 part-time/adjunct (0 women). *Students:* 14 full-time (5 women), 1 part-time; includes 4 minority (2 African Americans, 2 Hispanic Americans). 29 applicants, 38% accepted, 5 enrolled. In 2007, 2 master's, 3 doctorates awarded. *Median time to degree:* Of those who began their doctoral program in fall 1999, 100% received their degree in 8 years or less. *Degree requirements:* For master's, thesis; for doctorate, thesis/dissertation, essay. *Entrance requirements:* For master's and doctorate, GRE General Test, portfolio. Additional exam requirements/recommendations for international students: Required—TOEFL (minimum score 550 paper-based; 213 computer-based; 59 iBT). *Application deadline:* For fall admission, 2/1 priority date for domestic and international students; for spring admission, 11/1 priority date for domestic and international students. Applications are processed on a rolling basis. Application fee: $65. Electronic applications accepted. *Financial support:* In 2007–08, 12 students received support, including fellowships with full tuition reimbursements available (averaging $22,000 per year), 8 teaching assistantships with full tuition reimbursements available (averaging $10,000 per year); career-related internships or fieldwork, Federal Work-Study, and tuition waivers (partial) also available. Financial award application deadline: 2/1. *Unit head:* Dr. Dennis Kam, Chair, 305-284-6252, E-mail: d.kam@miami.edu. *Application contact:* Dr. Edward Paul Asmus, Associate Dean for Graduate Studies, 305-284-2241, Fax: 305-284-6475, E-mail: ed.asmus@miami.edu.

University of Miami, Graduate School, Frost School of Music, Department of Studio Music and Jazz, Coral Gables, FL 33124. Offers jazz composition (DMA); jazz pedagogy (MM); jazz performance (MM, DMA); studio jazz writing (MM). *Accreditation:* NASM. *Faculty:* 11 full-time (1 woman), 3 part-time/adjunct (0 women). *Students:* 29 full-time (2 women), 1 part-time; includes 6 minority (2 African Americans, 1 Asian American or Pacific Islander, 3 Hispanic Americans), 3 international. 55 applicants, 42% accepted, 9 enrolled. In 2007, 24 master's awarded. *Median time to degree:* Of those who began their doctoral program in fall 1999, 100% received their degree in 8 years or less. *Degree requirements:* For master's, thesis. *Entrance requirements:* For master's and doctorate, GRE General Test, portfolio. Additional exam requirements/recommendations for international students: Required—TOEFL (minimum score 550 paper-based; 213 computer-based; 59 iBT). *Application deadline:* For fall admission, 2/1 priority date for domestic and international students; for spring admission, 11/1 priority date for domestic and international students. Applications are processed on a rolling basis. Application fee: $65. Electronic applications accepted. *Financial support:* In 2007–08, 26 students received support, including fellowships with full tuition reimbursements available (averaging $22,000 per year), 7 teaching assistantships with full tuition reimbursements available (averaging $10,000 per year); career-related internships or fieldwork, Federal Work-Study, and tuition waivers (full and partial) also available. Financial award application deadline: 2/1. *Unit head:* Prof. Whitney Sidener, Chair and Director, 305-284-5813, E-mail: wsidener@miami.edu. *Application contact:* Dr. Edward Paul Asmus, Associate Dean for Graduate Studies, 305-284-2241, Fax: 305-284-6475, E-mail: ed.asmus@miami.edu.

University of Miami, Graduate School, Frost School of Music, Department of Vocal Performance, Coral Gables, FL 33124. Offers choral conducting (MM, DMA); vocal pedagogy (DMA); vocal performance (MM, DMA, AD). *Accreditation:* NASM. *Faculty:* 8 full-time (2 women), 6 part-time/adjunct (5 women). *Students:* 24 full-time (9 women), 1 (woman) part-time; includes 1 minority (Hispanic American), 4 international. 39 applicants, 51% accepted, 9 enrolled. In 2007, 2 master's, 1 doctorate awarded. *Median time to degree:* Of those who began their doctoral program in fall 1999, 100% received their degree in 8 years or less. *Degree requirements:* For master's, 2 foreign languages, thesis, recital paper; for doctorate, thesis/dissertation, essay. *Entrance requirements:* For master's and doctorate, GRE General Test, audition. Additional exam requirements/recommendations for international students: Required—TOEFL (minimum score 550 paper-based; 213 computer-based; 59 iBT). *Application deadline:* For fall admission, 2/1 priority date for domestic and international students; for spring admission, 11/1 priority date for domestic and international students. Applications are processed on a rolling basis. Application fee: $65. Electronic applications accepted. *Financial support:* In 2007–08, 22 students received support, including fellowships with full tuition reimbursements available (averaging $22,000 per year), 14 teaching assistantships with tuition reimbursements available (averaging $10,000 per year); research assistantships, tuition waivers (partial) also available. Financial award application deadline: 2/1. *Unit head:* Dr. David Alt, Chair and Director, 305-284-4886, E-mail: dalt@miami.edu. *Application contact:* Dr. Edward Paul Asmus, Associate Dean for Graduate Studies, 305-284-2241, Fax: 305-284-6475, E-mail: ed.asmus@miami.edu.

University of Michigan, Horace H. Rackham School of Graduate Studies, The School of Music, Theatre, and Dance, Ann Arbor, MI 48109. Offers MA, MFA, MM, A Mus D, PhD, Spec M, MBA/MM. *Accreditation:* NASM. *Entrance requirements:* For master's, audition, portfolio, interview. Additional exam requirements/recommendations for international students: Required—TOEFL (minimum score 560 paper-based; 237 computer-based). Electronic applications accepted.

University of Minnesota, Duluth, Graduate School, School of Fine Arts, Department of Music, Duluth, MN 55812-2496. Offers music education (MM); performance (MM). *Accreditation:* NASM. Part-time programs available. *Faculty:* 14 full-time (4 women), 2 part-time/adjunct (1 woman). *Students:* 6 full-time (2 women), 6 part-time (4 women). Average age 31. 1 applicant, 100% accepted, 1 enrolled. In 2007, 2 degrees awarded. *Degree requirements:* For master's, comprehensive exam, thesis (for some programs), recital (MM in performance). *Entrance requirements:* For master's, audition, minimum GPA of 3.0, sample of written work, interview, bachelor's degree in music, video of teaching. Additional exam requirements/recommendations for international students: Required—TOEFL (minimum score 550 paper-based; 213 computer-based). *Application deadline:* For fall admission, 7/15 for domestic students; for spring admission, 11/15 for domestic students. Applications are processed on a rolling basis. Application fee: $55 ($75 for international students). *Expenses:* Tuition, state resident: part-time $812 per credit. Tuition, nonresident: part-time $1,403 per credit. Tuition and fees vary according to program. *Financial support:* In 2007–08, 6 students received support, including 1 fellowship (averaging $4,500 per year), 5 teaching assistantships with tuition reimbursements available (averaging $6,000 per year); Federal Work-Study, institutionally sponsored loans, scholarships/grants, and unspecified assistantships also available. *Faculty research:* Band composition, music aesthetics, learning theory, value theory, music advocacy. *Unit head:* Dr. Judith Kritzmire, Director of Graduate Studies, 218-726-8260, Fax: 218-726-8210, E-mail: jkritzmire@d.umn.edu.

University of Minnesota, Twin Cities Campus, Graduate School, College of Liberal Arts, School of Music, Minneapolis, MN 55455-0213. Offers MA, MM, DMA, PhD. *Accreditation:* NASM. *Faculty:* 45 full-time (13 women), 48 part-time/adjunct (17 women). *Students:* 178 full-time (86 women), 40 part-time (17 women); includes 19 minority (5 African Americans, 2 American Indian/Alaska Native, 11 Asian Americans or Pacific Islanders, 1 Hispanic American), 41 international. 391 applicants, 30% accepted, 80 enrolled. In 2007, 63 master's, 37 doctorates awarded. *Degree requirements:* For master's, comprehensive exam, thesis (for some programs), foreign language (MA), recital (MM); for doctorate, comprehensive exam, thesis/dissertation (for some programs), 5 recitals (DMA); 2 foreign languages or computer languages, dissertation (PhD). *Entrance requirements:* For master's, GRE (MA); for doctorate, GRE (PhD). Additional exam requirements/recommendations for international students: Required—TOEFL (minimum score 550 paper-based; 213 computer-based; 79 iBT), IELTS (minimum score 7). *Application deadline:* For fall admission, 1/1 for domestic and international students; for spring admission, 10/15 for domestic and international students. Applications are processed on a rolling basis. Application fee: $55 ($75 for international students). Electronic applications accepted. *Financial support:* In 2007–08, 190 students received support, including 32 fellowships with partial tuition reimbursements available, 1 research assistantship with partial tuition reimbursement available, 94 teaching assistantships with partial tuition reimbursements available; Federal Work-Study, institutionally sponsored loans, scholarships/grants, health care benefits, tuition waivers (full and partial), and unspecified assistantships also available. Financial award application deadline: 2/9; financial award applicants required to submit FAFSA. *Unit head:* Jerry Luckhardt, Director, 612-626-1882, Fax: 612-626-2200. *Application contact:* Admissions Coordinator, 612-624-2847, Fax: 612-624-8001, E-mail: mnmusic@umn.edu.

University of Mississippi, Graduate School, College of Liberal Arts, Department of Music, Oxford, University, MS 38677. Offers MM, DA. *Accreditation:* NASM. *Faculty:* 27 full-time (6 women), 10 part-time/adjunct (7 women). *Students:* 39 full-time (15 women), 11 part-time (4 women); includes 11 minority (all African Americans), 4 international. In 2007, 8 master's, 3 doctorates awarded. *Degree requirements:* For master's, thesis (for some programs); for doctorate, thesis/dissertation. *Entrance requirements:* For master's, GRE General Test, minimum GPA of 3.0; for doctorate, GRE General Test. Additional exam requirements/recommendations for international students: Required—TOEFL. *Application deadline:* For fall admission, 4/1 for domestic students; for spring admission, 10/1 for domestic students. Applications are processed on a rolling basis. Application fee: $25. Electronic applications accepted. *Expenses:* Tuition, state resident: full-time $4,932. Tuition, nonresident: full-time $11,436. *Financial support:* Scholarships/grants available. Financial award application deadline: 3/1; financial award applicants required to submit FAFSA. *Unit head:* Dr. Charles Gates, Chairman, 662-915-7268, Fax: 662-915-7443, E-mail: music@olemiss.edu.

University of Missouri–Columbia, Graduate School, College of Arts and Sciences, School of Music, Columbia, MO 65211. Offers MA, MM. *Accreditation:* NASM. *Degree requirements:* For master's, 3 foreign languages, thesis. *Entrance requirements:* For master's, GRE General Test, minimum GPA of 3.0.

University of Missouri–Kansas City, Conservatory of Music, Kansas City, MO 64110-2499. Offers composition (MM, DMA); conducting (MM, DMA); music (MA); music education (MME, PhD); music history and literature (MM); music theory (MM); performance (MM, DMA). *Accreditation:* NASM. Part-time programs available. *Faculty:* 51 full-time (21 women), 32 part-time/adjunct (17 women). *Students:* 136 full-time (75 women), 120 part-time (56 women); includes 15 minority (7 African Americans, 1 American Indian/Alaska Native, 3 Asian Americans or Pacific Islanders, 4 Hispanic Americans), 59 international. Average age 29. 244 applicants, 48% accepted, 67 enrolled. In 2007, 47 master's, 14 doctorates awarded. *Median time to degree:* Of those who began their doctoral program in fall 1999, 62.2% received their degree in 8 years or less. *Degree requirements:* For master's, variable foreign language requirement, comprehensive exam, thesis (for some programs); for doctorate, variable foreign language requirement, comprehensive exam, thesis/dissertation or alternative. *Entrance requirements:* For master's, minimum GPA of 3.0 in major, auditions (performance); for doctorate, minimum graduate GPA of 3.5, auditions (performance degrees), portfolio of compositions. Additional exam requirements/recommendations for international students: Required—TOEFL (minimum score 550 paper-based; 213 computer-based). *Application deadline:* For fall admission, 1/15 priority date for domestic students, 1/15 for international students. Application fee: $35 ($50 for international students). *Expenses:* Tuition, state resident: part-time $287 per hour. Tuition, nonresident: part-time $741 per hour. Required fees: $31 per hour. Tuition and fees vary according to program. *Financial support:* In 2007–08, 135 students received support, including 43 teaching assistantships with partial tuition reimbursements available (averaging $8,256 per year); fellowships with partial tuition reimbursements available, career-related internships or fieldwork, Federal Work-Study, institutionally sponsored loans, scholarships/grants, tuition waivers (partial), and unspecified assistantships also available. Support available to part-time students. Financial award application deadline: 3/1; financial award applicants required to submit FAFSA. *Faculty research:* Electro-acoustic composition, affective music responses, American music theatre, Russian choral music, music therapy and Alzheimer's. Total annual research expenditures: $42,203. *Unit head:* Peter Witte, Dean, 816-235-2731, Fax: 816-235-5265. *Application contact:* James Elswick, Associate Director, 816-235-2932, Fax: 816-235-5264, E-mail: cadmissions@umkc.edu.

The University of Montana, Graduate School, School of Fine Arts, Department of Music, Missoula, MT 59812-0002. Offers music (MM), including composition/technology, music education, musical theater, performance. *Accreditation:* NASM. *Entrance requirements:* For master's, GRE General Test, GRE Subject Test, portfolio.

University of Montevallo, College of Fine Arts, Department of Music, Montevallo, AL 35115. Offers M Ed. *Accreditation:* NASM. Part-time programs available. *Degree requirements:* For master's, comprehensive exam, thesis or alternative. *Entrance requirements:* For master's, GRE General Test or MAT, audition, interview, minimum undergraduate GPA of 2.75 in last 60 hours or 2.5 overall. Additional exam requirements/recommendations for international students: Required—TOEFL (minimum score 550 paper-based).

University of Nebraska at Omaha, Graduate Studies and Research, College of Communication, Fine Arts and Media, Department of Music, Omaha, NE 68182. Offers MM. *Accreditation:* NASM. Part-time and evening/weekend programs available. *Faculty:* 12 full-time (2 women). *Students:* 13 full-time (9 women), 19 part-time (15 women); includes 2 minority (1 African American, 1 Asian American or Pacific Islander), 3 international. Average age 33. 16 applicants, 69% accepted, 10 enrolled. In 2007, 9 degrees awarded. *Degree requirements:* For master's, comprehensive exam, thesis (for some programs). *Entrance requirements:* For master's, departmental diagnostic exam, minimum GPA of 3.0. Additional exam requirements/recommendations for international students: Required—TOEFL (minimum score 500 paper-based; 173 computer-based; 61 iBT). *Application deadline:* For fall admission, 6/15 priority date for domestic students; for spring admission, 11/15 priority date for domestic students. Applications are processed on a rolling basis. Application fee: $45. Electronic applications accepted. *Financial support:* In 2007–08, 20 students received support; research assistantships with tuition reimbursements available, career-related internships or fieldwork, Federal Work-Study, institutionally sponsored loans, scholarships/grants, tuition waivers (partial), and unspecified assistantships available. Support available to part-time students. Financial award application deadline: 3/1; financial award applicants required to submit FAFSA. *Unit head:* Dr. Melissa Berke, Chairperson, 402-554-2251.

University of Nebraska–Lincoln, Graduate College, College of Fine and Performing Arts, School of Music, Lincoln, NE 68588. Offers MM, DMA. *Accreditation:* NASM. *Degree requirements:* For master's, thesis optional; for doctorate, comprehensive exam, thesis/dissertation. *Entrance requirements:* For master's and doctorate, audition. Additional exam requirements/recommendations for international students: Required—TOEFL. Electronic applications accepted. *Faculty research:* Mozart, Tchaikovsky, Josquin des Prez, practice of J. S. Bach's organ works, instructional strategies in music education.

University of Nevada, Las Vegas, Graduate College, College of Fine Arts, Department of Music, Las Vegas, NV 89154-9900. Offers applied music (performance) (MM); composition/theory (MM); music education (MM); performance studies (DMA). *Accreditation:* NASM. Part-time programs available. *Faculty:* 31 full-time (9 women), 10 part-time/adjunct (3 women). *Students:* 58 full-time (22 women), 44 part-time (23 women); includes 14 minority (4 African Americans, 5 Asian Americans or Pacific Islanders, 5 Hispanic Americans), 8 international. 56 applicants, 70% accepted, 31 enrolled. In 2007, 23 degrees awarded. *Degree requirements:* For master's, thesis optional, oral and/or written comprehensive exam; for doctorate, comprehensive exam, lecture-recital and document. *Entrance requirements:* For master's, minimum GPA of 3.0. Additional exam requirements/recommendations for international students: Required—TOEFL (minimum score 550 paper-based; 213 computer-based; 80 iBT). *Application deadline:* For fall admission, 6/15 for domestic students, 5/1 for international students; for spring admission, 11/15 for domestic students, 10/1 for international students. Application fee: $60 ($75 for international students). Electronic applications accepted. *Expenses:* Tuition, state resident: part-time $198 per credit. Tuition, nonresident: part-time $416 per credit. Required fees: $256 per semester. Tuition and fees vary according to course load and reciprocity agreements. *Financial support:* In 2007–08, 16 research assistantships (averaging $10,000 per year), 20 teaching assistantships with partial tuition reimbursements (averaging $10,000 per year) were awarded; career-related internships or fieldwork, Federal Work-Study, institutionally sponsored loans, scholarships/grants, health care benefits, and unspecified assistantships also available. Support available to part-time students. Financial award application deadline: 3/1. *Unit head:* Dr. Bill Bernatis, Interim Chair, 702-895-3332. *Application contact:* Graduate College Admissions Evaluator, 702-895-3320, Fax: 702-895-4180, E-mail: gradcollege@unlv.edu.

University of Nevada, Reno, Graduate School, College of Liberal Arts, Department of Music, Reno, NV 89557. Offers MA, MM. *Accreditation:* NASM. *Faculty:* 29. *Students:* 9 full-time (3 women), 10 part-time (5 women); includes 1 minority (Asian American or Pacific Islander), 1 international. Average age 32. 22 applicants, 73% accepted, 9 enrolled. In 2007, 10 degrees awarded. *Degree requirements:* For master's, thesis optional. *Entrance requirements:* For master's, minimum GPA of 2.75. Additional exam requirements/recommendations for international students: Required—TOEFL. *Application deadline:* For fall admission, 3/1 priority date for domestic students; for spring admission, 11/1 for domestic students. Applications are processed on a rolling basis. Application fee: $60 ($95 for international students). *Expenses:* Tuition, state resident: full-time $2,774; part-time $154 per credit. Tuition, nonresident: full-time $13,578; part-time $330 per credit. Required fees: $49 per semester. *Financial support:* In 2007–08, 10 teaching assistantships were awarded; Federal Work-Study and institutionally sponsored loans also available. Financial award application deadline: 3/1. *Faculty research:* Performance, conducting, music composition and arranging. *Unit head:* Dr. Andrea Lenz, Graduate Program Director, 775-784-6145.

University of New Hampshire, Graduate School, College of Liberal Arts, Department of Music, Durham, NH 03824. Offers music education (MA); music history (MA). *Accreditation:* NASM. *Faculty:* 15 full-time. *Students:* 8 full-time (4 women), 4 part-time (2 women), 1 international. Average age 35. 9 applicants, 89% accepted, 6 enrolled. In 2007, 5 degrees awarded. *Degree requirements:* For master's, one foreign language. *Entrance requirements:* For master's, audition. Additional exam requirements/recommendations for international students: Required—TOEFL (minimum score 550 paper-based; 213 computer-based; 80 iBT). *Application deadline:* For fall admission, 4/1 priority date for domestic students; for winter admission, 12/1 for domestic students. Applications are processed on a rolling basis. Application fee: $60. Electronic applications accepted. *Financial support:* In 2007–08, 4 teaching assistantships were awarded; fellowships, research assistantships, career-related internships or fieldwork, Federal Work-Study, scholarships/grants, and tuition waivers (full and partial) also available. Support available to part-time students. Financial award application deadline: 2/15. *Unit head:* Dr. Mark DeTurk, Chairperson, 603-862-3244. *Application contact:* Dr. Isabel Gray, Administrative Assistant, 603-862-2418, E-mail: grad.music@unh.edu.

University of New Mexico, Graduate School, College of Fine Arts, Department of Music, Albuquerque, NM 87131-2039. Offers M Mu. *Accreditation:* NASM. Part-time programs available. *Faculty:* 30 full-time (11 women), 24 part-time/adjunct (12 women). *Students:* 51 full-time (27 women), 35 part-time (22 women); includes 16 minority (3 African Americans, 1 American Indian/Alaska Native, 1 Asian American or Pacific Islander, 11 Hispanic Americans), 24 international. Average age 30. 68 applicants, 60% accepted, 33 enrolled. In 2007, 29 degrees awarded. *Degree requirements:* For master's, thesis (for some programs), oral exam, recital in some programs. *Entrance requirements:* For master's, placement exams in music history and theory. Additional exam requirements/recommendations for international students: Required—TOEFL (minimum score 550 paper-based; 213 computer-based). *Application deadline:* For fall admission, 7/1 for domestic students; for spring admission, 11/1 for domestic students. Application fee: $50. Electronic applications accepted. *Financial support:* In 2007–08, 30 students received support, including 20 teaching assistantships with tuition reimbursements available (averaging $6,437 per year); Federal Work-Study, scholarships/grants, and unspecified assistantships also available. Support available to part-time students. Financial award application deadline: 3/1; financial award applicants required to submit FAFSA. *Faculty research:* Opera, twentieth century and contemporary music, performance, conducting. Total annual research expenditures: $3,149. *Unit head:* Dr. Steven Block, Chair, 505-277-2127, Fax: 505-277-0708, E-mail: sblock@unm.edu. *Application contact:* Colleen Sheinberg, Graduate Coordinator, 505-277-8401, Fax: 505-277-0708, E-mail: colleens@unm.edu.

University of New Orleans, Graduate School, College of Liberal Arts, Department of Music, New Orleans, LA 70148. Offers MM. *Accreditation:* NASM. Evening/weekend programs available. *Students:* 25 (7 women). Average age 29. In 2007, 12 degrees awarded. *Degree requirements:* For master's, recital. *Entrance requirements:* For master's, GRE General Test, audition. Additional exam requirements/recommendations for international students: Required—TOEFL (minimum score 550 paper-based; 213 computer-based; 79 iBT). *Application deadline:* For fall admission, 7/1 priority date for domestic students, 6/1 for international students; for spring admission, 11/15 priority date for domestic students, 10/1 for international students. Applications are processed on a rolling basis. Application fee: $40. Electronic applications accepted. *Financial support:* Teaching assistantships, Federal Work-Study available. Financial award application deadline: 3/15; financial award applicants required to submit FAFSA. *Faculty research:* American jazz, Czech music, Hispanic music. *Unit head:* Dr. Robin Williams, Chairperson, 504-280-6789, Fax: 504-280-6098, E-mail: rhwillia@uno.edu. *Application contact:* Dr. Charles Blancq, Graduate Coordinator, 504-280-6786, Fax: 504-280-6098, E-mail: cblancq@uno.edu.

The University of North Carolina at Chapel Hill, Graduate School, College of Arts and Sciences, Department of Music, Chapel Hill, NC 27599. Offers MA, PhD. Terminal master's awarded for partial completion of doctoral program. *Degree requirements:* For master's, one foreign language, thesis, theory and keyboard exams; for doctorate, 2 foreign languages, comprehensive exam, thesis/dissertation, theory and keyboard exams. *Entrance requirements:* For master's and doctorate, GRE General Test, department diagnostic exam, minimum GPA of 3.0. Additional exam requirements/recommendations for international students: Required—TOEFL. Electronic applications accepted. Expenses: Contact institution. *Faculty research:* Music theory, ethnomusicology, music history.

The University of North Carolina at Greensboro, Graduate School, School of Music, Greensboro, NC 27412-5001. Offers composition (MM); education (MM); music education (PhD); performance (MM, DMA). *Accreditation:* NASM. *Faculty:* 56 full-time (14 women), 11 part-time/adjunct (5 women). *Students:* 138 full-time (79 women), 56 part-time (34 women); includes 26 minority (13 African Americans, 1 American Indian/Alaska Native, 10 Asian Americans or Pacific Islanders, 2 Hispanic Americans). 213 applicants, 41% accepted. *Degree requirements:* For master's, variable foreign language requirement, thesis (for some programs), recital; for doctorate, comprehensive exam, thesis/dissertation, diagnostic exam, recital. *Entrance requirements:* For master's, GRE General Test, NTE, audition; for doctorate, GRE General Test, GRE Subject Test (music), audition. Additional exam requirements/recommendations for international students: Required—TOEFL. *Application deadline:* For fall admission, 3/1 for domestic students. Application fee: $45. Electronic applications accepted. *Financial support:* Fellowships with full tuition reimbursements, research assistantships with full tuition reimbursements, teaching assistantships with full tuition reimbursements, unspecified assistantships available. *Unit head:* Dr. John J. Deal, Dean, 336-334-5789, Fax: 336-334-5497, E-mail: jjdeal@uncg.edu. *Application contact:* Michelle Harkleroad, Director of Graduate Admissions, 336-334-4884, Fax: 336-334-4424, E-mail: mbharkle@uncg.edu.

University of North Dakota, Graduate School, College of Arts and Sciences, Department of Music, Grand Forks, ND 58202. Offers music (M Mus); music education (M Mus, DMEd). *Accreditation:* NASM. Part-time programs available. *Faculty:* 15 full-time (6 women). *Students:* 4 full-time (all women), 6 part-time (2 women), 2 international. 5 applicants, 40% accepted, 1 enrolled. In 2007, 5 degrees awarded. *Degree requirements:* For master's, comprehensive exam, thesis or alternative. *Entrance requirements:* For master's, minimum GPA of 3.0. Additional exam requirements/recommendations for international students: Required—TOEFL (minimum score 550 paper-based; 213 computer-based; 79 iBT), IELTS (minimum score 7). *Application deadline:* For fall admission, 2/15 priority date for domestic and international students; for spring admission, 10/15 priority date for domestic and international students. Applications are processed on a rolling basis. Application fee: $35. Electronic applications accepted. *Expenses:* Tuition, state resident: full-time $4,050; part-time $225 per credit. Tuition, nonresident: full-time $10,818; part-time $601 per credit. Required fees: $110 per semester. Tuition and fees vary according to class time, campus/location, program and reciprocity agreements. *Financial support:* In 2007–08, 2 teaching assistantships with full tuition reimbursements (averaging $5,950 per year) were awarded; fellowships with full and partial tuition reimbursements, research assistantships with full and partial tuition reimbursements, Federal Work-Study, institutionally sponsored loans, scholarships/grants, health care benefits, tuition waivers (full and partial), and unspecified assistantships also available. Support available to part-time students. Financial award application deadline: 3/15; financial award applicants required to submit FAFSA. *Unit head:* Dr. Gary Towne, Graduate Director, 701-777-2644, Fax: 701-777-3320, E-mail: garytowne@und.nodak.edu. *Application contact:* Brenda Halle, Admissions Specialist, 701-777-2947, Fax: 701-777-3619, E-mail: brendahalle@mail.und.edu.

University of Northern Colorado, Graduate School, College of Performing and Visual Arts, School of Music, Greeley, CO 80639. Offers collaborative keyboard (MM); conducting (MM); instrumental performance (MM); jazz studies (MM); music conducting (DA); music education (MM, DA); music history and literature (MM, DA); music performance (DA); music theory and composition (MM, DA); vocal performance (MM). *Accreditation:* NASM; NCATE (one or more programs are accredited). Part-time programs available. *Faculty:* 30 full-time (8 women). *Students:* 68 full-time (29 women), 26 part-time (10 women); includes 5 minority (2 African Americans, 1 American Indian/Alaska Native, 2 Asian Americans or Pacific Islanders), 16 international. Average age 33. 67 applicants, 88% accepted, 31 enrolled. In 2007, 24 master's, 11 doctorates awarded. *Degree requirements:* For master's, comprehensive exam, thesis or alternative; for doctorate, comprehensive exam, thesis/dissertation. *Entrance requirements:* For master's, audition; for doctorate, GRE General Test, audition, 3 letters of recommendation. *Application deadline:* Applications are processed on a rolling basis. Application fee: $50 ($60 for international students). Electronic applications accepted. *Expenses:* Tuition, state resident: part-time $222 per credit. Tuition, nonresident: part-time $627 per credit. Required fees: $36 per credit. *Financial support:* In 2007–08, 32 research assistantships (averaging $5,308 per year), 4 teaching assistantships (averaging $11,620 per year) were awarded; fellowships, unspecified assistantships also available. Financial award application deadline: 3/1; financial award applicants required to submit FAFSA. *Unit head:* H. David Caffey, Director, 970-351-2679.

University of Northern Iowa, Graduate College, College of Humanities and Fine Arts, School of Music, Program in Music, Cedar Falls, IA 50614. Offers composition (MM); conducting (MM); music (MM); music history (MM); performance (MM). *Accreditation:* NASM. *Students:* 26 full-time (17 women), 6 part-time (4 women); includes 2 minority (1 African American, 1 Hispanic American), 10 international. 36 applicants, 67% accepted, 13 enrolled. In 2007, 12 degrees awarded. *Degree requirements:* For master's, comprehensive exam, thesis or alternative. *Entrance requirements:* For master's, written diagnostic exam in theory, music history, expository writing skills and in the area of claimed competency, portfolio, tape recordings of compositions, in person auditions, minimum GPA of 3.0. Additional exam requirements/recommendations for international students: Required—TOEFL (minimum score 500 paper-based; 180 computer-based; 61 iBT). *Application deadline:* For fall admission, 8/1 priority date for domestic students. Applications are processed on a rolling basis. Application fee: $30 ($50 for international students). Electronic applications accepted. *Expenses:* Tuition, state resident: full-time $6,246; part-time $694 per credit hour. Tuition, nonresident: full-time $14,554; part-time $694 per credit hour. Required fees: $838; $119 per semester. *Financial support:* Career-related internships or fieldwork, Federal Work-Study, and tuition waivers (full and partial) available. Support available to part-time students. Financial award application deadline: 2/1. *Unit head:* Dr. Rebecca Burkhardt, Coordinator, 319-273-6272, Fax: 319-273-7320, E-mail: rebecca.burkhardt@uni.edu.

University of North Texas, Robert B. Toulouse School of Graduate Studies, College of Music, Denton, TX 76203. Offers composition (MM, DMA); jazz studies (MM); music (MA); music education (MM, MME, PhD); music theory (MM, PhD); musicology (MM, PhD); performance (MM, DMA). *Accreditation:* NASM. *Faculty:* 98 full-time (21 women). *Students:* 392 full-time (179 women), 180 part-time (75 women); includes 74 minority (17 African Americans, 3 American Indian/Alaska Native, 20 Asian Americans or Pacific Islanders, 34 Hispanic Americans), 167 international. Average age 30. 486 applicants, 45% accepted, 137 enrolled. In 2007, 82 master's, 34 doctorates awarded. *Entrance requirements:* Additional exam requirements/recommendations for international students: Required—proof of English language proficiency; Recommended—TOEFL (minimum score 550 paper-based; 213 computer-based). *Application deadline:* For fall admission, 7/15 for domestic students; for spring admission, 11/15 for domestic students. Application fee: $50 ($75 for international students). *Financial support:* In 2007–08, 96 fellowships with partial tuition reimbursements (averaging $7,800 per year), 86 teaching assistantships (averaging $5,313 per year) were awarded; research assistantships, career-related internships or fieldwork, Federal Work-Study, institutionally sponsored loans, and scholarships/grants also available. Financial award application deadline: 4/1. *Faculty research:* Electro-acoustical music, intermedia, music and medicine, music performance. Total annual research expenditures: $7,000. *Unit head:* Dr. James C. Scott, Dean, 940-565-3704, Fax: 940-565-2002. *Application contact:* Becky Hughes, Admissions and Scholarship Services, 940-367-7771, Fax: 940-565-2002, E-mail: bhughes@music.unt.edu.

University of Oklahoma, Graduate College, College of Fine Arts, School of Music, Norman, OK 73019-0390. Offers choral conducting (M Mus); conducting (M Mus Ed, DMA); general (M Mus Ed); instrumental (M Mus Ed); instrumental conducting (M Mus); music composition (M Mus, DMA); music education (M Mus Ed, PhD); music theory (M Mus); musicology (M Mus); organ (M Mus, DMA); piano (M Mus, DMA); voice (M Mus, DMA); wind/percussion/string (M Mus, DMA). *Accreditation:* NASM. *Faculty:* 58 full-time (19 women). *Students:* 106 full-time (64 women), 62 part-time (37 women); includes 14 minority (2 African Americans, 4 American Indian/Alaska Native, 2 Asian Americans or Pacific Islanders, 6 Hispanic Americans), 17 international. 101 applicants, 77% accepted, 48 enrolled. In 2007, 28 master's, 15 doctorates awarded. *Degree requirements:* For master's, variable foreign language requirement, thesis (for some programs), departmental qualifying exam, oral and preliminary exams; for doctorate, variable foreign language requirement, thesis/dissertation, departmental qualifying exam, general and oral exams. *Entrance requirements:* For master's, audition, BA in music, minimum GPA of 3.0; for doctorate, audition, minimum GPA of 3.0. Additional exam requirements/recommendations for international students: Required—TOEFL (minimum score 550 paper-based; 213 computer-based). *Application deadline:* For fall admission, 6/1 priority date for domestic students, 4/1 for international students; for spring admission, 11/1 for domestic students, 9/1 for international students. Applications are processed on a rolling basis. Application fee: $40 ($90 for international students). Electronic applications accepted. *Expenses:* Tuition, state resident: full-time $3,451; part-time $144 per credit hour. Tuition, nonresident: full-time $12,432; part-time $518 per credit hour. Required fees: $1,925; $70 per credit hour. $122 per semester. *Financial support:* In 2007–08, 70 students received support, including 6 fellowships with full tuition reimbursements available (averaging $5,000 per year), 19 research assistantships with partial tuition reimbursements available (averaging $10,468 per year), 76 teaching assistantships with partial tuition reimbursements available (averaging $9,926 per

Music

University of Oklahoma (continued)

year); unspecified assistantships also available. Financial award application deadline: 4/7; financial award applicants required to submit FAFSA. *Faculty research:* Piano pedagogy; vocal and instrumental performance; music education. Total annual research expenditures: $31. *Unit head:* Dr. Steven Curtis, Director, 405-325-2081, Fax: 405-325-7574, E-mail: scurtis@ou.edu. *Application contact:* Jan Russell, Office Assistant, 405-325-5393, Fax: 405-325-7574, E-mail: jrussell@ou.edu.

University of Oregon, Graduate School, School of Music, Program in Music, Eugene, OR 97403. Offers composition (M Mus, DMA, PhD); conducting (M Mus); jazz studies (M Mus); music (MA), including music history, music theory; music history (PhD); music theory (PhD); performance (M Mus, DMA); piano pedagogy (M Mus). *Students:* 63 applicants, 86% accepted. In 2007, 10 master's, 5 doctorates awarded. *Entrance requirements:* For master's, minimum GPA of 3.0, audition (performance applicants), videotape or interview (conducting applicants); for doctorate, GRE General Test, minimum GPA of 3.0, audition (performance applicants), videotape or interview (conducting applicants). Additional exam requirements/recommendations for international students: Required—TOEFL. *Application deadline:* For fall admission, 7/1 for domestic students. *Financial support:* In 2007–08, 64 teaching assistantships were awarded. *Unit head:* Ann Tedards, Associate Dean, 541-346-5664. *Application contact:* Anne Merydith, Admissions Contact, 541-346-5664, E-mail: gradmus@uoregon.edu.

University of Ottawa, Faculty of Graduate and Postdoctoral Studies, Faculty of Arts, Department of Music, Ottawa, ON K1N 6N5, Canada. Offers music (M Mus, MA); orchestral studies (Certificate); piano pedagogy research (Certificate). *Degree requirements:* For master's, thesis optional. *Entrance requirements:* For master's, honors degree or equivalent, minimum B+ average. Electronic applications accepted. *Faculty research:* Performance, theory, musicology.

University of Pennsylvania, School of Arts and Sciences, Graduate Group in Music, Philadelphia, PA 19104. Offers AM, PhD. Terminal master's awarded for partial completion of doctoral program. *Degree requirements:* For master's, variable foreign language requirement; for doctorate, variable foreign language requirement, thesis/dissertation. *Entrance requirements:* For master's and doctorate, GRE General Test, GRE Subject Test, samples of previous work. Additional exam requirements/recommendations for international students: Required—TOEFL. Electronic applications accepted.

University of Pittsburgh, School of Arts and Sciences, Department of Music, Pittsburgh, PA 15260. Offers composition and theory (MA, PhD); ethnomusicology (MA, PhD); musicology (MA, PhD). Part-time programs available. *Faculty:* 11 full-time (3 women), 1 part-time/adjunct (0 women). *Students:* 34 full-time (14 women), 2 part-time (1 woman); includes 7 minority (2 African Americans, 4 Asian Americans or Pacific Islanders, 1 Hispanic American), 4 international. Average age 28. 52 applicants, 35% accepted, 6 enrolled. In 2007, 5 master's, 7 doctorates awarded. Terminal master's awarded for partial completion of doctoral program. *Median time to degree:* Of those who began their doctoral program in fall 1999, 80% received their degree in 8 years or less. *Degree requirements:* For master's, comprehensive exam, thesis, 1 foreign language (historical musicology); for doctorate, one foreign language, comprehensive exam, thesis/dissertation, 2 foreign languages (historical musicology). *Entrance requirements:* For master's and doctorate, GRE General Test, samples of work, references. Additional exam requirements/recommendations for international students: Required—TOEFL (minimum score 600 paper-based; 250 computer-based). *Application deadline:* For fall admission, 1/5 for domestic and international students. Application fee: $50. Electronic applications accepted. *Financial support:* In 2007–08, 25 students received support, including 6 fellowships with full tuition reimbursements available (averaging $16,500 per year), 2 research assistantships with full tuition reimbursements available (averaging $11,000 per year), 17 teaching assistantships with full tuition reimbursements available (averaging $14,000 per year); scholarships/grants, health care benefits, tuition waivers (partial), and unspecified assistantships also available. Financial award application deadline: 1/5. *Faculty research:* Composition, ethnomusicology, historical musicology, intercultural musicology, jazz. Total annual research expenditures:$100,000. *Unit head:* Dr. Mathew Rosenblum, Chairman, 412-624-4126, Fax: 412-624-4186, E-mail: rosenblu@pitt.edu. *Application contact:* Dr. Bell Yung, Director of Graduate Admissions, 412-624-4061, Fax: 412-624-4186, E-mail: byun@pitt.edu.

University of Pittsburgh, School of Arts and Sciences, Department of Theatre Arts, Pittsburgh, PA 15260. Offers performance pedagogy (MFA); theatre and performance studies (MA, PhD). *Accreditation:* NAST. *Faculty:* 5 full-time (3 women), 1 part-time/adjunct (0 women). *Students:* 26 full-time (12 women); includes 1 minority (Asian American or Pacific Islander) Average age 32. 48 applicants, 19% accepted, 5 enrolled. In 2007, 2 master's, 2 doctorates awarded. Terminal master's awarded for partial completion of doctoral program. *Degree requirements:* For master's, comprehensive exam; for doctorate, one foreign language, comprehensive exam, thesis/dissertation. *Entrance requirements:* For master's and doctorate, GRE General Test, samples of written work. Additional exam requirements/recommendations for international students: Required—TOEFL. *Application deadline:* For fall admission, 1/15 for domestic students; for winter admission, 10/15 priority date for domestic students. Application fee: $50. Electronic applications accepted. *Financial support:* In 2007–08, 19 students received support, including fellowships (averaging $9,665 per year), 6 research assistantships with full and partial tuition reimbursements available (averaging $8,500 per year), 12 teaching assistantships with full and partial tuition reimbursements available (averaging $10,500 per year); career-related internships or fieldwork, Federal Work-Study, institutionally sponsored loans, scholarships/grants, health care benefits, and unspecified assistantships also available. Support available to part-time students. Financial award application deadline: 1/15; financial award applicants required to submit FAFSA. *Faculty research:* American theatre, Renaissance theatre, Asian theatre, dramatic structure, performance theory. *Unit head:* Dr. Bruce McConachie, Chairman, 412-624-6156, Fax: 412-624-6338, E-mail: bamcco@pitt.edu. *Application contact:* Jami White, Graduate Secretary, 412-624-0466, Fax: 412-624-6338, E-mail: jsw17@pitt.edu.

University of Portland, Graduate School, College of Arts and Sciences, Department of Performing and Fine Arts, Program in Music, Portland, OR 97203-5798. Offers MA. *Accreditation:* NASM. Part-time and evening/weekend programs available. *Faculty:* 4 full-time (0 women). *Students:* 4 applicants, 100% accepted, 3 enrolled. In 2007, 1 degree awarded. *Degree requirements:* For master's, thesis optional. *Entrance requirements:* For master's, GRE General Test, minimum GPA of 3.0, resumé, 3 letters of recommendation, statement of goals, official transcripts. Additional exam requirements/recommendations for international students: Required—TOEFL (minimum score 600 paper-based; 100 iBT), IELTS (minimum score 8). *Application deadline:* For fall admission, 7/15 priority date for domestic and international students; for spring admission, 12/15 priority date for domestic and international students. Applications are processed on a rolling basis. Application fee: $50. *Expenses:* Tuition: Part-time $775 per semester hour. *Financial support:* Federal Work-Study, scholarships/grants, and tuition waivers (partial) available. Financial award application deadline: 3/1; financial award applicants required to submit FAFSA. *Unit head:* Dr. Roger Doyle, Director, 502-943-7382, E-mail: doyle@up.edu.

University of Redlands, College of Arts and Sciences, School of Music, Redlands, CA 92373-0999. Offers MM. *Accreditation:* NASM. Part-time programs available. *Faculty:* 13 full-time, 16 part-time/adjunct. *Students:* 4 full-time (0 women), 13 part-time (8 women); includes 4 minority (1 African American, 1 Asian American or Pacific Islander, 2 Hispanic Americans). Average age 25. In 2007, 4 degrees awarded. *Degree requirements:* For master's, comprehensive exam, thesis, 3 recitals, major conducted ensemble. *Entrance requirements:* For master's, GRE, bachelor's degree in music, minimum GPA of 2.75, audition, original scores. Additional exam requirements/recommendations for international students: Required—TOEFL (minimum score 550 paper-based). *Application deadline:* For fall admission, 8/9 for domestic students. Applications are processed on a rolling basis. Application fee: $40. *Expenses: Contact institution.* Tuition and fees vary according to course level, course load, degree level and program. *Financial support:* In 2007–08, 5 students received support. Health care benefits and unspecified assistantships available. Financial award application deadline: 3/2; financial award applicants required to submit FAFSA. *Faculty research:* Performance, composition. *Unit head:* Dr. Andrew Glendening, Director, 909-793-2121, Fax: 909-793-2029, E-mail: andrew_glendening@redlands.edu.

University of Regina, Faculty of Graduate Studies and Research, Faculty of Fine Arts, Department of Music, Regina, SK S4S 0A2, Canada. Offers music (M Mus); music theory (MA); musicology (MA, PhD). *Faculty:* 10 full-time (6 women). *Students:* 6 full-time (3 women), 2 part-time (both women). 3 applicants, 67% accepted, 2 enrolled. *Degree requirements:* For master's, thesis (for some programs), recital, oral exam; for doctorate, thesis/dissertation. *Entrance requirements:* For master's, B Mus or equivalent. Additional exam requirements/recommendations for international students: Required—TOEFL (minimum score 580 paper-based; 237 computer-based; 88 iBT). *Application deadline:* For fall admission, 3/15 for domestic students. Application fee: $85 ($100 for international students). *Financial support:* In 2007–08, 1 fellowship (averaging $15,750 per year), research assistantships (averaging $13,875 per year), teaching assistantships (averaging $13,060 per year) were awarded; scholarships/grants also available. Financial award application deadline: 6/15. *Faculty research:* Social status of 18th century musicians in the Habsburg Empire studies, electronic and computer music, piano performance. *Unit head:* Dr. Lynn Cavanagh, Head, 306-585-5507, Fax: 306-585-5780, E-mail: lynn.cavanagh@uregina.ca.

University of Rhode Island, Graduate School, College of Arts and Sciences, Department of Music, Kingston, RI 02881. Offers MM. *Accreditation:* NASM. In 2007, 4 degrees awarded. *Degree requirements:* For master's, thesis optional. *Application deadline:* For fall admission, 4/15 priority date for domestic students. Applications are processed on a rolling basis. Application fee: $35. *Expenses:* Tuition, state resident: full-time $6,936; part-time $385 per credit. Tuition, nonresident: full-time $19,044; part-time $1,058 per credit. Required fees: $1,508; $48 per credit. $30 per semester. One-time fee: $80 part-time. *Unit head:* Dr. Ronald Lee, Chairman, 401-874-2431.

University of Rochester, Eastman School of Music, Rochester, NY 14627-0250. Offers composition (MA, MM, DMA, PhD); conducting (MM, DMA); education (MA, PhD); jazz studies/contemporary media (MM); music education (MM, DMA); musicology (MA, PhD); pedagogy of music theory (MA); performance and literature (MM, DMA); piano accompanying and chamber music (MM, DMA); theory (MA, PhD). *Accreditation:* NASM. Part-time programs available. *Degree requirements:* For master's, thesis (for some programs); for doctorate, comprehensive exam (for some programs), thesis/dissertation (for some programs). *Entrance requirements:* For master's and doctorate, GRE. Expenses: Contact institution.

University of Saskatchewan, College of Graduate Studies and Research, College of Arts and Sciences, Department of Music, Saskatoon, SK S7N 5A2, Canada. Offers MA. *Degree requirements:* For master's, thesis. *Entrance requirements:* Additional exam requirements/recommendations for international students: Required—TOEFL.

University of South Africa, College of Human Sciences, Pretoria, South Africa. Offers adult education (M Ed); African languages (MA, PhD); African politics (MA, PhD); Afrikaans (MA, PhD); ancient history (MA, PhD); ancient Near Eastern studies (MA, PhD); anthropology (MA, PhD); applied linguistics (MA); Arabic (MA, PhD); archaeology (MA); art history (MA); Biblical archaeology (MA); Biblical studies (M Th, D Th, PhD); Christian spirituality (M Th, D Th); church history (M Th, D Th); classical studies (MA, PhD); clinical psychology (MA); communication (MA, PhD); comparative education (M Ed, Ed D); consulting psychology (D Admin, D Com, PhD); curriculum studies (M Ed, Ed D); development studies (M Admin, MA, D Admin, PhD); didactics (M Ed, Ed D); education (M Tech); education management (M Ed, Ed D); educational psychology (M Ed); English (MA); environmental education (M Ed); French (MA, PhD); German (MA, PhD); Greek (MA); guidance and counseling (M Ed); health studies (MA, PhD), including health sciences education (MA), health services management (MA), medical and surgical nursing science (critical care general) (MA), midwifery and neonatal nursing science (MA), trauma and emergency care (MA); history (MA, PhD); history of education (Ed D); inclusive education (M Ed, Ed D); information and communications technology policy and regulation (MA); information science (MA, MIS, PhD); international politics (MA, PhD); Islamic studies (MA, PhD); Italian (MA, PhD); Judaica (MA, PhD); linguistics (MA, PhD); mathematical education (M Ed); mathematics education (MA); missiology (M Th, D Th); modern Hebrew (MA, PhD); musicology (MA, MMus, D Mus, PhD); natural science education (M Ed); New Testament (M Th, D Th); Old Testament (D Th); pastoral therapy (M Th, D Th); philosophy (MA); philosophy of education (M Ed, Ed D); politics (MA, PhD); Portuguese (MA, PhD); practical theology (M Th, D Th); psychology (MA, MS, PhD); psychology of education (M Ed, Ed D); public health (MA); religious studies (MA, D Th, PhD); Romance languages (MA); Russian (MA, PhD); Semitic languages (MA, PhD); social behavior studies in HIV/AIDS (MA); social science (mental health) (MA); social science in development studies (MA); social science in psychology (MA); social science in social work (MA); social science in sociology (MA); social work (MSW, DSW, PhD); socio-education (M Ed, Ed D); sociolinguistics (MA); sociology (MA, PhD); Spanish (MA, PhD); systematic theology (M Th, D Th); TESOL (teaching English to speakers of other languages) (MA); theological ethics (M Th, D Th); theory of literature (MA, PhD); urban ministries (D Th); urban ministry (M Th).

University of South Carolina, The Graduate School, School of Music, Columbia, SC 29208. Offers composition (MM, DMA); conducting (MM, DMA); jazz studies (MM); music education (MM Ed, PhD); music history (MM); music performance (Certificate); music theory (MM); opera theater (MM); performance (MM, DMA); piano pedagogy (MM, DMA). *Accreditation:* NASM (one or more programs are accredited). Part-time programs available. *Faculty:* 46 full-time (14 women), 9 part-time/adjunct (4 women). *Students:* 115; includes 12 minority (9 African Americans, 1 Asian American or Pacific Islander, 2 Hispanic Americans), 13 international. Average age 28. 75 applicants, 73% accepted, 42 enrolled. In 2007, 29 master's, 12 doctorates, 2 other advanced degrees awarded. *Degree requirements:* For master's, 5 foreign languages, comprehensive exam, thesis (for some programs); for doctorate, one foreign language, comprehensive exam, thesis/dissertation; for Certificate, recitals. *Entrance requirements:* For master's and doctorate, GRE General Test or MAT, music diagnostic exam. Additional exam requirements/recommendations for international students: Required—TOEFL (minimum score 570 paper-based; 230 computer-based). *Application deadline:* For fall admission, 7/1 priority date for domestic students, 5/1 for international students; for spring admission, 11/15 priority date for domestic students, 9/1 for international students. Applications are processed on a rolling basis. Application fee: $40. Electronic applications accepted. *Expenses: Contact institution.* Tuition and fees vary according to program. *Financial support:* In 2007–08, 86 students received support, including 10 fellowships with partial tuition reimbursements available (averaging $1,500 per year), 50 teaching assistantships with partial tuition reimbursements available (averaging $4,500 per year). Financial award application deadline: 3/1. *Faculty research:* Music skills in pre-school children, evaluation of school performing ensembles. Total annual research expenditures: $20,000. *Unit head:* Dr. C. Tayloe Harding, Dean, 803-777-4336, Fax: 803-777-6508, E-mail: tharding@mozart.sc.edu. *Application contact:* Dr. Andrew D. Gowan, Graduate Director, 803-777-2838, Fax: 803-777-6508, E-mail: gradmusic@mozart.sc.edu.

The University of South Dakota, Graduate School, College of Fine Arts, Department of Music, Vermillion, SD 57069-2390. Offers MM. *Accreditation:* NASM. *Faculty:* 8 full-time (3 women), 2 part-time/adjunct (1 woman). *Students:* 21 (14 women). In 2007, 12 degrees awarded. *Degree requirements:* For master's, thesis or alternative. *Entrance requirements:* For master's, minimum GPA of 2.7, audition or performance tape. Additional exam requirements/recommendations for international students: Required—TOEFL (minimum score 550 paper-based; 213 computer-based; 79 iBT). *Application deadline:* Applications are processed on a rolling basis. Application fee: $35. Electronic applications accepted. *Financial support:* In 2007–08, research assistantships with partial tuition reimbursements (averaging $4,626 per year), teaching assistantships with partial tuition reimbursements (averaging $5,626 per year) were awarded; scholarships/grants also available. Financial award applicants required to submit FAFSA. *Unit head:* Dr. Larry Schou, Chair, 605-677-5274, Fax: 605-677-5988, E-mail:

ischou@usd.edu. *Application contact:* Dr. David Moskowitz, Graduate Director, 605-677-5716, Fax: 605-677-5988, E-mail: dmoskowi@usd.edu.

University of Southern California, Graduate School, School of Music, Program in Early Music Performance, Los Angeles, CA 90089. Offers MA. *Accreditation:* NASM. *Students:* 6 full-time (3 women), 1 (woman) part-time; includes 3 minority (1 African American, 1 Asian American or Pacific Islander, 1 Hispanic American). 8 applicants, 38% accepted. *Application deadline:* For fall admission, 1/12 priority date for domestic students. Application fee: $85. *Financial support:* In 2007–08, research assistantships (averaging $18,500 per year), teaching assistantships (averaging $18,500 per year) were awarded; fellowships, Federal Work-Study and institutionally sponsored loans also available. Support available to part-time students. Financial award application deadline: 2/15; financial award applicants required to submit FAFSA. *Unit head:* Adam Gilbert, Director, 213-740-3211.

University of Southern California, Graduate School, School of Music, Program in Music History and Literature, Los Angeles, CA 90089. Offers MA. *Accreditation:* NASM. *Students:* 1 full-time (0 women). 9 applicants, 11% accepted. In 2007, 3 degrees awarded. *Degree requirements:* For master's, 2 foreign languages. *Entrance requirements:* For master's, GRE General Test. *Application deadline:* For fall admission, 12/1 priority date for domestic students. Applications are processed on a rolling basis. Application fee: $85. *Financial support:* In 2007–08, research assistantships (averaging $18,500 per year), teaching assistantships (averaging $18,500 per year) were awarded; fellowships, Federal Work-Study and institutionally sponsored loans also available. Support available to part-time students. Financial award application deadline: 2/15; financial award applicants required to submit FAFSA. *Faculty research:* Medieval, Renaissance, baroque, classical, Romantic, twentieth-century music. *Unit head:* Bryan Simms, Chair, 213-740-3211. *Application contact:* Chris Sampson, Information Contact, 213-740-8984, E-mail: sampson@usc.edu.

University of Southern California, Graduate School, School of Music, Programs in Choral Music, Los Angeles, CA 90089. Offers MM, DMA. *Accreditation:* NASM. *Faculty:* 3 full-time (1 woman). *Students:* 23 full-time (11 women), 6 part-time (4 women); includes 5 minority (3 Asian Americans or Pacific Islanders, 2 Hispanic Americans), 3 international. 23 applicants, 48% accepted. In 2007, 2 master's, 1 doctorate awarded. *Degree requirements:* For doctorate, thesis/dissertation. *Entrance requirements:* For doctorate, GRE. *Application deadline:* For fall admission, 12/1 for domestic students. Application fee: $85. *Financial support:* In 2007–08, 10 students received support. Federal Work-Study, institutionally sponsored loans, and scholarships/grants available. Support available to part-time students. Financial award application deadline: 2/15; financial award applicants required to submit FAFSA. *Unit head:* Nick Strimple, Head, 213-740-2311.

University of Southern California, Graduate School, School of Music, Programs in Composition, Los Angeles, CA 90089. Offers MA, MM, DMA, PhD. *Accreditation:* NASM. *Students:* 18 full-time (3 women), 1 (woman) part-time; includes 5 minority (1 African American, 3 Asian Americans or Pacific Islanders, 1 Hispanic American), 3 international. 76 applicants, 21% accepted. In 2007, 2 master's, 1 doctorate awarded. *Degree requirements:* For doctorate, thesis/dissertation. *Entrance requirements:* For master's and doctorate, GRE General Test. *Application deadline:* For fall admission, 12/1 priority date for domestic students; for spring admission, 10/1 for domestic students. Application fee: $85. *Financial support:* In 2007–08, research assistantships (averaging $18,500 per year), teaching assistantships with full tuition reimbursements (averaging $18,500 per year) were awarded; fellowships, Federal Work-Study and institutionally sponsored loans also available. Support available to part-time students. Financial award application deadline: 2/15; financial award applicants required to submit FAFSA. *Unit head:* Donald Crockett, Chair, 213-740-7416, E-mail: lacross@usc.edu.

University of Southern California, Graduate School, School of Music, Programs in Jazz Studies, Los Angeles, CA 90089. Offers MM, DMA. *Accreditation:* NASM. Part-time programs available. *Students:* 16 full-time (3 women), 3 part-time (2 women); includes 4 minority (2 African Americans, 2 Asian Americans or Pacific Islanders), 1 international. 38 applicants, 37% accepted. In 2007, 12 master's, 2 doctorates awarded. *Degree requirements:* For master's, 2 recitals. *Application deadline:* For fall admission, 12/1 priority date for domestic students. Applications are processed on a rolling basis. Application fee: $85. *Financial support:* In 2007–08, research assistantships (averaging $18,500 per year), teaching assistantships with full tuition reimbursements (averaging $18,500 per year) were awarded; fellowships with partial tuition reimbursements, Federal Work-Study, institutionally sponsored loans, and scholarships/grants also available. Financial award application deadline: 2/15; financial award applicants required to submit FAFSA. *Faculty research:* Jazz improvisation, ear training, jazz history, music of black America. *Unit head:* Ronald McCurdy, Chair, 213-740-3119, E-mail: uscjazz@usc.edu. *Application contact:* Information Contact, 213-740-3119, E-mail: uscjazz@usc.edu.

University of Southern California, Graduate School, School of Music, Programs in Keyboard Collaborative Arts, Los Angeles, CA 90089. Offers MM, DMA, Graduate Certificate. *Students:* 57 full-time (42 women), 17 part-time (13 women); includes 22 minority (2 African Americans, 19 Asian Americans or Pacific Islanders, 1 Hispanic American), 31 international. 85 applicants, 39% accepted. In 2007, 10 master's, 12 doctorates awarded. *Application deadline:* For fall admission, 12/1 priority date for domestic students. Application fee: $85. *Financial support:* In 2007–08, research assistantships (averaging $18,500 per year), teaching assistantships (averaging $18,500 per year) were awarded. *Unit head:* Philip Placenti, Head, School of Music, 213-740-2311.

University of Southern California, Graduate School, School of Music, Programs in Organ Studies, Los Angeles, CA 90089. Offers MM, DMA, Graduate Certificate. *Students:* 7 full-time (5 women), 2 part-time (both women); includes 3 minority (1 African American, 2 Asian Americans or Pacific Islanders), 4 international. 5 applicants, 20% accepted. *Application deadline:* For fall admission, 12/1 priority date for domestic students. Application fee: $85. *Financial support:* In 2007–08, research assistantships (averaging $18,500 per year), teaching assistantships (averaging $18,500 per year) were awarded. *Unit head:* Ladd Thomas, Chair, 213-740-7703.

University of Southern California, Graduate School, School of Music, Programs in Strings, Los Angeles, CA 90089. Offers MM, DMA, Graduate Certificate. *Students:* 34 full-time (23 women), 7 part-time (5 women); includes 12 minority (2 African Americans, 9 Asian Americans or Pacific Islanders, 1 Hispanic American), 12 international. 87 applicants, 28% accepted. In 2007, 10 master's, 6 doctorates awarded. *Application deadline:* For fall admission, 12/1 priority date for domestic students. Application fee: $85. *Financial support:* In 2007–08, research assistantships (averaging $18,500 per year), teaching assistantships (averaging $18,500 per year) were awarded. *Unit head:* Philip Placenti, Head, School of Music, 213-740-2311.

University of Southern California, Graduate School, School of Music, Programs in Studio/Jazz Guitar, Los Angeles, CA 90089. Offers MM, DMA, Graduate Certificate. *Students:* 23 full-time (1 woman), 3 part-time; includes 6 minority (2 African Americans, 2 Asian Americans or Pacific Islanders, 2 Hispanic Americans), 1 international. 37 applicants, 27% accepted. In 2007, 5 master's, 6 doctorates awarded. *Application deadline:* For fall admission, 12/1 priority date for domestic students. Application fee: $85. *Financial support:* In 2007–08, research assistantships (averaging $18,500 per year), teaching assistantships (averaging $18,500 per year) were awarded. *Unit head:* Frank Potenza, Chair, 213-740-7399, E-mail: guitar@usc.edu.

University of Southern California, Graduate School, School of Music, Programs in Vocal Arts and Opera, Los Angeles, CA 90089. Offers MM, DMA, Graduate Certificate. *Students:* 23 full-time (16 women), 2 part-time (both women); includes 5 minority (2 Asian Americans or Pacific Islanders, 3 Hispanic Americans), 1 international. 118 applicants, 35% accepted. In 2007, 10 master's, 2 doctorates awarded. *Application deadline:* For fall admission, 12/1 priority date for domestic students. Application fee: $85. *Financial support:* In 2007–08, research assistantships (averaging $18,500 per year), teaching assistantships (averaging $18,500 per year) were awarded. *Unit head:* Elizabeth Hynes, Chair, 213-740-7704.

University of Southern California, Graduate School, School of Music, Programs in Winds and Percussion, Los Angeles, CA 90089. Offers MM, DMA, Graduate Certificate. *Students:* 57 full-time (27 women), 6 part-time (2 women); includes 11 minority (1 African American, 2 American Indian/Alaska Native, 6 Asian Americans or Pacific Islanders, 2 Hispanic Americans), 9 international. 143 applicants, 33% accepted. In 2007, 14 master's, 6 doctorates awarded. *Application deadline:* For fall admission, 12/1 priority date for domestic students. Application fee: $85. *Financial support:* In 2007–08, research assistantships (averaging $18,500 per year), teaching assistantships (averaging $18,500 per year) were awarded. *Unit head:* Terry Cravens, Chair, 213-740-7416, E-mail: lacross@usc.edu.

University of Southern Maine, College of Arts and Sciences, Program in Music, Portland, ME 04104-9300. Offers MM. *Accreditation:* NASM.

University of Southern Mississippi, Graduate School, College of Arts and Letters, School of Music, Hattiesburg, MS 39406-0001. Offers conducting (MM); history and literature (MM); music education (MME, PhD); performance (MM); performance and pedagogy (DMA); theory and composition (MM); woodwind performance (MM). *Accreditation:* NASM. *Faculty:* 37 full-time (12 women). *Students:* 64 full-time (24 women), 26 part-time (13 women); includes 12 minority (5 African Americans, 1 American Indian/Alaska Native, 1 Asian American or Pacific Islander, 5 Hispanic Americans), 18 international. Average age 30. 59 applicants, 56% accepted, 25 enrolled. In 2007, 21 master's, 5 doctorates awarded. Terminal master's awarded for partial completion of doctoral program. *Degree requirements:* For master's, comprehensive exam, thesis (for some programs); for doctorate, comprehensive exam, thesis/dissertation. *Entrance requirements:* For master's, GRE General Test, minimum GPA of 2.75 in last 60 hours; for doctorate, GRE General Test, minimum GPA of 3.5. Additional exam requirements/recommendations for international students: Required—TOEFL. *Application deadline:* For fall admission, 3/1 priority date for domestic students; for spring admission, 12/13 for domestic students. Applications are processed on a rolling basis. Application fee: $30. *Financial support:* In 2007–08, 58 teaching assistantships with full tuition reimbursements (averaging $6,344 per year) were awarded; research assistantships, Federal Work-Study, scholarships/grants, tuition waivers (partial), and unspecified assistantships also available. Financial award application deadline: 3/15. *Faculty research:* Music theory, composition. *Unit head:* Dr. Charles Elliott, Director, 601-266-5543, Fax: 601-266-6427, E-mail: celliott@usm.edu. *Application contact:* Graduate Coordinator, 601-266-5369, Fax: 601-266-6427.

University of South Florida, Graduate School, College of Visual and Performing Arts, School of Music, Tampa, FL 33620-9951. Offers chamber music (MM); composition (MM); conducting (MM); electro-acoustic music (MM); jazz studies (MM), including composition, performance; performance (MM), including percussion, piano, string, voice, wind; piano pedagogy (MM); theory (MM). *Accreditation:* NASM. Part-time and evening/weekend programs available. *Faculty:* 26 full-time (5 women), 9 part-time/adjunct (3 women). *Students:* 63 full-time (31 women), 39 part-time (19 women); includes 16 minority (5 African Americans, 5 Asian Americans or Pacific Islanders, 6 Hispanic Americans), 10 international. 80 applicants, 88% accepted, 42 enrolled. In 2007, 42 master's awarded. *Degree requirements:* For master's, comprehensive exam (for some programs), thesis. *Entrance requirements:* For master's, GRE General Test, diagnostic exam in theory and history, audition, portfolio. Additional exam requirements/recommendations for international students: Required—TOEFL (minimum score 550 paper-based; 213 computer-based). *Application deadline:* For fall admission, 8/1 priority date for domestic students, 6/1 for international students; for spring admission, 12/1 for domestic students, 10/1 for international students. Application fee: $30. *Financial support:* In 2007–08, 8 fellowships with full tuition reimbursements (averaging $7,640 per year), 34 teaching assistantships with full tuition reimbursements (averaging $4,486 per year) were awarded; research assistantships with full tuition reimbursements, career-related internships or fieldwork, Federal Work-Study, scholarships/grants, health care benefits, and unspecified assistantships also available. Financial award application deadline: 2/15. *Faculty research:* Medieval and Renaissance musicology, nonverbal conducting. *Unit head:* Dr. Wade P. Weast, Director, 813-974-2311, Fax: 813-974-8721, E-mail: wweast@arts.usf.edu. *Application contact:* Dr. William P. Hayden, Academic Advisor, 813-974-1753, Fax: 813-974-8721, E-mail: wphayden@arts.usf.edu.

The University of Tennessee, Graduate School, College of Arts and Sciences, Department of Theatre, Knoxville, TN 37996. Offers costume design (MFA); lighting design (MFA); performance (MFA); scene design (MFA); theatre technology (MFA). *Degree requirements:* For master's, thesis or alternative. *Entrance requirements:* For master's, audition, minimum GPA of 2.7. Additional exam requirements/recommendations for international students: Required—TOEFL. Electronic applications accepted.

The University of Tennessee, Graduate School, College of Arts and Sciences, School of Music, Knoxville, TN 37996. Offers accompanying (MM); choral conducting (MM); composition (MM); instrumental conducting (MM); jazz (MM); music education (MM); music theory (MM); musicology (MM); performance (MM); piano pedagogy and literature (MM). *Accreditation:* NASM. Part-time programs available. *Degree requirements:* For master's, thesis (for some programs). *Entrance requirements:* For master's, audition, minimum GPA of 2.7. Additional exam requirements/recommendations for international students: Required—TOEFL. Electronic applications accepted.

The University of Tennessee at Chattanooga, Graduate School, College of Arts and Sciences, Department of Music, Program in Music, Chattanooga, TN 37403-2598. Offers MM. *Accreditation:* NASM. Part-time and evening/weekend programs available. *Faculty:* 10 full-time (1 woman), 3 part-time/adjunct (2 women). *Students:* 4 full-time (1 woman), 12 part-time (9 women), 3 international. Average age 33. 8 applicants, 100% accepted, 5 enrolled. In 2007, 5 degrees awarded. *Degree requirements:* For master's, comprehensive exam, thesis or alternative, senior recital. *Entrance requirements:* For master's, GRE General Test or MAT, bachelor's degree in music, audition for placement. Additional exam requirements/recommendations for international students: Required—TOEFL (minimum score 550 paper-based; 213 computer-based; 79 iBT); Recommended—IELTS (minimum score 6). *Application deadline:* For fall admission, 8/1 priority date for domestic students, 6/1 for international students; for spring admission, 12/1 priority date for domestic students, 10/1 for international students. Applications are processed on a rolling basis. Application fee: $30 ($35 for international students). *Expenses:* Tuition, state resident: full-time $5,854; part-time $393 per hour. Tuition, nonresident: full-time $15,816; part-time $946 per hour. Required fees: $1,090; $256 per hour. *Financial support:* In 2007–08, 4 fellowships with full and partial tuition reimbursements (averaging $2,750 per year) were awarded; career-related internships or fieldwork, Federal Work-Study, institutionally sponsored loans, scholarships/grants, tuition waivers (partial), and unspecified assistantships also available. Support available to part-time students. Financial award application deadline: 4/1; financial award applicants required to submit FAFSA. *Faculty research:* Music education, conducting, opera, vocal instruction, orchestras. Total annual research expenditures: $25,000. *Unit head:* Dr. Monte C. Coulter, Coordinator, 423-425-4647, Fax: 423-425-4603, E-mail: monte-coulter@utc.edu. *Application contact:* Dr. Deborah E. Arfken, Dean of Graduate Studies, 423-425-4666, Fax: 423-425-5223, E-mail: deborah-arfken@utc.edu.

The University of Texas at Arlington, Graduate School, College of Liberal Arts, Department of Music, Arlington, TX 76019. Offers MM. *Accreditation:* NASM. Part-time and evening/weekend programs available. *Faculty:* 3 full-time (1 woman). *Students:* 8 full-time (3 women), 18 part-time (8 women); includes 6 minority (4 African Americans, 1 Asian American or Pacific Islander, 1 Hispanic American), 7 international. 13 applicants, 54% accepted, 5 enrolled. *Degree requirements:* For master's, comprehensive exam, thesis optional. *Entrance requirements:* For master's, 3 letters of recommendation, minimum GPA of 3.0 in last 60 hours of course work. Additional exam requirements/recommendations for international students: Required—TOEFL (minimum score 550 paper-based; 213 computer-based). Application fee: $35 ($50 for international students). *Expenses:* Tuition, state resident: full-time $5,934. Tuition, nonresident:

Music

The University of Texas at Arlington (continued)

full-time $10,938. *Financial support:* In 2007–08, 1 fellowship (averaging $1,000 per year), 1 research assistantship (averaging $6,000 per year), 4 teaching assistantships with partial tuition reimbursements (averaging $6,250 per year) were awarded; scholarships/grants also available. *Unit head:* Dr. John Burton, Chair, 817-272-3471, Fax: 817-272-3434. *Application contact:* Dr. Elizabeth Morrow, Assistant Chair/Graduate Advisor, 817-272-3471, Fax: 817-272-3434, E-mail: emorrow@uta.edu.

The University of Texas at Austin, Graduate School, College of Fine Arts, School of Music, Austin, TX 78712-1111. Offers M Music, DMA, PhD. *Accreditation:* NASM. Part-time programs available. *Degree requirements:* For master's, one foreign language, comprehensive exam, thesis (for some programs), recital for performance or composition majors; for doctorate, one foreign language, comprehensive exam, thesis/dissertation (for some programs), recital for performance or composition majors. *Entrance requirements:* For master's, GRE General Test (not required for performance or composition majors), audition (performance majors); for doctorate, GRE General Test (not required for performance or composition majors), audition (performance majors). Electronic applications accepted.

The University of Texas at El Paso, Graduate School, College of Liberal Arts, Department of Music, El Paso, TX 79968-0001. Offers music education (MM); music performance (MM). *Accreditation:* NASM. Part-time and evening/weekend programs available. *Degree requirements:* For master's, thesis. *Entrance requirements:* For master's, departmental exam. Additional exam requirements/recommendations for international students: Required—TOEFL. Electronic applications accepted.

The University of Texas at San Antonio, College of Liberal and Fine Arts, Department of Music, San Antonio, TX 78249-0617. Offers MM. *Accreditation:* NASM. Part-time programs available. *Faculty:* 10 full-time (4 women), 4 part-time/adjunct (3 women). *Students:* 8 full-time (5 women), 8 part-time (3 women); includes 6 minority (all Hispanic Americans) Average age 32. 9 applicants, 67% accepted, 6 enrolled. In 2007, 9 degrees awarded. *Degree requirements:* For master's, one foreign language, comprehensive exam, thesis (for some programs), recital. *Entrance requirements:* For master's, GRE, audition, 3 letters of recommendation. Additional exam requirements/recommendations for international students: Required—TOEFL (minimum score 500 paper-based; 173 computer-based). *Application deadline:* For fall admission, 7/1 for domestic students, 4/1 for international students; for spring admission, 11/1 for domestic students, 9/1 for international students. Applications are processed on a rolling basis. Application fee: $45 ($80 for international students). Electronic applications accepted. *Financial support:* In 2007–08, 5 teaching assistantships (averaging $5,180 per year) were awarded; career-related internships or fieldwork also available. Support available to part-time students. Financial award application deadline: 7/1. *Faculty research:* Computer applications to music, psychology and music, music composition, music performance. *Unit head:* Dr. Eugene Dowdy, Chair, 210-458-4354, E-mail: edowdy@utsa.edu. *Application contact:* Dr. David Heuser, Graduate Advisor, 210-458-4354, E-mail: dheuser@utsa.edu.

The University of Texas at Tyler, College of Arts and Sciences, Department of Music, Tyler, TX 75799-0001. Offers music (MAIS). Part-time programs available. *Faculty:* 7 full-time (2 women), 12 part-time/adjunct (5 women). *Students:* 1 full-time (0 women); minority (African American) Average age 39. *Degree requirements:* For master's, comprehensive exam. *Entrance requirements:* For master's, GRE General Test. *Application deadline:* For fall admission, 8/1 for domestic students; for spring admission, 12/1 for domestic students. Application fee: $0. Electronic applications accepted. *Expenses:* Tuition, state resident: part-time $627 per semester hour. Tuition, nonresident: part-time $908 per semester hour. Required fees: $107 per semester hour. Tuition and fees vary according to course load. *Financial support:* Fellowships, research assistantships, teaching assistantships available. Financial award application deadline: 7/1; financial award applicants required to submit FAFSA. *Faculty research:* Music education, piano pedagogy, applied music study, music history. Total annual research expenditures: $4,000. *Unit head:* Dr. Jeffrey D. Emge, Coordinator, 903-566-7304, Fax: 903-566-7062. *Application contact:* Pam Morrow, Assistant to Dean for Enrollment Management, 903-566-7205, Fax: 903-566-7068, E-mail: pmorrow@uttyler.edu.

The University of Texas–Pan American, College of Arts and Humanities, Department of Music, Edinburg, TX 78541-2999. Offers ethnomusicology (M Mus); interdisciplinary studies (MAIS); music education (M Mus); performance (M Mus). Part-time programs available. *Degree requirements:* For master's, comprehensive exam, thesis optional, recital (performance). *Entrance requirements:* For master's, audition for performance area, bachelor's degree in music. *Faculty research:* Music history, instrumental pedagogy, vocal pedagogy, music education, ethnomusicology.

The University of the Arts, College of Performing Arts, School of Music, Program in Jazz Studies, Philadelphia, PA 19102-4944. Offers MM. Part-time programs available. *Degree requirements:* For master's, professional internship, recital. *Entrance requirements:* For master's, audition. Additional exam requirements/recommendations for international students: Required—TOEFL (minimum score 550 paper-based; 213 computer-based).

See Close-Up on page 273.

University of the Pacific, Conservatory of Music, Stockton, CA 95211-0197. Offers MA, MM. *Accreditation:* NASM. *Faculty:* 4 full-time (3 women), 3 part-time/adjunct (2 women). *Students:* 7 full-time (4 women), 6 part-time (5 women); includes 2 minority (1 Asian American or Pacific Islander, 1 Hispanic American), 1 international. Average age 28. 13 applicants, 69% accepted, 3 enrolled. In 2007, 3 degrees awarded. *Entrance requirements:* For master's, GRE General Test. Additional exam requirements/recommendations for international students: Required—TOEFL (minimum score 475 paper-based; 150 computer-based). *Application deadline:* For fall admission, 3/1 priority date for domestic students; for spring admission, 10/1 priority date for domestic students. Applications are processed on a rolling basis. Application fee: $75. *Financial support:* Teaching assistantships, institutionally sponsored loans available. Support available to part-time students. Financial award application deadline: 3/1; financial award applicants required to submit FAFSA. *Unit head:* Dr. Steven Anderson, Dean, 209-946-2417. *Application contact:* Dr. Therese West, Chairperson, 209-946-3194.

The University of Toledo, College of Graduate Studies, College of Arts and Sciences, Department of Music, Toledo, OH 43606-3390. Offers performance (MMP). *Accreditation:* NASM. *Faculty:* 7. *Students:* 6 full-time (1 woman), 1 part-time, 1 international. Average age 33. 6 applicants, 67% accepted, 2 enrolled. In 2007, 3 degrees awarded. *Entrance requirements:* For master's, audition (performance), minimum A average in student teaching or teaching experience (music education). *Application deadline:* For fall admission, 1/15 priority date for domestic students. Application fee: $45. Electronic applications accepted. *Financial support:* In 2007–08, 9 teaching assistantships with full tuition reimbursements (averaging $6,000 per year) were awarded; research assistantships, Federal Work-Study, institutionally sponsored loans, scholarships/grants, tuition waivers (full), and unspecified assistantships also available. Support available to part-time students. Financial award application deadline: 4/1; financial award applicants required to submit FAFSA. *Unit head:* Dr. Timothy Brakel, Acting Chair, 419-530-2448, E-mail: timothy.brakel@utoledo.edu.

University of Toronto, School of Graduate Studies, Humanities Division, Faculty of Music, Toronto, ON M5S 1A1, Canada. Offers composition (Mus M, Mus Doc); music education (Mus M, PhD); music performance (DMA); musicology/theory (MA, PhD). Part-time programs available. *Faculty:* 29 full-time, 15 part-time/adjunct. *Students:* 215 full-time (122 women), 13 part-time, 16 international. 360 applicants, 45% accepted. In 2007, 5 degrees awarded. *Degree requirements:* For master's, comprehensive exam (for some programs), oral examination (Mus M in composition), 1 language (MA); for doctorate, thesis/dissertation (for some programs), recital of original works (Mus Doc), thesis (PhD). *Entrance requirements:* For master's, Bachelor of Music in area of specialization with minimum B average in final 2 years, original compositions (Mus M in composition); for doctorate, master's degree in area of specialization, minimum B+ average, at least 2 extended compositions (Mus Doc). *Application deadline:* For fall admission, 1/14 for domestic students. Application fee: $100 Canadian dollars. *Financial support:* In 2007–08, fellowships (averaging $10,000 Canadian dollars per year); teaching assistantships. *Unit head:* Prof. Russell Hartenberger, Interim Dean, 416-978-3761, Fax: 416-978-5771, E-mail: dean.music@utoronto.ca. *Application contact:* Susan Ironside, Graduate Administrator, 416-978-5772, Fax: 416-978-5771, E-mail: grad.music@utoronto.ca.

University of Trinity College, Faculty of Divinity, Toronto, ON M5S 1H8, Canada. Offers ministry (Diploma); ministry for church musicians (Diploma); theology (M Div, MTS, Th M, D Min, PhD, Th D, Diploma, L Th); M Div/MA. *Accreditation:* ATS. Part-time programs available. *Degree requirements:* For master's, 2 foreign languages, thesis (for some programs); for doctorate, 3 foreign languages, comprehensive exam, thesis/dissertation; for M Div, thesis/dissertation optional; for other advanced degree, thesis (for some programs). *Entrance requirements:* For M Div, interview; for master's, 1 language (modern or ancient), interview; for doctorate, 2 languages (modern and ancient). Additional exam requirements/recommendations for international students: Required—TOEFL, TWE. *Faculty research:* Interreligious dialogue, feminist theology, systematic theology, philosophy of religion, pastoral theology.

University of Utah, The Graduate School, College of Fine Arts, School of Music, Salt Lake City, UT 84112-1107. Offers M Mus, MA, DMA, PhD. *Accreditation:* NASM. *Faculty:* 29 full-time (11 women), 20 part-time/adjunct (9 women). *Students:* 66 full-time (39 women), 43 part-time (27 women); includes 10 minority (1 American Indian/Alaska Native, 4 Asian Americans or Pacific Islanders, 5 Hispanic Americans), 11 international. Average age 34. 76 applicants, 71% accepted, 43 enrolled. In 2007, 15 master's, 2 doctorates awarded. *Median time to degree:* Of those who began their doctoral program in fall 1999, 50% received their degree in 8 years or less. *Degree requirements:* For master's, one foreign language, thesis (for some programs), 2 recitals, final oral exam; for doctorate, one foreign language, thesis/dissertation, final oral exam, 4 recitals (DMA). *Entrance requirements:* For master's and doctorate, placement exams, minimum GPA of 3.0, audition. Additional exam requirements/recommendations for international students: Required—TOEFL (minimum score 500 paper-based; 173 computer-based; 61 iBT). *Application deadline:* For fall admission, 2/15 for domestic students, 1/15 for international students; for spring admission, 10/1 for domestic students, 9/1 for international students. Application fee: $45 ($65 for international students). *Financial support:* In 2007–08, 39 students received support, including 23 teaching assistantships with full and partial tuition reimbursements available (averaging $7,500 per year); fellowships with full and partial tuition reimbursements available, research assistantships with full and partial tuition reimbursements available, health care benefits and unspecified assistantships also available. Financial award application deadline: 2/15; financial award applicants required to submit FAFSA. *Faculty research:* Music education, conducting, musicology, composition, performance. Total annual research expenditures: $21,692. *Unit head:* Dr. Robert Walzel, Director, 801-581-6762, Fax: 801-581-5683, E-mail: robert.walzel@music.utah.edu. *Application contact:* Jill Wilson, Graduate Secretary/Recruitment, 801-585-6972, Fax: 801-581-5683, E-mail: jill.wilson@utah.edu.

University of Utah, The Graduate School, College of Humanities, Department of English, Salt Lake City, UT 84112-1107. Offers American studies (MA, PhD); British American literature (MA, PhD); creative writing (MFA, PhD); literature (PhD); rhetoric and composition (PhD). *Faculty:* 39 full-time (16 women). *Students:* 59 full-time (39 women), 23 part-time (14 women); includes 5 minority (2 African Americans, 1 American Indian/Alaska Native, 2 Asian Americans or Pacific Islanders), 1 international. Average age 33. 177 applicants, 23% accepted, 22 enrolled. In 2007, 14 master's, 7 doctorates awarded. *Median time to degree:* Of those who began their doctoral program in fall 1999, 83% received their degree in 8 years or less. *Degree requirements:* For master's, one foreign language, thesis (for some programs), written exam; for doctorate, 2 foreign languages, comprehensive exam, thesis/dissertation. *Entrance requirements:* For master's and doctorate, GRE General Test, minimum GPA of 3.2. Additional exam requirements/recommendations for international students: Required—TOEFL (minimum score 500 paper-based; 173 computer-based; 120 iBT). *Application deadline:* For fall admission, 12/15 for domestic and international students. Applications are processed on a rolling basis. Application fee: $45 ($65 for international students). Electronic applications accepted. *Financial support:* In 2007–08, 49 students received support, including 8 fellowships with full tuition reimbursements available (averaging $12,000 per year), 41 teaching assistantships with full tuition reimbursements available (averaging $12,000 per year); research assistantships, health care benefits also available. Financial award application deadline: 12/15; financial award applicants required to submit FAFSA. *Faculty research:* Poetics and modern poetry, 19th and 20th century British and American literature, the American west, environmental studies, critical theory and race and gender studies. Total annual research expenditures: $36,210. *Unit head:* Prof. Vincent P. Pecora, Chair, 801-581-6168, E-mail: v.pecora@utah.edu. *Application contact:* Prof. Matthew Potolsky, Director of Graduate Studies, 801-581-5245, E-mail: m.potolsky@utah.edu.

University of Victoria, Faculty of Graduate Studies, Faculty of Fine Arts, School of Music, Victoria, BC V8W 2Y2, Canada. Offers composition (M Mus); musicology (MA, PhD); musicology with performance (MA); performance (M Mus). *Faculty:* 19 full-time (4 women), 7 part-time/adjunct (5 women). *Students:* 29, 1 international. Average age 24. 54 applicants, 52% accepted, 14 enrolled. In 2007, 12 master's, 1 doctorate awarded. *Degree requirements:* For master's, 2 foreign languages, thesis; for doctorate, 2 foreign languages, thesis/dissertation, candidacy exam. *Entrance requirements:* For master's, theory placement test, audition or sample papers and compositions; for doctorate, audition or sample papers and compositions. Additional exam requirements/recommendations for international students: Required—TOEFL (minimum score 575 paper-based; 233 computer-based), IELTS (minimum score 7). *Application deadline:* For fall admission, 1/15 priority date for domestic students, 12/15 priority date for international students. Applications are processed on a rolling basis. Application fee: $75 ($125 for international students). Electronic applications accepted. *Expenses:* Tuition, state resident: full-time $3,110. International tuition: $3,700 full-time. Tuition and fees vary according to program. *Financial support:* In 2007–08, 2 fellowships (averaging $12,000 per year), 26 teaching assistantships (averaging $2,980 per year) were awarded; research assistantships, career-related internships or fieldwork and institutionally sponsored loans also available. Financial award application deadline: 2/15. *Faculty research:* Beethoven, Wagner, metrical structure in tonal music, French baroque, eighteenth century opera. *Unit head:* Dr. Gerald N. King, Director, 250-721-7902, Fax: 250-721-6597, E-mail: musdir@finearts.uvic.ca. *Application contact:* Dr. Michelle Fillion, Graduate Adviser, 250-721-7906, Fax: 250-721-6597, E-mail: mfillion@uvic.ca.

University of Virginia, College and Graduate School of Arts and Sciences, Department of Music, Charlottesville, VA 22903. Offers MA, PhD. *Faculty:* 15 full-time (3 women), 14 part-time/adjunct (5 women). *Students:* 29 full-time (11 women); includes 3 minority (1 American Indian/Alaska Native, 2 Asian Americans or Pacific Islanders), 4 international. Average age 30. 48 applicants, 21% accepted, 7 enrolled. In 2007, 1 degree awarded. *Degree requirements:* For master's, one foreign language, article length paper; for doctorate, one foreign language, comprehensive exam, thesis/dissertation. *Entrance requirements:* For master's, GRE General Test, GRE Subject Test. *Application deadline:* Applications are processed on a rolling basis. Application fee: $60. Electronic applications accepted. *Financial support:* Applicants required to submit FAFSA. *Unit head:* Bruce Holsinger, Chair, 434-924-3052, Fax: 434-924-6033, E-mail: bh9n@virginia.edu.

University of Washington, Graduate School, College of Arts and Sciences, School of Music, Seattle, WA 98195. Offers M Mus, MA, MM, DMA, PhD. *Accreditation:* NASM. Terminal master's awarded for partial completion of doctoral program. *Degree requirements:* For master's, variable foreign language requirement, thesis (for some programs); for doctorate, variable foreign language requirement, thesis/dissertation. *Entrance requirements:* For master's, GRE General Test, GRE Subject Test, minimum GPA of 3.0; for doctorate, GRE General Test, GRE Subject Test, minimum GPA of 3.0, sample of scholarly writing, videotape of teaching, 1 year of teaching experience. Additional exam requirements/recommendations for international students: Required—TOEFL. Electronic applications accepted. *Faculty research:* Music theory, composition, musicology, ethnomusicology, music performance.

The University of Western Ontario, Faculty of Graduate Studies, Faculty of Arts and Humanities, Don Wright Faculty of Music, London, ON N6A 5B8, Canada. Offers music (M Mus, PhD); popular music and culture (MA). Part-time programs available. *Faculty:* 34 full-time (6 women), 8 part-time/adjunct (2 women). *Students:* 49 full-time (32 women), 4 part-time (3 women). Average age 29. 70 applicants, 63% accepted. In 2007, 16 master's, 1 doctorate awarded. Terminal master's awarded for partial completion of doctoral program. *Degree requirements:* For master's, 2 foreign languages, thesis (for some programs), recital; for doctorate, 2 foreign languages, thesis/dissertation. *Entrance requirements:* For master's, honors degree in music; minimum A average in proposed area of concentration, B average overall; for doctorate, MA or equivalent. *Application deadline:* For fall admission, 2/1 priority date for domestic students. Applications are processed on a rolling basis. Application fee: $50. *Financial support:* In 2007–08, 32 students received support, including 32 teaching assistantships; institutionally sponsored loans, scholarships/grants, and tuition waivers (full) also available. Financial award application deadline: 2/1. *Faculty research:* Systematic musicology, musicology, theory, music education. *Unit head:* Dr. Robert Wood, Dean, 519-661-2111 Ext. 84008, E-mail: rwood@uwo.ca. *Application contact:* Shelly Koster, Graduate Assistant, 519-661-2111 Ext. 85354, Fax: 519-661-3531, E-mail: skoster@uwo.ca.

University of West Georgia, Graduate School, College of Arts and Sciences, Department of Music, Program in Performance, Carrollton, GA 30118. Offers M Mus. *Accreditation:* NASM. Part-time programs available. *Students:* 4 applicants, 100% accepted. *Degree requirements:* For master's, one foreign language, comprehensive exam, thesis optional, recitals. *Entrance requirements:* For master's, music qualifying exam, audition, minimum GPA of 2.5, performance evaluation. *Application deadline:* For fall admission, 7/18 priority date for domestic students; for spring admission, 11/27 for domestic students. Application fee: $30. Electronic applications accepted. *Expenses: Contact institution. Financial support:* In 2007–08, teaching assistantships with full tuition reimbursements (averaging $9,000 per year); career-related internships or fieldwork and unspecified assistantships also available. Financial award applicants required to submit FAFSA. *Faculty research:* Ethnomusicology, jazz performance, Latin American music, French music. *Application contact:* Dr. Charles W. Clark, Interim Dean, 678-839-6508, E-mail: cclark@westga.edu.

University of Wisconsin–Madison, Graduate School, College of Letters and Science, School of Music, Program in Composition, Madison, WI 53706-1380. Offers MM, DMA. *Accreditation:* NASM. *Degree requirements:* For doctorate, thesis/dissertation.

University of Wisconsin–Madison, Graduate School, College of Letters and Science, School of Music, Program in Conducting, Madison, WI 53706-1380. Offers choral (MM, DMA); instrumental (MM, DMA). *Accreditation:* NASM. *Degree requirements:* For doctorate, thesis/dissertation.

University of Wisconsin–Madison, Graduate School, College of Letters and Science, School of Music, Program in Ethnomusicology, Madison, WI 53706-1380. Offers MM, PhD. *Accreditation:* NASM. *Degree requirements:* For doctorate, 2 foreign languages, thesis/dissertation. *Entrance requirements:* For doctorate, GRE General Test.

University of Wisconsin–Madison, Graduate School, College of Letters and Science, School of Music, Program in Musicology, Madison, WI 53706-1380. Offers MA, MM, PhD. *Accreditation:* NASM. *Degree requirements:* For master's, thesis, 1 foreign language (MA); for doctorate, 2 foreign languages, thesis/dissertation. *Entrance requirements:* For master's, GRE General Test (MA); for doctorate, GRE General Test.

University of Wisconsin–Madison, Graduate School, College of Letters and Science, School of Music, Program in Performance, Madison, WI 53706-1380. Offers MM, DMA. *Accreditation:* NASM. *Degree requirements:* For doctorate, one foreign language, thesis/dissertation.

University of Wisconsin–Madison, Graduate School, College of Letters and Science, School of Music, Program in Theory, Madison, WI 53706-1380. Offers MA, MM, PhD. *Accreditation:* NASM. *Degree requirements:* For master's, thesis, 1 foreign language (MA); for doctorate, 2 foreign languages, thesis/dissertation. *Entrance requirements:* For master's, GRE General Test (MA); for doctorate, GRE General Test.

University of Wisconsin–Milwaukee, Graduate School, Peck School of the Arts, Department of Music, Milwaukee, WI 53201-0413. Offers MM, Certificate, MLIS/MM. *Accreditation:* NASM. Part-time programs available. *Faculty:* 19 full-time (6 women). *Students:* 38 full-time (17 women), 19 part-time (8 women); includes 4 minority (2 African Americans, 2 Hispanic Americans), 4 international. 44 applicants, 64% accepted, 16 enrolled. In 2007, 14 degrees awarded. *Degree requirements:* For master's, variable foreign language requirement, thesis or alternative. *Entrance requirements:* For master's, GRE General Test, GRE Subject Test, audition, interview. *Application deadline:* For fall admission, 1/1 priority date for domestic students; for spring admission, 9/1 for domestic students. Applications are processed on a rolling basis. Application fee: $45 ($75 for international students). *Expenses:* Tuition, state resident: part-time $530 per credit. Tuition, nonresident: part-time $1,428 per credit. Required fees: $19 per credit. $229 per term. Tuition and fees vary according to course load and program. *Financial support:* In 2007–08, 7 teaching assistantships were awarded; fellowships, research assistantships, career-related internships or fieldwork and unspecified assistantships also available. Support available to part-time students. Financial award application deadline: 4/15. *Unit head:* Timothy Noonan, Representative, 414-229-2286, Fax: 414-229-2776.

University of Wyoming, Graduate School, College of Arts and Sciences, Department of Music, Laramie, WY 82070. Offers music education (MME); performance (MM). *Accreditation:* NASM. *Faculty:* 12. *Students:* 10 full-time (4 women), 3 part-time (1 woman), 5 international. Average age 27. 16 applicants, 81% accepted. In 2007, 13 degrees awarded. *Degree requirements:* For master's, comprehensive exam, thesis, performance. *Entrance requirements:* For master's, minimum GPA of 3.0. Additional exam requirements/recommendations for international students: Required—TOEFL (minimum score 540 paper-based; 207 computer-based). *Application deadline:* For fall admission, 3/1 priority date for domestic and international students. Application fee: $50. Electronic applications accepted. *Financial support:* In 2007–08, 8 students received support, including 8 teaching assistantships with full tuition reimbursements available (averaging $10,384 per year); unspecified assistantships also available. Financial award application deadline: 3/1. *Unit head:* Dr. David Brinkman, Head, 307-766-5242, Fax: 307-766-5326, E-mail: brinkman@uwyo.edu.

Valdosta State University, Graduate School, College of the Fine Arts, Department of Music, Valdosta, GA 31698. Offers music education (MME); performance (MMP). *Accreditation:* NASM. Part-time programs available. *Faculty:* 9 full-time (3 women). *Students:* 6 full-time (4 women), 3 part-time (all women); includes 2 minority (1 African American, 1 Hispanic American). Average age 26. 4 applicants, 100% accepted, 4 enrolled. In 2007, 2 degrees awarded. *Degree requirements:* For master's, comprehensive written and/or oral exams. *Entrance requirements:* For master's, GRE General Test or MAT, portfolio, audition-MMP. Additional exam requirements/recommendations for international students: Required—TOEFL (minimum score 523 paper-based; 193 computer-based). *Application deadline:* For fall admission, 7/1 for domestic and international students; for spring admission, 11/15 for domestic and international students. Applications are processed on a rolling basis. Application fee: $40. *Expenses:* Tuition, state resident: part-time $147 per hour. Tuition, nonresident: part-time $586 per hour. Required fees: $520 per semester. Tuition and fees vary according to course level, course load, campus/location and program. *Financial support:* In 2007–08, 5 students received support, including 5 research assistantships with full tuition reimbursements available (averaging $2,452 per year); institutionally sponsored loans, scholarships/grants, and unspecified assistantships also available. Support available to part-time students. Financial award application deadline: 7/1; financial award applicants required to submit FAFSA. *Unit head:* Dr. James Schrader, Head, 229-333-5804, Fax: 229-259-5578.

Virginia Commonwealth University, Graduate School, School of the Arts, Department of Music, Richmond, VA 23284-9005. Offers education (MM). *Accreditation:* NASM. *Faculty:* 11 full-time (4 women). *Students:* 2 applicants, 0% accepted. In 2007, 12 degrees awarded. *Degree requirements:* For master's, departmental qualifying exam, recital. *Entrance requirements:* For master's, department examination, audition or tapes, portfolio. *Application deadline:* For fall admission, 7/1 for domestic students; for spring admission, 12/1 for domestic students. Application fee: $50. *Expenses:* Tuition, state resident: full-time $7,224; part-time $401 per credit. Tuition, nonresident: full-time $16,072; part-time $891 per credit. Required fees: $1,679; $63 per credit. Tuition and fees vary according to campus/location. *Financial support:* Fellowships, teaching assistantships, career-related internships or fieldwork, Federal Work-Study, and institutionally sponsored loans available. Support available to part-time students. Financial award application deadline: 3/15. *Faculty research:* Composition, conducting, education, performance. *Unit head:* Dr. John Guthmiller, Acting Chair, 804-828-1166, Fax: 804-828-6469, E-mail: jguthmil@vcu.edu.

See Close-Up on page 275.

Washington State University, Graduate School, College of Liberal Arts, School of Music and Theatre Arts, Pullman, WA 99164. Offers composition (MA); jazz (MA); music (MA); music education (MA); performance (MA). *Accreditation:* NASM. *Faculty:* 16. *Students:* 18 full-time (6 women), 2 part-time (1 woman); includes 1 minority (Hispanic American) Average age 30. 16 applicants, 44% accepted, 7 enrolled. In 2007, 11 degrees awarded. *Degree requirements:* For master's, comprehensive exam (for some programs), thesis (for some programs), oral exam. *Entrance requirements:* For master's, audition, minimum GPA of 3.0, 3 letters of recommendation, composition portfolio and recording (composition), writing sample and written philosophy (music education), writing sample (music history), in-depth audition (performance). Additional exam requirements/recommendations for international students: Required—TOEFL. *Application deadline:* For fall admission, 3/1 priority date for domestic students, 3/1 for international students; for spring admission, 9/1 for domestic students, 7/1 for international students. Applications are processed on a rolling basis. Application fee: $50. Electronic applications accepted. *Financial support:* In 2007–08, 20 students received support, including 1 fellowship (averaging $3,500 per year), research assistantships (averaging $13,917 per year), 11 teaching assistantships with full and partial tuition reimbursements available (averaging $13,056 per year); career-related internships or fieldwork, Federal Work-Study, institutionally sponsored loans, and tuition waivers (partial) also available. Financial award application deadline: 4/1; financial award applicants required to submit FAFSA. Total annual research expenditures: $4,950. *Unit head:* Dr. Gerald Berthiaume, Director, 509-335-2509, Fax: 509-335-4245, E-mail: berthia@wsu.edu. *Application contact:* Graduate School Admissions, 800-GRADWSU, Fax: 509-335-1949, E-mail: gradsch@wsu.edu.

Washington University in St. Louis, Graduate School of Arts and Sciences, Department of Music, St. Louis, MO 63130-4899. Offers MA, MM, PhD. Terminal master's awarded for partial completion of doctoral program. *Degree requirements:* For master's, thesis or alternative; for doctorate, thesis/dissertation. *Entrance requirements:* For master's and doctorate, departmental exam, GRE General Test. Electronic applications accepted.

Wayne State University, College of Fine, Performing and Communication Arts, Department of Music, Detroit, MI 48202. Offers choral conducting (MM); composition (MM); music (MA, MM); music education (MM); orchestral studies (Certificate); performance (MM); theory (MM). *Accreditation:* NASM. *Students:* 8 full-time (3 women), 21 part-time (11 women); includes 6 minority (3 African Americans, 1 American Indian/Alaska Native, 1 Asian American or Pacific Islander, 1 Hispanic American), 2 international. Average age 30. 18 applicants, 94% accepted, 13 enrolled. In 2007, 7 degrees awarded. *Degree requirements:* For master's, variable foreign language requirement. *Entrance requirements:* For master's, audition, interview. Additional exam requirements/recommendations for international students: Required—TOEFL (minimum score 550 paper-based; 213 computer-based); Recommended—TWE (minimum score 6). *Application deadline:* For fall admission, 4/1 for domestic students, 6/1 for international students; for winter admission, 10/1 for international students; for spring admission, 2/1 for international students. Applications are processed on a rolling basis. Application fee: $30 ($50 for international students). Electronic applications accepted. *Expenses:* Tuition, state resident: part-time $403 per credit hour. Tuition, nonresident: part-time $890 per credit hour. *Financial support:* In 2007–08, 12 students received support, including 1 teaching assistantship (averaging $18,000 per year); research assistantships, career-related internships or fieldwork, Federal Work-Study, institutionally sponsored loans, and scholarships/grants also available. Support available to part-time students. *Faculty research:* Teacher training, pedagogy, musicology, composition/theory, conducting/performance practice. *Unit head:* Dr. John Van Der Weg, Chair, 313-577-1800, Fax: 313-577-5420, E-mail: music.chair@wayne.edu. *Application contact:* Mary Wischusen, Graduate Director, 313-577-2612, E-mail: mary.wischusen@wayne.edu.

Webster University, Leigh Gerdine College of Fine Arts, Department of Music, St. Louis, MO 63119-3194. Offers church music (MM); composition (MM); conducting (MM); jazz studies (MM); music (MA); music education (MM); performance (MM); piano (MM). *Accreditation:* NASM. *Students:* 5 full-time (4 women), 18 part-time (8 women); includes 2 minority (1 African American, 1 Asian American or Pacific Islander), 1 international. Average age 28. In 2007, 6 degrees awarded. *Application deadline:* Applications are processed on a rolling basis. Application fee: $25 ($50 for international students). *Expenses:* Tuition: Full-time $9,360; part-time $520 per credit. *Financial support:* Teaching assistantships, Federal Work-Study available. Support available to part-time students. Financial award application deadline: 4/1; financial award applicants required to submit FAFSA. *Application contact:* Denise Harrell, Associate Director of Graduate and Evening Student Admissions, 314-968-6983, Fax: 314-968-7116, E-mail: gadmit@webster.edu.

Wesleyan University, Graduate Programs, Department of Music, Middletown, CT 06459-0260. Offers ethnomusicology (PhD); music (MA). *Faculty:* 7 full-time (1 woman), 6 part-time/adjunct (0 women). *Students:* 42 full-time (18 women); includes 4 minority (1 African American, 2 Asian Americans or Pacific Islanders, 1 Hispanic American), 13 international. Average age 30. In 2007, 6 master's, 1 doctorate awarded. *Degree requirements:* For master's, one foreign language, thesis; for doctorate, one foreign language, thesis/dissertation. *Entrance requirements:* For master's, GRE General Test, GRE Subject Test; for doctorate, GRE Subject Test. Additional exam requirements/recommendations for international students: Required—TOEFL. *Application deadline:* For fall admission, 1/15 for domestic and international students. Application fee: $50. Electronic applications accepted. *Financial support:* In 2007–08, 2 fellowships with tuition reimbursements, 23 teaching assistantships with tuition reimbursements were awarded. Financial award application deadline: 4/15; financial award applicants required to submit FAFSA. *Faculty research:* African, African-American, Indonesian, European, and Euro-American music. *Unit head:* Dr. Mark Slobin, Chair, 860-685-2606, E-mail: mslobin@wesleyan.edu. *Application contact:* Hope McNeil, Information Contact, 860-685-2650, Fax: 860-685-2651, E-mail: hmcneil@wesleyan.edu.

West Chester University of Pennsylvania, Office of Graduate Studies and Extended Education, College of Visual and Performing Arts, Department of Applied Music, West Chester, PA 19383. Offers accompanying (MM); performance (MM); piano pedagogy (MM, Certificate). Part-time and evening/weekend programs available. *Students:* 13 full-time (8 women), 9 part-time (5 women); includes 1 minority (Hispanic American) Average age 28. 14 applicants, 93% accepted, 10 enrolled. In 2007, 9 degrees awarded. *Degree requirements:* For master's, comprehensive exam, thesis optional, recital. *Entrance requirements:* For master's, GRE General Test, audition. Additional exam requirements/recommendations for international students: Required—TOEFL (minimum score 550 paper-based; 213 computer-based; 80 iBT). *Application deadline:* For fall admission, 4/15 priority date for domestic students; for spring admission, 10/15 for domestic students. Applications are processed on a rolling basis. Application fee: $35. *Expenses:* Tuition, state resident: part-time $345 per credit. Tuition, nonresident: part-time $552 per credit. Tuition and fees vary according to course load. *Financial support:* In 2007–08, 3 research assistantships with full and partial tuition reimbursements (averaging $5,000 per

Music

West Chester University of Pennsylvania (continued)
year) were awarded; unspecified assistantships also available. Support available to part-time students. Financial award application deadline: 2/15; financial award applicants required to submit FAFSA. *Unit head:* Dr. Chris Hanning, Interim Chair, 610-436-4178, E-mail: channing@wcupa.edu. *Application contact:* Dr. J. Bryan Burton, Graduate Coordinator, 610-436-2222, E-mail: jburton@wcupa.edu.

West Chester University of Pennsylvania, Office of Graduate Studies and Extended Education, College of Visual and Performing Arts, Department of Music History, West Chester, PA 19383. Offers MA. Part-time and evening/weekend programs available. *Students:* 1 full-time (0 women), 5 part-time (2 women). Average age 27. 3 applicants, 100% accepted, 2 enrolled. In 2007, 1 degree awarded. *Degree requirements:* For master's, comprehensive exam, thesis optional. *Entrance requirements:* For master's, GRE General Test, audition. Additional exam requirements/recommendations for international students: Required—TOEFL (minimum score 550 paper-based; 213 computer-based; 80 iBT). *Application deadline:* For fall admission, 4/15 priority date for domestic students; for spring admission, 10/15 for domestic students. Applications are processed on a rolling basis. Application fee: $35. *Expenses:* Tuition, state resident: part-time $345 per credit. Tuition, nonresident: part-time $552 per credit. Tuition and fees vary according to course load. *Financial support:* In 2007–08, research assistantships with full and partial tuition reimbursements (averaging $5,000 per year); unspecified assistantships also available. Support available to part-time students. Financial award application deadline: 2/15; financial award applicants required to submit FAFSA. *Faculty research:* Musicology, 18th-century European music. *Unit head:* Dr. Scott Balthazar, Chair, 610-436-2284, E-mail: sbalthazar@wcupa.edu. *Application contact:* Dr. J. Bryan Burton, Graduate Coordinator, 610-436-2222, E-mail: jburton@wcupa.edu.

West Chester University of Pennsylvania, Office of Graduate Studies and Extended Education, College of Visual and Performing Arts, Department of Music Theory, West Chester, PA 19383. Offers music: theory and composition (MM). Part-time and evening/weekend programs available. *Students:* 1 (woman) full-time, 2 part-time (1 woman), 1 international. Average age 42. In 2007, 1 degree awarded. *Degree requirements:* For master's, comprehensive exam, thesis optional. *Entrance requirements:* For master's, GRE General Test, audition. Additional exam requirements/recommendations for international students: Required—TOEFL (minimum score 550 paper-based; 213 computer-based; 80 iBT). *Application deadline:* For fall admission, 4/15 priority date for domestic students; for spring admission, 10/15 for domestic students. Applications are processed on a rolling basis. Application fee: $35. *Expenses:* Tuition, state resident: part-time $345 per credit. Tuition, nonresident: part-time $552 per credit. Tuition and fees vary according to course load. *Financial support:* In 2007–08, research assistantships with full and partial tuition reimbursements (averaging $5,000 per year); unspecified assistantships also available. Support available to part-time students. Financial award application deadline: 2/15; financial award applicants required to submit FAFSA. *Unit head:* Dr. Robert Maggio, Chair, 610-436-2646. *Application contact:* Dr. J. Bryan Burton, Graduate Coordinator, 610-436-2222, E-mail: jburton@wcupa.edu.

Western Carolina University, Graduate School, College of Fine and Performing Arts, School of Music, Cullowhee, NC 28723. Offers MM. Part-time programs available. *Faculty:* 5 full-time (1 woman). *Students:* 4 full-time (2 women), 1 part-time. Average age 26. 2 applicants, 100% accepted, 2 enrolled. In 2007, 4 degrees awarded. *Degree requirements:* For master's, comprehensive exam, thesis. *Entrance requirements:* For master's, GRE, appropriate undergraduate, live audition and/or interview, passing music entrance exam. Additional exam requirements/recommendations for international students: Required—TOEFL (minimum score 550 paper-based; 270 computer-based; 79 iBT). *Application deadline:* For fall admission, 5/1 priority date for domestic students; for spring admission, 9/1 priority date for domestic students. Application fee: $40. *Expenses:* Tuition, state resident: full-time $2,314. Tuition, nonresident: full-time $11,899. Required fees: $2,033. Tuition and fees vary according to course load. *Financial support:* In 2007–08, 5 students received support, including 3 research assistantships with full and partial tuition reimbursements available (averaging $7,000 per year), 2 teaching assistantships with full and partial tuition reimbursements available (averaging $7,000 per year); fellowships, institutionally sponsored loans, scholarships/grants, and unspecified assistantships also available. Financial award application deadline: 3/31; financial award applicants required to submit FAFSA. *Faculty research:* Music experiences for K-12 students, marching band, sound mixing for television, music technology, choral methods, music history. *Unit head:* Dr. William Peebles, Director, 828-227-7242, Fax: 828-227-7162, E-mail: wpeebles@email.wcu.edu. *Application contact:* Admissions Specialist for School of Music, 828-227-7398, Fax: 828-227-7480, E-mail: gradsch@email.wcu.edu.

Western Illinois University, School of Graduate Studies, College of Fine Arts and Communication, School of Music, Macomb, IL 61455-1390. Offers MM. *Accreditation:* NASM. Part-time programs available. *Students:* 22 full-time (11 women), 9 part-time (3 women); includes 1 minority (African American), 7 international. Average age 28. 19 applicants, 84% accepted. In 2007, 9 degrees awarded. *Degree requirements:* For master's, comprehensive exam, thesis or alternative. *Entrance requirements:* For master's, audition. Additional exam requirements/recommendations for international students: Required—TOEFL (minimum score 550 paper-based; 213 computer-based; 80 iBT). *Application deadline:* Applications are processed on a rolling basis. Application fee: $30. Electronic applications accepted. *Expenses:* Tuition, state resident: part-time $217 per credit hour. Tuition, nonresident: part-time $433 per credit hour. Required fees: $54 per credit hour. *Financial support:* In 2007–08, 21 students received support, including 21 research assistantships with full tuition reimbursements available (averaging $6,800 per year). Financial award applicants required to submit FAFSA. *Unit head:* Dr. Bart Shanklin, Director, 309-298-1544. *Application contact:* Dr. Barbara Baily, Director of Graduate Studies/Associate Provost, 309-298-1806, Fax: 309-298-2345, E-mail: grad-office@wiu.edu.

Western Michigan University, Graduate College, College of Fine Arts, Department of Art, Kalamazoo, MI 49008-5202. Offers graphic design (MFA); performing arts administration (MFA); textile design (MA, MFA). *Accreditation:* NASAD (one or more programs are accredited). *Degree requirements:* For master's, thesis or alternative.

Western Michigan University, Graduate College, College of Fine Arts, School of Music, Kalamazoo, MI 49008-5202. Offers MA, MM. *Accreditation:* NASM.

Western Oregon University, Graduate Programs, College of Liberal Arts and Sciences, Division of Creative Arts, Monmouth, OR 97361-1394. Offers contemporary music (MM). *Accreditation:* NASM. *Entrance requirements:* Additional exam requirements/recommendations for international students: Required—TOEFL (minimum score 550 paper-based; 213 computer-based; 79 iBT), IELTS (minimum score 7). *Expenses:* Tuition, state resident: full-time $9,648; part-time $346 per quarter. Tuition, nonresident: full-time $15,588; part-time $526 per quarter. Required fees: $374 per quarter. Tuition and fees vary according to course level and course load. *Unit head:* Dr. Diane Tarter, Chair, 503-838-8861.

Western Washington University, Graduate School, College of Fine and Performing Arts, Department of Music, Bellingham, WA 98225-5996. Offers M Mus. *Accreditation:* NASM. Part-time programs available. *Faculty:* 19. *Students:* 7 full-time (3 women), 1 (woman) part-time. 10 applicants, 50% accepted, 5 enrolled. In 2007, 2 degrees awarded. *Degree requirements:* For master's, thesis. *Entrance requirements:* For master's, GRE General Test, department placement exams, audition, portfolio, minimum GPA of 3.0 in last 60 semester hours or last 90 quarter hours of course work. Additional exam requirements/recommendations for international students: Required—TOEFL (minimum score 567 paper-based; 227 computer-based). *Application deadline:* For fall admission, 6/1 for domestic students; for winter admission, 10/1 for domestic students; for spring admission, 2/1 for domestic students. Applications are processed on a rolling basis. Application fee: $50. Electronic applications accepted. *Expenses:* Tuition, state resident: part-time $208 per credit. Tuition, nonresident: part-time $541 per credit. Required fees: $241 per quarter. One-time fee: $250 part-time. *Financial support:* In 2007–08, 2 teaching assistantships with partial tuition reimbursements (averaging $10,120 per year) were awarded; Federal Work-Study, institutionally sponsored loans, scholarships/grants, tuition waivers (partial), and unspecified assistantships also available. Support available to part-time students. Financial award application deadline: 2/15; financial award applicants required to submit FAFSA. *Faculty research:* Baroque opera, historical music of the Silk Road, original composition, 20th century orchestral music, 13th century polyphony. *Unit head:* Dr. David Feingold, Chair, 360-650-3130, Fax: 360-650-7538. *Application contact:* Dr. Edward Rutschman, Graduate Adviser, 360-650-3889, Fax: 360-650-7538.

Westminster Choir College of Rider University, Graduate Programs in Music, Princeton, NJ 08540-3899. Offers choral conducting (MM); composition (MM); music education (MM, MME); organ performance (MM); piano accompanying and coaching (MM); piano pedagogy and performance (MM); piano performance (MM); sacred music (MM); vocal pedagogy and performance (MM); vocal training (MVP). Part-time programs available. *Faculty:* 27 full-time (8 women), 29 part-time/adjunct (18 women). *Students:* 106 full-time (68 women), 24 part-time (16 women); includes 11 minority (4 African Americans, 6 Asian Americans or Pacific Islanders, 1 Hispanic American), 24 international. Average age 27. 127 applicants, 65% accepted, 54 enrolled. In 2007, 53 degrees awarded. *Degree requirements:* For master's, variable foreign language requirement, departmental qualifying exam. *Entrance requirements:* For master's, audition, interview, repertoire list, 2 letters of reference, resumé. Additional exam requirements/recommendations for international students: Required—TOEFL (minimum score 525 paper-based; 195 computer-based). *Application deadline:* Applications are processed on a rolling basis. Application fee: $50. Electronic applications accepted. *Expenses:* Tuition: Full-time $25,650; part-time $930 per credit. Required fees: $360; $22 per credit. *Financial support:* In 2007–08, 111 students received support, including 56 research assistantships (averaging $5,256 per year); career-related internships or fieldwork, Federal Work-Study, and unspecified assistantships also available. Support available to part-time students. Financial award application deadline: 3/1; financial award applicants required to submit FAFSA. *Unit head:* Robert L. Annis, Dean, 609-921-7100 Ext. 8206, Fax: 609-683-8856, E-mail: annis@rider.edu. *Application contact:* Kate Shields, Director of Admissions, 609-921-7100 Ext. 8103, Fax: 609-921-2538, E-mail: wccadmission@rider.edu.

West Texas A&M University, College of Fine Arts and Humanities, Department of Music and Dance, Program in Music, Canyon, TX 79016-0001. Offers MA. *Accreditation:* NASM. Part-time programs available. *Degree requirements:* For master's, comprehensive exam, thesis optional. *Entrance requirements:* For master's, GRE General Test. Additional exam requirements/recommendations for international students: Required—TOEFL (minimum score 550 paper-based). Electronic applications accepted.

West Texas A&M University, College of Fine Arts and Humanities, Department of Music and Dance, Program in Performance, Canyon, TX 79016-0001. Offers MM. *Accreditation:* NASM. Part-time programs available. *Degree requirements:* For master's, comprehensive exam, thesis optional. *Entrance requirements:* For master's, GRE General Test. Additional exam requirements/recommendations for international students: Required—TOEFL (minimum score 550 paper-based). Electronic applications accepted.

West Virginia University, College of Creative Arts, Division of Music, Morgantown, WV 26506. Offers music composition (MM, DMA); music education (MM, PhD); music history (MM); music performance (MM, DMA); music theory (MM). *Accreditation:* NASM. *Faculty:* 35 full-time (15 women), 11 part-time/adjunct (3 women). *Students:* 43 full-time (24 women), 31 part-time (16 women); includes 5 minority (2 African Americans, 1 American Indian/Alaska Native, 2 Asian Americans or Pacific Islanders), 19 international. Average age 32. 54 applicants, 65% accepted, 18 enrolled. In 2007, 17 master's, 10 doctorates awarded. *Degree requirements:* For master's, comprehensive exam, thesis (for some programs), recitals; for doctorate, variable foreign language requirement, comprehensive exam, thesis/dissertation, recitals (DMA). *Entrance requirements:* For master's, GRE General Test (music history), minimum GPA of 3.0, audition; for doctorate, GRE General Test (music education), minimum GPA of 3.0, audition. Additional exam requirements/recommendations for international students: Required—TOEFL. *Application deadline:* For fall admission, 3/15 priority date for domestic students, 2/15 priority date for international students; for spring admission, 10/15 for domestic students, 9/15 for international students. Applications are processed on a rolling basis. Application fee: $45. *Expenses:* Tuition, state resident: full-time $5,196; part-time $292 per credit hour. Tuition, nonresident: full-time $15,064; part-time $840 per credit hour. Tuition and fees vary according to program. *Financial support:* In 2007–08, 57 students received support, including 3 research assistantships with full and partial tuition reimbursements available (averaging $8,400 per year), 10 teaching assistantships with full and partial tuition reimbursements available (averaging $8,400 per year); Federal Work-Study, institutionally sponsored loans, and tuition waivers (partial) also available. Financial award application deadline: 2/1; financial award applicants required to submit FAFSA. *Faculty research:* Jazz history, seventeenth century French court music, nineteenth century composition theory. *Unit head:* Dr. Howard Keith Jackson, Chair, 304-293-4841, Fax: 304-293-7491, E-mail: keith.jackson@mail.wvu.edu. *Application contact:* Dr. Cynthia Anderson.

Wichita State University, Graduate School, College of Fine Arts, School of Music, Wichita, KS 67260. Offers music (MM); music education (MME). *Accreditation:* NASM. Part-time programs available. *Degree requirements:* For master's, one foreign language, thesis, recital, research project. *Entrance requirements:* For master's, GRE, audition, BM or BME. Additional exam requirements/recommendations for international students: Required—TOEFL. Electronic applications accepted.

William Paterson University of New Jersey, College of the Arts and Communication, Department of Music, Wayne, NJ 07470-8420. Offers MM. *Accreditation:* NASM. *Students:* 19 full-time (2 women), 15 part-time (3 women); includes 6 minority (2 African Americans, 2 Asian Americans or Pacific Islanders, 2 Hispanic Americans), 5 international. In 2007, 13 degrees awarded. *Entrance requirements:* For master's, audition, minimum GPA of 2.75. *Application deadline:* For fall admission, 3/1 for domestic students. Applications are processed on a rolling basis. Application fee: $50. Electronic applications accepted. *Financial support:* Research assistantships with full tuition reimbursements available. Financial award application deadline: 4/1; financial award applicants required to submit FAFSA. *Unit head:* Carol Frierson-Campbell, Head, 973-720-3639. *Application contact:* Danielle Liautaud, Director, 973-720-3579, Fax: 973-720-2035, E-mail: liautaudd@wpunj.edu.

Winthrop University, College of Visual and Performing Arts, Department of Music, Rock Hill, SC 29733. Offers conducting (MM); music education (MME); performance (MM). *Accreditation:* NASM. Part-time programs available. *Faculty:* 23 full-time (9 women), 16 part-time/adjunct (6 women). *Students:* 14 full-time (5 women), 16 part-time (5 women); includes 2 minority (both African Americans), 1 international. Average age 26. In 2007, 10 degrees awarded. *Degree requirements:* For master's, oral and written exams, recital (MM). *Entrance requirements:* For master's, GRE General Test, audition, minimum GPA of 3.0, 2 recitals. *Application deadline:* For fall admission, 7/15 priority date for domestic students; for spring admission, 12/1 for domestic students. Applications are processed on a rolling basis. Application fee: $50. Electronic applications accepted. *Expenses:* Tuition, state resident: full-time $9,834; part-time $412 per credit hour. Tuition, nonresident: full-time $18,280; part-time $763 per credit hour. *Financial support:* In 2007–08, 6 research assistantships with full tuition reimbursements (averaging $3,600 per year) were awarded; Federal Work-Study, scholarships/grants, and unspecified assistantships also available. Support available to part-time students. Financial award application deadline: 2/1; financial award applicants required to submit FAFSA. *Unit head:* Dr. Donald Rogers, Graduate Program Director, 803-323-2255, Fax: 803-323-2343, E-mail: rogersd@winthrop.edu. *Application contact:* Sharon B. Johnson, Director of Graduate Studies, 800-411-7041, Fax: 803-323-2292, E-mail: johnsons@winthrop.edu.

Wright State University, School of Graduate Studies, College of Liberal Arts, Department of Music, Dayton, OH 45435. Offers music education (M Mus); performance (M Mus). *Accreditation:* NASM. Part-time programs available. *Degree requirements:* For master's, thesis or alternative, oral exam. *Entrance requirements:* For master's, theory placement test, BA in music. Additional exam requirements/recommendations for international students: Required—TOEFL. *Faculty research:* General music, current needs, role of teacher, expectations in music education.

Yale University, Graduate School of Arts and Sciences, Department of Music, New Haven, CT 06520. Offers MA, PhD. *Accreditation:* NASM. Terminal master's awarded for partial completion of doctoral program. *Degree requirements:* For master's, one foreign language; for doctorate, 3 foreign languages, thesis/dissertation. *Entrance requirements:* For doctorate, GRE General Test, GRE Subject Test.

Yale University, School of Music, New Haven, CT 06520. Offers MM, MMA, DMA, AD, Certificate. *Accreditation:* NASM. *Faculty:* 22 full-time (7 women), 31 part-time/adjunct (5 women). *Students:* 220 full-time (93 women); includes 31 minority (3 African Americans, 21 Asian Americans or Pacific Islanders, 7 Hispanic Americans), 79 international. Average age 24. 1,181 applicants, 14% accepted, 114 enrolled. In 2007, 69 master's, 7 doctorates, 30 ADs awarded. Terminal master's awarded for partial completion of doctoral program. *Degree requirements:* For master's, one foreign language, thesis (for some programs), recitals; for doctorate, one foreign language, thesis/dissertation, oral and written exam, recitals; for other advanced degree, one foreign language, recitals. *Entrance requirements:* For master's, departmental exams, audition; for doctorate, GRE, departmental exams in history and theory of music, audition; for other advanced degree, departmental exams in history and theory of music, audition. Additional exam requirements/recommendations for international students: Required—TOEFL (minimum score 550 paper-based; 213 computer-based; 79 iBT). *Application deadline:* For fall admission, 12/1 for domestic and international students. Application fee: $100. Electronic applications accepted. *Expenses:* Contact institution. *Financial support:* In 2007–08, 220 students received support, including 220 fellowships (averaging $25,750 per year); Federal Work-Study, institutionally sponsored loans, and scholarships/grants also available. Financial award application deadline: 5/1; financial award applicants required to submit FAFSA. *Faculty research:* Performance, composition, conducting, music history and theory. *Unit head:* Robert Blocker, Dean, 203-432-4160, Fax: 203-432-7542. *Application contact:* Suzanne M. Stringer, Registrar and Financial Aid Administrator, 203-432-1962, Fax: 203-432-7448, E-mail: suzanne.stringer@yale.edu.

York University, Faculty of Graduate Studies, Faculty of Fine Arts, Program in Ethnomusicology and Musicology, Toronto, ON M3J 1P3, Canada. Offers composition (MA); musicology and ethnomusicology (MA, PhD). Part-time programs available. *Degree requirements:* For master's, one foreign language, thesis optional; for doctorate, 2 foreign languages, comprehensive exam, thesis/dissertation. *Entrance requirements:* For master's, portfolio. Electronic applications accepted.

Youngstown State University, Graduate School, College of Fine and Performing Arts, School of Music, Youngstown, OH 44555-0001. Offers music education (MM); music history and literature (MM); music theory and composition (MM); performance (MM). *Accreditation:* NASM. Part-time and evening/weekend programs available. *Degree requirements:* For master's, one foreign language, thesis optional, final qualifying exam. *Entrance requirements:* For master's, audition; GRE General Test or minimum GPA of 2.7. Additional exam requirements/ recommendations for international students: Required—TOEFL. *Faculty research:* Teaching education, use of computers, conducting.

Theater

American Conservatory Theater, Program in Acting, San Francisco, CA 94108-5800. Offers MFA, Certificate. Certificate open only to applicants with undergraduate degree from a non-accredited institution. *Faculty:* 9 full-time (3 women), 13 part-time/adjunct (8 women). *Students:* 46 full-time (21 women); includes 11 minority (all African Americans), 1 international. Average age 24. 318 applicants, 4% accepted, 14 enrolled. In 2007, 15 degrees awarded. *Degree requirements:* For master's, thesis (for some programs), performance. *Entrance requirements:* For master's, audition, interview, appropriate bachelor's degree, 2 letters of recommendation. *Application deadline:* For fall admission, 1/9 for domestic students. Application fee: $65. *Expenses:* Tuition: Full-time $15,980. Required fees: $510. Full-time tuition and fees vary according to student level. *Financial support:* In 2007–08, 42 students received support. Federal Work-Study, scholarships/grants, and tuition waivers (full and partial) available. Financial award application deadline: 2/16; financial award applicants required to submit FAFSA. *Unit head:* Melissa Smith, Conservatory Director, 415-439-2350, E-mail: mysmith@act-sf.org. *Application contact:* Dr. Jack F. Sharrar, Director of Academic Affairs, 415-439-2350, Fax: 415-834-3300, E-mail: jsharrar@act-sf.org.

Antioch University McGregor, Graduate Programs, Individualized Liberal and Professional Studies Program, Yellow Springs, OH 45387-1609. Offers liberal and professional studies (MA), including counseling, creative writing, education, film studies, liberal studies, management, modern literature, psychology, theatre, visual arts. Part-time and evening/weekend programs available. Postbaccalaureate distance learning degree programs offered (minimal on-campus study). *Faculty:* 2 full-time (1 woman), 3 part-time/adjunct (2 women). *Students:* Average age 40. 35 applicants, 63% accepted, 17 enrolled. In 2007, 31 degrees awarded. *Degree requirements:* For master's, thesis or alternative. *Entrance requirements:* For master's, resumé, 2 letters of reference. *Application deadline:* For fall admission, 8/25 for domestic students; for winter admission, 12/5 for domestic students; for spring admission, 3/8 for domestic students. Applications are processed on a rolling basis. Application fee: $50. Electronic applications accepted. *Expenses:* Contact institution. *Financial support:* Federal Work-Study available. Financial award applicants required to submit FAFSA. *Unit head:* Suzanne Fest, Chair, 937-769-1876, Fax: 937-769-1807, E-mail: sfest@mcgregor.edu. *Application contact:* Seth Gordon, Assistant Director of Admissions, 937-769-1800 Ext. 1825, Fax: 937-769-1804, E-mail: sgordon@mcgregor.edu.

See Close-Up on page 443.

Arcadia University, Graduate Studies, Department of Education, Glenside, PA 19038-3295. Offers art education (M Ed, MA Ed); biology education (MA Ed); chemistry education (MA Ed); child development (CAS); computer education (M Ed, CAS); computer education 7–12 (MA Ed); early childhood education (M Ed, CAS), including individualized (M Ed), master teacher (M Ed), research in child development (M Ed); educational leadership (M Ed, CAS); educational psychology (CAS); elementary education (M Ed, CAS); English education (MA Ed); environmental education (MA Ed, CAS); history education (MA Ed); language arts (M Ed, CAS); mathematics education (M Ed, MA Ed, CAS); music education (MA Ed); psychology (MA Ed); pupil personnel services (CAS); reading (M Ed, CAS); school library science (M Ed); science education (M Ed, CAS); secondary education (M Ed, CAS); special education (M Ed, D Ed, CAS); theater arts (MA Ed); written communication (MA Ed). *Accreditation:* NASAD. Part-time and evening/weekend programs available. Postbaccalaureate distance learning degree programs offered (minimal on-campus study). Electronic applications accepted.

Arizona State University, Graduate College, College of Fine Arts, Department of Theater, Tempe, AZ 85287. Offers MA, MFA, PhD. *Degree requirements:* For master's, thesis or alternative; for doctorate, thesis/dissertation. *Entrance requirements:* For master's, GRE or MAT.

Arkansas State University, Graduate School, College of Communications, Department of Communication Studies, Jonesboro, State University, AR 72467. Offers speech communications and theater (MA, SCCT). Part-time programs available. *Faculty:* 5 full-time (2 women). *Students:* 6 full-time (5 women), 2 part-time (1 woman); includes 2 minority (both African Americans) Average age 26. 6 applicants, 83% accepted, 5 enrolled. In 2007, 4 degrees awarded. *Degree requirements:* For master's, one foreign language, comprehensive exam, thesis or alternative. *Entrance requirements:* For master's, GRE General Test, appropriate bachelor's degree, writing sample, letter of recommendation, official transcript. Additional exam requirements/recommendations for international students: Required—TOEFL (minimum score 213 computer-based). *Application deadline:* Applications are processed on a rolling basis. Application fee: $30 ($40 for international students). Electronic applications accepted. *Expenses:* Tuition, state resident: full-time $3,528; part-time $196 per hour. Tuition, nonresident: full-time $8,928; part-time $496 per hour. Required fees: $842; $44 per hour. $25 per term. Tuition and fees vary according to course load and program. *Financial support:* Teaching assistantships, career-related internships or fieldwork, scholarships/grants, and unspecified assistantships available. Financial award application deadline: 7/1; financial award applicants required to submit FAFSA. *Faculty research:* Business and professional speech development, communication consulting, speech communication, interpersonal communication, organizational training and development. *Unit head:* Dr. Thomas Bagland, Chair, 870-972-3091, Fax: 870-972-3856, E-mail: tbaglan@astate.edu.

Arkansas State University, Graduate School, College of Fine Arts, Department of Theatre, Jonesboro, State University, AR 72467. Offers speech communication and theater (MA, SCCT). Part-time programs available. *Faculty:* 3 full-time (1 woman). *Students:* 1 (woman) full-time, 2 part-time (both women). Average age 29. In 2007, 1 degree awarded. *Degree requirements:* For master's, comprehensive exam, thesis or alternative; for SCCT, comprehensive exam. *Entrance requirements:* For master's, GRE General Test or MAT, appropriate bachelor's degree, official transcript; for SCCT, GRE General Test or MAT, interview, master's degree, official transcript. Additional exam requirements/recommendations for international students: Required—TOEFL (minimum score 213 computer-based). *Application deadline:* Applications are processed on a rolling basis. Application fee: $30 ($40 for international students). Electronic applications accepted. *Expenses:* Tuition, state resident: full-time $3,528; part-time $196 per hour. Tuition, nonresident: full-time $8,928; part-time $496 per hour. Required fees: $842; $44 per hour. $25 per term. Tuition and fees vary according to course load and program. *Financial support:* Teaching assistantships, scholarships/grants and unspecified assistantships available. Financial award application deadline: 7/1; financial award applicants required to submit FAFSA. *Faculty research:* Acting, costume design and technology, directing and stage, makeup design and technology, voice and movement. *Unit head:* Bobby Simpson, Chair, 870-972-2037, Fax: 870-972-2830, E-mail: bsimpson@astate.edu.

Baylor University, Graduate School, College of Arts and Sciences, Department of Theatre Arts, Waco, TX 76798. Offers directing (MFA). *Accreditation:* NAST. *Students:* 7 full-time (5 women). In 2007, 2 degrees awarded. *Degree requirements:* For master's, thesis. *Entrance requirements:* For master's, GRE General Test. *Application deadline:* Applications are processed on a rolling basis. Application fee: $25. *Financial support:* Fellowships, teaching assistantships, Federal Work-Study and institutionally sponsored loans available. *Unit head:* Dr. Marion Castleberry, Graduate Program Director, 254-710-1861, Fax: 254-710-1765, E-mail: marion_castleberry@baylor.edu. *Application contact:* Suzanne Keener, Administrative Assistant, 254-710-3588, Fax: 254-710-3870.

Bennington College, Graduate Programs, Program in Drama, Bennington, VT 05201. Offers MFA. Part-time programs available. *Faculty:* 7 full-time (4 women). *Students:* 6 applicants, 0% accepted. *Application deadline:* For fall admission, 2/1 for domestic students. Application fee: $60. *Expenses:* Tuition: Full-time $20,640; part-time $2,890 per course. One-time fee: $75 full-time. Tuition and fees vary according to program. *Financial support:* Unspecified assistantships available. Financial award application deadline: 4/1; financial award applicants required to submit FAFSA. *Unit head:* Kirk Jackson, Acting Director, 802-440-4545, E-mail: kjackson2@bennington.edu. *Application contact:* Ken Himmelman, Dean of Admissions and Financial Aid, 802-440-4312, Fax: 802-440-4320, E-mail: admissions@bennington.edu.

Bob Jones University, Graduate Programs, Greenville, SC 29614. Offers accountancy (MS); Bible (MA); Bible translation (MA); Biblical studies (Certificate); broadcast management (MS); business administration (MBA); church history (MA, PhD); church ministries (MA); church music (MM); cinema and video production (MA); counseling (MS); curriculum and instruction (Ed D); divinity (M Div); dramatic production (MA); educational leadership (MS, Ed D, Ed S); elementary education (M Ed, MAT); English (M Ed, MA, MAT); fine arts (MA); graphic design (MA); history (M Ed, MA); illustration (MA); interpretative speech (MA); mathematics (M Ed, MAT); medical missions (Certificate); ministry (MM, D Min); multi-categorical special education (M Ed, MAT); music (M Ed); New Testament interpretation (PhD); Old Testament interpretation (PhD); orchestral instrument performance (MM); organ performance (MM); pastoral studies (MA); personnel services (MS, Ed S); piano pedagogy (MM); piano performance (MM); platform arts (MA); radio and television broadcasting (MS); rhetoric and public address (MA); secondary education (M Ed); studio art (MA); teaching Bible (MA); theology (MA, PhD); voice performance (MM); youth ministries (MA); M Div/MM.

The Boston Conservatory, Graduate Division, Theater Division, Boston, MA 02215. Offers MM. Part-time programs available. *Faculty:* 13 full-time (9 women), 12 part-time/adjunct (8 women). *Students:* 16 full-time (10 women), 1 (woman) part-time; includes 1 Asian American or Pacific Islander. Average age 27. 42 applicants, 36% accepted, 7 enrolled. In 2007, 7 degrees awarded. *Degree requirements:* For master's, performances. *Entrance requirements:* For master's, audition. Additional exam requirements/recommendations for international students: Required—TOEFL (minimum score 580 paper-based; 237 computer-based). *Application deadline:* For fall admission, 12/1 for domestic and international students; for spring admission, 11/1 for domestic and international students. Application fee: $100. Electronic applications accepted. *Expenses:* Tuition: Full-time $26,700; part-time $1,170 per credit hour. Required fees: $110; $60 per year. *Financial support:* Federal Work-Study, institutionally sponsored loans, scholarships/grants, and work assistantships available. Financial award application deadline: 12/1; financial award applicants required to submit FAFSA. *Unit head:* Neil Donohoe, Division Director, 617-912-9144, Fax: 617-536-3176. *Application contact:* Director of Admissions, 617-912-9153, Fax: 617-912-9101, E-mail: admissions@bostonconservatory.edu.

Boston University, College of Fine Arts, School of Theatre, Boston, MA 02215. Offers costume design (MFA); costume production (MFA); directing (MFA); lighting design (MFA); scene design (MFA); technical production (MFA, Certificate); theatre crafts (Certificate); theatre education (MFA). *Faculty:* 16 full-time, 9 part-time/adjunct. *Students:* 38 full-time (18 women); includes 2 minority (both Hispanic Americans), 6 international. Average age 30. 93 applicants, 27% accepted, 12 enrolled. In 2007, 7 degrees awarded. *Entrance requirements:* For master's, interview, portfolio. Additional exam requirements/recommendations for international students: Required—TOEFL. *Application deadline:* For fall admission, 2/15 priority date for domestic and international students. Application fee: $60. *Expenses:* Tuition: Full-time $34,930; part-time $1,092 per credit. Tuition and fees vary according to class time, course level and program. *Financial support:* Fellowships, teaching assistantships available. Financial award application deadline: 2/15. *Unit head:* Jim Petosa, Director, 617-353-3390. *Application contact:* Mark Krone, Manager, Graduate Admissions, 617-353-3350, E-mail: arts@bu.edu.

See Close-Up on page 345.

Theater

Bowling Green State University, Graduate College, College of Arts and Sciences, Department of Theatre and Film, Bowling Green, OH 43403. Offers MA, PhD. *Accreditation:* NAST.Part-time programs available. *Faculty:* 13 full-time (4 women), 2 part-time/adjunct (both women). *Students:* 27 full-time (14 women), 6 part-time (5 women); includes 2 minority (1 African American, 1 American Indian/Alaska Native), 1 international. Average age 30. 24 applicants, 46% accepted, 4 enrolled. In 2007, 7 master's awarded. Terminal master's awarded for partial completion of doctoral program. *Degree requirements:* For master's, thesis or alternative; for doctorate, comprehensive exam, thesis/dissertation, 9 hour research tool. *Entrance requirements:* For master's and doctorate, GRE General Test. Additional exam requirements/recommendations for international students: Required—TOEFL. *Application deadline:* For fall admission, 1/15 for domestic students. Application fee: $30. Electronic applications accepted. *Financial support:* In 2007–08, 1 fellowship with full tuition reimbursement (averaging $14,707 per year), 4 research assistantships with full tuition reimbursements (averaging $10,925 per year), 20 teaching assistantships with full tuition reimbursements (averaging $10,421 per year) were awarded; Federal Work-Study and unspecified assistantships also available. Financial award applicants required to submit FAFSA. *Faculty research:* Theatre history, dramatic theory, cultural studies, performance studies, American theatre history. *Unit head:* Dr. Ronald Shields, Chair, 419-372-6812. *Application contact:* Dr. Jonathan Chambers, Graduate Coordinator, 419-372-9618.

Brandeis University, Graduate School of Arts and Sciences, Department of Theater Arts, Waltham, MA 02454-9110. Offers acting (MFA); design (MFA). *Faculty:* 11 full-time (6 women), 10 part-time/adjunct (5 women). *Students:* 27 full-time (19 women); includes 3 minority (2 African Americans, 1 Asian American or Pacific Islander), 1 international. Average age 26. 17 applicants, 71% accepted, 8 enrolled. In 2007, 8 master's awarded. *Entrance requirements:* For master's, resumé, portfolio (design), letters of recommendation, audition (acting). Additional exam requirements/recommendations for international students: Required—TOEFL (minimum score 600 paper-based; 250 computer-based; 100 iBT), IELTS (minimum score 7). *Application deadline:* For fall admission, 2/15 priority date for domestic students. Applications are processed on a rolling basis. Application fee: $55. Electronic applications accepted. *Financial support:* In 2007–08, 23 students received support, including 10 fellowships with partial tuition reimbursements available (averaging $10,800 per year), 3 research assistantships with tuition reimbursements available (averaging $5,000 per year), 10 teaching assistantships with partial tuition reimbursements available (averaging $3,000 per year); career-related internships or fieldwork, institutionally sponsored loans, scholarships/grants, and tuition waivers (full and partial) also available. Financial award application deadline: 4/15; financial award applicants required to submit CSS PROFILE or FAFSA. *Faculty research:* Acting, design, dramatic writing, dramaturgy. *Unit head:* Eric Hill, Chair, 781-736-3349, Fax: 781-736-3408, E-mail: ehill@brandeis.edu. *Application contact:* Alicia Hyland, Academic Administrator, 781-736-3340, Fax: 781-736-3408, E-mail: theater@brandeis.edu.

Brigham Young University, Graduate Studies, College of Fine Arts and Communications, Department of Theatre and Media Arts, Provo, UT 84602-1001. Offers production design (MFA); theatre and media arts (MA). MFA program accepts applications in odd-numbered years only. *Accreditation:* NAST (one or more programs are accredited). *Faculty:* 14 full-time (5 women). *Students:* 20 full-time (16 women), 4 part-time (2 women). Average age 33. 23 applicants, 61% accepted, 12 enrolled. In 2007, 5 degrees awarded. *Degree requirements:* For master's, comprehensive exam, thesis, oral defense, MA, 32 hours, MFA 60 hours. *Entrance requirements:* For master's, GRE General Test, writing samples, MFA—portfolio, interview. Additional exam requirements/recommendations for international students: Required—TOEFL (minimum score 580 paper-based; 237 computer-based; 85 iBT). *Application deadline:* For fall admission, 2/1 priority date for domestic and international students. Application fee: $50. Electronic applications accepted. *Financial support:* In 2007–08, 24 students received support, including 3 research assistantships with partial tuition reimbursements available (averaging $3,500 per year), 12 teaching assistantships with partial tuition reimbursements available (averaging $3,500 per year); career-related internships or fieldwork, institutionally sponsored loans, scholarships/grants, health care benefits, tuition waivers (partial), unspecified assistantships, and administrative aides also available. Support available to part-time students. *Faculty research:* Media library, children's media, theatre studies, costume and scenic design. *Unit head:* Dr. Rodger D. Sorensen, Department Chair, 801-422-8132, Fax: 801-422-0654, E-mail: rodger_sorensen@byu.edu. *Application contact:* Kim Poole, Secretary, 801-422-3750, Fax: 801-422-0654, E-mail: kim_poole@byu.edu.

Brooklyn College of the City University of New York, Division of Graduate Studies, Department of Theater, Brooklyn, NY 11210-2889. Offers acting (MFA); criticism and history (MA); design and technical production (MFA); directing (MFA); dramaturgy (MFA); performing arts management (MFA); theater (PhD). The department offers courses at Brooklyn College that are creditable toward the CUNY doctoral degree (with permission of the executive officer of the doctoral program). Part-time programs available. *Students:* 61 full-time (42 women), 15 part-time (11 women); includes 17 minority (10 African Americans, 3 Asian Americans or Pacific Islanders, 4 Hispanic Americans), 15 international. 125 applicants, 34% accepted, 31 enrolled. In 2007, 44 degrees awarded. *Degree requirements:* For master's, thesis, professional residency. *Entrance requirements:* For master's, audition or interview, 18 credits in theater, 2 letters of recommendation, essay. Additional exam requirements/recommendations for international students: Required—TOEFL. *Application deadline:* For fall admission, 2/1 for domestic and international students. Application fee: $125. Electronic applications accepted. *Financial support:* Career-related internships or fieldwork, Federal Work-Study, institutionally sponsored loans, and scholarships/grants available. Support available to part-time students. Financial award application deadline: 5/1; financial award applicants required to submit FAFSA. *Faculty research:* International Bibliography of Theater, Asian Theater Journal, multiculturalism and the arts, art education, arts collaboration. *Unit head:* Dr. Thomas Bullard, Chairperson, 718-951-5666, Fax: 718-951-4606, E-mail: tbullard@brooklyn.cuny.edu. *Application contact:* Hernan Sierra, Graduate Admissions Coordinator, 718-951-4536, Fax: 718-951-4506, E-mail: grads@brooklyn.cuny.edu.

Brown University, Graduate School, Department of Theatre, Speech, and Dance, Providence, RI 02912. Offers AM. *Degree requirements:* For master's, thesis or alternative. *Entrance requirements:* For master's, GRE General Test.

California Institute of the Arts, School of Theatre, Valencia, CA 91355-2340. Offers acting (MFA, Adv C); design and technology (Adv C); directing (MFA); performing arts design and technology (MFA); theater management (Adv C); theatre management (MFA); writing for performance (MFA). *Accreditation:* NAST. *Degree requirements:* For master's, thesis (for some programs), faculty review, performance or portfolio. *Entrance requirements:* For master's, audition or portfolio, interview. Additional exam requirements/recommendations for international students: Required—TOEFL. Electronic applications accepted.

California State University, Fullerton, Graduate Studies, College of the Arts, Department of Theatre and Dance, Fullerton, CA 92834-9480. Offers acting (MFA); acting and directing (MA); dance (MA); directing (MFA); dramatic literature/criticism (MA); oral interpretation (MA); playwriting (MA); technical theater (MA); technical theater and design (MFA); television (MA); theatre for children (MA); theatre history (MA). *Accreditation:* NASD; NAST (one or more programs are accredited). Part-time programs available. *Students:* 14 full-time (9 women), 2 part-time; includes 3 minority (1 African American, 1 Asian American or Pacific Islander, 1 Hispanic American), 1 international. Average age 27. 3 applicants, 0% accepted. In 2007, 8 degrees awarded. *Degree requirements:* For master's, oral and written exam, project or thesis. *Entrance requirements:* For master's, major in theatre or related field, audition or interview, minimum GPA of 2.5 in last 60 units of course work. Application fee: $55. *Financial support:* Teaching assistantships, career-related internships or fieldwork, Federal Work-Study, institutionally sponsored loans, and scholarships/grants available. Support available to part-time students. Financial award application deadline: 3/1. *Unit head:* Dr. Susan Hallman, Chair, 714-278-3628. *Application contact:* Gretchen Kanne, Adviser, 714-278-3628.

California State University, Long Beach, Graduate Studies, College of the Arts, Department of Theatre Arts, Long Beach, CA 90840. Offers theatre arts (professional performance/design) (MFA); theatre arts/drama (MA). *Accreditation:* NAST. Part-time programs available. *Faculty:* 11 full-time (5 women), 24 part-time/adjunct (12 women). *Students:* 41 full-time (25 women), 16 part-time (9 women); includes 10 minority (1 African American, 7 Asian Americans or Pacific Islanders, 2 Hispanic Americans). Average age 32. *Degree requirements:* For master's, thesis or alternative. *Application deadline:* For fall admission, 7/1 for domestic students; for spring admission, 12/1 for domestic students. Applications are processed on a rolling basis. Application fee: $55. Electronic applications accepted. *Financial support:* Research assistantships, teaching assistantships, Federal Work-Study, institutionally sponsored loans, scholarships/grants, and traineeships available. Financial award application deadline: 3/2. *Unit head:* Dr. Joanne L. Gordon, Chair, 562-985-7891, Fax: 562-985-2263, E-mail: jgordon@csulb.edu. *Application contact:* Barbara Matthews, Graduate Adviser, 562-985-4042, Fax: 562-985-2263, E-mail: jmatthew@csulb.edu.

California State University, Los Angeles, Graduate Studies, College of Arts and Letters, Department of Theater Arts and Dance, Los Angeles, CA 90032-8530. Offers theater arts (MA). Part-time and evening/weekend programs available. *Faculty:* 4 full-time (3 women). *Students:* 8 full-time (5 women), 12 part-time (7 women); includes 9 minority (3 African Americans, 2 Asian Americans or Pacific Islanders, 4 Hispanic Americans), 2 international. Average age 37. In 2007, 5 degrees awarded. *Degree requirements:* For master's, comprehensive exam, project or thesis. *Entrance requirements:* For master's, minimum GPA of 2.5, 30 units of course work in theater. Additional exam requirements/recommendations for international students: Required—TOEFL. *Application deadline:* For fall admission, 6/30 for domestic students; for spring admission, 2/1 for domestic students. Applications are processed on a rolling basis. Application fee: $55. *Financial support:* Federal Work-Study available. Support available to part-time students. Financial award application deadline: 3/1. *Faculty research:* Sondheim, Taiwanese theater, Australian theater, absurdism, dramaturgy. *Unit head:* Dr. Stephen Rothman, Acting Chair, 323-343-4110 Ext. 34130, Fax: 323-343-5567, E-mail: srothma@exchange.calstatela.edu.

California State University, Northridge, Graduate Studies, College of Arts, Media, and Communication, Department of Theatre, Northridge, CA 91330. Offers MA. *Accreditation:* NAST. *Faculty:* 11 full-time (5 women), 20 part-time/adjunct (10 women). *Students:* 4 full-time (all women), 19 part-time (9 women); includes 5 minority (3 African Americans, 2 Hispanic Americans). Average age 39. 18 applicants, 61% accepted, 7 enrolled. In 2007, 5 degrees awarded. *Degree requirements:* For master's, thesis. *Entrance requirements:* For master's, GRE General Test or minimum GPA of 3.0. Additional exam requirements/recommendations for international students: Required—TOEFL. *Application deadline:* For fall admission, 11/30 for domestic students. Application fee: $55. *Financial support:* Application deadline: 3/1. *Unit head:* Prof. Peter Grego, Chair, 818-677-3086.

California State University, Sacramento, Graduate Studies, College of Arts and Letters, Department of Theatre and Dance, Sacramento, CA 95819-6048. Offers MA. *Accreditation:* NAST. Part-time programs available. *Students:* 7 full-time (6 women), 7 part-time (5 women); includes 2 minority (both African Americans) Average age 33. 20 applicants, 50% accepted, 5 enrolled. *Degree requirements:* For master's, thesis or alternative, writing proficiency exam. *Entrance requirements:* For master's, GRE General Test, BA in drama or equivalent, minimum GPA of 2.5 during previous 2 years of course work. Additional exam requirements/recommendations for international students: Required—TOEFL. *Application deadline:* Applications are processed on a rolling basis. Application fee: $55. Electronic applications accepted. *Expenses:* Tuition, state resident: full-time $3,414. Tuition, nonresident: full-time $13,584; part-time $339 per unit. Required fees: $786; $393 per semester. *Financial support:* Research assistantships, teaching assistantships, career-related internships or fieldwork and Federal Work-Study available. Support available to part-time students. Financial award application deadline: 3/1. *Unit head:* Dr. Linda Goodrich, Chair, 916-278-6368 Ext. 4784, Fax: 916-278-5681.

California State University, Sacramento, Graduate Studies, College of Social Sciences and Interdisciplinary Studies, Liberal Arts Program, Sacramento, CA 95819-6048. Offers French (MA); German (MA); Spanish (MA); theater arts (MA). *Students:* 15 full-time (10 women), 24 part-time (17 women); includes 4 minority (2 African Americans, 1 American Indian/Alaska Native, 1 Asian American or Pacific Islander). Average age 37. 17 applicants, 88% accepted, 9 enrolled. *Degree requirements:* For master's, writing proficiency exam. *Entrance requirements:* Additional exam requirements/recommendations for international students: Required—TOEFL. *Application deadline:* Applications are processed on a rolling basis. Application fee: $55. Electronic applications accepted. *Expenses:* Tuition, state resident: full-time $3,414. Tuition, nonresident: full-time $13,584; part-time $339 per unit. Required fees: $786; $393 per semester. *Financial support:* Application deadline: 3/1. *Unit head:* Dr. Lindy Valdez, Coordinator, 916-278-6342.

California State University, San Bernardino, Graduate Studies, College of Arts and Letters, Department of Theatre Arts, San Bernardino, CA 92407-2397. Offers MA. *Accreditation:* NAST. *Students:* 7 full-time (5 women), 7 part-time (6 women); includes 7 minority (2 African Americans, 1 Asian American or Pacific Islander, 4 Hispanic Americans). Average age 33. 10 applicants, 70% accepted, 5 enrolled.Application fee: $55. *Unit head:* Dr. Kathryn Ervin, Interim Chair, 909-537-5876, E-mail: kervin@csusb.edu.

Carnegie Mellon University, College of Fine Arts, School of Drama, Pittsburgh, PA 15213-3890. Offers design (MFA); directing (MFA); dramatic writing (MFA); production technology and management (MFA). *Degree requirements:* For master's, thesis (for some programs). *Entrance requirements:* For master's, audition, portfolio review, interview. Additional exam requirements/recommendations for international students: Required—TOEFL. *Faculty research:* Developing voice and speech compact disc.

Case Western Reserve University, School of Graduate Studies, Department of Theater and Dance, Cleveland, OH 44106. Offers acting (MFA); contemporary dance (MFA); dance (MA); theater (MFA). *Faculty:* 8 full-time (3 women), 3 part-time/adjunct (0 women). *Students:* 20 full-time (10 women), 4 part-time (2 women); includes 1 minority (African American), 4 international. Average age 26. 17 applicants, 76% accepted, 10 enrolled. In 2007, 3 master's awarded. *Degree requirements:* For master's, thesis, oral presentation and defense, portfolio. *Entrance requirements:* For master's, audition, interview. Additional exam requirements/recommendations for international students: Required—TOEFL. *Application deadline:* For fall admission, 8/25 for domestic students. Applications are processed on a rolling basis. Application fee: $50. Electronic applications accepted. *Financial support:* Fellowships, career-related internships or fieldwork and tuition waivers (full and partial) available. Financial award application deadline: 3/1. *Faculty research:* Playwriting; history of theater; participation in professional area theaters in performing, design, acting, coaching. *Unit head:* Ron Wilson, Chairman, 216-368-6142, Fax: 216-368-5184, E-mail: ron.wilson@case.edu. *Application contact:* Scarlett Grala, Department Assistant II, 216-368-4868, Fax: 216-368-5184, E-mail: ksg@po.cwru.edu.

The Catholic University of America, School of Arts and Sciences, Department of Drama, Washington, DC 20064. Offers acting, directing, and playwriting (MFA); theatre history and criticism (MA). Part-time programs available. *Faculty:* 7 full-time (2 women), 9 part-time/adjunct (5 women). *Students:* 11 full-time (4 women), 20 part-time (12 women); includes 2 minority (1 African American, 1 Hispanic American). Average age 31. 27 applicants, 67% accepted, 13 enrolled. In 2007, 3 degrees awarded. *Degree requirements:* For master's, variable foreign language requirement, comprehensive exam, thesis (for some programs). *Entrance requirements:* For master's, GRE General Test, 3 letters of recommendation, audition, resumé. Additional exam requirements/recommendations for international students: Required—TOEFL (minimum score 580 paper-based; 237 computer-based). *Application deadline:* For fall admission, 2/1 priority date for domestic students; for spring admission, 11/15 priority date for domestic students. Applications are processed on a rolling basis. Application fee: $55. Electronic applications accepted. *Financial support:* Fellowships, research assistantships, teaching assistantships, career-related internships or fieldwork, Federal Work-Study, scholarships/

grants, tuition waivers (full and partial), and unspecified assistantships available. Support available to part-time students. Financial award application deadline: 2/1; financial award applicants required to submit FAFSA. *Faculty research:* Professional theater, Shakespearean stage history, feminist criticism, Strindberg theory, historiography. *Unit head:* Dr. Thomas Donahue, Chair, 202-319-5358, Fax: 202-319-5359, E-mail: donahuet@cua.edu.

Central Michigan University, College of Graduate Studies, College of Communication and Fine Arts, Department of Speech, Communication and Dramatic Arts, Concentration in Oral Interpretation, Mount Pleasant, MI 48859. Offers MA. *Degree requirements:* For master's, thesis or alternative. *Entrance requirements:* For master's, minimum GPA of 3.0 in last 15 hours of speech communication and dramatic arts courses, 2.7 in last 60 hours.

Central Michigan University, College of Graduate Studies, College of Communication and Fine Arts, Department of Speech, Communication and Dramatic Arts, Concentration in Theatre, Mount Pleasant, MI 48859. Offers MA. *Degree requirements:* For master's, thesis or alternative. *Entrance requirements:* For master's, minimum GPA of 3.0 in last 15 hours of speech communication and dramatic arts courses, 2.7 in last 60 hours.

Central Washington University, Graduate Studies, Research and Continuing Education, College of Arts and Humanities, Department of Theatre Arts, Ellensburg, WA 98926. Offers theatre production (MA). Part-time programs available. *Faculty:* 9 full-time (4 women). *Students:* 1 (woman) full-time, 5 part-time (2 women). In 2007, 10 degrees awarded. *Degree requirements:* For master's, thesis or alternative. *Entrance requirements:* For master's, minimum GPA of 3.0. Additional exam requirements/recommendations for international students: Required—TOEFL (minimum score 550 paper-based; 213 computer-based; 79 iBT). *Application deadline:* For fall admission, 4/1 for domestic students. Application fee: $50. Electronic applications accepted. *Expenses:* Tuition, state resident: full-time $2,209; part-time $221 per credit. Tuition, nonresident: full-time $4,939; part-time $442 per credit. Required fees: $207 per quarter. Tuition and fees vary according to degree level. *Financial support:* In 2007–08, 1 teaching assistantship with partial tuition reimbursement (averaging $8,100 per year) was awarded; research assistantships with partial tuition reimbursements, Federal Work-Study, health care benefits, and unspecified assistantships also available. Financial award application deadline: 3/1; financial award applicants required to submit FAFSA. *Unit head:* Prof. Scott Robinson, Chair, 509-963-1766. *Application contact:* Justine Eason, Admissions Program Coordinator, 509-963-3103, Fax: 509-963-1799, E-mail: masters@cwu.edu.

Christopher Newport University, Graduate Studies, Department of Teacher Preparation, Newport News, VA 23606-2998. Offers art (PK-12) (MAT); biology (6-12) (MAT); computer science (6-12) (MAT); elementary (PK-6) (MAT); English (6-12) (MAT); French (PK-12) (MAT); history (6-12) (MAT); history and social science (MAT); mathematics (6-12) (MAT); music (PK-12) (MAT), including choral, instrumental; physics (6-12) (MAT); Spanish (PK-12) (MAT); theater (PK-12) (MAT). Part-time and evening/weekend programs available. *Faculty:* 15 full-time (9 women), 7 part-time/adjunct (4 women). *Students:* 55 full-time (46 women), 20 part-time (12 women); includes 4 minority (3 African Americans, 1 Asian American or Pacific Islander). Average age 25. 14 applicants, 79% accepted, 11 enrolled. In 2007, 57 degrees awarded. *Degree requirements:* For master's, comprehensive exam, thesis or alternative. *Entrance requirements:* For master's, PRAXIS I, minimum GPA of 3.0. *Application deadline:* For fall admission, 5/1 priority date for domestic students; for spring admission, 11/1 for domestic students. Applications are processed on a rolling basis. Application fee: $45. Electronic applications accepted. *Expenses:* Tuition, state resident: full-time $5,886; part-time $327 per credit. Tuition, nonresident: full-time $10,998; part-time $611 per credit. *Financial support:* In 2007–08, 3 research assistantships with full and partial tuition reimbursements (averaging $2,000 per year) were awarded; career-related internships or fieldwork and Federal Work-Study also available. Support available to part-time students. Financial award application deadline: 3/1; financial award applicants required to submit FAFSA. *Faculty research:* Early literacy development, instructional innovations, professional teaching standards, multicultural issues, aesthetic education. *Unit head:* Dr. Marsha Sprague, Coordinator, 757-594-7388, Fax: 757-594-7304, E-mail: msprague@cnu.edu. *Application contact:* Lyn Sawyer, Associate Director, Graduate Admissions, 757-594-7544, Fax: 757-594-7649, E-mail: gradstdy@cnu.edu.

Columbia University, Graduate School of Arts and Sciences, Program in Theatre, New York, NY 10027. Offers M Phil, MA, PhD. *Faculty:* 12 full-time. *Students:* 20 full-time (10 women), 3 international. Average age 37. 22 applicants, 27% accepted. In 2007, 4 master's, 2 doctorates awarded. *Degree requirements:* For master's, one foreign language, thesis, written exam; for doctorate, 2 foreign languages, thesis/dissertation. *Entrance requirements:* For master's and doctorate, GRE General Test, writing sample. Additional exam requirements/recommendations for international students: Required—TOEFL. Application fee: $90. *Expenses:* Tuition: Part-time $1,452 per credit. Required fees: $152 per term. One-time fee: $75 part-time. Full-time tuition and fees vary according to course level, course load, degree level and program. *Financial support:* In 2007–08, 8 students received support; fellowships, teaching assistantships, Federal Work-Study and institutionally sponsored loans available. Support available to part-time students. Financial award application deadline: 1/5; financial award applicants required to submit FAFSA. *Unit head:* Steven Chaikelson, Chair, 212-854-1659, Fax: 212-854-3344, E-mail: secil@columbia.edu.

Columbia University, School of the Arts, Theatre Arts Division, New York, NY 10027. Offers acting (MFA); directing (MFA); dramaturgy (MFA); playwriting (MFA); stage management (MFA); theater management (MFA); JD/MFA. *Faculty:* 10 full-time (5 women), 30 part-time/adjunct (13 women). *Students:* 164 full-time (91 women); includes 31 minority (14 African Americans, 12 Asian Americans or Pacific Islanders, 5 Hispanic Americans). Average age 27. 274 applicants, 29% accepted, 52 enrolled. In 2007, 52 degrees awarded. *Degree requirements:* For master's, thesis, 2 internships. *Entrance requirements:* For master's, 3 letters of recommendation, resumé, other requirements vary by concentration. Additional exam requirements/recommendations for international students: Required—TOEFL (minimum score 600 paper-based; 250 computer-based; 100 iBT). *Application deadline:* For fall admission, 1/2 for domestic and international students. Application fee: $120. Electronic applications accepted. *Expenses:* Tuition: Part-time $1,452 per credit. Required fees: $152 per term. One-time fee: $75 part-time. Full-time tuition and fees vary according to course level, course load, degree level and program. *Financial support:* In 2007–08, 87 fellowships (averaging $6,067 per year), 8 research assistantships (averaging $33,399 per year) were awarded; career-related internships or fieldwork, Federal Work-Study, scholarships/grants, tuition waivers (partial), and unspecified assistantships also available. Financial award applicants required to submit FAFSA. *Unit head:* Steven Chaikelson, Chair, 212-854-3408, Fax: 212-554-3344, E-mail: theatre@columbia.edu. *Application contact:* Director of Admissions, 212-854-2134, E-mail: admissions-arts@columbia.edu.

See Close-Up on page 347.

Cornell University, Graduate School, Graduate Fields of Arts and Sciences, Field of Theatre Arts, Ithaca, NY 14853-0001. Offers drama and the theatre (PhD); theatre history (PhD); theatre theory and aesthetics (PhD). *Faculty:* 21 full-time (6 women). *Students:* 13 full-time (9 women); includes 1 minority (Hispanic American), 1 international. Average age 31. 2 applicants, 50% accepted, 1 enrolled. In 2007, 1 doctorate awarded. *Degree requirements:* For doctorate, 2 foreign languages, comprehensive exam, thesis/dissertation. *Entrance requirements:* For doctorate, GRE General Test, sample of written work, 3 letters of recommendation. Additional exam requirements/recommendations for international students: Required—TOEFL (minimum score 600 paper-based; 250 computer-based; 77 iBT). *Application deadline:* For fall admission, 1/15 for domestic students. Application fee: $70. Electronic applications accepted. *Financial support:* In 2007–08, 10 students received support, including 2 fellowships with full tuition reimbursements available, 8 teaching assistantships with full tuition reimbursements available; research assistantships with full tuition reimbursements available, institutionally sponsored loans, scholarships/grants, health care benefits, tuition waivers (full and partial), and unspecified assistantships also available. Financial award applicants required to submit FAFSA. *Faculty research:* Cultural studies and critical theory, seventeenth to twentieth-first century European and American theater, theory of the performing arts, film history and theory, feminism and theater. *Unit head:* Director of Graduate Studies, 607-254-2757, Fax: 607-254-2733. *Application contact:* Graduate Field Assistant, 607-254-2757, Fax: 607-254-2733, E-mail: theatre_grad@cornell.edu.

Dell'Arte School of Physical Theatre, MFA Program, Blue Lake, CA 95525. Offers ensemble based physical theatre (MFA). *Accreditation:* NAST. *Faculty:* 4 full-time (2 women), 6 part-time/adjunct (1 woman). *Students:* 22 full-time (13 women); includes 2 Asian Americans or Pacific Islanders, 2 Hispanic Americans. 42 applicants, 19% accepted, 6 enrolled. *Entrance requirements:* For master's, undergraduate degree, audition. *Application deadline:* For spring admission, 4/8 priority date for domestic and international students. Applications are processed on a rolling basis. Application fee: $35. Electronic applications accepted. *Expenses:* Tuition: Full-time $15,300. Required fees: $100. One-time fee: $500 full-time. *Financial support:* In 2007–08, 11 students received support. Career-related internships or fieldwork, institutionally sponsored loans, and scholarships/grants available. *Faculty research:* Physical Theatre, International Theatre, Ensemble, Divised. *Unit head:* Joan Schirle, Director, 707-668-5663, E-mail: joans@dellarte.com. *Application contact:* Joe Krienke, Recruitment Director, 707-668-5663 Ext. 27, E-mail: joe@dellarte.com.

DePaul University, The Theatre School, Chicago, IL 60604-2287. Offers acting (MFA, Certificate); directing (MFA). *Faculty:* 28 full-time (15 women), 42 part-time/adjunct (17 women). *Students:* 35 full-time (17 women); includes 5 minority (4 African Americans, 1 Hispanic American). Average age 28. 208 applicants, 11% accepted, 14 enrolled. In 2007, 9 degrees awarded. *Degree requirements:* For master's, comprehensive exam. *Entrance requirements:* For master's, audition or interview. Additional exam requirements/recommendations for international students: Required—TOEFL (minimum score 550 paper-based; 213 computer-based). *Application deadline:* For fall admission, 1/15 priority date for domestic and international students. Application fee: $35. Electronic applications accepted. *Expenses:* Contact institution. *Financial support:* In 2007–08, 26 fellowships (averaging $9,820 per year) were awarded; career-related internships or fieldwork, Federal Work-Study, and institutionally sponsored loans also available. Financial award application deadline: 2/15; financial award applicants required to submit FAFSA. *Unit head:* John Culbert, Chair, 773-325-7917 Ext. 7954, Fax: 773-325-7920, E-mail: jculbert@depaul.edu. *Application contact:* Jason Beck, Director of Admissions, 773-325-7999, Fax: 773-325-7920, E-mail: jbeck1@depaul.edu.

Drake University, School of Education, Department of Teaching and Learning, Program in Secondary Education, Des Moines, IA 50311-4516. Offers art (MAT); biology (MAT); business (MAT); chemistry (MAT); English (MAT); general science (MAT); history-American (MAT); history-world (MAT); journalism (MAT); mathematics (MAT); physical science (MAT); physics (MAT); sociology (MAT); speech (MAT); speech communication (MAT); theatre (MAT). Part-time programs available. *Faculty:* 10 full-time (3 women), 28 part-time/adjunct (16 women). *Students:* 13 full-time (7 women), 33 part-time (20 women). 41 applicants, 56% accepted. In 2007, 12 degrees awarded. *Degree requirements:* For master's, comprehensive exam, thesis (for some programs), internships (for some programs). *Entrance requirements:* For master's, GRE General Test, MAT, or Drake Writing Assessment, resumé, 2 letters of recommendation. Additional exam requirements/recommendations for international students: Required—TOEFL (minimum score 550 paper-based; 213 computer-based). *Application deadline:* For fall admission, 7/1 priority date for domestic students, 6/1 priority date for international students; for spring admission, 11/1 priority date for domestic students, 10/1 priority date for international students. Applications are processed on a rolling basis. Application fee: $25. Electronic applications accepted. *Expenses:* Tuition: Full-time $26,030; part-time $370 per credit hour. Required fees: $406; $40 per semester. Tuition and fees vary according to program. *Financial support:* Career-related internships or fieldwork and unspecified assistantships available. Support available to part-time students. *Faculty research:* Counseling and rehabilitation, behavioral supports, inquiry-based science methods, teacher quality enhancement. Total annual research expenditures: $1.5 million. *Application contact:* Ann J. Martin, Graduate Coordinator, 515-271-2034, Fax: 515-271-2831, E-mail: ann.martin@drake.edu.

Eastern Michigan University, Graduate School, College of Arts and Sciences, Department of Communication and Theatre Arts, Program in Arts Administration, Ypsilanti, MI 48197. Offers theatre arts-arts administration (MA). Part-time and evening/weekend programs available. Postbaccalaureate distance learning degree programs offered (minimal on-campus study). *Students:* 3 full-time (2 women), 10 part-time (9 women); includes 4 minority (3 African Americans, 1 Asian American or Pacific Islander), 2 international. Average age 33. In 2007, 1 degree awarded. *Entrance requirements:* Additional exam requirements/recommendations for international students: Required—TOEFL. *Application deadline:* Applications are processed on a rolling basis. Application fee: $35. *Expenses:* Tuition, state resident: full-time $8,952; part-time $373 per credit hour. Tuition, nonresident: full-time $17,634; part-time $735 per credit hour. Required fees: $896; $34 per credit hour. Tuition and fees vary according to course level, degree level and program. *Financial support:* Fellowships, research assistantships with full tuition reimbursements, teaching assistantships with full tuition reimbursements, career-related internships or fieldwork, Federal Work-Study, institutionally sponsored loans, scholarships/grants, tuition waivers (partial), and unspecified assistantships available. Support available to part-time students. Financial award applicants required to submit FAFSA. *Unit head:* Kenneth Stevens, Coordinator, 734-487-3130, Fax: 734-487-3443, E-mail: ken.stevens@emich.edu. *Application contact:* Dr. Lee Stille, Graduate Coordinator, 734-487-3131, Fax: 734-487-3443, E-mail: lee.stille@emich.edu.

Eastern Michigan University, Graduate School, College of Arts and Sciences, Department of Communication and Theatre Arts, Program in Drama/Theatre for the Young, Ypsilanti, MI 48197. Offers MA, MFA. Part-time programs available. Postbaccalaureate distance learning degree programs offered (minimal on-campus study). *Students:* 1 (woman) full-time, 24 part-time (21 women); includes 4 minority (all African Americans), 3 international. Average age 36. In 2007, 8 degrees awarded. *Degree requirements:* For master's, thesis optional. *Entrance requirements:* Additional exam requirements/recommendations for international students: Required—TOEFL. *Application deadline:* Applications are processed on a rolling basis. Application fee: $35. *Expenses:* Tuition, state resident: full-time $8,952; part-time $373 per credit hour. Tuition, nonresident: full-time $17,634; part-time $735 per credit hour. Required fees: $896; $34 per credit hour. Tuition and fees vary according to course level, degree level and program. *Financial support:* Fellowships, research assistantships with full tuition reimbursements, teaching assistantships with full tuition reimbursements, career-related internships or fieldwork, Federal Work-Study, institutionally sponsored loans, scholarships/grants, tuition waivers (partial), and unspecified assistantships available. Support available to part-time students. Financial award applicants required to submit FAFSA. *Unit head:* Dr. Christine Tanner, Coordinator, 734-487-0032, Fax: 734-487-3443, E-mail: christine.tanner@emich.edu. *Application contact:* Dr. Lee Stille, Graduate Coordinator, 734-487-3131, Fax: 734-487-3443, E-mail: lee.stille@emich.edu.

Eastern Michigan University, Graduate School, College of Arts and Sciences, Department of Communication and Theatre Arts, Program in Theatre, Ypsilanti, MI 48197. Offers interpretation/performance studies (MA); theatre arts (MA). Part-time and evening/weekend programs available. Postbaccalaureate distance learning degree programs offered (minimal on-campus study). *Students:* 4 full-time (2 women), 10 part-time (5 women); includes 1 minority (African American), 2 international. Average age 30. In 2007, 4 degrees awarded. *Degree requirements:* For master's, thesis or alternative. *Entrance requirements:* Additional exam requirements/recommendations for international students: Required—TOEFL. *Application deadline:* Applications are processed on a rolling basis. Application fee: $35. *Expenses:* Tuition, state resident: full-time $8,952; part-time $373 per credit hour. Tuition, nonresident: full-time $17,634; part-time $735 per credit hour. Required fees: $896; $34 per credit hour. Tuition and fees vary according to course level, degree level and program. *Financial support:* Fellowships, research assistantships with full tuition reimbursements, teaching assistantships with full tuition reimbursements, career-related internships or fieldwork, Federal Work-Study, institutionally sponsored loans, scholarships/grants, tuition waivers (partial), and unspecified assistantships available. Support available to part-time students. Financial award applicants required to submit FAFSA. *Unit*

Theater

Eastern Michigan University (continued)
head: Kenneth Stevens, Coordinator, 734-487-3130, Fax: 734-487-3443, E-mail: ken.stevens@emich.edu. *Application contact:* Dr. Lee Stille, Graduate Coordinator, 734-487-3131, Fax: 734-487-3443, E-mail: lee.stille@emich.edu.

Emerson College, Graduate Studies, School of the Arts, Department of Performing Arts, Program in Theatre Education, Boston, MA 02116-4624. Offers MA. Part-time programs available. *Faculty:* 22 full-time (11 women). *Students:* 59 full-time (45 women), 16 part-time (9 women). 72 applicants, 82% accepted, 35 enrolled. In 2007, 40 degrees awarded. *Degree requirements:* For master's, thesis optional. *Entrance requirements:* For master's, GRE General Test. Additional exam requirements/recommendations for international students: Required—TOEFL (minimum score 550 paper-based; 213 computer-based; 80 iBT), IELTS (minimum score 7). *Application deadline:* For fall admission, 3/1 priority date for domestic students; for spring admission, 11/1 priority date for domestic students. Applications are processed on a rolling basis. Application fee: $60 ($75 for international students). Electronic applications accepted. *Expenses:* Tuition: Full-time $16,800; part-time $840 per credit. Required fees: $60 per semester. One-time fee: $160. *Financial support:* In 2007–08, 1 fellowship with partial tuition reimbursement (averaging $14,000 per year), 11 research assistantships with partial tuition reimbursements (averaging $10,000 per year) were awarded; teaching assistantships with partial tuition reimbursements, career-related internships or fieldwork, Federal Work-Study, institutionally sponsored loans, scholarships/grants, and unspecified assistantships also available. Support available to part-time students. Financial award application deadline: 3/1; financial award applicants required to submit FAFSA. *Faculty research:* Theater. *Unit head:* Dr. Robert Colby, Director, 617-824-8780. *Application contact:* 617-824-8610, Fax: 617-824-8614, E-mail: gradapp@emerson.edu.

See Close-Up on page 349.

Florida Atlantic University, Dorothy F. Schmidt College of Arts and Letters, Department of Theatre, Boca Raton, FL 33431-0991. Offers MFA. *Degree requirements:* For master's, thesis, production. *Entrance requirements:* For master's, GRE General Test, minimum GPA of 3.0 during last 60 hours of undergraduate course work. *Faculty research:* Contemporary British theatre, Eastern European playwrights, Latin American drama.

Florida State University, Graduate Studies, School of Theatre, Tallahassee, FL 32306. Offers acting (MFA); directing (MFA); lighting, costume, and scenic design (MFA); technical production (MFA); theater management (MFA); theatre (MA, MS, PhD). *Accreditation:* NAST. *Faculty:* 20 full-time (10 women). *Students:* 102 full-time (49 women), 9 part-time (3 women); includes 11 minority (3 African Americans, 1 Asian American or Pacific Islander, 7 Hispanic Americans). Average age 25. 88 applicants, 43% accepted, 38 enrolled. In 2007, 28 master's, 2 doctorates awarded. *Median time to degree:* Of those who began their doctoral program in fall 1999, 0% received their degree in 8 years or less. *Degree requirements:* For master's, one foreign language, comprehensive exam (for some programs), thesis (for some programs); for doctorate, one foreign language, comprehensive exam, thesis/dissertation. *Entrance requirements:* For master's, GRE General Test, writing sample (MA), interview (MFA), minimum undergraduate GPA of 3.0, audition (MFA in acting), portfolio (MFA). Additional exam requirements/recommendations for international students: Required—TOEFL. *Application deadline:* For fall admission, 1/1 priority date for domestic and international students. Applications are processed on a rolling basis. Application fee: $30. *Expenses:* Tuition, state resident: part-time $248 per credit hour. Tuition, nonresident: part-time $880 per credit hour. Tuition and fees vary according to program. *Financial support:* In 2007–08, 1 fellowship with full tuition reimbursement (averaging $18,000 per year), 31 research assistantships with full tuition reimbursements (averaging $8,300 per year), 57 teaching assistantships with full tuition reimbursements (averaging $8,900 per year) were awarded; career-related internships or fieldwork, Federal Work-Study, institutionally sponsored loans, scholarships/grants, health care benefits, and unspecified assistantships also available. Financial award application deadline: 1/1; financial award applicants required to submit FAFSA. *Faculty research:* Gender theatre, performance theory, computers in theatre, dramaturgy, music theatre performance. *Unit head:* Cameron Jackson, Director, 850-644-7257, Fax: 850-644-7408, E-mail: ccjackson@admin.fsu.edu. *Application contact:* Barbara Thomas, Program Assistant, 850-644-7234, Fax: 850-644-7246, E-mail: bgthomas@admin.fsu.edu.

Fontbonne University, Graduate Programs, Department of Fine Arts, St. Louis, MO 63105-3098. Offers art (MA); fine arts (MFA); theater education (MA). Part-time and evening/weekend programs available. *Degree requirements:* For master's, thesis exhibit (MFA). *Entrance requirements:* For master's, minimum GPA of 3.0, portfolio.

The George Washington University, Columbian College of Arts and Sciences, Department of Theatre and Dance, Academy for Classical Acting, Washington, DC 20052. Offers MFA.

Graduate School and University Center of the City University of New York, Graduate Studies, Program in Theatre, New York, NY 10016-4039. Offers PhD. *Faculty:* 21 full-time (4 women). *Students:* 66 full-time (34 women), 5 part-time (3 women); includes 6 minority (all Hispanic Americans), 10 international. Average age 38. 58 applicants, 43% accepted, 10 enrolled. In 2007, 2 degrees awarded. *Degree requirements:* For doctorate, 2 foreign languages, thesis/dissertation. *Entrance requirements:* For doctorate, GRE General Test, writing sample. Additional exam requirements/recommendations for international students: Required—TOEFL. *Application deadline:* For fall admission, 3/1 for domestic students. Application fee: $125. Electronic applications accepted. *Financial support:* In 2007–08, 49 students received support, including 38 fellowships, 8 research assistantships, 12 teaching assistantships; career-related internships or fieldwork, Federal Work-Study, institutionally sponsored loans, and tuition waivers (full and partial) also available. Financial award application deadline: 2/1; financial award applicants required to submit FAFSA. *Unit head:* Dr. Glenn Burger, Executive Officer, 212-817-8871, Fax: 212-817-1538, E-mail: gburger@gc.cuny.edu.

Hollins University, Graduate Programs, Program in Playwriting, Roanoke, VA 24020-1603. Offers MFA. *Faculty:* 1 full-time (0 women), 1 part-time/adjunct (0 women). *Students:* 9 full-time (4 women). Average age 38. 17 applicants, 88% accepted, 9 enrolled. *Degree requirements:* For master's, thesis. *Entrance requirements:* For master's, letters of recommendation, writing samples. Additional exam requirements/recommendations for international students: Required—TOEFL (minimum score 550 paper-based; 213 computer-based). Application fee: $40. *Expenses:* Tuition: Part-time $265 per credit hour. Tuition and fees vary according to course load and program. *Unit head:* Todd Ristau, Director, 540-362-6386, E-mail: tristau@hollins.edu. *Application contact:* Cathy S. Koon, Manager of Graduate Services, 540-362-6326, Fax: 540-362-6288, E-mail: ckoon@hollins.edu.

Humboldt State University, Graduate Studies, College of Arts, Humanities, and Social Sciences, Department of Theatre, Film and Dance, Arcata, CA 95521-8299. Offers theatre arts/scenography (MFA); theatre arts/theatre production (MA). *Students:* 7 full-time (4 women), 2 part-time (both women); includes 1 minority (Hispanic American) Average age 35. 19 applicants, 53% accepted, 5 enrolled. In 2007, 1 degree awarded. *Degree requirements:* For master's, thesis or alternative, qualifying exam. *Entrance requirements:* For master's, minimum GPA of 2.5. Additional exam requirements/recommendations for international students: Required—TOEFL (minimum score 500 paper-based; 173 computer-based). *Application deadline:* For fall admission, 4/15 for domestic students. Applications are processed on a rolling basis. Application fee: $55. *Financial support:* Fellowships available. Financial award application deadline: 3/1; financial award applicants required to submit FAFSA. *Faculty research:* Physical theater, design, playwriting. *Unit head:* Bernadette Cheyne, Chair/Coordinator, 707-826-4606, Fax: 707-826-5494, E-mail: bmc3@humboldt.edu. *Application contact:* Ann Alter, Coordinator, 707-826-5495, Fax: 707-826-5494, E-mail: aea2@humboldt.edu.

Hunter College of the City University of New York, Graduate School, School of Arts and Sciences, Department of Theatre, New York, NY 10021-5085. Offers MA. Part-time and evening/weekend programs available. *Faculty:* 6 full-time (5 women). *Students:* 2 full-time (1 woman), 43 part-time (30 women); includes 5 minority (2 Asian Americans or Pacific Islanders, 3 Hispanic Americans). Average age 34. 22 applicants, 59% accepted, 7 enrolled. In 2007, 5 degrees awarded. *Degree requirements:* For master's, comprehensive exam, thesis. *Entrance requirements:* For master's, GRE General Test. Additional exam requirements/recommendations for international students: Required—TOEFL. *Application deadline:* For fall admission, 4/1 for domestic students, 2/1 for international students; for spring admission, 11/1 for domestic students, 9/1 for international students. Application fee: $125. *Expenses:* Tuition, state resident: full-time $6,400; part-time $270 per credit. Tuition, nonresident: part-time $500 per credit. One-time fee: $125 full-time. Tuition and fees vary according to program. *Financial support:* In 2007–08, 1 fellowship (averaging $3,000 per year), 4 teaching assistantships were awarded; research assistantships, career-related internships or fieldwork, Federal Work-Study, and tuition waivers (partial) also available. Support available to part-time students. Financial award application deadline: 4/15. *Faculty research:* Modern French mimes, acting techniques, directing, New York avant-garde theater and popular entertainment, playwriting. *Unit head:* Dr. Jonathan Kalb, Chairperson, 212-650-3789, Fax: 212-650-3584, E-mail: jonathan.kalb@hunter.cuny.edu.

Idaho State University, Office of Graduate Studies, College of Arts and Sciences, Program in Theatre and Dance, Pocatello, ID 83209. Offers theatre (MA). Part-time programs available. *Faculty:* 4 full-time (2 women). *Students:* 7 full-time (3 women), 3 part-time (2 women); includes 1 minority (Hispanic American) Average age 35. In 2007, 1 degree awarded. *Degree requirements:* For master's, comprehensive exam, thesis optional. *Entrance requirements:* For master's, GRE General Test, 35th percentile or above on one of the 3 sections of GRE. Additional exam requirements/recommendations for international students: Required—TOEFL (minimum score 550 paper-based; 213 computer-based; 80 iBT). *Application deadline:* For fall admission, 7/1 for domestic students, 6/1 for international students; for spring admission, 12/1 for domestic students, 11/1 for international students. Applications are processed on a rolling basis. Application fee: $55. *Expenses:* Tuition, state resident: full-time $2,882; part-time $259 per credit hour. Tuition, nonresident: full-time $11,566; part-time $379 per credit hour. Required fees: $2,278. Full-time tuition and fees vary according to program. Part-time tuition and fees vary according to course load. *Financial support:* In 2007–08, 2 teaching assistantships with full and partial tuition reimbursements (averaging $9,128 per year) were awarded; Federal Work-Study, institutionally sponsored loans, scholarships/grants, health care benefits, tuition waivers (full and partial), and unspecified assistantships also available. Support available to part-time students. Financial award application deadline: 1/1; financial award applicants required to submit FAFSA. *Faculty research:* Theatre history, technical theatre. *Unit head:* Dr. Sherri Dienstfrey, Chair, 208-282-3561, E-mail: diensher@isu.edu. *Application contact:* Ellen Combs, Graduate School Technical Records Specialist, 208-282-2150, Fax: 208-282-4847.

Illinois State University, Graduate School, College of Fine Arts, School of Theatre, Normal, IL 61790-2200. Offers MA, MFA, MS. *Accreditation:* NAST. Part-time programs available. *Faculty:* 20 full-time (12 women). *Students:* 19 full-time (12 women), 3 part-time (1 woman); includes 2 minority (1 African American, 1 Asian American or Pacific Islander), 2 international. 32 applicants, 25% accepted. In 2007, 13 degrees awarded. *Degree requirements:* For master's, variable foreign language requirement, thesis or alternative. *Entrance requirements:* For master's, sample of written work, minimum GPA of 3.0 in last 60 hours of course work. *Application deadline:* Applications are processed on a rolling basis. Application fee: $40. *Expenses:* Tuition, state resident: full-time $3,492; part-time $194 per credit hour. Tuition, nonresident: full-time $7,272; part-time $404 per credit hour. Required fees: $1,024; $57 per credit hour. *Financial support:* In 2007–08, 9 research assistantships (averaging $8,289 per year), 10 teaching assistantships (averaging $7,596 per year) were awarded; career-related internships or fieldwork, Federal Work-Study, institutionally sponsored loans, tuition waivers (full and partial), and unspecified assistantships also available. Financial award application deadline: 4/1. *Faculty research:* Illinois Shakespeare festival. Total annual research expenditures: $16,650. *Unit head:* Dr. John Poole, Acting Chair, 309-438-8783.

Indiana University Bloomington, University Graduate School, College of Arts and Sciences, Department of Theatre and Drama, Bloomington, IN 47405-7000. Offers acting (MFA); design and technology (MFA); directing (MFA); literature (MA, PhD); playwriting (MFA); theatre and drama (MAT); theatre history (MA, PhD); theory (MA, PhD). *Accreditation:* NAST. *Faculty:* 2 full-time (0 women), 2 part-time/adjunct (0 women). *Students:* 33 full-time (15 women), 8 part-time (3 women); includes 3 minority (1 American Indian/Alaska Native, 2 Hispanic Americans), 4 international. Average age 29. 41 applicants, 24% accepted, 10 enrolled. In 2007, 8 master's, 1 doctorate awarded. Terminal master's awarded for partial completion of doctoral program. *Median time to degree:* Of those who began their doctoral program in fall 1999, 100% received their degree in 8 years or less. *Degree requirements:* For master's, one foreign language, comprehensive exam, thesis, 30 credit hours; for doctorate, 2 foreign languages, comprehensive exam, thesis/dissertation, 90 credit hours, minor. *Entrance requirements:* For master's, GRE General Test, audition, interview, portfolio or script (MFA); for doctorate, GRE General Test. Additional exam requirements/recommendations for international students: Required—TOEFL (minimum score 550 paper-based; 213 computer-based; 80 iBT). *Application deadline:* For fall admission, 1/15 priority date for domestic students, 12/1 for international students. Application fee: $50 ($60 for international students). Electronic applications accepted. *Financial support:* In 2007–08, 38 students received support; fellowships with tuition reimbursements available, research assistantships with tuition reimbursements available, teaching assistantships with full tuition reimbursements available, career-related internships or fieldwork, Federal Work-Study, institutionally sponsored loans, scholarships/grants, health care benefits, and unspecified assistantships available. Financial award application deadline: 3/1. *Faculty research:* American, western European, world literature; history and theory; theatrical production, design and technology; acting; directing; playwriting. *Unit head:* Jonathan R. Michaelsen, Chairperson and Professor, 812-855-4535, Fax: 812-856-0698, E-mail: theatre@indiana.edu. *Application contact:* Barb Grinder, Administrative Secretary, 812-855-4503, Fax: 812-855-0698, E-mail: bgrinder@indiana.edu.

Kansas State University, Graduate School, College of Arts and Sciences, Department of Speech, Manhattan, KS 66506. Offers rhetoric/communication (MA); theatre (MA). *Faculty:* 14 full-time (8 women). *Students:* 44 full-time (26 women), 3 part-time (all women); includes 2 minority (1 African American, 1 Hispanic American), 2 international. Average age 23. 35 applicants, 86% accepted, 17 enrolled. In 2007, 1 degree awarded. *Degree requirements:* For master's, thesis or alternative. *Entrance requirements:* For master's, GRE General Test (recommended), minimum GPA of 3.0. Additional exam requirements/recommendations for international students: Required—TOEFL. *Application deadline:* For fall admission, 3/1 for domestic students, 2/1 priority date for international students; for spring admission, 10/1 for domestic students, 8/1 priority date for international students. Applications are processed on a rolling basis. Application fee: $30 ($55 for international students). *Financial support:* In 2007–08, 24 teaching assistantships with full tuition reimbursements (averaging $9,417 per year) were awarded; career-related internships or fieldwork, institutionally sponsored loans, and scholarships/grants also available. Support available to part-time students. Financial award application deadline: 3/1; financial award applicants required to submit FAFSA. *Faculty research:* Interpersonal/intercultural communication, political advertising, political rhetoric, deliberative democracy, persuasion, social influence, compliance-gaining. Total annual research expenditures: $2,748. *Unit head:* Charles Griffin, Head, 785-532-6860, Fax: 785-532-3714, E-mail: charlieg@ksu.edu. *Application contact:* William Schenck-Hamlin, Director, 785-532-6861, Fax: 785-532-3714, E-mail: billsh@ksu.edu.

Kent State University, College of the Arts, School of Theatre and Dance, Kent, OH 44242-0001. Offers acting (MFA); design and technology (MFA); theatre (MA, MFA). *Accreditation:* NAST. Part-time programs available. *Faculty:* 16 full-time. *Students:* 17 full-time (11 women), 1 part-time; includes 2 minority (1 African American, 1 American Indian/Alaska Native), 2 international. 9 applicants, 89% accepted. In 2007, 8 degrees awarded. *Degree requirements:* For master's, thesis. *Entrance requirements:* For master's, GRE General Test, minimum GPA of 2.75. Additional exam requirements/recommendations for international students: Required—TOEFL. *Application deadline:* For fall admission, 7/12 for domestic students; for spring admission, 11/29 for domestic students. Applications are processed on a rolling basis. Application fee: $30. Electronic applications accepted. *Financial support:* In 2007–08, 15 students received support, including teaching assistantships with full tuition reimbursements available (averaging $6,550 per year); research assistantships with full tuition reimbursements available, career-related internships or fieldwork, Federal Work-Study, health care benefits, tuition waivers (full), and unspecified assistantships also available. Financial award application deadline: 2/1. *Faculty research:* Scene design, costume design, lighting design, technical direction, musical theatre. *Unit head:* Cynthia R. Stillings, Director, 330-672-2082, E-mail: cstillin@kent.edu. *Application contact:* Rosemarie K. Bank, Coordinator of Graduate Studies, 330-672-2082, E-mail: rbank@kent.edu.

Lamar University, College of Graduate Studies, College of Fine Arts and Communication, Department of Music, Theatre, and Dance, Beaumont, TX 77710. Offers music education (MM Ed); music performance (MM); theatre (MS). *Accreditation:* NASM (one or more programs are accredited). *Faculty:* 11 full-time (4 women), 3 part-time/adjunct (1 woman). *Students:* 3 full-time (2 women), 4 part-time (all women). Average age 29. 5 applicants, 80% accepted, 2 enrolled. In 2007, 4 degrees awarded. *Degree requirements:* For master's, comprehensive exam, thesis optional. *Entrance requirements:* For master's, GRE General Test, theory placement exams, audition. Additional exam requirements/recommendations for international students: Required—TOEFL. *Application deadline:* For fall admission, 8/1 for domestic students; for spring admission, 12/1 for domestic students. Applications are processed on a rolling basis. Application fee: $25 ($50 for international students). *Expenses:* Tuition, state resident: part-time $348 per semester hour. Tuition, nonresident: part-time $626 per semester hour. Tuition and fees vary according to course load. *Financial support:* In 2007–08, 4 fellowships with tuition reimbursements (averaging $2,000 per year), 2 teaching assistantships were awarded; institutionally sponsored loans and tuition waivers (partial) also available. Support available to part-time students. Financial award application deadline: 4/1. *Faculty research:* Performance: ensembles and personal. *Unit head:* Dr. L. Randolph Babin, Chair, 409-880-8144, Fax: 409-880-8143, E-mail: babinlr@hal.lamar.edu. *Application contact:* Dr. Robert M. Culbertson, Adviser, 409-880-8073, Fax: 409-880-8143, E-mail: culbertsrm@hal.lamar.edu.

Lindenwood University, Graduate Programs, Division of Fine and Performing Arts, St. Charles, MO 63301-1695. Offers arts management (MA); communication arts (MA); studio art (MA, MFA); theatre (MA, MFA). Part-time programs available. *Faculty:* 19 full-time (9 women). *Students:* 17 full-time (11 women), 21 part-time (12 women); includes 3 minority (all African Americans), 3 international. Average age 34. In 2007, 23 degrees awarded. *Degree requirements:* For master's, thesis (for some programs). *Entrance requirements:* For master's, audition or interview, minimum GPA of 3.0. Additional exam requirements/recommendations for international students: Required—TOEFL (minimum score 550 paper-based; 213 computer-based; 80 iBT). *Application deadline:* For fall admission, 8/30 priority date for domestic and international students; for spring admission, 12/30 priority date for domestic and international students. Applications are processed on a rolling basis. Application fee: $30 ($100 for international students). Electronic applications accepted. *Expenses:* Tuition: Full-time $12,400; part-time $350 per hour. Full-time tuition and fees vary according to degree level and program. *Financial support:* Career-related internships or fieldwork, institutionally sponsored loans, tuition waivers (partial), and unspecified assistantships available. Financial award application deadline: 6/30; financial award applicants required to submit FAFSA. *Unit head:* Marsha Parker, Dean of Fine Arts, 636-949-4906, Fax: 636-949-4910, E-mail: mparker@lindenwood.edu. *Application contact:* Brett Barger, Dean of Evening Admissions and Extension Campuses, 636-949-4934, Fax: 636-949-4109, E-mail: adultadmissions@lindenwood.edu.

Long Island University, C.W. Post Campus, School of Visual and Performing Arts, Department of Theatre, Film, Dance and Arts Management, Brookville, NY 11548-1300. Offers interactive multimedia (MA); theatre (MA). Part-time and evening/weekend programs available. *Faculty:* 2 full-time (both women), 23 part-time/adjunct (13 women). *Students:* 18 full-time (12 women), 18 part-time (9 women); includes 7 minority (1 African American, 5 Asian Americans or Pacific Islanders, 1 Hispanic American), 3 international. Average age 31. 26 applicants, 65% accepted, 11 enrolled. In 2007, 4 degrees awarded. *Degree requirements:* For master's, thesis. *Entrance requirements:* For master's, placement exam. *Application deadline:* Applications are processed on a rolling basis. Application fee: $30. Electronic applications accepted. *Expenses:* Tuition: Part-time $825 per credit. Tuition and fees vary according to course load. *Financial support:* Career-related internships or fieldwork, Federal Work-Study, institutionally sponsored loans, scholarships/grants, and production assistantships available. Support available to part-time students. Financial award application deadline: 5/15; financial award applicants required to submit CSS PROFILE or FAFSA. *Faculty research:* Playwriting, intercultural dance and theatre, translation, Suzuki, set and costume design. *Unit head:* Dr. Cara Gargano, Chair, 516-299-2353, E-mail: cgargano@liu.edu. *Application contact:* Beth Carson, Director of Graduate and International Admissions, 516-299-2900 Ext. 3952, Fax: 516-299-2137, E-mail: enroll@cwpost.liu.edu.

Louisiana State University and Agricultural and Mechanical College, Graduate School, College of Music and Dramatic Arts, Department of Theatre, Baton Rouge, LA 70803. Offers acting (MFA); directing (MFA); theatre (PhD); theatre design/technology (MFA). *Accreditation:* NAST. *Faculty:* 18 full-time (8 women). *Students:* 23 full-time (12 women), 3 part-time (all women); includes 6 minority (3 African Americans, 2 Asian Americans or Pacific Islanders, 1 Hispanic American), 3 international. Average age 35. 12 applicants, 50% accepted, 6 enrolled. In 2007, 7 master's, 2 doctorates awarded. *Degree requirements:* For master's, thesis; for doctorate, one foreign language, thesis/dissertation. *Entrance requirements:* For master's, GRE General Test, audition, minimum GPA of 3.0; for doctorate, GRE General Test, minimum GPA of 3.0. Additional exam requirements/recommendations for international students: Required—TOEFL (minimum score 550 paper-based; 213 computer-based; 79 iBT). *Application deadline:* For fall admission, 1/25 priority date for domestic students, 5/15 for international students; for spring admission, 10/15 for international students. Applications are processed on a rolling basis. Application fee: $25. Electronic applications accepted. *Financial support:* In 2007–08, 24 students received support, including 5 fellowships with full and partial tuition reimbursements available (averaging $23,845 per year), 1 research assistantship with full and partial tuition reimbursement available (averaging $5,500 per year), 15 teaching assistantships with full and partial tuition reimbursements available (averaging $12,600 per year); Federal Work-Study, scholarships/grants, health care benefits, tuition waivers (full and partial), and unspecified assistantships also available. Support available to part-time students. Financial award application deadline: 6/15; financial award applicants required to submit FAFSA. *Faculty research:* Acting, American drama, arts administration, theatre history, dramatic theory/literature, black drama. *Unit head:* Dr. Michael Tick, Chair, 225-578-4174, Fax: 225-578-4135, E-mail: mtick1@lsu.edu. *Application contact:* James Murphy, Head, MFA Design/Tech, 225-578-3544.

Mary Baldwin College, Graduate Studies, Program in Shakespeare and Renaissance Literature in Performance, Staunton, VA 24401-3610. Offers acting (M Litt); directing (M Litt); Shakespeare and Renaissance literature in performance (MFA); teaching (M Litt). *Entrance requirements:* For master's, GRE (M Litt).

Massachusetts College of Art and Design, Graduate Programs, Program in Fine Arts, Boston, MA 02115-5882. Offers ceramics (MFA); design (MFA); fibers (MFA); film (MFA); glass (MFA); media and performing arts (MFA); metals (MFA); painting (MFA); photography (MFA); printmaking (MFA); sculpture (MFA). *Accreditation:* NASAD. *Faculty:* 10 full-time (5 women), 8 part-time/adjunct (6 women). *Students:* 80 full-time (46 women), 11 part-time (9 women); includes 7 minority (1 African American, 4 Asian Americans or Pacific Islanders, 2 Hispanic Americans), 13 international. Average age 34. 310 applicants, 26% accepted, 50 enrolled. In 2007, 37 degrees awarded. *Degree requirements:* For master's, thesis, exhibit. *Entrance requirements:* For master's, 12 units of course work in art history, portfolio, resumé. *Application deadline:* For fall admission, 2/1 for domestic students. Application fee: $75. *Expenses:* Tuition, state resident: full-time $16,260; part-time $542 per credit. Tuition, nonresident: full-time $16,260; part-time $542 per credit. *Financial support:* In 2007–08, 50 research assistantships (averaging $2,000 per year), 30 teaching assistantships (averaging $2,000 per year) were awarded; career-related internships or fieldwork, Federal Work-Study, and clerical/technical assistantships also available. Support available to part-time students. Financial award application deadline: 5/1; financial award applicants required to submit FAFSA. *Application contact:* George Creamer, Director, 617-879-7163, Fax: 617-879-7171, E-mail: creamer@massart.edu.

Miami University, Graduate School, School of Fine Arts, Department of Theatre, Oxford, OH 45056. Offers MA. *Accreditation:* NAST. *Degree requirements:* For master's, thesis (for some programs), final exam. *Entrance requirements:* For master's, minimum undergraduate GPA of 3.0 during previous 2 years or 2.75 overall.

Michigan State University, The Graduate School, College of Arts and Letters, Department of Theatre, East Lansing, MI 48824. Offers MA, MFA. *Entrance requirements:* Additional exam requirements/recommendations for international students: Required—TOEFL. Electronic applications accepted. *Expenses:* Tuition, state resident: part-time $379 per credit hour. Tuition, nonresident: part-time $800 per credit hour. Tuition and fees vary according to program.

Minnesota State University Mankato, College of Graduate Studies, College of Arts and Humanities, Department of Theatre and Dance, Mankato, MN 56001. Offers design/technology (MFA); performance (MFA); theatre arts (MA, MFA). *Students:* 12 full-time (5 women), 4 part-time (2 women). Average age 27. In 2007, 6 degrees awarded. *Degree requirements:* For master's, one foreign language, comprehensive exam, thesis. *Entrance requirements:* For master's, minimum GPA of 3.0 during previous 2 years, 3 letters of recommendation, resumé of theatre work, audition. Additional exam requirements/recommendations for international students: Required—TOEFL. *Application deadline:* For fall admission, 7/1 priority date for domestic students; for spring admission, 11/1 for domestic students. Applications are processed on a rolling basis. Application fee: $40. Electronic applications accepted. *Financial support:* Research assistantships with full tuition reimbursements, teaching assistantships with full tuition reimbursements, career-related internships or fieldwork, Federal Work-Study, institutionally sponsored loans, and unspecified assistantships available. Support available to part-time students. Financial award application deadline: 3/15; financial award applicants required to submit FAFSA. *Unit head:* Dr. Paul Hustoles, Chairperson, 507-389-2118. *Application contact:* 507-389-2321, E-mail: grad@mnsu.edu.

Missouri State University, Graduate College, College of Arts and Letters, Department of Theatre and Dance, Springfield, MO 65804-0094. Offers secondary education (MS Ed), including speech and theatre; theatre (MA). *Accreditation:* NAST. Part-time programs available. *Faculty:* 9 full-time (4 women). *Students:* 2 full-time (1 woman), 3 part-time (2 women); includes 1 minority (African American) Average age 30. 2 applicants, 100% accepted, 2 enrolled. In 2007, 1 degree awarded. *Degree requirements:* For master's, comprehensive exam, thesis or alternative. *Entrance requirements:* For master's, minimum GPA of 3.0 (MA), 9-12 teaching certification (MS Ed). Additional exam requirements/recommendations for international students: Required—TOEFL (minimum score 550 paper-based; 213 computer-based; 79 iBT). *Application deadline:* For fall admission, 7/20 for domestic students; for spring admission, 12/20 for domestic students. Applications are processed on a rolling basis. Application fee: $35. Electronic applications accepted. *Expenses:* Tuition, state resident: full-time $3,708; part-time $206 per credit hour. Tuition, nonresident: full-time $7,236; part-time $206 per credit hour. Required fees: $622. Full-time tuition and fees vary according to course level, course load, program and reciprocity agreements. *Financial support:* In 2007–08, 2 teaching assistantships with tuition reimbursements (averaging $7,050 per year) were awarded; research assistantships with tuition reimbursements, Federal Work-Study, institutionally sponsored loans, scholarships/grants, and unspecified assistantships also available. Financial award application deadline: 3/31; financial award applicants required to submit FAFSA. *Unit head:* Mark Biggs, Acting Head, 417-836-4400, Fax: 417-836-4234.

Montclair State University, The Office of Graduate Admissions and Support Services, School of the Arts, Department of Theatre and Dance, Montclair, NJ 07043-1624. Offers theatre (MA), including arts management, production/stage management, theatre studies. *Accreditation:* NAST. Part-time and evening/weekend programs available. *Faculty:* 7 full-time (3 women), 4 part-time/adjunct (2 women). *Students:* 9 full-time (8 women), 19 part-time (11 women); includes 4 minority (3 African Americans, 1 Hispanic American), 2 international. 16 applicants, 56% accepted, 6 enrolled. In 2007, 3 degrees awarded. *Degree requirements:* For master's, comprehensive exam, thesis or alternative. *Entrance requirements:* For master's, GRE General Test, minimum GPA of 3.0, undergraduate degree or work in theatre, oral interpretation, broadcasting, speech communication or media; 2 letters of recommendation. Additional exam requirements/recommendations for international students: Required—TOEFL (minimum score 83 computer-based). *Application deadline:* For fall admission, 6/1 for international students; for spring admission, 10/1 for international students. Applications are processed on a rolling basis. Application fee: $60. Electronic applications accepted. *Financial support:* In 2007–08, 1 research assistantship with full tuition reimbursement (averaging $7,000 per year) was awarded; Federal Work-Study, scholarships/grants, and unspecified assistantships also available. Support available to part-time students. Financial award application deadline: 3/1; financial award applicants required to submit FAFSA. *Unit head:* Dr. Jane Peterson, Chairperson, 973-655-4217, E-mail: peterson@mail.montclair.edu. *Application contact:* Dr. Jane Peterson, Adviser, 973-655-4109, E-mail: petersonj@mail.montclair.edu.

Naropa University, Graduate Programs, Program in Theater: Contemporary Performance, Boulder, CO 80302-6697. Offers MFA. *Faculty:* 2 full-time (1 woman), 1 (woman) part-time/adjunct. *Students:* 34 full-time (23 women); includes 6 minority (2 African Americans, 2 Asian Americans or Pacific Islanders, 2 Hispanic Americans). Average age 33. 38 applicants, 66% accepted, 19 enrolled. In 2007, 17 degrees awarded. *Entrance requirements:* For master's, interview, head shot. *Application deadline:* For fall admission, 1/15 for domestic and international students. Application fee: $60. *Expenses:* Tuition: Full-time $15,070; part-time $685 per credit. Required fees: $250 per semester. Tuition and fees vary according to course load. *Financial support:* In 2007–08, 18 students received support, including 1 research assistantship (averaging $3,000 per year), 2 teaching assistantships with partial tuition reimbursements available (averaging $3,000 per year); Federal Work-Study, scholarships/grants, health care benefits, tuition waivers (partial), and unspecified assistantships also available. Support available to part-time students. Financial award application deadline: 3/1; financial award applicants required to submit FAFSA. *Unit head:* Wendell Beavers, Director, Performing Arts, 303-245-4640. *Application contact:* Kate Levene, Assistant Director of Admissions, 303-245-4657, Fax: 303-546-3583, E-mail: klevene@naropa.edu.

See Close-Up on page 1449.

Naropa University, Graduate Programs, Program in Theater: Lecoq-Based Actor-Created Theater, Boulder, CO 80302-6697. Offers MFA. *Faculty:* 1 (woman) full-time. *Students:* Average age 27. 26 applicants, 81% accepted, 9 enrolled. In 2007, 7 degrees awarded. *Entrance requirements:* For master's, interview, head shot. *Application deadline:* For fall admission, 1/15 for domestic and international students. Application fee: $60. *Expenses:* Tuition: Full-time $15,070; part-time $685 per credit. Required fees: $250 per semester. Tuition and fees vary according to course load. *Financial support:* In 2007–08, 12 students received support. Scholarships/grants and tuition waivers (partial) available. Support available to part-time students. Financial award application deadline: 3/1. *Unit head:* Amy Russell, Chair, 303-482-1032, E-mail: london@naropa.edu. *Application contact:* Kate Levene, Assistant Director of Admissions, 303-245-4657, Fax: 303-546-3583, E-mail: klevene@naropa.edu.

See Close-Up on page 1449.

National Theatre Conservatory, Department of Acting, Denver, CO 80204-2157. Offers MFA, Certificate. *Entrance requirements:* For master's, audition/interview.

The New School: A University, The New School for Drama, New York, NY 10014. Offers acting (MFA); directing (MFA); playwriting (MFA). *Faculty:* 6 full-time (3 women), 31 part-time/adjunct (16 women). *Students:* 141 full-time (91 women), 8 part-time (5 women); includes 25 minority (15 African Americans, 1 Asian American or Pacific Islander, 9 Hispanic Americans), 29 international. Average age 27. In 2007, 54 degrees awarded. *Degree requirements:* For

Theater

The New School: A University (continued)

master's, thesis project. *Entrance requirements:* For master's, audition (acting), interview (directing and playwriting). Additional exam requirements/recommendations for international students: Required—TOEFL (minimum score 600 paper-based; 250 computer-based; 100 iBT). *Application deadline:* For fall admission, 1/10 priority date for domestic students. Application fee: $50. *Expenses: Contact institution. Financial support:* Federal Work-Study and scholarships/grants available. Financial award application deadline: 3/1; financial award applicants required to submit FAFSA. *Faculty research:* Translations of Vakhtangov, Metonymy and drama: essays on language and dramatic strategy; O'Neill, Sophocles. *Unit head:* Robert LuPone, Director, 212-229-5859 Ext. 2636, E-mail: luponer@newschool.edu. *Application contact:* Matthew Kelty, Director of Admissions, 212-229-5859, Fax: 212-229-5150, E-mail: keltym@newschool.edu.

See Close-Up on page 351.

New York University, Steinhardt School of Culture, Education and Human Development, Department of Music and Performing Arts Professions, Program in Educational Theatre, New York, NY 10012-1019. Offers educational theatre (Ed D, Advanced Certificate); educational theatre for colleges and communities (MA, PhD); educational theatre with English 7-12 (MA); teaching educational theatre, all grades (MA). Part-time and evening/weekend programs available. *Faculty:* 6 full-time (3 women). *Students:* 91 full-time (73 women), 46 part-time (36 women); includes 15 minority (5 African Americans, 1 American Indian/Alaska Native, 2 Asian Americans or Pacific Islanders, 7 Hispanic Americans), 9 international. 106 applicants, 87% accepted, 60 enrolled. In 2007, 72 master's, 6 doctorates awarded. Terminal master's awarded for partial completion of doctoral program. *Degree requirements:* For master's, thesis (for some programs); for doctorate, thesis/dissertation. *Entrance requirements:* For master's, audition; for doctorate, GRE General Test, interview; for Advanced Certificate, master's degree. Additional exam requirements/recommendations for international students: Required—TOEFL. *Application deadline:* For fall admission, 12/15 priority date for domestic and international students; for spring admission, 11/1 for domestic and international students. Applications are processed on a rolling basis. Application fee: $50. *Financial support:* Teaching assistantships with partial tuition reimbursements, career-related internships or fieldwork, Federal Work-Study, and scholarships/grants available. Support available to part-time students. Financial award application deadline: 2/1; financial award applicants required to submit FAFSA. *Faculty research:* Theatre for young audiences, drama in education, applied theatre, arts education assessment, reflective praxis. *Unit head:* Dr. Philip Taylor, Director, 212-998-5424, Fax: 212-995-4043. *Application contact:* 212-998-5030, Fax: 212-995-4328, E-mail: steinhardt.gradadmissions@nyu.edu.

New York University, Tisch School of the Arts and Graduate School of Arts and Science, Department of Performance Studies, New York, NY 10012-1019. Offers MA, PhD. *Faculty:* 12 full-time (7 women), 4 part-time/adjunct (3 women). *Students:* 93 full-time (71 women), 11 part-time (6 women); includes 19 minority (6 African Americans, 1 American Indian/Alaska Native, 6 Asian Americans or Pacific Islanders, 6 Hispanic Americans), 26 international. Average age 31. 203 applicants, 50% accepted, 60 enrolled. In 2007, 36 master's, 7 doctorates awarded. *Degree requirements:* For doctorate, one foreign language, comprehensive exam, thesis/dissertation, dissertation defense, qualifying exam. *Entrance requirements:* For master's, sample of written work; for doctorate, master's degree, writing sample. Additional exam requirements/recommendations for international students: Required—TOEFL or IELTS. *Application deadline:* For fall admission, 12/15 for domestic and international students. Application fee: $60. Electronic applications accepted. *Expenses: Contact institution. Financial support:* In 2007–08, 32 students received support, including 24 fellowships with full and partial tuition reimbursements available, 4 research assistantships, 4 teaching assistantships; Federal Work-Study, institutionally sponsored loans, tuition waivers (partial), and unspecified assistantships also available. Financial award application deadline: 2/15; financial award applicants required to submit CSS PROFILE or FAFSA. *Faculty research:* Performance theory, dance, folklore and festivals, postcolonial theory, anthropology and gender studies. *Unit head:* Jose Munoz, Chair, 212-998-1620, Fax: 212-995-4571, E-mail: performance.studies@nyu.edu. *Application contact:* Dan Sandford, Director of Graduate Admissions, 212-998-1918, Fax: 212-995-4060, E-mail: tisch.gradadmissions@nyu.edu.

New York University, Tisch School of the Arts, Graduate Acting Program, New York, NY 10012-1019. Offers MFA. *Faculty:* 9 full-time (6 women), 11 part-time/adjunct (5 women). *Students:* 52 full-time (23 women), 1 (woman) part-time; includes 14 minority (10 African Americans, 3 Asian Americans or Pacific Islanders, 1 Hispanic American), 2 international. Average age 26. 778 applicants, 2% accepted, 18 enrolled. In 2007, 18 degrees awarded. *Entrance requirements:* For master's, audition. *Application deadline:* For fall admission, 1/8 for domestic and international students. Application fee: $60. Electronic applications accepted. *Financial support:* In 2007–08, 30 students received support, including 4 fellowships with full and partial tuition reimbursements available; Federal Work-Study, institutionally sponsored loans, scholarships/grants, tuition waivers (full and partial), and unspecified assistantships also available. Financial award application deadline: 2/15; financial award applicants required to submit FAFSA. *Unit head:* Zelda Fichandler, Chair, 212-998-1964, Fax: 212-995-4067. *Application contact:* Dan Sandford, Director of Graduate Admissions, 212-998-1918, Fax: 212-995-4060, E-mail: tisch.gradadmissions@nyu.edu.

North Carolina School of the Arts, School of Design and Production, Winston-Salem, NC 27127-2188. Offers costume design (MFA); costume technology (MFA); film production design (MFA); scene design (MFA); scene painting/properties (MFA); sound design (MFA); technical direction (MFA); wig and make-up design (MFA). *Faculty:* 19 full-time (4 women), 16 part-time/adjunct (6 women). *Students:* 66 full-time (39 women); includes 4 minority (all Hispanic Americans), 2 international. Average age 25. 86 applicants, 77% accepted, 48 enrolled. In 2007, 14 degrees awarded. *Degree requirements:* For master's, project. *Entrance requirements:* For master's, interview, portfolio. *Application deadline:* For fall admission, 4/1 priority date for domestic students. Applications are processed on a rolling basis. Application fee: $60 ($100 for international students). Electronic applications accepted. *Expenses:* Tuition, state resident: full-time $3,636. Tuition, nonresident: full-time $15,220. Required fees: $1,688. *Financial support:* In 2007–08, 59 teaching assistantships with partial tuition reimbursements (averaging $1,500 per year) were awarded; career-related internships or fieldwork, Federal Work-Study, and unspecified assistantships also available. Support available to part-time students. Financial award application deadline: 3/15; financial award applicants required to submit FAFSA. *Unit head:* Joseph A. Tilford, Dean, 336-770-3214 Ext. 103, Fax: 336-770-3213. *Application contact:* Sheeler Lawson, Director of Admissions, 336-770-3290, Fax: 336-770-3370, E-mail: admissions@ncarts.edu.

Northern Illinois University, Graduate School, College of Visual and Performing Arts, School of Theatre and Dance, De Kalb, IL 60115-2854. Offers MFA. *Accreditation:* NAST. Part-time programs available. *Faculty:* 16 full-time (9 women). *Students:* 26 full-time (8 women); includes 2 minority (both African Americans), 3 international. Average age 28. 43 applicants, 49% accepted, 19 enrolled. In 2007, 17 degrees awarded. *Degree requirements:* For master's, comprehensive exam, final project and defense. *Entrance requirements:* For master's, minimum GPA of 2.75, audition or portfolio. Additional exam requirements/recommendations for international students: Required—TOEFL (minimum score 550 paper-based; 213 computer-based). *Application deadline:* For fall admission, 4/1 priority date for domestic students, 5/1 for international students; for spring admission, 10/15 priority date for domestic students, 10/1 for international students. Applications are processed on a rolling basis. Application fee: $30. Electronic applications accepted. *Expenses:* Tuition, area resident: Part-time $226 per credit hour. Tuition, state resident: full-time $5,424; part-time $225 per credit hour. Tuition, nonresident: full-time $10,848. Required fees: $2,416; $64 per credit hour. *Financial support:* In 2007–08, 2 research assistantships with full tuition reimbursements, 9 teaching assistantships with full tuition reimbursements were awarded; fellowships with full tuition reimbursements, career-related internships or fieldwork, Federal Work-Study, scholarships/grants, tuition waivers (full), and unspecified assistantships also available. Support available to part-time students. Financial award applicants required to submit FAFSA. *Faculty research:* Theatre history, choreography, performance art spectacles, storytelling, computer visualization of the ethical space. *Unit head:* Alexander Gelman, Director, 815-753-8253, Fax: 815-753-8415, E-mail: agelman@niu.edu. *Application contact:* Terrence McClellan, Information Contact, 815-753-8257, E-mail: tmcclell@niu.edu.

Northwestern University, The Graduate School, School of Communication, Department of Theatre, Evanston, IL 60208. Offers directing (MFA); stage design (MFA); theatre (MA). Admissions and degrees offered through The Graduate School. *Degree requirements:* For master's, thesis (MFA). *Entrance requirements:* For master's, GRE General Test. Additional exam requirements/recommendations for international students: Required—TOEFL. *Faculty research:* Critical analysis, theory and history of theatre and drama, philosophy of dance and movement, performance in multicultural contexts, storytelling, computer design process.

Northwestern University, The Graduate School, School of Communication, Interdisciplinary PhD Program in Theatre and Drama, Evanston, IL 60208. Offers PhD. Admissions and degree offered through The Graduate School. *Degree requirements:* For doctorate, thesis/dissertation, qualifying and final oral exams. *Entrance requirements:* For doctorate, GRE General Test, sample of written work. Additional exam requirements/recommendations for international students: Required—TOEFL. Electronic applications accepted. *Faculty research:* Theory and history of theatre and drama, performance theory, performance in multicultural contexts, critical analysis drama, theatre historiography.

The Ohio State University, Graduate School, College of the Arts, Department of Theatre, Columbus, OH 43210. Offers MA, MFA, PhD. *Accreditation:* NAST. *Faculty:* 22. *Students:* 32 full-time (15 women), 14 part-time (9 women); includes 7 minority (4 African Americans, 1 American Indian/Alaska Native, 1 Asian American or Pacific Islander, 1 Hispanic American), 5 international. Average age 30. In 2007, 17 master's, 3 doctorates awarded. *Degree requirements:* For master's, thesis (for some programs); for doctorate, one foreign language, thesis/dissertation. *Entrance requirements:* For master's, GRE General Test (MA); for doctorate, GRE General Test. Additional exam requirements/recommendations for international students: Recommended—TOEFL (minimum score 600 paper-based; 250 computer-based). *Application deadline:* For fall admission, 8/15 priority date for domestic students, 7/1 priority date for international students; for winter admission, 12/1 priority date for domestic students, 11/1 priority date for international students; for spring admission, 3/1 priority date for domestic students, 2/1 priority date for international students. Applications are processed on a rolling basis. Application fee: $40 ($50 for international students). Electronic applications accepted. *Financial support:* Fellowships, teaching assistantships, Federal Work-Study and institutionally sponsored loans available. Support available to part-time students. *Unit head:* Lesley K. Ferris, Graduate Studies Committee Chair, 614-292-5821, Fax: 614-292-3222, E-mail: ferris.36@osu.edu. *Application contact:* 614-292-9444, Fax: 614-292-3895, E-mail: domestic.grad@osu.edu.

Ohio University, Graduate College, College of Fine Arts, School of Theater, Athens, OH 45701-2979. Offers MA, MFA. *Accreditation:* NAST. *Faculty:* 14 full-time (5 women), 3 part-time/adjunct (1 woman). *Students:* 65 full-time (30 women), 4 part-time (all women); includes 7 minority (3 African Americans, 1 American Indian/Alaska Native, 3 Hispanic Americans), 19 international. 118 applicants, 29% accepted, 34 enrolled. In 2007, 31 master's awarded. *Median time to degree:* Of those who began their doctoral program in fall 1999, 90% received their degree in 8 years or less. *Degree requirements:* For master's, thesis or alternative. *Entrance requirements:* For master's, minimum GPA of 3.0. Additional exam requirements/recommendations for international students: Required—TOEFL. *Application deadline:* For fall admission, 3/1 priority date for domestic students. Applications are processed on a rolling basis. Application fee: $50 ($55 for international students). Electronic applications accepted. *Financial support:* In 2007–08, 59 students received support, including 46 research assistantships (averaging $7,348 per year); career-related internships or fieldwork, Federal Work-Study, institutionally sponsored loans, scholarships/grants, tuition waivers (full), and unspecified assistantships also available. Financial award application deadline: 2/15. *Faculty research:* Shakespearean performance, architecture, new plays, performance art, theory of comedy, playwriting. *Unit head:* William Fisher, Interim Director, 740-593-9194, Fax: 740-593-4817, E-mail: fisherw@ohio.edu. *Application contact:* Barbara M. Fiocchi, Administrative Assistant, 740-593-4818, Fax: 740-593-4817, E-mail: fiocchi@ohio.edu.

Oklahoma City University, Margaret E. Petree College of Performing Arts, Department of Theatre, Oklahoma City, OK 73106-1402. Offers costume design (MA); technical theater (MA); theater (MA); theater for young audiences (MA). Part-time programs available. *Faculty:* 4 full-time (2 women), 3 part-time/adjunct (0 women). *Students:* 3 full-time (all women), 1 (woman) part-time. Average age 28. 5 applicants, 60% accepted. In 2007, 2 degrees awarded. *Degree requirements:* For master's, thesis (for some programs). *Entrance requirements:* For master's, interview, audition, writing sample. Additional exam requirements/recommendations for international students: Required—TOEFL (minimum score 550 paper-based; 173 computer-based). *Application deadline:* For fall admission, 8/22 for domestic students; for spring admission, 1/15 for domestic students. Applications are processed on a rolling basis. Application fee: $30 ($70 for international students). *Expenses:* Tuition: Full-time $14,040; part-time $780 per hour. Required fees: $881; $32 per hour. *Financial support:* Fellowships with partial tuition reimbursements, career-related internships or fieldwork, Federal Work-Study, and institutionally sponsored loans available. Financial award application deadline: 8/1; financial award applicants required to submit FAFSA. *Faculty research:* Translation of plays, writing plays, dramaturgical research for plays and educational outreach materials. *Unit head:* Dr. Dan Childs, Chair, 405-208-5720, Fax: 405-208-5129, E-mail: dchilds@okcu.edu. *Application contact:* Leslie McKenzie, Director, Graduate Admissions, 800-633-7242, Fax: 405-208-5356, E-mail: gadmissions@okcu.edu.

Oklahoma State University, College of Arts and Sciences, Department of Theatre, Stillwater, OK 74078. Offers MA. *Accreditation:* NAST. *Faculty:* 8 full-time (4 women), 1 (woman) part-time/adjunct. *Students:* 5 full-time (3 women), 2 part-time (1 woman). Average age 27. 7 applicants, 29% accepted, 2 enrolled. In 2007, 2 degrees awarded. *Degree requirements:* For master's, creative component or thesis. *Entrance requirements:* For master's, GRE or GMAT. Additional exam requirements/recommendations for international students: Required—TOEFL. *Application deadline:* For fall admission, 3/1 priority date for international students; for spring admission, 8/1 priority date for international students. Applications are processed on a rolling basis. Application fee: $40 ($75 for international students). Electronic applications accepted. *Expenses:* Tuition, state resident: full-time $4,993; part-time $148 per credit hour. Tuition, nonresident: full-time $14,755; part-time $555 per credit hour. Tuition and fees vary according to program. *Financial support:* In 2007–08, 1 research assistantship (averaging $3,316 per year), 6 teaching assistantships (averaging $11,052 per year) were awarded; Federal Work-Study, scholarships/grants, health care benefits, and tuition waivers (partial) also available. Support available to part-time students. Financial award application deadline: 3/1. *Faculty research:* Historical scene painting and scenic art, Eastern European stage design, stage direction, voice and diction for the actor, stage choreography and dance. *Unit head:* Judith Cronk, Interim Head, 405-744-6094.

Pace University, Dyson College of Arts and Sciences, The Actors Studio MFA, New York, NY 10038. Offers MFA. *Faculty:* 3 full-time, 8 part-time/adjunct. *Students:* 63 full-time (36 women); includes 18 minority (12 African Americans, 2 Asian Americans or Pacific Islanders, 4 Hispanic Americans), 5 international. Average age 27. 116 applicants, 60% accepted, 39 enrolled. Application fee: $65. *Expenses:* Tuition: Part-time $856 per credit. Tuition and fees vary according to degree level and program. *Unit head:* Andreas Manolikakis, Head.

See Close-Up on page 353.

Penn State University Park, Graduate School, College of Arts and Architecture, School of Theatre, State College, University Park, PA 16802-1503. Offers MFA. *Accreditation:* NAST. *Expenses:* Tuition, state resident: full-time $14,738; part-time $614 per credit. Tuition, nonresident: full-time $26,050; part-time $1,085 per credit. Tuition and fees vary according to course load, program and student level. *Unit head:* Dan H. Carter, Director, 814-865-7586, Fax: 814-865-5754, E-mail: dhc4@psu.edu.

Pittsburg State University, Graduate School, College of Arts and Sciences, Department of Communication, Pittsburg, KS 66762. Offers applied communication (MA); communication education (MA); theatre (MA). *Degree requirements:* For master's, thesis or alternative.

Point Park University, Conservatory of Performing Arts, Pittsburgh, PA 15222-1984. Offers theatre arts-acting (MFA). *Faculty:* 4 full-time, 3 part-time/adjunct. *Students:* 5 full-time (3 women), 1 part-time. Average age 39. 1 applicant, 0% accepted. *Entrance requirements:* For master's, interview. *Application deadline:* Applications are processed on a rolling basis. Application fee: $30. Electronic applications accepted. *Expenses:* Tuition: Full-time $10,566; part-time $587 per credit. Required fees: $360; $20 per credit. *Financial support:* Teaching assistantships with full tuition reimbursements, scholarships/grants available. Financial award application deadline: 5/1; financial award applicants required to submit FAFSA. *Unit head:* Ronald Allan-Lindblom, Dean/Artistic Producing Director, 412-392-3454, Fax: 412-392-2424, E-mail: rlindblom@pointpark.edu. *Application contact:* Debbie P. Bateman, Director, Adult Academic Services, 412-392-3433, Fax: 412-392-6164, E-mail: dbateman@pointpark.edu.

Portland State University, Graduate Studies, School of Fine and Performing Arts, Department of Theater Arts, Portland, OR 97207-0751. Offers MA, MS, MA/MS. *Accreditation:* NAST. *Faculty:* 11 full-time (5 women), 10 part-time/adjunct (5 women). *Students:* 11 full-time (8 women), 5 part-time (2 women); includes 2 minority (1 Asian American or Pacific Islander, 1 Hispanic American), 2 international. Average age 33. 8 applicants, 88% accepted, 5 enrolled. In 2007, 4 degrees awarded. *Degree requirements:* For master's, variable foreign language requirement, thesis or alternative. *Entrance requirements:* For master's, minimum GPA of 3.0 in upper-division course work or 2.75 overall, 24 credits in theater arts. Additional exam requirements/recommendations for international students: Required—TOEFL (minimum score 550 paper-based; 213 computer-based). *Application deadline:* For fall admission, 3/1 priority date for domestic and international students. Applications are processed on a rolling basis. Application fee: $50. *Expenses:* Tuition, state resident: full-time $7,047. Tuition, nonresident: full-time $11,178. *Financial support:* Research assistantships, teaching assistantships with full tuition reimbursements, career-related internships or fieldwork, Federal Work-Study, and unspecified assistantships available. Support available to part-time students. Financial award application deadline: 3/1; financial award applicants required to submit FAFSA. *Faculty research:* Design, acting/directing, scene/costume technology, dramatic literature, theater history. Total annual research expenditures: $1,242. *Unit head:* Sarah Andrews-Collier, Chair, 503-725-4612, Fax: 503-725-4624, E-mail: andrews@pdx.edu. *Application contact:* Richard Wattenberg, Coordinator, 503-725-4602, Fax: 503-725-4624, E-mail: wattenbergr@pdx.edu.

Purchase College, State University of New York, Conservatory of Theatre Arts and Film, Purchase, NY 10577-1400. Offers theatre design (MFA); theatre technology (MFA). *Faculty:* 2 full-time (0 women), 15 part-time/adjunct (5 women). *Students:* 8 full-time (6 women). Average age 26. 14 applicants, 57% accepted, 2 enrolled. In 2007, 2 degrees awarded. *Degree requirements:* For master's, thesis or alternative, performance. *Entrance requirements:* For master's, BFA, interview, portfolio. *Application deadline:* For fall admission, 3/1 for domestic students. Application fee: $50. Electronic applications accepted. *Expenses:* Tuition, state resident: full-time $6,900; part-time $288 per credit. Tuition, nonresident: full-time $10,920; part-time $455 per credit. Required fees: $1,506; $125 per credit. Tuition and fees vary according to program. *Financial support:* In 2007–08, 7 students received support; fellowships, teaching assistantships, career-related internships or fieldwork, Federal Work-Study, scholarships/grants, and tuition waivers (partial) available. Support available to part-time students. Financial award application deadline: 3/15; financial award applicants required to submit FAFSA. *Faculty research:* Professional achievement: Broadway, opera, regional theatre, design and technology. *Unit head:* Gregory Taylor, Interim Dean, 914-251-6831, E-mail: gregory.taylor@purchase.edu. *Application contact:* Sabrina Johnston, Counselor, 914-251-6479, Fax: 914-251-6314, E-mail: admissn@purchase.edu.

Purdue University, Graduate School, College of Liberal Arts, Department of Visual and Performing Arts, West Lafayette, IN 47907. Offers art and design (MA); theatre (MA, MFA). *Accreditation:* NASAD; NAST. Part-time programs available. *Degree requirements:* For master's, terminal exhibit, project, or thesis. *Entrance requirements:* Additional exam requirements/recommendations for international students: Required—TOEFL. Electronic applications accepted. *Faculty research:* Design, fine arts, photography, acting, directing, theatre technology.

Regent University, Graduate School, School of Communication and the Arts, Virginia Beach, VA 23464-9800. Offers acting and directing (MFA); cinema arts (MA); communication (MA, PhD); fine arts (MFA); journalism (MA); script and screenwriting (MFA); television arts (MA); theatre arts (MA). Part-time programs available. Postbaccalaureate distance learning degree programs offered (minimal on-campus study). *Faculty:* 23 full-time (3 women), 12 part-time/adjunct (3 women). *Students:* 123 full-time (66 women), 145 part-time (83 women); includes 71 minority (54 African Americans, 2 American Indian/Alaska Native, 3 Asian Americans or Pacific Islanders, 12 Hispanic Americans), 14 international. Average age 33. 176 applicants, 66% accepted, 64 enrolled. In 2007, 60 master's, 15 doctorates awarded. *Degree requirements:* For master's, thesis or alternative; for doctorate, thesis/dissertation. *Entrance requirements:* For master's, GRE General Test or MAT, minimum undergraduate GPA of 3.0, writing sample, computer literacy survey, recommendation, resumé, interview, audition (MFA programs); for doctorate, GRE General Test, minimum graduate GPA of 3.0, writing sample, computer literacy survey, recommendation, interview, transcripts. Additional exam requirements/recommendations for international students: Required—TOEFL (minimum score 577 paper-based; 233 computer-based). *Application deadline:* For fall admission, 3/1 priority date for domestic students; for spring admission, 10/1 priority date for domestic students. Applications are processed on a rolling basis. Application fee: $50. Electronic applications accepted. *Expenses: Contact institution. Financial support:* In 2007–08, 247 students received support, including 5 fellowships with full and partial tuition reimbursements available (averaging $7,245 per year); scholarships/grants, tuition waivers (full and partial), and unspecified assistantships also available. Support available to part-time students. Financial award application deadline: 9/1; financial award applicants required to submit FAFSA. *Faculty research:* Southern gospel music, education and entertainment, celebrities and the media, journalism and ethics, C. S. Lewis. *Unit head:* Michael Patrick, Dean, 757-226-4970, Fax: 757-226-4279, E-mail: michpat@regent.edu. *Application contact:* Althea Bishard, Registrar and Executive Director of Enrollment and Academic Services, 800-373-5504, Fax: 757-226-4381, E-mail: admissions@regent.edu.

Rhode Island College, School of Graduate Studies, Faculty of Arts and Sciences, Department of Music, Theatre, and Dance, Providence, RI 02908-1991. Offers music education (MAT, MM Ed); theatre (MFA). Part-time and evening/weekend programs available. *Faculty:* 4 full-time (0 women), 15 part-time/adjunct (8 women). *Students:* 19 full-time (12 women), 7 part-time (5 women); includes 2 minority (1 African American, 1 Hispanic American). Average age 31. In 2007, 6 degrees awarded. *Degree requirements:* For master's, comprehensive exam, thesis, final project (MFA). *Entrance requirements:* For master's, GRE General Test or MAT, exams in music education, theory, history and literature, audition, 3 letters of recommendation, evidence of musicianship, interview. *Application deadline:* For fall admission, 4/1 for domestic students; for spring admission, 11/1 for domestic students. Applications are processed on a rolling basis. Application fee: $50. *Expenses:* Tuition, state resident: full-time $6,240; part-time $260 per credit hour. Tuition, nonresident: full-time $13,104; part-time $546 per credit hour. Required fees: $332; $14 per credit hour. One-time fee: $66 part-time. *Financial support:* Teaching assistantships with full tuition reimbursements, Federal Work-Study, scholarships/grants, health care benefits, and unspecified assistantships available. Support available to part-time students. Financial award application deadline: 5/15; financial award applicants required to submit FAFSA. *Unit head:* Dr. James Taylor, Chair, 401-456-8639, E-mail: jtaylor@ric.edu.

Roosevelt University, Graduate Division, Chicago College of Performing Arts, Theatre Conservatory, Chicago, IL 60605-1394. Offers directing and dramaturgy (MFA); musical theatre (MFA); theatre (MA, MFA); theatre-directing (MA); theatre-performance (MFA). MA is a special 3-summer program for high school teachers only. *Students:* 8 full-time (2 women), 7 part-time (2 women); includes 1 minority (African American) Average age 30. In 2007, 14 degrees awarded. *Degree requirements:* For master's, thesis production/performance. *Entrance requirements:* For master's, audition, interview, minimum GPA of 2.5. *Application deadline:* For fall admission, 6/1 priority date for domestic students; for spring admission, 9/1 for domestic students. Applications are processed on a rolling basis. Application fee: $25 ($35 for international students). *Financial support:* In 2007–08, 30 students received support, including 1 research assistantship; career-related internships or fieldwork, Federal Work-Study, scholarships/grants, and tuition waivers (full and partial) also available. Support available to part-time students. Financial award application deadline: 4/1. *Faculty research:* Brecht, Shakespeare, contemporary and new work, fully mounted theatre. *Unit head:* Joel Fink, Director, 312-341-3719, Fax: 312-341-8314. *Application contact:* Joanne Canyon-Heller, Coordinator of Graduate Admission, 877-APPLY RU, Fax: 312-281-3356, E-mail: applyru@roosevelt.edu.

Rowan University, Graduate School, College of Fine and Performing Arts, Program in Theatre, Glassboro, NJ 08028-1701. Offers MA. *Accreditation:* NAST. Part-time and evening/weekend programs available. *Faculty:* 2 full-time (1 woman). *Students:* Average age 47. 2 applicants, 50% accepted, 0 enrolled. *Entrance requirements:* Additional exam requirements/recommendations for international students: Required—TOEFL. *Application deadline:* Applications are processed on a rolling basis. Application fee: $50. Electronic applications accepted. *Expenses:* Tuition, nonresident: full-time $9,882; part-time $549 per credit. Required fees: $104,385 per credit. *Financial support:* Career-related internships or fieldwork, Federal Work-Study, and unspecified assistantships available. Support available to part-time students. *Unit head:* Dr. Philip Graneto, Adviser, 856-256-4392.

Rutgers, The State University of New Jersey, New Brunswick, Mason Gross School of the Arts, Department of Theater Arts, New Brunswick, NJ 08901-1281. Offers acting (MFA); design (MFA); directing (MFA); playwriting (MFA); stage management (MFA). *Degree requirements:* For master's, thesis (for some programs), performance project. *Entrance requirements:* For master's, audition, interview, portfolio. Electronic applications accepted. *Faculty research:* Faculty of working professional.

St. John's University, St. John's College of Liberal Arts and Sciences, Department of Speech, Communication Sciences and Theatre, Queens, NY 11439. Offers MA, Au D, Advanced Diploma. *Accreditation:* ASHA. Evening/weekend programs available. *Faculty:* 20 full-time (12 women), 40 part-time/adjunct (25 women). *Students:* 83 full-time (77 women), 75 part-time (71 women); includes 33 minority (15 African Americans, 1 American Indian/Alaska Native, 4 Asian Americans or Pacific Islanders, 13 Hispanic Americans), 2 international. Average age 27. 406 applicants, 26% accepted, 47 enrolled. In 2007, 60 degrees awarded. *Degree requirements:* For master's, comprehensive exam, thesis optional, internship. *Entrance requirements:* For master's, minimum GPA of 3.0. Additional exam requirements/recommendations for international students: Required—TOEFL (minimum score 500 paper-based; 173 computer-based; 61 iBT), IELTS (minimum score 6). *Application deadline:* For fall admission, 2/1 for domestic students, 5/1 priority date for international students; for spring admission, 10/1 for domestic students, 11/1 priority date for international students. Applications are processed on a rolling basis. Application fee: $40. Electronic applications accepted. *Expenses: Contact institution. Financial support:* Research assistantships, career-related internships or fieldwork and scholarships/grants available. Support available to part-time students. Financial award application deadline: 3/1; financial award applicants required to submit FAFSA. *Faculty research:* Bilingualism and adult and child language disorders, dysphagia speech motor control, electrophysiological measurement of hearing, central auditory processing disorders and auditory habilitation and rehabilitation. *Unit head:* Dr. Fredericka Bell-Berti, Chair, 718-990-6450, E-mail: bellf@stjohns.edu. *Application contact:* Beth Evans, Associate Vice President and Executive Director, Enrollment Management, 718-990-6999, Fax: 718-990-5686, E-mail: gradhelp@stjohns.edu.

San Diego State University, Graduate and Research Affairs, College of Professional Studies and Fine Arts, School of Theater, Television and Film, San Diego, CA 92182. Offers television, film, and new media production (MA); theatre arts (MA, MFA). *Accreditation:* NAST. Part-time programs available. *Students:* 39 full-time (20 women), 28 part-time (18 women); includes 7 minority (1 African American, 1 Asian American or Pacific Islander, 5 Hispanic Americans), 8 international. Average age 29. 53 applicants, 45% accepted, 19 enrolled. In 2007, 21 degrees awarded. *Degree requirements:* For master's, thesis. *Entrance requirements:* For master's, GRE General Test, 3 letters of recommendation, interview. Additional exam requirements/recommendations for international students: Required—TOEFL. *Application deadline:* For fall admission, 4/15 for domestic students, 4/15 priority date for international students. Applications are processed on a rolling basis. Application fee: $55. Electronic applications accepted. *Financial support:* In 2007–08, 5 teaching assistantships were awarded; career-related internships or fieldwork and unspecified assistantships also available. Financial award applicants required to submit FAFSA. Total annual research expenditures: $2,000. *Unit head:* Nick Reid, Director, 619-594-5091, Fax: 619-594-7431, E-mail: reid1@mail.sdsu.edu. *Application contact:* Paula Kalustian, Graduate Coordinator, 619-594-4757, Fax: 619-594-7431, E-mail: kalustia@mail.sdsu.edu.

San Francisco State University, Division of Graduate Studies, College of Creative Arts, Department of Theatre Arts, San Francisco, CA 94132-1722. Offers drama (MA); theatre arts (MFA), including design/technical production, performance. *Accreditation:* NAST. *Unit head:* Dr. Yukihiro Goto, Chair, 415-338-1341.

San Jose State University, Graduate Studies and Research, College of Humanities and the Arts, Department of Television, Radio, Film and Theatre, San Jose, CA 95192-0001. Offers theatre arts (MA). *Accreditation:* NAST. *Students:* 10 full-time (5 women), 25 part-time (16 women); includes 10 minority (6 African Americans, 1 Asian American or Pacific Islander, 3 Hispanic Americans), 3 international. Average age 36. 19 applicants, 74% accepted, 7 enrolled. In 2007, 4 degrees awarded. *Degree requirements:* For master's, written exam. *Entrance requirements:* Additional exam requirements/recommendations for international students: Required—TOEFL (minimum score 570 paper-based). *Application deadline:* For fall admission, 6/29 for domestic students; for spring admission, 11/30 for domestic students. Applications are processed on a rolling basis. Application fee: $59. Electronic applications accepted. *Financial support:* Scholarships/grants available. Financial award applicants required to submit FAFSA. *Unit head:* Dr. Mike Adams, Chair, 408-924-4545, Fax: 408-924-4574. *Application contact:* Dr. David Kahn, Graduate Coordinator, 408-924-4530, E-mail: dkahn@email.sjsu.edu.

Sarah Lawrence College, Graduate Studies, Program in Theater, Bronxville, NY 10708-5999. Offers MFA. *Faculty:* 25 part-time/adjunct (8 women). *Students:* 13 full-time (12 women), 2 part-time (1 woman); includes 2 minority (both African Americans), 3 international. Average age 34. 55 applicants, 31% accepted, 11 enrolled. In 2007, 13 degrees awarded. *Degree requirements:* For master's, portfolio. *Entrance requirements:* For master's, interview, minimum B average in undergraduate course work. Additional exam requirements/recommendations for international students: Required—TOEFL (minimum score 600 paper-based). *Application deadline:* For fall admission, 1/15 for domestic students. Application fee: $60. *Expenses:* Tuition: Part-time $1,034 per credit. Required fees: $430 per year. Tuition and fees vary according to program. *Financial support:* In 2007–08, 12 fellowships (averaging $5,117 per year) were awarded; career-related internships or fieldwork, scholarships/grants, and unspecified assistantships also available. Support available to part-time students. Financial award application deadline: 3/1. *Unit head:* Shirley Kaplan, Director, 914-395-2262. *Application contact:* Susan Guma, Dean of Graduate Studies, 914-395-2373, E-mail: sguma@mail.slc.edu.

See Close-Up on page 355.

Savannah College of Art and Design, Graduate School, Program in Production Design, Savannah, GA 31402-3146. Offers MA, MFA. Part-time programs available. *Faculty:* 2 full-time (0 women). *Students:* 4 full-time (3 women); includes 1 minority (African American) 6 applicants, 83% accepted, 2 enrolled. In 2007, 1 degree awarded. *Degree requirements:* For

Theater

Savannah College of Art and Design (continued)
master's, thesis. *Entrance requirements:* For master's, interview, portfolio. Additional exam requirements/recommendations for international students: Required—TOEFL (minimum score 450 paper-based; 133 computer-based). *Application deadline:* For fall admission, 4/1 priority date for domestic and international students. Applications are processed on a rolling basis. Application fee: $50. Electronic applications accepted. *Expenses:* Tuition: Full-time $24,840; part-time $552 per credit. One-time fee: $500 full-time. *Financial support:* Fellowships, career-related internships or fieldwork, Federal Work-Study, and scholarships/grants available. Financial award application deadline: 4/1; financial award applicants required to submit FAFSA. *Unit head:* Dr. Joseph Kline, Chair, 912-525-6648, Fax: 912-525-6935, E-mail: jkline@scad.edu. *Application contact:* Darrell Tutchton, Director of Graduate and International Enrollment, 912-525-5961, Fax: 912-525-5985, E-mail: admission@scad.edu.

Smith College, Graduate Programs, Department of Theatre, Northampton, MA 01063. Offers playwriting (MFA). Part-time programs available. *Faculty:* 8 full-time (5 women). *Students:* 1 (woman) full-time, 1 part-time. Average age 40. 4 applicants, 0% accepted. In 2007, 1 degree awarded. *Degree requirements:* For master's, one foreign language, thesis. *Entrance requirements:* Additional exam requirements/recommendations for international students: Required—TOEFL. *Application deadline:* For fall admission, 4/15 for domestic students, 1/15 for international students; for spring admission, 12/1 for domestic students. Application fee: $60. *Expenses:* Tuition: Full-time $33,940; part-time $1,060 per credit. Tuition and fees vary according to course load. *Financial support:* In 2007–08, 2 students received support. Institutionally sponsored loans and scholarships/grants available. Support available to part-time students. Financial award application deadline: 1/15; financial award applicants required to submit CSS PROFILE or FAFSA. *Unit head:* Leonard Berkman, Graduate Adviser, 413-585-3206, E-mail: lberkman@smith.edu. *Application contact:* Leonard Berkman, Graduate Adviser, 413-585-3206, E-mail: lberkman@smith.edu.

Southern Illinois University Carbondale, Graduate School, College of Liberal Arts, Theater Department, Carbondale, IL 62901-4701. Offers speech/theater (PhD); theater (MFA). *Accreditation:* NAST (one or more programs are accredited). Part-time programs available. *Faculty:* 8 full-time (4 women). *Students:* 16 full-time (8 women), 1 part-time; includes 1 minority (African American), 2 international. Average age 26. 27 applicants, 37% accepted, 9 enrolled. In 2007, 8 degrees awarded. *Degree requirements:* For master's, thesis; for doctorate, thesis/dissertation. *Entrance requirements:* For master's, minimum GPA of 2.7; for doctorate, minimum GPA of 3.25. Additional exam requirements/recommendations for international students: Required—TOEFL. *Application deadline:* For fall admission, 3/1 for domestic students. Applications are processed on a rolling basis. Application fee: $20. *Financial support:* In 2007–08, 13 research assistantships with full tuition reimbursements, 10 teaching assistantships with full tuition reimbursements were awarded; fellowships with full tuition reimbursements, career-related internships or fieldwork, Federal Work-Study, institutionally sponsored loans, and tuition waivers (full) also available. Support available to part-time students. Financial award application deadline: 3/15. *Faculty research:* Scenography, theater performance, theater history, dramatic criticism, theater technology, playwriting. *Unit head:* Dr. Mark K. Varns, Chair, 618-453-7588, E-mail: varns@siu.edu. *Application contact:* Dr. Ron Naverson, Director, 618-453-3076, E-mail: rnav@siu.edu.

Announcement: The Department of Theatre at Southern Illinois University Carbondale blends scholarship and practice in an academically based experience. The course work establishes a solid theoretical framework enhanced by a production season ensuring that students write, direct, and design as much as possible so they graduate with a full resume of experience and expertise in their areas of study. Faculty members bridge the academic and professional world by regularly working in professional theaters, writing articles and books and presenting at national and international conferences. The department maintains a newly renovated 520-seat proscenium theater and a flexible studio theater for productions.

See Close-Up on page 359.

Southern Methodist University, Meadows School of the Arts, Division of Theatre, Dallas, TX 75275. Offers acting (MFA); design (MFA). *Accreditation:* NAST. *Faculty:* 16 full-time (5 women), 3 part-time/adjunct (2 women). *Students:* 22 full-time (11 women); includes 3 minority (2 African Americans, 1 Asian American or Pacific Islander). Average age 25. 10 applicants, 90% accepted, 9 enrolled. In 2007, 8 degrees awarded. *Entrance requirements:* For master's, audition or interview. Additional exam requirements/recommendations for international students: Required—TOEFL (minimum score 550 paper-based; 213 computer-based; 80 iBT). *Application deadline:* For fall admission, 3/1 priority date for domestic and international students. Application fee: $75. *Financial support:* In 2007–08, 23 students received support, including 20 teaching assistantships (averaging $6,600 per year); scholarships/grants and unspecified assistantships also available. Financial award application deadline: 3/1; financial award applicants required to submit FAFSA. *Faculty research:* European lighting techniques. *Unit head:* Cecil O'Neal, Chair, 214-768-2558, Fax: 214-768-1136, E-mail: coneal@smu.edu. *Application contact:* Jean Cherry, Director of Graduate Admissions and Records, 214-768-3765, Fax: 214-768-3272, E-mail: jcherry@smu.edu.

Stanford University, School of Humanities and Sciences, Department of Drama, Stanford, CA 94305-9991. Offers PhD. *Degree requirements:* For doctorate, one foreign language, thesis/dissertation, qualifying exams. *Entrance requirements:* For doctorate, GRE General Test, summary of production experience. Additional exam requirements/recommendations for international students: Required—TOEFL. Electronic applications accepted.

State University of New York at Binghamton, Graduate School, School of Arts and Sciences, Department of Theater, Binghamton, NY 13902-6000. Offers MA. *Faculty:* 12 full-time (4 women), 9 part-time/adjunct (2 women). *Students:* 4 full-time (3 women), 2 part-time (1 woman). Average age 35. 12 applicants, 58% accepted, 2 enrolled. In 2007, 1 master's awarded. *Degree requirements:* For master's, thesis. *Entrance requirements:* For master's, GRE General Test, GRE Subject Test. Additional exam requirements/recommendations for international students: Required—TOEFL. *Application deadline:* For fall admission, 4/15 priority date for domestic students, 1/15 priority date for international students; for spring admission, 11/1 for domestic students, 10/1 priority date for international students. Applications are processed on a rolling basis. Application fee: $60. Electronic applications accepted. *Financial support:* In 2007–08, 3 students received support, including 1 fellowship (averaging $11,216 per year), 2 teaching assistantships with full and partial tuition reimbursements available (averaging $9,000 per year); career-related internships or fieldwork, Federal Work-Study, institutionally sponsored loans, and unspecified assistantships also available. Support available to part-time students. Financial award application deadline: 2/15. *Unit head:* Dr. John E. Vestal, Chairperson, 607-777-2360, E-mail: jvestal@binghamton.edu.

Stony Brook University, State University of New York, Graduate School, College of Arts and Sciences, Department of Theatre Arts, Program in Dramaturgy, Stony Brook, NY 11794. Offers MFA. *Students:* 10 full-time (7 women); includes 1 minority (Hispanic American), 1 international. Average age 29. 11 applicants, 91% accepted. In 2007, 4 degrees awarded. *Degree requirements:* For master's, one foreign language, thesis. *Entrance requirements:* For master's, GRE General Test. Additional exam requirements/recommendations for international students: Required—TOEFL. *Application deadline:* For fall admission, 1/15 for domestic students. Application fee: $60. *Application contact:* Michael Zelenak, Director of Graduate Studies, 631-632-7280.

See Close-Up on page 369.

Stony Brook University, State University of New York, Graduate School, College of Arts and Sciences, Department of Theatre Arts, Program in Theatre Arts, Stony Brook, NY 11794. Offers MA. Evening/weekend programs available. *Students:* 3 full-time (2 women), 4 part-time (2 women); includes 1 minority (Hispanic American), 1 international. Average age 35. 8 applicants, 88% accepted. In 2007, 1 degree awarded. *Degree requirements:* For master's, one foreign language, thesis. *Entrance requirements:* For master's, GRE General Test. Additional exam requirements/recommendations for international students: Required—TOEFL. *Application deadline:* For fall admission, 1/15 for domestic students. Application fee: $60. *Application contact:* Michael Zelenak, Director of Graduate Studies, 631-632-7280.

See Close-Up on page 369.

Temple University, Graduate School, School of Communications and Theater, Department of Theater, Philadelphia, PA 19122-6096. Offers acting (MFA); design (MFA); directing (MFA). *Accreditation:* NAST. Part-time programs available. *Degree requirements:* For master's, thesis (for some programs). *Entrance requirements:* For master's, minimum GPA of 3.0; audition/interview, portfolio, or samples of written work. Additional exam requirements/recommendations for international students: Required—TOEFL (minimum score 550 paper-based; 213 computer-based; 79 iBT). Electronic applications accepted.

Texas A&M University–Commerce, Graduate School, College of Arts and Sciences, Department of Communication and Theatre, Commerce, TX 75429-3011. Offers theatre (MA, MS). Part-time programs available. *Faculty:* 4 full-time (3 women). *Students:* 7 full-time (3 women), 8 part-time (3 women); includes 6 minority (3 African Americans, 2 American Indian/Alaska Native, 1 Hispanic American). Average age 36. In 2007, 1 degree awarded. *Degree requirements:* For master's, comprehensive exam, thesis (for some programs). *Entrance requirements:* For master's, GRE General Test. *Application deadline:* For fall admission, 6/1 priority date for domestic students; for spring admission, 11/1 priority date for domestic students. Applications are processed on a rolling basis. Application fee: $0 ($25 for international students). Electronic applications accepted. *Financial support:* In 2007–08, research assistantships (averaging $7,875 per year), teaching assistantships (averaging $7,875 per year) were awarded; Federal Work-Study, institutionally sponsored loans, and scholarships/grants also available. Financial award application deadline: 5/1; financial award applicants required to submit FAFSA. *Faculty research:* Theater history. Total annual research expenditures: $45,000. *Unit head:* Dr. John Hanners, Head, 903-886-5346, Fax: 903-468-3250, E-mail: john_hanners@tamu-commerce.edu. *Application contact:* Tammi Thompson, Graduate Admissions Adviser, 843-886-5167, Fax: 843-886-5165, E-mail: tammi_thompson@tamu-commerce.edu.

Texas State University–San Marcos, Graduate School, College of Fine Arts and Communication, Department of Theatre Arts and Dance, Program in Theatre Arts, San Marcos, TX 78666. Offers MA. Part-time and evening/weekend programs available. *Faculty:* 5 full-time (3 women), 1 part-time/adjunct (0 women). *Students:* 12 full-time (6 women), 9 part-time (8 women); includes 4 minority (1 African American, 3 Hispanic Americans), 1 international. Average age 34. 11 applicants, 82% accepted, 7 enrolled. In 2007, 5 degrees awarded. *Degree requirements:* For master's, comprehensive exam, thesis or alternative. *Entrance requirements:* For master's, GRE General Test, minimum GPA of 2.75 in last 60 hours of course work. Additional exam requirements/recommendations for international students: Required—TOEFL (minimum score 550 paper-based; 213 computer-based). *Application deadline:* For fall admission, 6/15 priority date for domestic students; for spring admission, 10/15 priority date for domestic students. Applications are processed on a rolling basis. Application fee: $40 ($90 for international students). Electronic applications accepted. *Expenses:* Tuition, state resident: full-time $3,780; part-time $210 per credit hour. Tuition, nonresident: full-time $8,784; part-time $488 per credit hour. Required fees: $493 per semester. Full-time tuition and fees vary according to course load. *Financial support:* In 2007–08, 19 students received support, including 11 teaching assistantships (averaging $4,384 per year); Federal Work-Study, institutionally sponsored loans, and unspecified assistantships also available. Support available to part-time students. Financial award application deadline: 4/1; financial award applicants required to submit FAFSA. *Faculty research:* Theatre history (especially nineteenth century American theatre), stage productions, playwriting. *Unit head:* Dr. Debra Charlton, Graduate Adviser, 512-245-2147, Fax: 512-245-8440, E-mail: dc21@txstate.edu.

Texas Tech University, Graduate School, College of Visual and Performing Arts, Department of Theatre and Dance, Lubbock, TX 79409. Offers fine arts (PhD); theatre arts (MA, MFA), including arts administration (MFA), design (MFA), performance/pedagogy (MFA), playwriting (MFA). *Accreditation:* NAST. Part-time programs available. *Faculty:* 9 full-time (5 women). *Students:* 35 full-time (18 women), 25 part-time (12 women); includes 5 minority (3 African Americans, 1 Asian American or Pacific Islander, 1 Hispanic American), 4 international. Average age 35. 32 applicants, 69% accepted, 16 enrolled. In 2007, 10 master's, 5 doctorates awarded. *Degree requirements:* For master's, variable foreign language requirement, thesis; for doctorate, thesis/dissertation. *Entrance requirements:* For master's and doctorate, GRE General Test. Additional exam requirements/recommendations for international students: Required—TOEFL (minimum score 550 paper-based; 213 computer-based). *Application deadline:* For fall admission, 3/1 priority date for international students; for spring admission, 11/1 priority date for international students. Applications are processed on a rolling basis. Application fee: $50 ($60 for international students). Electronic applications accepted. *Expenses:* Tuition, state resident: part-time $373 per credit hour. Tuition, nonresident: part-time $651 per credit hour. Tuition and fees vary according to program. *Financial support:* In 2007–08, 42 students received support, including 27 teaching assistantships with partial tuition reimbursements available (averaging $10,239 per year); research assistantships with partial tuition reimbursements available, Federal Work-Study and institutionally sponsored loans also available. Support available to part-time students. Financial award application deadline: 4/15; financial award applicants required to submit FAFSA. *Faculty research:* New student plays program, theatre planning, dramaturgy; feminist theatre; arts administration. *Unit head:* Prof. Frederick B. Christoffel, Chair, 806-742-3601 Ext. 228, Fax: 806-742-1338, E-mail: fred.christoffel@ttu.edu. *Application contact:* Dr. Linda Donahue, Graduate Adviser, 806-742-3601 Ext. 225, Fax: 806-742-1338, E-mail: linda.donahue@ttu.edu.

Texas Tech University, Graduate School, College of Visual and Performing Arts, Fine Arts Doctoral Program, Lubbock, TX 79409. Offers arts (PhD); music (PhD); theatre arts (PhD). *Accreditation:* NAST. *Students:* 40 full-time (16 women), 33 part-time (16 women); includes 8 minority (4 African Americans, 1 American Indian/Alaska Native, 1 Asian American or Pacific Islander, 2 Hispanic Americans), 9 international. Average age 37. 26 applicants, 62% accepted, 9 enrolled. In 2007, 10 degrees awarded. *Degree requirements:* For doctorate, thesis/dissertation. *Entrance requirements:* For doctorate, GRE General Test. Additional exam requirements/recommendations for international students: Required—TOEFL (minimum score 550 paper-based; 213 computer-based). *Application deadline:* For fall admission, 3/1 priority date for international students; for spring admission, 11/1 priority date for international students. Applications are processed on a rolling basis. Application fee: $50 ($60 for international students). Electronic applications accepted. *Expenses:* Tuition, state resident: part-time $373 per credit hour. Tuition, nonresident: part-time $651 per credit hour. Tuition and fees vary according to program. *Financial support:* Research assistantships with partial tuition reimbursements, teaching assistantships with partial tuition reimbursements available. Financial award application deadline: 4/15. *Faculty research:* Art criticism and theory, music, aesthetics, theatre arts. *Unit head:* Dr. Brian Steele, Director, 806-742-0700, Fax: 806-742-0695, E-mail: brian.steele@ttu.edu.

Texas Woman's University, Graduate School, College of Arts and Sciences, School of the Arts, Department of Music and Drama, Denton, TX 76201. Offers drama (MA); music (MA). *Accreditation:* NASM. Part-time programs available. *Students:* 45 full-time (35 women), 22 part-time (19 women); includes 10 minority (1 African American, 1 American Indian/Alaska Native, 1 Asian American or Pacific Islander, 7 Hispanic Americans), 9 international. Average age 32. In 2007, 14 master's awarded. *Degree requirements:* For master's, thesis optional, project recital. *Entrance requirements:* For master's, music history/theory placement exam, audition, interview, sample of professional work, licensure as a music therapist, piano and aural skills. Additional exam requirements/recommendations for international students: Required—TOEFL (minimum score 550 paper-based; 213 computer-based; 79 iBT). *Application deadline:* For fall admission, 4/1 for international students; for spring admission, 8/1 for international students. Applications are processed on a rolling basis. Application fee: $30 ($50 for international students). Electronic applications accepted. *Expenses:* Tuition, state resident: full-time $3,294; part-time $183 per credit. Tuition, nonresident: full-time $8,298; part-time $461 per credit. Required fees: $985; $55 per credit. Tuition and fees vary according to degree level. *Financial support:* In 2007–08, 9 teaching assistantships (averaging $9,684 per year) were awarded; career-related internships or fieldwork, Federal Work-Study, institutionally sponsored loans, scholarships/grants, traineeships, health care benefits, tuition waivers (partial), and unspecified assistantships also available. Support available to part-time students. Financial award application deadline: 3/1; financial award applicants required to submit FAFSA. *Faculty research:* Musical development in early childhood, little known or neglected compositions for flute (especially by women composers), relationship of visual art to piano music, pedagogical development of the singing voice, guided imagery and music. *Unit head:* Dr. James Chenevert, Chair, 940-898-2500, Fax: 940-898-2494, E-mail: jchenevert@mail.twu.edu. *Application contact:* Samuel Wheeler, Assistant Director of Admissions, 940-898-3188, Fax: 940-898-3081, E-mail: wheelersr@twu.edu.

Towson University, College of Graduate Studies and Research, Program in Theatre, Towson, MD 21252-0001. Offers MFA. *Accreditation:* NAST. *Faculty:* 5 full-time (2 women), 1 (woman) part-time/adjunct. *Students:* 13 full-time (10 women), 4 part-time; includes 6 minority (2 African Americans, 1 Asian American or Pacific Islander, 3 Hispanic Americans), 1 international. Average age 34. 5 applicants, 100% accepted, 4 enrolled. In 2007, 3 degrees awarded. *Degree requirements:* For master's, thesis. *Entrance requirements:* For master's, audition or portfolio, interview, minimum GPA of 3.0. *Application deadline:* For fall admission, 3/1 for domestic students. Application fee: $50. Electronic applications accepted. *Expenses:* Tuition, state resident: part-time $286 per credit. Tuition, nonresident: part-time $600 per credit. Required fees: $75 per credit. *Financial support:* In 2007–08, 1 fellowship with tuition reimbursement (averaging $10,000 per year), 1 teaching assistantship with tuition reimbursement (averaging $6,000 per year) were awarded; unspecified assistantships also available. Financial award application deadline: 4/1; financial award applicants required to submit FAFSA. *Faculty research:* Playwriting, directing, entrepreneurship in the arts, movement theatre, design, drama. *Unit head:* Stephen Nunns, Graduate Program Director, 410-704-3141. *Application contact:* 410-704-2501, Fax: 410-704-4675, E-mail: grads@towson.edu.

Tufts University, Graduate School of Arts and Sciences, Department of Drama and Dance, Medford, MA 02155. Offers dance (MA, PhD); drama (MA); dramatic literature and criticism (PhD); theater history (PhD). Part-time programs available. *Faculty:* 11 full-time, 8 part-time/adjunct. *Students:* 27 (18 women); includes 4 minority (1 African American, 3 Asian Americans or Pacific Islanders) 2 international. 37 applicants, 32% accepted, 4 enrolled. In 2007, 1 master's, 4 doctorates awarded. Terminal master's awarded for partial completion of doctoral program. *Degree requirements:* For master's, one foreign language, thesis; for doctorate, 2 foreign languages, thesis/dissertation, oral exam, written general exam. *Entrance requirements:* For master's and doctorate, GRE General Test, writing sample. Additional exam requirements/recommendations for international students: Required—TOEFL (minimum score 600 paper-based; 250 computer-based; 80 iBT). *Application deadline:* For fall admission, 1/15 for domestic students, 12/30 for international students. Applications are processed on a rolling basis. Application fee: $70. Electronic applications accepted. *Expenses:* Tuition: Full-time $35,052. *Financial support:* Fellowships with full and partial tuition reimbursements, teaching assistantships with full and partial tuition reimbursements, Federal Work-Study, scholarships/grants, and tuition waivers (partial) available. Support available to part-time students. Financial award application deadline: 1/15; financial award applicants required to submit FAFSA. *Unit head:* Dr. Barbara Grossman, Chair, 617-627-3524. *Application contact:* Dr. Laurence Senelick, Head, 617-627-3524.

Announcement: The department concentrates on theater and performance history and dramatic literature and criticism. First-year fellowships, assistantships, and research/travel stipends are available. Students have access to the Harvard Theatre Collection. There are opportunities as assistant directors and dramaturges on faculty-directed productions. Students regularly win scholarly awards and present papers at academic conferences. The program fosters close relationships between students and faculty members.

Tulane University, School of Liberal Arts, Department of Theatre and Dance, New Orleans, LA 70118-5669. Offers design and technical production (MFA). *Entrance requirements:* For master's, GRE General Test, minimum B average in undergraduate course work. Additional exam requirements/recommendations for international students: Required—TOEFL. Electronic applications accepted. *Faculty research:* Scene design, stage management, costume design, technical direction, lighting design.

Université de Sherbrooke, Faculty of Letters and Human Sciences, Department of Letters and Communications, Sherbrooke, QC J1K 2R1, Canada. Offers comparative Canadian literature (MA, PhD); French literature (MA, PhD); linguistics (MA); lit&erature de crèation (MA, PhD); theatre (MA). *Degree requirements:* For master's, thesis or alternative; for doctorate, thesis/dissertation. *Entrance requirements:* For master's, minimum GPA of 2.8; for doctorate, minimum GPA of 3.0.

Université du Québec à Montréal, Graduate Programs, Program in Dramatic Arts, Montréal, QC H3C 3P8, Canada. Offers MA. Part-time programs available. *Degree requirements:* For master's, thesis or alternative. *Entrance requirements:* For master's, appropriate bachelor's degree or equivalent, proficiency in French.

Université Laval, Faculty of Letters, Department of Literature, Programs in Literature and the Screen and Stage, Québec, QC G1K 7P4, Canada. Offers MA, PhD. Part-time programs available. Terminal master's awarded for partial completion of doctoral program. *Degree requirements:* For master's, thesis; for doctorate, comprehensive exam, thesis/dissertation. *Entrance requirements:* For master's and doctorate, linguistics exams, knowledge of French, knowledge of a second language. Electronic applications accepted.

University at Albany, State University of New York, College of Arts and Sciences, Department of Theatre, Albany, NY 12222-0001. Offers MA. *Students:* Average age 42. *Entrance requirements:* Additional exam requirements/recommendations for international students: Required—TOEFL (minimum score 550 paper-based; 213 computer-based). *Application deadline:* For fall admission, 8/1 for domestic students, 5/1 for international students. Applications are processed on a rolling basis. Application fee: $75. Electronic applications accepted. *Expenses:* Tuition, state resident: part-time $576 per credit. Tuition, nonresident: part-time $910 per credit. Tuition and fees vary according to program. *Financial support:* Application deadline: 4/1. *Unit head:* J. Kevin Doolen, Chair, 518-442-4200, Fax: 518-442-4206.

The University of Akron, Graduate School, College of Fine and Applied Arts, School of Dance, Theatre, and Arts Administration, Program in Theatre Arts, Akron, OH 44325. Offers MA. *Students:* 1 (woman) full-time. Average age 50. 4 applicants, 100% accepted. In 2007, 2 degrees awarded. *Degree requirements:* For master's, thesis optional. *Entrance requirements:* For master's, minimum GPA of 2.75, interview, personal statement. Additional exam requirements/recommendations for international students: Required—TOEFL (minimum score 550 paper-based; 213 computer-based; 79 iBT). *Application deadline:* For fall admission, 3/15 for domestic and international students. Applications are processed on a rolling basis. Application fee: $30 ($40 for international students). Electronic applications accepted. *Expenses:* Tuition, state resident: full-time $6,164; part-time $342 per credit. Tuition, nonresident: full-time $10,575; part-time $588 per credit. Required fees: $806; $43 per credit. $12 per term. Tuition and fees vary according to course load, degree level and program. *Unit head:* James Slowiak, Coordinator, 330-972-5909, E-mail: slowiak@uakron.edu.

The University of Alabama, Graduate School, College of Arts and Sciences, Department of Theatre and Dance, Tuscaloosa, AL 35487. Offers acting (MFA); costume design (MFA); directing (MFA); scene design/technical production (MFA); stage management (MFA); theatre (MFA); theatre management/administration (MFA). *Accreditation:* NAST. *Faculty:* 10 full-time (2 women). *Students:* 48 full-time (23 women), 1 (woman) part-time; includes 4 minority (all African Americans), 1 international. Average age 28. 34 applicants, 59% accepted, 20 enrolled. In 2007, 17 degrees awarded. *Degree requirements:* For master's, thesis project. *Entrance requirements:* For master's, auditions/portfolio review. *Application deadline:* For fall admission, 7/6 for domestic students. Applications are processed on a rolling basis. Application fee: $30. Electronic applications accepted. *Expenses:* Tuition, state resident: full-time $5,700. Tuition, nonresident: full-time $16,518. *Financial support:* In 2007–08, 25 research assistantships (averaging $14,544 per year), 21 teaching assistantships (averaging $10,908 per year) were awarded; Federal Work-Study and health care benefits also available. *Faculty research:* Arts management, theatre history, practice and production. *Unit head:* William Teague, Chairman and Professor, 205-348-5283, Fax: 205-348-9048, E-mail: wteague@theatre.as.ua.edu. *Application contact:* Pamela McCray, Recruiting Contact, 205-348-5283, Fax: 205-348-9048, E-mail: pmccray@bama.ua.edu.

University of Alberta, Faculty of Graduate Studies and Research, Department of Drama, Edmonton, AB T6G 2E1, Canada. Offers design (MFA); directing (MFA); drama (MA). *Degree requirements:* For master's, one foreign language, production thesis. *Faculty research:* Dramaturgy, history, theory and criticism, design.

The University of Arizona, Graduate College, College of Fine Arts, School of Theatre Arts, Tucson, AZ 85721. Offers MA, MFA. *Accreditation:* NAST. *Faculty:* 4. *Students:* 32 full-time (21 women), 1 international. Average age 29. 29 applicants, 41% accepted, 12 enrolled. In 2007, 23 degrees awarded. *Degree requirements:* For master's, comprehensive exam (for some programs), thesis (for some programs), production monograph. *Entrance requirements:* For master's, GRE, 3 letters of recommendation, statement of intent, portfolio. Additional exam requirements/recommendations for international students: Required—TOEFL (minimum score 550 paper-based; 213 computer-based). *Application deadline:* For fall admission, 2/15 for domestic students, 12/1 for international students. Applications are processed on a rolling basis. Application fee: $50. Electronic applications accepted. *Financial support:* In 2007–08, 2 fellowships with partial tuition reimbursements (averaging $10,000 per year), 13 teaching assistantships with partial tuition reimbursements (averaging $10,650 per year) were awarded; career-related internships or fieldwork, Federal Work-Study, institutionally sponsored loans, scholarships/grants, health care benefits, tuition waivers (full), and unspecified assistantships also available. Financial award application deadline: 3/1; financial award applicants required to submit FAFSA. *Faculty research:* Modern and contemporary theater, cultural studies, musical theater, women and theater. *Unit head:* Albert Tucci, Head, 520-621-7007, E-mail: tucci@email.arizona.edu. *Application contact:* Justine M. Collins, Assistant to Director, Administration, 520-621-7007, Fax: 520-621-2412, E-mail: jcollins@email.arizona.edu.

University of Arkansas, Graduate School, J. William Fulbright College of Arts and Sciences, Department of Drama, Fayetteville, AR 72701-1201. Offers MA, MFA. *Students:* 18 full-time (10 women), 5 part-time (1 woman); includes 3 minority (2 African Americans, 1 Hispanic American), 2 international. In 2007, 4 degrees awarded. *Degree requirements:* For master's, thesis optional. Application fee: $40 ($50 for international students). *Financial support:* In 2007–08, 17 fellowships with tuition reimbursements, 11 teaching assistantships were awarded; research assistantships, career-related internships or fieldwork and Federal Work-Study also available. Support available to part-time students. Financial award application deadline: 4/1; financial award applicants required to submit FAFSA. *Unit head:* Dr. Andrew Gibbs, Departmental Chairperson, 479-575-2953, Fax: 479-575-7602, E-mail: dagibbs@uark.edu.

The University of British Columbia, Faculty of Arts, Creative Writing Program, Vancouver, BC V6T 1Z1, Canada. Offers creative writing (MFA); creative writing and film (MFA); creative writing and theatre (MFA). Part-time programs available. Postbaccalaureate distance learning degree programs offered (minimal on-campus study). *Faculty:* 7 full-time (4 women), 14 part-time/adjunct (7 women). *Students:* 57 full-time (41 women), 90 part-time (67 women). 308 applicants, 22% accepted, 62 enrolled. In 2007, 24 degrees awarded. *Degree requirements:* For master's, thesis. *Entrance requirements:* For master's, sample of written work. Additional exam requirements/recommendations for international students: Required—TOEFL (minimum score 550 paper-based; 213 computer-based). *Application deadline:* For fall admission, 11/7 for domestic and international students; for winter admission, 9/12 for domestic and international students. Application fee: $90 Canadian dollars ($150 Canadian dollars for international students). Electronic applications accepted. *Expenses: Contact institution. Financial support:* In 2007–08, 13 students received support, including 5 fellowships (averaging $16,000 per year), research assistantships (averaging $1,500 per year), 2 teaching assistantships (averaging $3,000 per year); Federal Work-Study, institutionally sponsored loans, and unspecified assistantships also available. *Faculty research:* Writing of fiction; poetry, creative nonfiction, plays for stage, screen, television, radio, writing for children and translation, song lyrics and libretto. *Unit head:* Keith Maillard, Chair, 604-822-3058, Fax: 604-822-3616. *Application contact:* Bryan Wade, Residential Graduate Adviser, 604-822-3023, Fax: 604-822-3616, E-mail: bwade@interchange.ubc.ca.

The University of British Columbia, Faculty of Arts and Faculty of Graduate Studies, Department of Theatre and Film, Theatre Program, Vancouver, BC V6T 1Z1, Canada. Offers theatre (MA, PhD); theatre design (MFA); theatre directing (MFA). *Faculty:* 7 full-time (2 women). *Students:* 19 full-time (13 women); includes 3 minority (2 Asian Americans or Pacific Islanders, 1 Hispanic American), 1 international. Average age 28. 34 applicants, 15% accepted. In 2007, 3 master's, 1 doctorate awarded. *Degree requirements:* For master's, variable foreign language requirement, comprehensive exam, thesis; for doctorate, 2 foreign languages, comprehensive exam, thesis/dissertation. *Entrance requirements:* For master's, portfolio (MFA); for doctorate, MA or equivalent. Additional exam requirements/recommendations for international students: Required—TOEFL, TOEFL score of 550 paper-based, 213 computer-based required for MFA; score of 600 paper-based, 250 computer-based required for MA and PhD programs. *Application deadline:* For fall admission, 1/15 for domestic and international students. Application fee: $90 Canadian dollars ($150 Canadian dollars for international students). *Financial support:* In 2007–08, 1 fellowship (averaging $16,000 per year), research assistantships (averaging $5,161 per year), teaching assistantships (averaging $5,300 per year) were awarded; career-related internships or fieldwork and institutionally sponsored loans also available. Support available to part-time students. Financial award application deadline: 3/15. *Faculty research:* Dramatic literature, theatrical history, criticism, playwriting, directing. *Unit head:* Stephen Heatley, Chair, 604-822-0037, Fax: 604-822-5985, E-mail: sheatley@interchange.ubc.ca. *Application contact:* Karen Tong, Graduate Admissions, 604-822-3880 Ext. 0, Fax: 604-822-5985, E-mail: fwtheatr@interchange.ubc.ca.

University of Calgary, Faculty of Graduate Studies, Faculty of Fine Arts, Department of Drama, Calgary, AB T2N 1N4, Canada. Offers design and technical theatre (MFA); directing (MFA); playwriting (MFA); theatre studies (MFA). *Degree requirements:* For master's, thesis. *Entrance requirements:* For master's, bachelor's degree in drama, minimum GPA of 3.0, portfolio (design and playwriting). Additional exam requirements/recommendations for international students: Required—TOEFL. *Faculty research:* Popular theatre, collective creation, technical design, dramaturgy, directing styles.

University of California, Berkeley, Graduate Division, Group in Performance Studies, Berkeley, CA 94720-1500. Offers PhD. *Faculty:* 23 full-time. In 2007, 1 degree awarded. *Degree requirements:* For doctorate, one foreign language, thesis/dissertation, qualifying exam. *Entrance requirements:* For doctorate, GRE General Test, sample of critical writing, 3 letters of recommendation. Additional exam requirements/recommendations for international students: Required—TOEFL. *Application deadline:* For fall admission, 12/5 for domestic students. Application fee: $70 ($90 for international students). Electronic applications accepted. *Financial support:* Fellowships, teaching assistantships with tuition reimbursements, unspecified assistantships available. Financial award applicants required to submit FAFSA. *Faculty research:* Postcolonial performance, gender, sexuality, and performance; political performance; dramatic literature and theory; race, ethnicity, performance. *Unit head:* Shannon Jackson, Chair, 510-642-3895, E-mail: shjacks@berkeley.edu. *Application contact:* Mary Ajideh, Graduate Assistant for Admission, 510-642-1677, Fax: 510-643-9956, E-mail: phdprogram@theater.berkeley.edu.

Theater

University of California, Davis, Graduate Studies, Program in Dramatic Art, Davis, CA 95616. Offers acting (MFA); dramatic art (PhD). *Entrance requirements:* For master's, minimum GPA of 3.0, portfolio. Additional exam requirements/recommendations for international students: Required—TOEFL (minimum score 550 paper-based; 213 computer-based). Electronic applications accepted. *Faculty research:* Twentieth century performance and culture.

University of California, Davis, Graduate Studies, Program in Performance Studies, Davis, CA 95616. Offers dramatic art (PhD). *Degree requirements:* For doctorate, 2 foreign languages, thesis/dissertation. *Entrance requirements:* For doctorate, GRE, minimum GPA of 3.25. Additional exam requirements/recommendations for international students: Required—TOEFL (minimum score 550 paper-based; 213 computer-based). Electronic applications accepted.

University of California, Irvine, Office of Graduate Studies, Claire Trevor School of the Arts, Department of Drama, Irvine, CA 92697. Offers acting (MFA); design and stage management (MFA); directing (MFA); drama (MFA); drama and theatre (PhD). *Students:* 74 full-time (40 women); includes 6 minority (5 African Americans, 1 American Indian/Alaska Native), 4 international. In 2007, 15 master's, 2 doctorates awarded. *Degree requirements:* For master's, comprehensive exam, thesis; for doctorate, one foreign language, thesis/dissertation. *Entrance requirements:* For master's, audition, interview, or portfolio; minimum GPA of 3.0; for doctorate, GRE, minimum GPA of 3.5, critical writing samples. *Application deadline:* For fall admission, 1/15 priority date for domestic students; for winter admission, 10/15 priority date for domestic students. Applications are processed on a rolling basis. Application fee: $60. Electronic applications accepted. *Financial support:* Fellowships, teaching assistantships, institutionally sponsored loans, traineeships, health care benefits, and unspecified assistantships available. Financial award application deadline: 3/1; financial award applicants required to submit FAFSA. *Faculty research:* Costume, scenery, and lighting design; production; theatre history, literature, and criticism. *Unit head:* Dr. George C. Harvey, Chair, 949-824-6614, Fax: 949-824-4914, E-mail: gcharvey@uci.edu. *Application contact:* Felice Weis, Administrative Assistant, 949-824-6332, E-mail: fweis@uci.edu.

University of California, Los Angeles, Graduate Division, School of Theater, Film and Television, Department of Theater, Los Angeles, CA 90095. Offers theater (MA, MFA, PhD). *Accreditation:* NAST. *Faculty:* 16. *Students:* 92 full-time (49 women); includes 25 minority (9 African Americans, 1 American Indian/Alaska Native, 5 Asian Americans or Pacific Islanders, 10 Hispanic Americans), 8 international. Average age 28. 246 applicants, 16% accepted, 28 enrolled. In 2007, 24 master's, 4 doctorates awarded. *Degree requirements:* For master's, comprehensive exam or thesis; for doctorate, one foreign language, thesis/dissertation, oral and written exam. *Entrance requirements:* For master's, minimum GPA of 3.0, interview, portfolio, resumé, script, audition; for doctorate, GRE General Test, minimum undergraduate GPA of 3.0. *Application deadline:* For fall admission, 12/1 for domestic students. Application fee: $60 ($80 for international students). Electronic applications accepted. *Financial support:* In 2007–08, 72 fellowships with full and partial tuition reimbursements, 9 research assistantships with full and partial tuition reimbursements, 46 teaching assistantships with full and partial tuition reimbursements were awarded; career-related internships or fieldwork, Federal Work-Study, institutionally sponsored loans, scholarships/grants, traineeships, tuition waivers (full and partial), and unspecified assistantships also available. Financial award application deadline: 3/1; financial award applicants required to submit FAFSA. *Unit head:* William D. Ward, Chair, 310-825-8787. *Application contact:* Departmental Office, 310-825-8787, E-mail: info@tft.ucla.edu.

University of California, San Diego, Office of Graduate Studies, Department of Theatre and Dance, La Jolla, CA 92093. Offers acting (MFA); design (MFA); directing (MFA); drama and theatre (PhD); playwriting (MFA); stage management (MFA); theatre (PhD). *Degree requirements:* For master's, thesis. *Entrance requirements:* For master's, GRE General Test (directing, playwriting). Electronic applications accepted.

University of California, Santa Barbara, Graduate Division, College of Letters and Sciences, Division of Humanities and Fine Arts, Department of Theatre and Dance, Santa Barbara, CA 93106. Offers theater (MA, PhD); MA/PhD. *Faculty:* 6 full-time (2 women). *Students:* 22 full-time (16 women); includes 1 minority (Hispanic American), 1 international. Average age 32. 40 applicants, 20% accepted, 5 enrolled. In 2007, 3 master's, 1 doctorate awarded. Terminal master's awarded for partial completion of doctoral program. *Median time to degree:* Of those who began their doctoral program in fall 1999, 100% received their degree in 8 years or less. *Degree requirements:* For master's, variable foreign language requirement, comprehensive exam, thesis; for doctorate, one foreign language, comprehensive exam, thesis/dissertation. *Entrance requirements:* For master's and doctorate, GRE, sample of written work, 3 letters of recommendation, minimum 3.0 GPA. Additional exam requirements/recommendations for international students: Required—TOEFL (minimum score 600 paper-based; 250 computer-based; 80 iBT). *Application deadline:* For fall admission, 1/5 for domestic and international students. Application fee: $60. Electronic applications accepted. *Expenses:* Tuition, nonresident: full-time $14,888. Required fees: $10,108. *Financial support:* In 2007–08, 22 students received support, including 8 fellowships with full and partial tuition reimbursements available (averaging $14,700 per year), 13 teaching assistantships with full and partial tuition reimbursements available (averaging $16,400 per year); Federal Work-Study, scholarships/grants, traineeships, health care benefits, unspecified assistantships, and readers also available. Support available to part-time students. Financial award application deadline: 1/5; financial award applicants required to submit FAFSA. *Faculty research:* Spanish/Latin American drama, performance studies and European theatre history, East Asian and Russian studies, playwriting, Medieval theatre. *Unit head:* Prof. Simon Williams, Chair, 805-893-5515, E-mail: sjwill@dramadance.ucsb.edu. *Application contact:* Mary Tench, Graduate Program Assistant, 805-893-3147, Fax: 805-893-7029, E-mail: mtench@dramadance.ucsb.edu.

University of California, Santa Cruz, Division of Graduate Studies, Division of the Arts, Department of Theater Arts, Santa Cruz, CA 95064. Offers Certificate. *Faculty:* 9 full-time (4 women). *Students:* 14 full-time (7 women); includes 4 minority (1 American Indian/Alaska Native, 3 Hispanic Americans). 18 applicants, 100% accepted, 11 enrolled. In 2007, 5 degrees awarded. *Application deadline:* For fall admission, 3/1 for domestic students. Application fee: $60. *Expenses:* Tuition, nonresident: full-time $14,694. Required fees: $11,360. *Financial support:* Teaching assistantships, Federal Work-Study and institutionally sponsored loans available. Financial award application deadline: 2/1. *Unit head:* Mark Franko, Chairperson, 831-459-2974. *Application contact:* Judy L. Glass, Reporting Analyst for Graduate Admissions, 831-459-5906, Fax: 831-459-4843, E-mail: jlglass@ucsc.edu.

University of Central Florida, College of Arts and Humanities, Department of Theatre, Orlando, FL 32816. Offers acting (MA, MFA); design (MFA); musical theatre (MFA); theatre for young audiences (MFA). *Faculty:* 26 full-time (12 women), 6 part-time/adjunct (4 women). Application fee: $30. Electronic applications accepted. *Expenses:* Tuition, state resident: full-time $6,484. Tuition, nonresident: full-time $23,938. Tuition and fees vary according to program. *Financial support:* Fellowships, research assistantships, teaching assistantships available. *Unit head:* Dr. Steven Chicurel, Chair, 407-823-2399, Fax: 407-823-6446, E-mail: schicure@mail.ucf.edu.

University of Central Missouri, The Graduate School, College of Arts, Humanities and Social Sciences, Department of Theatre, Warrensburg, MO 64093. Offers MA. Part-time programs available. *Faculty:* 3 full-time (1 woman). *Students:* 12 full-time (6 women), 1 part-time, 2 international. Average age 30. 6 applicants, 83% accepted, 2 enrolled. In 2007, 2 degrees awarded. *Degree requirements:* For master's, comprehensive exam, research papers or thesis, oral exam. *Entrance requirements:* For master's, minimum GPA of 2.5 in major. Additional exam requirements/recommendations for international students: Required—TOEFL (minimum score 500 paper-based; 173 computer-based). *Application deadline:* For fall admission, 6/1 priority date for domestic students, 5/1 priority date for international students; for spring admission, 10/1 priority date for domestic students, 10/1 for international students. Applications are processed on a rolling basis. Application fee: $30 ($50 for international students). Electronic applications accepted. *Expenses:* Tuition, state resident: full-time $6,259; part-time $256 per credit hour. Tuition, nonresident: full-time $11,915; part-time $491 per credit hour. Required fees: $604; $20 per credit hour. *Financial support:* In 2007–08, 2 students received support; teaching assistantships with full tuition reimbursements available, Federal Work-Study, scholarships/grants, unspecified assistantships, and laboratory assistantships available. Support available to part-time students. Financial award application deadline: 3/1; financial award applicants required to submit FAFSA. *Faculty research:* Contemporary Theatre, Direct Theories, Performance Theories, Scenic Design, Design Technology. *Unit head:* Dr. Richard Herman, Chair, 660-543-8793, Fax: 660-543-8006, E-mail: rherman@ucmo.edu.

University of Cincinnati, Graduate School, College-Conservatory of Music, Divisions of Opera, Musical Theater, Drama, and Arts Administration, Cincinnati, OH 45221. Offers arts administration (MA); directing (MFA); theater design and production (MFA); voice and opera (MM, DMA); MBA/MA. *Accreditation:* NAST (one or more programs are accredited). *Faculty:* 25 full-time (6 women). *Students:* 53 full-time (35 women), 10 part-time (7 women); includes 22 minority (7 African Americans, 1 American Indian/Alaska Native, 9 Asian Americans or Pacific Islanders, 5 Hispanic Americans), 15 international. Average age 28. 71 applicants, 49% accepted. In 2007, 19 degrees awarded. *Degree requirements:* For master's, final project. *Entrance requirements:* For master's, GMAT (MA), audition/interview. Additional exam requirements/recommendations for international students: Required—TOEFL (minimum score 520 paper-based; 190 computer-based). *Application deadline:* For fall admission, 2/1 for domestic students. Applications are processed on a rolling basis. Application fee: $85. Electronic applications accepted. *Financial support:* In 2007–08, 31 teaching assistantships with full tuition reimbursements (averaging $4,897 per year) were awarded; fellowships, research assistantships, career-related internships or fieldwork, Federal Work-Study, scholarships/grants, tuition waivers (full), and unspecified assistantships also available. Financial award application deadline: 3/1. *Unit head:* R. Terrell Finney, Chair, 513-556-5803, Fax: 513-556-3399, E-mail: terrell.finney@uc.edu. *Application contact:* Paul R. Hillner, Assistant Dean for Admissions and Student Services, 513-556-5462, Fax: 513-556-1028, E-mail: paul.hillner@uc.edu.

University of Colorado at Boulder, Graduate School, College of Arts and Sciences, Department of Theatre and Dance, Boulder, CO 80309. Offers dance (MFA); theatre (MA, PhD). *Faculty:* 14. *Students:* 33 full-time (24 women), 8 part-time (6 women); includes 5 minority (3 African Americans, 2 Hispanic Americans), 1 international. Average age 36. 15 applicants, 80% accepted. In 2007, 8 master's, 5 doctorates awarded. Terminal master's awarded for partial completion of doctoral program. *Degree requirements:* For master's, comprehensive exam, thesis; for doctorate, one foreign language, thesis/dissertation. *Entrance requirements:* For master's, GRE General Test (MA), audition (MFA), minimum undergraduate GPA of 2.75. *Application deadline:* For fall admission, 1/15 priority date for domestic students, 12/1 for international students. Application fee: $50 ($60 for international students). *Financial support:* In 2007–08, 27 fellowships (averaging $4,240 per year) were awarded; tuition waivers (full) also available. Financial award application deadline: 1/15. *Faculty research:* Performance choreography; pedagogy administration; body therapies; multi-media forms; film, video, and cultural studies, non-concert forms, music, poetry writing, literature, kinesiology (dance); theater history, theory and literature . Total annual research expenditures: $22,500. *Unit head:* Bud Coleman, Chair, 303-492-5809, Fax: 303-492-7722, E-mail: bud.coleman@colorado.edu. *Application contact:* Graduate Program Assistant, 303-492-7356, Fax: 303-492-7722, E-mail: thtrdnce@colorado.edu.

University of Connecticut, Graduate School, School of Fine Arts, Department of Dramatic Arts, Field of Dramatic Arts, Storrs, CT 06269. Offers acting (MFA); costume design (MFA); lighting design (MFA); puppetry (MA, MFA); scenic design (MFA). *Faculty:* 16 full-time (4 women). *Students:* 30 full-time (14 women), 4 part-time (all women), 6 international. Average age 28. 15 applicants, 47% accepted, 5 enrolled. In 2007, 5 degrees awarded. *Degree requirements:* For master's, comprehensive exam. *Entrance requirements:* Additional exam requirements/recommendations for international students: Required—TOEFL (minimum score 550 paper-based; 213 computer-based). *Application deadline:* For fall admission, 2/1 priority date for domestic and international students; for spring admission, 11/1 for domestic students, 10/1 for international students. Applications are processed on a rolling basis. Application fee: $55. Electronic applications accepted. *Expenses:* Tuition, state resident: part-time $469 per credit hour. Tuition, nonresident: part-time $1,218 per credit hour. *Financial support:* In 2007–08, 23 research assistantships were awarded; fellowships, teaching assistantships with full tuition reimbursements, Federal Work-Study, scholarships/grants, health care benefits, and unspecified assistantships also available. Financial award application deadline: 2/1; financial award applicants required to submit FAFSA.

University of Delaware, College of Arts and Sciences, Department of Theatre, Professional Theatre Training Program, Newark, DE 19716. Offers acting (MFA); stage management (MFA); technical production (MFA). Students are matriculated into program once every three years. *Faculty:* 14 full-time (6 women). *Students:* 40 full-time (13 women); includes 8 minority (3 African Americans, 1 Asian American or Pacific Islander, 4 Hispanic Americans), 1 international. Average age 27. In 2007, 40 degrees awarded. *Entrance requirements:* For master's, audition, interview. *Application deadline:* For fall admission, 3/31 priority date for domestic students. Application fee: $60. Electronic applications accepted. *Financial support:* In 2007–08, 40 fellowships with full tuition reimbursements (averaging $11,250 per year) were awarded; career-related internships or fieldwork, institutionally sponsored loans, and health care benefits also available. Financial award application deadline: 3/31. *Faculty research:* Theatre training, acting, technical production, stage management. *Unit head:* Sanford Robbins, Chair, 302-831-2201, Fax: 302-831-3673, E-mail: srobbins@udel.edu. *Application contact:* Kristin Brady, Program Coordinator, 302-831-1083, Fax: 302-831-3673, E-mail: kbrady@udel.edu.

See Close-Up on page 371.

University of Florida, Graduate School, College of Fine Arts, School of Theatre and Dance, Gainesville, FL 32611. Offers theatre (MFA). *Accreditation:* NAST. *Faculty:* 18 full-time (7 women). *Students:* 40 (13 women); includes 8 minority (4 African Americans, 1 American Indian/Alaska Native, 3 Hispanic Americans) 1 international. In 2007, 11 degrees awarded. *Degree requirements:* For master's, thesis, creative project. *Entrance requirements:* For master's, audition/portfolio, bachelor's degree in theatre, interview, GRE General Test or minimum GPA of 3.0. Additional exam requirements/recommendations for international students: Required—TOEFL (minimum score 550 paper-based; 213 computer-based). *Application deadline:* For fall admission, 6/1 priority date for domestic students. Applications are processed on a rolling basis. Application fee: $30. Electronic applications accepted. *Expenses:* Tuition, state resident: full-time $7,478. Tuition, nonresident: full-time $22,603. *Financial support:* In 2007–08, 14 research assistantships with tuition reimbursements (averaging $9,804 per year), 19 teaching assistantships with tuition reimbursements (averaging $8,706 per year) were awarded; fellowships, career-related internships or fieldwork, Federal Work-Study, institutionally sponsored loans, and unspecified assistantships also available. *Faculty research:* Production, history of theatre, criticism. *Unit head:* Prof. Kevin Marshall, Chair, 352-273-0501, Fax: 352-392-5114, E-mail: kmarshall@arts.ufl.edu. *Application contact:* Dr. David Shelton, Graduate Coordinator, 352-273-0503, Fax: 352-392-5114, E-mail: dshelton@ufl.edu.

University of Georgia, Graduate School, College of Arts and Sciences, Department of Theatre and Film Studies, Athens, GA 30602. Offers theatre (MFA, PhD). *Accreditation:* NAST. *Faculty:* 13 full-time (4 women). *Students:* 34 full-time (21 women), 5 part-time (all women); includes 4 minority (2 African Americans, 2 Asian Americans or Pacific Islanders), 3 international. Average age 23. 50 applicants, 60% accepted, 24 enrolled. In 2007, 7 master's, 1 doctorate awarded. *Degree requirements:* For master's, comprehensive exam, written report; for doctorate, one foreign language, comprehensive exam, thesis/dissertation. *Entrance requirements:* For master's and doctorate, GRE General Test. Additional exam requirements/recommendations for international students: Required—TOEFL (minimum score 550 paper-based). *Application deadline:* For fall admission, 7/1 for domestic students, 4/15 for international students; for winter admission, 11/15 for domestic students, 10/15 for international students; for spring admission, 5/1 for domestic students, 2/15 for international students. Application fee: $50. Electronic applications accepted. *Financial support:* In 2007–08, research assistantships with full tuition reimbursements (averaging $10,089 per year), teaching assistantships with full tuition reimbursements (averaging $9,462 per year) were awarded; fellowships, health care benefits and unspecified assistantships also available. Financial award application deadline: 2/15. *Faculty research:* Digital media, African-American theatre, Indian theatre, history of animation, vaudeville and popular culture history. Total annual research expenditures:$375,984. *Unit head:* Dr. David Z. Saltz, Head, 706-542-2836, Fax: 706-542-2080, E-mail: saltz@uga.edu. *Application contact:* Dr. Freda Scott Giles, Graduate Coordinator, 706-542-2102, E-mail: fsgiles@uga.edu.

University of Guelph, Graduate Program Services, College of Arts, School of English and Theatre Studies, Program in Drama, Guelph, ON N1G 2W1, Canada. Offers MA. Part-time programs available. *Faculty:* 30 full-time (15 women). *Students:* 10 full-time (9 women). Average age 24. 17 applicants, 71% accepted, 8 enrolled. In 2007, 5 degrees awarded. *Degree requirements:* For master's, thesis (for some programs). *Entrance requirements:* For master's, 2 letters of reference, 4-year honours undergraduate degree in English or drama. Additional exam requirements/recommendations for international students: Required—TOEFL. *Application deadline:* For fall admission, 2/1 for domestic and international students. Application fee: $85. Electronic applications accepted. *Financial support:* In 2007–08, 3 research assistantships with tuition reimbursements (averaging $9,212 per year), 10 teaching assistantships with tuition reimbursements (averaging $9,212 per year) were awarded; scholarships/grants, health care benefits, tuition waivers (full), and unspecified assistantships also available. Financial award application deadline: 2/15. *Faculty research:* Canadian theatre, Renaissance, nineteenth and twentieth century drama and theatre, Shaw, theatre history, dramatic literature, performance theory. Total annual research expenditures: $500,000. *Application contact:* Dr. Daniel O'Quinn, Graduate Coordinator, 519-824-4120 Ext. 53250, Fax: 519-766-0844, E-mail: doquinn@uoguelph.ca.

University of Hawaii at Manoa, Graduate Division, Colleges of Arts and Sciences, College of Arts and Humanities, Department of Theatre and Dance, Honolulu, HI 96822. Offers dance (MA, MFA); theatre (MA, MFA, PhD). *Faculty:* 17 full-time (10 women), 4 part-time/adjunct (all women). *Students:* 53 full-time (38 women), 4 part-time (3 women); includes 8 minority (1 American Indian/Alaska Native, 7 Asian Americans or Pacific Islanders), 8 international. 55 applicants, 58% accepted, 26 enrolled. *Entrance requirements:* Additional exam requirements/recommendations for international students: Required—TOEFL. *Application deadline:* For fall admission, 2/1 for domestic students, 1/15 for international students; for spring admission, 9/1 for domestic students, 8/1 for international students. Application fee: $50. *Financial support:* In 2007–08, 1 research assistantship (averaging $16,824 per year), 15 teaching assistantships (averaging $13,609 per year) were awarded; fellowships, Federal Work-Study, institutionally sponsored loans, tuition waivers (full), and unspecified assistantships also available. Financial award application deadline: 2/1. *Faculty research:* Asian theatre, feminist theatre and dance, Russian theatre, Australian theatre.

Announcement: Hawaii offers exceptional programs that meld Western and Asian theater and dance. Includes research and performance in a multiracial environment; faculty of international repute; guest artists, teachers. 2008–09: Japanese Noh; 2009–10: Chinese Jingju. Study Western and Asian acting, design, directing, history, literature, contemporary theory, dance, youth theater, playwriting. PhD in Asian, Western, and comparative Asian-Western theater. Occasional touring.

University of Houston, College of Liberal Arts and Social Sciences, School of Theatre, Houston, TX 77204. Offers MA, MFA. Part-time programs available. *Faculty:* 10 full-time (2 women). *Students:* 32 full-time (20 women), 7 part-time (4 women); includes 9 minority (3 African Americans, 1 American Indian/Alaska Native, 1 Asian American or Pacific Islander, 4 Hispanic Americans), 1 international. Average age 30. 22 applicants, 100% accepted, 18 enrolled. In 2007, 7 degrees awarded. *Degree requirements:* For master's, thesis optional. *Entrance requirements:* For master's, GRE General Test. Application fee: $25. *Expenses:* Tuition, state resident: full-time $6,297; part-time $262 per credit. Tuition, nonresident: full-time $12,969; part-time $540 per credit. Required fees: $2,696. *Financial support:* In 2007–08, 25 teaching assistantships with full tuition reimbursements (averaging $9,100 per year) were awarded; fellowships with full tuition reimbursements, research assistantships with full tuition reimbursements, career-related internships or fieldwork, Federal Work-Study, institutionally sponsored loans, scholarships/grants, health care benefits, and unspecified assistantships also available. Support available to part-time students. Financial award application deadline: 2/1. *Unit head:* Steven Wallace, Chairperson, 713-743-3003, Fax: 713-749-1420.

University of Idaho, College of Graduate Studies, College of Letters, Arts and Social Sciences, Department of Theatre and Film, Moscow, ID 83844-2282. Offers theatre arts (MFA). *Students:* 29 (16 women). Average age 29. In 2007, 10 degrees awarded. *Entrance requirements:* For master's, minimum GPA of 2.8. *Application deadline:* For fall admission, 8/1 for domestic students; for spring admission, 12/15 for domestic students. Application fee: $55 ($60 for international students). *Financial support:* Research assistantships, teaching assistantships available. Financial award application deadline: 2/15. *Unit head:* Dr. Dean Fields Panttaja, Chair, 208-885-6465.

University of Illinois at Urbana–Champaign, Graduate College, College of Fine and Applied Arts, Department of Theatre, Champaign, IL 61820. Offers MA, MFA, PhD. *Accreditation:* NAST. *Faculty:* 15 full-time (5 women), 2 part-time/adjunct (both women). *Students:* 60 full-time (36 women), 2 part-time; includes 6 minority (5 African Americans, 1 Asian American or Pacific Islander), 5 international. 65 applicants, 28% accepted, 17 enrolled. In 2007, 9 master's, 2 doctorates awarded. *Degree requirements:* For doctorate, 2 foreign languages, thesis/dissertation. *Entrance requirements:* For master's, minimum GPA of 3.0, audition or portfolio. *Application deadline:* For fall admission, 3/1 for domestic students. Applications are processed on a rolling basis. Application fee: $60 ($75 for international students). Electronic applications accepted. *Financial support:* In 2007–08, 4 fellowships, 2 research assistantships, 24 teaching assistantships were awarded. Financial award application deadline: 2/15. *Unit head:* Thomas O. Mitchell, Head, 217-333-3538, Fax: 217-244-1861, E-mail: tomitch@uiuc.edu. *Application contact:* David Swinford, Admissions and Records Officer, 217-333-3538, Fax: 217-244-1861, E-mail: dswinfor@uiuc.edu.

The University of Iowa, Graduate College, College of Liberal Arts and Sciences, Department of Theatre Arts, Iowa City, IA 52242-1316. Offers MFA. *Accreditation:* NAST. *Faculty:* 13 full-time, 3 part-time/adjunct. *Students:* 46 full-time (29 women); includes 12 minority (7 African Americans, 4 Asian Americans or Pacific Islanders, 1 Hispanic American), 2 international. 94 applicants, 18% accepted, 16 enrolled. In 2007, 17 degrees awarded. *Degree requirements:* For master's, thesis, exam. *Entrance requirements:* For master's, GRE, minimum GPA of 3.0. Additional exam requirements/recommendations for international students: Required—TOEFL (minimum score 550 paper-based; 213 computer-based; 81 iBT). *Application deadline:* For fall admission, 3/1 for domestic and international students. Application fee: $60 ($85 for international students). Electronic applications accepted. *Expenses:* Tuition, state resident: part-time $349 per hour. Tuition, nonresident: part-time $349 per hour. Tuition and fees vary according to course load and program. *Financial support:* In 2007–08, 6 fellowships, 6 research assistantships with partial tuition reimbursements, 26 teaching assistantships with partial tuition reimbursements were awarded. Financial award applicants required to submit FAFSA. *Unit head:* Alan MacVey, Chair, 319-335-2700, Fax: 319-335-3568.

University of Kansas, Research and Graduate Studies, College of Liberal Arts and Sciences, Department of Theatre and Film, Lawrence, KS 66045. Offers theatre and film (MA, PhD); theatre-international theatre studies (MA). *Faculty:* 23. *Students:* 35 full-time (13 women), 3 part-time (1 woman); includes 2 minority (both Asian Americans or Pacific Islanders), 11 international. Average age 34. 30 applicants, 80% accepted, 8 enrolled. In 2007, 3 master's, 4 doctorates awarded. *Degree requirements:* For master's, thesis; for doctorate, one foreign language, comprehensive exam, thesis/dissertation. *Entrance requirements:* For master's, GRE General Test, minimum GPA of 3.2; for doctorate, GRE General Test, minimum GPA of 3.5, MA or MFA in Theatre, Film, or Related Field. Additional exam requirements/recommendations for international students: Required—TOEFL. *Application deadline:* For fall admission, 1/1 priority date for domestic students, 1/1 for international students. Application fee: $55 ($60 for international students). Electronic applications accepted. *Expenses:* Tuition, state resident: full-time $5,838. Tuition, nonresident: full-time $13,409. Tuition and fees vary according to program. *Financial support:* Fellowships with tuition reimbursements, teaching assistantships with full and partial tuition reimbursements, Federal Work-Study, scholarships/grants, and unspecified assistantships available. Financial award application deadline: 1/1. *Faculty research:* Film history, theatre history, film theory, cultural studies, performance studies. *Unit head:* John Staniunas, Chair, 785-864-3511, Fax: 785-864-5251. *Application contact:* Henry Bial, Director of Graduate Studies, 785-864-3511, Fax: 785-331-5251, E-mail: tfdgs@ku.edu.

University of Kentucky, Graduate School, College of Fine Arts, Program in Theatre, Lexington, KY 40506-0032. Offers MA. *Faculty:* 11 full-time (3 women). *Students:* 3 full-time (2 women), 7 part-time (5 women). Average age 31. 6 applicants, 50% accepted, 1 enrolled. In 2007, 4 degrees awarded. *Degree requirements:* For master's, comprehensive exam, thesis optional. *Entrance requirements:* For master's, GRE General Test, minimum undergraduate GPA of 2.75. Additional exam requirements/recommendations for international students: Required—TOEFL (minimum score 550 paper-based; 213 computer-based). *Application deadline:* For fall admission, 7/17 priority date for domestic students, 2/1 priority date for international students; for spring admission, 12/13 priority date for domestic students, 6/15 priority date for international students. Application fee: $50 ($65 for international students). Electronic applications accepted. *Expenses:* Tuition, state resident: part-time $437 per credit hour. Tuition, nonresident: part-time $931 per credit hour. *Financial support:* In 2007–08, 2 students received support, including 2 teaching assistantships with full tuition reimbursements available (averaging $9,548 per year); fellowships with full tuition reimbursements available, research assistantships with full tuition reimbursements available, Federal Work-Study, institutionally sponsored loans, scholarships/grants, traineeships, health care benefits, tuition waivers (partial), and unspecified assistantships also available. Support available to part-time students. Financial award application deadline: 3/15. *Faculty research:* Historical, critical, practical, theoretical, and experimental perspectives of acting, directing, design, performance, and dramaturgy. *Unit head:* Dr. Nelson Fields, Director of Graduate Studies, 859-257-7018, Fax: 859-257-3042, E-mail: nelson.fields@uky.edu. *Application contact:* Dr. Brian Jackson, Senior Associate Dean, 859-257-4667, Fax: 859-257-4676, E-mail: brian.jackson@uky.edu.

University of Louisville, Graduate School, College of Arts and Sciences, Department of Theatre Arts, Louisville, KY 40292-0001. Offers performance (MFA); production (MFA); theatre arts (MA). *Accreditation:* NAST. *Students:* 13 full-time (9 women), 1 (woman) part-time; includes 6 minority (all African Americans) Average age 29. In 2007, 3 degrees awarded. *Degree requirements:* For master's, thesis optional, performance project, monograph. *Entrance requirements:* For master's, GRE General Test, auditions or portfolio review. *Application deadline:* For spring admission, 4/15 priority date for domestic students. Applications are processed on a rolling basis. Application fee: $50. *Financial support:* In 2007–08, 11 teaching assistantships with full tuition reimbursements (averaging $12,000 per year) were awarded. *Unit head:* Dr. Russell Vandenbroucke, Chair, 502-852-8444, Fax: 502-852-7235, E-mail: r.vandenbrouke@louisville.edu.

University of Maryland, College Park, Graduate Studies, College of Arts and Humanities, Department of Theatre, College Park, MD 20742. Offers MA, MFA, PhD. *Accreditation:* NAST. *Faculty:* 15 full-time (7 women), 3 part-time/adjunct (all women). *Students:* 39 full-time (24 women), 1 part-time; includes 1 minority (Asian American or Pacific Islander), 1 international. 18 applicants, 22% accepted, 4 enrolled. In 2007, 2 master's, 3 doctorates awarded. *Degree requirements:* For master's, comprehensive exam, thesis optional; for doctorate, thesis/dissertation. *Entrance requirements:* For master's, GRE General Test, minimum GPA of 3.0, writing sample, portfolio (MFA), 3 letters of recommendation; for doctorate, GRE General Test, writing sample. Additional exam requirements/recommendations for international students: Required—TOEFL. *Application deadline:* For fall admission, 2/1 for domestic and international students. Applications are processed on a rolling basis. Application fee: $60. Electronic applications accepted. *Financial support:* In 2007–08, 2 fellowships with full tuition reimbursements (averaging $14,176 per year), 16 teaching assistantships with tuition reimbursements (averaging $13,765 per year) were awarded; research assistantships with tuition reimbursements, Federal Work-Study and scholarships/grants also available. Support available to part-time students. Financial award applicants required to submit FAFSA. *Faculty research:* Theatre aesthetics, performance, history/theory, design and production. *Unit head:* Dr. Dan M. Wagner, Chairman, 301-405-6675, Fax: 301-314-9599, E-mail: dmwagner@umd.edu. *Application contact:* Dean of Graduate School, 301-405-4190, Fax: 301-314-9305.

University of Massachusetts Amherst, Graduate School, College of Humanities and Fine Arts, Department of Theater, Amherst, MA 01003. Offers MFA. Part-time programs available. *Faculty:* 12 full-time (5 women). *Students:* 10 full-time (4 women), 4 part-time (3 women), 1 international. Average age 33. 1 applicant, 100% accepted, 0 enrolled. In 2007, 2 degrees awarded. *Degree requirements:* For master's, thesis. *Entrance requirements:* For master's, GRE General Test, resumé of production experience, two critical writing samples, original scripts or portfolios. Additional exam requirements/recommendations for international students: Required—TOEFL (minimum score 530 paper-based; 197 computer-based). *Application deadline:* For fall admission, 2/1 priority date for domestic and international students. Applications are processed on a rolling basis. Application fee: $50 ($65 for international students). Electronic applications accepted. *Expenses:* Tuition, state resident: full-time $2,640; part-time $110 per credit. Tuition, nonresident: full-time $9,936; part-time $414 per credit. Required fees: $7,455. One-time fee: $332. Tuition and fees vary according to course load, campus/location, program and reciprocity agreements. *Financial support:* In 2007–08, 15 teaching assistantships with full tuition reimbursements (averaging $13,376 per year) were awarded; fellowships with full tuition reimbursements, research assistantships with full tuition reimbursements, career-related internships or fieldwork, Federal Work-Study, scholarships/grants, traineeships, and unspecified assistantships also available. Support available to part-time students. Financial award application deadline: 2/1. *Unit head:* Dr. Harley Erdman, Director, 413-545-3490, Fax: 413-577-0025, E-mail: harley@theater.umass.edu.

University of Memphis, Graduate School, College of Communication and Fine Arts, Department of Theatre and Dance, Memphis, TN 38152. Offers theatre (MFA). *Accreditation:* NAST. *Faculty:* 8 full-time (4 women). *Students:* 15 full-time (8 women); includes 1 minority (African American), 1 international. Average age 30. 21 applicants, 29% accepted, 6 enrolled. In 2007, 7 degrees awarded. *Degree requirements:* For master's, comprehensive exam, practicum. *Entrance requirements:* For master's, minimum GPA of 3.0 in major, 2.5 overall. *Application deadline:* For fall admission, 8/1 for domestic students; for spring admission, 12/1 for domestic students. Applications are processed on a rolling basis. Application fee: $35 ($60 for international students). *Expenses:* Tuition, state resident: full-time $6,990; part-time $377 per hour. Tuition, nonresident: full-time $17,818; part-time $830 per hour. Tuition and fees vary according to course load and program. *Financial support:* In 2007–08, 12 research assistantships with full tuition reimbursements (averaging $5,400 per year), 4 teaching assistantships with full tuition reimbursements (averaging $4,050 per year) were awarded; career-related internships or fieldwork, Federal Work-Study, and institutionally sponsored loans also available. Financial award application deadline: 8/1. *Faculty research:* Theatre design, production management, Lessac vocal training, movement styles, directing. *Unit head:* Prof. Robert A. Hetherington, Chair, 901-678-2523, Fax: 901-678-1350, E-mail: rhether@memphis.edu. *Application contact:* Prof. Gloria D. Baxter, Coordinator, Graduate Studies, 901-678-2523, Fax: 901-678-1350, E-mail: gbaxter@memphis.edu.

University of Michigan, Horace H. Rackham School of Graduate Studies, The School of Music, Theatre, and Dance, Department of Theatre and Drama, Ann Arbor, MI 48109. Offers

Theater

University of Michigan (continued)

design (MFA); theatre (PhD). *Degree requirements:* For master's, thesis; for doctorate, one foreign language, thesis/dissertation, preliminary exam, qualifying exam. *Entrance requirements:* For master's, portfolio, interview, writing sample; for doctorate, GRE General Test, writing sample, interview. Additional exam requirements/recommendations for international students: Required—TOEFL (minimum score 600 paper-based; 250 computer-based). Electronic applications accepted. *Faculty research:* Silent film, avant-garde drama, popular entertainment.

University of Minnesota, Twin Cities Campus, Graduate School, College of Liberal Arts, Department of Theatre Arts and Dance, Minneapolis, MN 55455-0213. Offers design technology (MFA); theatre arts and dance (MA, PhD). *Accreditation:* NASD; NAST (one or more programs are accredited). *Faculty:* 15 full-time (6 women), 3 part-time/adjunct (2 women). *Students:* 26 full-time (17 women), 13 part-time (7 women); includes 9 minority (2 African Americans, 3 Asian Americans or Pacific Islanders, 4 Hispanic Americans), 2 international. Average age 31. 43 applicants, 23% accepted, 9 enrolled. In 2007, 4 master's, 3 doctorates awarded. Terminal master's awarded for partial completion of doctoral program. *Median time to degree:* Of those who began their doctoral program in fall 1999, 50% received their degree in 8 years or less. *Degree requirements:* For master's, thesis (for some programs), final creative project (MFA), foreign language (MA); for doctorate, one foreign language, thesis/dissertation, oral defense, written exams. *Entrance requirements:* For master's, GRE General Test, minimum GPA of 3.0, audition or portfolio; for doctorate, GRE General Test, minimum GPA of 3.0, writing sample, 1 foreign language. Additional exam requirements/recommendations for international students: Required—TOEFL (minimum score 550 paper-based; 213 computer-based; 79 iBT). *Application deadline:* For fall admission, 1/15 priority date for domestic and international students. Applications are processed on a rolling basis. Application fee: $55 ($75 for international students). Electronic applications accepted. *Financial support:* In 2007–08, 30 students received support, including 3 fellowships with full tuition reimbursements available (averaging $14,000 per year), 27 teaching assistantships with full tuition reimbursements available (averaging $12,253 per year); career-related internships or fieldwork, Federal Work-Study, scholarships/grants, health care benefits, tuition waivers (partial), and unspecified assistantships also available. Financial award application deadline: 4/15; financial award applicants required to submit FAFSA. *Faculty research:* Theatre history; Eastern European theatre; performance studies; medieval studies. Total annual research expenditures: $42,506. *Unit head:* Michal Kobialka, Chair, 612-625-0048, Fax: 612-625-6334, E-mail: kobia001@tc.umn.edu. *Application contact:* Ginni Arons, Graduate Studies Assistant, 612-625-5029, Fax: 612-625-6334, E-mail: theatre@tc.umn.edu.

University of Missouri–Columbia, Graduate School, College of Arts and Sciences, Department of Theatre, Columbia, MO 65211. Offers MA, PhD. Part-time programs available. *Degree requirements:* For doctorate, thesis/dissertation. *Entrance requirements:* For master's and doctorate, GRE General Test, minimum GPA of 3.0.

University of Missouri–Kansas City, College of Arts and Sciences, Theatre Department, Kansas City, MO 64110-2499. Offers acting (MFA); design technology (MFA); theatre (MA). *Accreditation:* NAST. *Faculty:* 15 full-time (4 women), 7 part-time/adjunct (2 women). *Students:* 74 full-time (33 women), 16 part-time (7 women); includes 13 minority (7 African Americans, 1 American Indian/Alaska Native, 1 Asian American or Pacific Islander, 4 Hispanic Americans), 2 international. Average age 27. 66 applicants, 52% accepted, 31 enrolled. In 2007, 19 degrees awarded. *Degree requirements:* For master's, thesis. *Entrance requirements:* For master's, audition or portfolio, interview. Additional exam requirements/recommendations for international students: Required—TOEFL. *Application deadline:* For fall admission, 3/1 priority date for domestic and international students; for spring admission, 11/1 priority date for domestic and international students. Applications are processed on a rolling basis. Application fee: $35 ($50 for international students). Electronic applications accepted. *Expenses:* Tuition, state resident: part-time $287 per hour. Tuition, nonresident: part-time $741 per hour. Required fees: $31 per hour. Tuition and fees vary according to program. *Financial support:* In 2007–08, 71 teaching assistantships with partial tuition reimbursements (averaging $9,726 per year) were awarded; fellowships with partial tuition reimbursements, career-related internships or fieldwork, Federal Work-Study, institutionally sponsored loans, and scholarships/grants also available. Financial award application deadline: 3/1; financial award applicants required to submit FAFSA. *Faculty research:* Contemporary Russian theatre, Shakespeare in performance, subtle energies in actor training, multi-channel sound, renovation of Zuni Pueblo historic Spanish mission. *Unit head:* Tom Mardikes, Chairperson, 816-235-2784, Fax: 816-235-6562, E-mail: markdikesa@umkc.edu. *Application contact:* Cindy Stofiel, Student Affairs Representative, 816-235-2702, Fax: 816-235-6562, E-mail: stofiel@umkc.edu.

The University of Montana, Graduate School, School of Fine Arts, Department of Drama/Dance, Missoula, MT 59812-0002. Offers fine arts (MA, MFA), including acting (MFA), design/technology (MFA), directing (MFA), drama (MA), integrated arts and education (MA), media arts (MFA). *Accreditation:* NAST (one or more programs are accredited). *Degree requirements:* For master's, thesis or alternative. *Entrance requirements:* For master's, GRE General Test, audition, portfolio, production notebook.

The University of Montana, Graduate School, School of Fine Arts, Department of Music, Missoula, MT 59812-0002. Offers music (MM), including composition/technology, music education, musical theater, performance. *Accreditation:* NASM. *Entrance requirements:* For master's, GRE General Test, GRE Subject Test, portfolio.

University of Nebraska at Omaha, Graduate Studies and Research, College of Communication, Fine Arts and Media, Department of Theatre, Omaha, NE 68182. Offers MA. Part-time programs available. *Faculty:* 6 full-time (3 women). *Students:* 3 full-time (all women), 4 part-time (3 women). Average age 31. 7 applicants, 71% accepted, 3 enrolled. In 2007, 9 degrees awarded. *Degree requirements:* For master's, comprehensive exam, thesis (for some programs). *Entrance requirements:* For master's, GRE General Test or MAT, minimum GPA of 3.0. Additional exam requirements/recommendations for international students: Required—TOEFL (minimum score 500 paper-based; 173 computer-based; 61 iBT). *Application deadline:* For fall admission, 7/31 priority date for domestic students; for spring admission, 12/1 priority date for domestic students. Applications are processed on a rolling basis. Application fee: $45. Electronic applications accepted. *Financial support:* In 2007–08, 7 students received support; fellowships, research assistantships with tuition reimbursements available, Federal Work-Study, institutionally sponsored loans, scholarships/grants, tuition waivers (full), and unspecified assistantships available. Support available to part-time students. Financial award application deadline: 3/1; financial award applicants required to submit FAFSA. *Unit head:* Sharon Sobel, Chairperson, 402-554-2406. *Application contact:* Dr. Cynthia Phaneuf, Student Contact, 402-554-2406.

University of Nebraska–Lincoln, Graduate College, College of Arts and Sciences, Department of Communication Studies, Lincoln, NE 68588. Offers communication studies and theatre arts (PhD); communications studies (MA). *Degree requirements:* For master's, thesis optional; for doctorate, comprehensive exam, thesis/dissertation. *Entrance requirements:* For master's and doctorate, GRE General Test, writing sample. Additional exam requirements/recommendations for international students: Required—TOEFL (minimum score 600 paper-based; 250 computer-based). Electronic applications accepted. *Faculty research:* Message strategies, gender communication, political communication, organizational communication, instructional communication.

University of Nebraska–Lincoln, Graduate College, College of Fine and Performing Arts, Department of Theatre Arts, Lincoln, NE 68588. Offers MFA. *Accreditation:* NAST. *Degree requirements:* For master's, thesis. *Entrance requirements:* For master's, audition, portfolio. Additional exam requirements/recommendations for international students: Required—TOEFL (minimum score 500 paper-based; 173 computer-based). Electronic applications accepted. *Faculty research:* American theatre history, British theatre history, modern American drama, contemporary performance, Elizabethan theatre history.

University of Nevada, Las Vegas, Graduate College, College of Fine Arts, Department of Theatre, Las Vegas, NV 89154-9900. Offers design/technology (MFA); directing (MFA); performance (MFA); playwriting (MFA); stage management (MFA); theatre (MA); theatre arts (MFA). *Accreditation:* NAST. Part-time programs available. *Faculty:* 18 full-time (4 women), 4 part-time/adjunct (1 woman). *Students:* 37 full-time (23 women), 3 part-time (2 women); includes 3 minority (1 American Indian/Alaska Native, 2 Hispanic Americans). 59 applicants, 34% accepted, 19 enrolled. In 2007, 19 degrees awarded. *Degree requirements:* For master's, thesis (for some programs), creative project. *Entrance requirements:* For master's, bachelor's degree in theatre arts, minimum GPA of 3.0. Additional exam requirements/recommendations for international students: Required—TOEFL (minimum score 550 paper-based; 213 computer-based; 80 iBT). *Application deadline:* For fall admission, 6/15 for domestic students, 5/1 for international students. Application fee: $60 ($75 for international students). Electronic applications accepted. *Expenses:* Tuition, state resident: part-time $198 per credit. Tuition, nonresident: part-time $416 per credit. Required fees: $256 per semester. Tuition and fees vary according to course load and reciprocity agreements. *Financial support:* In 2007–08, 16 research assistantships (averaging $10,000 per year), 15 teaching assistantships with partial tuition reimbursements (averaging $10,000 per year) were awarded; career-related internships or fieldwork, Federal Work-Study, institutionally sponsored loans, scholarships/grants, health care benefits, and unspecified assistantships also available. Support available to part-time students. Financial award application deadline: 3/1. *Unit head:* Jonathan Good, Chair, 702-895-3332. *Application contact:* Graduate College Admissions Evaluator, 702-895-3320, Fax: 702-895-4180, E-mail: gradcollege@unlv.edu.

University of New Mexico, Graduate School, College of Fine Arts, Department of Theatre and Dance, Albuquerque, NM 87131-2039. Offers dramatic writing (MFA); theater and dance (MA). *Accreditation:* NASD; NAST. *Faculty:* 12 full-time (7 women), 28 part-time/adjunct (18 women). *Students:* 16 full-time (11 women), 5 part-time (3 women); includes 7 minority (2 American Indian/Alaska Native, 1 Asian American or Pacific Islander, 4 Hispanic Americans), 1 international. Average age 35. 22 applicants, 200% accepted, 6 enrolled. In 2007, 1 master's awarded. *Degree requirements:* For master's, comprehensive exam (for some programs), thesis (for some programs). *Entrance requirements:* For master's, minimum GPA of 3.0, undergraduate major in theatre, dance or closely related field, 3 letters of recommendation, letter of intent. *Application deadline:* For fall admission, 4/15 for domestic students; for spring admission, 11/10 for domestic students. Application fee: $50. Electronic applications accepted. *Financial support:* In 2007–08, 14 students received support, including 5 research assistantships with partial tuition reimbursements available (averaging $8,000 per year), 6 teaching assistantships with partial tuition reimbursements available (averaging $8,000 per year); Federal Work-Study, health care benefits, tuition waivers (partial), and unspecified assistantships also available. Financial award application deadline: 3/1; financial award applicants required to submit FAFSA. *Faculty research:* Theater education and outreach, choreography, dramatic writing, dance history/criticism. *Unit head:* Susan Pearson, Chair, 505-277-4332, Fax: 505-277-8921, E-mail: speardav@unm.edu. *Application contact:* Christina Squire, Graduate Coordinator, 505-277-7362, Fax: 505-277-8921, E-mail: csquire@unm.edu.

University of New Orleans, Graduate School, College of Liberal Arts, Department of Film, Theatre and Communication Arts, New Orleans, LA 70148. Offers film production (MFA); theatre directing (MFA); theatre performance (MFA). *Accreditation:* NAST. *Students:* 110 (60 women). Average age 34. In 2007, 22 degrees awarded. *Degree requirements:* For master's, comprehensive exam, thesis. *Entrance requirements:* Additional exam requirements/recommendations for international students: Required—TOEFL (minimum score 550 paper-based; 213 computer-based; 79 iBT). *Application deadline:* For fall admission, 7/1 priority date for domestic students, 6/1 for international students; for spring admission, 11/15 priority date for domestic students, 10/1 for international students. Applications are processed on a rolling basis. Application fee: $40. Electronic applications accepted. *Financial support:* Teaching assistantships, career-related internships or fieldwork available. Financial award application deadline: 5/15; financial award applicants required to submit FAFSA. *Faculty research:* Mass communication theory, nineteenth- and twentieth-century theater history, film criticism and history. *Unit head:* Dr. Phillip Karnell, Chairperson, 504-280-6318, Fax: 504-280-6318, E-mail: pkarnell@uno.edu. *Application contact:* Dr. John McGowan-Hartmann, Graduate Coordinator, 504-280-6803, Fax: 504-280-6318, E-mail: jmcgowan@uno.edu.

The University of North Carolina at Chapel Hill, Graduate School, College of Arts and Sciences, Department of Dramatic Art, Chapel Hill, NC 27599. Offers acting (MFA); costume production (MFA); technical production (MFA). *Entrance requirements:* For master's, audition or portfolio.

The University of North Carolina at Charlotte, Graduate School, College of Education, Program in Teacher Education, Charlotte, NC 28223-0001. Offers art education (K-12) (MAT); dance education (K-12) (MAT); elementary education (K-6) (MAT); English as a second language (K-12) (MAT); foreign language education (K-12) (MAT); general teacher education (MAT); middle grades education (6-9) (MAT); music education (K-12) (MAT); secondary education (9-12) (MAT); special education (K-12) (MAT); theatre education (K-12) (MAT). *Students:* 19 full-time (15 women), 166 part-time (138 women); includes 24 minority (22 African Americans, 1 American Indian/Alaska Native, 1 Asian American or Pacific Islander), 2 international. Average age 32. 94 applicants, 89% accepted, 66 enrolled. In 2007, 90 degrees awarded. *Entrance requirements:* For master's, GRE or MAT. Additional exam requirements/recommendations for international students: Required—TOEFL (minimum score 557 paper-based; 220 computer-based). *Application deadline:* For fall admission, 7/1 for domestic students, 5/1 for international students; for spring admission, 11/1 for domestic students, 10/1 for international students. Applications are processed on a rolling basis. Application fee: $55. Electronic applications accepted. *Expenses:* Tuition, state resident: full-time $2,855. Tuition, nonresident: full-time $13,062. Required fees: $1,692. *Financial support:* Fellowships, research assistantships, teaching assistantships, career-related internships or fieldwork, Federal Work-Study, institutionally sponsored loans, scholarships/grants, and unspecified assistantships available. Support available to part-time students. Financial award application deadline: 4/1; financial award applicants required to submit FAFSA. *Unit head:* Dr. Kimberly J. Hartman, Coordinator, 704-687-8883, Fax: 704-687-6430, E-mail: khartman@email.uncc.edu. *Application contact:* Kathy B. Giddings, Director of Graduate Admissions, 704-687-3366, Fax: 704-687-3279, E-mail: agidding@uncc.edu.

The University of North Carolina at Greensboro, Graduate School, College of Arts and Sciences, Department of Theater, Greensboro, NC 27412-5001. Offers acting (MFA); design (MFA); directing (MFA); theater education (M Ed); theater for youth (MFA). *Accreditation:* NAST. *Faculty:* 11 full-time (4 women), 6 part-time/adjunct (3 women). *Students:* 23 full-time (14 women), 1 (woman) part-time. 43 applicants, 19% accepted. *Entrance requirements:* For master's, portfolio, interviews. *Application deadline:* For fall admission, 3/15 priority date for domestic students; for spring admission, 11/1 for domestic students. Applications are processed on a rolling basis. Electronic applications accepted. *Financial support:* Teaching assistantships available. *Unit head:* Jim Fisher, Head, 336-334-5576, Fax: 336-334-5100. *Application contact:* Michelle Harkleroad, Director of Graduate Admissions, 336-334-4884, Fax: 336-334-4424, E-mail: mbharkle@uncg.edu.

University of North Dakota, Graduate School, College of Arts and Sciences, Department of Theatre Arts, Grand Forks, ND 58202. Offers MA. *Accreditation:* NAST. *Faculty:* 4 full-time (3 women). *Students:* 1 (woman) full-time, 3 part-time (all women); includes 1 American Indian/Alaska Native. 2 applicants, 100% accepted, 2 enrolled. *Degree requirements:* For master's, comprehensive exam, thesis or alternative. *Entrance requirements:* For master's, minimum GPA of 3.0. Additional exam requirements/recommendations for international students: Required—TOEFL (minimum score 550 paper-based; 213 computer-based; 79 iBT), IELTS (minimum score 7). *Application deadline:* For fall admission, 2/15 priority date for domestic and international students; for spring admission, 10/15 priority date for domestic and international students. Applications are processed on a rolling basis. Application fee: $35. Electronic applications accepted. *Expenses:* Tuition, state resident: full-time $4,050; part-time $225 per credit.

Tuition, nonresident: full-time $10,818; part-time $601 per credit. Required fees: $110 per semester. Tuition and fees vary according to class time, campus/location, program and reciprocity agreements. *Financial support:* In 2007–08, 2 teaching assistantships with full tuition reimbursements (averaging $6,508 per year) were awarded; fellowships with full and partial tuition reimbursements, research assistantships with full and partial tuition reimbursements, Federal Work-Study, institutionally sponsored loans, scholarships/grants, and tuition waivers (full and partial) also available. Support available to part-time students. Financial award application deadline: 3/15; financial award applicants required to submit FAFSA. *Unit head:* Dr. Kathleen Mclennon, Graduate Director, 701-777-3446, Fax: 701-777-3522, E-mail: kathleenmclennon@mail.und.nodak.edu. *Application contact:* Brenda Halle, Admissions Specialist, 701-777-2947, Fax: 701-777-3619, E-mail: brendahalle@mail.und.edu.

University of Oklahoma, Graduate College, College of Fine Arts, School of Drama, Norman, OK 73019-0390. Offers acting (MFA); design (MFA); directing (MFA); drama (MA). *Accreditation:* NAST. *Faculty:* 7 full-time (5 women), 1 (woman) part-time/adjunct. *Students:* 13 full-time (5 women), 1 part-time; includes 2 minority (1 African American, 1 Asian American or Pacific Islander), 3 international. 10 applicants, 60% accepted, 6 enrolled. In 2007, 5 degrees awarded. *Degree requirements:* For master's, comprehensive exam, thesis (MA), departmental qualifying exam. *Entrance requirements:* For master's, BA with 36 hours in drama, auditions. Additional exam requirements/recommendations for international students: Required—TOEFL (minimum score 550 paper-based; 213 computer-based). *Application deadline:* For fall admission, 6/1 for domestic students, 4/1 for international students; for spring admission, 11/1 for domestic students, 9/1 for international students. Applications are processed on a rolling basis. Application fee: $40 ($90 for international students). Electronic applications accepted. *Expenses:* Tuition, state resident: full-time $3,451; part-time $144 per credit hour. Tuition, nonresident: full-time $12,432; part-time $518 per credit hour. Required fees: $1,925; $70 per credit hour. $122 per semester. *Financial support:* In 2007–08, 5 students received support, including research assistantships with partial tuition reimbursements available (averaging $9,397 per year), teaching assistantships with partial tuition reimbursements available (averaging $9,397 per year); unspecified assistantships also available. Financial award application deadline: 4/7; financial award applicants required to submit FAFSA. *Faculty research:* Directing, scenic design, costume, lighting acting. *Unit head:* Dr. Tom Orr, Director, 405-325-4021, Fax: 405-325-0400, E-mail: thorr@ou.edu. *Application contact:* Dr. Judith Pender, Graduate Liaison, 405-325-5319, Fax: 405-325-0400, E-mail: jmpender@ou.edu.

University of Oregon, Graduate School, College of Arts and Sciences, Department of Theater Arts, Eugene, OR 97403. Offers MA, MFA, MS, PhD. *Faculty:* 7 full-time (2 women), 1 part-time/adjunct (0 women). *Students:* 14 full-time (9 women), 3 part-time (2 women). 12 applicants, 17% accepted. In 2007, 3 master's, 1 doctorate awarded. *Degree requirements:* For master's, variable foreign language requirement, thesis or alternative; for doctorate, variable foreign language requirement, thesis/dissertation. *Entrance requirements:* For master's and doctorate, minimum GPA of 3.0. Additional exam requirements/recommendations for international students: Required—TOEFL. *Application deadline:* For fall admission, 3/1 for domestic students. Application fee: $50. *Financial support:* In 2007–08, 12 teaching assistantships were awarded; Federal Work-Study and institutionally sponsored loans also available. Financial award application deadline: 3/1. *Unit head:* John Schmor, Head, 541-346-4145. *Application contact:* May-Britt Jeremiah, Admissions Contact, 541-346-1979, E-mail: maybritt@uoregon.edu.

University of Ottawa, Faculty of Graduate and Postdoctoral Studies, Faculty of Arts, Department of Theatre, Ottawa, ON K1N 6N5, Canada. Offers directing for theatre (MA). Electronic applications accepted. *Faculty research:* Lamise en scéne.

University of Pittsburgh, School of Arts and Sciences, Department of Theatre Arts, Pittsburgh, PA 15260. Offers performance pedagogy (MFA); theatre and performance studies (MA, PhD). *Accreditation:* NAST. *Faculty:* 5 full-time (3 women), 1 part-time/adjunct (0 women). *Students:* 26 full-time (12 women); includes 1 minority (Asian American or Pacific Islander) Average age 32. 48 applicants, 19% accepted, 5 enrolled. In 2007, 2 master's, 2 doctorates awarded. Terminal master's awarded for partial completion of doctoral program. *Degree requirements:* For master's, comprehensive exam; for doctorate, one foreign language, comprehensive exam, thesis/dissertation. *Entrance requirements:* For master's and doctorate, GRE General Test, samples of written work. Additional exam requirements/recommendations for international students: Required—TOEFL. *Application deadline:* For fall admission, 1/15 for domestic students; for winter admission, 10/15 priority date for domestic students. Application fee: $50. Electronic applications accepted. *Financial support:* In 2007–08, 19 students received support, including fellowships (averaging $9,665 per year), 6 research assistantships with full and partial tuition reimbursements available (averaging $8,500 per year), 12 teaching assistantships with full and partial tuition reimbursements available (averaging $10,500 per year); career-related internships or fieldwork, Federal Work-Study, institutionally sponsored loans, scholarships/grants, health care benefits, and unspecified assistantships also available. Support available to part-time students. Financial award application deadline: 1/15; financial award applicants required to submit FAFSA. *Faculty research:* American theatre, Renaissance theatre, Asian theatre, dramatic structure, performance theory. *Unit head:* Dr. Bruce McConachie, Chairman, 412-624-6156, Fax: 412-624-6338, E-mail: bamcco@pitt.edu. *Application contact:* Jami White, Graduate Secretary, 412-624-0466, Fax: 412-624-6338, E-mail: jsw17@pitt.edu.

University of Portland, Graduate School, College of Arts and Sciences, Department of Performing and Fine Arts, Program in Drama, Portland, OR 97203-5798. Offers MFA. *Accreditation:* NAST. Part-time and evening/weekend programs available. *Faculty:* 3 full-time (1 woman). *Students:* 5 applicants, 40% accepted, 1 enrolled. In 2007, 3 degrees awarded. *Degree requirements:* For master's, thesis optional. *Entrance requirements:* For master's, GRE General Test, minimum GPA of 3.0, 3 letters of recommendation, resumé, statement of goals, official transcripts. Additional exam requirements/recommendations for international students: Required—TOEFL (minimum score 500 paper-based; 61 iBT), IELTS (minimum score 7). *Application deadline:* For fall admission, 7/15 priority date for domestic and international students; for spring admission, 12/15 priority date for domestic and international students. Applications are processed on a rolling basis. Application fee: $50. *Expenses:* Tuition: Part-time $775 per semester hour. *Financial support:* Federal Work-Study and scholarships/grants available. Financial award application deadline: 3/1; financial award applicants required to submit FAFSA. *Unit head:* Lawrence Larsen, Director, 503-943-7396, E-mail: larsen@up.edu.

University of San Diego, College of Arts and Sciences, Program in Dramatic Arts, San Diego, CA 92110-2492. Offers MFA. *Faculty:* 2 full-time (0 women), 1 part-time/adjunct (0 women). *Students:* 14 full-time (6 women); includes 4 minority (2 African Americans, 1 Asian American or Pacific Islander, 1 Hispanic American). Average age 28. 252 applicants, 3% accepted, 7 enrolled. In 2007, 6 degrees awarded. *Entrance requirements:* For master's, audition. Additional exam requirements/recommendations for international students: Required—TOEFL (minimum score 580 paper-based; 237 computer-based), TWE. *Application deadline:* For fall admission, 1/20 for domestic students. Application fee: $45. *Expenses:* Tuition: Part-time $1,095 per unit. Tuition and fees vary according to degree level and program. *Financial support:* In 2007–08, 14 students received support, including 14 fellowships with full tuition reimbursements available; career-related internships or fieldwork, Federal Work-Study, and institutionally sponsored loans also available. Financial award application deadline: 5/1; financial award applicants required to submit FAFSA. *Faculty research:* Drama, acting, instruction, voice and speech. *Unit head:* Richard Seer, Graduate Program Director, 619-260-4932, Fax: 619-231-5879. *Application contact:* Stephen Pultz, Director of Admissions, 619-260-4524, Fax: 619-260-4158, E-mail: grads@sandiego.edu.

University of Saskatchewan, College of Graduate Studies and Research, College of Arts and Sciences, Department of Drama, Saskatoon, SK S7N 5A2, Canada. Offers MA. *Degree requirements:* For master's, thesis. *Entrance requirements:* Additional exam requirements/recommendations for international students: Required—TOEFL.

University of South Carolina, The Graduate School, College of Arts and Sciences, Department of Theater and Dance, Columbia, SC 29208. Offers theater (MA, MAT, MFA). IMA and MAT offered in cooperation with the College of Education. *Accreditation:* NAST (one or more programs are accredited). *Faculty:* 18 full-time (6 women), 4 part-time/adjunct (3 women). *Students:* 23 full-time (11 women), 1 part-time; includes 1 minority (African American) Average age 25. In 2007, 15 degrees awarded. *Degree requirements:* For master's, comprehensive exam, thesis. *Entrance requirements:* For master's, GRE General Test, GRE or MAT (for MAT degree), audition, interview (for MFA degree). Additional exam requirements/recommendations for international students: Required—TOEFL. *Application deadline:* For fall admission, 3/1 priority date for domestic students. Applications are processed on a rolling basis. Application fee: $40. Electronic applications accepted. *Expenses:* Tuition, state resident: part-time $440 per hour. Tuition, nonresident: part-time $936 per hour. Required fees: $17 per hour. Tuition and fees vary according to program. *Financial support:* In 2007–08, 1 fellowship, 7 teaching assistantships with partial tuition reimbursements (averaging $6,750 per year) were awarded; career-related internships or fieldwork, Federal Work-Study, and unspecified assistantships also available. Financial award application deadline: 4/1. *Faculty research:* Computer assisted design, rhetoric of science and technology, Alexander Technique, script analysis, Lessac Method. *Unit head:* James W. Hunter, Chair, 803-777-1203, Fax: 803-777-6669, E-mail: hunter@sc.edu. *Application contact:* Nic W. Ularu, Director of Graduate Studies, 803-777-6892, Fax: 803-777-6669, E-mail: ularu@gwm.sc.edu.

University of South Carolina, The Graduate School, College of Education, Department of Instruction and Teacher Education, Program in Secondary Education, Columbia, SC 29208. Offers art education (IMA, MAT); business education (IMA, MAT); English (MAT); foreign language (MAT); health education (MAT); mathematics (MAT); science (IMA, MAT); secondary (Ed D); secondary education (MT, PhD); social studies (MAT); theatre and speech (MAT). IMA and MT offered jointly with the subject areas. *Accreditation:* NCATE. *Faculty:* 6 full-time (5 women), 7 part-time/adjunct (5 women). *Students:* 93 full-time (61 women), 35 part-time (22 women); includes 14 minority (10 African Americans, 1 American Indian/Alaska Native, 1 Asian American or Pacific Islander, 2 Hispanic Americans). 40 applicants, 50% accepted, 16 enrolled. In 2007, 108 master's, 1 doctorate awarded. *Degree requirements:* For master's, comprehensive exam, thesis (for some programs), foreign language (MA); for doctorate, one foreign language, comprehensive exam, thesis/dissertation. *Entrance requirements:* For master's, GRE General Test or MAT, teaching certificate (IMA, M Ed), interview; for doctorate, GRE General Test or MAT, interview. Application fee: $40. *Expenses:* Tuition, state resident: part-time $440 per hour. Tuition, nonresident: part-time $936 per hour. Required fees: $17 per hour. Tuition and fees vary according to program. *Faculty research:* Middle school programs, professional development, school collaboration. *Unit head:* Dr. Ed Dickey, Professor/Coordinator, 803-777-6235, Fax: 803-777-3193, E-mail: edickey@gwm.sc.edu. *Application contact:* 803-777-6732, Fax: 803-777-3068, E-mail: teach@gwm.sc.edu.

The University of South Dakota, Graduate School, College of Fine Arts, Department of Theatre, Vermillion, SD 57069-2390. Offers MA, MFA. *Accreditation:* NAST. *Faculty:* 7 full-time (3 women), 2 part-time/adjunct (1 woman). *Students:* 12 (6 women). In 2007, 5 degrees awarded. *Degree requirements:* For master's, thesis or alternative. *Entrance requirements:* For master's, GRE (MA), minimum GPA of 2.7, portfolio. Additional exam requirements/recommendations for international students: Required—TOEFL (minimum score 550 paper-based; 213 computer-based; 79 iBT). *Application deadline:* Applications are processed on a rolling basis. Application fee: $35. Electronic applications accepted. *Financial support:* In 2007–08, research assistantships with partial tuition reimbursements (averaging $4,626 per year), teaching assistantships with partial tuition reimbursements (averaging $4,626 per year) were awarded; unspecified assistantships also available. *Unit head:* Dr. Ron Moyer, Graduate Director/Chair, 605-677-5418, Fax: 605-677-5988, E-mail: theatre@usd.edu.

University of Southern California, Graduate School, School of Theatre, Program in Acting, Los Angeles, CA 90089. Offers MFA. Postbaccalaureate distance learning degree programs offered (minimal on-campus study). *Faculty:* 9 full-time (4 women), 3 part-time/adjunct (1 woman). *Students:* 22 full-time (9 women); includes 11 minority (7 African Americans, 1 Asian American or Pacific Islander, 3 Hispanic Americans), 2 international. 111 applicants, 11% accepted. *Entrance requirements:* For master's, 3 letters of recommendation, current headshot, audition. *Application deadline:* For fall admission, 1/11 for domestic students. Application fee: $85. *Financial support:* In 2007–08, 21 students received support. Federal Work-Study and tuition waivers (partial) available. *Unit head:* Dr. Andrew Robinson, Director, 213-821-4163, E-mail: sotmfa@usc.edu.

See Close-Up on page 373.

University of Southern California, Graduate School, School of Theatre, Program in Dramatic Writing, Los Angeles, CA 90089. Offers MFA. *Faculty:* 2 full-time (1 woman), 3 part-time/adjunct (2 women). *Students:* 10 full-time (3 women); includes 2 African Americans, 2 Asian Americans or Pacific Islanders, 1 international. 22 applicants, 18% accepted. In 2007, 3 degrees awarded. *Entrance requirements:* For master's, GRE General Test, 3 letters of recommendation, play in standard Samuel French of Final Draft stage format, a synopsis of the play. *Application deadline:* For fall admission, 1/11 for domestic students. Application fee: $85. *Financial support:* In 2007–08, 9 students received support, including teaching assistantships with full tuition reimbursements available (averaging $9,400 per year); fellowships with full tuition reimbursements available, career-related internships or fieldwork, Federal Work-Study, and scholarships/grants also available. Support available to part-time students. Financial award application deadline: 2/15; financial award applicants required to submit FAFSA. *Unit head:* Dr. Velina Hasu-Houston, Director, 213-740-2311.

See Close-Up on page 373.

University of Southern Mississippi, Graduate School, College of Arts and Letters, Department of Theatre and Dance, Hattiesburg, MS 39406-0001. Offers theatre (MFA). *Accreditation:* NAST. Part-time programs available. *Faculty:* 12 full-time (6 women). *Students:* 21 full-time (13 women); includes 4 minority (3 African Americans, 1 American Indian/Alaska Native). Average age 29. 14 applicants, 50% accepted, 7 enrolled. In 2007, 7 master's awarded. *Degree requirements:* For master's, comprehensive exam, thesis or alternative, creative project. *Entrance requirements:* For master's, GRE General Test, minimum GPA of 3.0. Additional exam requirements/recommendations for international students: Required—TOEFL. *Application deadline:* For fall admission, 3/1 priority date for domestic students, 3/1 for international students. Applications are processed on a rolling basis. Application fee: $30. *Financial support:* In 2007–08, 20 teaching assistantships with full tuition reimbursements (averaging $7,065 per year) were awarded; research assistantships, career-related internships or fieldwork, Federal Work-Study, and unspecified assistantships also available. Support available to part-time students. Financial award application deadline: 3/15. *Faculty research:* Technical design, acting. *Unit head:* Louis Rackoff, Chair, 601-266-4994, Fax: 601-266-6423.

The University of Tennessee, Graduate School, College of Arts and Sciences, Department of Theatre, Knoxville, TN 37996. Offers costume design (MFA); lighting design (MFA); performance (MFA); scene design (MFA); theatre technology (MFA). *Degree requirements:* For master's, thesis or alternative. *Entrance requirements:* For master's, audition, minimum GPA of 2.7. Additional exam requirements/recommendations for international students: Required—TOEFL. Electronic applications accepted.

The University of Texas at Austin, Graduate School, College of Fine Arts, Department of Theatre and Dance, Austin, TX 78712-1111. Offers dance (MFA); theatre (MA, MFA, PhD). *Accreditation:* NASD. *Degree requirements:* For master's, thesis; for doctorate, variable foreign language requirement, thesis/dissertation. *Entrance requirements:* For master's and doctorate, GRE General Test.

The University of Texas at El Paso, Graduate School, College of Liberal Arts, Department of Theatre Arts, El Paso, TX 79968-0001. Offers MA. Part-time and evening/weekend programs available. *Degree requirements:* For master's, thesis. *Entrance requirements:* For master's, GRE General Test. Additional exam requirements/recommendations for international students: Required—TOEFL. Electronic applications accepted.

Theater

The University of Texas–Pan American, College of Arts and Humanities, Department of Communications, Edinburg, TX 78541-2999. Offers communication (MA); theatre (MA). *Accreditation:* NAST. Part-time and evening/weekend programs available. *Degree requirements:* For master's, comprehensive exam, thesis or alternative. *Entrance requirements:* For master's, minimum GPA of 3.0. Additional exam requirements/recommendations for international students: Required—TOEFL. *Faculty research:* Rhetorical theory, intercultural and mass communication, American theatre, multicultural theatre and drama, television and film.

University of Toronto, School of Graduate Studies, Humanities Division, Centre for the Study of Drama, Toronto, ON M5S 1A1, Canada. Offers MA, PhD. Part-time programs available. *Faculty:* 29 full-time, 14 part-time/adjunct. *Students:* 76 full-time (49 women), 14 part-time, 5 international. 66 applicants, 67% accepted. In 2007, 9 master's, 3 doctorates awarded. *Degree requirements:* For doctorate, one foreign language, thesis/dissertation, language examination, qualifying examination, oral examination. *Entrance requirements:* For master's, minimum B+ average, significant coursework in drama and related disciplines, resumé, 2 letters of recommendation; for doctorate, minimum A- average, resumé, MA in drama; 2 letters of recommendation. *Application deadline:* For fall admission, 2/1 priority date for domestic students. Application fee: $100 Canadian dollars. *Unit head:* Prof. Stephen Johnson, Director, 416-9787981, Fax: 416-971-1378. *Application contact:* Robert Moses, Administrative Assistant, 416-978-7981, Fax: 416-971-1378, E-mail: graduate.drama@utoronto.ca.

University of Victoria, Faculty of Graduate Studies, Faculty of Fine Arts, Department of Theatre, Victoria, BC V8W 2Y2, Canada. Offers design (MFA); directing (MFA); theatre history (MA). *Students:* 6. Average age 31. 22 applicants, 32% accepted, 6 enrolled. *Degree requirements:* For master's, thesis. *Entrance requirements:* Additional exam requirements/recommendations for international students: Required—TOEFL (minimum score 575 paper-based; 233 computer-based), IELTS (minimum score 7). *Application deadline:* For fall admission, 2/1 priority date for domestic students, 12/15 priority date for international students. Applications are processed on a rolling basis. Application fee: $75 ($125 for international students). Electronic applications accepted. *Expenses:* Tuition, state resident: full-time $3,110. International tuition: $3,700 full-time. Tuition and fees vary according to program. *Financial support:* Application deadline: 2/15. *Unit head:* Prof. Brian Richmond, Chair, 250-721-7991, Fax: 250-721-6596, E-mail: brichmon@finearts.uvic.ca. *Application contact:* Connie te Kampe, Graduate Secretary, 250-721-7991, Fax: 250-721-6596, E-mail: theatre@uvic.ca.

University of Virginia, College and Graduate School of Arts and Sciences, Department of Drama, Charlottesville, VA 22903. Offers MFA. *Faculty:* 16 full-time (6 women), 2 part-time/adjunct (both women). *Students:* 16 full-time (9 women); includes 1 minority (Hispanic American) Average age 26. *Degree requirements:* For master's, thesis (for some programs). *Entrance requirements:* For master's, GRE General Test, minimum GPA of 3.0 in major. *Application deadline:* Applications are processed on a rolling basis. Application fee: $60. Electronic applications accepted. *Financial support:* Applicants required to submit FAFSA. *Unit head:* Tom Bloom, Chairman, 434-924-3326, Fax: 434-924-1447, E-mail: tab4p@virginia.edu.

University of Washington, Graduate School, College of Arts and Sciences, School of Drama, Seattle, WA 98195. Offers acting (MFA); costume design (MFA); directing (MFA); dramatic theory (PhD); lighting design (MFA); scenic design (MFA); theatre history (PhD). *Degree requirements:* For master's, thesis; for doctorate, one foreign language, comprehensive exam, thesis/dissertation. *Entrance requirements:* For master's, interview, minimum GPA of 3.0, portfolio; for doctorate, GRE General Test, minimum GPA of 3.0, writing sample. Additional exam requirements/recommendations for international students: Required—TOEFL. *Faculty research:* Semiotics, Suzuki actor training, modern American theatre, ethnic American theatre.

University of Wisconsin–Madison, Graduate School, College of Letters and Science, Department of Theatre and Drama, Madison, WI 53706-1380. Offers MA, MFA, PhD. *Accreditation:* NAST. Part-time programs available. *Degree requirements:* For master's, thesis; for doctorate, thesis/dissertation. *Entrance requirements:* For master's and doctorate, GRE. Electronic applications accepted. *Faculty research:* Theories and histories of dance, theatre and performance studies; Russian theatre and dance; postmodern performance; Holocaust drama; race and representation.

University of Wisconsin–Milwaukee, Graduate School, Peck School of the Arts, Program in Performing Arts, Milwaukee, WI 53201-0413. Offers dance (MFA); film (MFA); theatre (MFA). Part-time programs available. *Faculty:* 29 full-time (14 women). *Students:* 15 full-time (10 women), 3 part-time (all women); includes 1 minority (Hispanic American), 2 international. 32 applicants, 25% accepted, 6 enrolled. In 2007, 16 degrees awarded. *Degree requirements:* For master's, variable foreign language requirement, thesis or alternative. *Entrance requirements:* For master's, audition, interview. *Application deadline:* For fall admission, 1/1 priority date for domestic students; for spring admission, 9/1 for domestic students. Applications are processed on a rolling basis. Application fee: $45 ($75 for international students). *Expenses:* Tuition, state resident: part-time $530 per credit. Tuition, nonresident: part-time $1,428 per credit. Required fees: $19 per credit. $229 per term. Tuition and fees vary according to course load and program. *Financial support:* In 2007–08, 9 teaching assistantships were awarded; fellowships, research assistantships, career-related internships or fieldwork and unspecified assistantships also available. Support available to part-time students. Financial award application deadline: 4/15. *Unit head:* Simone Ferro, Representative, 414-229-4178, E-mail: sferro@uwm.edu.

University of Wisconsin–Superior, Graduate Division, Department of Communicating Arts, Superior, WI 54880-4500. Offers mass communication (MA); speech communication (MA); theater (MA). Part-time programs available. *Degree requirements:* For master's, comprehensive exam, thesis or alternative, position paper or project. *Entrance requirements:* For master's, minimum GPA of 2.75. *Faculty research:* Multimedia technology, ethics in journalism, diversity, electronic portfolio assessment.

Utah State University, School of Graduate Studies, College of Humanities, Arts and Social Sciences, Department of Theatre Arts, Logan, UT 84322. Offers advanced technical practice (MFA); design (MFA); theatre arts (MA, MFA). *Degree requirements:* For master's, variable foreign language requirement, thesis (for some programs), summer internship (MFA). *Entrance requirements:* For master's, GRE General Test or MAT, portfolio (MFA), minimum GPA of 3.0, interview, BS or 20 semester credit. Additional exam requirements/recommendations for international students: Required—TOEFL. *Faculty research:* Seventeenth and eighteenth century Spanish theatre, Greek and Roman theatre, interpretation of literature for performance.

Villanova University, Graduate School of Liberal Arts and Sciences, Department of Theatre, Villanova, PA 19085-1699. Offers MA. Part-time and evening/weekend programs available. *Faculty:* 6 full-time (2 women), 1 (woman) part-time/adjunct. *Students:* 21 full-time (14 women), 14 part-time (7 women); includes 3 minority (2 African Americans, 1 Hispanic American), 1 international. Average age 29. 26 applicants, 100% accepted. In 2007, 18 degrees awarded. *Degree requirements:* For master's, comprehensive exam. *Entrance requirements:* For master's, GRE, minimum GPA of 3.0. *Application deadline:* For fall admission, 8/1 priority date for domestic students; for spring admission, 12/1 for domestic students. Applications are processed on a rolling basis. Application fee: $50. Electronic applications accepted. *Financial support:* Research assistantships, Federal Work-Study and scholarships/grants available. Financial award applicants required to submit FAFSA. *Unit head:* Fr. Richard Cannuli, Chairperson, 610-519-4760.

Announcement: Graduate offerings include the 36-credit MA in theater and the 15-credit certificate in practical theater. Scholarly and creative studies in dramaturgy, script analysis, acting, directing, playwriting, solo performance, and scenography are supplemented with hands-on production work with professional directors and designers. Four professional-caliber productions are presented annually on the award-winning main stage. Acting scholarships and paid production assistantships are available.

Virginia Commonwealth University, Graduate School, School of the Arts, Department of Theatre, Richmond, VA 23284-9005. Offers acting (MFA); costume design (MFA); directing (MFA); pedagogy (MFA); scene design/technical theater (MFA). *Accreditation:* NAST. *Faculty:* 9 full-time (4 women). *Students:* 45 full-time (22 women), 9 part-time (4 women); includes 3 African Americans, 1 Hispanic American, 1 international. 35 applicants, 66% accepted, 14 enrolled. In 2007, 16 degrees awarded. *Degree requirements:* For master's, thesis (for some programs). *Entrance requirements:* For master's, audition, portfolio. *Application deadline:* For fall admission, 5/1 priority date for domestic students. Application fee: $50. *Expenses:* Tuition, state resident: full-time $7,224; part-time $401 per credit. Tuition, nonresident: full-time $16,072; part-time $891 per credit. Required fees: $1,679; $63 per credit. Tuition and fees vary according to campus/location. *Financial support:* Fellowships, teaching assistantships, career-related internships or fieldwork, Federal Work-Study, and institutionally sponsored loans available. Support available to part-time students. Financial award application deadline: 3/15. *Faculty research:* Dramatic literature, speech. *Unit head:* Dr. David S. Leong, Chair, 804-828-1514, Fax: 804-828-6741, E-mail: dsleong@vcu.edu.

See Close-Up on page 275.

Virginia Polytechnic Institute and State University, Graduate School, College of Liberal Arts and Human Sciences, Department of Theatre Arts, Blacksburg, VA 24061. Offers arts administration (MFA); costume design (MFA); lighting design (MFA); property management (MFA); scenic design (MFA); stage management (MFA); technical theatre (MFA). *Accreditation:* NAST. *Entrance requirements:* Additional exam requirements/recommendations for international students: Required—TOEFL (minimum score 550 paper-based; 213 computer-based). Electronic applications accepted.

Washington University in St. Louis, Graduate School of Arts and Sciences, Department of Performing Arts, St. Louis, MO 63130-4899. Offers MA. *Degree requirements:* For master's, thesis optional. *Entrance requirements:* For master's, GRE General Test, sample of written work. Electronic applications accepted.

Wayne State University, College of Fine, Performing and Communication Arts, Department of Theatre, Detroit, MI 48202. Offers MA, MFA, PhD. *Accreditation:* NAST. *Students:* 58 full-time (24 women), 3 part-time (all women); includes 11 minority (10 African Americans, 1 Hispanic American), 4 international. Average age 29. 24 applicants, 75% accepted, 16 enrolled. In 2007, 15 master's, 1 doctorate awarded. *Degree requirements:* For master's, thesis (for some programs); for doctorate, one foreign language, thesis/dissertation. *Entrance requirements:* For master's, minimum GPA of 3.0, auditions, interviews; for doctorate, GRE, MA with minimum GPA of 3.3; directing experience; recommendations; scholarly paper; statement of goals. Additional exam requirements/recommendations for international students: Required—TOEFL (minimum score 550 paper-based; 213 computer-based); Recommended—TWE (minimum score 6). *Application deadline:* For fall admission, 4/1 for domestic students, 6/1 for international students; for winter admission, 10/1 for international students; for spring admission, 2/1 for international students. Application fee: $30 ($50 for international students). Electronic applications accepted. *Expenses:* Tuition, state resident: part-time $403 per credit hour. Tuition, nonresident: part-time $890 per credit hour. *Financial support:* In 2007–08, 1 fellowship (averaging $13,901 per year), 43 research assistantships (averaging $12,922 per year), 4 teaching assistantships (averaging $13,372 per year) were awarded. *Faculty research:* Dramatic criticism, lighting design, acting, directing, scenography. *Unit head:* Blair Anderson, Chair, 313-577-3508, Fax: 313-577-0935, E-mail: ad5298@wayne.edu. *Application contact:* James Thomas, Professor, 313-577-0789, E-mail: jthomas@wayne.edu.

Western Illinois University, School of Graduate Studies, College of Fine Arts and Communication, Department of Theatre and Dance, Macomb, IL 61455-1390. Offers acting (MFA); costume design (MFA); directing (MFA); lighting design/theatre technology (MFA); scenic design (MFA). Part-time programs available. *Students:* 32 full-time (13 women), 4 part-time (1 woman); includes 4 minority (2 African Americans, 1 Asian American or Pacific Islander, 1 Hispanic American). Average age 28. 24 applicants, 63% accepted. In 2007, 6 degrees awarded. *Degree requirements:* For master's, comprehensive exam, thesis or alternative, creative project, written exam. *Entrance requirements:* For master's, audition or interview. Additional exam requirements/recommendations for international students: Required—TOEFL (minimum score 550 paper-based; 213 computer-based; 80 iBT). *Application deadline:* Applications are processed on a rolling basis. Application fee: $30. Electronic applications accepted. *Expenses:* Tuition, state resident: part-time $217 per credit hour. Tuition, nonresident: part-time $433 per credit hour. Required fees: $54 per credit hour. *Financial support:* In 2007–08, 29 students received support, including 25 research assistantships with full tuition reimbursements available (averaging $6,800 per year), 4 teaching assistantships with full tuition reimbursements available (averaging $7,840 per year). Financial award applicants required to submit FAFSA. *Unit head:* Dr. Jeannie Woods, Chairperson, 309-298-1543. *Application contact:* Dr. Barbara Baily, Director of Graduate Studies/Associate Provost, 309-298-1806, Fax: 309-298-2345, E-mail: grad-office@wiu.edu.

West Virginia University, College of Creative Arts, Division of Theatre and Dance, Morgantown, WV 26506. Offers acting (MFA); theatre design/technology (MFA). *Accreditation:* NAST. Part-time programs available. *Faculty:* 15 full-time (6 women), 3 part-time/adjunct (all women). *Students:* 11 full-time (7 women), 1 part-time; includes 2 minority (both African Americans) Average age 31. 2 applicants, 50% accepted, 1 enrolled. In 2007, 3 degrees awarded. *Degree requirements:* For master's, thesis, oral defense. *Entrance requirements:* For master's, minimum GPA of 3.0, audition or portfolio. Additional exam requirements/recommendations for international students: Required—TOEFL. *Application deadline:* For fall admission, 3/15 priority date for domestic students; for spring admission, 11/1 for domestic students. Applications are processed on a rolling basis. Application fee: $45. *Expenses:* Tuition, state resident: full-time $5,196; part-time $292 per credit hour. Tuition, nonresident: full-time $15,064; part-time $840 per credit hour. Tuition and fees vary according to program. *Financial support:* In 2007–08, 14 students received support, including 12 teaching assistantships; research assistantships, career-related internships or fieldwork, Federal Work-Study, institutionally sponsored loans, and tuition waivers (partial) also available. Financial award application deadline: 2/1; financial award applicants required to submit FAFSA. *Faculty research:* Professional directing, consulting, design. Total annual research expenditures: $2,104. *Unit head:* Joshua Blackmer Willliamson, Interim Chair, 304-293-4841 Ext. 3132, Fax: 304-293-2533, E-mail: joshua.williamson@mail.wvu.edu.

Yale University, School of Drama, New Haven, CT 06520. Offers MFA, DFA, Certificate, MBA/MFA. *Faculty:* 33 full-time (13 women), 57 part-time/adjunct (23 women). *Students:* 199 full-time (95 women); includes 32 minority (15 African Americans, 10 Asian Americans or Pacific Islanders, 7 Hispanic Americans), 20 international. Average age 27. 1,037 applicants, 8% accepted, 72 enrolled. *Degree requirements:* For master's, comprehensive exam (for some programs), thesis (for some programs); for doctorate, thesis/dissertation. *Entrance requirements:* For master's, in person audition (acting); portfolio, review (design); interview. Additional exam requirements/recommendations for international students: Required—TOEFL. *Application deadline:* For fall admission, 1/3 for domestic and international students. Application fee: $95. Electronic applications accepted. *Financial support:* Career-related internships or fieldwork, Federal Work-Study, institutionally sponsored loans, and scholarships/grants available. Financial award application deadline: 2/15; financial award applicants required to submit FAFSA. *Unit head:* James Bundy, Dean/Artistic Director, 203-432-1505. *Application contact:* Registrar's Office, 203-432-1507, Fax: 203-432-9668.

York University, Faculty of Graduate Studies, Faculty of Fine Arts, Program in Theatre, Toronto, ON M3J 1P3, Canada. Offers MFA. *Degree requirements:* For master's, thesis. Electronic applications accepted.

York University, Faculty of Graduate Studies, Faculty of Fine Arts, Program in Theatre Studies, Toronto, ON M3J 1P3, Canada. Offers MA, PhD.

Therapies—Dance, Drama, and Music

Antioch University New England, Graduate School, Department of Applied Psychology, Program in Dance/Movement Therapy and Counseling, Keene, NH 03431-3552. Offers M Ed, MA. *Faculty:* 9 full-time (7 women), 14 part-time/adjunct (9 women). *Students:* 45 full-time (44 women); includes 1 minority (Hispanic American), 2 international. Average age 29. 30 applicants, 77% accepted, 9 enrolled. In 2007, 20 degrees awarded. *Degree requirements:* For master's, thesis, internship, practicum. *Entrance requirements:* For master's, previous course work and work experience in psychology, experience in dance or movement. Additional exam requirements/recommendations for international students: Required—TOEFL (minimum score 600 paper-based; 250 computer-based). *Application deadline:* For fall admission, 7/15 for domestic and international students; for spring admission, 12/1 for domestic and international students. Applications are processed on a rolling basis. Application fee: $50. Electronic applications accepted. *Expenses: Contact institution.* Tuition and fees vary according to degree level, program and student level. *Financial support:* In 2007–08, 4 fellowships (averaging $1,050 per year) were awarded; Federal Work-Study and scholarships/grants also available. Financial award applicants required to submit FAFSA. *Faculty research:* Research attitudes and needs of dance/movement therapists. *Unit head:* Susan Loman, Director, 603-283-2137, Fax: 603-357-0718, E-mail: sloman@antiochne.edu. *Application contact:* Leatrice A. Oram, Co-Director of Admissions, 800-490-3310, Fax: 603-357-0718, E-mail: admissions@antiochne.edu.

Appalachian State University, Cratis D. Williams Graduate School, School of Music, Boone, NC 28608. Offers music education (MM); music performance (MM); music therapy (MMT). *Accreditation:* NASM. *Faculty:* 26 full-time (7 women). *Students:* 18 full-time (10 women), 9 part-time (4 women); includes 2 minority (1 African American, 1 Asian American or Pacific Islander), 2 international. 24 applicants, 75% accepted, 12 enrolled. In 2007, 6 master's awarded. *Degree requirements:* For master's, comprehensive exam, thesis or alternative. *Entrance requirements:* For master's, GRE General Test, 3 letters of ref + audition. Additional exam requirements/recommendations for international students: Required—TOEFL (minimum score 550 paper-based; 230 computer-based). *Application deadline:* For fall admission, 7/1 for domestic students, 1/1 for international students; for spring admission, 11/1 for domestic students, 6/1 for international students. Application fee: $50. *Expenses:* Tuition, state resident: part-time $127 per semester hour. Tuition, nonresident: part-time $597 per semester hour. Required fees: $18 per semester. *Financial support:* In 2007–08, 8 research assistantships (averaging $7,000 per year) were awarded; fellowships, teaching assistantships, career-related internships or fieldwork, Federal Work-Study, scholarships/grants, tuition waivers (partial), and unspecified assistantships also available. Financial award application deadline: 4/1. *Faculty research:* Music of the holocaust, Celtic folk music, early 19th century performance practice, hypermeter and phase rhythm, world music, music and psychoneuroimmunology. Total annual research expenditures: $45,853. *Unit head:* Dr. William Harbinson, Graduate Director and Associate Dean, 828-262-6446, E-mail: harbinsonwg@appstate.edu. *Application contact:* Dr. Nancy Schneeloch-Bingham, Graduate Program Director, 828-262-6463, E-mail: schneelochna@appstate.edu.

California Institute of Integral Studies, Graduate Programs, School of Professional Psychology, San Francisco, CA 94103. Offers clinical psychology (Psy D); community mental health (MA); drama therapy (MA); expressive arts therapy (MA); integral counseling psychology (MA); integral counseling, psychology-weekend (MA); psychology (Psy D), including clinical psychology; somatic psychology (MA). *Accreditation:* APA. Part-time programs available. *Faculty:* 28 full-time, 54 part-time/adjunct. *Students:* 591; includes 113 minority (19 African Americans, 3 American Indian/Alaska Native, 48 Asian Americans or Pacific Islanders, 43 Hispanic Americans). Average age 37. 383 applicants, 75% accepted, 155 enrolled. In 2007, 109 master's, 20 doctorates awarded. *Degree requirements:* For master's, comprehensive exam; for doctorate, comprehensive exam, thesis/dissertation. *Entrance requirements:* For master's, minimum GPA of 3.0, letters of recommendation, writing sample; for doctorate, GRE, MA in psychology or social work with appropriate practical experience for advanced standing, or BA with a minimum GPA of 3.1; letters of recommendation; writing sample. Additional exam requirements/recommendations for international students: Required—TOEFL. *Application deadline:* For fall admission, 2/1 priority date for domestic and international students; for spring admission, 10/15 priority date for domestic and international students. Applications are processed on a rolling basis. Application fee: $65. Electronic applications accepted. *Expenses:* Tuition: Full-time $16,930; part-time $780 per unit. Tuition and fees vary according to course load and program. *Financial support:* In 2007–08, 393 students received support; research assistantships with tuition reimbursements available, teaching assistantships with tuition reimbursements available, career-related internships or fieldwork, Federal Work-Study, institutionally sponsored loans, scholarships/grants, and tuition waivers (partial) available. Support available to part-time students. Financial award application deadline: 3/15; financial award applicants required to submit FAFSA. *Faculty research:* Somatic psychology, comparative psychology, art therapy, transpersonal psychology, eco-psychology. *Application contact:* David Townes, Senior Admissions Counselor, 415-575-6152, Fax: 415-575-1268, E-mail: dtownes@ciis.edu.

See Close-Up on page 1421.

Columbia College Chicago, Graduate School, Program in Dance/Movement Therapy, Chicago, IL 60605-1996. Offers MA, Certificate. Part-time programs available. *Faculty:* 2 full-time, 4 part-time/adjunct. *Students:* 4 full-time (all women), 64 part-time (63 women); includes 14 minority (6 African Americans, 1 American Indian/Alaska Native, 1 Asian American or Pacific Islander, 6 Hispanic Americans), 3 international. Average age 29. In 2007, 15 degrees awarded. *Degree requirements:* For master's, thesis, internship. *Entrance requirements:* For master's, movement assessment, interview, minimum GPA of 3.0. Additional exam requirements/recommendations for international students: Required—TOEFL (minimum score 550 paper-based; 213 computer-based). *Application deadline:* For fall admission, 3/1 for domestic students, 1/3 for international students. Application fee: $50. *Financial support:* Fellowships, career-related internships or fieldwork, Federal Work-Study, and scholarships/grants available. Support available to part-time students. Financial award application deadline: 8/13; financial award applicants required to submit FAFSA. *Unit head:* Susan Imus, Director, 312-344-7097, E-mail: simus@colum.edu. *Application contact:* Keith Cleveland, Acting Dean of the Graduate School, 312-344-7261, Fax: 312-344-8047, E-mail: kcleveland@colum.edu.

Drexel University, College of Nursing and Health Professions, Program in Creative Arts in Therapy, Specialization in Dance/Movement Therapy, Philadelphia, PA 19104-2875. Offers MA. Part-time programs available. *Degree requirements:* For master's, comprehensive exam, thesis. *Entrance requirements:* For master's, GRE General Test or MAT, audition, interview, minimum GPA of 2.75. Electronic applications accepted. *Faculty research:* Family nonverbal communication, early intervention, sexual abuse.

Drexel University, College of Nursing and Health Professions, Program in Creative Arts in Therapy, Specialization in Music Therapy, Philadelphia, PA 19104-2875. Offers MA. Part-time programs available. *Degree requirements:* For master's, comprehensive exam, thesis. *Entrance requirements:* For master's, GRE General Test or MAT, audition, interview, minimum GPA of 2.75. Electronic applications accepted. *Faculty research:* Early childhood intervention through creative art therapies, rhythm and dementia, music therapy and bulimia, assessment of adolescent suicide.

East Carolina University, Graduate School, College of Fine Arts and Communication, School of Music, Greenville, NC 27858-4353. Offers music education (MM); music therapy (MM); performance (MM); theory and composition (MM). *Accreditation:* NASM. Part-time programs available. *Faculty:* 37 full-time (10 women). *Students:* 37 full-time (20 women), 20 part-time (12 women); includes 6 minority (4 African Americans, 1 Asian American or Pacific Islander, 1 Hispanic American), 4 international. Average age 28. 24 applicants, 13% accepted, 3 enrolled. In 2007, 22 degrees awarded. *Degree requirements:* For master's, comprehensive exam, thesis optional. *Entrance requirements:* For master's, GRE General Test or MAT. Additional exam requirements/recommendations for international students: Required—TOEFL. *Application deadline:* For fall admission, 6/1 priority date for domestic students. Applications are processed on a rolling basis. Application fee: $50. *Financial support:* Fellowships, research assistantships, teaching assistantships, Federal Work-Study available. Support available to part-time students. Financial award application deadline: 6/1. *Unit head:* Dr. J. Christopher Buddo, Director, 252-328-6131. *Application contact:* Dean of Graduate School, 252-328-6012, Fax: 252-328-6071, E-mail: gradschool@ecu.edu.

Florida State University, Graduate Studies, College of Music, Tallahassee, FL 32306. Offers accompanying (MM); arts administration (MA); choral conducting (MM); composition (MM, DM); ethnomusicology (MM); general music (MA); instrumental accompanying (MM); instrumental conducting (MM); jazz studies (MM); music education (MM Ed, PhD); music theory (MM, PhD); music therapy (MM); musicology (MM, PhD), including ethnomusicology (PhD), historical musicology; opera (MM); performance (MM, DM); piano pedagogy (MM); piano technology (MA); vocal accompanying (MM). *Accreditation:* NASM. *Faculty:* 88 full-time, 13 part-time/adjunct. *Students:* 406 full-time (211 women); includes 98 minority (28 African Americans, 38 Asian Americans or Pacific Islanders, 32 Hispanic Americans). Average age 26. 525 applicants, 38% accepted, 145 enrolled. In 2007, 102 master's, 41 doctorates awarded. *Degree requirements:* For master's, comprehensive exam (for some programs), thesis (for some programs), departmental qualifying exam; for doctorate, comprehensive exam (for some programs), thesis/dissertation, departmental qualifying exam. *Entrance requirements:* For master's and doctorate, audition, GRE General Test or minimum GPA of 3.0. Additional exam requirements/recommendations for international students: Required—TOEFL (minimum score 550 paper-based; 213 computer-based). *Application deadline:* For fall admission, 7/1 for domestic students, 5/2 for international students; for spring admission, 11/3 for domestic students, 9/1 for international students. Applications are processed on a rolling basis. Application fee: $30. Electronic applications accepted. *Expenses:* Tuition, state resident: part-time $248 per credit hour. Tuition, nonresident: part-time $880 per credit hour. Tuition and fees vary according to program. *Financial support:* In 2007–08, 225 students received support, including 3 fellowships with full tuition reimbursements available (averaging $15,000 per year), 9 research assistantships with full tuition reimbursements available (averaging $4,000 per year), 173 teaching assistantships with full tuition reimbursements available (averaging $4,000 per year); career-related internships or fieldwork, Federal Work-Study, and tuition waivers (partial) also available. Support available to part-time students. Financial award application deadline: 2/28; financial award applicants required to submit FAFSA. *Unit head:* Don Gibson, Dean, 850-644-4361, Fax: 850-644-2033. *Application contact:* Dr. Seth Beckman, Assistant Dean for Academic Affairs/Director of Graduate Studies, 850-644-5848, Fax: 850-644-2033, E-mail: sbeckman@admin.fsu.edu.

Georgia College & State University, Graduate School, School of Health Sciences, Program in Music Therapy, Milledgeville, GA 31061. Offers MMT. *Students:* 4 full-time (3 women), 1 international. 5 applicants, 20% accepted, 1 enrolled. *Entrance requirements:* Additional exam requirements/recommendations for international students: Required—TOEFL. *Application deadline:* For fall admission, 7/15 priority date for domestic students. Applications are processed on a rolling basis. Application fee: $25. Electronic applications accepted. *Expenses:* Tuition, state resident: full-time $3,726. Tuition, nonresident: full-time $14,868. Required fees: $858. Tuition and fees vary according to campus/location. *Financial support:* In 2007–08, 1 research assistantship was awarded; career-related internships or fieldwork and Federal Work-Study also available. Support available to part-time students. Financial award application deadline: 3/1; financial award applicants required to submit FAFSA. *Unit head:* Dr. Chesley Mercado, Director, Music Therapy Program, 478-445-2645, Fax: 478-445-2645, E-mail: chesley.mercado@gcsu.edu.

Immaculata University, College of Graduate Studies, Program in Music Therapy, Immaculata, PA 19345. Offers MA. *Accreditation:* NASM. Part-time and evening/weekend programs available. *Students:* 1 (woman) full-time, 16 part-time (all women). Average age 33. 13 applicants, 85% accepted, 5 enrolled. In 2007, 3 degrees awarded. *Degree requirements:* For master's, comprehensive exam, thesis optional. *Entrance requirements:* For master's, GRE General Test or MAT, minimum GPA of 3.0. Additional exam requirements/recommendations for international students: Required—TOEFL. *Application deadline:* Applications are processed on a rolling basis. Application fee: $35. Electronic applications accepted. *Financial support:* Application deadline: 5/1. *Faculty research:* Biofeedback music laboratory, experimental music therapy, virtual arts therapies, sound beam. *Unit head:* Dr. Brian Abrams, Chair, 610-647-4400 Ext. 3490, Fax: 610-993-8550, E-mail: babrams@immaculata.edu. *Application contact:* 610-647-4400 Ext. 3211, Fax: 610-993-8550, E-mail: graduate@immaculata.edu.

Lesley University, Graduate School of Arts and Social Sciences, Division of Expressive Therapies, Cambridge, MA 02138-2790. Offers art (MA); dance (MA); expressive therapies (MA, PhD, CAGS); music (MA). *Faculty:* 9 full-time (8 women), 32 part-time/adjunct (27 women). *Students:* 174 full-time (161 women), 227 part-time (215 women); includes 4 minority (1 American Indian/Alaska Native, 1 Asian American or Pacific Islander, 2 Hispanic Americans), 22 international. Average age 32. 244 applicants, 88% accepted, 157 enrolled. In 2007, 138 master's, 1 doctorate awarded. Terminal master's awarded for partial completion of doctoral program. *Degree requirements:* For master's, internship, practicum; for doctorate, thesis/dissertation. *Entrance requirements:* For master's, art portfolio, performance DVD; for doctorate, GRE or MAT. Additional exam requirements/recommendations for international students: Required—TOEFL (minimum score 550 paper-based; 213 computer-based; 80 iBT). *Application deadline:* Applications are processed on a rolling basis. Application fee: $50. *Financial support:* In 2007–08, 24 students received support, including 1 teaching assistantship (averaging $7,298 per year); Federal Work-Study, scholarships/grants, and unspecified assistantships also available. Support available to part-time students. Financial award application deadline: 4/15; financial award applicants required to submit FAFSA. *Unit head:* Julia Byers, Director, 617-349-8121, E-mail: jbyers@lesley.edu. *Application contact:* Gilda Resmini-Walsh, Assistant Director, Advising and Student Services, 617-349-8444, E-mail: gresmini@lesley.edu.

See Close-Up on page 243.

Maryville University of Saint Louis, School of Health Professions, Program in Music Therapy, St. Louis, MO 63141-7299. Offers MMT. *Accreditation:* NASM. Part-time programs available. *Entrance requirements:* For master's, music audition, interview, minimum undergraduate GPA of 3.0, 3 letters of recommendation. Additional exam requirements/recommendations for international students: Required—TOEFL (minimum score 550 paper-based). *Application deadline:* Applications are processed on a rolling basis. Application fee: $35 ($50 for international students). Electronic applications accepted. *Expenses:* Tuition: Full-time $18,600; part-time $580 per credit. Required fees: $75 per semester. *Financial support:* Applicants required to submit FAFSA. *Unit head:* Dr. Cynthia Briggs, Director, 314-529-9441, E-mail: cbriggs@maryville.edu.

Marywood University, Academic Affairs, Insalaco College of Creative Arts and Management, Music Department, Program in Music Therapy, Scranton, PA 18509-1598. Offers MMT, Certificate. *Accreditation:* NASM. Part-time and evening/weekend programs available. *Degree requirements:* For master's, comprehensive exam, thesis or alternative. *Entrance requirements:* For master's, GRE Subject Test, audition. Additional exam requirements/recommendations for international students: Required—TOEFL (minimum score 550 paper-based; 213 computer-based). *Application deadline:* For fall admission, 4/15 priority date for domestic and international students; for spring admission, 11/15 priority date for domestic and international students. Applications are processed on a rolling basis. Application fee: $30. Electronic applications accepted. *Expenses:* Tuition: Full-time $15,290; part-time $695 per credit. Required fees: $990; $370 per term. Tuition and fees vary according to degree level. *Financial support:* Research assistantships with tuition reimbursements, career-related internships or fieldwork, scholarships/grants, tuition waivers (partial), unspecified assistantships, and tuition reductions

Therapies—Dance, Drama, and Music

Marywood University (continued)

available. Support available to part-time students. Financial award application deadline: 2/15; financial award applicants required to submit FAFSA. *Application contact:* Tammy Manka, Assistant Director of Graduate Admissions, 570-340-6002, E-mail: tmanka@marywood.edu.

Michigan State University, The Graduate School, College of Music, East Lansing, MI 48824. Offers music (PhD); music composition (M Mus, DMA); music conducting (M Mus, DMA); music education (M Mus); music performance (M Mus, DMA); music theory (M Mus); music therapy (M Mus); musicology (MA); piano pedagogy (M Mus). *Accreditation:* NASM. *Entrance requirements:* Additional exam requirements/recommendations for international students: Required—TOEFL. Electronic applications accepted. *Expenses:* Tuition, state resident: part-time $379 per credit hour. Tuition, nonresident: part-time $800 per credit hour. Tuition and fees vary according to program.

Montclair State University, The Office of Graduate Admissions and Support Services, School of the Arts, Department of Music, Montclair, NJ 07043-1624. Offers music (AD); music education (MA); music therapy (MA); performance (MA, Certificate); theory/composition (MA). *Accreditation:* NASM. Part-time and evening/weekend programs available. *Faculty:* 19 full-time (7 women), 57 part-time/adjunct (26 women). *Students:* 19 full-time (17 women), 33 part-time (19 women); includes 3 minority (2 African Americans, 1 Hispanic American), 9 international. 57 applicants, 39% accepted, 22 enrolled. In 2007, 12 master's, 2 other advanced degrees awarded. *Degree requirements:* For master's, comprehensive exam, compositions, recitals, or thesis. *Entrance requirements:* For master's, GRE General Test, audition; undergraduate degree in music or at least 40 semester hours of work in theory, music history, performance; 2 letters of recommendation; teaching certificate (MA in music education). Additional exam requirements/recommendations for international students: Required—TOEFL (minimum score 83 computer-based). *Application deadline:* For fall admission, 6/1 for international students; for spring admission, 10/1 for international students. Applications are processed on a rolling basis. Application fee: $60. Electronic applications accepted. *Financial support:* In 2007–08, 2 research assistantships with full tuition reimbursements (averaging $7,000 per year) were awarded; Federal Work-Study, scholarships/grants, and unspecified assistantships also available. Support available to part-time students. Financial award application deadline: 3/1; financial award applicants required to submit FAFSA. *Unit head:* Prof. Robert Aldridge, Chairperson, 973-655-7212.

Naropa University, Graduate Programs, Program in Somatic Counseling Psychotherapy, Concentration in Dance/Movement Therapy, Boulder, CO 80302-6697. Offers MA. Part-time programs available. *Faculty:* 3 full-time (2 women), 11 part-time/adjunct (8 women). *Students:* 16 full-time (all women), 2 part-time (1 woman); includes 3 minority (1 African American, 2 Hispanic Americans), 1 international. Average age 28. 30 applicants, 40% accepted, 7 enrolled. In 2007, 14 degrees awarded. *Degree requirements:* For master's, comprehensive exam, thesis, internship. *Entrance requirements:* For master's, in-person interview; course work in psychology, anatomy; experience in 3 forms of dance. Additional exam requirements/recommendations for international students: Required—TOEFL (minimum score 600 paper-based; 250 computer-based). *Application deadline:* For fall admission, 1/15 priority date for domestic and international students; for spring admission, 10/15 priority date for domestic students. Applications are processed on a rolling basis. Application fee: $60. Electronic applications accepted. *Expenses:* Tuition: Full-time $15,070; part-time $685 per credit. Required fees: $250 per semester. Tuition and fees vary according to course load. *Financial support:* In 2007–08, 10 students received support, including 1 research assistantship with partial tuition reimbursement available (averaging $3,000 per year), 1 teaching assistantship (averaging $3,000 per year); career-related internships or fieldwork, Federal Work-Study, scholarships/grants, health care benefits, tuition waivers (partial), and unspecified assistantships also available. Support available to part-time students. Financial award application deadline: 3/1; financial award applicants required to submit FAFSA. *Application contact:* Donna McIntyre, Admissions Counselor, 303-546-3555, Fax: 303-546-3583, E-mail: donna@naropa.edu.

See Close-Up on page 1449.

Nazareth College of Rochester, Graduate Studies, Department of Creative Arts Therapy, Program in Music Therapy, Rochester, NY 14618-3790. Offers MS. *Faculty:* 2 full-time (1 woman). *Students:* 5 full-time (3 women), 4 part-time (3 women). 6 applicants, 100% accepted, 6 enrolled. *Entrance requirements:* For master's, audition, minimum GPA of 3.0. *Application deadline:* For fall admission, 2/1 for domestic students; for spring admission, 10/1 for domestic students. Application fee: $40. *Financial support:* Research assistantships with partial tuition reimbursements available. Financial award application deadline: 3/1; financial award applicants required to submit FAFSA. *Unit head:* Dr. Bryan Hunter, Director, 585-389-2702, E-mail: bhunter7@naz.edu. *Application contact:* Judith G. Baker, Director, Graduate Admissions, 585-389-2050, Fax: 585-389-2817, E-mail: gradstudies@naz.edu.

New York University, Steinhardt School of Culture, Education and Human Development, Department of Music and Performing Arts Professions, Program in Drama Therapy, New York, NY 10012-1019. Offers MA. *Faculty:* 1 full-time (0 women). *Students:* 27 full-time (21 women), 8 part-time (7 women); includes 5 minority (2 African Americans, 1 Asian American or Pacific Islander, 2 Hispanic Americans), 4 international. 48 applicants, 35% accepted, 13 enrolled. In 2007, 12 degrees awarded. *Degree requirements:* For master's, thesis (for some programs). *Entrance requirements:* For master's, audition, interview. Additional exam requirements/recommendations for international students: Required—TOEFL. *Application deadline:* For fall admission, 12/15 priority date for domestic and international students; for spring admission, 11/1 for domestic and international students. Applications are processed on a rolling basis. Application fee: $50. *Financial support:* Career-related internships or fieldwork, Federal Work-Study, and scholarships/grants available. Support available to part-time students. Financial award application deadline: 2/1; financial award applicants required to submit FAFSA. *Faculty research:* Meaning of role in drama, therapy, and everyday life; clinical approaches to drama therapy; trauma effects on children. *Unit head:* Dr. Robert Landy, Director, 212-998-5424. *Application contact:* 212-998-5030, Fax: 212-995-4328, E-mail: steinhardt.gradadmissions@nyu.edu.

New York University, Steinhardt School of Culture, Education and Human Development, Department of Music and Performing Arts Professions, Program in Music Therapy, New York, NY 10012-1019. Offers MA, DA. Part-time and evening/weekend programs available. *Faculty:* 1 (woman) full-time. *Students:* 22 full-time (18 women), 26 part-time (20 women); includes 6 minority (2 African Americans, 3 Asian Americans or Pacific Islanders, 1 Hispanic American), 13 international. 65 applicants, 35% accepted, 21 enrolled. In 2007, 10 master's, 2 doctorates awarded. *Degree requirements:* For master's, thesis (for some programs). *Entrance requirements:* For master's, audition, interview. Additional exam requirements/recommendations for international students: Required—TOEFL. *Application deadline:* For fall admission, 12/15 priority date for domestic and international students; for spring admission, 11/1 for domestic and international students. Applications are processed on a rolling basis. Application fee: $50. *Financial support:* Career-related internships or fieldwork, Federal Work-Study, institutionally sponsored loans, and tuition waivers (partial) available. Support available to part-time students. Financial award application deadline: 2/1; financial award applicants required to submit FAFSA. *Faculty research:* Music therapy in special education, including autism and emotional disabilities. *Unit head:* Prof. Barbara Hesser, Director, 212-998-5424, Fax: 212-995-4043. *Application contact:* 212-998-5030, Fax: 212-995-4328, E-mail: steinhardt.gradadmissions@nyu.edu.

Ohio University, Graduate College, College of Fine Arts, School of Music, Athens, OH 45701-2979. Offers accompanying (MM); composition (MM); conducting (MM); history/literature (MM); music education (MM); music therapy (MM); performance (MM, Certificate); performance/pedagogy (MM); theory (MM). *Accreditation:* NASM. Postbaccalaureate distance learning degree programs offered (minimal on-campus study). *Faculty:* 35 full-time (10 women), 1 part-time/adjunct (0 women). *Students:* 31 full-time (15 women), 13 part-time (7 women); includes 2 minority (both African Americans), 12 international. 49 applicants, 55% accepted, 16 enrolled. In 2007, 22 degrees awarded. *Degree requirements:* For master's, thesis (for some programs), oral exam. *Entrance requirements:* For master's, audition, interview, and/or portfolio. Additional exam requirements/recommendations for international students: Required—TOEFL. *Application deadline:* For fall admission, 8/15 priority date for domestic students. Application fee: $50 ($55 for international students). *Financial support:* In 2007–08, 35 students received support, including 35 teaching assistantships with full and partial tuition reimbursements available (averaging $4,500 per year); career-related internships or fieldwork, Federal Work-Study, institutionally sponsored loans, and tuition waivers (full and partial) also available. Financial award application deadline: 3/15. *Unit head:* Dr. Michael Parkinson, Director, 740-593-4244, Fax: 740-593-1429, E-mail: parkinsw@ohio.edu. *Application contact:* Dr. Richard Wetzel, Graduate Chair, 740-593-1652, Fax: 740-593-1429, E-mail: wetzel@ohio.edu.

Pratt Institute, School of Art and Design, Programs in Creative Arts Therapy, Brooklyn, NY 11205-3899. Offers art therapy and creativity development (MPS); art therapy-special education (MPS); dance/movement therapy (MS). *Accreditation:* NASAD (one or more programs are accredited). Part-time programs available. *Faculty:* 3 full-time (all women), 19 part-time/adjunct (16 women). *Students:* 100 full-time (96 women), 2 part-time (both women); includes 18 minority (5 African Americans, 5 Asian Americans or Pacific Islanders, 8 Hispanic Americans), 4 international. Average age 31. 173 applicants, 35% accepted, 30 enrolled. In 2007, 31 degrees awarded. *Degree requirements:* For master's, thesis. *Entrance requirements:* For master's, bachelor's degree, transcripts, letters of recommendation, statement, portfolio. Additional exam requirements/recommendations for international students: Required—TOEFL (minimum score 600 paper-based; 250 computer-based). *Application deadline:* For fall admission, 2/1 for domestic students; for spring admission, 10/1 for domestic students. Applications are processed on a rolling basis. Application fee: $50 ($90 for international students). Electronic applications accepted. *Expenses:* Tuition: Full-time $25,680. Required fees: $1,106. Tuition and fees vary according to program. *Financial support:* Career-related internships or fieldwork, Federal Work-Study, institutionally sponsored loans, scholarships/grants, health care benefits, tuition waivers (full), and unspecified assistantships available. Support available to part-time students. Financial award application deadline: 2/1; financial award applicants required to submit FAFSA. *Faculty research:* Psychology and aesthetic interaction, art therapy and AIDS, art therapy and autism, art diagnosis. *Unit head:* Laurel Thompson, Chairperson, 718-636-4532, Fax: 718-636-3597, E-mail: lthompso@pratt.edu. *Application contact:* Young Hah, Director of Graduate Admissions, 718-636-3683, Fax: 718-399-4242, E-mail: yhah@pratt.edu.

See Close-Up on page 253.

Radford University, Graduate College, College of Visual and Performing Arts, Department of Music, Radford, VA 24142. Offers music (MA); music therapy (MS). *Accreditation:* NASM.Part-time programs available. *Faculty:* 12 full-time (4 women). *Students:* 7 full-time (6 women), 6 part-time (3 women); includes 1 minority (African American), 1 international. Average age 27. 13 applicants, 85% accepted, 5 enrolled. In 2007, 8 degrees awarded. *Degree requirements:* For master's, comprehensive exam, thesis or alternative. *Entrance requirements:* For master's, GRE General Test, GRE Subject Test (music), or PRAXIS II. Additional exam requirements/recommendations for international students: Required—TOEFL. *Application deadline:* For fall admission, 3/1 priority date for domestic students, 12/1 for international students; for spring admission, 10/1 for domestic students, 7/1 for international students. Applications are processed on a rolling basis. Application fee: $40. Electronic applications accepted. *Financial support:* In 2007–08, 11 students received support, including 5 research assistantships with partial tuition reimbursements available (averaging $8,000 per year), 6 teaching assistantships with partial tuition reimbursements available (averaging $8,700 per year); career-related internships or fieldwork, Federal Work-Study, institutionally sponsored loans, scholarships/grants, and unspecified assistantships also available. Financial award application deadline: 3/1; financial award applicants required to submit FAFSA. *Unit head:* Dr. Eugene C. Fellin, Chair, 540-831-5177, Fax: 540-831-6133, E-mail: efellin@radford.edu.

Saint Mary-of-the-Woods College, Program in Music Therapy, Saint Mary-of-the-Woods, IN 47876. Offers MA. *Accreditation:* NASM. Part-time programs available. Postbaccalaureate distance learning degree programs offered (minimal on-campus study). *Degree requirements:* For master's, thesis or alternative, qualifying exam, portfolio completion. *Entrance requirements:* For master's, diagnostic music exam, audition. Electronic applications accepted.

Shenandoah University, Shenandoah Conservatory, Winchester, VA 22601-5195. Offers arts administration (MS); church music (MM, Certificate); composition (MM); conducting (MM); dance (MA, MFA, MS); dance accompanying (MM); music (MS); music education (MME, DMA); music therapy (MMT, Certificate); pedagogy (MM); performance (MM, DMA, Artist Diploma); piano accompanying (MM). *Accreditation:* NASM. Part-time and evening/weekend programs available. *Faculty:* 35 full-time (17 women), 12 part-time/adjunct (6 women). *Students:* 69 full-time (39 women), 126 part-time (72 women); includes 5 minority (3 African Americans, 2 Hispanic Americans), 27 international. Average age 40. 90 applicants, 92% accepted, 59 enrolled. In 2007, 28 master's, 12 doctorates, 6 other advanced degrees awarded. *Degree requirements:* For master's, comprehensive exam (for some programs), thesis (for some programs), internship (MS), recital (MM), research teaching project or thesis (MME), project (MA); for doctorate, comprehensive exam, thesis/dissertation (for some programs), dissertation or teaching project, recital. *Entrance requirements:* For master's, audition, minimum GPA of 2.5, writing sample, resumé; for doctorate, audition, minimum GPA of 3.25, 2 letters of recommendation, writing sample, resumé. Additional exam requirements/recommendations for international students: Required—TOEFL (minimum score 527 paper-based; 197 computer-based; 71 iBT). *Application deadline:* Applications are processed on a rolling basis. Application fee: $30. Electronic applications accepted. *Expenses:* Tuition: Part-time $640 per credit. Part-time tuition and fees vary according to degree level and program. *Financial support:* In 2007–08, 154 students received support, including 23 teaching assistantships with partial tuition reimbursements available (averaging $5,440 per year); fellowships with partial tuition reimbursements available, career-related internships or fieldwork, institutionally sponsored loans, scholarships/grants, and unspecified assistantships also available. Support available to part-time students. Financial award application deadline: 3/15; financial award applicants required to submit FAFSA. *Faculty research:* Creative activity, performance practice, music therapy aging, composition, Motown music. Total annual research expenditures: $4,272. *Unit head:* Dr. Laurence A. Kaptain, Dean, 540-665-4600, Fax: 540-665-5402, E-mail: lkaptain@su.edu. *Application contact:* David Anthony, Dean of Admissions, 540-665-4581, Fax: 540-665-4627, E-mail: admit@su.edu.

See Close-Up on page 357.

Temple University, Graduate School, Esther Boyer College of Music and Dance, Department of Music Education and Therapy, Philadelphia, PA 19122-6096. Offers music education (MM, PhD); music therapy (MMT, PhD). *Accreditation:* NASM. Part-time and evening/weekend programs available. *Degree requirements:* For master's, thesis; for doctorate, thesis/dissertation. *Entrance requirements:* Additional exam requirements/recommendations for international students: Required—TOEFL. Electronic applications accepted. *Faculty research:* Music learning theory, guided imagery in music, computer learning theory.

University of Kansas, Research and Graduate Studies, School of Fine Arts, Department of Music and Dance, Program in Music Therapy, Lawrence, KS 66045. Offers MME. *Students:* 13 full-time (12 women), 15 part-time (13 women); includes 2 minority (both Asian Americans or Pacific Islanders), 12 international. Average age 27. 16 applicants, 69% accepted, 9 enrolled. In 2007, 3 degrees awarded. *Degree requirements:* For master's, comprehensive exam (for some programs), thesis or alternative. *Entrance requirements:* For master's, GRE General Test, video. Additional exam requirements/recommendations for international students: Required—TOEFL (minimum score 570 paper-based; 230 computer-based; 92 iBT), TOEFL or IELTS; Recommended—TWE. *Application deadline:* For fall admission, 3/15 priority date for domestic students, 3/15 for international students; for spring admission, 8/15 priority date for domestic students, 8/15 for international students. Applications are processed on a rolling basis. Application fee: $55 ($60 for international students). Electronic applications accepted.

Expenses: Tuition, state resident: full-time $5,838. Tuition, nonresident: full-time $13,409. Tuition and fees vary according to program. *Financial support:* Fellowships, research assistantships with partial tuition reimbursements, teaching assistantships with full and partial tuition reimbursements, institutionally sponsored loans, scholarships/grants, and unspecified assistantships available. Financial award application deadline: 12/15; financial award applicants required to submit FAFSA. *Faculty research:* Music therapy in health, wellness, gerontology, pediatrics, early intervention, autism and hospice; Orff music therapy; influence of music on behavior. *Application contact:* George L. Duerksen, Director of Graduate Studies, 785-864-9632, Fax: 785-864-9640, E-mail: gduerksen@ku.edu.

University of Miami, Graduate School, Frost School of Music, Department of Music Education and Music Therapy, Coral Gables, FL 33124. Offers music education (MM, PhD, Spec M); music therapy (MM). *Accreditation:* NASM. *Faculty:* 6 full-time (3 women), 1 part-time/adjunct (0 women). *Students:* 15 full-time (10 women), 3 part-time (1 woman); includes 3 minority (1 African American, 2 Hispanic Americans), 5 international. Average age 30. 20 applicants, 50% accepted, 7 enrolled. In 2007, 5 master's, 2 doctorates awarded. *Degree requirements:* For master's, thesis; for doctorate, thesis/dissertation, 2 research tools; for Spec M, thesis, research project. *Entrance requirements:* For master's and doctorate, GRE General Test. Additional exam requirements/recommendations for international students: Required—TOEFL (minimum score 550 paper-based; 213 computer-based; 59 iBT). *Application deadline:* For fall admission, 2/1 priority date for domestic and international students; for spring admission, 11/1 priority date for domestic and international students. Applications are processed on a rolling basis. Application fee: $65. Electronic applications accepted. *Financial support:* In 2007–08, 15 students received support, including fellowships with full tuition reimbursements available (averaging $22,000 per year), 8 teaching assistantships with full tuition reimbursements available (averaging $10,000 per year); career-related internships or fieldwork, Federal Work-Study, and tuition waivers (partial) also available. Financial award application deadline: 2/1. *Unit head:* Dr. Joyce Jordan, Chair and Director, 305-284-6252, E-mail: jjordan@miami.edu. *Application contact:* Dr. Edward Paul Asmus, Associate Dean for Graduate Studies, 305-284-2241, Fax: 305-284-6475, E-mail: ed.asmus@miami.edu.

University of the Pacific, Conservatory of Music, Program in Music Therapy, Stockton, CA 95211-0197. Offers MA. *Faculty:* 2 full-time (both women). *Students:* 4 full-time (3 women), 6 part-time (5 women), 1 international. Average age 30. 11 applicants, 64% accepted, 3 enrolled. In 2007, 1 degree awarded. *Degree requirements:* For master's, thesis (for some programs). *Entrance requirements:* For master's, GRE General Test. Additional exam requirements/recommendations for international students: Required—TOEFL (minimum score 475 paper-based; 150 computer-based). Application fee: $75. *Financial support:* Teaching assistantships, institutionally sponsored loans available. Support available to part-time students. Financial award application deadline: 3/1; financial award applicants required to submit FAFSA. *Unit head:* Dr. Therese West, Chairperson, 209-946-3194.

Wilfrid Laurier University, Faculty of Graduate Studies, Faculty of Music, Waterloo, ON N2L 3C5, Canada. Offers MMT. *Faculty:* 3 full-time, 3 part-time/adjunct. *Students:* 10 full-time. 16 applicants, 44% accepted, 6 enrolled. In 2007, 8 degrees awarded. *Entrance requirements:* For master's, 1 year program: 4 year honours BA in music therapy with a minimum B average in final year, grade 6 RCM and grade 10 performance ability. 2 Year program: 4 year honours BA in an allied area (music or psychology) with a minimum B average in final year, grade 6 RCM, grade 10 performance ability. Additional exam requirements/recommendations for international students: Required—TOEFL (minimum score 230 computer-based; 89 iBT). *Application deadline:* For fall admission, 2/1 priority date for domestic students. Application fee: $75. Electronic applications accepted. *Financial support:* Fellowships, research assistantships, teaching assistantships available. *Unit head:* Dr. Charles Morrison, Dean, 519-884-1970 Ext. 2285. *Application contact:* Jennifer Poppe, Student Contact, 519-884-0710 Ext. 3536, Fax: 519-884-1020, E-mail: gradstudies@wlu.ca.

BOSTON UNIVERSITY

College of Fine Arts

Programs of Study The Boston University (BU) College of Fine Arts (CFA) is a vibrant community of artists that brings together the School of Music, the School of Theatre, and the School of Visual Arts. Established in 1954, CFA offers professional training in the arts in a conservatory-style environment. Education at the College of Fine Arts begins on the BU campus and extends into Boston—a rich center of cultural, artistic, and intellectual activity—and reaches beyond the city to international programs as well. The three schools, while having separate faculties and programs of study, share a common goal of providing the best training in the arts and preparing students for professional work in music, the theater, or visual arts.

In the School of Music, the Master of Music degree is offered in composition, historical performance, music education, musicology, orchestral and choral conducting, performance, and theory. The School of Music also offers the Doctor of Musical Arts degree in composition, conducting, historical performance, music education, and performance; the Artist Diploma in conducting, historical performance, and performance; the Performance Diploma; and a Certificate in Opera Performance. The School of Music also offers an online Master of Music and a Doctor of Musical Arts program in music education.

In the School of Theatre, the Master of Fine Arts degree is available with majors in design, directing, production, stage and production management, and theater education.

In the School of Visual Arts, the Master of Fine Arts degree is offered with majors in art education, graphic design, museum education, painting, sculpture, and studio teaching.

Research Facilities The College of Fine Arts building includes a concert hall; a studio theater; a large exhibition gallery; studios for painting and sculpture; a music and visual arts library; theater classrooms; dance studios; opera rehearsal and coaching areas; three rehearsal halls for orchestra and choral groups; and outstanding recording facilities. The Boston University Theatre, an 890-seat theater, serves as the principle production space for the School of Theatre, the Huntington Theatre Company (a professional company in residence at Boston University), and the Opera Institute.

In addition to using the excellent facilities of Boston University's Mugar Library, graduate students may obtain permission to use other outstanding libraries in the Metropolitan Boston area, including the Boston Public Library.

Financial Aid The College of Fine Arts has a large merit scholarship fund, and a majority of graduate students receive scholarships and/or assistantships based on artistic merit and program needs. Also available are the Dean's Scholarship and numerous named-fund scholarships as well as loans and Federal Work-Study. The Opera Institute gives full tuition scholarships and stipends.

Cost of Study Most graduate students register for 8 credits per semester, which is considered full-time. The tuition is $1192 per credit hour, with additional fees for applied music instruction. The typical charge for most graduate students is approximately $9000 per semester ($18,000 per year).

Living and Housing Costs The University estimates the living costs for room and board to be approximately $12,000 per nine-month academic year. Most graduate students live off campus in the adjoining residential communities. The University maintains an off-campus housing listing.

Student Group There are approximately 13,123 graduate students at Boston University. Enrollment at the College of Fine Arts is 1,735 students, of whom approximately 500 are graduate students. College of Fine Arts graduate students come from twenty-seven countries and all fifty states.

Location Most of the University's schools and colleges line the south bank of the Charles River just west of downtown Boston. Students have at their disposal the exceptionally rich cultural resources of the Boston area. These cultural opportunities include the Boston Symphony Orchestra, the Museum of Fine Arts, Boston Ballet, the Theater District, and the Wang Center.

The University and The College Boston University is an internationally recognized institution of higher education and research, founded in 1839. Through its fifteen schools and colleges, thirteen of which offer advanced degrees, the University serves 31,697 students and 3,931 faculty members.

The College of Fine Arts has a long tradition of preparing students for careers in music, theater arts, and the visual arts. The College of Fine Arts began as the College of Music in 1873. The School of Visual Arts was founded in 1919 and the School of Theatre in 1950. The Muir String Quartet and Boston Baroque are in residence at the College of Fine Arts, and the Huntington Theatre Company is in residence at Boston University. The Boston University College of Fine Arts also runs the Tanglewood Institute in Lenox, Massachusetts. Students enjoy extended exposure to creative innovation and professional artistry through the resources provided by the College, the University, and the Boston artistic community.

Applying Application forms for admission and for financial aid may be obtained from the College. Early application for admission is urged, especially for those seeking financial aid. Requirements for entrance and application deadlines are provided in the Boston University College of Fine Arts bulletins available on request. Applicants may apply online at http://www.bu.edu/cfa.

Correspondence and Information

Graduate Admissions
College of Fine Arts
Boston University
855 Commonwealth Avenue
Boston, Massachusetts 02215

Phone: 617-353-3350
E-mail: arts@bu.edu
Web site: http://www.bu.edu/cfa

Boston University

THE FACULTY

Music
Aldo Abreu, M.M., Indiana. Recorder.
Ramelle Adams, M.F.A., Wisconsin. Dance/opera.
Laura Ahlbeck, M.M., Manhattan School of Music. Oboe.
Martin Amlin, Chairman, Theory and Composition; D.M.A., Rochester (Eastman). Theory and composition.
Steven Ansell, Muir String Quartet; Diploma, Curtis. Viola.
Sara Arneson, D.M.A., Michigan. Voice.
Edwin Barker, B.M., New England Conservatory. Double bass.
Jonathan Bass, Department Head, Piano; D.M.A., Indiana. Piano.
Penelope Bitzas, M.M., New England Conservatory. Voice.
Bonnie Black, M.A., Columbia. String pedagogy.
Deborah Burton, Ph.D., Michigan. Theory and composition
Lynn Chang, A.D., Harvard. Violin.
Peter Chapman, M.M., Boston University. Trumpet.
Maria Clodes-Jaguaribe, Mus.A.D., Boston University. Piano.
Victor Coelho, Associate Provost for Undergraduate Education, Musicology; Ph.D., UCLA. Musicology.
Bernadette Colley, Ed.D., Harvard. Music education.
Richard Cornell, Ph.D., Rochester (Eastman). Theory and composition.
Phyllis Curtin, Dean Emerita, College of Fine Arts; B.A., Wellesley; Mus.D. (hon.), New England Conservatory. Voice and opera.
Sharon Daniels, Director, Opera Programs; B.M., Chapman. Opera.
André de Quadros, Director, School of Music; M.Ed., Victorian College of Fine Arts, Melbourne (Australia). Music education.
James Demler, Performance certificate, Rochester (Eastman). Voice.
Anthony di Bonaventura, Diploma, Curtis. Piano.
Joy Douglass, Ph.D., Michigan. Music education.
Doriot Anthony Dwyer, B.M., Rochester (Eastman). Flute.
Jules Eskin, Chevalier du Violoncelle, Indiana. Principal cellist, Boston Symphony Orchestra since 1964. Cello.
Simon Estes, Juilliard. Voice.
Terry Everson, M.M., Ohio State. Trumpet.
John Ferrillo, Artist's Diploma, Curtis. Oboe.
Richard Flanagan, M.M., Boston University. Percussion.
Joseph Foley, M.M., Boston University. Trumpet.
Lukas Foss, Curtis. Theory and composition.
Sarah Freiberg, D.M.A., SUNY at Stony Brook. Baroque cello.
Edward Gazoulas, Graduate studies, Yale. Viola.
Timothy Genis, B.A., Juilliard. Percussion.
Ian Greitzer, M.M., New England Conservatory. Clarinet.
Ron Haroutunian, B.M., New England Conservatory. Bassoon.
Samuel Headrick, Ph.D., Rochester (Eastman). Theory and composition.
Brita Heimarck, Ph.D., Cornell. Ethnomusicology.
Gregg Henegar, studied with Sanford Berry, John Mack, and Myron Bloom. Bassoon.
Raphael Hillyer, M.M., Harvard. Viola.
Phyllis Elhady Hoffman, M.M., Boston University. Voice.
David Hoose, Director of Orchestral Activities; B.M., Oberlin. Orchestral conducting.
Laura Jeppesen, Yale. Viola da Gamba.
Linda Jiorle-Nagy, D.M.A., Boston University. Piano.
Ann Howard Jones, Director of Choral Conducting; D.M.A., Iowa. Choral conducting.
Patrick Jones, Department Head; Ph.D., Penn State. Music education.
Daniel Katzen, M.M., Northwestern. Horn.
Frank Kelley, M.M., Artist Certificate in Opera, Cincinnati Conservatory. Voice.
Bayla Keyes, M.M., Yale. Violin.
Shiela Kibbe-Hodgkins, Department Head, Collaborative Piano; M.M., Temple. Collaborative piano.
David Kopp, Ph.D., Brandeis. Theory and composition.
Christopher Kreuger, B.M., New England Conservatory. Baroque flute.
Michelle LaCourse, Department Head, Strings; M.M., Peabody Conservatory. Viola.
Lucia Lin, M.M., Rice. Violin.
Malcolm Lowe, A.D., Curtis. Violin.
Don Lucas, Department Head, Brass, Woodwinds, and Percussion; D.M.A., Houston. Trombone.
William Lumpkin, D.M.A., USC. Opera.
David Martins, M.M., Lowell. Conducting.
Dana Mazurkevich, A.D., M.M., Moscow Conservatory. Violin.
Yuri Mazurkevich, M.M., Moscow Conservatory. Violin.
Robert Merfeld, M.M., Juilliard. Collaborative piano
Ikuko Mizuno, M.M., Boston University. Violin.
John Muratore, M.M., New England Conservatory. Guitar.
Ketty Nez, D.M.A., Berkeley. Theory and composition.
Sandra Nicolucci, D.M.A., Boston University. Music education.
Craig Nordstrom, M.M., Catholic University. Clarinet.
James Orleans, B.M., Boston Conservatory. Double bass.
Susan Ormont, M.M., Yale. Voice.
Elizabeth Ostling, B.M., Curtis. Flute.
Anthony Palmer, Ph.D., UCLA. Music education.
Leslie Parnas, Curtis. Cello.
Martin Pearlman, M.M., Yale. Historical performance.
Thomas Peattie, Ph.D., Harvard. Musicology.
Ann Hobson Pilot, D.M.A., Bridgewater State. Harp.
Barbara Poeschl-Edrich, D.M.A., Boston University. Harp.
Jerrold Pope, Department Head, Voice; D.M.A., Rutgers. Voice.
Rick Ranti, Diploma, Curtis. Bassoon.
Michael Reynolds, B.M., Curtis. Cello.
Rhonda Rider, M.M., Yale. Cello.
Joshua Rifkin, M.F.A., Princeton. Musicology.
Thomas Rolfs, M.M., Northwestern. Trumpet.
Mike Roylance, Graduate studies, DePaul. Tuba.
Matthew Ruggiero, Ph.D., Boston University. Bassoon.
Eric Ruske, B.M., Northwestern. Horn.
Marc Schachman, D.M.A., Juilliard. Baroque oboe.
Todd Seeber, B.M., Boston University. Double bass.
Robert Sheena, M.M., Northwestern. Oboe and English horn.
Andrew Shenton, Ph.D., Harvard. Musicology.
Joel L. Sheveloff, Ph.D., Brandeis. Musicology.
Ethan Sloane, D.M.A., Yale. Clarinet.
Samuel Solomon, M.M., Juilliard. Percussion.
James Sommerville, Boston Symphony Orchestra. French horn.
Maria Spacagna, Mus.M., New England Conservatory. Voice.
Jane Starkman. Historical Performance.
Daniel Stepner, D.M.A., Yale. Baroque violin.
Peter Sykes, Department Head, Historical Performance; M.M., New England Conservatory. Harpsichord.
Linda Toote, B.M., Gold Diploma, Mannes College of Music. Flute.
Roman Totenberg, Gold Diploma, Warsaw Chopin Conservatory of Music, Berlin Academy of Music, Instrumental Academy of Paris. Violin.
Alison Voth, M.M., Manhattan School of Music. Opera.
John Wallace, M.A., Boston University. Theory and composition, music education.
Jeremy Yudkin, Ph.D., Stanford. Musicology.
Michael Zaretsky, Moscow Conservatory. Viola.
Peter Zazofsky, B.M., Graduate Certificate, Curtis. Violin.

Theater
Judy Braha, B.F.A., Carnegie-Mellon. Acting and directing.
Ilana M. Brownstein, M.F.A., Yale. Contemporary literature.
Judith Chaffee, M.F.A., Smith. Coordinator of Movement.
Mark Cohen, M.F.A., George Washington. Acting.
Lydia Diamond, B.S., Northwestern. Playwriting.
Ben Emerson, M.F.A., Boston University. Sound design.
Diane Fargo, M.F.A., Brandeis. Scene painting.
Sidney J. Friedman, Ph.D., Iowa. Theater arts.
Adam Godbout, B.F.A. Boston University. Vectorworks.
Christine Hamel, M.F.A., Boston. Voice, speech.
Paula Langton, M.F.A., Boston University. Voice and speech.
Nancy Leary, M.F.A., Boston University. Costume design and costume production.
Jonathan Lipsky, M.F.A., Iowa. Acting and playwriting.
Michael Maso, Ph.D., Cornell. Theater management.
James McCartney. Sound design.
J. Stratton McCrady, B.A., University of the South. Technical production.
Roger Meeker, B.A., Northern Iowa. Design and technical production.
James Noone, B.F.A., Boston University. Scene design.
Jim Petosa, Director, School of Theatre; M.A., Catholic University.
Penney Pinette, B.A., Mount Ida. Costume production.
Betsy Polatin, M.F.A., Boston University. Movement.
John Savage, M.F.A., North Carolina School of the Arts. Scene design.
Mark Stanley, M.F.A., Wisconsin–Madison. Lighting design.
Micki Taylor-Pinney, M.F.A., North Carolina at Greensboro. Coordinator of Dance.
Elaine Vaan Hogue, M.F.A., Boston University. Acting and directing.
Mariann Verheyen, M.F.A., Wisconsin. Costume design.
Denise Wallace, B.A., Bridgewater State. Costume crafts.

Visual Arts
Bryce Ambo, M.F.A., Yale. Graphic design.
Robert Burns, M.F.A., Yale. Graphic design.
Dana Clancy, M.F.A., Boston University. Painting.
Deborah Cornell, M.F.A., Norwich. Printmaking.
Jon Craine, studied at Yale. Graphic design.
Richard Doubleday, M.F.A., Boston University. Graphic design.
Stephen Frank, M.F.A., Rhode Island School of Design. Photography.
Howard Gerstein, B.F.A., Cincinnati. Ceramics.
Laura Giannitrapani, M.F.A., Boston University. Graphic design.
Diana Hampe, M.F.A., Boston University. Art education.
Hugh O'Donnell, H.Dip. A.D./M.A., Birmingham School of Art. Painting.
Alston Purvis, Department Head, Graphic Design; M.F.A., Yale. Graphic design.
Richard Raiselis, M.F.A., Temple. Painting.
Harold Reddicliffe, M.F.A., Maryland Institute. Painting.
Richard Ryan, M.F.A., Yale. Painting.
Barry Shauck, M.F.A., Maryland Institute College of Art. Art education.
Batu Siharulidze, State Academy of the Arts. Sculpture
Judith Simpson, Ph.D., Wisconsin. Art education.
Ruth Starratt, Ed.D., Columbia. Art education.
Scout Stevenson, B.A., Massachusetts. Graphic design.
Christopher Untalan, M.F.A., New York Academy of Art. Sculpture.
John Walker, Birmingham School of Art. Painting.

COLUMBIA UNIVERSITY

School of the Arts
Divisions of Film, Theatre Arts, Visual Arts, and Writing

Programs of Study

The School of the Arts offers M.F.A. degrees in film (directing, producing, and screenwriting), theater arts (acting, directing, dramaturgy, playwriting, stage management, and theater management), visual arts (digital media, drawing, new genres, painting, photography, printmaking, and sculpture), and writing (fiction, nonfiction, and poetry) and an M.A. degree in film studies. The School of the Arts accepts full-time students only. The Digital Media Center (DMC) offers a selection of courses in interactivity and advanced digital media applications. All DMC courses are interdisciplinary and open to School of the Arts students from all divisions. In addition, the Graduate School of Arts and Sciences offers the Ph.D. degree in drama and theater arts. The M.F.A. degree programs require 60 points of completed course work. All students take a core curriculum, which provides background in the history, theory, and literature of their field, and experience an understanding of the various disciplines taught within each division. During the first two years, students focus on workshops, lectures, and seminars in their particular disciplines. Students in film and theater arts partake in production crew work. Once the 60 points of course work are completed, each student concentrates on producing a thesis and/or completing internships under research arts status. The Division of Theatre Arts requires two professional internships; the Film and Writing Divisions recommend internships.

Research Facilities

The Film Division offers film and video production equipment, digital editing facilities, a sound stage, a screening room, and a film library. The Theatre Division offers two flexible-space theaters and two studios. In addition, there are various performing venues on campus that may be available for student productions. Each visual arts student is assigned a private studio (24-hour access) in Watson Hall on 115th Street and Prentis Hall on 125th Street. In addition, there are various spaces on campus where students have the opportunity to exhibit. The LeRoy Neiman Center for Print Studies provides the optimum environment to expose students to techniques in the production of intaglio, lithography, serigraphy, photography, and computer imaging. The University libraries house more than 6 million books, 4 million microfilms, and more than 26 million manuscripts. The library houses several special collections related to the arts, and it includes the Avery Architecture and Fine Arts Library. Students also have access to the Performing Arts Research Center of the New York Public Library at Lincoln Center as well as the vast holdings of the Central Research Library of the New York Public Library. There are dozens of special collections throughout New York City, such as the Film Study Center of the Museum of Modern Art, the Shubert Archives, and the Collections of the Players Club. New York City offers professional theaters, museums, galleries, movie theaters, concert halls, publishing companies, bookstores, and literary readings.

Financial Aid

The School seeks to work with students in arranging to cover costs through fellowships, scholarships, loans, and work-study. University scholarships, which are awarded by each division based upon merit, are limited. Departmental research assistantships, which carry tuition exemption plus a small stipend, are available, but generally only for second-year students. The Office of Student Affairs helps qualifying students arrange for federal financial aid.

Cost of Study

Tuition and fees for the 2007–08 school year were $39,800, based on full-time matriculation of 12 to 18 credits.

Living and Housing Costs

The University estimates that students need about $20,000 to cover living expenses and housing. University Apartment Housing is available to most graduate students, ranging from $565 to $1500 monthly, that offer furnished or unfurnished singles, suites, and studios to rent individually or to share. They also offer studio and one-bedroom apartments for married students.

Student Group

Columbia has an enrollment of approximately 22,000; 13,500 are graduate students. The School enrolled 778 full-time students in 2007–08: 318 students in film, 156 in theater arts, 256 in writing, and 48 in visual arts.

Location

Columbia University (including Barnard College and Teacher's College) occupies approximately eighteen square blocks in the Morningside Heights area of Manhattan. Its neighbors include Union Theological Seminary, Jewish Theological Seminary, the Manhattan School of Music, Riverside Church and the Interchurch Center, and the Cathedral of Saint John the Divine, the world's largest Gothic cathedral and home of a progressive arts program. Riverside Park and the Hudson River are a block away. The Upper West Side stretches south along Broadway for sixty blocks to Lincoln Center and beyond to the Theatre District and incorporates vital residential neighborhoods, some of the city's finest restaurants, and several theaters and museums, including the Apollo Theatre, the National Black Theatre, and City College.

The University and The School

Columbia, founded in 1754, is composed of fifteen undergraduate, graduate, and professional schools. In the late nineteenth century, Columbia became the first university to teach theater in the United States and, in 1914, the first to teach film courses. The School of Dramatic Arts and Painting and Sculpture was established in 1948, although the first drawing course was taught as early as 1881. These programs were joined by film, music composition, and writing in 1965 to form the School of the Arts. Columbia also offers undergraduate majors in dance, film studies, theater arts, visual arts, and writing.

Applying

Applications are accepted for the fall semester only. All deadlines are final. The application cost for fall 2008 is $100 for the online application and $120 for the paper application. The GRE is not required for application. International students are required to take the TOEFL prior to application; the minimum score required for admission is 600 on the written test, 250 on the computer-based test, and 100 on the Internet-based test.

Correspondence and Information

Admissions Office
School of the Arts
305 Dodge Hall, MC 1808
Columbia University
2960 Broadway
New York, New York 10027
Phone: 212-854-2134
E-mail: admissions-arts@columbia.edu
Web site: http://arts.columbia.edu

Columbia University

THE FACULTY

FILM
Jamal Joseph, Professor and Chair.
Bette Gordon, Associate Professor and Vice Chair.

Professors
Lewis Cole
Jane Gaines
Annette Insdorf
Nick Proferes
Janet Roach
Andrew Sarris

Associate Professors
Ira Deutchman
Bette Gordon
Jamal Joseph
Tom Kalin
Dan Kleinman
Richard Peña
James Schamus

Assistant Professors
Katherine Dieckmann
Trey Ellis
Eric Mendelsohn
Benjamin Ross

Adjunct Professors
Richard Brick
Lenore DeKoven
Leon Falk
Guy Gallo
Michael Hausman
Milena Jelinek
Peter Miner
Brendan Ward

Adjunct Associate Professors
David McKenna

Adjunct Assistant Professors
Chris Albers
Michael Barker
Henry Bean
Anthony Bregman
Adam Brooks
Joseph Cacaci
Patrick Downs
John Erman
John Fauer
David Ford
John Frankfurt
William Goldman
James V. Hart
Sabine Hoffman
Israel Horovitz
Malcolm Jamieson
David Jones
Jerome Kass
Chris Kelly
Jameel Khaja
Simon Kinberg
Alan Kingsberg
Sloane Klevin
Beth Kling
Darrell Larson
Christina Lazaridi
Andrew Lund
Mira Nair
Peter Parnell
Neil Pepe
Lee Percy
Frank Pugliese
Marie Reagan
Seth Rosenfeld
John Rubin
Maureen Ryan
Misael Sanchez
Malia Scotch-Marmo
Alex Sichel
Mary Jane Skalski
Edward Smith
Peter Sollett
Jeffrey Stanzler
Patrick Stettner
Fred Strype
Susanna Styron
Alan Taylor
Jim Taylor
Camilla Toniolo
Tzipi Trope
Adrien Weiss

Assistant Director of Instruction
Misael Sanchez

THEATER
Steven Chaikelson, Chair.

Professors
Arnold Aronson
Anne Bogart
Kristin Linklater
Andrei Serban

Associate Professors
Steven Chaikelson
Brian Kulick
Nikolaus Wolcz

Assistant Professor
Chuck Mee
Christian Parker

Adjunct Professors
Victoria Bailey
Bernard Gersten
Barry Grove
Paul Libin
Gerald Schoenfeld

Adjunct Associate Professors
Chris Boneau
James Leverett
Linda Winer

Adjunct Assistant Professors
Daniel Adamian
Barbara Allen
David Auster
Leslie Ayvazian
Robert Blacker
Gigi Bolt
Deborah Brevoort
Christopher Burney
Ben Cameron
Carolyn Casselman
Nancy Coyne
Beverly Emmons
Ragnar Freidank
James Freydberg
Robert Fried
David Grimm
Andy Hammerstein
Roy Harris
Hugh Hysell
Tom Kelly
Yurly Kordonskiy
Ruth Kreshka
Jeff Lee
Kelly Maurer
Maria Mileaf
Ira Mont
Gregory Mosher
Michael Naumann
Gene O'Donovan
Barney O'Hanlon
Frank Pugliese
William Russo
Micah Schraft
Larry Singer
David Stone
Livia Vanaver
Donna Walker-Kuhne
Dolphi Wertenbaker
J. Steven White
Robert Woodruff

Lecturers
Andrea Haring
Kelly Stuart
Ursula Wolcz

VISUAL ARTS
Gregory Amenoff, Chair.

Professors
Gregory Amenoff
Jon Kessler
Thomas Roma
Rirkrit Tiravanija
Kara Walker

Associate Professors
Tomas Vu Daniel

Assistant Professors
Dana Hoey
Gareth James
Blake Rayne
Paula Wilson

Adjunct Graduate Professors
Janine Antoni
Jackie Battenfield
Johanna Burton
Mark Dion
Liam Gillick
Rachel Harrison
Michael Joo
John Kelsey
John Miller
Matt Mullican
Jerry Saltz
Collier Schorr
Amy Sillman
Jeanne Silverthorne
Charline von Heyl

Visiting Graduate Critics
Vince Aletti
Gregg Bordowitz
Cecily Brown
Lynne Cooke
Liz Deschenes
Roe Ethridge
Jason Fox
Alfredo Jaar
John Kelsey
Jutta Koether
Christian Marclay
Allan McCollum
Sarah Morris
Dana Schutz
Gary Stephan
Cheyney Thompson
Steven Westfall
Terry Winters
Andrea Zittel

WRITING
Ben Marcus, Chair.

Professors
Lucie Brock-Broido
Nicholas Christopher
Richard Howard
Michael Janeway
Margo Jefferson
Binnie Kirshenbaum
Richard Locke
David Plante
Michael Scammell
Alan Ziegler

Associate Professors
Lis Harris
Jaime Manrique
Ben Marcus
Patricia O'Toole

Assistant Professors
Stacy D'Erasmo
Timothy Donnelly
Sam Lipsyte
Gary Shteyngart

Adjunct Professors
Eamon Grennan
Edith Grossman
Maureen Howard
Marie Howe
Phillip Lopate
Alice Quinn
Brenda Wineapple
James Wood

Adjunct Associate Professors
Steven O'Connor
Ben Taylor

Adjunct Assistant Professors
Esther Allen
Jonathan Dee
David Ebershoff
Darcy Frey
Samantha Gillison
Claire Harman
Bob Holman
Paul LaFarge
Victor LaValle
Ethan Nosowsky
Victoria Redel
Leslie Sharpe
Darcey Steinke
Rene Steinke
Bill Wadsworth
Mark Wunderlich

EMERSON COLLEGE

School of the Arts
Master of Arts in Theatre Education

Programs of Study As a premier performing arts school in the heart of Boston's theater community, Emerson offers three streams of study in theater education, allowing students to explore themselves as both artists and educators. Theater teacher education prepares M.A. candidates to teach drama to children grades pre-K through 12. Theater and community explores the uses of theater in a variety of settings, such as community theater, recreation and arts centers, museums, and professional theater for young audiences. Theater education prepares students to go on to pursue a doctorate and teach at the college level.

As students cultivate their own talents, they are joined by world-renowned Emerson faculty members—distinguished directors, producers, writers, actors, performance artists, and educators. In demand nationwide, Emerson's graduates are employed as theater teachers, community theater producers and directors, and as coordinators of educational outreach programs. For more information about Emerson's M.A. in theater education, interested students should visit http://admission.emerson.edu/admission/graduate/academics/te.cfm.

Research Facilities Emerson College offers theater education students the opportunity to hone their craft in the Cutler Majestic Theatre, a 100-year-old, 1,200-seat facility that is the home of fourteen of New England's leading art troupes as well as Emerson College student theatrical productions. In 2003, Emerson opened the eleven-story, state-of-the-art Tufte Performance and Production Center adjacent to the Cutler Majestic Theatre. The new theater enhances the studies of students enrolled in the theater program by giving them access to the latest in sound and lighting technology for dramatic purposes.

The Emerson College library has more than 200,000 volumes, 20,000 journals (paper and electronic), 8,000 e-books, 10,000 nonprint materials, and 10,000 microforms in its collection that focus on the communication studies and performing arts. Through membership in the Fenway Library Consortium, graduate students have access to more than 2 million volumes. Computer-assisted reference services provide bibliographic databases through Dialog, BRS, and other online services. The Online Computer Library Center is used for student research support.

M.A. candidates gain valuable hands-on experience in the Media Services Center, which provides students with access to approximately 2,400 films, videos, laser discs, and DVDs. The center is the home of audio, video, and multimedia production facilities; a video studio; and several nonlinear editing suites comparable to those of any television studio in a major U.S. city.

Financial Aid Emerson College offers several financial assistance programs that make graduate education possible: merit-based awards (domestic and international applicants), low-interest federal loans (domestic applicants only), federal work-study (domestic applicants only), private loans (domestic and international applicants), student employment (domestic and international applicants), and alternative payment plans (domestic and international applicants). For detailed information, students should visit the Office of Student Financial Services Web site at http://www.emerson.edu/financial_services.

Cost of Study Tuition for the 2008–09 academic year is $886 per credit hour. Other fees vary and may apply.

Living and Housing Costs Though on-campus housing is not available for its graduate students, the Emerson College Office of Off-Campus Student Services offers assistance in finding housing, including: local apartment listings, realtor lists, temporary accommodations, search tips, pertinent neighborhood information, a roommate networking service, and more. Costs for housing are comparable to those of rental properties available in larger East Coast cities.

Student Group More than 950 graduate students representing forty-five states and sixty countries are enrolled in Emerson programs.

Student Outcomes For the last few years, the theater education program has had a 95 percent placement rate. Among the recent employers are public and private schools, the Huntington Theatre Company, the North Shore Music Theatre, and the Wang Center for the Performing Arts.

Location Situated in the heart of downtown Boston, Emerson offers access to the vast resources of a city that is the home of the nation's finest educational institutions and an international hub of culture, media production, writing, publishing, communication, commerce, and medical innovation. Boston is a career launching pad for Emerson's students, many of whom intern or work at world-renowned organizations throughout the city. Emerson students from around the country and world absorb the city's unique blend of local and global culture, and many find that Boston is an education in itself.

The College Emerson College, founded in 1880 by Charles Wesley Emerson, has expanded upon its original mission of promoting the study of oratory and the performing arts by offering some of the nation's most distinctive graduate programs in communication.

Applying Emerson's graduate programs welcome applicants from across the United States and around the world. Admission is competitive and selective. Emerson is looking for students whose academic and professional backgrounds, communication skills, and passion for the field meet the demands of their chosen program and promise a successful career.

The application deadline is June 1 for domestic applicants and May 1 for international applicants. Applications that are not complete by the final deadline are not reviewed by the admission committee. Applicants are responsible for ensuring the completion of their application. Application fees are nonrefundable; application forms and supporting materials become the property of the Office of Graduate Admission once they are sent to the office, and they will not be returned.

All application materials, with the exception of GRE test scores, must be submitted together in one package to ensure a timely review. A complete application includes the application form (students may apply online or they may download the PDF version), the application fee ($60 for domestic applicants; $75 for international applicants), official transcripts from all colleges/universities previously attended, three sealed letters of recommendation (by persons best able to assess academic and professional qualifications, including motivation, goals, and potential), GRE test scores, an essay, an artistic resume, and a professional resume. Applicants whose native language is not English must provide evidence of English proficiency by submitting official TOEFL or IELTS test results. (Applicants from India and the Philippines are considered nonnative English speakers and are required to take the TOEFL.) Emerson College's school code for the TOEFL is 3367; no department code is needed. For more information about these tests, prospective student can visit http://www.toefl.org or http://www.ielts.org. Minimum TOEFL scores are 550 paper-based, 213 computer-based, and 80 Internet-based. The minimum IELTS score is 6.5. Applicants who do not meet this requirement are not reviewed for admission.

Decisions are made on complete applications within six to eight weeks.

Deadlines for merit-based and federal aid applications for fall are March 1 and April 1, respectively. For more information about financing a graduate education, students should visit: http://www.emerson.edu/financial_services/info-grad.cfm/.

Correspondence and Information

Office of Graduate Admission
Emerson College
120 Boylston Street
Boston, Massachusetts 02116-4624

Phone: 617-824-8610
Fax: 617-824-8614
E-mail: gradapp@emerson.edu
Web site: http://admission.emerson.edu/admission/graduate

Emerson College

THE FACULTY AND THEIR RESEARCH

Melia Bensussen, Acting Chair and Associate Professor; B.A., Brown. Ms. Bensussen is producing director of Emerson Stage and teaches directing. She was awarded an OBIE for outstanding direction in 1999. In New York, she has worked at Playwrights Horizons, Primary Stages, Manhattan Class Company, Bay Street (Sag Harbor, New York), The Women's Project, the WPA, and the New York Shakespeare Festival (where she was the artist-in-residence), among others. She was twice given directing awards by the Princess Grace Foundation-USA and is a recipient of their Statuette Award. Her edition of the Langston Hughes translation of Garcia Lorca's *Blood Wedding* is in its fifth printing by Theatre Communications Group.

Robert Colby, Associate Professor, Graduate Program Director, and Program Director of Teacher Education; Ed.D., Harvard. Dr. Colby teaches in the areas of theater education and theater for young audiences, and directing. His productions for young audiences have toured extensively throughout the New England area and have been showcased at regional and national conferences. He has published in *Children's Theatre Review*, *Youth Theatre Journal*, and *2D: Drama/Dance*. In 2003 he was recognized for his contributions to the field of theater education with the Lin Wright Special Recognition Award given by the American Alliance for Theatre and Education.

Mary Ellen Adams, Assistant Professor; M.S., Emerson. Ms. Adams teaches in the design/technology area with a specialty in makeup, crafts, and puppetry. She received her training in makeup for theater from Jack Stein, and for film, television, and special effects with Vincent Kehoe at the Research Council of Makeup Artists. Her professional work includes design responsibilities at major Boston television stations, and historical productions for Sudbury Militia and Minuteman National Park in Lexington, Massachusetts. She continues to serve as consultant to local educational, community, and regional theater companies. She has also conducted workshops for the Puppeteers of New England and New England Theatre Conference. At the College, she has designed and executed costumes, specialty headgear, makeup, and puppets for department productions.

Kathleen Donohue, Associate Professor; M.F.A., Iowa. Ms. Donohue has worked professionally in both television and theater. She has taught acting workshops for the International Association for the Study of Dreams in Delphi, Greece, and produced and performed in *Living In Exile—A Retelling of the Iliad* in Edinburgh, Scotland, after having toured the show at institutions including the Remis Theatre of the Museum of Fine Arts, Boston, and the Philadelphia Museum of Art. Professor Donohue produced the Clauder Competition in Playwrighting and has written and performed her own one-woman shows. From 1990 to 1996 she was artistic director for TheatreWorks of Boston, Inc. Kathleen is a member of the Actors' Equity Association and took the Advanced Training Program at The Goodman School of the Chicago Art Institute.

Sarah Hickler, Assistant Professor; M.F.A., Boston University. Ms. Hickler creates movement/theater work, including solo, group, improvisational, collaborative, and interdisciplinary performances. Her work has been presented at Lincoln Center in New York City, Austin Arts Center, Trinity College in Hartford, the Institute of Contemporary Art, EventWorks, Mobius in Boston, the Dance Complex, Margaret Jewett Hall, and the Cambridge Multicultural Arts Center in Cambridge. She is a former member of the Mobius Artists Group, an internationally acclaimed group known for experimental work. She is a member of Shakespeare and Company, Lenox, Massachusetts, and has worked on productions at the Los Angeles Women's Shakespeare Company.

Timothy Jozwick, Assistant Professor; M.F.A., Carnegie Mellon. Mr. Jozwick's design work has been produced for stage, television, and film. In addition to his responsibilities with Emerson Stage, he serves as a resident designer for Chamber Repertory Theatre. His work has been featured at Michigan Opera, the Indianapolis Opera, the Repertory Theatre of Saint Louis, the Goodspeed Opera, the Memphis Opera, the Opera Theatre of Syracuse, and the Dayton Opera. Tim's exhibit designs have been installed in the Museum of Science, Boston, the California Museum of Science, the Franklin Institute, the Chicago Museum of Science, the Ohio Center for Science and Industry, the Science Museum of Minnesota, and the City Museum of Saint Louis. Tim is also the recipient of a regional Emmy Award, and he was the art director for a film documentary that went on to win the National Golden Eagle Award. Tim is a member of United Scenic Artists.

David Krasner, Head of Acting and Associate Professor; Ph.D., Tufts. David Krasner is the former Director of Undergraduate Theater Studies at Yale University (1997 to 2007) and the former Head of the M.F.A. Directing Program at Southern Illinois University (1995 to 1997). He taught acting, voice, speech, and movement at the New York branch of American Academy of Dramatic Arts from 1978 to 1987, while simultaneously acting in New York. He has appeared as an actor in numerous off- and off-off-Broadway productions of plays by Shakespeare, Brecht, O'Neill, and dozens of new works at Playwrights Horizons, New York Theatre Workshop, Ensemble Studio Theatre, and the Theatre Exchange. He has published several books on theater, drama, and performance, particularity on African American theater, dramatic theory and criticism, and acting. He has authored articles on method acting for twentieth-century acting training, and is the editor of the book *Method Acting Reconsidered*.

Robbie McCauley, Associate Professor; M.A., NYU. Ms. McCauley is an OBIE Award playwright and a nationally recognized performance artist and director. An AUDELCO Award recipient for acting, her directing credits include the premier of Daniel Alexander Jones' *Bel Canto*, co-produced with the Theater Offensive and Wheelock Family Theatre. One of the early cast members of Ntozake Shange's *for colored girls who have considered suicide when the rainbow is enuf*, Ms. McCauley went on to write and perform regularly in cities across the country, striving to facilitate dialogues on race between local whites and blacks. She is anthologized in several books including *Extreme Exposure*, by Jo Bonney, ed.; *Moon Marked* and *Touched by Sun*, by Sydne Mahone, ed.; and *Out of Character*, by Mark Russell, ed.

Joshua Polster, Assistant Professor; Ph.D., Washington (Seattle). Dr. Polster teaches theater history, dramatic theory, and criticism. His articles have appeared in *Law and Literature*, *The Arthur Miller Journal*, *Texas Theatre Journal*, and *Theatre Tours*. His scholarship earned him a *Modern Language Quarterly* grant and the Michael Quinn Prize. Dr. Polster recently completed his manuscript *Rethinking Arthur Miller: Symbol and Structure*. He has presented papers at the American Society for Theatre Research Conference, Mid-American Theatre Conference, Comparative Drama Conference, and International Arthur Miller Conference. He has taught at Roosevelt University, Columbia College and the Chicago Center for the Performing Arts. In addition to his scholarship and teaching, Dr. Polster has directed critically acclaimed plays in London and Chicago. He was the Assistant Director of the Nuffield Theatre in Southampton, England, the Assistant Artistic Administrator at the Goodman Theatre, and the Artistic Director of the Steep Theatre Company in Chicago.

Maureen Shea, Professor and Chairperson; Ph.D., Ohio State. Dr. Shea teaches in the areas of directing, dramatic literature, and theater history. She has collaborated with playwrights and composers on a number of new works, including staged readings at the Philadelphia Drama Guild, the Coyote Theatre Company, the Nora Theatre Company, the Theatre Offensive, and workshop productions and staged readings for Next Stage Inc., New Voices, and Word of Mouth in Cambridge, Somerville, and Boston, Massachusetts. Her production of *How I Got That Story* was presented at the Kennedy Center for the Performing Arts as a national finalist in the American College Theatre Festival. She has been an artist-in-residence at the Iowa Playwrights Lab and at the Toneelacademie in Maastricht, the Netherlands. She was an associate director of the Company of Women, an all female Shakespeare Company. She is a member of the Society of Stage Directors and Choreographers.

Scott Wheeler, Associate Professor; Ph.D., Brandeis. Dr. Wheeler is a composer and conductor. As a composer, he has received awards from the Guggenheim Foundation, the Koussevitsky Foundation, the Fromm Foundation, Tanglewood, the National Endowment for the Arts, and many others. As a conductor, Scott Wheeler can be heard on several recent CDs conducting the Boston-based Dinosaur Annex Music Ensemble, of which he is co-artistic director, and on a recent Newport Classic CD, conducting members of the Orchestra of St. Luke's. Recent musical compositions include *The Little Dragon* and *The Construction of Boston*.

Artists-in-Residence and Production Experts

Bonnie J. Baggesen, Production Manager, Department and Emerson Stage; M.F.A., Columbia. Ms. Baggesen teaches stage management. Prior to Emerson, she was the production manager for The Acting Company, a national touring company, and has stage managed in regional and commercial theater. Her regional credits include Trinity Repertory Company, Playmakers Repertory Company at UNC at Chapel Hill, and Rites and Reason Theatre at Brown University. Her touring credits include national tours of *Damn Yankees* with Jerry Lewis and *Sunset Boulevard* with Petula Clark. In addition, she has taught stage management at Rhode Island College. While earning an M.F.A. in theater management and producing at Columbia University, Ms. Baggesen continued to stage-manage by substituting on *The Lion King*, *Search for Signs of Intelligent Life*, and other Broadway shows.

Amelia Broome, Artist-in-Residence; M.A. West Florida; M.F.A., Boston University. Ms. Broome is a vocal and dialect coach and has more than twenty years of experience performing leading roles in opera, operetta, musical theater, and plays throughout New England, Georgia, Florida, and Canada. In Boston she has performed with Longwood Opera, Janus Opera, and Boston Lyric Opera. Amelia is a certified Linklater voice teacher.

Ken Cheeseman, Artist-in-Residence; Professional Training, University of Rhode Island Trinity Repertory Conservatory. Mr. Cheeseman studied at the International Film Workshops with feature film directors Mark Rydell, Alex Singer, Peter Werner, and Kevin Reynolds, and studied improvisation with Keith Johnstone. He received the grant "Partners in Production" to produce television programs with Boston's Deaf Community. He is director of educational services for the Boston Shakespeare Company and has hosted two children's television shows, *Story Shop* and *The Lil' Iguana Show*, winners of New England Emmy and Massachusetts Broadcast Awards. He has appeared in films including: *Domino One*, *Mystic River*, *Sundown*, *Big Night*, *Blue Diner*, *Next Stop Wonderland*, *State and Main*, *The Crucible*, *Malice*, *Housesitter*, *In Dreams*, and *The Proposition*, and the television shows *Monk* and *Law and Order: CI*. He is a member of the American Repertory Theatre and Trinity Rep and has worked at regional theaters around the country as well as off-Broadway in New York.

Stephen Terrell, Head of Musical Theatre and Artist-in-Residence; B.A. Mr. Terrell is a director and choreographer with an extensive background in musical theater, opera, and contemporary and classical theater. His work has been seen at off-Broadway's Minetta Lane Theatre, Goodspeed Opera House (Connecticut Critics' Circle Award, Best Choreographer), and the Texas Shakespeare Festival, where he is a founding member and resident director. His work in opera includes productions for the Paris Opera and the Teatro alla Scala in Milan, Teatro Real in Madrid; and Bunkamura Theatre in Tokyo, among others. A former actor-singer-dancer, Mr. Terrell appeared in shows on- and off-Broadway, at Radio City Music Hall, and at numerous theaters across the country.

Rafael Jaen, Resident Costume Designer; M.A., Emerson. Mr. Jaen teaches costume design and the history of fashion and decor. He has been designing costumes in projects produced in the United States, Spain, Scotland, and Venezuela. Mr. Jaen is currently the Costume Area Head and Costume Design Resident at Emerson. Recently he has chaired portfolio development workshops at the USITT Annual Conference and Stage Expo and was a guest speaker at the MIT Theater Design Symposium. He is a member of the United States Institute for Theatre Technology (USITT) where he is chair of costume portfolio reviews. He is also is a member of the United Scenic Artist (USA) Chapter 829.

Technical Staff

Keith Cornelius, Scene Shop/Technical Supervisor. Mr. Cornelius has served as the technical director for more than 150 productions and is also a lighting and sound designer. He has worked at the Appletree Theatre, the Connecticut Opera, the University of Tennessee at Knoxville, and the University of Tulsa. He has been published in the *USITT Biennial Technical Exposition Catalogue* and *Theatre Crafts*, and is a member of the United States Institute for Theatre Technology.

Ron J. De Marco, Properties Supervisor and Assistant Technical Director; B.A., North Central College. Mr. De Marco came to Emerson from Chicago, and his work has included technical director, stage manager, sound engineer, property designer, master electrician, special effects engineer, and changeover crew with companies such as Shakespeare Repertory, Light Opera Works, Theatre BAM!, Pegasus Players, Drury Lane, Northlight, Goodman, Steppenwolf, City Lit, Remy Bummpo, and Coyote Theatres. He has also led workshops in scenic design and construction for the Wisconsin Area Community Theatre Festival and for The Company Theatre in Norwell, Massachusetts. Ron is a member of USITT.

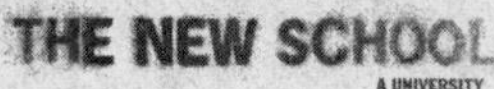

THE NEW SCHOOL: A UNIVERSITY

The New School for Drama

Program of Study

The New School for Drama offers a three-year intensive program dedicated to training artists in the fields of playwriting, directing, and acting. Students who successfully complete the program are awarded a Master of Fine Arts degree in playwriting, directing, or acting. The program is progressive—students begin with a course of self-discovery, explore technical craftsmanship in the second year, and finish by writing, directing, and acting in full productions, as well as developing a business plan for the transition from student to professional artist.

The actor is encouraged to stretch the fabric of his or her talent through a combination of disciplines—including the rigor of the Alexander Technique, an exacting voice and speech curriculum that universally coordinates several systems of training, as well as the acting techniques of Stanislavski. The playwright, through one-act festivals and main-stage productions, is trained within the context of real-world conditions that augment and enhance his or her individuality. The director is encouraged to learn what the word story means and how to express, conceive, and create visionary theater through main-stage and one-act productions.

The program at The New School for Drama relies on collaboration within each class. Playwrights work on their scripts in rehearsals and benefit from hearing and seeing their work performed. Directing and acting students work closely together as well. Playwrights, actors, and directors are all often represented (by both students and teachers) in rehearsals or in the classroom, giving them a glimpse of what it means to develop a new play. This crossover within a class lets students learn from their peers as well as from the instructors and allows students to develop important and long-lasting professional connections. A faculty of working professionals, through the discovery process, nurtures and guides each student's unique and original voice. Ultimately, students gain a rooted sense of who they are as individuals and how they may join, collaboratively, in finding their individual and collective artistic expression.

Research Facilities

The Herbert Robinson Drama Book and Script Collection contains more than 3,000 plays, screenplays, and books on film, theater history, and criticism.

A resource library of periodical, reference, and job-list materials is located in the Office of Career Development. In addition to such magazines as *Backstage, American Theatre,* and *ArtSearch,* the library contains information ranging from fellowship resources to directories of theaters, talent and casting agencies, and many other professional organizations. There is also a listing of internship opportunities, updated at the beginning of each week. The library also hosts an extensive lending library of plays, craft books, biographies, and industry guides—all for student use.

Financial Aid

Financial aid is available to matriculated degree candidates at The New School for Drama. Scholarships are merit-based, and assistance is granted on the basis of performance, starting with the audition or interview during the application phase and taking into account classroom performance and academic citizenship throughout the three years. All applicants for financial aid who are U.S. citizens or permanent residents must file the Free Application for Federal Student Assistance (FAFSA) each year in order to qualify for federally funded educational loans. International applicants may be considered for scholarships. Additional information is available from the Office of Financial Services at 212-229-8930.

Cost of Study

Tuition in 2008–09 is $16,195 per term, and fees are approximately $200 each term.

Living and Housing Costs

The University Housing Office maintains a comprehensive resource center with apartment listings. University-run apartments and residence halls are also available. The cost of housing, food, transportation, books, and living expenses averages $17,000 annually. For more information, students should go online to http://www.newschool.edu/studentservices.

Student Group

There are 170 students in the program; 169 attend on a full-time basis. Of these students, 108 are women, 32 are members of minority groups, and 27 are international students.

Location

With theater in the air and on its streets, as well as on its hundreds of stages, New York City provides an unrivaled curriculum in observation and a wealth of professional opportunities. Students are encouraged to take advantage of the museums, performance venues, and other cultural institutions that are only a walk or subway ride away. An extension of the classroom, the city also offers excellent professional and networking opportunities.

The University and The School

The New School pioneered the idea of lifelong university-level education for adults. It was created for teachers and students from different backgrounds who were willing to take risks for their intellectual and political beliefs. The New School for Drama has a legacy of vision. Artistic voices as distinctive as Tennessee Williams and Marlon Brando found their singularity at The New School, under the wing of Dramatic Workshop founder Erwin Piscator and a faculty that included Stella Adler and Lee Strasberg. Since 1994, the University has offered the M.F.A. in dramatic arts. Through its interrelated program of acting, directing, and playwriting, The New School for Drama is creative in its simplicity and original in its vision. The New School is forging the next generation of artists capable of meeting expectations of storytelling and of touching what is human about art.

A privately supported institution, The New School is accredited by the Commission on Higher Education of the Middle States Association of Colleges and Schools and chartered as a university by the Regents of the State of New York.

The eight schools that make up The New School are The New School for General Studies, The New School for Social Research, Milano The New School for Management and Urban Policy, Parsons The New School for Design, Eugene Lang College The New School for Liberal Arts, Mannes College The New School for Music, The New School for Drama, and The New School for Jazz and Contemporary Music.

Applying

An applicant to The New School for Drama must hold a bachelor's degree from an accredited college or university. A completed application, the $50 application fee, a statement of purpose, an artistic resume and a headshot, official transcripts of all undergraduate and graduate studies, and two letters of recommendation should be submitted to the University Admissions Office by January 10. Applicants are invited to audition based on application submissions.

Correspondence and Information

Office of Admissions
The New School for Drama
The New School
151 Bank Street
New York, New York 10014

Phone: 212-229-5859
E-mail: studentinfo@newschool.edu
Web site: http://www.newschool.edu/drama

The New School: A University

THE FACULTY

School Directors and Department Chairs

Robert LuPone, Director. A member of the Actors Studio, Mr. LuPone appeared on Broadway in *True West, A Thousand Clowns, A View from the Bridge, Late Nite Comic, Zoya's Apartment, Swing, St. Joan,* and *Nefertiti* and as Zach in *A Chorus Line.* Television credits include *Law & Order, Crossing Jordan, Swift Justice, Guiding Light, Mia—Child of Hollywood, American Tragedy, Palookaville, Sex and the City,* and Dr. Cusimano in *The Sopranos.* He received an Emmy nomination for his portrayal of Zach Grayson on *All My Children.* Film credits include *Nick of Time, Dead Presidents, The Doors, Jesus Christ Superstar, The Door in the Floor,* and the upcoming *Indocumentos.* LuPone is president of the board of ART/NY and artistic director of MCC Theater in New York City.

Paul Rudd, Associate Director. Mr. Rudd worked as a professional actor and director from 1967 to 1986 in New York City, both on- and off-Broadway, and in regional theaters around the country. His credits include the New York Shakespeare Festival/Public Theater, the Lincoln Center Theater, the Roundabout Theater, the Circle-in-the-Square, the Hudson Guild Theater, the Longwharf Theater, the Hartford Stage the Company, the Arena Stage, the American Repertory Theater, the Goodman Theater, the South Coast Repertory, and the San Diego Shakespeare Festival. Primarily a theater actor, Rudd has also worked in television and film productions of *End of Summer, A Family Reunion,* and *Beulah Land.* His roles include the central character of Brian Mallory in *Beacon Hill,* JFK in *Johnny We Hardly Knew Ye,* and guest appearances in episodes of *Moonlighting, Knot's Landing, Hart to Hart,* and *Murder, She Wrote.*

Ron Leibman, Chair of the Acting Department. A member of the Actors Studio, Mr. Leibman received the Tony Award and Drama Desk Award as Best Actor in Tony Kushner's Pulitzer Prize–winning *Angels in America.* Leibman won the Emmy Award as Best Actor for his work on *Kaz,* which he also created. Leibman has won Drama Desk Awards for *We Bombed in New Haven* (for which he also won a Theatre World Award), *Room Service, A Dybbuk,* and *Transfers,* and he won Obie Awards for his performance as Shylock in the New York Shakespeare Festival's *Merchant of Venice* and for his role in *Transfers.* Other Broadway appearances include *Rumors* and *I Ought To Be in Pictures* (both by Neil Simon), *Cop-Out* by John Guare, *The Deputy,* and *Dear Me, the Sky Is Falling.* His film work includes roles in *Norma Rae, Night Falls on Manhattan, Where's Poppa?, Slaughterhouse Five, Super Cops, The Hot Rock, Personal Velocity* (Sundance Grand Jury Prize winner), Paul Schrader's *Auto Focus,* and *Garden State.* Television credits include *Friends* (as Rachel's father), *Christmas Eve* (Golden Globe winner), *Central Park West, Law & Order,* a recurring role on *The Sopranos,* and numerous miniseries.

Pippin Parker, Chair of the Playwriting Department. Mr. Parker is a writer, director, and dramaturge. He is also a founding member and former artistic director of the Naked Angels theater company. His plays include *Anesthesia, Assisted Living,* and numerous one acts that have been produced in New York and Los Angeles. His radio play *A Gift* was broadcast on NPR's *The Next Big Thing.* Television credits include *The High Life* for HBO and the animated series *The Tick.* He was recently artistic director for the Naked Angels/Culture Project series, *The Democracy Project.*

Elinor Renfield, Chair of the Directing Department. Ms. Renfield began her training as a dancer with the Martha Graham Company in the 1950s. She attended the "old" High School of the Performing Arts and the Central School of Speech and Drama in London and earned an M.A. in theater at City University of New York. She has directed more than twenty-five new American plays since 1976 at the New York Shakespeare Festival, Playwrights Horizon, the American Place Theater, Ensemble Studio Theater, Theater for the New City, and Café La Mama. Her production of *Johnny Got His Gun* at the Circle Repertory won an Obie Award; her production of *The Diary of Anne Frank* won the Boston Theater Award; and her production of *Passion Play* by Peter Nichols at the Arena Stage in Washington, D.C., was nominated for a Helen Hayes Award. On Broadway, Renfield directed *Open Admissions* by Shirley Lauro at the Music Box.

Nova Thomas, Chair of the Voice and Speech Program. Ms. Thomas is an internationally acclaimed opera singer whose work has been characterized as "ravishing in sound and magical in stage appearance" (*OPERA*). Her roles have included Violetta in *La Traviata,* Leonora in *Il Trovatore,* Mimì in *La Bohème,* Desdemona in *Otello,* Lady Macbeth in *Macbeth,* all four heroines of *Les Contes d'Hoffman,* and the title roles of *Madama Butterfly, Norma, Anna Bolena, Tosca, Aida,* and *Turandot.* Her performances have taken her to the opera houses throughout the United States and the world. She has recorded the title role of *The Bohemian Girl* for DECCA records. A member of The New School for Drama faculty since its first year, she has coauthored and developed a three-year curriculum of voice and speech training uniquely designed to parallel and partner the Stanislavski-inspired system of training. Ms. Thomas serves on the national board of directors for the General H. Hugh Shelton Leadership Initiative, as well as several national scholarship committees. She is a recipient of The New School's Excellence in Teaching Award and the winner of a Lifetime Achievement Award from her home state of North Carolina for her contributions to the arts.

Tom Vasiliades, Chair of the Movement Program. Mr. Vasiliades trained and was certified at the American Center for the Alexander Technique in New York City. He is a member of the American Society for the Alexander Technique, Alexander Technique International, and the Society of Teachers for the Alexander Technique. After graduating from the American Center, he continued training in New York and London. He did postgraduate work with Barbara Kent, Glynn Macdonald, John Nicholls, Peggy Williams, and Walter Carrington, who carried on the training course after F.M. Alexander's death. Since the late 1970s, he has acted at regional theaters and in New York and in film and television. He has directed plays and produced two plays in New York, *The Sin Eaters* and *Triptych.* He has taught the Alexander Technique to many performers, including members of the Broadway cast of *Private Lives* with Alan Rickman and Lindsay Duncan.

ACTING

Ron Leibman, Chair.
Marcia Haufrecht
Gene Lasko
Karen Ludwig
Joseph Ragno
Paul Rudd
Arthur Storch
Mimi Turque
Robert Walden

Movement

Tom Vasiliades, Chair.
Teva Bjerken
Judith Grodowitz
Brendan McCall
Cynthia Reynolds
Rick Sordelet
Jean Taylor

Voice and Speech

Nova Thomas, Chair
Keith Buhl
Susan Cameron
Patricia Fletcher
Alba Quezada
Christopher Roselli

DIRECTING

Elinor Renfield, Chair.
Casey Biggs
Lou Jacob
Dorothy Lyman
Austin Pendleton
Jamie Richards

Design

Jack O'Connor
Jamie Richards

PLAYWRITING

Pippin Parker, Chair
Nicole Burdette
Laura Maria Censabella
Frank Pugliese
Christopher Shinn
Michael Weller

Script Analysis

Stephen Willems

Theater History

Jane Ann Crum
Beowulf Boritt
Donald Holder

PACE UNIVERSITY

The Actors Studio M.F.A.

Program of Study

The Actors Studio M.F.A. is a full-time, three-year program, with no part-time, noncredit, or summer classes available. As the only M.F.A. theater program officially sanctioned by the Actors Studio, the entire curriculum has been designed and supervised by the leadership of the Actors Studio through its Curriculum Advisory Committee, which includes the presidents, Ellen Burstyn, Harvey Keitel, and Al Pacino. Tracks are available in acting, directing, and playwriting.

All M.F.A. candidates study and practice together—beginning at the same place as they learn a shared "language" and technique. On parallel tracks to that "ensemble" experience, every student undergoes intensive—and intense—training in his or her own discipline, at the hands of one of the most distinguished acting, directing, and writing faculties ever assembled. Students have the opportunity to develop their craft not only in their classes but also in a variety of public performing events.

From the beginning, all students participate in the Craft Seminars, where the most accomplished members of the Actors Studio share their knowledge and experiences. Many Actors Studio artists also teach in the intensive Friday Workshop sessions. While the Actors Studio is a private space, accessible only to members, M.F.A. candidates have the rare privilege of attending a number of the Studio's closed-door sessions as observers. On numerous occasions, students have the opportunity to spend an evening with some of the world's most distinguished creative and performing artists in the *Inside the Actors Studio* seminars. After graduation for one year, all students have the privilege, of the status of working finalists at the Actors Studio itself, which means they are eligible to attend sessions and take a final audition for studio membership, bypassing the usual preliminary audition.

In the first week of their first semester, students are introduced to the communal world of the theater, and all of the students and teachers spend three days together in an informal introduction to the program's philosophy, process, and intentions. Students encounter another unique feature of the program as they set out on a side-by-side journey—actors, directors, playwrights together learning the common language that will enable them to collaborate productively, harmoniously, and seamlessly. Armed with the technical fundamentals they are likely to use for the rest of their educational and professional careers, second-year students move from the preparation of their instrument (themselves) to the preparation of the role. In the final year, course work continues, with the focus on the project that brings together three years of work in weeks of graduation performance nights. The Repertory Season is a semester-long series of evenings of scenes, one-act plays, and, if possible, one full-length play—all new works written by student playwrights, directed by student directors, acted by student actors, and presented in repertory. The center of the third year is the Process Lab, which continues to build on the work of the student's second year.

Research Facilities

Inside the Actors Studio, the hit Bravo television show hosted by James Lipton, is filmed in the University's Michael Schimmel Center for the Arts, a 743-seat theater located on Spruce Street between Park Row and Gold Street, near the foot of the Brooklyn Bridge. The largest in lower Manhattan, the center also provides performance space for the Grammy in the Schools program, exhibit space for the Accademia di Belle Arti in Florence, and a wealth of other arts events.

The Pace University Library is a comprehensive teaching library and student-learning center, a virtual library that combines strong core collections with access to Internet resources to support the broad and diversified curricula. Reciprocal borrowing and access accords, traditional interlibrary loan services, and commercial document-delivery options supplement the library's collection. Pace offers instructional services librarians, a state-of-the-art electronic classroom, digital reference services, and multimedia applications. Recognized as one of America's most wired universities, Pace supports high-speed Internet and Internet2 access on every campus. Residence facilities are wired, and most public areas are enabled for wireless connectivity.

Financial Aid

Pace participates in all major federal and state financial aid programs, such as Direct Loans, the New York State Tuition Assistance Program (TAP), and Federal Perkins Loans. All students are encouraged to apply for these programs by filing the Free Application for Federal Student Aid (FAFSA).

Cost of Study

Tuition for the 2006–07 academic year was $29,000.

Living and Housing Costs

Residence facilities are available on campus. Double-occupancy rooms cost approximately $10,000 for the 2007–08 academic year. University-operated, off-campus housing is available in proximity of the New York City campus.

Student Group

There are 535 graduate students enrolled in the Dyson College of Arts and Sciences, of which the Actors Studio is a part.

Location

Located in downtown Manhattan, Pace University is one of the reasons that lower Manhattan is quickly becoming a magnet for performing and visual arts in New York City. Currently celebrating its 100th year, Pace is an active partner with the Tribeca Film and Theatre Festivals, the New York International Fringe Festival, and the River-to-River Summer Stars Series. Pace University's downtown campus is served by at least twelve subway lines and numerous bus routes.

The University

Founded in 1906, Pace University is a private, nonsectarian, coeducational institution. Originally founded as a school of accounting, Pace Institute was designated Pace College in 1973. Through growth and various successes, it was renamed Pace University, as approved by the New York State Board of Regents. Today, Pace offers comprehensive undergraduate, graduate, doctoral, and professional programs at several campus locations through six schools and colleges.

Applying

The M.F.A. program is open to qualified candidates who have earned a bachelor's degree or the international equivalent from an accredited college or university. Students must submit the completed application, the $65 application fee, a personal statement, an artistic resume, two letters of recommendation (one academic and one personal), and official college or university transcripts. In addition, actors must send in headshots; directors, portfolios; and playwrights, writing samples. International students are required to submit TOEFL scores (at least 570 on the paper-based test, 230 on the computer-based test, or 88–89 on the Internet-based test) and a financial affidavit. The priority application deadline is February 12; the general application deadline is April 10. Select candidates are invited to interview or audition based on the quality of their application materials.

Correspondence and Information

Office of Graduate Admission
Pace University
1 Pace Plaza
New York, New York 10038

Phone: 212-346-1531
Fax: 212-346-1585
E-mail: ActorsStudioMFA@pace.edu
Web site: http://appserv.pace.edu/execute/page.cfm?doc_id=20051

Pace University

THE FACULTY AND THEIR BACKGROUNDS

Susan Aston, Acting. A teacher, coach, and actress in New York City, Aston was a charter member of the core acting faculty at the Actors Studio Drama School, teaching scene study, basic technique, and workshops. At New York's School of Visual Arts, Aston taught the Acting for Directors course. She is most noted for her work with James Gandolfini on *The Sopranos,* having coached his Emmy, Golden Globe, and SAG award-winning performances. As an actress, she appeared on stage with James Gandolfini, Jessica Lange, and Alec Baldwin. In film, she acted with Demi Moore and Robert Duvall and was directed by Ridley Scott and Bruce Beresford. She has coached performances on *All the King's Men, Lonely Hearts, The Castle, The Mexican, Romance and Cigarettes, Fever Pitch, Law & Order,* and Showtime's *Brotherhood.* Aston was honored by the Academy of Television Arts and Sciences at the 2002–03 Primetime Emmy Awards. She is a lifetime member of the Actors Studio.

Edward Allan Baker, Playwriting. Baker is a published and frequently produced New York City playwright with thirty-two plays to his credit—most notably, *Dolores,* which starred Joan Allen and is included in *The Best Short Plays of 1989; North of Providence; Prairie Avenue,* which starred Ed Harris; *Rosemary with Ginger;* and *Face Divided,* which starred Sam Rockwell. He has written for HBO and Showtime, attended the Sundance Film Institute, and taught playwriting for more than twenty years. Baker was recently presented with the 25th Anniversary Award for Theatrical Excellence by the Ensemble Studio Theatre of New York.

Michael Billingsley, M.F.A., Pace; Movement. Billingsley began his martial arts training as soon as he could walk and has continued ever since. Raised in his father's tae kwon do school, he was awarded his first-degree black belt from the Jhoon Rhee Institute at age 17. Other styles he has studied include capoeira, tai chi, jujitsu, and escrima. Billingsley is a senior instructor with Kids Kicking Cancer, teaching martial arts and meditation techniques as a form of pain management for children in hospitals throughout New York City. Billingsley has performed in theater and films produced in New York, San Francisco, Los Angeles, and Atlanta. As a founding member of Woken Glacier Theater Company, he holds membership in Actors' Equity Association and the Screen Actors Guild. Billingsley is a lifetime member of the Actors Studio.

Bill Coco, Director, Theater History Department; Ph.D., Columbia; Theater History and History of Directing. A dramaturge, translator, magazine and book editor, and teacher, Coco was principal dramaturge for the late director Joseph Chaikin on fifteen productions for the stage, radio, and audio recording. His has written for *TDR: The Drama Review, Performance, Scripts, Theatre Journal,* and *Performing Arts Journal (PAJ).* He was associate editor of *TDR* and a founding editor of *Performance* and *Scripts,* which were published by Joseph Papp at the New York Shakespeare Festival Public Theater. He was also contributing editor for *PAJ* and the Yale School of Drama's Theater. His translations include Sophocles' *Elektra,* produced at the Actors Studio, and Strindberg's *Dance of Death* (co-translated with Peter Stormare) at Arena Stage in Washington, D.C. His productions with Chaikin include premieres and performances of plays by Jean-Claude van Itallie, Sam Shepard, Adrienne Kennedy, Moliere, and Ionesco and four plays by Beckett, at such venues as the NYSF Public Theater, Signature Theater (Shepard and Kennedy seasons), the Mark Taper Forum in Los Angeles, and the Juilliard School. He coedited, with Gloria Brim Beckerman, Bernard Beckerman's posthumous book *Theatrical Presentation: Performer, Audience and Act.*

Elizabeth Kemp, Director, Acting Department; Acting. A longtime member of the Actors Studio, Kemp has worked extensively in theater on Broadway and Off-Broadway as well as in film and television. As an actress, she has worked opposite Tom Hanks, Christopher Reeve, and Kevin Kline. She was a favorite of Elia Kazan, who chose her to play Baby Doll for Tennessee Williams in the world premiere of one of his last plays, *Tiger Tail.* As a director, she has worked in New York and Paris. As a teacher and coach, she has taught privately for many years. She taught at the Lee Strasberg Institute and was one of the original faculty members of the Actors Studio Drama School. She has taught her Character Dream workshops around the world and is the personal acting coach to many leading actors, including recipients of the Oscar and Cesar Awards.

Shawn Lewis, M.F.A., NYU; Design. Based in New York City, Lewis has worked as a set designer for more than fifty productions throughout the United States and abroad, designing plays, musicals, opera, and film. Currently, she is designing *Frankenstein: The Rock Musical* and *Forever Plaid* in Canada. Her most recent productions include, in film, the indie feature *Whiskey Story* and, in theater, *Mountains in the Bering* (Ensemble Studio Theatre), *The Miracle Worker* (National School of Drama), *The Death of Cartula* (Cuba), *Cheri* (the Actors Studio), *Les Miserables* (Kodesh), *Spring Storm* (Lobo), and *Jazz Reach* (Kennedy Center, Washington, D.C.). Lewis's mentor has been Tony Walton, with whom she started teaching in 1996 at the Actors Studio Drama School. As a resident scenic designer there, she designed more than 400 one-act productions. In addition, she has taught master's-level classes in set design at the University of North Carolina and Yale. She is a member of the League of Professional Theater Women and of United Scenic Artists.

Susan Main, M.F.A., Boston University; Voice. An actress and designated Linklater voice teacher, Main has taught voice and/or movement on the faculties of the Linklater Center for Voice and Language in New York City, NYU Cap 21, Emerson College, MIT, Boston Conservatory, and Southwick Studios. She has taught workshops in Italy and served as a voice and movement coach for theater companies in Italy and Portugal. In 2005, she served as script supervisor/assistant director on the documentary *Vox Erotica,* filmed in Stromboli, Italy, and featuring Kristin Linklater.

Andreas Manolikakis, Chair of M.F.A. Program; M.F.A., Paris VIII (Vincennes); Acting and Directing. Manolikakis was chair of the directing department at the Actors Studio Drama School, where he taught acting and directing from 1995 to 2005. He has taught workshops in acting, directing, and script analysis in Athens, Berlin, and Paris (at the French national film school La FEMIS, the Conservatoire National Supérieur d'Art Dramatique, and L'Escalier 4). He translated into Greek and published in Athens in 1997 Nikolai Gorchakov's Russian classic *The Vakhtangov School of Stage Art,* which has become a required text for the theater department of the University of Athens. He has lectured at L'Escalier 4 in Paris, the University of Athens, the National Theater, the University of Northern Greece, the Drama School of the National Theater of Greece, and the National Organization of Theater Studies in Athens on method acting and Greek tragedy, method acting and directing, and Stanislavski and Vakhtangov. He directed and acted in numerous plays from the Greek and international repertoire for the New Hellenic Stage of New York, which he founded in 1983. He is also the author of *The Classmates,* a thirteen-episode television series produced by the National Greek Television ET3. Manolikakis studied with Marcel Marceau at his International School of Mime in Paris. At the Actors Studio, he is a lifetime member and is a member of the board of directors.

Rebecca DuMaine Miller, M.F.A., Rutgers; Neutral American Speech. A New York–based actress and designated Linklater voice teacher, DuMaine Miller has acted onstage in New York, regionally, and on television and radio. She has taught voice and speech at Rutgers, the New Actors Workshop, Circle in the Square, the William Esper Studio, SUNY at Purchase, and NYU. DuMaine Miller coaches actors and corporate clients privately in dialects, accent reduction, and text.

Brian Rhinehart, Ph.D., Florida; Directing. Rhinehart has taught acting, directing, playwriting, and script analysis at such schools as Baruch College, Marymount Manhattan College, Eugene Lang College The New School for Liberal Arts, and Kean University. A member of the 2006 Lincoln Center Theater Directors Lab, Rhinehart was recently awarded an Artist in Residence grant through The Field (The Silo Project, 2006) and was Resident Artist at the Kraine Theater from 2003 to 2005. In 2001, he was named Best Director of the New York International Fringe Festival for *Einstein's Dreams,* and in 1998 he was awarded Best Director for *Escape Artist* in the Drop Your Shorts: Short Play Festival at the Trilogy Theatre. He has acted in more than fifty productions, and the plays he has written or cowritten have been seen at the Fringe Festival and in a variety of off-off Broadway venues. He is a reviewer for OffBroadway.Com, a member of Actors Equity Association, and an associate member of the Society of Stage Directors and Choreographers.

SARAH LAWRENCE COLLEGE

Master of Fine Arts Programs

Programs of Study

Sarah Lawrence College offers advanced dance, theater, and writing students the opportunity to study with an outstanding faculty as they pursue the Master of Fine Arts degree at one of the nation's most selective liberal arts colleges. These programs follow the College's philosophy, which stresses a high degree of individual development that is essentially exploratory and noncompetitive in nature. Small seminar classes with individual student-faculty conferences allow close collaboration with faculty members in all three programs, and the opportunity for fieldwork is extensive and varied.

The dance and theater programs require two years of full-time study and completion of 36 course credits. The writing program offers both full-time and part-time study.

The program in dance is based on the premise that dance is a unique art form, calling for the integration of body, mind, and spirit. Daily modern and ballet technique classes are required of all graduate students. Basic physical skills, strength, and control are required for the central focus of the program—the creative use of the dance medium. The student is exposed to vital aspects of the art as a performer, creator, and observer, with music as an integral part. The curriculum centers on choreography, dance improvisation, music improvisation, composition, and the teaching of dance. Course work is offered with undergraduate dancers, and the dance program offers students an opportunity to grow under the guidance of an excellent faculty of dancers and dance scholars with professional experience in the New York area and abroad.

The theater program is based on the principle that learning comes through practical application, personal experience, and intensive workshops. Working with a faculty of New York City theater professionals, students explore playwriting, acting, directing, design, and technical work in small seminars, private tutorials, and collaborative projects.

The writing program offers an uncommon opportunity for students to develop as poets, creative nonfiction writers, or fiction writers under the close supervision of a nationally renowned faculty. At the center of the course of study are four successive seminars that students take during their two years in the program. In addition to the lively exchanges in these seminars, students participate in individual conferences with faculty members every two weeks. This distinctive aspect of the Sarah Lawrence program provides further intensive scrutiny of students' writing and helps them create the substantial body of work needed to fulfill the program's requirements.

Research Facilities

The College's facilities include classrooms, laboratories, a computer center, and a state-of-the-art sports center; a library with 202,265 books and 880 periodicals, which is linked by computer to more than 6,000 other libraries; the Performing Arts Center, which consists of four theaters, a dance studio, and a concert hall; a music building, including a music library; and the Center for Graduate Studies.

Financial Aid

Graduate students are welcome to apply for financial aid. There are two required forms for U.S. citizens (and other federally eligible students) and one form for international students. U.S. citizens should complete the Free Application for Federal Student Aid (FAFSA) and the Financial Aid PROFILE. International students may use the College's International Application for Financial Aid. There are links to all three forms at http://www.sarahlawrence.edu/finaid. March 1 is the College's preferential filing date. It is important that all applicants for financial aid complete either the PROFILE or the international application for aid at the same time as their application for admission. All financial aid is awarded on the basis of need. Students who complete the appropriate forms in a timely manner are automatically considered for all aid resources administered by Sarah Lawrence College. Grants (gift aid) and student loans comprise the two elements of a Sarah Lawrence financial aid package. Every federally eligible aid recipient is offered a student loan. Students are not required to accept the loan in order to receive Sarah Lawrence College gift aid. International students are advised to investigate financing opportunities offered by their government or private institutions. Detailed descriptions and a thorough explanation of financial aid procedures are available in *Financing Your Graduate Education at Sarah Lawrence College*, published and updated by the Office of Graduate Studies. A copy of the booklet is mailed to all students who apply to a graduate studies program.

Cost of Study

In 2008–09, tuition for the M.F.A. varies according to program. For more information, prospective students should visit http://www.slc.edu/student-accounts/Graduate_Tuition_and_Costs.php.

Living and Housing Costs

Estimated expenses for off-campus housing and food are $15,390 per year.

Student Group

Sarah Lawrence attracts students who seek a creative education and are eager to take responsibility for it. The College draws its graduate students from forty-nine states and thirty-one countries. Graduate programs are deliberately kept small. There are approximately 320 graduate students.

Location

The College is situated in the Bronxville/Yonkers suburban community in southern Westchester County, just 15 miles north of midtown Manhattan in New York City. Highways and a commuter railroad make it possible to reach the city in about 30 minutes, enabling students to take advantage of its social and cultural riches and its internship possibilities.

The College

Founded in 1926, Sarah Lawrence is a small, liberal arts college for men and women. It is a lively community of students, scholars, and artists, nationally renowned for its distinctive academic structure that combines small classes with individual student-faculty conferences.

Applying

Applicants for graduate studies must have received a Bachelor of Arts or an equivalent degree from an accredited college or university and have at least a 3.0 grade point average. Applicants should write to the College address to request information on a specific program.

Applicants are asked to complete the application form and to furnish transcripts of all undergraduate work and two letters of recommendation, preferably from former teachers. Personal interviews may be arranged with the program directors and with the director of graduate studies. The creative writing and the performing arts programs require demonstration of the candidate's ability. GRE scores are not required. Application deadlines vary according to the program. Students should visit the Web site at http://www.slc.edu/graduate/index.php.

Correspondence and Information

Susan Guma
Dean of Graduate Studies
Sarah Lawrence College
1 Mead Way
Bronxville, New York 10708

Phone: 914-395-2371
Fax: 914-395-2664
E-mail: grad@sarahlawrence.edu
Web site: http://www.sarahlawrence.edu

Sarah Lawrence College

THE FACULTY

Dance
Sara Rudner, Director; M.F.A., Bennington.
Emmy Devine, B.A., Connecticut.
Dan Hurlin, B.A., Sarah Lawrence.
Rose Anne Thom, B.A., McGill.
John Yannelli, M.F.A., Sarah Lawrence.

Theater
John Dillon, Director; M.F.A., Columbia (Danforth and Woodrow Wilson Fellow).
Ernest H. Abuba, Member, Ensemble Studio Theatre; Rockefeller Foundation Fellowship.
Edward Allen Baker, B.A., Rhode Island.
Lynn Book, M.F.A., Art Institute of Chicago.
Kevin Confoy, B.A., Rutgers.
Michael Early, M.F.A., Yale.
June Ekman, B.A., Goddard, Illinois; ACAT. Alexander Technique.
Christine Farrell, M.F.A., Columbia.
Nancy Franklin, Member, Actors Studio and Ensemble Studio Theatre.
Dan Hurlin, B.A., Sarah Lawrence.
Chris Jones, M.F.A., Carnegie Mellon.
Shirley Kaplan, A.A., Briarcliff, Academie de la Grande Chaumiere (Paris).
Doug MacHugh, M.F.A., Sarah Lawrence.
Greg MacPherson, B.A., Vermont.
John McCormack, B.A., Hamilton.
William D. McRee, M.F.A., Sarah Lawrence.
Cassandra Medley, Michigan.
Carol Ann Pelletier, B.A., Brandeis.
Paul Rudd, B.A., Fairfield.
Fanchon Miller Scheier, M.F.A., Sarah Lawrence.
Stuart Spencer, B.A., Lawrence Tech.
Sterling Swann, B.A., Vassar.
John Yannelli, M.F.A., Sarah Lawrence.

Writing/Creative Nonfiction
Vijay Seshadri, Director; M.F.A., Columbia.
Jo Ann Beard, M.A., Iowa.
Rachel Cohen, A.B., Harvard.
Stephen O'Connor, M.A., Berkeley.
Penny Wolfson, M.F.A., Sarah Lawrence.

Writing/Fiction
Brian Morton, Director; B.A., Sarah Lawrence.
Jo Ann Beard, M.A., Iowa.
Melvin Jules Bukiet, M.F.A., Columbia.
Carolyn Ferrell, M.A., CUNY, City College.
Myra Goldberg, M.A., CUNY Graduate Center.
Joshua Henkin, M.F.A., Michigan.
Kathleen Hill, Ph.D., Wisconsin.
William Melvin Kelley, Writer; Harvard.
Mary La Chapelle, M.F.A., Vermont.
Paul Lisicky, M.A., Rutgers.
Mary Morris, M.Phil., Columbia.
Dennia Nurkse, B.A., Harvard.
Victoria Redel, M.F.A., Iowa.
Lucy Rosenthal, M.F.A., Yale.
Joan Silber, M.A., NYU.

Writing/Poetry
Kate Knapp Johnson, Director; M.F.A., Sarah Lawrence.
Laure-Anne Bosselaar, M.F.A., National Institute for Performing Arts (Belgium).
Suzanne Gardinier, M.F.A., Columbia.
Marie Howe, M.F.A., Columbia.
Joan Larkin, M.A., Arizona.
Thomas Lux, B.A., Emerson; Iowa Writers Workshop.
Kevin Pilkington, M.A., Georgetown.
Victoria Redel, M.F.A., Iowa.
Vijay Seshadri, M.F.A., Columbia.

The Performing Arts Center houses a wide range of facilities, including the 117-seat Workshop Theatre and the 400-seat Reisinger Concert Hall.

SHENANDOAH UNIVERSITY

Shenandoah Conservatory

Programs of Study Shenandoah Conservatory offers intense, specialized, professional training in music, theater, and dance. Students work with a faculty of active professionals as they develop artistically and intellectually for careers in the performing arts.

Master's degrees include the Master of Music Education, the Master of Music in church music (with sequences in organ, voice, and conducting), the Master of Music in composition, the Master of Music in conducting, the Master of Music in dance accompanying, the Master of Music in pedagogy, the Master of Music in performance, the Master of Music in collaborative piano, the Master of Music Therapy, the Master of Science in arts administration, the Master of Science in dance with initial teacher licensure, and the Master of Science in music with initial teacher licensure (choral or instrumental).

Doctoral degrees include the Doctor of Musical Arts in music education, the Doctor of Musical Arts in pedagogy, and the Doctor of Musical Arts in performance.

Certificates are available in church music and music therapy, and the Artist Diploma is offered as a post-master's certificate. More information about each program can be found online or obtained by contacting the Conservatory.

Research Facilities The Shenandoah Conservatory comprises state-of-the-art facilities that were completed in 1998. These include the $18-million Ohrstrom-Bryant Theatre, the Glaize Studio Theater, and Ruebush Hall, which houses faculty members' studios, practice and rehearsal rooms, scene and costume shops, and a $1.5-million recording studio. Other conservatory resources on campus are the Goodson Recital Hall, the Armstrong Hall, the Armstrong Concert Hall, and the Smith Library's music collection, which includes more than 10,000 recordings and 15,000 scores.

Financial Aid Shenandoah University is proud to offer a wide variety of scholarships and assistantships. Shenandoah also participates in all federal grant and loan programs through the Free Application for Federal Student Aid (FAFSA). Shenandoah University offers institutional grants to help students with need greater than all other resources, such as the federal awards. The Commonwealth of Virginia awards non-need-based tuition grants, referred to as the Virginia Tuition Assistance Grants (VTAG), for residents of Virginia who attend private colleges in Virginia on a full-time basis.

Cost of Study In 2008–09, tuition is $670 per credit. Fees are additional.

Living and Housing Costs Room and board costs range from $3715 to $4175 per term, depending on the meal plan chosen. Off-campus housing is also available.

Student Group The University attracts students from throughout the region and around the globe. Total enrollment is approximately 3,400 students. Of these, 57 percent are from Virginia; the remaining students represent forty-five states and forty-one countries. Forty-five percent of the students are men. The Conservatory enrolls approximately 700 students, with 500 in full-time status and 200 in part-time status.

Location The Shenandoah campus is located 72 miles west of Washington, D.C., in the historic Shenandoah Valley of Virginia. The University is on the southeast edge of the city of Winchester, Virginia. Winchester–Frederick County, rich in history, is a vigorous community of approximately 70,000 people. Shenandoah's students have the distinct advantage of being on a small campus near large metropolitan cultural centers.

The University Shenandoah University, established in 1875, is a comprehensive Level V private university. The University offers more than sixty programs of study at the undergraduate, master's, doctoral, and professional levels at the main campus in Winchester, the Health Professions Building on the campus of the Winchester Medical Center, and the Northern Virginia Campus in Leesburg. There are 116 full-time and 114 part-time faculty members. Sixty-four of Shenandoah Conservatory's full-time faculty members hold the terminal degree in their fields. The student-faculty ratio is 10:1.

Applying Students must submit the completed application, the $30 application fee, and official transcripts. All applicants, except those for the music education program, must complete a live audition. On-campus auditions are scheduled throughout the fall and spring. Regional auditions are held in selected cities in the eastern United States in January and February. Videotaped auditions are permitted in special circumstances. Applications are processed on a rolling basis, but students accepted before March 1 have better opportunities for scholarships and financial aid.

Correspondence and Information

Office of Admissions
Shenandoah University
1460 University Avenue
Winchester, Virginia 22601
Phone: 540-665-4600
Fax: 540-665-4627
E-mail: admit@su.edu
Web site: http://www.su.edu/conservatory/index.cfm

Shenandoah University

THE FACULTY

Jennifer F. Adams, Associate Professor of Theatre/Costuming; M.F.A., Illinois.
Charlotte Nelson Aiosa, Professor of Music; D.M.A., Michigan.
Thomas Albert, Professor of Music; D.M.A., Illinois.
Alan Arnett, Assistant Professor and Christina Halpin Endowed Chair of Dance; M.F.A., SMU.
Frances Lapp Averitt, Professor of Music; D.M., Florida State.
William E. Averitt, Professor of Music; D.M., Florida State.
Barbara Boddé Bauer, Adjunct Assistant Professor of Theatre; M.F.A., South Carolina.
Donald B. Black, Professor of Music; M.F.A., Ohio.
Elizabeth Blakeslee, Adjunct Assistant Professor of Music; M.M., Virginia Commonwealth.
Sue M. Boyd, Professor of Music; D.M.A., Catholic University.
William McConnell Bozman, Professor of Theatre; M.F.A., Wayne State.
Michael Bunn, Adjunct Associate Professor of Music; M.M., Johns Hopkins (Peabody).
Elizabeth Caluda, Professor of Music; D.M.A., Catholic University.
Glenn Caluda, Professor of Music; Ph.D., LSU.
Todd Campbell, Assistant Professor of Music; M.M., West Virginia.
Ting-Yu Chen, Assistant Professor of Dance; M.F.A., Ohio State.
Warren C. Coker, Adjunct Instructor of Music; B.M., North Carolina at Greensboro.
Charlotte A. Collins, Professor of Music and Dean of Shenandoah Conservatory; Ed.D., Michigan.
Irma Collins, Adjunct Professor of Music; D.M.A., Temple.
Judy Connelly, Adjunct Assistant Professor of Music; M.M., West Virginia.
Steven L. Cooksey, Professor of Music; Ph.D., Washington (St. Louis).
Shan Dai, Adjunct Assistant Professor of Dance; B.A., Beijing Dance College (China).
Michael DeLalla, Adjunct Assistant Professor of Music; M.M.E., Shenandoah.
Constance DeVereaux, Associate Professor of Arts Administration; Ph.D., Claremont.
James T. Dickey III, Adjunct Associate Professor of Music; M.M., Johns Hopkins (Peabody).
Lee Ann Dranesfield, Adjunct Assistant Professor of Music; M.M., Oregon.
Karen Follett, Lecturer of Music; M.M., Shenandoah.
Michael Forest, Associate Professor of Music; M.M.E., Shenandoah.
Craig Fraedrich, Adjunct Associate Professor of Music; M.M., Arizona State.
Wade Fransen, Assistant Professor of Theatre; Ph.D., Texas Tech.
Kimberly Gibilisco, Assistant Professor of Dance; M.A., NYU.
RT Good III, Associate Professor of Arts Management and Dean of the School of Continuing Education; Ed.D., Nova Southeastern.
Jereme S. Goshorn, Adjunct Instructor of Dance.
Jennifer Green, Instructor of Arts; B.A., Mary Washington.
Kathryn Green, Associate Professor of Music; D.M.A., Cincinnati.
Donna Gullstrand, Professor of Music; M.M., Illinois at Urbana-Champaign.
Erica Helm, Associate Professor of Dance; M.F.A., SMU.
Lori Horne, Adjunct Assistant Professor of Music; M.M., Shenandoah.
William J. Ingham, Assistant Professor of Theatre; M.F.A., Florida State.
Byron Jones, Adjunct Assistant Professor of Music; M.A., Massachusetts; M.M., Maryland.
Karen Keating, Associate Professor of Music/Theory; D.M.A., Shenandoah.
Wayne N. Kemp, Adjunct Associate Professor of Music; D.M.A., Catholic University.
C. Bryan Kidd, Adjunct Associate Professor of Music; B.M.E., Shenandoah.
David B. Langan, Adjunct Associate Professor of Music; M.M., Indiana.
Robert Larson, Assistant Professor of Music and Harrison Chair in Piano; M.A., Oregon.
James E. Latten, Adjunct Assistant Professor of Music; M.M.Ed., Indiana.
Doris Lederer, Adjunct Associate Professor of Music; Diploma, Curtis.
Anne Lipe, Adjunct Associate Professor of Music; Ph.D., Maryland.
Michael J. Maher, Adjunct Assistant Professor of Music; M.A., Rollins; M.M., Oberlin.
Jennifer Marlowe, Adjunct Assistant Professor of Music; M.M., M.M.Ed., Shenandoah.
Brian McCurdy, Adjunct Assistant Professor of Music; M.M., Maryland.
J. Thomas Mitts, Adjunct Associate Professor of Music; D.M.A., Iowa.
Kelly D. Moon, Adjunct Instructor of Dance; B.F.A., Shenandoah.
Medea Namoradze-Ruhadze, Associate Professor of Music; D.S.S., Tbilisi State Conservatory (Georgia).
Scott Nelson, Associate Professor of Music; D.M.A., Cincinnati.
Dudley Oakes, Adjunct Associate Professor of Music; D.M.A., Michigan.
Janette Ogg, Professor of Music; D.M., Florida State.
Golder O'Neill, Assistant Professor of Music; M.M.E., Shenandoah.
Sandor Ostlund, Associate Professor of Music; D.M.A., Rice.
William J. Pierson, Associate Professor of Theatre; M.F.A., Illinois State.
Susan M. Pike, Adjunct Instructor of Theatre; M.F.A., Catholic University.
Joel Puckett, Adjunct Assistant Professor of Music; B.S., Shenandoah.
Adrien Ré, Adjunct Assistant Professor of Music; D.M.A., Ball State.
Lisa Reagan, Adjunct Assistant Professor of Music; M.M., Maryland.
Carlos Dos Reis, Adjunct Instructor of Music; M.M., Shenandoah.
Susan Rider, Adjunct Associate Professor of Music; D.M., Indiana.
Michael J. Rohrbacher, Associate Professor of Music Therapy; Ph.D., Maryland.
Suzanne M. Rohrbacher, Assistant Professor of Music Therapy; M.M., Catholic University.
Charlene Romano, Adjunct Lecturer of Music; M.M., San Francisco State.
Jena Root, Assistant Professor of Music; Ph.D., Minnesota.
James Carlton Rowe, Adjunct Assistant Professor of Music; M.M., Catholic University.
LaVerne Sargent, Adjunct Assistant Professor of Music; M.S., Illinois; M.M., Shenandoah.
Philip Sargent, Associate Professor of Music; D.M.A., Illinois.
Daniel J. Schoemmel, Adjunct Assistant Professor of Music; M.M.E., Shenandoah.
Robyn Hart Schroth, Adjunct Assistant Professor of Dance; M.A., George Washington.
Robert Shafer, Professor of Music and Artist-in-Residence; M.M., Catholic University.
Clyde Thomas Shaw, Associate Professor of Music; M.M., SUNY at Binghamton.
Katerina Souvorova, Adjunct Assistant Professor of Music; M.M., Conservatory of Belarus.
John B. Spirtas, Adjunct Associate Professor of Music; M.M., New England Conservatory.
Aimé Sposato, Professor of Music; D.M.A., West Virginia.
Robert Strain, Adjunct Instructor of Music; M.M., Shenandoah.
Bard Suverkrop, Professor of Music; M.M., Cincinnati.
Elizabeth Temple, Professor of Music; M.M., West Virginia.
Kirsten Trump, Assistant Professor of Theatre; M.F.A., West Virginia.
Stafford Turner, Associate Professor of Music; D.M.A., Cincinnati.
James Vaughn, Adjunct Instructor of Music; B.M., Michigan.
Jan Wagner, Associate Professor of Music; Diploma and Korrepetitions Praxis, Academy of Music Hochschule (Austria).
Karen Walker, Associate Professor of Music; D.M.A., Catholic University.
Edrie Means Weekly, Adjunct Associate Professor of Music; M.M., Houston.
Wayne Wells, Assistant Professor of Music; M.M., Maryland.
Diana Fenni White, Adjunct Assistant Professor; M.M., Michigan.
Richard Whitehead, Adjunct Assistant Professor; B.A., Miami (Florida).
Cheryl N. Yancey, Associate Professor of Costume Design; M.F.A., George Washington.
Alphonso Young, Adjunct Assistant Professor; M.M., Miami (Florida).
David Zerull, Associate Professor of Music Education; M.M., Bowling Green State; Ph.D., Northwestern.
Antony Zwerdling, M.M., Boston University.

SOUTHERN ILLINOIS UNIVERSITY CARBONDALE

Department of Theater

Programs of Study

The Department of Theater at Southern Illinois University Carbondale (SIUC) blends scholarship and practice in an academically based theater experience. The Department offers an M.F.A. in Theater with concentrations in directing, playwriting, costume, lighting, scenic design, and technical direction. The interdisciplinary Ph.D. program, with emphasis on theater history or playwriting, is administered through the Department of Speech Communication. The doctoral program allows students to explore a broad range of course work in the theater/speech communication arts, including American theater history, theory and criticism, dramaturgy, playwriting, intercultural communication, and pedagogy. Methodology classes are drawn from departments across the campus. Classes are small, providing many opportunities to work closely with faculty on a one-to-one basis. Courses of study are tailor made for each student.

The Department maintains two theaters. The McLeod Theater, a proscenium stage seating 520, was recently renovated with new rigging, sound and lighting control, and inventories. The Christian H. Moe Laboratory Theater, a flexible studio space seating up to 110, was also recently renovated with new lighting and sound systems, risers, and seating. The academic season in both theaters is designed to highlight contemporary theater and original works as well as the major historical periods of theater. Musicals and operas are fully produced and orchestrated in conjunction with the School of Music. The professional summer stock company (McLeod Summer Playhouse) offers a variety of plays and musicals. All of these productions provide opportunities for hands-on experience in all graduate programs.

Members of the Department of Theater faculty embrace both the academic and professional theater communities, regularly writing, performing, directing, designing for professional regional theaters, publishing articles and books, and presenting papers at national and international conferences. The faculty are all members of their respective professional unions and associations. Faculty members actively prepare students for academic and professional careers through internships, conferences, and summer theater experiences.

Research Facilities

Southern Illinois University Carbondale offers outstanding research facilities. In addition to containing more than 2 million volumes, nearly 3 million microforms, and 12,000 current periodicals, Morris Library is also at the forefront of providing electronic access to information via its own network, the University's network, and the Internet. Multiple computer stations on each floor allow patrons to obtain information, often in full text, from local, state, national, and international sources. The library is a member of Illinet Online (IO), the statewide library automated catalog, circulation, and interlibrary loan system, and the national Online Computer Library Center (OCLC), the world's largest bibliographic network. Library holdings include a variety of special collections, including the papers of Mordecai Gorelik, John Howard Lawson, and others.

Financial Aid

Financial aid is available in many forms. The Department offers assistantships, fellowships, several scholarships, and a variety of work-study programs. Fellowships for promising minority students are available through the Proactive Recruitment of Multicultural Professionals for Tomorrow (PROMPT) Program, the Graduate Dean's Fellowship (GDF), the Illinois Minority Graduate Incentive Program (IMGIP), and the Illinois Consortium for Educational Opportunity Program (ICEOP). Assistantships and fellowships carry tuition scholarships. Student employment, loans, and other tuition scholarships are also available. About 70 percent of all graduate students receive some form of SIUC financial aid.

Cost of Study

In-state graduate tuition is $313.90 per credit hour in 2008–09. Out-of-state tuition is 2.5 times the in-state tuition rate ($784.75 per credit hour). Graduate students with at least a 25 percent appointment as a graduate assistant receive a tuition scholarship. Fees vary from $511.26 (1 credit hour) to $1416.05 (12 credit hours). Students with a graduate assistantship receive a 25 percent reduction in the Primary Care Medical Fee.

Living and Housing Costs

For married couples, students with families, and single graduate students, the University has 690 efficiency and one-, two-, three-, and four-bedroom apartments that rent for $484 to $686 per month in 2008–09. Residence halls for single graduate students are also available, as are accessible residence hall rooms and apartments for students with disabilities.

Student Group

The University's total enrollment exceeds 21,000, including more than 4,000 graduate students. Men and women come from all fifty states and more than 100 other countries. About 53 percent of the graduate students are women, 23 percent are international, and 13 percent are American minorities.

Location

SIUC is 350 miles south of Chicago and 100 miles southeast of St. Louis. Nestled in rolling hills bordered by the Ohio and Mississippi Rivers and enhanced by a mild climate, the area has state parks, national forests and wildlife refuges, and large lakes for outdoor recreation. Cultural offerings include theater, opera, concerts, art exhibits, and cinema. Educational facilities for the families of students are excellent.

The University and The Department

Southern Illinois University Carbondale is a comprehensive public university with a variety of general and professional education programs. The University offers associate, bachelor's, master's, and doctoral degrees and the J.D. and M.D. degrees. The University is fully accredited by the North Central Association of Colleges and Schools. The Graduate School has an essential role in the development and coordination of graduate instruction and research programs. The Graduate Council has academic responsibility for determining graduate standards, recommending new graduate programs and research centers, and establishing policies to facilitate the research effort. Southern Illinois University Carbondale is a state-funded university founded in 1869. The University is an accredited institutional member of the National Association of Schools of Theater.

Applying

Applications should be requested from the address given in the Correspondence and Information section. Each application must include a completed Departmental and Graduate School application form, three letters of recommendation, official transcripts from all colleges and universities previously attended, a personal statement of career goals, and GRE scores as well as a portfolio of theater work in the student's area of interest. The deadline for application is February 1 for the following fall. All materials should be sent directly to the Department of Theater.

Correspondence and Information

Dr. Ronald Naversen, Director of Graduate Studies
Department of Theater
Mail Code 6608
Southern Illinois University Carbondale
Carbondale, Illinois 62901

Phone: 618-453-5741
Fax: 618-453-7582
E-mail: rnav@siu.edu
Web site: http://www.siu.edu/~mcleod/

Southern Illinois University Carbondale

THE FACULTY AND THEIR RESEARCH

Susan Patrick Benson, Assistant Professor; M.F.A. (acting), Rutgers. Acting and voice.
Mary Bogumil, Associate Professor; Ph.D. (English), South Florida. Dramatic literature.
Anne Fletcher, Associate Professor; Ph.D. (theater history), Tufts. History and dramaturgy.
Robert Holcombe, Associate Professor and Technical Director; M.F.A. (technical direction), Ohio. Theater health and safety.
Tom Kidd, Assistant Professor; M.F.A. (directing), Southern Illinois Carbondale. Acting and voice.
Lori Merrill-Fink, Associate Professor and Director of the University Honors Program; M.F.A. (acting), Arizona. Movement and acting.
Ronald Naversen, Professor; M.F.A. (scenic design), Carnegie-Mellon; Ph.D. (theater history), Southern Illinois Carbondale. Scene design painting and properties.
Olusegun Ojewuyi, Assistant Professor; M.F.A. (directing), Yale. Acting and directing.
David Rush, Professor; Ph.D., Illinois. Playwriting and analysis.
Mark K. Varns, Associate Professor and Chair; M.F.A. (technical direction), Kansas. Lighting design and technical direction.
Kathryn Wagner, Associate Professor; M.F.A. (costume design), Rutgers. Costume design and technology.

STONY BROOK UNIVERSITY, STATE UNIVERSITY OF NEW YORK

Department of Music
Graduate Programs in Composition

Programs of Study

The Department of Music at Stony Brook offers M.A. and Ph.D. degrees in composition. Students in the M.A. in composition program take a series of core courses in their discipline, including work in analysis—analysis of twentieth-century music or an advanced course in twentieth-century theory or analysis, such as topics in theory or topics in analysis. The first year often involves one or two semesters of intensive ear-training in foundations of musicianship and/or graduate musicianship. In addition to regular composition lessons (advanced composition), composers often take an intensive review of tonal harmony and counterpoint and an introduction to electronic music. Other electives often taken are a workshop in instrumentation and orchestration, introduction to computer music, and advanced projects in computer music. In the second year of the master's program, composers develop a portfolio to be reviewed by the composition faculty and take comprehensive examinations in musical analysis, which are written essays on two assigned compositions, one tonal and the other post-tonal.

Students admitted at the M.A. level are provisionally admitted to the Ph.D. program; they usually spend two years at the master's level, although it is possible to advance faster. The end of master's-level work is an "articulation point." Students continue into the Ph.D. program if all master's-level work is satisfactorily completed, and upon recommendation of the faculty.

In the first year of study, Ph.D. students are assigned a directing committee of 3 to 4 faculty members, with whom they create their own curriculum by drawing up a doctoral contract. The contract lists courses to be taken and projected work and includes a number of compositions demonstrating fluency in working with a variety of contemporary performance media. The contract also requires foreign language competence (a reading knowledge of French, German, Italian, or Spanish) and the presentation of a public colloquium on a topic of significant interest in twentieth- or twenty-first-century music. Students who did not complete their master's degree at Stony Brook must also take the comprehensive exam in analysis required of master's students. Prior to advancing to candidacy (normally after three years), students must submit a prospectus outlining the nature and aims of the dissertation (an extended composition for composers) and pass a preliminary examination that demonstrates preparation in the area of the dissertation composition. Students who successfully complete the Ph.D. in composition are well qualified to teach composition or related subjects at the college level, or to pursue a career as a freelance composer.

Research Facilities

The Department of Music has fully equipped electronic (analog) and computer (digital) music studios. There is an e-media digital arts site in the Music Building, which is shared by music, theater arts, and art students and a Laboratory for Technology in the Arts, which is an interdisciplinary studio for music, art, and theater arts housed in the Theater Arts Department. In addition, student composers have the opportunity to have their compositions performed by advanced instrumental and vocal students in the M.M. and D.M.A. programs. The music library contains an extensive research collection of books, periodicals, scores, microfilms, and recordings and includes an excellent listening facility.

Financial Aid

The Department of Music offers competitively based tuition scholarships with traineeship or free-standing tuition scholarships without traineeship. Full-time Graduate School traineeships (teaching assistantships, graduate assistantships) are $12,664 per year, three-quarter-time are $9498 per year, and half-time are $6332 per year. Graduate Council Fellowships are restricted to U.S. citizens and permanent residents and carry a stipend of $15,630 plus a full tuition scholarship; ten are awarded campuswide each year. W. Burghardt Turner Fellowships carry a stipend of $10,000 plus a full-tuition scholarship; twenty are awarded campuswide each year to U.S. citizens or permanent residents who are Native American, African American, or Hispanic American. Federal and state aid includes Veterans Administration educational benefits, Federal Work-Study, subsidized and unsubsidized Federal Stafford Student Loans, Federal Perkins Loans, and Tuition Assistance Program (TAP).

Cost of Study

In 2008–09, full-time tuition at 12 credits for entering in-state residents is $3450 per semester, while out-of-state residents and international students pay $5460. Doctoral students who have already earned a master's degree take 9 credits per semester; for them the tuition was $2592 per semester for in-state residents and $4095 per semester for out-of-state and international students. Additional fees for each semester, including (but not limited to) the infirmary, activity, technology, and transportation fees, total about $875. International students also pay a service fee of approximately $35 per semester and an orientation fee of $50. Fees for the mandatory Student Health Insurance Plan vary depending on citizenship and employment status.

Living and Housing Costs

For 2008–09, Stony Brook calculates the cost of education excluding tuition, fees, and insurance at $14,228 per year. On-campus apartments range in cost from approximately $336 per month to approximately $1456 per month, depending on the size of the unit and the number of students sharing the space. Off-campus housing options include rooms, houses, and apartments that can be rented from approximately $350 to $2500 per month. Costs including books, food, and transportation may vary depending on academic program and/or personal circumstances.

Student Group

There are 25 students in the M.A. and Ph.D. programs in composition. Of these, 18 are men and 7 are women; 6 are international students. The composition faculty members look for evidence of creativity and originality as demonstrated in scores and tapes or recordings submitted by applicants to the M.A. and Ph.D. programs. The entire composition faculty reviews and evaluates these materials.

Student Outcomes

Oded Zehavi and Isabel Soveral, both of whom received their Ph.D.'s in composition in 1994, are now Chair of the Composition Department at Haifa University in Israel and Chair of the Department of Music at the University of Aveiro in Portugal, respectively. Gregory Glancey (Ph.D. composition) is Assistant Professor of Music and Assistant Chair of the music department at Vanguard University of Southern California. Other recent graduates hold faculty positions at American universities, including the University of Wisconsin–Madison and Pomona College.

Location

The University is located on the North Shore of Long Island, about 60 miles east of New York City. The campus is nestled amid fields and woodlands, with Long Island Sound just minutes to the north and the Atlantic Ocean a 45-minute drive to the south. The Long Island Railroad connects New York City with the Stony Brook campus. Three major highways lead to New York City, and bus service is available on campus and to various points on Long Island. Other transportation options include ferry, airplane, taxi, and limousine.

The University and The Department

Established in 1957 as part of the State University of New York system, Stony Brook is now recognized as one of the nation's finest public universities. Stony Brook is classified as Research University (very high research activity) by the Carnegie Foundation. This distinction, granted to fewer than 2 percent of all colleges and universities nationwide, reflects Stony Brook's high volume of federally sponsored research, high percentage of doctoral students, and emphasis on scholarship. A study published by Johns Hopkins University Press placed Stony Brook among the top three public research universities in the country—second only to the University of California at Berkeley and tied for second with the University of California, Santa Barbara—in research per faculty member.

Stony Brook's music programs have grown out of an unusual partnership between the academy and the conservatory and are designed to favor interaction among musical disciplines that have traditionally been kept separate. The Department believes that a sound education for any musician must involve a solid theoretical grasp of musical structure, an understanding of the historical and cultural forces that shape music, and practical experience with music making on a professional level. The program in composition is enriched by daily contact with students and faculty members in the performance programs. Interdisciplinary studies are central to the educational philosophy of the Department. A number of courses are team-taught by 2 or more faculty members, examining topics from several disciplinary viewpoints. The Department frequently offers courses in collaboration with the Departments of Philosophy, Comparative Studies, Theatre Arts, and Art, as well as the programs in cultural studies and women's studies and in Stony Brook's Humanities Institute.

Applying

Admission and financial aid applications should be filed by January 15 for fall admission. Applications should be completed online. This can be done at the Graduate School's Web site at http://www.grad.sunysb.edu. Admissions and support decisions are made during the first week in March, and applicants receive notification no later than March 15. April 15 is the deadline to respond to offers of admission and support.

Correspondence and Information

Judith Lochhead, Graduate Program Director
Department of Music
Staller Center 3307
Stony Brook University, State University of New York
Stony Brook, New York 11794-5475
Phone: 631-632-7330
E-mail: judith.lochhead@stonybrook.edu

Josephine Goykin, Graduate Program Coordinator
Department of Music
Staller Center 3304
Stony Brook University, State University of New York
Stony Brook, New York 11794-5475
Phone: 631-632-7330
Web site: http://www.stonybrook.edu/music

Stony Brook University, State University of New York

THE FACULTY AND THEIR RESEARCH

Perry Goldstein, Associate Professor and Undergraduate Director; Ph.D., Columbia, 1986. Composition, coordinator of musicianship.
Daria Semegen, Associate Professor and Director of the Electronic Music Studio; M.M., Yale, 1971. Composition, electronic music, composition, history, aesthetics of electronic music.
Sheila Silver, Professor; Ph.D., Brandeis, 1976. Composition, analysis, instrumentation and orchestration.
Daniel Weymouth, Associate Professor, Department Chair, Director of the Computer Music Studio, and Co-Director, Laboratory for Technology in the Arts; Ph.D., Berkeley, 1992. Composition, analysis, computer music, multimedia and performance technologies.
Peter Winkler, Professor; M.F.A., Princeton, 1967. Composition, history and theory of popular music.

STONY BROOK UNIVERSITY, STATE UNIVERSITY OF NEW YORK

Department of Music
Ethnomusicology Program

Programs of Study

In 2005, the Department of Music at Stony Brook University inaugurated a graduate program in ethnomusicology, offering studies at the master's and doctoral levels. Ethnomusicology as a field examines practices of music making worldwide, in various settings and at all social levels. Its methodology combines critical and analytical perspectives with ethnographic inquiry in the form of field research. In their analyses, ethnomusicologists emphasize both the particularities of music sound and the specific historical and social contexts in which music making takes place. At Stony Brook, the graduate curriculum in ethnomusicology balances course work in specific musical genres and world areas with intensive theoretical and methodological training. Students work closely with faculty members within a system that emphasizes individual mentoring and rounded professional training at all stages of graduate study. The ethnomusicology faculty members look for evidence of original thought, competence in history and theory, and writing skill, as demonstrated in essays submitted by applicants. The entire musicology faculty reviews and evaluates these materials.

Students in the Master of Arts in ethnomusicology program combine elective courses with core courses in ethnomusicology. At the doctoral level, each student devises a unique program of study in consultation with a directing committee, whose members help to oversee the student's progress toward completion of degree requirements. Because of the interdisciplinary character of the field, students are encouraged to take courses in fields such as anthropology, sociology, history, cultural studies, philosophy, or women's studies. In addition to their degree in ethnomusicology, students may choose to earn an advanced certificate in cultural studies, women's studies, or philosophy. The first year often involves one or two semesters of intensive ear training in foundations of musicianship and/or graduate musicianship. In the second year of the master's program, students write a short thesis and take comprehensive examinations in history (written) and musical analysis (an oral exam on two assigned compositions, one tonal and the other posttonal). Students admitted at the M.A. level are provisionally admitted to the Ph.D. program; they usually spend two years at the master's level, although it is possible to advance faster. The end of master's-level work is an "articulation point." Students continue into the Ph.D. program if all master's-level work is satisfactorily completed and upon recommendation of the faculty.

In their first year of study, Ph.D. students are assigned a directing committee of 3 to 4 faculty members, with whom they create their own curriculum by drawing up a doctoral contract. The contract lists courses to be taken and projected work (a number of essays demonstrating proficiency in various aspects of ethnomusicological research, analysis, or criticism). The essays normally grow out of course work in particular seminars. The contract also requires a reading knowledge of two languages—one major European language other than English and another relevant to the student's research—and the presentation of a public lecture or colloquium on a topic determined by the student in consultation with their directing committee. Students who did not complete their master's degree at Stony Brook must also take the comprehensive exams required of master's studies. Prior to advancing to candidacy (normally after three years in the program), ethnomusicology candidates take an exam in their field of interest and present a prospectus for their dissertation. Students who successfully complete the Ph.D. program in ethnomusicology are well prepared to assume teaching positions in colleges or universities and are able to teach a variety of nonmajor, major, and graduate courses in ethnomusicology.

Research Facilities

The music library contains an extensive research collection of books, periodicals, scores, microfilms, and recordings and includes an excellent listening facility. Other resources open to students are the Stony Brook Humanities Institute and the programs in cultural studies and women's studies.

Financial Aid

The Department offers competitively based tuition scholarships in conjunction with traineeships and free-standing tuition scholarships without traineeships. Full-time Graduate School traineeships (teaching and graduate assistantships) are $12,664 per year, three-quarter-time are $9498 per year, and half-time are $6334 per year. Graduate Council Fellowships are restricted to U.S. citizens and permanent residents and carry a stipend of $15,630 plus a full-tuition scholarship; ten are awarded campuswide each year. W. Burghardt Turner Fellowships carry a stipend of $10,000 plus a full-tuition scholarship; twenty are awarded campuswide each year to U.S. citizens or permanent residents who are Native American, African American, or Hispanic American. Federal and state aid includes Veteran Administration educational benefits, Federal Work-Study, subsidized and unsubsidized Federal Stafford Student Loans, Federal Perkins Loans, and the Tuition Assistance Program (TAP).

Cost of Study

In 2008–09, full-time tuition at 12 credits for entering in-state residents is $3450 per semester, while out-of-state residents and international students pay $5460. Doctoral students who have already earned a master's degree take 9 credits per semester; for them the tuition was $2592 per semester for in-state residents and $4095 per semester for out-of-state and international students. Additional fees for each semester, including (but not limited to) the infirmary, activity, technology, and transportation fees, total about $875. International students also pay a service fee of approximately $35 per semester and an orientation fee of $50. Fees for the mandatory Student Health Insurance Plan vary depending on citizenship and employment status.

Living and Housing Costs

For 2008–09, Stony Brook calculates the cost of education excluding tuition, fees, and insurance at $14,228 per year. On-campus apartments range in cost from approximately $336 per month to approximately $1456 per month, depending on the size of the unit and the number of students sharing the space. Off-campus housing options include rooms, houses, and apartments that can be rented from approximately $350 to $2500 per month. Costs including books, food, and transportation may vary depending on academic program and/or personal circumstances.

Student Group

As this is a new program, the M.A. and Ph.D. programs in ethnomusicology currently have 3 students: 1 man and 2 women.

Location

The University is located on the North Shore of Long Island, about 60 miles east of New York City. The campus is nestled amid fields and woodlands, with Long Island Sound just minutes to the north and the Atlantic Ocean a 45-minute drive to the south. The Long Island Railroad connects New York City with the Stony Brook campus. Three major highways lead to New York City, and bus service is available on campus and to various points on Long Island. Other transportation options include ferry, airplane, taxi, and limousine.

The University and The Department

Established in 1957 as part of the State University of New York system, Stony Brook is now recognized as one of the nation's finest public universities. Stony Brook is classified as Research University (very high research activity) by the Carnegie Foundation. This distinction, granted to fewer than 2 percent of all colleges and universities nationwide, reflects Stony Brook's high volume of federally sponsored research, high percentage of doctoral students, and emphasis on scholarship. A 1997 study published by Johns Hopkins University Press placed Stony Brook among the top three public research universities in the country—second only to the University of California at Berkeley and tied for second with the University of California, Santa Barbara—in research per faculty member. Stony Brook's music programs have grown out of an unusual partnership between the academy and the conservatory. Degree programs are designed to favor interaction among musical disciplines that have traditionally been kept separate. The Department believes that a sound education for any musician must involve a solid theoretical grasp of musical structure, an understanding of the historical and cultural forces that shape music, and practical experience with music making on a professional level. The program in history/theory is enriched by daily contact with students and faculty members in the performance programs. Interdisciplinary studies are central to the educational philosophy of the Department. A number of courses are team-taught by 2 or more faculty members, examining topics from several disciplinary viewpoints. The Department frequently offers courses in collaboration with the Departments of Philosophy, Comparative Studies, Theatre Arts, and Art, as well as the programs in cultural studies and women's studies and in Stony Brook's Humanities Institute.

Applying

Admission and financial aid applications should be filed by January 15 for fall admission. Applications should be completed online. This can be done at the Graduate School's Web site at http://www.grad.sunysb.edu. Admissions and support decisions are made during the first week in March, and applicants receive notification no later than March 15. April 15 is the deadline to respond to offers of admission and support.

Correspondence and Information

Judith Lochhead, Graduate Program Director
Department of Music
Staller Center 3307
Stony Brook University, State University of New York
Stony Brook, New York 11794-5475
Phone: 631-632-7330
E-mail: judith.lochhead@stonybrook.edu

Josephine Goykin, Graduate Program Coordinator
Department of Music
Staller Center 3304
Stony Brook University, State University of New York
Stony Brook, New York 11794-5475
Phone: 631-632-7330
Web site: http://www.stonybrook.edu/music

Stony Brook University, State University of New York

THE FACULTY AND THEIR RESEARCH

Sarah Fuller, Professor; Ph.D., Berkeley, 1969. Medieval and Renaissance music, history of music theory.
David Lawton, Professor; Ph.D., Berkeley, 1973. Opera workshop, nineteenth-century opera.
Judith Lochhead, Professor; Ph.D., SUNY at Stony Brook, 1982. Theory and history of recent music, phenomenology and music, performance and analysis.
Ryan Minor, Assistant Professor; Ph.D., Chicago, 2005. Nineteenth-century music history, music and nationalism.
Frederick Moehn, Assistant Professor; Ph.D., NYU, 2001. Ethnomusicology, Brazilian music, popular music and jazz.
Benjamin Steege, Assistant Professor; Ph.D., Harvard, 2007. Early twentieth-century history and theory, music and technology, music theory.
Jane Sugarman, Associate Professor; Ph.D., UCLA, 1993. Ethnomusicology, music of southeastern Europe and the Middle East, gender studies.
Peter Winkler, Professor; M.F.A., Princeton, 1967. Composition, American popular music, folk music, jazz.

STONY BROOK UNIVERSITY, STATE UNIVERSITY OF NEW YORK

Department of Music
Music History / Theory Program

Programs of Study

The Department of Music at Stony Brook offers M.A. and Ph.D. degrees in music history/theory. Students in the Master of Arts in history/theory program take a series of core courses in their discipline, including work in theory, analysis, and history. The first year often involves one or two semesters of intensive ear-training in foundations of musicianship and/or graduate musicianship. Historians also take an introduction to music research during the first semester of study. In the second year of the master's program, historians write a short thesis and take comprehensive examinations in history (written) and musical analysis (an oral on two assigned compositions, one tonal and the other post-tonal).

Students admitted at the M.A. level are provisionally admitted to the Ph.D. program; they usually spend two years at the master's level, although it is possible to advance faster. The end of master's-level work is an "articulation point." Students continue into the Ph.D. program if all master's-level work is satisfactorily completed and upon recommendation of the faculty.

In their first year of study, Ph.D. students are assigned a directing committee of 3 to 4 faculty members, with whom they create their own curriculum by drawing up a doctoral contract. The contract lists courses to be taken and projected work (a number of essays demonstrating proficiency in various aspects of musicological research, analysis, or criticism). The essays normally grow out of course work in particular seminars. The contract also requires a reading knowledge of German and French and the presentation of a public lecture or colloquium on a topic determined by the student in consultation with their directing committee. Students who did not complete their master's degree at Stony Brook must also take the comprehensive exams required of master's studies. Prior to advancing to candidacy (normally after three years in the program), history/theory candidates take an exam in their field of interest and present a prospectus for their dissertation. Students who successfully complete the Ph.D. program in the history and theory of music are well prepared to assume teaching positions in colleges or universities and are able to teach a variety of nonmajor, major, and graduate courses in music history and/or theory.

Research Facilities

The music library contains an extensive research collection of books, periodicals, scores, microfilms, and recordings and includes an excellent listening facility. Other resources open to history/theory students are the Stony Brook Humanities Institute and the programs in cultural studies and women's studies.

Financial Aid

The Department offers competitively based tuition scholarships with traineeship or free-standing tuition scholarships without traineeship.. Full-time Graduate School traineeships (teaching and graduate assistantships) are $12,664 per year, three-quarter-time are $9498 per year, and half-time are $6332 per year. Graduate Council Fellowships are restricted to U.S. citizens and permanent residents and carry a stipend of $15,630 plus a full tuition scholarship; ten are awarded campuswide each year. W. Burghardt Turner Fellowships carry a stipend of $10,000 plus a full-tuition scholarship; twenty are awarded campuswide each year to U.S. citizens or permanent residents who are Native American, African American, or Hispanic American. Federal and state aid includes Veterans Administration educational benefits, Federal Work-Study, subsidized and unsubsidized Federal Stafford Student Loans, Federal Perkins Loans, and Tuition Assistance Program (TAP).

Cost of Study

In 2008–09, full-time tuition at 12 credits for entering in-state residents is $3450 per semester, while out-of-state residents and international students pay $5460. Doctoral students who have already earned a master's degree take 9 credits per semester; for them the tuition was $2592 per semester for in-state residents and $4095 per semester for out-of-state and international students. Additional fees for each semester, including (but not limited to) the infirmary, activity, technology, and transportation fees, total about $875. International students also pay a service fee of approximately $35 per semester and an orientation fee of $50. Fees for the mandatory Student Health Insurance Plan vary depending on citizenship and employment status.

Living and Housing Costs

For 2008–09, Stony Brook calculates the cost of education excluding tuition, fees, and insurance at $14,228 per year. On-campus apartments range in cost from approximately $336 per month to approximately $1456 per month, depending on the size of the unit and the number of students sharing the space. Off-campus housing options include rooms, houses, and apartments that can be rented from approximately $350 to $2500 per month. Costs including books, food, and transportation may vary depending on academic program and/or personal circumstances.

Student Group

In the M.A. and Ph.D. programs in history/theory there are 17 students, 5 men, 12 women, and 5 international students. The music history faculty members look for evidence of original thought, competence in history and theory, and writing skill, as demonstrated in essays submitted by applicants. The entire history/theory faculty reviews and evaluates these materials.

Student Outcomes

Lisa Barg (Ph.D. in history/theory, 2001) is an Assistant Professor in the department of theory at McGill University; Theo Cateforis (Ph.D. 2000) is an Assistant Professor at Syracuse University. Jennifer Bain (Ph.D. in history/theory, 2001) is now an Assistant Professor at Dalhousie University in Halifax, Nova Scotia. Stephen Cahn and Stephen Meyer, both of whom received their Ph.D.'s in history/theory in 1996, are now faculty members at the University of Cincinnati and Syracuse University, respectively. Recent graduates have found faculty positions at American and international universities and colleges, including Handong University (Korea) and the University of Western Ontario.

Location

The University is located on the North Shore of Long Island, about 60 miles east of New York City. The campus is nestled amid fields and woodlands, with Long Island Sound just minutes to the north, and the Atlantic Ocean is a 45-minute drive to the south. The Long Island Railroad connects New York City with the Stony Brook campus. Three major highways lead to New York City, and bus service is available on campus and to various points on Long Island. Other transportation options include ferry, airplane, taxi, and limousine.

The University and The Department

Established in 1957 as part of the State University of New York system, Stony Brook is now recognized as one of the nation's finest public universities. Stony Brook is classified as Research University (very high research activity) by the Carnegie Foundation. This distinction, granted to fewer than 2 percent of all colleges and universities nationwide, reflects Stony Brook's high volume of federally sponsored research, high percentage of doctoral students, and emphasis on scholarship. A 1997 study published by Johns Hopkins University Press placed Stony Brook among the top three public research universities in the country—second only to the University of California at Berkeley and tied for second with the University of California, Santa Barbara—in research per faculty member.

Stony Brook's music programs have grown out of an unusual partnership between the academy and the conservatory and are designed to favor interaction among musical disciplines that have traditionally been kept separate. The Department believes that a sound education for any musician must involve a solid theoretical grasp of musical structure, an understanding of the historical and cultural forces that shape music, and practical experience with music making on a professional level. The program in composition is enriched by daily contact with students and faculty members in the performance programs. Interdisciplinary studies are central to the educational philosophy of the Department. A number of courses are team-taught by 2 or more faculty members, examining topics from several disciplinary viewpoints. The Department frequently offers courses in collaboration with the Departments of Philosophy, Comparative Studies, Theatre Arts, and Art, as well as the programs in cultural studies and women's studies and in Stony Brook's Humanities Institute.

Applying

Admission and financial aid applications should be filed by January 15 for fall admission. Applications should be completed online. This can be done at the Graduate School's Web site at http://www.grad.sunysb.edu. Admissions and support decisions are made during the first week in March, and applicants receive notification no later than March 15. April 15 is the deadline to respond to offers of admission and support.

Correspondence and Information

Judith Lochhead, Graduate Program Director
Department of Music
Staller Center 3307
Stony Brook University, State University of New York
Stony Brook, New York 11794-5475
Phone: 631-632-7330
E-mail: judith.lochhead@stonybrook.edu

Josephine Goykin, Graduate Program Coordinator
Department of Music
Staller Center 3304
Stony Brook University, State University of New York
Stony Brook, New York 11794-5475
Phone: 631-632-7330
Web site: http://www.stonybrook.edu/music

Stony Brook University, State University of New York

THE FACULTY AND THEIR RESEARCH

Sarah Fuller, Professor; Ph.D., Berkeley, 1969. Medieval and Renaissance music, history of music theory.

David Lawton, Professor; Ph.D., California, 1973. Opera workshop, nineteenth-century opera.

Judith Lochhead, Professor and Graduate Studies Director; Ph.D., SUNY at Stony Brook, 1982. Theory and history of recent music, phenomenology and music, performance and analysis.

Ryan Minor, Assistant Professor; Ph.D., Chicago, 2005. Nineteenth-century music history, music and nationalism.

Frederick Moehn, Assistant Professor; Ph.D., NYU, 2001. Ethnomusicology, Brazilian music, popular music and jazz.

Jane Sugarman, Associate Professor; Ph.D., UCLA, 1993. Ethnomusicology, musics of Southeastern Europe and the Middle East, gender studies.

Benjamin Steege, Assistant Professor; Ph.D., Harvard, 2007. Early twentieth-century history and theory, music and technology, music theory.

Peter Winkler, Professor; M.F.A., Princeton, 1967. Composition, history and theory of popular music.

STONY BROOK UNIVERSITY, STATE UNIVERSITY OF NEW YORK

Department of Music
Graduate Programs in Performance

Programs of Study

The Department of Music at Stony Brook University offers the Master of Music (M.M.) and Doctor of Musical Arts (D.M.A.) degrees in performance. Areas of performance represented are choral conducting, piano, voice, harpsichord, and guitar as well as the following orchestral instruments: flute, oboe, clarinet, bassoon, horn, trumpet, trombone, percussion, violin, viola, cello, and double bass. First-year M.M. students typically take one or two semesters of intensive ear-training. These students must also take one history course and one theory course for the degree; beyond that the focus of the program is on performance. Chamber music is required during the first two semesters of the program. Participation in the graduate orchestra is required of all orchestral musicians. Entering students in voice are expected to have a basic proficiency equivalent to one year each of college-level Italian, French, and German. A knowledge of French or German is required of harpsichord students. During the second year, M.M. students must pass a jury examination and present a public recital. All areas of study listed for the M.M. are also available to the D.M.A. in performance. D.M.A. students must have a master's degree either from Stony Brook or another institution. Under special circumstances, master's students may begin work on their doctoral degree before they have completed all master's requirements. Students admitted at the M.M. level are provisionally admitted to the D.M.A. program; they usually spend two years at the master's level, although it is possible to advance faster. The end of the master's-level work is an "articulation point." Students continue into the D.M.A. program if all master's-level work is satisfactorily completed and upon recommendation of the faculty.

In the first year of study, D.M.A. students create their own curriculum by drawing up a doctoral contract with a committee consisting of their major teacher and their academic adviser. The contract lists courses to be taken, projected topics for their doctoral research paper and lecture-recital, and a sketch of the repertoire for their four required contract recitals. The D.M.A. also has a foreign language requirement (the equivalent of one year of college-level study of French, German, or Italian for all instrumentalists except harpsichordists; this requirement can be satisfied either by taking and passing an exam given each fall or by taking a class). Students in harpsichord must demonstrate the equivalent of one year of college-level study in any two of the following languages: French, German, or Italian. Voice students must pass reading/translation examinations in any two of the following languages: French, German, Italian, or Russian. Many students study a language in their first year. In subsequent years, students complete the requirements of their contracts. As in the M.M. program, students are required to take chamber music during the first two semesters, and participation in graduate orchestra is required of all orchestral musicians. D.M.A. students can advance to candidacy (typically after two years in the program) after they have given three recitals, a lecture-recital, passed a preliminary jury, passed at least one language requirement, taken one history and one theory course, had the research paper from one of these courses approved after revision, and passed a doctoral jury examination. The fourth contract recital may be given after the student advances to doctoral candidacy. The last stage of the degree is a final doctoral recital and oral exam (an examination covering the contents of the recital by a special faculty committee). Students who successfully complete the D.M.A. degree are well-prepared to assume teaching and performing positions at colleges, universities, and conservatories, or to work as freelance musicians.

Research Facilities

Stony Brook's Staller Center for the Arts includes an acoustically excellent theater-concert hall (1,100 seats) and a more intimate recital hall (400 seats), both furnished with digital recording equipment. The music building contains a full range of rehearsal and teaching facilities, over seventy practice rooms and studios for graduate students, and more than forty Steinway grand pianos. The Department also has a collection of early instruments and organs, a virginal, a consort of viols, several Baroque string instruments and a collection of Baroque bows, as well as some Renaissance and Baroque wind instruments. The computer music studio is available for interactive work and also contains CD-burning equipment.

Financial Aid

The Department of Music offers competitively based tuition scholarships with traineeship or free-standing tuition scholarships without traineeship. Full-time Graduate School traineeships (teaching assistantships, graduate assistantships) are approximately $12,664 per year, three-quarter-time are $9498 per year, and half-time are $6332 per year. Graduate Council Fellowships are restricted to U.S. citizens and permanent residents and carry a stipend of $15,630 plus a full-tuition scholarship; ten are awarded campuswide each year. W. Burghardt Turner Fellowships carry a stipend of $10,000 plus a full-tuition scholarship; twenty are awarded campuswide each year to U.S. citizens or permanent residents who are Native American, African American, or Hispanic American. Federal and state aid includes Veterans Administration educational benefits, Federal Work-Study, subsidized and unsubsidized Federal Stafford Student Loans, Federal Perkins Loans, and Tuition Assistance Program (TAP), state-funded grants only available to U.S. citizens who are New York State residents.

The Graduate School maintains a database of external funding opportunities from private, public, and noninstitutional sources. Many foreign governments also offer scholarships for study in the U.S. The Department of Music also awards several fellowships or scholarships from its own funds, including the Sidney Gelber Fellowship, the Thomas G. Neumiller Scholarship (for voice students), and the Samuel Baron Prize, which is awarded every two years to an outstanding flutist or woodwind player.

Cost of Study

In 2008–09, full-time tuition at 12 credits for entering in-state residents is $3450 per semester, while out-of-state residents and international students pay $5460. Doctoral students who have already earned a master's degree take 9 credits per semester; for them the tuition was $2592 per semester for in-state residents and $4095 per semester for out-of-state and international students. Additional fees for each semester, including (but not limited to) the infirmary, activity, technology, and transportation fees, total about $875. International students also pay a service fee of approximately $35 per semester and an orientation fee of $50. Fees for the mandatory Student Health Insurance Plan vary depending on citizenship and employment status.

Living and Housing Costs

For 2008–09, Stony Brook calculates the cost of education excluding tuition, fees, and insurance at $14,228 per year. On-campus apartments range in cost from approximately $336 per month to approximately $1456 per month, depending on the size of the unit and the number of students sharing the space. Off-campus housing options include rooms, houses, and apartments that can be rented from approximately $350 to $2500 per month. Costs including books, food, and transportation may vary depending on academic program and/or personal circumstances.

Student Group

In the M.M. and D.M.A. programs in performance, 177 students are enrolled, of whom 69 are men, 108 are women, and 70 are international students. Performance faculty members evaluate applicants through a live audition, and generally, all faculty members in the area of the applicant's instrument hear the audition. Since the D.M.A. programs also have a significant academic component, the Graduate Studies Committee reviews every D.M.A. applicant's academic potential by evaluating their transcripts and sample essays.

Student Outcomes

Recent graduates have joined symphony orchestras, including the St. Louis Symphony Orchestra, the Netherlands Ballet Orchestra, the Brooklyn Philharmonic, Washington Symphony Orchestra, and the Grand Rapids Symphony. Others hold faculty positions at colleges, universities, or conservatories, including California State University, Sacramento; University of Michigan; the Escuela Superior de Musica in Naucalpan, Mexico; the College of St. Catherine in Montreal, Quebec; the Musikhochschule des Saarlandes in Saarbruecken, Germany; the New England Conservatory; and the University of Oklahoma.

Location

The University is located on the North Shore of Long Island, about 60 miles east of New York City. The campus is nestled amid fields and woodlands, with Long Island Sound just minutes to the north and the Atlantic Ocean a 45-minute drive to the south. The Long Island Railroad connects New York City with the Stony Brook campus. Other nearby transportation facilities include a ferry, airports, and highways and bus, taxi, and limousine service.

The University and The Department

Established in 1957 as part of the State University of New York system, Stony Brook is now recognized as one of the nation's finest public universities. Stony Brook is classified by the Carnegie Foundation as one of the Doctoral/Research Universities—Extensive. A 1997 study published by Johns Hopkins University Press placed Stony Brook among the top three public research universities in the country—second only to the University of California at Berkeley and tied for second with the University of California at Santa Barbara—in research per faculty member.

Stony Brook's music programs have grown out of an unusual partnership between the academy and the conservatory and are designed to favor interaction among musical disciplines that have traditionally been kept separate. The Department believes that a sound education for any musician must involve a solid theoretical grasp of musical structure, an understanding of the historical and cultural forces that shape music and practical experience with music making on a professional level. The Department frequently offers courses in collaboration with the Departments of Philosophy, Comparative Studies, Theatre Arts, and Art; the programs in cultural studies and women's studies; and Stony Brook's Humanities Institute.

Applying

Admission and financial aid applications should be filed by January 15 for fall admission. Applications should be completed online. This can be done at the Graduate School's Web site at http://www.grad.sunysb.edu. Admissions and support decisions are made during the first week in March, and applicants receive notification no later than March 15.

Correspondence and Information

Judith Lochhead, Graduate Program Director
Department of Music
Staller Center 3307
Stony Brook, New York 11794-5475
Phone: 631-632-7330
E-mail: judith.lochhead@stonybrook.edu

Josephine Goykin, Graduate Program Coordinator
Department of Music
Staller Center 3304
Stony Brook, New York 11794-5475
Phone: 631-632-7330
Web site: http://www.stonybrook.edu/music

Stony Brook University, State University of New York

THE FACULTY AND THEIR RESEARCH

Faculty members have studied under noted musicians such as James Chambers, Raphael Druian, Josef Gingold, Sophocles Papas, Oscar Shurnsky, and Forrest Standley. The Emerson String Quartet is Stony Brook's quartet-in-residence. Members include Philip Setzer and Eugene Drucker (violins), Lawrence Dutton (viola), and David Finckel (cello).

Ray Andersen, Professor of Jazz Studies.
Elaine Bonazzi, Performing Artist in Residence; B.M., Rochester (Eastman). Voice, vocal repertory.
Colin Carr, Professor; Diploma, Yehudi Menuhin School, 1974. Cello, cello repertory, chamber music.
Joseph Carver, Assistant Professor; D.M.A., SUNY at Stony Brook, 1992. Double bass, chamber music, orchestral repertory.
Kevin Cobb, Artist-in-Residence; M.M., Julliard, 1995. Trumpet, chamber music, brass ensemble repertory.
Christina Dahl, Assistant Professor; M.M., Peabody Conservatory, 1989. Piano, accompaniment, chamber music.
Susan Deaver, Director of the University Orchestra; D.M.A., Manhattan School of Music, 1994.
Larry Dutton, Performing Artist in Residence and Member of the Emerson String Quartet; M.M., Juilliard.
Bruce Engel, Director of the University Wind Ensemble; M.M., Juilliard, 1974. Conducting.
Pamela Frank, Performing Artist in Residence. Violin and chamber music.
Daniel Gilbert, Performing Artist in Residence; Professional Studies Certificate, Juilliard, 1989. Clarinet, chamber music, orchestral repertory.
Arthur Haas, Professor; M.A., UCLA, 1974. Harpsichord, performance of early music.
Gilbert Kalish, Professor; B.A., Columbia, 1956. Piano, chamber music, twentieth-century repertory for piano.
Eduardo Leandro, Performing Artist in Residence; M.M., Yale, 1999. Percussion.
Timothy Long, Assistant Professor; M.M., Rochester (Eastman). Vocal coach, conducting.
Frank Morelli, Performing Artist in Residence; D.M.A., Julliard, 1980. Bassoon and chamber music.
Timothy Mount, Professor and Director of Choral Music; D.M.A., USC, 1981. Choral conducting.
Katherine Murdock, Performing Artist in Residence; B.M., Boston University, 1977. Viola, chamber music.
Michael Powell, Performing Artist in Residence; B.Mus., Wichita State, 1973. Trombone, chamber music.
William Purvis, Performing Artist in Residence; B.A., Haverford, 1971. Pupil of Forrest Standley and James Chambers. Horn, chamber music.
Philip Setzer, Performing Artist in Residence and Member of the Emerson String Quartet. Pupil of Josef Gingold, Raphael Druian, and Oscar Shumsky. Violin, violin repertory, chamber music.
Stephen Taylor, Performing Artist in Residence. Diploma, Juilliard, 1974. Oboe, chamber music.
Chris Pedro Trakas, Performing Artist in Residence. Voice and opera studies.
Jerry Willard, Performing Artist in Residence. Pupil of Sophocles Papas. Guitar, lute.
Carol Wincenc, Performing Artist in Residence; M.M., Juilliard, 1972. Flute, chamber music.

STONY BROOK UNIVERSITY, STATE UNIVERSITY OF NEW YORK

Program in Theatre Arts

Programs of Study

The Department of Theatre Arts at Stony Brook University, State University of New York offers two graduate programs: a 30-credit Master of Arts (M.A.) degree in theater and a 60-credit Master of Fine Arts (M.F.A.) degree in dramaturgy. The goals of the M.A. program are to study the dramatic tradition and the history of the performing arts, to develop an understanding of the vital relationship between theater theory and onstage practice, and to prepare students to be qualified to matriculate in programs of study at the M.F.A. or Ph.D. level.

Founded in 1984, the small, rigorously selective, and intellectually challenging three-year professional M.F.A. program has been at the forefront of the study and practice of dramaturgy in America. Stony Brook seeks to find and nurture dramaturgical collaborators who are skilled in numerous practical sides of the theater. Student dramaturgs and faculty members work as colleagues in the heart of the production process—not as critics working from the outside. Dramaturgs at Stony Brook also act, write, produce, and stage plays in addition to the more traditional dramaturgy work. In this practical environment of "making theater" (dramatourgos, in Greek), students study production dramaturgy, marketing, performance, new play development, and every aspect of theater life.

Stony Brook University's graduate program in dramaturgy is the home of theatrical innovation for the twenty-first century. In this program, there is very little time to ponder the death of the theater when every moment is filled with the discovery, invention, and creation of new venues and theatrical opportunities. This is a place where artists can grow and learn to channel their own voices and nurture the voices of others in the spirit and practice of the collaborative arts.

Research Facilities

The Department of Theatre Arts is located in the Staller Center for the Arts, one of Suffolk County's premier cultural institutions. The department operates two large (180 seats each) and one small (sixty seats) black box theaters in the Staller Center. Additional theater spaces are also available on campus. The Stony Brook Cabaret is run by the graduate students in the Dramaturgy Program. Students may develop, devise, write, direct, or commission new and unusual work in this theatrical laboratory. Each year, four to eight productions are presented in spaces on and off campus. The department also has a Laboratory for Technology in the Arts and an electronic classroom.

Financial Aid

Full-time teaching and graduate assistantships carry stipends of $15,145 per year. Graduate Council Fellowships are restricted to U.S. citizens and permanent residents and carry a stipend of $15,975, plus a full tuition scholarship; ten are awarded campuswide each year. W. Burghardt Turner Fellowships carry a stipend of $17,572, plus a full-tuition scholarship; twenty are awarded each year to U.S. citizens or permanent residents who are Native American, African-American, or Hispanic American. Federal and state aid includes Veterans Administration educational benefits, Federal Work-Study, subsidized and unsubsidized Federal Stafford Student Loans, Federal Perkins Loans, and the Tuition Assistance Program (TAP).

Cost of Study

In 2008–09, full-time tuition at 12 credits for entering in-state residents is $3450 per semester, while out-of-state residents and international students pay $5460. Additional fees for each semester, including (but not limited to) the infirmary, activity, technology, and transportation fees, total about $875. International students also pay a service fee of approximately $35 per semester and an orientation fee of $50. Fees for the mandatory Student Health Insurance Plan vary depending on citizenship and employment status.

Living and Housing Costs

For 2008–09, Stony Brook calculates the cost of education excluding tuition, fees, and insurance at $14,228 per year. On-campus apartments range in cost from approximately $336 per month to approximately $1456 per month, depending on the size of the unit and the number of students sharing the space. Off-campus housing options include rooms, houses, and apartments that can be rented from approximately $350 to $2500 per month. Costs including books, food, and transportation may vary depending on academic program and/or personal circumstances.

Student Group

There are typically 15 to 20 graduate students in the program, most of whom are full-time students seeking the M.F.A. degree. About 70 percent of the students are women. While most come from the United States, there is a significant number of international students from such countries as Austria, Bosnia, Chile, Germany, Korea, the People's Republic of China, and Russia. The faculty looks for students who are intellectually and emotionally mature and who have a strong desire to engage in the practice of theater.

Student Outcomes

Dramaturgy at Stony Brook is a dynamic process that is different for each individual. Graduates have not only pursued careers as dramaturgs and literary managers, but also in other areas of the theater, the arts, and the media; many have also taken teaching positions at the university level. Professional dramaturgs often become directors, producers, administrators, drama critics, teachers, or playwrights, and many combine two or three different careers. For students with a wide range of interests in theater practice, the Stony Brook program offers numerous opportunities to pursue individual development within a professional orientation.

Location

The University is located on the North Shore of Long Island, about 60 miles east of New York City. The campus is nestled amid fields and woodlands, with Long Island Sound just minutes to the north, and the Atlantic Ocean is a 45-minute drive to the south. The Long Island Railroad connects New York City with the Stony Brook campus. Three major highways lead to New York City, and bus service is available on campus to various points on Long Island. Other transportation options include ferry, airplane, taxi, and limousine.

The University and The Department

Established in 1957 as part of the State University of New York system, Stony Brook is now recognized as one of the nation's finest public universities. Stony Brook is classified by the Carnegie Foundation as one of the Doctoral/Research Universities–Extensive. This distinction, granted to fewer than 2 percent of all colleges and universities nationwide, reflects Stony Brook's high volume of federally sponsored research, its high percentage of doctoral students, and its emphasis on scholarship. A 1997 study published by the Johns Hopkins University Press placed Stony Brook among the top three public research universities in the country—second only to the University of California, Berkeley and tied for second with the University of California, Santa Barbara—in research per faculty member.

Graduate study in this department is unique in a number of ways. First, the programs incorporate multicultural study, including both eastern and western drama and theater. Second, the program puts practical theater work and the production process at the center of the curriculum, offering graduate students numerous opportunities to produce their work in actual theater productions. Third, the program reflects the interdisciplinary nature of the theater arts. Among the faculty members are practicing directors, designers, actors, playwrights, and dramaturgs, all of whom work closely with graduate students. Finally, there is a strong emphasis placed on new technologies and interactive media studies.

Applying

Admission and financial aid applications should be filed by January 15 for fall admission. Application materials are available from the Web site at http://www.grad.sunysb.edu. Admissions and support decisions are made during the first week in March, and applicants receive notification no later than March 15. April 15 is the deadline to respond to offers of admission and support. Interested students should request information and application forms as early as possible, especially if they plan to apply for financial aid.

Correspondence and Information

Steve Marsh, Director of Graduate Studies
Department of Theatre Arts
Stony Brook University, State University of New York
Stony Brook, New York 11794-5450

Phone: 631-632-7300
Fax: 631-632-7258
E-mail: Steve.Marsh@stonybrook.edu
Web site: http://ws.cc.sunysb.edu/theatrearts/

Stony Brook University, State University of New York

THE FACULTY AND THEIR RESEARCH

Philip Baldwin, Associate Professor; M.F.A., Yale, 1987. Scene design, interactive media, cultural studies.
David Barnett, Technical Director and Instructor; B.A., Stony Brook, SUNY, 1985.
Joe Jeffreys, Adjunct Professor; Ph.D., NYU, 1996. Theater history and criticism.
Maxine Kern, Adjunct Professor; M.A ., Washington (Seattle); M.F.A., Massachusetts Amherst. American theater history.
Theresa Kim, Associate Professor Emeritus; Ph.D., NYU, 1988. Asian history, acting, Eastern styles.
Valeri Lantz-Gefroh, Head of Acting Program; M.F.A., Stony Brook, SUNY, 2003. Acting, directing.
John Lutterbie, Associate Professor and Associate Director of the Humanities Institute; Ph.D., Washington (Seattle), 1983. Theater history, performance theory and criticism, dramaturgy, directing.
Nick Mangano, Professor and Chair; M.F.A., Columbia. Directing.
Steve Marsh, Director of Graduate Studies and Literary Manager; M.F.A., Stony Brook, SUNY, 1999. Literary management, dramaturgy, acting.
Deborah Mayo, Associate Professor; M.F.A., Yale, 1973. Acting.
Peggy Morin, Lecturer; M.F.A., Stony Brook, SUNY, 1999; J.D. California, Hastings. Costume design.
Norman L. Prusslin, Adjunct Professor and WUSB Director; B.A., Stony Brook, SUNY, 1973. Broadcast management.
Amy Sullivan, Associate Professor; M.F.A., North Carolina at Greensboro, 1980. Dance, with emphasis on performance and choreography.
Michael X. Zelenak, Associate Professor; D.F.A., Yale, 1990. Dramaturgy, criticism, and theater history.

UNIVERSITY OF DELAWARE

Department of Theatre
Professional Theatre Training Program

Program of Study

The Department of Theatre offers graduate study leading to a Master of Fine Arts degree with concentrations in acting, technical production, and stage management. The Professional Theatre Training Program (PTTP) involves intensive studio work designed to prepare students for creative careers in the professional theater and thereby contribute to its growth and improve its quality.

Once every four years, a group of exceptionally talented students is selected for admission to the Professional Theatre Training Program. Each student in the PTTP participates in an intense curriculum in one of the three concentrations for three years. Each curriculum is skill oriented and is carefully designed to provide the skills, abilities, and experiences necessary to begin a successful career in theater. Students work exclusively within their area in an intensive program of studio classes and production experiences and continue working with one another throughout the three years of training. Because there is only one class enrolled at a time, the faculty is able to focus its full energies on the development of each student. In all three years, students enjoy multiple production opportunities. The PTTP adheres to the University's Academic Probation Policy. In addition, students must maintain a minimum grade of B in specific courses by the end of the third semester and every semester thereafter. Although graduates find themselves well prepared for employment in many styles and mediums, the program is specifically designed to train through plays from the classic repertoire and seeks students with a particular commitment to, and appetite for, the acknowledged masterworks of dramatic literature.

Research Facilities

In 2006, the PTTP began performing in the brand-new Louise and David Roselle Center for the Arts, which includes the Thompson Theatre, a 450-seat state-of-the-art proscenium theater, as well as a flexible studio theater. The program continues to use Hartshorn Hall, which has the capacity to seat up to 350 people and is a flexible space that can accommodate arena, thrust, and proscenium stages. Hartshorn Hall also houses rehearsal space, a dance studio, a computer-aided design (CAD) laboratory, and the stage management and technical production offices. The Box Office, Costume Shop, and faculty offices are also located in Hartshorn. The Scene, Prop, and Paint Shops are located at another site on Wyoming Road.

Financial Aid

Financial aid, in the form of stipends, tuition waivers, and fellowships, is available to needy students in the program. Applicants who require financial aid to attend must indicate that on their application form. In 2008–09, stipends are approximately $7300 per semester. Federal Stafford Student Loans are available through the assistance of the Financial Aid Office; in order to be eligible for need-based programs, students must file a Free Application for Federal Student Aid (FAFSA) by March 1. Students should begin the application procedure in the previous fall for the fall semester.

Cost of Study

In 2008–09, tuition for Delaware residents is $7780 per year; for nonresidents, tuition is $21,106 per year. Students are required to pay the $466 health service fee, the $233 student center fee, the $180 comprehensive student fee, and the $50 registration fee each year. Initial required expenses for the first year are between $200 and $500, depending on the area of concentration. Required expenses for all areas are between $100 and $1000 in the second and third years. For the acting area, recommended, but not required, activities and equipment for the entire three-year period amount to $4000.

All University of Delaware students are required to have health insurance, which can be purchased through the University at a reduced group rate. An application and brochure describing these plans are distributed to all students before the fall semester and are available upon request at the Student Health Service.

Living and Housing Costs

The 2008–09 cost for a room in a double-occupancy graduate apartment is $500 to $600 per month. Local housing ranges from $400 per month for a room in a shared three-bedroom house to $800 per month in a two-bedroom unfurnished apartment. Room and board for the 2008 calendar year were approximately $7500. Additional miscellaneous expenses are approximately $2000.

Student Group

In 2007, the PTTP graduated a class of 40 students, made up of 27 men and 13 women. Upon entering the PTTP, 95 percent of students received some financial aid. Recent PTTP graduates have worked at leading theaters across the United States, including the Oregon Shakespeare Festival, Milwaukee Repertory Theater, Arena Stage, Guthrie Theater, McCarter Theatre, Goodman Theatre, and Alliance Theatre, as well as in featured roles on Broadway and in film and television. In recent years, PTTP graduates have been nominated for Tony, Emmy, and Obie awards. In the 2002 theater season, 82 percent of PTTP alumni worked in the theater, compared to 41 percent of Equity members.

Location

The University of Delaware is located in the residential community of Newark, a suburban area of approximately 26,000 people. Newark is close to many of the professional theaters of the Northeast. New York, Philadelphia, Baltimore, Princeton, and Washington, D.C., with their many regional, repertory, and commercial theater companies, are all within a short distance of the campus.

The University

The University of Delaware was founded in 1743 as a small private academy. Today, as one of the oldest land-grant institutions in the nation, the University of Delaware is recognized as a major state-assisted private university. The beautifully landscaped Newark campus consists of 1,100 acres and a $499-million physical plant of 318 buildings that includes classrooms and laboratories, the recently expanded Morris Library, residence and dining halls, and athletic and student activity facilities.

Applying

In addition to specific audition and interview criteria for admission to each concentration, all students must submit an application for admission, accompanied by a $60 nonrefundable application fee. Applicants must provide three letters of reference, a resume detailing professional theater experience, and two official academic transcripts. Interested students should contact the Department of Theatre for application information, audition format, and interview requirements. The next auditions and interviews are scheduled to be held in the winter/spring of 2012 for entrance in fall 2012.

Correspondence and Information

Kristin Brady, Program Coordinator
Professional Theatre Training Program
Department of Theatre
University of Delaware
Newark, Delaware 19716-2530
Phone: 302-831-2201
Web site: http://www.udel.edu/theatre

University of Delaware

THE FACULTY AND THEIR RESEARCH

Peter Brakhage, Technical Director. Technical production.
Joann Browning, Associate Professor and Associate Chair; M.F.A., SMU. Stage movement and dance.
William Browning, Professor; M.F.A., Iowa. Technical production.
Deena Burke, Associate Professor; B.F.A., Juilliard.
Rick Cunningham, Associate Professor; M.F.A., Tulane. Stage management.
Stephanie Hansen, Assistant Professor; M.F.A., San Diego State. Technical production.
Heinz-Uwe Haus, Professor; Ph.D., Humboldt (Berlin).
Leslie Reidel, Professor; M.F.A., Temple. Acting, directing.
Sanford Robbins, Professor and Chair; M.F.A., Carnegie Mellon. Acting, directing.
Eileen Smitheimer, Associate Professor; B.A., Purdue. Technical production.
Fritz Szabo, Assistant Professor; M.F.A., Syracuse. Technical production.
Steve Tague, Assistant Professor; M.F.A., Wisconsin–Milwaukee. Acting.
Jewel Walker, Professor. Acting, directing, stage movement.

Guest Artist Faculty in Residence, 1989–2007
John Amos, Film and television actor.
Harriet Bass, New York casting director, Bass-Vasiglio Casting.
Peter Bennett, Award-winning director.
Charles Berliner, Costume designer for theater, television, film, and fashion.
Les Bisno, Composer.
Alexander Borovsky, Designer for the Moscow Art Theatre.
Dr. Dohyun Choe, Sugi master.
James Cromwell, Academy Award–nominated actor.
Jeffrey Dreisbach, Director of the Connecticut School of Broadcasting.
Don Evans, Playwright of *Cootch* and of plays produced at the National Black Theatre, the Crossroads Theatre, and the Negro Ensemble Company.
Rolf Fjelde, Author/translator/dramaturg; translator of Ibsen's plays; faculty member of the Juilliard School and Pratt Institute; President, Ibsen Society of America.
Alexander Galin, Russian playwright and author of *The Roof.*
Jack Going, Nationally known regional theater director.
Adrian Hall, Regional theater pioneer, founder of Trinity Repertory Company, and artistic director for Trinity Repertory and the Dallas Theatre Center.
Joseph Hanreddy, Artistic director, Milwaukee Repertory Theatre.
Richard Isackes, Scene designer for regional theater, CBS, and NBC; two-time winner of the Boston Drama Critics award for best scene design.
Cherry Jones, Tony Award–winning actress.
Tero Kiiskinen, Finnish designer for such theaters as the National Theatre of Finland and City Theatre of Stockholm.
Stephanie Klapper, New York casting director.
Ko-Thi Dance Company.
Jussi Kylatasku, Finnish playwright, novelist, and poet; winner of the Tampere International Theatre Festival Award and the Lea Award for Best Play in Finland.
Mark Lamos, Tony Award–nominated director.
Arnie Levine, Costume designer at the New York City Ballet and the Paris Opera Ballet.
Joan MacIntosh, Broadway and film actress.
Ada Brown Mather, Shakespearean verse expert and director.
Robert McBroom, Scene designer for regional theater, including New York Lyric Opera, St. Louis Repertory, Cape Cod Playhouse, Intar, and Bel Canto Opera.
Pat McCorkle, New York casting director, McCorkle Casting.
Ethan McSweeny, New York and regional theater director.
Charles Morey, Artistic director, Pioneer Theatre Company.
Pilobolus Dance Company.
Joan Powell, Professional cutter and draper.
Claude Purdy, Director at regional theaters, including the Guthrie, Cleveland Playhouse, Pittsburgh Public Theatre, and American Conservatory Theatre.
Richard Ramos, Nationally known director and stage and film actor.
Mark Redanty, New York talent agent.
Paul Roche, Internationally known poet, author, and translator of *The Oedipus Plays of Sophocles* and *The Orestes Plays.*
Roy Hart Theatre of France, Obie Award–winning theater ensemble and voice teachers.
Mark Schlegel, New York talent agent.
Paule Stein, Costume, scenic, and mask designer for the National Theatre of France.
Leroy Stoner, Lighting designer.
J. R. Sullivan, Regional theater director.
Tadashi Suzuki, Artistic director of the Suzuki Company of Toga (SCOT), Japan.
Oleg Tabakov, Director of the Moscow Art Theatre.
Robert Taylor, Artistic director of the IAT Renaissance Theatre.
Mikko Viherjuuri, Finnish director for the National Theatre of Finland and Tampere Worker's Theatre; served as artistic director for the Kuopio City Theatre.
Andrew Wade, Royal Shakespeare Company.
Kenneth Washington, Director of Company Development at Guthrie Theatre.
Paul Wonsek, Scenic designer for, among others, the St. Louis Municipal Opera, Buffalo Theatre, Walnut Street Theatre, and off-Broadway.
Liz Woodman, New York casting director.
William Woodman, Former artistic director of the Goodman Theatre; director for Denver Center Theater Company, McCarter Theatre, and Syracuse Stage.
Collier Woods, Lighting designer for such theaters as the Dance Theatre of Harlem, Pennsylvania Opera, Intiman Theatre, and Empty Space Theatre.
Anthony Zerbe, Stage and film actor.

UNIVERSITY OF SOUTHERN CALIFORNIA

School of Theatre

Programs of Study

The University of Southern California (USC) School of Theatre currently offers M.F.A. degrees in acting and dramatic writing.

The M.F.A. program in acting requires 72 units of course work, while the M.F.A. program in dramatic writing requires 64 units.

USC School of Theatre offers conservatory-style training that combines rigorous academics with a rich artistic environment. The programs provide students with opportunities to develop and exercise their craft in a setting that parallels the professional theater world through practical and hands-on experience.

The graduate programs in acting and dramatic writing are intensive, three-year programs taught by a faculty comprising first-rate master teachers and theater professionals working at the highest level in their respective fields. The School of Theatre faculty members have strong ties in the theater world and are sought out by leaders in the industry, the arts, and the media for their expertise.

The USC School of Theatre encourages students to fully explore their creative possibilities. The quality of programs and the lasting relationships students forge with faculty members and peers make USC a nurturing environment for developing theater skills and knowledge. A theater education at the University of Southern California is a unique and invaluable experience.

Research Facilities

The School operates the Bing Theatre, a modern proscenium 550-seat house; the Massman Theatre, an intimate studio seating 50–70; the Scene Dock Theatre, offering flexible seating for 99; and the Village Gate, a cabaret-style space that seats 70.

Financial Aid

In 2007, USC awarded $297 million in need-based grants, merit scholarships, loans, and work-study through a combination of state, federal, university, and private funds. The School of Theatre offers a range of graduate assistantships that provide 8–12 units of tuition remission per semester. In addition, students who qualify for teaching assistantships receive a stipend, payable over a nine-month period, that ranges from $2500 to $16,000. Graduate students are also eligible for various types of need-based assistance, generally provided through student loan programs and college work-study employment.

Cost of Study

Based on the 2008–09 academic year, tuition and fees are approximately $32,000 for two semesters (12 to 18 units per semester).

Living and Housing Costs

The University estimates that students need approximately $16,000 per year if residing in on-campus housing or renting off-campus housing. The University Housing Office reserves numerous apartments for graduate students. All apartments are furnished and accommodate 1, 2, or 4 students.

Student Group

The School of Theatre consists of 500 students, of whom 33 are graduate students. Students are able to take advantage of a variety of student organizations, including Theatre for Youth, Brand New Theatre, and other groups creating new theatrical work. Every spring semester the School presents Blueprints: The MFA in Dramatic Writing Playwrights Workshop, featuring the second-year writing students, and Under Construction: The Master of Fine Arts Play Project, featuring the third-year writing students.

Location

The location of USC in Los Angeles—in the heart of the entertainment industry near major motion picture studios, performing arts centers, museums, and vibrant resident theatres—offers enrichment for the artist and the young professional that make the School of Theatre distinctive among colleges and universities in the United States.

The University and The School

The University of Southern California was founded in 1880. The School of Theatre is one of the premiere theater schools in the United States. Founded in 1945 by playwright and director William C. DeMille, the School is recognized internationally as a leader in theater education. The School blends artistic training in a conservatory environment with all the academic advantages of a major research university.

Applying

Applications are accepted for the fall semester only. The deadline for all M.F.A. programs is January 9, 2009. All applicants are required to submit a School of Theatre supplementary application, three letters of recommendation, an unofficial copy of transcripts, and a statement of purpose. Acting applicants must also submit a current headshot and a non-refundable $40 audition fee. Auditions are held in Los Angeles, New York, Chicago, and San Francisco. Dramatic writing applicants must also submit a play in standard Samuel French or Final Draft stage format, a synopsis of the play, and a GRE report. Applicants are encouraged to apply early since the number of students accepted is limited.

Correspondence and Information

Sergio Ramirez
School of Theatre
University of Southern California
1029 Childs Way, DRC 107
Los Angeles, California 90089-0791
Phone: 213-821-4163
E-mail: sotmfa@usc.edu
Web site: http://theatre.usc.edu/mfa

University of Southern California

THE FACULTY AND THEIR AREAS OF FOCUS

Madeline Puzo, Dean.
Andrew J. Robinson, Senior Lecturer and Director of M.F.A. Acting; London Academy of Music and Dramatic Art.
Velina Hasu Houston, Associate Dean and Director of M.F.A. Dramatic Writing; M.F.A., UCLA.
Luis Alfaro, Adjunct Faculty. Dramatic writing.
David Bridel, Senior Lecturer; Hull University. Acting.
Paula Cizmar, Adjunct Faculty. Dramatic writing.
Charlotte Cornwell, Senior Lecturer; Webber Douglas Academy of Dramatic Art. Acting.
Oliver Mayer, Assistant Professor; M.F.A., Columbia. Dramatic writing.
Natsuko Ohama, Lecturer. Acting.
Jack Rowe, Senior Lecturer and Associate Dean; B.A., USC. Acting.

ACADEMIC AND PROFESSIONAL PROGRAMS IN THE HUMANITIES

Section 7
History

This section contains a directory of institutions offering graduate work in history, followed by in-depth entries submitted by institutions that chose to prepare detailed program descriptions. Additional information about programs listed in the directory but not augmented by an in-depth entry may be obtained by writing directly to the dean of a graduate school or chair of a department at the address given in the directory.

For programs offering related work, see also in this book *Area and Cultural Studies, Architecture, Humanities, Political Science and International Affairs,* and *Sociology, Anthropology, and Archaeology.*

CONTENTS

Program Directories

Announcements

Close-Ups

See also:

History

Adams State College, The Graduate School, Department of History, Government and Philosophy, Alamosa, CO 81102. Offers history (MA). Application fee: $30. *Unit head:* Dr. Edward Crowther, Chair, 719-587-7771, Fax: 719-587-7176, E-mail: aschgp@adams.edu.

American Public University System, AMU/APU Graduate Programs, Charles Town, WV 25414. Offers air warfare (MA Military Studies); American Revolution (MA Military Studies); business administration (MBA); Civil War (MA Military Studies); criminal justice (MA); defense management (MA Military Studies); emergency and disaster management (MA); environmental policy and management (MS); fire science management (MA); global engagement (MA); history (MA); homeland security (MA); humanities (MA); intelligence (MA Military Studies, MA Strategic Intelligence); international peace and conflict resolution (MA); international relations and conflict resolution (MA); joint warfare (MA Military Studies); land warfare international perspective (MA Military Studies); management (MA); military history (MA); military leadership (MA Military Studies); national security studies (MA); naval warfare international (MA Military Studies); naval warfare US (MA Military Studies); political science (MA); public administration (MA); public health (MA); security management (MA); space studies (MS); special ops/LIC (MA Military Studies); sports management (MA); transportation and logistics management (MA); transportation management (MA); unconventional warfare (MA Military Studies); World War II (MA Military Studies). Programs offered via distance learning only. Part-time and evening/weekend programs available. Postbaccalaureate distance learning degree programs offered (no on-campus study). *Faculty:* 10 full-time (3 women), 188 part-time/adjunct (57 women). *Students:* 340 full-time (98 women), 3,567 part-time (790 women); includes 615 minority (317 African Americans, 28 American Indian/Alaska Native, 85 Asian Americans or Pacific Islanders, 185 Hispanic Americans), 20 international. Average age 36. 2,123 applicants, 100% accepted, 893 enrolled. In 2007, 829 degrees awarded. *Degree requirements:* For master's, comprehensive exam. *Entrance requirements:* For master's, bachelor's degree or equivalent, minimum GPA of 2.7 in last 60 hours of course work. *Application deadline:* Applications are processed on a rolling basis. Application fee: $0. Electronic applications accepted. *Expenses:* Tuition: Part-time $275 per semester hour. *Financial support:* Applicants required to submit FAFSA. *Faculty research:* Military history, criminal justice, management performance, national security. *Unit head:* Dr. Frank McCluskey, Provost, 877-468-6268, Fax: 304-724-3780. *Application contact:* Terry Grant, Director of Enrollment Management, 877-468-6268, Fax: 304-724-3780, E-mail: info@apus.edu.

American University, College of Arts and Sciences, Department of History, Washington, DC 20016-8001. Offers MA, PhD. Part-time and evening/weekend programs available. *Faculty:* 19 full-time (8 women), 6 part-time/adjunct (2 women). *Students:* 37 full-time (19 women), 61 part-time (33 women); includes 10 minority (4 African Americans, 1 American Indian/Alaska Native, 2 Asian Americans or Pacific Islanders, 3 Hispanic Americans), 4 international. Average age 32. 130 applicants, 68% accepted, 30 enrolled. In 2007, 19 master's, 3 doctorates awarded. *Degree requirements:* For master's, comprehensive exam, thesis or alternative, Tools of research in foreign language, methods, history or methodology; for doctorate, thesis/dissertation, Tools of research; 2 seminars; 2 colloquia. *Entrance requirements:* For master's, GRE General Test, writing sample; for doctorate, GRE General Test, sample of written work. Additional exam requirements/recommendations for international students: Required—TOEFL (minimum score 550 paper-based; 213 computer-based). *Application deadline:* For fall admission, 2/1 priority date for domestic students; for spring admission, 10/1 priority date for domestic students. Application fee: $50. *Expenses:* Tuition: Full-time $19,998; part-time $1,111 per credit hour. Required fees: $380. Tuition and fees vary according to program. *Financial support:* In 2007–08, 20 students received support; fellowships, research assistantships, teaching assistantships, career-related internships or fieldwork, institutionally sponsored loans, tuition waivers (full and partial), and unspecified assistantships available. Financial award application deadline: 2/1. *Faculty research:* U.S. political and diplomatic history, modern European history, U.S. social and cultural history, recent U.S. history, early republic, modern Europe. *Unit head:* Dr. Robert Griffith, Chair, 202-885-2419, Fax: 202-885-6166.

American University of Beirut, Graduate Programs, Faculty of Arts and Sciences, Beirut, Lebanon. Offers anthropology (MA); Arabic language and literature (MA); archaeology (MA); biology (MS); chemistry (MS); computer science (MS); economics (MA); education (MA); English language (MA); English literature (MA); environmental policy planning (MSES); financial economics (MAFE); geology (MS); history (MA); mathematics (MA, MS); Middle Eastern studies (MA); philosophy (MA); physics (MS); political studies (MA); psychology (MA); public administration (MA); sociology (MA); statistics (MA, MS). Part-time programs available. *Faculty:* 108 full-time (29 women), 5 part-time/adjunct (3 women). *Students:* 134 full-time (92 women), 228 part-time (167 women). Average age 25. 319 applicants, 67% accepted, 91 enrolled. In 2007, 144 degrees awarded. *Degree requirements:* For master's, one foreign language, comprehensive exam, thesis (for some programs). *Entrance requirements:* For master's, GRE, letter of recommendation. Additional exam requirements/recommendations for international students: Required—TOEFL (minimum score 600 paper-based; 250 computer-based; 100 iBT), IELTS (minimum score 8). *Application deadline:* For fall admission, 4/30 for domestic and international students; for spring admission, 11/1 for domestic and international students. Application fee: $50. *Expenses:* Tuition: Full-time $9,954; part-time $553 per credit. Tuition and fees vary according to course load and program. *Financial support:* In 2007–08, 28 students received support. Career-related internships or fieldwork, institutionally sponsored loans, scholarships/grants, health care benefits, and unspecified assistantships available. Financial award application deadline: 2/4; financial award applicants required to submit FAFSA. *Faculty research:* String theory and supergravity; computer graphics; algebra and number theory; popular Arabic literature; marine and freshwater biology; integrating science, math and technology. Total annual research expenditures: $132,270. *Unit head:* Khalil Bitar, Dean, 961-1374374 Ext. 3800, Fax: 961-1744461, E-mail: kmb@aub.edu.lb. *Application contact:* Dr. Salim Kanaan, Director, Admissions Office, 961-1350000 Ext. 2594, Fax: 961-1750775, E-mail: sk00@aub.edu.lb.

Andrews University, School of Graduate Studies, College of Arts and Sciences, Department of History, Berrien Springs, MI 49104. Offers MA, MAT. Part-time programs available. *Degree requirements:* For master's, variable foreign language requirement, thesis optional. *Entrance requirements:* For master's, GRE Subject Test. *Faculty research:* American intellectual history, Civil War, American church history, modern German history.

Angelo State University, College of Graduate Studies, College of Liberal and Fine Arts, Department of History, San Angelo, TX 76909. Offers MA. Part-time and evening/weekend programs available. *Faculty:* 3 full-time (0 women). *Students:* Average age 35. 3 applicants, 100% accepted, 2 enrolled. In 2007, 2 degrees awarded. *Degree requirements:* For master's, comprehensive exam, thesis optional. *Entrance requirements:* For master's, GRE General Test. Additional exam requirements/recommendations for international students: Required—TOEFL or IELTS. *Application deadline:* For fall admission, 7/15 priority date for domestic students, 6/10 for international students; for spring admission, 12/8 for domestic students, 11/1 for international students. Applications are processed on a rolling basis. Application fee: $40 ($50 for international students). Electronic applications accepted. *Financial support:* In 2007–08, 4 students received support. Federal Work-Study, scholarships/grants, and unspecified assistantships available. Support available to part-time students. Financial award application deadline: 3/1. *Unit head:* Dr. Virginia Noelke, Department Head, 325-942-2115. *Application contact:* Dr. Shirley Eoff, Graduate Advisor, 325-942-2118, E-mail: shirley.eoff@angelo.edu.

Appalachian State University, Cratis D. Williams Graduate School, Department of History, Boone, NC 28608. Offers history (MA); history education (MA); public history (MA). Part-time programs available. *Faculty:* 28 full-time (8 women). *Students:* 20 full-time (8 women), 23 part-time (9 women); includes 3 minority (1 American Indian/Alaska Native, 1 Asian American or Pacific Islander, 1 Hispanic American), 1 international. 25 applicants, 84% accepted, 15 enrolled. In 2007, 5 master's awarded. *Degree requirements:* For master's, one foreign language, comprehensive exam, thesis (for some programs). *Entrance requirements:* For master's, GRE General Test, 3 letters of recommendation. Additional exam requirements/recommendations for international students: Required—TOEFL (minimum score 570 paper-based; 230 computer-based; 79 iBT), IELTS (minimum score 7), TOEFL or IELTS. *Application deadline:* For fall admission, 7/1 for domestic students, 1/1 for international students; for spring admission, 11/1 for domestic students, 6/1 for international students. Applications are processed on a rolling basis. Application fee: $50. Electronic applications accepted. *Expenses:* Tuition, state resident: part-time $127 per semester hour. Tuition, nonresident: part-time $597 per semester hour. Required fees: $18 per semester. *Financial support:* In 2007–08, 4 research assistantships (averaging $10,000 per year), 7 teaching assistantships (averaging $7,500 per year) were awarded; fellowships, career-related internships or fieldwork, Federal Work-Study, scholarships/grants, and unspecified assistantships also available. Financial award application deadline: 4/1. *Faculty research:* Women's history, social/cultural history, US history, Latin America, medieval studies. Total annual research expenditures: $4,370. *Unit head:* Dr. Michael Krenn, Chairperson, 828-262-2282, E-mail: krennml@appstate.edu. *Application contact:* Dr. James Goff, Director, 828-262-6019, E-mail: goffjr@appstate.edu.

Arizona State University, Graduate College, College of Liberal Arts and Sciences, Division of Humanities, Department of History, Tempe, AZ 85287. Offers Asian history (MA, PhD); British history (MA, PhD); European history (MA, PhD); Latin American studies (MA, PhD); public history (MA); U.S. history (PhD); U.S. western history (MA). *Degree requirements:* For master's, thesis or alternative; for doctorate, 2 foreign languages, thesis/dissertation. *Entrance requirements:* For master's and doctorate, GRE.

Arkansas State University, Graduate School, College of Humanities and Social Sciences, Department of History, Jonesboro, State University, AR 72467. Offers history (MA, SCCT); social science (MSE). Part-time programs available. *Faculty:* 14 full-time (7 women), 2 part-time/adjunct (both women). *Students:* 12 full-time (5 women), 27 part-time (19 women); includes 6 minority (4 African Americans, 2 Hispanic Americans). Average age 35. 13 applicants, 100% accepted, 13 enrolled. In 2007, 11 degrees awarded. *Degree requirements:* For master's, comprehensive exam, thesis or alternative; for SCCT, comprehensive exam. *Entrance requirements:* For master's, GRE General Test or MAT, GMAT, appropriate bachelor's degree, letters of reference, official transcript; for SCCT, GRE General Test or MAT, interview, master's degree, letters of reference, official transcript. Additional exam requirements/recommendations for international students: Required—TOEFL (minimum score 213 computer-based). *Application deadline:* Applications are processed on a rolling basis. Application fee: $30 ($40 for international students). Electronic applications accepted. *Expenses:* Tuition, state resident: full-time $3,528; part-time $196 per hour. Tuition, nonresident: full-time $8,928; part-time $496 per hour. Required fees: $842; $44 per hour. $25 per term. Tuition and fees vary according to course load and program. *Financial support:* Scholarships/grants and unspecified assistantships available. Financial award application deadline: 7/1; financial award applicants required to submit FAFSA. *Faculty research:* U.S. history, women's history, Islamic history, Eurasian perspectives, history of criminal justice. *Unit head:* Dr. Pamela Hronek, Chair, 870-972-3046, Fax: 870-972-2880, E-mail: phronek@astate.edu.

Arkansas Tech University, Graduate School, School of Liberal and Fine Arts, Russellville, AR 72801. Offers communication (MLA); English (M Ed, MA); fine arts (MLA); history (MA); multi-media journalism (MA); social science (MLA); social studies (M Ed); Spanish (MA, MLA); teaching English as a second language (MA, MLA). Part-time programs available. *Students:* 54 full-time (43 women), 79 part-time (54 women); includes 11 minority (3 African Americans, 1 American Indian/Alaska Native, 1 Asian American or Pacific Islander, 6 Hispanic Americans), 29 international. Average age 33. In 2007, 71 degrees awarded. *Degree requirements:* For master's, project. *Entrance requirements:* For master's, GRE General Test or MAT. Additional exam requirements/recommendations for international students: Required—TOEFL (minimum score 500 paper-based; 173 computer-based; 61 iBT). *Application deadline:* For fall admission, 3/1 priority date for domestic students, 5/1 priority date for international students; for winter admission, 10/1 priority date for international students; for spring admission, 10/1 priority date for domestic and international students. Applications are processed on a rolling basis. Application fee: $0 ($30 for international students). Electronic applications accepted. *Expenses:* Tuition, state resident: full-time $3,150; part-time $175 per hour. Tuition, nonresident: full-time $6,300; part-time $350 per hour. Required fees: $384; $8 per hour. $120 per term. Tuition and fees vary according to course load. *Financial support:* In 2007–08, teaching assistantships with full tuition reimbursements (averaging $4,000 per year); career-related internships or fieldwork, Federal Work-Study, scholarships/grants, health care benefits, and unspecified assistantships also available. Support available to part-time students. Financial award application deadline: 4/15; financial award applicants required to submit FAFSA. *Unit head:* Dr. Georgena Duncan, Dean, 479-968-0266, Fax: 479-968-0275, E-mail: georgena.duncan@atu.edu. *Application contact:* Dr. Eldon G. Clary, Dean of Graduate School, 479-968-0398, Fax: 479-964-0542, E-mail: graduate.school@atu.edu.

Armstrong Atlantic State University, School of Graduate Studies, Program in History, Savannah, GA 31419-1997. Offers MA. Part-time and evening/weekend programs available. *Faculty:* 15 full-time (4 women). *Students:* 5 full-time (4 women), 18 part-time (8 women); includes 1 African American, 1 Hispanic American. Average age 33. In 2007, 7 degrees awarded. *Degree requirements:* For master's, one foreign language, comprehensive exam, thesis (for some programs). *Entrance requirements:* For master's, GRE General Test, minimum GPA of 3.0, letters of recommendation, BA in history or equivalent. Additional exam requirements/recommendations for international students: Required—TOEFL (minimum score 523 paper-based; 193 computer-based). *Application deadline:* For fall admission, 7/1 priority date for domestic and international students; for spring admission, 11/15 priority date for domestic and international students. Applications are processed on a rolling basis. Application fee: $30. Electronic applications accepted. *Expenses:* Tuition, state resident: full-time $3,228; part-time $135 per hour. Tuition, nonresident: full-time $12,904; part-time $538 per hour. Required fees: $278 per term. *Financial support:* In 2007–08, research assistantships with partial tuition reimbursements (averaging $2,500 per year); career-related internships or fieldwork, Federal Work-Study, and unspecified assistantships also available. Support available to part-time students. Financial award applicants required to submit FAFSA. *Faculty research:* Public history; European, Latin American, African, and United State history. *Unit head:* Dr. June Hopkins, Interim Department Head, 912-927-5283, E-mail: june.hopkins@armstrong.edu. *Application contact:* Dr. Christopher Hendricks, Graduate Coordinator, 912-921-5833, E-mail: hendrich@mail.armstrong.edu.

Ashland Theological Seminary, Graduate Programs, Ashland, OH 44805. Offers biblical and theological studies (MA, MAR), including New Testament (MA), Old Testament (MA); Christian ministry (MAPT); Christian studies (Diploma); clinical pastoral counseling (MACPC); historical studies (MA); ministry (D Min); pastoral counseling (MAPC); pastoral ministry (M Div); theological studies (MA). *Accreditation:* ATS. Part-time programs available. *Degree requirements:* For master's, comprehensive exam (for some programs), thesis (for some programs); for doctorate, thesis/dissertation; for M Div, 2 foreign languages. *Entrance requirements:* For M Div, minimum GPA of 2.75; for master's, minimum undergraduate GPA of 2.75; for doctorate, M Div, minimum undergraduate GPA of 3.0. Additional exam requirements/recommendations for international students: Required—TOEFL (minimum score 550 paper-based). Electronic applications accepted. *Faculty research:* Semitic languages and linguistics, rhetorical and social-scientific criticism, Anabaptist studies, inner spiritual healing, African-American clergy in film and literature.

Ashland University, College of Arts and Sciences, Program in American History and Government, Ashland, OH 44805-3702. Offers MAHG. Part-time programs available. *Faculty:* 4 full-time (0 women), 12 part-time/adjunct (0 women). *Students:* 38 full-time (17 women), 38 part-time (16 women); includes 3 minority (2 Asian Americans or Pacific Islanders, 1

Hispanic American). Average age 38. *Degree requirements:* For master's, thesis optional. *Entrance requirements:* For master's, minimum GPA of 3.0. *Application deadline:* Applications are processed on a rolling basis. Application fee: $30. Electronic applications accepted. *Expenses: Contact institution. Financial support:* In 2007–08, 25 students received support. Application deadline: 4/15. *Faculty research:* American founding, civil war, progressives. *Unit head:* Dr. Peter W. Schramm, Executive Director, Ashbrook Center, 419-289-5414, Fax: 419-289-5425, E-mail: pschramm@ashland.edu. *Application contact:* Roger L. Beckett, Deputy Director, Ashbrook Center, 419-289-5413, Fax: 419-289-5425, E-mail: rbeckett@ashland.edu.

Auburn University, Graduate School, College of Liberal Arts, Department of History, Auburn University, AL 36849. Offers MA, PhD. Part-time programs available. *Faculty:* 23 full-time (9 women). *Students:* 27 full-time (6 women), 48 part-time (17 women); includes 4 minority (1 African American, 3 Hispanic Americans), 1 international. Average age 37. 51 applicants, 55% accepted, 12 enrolled. In 2007, 9 master's, 3 doctorates awarded. *Degree requirements:* For master's, thesis, oral exam; for doctorate, 2 foreign languages, thesis/dissertation. *Entrance requirements:* For master's, GRE General Test; for doctorate, GRE General Test, master's degree with thesis. *Application deadline:* For fall admission, 7/7 for domestic students; for spring admission, 11/24 for domestic students. Applications are processed on a rolling basis. Application fee: $25 ($50 for international students). Electronic applications accepted. *Financial support:* Teaching assistantships, Federal Work-Study available. Support available to part-time students. Financial award application deadline: 3/15. *Unit head:* Dr. Tony Carey, Chair, 334-844-4360. *Application contact:* Dr. Joe Pittman, Interim Dean of the Graduate School, 334-844-4700.

Ball State University, Graduate School, College of Sciences and Humanities, Department of History, Muncie, IN 47306-1099. Offers MA. *Faculty:* 24. *Students:* 11 full-time (3 women), 19 part-time (6 women); includes 3 minority (1 African American, 1 Asian American or Pacific Islander, 1 Hispanic American). Average age 26. 31 applicants, 71% accepted, 17 enrolled. In 2007, 3 degrees awarded. Application fee: $25 ($35 for international students). *Expenses:* Tuition, state resident: full-time $6,864. Tuition, nonresident: full-time $17,932. Required fees: $1,866. *Financial support:* In 2007–08, 5 teaching assistantships with full tuition reimbursements (averaging $10,176 per year) were awarded. Financial award application deadline: 3/1. *Faculty research:* European, British, and American history. *Application contact:* Dr. James Connolly, Graduate Program Director, 765-285-8700, Fax: 765-285-5612, E-mail: jconnoll@bsu.edu.

Baylor University, Graduate School, College of Arts and Sciences, Department of History, Waco, TX 76798. Offers MA. Part-time and evening/weekend programs available. *Students:* 21 full-time (9 women), 1 (woman) part-time; includes 1 minority (Hispanic American), 1 international. In 2007, 5 degrees awarded. *Degree requirements:* For master's, comprehensive exam, thesis, foreign language translation exam. *Entrance requirements:* For master's, GRE General Test, 24 semester hours in history. *Application deadline:* For fall admission, 8/1 for domestic students. Applications are processed on a rolling basis. Application fee: $25. *Financial support:* Fellowships, research assistantships, Federal Work-Study and institutionally sponsored loans available. Financial award application deadline: 4/15. *Faculty research:* U.S. women's history, naval history, Chinese missions, late nineteenth century Germany, twentieth century urban U.S. *Unit head:* Dr. Patricia Wallace, Graduate Program Director, 254-710-2667, Fax: 254-710-2551, E-mail: patricia_wallace@baylor.edu. *Application contact:* Suzanne Keener, Administrative Assistant, 254-710-3588, Fax: 254-710-3870.

Bob Jones University, Graduate Programs, Greenville, SC 29614. Offers accountancy (MS); Bible (MA); Bible translation (MA); Biblical studies (Certificate); broadcast management (MS); business administration (MBA); church history (MA, PhD); church ministries (MA); church music (MM); cinema and video production (MA); counseling (MS); curriculum and instruction (Ed D); divinity (M Div); dramatic production (MA); educational leadership (MS, Ed D, Ed S); elementary education (M Ed, MAT); English (M Ed, MA, MAT); fine arts (MA); graphic design (MA); history (M Ed, MA); illustration (MA); interpretative speech (MA); mathematics (M Ed, MAT); medical missions (Certificate); ministry (MM, D Min); multi-categorical special education (M Ed, MAT); music (M Ed); New Testament interpretation (PhD); Old Testament interpretation (PhD); orchestral instrument performance (MM); organ performance (MM); pastoral studies (MA); personnel services (MS, Ed S); piano pedagogy (MM); piano performance (MM); platform arts (MA); radio and television broadcasting (MS); rhetoric and public address (MA); secondary education (M Ed); studio art (MA); teaching Bible (MA); theology (MA, PhD); voice performance (MM); youth ministries (MA); M Div/MM.

Boise State University, Graduate College, College of Social Sciences and Public Affairs, Department of History, Boise, ID 83725-0399. Offers MA. Part-time programs available. *Degree requirements:* For master's, thesis. *Entrance requirements:* For master's, GRE General Test, minimum GPA of 3.0. Electronic applications accepted. *Faculty research:* Public history, American social and cultural history, European history, Third World history.

Boston College, Graduate School of Arts and Sciences, Department of History, Chestnut Hill, MA 02467-3800. Offers European national studies (MA); history (MA, PhD); medieval studies (MA). *Students:* 70 full-time (35 women), 10 part-time (6 women); includes 8 minority (2 African Americans, 3 Asian Americans or Pacific Islanders, 3 Hispanic Americans), 6 international. 192 applicants, 25% accepted, 25 enrolled. In 2007, 16 master's, 7 doctorates awarded. Terminal master's awarded for partial completion of doctoral program. *Degree requirements:* For master's, one foreign language, comprehensive exam, thesis optional; for doctorate, 2 foreign languages, comprehensive exam, thesis/dissertation. *Entrance requirements:* For master's and doctorate, GRE General Test, writing sample. Additional exam requirements/recommendations for international students: Required—TOEFL (minimum score 590 paper-based; 250 computer-based; 91 iBT). *Application deadline:* For fall admission, 1/15 for domestic students. Application fee: $70. Electronic applications accepted. *Financial support:* Fellowships with full tuition reimbursements, research assistantships with full tuition reimbursements, teaching assistantships with full tuition reimbursements, Federal Work-Study and scholarships/grants available. Support available to part-time students. Financial award application deadline: 3/1; financial award applicants required to submit FAFSA. *Faculty research:* Modern and early modern European, U.S., Russian, and Soviet history; European and U.S. intellectual history. *Unit head:* Dr. Marilynn Johnson, Chairperson, 617-552-3781. *Application contact:* Dr. David Quigley, Director of Graduate Studies, 617-552-2267, E-mail: david.quigley@bc.edu.

Boston University, Graduate School of Arts and Sciences, Department of History, Boston, MA 02215. Offers MA, PhD. *Students:* 42 full-time (22 women), 11 part-time (8 women); includes 2 minority (1 African American, 1 Hispanic American), 5 international. Average age 34. 124 applicants, 41% accepted, 10 enrolled. In 2007, 7 master's, 2 doctorates awarded. Terminal master's awarded for partial completion of doctoral program. *Degree requirements:* For master's, one foreign language; for doctorate, 2 foreign languages, comprehensive exam, thesis/dissertation. *Entrance requirements:* For master's and doctorate, GRE General Test, 2 letters of recommendation. Additional exam requirements/recommendations for international students: Required—TOEFL (minimum score 550 paper-based; 213 computer-based). *Application deadline:* For fall admission, 2/15 for domestic and international students. Application fee: $70. *Expenses:* Tuition: Full-time $34,930; part-time $1,092 per credit. Tuition and fees vary according to class time, course level and program. *Financial support:* In 2007–08, 28 students received support, including 2 fellowships with full tuition reimbursements available (averaging $18,000 per year), 1 research assistantship with full tuition reimbursement available (averaging $16,500 per year), 10 teaching assistantships with full tuition reimbursements available (averaging $16,500 per year); Federal Work-Study, scholarships/grants, and unspecified assistantships also available. Support available to part-time students. Financial award application deadline: 1/15; financial award applicants required to submit FAFSA. *Unit head:* Charles Dellheim, Chairman, 617-353-2550, Fax: 617-353-2556, E-mail: dellheim@bu.edu. *Application contact:* James T. Dutton, Department Administrator, 617-353-2555, Fax: 617-353-2556, E-mail: jtdutton@bu.edu.

Bowling Green State University, Graduate College, College of Arts and Sciences, Department of History, Bowling Green, OH 43403. Offers history (MA, MAT, PhD); public history (MA); MA/MA. Part-time programs available. *Faculty:* 23 full-time (8 women), 11 part-time/adjunct (2 women). *Students:* 46 full-time (24 women), 6 part-time (1 woman); includes 3 African Americans, 1 Hispanic American, 3 international. Average age 31. 41 applicants, 51% accepted, 11 enrolled. In 2007, 2 master's awarded. *Degree requirements:* For master's, thesis or alternative; for doctorate, one foreign language, comprehensive exam, thesis/dissertation. *Entrance requirements:* For master's and doctorate, GRE General Test. Additional exam requirements/recommendations for international students: Required—TOEFL. *Application deadline:* For fall admission, 2/15 priority date for domestic students. Application fee: $30. Electronic applications accepted. *Financial support:* In 2007–08, 2 fellowships with full tuition reimbursements (averaging $14,707 per year), 10 research assistantships with full tuition reimbursements (averaging $8,320 per year), 18 teaching assistantships with full tuition reimbursements (averaging $11,205 per year) were awarded; Federal Work-Study and unspecified assistantships also available. Financial award applicants required to submit FAFSA. *Faculty research:* Policy history, modern Europe, recent United States history, East Asia, Latin America. *Unit head:* Dr. Scott Martin, Chair, 419-372-2030. *Application contact:* Dr. Walter Grunden, Graduate Coordinator, 419-372-8639.

Brandeis University, Graduate School of Arts and Sciences, Department of History, Program in American History, Waltham, MA 02454-9110. Offers MA, PhD. Part-time programs available. *Faculty:* 15 full-time (4 women), 1 part-time/adjunct (0 women). *Students:* 33 full-time (15 women), 3 international. Average age 30. 58 applicants, 29% accepted, 7 enrolled. In 2007, 6 master's, 3 doctorates awarded. Terminal master's awarded for partial completion of doctoral program. *Degree requirements:* For master's, one foreign language, thesis, colloquia, directed research, seminars; for doctorate, one foreign language, comprehensive exam, thesis/dissertation, colloquia, directed research, seminars. *Entrance requirements:* For master's and doctorate, GRE General Test, resumé, writing sample, letters of recommendation, statement of purpose. Additional exam requirements/recommendations for international students: Required—TOEFL (minimum score 600 paper-based; 250 computer-based; 100 iBT), IELTS (minimum score 7). *Application deadline:* For fall admission, 1/15 for domestic students. Application fee: $55. Electronic applications accepted. *Financial support:* In 2007–08, 19 students received support, including 14 fellowships with full tuition reimbursements available (averaging $18,500 per year), 5 teaching assistantships (averaging $3,000 per year); research assistantships, scholarships/grants, health care benefits, and tuition waivers (full and partial) also available. Support available to part-time students. Financial award application deadline: 4/15; financial award applicants required to submit CSS PROFILE or FAFSA. *Faculty research:* American polity, social history, cultural, legal, colonial. *Unit head:* Dr. Michael Willrich, Program Chair, 781-736-2292, Fax: 781-736-2273, E-mail: willrich@brandeis.edu.

Brandeis University, Graduate School of Arts and Sciences, Department of History, Program in Comparative History, Waltham, MA 02454-9110. Offers MA, PhD. Part-time programs available. *Faculty:* 15 full-time (4 women), 1 part-time/adjunct (0 women). *Students:* 33 full-time (15 women); includes 1 minority (Hispanic American), 3 international. Average age 28. 35 applicants, 106% accepted, 9 enrolled. In 2007, 7 master's, 3 doctorates awarded. Terminal master's awarded for partial completion of doctoral program. *Degree requirements:* For master's, one foreign language, thesis, colloquia, seminar, research paper; for doctorate, 2 foreign languages, comprehensive exam, thesis/dissertation, colloquia, seminar, research paper. *Entrance requirements:* For master's and doctorate, GRE General Test, sample of written work, resumé, letters of recommendation, statement of purpose. Additional exam requirements/recommendations for international students: Required—TOEFL (minimum score 600 paper-based; 250 computer-based; 100 iBT), IELTS (minimum score 7). *Application deadline:* For fall admission, 1/15 for domestic students. Application fee: $55. Electronic applications accepted. *Financial support:* In 2007–08, 11 fellowships with tuition reimbursements (averaging $16,500 per year), teaching assistantships (averaging $3,000 per year) were awarded; research assistantships, scholarships/grants, health care benefits, and tuition waivers (full and partial) also available. Financial award application deadline: 4/15; financial award applicants required to submit CSS PROFILE or FAFSA. *Faculty research:* Early modern Europe, modern Europe, intellectual history, medieval. *Unit head:* Dr. Govind Sreenivasan, Program Chair, 781-736-2377, Fax: 781-736-2273, E-mail: sreenivsan@brandeis.edu.

Brock University, Faculty of Graduate Studies, Faculty of Humanities, Program in History, St. Catharines, ON L2S 3A1, Canada. Offers MA. Part-time programs available. *Degree requirements:* For master's, thesis optional. *Entrance requirements:* For master's, honors degree in history. Additional exam requirements/recommendations for international students: Required—TOEFL (minimum score 550 paper-based; 213 computer-based; 80 iBT), IELTS (minimum score 7), TWE (minimum score 4). Electronic applications accepted.

Brooklyn College of the City University of New York, Division of Graduate Studies, Department of History, Brooklyn, NY 11210-2889. Offers MA, PhD. The department offers courses at Brooklyn College that are creditable toward the CUNY doctoral degree (with permission of the executive officer of the doctoral program). Part-time and evening/weekend programs available. *Students:* 1 (woman) full-time, 55 part-time (27 women); includes 14 minority (8 African Americans, 2 Asian Americans or Pacific Islanders, 4 Hispanic Americans). 26 applicants, 92% accepted, 15 enrolled. In 2007, 7 degrees awarded. *Degree requirements:* For master's, 30 credits. *Entrance requirements:* For master's, 12 credits in history, minimum GPA of 3.0 in major, 2 letters of recommendation. Additional exam requirements/recommendations for international students: Required—TOEFL. *Application deadline:* For fall admission, 3/1 priority date for domestic students, 2/1 priority date for international students; for spring admission, 11/1 priority date for domestic students, 10/1 priority date for international students. Applications are processed on a rolling basis. Application fee: $125. Electronic applications accepted. *Financial support:* Federal Work-Study, institutionally sponsored loans, and scholarships/grants available. Support available to part-time students. Financial award application deadline: 5/1; financial award applicants required to submit FAFSA. *Faculty research:* Modern European, U.S., medieval, women's, Asian, and Caribbean history. *Unit head:* Dr. David Troyansky, Chairperson, 718-951-5303, E-mail: troyansky@brooklyn.cuny.edu. *Application contact:* Hernan Sierra, Graduate Admissions Coordinator, 718-951-4536, Fax: 718-951-4506, E-mail: grads@brooklyn.cuny.edu.

Brown University, Graduate School, Department of History, Providence, RI 02912. Offers AM, PhD. *Degree requirements:* For master's, thesis or alternative; for doctorate, variable foreign language requirement, thesis/dissertation, preliminary exam.

Buffalo State College, State University of New York, Graduate Studies and Research, Faculty of Natural and Social Sciences, Department of History and Social Studies, Buffalo, NY 14222-1095. Offers history (MA); secondary education (MS Ed), including social studies. Part-time and evening/weekend programs available. *Degree requirements:* For master's, one foreign language, thesis (for some programs), project (MS Ed). *Entrance requirements:* For master's, minimum GPA of 2.75, 30 hours in history (MA), 36 hours in history or social sciences (MS Ed). Additional exam requirements/recommendations for international students: Required—TOEFL (minimum score 550 paper-based; 213 computer-based).

Butler University, College of Liberal Arts and Sciences, Department of History, Indianapolis, IN 46208-3485. Offers MA. Part-time programs available. *Faculty:* 2 full-time (1 woman). *Students:* Average age 38. 2 applicants, 100% accepted, 0 enrolled. In 2007, 1 degree awarded. *Degree requirements:* For master's, thesis or alternative. *Entrance requirements:* For master's, GRE General Test, minimum GPA of 3.25 in undergraduate major. *Application deadline:* For fall admission, 8/15 priority date for domestic students. Applications are processed on a rolling basis. Application fee: $35. Electronic applications accepted. *Expenses:* Tuition: Full-time $6,300; part-time $350 per credit. Tuition and fees vary according to program. *Financial support:* Institutionally sponsored loans available. Support available to part-time students. Financial award applicants required to submit FAFSA. *Faculty research:* Gender issues in Africa, Indiana history, transnational migration, French Revolution. *Unit head:* Dr. Scott Swanson, Head, 317-940-9680, E-mail: sswanson@butler.edu.

History

California Polytechnic State University, San Luis Obispo, College of Liberal Arts, Department of History, San Luis Obispo, CA 93407. Offers MA. Part-time programs available. *Faculty:* 2 full-time (0 women). *Students:* 7 full-time (2 women), 23 part-time (3 women); includes 5 minority (1 Asian American or Pacific Islander, 4 Hispanic Americans). 20 applicants, 75% accepted, 12 enrolled. *Degree requirements:* For master's, comprehensive exam (for some programs), thesis (for some programs). *Entrance requirements:* For master's, minimum GPA of 3.0 in last 90 quarter units of course work, writing sample. Additional exam requirements/recommendations for international students: Required—TOEFL (minimum score 550 paper-based; 213 computer-based), TWE (minimum score 4.5). *Application deadline:* For fall admission, 5/1 for domestic students, 11/30 for international students; for winter admission, 10/1 for domestic students, 6/30 for international students; for spring admission, 1/15 for domestic students. Applications are processed on a rolling basis. Application fee: $55. Electronic applications accepted. *Expenses:* Tuition, nonresident: part-time $226 per unit. Required fees: $1,777 per quarter. *Financial support:* Federal Work-Study and scholarships/grants available. Support available to part-time students. Financial award application deadline: 3/2; financial award applicants required to submit FAFSA. *Unit head:* Dr. George Cotkin, Graduate Coordinator, 805-756-2763, Fax: 805-756-5055, E-mail: gcotkin@calpoly.edu.

California State Polytechnic University, Pomona, Academic Affairs, College of Letters, Arts, and Social Sciences, Program in History, Pomona, CA 91768-2557. Offers MA. *Students:* 3 full-time (2 women), 10 part-time (2 women); includes 2 minority (1 African American, 1 Hispanic American). Average age 32. 7 applicants, 43% accepted, 2 enrolled. In 2007, 5 degrees awarded. *Degree requirements:* For master's, comprehensive exam (for some programs), thesis (for some programs). *Application deadline:* For fall admission, 5/1 priority date for domestic students; for winter admission, 10/15 priority date for domestic students; for spring admission, 1/20 priority date for domestic students. Applications are processed on a rolling basis. Application fee: $55. Electronic applications accepted. *Expenses:* Tuition, nonresident: full-time $7,232; part-time $226 per unit. Required fees: $3,920. One-time fee: $2,486 part-time. *Unit head:* Dr. Daniel K. Lewis, Chair, 909-869-3869, E-mail: dklewis@csupomona.edu.

California State University, Bakersfield, Division of Graduate Studies, School of Humanities and Social Sciences, Program in History, Bakersfield, CA 93311-1022. Offers MA. *Degree requirements:* For master's, comprehensive exam or thesis. *Entrance requirements:* For master's, 2 letters of recommendation. *Faculty research:* American, European, Latin American, and modern Chinese history.

California State University, Chico, Graduate School, College of Humanities and Fine Arts, Department of History, Chico, CA 95929-0735. Offers MA. Part-time programs available. *Students:* 7 full-time (3 women), 4 part-time; includes 1 minority (American Indian/Alaska Native). Average age 32. 12 applicants, 58% accepted, 4 enrolled. In 2007, 6 degrees awarded. *Degree requirements:* For master's, thesis or alternative, oral exam. *Entrance requirements:* For master's, GRE General Test, 2 letters of recommendation, writing sample, statement of purpose. Additional exam requirements/recommendations for international students: Required—TOEFL (minimum score 550 paper-based; 213 computer-based; 80 iBT), IELTS (minimum score 7). *Application deadline:* For fall admission, 3/1 priority date for domestic students, 3/1 for international students; for spring admission, 9/15 priority date for domestic students, 9/15 for international students. Applications are processed on a rolling basis. Application fee: $55. Electronic applications accepted. *Unit head:* Dr. Kate Transchel, Graduate Coordinator, 530-898-6417, E-mail: ktranschel@csuchico.edu. *Application contact:* Dr. Kate Transchel, Graduate Coordinator, 530-898-6417, E-mail: ktranschel@csuchico.edu.

California State University, East Bay, Academic Programs and Graduate Studies, College of Letters, Arts, and Social Sciences, Department of History, Hayward, CA 94542-3000. Offers MA. Part-time and evening/weekend programs available. *Faculty:* 9 full-time (5 women), 2 part-time/adjunct (0 women). *Students:* 7 full-time (4 women), 33 part-time (15 women); includes 12 minority (4 African Americans, 1 American Indian/Alaska Native, 3 Asian Americans or Pacific Islanders, 4 Hispanic Americans), 1 international. Average age 39. 30 applicants, 77% accepted, 13 enrolled. In 2007, 6 degrees awarded. *Degree requirements:* For master's, one foreign language, comprehensive exam, thesis optional, project or thesis. *Entrance requirements:* For master's, minimum GPA of 3.0 in field. Additional exam requirements/recommendations for international students: Required—TOEFL (minimum score 550 paper-based; 213 computer-based). *Application deadline:* For fall admission, 5/31 for domestic students, 4/30 for international students; for winter admission, 9/30 for domestic and international students; for spring admission, 12/31 for domestic students, 11/30 for international students. Applications are processed on a rolling basis. Application fee: $55. Electronic applications accepted. *Expenses:* Required fees: $3,987; $851 per quarter. *Financial support:* Career-related internships or fieldwork, Federal Work-Study, and institutionally sponsored loans available. Support available to part-time students. Financial award application deadline: 3/2. *Unit head:* Dr. Dee Andrews, Chair, 510-885-3207, Fax: 510-885-4791. *Application contact:* My Huynh, Graduate Prospect Specialist, 510-885-2989, Fax: 510-885-4059, E-mail: my.huynh@csueastbay.edu.

California State University, Fresno, Division of Graduate Studies, College of Social Sciences, Department of History, Fresno, CA 93740-8027. Offers history-teaching option (MA); history-traditional track (MA). Part-time and evening/weekend programs available. *Faculty:* 11 full-time (6 women). *Students:* 41; includes 11 minority (1 African American, 10 Hispanic Americans). Average age 28. 2 applicants. In 2007, 4 degrees awarded. *Degree requirements:* For master's, thesis or alternative. *Entrance requirements:* For master's, GRE General Test, minimum GPA of 3.0. Additional exam requirements/recommendations for international students: Required—TOEFL. *Application deadline:* For fall admission, 5/1 for domestic and international students; for spring admission, 10/1 for domestic and international students. Applications are processed on a rolling basis. Application fee: $55. Electronic applications accepted. *Financial support:* Teaching assistantships, career-related internships or fieldwork, Federal Work-Study, scholarships/grants, and unspecified assistantships available. Support available to part-time students. Financial award application deadline: 3/1; financial award applicants required to submit FAFSA. *Faculty research:* International education, classical art history, improving teacher quality. *Unit head:* Dr. Michelle Den Beste, Chair, 559-278-2153, Fax: 559-278-5321, E-mail: michelle_denbeste@csufresno.edu. *Application contact:* Dr. Maritere Lopez, Graduate Program Coordinator, 559-278-2153, Fax: 559-278-5321, E-mail: mariterel@csufresno.edu.

California State University, Fullerton, Graduate Studies, College of Humanities and Social Sciences, Department of History, Fullerton, CA 92834-9480. Offers MA. Part-time programs available. *Students:* 23 full-time (7 women), 86 part-time (37 women); includes 32 minority (3 African Americans, 5 Asian Americans or Pacific Islanders, 24 Hispanic Americans), 1 international. Average age 32. 52 applicants, 60% accepted, 27 enrolled. In 2007, 34 degrees awarded. *Degree requirements:* For master's, comprehensive exam, project or thesis. *Entrance requirements:* For master's, undergraduate major in history or related field, minimum GPA of 3.0. Application fee: $55. *Financial support:* Teaching assistantships, career-related internships or fieldwork, Federal Work-Study, institutionally sponsored loans, and scholarships/grants available. Support available to part-time students. Financial award application deadline: 3/1. *Unit head:* Dr. William Haddad, Chair, 714-278-3474. *Application contact:* Dr. David Van Deventer, Adviser, 714-278-3474.

California State University, Long Beach, Graduate Studies, College of Liberal Arts, Department of History, Long Beach, CA 90840. Offers MA. Part-time and evening/weekend programs available. *Faculty:* 30 full-time (15 women), 34 part-time/adjunct (14 women). *Students:* 9 full-time (4 women), 53 part-time (23 women); includes 17 minority (3 African Americans, 2 American Indian/Alaska Native, 4 Asian Americans or Pacific Islanders, 8 Hispanic Americans). Average age 35. *Degree requirements:* For master's, one foreign language, comprehensive exam or thesis. *Application deadline:* For fall admission, 7/1 for domestic students; for spring admission, 12/1 for domestic students. Applications are processed on a rolling basis. Application fee: $55. Electronic applications accepted. *Financial support:* Research assistantships, Federal Work-Study, institutionally sponsored loans, and scholarships/grants available. Financial award application deadline: 3/2. *Faculty research:* All periods of European and American history, recent Asian and African history. *Unit head:* Dr. Nancy L Quam-Wickham, Graduate Advisor, 562-985-4449, Fax: 562-985-5431, E-mail: quamwick@csulb.edu. *Application contact:* Dr. Houri Berberian, Information Contact, 562-985-4431, Fax: 562-985-5431.

California State University, Los Angeles, Graduate Studies, College of Natural and Social Sciences, Department of History, Los Angeles, CA 90032-8530. Offers MA. Part-time and evening/weekend programs available. *Faculty:* 4 full-time (1 woman), 1 part-time/adjunct (0 women). *Students:* 36 full-time (10 women), 73 part-time (31 women); includes 61 minority (5 African Americans, 2 American Indian/Alaska Native, 5 Asian Americans or Pacific Islanders, 49 Hispanic Americans), 10 international. Average age 33. In 2007, 7 degrees awarded. *Degree requirements:* For master's, one foreign language, comprehensive exam or thesis. *Entrance requirements:* For master's, minimum GPA of 3.0, undergraduate major in history. Additional exam requirements/recommendations for international students: Required—TOEFL. *Application deadline:* For fall admission, 6/30 for domestic students; for spring admission, 2/1 for domestic students. Applications are processed on a rolling basis. Application fee: $55. *Financial support:* Federal Work-Study available. Support available to part-time students. Financial award application deadline: 3/1. *Faculty research:* Ancient and modern Europe, the Middle East, Latin America, U.S. history-Bill of Rights. *Unit head:* Dr. Cheryl A. Koos, Chair, 323-343-2020, Fax: 323-343-6431, E-mail: ckoos@calstatela.edu.

California State University, Northridge, Graduate Studies, College of Social and Behavioral Sciences, Department of History, Northridge, CA 91330. Offers MA. *Faculty:* 15 full-time (6 women), 16 part-time/adjunct (6 women). *Students:* 36 full-time (16 women), 81 part-time (42 women); includes 31 minority (5 African Americans, 5 Asian Americans or Pacific Islanders, 21 Hispanic Americans). Average age 35. 63 applicants, 83% accepted, 33 enrolled. In 2007, 31 degrees awarded. *Degree requirements:* For master's, one foreign language. *Entrance requirements:* For master's, GRE General Test or minimum GPA of 3.0, 2 letters of recommendation. Additional exam requirements/recommendations for international students: Required—TOEFL. *Application deadline:* For fall admission, 5/15 for domestic students; for spring admission, 11/1 for domestic students. Application fee: $55. *Financial support:* Fellowships, scholarships/grants available. Financial award application deadline: 3/1. *Unit head:* Dr. Thomas R. Maddux, Chair, 818-677-3566, E-mail: thomas.maddux@csun.edu. *Application contact:* Prof. Jeffrey Auerbach, Graduate Coordinator, 818-677-3566.

California State University, Stanislaus, College of Humanities and Social Sciences, Department of History, Turlock, CA 95382. Offers history (MA); international relations (MA); secondary school teachers (MA). Part-time programs available. *Faculty:* 9. *Students:* 4 full-time (2 women), 19 part-time (7 women); includes 5 minority (1 African American, 1 Asian American or Pacific Islander, 3 Hispanic Americans). Average age 36. 18 applicants, 100% accepted, 9 enrolled. *Degree requirements:* For master's, one foreign language, comprehensive exam, thesis or alternative. *Entrance requirements:* For master's, GRE General Test, minimum undergraduate GPA of 3.0, personal statement. Additional exam requirements/recommendations for international students: Required—TOEFL (minimum score 550 paper-based; 213 computer-based). Application fee: $55. Electronic applications accepted. *Expenses:* Tuition, nonresident: full-time $10,170; part-time $339 per unit. Required fees: $3,972; $2,538 per term. $1,165 per semester. *Financial support:* Fellowships, Federal Work-Study available. Financial award application deadline: 3/2; financial award applicants required to submit FAFSA. *Faculty research:* History of Ancient Greece, history and ecology of the central valley, acculturation and gender. *Application contact:* Dr. Samuel Relgalado, Chair, 209-667-3238, Fax: 209-667-3132.

Cardinal Stritch University, College of Arts and Sciences, Department of History, Milwaukee, WI 53217-3985. Offers MA. Part-time programs available. *Degree requirements:* For master's, comprehensive exam, research project. *Entrance requirements:* For master's, minimum GPA of 3.0, 2 letters of recommendation. Electronic applications accepted.

Carleton University, Faculty of Graduate Studies, Faculty of Arts and Social Sciences, Department of History, Ottawa, ON K1S 5B6, Canada. Offers MA, PhD. *Degree requirements:* For master's, one foreign language, thesis; for doctorate, one foreign language, thesis/dissertation. *Entrance requirements:* For master's, honors degree; for doctorate, master's degree. Additional exam requirements/recommendations for international students: Required—TOEFL. Application fee: $77. *Financial support:* Fellowships, research assistantships, teaching assistantships, institutionally sponsored loans, scholarships/grants, and unspecified assistantships available. *Faculty research:* Canadian, American, British, modern French, and modern Russian history; international, medieval, and European intellectual history; women's history. *Unit head:* A.B. McKillop, Chair, 613-520-2600 Ext. 2828, Fax: 613-520-2819, E-mail: chair_history@carleton.ca. *Application contact:* Dominique Marshall, Supervisor of Graduate Studies, 613-520-2600 Ext. 2828, Fax: 613-520-2819, E-mail: grad_history@carleton.ca.

Carnegie Mellon University, College of Humanities and Social Sciences, Department of History, Pittsburgh, PA 15213-3891. Offers history (MA, MS); history and policy (MA, PhD); social and cultural history (PhD). Part-time programs available. *Degree requirements:* For doctorate, oral and written comprehensive exams, dissertation defense. *Entrance requirements:* For doctorate, GRE General Test. Additional exam requirements/recommendations for international students: Required—TOEFL. Electronic applications accepted. *Faculty research:* Anthropology and history, African American history, technology/environment, cultural history analysis.

Case Western Reserve University, School of Graduate Studies, Department of History, Cleveland, OH 44106. Offers MA, PhD. Part-time programs available. *Faculty:* 15 full-time (6 women), 4 part-time/adjunct (2 women). *Students:* 5 full-time (2 women), 21 part-time (10 women); includes 2 minority (1 African American, 1 Asian American or Pacific Islander). 18 applicants, 61% accepted, 3 enrolled. In 2007, 2 master's awarded. Terminal master's awarded for partial completion of doctoral program. *Degree requirements:* For master's, thesis; for doctorate, thesis/dissertation. *Entrance requirements:* For master's and doctorate, GRE General Test. Additional exam requirements/recommendations for international students: Required—TOEFL. *Application deadline:* For fall admission, 3/1 for domestic students. Application fee: $50. Electronic applications accepted. *Financial support:* Fellowships, research assistantships, teaching assistantships, career-related internships or fieldwork, tuition waivers (full and partial), and unspecified assistantships available. Financial award application deadline: 3/1. *Faculty research:* American social history, social policy history, history of technology and science. *Unit head:* Jonathan Sadowsky, Chair, 216-368-2622, Fax: 216-368-4681, E-mail: jonathan.sadowsky@case.edu. *Application contact:* Marissa Ross, Admissions, 216-368-2380, Fax: 216-368-4681, E-mail: mar14@case.edu.

The Catholic University of America, School of Arts and Sciences, Department of History, Washington, DC 20064. Offers MA, PhD, JD/MA, MSLS/MA. Part-time programs available. *Faculty:* 14 full-time (6 women), 2 part-time/adjunct (0 women). *Students:* 15 full-time (9 women), 24 part-time (11 women); includes 1 minority (Asian American or Pacific Islander), 3 international. Average age 35. 36 applicants, 81% accepted, 8 enrolled. In 2007, 9 degrees awarded. *Degree requirements:* For master's, one foreign language, comprehensive exam, thesis or alternative; for doctorate, 2 foreign languages, comprehensive exam, thesis/dissertation, oral exams. *Entrance requirements:* For master's and doctorate, GRE General Test, 3 letters of recommendation. Additional exam requirements/recommendations for international students: Required—TOEFL (minimum score 580 paper-based; 237 computer-based). *Application deadline:* For fall admission, 2/1 priority date for domestic students; for spring admission, 11/15 priority date for domestic students. Applications are processed on a rolling basis. Application fee: $55. Electronic applications accepted. *Financial support:* Teaching assistantships, career-related internships or fieldwork, Federal Work-Study, scholarships/grants, tuition waivers (full and partial), and unspecified assistantships available. Financial award application deadline: 2/1; financial award applicants required to submit FAFSA. *Faculty research:* Medieval family law, U.S. liberalism, capitalism in Europe, Mexican rural society, urbanization in France. *Unit head:* Dr. Leslie Tentler, Chair, 202-319-5484, Fax: 202-319-5569, E-mail: tentler@cua.edu.

Central Connecticut State University, School of Graduate Studies, School of Arts and Sciences, Department of History, New Britain, CT 06050-4010. Offers history (MA, Certificate); public history (MA). Part-time and evening/weekend programs available. *Faculty:* 18 full-time (9 women), 21 part-time/adjunct (7 women). *Students:* 22 full-time (13 women), 38 part-time (15 women); includes 2 minority (both African Americans) Average age 33. 50 applicants, 40% accepted, 13 enrolled. In 2007, 9 master's, 2 other advanced degrees awarded. *Degree requirements:* For master's, thesis or alternative, comprehensive exam or special project. *Entrance requirements:* For master's, minimum GPA of 2.7. Additional exam requirements/recommendations for international students: Required—TOEFL. *Application deadline:* For fall admission, 5/1 for domestic students; for spring admission, 12/1 for domestic students. Applications are processed on a rolling basis. Application fee: $50. Electronic applications accepted. *Expenses:* Tuition, area resident: Full-time $4,169. Tuition, state resident: full-time $6,253. Tuition, nonresident: full-time $11,614; part-time $400 per credit. Required fees: $3,322. One-time fee: $62 part-time. Tuition and fees vary according to degree level and program. *Financial support:* In 2007–08, 7 students received support, including 1 research assistantship; career-related internships or fieldwork, Federal Work-Study, scholarships/grants, and unspecified assistantships also available. Support available to part-time students. Financial award application deadline: 3/1; financial award applicants required to submit FAFSA. *Faculty research:* American West, African history, Eastern Europe, modern Middle East, East Asia. *Unit head:* Dr. Glenn Sunshine, Chair, 860-832-2800.

Central European University, Graduate Studies, Department of History, Budapest, Hungary. Offers MA, PhD. *Faculty:* 8 full-time (2 women), 13 part-time/adjunct (1 woman). *Students:* 100 full-time (55 women). Average age 26. 148 applicants, 33% accepted, 48 enrolled. In 2007, 27 master's, 7 doctorates awarded. Terminal master's awarded for partial completion of doctoral program. *Median time to degree:* Of those who began their doctoral program in fall 1999, 71% received their degree in 8 years or less. *Degree requirements:* For master's, one foreign language, thesis; for doctorate, one foreign language, comprehensive exam, thesis/dissertation. *Entrance requirements:* For master's and doctorate, interview. Additional exam requirements/recommendations for international students: Required—TOEFL (minimum score 570 paper-based; 230 computer-based). *Application deadline:* For fall admission, 1/5 for domestic and international students. Application fee: $0. Electronic applications accepted. Tuition charges are reported in euros. *Expenses:* Tuition: Full-time 10,000 euros; part-time 315 euros per credit. *Financial support:* In 2007–08, 46 students received support, including 38 fellowships with full and partial tuition reimbursements available (averaging $5,000 per year); career-related internships or fieldwork, institutionally sponsored loans, scholarships/grants, and tuition waivers (full and partial) also available. *Faculty research:* Early modern intellectual history; history of ideas; contemporary historiography comparative history of empires, symbolic geography, history of cultural and religious co-existence. *Unit head:* Dr. Lazlo Kontler, Head, 361-327-3022, Fax: 361-327-3191, E-mail: history@ceu.hu. *Application contact:* Zsuzsanna Macht, Coordinator, 361-327-3022, Fax: 361-235-6145, E-mail: history@ceu.hu.

Central Michigan University, College of Graduate Studies, College of Humanities and Social and Behavioral Sciences, Department of History, Mount Pleasant, MI 48859. Offers MA, PhD. Offered jointly with the University of Stratclyde, Scotland. *Degree requirements:* For master's, thesis or alternative. *Entrance requirements:* For master's, minimum GPA of 3.0 in history, 2.7 overall; for doctorate, GRE Subject Test, MA in history, minimum GPA of 3.3. *Faculty research:* U.S. social history; modern Europe (England, France, Germany); Latin America; medieval European, ancient Near Eastern, and Mediterranean history.

See Close-Up on page 415.

Central Washington University, Graduate Studies, Research and Continuing Education, College of Arts and Humanities, Department of History, Ellensburg, WA 98926. Offers MA. *Faculty:* 10 full-time (3 women). *Students:* 14 full-time (6 women), 7 part-time (2 women); includes 1 minority (American Indian/Alaska Native), 1 international. 6 applicants, 67% accepted, 3 enrolled. In 2007, 7 degrees awarded. *Degree requirements:* For master's, thesis or alternative. *Entrance requirements:* For master's, GRE General Test, minimum GPA of 3.0. Additional exam requirements/recommendations for international students: Required—TOEFL (minimum score 550 paper-based; 213 computer-based; 79 iBT). *Application deadline:* For fall admission, 4/1 priority date for domestic students; for winter admission, 10/1 for domestic students; for spring admission, 1/1 for domestic students. Application fee: $50. Electronic applications accepted. *Expenses:* Tuition, state resident: full-time $2,209; part-time $221 per credit. Tuition, nonresident: full-time $4,939; part-time $442 per credit. Required fees: $207 per quarter. Tuition and fees vary according to degree level. *Financial support:* In 2007–08, 1 research assistantship with partial tuition reimbursement (averaging $8,100 per year), 6 teaching assistantships with partial tuition reimbursements (averaging $8,100 per year) were awarded; Federal Work-Study, health care benefits, and unspecified assistantships also available. Financial award application deadline: 3/1; financial award applicants required to submit FAFSA. *Unit head:* Dr. Karen Blair, Chair, 509-963-1655. *Application contact:* Justine Eason, Admissions Program Coordinator, 509-963-3103, Fax: 509-963-1799, E-mail: masters@cwu.edu.

Centro de Estudios Avanzados de Puerto Rico y el Caribe, Graduate Program in Puerto Rican and Caribbean Studies, Old San Juan, PR 00902-3970. Offers Puerto Rican and Caribbean history (MA, PhD); Puerto Rican and Caribbean literature (MA, PhD); Puerto Rican studies (MA). Part-time and evening/weekend programs available. *Degree requirements:* For master's, comprehensive exam, thesis; for doctorate, 2 foreign languages, comprehensive exam, thesis/dissertation. *Entrance requirements:* For master's and doctorate, interview. *Faculty research:* Literature, history, art, folklore, and culture of Puerto Rico and Caribbean countries.

Chicago State University, School of Graduate and Professional Studies, College of Arts and Sciences, Department of History, Philosophy, and Political Science, Chicago, IL 60628. Offers MA. Part-time and evening/weekend programs available. *Degree requirements:* For master's, thesis optional. *Entrance requirements:* For master's, minimum GPA of 2.75. Electronic applications accepted. *Faculty research:* Gregory the Great-use in later Middle Ages, Renaissance alchemy, Liberian wars, Waldo Frank, Sangalan oral traditions.

Christopher Newport University, Graduate Studies, Department of Teacher Preparation, Newport News, VA 23606-2998. Offers art (PK-12) (MAT); biology (6-12) (MAT); computer science (6-12) (MAT); elementary (PK-6) (MAT); English (6-12) (MAT); French (PK-12) (MAT); history (6-12) (MAT); history and social science (MAT); mathematics (6-12) (MAT); music (PK-12) (MAT), including choral, instrumental; physics (6-12) (MAT); Spanish (PK-12) (MAT); theater (PK-12) (MAT). Part-time and evening/weekend programs available. *Faculty:* 15 full-time (9 women), 7 part-time/adjunct (4 women). *Students:* 55 full-time (46 women), 20 part-time (12 women); includes 4 minority (3 African Americans, 1 Asian American or Pacific Islander). Average age 25. 14 applicants, 79% accepted, 11 enrolled. In 2007, 57 degrees awarded. *Degree requirements:* For master's, comprehensive exam, thesis or alternative. *Entrance requirements:* For master's, PRAXIS I, minimum GPA of 3.0. *Application deadline:* For fall admission, 5/1 priority date for domestic students; for spring admission, 11/1 for domestic students. Applications are processed on a rolling basis. Application fee: $45. Electronic applications accepted. *Expenses:* Tuition, state resident: full-time $5,886; part-time $327 per credit. Tuition, nonresident: full-time $10,998; part-time $611 per credit. *Financial support:* In 2007–08, 3 research assistantships with full and partial tuition reimbursements (averaging $2,000 per year) were awarded; career-related internships or fieldwork and Federal Work-Study also available. Support available to part-time students. Financial award application deadline: 3/1; financial award applicants required to submit FAFSA. *Faculty research:* Early literacy development, instructional innovations, professional teaching standards, multicultural issues, aesthetic education. *Unit head:* Dr. Marsha Sprague, Coordinator, 757-594-7388, Fax: 757-594-7304, E-mail: msprague@cnu.edu. *Application contact:* Lyn Sawyer, Associate Director, Graduate Admissions, 757-594-7544, Fax: 757-594-7649, E-mail: gradstdy@cnu.edu.

The Citadel, The Military College of South Carolina, Citadel Graduate College, Department of History, Charleston, SC 29409. Offers MA. Evening/weekend programs available. *Students:* 1 full-time (0 women), 18 part-time (7 women); includes 1 minority (Hispanic American), 1 international. Average age 33. In 2007, 1 degree awarded. *Degree requirements:* For master's, thesis optional. *Entrance requirements:* For master's, GRE General Test, MAT. Additional exam requirements/recommendations for international students: Required—TOEFL (minimum score 550 paper-based; 213 computer-based). *Application deadline:* Applications are processed on a rolling basis. Application fee: $30. *Expenses:* Tuition, state resident: part-time $280 per credit hour. Tuition, nonresident: part-time $503 per credit hour. *Financial support:* Fellowships available. Financial award application deadline: 7/1; financial award applicants required to submit FAFSA. *Unit head:* Dr. Winfred B. Moore, Director, 843-953-5073, E-mail: bo.moore@citadel.edu. *Application contact:* Dr. Raymond S. Jones, Associate Dean, Citadel Graduate College, 843-953-5089, Fax: 843-953-7630, E-mail: ray.jones@citadel.edu.

City College of the City University of New York, Graduate School, College of Liberal Arts and Science, Division of the Humanities and Arts, Department of History, New York, NY 10031-9198. Offers MA. Part-time programs available. *Students:* 2 full-time (1 woman), 28 part-time (12 women); includes 23 minority (9 African Americans, 1 American Indian/Alaska Native, 5 Asian Americans or Pacific Islanders, 8 Hispanic Americans), 3 international. 13 applicants, 85% accepted, 11 enrolled. In 2007, 8 degrees awarded. *Degree requirements:* For master's, one foreign language, comprehensive exam, thesis. *Entrance requirements:* For master's, GRE. Additional exam requirements/recommendations for international students: Required—TOEFL (minimum score 500 paper-based; 173 computer-based). *Application deadline:* For fall admission, 5/1 for domestic students; for spring admission, 11/1 for domestic students. Application fee: $125. *Financial support:* Federal Work-Study and institutionally sponsored loans available. Support available to part-time students. *Faculty research:* Latin American, European, Asian, urban, and architectural history. *Unit head:* Darren Staloff, Chair, 212-650-7457, Fax: 212-650-7179, E-mail: dstaloff@ccny.cuny.edu. *Application contact:* Andreas Killen, Graduate Adviser, 212-650-7454, Fax: 212-650-7179.

Claremont Graduate University, Graduate Programs, School of Arts and Humanities, Department of History, Claremont, CA 91711-6160. Offers Africana history (Certificate); American studies and U.S. history (MA, PhD); archival studies (MA); early modern studies (MA, PhD); European studies (MA, PhD); oral history (MA, PhD); MBA/MA; MBA/PhD. *Faculty:* 3 full-time (2 women), 1 part-time/adjunct (0 women). *Students:* 74 full-time (40 women), 8 part-time (3 women); includes 15 minority (1 African American, 2 Asian Americans or Pacific Islanders, 12 Hispanic Americans), 2 international. Average age 37. In 2007, 8 master's, 8 doctorates awarded. *Degree requirements:* For master's, 2 foreign languages, thesis; for doctorate, 2 foreign languages, comprehensive exam, thesis/dissertation. *Entrance requirements:* For master's and doctorate, GRE General Test. *Application deadline:* For fall admission, 2/15 priority date for domestic students. Applications are processed on a rolling basis. Electronic applications accepted. *Expenses:* Tuition: Full-time $31,640; part-time $1,376 per unit. Required fees: $145 per semester. Tuition and fees vary according to course load, degree level and program. *Financial support:* Fellowships, research assistantships, Federal Work-Study and institutionally sponsored loans available. Support available to part-time students. Financial award application deadline: 2/15; financial award applicants required to submit FAFSA. *Faculty research:* Intellectual and social history, cultural studies, gender studies, Western history, Chicano history. *Unit head:* Janet Farrell Brodie, Chair, 909-621-8880, Fax: 909-621-8609, E-mail: janet.brodie@cgu.edu.

Clark Atlanta University, School of Arts and Sciences, Department of History, Atlanta, GA 30314. Offers MA, DAH. Part-time programs available. *Faculty:* 4 part-time/adjunct (2 women). *Students:* 1 (woman) full-time, 11 part-time (5 women); 11 African Americans, 1 Asian American or Pacific Islander. Average age 35. 3 applicants, 100% accepted, 1 enrolled. In 2007, 3 degrees awarded. *Degree requirements:* For master's, one foreign language, thesis. *Entrance requirements:* For master's, GRE General Test, minimum GPA of 2.5. Additional exam requirements/recommendations for international students: Required—TOEFL (minimum score 550 paper-based; 173 computer-based). *Application deadline:* For fall admission, 4/1 for domestic and international students; for spring admission, 11/1 for domestic and international students. Applications are processed on a rolling basis. Application fee: $40 ($55 for international students). Electronic applications accepted. *Expenses:* Tuition: Full-time $11,664; part-time $648 per credit hour. Required fees: $550; $275 per semester. *Financial support:* Career-related internships or fieldwork, Federal Work-Study, scholarships/grants, and unspecified assistantships available. Support available to part-time students. Financial award application deadline: 4/30; financial award applicants required to submit FAFSA. *Faculty research:* Education for public service. *Unit head:* Dr. Barbara Moss, Chairperson, 404-880-8372, E-mail: bmoss@cau.edu. *Application contact:* Michelle Clark-Davis, Graduate Program Admissions, 404-880-8709, E-mail: mdowis@cau.edu.

Clark University, Graduate School, Department of History, Worcester, MA 01610-1477. Offers history (MA, CAGS); holocaust history (PhD). *Faculty:* 10 full-time (4 women), 2 part-time/adjunct (0 women). *Students:* 19 full-time (11 women), 4 international. Average age 29. 54 applicants, 28% accepted, 13 enrolled. In 2007, 3 master's, 1 doctorate awarded. *Degree requirements:* For master's, thesis, oral exam; for doctorate, thesis/dissertation. *Entrance requirements:* Additional exam requirements/recommendations for international students: Required—TOEFL. *Application deadline:* For fall admission, 2/1 priority date for domestic students. Applications are processed on a rolling basis. Application fee: $55. *Expenses:* Tuition: Full-time $32,600; part-time $1,019 per credit. Required fees: $30. Tuition and fees vary according to program. *Financial support:* In 2007–08, fellowships with full and partial tuition reimbursements (averaging $11,850 per year), research assistantships with full and partial tuition reimbursements (averaging $11,850 per year), 3 teaching assistantships with full and partial tuition reimbursements (averaging $11,850 per year) were awarded; tuition waivers (full and partial) also available. *Faculty research:* American political history, comparative history, modern German and European history, Holocaust history, American family history. Total annual research expenditures: $70,000. *Unit head:* Dr. Drew McCoy, Chair, 508-793-7288. *Application contact:* Diane Fenner, Academic Secretary, 508-793-7288, Fax: 508-793-8816, E-mail: history@clarku.edu.

Clemson University, Graduate School, College of Architecture, Arts, and Humanities, Department of History, Clemson, SC 29634. Offers MA. Part-time programs available. *Faculty:* 23 full-time (6 women). *Students:* 24 full-time (10 women), 13 part-time (6 women); includes 1 minority (Asian American or Pacific Islander) 30 applicants, 43% accepted, 8 enrolled. In 2007, 11 degrees awarded. *Degree requirements:* For master's, one foreign language, thesis. *Entrance requirements:* For master's, GRE General Test. Additional exam requirements/recommendations for international students: Required—TOEFL. *Application deadline:* For fall admission, 6/1 for domestic students, 4/15 for international students; for spring admission, 9/15 for international students. Application fee: $55. *Financial support:* In 2007–08, 18 teaching assistantships (averaging $9,575 per year) were awarded; career-related internships or fieldwork also available. Financial award application deadline: 2/15; financial award applicants required to submit FAFSA. *Faculty research:* American, European, British, and Third World history. *Unit head:* Dr. Thomas Kuehn, Chair, 864-656-5361, Fax: 864-656-1015, E-mail: tjkuehn@clemson.edu. *Application contact:* Dr. Steve Marks, Graduate Coordinator, 864-656-5355, Fax: 864-656-1015, E-mail: msteven@clemson.edu.

Cleveland State University, College of Graduate Studies, College of Liberal Arts and Social Sciences, Department of History, Cleveland, OH 44115. Offers history (MA); museum studies (MA). Part-time and evening/weekend programs available. *Faculty:* 21 full-time (8 women), 2 part-time/adjunct (0 women). *Students:* 8 full-time (3 women), 20 part-time (12 women); includes 2 minority (both African Americans) Average age 34. 23 applicants, 61% accepted, 9 enrolled. In 2007, 14 degrees awarded. *Degree requirements:* For master's, thesis optional. *Entrance requirements:* For master's, minimum GPA of 3.0, bachelor's degree in history. Additional exam requirements/recommendations for international students: Required—TOEFL (minimum score 525 paper-based; 197 computer-based). *Application deadline:* For fall admission, 7/15 priority date for domestic students. Applications are processed on a rolling basis. Application fee: $30. Electronic applications accepted. *Financial support:* In 2007–08, 7 students received support, including research assistantships with full tuition reimbursements

History

Cleveland State University (continued)
available (averaging $8,600 per year); career-related internships or fieldwork and unspecified assistantships also available. *Faculty research:* African diaspora, social history and the city, early modern Europe, local history. *Unit head:* Dr. Joyce M. Mastboom, Chairperson, 216-687-3920, Fax: 216-687-5592, E-mail: j.mastboom@csuohio.edu. *Application contact:* Dr. Robert S. Shelton, Graduate Director, 216-687-3927, E-mail: r.s.shelton@csuohio.edu.

The College at Brockport, State University of New York, School of Letters and Sciences, Department of History, Brockport, NY 14420-2997. Offers MA. Part-time and evening/weekend programs available. *Students:* 22 full-time (8 women), 28 part-time (10 women); includes 1 minority (African American) 23 applicants, 78% accepted, 17 enrolled. In 2007, 19 degrees awarded. *Degree requirements:* For master's, thesis or alternative. *Entrance requirements:* For master's, GRE General Test (recommended), minimum GPA of 3.0, writing sample, letters of recommendation. Additional exam requirements/recommendations for international students: Required—TOEFL (minimum score 550 paper-based; 213 computer-based; 79 iBT). *Application deadline:* For fall admission, 7/15 for domestic and international students; for spring admission, 11/15 for domestic and international students. Application fee: $50. *Expenses:* Tuition, state resident: full-time $6,900; part-time $288 per credit. Tuition, nonresident: full-time $10,920; part-time $455 per credit. Required fees: $738; $31 per credit. *Financial support:* In 2007–08, 1 fellowship with tuition reimbursement (averaging $1,600 per year), 1 teaching assistantship with tuition reimbursement (averaging $6,000 per year) were awarded; Federal Work-Study, scholarships/grants, and unspecified assistantships also available. Support available to part-time students. Financial award application deadline: 3/15; financial award applicants required to submit FAFSA. *Faculty research:* American history, women's history, European history, world history, cultural history. *Unit head:* Dr. Jennifer M. Lloyd, Chairperson, 585-395-2377, Fax: 585-395-2620, E-mail: jlloyd@brockport.edu. *Application contact:* Dr. Morag Martin, Graduate Director, 585-395-5690, Fax: 585-395-2620, E-mail: mmartin@brockport.edu.

College of Charleston, Graduate School, School of Humanities and Social Sciences, Program in History, Charleston, SC 29424-0001. Offers MA. Part-time and evening/weekend programs available. *Faculty:* 22 full-time (3 women), 12 part-time/adjunct (5 women). *Students:* 13 full-time (3 women), 15 part-time (6 women); includes 4 minority (3 African Americans, 1 Hispanic American), 2 international. Average age 29. 19 applicants, 68% accepted, 11 enrolled. In 2007, 9 degrees awarded. *Degree requirements:* For master's, comprehensive exam, thesis optional. *Entrance requirements:* For master's, GRE General Test or MAT, writing sample. Additional exam requirements/recommendations for international students: Required—TOEFL. *Application deadline:* For fall admission, 3/1 for domestic students; for spring admission, 10/15 for domestic students. Applications are processed on a rolling basis. Application fee: $35. Electronic applications accepted. *Expenses:* Tuition, state resident: full-time $7,778; part-time $324 per hour. Tuition, nonresident: full-time $18,732; part-time $781 per hour. *Financial support:* Research assistantships, career-related internships or fieldwork and Federal Work-Study available. Financial award application deadline: 6/1; financial award applicants required to submit FAFSA. *Faculty research:* Modern west Africa, Labor history, Southern women's education, Native Americans, the Atlantic world. *Unit head:* Dr. William Scott Poole, Director, 843-953-4862, Fax: 843-953-6349, E-mail: poolews@cofc.edu. *Application contact:* Susan Hallatt, Assistant Director of Graduate Admissions, 843-953-5614, Fax: 843-953-1434, E-mail: hallatts@cofc.edu.

The College of Saint Rose, Graduate Studies, School of Arts and Humanities, Program in History/Political Science, Albany, NY 12203-1419. Offers MA. Part-time and evening/weekend programs available. *Faculty:* 13 full-time (7 women), 15 part-time/adjunct (6 women). *Students:* 8 full-time (3 women), 14 part-time (5 women); includes 1 minority (Asian American or Pacific Islander) Average age 34. 12 applicants, 83% accepted, 10 enrolled. *Degree requirements:* For master's, final paper/project, thesis or comprehensive exam. *Entrance requirements:* For master's, minimum undergraduate GPA of 3.0, 12 undergraduate credits in US history and/or political science. Additional exam requirements/recommendations for international students: Required—TOEFL (minimum score 550 paper-based; 213 computer-based). *Application deadline:* For fall admission, 7/15 priority date for domestic and international students; for spring admission, 11/15 priority date for domestic and international students. Applications are processed on a rolling basis. Application fee: $35. Electronic applications accepted. *Financial support:* Career-related internships or fieldwork, scholarships/grants, tuition waivers (partial), and unspecified assistantships available. Support available to part-time students. Financial award application deadline: 3/1; financial award applicants required to submit FAFSA. *Unit head:* Dr. Angela Ledford, Graduate Coordinator, 518-458-5326, Fax: 518-454-2862, E-mail: ledforda@strose.edu. *Application contact:* Susan Patterson, Assistant Vice President for Graduate Admission, 518-454-5136, Fax: 518-458-5479, E-mail: ace@strose.edu.

College of Staten Island of the City University of New York, Graduate Programs, Program in History, Staten Island, NY 10314-6600. Offers MA. Part-time and evening/weekend programs available. *Faculty:* 4 full-time (1 woman). *Students:* 2 full-time (1 woman), 14 part-time (5 women); includes 2 minority (1 African American, 1 Hispanic American). Average age 34. 11 applicants, 82% accepted, 7 enrolled. In 2007, 9 degrees awarded. *Degree requirements:* For master's, thesis. *Entrance requirements:* For master's, minimum GPA of 3.0, 2 academic letters of recommendation, minimum GPA in undergraduate history courses of 3.0, letter explaining interest. Additional exam requirements/recommendations for international students: Required—TOEFL (minimum score 550 paper-based; 213 computer-based; 79 iBT). *Application deadline:* Applications are processed on a rolling basis. Application fee: $125. Electronic applications accepted. *Expenses:* Tuition, state resident: part-time $270 per credit. Tuition, nonresident: part-time $500 per credit. Required fees: $38 per semester. One-time fee: $15 part-time. Tuition and fees vary according to course load. *Financial support:* In 2007–08, 1 student received support. Career-related internships or fieldwork and Federal Work-Study available. Financial award application deadline: 4/1; financial award applicants required to submit CSS PROFILE or FAFSA. *Faculty research:* Creoles in Alaska, 1800-1900; African travel narratives and their readers in eighteenth century America. *Unit head:* Dr. Stephen Stearns, Interim Coordinator, 718-982-9639, Fax: 718-982-2864, E-mail: historymakers@mail.csi.cuny.edu. *Application contact:* Sasha Spence, Assistant Director of Graduate Recruitment Admissions, 718-982-2699, Fax: 718-982-2500, E-mail: spence@mail.csi.cuny.edu.

The College of William and Mary, Faculty of Arts and Sciences, Lyon Gardiner Tyler Department of History, Williamsburg, VA 23187-8795. Offers MA, PhD. *Faculty:* 34 full-time (12 women), 6 part-time/adjunct (3 women). *Students:* 60 full-time (33 women); includes 1 minority (African American), 4 international. Average age 28. 155 applicants, 30% accepted, 25 enrolled. In 2007, 9 master's, 7 doctorates awarded. Terminal master's awarded for partial completion of doctoral program. *Median time to degree:* Of those who began their doctoral program in fall 1999, 25% received their degree in 8 years or less. *Degree requirements:* For master's, one foreign language, comprehensive exam, thesis; for doctorate, one foreign language, comprehensive exam, thesis/dissertation. *Entrance requirements:* For master's and doctorate, GRE General Test, minimum GPA of 3.0. Additional exam requirements/recommendations for international students: Required—TOEFL. *Application deadline:* For fall admission, 12/5 for domestic and international students. Application fee: $45. Electronic applications accepted. *Expenses:* Tuition, state resident: full-time $6,250; part-time $275 per credit hour. Tuition, nonresident: part-time $760 per credit hour. Required fees: $3,550. Tuition and fees vary according to program. *Financial support:* In 2007–08, 46 students received support, including 2 fellowships with full tuition reimbursements available (averaging $14,000 per year), 33 research assistantships with full tuition reimbursements available (averaging $14,000 per year), 11 teaching assistantships with full tuition reimbursements available (averaging $14,000 per year); career-related internships or fieldwork also available. Financial award application deadline: 2/1; financial award applicants required to submit FAFSA. *Faculty research:* American history, comparative history. Total annual research expenditures: $145,218. *Unit head:* Dr. Philip Daileader, Chair, 757-221-3725, Fax: 757-221-2111, E-mail: phdail@wm.edu. *Application contact:* Dr. Leisa Meyer, Director of Graduate Studies, 757-221-3737, Fax: 757-221-2111, E-mail: ldmeyer@wm.edu.

Colorado State University, Graduate School, College of Liberal Arts, Department of History, Fort Collins, CO 80523-0015. Offers MA. Part-time programs available. *Faculty:* 21 full-time (9 women). *Students:* 35 full-time (20 women), 7 part-time (3 women); includes 4 minority (1 American Indian/Alaska Native, 3 Hispanic Americans). Average age 29. 45 applicants, 71% accepted, 25 enrolled. In 2007, 11 master's awarded. *Degree requirements:* For master's, one foreign language, thesis (for some programs), written and oral exams. *Entrance requirements:* For master's, GRE General Test, minimum GPA of 3.0, minimum 21 credits in history. Additional exam requirements/recommendations for international students: Required—TOEFL. *Application deadline:* For fall admission, 2/1 priority date for domestic and international students; for spring admission, 11/1 for domestic and international students. Application fee: $50. Electronic applications accepted. *Expenses:* Tuition, state resident: full-time $4,887; part-time $272 per credit. Tuition, nonresident: full-time $16,425; part-time $913 per credit. Required fees: $1,379; $75 per credit. *Financial support:* In 2007–08, 22 teaching assistantships with tuition reimbursements (averaging $11,478 per year) were awarded; fellowships, career-related internships or fieldwork, Federal Work-Study, institutionally sponsored loans, scholarships/grants, traineeships, and unspecified assistantships also available. Financial award application deadline: 3/1; financial award applicants required to submit FAFSA. *Faculty research:* U.S. history, world history, gender history, European history, environmental history. Total annual research expenditures: $49,745. *Unit head:* Dr. Douglas Yarrington, Professor and Chair, 970-491-6334, Fax: 970-491-2941, E-mail: doug.yarrington@colostate.edu. *Application contact:* Robin Troxell, Graduate Studies Administrator, 970-491-6334, Fax: 970-491-2941, E-mail: robin.troxell@colostate.edu.

Columbia University, Graduate School of Arts and Sciences, Division of Social Sciences, Department of History, New York, NY 10027. Offers American history (M Phil, MA, PhD); history (M Phil, MA, PhD); JD/MA; JD/PhD. Part-time programs available. *Faculty:* 63 full-time, 6 part-time/adjunct. *Students:* 223 full-time (103 women), 25 part-time (8 women). Average age 34. 443 applicants, 44% accepted. In 2007, 15 master's, 28 doctorates awarded. *Degree requirements:* For master's, one foreign language, thesis; for doctorate, variable foreign language requirement, thesis/dissertation. *Entrance requirements:* For master's and doctorate, GRE General Test, writing sample. Additional exam requirements/recommendations for international students: Required—TOEFL. Application fee: $90. *Expenses:* Tuition: Part-time $1,452 per credit. Required fees: $152 per term. One-time fee: $75 part-time. Full-time tuition and fees vary according to course level, course load, degree level and program. *Financial support:* Fellowships, teaching assistantships, Federal Work-Study and institutionally sponsored loans available. Support available to part-time students. Financial award application deadline: 1/5; financial award applicants required to submit FAFSA. *Unit head:* Mark L. Von Hagen, Chair, 212-854-6598, Fax: 212-932-0602, E-mail: mlv2@columbia.edu.

Concordia University, School of Graduate Studies, Faculty of Arts and Science, Department of History, Montréal, QC H3G 1M8, Canada. Offers MA, PhD. *Degree requirements:* For master's, one foreign language, thesis optional; for doctorate, one foreign language, comprehensive exam, thesis/dissertation. *Entrance requirements:* For master's, honors degree in history or equivalent. *Faculty research:* Canadian history, European social history, Canadian-American relations.

Converse College, School of Education and Graduate Studies, Program in Liberal Arts, Spartanburg, SC 29302-0006. Offers English (MLA); history (MLA); political science (MLA). *Degree requirements:* For master's, capstone paper. *Entrance requirements:* For master's, minimum GPA of 3.0, 2 recommendations.

Cornell University, Graduate School, Graduate Fields of Arts and Sciences, Field of History, Ithaca, NY 14853-0001. Offers African history (MA, PhD); American history (MA, PhD); ancient history (MA, PhD); early modern European history (MA, PhD); English history (MA, PhD); French history (MA, PhD); German history (MA, PhD); history of science (MA, PhD); Latin American history (MA, PhD); medieval Chinese history (MA, PhD); medieval history (MA, PhD); modern Chinese history (MA, PhD); modern European history (MA, PhD); modern Japanese history (MA, PhD); premodern Islamic history (MA, PhD); premodern Japanese history (MA, PhD); Renaissance history (MA, PhD); Russian history (MA, PhD); Southeast Asian history (MA, PhD). *Faculty:* 56 full-time (14 women). *Students:* 63 full-time (29 women); includes 11 minority (6 African Americans, 2 Asian Americans or Pacific Islanders, 3 Hispanic Americans), 20 international. Average age 31. 201 applicants, 6% accepted, 10 enrolled. In 2007, 11 master's, 11 doctorates awarded. Terminal master's awarded for partial completion of doctoral program. *Degree requirements:* For master's, thesis; for doctorate, 2 foreign languages, comprehensive exam, thesis/dissertation, 1 year of teaching experience. *Entrance requirements:* For master's and doctorate, GRE General Test, writing sample, 3 letters of recommendation. Additional exam requirements/recommendations for international students: Required—TOEFL (minimum score 550 paper-based; 213 computer-based; 77 iBT). *Application deadline:* For fall admission, 1/15 for domestic students. Application fee: $70. Electronic applications accepted. *Financial support:* In 2007–08, 54 students received support, including 26 fellowships with full tuition reimbursements available, 28 teaching assistantships with full tuition reimbursements available; research assistantships with full tuition reimbursements available, institutionally sponsored loans, scholarships/grants, health care benefits, tuition waivers (full and partial), and unspecified assistantships also available. Financial award applicants required to submit FAFSA. *Unit head:* Director of Graduate Studies, 607-255-6738, Fax: 607-255-0469. *Application contact:* Graduate Field Assistant, 607-255-6738, Fax: 607-255-0469, E-mail: history_grad_info@cornell.edu.

Dalhousie University, Faculty of Arts and Social Science, Department of History, Halifax, NS B3H 4R2, Canada. Offers MA, PhD. Part-time programs available. *Faculty:* 16 full-time (3 women), 4 part-time/adjunct (1 woman). *Students:* 23 full-time (15 women). 32 applicants, 38% accepted. In 2007, 4 master's, 2 doctorates awarded. *Degree requirements:* For master's, thesis; for doctorate, thesis/dissertation. *Entrance requirements:* For doctorate, MA. Additional exam requirements/recommendations for international students: Required—TOEFL. *Application deadline:* For fall admission, 6/1 for domestic students. Applications are processed on a rolling basis. Application fee: $60. *Financial support:* Fellowships, research assistantships, teaching assistantships available. *Faculty research:* African, British, Russian, Canadian and Medieval history. *Unit head:* Dr. Shirley Tillotson, Chair, 902-494-2011, Fax: 902-494-3349, E-mail: history@dal.ca. *Application contact:* Dr. Krista Kesselring, Graduate Coordinator, 902-494-3623, Fax: 902-494-3349.

DePaul University, College of Liberal Arts and Sciences, Department of History, Chicago, IL 60604-2287. Offers MA. Part-time and evening/weekend programs available. *Faculty:* 27 full-time (11 women), 12 part-time/adjunct (6 women). *Students:* 12 full-time (9 women), 19 part-time (6 women); includes 1 minority (African American) Average age 29. 28 applicants, 93% accepted, 12 enrolled. In 2007, 6 degrees awarded. *Degree requirements:* For master's, thesis optional. *Entrance requirements:* For master's, GRE General Test, bachelor's degree in social science or history, or history minor. Additional exam requirements/recommendations for international students: Required—TOEFL. *Application deadline:* 4/1 priority date for domestic and international students. Applications are processed on a rolling basis. Application fee: $25. Electronic applications accepted. *Financial support:* In 2007–08, 3 students received support, including fellowships (averaging $7,000 per year); career-related internships or fieldwork, scholarships/grants, and tuition waivers (full) also available. *Faculty research:* U.S., Europe, Latin America, Asia, Africa. *Unit head:* Dr. Warren C. Schultz, Chairperson, 773-325-1561, Fax: 773-325-4764, E-mail: wschultz@depaul.edu. *Application contact:* Dr. Roshanna P. Sylvester, Graduate Director, 773-325-7825, Fax: 773-325-4764, E-mail: rsylvest@depaul.edu.

Drake University, School of Education, Department of Teaching and Learning, Program in Secondary Education, Des Moines, IA 50311-4516. Offers art (MAT); biology (MAT); business (MAT); chemistry (MAT); English (MAT); general science (MAT); history-American (MAT); history-world (MAT); journalism (MAT); mathematics (MAT); physical science (MAT); physics

(MAT); sociology (MAT); speech (MAT); speech communication (MAT); theatre (MAT). Part-time programs available. *Faculty:* 10 full-time (3 women), 28 part-time/adjunct (16 women). *Students:* 13 full-time (7 women), 33 part-time (20 women). 41 applicants, 56% accepted. In 2007, 12 degrees awarded. *Degree requirements:* For master's, comprehensive exam, thesis (for some programs), internships (for some programs). *Entrance requirements:* For master's, GRE General Test, MAT, or Drake Writing Assessment, resumé, 2 letters of recommendation. Additional exam requirements/recommendations for international students: Required—TOEFL (minimum score 550 paper-based; 213 computer-based). *Application deadline:* For fall admission, 7/1 priority date for domestic students, 6/1 priority date for international students; for spring admission, 11/1 priority date for domestic students, 10/1 priority date for international students. Applications are processed on a rolling basis. Application fee: $25. Electronic applications accepted. *Expenses:* Tuition: Full-time $26,030; part-time $370 per credit hour. Required fees: $406; $40 per semester. Tuition and fees vary according to program. *Financial support:* Career-related internships or fieldwork and unspecified assistantships available. Support available to part-time students. *Faculty research:* Counseling and rehabilitation, behavioral supports, inquiry-based science methods, teacher quality enhancement. Total annual research expenditures: $1.5 million. *Application contact:* Ann J. Martin, Graduate Coordinator, 515-271-2034, Fax: 515-271-2831, E-mail: ann.martin@drake.edu.

Drew University, Caspersen School of Graduate Studies, Program in Modern History and Literature, Madison, NJ 07940-1493. Offers MA, PhD. Part-time and evening/weekend programs available. Terminal master's awarded for partial completion of doctoral program. *Degree requirements:* For master's, one foreign language, thesis; for doctorate, 2 foreign languages, comprehensive exam, thesis/dissertation. *Entrance requirements:* For master's and doctorate, GRE General Test. *Faculty research:* History of the book, modern American history/European history, cultural and intellectual history, eighteenth- to twentieth-century history and literature, history of science.

Duke University, Graduate School, Department of History, Durham, NC 27708. Offers history (AM, PhD); Latin American studies (PhD); JD/AM; MD/PhD. *Faculty:* 37 full-time. *Students:* 63 full-time (34 women); includes 10 minority (8 African Americans, 1 American Indian/Alaska Native, 1 Asian American or Pacific Islander), 15 international. 204 applicants, 11% accepted, 10 enrolled. In 2007, 10 master's, 10 doctorates awarded. *Degree requirements:* For doctorate, 2 foreign languages, thesis/dissertation. *Entrance requirements:* For doctorate, GRE General Test. Additional exam requirements/recommendations for international students: Required—TOEFL (minimum score 550 paper-based; 213 computer-based; 83 iBT), IELTS (minimum score 7). *Application deadline:* For fall admission, 12/15 priority date for domestic and international students. Application fee: $75. Electronic applications accepted. *Financial support:* Fellowships, research assistantships, teaching assistantships, Federal Work-Study available. Financial award application deadline: 12/31. *Unit head:* John Thompson, Director of Graduate Studies, 919-681-5746, Fax: 919-681-7670, E-mail: rmennis@duke.edu.

Duquesne University, Graduate School of Liberal Arts, Department of History, Pittsburgh, PA 15282-0001. Offers archival, museum, and editing studies (MA); history (MA). Part-time and evening/weekend programs available. *Faculty:* 6 full-time (1 woman), 3 part-time/adjunct (1 woman). *Students:* 35 full-time (18 women), 10 part-time (5 women). Average age 26. In 2007, 15 degrees awarded. *Degree requirements:* For master's, comprehensive exam (for some programs), thesis optional. *Entrance requirements:* For master's, GRE General Test, writing sample. Additional exam requirements/recommendations for international students: Required—TOEFL. *Application deadline:* For fall admission, 8/15 for domestic students, 5/1 for international students; for spring admission, 11/1 priority date for domestic students. Applications are processed on a rolling basis. Application fee: $50. *Expenses:* Tuition: Part-time $774 per credit. Required fees: $74 per credit. Tuition and fees vary according to program. *Financial support:* In 2007–08, 4 research assistantships with full tuition reimbursements (averaging $4,800 per year) were awarded; career-related internships or fieldwork, Federal Work-Study, scholarships/grants, tuition waivers (full and partial), and unspecified assistantships also available. Support available to part-time students. Financial award application deadline: 5/1. *Faculty research:* American studies, immigration history, local social history, applied history, Eastern European history. *Unit head:* Dr. Holly Mayer, Chair, 412-396-6470.

East Carolina University, Graduate School, Thomas Harriot College of Arts and Sciences, Department of History, Greenville, NC 27858-4353. Offers American history (MA); European history (MA); maritime history (MA). Part-time and evening/weekend programs available. *Faculty:* 27 full-time (4 women). *Students:* 30 full-time (14 women), 26 part-time (14 women); includes 4 minority (2 African Americans, 2 Hispanic Americans), 3 international. Average age 31. 14 applicants, 50% accepted, 3 enrolled. In 2007, 13 degrees awarded. *Degree requirements:* For master's, one foreign language, comprehensive exam, thesis. *Entrance requirements:* For master's, GRE General Test, GRE Subject Test. Additional exam requirements/recommendations for international students: Required—TOEFL. *Application deadline:* For fall admission, 6/1 priority date for domestic students; for spring admission, 10/15 for domestic students. Applications are processed on a rolling basis. Application fee: $50. *Financial support:* Fellowships, research assistantships with partial tuition reimbursements, teaching assistantships with partial tuition reimbursements, Federal Work-Study available. Support available to part-time students. Financial award application deadline: 6/1. *Unit head:* Dr. Michael Palmer, Chair, 252-328-1046, E-mail: palmerm@ecu.edu. *Application contact:* Dr. Carl Swanson, Director of Graduate Studies, 252-328-6485, E-mail: swansonc@ecu.edu.

Eastern Illinois University, Graduate School, College of Arts and Humanities, Department of History, Charleston, IL 61920-3099. Offers historical administration (MA); history (MA). *Faculty:* 14 full-time (2 women). In 2007, 17 degrees awarded. *Application deadline:* For fall admission, 7/31 priority date for domestic students. Applications are processed on a rolling basis. Application fee: $30. *Expenses:* Tuition, state resident: part-time $218 per hour. Tuition, nonresident: part-time $654 per hour. *Financial support:* In 2007–08, research assistantships with tuition reimbursements (averaging $7,200 per year), 9 teaching assistantships with tuition reimbursements (averaging $7,200 per year) were awarded; career-related internships or fieldwork also available. *Unit head:* Dr. Anita Shelton, Chairperson, 217-581-3310, Fax: 217-581-2722, E-mail: ashelton@eiu.edu. *Application contact:* Dr. Ed Wehrle, Graduate Coordinator, 217-581-6372, Fax: 217-581-2722, E-mail: efwehrle@eiu.edu.

Eastern Kentucky University, The Graduate School, College of Arts and Sciences, Department of History, Richmond, KY 40475-3102. Offers MA. Part-time programs available. *Faculty:* 4 full-time (0 women). *Students:* 8 full-time (1 woman), 11 part-time (3 women). Average age 29. 25 applicants, 48% accepted. In 2007, 9 degrees awarded. *Degree requirements:* For master's, comprehensive exam, thesis optional. *Entrance requirements:* For master's, GRE General Test, GRE Subject Test, minimum GPA of 2.5. Application fee: $35. *Financial support:* In 2007–08, research assistantships (averaging $6,500 per year), teaching assistantships (averaging $6,500 per year) were awarded; Federal Work-Study also available. Support available to part-time students. *Faculty research:* Twentieth-century U.S. history, Kentucky history, British history, world history, Eastern Europe. *Unit head:* Dr. David K. Coleman, Chair, 859-622-1287, Fax: 859-622-1357. *Application contact:* Dr. Todd E. Hartch, Coordinator of Graduate Program, Associate Professor, 859-622-1367, E-mail: todd.hartch@eku.edu.

Eastern Michigan University, Graduate School, College of Arts and Sciences, Department of History and Philosophy, Program in History, Ypsilanti, MI 48197. Offers history (MA); state and local history (Graduate Certificate). Part-time and evening/weekend programs available. Postbaccalaureate distance learning degree programs offered (minimal on-campus study). *Students:* 5 full-time (1 woman), 42 part-time (18 women); includes 7 minority (5 African Americans, 1 Asian American or Pacific Islander, 1 Hispanic American). Average age 34. In 2007, 12 degrees awarded. *Degree requirements:* For master's, thesis optional. *Entrance requirements:* Additional exam requirements/recommendations for international students: Required—TOEFL. *Application deadline:* Applications are processed on a rolling basis. Application fee: $35. *Expenses:* Tuition, state resident: full-time $8,952; part-time $373 per credit hour. Tuition, nonresident: full-time $17,634; part-time $735 per credit hour. Required fees: $896; $34 per credit hour. Tuition and fees vary according to course level, degree level and program. *Financial support:* Fellowships, research assistantships with full tuition reimbursements, teaching assistantships with full tuition reimbursements, career-related internships or fieldwork, Federal Work-Study, institutionally sponsored loans, scholarships/grants, tuition waivers (partial), and unspecified assistantships available. Support available to part-time students. Financial award applicants required to submit FAFSA. *Application contact:* Dr. Ronald Delph, Coordinator, 734-487-0053, E-mail: rdelph@emich.edu.

Eastern Washington University, Graduate Studies, College of Social and Behavioral Sciences, Department of History, Cheney, WA 99004-2431. Offers MA. *Degree requirements:* For master's, comprehensive exam, thesis optional. *Entrance requirements:* For master's, minimum GPA of 3.0.

East Stroudsburg University of Pennsylvania, Graduate School, College of Arts and Sciences, Department of History, East Stroudsburg, PA 18301-2999. Offers M Ed, MA. Part-time and evening/weekend programs available. *Faculty:* 7 full-time (1 woman). *Students:* 12 full-time (6 women), 18 part-time (11 women); includes 1 minority (African American) Average age 32. In 2007, 8 degrees awarded. *Degree requirements:* For master's, variable foreign language requirement, comprehensive exam, thesis (for some programs). *Entrance requirements:* Additional exam requirements/recommendations for international students: Required—TOEFL (minimum score 560 paper-based; 220 computer-based; 83 iBT). *Application deadline:* For fall admission, 7/31 priority date for domestic students, 5/1 priority date for international students; for spring admission, 11/30 for domestic students, 10/1 for international students. Applications are processed on a rolling basis. Application fee: $50. *Expenses:* Tuition, state resident: full-time $6,214; part-time $345 per credit. Tuition, nonresident: full-time $9,944; part-time $552 per credit. Required fees: $1,441; $120 per credit. *Financial support:* In 2007–08, 7 research assistantships with full and partial tuition reimbursements (averaging $1,966 per year) were awarded; Federal Work-Study and institutionally sponsored loans also available. Financial award application deadline: 3/1; financial award applicants required to submit FAFSA. *Unit head:* Dr. Lawrence Squeri, Graduate Coordinator, 570-422-3284, Fax: 570-422-3506, E-mail: lsqueri@po-box.esu.edu. *Application contact:* Dr. Henry Gardner, Associate Provost for Enrollment Management, 570-422-2870, Fax: 570-422-2843, E-mail: hgardner@po-box.esu.edu.

East Tennessee State University, School of Graduate Studies, College of Arts and Sciences, Department of History, Johnson City, TN 37614. Offers MA. Part-time and evening/weekend programs available. *Degree requirements:* For master's, comprehensive exam, thesis or alternative. *Entrance requirements:* For master's, GRE, bachelor's degree in history, minimum GPA of 3.0. Additional exam requirements/recommendations for international students: Required—TOEFL (minimum score 550 paper-based; 213 computer-based). *Faculty research:* Post-World War II German occupation, biographies of Eleanor Copenhaver Anderson and Harry M. Candill, the Miss America Pageant, encyclopedia of colonialism, the new Georgia campaign in the Pacific war.

Emory & Henry College, Graduate Programs, Emory, VA 24327-0947. Offers American history (MA Ed); professional studies (M Ed); reading specialist (MA Ed). Part-time and evening/weekend programs available. *Faculty:* 3 full-time (1 woman). *Students:* Average age 37. 15 applicants, 100% accepted, 15 enrolled. In 2007, 68 degrees awarded. *Entrance requirements:* For master's, GRE or PRAXIS I, recommendations, writing sample, official transcripts. *Application deadline:* Applications are processed on a rolling basis. Application fee: $30. *Expenses:* Tuition: Part-time $285 per semester hour. *Financial support:* Applicants required to submit FAFSA. *Unit head:* Dr. Jack Roper, Director of Graduate Studies, 276-944-6188, Fax: 276-944-5223, E-mail: jroper@ehc.edu.

Emory University, Graduate School of Arts and Sciences, Department of History, Atlanta, GA 30322-1100. Offers PhD. *Degree requirements:* For doctorate, 2 foreign languages, comprehensive exam, thesis/dissertation. *Entrance requirements:* For doctorate, GRE General Test, minimum GPA of 3.0. Electronic applications accepted. *Faculty research:* U.S., modern Europe, early modern Europe, medieval Europe, Latin America, Africa.

Emporia State University, School of Graduate Studies, College of Liberal Arts and Sciences, Department of Social Sciences, Program in History, Emporia, KS 66801-5087. Offers American history (MA); world history (MA). *Students:* 4 full-time (1 woman), 23 part-time (9 women); includes 3 minority (2 African Americans, 1 Hispanic American). 5 applicants, 100% accepted, 5 enrolled. In 2007, 9 degrees awarded. *Degree requirements:* For master's, comprehensive exam or thesis. *Entrance requirements:* For master's, 12 credit hours in history, minimum undergraduate GPA of 2.5, writing sample. Additional exam requirements/recommendations for international students: Required—TOEFL. *Application deadline:* For fall admission, 8/15 priority date for domestic students. Applications are processed on a rolling basis. Application fee: $30 ($75 for international students). Electronic applications accepted. *Expenses:* Tuition, state resident: part-time $157 per credit hour. Tuition, nonresident: part-time $475 per credit hour. Required fees: $47 per credit hour. Tuition and fees vary according to campus/location. *Financial support:* Federal Work-Study, institutionally sponsored loans, health care benefits, and unspecified assistantships available. Financial award application deadline: 3/15; financial award applicants required to submit FAFSA. *Faculty research:* Great Plains history. *Application contact:* Dr. Deborah Gerish, Assistant Professor, 620-341-5579, E-mail: dgerish@emporia.edu.

Fairleigh Dickinson University, Metropolitan Campus, University College: Arts, Sciences, and Professional Studies, School of History, Political and International Studies, Program in History, Teaneck, NJ 07666-1914. Offers MA. *Students:* Average age 24. 2 applicants, 50% accepted, 0 enrolled. *Application deadline:* Applications are processed on a rolling basis. Application fee: $40. *Expenses:* Tuition: Part-time $869 per credit. Tuition and fees vary according to degree level, campus/location and program. *Unit head:* Dr. Faramarz S. Fatemi, Director, School of History, Political and International Studies, 201-692-2272, Fax: 201-692-9096, E-mail: fatemi@fdu.edu.

Fayetteville State University, Graduate School, Department of Geography, History and Political Science, Fayetteville, NC 28301-4298. Offers history (MA); political science (MA). Part-time and evening/weekend programs available. *Faculty:* 6 full-time (1 woman). *Students:* 6 full-time (3 women), 9 part-time (4 women); includes 10 minority (all African Americans) Average age 40. 2 applicants, 100% accepted, 2 enrolled. In 2007, 11 degrees awarded. *Degree requirements:* For master's, comprehensive exam, internship. *Entrance requirements:* For master's, GRE General Test. *Application deadline:* For fall admission, 7/1 for domestic students; for spring admission, 12/1 for domestic students. Applications are processed on a rolling basis. Application fee: $25. Electronic applications accepted. *Expenses:* Tuition, state resident: full-time $2,118; part-time $265 per credit hour. Tuition, nonresident: full-time $11,708; part-time $1,464 per credit hour. Required fees: $1,218; $152 per credit hour. *Unit head:* Dr. Adeguke Ademiluyi, Chairperson, 910-672-1137, E-mail: aademiluyi@uncfsu.edu.

Fitchburg State College, Division of Graduate and Continuing Education, Programs in History and Teaching History (Secondary Level), Fitchburg, MA 01420-2697. Offers MA, MAT, Certificate. *Accreditation:* NCATE. Part-time and evening/weekend programs available. *Students:* 2 full-time (0 women), 22 part-time (9 women); includes 2 minority (1 African American, 1 Hispanic American). Average age 35. 7 applicants, 71% accepted, 4 enrolled. In 2007, 4 degrees awarded. *Entrance requirements:* For master's, GRE General Test or MAT, appropriate bachelor's degree, letters of recommendation, resumé. Additional exam requirements/recommendations for international students: Required—TOEFL (minimum score 550 paper-based; 213 computer-based; 79 iBT). *Application deadline:* Applications are processed on a rolling basis. Application fee: $25 ($50 for international students). *Expenses:* Tuition, nonresident: part-time $150 per credit. Required fees: $109 per credit. *Financial support:* In 2007–08, research assistantships with partial tuition reimbursements (averaging $5,500 per year); Federal Work-Study, scholarships/grants, and unspecified assistantships also available. Support available to part-time students. Financial award application deadline: 3/1; financial award applicants required to submit FAFSA. *Unit head:* Dr. Laura Baker, Chair, 978-665-3379, Fax: 978-665-3658, E-mail:

History

Fitchburg State College (continued)
gce@fsc.edu. *Application contact:* Director of Admissions, 978-665-3144, Fax: 978-665-4540, E-mail: admissions@fsc.edu.

Florida Agricultural and Mechanical University, Division of Graduate Studies, Research, and Continuing Education, College of Arts and Sciences, Division of History and Political Sciences, Program in Applied Social Science, Tallahassee, FL 32307-3200. Offers African American history (MASS); criminal justice (MASS); economics (MASS); history (MASS); political science (MASS); public administration (MASS); public management (MASS); social work (MASS); sociology (MASS). Part-time programs available. *Degree requirements:* For master's, thesis optional. *Entrance requirements:* For master's, GRE General Test, minimum GPA of 3.0. *Faculty research:* Southern history, black history, election trends, presidential history.

Florida Atlantic University, Dorothy F. Schmidt College of Arts and Letters, Department of History, Boca Raton, FL 33431-0991. Offers MA. Part-time programs available. *Degree requirements:* For master's, one foreign language, thesis optional. *Entrance requirements:* For master's, GRE General Test, minimum GPA of 3.0. Electronic applications accepted. *Faculty research:* Twentieth century America, U.S. urban history, Florida history, history of socialism, Latin America.

Florida Gulf Coast University, College of Arts and Sciences, Program in History, Fort Myers, FL 33965-6565. Offers MA. Part-time and evening/weekend programs available. *Faculty:* 82 full-time (31 women), 103 part-time/adjunct (46 women). *Students:* Average age 37. 17 applicants, 82% accepted, 10 enrolled. *Entrance requirements:* Additional exam requirements/recommendations for international students: Required—TOEFL (minimum score 550 paper-based; 213 computer-based). *Application deadline:* For fall admission, 2/15 priority date for domestic students; for spring admission, 10/1 for domestic students. Applications are processed on a rolling basis. Electronic applications accepted. *Expenses:* Tuition, state resident: full-time $4,542. Tuition, nonresident: full-time $19,449. Required fees: $1,297. *Unit head:* Eric Strahorn, Head, 239-590-7214, E-mail: estraho@fgcu.edu.

Florida International University, College of Arts and Sciences, Department of History, Miami, FL 33199. Offers MA, PhD. Part-time and evening/weekend programs available. *Faculty:* 20 full-time (10 women), 3 part-time/adjunct (all women). *Students:* 34 full-time (13 women), 56 part-time (27 women); includes 41 minority (7 African Americans, 1 American Indian/Alaska Native, 1 Asian American or Pacific Islander, 32 Hispanic Americans), 5 international. Average age 36. 74 applicants, 68% accepted, 36 enrolled. In 2007, 10 master's, 3 doctorates awarded. *Degree requirements:* For master's, thesis optional; for doctorate, comprehensive exam, thesis/dissertation. *Entrance requirements:* For master's, GRE General Test, minimum 3.0 average, 2 letters of recommendation; for doctorate, GRE General Test, minimum GPA of 3.25, 2 letters of recommendation. Additional exam requirements/recommendations for international students: Required—TOEFL. *Application deadline:* For fall admission, 2/15 priority date for domestic students; for spring admission, 10/1 for domestic students. Applications are processed on a rolling basis. Application fee: $30. *Expenses:* Tuition, state resident: full-time $6,106. Tuition, nonresident: full-time $15,528. Required fees: $284. *Financial support:* Teaching assistantships, Federal Work-Study, institutionally sponsored loans, and scholarships/grants available. Support available to part-time students. *Faculty research:* European social history, American culture, Latin American culture and social history, Holocaust education. *Unit head:* Dr. Noble David Cook, Chairperson, 305-348-2328, Fax: 305-348-3561, E-mail: noble.cook@fiu.edu.

Florida State University, Graduate Studies, College of Arts and Sciences, Department of History, Tallahassee, FL 32306. Offers historical administration (MA); history (MA, PhD). Part-time programs available. *Faculty:* 28 full-time (10 women). *Students:* 85 full-time (36 women), 54 part-time (23 women); includes 19 minority (10 African Americans, 2 Asian Americans or Pacific Islanders, 7 Hispanic Americans), 4 international. Average age 26. 72 applicants, 74% accepted, 27 enrolled. In 2007, 13 master's, 7 doctorates awarded. *Median time to degree:* Of those who began their doctoral program in fall 1999, 0% received their degree in 8 years or less. *Degree requirements:* For master's, one foreign language, comprehensive exam (for some programs), thesis (for some programs), internships; for doctorate, one foreign language, comprehensive exam, thesis/dissertation. *Entrance requirements:* For master's, GRE General Test, minimum GPA of 3.3, minimum 18 hours of course work in history; for doctorate, GRE General Test, minimum GPA of 3.3 (undergraduate), 3.65 (graduate). Additional exam requirements/recommendations for international students: Required—TOEFL (minimum score 550 paper-based; 213 computer-based; 80 iBT). *Application deadline:* For fall admission, 1/10 for domestic students; for spring admission, 10/1 for domestic students. Applications are processed on a rolling basis. Application fee: $30. Electronic applications accepted. *Expenses:* Tuition, state resident: part-time $248 per credit hour. Tuition, nonresident: part-time $880 per credit hour. Tuition and fees vary according to program. *Financial support:* In 2007–08, 66 students received support, including 8 fellowships with full tuition reimbursements available (averaging $9,000 per year), 10 research assistantships with full tuition reimbursements available (averaging $9,000 per year), 24 teaching assistantships with full tuition reimbursements available (averaging $10,500 per year); Federal Work-Study, institutionally sponsored loans, scholarships/grants, and unspecified assistantships also available. Financial award application deadline: 1/10; financial award applicants required to submit FAFSA. *Faculty research:* Southern and Caribbean studies, Napoleon and the French Revolution, modern Europe, Latin America, U.S. intellectual and cultural history. *Unit head:* Dr. Neil Jumonville, Chairman, 850-644-5888, Fax: 850-644-6402, E-mail: njumonville@fsu.edu. *Application contact:* Chris Pignatiello, Academic Support Assistant, 850-644-2610, Fax: 850-644-6402, E-mail: cpignatiello@fsu.edu.

Fordham University, Graduate School of Arts and Sciences, Department of History, New York, NY 10458. Offers MA, PhD. Part-time and evening/weekend programs available. *Faculty:* 32 full-time (14 women). *Students:* 44 full-time (20 women), 26 part-time (15 women); includes 6 minority (3 African Americans, 1 Asian American or Pacific Islander, 2 Hispanic Americans), 2 international. Average age 31. 101 applicants, 72% accepted, 24 enrolled. In 2007, 13 master's awarded. Terminal master's awarded for partial completion of doctoral program. *Median time to degree:* Of those who began their doctoral program in fall 1999, 25% received their degree in 8 years or less. *Degree requirements:* For master's, one foreign language, thesis optional; for doctorate, 2 foreign languages, comprehensive exam, thesis/dissertation. *Entrance requirements:* For master's and doctorate, GRE General Test. Additional exam requirements/recommendations for international students: Required—TOEFL (minimum score 650 paper-based; 280 computer-based). *Application deadline:* For fall admission, 1/4 priority date for domestic students; for spring admission, 11/1 for domestic students. Application fee: $70. Electronic applications accepted. *Expenses:* Tuition: Full-time $23,880; part-time $995 per credit. *Financial support:* In 2007–08, 17 students received support, including 2 fellowships with tuition reimbursements available (averaging $22,225 per year), 9 research assistantships with tuition reimbursements available (averaging $17,172 per year), 6 teaching assistantships with tuition reimbursements available (averaging $16,075 per year); institutionally sponsored loans, tuition waivers (full and partial), and unspecified assistantships also available. Financial award application deadline: 1/4; financial award applicants required to submit FAFSA. *Unit head:* Dr. Doran Ben-Atar, Chair, 718-817-3925, Fax: 718-817-4680. *Application contact:* Charlene Dundie, Director of Graduate Admissions, 718-817-4420, Fax: 718-817-3566, E-mail: dundie@fordham.edu.

Fort Hays State University, Graduate School, College of Arts and Sciences, Department of History, Hays, KS 67601-4099. Offers MA. *Faculty:* 7 full-time (1 woman). *Students:* 4 full-time (2 women), 5 part-time (3 women). Average age 34. 3 applicants, 67% accepted. In 2007, 7 degrees awarded. *Degree requirements:* For master's, comprehensive exam, thesis or alternative. *Entrance requirements:* For master's, minimum undergraduate GPA of 3.0. Additional exam requirements/recommendations for international students: Required—TOEFL (minimum score 550 paper-based; 213 computer-based). *Application deadline:* For fall admission, 7/1 priority date for domestic students. Applications are processed on a rolling basis. Application fee: $35. Electronic applications accepted. *Expenses:* Tuition, state resident: part-time $155 per credit hour. Tuition, nonresident: part-time $409 per credit hour. Tuition and fees vary according to class time, course level, course load, degree level, campus/location and program. *Financial support:* In 2007–08, 4 teaching assistantships (averaging $7,000 per year) were awarded; research assistantships, career-related internships or fieldwork, institutionally sponsored loans, and tuition waivers (full and partial) also available. Support available to part-time students. *Faculty research:* Seventeenth century English legal history, Native American history, immigration history, Volga German settlement. *Unit head:* Dr. Raymond Wilson, Chair, 785-628-4248, E-mail: rwilson@fhsu.edu.

George Mason University, College of Humanities and Social Sciences, Department of History and Art History, Program in History, Fairfax, VA 22030. Offers MA, PhD. Evening/weekend programs available. *Degree requirements:* For master's, comprehensive exam; for doctorate, comprehensive exam, thesis/dissertation. *Entrance requirements:* For master's, GRE, 2 letters of recommendation, resumé; for doctorate, GRE, 3 letters of recommendation.

George Mason University, Graduate School of Education, Programs in Curriculum and Instruction, Fairfax, VA 22030. Offers early childhood education (M Ed); English as a second language (M Ed); gifted child education (M Ed); history (M Ed); instructional technology (M Ed); library media (M Ed); literacy and reading (M Ed); mathematics (M Ed); physical education (M Ed); science (M Ed); secondary education (M Ed); special education (M Ed, Graduate Certificate); teacher leadership (M Ed). Part-time and evening/weekend programs available. *Faculty:* 108 full-time (70 women), 193 part-time/adjunct (140 women). *Students:* 185 full-time (157 women), 819 part-time (646 women); includes 116 minority (30 African Americans, 3 American Indian/Alaska Native, 42 Asian Americans or Pacific Islanders, 41 Hispanic Americans), 35 international. Average age 33. 501 applicants, 71% accepted, 310 enrolled. In 2007, 360 master's, 7 other advanced degrees awarded. *Entrance requirements:* For master's, minimum GPA of 3.0 in last 60 hours. *Application deadline:* For fall admission, 5/1 for domestic students; for spring admission, 11/1 for domestic students. Application fee: $60 ($75 for international students). Electronic applications accepted. *Financial support:* Career-related internships or fieldwork available. Support available to part-time students. Financial award application deadline: 3/1; financial award applicants required to submit FAFSA. *Unit head:* Martin E. Ford, Senior Associate Dean, 703-993-2004.

Georgetown University, Graduate School of Arts and Sciences, Department of History, Washington, DC 20057-1035. Offers MA, PhD, MA/PhD. *Degree requirements:* For doctorate, 2 foreign languages, comprehensive exam, thesis/dissertation. *Entrance requirements:* For master's and doctorate, GRE General Test. Additional exam requirements/recommendations for international students: Required—TOEFL.

The George Washington University, Columbian College of Arts and Sciences, Department of History, Washington, DC 20052. Offers MA, PhD. Part-time and evening/weekend programs available. Terminal master's awarded for partial completion of doctoral program. *Degree requirements:* For master's, one foreign language, comprehensive exam, thesis or alternative; for doctorate, 2 foreign languages, thesis/dissertation, general exam. *Entrance requirements:* For master's and doctorate, GRE General Test, minimum GPA of 3.0. Additional exam requirements/recommendations for international students: Required—TOEFL (minimum score 550 paper-based; 213 computer-based). Electronic applications accepted.

Georgia College & State University, Graduate School, School of Liberal Arts and Sciences, Department of History and Geography, Program in History, Milledgeville, GA 31061. Offers MA. *Faculty:* 14 full-time (4 women). *Students:* 5 full-time (4 women), 3 part-time (1 woman); includes 1 minority (African American) Average age 29. 12 applicants, 33% accepted, 3 enrolled. In 2007, 4 degrees awarded. *Expenses:* Tuition, state resident: full-time $3,726. Tuition, nonresident: full-time $14,868. Required fees: $858. Tuition and fees vary according to campus/location. *Financial support:* In 2007–08, 6 research assistantships were awarded. *Unit head:* Dr. John Fair, Head, 478-445-5004.

Georgia Southern University, Jack N. Averitt College of Graduate Studies, College of Liberal Arts and Social Sciences, Department of History, Statesboro, GA 30460. Offers MA. Part-time programs available. *Students:* 15 full-time (6 women), 9 part-time (4 women); includes 1 minority (African American) Average age 29. 12 applicants, 83% accepted, 6 enrolled. In 2007, 5 degrees awarded. *Degree requirements:* For master's, one foreign language, thesis optional, terminal exams. *Entrance requirements:* For master's, GRE General Test, minimum GPA of 3.0, undergraduate major in history or equivalent, letters of reference. Additional exam requirements/recommendations for international students: Required—TOEFL (minimum score 550 paper-based; 213 computer-based; 80 iBT). *Application deadline:* For fall admission, 3/1 priority date for domestic and international students; for spring admission, 10/1 priority date for domestic students, 10/1 for international students. Applications are processed on a rolling basis. Application fee: $50. Electronic applications accepted. *Expenses:* Tuition, state resident: full-time $3,516; part-time $147 per semester hour. Tuition, nonresident: full-time $14,060; part-time $586 per semester hour. Required fees: $562 per term. *Financial support:* In 2007–08, 14 students received support, including research assistantships with partial tuition reimbursements available (averaging $6,850 per year), teaching assistantships with partial tuition reimbursements available (averaging $6,850 per year); career-related internships or fieldwork, Federal Work-Study, scholarships/grants, tuition waivers (partial), and unspecified assistantships also available. Support available to part-time students. Financial award application deadline: 4/15; financial award applicants required to submit FAFSA. *Faculty research:* Women's/gender history, American South, Europe, history of religion. *Unit head:* Dr. Sandra Peacock, Chair, 912-478-5586, Fax: 912-478-0377, E-mail: speacock@georgiasouthern.edu. *Application contact:* 912-478-5384, Fax: 912-478-0740, E-mail: gradadmissions@georgiasouthern.edu.

Georgia State University, College of Arts and Sciences, Department of History, Program in History, Atlanta, GA 30303-3083. Offers MA, PhD. Part-time and evening/weekend programs available. *Degree requirements:* For master's, one foreign language, thesis, exam; for doctorate, 2 foreign languages, thesis/dissertation, exam. *Entrance requirements:* For master's, GRE General Test; for doctorate, GRE General Test, sample of written work. Additional exam requirements/recommendations for international students: Required—TOEFL. *Application deadline:* For fall admission, 4/15 for domestic students; for spring admission, 11/15 for domestic students. Applications are processed on a rolling basis. Application fee: $50. Electronic applications accepted. *Expenses:* Tuition, state resident: part-time $221 per credit hour. *Financial support:* In 2007–08, research assistantships with full tuition reimbursements (averaging $6,750 per year), teaching assistantships with full tuition reimbursements (averaging $14,250 per year) were awarded; Federal Work-Study, scholarships/grants, and health care benefits also available. Financial award application deadline: 3/1; financial award applicants required to submit FAFSA. *Faculty research:* World, U.S. South, cultural history, public history, labor. Total annual research expenditures: $140,000.

Graduate School and University Center of the City University of New York, Graduate Studies, Program in History, New York, NY 10016-4039. Offers PhD. *Faculty:* 75 full-time (18 women). *Students:* 132 full-time (57 women), 4 part-time (3 women); includes 11 minority (3 African Americans, 2 Asian Americans or Pacific Islanders, 6 Hispanic Americans), 12 international. Average age 36. 130 applicants, 55% accepted, 32 enrolled. In 2007, 10 degrees awarded. *Degree requirements:* For doctorate, one foreign language, thesis/dissertation. *Entrance requirements:* For doctorate, GRE General Test, writing sample (15 pages). Additional exam requirements/recommendations for international students: Required—TOEFL. *Application deadline:* For fall admission, 1/15 for domestic students. Application fee: $125. Electronic applications accepted. *Financial support:* In 2007–08, 86 students received support, including 71 fellowships, 12 research assistantships, 13 teaching assistantships; career-related internships or fieldwork, Federal Work-Study, institutionally sponsored loans, and tuition waivers (full and partial) also available. Financial award application deadline: 2/1; financial award applicants required to submit FAFSA. *Unit head:* Dr. Joshua Freeman, Executive Officer, 212-817-8430, Fax: 212-817-1523.

Hardin-Simmons University, Graduate School, Cynthia Ann Parker College of Liberal Arts, Department of History, Abilene, TX 79698-0001. Offers MA. Part-time programs available. *Faculty:* 5 full-time (2 women). *Students:* Average age 31. 4 applicants, 50% accepted, 2 enrolled. *Degree requirements:* For master's, one foreign language, comprehensive exam, thesis or alternative. *Entrance requirements:* For master's, GRE, minimum undergraduate GPA of 3.0 in history, 2.7 overall; 18 upper-level hours of course work in history; letters of recommendation; resumé; writing sample. Additional exam requirements/recommendations for international students: Required—TOEFL (minimum score 550 paper-based; 213 computer-based). *Application deadline:* For fall admission, 8/15 priority date for domestic students; for spring admission, 1/5 priority date for domestic students. Applications are processed on a rolling basis. Application fee: $50 ($100 for international students). *Expenses:* Tuition: Full-time $9,810; part-time $545 per hour. Required fees: $590; $75 per semester. One-time fee: $50 part-time. *Financial support:* In 2007–08, 5 students received support; fellowships, scholarships/grants available. Support available to part-time students. Financial award application deadline: 6/30; financial award applicants required to submit FAFSA. *Faculty research:* Vietnam, diplomatic history, Texas politics, Mexico and NAFTA, classical warfare. *Unit head:* Dr. Mark Beasley, Program Director, 325-670-1279, Fax: 325-670-1526, E-mail: mbeasley@hsutx.edu. *Application contact:* Dr. Gary Stanlake, Dean of Graduate Studies, 325-670-1298, Fax: 325-670-1564, E-mail: gradoff@hsutx.edu.

Harvard University, Graduate School of Arts and Sciences, Department of History, Cambridge, MA 02138. Offers African history (PhD); American history (PhD); ancient, medieval, early modern, and modern Europe (PhD), including Central Europe, Russia, Southeastern Europe, Western Europe; diplomatic history (PhD); East Asian history (PhD); economic and social history (PhD); intellectual history (PhD); Latin American history (PhD); Near Eastern history (PhD); oceanic history (PhD). *Degree requirements:* For doctorate, variable foreign language requirement, thesis/dissertation, oral general exam. *Entrance requirements:* For doctorate, GRE General Test, proficiency in 2 languages. Additional exam requirements/recommendations for international students: Required—TOEFL. *Expenses:* Tuition: Full-time $31,456. Full-time tuition and fees vary according to program and student level.

High Point University, Norcross Graduate School, High Point, NC 27262-3598. Offers business administration (MBA); educational leadership (M Ed); elementary education (M Ed); history (MA); nonprofit management (MA); special education (M Ed); sport studies (MS). *Accreditation:* ACBSP; NCATE. Part-time and evening/weekend programs available. *Faculty:* 36 full-time (13 women). *Students:* 47 full-time (20 women), 271 part-time (161 women); includes 107 minority (100 African Americans, 1 Asian American or Pacific Islander, 6 Hispanic Americans), 19 international. Average age 33. 249 applicants, 69% accepted, 141 enrolled. In 2007, 78 degrees awarded. *Degree requirements:* For master's, comprehensive exam (for some programs), thesis (for some programs). *Entrance requirements:* For master's, GMAT (MBA), GRE, MAT, minimum GPA of 3.0. Additional exam requirements/recommendations for international students: Required—TOEFL (minimum score 550 paper-based). *Application deadline:* For fall admission, 4/15 priority date for domestic and international students; for spring admission, 10/15 priority date for domestic and international students. Applications are processed on a rolling basis. Application fee: $50. Electronic applications accepted. *Expenses:* Tuition: Full-time $9,270; part-time $515 per credit. Required fees: $160; $80 per term. Tuition and fees vary according to course load and program. *Financial support:* In 2007–08, 190 students received support. Federal Work-Study available. Support available to part-time students. Financial award application deadline: 3/1; financial award applicants required to submit FAFSA. *Application contact:* Dr. Alberta Haynes Herron, Dean of Norcross Graduate School, 336-841-9198, Fax: 336-888-6378, E-mail: aherron@highpoint.edu.

Howard University, Graduate School, Department of History, Washington, DC 20059-0002. Offers African diaspora (MA, PhD); African history (MA, PhD); Latin America and the Caribbean (MA, PhD); public history (MA); United States history (MA, PhD). Part-time programs available. Terminal master's awarded for partial completion of doctoral program. *Degree requirements:* For master's, one foreign language, thesis optional; for doctorate, 2 foreign languages, comprehensive exam, thesis/dissertation. *Entrance requirements:* For master's, GRE General Test, minimum GPA of 3.0, 3 letters of recommendation; for doctorate, GRE General Test, minimum GPA of 3.5, 3 letters of recommendation. Additional exam requirements/recommendations for international students: Required—TOEFL. Electronic applications accepted. *Expenses:* Tuition: Full-time $16,175; part-time $899 per credit hour. Required fees: $805. *Faculty research:* Africa diaspora, U.S. diplomatic relations, Caribbean economic history.

Hunter College of the City University of New York, Graduate School, School of Arts and Sciences, Department of History, New York, NY 10021-5085. Offers MA. *Faculty:* 10 full-time (4 women), 2 part-time/adjunct (1 woman). *Students:* 1 full-time (0 women), 41 part-time (15 women); includes 3 minority (1 Asian American or Pacific Islander, 2 Hispanic Americans). Average age 37. 23 applicants, 61% accepted, 4 enrolled. In 2007, 10 degrees awarded. *Degree requirements:* For master's, one foreign language, comprehensive exam, thesis, essay, language exam. *Entrance requirements:* For master's, GRE General Test, minimum of 18 credits in undergraduate history or related field. Additional exam requirements/recommendations for international students: Required—TOEFL. *Application deadline:* For fall admission, 4/1 for domestic students, 2/1 for international students; for spring admission, 11/1 for domestic students, 9/1 for international students. Application fee: $125. *Expenses:* Tuition, state resident: full-time $6,400; part-time $270 per credit. Tuition, nonresident: part-time $500 per credit. One-time fee: $125 full-time. Tuition and fees vary according to program. *Financial support:* Federal Work-Study, scholarships/grants, and tuition waivers (partial) available. Support available to part-time students. *Unit head:* Dr. Barbara Welter, Chair and Graduate Advisor, 212-772-5487, E-mail: bwelter@hunter.cuny.edu. *Application contact:* William Zlata, Director for Graduate Admissions, 212-772-4482, Fax: 212-650-3336, E-mail: admissions@hunter.cuny.edu.

Idaho State University, Office of Graduate Studies, College of Arts and Sciences, Department of History, Pocatello, ID 83209. Offers historical resources management (MA). Part-time programs available. *Faculty:* 7 full-time (2 women), 1 (woman) part-time/adjunct. *Students:* 3 full-time (1 woman), 2 part-time (1 woman), 1 international. Average age 42. *Degree requirements:* For master's, comprehensive exam, thesis optional, minimum of 30 credits, internship. *Entrance requirements:* For master's, GRE, 3 letters of recommendation, minimum of 18 upper division history credits, statement of interest in historical studies. Additional exam requirements/recommendations for international students: Required—TOEFL (minimum score 550 paper-based; 213 computer-based; 80 iBT). *Application deadline:* For fall admission, 7/1 for domestic students, 6/1 for international students; for spring admission, 12/1 for domestic students, 11/1 for international students. Applications are processed on a rolling basis. Application fee: $55. Electronic applications accepted. *Expenses:* Tuition, state resident: full-time $2,882; part-time $259 per credit hour. Tuition, nonresident: full-time $11,566; part-time $379 per credit hour. Required fees: $2,278. Full-time tuition and fees vary according to program. Part-time tuition and fees vary according to course load. *Financial support:* In 2007–08, 2 research assistantships (averaging $9,128 per year) were awarded; career-related internships or fieldwork, Federal Work-Study, institutionally sponsored loans, scholarships/grants, health care benefits, and unspecified assistantships also available. Support available to part-time students. Financial award applicants required to submit FAFSA. *Faculty research:* Geographic information systems, gender issues. *Unit head:* Dr. Laura Woodworth-Ney, Chairman, 208-282-2379, E-mail: woodlaur@isu.edu. *Application contact:* Ellen Combs, Graduate School Technical Records Specialist, 208-282-2150, Fax: 208-282-4847.

Illinois State University, Graduate School, College of Arts and Sciences, Department of History, Normal, IL 61790-2200. Offers MA, MS. *Faculty:* 19 full-time (6 women). *Students:* 17 full-time (7 women), 24 part-time (11 women); includes 4 minority (2 Asian Americans or Pacific Islanders, 2 Hispanic Americans), 1 international. 20 applicants, 100% accepted. In 2007, 18 degrees awarded. *Degree requirements:* For master's, thesis or alternative. *Entrance requirements:* For master's, GRE General Test, minimum GPA of 2.6 in last 60 hours of course work. *Application deadline:* Applications are processed on a rolling basis. Application fee: $40. *Expenses:* Tuition, state resident: full-time $3,492; part-time $194 per credit hour. Tuition, nonresident: full-time $7,272; part-time $404 per credit hour. Required fees: $1,024; $57 per credit hour. *Financial support:* In 2007–08, 18 teaching assistantships (averaging $7,335 per year) were awarded; tuition waivers (full) also available. Financial award application deadline: 4/1. *Unit head:* Dr. William Biles, Chairperson, 309-438-5641.

Indiana State University, School of Graduate Studies, College of Arts and Sciences, Department of History, Terre Haute, IN 47809-1401. Offers MA, MS. Part-time and evening/weekend programs available. *Faculty:* 10 full-time (3 women), 3 part-time/adjunct (1 woman). *Students:* 11 full-time (3 women), 6 part-time (2 women). Average age 33. 5 applicants, 100% accepted, 2 enrolled. In 2007, 7 degrees awarded. *Degree requirements:* For master's, comprehensive exam (for some programs), thesis or alternative. *Entrance requirements:* For master's, equivalent of minor in geography or geology. Additional exam requirements/recommendations for international students: Required—TOEFL (minimum score 550 paper-based). *Application deadline:* For fall admission, 7/1 priority date for domestic students; for spring admission, 11/1 priority date for domestic students. Applications are processed on a rolling basis. Application fee: $35. *Expenses:* Tuition, state resident: full-time $7,056; part-time $294 per semester hour. Tuition, nonresident: full-time $14,016; part-time $584 per semester hour. Required fees: $175 per semester. *Financial support:* In 2007–08, 6 research assistantships with partial tuition reimbursements (averaging $7,000 per year) were awarded; teaching assistantships, Federal Work-Study, tuition waivers (partial), and unspecified assistantships also available. Financial award application deadline: 3/1; financial award applicants required to submit FAFSA. *Unit head:* Dr. Christopher Olsen, Chairperson, 812-237-2710.

Indiana University Bloomington, University Graduate School, College of Arts and Sciences, Department of History, Bloomington, IN 47405-7000. Offers MA, MAT, PhD, MA/MLS. *Faculty:* 44 full-time (12 women), 34 part-time/adjunct (15 women). *Students:* 79 full-time (37 women), 56 part-time (36 women); includes 23 minority (8 African Americans, 1 American Indian/Alaska Native, 3 Asian Americans or Pacific Islanders, 11 Hispanic Americans), 19 international. Average age 32. 218 applicants, 10% accepted, 21 enrolled. In 2007, 15 master's, 11 doctorates awarded. Terminal master's awarded for partial completion of doctoral program. *Median time to degree:* Of those who began their doctoral program in fall 1999, 29% received their degree in 8 years or less. *Degree requirements:* For master's, one foreign language, thesis optional; for doctorate, one foreign language, comprehensive exam, thesis/dissertation. *Entrance requirements:* For master's and doctorate, GRE General Test. Additional exam requirements/recommendations for international students: Required—TOEFL. *Application deadline:* For fall admission, 1/2 for domestic students, 12/1 for international students. Application fee: $50 ($60 for international students). Electronic applications accepted. *Financial support:* Fellowships with full tuition reimbursements, research assistantships with full tuition reimbursements, teaching assistantships with full tuition reimbursements, career-related internships or fieldwork, Federal Work-Study, institutionally sponsored loans, scholarships/grants, traineeships, health care benefits, and unspecified assistantships available. *Faculty research:* Medieval and early modern Europe, Russia, Latin America, Middle East, Great Britain, United States, Africa and African Dispora, Europe, eastern Europe. *Unit head:* Dr. Claude Clegg, Chairman, 812-855-3236, Fax: 812-855-3378, E-mail: cclegg@indiana.edu. *Application contact:* Mary Medley-Byers, Admissions Secretary, 812-855-8233, Fax: 812-855-3378, E-mail: histadm@indiana.edu.

Indiana University of Pennsylvania, School of Graduate Studies and Research, College of Humanities and Social Sciences, Department of History, Program in History, Indiana, PA 15705-1087. Offers MA. Part-time programs available. *Faculty:* 11 full-time (4 women). *Students:* 15 full-time (10 women), 5 part-time. Average age 29. 21 applicants, 33% accepted, 5 enrolled. In 2007, 4 degrees awarded. *Degree requirements:* For master's, thesis optional. *Entrance requirements:* For master's, GRE, 2 letters of recommendation. Additional exam requirements/recommendations for international students: Required—TOEFL. *Application deadline:* For spring admission, 11/1 for domestic students. Applications are processed on a rolling basis. Application fee: $30. *Expenses:* Tuition, state resident: full-time $6,214; part-time $345 per credit. Tuition, nonresident: full-time $9,944; part-time $552 per credit. Required fees: $43 per credit. One-time fee: $140 part-time. Tuition and fees vary according to course load. *Financial support:* In 2007–08, 5 research assistantships with full and partial tuition reimbursements (averaging $5,290 per year) were awarded; fellowships, Federal Work-Study also available. Support available to part-time students. Financial award application deadline: 3/15; financial award applicants required to submit FAFSA. *Unit head:* Dr. Tami Whited, Graduate Coordinator, 724-357-2573, E-mail: twhited@iup.edu.

Indiana University–Purdue University Indianapolis, Department of History, Indianapolis, IN 46202-2896. Offers history (MA); public history (MA); MA/MLS. Part-time and evening/weekend programs available. *Faculty:* 14 full-time (6 women). *Students:* 11 full-time (6 women), 28 part-time (16 women); includes 1 minority (African American) Average age 30. In 2007, 11 degrees awarded. *Degree requirements:* For master's, one foreign language, thesis. *Entrance requirements:* For master's, GRE General Test, minimum GPA of 3.0. *Application deadline:* For fall admission, 2/1 priority date for domestic students. Applications are processed on a rolling basis. Application fee: $50 ($60 for international students). *Expenses:* Tuition, state resident: full-time $5,818; part-time $242 per credit hour. Tuition, nonresident: full-time $17,106; part-time $713 per credit hour. Required fees: $629. Tuition and fees vary according to course load, campus/location and program. *Financial support:* In 2007–08, 1 fellowship with full tuition reimbursement (averaging $10,000 per year), 19 teaching assistantships with full tuition reimbursements (averaging $8,612 per year) were awarded; research assistantships with full tuition reimbursements, career-related internships or fieldwork also available. *Unit head:* Robert Barrows, Chair, 317-274-2457. *Application contact:* Mary Gelzleichter, Graduate Secretary, 317-274-5840, Fax: 317-278-7800, E-mail: mgelzlei@iupui.edu.

Inter American University of Puerto Rico, Metropolitan Campus, Faculty of Liberal Arts, Program in History, San Juan, PR 00919-1293. Offers MA.

Iona College, School of Arts and Science, Program in History, New Rochelle, NY 10801-1890. Offers MA. Part-time and evening/weekend programs available. *Faculty:* 7 full-time (1 woman). *Students:* 5 full-time (all women), 15 part-time (6 women); includes 3 minority (1 African American, 2 Hispanic Americans). Average age 28. 10 applicants, 80% accepted, 5 enrolled. In 2007, 3 degrees awarded. *Degree requirements:* For master's, one foreign language, thesis. *Entrance requirements:* For master's, undergraduate major in history or related field, minimum GPA of 3.0. Additional exam requirements/recommendations for international students: Required—TOEFL (minimum score 550 paper-based; 213 computer-based). *Application deadline:* Applications are processed on a rolling basis. Application fee: $50. Electronic applications accepted. *Expenses:* Tuition: Part-time $712 per credit. Required fees: $150 per term. *Financial support:* Unspecified assistantships available. *Faculty research:* Global studies, American diplomacy, Native Americans, foreign policy, Armenian history. *Unit head:* Dr. James Carroll, Chairman, 914-633-2694, E-mail: jcarroll@iona.edu. *Application contact:* Veronica Jarek-Prinz, Director of Graduate Admissions, 914-633-2420, Fax: 914-633-2277, E-mail: vjarekprinz@iona.edu.

Iowa State University of Science and Technology, Graduate College, College of Liberal Arts and Sciences, Department of History, Ames, IA 50011. Offers agricultural history and rural studies (PhD); history (MA); history of technology and science (MA, PhD). *Faculty:* 16 full-time (4 women). *Students:* 29 full-time (12 women), 14 part-time (3 women); includes 2 minority (1 African American, 1 Hispanic American), 3 international. 23 applicants, 87% accepted, 11 enrolled. In 2007, 8 master's, 3 doctorates awarded. *Degree requirements:* For master's, thesis or alternative; for doctorate, thesis/dissertation. *Entrance requirements:* For master's and doctorate, GRE General Test. Additional exam requirements/recommendations for international students: Required—TOEFL (paper-based 600; computer-based 250; iBT 79) or IELTS (7.0). *Application deadline:* For fall admission, 1/15 priority date for domestic and international students. Applications are processed on a rolling basis. Application fee: $30 ($70 for international students). Electronic applications accepted. *Financial support:* In 2007–08,

History

Iowa State University of Science and Technology (continued)

research assistantships with partial tuition reimbursements (averaging $15,660 per year), 18 teaching assistantships with full and partial tuition reimbursements (averaging $15,829 per year) were awarded; scholarships/grants, health care benefits, and unspecified assistantships also available. *Unit head:* Dr. Charles Dobbs, Chair, 515-294-7266, Fax: 515-294-6390, E-mail: cdobbs@iastate.edu. *Application contact:* Dr. Christopher Curtis, Information Contact, 515-294-7266, Fax: 515-294-6390.

Jackson State University, Graduate School, School of Liberal Arts, Department of History, Jackson, MS 39217. Offers MA. Part-time and evening/weekend programs available. *Degree requirements:* For master's, comprehensive exam, thesis or alternative. *Entrance requirements:* For master's, GRE General Test. Additional exam requirements/recommendations for international students: Required—TOEFL.

Jacksonville State University, College of Graduate Studies and Continuing Education, College of Arts and Sciences, Department of History, Jacksonville, AL 36265-1602. Offers MA. *Faculty:* 10 full-time (2 women). *Students:* 8 full-time (0 women), 15 part-time (5 women); includes 2 minority (both African Americans), 1 international. In 2007, 10 degrees awarded. *Degree requirements:* For master's, thesis optional. *Entrance requirements:* For master's, GRE General Test or MAT. *Application deadline:* Applications are processed on a rolling basis. Application fee: $20. *Financial support:* In 2007–08, 1 teaching assistantship was awarded. Support available to part-time students. Financial award application deadline: 4/1. *Unit head:* Dr. Harvy Jackson, Head, 256-782-5622. *Application contact:* 256-782-5329, Fax: 256-782-5321, E-mail: graduate@jsu.edu.

James Madison University, The Graduate School, College of Arts and Letters, Department of History, Harrisonburg, VA 22807. Offers MA. Part-time programs available. *Faculty:* 15 full-time (3 women), 3 part-time/adjunct (1 woman). *Students:* 25 full-time (8 women), 16 part-time (3 women); includes 1 minority (African American) Average age 27. In 2007, 13 degrees awarded. *Degree requirements:* For master's, one foreign language, comprehensive exam, thesis, reading exam in a language. *Entrance requirements:* For master's, GRE General Test, GRE Subject Test, 2 letters of recommendation. Additional exam requirements/recommendations for international students: Required—TOEFL. *Application deadline:* For fall admission, 1/15 for domestic students. Applications are processed on a rolling basis. Application fee: $55. Electronic applications accepted. *Expenses:* Tuition, state resident: full-time $6,720; part-time $280 per credit hour. Tuition, nonresident: full-time $19,104; part-time $796 per credit hour. *Financial support:* In 2007–08, 12 students received support, including 3 teaching assistantships with full tuition reimbursements available (averaging $8,494 per year); Federal Work-Study, unspecified assistantships, and 9 graduate assistantships ($7,237) also available. Financial award application deadline: 3/1; financial award applicants required to submit FAFSA. *Unit head:* Dr. Michael J. Galgano, Academic Unit Head, 540-568-6132.

John Carroll University, Graduate School, Department of History, University Heights, OH 44118-4581. Offers MA. Part-time and evening/weekend programs available. *Faculty:* 10 full-time (3 women). *Students:* 3 full-time (1 woman), 5 part-time (1 woman). 14 applicants, 57% accepted, 3 enrolled. In 2007, 2 degrees awarded. *Degree requirements:* For master's, comprehensive exam, thesis (for some programs), research essay or thesis. *Entrance requirements:* For master's, GRE General Test, minimum 2.5 GPA average. Additional exam requirements/recommendations for international students: Required—TOEFL. *Application deadline:* For fall admission, 8/15 priority date for domestic students; for spring admission, 1/3 for domestic students. Applications are processed on a rolling basis. Application fee: $25 ($35 for international students). Electronic applications accepted. *Financial support:* In 2007–08, 2 students received support, including 2 teaching assistantships with full tuition reimbursements available (averaging $8,400 per year); scholarships/grants and tuition waivers (partial) also available. Financial award application deadline: 3/1; financial award applicants required to submit FAFSA. *Faculty research:* Social history of Cleveland, early national Pennsylvania, modern Japanese journalism, Catholic Reformation. *Unit head:* Dr. Anne Kugler, Chairperson, 216-397-4770, E-mail: akugler@jcu.edu. *Application contact:* Dr. David W. Robson, Director of Graduate Studies, 216-397-4771, Fax: 216-397-4175, E-mail: robson@jcu.edu.

The Johns Hopkins University, Zanvyl Krieger School of Arts and Sciences, Department of History, Baltimore, MD 21218-2699. Offers PhD. *Faculty:* 68 full-time (30 women). *Students:* 72 full-time (37 women); includes 3 minority (2 Asian Americans or Pacific Islanders, 1 Hispanic American), 16 international. Average age 26. 120 applicants, 18% accepted, 12 enrolled. In 2007, 10 doctorates awarded. *Median time to degree:* Of those who began their doctoral program in fall 1999, 50% received their degree in 8 years or less. *Degree requirements:* For doctorate, variable foreign language requirement, comprehensive exam, thesis/dissertation. *Entrance requirements:* For doctorate, GRE General Test. Additional exam requirements/recommendations for international students: Required—TOEFL. *Application deadline:* For fall admission, 12/1 for domestic and international students. Application fee: $60. Electronic applications accepted. *Financial support:* In 2007–08, 53 students received support, including 31 fellowships with full tuition reimbursements available (averaging $16,000 per year), 2 research assistantships with full tuition reimbursements available (averaging $16,000 per year), 20 teaching assistantships with full tuition reimbursements available (averaging $16,000 per year); Federal Work-Study and institutionally sponsored loans also available. Financial award application deadline: 4/15; financial award applicants required to submit FAFSA. *Faculty research:* American, European, Latin American, Chinese, and African history. *Unit head:* Dr. Gabrielle Spiegel, Chair, 410-516-5075, Fax: 410-516-7586, E-mail: spiegel@jhu.edu. *Application contact:* Megan B. Zeller, Senior Administrative Coordinator, 410-516-5296, Fax: 410-516-7586, E-mail: mzeller4@jhu.edu.

Kansas State University, Graduate School, College of Arts and Sciences, Department of History, Manhattan, KS 66506. Offers MA, PhD. Part-time programs available. *Faculty:* 18 full-time (6 women), 1 part-time/adjunct (0 women). *Students:* 59 full-time (16 women), 31 part-time (6 women); includes 3 minority (1 African American, 2 Asian Americans or Pacific Islanders), 1 international. Average age 25. 51 applicants, 61% accepted, 12 enrolled. In 2007, 4 master's, 4 doctorates awarded. *Degree requirements:* For master's, thesis (for some programs); for doctorate, one foreign language, thesis/dissertation, qualifying exam. *Entrance requirements:* For master's, GRE General Test or MAT, minimum undergraduate GPA of 3.0; for doctorate, GRE General Test or MAT. Additional exam requirements/recommendations for international students: Required—TOEFL (minimum score 600 paper-based). *Application deadline:* For fall admission, 5/1 for domestic students, 2/1 priority date for international students; for spring admission, 11/1 for domestic students, 8/1 priority date for international students. Applications are processed on a rolling basis. Application fee: $30 ($55 for international students). *Financial support:* In 2007–08, 4 research assistantships (averaging $9,658 per year), 12 teaching assistantships with full tuition reimbursements (averaging $8,904 per year) were awarded; career-related internships or fieldwork, Federal Work-Study, institutionally sponsored loans, and scholarships/grants also available. Support available to part-time students. Financial award application deadline: 3/1; financial award applicants required to submit FAFSA. *Faculty research:* Environmental history, history of Christianity, American social history, history of war and society, history of international relations and diplomacy. Total annual research expenditures: $10,171. *Unit head:* Sue Zschoche, Head, 785-532-6730, Fax: 785-532-7004, E-mail: suez@ksu.edu. *Application contact:* Louise Breen, Director, 785-532-6730, Fax: 785-532-7004, E-mail: breen@ksu.edu.

Kent State University, College of Arts and Sciences, Department of History, Kent, OH 44242-0001. Offers MA, PhD. Part-time programs available. *Faculty:* 25 full-time (10 women). *Students:* 52 full-time (24 women), 15 part-time (9 women); includes 5 minority (4 African Americans, 1 American Indian/Alaska Native), 1 international. Average age 33. 15 applicants, 40% accepted. In 2007, 11 degrees awarded. *Degree requirements:* For master's, variable foreign language requirement, thesis optional; for doctorate, variable foreign language requirement, thesis/dissertation. *Entrance requirements:* For master's, GRE General Test, GRE Subject Test, minimum GPA of 2.75; for doctorate, GRE General Test, GRE Subject Test, minimum GPA of 3.0. Additional exam requirements/recommendations for international students: Required—TOEFL. *Application deadline:* For fall admission, 7/12 for domestic students; for spring admission, 11/29 for domestic students. Applications are processed on a rolling basis. Application fee: $30. Electronic applications accepted. *Financial support:* In 2007–08, 21 students received support; fellowships with full tuition reimbursements available, research assistantships with full tuition reimbursements available, teaching assistantships with full tuition reimbursements available, Federal Work-Study, institutionally sponsored loans, and tuition waivers (full) available. Financial award application deadline: 2/1. *Faculty research:* African American, civil war, British empire, Latin America, public history. *Unit head:* Dr. John R. Jameson, Chairman, 330-672-2882, Fax: 330-672-2943, E-mail: jjameson@kent.edu. *Application contact:* Dr. Kim Gruenwald, Graduate Coordinator, 330-672-2882, Fax: 330-672-2943, E-mail: kgruenwa@kent.edu.

Lakehead University, Graduate Studies, Department of History, Thunder Bay, ON P7B 5E1, Canada. Offers MA. Part-time programs available. *Degree requirements:* For master's, one foreign language, thesis. *Entrance requirements:* For master's, minimum B average. Additional exam requirements/recommendations for international students: Required—TOEFL. *Faculty research:* Canadian history, British history, Russian/German history, women's studies.

Lamar University, College of Graduate Studies, College of Arts and Sciences, Department of History, Beaumont, TX 77710. Offers MA. Part-time programs available. *Faculty:* 5 full-time (1 woman), 1 part-time/adjunct (0 women). *Students:* 2 full-time (0 women), 8 part-time (2 women). Average age 47. 12 applicants, 50% accepted, 4 enrolled. In 2007, 3 degrees awarded. *Degree requirements:* For master's, comprehensive exam (for some programs), thesis (for some programs). *Entrance requirements:* For master's, GRE General Test, minimum GPA of 2.5 in last 60 hours of undergraduate course work. Additional exam requirements/recommendations for international students: Required—TOEFL. *Application deadline:* For fall admission, 8/1 for domestic students; for spring admission, 12/1 for domestic students. Applications are processed on a rolling basis. Application fee: $25 ($50 for international students). *Expenses:* Tuition, state resident: part-time $348 per semester hour. Tuition, nonresident: part-time $626 per semester hour. Tuition and fees vary according to course load. *Financial support:* In 2007–08, fellowships (averaging $1,000 per year), teaching assistantships (averaging $2,000 per year) were awarded. Financial award application deadline: 4/1. *Faculty research:* Old South, nineteenth century reform, twentieth century U.S., religion in America's South, Renaissance/early modern Europe. *Unit head:* Dr. John Storey, Chair, 409-880-8511, Fax: 409-880-8710, E-mail: storeyjw@hal.lamar.edu. *Application contact:* Dr. Howell H. Gwin, Graduate Adviser, 409-880-8530, Fax: 409-880-8710, E-mail: gwinhh@hal.lamar.edu.

La Salle University, School of Arts and Sciences, Program in History, Philadelphia, PA 19141-1199. Offers MA. Part-time programs available. *Faculty:* 6 full-time (0 women), 3 part-time/adjunct (1 woman). *Students:* 1 full-time (0 women), 33 part-time (11 women); includes 3 minority (all African Americans) Average age 32. 23 applicants, 100% accepted, 11 enrolled. In 2007, 5 degrees awarded. *Application deadline:* Applications are processed on a rolling basis. Application fee: $35. *Expenses:* Tuition: Full-time $16,300; part-time $550 per credit. Required fees: $85 per term. Tuition and fees vary according to program. *Financial support:* In 2007–08, 21 students received support; fellowships available. Financial award applicants required to submit FAFSA. *Unit head:* Dr. George B. Stow, Director, 215-951-1097, E-mail: grahis@lasalle.edu.

Laurentian University, School of Graduate Studies and Research, Programme in History, Sudbury, ON P3E 2C6, Canada. Offers MA. Part-time programs available. *Degree requirements:* For master's, thesis or alternative. *Entrance requirements:* For master's, honors degree with minimum second class. *Faculty research:* Franco-Ontarian history, northern Ontarian history, Canadian social history, European social history, Franco-Canadian history.

Lehigh University, College of Arts and Sciences, Department of History, Bethlehem, PA 18015-3094. Offers MA, PhD. *Faculty:* 14 full-time (5 women), 1 (woman) part-time/adjunct. *Students:* 22 full-time (7 women), 22 part-time (7 women); includes 1 minority (Asian American or Pacific Islander) Average age 29. 35 applicants, 49% accepted, 12 enrolled. In 2007, 2 master's, 3 doctorates awarded. *Degree requirements:* For master's, comprehensive exam or thesis; for doctorate, thesis/dissertation. *Entrance requirements:* For master's, GRE General Test, recommendations; for doctorate, GRE General Test, recommendations, writing samples. Additional exam requirements/recommendations for international students: Required—TOEFL. *Application deadline:* For winter admission, 1/15 priority date for domestic and international students. Applications are processed on a rolling basis. Application fee: $65. Electronic applications accepted. *Financial support:* In 2007–08, 7 students received support, including fellowships with full tuition reimbursements available (averaging $20,000 per year), research assistantships with full tuition reimbursements available (averaging $15,600 per year), teaching assistantships with full tuition reimbursements available (averaging $15,600 per year); career-related internships or fieldwork, Federal Work-Study, institutionally sponsored loans, scholarships/grants, tuition waivers (full and partial), and unspecified assistantships also available. Support available to part-time students. Financial award application deadline: 1/15. *Faculty research:* Colonial America, modern America, history of technology . Total annual research expenditures: $4,758. *Unit head:* Dr. Michael Baylor, Chairman, 610-758-3360, Fax: 610-758-6554, E-mail: mgb2@lehigh.edu. *Application contact:* Dr. John K. Smith, Graduate Coordinator, 610-758-3365, Fax: 610-758-6554, E-mail: jks0@lehigh.edu.

Lehman College of the City University of New York, Division of Arts and Humanities, Department of History, Bronx, NY 10468-1589. Offers MA. Part-time and evening/weekend programs available. *Degree requirements:* For master's, comprehensive exam, thesis. *Entrance requirements:* For master's, 18 undergraduate credits in history, minimum GPA of 2.7.

Lincoln University, School of Graduate Studies and Continuing Education, College of Liberal Arts, Education and Journalism, Department of Social and Behavioral Sciences, Jefferson City, MO 65102. Offers history (MA); social science (MA), including history, political science, sociology; sociology (MA); sociology/criminal justice (MA). Part-time and evening/weekend programs available. *Faculty:* 12 part-time/adjunct (4 women). *Students:* 13 full-time (9 women), 17 part-time (7 women); includes 16 minority (13 African Americans, 1 American Indian/Alaska Native, 2 Hispanic Americans), 3 international. Average age 33. 9 applicants, 89% accepted, 5 enrolled. In 2007, 6 degrees awarded. *Degree requirements:* For master's, comprehensive exam, thesis optional. *Entrance requirements:* For master's, GRE General Test or MAT, 15 undergraduate hours of course work in social science including 6 hours upper-division, with 9 hours in the area of concentration; see parent units for general requirements. Additional exam requirements/recommendations for international students: Required—TOEFL (minimum score 500 paper-based; 173 computer-based; 61 iBT). *Application deadline:* For fall admission, 7/1 priority date for domestic and international students; for spring admission, 12/1 priority date for domestic and international students. Applications are processed on a rolling basis. Application fee: $20. *Expenses:* Tuition, state resident: full-time $5,400; part-time $225 per credit hour. Tuition, nonresident: full-time $10,020; part-time $417 per credit hour. Required fees: $360; $15 per credit hour. $20 per semester. *Financial support:* Federal Work-Study and scholarships/grants available. Financial award application deadline: 4/1; financial award applicants required to submit FAFSA. *Faculty research:* Suicide prevention. *Unit head:* Dr. Antonio Holland, Department Head, 573-681-5145, Fax: 573-681-5150, E-mail: hollanda@lincolnu.edu.

Long Island University, Brooklyn Campus, Richard L. Conolly College of Liberal Arts and Sciences, Program in Social Science, Brooklyn, NY 11201-8423. Offers history (MS); United Nations studies (Certificate). Part-time and evening/weekend programs available. *Entrance requirements:* For master's, 2 letters of recommendation. Additional exam requirements/recommendations for international students: Required—TOEFL (minimum score 500 paper-based; 173 computer-based). Electronic applications accepted.

Long Island University, C.W. Post Campus, College of Liberal Arts and Sciences, Department of History, Brookville, NY 11548-1300. Offers MA. Part-time and evening/weekend programs available. *Faculty:* 4 full-time (1 woman), 5 part-time/adjunct (0 women). *Students:* 4 full-time (2 women), 21 part-time (11 women); includes 3 minority (1 Asian American or Pacific

Islander, 2 Hispanic Americans). Average age 29. 16 applicants, 81% accepted, 8 enrolled. In 2007, 4 degrees awarded. *Degree requirements:* For master's, comprehensive exam or thesis. *Entrance requirements:* For master's, bachelor's degree in history, minimum GPA of 3.0. *Application deadline:* Applications are processed on a rolling basis. Application fee: $30. Electronic applications accepted. *Expenses:* Tuition: Part-time $825 per credit. Tuition and fees vary according to course load. *Financial support:* Research assistantships, career-related internships or fieldwork, Federal Work-Study, and institutionally sponsored loans available. Support available to part-time students. Financial award application deadline: 5/15; financial award applicants required to submit CSS PROFILE or FAFSA. *Faculty research:* American slavery, women's studies, military history. *Unit head:* Dr. Jeanie Attie, Chair, 516-299-2407, Fax: 516-299-4140, E-mail: jeanie.attie@ciu.edu. *Application contact:* Dr. Carol Bauer, Graduate Advisor, 516-299-2407.

Louisiana State University and Agricultural and Mechanical College, Graduate School, College of Arts and Sciences, Department of History, Baton Rouge, LA 70803. Offers MA, PhD. Part-time programs available. *Faculty:* 24 full-time (6 women). *Students:* 47 full-time (13 women), 18 part-time (10 women); includes 6 minority (5 African Americans, 1 Asian American or Pacific Islander), 2 international. Average age 33. 56 applicants, 41% accepted, 14 enrolled. In 2007, 16 master's, 1 doctorate awarded. Terminal master's awarded for partial completion of doctoral program. *Degree requirements:* For master's, thesis (for some programs), oral exam; for doctorate, one foreign language, thesis/dissertation, comprehensive written and oral exams. *Entrance requirements:* For master's and doctorate, GRE General Test, minimum GPA of 3.0. Additional exam requirements/recommendations for international students: Required—TOEFL (minimum score 550 paper-based; 213 computer-based; 79 iBT). *Application deadline:* For fall admission, 1/25 priority date for domestic students, 5/15 for international students; for spring admission, 10/15 for international students. Applications are processed on a rolling basis. Application fee: $25. Electronic applications accepted. *Financial support:* In 2007–08, 46 students received support, including 1 research assistantship with partial tuition reimbursement available (averaging $13,910 per year), 30 teaching assistantships with partial tuition reimbursements available (averaging $12,233 per year); fellowships with full tuition reimbursements available, career-related internships or fieldwork, Federal Work-Study, institutionally sponsored loans, health care benefits, and unspecified assistantships also available. Support available to part-time students. Financial award application deadline: 1/15; financial award applicants required to submit FAFSA. *Faculty research:* U.S. South, Civil War; modern Europe, British; medieval history. Total annual research expenditures: $8,000. *Unit head:* Dr. Gaines Foster, Chair, 225-578-4471, Fax: 225-578-4909, E-mail: hyfost@lsu.edu. *Application contact:* Dr. Victor Stater, Adviser, 225-578-4505, Fax: 225-578-4909, E-mail: stater@lsu.edu.

Louisiana Tech University, Graduate School, College of Liberal Arts, Department of History, Ruston, LA 71272. Offers MA. Part-time programs available. *Degree requirements:* For master's, thesis or alternative. *Entrance requirements:* For master's, GRE General Test. *Application deadline:* For fall admission, 7/29 for domestic students; for spring admission, 2/3 for domestic students. Application fee: $20 ($30 for international students). *Financial support:* Fellowships available. Financial award application deadline: 2/1. *Unit head:* Dr. Stephen Webre, Head, 318-257-2872, Fax: 318-257-3935, E-mail: swebre@gans.latech.edu.

Loyola University Chicago, Graduate School, Department of History, Chicago, IL 60611-2196. Offers history (MA, PhD); public library (MA). Part-time and evening/weekend programs available. *Faculty:* 21 full-time (8 women), 4 part-time/adjunct (3 women). *Students:* 75 full-time (46 women), 34 part-time (13 women); includes 10 minority (4 African Americans, 1 Asian American or Pacific Islander, 5 Hispanic Americans). Average age 33. 132 applicants, 57% accepted, 28 enrolled. In 2007, 19 master's, 5 doctorates awarded. Terminal master's awarded for partial completion of doctoral program. *Median time to degree:* Of those who began their doctoral program in fall 1999, 14% received their degree in 8 years or less. *Degree requirements:* For master's, one foreign language, comprehensive exam, essay; for doctorate, 2 foreign languages, comprehensive exam, thesis/dissertation. *Entrance requirements:* For master's, GRE General Test, research paper; for doctorate, GRE General Test, seminar paper or master's thesis. Additional exam requirements/recommendations for international students: Required—TOEFL (minimum score 550 paper-based; 213 computer-based), IELTS. *Application deadline:* For fall admission, 5/1 for domestic students; for spring admission, 10/1 for domestic students. Applications are processed on a rolling basis. Application fee: $50. Electronic applications accepted. *Expenses:* Tuition: Full-time $12,780; part-time $710 per credit hour. Required fees: $55 per semester. Full-time tuition and fees vary according to program. *Financial support:* In 2007–08, 7 fellowships with full tuition reimbursements (averaging $14,500 per year), 10 teaching assistantships with full tuition reimbursements (averaging $15,000 per year) were awarded; research assistantships with full tuition reimbursements, Federal Work-Study also available. Financial award application deadline: 1/1; financial award applicants required to submit FAFSA. *Faculty research:* Medieval and early modern Europe, U.S. public history, U.S. urban history, gender history, Britain and Ireland. *Unit head:* Barbara Rosenwein, Chair, 773-508-2215, Fax: 773-508-2153, E-mail: brosen@luc.edu. *Application contact:* Dr. Suzanne Kaufman, Director, Graduate Programs, 773-508-2233, Fax: 773-508-2153, E-mail: skaufma@luc.edu.

Marquette University, Graduate School, College of Arts and Sciences, Department of History, Milwaukee, WI 53201-1881. Offers European history (MA, PhD); medieval history (MA); Renaissance and Reformation (MA); United States history (MA, PhD). Part-time programs available. *Faculty:* 20 full-time (4 women), 2 part-time/adjunct (0 women). *Students:* 52. Average age 31. 39 applicants, 56% accepted, 12 enrolled. In 2007, 9 master's, 5 doctorates awarded. Terminal master's awarded for partial completion of doctoral program. *Degree requirements:* For master's, comprehensive exam, thesis or alternative; for doctorate, one foreign language, thesis/dissertation, qualifying exam. *Entrance requirements:* For master's, GRE General Test, GRE Subject Test; for doctorate, GRE General Test, writing sample. Additional exam requirements/recommendations for international students: Required—TOEFL. Application fee: $40. *Financial support:* In 2007–08, 4 fellowships, 5 research assistantships, 15 teaching assistantships were awarded; Federal Work-Study, institutionally sponsored loans, scholarships/grants, and tuition waivers (full and partial) also available. Support available to part-time students. Financial award application deadline: 2/15. *Faculty research:* Social history, political history, diplomatic history, history of science, religious history. Total annual research expenditures: $44,005. *Unit head:* James Marten, Chair, 414-288-7901, Fax: 414-288-1578.

Marshall University, Academic Affairs Division, College of Liberal Arts, Department of History, Huntington, WV 25755. Offers MA. *Faculty:* 14 full-time (3 women), 10 part-time/adjunct (1 woman). *Students:* 25 full-time (14 women), 14 part-time (3 women), 2 international. Average age 32. In 2007, 10 degrees awarded. *Degree requirements:* For master's, thesis optional. Application fee: $40. *Unit head:* Dr. David Mills, Chairperson, 304-696-2725, Fax: 304-696-2957, E-mail: milld@marshall.edu. *Application contact:* Information Contact, 304-746-1900, Fax: 304-746-1902, E-mail: services@marshall.edu.

McGill University, Faculty of Graduate and Postdoctoral Studies, Faculty of Arts, Department of History, Montréal, QC H3A 2T5, Canada. Offers history (MA, PhD); history of medicine (MA). *Faculty:* 36 full-time (9 women), 22 part-time/adjunct (8 women). *Students:* 72 full-time (29 women), 1 (woman) part-time. 182 applicants, 45% accepted, 31 enrolled. In 2007, 25 master's, 2 doctorates awarded.

McMaster University, School of Graduate Studies, Faculty of Humanities, Department of History, Hamilton, ON L8S 4M2, Canada. Offers MA, PhD. Part-time programs available. *Faculty:* 22 full-time. *Students:* 54 full-time, 4 part-time. 86 applicants, 26% accepted. *Degree requirements:* For master's, one foreign language, thesis or alternative; for doctorate, one foreign language, comprehensive exam, thesis/dissertation. *Entrance requirements:* For master's, honors BA in history, minimum B+ average. Additional exam requirements/recommendations for international students: Required—TOEFL (minimum score 580 paper-based; 237 computer-based). *Application deadline:* For fall admission, 2/15 priority date for domestic students. Applications are processed on a rolling basis. Application fee: $90. *Financial support:* In 2007–08, fellowships (averaging $7,500 per year), 27 teaching assistantships (averaging $8,440 per year) were awarded; institutionally sponsored loans and scholarships/grants also available. *Faculty research:* Canadian, European, British, U.S. history; ancient history. Total annual research expenditures: $86,000. *Unit head:* Dr. Kenneth Cruikshank, Chair, 905-525-9140 Ext. 24850, Fax: 905-777-0158, E-mail: cruiksha@mcmaster.ca. *Application contact:* Wendy Benedetti, Administrative Coordinator, 905-525-9140 Ext. 24416, Fax: 905-777-0158, E-mail: histdept@mcmaster.ca.

Memorial University of Newfoundland, School of Graduate Studies, Department of History, St. John's, NL A1C 5S7, Canada. Offers MA, PhD. Part-time programs available. *Degree requirements:* For master's, thesis or comprehensive exam; for doctorate, one foreign language, comprehensive exam, thesis/dissertation, oral defense of thesis. *Entrance requirements:* For master's, honors degree or equivalent; for doctorate, master's degree. Electronic applications accepted. *Faculty research:* Canadian history, maritime history, Newfoundland history, social history, labor history.

Miami University, Graduate School, College of Arts and Sciences, Department of History, Oxford, OH 45056. Offers MA, PhD. Part-time programs available. *Degree requirements:* For master's, comprehensive exam, thesis, final exam; for doctorate, comprehensive exam, thesis/dissertation, final exam. *Entrance requirements:* For master's, minimum undergraduate GPA of 3.0 during previous 2 years or 2.75 overall. Additional exam requirements/recommendations for international students: Required—TOEFL (minimum score 550 paper-based; 213 computer-based), TWE (minimum score 4). Electronic applications accepted.

Michigan State University, The Graduate School, College of Arts and Letters, Department of History, East Lansing, MI 48824. Offers history (MA, PhD); history-secondary school teaching (MA). *Entrance requirements:* Additional exam requirements/recommendations for international students: Required—TOEFL. Electronic applications accepted. *Expenses:* Tuition, state resident: part-time $379 per credit hour. Tuition, nonresident: part-time $800 per credit hour. Tuition and fees vary according to program.

Middle Tennessee State University, College of Graduate Studies, College of Liberal Arts, Department of History, Program in History, Murfreesboro, TN 37132. Offers MA. Part-time and evening/weekend programs available. Postbaccalaureate distance learning degree programs offered. *Students:* 4 full-time (all women), 58 part-time (35 women); includes 1 minority (American Indian/Alaska Native). 24 applicants, 79% accepted. In 2007, 7 degrees awarded. *Degree requirements:* For master's, one foreign language, comprehensive exam, thesis. *Entrance requirements:* For master's, GRE. Additional exam requirements/recommendations for international students: Required—TOEFL (paper-based 525; computer-based 195; IBT 71) or IELTS (6.0). *Financial support:* Application deadline: 5/1. *Unit head:* Dr. John McDaniel, Dean, College of Liberal Arts, 615-898-2534, Fax: 615-898-5907, E-mail: mcdaniel@mtsu.edu.

Midwestern State University, Graduate Studies, College of Humanities and Social Sciences, Department of History, Wichita Falls, TX 76308. Offers MA. Part-time programs available. *Degree requirements:* For master's, one foreign language. *Entrance requirements:* For master's, GRE General Test. Additional exam requirements/recommendations for international students: Required—TOEFL (minimum score 550 paper-based; 213 computer-based). Electronic applications accepted. *Faculty research:* Conservation, Spanish borderlands, Jacksonian era, New Deal, Texas and the Southwest.

Millersville University of Pennsylvania, Graduate School, School of Humanities and Social Sciences, Department of History, Millersville, PA 17551-0302. Offers MA. Part-time and evening/weekend programs available. *Faculty:* 11 full-time (4 women), 5 part-time/adjunct (3 women). *Students:* 2 full-time (1 woman), 22 part-time (10 women); includes 3 minority (1 African American, 1 Asian American or Pacific Islander, 1 Hispanic American). Average age 32. 9 applicants, 67% accepted, 4 enrolled. In 2007, 1 degree awarded. *Degree requirements:* For master's, comprehensive exam, thesis optional, departmental exam. *Entrance requirements:* For master's, GRE (preferred) or MAT, 24 credits of undergraduate course work in history, minimum GPA of 2.75 in history. Additional exam requirements/recommendations for international students: Required—TOEFL (minimum score 500 paper-based; 183 computer-based). *Application deadline:* For fall admission, 2/1 priority date for domestic students; for winter admission, 10/1 priority date for domestic students; for spring admission, 10/1 priority date for domestic students. Applications are processed on a rolling basis. Application fee: $40. Electronic applications accepted. *Expenses:* Tuition, state resident: full-time $6,214; part-time $345 per credit. Tuition, nonresident: full-time $9,944; part-time $552 per credit. Required fees: $1,442. Tuition and fees vary according to course load. *Financial support:* In 2007–08, 2 students received support, including 2 research assistantships with full tuition reimbursements available (averaging $5,200 per year); institutionally sponsored loans and unspecified assistantships also available. Financial award application deadline: 3/15; financial award applicants required to submit FAFSA. *Faculty research:* Social history of music, Vietnam War, women in Africa, Colonial Caribbean, Colonial New England. *Unit head:* Dr. Francis Bremer, Chair, 717-872-3548, Fax: 717-871-2485, E-mail: francis.bremer@millersville.edu. *Application contact:* Dr. Victor S. DeSantis, Dean of Graduate Studies, 717-872-3099, Fax: 717-871-2022, E-mail: victor.desantis@millersville.edu.

Minnesota State University Mankato, College of Graduate Studies, College of Social and Behavioral Sciences, Department of History, Mankato, MN 56001. Offers history (MA, MS); social studies (MS); teaching history (MS, MT). *Students:* 3 full-time (1 woman), 17 part-time (6 women). Average age 35. In 2007, 7 degrees awarded. *Degree requirements:* For master's, one foreign language, comprehensive exam, thesis or alternative. *Entrance requirements:* For master's, minimum GPA of 3.0 during previous 2 years. Additional exam requirements/recommendations for international students: Required—TOEFL. *Application deadline:* For fall admission, 7/1 priority date for domestic students; for spring admission, 11/1 for domestic students. Applications are processed on a rolling basis. Application fee: $40. Electronic applications accepted. *Financial support:* Research assistantships, teaching assistantships with full tuition reimbursements, career-related internships or fieldwork, Federal Work-Study, institutionally sponsored loans, and unspecified assistantships available. Support available to part-time students. Financial award application deadline: 3/15. *Faculty research:* Charivaris, Lindbergh in the U.S., Dutch trade to South America in the seventeenth and eighteenth centuries. *Unit head:* Dr. Matt Loayza, Graduate Coordinator, 507-389-1618. *Application contact:* 507-389-2321, E-mail: grad@mnsu.edu.

Mississippi College, Graduate School, College of Arts and Sciences, School of Humanities and Social Sciences, Department of History and Political Science, Clinton, MS 39058. Offers administration of justice (MSS); history (M Ed, MA, MSS); paralegal studies (Certificate); political science (MSS); social sciences (M Ed, MSS). Part-time programs available. *Faculty:* 5 full-time (1 woman), 2 part-time/adjunct (0 women). *Students:* 12 full-time (7 women), 17 part-time (14 women); includes 7 minority (6 African Americans, 1 American Indian/Alaska Native), 1 international. Average age 27. In 2007, 5 master's, 2 other advanced degrees awarded. *Degree requirements:* For master's, one foreign language, comprehensive exam, thesis (for some programs). *Entrance requirements:* For master's, GRE or NTE, minimum GPA of 2.5. Additional exam requirements/recommendations for international students: Recommended—IELTS. *Application deadline:* For fall admission, 8/15 priority date for domestic students. Applications are processed on a rolling basis. Application fee: $25. Electronic applications accepted. *Expenses:* Tuition: Full-time $7,470; part-time $415 per hour. Required fees: $1,160 per term. Part-time tuition and fees vary according to course load and degree level. *Financial support:* Teaching assistantships, Federal Work-Study, scholarships/grants, and unspecified assistantships available. Support available to part-time students. Financial award application deadline: 4/1; financial award applicants required to submit FAFSA. *Unit head:* Dr. Kirk Ford, Chair, 601-925-3326, E-mail: ford@mc.edu.

Mississippi State University, College of Arts and Sciences, Department of History, Mississippi State, MS 39762. Offers MA, PhD. Part-time programs available. *Faculty:* 15 full-time (6

History

Mississippi State University (continued)

women), 1 part-time/adjunct (0 women). *Students:* 27 full-time (7 women), 8 part-time (1 woman); includes 1 minority (African American) Average age 32. 17 applicants, 76% accepted, 9 enrolled. In 2007, 8 master's, 1 doctorate awarded. *Degree requirements:* For master's, one foreign language, comprehensive exam, thesis optional; for doctorate, 2 foreign languages, thesis/dissertation, comprehensive oral and written exam. *Entrance requirements:* For master's, minimum GPA of 3.0; for doctorate, GRE General Test, writing sample, minimum graduate GPA of 3.0. Additional exam requirements/recommendations for international students: Required—TOEFL. *Application deadline:* For fall admission, 4/1 for domestic students; for spring admission, 11/1 for domestic students. Applications are processed on a rolling basis. Application fee: $30. *Expenses:* Tuition, state resident: full-time $4,978; part-time $274 per hour. Tuition, nonresident: full-time $11,469; part-time $635 per hour. *Financial support:* In 2007–08, 19 teaching assistantships with full tuition reimbursements (averaging $9,648 per year) were awarded; research assistantships, Federal Work-Study, institutionally sponsored loans, scholarships/grants, and unspecified assistantships also available. Financial award applicants required to submit FAFSA. *Faculty research:* U.S. political, diplomatic, military, social, and cultural history; modern Europe; Latin America; Asian history; African history. *Unit head:* Dr. Alan I. Marcus, Head, 662-325-3604, Fax: 662-325-1139, E-mail: aim10@msstate.edu. *Application contact:* Dr. William A. Person, Interim Associate Vice President for Academic Affairs/Interim Dean of Graduate Studies, 662-325-7400, Fax: 662-325-1967, E-mail: grad@grad.msstate.edu.

Missouri State University, Graduate College, College of Humanities and Public Affairs, Department of History, Springfield, MO 65804-0094. Offers history (MA); secondary education (MS Ed), including history, social science. Part-time programs available. *Faculty:* 17 full-time (2 women). *Students:* 13 full-time (8 women), 44 part-time (19 women); includes 3 minority (1 Asian American or Pacific Islander, 2 Hispanic Americans). Average age 34. 20 applicants, 95% accepted, 14 enrolled. In 2007, 9 degrees awarded. *Degree requirements:* For master's, comprehensive exam, thesis or alternative. *Entrance requirements:* For master's, minimum GPA of 2.75, 24 hours of undergraduate course work in history (MA), 9-12 teaching certification (MS Ed). Additional exam requirements/recommendations for international students: Required—TOEFL (minimum score 550 paper-based; 213 computer-based; 79 iBT), IELTS (minimum score 6). *Application deadline:* For fall admission, 7/20 priority date for domestic students; for spring admission, 12/20 priority date for domestic students. Applications are processed on a rolling basis. Application fee: $35. Electronic applications accepted. *Expenses:* Tuition, state resident: full-time $3,708; part-time $206 per credit hour. Tuition, nonresident: full-time $7,236; part-time $206 per credit hour. Required fees: $622. Full-time tuition and fees vary according to course level, course load, program and reciprocity agreements. *Financial support:* In 2007–08, 5 teaching assistantships with full tuition reimbursements (averaging $9,360 per year) were awarded; research assistantships with full tuition reimbursements, Federal Work-Study, scholarships/grants, and unspecified assistantships also available. Support available to part-time students. Financial award application deadline: 3/31; financial award applicants required to submit FAFSA. *Faculty research:* Recent U.S. history, Native American history, legal history, women's history, ancient Near East. *Unit head:* Michael Sheng, Head, 417-836-5511, Fax: 417-836-5523, E-mail: history@missouristate.edu.

Monmouth University, Graduate School, Department of History, West Long Branch, NJ 07764-1898. Offers MA. Part-time and evening/weekend programs available. *Faculty:* 13 full-time (2 women). *Students:* 8 full-time (4 women), 46 part-time (19 women); includes 4 minority (all Hispanic Americans) Average age 35. 25 applicants, 100% accepted, 14 enrolled. In 2007, 20 degrees awarded. *Degree requirements:* For master's, comprehensive exam, thesis or alternative. *Entrance requirements:* For master's, minimum GPA of 3.0 in major, 2.5 overall. Additional exam requirements/recommendations for international students: Required—TOEFL (minimum score 550 paper-based; 213 computer-based; 79 iBT), IELTS (minimum score 5), MELAB 77, Cambridge A, B, C. *Application deadline:* For fall admission, 7/15 priority date for domestic students, 6/1 for international students; for spring admission, 11/15 priority date for domestic students, 11/1 for international students. Applications are processed on a rolling basis. Application fee: $50. Electronic applications accepted. *Financial support:* In 2007–08, 36 students received support, including 33 fellowships (averaging $1,380 per year), 6 research assistantships (averaging $4,902 per year); career-related internships or fieldwork, scholarships/grants, tuition waivers (partial), and unspecified assistantships also available. Support available to part-time students. Financial award application deadline: 3/1; financial award applicants required to submit FAFSA. *Faculty research:* U.S. business; labor; British, German, and French Revolutions; Soviet Union; Africa. *Unit head:* Dr. Christopher DeRosa, Director, 732-571-4495, Fax: 732-263-5112, E-mail: cderosa@monmouth.edu. *Application contact:* Kevin Roane, Director, Office of Graduate Admission, 732-571-3452, Fax: 732-263-5123, E-mail: gradadm@monmouth.edu.

Montana State University, College of Graduate Studies, College of Letters and Science, Department of History, Bozeman, MT 59717. Offers MA, PhD. Part-time programs available. *Faculty:* 20 full-time (7 women), 8 part-time/adjunct (3 women). *Students:* 3 full-time (2 women), 23 part-time (11 women); includes 1 minority (Asian American or Pacific Islander) Average age 40. 24 applicants, 54% accepted, 9 enrolled. In 2007, 6 degrees awarded. *Degree requirements:* For master's and doctorate, comprehensive exam. *Entrance requirements:* For master's and doctorate, GRE General Test. Additional exam requirements/recommendations for international students: Required—TOEFL (minimum score 550 paper-based; 213 computer-based). *Application deadline:* For fall admission, 7/15 priority date for domestic students, 5/15 priority date for international students; for spring admission, 12/1 priority date for domestic students, 10/1 priority date for international students. Applications are processed on a rolling basis. Application fee: $30. Electronic applications accepted. *Expenses:* Tuition, state resident: full-time $5,176. Tuition, nonresident: full-time $13,070. *Financial support:* In 2007–08, 11 students received support, including 2 research assistantships with full tuition reimbursements available (averaging $15,000 per year), 9 teaching assistantships with full tuition reimbursements available. Financial award application deadline: 3/1; financial award applicants required to submit FAFSA. *Faculty research:* U.S. West, environmental history, science and technology history. Total annual research expenditures: $317,293. *Unit head:* Dr. Brett Walker, Head, 406-994-4395, Fax: 406-994-6879, E-mail: bwalker@montana.edu.

Montclair State University, The Office of Graduate Admissions and Support Services, College of Humanities and Social Sciences, Department of History, Montclair, NJ 07043-1624. Offers social sciences (MA), including history; social studies (Certificate). Part-time and evening/weekend programs available. *Faculty:* 15 full-time (6 women). *Students:* 5 full-time (0 women), 35 part-time (7 women); includes 1 minority (Hispanic American) 32 applicants, 34% accepted, 10 enrolled. In 2007, 11 master's, 3 other advanced degrees awarded. *Degree requirements:* For master's, comprehensive exam. *Entrance requirements:* For master's, GRE General Test, 2 letters of recommendation. Additional exam requirements/recommendations for international students: Required—TOEFL (minimum score 550 paper-based; 213 computer-based). *Application deadline:* For fall admission, 6/1 for international students; for spring admission, 11/1 for international students. Applications are processed on a rolling basis. Application fee: $60. Electronic applications accepted. *Financial support:* Research assistantships with full tuition reimbursements, Federal Work-Study, scholarships/grants, and unspecified assistantships available. Support available to part-time students. Financial award application deadline: 3/1. *Unit head:* Dr. Michael Whelan, Chairperson, 973-655-7848.

Morgan State University, School of Graduate Studies, College of Liberal Arts, Department of History and Geography, Baltimore, MD 21251. Offers African-American studies (MA); history (MA, PhD). Part-time and evening/weekend programs available. *Faculty:* 8 full-time. *Students:* 34 (16 women); includes 30 minority (all African Americans) 20 applicants, 75% accepted. *Degree requirements:* For master's, comprehensive exam, thesis; for doctorate, comprehensive exam, thesis/dissertation. *Entrance requirements:* For master's, minimum GPA of 2.5; for doctorate, GRE or MAT. Additional exam requirements/recommendations for international students: Required—TOEFL (minimum score 550 paper-based; 213 computer-based). *Application deadline:* For fall admission, 2/1 priority date for domestic students; for spring admission, 10/1 priority date for domestic students. Applications are processed on a rolling basis. Application fee: $0. *Financial support:* In 2007–08, 2 fellowships were awarded; research assistantships. Financial award application deadline: 2/1. *Faculty research:* Women's history, African diaspora history, urban history. *Unit head:* Dr. Annette Palmer, Chair, 443-885-3190, E-mail: annette.palmer@morgan.edu. *Application contact:* Dr. Mark Garrison, Associate Dean, 443-885-3185, Fax: 443-885-8226, E-mail: mark.garrison@morgan.edu.

Murray State University, College of Humanities and Fine Arts, Program in History, Murray, KY 42071. Offers MA. Part-time programs available. *Degree requirements:* For master's, one foreign language, comprehensive exam, thesis (for some programs). *Entrance requirements:* For master's, GRE General Test. Additional exam requirements/recommendations for international students: Required—TOEFL.

Nebraska Wesleyan University, University College, Program in Historical Studies, Lincoln, NE 68504-2796. Offers MA. Part-time programs available. *Faculty:* 1 full-time (0 women), 1 part-time/adjunct (0 women). *Students:* Average age 38. In 2007, 15 degrees awarded. Application fee: $50. *Expenses:* Contact institution. *Unit head:* Dr. Kevin Bower, Program Director, 402-465-2461, E-mail: kbower@nebrwesleyan.edu.

New Jersey Institute of Technology, Office of Graduate Studies, College of Science and Liberal Arts, Federated Department of History, Newark, NJ 07102. Offers MA, MAT. Part-time and evening/weekend programs available. *Faculty:* 6 full-time (1 woman), 3 part-time/adjunct (0 women). *Entrance requirements:* For master's, GRE General Test, minimum B average in undergraduate course work. Additional exam requirements/recommendations for international students: Required—TOEFL (minimum score 550 paper-based; 213 computer-based). *Application deadline:* For fall admission, 6/5 priority date for domestic students; for spring admission, 10/15 for domestic students. Applications are processed on a rolling basis. Application fee: $60. Electronic applications accepted. *Expenses:* Tuition, state resident: full-time $12,730. Tuition, nonresident: full-time $18,090. Tuition and fees vary according to course load and campus/location. *Financial support:* Fellowships with full and partial tuition reimbursements, research assistantships with full and partial tuition reimbursements, teaching assistantships with full and partial tuition reimbursements, career-related internships or fieldwork, Federal Work-Study, institutionally sponsored loans, and unspecified assistantships available. Financial award application deadline: 3/15. *Unit head:* Dr. Richard B. Scherl, Chair, 973-596-3377, Fax: 973-762-3039, E-mail: richard.b.scherl@njit.edu. *Application contact:* Kathryn Kelly, Director of Admissions, 973-596-3300, Fax: 973-596-3461, E-mail: admissions@njit.edu.

New Mexico State University, Graduate School, College of Arts and Sciences, Department of History, Las Cruces, NM 88003-8001. Offers history (MA); public history (MA). Part-time programs available. *Faculty:* 10 full-time (5 women), 1 part-time/adjunct (0 women). *Students:* 38 full-time (20 women), 12 part-time (4 women); includes 1 American Indian/Alaska Native, 14 Hispanic Americans. Average age 34. 29 applicants, 72% accepted, 14 enrolled. In 2007, 8 degrees awarded. *Degree requirements:* For master's, thesis (for some programs). *Entrance requirements:* For master's, 12 undergraduate history credits. *Application deadline:* For fall admission, 7/1 priority date for domestic students; for spring admission, 11/1 for domestic students. Applications are processed on a rolling basis. Application fee: $30 ($50 for international students). Electronic applications accepted. *Expenses:* Tuition, state resident: full-time $3,602; part-time $199 per credit. Tuition, nonresident: full-time $13,380; part-time $607 per credit. Required fees: $1,178. *Financial support:* In 2007–08, 3 research assistantships with partial tuition reimbursements, 9 teaching assistantships with partial tuition reimbursements were awarded; fellowships, career-related internships or fieldwork, Federal Work-Study, and health care benefits also available. Support available to part-time students. Financial award application deadline: 3/1. *Faculty research:* U.S. Southwestern and border history, Latin American history, U.S. women's history, European history, history of science, U.S. diplomatic history, East Asian history. *Unit head:* Dr. Jeffrey P Brown, Head, 575-646-4601, Fax: 575-646-6096, E-mail: jbrown@nmsu.edu. *Application contact:* Dr. Jamie Bronstein, Director of Graduate Studies, 575-646-4612, Fax: 575-646-6096, E-mail: jbronste@nmsu.edu.

The New School: A University, The New School for Social Research, Committee on Historical Studies, New York, NY 10011. Offers MA, PhD. Part-time and evening/weekend programs available. *Faculty:* 8 full-time (4 women). *Students:* 14 full-time (5 women), 3 part-time (all women); includes 4 minority (3 Asian Americans or Pacific Islanders, 1 Hispanic American), 1 international. Average age 30. In 2007, 5 degrees awarded. Terminal master's awarded for partial completion of doctoral program. *Degree requirements:* For master's, thesis optional, exam or paper; for doctorate, variable foreign language requirement, thesis/dissertation, qualifying exam. *Entrance requirements:* For master's, GRE General Test; for doctorate, GRE General Test, MA. Additional exam requirements/recommendations for international students: Required—TOEFL (minimum score 600 paper-based; 250 computer-based; 100 iBT). *Application deadline:* For fall admission, 1/15 priority date for domestic students. Applications are processed on a rolling basis. Application fee: $50. *Financial support:* Fellowships, research assistantships, teaching assistantships, career-related internships or fieldwork, Federal Work-Study, scholarships/grants, and tuition waivers (full and partial) available. Support available to part-time students. Financial award application deadline: 3/1; financial award applicants required to submit FAFSA. *Faculty research:* Social movements, systemic change, culture and history. *Unit head:* Dr. David Plotke, Chair, 212-229-5747 Ext. 3087, Fax: 212-229-5315, E-mail: plotked@newschool.edu. *Application contact:* Robert MacDonald, Director of Admissions, 800-523-5710 Ext. 3007, Fax: 212-989-7102, E-mail: macdonar@newschool.edu.

See Close-Up on page 1653.

New York University, Graduate School of Arts and Science, Department of History, New York, NY 10012-1019. Offers African diaspora (PhD); African history (PhD); archival management and historical editing (Advanced Certificate); Atlantic history (PhD); French studies/history (PhD); Hebrew and Judaic studies/history (PhD); history (MA, PhD), including Europe (PhD), Latin American and the Caribbean (PhD), United States (PhD), women's history (MA); Middle Eastern history (MA); Middle Eastern studies/history (PhD); public history (Advanced Certificate); world history (MA); JD/MA; MA/Advanced Certificate. Part-time programs available. *Faculty:* 43 full-time (19 women), 18 part-time/adjunct. *Students:* 106 full-time (68 women), 48 part-time (34 women); includes 29 minority (18 African Americans, 4 Asian Americans or Pacific Islanders, 7 Hispanic Americans), 26 international. Average age 31. 413 applicants, 19% accepted, 40 enrolled. In 2007, 17 master's, 7 doctorates awarded. Terminal master's awarded for partial completion of doctoral program. *Degree requirements:* For master's, seminar paper; for doctorate, one foreign language, thesis/dissertation, oral and written exams; for Advanced Certificate, internship. *Entrance requirements:* For master's, GRE General Test, minimum GPA of 3.0, writing sample; for doctorate, GRE. Additional exam requirements/recommendations for international students: Required—TOEFL. *Application deadline:* For fall admission, 12/12 for domestic students. Application fee: $85. *Financial support:* Fellowships with tuition reimbursements, research assistantships, teaching assistantships with tuition reimbursements, career-related internships or fieldwork, Federal Work-Study, institutionally sponsored loans, scholarships/grants, health care benefits, and unspecified assistantships available. Financial award application deadline: 12/12; financial award applicants required to submit FAFSA. *Faculty research:* African, East Asian, Medieval, early modern, and modern European history; U.S. history; African and African diaspora; Latin American history; Atlantic World. *Unit head:* Michael Gomez, Chair, 212-998-8600, Fax: 212-995-4017, E-mail: history.dept@nyu.edu. *Application contact:* Gregory Grandin, Director of Graduate Studies, 212-998-8600, Fax: 212-995-4017, E-mail: history.dept@nyu.edu.

North Carolina Central University, Division of Academic Affairs, College of Arts and Sciences, Department of History, Durham, NC 27707-3129. Offers MA. Part-time and evening/weekend programs available. *Degree requirements:* For master's, one foreign language, comprehensive exam, thesis. *Entrance requirements:* For master's, GRE, minimum GPA of 3.0 in major, 2.5 overall. Additional exam requirements/recommendations for international students: Required—TOEFL.

North Carolina State University, Graduate School, College of Humanities and Social Sciences, Department of History, Raleigh, NC 27695. Offers history (MA); public history (MA). Part-time and evening/weekend programs available. *Degree requirements:* For master's, thesis. *Entrance requirements:* For master's, GRE General Test. Electronic applications accepted. *Faculty research:* History of the United States, Europe, Asia Africa and the Middle East; history of science; intellectual, cultural, social, environmental and political history.

North Dakota State University, College of Graduate and Interdisciplinary Studies, College of Arts, Humanities and Social Sciences, Department of History, Fargo, ND 58105. Offers MA, MS, PhD. Part-time and evening/weekend programs available. *Faculty:* 9 full-time (1 woman), 2 part-time/adjunct (0 women). *Students:* 13 full-time (7 women), 13 part-time (5 women); includes 1 minority (Hispanic American) Average age 27. 11 applicants, 91% accepted, 10 enrolled. In 2007, 1 degree awarded. *Degree requirements:* For master's, one foreign language, comprehensive exam, thesis optional; for doctorate, 2 foreign languages, comprehensive exam, thesis/dissertation. *Entrance requirements:* For master's and doctorate, GRE General Test. Additional exam requirements/recommendations for international students: Required—TOEFL (minimum score 600 paper-based; 250 computer-based; 100 iBT). *Application deadline:* For fall admission, 2/10 priority date for domestic and international students. Applications are processed on a rolling basis. Application fee: $45 ($60 for international students). *Expenses:* Tuition, state resident: full-time $5,376; part-time $224 per credit. Tuition, nonresident: full-time $14,354; part-time $598 per credit. Required fees: $962; $40 per credit. Part-time tuition and fees vary according to course load and reciprocity agreements. *Financial support:* In 2007–08, 9 students received support, including 1 fellowship with tuition reimbursement available (averaging $15,000 per year), 2 research assistantships with full tuition reimbursements available (averaging $9,400 per year), 4 teaching assistantships with full tuition reimbursements available (averaging $8,200 per year); career-related internships or fieldwork, Federal Work-Study, institutionally sponsored loans, and tuition waivers also available. Financial award application deadline: 3/15. *Faculty research:* Recent U.S., modern English, early modern European, North Dakota, Latin American, and Great Plains history. *Unit head:* Dr. John K. Cox, Head, 701-231-8654, Fax: 701-231-1047, E-mail: john.cox.l@ndsu.edu. *Application contact:* Dr. Jim Norris, Graduate Coordinator, 701-231-8827, Fax: 701-231-1047, E-mail: jim.norris@nodak.edu.

Northeastern Illinois University, Graduate College, College of Arts and Sciences, Department of History, Program in History, Chicago, IL 60625-4699. Offers MA. Part-time and evening/weekend programs available. *Faculty:* 11 full-time (3 women), 3 part-time/adjunct (0 women). *Students:* 1 full-time (0 women), 29 part-time (12 women); includes 5 minority (2 African Americans, 3 Hispanic Americans). Average age 38. 15 applicants, 73% accepted, 7 enrolled. In 2007, 5 degrees awarded. *Degree requirements:* For master's, comprehensive exam, thesis optional, minimum GPA of 3.0. *Entrance requirements:* For master's, 24 undergraduate hours in history, minimum GPA of 2.75. Additional exam requirements/recommendations for international students: Required—TOEFL (minimum score 550 paper-based; 213 computer-based; 80 iBT). *Application deadline:* For fall admission, 4/1 priority date for domestic students; for spring admission, 8/15 for domestic students. Applications are processed on a rolling basis. Application fee: $25. Electronic applications accepted. *Expenses:* Tuition, state resident: part-time $243 per credit hour. Tuition, nonresident: part-time $443 per credit hour. *Financial support:* In 2007–08, 21 students received support, including 3 research assistantships with full tuition reimbursements available (averaging $6,600 per year); career-related internships or fieldwork, Federal Work-Study, institutionally sponsored loans, scholarships/grants, tuition waivers (full and partial), and unspecified assistantships also available. Support available to part-time students. Financial award applicants required to submit FAFSA. *Faculty research:* Africa; East Asia; European medieval, early-modern, and modern history; U.S. social, cultural, and intellectual history.

Northeastern University, College of Arts and Sciences, Department of History, Boston, MA 02115-5096. Offers history (MA); public history (MA); world history (PhD). Part-time and evening/weekend programs available. *Faculty:* 14 full-time (4 women), 4 part-time/adjunct. *Students:* 53 full-time (32 women), 4 part-time. 97 applicants, 49% accepted. In 2007, 9 master's, 1 doctorate awarded. Terminal master's awarded for partial completion of doctoral program. *Degree requirements:* For master's, one foreign language, thesis or alternative, project; for doctorate, thesis/dissertation. *Entrance requirements:* For master's and doctorate, GRE General Test. *Application deadline:* For fall admission, 2/1 for domestic students. Application fee: $50. Electronic applications accepted. *Financial support:* In 2007–08, 13 teaching assistantships with tuition reimbursements (averaging $14,035 per year) were awarded; research assistantships with tuition reimbursements, career-related internships or fieldwork, scholarships/grants, and tuition waivers (full and partial) also available. Financial award application deadline: 2/1; financial award applicants required to submit FAFSA. *Faculty research:* World history, U.S. social history. *Unit head:* Dr. Laura Frader, Chair, 617-373-2660, Fax: 617-373-2661. *Application contact:* Dr. Christina Gilmartin, Graduate Coordinator, 617-373-2660, Fax: 617-373-2661.

See Close-Up on page 417.

Northern Arizona University, Graduate College, College of Arts and Letters, Department of History, Flagstaff, AZ 86011. Offers MA, PhD. Part-time programs available. *Degree requirements:* For master's, thesis or departmental qualifying exam; for doctorate, thesis/dissertation. *Entrance requirements:* For master's and doctorate, GRE General Test. *Faculty research:* Twentieth-century U.S., U.S. trans-Mississippi West, Arizona and the Southwest, women's history, U.S. intellectual history.

Northern Illinois University, Graduate School, College of Liberal Arts and Sciences, Department of History, De Kalb, IL 60115-2854. Offers MA, PhD. Part-time programs available. *Faculty:* 18 full-time (8 women), 2 part-time/adjunct (0 women). *Students:* 28 full-time (8 women), 40 part-time (16 women); includes 4 minority (2 African Americans, 1 American Indian/Alaska Native, 1 Asian American or Pacific Islander), 4 international. Average age 34. 66 applicants, 53% accepted, 18 enrolled. In 2007, 13 master's, 3 doctorates awarded. Terminal master's awarded for partial completion of doctoral program. *Degree requirements:* For master's, variable foreign language requirement, comprehensive exam, thesis optional, research seminars; for doctorate, variable foreign language requirement, thesis/dissertation, candidacy exam, dissertation defense, research seminars. *Entrance requirements:* For master's, GRE General Test, minimum GPA of 2.75; for doctorate, GRE General Test, minimum undergraduate GPA of 2.75, graduate GPA of 3.2. Additional exam requirements/recommendations for international students: Required—TOEFL (minimum score 550 paper-based; 213 computer-based). *Application deadline:* For fall admission, 6/1 for domestic students, 5/1 for international students; for spring admission, 11/1 for domestic students, 10/1 for international students. Applications are processed on a rolling basis. Application fee: $30. Electronic applications accepted. *Expenses:* Tuition, area resident: Part-time $226 per credit hour. Tuition, state resident: full-time $5,424; part-time $225 per credit hour. Tuition, nonresident: full-time $10,848. Required fees: $2,416; $64 per credit hour. *Financial support:* In 2007–08, 21 teaching assistantships with full tuition reimbursements were awarded; fellowships with full tuition reimbursements, research assistantships with full tuition reimbursements, career-related internships or fieldwork, Federal Work-Study, scholarships/grants, tuition waivers (full), and unspecified assistantships also available. Support available to part-time students. Financial award applicants required to submit FAFSA. *Faculty research:* History of the Carolingian empire, world history of early modern Europe, modern Irish history, history of the Ming dynasty. *Unit head:* Dr. Kenton Clymer, Chair, 815-753-6819, Fax: 815-753-6302, E-mail: kclymer@niu.edu. *Application contact:* Dr. Heide Fehrenbach, Assistant Chair and Director of Graduate Studies, 815-753-6699, E-mail: hfehrenboch@niu.edu.

Northwestern University, The Graduate School, Judd A. and Marjorie Weinberg College of Arts and Sciences, Department of History, Evanston, IL 60208. Offers PhD, JD/PhD. Admissions and degrees offered through The Graduate School. *Degree requirements:* For doctorate, variable foreign language requirement, thesis/dissertation, major and minor field exams. *Entrance requirements:* For doctorate, sample of written work. Additional exam requirements/recommendations for international students: Required—TOEFL. Electronic applications accepted. *Faculty research:* Medieval and early modern Europe, Africa, race and slavery, Atlantic history, gender.

Northwest Missouri State University, Graduate School, College of Arts and Sciences, Department of History, Humanities, and Political Science, Maryville, MO 64468-6001. Offers history (MA); teaching history (MS Ed). Part-time programs available. *Faculty:* 5 full-time (1 woman). *Students:* 7 full-time (4 women), 5 part-time (1 woman); includes 1 minority (Asian American or Pacific Islander) 4 applicants, 100% accepted, 1 enrolled. In 2007, 5 degrees awarded. *Degree requirements:* For master's, comprehensive exam, thesis. *Entrance requirements:* For master's, GRE General Test, undergraduate major/minor in social studies/humanities, minimum undergraduate GPA of 2.5, writing sample. Additional exam requirements/recommendations for international students: Required—TOEFL (minimum score 550 paper-based; 213 computer-based). *Application deadline:* For fall admission, 7/1 for domestic and international students; for spring admission, 11/15 for domestic and international students. Applications are processed on a rolling basis. Application fee: $0 ($50 for international students). *Financial support:* In 2007–08, 2 research assistantships with full tuition reimbursements (averaging $6,000 per year) were awarded. Financial award application deadline: 3/1; financial award applicants required to submit FAFSA. *Unit head:* Dr. Richard Frucht, Chairperson, 660-562-1614. *Application contact:* Dr. Frances Shipley, Dean of Graduate School, 660-562-1145, Fax: 660-562-1096, E-mail: gradsch@nwmissouri.edu.

Oakland University, Graduate Study and Lifelong Learning, College of Arts and Sciences, Department of History, Rochester, MI 48309-4401. Offers MA. Part-time and evening/weekend programs available. *Faculty:* 10 full-time (3 women). *Students:* 5 full-time (2 women), 15 part-time (3 women). Average age 37. 8 applicants, 75% accepted, 5 enrolled. In 2007, 3 degrees awarded. *Entrance requirements:* For master's, minimum GPA of 3.0 for unconditional admission. Additional exam requirements/recommendations for international students: Required—TOEFL (minimum score 550 paper-based; 213 computer-based). *Application deadline:* For fall admission, 7/15 priority date for domestic students, 5/1 for international students; for winter admission, 12/1 priority date for domestic students, 9/1 for international students; for spring admission, 3/15 priority date for domestic students. Applications are processed on a rolling basis. Application fee: $35. Electronic applications accepted. *Expenses:* Tuition, state resident: full-time $9,936; part-time $414 per credit. Tuition, nonresident: full-time $17,202; part-time $716 per credit. *Financial support:* Federal Work-Study, institutionally sponsored loans, and tuition waivers (full) available. Financial award application deadline: 3/1; financial award applicants required to submit FAFSA. *Unit head:* Dr. Karen Miller, Chair, 248-370-3510, Fax: 248-370-3528.

The Ohio State University, Graduate School, College of Humanities, Department of History, Columbus, OH 43210. Offers MA, PhD. *Faculty:* 73. *Students:* 112 full-time (46 women), 15 part-time (5 women); includes 17 minority (9 African Americans, 2 American Indian/Alaska Native, 6 Hispanic Americans), 19 international. Average age 30. In 2007, 21 master's, 14 doctorates awarded. *Degree requirements:* For master's, thesis optional; for doctorate, variable foreign language requirement, thesis/dissertation. *Entrance requirements:* For master's and doctorate, GRE General Test. Additional exam requirements/recommendations for international students: Required—TOEFL (minimum score 600 paper-based; 250 computer-based). *Application deadline:* For fall admission, 8/15 priority date for domestic students, 7/1 priority date for international students; for winter admission, 12/1 priority date for domestic students, 11/1 priority date for international students; for spring admission, 3/1 priority date for domestic students, 2/1 priority date for international students. Applications are processed on a rolling basis. Application fee: $40 ($50 for international students). Electronic applications accepted. *Financial support:* Fellowships, research assistantships, teaching assistantships, Federal Work-Study, institutionally sponsored loans, and unspecified assistantships available. Support available to part-time students. *Unit head:* Margaret Newell, Graduate Studies Committee Chair, 614-247-2674, E-mail: newell.20@osu.edu. *Application contact:* 614-247-9444, Fax: 614-292-3895, E-mail: domestic.grad@osu.edu.

Ohio University, Graduate College, College of Arts and Sciences, Department of History, Athens, OH 45701-2979. Offers MA, PhD. *Faculty:* 24 full-time (7 women). *Students:* 48 full-time (13 women); includes 1 Asian American or Pacific Islander, 1 Hispanic American. 57 applicants, 46% accepted, 14 enrolled. In 2007, 8 master's, 5 doctorates awarded. *Median time to degree:* Of those who began their doctoral program in fall 1999, 100% received their degree in 8 years or less. *Degree requirements:* For master's, one foreign language, thesis optional; for doctorate, 2 foreign languages, comprehensive exam, thesis/dissertation. *Entrance requirements:* For master's, GRE, minimum GPA of 3.0; for doctorate, GRE, minimum GPA of 3.0, completed M.A. Additional exam requirements/recommendations for international students: Required—TOEFL (minimum score 550 paper-based; 213 computer-based), IELTS (minimum score 7), TWE (minimum score 5). *Application deadline:* For fall admission, 2/1 for domestic and international students. Applications are processed on a rolling basis. Application fee: $50 ($55 for international students). Electronic applications accepted. *Financial support:* In 2007–08, 40 students received support, including 8 fellowships with tuition reimbursements available (averaging $12,350 per year), 30 teaching assistantships with tuition reimbursements available (averaging $12,367 per year); Federal Work-Study, institutionally sponsored loans, and tuition waivers (full) also available. Financial award application deadline: 2/1. *Faculty research:* U.S. foreign relations, modern Europe, Latin America, southeast Asia, U.S. women. *Unit head:* Dr. Norman J.W. Goda, Chair, 740-593-4334, Fax: 740-593-0259, E-mail: goda@ohio.edu. *Application contact:* Chester Pack, Graduate Chair, 740-593-4335, Fax: 740-593-0259, E-mail: pach@ohio.edu.

Oklahoma State University, College of Arts and Sciences, Department of History, Stillwater, OK 74078. Offers applied history (MA); history (MA, PhD). *Faculty:* 23 full-time (6 women), 3 part-time/adjunct (1 woman). *Students:* 19 full-time (5 women), 38 part-time (15 women); includes 9 minority (6 American Indian/Alaska Native, 2 Asian Americans or Pacific Islanders, 1 Hispanic American), 1 international. Average age 37. 45 applicants, 49% accepted, 15 enrolled. In 2007, 7 master's, 4 doctorates awarded. *Degree requirements:* For master's, variable foreign language requirement, thesis or report; for doctorate, 2 foreign languages, thesis/dissertation. *Entrance requirements:* For master's and doctorate, GRE General Test or GMAT. Additional exam requirements/recommendations for international students: Required—TOEFL. *Application deadline:* For fall admission, 3/1 priority date for international students; for spring admission, 8/1 priority date for international students. Applications are processed on a rolling basis. Application fee: $40 ($75 for international students). Electronic applications accepted. *Expenses:* Tuition, state resident: full-time $4,993; part-time $148 per credit hour. Tuition, nonresident: full-time $14,755; part-time $555 per credit hour. Tuition and fees vary according to program. *Financial support:* In 2007–08, 27 teaching assistantships (averaging $12,675 per year) were awarded; career-related internships or fieldwork, Federal Work-Study, scholarships/grants, health care benefits, tuition waivers (partial), and unspecified assistantships also available. Support available to part-time students. Financial award application deadline: 3/1. *Faculty research:* U.S. history, The American West, Native American history, modern European history, women's history. *Unit head:* Dr. Elizabeth A. Williams, Head, 405-744-5678, E-mail: williea@okstate.edu.

Old Dominion University, College of Arts and Letters, Program in History, Norfolk, VA 23529. Offers MA. Part-time and evening/weekend programs available. *Faculty:* 16 full-time (7 women). *Students:* 15 full-time (4 women), 29 part-time (12 women); includes 3 minority (all African Americans) Average age 31. 41 applicants, 80% accepted, 20 enrolled. In 2007, 16 degrees awarded. *Degree requirements:* For master's, comprehensive exam, thesis optional. *Entrance requirements:* For master's, GRE General Test, 24 credits in history with minimum GPA of 3.0. *Application deadline:* For fall admission, 6/1 for domestic students; for spring admission, 11/1 for domestic students. Applications are processed on a rolling basis. Application fee: $40. Electronic applications accepted. *Expenses:* Tuition, state resident: part-time $304 per credit hour. Tuition, nonresident: part-time $761 per credit hour. *Financial*

History

Old Dominion University (continued)

support: In 2007–08, 1 fellowship with full tuition reimbursement (averaging $8,000 per year), 6 teaching assistantships with partial tuition reimbursements (averaging $8,000 per year) were awarded; career-related internships or fieldwork and scholarships/grants also available. Support available to part-time students. Financial award application deadline: 2/15; financial award applicants required to submit FAFSA. *Faculty research:* History: maritime, American, European, modern Asia, and Africa. *Unit head:* Dr. Jane T. Merritt, Graduate Program Director, 757-683-3949, Fax: 757-683-5644, E-mail: histgpd@odu.edu.

Oregon State University, Graduate School, College of Liberal Arts, Department of History, Corvallis, OR 97331. Offers MA, MS, PhD. *Expenses:* Tuition, state resident: full-time $9,126; part-time $338 per credit. Tuition, nonresident: full-time $14,796; part-time $548 per credit. Required fees: $1,447. *Unit head:* Dr. Paul L. Farber, Chair, 541-737-1273, Fax: 541-737-1257, E-mail: pfarber@oregonstate.edu.

Penn State University Park, Graduate School, College of the Liberal Arts, Department of History, State College, University Park, PA 16802-1503. Offers MA, PhD. *Expenses:* Tuition, state resident: full-time $14,738; part-time $614 per credit. Tuition, nonresident: full-time $26,050; part-time $1,085 per credit. Tuition and fees vary according to course load, program and student level. *Unit head:* Dr. Sally A. McMurry, Head, 814-865-6097, Fax: 814-863-7840, E-mail: sam9@psu.edu. *Application contact:* Matthew Restall, Director of Graduate Studies, E-mail: mxr40@psu.edu.

Pepperdine University, Seaver College, Humanities Division, Malibu, CA 90263. Offers American studies (MA); history (MA). *Degree requirements:* For master's, oral and written exams. *Entrance requirements:* For master's, GRE General Test, undergraduate major or 15 upper-division units in history. Additional exam requirements/recommendations for international students: Required—TOEFL.

Pittsburg State University, Graduate School, College of Arts and Sciences, Department of History, Pittsburg, KS 66762. Offers MA. *Degree requirements:* For master's, thesis or alternative.

Pontifical Catholic University of Puerto Rico, College of Arts and Humanities, Department of History, Ponce, PR 00717-0777. Offers MA. *Entrance requirements:* For master's, GRE General Test, minimum GPA of 2.75, 2 letters of recommendation.

Portland State University, Graduate Studies, College of Liberal Arts and Sciences, Department of History, Portland, OR 97207-0751. Offers MA. Part-time programs available. *Faculty:* 19 full-time (6 women), 7 part-time/adjunct (4 women). *Students:* 23 full-time (7 women), 27 part-time (11 women); includes 3 minority (1 American Indian/Alaska Native, 1 Asian American or Pacific Islander, 1 Hispanic American). Average age 34. 29 applicants, 59% accepted, 10 enrolled. In 2007, 12 degrees awarded. *Degree requirements:* For master's, one foreign language, thesis, oral and written exams. *Entrance requirements:* For master's, GRE General Test, minimum GPA of 3.50 in upper division history courses, 2 letters of recommendation, BA/BS in history. Additional exam requirements/recommendations for international students: Required—TOEFL (minimum score 550 paper-based; 213 computer-based). *Application deadline:* For fall admission, 4/1 for domestic students, 3/1 for international students; for winter admission, 9/1 for domestic students, 6/1 for international students; for spring admission, 11/1 for domestic and international students. Application fee: $50. *Expenses:* Tuition, state resident: full-time $7,047. Tuition, nonresident: full-time $11,178. *Financial support:* In 2007–08, 2 research assistantships with full tuition reimbursements (averaging $11,000 per year) were awarded; teaching assistantships with full tuition reimbursements, career-related internships or fieldwork, Federal Work-Study, scholarships/grants, and unspecified assistantships also available. Support available to part-time students. Financial award application deadline: 3/1; financial award applicants required to submit FAFSA. *Faculty research:* Germany and Modern Europe, early modern France and England, Mexico in the 1920's, eighteenth century France, Reformation, U.S. cultural history. *Unit head:* Dr. Linda Walton, Head, 503-725-3917, Fax: 503-725-3953. *Application contact:* Dr. Richard Beyler, Graduate Coordinator, 503-725-3996, Fax: 503-725-3953, E-mail: beylerr@pdx.edu.

Prescott College, Graduate Programs, Program in Humanities, Prescott, AZ 86301. Offers humanities (MA); Southwestern regional history (MA). Part-time programs available. Post-baccalaureate distance learning degree programs offered (minimal on-campus study). *Faculty:* 1 (woman) full-time, 43 part-time/adjunct (25 women). *Students:* 19 full-time (12 women), 30 part-time (25 women); includes 9 minority (6 African Americans, 1 American Indian/Alaska Native, 2 Hispanic Americans), 1 international. Average age 41. 25 applicants, 76% accepted, 13 enrolled. In 2007, 18 degrees awarded. *Degree requirements:* For master's, thesis, fieldwork or internship, practicum. *Entrance requirements:* For master's, 2 letters of recommendation, resumé. Additional exam requirements/recommendations for international students: Required—TOEFL (minimum score 550 paper-based; 213 computer-based). *Application deadline:* For fall admission, 5/1 priority date for domestic and international students; for spring admission, 11/1 priority date for domestic and international students. Applications are processed on a rolling basis. Application fee: $40. Electronic applications accepted. *Expenses:* Tuition: Full-time $6,480; part-time $540 per credit. *Financial support:* Career-related internships or fieldwork and Federal Work-Study available. Financial award applicants required to submit FAFSA. *Unit head:* Joan Clingan, Chair, 928-350-3208. *Application contact:* Kerstin Alicki, Admissions Counselor, 877-350-2102, Fax: 928-776-5242, E-mail: admissions@prescott.edu.

Princeton University, Graduate School, Department of Classics, Princeton, NJ 08544-1019. Offers ancient history (PhD); classical archaeology (PhD); classical philosophy (PhD); history, archaeology and religions of the ancient world (PhD). *Degree requirements:* For doctorate, thesis/dissertation. *Entrance requirements:* For doctorate, GRE General Test, sample of written work. Additional exam requirements/recommendations for international students: Required—TOEFL (minimum score 600 paper-based; 250 computer-based). Electronic applications accepted.

Princeton University, Graduate School, Department of History, Princeton, NJ 08544-1019. Offers community college history teaching (PhD); history (PhD); history of science (PhD). *Degree requirements:* For doctorate, variable foreign language requirement, comprehensive exam, thesis/dissertation. *Entrance requirements:* For doctorate, GRE General Test, sample of written work. Additional exam requirements/recommendations for international students: Required—TOEFL (minimum score 600 paper-based; 250 computer-based). Electronic applications accepted. *Faculty research:* World comparative, Europe-early modern, modern, late antique, medieval.

Providence College, Graduate Studies, Department of History, Providence, RI 02918. Offers MA. Part-time and evening/weekend programs available. *Faculty:* 5 full-time (1 woman), 4 part-time/adjunct (1 woman). *Students:* 20 full-time (7 women), 47 part-time (18 women). Average age 32. 14 applicants, 100% accepted. In 2007, 32 degrees awarded. *Degree requirements:* For master's, comprehensive exam, thesis optional. *Entrance requirements:* Additional exam requirements/recommendations for international students: Required—TOEFL (minimum score 550 paper-based; 213 computer-based; 79 iBT). *Application deadline:* For fall admission, 8/1 for domestic students; for spring admission, 12/31 for domestic students. Applications are processed on a rolling basis. Application fee: $55. *Expenses:* Tuition: Full-time $6,783; part-time $969 per course. *Financial support:* In 2007–08, 7 research assistantships with full tuition reimbursements (averaging $8,400 per year) were awarded; career-related internships or fieldwork, institutionally sponsored loans, and unspecified assistantships also available. Support available to part-time students. Financial award application deadline: 8/1; financial award applicants required to submit FAFSA. *Faculty research:* General American history, eighteenth and nineteenth century British history, Eastern European history, medieval history, church history. *Unit head:* Dr. Paul O'Malley, Director, 401-865-2193, Fax: 401-865-1193, E-mail: pomalley@providence.edu. *Application contact:* Phyllis S. Cardullo, Senior Administrator Coordinator, 401-865-2193, Fax: 401-865-1193, E-mail: pcardull@providence.edu.

Purdue University, Graduate School, College of Liberal Arts, Department of History, West Lafayette, IN 47907. Offers MA, PhD. Part-time programs available. *Degree requirements:* For master's, thesis optional; for doctorate, 2 foreign languages, thesis/dissertation. *Entrance requirements:* For master's and doctorate, GRE General Test, sample of written work. Additional exam requirements/recommendations for international students: Required—TOEFL. Electronic applications accepted. *Faculty research:* U.S. history, early modern and modern European history, global women's history, U.S. minority history, medieval history.

Purdue University Calumet, Graduate School, School of Liberal Arts and Sciences, Department of History and Political Science, Hammond, IN 46323-2094. Offers MA. Part-time and evening/weekend programs available. *Entrance requirements:* Additional exam requirements/recommendations for international students: Required—TOEFL. *Faculty research:* Mid-east, German history, US regional history, US social history, holocaust.

Queens College of the City University of New York, Division of Graduate Studies, Social Science Division, Department of History, Flushing, NY 11367-1597. Offers MA. Part-time and evening/weekend programs available. *Faculty:* 24 full-time (12 women). *Students:* 4 full-time (1 woman), 56 part-time (25 women). 78 applicants, 88% accepted, 43 enrolled. In 2007, 5 degrees awarded. *Degree requirements:* For master's, one foreign language, comprehensive exam, thesis. *Entrance requirements:* For master's, minimum GPA of 3.0. Additional exam requirements/recommendations for international students: Required—TOEFL. *Application deadline:* For fall admission, 4/1 for domestic students; for spring admission, 11/1 for domestic students. Applications are processed on a rolling basis. Application fee: $125. *Financial support:* Career-related internships or fieldwork, Federal Work-Study, institutionally sponsored loans, and tuition waivers (partial) available. Support available to part-time students. Financial award application deadline: 4/1; financial award applicants required to submit FAFSA. *Faculty research:* Ancient, modern European, medieval, and American history. *Unit head:* Dr. Frank Warren, Chairperson, 718-997-5350, E-mail: frank_warren@qc.edu. *Application contact:* Dr. Jon Peterson, Graduate Adviser, 718-997-5350, E-mail: jon_peterson@qc.edu.

Rhode Island College, School of Graduate Studies, Faculty of Arts and Sciences, Department of History, Providence, RI 02908-1991. Offers MA. Part-time and evening/weekend programs available. *Faculty:* 10 full-time (3 women). *Students:* 1 full-time (0 women), 5 part-time. Average age 35. In 2007, 1 degree awarded. *Degree requirements:* For master's, oral exam or thesis. *Entrance requirements:* For master's, GRE General Test and GRE Subject Test or MAT, 3 letters of recommendation, interview. *Application deadline:* For fall admission, 4/1 for domestic students; for spring admission, 11/1 for domestic students. Applications are processed on a rolling basis. Application fee: $50. *Expenses:* Tuition, state resident: full-time $6,240; part-time $260 per credit hour. Tuition, nonresident: full-time $13,104; part-time $546 per credit hour. Required fees: $332; $14 per credit hour. One-time fee: $66 part-time. *Financial support:* Teaching assistantships with full tuition reimbursements, Federal Work-Study, scholarships/grants, health care benefits, and unspecified assistantships available. Support available to part-time students. Financial award application deadline: 5/15; financial award applicants required to submit FAFSA. *Unit head:* Dr. Joanne Schneider, Chair, 401-456-8039.

Rice University, Graduate Programs, School of Humanities, Department of History, Houston, TX 77251-1892. Offers MA, PhD. Terminal master's awarded for partial completion of doctoral program. *Degree requirements:* For doctorate, one foreign language, comprehensive exam, thesis/dissertation. *Entrance requirements:* For master's and doctorate, GRE General Test, minimum GPA of 3.0. Additional exam requirements/recommendations for international students: Required—TOEFL (minimum score 600 paper-based; 250 computer-based; 90 iBT). *Faculty research:* Modern European and American military, modern British history, U.S. South, world history.

Roosevelt University, Graduate Division, College of Arts and Sciences, Department of History, Art, and Philosophy, Chicago, IL 60605-1394. Offers history (MA). Part-time and evening/weekend programs available. *Students:* 11 full-time (6 women), 35 part-time (17 women); includes 11 minority (7 African Americans, 1 Asian American or Pacific Islander, 3 Hispanic Americans). Average age 37. 32 applicants, 44% accepted, 11 enrolled. In 2007, 13 degrees awarded. *Degree requirements:* For master's, thesis or alternative. *Application deadline:* For fall admission, 6/1 priority date for domestic students. Applications are processed on a rolling basis. Application fee: $25 ($35 for international students). *Financial support:* Application deadline: 2/15. *Faculty research:* American social history, Holocaust, European history, African-American history, popular culture. *Unit head:* Susan Weininger, Head, 312-341-3711, E-mail: sweining@roosevelt.edu. *Application contact:* Joanne Canyon-Heller, Coordinator of Graduate Admission, 877-APPLY RU, Fax: 312-281-3356, E-mail: applyru@roosevelt.edu.

Rutgers, The State University of New Jersey, Camden, Graduate School of Arts and Sciences, Program in American and Public History, Camden, NJ 08102-1401. Offers MA. Part-time and evening/weekend programs available. *Entrance requirements:* For master's, GRE General Test. Electronic applications accepted. *Faculty research:* Women's history, military history, Afro-American history, urban history, history of technology.

Rutgers, The State University of New Jersey, Newark, Graduate School, Program in History, Newark, NJ 07102. Offers MA, MAT. Part-time and evening/weekend programs available. *Degree requirements:* For master's, one foreign language, comprehensive exam, thesis optional. *Entrance requirements:* For master's, GRE, minimum undergraduate B average. *Faculty research:* Global history, American history, American diplomatic and legal history, women's history, history of technology, environment and medicine.

Rutgers, The State University of New Jersey, New Brunswick, Graduate School, Program in History, New Brunswick, NJ 08901-1281. Offers African-American history (PhD); early American history (PhD); early modern European history (PhD); east Asian history (PhD); global and comparative history (PhD); history (PhD); history of diplomacy and foreign relations (PhD); history of technology, environment and health (PhD); history of the Atlantic cultures and African diaspora (PhD); Latin American history (PhD); medieval history (PhD); modern European history (PhD); nineteenth and twentieth century American history (PhD); women's and gender history (PhD). *Degree requirements:* For doctorate, thesis/dissertation. *Entrance requirements:* For doctorate, GRE General Test, sample of written work. Electronic applications accepted. *Faculty research:* American history, European history, Afro-American history, women's history, Latin American history.

St. Cloud State University, School of Graduate Studies, College of Social Sciences, Department of History, St. Cloud, MN 56301-4498. Offers MA, MS. Part-time programs available. *Faculty:* 12 full-time (3 women). *Students:* 7 full-time (2 women), 16 part-time (9 women), 1 international. 8 applicants, 88% accepted. In 2007, 3 degrees awarded. *Degree requirements:* For master's, thesis or alternative. *Entrance requirements:* For master's, GRE General Test, GRE Subject Test, minimum GPA of 2.75. Additional exam requirements/recommendations for international students: Required—MELAB; Recommended—TOEFL (minimum score 550 paper-based; 213 computer-based), IELTS (minimum score 7). *Application deadline:* For fall admission, 6/1 priority date for domestic students, 4/1 for international students; for spring admission, 10/1 priority date for domestic students, 8/1 for international students. Applications are processed on a rolling basis. Application fee: $35. *Expenses:* Tuition, state resident: part-time $267 per credit. Tuition, nonresident: part-time $418 per credit. Required fees: $28 per credit. *Financial support:* Federal Work-Study, scholarships/grants, and unspecified assistantships available. Financial award application deadline: 3/1. *Unit head:* Dr. Peter Nayenga, Chairperson, 320-308-3165, Fax: 320-308-5198. *Application contact:* Linda Lou Krueger, School of Graduate Studies, 320-308-2113, Fax: 320-308-5371, E-mail: lekrueger@stcloudstate.edu.

St. John's University, St. John's College of Liberal Arts and Sciences, Department of History, Queens, NY 11439. Offers history (MA); modern world history (DA). Part-time and evening/weekend programs available. *Faculty:* 18 full-time (7 women), 15 part-time/adjunct (2 women). *Students:* 9 full-time (4 women), 40 part-time (14 women); includes 14 minority (4 African

Americans, 2 Asian Americans or Pacific Islanders, 8 Hispanic Americans), 9 international. Average age 34. 33 applicants, 82% accepted, 15 enrolled. In 2007, 10 master's, 4 doctorates awarded. *Median time to degree:* Of those who began their doctoral program in fall 1999, 100% received their degree in 8 years or less. *Degree requirements:* For master's, one foreign language, comprehensive exam, thesis optional; for doctorate, one foreign language, comprehensive exam, thesis/dissertation, internship, practicum. *Entrance requirements:* For master's, minimum GPA of 3.0; for doctorate, interview; minimum GPA of 3.5 in history, 3.0 overall; writing sample. Additional exam requirements/recommendations for international students: Required—TOEFL (minimum score 500 paper-based; 173 computer-based; 61 iBT), IELTS (minimum score 6). *Application deadline:* For fall admission, 5/1 priority date for domestic and international students; for spring admission, 11/1 priority date for domestic and international students. Applications are processed on a rolling basis. Application fee: $40. Electronic applications accepted. *Financial support:* Fellowships, research assistantships, scholarships/grants available. Support available to part-time students. Financial award application deadline: 3/1; financial award applicants required to submit FAFSA. *Faculty research:* European economic history, history of East Asian culture, Irish history. *Unit head:* Dr. Mauricio Borrero, Chair, 718-990-6228, E-mail: borrerom@stjohns.edu. *Application contact:* Beth Evans, Associate Vice President and Executive Director, Enrollment Management, 718-990-6999, Fax: 718-990-5686, E-mail: gradhelp@stjohns.edu.

Saint Louis University, Graduate School, College of Arts and Sciences and Graduate School, Department of History, St. Louis, MO 63103-2097. Offers MA, MA-R, PhD. Part-time programs available. *Faculty:* 18 full-time (2 women). *Students:* 22 full-time (6 women), 17 part-time (6 women); includes 2 minority (both Hispanic Americans) Average age 36. 47 applicants, 43% accepted, 8 enrolled. In 2007, 3 master's, 3 doctorates awarded. *Median time to degree:* Of those who began their doctoral program in fall 1999, 60% received their degree in 8 years or less. *Degree requirements:* For master's, one foreign language, comprehensive exam, thesis optional, comprehensive oral exam; for doctorate, 2 foreign languages, comprehensive exam, thesis/dissertation, preliminary oral and written exams. *Entrance requirements:* For master's and doctorate, GRE General Test, letters of recommendation, resumé, writing sample, goal statement, transcripts. Additional exam requirements/recommendations for international students: Required—TOEFL (minimum score 525 paper-based; 194 computer-based). *Application deadline:* For fall admission, 2/1 for domestic and international students. Applications are processed on a rolling basis. Application fee: $40. Electronic applications accepted. *Expenses:* Tuition: Part-time $845 per credit hour. Required fees: $105 per semester. *Financial support:* In 2007–08, 26 students received support, including 5 research assistantships with full tuition reimbursements available (averaging $12,000 per year), 10 teaching assistantships with full tuition reimbursements available (averaging $12,000 per year); Federal Work-Study, scholarships/grants, traineeships, health care benefits, and unspecified assistantships also available. Support available to part-time students. Financial award application deadline: 2/1; financial award applicants required to submit FAFSA. *Faculty research:* Medieval Europe, Crusades, Byzantine Empire, US West and Borderlands, Early Modern Europe. Total annual research expenditures: $50,000. *Unit head:* Dr. Michal J. Rozbicki, Chairperson, 314-977-2910, Fax: 314-977-1603, E-mail: rozbicmj@slu.edu. *Application contact:* Gary U. Behrman, Associate Dean of Graduate School Admissions, 314-977-3827, Fax: 314-977-3943, E-mail: behrmang@slu.edu.

Saint Mary's University, Faculty of Arts, Department of History, Halifax, NS B3H 3C3, Canada. Offers MA. Part-time programs available. *Degree requirements:* For master's, one foreign language, comprehensive exam, thesis. *Entrance requirements:* For master's, honors degree. Expenses: Contact institution. *Faculty research:* Atlantic Canada, British Empire, history of science, South Africa.

Salem State College, Graduate School, Program in History, Salem, MA 01970-5353. Offers MA, MAT. Part-time and evening/weekend programs available. *Faculty:* 1 part-time/adjunct (0 women). *Students:* 10 full-time (2 women), 53 part-time (24 women); includes 1 minority (Hispanic American) Average age 31. In 2007, 17 degrees awarded. *Degree requirements:* For master's, one foreign language, thesis optional. *Entrance requirements:* For master's, GRE General Test, MAT. *Application deadline:* Applications are processed on a rolling basis. Application fee: $35. *Unit head:* Emerson Baker, Associate Professor, 978-542-6321, Fax: 978-542-7215, E-mail: ebaker@salemstate.edu.

Salisbury University, Graduate Division, Program in History, Salisbury, MD 21801-6837. Offers MA. Part-time and evening/weekend programs available. *Faculty:* 10 full-time (3 women). *Students:* 8 full-time (1 woman), 12 part-time (5 women); includes 1 minority (African American) Average age 31. 9 applicants, 100% accepted, 6 enrolled. In 2007, 10 degrees awarded. *Degree requirements:* For master's, thesis optional, 2 research and 3 reading seminars, final and oral exam. *Entrance requirements:* For master's, GRE General Test, minimum GPA of 3.0, 3 letters of recommendation. Additional exam requirements/recommendations for international students: Required—TOEFL (minimum score 550 paper-based; 213 computer-based). *Application deadline:* For fall admission, 8/1 for domestic students; for spring admission, 1/1 for domestic students. Applications are processed on a rolling basis. Application fee: $45. Electronic applications accepted. *Expenses:* Tuition, state resident: part-time $260 per credit hour. Tuition, nonresident: part-time $556 per credit hour. *Financial support:* Career-related internships or fieldwork and scholarships/grants available. Support available to part-time students. Financial award applicants required to submit FAFSA. *Faculty research:* History of science and technology, U. S. foreign relations, Maryland history, African-American history, medieval history. *Unit head:* Dr. Maarten L. Pereboom, Director, 410-543-6454, Fax: 410-547-5038, E-mail: mlbereboom@salisbury.edu. *Application contact:* Mia C. Vye, Administrative Assistant II, 410-548-4499, Fax: 410-547-5038, E-mail: mcvye@salisbury.edu.

Sam Houston State University, College of Humanities and Social Sciences, Department of History, Huntsville, TX 77341. Offers MA. Part-time and evening/weekend programs available. *Faculty:* 20 full-time (7 women). *Students:* 13 full-time (4 women), 47 part-time (11 women); includes 3 Hispanic Americans. Average age 36. In 2007, 11 degrees awarded. *Entrance requirements:* For master's, GRE General Test. Additional exam requirements/recommendations for international students: Required—TOEFL (minimum score 550 paper-based; 213 computer-based). Application fee: $20. *Expenses:* Tuition, state resident: full-time $5,026; part-time $184 per semester hour. Tuition, nonresident: full-time $10,586; part-time $462 per semester hour. Required fees: $494 per semester. *Financial support:* Teaching assistantships, Federal Work-Study and institutionally sponsored loans available. Support available to part-time students. Financial award application deadline: 5/31; financial award applicants required to submit FAFSA. *Unit head:* Dr. Terry Bilhartz, Chair, 936-294-1483, Fax: 936-294-3938, E-mail: his_tdb@shsu.edu.

San Diego State University, Graduate and Research Affairs, College of Arts and Letters, Department of History, San Diego, CA 92182. Offers MA. *Students:* 40 full-time (14 women), 43 part-time (15 women); includes 20 minority (1 African American, 1 American Indian/Alaska Native, 9 Asian Americans or Pacific Islanders, 9 Hispanic Americans). Average age 30. 65 applicants, 69% accepted, 37 enrolled. In 2007, 14 degrees awarded. *Degree requirements:* For master's, one foreign language. *Entrance requirements:* For master's, GRE General Test, bachelor's degree in related field. Additional exam requirements/recommendations for international students: Required—TOEFL. *Application deadline:* For fall admission, 4/1 for domestic students, 4/1 priority date for international students; for spring admission, 11/1 for domestic students, 10/1 priority date for international students. Applications are processed on a rolling basis. Application fee: $55. Electronic applications accepted. *Financial support:* In 2007–08, 15 teaching assistantships were awarded; fellowships, career-related internships or fieldwork also available. Financial award applicants required to submit FAFSA. *Faculty research:* Latin American history, Filipino history. Total annual research expenditures: $144,000. *Unit head:* Joanne Ferraro, Chair, 619-594-5262, Fax: 619-594-4998, E-mail: jferraro@sciences.mail.sdsu.edu. *Application contact:* Dr. Lawrence Baron, Graduate Advisor, 619-594-6595, Fax: 619-594-4998.

San Francisco State University, Division of Graduate Studies, College of Behavioral and Social Sciences, Department of History, San Francisco, CA 94132-1722. Offers MA. *Unit head:* Dr. Barbara Loomis, Chair, 415-338-1604. *Application contact:* Dr. Jarbel Rodriguez, Graduate Coordinator, 415-338-1604, E-mail: jarbel@sfsu.edu.

San Jose State University, Graduate Studies and Research, College of Social Sciences, Department of History, San Jose, CA 95192-0001. Offers history (MA); history education (MA). *Students:* 10 full-time (4 women), 45 part-time (22 women); includes 6 minority (1 African American, 3 Asian Americans or Pacific Islanders, 2 Hispanic Americans), 1 international. Average age 38. 67 applicants, 78% accepted, 24 enrolled. In 2007, 14 degrees awarded. *Degree requirements:* For master's, comprehensive exam, thesis or alternative. *Entrance requirements:* For master's, bachelor's degree or 15 units of course work in history, minimum GPA of 3.0. *Application deadline:* For fall admission, 2/15 for domestic students. Applications are processed on a rolling basis. Application fee: $59. Electronic applications accepted. *Financial support:* Fellowships available. Financial award applicants required to submit FAFSA. *Unit head:* Jonathan P. Roth, Chair, 408-924-5500, Fax: 408-924-5531. *Application contact:* Patricia Evridge Hill, Graduate Adviser, 408-924-5755.

Sarah Lawrence College, Graduate Studies, Program in Women's History, Bronxville, NY 10708-5999. Offers MA. Part-time programs available. *Faculty:* 9 part-time/adjunct (8 women). *Students:* 16 full-time (14 women), 6 part-time (all women); includes 5 minority (1 African American, 1 Asian American or Pacific Islander, 3 Hispanic Americans). Average age 27. 35 applicants, 80% accepted, 12 enrolled. In 2007, 14 degrees awarded. *Degree requirements:* For master's, thesis. *Entrance requirements:* For master's, previous course work in history, minimum B average in undergraduate course work. Additional exam requirements/recommendations for international students: Required—TOEFL (minimum score 600 paper-based). *Application deadline:* For fall admission, 2/1 priority date for domestic students. Applications are processed on a rolling basis. Application fee: $60. *Expenses:* Tuition: Part-time $1,034 per credit. Required fees: $430 per year. Tuition and fees vary according to program. *Financial support:* In 2007–08, 15 fellowships (averaging $3,433 per year) were awarded; career-related internships or fieldwork also available. Support available to part-time students. Financial award application deadline: 3/1. *Unit head:* Priscilla Murolo, Director, 914-395-2405. *Application contact:* Susan Guma, Dean of Graduate Studies, 914-395-2373, E-mail: sguma@mail.slc.edu.

See Close-Up on page 805.

Seton Hall University, College of Arts and Sciences, Department of History, South Orange, NJ 07079-2697. Offers Catholic history (MA); European history (MA); global history (MA); US history (MA). Electronic applications accepted. *Faculty research:* Latin America Renaissance, Italy, Italian-American, urban African-American, law.

See Close-Up on page 419.

Shippensburg University of Pennsylvania, School of Graduate Studies, College of Arts and Sciences, Department of History and Philosophy, Shippensburg, PA 17257-2299. Offers applied history (MA, Certificate). Part-time and evening/weekend programs available. *Faculty:* 7 full-time (3 women). *Students:* 18 full-time (9 women), 17 part-time (7 women); includes 2 minority (1 African American, 1 Asian American or Pacific Islander). Average age 30. 29 applicants, 83% accepted, 13 enrolled. In 2007, 15 degrees awarded. *Degree requirements:* For master's, thesis or internship. *Entrance requirements:* For master's, interview if undergraduate GPA less than 2.75. Additional exam requirements/recommendations for international students: Required—TOEFL (minimum score 560 paper-based; 220 computer-based). *Application deadline:* For fall admission, 3/1 for international students; for spring admission, 7/1 for international students. Applications are processed on a rolling basis. Application fee: $30. Electronic applications accepted. *Expenses:* Tuition, state resident: part-time $345 per credit. Tuition, nonresident: part-time $552 per credit. Required fees: $28 per credit. Tuition and fees vary according to course load. *Financial support:* In 2007–08, 10 research assistantships with full tuition reimbursements (averaging $3,575 per year) were awarded; career-related internships or fieldwork, scholarships/grants, and unspecified assistantships also available. Support available to part-time students. Financial award application deadline: 3/1; financial award applicants required to submit FAFSA. *Unit head:* Dr. David Godshalk, Chairperson, 717-477-1621, Fax: 717-477-4062, E-mail: dfgods@ship.edu. *Application contact:* Renee Payne, Associate Dean of Graduate Admissions, 717-477-1231, Fax: 717-477-4016, E-mail: rmpayn@ship.edu.

Simon Fraser University, Graduate Studies, Faculty of Arts and Social Sciences, Department of History, Burnaby, BC V5A 1S6, Canada. Offers MA, PhD. *Degree requirements:* For master's, one foreign language, thesis or alternative, project; for doctorate, one foreign language, comprehensive exam, thesis/dissertation. *Entrance requirements:* For master's, minimum GPA of 3.0; for doctorate, minimum GPA of 3.5. Additional exam requirements/recommendations for international students: Required—TOEFL or IELTS. *Faculty research:* Colonialism and imperialism, Canadian history, Middle East and Islam labor, Victorian intellect.

Slippery Rock University of Pennsylvania, Graduate Studies (Recruitment), College of Humanities, Fine and Performing Arts, Department of History, Slippery Rock, PA 16057-1383. Offers MA. Part-time and evening/weekend programs available. *Degree requirements:* For master's, comprehensive exam (for some programs), thesis (for some programs). *Entrance requirements:* For master's, GRE General Test, MAT, minimum GPA of 2.75. Additional exam requirements/recommendations for international students: Required—TOEFL (minimum score 550 paper-based; 213 computer-based). *Application deadline:* For fall admission, 7/1 priority date for domestic and international students; for spring admission, 11/1 priority date for domestic and international students. Applications are processed on a rolling basis. Application fee: $25. Electronic applications accepted. *Expenses:* Tuition, state resident: part-time $345 per credit hour. Tuition, nonresident: part-time $552 per credit hour. Required fees: $142 per credit hour. *Financial support:* Career-related internships or fieldwork, Federal Work-Study, scholarships/grants, and unspecified assistantships available. Support available to part-time students. Financial award application deadline: 5/1; financial award applicants required to submit FAFSA. *Unit head:* Dr. David Dixon, Graduate Coordinator, 724-738-2408, Fax: 724-738-4762, E-mail: larry.rotge@sru.edu. *Application contact:* April Longwell, Interim Director of Graduate Studies, 724-738-2051 Ext. 2116, Fax: 724-738-2146, E-mail: graduate.studies@sru.edu.

Smith College, Graduate Programs, Department of History, Northampton, MA 01063. Offers MAT. *Faculty:* 11 full-time (5 women). *Students:* 1 applicant, 100% accepted, 0 enrolled. In 2007, 2 degrees awarded. *Entrance requirements:* For master's, GRE General Test. Additional exam requirements/recommendations for international students: Required—TOEFL. *Application deadline:* For fall admission, 4/15 for domestic students, 1/15 for international students; for spring admission, 12/1 for domestic students. Application fee: $60. *Expenses:* Tuition: Full-time $33,940; part-time $1,060 per credit. Tuition and fees vary according to course load. *Financial support:* Institutionally sponsored loans and scholarships/grants available. Support available to part-time students. Financial award application deadline: 1/15; financial award applicants required to submit CSS PROFILE or FAFSA. *Unit head:* Ernest Benz, Associate Professor, 413-585-3716.

Sonoma State University, School of Social Sciences, Department of History, Rohnert Park, CA 94928-3609. Offers MA. Part-time programs available. *Faculty:* 3 full-time (2 women). *Students:* 12 full-time (3 women), 5 part-time (all women); includes 2 minority (1 American Indian/Alaska Native, 1 Asian American or Pacific Islander). Average age 32. 12 applicants, 58% accepted, 7 enrolled. In 2007, 8 master's awarded. *Degree requirements:* For master's, thesis or alternative. *Entrance requirements:* For master's, GRE General Test or GRE Subject Test, minimum GPA of 3.0. *Application deadline:* For fall admission, 11/30 for domestic students; for spring admission, 8/31 for domestic students. Application fee: $55. *Financial support:* In 2007–08, 8 research assistantships (averaging $500 per year), 5 teaching assistantships were awarded; fellowships, career-related internships or fieldwork and Federal Work-

History

Sonoma State University (continued)

Study also available. Financial award application deadline: 3/2. *Faculty research:* Public historical studies. *Unit head:* Dr. Michelle Jolly, Chair, 707-664-2462, E-mail: michelle.jolly@sonoma.edu.

Southeastern Louisiana University, College of Arts, Humanities and Social Sciences, Department of History and Political Science, Hammond, LA 70402. Offers history (MA). Part-time programs available. *Faculty:* 10 full-time (3 women). *Students:* 6 full-time (3 women), 37 part-time (19 women); includes 2 minority (both African Americans), 1 international. Average age 31. 11 applicants, 91% accepted, 10 enrolled. In 2007, 3 degrees awarded. *Degree requirements:* For master's, comprehensive exam, thesis optional. *Entrance requirements:* For master's, GRE General Test, 30 undergraduate credits in history, minimum GPA of 2.5. Additional exam requirements/recommendations for international students: Required—TOEFL (minimum score 500 paper-based; 173 computer-based). *Application deadline:* For fall admission, 7/15 priority date for domestic students, 6/1 priority date for international students; for spring admission, 12/1 priority date for domestic students, 10/1 priority date for international students. Applications are processed on a rolling basis. Application fee: $20 ($30 for international students). Electronic applications accepted. *Expenses:* Tuition, state resident: full-time $2,216; part-time $123 per credit. Tuition, nonresident: full-time $6,716; part-time $373 per credit. Required fees: $1,105; $61 per credit. *Financial support:* In 2007–08, 2 research assistantships with full tuition reimbursements (averaging $6,750 per year) were awarded; career-related internships or fieldwork, Federal Work-Study, institutionally sponsored loans, unspecified assistantships, and administrative assistantships also available. Support available to part-time students. Financial award application deadline: 5/1; financial award applicants required to submit FAFSA. *Faculty research:* American history, British history, southern history, public history, European history. *Unit head:* Dr. William B. Robison, Department Head, 985-549-2109, Fax: 985-549-2012, E-mail: wrobison@selu.edu. *Application contact:* Sandra Meyers, Graduate Admissions Analyst, 985-549-2066, Fax: 985-549-5632, E-mail: admissions@selu.edu.

Southeast Missouri State University, School of Graduate Studies, Department of History, Cape Girardeau, MO 63701-4799. Offers MA. Part-time and evening/weekend programs available. *Faculty:* 9 full-time (1 woman). *Students:* 5 full-time (2 women), 38 part-time (28 women); includes 1 minority (African American) Average age 38. 3 applicants, 67% accepted. In 2007, 4 degrees awarded. *Degree requirements:* For master's, comprehensive exam (for some programs), thesis or alternative. *Entrance requirements:* For master's, GRE, minimum GPA of 2.75. Additional exam requirements/recommendations for international students: Required—TOEFL (minimum score 550 paper-based; 213 computer-based). *Application deadline:* For fall admission, 8/1 for domestic students, 6/1 for international students; for spring admission, 11/21 for domestic students, 10/1 for international students. Applications are processed on a rolling basis. Application fee: $25 ($100 for international students). Electronic applications accepted. *Expenses:* Tuition, state resident: part-time $224 per credit hour. Tuition, nonresident: part-time $395 per credit hour. Tuition and fees vary according to course load and program. *Financial support:* In 2007–08, 13 students received support, including 3 research assistantships with full tuition reimbursements available (averaging $7,600 per year), 2 teaching assistantships with full tuition reimbursements available (averaging $7,600 per year); career-related internships or fieldwork and unspecified assistantships also available. Financial award applicants required to submit FAFSA. *Unit head:* Dr. Joseph Werne, Interim Chairperson, 573-651-2179. *Application contact:* Marsha L. Arant, Senior Administrative Assistant, Office of Graduate Studies, 573-651-2192, Fax: 573-651-2001, E-mail: marant@semo.edu.

Southern Connecticut State University, School of Graduate Studies, School of Arts and Sciences, Department of History, New Haven, CT 06515-1355. Offers MA, MS, MLS/MA. Part-time and evening/weekend programs available. *Faculty:* 5 full-time. *Students:* 27 full-time (12 women), 47 part-time (23 women); includes 6 minority (2 African Americans, 2 Asian Americans or Pacific Islanders, 2 Hispanic Americans). 65 applicants, 42% accepted, 22 enrolled. In 2007, 6 degrees awarded. *Degree requirements:* For master's, one foreign language, thesis. *Entrance requirements:* For master's, interview, undergraduate major or minor in history. *Application deadline:* For fall admission, 7/15 priority date for domestic students. Applications are processed on a rolling basis. Application fee: $50. Electronic applications accepted. *Financial support:* Career-related internships or fieldwork available. Financial award application deadline: 4/15; financial award applicants required to submit FAFSA. *Unit head:* Dr. Steven Judd, Chairperson, 203-392-5605, Fax: 203-392-5670, E-mail: judds1@southernct.edu. *Application contact:* Dr. Polly Beals, Graduate Coordinator, 203-392-5607, Fax: 203-392-5670, E-mail: bealsp1@southernct.edu.

Southern Illinois University Carbondale, Graduate School, College of Liberal Arts, Department of History, Carbondale, IL 62901-4701. Offers MA, PhD. Part-time programs available. *Faculty:* 23 full-time (8 women). *Students:* 9 full-time (3 women), 37 part-time (10 women); includes 3 minority (1 African American, 2 American Indian/Alaska Native), 3 international. 32 applicants, 28% accepted, 4 enrolled. In 2007, 8 master's, 2 doctorates awarded. *Degree requirements:* For master's, one foreign language, research papers or thesis, written exams; for doctorate, 2 foreign languages, thesis/dissertation. *Entrance requirements:* For master's, GRE General Test, minimum GPA of 3.0; for doctorate, GRE General Test, minimum GPA of 3.25. Additional exam requirements/recommendations for international students: Required—TOEFL. *Application deadline:* For fall admission, 2/1 priority date for domestic students. Applications are processed on a rolling basis. Application fee: $20. *Financial support:* In 2007–08, 33 students received support, including 4 fellowships with full tuition reimbursements available, 5 research assistantships with full tuition reimbursements available, 18 teaching assistantships with full tuition reimbursements available; career-related internships or fieldwork, Federal Work-Study, institutionally sponsored loans, and tuition waivers (full) also available. Support available to part-time students. Financial award application deadline: 2/1. *Faculty research:* American, Asian, European, and Latin American history, global history. *Unit head:* Dr. Michael C. Batinski, Interim chair, 618-453-7862, E-mail: batinski@siu.edu. *Application contact:* Chasity Wright, Administrative Clerk, 618-453-7863, E-mail: cwright@siu.edu.

Announcement: The MA in history gives special attention to teacher preparation, including the area of world history. Most students holding teaching assistantships are required to do grading and teach discussion sessions. In addition, students attend a weeklong teacher-training session before classes start in the fall and take a 1-hour practicum in teaching the first year they hold an assistantship. This preparation gives graduates a competitive edge in the job search.

See Close-Up on page 421.

Southern Illinois University Edwardsville, Graduate Studies and Research, College of Arts and Sciences, Department of Historical Studies, Program in History, Edwardsville, IL 62026-0001. Offers MA. Part-time and evening/weekend programs available. *Students:* 16 full-time (11 women), 19 part-time (7 women); includes 4 minority (all African Americans) 14 applicants, 86% accepted. In 2007, 2 degrees awarded. *Degree requirements:* For master's, one foreign language, thesis or alternative, final exam. *Entrance requirements:* For master's, GRE. Additional exam requirements/recommendations for international students: Required—TOEFL. *Application deadline:* For fall admission, 7/20 for domestic students, 6/1 for international students; for spring admission, 12/14 for domestic students, 10/1 for international students. Application fee: $30. Electronic applications accepted. *Financial support:* In 2007–08, 1 fellowship was awarded; research assistantships. Financial award application deadline: 3/1. *Unit head:* Dr. Carole Frick, Director, 618-650-3237, E-mail: cfrick@siue.edu.

Southern Methodist University, Dedman College, Clements Department of History, Dallas, TX 75275. Offers MA, PhD. Part-time programs available. *Faculty:* 21 full-time (6 women), 3 part-time/adjunct (2 women). *Students:* 29 full-time (11 women), 3 part-time (1 woman); includes 8 minority (1 African American, 7 Hispanic Americans), 3 international. Average age 30. 29 applicants, 48% accepted, 7 enrolled. In 2007, 4 master's, 3 doctorates awarded. Terminal master's awarded for partial completion of doctoral program. *Degree requirements:* For master's, one foreign language, thesis, oral exam, thesis defense; for doctorate, one foreign language, thesis/dissertation, oral exam, dissertation defense. *Entrance requirements:* For master's and doctorate, GRE General Test, minimum GPA of 3.0, 12 undergraduate hours in advanced level history, writing sample. Additional exam requirements/recommendations for international students: Required—TOEFL. *Application deadline:* For fall admission, 2/1 priority date for domestic and international students. Applications are processed on a rolling basis. Application fee: $60. Electronic applications accepted. *Financial support:* In 2007–08, 23 students received support, including 22 fellowships with full tuition reimbursements available (averaging $17,000 per year); career-related internships or fieldwork, institutionally sponsored loans, scholarships/grants, health care benefits, and tuition waivers (full and partial) also available. Financial award application deadline: 2/1; financial award applicants required to submit FAFSA. *Faculty research:* U.S. history, European history, Latin America, Africa/Middle East, China. *Unit head:* Dr. James K. Hopkins, Chair, 214-768-2977, Fax: 214-768-2404, E-mail: hist@mail.smu.edu. *Application contact:* Dr. Sherry L. Smith, Graduate Director, 214-768-1312, Fax: 214-768-2404, E-mail: hist@smu.edu.

Southern University and Agricultural and Mechanical College, Graduate School, College of Arts and Humanities, Department of History, Baton Rouge, LA 70813. Offers social sciences (MA). Part-time programs available. *Faculty:* 10 full-time (4 women). *Students:* 23 full-time (16 women), 42 part-time (35 women); all minorities (63 African Americans, 1 American Indian/Alaska Native, 1 Asian American or Pacific Islander). Average age 25. 27 applicants, 67% accepted, 15 enrolled. In 2007, 18 degrees awarded. *Degree requirements:* For master's, thesis. *Entrance requirements:* For master's, GRE General Test. Additional exam requirements/recommendations for international students: Required—TOEFL (minimum score 525 paper-based; 193 computer-based). *Application deadline:* For fall admission, 4/15 priority date for domestic and international students; for spring admission, 11/1 priority date for domestic and international students. Applications are processed on a rolling basis. Application fee: $25. *Financial support:* In 2007–08, research assistantships (averaging $7,000 per year); scholarships/grants and unspecified assistantships also available. Financial award application deadline: 4/15; financial award applicants required to submit FAFSA. Total annual research expenditures: $230,000. *Unit head:* Dr. Raymond Lockett, Chairman, 225-771-3260, Fax: 225-771-5861.

Stanford University, School of Humanities and Sciences, Department of History, Stanford, CA 94305-9991. Offers MA, PhD. Terminal master's awarded for partial completion of doctoral program. *Degree requirements:* For doctorate, variable foreign language requirement, thesis/dissertation, oral exam. *Entrance requirements:* For master's and doctorate, GRE General Test. Additional exam requirements/recommendations for international students: Required—TOEFL. Electronic applications accepted.

State University of New York at Binghamton, Graduate School, School of Arts and Sciences, Department of History, Binghamton, NY 13902-6000. Offers MA, PhD. Part-time programs available. *Faculty:* 25 full-time (8 women), 2 part-time/adjunct (0 women). *Students:* 68 full-time (36 women), 41 part-time (29 women); includes 7 minority (1 African American, 1 Asian American or Pacific Islander, 5 Hispanic Americans), 14 international. Average age 32. 78 applicants, 60% accepted, 20 enrolled. In 2007, 13 master's, 6 doctorates awarded. Terminal master's awarded for partial completion of doctoral program. *Degree requirements:* For master's, one foreign language, thesis or alternative, written exam; for doctorate, variable foreign language requirement, comprehensive exam, thesis/dissertation. *Entrance requirements:* For master's and doctorate, GRE General Test, GRE Subject Test. Additional exam requirements/recommendations for international students: Required—TOEFL. *Application deadline:* For fall admission, 4/15 priority date for domestic students, 1/15 priority date for international students; for spring admission, 11/1 for domestic students, 10/1 priority date for international students. Applications are processed on a rolling basis. Application fee: $60. Electronic applications accepted. *Financial support:* In 2007–08, 42 students received support, including 6 fellowships with full tuition reimbursements available (averaging $8,000 per year), 2 research assistantships with full tuition reimbursements available (averaging $15,300 per year), 30 teaching assistantships with full tuition reimbursements available (averaging $14,700 per year); career-related internships or fieldwork, Federal Work-Study, institutionally sponsored loans, tuition waivers (full and partial), and unspecified assistantships also available. Support available to part-time students. Financial award application deadline: 2/15. *Unit head:* Dr. Howard G. Brown, Chairperson, 607-777-6025, E-mail: hgbrown@binghamton.edu.

State University of New York at Oswego, Graduate Studies, College of Arts and Sciences, Department of History, Oswego, NY 13126. Offers MA. Part-time programs available. *Faculty:* 12 full-time, 1 part-time/adjunct. *Students:* 6 full-time (2 women), 9 part-time (2 women). Average age 25. 11 applicants, 91% accepted. In 2007, 7 degrees awarded. *Degree requirements:* For master's, thesis optional. *Entrance requirements:* For master's, writing sample. Additional exam requirements/recommendations for international students: Required—TOEFL (minimum score 560 paper-based; 220 computer-based). *Application deadline:* For fall admission, 4/1 for domestic students; for spring admission, 10/1 for domestic students. Applications are processed on a rolling basis. Application fee: $50. *Expenses:* Tuition, state resident: full-time $6,900; part-time $288 per credit. Tuition, nonresident: full-time $10,920; part-time $455 per credit. Required fees: $607; $32 per credit. $225 per term. Tuition and fees vary according to degree level. *Financial support:* In 2007–08, 2 students received support, including 2 teaching assistantships with full tuition reimbursements available (averaging $3,800 per year); career-related internships or fieldwork, Federal Work-Study, institutionally sponsored loans, scholarships/grants, health care benefits, and unspecified assistantships also available. Support available to part-time students. Financial award application deadline: 4/1; financial award applicants required to submit FAFSA. *Unit head:* Dr. Ming-Te Pan, Chair, 315-312-2170, E-mail: pan@oswego.edu. *Application contact:* Dr. Ming-Te Pan, Graduate Program Coordinator, 315-312-3441, E-mail: pan@oswego.edu.

State University of New York College at Cortland, Graduate Studies, School of Arts and Sciences, Department of History, Cortland, NY 13045. Offers MA, MS Ed. Part-time and evening/weekend programs available. *Degree requirements:* For master's, one foreign language, comprehensive exam (for some programs), thesis (for some programs). *Entrance requirements:* For master's, GRE General Test, GRE Subject Test. Additional exam requirements/recommendations for international students: Required—TOEFL.

Stephen F. Austin State University, Graduate School, College of Liberal Arts, Department of History, Nacogdoches, TX 75962. Offers MA. Part-time and evening/weekend programs available. *Degree requirements:* For master's, comprehensive exam. *Entrance requirements:* For master's, GRE General Test. Additional exam requirements/recommendations for international students: Required—TOEFL. *Faculty research:* U.S.-Third World foreign policy, racial attitudes of antebellum Southern whites, naval warfare in World War II, demography of East Texas, medieval sermons.

Stony Brook University, State University of New York, Graduate School, College of Arts and Sciences, Department of History, Stony Brook, NY 11794. Offers MA, PhD. Evening/weekend programs available. *Faculty:* 24 full-time (12 women), 1 (woman) part-time/adjunct. *Students:* 92 full-time (40 women), 13 part-time (3 women); includes 14 minority (7 African Americans, 1 American Indian/Alaska Native, 2 Asian Americans or Pacific Islanders, 4 Hispanic Americans), 22 international. Average age 33. 60 applicants, 42% accepted. In 2007, 13 master's, 6 doctorates awarded. *Degree requirements:* For doctorate, thesis/dissertation. *Entrance requirements:* For master's and doctorate, GRE General Test. Additional exam requirements/recommendations for international students: Required—TOEFL. *Application deadline:* For fall admission, 1/15 for domestic students. Application fee: $60. *Financial support:* In 2007–08, 2 fellowships, 43 teaching assistantships were awarded; research assistantships. *Faculty research:* Social, cultural, and political history. Total annual research expenditures: $6,750. *Unit head:* Dr. Ned Landsman, Chair, 631-632-7500. *Application contact:* Frances Arnetta, Graduate Coordinator, 631-632-7511, Fax: 631-632-7367, E-mail: farnetta@notes.cc.sunysb.edu.

Announcement: In the 2000 National Doctoral Program Survey, which ranks the nation's 50-plus full history programs based on student satisfaction, the Stony Brook Department of History tied for first place. Department faculty also ranked 4th nationally in a 2000 survey of historians' publication impact and prestigious awards.

See Close-Up on page 423.

Sul Ross State University, School of Arts and Sciences, Department of Behavioral and Social Sciences, Program in History, Alpine, TX 79832. Offers MA. Part-time and evening/weekend programs available. *Degree requirements:* For master's, thesis optional. *Entrance requirements:* For master's, GRE General Test, minimum GPA of 2.5 in last 60 hours of undergraduate work. *Faculty research:* Borderland/Southwestern studies, British studies, women's history, Native American studies, local history.

Syracuse University, Graduate School, Maxwell School of Citizenship and Public Affairs, Department of History, Syracuse, NY 13244. Offers MA, PhD. Part-time programs available. *Students:* 41 full-time (16 women), 12 part-time (7 women); includes 5 minority (3 African Americans, 1 American Indian/Alaska Native, 1 Asian American or Pacific Islander), 7 international. 50 applicants, 22% accepted, 4 enrolled. In 2007, 6 master's, 3 doctorates awarded. Terminal master's awarded for partial completion of doctoral program. *Degree requirements:* For master's, comprehensive exam, thesis or alternative; for doctorate, 2 foreign languages, comprehensive exam, thesis/dissertation. *Entrance requirements:* For master's and doctorate, GRE General Test. Additional exam requirements/recommendations for international students: Required—TOEFL. *Application deadline:* For fall admission, 2/1 priority date for domestic students. Applications are processed on a rolling basis. Application fee: $75. Electronic applications accepted. *Expenses:* Tuition: Full-time $18,216; part-time $1,012 per credit. Required fees: $980. Tuition and fees vary according to program. *Financial support:* Fellowships with full and partial tuition reimbursements, research assistantships with tuition reimbursements, teaching assistantships with full and partial tuition reimbursements, tuition waivers (partial) available. Financial award applicants required to submit FAFSA. *Faculty research:* American, Medieval, European, South East Asia, Russian. *Unit head:* Dr. Criage Chompion, Chair, 315-443-2594, Fax: 315-443-5876. *Application contact:* Pat Bohrer, Information Contact, 315-443-2210, E-mail: pabohrer@syr.edu.

Tarleton State University, College of Graduate Studies, College of Liberal and Fine Arts, Department of Social Sciences, Stephenville, TX 76402. Offers history (MA); political science (MA). Part-time and evening/weekend programs available. Postbaccalaureate distance learning degree programs offered (minimal on-campus study). *Faculty:* 8 full-time (1 woman), 3 part-time/adjunct (0 women). *Students:* 7 full-time (2 women), 28 part-time (10 women); includes 6 minority (2 African Americans, 1 American Indian/Alaska Native, 3 Hispanic Americans), 1 international. Average age 37. 15 applicants, 93% accepted, 10 enrolled. In 2007, 3 degrees awarded. *Degree requirements:* For master's, variable foreign language requirement, comprehensive exam, thesis optional. *Entrance requirements:* For master's, GRE General Test, minimum GPA of 3.0. Additional exam requirements/recommendations for international students: Required—TOEFL (minimum score 550 paper-based; 213 computer-based). *Application deadline:* For fall admission, 8/5 priority date for domestic students; for spring admission, 12/1 for domestic students. Applications are processed on a rolling basis. Application fee: $25 ($125 for international students). Electronic applications accepted. *Expenses:* Tuition, state resident: full-time $2,520; part-time $140 per credit hour. Tuition, nonresident: full-time $7,344; part-time $408 per credit hour. Required fees: $948; $39 per credit hour. *Financial support:* Research assistantships, teaching assistantships, career-related internships or fieldwork and Federal Work-Study available. Support available to part-time students. Financial award application deadline: 5/1; financial award applicants required to submit FAFSA. *Unit head:* Dr. Dean A. Minix, Interim Department Head, 254-968-9141, Fax: 254-968-9798, E-mail: minix@tarleton.edu.

Teachers College, Columbia University, Graduate Faculty of Education, Department of Arts and Humanities, Program in History and Education, New York, NY 10027-6696. Offers Ed M, MA, Ed D, PhD. *Faculty:* 1 (woman) full-time. *Students:* 2 full-time (1 woman), 14 part-time (8 women); includes 4 minority (3 African Americans, 1 Asian American or Pacific Islander). Average age 37. 12 applicants, 8% accepted, 1 enrolled. In 2007, 3 master's awarded. *Degree requirements:* For doctorate, thesis/dissertation. *Entrance requirements:* For master's, sample of historical writing (Ed M); for doctorate, sample of historical writing. *Application deadline:* For fall admission, 5/15 for domestic students; for spring admission, 12/1 for domestic students. Application fee: $70. *Financial support:* Career-related internships or fieldwork, Federal Work-Study, institutionally sponsored loans, and tuition waivers (full and partial) available. Support available to part-time students. Financial award application deadline: 2/1. *Faculty research:* History of American education. *Application contact:* Mark E. Stearns, Associate Director of Admission, 212-678-3710, Fax: 212-678-4171.

See Close-Up on page 267.

Temple University, Graduate School, College of Liberal Arts, Department of History, Philadelphia, PA 19122-6096. Offers MA, PhD. Part-time and evening/weekend programs available. Terminal master's awarded for partial completion of doctoral program. *Degree requirements:* For doctorate, one foreign language, thesis/dissertation. *Entrance requirements:* For master's and doctorate, GRE General Test, minimum GPA of 3.0. Additional exam requirements/recommendations for international students: Required—TOEFL (minimum score 550 paper-based; 213 computer-based; 79 iBT). Electronic applications accepted. *Faculty research:* Third World; American military and diplomatic history; American social, cultural, and public history, European history.

Texas A&M International University, Office of Graduate Studies and Research, College of Arts and Sciences, Department of Social Sciences, Laredo, TX 78041-1900. Offers history (MA); political science (MA); public administration (MPA). *Faculty:* 8 full-time (3 women), 2 part-time/adjunct (1 woman). *Students:* 14 full-time (8 women), 65 part-time (34 women); includes 68 minority (1 Asian American or Pacific Islander, 67 Hispanic Americans), 4 international. Average age 34. 35 applicants, 97% accepted, 23 enrolled. In 2007, 10 degrees awarded. *Degree requirements:* For master's, thesis (for some programs). *Entrance requirements:* For master's, GRE General Test. Additional exam requirements/recommendations for international students: Required—TOEFL (minimum score 550 paper-based; 213 computer-based). *Application deadline:* For fall admission, 7/15 priority date for domestic students; for spring admission, 11/12 for domestic students. Applications are processed on a rolling basis. Application fee: $25. *Financial support:* In 2007–08, 29 students received support. Application deadline: 11/1. *Unit head:* Dr. William W. Riggs, Chair, 956-328-2540, E-mail: wriggs@tamiu.edu. *Application contact:* Rosie Espinoza-Dickinson, Director of Admissions, 956-326-2200, Fax: 956-326-2199, E-mail: enroll@tamiu.edu.

Texas A&M University, College of Liberal Arts, Department of History, College Station, TX 77843. Offers MA, PhD. Part-time programs available. *Faculty:* 24. *Students:* 39 full-time (11 women), 29 part-time (7 women); includes 8 minority (4 African Americans, 4 Hispanic Americans), 2 international. Average age 32. 69 applicants, 42% accepted, 8 enrolled. In 2007, 11 master's, 2 doctorates awarded. Terminal master's awarded for partial completion of doctoral program. *Degree requirements:* For master's, one foreign language, thesis optional; for doctorate, 2 foreign languages, thesis/dissertation. *Entrance requirements:* For master's and doctorate, GRE General Test. Additional exam requirements/recommendations for international students: Required—TOEFL. *Application deadline:* For fall admission, 3/1 for domestic students. Application fee: $50 ($75 for international students). *Expenses:* Tuition, state resident: full-time $6,129. Tuition, nonresident: full-time $11,689. Tuition and fees vary according to course load. *Financial support:* In 2007–08, fellowships (averaging $4,000 per year); research assistantships, teaching assistantships with partial tuition reimbursements. Financial award application deadline: 2/1. *Faculty research:* Recent U.S. history, southwest, border studies, military history, Europe. *Unit head:* Dr. Walter L. Buenger, Head, 979-845-7151, Fax: 979-862-4314. *Application contact:* Albert S. Broussard, Coordinator, 979-845-7130, Fax: 979-862-4314.

Texas A&M University–Commerce, Graduate School, College of Arts and Sciences, Department of History, Commerce, TX 75429-3011. Offers history (MA, MS); social sciences (M Ed, MS). Part-time programs available. *Faculty:* 4 full-time (2 women). *Students:* Average age 36. In 2007, 1 degree awarded. *Degree requirements:* For master's, comprehensive exam, thesis (for some programs). *Entrance requirements:* For master's, GRE General Test. *Application deadline:* For fall admission, 6/1 priority date for domestic students; for spring admission, 11/1 priority date for domestic students. Applications are processed on a rolling basis. Application fee: $0 ($25 for international students). Electronic applications accepted. *Financial support:* In 2007–08, research assistantships (averaging $7,875 per year), teaching assistantships (averaging $7,875 per year) were awarded; Federal Work-Study, institutionally sponsored loans, and scholarships/grants also available. Financial award application deadline: 5/1; financial award applicants required to submit FAFSA. *Faculty research:* American foreign policy, colonial America, Texas politics, Medieval England. *Unit head:* Dr. Judy Ford, Interim Head, 903-886-5226, Fax: 903-468-3230, E-mail: judy_ford@tamu_commerce.edu. *Application contact:* Tammi Thompson, Graduate Admissions Adviser, 843-886-5167, Fax: 843-886-5165, E-mail: tammi_thompson@tamu-commerce.edu.

Texas A&M University–Corpus Christi, Graduate Studies and Research, College of Liberal Arts, Corpus Christi, TX 78412-5503. Offers English (MA); history (MA); psychology (MA); public administration (MPA); studio arts (MA, MFA). Part-time and evening/weekend programs available. *Students:* 49 full-time (28 women), 119 part-time (76 women); includes 64 minority (5 African Americans, 1 American Indian/Alaska Native, 2 Asian Americans or Pacific Islanders, 56 Hispanic Americans), 7 international. 101 applicants, 73% accepted, 55 enrolled. In 2007, 52 degrees awarded. *Degree requirements:* For master's, comprehensive exam, thesis (for some programs). *Entrance requirements:* For master's, GRE General Test. Additional exam requirements/recommendations for international students: Required—TOEFL. *Application deadline:* For fall admission, 7/15 priority date for domestic students, 5/1 priority date for international students; for spring admission, 11/15 priority date for domestic students, 9/1 priority date for international students. Applications are processed on a rolling basis. Application fee: $30 ($50 for international students). Electronic applications accepted. *Expenses:* Tuition, state resident: part-time $63 per credit hour. Tuition, nonresident: part-time $341 per credit hour. Tuition and fees vary according to course load. *Financial support:* Research assistantships, teaching assistantships, career-related internships or fieldwork, Federal Work-Study, institutionally sponsored loans, scholarships/grants, health care benefits, and unspecified assistantships available. Support available to part-time students. Financial award application deadline: 3/15; financial award applicants required to submit FAFSA. *Unit head:* Dr. Richard Gigliotti, Dean, 361-825-2659, Fax: 361-825-5844, E-mail: richard.gigliotti@tamucc.edu. *Application contact:* Maria Martinez, Graduate Admissions Coordinator, 361-825-2177, Fax: 361-825-2755, E-mail: gradweb@tamucc.edu.

Texas A&M University–Kingsville, College of Graduate Studies, College of Arts and Sciences, Program in History and Political Science, Kingsville, TX 78363. Offers MA, MS. Part-time and evening/weekend programs available. *Degree requirements:* For master's, comprehensive exam, thesis or alternative. *Entrance requirements:* For master's, GRE General Test. Additional exam requirements/recommendations for international students: Required—TOEFL.

Texas A&M University–Texarkana, Graduate Studies and Research, College of Arts and Sciences and Education, Texarkana, TX 75505-5518. Offers adult education (MS); curriculum and instruction (MS); education (MS); educational administration (M Ed); English (MA); history (MS); instructional technology (MS); interdisciplinary studies (MS); special education (M Ed, MS). Part-time and evening/weekend programs available. *Students:* 273. Average age 32. In 2007, 86 degrees awarded. *Degree requirements:* For master's, comprehensive exam (for some programs), thesis optional. *Entrance requirements:* For master's, minimum GPA of 2.5 on last 60 hours of bachelor's degree. Additional exam requirements/recommendations for international students: Required—TOEFL. *Application deadline:* For fall admission, 7/15 priority date for domestic students; for spring admission, 12/1 priority date for domestic students. Applications are processed on a rolling basis. Application fee: $0 ($25 for international students). Electronic applications accepted. *Financial support:* Career-related internships or fieldwork and scholarships/grants available. Financial award applicants required to submit FAFSA. *Application contact:* Patricia E. Black, Director of Admissions and Registrar, 903-223-3068, Fax: 903-223-3140, E-mail: pat.black@tamut.edu.

Texas Christian University, AddRan College of Humanities and Social Sciences, Department of History, Fort Worth, TX 76129-0002. Offers MA, PhD. Part-time and evening/weekend programs available. *Degree requirements:* For master's, one foreign language, thesis; for doctorate, one foreign language, thesis/dissertation, qualifying exams. *Entrance requirements:* For master's and doctorate, GRE General Test. Additional exam requirements/recommendations for international students: Required—TOEFL. *Application deadline:* For fall admission, 3/1 for domestic students; for spring admission, 12/1 for domestic students. Applications are processed on a rolling basis. Application fee: $0. *Expenses:* Tuition: Part-time $865 per credit hour. Required fees: $48 per year. *Financial support:* Fellowships, teaching assistantships, unspecified assistantships available. Financial award application deadline: 3/1. *Unit head:* Dr. Kenneth Stevens, Chairperson, 817-257-7288, E-mail: k.stevens@tcu.edu. *Application contact:* Dr. Mike Butler, Associate Dean, AddRan College of Humanities and Social Sciences, E-mail: m.butler@tcu.edu.

Texas Southern University, Graduate School, College of Liberal Arts and Behavioral Sciences, Department of History and Geography, Houston, TX 77004-4584. Offers history (MA). Part-time and evening/weekend programs available. *Faculty:* 7 full-time (3 women). *Students:* 2 full-time (1 woman), 7 part-time (2 women); all minorities (all African Americans) Average age 36. 7 applicants, 86% accepted, 4 enrolled. *Degree requirements:* For master's, comprehensive exam, thesis optional. *Entrance requirements:* For master's, GRE General Test, minimum GPA of 2.5. Additional exam requirements/recommendations for international students: Required—TOEFL. *Application deadline:* For fall admission, 7/15 priority date for domestic students. Applications are processed on a rolling basis. Application fee: $50 ($75 for international students). *Financial support:* Research assistantships, teaching assistantships, Federal Work-Study and institutionally sponsored loans available. Financial award application deadline: 5/1. *Faculty research:* American, Colonial, African, Asian, and African-American history. *Unit head:* Dr. Ethopia Keleta, Chair, 713-313-7324, Fax: 713-313-4236, E-mail: keleta_ex@tsu.edu.

Texas State University–San Marcos, Graduate School, College of Liberal Arts, Department of History, San Marcos, TX 78666. Offers M Ed, MA. Part-time programs available. *Faculty:* 7 full-time (4 women), 4 part-time/adjunct (1 woman). *Students:* 32 full-time (9 women), 36 part-time (14 women); includes 15 minority (1 African American, 14 Hispanic Americans). Average age 32. 33 applicants, 94% accepted, 23 enrolled. In 2007, 14 degrees awarded. *Degree requirements:* For master's, comprehensive exam, thesis (for some programs). *Entrance requirements:* For master's, GRE General Test, minimum GPA of 3.0 in history. Additional exam requirements/recommendations for international students: Required—TOEFL (minimum score 550 paper-based; 213 computer-based). *Application deadline:* For fall admission, 6/15 priority date for domestic students, 6/1 for international students; for spring admission, 10/15 priority date for domestic students, 10/1 for international students. Applications are processed on a rolling basis. Application fee: $40 ($90 for international students). Electronic applications accepted. *Expenses:* Tuition, state resident: full-time $3,780; part-time $210 per credit hour. Tuition, nonresident: full-time $8,784; part-time $488 per credit hour. Required fees: $493 per semester. Full-time tuition and fees vary according to course load. *Financial support:* In 2007–08, 51 students received support, including 3 research assistantships (averaging $5,643 per year), 30 teaching assistantships (averaging $5,112 per year); Federal Work-Study and institutionally sponsored loans also available. Support available to part-time students. Financial

History

Texas State University–San Marcos (continued)

award application deadline: 4/1; financial award applicants required to submit FAFSA. *Faculty research:* American women, Texas and the Southwest, Hispanic Southwest, American conservative movement, Mexico and Brazil. Total annual research expenditures: $4,815. *Unit head:* Dr. J. F. dela Teja, Chair, 512-245-2142, Fax: 512-245-3043. *Application contact:* Dr. Mary Brennan, Graduate Adviser, 512-245-2110, Fax: 512-245-3043, E-mail: mb18@txstate.edu.

Texas Tech University, Graduate School, College of Arts and Sciences, Department of History, Lubbock, TX 79409. Offers MA, PhD. Part-time programs available. *Faculty:* 19 full-time (4 women), 2 part-time/adjunct (1 woman). *Students:* 47 full-time (19 women), 29 part-time (9 women); includes 11 minority (1 African American, 2 Asian Americans or Pacific Islanders, 8 Hispanic Americans), 4 international. Average age 33. 44 applicants, 59% accepted, 10 enrolled. In 2007, 10 master's, 3 doctorates awarded. *Degree requirements:* For master's, one foreign language; for doctorate, 2 foreign languages, thesis/dissertation. *Entrance requirements:* For master's and doctorate, GRE General Test. Additional exam requirements/recommendations for international students: Required—TOEFL (minimum score 550 paper-based; 213 computer-based). *Application deadline:* For fall admission, 3/1 priority date for international students; for spring admission, 11/1 priority date for international students. Applications are processed on a rolling basis. Application fee: $50 ($60 for international students). Electronic applications accepted. *Expenses:* Tuition, state resident: part-time $373 per credit hour. Tuition, nonresident: part-time $651 per credit hour. Tuition and fees vary according to program. *Financial support:* In 2007–08, 56 students received support, including 1 research assistantship with partial tuition reimbursement available (averaging $11,000 per year), 34 teaching assistantships with partial tuition reimbursements available (averaging $12,308 per year); Federal Work-Study and institutionally sponsored loans also available. Support available to part-time students. Financial award application deadline: 4/15; financial award applicants required to submit FAFSA. *Faculty research:* History of U.S. Southwest/West, the borderlands, history of Vietnam War and US military history, history of Hispanics/Latinos and other U.S. minorities, history of Europe. *Unit head:* Randy McBee, Chair, 806-742-1004, Fax: 806-742-1060, E-mail: randy.mcbee@ttu.edu. *Application contact:* Dr. Gretchen Adams, Graduate Adviser, 806-742-3744, Fax: 806-742-1060.

Texas Woman's University, Graduate School, College of Arts and Sciences, Department of History and Government, Denton, TX 76201. Offers government (MA); history (MA). Part-time and evening/weekend programs available. *Students:* 9 full-time (all women), 30 part-time (25 women); includes 9 minority (5 African Americans, 1 Asian American or Pacific Islander, 3 Hispanic Americans). Average age 35. In 2007, 16 master's awarded. *Degree requirements:* For master's, thesis. *Entrance requirements:* For master's, minimum GPA of 3.3, writing sample/portfolio. Additional exam requirements/recommendations for international students: Required—TOEFL (minimum score 550 paper-based; 213 computer-based; 79 iBT). *Application deadline:* For fall admission, 4/1 for international students; for spring admission, 8/1 for international students. Applications are processed on a rolling basis. Application fee: $30 ($50 for international students). Electronic applications accepted. *Expenses:* Tuition, state resident: full-time $3,294; part-time $183 per credit. Tuition, nonresident: full-time $8,298; part-time $461 per credit. Required fees: $985; $55 per credit. Tuition and fees vary according to degree level. *Financial support:* In 2007–08, 14 teaching assistantships (averaging $9,684 per year) were awarded; career-related internships or fieldwork, Federal Work-Study, institutionally sponsored loans, scholarships/grants, traineeships, health care benefits, and unspecified assistantships also available. Support available to part-time students. Financial award application deadline: 3/1; financial award applicants required to submit FAFSA. *Faculty research:* Recent American history, civil liberties, military history, legal studies, women and politics. *Unit head:* Dr. Barbara Presnall, Interim Chair, 940-898-2133, Fax: 940-898-2130, E-mail: bpresnall@twu.edu. *Application contact:* Samuel Wheeler, Assistant Director of Admissions, 940-898-3188, Fax: 940-898-3081, E-mail: wheelersr@twu.edu.

Trent University, Graduate Studies, Program in Methodologies for the Study of Western History and Culture, Peterborough, ON K9J 7B8, Canada. Offers MA. Part-time programs available. *Degree requirements:* For master's, thesis. *Entrance requirements:* For master's, honors degree. *Faculty research:* Foundations and structures of modern knowledge in its historical and cultural contexts.

Trinity Western University, Faculty of Graduate Studies, Program in Interdisciplinary Humanities, Langley, BC V2Y 1Y1, Canada. Offers general humanities (MAIH); specialized (MAIH), including English, history, philosophy. Part-time and evening/weekend programs available. Postbaccalaureate distance learning degree programs offered (minimal on-campus study). *Faculty:* 19 full-time (6 women), 3 part-time/adjunct (0 women). *Students:* 9 full-time (4 women), 24 part-time (13 women). Average age 30. 16 applicants, 75% accepted, 9 enrolled. In 2007, 2 degrees awarded. *Degree requirements:* For master's, 36 semester hours. *Entrance requirements:* For master's, strong undergraduate degree in Humanities or English, History or Philosophy. *Application deadline:* For fall admission, 5/15 priority date for domestic students; for winter admission, 11/1 priority date for domestic students. Application fee: $40. *Financial support:* In 2007–08, 12 students received support, including 3 fellowships (averaging $17,500 per year), 1 research assistantship (averaging $12,000 per year); career-related internships or fieldwork, scholarships/grants, and traineeships also available. Financial award application deadline: 4/1. *Faculty research:* Literary theory, gender, medieval and early modern literature, philosophy of religion, Thomas Merton's poetics. Total annual research expenditures: $145,000 Canadian dollars. *Unit head:* Dr. Bob Burkinshaw, Director, 604-888-7511 Ext. 3111, Fax: 604-513-2143, E-mail: burkinsh@twu.ca. *Application contact:* Vic Cornish, Director, Graduate Admissions, 604-888-7511 Ext. 3130, Fax: 604-513-2064, E-mail: vic.cornish@twu.edu.

Tufts University, Graduate School of Arts and Sciences, Department of History, Medford, MA 02155. Offers MA, PhD. *Faculty:* 18 full-time, 2 part-time/adjunct. *Students:* 22 (16 women); includes 4 minority (3 Asian Americans or Pacific Islanders, 1 Hispanic American) 2 international. 63 applicants, 33% accepted, 10 enrolled. In 2007, 8 degrees awarded. Terminal master's awarded for partial completion of doctoral program. *Degree requirements:* For master's, one foreign language; for doctorate, thesis/dissertation. *Entrance requirements:* For master's and doctorate, GRE General Test, writing sample. Additional exam requirements/recommendations for international students: Required—TOEFL (minimum score 550 paper-based; 213 computer-based; 80 iBT). *Application deadline:* For fall admission, 1/15 for domestic students, 12/30 for international students. Applications are processed on a rolling basis. Application fee: $70. Electronic applications accepted. *Expenses:* Tuition: Full-time $35,052. *Financial support:* Fellowships, teaching assistantships with full and partial tuition reimbursements, Federal Work-Study, scholarships/grants, and tuition waivers (partial) available. Financial award application deadline: 1/15; financial award applicants required to submit FAFSA. *Unit head:* Howard Malchow, Chair, 617-627-3558, Fax: 617-627-3479. *Application contact:* Steve Marrone, Information Contact, 617-627-2781.

Tulane University, School of Liberal Arts, Department of History, New Orleans, LA 70118-5669. Offers MA, PhD. *Degree requirements:* For master's, one foreign language, thesis; for doctorate, variable foreign language requirement, thesis/dissertation. *Entrance requirements:* For master's, GRE General Test, minimum B average in undergraduate course work; for doctorate, GRE General Test. Additional exam requirements/recommendations for international students: Required—TOEFL. Electronic applications accepted.

Union Institute & University, Online MA Programs, Cincinnati, OH 45206-1925. Offers health and wellness (MA); history and culture (MA); leadership (MA); literature and writing (MA); psychology (MA). Part-time programs available. Postbaccalaureate distance learning degree programs offered (no on-campus study). *Faculty:* 3 full-time (1 woman), 15 part-time/adjunct (11 women). *Students:* 204 full-time (143 women); includes 19 minority (14 African Americans, 2 American Indian/Alaska Native, 3 Hispanic Americans). Average age 39. In 2007, 46 degrees awarded. *Degree requirements:* For master's, thesis. *Application deadline:* Applications are processed on a rolling basis. Application fee: $50. *Expenses:* Contact institution. *Financial support:* Career-related internships or fieldwork and tuition waivers available. Financial award applicants required to submit FAFSA. *Unit head:* Dr. Brian Webb, Assistant Vice President, Academic Affairs, 802-828-8777, E-mail: brian.webb@tui.edu.

Universidad Adventista de las Antillas, EGECED Department, Mayagüez, PR 00681-0118. Offers curriculum and instruction (MA), including elementary, secondary biology, secondary history, secondary Spanish; education (MA), including ESL (elementary school level), ESL (high school level), school administration and supervision. *Faculty:* 10 part-time/adjunct (5 women). *Students:* 12 full-time (11 women), 29 part-time (24 women); all minorities (all Hispanic Americans) Average age 30. 60 applicants, 88% accepted, 28 enrolled. In 2007, 5 degrees awarded. *Degree requirements:* For master's, comprehensive exam (for some programs), thesis (for some programs). *Entrance requirements:* For master's, EXADEP or GRE, recommendations, transcripts (original). Application fee: $175. Electronic applications accepted. *Expenses:* Tuition: Part-time $175 per credit. *Financial support:* Fellowships, Federal Work-Study available. *Unit head:* Dr. Zilma Sepulveda, Director, 787-834-9595 Ext. 2282, Fax: 787-834-9595, E-mail: zsantiago@uaa.edu. *Application contact:* Prof. Evelyn del Valle, Admissions Department Director, 787-834-9595 Ext. 2261, Fax: 787-834-9597, E-mail: admissions@uaa.edu.

Université de Moncton, Faculty of Arts and Social Sciences, Department of History and Geography, Moncton, NB E1A 3E9, Canada. Offers history (MA). *Degree requirements:* For master's, thesis, proficiency in English and French. *Entrance requirements:* For master's, honors degree in history, minimum GPA of 2.7. Electronic applications accepted. *Faculty research:* Economic and social history (Canada, France, Acadia), sociocultural history, women's history, labor history, history of the press.

Université de Montréal, Faculty of Arts and Sciences, Department of History, Montréal, QC H3C 3J7, Canada. Offers MA, PhD. *Faculty:* 23 full-time (5 women), 9 part-time/adjunct (2 women). *Students:* 143 full-time (68 women), 6 part-time (1 woman). 52 applicants, 62% accepted, 31 enrolled. In 2007, 32 master's, 2 doctorates awarded. *Degree requirements:* For master's, thesis; for doctorate, thesis/dissertation, general exam. *Entrance requirements:* For doctorate, master's degree in related field. *Application deadline:* For fall admission, 2/1 priority date for domestic students; for winter admission, 11/1 priority date for domestic students; for spring admission, 2/1 priority date for domestic students. Applications are processed on a rolling basis. Application fee: $100. Electronic applications accepted. *Financial support:* In 2007–08, 15 fellowships (averaging $3,000 per year), 20 research assistantships (averaging $5,000 per year), 30 teaching assistantships (averaging $2,000 per year) were awarded; institutionally sponsored loans also available. Support available to part-time students. *Faculty research:* Preindustrial Quebec, Quebec working class, Quebec intellectual, diffusion of scientific thought, history of medicine. Total annual research expenditures: $550,000. *Unit head:* Michael J. Carley, Director, 514-343-6238, Fax: 514-343-2483, E-mail: michael.j.carley@umontreal.ca. *Application contact:* Ollivier Hubert, Graduate Chairman, 514-343-6111, Fax: 514-343-7108, E-mail: ollivier.hubert@umontreal.ca.

Université de Sherbrooke, Faculty of Letters and Human Sciences, Department of Human Sciences, Sherbrooke, QC J1K 2R1, Canada. Offers history (MA); philosophy (MA). *Degree requirements:* For master's, thesis. *Entrance requirements:* For master's, minimum GPA of 2.75. *Faculty research:* Political, social, and urban history; history of women.

Université du Québec à Montréal, Graduate Programs, Program in History, Montréal, QC H3C 3P8, Canada. Offers MA, PhD. Part-time programs available. *Degree requirements:* For master's, thesis; for doctorate, thesis/dissertation. *Entrance requirements:* For master's, appropriate bachelor's degree or equivalent, proficiency in French; for doctorate, appropriate master's degree or equivalent, proficiency in French.

Université Laval, Faculty of Letters, Department of History, Programs in History, Québec, QC G1K 7P4, Canada. Offers MA, PhD. Terminal master's awarded for partial completion of doctoral program. *Degree requirements:* For master's, thesis (for some programs); for doctorate, comprehensive exam, thesis/dissertation. *Entrance requirements:* For master's and doctorate, English exam (comprehension of written English), knowledge of French. Electronic applications accepted.

Université Laval, Faculty of Letters, Department of Literature, Programs in Ancient Civilization, Québec, QC G1K 7P4, Canada. Offers MA, PhD. Part-time programs available. Terminal master's awarded for partial completion of doctoral program. *Degree requirements:* For master's, thesis; for doctorate, comprehensive exam, thesis/dissertation. *Entrance requirements:* For master's and doctorate, English test (comprehension of written English), knowledge of French, knowledge of an ancient language. Electronic applications accepted.

University at Albany, State University of New York, College of Arts and Sciences, Department of History, Albany, NY 12222-0001. Offers history (MA, PhD); public history (Certificate). Part-time programs available. *Students:* 77 full-time (37 women), 70 part-time (29 women). Average age 34. In 2007, 31 master's, 4 doctorates awarded. *Degree requirements:* For master's, variable foreign language requirement, exam, research paper or thesis; for doctorate, thesis/dissertation. *Entrance requirements:* For master's, minimum GPA of 3.0; for doctorate, GRE General Test, minimum GPA of 3.0. Additional exam requirements/recommendations for international students: Required—TOEFL (minimum score 550 paper-based; 213 computer-based). *Application deadline:* For fall admission, 3/1 for domestic students, 5/1 for international students; for spring admission, 11/1 for international students. Applications are processed on a rolling basis. Application fee: $75. Electronic applications accepted. *Expenses:* Tuition, state resident: part-time $576 per credit. Tuition, nonresident: part-time $910 per credit. Tuition and fees vary according to program. *Financial support:* Teaching assistantships, career-related internships or fieldwork available. Financial award application deadline: 3/1. *Faculty research:* American history (all phases); public policy; European history (Medieval to modern); Asian, African, and Latin American history. *Unit head:* Richard Hamm, Chair, 518-442-5300.

University at Buffalo, the State University of New York, Graduate School, College of Arts and Sciences, Department of History, Buffalo, NY 14260. Offers MA, PhD. Part-time programs available. Terminal master's awarded for partial completion of doctoral program. *Degree requirements:* For master's, project; for doctorate, variable foreign language requirement, thesis/dissertation, general exam. *Entrance requirements:* For master's and doctorate, GRE General Test. Additional exam requirements/recommendations for international students: Required—TOEFL. Electronic applications accepted. *Faculty research:* Early modern and modern European social, cultural and intellectual history; American social, cultural and political history; north and south Atlantic world history; Latin America; East Asian history; women's and gender history.

The University of Akron, Graduate School, Buchtel College of Arts and Sciences, Department of History, Akron, OH 44325. Offers MA, PhD. Part-time programs available. *Faculty:* 14 full-time (5 women), 3 part-time/adjunct (1 woman). *Students:* 21 full-time (10 women), 14 part-time (6 women); includes 3 minority (2 African Americans, 1 American Indian/Alaska Native), 3 international. Average age 36. 34 applicants, 71% accepted, 13 enrolled. In 2007, 6 master's, 1 doctorate awarded. *Degree requirements:* For master's, one foreign language, thesis optional, written exams, seminars; for doctorate, 2 foreign languages, comprehensive exam, thesis/dissertation, written exams, oral exams. *Entrance requirements:* For master's, GRE, minimum GPA of 3.0, writing sample, letters of recommendation, letter of intent; for doctorate, GRE, minimum GPA of 3.5, writing sample, letters of recommendation. Additional exam requirements/recommendations for international students: Required—TOEFL (minimum score 580 paper-based; 237 computer-based; 92 iBT). *Application deadline:* For fall admission, 2/1 for domestic and international students. Applications are processed on a rolling basis. Application fee: $30 ($40 for international students). Electronic applications accepted. *Expenses:* Tuition, state resident: full-time $6,164; part-time $342 per credit. Tuition, nonresident: full-time $10,575; part-time $588 per credit. Required fees: $806; $43 per credit. $12 per term. Tuition and fees vary according to course load, degree level and program. *Financial support:* In 2007–08, 4 fellowships with full tuition reimbursements, 1 research assistantship with full tuition reimbursement, 13 teaching assistantships with full tuition reimbursements were awarded; career-related internships or fieldwork, Federal Work-Study, and tuition waivers (full) also available. Support available to part-time students. *Faculty research:* European, American, and world history;. Total annual research expenditures: $99,132. *Unit head:* Dr. Walter Hixson, Interim Chair, 330-972-7007, E-mail: whixson@uakron.edu.

The University of Alabama, Graduate School, College of Arts and Sciences, Department of History, Tuscaloosa, AL 35487. Offers MA, PhD. *Faculty:* 22 full-time (3 women). *Students:* 51 full-time (10 women), 14 part-time (9 women); includes 3 minority (1 African American, 1 Asian American or Pacific Islander, 1 Hispanic American), 1 international. Average age 28. 59 applicants, 53% accepted, 16 enrolled. In 2007, 12 master's, 4 doctorates awarded. Terminal master's awarded for partial completion of doctoral program. *Median time to degree:* Of those who began their doctoral program in fall 1999, 67% received their degree in 8 years or less. *Degree requirements:* For master's, one foreign language, thesis optional, oral exam; for doctorate, 2 foreign languages, comprehensive exam, thesis/dissertation, oral exams, written exam. *Entrance requirements:* For master's and doctorate, GRE General Test. *Application deadline:* For fall admission, 5/1 for domestic students. Applications are processed on a rolling basis. Application fee: $30. *Expenses:* Tuition, state resident: full-time $5,700. Tuition, nonresident: full-time $16,518. *Financial support:* In 2007–08, 29 students received support, including 6 fellowships with full tuition reimbursements available (averaging $10,000 per year), research assistantships (averaging $10,000 per year), 23 teaching assistantships with full tuition reimbursements available (averaging $10,200 per year); institutionally sponsored loans and unspecified assistantships also available. Financial award application deadline: 1/15. *Faculty research:* U.S., modern European, Latin American, military, and southern U.S. history. *Unit head:* Dr. Michael Mendle, Chair, 205-348-7103. *Application contact:* Dr. Lisa Lindquist Dorr, Graduate Director, 205-348-1859, E-mail: ldorr@bama.ua.edu.

The University of Alabama at Birmingham, School of Social and Behavioral Sciences, Department of History, Birmingham, AL 35294. Offers MA. Part-time programs available. *Students:* 13 full-time (6 women), 14 part-time (4 women); includes 3 minority (all African Americans) Average age 33. In 2007, 7 degrees awarded. *Degree requirements:* For master's, variable foreign language requirement, thesis or alternative. *Entrance requirements:* For master's, GRE General Test or MAT. *Application deadline:* Applications are processed on a rolling basis. Application fee: $35 ($60 for international students). Electronic applications accepted. *Financial support:* In 2007–08, 4 research assistantships, 5 teaching assistantships were awarded; institutionally sponsored loans also available. *Faculty research:* History of Europe, United States, Latin America, American South. *Unit head:* Dr. James F. Tent, Chair, 205-934-5634, Fax: 205-975-8360.

The University of Alabama in Huntsville, School of Graduate Studies, College of Liberal Arts, Department of History, Huntsville, AL 35899. Offers MA. Part-time and evening/weekend programs available. *Faculty:* 4 full-time (1 woman). *Students:* 4 full-time (2 women), 9 part-time (3 women). Average age 33. 5 applicants, 80% accepted, 4 enrolled. In 2007, 4 degrees awarded. *Degree requirements:* For master's, one foreign language, comprehensive exam, thesis or alternative, oral and written exams. *Entrance requirements:* For master's, GRE General Test, minimum GPA of 3.0, bachelor's degree in history or related area. Additional exam requirements/recommendations for international students: Required—TOEFL (minimum score 500 paper-based; 173 computer-based; 62 iBT). *Application deadline:* For fall admission, 7/18 for domestic students, 4/1 for international students; for spring admission, 11/30 for domestic students, 9/1 for international students. Applications are processed on a rolling basis. Application fee: $40 ($50 for international students). *Expenses:* Tuition, state resident: full-time $6,548; part-time $276 per credit hour. Tuition, nonresident: full-time $13,466; part-time $565 per credit hour. *Financial support:* In 2007–08, 4 students received support, including 1 research assistantship with full and partial tuition reimbursement available (averaging $8,460 per year); fellowships with full and partial tuition reimbursements available, teaching assistantships with full and partial tuition reimbursements available, career-related internships or fieldwork, Federal Work-Study, institutionally sponsored loans, scholarships/grants, health care benefits, and unspecified assistantships also available. Support available to part-time students. Financial award application deadline: 4/1; financial award applicants required to submit FAFSA. *Faculty research:* American and European history, U.S. diplomatic history, Old South, ancient and medieval history. *Unit head:* Dr. Andrew Dunar, Chair, 256-824-6312, Fax: 256-824-6477, E-mail: dunara@uah.edu.

University of Alberta, Faculty of Graduate Studies and Research, Department of History and Classics, Edmonton, AB T6G 2E1, Canada. Offers ancient history (PhD); classical archaeology (MA, PhD); classical literature (PhD); classics (MA); history (MA, PhD). Part-time and evening/weekend programs available. *Degree requirements:* For master's, one foreign language, thesis (for some programs); for doctorate, one foreign language, thesis/dissertation. *Entrance requirements:* For master's, minimum B+ average; for doctorate, minimum A- average. Additional exam requirements/recommendations for international students: Required—TOEFL (minimum score 580 paper-based; 237 computer-based). Electronic applications accepted. *Faculty research:* Western Canada, classical archaeology, Britain, Eastern Europe, East Asia.

The University of Arizona, Graduate College, College of Social and Behavioral Sciences, Department of History, Tucson, AZ 85721. Offers MA, PhD. Part-time programs available. *Faculty:* 33. *Students:* 59 full-time (33 women), 21 part-time (11 women); includes 15 minority (2 American Indian/Alaska Native, 1 Asian American or Pacific Islander, 12 Hispanic Americans), 11 international. Average age 33. 96 applicants, 17% accepted, 10 enrolled. In 2007, 2 master's, 10 doctorates awarded. Terminal master's awarded for partial completion of doctoral program. *Degree requirements:* For master's, one foreign language, comprehensive exam, thesis optional; for doctorate, 2 foreign languages, comprehensive exam, thesis/dissertation. *Entrance requirements:* For master's, GRE, minimum GPA of 3.0, 3 letters of recommendation, writing sample; for doctorate, GRE General Test, minimum GPA of 3.0, 3 letters of recommendation, 2 writing samples. Additional exam requirements/recommendations for international students: Required—TOEFL (minimum score 550 paper-based). *Application deadline:* Applications are processed on a rolling basis. Application fee: $50. Electronic applications accepted. *Financial support:* In 2007–08, 72 students received support, including 1 fellowship with full tuition reimbursement available (averaging $10,000 per year), 2 research assistantships with full tuition reimbursements available (averaging $12,692 per year), 29 teaching assistantships with full tuition reimbursements available (averaging $12,692 per year); career-related internships or fieldwork, Federal Work-Study, institutionally sponsored loans, scholarships/grants, tuition waivers (full and partial), and unspecified assistantships also available. Financial award application deadline: 2/1. *Faculty research:* Latin American history, European history, U.S. history, women's history, global/environmental history. Total annual research expenditures: $45,857. *Unit head:* Dr. Kevin Gosner, Head, 520-621-1168, Fax: 520-621-2422, E-mail: kgosner@u.arizona.edu. *Application contact:* Gina M. Wasson, Information Contact, 520-621-5860, Fax: 520-621-2422, E-mail: gmus@u.arizona.edu.

University of Arkansas, Graduate School, J. William Fulbright College of Arts and Sciences, Department of History, Fayetteville, AR 72701-1201. Offers MA, PhD. Part-time programs available. *Students:* 24 full-time (6 women), 55 part-time (16 women); includes 3 minority (all African Americans), 4 international. In 2007, 7 master's, 2 doctorates awarded. *Degree requirements:* For master's, thesis optional; for doctorate, 2 foreign languages, thesis/dissertation. *Entrance requirements:* For master's, GRE General Test; for doctorate, GRE General Test, GRE Subject Test. Application fee: $40 ($50 for international students). *Financial support:* In 2007–08, 9 fellowships with tuition reimbursements, 8 research assistantships, 13 teaching assistantships were awarded; career-related internships or fieldwork and Federal Work-Study also available. Support available to part-time students. Financial award application deadline: 4/1; financial award applicants required to submit FAFSA. *Unit head:* Dr. Jeannie Whayne, Departmental Chairperson, 479-575-3001, Fax: 479-575-2775, E-mail: jwhayne@uark.edu. *Application contact:* Richard Sonn, Graduate Coordinator, 479-575-3001, Fax: 479-575-2775, E-mail: rsonn@uark.edu.

The University of British Columbia, Faculty of Arts and Faculty of Graduate Studies, Department of History, Vancouver, BC V6T 1Z1, Canada. Offers MA, PhD. Part-time programs available. *Faculty:* 35 full-time (10 women). *Students:* 61 full-time (25 women). Average age 24. 107 applicants, 56% accepted, 25 enrolled. In 2007, 6 master's, 1 doctorate awarded. *Median time to degree:* Of those who began their doctoral program in fall 1999, 95% received their degree in 8 years or less. *Degree requirements:* For master's, one foreign language, thesis, six 3-credit courses; for doctorate, one foreign language, comprehensive exam, thesis/dissertation, four 3-credit courses. *Entrance requirements:* Additional exam requirements/recommendations for international students: Required—TOEFL (minimum score 570 paper-based; 230 computer-based). *Application deadline:* For fall admission, 1/12 for domestic and international students. Applications are processed on a rolling basis. Application fee: $90 Canadian dollars ($150 Canadian dollars for international students). Electronic applications accepted. *Financial support:* In 2007–08, 51 students received support, including 18 fellowships with partial tuition reimbursements available (averaging $17,500 per year), 10 research assistantships with partial tuition reimbursements available (averaging $5,000 per year), 28 teaching assistantships with partial tuition reimbursements available (averaging $490 per year); tuition waivers (partial) also available. Financial award application deadline: 9/21. *Faculty research:* Canadian, British, European, modern Chinese and Japanese history; international relations. *Unit head:* Dr. Daniel F. Vickers, Head, 604-827-3560, Fax: 604-822-6658, E-mail: dvickers@interchange.ubc.ca. *Application contact:* Dr. Tamara G. Myers, Graduate Advisor, 604-822-5161, Fax: 604-822-6658, E-mail: tamara.myers@ubc.ca.

University of Calgary, Faculty of Graduate Studies, Faculty of Social Sciences, Department of History, Calgary, AB T2N 1N4, Canada. Offers MA, PhD. Part-time programs available. *Degree requirements:* For master's, one foreign language, thesis; for doctorate, one foreign language, thesis/dissertation, 3 written comprehensive exams, oral candidacy exam. *Entrance requirements:* For master's, minimum GPA of 3.4, writing sample; for doctorate, sample of written work, master's degree in history. Electronic applications accepted. *Faculty research:* Military history, Canadian history, Latin American history, gender/women's history, native history.

University of California, Berkeley, Graduate Division, College of Letters and Science, Department of History, Berkeley, CA 94720-1500. Offers PhD, MA/PhD. *Faculty:* 45 full-time (22 women), 2 part-time/adjunct (0 women). *Students:* 218 full-time (94 women); includes 37 minority (6 African Americans, 1 American Indian/Alaska Native, 17 Asian Americans or Pacific Islanders, 13 Hispanic Americans), 20 international. 342 applicants, 20% accepted, 28 enrolled. In 2007, 23 doctorates awarded. *Degree requirements:* For doctorate, variable foreign language requirement, comprehensive exam, thesis/dissertation. *Entrance requirements:* For doctorate, GRE General Test, minimum GPA of 3.0, 3 letters of recommendation, 2 copies of transcripts, statement of purpose, writing sample (not to exceed 10 pages). Additional exam requirements/recommendations for international students: Required—TOEFL (minimum score 570 paper-based; 230 computer-based; 68 iBT). *Application deadline:* For fall admission, 12/1 for domestic and international students. Application fee: $60 ($80 for international students). Electronic applications accepted. *Financial support:* In 2007–08, 177 students received support, including 70 fellowships with full and partial tuition reimbursements available (averaging $17,000 per year), research assistantships with partial tuition reimbursements available (averaging $3,200 per year), 107 teaching assistantships with partial tuition reimbursements available (averaging $8,200 per year); Federal Work-Study, institutionally sponsored loans, scholarships/grants, health care benefits, tuition waivers (full and partial), and unspecified assistantships also available. Financial award application deadline: 12/1; financial award applicants required to submit FAFSA. *Unit head:* Mary Elizabeth Berry, Chair, 510-642-3402, Fax: 510-643-5323, E-mail: histadm@berkeley.edu. *Application contact:* Barbara Hayashida, Graduate Admissions Coordinator, 510-642-2378, Fax: 510-643-5323, E-mail: histadm@berkeley.edu.

University of California, Berkeley, Graduate Division, Group in Ancient History and Mediterranean Archaeology, Berkeley, CA 94720-1500. Offers MA, PhD. *Degree requirements:* For master's, one foreign language, exam or thesis; for doctorate, 2 foreign languages, thesis/dissertation, qualifying exam. *Entrance requirements:* For master's and doctorate, GRE General Test, minimum GPA of 3.0, 3 letters of recommendation. Additional exam requirements/recommendations for international students: Required—TOEFL (minimum score 570 paper-based; 230 computer-based), TWE. *Application deadline:* For fall admission, 12/15 for domestic students. Application fee: $70 ($90 for international students). *Financial support:* Fellowships, research assistantships, teaching assistantships, career-related internships or fieldwork and unspecified assistantships available. *Unit head:* Erich Gruen, Chair, 510-642-1489, E-mail: gruene@berkeley.edu. *Application contact:* Janet A. Yonan, Student Affairs Officer, 510-643-8741, Fax: 510-643-2959, E-mail: casmaadm@berkeley.edu.

University of California, Davis, Graduate Studies, Program in History, Davis, CA 95616. Offers MA, PhD. Terminal master's awarded for partial completion of doctoral program. *Degree requirements:* For master's, one foreign language, comprehensive exam (for some programs), thesis (for some programs); for doctorate, 2 foreign languages, thesis/dissertation. *Entrance requirements:* For master's, GRE General Test, minimum GPA of 3.0, writing sample; for doctorate, GRE General Test, master's degree, writing sample. Additional exam requirements/recommendations for international students: Required—TOEFL (minimum score 550 paper-based; 213 computer-based). Electronic applications accepted. *Faculty research:* American social, cultural, and western history; modern and early history; modern European, East Asian, and Latin American history; history of science and medicine; cross-cultural history of women.

University of California, Irvine, Office of Graduate Studies, School of Humanities, Department of History, Irvine, CA 92697. Offers MA, PhD. *Students:* 94 full-time (48 women), 2 part-time; includes 20 minority (1 African American, 7 Asian Americans or Pacific Islanders, 12 Hispanic Americans), 6 international. In 2007, 15 master's, 4 doctorates awarded. *Degree requirements:* For doctorate, thesis/dissertation. *Entrance requirements:* For master's and doctorate, GRE General Test, minimum GPA of 3.0. Additional exam requirements/recommendations for international students: Required—TOEFL (minimum score 550 paper-based; 213 computer-based). *Application deadline:* For fall admission, 1/15 priority date for domestic students; for winter admission, 10/15 priority date for domestic students. Application fee: $60. Electronic applications accepted. *Financial support:* Fellowships, research assistantships with full tuition reimbursements, teaching assistantships, institutionally sponsored loans, traineeships, health care benefits, and unspecified assistantships available. Financial award application deadline: 3/1; financial award applicants required to submit FAFSA. *Faculty research:* European, U.S., Latin American, ancient, and East Asian history. *Unit head:* Kenneth Pomeranz, Chair, 949-824-5169, Fax: 949-824-2865, E-mail: klpomera@uci.edu. *Application contact:* Carol Roberts, Graduate Administrator, 949-824-5891, Fax: 949-824-2865, E-mail: carol@uci.edu.

University of California, Los Angeles, Graduate Division, College of Letters and Science, Department of History, Los Angeles, CA 90095. Offers MA, PhD, MLIS/MA. *Students:* 195 full-time (95 women); includes 32 minority (11 African Americans, 3 American Indian/Alaska Native, 4 Asian Americans or Pacific Islanders, 14 Hispanic Americans), 22 international. Average age 31. 330 applicants, 23% accepted, 25 enrolled. In 2007, 19 master's, 27 doctorates awarded. Terminal master's awarded for partial completion of doctoral program. *Degree requirements:* For master's, one foreign language, comprehensive exam; for doctorate, variable foreign language requirement, thesis/dissertation, oral and written qualifying exams. *Entrance requirements:* For master's, GRE General Test, minimum GPA of 3.0, degree objective of Ph.D; for doctorate, GRE General Test, minimum undergraduate GPA of 3.0. *Application deadline:* For fall admission, 12/1 for domestic students. Application fee: $60. Electronic applications accepted. *Expenses:* Tuition, nonresident: full-time $5,728. Required fees:$8,966. Full-time tuition and fees vary according to program and student level. *Financial support:* In 2007–08, 134 fellowships with full and partial tuition reimbursements, 54 research assistantships with full and partial tuition reimbursements, 121 teaching assistantships with full and partial tuition reimbursements were awarded; Federal Work-Study, institutionally sponsored loans, scholarships/grants, and tuition waivers (full and partial) also available. Financial award application deadline: 3/1; financial award applicants required to submit FAFSA. *Unit head:* Dr.

History

University of California, Los Angeles (continued)

Edward Alpers, Chair, 310-206-9043. *Application contact:* Departmental Office, 310-206-2627, E-mail: gradoffice@history.ucla.edu.

University of California, Riverside, Graduate Division, Department of History, Riverside, CA 92521-0102. Offers archival management (MA); historic preservation (MA); history (MA, PhD); museum curatorship (MA). Part-time programs available. *Faculty:* 28 full-time (12 women). *Students:* 76 full-time (36 women), 1 (woman) part-time; includes 12 minority (1 African American, 2 American Indian/Alaska Native, 5 Asian Americans or Pacific Islanders, 4 Hispanic Americans), 1 international. Average age 31. 63 applicants, 49% accepted, 21 enrolled. In 2007, 12 master's, 6 doctorates awarded. Terminal master's awarded for partial completion of doctoral program. *Median time to degree:* Of those who began their doctoral program in fall 1999, 50% received their degree in 8 years or less. *Degree requirements:* For master's, one foreign language, comprehensive exam, internship report and oral exams, or thesis; for doctorate, 2 foreign languages, thesis/dissertation, qualifying exams, teaching experience. *Entrance requirements:* For master's, GRE General Test, minimum GPA of 3.2; for doctorate, GRE General Test, MA in history, minimum GPA of 3.2. Additional exam requirements/recommendations for international students: Required—TOEFL (minimum score 550 paper-based; 213 computer-based; 80 iBT). *Application deadline:* For fall admission, 5/1 for domestic students, 2/1 for international students. Applications are processed on a rolling basis. Application fee: $60 ($75 for international students). Electronic applications accepted. *Financial support:* In 2007–08, 56 students received support, including fellowships with full tuition reimbursements available (averaging $13,000 per year), teaching assistantships with partial tuition reimbursements available (averaging $16,500 per year); career-related internships or fieldwork, Federal Work-Study, institutionally sponsored loans, health care benefits, and tuition waivers (full and partial) also available. Financial award application deadline: 1/5; financial award applicants required to submit FAFSA. *Faculty research:* Native American history, United States, public history, Russia, Europe. *Unit head:* Dr. Robert Patch, Chair, 951-827-5401 Ext. 11437, Fax: 951-827-5299, E-mail: history@ucr.edu.

University of California, San Diego, Office of Graduate Studies, Department of History, La Jolla, CA 92093. Offers history (MA, PhD); Judaic studies (MA); science studies (PhD). *Degree requirements:* For doctorate, thesis/dissertation. *Entrance requirements:* For master's and doctorate, GRE General Test. Electronic applications accepted.

University of California, Santa Barbara, Graduate Division, College of Letters and Sciences, Division of Humanities and Fine Arts, Department of History, Santa Barbara, CA 93106. Offers history (PhD), including European medieval studies, global studies, public history, technology and society, women's studies; MA/PhD. *Faculty:* 44 full-time (19 women), 7 part-time/adjunct (3 women). *Students:* 122 full-time (66 women); includes 26 minority (3 African Americans, 6 Asian Americans or Pacific Islanders, 17 Hispanic Americans), 8 international. Average age 34. 139 applicants, 38% accepted, 21 enrolled. In 2007, 16 doctorates awarded. Terminal master's awarded for partial completion of doctoral program. *Median time to degree:* Of those who began their doctoral program in fall 1999, 47% received their degree in 8 years or less. *Degree requirements:* For doctorate, one foreign language, comprehensive exam, thesis/dissertation, one or more languages depending on field of study. *Entrance requirements:* For doctorate, GRE. Additional exam requirements/recommendations for international students: Required—TOEFL (minimum score 550 paper-based; 213 computer-based; 80 iBT). *Application deadline:* For fall admission, 12/5 for domestic and international students. Application fee: $60. Electronic applications accepted. *Expenses:* Tuition, nonresident: full-time $14,888. Required fees: $10,108. *Financial support:* In 2007–08, 109 students received support, including 44 fellowships with full and partial tuition reimbursements available (averaging $9,600 per year), 40 teaching assistantships with partial tuition reimbursements available (averaging $16,391 per year); research assistantships, Federal Work-Study, scholarships/grants, traineeships, health care benefits, tuition waivers (full and partial), and unspecified assistantships also available. Financial award application deadline: 12/5. *Faculty research:* Europe, U. S., Latin America, Middle East, East Asia. *Unit head:* Kenneth J. Mouré, Chair, 805-893-8156, Fax: 805-893-8795, E-mail: moure@history.ucrb.edu. *Application contact:* Deborah Johnson, Graduate Program Assistant, 805-893-2224, Fax: 805-893-8795, E-mail: deborahj@history.ucsb.edu.

University of California, Santa Cruz, Division of Graduate Studies, Division of Humanities, Department of History, Santa Cruz, CA 95064. Offers MA, PhD. *Faculty:* 30 full-time (11 women). *Students:* 31 full-time (16 women), 1 (woman) part-time; includes 8 minority (1 African American, 3 Asian Americans or Pacific Islanders, 4 Hispanic Americans), 3 international. 50 applicants, 40% accepted, 15 enrolled. In 2007, 9 master's, 3 doctorates awarded. *Degree requirements:* For doctorate, variable foreign language requirement, thesis/dissertation, qualifying exam. *Application deadline:* For fall admission, 12/15 for domestic students. Application fee: $60. *Expenses:* Tuition, nonresident: full-time $14,694. Required fees: $11,360. *Financial support:* Fellowships, teaching assistantships, career-related internships or fieldwork, Federal Work-Study, and institutionally sponsored loans available. Financial award application deadline: 1/15. *Faculty research:* Comparative, interdisciplinary approach to history; the Americas, Asia, the Islamic world, and Europe since 1500; society history. *Unit head:* Mark Traugott, Chairperson, 831-459-2465, Fax: 831-459-2555, E-mail: traugott@ucsc.edu. *Application contact:* Judy L. Glass, Reporting Analyst for Graduate Admissions, 831-459-5906, Fax: 831-459-4843, E-mail: jlglass@ucsc.edu.

University of Central Arkansas, Graduate School, College of Liberal Arts, Department of History, Conway, AR 72035-0001. Offers MA. Part-time programs available. *Faculty:* 15 full-time (4 women). *Students:* 15 full-time (8 women), 19 part-time (8 women); includes 2 minority (1 American Indian/Alaska Native, 1 Hispanic American), 2 international. 17 applicants, 100% accepted, 17 enrolled. In 2007, 3 degrees awarded. *Degree requirements:* For master's, one foreign language, comprehensive exam, thesis optional. *Entrance requirements:* For master's, GRE General Test, minimum GPA of 2.7. Additional exam requirements/recommendations for international students: Required—TOEFL (minimum score 550 paper-based; 213 computer-based). *Application deadline:* For fall admission, 3/1 priority date for domestic students; for spring admission, 10/1 priority date for domestic students. Applications are processed on a rolling basis. Application fee: $25 ($40 for international students). *Expenses:* Tuition, state resident: full-time $4,513; part-time $240 per credit. Tuition, nonresident: full-time $8,805; part-time $440 per credit. International tuition: $9,700 full-time. Required fees: $100 per term. *Financial support:* Federal Work-Study, scholarships/grants, and unspecified assistantships available. Financial award application deadline: 2/15; financial award applicants required to submit FAFSA. *Faculty research:* History Day, Russian culture. *Unit head:* Dr. Ken Barnes, Chairperson, 501-450-5631, Fax: 501-450-5185, E-mail: kennethb@uca.edu. *Application contact:* Brenda Herring, Admissions Assistant, 501-450-5065, Fax: 501-450-5678, E-mail: bherring@uca.edu.

University of Central Florida, College of Arts and Humanities, Department of History, Orlando, FL 32816. Offers MA. Part-time and evening/weekend programs available. *Faculty:* 31 full-time (14 women), 20 part-time/adjunct (6 women). *Students:* Average age 34. *Degree requirements:* For master's, thesis, written exam. *Entrance requirements:* For master's, GRE General Test, minimum GPA of 3.0 in last 60 hours. Additional exam requirements/recommendations for international students: Required—TOEFL. *Application deadline:* For fall admission, 7/15 for domestic students; for spring admission, 12/1 for domestic students. Electronic applications accepted. *Expenses:* Tuition, state resident: full-time $6,484. Tuition, nonresident: full-time $23,938. Tuition and fees vary according to program. *Financial support:* Fellowships with partial tuition reimbursements, research assistantships with partial tuition reimbursements, teaching assistantships with partial tuition reimbursements, career-related internships or fieldwork, Federal Work-Study, institutionally sponsored loans, tuition waivers (partial), and unspecified assistantships available. Financial award application deadline: 3/1; financial award applicants required to submit FAFSA. *Unit head:* Dr. Rosalind Beiler, Interim Chair, 407-823-6467, E-mail: beiler@pegasus.cc.ucf.edu. *Application contact:* Hong Zhang, Graduate Program Director, 407-823-2224.

University of Central Missouri, The Graduate School, College of Arts, Humanities and Social Sciences, Department of History and Anthropology, Warrensburg, MO 64093. Offers history (MA). Part-time programs available. *Faculty:* 14 full-time (6 women). *Students:* 3 full-time (1 woman), 11 part-time (7 women); includes 2 minority (1 African American, 1 American Indian/Alaska Native). Average age 36. 3 applicants, 67% accepted, 2 enrolled. In 2007, 1 degree awarded. *Degree requirements:* For master's, comprehensive exam. *Entrance requirements:* For master's, GRE Subject Test, 20 undergraduate hours of course work in history, minimum GPA of 2.75. Additional exam requirements/recommendations for international students: Required—TOEFL (minimum score 500 paper-based; 173 computer-based). *Application deadline:* For fall admission, 6/1 priority date for domestic students, 5/1 priority date for international students; for spring admission, 10/1 priority date for domestic students, 10/1 for international students. Applications are processed on a rolling basis. Application fee: $30 ($50 for international students). *Expenses:* Tuition, state resident: full-time $6,259; part-time $256 per credit hour. Tuition, nonresident: full-time $11,915; part-time $491 per credit hour. Required fees: $604; $20 per credit hour. *Financial support:* In 2007–08, 1 student received support. Federal Work-Study, scholarships/grants, unspecified assistantships, and administrative assistantships available. Support available to part-time students. Financial award application deadline: 3/1; financial award applicants required to submit FAFSA. *Faculty research:* American History, World History, Public History. Total annual research expenditures: $15,000. *Unit head:* Dr. John Sheets, Chair, 660-543-4404, Fax: 660-543-8006, E-mail: sheets@ucmo.edu.

University of Central Oklahoma, College of Graduate Studies and Research, College of Liberal Arts, Department of History, Edmond, OK 73034-5209. Offers history (MA); museum studies (MA); social studies teaching (MA); Southwestern studies (MA). Part-time programs available. *Faculty:* 12 full-time (3 women). *Students:* 12 full-time (6 women), 15 part-time (9 women); includes 1 minority (Hispanic American) Average age 32. 10 applicants, 100% accepted. In 2007, 8 degrees awarded. *Degree requirements:* For master's, thesis optional. *Entrance requirements:* Additional exam requirements/recommendations for international students: Required—TOEFL (minimum score 550 paper-based; 213 computer-based). *Application deadline:* For fall admission, 7/1 for international students; for spring admission, 11/1 for international students. Applications are processed on a rolling basis. Application fee: $25. Electronic applications accepted. *Expenses:* Tuition, state resident: full-time $3,516; part-time $147 per hour. Tuition, nonresident: full-time $9,054; part-time $377 per hour. Required fees: $433; $18 per hour. *Financial support:* Career-related internships or fieldwork, Federal Work-Study, and unspecified assistantships available. Financial award application deadline: 3/31; financial award applicants required to submit FAFSA. *Faculty research:* China, Russia, civil war, American naval logistics. *Unit head:* Dr. Stanley Adamial, Chairman, 405-974-5451, Fax: 405-974-3823. *Application contact:* Dr. Carolyn Pool, Director, 405-974-5671, Fax: 405-974-3823, E-mail: cpool@ucok.edu.

University of Chicago, Division of Social Sciences, Department of History, Chicago, IL 60637-1513. Offers PhD. *Students:* 268. In 2007, 37 degrees awarded. *Degree requirements:* For doctorate, variable foreign language requirement, thesis/dissertation, oral exams in 3 fields. *Entrance requirements:* For doctorate, GRE General Test. Additional exam requirements/recommendations for international students: Required—TOEFL, IELTS (minimum score 7). *Application deadline:* For fall admission, 12/10 for domestic and international students. Application fee: $55. Electronic applications accepted. *Financial support:* Fellowships, teaching assistantships, Federal Work-Study, institutionally sponsored loans, scholarships/grants, traineeships, health care benefits, and unspecified assistantships available. Financial award application deadline: 12/15. *Unit head:* Prof. Bruce Cumings, Chair, 773-702-8397. *Application contact:* Office of the Dean of Students, 773-702-8415.

University of Cincinnati, Graduate School, McMicken College of Arts and Sciences, Department of History, Cincinnati, OH 45221. Offers MA, PhD. *Faculty:* 19 full-time (8 women), 15 part-time/adjunct (4 women). *Students:* 29 full-time (19 women), 14 part-time (6 women); includes 3 minority (2 Asian Americans or Pacific Islanders, 1 Hispanic American), 1 international. Average age 35. 62 applicants, 39% accepted, 18 enrolled. In 2007, 18 master's, 2 doctorates awarded. Terminal master's awarded for partial completion of doctoral program. *Median time to degree:* Of those who began their doctoral program in fall 1999, 100% received their degree in 8 years or less. *Degree requirements:* For master's, comprehensive exam, thesis optional; for doctorate, comprehensive exam, thesis/dissertation. *Entrance requirements:* For master's, GRE General Test, BA in history; for doctorate, GRE General Test, MA in history. Additional exam requirements/recommendations for international students: Required—TOEFL (minimum score 600 paper-based). *Application deadline:* For fall admission, 1/1 priority date for domestic and international students. Applications are processed on a rolling basis. Application fee: $40. Electronic applications accepted. *Financial support:* In 2007–08, 2 fellowships with full tuition reimbursements (averaging $12,500 per year), 24 teaching assistantships with full tuition reimbursements (averaging $10,586 per year) were awarded; career-related internships or fieldwork, scholarships/grants, tuition waivers (partial), and unspecified assistantships also available. Financial award application deadline: 1/1. *Faculty research:* US cultural and social history, women's history, US and British intellectual history, modern Europe. *Unit head:* Dr. Man Bun Kwan, Head, 513-556-0917, E-mail: kwanmb@uc.edu. *Application contact:* Dr. Martin Francis, Graduate Program Director, 513-556-2062, E-mail: martin.francis.uc.edu.

University of Colorado at Boulder, Graduate School, College of Arts and Sciences, Department of History, Boulder, CO 80309. Offers MA, PhD. *Faculty:* 30. *Students:* 32 full-time (9 women), 25 part-time (16 women); includes 5 minority (1 American Indian/Alaska Native, 1 Asian American or Pacific Islander, 3 Hispanic Americans). Average age 37. 40 applicants, 95% accepted. In 2007, 13 master's, 5 doctorates awarded. Terminal master's awarded for partial completion of doctoral program. *Degree requirements:* For master's, comprehensive exam, thesis optional; for doctorate, one foreign language, thesis/dissertation. *Entrance requirements:* For master's, GRE General Test, minimum undergraduate GPA of 2.75; for doctorate, GRE General Test. *Application deadline:* For fall admission, 1/1 priority date for domestic students, 1/1 for international students. Application fee: $50 ($60 for international students). *Financial support:* In 2007–08, 15 fellowships (averaging $9,964 per year), 2 research assistantships (averaging $13,002 per year) were awarded; tuition waivers (full) also available. *Faculty research:* History of the American West; early American history; history of women and gender; American political, social and intellectual history; early modern and modern European social history. Total annual research expenditures: $65,456. *Unit head:* Peter Boag, Chair, 303-492-6683, Fax: 303-492-1868, E-mail: peter.boag@colorado.edu. *Application contact:* Graduate Secretary, 303-492-2352, Fax: 303-492-1868, E-mail: history@colorado.edu.

University of Colorado at Colorado Springs, Graduate School, College of Letters, Arts and Sciences, Department of History, Colorado Springs, CO 80933-7150. Offers MA. Part-time and evening/weekend programs available. *Faculty:* 5 full-time (1 woman). *Students:* 52 full-time (18 women), 40 part-time (28 women); includes 10 minority (2 African Americans, 2 American Indian/Alaska Native, 6 Hispanic Americans). Average age 34. 15 applicants, 87% accepted, 12 enrolled. In 2007, 5 degrees awarded. *Degree requirements:* For master's, portfolio of 3-4 research projects, oral exam. *Entrance requirements:* For master's, minimum GPA of 2.75, writing sample. *Application deadline:* For fall admission, 3/1 for domestic students; for spring admission, 10/15 for domestic students. Applications are processed on a rolling basis. Application fee: $60 ($75 for international students). *Financial support:* Teaching assistantships available. *Faculty research:* U.S. to 1865, Latin America, India, medieval and modern Europe. Total annual research expenditures: $10,972. *Unit head:* Dr. Robert E. Sackett, Chair, 719-262-4079, Fax: 719-262-4068, E-mail: rsackett@uccs.edu. *Application contact:* Dr. Debbie Scott, Administrative Assistant, 719-262-4069, Fax: 719-262-4068, E-mail: dscott@uccs.edu.

University of Colorado Denver, College of Liberal Arts and Sciences, Department of History, Denver, CO 80217-3364. Offers MA. Part-time and evening/weekend programs available.

Faculty: 17 full-time (6 women). *Students:* 10 full-time (5 women), 54 part-time (29 women); includes 5 minority (2 African Americans, 3 Hispanic Americans). Average age 39. 29 applicants, 69% accepted, 12 enrolled. In 2007, 20 degrees awarded. *Degree requirements:* For master's, comprehensive exam, thesis. *Entrance requirements:* For master's, GRE General Test, interview, minimum GPA of 3.25. Additional exam requirements/recommendations for international students: Required—TOEFL (minimum score 525 paper-based; 197 computer-based). *Application deadline:* For fall admission, 4/1 for domestic students; for spring admission, 10/1 for domestic students. Applications are processed on a rolling basis. Application fee: $50 ($75 for international students). Electronic applications accepted. *Financial support:* Research assistantships, teaching assistantships, Federal Work-Study available. Financial award application deadline: 4/1; financial award applicants required to submit FAFSA. *Unit head:* Myra Rich, Chair, 303-556-8316, Fax: 303-556-6037, E-mail: myra.rich@cudenver.edu. *Application contact:* Sue Sethney, Program Assistant, 303-556-4830, Fax: 303-556-6037, E-mail: sue.sethney@cudenver.edu.

University of Connecticut, Graduate School, College of Liberal Arts and Sciences, Department of History, Field of History, Storrs, CT 06269. Offers MA, PhD. *Faculty:* 40 full-time (17 women). *Students:* 52 full-time (22 women), 14 part-time (4 women); includes 12 minority (5 African Americans, 1 American Indian/Alaska Native, 1 Asian American or Pacific Islander, 5 Hispanic Americans), 5 international. Average age 36. 99 applicants, 19% accepted, 17 enrolled. In 2007, 11 degrees awarded. Terminal master's awarded for partial completion of doctoral program. *Degree requirements:* For master's, comprehensive exam; for doctorate, thesis/dissertation. *Entrance requirements:* For master's and doctorate, GRE General Test. Additional exam requirements/recommendations for international students: Required—TOEFL (minimum score 550 paper-based; 213 computer-based). *Application deadline:* For fall admission, 2/1 priority date for domestic and international students; for spring admission, 11/1 for domestic students, 10/1 for international students. Applications are processed on a rolling basis. Application fee: $55. Electronic applications accepted. *Expenses:* Tuition, state resident: part-time $469 per credit hour. Tuition, nonresident: part-time $1,218 per credit hour. *Financial support:* In 2007–08, 2 research assistantships with full tuition reimbursements, 50 teaching assistantships with full tuition reimbursements were awarded; fellowships, Federal Work-Study, scholarships/grants, health care benefits, and unspecified assistantships also available. Financial award application deadline: 2/1; financial award applicants required to submit FAFSA. *Application contact:* Dee Gosline, Administrative Assistant, 860-486-3717, Fax: 860-486-0641, E-mail: diedra.gosline@uconn.edu.

University of Delaware, College of Arts and Sciences, Department of History, Hagley Program in the History of Technology and Industrialization, Newark, DE 19716. Offers MA, PhD. *Degree requirements:* For master's, thesis optional; for doctorate, comprehensive exam, thesis/dissertation. *Entrance requirements:* For master's and doctorate, interview. *Application deadline:* For fall admission, 1/15 for domestic students. Electronic applications accepted. *Financial support:* Fellowships available. *Unit head:* Dr. Arwen Mohun, Director, 302-831-8226.

University of Florida, Graduate School, College of Liberal Arts and Sciences, Department of History, Gainesville, FL 32611. Offers MA, PhD, JD/MA, JD/PhD. *Faculty:* 37 full-time (13 women), 1 (woman) part-time/adjunct. *Students:* 92 (35 women); includes 10 minority (4 African Americans, 1 American Indian/Alaska Native, 1 Asian American or Pacific Islander, 4 Hispanic Americans) 8 international. In 2007, 16 master's, 7 doctorates awarded. *Degree requirements:* For doctorate, thesis/dissertation. *Entrance requirements:* For master's and doctorate, GRE General Test, minimum GPA of 3.0. Additional exam requirements/recommendations for international students: Required—TOEFL (minimum score 550 paper-based; 213 computer-based). *Application deadline:* For fall admission, 2/1 priority date for domestic students. Applications are processed on a rolling basis. Application fee: $30. Electronic applications accepted. *Expenses:* Tuition, state resident: full-time $7,478. Tuition, nonresident: full-time $22,603. *Financial support:* In 2007–08, 10 research assistantships (averaging $18,163 per year), 34 teaching assistantships (averaging $15,266 per year) were awarded; fellowships, career-related internships or fieldwork and unspecified assistantships also available. *Faculty research:* U.S. history, Florida studies, Latin American history, African history. *Unit head:* Joe Spillane, Chair, 352-392-0271 Ext. 227. *Application contact:* Dr. Jeffrey Needell, Coordinator, 352-392-8328, Fax: 352-392-6927, E-mail: jneedell@history.ufl.edu.

University of Georgia, Graduate School, College of Arts and Sciences, Department of History, Athens, GA 30602. Offers MA, PhD. *Faculty:* 31 full-time (8 women). *Students:* 48 full-time (21 women), 13 part-time (4 women); includes 4 African Americans, 1 American Indian/Alaska Native, 3 international. 131 applicants, 27% accepted, 10 enrolled. In 2007, 10 master's, 3 doctorates awarded. *Degree requirements:* For master's, one foreign language, thesis; for doctorate, one foreign language, thesis/dissertation. *Entrance requirements:* For master's and doctorate, GRE General Test. *Application deadline:* For fall admission, 7/1 priority date for domestic students; for spring admission, 11/15 for domestic students. Application fee: $50. Electronic applications accepted. *Financial support:* Fellowships, research assistantships, teaching assistantships, unspecified assistantships available. *Unit head:* Dr. Robert Antonio Pratt, Head, 706-542-2510, E-mail: rapratt@uga.edu. *Application contact:* Dr. Karl F. Friday, Graduate Coordinator, 706-542-2537, Fax: 706-542-4367, E-mail: kfriday@uga.edu.

University of Guelph, Graduate Program Services, College of Arts, Department of History, Guelph, ON N1G 2W1, Canada. Offers MA, PhD. Part-time programs available. *Faculty:* 26 full-time (11 women), 2 part-time/adjunct (1 woman). *Students:* 53 full-time (32 women), 5 part-time (1 woman); includes 1 minority (American Indian/Alaska Native), 5 international. Average age 23. 68 applicants, 57% accepted, 27 enrolled. In 2007, 11 master's, 1 doctorate awarded. *Median time to degree:* Of those who began their doctoral program in fall 1999, 100% received their degree in 8 years or less. *Degree requirements:* For master's, one foreign language, thesis (for some programs); for doctorate, one foreign language, thesis/dissertation, 3 qualifying fields. *Entrance requirements:* For master's, minimum B+ average during previous 2 years of course work; for doctorate, minimum A- average in MA. Additional exam requirements/recommendations for international students: Required—TOEFL (minimum score 550 paper-based; 219 computer-based). *Application deadline:* For fall admission, 2/1 priority date for domestic and international students. Application fee: $80. Electronic applications accepted. *Financial support:* In 2007–08, 19 fellowships with full tuition reimbursements (averaging $2,000 per year), 3 research assistantships with full and partial tuition reimbursements (averaging $5,107 per year), 55 teaching assistantships with full and partial tuition reimbursements (averaging $5,107 per year) were awarded; tuition waivers (full) also available. Financial award application deadline: 2/1. *Faculty research:* Gender and family, Scottish history, rural and urban community studies, eighteenth century England, Canadian legal and social history, modern Europe. Total annual research expenditures: $542,888. *Unit head:* Dr. Peter A. Goddard, Graduate Coordinator, 519-824-4120 Ext. 54460, Fax: 519-766-9516, E-mail: pgoddard@uoguelph.ca. *Application contact:* Dr. D. Monod, Graduate Coordinator, 519-824-4120 Ext. 53556, Fax: 519-766-9516, E-mail: dmonod@wlu.ca.

University of Hawaii at Manoa, Graduate Division, Colleges of Arts and Sciences, College of Arts and Humanities, Department of History, Honolulu, HI 96822. Offers MA, PhD. Part-time programs available. *Faculty:* 26 full-time (6 women). *Students:* 48 full-time (18 women), 10 part-time (5 women); includes 14 minority (1 American Indian/Alaska Native, 12 Asian Americans or Pacific Islanders, 1 Hispanic American), 8 international. Average age 36. 57 applicants, 46% accepted, 12 enrolled. *Median time to degree:* Of those who began their doctoral program in fall 1999, 50% received their degree in 8 years or less. *Degree requirements:* For master's, 2 foreign languages, thesis optional; for doctorate, 2 foreign languages, comprehensive exam, thesis/dissertation. *Entrance requirements:* For master's, GRE, minimum GPA of 3.0, writing sample; for doctorate, GRE, MA, sample of written work. Additional exam requirements/recommendations for international students: Required—TOEFL (minimum score 580 paper-based; 237 computer-based; 92 iBT), IELTS (minimum score 5). *Application deadline:* For fall admission, 1/1 for domestic and international students. Application fee: $50. *Financial support:* In 2007–08, 18 teaching assistantships (averaging $13,842 per year) were awarded; research assistantships, scholarships/grants and tuition waivers (full) also available. Financial award application deadline: 2/1. *Faculty research:* Asian, Pacific, world, American and European history. Total annual research expenditures: $365,083. *Application contact:* Mark McNally, Graduate Chair, 808-956-8358, Fax: 808-956-9600, E-mail: gradhist@hawaii.edu.

University of Houston, College of Liberal Arts and Social Sciences, Department of History, Houston, TX 77204. Offers history (MA, PhD); public history (MA). Part-time programs available. *Faculty:* 25 full-time (9 women). *Students:* 59 full-time (27 women), 38 part-time (20 women); includes 18 minority (3 African Americans, 2 American Indian/Alaska Native, 2 Asian Americans or Pacific Islanders, 11 Hispanic Americans), 2 international. Average age 36. 29 applicants, 69% accepted, 9 enrolled. In 2007, 7 master's, 5 doctorates awarded. Terminal master's awarded for partial completion of doctoral program. *Degree requirements:* For master's, one foreign language, thesis (for some programs); for doctorate, one foreign language, thesis/dissertation. *Entrance requirements:* For master's, GRE General Test, minimum GPA of 3.3; for doctorate, GRE General Test, minimum GPA of 3.67. Additional exam requirements/recommendations for international students: Required—TOEFL. *Application deadline:* For fall admission, 1/15 for domestic students; for spring admission, 11/1 for domestic students. Application fee: $25 ($100 for international students). *Expenses:* Tuition, state resident: full-time $6,297; part-time $262 per credit. Tuition, nonresident: full-time $12,969; part-time $540 per credit. Required fees: $2,696. *Financial support:* In 2007–08, 7 research assistantships with full tuition reimbursements (averaging $9,800 per year), 34 teaching assistantships with full tuition reimbursements (averaging $9,800 per year) were awarded; fellowships with full tuition reimbursements, career-related internships or fieldwork, Federal Work-Study, institutionally sponsored loans, scholarships/grants, health care benefits, and unspecified assistantships also available. Support available to part-time students. Financial award application deadline: 2/1. *Faculty research:* U.S., Latin American, European, social, and women's history. *Unit head:* Robert Buzzanco, Chairperson, 713-743-3008, Fax: 713-743-3216.

University of Houston–Clear Lake, School of Human Sciences and Humanities, Programs in Humanities and Fine Arts, Houston, TX 77058-1098. Offers history (MA); humanities (MA); literature (MA). Part-time and evening/weekend programs available. Postbaccalaureate distance learning degree programs offered (minimal on-campus study). *Degree requirements:* For master's, thesis or alternative. *Entrance requirements:* For master's, GRE General Test. Additional exam requirements/recommendations for international students: Required—TOEFL (minimum score 550 paper-based; 213 computer-based). *Faculty research:* Digital media studies, Latin American history, labor history, Chaucer evolution versus creationism debate.

University of Idaho, College of Graduate Studies, College of Letters, Arts and Social Sciences, Department of History, Moscow, ID 83844-2282. Offers MA, MAT, PhD. *Students:* 23 (7 women). Average age 39. In 2007, 2 master's, 2 doctorates awarded. *Degree requirements:* For doctorate, thesis/dissertation. *Entrance requirements:* For master's, minimum GPA of 2.8; for doctorate, minimum undergraduate GPA of 2.8, 3.0 graduate. *Application deadline:* For fall admission, 8/1 for domestic students; for spring admission, 12/15 for domestic students. Application fee: $55 ($60 for international students). *Financial support:* Research assistantships, teaching assistantships available. Financial award application deadline: 2/15. *Unit head:* Dr. Richard Spence, Chair, 208-885-6228.

University of Illinois at Chicago, Graduate College, College of Liberal Arts and Sciences, Department of History, Chicago, IL 60607-7128. Offers MA, MAT, PhD. Part-time and evening/weekend programs available. *Degree requirements:* For master's, one foreign language, comprehensive exam; for doctorate, 2 foreign languages, comprehensive exam, thesis/dissertation. *Entrance requirements:* For master's and doctorate, GRE General Test, previous course work in a foreign language, minimum GPA of 3.0. Additional exam requirements/recommendations for international students: Required—TOEFL. Electronic applications accepted. *Faculty research:* American urban and immigration history, early modern European history, Eastern European history.

University of Illinois at Springfield, Graduate Programs, College of Liberal Arts and Sciences, Program in History, Springfield, IL 62703-5407. Offers MA. Part-time and evening/weekend programs available. *Faculty:* 8 full-time (3 women). *Students:* 15 full-time (6 women), 30 part-time (18 women); includes 3 minority (2 African Americans, 1 Hispanic American). Average age 33. 29 applicants, 72% accepted, 15 enrolled. In 2007, 11 degrees awarded. *Degree requirements:* For master's, thesis or internship, project. *Entrance requirements:* For master's, BA in history or related field, minimum GPA of 3.0, writing sample, statement of purpose. Additional exam requirements/recommendations for international students: Required—TOEFL (minimum score 550 paper-based; 213 computer-based). *Application deadline:* Applications are processed on a rolling basis. Application fee: $50 ($60 for international students). Electronic applications accepted. *Expenses:* Tuition, state resident: full-time $5,424; part-time $226 per credit hour. Tuition, nonresident: part-time $553 per credit hour. Required fees: $618 per term. *Financial support:* In 2007–08, research assistantships with full tuition reimbursements (averaging $7,988 per year), teaching assistantships with full tuition reimbursements (averaging $7,988 per year) were awarded; career-related internships or fieldwork, Federal Work-Study, scholarships/grants, health care benefits, and unspecified assistantships also available. Support available to part-time students. Financial award application deadline: 11/15; financial award applicants required to submit FAFSA. *Unit head:* Dr. William Siles, Program Administrator, 217-206-7432, Fax: 217-206-6217, E-mail: siles.william@uis.edu.

University of Illinois at Urbana–Champaign, Graduate College, College of Liberal Arts and Sciences, Department of History, Champaign, IL 61820. Offers MA, PhD. *Faculty:* 41 full-time (16 women), 1 part-time/adjunct (0 women). *Students:* 95 full-time (37 women), 24 part-time (14 women); includes 22 minority (16 African Americans, 5 Asian Americans or Pacific Islanders, 1 Hispanic American), 20 international. 166 applicants, 9% accepted, 15 enrolled. In 2007, 8 master's, 7 doctorates awarded. *Degree requirements:* For master's, one foreign language; for doctorate, 2 foreign languages, thesis/dissertation. *Entrance requirements:* For master's, GRE General Test, minimum GPA of 3.0. *Application deadline:* For fall admission, 1/5 for domestic students. Applications are processed on a rolling basis. Application fee: $60 ($75 for international students). Electronic applications accepted. *Financial support:* In 2007–08, 48 fellowships, 16 research assistantships, 55 teaching assistantships were awarded; tuition waivers (full and partial) also available. Financial award application deadline: 2/15. *Unit head:* Antoinette Burton, Chairperson, 217-244-2075, Fax: 217-333-2297, E-mail: aburton@uiuc.edu. *Application contact:* Elaine B. Sampson, Staff Secretary, 217-244-2591, Fax: 217-333-2297, E-mail: esampson@uiuc.edu.

University of Indianapolis, Graduate Programs, College of Arts and Sciences, Department of History and Political Science, Indianapolis, IN 46227-3697. Offers history (MA); international relations (MA). Part-time and evening/weekend programs available. *Faculty:* 5 full-time (2 women). *Students:* 3 full-time (2 women), 28 part-time (15 women); includes 4 minority (3 African Americans, 1 Hispanic American), 2 international. Average age 30. *Degree requirements:* For master's, thesis optional. *Entrance requirements:* For master's, GRE Subject Test, minimum GPA of 3.0, 3 letters of recommendation, statement of purpose. Additional exam requirements/recommendations for international students: Required—TOEFL (minimum score 550 paper-based; 213 computer-based). *Application deadline:* Applications are processed on a rolling basis. Application fee: $30. Electronic applications accepted. *Financial support:* Federal Work-Study available. Financial award application deadline: 5/1; financial award applicants required to submit FAFSA. *Unit head:* Dr. Lawrence Sondhaus, Chairperson, 317-788-2196, Fax: 317-788-3480, E-mail: sondhaus@uindy.edu.

The University of Iowa, Graduate College, College of Liberal Arts and Sciences, Department of History, Iowa City, IA 52242-1316. Offers MA, PhD. *Faculty:* 27 full-time, 11 part-time/adjunct. *Students:* 21 full-time (11 women), 68 part-time (38 women); includes 12 minority (6 African Americans, 1 American Indian/Alaska Native, 1 Asian American or Pacific Islander, 4 Hispanic Americans), 11 international. 110 applicants, 16% accepted, 12 enrolled. In 2007, 8 master's, 3 doctorates awarded. *Degree requirements:* For master's, thesis optional, exam; for doctorate, comprehensive exam, thesis/dissertation. *Entrance requirements:* For master's and

History

The University of Iowa (continued)

doctorate, GRE General Test, minimum GPA of 3.0. Additional exam requirements/recommendations for international students: Required—TOEFL (minimum score 550 paper-based; 213 computer-based; 81 iBT). *Application deadline:* For fall admission, 1/10 for domestic and international students. Application fee: $60 ($85 for international students). Electronic applications accepted. *Expenses:* Tuition, state resident: part-time $349 per hour. Tuition, nonresident: part-time $349 per hour. Tuition and fees vary according to course load and program. *Financial support:* In 2007–08, 5 fellowships, 2 research assistantships with partial tuition reimbursements, 47 teaching assistantships with partial tuition reimbursements were awarded. Financial award applicants required to submit FAFSA. *Unit head:* Colin Gordon, Chair, 319-335-2303, Fax: 319-335-2293.

University of Kansas, Research and Graduate Studies, College of Liberal Arts and Sciences, Department of History, Lawrence, KS 66045. Offers MA, PhD. Part-time programs available. *Faculty:* 34. *Students:* 77 full-time (32 women), 47 part-time (19 women); includes 16 minority (3 African Americans, 4 American Indian/Alaska Native, 4 Asian Americans or Pacific Islanders, 5 Hispanic Americans), 11 international. Average age 36. 102 applicants, 29% accepted, 19 enrolled. In 2007, 17 master's, 9 doctorates awarded. *Degree requirements:* For master's, one foreign language, 2 professional quality papers; for doctorate, 2 foreign languages, comprehensive exam, thesis/dissertation. *Entrance requirements:* For master's and doctorate, GRE General Test, minimum GPA of 3.0. Additional exam requirements/recommendations for international students: Required—TOEFL. *Application deadline:* For fall admission, 12/1 for domestic and international students. Application fee: $55 ($60 for international students). Electronic applications accepted. *Expenses:* Tuition, state resident: full-time $5,838. Tuition, nonresident: full-time $13,409. Tuition and fees vary according to program. *Financial support:* Fellowships with full and partial tuition reimbursements, research assistantships with full and partial tuition reimbursements, teaching assistantships with full and partial tuition reimbursements, Federal Work-Study and unspecified assistantships available. Financial award application deadline: 12/1. *Faculty research:* Environment, military, early modern, East Asia, Russia/East Europe. *Unit head:* William Tsutsui, Chair, 785-864-9441, Fax: 785-864-5046, E-mail: btsutsui@ku.edu. *Application contact:* Ellen Garber, Graduate Program Administrator, 785-864-9438, Fax: 785-864-5046.

University of Kentucky, Graduate School, College of Arts and Sciences, Program in History, Lexington, KY 40506-0032. Offers MA, PhD. Part-time programs available. *Faculty:* 29 full-time (11 women). *Students:* 82 full-time (37 women), 15 part-time (7 women); includes 4 minority (3 African Americans, 1 Hispanic American). Average age 34. 87 applicants, 43% accepted, 22 enrolled. In 2007, 9 master's, 1 doctorate awarded. *Median time to degree:* Of those who began their doctoral program in fall 1999, 64% received their degree in 8 years or less. *Degree requirements:* For master's, one foreign language, comprehensive exam, thesis optional; for doctorate, variable foreign language requirement, comprehensive exam, thesis/dissertation. *Entrance requirements:* For master's, GRE General Test, minimum undergraduate GPA of 2.75; for doctorate, GRE General Test, minimum graduate GPA of 3.0. Additional exam requirements/recommendations for international students: Required—TOEFL (minimum score 550 paper-based; 213 computer-based). *Application deadline:* For fall admission, 7/17 priority date for domestic students, 2/1 priority date for international students; for spring admission, 12/13 priority date for domestic students, 6/15 priority date for international students. Application fee: $50 ($65 for international students). Electronic applications accepted. *Expenses:* Tuition, state resident: part-time $437 per credit hour. Tuition, nonresident: part-time $931 per credit hour. *Financial support:* In 2007–08, 36 students received support, including 9 fellowships with full tuition reimbursements available (averaging $2,884 per year), 4 research assistantships with full tuition reimbursements available (averaging $4,850 per year), 27 teaching assistantships with full tuition reimbursements available (averaging $12,500 per year); Federal Work-Study, institutionally sponsored loans, tuition waivers (partial), and unspecified assistantships also available. Support available to part-time students. Financial award application deadline: 3/15. *Faculty research:* English, British, European history; U.S. social, political and diplomatic history; U.S. early national history; U.S. Southern history; Native American and African-American history. *Unit head:* Dr. Eric Christianson, Director of Graduate Studies, 859-257-4341, Fax: 859-323-3885, E-mail: ehchri01@pop.uky.edu. *Application contact:* Dr. Brian Jackson, Senior Associate Dean, 859-257-4667, Fax: 859-257-4676, E-mail: brian.jackson@uky.edu.

University of Lethbridge, School of Graduate Studies, Lethbridge, AB T1K 3M4, Canada. Offers accounting (MScM); addictions counseling (M Sc); agricultural biotechnology (M Sc); agricultural studies (M Sc, MA); anthropology (MA); archaeology (MA); art (MA); biochemistry (M Sc); biological sciences (M Sc); biomolecular science (PhD); biosystems and biodiversity (PhD); Canadian studies (MA); chemistry (M Sc); computer science (M Sc); computer science and geographical information science (M Sc); counseling psychology (M Ed); dramatic arts (MA); earth, space, and physical science (PhD); economics (MA); educational leadership (M Ed); English (MA); environmental science (M Sc); evolution and behavior (PhD); exercise science (M Sc); finance (MScM); French (MA); French/German (MA); French/Spanish (MA); general education (M Ed); general management (MScM); geography (M Sc, MA); German (MA); health sciences (M Sc, MA); history (MA); human resource management and labour relations (MScM); individualized multidisciplinary (M Sc, MA); information systems (MScM); international management (MScM); kinesiology (M Sc, MA); management (M Sc, MA); marketing (MScM); mathematics (M Sc); music (MA); Native American studies (MA); neuroscience (M Sc, PhD); new media (MA); nursing (M Sc); philosophy (MA); physics (M Sc); policy and strategy (MScM); political science (MA); psychology (M Sc, MA); religious studies (MA); sociology (MA); theoretical and computational science (PhD); urban and regional studies (MA). Part-time and evening/weekend programs available. *Students:* 215 full-time, 98 part-time. In 2007, 87 master's, 1 doctorate awarded. *Degree requirements:* For doctorate, comprehensive exam, thesis/dissertation. *Entrance requirements:* For master's, GMAT (M Sc in management), bachelor's degree in related field, minimum GPA of 3.0 during previous 20 graded semester courses, 2 years teaching or related experience (M Ed); for doctorate, master's degree, minimum graduate GPA of 3.5. Additional exam requirements/recommendations for international students: Required—TOEFL. Application fee: $60 Canadian dollars. *Financial support:* Fellowships, research assistantships, teaching assistantships, scholarships/grants, health care benefits, and unspecified assistantships available. *Faculty research:* Movement and brain plasticity, gibberellin physiology, photosynthesis, carbon cycling, molecular properties of main-group ring components. *Unit head:* Dr. Jo-Anne Fiske, Interim Dean, 403-329-2121, Fax: 403-329-2097. *Application contact:* Jennifer Geddes, Graduate Liaison Officer, 403-329-2762, Fax: 403-329-5159, E-mail: jennifer.geddes@uleth.ca.

University of Louisiana at Lafayette, Graduate School, College of Liberal Arts, Department of History and Geography, Lafayette, LA 70504. Offers history (MA). Part-time programs available. *Degree requirements:* For master's, one foreign language, thesis or alternative. *Entrance requirements:* For master's, GRE General Test, minimum GPA of 2.75. Additional exam requirements/recommendations for international students: Required—TOEFL (minimum score 550 paper-based; 213 computer-based). Electronic applications accepted.

University of Louisiana at Monroe, Graduate Studies and Research, College of Arts and Sciences, Department of History, Monroe, LA 71209-0001. Offers MA. Part-time and evening/weekend programs available. *Faculty:* 4 full-time (0 women). *Students:* 14 full-time (4 women), 20 part-time (8 women); includes 7 African Americans. Average age 30. In 2007, 7 degrees awarded. *Degree requirements:* For master's, thesis optional. *Entrance requirements:* For master's, GRE General Test, minimum undergraduate GPA of 2.5. Additional exam requirements/recommendations for international students: Required—TOEFL (minimum score 500 paper-based; 173 computer-based; 61 iBT). *Application deadline:* For fall admission, 8/22 priority date for domestic students, 7/1 for international students; for winter admission, 12/12 priority date for domestic students; for spring admission, 1/17 for domestic students, 11/1 for international students. Applications are processed on a rolling basis. Application fee: $20 ($30 for international students). Electronic applications accepted. *Expenses:* Tuition, state resident: full-time $2,220. Tuition, nonresident: full-time $8,172. *Financial support:* In 2007–08, 7 research assistantships with full tuition reimbursements (averaging $2,500 per year) were awarded; teaching assistantships with full tuition reimbursements, career-related internships or fieldwork, Federal Work-Study, and unspecified assistantships also available. Financial award application deadline: 4/1; financial award applicants required to submit FAFSA. *Faculty research:* Early Louisiana settlements, Soviet history, Louisiana 'Tigers" in Civil War, Anglo-American relations, U.S./East European relations. *Unit head:* Dr. Gordon E. Harvey, Head, 318-342-1538, E-mail: harvey@ulm.edu.

University of Louisville, Graduate School, College of Arts and Sciences, Department of History, Louisville, KY 40292-0001. Offers MA. *Students:* 7 full-time (4 women), 16 part-time (6 women); includes 2 minority (both American Indian/Alaska Native). Average age 32. In 2007, 7 degrees awarded. *Degree requirements:* For master's, one foreign language, thesis (for some programs). *Entrance requirements:* For master's, GRE General Test. *Application deadline:* Applications are processed on a rolling basis. Application fee: $50. *Financial support:* In 2007–08, 2 teaching assistantships with tuition reimbursements (averaging $12,000 per year) were awarded. *Unit head:* Dr. John McLeod, Chair, 502-852-6817, Fax: 502-852-0770, E-mail: john.mcleod@louisville.edu.

University of Maine, Graduate School, College of Liberal Arts and Sciences, Department of History, Orono, ME 04469. Offers MA, PhD. *Faculty:* 18 full-time. *Students:* 27 full-time (9 women), 25 part-time (14 women); includes 5 minority (2 African Americans, 2 American Indian/Alaska Native, 1 Hispanic American), 2 international. Average age 38. 43 applicants, 72% accepted, 19 enrolled. In 2007, 8 master's, 4 doctorates awarded. Terminal master's awarded for partial completion of doctoral program. *Degree requirements:* For master's, variable foreign language requirement, thesis optional; for doctorate, one foreign language, thesis/dissertation. *Entrance requirements:* For master's and doctorate, GRE General Test. Additional exam requirements/recommendations for international students: Required—TOEFL. *Application deadline:* For fall admission, 2/1 priority date for domestic students. Applications are processed on a rolling basis. Application fee: $60. Electronic applications accepted. *Financial support:* In 2007–08, 1 fellowship with tuition reimbursement (averaging $9,010 per year), 3 research assistantships with tuition reimbursements (averaging $9,010 per year), 9 teaching assistantships with tuition reimbursements (averaging $9,010 per year) were awarded; career-related internships or fieldwork, Federal Work-Study, and tuition waivers (full and partial) also available. Support available to part-time students. Financial award application deadline: 3/1. *Faculty research:* Canadian labor and working classes; American social, cultural, and urban history. *Unit head:* Dr. Scott See, Chair, 207-581-1908, Fax: 207-581-1817. *Application contact:* Scott G. Delcourt, Associate Dean of the Graduate School, 207-581-3219, Fax: 207-581-3232, E-mail: graduate@maine.edu.

University of Manitoba, Faculty of Graduate Studies, Faculty of Arts, Department of History, Winnipeg, MB R3T 2N2, Canada. Offers MA, PhD. *Degree requirements:* For master's, thesis; for doctorate, one foreign language, thesis/dissertation.

University of Maryland, Baltimore County, Graduate School, College of Arts, Humanities and Social Sciences, Department of History, Baltimore, MD 21250. Offers historical studies (MA). Part-time and evening/weekend programs available. *Faculty:* 18 full-time (10 women), 10 part-time/adjunct (2 women). *Students:* 10 full-time (8 women), 56 part-time (29 women); includes 3 minority (1 African American, 2 Asian Americans or Pacific Islanders), 1 international. Average age 30. 37 applicants, 65% accepted, 14 enrolled. In 2007, 15 degrees awarded. *Degree requirements:* For master's, thesis or alternative. *Entrance requirements:* For master's, GRE General Test, minimum GPA of 3.0. Additional exam requirements/recommendations for international students: Required—TOEFL. *Application deadline:* For fall admission, 4/1 priority date for domestic students, 1/1 for international students; for spring admission, 11/1 priority date for domestic students, 5/1 for international students. Applications are processed on a rolling basis. Application fee: $50. Electronic applications accepted. *Financial support:* In 2007–08, 10 students received support, including research assistantships with tuition reimbursements available (averaging $11,324 per year), teaching assistantships with tuition reimbursements available (averaging $11,324 per year); career-related internships or fieldwork, health care benefits, tuition waivers (partial), and unspecified assistantships also available. Financial award application deadline: 3/30; financial award applicants required to submit FAFSA. *Faculty research:* Archival administration, historical editing. Total annual research expenditures:$50,000. *Unit head:* Dr. Constantine Vaporis, Director, 410-455-2092, Fax: 410-455-1045, E-mail: vaporis@umbc.edu. *Application contact:* Carla Ison, Administrative Assistant, 410-455-2312, Fax: 410-455-1045, E-mail: ison@umbc.edu.

University of Maryland, College Park, Graduate Studies, College of Arts and Humanities, Department of History, College Park, MD 20742. Offers MA, PhD. *Faculty:* 45 full-time (15 women), 14 part-time/adjunct (3 women). *Students:* 107 full-time (48 women), 25 part-time (8 women); includes 17 minority (10 African Americans, 4 Asian Americans or Pacific Islanders, 3 Hispanic Americans), 15 international. 242 applicants, 25% accepted, 23 enrolled. In 2007, 16 master's, 8 doctorates awarded. *Median time to degree:* Of those who began their doctoral program in fall 1999, 15% received their degree in 8 years or less. *Degree requirements:* For master's, comprehensive exam, thesis optional; for doctorate, one foreign language, thesis/dissertation, oral and written exams. *Entrance requirements:* For master's, GRE General Test, minimum GPA of 3.25, writing sample, 3 letters of recommendation; for doctorate, GRE General Test, minimum GPA of 3.5. Additional exam requirements/recommendations for international students: Required—TOEFL. *Application deadline:* For fall admission, 12/15 for domestic students, 2/1 for international students. Applications are processed on a rolling basis. Application fee: $60. Electronic applications accepted. *Financial support:* In 2007–08, 10 fellowships with full tuition reimbursements (averaging $14,169 per year), 24 research assistantships with tuition reimbursements (averaging $16,426 per year), 48 teaching assistantships (averaging $16,005 per year) were awarded; career-related internships or fieldwork, Federal Work-Study, and scholarships/grants also available. Support available to part-time students. Financial award applicants required to submit FAFSA. *Faculty research:* Ancient, British, East Asian, Latin American, and diplomatic history; papers of Samuel Gompers; Freedman and Southern Society; Caesarea excavations; Folger Institute. Total annual research expenditures: $376,618. *Unit head:* Dr. Richard N. Price, Chair, 301-405-4260, Fax: 301-314-9652, E-mail: rnp@umd.edu. *Application contact:* John Mollish, Director, Graduate Admissions and Records, 301-405-4198, Fax: 301-314-9305.

University of Maryland, College Park, Graduate Studies, Interdepartmental Programs, Program in History, Library, and Information Services, College Park, MD 20742. Offers MA/MLS. *Students:* 16 full-time (13 women), 2 part-time (both women); includes 1 minority (African American), 2 international. 22 applicants, 55% accepted, 5 enrolled. *Entrance requirements:* Additional exam requirements/recommendations for international students: Required—TOEFL. *Application deadline:* For fall admission, 12/15 for domestic students, 2/1 for international students. Applications are processed on a rolling basis. Application fee: $60. Electronic applications accepted. *Financial support:* In 2007–08, 1 research assistantship (averaging $15,542 per year), 7 teaching assistantships (averaging $14,569 per year) were awarded; fellowships also available. Financial award applicants required to submit FAFSA. *Unit head:* Dr. Diane Barlow, Associate Dean, 301-405-2042, Fax: 301-314-9145, E-mail: dbarlow@umd.edu. *Application contact:* Dean of Graduate School, 301-405-0358, Fax: 301-314-9305.

University of Massachusetts Amherst, Graduate School, College of Humanities and Fine Arts, Department of History, Amherst, MA 01003. Offers ancient history (MA); British Empire history (MA); European (medieval and modern) history (MA, PhD); Islamic history (MA); Latin American history (MA, PhD); modern global history (MA); public history (MA); science and technology history (MA); U.S. history (MA, PhD). Part-time programs available. *Faculty:* 30 full-time (13 women). *Students:* 21 full-time (10 women), 41 part-time (23 women); includes 5 minority (3 African Americans, 1 American Indian/Alaska Native, 1 Hispanic American), 4 international. Average age 32. 159 applicants, 34% accepted, 25 enrolled. In 2007, 13 master's, 2 doctorates awarded. Terminal master's awarded for partial completion of doctoral program. *Degree requirements:* For master's, one foreign language, thesis or alternative; for doctorate, one foreign language, thesis/dissertation. *Entrance requirements:* For master's and doctorate, GRE General Test, writing sample. Additional exam requirements/recommendations for international students: Required—TOEFL (minimum score 530 paper-based; 197 computer-based). *Application deadline:* For fall admission, 1/2 priority date for domestic and international students. Applications are processed on a rolling basis. Application fee: $50 ($65 for international students). Electronic applications accepted. *Expenses:* Tuition, state resident: full-time $2,640; part-time $110 per credit. Tuition, nonresident: full-time $9,936; part-time $414 per credit. Required fees: $7,455. One-time fee: $332. Tuition and fees vary according to course load, campus/location, program and reciprocity agreements. *Financial support:* In 2007–08, 1 fellowship with full tuition reimbursement (averaging $16,000 per year), 1 research assistantship with full tuition reimbursement (averaging $704 per year), 36 teaching assistantships with full tuition reimbursements (averaging $12,076 per year) were awarded; career-related internships or fieldwork, Federal Work-Study, scholarships/grants, traineeships, and unspecified assistantships also available. Support available to part-time students. Financial award application deadline: 2/1. *Unit head:* Dr. Audrey L. Altstadt, Chair, 413-545-2378, Fax: 413-545-6137.

University of Massachusetts Boston, Office of Graduate Studies, College of Liberal Arts, Program in History, Boston, MA 02125-3393. Offers archival methods (MA); historical archaeology (MA); history (MA). Part-time and evening/weekend programs available. *Degree requirements:* For master's, thesis, oral exam. *Entrance requirements:* For master's, minimum GPA of 2.75. *Faculty research:* European intellectual history, American labor and social history in 19th century, colonial American Revolution, Afro-American Cold War.

University of Memphis, Graduate School, College of Arts and Sciences, Department of History, Memphis, TN 38152. Offers MA, PhD. Part-time programs available. *Faculty:* 21 full-time (5 women), 1 part-time/adjunct (0 women). *Students:* 60 full-time (28 women), 47 part-time (22 women); includes 18 minority (all African Americans), 2 international. Average age 38. 43 applicants, 77% accepted, 13 enrolled. In 2007, 10 master's, 2 doctorates awarded. Terminal master's awarded for partial completion of doctoral program. *Degree requirements:* For master's, comprehensive exam, thesis or alternative; for doctorate, one foreign language, comprehensive exam, thesis/dissertation. *Entrance requirements:* For master's, GRE General Test or MAT, minimum GPA of 3.0 in history, 18 undergraduate hours of course work in history; for doctorate, GRE General Test, GRE Subject Test, MA in history, minimum GPA of 3.25. *Application deadline:* For fall admission, 8/1 for domestic students; for spring admission, 12/1 for domestic students. Applications are processed on a rolling basis. Application fee: $35 ($60 for international students). Electronic applications accepted. *Expenses:* Tuition, state resident: full-time $6,990; part-time $377 per hour. Tuition, nonresident: full-time $17,818; part-time $830 per hour. Tuition and fees vary according to course load and program. *Financial support:* In 2007–08, 14 research assistantships with full tuition reimbursements (averaging $3,350 per year), 26 teaching assistantships with full tuition reimbursements (averaging $3,700 per year) were awarded; career-related internships or fieldwork and scholarships/grants also available. Financial award application deadline: 2/15. *Faculty research:* African/African-American history, mid-south regional studies, social cultural history, ancient Egyptian history. Total annual research expenditures: $36,442. *Unit head:* Dr. Janann Sherman, Chairman, 901-678-2515, Fax: 907-678-2720, E-mail: sherman@memphis.edu. *Application contact:* Dr. James M. Blythe, Coordinator of Graduate Studies, 901-678-3381, Fax: 901-678-2720, E-mail: jmblythe@memphis.edu.

University of Miami, Graduate School, College of Arts and Sciences, Department of History, Coral Gables, FL 33124. Offers MA, PhD. Part-time programs available. *Faculty:* 20 full-time (7 women), 1 part-time/adjunct (0 women). *Students:* 22 full-time (15 women); includes 8 minority (5 African Americans, 3 Hispanic Americans), 2 international. Average age 35. 20 applicants, 55% accepted, 6 enrolled. In 2007, 3 master's, 1 doctorate awarded. Terminal master's awarded for partial completion of doctoral program. *Degree requirements:* For master's, one foreign language, comprehensive exam, thesis optional; for doctorate, one foreign language, comprehensive exam, thesis/dissertation. *Entrance requirements:* For master's and doctorate, GRE General Test, GRE Subject Test. Additional exam requirements/recommendations for international students: Required—TOEFL (minimum score 550 paper-based; 213 computer-based; 59 iBT). *Application deadline:* For fall admission, 1/20 priority date for domestic students, 1/20 for international students. Applications are processed on a rolling basis. Application fee: $50. Electronic applications accepted. *Financial support:* In 2007–08, 22 students received support, including 4 fellowships with full tuition reimbursements available (averaging $18,000 per year), 13 teaching assistantships with full tuition reimbursements available (averaging $16,000 per year); research assistantships, career-related internships or fieldwork, institutionally sponsored loans, and scholarships/grants also available. Financial award application deadline: 1/20; financial award applicants required to submit FAFSA. *Faculty research:* Latin American, European, U.S., and public history. *Unit head:* Dr. Guido A. Ruggiero, Chairman, 305-284-3660, Fax: 305-284-3558, E-mail: gruggiero@miami.edu. *Application contact:* Dr. Michael Miller, Director of Graduate Studies, 305-284-3660, Fax: 305-284-3558, E-mail: mbmiller@miami.edu.

University of Michigan, Horace H. Rackham School of Graduate Studies, College of Literature, Science, and the Arts, Department of History, Ann Arbor, MI 48109. Offers PhD. *Faculty:* 75 full-time (27 women), 13 part-time/adjunct (5 women). *Students:* 207 full-time (101 women); includes 47 minority (17 African Americans, 1 American Indian/Alaska Native, 14 Asian Americans or Pacific Islanders, 15 Hispanic Americans), 31 international. Average age 32. 350 applicants, 11% accepted, 22 enrolled. In 2007, 12 doctorates awarded. *Median time to degree:* Of those who began their doctoral program in fall 1999, 35% received their degree in 8 years or less. *Degree requirements:* For doctorate, 2 foreign languages, thesis/dissertation, oral defense of dissertation, preliminary exam. *Entrance requirements:* For doctorate, GRE General Test, writing sample. Additional exam requirements/recommendations for international students: Required—TOEFL. *Application deadline:* For fall admission, 12/1 for domestic and international students. Application fee: $60 ($75 for international students). Electronic applications accepted. *Financial support:* In 2007–08, 135 students received support, including 71 fellowships with tuition reimbursements available (averaging $15,200 per year), 1 research assistantship (averaging $15,600 per year), 63 teaching assistantships with tuition reimbursements available (averaging $15,600 per year). Financial award application deadline: 3/1. *Faculty research:* Europe, Latin America, Africa, Asia, United States . Total annual research expenditures: $36,400. *Unit head:* Dr. Mary Kelley, Chair, 734-764-6305, Fax: 734-647-4881. *Application contact:* Diana Y. Denney, Graduate Program Coordinator, 734-764-2559, Fax: 734-647-4881, E-mail: dianad@umich.edu.

University of Michigan, Horace H. Rackham School of Graduate Studies, College of Literature, Science, and the Arts, Department of Women's Studies, Ann Arbor, MI 48109. Offers English and women's studies (PhD); history and women's studies (PhD); lesbian, gay, bisexual, transgender, queer (LGBTQ) studies (Certificate); psychology and women's studies (PhD); sociology and women's studies (PhD); women's studies (Certificate). *Faculty:* 71 full-time (68 women). *Students:* 70 full-time (69 women); includes 12 minority (4 African Americans, 5 Asian Americans or Pacific Islanders, 3 Hispanic Americans), 9 international. Average age 30. 140 applicants, 9% accepted. In 2007, 6 doctorates, 5 other advanced degrees awarded. *Degree requirements:* For doctorate, variable foreign language requirement, thesis/dissertation. *Entrance requirements:* For doctorate, GRE General Test, previous undergraduate course work in women's studies. *Application deadline:* For fall admission, 12/15 for domestic students. Application fee: $60 ($75 for international students). Electronic applications accepted. *Financial support:* In 2007–08, 23 fellowships with full tuition reimbursements (averaging $16,000 per year), 19 teaching assistantships with full and partial tuition reimbursements (averaging $15,199 per year) were awarded; career-related internships or fieldwork, institutionally sponsored loans, scholarships/grants, traineeships, health care benefits, and unspecified assistantships also available. *Faculty research:* Gender issues; LGBTQ studies; sexuality; women and science; global feminism. *Unit head:* Valerie Traub, Chair, 734-763-2047, Fax: 734-647-4943, E-mail: traubv@umich.edu. *Application contact:* Jen Sarafin, Graduate Student Services Coordinator, 734-763-2047, Fax: 734-647-4943, E-mail: jsarafin@umich.edu.

University of Michigan, Horace H. Rackham School of Graduate Studies, College of Literature, Science, and the Arts, Doctoral Program in Anthropology and History, Ann Arbor, MI 48109. Offers PhD. *Faculty:* 43 full-time (22 women). *Students:* 26 full-time (12 women); includes 6 minority (2 African Americans, 2 Asian Americans or Pacific Islanders, 2 Hispanic Americans), 12 international. Average age 33. 51 applicants, 20% accepted, 4 enrolled. In 2007, 4 doctorates awarded. *Median time to degree:* Of those who began their doctoral program in fall 1999, 75% received their degree in 8 years or less. *Degree requirements:* For doctorate, 2 foreign languages, thesis/dissertation, oral defense of dissertation, preliminary exam. *Entrance requirements:* For doctorate, GRE General Test, writing sample. Additional exam requirements/recommendations for international students: Required—TOEFL. *Application deadline:* For fall admission, 12/1 for domestic and international students. Application fee: $60 ($75 for international students). Electronic applications accepted. *Financial support:* In 2007–08, 14 students received support, including 8 fellowships with full tuition reimbursements available (averaging $15,500 per year), 6 teaching assistantships with full tuition reimbursements available (averaging $15,600 per year); research assistantships with full tuition reimbursements available, institutionally sponsored loans, scholarships/grants, and traineeships also available. Financial award application deadline: 3/1. *Faculty research:* Historical anthropology. *Unit head:* Paul Christopher Johnson, Director, 734-764-1817. *Application contact:* Diana Y. Denney, Graduate Program Coordinator, 734-764-2559, Fax: 734-647-4881, E-mail: dianad@umich.edu.

University of Michigan, Horace H. Rackham School of Graduate Studies, College of Literature, Science, and the Arts, Interdepartmental Program in Greek and Roman History, Ann Arbor, MI 48109. Offers PhD, Certificate. *Faculty:* 4 full-time (1 woman), 17 part-time/adjunct (7 women). *Students:* 9 full-time (4 women). Average age 27. 28 applicants, 7% accepted, 2 enrolled. *Degree requirements:* For doctorate, 4 foreign languages, comprehensive exam, thesis/dissertation, oral defense of dissertation, dissertation prospectus, preliminary exams. *Entrance requirements:* For doctorate, GRE, knowledge of classical Greek and Latin. Additional exam requirements/recommendations for international students: Required—TOEFL (minimum score 560 paper-based; 220 computer-based). *Application deadline:* For fall admission, 12/15 for domestic and international students. Application fee: $60 ($75 for international students). Electronic applications accepted. *Financial support:* In 2007–08, 9 students received support, including 4 fellowships with full tuition reimbursements available (averaging $15,200 per year), 7 teaching assistantships with full tuition reimbursements available (averaging $15,199 per year); career-related internships or fieldwork, Federal Work-Study, institutionally sponsored loans, scholarships/grants, traineeships, health care benefits, and unspecified assistantships also available. Financial award application deadline: 3/15. *Faculty research:* Greek history, Roman history. *Unit head:* Raymond Van Dam, Professor, 734-763-1193, E-mail: rvandam@umich.edu. *Application contact:* Michelle M. Biggs, Graduate Coordinator, 734-647-2330, Fax: 734-763-4959, E-mail: mbiggs@umich.edu.

University of Minnesota, Twin Cities Campus, Graduate School, College of Liberal Arts, Department of Classical and Near Eastern Studies, Minneapolis, MN 55455-0213. Offers ancient and medieval art and archaeology (MA, PhD); classics (MA, PhD); Greek (MA, PhD); Latin (MA, PhD); religions in antiquity (MA). Part-time programs available. *Faculty:* 12 full-time (2 women), 3 part-time/adjunct (2 women). *Students:* 24 full-time (10 women), 8 part-time (2 women); includes 1 minority (African American), 1 international. Average age 29. 37 applicants, 32% accepted, 9 enrolled. In 2007, 4 master's, 1 doctorate awarded. Terminal master's awarded for partial completion of doctoral program. *Degree requirements:* For master's, 2 foreign languages, comprehensive exam, thesis or alternative; for doctorate, variable foreign language requirement, comprehensive exam, thesis/dissertation. *Entrance requirements:* For master's and doctorate, GRE, 3 letters of recommendation, department application, writing sample, copies of transcripts, personal statement. Additional exam requirements/recommendations for international students: Required—TOEFL. *Application deadline:* For fall admission, 1/4 for domestic students. Application fee: $55 ($75 for international students). Electronic applications accepted. *Financial support:* In 2007–08, 10 fellowships with full and partial tuition reimbursements (averaging $11,165 per year), 4 research assistantships (averaging $23,166 per year), 20 teaching assistantships (averaging $23,357 per year) were awarded; career-related internships or fieldwork, Federal Work-Study, institutionally sponsored loans, and tuition waivers (full and partial) also available. Support available to part-time students. Financial award application deadline: 1/4. *Faculty research:* Greek and Latin literature, archaeology, religions in antiquity, ancient Near East. Total annual research expenditures: $14,849. *Unit head:* George A. Sheets, Chair, 612-625-3326, Fax: 612-624-4894, E-mail: gasheets@umn.edu. *Application contact:* Victoria Keller, Administrative Assistant, Fax: 612-624-4894, E-mail: kell0801@umn.edu.

University of Minnesota, Twin Cities Campus, Graduate School, College of Liberal Arts, Department of History, Minneapolis, MN 55455-0213. Offers MA, PhD. *Faculty:* 36 full-time (20 women), 20 part-time/adjunct (11 women). *Students:* 111 full-time (46 women), 22 part-time (11 women); includes 26 minority (8 African Americans, 2 American Indian/Alaska Native, 12 Asian Americans or Pacific Islanders, 4 Hispanic Americans), 25 international. Average age 31. 177 applicants, 25% accepted, 24 enrolled. In 2007, 7 master's, 10 doctorates awarded. *Median time to degree:* Of those who began their doctoral program in fall 1999, 50% received their degree in 8 years or less. *Degree requirements:* For master's, one foreign language, comprehensive exam, thesis or alternative; for doctorate, 2 foreign languages, comprehensive exam, thesis/dissertation. *Entrance requirements:* For doctorate, GRE General Test, writing sample, letters of recommendation. Additional exam requirements/recommendations for international students: Required—TOEFL (minimum score 550 paper-based; 213 computer-based). *Application deadline:* For fall admission, 12/1 for domestic and international students. Application fee: $55 ($75 for international students). Electronic applications accepted. *Financial support:* In 2007–08, 18 fellowships with full tuition reimbursements (averaging $14,000 per year), 25 research assistantships with full tuition reimbursements (averaging $14,000 per year), 58 teaching assistantships with full tuition reimbursements (averaging $14,000 per year) were awarded; career-related internships or fieldwork, Federal Work-Study, scholarships/grants, health care benefits, tuition waivers (full and partial), and unspecified assistantships also available. Financial award application deadline: 12/1. *Faculty research:* Early and modern U.S.; medieval, early modern and modern Europe; Africa; East and South Asia; Latin America . Total annual research expenditures: $270,491. *Unit head:* Eric Weitz, Chair, 612-624-2800, Fax: 612-624-7096, E-mail: weitz004@umn.edu. *Application contact:* Barbara Welke, Director of Graduate Studies, 612-624-5840, Fax: 612-624-7096, E-mail: histdgs@umn.edu.

University of Mississippi, Graduate School, College of Liberal Arts, Department of History, Oxford, University, MS 38677. Offers MA, PhD. *Faculty:* 23 full-time (10 women), 3 part-time/adjunct (1 woman). *Students:* 41 full-time (18 women), 10 part-time (4 women); includes 10 minority (all African Americans), 1 international. In 2007, 4 master's, 5 doctorates awarded. *Degree requirements:* For doctorate, thesis/dissertation. *Entrance requirements:* For master's, GRE General Test, GRE Subject Test, minimum GPA of 3.0; for doctorate, GRE General Test, GRE Subject Test. Additional exam requirements/recommendations for international students: Required—TOEFL. *Application deadline:* For fall admission, 1/15 for domestic students; for spring admission, 11/1 for domestic students. Applications are processed on a rolling basis. Application fee: $25. Electronic applications accepted. *Expenses:* Tuition, state resident: full-time $4,932. Tuition, nonresident: full-time $11,436. *Financial support:* Scholarships/grants available. Financial award application deadline: 3/1; financial award applicants required to submit FAFSA. *Unit head:* Dr. Joseph P. Ward, Chair, 662-915-7148, Fax: 662-915-7938.

University of Missouri–Columbia, Graduate School, College of Arts and Sciences, Department of History, Columbia, MO 65211. Offers MA, PhD. *Degree requirements:* For master's, thesis; for doctorate, 2 foreign languages, thesis/dissertation. *Entrance requirements:* For master's and doctorate, GRE General Test, minimum GPA of 3.0.

University of Missouri–Kansas City, College of Arts and Sciences, Department of History, Kansas City, MO 64110-2499. Offers MA, PhD. PhD offered through the School of Graduate Studies. Part-time programs available. *Faculty:* 16 full-time (7 women), 6 part-time/adjunct (2 women). *Students:* 5 full-time (2 women), 23 part-time (14 women). Average age

History

University of Missouri–Kansas City (continued)

33. 14 applicants, 79% accepted, 7 enrolled. In 2007, 4 degrees awarded. *Degree requirements:* For master's, thesis optional; for doctorate, one foreign language, thesis/dissertation. *Entrance requirements:* For master's, GRE General Test, minimum GPA of 3.0, 2 writing samples, 3 letters of recommendation; for doctorate, GRE General Test. Additional exam requirements/recommendations for international students: Required—TOEFL. *Application deadline:* For fall admission, 3/15 for domestic and international students; for spring admission, 10/1 priority date for domestic students, 10/1 for international students. Applications are processed on a rolling basis. Application fee: $35 ($50 for international students). Electronic applications accepted. *Expenses:* Tuition, state resident: part-time $287 per hour. Tuition, nonresident: part-time $741 per hour. Required fees: $31 per hour. Tuition and fees vary according to program. *Financial support:* In 2007–08, 1 research assistantship with tuition reimbursement (averaging $9,880 per year), 4 teaching assistantships with partial tuition reimbursements (averaging $14,020 per year) were awarded; fellowships with partial tuition reimbursements, career-related internships or fieldwork, Federal Work-Study, institutionally sponsored loans, and tuition waivers (full and partial) also available. Support available to part-time students. Financial award application deadline: 3/1; financial award applicants required to submit FAFSA. *Faculty research:* U.S. history, Europe, women and gender, religious studies, history of science. *Unit head:* Dr. Louis W. Potts, Chairperson, 816-235-2873, Fax: 816-235-2873, E-mail: pottsle@umkc.edu. *Application contact:* Dr. Carla Klausner, Principal Graduate Adviser, 816-235-5723, Fax: 816-235-5723, E-mail: klausnerc@umkc.edu.

The University of Montana, Graduate School, College of Arts and Sciences, Department of History, Missoula, MT 59812-0002. Offers MA, PhD. *Degree requirements:* For master's, thesis or additional course work/professional paper. *Entrance requirements:* For master's, GRE General Test. Additional exam requirements/recommendations for international students: Required—TOEFL.

University of Nebraska at Kearney, College of Graduate Study, College of Natural and Social Sciences, Department of History, Kearney, NE 68849-0001. Offers history (MA). Part-time and evening/weekend programs available. *Degree requirements:* For master's, thesis optional. *Entrance requirements:* For master's, GRE General Test, writing sample. Additional exam requirements/recommendations for international students: Required—TOEFL (minimum score 550 paper-based; 213 computer-based). Electronic applications accepted. *Faculty research:* Military history, labor history/labor and the law, state formation and nationalism, American intellectual history, Civil War and Reconstruction.

University of Nebraska at Omaha, Graduate Studies and Research, College of Arts and Sciences, Department of History, Omaha, NE 68182. Offers MA. Part-time and evening/weekend programs available. *Faculty:* 15 full-time (6 women). *Students:* 8 full-time (1 woman), 63 part-time (29 women); includes 4 minority (2 African Americans, 2 Asian Americans or Pacific Islanders). Average age 32. 28 applicants, 75% accepted, 15 enrolled. In 2007, 7 degrees awarded. *Degree requirements:* For master's, comprehensive exam, thesis (for some programs). *Entrance requirements:* For master's, minimum GPA of 3.0, 21 hours of course work in history, statement of purpose, 2 letters of recommendation. Additional exam requirements/recommendations for international students: Required—TOEFL (minimum score 500 paper-based; 173 computer-based; 61 iBT). *Application deadline:* For fall admission, 7/1 priority date for domestic students; for spring admission, 12/1 priority date for domestic students. Applications are processed on a rolling basis. Application fee: $45. Electronic applications accepted. *Financial support:* In 2007–08, 43 students received support; fellowships, research assistantships with tuition reimbursements available, teaching assistantships with tuition reimbursements available, Federal Work-Study, institutionally sponsored loans, scholarships/grants, tuition waivers (partial), and unspecified assistantships available. Support available to part-time students. Financial award application deadline: 3/1; financial award applicants required to submit FAFSA. *Unit head:* Dr. Bruce Garver, Chairperson, 402-554-2593. *Application contact:* Dr. Michael Tate, Student Contact, 402-554-2593.

University of Nebraska–Lincoln, Graduate College, College of Arts and Sciences, Department of History, Lincoln, NE 68588. Offers MA, PhD. *Degree requirements:* For master's, thesis optional; for doctorate, one foreign language, comprehensive exam, thesis/dissertation. *Entrance requirements:* For master's and doctorate, GRE General Test, GRE Subject Test, writing sample. Additional exam requirements/recommendations for international students: Required—TOEFL (minimum score 575 paper-based; 233 computer-based). Electronic applications accepted. *Faculty research:* Military history, indigenous peoples, German history, American history (American West society and culture).

University of Nevada, Las Vegas, Graduate College, College of Liberal Arts, Department of History, Las Vegas, NV 89154-9900. Offers MA, PhD. Part-time programs available. *Faculty:* 26 full-time (9 women), 4 part-time/adjunct (2 women). *Students:* 31 full-time (14 women), 50 part-time (20 women); includes 5 minority (2 Asian Americans or Pacific Islanders, 3 Hispanic Americans), 1 international. 36 applicants, 39% accepted, 9 enrolled. In 2007, 12 degrees awarded. *Degree requirements:* For master's, one foreign language, comprehensive exam (for some programs), thesis (for some programs), written exam; for doctorate, 2 foreign languages, comprehensive exam, thesis/dissertation, oral exam. *Entrance requirements:* For master's, minimum GPA of 3.3 in field, 3.0 overall; for doctorate, GRE General Test, minimum undergraduate GPA of 3.0, graduate 3.5. Additional exam requirements/recommendations for international students: Required—TOEFL (minimum score 550 paper-based; 213 computer-based; 80 iBT). *Application deadline:* For fall admission, 2/1 for domestic and international students; for spring admission, 11/1 for domestic students, 10/1 for international students. Application fee: $60 ($75 for international students). Electronic applications accepted. *Expenses:* Tuition, state resident: part-time $198 per credit. Tuition, nonresident: part-time $416 per credit. Required fees: $256 per semester. Tuition and fees vary according to course load and reciprocity agreements. *Financial support:* In 2007–08, 4 research assistantships with partial tuition reimbursements (averaging $11,000 per year), 20 teaching assistantships with partial tuition reimbursements (averaging $10,000 per year) were awarded; career-related internships or fieldwork, Federal Work-Study, institutionally sponsored loans, scholarships/grants, health care benefits, and unspecified assistantships also available. Support available to part-time students. Financial award application deadline: 3/1. *Unit head:* Dr. Eugene Moehring, Chair, 702-895-3349. *Application contact:* Graduate College Admissions Evaluator, 702-895-3320, Fax: 702-895-4180, E-mail: gradcollege@unlv.edu.

University of Nevada, Reno, Graduate School, College of Liberal Arts, Department of History, Reno, NV 89557. Offers MA, PhD. *Faculty:* 18. *Students:* 5 full-time (all women), 24 part-time (10 women); includes 4 minority (2 African Americans, 2 Hispanic Americans), 1 international. Average age 38. 18 applicants, 22% accepted, 4 enrolled. In 2007, 5 master's, 2 doctorates awarded. Terminal master's awarded for partial completion of doctoral program. *Degree requirements:* For master's, thesis optional; for doctorate, one foreign language, thesis/dissertation. *Entrance requirements:* For master's, GRE General Test, GRE Subject Test, minimum GPA of 2.75; for doctorate, GRE General Test, GRE Subject Test, minimum GPA of 3.0. Additional exam requirements/recommendations for international students: Required—TOEFL. *Application deadline:* For fall admission, 3/1 priority date for domestic students; for spring admission, 10/15 for domestic students. Applications are processed on a rolling basis. Application fee: $60 ($95 for international students). *Expenses:* Tuition, state resident: full-time $2,774; part-time $154 per credit. Tuition, nonresident: full-time $13,578; part-time $330 per credit. Required fees: $49 per semester. *Financial support:* In 2007–08, 11 teaching assistantships were awarded; research assistantships, Federal Work-Study and institutionally sponsored loans also available. Financial award application deadline: 3/1. *Faculty research:* History of medicine, science, environmental history, western America, social/cultural history. *Unit head:* Dr. Barbara Walker, Graduate Program Director, 775-784-6855.

University of New Brunswick Fredericton, School of Graduate Studies, Faculty of Arts, Department of History, Fredericton, NB E3B 5A3, Canada. Offers MA, PhD. Part-time programs available. *Faculty:* 18 full-time (5 women), 2 part-time/adjunct (0 women). *Students:* 65 full-time (25 women), 9 part-time (4 women). In 2007, 12 master's, 1 doctorate awarded. *Degree requirements:* For master's, thesis; for doctorate, thesis/dissertation. *Entrance requirements:* For master's, minimum GPA of 3.0, resumé, writing sample and/or statement of research interests; for doctorate, minimum GPA of 3.0, statement of research interests, writing sample. Additional exam requirements/recommendations for international students: Required—TOEFL, TWE. *Application deadline:* For fall admission, 3/1 priority date for domestic students. Applications are processed on a rolling basis. Application fee: $50 Canadian dollars. *Financial support:* In 2007–08, 1 fellowship (averaging $4,000 per year), 19 research assistantships, 17 teaching assistantships were awarded; scholarships/grants also available. *Faculty research:* Canadian history, colonial North America, military/international, women's/gender history. *Unit head:* Dr. Steve Turner, Director of Graduate Studies (Acting), 506-452-6158, Fax: 506-453-5068, E-mail: waite@unb.ca. *Application contact:* Elizabeth Adshade, Graduate Secretary, 506-458-7471, Fax: 506-453-5068, E-mail: eliz@unb.ca.

University of New Hampshire, Graduate School, College of Liberal Arts, Department of History, Durham, NH 03824. Offers history (MA, PhD); museum studies (MA). Part-time programs available. *Faculty:* 26 full-time. *Students:* 29 full-time (22 women), 24 part-time (14 women); includes 3 minority (2 American Indian/Alaska Native, 1 Asian American or Pacific Islander), 2 international. Average age 35. 75 applicants, 43% accepted, 12 enrolled. In 2007, 8 master's, 3 doctorates awarded. *Degree requirements:* For master's, thesis or alternative; for doctorate, 2 foreign languages, thesis/dissertation. *Entrance requirements:* For master's and doctorate, GRE General Test. Additional exam requirements/recommendations for international students: Required—TOEFL (minimum score 550 paper-based; 213 computer-based; 80 iBT). *Application deadline:* For fall admission, 2/15 priority date for domestic students, 2/15 for international students. Applications are processed on a rolling basis. Application fee: $60. Electronic applications accepted. *Financial support:* In 2007–08, 1 research assistantship, 15 teaching assistantships were awarded; fellowships, career-related internships or fieldwork, Federal Work-Study, scholarships/grants, and tuition waivers (full and partial) also available. Support available to part-time students. Financial award application deadline: 2/15. *Unit head:* Dr. Janet Polasky, Chairperson, 603-862-3789. *Application contact:* Susan Kilday, Administrative Assistant, 603-862-1764, E-mail: history.grad@unh.edu.

University of New Mexico, Graduate School, College of Arts and Sciences, Department of History, Albuquerque, NM 87131-2039. Offers MA, PhD. Part-time programs available. *Faculty:* 24 full-time (12 women), 3 part-time/adjunct (1 woman). *Students:* 68 full-time (31 women), 38 part-time (16 women); includes 23 minority (3 American Indian/Alaska Native, 20 Hispanic Americans), 2 international. Average age 35. 69 applicants, 67% accepted, 20 enrolled. In 2007, 12 master's, 6 doctorates awarded. *Degree requirements:* For master's, one foreign language, comprehensive exam, thesis optional; for doctorate, one foreign language, comprehensive exam, thesis/dissertation. *Entrance requirements:* For master's, GRE, BA in history or equivalent; for doctorate, GRE, MA in history or equivalent. Additional exam requirements/recommendations for international students: Required—TOEFL. *Application deadline:* For fall admission, 1/15 for domestic students; for spring admission, 10/15 for domestic students. Application fee: $50. Electronic applications accepted. *Financial support:* In 2007–08, 42 students received support, including 23 teaching assistantships with full tuition reimbursements available (averaging $11,600 per year); institutionally sponsored loans, scholarships/grants, and health care benefits also available. Financial award application deadline: 1/15; financial award applicants required to submit FAFSA. *Faculty research:* Western U.S. history, Latin American history, European and American history, Asian history, comparative gender and women's history. Total annual research expenditures: $59,355. *Unit head:* Patricia Risso, Chair, 505-277-2451, Fax: 505-277-6023, E-mail: prisso@unm.edu. *Application contact:* Yolanda Martinez, Department Administrator, 505-277-2451, Fax: 505-277-6023, E-mail: history@unm.edu.

University of New Orleans, Graduate School, College of Liberal Arts, Department of History, New Orleans, LA 70148. Offers history (MA); history teaching (MAHT). *Students:* 36 (18 women). Average age 34. In 2007, 6 degrees awarded. *Degree requirements:* For master's, one foreign language, thesis (for some programs). *Entrance requirements:* For master's, GRE General Test. Additional exam requirements/recommendations for international students: Required—TOEFL (minimum score 550 paper-based; 213 computer-based; 79 iBT). *Application deadline:* For fall admission, 7/1 priority date for domestic students, 6/1 for international students; for spring admission, 11/15 priority date for domestic students, 10/1 for international students. Applications are processed on a rolling basis. Application fee: $40. Electronic applications accepted. *Financial support:* Research assistantships available. Financial award application deadline: 3/15; financial award applicants required to submit FAFSA. *Faculty research:* Recent U.S. political, military, urban, regional, and legal history. *Unit head:* Dr. Gunter Bischoft, Chairperson, 504-280-6611, Fax: 504-280-6883, E-mail: gjbischo@uno.edu. *Application contact:* Dr. Molly Mitchell, Graduate Coordinator, Fax: 504-280-6883, E-mail: mnmitche@uno.edu.

University of North Alabama, College of Arts and Sciences, Department of History, Florence, AL 35632-0001. Offers MA. *Students:* 5 full-time (2 women), 12 part-time (3 women). *Expenses:* Tuition, state resident: part-time $170 per credit hour. Tuition, nonresident: part-time $340 per credit hour. *Unit head:* Dr. Daniel Heimmermann, Chair, 256-765-4541.

The University of North Carolina at Chapel Hill, Graduate School, College of Arts and Sciences, Department of History, Chapel Hill, NC 27599. Offers MA, PhD. Terminal master's awarded for partial completion of doctoral program. *Degree requirements:* For master's, one foreign language, thesis, oral thesis defense; for doctorate, 2 foreign languages, comprehensive exam, thesis/dissertation, oral dissertation defense. *Entrance requirements:* For master's and doctorate, GRE General Test, minimum GPA of 3.0. Electronic applications accepted.

The University of North Carolina at Charlotte, Graduate School, College of Arts and Sciences, Department of History, Charlotte, NC 28223-0001. Offers MA. Part-time and evening/weekend programs available. *Faculty:* 24 full-time (9 women). *Students:* 10 full-time (3 women), 33 part-time (17 women); includes 4 minority (2 African Americans, 1 American Indian/Alaska Native, 1 Hispanic American), 1 international. Average age 30. 33 applicants, 73% accepted, 17 enrolled. In 2007, 15 degrees awarded. *Degree requirements:* For master's, thesis or comprehensive exam. *Entrance requirements:* For master's, GRE General Test, minimum GPA of 3.0 in undergraduate major, 2.75 overall. Additional exam requirements/recommendations for international students: Required—TOEFL (minimum score 557 paper-based; 220 computer-based). *Application deadline:* For fall admission, 7/1 for domestic students, 5/1 for international students; for spring admission, 11/1 for domestic students, 10/1 for international students. Applications are processed on a rolling basis. Application fee: $55. Electronic applications accepted. *Expenses:* Tuition, state resident: full-time $2,855. Tuition, nonresident: full-time $13,062. Required fees: $1,692. *Financial support:* In 2007–08, 2 fellowships (averaging $4,000 per year), 2 research assistantships (averaging $9,000 per year), 10 teaching assistantships (averaging $9,000 per year) were awarded; career-related internships or fieldwork, Federal Work-Study, institutionally sponsored loans, scholarships/grants, and unspecified assistantships also available. Support available to part-time students. Financial award application deadline: 4/1; financial award applicants required to submit FAFSA. *Faculty research:* Southern (U.S.) history, Latin American history, race and gender history, urban history, history of science, medicine, technology. Total annual research expenditures: $175,000. *Unit head:* Dr. John Smail, Chair, 704-687-4633, Fax: 704-687-3218, E-mail: jsmail@email.uncc.edu. *Application contact:* Kathy B. Giddings, Director of Graduate Admissions, 704-687-3366, Fax: 704-687-3279, E-mail: agidding@uncc.edu.

The University of North Carolina at Greensboro, Graduate School, College of Arts and Sciences, Department of History, Greensboro, NC 27412-5001. Offers historic preservation (Certificate); history (MA); museum studies (Certificate); U.S. history (PhD). Part-time programs available. *Faculty:* 23 full-time (8 women). *Students:* 62 full-time (38 women), 11 part-time (4 women); includes 8 minority (5 African Americans, 1 Asian American or Pacific Islander, 2 Hispanic Americans). 136 applicants, 31% accepted. In 2007, 15 degrees awarded. *Entrance requirements:* For master's, GRE General Test. Additional exam requirements/

recommendations for international students: Required—TOEFL. *Application deadline:* For fall admission, 3/1 for domestic students; for spring admission, 11/1 for domestic students. Electronic applications accepted. *Financial support:* Fellowships with full tuition reimbursements, research assistantships with full tuition reimbursements, teaching assistantships with full tuition reimbursements, career-related internships or fieldwork, Federal Work-Study, scholarships/grants, traineeships, and unspecified assistantships available. Support available to part-time students. *Faculty research:* Simultaneous discovery in science, progressive social reform, Robert Mayer. *Unit head:* Dr. Chuck Bolton, Head, 336-334-5910, Fax: 336-334-5910, E-mail: ccbolton@uncg.edu. *Application contact:* Michelle Harkleroad, Director of Graduate Admissions, 336-334-4884, Fax: 336-334-4424, E-mail: mbharkle@uncg.edu.

The University of North Carolina Wilmington, College of Arts and Sciences, Department of History, Wilmington, NC 28403-3297. Offers MA. Part-time programs available. *Students:* 14 full-time (8 women), 24 part-time (11 women); includes 1 minority (African American) Average age 28. 28 applicants, 64% accepted, 14 enrolled. In 2007, 6 master's awarded. *Degree requirements:* For master's, comprehensive exam, thesis. *Entrance requirements:* For master's, GRE General Test, minimum B average in undergraduate major. *Application deadline:* For fall admission, 6/1 for domestic students. Applications are processed on a rolling basis. Application fee: $45. *Expenses:* Tuition, state resident: full-time $2,714. Tuition, nonresident: full-time $12,579. Required fees: $1,985. *Financial support:* In 2007–08, 14 teaching assistantships were awarded; career-related internships or fieldwork and Federal Work-Study also available. Support available to part-time students. Financial award application deadline: 3/15. *Unit head:* Dr. Susan P. McCaffray, Chair, 910-962-3308, Fax: 910-962-7011, E-mail: mccaffrays@uncw.edu. *Application contact:* Dr. Robert D. Roer, Dean, Graduate School, 910-962-4117, Fax: 910-962-3787, E-mail: roer@uncw.edu.

University of North Dakota, Graduate School, College of Arts and Sciences, Department of History, Grand Forks, ND 58202. Offers MA, DA, PhD. *Faculty:* 8 full-time (2 women). *Students:* 16 full-time (4 women), 4 part-time (1 woman). 19 applicants, 37% accepted, 7 enrolled. In 2007, 4 master's, 1 doctorate awarded. *Degree requirements:* For master's, thesis, final exam; for doctorate, comprehensive exam, thesis/dissertation, final exam. *Entrance requirements:* For master's, minimum GPA of 3.0; for doctorate, minimum GPA of 3.5. Additional exam requirements/recommendations for international students: Required—TOEFL (minimum score 550 paper-based; 213 computer-based; 79 iBT), IELTS (minimum score 7). *Application deadline:* For fall admission, 2/15 priority date for domestic and international students; for spring admission, 10/15 priority date for domestic and international students. Applications are processed on a rolling basis. Application fee: $35. Electronic applications accepted. *Expenses:* Tuition, state resident: full-time $4,050; part-time $225 per credit. Tuition, nonresident: full-time $10,818; part-time $601 per credit. Required fees: $110 per semester. Tuition and fees vary according to class time, campus/location, program and reciprocity agreements. *Financial support:* In 2007–08, 12 teaching assistantships with full and partial tuition reimbursements (averaging $6,626 per year) were awarded; fellowships with full and partial tuition reimbursements, research assistantships with full and partial tuition reimbursements, career-related internships or fieldwork, Federal Work-Study, institutionally sponsored loans, scholarships/grants, health care benefits, tuition waivers (full and partial), and unspecified assistantships also available. Support available to part-time students. Financial award application deadline: 3/15; financial award applicants required to submit FAFSA. *Faculty research:* U.S. history, Latin America, Russia, modern Europe, women studies. *Unit head:* Dr. Gordon L. Iseminger, Graduate Director, 701-777-2688, Fax: 701-777-4636, E-mail: history_und@mail.und.nodak.edu. *Application contact:* Brenda Halle, Admissions Specialist, 701-777-2947, Fax: 701-777-3618, E-mail: brandahalle@mail.und.edu.

University of Northern British Columbia, Office of Graduate Studies, Prince George, BC V2N 4Z9, Canada. Offers business administration (Diploma); community health science (M Sc); disability management (MA); education (M Ed); first nations studies (MA); gender studies (MA); history (MA); interdisciplinary studies (MA); international studies (MA); mathematical, computer and physical sciences (M Sc); natural resources and environmental studies (M Sc, MA, MNRES, PhD); political science (MA); psychology (M Sc, PhD); social work (MSW). Part-time and evening/weekend programs available. Postbaccalaureate distance learning degree programs offered (no on-campus study). *Degree requirements:* For master's, thesis; for doctorate, thesis/dissertation. *Entrance requirements:* For master's, GRE, minimum B average in undergraduate course work; for doctorate, candidacy exam, minimum A average in graduate course work.

University of Northern Colorado, Graduate School, College of Humanities and Social Sciences, Program in History, Greeley, CO 80639. Offers MA. Part-time programs available. *Faculty:* 11 full-time (3 women). *Students:* 5 full-time (3 women), 8 part-time (1 woman); includes 2 minority (1 African American, 1 Hispanic American). Average age 36. 8 applicants, 100% accepted, 5 enrolled. In 2007, 5 degrees awarded. *Degree requirements:* For master's, comprehensive exam, thesis or alternative. *Entrance requirements:* For master's, GRE, 3 letters of recommendation. *Application deadline:* Applications are processed on a rolling basis. Application fee: $50 ($60 for international students). Electronic applications accepted. *Expenses:* Tuition, state resident: part-time $222 per credit. Tuition, nonresident: part-time $627 per credit. Required fees: $36 per credit. *Financial support:* In 2007–08, 1 teaching assistantship (averaging $2,518 per year) was awarded. Financial award application deadline: 3/1; financial award applicants required to submit FAFSA. *Unit head:* Dr. Michael Welsh, Program Coordinator, 970-351-2905, Fax: 970-351-2199.

University of Northern Colorado, Graduate School, College of Humanities and Social Sciences, School of History, Philosophy and Political Science, Greeley, CO 80639. Offers history (MA). Part-time programs available. *Faculty:* 11 full-time (3 women). *Students:* 5 full-time (3 women), 8 part-time (1 woman); includes 2 minority (1 African American, 1 Hispanic American). Average age 36. 8 applicants, 100% accepted, 5 enrolled. In 2007, 5 degrees awarded. *Degree requirements:* For master's, comprehensive exam, thesis or alternative. *Entrance requirements:* For master's, GRE, 3 letters of reference. *Application deadline:* Applications are processed on a rolling basis. Application fee: $50 ($60 for international students). Electronic applications accepted. *Expenses:* Tuition, state resident: part-time $222 per credit. Tuition, nonresident: part-time $627 per credit. Required fees: $36 per credit. *Financial support:* In 2007–08, 1 teaching assistantship (averaging $2,518 per year) was awarded; fellowships, research assistantships, unspecified assistantships also available. Financial award application deadline: 3/1; financial award applicants required to submit FAFSA. *Unit head:* Dr. Barry Rothaus, Director, 970-351-2905, Fax: 970-351-2199.

University of Northern Iowa, Graduate College, College of Social and Behavioral Sciences, Department of History, Cedar Falls, IA 50614. Offers MA. Part-time programs available. *Students:* 15 full-time (8 women), 8 part-time (4 women); includes 2 minority (both African Americans) 18 applicants, 67% accepted, 9 enrolled. In 2007, 6 degrees awarded. *Degree requirements:* For master's, comprehensive exam (for some programs), thesis or alternative. *Entrance requirements:* For master's, minimum GPA of 3.2. Additional exam requirements/recommendations for international students: Required—TOEFL (minimum score 500 paper-based; 180 computer-based; 61 iBT). *Application deadline:* For fall admission, 8/1 priority date for domestic students. Applications are processed on a rolling basis. Application fee: $30 ($50 for international students). Electronic applications accepted. *Expenses:* Tuition, state resident: full-time $6,246; part-time $694 per credit hour. Tuition, nonresident: full-time $14,554; part-time $694 per credit hour. Required fees: $838; $119 per semester. *Financial support:* Career-related internships or fieldwork, Federal Work-Study, scholarships/grants, and tuition waivers (full and partial) available. Support available to part-time students. Financial award application deadline: 2/1. *Unit head:* Dr. Robert Martin, Head, 319-273-2097, Fax: 319-273-5846, E-mail: robert.martin@uni.edu.

University of North Florida, College of Arts and Sciences, Department of History, Jacksonville, FL 32224-2645. Offers European history (MA); US history (MA). Part-time programs available. *Faculty:* 15 full-time (5 women). *Students:* 18 full-time (10 women), 23 part-time (12 women). Average age 35. 20 applicants, 50% accepted, 9 enrolled. In 2007, 12 degrees awarded. *Degree requirements:* For master's, comprehensive exam (for some programs), thesis optional. *Entrance requirements:* For master's, GRE General Test, 3 letters of recommendation, minimum GPA of 3.0 in last 60 hours of course work. Additional exam requirements/recommendations for international students: Required—TOEFL (minimum score 500 paper-based; 173 computer-based). *Application deadline:* For fall admission, 7/1 priority date for domestic students, 5/1 for international students; for spring admission, 11/1 priority date for domestic students, 10/1 for international students. Applications are processed on a rolling basis. Application fee: $30. Electronic applications accepted. *Expenses:* Tuition, state resident: part-time $266 per credit hour. Tuition, nonresident: part-time $858 per credit hour. One-time fee: $35 part-time. Tuition and fees vary according to program. *Financial support:* In 2007–08, 19 students received support, including 14 teaching assistantships (averaging $4,352 per year); career-related internships or fieldwork, Federal Work-Study, and tuition waivers (partial) also available. Support available to part-time students. Financial award application deadline: 4/1; financial award applicants required to submit FAFSA. Total annual research expenditures: $2,094. *Unit head:* Dr. Dale Clifford, E-mail: clifford@unf.edu. *Application contact:* Dr. Phil Kaplan, Graduate Coordinator, 904-620-1863, Fax: 904-620-1018, E-mail: pkaplan@unf.edu.

University of North Texas, Robert B. Toulouse School of Graduate Studies, College of Arts and Sciences, Department of History, Denton, TX 76203. Offers MA, MS, PhD. Part-time programs available. *Faculty:* 28 full-time (7 women). *Students:* 36 full-time (12 women), 76 part-time (27 women); includes 12 minority (3 African Americans, 3 Asian Americans or Pacific Islanders, 6 Hispanic Americans), 3 international. Average age 34. 80 applicants, 54% accepted, 29 enrolled. In 2007, 13 master's awarded. Terminal master's awarded for partial completion of doctoral program. *Degree requirements:* For master's, one foreign language, comprehensive exam, thesis or alternative; for doctorate, 2 foreign languages, comprehensive exam, thesis/dissertation. *Entrance requirements:* For master's and doctorate, GRE General Test. Additional exam requirements/recommendations for international students: Required—proof of English language proficiency required for non-native English speakers; Recommended—TOEFL (minimum score 550 paper-based; 213 computer-based). *Application deadline:* For fall admission, 7/15 for domestic students; for spring admission, 11/15 for domestic students. Application fee: $50 ($75 for international students). *Financial support:* In 2007–08, 21 fellowships with tuition reimbursements (averaging $26,000 per year), 26 teaching assistantships were awarded; career-related internships or fieldwork, Federal Work-Study, and institutionally sponsored loans also available. Financial award application deadline: 2/15. *Faculty research:* U.S. local, Texas, women and European history. Total annual research expenditures: $4,530. *Unit head:* Dr. Adrian Lewis, Chair, 940-565-2288, Fax: 940-369-8838, E-mail: arl0008@unt.edu. *Application contact:* Dr. Ken Johnson, Graduate Advisor, 940-565-4208, Fax: 940-369-8838, E-mail: krj@unt.edu.

University of Notre Dame, Graduate School, College of Arts and Letters, Division of Humanities, Department of History, Notre Dame, IN 46556. Offers MA, PhD. *Faculty:* 31 full-time (9 women). *Students:* 64 full-time (23 women); includes 7 minority (1 African American, 1 American Indian/Alaska Native, 2 Asian Americans or Pacific Islanders, 3 Hispanic Americans), 9 international. 185 applicants, 12% accepted, 17 enrolled. In 2007, 5 master's, 5 doctorates awarded. *Median time to degree:* Of those who began their doctoral program in fall 1999, 84% received their degree in 8 years or less. *Degree requirements:* For doctorate, one foreign language, thesis/dissertation, candidacy exam. *Entrance requirements:* For doctorate, GRE General Test. Additional exam requirements/recommendations for international students: Required—TOEFL (minimum score 600 paper-based; 250 computer-based; 80 iBT). *Application deadline:* For fall admission, 1/4 priority date for domestic students, 1/4 for international students. Application fee: $50. Electronic applications accepted. *Financial support:* In 2007–08, 11 fellowships with full tuition reimbursements (averaging $22,000 per year), research assistantships with full tuition reimbursements (averaging $16,000 per year), 38 teaching assistantships with full tuition reimbursements (averaging $16,000 per year) were awarded; tuition waivers (full) also available. Financial award application deadline: 1/15. *Faculty research:* U.S., modern European and medieval history; history of European and U.S. religions; U.S. and European intellectual and cultural history; history of Central Europe. *Unit head:* Dr. Thomas Kselman, Director of Graduate Studies, 574-631-7266, Fax: 574-631-4268, E-mail: history.1@nd.edu. *Application contact:* Dr. Jarren Gonzales, Director of Graduate Admissions, 574-631-7706, Fax: 574-631-4183.

University of Oklahoma, Graduate College, College of Arts and Sciences, Department of History, Norman, OK 73019-0390. Offers MA, PhD. Part-time and evening/weekend programs available. *Faculty:* 34 full-time (10 women), 1 (woman) part-time/adjunct. *Students:* 35 full-time (16 women), 18 part-time (8 women); includes 9 minority (5 American Indian/Alaska Native, 2 Asian Americans or Pacific Islanders, 2 Hispanic Americans). 21 applicants, 76% accepted, 10 enrolled. In 2007, 1 master's, 6 doctorates awarded. Terminal master's awarded for partial completion of doctoral program. *Degree requirements:* For master's, one foreign language, thesis or alternative, oral and written exams; for doctorate, 2 foreign languages, thesis/dissertation, oral and written exams. *Entrance requirements:* For master's, GRE General Test, BA with 20 hours in history; for doctorate, GRE General Test. Additional exam requirements/recommendations for international students: Required—TOEFL (minimum score 550 paper-based; 213 computer-based). *Application deadline:* For fall admission, 4/1 for domestic and international students; for spring admission, 11/1 for domestic students, 9/1 for international students. Applications are processed on a rolling basis. Application fee: $40 ($90 for international students). Electronic applications accepted. *Expenses:* Tuition, state resident: full-time $3,451; part-time $144 per credit hour. Tuition, nonresident: full-time $12,432; part-time $518 per credit hour. Required fees: $1,925; $70 per credit hour. $122 per semester. *Financial support:* In 2007–08, 28 students received support, including 8 fellowships with full tuition reimbursements available (averaging $4,125 per year), 3 research assistantships with partial tuition reimbursements available (averaging $18,985 per year), 25 teaching assistantships with partial tuition reimbursements available (averaging $13,503 per year); scholarships/grants, health care benefits, tuition waivers (partial), and unspecified assistantships also available. Financial award application deadline: 1/31. *Faculty research:* Ethnohistory, environment, Western and Latin American history. Total annual research expenditures:$194,130. *Unit head:* Dr. Robert L. Griswold, Chair, 405-325-6002, Fax: 405-325-4503, E-mail: rgriswold@ou.edu. *Application contact:* Dr. Terry Rugeley, Professor, 405-625-6002, Fax: 405-325-4503, E-mail: trugeley@ou.edu.

University of Oregon, Graduate School, College of Arts and Sciences, Department of History, Eugene, OR 97403. Offers MA, PhD. *Faculty:* 20 full-time (6 women), 3 part-time/adjunct (1 woman). *Students:* 21 full-time (8 women), 3 part-time (1 woman); includes 2 minority (1 Asian American or Pacific Islander, 1 Hispanic American), 6 international. 85 applicants, 15% accepted. In 2007, 12 master's, 2 doctorates awarded. *Degree requirements:* For master's, one foreign language, thesis or alternative, written exam; for doctorate, 2 foreign languages, thesis/dissertation, oral and written exams. *Entrance requirements:* For master's and doctorate, GRE General Test, minimum GPA of 3.0. Additional exam requirements/recommendations for international students: Required—TOEFL. *Application deadline:* For fall admission, 1/7 for domestic students. Application fee: $50. *Financial support:* In 2007–08, 23 teaching assistantships were awarded; Federal Work-Study and institutionally sponsored loans also available. Financial award application deadline: 2/1. *Faculty research:* U.S., European, East and Southeast Asian, Latin American, and ancient history. *Unit head:* John McCole, Head, 541-346-1265, Fax: 541-346-4895. *Application contact:* Rebecca Lynn, Admissions Contact, 541-346-5900, Fax: 540-346-4895, E-mail: rlynn@uoregon.edu.

University of Ottawa, Faculty of Graduate and Postdoctoral Studies, Faculty of Arts, Department of History, Ottawa, ON K1N 6N5, Canada. Offers MA, PhD. *Degree requirements:* For master's, 2 foreign languages, thesis or alternative; for doctorate, 2 foreign languages, thesis/dissertation, oral exam. *Entrance requirements:* For master's, honors degree or equivalent, minimum B average; for doctorate, master's degree, minimum B+ average. Electronic applications accepted. *Faculty research:* Canadian history.

History

University of Pennsylvania, School of Arts and Sciences, Graduate Group in Ancient History, Philadelphia, PA 19104. Offers AM, PhD. *Degree requirements:* For doctorate, 4 foreign languages, thesis/dissertation. Electronic applications accepted.

University of Pennsylvania, School of Arts and Sciences, Graduate Group in History, Philadelphia, PA 19104. Offers AM, PhD. Terminal master's awarded for partial completion of doctoral program. *Degree requirements:* For master's, thesis; for doctorate, one foreign language, thesis/dissertation. *Entrance requirements:* For master's and doctorate, GRE General Test. Additional exam requirements/recommendations for international students: Required—TOEFL. Electronic applications accepted.

University of Pittsburgh, School of Arts and Sciences, Department of History, Pittsburgh, PA 15260. Offers MA, PhD. Part-time programs available. *Faculty:* 24 full-time (6 women), 10 part-time/adjunct (2 women). *Students:* 38 full-time (19 women); includes 10 minority (3 African Americans, 2 Asian Americans or Pacific Islanders, 5 Hispanic Americans). 111 applicants, 14% accepted, 11 enrolled. In 2007, 4 master's, 4 doctorates awarded. Terminal master's awarded for partial completion of doctoral program. *Median time to degree:* Of those who began their doctoral program in fall 1999, 33% received their degree in 8 years or less. *Degree requirements:* For master's, one foreign language, oral exam, 1 seminar paper; for doctorate, 2 foreign languages, comprehensive exam, thesis/dissertation. *Entrance requirements:* For master's and doctorate, GRE General Test. Additional exam requirements/recommendations for international students: Required—TOEFL. *Application deadline:* For fall admission, 1/15 for domestic and international students. Application fee: $50. Electronic applications accepted. *Financial support:* In 2007–08, 5 fellowships with tuition reimbursements (averaging $13,995 per year), 24 teaching assistantships with tuition reimbursements (averaging $14,777 per year) were awarded; Federal Work-Study, scholarships/grants, and tuition waivers (full and partial) also available. Financial award application deadline: 1/15. *Faculty research:* Western Europe, Latin America, Russia, Eastern Europe, U.S., East Asia. *Unit head:* Dr. Marcus Rediker, Chairman, 412-648-7452, Fax: 412-648-9074. *Application contact:* Molly Estes, Graduate Secretary, 412-648-7454, Fax: 412-648-9074, E-mail: wid2@pitt.edu.

University of Puerto Rico, Río Piedras, College of Humanities, Department of History, San Juan, PR 00931-3300. Offers MA, PhD. Part-time programs available. *Students:* 63 full-time (20 women), 51 part-time (23 women). Average age 37. In 2007, 2 master's, 3 doctorates awarded. *Degree requirements:* For master's, one foreign language, comprehensive exam, thesis; for doctorate, one foreign language, comprehensive exam, thesis/dissertation. *Entrance requirements:* For master's, PAEG or GRE, interview, minimum GPA of 3.0, 2 letters of recommendation; for doctorate, PAEG or GRE, interview, master's degree, minimum GPA of 3.0, 2 letters of recommendation. *Application deadline:* For fall admission, 2/1 for domestic and international students. Application fee: $17. *Expenses:* Tuition, state resident: full-time $1,808; part-time $113 per credit. Tuition, nonresident: full-time $5,248; part-time $328 per credit. Required fees: $72 per term. *Financial support:* Fellowships, research assistantships, teaching assistantships, Federal Work-Study, institutionally sponsored loans, and tuition waivers (partial) available. Financial award application deadline: 5/31. *Unit head:* Dr. Marcial Ocasio, Director, 787-764-0000 Ext. 3775, Fax: 787-763-5879.

University of Regina, Faculty of Graduate Studies and Research, Faculty of Arts, Department of History, Regina, SK S4S 0A2, Canada. Offers MA, PhD. *Faculty:* 13 full-time (2 women). *Students:* 8 full-time (3 women), 2 part-time. 6 applicants, 67% accepted, 3 enrolled. In 2007, 2 degrees awarded. *Degree requirements:* For master's, thesis. *Entrance requirements:* Additional exam requirements/recommendations for international students: Required—TOEFL (minimum score 580 paper-based; 237 computer-based; 88 iBT). *Application deadline:* Applications are processed on a rolling basis. Application fee: $85 ($100 for international students). Electronic applications accepted. *Financial support:* In 2007–08, 3 fellowships (averaging $15,750 per year), 1 research assistantship (averaging $13,875 per year), 2 teaching assistantships (averaging $13,060 per year) were awarded; scholarships/grants also available. Financial award application deadline: 6/15. *Faculty research:* Canadian, English, United States, European, Asian history, British history, and Latin-American. *Unit head:* Dr. Thomas Bredohl, Head, 306-585-4155, Fax: 306-585-4827, E-mail: thomas.bredohl@uregina.ca. *Application contact:* Dr. William Brennan, Graduate Program Coordinator, 306-585-4214, E-mail: william.brennan@uregina.ca.

University of Rhode Island, Graduate School, College of Arts and Sciences, Department of History, Kingston, RI 02881. Offers MA. In 2007, 1 degree awarded. *Degree requirements:* For master's, thesis optional. *Application deadline:* For fall admission, 7/15 priority date for domestic students; for spring admission, 11/15 for domestic students. Applications are processed on a rolling basis. Application fee: $35. *Expenses:* Tuition, state resident: full-time $6,936; part-time $385 per credit. Tuition, nonresident: full-time $19,044; part-time $1,058 per credit. Required fees: $1,508; $48 per credit. $30 per semester. One-time fee: $80 part-time. *Financial support:* Application deadline: 2/1. *Unit head:* Dr. Marie Jenkins Schwartz, Chair, 401-874-4090, E-mail: schwartz@uri.edu.

University of Rochester, The College, Arts and Sciences, Department of History, Rochester, NY 14627-0250. Offers MA, PhD. Terminal master's awarded for partial completion of doctoral program. *Degree requirements:* For master's, one foreign language, thesis or alternative; for doctorate, 2 foreign languages, thesis/dissertation, comprehensive oral exam, qualifying exam. *Entrance requirements:* For master's and doctorate, GRE General Test, sample of written work. Additional exam requirements/recommendations for international students: Required—TOEFL.

University of San Diego, College of Arts and Sciences, Department of History, San Diego, CA 92110-2492. Offers MA. Part-time and evening/weekend programs available. *Faculty:* 3 full-time (1 woman). *Students:* 7 full-time (2 women), 16 part-time (9 women); includes 3 minority (all Hispanic Americans) Average age 30. 15 applicants, 80% accepted, 7 enrolled. In 2007, 6 degrees awarded. *Degree requirements:* For master's, one foreign language, thesis. *Entrance requirements:* For master's, GRE General Test, minimum GPA of 3.0. Additional exam requirements/recommendations for international students: Required—TOEFL (minimum score 580 paper-based; 237 computer-based), TWE. *Application deadline:* For fall admission, 5/1 priority date for domestic students; for spring admission, 11/15 for domestic students. Applications are processed on a rolling basis. Application fee: $45. Electronic applications accepted. *Expenses:* Tuition: Part-time $1,095 per unit. Tuition and fees vary according to degree level and program. *Financial support:* Career-related internships or fieldwork, Federal Work-Study, institutionally sponsored loans, tuition waivers (partial), and unspecified assistantships available. Support available to part-time students. Financial award application deadline: 5/1; financial award applicants required to submit FAFSA. *Unit head:* Dr. Michael Gonzalez, Graduate Program Director, 619-260-4756, Fax: 619-260-2272, E-mail: michaelg@sandiego.edu. *Application contact:* Stephen Pultz, Director of Admissions, 619-260-4524, Fax: 619-260-4158, E-mail: grads@sandiego.edu.

University of Saskatchewan, College of Graduate Studies and Research, College of Arts and Sciences, Department of History, Saskatoon, SK S7N 5A2, Canada. Offers MA, PhD. Part-time programs available. *Degree requirements:* For master's, thesis; for doctorate, thesis/dissertation. *Entrance requirements:* Additional exam requirements/recommendations for international students: Required—TOEFL.

The University of Scranton, Graduate School, Department of History, Scranton, PA 18510. Offers MA. Part-time and evening/weekend programs available. *Degree requirements:* For master's, comprehensive exam, thesis (for some programs), capstone experience. *Entrance requirements:* For master's, minimum GPA of 2.75. Additional exam requirements/recommendations for international students: Required—TOEFL (minimum score 500 paper-based; 173 computer-based), IELTS (minimum score 6). *Faculty research:* American, European, Latin American, Russian, and Chinese history.

University of South Africa, College of Human Sciences, Pretoria, South Africa. Offers adult education (M Ed); African languages (MA, PhD); African politics (MA, PhD); Afrikaans (MA, PhD); ancient history (MA, PhD); ancient Near Eastern studies (MA, PhD); anthropology (MA, PhD); applied linguistics (MA); Arabic (MA, PhD); archaeology (MA); art history (MA); Biblical archaeology (MA); Biblical studies (M Th, D Th, PhD); Christian spirituality (M Th, D Th); church history (M Th, D Th); classical studies (MA, PhD); clinical psychology (MA); communication (MA, PhD); comparative education (M Ed, Ed D); consulting psychology (D Admin, D Com, PhD); curriculum studies (M Ed, Ed D); development studies (M Admin, MA, D Admin, PhD); didactics (M Ed, Ed D); education (M Tech); education management (M Ed, Ed D); educational psychology (M Ed); English (MA); environmental education (M Ed); French (MA, PhD); German (MA, PhD); Greek (MA); guidance and counseling (M Ed); health studies (MA, PhD), including health sciences education (MA), health services management (MA), medical and surgical nursing science (critical care general) (MA), midwifery and neonatal nursing science (MA), trauma and emergency care (MA); history (MA, PhD); history of education (Ed D); inclusive education (M Ed, Ed D); information and communications technology policy and regulation (MA); information science (MA, MIS, PhD); international politics (MA, PhD); Islamic studies (MA, PhD); Italian (MA, PhD); Judaica (MA, PhD); linguistics (MA, PhD); mathematical education (M Ed); mathematics education (MA); missiology (M Th, D Th); modern Hebrew (MA, PhD); musicology (MA, MMus, D Mus, PhD); natural science education (M Ed); New Testament (M Th, D Th); Old Testament (D Th); pastoral therapy (M Th, D Th); philosophy (MA); philosophy of education (M Ed, Ed D); politics (MA, PhD); Portuguese (MA, PhD); practical theology (M Th, D Th); psychology (MA, MS, PhD); psychology of education (M Ed, Ed D); public health (MA); religious studies (MA, D Th, PhD); Romance languages (MA); Russian (MA, PhD); Semitic languages (MA, PhD); social behavior studies in HIV/AIDS (MA); social science (mental health) (MA); social science in development studies (MA); social science in psychology (MA); social science in social work (MA); social science in sociology (MA); social work (MSW, DSW, PhD); socio-education (M Ed, Ed D); sociolinguistics (MA); sociology (MA, PhD); Spanish (MA, PhD); systematic theology (M Th, D Th); TESOL (teaching English to speakers of other languages) (MA); theological ethics (M Th, D Th); theory of literature (MA, PhD); urban ministries (D Th); urban ministry (M Th).

University of South Alabama, Graduate School, College of Arts and Sciences, Department of History, Mobile, AL 36688-0002. Offers MA. Part-time and evening/weekend programs available. *Faculty:* 5 full-time (0 women), 9 part-time/adjunct (5 women). *Students:* 15 full-time (2 women), 7 part-time (3 women); includes 3 minority (all African Americans) 14 applicants, 71% accepted, 8 enrolled. In 2007, 3 degrees awarded. *Degree requirements:* For master's, one foreign language, comprehensive exam, thesis optional. *Entrance requirements:* For master's, GRE General Test, GRE Subject Test, 21 hours of course work in history, minimum GPA of 3.0. *Application deadline:* For fall admission, 9/1 priority date for domestic students. Applications are processed on a rolling basis. Application fee: $25. *Expenses:* Tuition, state resident: full-time $4,224; part-time $176 per credit hour. Tuition, nonresident: full-time $8,448; part-time $352 per credit hour. Required fees: $802. Full-time tuition and fees vary according to program and student level. *Financial support:* Fellowships, research assistantships available. Support available to part-time students. Financial award application deadline: 4/1. *Unit head:* Dr. Clarence Mohr, Chair, 251-460-6210.

University of South Carolina, The Graduate School, College of Arts and Sciences, Department of History, Columbia, SC 29208. Offers history (MA, PhD); public history (MA, Certificate), including archives (MA), historic preservation (MA), museum (MA), museum management (Certificate); MLIS/MA. IMA and MAT offered in cooperation with the College of Education. Part-time programs available. *Faculty:* 38 full-time (7 women). *Students:* 35 full-time (17 women), 5 part-time (all women); includes 2 minority (both African Americans) Average age 33. 127 applicants, 8% accepted, 13 enrolled. In 2007, 3 master's, 3 doctorates awarded. Terminal master's awarded for partial completion of doctoral program. *Degree requirements:* For master's, one foreign language, thesis; for doctorate, one foreign language, thesis/dissertation. *Entrance requirements:* For master's and doctorate, GRE General Test. Additional exam requirements/recommendations for international students: Required—TOEFL. *Application deadline:* For fall admission, 1/5 for domestic students. Application fee: $40. Electronic applications accepted. *Expenses:* Tuition, state resident: part-time $440 per hour. Tuition, nonresident: part-time $936 per hour. Required fees: $17 per hour. Tuition and fees vary according to program. *Financial support:* In 2007–08, 26 teaching assistantships with tuition reimbursements (averaging $14,250 per year) were awarded; fellowships with partial tuition reimbursements, research assistantships with partial tuition reimbursements, career-related internships or fieldwork, Federal Work-Study, and institutionally sponsored loans also available. Financial award application deadline: 1/5. *Faculty research:* U.S. history; European history; Latin American history; history of science and technology. Total annual research expenditures: $15,000. *Unit head:* Lacy K. Ford, Chair, 803-777-5195, Fax: 803-777-4494, E-mail: ford@gwm.sc.edu. *Application contact:* Thomas Brown, Director of Graduate Studies, 803-777-2341, Fax: 803-777-4494, E-mail: browntj@gwm.sc.edu.

The University of South Dakota, Graduate School, College of Arts and Sciences, Department of History, Vermillion, SD 57069-2390. Offers MA, JD/MA. Part-time programs available. *Faculty:* 8 full-time (2 women). *Students:* 19 (5 women). In 2007, 3 degrees awarded. *Degree requirements:* For master's, thesis (for some programs). *Entrance requirements:* For master's, GRE General Test, minimum GPA of 2.7. Additional exam requirements/recommendations for international students: Required—TOEFL (minimum score 550 paper-based; 213 computer-based; 79 iBT). *Application deadline:* Applications are processed on a rolling basis. Application fee: $35. Electronic applications accepted. *Financial support:* In 2007–08, research assistantships with partial tuition reimbursements (averaging $4,626 per year), teaching assistantships with partial tuition reimbursements (averaging $4,626 per year) were awarded; Federal Work-Study, scholarships/grants, and unspecified assistantships also available. Financial award applicants required to submit FAFSA. *Unit head:* Dr. Judith Sebesta, Chair, 605-677-5218, Fax: 605-677-5568, E-mail: history@usd.edu. *Application contact:* Dr. Robert Hilderbrand, Graduate Student Advisor, 605-677-5218, Fax: 605-677-5568, E-mail: history@usd.edu.

University of Southern California, Graduate School, College of Letters, Arts and Sciences, Department of History, Los Angeles, CA 90089. Offers PhD. *Faculty:* 32 full-time (17 women). *Students:* 59 full-time (34 women); includes 11 minority (1 Asian American or Pacific Islander, 10 Hispanic Americans), 12 international. 81 applicants, 20% accepted. In 2007, 6 doctorates awarded. Terminal master's awarded for partial completion of doctoral program. *Degree requirements:* For doctorate, 2 foreign languages, thesis/dissertation. *Entrance requirements:* For doctorate, GRE General Test. *Application deadline:* For fall admission, 12/1 for domestic students. Application fee: $85. *Financial support:* In 2007–08, 55 students received support, including fellowships with full tuition reimbursements available (averaging $20,000 per year), research assistantships with full tuition reimbursements available (averaging $18,800 per year), teaching assistantships with full tuition reimbursements available (averaging $18,800 per year); scholarships/grants also available. Financial award application deadline: 2/15; financial award applicants required to submit FAFSA. *Faculty research:* U.S., Latin America, Europe, Middle East, Central and East Asia. *Unit head:* Dr. Steven Ross, Chair, 213-740-2311, E-mail: history@usc.edu. *Application contact:* Karen Halhumen, Information Contact, 213-740-2311.

University of Southern Mississippi, Graduate School, College of Arts and Letters, Department of History, Hattiesburg, MS 39406-0001. Offers MA, MS, PhD. Part-time programs available. *Faculty:* 19 full-time (6 women). *Students:* 33 full-time (6 women), 30 part-time (12 women); includes 4 minority (2 African Americans, 1 Asian American or Pacific Islander, 1 Hispanic American), 2 international. Average age 34. 35 applicants, 60% accepted, 16 enrolled. In 2007, 2 master's, 2 doctorates awarded. *Degree requirements:* For master's, one foreign language, comprehensive exam, thesis (for some programs); for doctorate, 2 foreign languages, comprehensive exam, thesis/dissertation. *Entrance requirements:* For master's, GRE General Test, minimum GPA of 3.0 in field of study, 2.75 in last 2 years; for doctorate, GRE General Test, minimum GPA of 3.5. Additional exam requirements/recommendations for international students: Required—TOEFL. *Application deadline:* For fall admission, 3/1 priority date for domestic students, 3/1 for international students. Applications are processed on a rolling basis. Application fee: $30. *Financial support:* In 2007–08, 1 research assistantship (averaging $7,840 per year), 26 teaching assistantships with full tuition reimbursements (averaging $7,840 per year) were awarded; fellowships with full tuition reimbursements, Federal Work-Study, scholarships/grants, and unspecified assistantships also available. Financial award application deadline: 3/15. *Faculty research:* Civil War, civil rights, modern European history, war history. *Unit head:* Dr. Phyllis Jestice, Chair, 601-266-4333, Fax: 601-266-4334. *Application contact:* Dr. Michael Niebarg, Graduate Coordinator, 601-266-4333, Fax: 601-266-4334.

University of South Florida, Graduate School, College of Arts and Sciences, Department of History, Tampa, FL 33620-9951. Offers MA. Part-time and evening/weekend programs available. *Faculty:* 16 full-time (6 women). *Students:* 23 full-time (11 women), 46 part-time (14 women); includes 8 minority (2 African Americans, 1 Asian American or Pacific Islander, 5 Hispanic Americans). 32 applicants, 59% accepted, 12 enrolled. In 2007, 10 degrees awarded. *Degree requirements:* For master's, thesis optional. *Entrance requirements:* For master's, GRE General Test, minimum GPA of 3.0 in last 60 hours, 2 letters of recommendation. *Application deadline:* For fall admission, 6/1 priority date for domestic students, 6/1 for international students; for spring admission, 10/15 priority date for domestic students, 10/1 for international students. Applications are processed on a rolling basis. Application fee: $30. Electronic applications accepted. *Financial support:* Application deadline: 4/1. *Faculty research:* U.S. history, European history, Latin American history, medieval history, ancient history. Total annual research expenditures: $139,616. *Unit head:* Dr. William M. Murray, Chairperson, 813-974-6209, Fax: 813-974-6228, E-mail: wmurray@cas.usf.edu. *Application contact:* Dr. Robert P. Ingalls, Graduate Advisor, 813-974-6233, Fax: 813-974-6228, E-mail: ingalls@cas.usf.edu.

The University of Tennessee, Graduate School, College of Arts and Sciences, Department of History, Knoxville, TN 37996. Offers American history (PhD); European history (PhD); history (MA). Part-time programs available. *Degree requirements:* For master's, thesis or alternative; for doctorate, one foreign language, thesis/dissertation. *Entrance requirements:* For master's and doctorate, GRE General Test, minimum GPA of 2.7. Additional exam requirements/recommendations for international students: Required—TOEFL. Electronic applications accepted.

The University of Texas at Arlington, Graduate School, College of Liberal Arts, Department of History, Arlington, TX 76019. Offers history (MA); transatlantic history (PhD). Part-time and evening/weekend programs available. *Faculty:* 10 full-time (2 women). *Students:* 34 full-time (13 women), 79 part-time (24 women); includes 15 minority (5 African Americans, 2 American Indian/Alaska Native, 2 Asian Americans or Pacific Islanders, 6 Hispanic Americans), 7 international. 36 applicants, 69% accepted, 24 enrolled. In 2007, 10 master's, 5 doctorates awarded. *Degree requirements:* For master's, one foreign language, comprehensive exam (for some programs), thesis (for some programs); for doctorate, one foreign language, comprehensive exam, thesis/dissertation. *Entrance requirements:* For master's, GRE General Test, minimum GPA of 3.0 in last 60 hours, 3 letters of recommendation; for doctorate, GRE General Test, minimum graduate GPA of 3.5, 3 letters of recommendation, academic writing sample. Additional exam requirements/recommendations for international students: Required—TOEFL (minimum score 550 paper-based; 213 computer-based). *Application deadline:* For fall admission, 6/16 for domestic students. Applications are processed on a rolling basis. Application fee: $35 ($50 for international students). *Expenses:* Tuition, state resident: full-time $5,934. Tuition, nonresident: full-time $10,938. *Financial support:* In 2007–08, 7 fellowships with full tuition reimbursements, 3 research assistantships (averaging $9,467 per year), 16 teaching assistantships (averaging $12,000 per year) were awarded; career-related internships or fieldwork also available. Financial award application deadline: 5/1; financial award applicants required to submit FAFSA. *Unit head:* Dr. Robert Fairbanks, Chair, 817-272-2861, Fax: 817-272-2852, E-mail: history@uta.edu. *Application contact:* Dr. Thomas Adam, Graduate Advisor, 817-272-2861, Fax: 817-272-2852, E-mail: adam@uta.edu.

The University of Texas at Austin, Graduate School, College of Liberal Arts, Department of History, Austin, TX 78712-1111. Offers MA, PhD. *Degree requirements:* For doctorate, thesis/dissertation. *Entrance requirements:* For master's and doctorate, GRE General Test. Electronic applications accepted. *Faculty research:* U.S., Latin American, European, African, Asian, and Middle Eastern history.

The University of Texas at Brownsville, Graduate Studies, College of Liberal Arts, Department of History, Brownsville, TX 78520-4991. Offers MAIS. Part-time and evening/weekend programs available. *Degree requirements:* For master's, comprehensive exam, thesis optional. *Entrance requirements:* For master's, GRE General Test. Additional exam requirements/recommendations for international students: Required—TOEFL.

The University of Texas at El Paso, Graduate School, College of Liberal Arts, Department of History, El Paso, TX 79968-0001. Offers border history (MA); history (MA, PhD). Part-time and evening/weekend programs available. *Degree requirements:* For master's, thesis optional; for doctorate, thesis/dissertation. *Entrance requirements:* For master's and doctorate, GRE General Test, minimum GPA of 3.0 in major. Additional exam requirements/recommendations for international students: Required—TOEFL. Electronic applications accepted.

The University of Texas at San Antonio, College of Liberal and Fine Arts, Department of History, San Antonio, TX 78249-0617. Offers MA. Part-time and evening/weekend programs available. *Faculty:* 11 full-time (4 women). *Students:* 18 full-time (7 women), 59 part-time (28 women); includes 30 minority (2 African Americans, 1 American Indian/Alaska Native, 3 Asian Americans or Pacific Islanders, 24 Hispanic Americans). Average age 37. 41 applicants, 80% accepted, 32 enrolled. In 2007, 21 degrees awarded. *Degree requirements:* For master's, comprehensive exam, thesis optional. *Entrance requirements:* For master's, GRE, minimum GPA of 3.0 in last 60 hours. Additional exam requirements/recommendations for international students: Required—TOEFL (minimum score 500 paper-based; 173 computer-based). *Application deadline:* For fall admission, 7/1 for domestic students, 4/1 for international students; for spring admission, 11/1 for domestic students, 9/1 for international students. Applications are processed on a rolling basis. Application fee: $45 ($80 for international students). Electronic applications accepted. *Financial support:* In 2007–08, 4 research assistantships (averaging $2,805 per year) were awarded; career-related internships or fieldwork, Federal Work-Study, scholarships/grants, and unspecified assistantships also available. Total annual research expenditures: $55,726. *Unit head:* Dr. John Reynolds, Chair, 210-458-4033, Fax: 210-458-4796, E-mail: history@utsa.edu. *Application contact:* Dr. Anne Hardgrove, Graduate Advisor, 210-458-7402, E-mail: ahardgrove@utsa.edu.

The University of Texas at Tyler, College of Arts and Sciences, Department of History, Tyler, TX 75799-0001. Offers history (MA). Part-time and evening/weekend programs available. *Faculty:* 5 full-time (1 woman). *Students:* 4 full-time (2 women), 11 part-time (5 women); includes 1 Hispanic American. Average age 38. 5 applicants, 100% accepted, 4 enrolled. In 2007, 1 degree awarded. *Degree requirements:* For master's, one foreign language, comprehensive exam, thesis optional. *Entrance requirements:* For master's, GRE General Test, minimum GPA of 3.0. *Application deadline:* Applications are processed on a rolling basis. Application fee: $0. Electronic applications accepted. *Expenses:* Tuition, state resident: part-time $627 per semester hour. Tuition, nonresident: part-time $908 per semester hour. Required fees: $107 per semester hour. Tuition and fees vary according to course load. *Financial support:* Federal Work-Study and unspecified assistantships available. Support available to part-time students. Financial award application deadline: 7/1; financial award applicants required to submit FAFSA. *Faculty research:* Early and modern U.S. history, early modern and modern European history. *Unit head:* Dr. Vincent J. Falzone, Chair, 903-566-7395, Fax: 903-565-5700, E-mail: vfalzone@mail.uttyl.edu. *Application contact:* Pam Morrow, Assistant to Dean for Enrollment Management, 903-566-7205, Fax: 903-566-7068, E-mail: pmorrow@uttyler.edu.

The University of Texas of the Permian Basin, Office of Graduate Studies, College of Arts and Sciences, Department of Humanities and Fine Arts, Program in History, Odessa, TX 79762-0001. Offers MA. Part-time and evening/weekend programs available. *Degree requirements:* For master's, comprehensive exam (for some programs), thesis (for some programs). *Entrance requirements:* For master's, GRE General Test. Additional exam requirements/recommendations for international students: Required—TOEFL (minimum score 550 paper-based; 213 computer-based).

The University of Texas–Pan American, College of Arts and Humanities, Department of History, Edinburg, TX 78541-2999. Offers MA, MAIS. Part-time and evening/weekend programs available. *Degree requirements:* For master's, comprehensive exam, thesis or alternative. *Entrance requirements:* For master's, GRE General Test, minimum GPA of 3.0. *Faculty research:* Texas-Mexican legacy, modern America, Southwest, labor, modern Europe.

The University of Toledo, College of Graduate Studies, College of Arts and Sciences, Department of History, Toledo, OH 43606-3390. Offers MA, PhD. Part-time programs available. *Faculty:* 23. *Students:* 19 full-time (10 women), 10 part-time (4 women); includes 1 minority (African American) Average age 32. 31 applicants, 55% accepted, 12 enrolled. In 2007, 7 master's, 2 doctorates awarded. *Degree requirements:* For doctorate, one foreign language, thesis/dissertation, oral and written exams. *Entrance requirements:* For master's, GRE General Test, minimum GPA of 2.7; for doctorate, GRE General Test, minimum GPA of 3.0. *Application deadline:* For fall admission, 1/15 priority date for domestic students. Applications are processed on a rolling basis. Application fee: $45. Electronic applications accepted. *Financial support:* In 2007–08, 18 teaching assistantships with full tuition reimbursements (averaging $9,400 per year) were awarded; Federal Work-Study, institutionally sponsored loans, scholarships/grants, tuition waivers (full), and unspecified assistantships also available. Financial award application deadline: 4/1; financial award applicants required to submit FAFSA. *Faculty research:* U.S. diplomatic history, U.S. history, urban history, public history, European history. *Unit head:* Dr. William O'Neal, Interim Chair, 419-530-2242, E-mail: william.oneal@utoledo.edu.

See Close-Up on page 425.

University of Toronto, School of Graduate Studies, Humanities Division, Department of History, Toronto, ON M5S 1A1, Canada. Offers MA, PhD. Part-time programs available. *Faculty:* 81 full-time, 4 part-time/adjunct. *Students:* 166 full-time (88 women), 6 part-time, 34 international. 381 applicants, 38% accepted. In 2007, 26 master's, 7 doctorates awarded. *Degree requirements:* For master's, one foreign language, thesis optional, thesis or research essay, French language exam; for doctorate, comprehensive exam, thesis/dissertation, oral examination/thesis defense. *Entrance requirements:* For master's, minimum B+ average or GPA of 3.3, 6 full academic year history courses; for doctorate, MA in history, minimum A– average or GPA of 3.7. *Application deadline:* For fall admission, 1/15 for domestic students. Application fee: $100 Canadian dollars. *Financial support:* Teaching assistantships available. *Unit head:* Prof. Jane Abray, Chair, 416-978-3369, Fax: 416-978-4810. *Application contact:* Davina Joseph, Graduate Administrator, 416-978-3369, Fax: 416-978-4810, E-mail: histgrad@chass.utoronto.ca.

University of Tulsa, Graduate School, College of Arts and Sciences, Department of History, Tulsa, OK 74104-3189. Offers MA, MTA, JD/MA. Part-time programs available. *Faculty:* 13 full-time (5 women). *Students:* 6 full-time (all women), 13 part-time (5 women); includes 1 minority (American Indian/Alaska Native). Average age 36. 21 applicants, 67% accepted, 11 enrolled. In 2007, 7 degrees awarded. *Degree requirements:* For master's, one foreign language, comprehensive exam or oral defense of thesis. *Entrance requirements:* For master's, GRE General Test, writing sample. Additional exam requirements/recommendations for international students: Required—TOEFL (minimum score 575 paper-based; 231 computer-based; 91 iBT), IELTS (minimum score 7). *Application deadline:* Applications are processed on a rolling basis. Application fee: $40. Electronic applications accepted. *Expenses:* Tuition: Full-time $14,004; part-time $778 per credit hour. Required fees: $60; $30 per term. Tuition and fees vary according to course load. *Financial support:* In 2007–08, 8 students received support, including 2 fellowships with full and partial tuition reimbursements available (averaging $13,700 per year), 1 research assistantship (averaging $10,734 per year), 5 teaching assistantships with full and partial tuition reimbursements available (averaging $10,734 per year); Federal Work-Study, scholarships/grants, tuition waivers (full and partial), and unspecified assistantships also available. Support available to part-time students. Financial award application deadline: 2/1; financial award applicants required to submit FAFSA. *Faculty research:* England, France, Latin America, and Russia; diplomatic history; 19th century American history; women's history, cultural history. *Unit head:* Dr. Thomas Buoye, Chairperson, 918-631-2825, Fax: 918-631-2057, E-mail: thomas-buoye@utulsa.edu. *Application contact:* Dr. Christine Ruane, Adviser, 918-631-3814, Fax: 918-631-2057, E-mail: christine-ruane@utulsa.edu.

University of Utah, The Graduate School, College of Humanities, Department of History, Salt Lake City, UT 84112-1107. Offers MA, MS, PhD. Part-time and evening/weekend programs available. *Faculty:* 31 full-time (9 women), 1 part-time/adjunct (0 women). *Students:* 35 full-time (10 women), 28 part-time (14 women); includes 3 minority (all Asian Americans or Pacific Islanders), 1 international. Average age 34. 62 applicants, 53% accepted, 17 enrolled. In 2007, 15 master's, 5 doctorates awarded. Terminal master's awarded for partial completion of doctoral program. *Degree requirements:* For master's, one foreign language, thesis (for some programs); for doctorate, 2 foreign languages, comprehensive exam, thesis/dissertation. *Entrance requirements:* For master's, GRE General Test, minimum GPA of 3.2; for doctorate, GRE General Test, minimum graduate GPA of 3.6. Additional exam requirements/recommendations for international students: Required—TOEFL (minimum score 500 paper-based; 173 computer-based). *Application deadline:* For fall admission, 1/15 for domestic and international students. Application fee: $45 ($65 for international students). Electronic applications accepted. *Financial support:* In 2007–08, 13 students received support, including 3 fellowships (averaging $12,000 per year), 14 teaching assistantships with full tuition reimbursements available (averaging $11,000 per year); career-related internships or fieldwork also available. Financial award application deadline: 1/15; financial award applicants required to submit FAFSA. *Faculty research:* U.S. history, European history, U.S. African-American studies, Middle East, Latin America. Total annual research expenditures: $66,787. *Unit head:* Dr. James Lehning, Chair, 801-581-5685, Fax: 801-585-0580, E-mail: jim.lehning@utah.edu. *Application contact:* Sarah Orton, Graduate Secretary, 801-581-5201, Fax: 801-585-0580, E-mail: sarah.orton@history.utah.edu.

University of Utah, The Graduate School, College of Humanities, Program in Middle East Studies, Salt Lake City, UT 84112-1107. Offers anthropology (MA); Arabic (MA, PhD); Arabic and linguistics (MA, PhD); Hebrew (MA); history (MA, PhD); Persian (MA, PhD); political science (MA, PhD); Turkish (MA). *Faculty:* 12 full-time (3 women). *Students:* 26 full-time (12 women), 10 part-time (2 women); includes 1 minority (Asian American or Pacific Islander), 10 international. Average age 36. 36 applicants, 78% accepted, 10 enrolled. In 2007, 6 master's awarded. Terminal master's awarded for partial completion of doctoral program. *Median time to degree:* Of those who began their doctoral program in fall 1999, 100% received their degree in 8 years or less. *Degree requirements:* For master's, 2 foreign languages, comprehensive exam, thesis optional; for doctorate, 3 foreign languages, comprehensive exam, thesis/dissertation. *Entrance requirements:* For master's, GRE General Test, minimum GPA of 3.2; for doctorate, GRE General Test, MA in Middle East studies or equivalent, minimum GPA of 3.2. Additional exam requirements/recommendations for international students: Required—TOEFL (minimum score 580 paper-based; 237 computer-based; 92 iBT). *Application deadline:* For fall admission, 1/15 for domestic and international students; for spring admission, 9/15 for domestic and international students. Application fee: $45 ($65 for international students). *Financial support:* In 2007–08, 17 students received support, including 14 fellowships with full tuition reimbursements available (averaging $14,000 per year), 2 teaching assistantships with full tuition reimbursements available (averaging $12,000 per year); unspecified assistantships also available. Financial award application deadline: 1/15. *Faculty research:* Arabic literature and linguistics, Islamic studies, Middle East history, political science, Judaic studies. *Unit head:* Dr. Ibrahim A. Karawan, Director, 801-581-6181, Fax: 801-581-6183, E-mail: ibrahim.

History

University of Utah (continued)
karawan@poli-sci.utah.edu. *Application contact:* Peter von Sivers, Director of Graduate Studies, 801-581-8073, Fax: 801-581-6183, E-mail: peter.vonsivers@utah.edu.

University of Vermont, Graduate College, College of Arts and Sciences, Department of History, Burlington, VT 05405. Offers MA. *Students:* 23 (11 women); includes 1 minority (American Indian/Alaska Native). 29 applicants, 59% accepted, 7 enrolled. In 2007, 2 degrees awarded. *Degree requirements:* For master's, thesis. *Entrance requirements:* For master's, GRE General Test, sample project. Additional exam requirements/recommendations for international students: Required—TOEFL (minimum score 550 paper-based; 213 computer-based; 80 iBT). *Application deadline:* For fall admission, 3/1 priority date for domestic students. Applications are processed on a rolling basis. Application fee: $40. Electronic applications accepted. *Financial support:* Fellowships, research assistantships, teaching assistantships, career-related internships or fieldwork available. Financial award application deadline: 3/1. *Faculty research:* American, European, and Asian history. *Unit head:* Chair, 802-656-3180. *Application contact:* Paul Deslandes, Coordinator, 802-656-3180.

University of Victoria, Faculty of Graduate Studies, Faculty of Humanities, Department of History, Victoria, BC V8W 2Y2, Canada. Offers MA, PhD. Part-time programs available. *Faculty:* 25 full-time (7 women), 3 part-time/adjunct (1 woman). *Students:* 64, 2 international. Average age 29. 71 applicants, 42% accepted, 19 enrolled. In 2007, 8 master's, 1 doctorate awarded. *Degree requirements:* For master's, one foreign language, thesis; for doctorate, one foreign language, comprehensive exam, thesis/dissertation. *Entrance requirements:* Additional exam requirements/recommendations for international students: Required—TOEFL (minimum score 600 paper-based; 250 computer-based), TWE. *Application deadline:* For fall admission, 1/15 for domestic students, 12/15 priority date for international students. Applications are processed on a rolling basis. Application fee: $75 ($125 for international students). Electronic applications accepted. *Expenses:* Tuition, state resident: full-time $3,110. International tuition: $3,700 full-time. Tuition and fees vary according to program. *Financial support:* In 2007–08, 28 fellowships, 9 research assistantships, 29 teaching assistantships were awarded; career-related internships or fieldwork, institutionally sponsored loans, and scholarships/grants also available. Financial award application deadline: 2/1. *Faculty research:* Canadian social history, Canadian gender history, Canadian native history, Canadian military history, British Columbian history, Western history, medieval history, world history. *Unit head:* Dr. Thomas J. Saunders, Chair, 250-721-7381, Fax: 250-721-8772, E-mail: histchr@uvic.ca. *Application contact:* Dr. Elizabeth Vibert, Graduate Adviser, 250-721-7286, Fax: 250-721-8772, E-mail: evibert@uvic.ca.

University of Virginia, College and Graduate School of Arts and Sciences, Department of History, Charlottesville, VA 22903. Offers MA, PhD, JD/MA. *Faculty:* 39 full-time (6 women), 4 part-time/adjunct (1 woman). *Students:* 110 full-time (35 women), 1 part-time; includes 6 minority (3 African Americans, 3 Hispanic Americans), 8 international. Average age 30. 219 applicants, 28% accepted, 25 enrolled. In 2007, 21 master's, 5 doctorates awarded. *Degree requirements:* For master's, one foreign language, thesis; for doctorate, variable foreign language requirement, comprehensive exam, thesis/dissertation. *Entrance requirements:* For master's and doctorate, GRE General Test, GRE Subject Test. *Application deadline:* Applications are processed on a rolling basis. Application fee: $60. Electronic applications accepted. *Financial support:* Applicants required to submit FAFSA. *Unit head:* Duane J. Osheim, Chair, 434-924-7146, Fax: 434-924-7891, E-mail: history@virginia.edu.

University of Washington, Graduate School, College of Arts and Sciences, Department of History, Seattle, WA 98195. Offers MA, PhD. Part-time programs available. *Degree requirements:* For master's, one foreign language, comprehensive exam, thesis optional; for doctorate, one foreign language, comprehensive exam, thesis/dissertation. *Entrance requirements:* For master's and doctorate, GRE, minimum GPA of 3.0. Additional exam requirements/recommendations for international students: Required—TOEFL. Electronic applications accepted. *Faculty research:* U.S., Asia, Europe, comparative history.

University of Waterloo, Graduate Studies, Faculty of Arts, Department of Classical Studies, Waterloo, ON N2L 3G1, Canada. Offers ancient Mediterranean cultures (MA). *Degree requirements:* For master's, one foreign language. *Entrance requirements:* For master's, BA, B+. Application fee: $75. *Financial support:* Fellowships, research assistantships, teaching assistantships available. *Faculty research:* Ancient history, philosophy, anthropology, religion, culture. *Unit head:* Dr. Riemer Faber, Chair, Classical Studies, E-mail: rfarber@uwaterloo.ca. *Application contact:* Dr. David Porreca, Graduate Officer, E-mail: dporreca@uwaterloo.ca.

University of Waterloo, Graduate Studies, Faculty of Arts, Department of History, Waterloo, ON N2L 3G1, Canada. Offers MA, PhD. Part-time and evening/weekend programs available. *Faculty:* 12 full-time (4 women), 7 part-time/adjunct (3 women). *Students:* 62. 111 applicants, 63% accepted, 16 enrolled. In 2007, 13 master's, 2 doctorates awarded. *Degree requirements:* For master's, one foreign language, thesis optional; for doctorate, one foreign language, thesis/dissertation. *Entrance requirements:* For master's, honors degree, minimum B+ average, resumé; for doctorate, master's degree, minimum A average, resumé, writing sample. Additional exam requirements/recommendations for international students: Required—TOEFL, TWE. *Application deadline:* For fall admission, 2/1 priority date for domestic students. Application fee: $75 Canadian dollars. Electronic applications accepted. *Financial support:* Research assistantships, teaching assistantships, career-related internships or fieldwork and scholarships/grants available. *Faculty research:* Canadian, British, international, modern, European, and U.S. history; women's history; imperialism and slavery. *Unit head:* Dr. P. J. Harrigan, Chair, 519-888-4567 Ext. 3768, Fax: 519-746-2658, E-mail: harrigan@watarts.uwaterloo.ca. *Application contact:* Dr. Bruce Muirhead, Associate Dean of the Arts, Graduate Studies and Research, 519-888-4567 Ext. 33133, Fax: 519-725-1749, E-mail: muirhead@watarts.uwaterloo.ca.

The University of Western Ontario, Faculty of Graduate Studies, Social Sciences Division, Department of History, London, ON N6A 5B8, Canada. Offers MA, PhD. Part-time programs available. *Faculty:* 35 full-time (7 women). *Students:* 51 full-time (26 women), 2 part-time (1 woman), 1 international. 67 applicants, 36% accepted. In 2007, 5 master's, 2 doctorates awarded. *Degree requirements:* For master's, one foreign language, thesis (for some programs); for doctorate, one foreign language, thesis/dissertation. *Entrance requirements:* For master's, minimum B+ average on last 10 senior courses; for doctorate, minimum A-average on MA or last year honors degree. Additional exam requirements/recommendations for international students: Required—TOEFL. *Application deadline:* For fall admission, 2/1 for domestic and international students. Applications are processed on a rolling basis. Application fee: $50. *Financial support:* In 2007–08, 37 students received support, including teaching assistantships (averaging $9,000 Canadian dollars per year); fellowships with tuition reimbursements available, career-related internships or fieldwork also available. Financial award application deadline: 4/1. *Faculty research:* Canadian, U.S., Britain, Modern Europe, British Empire and Commonwealth Latin America. Total annual research expenditures: $115,667. *Unit head:* Dr. J. J. B. Forster, Chair, 519-661-2111 Ext. 83647, Fax: 519-661-3010, E-mail: chair-history@uwo.ca. *Application contact:* Chris Speed, Graduate Affairs Assistant, 519-661-3646, Fax: 519-661-3010, E-mail: speed@uwo.ca.

University of West Florida, College of Arts and Sciences: Arts, Department of History, Pensacola, FL 32514-5750. Offers historic preservation (MA); history (MA); public history (MA). Part-time and evening/weekend programs available. *Faculty:* 6 full-time (2 women), 2 part-time/adjunct (both women). *Students:* 15 full-time (9 women), 27 part-time (14 women); includes 5 minority (2 African Americans, 2 American Indian/Alaska Native, 1 Hispanic American), 1 international. Average age 33. 22 applicants, 100% accepted, 15 enrolled. In 2007, 14 degrees awarded. *Degree requirements:* For master's, thesis or alternative. *Entrance requirements:* For master's, GRE General Test, minimum GPA of 3.0, minimum 15 hours of upper-level history courses. Additional exam requirements/recommendations for international students: Required—TOEFL (minimum score 550 paper-based; 213 computer-based). *Application deadline:* For fall admission, 6/1 for domestic students, 5/15 for international students; for spring admission, 11/1 for domestic students, 10/1 for international students. Applications are processed on a rolling basis. Application fee: $30. *Expenses:* Tuition, state resident: full-time $6,054; part-time $252 per credit. Tuition, nonresident: full-time $21,886; part-time $912 per credit. *Financial support:* In 2007–08, 3 research assistantships with partial tuition reimbursements (averaging $5,640 per year) were awarded; fellowships, teaching assistantships with partial tuition reimbursements, Federal Work-Study, institutionally sponsored loans, scholarships/grants, and unspecified assistantships also available. Financial award application deadline: 4/15; financial award applicants required to submit FAFSA. *Unit head:* Dr. John J. Clune, Chairperson, 850-474-2680.

University of West Georgia, Graduate School, College of Arts and Sciences, Department of History, Program in History, Carrollton, GA 30118. Offers MA. *Students:* 23 full-time (14 women), 15 part-time (7 women); includes 3 African Americans, 1 Hispanic American. Average age 33. In 2007, 8 degrees awarded. Application fee: $30. *Expenses:* Tuition, state resident: full-time $2,448; part-time $136 per semester hour. Tuition, nonresident: full-time $9,774; part-time $543 per semester hour. Required fees: $26 per semester hour. $173 per semester. *Application contact:* Dr. Charles W. Clark, Interim Dean, 678-839-6508, E-mail: cclark@westga.edu.

University of Windsor, Faculty of Graduate Studies, Faculty of Arts and Social Sciences, Department of History, Windsor, ON N9B 3P4, Canada. Offers MA. Part-time programs available. *Faculty:* 9 full-time (4 women). *Students:* 26 full-time (13 women). 46 applicants, 54% accepted. In 2007, 5 degrees awarded. *Degree requirements:* For master's, thesis (for some programs). *Entrance requirements:* For master's, minimum B average. Additional exam requirements/recommendations for international students: Required—TOEFL (minimum score 600 paper-based; 250 computer-based). *Application deadline:* For fall admission, 7/1 priority date for domestic students. Applications are processed on a rolling basis. Application fee: $55. Electronic applications accepted. *Financial support:* In 2007–08, 17 teaching assistantships (averaging $8,901 per year) were awarded; Federal Work-Study, tuition waivers (full and partial), unspecified assistantships, and bursary also available. Financial award application deadline: 2/15. *Faculty research:* Gender history, social-history questions about class gender and national identity, divorce in France: 1792-1816, gender and sexuality in Western Europe during the high and later Middle Ages, U.S.-Canadian comparisons in women's history. *Unit head:* Dr. Peter Way, Head, 519-253-4232 Ext. 2318, E-mail: peterway@uwindsor.ca. *Application contact:* Applicant Services, 519-253-3000 Ext. 7014, Fax: 519-971-3653, E-mail: gradadmit@uwindsor.ca.

The University of Winnipeg, Graduate Studies, Department of History, Winnipeg, MB R3B 2E9, Canada. Offers MA. Part-time and evening/weekend programs available. *Degree requirements:* For master's, one foreign language, comprehensive exam or thesis. *Faculty research:* Canadian social history, European diplomacy, Indian history, colonial America, medieval history.

University of Wisconsin–Eau Claire, College of Arts and Sciences, Department of History, Eau Claire, WI 54702-4004. Offers MA. *Faculty:* 11 full-time (4 women). *Students:* 16 full-time (6 women), 9 part-time (6 women); includes 6 minority (3 American Indian/Alaska Native, 3 Asian Americans or Pacific Islanders). Average age 29. 9 applicants, 89% accepted, 7 enrolled. In 2007, 6 degrees awarded. *Degree requirements:* For master's, thesis optional, 30-credit with thesis, 33-credit non-thesis. *Entrance requirements:* For master's, minimum GPA of 3.15 during last 2 years, minimum GPA of 3.3 in history, or 3.0 overall, research paper. *Application deadline:* For fall admission, 3/1 for domestic students; for spring admission, 12/1 for domestic students. Applications are processed on a rolling basis. Application fee: $45. Electronic applications accepted. *Expenses:* Tuition, state resident: full-time $6,870; part-time $381 per credit. Tuition, nonresident: full-time $17,480; part-time $971 per credit. Tuition and fees vary according to reciprocity agreements. *Financial support:* In 2007–08, 15 students received support, including fellowships (averaging $1,000 per year), 3 teaching assistantships (averaging $6,000 per year); Federal Work-Study also available. Financial award application deadline: 4/15; financial award applicants required to submit FAFSA. *Unit head:* Dr. John Mann, Interim Program Director, 715-836-5850, Fax: 715-836-3540, E-mail: mannjw@uwec.edu.

University of Wisconsin–Madison, Graduate School, College of Letters and Science, Department of History, Madison, WI 53706-1380. Offers MA, PhD. Terminal master's awarded for partial completion of doctoral program. *Degree requirements:* For master's, thesis (for some programs); for doctorate, variable foreign language requirement, thesis/dissertation. *Entrance requirements:* For master's and doctorate, GRE General Test. Additional exam requirements/recommendations for international students: Required—Michigan English Language Assessment Battery or TOEFL. Electronic applications accepted. *Faculty research:* American, African, European, Asian, Latin American, and Middle Eastern history.

University of Wisconsin–Milwaukee, Graduate School, College of Letters and Sciences, Department of History, Milwaukee, WI 53201-0413. Offers MA, PhD, MLIS/MA. Part-time programs available. *Faculty:* 33 full-time (12 women). *Students:* 27 full-time (15 women), 41 part-time (14 women); includes 6 minority (2 African Americans, 1 American Indian/Alaska Native, 3 Hispanic Americans). 70 applicants, 64% accepted, 15 enrolled. In 2007, 17 master's awarded. *Degree requirements:* For master's, thesis or alternative. *Entrance requirements:* For master's, GRE General Test. *Application deadline:* For fall admission, 1/1 priority date for domestic students; for spring admission, 9/1 for domestic students. Applications are processed on a rolling basis. Application fee: $45 ($75 for international students). *Expenses:* Tuition, state resident: part-time $530 per credit. Tuition, nonresident: part-time $1,428 per credit. Required fees: $19 per credit. $229 per term. Tuition and fees vary according to course load and program. *Financial support:* In 2007–08, 22 teaching assistantships were awarded; fellowships, research assistantships, career-related internships or fieldwork and unspecified assistantships also available. Support available to part-time students. Financial award application deadline: 4/15. *Unit head:* Martha Carlin, Representative, 414-229-4361, Fax: 414-229-2435, E-mail: carlin@uwm.edu.

University of Wisconsin–Stevens Point, College of Letters and Science, Department of History, Stevens Point, WI 54481-3897. Offers MST. *Degree requirements:* For master's, thesis or alternative. *Application deadline:* For fall admission, 5/1 priority date for domestic students. Applications are processed on a rolling basis. Application fee: $45. *Expenses:* Tuition, state resident: full-time $6,161. Tuition, nonresident: full-time $16,771. Required fees: $884. Tuition and fees vary according to course load. *Financial support:* Federal Work-Study and unspecified assistantships available. Financial award application deadline: 5/1; financial award applicants required to submit FAFSA. *Unit head:* Dr. Greg Summers, Chair, 715-346-2334, Fax: 715-346-4489.

University of Wyoming, Graduate School, College of Arts and Sciences, Department of History, Laramie, WY 82070. Offers MA, MAT. Part-time programs available. *Faculty:* 11 full-time (4 women). *Students:* 17 full-time (7 women), 10 part-time (4 women); includes 1 minority (Hispanic American), 2 international. Average age 31. 20 applicants, 75% accepted, 11 enrolled. In 2007, 5 degrees awarded. *Degree requirements:* For master's, one foreign language, thesis (for some programs). *Entrance requirements:* For master's, GRE General Test, minimum GPA of 3.0, 12 semester hours of undergraduate course work in history. Additional exam requirements/recommendations for international students: Required—TOEFL. *Application deadline:* For fall admission, 2/1 priority date for domestic and international students. Applications are processed on a rolling basis. Application fee: $50. Electronic applications accepted. *Financial support:* In 2007–08, 9 students received support, including 7 teaching assistantships with tuition reimbursements available (averaging $10,062 per year); career-related internships or fieldwork, Federal Work-Study, institutionally sponsored loans, and health care benefits also available. Financial award application deadline: 3/1; financial award applicants required to submit FAFSA. *Faculty research:* American West, Native American history, nineteenth and twentieth century U.S. history, European history, Asian studies. Total annual research expenditures: $13,000. *Unit head:* Dr. Mark D. Potter, Head, 307-766-5101, Fax: 307-766-5192, E-mail: mpotter@uwyo.edu. *Application contact:* Douglas R. Johnson, Office Associate, 307-766-5101, E-mail: djohnson@uwyo.edu.

Utah State University, School of Graduate Studies, College of Humanities, Arts and Social Sciences, Department of History, Logan, UT 84322. Offers MA, MS. Part-time and evening/weekend programs available. *Degree requirements:* For master's, one foreign language, thesis. *Entrance requirements:* For master's, GRE General Test, minimum GPA of 3.0. Additional exam requirements/recommendations for international students: Required—TOEFL. Electronic applications accepted. *Faculty research:* U.S. race and ethnicity, early modern and modern Europe, environmental history, western regional history.

Valdosta State University, Graduate School, College of Arts and Sciences, Department of History, Valdosta, GA 31698. Offers MA. Part-time programs available. *Faculty:* 11 full-time (3 women). *Students:* 2 full-time (0 women), 3 part-time (2 women). Average age 23. 2 applicants, 0% accepted. In 2007, 1 degree awarded. *Degree requirements:* For master's, one foreign language, thesis optional, comprehensive written and/or oral exams. *Entrance requirements:* For master's, GRE General Test, minimum GPA of 2.5. Additional exam requirements/recommendations for international students: Required—TOEFL (minimum score 523 paper-based; 193 computer-based). *Application deadline:* For fall admission, 5/15 for domestic and international students; for spring admission, 11/15 for domestic and international students. Applications are processed on a rolling basis. Application fee: $40. Electronic applications accepted. *Expenses:* Tuition, state resident: part-time $147 per hour. Tuition, nonresident: part-time $586 per hour. Required fees: $520 per semester. Tuition and fees vary according to course level, course load, campus/location and program. *Financial support:* In 2007–08, 1 research assistantship with full tuition reimbursement (averaging $2,452 per year), 1 teaching assistantship with full tuition reimbursement (averaging $2,800 per year) were awarded; scholarships/grants and unspecified assistantships also available. Support available to part-time students. Financial award application deadline: 7/1; financial award applicants required to submit FAFSA. *Faculty research:* Georgia history, U.S. history, Napoleonic France, American diplomatic history, English history. *Unit head:* Dr. Paul Riggs, Head, 229-333-5947, Fax: 229-249-4865.

Valparaiso University, Graduate Division, Program in Liberal Studies, Concentration in History, Valparaiso, IN 46383. Offers MALS, Post-Master's Certificate, JD/MALS. Part-time and evening/weekend programs available. *Students:* 6 full-time (3 women), 6 part-time (3 women); includes 1 minority (Asian American or Pacific Islander) Average age 26. *Entrance requirements:* For master's, minimum GPA of 3.0. Additional exam requirements/recommendations for international students: Required—TOEFL (minimum score 550 paper-based; 213 computer-based). *Application deadline:* Applications are processed on a rolling basis. Application fee: $30 ($50 for international students). Electronic applications accepted. *Financial support:* Available to part-time students. Applicants required to submit FAFSA. *Faculty research:* Regional Chinese history, British history, Martin Luther, Latin American history, African history. *Application contact:* Jamie Haney, Coordinator of Recruitment Activities, 219-464-5313, Fax: 219-464-5381, E-mail: jamie.haney@valpo.edu.

Vanderbilt University, Graduate School, Department of History, Nashville, TN 37240-1001. Offers MA, MAT, PhD. *Faculty:* 34 full-time (9 women). *Students:* 39 full-time (18 women), 6 part-time (3 women); includes 8 minority (5 African Americans, 1 Asian American or Pacific Islander, 2 Hispanic Americans), 8 international. Average age 30. 131 applicants, 15% accepted, 11 enrolled. In 2007, 3 master's, 3 doctorates awarded. *Degree requirements:* For master's, one foreign language, thesis; for doctorate, one foreign language, thesis/dissertation, final and qualifying exams. *Entrance requirements:* For master's and doctorate, GRE General Test, sample of written work (recommended). *Application deadline:* For fall admission, 1/15 for domestic and international students. Application fee: $0. Electronic applications accepted. *Financial support:* Fellowships with full tuition reimbursements, teaching assistantships with full tuition reimbursements, Federal Work-Study, institutionally sponsored loans, and health care benefits available. Financial award application deadline: 1/15; financial award applicants required to submit CSS PROFILE or FAFSA. *Faculty research:* Southern American history, recent U.S. history, intellectual and cultural history, European history, Latin American history. *Unit head:* Elizabeth Lunback, Chair, 615-322-2575, Fax: 615-343-6002. *Application contact:* Katherine B. Crawford, Director of Graduate Studies, 615-322-2755, Fax: 615-343-6002, E-mail: kathering.b.crawford@vanderbilt.edu.

Villanova University, Graduate School of Liberal Arts and Sciences, Department of History, Villanova, PA 19085-1699. Offers MA. Part-time and evening/weekend programs available. *Faculty:* 9 full-time (4 women). *Students:* 20 full-time (10 women), 49 part-time (20 women); includes 6 minority (4 African Americans, 2 Hispanic Americans), 3 international. Average age 27. 66 applicants, 76% accepted. In 2007, 24 degrees awarded. *Degree requirements:* For master's, comprehensive exam, thesis optional. *Entrance requirements:* For master's, GRE General Test, minimum GPA of 3.0. *Application deadline:* For fall admission, 5/1 for domestic and international students; for spring admission, 11/15 for domestic and international students. Applications are processed on a rolling basis. Application fee: $50. Electronic applications accepted. *Financial support:* Research assistantships, Federal Work-Study and scholarships/grants available. Financial award applicants required to submit FAFSA. *Unit head:* Dr. Adele Lindenmeyr, Chairperson, 610-519-4660.

See Close-Up on page 427.

Virginia Commonwealth University, Graduate School, College of Humanities and Sciences, Department of History, Richmond, VA 23284-9005. Offers MA. Part-time programs available. *Faculty:* 16 full-time (4 women). *Students:* 15 full-time (8 women), 26 part-time (10 women); includes 4 minority (1 African American, 1 American Indian/Alaska Native, 2 Asian Americans or Pacific Islanders). 33 applicants, 64% accepted, 10 enrolled. In 2007, 11 degrees awarded. *Degree requirements:* For master's, thesis optional. *Entrance requirements:* For master's, GRE General Test, 30 undergraduate credits in history. *Application deadline:* For fall admission, 3/1 for domestic students; for spring admission, 12/1 for domestic students. Application fee: $50. *Expenses:* Tuition, state resident: full-time $7,224; part-time $401 per credit. Tuition, nonresident: full-time $16,072; part-time $891 per credit. Required fees: $1,679; $63 per credit. Tuition and fees vary according to campus/location. *Financial support:* Research assistantships, teaching assistantships available. *Unit head:* Dr. Bernard Moitt, Chair, 804-828-9755, Fax: 804-828-7085, E-mail: bmoitt@vcu.edu. *Application contact:* Dr. John E. Herman, Director, 804-828-2856, Fax: 804-828-7085, E-mail: jeherman@vcu.edu.

See Close-Up on page 457.

Virginia Commonwealth University, Graduate School, School of the Arts, Department of Art History, Richmond, VA 23284-9005. Offers architectural history (MA); art history (MA, PhD); historical studies (MA); museum studies (MA). *Accreditation:* NASAD. *Faculty:* 10 full-time (4 women). *Students:* 19 full-time (18 women), 24 part-time (20 women); includes 6 minority (2 African Americans, 2 Asian Americans or Pacific Islanders, 2 Hispanic Americans), 1 international. 54 applicants, 50% accepted, 13 enrolled. In 2007, 15 master's, 4 doctorates awarded. *Degree requirements:* For master's, thesis; for doctorate, comprehensive exam, thesis/dissertation. *Entrance requirements:* For master's and doctorate, GRE General Test. *Application deadline:* For fall admission, 1/15 for domestic students. Application fee: $50. *Expenses:* Tuition, state resident: full-time $7,224; part-time $401 per credit. Tuition, nonresident: full-time $16,072; part-time $891 per credit. Required fees: $1,679; $63 per credit. Tuition and fees vary according to campus/location. *Financial support:* Fellowships, teaching assistantships, career-related internships or fieldwork, Federal Work-Study, and institutionally sponsored loans available. Support available to part-time students. Financial award application deadline: 3/15. *Faculty research:* Modern, nineteenth century, Renaissance, American, and Medieval art. *Unit head:* Dr. James Farmer, Coordinator of Graduate Studies, 804-828-2784, Fax: 804-828-7468, E-mail: jfarmer@saturn.vcu.edu.

See Close-Up on page 275.

Virginia Polytechnic Institute and State University, Graduate School, College of Liberal Arts and Human Sciences, Department of History, Blacksburg, VA 24061. Offers MA. Part-time programs available. *Entrance requirements:* For master's, GRE General Test. Additional exam requirements/recommendations for international students: Required—TOEFL (minimum score 600 paper-based; 250 computer-based). Electronic applications accepted. *Faculty research:* History of the U.S.; race, class and gender; European (area studies); history of science and technology.

Virginia State University, School of Graduate Studies, Research, and Outreach, School of Liberal Arts and Education, Department of History, Petersburg, VA 23806-0001. Offers MA. *Degree requirements:* For master's, one foreign language, thesis (for some programs). *Entrance requirements:* For master's, GRE General Test, minimum GPA of 2.5.

Washington College, Graduate Programs, Department of History, Chestertown, MD 21620-1197. Offers MA. Part-time and evening/weekend programs available.

Washington State University, Graduate School, College of Liberal Arts, Department of History, Pullman, WA 99164. Offers early and modern European history (MA, PhD); environmental history (MA, PhD); Latin American history (MA, PhD); modern East Asia history (MA, PhD); public history (MA, PhD); US history (MA, PhD); women's history (MA, PhD); world history (MA, PhD). Part-time programs available. *Faculty:* 24. *Students:* 45 full-time (28 women), 8 part-time (4 women); includes 2 minority (both Hispanic Americans), 2 international. Average age 33. 64 applicants, 41% accepted, 15 enrolled. In 2007, 8 master's, 2 doctorates awarded. *Degree requirements:* For master's, comprehensive exam (for some programs), thesis, oral exam; for doctorate, one foreign language, comprehensive exam, thesis/dissertation, oral and written exam. *Entrance requirements:* For master's, GRE General Test, minimum GPA of 3.3, language background form, writing sample; for doctorate, GRE General Test, minimum GPA of 3.5, language background form, writing sample. Additional exam requirements/recommendations for international students: Required—TOEFL (minimum score 550 paper-based). *Application deadline:* For fall admission, 2/1 for domestic and international students; for spring admission, 11/1 for domestic and international students. Applications are processed on a rolling basis. Application fee: $50. Electronic applications accepted. *Financial support:* In 2007–08, 30 students received support, including 1 fellowship with partial tuition reimbursement available (averaging $3,000 per year), research assistantships with full and partial tuition reimbursements available (averaging $13,917 per year), 28 teaching assistantships with full and partial tuition reimbursements available (averaging $13,056 per year); career-related internships or fieldwork, Federal Work-Study, institutionally sponsored loans, scholarships/grants, and health care benefits also available. Financial award application deadline: 4/1; financial award applicants required to submit FAFSA. *Faculty research:* Public, world, environmental, women and U.S. history. Total annual research expenditures: $44,501. *Unit head:* Dr. John Kicza, Co-Chair, 509-335-5002, Fax: 509-335-4171, E-mail: jekicza@wsu.edu. *Application contact:* Graduate Studies Director, 509-335-4030, Fax: 509-335-4171, E-mail: kale@wsu.edu.

Washington State University, Graduate School, College of Liberal Arts, Program in American Studies, Pullman, WA 99164. Offers ethnic studies (MA, PhD); feminist studies (MA, PhD); history (MA, PhD); literature (MA, PhD). *Faculty:* 39. *Students:* 27 full-time (19 women), 4 part-time (2 women); includes 17 minority (6 African Americans, 4 American Indian/Alaska Native, 2 Asian Americans or Pacific Islanders, 5 Hispanic Americans), 3 international. Average age 35. 78 applicants, 15% accepted, 12 enrolled. In 2007, 5 master's, 1 doctorate awarded. *Degree requirements:* For master's, one foreign language, comprehensive exam (for some programs), thesis optional, oral exam; for doctorate, one foreign language, comprehensive exam (for some programs), thesis/dissertation, oral exam. *Entrance requirements:* For master's and doctorate, GRE General Test, minimum GPA of 3.0, writing sample, 3 letters of recommendation. Additional exam requirements/recommendations for international students: Required—TOEFL. *Application deadline:* For fall admission, 2/1 priority date for domestic students, 3/1 for international students; for spring admission, 7/1 for international students. Applications are processed on a rolling basis. Application fee: $50. *Financial support:* In 2007–08, 24 students received support, including 1 fellowship (averaging $6,950 per year), 3 research assistantships with full and partial tuition reimbursements available (averaging $13,917 per year), 17 teaching assistantships with full and partial tuition reimbursements available (averaging $13,056 per year); career-related internships or fieldwork, Federal Work-Study, institutionally sponsored loans, tuition waivers (partial), and teaching associateships also available. Financial award application deadline: 3/1; financial award applicants required to submit FAFSA. *Faculty research:* The American West in multicultural perspective; nineteenth century historical, literary, and cultural studies; comparative American ethnic literatures and cultures; American cultures and the environment; American rhetoric. *Unit head:* Dr. Noel Sturgeon, Director, 509-335-1560, E-mail: reedtv@wsu.edu. *Application contact:* Graduate School Admissions, 800-GRADWSU, Fax: 509-335-1949, E-mail: gradsch@wsu.edu.

Washington State University Vancouver, Graduate Programs, Program in History, Vancouver, WA 98686. Offers MA. Part-time programs available. *Faculty:* 5 full-time (all women). *Students:* 4 full-time (3 women), 3 part-time (1 woman), 1 international. Average age 32. 5 applicants, 80% accepted, 2 enrolled. *Degree requirements:* For master's, comprehensive exam (for some programs), thesis. *Entrance requirements:* For master's, GRE, minimum GPA of 3.0, writing sample, language background form, preferred field of study form, 3 letters of recommendation. Additional exam requirements/recommendations for international students: Required—TOEFL (minimum score 550 paper-based; 213 computer-based). *Application deadline:* For fall admission, 7/15 for domestic students, 3/1 for international students; for spring admission, 10/15 for domestic students, 7/1 for international students. Application fee: $50. *Financial support:* In 2007–08, 4 students received support, including 1 teaching assistantship with full and partial tuition reimbursement available (averaging $13,056 per year); career-related internships or fieldwork, Federal Work-Study, and unspecified assistantships also available. *Faculty research:* Immigration, gender, slavery, labor, public history. *Unit head:* Dr. Amy Wharton, Co-Director, 360-546-9617, E-mail: wharton@wsu.edu.

Washington University in St. Louis, Graduate School of Arts and Sciences, Department of History, St. Louis, MO 63130-4899. Offers American history (MA, PhD); Asian history (MA, PhD); British history (MA, PhD); European history (MA, PhD); Jewish, Islamic, and Near Eastern studies (MA), including Islamic and Near Eastern studies, Jewish studies; Latin American history (MA, PhD); Middle Eastern history (MA, PhD). Terminal master's awarded for partial completion of doctoral program. *Degree requirements:* For master's, one foreign language, thesis (for some programs); for doctorate, 2 foreign languages, thesis/dissertation. *Entrance requirements:* For master's and doctorate, GRE General Test. Electronic applications accepted.

Wayne State University, College of Liberal Arts and Sciences, Department of History, Detroit, MI 48202. Offers MA, PhD, JD/MA. Evening/weekend programs available. *Students:* 31 full-time (16 women), 37 part-time (16 women); includes 10 minority (8 African Americans, 1 Asian American or Pacific Islander, 1 Hispanic American), 4 international. Average age 32. 30 applicants, 43% accepted, 7 enrolled. In 2007, 6 master's, 2 doctorates awarded. *Degree requirements:* For doctorate, 2 foreign languages, thesis/dissertation, qualifying exam in 4 fields of history. *Entrance requirements:* For master's, GRE General Test, GRE Subject Test, minimum GPA of 3.0 in history, 2.75 overall; for doctorate, GRE General Test, GRE Subject Test, minimum GPA of 3.0. Additional exam requirements/recommendations for international students: Required—TOEFL (minimum score 550 paper-based; 213 computer-based); Recommended—TWE (minimum score 6). *Application deadline:* For fall admission, 7/1 priority date for domestic students, 6/1 for international students; for winter admission, 10/1 for international students; for spring admission, 2/1 for international students. Applications are processed on a rolling basis. Application fee: $30 ($50 for international students). Electronic applications accepted. *Expenses:* Tuition, state resident: part-time $403 per credit hour. Tuition, nonresident: part-time $890 per credit hour. *Financial support:* In 2007–08, 2 fellowships with tuition reimbursements (averaging $13,001 per year), 6 teaching assistantships with tuition reimbursements (averaging $13,672 per year) were awarded; research assistantships, institutionally sponsored loans also available. Support available to part-time students. Financial award application deadline: 3/1. *Faculty research:* Labor and social history; citizenship and governance; modern U.S. history; early modern and modern European history; African-

History

Wayne State University (continued)

American history. *Unit head:* Dr. Marc Kruman, Chair, 313-577-2525, Fax: 313-577-6987, E-mail: aa1277@wayne.edu. *Application contact:* Mel Small, Graduate Director, 313-577-6138, E-mail: m.small@wayne.edu.

West Chester University of Pennsylvania, Office of Graduate Studies and Extended Education, College of Arts and Sciences, Department of History, West Chester, PA 19383. Offers history (M Ed, MA); holocaust and genocide studies (MA, Certificate). Part-time and evening/weekend programs available. *Students:* 13 full-time (6 women), 27 part-time (12 women); includes 3 minority (1 African American, 2 Hispanic Americans). Average age 31. 35 applicants, 100% accepted, 14 enrolled. In 2007, 17 degrees awarded. *Degree requirements:* For master's, comprehensive exam, thesis optional. *Entrance requirements:* Additional exam requirements/recommendations for international students: Required—TOEFL (minimum score 550 paper-based; 213 computer-based; 80 iBT). *Application deadline:* For fall admission, 4/15 priority date for domestic students; for spring admission, 10/15 for domestic students. Applications are processed on a rolling basis. Application fee: $35. *Expenses:* Tuition, state resident: part-time $345 per credit. Tuition, nonresident: part-time $552 per credit. Tuition and fees vary according to course load. *Financial support:* In 2007–08, 4 research assistantships with full and partial tuition reimbursements (averaging $5,000 per year) were awarded; unspecified assistantships also available. Support available to part-time students. Financial award application deadline: 2/15. *Faculty research:* Oral histories, siege of Leningrad. *Unit head:* Dr. Thomas Legg, Chair, 610-436-2201, E-mail: tlegg@wcupa.edu. *Application contact:* Dr. Maria Boes, Graduate Coordinator, 610-436-2201, E-mail: mboes@wcupa.edu.

Western Carolina University, Graduate School, College of Arts and Sciences, Department of History, Cullowhee, NC 28723. Offers MA. Part-time and evening/weekend programs available. *Faculty:* 11 full-time (4 women), 2 part-time/adjunct (0 women). *Students:* 9 full-time (4 women), 9 part-time (5 women); includes 1 minority (Asian American or Pacific Islander) Average age 34. 13 applicants, 85% accepted, 6 enrolled. In 2007, 3 degrees awarded. *Degree requirements:* For master's, one foreign language, comprehensive exam, thesis or alternative. *Entrance requirements:* For master's, GRE General Test, appropriate undergraduate, 3 letters of recommendation. Additional exam requirements/recommendations for international students: Required—TOEFL (minimum score 550 paper-based; 270 computer-based; 79 iBT). *Application deadline:* For fall admission, 5/1 priority date for domestic students; for spring admission, 9/1 priority date for domestic students. Applications are processed on a rolling basis. Application fee: $40. *Expenses:* Tuition, state resident: full-time $2,314. Tuition, nonresident: full-time $11,899. Required fees: $2,033. Tuition and fees vary according to course load. *Financial support:* In 2007–08, 9 students received support, including 9 research assistantships with full and partial tuition reimbursements available (averaging $8,000 per year); fellowships, teaching assistantships with full and partial tuition reimbursements available, career-related internships or fieldwork, institutionally sponsored loans, scholarships/grants, and unspecified assistantships also available. Financial award application deadline: 3/31; financial award applicants required to submit FAFSA. *Faculty research:* Social and economic history of the American South, Islamic world history, German history, social and political protest, medieval social history. *Unit head:* Dr. Richard Starnes, Head, 828-227-7243, Fax: 828-227-7647, E-mail: starnes@email.wcu.edu. *Application contact:* Admissions Specialist for History, 828-227-7398, Fax: 828-227-7480, E-mail: gradsch@email.wcu.edu.

Western Connecticut State University, Division of Graduate Studies, School of Arts and Sciences, Department of History, Danbury, CT 06810-6885. Offers MA. Part-time and evening/weekend programs available. *Faculty:* 5 full-time (2 women). *Students:* 2 full-time (1 woman), 33 part-time (10 women); includes 1 minority (Asian American or Pacific Islander) Average age 39. 16 applicants, 94% accepted, 10 enrolled. In 2007, 20 degrees awarded. *Degree requirements:* For master's, comprehensive exam, thesis or research project. *Entrance requirements:* For master's, minimum GPA of 2.5. *Application deadline:* For fall admission, 8/5 priority date for domestic students; for spring admission, 1/5 priority date for domestic students. Applications are processed on a rolling basis. Application fee: $50. *Expenses:* Tuition, state resident: full-time $4,169. Tuition, nonresident: full-time $11,614. Required fees: $3,278. *Financial support:* Available to part-time students. Application deadline: 5/1; *Unit head:* Dr. Michael Nolan, Assistant Professor, 203-837-8483. *Application contact:* Chris Shankle, Associate Director of Graduate Admissions, 203-837-8244, Fax: 203-837-8338, E-mail: shanklec@wcsu.edu.

Western Illinois University, School of Graduate Studies, College of Arts and Sciences, Department of History, Macomb, IL 61455-1390. Offers MA. Part-time programs available. *Students:* 18 full-time (6 women), 19 part-time (5 women); includes 2 minority (both African Americans) Average age 32. 20 applicants, 95% accepted. In 2007, 9 degrees awarded. *Degree requirements:* For master's, thesis or alternative. *Entrance requirements:* For master's, minimum GPA of 2.75. Additional exam requirements/recommendations for international students: Required—TOEFL (minimum score 550 paper-based; 213 computer-based; 80 iBT). *Application deadline:* Applications are processed on a rolling basis. Application fee: $30. Electronic applications accepted. *Expenses:* Tuition, state resident: part-time $217 per credit hour. Tuition, nonresident: part-time $433 per credit hour. Required fees: $54 per credit hour. *Financial support:* In 2007–08, 7 students received support, including 7 research assistantships with full tuition reimbursements available (averaging $6,800 per year). Financial award applicants required to submit FAFSA. *Unit head:* Dr. Virginia Boynton, Interim Chairperson, 309-298-1053. *Application contact:* Dr. Barbara Baily, Director of Graduate Studies/Associate Provost, 309-298-1806, Fax: 309-298-2345, E-mail: grad-office@wiu.edu.

Western Kentucky University, Graduate Studies, Potter College of Arts and Letters, Department of History, Bowling Green, KY 42101. Offers MA, MA Ed. Part-time and evening/weekend programs available. Postbaccalaureate distance learning degree programs offered. *Degree requirements:* For master's, comprehensive exam, thesis optional, final exam. *Entrance requirements:* For master's, GRE General Test, minimum GPA of 2.75. Additional exam requirements/recommendations for international students: Required—TOEFL (minimum score 555 paper-based; 213 computer-based; 79 iBT). *Faculty research:* U.S.A, Europe, China, India, Latin America.

Western Michigan University, Graduate College, College of Arts and Sciences, Department of History, Kalamazoo, MI 49008-5202. Offers MA, PhD. *Degree requirements:* For master's, thesis optional, oral exams; for doctorate, thesis/dissertation, oral exam. *Entrance requirements:* For doctorate, GRE General Test.

Western Washington University, Graduate School, College of Humanities and Social Sciences, Department of History, Bellingham, WA 98225-5996. Offers MA. Part-time programs available. *Faculty:* 18. *Students:* 14 full-time (3 women), 6 part-time (4 women); includes 1 minority (Asian American or Pacific Islander) 26 applicants, 81% accepted, 12 enrolled. In 2007, 12 degrees awarded. *Degree requirements:* For master's, one foreign language, comprehensive exam, thesis (for some programs). *Entrance requirements:* For master's, GRE General Test, minimum GPA of 3.0 in last 60 semester hours or last 90 quarter hours. Additional exam requirements/recommendations for international students: Required—TOEFL (minimum score 567 paper-based; 227 computer-based). *Application deadline:* For fall admission, 6/1 for domestic students; for winter admission, 10/1 for domestic students; for spring admission, 2/1 for domestic students. Applications are processed on a rolling basis. Application fee: $50. Electronic applications accepted. *Expenses:* Tuition, state resident: part-time $208 per credit. Tuition, nonresident: part-time $541 per credit. Required fees: $241 per quarter. One-time fee: $250 part-time. *Financial support:* In 2007–08, 7 teaching assistantships with partial tuition reimbursements (averaging $9,339 per year) were awarded; career-related internships or fieldwork, Federal Work-Study, institutionally sponsored loans, scholarships/grants, tuition waivers (partial), and unspecified assistantships also available. Support available to part-time students. Financial award application deadline: 2/15; financial award applicants required to submit FAFSA. *Unit head:* Kathleen Kennedy, Chair, 360-650-3429, Fax: 360-650-7789. *Application contact:* Dr. Leonard M. Helfgott, Graduate Adviser, 360-650-3095, E-mail: helfgott@cc.wwu.edu.

Westfield State College, Division of Graduate and Continuing Education, Department of History, Westfield, MA 01086. Offers M Ed. Part-time and evening/weekend programs available. *Degree requirements:* For master's, thesis. *Entrance requirements:* For master's, GRE General Test or MAT, minimum undergraduate GPA of 2.7.

West Texas A&M University, College of Education and Social Sciences, Department of History and Political Science, Program in History, Canyon, TX 79016-0001. Offers MA. Part-time and evening/weekend programs available. *Degree requirements:* For master's, comprehensive exam, thesis optional. *Entrance requirements:* For master's, GRE General Test. Additional exam requirements/recommendations for international students: Required—TOEFL (minimum score 550 paper-based). Electronic applications accepted. *Faculty research:* John B. Stetson Jr. (an American businessman in Warsaw), creation of kokugo in late Meiji Japan, canon law on cyberspace, Russian and American frontiers, Texas women of two cultures.

West Virginia University, Eberly College of Arts and Sciences, Department of History, Morgantown, WV 26506. Offers African history (MA, PhD); African-American history (MA, PhD); American history (MA, PhD); Appalachian/regional history (MA, PhD); East Asian history (MA, PhD); European history (MA, PhD); history of science and technology (MA, PhD); Latin American history (MA). Part-time programs available. *Faculty:* 19 full-time (5 women), 12 part-time/adjunct (4 women). *Students:* 43 full-time (17 women), 30 part-time (11 women); includes 5 minority (1 African American, 1 American Indian/Alaska Native, 2 Asian Americans or Pacific Islanders, 1 Hispanic American), 7 international. Average age 33. 70 applicants, 59% accepted, 17 enrolled. In 2007, 8 master's, 3 doctorates awarded. *Median time to degree:* Of those who began their doctoral program in fall 1999, 75% received their degree in 8 years or less. *Degree requirements:* For master's, one foreign language, thesis (for some programs), oral exam, thesis defense; for doctorate, one foreign language, comprehensive exam, thesis/dissertation, dissertation defense. *Entrance requirements:* For master's, GRE General Test, minimum GPA of 3.0; for doctorate, GRE General Test. Additional exam requirements/recommendations for international students: Required—TOEFL (minimum score 550 paper-based), IELTS (minimum score 7). *Application deadline:* For fall admission, 12/31 for domestic students; for spring admission, 10/1 for domestic students. Applications are processed on a rolling basis. Application fee: $45. Electronic applications accepted. *Expenses:* Tuition, state resident: full-time $5,196; part-time $292 per credit hour. Tuition, nonresident: full-time $15,064; part-time $840 per credit hour. Tuition and fees vary according to program. *Financial support:* In 2007–08, 60 students received support, including 5 fellowships with full tuition reimbursements available (averaging $3,000 per year), 1 research assistantship with full tuition reimbursement available (averaging $7,200 per year), 8 teaching assistantships with full tuition reimbursements available (averaging $12,000 per year); career-related internships or fieldwork, Federal Work-Study, institutionally sponsored loans, health care benefits, tuition waivers (full and partial), and graduate administrative assistantships also available. Financial award application deadline: 12/31; financial award applicants required to submit FAFSA. *Faculty research:* U.S., Appalachia, modern Europe, Africa, colonial and post-colonial societies. Total annual research expenditures: $93,327. *Unit head:* Dr. Steven M. Zdatny, Chair, 304-293-2421 Ext. 5241, Fax: 304-293-3616, E-mail: steve.zdatny@mail.wvu.edu. *Application contact:* Dr. Greg A. Good, Director of Graduate Studies, 304-293-2421 Ext. 5247, Fax: 304-293-3616, E-mail: greg.good@mail.wvu.edu.

Wichita State University, Graduate School, Fairmount College of Liberal Arts and Sciences, Department of History, Wichita, KS 67260. Offers MA. Part-time programs available. *Degree requirements:* For master's, one foreign language, comprehensive exam or thesis. *Entrance requirements:* For master's, GRE. Additional exam requirements/recommendations for international students: Required—TOEFL. Electronic applications accepted. *Faculty research:* U.S. history, European history, public history.

Wilfrid Laurier University, Faculty of Graduate Studies, Faculty of Arts, Department of History, Waterloo, ON N2L 3C5, Canada. Offers MA, PhD. *Faculty:* 20 full-time, 1 part-time/adjunct. *Students:* 35 full-time, 2 part-time. 138 applicants, 19% accepted, 14 enrolled. In 2007, 11 master's, 1 doctorate awarded. *Degree requirements:* For master's, thesis optional; for doctorate, thesis/dissertation. *Entrance requirements:* For master's, honors BA degree or the equivalent in history, minimum B+ average in undergraduate course work, exclusive of first year level courses; for doctorate, MA in history, minimum A-average. Additional exam requirements/recommendations for international students: Required—TOEFL (minimum score 230 computer-based; 89 iBT). *Application deadline:* For fall admission, 2/1 priority date for domestic students. Application fee: $75. Electronic applications accepted. *Financial support:* Fellowships, research assistantships, teaching assistantships available. *Faculty research:* Canadian, early modern European, modern European, Scottish, race/class/imperialism/slavery, British, urban and rural, science/medicine/technology, gender/women's/family, international, United States. *Unit head:* Dr. Joyce Lorimer, Chairperson, 519-884-0710 Ext. 3331, E-mail: jlorimer@wlu.ca. *Application contact:* Jennifer Poppe, Student Contact, 519-884-0710 Ext. 3536, Fax: 519-884-1020, E-mail: gradstudies@wlu.ca.

William Paterson University of New Jersey, College of the Humanities and Social Sciences, Department of History, Wayne, NJ 07470-8420. Offers MA. *Students:* 3 full-time (2 women), 21 part-time (7 women). In 2007, 2 degrees awarded. *Entrance requirements:* For master's, GRE. *Application deadline:* Applications are processed on a rolling basis. Application fee: $50. Electronic applications accepted. *Financial support:* Research assistantships with full tuition reimbursements, teaching assistantships with full tuition reimbursements available. Financial award application deadline: 4/1; financial award applicants required to submit FAFSA. *Unit head:* Krista O'Donnell, Graduate Program Director, 973-720-2146. *Application contact:* Danielle Liautaud, Director, 973-720-3579, Fax: 973-720-2035, E-mail: liautaudd@wpunj.edu.

Winthrop University, College of Arts and Sciences, Department of History, Rock Hill, SC 29733. Offers MA. Part-time programs available. *Faculty:* 8 full-time (1 woman), 1 part-time/adjunct (0 women). *Students:* 2 full-time (1 woman), 4 part-time (1 woman). Average age 30. In 2007, 6 degrees awarded. *Degree requirements:* For master's, one foreign language, thesis optional. *Entrance requirements:* For master's, GRE General Test or PRAXIS, 24 hours of history at the undergraduate level. *Application deadline:* For fall admission, 7/15 priority date for domestic students; for spring admission, 12/1 for domestic students. Applications are processed on a rolling basis. Application fee: $50. Electronic applications accepted. *Expenses:* Tuition, state resident: full-time $9,834; part-time $412 per credit hour. Tuition, nonresident: full-time $18,280; part-time $763 per credit hour. *Financial support:* In 2007–08, 1 research assistantship with full tuition reimbursement (averaging $3,600 per year) was awarded; Federal Work-Study, scholarships/grants, and unspecified assistantships also available. Support available to part-time students. Financial award application deadline: 2/1; financial award applicants required to submit FAFSA. *Unit head:* Dr. Sarah Stellings, Graduate Program Director, 803-323-2183, E-mail: stellings@winthrop.edu. *Application contact:* 800-411-7041, Fax: 580-323-2292, E-mail: graduatestu@winthrop.edu.

Wright State University, School of Graduate Studies, College of Liberal Arts, Department of History, Dayton, OH 45435. Offers MA. *Degree requirements:* For master's, thesis optional. *Entrance requirements:* For master's, GRE General Test, minimum GPA of 3.0 in history, 2.7 overall. Additional exam requirements/recommendations for international students: Required—TOEFL. *Faculty research:* U.S. religions; women's, Southern, European, and archival history.

Yale University, Graduate School of Arts and Sciences, Department of History, New Haven, CT 06520. Offers MA, PhD. Terminal master's awarded for partial completion of doctoral program. *Degree requirements:* For master's, one foreign language; for doctorate, 2 foreign languages, thesis/dissertation. *Entrance requirements:* For doctorate, GRE General Test.

York University, Faculty of Graduate Studies, Faculty of Arts, Program in History, Toronto, ON M3J 1P3, Canada. Offers MA, PhD. Part-time programs available. *Degree requirements:* For master's, thesis or alternative; for doctorate, one foreign language, comprehensive exam, thesis/dissertation, qualifying exam. Electronic applications accepted.

Youngstown State University, Graduate School, College of Arts and Sciences, Department of History, Youngstown, OH 44555-0001. Offers MA. Part-time programs available. *Degree requirements:* For master's, thesis optional, oral and written exams. *Entrance requirements:* For master's, minimum GPA of 2.75. Additional exam requirements/recommendations for international students: Required—TOEFL. *Faculty research:* Holocaust, Marxism, nineteenth- and twentieth-century United States, historic preservation, revolutionary France.

History of Medicine

Duke University, Graduate School, Department of History, Program in Medical Historian Training, Durham, NC 27708-0586. Offers MD/PhD. *Application deadline:* For fall admission, 12/31 for domestic students. Application fee: $75. *Financial support:* Application deadline:12/31. *Unit head:* Dr. Peter English, Director, 919-684-8206.

McGill University, Faculty of Graduate and Postdoctoral Studies, Faculty of Arts, Department of History, Montréal, QC H3A 2T5, Canada. Offers history (MA, PhD); history of medicine (MA). *Faculty:* 36 full-time (9 women), 22 part-time/adjunct (8 women). *Students:* 72 full-time (29 women), 1 (woman) part-time. 182 applicants, 45% accepted, 31 enrolled. In 2007, 25 master's, 2 doctorates awarded.

McGill University, Faculty of Graduate and Postdoctoral Studies, Faculty of Medicine, Department of Social Studies in Medicine, Montréal, QC H3A 2T5, Canada. Offers medical anthropology (MA, PhD); medical history (MA, PhD); medical sociology (MA, PhD). *Faculty:* 7 full-time (2 women), 3 part-time/adjunct (1 woman).

Rutgers, The State University of New Jersey, New Brunswick, Graduate School, Program in History, New Brunswick, NJ 08901-1281. Offers African-American history (PhD); early American history (PhD); early modern European history (PhD); east Asian history (PhD); global and comparative history (PhD); history (PhD); history of diplomacy and foreign relations (PhD); history of technology, environment and health (PhD); history of the Atlantic cultures and African diaspora (PhD); Latin American history (PhD); medieval history (PhD); modern European history (PhD); nineteenth and twentieth century American history (PhD); women's and gender history (PhD). *Degree requirements:* For doctorate, thesis/dissertation. *Entrance requirements:* For doctorate, GRE General Test, sample of written work. Electronic applications accepted. *Faculty research:* American history, European history, Afro-American history, women's history, Latin American history.

Uniformed Services University of the Health Sciences, School of Medicine, Programs in Biomedical Sciences, Department of Medical History, Bethesda, MD 20814-4799. Offers MMH. Available to active duty military only. *Faculty:* 3 full-time (2 women), 2 part-time/adjunct (0 women). *Degree requirements:* For master's, comprehensive exam, thesis or alternative. *Entrance requirements:* For master's, GRE General Test, US citizenship, active military duty. *Application deadline:* For fall admission, 1/15 priority date for domestic students. Applications are processed on a rolling basis. Application fee: $0. *Unit head:* Dr. Dale Smith, Chair, 301-295-3427, E-mail: dcsmith@usuhs.mil. *Application contact:* Janet M. Anastasi, Graduate Program Coordinator, 301-295-9474, Fax: 301-295-6772, E-mail: janastasi@usuhs.mil.

University of Minnesota, Twin Cities Campus, Graduate School, Program in the History of Science, Technology and Medicine, Minneapolis, MN 55455-0213. Offers MA, PhD. Part-time programs available. *Faculty:* 10 full-time (4 women), 5 part-time/adjunct (2 women). *Students:* 25 full-time (16 women), 6 part-time (4 women), 4 international. Average age 29. 14 applicants, 64% accepted, 3 enrolled. In 2007, 1 master's, 3 doctorates awarded. *Degree requirements:* For master's, one foreign language, thesis or alternative; for doctorate, 2 foreign languages, thesis/dissertation. *Entrance requirements:* For master's and doctorate, GRE General Test. *Application deadline:* For fall admission, 12/31 priority date for domestic students, 12/31 for international students. Applications are processed on a rolling basis. Application fee: $0. *Financial support:* In 2007–08, 2 fellowships with full tuition reimbursements (averaging $13,500 per year), 2 teaching assistantships with full tuition reimbursements were awarded; institutionally sponsored loans and tuition waivers (full) also available. Financial award application deadline: 1/15. *Faculty research:* History of infectious diseases, history of public health, history of evolutionary biology, history of infertility, women in science. Total annual research expenditures: $45,000. *Unit head:* John M. Eyler, Professor, 612-624-5921, E-mail: eyler001@umn.edu.

Yale University, Graduate School of Arts and Sciences, Department of History of Medicine and the Life Sciences, New Haven, CT 06520. Offers MS, PhD. *Degree requirements:* For doctorate, 2 foreign languages, thesis/dissertation. *Entrance requirements:* For doctorate, GRE General Test.

History of Science and Technology

Arizona State University, Graduate College, College of Liberal Arts and Sciences, Department of Biology, Program in History and Philosophy of Biology, Tempe, AZ 85287. Offers MS, PhD. Terminal master's awarded for partial completion of doctoral program. *Degree requirements:* For master's, thesis; for doctorate, thesis/dissertation, oral exam. *Entrance requirements:* For master's, GRE General Test, GRE Subject Test. Additional exam requirements/recommendations for international students: Required—TOEFL (minimum score 600 paper-based; 250 computer-based).

Brown University, Graduate School, Department of History of Mathematics, Providence, RI 02912. Offers AM, PhD. *Degree requirements:* For master's, 2 foreign languages, thesis or alternative; for doctorate, 2 foreign languages, thesis/dissertation or alternative.

Cornell University, Graduate School, Graduate Fields of Arts and Sciences, Field of History, Ithaca, NY 14853-0001. Offers African history (MA, PhD); American history (MA, PhD); ancient history (MA, PhD); early modern European history (MA, PhD); English history (MA, PhD); French history (MA, PhD); German history (MA, PhD); history of science (MA, PhD); Latin American history (MA, PhD); medieval Chinese history (MA, PhD); medieval history (MA, PhD); modern Chinese history (MA, PhD); modern European history (MA, PhD); modern Japanese history (MA, PhD); premodern Islamic history (MA, PhD); premodern Japanese history (MA, PhD); Renaissance history (MA, PhD); Russian history (MA, PhD); Southeast Asian history (MA, PhD). *Faculty:* 56 full-time (14 women). *Students:* 63 full-time (29 women); includes 11 minority (6 African Americans, 2 Asian Americans or Pacific Islanders, 3 Hispanic Americans), 20 international. Average age 31. 201 applicants, 6% accepted, 10 enrolled. In 2007, 11 master's, 11 doctorates awarded. Terminal master's awarded for partial completion of doctoral program. *Degree requirements:* For master's, thesis; for doctorate, 2 foreign languages, comprehensive exam, thesis/dissertation, 1 year of teaching experience. *Entrance requirements:* For master's and doctorate, GRE General Test, writing sample, 3 letters of recommendation. Additional exam requirements/recommendations for international students: Required—TOEFL (minimum score 550 paper-based; 213 computer-based; 77 iBT). *Application deadline:* For fall admission, 1/15 for domestic students. Application fee: $70. Electronic applications accepted. *Financial support:* In 2007–08, 54 students received support, including 26 fellowships with full tuition reimbursements available, 28 teaching assistantships with full tuition reimbursements available; research assistantships with full tuition reimbursements available, institutionally sponsored loans, scholarships/grants, health care benefits, tuition waivers (full and partial), and unspecified assistantships also available. Financial award applicants required to submit FAFSA. *Unit head:* Director of Graduate Studies, 607-255-6738, Fax: 607-255-0469. *Application contact:* Graduate Field Assistant, 607-255-6738, Fax: 607-255-0469, E-mail: history_grad_info@cornell.edu.

Cornell University, Graduate School, Graduate Fields of Arts and Sciences, Field of Science and Technology Studies, Ithaca, NY 14853-0001. Offers history and philosophy of science and technology (MA, PhD); social studies of science and technology (MA, PhD). *Faculty:* 30 full-time. *Students:* 24 full-time (15 women); includes 4 minority (1 African American, 3 Asian Americans or Pacific Islanders), 10 international. Average age 31. 54 applicants, 11% accepted, 4 enrolled. In 2007, 3 master's, 2 doctorates awarded. Terminal master's awarded for partial completion of doctoral program. *Degree requirements:* For master's, one foreign language, thesis; for doctorate, one foreign language, comprehensive exam, thesis/dissertation. *Entrance requirements:* For master's and doctorate, GRE General Test, writing sample, 3 letters of recommendation. Additional exam requirements/recommendations for international students: Required—TOEFL (minimum score 550 paper-based; 213 computer-based; 77 iBT). *Application deadline:* For fall admission, 1/10 for domestic students. Application fee: $70. Electronic applications accepted. *Financial support:* In 2007–08, 21 students received support, including 9 fellowships with full tuition reimbursements available, 1 research assistantship with full tuition reimbursement available, 11 teaching assistantships with full tuition reimbursements available; institutionally sponsored loans, scholarships/grants, health care benefits, tuition waivers (full and partial), and unspecified assistantships also available. Financial award applicants required to submit FAFSA. *Faculty research:* History, philosophy, sociology, politics, and policy of science and technology; gender, legal order, environment, and communication. *Unit head:* Director of Graduate Studies, 607-255-6234. *Application contact:* Graduate Field Assistant, 607-255-6234, E-mail: stsgradfield@cornell.edu.

Drexel University, College of Arts and Sciences, Department of History and Politics, Philadelphia, PA 19104-2875. Offers science, technology and society (MS). Part-time programs available. *Entrance requirements:* For master's, GRE. Additional exam requirements/recommendations for international students: Required—TOEFL. Electronic applications accepted.

Georgia Institute of Technology, Graduate Studies and Research, Ivan Allen College of Policy and International Affairs, Program in History of Technology, Atlanta, GA 30332-0001. Offers MSHT, PhD. Terminal master's awarded for partial completion of doctoral program. *Degree requirements:* For master's, research paper; for doctorate, one foreign language, comprehensive exam, thesis/dissertation. *Entrance requirements:* Additional exam requirements/recommendations for international students: Required—TOEFL. Electronic applications accepted. *Faculty research:* Industrialization, labor history, modern Europe, social history, sociology of science.

Harvard University, Graduate School of Arts and Sciences, Department of the History of Science, Cambridge, MA 02138. Offers AM, PhD. Terminal master's awarded for partial completion of doctoral program. *Degree requirements:* For master's, one foreign language; for doctorate, 2 foreign languages, thesis/dissertation. *Entrance requirements:* For master's and doctorate, GRE General Test. Additional exam requirements/recommendations for international students: Required—TOEFL. *Expenses:* Tuition: Full-time $31,456. Full-time tuition and fees vary according to program and student level.

Indiana University Bloomington, University Graduate School, College of Arts and Sciences, Department of History and Philosophy of Science, Bloomington, IN 47405-7000. Offers MA, PhD, MLS/MA. Part-time programs available. *Faculty:* 9 full-time (2 women). *Students:* 26 full-time (5 women), 8 part-time (2 women); includes 4 minority (1 Asian American or Pacific Islander, 3 Hispanic Americans), 6 international. Average age 30. 30 applicants, 67% accepted, 10 enrolled. In 2007, 3 master's, 1 doctorate awarded. Terminal master's awarded for partial completion of doctoral program. *Median time to degree:* Of those who began their doctoral program in fall 1999, 33% received their degree in 8 years or less. *Degree requirements:* For master's, one foreign language, thesis optional; for doctorate, 2 foreign languages, thesis/dissertation. *Entrance requirements:* For master's and doctorate, GRE General Test. Additional exam requirements/recommendations for international students: Required—TOEFL. *Application deadline:* For fall admission, 1/15 priority date for domestic students, 12/15 for international students; for spring admission, 9/1 priority date for domestic students, 9/1 for international students. Applications are processed on a rolling basis. Application fee: $50 ($60 for international students). Electronic applications accepted. *Financial support:* Fellowships with full tuition reimbursements, research assistantships with full tuition reimbursements, teaching assistantships with full tuition reimbursements, Federal Work-Study and institutionally sponsored loans available. Support available to part-time students. Financial award application deadline: 3/1; financial award applicants required to submit FAFSA. *Faculty research:* History of scientific ideas, instruments, and institutions; foundations of physics; scientific methodology; relationship between history of science and history of philosophy. *Unit head:* William Newman, Chair, 812-855-3071. *Application contact:* Becky Wood, Graduate Secretary, 812-855-9334, Fax: 812-855-3631, E-mail: hpscdept@ucs.indiana.edu.

Iowa State University of Science and Technology, Graduate College, College of Liberal Arts and Sciences, Department of History, Ames, IA 50011. Offers agricultural history and rural studies (PhD); history (MA); history of technology and science (MA, PhD). *Faculty:* 16 full-time (4 women). *Students:* 29 full-time (12 women), 14 part-time (3 women); includes 2 minority (1 African American, 1 Hispanic American), 3 international. 23 applicants, 87% accepted, 11 enrolled. In 2007, 8 master's, 3 doctorates awarded. *Degree requirements:* For master's, thesis or alternative; for doctorate, thesis/dissertation. *Entrance requirements:* For master's and doctorate, GRE General Test. Additional exam requirements/recommendations for international students: Required—TOEFL (paper-based 600; computer-based 250; iBT 79) or IELTS (7.0). *Application deadline:* For fall admission, 1/15 priority date for domestic and international students. Applications are processed on a rolling basis. Application fee: $30 ($70 for international students). Electronic applications accepted. *Financial support:* In 2007–08, research assistantships with partial tuition reimbursements (averaging $15,660 per year), 18

History of Science and Technology

Iowa State University of Science and Technology (continued)
teaching assistantships with full and partial tuition reimbursements (averaging $15,829 per year) were awarded; scholarships/grants, health care benefits, and unspecified assistantships also available. *Unit head:* Dr. Charles Dobbs, Chair, 515-294-7266, Fax: 515-294-6390, E-mail: cdobbs@iastate.edu. *Application contact:* Dr. Christopher Curtis, Information Contact, 515-294-7266, Fax: 515-294-6390.

The Johns Hopkins University, Zanvyl Krieger School of Arts and Sciences, Department of the History of Science and Technology, Baltimore, MD 21218-2699. Offers MA, PhD. *Faculty:* 6 full-time (3 women), 8 part-time/adjunct (3 women). *Students:* 7 full-time (4 women), 1 part-time, 2 international. Average age 29. 18 applicants, 17% accepted, 1 enrolled. In 2007, 3 doctorates awarded. Terminal master's awarded for partial completion of doctoral program. *Median time to degree:* Of those who began their doctoral program in fall 1999, 100% received their degree in 8 years or less. *Degree requirements:* For master's, one foreign language, thesis; for doctorate, 2 foreign languages, thesis/dissertation. *Entrance requirements:* For doctorate, GRE General Test. Additional exam requirements/recommendations for international students: Required—TOEFL (minimum score 600 paper-based; 250 computer-based). *Application deadline:* For fall admission, 1/17 for domestic and international students. Applications are processed on a rolling basis. Application fee: $60. Electronic applications accepted. *Financial support:* In 2007–08, 6 students received support, including fellowships with full tuition reimbursements available (averaging $18,000 per year), teaching assistantships with full tuition reimbursements available (averaging $18,000 per year); research assistantships, career-related internships or fieldwork, Federal Work-Study, and institutionally sponsored loans also available. Financial award application deadline: 1/31; financial award applicants required to submit FAFSA. *Faculty research:* History of physical and biomedical sciences, history of technology, history of medicine (seventeenth–twentieth centuries). *Unit head:* Dr. Sharon Kingsland, Chair, 410-516-7501, Fax: 410-516-7502, E-mail: sharon@jhu.edu. *Application contact:* Danielle Stout, Academic Program Coordinator, 410-516-7501, Fax: 410-516-7502, E-mail: danielle@jhu.edu.

Massachusetts Institute of Technology, School of Humanities, Arts, and Social Sciences, Program in Science, Technology, and Society, Cambridge, MA 02139-4307. Offers history, anthropology, and science, technology and society (PhD). *Faculty:* 11 full-time (4 women). *Students:* 28 full-time (16 women); includes 4 minority (2 American Indian/Alaska Native, 2 Asian Americans or Pacific Islanders), 5 international. Average age 30. 93 applicants, 8% accepted, 6 enrolled. In 2007, 7 doctorates awarded. *Degree requirements:* For doctorate, comprehensive exam, thesis/dissertation. *Entrance requirements:* For doctorate, GRE General Test. Additional exam requirements/recommendations for international students: Required—TOEFL (minimum score 577 paper-based; 233 computer-based). *Application deadline:* For fall admission, 1/1 for domestic and international students. Application fee: $70. Electronic applications accepted. *Expenses:* Tuition: Full-time $34,760; part-time $545 per unit. Required fees: $236. *Financial support:* In 2007–08, 25 students received support, including 17 fellowships with tuition reimbursements available (averaging $25,765 per year), 1 research assistantship, 5 teaching assistantships with tuition reimbursements available (averaging $27,000 per year); Federal Work-Study, institutionally sponsored loans, scholarships/grants, traineeships, health care benefits, and unspecified assistantships also available. *Faculty research:* History of science; history of technology; sociology of science and technology; anthropology of science and technology; science, technology, and society. Total annual research expenditures:$563,000. *Unit head:* Prof. David A. Mindell, Director, 617-253-4062, Fax: 617-258-8118. *Application contact:* Karen Gardner, Student Contact, 617-253-9759, Fax: 617-258-8118, E-mail: hasts@mit.edu.

Polytechnic Institute of NYU, Department of Humanities and Social Sciences, Major in History of Science, Brooklyn, NY 11201-2990. Offers MS. Part-time and evening/weekend programs available. *Students:* 1 applicant, 0% accepted. *Degree requirements:* For master's, comprehensive exam (for some programs), thesis (for some programs). *Entrance requirements:* Additional exam requirements/recommendations for international students: Required—TOEFL (minimum score 550 paper-based; 213 computer-based); Recommended—IELTS (minimum score 7). *Application deadline:* For fall admission, 7/15 priority date for domestic students, 4/1 priority date for international students; for spring admission, 12/15 priority date for domestic students, 10/1 priority date for international students. Applications are processed on a rolling basis. Application fee: $55. Electronic applications accepted. *Expenses:* Tuition: Full-time $18,486; part-time $1,027 per credit. Required fees: $352 per semester.

Princeton University, Graduate School, Department of History, Program in History of Science, Princeton, NJ 08544-1019. Offers PhD. *Degree requirements:* For doctorate, 2 foreign languages, thesis/dissertation. *Entrance requirements:* For doctorate, GRE General Test, sample of written work, 3 letters of recommendation. Additional exam requirements/recommendations for international students: Required—TOEFL (minimum score 600 paper-based; 250 computer-based). Electronic applications accepted. *Faculty research:* Early modern science, history of modern life sciences, history of physical sciences, history of modern technology, science and medicine in European expansion and colonialism.

Rensselaer Polytechnic Institute, Graduate School, School of Humanities and Social Sciences, Department of Science and Technology Studies, Troy, NY 12180-3590. Offers MS, PhD. Part-time programs available. *Faculty:* 15 full-time (6 women). *Students:* Average age 27. 47 applicants, 49% accepted, 7 enrolled. In 2007, 9 degrees awarded. Terminal master's awarded for partial completion of doctoral program. *Median time to degree:* Of those who began their doctoral program in fall 1999, 100% received their degree in 8 years or less. *Degree requirements:* For master's, thesis (for some programs); for doctorate, comprehensive exam, thesis/dissertation. *Entrance requirements:* For master's and doctorate, GRE General Test. Additional exam requirements/recommendations for international students: Required—TOEFL (minimum score 600 paper-based; 250 computer-based). *Application deadline:* For fall admission, 1/15 priority date for domestic students, 1/15 for international students. Applications are processed on a rolling basis. Application fee: $75. Electronic applications accepted. *Expenses:* Tuition: Full-time $34,900; part-time $1,454 per credit. Required fees: $1,802. *Financial support:* In 2007–08, 22 students received support, including 6 fellowships (averaging $20,000 per year), 2 research assistantships with full tuition reimbursements available (averaging $14,500 per year), 8 teaching assistantships with full tuition reimbursements available (averaging $14,500 per year); career-related internships or fieldwork, institutionally sponsored loans, and tuition waivers (partial) also available. Financial award application deadline: 1/15. *Faculty research:* Communities and technology, social dimensions of IT and biotechnology, ethics and policy, design. Total annual research expenditures: $75,000. *Unit head:* Dr. Sharon Anderson-Gold, Chair, 518-276-8837, Fax: 518-276-2659, E-mail: anders@rpi.edu. *Application contact:* Dr. Edward J. Woodhouse, Director of Graduate Studies, 518-276-8506, Fax: 518-276-2659, E-mail: woodhouse@rpi.edu.

Rutgers, The State University of New Jersey, New Brunswick, Graduate School, Program in History, New Brunswick, NJ 08901-1281. Offers African-American history (PhD); early American history (PhD); early modern European history (PhD); east Asian history (PhD); global and comparative history (PhD); history (PhD); history of diplomacy and foreign relations (PhD); history of technology, environment and health (PhD); history of the Atlantic cultures and African diaspora (PhD); Latin American history (PhD); medieval history (PhD); modern European history (PhD); nineteenth and twentieth century American history (PhD); women's and gender history (PhD). *Degree requirements:* For doctorate, thesis/dissertation. *Entrance requirements:* For doctorate, GRE General Test, sample of written work. Electronic applications accepted. *Faculty research:* American history, European history, Afro-American history, women's history, Latin American history.

Uniformed Services University of the Health Sciences, School of Medicine, Programs in Biomedical Sciences, Bethesda, MD 20814-4799. Offers emerging infectious diseases (PhD); medical and clinical psychology (PhD), including clinical psychology, medical psychology; medical history (MMH); microbiology and immunology (PhD); molecular and cell biology (PhD); neuroscience (PhD); preventive medicine and biometrics (MPH, MSPH, MTMH, Dr PH, PhD), including environmental health science (PhD), medical zoology (PhD), public health (MPH, MSPH, Dr PH), tropical medicine and hygiene (MTMH). *Faculty:* 372 full-time (119 women), 4,044 part-time/adjunct (908 women). *Students:* 154 full-time (76 women); includes 31 minority (6 African Americans, 4 American Indian/Alaska Native, 14 Asian Americans or Pacific Islanders, 7 Hispanic Americans), 9 international. Average age 28. 244 applicants, 41% accepted, 69 enrolled. In 2007, 55 master's, 10 doctorates awarded. Terminal master's awarded for partial completion of doctoral program. *Median time to degree:* Of those who began their doctoral program in fall 1999, 100% received their degree in 8 years or less. *Degree requirements:* For master's, comprehensive exam, thesis or alternative; for doctorate, comprehensive exam, thesis/dissertation, qualifying exam. *Entrance requirements:* For master's, GRE General Test; for doctorate, GRE General Test, minimum GPA of 3.0. Additional exam requirements/recommendations for international students: Required—TOEFL. *Application deadline:* For fall admission, 1/15 priority date for domestic students. Applications are processed on a rolling basis. Application fee: $0. *Financial support:* In 2007–08, fellowships with full tuition reimbursements (averaging $25,000 per year), research assistantships with full tuition reimbursements (averaging $25,000 per year) were awarded; career-related internships or fieldwork and tuition waivers (full) also available. *Unit head:* Dr. Eleanor S. Metcalf, Associate Dean, 301-295-1104, E-mail: emetcalf@usuhs.mil. *Application contact:* Janet M. Anastasi, Graduate Program Coordinator, 301-295-9474, Fax: 301-295-6772, E-mail: janastasi@usuhs.mil.

University of California, Berkeley, Graduate Division, College of Letters and Science, Group in Logic and the Methodology of Science, Berkeley, CA 94720-1500. Offers PhD. *Degree requirements:* For doctorate, qualifying exam, oral defense of dissertation. *Entrance requirements:* For doctorate, GRE General Test, minimum GPA of 3.5, 3 letters of recommendation. *Application deadline:* For fall admission, 12/14 for domestic students. Application fee: $70 ($90 for international students). *Financial support:* Fellowships, research assistantships, teaching assistantships, tuition waivers (full and partial) and unspecified assistantships available. *Faculty research:* Set theory, recursion theory, theoretical computer science, philosophy of mathematics, philosophy of language. *Unit head:* Paolo Mancosu, Chair, 510-642-5033, E-mail: mancosu@socrates.berkeley.edu. *Application contact:* Barbara F. Waller, Student Affairs Officer, 510-642-0665, E-mail: barb@math.berkeley.edu.

University of California, San Diego, Office of Graduate Studies, Department of History, La Jolla, CA 92093. Offers history (MA, PhD); Judaic studies (MA); science studies (PhD). *Degree requirements:* For doctorate, thesis/dissertation. *Entrance requirements:* For master's and doctorate, GRE General Test. Electronic applications accepted.

University of California, San Francisco, Graduate Division, Department of History of Health Sciences, San Francisco, CA 94143. Offers MA, PhD, MD/PhD. *Faculty:* 3 full-time. *Students:* 7 full-time (5 women); includes 2 minority (both Asian Americans or Pacific Islanders) 3 applicants, 0% accepted.Terminal master's awarded for partial completion of doctoral program. *Degree requirements:* For master's, 2 foreign languages, thesis; for doctorate, 2 foreign languages, thesis/dissertation. *Entrance requirements:* For master's and doctorate, GRE General Test. *Application deadline:* For fall admission, 2/1 for domestic students. Application fee: $40. *Financial support:* Fellowships, research assistantships, teaching assistantships available. Financial award application deadline: 1/10. *Unit head:* Dorothy Porter, Chair, 415-476-8826, E-mail: porterd@dahsm.ucsf.edu. *Application contact:* Kimberly Bissell, Program Assistant, 415-476-7223, Fax: 415-476-6715.

University of Delaware, College of Arts and Sciences, Department of History, Hagley Program in the History of Technology and Industrialization, Newark, DE 19716. Offers MA, PhD. *Degree requirements:* For master's, thesis optional; for doctorate, comprehensive exam, thesis/dissertation. *Entrance requirements:* For master's and doctorate, interview. *Application deadline:* For fall admission, 1/15 for domestic students. Electronic applications accepted. *Financial support:* Fellowships available. *Unit head:* Dr. Arwen Mohun, Director, 302-831-8226.

University of Massachusetts Amherst, Graduate School, College of Humanities and Fine Arts, Department of History, Amherst, MA 01003. Offers ancient history (MA); British Empire history (MA); European (medieval and modern) history (MA, PhD); Islamic history (MA); Latin American history (MA, PhD); modern global history (MA); public history (MA); science and technology history (MA); U.S. history (MA, PhD). Part-time programs available. *Faculty:* 30 full-time (13 women). *Students:* 21 full-time (10 women), 41 part-time (23 women); includes 5 minority (3 African Americans, 1 American Indian/Alaska Native, 1 Hispanic American), 4 international. Average age 32. 159 applicants, 34% accepted, 25 enrolled. In 2007, 13 master's, 2 doctorates awarded. Terminal master's awarded for partial completion of doctoral program. *Degree requirements:* For master's, one foreign language, thesis or alternative; for doctorate, one foreign language, thesis/dissertation. *Entrance requirements:* For master's and doctorate, GRE General Test, writing sample. Additional exam requirements/recommendations for international students: Required—TOEFL (minimum score 530 paper-based; 197 computer-based). *Application deadline:* For fall admission, 1/2 priority date for domestic and international students. Applications are processed on a rolling basis. Application fee: $50 ($65 for international students). Electronic applications accepted. *Expenses:* Tuition, state resident: full-time $2,640; part-time $110 per credit. Tuition, nonresident: full-time $9,936; part-time $414 per credit. Required fees: $7,455. One-time fee: $332. Tuition and fees vary according to course load, campus/location, program and reciprocity agreements. *Financial support:* In 2007–08, 1 fellowship with full tuition reimbursement (averaging $16,000 per year), 1 research assistantship with full tuition reimbursement (averaging $704 per year), 36 teaching assistantships with full tuition reimbursements (averaging $12,076 per year) were awarded; career-related internships or fieldwork, Federal Work-Study, scholarships/grants, traineeships, and unspecified assistantships also available. Support available to part-time students. Financial award application deadline: 2/1. *Unit head:* Dr. Audrey L. Altstadt, Chair, 413-545-2378, Fax: 413-545-6137.

University of Minnesota, Twin Cities Campus, Institute of Technology, Program in History of Science and Technology, Minneapolis, MN 55455-0213. Offers MA, PhD. Terminal master's awarded for partial completion of doctoral program. *Degree requirements:* For master's, one foreign language; for doctorate, 2 foreign languages, thesis/dissertation. *Entrance requirements:* For master's and doctorate, GRE General Test. *Faculty research:* History of physics, biology, and technology.

University of Notre Dame, Graduate School, College of Arts and Letters, Division of Humanities, Program in History and Philosophy of Science, Notre Dame, IN 46556. Offers MA, PhD. *Faculty:* 24 full-time (6 women). *Students:* 19 full-time (10 women); includes 1 minority (Hispanic American), 1 international. 32 applicants, 13% accepted, 4 enrolled. In 2007, 3 master's, 2 doctorates awarded. *Median time to degree:* Of those who began their doctoral program in fall 1999, 67% received their degree in 8 years or less. *Degree requirements:* For doctorate, 2 foreign languages, comprehensive exam, thesis/dissertation, candidacy exam. *Entrance requirements:* For doctorate, GRE General Test. Additional exam requirements/recommendations for international students: Required—TOEFL (minimum score 600 paper-based; 250 computer-based; 80 iBT). *Application deadline:* For fall admission, 1/15 priority date for domestic students. Application fee: $50. Electronic applications accepted. *Financial support:* In 2007–08, 5 fellowships with full tuition reimbursements (averaging $22,000 per year), 13 teaching assistantships with full tuition reimbursements (averaging $16,000 per year) were awarded; research assistantships with full tuition reimbursements, scholarships/grants and tuition waivers (full) also available. Financial award application deadline: 2/1. *Faculty research:* Philosophy of physics, science and ethics, history and philosophy of biology, history of medicine and technology, history and philosophy of economics. *Unit head:* Dr. Vaughn McKim, Director, 574-631-5015, Fax: 574-631-3958. *Application contact:* Dr. Jarren Gonzales, Director of Graduate Admissions, 574-631-7706, Fax: 574-631-4183.

University of Oklahoma, Graduate College, College of Arts and Sciences, Department of History of Science, Norman, OK 73019-0390. Offers MA, PhD. *Faculty:* 11 full-time (4 women). *Students:* 12 full-time (4 women), 3 part-time (1 woman). 9 applicants, 33% accepted, 1 enrolled. In 2007, 3 master's, 1 doctorate awarded. Terminal master's awarded for partial completion of doctoral program. *Degree requirements:* For master's, one foreign language, thesis (for some programs); for doctorate, 2 foreign languages, thesis/dissertation. *Entrance requirements:* For master's, GRE, minimum GPA of 3.0 in last 60 hours, 3 letters of reference, writing sample; for doctorate, GRE. Additional exam requirements/recommendations for international students: Required—TOEFL (minimum score 550 paper-based; 213 computer-based). *Application deadline:* For fall admission, 1/15 priority date for domestic students, 4/1 for international students; for spring admission, 11/1 for domestic students, 9/1 for international students. Application fee: $40 ($90 for international students). Electronic applications accepted. *Expenses:* Tuition, state resident: full-time $3,451; part-time $144 per credit hour. Tuition, nonresident: full-time $12,432; part-time $518 per credit hour. Required fees: $1,925; $70 per credit hour. $122 per semester. *Financial support:* In 2007–08, 5 students received support, including 3 fellowships with full tuition reimbursements available (averaging $5,000 per year), 4 research assistantships (averaging $15,720 per year), 6 teaching assistantships with partial tuition reimbursements available (averaging $14,048 per year); Federal Work-Study, institutionally sponsored loans, scholarships/grants, health care benefits, and unspecified assistantships also available. Financial award applicants required to submit FAFSA. *Faculty research:* Science and religion, Medieval science, Medieval and early modern science, history of technology, history of science in America, natural and social sciences in the modern world. Total annual research expenditures: $106,333. *Unit head:* Steven Livesey, Professor and Department Chair, 405-325-2213, Fax: 405-325-2363, E-mail: slivesey@ou.edu.

University of Pennsylvania, School of Arts and Sciences, Graduate Group in the History and Sociology of Science, Philadelphia, PA 19104. Offers AM, PhD. *Degree requirements:* For master's, thesis or alternative; for doctorate, 2 foreign languages, thesis/dissertation. *Entrance requirements:* For master's and doctorate, GRE General Test. Additional exam requirements/recommendations for international students: Required—TOEFL. Electronic applications accepted.

University of Pittsburgh, School of Arts and Sciences, Department of History and Philosophy of Science, Pittsburgh, PA 15260. Offers MA, PhD. *Faculty:* 8 full-time (1 woman), 2 part-time/adjunct (0 women). *Students:* 23 full-time (4 women); includes 1 minority (Asian American or Pacific Islander), 4 international. Average age 29. 52 applicants, 19% accepted, 5 enrolled. In 2007, 4 degrees awarded. Terminal master's awarded for partial completion of doctoral program. *Median time to degree:* Of those who began their doctoral program in fall 1999, 83% received their degree in 8 years or less. *Degree requirements:* For master's, one foreign language, comprehensive exam; for doctorate, 2 foreign languages, comprehensive exam, thesis/dissertation. *Entrance requirements:* For master's and doctorate, GRE General Test. Additional exam requirements/recommendations for international students: Required—TOEFL (minimum score 550 paper-based; 213 computer-based). *Application deadline:* For fall admission, 1/10 for domestic and international students. Application fee: $50. Electronic applications accepted. *Financial support:* In 2007–08, 25 students received support, including 10 fellowships with full tuition reimbursements available (averaging $20,304 per year), 11 teaching assistantships with full tuition reimbursements available (averaging $15,070 per year); health care benefits also available. Financial award application deadline: 1/10. *Faculty research:* History and philosophy of biology, psychology, neuroscience; history and philosophy of physics; early modern science; rhetoric of science; philosophy of social science. *Unit head:* Dr. Sandra Mitchell, Chairman, 412-624-5896, Fax: 412-624-6825, E-mail: smitchel@pitt.edu. *Application contact:* Joann McIntyre, Graduate Admissions Secretary, 412-624-5896, Fax: 412-624-6825, E-mail: vanna@pitt.edu.

University of Toronto, School of Graduate Studies, Humanities Division, Institute for the History and Philosophy of Science and Technology, Toronto, ON M5S 1A1, Canada. Offers MA, PhD. Part-time programs available. *Faculty:* 31 full-time, 1 part-time/adjunct. *Students:* 48 full-time (19 women), 4 part-time, 8 international. 57 applicants, 53% accepted. In 2007, 9 degrees awarded. *Degree requirements:* For master's, one foreign language, thesis optional, reading ability in French or German; for doctorate, 2 foreign languages, thesis/dissertation, reading knowledge examinations, thesis defense. *Entrance requirements:* For master's, 2 letters of reference; for doctorate, 2 letters of reference, MA in history and philosophy of science and technology, minimum A– average. Additional exam requirements/recommendations for international students: Required—TOEFL (minimum score 580 paper-based; 237 computer-based), TWE (minimum score 5). *Application deadline:* For fall admission, 2/1 for domestic students. Application fee: $100 Canadian dollars. *Financial support:* Fellowships, research assistantships, teaching assistantships available. *Unit head:* Prof. R. Paul Thompson, Director, 416-978-6280, Fax: 416-978-3003, E-mail: p.thompson@utoronto.ca. *Application contact:* Muna Salloum, Executive Assistant to the Director, 416-978-5131, Fax: 416-978-3003, E-mail: muna.salloum@utoronto.ca.

University of Wisconsin–Madison, Graduate School, College of Letters and Science, Department of History of Science, Madison, WI 53706-1380. Offers MA, PhD. Terminal master's awarded for partial completion of doctoral program. *Degree requirements:* For master's, thesis; for doctorate, 2 foreign languages, thesis/dissertation. *Entrance requirements:* For master's and doctorate, GRE General Test. Electronic applications accepted. *Faculty research:* History of biology, physical sciences, technology, medicine.

Virginia Polytechnic Institute and State University, Graduate School, College of Liberal Arts and Human Sciences, Program in Science and Technology Studies, Blacksburg, VA 24061. Offers MS, PhD. *Entrance requirements:* Additional exam requirements/recommendations for international students: Required—TOEFL (minimum score 550 paper-based; 213 computer-based). Electronic applications accepted.

West Virginia University, Eberly College of Arts and Sciences, Department of History, Morgantown, WV 26506. Offers African history (MA, PhD); African-American history (MA, PhD); American history (MA, PhD); Appalachian/regional history (MA, PhD); East Asian history (MA, PhD); European history (MA, PhD); history of science and technology (MA, PhD); Latin American history (MA). Part-time programs available. *Faculty:* 19 full-time (5 women), 12 part-time/adjunct (4 women). *Students:* 43 full-time (17 women), 30 part-time (11 women); includes 5 minority (1 African American, 1 American Indian/Alaska Native, 2 Asian Americans or Pacific Islanders, 1 Hispanic American), 7 international. Average age 33. 70 applicants, 59% accepted, 17 enrolled. In 2007, 8 master's, 3 doctorates awarded. *Median time to degree:* Of those who began their doctoral program in fall 1999, 75% received their degree in 8 years or less. *Degree requirements:* For master's, one foreign language, thesis (for some programs), oral exam, thesis defense; for doctorate, one foreign language, comprehensive exam, thesis/dissertation, dissertation defense. *Entrance requirements:* For master's, GRE General Test, minimum GPA of 3.0; for doctorate, GRE General Test. Additional exam requirements/recommendations for international students: Required—TOEFL (minimum score 550 paper-based), IELTS (minimum score 7). *Application deadline:* For fall admission, 12/31 for domestic students; for spring admission, 10/1 for domestic students. Applications are processed on a rolling basis. Application fee: $45. Electronic applications accepted. *Expenses:* Tuition, state resident: full-time $5,196; part-time $292 per credit hour. Tuition, nonresident: full-time $15,064; part-time $840 per credit hour. Tuition and fees vary according to program. *Financial support:* In 2007–08, 60 students received support, including 5 fellowships with full tuition reimbursements available (averaging $3,000 per year), 1 research assistantship with full tuition reimbursement available (averaging $7,200 per year), 8 teaching assistantships with full tuition reimbursements available (averaging $12,000 per year); career-related internships or fieldwork, Federal Work-Study, institutionally sponsored loans, health care benefits, tuition waivers (full and partial), and graduate administrative assistantships also available. Financial award application deadline: 12/31; financial award applicants required to submit FAFSA. *Faculty research:* U.S., Appalachia, modern Europe, Africa, colonial and post-colonial societies. Total annual research expenditures: $93,327. *Unit head:* Dr. Steven M. Zdatny, Chair, 304-293-2421 Ext. 5241, Fax: 304-293-3616, E-mail: steve.zdatny@mail.wvu.edu. *Application contact:* Dr. Greg A. Good, Director of Graduate Studies, 304-293-2421 Ext. 5247, Fax: 304-293-3616, E-mail: greg.good@mail.wvu.edu.

Yale University, Graduate School of Arts and Sciences, Department of History of Medicine and the Life Sciences, New Haven, CT 06520. Offers MS, PhD. *Degree requirements:* For doctorate, 2 foreign languages, thesis/dissertation. *Entrance requirements:* For doctorate, GRE General Test.

Medieval and Renaissance Studies

The Catholic University of America, School of Arts and Sciences, Program in Medieval and Byzantine Studies, Washington, DC 20064. Offers Byzantine studies (MA, Certificate); medieval studies (MA, PhD, Certificate). Part-time programs available. *Students:* 5 full-time (1 woman), 4 part-time (3 women). Average age 32. 1 applicant, 100% accepted, 1 enrolled.Terminal master's awarded for partial completion of doctoral program. *Degree requirements:* For master's, 2 foreign languages, comprehensive exam, thesis or alternative; for doctorate, 3 foreign languages, comprehensive exam, thesis/dissertation. *Entrance requirements:* For master's and doctorate, GRE General Test, 3 letters of recommendation, writing sample. Additional exam requirements/recommendations for international students: Required—TOEFL (minimum score 580 paper-based; 237 computer-based). *Application deadline:* For fall admission, 2/1 priority date for domestic students; for spring admission, 11/15 priority date for domestic students. Applications are processed on a rolling basis. Application fee: $55. Electronic applications accepted. *Financial support:* Fellowships, career-related internships or fieldwork, Federal Work-Study, scholarships/grants, tuition waivers (full and partial), and unspecified assistantships available. Support available to part-time students. Financial award application deadline: 2/1; financial award applicants required to submit FAFSA. *Unit head:* Dr. Timothy B. Noone, Director, 202-319-5794, Fax: 202-319-6609, E-mail: noonet@cua.edu.

Central European University, Graduate Studies, School of Social Sciences and Humanities, Budapest, Hungary. Offers economics (MA, PhD); gender studies (MA, PhD); international relations and European studies (MA, PhD); mathematics and its applications (MS, PhD); medieval studies (MA, PhD); nationalism studies (MA, PhD); philosophy (MA, PhD); political science (MA, PhD); public policy (MA, PhD); sociology and social anthropology (MA, PhD). *Faculty:* 75 full-time (25 women), 46 part-time/adjunct (10 women). *Students:* 625 full-time (355 women). Average age 26. 2,500 applicants, 31% accepted, 540 enrolled. In 2007, 325 master's, 20 doctorates awarded. Terminal master's awarded for partial completion of doctoral program. *Degree requirements:* For master's, one foreign language, thesis; for doctorate, one foreign language, comprehensive exam, thesis/dissertation. *Entrance requirements:* For master's, CEU subject tests, interview; for doctorate, GRE, CEU subject test, interview. Additional exam requirements/recommendations for international students: Required—TOEFL (minimum score 570 paper-based; 230 computer-based). *Application deadline:* For fall admission, 1/15 priority date for domestic and international students. Application fee: $0. Electronic applications accepted. Tuition charges are reported in euros. *Expenses:* Tuition: Full-time 10,000 euros; part-time 315 euros per credit. *Financial support:* In 2007–08, 402 students received support, including 350 fellowships with full and partial tuition reimbursements available (averaging $5,000 per year); career-related internships or fieldwork, institutionally sponsored loans, and scholarships/grants also available. Financial award application deadline: 1/5. *Faculty research:* Civil society, fiscal decentralization, party politics, political philosophy (especially Liberalism, theory of Democracy). Total annual research expenditures: $35,000. *Unit head:* Dr. Howard Michael Robinson, Provost, 361-327-3003, Fax: 361-327-3211, E-mail: robinson@ceu.hu. *Application contact:* Zsuzsanna Jaszberenyi, Admissions Officer, 361-327-3009, Fax: 361-327-3211, E-mail: admissions@ceu.hu.

See Close-Up on page 447.

Columbia University, Graduate School of Arts and Sciences, Program in Liberal Studies, New York, NY 10027. Offers American studies (MA); East Asian studies (MA); human rights studies (MA); Islamic culture studies (MA); Jewish studies (MA); medieval studies (MA); modern European studies (MA); South Asian studies (MA). Part-time and evening/weekend programs available. *Faculty:* 5 part-time/adjunct (2 women). *Students:* 7 full-time (2 women), 75 part-time (51 women); includes 5 minority (1 African American, 3 Asian Americans or Pacific Islanders, 1 Hispanic American), 8 international. Average age 41. 39 applicants, 77% accepted. In 2007, 20 degrees awarded. *Degree requirements:* For master's, thesis. Application fee: $90. *Expenses:* Tuition: Part-time $1,452 per credit. Required fees: $152 per term. One-time fee: $75 part-time. Full-time tuition and fees vary according to course level, course load, degree level and program. *Unit head:* Kristin Balicki, Program Coordinator, 212-854-4932, Fax: 212-854-4912, E-mail: knb2110@columbia.edu.

Cornell University, Graduate School, Graduate Fields of Arts and Sciences, Field of Archaeology, Ithaca, NY 14853-0001. Offers environmental archaeology (MA); historical archaeology (MA); Latin American archaeology (MA); medieval archaeology (MA); Mediterranean and Near Eastern archaeology (MA); Stone Age archaeology (MA). *Faculty:* 14 full-time (3 women). *Students:* 2 full-time (both women). Average age 26. 19 applicants, 5% accepted, 1 enrolled. In 2007, 2 degrees awarded. *Degree requirements:* For master's, one foreign language, thesis. *Entrance requirements:* For master's, GRE General Test, 3 letters of recommendation, sample of written work. Additional exam requirements/recommendations for international students: Required—TOEFL (minimum score 550 paper-based; 213 computer-based; 77 iBT). *Application deadline:* For fall admission, 1/15 for domestic students. Application fee: $70. Electronic applications accepted. *Financial support:* In 2007–08, 2 students received support, including 2 teaching assistantships with full tuition reimbursements available; fellowships with full tuition reimbursements available, research assistantships with full tuition reimbursements available, institutionally sponsored loans, scholarships/grants, health care benefits, tuition waivers (full and partial), and unspecified assistantships also available. Financial award applicants required to submit FAFSA. *Faculty research:* Anatolia, Lydia, Sardis, classical and Hellenistic Greece; science in archaeology; North American Indians; Stone Age Africa; Maya trade. *Unit head:* Director of Graduate Studies, 607-255-6768, E-mail: blj7@cornell.edu. *Application contact:* Graduate Field Assistant, 607-255-6768, E-mail: dsd6@cornell.edu.

Cornell University, Graduate School, Graduate Fields of Arts and Sciences, Field of English Language and Literature, Ithaca, NY 14853-0001. Offers African-American literature (PhD); American literature after 1865 (PhD); American literature to 1865 (PhD); American studies (PhD); colonial and postcolonial literature (PhD); creative writing (MFA); cultural studies (PhD); dramatic literature (PhD); English poetry (PhD); English Renaissance to 1660 (PhD); lesbian, bisexual, and gay literature studies (PhD); literary criticism and theory (PhD); nineteenth century (PhD); Old and Middle English (PhD); prose fiction (PhD); Restoration and eighteenth century (PhD); twentieth century (PhD); women's literature (PhD); MFA/PhD. *Faculty:* 59 full-time (28 women). *Students:* 97 full-time (53 women); includes 20 minority (7 African Americans, 3 American Indian/Alaska Native, 5 Asian Americans or Pacific Islanders, 5 Hispanic

Medieval and Renaissance Studies

Cornell University (continued)

Americans), 13 international. Average age 28. 759 applicants, 7% accepted, 21 enrolled. In 2007, 29 master's, 8 doctorates awarded. Terminal master's awarded for partial completion of doctoral program. *Degree requirements:* For master's, one foreign language, thesis; for doctorate, one foreign language, comprehensive exam, thesis/dissertation, teaching experience. *Entrance requirements:* For master's, GRE General Test, 3 letters of recommendation, creative writing sample; for doctorate, GRE General Test, GRE Subject Test (English), 3 letters of recommendation, writing sample. Additional exam requirements/recommendations for international students: Required—TOEFL (minimum score 600 paper-based; 250 computer-based; 77 iBT). *Application deadline:* For fall admission, 1/10 for domestic students. Application fee: $70. Electronic applications accepted. *Financial support:* In 2007–08, 92 students received support, including 32 fellowships with full tuition reimbursements available, 60 teaching assistantships with full tuition reimbursements available; research assistantships with full tuition reimbursements available, institutionally sponsored loans, scholarships/grants, health care benefits, tuition waivers (full and partial), and unspecified assistantships also available. Financial award applicants required to submit FAFSA. *Faculty research:* English and American literature, women's writing, ethnic and post-colonial literature, critical theory, medievalism. *Unit head:* Director of Graduate Studies, 607-255-7989, Fax: 607-255-6661. *Application contact:* Graduate Field Assistant, 607-255-7989, Fax: 607-255-6661, E-mail: english_grad@cornell.edu.

Cornell University, Graduate School, Graduate Fields of Arts and Sciences, Field of History, Ithaca, NY 14853-0001. Offers African history (MA, PhD); American history (MA, PhD); ancient history (MA, PhD); early modern European history (MA, PhD); English history (MA, PhD); French history (MA, PhD); German history (MA, PhD); history of science (MA, PhD); Latin American history (MA, PhD); medieval Chinese history (MA, PhD); medieval history (MA, PhD); modern Chinese history (MA, PhD); modern European history (MA, PhD); modern Japanese history (MA, PhD); premodern Islamic history (MA, PhD); premodern Japanese history (MA, PhD); Renaissance history (MA, PhD); Russian history (MA, PhD); Southeast Asian history (MA, PhD). *Faculty:* 56 full-time (14 women). *Students:* 63 full-time (29 women); includes 11 minority (6 African Americans, 2 Asian Americans or Pacific Islanders, 3 Hispanic Americans), 20 international. Average age 31. 201 applicants, 6% accepted, 10 enrolled. In 2007, 11 master's, 11 doctorates awarded. Terminal master's awarded for partial completion of doctoral program. *Degree requirements:* For master's, thesis; for doctorate, 2 foreign languages, comprehensive exam, thesis/dissertation, 1 year of teaching experience. *Entrance requirements:* For master's and doctorate, GRE General Test, writing sample, 3 letters of recommendation. Additional exam requirements/recommendations for international students: Required—TOEFL (minimum score 550 paper-based; 213 computer-based; 77 iBT). *Application deadline:* For fall admission, 1/15 for domestic students. Application fee: $70. Electronic applications accepted. *Financial support:* In 2007–08, 54 students received support, including 26 fellowships with full tuition reimbursements available, 28 teaching assistantships with full tuition reimbursements available; research assistantships with full tuition reimbursements available, institutionally sponsored loans, scholarships/grants, health care benefits, tuition waivers (full and partial), and unspecified assistantships also available. Financial award applicants required to submit FAFSA. *Unit head:* Director of Graduate Studies, 607-255-6738, Fax: 607-255-0469. *Application contact:* Graduate Field Assistant, 607-255-6738, Fax: 607-255-0469, E-mail: history_grad_info@cornell.edu.

Cornell University, Graduate School, Graduate Fields of Arts and Sciences, Field of History of Art and Archaeology, Ithaca, NY 14853. Offers American art (PhD); ancient art and archaeology (PhD); Asian art (PhD); baroque art (PhD); medieval art (PhD); modern art (PhD); Renaissance art (PhD); Southeast Asian art (PhD); theory and criticism (PhD). *Faculty:* 21 full-time (14 women). *Students:* 22 full-time (17 women); includes 6 minority (2 African Americans, 2 Asian Americans or Pacific Islanders, 2 Hispanic Americans), 6 international. Average age 32. 61 applicants, 15% accepted, 4 enrolled. In 2007, 2 doctorates awarded. *Degree requirements:* For doctorate, one foreign language, comprehensive exam, thesis/dissertation, general exams in 3 areas. *Entrance requirements:* For doctorate, GRE General Test, sample of written work, 3 letters of recommendation. Additional exam requirements/recommendations for international students: Required—TOEFL (minimum score 550 paper-based; 213 computer-based; 77 iBT). *Application deadline:* For fall admission, 1/15 for domestic students. Application fee: $70. Electronic applications accepted. *Financial support:* In 2007–08, 17 students received support, including 10 fellowships with full tuition reimbursements available, 7 teaching assistantships with full tuition reimbursements available; research assistantships with full tuition reimbursements available, institutionally sponsored loans, scholarships/grants, health care benefits, tuition waivers (full and partial), and unspecified assistantships also available. Financial award applicants required to submit FAFSA. *Unit head:* Director of Graduate Studies, 607-255-4905, Fax: 607-255-0566, E-mail: art_history@cornell.edu. *Application contact:* Director of Graduate Studies, 607-255-4905, Fax: 607-255-0566, E-mail: art_history@cornell.edu.

Cornell University, Graduate School, Graduate Fields of Arts and Sciences, Field of Medieval Studies, Ithaca, NY 14853-0001. Offers medieval archaeology (PhD); medieval art (PhD); medieval history (PhD); medieval literature (PhD); medieval music (PhD); medieval philology and linguistics (PhD); medieval philosophy (PhD). *Faculty:* 36 full-time (12 women). *Students:* 16 full-time (10 women), 2 international. Average age 29. 23 applicants, 17% accepted, 2 enrolled. *Degree requirements:* For doctorate, 3 foreign languages, comprehensive exam, thesis/dissertation, teaching experience. *Entrance requirements:* For doctorate, GRE General Test, 3 letters of recommendation, proficiency in Latin (recommended), 20 page writing sample on a Medieval topic. Additional exam requirements/recommendations for international students: Required—TOEFL (minimum score 600 paper-based; 250 computer-based; 77 iBT). *Application deadline:* For fall admission, 1/15 for domestic students. Application fee: $70. Electronic applications accepted. *Financial support:* In 2007–08, 16 students received support, including 7 fellowships with full tuition reimbursements available, 9 teaching assistantships with full tuition reimbursements available; research assistantships with full tuition reimbursements available, institutionally sponsored loans, scholarships/grants, health care benefits, tuition waivers (full and partial), and unspecified assistantships also available. Financial award applicants required to submit FAFSA. *Faculty research:* Interdisciplinary study of medieval culture, languages, literatures, history, archaeology. *Unit head:* Director of Graduate Studies, 607-255-8545. *Application contact:* Graduate Field Assistant, 607-255-8545, E-mail: medievalst@cornell.edu.

Duke University, Graduate School, Program in Medieval and Renaissance Studies, Durham, NC 27708. Offers Certificate. *Application deadline:* For fall admission, 12/31 for domestic students. Application fee: $75. *Financial support:* Application deadline: 12/31. *Unit head:* Marc Schachter, Director, 919-660-2421, E-mail: schachte@duke.edu.

Fordham University, Graduate School of Arts and Sciences, Center for Medieval Studies, New York, NY 10458. Offers MA, Certificate. Part-time and evening/weekend programs available. *Students:* Average age 28. 20 applicants, 85% accepted, 3 enrolled. In 2007, 8 degrees awarded. *Degree requirements:* For master's, thesis. *Entrance requirements:* For master's, GRE General Test. Additional exam requirements/recommendations for international students: Required—TOEFL (minimum score 650 paper-based; 280 computer-based). *Application deadline:* For fall admission, 1/4 priority date for domestic students; for spring admission, 11/1 for domestic students. Application fee: $70. Electronic applications accepted. *Expenses:* Tuition: Full-time $23,880; part-time $995 per credit. *Financial support:* In 2007–08, 4 students received support, including 4 research assistantships with tuition reimbursements available (averaging $11,187 per year); fellowships with tuition reimbursements available, institutionally sponsored loans, tuition waivers (full and partial), and unspecified assistantships also available. Financial award application deadline: 1/4; financial award applicants required to submit FAFSA. *Faculty research:* Medieval literature, Medieval history, Medieval philosophy, Medieval theology, Medieval fine arts, Anglo-Norman. Total annual research expenditures: $77,440. *Unit head:* Dr. Maryanne Kowaleski, Director, 718-817-4655, E-mail: kowaleski@fordham.edu. *Application contact:* Charlene Dundie, Director of Graduate Admissions, 718-817-4420, Fax: 718-817-3566, E-mail: dundie@fordham.edu.

Graduate School and University Center of the City University of New York, Graduate Studies, Interdisciplinary Studies, New York, NY 10016-4039. Offers language in social context (PhD); medieval studies (PhD); public policy (MA, PhD); urban studies (MA, PhD); women's studies (MA, PhD). Terminal master's awarded for partial completion of doctoral program. *Degree requirements:* For master's, thesis; for doctorate, comprehensive exam, thesis/dissertation. *Entrance requirements:* For master's and doctorate, GRE General Test. *Application deadline:* For fall admission, 2/1 for domestic students. Application fee: $40. *Financial support:* Application deadline: 2/1. *Unit head:* Chairman, 212-642-2430.

Harvard University, Graduate School of Arts and Sciences, Department of English and American Literature and Language, Cambridge, MA 02138. Offers critical theory (PhD); eighteenth-century literature (PhD); literature: nineteenth-century to the present (PhD); medieval literature and language (PhD); modern British and American literature (PhD); Renaissance literature (PhD). Terminal master's awarded for partial completion of doctoral program. *Degree requirements:* For doctorate, 2 foreign languages, thesis/dissertation, oral exam. *Entrance requirements:* For doctorate, GRE General Test, GRE Subject Test, writing sample. Additional exam requirements/recommendations for international students: Required—TOEFL. *Expenses:* Tuition: Full-time $31,456. Full-time tuition and fees vary according to program and student level. *Faculty research:* Old and Middle English language and literature, drama, creative writing, transition to Romanticism, history and theory of criticism.

Indiana University Bloomington, University Graduate School, College of Arts and Sciences, Department of Germanic Studies, Bloomington, IN 47405-7000. Offers German literature and studies (PhD); German studies (MA, PhD), including German and business studies (MA), German literature and culture (MA), German literature and linguistics (MA); medieval German studies (PhD); teaching German (MAT). *Faculty:* 12 full-time (3 women), 6 part-time/adjunct (2 women). *Students:* 27 full-time (15 women), 8 part-time (3 women); includes 1 minority (African American), 9 international. Average age 31. 26 applicants, 35% accepted, 9 enrolled. In 2007, 3 master's, 6 doctorates awarded. Terminal master's awarded for partial completion of doctoral program. *Median time to degree:* Of those who began their doctoral program in fall 1999, 86% received their degree in 8 years or less. *Degree requirements:* For master's, one foreign language; for doctorate, one foreign language, comprehensive exam, thesis/dissertation. *Entrance requirements:* For master's, GRE General Test, BA in German or equivalent; for doctorate, GRE General Test, MA in German or equivalent. Additional exam requirements/recommendations for international students: Required—TOEFL. *Application deadline:* For fall admission, 1/15 priority date for domestic students, 12/15 for international students; for spring admission, 9/1 priority date for domestic students, 9/1 for international students. Applications are processed on a rolling basis. Application fee: $50 ($60 for international students). *Financial support:* Fellowships with full and partial tuition reimbursements, research assistantships, teaching assistantships with full tuition reimbursements, Federal Work-Study, institutionally sponsored loans, scholarships/grants, and unspecified assistantships available. Support available to part-time students. Financial award application deadline: 1/15; financial award applicants required to submit FAFSA. *Faculty research:* German (and European) literature: medieval to modern/postmodern, German and culture studies, Germanic philology, literary theory, literature and the other arts. *Unit head:* Kari Ellen Gade, Director of Graduate Studies, 812-855-8138, Fax: 812-855-8292, E-mail: gade@indiana.edu. *Application contact:* Michelle Dunbar, Graduate Secretary, 812-855-7947, E-mail: germanic@indiana.edu.

Marquette University, Graduate School, College of Arts and Sciences, Department of History, Milwaukee, WI 53201-1881. Offers European history (MA, PhD); medieval history (MA); Renaissance and Reformation (MA); United States history (MA, PhD). Part-time programs available. *Faculty:* 20 full-time (4 women), 2 part-time/adjunct (0 women). *Students:* 52. Average age 31. 39 applicants, 56% accepted, 12 enrolled. In 2007, 9 master's, 5 doctorates awarded. Terminal master's awarded for partial completion of doctoral program. *Degree requirements:* For master's, comprehensive exam, thesis or alternative; for doctorate, one foreign language, thesis/dissertation, qualifying exam. *Entrance requirements:* For master's, GRE General Test, GRE Subject Test; for doctorate, GRE General Test, writing sample. Additional exam requirements/recommendations for international students: Required—TOEFL. Application fee: $40. *Financial support:* In 2007–08, 4 fellowships, 5 research assistantships, 15 teaching assistantships were awarded; Federal Work-Study, institutionally sponsored loans, scholarships/grants, and tuition waivers (full and partial) also available. Support available to part-time students. Financial award application deadline: 2/15. *Faculty research:* Social history, political history, diplomatic history, history of science, religious history. Total annual research expenditures: $44,005. *Unit head:* James Marten, Chair, 414-288-7901, Fax: 414-288-1578.

Rutgers, The State University of New Jersey, New Brunswick, Graduate School, Program in History, New Brunswick, NJ 08901-1281. Offers African-American history (PhD); early American history (PhD); early modern European history (PhD); east Asian history (PhD); global and comparative history (PhD); history (PhD); history of diplomacy and foreign relations (PhD); history of technology, environment and health (PhD); history of the Atlantic cultures and African diaspora (PhD); Latin American history (PhD); medieval history (PhD); modern European history (PhD); nineteenth and twentieth century American history (PhD); women's and gender history (PhD). *Degree requirements:* For doctorate, thesis/dissertation. *Entrance requirements:* For doctorate, GRE General Test, sample of written work. Electronic applications accepted. *Faculty research:* American history, European history, Afro-American history, women's history, Latin American history.

Southern Methodist University, Dedman College, Program in Medieval Studies, Dallas, TX 75275. Offers MA. Part-time programs available. *Students:* 3 full-time (2 women), 2 part-time (1 woman); includes 1 minority (Asian American or Pacific Islander) Average age 28. In 2007, 1 degree awarded. *Degree requirements:* For master's, 2 foreign languages, thesis. *Entrance requirements:* For master's, GRE General Test, minimum GPA of 3.0. *Application deadline:* Applications are processed on a rolling basis. Application fee: $60. Electronic applications accepted. *Financial support:* Federal Work-Study and institutionally sponsored loans available. *Faculty research:* Byzantine culture, medieval Europe, Arthurian literature, Chaucer, romance. *Unit head:* Dr. Bonnie Wheeler, Director, 214-768-2949, Fax: 214-768-1234, E-mail: bwheeler@smu.edu.

Tufts University, Graduate School of Arts and Sciences, Department of Drama and Dance, Medford, MA 02155. Offers dance (MA, PhD); drama (MA); dramatic literature and criticism (PhD); theater history (PhD). Part-time programs available. *Faculty:* 11 full-time, 8 part-time/adjunct. *Students:* 27 (18 women); includes 4 minority (1 African American, 3 Asian Americans or Pacific Islanders) 2 international. 37 applicants, 32% accepted, 4 enrolled. In 2007, 1 master's, 4 doctorates awarded. Terminal master's awarded for partial completion of doctoral program. *Degree requirements:* For master's, one foreign language, thesis; for doctorate, 2 foreign languages, thesis/dissertation, oral exam, written general exam. *Entrance requirements:* For master's and doctorate, GRE General Test, writing sample. Additional exam requirements/recommendations for international students: Required—TOEFL (minimum score 600 paper-based; 250 computer-based; 80 iBT). *Application deadline:* For fall admission, 1/15 for domestic students, 12/30 for international students. Applications are processed on a rolling basis. Application fee: $70. Electronic applications accepted. *Expenses:* Tuition: Full-time $35,052. *Financial support:* Fellowships with full and partial tuition reimbursements, teaching assistantships with full and partial tuition reimbursements, Federal Work-Study, scholarships/grants, and tuition waivers (partial) available. Support available to part-time students. Financial award application deadline: 1/15; financial award applicants required to submit FAFSA. *Unit head:* Dr. Barbara Grossman, Chair, 617-627-3524. *Application contact:* Dr. Laurence Senelick, Head, 617-627-3524.

University of California, Santa Barbara, Graduate Division, College of Letters and Sciences, Division of Humanities and Fine Arts, Department of History, Santa Barbara, CA 93106. Offers history (PhD), including European medieval studies, global studies, public history, technology and society, women's studies; MA/PhD. *Faculty:* 44 full-time (19 women), 7 part-time/adjunct (3 women). *Students:* 122 full-time (66 women); includes 26 minority (3 African Americans, 6 Asian Americans or Pacific Islanders, 17 Hispanic Americans), 8 international. Average age 34. 139 applicants, 38% accepted, 21 enrolled. In 2007, 16 doctorates awarded. Terminal master's awarded for partial completion of doctoral program. *Median time to degree:* Of those who began their doctoral program in fall 1999, 47% received their degree in 8 years or less. *Degree requirements:* For doctorate, one foreign language, comprehensive exam, thesis/dissertation, one or more languages depending on field of study. *Entrance requirements:* For doctorate, GRE. Additional exam requirements/recommendations for international students: Required—TOEFL (minimum score 550 paper-based; 213 computer-based; 80 iBT). *Application deadline:* For fall admission, 12/5 for domestic and international students. Application fee: $60. Electronic applications accepted. *Expenses:* Tuition, nonresident: full-time $14,888. Required fees: $10,108. *Financial support:* In 2007–08, 109 students received support, including 44 fellowships with full and partial tuition reimbursements available (averaging $9,600 per year), 40 teaching assistantships with partial tuition reimbursements available (averaging $16,391 per year); research assistantships, Federal Work-Study, scholarships/grants, traineeships, health care benefits, tuition waivers (full and partial), and unspecified assistantships also available. Financial award application deadline: 12/5. *Faculty research:* Europe, U. S., Latin America, Middle East, East Asia. *Unit head:* Kenneth J. Mouré, Chair, 805-893-8156, Fax: 805-893-8795, E-mail: moure@history.ucrb.edu. *Application contact:* Deborah Johnson, Graduate Program Assistant, 805-893-2224, Fax: 805-893-8795, E-mail: deborahj@history.ucsb.edu.

University of Colorado at Boulder, Graduate School, College of Arts and Sciences, Department of Spanish and Portuguese, Boulder, CO 80309. Offers Hispanic linguistics (MA); medieval/early modern Hispanic literatures (PhD); Spanish literature (MA, PhD), including 18th and 19th century peninsular literature (MA), Golden Age (MA), medieval Iberian literature (MA). Part-time programs available. *Faculty:* 14. *Students:* 28 full-time (19 women), 14 part-time (10 women); includes 12 minority (all Hispanic Americans), 18 international. Average age 32. 17 applicants, 88% accepted. In 2007, 5 master's, 4 doctorates awarded. Terminal master's awarded for partial completion of doctoral program. *Degree requirements:* For master's, one foreign language, comprehensive exam, thesis or alternative; for doctorate, 2 foreign languages, thesis/dissertation. *Entrance requirements:* For master's, minimum undergraduate GPA of 2.75. *Application deadline:* For fall admission, 12/15 priority date for domestic students, 12/15 for international students. Applications are processed on a rolling basis. Application fee: $50 ($60 for international students). *Financial support:* In 2007–08, 41 fellowships with full tuition reimbursements (averaging $1,663 per year) were awarded; tuition waivers (full) also available. Financial award application deadline: 12/15. *Faculty research:* Spanish peninsular and Spanish-American literatures; Hispanic linguistics; Medieval, Golden Age, eighteenth and nineteenth century literatures. Total annual research expenditures: $6,076. *Unit head:* Ricardo Laudiera, Chair, 303-492-5386, Fax: 303-492-3699, E-mail: laudiera@colorado.edu. *Application contact:* Graduate Program Assistant, 303-492-7308, Fax: 303-492-3699, E-mail: spanport@colorado.edu.

University of Connecticut, Graduate School, College of Liberal Arts and Sciences, Field of Medieval Studies, Storrs, CT 06269. Offers MA, PhD. *Faculty:* 18 full-time (6 women). *Students:* 17 full-time (11 women), 2 part-time; includes 1 minority (African American) Average age 31. 23 applicants, 22% accepted, 4 enrolled. In 2007, 3 master's, 1 doctorate awarded. Terminal master's awarded for partial completion of doctoral program. *Degree requirements:* For master's, comprehensive exam; for doctorate, 3 foreign languages, thesis/dissertation. *Entrance requirements:* For master's and doctorate, GRE General Test, GRE Subject Test. Additional exam requirements/recommendations for international students: Required—TOEFL (minimum score 550 paper-based; 213 computer-based). *Application deadline:* For fall admission, 2/1 priority date for domestic and international students; for spring admission, 11/1 for domestic students, 10/1 for international students. Applications are processed on a rolling basis. Application fee: $55. Electronic applications accepted. *Expenses:* Tuition, state resident: part-time $469 per credit hour. Tuition, nonresident: part-time $1,218 per credit hour. *Financial support:* In 2007–08, 3 research assistantships with full tuition reimbursements, 13 teaching assistantships with full tuition reimbursements were awarded; fellowships, Federal Work-Study, scholarships/grants, health care benefits, and unspecified assistantships also available. Financial award application deadline: 2/1; financial award applicants required to submit FAFSA. *Unit head:* Robert Hasenfratz, Co-Director, 860-486-1525, Fax: 860-486-1530, E-mail: robert.hasenfratz@uconn.edu.

See Close-Up on page 587.

University of Guelph, Graduate Program Services, College of Arts, School of English and Theatre Studies, Joint Program in Literary Studies/Theatre Studies in English, Guelph, ON N1G 2W1, Canada. Offers PhD. Part-time programs available. *Faculty:* 30 full-time (15 women). *Students:* 22 full-time (10 women), 1 (woman) part-time; includes 1 African American, 1 Asian American or Pacific Islander. 31 applicants, 35% accepted, 6 enrolled. In 2007, 1 degree awarded. *Degree requirements:* For doctorate, one foreign language, comprehensive exam, thesis/dissertation. *Entrance requirements:* For doctorate, MA, 3 letters of reference, writing samples, resumé, minimum A- average in graduate course work. Additional exam requirements/recommendations for international students: Required—TOEFL. *Application deadline:* For fall admission, 2/1 priority date for domestic students, 2/1 for international students. Application fee: $85. Electronic applications accepted. *Financial support:* In 2007–08, 6 students received support, including research assistantships (averaging $9,212 per year), teaching assistantships (averaging $9,212 per year); tuition waivers (full) also available. Financial award application deadline: 2/15. *Faculty research:* Canadian studies, Early Modern studies, Postcolonial studies, studies in gender and genre, 19th Century studies. Total annual research expenditures: $500,000. *Application contact:* Dr. Daniel O'Quinn, Graduate Coordinator, 519-824-4120 Ext. 53250, Fax: 519-766-0844, E-mail: doquinn@uoguelph.ca.

University of Michigan, Horace H. Rackham School of Graduate Studies, College of Literature, Science, and the Arts, Program in Medieval and Early Modern Studies, Ann Arbor, MI 48109. Offers Certificate. *Students:* 2 applicants, 100% accepted, 2 enrolled. *Entrance requirements:* For degree, acceptance by Rackham Graduate School and A- average grade. *Financial support:* In 2007–08, 3 fellowships (averaging $750 per year) were awarded; scholarships/grants also available. *Unit head:* Karla Taylor, Associate Professor of English and Director, 734-764-6363, Fax: 734-647-4881, E-mail: kttaylor@umich.edu. *Application contact:* Terre Fisher, Programs Coordinator, 734-763-2016, Fax: 734-647-4881, E-mail: teif@umich.edu.

University of Minnesota, Twin Cities Campus, Graduate School, College of Liberal Arts, Department of German, Scandinavian, and Dutch, Minneapolis, MN 55455-0213. Offers Germanic studies: German and Scandinavian studies track (PhD); Germanic studies: German track (MA, PhD); Germanic studies: Germanic medieval studies track (MA, PhD); Germanic studies: Scandinavian studies track (MA); Germanic studies: teaching track (MA). Part-time programs available. *Faculty:* 19 full-time (8 women). *Students:* 22 full-time (14 women), 6 part-time (4 women); includes 2 minority (1 African American, 1 Hispanic American), 10 international. 31 applicants, 61% accepted, 8 enrolled. In 2007, 1 master's, 6 doctorates awarded. Terminal master's awarded for partial completion of doctoral program. *Degree requirements:* For doctorate, 2 foreign languages, thesis/dissertation. *Entrance requirements:* For master's, GRE General Test, BA in German, Scandinavian, or equivalent; for doctorate, GRE General Test, MA in German, Scandinavian, or equivalent. Additional exam requirements/recommendations for international students: Required—TOEFL (minimum score 550 paper-based; 213 computer-based; 79 iBT). *Application deadline:* For fall admission, 12/15 for domestic and international students. Application fee: $55 ($75 for international students). Electronic applications accepted. *Financial support:* In 2007–08, 85 fellowships with full tuition reimbursements (averaging $18,000 per year), 1 research assistantship with full tuition reimbursement (averaging $11,985 per year), 14 teaching assistantships with full tuition reimbursements (averaging $12,839 per year) were awarded; career-related internships or fieldwork, Federal Work-Study, institutionally sponsored loans, scholarships/grants, health care benefits, and unspecified assistantships also available. Support available to part-time students. Financial award application deadline: 1/10. *Faculty research:* Cultural studies, literary theory, feminist criticism, film, Germanic philology. *Unit head:* Prof. Charlotte Melin, Chair, 612-625-2080, Fax: 612-624-8297, E-mail: melin005@umn.edu. *Application contact:* Director of Graduate Studies, 612-625-9034, Fax: 612-624-8297, E-mail: gsd@umn.edu.

University of Notre Dame, Graduate School, College of Arts and Letters, Division of Humanities, Medieval Institute, Notre Dame, IN 46556. Offers MMS, PhD. *Faculty:* 51 full-time (20 women). *Students:* 32 full-time (12 women); includes 1 minority (Hispanic American), 3 international. 83 applicants, 11% accepted, 6 enrolled. In 2007, 5 master's, 1 doctorate awarded. Terminal master's awarded for partial completion of doctoral program. *Median time to degree:* Of those who began their doctoral program in fall 1999, 65% received their degree in 8 years or less. *Degree requirements:* For master's, 3 foreign languages, comprehensive exam; for doctorate, 3 foreign languages, thesis/dissertation, candidacy exam. *Entrance requirements:* For master's and doctorate, GRE General Test. Additional exam requirements/recommendations for international students: Required—TOEFL (minimum score 600 paper-based; 250 computer-based; 80 iBT). *Application deadline:* For fall admission, 1/15 for domestic and international students. Application fee: $50. Electronic applications accepted. *Financial support:* In 2007–08, 7 fellowships with full tuition reimbursements (averaging $22,000 per year), 10 teaching assistantships with full tuition reimbursements (averaging $16,000 per year) were awarded; research assistantships with full tuition reimbursements, tuition waivers (full) also available. Financial award application deadline: 2/1. *Faculty research:* Medieval history, vernacular literatures, theology, philosophy, Ambrosiana manuscripts and drawings. *Unit head:* Dr. Thomas Noble, Director, 574-631-6603, Fax: 574-631-8644. *Application contact:* Dr. Jarren Gonzales, Director of Graduate Admissions, 574-631-7706, Fax: 574-631-4183.

University of Toronto, School of Graduate Studies, Humanities Division, Centre for Medieval Studies, Toronto, ON M5S 1A1, Canada. Offers MA, PhD. Part-time programs available. *Faculty:* 51 full-time, 12 part-time/adjunct. *Students:* 105 full-time (63 women), 1 part-time, 60 international. 166 applicants, 43% accepted. In 2007, 19 master's, 1 doctorate awarded. *Degree requirements:* For master's, one foreign language, thesis optional, 4 courses or 3 courses and a thesis; for doctorate, 3 foreign languages, thesis/dissertation, proficiency in Latin, German and French. *Entrance requirements:* For master's, letters of reference, minimum B+ average, course work in the medieval period; for doctorate, letters of reference, passing score on MA Latin examination. Additional exam requirements/recommendations for international students: Required—TOEFL (minimum score 580 paper-based; 237 computer-based), TWE (minimum score 5). *Application deadline:* For fall admission, 1/20 for domestic students. Application fee: $100 Canadian dollars. *Unit head:* Prof. Lawrin Armstrong, Acting Director, 416-978-5422, Fax: 416-971-1398. *Application contact:* Grace Desa, Graduate Administrator, 416-978-4884, Fax: 416-971-1398, E-mail: medieval@chass.utoronto.ca.

Western Michigan University, Graduate College, College of Arts and Sciences, Medieval Studies, Kalamazoo, MI 49008-5202. Offers MA. *Degree requirements:* For master's, one foreign language, thesis optional, oral exam.

Yale University, Graduate School of Arts and Sciences, Interdisciplinary Program in Medieval Studies, New Haven, CT 06520. Offers MA, PhD. *Entrance requirements:* For doctorate, GRE General Test.

Yale University, Graduate School of Arts and Sciences, Program in Renaissance Studies, New Haven, CT 06520. Offers PhD. *Degree requirements:* For doctorate, 3 foreign languages. *Entrance requirements:* For doctorate, GRE General Test.

Public History

Appalachian State University, Cratis D. Williams Graduate School, Department of History, Boone, NC 28608. Offers history (MA); history education (MA); public history (MA). Part-time programs available. *Faculty:* 28 full-time (8 women). *Students:* 20 full-time (8 women), 23 part-time (9 women); includes 3 minority (1 American Indian/Alaska Native, 1 Asian American or Pacific Islander, 1 Hispanic American), 1 international. 25 applicants, 84% accepted, 15 enrolled. In 2007, 5 master's awarded. *Degree requirements:* For master's, one foreign language, comprehensive exam, thesis (for some programs). *Entrance requirements:* For master's, GRE General Test, 3 letters of recommendation. Additional exam requirements/recommendations for international students: Required—TOEFL (minimum score 570 paper-based; 230 computer-based; 79 iBT), IELTS (minimum score 7), TOEFL or IELTS. *Application deadline:* For fall admission, 7/1 for domestic students, 1/1 for international students; for spring admission, 11/1 for domestic students, 6/1 for international students. Applications are processed on a rolling basis. Application fee: $50. Electronic applications accepted. *Expenses:* Tuition, state resident: part-time $127 per semester hour. Tuition, nonresident: part-time $597 per semester hour. Required fees: $18 per semester. *Financial support:* In 2007–08, 4 research assistantships (averaging $10,000 per year), 7 teaching assistantships (averaging $7,500 per year) were awarded; fellowships, career-related internships or fieldwork, Federal Work-Study, scholarships/grants, and unspecified assistantships also available. Financial award application deadline: 4/1. *Faculty research:* Women's history, social/cultural history, US history, Latin America, medieval studies. Total annual research expenditures: $4,370. *Unit head:* Dr. Michael Krenn, Chairperson, 828-262-2282, E-mail: krennml@appstate.edu. *Application contact:* Dr. James Goff, Director, 828-262-6019, E-mail: goffjr@appstate.edu.

Arizona State University, Graduate College, College of Liberal Arts and Sciences, Division of Humanities, Department of History, Tempe, AZ 85287. Offers Asian history (MA, PhD); British history (MA, PhD); European history (MA, PhD); Latin American studies (MA, PhD); public history (MA); U.S. history (PhD); U.S. western history (MA). *Degree requirements:* For master's, thesis or alternative; for doctorate, 2 foreign languages, thesis/dissertation. *Entrance requirements:* For master's and doctorate, GRE.

California State University, Sacramento, Graduate Studies, College of Arts and Letters, Department of History, Sacramento, CA 95819-6048. Offers public history (MA). Part-time programs available. *Students:* 26 full-time (16 women), 58 part-time (37 women); includes 13 minority (3 African Americans, 2 American Indian/Alaska Native, 3 Asian Americans or Pacific Islanders, 5 Hispanic Americans). Average age 34. 69 applicants, 70% accepted, 33 enrolled. *Degree requirements:* For master's, thesis or alternative, writing proficiency exam. *Entrance requirements:* For master's, GRE General Test, minimum GPA of 3.25 in history, 3.0 overall during previous 2 years; BA in history or equivalent. Additional exam requirements/recommendations for international students: Required—TOEFL. *Application deadline:* Applica-

Public History

California State University, Sacramento (continued)
tions are processed on a rolling basis. Application fee: $55. Electronic applications accepted. *Expenses:* Tuition, state resident: full-time $3,414. Tuition, nonresident: full-time $13,584; part-time $339 per unit. Required fees: $786; $393 per semester. *Financial support:* Career-related internships or fieldwork and Federal Work-Study available. Support available to part-time students. Financial award application deadline: 3/1. *Unit head:* Chris Castaneda, Chair, 916-278-6206.

Eastern Illinois University, Graduate School, College of Arts and Humanities, Department of History, Charleston, IL 61920-3099. Offers historical administration (MA); history (MA). *Faculty:* 14 full-time (2 women). In 2007, 17 degrees awarded. *Application deadline:* For fall admission, 7/31 priority date for domestic students. Applications are processed on a rolling basis. Application fee: $30. *Expenses:* Tuition, state resident: part-time $218 per hour. Tuition, nonresident: part-time $654 per hour. *Financial support:* In 2007–08, research assistantships with tuition reimbursements (averaging $7,200 per year), 9 teaching assistantships with tuition reimbursements (averaging $7,200 per year) were awarded; career-related internships or fieldwork also available. *Unit head:* Dr. Anita Shelton, Chairperson, 217-581-3310, Fax: 217-581-2722, E-mail: ashelton@eiu.edu. *Application contact:* Dr. Ed Wehrle, Graduate Coordinator, 217-581-6372, Fax: 217-581-2722, E-mail: efwehrle@eiu.edu.

Florida State University, Graduate Studies, College of Arts and Sciences, Department of History, Tallahassee, FL 32306. Offers historical administration (MA); history (MA, PhD). Part-time programs available. *Faculty:* 28 full-time (10 women). *Students:* 85 full-time (36 women), 54 part-time (23 women); includes 19 minority (10 African Americans, 2 Asian Americans or Pacific Islanders, 7 Hispanic Americans), 4 international. Average age 26. 72 applicants, 74% accepted, 27 enrolled. In 2007, 13 master's, 7 doctorates awarded. *Median time to degree:* Of those who began their doctoral program in fall 1999, 0% received their degree in 8 years or less. *Degree requirements:* For master's, one foreign language, comprehensive exam (for some programs), thesis (for some programs), internships; for doctorate, one foreign language, comprehensive exam, thesis/dissertation. *Entrance requirements:* For master's, GRE General Test, minimum GPA of 3.3, minimum 18 hours of course work in history; for doctorate, GRE General Test, minimum GPA of 3.3 (undergraduate), 3.65 (graduate). Additional exam requirements/recommendations for international students: Required—TOEFL (minimum score 550 paper-based; 213 computer-based; 80 iBT). *Application deadline:* For fall admission, 1/10 for domestic students; for spring admission, 10/1 for domestic students. Applications are processed on a rolling basis. Application fee: $30. Electronic applications accepted. *Expenses:* Tuition, state resident: part-time $248 per credit hour. Tuition, nonresident: part-time $880 per credit hour. Tuition and fees vary according to program. *Financial support:* In 2007–08, 66 students received support, including 8 fellowships with full tuition reimbursements available (averaging $9,000 per year), 10 research assistantships with full tuition reimbursements available (averaging $9,000 per year), 24 teaching assistantships with full tuition reimbursements available (averaging $10,500 per year); Federal Work-Study, institutionally sponsored loans, scholarships/grants, and unspecified assistantships also available. Financial award application deadline: 1/10; financial award applicants required to submit FAFSA. *Faculty research:* Southern and Caribbean studies, Napoleon and the French Revolution, modern Europe, Latin America, U.S. intellectual and cultural history. *Unit head:* Dr. Neil Jumonville, Chairman, 850-644-5888, Fax: 850-644-6402, E-mail: njumonville@fsu.edu. *Application contact:* Chris Pignatiello, Academic Support Assistant, 850-644-2610, Fax: 850-644-6402, E-mail: cpignatiello@fsu.edu.

Indiana University–Purdue University Indianapolis, Department of History, Indianapolis, IN 46202-2896. Offers history (MA); public history (MA); MA/MLS. Part-time and evening/weekend programs available. *Faculty:* 14 full-time (6 women). *Students:* 11 full-time (6 women), 28 part-time (16 women); includes 1 minority (African American) Average age 30. In 2007, 11 degrees awarded. *Degree requirements:* For master's, one foreign language, thesis. *Entrance requirements:* For master's, GRE General Test, minimum GPA of 3.0. *Application deadline:* For fall admission, 2/1 priority date for domestic students. Applications are processed on a rolling basis. Application fee: $50 ($60 for international students). *Expenses:* Tuition, state resident: full-time $5,818; part-time $242 per credit hour. Tuition, nonresident: full-time $17,106; part-time $713 per credit hour. Required fees: $629. Tuition and fees vary according to course load, campus/location and program. *Financial support:* In 2007–08, 1 fellowship with full tuition reimbursement (averaging $10,000 per year), 19 teaching assistantships with full tuition reimbursements (averaging $8,612 per year) were awarded; research assistantships with full tuition reimbursements, career-related internships or fieldwork also available. *Unit head:* Robert Barrows, Chair, 317-274-2457. *Application contact:* Mary Gelzleichter, Graduate Secretary, 317-274-5840, Fax: 317-278-7800, E-mail: mgelzlei@iupui.edu.

Loyola University Chicago, Graduate School, Department of History, Chicago, IL 60611-2196. Offers history (MA, PhD); public library (MA). Part-time and evening/weekend programs available. *Faculty:* 21 full-time (8 women), 4 part-time/adjunct (3 women). *Students:* 75 full-time (46 women), 34 part-time (13 women); includes 10 minority (4 African Americans, 1 Asian American or Pacific Islander, 5 Hispanic Americans). Average age 33. 132 applicants, 57% accepted, 28 enrolled. In 2007, 19 master's, 5 doctorates awarded. Terminal master's awarded for partial completion of doctoral program. *Median time to degree:* Of those who began their doctoral program in fall 1999, 14% received their degree in 8 years or less. *Degree requirements:* For master's, one foreign language, comprehensive exam, essay; for doctorate, 2 foreign languages, comprehensive exam, thesis/dissertation. *Entrance requirements:* For master's, GRE General Test, research paper; for doctorate, GRE General Test, seminar paper or master's thesis. Additional exam requirements/recommendations for international students: Required—TOEFL (minimum score 550 paper-based; 213 computer-based), IELTS. *Application deadline:* For fall admission, 5/1 for domestic students; for spring admission, 10/1 for domestic students. Applications are processed on a rolling basis. Application fee: $50. Electronic applications accepted. *Expenses:* Tuition: Full-time $12,780; part-time $710 per credit hour. Required fees: $55 per semester. Full-time tuition and fees vary according to program. *Financial support:* In 2007–08, 7 fellowships with full tuition reimbursements (averaging $14,500 per year), 10 teaching assistantships with full tuition reimbursements (averaging $15,000 per year) were awarded; research assistantships with full tuition reimbursements, Federal Work-Study also available. Financial award application deadline: 1/1; financial award applicants required to submit FAFSA. *Faculty research:* Medieval and early modern Europe, U.S. public history, U.S. urban history, gender history, Britain and Ireland. *Unit head:* Barbara Rosenwein, Chair, 773-508-2215, Fax: 773-508-2153, E-mail: brosen@luc.edu. *Application contact:* Dr. Suzanne Kaufman, Director, Graduate Programs, 773-508-2233, Fax: 773-508-2153, E-mail: skaufma@luc.edu.

Middle Tennessee State University, College of Graduate Studies, College of Liberal Arts, Department of History, Program in Public History, Murfreesboro, TN 37132. Offers PhD. Part-time and evening/weekend programs available. Postbaccalaureate distance learning degree programs offered. *Students:* 34 applicants, 88% accepted. In 2007, 1 degree awarded. *Degree requirements:* For doctorate, one foreign language, comprehensive exam, thesis/dissertation. *Entrance requirements:* For doctorate, GRE. Additional exam requirements/recommendations for international students: Required—TOEFL (paper-based 525; computer-based 195; IBT 71) or IELTS (6.0). *Financial support:* Application deadline: 5/1. *Unit head:* Dr. John McDaniel, Dean, College of Liberal Arts, 615-898-2534, Fax: 615-898-5907, E-mail: mcdaniel@mtsu.edu.

New York University, Graduate School of Arts and Science, Department of History, New York, NY 10012-1019. Offers African diaspora (PhD); African history (PhD); archival management and historical editing (Advanced Certificate); Atlantic history (PhD); French studies/history (PhD); Hebrew and Judaic studies/history (PhD); history (MA, PhD), including Europe (PhD), Latin American and the Caribbean (PhD), United States (PhD), women's history (MA); Middle Eastern history (MA); Middle Eastern studies/history (PhD); public history (Advanced Certificate); world history (MA); JD/MA; MA/Advanced Certificate. Part-time programs available. *Faculty:* 43 full-time (19 women), 18 part-time/adjunct. *Students:* 106 full-time (68 women), 48 part-time (34 women); includes 29 minority (18 African Americans, 4 Asian Americans or Pacific Islanders, 7 Hispanic Americans), 26 international. Average age 31. 413 applicants, 19% accepted, 40 enrolled. In 2007, 17 master's, 7 doctorates awarded. Terminal master's awarded for partial completion of doctoral program. *Degree requirements:* For master's, seminar paper; for doctorate, one foreign language, thesis/dissertation, oral and written exams; for Advanced Certificate, internship. *Entrance requirements:* For master's, GRE General Test, minimum GPA of 3.0, writing sample; for doctorate, GRE. Additional exam requirements/recommendations for international students: Required—TOEFL. *Application deadline:* For fall admission, 12/12 for domestic students. Application fee: $85. *Financial support:* Fellowships with tuition reimbursements, research assistantships, teaching assistantships with tuition reimbursements, career-related internships or fieldwork, Federal Work-Study, institutionally sponsored loans, scholarships/grants, health care benefits, and unspecified assistantships available. Financial award application deadline: 12/12; financial award applicants required to submit FAFSA. *Faculty research:* African, East Asian, Medieval, early modern, and modern European history; U.S. history; African and African diaspora; Latin American history; Atlantic World. *Unit head:* Michael Gomez, Chair, 212-998-8600, Fax: 212-995-4017, E-mail: history.dept@nyu.edu. *Application contact:* Gregory Grandin, Director of Graduate Studies, 212-998-8600, Fax: 212-995-4017, E-mail: history.dept@nyu.edu.

North Carolina State University, Graduate School, College of Humanities and Social Sciences, Department of History, Program in Public History, Raleigh, NC 27695. Offers MA. *Degree requirements:* For master's, thesis optional. *Entrance requirements:* For master's, GRE General Test. Electronic applications accepted.

Northeastern University, College of Arts and Sciences, Department of History, Boston, MA 02115-5096. Offers history (MA); public history (MA); world history (PhD). Part-time and evening/weekend programs available. *Faculty:* 14 full-time (4 women), 4 part-time/adjunct. *Students:* 53 full-time (32 women), 4 part-time. 97 applicants, 49% accepted. In 2007, 9 master's, 1 doctorate awarded. Terminal master's awarded for partial completion of doctoral program. *Degree requirements:* For master's, one foreign language, thesis or alternative, project; for doctorate, thesis/dissertation. *Entrance requirements:* For master's and doctorate, GRE General Test. *Application deadline:* For fall admission, 2/1 for domestic students. Application fee: $50. Electronic applications accepted. *Financial support:* In 2007–08, 13 teaching assistantships with tuition reimbursements (averaging $14,035 per year) were awarded; research assistantships with tuition reimbursements, career-related internships or fieldwork, scholarships/grants, and tuition waivers (full and partial) also available. Financial award application deadline: 2/1; financial award applicants required to submit FAFSA. *Faculty research:* World history, U.S. social history. *Unit head:* Dr. Laura Frader, Chair, 617-373-2660, Fax: 617-373-2661. *Application contact:* Dr. Christina Gilmartin, Graduate Coordinator, 617-373-2660, Fax: 617-373-2661.

See Close-Up on page 417.

Rutgers, The State University of New Jersey, Camden, Graduate School of Arts and Sciences, Program in American and Public History, Camden, NJ 08102-1401. Offers MA. Part-time and evening/weekend programs available. *Entrance requirements:* For master's, GRE General Test. Electronic applications accepted. *Faculty research:* Women's history, military history, Afro-American history, urban history, history of technology.

Shippensburg University of Pennsylvania, School of Graduate Studies, College of Arts and Sciences, Department of History and Philosophy, Shippensburg, PA 17257-2299. Offers applied history (MA, Certificate). Part-time and evening/weekend programs available. *Faculty:* 7 full-time (3 women). *Students:* 18 full-time (9 women), 17 part-time (7 women); includes 2 minority (1 African American, 1 Asian American or Pacific Islander). Average age 30. 29 applicants, 83% accepted, 13 enrolled. In 2007, 15 degrees awarded. *Degree requirements:* For master's, thesis or internship. *Entrance requirements:* For master's, interview if undergraduate GPA less than 2.75. Additional exam requirements/recommendations for international students: Required—TOEFL (minimum score 560 paper-based; 220 computer-based). *Application deadline:* For fall admission, 3/1 for international students; for spring admission, 7/1 for international students. Applications are processed on a rolling basis. Application fee: $30. Electronic applications accepted. *Expenses:* Tuition, state resident: part-time $345 per credit. Tuition, nonresident: part-time $552 per credit. Required fees: $28 per credit. Tuition and fees vary according to course load. *Financial support:* In 2007–08, 10 research assistantships with full tuition reimbursements (averaging $3,575 per year) were awarded; career-related internships or fieldwork, scholarships/grants, and unspecified assistantships also available. Support available to part-time students. Financial award application deadline: 3/1; financial award applicants required to submit FAFSA. *Unit head:* Dr. David Godshalk, Chairperson, 717-477-1621, Fax: 717-477-4062, E-mail: dfgods@ship.edu. *Application contact:* Renee Payne, Associate Dean of Graduate Admissions, 717-477-1231, Fax: 717-477-4016, E-mail: rmpayn@ship.edu.

Simmons College, Graduate School of Library and Information Science and College of Arts and Sciences Graduate Studies, Program in History and Archives Management, Boston, MA 02115. Offers MS/MA. *Faculty:* 6 full-time (3 women), 2 part-time/adjunct (1 woman). *Students:* 20 full-time (15 women), 17 part-time (14 women); includes 1 Asian American or Pacific Islander. Average age 27. *Application deadline:* For fall admission, 3/1 priority date for domestic students; for spring admission, 11/1 priority date for domestic students. Applications are processed on a rolling basis. Application fee: $35. Electronic applications accepted. *Expenses: Contact institution. Financial support:* In 2007–08, 17 students received support, including 1 fellowship (averaging $11,785 per year); scholarships/grants also available. Financial award application deadline: 3/1; financial award applicants required to submit FAFSA. *Faculty research:* History of women/gender, American history, cultural history, world history, modern Europe. *Unit head:* Laura Prieto, Co-Director, 617-521-2253, Fax: 617-521-3192, E-mail: laura.prieto@simmons.edu. *Application contact:* Christine Leland, Assistant Director of Admissions, 617-521-2801, Fax: 617-521-3192, E-mail: leland@simmons.edu.

Sonoma State University, School of Social Sciences, Program in Cultural Resources Management, Rohnert Park, CA 94928-3609. Offers MA. Part-time programs available. *Faculty:* 3 full-time (1 woman). *Students:* 20 full-time (14 women), 2 part-time (both women); includes 3 minority (1 African American, 1 Asian American or Pacific Islander, 1 Hispanic American), 1 international. Average age 33. 28 applicants, 43% accepted, 11 enrolled. *Degree requirements:* For master's, thesis. *Entrance requirements:* For master's, minimum GPA of 3.0. *Application deadline:* For fall admission, 1/31 for domestic students. Application fee: $55. *Financial support:* Career-related internships or fieldwork, scholarships/grants, traineeships, and unspecified assistantships available. Financial award application deadline: 3/2. *Faculty research:* Identification, evaluation, and preservation of cultural resources. *Unit head:* Dr. John D. Wingard, Chair, Anthropology Department, 707-664-2319, Fax: 707-664-2505, E-mail: john.wingard@sonoma.edu. *Application contact:* Margaret Purser, Coordinator, 707-664-3164, Fax: 707-664-2505, E-mail: margaret.purser@sonoma.edu.

University at Albany, State University of New York, College of Arts and Sciences, Department of History, Albany, NY 12222-0001. Offers history (MA, PhD); public history (Certificate). Part-time programs available. *Students:* 77 full-time (37 women), 70 part-time (29 women). Average age 34. In 2007, 31 master's, 4 doctorates awarded. *Degree requirements:* For master's, variable foreign language requirement, exam, research paper or thesis; for doctorate, thesis/dissertation. *Entrance requirements:* For master's, minimum GPA of 3.0; for doctorate, GRE General Test, minimum GPA of 3.0. Additional exam requirements/recommendations for international students: Required—TOEFL (minimum score 550 paper-based; 213 computer-based). *Application deadline:* For fall admission, 3/1 for domestic students, 5/1 for international students; for spring admission, 11/1 for international students. Applications are processed on a rolling basis. Application fee: $75. Electronic applications accepted. *Expenses:* Tuition, state resident: part-time $576 per credit. Tuition, nonresident: part-time $910 per credit. Tuition and fees vary according to program. *Financial support:* Teaching assistantships, career-related internships or fieldwork available. Financial award application deadline: 3/1. *Faculty research:*

American history (all phases); public policy; European history (Medieval to modern); Asian, African, and Latin American history. *Unit head:* Richard Hamm, Chair, 518-442-5300.

University of Arkansas at Little Rock, Graduate School, College of Arts, Humanities, and Social Science, Department of History, Little Rock, AR 72204-1099. Offers public history (MA). Part-time programs available. *Students:* Average age 33. *Degree requirements:* For master's, oral exam. *Entrance requirements:* For master's, GRE General Test, minimum GPA of 3.25 in history, 2.7 overall; 18 hours of art history. *Application deadline:* Applications are processed on a rolling basis. *Financial support:* Research assistantships with tuition reimbursements, teaching assistantships with tuition reimbursements, career-related internships or fieldwork, Federal Work-Study, institutionally sponsored loans, and unspecified assistantships available. Support available to part-time students. *Faculty research:* Historic preservation and restoration, museum studies, archives. *Application contact:* Dr. Johanna M. Lewis, Coordinator, 501-569-3059, E-mail: jmlewis@ualr.edu.

The University of British Columbia, Faculty of Arts, School of Library, Archival and Information Studies, Program in Archival Studies, Vancouver, BC V6T 1Z1, Canada. Offers MAS. *Faculty:* 4 full-time (3 women), 6 part-time/adjunct (5 women). *Students:* 23 full-time (16 women). Average age 32. 37 applicants, 54% accepted, 11 enrolled. In 2007, 9 degrees awarded. *Degree requirements:* For master's, thesis optional. *Entrance requirements:* For master's, minimum GPA of 3.3 in undergraduate upper-division courses. Additional exam requirements/recommendations for international students: Required—TOEFL (minimum score 600 paper-based; 250 computer-based; 100 iBT). *Application deadline:* For fall admission, 2/1 for domestic and international students. Application fee: $90 Canadian dollars ($150 Canadian dollars for international students). Electronic applications accepted. *Financial support:* In 2007–08, 9 students received support, including 6 research assistantships (averaging $625 per year); fellowships, Federal Work-Study, institutionally sponsored loans, scholarships/grants, health care benefits, tuition waivers (partial), and unspecified assistantships also available. *Faculty research:* Diplomatics, electronic record, appraisal, descriptive standards, preservation.

The University of British Columbia, Faculty of Arts, School of Library, Archival and Information Studies, Program in Library, Archival and Information Studies, Vancouver, BC V6T 1Z1, Canada. Offers PhD. *Faculty:* 13 full-time (10 women), 34 part-time/adjunct (27 women). *Students:* 15 full-time (12 women). Average age 40. 6 applicants, 33% accepted, 1 enrolled. *Degree requirements:* For doctorate, thesis/dissertation. *Entrance requirements:* For doctorate, GRE, minimum GPA of 3.3 in MAS or MLIS. Other master's may be considered. Additional exam requirements/recommendations for international students: Required—TOEFL (minimum score 600 paper-based; 250 computer-based; 100 iBT). *Application deadline:* For fall admission, 2/1 for domestic and international students. Application fee: $90 Canadian dollars ($150 Canadian dollars for international students). Electronic applications accepted. *Financial support:* In 2007–08, 11 students received support, including 2 fellowships (averaging $12,500 Canadian dollars per year), 9 research assistantships (averaging $3,255 Canadian dollars per year); Federal Work-Study, institutionally sponsored loans, scholarships/grants, health care benefits, and unspecified assistantships also available. *Faculty research:* Computer systems/database design; library and archival management; archival description and organization; children's literature and youth services; interactive information retrieval. *Application contact:* Graduate Admissions Secretary, 604-822-2404, Fax: 604-822-6006, E-mail: slais.admissions@ubc.ca.

University of Houston, College of Liberal Arts and Social Sciences, Department of History, Houston, TX 77204. Offers history (MA, PhD); public history (MA). Part-time programs available. *Faculty:* 25 full-time (9 women). *Students:* 59 full-time (27 women), 38 part-time (20 women); includes 18 minority (3 African Americans, 2 American Indian/Alaska Native, 2 Asian Americans or Pacific Islanders, 11 Hispanic Americans), 2 international. Average age 36. 29 applicants, 69% accepted, 9 enrolled. In 2007, 7 master's, 5 doctorates awarded. Terminal master's awarded for partial completion of doctoral program. *Degree requirements:* For master's, one foreign language, thesis (for some programs); for doctorate, one foreign language, thesis/dissertation. *Entrance requirements:* For master's, GRE General Test, minimum GPA of 3.3; for doctorate, GRE General Test, minimum GPA of 3.67. Additional exam requirements/recommendations for international students: Required—TOEFL. *Application deadline:* For fall admission, 1/15 for domestic students; for spring admission, 11/1 for domestic students. Application fee: $25 ($100 for international students). *Expenses:* Tuition, state resident: full-time $6,297; part-time $262 per credit. Tuition, nonresident: full-time $12,969; part-time $540 per credit. Required fees: $2,696. *Financial support:* In 2007–08, 7 research assistantships with full tuition reimbursements (averaging $9,800 per year), 34 teaching assistantships with full tuition reimbursements (averaging $9,800 per year) were awarded; fellowships with full tuition reimbursements, career-related internships or fieldwork, Federal Work-Study, institutionally sponsored loans, scholarships/grants, health care benefits, and unspecified assistantships also available. Support available to part-time students. Financial award application deadline: 2/1. *Faculty research:* U.S., Latin American, European, social, and women's history. *Unit head:* Robert Buzzanco, Chairperson, 713-743-3008, Fax: 713-743-3216.

University of Illinois at Springfield, Graduate Programs, College of Liberal Arts and Sciences, Program in History, Springfield, IL 62703-5407. Offers MA. Part-time and evening/weekend programs available. *Faculty:* 8 full-time (3 women). *Students:* 15 full-time (6 women), 30 part-time (18 women); includes 3 minority (2 African Americans, 1 Hispanic American). Average age 33. 29 applicants, 72% accepted, 15 enrolled. In 2007, 11 degrees awarded. *Degree requirements:* For master's, thesis or internship, project. *Entrance requirements:* For master's, BA in history or related field, minimum GPA of 3.0, writing sample, statement of purpose. Additional exam requirements/recommendations for international students: Required—TOEFL (minimum score 550 paper-based; 213 computer-based). *Application deadline:* Applications are processed on a rolling basis. Application fee: $50 ($60 for international students). Electronic applications accepted. *Expenses:* Tuition, state resident: full-time $5,424; part-time $226 per credit hour. Tuition, nonresident: part-time $553 per credit hour. Required fees: $618 per term. *Financial support:* In 2007–08, research assistantships with full tuition reimbursements (averaging $7,988 per year), teaching assistantships with full tuition reimbursements (averaging $7,988 per year) were awarded; career-related internships or fieldwork, Federal Work-Study, scholarships/grants, health care benefits, and unspecified assistantships also available. Support available to part-time students. Financial award application deadline: 11/15; financial award applicants required to submit FAFSA. *Unit head:* Dr. William Siles, Program Administrator, 217-206-7432, Fax: 217-206-6217, E-mail: siles.william@uis.edu.

University of Massachusetts Amherst, Graduate School, College of Humanities and Fine Arts, Department of History, Amherst, MA 01003. Offers ancient history (MA); British Empire history (MA); European (medieval and modern) history (MA, PhD); Islamic history (MA); Latin American history (MA, PhD); modern global history (MA); public history (MA); science and technology history (MA); U.S. history (MA, PhD). Part-time programs available. *Faculty:* 30 full-time (13 women). *Students:* 21 full-time (10 women), 41 part-time (23 women); includes 5 minority (3 African Americans, 1 American Indian/Alaska Native, 1 Hispanic American), 4 international. Average age 32. 159 applicants, 34% accepted, 25 enrolled. In 2007, 13 master's, 2 doctorates awarded. Terminal master's awarded for partial completion of doctoral program. *Degree requirements:* For master's, one foreign language, thesis or alternative; for doctorate, one foreign language, thesis/dissertation. *Entrance requirements:* For master's and doctorate, GRE General Test, writing sample. Additional exam requirements/recommendations for international students: Required—TOEFL (minimum score 530 paper-based; 197 computer-based). *Application deadline:* For fall admission, 1/2 priority date for domestic and international students. Applications are processed on a rolling basis. Application fee: $50 ($65 for international students). Electronic applications accepted. *Expenses:* Tuition, state resident: full-time $2,640; part-time $110 per credit. Tuition, nonresident: full-time $9,936; part-time $414 per credit. Required fees: $7,455. One-time fee: $332. Tuition and fees vary according to course load, campus/location, program and reciprocity agreements. *Financial support:* In 2007–08, 1 fellowship with full tuition reimbursement (averaging $16,000 per year), 1 research assistantship with full tuition reimbursement (averaging $704 per year), 36 teaching assistantships with full tuition reimbursements (averaging $12,076 per year) were awarded; career-related internships or fieldwork, Federal Work-Study, scholarships/grants, traineeships, and unspecified assistantships also available. Support available to part-time students. Financial award application deadline: 2/1. *Unit head:* Dr. Audrey L. Altstadt, Chair, 413-545-2378, Fax: 413-545-6137.

University of Massachusetts Boston, Office of Graduate Studies, College of Liberal Arts, Program in History, Boston, MA 02125-3393. Offers archival methods (MA); historical archaeology (MA); history (MA). Part-time and evening/weekend programs available. *Degree requirements:* For master's, thesis, oral exam. *Entrance requirements:* For master's, minimum GPA of 2.75. *Faculty research:* European intellectual history, American labor and social history in 19th century, colonial American Revolution, Afro-American Cold War.

University of South Carolina, The Graduate School, College of Arts and Sciences, Department of History, Program in Public History, Columbia, SC 29208. Offers archives (MA); historic preservation (MA); museum (MA); museum management (Certificate); MLIS/MA. *Faculty:* 3 full-time (2 women). *Students:* 10 full-time (7 women), 3 part-time (2 women); includes 1 minority (Hispanic American) Average age 26. 34 applicants, 18% accepted. In 2007, 13 degrees awarded. *Degree requirements:* For master's, one foreign language, thesis, internship. *Entrance requirements:* For master's, GRE General Test, writing sample. Additional exam requirements/recommendations for international students: Required—TOEFL. *Application deadline:* For fall admission, 1/5 for domestic students. Application fee: $40. Electronic applications accepted. *Expenses:* Tuition, state resident: part-time $440 per hour. Tuition, nonresident: part-time $936 per hour. Required fees: $17 per hour. Tuition and fees vary according to program. *Financial support:* In 2007–08, 12 teaching assistantships with partial tuition reimbursements (averaging $11,000 per year) were awarded; fellowships with partial tuition reimbursements, research assistantships with partial tuition reimbursements, career-related internships or fieldwork, Federal Work-Study, and institutionally sponsored loans also available. Financial award application deadline: 1/5. *Faculty research:* Museum studies, historic preservation, archives administration. *Application contact:* Robert R. Weyeneth, Co-Director, 803-777-5195, Fax: 803-777-4494, E-mail: weyeneth@sc.edu.

The University of Texas at Austin, Graduate School, College of Liberal Arts, Department of Anthropology, Program in Folklore and Public Culture, Austin, TX 78712-1111. Offers MA, PhD. Part-time programs available. Terminal master's awarded for partial completion of doctoral program. *Degree requirements:* For master's, one foreign language, thesis, report; for doctorate, one foreign language, thesis/dissertation. *Entrance requirements:* For master's and doctorate, GRE General Test. Electronic applications accepted. *Faculty research:* Expressive culture, gender, genre, folklore and culture of British Isles, ethnography of speaking.

University of West Florida, College of Arts and Sciences: Arts, Department of History, Pensacola, FL 32514-5750. Offers historic preservation (MA); history (MA); public history (MA). Part-time and evening/weekend programs available. *Faculty:* 6 full-time (2 women), 2 part-time/adjunct (both women). *Students:* 15 full-time (9 women), 27 part-time (14 women); includes 5 minority (2 African Americans, 2 American Indian/Alaska Native, 1 Hispanic American), 1 international. Average age 33. 22 applicants, 100% accepted, 15 enrolled. In 2007, 14 degrees awarded. *Degree requirements:* For master's, thesis or alternative. *Entrance requirements:* For master's, GRE General Test, minimum GPA of 3.0, minimum 15 hours of upper-level history courses. Additional exam requirements/recommendations for international students: Required—TOEFL (minimum score 550 paper-based; 213 computer-based). *Application deadline:* For fall admission, 6/1 for domestic students, 5/15 for international students; for spring admission, 11/1 for domestic students, 10/1 for international students. Applications are processed on a rolling basis. Application fee: $30. *Expenses:* Tuition, state resident: full-time $6,054; part-time $252 per credit. Tuition, nonresident: full-time $21,886; part-time $912 per credit. *Financial support:* In 2007–08, 3 research assistantships with partial tuition reimbursements (averaging $5,640 per year) were awarded; fellowships, teaching assistantships with partial tuition reimbursements, Federal Work-Study, institutionally sponsored loans, scholarships/grants, and unspecified assistantships also available. Financial award application deadline: 4/15; financial award applicants required to submit FAFSA. *Unit head:* Dr. John J. Clune, Chairperson, 850-474-2680.

Washington State University, Graduate School, College of Liberal Arts, Department of History, Pullman, WA 99164. Offers early and modern European history (MA, PhD); environmental history (MA, PhD); Latin American history (MA, PhD); modern East Asia history (MA, PhD); public history (MA, PhD); US history (MA, PhD); women's history (MA, PhD); world history (MA, PhD). Part-time programs available. *Faculty:* 24. *Students:* 45 full-time (28 women), 8 part-time (4 women); includes 2 minority (both Hispanic Americans), 2 international. Average age 33. 64 applicants, 41% accepted, 15 enrolled. In 2007, 8 master's, 2 doctorates awarded. *Degree requirements:* For master's, comprehensive exam (for some programs), thesis, oral exam; for doctorate, one foreign language, comprehensive exam, thesis/dissertation, oral and written exam. *Entrance requirements:* For master's, GRE General Test, minimum GPA of 3.3, language background form, writing sample; for doctorate, GRE General Test, minimum GPA of 3.5, language background form, writing sample. Additional exam requirements/recommendations for international students: Required—TOEFL (minimum score 550 paper-based). *Application deadline:* For fall admission, 2/1 for domestic and international students; for spring admission, 11/1 for domestic and international students. Applications are processed on a rolling basis. Application fee: $50. Electronic applications accepted. *Financial support:* In 2007–08, 30 students received support, including 1 fellowship with partial tuition reimbursement available (averaging $3,000 per year), research assistantships with full and partial tuition reimbursements available (averaging $13,917 per year), 28 teaching assistantships with full and partial tuition reimbursements available (averaging $13,056 per year); career-related internships or fieldwork, Federal Work-Study, institutionally sponsored loans, scholarships/grants, and health care benefits also available. Financial award application deadline: 4/1; financial award applicants required to submit FAFSA. *Faculty research:* Public, world, environmental, women and U.S. history. Total annual research expenditures: $44,501. *Unit head:* Dr. John Kicza, Co-Chair, 509-335-5002, Fax: 509-335-4171, E-mail: jekicza@wsu.edu. *Application contact:* Graduate Studies Director, 509-335-4030, Fax: 509-335-4171, E-mail: kale@wsu.edu.

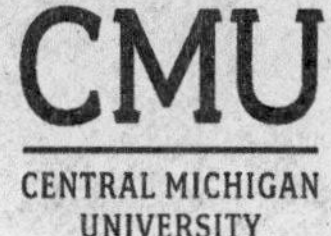

CENTRAL MICHIGAN UNIVERSITY

Department of History

Programs of Study At Central Michigan University (CMU), the Department of History's graduate program encompasses a wide array of research interests, collaborations, and approaches. Through graduate student and faculty exchanges with partner universities and through the activities of the Center for Transnational and Comparative History (CTCH), the program provides a distinctive setting and a rich cultural community for graduate training. It provides international academic study and dialogue among graduate students and faculty members from both CMU and its distinguished foreign partners. The goal is to cultivate graduate student and faculty research and to foster historical investigation of human experience in a transnational and comparative learning and research environment. Graduates are expected to become successful university scholars and teachers, leading figures in the governmental and private sectors, and successful professionals in a host of other fields in the United States and abroad.

The Department offers a Master of Arts in history, a joint M.A./Ph.D. in history (in consortium with partner universities), and graduate certificates in European, modern, and U.S. history. For the M.A. in history, which requires at least 30 semester hours, students must complete a minimum of 6 hours of history research and writing courses, either through a thesis or seminars. The former includes an oral examination in the field of the thesis. Students who choose the latter option must submit two research papers as evidence of scholarship. These papers must be prepared in connection with a seminar, an independent research course, or a graduate-level course in the Department of History. In the 36-semester-hour M.A./Ph.D. program in history, students are expected to study abroad—at the Erasmus University of Rotterdam, the Netherlands; the Friedrich Schiller University of Jena, Germany; the University of Strathclyde in Glasgow, Scotland; or the Autonomous University of Puebla, Mexico—for at least two academic semesters, usually in one academic year. All certificate programs require a minimum of 18 semester hours, which can be transferred toward the M.A. in history degree.

In addition to coordinating the transnational M.A./Ph.D. programs, the CTCH holds a multitude of other activities, such as a yearly speaker series with leading academics and people of public interest from around the world. The CTCH also hosts yearly conferences on transnational and comparative topics. The CTCH acts as a cultural, business, and political conduit that mediates academic knowledge and study with matters of important national and international concern.

Research Facilities The University's library system includes off-campus library services, the Clarke Historical Library, and the main library, with numerous books and publications, electronic and paper journals, and access to several databases. The original goal of the Clarke Library was to document all aspects of the history of Michigan and the Old Northwest Territory. Collecting material regarding the state and the Old Northwest Territory remains a fundamental focus of the library. The collection includes more than 65,000 volumes, 2,500 manuscript collections, 11,000 reels of microfilm, 16,000 visual images, and 3,000 maps. There are three large public computer labs on campus that contain 400 PC and Mac workstations, and the library offers more than 300 public workstations that are distributed throughout the facility. A large selection of general software is available, including Adobe Photoshop, Microsoft Office, SPSS, SAS, and Minitab.

Financial Aid Funding sources include University and Departmental fellowships, graduate research and teaching assistantships, and grants for research and presentation. More information is available at http://www.chsbs.cmich.edu/ctch/funding.htm.

Cost of Study For the 2007–08 academic year, tuition was $388 per credit for Michigan residents and $719 per credit for out-of-state students.

Living and Housing Costs Single-student and one- to three-bedroom family apartments are available in apartment complexes on the campus. Rent includes electricity, gas, water, heat, telephone, cable TV, and other such services as the University deems appropriate. Off-campus housing is available from $250 per month, depending on the neighborhood, number of roommates, and size of apartment.

Student Group There are 15 full-time and 14 part-time students, 10 of whom are women. The average age is 32.

Location Mount Pleasant is located in Michigan's Lower Peninsula. The downtown district features specialty stores and boutiques of all types within walking distance of the campus. Thirteen golf courses are located within a 30-minute drive, and surrounding state preserves are frequented by local hunters. Eleven parks covering 300 acres—plus another 900 acres in Isabella County—offer venues for swimming, canoeing, hiking, camping, and cross-country skiing.

The University and The Department Central Michigan University opened its doors in 1892 to formally train teachers in the state. Bachelor's degrees were first awarded in 1918, and graduate courses were first offered in 1938. Today the University enrolls more than 28,000 students in more than 200 programs leading to twenty-seven degrees at the bachelor's, master's, specialist, and doctoral levels. The University's $50-million New Vision of Excellence Campaign is a broadly focused initiative to raise academic standards, strengthen discovery and creative activity, and enhance learning-environment facilities and technology.

The Department of History offers an extensive array of undergraduate and graduate courses reflecting the historical depth, range, and diversity of the human experience. Through learning and research, the Department trains students in historical interpretation and analysis. The objective is to provide a foundation for numerous professions, including business, government, journalism, and law; to train professionals in primary, secondary, and higher education; and to encourage and support advanced scholarship in historical studies.

Applying Specific requirements vary by program; students should contact the Department for details. In general, students must submit the completed application, the nonrefundable application fee ($35 for U.S. citizens and resident aliens, $45 for international applicants), and official transcripts from each college or university attended. The deadlines for the M.A. and certificate programs are July 15 for the fall and November 1 for the spring. The M.A./Ph.D. application deadline is December 1.

Correspondence and Information

Jennifer Banister, Secretary
Center for Transnational and Comparative History
Central Michigan University
242B Powers Hall
Mount Pleasant, Michigan 48859
Phone: 989-774-4313
Fax: 989-774-2806
E-mail: ctch@cmich.edu
Web site: http://www.chsbs.cmich.edu/history.grad

Central Michigan University

THE FACULTY AND THEIR RESEARCH

Thomas Benjamin, Ph.D., Michigan State. Latin America, Atlantic history, Mexico.
The Atlantic World: Europeans, Africans and Indians & Their Shared History, 1400–1900. Cambridge: Cambridge University Press, 2007.
Andrew D. Devenney, Ph.D., Central Michigan. Modern Britain and Ireland, European integration, urban history.
One Britain, One Europe, One World: Arthur Woodburn and the Last Throes of Socialist Internationalism in Scotland, 1960–1970. Midwest Conference on British Studies, Wright State University, Dayton, Ohio, September 2007.
Kathleen G. Donohue, Ph.D., Virginia. Twentieth-century United States.
Freedom from Want: American Liberalism and the Idea of the Consumer. Baltimore: Johns Hopkins Press, 2003.
Randall J. Doyle, Ph.D., Idaho. U.S. history, East Asian history, Australian history.
America and China: Asia-Pacific Rim Hegemony in the Twenty-First Century. Lanham, Md.: Lexington Books, 2007.
Carrie Euler, Ph.D., Johns Hopkins. Late medieval/early modern Europe, Renaissance/Reformation, England.
Anabaptism and Anti-Anabaptism in the early English Reformation: Defining Protestant heresy and orthodoxy during the reign of Edward VI. In *Heresy, Literature, and Politics in Early Modern England,* pp. 40–58, eds. D. Loewenstein and J. Marshall. Cambridge: Cambridge University Press, 2006.
Michael Federspiel. U.S. history, history education.
Focus on the questions in high school. In *Uncovering Our History: Teaching with Primary Sources*, ed. S. Veccia. Chicago: American Library Association, 2004.
Solomon Addis Getahun, Ph.D., Michigan State. African history, Ethiopia, urban history.
Determinants of Ethiopian refugee flow in the Horn of Africa, 1970–2000. In *The Human Cost of African Migrations*, pp. 359–80, eds. T. Falola and N. Afolabi. New York: Routledge, 2007.
Jennifer R. Green, Ph.D., Boston University. Nineteenth-century United States, Civil War.
Networks of military educators: Middle-class stability and professionalization in the late antebellum South. *J. South. Hist.* 63, February 2007.
Mitchell K. Hall, Ph.D., Kentucky. Twentieth-century United States, Vietnam War.
Crossroads: American Popular Culture and the Vietnam Generation. Lanham, Md.: Rowman & Littlefield, 2005.
Timothy D. Hall, Ph.D., Northwestern. Colonial and Revolutionary America.
Closing the gap between professors and teachers: "Uncoverage" as a model of professional development for history teachers. *Hist. Teach.* 2007. With Scott.
Doina Pasca Harsanyi, Ph.D., North Carolina at Chapel Hill. Enlightenment, French and American history.
The memoirs of Alexandre de Lameth and the reconciliation between nobility and revolution. In *The French Nobility and the Eighteenth Century: Reassessments and New Approaches,* ed. J. Smith. University Park, Pa.: Penn State University Press, 2006.
Eric A. Johnson, Ph.D., Pennsylvania. Modern Europe, Germany, Holocaust, social science, history.
What We Knew: Terror, Mass Murder, and Everyday Life in Nazi Germany. New York: Basic Books, 2005.
Stephen Jones. U.S. history, African American history.
David Macleod, Ph.D., Wisconsin–Madison. Nineteenth- and twentieth-century United States.
Mapping in Michigan and the Great Lakes Region. East Lansing: Michigan State University Press, 2007.
William McDaid. U.S. history, military history.
Timothy M. O'Neil, Ph.D., Wayne State. European labor history, Ireland.
Patrick H. O'Brien: The workingman's advocate: The copper country years, 1868–1922. In *New Perspectives on Michigan's Copper Country,* pp. 138–65, eds. K. Hoagland and T. Reynolds. Houghton: Michigan Technological University, 2005.
William S. Pretzer, Ph.D., Northern Illinois. American labor and technological history, public history, museum studies.
Of the paper cap and inky apron: The labor history of journeymen printers. In *An Extensive Republic: Print, Culture, and Society in the New Nations,* vol. 2 of *A History of the Book in America,* eds. R. Gross and M. Kelly. New York: Cambridge University Press, in press.
Benjamin Ramirez-shkwegnaabi, Ph.D., Wisconsin. Nineteenth-century U.S., Native American history.
The dynamics of American Indian diplomacy in the Great Lakes region. *Am. Indian Cult. Res. J.* 27(4):53–77, 2003.
John F. Robertson, Ph.D., Pennsylvania. Ancient Near East, Islamic Middle East.
Cursed Cradle: A Short History of Mesopotamia/Iraq. Oxford: One World Publications, in press.
David Rutherford, Ph.D., Michigan–Ann Arbor. Medieval/early modern Europe, Italian Renaissance.
Early Renaissance Invective and the Controversies of Antonio da Rho. Renaissance text series 19. Tempe, Ariz.: Renaissance Society of America, 2005.
Stephen P. Scherer, Ph.D., Ohio State. Modern Europe, Russia, historiography.
A comparison of Swedenborg and Skovoroda's biblical thought. *Logos J. E. Christ. Stud.,* 2005.
James A. Schmiechen, Ph.D., Illinois at Urbana-Champaign. Modern Britain, urban history, history of architecture.
Snapshots: A Saugatuck Album. A Photographic History of Saugatuck, Michigan. Saugatuck-Douglas Historical Society Fund, 2003.
Gregory Smith, Ph.D., Harvard. Ancient Mediterranean, late antiquity, early Middle Ages, Byzantium.
The Myth of the Vaginal Soul. *Greek Roman & Byzantine Studies* 44:199–225, 2004.
David Snyder, Ph.D., Southern Illinois. U.S. history, U.S. foreign policy.
Catherine Tobin, Ph.D., Notre Dame. Nineteenth-century U.S. history, immigration.

NORTHEASTERN UNIVERSITY

Department of History

Programs of Study

The Ph.D. program in world history trains research historians who plan to teach at the college or university level. Systematic training in theoretical and methodological approaches to world history is a distinctive feature of the program. Students gain experience teaching at the university level as teaching assistants and as instructors of their own courses. Emphasizing global approaches to historical study, the program encourages students to think beyond national boundaries and comparatively and to investigate themes that span geographically dispersed areas of the world, such as trade, migrations, religions, state formation, colonialism, and postcolonialism. Studies may include long-term historical processes, major global transformations, interactions between states, and colonial societies.

The Department also offers a Master of Arts (M.A.) program with an emphasis on world history. Candidates for the M.A., like Ph.D. candidates, examine African, Asian, European, or U.S. history in a global context. M.A. candidates may also develop expertise in public history, receiving a Department certificate in public history in addition to the master's degree. Candidates for the M.A. with certificate in public history meet the same basic requirements as other M.A. candidates, along with public history courses and fieldwork in historical agencies, historical sites, and museums. Both M.A. programs emphasize the theories and methodologies of historical scholarship.

The Graduate School of Arts and Sciences' School of Education offers a Master of Arts in Teaching (M.A.T.) program designed to meet the Massachusetts requirements for teacher training for secondary and junior high school history teachers. Students may concentrate on history or on history and social studies in this program, whose focus is at once urban and global.

Research Facilities

Snell Library supports all graduate and research programs, including an extensive collection of nonprint historical materials. The Boston Public Library, the second-largest public library collection in the United States, with extensive resources in many fields of history, is a few minutes' walk from the campus. Northeastern students have access to some fifteen major academic and research libraries through the Boston Library Consortium. Graduate students at Northeastern also benefit from access to selected libraries of Harvard University.

Financial Aid

Graduate assistantships that pay stipends and cover tuition and fees are available to the most qualified graduate students. Full-time Ph.D. students typically receive five years of support, consisting of a tuition waiver and an assistantship. Some doctoral students may be eligible for the Provost's University Excellence Fellowship, which provides additional financial support beyond normal graduate assistantships. Full and partial tuition-only assistantships are also available to promising candidates in the M.A. program.

Cost of Study

Tuition for the 2008–09 academic year is $1035 per credit hour. Yearly tuition and fees are approximately $18,900 at the rate of two courses per semester. Tuition, fees, and degree requirements are subject to revision by the University at any time.

Living and Housing Costs

On-campus housing for graduate students is limited and granted on a first-come, first-served basis. For more information about on- and off-campus housing, students should go to http://www.housing.neu.edu.

Student Group

The current group of more than 50 graduate students is globally diverse. Currently, 24 students are enrolled in the Ph.D. program.

Student Outcomes

In recent years, one third of M.A. graduates have gone on to doctoral programs at major research universities and others into a variety of careers in education, communications, government, or business. Two thirds of recent M.A. graduates in public history have taken full-time professional positions in fields related to their studies. Some M.A. students have been accepted into the doctoral program in world history. All students who have received the Ph.D. are employed in full-time teaching positions.

Location

Northeastern University is located in the Fenway section of Boston, an intellectually vital city with profuse academic, scientific, and cultural opportunities and resources. The Museum of Fine Arts and Symphony Hall are both adjacent to the Northeastern University campus.

The University

Northeastern is a privately endowed nonsectarian institution of higher education established in 1898 and is one of the largest private universities in the United States. Located in the center of Boston's thriving educational and cultural life on the Avenue of the Arts, Northeastern University offers a wide spectrum of opportunities in graduate and professional education.

Applying

The priority deadline for applications is February 1. Graduate Record Examinations (GRE) scores are required of all applicants, as are TOEFL scores for international applicants whose first language is not English.

Correspondence and Information

Graduate Programs
Department of History
249 Meserve Hall
Northeastern University
Boston, Massachusetts 02115-5000

Phone: 617-373-4449
Fax: 617-373-2661
E-mail: gradhistory@neu.edu
Web site: http://www.history.neu.edu

Northeastern University

THE FACULTY AND THEIR RESEARCH

Philip N. Backstrom Jr., Ph.D., Boston University (Emeritus). Modern British and twentieth-century European history.
Ronald W. Bailey, Ph.D., Stanford (joint appointment with African-American Studies). African American history.
Timothy S. Brown, Ph.D., Berkeley. Modern German history, imperialism, transnational social and cultural movements.
Jeffrey Burds, Ph.D., Yale. Russian and Ukrainian studies.
Ballard C. Campbell, Ph.D., Wisconsin. American history, government and politics.
William M. Fowler Jr., Ph.D., Notre Dame. American Colonial, Revolution, maritime, and naval history; Boston history; Atlantic history.
Laura L. Frader, Chair; Ph.D., Rochester. European history, French history, women's and gender history, empire and colonialism.
James W. Fraser, Ph.D., Columbia (Emeritus). American education.
Richard M. Freeland, Ph.D., Pennsylvania. American foreign policy and American education.
Christina Gilmartin, Graduate Coordinator; Ph.D., Pennsylvania. Chinese history and gender studies.
Harvey Green, Ph.D., Rutgers. American cultural history, public history, American housing and material life, American literary history.
Robert L. Hall, Ph.D., Florida State (joint appointment with African-American Studies). African American history; American Colonial, social, and cultural history.
Tom Havens, Ph.D., Berkeley. Japanese culture.
Gerald H. Herman, M.A., Northeastern. European cultural history, science and technology, contemporary history, war in the twentieth century, media history.
Ilham Khuri-Makdisi, Ph.D., Harvard. Modern Middle East, Islam, Diaspora, Arabic cultural and intellectual history.
Katherine A. Luongo, Ph.D., Michigan. African and South Asian history.
Patrick Manning, Ph.D., Wisconsin (Emeritus). African history and world history; economic, social, and demographic history.
Clay McShane, Ph.D., Wisconsin. Urban history, recent United States history, social history.
Anthony N. Penna, D.A., Carnegie Mellon. Environmental history, American education, recent United States and world history.
John Post, Ph.D., Boston University (Emeritus). Modern Western economic history, population history, twentieth-century world history.
Harlow L. Robinson, Ph.D., Berkeley (joint appointment with Modern Languages). Russian culture, music, film.
Raymond H. Robinson, Ph.D., Harvard. American history, history of media in America, American elites, history of American transportation, American historiography.
Anna Suranyi, Ph.D., UCLA. Early modern British history, British empire, Atlantic history.
Charissa J. Threat, Ph.D., Iowa. African American history, African American women's history.
Karin Velez, Ph.D., Princeton. Early modern Iberian Atlantic history, world history.

Northeastern University is an Equal Opportunity/Affirmative Action educational institution and employer.

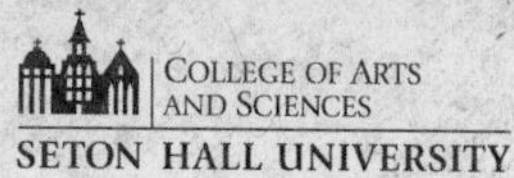

SETON HALL UNIVERSITY

Department of History

Programs of Study

The Department of History, located in the College of Arts and Sciences at Seton Hall University, offers a Master of Arts (M.A.) degree program with four concentrations: United States, European, global, and Catholic history. The program requires successful completion of ten courses (30 credits). All students must take an introductory course called The Historian's Craft, a minimum of one Program in Directed Readings (PDR) course, four courses in the chosen area of concentration, and electives in other areas. Advanced graduate students may choose either to conduct two semesters of thesis research and writing or to complete comprehensive written and oral examinations in the final semester of study.

The master's program requires all students to pass a foreign language translation exam (proving reading knowledge) or demonstrate mastery of advanced statistical methods.

This program is particularly attractive to K–12 teachers who are interested in an advanced degree in their field, as well as librarians and other professionals desiring a second advanced degree. It also provides a solid basis for those interested in continuing in a doctoral program.

Seton Hall University undergraduates who have completed 75 credits toward their undergraduate degree in history, with at least 21 credits in history (at least seven courses) are eligible to apply to the combined B.A./M.A. program option and complete both degrees in five years.

More information about graduate study in history at Seton Hall is available at http://www.shu.edu/academics/artsci/ma-history/.

Research Facilities

Students have access to the Seton Hall's Walsh Library as well as libraries at area colleges and the many important research facilities in New York City. The Walsh Library is a pioneer in electronic research facilities, making numerous online databases, journals, and resources available both on and off campus.

Financial Aid

Students may apply for graduate assistantships in the Department of History. Graduate assistants work for the Department or individual professors on special projects. The assistantships offer tuition remission and a stipend. Students should contact the Department of History for information about these graduate assistantships.

Additional graduate assistantships are available through the Office of Graduate Programs. Graduate assistants work in a variety of campus positions and receive tuition benefits and a stipend. For more information, students should visit http://www.shu.edu/applying/graduate/grad-finaid.cfm.

Cost of Study

Tuition is $875 per credit; all courses are 3 credits. Fees are $305 per semester for full-time students and $185 per semester for part-time students. Students not on assistantships may, for a fee, lease an IBM laptop computer. All students have access to free computer training.

Living and Housing Costs

Housing and living costs in South Orange are comparable to most suburbs of major cities, with studio and one-bedroom apartments renting for $750 to $1000 per month.

Student Group

The M.A. program enrolls approximately 20 full-time and part-time students. Entering classes consist of 8 to 10 students per year.

Location

Seton Hall University, located in South Orange, New Jersey, is only 14 miles by train, bus, or car from New York City, offering students a unique cosmopolitan location complete with cultural, employment, and internship opportunities.

The University and The Department

Seton Hall is New Jersey's largest Catholic university. The University's diverse academic program is characterized by a strong teaching faculty and a wide range of academic choices. Students benefit from the personal attention generated by small classes and a low student-faculty ratio. At Seton Hall, students find people who are willing to listen, offer support, and help them get the most out of their education.

The Department of History's faculty is distinguished by excellent scholarship and teaching. Faculty members regularly publish books and articles and participate in local, regional, and international conferences.

Applying

Applicants, other than dual-degree candidates, must have a baccalaureate degree, preferably in history or a history-related field, such as political science, geography, or economics. Students who have majored in other fields may be asked to take up to four undergraduate courses in history. Applicants must submit the Seton Hall University Graduate Application (available through a link on the Web site of the M.A. in History program at http://www.shu.edu/academics/artsci/ma-history/) as well as a personal statement, three letters of recommendation, and scores on the Graduate Record Examinations (GRE).

Candidates applying for a graduate assistantship can find the online application at http://www.shu.edu/applying/graduate/grad-finaid.cfm. This application should be submitted with a statement of interest in the position and a writing sample. Students should contact the Department of History for more information on graduate assistantships.

Correspondence and Information

Dr. Dermot Quinn, Director of Graduate Studies
Department of History
College of Arts and Sciences
Fahy Hall, Room 339
Seton Hall University
400 South Orange Avenue
South Orange, New Jersey 07079
Phone: 973-275-2984
Fax: 973-761-7798
E-mail: quinnder@shu.edu
Web site: http://www.shu.edu/academics/artsci/ma-history/

Seton Hall University

THE GRADUATE FACULTY AND THEIR RESEARCH

Tracey E. Billado, Ph.D., Emory. Medieval.
William J. Connell, Ph.D., Berkeley. Renaissance, Italy, Italian American.
Howard Eissenstat, Ph.D., UCLA. Middle East.
Larry A. Greene, Ph.D., Columbia. United States, urban, African American.
Williamjames Hull Hoffer, J.D., Harvard; Ph.D., Johns Hopkins. United States, law, economy.
Nathaniel Knight, Ph.D., Columbia. Russia/Soviet Union, Eastern Europe.
Daniel J. Leab, Ph.D., Columbia. United States, labor, film.
Maxine N. Lurie, Ph.D., Wisconsin. United States, colonial and revolutionary, New Jersey.
Maxim Matusevich, Ph.D., Illinois at Urbana-Champaign. Global, Africa.
James P. McCartin, Ph.D., Notre Dame. United States, Catholic, religion and culture.
Mark C. Molesky, Ph.D., Harvard. Germany, France, intellectual.
Dermot A. Quinn, D.Phil., Oxford. England, Ireland, intellectual.
Thomas F. Rzeznik, Ph.D., Notre Dame. American religious.
Kirsten Schultz, Ph.D., NYU. Immigration, Latin America.

SOUTHERN ILLINOIS UNIVERSITY CARBONDALE

Department of History
Ph.D. Program

Program of Study

The Department of History offers a Ph.D. degree in selected fields of United States, European, and Latin American history. In addition to these fields, students may select secondary fields in East Asian and African history. It is possible to complete all requirements for the Ph.D. degree in three to four years of full-time study after the M.A. Most students spend two years completing classroom studies; thereafter, the time required for the completion of the dissertation varies considerably with the topic and the student. Ph.D. students are also encouraged to do internship work toward the development of career-related professional skills. Internships include teaching, training in innovative instructional technologies, editing at the Southern Illinois University Press, public history at the University museum, archive management at Morris Library, and similar approved activities at other venues.

The Department of History's graduate student body is small (between 55 and 65 students), allowing for close working relationships between faculty members and students. The faculty members are particularly strong in national and ethnic identity studies, local and regional studies, business and labor history, American studies, and gender and women's history. Students take regular courses and seminars in these and other areas, and they also arrange independent study courses and internships. Southern Illinois University Carbondale (SIUC) also has a cooperative Ph.D. program with SIU at Edwardsville (SIUE), which allows students to take courses on both campuses.

Students benefit from Departmental support for publishing and for travel to conferences. They may also participate in a very active History Graduate Student Association that provides a sense of community and a vehicle for organizing activities on campus.

Research Facilities

The Morris Library, with its collection of more than 2 million printed volumes and 4 million microfilm units, provides excellent support for research. More than one fourth of its holdings are in history or related areas, and it is particularly strong in U.S., European, and Latin American history. The library's special collections hold rare printed works and manuscripts to support historical research on many topics, including Irish studies, First Amendment freedoms, theater history, and Illinois history. The University is also home to the Ulysses S. Grant Association, the John Dewey Center, the Center for Irish Studies, and the Illinois Regional Archives Depository.

Financial Aid

Most qualified Ph.D. students receive support in the form of fellowships through programs such as the Illinois Minority Graduate Incentive Program (IMGIP) and the Illinois Consortium for Educational Opportunities Program (ICEOP) or through graduate fellowships, Morris Doctoral Fellowships, and dissertation research awards. Teaching assistantships or research assistantships are also available. All carry stipends (minimum of $11,000 for nine months) and remission of tuition. A maximum of forty-eight months of assistance is allowed. Application for these awards should be submitted by January 15.

Cost of Study

In-state graduate tuition is $313.90 per credit hour in 2008–09. Out-of-state tuition is 2.5 times the in-state tuition rate ($784.75 per credit hour). Graduate students with at least a 25 percent appointment as a graduate assistant receive a tuition scholarship. Fees vary from $511.26 (1 credit hour) to $1416.05 (12 credit hours). Students with a graduate assistantship receive a 25 percent reduction in the Primary Care Medical Fee.

Living and Housing Costs

For married couples, students with families, and single graduate students, the University has 690 efficiency and one-, two-, three-, and four-bedroom apartments that rent for $484 to $686 per month in 2008–09. Residence halls for single graduate students are also available, as are accessible residence hall rooms and apartments for students with disabilities.

Student Group

This program admits students seeking careers in academia and other areas of the workplace. There are between 30 and 35 students in the Ph.D. program (approximately 35 percent women), with at least half receiving financial assistance. Roughly one fourth of the students are part-time.

Student Outcomes

Graduates of the Ph.D. program in history have been very successful at obtaining tenure-track jobs with colleges and universities as well as jobs with museums and publications and editorial projects.

Location

SIUC is 350 miles south of Chicago and 100 miles southeast of St. Louis. Nestled in rolling hills bordered by the Ohio and Mississippi Rivers and enhanced by a mild climate, the area has state parks, national forests and wildlife refuges, and large lakes for outdoor recreation. Cultural offerings include theater, opera, concerts, art exhibits, and cinema. Educational facilities available for the families of students are excellent.

The University

Southern Illinois University Carbondale is a comprehensive public university with a variety of general and professional education programs. The University offers associate, bachelor's, master's, and doctoral degrees as well as the J.D. and M.D. degrees. The University is fully accredited by the North Central Association of Colleges and Schools. The Graduate School has an essential role in the development and coordination of graduate instruction and research programs. The Graduate Council has academic responsibility for determining graduate standards, recommending new graduate programs and research centers, and establishing policies to facilitate the research effort.

Applying

Applications should be requested from and sent to the Department. Each application must include the standard application forms, transcripts of all postsecondary school work, official GRE scores, three letters of recommendation, a statement of professional goals and interests, and the application fee. The deadline for application materials is January 15 for the following fall. Admission requires a grade point average in graduate work of at least 3.25 (A = 4.0).

Direct entry into the Ph.D. program from baccalaureate studies is possible for students of exceptional ability. This is demonstrated through extensive undergraduate course work of superior quality, excellent GRE scores, previous research experience, and letters of recommendation.

Correspondence and Information

Chasity Wright
Department of History
Southern Illinois University
Carbondale, Illinois 62901-4519
Phone: 618-453-4391
E-mail: cwright@siu.edu
histgrad@siu.edu
Web site: http://www.siu.edu/~histsiu

Southern Illinois University Carbondale

THE FACULTY AND THEIR RESEARCH

(The number in parentheses in each entry represents the year in which the person joined the faculty.)

Jane H. Adams, Associate Professor; Ph.D., Illinois at Urbana-Champaign, 1987 (1987). U.S. rural, gender, social movements.
Howard W. Allen, Professor Emeritus; Ph.D., Washington (Seattle), 1959 (1962).
James Smith Allen, Professor; Ph.D., Tufts, 1979 (1991). European, modern France, social and cultural.
Harry Ammon, Professor Emeritus; Ph.D., Virginia, 1948 (1950).
Jo Ann E. Argersinger, Professor; Ph.D., George Washington, 1980 (1998). U.S. labor.
Peter H. Argersinger, Professor; Ph.D., Wisconsin–Madison, 1970 (1998). U.S. political and rural, Gilded Age.
H. Arnold Barton, Professor Emeritus; Ph.D., Princeton, 1962 (1970).
Michael C. Batinski, Professor Emeritus; Ph.D., Northwestern, 1969 (1968). Early America.
Jonathan J. Bean, Professor; Ph.D., Ohio State, 1994 (1995). U.S. economic and business.
Dale R. Bengtson, Assistant Professor Emeritus; Ph.D., Hartford Seminary Foundation, 1971 (1973). History of religions.
Getahun Benti, Associate Professor; Ph.D., Michigan State, 2000 (2001). Modern Africa, urbanization-migration.
Michael Brown, Assistant Professor; Ph.D., Georgia, 2004 (2004). African American and Atlantic history.
Kay J. Carr, Associate Professor; Ph.D., Chicago, 1987 (1989). U.S. social, nineteenth century, Illinois, frontier, historical geography.
M. Browning Carrott, Professor Emeritus; Ph.D., Northwestern, 1966 (1967).
David E. Conrad, Professor Emeritus; Ph.D., Oklahoma, 1962 (1967).
Donald S. Detwiler, Professor Emeritus; D.Phil., Göttingen (Germany), 1961 (1967).
John E. Dotson, Professor Emeritus; Ph.D., Johns Hopkins, 1969 (1970). European medieval and renaissance, Italy, maritime.
Mariola Espinonsa, Assistant Professor; Ph.D., North Carolina, 2003 (2003). Latin American history.
Germaine Etienne, Assistant Professor; Ph.D., Massachusetts, 2004 (2004). African American history.
Charles F. Fanning, Professor Emeritus; Ph.D., Pennsylvania, 1972 (1993). Ireland, Irish American, immigration and ethic studies.
Robert L. Gold, Professor Emeritus; Ph.D., Iowa, 1964 (1965).
John S. Haller Jr., Professor; Ph.D., Maryland, 1968 (1990). U.S. intellectual history, history of medicine and pharmacology.
Holly S. Hurlburt, Associate Professor; Ph.D., Syracuse, 2000 (2001). Early modern Europe, Italy, women and gender.
Robbie Lieberman, Professor; Ph.D., Michigan, 1984 (1991). Contemporary U.S., war and peace, social movements.
James B. Murphy, Associate Professor Emeritus; Ph.D., LSU, 1968 (1968).
Edward J. O'Day, Associate Professor Emeritus; A.M., Indiana, 1956 (1962).
Lon R. Shelby, Professor Emeritus; Ph.D., North Carolina, 1962 (1961).
John Y. Simon, Professor; Ph.D., Harvard, 1961 (1964). Civil War and Reconstruction, Illinois.
Joseph Sramek, Assistant Professor; Ph.D., CUNY Graduate Center, 2007 (2007). South Asia and British Empire.
Rachel Stocking, Associate Professor; Ph.D., Stanford, 1994 (1994). Ancient and early medieval European, cultural and political, Spain.
Henry S. Vyverberg, Professor Emeritus; Ph.D., Harvard, 1950 (1968).
Theodore R. Weeks, Professor; Ph.D., Berkeley, 1992 (1993). Russia/USSR East Central Europe, cultural and political, nationalism.
David P. Werlich, Professor Emeritus; Ph.D., Minnesota, 1968 (1968). Latin American Andean region.
Jonathan S. Wiesen, Associate Professor; Ph.D., Brown, 1997 (1998). Modern Europe, Germany, Jewish.
David L. Wilson, Professor; Ph.D., Tennessee, 1974 (1974). United States foreign relations.
Hale Yilmaz, Assistant Professor; Ph.D., Utah, 2006 (2006). Middle East.
Gray Whaley, Assistant Professor; Ph.D., Oregon, 2002 (2002). Native America.
Natasha Zaretsky, Associate Professor; Ph.D., Brown, 2002 (2002). United States, cultural, family and gender.

SIUE Cooperative Ph.D. Faculty

Stefan Bradley, Assistant Professor; Ph.D., Missouri–Columbia, 2003. African Americans.
Anthony Cheeseboro, Assistant Professor; Ph.D., Michigan State, 1993. History of development, agriculture, and slavery.
Ching-chih Chen, Professor Emeritus; Ph.D., Harvard, 1973.
Leigh Anne Eubanks, Instructor; Ph.D. candidate, Cornell. Modern Europe.
Carole C. Frick, Associate Professor; Ph.D., UCLA, 1995. Renaissance/reformation and early modern history.
Stephen L. Hansen, Associate Professor; Ph.D., Illinois at Chicago, 1978. Civil War.
Alex Haskell, Assistant Professor; Ph.D., Johns Hopkins, 2004. Colonial U.S.
Christienne L. Hinz, Assistant Professor; Ph.D., Ohio State, 2001 (2001). Japanese history, business history, world history, women's history.
Thomas Jordan, Assistant Professor; Ph.D., Illinois at Urbana-Champaign, 1999. Latin America.
Rowena McClinton, Associate Professor; Ph.D., Kentucky, 1996. Native American history, antebellum South and United States history since 1865.
Laura Milsk, Assistant Professor; Ph.D., Loyola Chicago, 2003. Museum studies.
Michael Moore, Assistant Professor, Ph.D., Michigan, 1996. Medieval Europe.
Norman E. Nordhauser, Professor Emeritus; Ph.D., Stanford, 1970. American economic history, history of American business.
Ellen Nore, Associate Professor; Ph.D., Stanford, 1980. Illinois history, women's history, progressive intellectuals, historiography.
Shirley J. Portwood, Professor; Ph.D., Washington (St. Louis), 1982. African-American and women's history.
Eric Ruckh, Assistant Professor; Ph.D., California, Irvine, 1997. Critical theory.
Stephen E. Tamari, Assistant Professor; Ph.D., Georgetown, 1998 (2001). Middle East history, Ottoman Empire, Arab world, Arab-Israeli conflict.
John A. Taylor, Professor; Ph.D., Chicago. Britain and Colonial U.S.
Allison K. Thomason, Assistant Professor; Ph.D., Columbia, 1999. Ancient Near-Eastern and Greco-Roman history.
Anne Valk, Associate Professor; Ph.D., Duke, 1996. Public history, oral history, women's history, twentieth-century United States.
James J. Weingartner, Professor Emeritus; Ph.D., Wisconsin, 1967. Nazi Germany, the Holocaust, war crimes, World War II.

STONY BROOK UNIVERSITY, STATE UNIVERSITY OF NEW YORK

Department of History

Programs of Study

The Department of History at Stony Brook offers the M.A. and Ph.D. degrees in history. The graduate program pivots around several thematic clusters that transcend traditional geographic and period boundaries and that capture the ways in which the faculty members' current interests converge. These thematic areas are: women, gender, sexuality, and reproduction; nation, state, and civil society; empire, modernity and globalization; and environment, science, and health. From the outset, students are prepared to balance area and period specialties with thematic, comparative, and theoretical perspectives. Students start out in their first year with the core seminar, which is taken with the rest of the incoming class and offers an initial experience with the analytic, theme-centered history that they will pursue in their chosen specialties of period and place. Through field seminars, students also learn the classic as well as state-of-the-art scholarship in their specialties. The rest of their courses include the thematic seminars, involving cross-national study of one important aspect of a thematic cluster, which provide all students with analytic tools and comparative frameworks with which to pursue individual research and reading. Among the required as well as optional courses are research seminars, which are flexibly designed to give students guidance and feedback in their individual research projects, as well as more individually tailored workshops.

M.A. students choose from among these courses to complete their 30 course credits (normally 3 credits per course). An oral exam completes their degree requirements. Doctoral students usually complete their course as well as additional requirements—competence in the appropriate languages, a dissertation prospectus, their oral examination—by the end of the third year. They then plunge into full-time dissertation work.

Financial Aid

Stony Brook offers University tuition scholarships, Graduate School assistantships, and Graduate Council Fellowships. Graduate School assistantships are $17,145 per year. Graduate Council Fellowships are restricted to U.S. citizens and permanent residents and carry a stipend of $17,573 plus a full-tuition scholarship; ten are awarded campuswide each year. W. Burghardt Turner Fellowships carry a stipend of $17,573 plus a full-tuition scholarship; twenty are awarded each year to U.S. citizens or permanent residents who are Native American, African American, or Hispanic American. Federal and state aid includes Veterans Administration educational benefits, Federal Work-Study, subsidized and unsubsidized Federal Stafford Loans, Federal Perkins Loans, and Tuition Assistance Program (TAP).

The Department of History also awards a generous Frankel Fellowship to its top incoming student.

Cost of Study

In 2008–09, full-time tuition at 12 credits for entering in-state residents is $3450 per semester, while out-of-state residents and international students pay $5460. Additional fees for each semester, including (but not limited to) the infirmary, activity, technology, and transportation fees, total about $875. International students also pay a service fee of approximately $35 per semester and an orientation fee of $50. Fees for the mandatory Student Health Insurance Plan vary depending on citizenship and employment status.

Living and Housing Costs

For 2008–09, Stony Brook calculates the cost of education excluding tuition, fees, and insurance at $14,228 per year. On-campus apartments range in cost from approximately $336 per month to approximately $1456 per month, depending on the size of the unit and the number of students sharing the space. Off-campus housing options include rooms, houses, and apartments that can be rented from approximately $350 to $2500 per month. Costs including books, food, and transportation may vary depending on academic program and/or personal circumstances.

Student Group

For 2007–08, the entering class had 13 doctoral and 2 master's students. Of these, 8 are men and 7 are women, and 4 of the doctoral students are international students. The program has a total of 104 doctoral and 30 master's students.

Student Outcomes

Recent doctoral graduates hold academic positions at George Washington University, Boston College, Purdue University, Ohio State University, University of California, and Pennsylvania State University. Both doctoral and master's graduates have also moved into a diversity of nonacademic positions, from university administration, to public school teaching, to archival work, to positions in business and government.

Location

The University is located on the North Shore of Long Island, about 60 miles east of New York City. The Long Island Railroad connects New York City with the Stony Brook campus, and bus service is available on campus and to various points on Long Island.

The University and The Department

Established in 1957 as part of the State University of New York system, Stony Brook is now recognized as one of the nation's finest public universities. Stony Brook is classified by the Carnegie Foundation as a Doctoral/Research University–Extensive, the highest distinction granted to fewer than 2 percent of all colleges and universities nationwide, reflecting Stony Brook's high volume of federally sponsored research, high percentage of doctoral students, and emphasis on scholarship. A book published by Johns Hopkins University Press (*The Rise of American Research Universities: Elites and Challengers in the Postwar Era,* by Hugh Davis Graham and Nancy Diamond, 1997) placed Stony Brook among the top three public research universities in the country—second only to the University of California at Berkeley and tied for second with the University of California, Santa Barbara—in research per faculty member.

Building on a decades-long tradition of postgraduate training, the Stony Brook history department has also recently leaped to the forefront of innovation in graduate instruction. Starting in 1998, the department reoriented the curriculum in ways that its own scholarship and the history profession were already moving. Now, alongside a thorough grounding in their choice of geographic and chronological specialty, a student's course of study revolves around processes, topics, and themes that transcend national or regional boundaries. The thematic history the department teaches enables communication between specialists as well as more comparative and analytic approaches. It is also an increasing advantage in the job market, where the demand for those who can teach global as well as, for example, U.S. or Latin American history, continues to rise.

In addition to placing the curriculum in the forefront of current historical interests, reshaping the doctoral offerings around these thematic clusters also connects the doctoral program to strengths in Stony Brook outside the history department. For example, the department's interest in women, gender, and sexuality links it to women's studies; its versatility in Latin American issues joins it to Africana studies, to Hispanic languages and literature, and to the English and sociology departments. The department's strengths in environmental history link it to the many faculty members from natural and social sciences and humanities involved in the environmental studies program; its focus on the social history of medicine connects us to the Medical School; its interest in race and ethnicity links it to Africana Studies and the Latin American Center; and its strength in cultural studies connects the department to a whole range of departments in the humanities. The history department strongly encourages this kind of interdisciplinary work.

Applying

Admission and financial aid applications should be filed by January 15 for fall admission. Application materials are available from the Web site at http://www.grad.sunysb.edu. Admissions and support decisions are made during the first week in March, and applicants receive notification no later than March 15. April 15 is the deadline to respond to offers of admission and support.

Correspondence and Information

Brooke Larson
Graduate Program Director
Department of History
SBS Building, 3rd Floor, S-333
Stony Brook University, State University of New York
Stony Brook, New York 11794-4348
Phone: 631-632-7489
E-mail: brooke.larson@stonybrook.edu
Web site: http://www.sunysb.edu/history

Josephine Goykin
Graduate Program Coordinator
Department of History
SBS Building, 3rd Floor, S303
Stony Brook University, State University of New York
Stony Brook, New York 11794-4348
Phone: 631-632-7490
E-mail: josephine.goykin@stonybrook.edu

Stony Brook University, State University of New York

THE FACULTY AND THEIR RESEARCH

Professors

Jennifer Andrerson, Ph.D., NYU, 2007. Early American and Atlantic history.
Charles Backfish, M.A., NYU, 1968. Social studies education.
Michael Barnhart, Ph.D., Harvard, 1980. U.S. foreign policy, twentieth-century U.S. history, modern Japan.
Eric Beverly, Ph.D., Harvard, 2007. South Asia, comparative colonialism.
Karl S. Bottigheimer (Emeritus), Ph.D., Berkeley, 1965. Tudor-Stuart England and Ireland, early modern Europe, modern Ireland.
David Burner (Emeritus), Ph.D., Columbia, 1965. Twentieth-century U.S. political and social history.
Themis Chronopoulos, Ph.D., Brown, 2004. U.S. urban history, race, and ethnicity; popular culture; public policy; world cities.
Alix Cooper, Ph.D., Harvard, 1998. Early modern Europe/world; history of science, medicine, and technology; environmental history; cross-cultural encounters.
Ruth Schwarz Cowan (Emerita), Ph.D., Johns Hopkins, 1969: Modern sciences, technology and medicine.
Jared Farmer, Ph.D., Stamford, 2005. Environmental history and policy, U.S. cultural history, and U.S. West.
Larry Frohman, Ph.D., Berkeley, 1992. European intellectual history, welfare and social policy, social studies education.
Elizabeth Garber (Emerita), Ph.D., Case Western Reserve, 1966. Social and intellectual history of science, nineteenth- and twentieth-century physics, European intellectual and social history.
Robert Goldenberg, Ph.D., Brown, 1974. Jewish history and religion in late antiquity, rabbinic literature and exegesis, history of Jewish thought, rabbinic hermeneutics, ancient history.
Paul Gootenberg, Ph.D., Chicago, 1985. Modern Latin America (Andes and Mexico), economic, state formation, commodities, drugs.
Susan Hinely, J.D., Harvard, 1983; Ph.D., Stanford, 1987. European history and women's history.
Young-Sun Hong, Ph.D., Michigan, 1989. Modern Germany, social theory, culture and politics in Germany, culture and politics in modern Europe, gender history.
Richard Kuisel (Emeritus), Ph.D., Berkeley, 1963. Contemporary Europe, political and economic history, modern France.
Ned Landsman, Chairperson; Ph.D., Pennsylvania, 1979. Early American history, Atlantic history.
Brooke Larson, Ph.D., Columbia, 1978. Colonial and modern Latin America, Andean rural societies; race, ethnicity, and nation-making.
Herman Lebovics, Ph.D., Yale, 1965. Modern Europe, intellectual and cultural history, Germany and France.
Helen Lemay (Emeritus), Ph.D., Columbia, 1972. Medieval and Renaissance intellectual history, paleography, history of science and medicine, women's history.
Shirley Lim, Ph.D., UCLA, 1998. Asian American women's cultural history.
Sara Lipton, Ph.D., Yale, 1991. Medieval cultural and religious history, Jewish-Christian relations, gender.
Iona Man-Cheong, Ph.D., Yale, 1991. Modern China, late imperial China, women and gender, Chinese Diaspora.
Gary J. Marker, Ph.D., Berkeley, 1977. Russian social and intellectual history, history of printing, European labor history.
April Masten, Ph.D., Rutgers, 1999. U.S. nineteenth-century cultural history.
Wilbur R. Miller, Ph.D., Columbia, 1973. U.S. social and political history, Civil War and Reconstruction, crime and criminal justice history.
Janis Mimura, Ph.D., Berkeley, 2002. Modern Japan.
Kathleen Banks Nutter, Ph.D., Massachusetts, 1998. Twentieth century U.S., labor and women.
Donna J. Rilling, Ph.D., Pennsylvania, 1993. Early national U.S. history; business, legal, urban, and labor history.
Alice Ritscherle, Ph.D., Michigan, 2005. Modern British social and cultural colonialism and imperialism, modern Ireland.
Joel T. Rosenthal (Emeritus), Ph.D., Chicago, 1963. Medieval history, medieval England, social history.
Wolf Schäfer, Dr.Phil., Bremen (Germany), 1983. History of technoscience, social history, global history.
Eli Seifman (Emeritus), Ph.D., NYU, 1965. U.S. social history, history of education, People's Republic of China.
Christopher Sellers, Graduate Director; Ph.D., Yale, 1992; M.D., North Carolina at Chapel Hill, 1992. U.S. environmental, industrial, and cultural history; history of medicine and the body.
Nancy J. Tomes, Ph.D., Pennsylvania, 1978. American social and cultural history, medicine, nursing and psychiatry, women and the family.
Fred Weinstein (Emeritus), Ph.D., Berkeley, 1962. Theory in history, Russian and European history.
Kathleen Wilson, Ph.D., Yale, 1985. British social, cultural, and political studies, seventeenth to nineteenth centuries; cultures of imperialism; gender studies; cultural, feminist, and postcolonial theory.
John A. Williams (Emeritus), Ph.D., Wisconsin, 1963. British Empire, Africa, the Commonwealth, expansion of Europe.
Judith Wishnia (Emerita), Ph.D., SUNY at Stony Brook, 1978: Modern Europe, France, labor history, women's history.
Paul Zimansky, Ph.D., Chicago, 1980. Near Eastern languages and civilizations, Near Eastern archaeology and history.

Associate Professors

Floris B. Cash, Ph.D., SUNY at Stony Brook, 1986. African American history, African American women's studies.
Leslie H. Owens, Ph.D., California, Riverside, 1972. African American history, U.S. Southern history.
Peniel E. Joseph, Ph.D., Temple, 2000. African American history; Civil Rights Black Power Movements; Black cultural, social, political, and intellectual history; Black feminism; African Diaspora; global studies; race and urban history.
Ian Roxborough (Emeritus), Ph.D., Wisconsin, 1977. Sociology, social history of Latin America, modern Mexico.
Warren Sanderson, Ph.D., Stanford, 1974. U.S. economic history, demography.
Olufemi Vaughan, Ph.D., Oxford, 1989. African politics and history, international relations.

UNIVERSITY OF TOLEDO

Department of History

Programs of Study

The mission of the Department of History at the University of Toledo is to provide the highest possible quality of instruction, to prepare historians and teachers as intellectually broadly as possible, to train students in the discipline of history, acquaint them with the profession, and promote a greater public understanding and awareness of the past.

The Ph.D. requires a minimum of 62 hours beyond the master's degree, including 24 hours for the dissertation. Students must complete a minimum of two seminars and a course in historiography. Additional requirements are listed in the Guidelines for Graduate Study in History. Examinations are given in one general field, one major area of concentration within the general field, and one minor area outside of the general field. Upon passing all examinations, each student must complete an acceptable dissertation. A maximum of seven years is allowed between matriculation and completion of all requirements for the degree.

Students may earn a Master of Arts (M.A.) degree by completing 30 graduate credits with a thesis or 36 graduate credits without a thesis. At least 18 hours must be earned in the major subject area; of these, 6 hours must be in 6990-level courses. Those students who choose to write a thesis must first receive approval from an advisory committee before defending it. Students who plan to pursue doctoral degrees should enroll in the thesis program, which concludes with an oral examination that covers the thesis and course work. The nonthesis program concludes with a written exam. Candidates must also successfully complete one course in historiography and one seminar. Students must maintain a minimum 3.0 average in all graduate work.

The Master of Arts and Education degree in history requires at least 21 hours of graduate credit in history, including American or European historiography and a seminar as well as a comprehensive written and oral examination.

Research Facilities

The William S. Carlson Library houses more than 1.6 million volumes and 3,000 periodicals, including more than 5,000 electronic journals. The University Libraries have a fully electronic catalog and circulation service that is available through any terminal on or off campus. The University Library network is connected to a statewide university library network, which provides access to the collections of all other university and college libraries in the state of Ohio as well as numerous research databases such as ISI. Tucker Hall, home of the Department of History, includes a large computer lab and a state-of-the-art enhanced classroom.

Financial Aid

The out-of-state tuition surcharge normally charged to out-of-state and international students is waived for students whose permanent address is within one of the following Michigan counties: Hillsdale, Lenawee, Macomb, Oakland, Washtenaw, and Wayne. In addition, the University of Toledo offers an out-of-state tuition surcharge waiver to cities and regions that are a part of the Sister Cities Agreement. These regions include Toledo, Spain; Londrina, Brazil; Qinhuangdao, China; Csongrad County, Hungary; Delmenhorst, Germany; Toyohashi, Japan; Tanga, Tanzania; Bekaa Valley, Lebanon; and Poznan, Poland. The University of Toledo Graduate College offers a variety of memorial and minority scholarship awards, including the Ronald E. McNair Postbaccalaureate Achievement Scholarship, the Graduate Minority Assistantship Award, and two full University fellowships.

Cost of Study

The graduate tuition rate is available at the Graduate School office.

Living and Housing Costs

The University of Toledo has a diverse offering of student housing options, including suite-style and traditional residential halls. Housing is offered to graduate students through Residence Life or contracted individually by the student. Affordable, high-quality off-campus apartment-style housing within walking distance of campus is abundant.

Student Group

There are approximately 20,000 students at the University of Toledo. About 4,000 are graduate and professional students. The University has a rich diversity of student organizations. Students join groups that are organized around common cultural, religious, athletic, and educational interests.

Student Outcomes

Graduates of the program are prepared to enter careers as historians or teachers in a wide variety of settings.

Location

The University of Toledo has several campus sites in the city of Toledo. Most graduate students take classes on the Main campus, which is located in suburban western Toledo. With a population of more than 330,000, Toledo is the fiftieth-largest city in the United States. It is located on the western shores of Lake Erie, within a 2-hour drive of Cleveland and Detroit.

The University

The University of Toledo was founded by Jessup W. Scott in 1872 as a municipal institution and became part of the state of Ohio's system of higher education in 1967. On July 1, 2006, the University of Toledo merged with the Medical University of Ohio becoming one of only seventeen American universities to offer professional and graduate academic programs in medicine, law, pharmacy, nursing, health sciences, engineering, and business.

Applying

Admission to the program requires a baccalaureate degree in history from an accredited institution with a minimum GPA of 3.0, a completed application form, three copies of transcripts from each university previously attended, three letters of recommendation, a statement of purpose, copies of GMAT or GRE test scores, and a nonrefundable $40 application fee.

Correspondence and Information

Dr. William O'Neal, Director of Graduate Studies
Chair, Department of History
University of Toledo
2801 West Bancroft Street
Toledo, Ohio 43606-3390

Phone: 419-530-2242
E-mail: william.oneal@utoledo.edu
Web site: http://www.utoledo.edu/as/history/index.html

University of Toledo

THE FACULTY AND THEIR RESEARCH

Glenn J. Ames, Professor; Ph.D., Minnesota. The French experience in Asia; economy of Portuguese Asia after 1640; indigenous dominance in the economy of Portuguese Monsoon Asia, 1600–1700.

Diane F. Britton, Professor; Ph.D., Washington State. Community building, memory, interpretation of history for public audiences.

Cynthia J. Ingham, Assistant Professor of History; Ph.D., Kansas. U.S. colonial and revolutionary history.

Michael Jakobson, Professor; Ph.D., Minnesota. Origins and history of the Gulag.

Peter Linebaugh, Professor; Ph.D., Warwick (England). Social history of crime and the death penalty in eighteenth-century England.

Charles Beatty Medina, Assistant Professor; Ph.D., Brown. Latin American history; African diaspora in Latin America, with a concentration on maroon societies and African resistance to colonial rule.

William J. O'Neal, Professor; Ph.D., Missouri–Columbia. Greek and Roman constitutional histories and the manuscript studies of neo-classical Latin.

Larry D. Wilcox, Professor; Ph.D., Virginia. Modern Europe, the contemporary world, modern Germany, Europe since 1870, the Holocaust, visual representations of World War II and the Holocaust.

Emeritus Professors

Alfred A. Cave, Ph.D., Florida. Ethnohistory of colonial America, Jacksonian America.

Charles N. Glaab, Ph.D., Missouri. American urban history; business, cultural, and urban history; progressivism and American historiography.

William D. Hoover, Ph.D., Michigan. Nineteenth- and twentieth-century Japan and China, nineteenth-century entrepreneurs, prewar Japanese internationalism and pacifism, journalist-publicist Kawakami Kiyoshi, postwar Japanese historiography.

Ronald Lora, Ph.D., Ohio State. American intellectual history and recent political and cultural history, intellectual history and conservatism.

Roger Ray, Ph.D., Duke. Intellectual and ecclesiastical history of England and France before 1300, medieval historiography, writings of the Venerable Bede.

Robert Freeman Smith, Ph.D, Wisconsin. Military and foreign relations.

VILLANOVA UNIVERSITY

Graduate Studies in Liberal Arts and Sciences
Department of History

Program of Study

Villanova University is one of relatively few academic institutions in the country that offer only an M.A. degree in history, rather than the M.A. and Ph.D. The program seeks to encourage students' love of history and strengthen their analytical and interpretive skills to meet diverse career goals.

Over the course of an academic year (fall and spring semesters and a summer term), twenty-one different graduate seminars are typically offered that cover a broad range of historical periods, themes, and regions. The average class size is 11 to 12 students. During the fall and spring semesters, classes meet once a week for 2 hours in the late afternoon or early evening. During the summer, classes meet one evening each week for eight weeks. The program is especially strong in European and American history, but thematic and non-Western topics are an important part of the curriculum. Villanova has a cooperative agreement with the Department of History at Temple University, where Villanova students may also take graduate seminars.

Program requirements include the successful completion of ten graduate courses and a passing score on the comprehensive examination. There is no formal language requirement. Students may begin taking courses in the fall, spring, or summer sessions and may take courses on a part-time (one course per session) or full-time basis. As many as two graduate courses in related disciplines, such as literature or political science, may be taken at Villanova. Students may also transfer a maximum of 6 credits for graduate courses taken at other institutions.

Research Facilities

The University Library contains more than 780,000 volumes and 5,600 current periodicals. The Philadelphia region, with its numerous other colleges and universities, museums, historical societies, and archival collections, offers a rich cultural and institutional environment for study and research in history.

Financial Aid

The Department has graduate assistantships and tuition scholarships for 15 full-time students. Graduate assistantships are awarded on a competitive basis. The assistantship in history included a waiver of all tuition and academic fees and a stipend of $6328 in 2007–08. A number of tuition scholarships are also available that provide a waiver of all tuition and academic fees.

In addition, the office of the director of financial aid administers the Federal Stafford Student Loan, the unsubsidized Federal Stafford Student Loan, and the Federal Supplemental Loans for Students.

Cost of Study

Graduate tuition was $585 per credit hour in 2007–08. In addition, there are a one-time application fee of $50 and a University fee of $30 each semester.

Living and Housing Costs

The area surrounding the University offers a wide selection of living quarters that are convenient to the campus, which is served by two suburban rail lines and buses. The University does not maintain accommodations for graduate students, but second-year students are eligible for positions as resident counselors in the dormitories.

Student Group

There is no typical graduate student in history at Villanova. The students comprise a large and diverse yet very congenial community. Many students enter the program directly from their undergraduate college. Others are completing graduate work in history while also engaged in careers in government service, law, business, or teaching. In any given semester, between 50 and 60 students take courses, approximately one third of whom are part-time students.

Student Outcomes

Many students continue to study toward a Ph.D. in history; recent graduates may be found in doctoral programs at Temple, Indiana Bloomington, the College of William and Mary, the University of Madrid, Brandeis, and other institutions. Other graduates pursue history-related careers in libraries, archives, or museums. Many have gone on to teaching or educational administration at the secondary or college level in places as diverse as Kuwait and West Point. Still other graduates work for government or nonprofit organizations, newspapers, or corporations.

Location

Located in the heart of the Delaware Valley's Main Line, the University occupies more than 200 handsomely landscaped acres in the town of Villanova, 12 miles west of Philadelphia. The location combines the advantages of a tranquil suburban setting with proximity to a large metropolitan city known for its outstanding historical, educational, and cultural resources.

The University

Villanova University is a private institution founded in 1842 by the Augustinian Fathers. Graduate programs were first administered separately in 1931. Currently, there are five academic units in addition to Graduate Studies: the Colleges of Arts and Sciences, Commerce and Finance, Engineering, and Nursing and the School of Law.

Applying

Applicants should have at least 18 undergraduate credits and a 3.0 average in history. The Graduate Record Examinations General Test is required for admission to the program. International applicants must take the TOEFL examination. Application deadlines are March 1 for fall admission, November 15 for spring admission, and May 1 for summer admission. The deadline is March 1 for those applying for a graduate assistantship.

Application forms and other information may be obtained from either the Department of History or the Office of Graduate Studies in the College of Liberal Arts and Sciences, Villanova University, 800 Lancaster Avenue, Villanova, Pennsylvania 19085 (phone: 610-519-7090, fax: 610-519-7096, e-mail: gradinformation@villanova.edu). Online submission of applications is also possible at http://www.villanova.edu/artsci/college/academics/graduate/.

Correspondence and Information

To discuss situation, qualifications, and goals:

Dr. R. Emmet McLaughlin, Director of the History Graduate Program
Department of History
Villanova University
Villanova, Pennsylvania 19085-1696

Phone: 610-519-4660
E-mail: emmet.mclaughlin@villanova.edu
Web site: http://www.villanova.edu/artsci/history/

Villanova University

THE FACULTY AND THEIR RESEARCH

Marc Gallicchio, Professor and Chair; Ph.D., Temple, 1986. U.S. foreign relations, American political and military history.
Hibba Abugideiri, Assistant Professor; Ph.D., Georgetown, 2001. Middle East history.
Craig Bailey, Assistant Professor; Ph.D., London, 2004. History of Ireland and Britain.
Jessey J. C. Choo, Assistant Professor; Ph.D., Princeton, 2007. History of pre-modern Asia.
Judith Ann Giesberg, Assistant Professor; Ph.D., Boston College, 1997. U.S. women's history.
Christopher Haas, Associate Professor; Ph.D., Michigan, 1988. Greece, Rome, late antiquity, early Christianity history.
Jeffrey A. Johnson, Professor; Ph.D., Princeton, 1980. History of science and technology.
Maghan Keita, Professor; Ph.D., Howard, 1988. African and world history.
Catherine Kerrison, Associate Professor; Ph.D., William and Mary, 1999. Colonial and revolutionary America, U.S. women's history.
Elizabeth Kolsky, Assistant Professor; Ph.D., Columbia, 2002. South Asian history.
Adele Lindenmeyr, Professor; Ph.D., Princeton, 1980. Russia and Soviet history, environmental history.
Lawrence Little, Associate Professor; Ph.D., Ohio State, 1993. African-American history.
Timothy McCall, Assistant Professor; Ph.D., Michigan, 2005. History of Renaissance art.
R. Emmet McLaughlin, Professor; Ph.D., Yale, 1980. Renaissance and Reformation history, early modern European history.
Charlene Mires, Associate Professor; Ph.D., Temple, 1997. American history, material culture, public history.
Paul Rosier, Associate Professor; Ph.D., Rochester, 1998. Modern and Native American history.
Rev. Joseph G. Ryan, O.S.A., Assistant Professor; Ph.D., American, 1997. American history, history of medicine.
Holly Sanders, Assistant Professor; Ph.D., Princeton, 2005. History of modern Asia.
Paul R. Steege, Associate Professor; Ph.D., Chicago, 1999. Post-1945 European history.
Rebecca L. Winer, Associate Professor; Ph.D., UCLA, 1996. Medieval Europe, European women's history, Jewish history.

Section 8
Humanities

This section contains a directory of institutions offering graduate work in humanities, followed by in-depth entries submitted by institutions that chose to prepare detailed program descriptions. Additional information about programs listed in the directory but not augmented by an in-depth entry may be obtained by writing directly to the dean of a graduate school or chair of a department at the address given in the directory.

For programs offering related work, see also in this book *Area and Cultural Studies, Geography, Interdisciplinary Studies, Philosophy, Political Science and International Affairs, Religious Studies,* and *Sociology, Anthropology, and Archaeology.* In another guide in this series:

Graduate Programs in Engineering & Applied Sciences
See *Management of Engineering and Technology*

CONTENTS

Program Directories

Close-Ups

See also:

Humanities

American Public University System, AMU/APU Graduate Programs, Charles Town, WV 25414. Offers air warfare (MA Military Studies); American Revolution (MA Military Studies); business administration (MBA); Civil War (MA Military Studies); criminal justice (MA); defense management (MA Military Studies); emergency and disaster management (MA); environmental policy and management (MS); fire science management (MA); global engagement (MA); history (MA); homeland security (MA); humanities (MA); intelligence (MA Military Studies, MA Strategic Intelligence); international peace and conflict resolution (MA); international relations and conflict resolution (MA); joint warfare (MA Military Studies); land warfare international perspective (MA Military Studies); management (MA); military history (MA); military leadership (MA Military Studies); national security studies (MA); naval warfare international (MA Military Studies); naval warfare US (MA Military Studies); political science (MA); public administration (MA); public health (MA); security management (MA); space studies (MS); special ops/LIC (MA Military Studies); sports management (MA); transportation and logistics management (MA); transportation management (MA); unconventional warfare (MA Military Studies); World War II (MA Military Studies). Programs offered via distance learning only. Part-time and evening/weekend programs available. Postbaccalaureate distance learning degree programs offered (no on-campus study). *Faculty:* 10 full-time (3 women), 188 part-time/adjunct (57 women). *Students:* 340 full-time (98 women), 3,567 part-time (790 women); includes 615 minority (317 African Americans, 28 American Indian/Alaska Native, 85 Asian Americans or Pacific Islanders, 185 Hispanic Americans), 20 international. Average age 36. 2,123 applicants, 100% accepted, 893 enrolled. In 2007, 829 degrees awarded. *Degree requirements:* For master's, comprehensive exam. *Entrance requirements:* For master's, bachelor's degree or equivalent, minimum GPA of 2.7 in last 60 hours of course work. *Application deadline:* Applications are processed on a rolling basis. Application fee: $0. Electronic applications accepted. *Expenses:* Tuition: Part-time $275 per semester hour. *Financial support:* Applicants required to submit FAFSA. *Faculty research:* Military history, criminal justice, management performance, national security. *Unit head:* Dr. Frank McCluskey, Provost, 877-468-6268, Fax: 304-724-3780. *Application contact:* Terry Grant, Director of Enrollment Management, 877-468-6268, Fax: 304-724-3780, E-mail: info@apus.edu.

Arcadia University, Graduate Studies, Program in Humanities, Glenside, PA 19038-3295. Offers fine arts, theater, and music (MAH); history, philosophy, and religion (MAH); literature and language (MAH). Part-time programs available. *Degree requirements:* For master's, thesis or alternative.

Arizona State University, Graduate College, College of Liberal Arts and Sciences, Division of Humanities, Interdisciplinary Program in the Humanities, Tempe, AZ 85287. Offers MA. *Degree requirements:* For master's, one foreign language, thesis. *Entrance requirements:* For master's, GRE.

Brigham Young University, Graduate Studies, College of Humanities, Department of Humanities, Classics, and Comparative Literature, Provo, UT 84602-1001. Offers comparative literature (MA); comparative studies (MA); humanities (MA). *Faculty:* 26 full-time (4 women). *Students:* 27 full-time (14 women). Average age 27. 15 applicants, 80% accepted, 6 enrolled. In 2007, 5 degrees awarded. *Degree requirements:* For master's, 2 foreign languages, thesis. *Entrance requirements:* For master's, GRE, minimum GPA of 3.0 in last 60 hours. *Application deadline:* For fall admission, 3/1 for domestic and international students. Application fee: $50. Electronic applications accepted. *Financial support:* In 2007–08, 27 students received support, including 7 research assistantships (averaging $4,680 per year), 29 teaching assistantships (averaging $65,678 per year); fellowships, career-related internships or fieldwork, institutionally sponsored loans, scholarships/grants, tuition waivers (full and partial), and student instructorships also available. Support available to part-time students. *Unit head:* Dr. Michael J. Call, Chair, 801-422-2550, Fax: 801-422-0305, E-mail: michael_call@byu.edu. *Application contact:* Carolyn Hone, Graduate Secretary for Humanities and Comparative Literature, 801-422-4430, Fax: 801-422-0305, E-mail: carolyn_hone@byu.edu.

California Institute of Integral Studies, Graduate Programs, School of Consciousness and Transformation, San Francisco, CA 94103. Offers cultural anthropology and social transformation (MA); East-West psychology (MA, PhD); integrative health studies (MA); philosophy and religion (MA, PhD), including Asian and comparative studies, philosophy, cosmology, and consciousness, social and cultural anthropology (PhD), transformative leadership (MA), transformative studies (PhD), women's spirituality, women's spirituality flex format; social and cultural anthropology (PhD); transformative leadership (MA); transformative studies (PhD). Part-time and evening/weekend programs available. Postbaccalaureate distance learning degree programs offered (minimal on-campus study). *Faculty:* 30 full-time, 28 part-time/adjunct. *Students:* 456; includes 92 minority (32 African Americans, 3 American Indian/Alaska Native, 40 Asian Americans or Pacific Islanders, 17 Hispanic Americans), 1 international. Average age 37. 206 applicants, 93% accepted, 114 enrolled. In 2007, 26 degrees awarded. Terminal master's awarded for partial completion of doctoral program. *Degree requirements:* For master's, comprehensive exam (for some programs), thesis optional; for doctorate, comprehensive exam, thesis/dissertation. *Entrance requirements:* For master's, minimum GPA of 3.0, letters of recommendation, writing sample; for doctorate, master's degree, minimum GPA of 3.0, letters of recommendation, writing sample. Additional exam requirements/recommendations for international students: Required—TOEFL. *Application deadline:* For fall admission, 2/15 priority date for domestic and international students; for spring admission, 10/15 priority date for domestic and international students. Applications are processed on a rolling basis. Application fee: $65. Electronic applications accepted. *Expenses:* Tuition: Full-time $16,930; part-time $780 per unit. Tuition and fees vary according to course load and program. *Financial support:* In 2007–08, 292 students received support; research assistantships, teaching assistantships, career-related internships or fieldwork, Federal Work-Study, institutionally sponsored loans, scholarships/grants, and tuition waivers (partial) available. Support available to part-time students. Financial award application deadline: 3/15; financial award applicants required to submit FAFSA. *Faculty research:* Altered states of consciousness, dreams, cosmology, postcolonial studies, integrative health studies. *Application contact:* Allyson Werner, Senior Admissions Counselor, 415-575-6155, Fax: 415-575-1268.

See Close-Up on page 445.

California State University, Dominguez Hills, College of Arts and Humanities, Program in the Humanities, Carson, CA 90747-0001. Offers MA. Part-time and evening/weekend programs available. *Faculty:* 5 full-time (2 women), 4 part-time/adjunct (3 women). *Students:* 7 full-time (5 women), 13 part-time (9 women); includes 9 minority (6 African Americans, 3 Hispanic Americans). Average age 40. 10 applicants, 70% accepted, 5 enrolled. In 2007, 5 degrees awarded. *Degree requirements:* For master's, thesis or alternative. *Entrance requirements:* For master's, minimum GPA of 3.0. *Application deadline:* For fall admission, 6/1 for domestic students. Applications are processed on a rolling basis. Application fee: $55. *Financial support:* Institutionally sponsored loans available. Support available to part-time students. Financial award application deadline: 8/1. *Faculty research:* African American music, postmodernism, cities of antiquity, Faust, African studies. *Unit head:* Dr. Lorna Fitzsimmons, Coordinator, 310-243-3036, E-mail: lfitzsimmons@csudh.edu.

California State University, Dominguez Hills, College of Extended and International Education, Humanities External Degree Program, Carson, CA 90747-0001. Offers MA. Part-time and evening/weekend programs available. Postbaccalaureate distance learning degree programs offered. *Faculty:* 8 full-time (4 women), 34 part-time/adjunct (13 women). *Students:* 7 full-time (3 women), 505 part-time (263 women); includes 53 minority (17 African Americans, 5 American Indian/Alaska Native, 7 Asian Americans or Pacific Islanders, 24 Hispanic Americans), 13 international. Average age 43. 70 applicants, 94% accepted, 49 enrolled. In 2007, 54 degrees awarded. *Degree requirements:* For master's, thesis, advancement to candidacy essays. *Entrance requirements:* Additional exam requirements/recommendations for international students: Required—TOEFL. *Application deadline:* For fall admission, 6/1 for domestic and international students; for winter admission, 3/1 for domestic and international students; for spring admission, 11/1 for domestic and international students. Application fee: $55. *Expenses:* Contact institution. *Financial support:* Applicants required to submit FAFSA. *Faculty research:* 19th and 20th century literature, Arab history, Greek philosophy, ancient history, East Asian, Soviet cultural history, Native American history and culture, feminist studies. *Unit head:* Dr. Patricia Cherin, Coordinator, 310-243-3191, Fax: 310-516-4399, E-mail: huxonline@csudh.edu. *Application contact:* Lisa Ayers, Program Assistant, 310-243-3190, Fax: 310-516-4399, E-mail: layers@csudh.edu.

Carlow University, Humanities Division, Pittsburgh, PA 15213-3165. Offers creative writing (MFA), including fiction, nonfiction, poetry. Part-time and evening/weekend programs available. *Degree requirements:* For master's, thesis or alternative. *Entrance requirements:* For master's, minimum GPA of 3.0, resumé. Additional exam requirements/recommendations for international students: Required—TOEFL (minimum score 550 paper-based; 213 computer-based).

Central European University, Graduate Studies, School of Social Sciences and Humanities, Budapest, Hungary. Offers economics (MA, PhD); gender studies (MA, PhD); international relations and European studies (MA, PhD); mathematics and its applications (MS, PhD); medieval studies (MA, PhD); nationalism studies (MA, PhD); philosophy (MA, PhD); political science (MA, PhD); public policy (MA, PhD); sociology and social anthropology (MA, PhD). *Faculty:* 75 full-time (25 women), 46 part-time/adjunct (10 women). *Students:* 625 full-time (355 women). Average age 26. 2,500 applicants, 31% accepted, 540 enrolled. In 2007, 325 master's, 20 doctorates awarded. Terminal master's awarded for partial completion of doctoral program. *Degree requirements:* For master's, one foreign language, thesis; for doctorate, one foreign language, comprehensive exam, thesis/dissertation. *Entrance requirements:* For master's, CEU subject tests, interview; for doctorate, GRE, CEU subject test, interview. Additional exam requirements/recommendations for international students: Required—TOEFL (minimum score 570 paper-based; 230 computer-based). *Application deadline:* For fall admission, 1/15 priority date for domestic and international students. Application fee: $0. Electronic applications accepted. Tuition charges are reported in euros. *Expenses:* Tuition: Full-time 10,000 euros; part-time 315 euros per credit. *Financial support:* In 2007–08, 402 students received support, including 350 fellowships with full and partial tuition reimbursements available (averaging $5,000 per year); career-related internships or fieldwork, institutionally sponsored loans, and scholarships/grants also available. Financial award application deadline: 1/5. *Faculty research:* Civil society, fiscal decentralization, party politics, political philosophy (especially Liberalism, theory of Democracy). Total annual research expenditures: $35,000. *Unit head:* Dr. Howard Michael Robinson, Provost, 361-327-3003, Fax: 361-327-3211, E-mail: robinson@ceu.hu. *Application contact:* Zsuzsanna Jaszberenyi, Admissions Officer, 361-327-3009, Fax: 361-327-3211, E-mail: admissions@ceu.hu.

See Close-Up on page 447.

Central Michigan University, Central Michigan University Off-Campus Programs, Program in Humanities, Mount Pleasant, MI 48859. Offers MA. Part-time and evening/weekend programs available. *Entrance requirements:* For master's, minimum GPA of 2.7 in major. Additional exam requirements/recommendations for international students: Required—TOEFL. *Application deadline:* Applications are processed on a rolling basis. Application fee: $50. Electronic applications accepted. *Financial support:* Scholarships/grants available. Support available to part-time students. Financial award applicants required to submit FAFSA. *Unit head:* Dr. Ronald Primeau, Director, 989-774-3117, Fax: 989-774-7106, E-mail: ronald.r.primeau@cmich.edu. *Application contact:* 877-268-4636, E-mail: cmuoffcampus@cmich.edu.

See Close-Up on page 449.

Central Michigan University, College of Graduate Studies, College of Humanities and Social and Behavioral Sciences, Program in Humanities, Mount Pleasant, MI 48859. Offers MA. *Degree requirements:* For master's, thesis or alternative. *Entrance requirements:* For master's, 20 hours of course work in humanities, minimum GPA of 2.7.

See Close-Up on page 449.

Claremont Graduate University, Graduate Programs, School of Arts and Humanities, Claremont, CA 91711-6160. Offers M Phil, MA, MFA, DCM, DMA, PhD, Certificate, MA/PhD, MBA/MA, MBA/PhD. Part-time programs available. *Faculty:* 16 full-time (6 women), 29 part-time/adjunct (11 women). *Students:* 361 full-time (209 women), 48 part-time (24 women); includes 89 minority (13 African Americans, 4 American Indian/Alaska Native, 32 Asian Americans or Pacific Islanders, 40 Hispanic Americans), 28 international. Average age 35. In 2007, 77 master's, 22 doctorates, 1 other advanced degree awarded. *Degree requirements:* For doctorate, 2 foreign languages, comprehensive exam, thesis/dissertation, oral and written qualifying exams, oral defense of dissertation, recitals. *Entrance requirements:* For doctorate, GRE General Test. *Application deadline:* For fall admission, 2/15 priority date for domestic students. Applications are processed on a rolling basis. Electronic applications accepted. *Expenses:* Tuition: Full-time $31,640; part-time $1,376 per unit. Required fees: $145 per semester. Tuition and fees vary according to course load, degree level and program. *Financial support:* Fellowships, research assistantships, teaching assistantships, Federal Work-Study and institutionally sponsored loans available. Support available to part-time students. Financial award application deadline: 2/15; financial award applicants required to submit FAFSA. *Unit head:* Marc Redfield, Interim Dean, 909-607-3337, Fax: 909-607-1221, E-mail: marc.redfield@cgu.edu. *Application contact:* Justin Evans, Admissions Coordinator, 909-607-1278, Fax: 909-607-1221, E-mail: humanities@cgu.edu.

College of the Humanities and Sciences, Harrison Middleton University, Graduate Program, Tempe, AZ 85282. Offers education (MA, Ed D); humanities (MA); imaginative literature (MA); jurisprudence (MA); natural science (MA); philosophy and religion (MA); social science (MA). Part-time and evening/weekend programs available. Postbaccalaureate distance learning degree programs offered (no on-campus study).

Concordia University, School of Graduate Studies, Faculty of Arts and Science, Program in Humanities, Montréal, QC H3G 1M8, Canada. Offers PhD. *Degree requirements:* For doctorate, one foreign language, comprehensive exam, thesis/dissertation.

Dominican University of California, Graduate Programs, School of Arts and Sciences, Program in Humanities, San Rafael, CA 94901-2298. Offers MA. Part-time programs available. *Faculty:* 7 full-time (3 women), 3 part-time/adjunct (1 woman). *Students:* 4 full-time (3 women), 38 part-time (28 women); includes 4 minority (1 African American, 1 American Indian/Alaska Native, 2 Hispanic Americans). Average age 46. 15 applicants, 53% accepted, 8 enrolled. In 2007, 9 master's awarded. *Degree requirements:* For master's, thesis or alternative. *Entrance requirements:* For master's, minimum GPA of 3.0, interview. Additional exam requirements/recommendations for international students: Required—TOEFL (minimum score 550 paper-based; 213 computer-based). *Application deadline:* Applications are processed on a rolling basis. Application fee: $40. Electronic applications accepted. *Financial support:* In 2007–08, 18 students received support, including 7 fellowships (averaging $1,000 per year); scholarships/grants also available. Support available to part-time students. Financial award applicants required to submit FAFSA. *Unit head:* Dr. Craig Singleton, Director, 415-485-3275, Fax: 415-485-3205, E-mail: singleton@dominican.edu. *Application contact:* Shannon Lovelace, Assistant Director, 415-485-3246, Fax: 415-485-3214.

Drew University, Caspersen School of Graduate Studies, Program in Medical Humanities, Madison, NJ 07940-1493. Offers MMH, DMH, CMH. Part-time and evening/weekend programs available. *Degree requirements:* For master's, thesis; for doctorate, comprehensive exam. *Faculty research:* Biomedical ethics, medical narrative, history of medicine, medicine and the arts.

Duke University, Graduate School, Program in Humanities, Durham, NC 27708. Offers AM, JD/AM. Part-time programs available. *Students:* 9 full-time (5 women); includes 1 minority (African American), 1 international. 7 applicants, 71% accepted, 3 enrolled. In 2007, 5 degrees awarded. *Entrance requirements:* For master's, GRE General Test. Additional exam requirements/recommendations for international students: Required—TOEFL (minimum score 550 paper-based; 213 computer-based; 83 iBT), IELTS (minimum score 7). *Application deadline:* For fall admission, 12/15 priority date for domestic and international students; for spring admission, 11/1 for domestic students. Application fee: $75. *Financial support:* Application deadline: 12/31. *Unit head:* Dr. David Bell, Director, 919-681-3252, Fax: 919-684-2277, E-mail: jgw2@duke.edu.

Florida State University, Graduate Studies, College of Arts and Sciences, Department of Interdisciplinary Humanities, Tallahassee, FL 32306. Offers American and Florida studies (MA, Certificate); interdisciplinary humanities (PhD). Part-time programs available. *Faculty:* 34 full-time (7 women), 3 part-time/adjunct (2 women). *Students:* 73 full-time (38 women), 22 part-time (10 women); includes 26 minority (8 African Americans, 1 American Indian/Alaska Native, 5 Asian Americans or Pacific Islanders, 12 Hispanic Americans). Average age 30. 9 applicants, 44% accepted, 4 enrolled. In 2007, 10 master's, 3 doctorates awarded. Terminal master's awarded for partial completion of doctoral program. *Degree requirements:* For master's, one foreign language; for doctorate, 2 foreign languages, thesis/dissertation. *Entrance requirements:* For master's, GRE General Test (minimum score: 1100), minimum GPA of 3.0; for doctorate, GRE General Test, minimum GPA of 3.0. Additional exam requirements/recommendations for international students: Required—TOEFL (minimum score 550 paper-based; 213 computer-based). *Application deadline:* For fall admission, 2/8 for domestic students, 2/15 for international students; for winter admission, 2/15 for domestic and international students; for spring admission, 10/15 for domestic and international students. Applications are processed on a rolling basis. Application fee: $0. Electronic applications accepted. *Expenses:* Tuition, state resident: part-time $248 per credit hour. Tuition, nonresident: part-time $880 per credit hour. Tuition and fees vary according to program. *Financial support:* In 2007–08, 2 fellowships with partial tuition reimbursements, 4 research assistantships with partial tuition reimbursements (averaging $9,000 per year), 25 teaching assistantships with partial tuition reimbursements (averaging $9,000 per year) were awarded; Federal Work-Study also available. Financial award applicants required to submit FAFSA. *Unit head:* Dr. David F. Johnson, Director, 850-644-2726, Fax: 850-644-1139, E-mail: djohnson@english.fsu.edu. *Application contact:* William Rutledge, Program Assistant, 850-644-9121, Fax: 850-644-1139, E-mail: ww84450@garnet.acns.fsu.edu.

Hofstra University, College of Liberal Arts and Sciences, Department of Comparative Arts and Culture, Hempstead, NY 11549. Offers MA. Part-time programs available. *Faculty:* 6 full-time (1 woman), 2 part-time/adjunct (1 woman). *Students:* 6 full-time (all women), 9 part-time (4 women); includes 2 minority (both Asian Americans or Pacific Islanders), 1 international. Average age 36. 6 applicants, 83% accepted, 3 enrolled. *Degree requirements:* For master's, comprehensive exam, thesis. *Entrance requirements:* For master's, letter of recommendation, interview, essay. Additional exam requirements/recommendations for international students: Required—TOEFL (minimum score 550 paper-based; 213 computer-based). *Application deadline:* Applications are processed on a rolling basis. Application fee: $60. Electronic applications accepted. *Expenses:* Tuition: Full-time $14,220; part-time $820 per credit. Required fees: $970; $165 per term. Tuition and fees vary according to program. *Financial support:* In 2007–08, 10 students received support, including 3 fellowships with tuition reimbursements available (averaging $2,667 per year), 1 research assistantship with full and partial tuition reimbursement available (averaging $13,320 per year); Federal Work-Study, institutionally sponsored loans, scholarships/grants, and tuition waivers (full and partial) also available. Support available to part-time students. Financial award applicants required to submit FAFSA. *Faculty research:* Postmodern theory, literacy studies; film; art and architecture; modernism. *Unit head:* Prof. Laurie Fendrich, Chairperson, 516-463-7150, E-mail: laurie.fendrich@hofstra.edu. *Application contact:* Carol Drummer, Dean of Graduate Admissions, 516-463-4876, Fax: 516-463-4664, E-mail: gradstudent@hofstra.edu.

Hollins University, Graduate Programs, Program in Liberal Studies, Roanoke, VA 24020-1603. Offers humanities (MALS); interdisciplinary studies (MALS); justice and legal studies (MALS); liberal studies (CAS); social science (MALS); visual and performing arts (MALS). Part-time and evening/weekend programs available. *Faculty:* 9 full-time (2 women), 12 part-time/adjunct (5 women). *Students:* 20 full-time (17 women), 89 part-time (74 women); includes 15 minority (11 African Americans, 1 American Indian/Alaska Native, 2 Asian Americans or Pacific Islanders, 1 Hispanic American). Average age 39. 30 applicants, 93% accepted, 20 enrolled. In 2007, 48 degrees awarded. *Degree requirements:* For master's, thesis. *Entrance requirements:* For master's, letters of recommendation, interview. Additional exam requirements/recommendations for international students: Required—TOEFL (minimum score 550 paper-based; 213 computer-based). *Application deadline:* For fall admission, 7/1 priority date for domestic and international students; for spring admission, 12/10 priority date for domestic and international students. Applications are processed on a rolling basis. Application fee: $40. Electronic applications accepted. *Expenses:* Tuition: Part-time $265 per credit hour. Tuition and fees vary according to course load and program. *Financial support:* In 2007–08, 53 students received support, including 4 fellowships (averaging $1,060 per year); Federal Work-Study and scholarships/grants also available. Support available to part-time students. Financial award application deadline: 7/15; financial award applicants required to submit FAFSA. *Faculty research:* Elderly blacks, film, feminist economics, U.S. voting patterns, Wagner, diversity. *Unit head:* Dr. Edward A. Lynch, Director, 540-362-6475, Fax: 540-362-6288, E-mail: elynch@hollins.edu. *Application contact:* Cathy S. Koon, Manager of Graduate Services, 540-362-6326, Fax: 540-362-6288, E-mail: ckoon@hollins.edu.

Hood College, Graduate School, Program in Humanities, Frederick, MD 21701-8575. Offers MA. *Entrance requirements:* For master's, minimum GPA of 2.5.

Instituto Tecnológico y de Estudios Superiores de Monterrey, Campus Central de Veracruz, Graduate Programs, Córdoba, Mexico. Offers administration (MA); administration of information technologies (MTI); computer sciences (MCC); education (MEE); educational institution administration (MAD); educational technology (MTE); electronic commerce (MCE); finance (MAF); humanistic studies (MEH); international business for Latin America (MNL); marketing (MMT); science (MCP); technology management (MTT). Part-time and evening/weekend programs available. Postbaccalaureate distance learning degree programs offered (minimal on-campus study). *Degree requirements:* For master's, thesis (for some programs). *Entrance requirements:* For master's, PAEP College Board. Electronic applications accepted.

Instituto Tecnológico y de Estudios Superiores de Monterrey, Campus Ciudad de México, Virtual University Division, Ciudad de Mexico, Mexico. Offers administration of information technologies (MA); computer sciences (MA); education (MA, PhD); educational technology (MA); environmental engineering (MA); environmental systems (MA); humanistic studies (MA); industrial engineering (MA); international business for Latin America (MA); quality systems (MA); quality systems and productivity (MA). Part-time and evening/weekend programs available. Postbaccalaureate distance learning degree programs offered (minimal on-campus study). *Entrance requirements:* For master's and doctorate, Instituto entrance exam. Additional exam requirements/recommendations for international students: Required—TOEFL.

Instituto Tecnológico y de Estudios Superiores de Monterrey, Campus Estado de México, Professional and Graduate Division, Estado de Mexico, Mexico. Offers administration of information technologies (MITA); architecture (M Arch); business administration (GMBA, MBA); computer sciences (MCS, PhD); education (M Ed); educational institution administration (MAD); educational technology and innovation (PhD); electronic commerce (MEC); environmental systems (MS); finance (MAF); humanistic studies (MHS); information sciences and knowledge management (MISKM); information systems (MS); manufacturing systems (MS); marketing (MEM); quality systems and productivity (MS); science and materials engineering (PhD); telecommunications management (MTM). Part-time programs available. Postbaccalaureate distance learning degree programs offered (minimal on-campus study). *Degree requirements:* For master's, one foreign language, thesis (for some programs); for doctorate, one foreign language, thesis/dissertation. *Entrance requirements:* For master's, E-PAEP 500, interview; for doctorate, E-PAEP 500, research proposal. Additional exam requirements/recommendations for international students: Required—TOEFL (minimum score 550 paper-based). *Faculty research:* Surface treatments by plasmas, mechanical properties, robotics, graphical computing, mechatronics security protocols.

Instituto Tecnológico y de Estudios Superiores de Monterrey, Campus Irapuato, Graduate Programs, Irapuato, Mexico. Offers administration (MBA); administration of information technology (MAIT); administration of telecommunications (MAT); architecture (M Arch); computer science (MCS); education (M Ed); educational administration (MEA); educational innovation and technology (DEIT); educational technology (MET); electronic commerce (MBA); environmental administration and planning (MEAP); environmental systems (MES); finances (MBA); humanistic studies (MHS); international management for Latin American executives (MIMLAE); library and information science (MLIS); manufacturing quality management (MMQM); marketing research (MBA).

John Carroll University, Graduate School, Program in Humanities, University Heights, OH 44118-4581. Offers MA. Part-time and evening/weekend programs available. *Faculty:* 1 full-time (0 women), 1 part-time/adjunct (0 women). *Students:* 2 full-time (both women), 13 part-time (7 women). Average age 36. 12 applicants, 83% accepted, 5 enrolled. In 2007, 13 degrees awarded. *Degree requirements:* For master's, thesis optional, comprehensive research essay. *Entrance requirements:* For master's, minimum GPA of 2.75, interview. *Application deadline:* For fall admission, 8/15 priority date for domestic students; for spring admission, 1/3 for domestic students. Applications are processed on a rolling basis. Application fee: $25 ($35 for international students). Electronic applications accepted. *Financial support:* In 2007–08, 5 students received support. Application deadline: 3/1; *Faculty research:* Modern French history, modern American Catholic history. *Unit head:* Dr. W. Francis Ryan, Director, 216-397-4780, Fax: 216-397-4175, E-mail: wryan@jcu.edu.

Laura and Alvin Siegal College of Judaic Studies, Graduate Programs, Beachwood, OH 44122-7116. Offers humanities (MA), including Holocaust studies; religious education (MAJS), including Jewish education, Judaic studies. Part-time and evening/weekend programs available. Postbaccalaureate distance learning degree programs offered (no on-campus study). *Degree requirements:* For master's, one foreign language, thesis. *Entrance requirements:* For master's, interview.

Laurentian University, School of Graduate Studies and Research, Programme in Humanities: Interpretation and Values, Sudbury, ON P3E 2C6, Canada. Offers MA. Part-time programs available. *Faculty research:* Modern Canadian literature; aboriginal languages and cultures; relation between ethics, religion, and the arts; narrative conventions; Renaissance drama and Reformation literature, Biblical and philosophical hermeneutics.

Marshall University, Academic Affairs Division, College of Liberal Arts, Program in Humanities, Huntington, WV 25755. Offers MA. Part-time and evening/weekend programs available. *Faculty:* 8 full-time (2 women), 5 part-time/adjunct (2 women). *Students:* 7 full-time (4 women), 13 part-time (10 women); includes 1 minority (American Indian/Alaska Native). Average age 35. In 2007, 5 degrees awarded. *Degree requirements:* For master's, thesis, comprehensive assessment. *Entrance requirements:* For master's, GRE General Test, MAT, bachelor's degree in humanities, minimum undergraduate GPA of 3.0. Application fee: $40. *Financial support:* Applicants required to submit FAFSA. *Unit head:* Dr. Luke Eric Lassiter, Chairperson, 304-746-1923, E-mail: lassiter@marshall.edu. *Application contact:* Information Contact, 304-746-1900, Fax: 304-746-1902, E-mail: services@marshall.edu.

Marymount University, School of Arts and Sciences, Program in Humanities, Arlington, VA 22207-4299. Offers humanities (MA); humanities: teaching licensure in secondary English (MA). Part-time and evening/weekend programs available. *Students:* Average age 30. 3 applicants, 67% accepted, 2 enrolled. *Degree requirements:* For master's, thesis or alternative. *Entrance requirements:* For master's, GRE or MAT and PRAXIS I or SAT/ACT (for teaching licensure), interview, 2 letters of recommendation, essay. Additional exam requirements/recommendations for international students: Required—TOEFL (minimum score 600 paper-based; 250 computer-based; 100 iBT). *Application deadline:* Applications are processed on a rolling basis. Application fee: $40. Electronic applications accepted. *Expenses:* Tuition: Full-time $11,790; part-time $655 per credit. Required fees: $121; $6.7 per credit. *Financial support:* Career-related internships or fieldwork, scholarships/grants, and unspecified assistantships available. Support available to part-time students. Financial award applicants required to submit FAFSA.

Massachusetts Institute of Technology, School of Humanities, Arts, and Social Sciences, Program in Writing and Humanistic Studies, Cambridge, MA 02139-4307. Offers science writing (SM). *Faculty:* 7 full-time (2 women), 1 part-time/adjunct (0 women). *Students:* 7 full-time (6 women), 1 international. Average age 24. 37 applicants, 30% accepted, 7 enrolled. In 2007, 6 degrees awarded. *Degree requirements:* For master's, thesis, internship. *Entrance requirements:* For master's, GRE General Test. Application fee: $70. Electronic applications accepted. *Expenses:* Tuition: Full-time $34,760; part-time $545 per unit. Required fees: $236. *Financial support:* In 2007–08, 7 students received support, including 7 fellowships with tuition reimbursements available (averaging $28,560 per year); career-related internships or fieldwork, Federal Work-Study, institutionally sponsored loans, scholarships/grants, health care benefits, and unspecified assistantships also available. *Unit head:* Prof. James Paradis, Head, 617-253-7894, Fax: 617-253-6910.

Memorial University of Newfoundland, School of Graduate Studies, Interdisciplinary Programs in Humanities, St. John's, NL A1C 5S7, Canada. Offers M Phil. *Degree requirements:* For master's, comprehensive exam, journal. *Entrance requirements:* For master's, honors bachelor's degree. Electronic applications accepted. *Faculty research:* Western language, philosophy, literature, and history.

Michigan State University, College of Human Medicine and The Graduate School, Graduate Programs in Human Medicine, Program in Bioethics, Humanities, and Society, East Lansing, MI 48824. Offers MA. *Degree requirements:* For master's, thesis or alternative, oral defense of thesis. *Entrance requirements:* Additional exam requirements/recommendations for international students: Required—TOEFL (minimum score 550 paper-based; 213 computer-based), Michigan State University ELT (85), Michigan ELAB (83). Electronic applications accepted. *Expenses:* Tuition, state resident: part-time $379 per credit hour. Tuition, nonresident: part-time $800 per credit hour. Tuition and fees vary according to program.

Mount St. Mary's College, Graduate Division, Program in Humanities, Los Angeles, CA 90049-1599. Offers MA. *Students:* 1 (woman) full-time, 93 part-time (73 women); includes 42 minority (8 African Americans, 1 American Indian/Alaska Native, 8 Asian Americans or Pacific Islanders, 25 Hispanic Americans). Average age 41. In 2007, 19 degrees awarded. *Entrance requirements:* Additional exam requirements/recommendations for international students: Required—TOEFL. *Application deadline:* For fall admission, 7/15 priority date for domestic students; for spring admission, 11/15 priority date for domestic students. Application fee: $50. *Expenses:* Tuition: Part-time $662 per unit. *Unit head:* Dr. Millie Kidd, Head, 310-954-4284. *Application contact:* Jessica M. Bibeau, Director of Graduate Admission, 213-477-2800 Ext. 2798, Fax: 213-477-2797, E-mail: jbibeau@msmc.la.edu.

National University, Academic Affairs, College of Letters and Sciences, Department of Art and Humanities, La Jolla, CA 92037-1011. Offers creative writing (MFA); English (MA). Part-time and evening/weekend programs available. Postbaccalaureate distance learning degree programs offered (no on-campus study). *Faculty:* 18 full-time (6 women), 219 part-time/adjunct (120 women). *Students:* 139 full-time (101 women), 353 part-time (250 women); includes 91

Humanities

National University (continued)

minority (41 African Americans, 4 American Indian/Alaska Native, 15 Asian Americans or Pacific Islanders, 31 Hispanic Americans). Average age 37. 371 applicants, 330 enrolled. In 2007, 100 degrees awarded. *Degree requirements:* For master's, thesis (for some programs). *Entrance requirements:* For master's, interview, minimum GPA of 2.5. Additional exam requirements/recommendations for international students: Required—TOEFL (minimum score 550 paper-based; 213 computer-based; 80 iBT), IELTS (minimum score 6). *Application deadline:* Applications are processed on a rolling basis. Application fee: $60 ($65 for international students). Electronic applications accepted. *Expenses:* Tuition: Full-time $8,262; part-time $306 per unit. One-time fee: $60. *Financial support:* Career-related internships or fieldwork, institutionally sponsored loans, scholarships/grants, and tuition waivers (partial) available. Support available to part-time students. Financial award application deadline: 6/30; financial award applicants required to submit FAFSA. *Unit head:* Dr. Janet Baker, Chair, 858-642-8472, Fax: 858-642-8715, E-mail: jbaker@nu.edu. *Application contact:* Dominick Giovanniello, Associate Regional Dean—San Diego, 800-NAT-UNIV, Fax: 858-642-8709, E-mail: dgiovann@nu.edu.

New York University, Graduate School of Arts and Science, Draper Interdisciplinary Program in Humanities and Social Thought, New York, NY 10012-1019. Offers humanities and social thought (MA); religion (Advanced Certificate); social theory (Advanced Certificate). Part-time programs available. *Faculty:* 6 full-time (3 women). *Students:* 87 full-time (58 women), 130 part-time (85 women); includes 32 minority (7 African Americans, 13 Asian Americans or Pacific Islanders, 12 Hispanic Americans), 12 international. Average age 28. 259 applicants, 56% accepted, 88 enrolled. In 2007, 64 degrees awarded. *Degree requirements:* For master's, thesis, comprehensive exam or essay. *Entrance requirements:* For degree, master's degree. Additional exam requirements/recommendations for international students: Required—TOEFL. *Application deadline:* For fall admission, 7/1 for domestic students; for spring admission, 12/1 for domestic students. Applications are processed on a rolling basis. Application fee: $85. *Financial support:* Teaching assistantships with tuition reimbursements, Federal Work-Study, institutionally sponsored loans, and tuition waivers (partial) available. Financial award application deadline: 7/1; financial award applicants required to submit FAFSA. *Faculty research:* Art world, gender politics, global histories, literary cultures, the city. *Unit head:* Robin Nagle, Director, 212-998-8070, Fax: 212-995-4691, E-mail: draper.program@nyu.edu. *Application contact:* Robert Dimit, Associate Director, 212-998-8070, Fax: 212-995-4691, E-mail: draper.program@nyu.edu.

Nova Southeastern University, Graduate School of Humanities and Social Sciences, Department of Multi-Disciplinary Studies, Fort Lauderdale, FL 33314-7796. Offers college student affairs (MS); college student personnel administration (Certificate); cross-disciplinary studies (MA). Part-time programs available. Postbaccalaureate distance learning degree programs offered (no on-campus study). *Faculty:* 4 part-time/adjunct (2 women). *Students:* 24 full-time (15 women), 35 part-time (29 women); includes 24 minority (20 African Americans, 4 Hispanic Americans), 2 international. 45 applicants, 67% accepted, 30 enrolled. In 2007, 7 master's awarded. *Degree requirements:* For master's, comprehensive exam, thesis optional, portfolio. *Entrance requirements:* For master's, interview, minimum GPA of 3.0. Additional exam requirements/recommendations for international students: Required—TOEFL. *Application deadline:* For fall admission, 7/1 priority date for domestic and international students; for winter admission, 11/1 priority date for domestic and international students; for spring admission, 3/1 priority date for domestic and international students. Applications are processed on a rolling basis. Electronic applications accepted. *Financial support:* In 2007–08, 20 research assistantships with tuition reimbursements (averaging $13,000 per year) were awarded; career-related internships or fieldwork, Federal Work-Study, institutionally sponsored loans, and scholarships/grants also available. Financial award applicants required to submit CSS PROFILE. *Unit head:* Dr. Judith McKay, Senior Associate Dean, 954-262-3060, Fax: 954-262-3893, E-mail: mckayj@nsu.nova.edu. *Application contact:* Marcia Arango, Student Recruitment Coordinator, 954-262-3006, Fax: 954-262-3968, E-mail: marango@nsu.nova.edu.

See Close-Up on page 953.

Old Dominion University, College of Arts and Letters, Program in Humanities, Norfolk, VA 23529. Offers MA. Part-time and evening/weekend programs available. *Faculty:* 2 full-time (1 woman). *Students:* 10 full-time (6 women), 14 part-time (11 women); includes 4 minority (3 African Americans, 1 Hispanic American), 1 international. Average age 32. 27 applicants, 96% accepted. In 2007, 10 degrees awarded. *Degree requirements:* For master's, thesis optional, project. *Entrance requirements:* For master's, GRE General Test, minimum GPA of 3.0. *Application deadline:* For fall admission, 7/1 for domestic students; for spring admission, 10/1 for domestic students. Applications are processed on a rolling basis. Application fee: $40. Electronic applications accepted. *Expenses:* Tuition, state resident: part-time $304 per credit hour. Tuition, nonresident: part-time $761 per credit hour. *Financial support:* In 2007–08, 3 students received support, including 1 fellowship (averaging $4,000 per year), 2 research assistantships with tuition reimbursements available (averaging $8,000 per year); career-related internships or fieldwork, scholarships/grants, and unspecified assistantships also available. Financial award application deadline: 2/15; financial award applicants required to submit FAFSA. *Faculty research:* Media studies, communications, cultural studies, gender studies, American literature. *Unit head:* Dr. Dana Heller, Graduate Program Director, 757-683-3719, Fax: 757-683-6191, E-mail: humgpd@odu.edu.

Penn State Harrisburg, Graduate School, School of Humanities, Middletown, PA 17057-4898. Offers American studies (MA); humanities (MA). Evening/weekend programs available. *Unit head:* Kathryn Robinson, Director, 717-948-6189, E-mail: kdr12@psu.edu.

Pepperdine University, Seaver College, Humanities Division, Malibu, CA 90263. Offers American studies (MA); history (MA). *Degree requirements:* For master's, oral and written exams. *Entrance requirements:* For master's, GRE General Test, undergraduate major or 15 upper-division units in history. Additional exam requirements/recommendations for international students: Required—TOEFL.

Polytechnic Institute of NYU, Department of Humanities and Social Sciences, Brooklyn, NY 11201-2990. Offers environment-behavior studies (MS); history of science (MS); integrated digital media (MS, Graduate Certificate); technical communication (Graduate Certificate); technical writing and specialized journalism (MS). Part-time and evening/weekend programs available. *Faculty:* 5 full-time (2 women), 6 part-time/adjunct (3 women). *Students:* 23 full-time (8 women), 15 part-time (4 women); includes 12 minority (7 African Americans, 4 Asian Americans or Pacific Islanders, 1 Hispanic American), 5 international. Average age 32. 48 applicants, 75% accepted, 20 enrolled. In 2007, 11 degrees awarded. *Degree requirements:* For master's, comprehensive exam (for some programs), thesis (for some programs). *Entrance requirements:* Additional exam requirements/recommendations for international students: Required—TOEFL (minimum score 550 paper-based; 213 computer-based); Recommended—IELTS (minimum score 7). *Application deadline:* For fall admission, 7/15 priority date for domestic students, 4/1 priority date for international students; for spring admission, 12/15 priority date for domestic students, 10/1 priority date for international students. Applications are processed on a rolling basis. Application fee: $55. Electronic applications accepted. *Expenses:* Tuition: Full-time $18,486; part-time $1,027 per credit. Required fees: $352 per semester. *Financial support:* Fellowships, research assistantships, teaching assistantships, career-related internships or fieldwork and institutionally sponsored loans available. Support available to part-time students. Financial award applicants required to submit FAFSA. *Faculty research:* Trade magazine journalism, technical writing, financial reporting, medical and science reporting, industrial advertising and public relations. Total annual research expenditures: $10,199. *Unit head:* Dr. Harold Sjursen, Head, 718-260-3597, Fax: 718-260-3289, E-mail: hsjursen@poly.edu. *Application contact:* Anthea Jeffrey, Graduate Admissions, 718-260-3200, Fax: 718-260-3624, E-mail: gradinfo@poly.edu.

Prescott College, Graduate Programs, Program in Humanities, Prescott, AZ 86301. Offers humanities (MA); Southwestern regional history (MA). Part-time programs available. Postbaccalaureate distance learning degree programs offered (minimal on-campus study). *Faculty:* 1 (woman) full-time, 43 part-time/adjunct (25 women). *Students:* 19 full-time (12 women), 30 part-time (25 women); includes 9 minority (6 African Americans, 1 American Indian/Alaska Native, 2 Hispanic Americans), 1 international. Average age 41. 25 applicants, 76% accepted, 13 enrolled. In 2007, 18 degrees awarded. *Degree requirements:* For master's, thesis, fieldwork or internship, practicum. *Entrance requirements:* For master's, 2 letters of recommendation, resumé. Additional exam requirements/recommendations for international students: Required—TOEFL (minimum score 550 paper-based; 213 computer-based). *Application deadline:* For fall admission, 5/1 priority date for domestic and international students; for spring admission, 11/1 priority date for domestic and international students. Applications are processed on a rolling basis. Application fee: $40. Electronic applications accepted. *Expenses:* Tuition: Full-time $6,480; part-time $540 per credit. *Financial support:* Career-related internships or fieldwork and Federal Work-Study available. Financial award applicants required to submit FAFSA. *Unit head:* Joan Clingan, Chair, 928-350-3208. *Application contact:* Kerstin Alicki, Admissions Counselor, 877-350-2102, Fax: 928-776-5242, E-mail: admissions@prescott.edu.

Salve Regina University, Graduate Studies, Program in Humanities, Newport, RI 02840-4192. Offers MA, PhD. Part-time and evening/weekend programs available. Postbaccalaureate distance learning degree programs offered. *Degree requirements:* For master's, thesis optional; for doctorate, one foreign language, comprehensive exam, thesis/dissertation. *Entrance requirements:* For master's, GMAT, GRE General Test, or MAT; for doctorate, GRE. Additional exam requirements/recommendations for international students: Required—TOEFL or IELTS. Electronic applications accepted.

Sam Houston State University, College of Humanities and Social Sciences, Huntsville, TX 77341. Offers MA, MPA, PhD. *Faculty:* 95 full-time (43 women). *Students:* 115 full-time (49 women), 134 part-time (52 women); includes 39 minority (9 African Americans, 2 American Indian/Alaska Native, 10 Asian Americans or Pacific Islanders, 18 Hispanic Americans), 3 international. Average age 31. In 2007, 70 master's, 6 doctorates awarded. *Entrance requirements:* For master's, GRE General Test. *Expenses:* Tuition, state resident: full-time $5,026; part-time $184 per semester hour. Tuition, nonresident: full-time $10,586; part-time $462 per semester hour. Required fees: $494 per semester. *Unit head:* Dr. John deCastro, Dean, 936-294-2200, Fax: 936-294-2207, E-mail: jmd018@shsu.edu.

San Francisco State University, Division of Graduate Studies, College of Humanities, Department of Humanities, San Francisco, CA 94132-1722. Offers MA. Part-time and evening/weekend programs available. *Unit head:* Dr. Saul Steier, Chair, 415-338-1830. *Application contact:* Dr. Mary Scott, Graduate Coordinator, 415-338-2165, E-mail: mscott@sfsu.edu.

Stanford University, School of Humanities and Sciences, Department of Humanities, Stanford, CA 94305-9991. Offers MA. *Degree requirements:* For master's, one foreign language, thesis. *Entrance requirements:* For master's, GRE General Test. Additional exam requirements/recommendations for international students: Required—TOEFL. Electronic applications accepted.

Texas Tech University, Graduate School, College of Arts and Sciences, Department of Classical and Modern Languages and Literatures, Lubbock, TX 79409. Offers applied linguistics (MA); classics (MA); German (MA); Romance language (MA); Romance languages-French (MA); Romance languages-Spanish (MA, PhD). Part-time programs available. *Faculty:* 23 full-time (9 women), 1 (woman) part-time/adjunct. *Students:* 76 full-time (43 women), 24 part-time (16 women); includes 26 minority (1 African American, 2 Asian Americans or Pacific Islanders, 23 Hispanic Americans), 18 international. Average age 32. 69 applicants, 84% accepted, 27 enrolled. In 2007, 13 master's, 2 doctorates awarded. *Degree requirements:* For doctorate, thesis/dissertation. *Entrance requirements:* For master's and doctorate, GRE General Test. Additional exam requirements/recommendations for international students: Required—TOEFL (minimum score 550 paper-based; 213 computer-based). *Application deadline:* For fall admission, 3/1 priority date for international students; for spring admission, 11/1 priority date for international students. Applications are processed on a rolling basis. Application fee: $50 ($60 for international students). Electronic applications accepted. *Expenses:* Tuition, state resident: part-time $373 per credit hour. Tuition, nonresident: part-time $651 per credit hour. Tuition and fees vary according to program. *Financial support:* In 2007–08, 44 students received support, including 70 teaching assistantships with partial tuition reimbursements available (averaging $11,627 per year); research assistantships with partial tuition reimbursements available, Federal Work-Study and institutionally sponsored loans also available. Support available to part-time students. Financial award application deadline: 4/15; financial award applicants required to submit FAFSA. *Faculty research:* Literature, comparative literature, linguistics, culture, pedagogy. *Unit head:* Dr. Julian Frederick Suppe, Chair and Professor, 806-742-4355, Fax: 806-742-3306, E-mail: frederick.suppe@ttu.edu. *Application contact:* Liz Hildebrand, Senior Advisor, 806-742-4055, Fax: 806-742-3306, E-mail: liz.hildebrand@ttu.edu.

Tiffin University, Program in Humanities, Tiffin, OH 44883-2161. Offers MH. *Entrance requirements:* For master's, work experience. Additional exam requirements/recommendations for international students: Required—TOEFL (minimum score 550 paper-based; 213 computer-based).

Towson University, College of Graduate Studies and Research, Program in Humanities, Towson, MD 21252-0001. Offers MA. Part-time and evening/weekend programs available. *Students:* 4 full-time (2 women), 8 part-time (6 women); includes 1 minority (African American) Average age 26. 5 applicants, 80% accepted, 5 enrolled. In 2007, 4 degrees awarded. *Degree requirements:* For master's, thesis or alternative. *Entrance requirements:* For master's, 2 letters of recommendation, minimum GPA of 3.0, research paper, letter of intent. Additional exam requirements/recommendations for international students: Required—TOEFL. *Application deadline:* Applications are processed on a rolling basis. Application fee: $50. Electronic applications accepted. *Expenses:* Tuition, state resident: part-time $286 per credit. Tuition, nonresident: part-time $600 per credit. Required fees: $75 per credit. *Financial support:* Application deadline: 4/1; *Unit head:* H. George Hahn, Graduate Program Director, 410-704-5198, E-mail: ghahn@towson.edu. *Application contact:* 410-704-2501, Fax: 410-704-4675, E-mail: grads@towson.edu.

Trinity Western University, Faculty of Graduate Studies, Program in Interdisciplinary Humanities, Langley, BC V2Y 1Y1, Canada. Offers general humanities (MAIH); specialized (MAIH), including English, history, philosophy. Part-time and evening/weekend programs available. Postbaccalaureate distance learning degree programs offered (minimal on-campus study). *Faculty:* 19 full-time (6 women), 3 part-time/adjunct (0 women). *Students:* 9 full-time (4 women), 24 part-time (13 women). Average age 30. 16 applicants, 75% accepted, 9 enrolled. In 2007, 2 degrees awarded. *Degree requirements:* For master's, 36 semester hours. *Entrance requirements:* For master's, strong undergraduate degree in Humanities or English, History or Philosophy. *Application deadline:* For fall admission, 5/15 priority date for domestic students; for winter admission, 11/1 priority date for domestic students. Application fee: $40. *Financial support:* In 2007–08, 12 students received support, including 3 fellowships (averaging $17,500 per year), 1 research assistantship (averaging $12,000 per year); career-related internships or fieldwork, scholarships/grants, and traineeships also available. Financial award application deadline: 4/1. *Faculty research:* Literary theory, gender, medieval and early modern literature, philosophy of religion, Thomas Merton's poetics. Total annual research expenditures: $145,000 Canadian dollars. *Unit head:* Dr. Bob Burkinshaw, Director, 604-888-7511 Ext. 3111, Fax: 604-513-2143, E-mail: burkinsh@twu.ca. *Application contact:* Vic Cornish, Director, Graduate Admissions, 604-888-7511 Ext. 3130, Fax: 604-513-2064, E-mail: vic.cornish@twu.edu.

Universidad Nacional Pedro Henriquez Urena, Graduate School, Santo Domingo, Dominican Republic. Offers accounting and auditing (M Acct); animal production (M Agr); business administration (MBA, PhD); Caribbean tropical architecture (M Arch); conservation of monuments and cultural goods (M Arch); economics (M Econ); education (PhD); environmental engineering (MEE); horticulture (M Agr); hospital administration (PhD); humanities (PhD); international relations (MPS); management of natural resources (MNRM); project management (M Man, MPM); public administration (MPS); sanitary engineering (ME); social science (PhD); veterinary medicine (DVM).

University of California, Santa Cruz, Division of Graduate Studies, Division of Humanities, Program in the History of Consciousness, Santa Cruz, CA 95064. Offers PhD. *Faculty:* 7 full-time (4 women). *Students:* 62 full-time (42 women), 3 part-time (2 women); includes 15 minority (4 African Americans, 2 American Indian/Alaska Native, 6 Asian Americans or Pacific Islanders, 3 Hispanic Americans), 6 international. 174 applicants, 13% accepted, 10 enrolled. In 2007, 7 doctorates awarded. *Degree requirements:* For doctorate, one foreign language, thesis/dissertation, qualifying exam. *Entrance requirements:* Additional exam requirements/recommendations for international students: Required—TOEFL (minimum score 550 paper-based; 220 computer-based). *Application deadline:* For fall admission, 12/1 for domestic students. Application fee: $60. *Expenses:* Tuition, nonresident: full-time $14,694. Required fees: $11,360. *Financial support:* Fellowships, teaching assistantships, Federal Work-Study, institutionally sponsored loans, scholarships/grants, and unspecified assistantships available. Financial award application deadline: 12/15. *Faculty research:* Interdisciplinary humanities and social sciences, political theory, cultural theory, feminist studies, literary theory. *Unit head:* Chairperson, 831-459-4310. *Application contact:* Judy L. Glass, Reporting Analyst for Graduate Admissions, 831-459-5906, Fax: 831-459-4843, E-mail: jlglass@ucsc.edu.

University of Chicago, Division of the Humanities, Master of Arts Program in the Humanities, Chicago, IL 60637-1513. Offers MA. MAPH students take courses from faculty members of all departments at University of Chicago. Part-time programs available. *Faculty:* 158 full-time. *Students:* 132 full-time (72 women); includes 11 minority (5 African Americans, 1 American Indian/Alaska Native, 5 Hispanic Americans), 3 international. Average age 26. 749 applicants, 33% accepted, 139 enrolled. In 2007, 110 degrees awarded. *Degree requirements:* For master's, thesis. *Entrance requirements:* For master's, GRE General Test. Additional exam requirements/recommendations for international students: Required—TOEFL (minimum score 600 paper-based; 260 computer-based). *Application deadline:* For fall admission, 12/15 priority date for domestic and international students. Application fee: $55. Electronic applications accepted. *Financial support:* In 2007–08, 100 students received support, including 8 fellowships with partial tuition reimbursements available (averaging $12,000 per year); Federal Work-Study, institutionally sponsored loans, and tuition waivers (partial) also available. Financial award application deadline: 12/15; financial award applicants required to submit FAFSA. *Unit head:* Prof. Mark Miller, Co-Director, 773-834-1201, E-mail: ma-humanities@uchicago.edu. *Application contact:* Program Coordinator, 773-834-1201, Fax: 773-834-7526, E-mail: ma-humanities@uchicago.edu.

University of Colorado Denver, College of Liberal Arts and Sciences, Program in Humanities, Denver, CO 80217-3364. Offers MH. Part-time and evening/weekend programs available. *Students:* 7 full-time (5 women), 51 part-time (27 women); includes 8 minority (4 Asian Americans or Pacific Islanders, 4 Hispanic Americans). 21 applicants, 67% accepted, 12 enrolled. In 2007, 11 degrees awarded. *Degree requirements:* For master's, thesis or alternative. *Entrance requirements:* For master's, GRE or MAT, interview, minimum GPA of 2.75, writing sample. Additional exam requirements/recommendations for international students: Required—TOEFL (minimum score 525 paper-based; 197 computer-based). *Application deadline:* For fall admission, 5/15 for domestic students; for spring admission, 10/15 for domestic students. Applications are processed on a rolling basis. Application fee: $50 ($75 for international students). Electronic applications accepted. *Financial support:* Research assistantships, teaching assistantships, Federal Work-Study available. Financial award application deadline: 4/1; financial award applicants required to submit FAFSA. *Unit head:* Myra Bookman, Director, 303-556-2496, Fax: 303-556-8100, E-mail: myra.bookman@cudenver.edu.

University of Dallas, Braniff Graduate School of Liberal Arts, Program in Humanities, Irving, TX 75062-4736. Offers M Hum, MA. Part-time programs available. *Faculty:* 2 full-time (0 women), 6 part-time/adjunct (1 woman). *Students:* 27 full-time (9 women), 49 part-time (25 women); includes 11 minority (2 African Americans, 2 American Indian/Alaska Native, 4 Asian Americans or Pacific Islanders, 3 Hispanic Americans), 2 international. Average age 32. 33 applicants, 100% accepted, 24 enrolled. In 2007, 16 degrees awarded. *Degree requirements:* For master's, one foreign language, comprehensive exam, thesis (for some programs). *Entrance requirements:* For master's, GRE General Test. Additional exam requirements/recommendations for international students: Required—TOEFL. *Application deadline:* For fall admission, 2/15 priority date for domestic students; for spring admission, 11/15 for domestic students. Applications are processed on a rolling basis. Application fee: $50. *Expenses:* Tuition: Part-time $600 per credit. Required fees: $15 per credit. *Financial support:* In 2007–08, 75 students received support. Scholarships/grants available. Financial award application deadline: 2/15. *Faculty research:* Classical epic poetry, scholastic poetry, Renaissance drama, nineteenth and twentieth century Continental philosophy. *Application contact:* Graduate Coordinator, 972-721-5106, Fax: 972-721-5280, E-mail: graduate@acad.udallas.edu.

University of Houston–Clear Lake, School of Human Sciences and Humanities, Programs in Humanities and Fine Arts, Houston, TX 77058-1098. Offers history (MA); humanities (MA); literature (MA). Part-time and evening/weekend programs available. Postbaccalaureate distance learning degree programs offered (minimal on-campus study). *Degree requirements:* For master's, thesis or alternative. *Entrance requirements:* For master's, GRE General Test. Additional exam requirements/recommendations for international students: Required—TOEFL (minimum score 550 paper-based; 213 computer-based). *Faculty research:* Digital media studies, Latin American history, labor history, Chaucer evolution versus creationism debate.

University of Louisville, Graduate School, College of Arts and Sciences, Department of Humanities, Louisville, KY 40292-0001. Offers MA, PhD, MA/JD. *Students:* 24 full-time (16 women), 66 part-time (42 women); includes 8 minority (5 African Americans, 2 Asian Americans or Pacific Islanders, 1 Hispanic American), 24 international. Average age 37. In 2007, 9 master's, 2 doctorates awarded. *Degree requirements:* For master's, one foreign language, comprehensive exam (for some programs), thesis (for some programs), internship, project; for doctorate, 2 foreign languages, thesis/dissertation, internship. *Entrance requirements:* For master's, GRE General Test; for doctorate, GRE General Test, letters of recommendation, writing sample. *Application deadline:* Applications are processed on a rolling basis. Application fee: $50. *Financial support:* In 2007–08, 10 teaching assistantships with tuition reimbursements (averaging $18,000 per year) were awarded; institutionally sponsored loans, scholarships/grants, and tuition waivers (partial) also available. *Unit head:* Elaine O. Wise, Chair, 502-852-7149, Fax: 502-852-0078, E-mail: elaine.wise@louisville.edu.

The University of Texas at Arlington, Graduate School, College of Liberal Arts, Graduate Humanities Program, Arlington, TX 76019. Offers MA. Part-time and evening/weekend programs available. *Faculty:* 1 full-time (0 women). *Students:* 4 full-time (1 woman), 16 part-time (4 women); includes 4 minority (3 African Americans, 1 Hispanic American), 2 international. In 2007, 2 degrees awarded. *Degree requirements:* For master's, one foreign language, thesis optional. *Entrance requirements:* For master's, GRE General Test. Additional exam requirements/recommendations for international students: Required—TOEFL (minimum score 550 paper-based; 213 computer-based). *Application deadline:* For fall admission, 6/16 for domestic students. Applications are processed on a rolling basis. Application fee: $35 ($50 for international students). *Expenses:* Tuition, state resident: full-time $5,934. Tuition, nonresident: full-time $10,938. *Financial support:* In 2007–08, 1 fellowship (averaging $1,000 per year), 1 teaching assistantship (averaging $7,500 per year) were awarded. Financial award application deadline: 6/1; financial award applicants required to submit FAFSA. *Unit head:* Dr. Susan Hekman, Graduate Advisor, 817-272-2389, Fax: 817-272-5807, E-mail: hekman@uta.edu.

The University of Texas at Dallas, School of Arts and Humanities, Richardson, TX 75083-0688. Offers arts and technology (MFA); humanities (MA, MAT, PhD), including aesthetic studies, arts and technology (MA), historical studies (MA), history of ideas, studies in literature. Part-time and evening/weekend programs available. *Faculty:* 49 full-time (14 women), 4 part-time/adjunct (1 woman). *Students:* 192 full-time (104 women), 217 part-time (118 women); includes 98 minority (33 African Americans, 3 American Indian/Alaska Native, 28 Asian Americans or Pacific Islanders, 34 Hispanic Americans), 29 international. Average age 37. 161 applicants, 75% accepted, 86 enrolled. In 2007, 76 master's, 13 doctorates awarded. *Degree requirements:* For master's, one foreign language, portfolio; for doctorate, one foreign language, thesis/dissertation. *Entrance requirements:* For master's and doctorate, GRE General Test, minimum GPA of 3.0 in undergraduate course work in field. Additional exam requirements/recommendations for international students: Required—TOEFL (minimum score 550 paper-based; 213 computer-based). *Application deadline:* For fall admission, 7/15 for domestic students; for spring admission, 11/15 for domestic students. Applications are processed on a rolling basis. Application fee: $50 ($100 for international students). Electronic applications accepted. *Expenses:* Tuition, state resident: full-time $7,052. Tuition, nonresident: full-time $12,632. Tuition and fees vary according to course load. *Financial support:* In 2007–08, 1 research assistantship with tuition reimbursement (averaging $11,700 per year), 73 teaching assistantships with tuition reimbursements (averaging $9,750 per year) were awarded; fellowships, Federal Work-Study, institutionally sponsored loans, scholarships/grants, and unspecified assistantships also available. Support available to part-time students. Financial award application deadline: 4/30; financial award applicants required to submit FAFSA. *Faculty research:* Translation, science and the arts and humanities, intellectual and philosophical history, cultural studies. Total annual research expenditures: $368,048. *Unit head:* Dr. Dennis M. Kratz, Dean, 972-883-2984, Fax: 972-883-2989, E-mail: dkratz@utdallas.edu. *Application contact:* Dr. W. Jackson Rushing, Associate Dean of Graduate Studies, 972-883-2226, Fax: 972-883-2989, E-mail: jackson.rushing@utdallas.edu.

The University of Texas Medical Branch, Graduate School of Biomedical Sciences, Program in Medical Humanities, Galveston, TX 77555. Offers MA, PhD. *Students:* 16 full-time (9 women), 2 part-time (both women); includes 3 minority (1 Asian American or Pacific Islander, 2 Hispanic Americans). Average age 42. In 2007, 2 master's, 3 doctorates awarded. *Degree requirements:* For master's, thesis; for doctorate, thesis/dissertation. *Entrance requirements:* For master's and doctorate, GRE General Test, writing sample. Additional exam requirements/recommendations for international students: Required—TOEFL (minimum score 550 paper-based; 213 computer-based). Application fee: $30 ($75 for international students). Electronic applications accepted. *Expenses:* Tuition, state resident: part-time $50 per credit hour. Tuition, nonresident: part-time $328 per credit hour. *Financial support:* In 2007–08, fellowships (averaging $25,000 per year), research assistantships with full tuition reimbursements (averaging $25,000 per year) were awarded; institutionally sponsored loans also available. Financial award applicants required to submit FAFSA. *Unit head:* Dr. Anne Hudson Jones, Director, 409-772-2376, Fax: 409-772-5640, E-mail: ahjones@utmb.edu. *Application contact:* Donna A. Vickers, Administrative Coordinator, 409-772-9396, Fax: 409-772-5640, E-mail: davicker@utmb.edu.

University of West Florida, College of Arts and Sciences: Arts, Program in Interdisciplinary Humanities, Pensacola, FL 32514-5750. Offers MA. Part-time and evening/weekend programs available. *Faculty:* 2 full-time (0 women). *Students:* 1 full-time (0 women), 7 part-time (2 women). Average age 36. 2 applicants, 0% accepted. In 2007, 10 degrees awarded. *Degree requirements:* For master's, thesis. *Entrance requirements:* For master's, GRE General Test, minimum GPA of 3.0 in last 60 hours. Additional exam requirements/recommendations for international students: Required—TOEFL (minimum score 550 paper-based; 213 computer-based). *Application deadline:* For fall admission, 6/1 for domestic students, 5/15 for international students; for spring admission, 11/1 for domestic students, 10/1 for international students. Applications are processed on a rolling basis. Application fee: $30. *Expenses:* Tuition, state resident: full-time $6,054; part-time $252 per credit. Tuition, nonresident: full-time $21,886; part-time $912 per credit. *Financial support:* Fellowships, research assistantships with partial tuition reimbursements, teaching assistantships, institutionally sponsored loans, scholarships/grants, and unspecified assistantships available. Financial award application deadline: 4/15; financial award applicants required to submit FAFSA. *Unit head:* Dr. Sally Ferguson, Chairperson, 850-474-2676.

Virginia Commonwealth University, Graduate School, College of Humanities and Sciences, Richmond, VA 23284-9005. Offers MA, MFA, MPA, MS, MURP, PhD, CASR, CCJA, CPM, CURP, Certificate, Graduate Certificate, JD/MURP, MSW/Certificate. Part-time and evening/weekend programs available. *Students:* 776 full-time, 2,853 part-time; includes 469 minority (320 African Americans, 11 American Indian/Alaska Native, 94 Asian Americans or Pacific Islanders, 44 Hispanic Americans), 525 international. 1,529 applicants, 42% accepted, 395 enrolled.Application fee: $50. *Expenses:* Tuition, state resident: full-time $7,224; part-time $401 per credit. Tuition, nonresident: full-time $16,072; part-time $891 per credit. Required fees: $1,679; $63 per credit. Tuition and fees vary according to campus/location. *Financial support:* Fellowships, research assistantships, teaching assistantships, career-related internships or fieldwork, Federal Work-Study, institutionally sponsored loans, scholarships/grants, and tuition waivers (full and partial) available. Support available to part-time students. *Unit head:* Dr. Robert D. Holsworth, Dean, 804-828-1674.

See Close-Up on page 457.

Wright State University, School of Graduate Studies, College of Liberal Arts, Interdisciplinary Program in Humanities, Dayton, OH 45435. Offers M Hum. *Degree requirements:* For master's, thesis or alternative. *Entrance requirements:* Additional exam requirements/recommendations for international students: Required—TOEFL.

York University, Faculty of Graduate Studies, Faculty of Arts, Program in Humanities, Toronto, ON M3J 1P3, Canada. Offers MA, PhD. Part-time programs available. *Degree requirements:* For master's, thesis or alternative; for doctorate, comprehensive exam, thesis/dissertation. *Entrance requirements:* Additional exam requirements/recommendations for international students: Required—TOEFL (minimum score 600 paper-based; 250 computer-based). Electronic applications accepted.

Liberal Studies

Abilene Christian University, Graduate School, Interdisciplinary Program in the Liberal Arts, Abilene, TX 79699-9100. Offers MLA. Part-time programs available. *Students:* 3 full-time (2 women), 7 part-time (4 women), 1 international. 5 applicants, 80% accepted, 4 enrolled. *Degree requirements:* For master's, comprehensive exam, thesis or alternative. *Entrance requirements:* For master's, GRE General Test, MAT. *Application deadline:* For fall admission, 4/1 priority date for domestic students; for spring admission, 11/1 for domestic students. Applications are processed on a rolling basis. Application fee: $40 ($45 for international students). Electronic applications accepted. *Expenses:* Tuition: Full-time $13,368; part-time $557 per hour. Required fees: $700; $34 per hour. $10 per semester. Tuition and fees vary according to degree level and campus/location. *Financial support:* Federal Work-Study available. Support available to part-time students. Financial award application deadline: 4/1. *Unit head:* Dr. David Merrell, Graduate Adviser, 325-674-2035, Fax: 325-674-6844, E-mail: merrelld@acu.edu. *Application contact:* William Horn, Graduate Admissions Counselor, 325-674-2656, Fax: 325-674-6717, E-mail: gradinfo@acu.edu.

Alaska Pacific University, Graduate Programs, Liberal Studies Department, Anchorage, AK 99508-4672. Offers self-designed study (MA). *Students:* 6 full-time (all women), 13 part-time (11 women); includes 1 minority (American Indian/Alaska Native), 1 international. Average age 43. In 2007, 7 degrees awarded. *Expenses:* Tuition: Full-time $12,510. One-time fee: $110 full-time. *Unit head:* Dr. Lynn Paulson, Chair, 907-564-8233, E-mail: lep@alaskapacific.edu.

Albertus Magnus College, Liberal Studies Program, New Haven, CT 06511-1189. Offers MALS. Part-time and evening/weekend programs available. *Faculty:* 5 full-time (3 women), 4 part-time/adjunct (2 women). *Students:* Average age 39. 5 applicants, 60% accepted, 3 enrolled. In 2007, 3 degrees awarded. *Degree requirements:* For master's, thesis. *Entrance requirements:* For master's, interview, writing sample. *Application deadline:* For fall admission, 8/31 priority date for domestic students; for spring admission, 1/10 for domestic students. Applications are processed on a rolling basis. Application fee: $25. *Financial support:* Available to part-time students. Application deadline: 8/17. *Unit head:* Dr. Paul Robichaud, Director, 203-773-8556, Fax: 203-773-3117, E-mail: probichaud@albertus.edu.

Alvernia College, Graduate and Continuing Studies, Department of Liberal Studies, Reading, PA 19607-1799. Offers MALS. Part-time and evening/weekend programs available. *Degree requirements:* For master's, thesis optional. *Entrance requirements:* For master's, MAT or GRE (alumni excluded). Electronic applications accepted.

Antioch University McGregor, Graduate Programs, Individualized Liberal and Professional Studies Program, Yellow Springs, OH 45387-1609. Offers liberal and professional studies (MA), including counseling, creative writing, education, film studies, liberal studies, management, modern literature, psychology, theatre, visual arts. Part-time and evening/weekend programs available. Postbaccalaureate distance learning degree programs offered (minimal on-campus study). *Faculty:* 2 full-time (1 woman), 3 part-time/adjunct (2 women). *Students:* Average age 40. 35 applicants, 63% accepted, 17 enrolled. In 2007, 31 degrees awarded. *Degree requirements:* For master's, thesis or alternative. *Entrance requirements:* For master's, resumé, 2 letters of reference. *Application deadline:* For fall admission, 8/25 for domestic students; for winter admission, 12/5 for domestic students; for spring admission, 3/8 for domestic students. Applications are processed on a rolling basis. Application fee: $50. Electronic applications accepted. *Expenses: Contact institution. Financial support:* Federal Work-Study available. Financial award applicants required to submit FAFSA. *Unit head:* Suzanne Fest, Chair, 937-769-1876, Fax: 937-769-1807, E-mail: sfest@mcgregor.edu. *Application contact:* Seth Gordon, Assistant Director of Admissions, 937-769-1800 Ext. 1825, Fax: 937-769-1804, E-mail: sgordon@mcgregor.edu.

See Close-Up on page 443.

Armstrong Atlantic State University, School of Graduate Studies, Program in Liberal and Professional Studies, Savannah, GA 31419-1997. Offers MALPS. Part-time programs available. *Faculty:* 1 (woman) full-time. *Students:* 6 full-time (4 women), 19 part-time (16 women); includes 3 minority (2 African Americans, 1 Hispanic American). Average age 34. *Degree requirements:* For master's, comprehensive exam, project. *Entrance requirements:* For master's, GRE, minimum GPA of 2.5, letters of recommendation. Additional exam requirements/recommendations for international students: Required—TOEFL (minimum score 523 paper-based; 193 computer-based). *Application deadline:* For fall admission, 7/1 priority date for domestic and international students; for spring admission, 11/15 priority date for domestic and international students. Application fee: $30. *Expenses:* Tuition, state resident: full-time $3,228; part-time $135 per hour. Tuition, nonresident: full-time $12,904; part-time $538 per hour. Required fees: $278 per term. *Financial support:* In 2007–08, research assistantships with partial tuition reimbursements (averaging $2,500 per year); scholarships/grants and unspecified assistantships also available. Financial award applicants required to submit FAFSA. *Unit head:* Dr. Richard Nordquist, Director, 912-921-5991, E-mail: richard.nordquist@armstrong.edu. *Application contact:* Peggy Williams, Degree Program Assistant, 912-921-5991, E-mail: peggy.williams@armstrong.edu.

Auburn University Montgomery, School of Liberal Arts, Montgomery, AL 36124-4023. Offers MLA. Part-time and evening/weekend programs available. *Faculty:* 23 full-time (8 women). *Students:* 6 full-time (5 women), 20 part-time (16 women); includes 5 minority (3 African Americans, 2 Asian Americans or Pacific Islanders). Average age 33. In 2007, 7 degrees awarded. *Degree requirements:* For master's, thesis. *Entrance requirements:* For master's, GRE or MAT. *Application deadline:* Applications are processed on a rolling basis. Application fee: $25. Electronic applications accepted. *Expenses:* Tuition, state resident: full-time $4,536; part-time $189 per credit hour. Tuition, nonresident: full-time $13,608; part-time $567 per credit hour. Required fees: $234. *Financial support:* In 2007–08, 2 teaching assistantships were awarded; career-related internships or fieldwork and scholarships/grants also available. Support available to part-time students. Financial award application deadline: 3/1; financial award applicants required to submit FAFSA. *Unit head:* Dr. Steven Daniell, Interim Dean, 334-244-3382, Fax: 334-244-3740. *Application contact:* Dr. Susan L. Willis, Graduate Coordinator, 334-244-3406, Fax: 334-244-3740, E-mail: swillis1@mail.aum.edu.

Baker University, School of Professional and Graduate Studies, Program in Liberal Arts, Baldwin City, KS 66006-0065. Offers MLA. Program also offered in Overland Park, KS. Part-time and evening/weekend programs available. *Students:* 19 full-time (15 women), 74 part-time (57 women); includes 17 minority (10 African Americans, 4 American Indian/Alaska Native, 3 Hispanic Americans). Average age 38. In 2007, 40 degrees awarded. *Degree requirements:* For master's, portfolio of learning. *Entrance requirements:* Additional exam requirements/recommendations for international students: Required—TOEFL (minimum score 600 paper-based; 250 computer-based). *Application deadline:* Applications are processed on a rolling basis. Application fee: $20. *Expenses:* Tuition: Full-time $10,800; part-time $100 per credit hour. Required fees: $130; $130 per year. Tuition and fees vary according to program. *Financial support:* Applicants required to submit FAFSA. *Application contact:* Dr. Cindy Hoss, Assistant Dean for Instruction and Curriculum, 913-491-4432, Fax: 913-491-0470, E-mail: choss@bakeru.edu.

Barry University, School of Arts and Sciences, Interdisciplinary Program, Miami Shores, FL 33161-6695. Offers MA. *Students:* 1 (woman) full-time, 5 part-time (4 women); includes 5 minority (3 African Americans, 2 Hispanic Americans). *Unit head:* Dr. Aphrodite Alexandrakis, Director, 305-899-3349, Fax: 305-899-3466, E-mail: aalexandrakis@mail.barry.edu. *Application contact:* Dave Fletcher, Director of Graduate Admissions, 305-899-3113, Fax: 305-899-2971, E-mail: dfletcher@mail.barry.edu.

Boston University, Metropolitan College (Continuing Education), Department of Liberal Studies, Boston, MA 02215. Offers interdisciplinary studies (MLA). Part-time and evening/weekend programs available. *Students:* Average age 29. 4 applicants, 100% accepted, 4 enrolled. *Degree requirements:* For master's, thesis. *Entrance requirements:* For master's, interview. Additional exam requirements/recommendations for international students: Required—TOEFL (minimum score 560 paper-based). *Application deadline:* Applications are processed on a rolling basis. Application fee: $70. Electronic applications accepted. *Expenses:* Tuition: Full-time $34,930; part-time $1,092 per credit. Tuition and fees vary according to class time, course level and program. *Financial support:* Research assistantships with partial tuition reimbursements, scholarships/grants available. Support available to part-time students. *Faculty research:* Arts and gastronomy. *Unit head:* Daniel Ranall, Interim Chair, 617-358-0005, Fax: 617-358-1230, E-mail: dranalli@bu.edu.

Bradley University, Graduate School, College of Liberal Arts and Sciences, Program in Liberal Studies, Peoria, IL 61625-0002. Offers MLS. Part-time and evening/weekend programs available. In 2007, 6 degrees awarded. *Degree requirements:* For master's, comprehensive exam, colloquium. *Entrance requirements:* For master's, 2 letters of recommendation. Additional exam requirements/recommendations for international students: Required—TOEFL (minimum score 550 paper-based; 213 computer-based; 79 iBT). *Application deadline:* For fall admission, 5/15 priority date for domestic and international students; for spring admission, 10/15 priority date for domestic and international students. Applications are processed on a rolling basis. *Expenses: Contact institution. Financial support:* Scholarships/grants and tuition waivers (partial) available. Financial award application deadline: 4/1. *Unit head:* Dr. Max H. Taylor, Director, 309-677-3026, E-mail: mtaylor@bradley.edu.

Brooklyn College of the City University of New York, Division of Graduate Studies, Liberal Studies Program, Brooklyn, NY 11210-2889. Offers MA. Part-time programs available. *Students:* 1 (woman) full-time, 14 part-time (10 women); includes 6 minority (5 African Americans, 1 Hispanic American), 2 international. 10 applicants, 70% accepted, 2 enrolled. In 2007, 10 degrees awarded. *Degree requirements:* For master's, thesis or alternative, final project. *Entrance requirements:* For master's, interview, 2 letters of recommendation, essay. Additional exam requirements/recommendations for international students: Required—TOEFL. *Application deadline:* For fall admission, 3/1 priority date for domestic students, 2/1 priority date for international students; for spring admission, 11/1 priority date for domestic students, 10/1 priority date for international students. Applications are processed on a rolling basis. Application fee: $125. Electronic applications accepted. *Financial support:* Federal Work-Study, institutionally sponsored loans, and scholarships/grants available. Support available to part-time students. Financial award application deadline: 5/1; financial award applicants required to submit FAFSA. *Faculty research:* Language acquisition, Judaic biography, ecocriticism. *Unit head:* Dr. George Brinton, Director, 718-951-5281, E-mail: gabbc@brooklyn.cuny.edu. *Application contact:* Hernan Sierra, Graduate Admissions Coordinator, 718-951-4536, Fax: 718-951-4506, E-mail: grads@brooklyn.cuny.edu.

Brooklyn College of the City University of New York, Division of Graduate Studies, School of Education, Program in Childhood Education, Brooklyn, NY 11210-2889. Offers bilingual education (MS Ed); liberal arts (MS Ed); mathematics (MS Ed); science/environmental education (MS Ed). Part-time and evening/weekend programs available. *Students:* 16 full-time (13 women), 257 part-time (219 women); includes 136 minority (77 African Americans, 13 Asian Americans or Pacific Islanders, 46 Hispanic Americans), 8 international. 167 applicants, 87% accepted, 90 enrolled. In 2007, 145 degrees awarded. *Entrance requirements:* For master's, LAST, interview, previous course work in education, writing sample, resumé, 2 letters of recommendation. Additional exam requirements/recommendations for international students: Required—TOEFL. *Application deadline:* For fall admission, 3/1 priority date for domestic students, 2/1 priority date for international students; for spring admission, 11/1 priority date for domestic students, 10/1 priority date for international students. Applications are processed on a rolling basis. Application fee: $125. Electronic applications accepted. *Financial support:* Career-related internships or fieldwork, Federal Work-Study, institutionally sponsored loans, and scholarships/grants available. Support available to part-time students. Financial award application deadline: 5/1; financial award applicants required to submit FAFSA. *Faculty research:* Emotional intelligence, multiculturalism, arts immersion, the Holocaust. *Unit head:* Dr. Sharon O'Connor-Petruso, Program Head, 718-951-5214. *Application contact:* Hernan Sierra, Graduate Admissions Coordinator, 718-951-4536, Fax: 718-951-4506, E-mail: grads@brooklyn.cuny.edu.

California State University, Sacramento, Graduate Studies, College of Social Sciences and Interdisciplinary Studies, Liberal Arts Program, Sacramento, CA 95819-6048. Offers French (MA); German (MA); Spanish (MA); theater arts (MA). *Students:* 15 full-time (10 women), 24 part-time (17 women); includes 4 minority (2 African Americans, 1 American Indian/Alaska Native, 1 Asian American or Pacific Islander). Average age 37. 17 applicants, 88% accepted, 9 enrolled. *Degree requirements:* For master's, writing proficiency exam. *Entrance requirements:* Additional exam requirements/recommendations for international students: Required—TOEFL. *Application deadline:* Applications are processed on a rolling basis. Application fee: $55. Electronic applications accepted. *Expenses:* Tuition, state resident: full-time $3,414. Tuition, nonresident: full-time $13,584; part-time $339 per unit. Required fees: $786; $393 per semester. *Financial support:* Application deadline: 3/1. *Unit head:* Dr. Lindy Valdez, Coordinator, 916-278-6342.

Cardinal Stritch University, College of Arts and Sciences, Milwaukee, WI 53217-3985. Offers MA, MM. Part-time and evening/weekend programs available. *Degree requirements:* For master's, thesis.

Clark University, Graduate School, College of Professional and Continuing Education, Program in Liberal Studies, Worcester, MA 01610-1477. Offers MALA. Part-time and evening/weekend programs available. *Students:* 1 (woman) full-time, 8 part-time (4 women), 1 international. Average age 58. 3 applicants, 100% accepted, 3 enrolled. In 2007, 3 degrees awarded. *Degree requirements:* For master's, thesis optional. *Application deadline:* For fall admission, 2/15 priority date for domestic students. Applications are processed on a rolling basis. Application fee: $40. Electronic applications accepted. *Expenses:* Tuition: Full-time $32,600; part-time $1,019 per credit. Required fees: $30. Tuition and fees vary according to program. *Financial support:* Career-related internships or fieldwork available. Support available to part-time students. *Unit head:* Max E. Hess, Director of Graduate Studies, 508-793-7217, Fax: 508-793-7232. *Application contact:* Julia Parent, Director of Marketing, Communications, and Admissions, 508-793-7217, Fax: 508-793-7232, E-mail: jparent@clarku.edu.

Clayton State University, School of Graduate Studies, Program in Liberal Studies, Morrow, GA 30260-0285. Offers MALS.

The College at Brockport, State University of New York, School of Letters and Sciences, Program in Liberal Studies, Brockport, NY 14420-2997. Offers MA. Part-time programs available. *Students:* 2 full-time (1 woman), 44 part-time (22 women); includes 3 minority (all African Americans) 12 applicants, 100% accepted, 12 enrolled. In 2007, 23 degrees awarded. *Degree requirements:* For master's, portfolio. *Entrance requirements:* For master's, minimum GPA of 3.0, letters of recommendation, written statement of programmatic focus. Additional exam requirements/recommendations for international students: Required—TOEFL (minimum score 550 paper-based; 213 computer-based; 79 iBT). *Application deadline:* For fall admission, 6/15 for domestic and international students; for spring admission, 10/15 for domestic and international students. Application fee: $50. *Expenses:* Tuition, state resident: full-time $6,900; part-time $288 per credit. Tuition, nonresident: full-time $10,920; part-time $455 per credit. Required fees: $738; $31 per credit. *Financial support:* Federal Work-Study, scholarships/grants, and unspecified assistantships available. Financial award application deadline: 3/15; financial award applicants required to submit FAFSA. *Unit head:* Dr. Kalathur Rajasethupathy, Director, 585-395-2262, Fax: 585-395-2172, E-mail: kraja@brockport.edu.

College of Notre Dame of Maryland, Graduate Studies, Program in Liberal Studies, Baltimore, MD 21210-2476. Offers MA. Part-time and evening/weekend programs available. *Students:* 1 (woman) full-time, 14 part-time (12 women). *Degree requirements:* For master's, thesis or alternative. *Entrance requirements:* For master's, minimum GPA of 3.0. Additional exam requirements/recommendations for international students: Required—TOEFL (minimum score 500 paper-based; 173 computer-based; 61 iBT). *Application deadline:* For fall admission, 7/5 for domestic students; for winter admission, 11/5 for domestic students; for spring admission, 12/5 for domestic students. Applications are processed on a rolling basis. Application fee: $45. Electronic applications accepted. *Financial support:* Career-related internships or fieldwork and institutionally sponsored loans available. Support available to part-time students. Financial award application deadline: 6/30; financial award applicants required to submit FAFSA. *Unit head:* Dr. Joseph Dirienzi, Head, 410-532-5702, Fax: 410-532-5333, E-mail: jdirienzi@ndm.edu. *Application contact:* Erica D. Jones, Graduate Admissions Coordinator, 410-532-5317, Fax: 410-532-5333, E-mail: gradadm@ndm.edu.

College of Staten Island of the City University of New York, Graduate Programs, Program in Liberal Studies, Staten Island, NY 10314-6600. Offers MA. Evening/weekend programs available. *Faculty:* 4 full-time (1 woman). *Students:* Average age 34. 13 applicants, 92% accepted, 7 enrolled. In 2007, 18 degrees awarded. *Degree requirements:* For master's, thesis, 30 credits. *Entrance requirements:* For master's, minimum undergraduate GPA of 3.0, interview. Additional exam requirements/recommendations for international students: Required—TOEFL (minimum score 550 paper-based; 213 computer-based; 79 iBT). *Application deadline:* Applications are processed on a rolling basis. Application fee: $125. Electronic applications accepted. *Expenses:* Tuition, state resident: part-time $270 per credit. Tuition, nonresident: part-time $500 per credit. Required fees: $38 per semester. One-time fee: $15 part-time. Tuition and fees vary according to course load. *Financial support:* Fellowships, research assistantships, teaching assistantships available. Financial award application deadline: 4/1; financial award applicants required to submit CSS PROFILE or FAFSA. *Unit head:* Dr. Howard Weiner, Acting Coordinator, 718-982-2868, E-mail: mals@mail.csi.cuny.edu. *Application contact:* Sasha Spence, Assistant Director of Graduate Recruitment Admissions, 718-982-2699, Fax: 718-982-2500, E-mail: spence@mail.csi.cuny.edu.

Columbia University, Graduate School of Arts and Sciences, Program in Liberal Studies, New York, NY 10027. Offers American studies (MA); East Asian studies (MA); human rights studies (MA); Islamic culture studies (MA); Jewish studies (MA); medieval studies (MA); modern European studies (MA); South Asian studies (MA). Part-time and evening/weekend programs available. *Faculty:* 5 part-time/adjunct (2 women). *Students:* 7 full-time (2 women), 75 part-time (51 women); includes 5 minority (1 African American, 3 Asian Americans or Pacific Islanders, 1 Hispanic American), 8 international. Average age 41. 39 applicants, 77% accepted. In 2007, 20 degrees awarded. *Degree requirements:* For master's, thesis. Application fee: $90. *Expenses:* Tuition: Part-time $1,452 per credit. Required fees: $152 per term. One-time fee: $75 part-time. Full-time tuition and fees vary according to course level, course load, degree level and program. *Unit head:* Kristin Balicki, Program Coordinator, 212-854-4932, Fax: 212-854-4912, E-mail: knb2110@columbia.edu.

Concordia University Chicago, College of Arts and Sciences, Program in Liberal Studies, River Forest, IL 60305-1499. Offers MA. *Entrance requirements:* Additional exam requirements/recommendations for international students: Required—TOEFL (minimum score 550 paper-based; 195 computer-based). Electronic applications accepted.

Converse College, School of Education and Graduate Studies, Program in Liberal Arts, Spartanburg, SC 29302-0006. Offers English (MLA); history (MLA); political science (MLA). *Degree requirements:* For master's, capstone paper. *Entrance requirements:* For master's, minimum GPA of 3.0, 2 recommendations.

Creighton University, Graduate School, College of Arts and Sciences, Program in Liberal Studies, Omaha, NE 68178-0001. Offers MLS. Part-time and evening/weekend programs available. *Students:* 4 full-time (3 women), 8 part-time (6 women); includes 1 minority (African American) 4 applicants, 75% accepted, 3 enrolled. In 2007, 1 degree awarded. *Degree requirements:* For master's, thesis (for some programs). *Entrance requirements:* For master's, 3 letters of recommendation. Additional exam requirements/recommendations for international students: Required—TOEFL (minimum score 550 paper-based; 213 computer-based; 80 iBT). *Application deadline:* For fall admission, 3/1 priority date for domestic and international students; for winter admission, 12/1 priority date for domestic and international students; for spring admission, 4/1 priority date for domestic and international students. Applications are processed on a rolling basis. Application fee: $50. Electronic applications accepted. *Financial support:* Available to part-time students. Applicants required to submit FAFSA. *Unit head:* Dr. Richard J. White, Director, 402-280-2642. *Application contact:* LuAnn M. Schwery, Assistant Dean, 402-280-2870, Fax: 402-280-5762, E-mail: schwery@creighton.edu.

Dallas Baptist University, College of Adult Education, Liberal Arts Program, Dallas, TX 75211-9299. Offers arts (MLA); Christian ministry (MLA); English (MLA); English as a second language (MLA); fine arts (MLA); history (MLA); missions (MLA); political science (MLA). Part-time and evening/weekend programs available. *Faculty:* 55 full-time (22 women), 114 part-time/adjunct (44 women). *Students:* 2 full-time, 41 part-time. 16 applicants, 56% accepted, 7 enrolled. In 2007, 17 degrees awarded. *Entrance requirements:* For master's, minimum GPA of 3.0. Additional exam requirements/recommendations for international students: Required—TOEFL. *Application deadline:* Applications are processed on a rolling basis. Application fee: $25. Electronic applications accepted. *Expenses:* Tuition: Full-time $9,144; part-time $508 per credit hour. *Financial support:* Federal Work-Study, institutionally sponsored loans, scholarships/grants, and tuition waivers (full and partial) available. Support available to part-time students. Financial award applicants required to submit FAFSA. *Faculty research:* Milton and seventeenth century Puritans, inter-Biblical years, nineteenth century literature, Latin American and Texas history. *Unit head:* Dr. David Stricklin, Acting Director, 214-333-5496, Fax: 214-333-5558, E-mail: graduate@dbu.edu. *Application contact:* Kit P. Montgomery, Director of Graduate Programs, 214-333-5242, Fax: 214-333-5579, E-mail: graduate@dbu.edu.

Dartmouth College, Arts and Sciences Graduate Programs, Program in Liberal Studies, Hanover, NH 03755. Offers MALS. Part-time programs available. *Faculty:* 19 full-time (4 women). *Students:* 39 full-time (24 women), 27 part-time (18 women); includes 6 minority (2 African Americans, 1 Asian American or Pacific Islander, 3 Hispanic Americans), 7 international. Average age 29. 85 applicants, 62% accepted, 35 enrolled. In 2007, 49 degrees awarded. *Degree requirements:* For master's, thesis. *Entrance requirements:* Additional exam requirements/recommendations for international students: Required—TOEFL. *Application deadline:* For fall admission, 2/15 for domestic students; for winter admission, 7/15 for domestic students; for spring admission, 7/15 for domestic students. Application fee: $50. *Financial support:* Federal Work-Study, institutionally sponsored loans, scholarships/grants, and tuition waivers (full and partial) available. Support available to part-time students. Financial award application deadline: 4/2. *Unit head:* Dr. Donald Pease, Chair, 603-646-3592. *Application contact:* Lauren E. Clarke, Executive Director, 603-646-3592, Fax: 603-646-3590, E-mail: lauren.e.clarke@dartmouth.edu.

See Close-Up on page 451.

DePaul University, College of Liberal Arts and Sciences, Department of Liberal Studies, Chicago, IL 60604-2287. Offers MA. Part-time and evening/weekend programs available. *Faculty:* 17 full-time (10 women). *Students:* 53 full-time (41 women), 90 part-time (65 women); includes 27 minority (12 African Americans, 4 Asian Americans or Pacific Islanders, 11 Hispanic Americans), 2 international. Average age 36. 18 applicants, 78% accepted. In 2007, 7 master's awarded. *Degree requirements:* For master's, thesis, integrating project. *Entrance requirements:* For master's, interview. Additional exam requirements/recommendations for international students: Required—TOEFL. *Application deadline:* For fall admission, 7/15 priority date for domestic students; for winter admission, 10/15 priority date for domestic students; for spring admission, 2/15 priority date for domestic students. Applications are processed on a rolling basis. Application fee: $25. *Financial support:* Fellowships with partial tuition reimbursements, tuition waivers (partial) available. *Unit head:* Dr. David Gitomer, Director, 773-325-7840, E-mail: dgitomer@wppost.depaul.edu.

Dowling College, Programs in Arts and Sciences, Oakdale, NY 11769-1999. Offers integrated math and science (MS); liberal studies (MA). Part-time and evening/weekend programs available. *Faculty:* 13 full-time (4 women), 4 part-time/adjunct (3 women). *Students:* 6 full-time (all women), 10 part-time (all women); includes 1 minority (Hispanic American) Average age 26. 20 applicants, 50% accepted, 6 enrolled. In 2007, 2 degrees awarded. *Degree requirements:* For master's, comprehensive exam, thesis. *Entrance requirements:* For master's, minimum undergraduate GPA of 3.0, 2 letters of recommendation. Additional exam requirements/recommendations for international students: Required—TOEFL (minimum score 550 paper-based). *Application deadline:* For fall admission, 9/1 priority date for domestic students; for winter admission, 1/1 priority date for domestic students; for spring admission, 2/1 priority date for domestic students. Applications are processed on a rolling basis. Application fee: $25. Electronic applications accepted. *Expenses:* Tuition: Full-time $17,452; part-time $606 per credit. Required fees: $2,908; $538 per term. One-time fee: $55. *Financial support:* In 2007–08, 4 students received support, including 1 research assistantship (averaging $2,001 per year); Federal Work-Study, scholarships/grants, and unspecified assistantships also available. Support available to part-time students. Financial award application deadline: 6/30; financial award applicants required to submit FAFSA. *Unit head:* Dr. Paul Abramson, Dean, 631-244-3162, Fax: 631-244-1035, E-mail: abramsop@dowling.edu.

Duke University, Graduate School, Program in Liberal Studies, Durham, NC 27708. Offers AM. Part-time and evening/weekend programs available. *Degree requirements:* For master's, thesis or alternative, final project. *Entrance requirements:* For master's, interview. Additional exam requirements/recommendations for international students: Required—IELTS (preferred) or TOEFL. Electronic applications accepted.

Duquesne University, School of Leadership and Professional Advancement, Pittsburgh, PA 15282-0001. Offers community leadership (MS); leadership and business ethics (MS); leadership and information technology (MS); leadership and liberal studies (MA); sports leadership (MS). Postbaccalaureate distance learning degree programs offered. *Expenses:* Tuition: Part-time $774 per credit. Required fees: $74 per credit. Tuition and fees vary according to program. *Unit head:* Shawn Gearing, Senior Academic Advisor, 412-396-5558, E-mail: gearing@duq.edu.

East Tennessee State University, School of Graduate Studies, Division of Cross-Disciplinary Studies, Johnson City, TN 37614. Offers liberal studies (MALS). *Entrance requirements:* For master's, GRE. Additional exam requirements/recommendations for international students: Required—TOEFL (minimum score 550 paper-based; 213 computer-based).

Excelsior College, School of Liberal Arts, Albany, NY 12203-5159. Offers liberal studies (MA). Part-time and evening/weekend programs available. Postbaccalaureate distance learning degree programs offered (no on-campus study). *Faculty:* 2 full-time (both women), 35 part-time/adjunct (20 women). *Students:* Average age 49. 150 applicants, 67% accepted. In 2007, 35 degrees awarded. *Degree requirements:* For master's, thesis or alternative. *Application deadline:* Applications are processed on a rolling basis. Application fee: $100. Electronic applications accepted. *Expenses:* Tuition: Part-time $390 per credit. Required fees: $215 per year. *Financial support:* In 2007–08, 2 fellowships (averaging $2,000 per year) were awarded; career-related internships or fieldwork, scholarships/grants, and traineeships also available. Total annual research expenditures: $50,000. *Unit head:* Dr. Janet L. Shideler, Associate Dean, 518-464-8500, Fax: 518-464-8777, E-mail: mlsadmin@excelsior.edu. *Application contact:* Susan Carlson, Administrative Assistant, 518-464-8500 Ext. 1323, Fax: 518-464-8777, E-mail: mls@excelsior.edu.

Florida Atlantic University, Dorothy F. Schmidt College of Arts and Letters, Department of Liberal Studies, Boca Raton, FL 33431-0991. Offers MLBLST. *Degree requirements:* For master's, thesis or alternative. *Entrance requirements:* For master's, GRE General Test.

Florida International University, College of Arts and Sciences, Program in Liberal Studies, Miami, FL 33199. Offers MA. *Faculty:* 11 full-time (4 women). *Students:* 2 full-time (both women), 3 part-time (2 women); includes 2 minority (1 African American, 1 Hispanic American), 1 international. Average age 34. 11 applicants, 27% accepted, 3 enrolled. In 2007, 6 degrees awarded. *Entrance requirements:* For master's, minimum GPA of 3.0, letters of recommendation. Additional exam requirements/recommendations for international students: Required—TOEFL (minimum score 550 paper-based; 213 computer-based). *Application deadline:* For fall admission, 6/1 for domestic students, 4/1 for international students; for spring admission, 10/1 for domestic students, 9/1 for international students. Applications are processed on a rolling basis. Application fee: $30. Electronic applications accepted. *Expenses:* Tuition, state resident: full-time $6,106. Tuition, nonresident: full-time $15,528. Required fees: $284. *Financial support:* Teaching assistantships available. *Unit head:* Dr. Kiriake Yerohemona, Graduate Program Director, 305-348-7563, Fax: 305-348-1799, E-mail: kiriake.xerohemona@fiu.edu.

Fordham University, Graduate School of Arts and Sciences, Program in Humanities and Sciences, New York, NY 10458. Offers MA. Part-time and evening/weekend programs available. *Students:* 9 full-time (3 women), 20 part-time (13 women); includes 1 minority (Asian American or Pacific Islander), 1 international. Average age 26. 29 applicants, 83% accepted, 2 enrolled. In 2007, 5 degrees awarded. *Degree requirements:* For master's, final paper. *Entrance requirements:* Additional exam requirements/recommendations for international students: Required—TOEFL (minimum score 650 paper-based; 280 computer-based). *Application deadline:* For fall admission, 1/4 priority date for domestic students; for spring admission, 11/1 for domestic students. Application fee: $70. Electronic applications accepted. *Expenses:* Tuition: Full-time $23,880; part-time $995 per credit. *Financial support:* Fellowships, institutionally sponsored loans and tuition waivers (full and partial) available. Financial award application deadline: 1/4; financial award applicants required to submit FAFSA. *Unit head:* Dr. Hugo Benavides, Director, 718-817-4407, E-mail: benavides@fordham.edu. *Application contact:* Charlene Dundie, Director of Graduate Admissions, 718-817-4420, Fax: 718-817-3566, E-mail: dundie@fordham.edu.

Fort Hays State University, Graduate School, College of Arts and Sciences, Center for Interdisciplinary Studies, Hays, KS 67601-4099. Offers liberal studies (MLS). Postbaccalaureate distance learning degree programs offered (minimal on-campus study). *Faculty:* 2 full-time (0 women). *Students:* 41 full-time (25 women), 252 part-time (133 women); includes 47 minority (25 African Americans, 4 American Indian/Alaska Native, 9 Asian Americans or Pacific Islanders, 9 Hispanic Americans). 93 applicants, 70% accepted. In 2007, 64 degrees awarded. *Degree requirements:* For master's, comprehensive exam, thesis or alternative. *Entrance requirements:* Additional exam requirements/recommendations for international students: Required—TOEFL (minimum score 550 paper-based; 213 computer-based). *Application deadline:* For fall admission, 7/1 priority date for domestic students. Applications are processed on a rolling basis. Application fee: $35. Electronic applications accepted. *Expenses:* Tuition, state resident: part-time $155 per credit hour. Tuition, nonresident: part-time $409 per credit hour. Tuition and fees vary according to class time, course level, course load, degree level, campus/location and program. *Unit head:* Dr. Art Morin, Director, 785-628-5578, E-mail: amorin@fhsu.edu.

Georgetown University, Graduate School of Arts and Sciences, School for Summer and Continuing Education, Washington, DC 20057. Offers MALS. *Entrance requirements:* Additional exam requirements/recommendations for international students: Required—TOEFL.

Graduate School and University Center of the City University of New York, Graduate Studies, Program in Liberal Studies, New York, NY 10016-4039. Offers MA. *Students:* 3 full-time (2 women), 95 part-time (60 women); includes 8 minority (2 Asian Americans or Pacific Islanders, 6 Hispanic Americans), 6 international. Average age 35. 47 applicants, 81% accepted, 27 enrolled. In 2007, 15 degrees awarded. *Degree requirements:* For master's, thesis. *Entrance requirements:* For master's, GRE General Test. Additional exam requirements/

Liberal Studies

Graduate School and University Center of the City University of New York (continued)

recommendations for international students: Required—TOEFL. *Application deadline:* For fall admission, 4/15 for domestic students; for spring admission, 11/15 for domestic students. Application fee: $125. Electronic applications accepted. *Financial support:* In 2007–08, 24 students received support; fellowships, Federal Work-Study, institutionally sponsored loans, and tuition waivers (full and partial) available. Financial award application deadline: 2/1; financial award applicants required to submit FAFSA. *Unit head:* Dr. Joseph Dauben, Executive Officer, 212-817-8481, Fax: 212-817-1525.

Hamline University, Graduate School of Liberal Studies, St. Paul, MN 55104-1284. Offers MALS, MFA, CALS. Part-time and evening/weekend programs available. *Faculty:* 4 full-time (3 women), 7 part-time/adjunct (6 women). *Students:* 71 full-time (58 women), 154 part-time (112 women); includes 8 minority (5 African Americans, 1 American Indian/Alaska Native, 1 Asian American or Pacific Islander, 1 Hispanic American), 3 international. Average age 38. 64 applicants, 64% accepted, 29 enrolled. In 2007, 39 degrees awarded. *Degree requirements:* For master's, thesis. *Entrance requirements:* For master's, 20 page writing sample (MFA), official transcripts, letters of recommendation. Additional exam requirements/recommendations for international students: Required—TOEFL (minimum score 550 paper-based), TWE (minimum score 5). *Application deadline:* For fall admission, 3/1 priority date for domestic students; for spring admission, 9/1 priority date for domestic students. Applications are processed on a rolling basis. Application fee: $30. Electronic applications accepted. *Expenses: Contact institution.* One-time fee: $175 part-time. *Financial support:* Federal Work-Study available. Financial award applicants required to submit FAFSA. *Unit head:* Mary Francòis Rockcastle, Dean, 651-523-2047, Fax: 651-523-2490, E-mail: mrockcastle@hamline.edu. *Application contact:* Rae A. Lenway, Director, Graduate Recruitment and Admission, 651-523-2900, Fax: 651-523-3058, E-mail: rlenway@hamline.edu.

Harvard University, Extension School, Cambridge, MA 02138-3722. Offers applied sciences (CAS); biotechnology (ALM); educational technologies (ALM); educational technology (CET); English for graduate and professional studies (DGP); environmental management (ALM, CEM); information technology (ALM); journalism (ALM); liberal arts (ALM); management (ALM, CM); mathematics for teaching (ALM); museum studies (ALM); premedical studies (Diploma); publication and communication (CPC). Part-time and evening/weekend programs available. *Faculty:* 242 part-time/adjunct. *Students:* Average age 35. In 2007, 190 master's, 78 other advanced degrees awarded. *Degree requirements:* For master's, thesis. *Entrance requirements:* For master's, 3 completed graduate courses with grade of B or higher. Additional exam requirements/recommendations for international students: Required—TOEFL (minimum score 600 paper-based; 250 computer-based), TWE (minimum score 5). *Application deadline:* Applications are processed on a rolling basis. Application fee: $75. *Expenses: Contact institution.* Full-time tuition and fees vary according to program and student level. *Financial support:* In 2007–08, 198 students received support. Scholarships/grants available. Support available to part-time students. Financial award application deadline: 8/6; financial award applicants required to submit FAFSA. *Unit head:* Michael Shinagel, Dean, 617-495-1000. *Application contact:* Program Director, 617-495-4024, Fax: 617-495-9176.

Henderson State University, Graduate Studies, Ellis College of Arts and Sciences, Arkadelphia, AR 71999-0001. Offers MLA. Part-time programs available. *Entrance requirements:* For master's, minimum GPA of 2.7, interview.

Hollins University, Graduate Programs, Program in Liberal Studies, Roanoke, VA 24020-1603. Offers humanities (MALS); interdisciplinary studies (MALS); justice and legal studies (MALS); liberal studies (CAS); social science (MALS); visual and performing arts (MALS). Part-time and evening/weekend programs available. *Faculty:* 9 full-time (2 women), 12 part-time/adjunct (5 women). *Students:* 20 full-time (17 women), 89 part-time (74 women); includes 15 minority (11 African Americans, 1 American Indian/Alaska Native, 2 Asian Americans or Pacific Islanders, 1 Hispanic American). Average age 39. 30 applicants, 93% accepted, 20 enrolled. In 2007, 48 degrees awarded. *Degree requirements:* For master's, thesis. *Entrance requirements:* For master's, letters of recommendation, interview. Additional exam requirements/recommendations for international students: Required—TOEFL (minimum score 550 paper-based; 213 computer-based). *Application deadline:* For fall admission, 7/1 priority date for domestic and international students; for spring admission, 12/10 priority date for domestic and international students. Applications are processed on a rolling basis. Application fee: $40. Electronic applications accepted. *Expenses:* Tuition: Part-time $265 per credit hour. Tuition and fees vary according to course load and program. *Financial support:* In 2007–08, 53 students received support, including 4 fellowships (averaging $1,060 per year); Federal Work-Study and scholarships/grants also available. Support available to part-time students. Financial award application deadline: 7/15; financial award applicants required to submit FAFSA. *Faculty research:* Elderly blacks, film, feminist economics, U.S. voting patterns, Wagner, diversity. *Unit head:* Dr. Edward A. Lynch, Director, 540-362-6475, Fax: 540-362-6288, E-mail: elynch@hollins.edu. *Application contact:* Cathy S. Koon, Manager of Graduate Services, 540-362-6326, Fax: 540-362-6288, E-mail: ckoon@hollins.edu.

Houston Baptist University, College of Arts and Humanities, Program in Liberal Arts, Houston, TX 77074-3298. Offers MLA. Part-time and evening/weekend programs available. *Faculty:* 10 full-time (5 women), 4 part-time/adjunct (1 woman). *Students:* 3 full-time (all women), 40 part-time (25 women); includes 13 minority (9 African Americans, 2 Asian Americans or Pacific Islanders, 2 Hispanic Americans), 1 international. Average age 39. 25 applicants, 80% accepted, 15 enrolled. In 2007, 10 degrees awarded. *Entrance requirements:* For master's, interview, minimum GPA of 2.5, writing sample. Additional exam requirements/recommendations for international students: Required—TOEFL (minimum score 550 paper-based; 213 computer-based). *Application deadline:* For fall admission, 7/1 priority date for domestic and international students; for winter admission, 10/1 priority date for domestic and international students; for spring admission, 1/1 priority date for domestic and international students. Applications are processed on a rolling basis. Application fee: $25 ($100 for international students). *Expenses:* Tuition: Part-time $1,416 per course. Required fees: $190 per quarter. *Financial support:* Federal Work-Study available. Support available to part-time students. Financial award application deadline: 3/1; financial award applicants required to submit FAFSA. *Unit head:* Dr. Christopher Hammons, Director, 281-649-3270, Fax: 281-649-3012, E-mail: chammons@hbu.edu. *Application contact:* Jennie Hedger, Secretary, 281-649-3269, Fax: 281-649-3012, E-mail: jhedger@hbu.edu.

Indiana University Kokomo, School of Arts and Sciences, Kokomo, IN 46904-9003. Offers liberal studies (MALS). *Faculty:* 32 full-time (10 women). *Students:* 5 full-time (all women), 14 part-time (10 women); includes 2 minority (1 African American, 1 Hispanic American). Average age 39. In 2007, 2 degrees awarded. *Degree requirements:* For master's, thesis. *Entrance requirements:* For master's, minimum GPA of 3.0. Additional exam requirements/recommendations for international students: Required—TOEFL. *Application deadline:* For fall admission, 4/15 priority date for domestic students; for spring admission, 10/15 priority date for domestic students. Applications are processed on a rolling basis. Application fee: $50. *Expenses:* Tuition, state resident: full-time $4,698; part-time $196 per credit hour. Tuition, nonresident: full-time $10,746; part-time $448 per credit hour. Required fees: $397; $397 per year. Full-time tuition and fees vary according to course load, campus/location and program. *Faculty research:* Bibliography and textual studies, comparative literature, current global issues/political science. *Unit head:* Dr. Susan Sciame-Giesecke, Dean, 765-455-9258, Fax: 765-455-9566, E-mail: sgieseck@iuk.edu.

Indiana University–Purdue University Fort Wayne, College of Arts and Sciences, Program in Liberal Studies, Fort Wayne, IN 46805-1499. Offers MLS. Part-time programs available. *Students:* 4 full-time (3 women), 14 part-time (6 women); includes 4 minority (all African Americans) Average age 35. 6 applicants, 100% accepted, 5 enrolled. In 2007, 6 degrees awarded. *Entrance requirements:* For master's, minimum GPA of 3.0, major or minor in related area. Additional exam requirements/recommendations for international students: Required—TOEFL (minimum score 550 paper-based; 213 computer-based; 77 iBT). *Application deadline:* For fall admission, 8/1 for domestic students; for spring admission, 12/1 for domestic students. Applications are processed on a rolling basis. Application fee: $30. *Expenses:* Tuition, state resident: full-time $4,203; part-time $234 per credit. Tuition, nonresident: full-time $9,761; part-time $542 per credit. Required fees: $466; $26 per credit. Tuition and fees vary according to course load. *Financial support:* Scholarships/grants available. Support available to part-time students. Financial award application deadline: 3/1; financial award applicants required to submit FAFSA. *Unit head:* Dr. Michael E. Kaufmann, Director, 260-481-6760, Fax: 260-481-6985, E-mail: kaufmann@ipfw.edu.

Indiana University–Purdue University Indianapolis, School of Liberal Arts, Indianapolis, IN 46202-2896. Offers MA, MS, XMA, PhD, Certificate, JD/MA, MA/MA, MD/MA, MPA/MA, MSN/MA. *Students:* 86 full-time (59 women), 230 part-time (146 women); includes 45 minority (24 African Americans, 2 American Indian/Alaska Native, 13 Asian Americans or Pacific Islanders, 6 Hispanic Americans), 24 international. Average age 32. *Expenses:* Tuition, state resident: full-time $5,818; part-time $242 per credit hour. Tuition, nonresident: full-time $17,106; part-time $713 per credit hour. Required fees: $629. Tuition and fees vary according to course load, campus/location and program. *Unit head:* Robert W. White, Dean, School of Liberal Arts, 317-274-8448. *Application contact:* Director of Research and Graduate Programs, 317-274-8305.

Indiana University South Bend, College of Liberal Arts and Sciences, South Bend, IN 46634-7111. Offers applied mathematics and computer science (MS); applied psychology (MA); English (MA); liberal studies (MLS). Part-time and evening/weekend programs available. *Faculty:* 79 full-time (33 women). *Students:* 11 full-time (6 women), 71 part-time (44 women); includes 14 minority (8 African Americans, 1 American Indian/Alaska Native, 3 Asian Americans or Pacific Islanders, 2 Hispanic Americans), 8 international. Average age 37. In 2007, 24 degrees awarded. *Degree requirements:* For master's, thesis (for some programs). *Entrance requirements:* For master's, minimum GPA of 3.0. Additional exam requirements/recommendations for international students: Required—TOEFL. *Application deadline:* For fall admission, 7/31 priority date for domestic students, 7/1 priority date for international students; for spring admission, 3/31 priority date for domestic students, 11/1 priority date for international students. Applications are processed on a rolling basis. Application fee: $46 ($58 for international students). *Expenses:* Tuition, state resident: full-time $4,762; part-time $198 per credit hour. Tuition, nonresident: full-time $11,720; part-time $488 per credit hour. Required fees: $422; $422 per year. Full-time tuition and fees vary according to course load, campus/location and program. *Financial support:* In 2007–08, 5 students received support, including 5 teaching assistantships; Federal Work-Study also available. Support available to part-time students. *Faculty research:* Artificial intelligence, bioinformatics, English language and literature, creative writing, computer networks. Total annual research expenditures: $127,000. *Unit head:* Dr. Lynn R. Williams, Dean, 574-520-4322, Fax: 574-520-4528, E-mail: lwilliam@iusb.edu.

Indiana University Southeast, Program in Liberal Studies, New Albany, IN 47150-6405. Offers MLS. *Students:* 1 (woman) full-time, 32 part-time (21 women); includes 5 minority (4 African Americans, 1 Hispanic American). Average age 41. In 2007, 2 degrees awarded. *Degree requirements:* For master's, thesis or alternative. *Entrance requirements:* For master's, 3 letters of recommendation. Application fee: $35. *Expenses:* Tuition, state resident: full-time $4,800; part-time $200 per credit hour. Tuition, nonresident: full-time $10,910; part-time $455 per credit hour. Required fees: $442; $442 per year. Full-time tuition and fees vary according to course load, campus/location and program. *Unit head:* Dr. Sandra S. French, Director, 812-941-2393, E-mail: sfrench@ius.edu. *Application contact:* Debra Voyles, Administrative Assistant, 812-941-2604, E-mail: davoyles@ius.edu.

Jacksonville State University, College of Graduate Studies and Continuing Education, College of Arts and Sciences, Department of Liberal Studies, Jacksonville, AL 36265-1602. Offers MA. *Students:* 1 (woman) full-time, 22 part-time (11 women); includes 10 minority (all African Americans) In 2007, 6 degrees awarded. *Financial support:* Application deadline: 4/1.

The Johns Hopkins University, Zanvyl Krieger School of Arts and Sciences, Advanced Academic Programs, Program in Liberal Arts, Washington, DC 20036. Offers MA, Certificate. Part-time and evening/weekend programs available. *Students:* 35 applicants, 63% accepted, 22 enrolled. *Degree requirements:* For master's, thesis. *Entrance requirements:* Additional exam requirements/recommendations for international students: Required—TOEFL (minimum score 250 computer-based; 100 iBT). *Application deadline:* For fall admission, 5/31 priority date for domestic students, 4/30 priority date for international students; for spring admission, 10/31 priority date for domestic and international students. Applications are processed on a rolling basis. Application fee: $70. Electronic applications accepted. *Financial support:* Applicants required to submit FAFSA. *Unit head:* Dr. Melissa Hilbish, Associate Program Chair, 410-516-4640, E-mail: mhilbish@jhu.edu. *Application contact:* Rachel C. Jenkins, Admissions Manager, 202-452-1941, Fax: 202-452-1970, E-mail: aapadmissions@jhu.edu.

See Close-Up on page 453.

Kean University, School of Visual and Performing Arts, Program in Liberal Studies, Union, NJ 07083. Offers MA. Part-time and evening/weekend programs available. *Students:* 4 full-time (3 women), 19 part-time (12 women); includes 4 African Americans, 1 Hispanic American. Average age 37. 8 applicants, 100% accepted, 5 enrolled. In 2007, 4 degrees awarded. *Degree requirements:* For master's, comprehensive exam, thesis, final project. *Entrance requirements:* For master's, 3 letters of recommendation, minimum GPA of 3.0, interview, essay. *Application deadline:* For fall admission, 5/1 for domestic students; for spring admission, 11/1 for domestic students. Application fee: $60 ($150 for international students). Electronic applications accepted. *Expenses:* Tuition, state resident: full-time $9,384; part-time $391 per credit. Tuition, nonresident: full-time $12,720; part-time $530 per credit. Required fees: $2,382; $99 per credit. Part-time tuition and fees vary according to course load. *Financial support:* In 2007–08, 3 research assistantships with full tuition reimbursements (averaging $3,217 per year) were awarded; unspecified assistantships also available. *Unit head:* Dr. John C. Gruesser, Program Coordinator, 908-737-4192, E-mail: jgruesse@kean.edu. *Application contact:* Joanne Morris, Director of Graduate Admissions, 908-737-3355, Fax: 908-737-3354, E-mail: grad-adm@kean.edu.

Kent State University, College of Arts and Sciences, Program in Liberal Studies, Kent, OH 44242-0001. Offers MLS. Part-time programs available. *Students:* 9 full-time (7 women), 18 part-time (10 women); includes 6 minority (5 African Americans, 1 Asian American or Pacific Islander). 15 applicants, 100% accepted. In 2007, 7 degrees awarded. *Degree requirements:* For master's, thesis. *Entrance requirements:* For master's, minimum GPA of 2.75. *Application deadline:* For fall admission, 7/12 for domestic students; for spring admission, 11/29 for domestic students. Applications are processed on a rolling basis. Application fee: $30. Electronic applications accepted. *Financial support:* Institutionally sponsored loans available. *Unit head:* Dr. Alison J. Smith, Director, 330-672-9878, Fax: 330-672-2938.

Lake Forest College, Graduate Program in Liberal Studies, Lake Forest, IL 60045-2399. Offers MLS. Part-time and evening/weekend programs available. *Faculty:* 15 full-time (6 women), 1 part-time/adjunct (0 women). *Students:* 1 full-time (0 women), 41 part-time (23 women); includes 3 minority (2 African Americans, 1 Asian American or Pacific Islander). Average age 40. 27 applicants, 59% accepted, 10 enrolled. In 2007, 8 degrees awarded. *Degree requirements:* For master's, thesis optional, 8 courses completed. *Entrance requirements:* For master's, interview, application, essay. *Application deadline:* For fall admission, 7/1 priority date for domestic students; for spring admission, 12/1 priority date for domestic students. Applications are processed on a rolling basis. Application fee: $20. *Expenses:* Tuition: Full-time $7,600; part-time $1,900 per course. *Financial support:* In 2007–08, 8 students received support. Partial tuition waivers for full-time teachers available. Financial award application deadline: 7/1; financial award applicants required to submit FAFSA. *Faculty research:* Latin American film, the European Left, solid state chemistry, cast iron architecture, concepts of education in 19th century America. *Unit head:* Prof. D. L. LeMahieu, Director, 847-735-5133,

Fax: 847-735-6291, E-mail: lemahieu@lakeforest.edu. *Application contact:* Prof. Carol Gayle, Associate Director, Graduate Program in Liberal Studies, 847-735-5083, Fax: 847-735-6291, E-mail: gayle@lakeforest.edu.

Lock Haven University of Pennsylvania, Office of Graduate Studies, Department of Liberal Arts, Lock Haven, PA 17745-2390. Offers MLA. *Degree requirements:* For master's, thesis. *Entrance requirements:* For master's, minimum undergraduate GPA of 3.0. Additional exam requirements/recommendations for international students: Required—TOEFL. Electronic applications accepted.

Louisiana State University and Agricultural and Mechanical College, Graduate School, College of Arts and Sciences, Interdepartmental Program in the Liberal Arts, Baton Rouge, LA 70803. Offers MALA. Part-time and evening/weekend programs available. *Faculty:* 1 full-time (0 women). *Students:* 8 full-time (3 women), 18 part-time (12 women); includes 2 minority (both African Americans) Average age 36. 5 applicants, 100% accepted. In 2007, 21 master's awarded. *Degree requirements:* For master's, project or thesis. *Entrance requirements:* For master's, GRE General Test, minimum GPA of 3.0. Additional exam requirements/recommendations for international students: Required—TOEFL (minimum score 550 paper-based; 213 computer-based; 79 iBT). *Application deadline:* For fall admission, 1/25 priority date for domestic students, 5/15 for international students; for spring admission, 10/15 for international students. Applications are processed on a rolling basis. Application fee: $25. Electronic applications accepted. *Financial support:* In 2007–08, 13 students received support; fellowships with full tuition reimbursements available, research assistantships with partial tuition reimbursements available, teaching assistantships with partial tuition reimbursements available, Federal Work-Study and health care benefits available. Financial award applicants required to submit FAFSA. *Unit head:* Dr. William Clark, Director, 225-578-3183, Fax: 225-578-6447.

Louisiana State University in Shreveport, College of Liberal Arts, Program in Liberal Arts, Shreveport, LA 71115-2399. Offers MA. Part-time and evening/weekend programs available. *Faculty:* 28 full-time (13 women). *Students:* 7 full-time (6 women), 39 part-time (27 women); includes 8 minority (6 African Americans, 1 Asian American or Pacific Islander, 1 Hispanic American). Average age 38. 24 applicants, 79% accepted, 12 enrolled. In 2007, 6 degrees awarded. *Degree requirements:* For master's, comprehensive exam, thesis or alternative, 33 credit-hour curriculum. *Entrance requirements:* For master's, interview, minimum GPA of 3.0 during final 2 years of course work, statement of purpose. Additional exam requirements/recommendations for international students: Required—TOEFL (minimum score 500 paper-based; 173 computer-based; 61 iBT). *Application deadline:* For fall admission, 6/30 for domestic and international students; for spring admission, 11/30 for domestic and international students. Applications are processed on a rolling basis. Application fee: $10. *Financial support:* In 2007–08, 3 students received support, including 3 research assistantships with partial tuition reimbursements available (averaging $30,000 per year). *Unit head:* Dr. Helen Taylor, Program Director, 318-797-5211, Fax: 318-797-5358, E-mail: helen.taylor@lsus.edu.

Loyola College in Maryland, Graduate Programs, College of Arts and Sciences, Program in Liberal Studies, Baltimore, MD 21210-2699. Offers MMS. Part-time and evening/weekend programs available. *Entrance requirements:* For master's, GRE General Test, GRE Subject Test (recommended). Additional exam requirements/recommendations for international students: Required—TOEFL (minimum score 550 paper-based; 213 computer-based).

See Close-Up on page 455.

Madonna University, Program in Liberal Studies, Livonia, MI 48150-1173. Offers MALS.

Manhattanville College, Graduate Programs, Humanities and Social Sciences Programs, Program in Liberal Studies, Purchase, NY 10577-2132. Offers MA. Part-time and evening/weekend programs available. *Degree requirements:* For master's, thesis. *Entrance requirements:* For master's, interview, 2 letters of recommendation.

McDaniel College, Graduate and Professional Studies, Program in Liberal Studies, Westminster, MD 21157-4390. Offers MLA. Part-time and evening/weekend programs available. *Degree requirements:* For master's, final project. *Entrance requirements:* For master's, letters of reference (3). Additional exam requirements/recommendations for international students: Required—TOEFL (minimum score 213 computer-based).

Metropolitan State University, College of Arts and Sciences, St. Paul, MN 55106-5000. Offers computer science (MS); liberal studies (MA); technical communication (MS). Part-time and evening/weekend programs available. *Faculty:* 12 full-time (7 women), 4 part-time/adjunct (3 women). *Students:* 17 full-time (13 women), 51 part-time (31 women); includes 8 minority (2 African Americans, 2 American Indian/Alaska Native, 2 Asian Americans or Pacific Islanders, 2 Hispanic Americans), 6 international. Average age 39. In 2007, 21 degrees awarded. *Entrance requirements:* For master's, BA/BS; 2.75 GPA; resum&e. Additional exam requirements/recommendations for international students: Required—TOEFL (minimum score 550 paper-based; 213 computer-based). *Application deadline:* For fall admission, 8/1 priority date for domestic students, 3/15 for international students; for winter admission, 10/15 for international students; for spring admission, 12/1 priority date for domestic students, 3/15 for international students. Application fee: $20. *Expenses:* Tuition, state resident: full-time $5,080; part-time $254 per credit. Tuition, nonresident: full-time $10,160; part-time $508 per credit. Required fees: $189; $34 per credit. *Financial support:* Applicants required to submit FAFSA. *Faculty research:* Computer security, software engineering, distributed systems, document design, diffusing of innovations, social issues and communication technology. *Unit head:* Dr. Ed Malecki, Dean, 651-793-1443, Fax: 651-793-1446, E-mail: ed.malecki@metrostate.edu.

Minnesota State University Moorhead, Graduate Studies, College of Arts and Humanities, Program in Liberal Studies, Moorhead, MN 56563-0002. Offers MLA. Part-time and evening/weekend programs available. *Degree requirements:* For master's, thesis, final oral exam. *Entrance requirements:* For master's, minimum GPA of 2.75. Additional exam requirements/recommendations for international students: Required—TOEFL (minimum score 570 paper-based; 230 computer-based). Electronic applications accepted.

Mississippi College, Graduate School, Program in Liberal Studies, Clinton, MS 39058. Offers MLS. Part-time programs available. In 2007, 1 degree awarded. *Degree requirements:* For master's, comprehensive exam, thesis optional. *Entrance requirements:* For master's, GRE, minimum GPA of 2.5. Additional exam requirements/recommendations for international students: Recommended—IELTS. Application fee: $25. *Expenses:* Tuition: Full-time $7,470; part-time $415 per hour. Required fees: $1,160 per term. Part-time tuition and fees vary according to course load and degree level. *Financial support:* Federal Work-Study and unspecified assistantships available. Support available to part-time students. Financial award application deadline: 4/1; financial award applicants required to submit FAFSA. *Unit head:* Dr. Debbie C. Norris, Graduate Dean, 601-925-3260, Fax: 601-925-3889, E-mail: dnorris@mc.edu.

Monmouth University, Graduate School, Program in Liberal Arts, West Long Branch, NJ 07764-1898. Offers MA. Part-time and evening/weekend programs available. *Faculty:* 10 full-time (4 women), 2 part-time/adjunct (both women). *Students:* 3 full-time (1 woman), 15 part-time (11 women); includes 2 minority (1 African American, 1 Hispanic American), 2 international. Average age 37. 7 applicants, 100% accepted, 5 enrolled. In 2007, 6 degrees awarded. *Degree requirements:* For master's, thesis or alternative, project. *Entrance requirements:* For master's, minimum GPA of 3.0 in major, 2.5 overall. Additional exam requirements/recommendations for international students: Required—TOEFL (minimum score 550 paper-based; 213 computer-based; 79 iBT), IELTS (minimum score 5), MELAB 77, Cambridge A, B, C. *Application deadline:* For fall admission, 7/15 priority date for domestic students, 6/1 for international students; for spring admission, 11/15 priority date for domestic students, 11/1 for international students. Applications are processed on a rolling basis. Application fee: $50. Electronic applications accepted. *Financial support:* In 2007–08, 5 students received support, including 5 fellowships (averaging $1,050 per year), 1 research assistantship (averaging $14,706 per year); career-related internships or fieldwork, scholarships/grants, tuition waivers (partial), and unspecified assistantships also available. Support available to part-time students. Financial award application deadline: 3/1; financial award applicants required to submit FAFSA. *Faculty research:* Labor history, war and society, technology, historical archeology, art and society. *Unit head:* Dr. Richard Veit, Director, 732-571-4496, Fax: 732-263-5192, E-mail: rveit@monmouth.edu. *Application contact:* Kevin Roane, Director, Office of Graduate Admission, 732-571-3452, Fax: 732-263-5123, E-mail: gradadm@monmouth.edu.

Nazareth College of Rochester, Graduate Studies, Department of Liberal Studies, Rochester, NY 14618-3790. Offers MA. *Faculty:* 2 part-time/adjunct (1 woman). *Students:* Average age 30. 19 applicants, 100% accepted, 19 enrolled. In 2007, 13 degrees awarded. *Entrance requirements:* For master's, minimum GPA of 3.0. *Application deadline:* For fall admission, 8/1 priority date for domestic students; for spring admission, 11/1 priority date for domestic students. Application fee: $40. *Financial support:* Research assistantships with partial tuition reimbursements available. Financial award application deadline: 3/1; financial award applicants required to submit FAFSA. *Unit head:* Dr. Monica Weis, Director, 585-389-2637, Fax: 585-389-2817, E-mail: mweis9@naz.edu. *Application contact:* Judith G. Baker, Director, Graduate Admissions, 585-389-2050, Fax: 585-389-2817, E-mail: gradstudies@naz.edu.

The New School: A University, The New School for Social Research, Committee on Liberal Studies, New York, NY 10011. Offers MA. Part-time and evening/weekend programs available. *Faculty:* 5 full-time (4 women), 5 part-time/adjunct (2 women). *Students:* 25 full-time (16 women), 23 part-time (16 women); includes 6 minority (3 African Americans, 1 Asian American or Pacific Islander, 2 Hispanic Americans), 9 international. Average age 27. In 2007, 19 degrees awarded. *Degree requirements:* For master's, thesis. *Entrance requirements:* For master's, GRE General Test. Additional exam requirements/recommendations for international students: Required—TOEFL (minimum score 600 paper-based; 250 computer-based; 100 iBT). *Application deadline:* For fall admission, 1/15 priority date for domestic students. Applications are processed on a rolling basis. Application fee: $50. *Financial support:* Fellowships, research assistantships, teaching assistantships, career-related internships or fieldwork, Federal Work-Study, scholarships/grants, and tuition waivers (full and partial) available. Financial award application deadline: 3/1; financial award applicants required to submit FAFSA. *Faculty research:* Intellectual history, public intellectuals, popular culture. *Unit head:* Dr. Elzbieta Matynia, Director, 212-229-5580 Ext. 3138, E-mail: matynia@newschool.edu. *Application contact:* Robert MacDonald, Director of Admissions, 800-523-5710 Ext. 3007, Fax: 212-989-7102, E-mail: macdonar@newschool.edu.

See Close-Up on page 1653.

North Carolina State University, Graduate School, College of Humanities and Social Sciences, Program in Liberal Studies, Raleigh, NC 27695. Offers MA. Part-time and evening/weekend programs available. *Degree requirements:* For master's, thesis optional. Electronic applications accepted. *Faculty research:* Humanities, social sciences, sciences.

North Central College, Graduate Programs, Department of Liberal Studies, Naperville, IL 60566-7063. Offers MALS. Part-time and evening/weekend programs available. *Faculty:* 4 full-time (2 women), 1 (woman) part-time/adjunct. *Students:* 6 full-time (3 women), 16 part-time (11 women); includes 2 minority (1 American Indian/Alaska Native, 1 Hispanic American). Average age 33. In 2007, 8 degrees awarded. *Degree requirements:* For master's, project. *Entrance requirements:* For master's, interview. *Application deadline:* For fall admission, 8/15 for domestic students; for winter admission, 12/1 for domestic students; for spring admission, 2/1 for domestic students. Applications are processed on a rolling basis. Application fee: $25. *Expenses: Contact institution.* Tuition and fees vary according to program. *Financial support:* Scholarships/grants available. Support available to part-time students. *Unit head:* Dr. Richard Guzman, Head, 630-637-5285. *Application contact:* Martha Stolze, Director and Graduate and Continuing Education Admissions, 630-637-5840, Fax: 630-637-5844, E-mail: mastolze@noctrl.edu.

Northern Arizona University, Graduate College, College of Arts and Letters, Program in Liberal Studies, Flagstaff, AZ 86011. Offers MLS. Part-time programs available.

Northern Kentucky University, Office of Graduate Programs, College of Arts and Sciences, Program in Liberal Studies, Highland Heights, KY 41099. Offers MALS. Part-time and evening/weekend programs available. Postbaccalaureate distance learning degree programs offered (no on-campus study). *Faculty:* 1 (woman) full-time, 1 part-time/adjunct (0 women). *Students:* 4 full-time (3 women), 40 part-time (25 women); includes 6 minority (4 African Americans, 1 Asian American or Pacific Islander, 1 Hispanic American), 1 international. Average age 40. 21 applicants, 62% accepted, 12 enrolled. In 2007, 3 degrees awarded. *Degree requirements:* For master's, thesis. *Entrance requirements:* For master's, minimum GPA of 3.0, resumé, 2 letters of recommendation, 1 letter of intent. Additional exam requirements/recommendations for international students: Required—TOEFL (minimum score 550 paper-based; 213 computer-based; 79 iBT), Michigan English Language Assessment Battery (must be taken at NKU). *Application deadline:* For fall admission, 7/1 priority date for domestic students, 6/1 for international students; for spring admission, 11/1 priority date for domestic students, 10/1 for international students. Applications are processed on a rolling basis. Application fee: $40. Electronic applications accepted. *Financial support:* Unspecified assistantships available. *Faculty research:* Civic engagement, education and diversity. *Unit head:* Dr. Debra Meyers, MALS Director, 859-572-5831, Fax: 859-572-6185, E-mail: meyersde@nku.edu. *Application contact:* Dr. Peg Griffin, Director of Graduate Programs, 859-572-1555, Fax: 859-572-6670, E-mail: gradprog@nku.edu.

Northwestern University, The Graduate School, Interdepartmental Degree Programs, Interdisciplinary Program in Liberal Studies, Evanston, IL 60208. Offers MA. Admissions and degree offered through The Graduate School. Part-time and evening/weekend programs available. *Degree requirements:* For master's, thesis. *Entrance requirements:* For master's, writing sample. Additional exam requirements/recommendations for international students: Required—TOEFL. *Faculty research:* Urban and social history, literary criticism and comparative literature, women's studies, media and film criticism, philosophy.

Oakland University, Graduate Study and Lifelong Learning, College of Arts and Sciences, Program in Liberal Studies, Rochester, MI 48309-4401. Offers MA. *Students:* 5 full-time (all women), 14 part-time (12 women); includes 1 minority (American Indian/Alaska Native). Average age 45. 7 applicants, 57% accepted, 2 enrolled. In 2007, 2 degrees awarded. *Entrance requirements:* For master's, minimum GPA of 3.0 for unconditional admission. Additional exam requirements/recommendations for international students: Required—TOEFL (minimum score 550 paper-based; 213 computer-based). *Application deadline:* For fall admission, 7/15 priority date for domestic students, 5/1 priority date for international students; for winter admission, 12/1 priority date for domestic students, 9/1 priority date for international students; for spring admission, 3/15 priority date for domestic students. Applications are processed on a rolling basis. Application fee: $35. Electronic applications accepted. *Expenses:* Tuition, state resident: full-time $9,936; part-time $414 per credit. Tuition, nonresident: full-time $17,202; part-time $716 per credit. *Financial support:* Application deadline: 3/1; *Unit head:* Dr. Natalie B. Cole, Coordinator, 248-370-2539, Fax: 248-370-4429, E-mail: cole@oakland.edu.

Occidental College, Graduate Studies, Department of Education, Program in Elementary Education, Los Angeles, CA 90041-3314. Offers liberal studies (MAT). Part-time programs available. *Faculty:* 3 full-time (2 women), 3 part-time/adjunct (2 women). *Students:* 4 full-time (all women), 2 part-time (both women); includes 5 minority (2 Asian Americans or Pacific Islanders, 3 Hispanic Americans). Average age 25. 5 applicants, 100% accepted, 5 enrolled. In 2007, 4 degrees awarded. *Degree requirements:* For master's, final exam, graduate synthesis paper. *Entrance requirements:* For master's, GRE General Test, minimum GPA of 3.0. Additional exam requirements/recommendations for international students: Required—TOEFL (minimum score 625 paper-based; 263 computer-based). *Application deadline:* For fall admission, 3/1 for domestic and international students; for spring admission, 10/1 for domestic and international

Liberal Studies

Occidental College (continued)

students. Applications are processed on a rolling basis. Application fee: $50. *Expenses:* *Contact institution.* Tuition and fees vary according to program. *Financial support:* Fellowships, Federal Work-Study, institutionally sponsored loans, and scholarships/grants available. Support available to part-time students. Financial award application deadline: 3/1; financial award applicants required to submit FAFSA. *Unit head:* Chair, 323-259-2781, E-mail: edudept@oxy.edu. *Application contact:* Angela Allen, Credential Analyst/Department Services Coordinator, 323-259-2781, E-mail: edudept@oxy.edu.

Ohio Dominican University, Graduate Programs, Program in Liberal Studies, Columbus, OH 43219-2099. Offers MA. Part-time and evening/weekend programs available. *Students:* 1 (woman) full-time, 16 part-time (11 women); includes 3 minority (all African Americans) Average age 32. In 2007, 1 degree awarded. *Degree requirements:* For master's, comprehensive exam or thesis. *Entrance requirements:* For master's, minimum undergraduate GPA of 3.0, 3 letters of recommendation. Additional exam requirements/recommendations for international students: Required—TOEFL (minimum score 550 paper-based; 213 computer-based). *Application deadline:* For fall admission, 7/15 priority date for domestic and international students; for spring admission, 12/15 priority date for domestic and international students. Applications are processed on a rolling basis. Application fee: $25. *Expenses:* Tuition: Part-time $450 per credit hour. Required fees: $10 per semester. *Financial support:* Applicants required to submit FAFSA. *Unit head:* Jeremy Glaizer, Director of MA in Liberal Studies, 614-251-4756, E-mail: glaizerj@ohiodominican.edu. *Application contact:* Jill M. Westerfeld, Graduate Admissions Recruiter, 614-251-4725, Fax: 614-251-4634, E-mail: westerfj@ohiodominican.edu.

Oklahoma City University, Petree College of Arts and Sciences, Program in Liberal Arts, Oklahoma City, OK 73106-1402. Offers art (MLA); general studies (MLA); leadership/management (MLA); literature (MLA); mass communications (MLA); philosophy (MLA); writing (MLA). Part-time and evening/weekend programs available. *Faculty:* 18 full-time (7 women), 14 part-time/adjunct (4 women). *Students:* 24 full-time (18 women), 23 part-time (17 women); includes 6 minority (3 African Americans, 1 American Indian/Alaska Native, 1 Asian American or Pacific Islander, 1 Hispanic American), 14 international. Average age 31. 20 applicants, 95% accepted. In 2007, 13 degrees awarded. *Degree requirements:* For master's, comprehensive exam, thesis optional. *Entrance requirements:* Additional exam requirements/recommendations for international students: Required—TOEFL. *Application deadline:* For fall admission, 8/22 for domestic students; for spring admission, 1/15 for domestic students. Applications are processed on a rolling basis. Application fee: $30 ($70 for international students). *Expenses:* Tuition: Full-time $14,040; part-time $780 per hour. Required fees: $881; $32 per hour. *Financial support:* Fellowships with partial tuition reimbursements, career-related internships or fieldwork, Federal Work-Study, institutionally sponsored loans, and tuition waivers (partial) available. Support available to part-time students. Financial award application deadline: 8/1; financial award applicants required to submit FAFSA. *Unit head:* Dr. Regina Benuett, Director, 405-208-5178, Fax: 405-208-5451, E-mail: rebeunett@okcu.edu. *Application contact:* Leslie McKenzie, Director, Graduate Admissions, 800-633-7242, Fax: 405-208-5356, E-mail: gadmissions@okcu.edu.

Queens College of the City University of New York, Division of Graduate Studies, Social Science Division, Program in Liberal Studies, Flushing, NY 11367-1597. Offers MALS. Part-time and evening/weekend programs available. *Faculty:* 4 full-time (0 women). *Students:* 16 applicants, 94% accepted, 6 enrolled. In 2007, 8 degrees awarded. *Degree requirements:* For master's, thesis. *Entrance requirements:* For master's, minimum GPA of 3.0. Additional exam requirements/recommendations for international students: Required—TOEFL. *Application deadline:* For fall admission, 4/1 for domestic students; for spring admission, 11/1 for domestic students. Applications are processed on a rolling basis. Application fee: $125. *Financial support:* Career-related internships or fieldwork, Federal Work-Study, institutionally sponsored loans, and tuition waivers (partial) available. Support available to part-time students. Financial award application deadline: 4/1; financial award applicants required to submit FAFSA. *Unit head:* Dr. Nick Jordan, Graduate Adviser, 718-997-5350. *Application contact:* Mario Caruso, Director of Graduate Admissions, 718-997-5200, Fax: 718-997-5193, E-mail: graduate_admissions@qc.edu.

Ramapo College of New Jersey, Program in Liberal Studies, Mahwah, NJ 07430-1680. Offers MALS. Part-time and evening/weekend programs available. *Faculty:* 15 part-time/adjunct (7 women). *Students:* 49 (31 women); includes 23 minority (2 African Americans, 1 Asian American or Pacific Islander, 20 Hispanic Americans). 17 applicants, 100% accepted, 14 enrolled. In 2007, 13 degrees awarded. *Degree requirements:* For master's, thesis. *Entrance requirements:* For master's, minimum undergraduate GPA of 3.0, 2 letters of recommendation. Additional exam requirements/recommendations for international students: Required—TOEFL. *Application deadline:* For fall admission, 9/1 priority date for domestic and international students; for spring admission, 1/30 priority date for domestic and international students. Applications are processed on a rolling basis. Application fee: $55. Electronic applications accepted. *Expenses:* Tuition, state resident: part-time $472 per unit. Tuition, nonresident: part-time $607 per unit. Required fees: $44 per unit. *Financial support:* Tuition waivers (full) available. Financial award applicants required to submit FAFSA. *Faculty research:* History of science, women's studies, Native American studies, theology, genocide studies. *Unit head:* Dr. Anthony T. Padovano, Director, 201-684-7430, Fax: 201-684-7973, E-mail: apadovan@ramapo.edu. *Application contact:* Melissa C. Kupfer, MALS Secretary, 201-684-7709, Fax: 201-684-7973, E-mail: mkupfer@ramapo.edu.

Reed College, Graduate Program in Liberal Studies, Portland, OR 97202-8199. Offers MALS. Part-time and evening/weekend programs available. *Faculty:* 16 part-time/adjunct (5 women). *Students:* Average age 37. 19 applicants, 37% accepted, 6 enrolled. In 2007, 6 degrees awarded. *Degree requirements:* For master's, thesis, oral defense of thesis. *Entrance requirements:* For master's, interview, letters of recommendation. *Application deadline:* For fall admission, 7/1 priority date for domestic students; for spring admission, 12/1 priority date for domestic students. Applications are processed on a rolling basis. Application fee: $60. *Expenses:* Tuition: Part-time $3,280 per unit. Part-time tuition and fees vary according to program. *Financial support:* In 2007–08, 4 students received support. Scholarships/grants and health care benefits available. Support available to part-time students. Financial award application deadline: 5/1; financial award applicants required to submit CSS PROFILE or FAFSA. *Unit head:* Barbara A. Amen, Director, Graduate Studies, 503-777-7259, Fax: 503-517-7345, E-mail: bamen@reed.edu.

Rollins College, Hamilton Holt School, Program in Liberal Studies, Winter Park, FL 32789-4499. Offers MLS. Part-time and evening/weekend programs available. *Students:* 2 full-time (1 woman), 75 part-time (46 women); includes 8 minority (3 African Americans, 5 Hispanic Americans). Average age 41. In 2007, 15 degrees awarded. *Degree requirements:* For master's, thesis. *Entrance requirements:* For master's, GRE or MAT, interview. Additional exam requirements/recommendations for international students: Required—TOEFL. *Application deadline:* For fall admission, 12/1 for domestic students; for spring admission, 4/1 for domestic students. Application fee: $50. Electronic applications accepted. *Expenses:* *Contact institution.* *Financial support:* Institutionally sponsored loans and scholarships/grants available. Support available to part-time students. *Unit head:* Dr. Robert Smither, Director, 407-646-2237, Fax: 407-646-2363. *Application contact:* Claire Thiebault, Coordinator of Records and Registration, 407-646-2653, Fax: 407-646-1551, E-mail: cthiebault@rollins.edu.

Rutgers, The State University of New Jersey, Camden, Graduate School of Arts and Sciences, Program in Liberal Studies, Camden, NJ 08102-1401. Offers MA. Part-time and evening/weekend programs available.

Rutgers, The State University of New Jersey, Newark, Graduate School, Program in Liberal Studies, Newark, NJ 07102. Offers MALS. Part-time and evening/weekend programs available. *Degree requirements:* For master's, thesis. *Entrance requirements:* For master's, GRE, minimum B average. Electronic applications accepted.

St. Edward's University, New College, Program in Liberal Arts, Austin, TX 78704. Offers MLA, Certificate. Part-time and evening/weekend programs available. *Faculty:* 24 full-time (9 women), 4 part-time/adjunct (1 woman). *Students:* 8 full-time (7 women), 76 part-time (47 women); includes 21 minority (4 African Americans, 1 American Indian/Alaska Native, 16 Hispanic Americans), 1 international. Average age 33. 37 applicants, 86% accepted, 30 enrolled. In 2007, 35 degrees awarded. *Degree requirements:* For master's, minimum 24 resident hours. *Entrance requirements:* For master's, minimum GPA of 2.75 in last 60 hours of course work, interview. Additional exam requirements/recommendations for international students: Required—TOEFL (minimum score 550 paper-based; 213 computer-based; 79 iBT). *Application deadline:* For fall admission, 8/1 for domestic students, 7/1 for international students; for spring admission, 12/1 for domestic students, 11/1 for international students. Applications are processed on a rolling basis. Application fee: $45 ($50 for international students). Electronic applications accepted. *Expenses:* Tuition: Full-time $12,672; part-time $704 per credit hour. Full-time tuition and fees vary according to program. Part-time tuition and fees vary according to course load. *Financial support:* In 2007–08, 3 students received support. Scholarships/grants available. Financial award applicants required to submit FAFSA. *Unit head:* Dr. Paula Marks, Director, 512-448-8702, Fax: 512-448-8492, E-mail: paulam@stewards.edu. *Application contact:* Kay L. Arnold, Graduate Admissions Coordinator, 512-233-1636, Fax: 512-428-1032, E-mail: kayla@stedwards.edu.

St. John's College, Graduate Institute in Liberal Education, Annapolis, MD 21404. Offers liberal arts (MALA). Evening/weekend programs available. *Faculty:* 13 full-time (2 women), 5 part-time/adjunct (1 woman). *Students:* 76 full-time (32 women), 6 part-time (4 women); includes 4 minority (1 African American, 1 American Indian/Alaska Native, 1 Asian American or Pacific Islander, 1 Hispanic American). Average age 30. 106 applicants, 68% accepted, 41 enrolled. In 2007, 62 degrees awarded. *Degree requirements:* For master's, thesis optional. *Entrance requirements:* Additional exam requirements/recommendations for international students: Required—TOEFL (minimum score 650 paper-based; 250 computer-based; 112 iBT), TWE (minimum score 5). *Application deadline:* For fall admission, 5/1 priority date for domestic and international students; for winter admission, 10/1 priority date for domestic and international students; for spring admission, 3/15 priority date for domestic and international students. Applications are processed on a rolling basis. Application fee: $0. *Expenses:* Tuition: Full-time $13,272. Required fees: $600. One-time fee: $90 full-time. *Financial support:* In 2007–08, 63 students received support, including 11 fellowships (averaging $7,000 per year); Federal Work-Study and scholarships/grants also available. Financial award applicants required to submit FAFSA. *Unit head:* Marilyn Higuera, Director, 410-626-2542, Fax: 410-626-2880.

St. John's College, Graduate Institute in Liberal Education, Program in Liberal Arts, Santa Fe, NM 87505-4599. Offers MA. Evening/weekend programs available. *Entrance requirements:* For master's, 2 letters of recommendation. Additional exam requirements/recommendations for international students: Required—TOEFL, TWE.

St. John's University, St. John's College of Liberal Arts and Sciences, Program in Liberal Studies, Queens, NY 11439. Offers MA. Part-time and evening/weekend programs available. *Faculty:* 22 full-time (4 women), 26 part-time/adjunct (4 women). *Students:* 1 (woman) full-time, 59 part-time (33 women); includes 11 minority (4 African Americans, 1 American Indian/Alaska Native, 3 Asian Americans or Pacific Islanders, 3 Hispanic Americans), 3 international. Average age 35. 51 applicants, 78% accepted, 31 enrolled. In 2007, 2 degrees awarded. *Entrance requirements:* Additional exam requirements/recommendations for international students: Required—TOEFL (minimum score 500 paper-based; 173 computer-based; 61 iBT), IELTS (minimum score 6). *Application deadline:* For fall admission, 5/1 priority date for domestic and international students; for spring admission, 11/1 priority date for domestic and international students. *Financial support:* Career-related internships or fieldwork and scholarships/grants available. Support available to part-time students. *Unit head:* Fr. Jean-Pierre Ruiz, Director, 718-990-6467, E-mail: ruizj@stjohns.edu. *Application contact:* Beth Evans, Associate Vice President and Executive Director, Enrollment Management, 718-990-6999, Fax: 718-990-5686, E-mail: gradhelp@stjohns.edu.

Saint Mary's College of California, School of Liberal Arts, Graduate Liberal Studies Program, Moraga, CA 94575. Offers MA. Not accepting new students at this time. Part-time and evening/weekend programs available. *Faculty:* 18 part-time/adjunct (9 women). *Students:* 45 (35 women); includes 9 minority (1 African American, 5 Asian Americans or Pacific Islanders, 3 Hispanic Americans). Average age 45. 26 applicants, 85% accepted, 22 enrolled. In 2007, 5 degrees awarded. *Degree requirements:* For master's, thesis or final project. *Entrance requirements:* For master's, interview. *Application deadline:* For fall admission, 7/1 for domestic students. Applications are processed on a rolling basis. Application fee: $50. *Expenses:* *Contact institution.* *Financial support:* In 2007–08, 36 students received support. Federal Work-Study, institutionally sponsored loans, and scholarships/grants available. Financial award application deadline: 6/1; financial award applicants required to submit FAFSA. *Faculty research:* Philosophy, theology, classics, theatre, literature. *Unit head:* Linda E. Saulsby, Acting Director, 925-631-4574, Fax: 925-631-8312, E-mail: lsaulsby@stmarys-ca.edu. *Application contact:* Nancy Wells Brewer, Admissions Counselor, 925-631-8265, Fax: 925-631-8312, E-mail: nbrewer@stmarys-ca.edu.

San Diego State University, Graduate and Research Affairs, College of Arts and Letters, Program in Liberal Arts and Sciences, San Diego, CA 92182. Offers MA. Part-time and evening/weekend programs available. *Students:* 7 full-time (6 women), 10 part-time (6 women); includes 7 minority (1 African American, 1 Asian American or Pacific Islander, 5 Hispanic Americans), 2 international. Average age 29. 2 applicants, 100% accepted, 1 enrolled. In 2007, 6 degrees awarded. *Degree requirements:* For master's, thesis. *Entrance requirements:* For master's, GRE General Test. Additional exam requirements/recommendations for international students: Required—TOEFL. *Application deadline:* For fall admission, 5/1 for domestic and international students; for spring admission, 11/1 for domestic students, 10/1 for international students. Applications are processed on a rolling basis. Application fee: $55. Electronic applications accepted. *Financial support:* In 2007–08, 1 research assistantship was awarded; Federal Work-Study and institutionally sponsored loans also available. Support available to part-time students. Financial award application deadline: 3/2; financial award applicants required to submit FAFSA. *Unit head:* Dr. Alan Kilpatrick, Director, 619-594-1679, Fax: 619-594-2646, E-mail: akilpatr@mail.sdsu.edu.

Simon Fraser University, Graduate Studies, Faculty of Arts and Social Sciences, Program in Liberal Studies, Burnaby, BC V5A 1S6, Canada. Offers MALS. Part-time and evening/weekend programs available. *Degree requirements:* For master's, thesis or alternative. *Entrance requirements:* For master's, minimum GPA of 3.0. Additional exam requirements/recommendations for international students: Required—TOEFL or IELTS. *Faculty research:* Humanities, psychology, history, women's studies, English.

Skidmore College, Liberal Studies Program, Saratoga Springs, NY 12866-1632. Offers MA. Part-time programs available. Postbaccalaureate distance learning degree programs offered (minimal on-campus study). *Faculty:* 78 full-time (38 women), 3 part-time/adjunct (1 woman). *Students:* Average age 42. 32 applicants, 59% accepted, 14 enrolled. In 2007, 6 degrees awarded. *Degree requirements:* For master's, thesis. *Application deadline:* For fall admission, 6/1 priority date for domestic and international students; for spring admission, 10/1 priority date for domestic and international students. Applications are processed on a rolling basis. Application fee: $60. Electronic applications accepted. *Expenses:* Tuition: Part-time $3,300 per year. *Financial support:* In 2007–08, 4 students received support. Career-related internships or fieldwork and scholarships/grants available. Support available to part-time students. Financial award applicants required to submit FAFSA. *Unit head:* Dr. John Anzalone, Director, 518-580-5480, Fax: 518-580-5486. *Application contact:* Information Contact, 518-580-5480, Fax: 518-580-5486, E-mail: mals@skidmore.edu.

Spring Hill College, Graduate Programs, Program in Liberal Arts, Mobile, AL 36608-1791. Offers MLA. Part-time and evening/weekend programs available. *Faculty:* 7 full-time (3 women), 2 part-time/adjunct (1 woman). *Students:* 1 (woman) full-time, 29 part-time (19 women);

includes 9 minority (all African Americans) Average age 36. In 2007, 4 degrees awarded. *Degree requirements:* For master's, capstone course. *Entrance requirements:* For master's, minimum undergraduate GPA of 3.0. Additional exam requirements/recommendations for international students: Required—TOEFL (minimum score 550 paper-based; 213 computer-based). *Application deadline:* For fall admission, 8/1 priority date for domestic students, 6/1 priority date for international students; for spring admission, 12/1 priority date for domestic students, 11/1 priority date for international students. Applications are processed on a rolling basis. Application fee: $25 ($35 for international students). Electronic applications accepted. *Expenses: Contact institution. Financial support:* In 2007–08, 26 students received support. Career-related internships or fieldwork and scholarships/grants available. Support available to part-time students. Financial award applicants required to submit FAFSA. *Unit head:* Dr. Alexander R. Landi, Director, Master of Liberal Arts Program, 251-380-3056, Fax: 251-460-2115, E-mail: landi@shc.edu. *Application contact:* Joyce Genz, Dean of Continuing Studies and Director of Graduate Programs, 251-380-3094, Fax: 251-460-2190, E-mail: grad@shc.edu.

State University of New York at Plattsburgh, School of Business and Economics, Program in Liberal Studies, Plattsburgh, NY 12901-2681. Offers MA. *Faculty:* 4 full-time (1 woman), 3 part-time/adjunct (1 woman). *Students:* 18 full-time (8 women), 38 part-time (24 women); includes 2 Asian Americans or Pacific Islanders, 2 international. Average age 34. 18 applicants, 89% accepted, 13 enrolled. In 2007, 21 degrees awarded. *Expenses:* Tuition, state resident: full-time $6,900; part-time $288 per credit hour. Tuition, nonresident: full-time $10,920; part-time $455 per credit hour. Required fees: $1,036. *Unit head:* Dr. Suzanne Catana, Coordinator, 518-792-5425, E-mail: catanasl@plattsburgh.edu. *Application contact:* Sharon Derr, Assistant Director, Graduate Admission, 518-564-4723, Fax: 518-564-4722, E-mail: derrsl@plattsburgh.edu.

State University of New York Empire State College, Graduate Studies, Program in Liberal Studies, Saratoga Springs, NY 12866-4391. Offers MA. Part-time and evening/weekend programs available. Postbaccalaureate distance learning degree programs offered (minimal on-campus study). *Degree requirements:* For master's, thesis. *Entrance requirements:* Additional exam requirements/recommendations for international students: Required—TOEFL (minimum score 600 paper-based; 250 computer-based). Electronic applications accepted.

Stony Brook University, State University of New York, School of Professional Development, Stony Brook, NY 11794. Offers biology -grade 7-12 (MAT); chemistry-grade 7-12 (MAT); coaching (Certificate); earth science-grade 7-12 (MAT); educational computing (Certificate); educational leadership (Advanced Certificate); English-grade 7-12 (MAT); environmental management (Certificate); French-grade 7-12 (MAT); German-grade 7-12 (MAT); human resource management (Certificate); information systems management (Certificate); Italian-grade 7-12 (MAT); liberal studies (MA); liberal studies online (MA); mathematics-grade 7-12 (MAT); operation research (Certificate); physics-grade 7-12 (MAT); school district business leadership (Advanced Certificate); social science and the professions (MPS), including environmental waste management, human resource management; social studies-grade 7-12 (MAT); Spanish-grade 7-12 (MAT). Part-time and evening/weekend programs available. Postbaccalaureate distance learning degree programs offered. *Faculty:* 1 full-time (0 women), 118 part-time/adjunct (45 women). *Students:* 322 full-time (202 women), 1,188 part-time (728 women); includes 164 minority (69 African Americans, 2 American Indian/Alaska Native, 29 Asian Americans or Pacific Islanders, 64 Hispanic Americans), 11 international. Average age 28. In 2007, 738 master's, 405 other advanced degrees awarded. *Degree requirements:* For master's, one foreign language, thesis or alternative. *Application deadline:* Applications are processed on a rolling basis. Application fee: $62. *Financial support:* In 2007–08, 5 teaching assistantships were awarded; fellowships, research assistantships, career-related internships or fieldwork also available. Support available to part-time students. *Unit head:* Dr. Paul J. Edelson, Dean, 631-632-7052, Fax: 631-632-9046, E-mail: paul.edelson@stonybrook.edu.

Tarleton State University, College of Graduate Studies, Program in Liberal Studies, Stephenville, TX 76402. Offers MS. Part-time and evening/weekend programs available. *Students:* Average age 31. 1 applicant, 100% accepted, 0 enrolled. In 2007, 2 degrees awarded. *Entrance requirements:* Additional exam requirements/recommendations for international students: Required—TOEFL (minimum score 550 paper-based; 213 computer-based). *Application deadline:* For fall admission, 8/5 priority date for domestic students; for spring admission, 12/1 for domestic students. Applications are processed on a rolling basis. Application fee: $25 ($125 for international students). Electronic applications accepted. *Expenses:* Tuition, state resident: full-time $2,520; part-time $140 per credit hour. Tuition, nonresident: full-time $7,344; part-time $408 per credit hour. Required fees: $948; $39 per credit hour. *Financial support:* Application deadline: 5/1; *Application contact:* Information Contact, 254-968-9104, Fax: 254-968-9670, E-mail: gradoffice@tarleton.edu.

Temple University, Graduate School, College of Liberal Arts, Program in Liberal Arts, Philadelphia, PA 19122-6096. Offers MLA. Part-time and evening/weekend programs available. *Degree requirements:* For master's, thesis, qualifying paper. *Entrance requirements:* Additional exam requirements/recommendations for international students: Required—TOEFL (minimum score 550 paper-based; 213 computer-based; 79 iBT). Electronic applications accepted.

Texas Christian University, Graduate Studies, Fort Worth, TX 76129-0002. Offers MLA. Part-time and evening/weekend programs available. *Entrance requirements:* Additional exam requirements/recommendations for international students: Required—TOEFL. *Application deadline;* For fall admission, 3/1 for domestic students; for spring admission, 12/1 for domestic students. Applications are processed on a rolling basis. Application fee: $0. *Expenses:* Tuition: Part-time $865 per credit hour. Required fees: $48 per year. *Financial support:* Application deadline: 3/1. *Unit head:* Dr. Don Coerver, Director, 817-257-6290, E-mail: d.coerver@tcu.edu.

Thomas Edison State College, Heavin School of Arts and Sciences, Program in Liberal Studies, Trenton, NJ 08608-1176. Offers homeland security (MALS); human resource management (MALS); online learning and teaching (MALS); organizational leadership (MALS). Part-time programs available. Postbaccalaureate distance learning degree programs offered (no on-campus study). *Students:* Average age 45. 16 applicants, 26 enrolled. In 2007, 13 degrees awarded. *Degree requirements:* For master's, capstone project. *Entrance requirements:* Additional exam requirements/recommendations for international students: Required—TOEFL (minimum score 550 paper-based; 213 computer-based; 79 iBT). *Application deadline:* For fall admission, 8/15 priority date for domestic and international students; for winter admission, 11/15 priority date for domestic and international students; for spring admission, 2/15 priority date for domestic and international students. Applications are processed on a rolling basis. Application fee: $75. Electronic applications accepted. *Expenses:* Tuition, state resident: part-time $440 per credit. Tuition, nonresident: part-time $440 per credit. Part-time tuition and fees vary according to program. *Financial support:* Applicants required to submit FAFSA. *Application contact:* David Hoftiezer, Director of Admissions, 888-442-8372, Fax: 609-984-8447, E-mail: admissions@tesc.edu.

Towson University, College of Graduate Studies and Research, Program in Professional Studies, Towson, MD 21252-0001. Offers MA. Part-time and evening/weekend programs available. *Faculty:* 10 full-time (5 women). *Students:* 6 full-time (4 women), 24 part-time (17 women); includes 13 minority (11 African Americans, 1 Asian American or Pacific Islander, 1 Hispanic American), 3 international. Average age 32. 12 applicants, 83% accepted, 9 enrolled. In 2007, 20 degrees awarded. *Degree requirements:* For master's, thesis optional, exam. *Entrance requirements:* For master's, minimum GPA of 3.0, admission essay, official transcripts. *Application deadline:* Applications are processed on a rolling basis. Application fee: $50. Electronic applications accepted. *Expenses:* Tuition, state resident: part-time $286 per credit. Tuition, nonresident: part-time $600 per credit. Required fees: $75 per credit. *Financial support:* Federal Work-Study and unspecified assistantships available. Financial award application deadline: 4/1; financial award applicants required to submit FAFSA. *Faculty research:* History, World War II, counseling, marriage and family, human development. *Unit head:* Dr. James Smith, Graduate Program Director, 410-704-2128, E-mail: jsmith@towson.edu. *Application contact:* 410-704-2501, Fax: 410-704-4678, E-mail: grads@towson.edu.

Tulane University, Program in Liberal Arts, New Orleans, LA 70118-5669. Offers MLA. Part-time programs available. *Degree requirements:* For master's, thesis. *Entrance requirements:* For master's, GRE General Test, minimum B average in undergraduate course work. Additional exam requirements/recommendations for international students: Required—TOEFL.

University at Albany, State University of New York, College of Arts and Sciences, Liberal Studies Program, Albany, NY 12222-0001. Offers MA. *Students:* 39 full-time (19 women), 8 part-time (6 women). Average age 30. In 2007, 12 degrees awarded. *Entrance requirements:* Additional exam requirements/recommendations for international students: Required—TOEFL (minimum score 550 paper-based; 213 computer-based). *Application deadline:* For fall admission, 4/1 for domestic students, 5/1 for international students. Applications are processed on a rolling basis. Application fee: $75. Electronic applications accepted. *Expenses:* Tuition, state resident: part-time $576 per credit. Tuition, nonresident: part-time $910 per credit. Tuition and fees vary according to program. *Financial support:* Application deadline: 4/1. *Unit head:* Dr. Leonard Slade, Director, 518-442-4010.

University of Arkansas at Little Rock, Graduate School, College of Arts, Humanities, and Social Science, Department of Philosophy and Liberal Studies, Little Rock, AR 72204-1099. Offers MALS. *Entrance requirements:* For master's, GRE. *Application deadline:* Applications are processed on a rolling basis. *Financial support:* Research assistantships with tuition reimbursements, teaching assistantships with tuition reimbursements available. *Unit head:* Dr. Jan Thomas, Chair, 501-569-3312, E-mail: jlthomas@ualr.edu. *Application contact:* Dr. Angela Hunter, Information Contact, 501-683-7066, E-mail: anhunter@ualr.edu.

University of Delaware, College of Arts and Sciences, Program in Liberal Studies, Newark, DE 19716. Offers MALS. Part-time and evening/weekend programs available. *Faculty:* 10 full-time (4 women), 3 part-time/adjunct (2 women). *Students:* 8 full-time (7 women), 38 part-time (23 women); includes 2 minority (1 African American, 1 Hispanic American). Average age 47. 11 applicants, 73% accepted, 8 enrolled. In 2007, 13 degrees awarded. *Degree requirements:* For master's, thesis. *Application deadline:* For fall admission, 4/1 priority date for domestic students. Applications are processed on a rolling basis. Application fee: $60. Electronic applications accepted. *Financial support:* Tuition waivers (full) and employee tuition benefit program available. *Faculty research:* British Raj, medical and scientific ethics, Jewish-American novelists, intellectual freedom. *Unit head:* Dr. Joan Del Fattore, Director, 302-831-6075, Fax: 302-831-4461. *Application contact:* Maryanne Brown-Mackay, Administrative Assistant, 302-831-6075, Fax: 302-831-4461, E-mail: brownmac@udel.edu.

University of Denver, University College, Denver, CO 80208. Offers applied communication (MAS, MPS, Certificate); computer information systems (MAS, Certificate); environmental policy and management (MAS, Certificate); geographic information systems (MAS, Certificate); human resource administration (MPS, Certificate); knowledge and information technologies (MAS); liberal studies (MLS, Certificate); modern languages (MLS, Certificate); organizational leadership (MPS, Certificate); security management (Certificate); technology management (MAS, Certificate), including 21st century strategic management (MAS), international markets (MAS), project management (MAS), research and development management (MAS); telecommunications (MAS, Certificate), including broadband (MAS), telecommunications management and policy (MAS), telecommunications technology (MAS), wireless networks (MAS). Part-time and evening/weekend programs available. Postbaccalaureate distance learning degree programs offered (no on-campus study). *Students:* 29 full-time (15 women), 524 part-time (304 women); includes 92 minority (37 African Americans, 3 American Indian/Alaska Native, 17 Asian Americans or Pacific Islanders, 35 Hispanic Americans), 53 international. Average age 36. 625 applicants, 97% accepted, 359 enrolled. In 2007, 151 master's, 2 Certificates awarded. *Entrance requirements:* Additional exam requirements/recommendations for international students: Required—TOEFL (minimum score 550 paper-based; 213 computer-based). *Application deadline:* Applications are processed on a rolling basis. Application fee: $75. Electronic applications accepted. *Expenses: Contact institution. Financial support:* Applicants required to submit FAFSA. *Unit head:* Dr. James Davis, Dean, 303-871-2291, Fax: 303-871-4047, E-mail: jdavis@du.edu. *Application contact:* Information Contact, 303-871-3069.

University of Detroit Mercy, College of Liberal Arts and Education, Program in Liberal Studies, Detroit, MI 48221. Offers MALS. Part-time programs available.

The University of Findlay, Graduate and Professional Studies, College of Liberal Arts, Program in Liberal Studies, Findlay, OH 45840-3653. Offers MALS. Part-time and evening/weekend programs available. *Students:* 11 full-time (3 women), 11 part-time (8 women); includes 4 minority (1 African American, 1 American Indian/Alaska Native, 1 Asian American or Pacific Islander, 1 Hispanic American), 7 international. Average age 35. 8 applicants, 63% accepted, 5 enrolled. In 2007, 10 degrees awarded. *Degree requirements:* For master's, thesis, cumulative project. *Entrance requirements:* For master's, minimum undergraduate GPA of 2.5 in last 64 hours of course work, 3 letters of recommendation, essay. Additional exam requirements/recommendations for international students: Required—TOEFL (minimum score 550 paper-based). *Application deadline:* Applications are processed on a rolling basis. Application fee: $25. Electronic applications accepted. *Expenses:* Tuition: Full-time $17,460; part-time $485 per credit. Required fees: $90 per term. Tuition and fees vary according to program. *Financial support:* In 2007–08, 8 students received support, including 2 teaching assistantships with full tuition reimbursements available (averaging $6,000 per year); unspecified assistantships also available. Financial award application deadline: 4/1; financial award applicants required to submit FAFSA. *Application contact:* Heather Riffle, Assistant to the Dean, Graduate and Professional Studies, 419-434-4640, Fax: 419-434-5517, E-mail: riffle@findlay.edu.

University of Maine, Graduate School, Program in Liberal Studies, Orono, ME 04469. Offers MA. Part-time and evening/weekend programs available. *Students:* 15 full-time (8 women), 16 part-time (12 women); includes 1 minority (American Indian/Alaska Native). Average age 40. 9 applicants, 78% accepted, 5 enrolled. In 2007, 4 master's awarded. *Degree requirements:* For master's, project. *Entrance requirements:* Additional exam requirements/recommendations for international students: Required—TOEFL. *Application deadline:* For fall admission, 4/1 for domestic students; for spring admission, 11/1 for domestic students. Applications are processed on a rolling basis. Application fee: $60. Electronic applications accepted. *Financial support:* Federal Work-Study and institutionally sponsored loans available. Financial award application deadline: 3/1.

University of Memphis, Graduate School, University College, Memphis, TN 38152. Offers liberal studies (MALS); merchandising and consumer science (MS), including consumer science and education; strategic leadership (MPS). Part-time and evening/weekend programs available. *Faculty:* 6 full-time (3 women). *Students:* 12 full-time (8 women), 63 part-time (48 women); includes 44 African Americans, 2 Asian Americans or Pacific Islanders. Average age 41. 52 applicants, 58% accepted, 21 enrolled. In 2007, 26 degrees awarded. *Degree requirements:* For master's, comprehensive exam, thesis (for some programs). *Entrance requirements:* For master's, GRE General Test (MS) or MAT, interview (MALS). Additional exam requirements/recommendations for international students: Required—TOEFL (minimum score 550 paper-based; 210 computer-based). *Application deadline:* For fall admission, 7/1 for domestic students, 5/1 for international students; for spring admission, 11/1 for domestic students, 9/15 for international students. Applications are processed on a rolling basis. Application fee: $35 ($60 for international students). Electronic applications accepted. *Expenses:* Tuition, state resident: full-time $6,990; part-time $377 per hour. Tuition, nonresident: full-time $17,818; part-time $830 per hour. Tuition and fees vary according to course load and program. *Financial support:* In 2007–08, 5 research assistantships with full tuition reimbursements (averaging $7,400 per year), 1 teaching assistantship (averaging $2,625 per year) were awarded; unspecified assistantships also available. Financial award application deadline: 4/1; financial award applicants required to submit FAFSA. *Faculty research:* Media ethics, history of psychiatry, public relations. Total annual research expenditures: $16,430. *Unit head:* Dr. Dan Lattimore, Dean,

Liberal Studies

University of Memphis (continued)
901-678-2991. *Application contact:* Dr. David Arant, Coordinator of Graduate Studies, 901-678-4596, Fax: 901-678-4913, E-mail: darant@memphis.edu.

University of Miami, Graduate School, College of Arts and Sciences, Program in Liberal Studies, Coral Gables, FL 33124. Offers MALS. Part-time and evening/weekend programs available. *Faculty:* 15 full-time (3 women). *Students:* 4 full-time (3 women), 45 part-time (36 women); includes 18 minority (3 African Americans, 1 Asian American or Pacific Islander, 14 Hispanic Americans), 2 international. Average age 39. 14 applicants, 86% accepted, 12 enrolled. In 2007, 23 degrees awarded. *Degree requirements:* For master's, thesis or alternative. *Entrance requirements:* For master's, minimum GPA of 3.0. Additional exam requirements/recommendations for international students: Required—TOEFL. *Application deadline:* For fall admission, 7/28 priority date for domestic students; for spring admission, 12/1 priority date for domestic students. Applications are processed on a rolling basis. Application fee: $50. Electronic applications accepted. *Expenses: Contact institution. Financial support:* In 2007–08, 36 students received support. Institutionally sponsored loans available. Support available to part-time students. Financial award applicants required to submit FAFSA. *Unit head:* Dr. Eugene Clasby, Director, 305-284-3809, Fax: 305-284-2796, E-mail: gclasby@miami.edu. *Application contact:* Priscilla L. Keane, Program Coordinator, 305-284-6731, Fax: 305-284-2796, E-mail: pkeane@miami.edu.

University of Michigan–Dearborn, College of Arts, Sciences, and Letters, Program in Liberal Studies, Dearborn, MI 48128-1491. Offers MA. Part-time and evening/weekend programs available. *Faculty:* 14 full-time (7 women). *Students:* Average age 45. 11 applicants, 82% accepted, 7 enrolled. In 2007, 10 degrees awarded. *Degree requirements:* For master's, thesis or alternative, capstone course. *Entrance requirements:* For master's, minimum GPA of 3.0, writing sample, interview, statement of purpose. Additional exam requirements/recommendations for international students: Required—TOEFL (minimum score 560 paper-based; 220 computer-based). *Application deadline:* For fall admission, 8/1 priority date for domestic students; for winter admission, 12/1 priority date for domestic students; for spring admission, 4/1 for domestic students. Applications are processed on a rolling basis. Application fee: $60 ($75 for international students). Electronic applications accepted. *Expenses:* Tuition, state resident: part-time $318 per credit hour. Tuition, nonresident: part-time $722 per credit hour. Tuition and fees vary according to course load and program. *Financial support:* Scholarships/grants available. Support available to part-time students. Financial award application deadline: 4/1; financial award applicants required to submit FAFSA. *Faculty research:* History of science studies, consciousness, memory studies, early American history, environmental studies. *Unit head:* Dr. Kathleen Wider, Director, 313-593-4938, Fax: 313-583-6498, E-mail: kwider@umd.umich.edu. *Application contact:* Carol Ligienza, Administrative Coordinator, CASL Graduate Programs, 313-593-1183, Fax: 313-583-6498, E-mail: caslgrad@umd.umich.edu.

University of Minnesota, Duluth, Graduate School, College of Liberal Arts, Department of Sociology/Anthropology, Liberal Studies Program, Duluth, MN 55812-2496. Offers MLS. Part-time and evening/weekend programs available. *Faculty:* 23 part-time/adjunct (9 women). *Students:* 6 full-time (4 women), 18 part-time (12 women); includes 1 minority (Asian American or Pacific Islander) Average age 35. In 2007, 2 degrees awarded. *Expenses:* Tuition, state resident: part-time $812 per credit. Tuition, nonresident: part-time $1,403 per credit. Tuition and fees vary according to program. *Financial support:* Scholarships/grants available. *Faculty research:* Nature of knowledge, cultural studies, language, literature, sociology. *Unit head:* Dr. Gesa Zinn, Graduate Director, 218-726-8990, Fax: 218-726-8109, E-mail: gzinn@d.umn.edu.

University of New Hampshire, Graduate School, College of Liberal Arts, Program in Liberal Studies, Durham, NH 03824. Offers MALS. *Faculty:* 2 full-time. *Students:* 1 full-time (0 women), 21 part-time (17 women). Average age 39. 10 applicants, 90% accepted, 6 enrolled. In 2007, 8 degrees awarded. *Entrance requirements:* Additional exam requirements/recommendations for international students: Required—TOEFL (minimum score 550 paper-based; 213 computer-based; 80 iBT). *Application deadline:* For fall admission, 4/1 for domestic and international students; for winter admission, 12/1 for domestic students. Applications are processed on a rolling basis. Application fee: $60. Electronic applications accepted. *Financial support:* In 2007–08, 1 fellowship was awarded; research assistantships, teaching assistantships. Financial award application deadline: 2/15. *Unit head:* Dr. Warren Brown, Chairperson, 603-862-3225, E-mail: liberal.studies@unh.edu.

The University of North Carolina at Asheville, Graduate Studies, Asheville, NC 28804-3299. Offers MLA. Part-time and evening/weekend programs available. *Faculty:* 8 full-time (4 women), 4 part-time/adjunct (1 woman). *Students:* 3 full-time (all women), 20 part-time (18 women). Average age 43. 9 applicants, 67% accepted, 4 enrolled. In 2007, 9 degrees awarded. *Degree requirements:* For master's, thesis. *Application deadline:* For fall admission, 4/15 for domestic students; for spring admission, 11/15 for domestic students. Applications are processed on a rolling basis. Application fee: $50. *Expenses:* Tuition, state resident: full-time $2,705. Tuition, nonresident: full-time $13,569. Required fees: $1,857. *Financial support:* Federal Work-Study and institutionally sponsored loans available. Support available to part-time students. Financial award application deadline: 5/1; financial award applicants required to submit FAFSA. *Unit head:* Dr. Bill Spellman, Director, 828-250-2399, E-mail: spellman@unca.edu.

The University of North Carolina at Charlotte, Graduate School, College of Arts and Sciences, Program in Liberal Studies, Charlotte, NC 28223-0001. Offers MA. *Students:* 4 full-time (all women), 19 part-time (12 women); includes 4 minority (all African Americans), 1 international. Average age 36. 8 applicants, 88% accepted, 6 enrolled. In 2007, 3 degrees awarded. *Degree requirements:* For master's, comprehensive exam or project. *Entrance requirements:* For master's, GRE General Test or MAT, minimum GPA of 3.0 during previous 2 years, 2.75 overall. Additional exam requirements/recommendations for international students: Required—TOEFL (minimum score 557 paper-based; 220 computer-based). *Application deadline:* For fall admission, 7/1 for domestic students, 5/1 for international students; for spring admission, 11/1 for domestic students, 10/1 for international students. Applications are processed on a rolling basis. Application fee: $55. Electronic applications accepted. *Expenses:* Tuition, state resident: full-time $2,855. Tuition, nonresident: full-time $13,062. Required fees: $1,692. *Financial support:* Fellowships, research assistantships, teaching assistantships, career-related internships or fieldwork, Federal Work-Study, institutionally sponsored loans, scholarships/grants, and unspecified assistantships available. Support available to part-time students. Financial award application deadline: 4/1; financial award applicants required to submit FAFSA. *Unit head:* Dr. Alan Rauch, Director, 704-687-4312, Fax: 704-687-4347, E-mail: arauch@email.uncc.edu. *Application contact:* Kathy B. Giddings, Director of Graduate Admissions, 704-687-3366, Fax: 704-687-3279, E-mail: agidding@uncc.edu.

The University of North Carolina at Greensboro, Graduate School, Program in Liberal Studies, Greensboro, NC 27412-5001. Offers MALS. *Students:* 40 full-time (2 women), 105 part-time (all women); includes 23 minority (22 African Americans, 1 Hispanic American). *Application deadline:* For fall admission, 6/15 for domestic students; for spring admission, 10/15 for domestic students. Applications are processed on a rolling basis. Application fee: $45. Electronic applications accepted. *Unit head:* Kathleen Forbes, Director, 336-334-5414, Fax: 336-334-5628. *Application contact:* Michelle Harkleroad, Director of Graduate Admissions, 336-334-4884, Fax: 336-334-4424, E-mail: mbharkle@uncg.edu.

The University of North Carolina Wilmington, College of Arts and Sciences, Interdisciplinary Program in Liberal Studies, Wilmington, NC 28403-3297. Offers MALS. Part-time programs available. *Students:* 11 full-time (7 women), 61 part-time (43 women); includes 13 minority (11 African Americans, 1 Asian American or Pacific Islander, 1 Hispanic American), 1 international. Average age 38. 36 applicants, 81% accepted, 22 enrolled. In 2007, 33 degrees awarded. *Degree requirements:* For master's, final project. *Entrance requirements:* For master's, minimum GPA of 3.0, writing sample. *Application deadline:* For fall admission, 3/15 for domestic students. Application fee: $45. *Expenses:* Tuition, state resident: full-time $2,714. Tuition, nonresident: full-time $12,579. Required fees: $1,985. *Financial support:* In 2007–08, 3 teaching assistantships were awarded. Financial award application deadline:3/15. *Unit head:* Dr. Herb Berg, Director, 910-962-3299. *Application contact:* Dr. Robert D. Roer, Dean, Graduate School, 910-962-4117, Fax: 910-962-3787, E-mail: roer@uncw.edu.

University of Oklahoma, Graduate College, College of Liberal Studies, Norman, OK 73019-0390. Offers administrative leadership (MLS); integrated studies (MLS); interprofessional human and health services (MLS); museum studies (MLS). Part-time programs available. Post-baccalaureate distance learning degree programs offered (no on-campus study). *Faculty:* 11 full-time (6 women), 13 part-time/adjunct (3 women). *Students:* 16 full-time (8 women), 264 part-time (153 women); includes 59 minority (32 African Americans, 12 American Indian/Alaska Native, 6 Asian Americans or Pacific Islanders, 9 Hispanic Americans). 117 applicants, 96% accepted, 71 enrolled. In 2007, 52 degrees awarded. *Degree requirements:* For master's, thesis, research project, internship. *Entrance requirements:* For master's, minimum GPA of 3.0 in last 60 hours, writing sample. Additional exam requirements/recommendations for international students: Required—TOEFL (minimum score 550 paper-based; 213 computer-based). *Application deadline:* For fall admission, 7/15 priority date for domestic students, 4/1 for international students; for spring admission, 12/1 for domestic students, 9/1 for international students. Applications are processed on a rolling basis. Application fee: $40 ($90 for international students). Electronic applications accepted. *Expenses:* Tuition, state resident: full-time $3,451; part-time $144 per credit hour. Tuition, nonresident: full-time $12,432; part-time $518 per credit hour. Required fees: $1,925; $70 per credit hour. $122 per semester. *Financial support:* In 2007–08, 112 students received support. Career-related internships or fieldwork, scholarships/grants, and tuition waivers (partial) available. Support available to part-time students. Financial award applicants required to submit FAFSA. *Faculty research:* Distance education, adult learning processes, student satisfaction, administrative leadership, organizations, museum studies. *Unit head:* Dr. James Pappas, Dean and Vice President, 405-325-1061, Fax: 405-325-7132, E-mail: jpappas@ou.edu. *Application contact:* Dr. Julie Raadschelders, MA Program Coordinator, 405-325-1061, Fax: 405-325-9632, E-mail: jraadschelders@ou.edu.

University of Pennsylvania, School of Arts and Sciences, College of General Studies, Program of Individualized Study, Philadelphia, PA 19104. Offers MLA.

University of St. Thomas, Program in Liberal Arts, Houston, TX 77006-4696. Offers MLA. Part-time and evening/weekend programs available. *Faculty:* 35 full-time (15 women), 12 part-time/adjunct (7 women). *Students:* 20 full-time (13 women), 122 part-time (88 women); includes 53 minority (16 African Americans, 2 Asian Americans or Pacific Islanders, 35 Hispanic Americans), 7 international. Average age 36. 37 applicants, 95% accepted, 35 enrolled. In 2007, 50 degrees awarded. *Degree requirements:* For master's, thesis optional. *Entrance requirements:* For master's, minimum GPA of 2.5. Additional exam requirements/recommendations for international students: Required—TOEFL (minimum score 550 paper-based; 213 computer-based). *Application deadline:* Applications are processed on a rolling basis. Application fee: $35. *Financial support:* In 2007–08, 64 students received support. Federal Work-Study and scholarships/grants available. Support available to part-time students. Financial award application deadline: 3/1; financial award applicants required to submit FAFSA. *Unit head:* Dr. Ravi Srinivas, Dean, 713-525-6924, Fax: 713-525-3804, E-mail: srinivas@stthom.edu.

University of Southern Indiana, Graduate Studies, College of Liberal Arts, Program in Liberal Studies, Evansville, IN 47712-3590. Offers MA. Part-time and evening/weekend programs available. *Faculty:* 12 full-time (4 women), 4 part-time/adjunct (2 women). *Students:* 5 full-time (1 woman), 33 part-time (22 women); includes 3 minority (2 African Americans, 1 American Indian/Alaska Native), 2 international. Average age 38. 8 applicants, 100% accepted, 8 enrolled. In 2007, 4 degrees awarded. *Entrance requirements:* For master's, minimum GPA of 2.5, resumé, interview. Additional exam requirements/recommendations for international students: Required—TOEFL (minimum score 550 paper-based; 213 computer-based; 79 iBT), IELTS (minimum score 6). *Application deadline:* For fall admission, 8/15 priority date for domestic students, 3/1 priority date for international students. Applications are processed on a rolling basis. Application fee: $25. *Expenses:* Tuition, state resident: full-time $4,374; part-time $243 per credit. Tuition, nonresident: full-time $8,622; part-time $479 per credit. Required fees: $220; $23 per term. Tuition and fees vary according to course load and reciprocity agreements. *Financial support:* In 2007–08, 26 students received support. Federal Work-Study, scholarships/grants, tuition waivers (full and partial), and unspecified assistantships available. Financial award application deadline: 3/1; financial award applicants required to submit FAFSA. *Unit head:* Dr. Thomas M. Rivers, Director, 812-464-1753, E-mail: trivers@usi.edu.

University of South Florida, Graduate School, College of Arts and Sciences, Department of Humanities and American Studies, Program in Liberal Arts, Tampa, FL 33620-9951. Offers MLA. *Degree requirements:* For master's, thesis. *Entrance requirements:* For master's, GRE, minimum GPA of 3.0.

The University of Toledo, College of Graduate Studies, College of Arts and Sciences, Master of Liberal Studies Program, Toledo, OH 43606-3390. Offers MLS. Part-time and evening/weekend programs available. *Students:* 12 full-time (7 women), 50 part-time (35 women); includes 21 minority (all African Americans) Average age 40. 27 applicants, 74% accepted, 10 enrolled. In 2007, 6 degrees awarded. *Degree requirements:* For master's, thesis. *Entrance requirements:* For master's, interview, minimum GPA of 2.7. *Application deadline:* For fall admission, 7/15 priority date for domestic students. Applications are processed on a rolling basis. Application fee: $45. Electronic applications accepted. *Financial support:* In 2007–08, 4 students received support; teaching assistantships with full tuition reimbursements available, Federal Work-Study, institutionally sponsored loans, scholarships/grants, and unspecified assistantships available. Support available to part-time students. Financial award application deadline: 4/1; financial award applicants required to submit FAFSA. *Unit head:* Dr. Lawrence Anderson, Chair, 419-530-7257, E-mail: lawrence.anderson@utoledo.edu.

University of Wisconsin–Milwaukee, Graduate School, College of Letters and Sciences, Interdepartmental Program in Liberal Studies, Milwaukee, WI 53201-0413. Offers MLS. *Faculty:* 10 full-time (3 women). *Students:* 7 full-time (5 women), 16 part-time (10 women); includes 4 minority (3 African Americans, 1 Hispanic American). 17 applicants, 88% accepted, 8 enrolled. In 2007, 9 degrees awarded. Application fee: $45 ($75 for international students). *Expenses:* Tuition, state resident: part-time $530 per credit. Tuition, nonresident: part-time $1,428 per credit. Required fees: $19 per credit. $229 per term. Tuition and fees vary according to course load and program. *Financial support:* Fellowships available. *Unit head:* Jeffrey Hayes, Representative, 414-229-5963, E-mail: jhayes@uwm.edu.

Ursuline College, School of Graduate Studies, Program in Liberal Studies, Pepper Pike, OH 44124-4398. Offers MALS. *Students:* Average age 43. In 2007, 3 degrees awarded. *Degree requirements:* For master's, thesis. *Entrance requirements:* For master's, minimum undergraduate GPA of 3.0. Additional exam requirements/recommendations for international students: Required—TOEFL (minimum score 500 paper-based; 173 computer-based). *Application deadline:* For fall admission, 8/1 priority date for domestic students. Applications are processed on a rolling basis. Application fee: $25. Electronic applications accepted. *Expenses:* Tuition: Full-time $13,356; part-time $742 per credit hour. Required fees: $200; $60 per semester. Tuition and fees vary according to program. *Financial support:* In 2007–08, 5 students received support. Federal Work-Study available. Financial award application deadline: 3/1; financial award applicants required to submit FAFSA. *Unit head:* Dr. Tim Kinsella, Director, 440-646-8389, Fax: 440-684-6088, E-mail: tkinsell@ursuline.edu. *Application contact:* Jo Mann, Secretary, 440-646-8119, Fax: 440-684-6088, E-mail: gradsch@ursuline.edu.

Utica College, Liberal Studies Program, Utica, NY 13502-4892. Offers MS. Part-time and evening/weekend programs available. *Faculty:* 19 full-time (8 women). *Students:* 3 full-time (2 women), 35 part-time (27 women); includes 2 minority (1 African American, 1 Asian American or Pacific Islander). Average age 32. 10 applicants, 100% accepted, 9 enrolled. *Degree requirements:* For master's, comprehensive exam or thesis. *Entrance requirements:* For master's, minimum GPA of 3.0. Additional exam requirements/recommendations for international students:

Required—TOEFL (minimum score 525 paper-based; 195 computer-based). *Application deadline:* Applications are processed on a rolling basis. Application fee: $50. Electronic applications accepted. *Expenses: Contact institution. Financial support:* In 2007–08, 18 students received support. Career-related internships or fieldwork, scholarships/grants, tuition waivers (partial), and unspecified assistantships available. Support available to part-time students. Financial award application deadline: 3/15; financial award applicants required to submit FAFSA. *Unit head:* Dr. Alan Bessette, Coordinator, Liberal Studies, 315-792-3132, E-mail: abessette@utica.edu. *Application contact:* John D. Rowe, Director of Graduate Admissions, 315-792-3824, Fax: 315-792-3003, E-mail: jrowe@utica.edu.

Valparaiso University, Graduate Division, Program in Liberal Studies, Concentration in Human Behavior and Society, Valparaiso, IN 46383. Offers MALS, Post-Master's Certificate, JD/MALS. Part-time and evening/weekend programs available. *Students:* 8 full-time (2 women), 8 part-time (3 women); includes 3 minority (all African Americans) Average age 31. In 2007, 5 degrees awarded. *Entrance requirements:* For master's, minimum GPA of 3.0. Additional exam requirements/recommendations for international students: Required—TOEFL (minimum score 550 paper-based; 213 computer-based). *Application deadline:* Applications are processed on a rolling basis. Application fee: $30 ($50 for international students). Electronic applications accepted. *Financial support:* Available to part-time students. Applicants required to submit FAFSA. *Application contact:* Jamie Haney, Coordinator of Recruitment Activities, 219-464-5313, Fax: 219-464-5381, E-mail: jamie.haney@valpo.edu.

Valparaiso University, Graduate Division, Program in Liberal Studies, Individualized Program, Valparaiso, IN 46383. Offers MALS, JD/MALS. Part-time and evening/weekend programs available. *Students:* 2 full-time (1 woman), 5 part-time (all women); includes 1 minority (African American) Average age 37. In 2007, 2 degrees awarded. *Entrance requirements:* For master's, minimum GPA of 3.0. Additional exam requirements/recommendations for international students: Required—TOEFL (minimum score 550 paper-based; 213 computer-based). *Application deadline:* Applications are processed on a rolling basis. Application fee: $30 ($50 for international students). Electronic applications accepted. *Financial support:* Available to part-time students. Applicants required to submit FAFSA. *Application contact:* Jamie Haney, Coordinator of Recruitment Activities, 219-464-5313, Fax: 219-464-5381, E-mail: jamie.haney@valpo.edu.

Vanderbilt University, Graduate School, Program in Liberal Arts and Science, Nashville, TN 37240-1001. Offers MLAS. Part-time programs available. *Students:* 1 (woman) full-time, 79 part-time (46 women); includes 2 minority (both African Americans) Average age 45. 27 applicants, 74% accepted, 18 enrolled. In 2007, 8 degrees awarded. *Degree requirements:* For master's, thesis optional. *Entrance requirements:* For master's, GRE General Test. *Application deadline:* For fall admission, 1/15 priority date for domestic students, 1/15 for international students; for spring admission, 11/15 for domestic and international students. Applications are processed on a rolling basis. Application fee: $0. *Financial support:* Institutionally sponsored loans and tuition waivers (partial) available. *Unit head:* Martin Rapisarda, Associate Dean and Director, 615-343-3140, Fax: 615-343-8453, E-mail: martin.rapisarda@vanderbilt.edu.

Villanova University, Graduate School of Liberal Arts and Sciences, Program in Liberal Studies, Villanova, PA 19085-1699. Offers MA. Part-time and evening/weekend programs available. *Faculty:* 6 full-time (1 woman). *Students:* 8 full-time (6 women), 25 part-time (17 women); includes 1 minority (African American) Average age 40. 9 applicants, 78% accepted. In 2007, 16 degrees awarded. *Degree requirements:* For master's, comprehensive exam. *Entrance requirements:* For master's, minimum GPA of 3.0. *Application deadline:* For fall admission, 8/1 for domestic and international students; for spring admission, 12/1 for domestic and international students. Applications are processed on a rolling basis. Application fee: $50. Electronic applications accepted. *Financial support:* Research assistantships, Federal Work-Study available. Financial award applicants required to submit FAFSA. *Unit head:* Dr. Eugene McCarraher, Director, 610-519-4796, Fax: 610-519-4639, E-mail: eugene.mccarraher@villanova.edu.

Wake Forest University, Graduate School of Arts and Sciences, Liberal Studies Program, Winston-Salem, NC 27109. Offers MALS. Part-time programs available. *Students:* 23 full-time (14 women), 43 part-time (29 women); includes 9 minority (all African Americans), 1 international. Average age 41. 10 applicants, 80% accepted, 8 enrolled. In 2007, 11 master's awarded. *Degree requirements:* For master's, thesis. *Entrance requirements:* Additional exam requirements/recommendations for international students: Required—TOEFL (minimum score 213 computer-based; 79 iBT). *Application deadline:* Applications are processed on a rolling basis. Application fee: $35. *Financial support:* In 2007–08, 26 students received support. *Unit head:* Dr. Cecilia H. Solano, Director, 336-758-5410, Fax: 336-758-4230, E-mail: solano@wfu.edu.

Washburn University, College of Arts and Sciences, Program in Liberal Studies, Topeka, KS 66621. Offers MLS. Part-time and evening/weekend programs available. *Students:* 2 full-time (0 women), 8 part-time (6 women). Average age 42. In 2007, 2 degrees awarded. *Degree requirements:* For master's, thesis, 15 seminar hours. *Entrance requirements:* For master's, minimum GPA of 3.0. *Application deadline:* For fall admission, 4/15 priority date for domestic students; for spring admission, 11/15 priority date for domestic students. Applications are processed on a rolling basis. Application fee: $0. Electronic applications accepted. *Expenses:* Tuition, state resident: full-time $4,590; part-time $255 per credit hour. Tuition, nonresident: full-time $9,360; part-time $520 per credit hour. Required fees: $86; $43 per semester. Tuition and fees vary according to program. *Financial support:* Career-related internships or fieldwork, Federal Work-Study, and scholarships/grants available. Support available to part-time students. Financial award application deadline: 2/15; financial award applicants required to submit FAFSA. *Faculty research:* European architecture/history, British cultural studies movement, American military strategy/history. *Unit head:* Dr. Maureen Godman, Director, 785-670-1917, E-mail: mo.godman@washburn.edu.

Wesleyan University, Graduate Liberal Studies Program, Middletown, CT 06459-0260. Offers MALS, CAS. Part-time and evening/weekend programs available. *Faculty:* 20 part-time/adjunct (8 women). *Students:* Average age 40. 215 applicants, 100% accepted. In 2007, 58 master's awarded. *Degree requirements:* For master's, thesis optional; for CAS, thesis. *Entrance requirements:* For master's, application; for CAS, application, master's degree. Additional exam requirements/recommendations for international students: Required—TOEFL. *Application deadline:* For fall admission, 9/10 for domestic students; for spring admission, 1/28 for domestic students. Applications are processed on a rolling basis. Application fee: $100. *Expenses: Contact institution. Financial support:* In 2007–08, 63 students received support. Scholarships/grants available. Support available to part-time students. *Faculty research:* Interdisciplinary studies. *Unit head:* Dr. Karen Anderson, Associate Dean of Continuing Studies and Director, GLSP, 860-685-3977, Fax: 860-685-2901, E-mail: kanderson@wesleyan.edu. *Application contact:* Jennifer M. Curran, Assistant Director, Admissions and Outreach, 860-685-3338, Fax: 860-685-2901, E-mail: jcurran@wesleyan.edu.

Western Illinois University, School of Graduate Studies, College of Arts and Sciences, Program in Liberal Arts and Sciences, Macomb, IL 61455-1390. Offers MLAS. *Degree requirements:* For master's, thesis or alternative. *Entrance requirements:* Additional exam requirements/recommendations for international students: Required—TOEFL (minimum score 550 paper-based; 213 computer-based; 80 iBT). *Application deadline:* Applications are processed on a rolling basis. Application fee: $30. Electronic applications accepted. *Expenses:* Tuition, state resident: part-time $217 per credit hour. Tuition, nonresident: part-time $433 per credit hour. Required fees: $54 per credit hour. *Application contact:* Dr. Barbara Baily, Director of Graduate Studies/Associate Provost, 309-298-1806, Fax: 309-298-2345, E-mail: grad-office@wiu.edu.

West Virginia University, Eberly College of Arts and Sciences, Interdisciplinary Program in Liberal Studies, Morgantown, WV 26506. Offers MALS. Part-time programs available. *Students:* 2 full-time (both women), 1 part-time. Average age 33. 5 applicants, 60% accepted, 2 enrolled. In 2007, 2 degrees awarded. *Degree requirements:* For master's, thesis or alternative. *Entrance requirements:* For master's, GRE General Test, minimum GPA of 3.0. Additional exam requirements/recommendations for international students: Required—TOEFL. *Application deadline:* For fall admission, 3/1 priority date for domestic students; for spring admission, 10/1 for domestic students. Applications are processed on a rolling basis. Application fee: $45. *Expenses:* Tuition, state resident: full-time $5,196; part-time $292 per credit hour. Tuition, nonresident: full-time $15,064; part-time $840 per credit hour. Tuition and fees vary according to program. *Financial support:* In 2007–08, 3 students received support, including 1 research assistantship with full tuition reimbursement available (averaging $8,500 per year), 2 teaching assistantships with full tuition reimbursements available (averaging $8,500 per year); Federal Work-Study, institutionally sponsored loans, and tuition waivers (full and partial) also available. Financial award application deadline: 2/1; financial award applicants required to submit FAFSA.

Wichita State University, Graduate School, Fairmount College of Liberal Arts and Sciences, Interdisciplinary Program in Liberal Studies, Wichita, KS 67260. Offers environmental science (MS). Participating faculty are from the Departments of Minority Studies, Philosophy, Religion, Social Work, and Women's Studies. Part-time programs available. *Degree requirements:* For master's, thesis optional, project. *Entrance requirements:* For master's, GRE, minimum GPA of 2.75. Additional exam requirements/recommendations for international students: Required—TOEFL. Electronic applications accepted.

Widener University, College of Arts and Sciences, Program in Liberal Studies, Chester, PA 19013-5792. Offers MA. Part-time and evening/weekend programs available. *Faculty:* 4 full-time (1 woman). *Students:* Average age 40. 3 applicants, 100% accepted. *Degree requirements:* For master's, thesis, project. *Entrance requirements:* For master's, interview, minimum undergraduate GPA of 3.0. *Application deadline:* Applications are processed on a rolling basis. Application fee: $25 ($300 for international students). *Expenses: Contact institution.* Tuition and fees vary according to course load and program. *Financial support:* Federal Work-Study and tuition waivers (full and partial) available. Financial award application deadline: 5/1. *Faculty research:* Contemporary analytical metaphysics, popular culture, British art, American literature, folklore. *Unit head:* Dr. Kenneth Skinner, Director, 610-499-4287, Fax: 610-499-4605, E-mail: kenneth.a.skinner@widener.edu.

Winthrop University, College of Arts and Sciences, Program in Liberal Arts, Rock Hill, SC 29733. Offers MLA. Part-time programs available. *Faculty:* 3 part-time/adjunct (1 woman). *Students:* 3 full-time (1 woman), 20 part-time (15 women); includes 2 minority (both African Americans) Average age 42. In 2007, 2 degrees awarded. *Entrance requirements:* For master's, interview, minimum GPA of 3.0, 3-4 page essay. *Application deadline:* For fall admission, 7/15 priority date for domestic students; for spring admission, 12/1 for domestic students. Applications are processed on a rolling basis. Application fee: $50. Electronic applications accepted. *Expenses:* Tuition, state resident: full-time $9,834; part-time $412 per credit hour. Tuition, nonresident: full-time $18,280; part-time $763 per credit hour. *Financial support:* Federal Work-Study, scholarships/grants, and unspecified assistantships available. Support available to part-time students. Financial award application deadline: 2/1; financial award applicants required to submit FAFSA. *Unit head:* Dr. David L. Rankin, Graduate Program Director, 803-323-2368, Fax: 803-323-2347, E-mail: rankind@winthrop.edu. *Application contact:* 800-411-7041, Fax: 803-323-2292, E-mail: graduatestu@winthrop.edu.

ANTIOCH UNIVERSITY MCGREGOR

Graduate Programs

Programs of Study

Antioch University McGregor offers Master of Arts (M.A.) degrees in community change and civic leadership, conflict analysis and management, creative writing, visual and performing arts, and a student's field of choice through the Individualized Master of Arts (IMA) Program. All programs combine a limited residency with online course work.

A Master of Arts through the individualized program allows motivated and ambitious students to design a Master of Arts degree in the humanities, liberal arts, social sciences, or the visual and performing arts, including creative writing. Students often pursue unique or emerging interdisciplinary fields that may meet their specialized interests and/or professional backgrounds. Students may also earn credit for prior experiential learning through a rigorous portfolio process. This is a limited-residency program with flexibility of design as a distance learning program or as a program local to the student, depending on the student's preferences and academic resources.

Two concentrations are offered through the IMA program: community change and civic leadership (CCCL) and integral knowledge systems (IKS). Both concentrations provide online courses and a recommended curriculum that may be tailored to meet an individual's specific interest. The CCCL program focuses on the development of leadership as a necessary and sustainable community resource. IKS seeks to place the developments made by science (social and physical) into a broader framework of the spirit. In addition, the courses within these two disciplines are available to all students enrolled in the IMA program or to non-degree-seeking students.

McGregor's graduate programs in conflict analysis and management are internationally recognized, with a reputation for graduating students who are highly skilled and knowledgeable theorist-practitioners. Students may pursue a graduate certificate option (four quarters) as well as an eight-quarter Master of Arts with an optional individualized concentration. Students attend three 8-day residencies, participate in online courses, and complete a practicum. Students may bring in up to 5 quarter credit hours of prior learning.

Research Facilities

Students have access to the Olive Kettering Library, which is located in Yellow Springs, Ohio. The library houses a collection of more than 325,000 volumes, including extensive files of bound periodicals, many of which date back to the nineteenth century. In addition, students gain access to OhioLINK, a consortium of all the public colleges and universities in Ohio, as well as OPAL, the private college consortium in Ohio. With more than sixty colleges and universities in Ohio, students have access to all online journals and resources maintained by each of the schools. Students also have access to We Deliver!, Antioch's interlibrary loan/document delivery service for documents and books unavailable through OhioLink or OPAL.

Financial Aid

Antioch participates in the Federal Stafford Student Loan, Federal Perkins Loan, and Federal Work-Study Programs. Other payment options are available. Approximately 50 percent of students receive financial aid.

Cost of Study

Each program of study differs in cost, depending on the number of credits needed to graduate. Antioch is a moderately priced, private higher education institution. Average tuition costs to complete a graduate degree program range from $19,000 to $25,000.

Living and Housing Costs

The University does not offer on-campus housing. Students commute or are enrolled in limited-residency programs.

Student Group

Most students are working professionals. Student activities focus on events organized within the academic programs.

Location

Antioch University McGregor is located in Yellow Springs, Ohio.

The University

Founded in 1852, Antioch University has had a proud history of progressive education for more than 150 years. Under the guidance of Horace Mann, the father of public education, Antioch was the first college to offer equal opportunities to women and one of the first colleges to admit African-American students. Antioch continued to break ground by including community participation and service as an integral part of the higher education curriculum. In 1996, Antioch received the prestigious John D. and Catherine T. MacArthur Foundation Award for creative genius in recognition of its history of innovative education. Today, Antioch University has six campuses across the United States: Antioch College and Antioch University McGregor in Yellow Springs, Ohio; Antioch University Seattle in Washington; Antioch New England Graduate School in New Hampshire; and Antioch Southern California in Los Angeles and in Santa Barbara.

Applying

Applications are accepted throughout the year. Financial aid applications should be submitted six weeks before the quarter begins to ensure timely receipt of aid, loans, and grants. Applicants must take part in a personal interview with the Admissions Committee. GRE and GMAT scores are not required for admission. Applications may be submitted online at Antioch University McGregor's Web site.

Correspondence and Information

Office of Student and Alumni Services
Antioch University McGregor
900 Dayton Street
Yellow Springs, Ohio 45387
Phone: 937-769-1818
Fax: 937-769-1804
E-mail: sas@mcgregor.edu
Web site: http://www.mcgregor.edu

Antioch University McGregor

THE FACULTY AND THEIR RESEARCH

Prospective students should visit the University's Web site for a complete list of faculty members' research interests and a listing of associated faculty members by program.

CALIFORNIA INSTITUTE OF INTEGRAL STUDIES

School of Consciousness and Transformation

Programs of Study

The mission of the School of Consciousness and Transformation at California Institute of Integral Studies (CIIS) is to conduct scholarly, interdisciplinary inquiry in the fields of anthropology, philosophy, East-West psychology, religion, transformative studies and leadership, integrative health studies, and women's spirituality. This mode of inquiry appreciates and challenges received traditions, enriching them with perspectives taken from feminist theory, ecological thought, consciousness studies, critical social theory, and new scientific paradigms. The School aims to support personal growth and development and to promote social action. The founding vision of an integral approach to education continues to inspire the School. Academic programs embody this integral vision by respecting the spiritual dimension of experience, incorporating different ways of knowing, and exposing students to the worldviews of diverse cultures.

Asian and Comparative Studies: M.A. and Ph.D. in philosophy and religion with a concentration in Asian and comparative studies. The Asian and comparative studies concentration offers a wide-ranging course of study in the world's spiritual and philosophical traditions. Students gain practical skills in research, teaching, language, translation, and cross-cultural communication. Areas of emphasis include Hinduism, Buddhism, and Chinese philosophy.

East-West Psychology: M.A. and Ph.D. in East-West psychology and, new for the 2007–08 year, a two-semester Advanced Certificate Program in Spiritual Counseling. Guided by an interest in pluralism, dialogue, and spiritual transformation, the East-West psychology program offers contemporary inquiry into Eastern and Western psychological and spiritual traditions while providing a larger context for productive explorations in transpersonal psychology, consciousness studies, depth psychology, spiritual counseling, and ecopsychology.

Integrative Health Studies: M.A. in integrative health studies. This nonclinical degree prepares its graduates to take leadership roles in the new field of integrative health, an exciting collaboration that combines the therapeutic treatment modalities of Western allopathic medicine with complementary and alternative healing systems, mind-body medicine, and spiritual healing traditions. The core curriculum includes the underlying methodology and philosophy foundational to complementary and alternative health-care systems and introduces new ideas in quantum physics that are bringing scientific and spiritual forms of healing together. Classes are offered in medical anthropology; global health issues; health policy and planning; grant writing; diversity training with program planning, evaluation, and assessment; and communication and health education.

Philosophy, Cosmology, and Consciousness: M.A. and Ph.D. in philosophy and religion with a concentration in philosophy, cosmology, and consciousness. The philosophy, cosmology, and consciousness concentration addresses the complex relations between philosophy, religion, science, and art as these practices converge to shape the view of self and the world. The program provides a solid foundation in the larger Western intellectual tradition, including ancient and esoteric thought and contemporary ecological, cosmological, evolutionary, religious, transpersonal, and feminist studies.

Social and Cultural Anthropology: M.A. in cultural anthropology and social transformation, emphasis in gender, ecology, and society; Ph.D. in social and cultural anthropology. CIIS's anthropology programs foster an interdisciplinary understanding of global systems through scholarship and action from perspectives that are sensitive to dynamics of power. They emphasize global ecology, social justice, postcolonial thought, critical social theory, and the integration of activism and scholarship. Students who have completed studies in the gender, ecology, and society program are eligible to apply to the social and cultural anthropology program, where they study the principles, theories, methods, actions, and interventions of anthropology-as-social-critique. Students in both programs benefit from close mentoring relationships with faculty members and have carried out research projects around the globe in such areas as sustainable development organizations, the homeless, land-use disputes, and social justice.

Transformative Studies: Ph.D. in transformative studies (online). Transformative studies provides students with the platform to pursue cutting-edge research in a field of their choosing. Under the mentorship of an adviser and in conjunction with a collaborative community of learners, students create a work of scholarship that is original, personally meaningful, and transdisciplinary. Students are exposed to a plurality of perspectives and disciplines and learn how to excavate the underlying assumptions and paradigms informing them. Students learn ways of inquiry that connect and contextualize in order to integrate different, even divergent, perspectives in a coherent way.

Transformative Leadership: M.A. in transformative leadership (online). In an era of complexity, challenges, and opportunities, there is a critical need for skilled leaders in a wide array of disciplines and settings—from education and the environment to businesses and local communities. The transformative leadership online M.A. program is for individuals who have the initiative, passion, and vision to facilitate positive social change and to make a significant contribution to the world. Transformative leadership students recognize that effective leadership requires specific skills in conflict resolution, group dynamics, and creative thinking. Also important is the ability to reflect on why change is needed, how it is conducted, and who is engaged in the process. The program invites students to engage in a profound questioning of these assumptions, along with their implications and applications to practice. Reflection and theory are united with practice by focusing on the development of capacities to envision, initiate, and engage in transformative change processes.

Women's Spirituality: M.A. and Ph.D. in philosophy and religion with a concentration in women's spirituality. One of the first accredited graduate programs in women's spirituality in the world, this program offers an experiential learning community that celebrates the contribution women have made in shaping and defining the spiritual throughout history and across cultures.

Research Facilities

The Laurance S. Rockefeller Library has collections of approximately 35,000 volumes (including numerous e-books), 290 periodicals (including electronic journals), 1,000 audiovisual materials (including audiocassettes, videotapes, and compact discs), and almost 1,000 CIIS dissertations and master's theses. The collections are especially strong in the areas of transpersonal and multicultural psychology, spirituality (particularly women's spirituality, Buddhism, Hinduism, Taoism, Confucianism, and wisdom traditions), integral studies, and studies of consciousness. Special collections include Alan Watts' and Haridas Chaudhuri's personal collections, the Langley-Porter collection of psychology and psychiatry, the Rogo collection of parapsychology, and a CIIS Institute Authors' collection.

Financial Aid

Financial assistance is awarded primarily on the basis of need. Financial aid consists of scholarships, loans, grants, and Federal Work-Study Program awards. There are a limited number of Institute scholarships. International students may obtain nonimmigrant visas and are eligible for part-time employment on the campus.

Cost of Study

In 2007–08, full-time annual tuition and fees were $14,040 for M.A. programs and $16,650 for doctoral programs.

Living and Housing Costs

There is no on-campus housing. Living expenses are about $1200 per month. Information about living and housing costs can be found on the CIIS Web site at http://www.ciis.edu/students/housing.

Student Group

Total enrollment in 2007–08 was 1,149. About 20 percent are students of color; 9 percent, international; and 75 percent, women.

The Institute

Founded in 1968 by the Indian philosopher, educator, and humanist Haridas Chaudhuri, California Institute of Integral Studies is a WASC-accredited institution of higher education and research dedicated to integrating mind, body, and spirit in service to individuals, communities, and the Earth. Certain programs offer online options or a combination of online and monthly weekend meetings. The Institute is defined by its value of cultural diversity as well as cultural coherence, multiple ways of knowing, spiritual development, a sense of community, emancipatory ideals, and ecological sustainability.

Applying

Decisions regarding admission are based on the potential for success in the chosen field of study by considering past academic achievement and motivation for educational and personal development and the congruence of the applicant's worldview with the Institute's mission and vision. Applicants to the M.A. programs must have earned a bachelor's degree from a regionally accredited institution. A grade point average of 3.0 or higher is strongly recommended for all programs. Applicants to the Ph.D. and Psy.D. programs must have earned an M.A., preferably in a related discipline, with a minimum 3.1 GPA. Academic transcripts, the autobiographical and goal statements, a writing sample (if required), letters of recommendation (if required), and an interview are all considered in the admissions committee's decision. The GRE (Graduate Record Examinations) is required for the Psy.D. program only. For specific program requirements, students should visit http://www.ciis.edu.

Correspondence and Information

Office of Admissions
California Institute of Integral Studies
1453 Mission Street
San Francisco, California 94103

Phone: 415-575-6154
Fax: 415-575-1268
E-mail: admissions@ciis.edu
Web site: http://www.ciis.edu

California Institute of Integral Studies

THE FACULTY AND THEIR RESEARCH

Asian Comparative Studies

Steven Goodman, Program Co-Director; Ph.D., Saskatchewan, 1984. Indo-Tibetan Buddhism, comparative philosophy, classical Tibetan language, Mahayana Buddhism, poetics.

Jim Ryan, Program Co-Director; Ph.D., Berkeley, 1985. Sanskrit, Hindi and Tamil, Hindu Tantrism, Jainism.

Rina Sircar, Haridas Chaudhuri Professor of South Asian and Comparative Philosophy; Ph.D., Gujarat (India), 1974; Ph.D., California Institute of Integral Studies, 1976. Buddhism, mindfulness, healing in the Theravada forest tradition, Pali language.

Yi Wu, Ph.D., University of Chinese Culture, 1970. Chinese philosophy, religion, and literature; Chinese language.

East-West Psychology

Brendan Collins, Ph.D., US International, 1977. Contemporary psychology, psychoanalysis, Western mystical and contemplative traditions.

Daniel Deslauriers, Ph.D., Montreal, 1989. Cross-cultural approaches to dreams, altered states, meditation, body-mind integrative practice.

Jorge Ferrer, Ph.D., California Institute of Integral Studies, 1999. Transpersonal psychology, epistemology, Buddhism and social engagement, sexuality and spirituality.

Janis Phelps, Ph.D., Connecticut, 1986. Child development, clinical studies in enhanced expectancies and treatment, mind-body wellness, Eastern disciplines, interaction of meditation and creativity.

Carol Whitfield, Ph.D., Graduate Theological Union, 1992; Ph.D., San Francisco School of Psychology, 1997. Synthesis of Western psychology and Eastern spirituality, Jungian psychotherapy.

Integrative Health Studies

Michael Denney, M.D., Ph.D., Pacifica Graduate. Fundamentals of integrative health studies, science, spirituality and healing, ethics of the healing relationship, psychosomatic counseling, holistic health and healing, alternative and complementary medicine and science.

Mutombo Mpanya, Ph.D., Michigan, 1982. Global health, medical anthropology, health policy and planning, health costs, nutrition.

Ricki Pollycove, M.H.S., Berkeley, 1975; M.D., California, San Francisco, 1977. Integrative health approaches to women in midlife; integrative anatomy and physiology; psychosocial-spiritual healing; complementary, supportive, and therapeutic care as adjuncts in the treatment of breast cancer.

Arisika Razak, M.P.H., Berkeley, 1978; RN. Contemporary issues in women's health, women's embodiment of healing and sexuality, health issues of women of color, women's spirituality, diversity.

Julia Zarcone, M.A., San Francisco State; CMT; Rosen Method Bodywork practitioner. Psychosocial treatment and trauma research.

Philosophy, Cosmology, and Consciousness

Sean Kelly, Ph.D., Ottawa, 1988. Transpersonal theory, Jungian thought, new paradigm studies.

Robert McDermott, Ph.D., Boston University, 1969. American philosophy, evolution of consciousness, modern spiritual masters, Rudolf Steiner.

Brian Swimme, Ph.D., Oregon, 1978. Evolutionary cosmology, science and spirituality, the role of humanity in the unfolding story of Earth.

Richard Tarnas, Ph.D., Saybrook Institute, 1976. History of Western thought and culture, depth psychology, archetypal studies, philosophy.

David Ulansey, Ph.D., Princeton, 1984. Ancient Mediterranean religions, evolution of consciousness, metaphysics of cyberspace.

Social and Cultural Anthropology

Matthew Bronson, M.A., Berkeley, 1982. Accelerative teacher/trainer, intercultural communications, human learning potential, influence of indigenous languages on Spanish, linguistic analysis of discourses.

Angana Chatterji, Ph.D., California Institute of Integral Studies. Anthropology of development, participatory development, environmental management, gender, policy, research, postcolonial critique.

Mutombo Mpanya, Ph.D., Michigan, 1982. Twenty years with international development agencies in African countries, management of natural resources, economics, globalization, nonprofit sector.

Richard Shapiro, M.A., Ph.D. candidate, New School, 1981. Emancipatory education; cross-cultural study of subjectivity, gender, and European thought.

Transformative Studies/Transformative Leadership

Allan Combs, Ph.D. (neural psychology), Georgia, 1977. Integral psychology and philosophy; evolution of consciousness and spirituality; transformation of consciousness, dreaming, mind and brain, chaos, and complexity.

Riane Eisler, J.D., UCLA, 1965; President, Center for Partnership Studies. Developed study of relational dynamics, cultural transformation theory, and other new approaches to understanding systems maintenance and transformation; author of *The Power of Partnership,* among many other works introducing the new social categories of the partnership and domination systems as two underlying possibilities for structuring beliefs, institutions, and relations.

Ursula Fahim, Ph.D. (transformative learning and change), California Institute of Integral Studies, 2003. Women's leadership, inquiry and research methodologies, group process, collaborative creativity, intercultural communication.

Joanne Gozawa, Ph.D., California Institute of Integral Studies, 2000. Organic inquiry, learning community, transformative learning.

Constance Jones, Ph.D., Emory, 1977. History of Hindu movements in the United States, transformational learning, sociology of religion, new religious movements in the United States.

Bradford Keeney, Ph.D. (family therapy), Purdue, 1981. Ecstatic transformation, shaking medicine, wild conversation and absurd performance, n/om leadership, radical creativity, extreme improvisation.

Alfonso Montuori, Ph.D., Saybrook Institute, 1991. Systems and complexity theory, creativity, postmodernism, social change, cross-cultural theory.

Linda Jean Shepherd, Ph.D. (biochemistry), Penn State, 1976. Integral science, feminism, Jungian studies, ethnobotany, herbal studies, sustainability, building bridges between science and spirituality. Author of *Lifting the Veil: The Feminine Face of Science.*

Shoshana Simons, Ph.D. (human and organizational systems), Fielding Institute. Narrative and relational-constructionist approaches to systems change; integration of expressive arts in transformational work; intercultural communications in groups and organizations; social-emotional learning in education and leadership; race, gender, class, and sexuality issues.

Women's Spirituality

Lucia Chiavola Birnbaum, Ph.D., Berkeley, 1964. Feminist and cultural history and/or vernacular history of women and other subaltern classes.

Mara Lynn Keller, Ph.D., Yale, 1971. Ancient goddess cultures of Crete and Greece, holistic philosophy, ecofeminism, peace issues.

Arisika Razak, M.P.H., Berkeley, 1978. Reproductive health, ritual, embodiment of the sacred, perinatal care of African American women.

Charlene Spretnak, M.A., Berkeley, 1981. Women's spirituality, spirituality and art, ecological postmodernism, embodied/embedded philosophy and literature.

CENTRAL EUROPEAN UNIVERSITY

Graduate Programs in Social Sciences

Programs of Study Central European University (CEU) offers graduate degrees in economics, environmental sciences and policy, gender studies, history, international relations and European studies, legal studies, mathematics and its applications, medieval studies, nationalism studies, philosophy, political science, public policy, and sociology and social anthropology. In addition, the CEU Business School offers an M.B.A., a Master of Science in information technology management, and executive programs. CEU typically has two types of master's degree programs: one-year master's programs, which take ten months to complete and normally require four years of undergraduate study, and Bologna-type two-year programs, which are specially designed for graduates of three-year undergraduate programs. CEU is a partner institution in several Erasmus Mundus consortia, offering the following two-year master's degree programs: environmental sciences, policy, and management (MESPOM); the Joint European Master in Women's and Gender Studies (GEMMA); and public policy (Mundus MAPP). Doctoral programs are offered on a full-time basis only and take three to six years to complete. A graduate research–intensive university, CEU promotes a combined emphasis on scholarship, research, and social engagement. Through both disciplinary depth and a strong comparative and transdisciplinary approach, studies at CEU focus on the diverse and changing social, economic, and political aspects and needs of societies in transition.

Research Facilities The dissemination and pursuit of knowledge at CEU rests on the idea that nearly all of the major problems facing humanity today—e.g., poverty, climate change, democratization—require interdisciplinary cooperation from academics, experts, and policy makers. Much of this work is accomplished by programs conducted at the Research Centers of CEU. Thus, beyond the creation of knowledge in their respective academic disciplines, both CEU faculty members and accomplished visiting scholars engaged by these centers continually explore the sociocultural context of the contemporary state of learning.

The CEU library is the largest English-language academic library in the region. It collects materials in the fields of arts and literature, business studies, economics, environmental sciences, gender studies, history, international relations, legal studies, medieval studies, philosophy, political sciences, and social sciences. The library currently holds more than 250,000 documents in various formats, including 135,000 monographs, 1,600 periodical titles, and more than 10,000 papers, essays, and various research documents published by select academic and research institutions. The library offers access to a number of online sources, such as EBSCO Electronic Journals Service, Economist Intelligence Unit's Country Reports, International Financial Statistics (IFS), Westlaw International, and others.

The Open Society Archives (OSA) at CEU is another resource for the study and understanding of recent history—more specifically, the fascist and communist attempts to radically alter the course of human history. OSA is probably the richest international textual and audiovisual archive of the period of communism, a notable repository of documents from the era of the Cold War, and holds one of the largest collections of propaganda from the post–World War II period.

Financial Aid CEU provides full and partial financial assistance to the majority of its students, regardless of their nationality. The full CEU fellowship is an award that covers tuition and fees and medical insurance and provides a scholarship for living expenses. Candidates admitted into the CEU doctoral programs are eligible to receive the full CEU fellowship for three years, as well as institutional research support grants and study-abroad funding. For students enrolled in the master's programs, CEU has established a diversified financial aid program, which offers full or partial financial assistance.

Financial aid is awarded primarily on the basis of merit.

Cost of Study The tuition fee in 2008–09 is €10,000.

Living and Housing Costs Students need to budget approximately €6200 per academic year to cover their living costs in Budapest. These include housing in a shared apartment (or in the residence center), meals, local transportation, and incidentals. Travel, recreation, and other expenses vary with the individual and need to be budgeted separately. Information about the estimated cost of living is available at http://www.ceu.hu/studentlife/students/costofliving.

Student Group One of the main characteristics of CEU's student body is the lack of a dominant national culture. Most of the students come from the countries in Central and Eastern Europe and the former Soviet Union. In addition, CEU has enrolled students from Western Europe, North America, Central and South America, Africa, and Asia. In 2007–08, CEU enrolled approximately 1,300 students from more than eighty countries. Students are admitted on the basis of merit, without any specific country quotas. The University admits those with the highest academic achievement who share its mission and CEU's curriculum, which is tuned to that mission. In addition, CEU is looking to attract students with a sense of social responsibility who are transnationally inclined and have the potential to work for open and democratic societies.

Student Outcomes CEU students—who now come from more than eighty countries around the world—represent a lively multicultural group of talented and motivated young scholars. They share a commitment to working for open and democratic societies and a desire to contribute to the public good. As of 2008, 27 percent of CEU's master's graduates are enrolled in doctoral and other graduate programs, and 73 percent have entered a professional career. Of those, 36 percent are employed in education and research institutions, 31 percent are in the business sector, 20 percent are in international organizations and public interest and advocacy groups, and 13 percent are in government.

Location The University is located in Budapest, the political, cultural, intellectual, and economic center of Hungary. A city of outstanding architectural elegance, Budapest is brimming with restaurants, cafés, clubs, and shops. It offers something for everyone, including medieval and Roman areas, theaters and concert halls, sports facilities, and plenty of opportunities for recreation.

The University Central European University is a U.S.-style graduate university with a focus on the social sciences and the humanities, accredited both in the United States and in Hungary, and located in Budapest, in the heart of Europe. The University is oriented to interdisciplinary research on, and the study of, social change and the policy implications of transition to open societies. In addition, emphasis is placed on European Union affairs, as well as on the special features of non-Western democracies.

Through their international experience at CEU, and exposure to a multitude of different—and sometimes opposing—points of view, students at the University develop a deep understanding of the intellectual and practical challenges arising along the shifting boundary between the local and the universal. They leave CEU with the knowledge and skills that enable them to pursue careers in academia, the government and the nongovernmental sectors, international organizations and research institutes, and missions of the United Nations, as well as business organizations at the national and international levels.

Applying The application deadlines for 2009–10 are in January 2009. Details on the admission process are available at http://www.ceu.hu/admissions.

Application forms are submitted online through the CEU Web site. A complete application package typically includes a statement of purpose or research outline, resume, academic records, two letters of recommendation, and proof of English language proficiency. Special requirements and subject tests may be requested by particular departments.

Correspondence and Information
Admissions Office
Central European University
Nador u.9
1051 Budapest
Hungary
Phone: 36-1-327-3009, 3272, 3210, or 3208
Fax: 36-1-327-3211
E-mail: admissions@ceu.hu
Web site: http://www.ceu.hu

Central European University

THE FACULTY AND THEIR RESEARCH

More than 200 professors from around the world teach at CEU. They come from countries including Albania, Australia, Austria, Belarus, Belgium, Bulgaria, Canada, Croatia, Cyprus, Denmark, Estonia, France, Germany, Hungary, Israel, Italy, Lebanon, Luxembourg, Malaysia, the Netherlands, Nigeria, New Zealand, Poland, Romania, Russia, Serbia, Slovakia, Slovenia, Switzerland, Turkey, Ukraine, the United Kingdom, and the United States. Among the faculty members are a large number of visiting professors who teach courses and give frequent lectures and seminars, thus giving students access to highly respected academics from other institutions.

Attracted by the University's academic excellence, by its social values and willingness to encourage intellectual risks, both renowned senior scholars and talented young faculty members have recognized CEU as an institution ready to organize resources and structures around promising new ideas. Even as CEU becomes increasingly global, the faculty's scholarship reflects its roots in this region. Their richly varied experiences have led naturally to a distinction found in both teaching and research at the University: an emphasis on the interplay between universal principles and local circumstances in shaping change.

SELECTED FACULTY

Yehuda Elkana, CEU President and Rector; Ph.D., Brandeis, 1968. Taught at Harvard, Tel Aviv, and Hebrew Universities and was a full Professor for the Philosophy of Science at the ETH Zurich; currently, a permanent Fellow at the Wissenschaftskolleg zu Berlin; throughout his academic career has served as the Chairman of Department of History and Philosophy of Science at the Hebrew University, as Director of the Cohn Institute for the History and Philosophy of Science and Ideas at Tel Aviv University, and Director of the Van Leer Jerusalem Institute; was elected in 2001 to serve on the Board of Trustees of the Carnegie Foundation for the Advancement of Teaching for a period of four years.
Howard Robinson, CEU University Professor and Provost; Ph.D., Liverpool. Professor of philosophy at CEU and Honorary Research Fellow in the Department of Philosophy at the University of Liverpool; specializes in metaphysics, including the philosophy of religion and the philosophy of mind; has an interest in the history of philosophy.
Aziz Al-Azmeh, CEU University Professor; Ph.D., Oxford.
Peter Balazs, Professor; Ph.D., Hungarian Academy of Sciences.
Karoly Bard, Professor and Pro-Rector for Hungarian and European Union Affairs; Ph.D., Hungarian Academy of Sciences.
Andras Bozoki, Professor; Ph.D., Hungarian Academy of Sciences.
Rogers Brubaker, Recurrent Visiting Professor; Ph.D., Columbia.
Ayse Caglar, Professor; Ph.D., McGill.
László Csaba, Professor; Ph.D., Hungarian Academy of Sciences.
Francisca de Haan, Professor; Ph.D., Erasmus.
Nenad Dimitrijevic, Associate Professor; Ph.D., Novi Sad (Serbia).
John Earle, Professor; Ph.D., Stanford.
Béla Greskovits, Professor; Ph.D., Hungarian Academy of Sciences.
Julius Horvath, Professor; Ph.D., Southern Illinois at Carbondale.
Ferenc Huoranszki, Professor; Ph.D., Hungarian Academy of Sciences.
János Kis, CEU University Professor; M.A., Eötvös Loránd (Budapest).
Gábor Klaniczay, CEU University Professor; Ph.D., Hungarian Academy of Sciences.
László Kontler, Professor; Ph.D., Hungarian Academy of Sciences.
János Kornai, CEU Distinguished Research Professor; Dr.Oec., Karl Marx (Budapest); Dr.Sc., Hungarian Academy of Sciences.
Andras Kovacs, Professor; Ph.D., Eötvös Loránd (Budapest).
Maria Kovacs, Professor; Ph.D., Hungarian Academy of Sciences.
Will Kymlicka, Recurrent Visiting Professor; D.Phil., Oxford.
Jozsef Laszlovszky, Professor; Ph.D., Hungarian Academy of Sciences.
László Mátyás, CEU University Professor; Ph.D., Hungarian Academy of Sciences.
Stefan Messmann, Professor; Ph.D., Fribourg (Switzerland).
Ruben Mnatsakanian, Professor; Ph.D., Moscow State.
Gheorghe Morosanu, Professor; Ph.D., Alexandru Ioan Cuza (Romania).
Wiktor Osiatynski, CEU University Professor; Ph.D., Polish Academy of Sciences.
Anton Pelinka, Professor; J.D., Vienna.
Istvan Perczel, Professor; Ph.D., Hungarian Academy of Sciences.
András Sajó, CEU University Professor; Ph.D., Hungarian Academy of Sciences.
Judit Sandor, Professor; Ph.D., Hungarian Academy of Sciences.
Diana Urge-Vorsatz, Professor; Ph.D., Berkeley.
Tibor Várady, CEU University Professor; S.J.D., Harvard.
Susan Zimmermann, Professor; Dr.habil., Linz (Austria); Dr.habil., Eötvös Loránd (Budapest).

SELECTED AREAS OF RESEARCH

Economics: Monetary economics; international macroeconomics; applied econometrics; labor economics; corporate governance; pension economics; stochastic analysis and mathematical finance; health economics; comparative economic institutions; macroeconomics; European integration.

Environmental Sciences and Policy: Management of ecological systems (special reference to freshwaters); state-of-the-environment assessments; environmental policy and law in countries in transition; environmental management and audit.

Gender Studies: Feminist theories and epistemology; interdisciplinary; intersections with race, class, and sexuality; local and transnational women's movement; comparative analysis; gender and post-state socialist societies; cultural studies; queer theory; globalization and postcolonialism; labor; literary studies; gender, nation, and state.

History: Interdisciplinary, transnational, comparative history of Europe, with a focus on Central Europe, Southeastern Europe, and Eastern Europe.

International Relations and European Studies: Ethnic conflicts; international refugee law; CIS member states foreign policy; international relations theory; international political theory; leading sectors and the variety of transnational capitalism in Eastern Europe; politics of economic policy making; political economy of international monetary relations; political economy of the European Union; European governance; European constitution; European cultural policy.

Legal Studies: Public law; free speech problems in a post-totalitarian context; constitutional transplant; institutional, constitutional, and human rights in the European Union law; data protection law; biotechnical and human rights; biomedical law and reproductive rights; international commercial arbitration; law and ethnicity; language and translation in international dispute settlement; Islamic banking and finance; southeastern European investment law; enforcement of contracts in Eastern Europe; transplant of war criminal law to the Balkans from Germany; comparative secured transactions law and the related reforms of the laws of emerging markets; comparative mortgage and housing programs; capital markets and securities regulation in emerging markets.

Mathematics and Its Applications: Algebra; algebraic geometry; approximation theory; combinatorics; computational geometry; computing; cryptology; evolutional equations; dynamical systems; differential geometry; ergodic theory; fractals; functional analysis; graph theory; homological algebra; information theory; logic; number theory; numerical analysis; optimization; partial differential equations; probability theory; set theory; statistics; stochastic processes.

Medieval Studies: Social, cultural, and religious history of medieval east-central and southeastern Europe, such as nobility, law collections, rulership, urban evolution, Jewish minorities, cultural heritage, historical-environmental studies, monastic culture, hagiography, patristic traditions, interactions between medieval Latin and Greek Christianity and Slavia Orthodoxy, Christianity and Islam, and the broader world of Christian oikumene. Research projects are based on working with digitalized visual resources, manuscripts (Latin, Slavonic, Greek, and Siriac), and archaeological documentation.

Nationalism Studies: Empirical, theoretical, and normative issues connected to nationalism, self-determination and state-formation, ethnic conflict, minority protection, language and citizenship rights, constitutional design, and parliamentary mechanisms in ethnically divided societies.

Philosophy: History of philosophy ancient and modern; philosophy of language and logic, especially the nature of quantification, and semantics of externalism; philosophy of mind, especially dualism, the mind-body problem, and perception; metaphysics, especially agency, free will, causation, and idealism; political philosophy, especially liberalism, theory of democracy, and epistemology.

Political Science: Democratization and political economy (especially concerning eastern Europe and the EU); comparative and survey methods; analytical political theory; constitutional theory; normative and applied ethics; political obligation; democratic theory; discourse analysis; peacekeeping; media policy; bioethics; party politics; church-state relations; voting behavior.

Public Policy: Globalization; European integration and policy making; governance and policy reform; local government management; fiscal decentralization; comparative public budgeting; public finance; intergovernmental finance; public integrity; equal opportunity policies; rural development; economic culture; urban public transport management and policy; media and telecommunications policy; social policy; public-sector management; social network analysis; game theory.

Sociology and Social Anthropology: Empirical research using a wide variety of methodologies. Special research fields include comparative approaches to the theory and practice of development; modernity; globalization; state; politics of culture; migration; memory; civil society; inequalities; gender; the city and urban processes.

CENTRAL MICHIGAN UNIVERSITY

Master of Arts in Humanities

Program of Study

Central Michigan University (CMU) offers the Master of Arts in humanities, a 30-semester-hour program designed to integrate the study of the humanities in an interdisciplinary format. Because the various areas of the humanities are naturally interrelated, they are best understood and appreciated from an interdisciplinary perspective. This degree program is appropriate for teachers in all areas of the humanities, for preprofessional students, and for generalists. The Master of Arts in humanities was designed for those more interested in synthesis than specialization; the format emphasizes connection rather than fragmentation.

The courses are generally selected from such traditional areas of the humanities as history, literature, philosophy, religion, music, and art; they may, however, also include such areas as women's studies and anthropology. Courses for the degree are thematically woven into a study of the changing role of the humanities in contemporary society. To complete the requirements, students must either enroll in 6 more hours of course work or complete a thesis.

The program is flexible enough to meet the needs of a great variety of students. It is an appropriate degree choice for students seeking a graduate degree that offers educational development or a focus on interdisciplinary knowledge. Students interested in certification or additional endorsements should contact the Teacher Certification Office.

Research Facilities

The University's library system includes off-campus library services, the Clarke Historical Library, and the main library, with numerous books and publications, electronic and paper journals, and access to several databases. The original goal of the Clarke Library was to document all aspects of the history of Michigan and the Old Northwest Territory. Collecting material regarding the state and the Old Northwest Territory remains a fundamental focus of the library. The collection includes more than 65,000 volumes, 2,500 manuscript collections, 11,000 reels of microfilm, 16,000 visual images, and 3,000 maps. There are three large public computer labs on campus that contain 400 PC and Mac workstations, and the library offers more than 300 public workstations that are distributed throughout the facility. A large selection of general software is available, including Adobe Photoshop, Microsoft Office, SPSS, SAS, and Minitab.

CMU's off-campus library program is the most comprehensive and sophisticated of its type. More than $1 million is invested annually to keep it that way, because the University believes that high-quality, convenient library support is critical to delivering high-quality, convenient academic programs. Off-Campus Library Services have full-time librarians located on campus and in regional offices around the country who are available to provide students with reference and referral assistance. Additional support staff and document-delivery specialists work specifically to meet off-campus students' needs. Students can use a toll-free number, fax, e-mail, or a Web form to request reference assistance, book loans, and copies of journal articles. Books and copies of journal articles are sent within 24 to 48 hours after the request is received. A growing number of full-text sources are also available on the Web, so students can print the information they need immediately.

Financial Aid

Many students are concerned about financing their education. CMU wants to make the financial aid process as simple as possible. The program director can explain to interested students the options offered through CMU. Financial aid specialists are also available by telephone at 800-950-1144 Ext. 1260 to answer any questions students might have.

Cost of Study

For the 2007–08 academic year, tuition was $403 per credit hour.

Living and Housing Costs

Single-student and one- to three-bedroom family apartments are available in apartment complexes on the campus. Rent includes electricity, gas, water, heat, telephone, cable TV, and other such services as the University deems appropriate. Off-campus housing is available from $250 per month, depending on the neighborhood, number of roommates, and size of apartment.

Student Group

The M.A. degree in humanities draws students from many different disciplines. Students are teachers, community college instructors, businessmen and businesswomen, writers, nurses, bartenders, accountants—in short, all kinds of people with a passion for banishing ignorance with knowledge and celebrating the intricacies of nature. More than 75 percent of M.A. in humanities alumni are employed in a job related to their degree. Most are in the teaching professions; however, a variety of positions in finance, marketing research, and writing are also represented.

Location

Mount Pleasant is located in Michigan's Lower Peninsula. The downtown district features specialty stores and boutiques of all types within walking distance of the campus. Thirteen golf courses are located within a 30-minute drive, while surrounding state preserves are frequented by local hunters. Eleven parks covering 300 acres—plus another 900 acres in Isabella County—offer venues for swimming, canoeing, hiking, camping, and cross-country skiing.

The University

Central Michigan University opened its doors in 1892 to formally train teachers in the state. Bachelor's degrees were first awarded in 1918, and graduate courses were first offered in 1938. Today the University enrolls more than 28,000 students in more than 200 programs leading to twenty-seven degrees at the bachelor's, master's, specialist, and doctoral levels. The University's $50-million New Vision of Excellence Campaign is a broadly focused initiative to raise academic standards, strengthen discovery and creative activity, and enhance learning-environment facilities and technology.

Applying

Applicants holding a four-year baccalaureate or equivalent degree from a college or university of recognized standing may be granted regular admission. In addition to the University's general admission requirements (a baccalaureate degree and an overall minimum GPA of 2.7), applicants must have a minimum of 20 hours of course work in areas of the humanities (history, literature, philosophy, etc.), with a minimum GPA of 2.7. In general, students must submit the completed application, the $50 nonrefundable application fee, and official transcripts from each college or university attended. The deadline for submitting admission applications is July 1.

Correspondence and Information

Ronald Primeau
Director, M.A. in Humanities
Central Michigan University
802 Industrial Drive
Mount Pleasant, Michigan 48859
Phone: 989-774-3117
Fax: 989-774-7106
E-mail: ronald.r.primeau@cmich.edu
Web site: http://www.cmich.edu

Central Michigan University

THE FACULTY AND THEIR RESEARCH

Instructors come from CMU's main campus and from other distinguished universities. They are committed to the concept of interdisciplinary studies. Faculty members are selected to teach in the M.A. in humanities program based on their ability to connect ideas and philosophies from a variety of subject areas and to foster that ability in their students.

For more information, students should contact the program director, Ronald Primeau, at 989-774-3117 or ronald.r.primeau@cmich.edu.

DARTMOUTH COLLEGE

Master of Arts in Liberal Studies

Program of Study

The Dartmouth Master of Arts in Liberal Studies (M.A.L.S.) Program was designed for individuals who want to engage in self-directed study in the liberal arts at the graduate level. A fundamental principle of liberal studies is the examination of accepted premises in traditional disciplines, and the M.A.L.S. Program affords students the opportunity to combine disparate disciplines in order to forge new areas of scholarly inquiry. Courses offered through the program have combined such disciplines as psychology and philosophy, history and sociology, art history and literature, geography and history, and many others. In addition, the program features courses that demonstrate breadth within a single discipline.

Candidates for the M.A.L.S. degree complete eight courses, three of which must be interdisciplinary; two summer symposia; and a thesis. At least one of the eight courses must be an independent study. A research methods course is offered in the summer as an alternative to the symposium. M.A.L.S. students pursue a self-designed liberal studies curriculum with the guidance of a faculty adviser and a faculty thesis committee. The program also offers concentrations in cultural studies, creative writing, and globalization studies. Each concentration consists of three courses in the area of concentration; three interdisciplinary M.A.L.S. courses; an independent study, also in the area of concentration; and one elective. Cultural studies courses encompass the subjects of race, class, gender, post-Colonial studies, and performance/media studies. Creative writing majors may pursue workshops in the genres of fiction, nonfiction, poetry, journalism, screenwriting, oral history, or playwriting. The globalization studies track combines history, politics, economics, sociology, and anthropology, and students may elect a regional focus. Candidates intending to concentrate in one of these areas should indicate their interest on their application but will be formally considered as concentrators after completing two M.A.L.S. courses.

Candidates for the M.A.L.S. Program may attend the program year-round on a full-time basis, part-time, summers only (for teachers and other professionals), or in a combination of these patterns. Students have six years from the time of entry to complete degree requirements. The program generally takes six to eight terms (1½ to 2 years) with full-time attendance, including thesis research and writing. After course work and the symposium requirements are fulfilled, students may remain on campus and formally enroll in thesis research, or they may work independently on their thesis off campus.

Research Facilities

Dartmouth's extensive facilities are available to all graduate students and visitors year-round. The College library's collection of more than a million volumes, the rich variety of computer network services, the Hopkins Center for the Performing Arts, the Hood Museum, Alumni Gym, and numerous other facilities and services offer many advantages to M.A.L.S. students. Resources that provide opportunities for students to engage in community activism, international and public affairs activities, and intellectual forums with guest speakers, debates, discussion groups, and student organizations include the Tucker Foundation, the John Sloan Dickey Center for International Affairs, the Nelson A. Rockefeller Center for Public Affairs, the Ethics Institute, the Humanities Center, and the Women's Resource Center, among many others.

Financial Aid

Financial assistance is available to M.A.L.S. students in the form of tuition scholarships and loans. Teachers on the elementary and secondary school levels are considered a priority group for financial aid decisions; they are also encouraged to seek staff development funds from their home school. Many U.S. citizens are eligible for Federal Stafford Student Loans, Federal Perkins Loans, or veterans' benefits. Limited scholarship assistance is available for qualified international students. Both the Dartmouth Graduate Financial Aid Form and a link to the FAFSA form are available through Dartmouth's Web site. Inquiries about financial aid should be directed to the Executive Director of the program.

Cost of Study

Tuition for the M.A.L.S. Program is charged based upon enrollment per quarter, due to the flexible study options. Because Dartmouth College is on the quarter system, two courses are considered full-time study. During the 2007–08 academic year, the tuition per course was $4662. For two courses in one term, the tuition was $8159, and for three courses, $11,655. There is no charge for the summer symposium, research methods, or the writing workshop. Thesis research enrollment tuition is subsidized by the program for up to four terms.

Living and Housing Costs

During the summer, the M.A.L.S. Program provides a dormitory for full-time students at a rate of approximately $2000 for the ten-week summer term. Local furnished apartments rent for an average of $700 per month. Married students have access to unfurnished apartments owned by Dartmouth that rent for $550 to $700 per month.

Student Group

The M.A.L.S. Program offers enrollment on a full-time, part-time, or summers-only basis to accommodate both full-time graduate students and working professionals. Originally designed as a program for teachers to expand their cross-disciplinary knowledge, M.A.L.S. now satisfies a broad spectrum of academic and professional needs. M.A.L.S. has a typical enrollment of 75 to 90 students during the traditional academic year, with approximately 100 to 120 in the summer session.

Location

Dartmouth is located in Hanover, New Hampshire, a small New England town dating back to a few years before the College's founding in 1769. Situated in the Upper Valley of the Connecticut River between the White Mountains of New Hampshire and the Green Mountains of Vermont, Hanover combines the advantages of a rural setting with the resources of a university. The Dartmouth campus is about 2 hours by car from Boston and 3½ hours from Montreal. Local airports include Lebanon-Hanover, Manchester, and Burlington, and there is an Amtrak station approximately 15 minutes from campus in White River Junction, Vermont.

The Program and The College

The M.A.L.S. Program is in the Faculty of Arts and Sciences, which offers fifteen graduate programs in the natural sciences, social sciences, and humanities. Graduate programs are also offered by Dartmouth's professional schools, which include Dartmouth Medical School, Amos Tuck School of Business, and Thayer School of Engineering. All graduate programs maintain a favorable student-faculty ratio.

Applying

The M.A.L.S. applications committee requires the completion of an application form, three letters of professional/academic reference, a statement of purpose, and academic transcripts. Writing samples are optional but are recommended for candidates interested in the creative writing concentration. Submission of GRE scores is also optional. Applicants are strongly urged to schedule an admissions interview prior to the application deadline. Telephone interviews are also acceptable for people outside of the immediate area. Application deadlines are February 15 (for summer or fall enrollment) and July 15 (for winter or spring entry.)

Correspondence and Information

M.A.L.S. Program
Dartmouth College
116 Wentworth, HB 6092
Hanover, New Hampshire 03755-3526

Phone: 603-646-3592
Fax: 603-646-3590
E-mail: mals.program@dartmouth.edu
Web site: http://www.dartmouth.edu/~mals

Dartmouth College

THE FACULTY

Brock Brower, M.A., Oxford; Visiting Lecturer of Journalism.
Raúl Bueno, Ph.D., San Agustin (Peru); Professor of Spanish and Portuguese.
George Demko, Ph.D., Penn State; Professor Emeritus of Geography.
Ronald Edsforth, Ph.D., Michigan; Visiting Professor of History.
Carl B. Estabrook, Ph.D., Brown; Associate Professor of History.
Harvey Frommer, Ph.D., NYU; Visiting Professor of Liberal Studies.
Myrna Katz Frommer, Ph.D., NYU; Visiting Assistant Professor of Liberal Studies.
Cecilia Gaposchkin, Ph.D., Berkeley; Assistant Dean of Premajor Advising.
Jay Hull, Ph.D., Duke; Professor of Psychology.
Phyllis Katz, Ph.D., Columbia; Senior Lecturer in Classics and Women's Studies.
Barbara S. Kreiger, Ph.D., Brandeis; Senior Lecturer in English.
Sydney Lea, Ph.D., Yale; Visiting Professor of Poetry.
Alan Lelchuk, Ph.D., Stanford; Adjunct Professor of Liberal Studies.
Patricia McKee, Ph.D., Brandeis; Professor of English.
Klaus Milich; Ph.D., Humboldt (Berlin); Visiting Lecturer of American Literary and Cultural Studies.
Hua-yuan Mowry, Ph.D., Berkeley; Associate Professor of Chinese Language and Literature.
Misagh Parsa, Ph.D., Michigan; Professor of Sociology.
Donald E. Pease Jr., Ph.D., Chicago; Professor of English.
William Phillips, M.F.A., USC; Visiting Associate Professor of Film.
Thomas Powers, Visiting Lecturer of Nonfiction Writing.
Regine Rosenthal, Ph.D., Munich; Visiting Professor of American and Jewish Studies.
Diederik Vandewalle, Ph.D., Columbia; Associate Professor of Government.
Keith Walker, Ph.D., Yale; Associate Professor of French and Italian and Liberal Studies.
Christopher Wren, M.A., Columbia; Visiting Professor of Journalism.

Administration
Lauren E. Clarke, Executive Director.
Carole Webber, Administrative Assistant.
Wole P. Ojurongbe, Administrator/Registrar.
Donald E. Pease Jr., Academic Chair.

Dartmouth Hall.

THE JOHNS HOPKINS UNIVERSITY

Zanvyl Krieger School of Arts and Sciences
Advanced Academic Programs
Master of Liberal Arts

Program of Study

Established in 1962, the Johns Hopkins Master of Liberal Arts (M.L.A.) Program has gained national recognition for the quality of its teaching and the breadth of its course offerings. The multicultural and interdisciplinary focus in this program encourages students to develop the knowledge and skill necessary to explore issues and ideas from a variety of perspectives and disciplines. The ten-course program enables students to continue their intellectual growth and further their professional goals. Students can focus on specific areas of learning or explore a wide range of engaging subjects in political science, art history, world religions and philosophy, history, music, literature, and science and technology.

The program features small, interactive seminars led by distinguished Johns Hopkins faculty members and leading experts from cultural, artistic, government, and academic institutions in the region, including the Walters Art Museum, the Peabody Institute, the State Department, and the Maryland State Archives.

The M.L.A. Program is part of the Johns Hopkins University Center for Liberal Arts, which also offers noncredit courses for adults and seniors.

Research Facilities

The Sheridan Libraries encompass the Milton S. Eisenhower Library and its collections at the Albert D. Hutzler Reading Room, the John Work Garrett Library at Evergreen House, and the George Peabody Library at Mt. Vernon Place. Together, these collections provide the major research library resources for the University. The Milton S. Eisenhower Library, the University's principal research library, includes specialized facilities and collections in medicine, public health, engineering, international affairs, and music. The Sheridan Libraries collections contain more than 2.6 million books, over 30,000 print and electronic journal subscriptions, more than 600,000 e-books, over 7,000 videos and DVDs, 215,000 maps, and 4.1 million microforms. University students have access to the libraries at five academic centers in the Baltimore-Washington metropolitan area. In addition, the interlibrary loan department makes the research collection of the nation available to faculty members and students.

Financial Aid

Federal financial aid in the form of student loans is available on a limited basis to degree candidates who are enrolled in two or more courses per semester or term. More information is available from the Office of Student Financial Services.

Cost of Study

Tuition is $1720 per course in 2008–09. Ten courses are required to complete the degree.

Living and Housing Costs

Students make their own arrangements for housing.

Student Group

Students study with and learn from other adults of diverse backgrounds, perspectives, and interests, and the seminars provide a challenging and nurturing environment.

Location

The program is housed at the Johns Hopkins University Homewood campus located in Baltimore, which is the main campus for the Krieger School of Arts and Sciences, Whiting School of Engineering, Carey Business School, and School of Education.

The University and The School

Privately endowed, the Johns Hopkins University was founded in 1876 as the first true American university based on the European model—a graduate institution with an associated preparatory college, a place where knowledge would be created and assembled as well as taught. The Zanvyl Krieger School of Arts and Sciences is at the heart of a small but unusually diverse coeducational university. The core institution of the Johns Hopkins complex of schools, centers, and institutes, the School recognizes the intellectual strength and education requirements of working adults. Through the Advanced Academic Programs, the School offers a Hopkins education to those wishing to attend graduate school.

Applying

Students must submit the completed application form, the nonrefundable application fee, official transcripts of all previous college work, a resume, and one letter of recommendation.

Students may apply throughout the year and begin study during any of the three terms. When an application is received, every effort is made to render a decision and notify an applicant in time for the upcoming term. For more information, students should visit http://advanced.jhu.edu/admissions.

Correspondence and Information

Advanced Academic Programs
Zanvyl Krieger School of Arts and Sciences
The Johns Hopkins University
1717 Massachusetts Avenue, NW, Suite 101
Washington, D.C. 20036-1717
Phone: 800-847-3330 (toll-free)
E-mail: advanced@jhu.edu
Web site: http://mla.jhu.edu

The Johns Hopkins University

ADVISORY BOARD AND FACULTY

Advisory Board
P. Kyle McCarter Jr., William Foxwell Albright Professor of Biblical and Ancient Near Eastern Studies and Chair, M.L.A. Program.
Mark Blyth, Professor of Political Science.
Neil Hertz, Professor of Humanities.
Edward Papenfuse, Maryland State Archivist.
Gary Vikan, Director of the Walters Art Museum.
Ronald G. Walters, Professor of History.
Susan F. Weiss, Faculty Member in Musicology, Peabody Conservatory of Music.

Ex Officio
Melissa Hilbish, Associate Program Chair.

Faculty
Martina Bagnoli, Associate Curator, Department of Manuscripts and Rare Books, Walters Art Museum.
Stephen F. Barker, Ph.D., Professor of Philosophy Emeritus, Johns Hopkins University.
Matt Belzer, Director, Homewood Jazz Ensembles, Johns Hopkins University.
Mark Blyth, Ph.D., Associate Professor of Political Science, Johns Hopkins University.
D. Duane Cummins, Ph.D., Visiting Scholar in American History, Johns Hopkins University, and President Emeritus, Bethany College.
David C. Dougherty, Ph.D., Lecturer.
William J. Evitts, Ph.D., Lecturer.
George W. Fisher, Ph.D., Professor Emeritus of Geology, Earth and Planetary Sciences Department, Johns Hopkins University.
B. N. Hebbar, Ph.D., Professor of Religion, George Washington University.
Richard Conn Henry, Professor of Physics and Astronomy, Zanvyl Krieger School of Arts and Sciences, Johns Hopkins University.
Neil Hertz, M.A., Professor of Humanities Emeritus, Johns Hopkins University.
Melissa Hilbish, Ph.D., Director, Center for Liberal Arts, Advanced Academic Programs, Johns Hopkins University.
Paul Kramer, Ph.D., Assistant Professor of History, Zanvyl Krieger School of Arts and Sciences, Johns Hopkins University.
Trevor Lipscombe, Ph.D., Editor-in-Chief, Johns Hopkins University Press.
P. Kyle McCarter Jr., Ph.D., William F. Albright Professor of Biblical and Ancient Near Eastern Studies, Zanvyl Krieger School of Arts and Sciences, and Program Chair, Master of Liberal Arts Program, Advanced Academic Programs, Johns Hopkins University.
Susan Foster McCarter, Ph.D., Adjunct Assistant Professor, Johns Hopkins University, and Adjunct Professor, York College of Pennsylvania.
William Noel, Ph.D., Curator, Department of Manuscripts and Rare Books, Walters Art Museum.
Nancy R. Norris-Kniffin, Ph.D., Lecturer.
Edward C. Papenfuse, Ph.D., State Archivist and Commissioner of Land Patents, State of Maryland.
Jonathan Pevsner, Ph.D., Associate Professor, Kennedy Krieger Institute and Johns Hopkins School of Medicine.
Harold K. Resnick, Ph.D., Management Consultant, Basehart Inc.
Bruce C. Robertson, Ph.D., Associate Investigator, Institute for Genomic Research.
Elizabeth Rodini, Ph.D., Associate Director, Program in Museums, and Society Senior Lecturer, History of Art Department, Johns Hopkins University.
Diane Scheper, Lecturer.
George L. Scheper, Ph.D., Professor Emeritus and Coordinator of Humanities, Community College of Baltimore County.
Adam Sheingate, Ph.D., Associate Professor, Department of Political Science, Johns Hopkins University.
Linda Skalet, Ph.D., Independent Art Historian.
E. Ray Sprenkle, D.M.A., Faculty, Peabody Institute, Johns Hopkins University.
Gary Vikan, Ph.D., Director, Walters Art Museum.
Ronald G. Walters, Ph.D., Professor of History, Johns Hopkins University.
Susan Zimmerman, Ph.D., Associate Professor of English, Queens College, CUNY.
Nancy E. Zinn, Ph.D., Associate Director for Collections and Exhibitions, Walters Art Museum.

LOYOLA COLLEGE IN MARYLAND

Graduate Liberal Studies Program

Program of Study

Loyola College's Master of Arts graduate program in liberal studies presents a unique opportunity for students with a broad spectrum of interests and experiences to engage in an intellectual dialogue that examines a wide range of issues through multiple viewpoints, perspectives, and academic disciplines. Though traditional in its emphasis on academic rigor, the program is innovative in that it encourages students to focus on breadth of reading and study rather than engage in specialized research.

Courses fall into one of three modules. Courses in historical approaches emphasize the origin, evolution, and development of ideas and movements crucial to the modern American experience. Courses in themes in the modern experience are organized around the structure of an idea or institution, specifically how central elements of the structure contribute to the uniqueness and relevance of the idea or institution. Courses in the creative process stress the importance of discovering new forms of expression, particularly film, paint, and other media, to communicate one's ideas. Students are required to complete at least one course from each of these modules.

The Master of Arts degree requires completion of twelve courses, or 36 credits. Students may choose to take all their required credits within the program, or they may apply three courses taken in another department to the degree. Some students choose to complete a capstone project in which they engage in extended, cross-disciplinary research and present a sustained composition and a public presentation. All courses are limited to 15 students, providing an opportunity for each student to participate in rigorous discussion and in-depth analysis of topics relevant to the course.

Research Facilities

The Loyola Notre Dame Library contains approximately 463,000 books and bound periodical volumes; over 11,000 videos, DVDs, and CDs; and 989 print periodical subscriptions. The library's Web site serves as a gateway to a variety of Internet resources, including numerous databases such as ERIC, Lexis-Nexis Academic Universe, Maryland Digital Library, Cambridge Scientific, and Business Source Premier, as well as full-text articles from over 23,000 periodicals.

Financial Aid

A variety of financial assistance is available to graduate students. Graduate assistants work 10–20 hours per week in faculty and administrative departments in exchange for a stipend and tuition remission. A number of scholarships are available from the College; award amounts, entry requirements, and eligibility criteria vary. Federal Stafford Loans provide up to $8500 per year in subsidized loans or $20,500 in unsubsidized loans. The Federal Graduate PLUS Loan Program allows students to borrow up to the full cost of attendance, less other aid received. Other loans may be available from alternative sources. Some students may be eligible for federal work-study.

Cost of Study

In 2007–08, tuition is $415 per credit hour. Other costs include a $10 parking fee (Baltimore campus only) and a $25 registration fee per semester.

Living and Housing Costs

The College does not offer on-campus housing for graduate students, except those who work as resident assistants as part of their financial aid package. However, off-campus housing is available. Students can expect to spend $400–$1000 per month for a 1-bedroom apartment and $850–$1300 for a 2-bedroom apartment, depending on size and location.

Student Group

About 20 students complete the program every year. These students come from a wide range of social, economic, national, and academic backgrounds, including professionals whose specialized education did not allow for liberal arts courses; teachers, librarians, and government workers who seek additional course work; and intellectually curious people.

Location

Baltimore is one of the most visited cities in the nation, with 12 million visitors each year. The city has a variety of museums, art galleries, theaters, and music venues, as well as annual festivals. The Inner Harbor, a popular waterfront attraction, is surrounded by historic neighborhoods with unique shops and restaurants for every style and taste.

The University

Founded by Jesuits in 1852, Loyola College remains committed to the ideals embodied by the priests and brothers of the Society of Jesus, which include an emphasis on academic excellence, the importance of the liberal arts, and the education of the whole person. The College enrolls approximately 6,100 students in a broad spectrum of programs that are practitioner-oriented and designed for professionals seeking a greater level of expertise and satisfaction in their careers.

Applying

Prospective students must submit a completed application form, official transcripts from each college attended, a current resume, one professional or academic recommendation, an essay responding to the question on the application form, and a nonrefundable $50 application fee. Students who have been accepted are invited for an interview. The deadlines to apply are August 1 for fall admission, December 1 for spring admission, and May 1 for summer admission.

Correspondence and Information

Office of Graduate Admission
Loyola College in Maryland
4501 North Charles Street
Baltimore, Maryland 21210
Phone: 410-617-2587
800-221-9107 Ext. 5020 (toll-free)
Fax: 410-617-2002
E-mail: graduate@loyola.edu
Web site: http://graduate.loyola.edu/lsgrad/info

Loyola College in Maryland

THE FACULTY AND THEIR RESEARCH

David R. Belz, Professor of Writing; M.A., St. John's College (Annapolis).
Donald R. Boomgaarden, Instructor; Ph.D., Rochester (Eastman). Eighteenth-century musical thought and music theory.
Richard Boothby, Professor of Philosophy; Ph.D., Boston University. Contemporary continental philosophy, especially psychoanalysis, phenomenology, and existentialism.
Steven Burr, Instructor; Ph.D., Georgetown. Existentialist attempts to characterize and confront the "human condition," especially the works of Friedrich Nietzsche, Martin Heidegger, and Albert Camus.
Russell J. Cook, Professor and Chair of Communication; Ph.D., Ohio. News, videographic culture, cinema, philosophy, educational computing, art.
John DiJoseph, Instructor; Ph.D., Catholic University.
Charles Donahue, Affiliate Professor of History; Ph.D., Union Theological Seminary (New York). Religious history of the Civil Rights Movement.
Randall Donaldson, Associate Professor of Modern Languages (German) and Literature and Director of Graduate Program; Ph.D., Johns Hopkins.
Michael Goff, Instructor; Ph.D., Georgetown. American national government, the U.S. presidency, the presidential nomination and election process, political fund-raising and campaigns.
Christopher Lonegan, Instructor; M.F.A., Pennsylvania Academy of Fine Arts.
Brian Murray, Professor of Communication.
Arthur Sutherland, Instructor of Theology. Ph.D., Princeton Theological Seminary. Hospitality, autobiography, systematic theology.

VIRGINIA COMMONWEALTH UNIVERSITY

College of Humanities and Sciences

Programs of Study

The faculty and staff of the College of Humanities and Sciences are dedicated to excellence in their teaching, research, and public service. The mission of Virginia Commonwealth University provides the framework for their pursuit of excellence.

Teaching and learning are central to the College, and the College is central to the educational and intellectual life of VCU. The College meets the educational needs of a diverse student body. It provides general education for all undergraduate students of the University; preparatory programs for the health sciences, engineering, and law; and education in the liberal arts and sciences for future teachers. The College offers comprehensive undergraduate, graduate, and professional programs of study that link a foundation of understanding and knowledge with skills on which students can build careers, become responsible citizens, and continue lifelong learning.

Scholarship, creative work, and professional accomplishment are essential to teaching and learning. The faculty and staff members of the College are responsible for advancing understanding and increasing knowledge for its own sake, for the educational benefit of their students, and for the good of the larger community.

In both teaching and research, the College of Humanities and Sciences takes seriously the responsibilities of being part of a public, urban university. Through service and public teaching, it meets the challenges and opportunities afforded by its metropolitan environment and by its location in the capital of the commonwealth.

The College achieves national and international recognition through the success of its students, through the advancement of the disciplines and professions represented by its programs, and through the individual and collaborative research of its faculty.

Graduate programs in the College of Humanities and Sciences include VCU Brandcenter (M.S.); Biology (M.S.); Chemistry (M.S., Ph.D.); Chemical Physics (Ph.D.); Computer Science (M.S.); Creative Writing (M.F.A.); Criminal Justice (M.S.); Forensic Science (M.S.); English (M.A.); Homeland Security (M.A.); History (M.A.); Mass Communications–Multimedia Journalism and Strategic Public Relations (M.S.); Mathematical Sciences–Applied Mathematics, Mathematics, Operations Research, Statistics (M.S.); Media, Art and Text (Ph.D.); Physics (M.S.); Psychology (M.S., Ph.D.); Public Administration (M.P.A.); Public Policy and Administration (Ph.D); Sociology (M.S.); and Urban and Regional Planning (M.U.R.P.)

From postbaccalaureate certificates to master's and doctoral degrees, graduate education in the College emphasizes scholarship and research—whether it be carried into the professional sector or academia. Applicants must apply to programs within the College through the School of Graduate Studies.

Research Facilities

VCU libraries provide a combined capacity of more than 1.7 million volumes and 10,200 periodical titles and an online bibliographic search service accessing hundreds of databases. In addition, the Virginia State and Richmond Public Libraries are within walking distance of both VCU campuses. Academic Computing provides a variety of microcomputer, minicomputer, and mainframe computing services to support the research and instructional endeavors of its faculty members and students, including consultation, instruction, and computer acquisition.

Financial Aid

The College of Humanities and Sciences is committed to rewarding academic excellence. Each year, through the generosity of donors, the financial burdens of pursuing a graduate degree are eased for many students through scholarships. Information regarding these scholarships can be found at http://www.has.vcu.edu/students/grad_edu/assistantships.html

In addition, need-based financial aid is awarded through the Office of Financial Aid, and graduate students at VCU are eligible for a number of University-sponsored financing options, including scholarships, employment opportunities, and fellowships and teaching assistantships. All forms of graduate student support are reported to the Office of Financial Aid and are considered when determining need-based support.

A number of assistantships, fellowships, and scholarships are awarded each year to new and continuing graduate students on the basis of a variety of criteria. Awards vary by program, and selection is made at the department level; therefore, inquiry about such awards should be made directly to the director of the program.

Students may contact the Office of Financial Aid at 804-828-6669 (Monroe Park Campus) or 804-828-2702 (MCV Campus) or visit http://www.vcu.edu/enroll/finaid/ for current information on financial aid programs, policies, and procedures.

Cost of Study

For full-time graduate study (9–15 credits) in 2008–09, Virginia residents pay tuition and fees of $4739 per semester; nonresidents, $9106 per semester. For part-time graduate study, Virginia residents pay tuition and fees of $495 per hour; nonresidents, $978 per hour.

For full-time doctoral study (9–15 credits) in 2008–09, Virginia residents pay tuition and fees of $4523 per semester; nonresidents, $8947 per semester. For part-time graduate study, Virginia residents pay tuition and fees of $471 per hour; nonresidents, $960 per hour.

Some programs require additional fees. On the Medical College of Virginia (MCV) campus, tuition, fees, and other expenses vary in the Medicine, Pharmacy, Nurse Anesthesia, Dentistry, and School of Allied Health programs

Living and Housing Costs

Graduate student housing is available on both the MCV campus and the academic campus of Virginia Commonwealth University. Many graduate students live in off-campus housing, which is reasonably priced and readily available in a variety of styles and settings in nearby residential areas or within easy commuting distance. On-campus housing information is available on the Web at http://www.housing.vcu.edu/. Off-campus housing information is available at http://www.usca.vcu.edu/offcampus/.

Student Group

VCU enrolls nearly 32,000 students, 8,149 of whom are graduate students. More than 200 clubs and organizations reflect the diverse social, recreational, educational, political, and religious interests of the student body.

Location

Richmond is Virginia's capital and a major East Coast financial and manufacturing center that offers students a wide range of cultural, educational, and recreational activities. Richmond is located in central Virginia at the intersection of Interstates 95 and 64, 2 hours south of Washington, D.C., and nestled between the Blue Ridge Mountains and the Atlantic coast. The Richmond region is easily accessible by plane, car, and train. With nearly 1 million residents, the historic city of Richmond combines big-city offerings with small-town hospitality. Applicants are encouraged to explore http://www.visit.richmond.com/ for more information on the city.

The University and The School

Virginia Commonwealth University is a state-supported coeducational university with a graduate school, a major teaching hospital, and twelve academic and professional units that offer sixty-two undergraduate, sixty-nine master's, forty postbaccalaureate and post-master's certificate programs, and thirty-one Ph.D. programs. VCU also offers M.D., D.D.S., D.P.T., and Pharm.D. programs as well as cooperative degree programs with other major Virginia colleges and universities. The academic campus is located in Richmond's historic Fan District. The health sciences campus and hospital are located 2 miles east in the downtown business district. A University bus service provides free intercampus transportation for faculty members and students.

With more than $211 million in annual research funding, VCU is classified as one of the nation's top research universities by the Carnegie Foundation for the Advancement of Teaching. More than 32,000 undergraduate, certificate, graduate, post-master's, professional, and doctoral students are enrolled in 205 academic programs, sixty-five of which are unique in the commonwealth of Virginia. The faculty members represent the finest American and international graduate institutions and enhance the University's position among the important institutions of higher learning in the United States and the world via their work in the classroom, laboratory, studio, and clinic and in their scholarly publications.

Applying

Admission procedures and program requirements are detailed in the Graduate Bulletin. Application deadlines and materials, including the application and the Graduate Bulletin, are available online at the Graduate School Web site at http://www.graduate.vcu.edu. Virginia Commonwealth University is an equal opportunity/affirmative action institution providing access to education and employment without regard to age, race, color, national origin, gender, religion, sexual orientation, veteran's status, political affiliation, or disability.

Correspondence and Information

Katherine Mangum
Director, Student Recruitment
Harrison House, Room 111
Virginia Commonwealth University
816 W. Franklin Street
P.O. Box 842019
Richmond, Virginia 23284-2019
Phone: 804-828-1674
E-mail: klmangum@vcu.edu
Web site: http://www.has.vcu.edu

Virginia Commonwealth University

THE FACULTY

For more information about faculty in a specific area of interest, students should visit http://www.has.vcu.edu. Each program offers a complete listing of faculty and staff members.

Section 9
Language and Literature

This section contains a directory of institutions offering graduate work in language and literature, followed by in-depth entries submitted by institutions that chose to prepare detailed program descriptions. Additional information about programs listed in the directory but not augmented by an in-depth entry may be obtained by writing directly to the dean of a graduate school or chair of a department at the address given in the directory.

For programs offering related work, see also in this book *Area and Cultural Studies, Communication and Media, Political Science and International Affairs,* and *Sociology, Anthropology, and Archaeology.* In another guide in this series:

Graduate Programs in Business, Education, Health, Information Studies, Law & Social Work

See *Special Focus* and *Subject Areas*

CONTENTS

Asian Languages

Columbia University, Graduate School of Arts and Sciences, Division of Humanities, Department of East Asian Languages and Cultures, New York, NY 10027. Offers East Asian languages and cultures (M Phil, MA, PhD); Oriental studies (M Phil, MA, PhD). *Faculty:* 17 full-time, 17 part-time/adjunct. *Students:* 68 full-time (39 women), 5 part-time (3 women); includes 9 minority (all Asian Americans or Pacific Islanders), 15 international. Average age 32. 162 applicants, 31% accepted. In 2007, 11 master's, 7 doctorates awarded. *Degree requirements:* For master's, one foreign language, comprehensive exam, thesis; for doctorate, 2 foreign languages, thesis/dissertation. *Entrance requirements:* For master's and doctorate, GRE General Test. Additional exam requirements/recommendations for international students: Required—TOEFL. Application fee: $90. *Expenses:* Tuition: Part-time $1,452 per credit. Required fees: $152 per term. One-time fee: $75 part-time. Full-time tuition and fees vary according to course level, course load, degree level and program. *Financial support:* Fellowships, teaching assistantships, institutionally sponsored loans available. Support available to part-time students. Financial award application deadline: 1/5; financial award applicants required to submit FAFSA. *Unit head:* Robert Hymes, Chair, 212-854-2574, Fax: 212-678-8629, E-mail: hymes@columbia.edu.

Columbia University, Graduate School of Arts and Sciences, Division of Humanities, Department of Middle East Languages and Cultures, New York, NY 10027. Offers Hebrew language and literature (M Phil, MA, PhD); Middle Eastern languages and cultures (M Phil, MA, PhD); South Asian languages and cultures (M Phil, MA, PhD). Part-time programs available. *Faculty:* 22 full-time, 11 part-time/adjunct. *Students:* 52 full-time (25 women), 4 part-time (3 women); includes 4 minority (3 Asian Americans or Pacific Islanders, 1 Hispanic American), 12 international. Average age 35. 42 applicants, 48% accepted. In 2007, 2 master's, 5 doctorates awarded. *Degree requirements:* For master's, thesis, oral and written exams; for doctorate, 3 foreign languages, thesis/dissertation. *Entrance requirements:* For master's and doctorate, GRE General Test. Additional exam requirements/recommendations for international students: Required—TOEFL. Application fee: $90. *Expenses:* Tuition: Part-time $1,452 per credit. Required fees: $152 per term. One-time fee: $75 part-time. Full-time tuition and fees vary according to course level, course load, degree level and program. *Financial support:* Fellowships, teaching assistantships, Federal Work-Study and institutionally sponsored loans available. Support available to part-time students. Financial award application deadline: 1/5; financial award applicants required to submit FAFSA. *Faculty research:* Indo-Iranian, Turkish, central Asian, and Armenian studies; Arabic and ancient Semitics. *Unit head:* Sheldon Pollock, Chair, 212-854-6781, Fax: 212-854-5517, E-mail: sp2356@columbia.edu.

Cornell University, Graduate School, Graduate Fields of Arts and Sciences, Field of East Asian Literature, Ithaca, NY 14853-0001. Offers Asian religions (MA, PhD); Chinese linguistics (MA, PhD); Chinese philology (MA, PhD); classical Chinese literature (MA, PhD); classical Japanese literature (MA, PhD); Japanese linguistics (MA, PhD); Korean literature (MA, PhD); modern Chinese literature (MA, PhD); modern Japanese literature (MA, PhD). *Faculty:* 12 full-time (4 women). *Students:* 20 full-time (10 women); includes 4 minority (all Asian Americans or Pacific Islanders), 11 international. Average age 32. 41 applicants, 15% accepted, 3 enrolled. In 2007, 1 master's, 4 doctorates awarded. *Degree requirements:* For master's, 2 foreign languages, thesis, teaching experience; for doctorate, 2 foreign languages, comprehensive exam, thesis/dissertation, teaching experience. *Entrance requirements:* For master's and doctorate, GRE General Test, 3 years of study in Chinese, Japanese, Korean, or Vietnamese, 3 letters of recommendation, academic writing sample. Additional exam requirements/recommendations for international students: Required—TOEFL (minimum score 600 paper-based; 250 computer-based; 77 iBT). *Application deadline:* For fall admission, 1/10 priority date for domestic students. Application fee: $70. Electronic applications accepted. *Financial support:* In 2007–08, 19 students received support, including 15 fellowships with full tuition reimbursements available, 4 teaching assistantships with full tuition reimbursements available; research assistantships with full tuition reimbursements available, institutionally sponsored loans, scholarships/grants, health care benefits, tuition waivers (full and partial), and unspecified assistantships also available. Financial award applicants required to submit FAFSA. *Faculty research:* Vietnamese literature; Chinese literature, drama, and film; Japanese theater and literature; popular culture in East Asia; Korean literature; Asian linguistics. *Unit head:* Director of Graduate Studies, 607-255-9099. *Application contact:* Graduate Field Assistant, 607-255-9099, E-mail: east_asian_lit@cornell.edu.

Cornell University, Graduate School, Graduate Fields of Arts and Sciences, Field of Linguistics, Ithaca, NY 14853-0001. Offers applied linguistics (MA, PhD); East Asian linguistics (MA, PhD); English linguistics (MA, PhD); general linguistics (MA, PhD); Germanic linguistics (MA, PhD); Indo-European linguistics (MA, PhD); phonetics (MA, PhD); phonological theory (MA, PhD); Romance linguistics (MA, PhD); second language acquisition (MA, PhD); semantics (MA, PhD); Slavic linguistics (MA, PhD); sociolinguistics (MA, PhD); South Asian linguistics (MA, PhD); Southeast Asian linguistics (MA, PhD); syntactic theory (MA, PhD). *Faculty:* 19 full-time. *Students:* 31 full-time (16 women); includes 1 minority (Hispanic American), 19 international. Average age 28. 89 applicants, 17% accepted, 8 enrolled. In 2007, 2 master's, 1 doctorate awarded. Terminal master's awarded for partial completion of doctoral program. *Degree requirements:* For master's, one foreign language, thesis; for doctorate, one foreign language, comprehensive exam, thesis/dissertation. *Entrance requirements:* For master's and doctorate, GRE General Test, 2 letters of recommendation. Additional exam requirements/recommendations for international students: Required—TOEFL (minimum score 600 paper-based; 250 computer-based; 77 iBT). *Application deadline:* For fall admission, 1/15 for domestic students. Application fee: $70. Electronic applications accepted. *Financial support:* In 2007–08, 30 students received support, including 14 fellowships with full tuition reimbursements available, 2 research assistantships with full tuition reimbursements available, 14 teaching assistantships with full tuition reimbursements available; institutionally sponsored loans, scholarships/grants, health care benefits, tuition waivers (full and partial), and unspecified assistantships also available. Financial award applicants required to submit FAFSA. *Faculty research:* Phonology and phonetics; syntax and semantics; historical linguistics; philosophy of language; language acquisition. *Unit head:* Director of Graduate Studies, 607-255-1105. *Application contact:* Graduate Field Assistant, 607-255-1105, E-mail: lingfield@cornell.edu.

Harvard University, Graduate School of Arts and Sciences, Department of East Asian Languages and Civilizations, Cambridge, MA 02138. Offers Chinese (PhD); Japanese (PhD); Korean (PhD); Mongolian (PhD); Vietnamese (PhD). Terminal master's awarded for partial completion of doctoral program. *Degree requirements:* For doctorate, 3 foreign languages, thesis/dissertation, general exams. *Entrance requirements:* For doctorate, GRE General Test. Additional exam requirements/recommendations for international students: Required—TOEFL. *Expenses:* Tuition: Full-time $31,456. Full-time tuition and fees vary according to program and student level. *Faculty research:* Central Asian literature, religion, and premodern history.

Harvard University, Graduate School of Arts and Sciences, Department of Sanskrit and Indian Studies, Cambridge, MA 02138. Offers Indian philosophy (AM, PhD); Pali (AM, PhD); Sanskrit (AM, PhD); Tibetan (AM, PhD); Urdu (AM, PhD). Terminal master's awarded for partial completion of doctoral program. *Degree requirements:* For master's, 3 foreign languages; for doctorate, 3 foreign languages, thesis/dissertation. *Entrance requirements:* For master's, GRE General Test; for doctorate, GRE General Test, proficiency in French and German. Additional exam requirements/recommendations for international students: Required—TOEFL. *Expenses:* Tuition: Full-time $31,456. Full-time tuition and fees vary according to program and student level.

Indiana University Bloomington, University Graduate School, College of Arts and Sciences, Department of East Asian Languages and Cultures, Bloomington, IN 47405-7000. Offers Chinese (MA, PhD); East Asian languages and cultures (PhD); East Asian studies (MA); Japanese (MA, PhD); language pedagogy (MA). Part-time programs available. *Faculty:* 7 full-time (2 women). *Students:* 19 full-time (12 women), 6 part-time (3 women); includes 3 minority (1 African American, 1 Asian American or Pacific Islander, 1 Hispanic American), 6 international. Average age 32. 77 applicants, 25% accepted, 10 enrolled. In 2007, 7 master's, 1 doctorate awarded. *Degree requirements:* For master's, 2 foreign languages, thesis; for doctorate, 2 foreign languages, thesis/dissertation. *Entrance requirements:* Additional exam requirements/recommendations for international students: Required—TOEFL. *Application deadline:* For fall admission, 1/15 for domestic students, 12/15 for international students; for spring admission, 9/1 for domestic and international students. Applications are processed on a rolling basis. Application fee: $50 ($60 for international students). Electronic applications accepted. *Financial support:* Fellowships, teaching assistantships, Federal Work-Study and tuition waivers (full) available. Financial award application deadline: 3/1. *Faculty research:* Postwar/postmodern Japanese fiction, modern Chinese film and literature, classical Chinese literature and philosophy, Chinese and Japanese linguistics and pedagogy, East Asian politics. *Unit head:* Robert Eno, Chair, 812-855-0856, E-mail: eno@indiana.edu. *Application contact:* Edith Sarra, Director of Graduate Studies, 812-855-4031, Fax: 812-855-6402, E-mail: eserra@indiana.edu.

Naropa University, Graduate Programs, Program in Indo-Tibetan Buddhism with Language, Boulder, CO 80302-6697. Offers MA. *Faculty:* 6 full-time (2 women), 19 part-time/adjunct (8 women). *Students:* 12 full-time (3 women), 3 part-time (2 women); includes 1 minority (Hispanic American), 1 international. Average age 32. 20 applicants, 70% accepted, 7 enrolled. In 2007, 5 degrees awarded. *Degree requirements:* For master's, comprehensive exam, thesis. *Entrance requirements:* For master's, writing sample, interview (by phone or in-person). Additional exam requirements/recommendations for international students: Required—TOEFL (minimum score 600 paper-based; 250 computer-based). *Application deadline:* For fall admission, 1/15 priority date for domestic and international students; for spring admission, 10/15 priority date for domestic students. Applications are processed on a rolling basis. Application fee: $60. Electronic applications accepted. *Expenses:* Tuition: Full-time $15,070; part-time $685 per credit. Required fees: $250 per semester. Tuition and fees vary according to course load. *Financial support:* In 2007–08, 11 students received support, including 1 research assistantship with partial tuition reimbursement available (averaging $3,000 per year), 5 teaching assistantships with partial tuition reimbursements available (averaging $3,000 per year); career-related internships or fieldwork, Federal Work-Study, scholarships/grants, tuition waivers (partial), and unspecified assistantships also available. Support available to part-time students. Financial award application deadline: 3/1; financial award applicants required to submit FAFSA. *Unit head:* Roger Dorris, Co-Chair, 303-546-0937. *Application contact:* Donna McIntyre, Admissions Counselor, 303-546-3555, Fax: 303-546-3583, E-mail: donna@naropa.edu.

See Close-Up on page 1449.

The Ohio State University, Graduate School, College of Humanities, Department of East Asian Languages and Literatures, Columbus, OH 43210. Offers Chinese (MA, PhD); Japanese (MA, PhD). *Faculty:* 22. *Students:* 49 full-time (31 women), 6 part-time (1 woman); includes 6 minority (5 Asian Americans or Pacific Islanders, 1 Hispanic American), 24 international. Average age 28. In 2007, 11 master's, 1 doctorate awarded. *Degree requirements:* For master's, thesis optional; for doctorate, thesis/dissertation. *Entrance requirements:* For master's and doctorate, GRE (if applying for financial aid). Additional exam requirements/recommendations for international students: Required—TOEFL (minimum score 577 paper-based; 233 computer-based). *Application deadline:* For fall admission, 8/15 priority date for domestic students, 7/1 priority date for international students; for winter admission, 12/1 priority date for domestic students, 11/1 priority date for international students; for spring admission, 3/1 priority date for domestic students, 2/1 priority date for international students. Applications are processed on a rolling basis. Application fee: $40 ($50 for international students). Electronic applications accepted. *Financial support:* Fellowships, research assistantships, teaching assistantships, Federal Work-Study, institutionally sponsored loans, and unspecified assistantships available. Support available to part-time students. *Unit head:* Mineharu Nakayama, Graduate Studies Committee Chair, 614-292-5816, Fax: 614-292-3225, E-mail: nakayama.1@osu.edu. *Application contact:* Graduate Admissions, 614-292-9444, Fax: 614-292-3895, E-mail: domestic.grad@osu.edu.

St. John's College, Graduate Institute in Liberal Education, Program in Eastern Classics, Santa Fe, NM 87505-4599. Offers MA. Part-time and evening/weekend programs available. *Entrance requirements:* For master's, 2 letters of recommendation. Additional exam requirements/recommendations for international students: Required—TOEFL, TWE. Expenses: Contact institution.

University of California, Berkeley, Graduate Division, College of Letters and Science, Department of South and Southeast Asian Studies, Berkeley, CA 94720-1500. Offers Hindi (MA, PhD); Indonesian (MA, PhD); Sanskrit (MA, PhD); Tamil (MA, PhD). *Faculty:* 6 full-time, 14 part-time/adjunct. Terminal master's awarded for partial completion of doctoral program. *Degree requirements:* For master's, 2 foreign languages, thesis; for doctorate, 2 foreign languages, thesis/dissertation, oral qualifying exam. *Entrance requirements:* For master's and doctorate, GRE General Test, minimum GPA of 3.0, 3 letters of recommendation. *Application deadline:* For fall admission, 12/3 for domestic students. Application fee: $70 ($90 for international students). Electronic applications accepted. *Financial support:* Fellowships, research assistantships, teaching assistantships, unspecified assistantships available. *Unit head:* George Hart, Chair, 510-642-8169, E-mail: ghart@socrates.berkeley.edu. *Application contact:* Lee Amazonas, Student Affairs Officer, 510-642-4219, E-mail: casmauga@berkeley.edu.

University of California, Irvine, Office of Graduate Studies, School of Humanities, Department of East Asian Languages and Literatures, Irvine, CA 92697. Offers Chinese (MA, PhD); East Asian languages and literatures (MA, PhD); Japanese (MA, PhD). *Students:* 14 full-time (12 women); includes 1 minority (Asian American or Pacific Islander), 10 international. In 2007, 1 master's, 1 doctorate awarded. *Degree requirements:* For doctorate, thesis/dissertation. *Entrance requirements:* For master's, GRE, minimum GPA of 3.0; for doctorate, GRE General Test, minimum GPA of 3.0. Additional exam requirements/recommendations for international students: Required—TOEFL (minimum score 550 paper-based; 213 computer-based). *Application deadline:* For fall admission, 1/15 priority date for domestic students; for winter admission, 10/15 priority date for domestic students; for spring admission, 1/15 for domestic students. Application fee: $60. Electronic applications accepted. *Financial support:* Fellowships with tuition reimbursements, research assistantships with full tuition reimbursements, teaching assistantships with partial tuition reimbursements, institutionally sponsored loans, traineeships, health care benefits, and unspecified assistantships available. Financial award application deadline: 3/1; financial award applicants required to submit FAFSA. *Faculty research:* Chinese, Japanese, and Korean literature and culture; language and textual analysis; historical, social, and cultural dimensions of literary study. *Unit head:* Michael Fuller, Interim Chair, 949-824-2151. *Application contact:* Angie Agsalog, Graduate Staff Contact, 949-824-1601, Fax: 949-824-3248, E-mail: aagsalog@uci.edu.

University of California, Los Angeles, Graduate Division, College of Letters and Science, Department of Asian Languages and Cultures, Los Angeles, CA 90095. Offers MA, PhD. *Faculty:* 15. *Students:* 34 full-time (20 women); includes 20 minority (all Asian Americans or Pacific Islanders), 19 international. Average age 26. 70 applicants, 21% accepted, 8 enrolled. In 2007, 1 master's, 7 doctorates awarded. Terminal master's awarded for partial completion of doctoral program. *Degree requirements:* For master's, one foreign language, comprehensive exam, comprehensive exam or thesis; for doctorate, 2 foreign languages, thesis/dissertation, oral and written qualifying exams. *Entrance requirements:* For master's, GRE General Test, minimum GPA of 3.0, sample of written work; for doctorate, GRE General Test, minimum undergraduate GPA of 3.0, sample of research writing or thesis in English. Additional exam requirements/recommendations for international students: Required—TOEFL. *Application deadline:* For fall admission, 12/15 for domestic students. Application fee: $60. Electronic applications accepted. *Expenses:* Tuition, nonresident: full-time $5,728. Required fees:$8,966. Full-time tuition and fees vary according to program and student level. *Financial support:* In 2007–08, 6 fellowships with full and partial tuition reimbursements, 20 research assistantships with full and partial tuition reimbursements, 27 teaching assistantships with full and partial tuition reimbursements were awarded; Federal Work-Study, institutionally sponsored loans, and tuition waivers (full and partial) also available. Financial award application deadline: 3/1; financial award applicants required to submit FAFSA. *Unit head:* Dr. John Duncan, Chair, 310-206-8235. *Application contact:* Departmental Office, 310-206-8235, E-mail: alcgen@humnet.ucla.edu.

University of California, Santa Barbara, Graduate Division, College of Letters and Sciences, Division of Humanities and Fine Arts, Department of East Asian Languages and Cultural Studies, Santa Barbara, CA 93106. Offers Asian studies (MA), including East Asian languages and cultural studies; East Asian languages and cultural studies (PhD). *Faculty:* 10 full-time (5 women), 6 part-time/adjunct (2 women). *Students:* 12 full-time (8 women); includes 2 minority (both Asian Americans or Pacific Islanders), 5 international. Average age 28. 73 applicants, 30% accepted, 5 enrolled. In 2007, 7 degrees awarded. *Degree requirements:* For master's, one foreign language, thesis or alternative. *Entrance requirements:* For master's and doctorate, GRE. Additional exam requirements/recommendations for international students: Required—TOEFL (minimum score 550 paper-based; 213 computer-based; 80 iBT). *Application deadline:* For fall admission, 4/1 for domestic and international students. Application fee: $60. Electronic applications accepted. *Expenses:* Tuition, nonresident: full-time $14,888. Required fees: $10,108. *Financial support:* In 2007–08, 11 students received support, including 5 fellowships with full and partial tuition reimbursements available (averaging $15,300 per year), 6 teaching assistantships with partial tuition reimbursements available; research assistantships, Federal Work-Study, institutionally sponsored loans, scholarships/grants, health care benefits, and unspecified assistantships also available. Financial award application deadline: 12/15; financial award applicants required to submit FAFSA. *Faculty research:* Chinese literature, Chinese film, Japanese society, Japanese literature, East Asian cultural studies. *Unit head:* Dr. William Powell, Chair, 805-893-4455, Fax: 805-893-3011, E-mail: bpowell@religion.ucsb.edu. *Application contact:* Dr. Ronald Egan, Faculty Graduate Advisor, 805-893-3770, Fax: 805-893-3011, E-mail: ronegan@eastasian.ucsb.edu.

University of California, Santa Barbara, Graduate Division, College of Letters and Sciences, Division of Humanities and Fine Arts, Program in Comparative Literature, Santa Barbara, CA 93106. Offers comparative literature (PhD); East Asian literatures (PhD); women's studies (PhD); MA/PhD. *Faculty:* 22 full-time (18 women). *Students:* 25 full-time (19 women); includes 4 minority (2 Asian Americans or Pacific Islanders, 2 Hispanic Americans), 4 international. Average age 31. 33 applicants, 39% accepted, 8 enrolled. In 2007, 4 doctorates awarded. Terminal master's awarded for partial completion of doctoral program. *Median time to degree:* Of those who began their doctoral program in fall 1999, 25% received their degree in 8 years or less. *Degree requirements:* For doctorate, 2 foreign languages, comprehensive exam, thesis/dissertation. *Entrance requirements:* For doctorate, GRE, samples of written work, study of literature in at least 2 approved languages, demonstration of foreign language proficiency. Additional exam requirements/recommendations for international students: Required—TOEFL (minimum score 550 paper-based; 213 computer-based; 80 iBT). *Application deadline:* For fall admission, 12/15 for domestic and international students. Application fee: $60. Electronic applications accepted. *Expenses:* Tuition, nonresident: full-time $14,888. Required fees: $10,108. *Financial support:* In 2007–08, 25 students received support, including 11 fellowships with full and partial tuition reimbursements available (averaging $13,200 per year), 7 teaching assistantships with full and partial tuition reimbursements available (averaging $16,389 per year); Federal Work-Study, institutionally sponsored loans, scholarships/grants, and health care benefits also available. Financial award application deadline: 12/15; financial award applicants required to submit FAFSA. *Faculty research:* Interdisciplinary studies, literary theory, cultural studies, early-modern and modern literature, critical theory. *Unit head:* Prof. Elisabeth Weber, Chair, 805-893-2295, E-mail: weber@gss.ucsb.edu. *Application contact:* Sierra Gray, Graduate Program Assistant, 805-893-2131, Fax: 805-893-2374, E-mail: sierra@gss.ucsb.edu.

University of Chicago, Division of the Humanities, Department of East Asian Languages and Civilizations, Chicago, IL 60637-1513. Offers AM, PhD. *Students:* 48. 65 applicants, 14% accepted, 4 enrolled.Terminal master's awarded for partial completion of doctoral program. *Degree requirements:* For master's, one foreign language, thesis; for doctorate, 2 foreign languages, thesis/dissertation. *Entrance requirements:* For master's and doctorate, GRE General Test. Additional exam requirements/recommendations for international students: Required—TOEFL. *Application deadline:* For fall admission, 12/15 for domestic students. Application fee: $55. *Financial support:* Fellowships, Federal Work-Study available. Financial award application deadline: 12/15; financial award applicants required to submit FAFSA. *Unit head:* Dr. Edward Shaughnessy, Chair, 773-702-1255.

University of Chicago, Division of the Humanities, Department of South Asian Languages and Civilizations, Chicago, IL 60637-1513. Offers South Asian languages and civilizations (AM, PhD), including Bengali (PhD), Hindi (PhD), Sanskrit (PhD), Tamil (PhD), Urdu (PhD). *Students:* 27. 27 applicants, 33% accepted, 5 enrolled.Terminal master's awarded for partial completion of doctoral program. *Degree requirements:* For master's, one foreign language, thesis; for doctorate, 2 foreign languages, thesis/dissertation. *Entrance requirements:* For master's and doctorate, GRE General Test. Additional exam requirements/recommendations for international students: Required—TOEFL. *Application deadline:* For fall admission, 12/15 for domestic students. Application fee: $55. *Financial support:* Fellowships, Federal Work-Study available. Financial award application deadline: 12/15; financial award applicants required to submit FAFSA. *Unit head:* Dr. Steven Collins, Chair, 773-702-8373.

University of Hawaii at Manoa, Graduate Division, Colleges of Arts and Sciences, College of Language, Linguistics and Literature, Department of East Asian Languages and Literatures, Program in Korean, Honolulu, HI 96822. Offers MA, PhD. Part-time programs available. *Faculty:* 6 full-time (3 women). *Students:* 17 full-time (15 women), 5 part-time (1 woman); includes 7 minority (all Asian Americans or Pacific Islanders), 14 international. 11 applicants, 64% accepted, 4 enrolled. *Median time to degree:* Of those who began their doctoral program in fall 1999, 0% received their degree in 8 years or less. *Degree requirements:* For master's, 2 foreign languages, thesis optional; for doctorate, 2 foreign languages, comprehensive exam, thesis/dissertation. *Entrance requirements:* For master's and doctorate, GRE General Test. Additional exam requirements/recommendations for international students: Required—TOEFL (minimum score 560 paper-based; 220 computer-based; 83 iBT), IELTS (minimum score 5). *Application deadline:* For fall admission, 2/1 for domestic and international students; for spring admission, 9/1 for domestic and international students. Application fee: $50. *Financial support:* In 2007–08, 6 teaching assistantships (averaging $14,212 per year) were awarded; research assistantships. *Application contact:* Leon Serafim, Graduate Chair, 808-956-2069, Fax: 808-956-9515, E-mail: serafim@hawaii.edu.

University of Illinois at Urbana–Champaign, Graduate College, College of Liberal Arts and Sciences, School of Literatures, Cultures and Linguistics, Department of East Asian Languages and Cultures, Champaign, IL 61820. Offers Asian studies (MA); East Asian languages and cultures (PhD). *Faculty:* 15 full-time (5 women), 1 (woman) part-time/adjunct. *Students:* 28 full-time (23 women), 11 part-time (8 women); includes 5 minority (1 American Indian/Alaska Native, 4 Asian Americans or Pacific Islanders), 25 international. 59 applicants, 19% accepted, 8 enrolled. In 2007, 4 master's awarded. *Degree requirements:* For master's, one foreign language; for doctorate, thesis/dissertation. *Entrance requirements:* For master's, GRE General Test, minimum GPA of 3.0. Additional exam requirements/recommendations for international students: Required—TOEFL. *Application deadline:* For fall admission, 1/16 for domestic students; for spring admission, 1/16 for domestic students. Application fee: $60 ($75 for international students). Electronic applications accepted. *Financial support:* In 2007–08, 8 fellowships, 3 research assistantships, 27 teaching assistantships were awarded; tuition waivers (full and partial) also available. Financial award application deadline: 2/15. *Unit head:* Karen Kelsky, Head, 217-244-9077, Fax: 217-244-2223, E-mail: kelsky@uiuc.edu. *Application contact:* Brian Ruppert, Director of Graduate Studies, 217-244-4012, Fax: 217-244-2223, E-mail: ruppert@uiuc.edu.

University of Kansas, Research and Graduate Studies, College of Liberal Arts and Sciences, Department of East Asian Languages and Cultures, Lawrence, KS 66045. Offers MA. Part-time programs available. *Faculty:* 8. *Students:* 8 full-time (2 women), 3 part-time (all women); includes 1 minority (Asian American or Pacific Islander), 2 international. Average age 30. 15 applicants, 53% accepted, 4 enrolled. In 2007, 2 degrees awarded. *Degree requirements:* For master's, one foreign language, thesis. *Entrance requirements:* For master's, GRE. Additional exam requirements/recommendations for international students: Required—TOEFL. *Application deadline:* For fall admission, 5/1 priority date for domestic students; for spring admission, 11/30 priority date for domestic students. Applications are processed on a rolling basis. Application fee: $55 ($60 for international students). Electronic applications accepted. *Expenses:* Tuition, state resident: full-time $5,838. Tuition, nonresident: full-time $13,409. Tuition and fees vary according to program. *Financial support:* Fellowships, teaching assistantships with full and partial tuition reimbursements, unspecified assistantships available. Financial award application deadline: 2/1. *Faculty research:* Gender relations in literature, ancient Chinese law, visual culture of modern Japan, Japanese language pedagogy, Chinese paleography, Korean shananism, folklore, traditional Chinese and Japenese literature, Chinese linguistics and language pedagogy. *Unit head:* Keith McMahon, Chair and Graduate Director, 785-864-3100, E-mail: kmcmahon@ku.edu. *Application contact:* Georgia Damis, Graduate Secretary, 785-864-3100, Fax: 785-864-4298, E-mail: ealc@ku.edu.

University of Michigan, Horace H. Rackham School of Graduate Studies, College of Literature, Science, and the Arts, Department of Asian Languages and Cultures, Ann Arbor, MI 48109. Offers MA, PhD. Terminal master's awarded for partial completion of doctoral program. *Degree requirements:* For master's, variable foreign language requirement, thesis; for doctorate, 2 foreign languages, thesis/dissertation, oral defense of dissertation, preliminary exam. *Entrance requirements:* For master's and doctorate, GRE General Test. Additional exam requirements/recommendations for international students: Required—TOEFL (minimum score 600 paper-based; 250 computer-based). Electronic applications accepted. *Faculty research:* Literature, linguistics, religion, philosophy, music, cinema.

University of Minnesota, Twin Cities Campus, Graduate School, College of Liberal Arts, Department of Asian Languages and Literatures, Minneapolis, MN 55455-0213. Offers Asian literatures, cultures, and media (PhD). *Faculty:* 9 full-time (4 women), 5 part-time/adjunct (all women). *Students:* 10 full-time (3 women); includes 2 minority (1 African American, 1 Hispanic American), 8 international. Average age 23. 40 applicants, 23% accepted, 5 enrolled. *Degree requirements:* For doctorate, comprehensive exam, thesis/dissertation. *Entrance requirements:* For doctorate, GRE, 3 letters of recommendation. Additional exam requirements/recommendations for international students: Required—TOEFL (minimum score 550 paper-based; 213 computer-based), IELTS (minimum score 7). *Application deadline:* For fall admission, 1/2 for domestic and international students. Application fee: $55 ($75 for international students). Electronic applications accepted. *Financial support:* In 2007–08, 2 students received support, including 2 fellowships with full tuition reimbursements available (averaging $16,000 per year). Financial award application deadline: 1/5. *Faculty research:* Gender studies, post-colonial theory, poetics and poetic theory, film studies, post modernist thought. Total annual research expenditures: $2,500. *Unit head:* Ray Wakefield, Interim Chair, 612-625-0122, E-mail: allchair@umn.edu. *Application contact:* Prof. Paul Rouzer, Director of Graduate Studies, 612-625-2564, Fax: 612-624-5513, E-mail: prouzer@umn.edu.

University of Oregon, Graduate School, College of Arts and Sciences, Department of East Asian Languages and Literature, Eugene, OR 97403. Offers Chinese (MA, PhD); Japanese (MA, PhD). *Faculty:* 15 full-time (9 women), 1 part-time/adjunct (0 women). *Students:* 15 full-time (12 women), 2 part-time (1 woman); includes 1 minority (Asian American or Pacific Islander), 12 international. 29 applicants, 21% accepted. In 2007, 10 degrees awarded. *Entrance requirements:* Additional exam requirements/recommendations for international students: Required—TOEFL. *Application deadline:* For fall admission, 2/15 for domestic students. Application fee: $50. *Financial support:* In 2007–08, 20 teaching assistantships were awarded. Financial award application deadline: 3/1. *Faculty research:* Linguistics, pedagogy. *Unit head:* Stephen Durrant, Head, 541-346-4008. *Application contact:* Michael Bardossi, Admissions Contact, 541-346-4066, E-mail: bardossm@oregon.uoregon.edu.

University of Southern California, Graduate School, College of Letters, Arts and Sciences, Department of East Asian Languages and Cultures, Los Angeles, CA 90089. Offers MA, PhD. *Faculty:* 13 full-time (5 women). *Students:* 20 full-time (14 women); includes 5 minority (1 African American, 4 Asian Americans or Pacific Islanders), 11 international. 45 applicants, 24% accepted. In 2007, 3 master's, 1 doctorate awarded. *Degree requirements:* For master's, one foreign language, thesis; for doctorate, 2 foreign languages, thesis/dissertation. *Entrance requirements:* For master's and doctorate, GRE General Test. *Application deadline:* For fall admission, 12/20 for domestic students. Application fee: $85. *Financial support:* In 2007–08, 18 students received support, including fellowships with tuition reimbursements available (averaging $19,000 per year), teaching assistantships with tuition reimbursements available (averaging $18,570 per year); scholarships/grants also available. Financial award application deadline: 2/15; financial award applicants required to submit FAFSA. *Faculty research:* Premodern Chinese history, modern and classical Chinese literature, Japanese, Korea. *Unit head:* Dr. Xiabing Tang, Chair, 213-740-3707, Fax: 213-740-9295, E-mail: ealc@usc.edu. *Application contact:* Josephine Le, Information Contact, 213-740-2311.

University of Southern California, Graduate School, College of Letters, Arts and Sciences, Department of Linguistics, Los Angeles, CA 90089. Offers East Asian linguistics (PhD); Hispanic linguistics (PhD); linguistics (PhD). *Faculty:* 18 full-time (11 women). *Students:* 40 full-time (23 women), 4 part-time (3 women); includes 7 minority (4 Asian Americans or Pacific Islanders, 3 Hispanic Americans), 20 international. 62 applicants, 31% accepted. In 2007, 10 doctorates awarded. *Degree requirements:* For doctorate, 2 foreign languages, thesis/dissertation. *Entrance requirements:* For doctorate, GRE General Test. *Application deadline:* For fall admission, 12/1 priority date for domestic students. Application fee: $85. *Financial support:* In 2007–08, fellowships with full tuition reimbursements (averaging $19,000 per year), research assistantships with full tuition reimbursements (averaging $19,000 per year), teaching assistantships with full tuition reimbursements (averaging $19,000 per year) were awarded. Financial award application deadline: 2/15; financial award applicants required to submit FAFSA. *Faculty research:* Syntax, phonology, phonetics, semantics, sociolinguistics, psycholinguistics. *Unit head:* Dr. James Higginbotham, Chair, 213-740-2986, E-mail: lingdept@usc.edu. *Application contact:* Joyce Perez, Information Contact, 213-740-2311.

The University of Texas at Austin, Graduate School, College of Liberal Arts, Department of Asian Studies, Austin, TX 78712-1111. Offers Asian cultures and languages (MA, PhD). Part-time programs available. *Degree requirements:* For master's, thesis; for doctorate, 3 foreign languages, thesis/dissertation. *Entrance requirements:* For master's and doctorate, GRE General Test. Electronic applications accepted. *Faculty research:* Modern Taiwanese fiction, modern Japanese literature, religious studies in South Asia during classical period.

University of Washington, Graduate School, College of Arts and Sciences, Department of Asian Languages and Literature, Seattle, WA 98195. Offers Chinese language and literature (MA, PhD); Japanese language and literature (MA, PhD); South Asian language and literature (MA, PhD). *Degree requirements:* For master's, 2 foreign languages, general exam, thesis or 2 research papers; for doctorate, 3 foreign languages, thesis/dissertation, general exam. *Entrance requirements:* For master's, GRE, minimum GPA of 3.0; for doctorate, GRE, master's degree in related field, minimum GPA of 3.0. Additional exam requirements/recommendations for international students: Required—TOEFL. Electronic applications accepted. *Faculty research:* Textual, linguistic, philological, and literary study of languages and literatures of Asia.

Asian Languages

University of Wisconsin–Madison, Graduate School, College of Letters and Science, Department of Languages and Cultures of Asia, Madison, WI 53706-1380. Offers MA, PhD. Part-time programs available. Terminal master's awarded for partial completion of doctoral program. *Degree requirements:* For master's, one foreign language, thesis or alternative; for doctorate, 2 foreign languages, thesis/dissertation. *Entrance requirements:* For master's, minimum GPA of 3.0; for doctorate, minimum GPA of 3.25, master's degree. Electronic applications accepted. *Faculty research:* Literature, folklore, religion.

Washington University in St. Louis, Graduate School of Arts and Sciences, Department of Asian and Near Eastern Languages and Literatures, St. Louis, MO 63130-4899. Offers Asian language (MA); Asian studies (MA); Chinese (PhD); comparative literature (MA, PhD); Japanese (PhD). Terminal master's awarded for partial completion of doctoral program. *Degree requirements:* For master's, thesis optional; for doctorate, thesis/dissertation. *Entrance requirements:* For master's and doctorate, GRE General Test. Electronic applications accepted.

Washington University in St. Louis, Graduate School of Arts and Sciences, Program in East Asian Studies, St. Louis, MO 63130-4899. Offers art history (PhD); Chinese (MA); Chinese and comparative literature (PhD); East Asian studies (MA); history (PhD); Japanese (MA); Japanese and comparative literature (PhD); JD/MA; MBA/MA. PhD offered through specific departments. *Entrance requirements:* For master's and doctorate, GRE General Test. Electronic applications accepted.

See Close-Up on page 815.

Yale University, Graduate School of Arts and Sciences, Department of East Asian Languages and Literatures, New Haven, CT 06520. Offers PhD. *Degree requirements:* For doctorate, 2 foreign languages, thesis/dissertation. *Entrance requirements:* For doctorate, GRE General Test.

Celtic Languages

Harvard University, Graduate School of Arts and Sciences, Department of Celtic Languages and Literatures, Cambridge, MA 02138. Offers Irish (PhD); Welsh (PhD). *Degree requirements:* For doctorate, thesis/dissertation, proficiency in 2 Celtic languages; reading knowledge of French, German, and Latin. *Entrance requirements:* For doctorate, GRE General Test. Additional exam requirements/recommendations for international students: Required—TOEFL. *Expenses:* Tuition: Full-time $31,456. Full-time tuition and fees vary according to program and student level.

Chinese

Cornell University, Graduate School, Graduate Fields of Arts and Sciences, Field of East Asian Literature, Ithaca, NY 14853-0001. Offers Asian religions (MA, PhD); Chinese linguistics (MA, PhD); Chinese philology (MA, PhD); classical Chinese literature (MA, PhD); classical Japanese literature (MA, PhD); Japanese linguistics (MA, PhD); Korean literature (MA, PhD); modern Chinese literature (MA, PhD); modern Japanese literature (MA, PhD). *Faculty:* 12 full-time (4 women). *Students:* 20 full-time (10 women); includes 4 minority (all Asian Americans or Pacific Islanders), 11 international. Average age 32. 41 applicants, 15% accepted, 3 enrolled. In 2007, 1 master's, 4 doctorates awarded. *Degree requirements:* For master's, 2 foreign languages, thesis, teaching experience; for doctorate, 2 foreign languages, comprehensive exam, thesis/dissertation, teaching experience. *Entrance requirements:* For master's and doctorate, GRE General Test, 3 years of study in Chinese, Japanese, Korean, or Vietnamese, 3 letters of recommendation, academic writing sample. Additional exam requirements/recommendations for international students: Required—TOEFL (minimum score 600 paper-based; 250 computer-based; 77 iBT). *Application deadline:* For fall admission, 1/10 priority date for domestic students. Application fee: $70. Electronic applications accepted. *Financial support:* In 2007–08, 19 students received support, including 15 fellowships with full tuition reimbursements available, 4 teaching assistantships with full tuition reimbursements available; research assistantships with full tuition reimbursements available, institutionally sponsored loans, scholarships/grants, health care benefits, tuition waivers (full and partial), and unspecified assistantships also available. Financial award applicants required to submit FAFSA. *Faculty research:* Vietnamese literature; Chinese literature, drama, and film; Japanese theater and literature; popular culture in East Asia; Korean literature; Asian linguistics. *Unit head:* Director of Graduate Studies, 607-255-9099. *Application contact:* Graduate Field Assistant, 607-255-9099, E-mail: east_asian_lit@cornell.edu.

Harvard University, Graduate School of Arts and Sciences, Department of East Asian Languages and Civilizations, Cambridge, MA 02138. Offers Chinese (PhD); Japanese (PhD); Korean (PhD); Mongolian (PhD); Vietnamese (PhD). Terminal master's awarded for partial completion of doctoral program. *Degree requirements:* For doctorate, 3 foreign languages, thesis/dissertation, general exams. *Entrance requirements:* For doctorate, GRE General Test. Additional exam requirements/recommendations for international students: Required—TOEFL. *Expenses:* Tuition: Full-time $31,456. Full-time tuition and fees vary according to program and student level. *Faculty research:* Central Asian literature, religion, and premodern history.

Indiana University Bloomington, University Graduate School, College of Arts and Sciences, Department of East Asian Languages and Cultures, Bloomington, IN 47405-7000. Offers Chinese (MA, PhD); East Asian languages and cultures (PhD); East Asian studies (MA); Japanese (MA, PhD); language pedagogy (MA). Part-time programs available. *Faculty:* 7 full-time (2 women). *Students:* 19 full-time (12 women), 6 part-time (3 women); includes 3 minority (1 African American, 1 Asian American or Pacific Islander, 1 Hispanic American), 6 international. Average age 32. 77 applicants, 25% accepted, 10 enrolled. In 2007, 7 master's, 1 doctorate awarded. *Degree requirements:* For master's, 2 foreign languages, thesis; for doctorate, 2 foreign languages, thesis/dissertation. *Entrance requirements:* Additional exam requirements/recommendations for international students: Required—TOEFL. *Application deadline:* For fall admission, 1/15 for domestic students, 12/15 for international students; for spring admission, 9/1 for domestic and international students. Applications are processed on a rolling basis. Application fee: $50 ($60 for international students). Electronic applications accepted. *Financial support:* Fellowships, teaching assistantships, Federal Work-Study and tuition waivers (full) available. Financial award application deadline: 3/1. *Faculty research:* Postwar/postmodern Japanese fiction, modern Chinese film and literature, classical Chinese literature and philosophy, Chinese and Japanese linguistics and pedagogy, East Asian politics. *Unit head:* Robert Eno, Chair, 812-855-0856, E-mail: eno@indiana.edu. *Application contact:* Edith Sarra, Director of Graduate Studies, 812-855-4031, Fax: 812-855-6402, E-mail: eserra@indiana.edu.

Middlebury College, Language Schools, Chinese School, Middlebury, VT 05753-6002. Offers MA. *Faculty:* 1 full-time (0 women). *Students:* 17 full-time (14 women); includes 11 minority (all Asian Americans or Pacific Islanders) Average age 34. 35 applicants, 60% accepted, 17 enrolled. *Degree requirements:* For master's, one foreign language. *Entrance requirements:* For master's, 3 letters of rec, writing sample. Additional exam requirements/recommendations for international students: Required—TOEFL. *Application deadline:* Applications are processed on a rolling basis. Application fee: $55. Electronic applications accepted. *Financial support:* Fellowships, scholarships/grants available. *Unit head:* Dr. Jianhua Bai, Director, 802-443-5520, Fax: 802-443-2075, E-mail: jbai@middlebury.edu. *Application contact:* Anna Sun, Coordinator, 802-443-5520, Fax: 802-443-2075, E-mail: sun@middlebury.edu.

The Ohio State University, Graduate School, College of Humanities, Department of East Asian Languages and Literatures, Columbus, OH 43210. Offers Chinese (MA, PhD); Japanese (MA, PhD). *Faculty:* 22. *Students:* 49 full-time (31 women), 6 part-time (1 woman); includes 6 minority (5 Asian Americans or Pacific Islanders, 1 Hispanic American), 24 international. Average age 28. In 2007, 11 master's, 1 doctorate awarded. *Degree requirements:* For master's, thesis optional; for doctorate, thesis/dissertation. *Entrance requirements:* For master's and doctorate, GRE (if applying for financial aid). Additional exam requirements/recommendations for international students: Required—TOEFL (minimum score 577 paper-based; 233 computer-based). *Application deadline:* For fall admission, 8/15 priority date for domestic students, 7/1 priority date for international students; for winter admission, 12/1 priority date for domestic students, 11/1 priority date for international students; for spring admission, 3/1 priority date for domestic students, 2/1 priority date for international students. Applications are processed on a rolling basis. Application fee: $40 ($50 for international students). Electronic applications accepted. *Financial support:* Fellowships, research assistantships, teaching assistantships, Federal Work-Study, institutionally sponsored loans, and unspecified assistantships available. Support available to part-time students. *Unit head:* Mineharu Nakayama, Graduate Studies Committee Chair, 614-292-5816, Fax: 614-292-3225, E-mail: nakayama.1@osu.edu. *Application contact:* Graduate Admissions, 614-292-9444, Fax: 614-292-3895, E-mail: domestic.grad@osu.edu.

San Francisco State University, Division of Graduate Studies, College of Humanities, Department of Foreign Languages and Literatures, Program in Chinese, San Francisco, CA 94132-1722. Offers MA. *Application deadline:* Applications are processed on a rolling basis. *Unit head:* Dr. Chris Wen-Chao Li, Program Coordinator, 415-338-1421, E-mail: wenchao@sfsu.edu.

Stanford University, School of Humanities and Sciences, Department of Asian Languages, Stanford, CA 94305-9991. Offers Chinese (MA, PhD); Japanese (MA, PhD). Terminal master's awarded for partial completion of doctoral program. *Degree requirements:* For master's, one foreign language, thesis or an annotated translation of a literary or historical text; for doctorate, 2 foreign languages, thesis/dissertation, field exams. *Entrance requirements:* For master's and doctorate, GRE General Test. Additional exam requirements/recommendations for international students: Required—TOEFL. Electronic applications accepted.

University of Alberta, Faculty of Graduate Studies and Research, Department of East Asian Studies, Edmonton, AB T6G 2E1, Canada. Offers Chinese literature (MA); East Asian interdisciplinary studies (MA); Japanese literature (MA). Part-time programs available. *Degree requirements:* For master's, one foreign language, thesis. *Entrance requirements:* Additional exam requirements/recommendations for international students: Required—TOEFL. Electronic applications accepted. *Faculty research:* Classical Chinese poetry and poetics, Chinese philosophy, modern/contemporary Chinese literature, modern Japanese literature and culture, Japanese women's writing.

University of California, Berkeley, Graduate Division, College of Letters and Science, Department of East Asian Languages and Cultures, Berkeley, CA 94720-1500. Offers Chinese language (PhD); Japanese language (PhD). *Degree requirements:* For doctorate, one foreign language, thesis/dissertation, oral qualifying exam. *Entrance requirements:* For doctorate, GRE General Test, minimum GPA of 3.0, MA thesis, 3 letters of recommendation. *Application deadline:* For fall admission, 12/8 for domestic students. Application fee: $70 ($90 for international students). Electronic applications accepted. *Financial support:* Fellowships, research assistantships, teaching assistantships, Federal Work-Study, institutionally sponsored loans, and unspecified assistantships available. Financial award applicants required to submit FAFSA. *Faculty research:* Chinese and Japanese modern and classical texts, prose, and poetry; Chinese and Japanese linguistics. *Unit head:* Dr. Alan Tansman, Chair, 510-643-4311, Fax: 510-642-6031, E-mail: tansman@berkeley.edu. *Application contact:* Information Contact, 510-642-3480, E-mail: ealang@berkeley.edu.

University of California, Irvine, Office of Graduate Studies, School of Humanities, Department of East Asian Languages and Literatures, Irvine, CA 92697. Offers Chinese (MA, PhD); East Asian languages and literatures (MA, PhD); Japanese (MA, PhD). *Students:* 14 full-time (12 women); includes 1 minority (Asian American or Pacific Islander), 10 international. In 2007, 1 master's, 1 doctorate awarded. *Degree requirements:* For doctorate, thesis/dissertation. *Entrance requirements:* For master's, GRE, minimum GPA of 3.0; for doctorate, GRE General Test, minimum GPA of 3.0. Additional exam requirements/recommendations for international students: Required—TOEFL (minimum score 550 paper-based; 213 computer-based). *Application deadline:* For fall admission, 1/15 priority date for domestic students; for winter admission, 10/15 priority date for domestic students; for spring admission, 1/15 for domestic students. Application fee: $60. Electronic applications accepted. *Financial support:* Fellowships with tuition reimbursements, research assistantships with full tuition reimbursements, teaching assistantships with partial tuition reimbursements, institutionally sponsored loans, traineeships, health care benefits, and unspecified assistantships available. Financial award application deadline: 3/1; financial award applicants required to submit FAFSA. *Faculty research:* Chinese, Japanese, and Korean literature and culture; language and textual analysis; historical, social, and cultural dimensions of literary study. *Unit head:* Michael Fuller, Interim Chair, 949-824-2151. *Application contact:* Angie Agsalog, Graduate Staff Contact, 949-824-1601, Fax: 949-824-3248, E-mail: aagsalog@uci.edu.

University of Colorado at Boulder, Graduate School, College of Arts and Sciences, Department of East Asian Languages and Civilizations, Boulder, CO 80309. Offers Chinese (MA, PhD); Japanese (MA, PhD). Part-time programs available. *Faculty:* 9. *Students:* 29 full-time (15 women), 6 part-time (4 women); includes 5 minority (all Asian Americans or Pacific Islanders), 12 international. Average age 29. 25 applicants, 64% accepted. In 2007, 6 degrees awarded. *Degree requirements:* For master's, comprehensive exam. *Entrance requirements:* For master's,

BA in Chinese or Japanese, minimum undergraduate GPA of 3.0. Additional exam requirements/recommendations for international students: Required—TOEFL. *Application deadline:* For fall admission, 1/1 priority date for domestic students, 12/1 for international students; for spring admission, 10/1 for domestic students, 9/1 for international students. Applications are processed on a rolling basis. Application fee: $50 ($60 for international students). *Financial support:* In 2007–08, 12 fellowships (averaging $3,372 per year), 2 research assistantships (averaging $10,564 per year) were awarded; career-related internships or fieldwork and Federal Work-Study also available. Financial award application deadline: 2/1. *Faculty research:* Chinese and Japanese modern and classical literature, religions, linguistics, language pedagogy, pre-modern and contemporary fiction, sociolinguistics. Total annual research expenditures: $1.1 million. *Unit head:* Michael Breed, Chair, 303-492-7241, Fax: 303-492-7272, E-mail: michael.breed@colorado.edu. *Application contact:* Graduate Secretary, 303-492-6639, Fax: 303-492-7272, E-mail: ealc@colorado.edu.

University of Hawaii at Manoa, Graduate Division, Colleges of Arts and Sciences, College of Language, Linguistics and Literature, Department of East Asian Languages and Literatures, Program in Chinese, Honolulu, HI 96822. Offers MA, PhD. Part-time programs available. *Faculty:* 8 full-time (2 women). *Students:* 15 full-time (11 women), 2 part-time (1 woman); includes 2 minority (both Asian Americans or Pacific Islanders), 12 international. 27 applicants, 74% accepted, 7 enrolled. *Median time to degree:* Of those who began their doctoral program in fall 1999, 50% received their degree in 8 years or less. *Degree requirements:* For master's, 2 foreign languages, thesis optional; for doctorate, 2 foreign languages, comprehensive exam, thesis/dissertation. *Entrance requirements:* For master's and doctorate, GRE General Test. Additional exam requirements/recommendations for international students: Required—TOEFL (minimum score 560 paper-based; 220 computer-based; 83 iBT), IELTS (minimum score 5). *Application deadline:* For fall admission, 2/1 for domestic and international students; for spring admission, 9/1 for domestic and international students. Application fee: $50. *Financial support:* In 2007–08, 5 teaching assistantships (averaging $14,165 per year) were awarded; research assistantships. *Application contact:* Leon Serafim, Graduate Chair, 808-956-2069, Fax: 808-956-9515, E-mail: serafim@hawaii.edu.

University of Hawaii at Manoa, Graduate Division, School of Pacific and Asian Studies, Program in Asian Studies, Concentration in Chinese Studies, Honolulu, HI 96822. Offers Graduate Certificate. Part-time programs available. *Students:* 3 full-time (1 woman); includes 1 minority (Asian American or Pacific Islander) *Degree requirements:* For Graduate Certificate, one foreign language. *Entrance requirements:* For degree, GRE. Additional exam requirements/recommendations for international students: Required—TOEFL (minimum score 560 paper-based; 220 computer-based; 83 iBT), IELTS (minimum score 5). *Financial support:* In 2007–08, 1 research assistantship (averaging $15,552 per year), 1 teaching assistantship (averaging $13,296 per year) were awarded. Total annual research expenditures: $144,877. *Application contact:* Dr. Ricardo D. Trimillos, Graduate Field Chairperson, 808-956-7814, Fax: 808-956-2682, E-mail: rtrimil@hawaii.edu.

University of Massachusetts Amherst, Graduate School, College of Humanities and Fine Arts, Department of Asian Languages and Literatures, Program in Chinese, Amherst, MA 01003. Offers MA. *Students:* 9 full-time (5 women), 9 part-time (8 women); includes 8 minority (1 African American, 7 Asian Americans or Pacific Islanders), 5 international. Average age 34. 21 applicants, 81% accepted, 6 enrolled. In 2007, 1 degree awarded. *Degree requirements:* For master's, thesis, general exam. *Entrance requirements:* For master's, GRE General Test, minimum GPA of 3.0. Additional exam requirements/recommendations for international students: Required—TOEFL (minimum score 530 paper-based; 197 computer-based). *Application deadline:* For fall admission, 2/1 priority date for domestic and international students. Applications are processed on a rolling basis. Application fee: $50 ($65 for international students). Electronic applications accepted. *Expenses:* Tuition, state resident: full-time $2,640; part-time $110 per credit. Tuition, nonresident: full-time $9,936; part-time $414 per credit. Required fees: $7,455. One-time fee: $332. Tuition and fees vary according to course load, campus/location, program and reciprocity agreements. *Financial support:* Fellowships with full tuition reimbursements, research assistantships with full tuition reimbursements, teaching assistantships with full tuition reimbursements, career-related internships or fieldwork, Federal Work-Study, scholarships/grants, traineeships, and unspecified assistantships available. Support available to part-time students. Financial award application deadline: 2/1. *Unit head:* Dr. Donald Gjertson, Director, 413-545-0886, Fax: 413-545-4975. *Application contact:* Information Contact, 413-545-0886, Fax: 413-545-4975.

University of Oregon, Graduate School, College of Arts and Sciences, Department of East Asian Languages and Literature, Eugene, OR 97403. Offers Chinese (MA, PhD); Japanese (MA, PhD). *Faculty:* 15 full-time (9 women), 1 part-time/adjunct (0 women). *Students:* 15 full-time (12 women), 2 part-time (1 woman); includes 1 minority (Asian American or Pacific Islander), 12 international. 29 applicants, 21% accepted. In 2007, 10 degrees awarded. *Entrance requirements:* Additional exam requirements/recommendations for international students: Required—TOEFL. *Application deadline:* For fall admission, 2/15 for domestic students. Application fee: $50. *Financial support:* In 2007–08, 20 teaching assistantships were awarded. Financial award application deadline: 3/1. *Faculty research:* Linguistics, pedagogy. *Unit head:* Stephen Durrant, Head, 541-346-4008. *Application contact:* Michael Bardossi, Admissions Contact, 541-346-4066, E-mail: bardossm@oregon.uoregon.edu.

University of Washington, Graduate School, College of Arts and Sciences, Department of Asian Languages and Literature, Seattle, WA 98195. Offers Chinese language and literature (MA, PhD); Japanese language and literature (MA, PhD); South Asian language and literature (MA, PhD). *Degree requirements:* For master's, 2 foreign languages, general exam, thesis or 2 research papers; for doctorate, 3 foreign languages, thesis/dissertation, general exam. *Entrance requirements:* For master's, GRE, minimum GPA of 3.0; for doctorate, GRE, master's degree in related field, minimum GPA of 3.0. Additional exam requirements/recommendations for international students: Required—TOEFL. Electronic applications accepted. *Faculty research:* Textual, linguistic, philological, and literary study of languages and literatures of Asia.

University of Wisconsin–Madison, Graduate School, College of Letters and Science, Department of East Asian Languages and Literature, Program in Chinese, Madison, WI 53706-1380. Offers MA, PhD. Part-time programs available. Terminal master's awarded for partial completion of doctoral program. *Degree requirements:* For master's, one foreign language, seminars, written exam; for doctorate, 3 foreign languages, thesis/dissertation, seminars, preliminary exams, oral exam. *Entrance requirements:* For master's, bachelor's degree or equivalent in Chinese; for doctorate, master's degree or equivalent in Chinese. Electronic applications accepted. *Faculty research:* Chinese historical and modern linguistics, classical Chinese literary and cultural history, modern Chinese literary and cultural history, Chinese paleography.

Washington University in St. Louis, Graduate School of Arts and Sciences, Department of Asian and Near Eastern Languages and Literatures, St. Louis, MO 63130-4899. Offers Asian language (MA); Asian studies (MA); Chinese (PhD); comparative literature (MA, PhD); Japanese (PhD). Terminal master's awarded for partial completion of doctoral program. *Degree requirements:* For master's, thesis optional; for doctorate, thesis/dissertation. *Entrance requirements:* For master's and doctorate, GRE General Test. Electronic applications accepted.

Washington University in St. Louis, Graduate School of Arts and Sciences, Program in East Asian Studies, St. Louis, MO 63130-4899. Offers art history (PhD); Chinese (MA); Chinese and comparative literature (PhD); East Asian studies (MA); history (PhD); Japanese (MA); Japanese and comparative literature (PhD); JD/MA; MBA/MA. PhD offered through specific departments. *Entrance requirements:* For master's and doctorate, GRE General Test. Electronic applications accepted.

See Close-Up on page 815.

Classics

Boston College, Graduate School of Arts and Sciences, Department of Classics, Chestnut Hill, MA 02467-3800. Offers classics (MA); Greek (MA); Latin (MA). Part-time programs available. *Students:* 8 full-time (6 women), 4 part-time (2 women). 18 applicants, 56% accepted, 4 enrolled. In 2007, 2 degrees awarded. *Degree requirements:* For master's, one foreign language, thesis optional. *Entrance requirements:* Additional exam requirements/recommendations for international students: Required—TOEFL (minimum score 590 paper-based; 250 computer-based; 91 iBT). *Application deadline:* For fall admission, 1/15 for domestic students. Application fee: $70. *Financial support:* Federal Work-Study, scholarships/grants, and tuition waivers (full and partial) available. Support available to part-time students. Financial award application deadline: 3/1; financial award applicants required to submit FAFSA. *Faculty research:* Classical philology, ancient history, modern Greek. *Unit head:* Dr. Gail Hoffman, Chairperson, 617-552-2236, E-mail: hoffmaga@bc.edu.

Boston University, Graduate School of Arts and Sciences, Department of Classical Studies, Boston, MA 02215. Offers MA, PhD, MA/PhD. *Faculty:* 14 full-time (5 women), 2 part-time/adjunct (0 women). *Students:* 18 full-time (5 women), 3 part-time (all women). Average age 29. 35 applicants, 40% accepted, 3 enrolled. In 2007, 2 master's awarded. Terminal master's awarded for partial completion of doctoral program. *Degree requirements:* For master's, one foreign language, comprehensive exam; for doctorate, 2 foreign languages, comprehensive exam, thesis/dissertation. *Entrance requirements:* For master's and doctorate, GRE General Test, 3 letters of recommendation, scholarly writing sample, personal statement. Additional exam requirements/recommendations for international students: Required—TOEFL (minimum score 550 paper-based; 213 computer-based; 84 iBT). *Application deadline:* For fall admission, 7/1 for domestic and international students; for spring admission, 10/15 for domestic and international students. Application fee: $70. Electronic applications accepted. *Expenses:* Tuition: Full-time $34,930; part-time $1,092 per credit. Tuition and fees vary according to class time, course level and program. *Financial support:* In 2007–08, 10 students received support, including 1 fellowship with full tuition reimbursement available (averaging $18,000 per year), 7 teaching assistantships with full tuition reimbursements available (averaging $16,500 per year); research assistantships, career-related internships or fieldwork, Federal Work-Study, institutionally sponsored loans, scholarships/grants, health care benefits, and first-year scholarships also available. Support available to part-time students. Financial award application deadline: 1/15; financial award applicants required to submit FAFSA. *Faculty research:* Homer and Hesiod, tragedy and comedy, classical tradition, fifth century Athenian history, empire literature and history. *Unit head:* Dr. Loren J. Samons, Interim Chairman, 617-353-2427, Fax: 617-353-1610, E-mail: sscully@bu.edu. *Application contact:* Stacy Fox, Department Administrator, 617-353-2426, E-mail: sfox@bu.edu.

Boston University, School of Education, Department of Curriculum and Teaching, Program in Latin and Classical Studies, Boston, MA 02215. Offers MAT. *Students:* 2 full-time (both women), 1 (woman) part-time. Average age 25. 5 applicants, 100% accepted, 2 enrolled. *Degree requirements:* For master's, comprehensive exam, thesis optional. *Entrance requirements:* For master's, GRE General Test or MAT. Additional exam requirements/recommendations for international students: Required—TOEFL. *Application deadline:* For fall admission, 2/15 priority date for domestic students; for winter admission, 10/1 priority date for domestic students. Applications are processed on a rolling basis. Application fee: $70. Electronic applications accepted. *Expenses:* Tuition: Full-time $34,930; part-time $1,092 per credit. Tuition and fees vary according to class time, course level and program. *Financial support:* Application deadline: 2/15. *Application contact:* 617-353-4237, Fax: 617-353-8937, E-mail: sedgrad@bu.edu.

Brandeis University, Graduate School of Arts and Sciences, Program in Classics, Waltham, MA 02454-9110. Offers Graduate Certificate. Part-time programs available. *Faculty:* 5 full-time (4 women). *Entrance requirements:* Additional exam requirements/recommendations for international students: Required—TOEFL (minimum score 600 paper-based; 250 computer-based; 100 iBT), IELTS (minimum score 7). *Application deadline:* Applications are processed on a rolling basis. Application fee: $55. Electronic applications accepted. *Financial support:* Scholarships/grants available. Support available to part-time students. Financial award application deadline: 4/15; financial award applicants required to submit CSS PROFILE. *Unit head:* Dr. Ann Olga Koluski-Ostrow, Chair, Graduate Certificate Program, 781-736-2183, E-mail: aoko@brandeis.edu.

Brock University, Faculty of Graduate Studies, Faculty of Humanities, Program in Classics, St. Catharines, ON L2S 3A1, Canada. Offers MA. Part-time programs available. *Degree requirements:* For master's, thesis. *Entrance requirements:* For master's, honors degree. Additional exam requirements/recommendations for international students: Required—TOEFL (minimum score 550 paper-based; 213 computer-based; 80 iBT), IELTS (minimum score 7), TWE (minimum score 4). Electronic applications accepted.

Brown University, Graduate School, Department of Classics, Providence, RI 02912. Offers AM, PhD. *Degree requirements:* For master's, one foreign language, thesis; for doctorate, 2 foreign languages, thesis/dissertation. *Entrance requirements:* For master's and doctorate, GRE General Test. *Faculty research:* Philology, archaeology, Sanskrit.

Bryn Mawr College, Graduate School of Arts and Sciences, Department of Greek, Latin, and Classical Studies, Bryn Mawr, PA 19010-2899. Offers MA, PhD. Part-time programs available. *Faculty:* 5. *Students:* 6 full-time (2 women), 11 part-time (6 women). 19 applicants, 21% accepted, 0 enrolled. In 2007, 1 degree awarded. *Degree requirements:* For master's, 2 foreign languages, thesis; for doctorate, 3 foreign languages, comprehensive exam, thesis/dissertation. *Entrance requirements:* For master's and doctorate, GRE General Test. Additional exam requirements/recommendations for international students: Required—TOEFL (minimum score 600 paper-based; 250 computer-based). *Application deadline:* For fall admission, 1/3 for domestic and international students. Application fee: $30. *Financial support:* Fellowships with full tuition reimbursements, teaching assistantships with partial tuition reimbursements, Federal Work-Study, scholarships/grants, and tuition waivers (full and partial) available. Support available to part-time students. Financial award application deadline: 1/3. *Unit head:* Dr. Richard Hamilton, Chairman, 610-526-5399, E-mail: rhamilto@brynmawr.edu. *Application contact:* Lea R. Miller, Secretary, 610-526-5072, Fax: 610-526-5076, E-mail: lrmiller@brynmawr.edu.

See Close-Up on page 563.

The Catholic University of America, School of Arts and Sciences, Department of Greek and Latin, Washington, DC 20064. Offers classics (MA); Greek and Latin (PhD); Latin (MA); MSLS/MA.

Classics

The Catholic University of America (continued)

Part-time programs available. *Faculty:* 5 full-time (1 woman), 2 part-time/adjunct (1 woman). *Students:* 6 full-time (2 women), 5 part-time (2 women), 1 international. Average age 39. 13 applicants, 69% accepted, 3 enrolled. In 2007, 2 master's, 1 doctorate awarded. Terminal master's awarded for partial completion of doctoral program. *Degree requirements:* For master's, one foreign language, comprehensive exam; for doctorate, 2 foreign languages, comprehensive exam, thesis/dissertation. *Entrance requirements:* For master's and doctorate, GRE General Test, 3 letters of recommendation, writing sample. Additional exam requirements/recommendations for international students: Required—TOEFL (minimum score 580 paper-based; 237 computer-based). *Application deadline:* For fall admission, 2/1 priority date for domestic students; for spring admission, 11/15 priority date for domestic students. Applications are processed on a rolling basis. Application fee: $55. Electronic applications accepted. *Financial support:* Fellowships, teaching assistantships, career-related internships or fieldwork, Federal Work-Study, scholarships/grants, tuition waivers (full and partial), and unspecified assistantships available. Support available to part-time students. Financial award application deadline: 2/1; financial award applicants required to submit FAFSA. *Faculty research:* Greek and Latin patristics, medieval Latin, computers and classics, late antique history, late antique Byzantine art history. *Unit head:* Dr. Frank A. C. Mantello, Chair, 202-319-5216, Fax: 202-319-5297, E-mail: mantello@cua.edu.

Columbia University, Graduate School of Arts and Sciences, Division of Humanities, Department of Classics, New York, NY 10027. Offers M Phil, MA, PhD. *Faculty:* 15 full-time, 1 part-time/adjunct. *Students:* 21 full-time (11 women), 3 part-time (1 woman); includes 3 minority (1 Asian American or Pacific Islander, 2 Hispanic Americans), 5 international. Average age 31. 37 applicants, 59% accepted. In 2007, 7 master's, 3 doctorates awarded. *Degree requirements:* For master's, one foreign language, seminar paper; for doctorate, 3 foreign languages, thesis/dissertation. *Entrance requirements:* For master's, GRE General Test, reading knowledge of Greek or Latin; for doctorate, GRE General Test, reading knowledge of Greek and Latin. Additional exam requirements/recommendations for international students: Required—TOEFL. Application fee: $90. *Expenses:* Tuition: Part-time $1,452 per credit. Required fees: $152 per term. One-time fee: $75 part-time. Full-time tuition and fees vary according to course level, course load, degree level and program. *Financial support:* Fellowships, teaching assistantships, Federal Work-Study and institutionally sponsored loans available. Support available to part-time students. Financial award application deadline: 1/5; financial award applicants required to submit FAFSA. *Faculty research:* Greek and Latin literature, ancient philosophy. *Unit head:* Gareth Williams, Chair, 212-854-2850, Fax: 212-854-7856.

Cornell University, Graduate School, Graduate Fields of Arts and Sciences, Field of Classics, Ithaca, NY 14853-0001. Offers ancient history (PhD); ancient philosophy (PhD); classical archaeology (PhD); classical myth (PhD); classical rhetoric (PhD); Greek and Latin language and linguistics (PhD); Greek language and literature (PhD); Indo-European linguistics (PhD); Latin language and literature (PhD); medieval and Renaissance Latin literature (PhD). *Faculty:* 27 full-time (6 women). *Students:* 18 full-time (3 women), 7 international. Average age 27. 66 applicants, 11% accepted, 5 enrolled. In 2007, 1 doctorate awarded. *Degree requirements:* For doctorate, 2 foreign languages, comprehensive exam, thesis/dissertation. *Entrance requirements:* For doctorate, GRE General Test, 3 letters of recommendation, sample of written work. Additional exam requirements/recommendations for international students: Required—TOEFL (minimum score 550 paper-based; 213 computer-based; 77 iBT). *Application deadline:* For fall admission, 1/15 for domestic students. Application fee: $70. Electronic applications accepted. *Financial support:* In 2007–08, 17 students received support, including 11 fellowships with full tuition reimbursements available, 6 teaching assistantships with full tuition reimbursements available; research assistantships with full tuition reimbursements available, institutionally sponsored loans, scholarships/grants, health care benefits, tuition waivers (full and partial), and unspecified assistantships also available. Financial award applicants required to submit FAFSA. *Faculty research:* Greek and Roman literature, ancient philosophy, Greek and Roman archaeology, ancient history, Indo-European linguistics. *Unit head:* Director of Graduate Studies, 607-255-3354. *Application contact:* Graduate Field Assistant, 607-255-3354, E-mail: classics@cornell.edu.

Dalhousie University, Faculty of Arts and Social Science, Department of Classics, Halifax, NS B3H 4R2, Canada. Offers MA, PhD. *Faculty:* 7 full-time (1 woman), 3 part-time/adjunct (2 women). *Students:* 10 full-time (2 women), 1 (woman) part-time. Average age 25. 10 applicants, 50% accepted. In 2007, 3 master's, 1 doctorate awarded. *Degree requirements:* For master's, 3 foreign languages, thesis; for doctorate, 4 foreign languages, thesis/dissertation. *Entrance requirements:* For doctorate, MA. Additional exam requirements/recommendations for international students: Required—TOEFL. *Application deadline:* For fall admission, 6/1 for domestic students. Applications are processed on a rolling basis. Application fee: $60. *Financial support:* In 2007–08, 10 students received support, including 5 fellowships (averaging $8,900 per year), 3 research assistantships (averaging $16,000 per year), 10 teaching assistantships (averaging $2,500 per year). *Faculty research:* Greek and Latin poetry, Hellenistic and early Christian history, Greek philosophy, Aristotelianism, late Roman Empire history. Total annual research expenditures: $8,000. *Unit head:* Prof. Wayne Hankey, Chair, 902-494-3468, Fax: 902-494-2467, E-mail: claswww@is.dal.ca. *Application contact:* Dr. Peter O'Brien, Graduate Coordinator, 902-494-2295, Fax: 902-494-2467, E-mail: peter.obrien@dal.ca.

Duke University, Graduate School, Department of Classical Studies, Durham, NC 27708-0586. Offers PhD. *Faculty:* 10 full-time. *Students:* 22 full-time (7 women); includes 1 minority (Asian American or Pacific Islander), 5 international. 34 applicants, 38% accepted, 7 enrolled. *Degree requirements:* For doctorate, 2 foreign languages, thesis/dissertation. *Entrance requirements:* For doctorate, GRE General Test. Additional exam requirements/recommendations for international students: Required—TOEFL (minimum score 550 paper-based; 213 computer-based; 83 iBT), IELTS (minimum score 7). *Application deadline:* For fall admission, 12/15 priority date for domestic and international students. Application fee: $75. Electronic applications accepted. *Financial support:* Teaching assistantships, Federal Work-Study available. Financial award application deadline: 12/31. *Faculty research:* Greek Bronze Age; classical and Roman archaeology; Pompeii and Hadrian; epigraphy, papyrology, and Latin paleography. *Unit head:* Mary Tolly Boatwright, Director of Graduate Studies, 919-681-4292, Fax: 919-681-4262, E-mail: cathy.puckett@duke.edu.

Florida State University, Graduate Studies, College of Arts and Sciences, Department of Classics, Tallahassee, FL 32306. Offers classical archaeology (MA); classical civilization (MA); classics (MA, PhD), including archaeology (PhD), literature and languages (PhD); Greek (MA); Greek and Latin (MA); Latin (MA). Part-time programs available. *Faculty:* 13 full-time (3 women), 3 part-time/adjunct (1 woman). *Students:* 45 full-time (21 women), 3 part-time (all women). Average age 25. 48 applicants, 75% accepted, 13 enrolled. In 2007, 15 master's, 1 doctorate awarded. *Median time to degree:* Of those who began their doctoral program in fall 1999, 50% received their degree in 8 years or less. *Degree requirements:* For master's, one foreign language, comprehensive exam (for some programs), thesis (for some programs); for doctorate, 2 foreign languages, comprehensive exam, thesis/dissertation. *Entrance requirements:* For master's, GRE General Test, minimum GPA of 3.0; for doctorate, GRE General Test. Additional exam requirements/recommendations for international students: Required—TOEFL. *Application deadline:* For fall admission, 1/15 priority date for domestic students, 2/15 for international students. Applications are processed on a rolling basis. Application fee: $30. Electronic applications accepted. *Expenses:* Tuition, state resident: part-time $248 per credit hour. Tuition, nonresident: part-time $880 per credit hour. Tuition and fees vary according to program. *Financial support:* In 2007–08, 37 students received support, including fellowships with full tuition reimbursements available (averaging $18,000 per year), 2 research assistantships with full tuition reimbursements available (averaging $10,000 per year), 28 teaching assistantships with full tuition reimbursements available (averaging $9,275 per year); Federal Work-Study and institutionally sponsored loans also available. Support available to part-time students. Financial award application deadline: 1/15; financial award applicants required to submit FAFSA. *Faculty research:* Greek and Latin literature, mythology, classical archaeology, history, Roman religion. Total annual research expenditures: $100,000. *Unit head:* Dr. Daniel J. Pullen, Chairman, 850-644-0304, Fax: 850-644-4073, E-mail: dpullen@fsu.edu. *Application contact:* Dr. Nancy de Grummond, Admissions Director, 850-644-0305, Fax: 850-644-0303, E-mail: ndegrummond@fsu.edu.

Fordham University, Graduate School of Arts and Sciences, Department of Classical Languages and Literatures, New York, NY 10458. Offers classical Greek and Latin literature (MA); classics (PhD). Part-time and evening/weekend programs available. *Faculty:* 7 full-time (1 woman). *Students:* 9 full-time (3 women), 8 part-time (2 women); includes 1 minority (Asian American or Pacific Islander), 1 international. Average age 29. 10 applicants, 80% accepted, 1 enrolled. In 2007, 1 master's awarded. Terminal master's awarded for partial completion of doctoral program. *Median time to degree:* Of those who began their doctoral program in fall 1999, 33% received their degree in 8 years or less. *Degree requirements:* For master's, one foreign language, comprehensive exam; for doctorate, 2 foreign languages, comprehensive exam, thesis/dissertation. *Entrance requirements:* For master's and doctorate, GRE General Test. Additional exam requirements/recommendations for international students: Required—TOEFL (minimum score 650 paper-based; 280 computer-based). *Application deadline:* For fall admission, 1/4 priority date for domestic students; for spring admission, 11/1 for domestic students. Application fee: $70. Electronic applications accepted. *Expenses:* Tuition: Full-time $23,880; part-time $995 per credit. *Financial support:* In 2007–08, 6 students received support, including 1 fellowship with tuition reimbursement available (averaging $21,100 per year), 3 research assistantships with tuition reimbursements available (averaging $18,500 per year), 2 teaching assistantships with tuition reimbursements available (averaging $20,000 per year); Federal Work-Study, institutionally sponsored loans, scholarships/grants, tuition waivers (full and partial), and unspecified assistantships also available. Support available to part-time students. Financial award application deadline: 1/4; financial award applicants required to submit FAFSA. *Unit head:* Dr. Robert Penella, Chair, 718-817-3132, Fax: 718-817-3134, E-mail: penella@fordham.edu. *Application contact:* Charlene Dundie, Director of Graduate Admissions, 718-817-4420, Fax: 718-817-3566, E-mail: dundie@fordham.edu.

Graduate School and University Center of the City University of New York, Graduate Studies, Program in Classics, New York, NY 10016-4039. Offers MA, PhD. *Faculty:* 14 full-time (5 women). *Students:* 13 full-time (6 women), 10 part-time (1 woman); includes 1 minority (Hispanic American), 1 international. Average age 42. 10 applicants, 70% accepted, 3 enrolled. *Degree requirements:* For master's, 2 foreign languages, thesis; for doctorate, 2 foreign languages, thesis/dissertation. *Entrance requirements:* For master's and doctorate, GRE General Test. Additional exam requirements/recommendations for international students: Required—TOEFL. *Application deadline:* For fall admission, 4/15 for domestic students. Application fee: $125. Electronic applications accepted. *Financial support:* In 2007–08, 9 students received support, including 9 fellowships, 1 teaching assistantship; research assistantships, career-related internships or fieldwork, Federal Work-Study, institutionally sponsored loans, and tuition waivers (full and partial) also available. Financial award application deadline: 2/1; financial award applicants required to submit FAFSA. *Unit head:* Dr. Dee Clayman, Executive Officer, 212-817-8151, Fax: 212-817-1508.

Graduate School and University Center of the City University of New York, Graduate Studies, Program in Comparative Literature, New York, NY 10016-4039. Offers comparative literature (MA, PhD), including classics (PhD), German (PhD), Italian (PhD). *Faculty:* 16 full-time (3 women). *Students:* 98 full-time (59 women), 11 part-time (9 women); includes 7 minority (2 Asian Americans or Pacific Islanders, 5 Hispanic Americans), 26 international. Average age 36. 66 applicants, 35% accepted, 14 enrolled. In 2007, 6 master's, 5 doctorates awarded. Terminal master's awarded for partial completion of doctoral program. *Degree requirements:* For master's, 2 foreign languages, comprehensive exam, thesis; for doctorate, 3 foreign languages, comprehensive exam, thesis/dissertation. *Entrance requirements:* For master's and doctorate, GRE General Test. Additional exam requirements/recommendations for international students: Required—TOEFL. *Application deadline:* For fall admission, 4/15 for domestic students; for spring admission, 11/15 for domestic students. Application fee: $125. Electronic applications accepted. *Financial support:* In 2007–08, 63 students received support, including 53 fellowships, 5 research assistantships, 14 teaching assistantships; career-related internships or fieldwork, Federal Work-Study, institutionally sponsored loans, and tuition waivers (full and partial) also available. Financial award application deadline: 2/1; financial award applicants required to submit FAFSA. *Unit head:* Dr. Andre Aciman, Executive Officer, 212-817-8170, Fax: 212-817-1509, E-mail: aaciman@gc.cuny.edu.

Harvard University, Graduate School of Arts and Sciences, Department of the Classics, Cambridge, MA 02138. Offers Byzantine Greek (PhD); classical archaeology (PhD); classical philology (PhD); classical philosophy (PhD); medieval Latin (PhD). *Degree requirements:* For doctorate, 4 foreign languages, thesis/dissertation, preliminary and special exams. *Entrance requirements:* For doctorate, GRE General Test. Additional exam requirements/recommendations for international students: Required—TOEFL. *Expenses:* Tuition: Full-time $31,456. Full-time tuition and fees vary according to program and student level.

Heritage Christian University, Graduate Programs, Florence, AL 35630. Offers counseling (MM); Greek (MA); ministry (MM); New Testament (MA). *Degree requirements:* For master's, practicum (MM), major research paper (MA). *Entrance requirements:* For master's, MAT or GRE, bachelor's degree in Bible from an accredited college or university, minimum GPA of 2.75, 3 letters of recommendation.

Hunter College of the City University of New York, Graduate School, School of Arts and Sciences, Department of Classical and Oriental Studies, Program in Teaching Latin, New York, NY 10021-5085. Offers MA. Part-time and evening/weekend programs available. *Faculty:* 2 full-time (1 woman). *Students:* 1 (woman) full-time, 14 part-time (9 women). Average age 34. 10 applicants, 100% accepted, 9 enrolled. In 2007, 1 degree awarded. *Degree requirements:* For master's, one foreign language, comprehensive exam. *Entrance requirements:* For master's, undergraduate major in Latin or equivalent with a minimum GPA of 3.0, 2.8 overall; interview, 2 letters of recommendation. Additional exam requirements/recommendations for international students: Required—TOEFL. *Application deadline:* For fall admission, 4/28 for domestic students; for spring admission, 11/21 for domestic students. Application fee: $125. *Expenses:* Tuition, state resident: full-time $6,400; part-time $270 per credit. Tuition, nonresident: part-time $500 per credit. One-time fee: $125 full-time. Tuition and fees vary according to program. *Financial support:* Federal Work-Study, scholarships/grants, and tuition waivers (partial) available. Support available to part-time students. Financial award application deadline: 4/15. *Faculty research:* Late antique religion and social history, women in antiquity, Horace and lyric poetry, Roman comedy, Latin prose. *Unit head:* Dr. Ronnie Aucona, Director, 212-772-4960, E-mail: rancona@hunter.cuny.edu.

Indiana University Bloomington, University Graduate School, College of Arts and Sciences, Department of Classical Studies, Bloomington, IN 47405-7000. Offers MA, MAT, PhD. Part-time programs available. *Faculty:* 5 full-time (3 women). *Students:* 25 full-time (15 women), 7 part-time (3 women); includes 1 minority (Asian American or Pacific Islander), 2 international. Average age 30. 24 applicants, 50% accepted, 9 enrolled. In 2007, 6 master's, 1 doctorate awarded. *Median time to degree:* Of those who began their doctoral program in fall 1999, 50% received their degree in 8 years or less. *Degree requirements:* For master's, 2 foreign languages; for doctorate, 3 foreign languages, thesis/dissertation. *Entrance requirements:* For master's and doctorate, GRE, minimum GPA of 3.0. Additional exam requirements/recommendations for international students: Required—TOEFL. *Application deadline:* For fall admission, 1/15 priority date for domestic students, 12/15 for international students; for spring admission, 9/1 priority date for domestic students, 9/1 for international students. Applications are processed on a rolling basis. Application fee: $50 ($60 for international students). *Financial support:* Fellowships with full tuition reimbursements, teaching assistantships with full tuition reimbursements, Federal Work-Study available. *Faculty research:* Roman literature (particularly Empire and late Latin), Greek drama, Homer, history of ideas, papyrology. *Unit head:* Prof.

Matthew Christ, Chair, 812-855-6651. *Application contact:* Yvette Rollins, Graduate Secretary, 812-855-6651, E-mail: rollinsy@indiana.edu.

The Johns Hopkins University, Zanvyl Krieger School of Arts and Sciences, Department of Classics, Baltimore, MD 21218-2699. Offers PhD. *Faculty:* 6 full-time (1 woman), 1 part-time/adjunct (0 women). *Students:* 20 full-time (12 women), 7 international. Average age 27. 29 applicants, 17% accepted, 4 enrolled. In 2007, 1 doctorate awarded. Terminal master's awarded for partial completion of doctoral program. *Median time to degree:* Of those who began their doctoral program in fall 1999, 100% received their degree in 8 years or less. *Degree requirements:* For doctorate, 4 foreign languages, thesis/dissertation. *Entrance requirements:* For doctorate, GRE General Test. Additional exam requirements/recommendations for international students: Required—TOEFL (minimum score 600 paper-based; 250 computer-based), IELTS (minimum score 7). *Application deadline:* For fall admission, 1/15 for domestic and international students. Application fee: $75. Electronic applications accepted. *Financial support:* In 2007–08, 20 students received support, including 18 fellowships with full tuition reimbursements available (averaging $17,000 per year), 5 teaching assistantships with full tuition reimbursements available (averaging $17,000 per year); research assistantships with full tuition reimbursements available, career-related internships or fieldwork, institutionally sponsored loans, and tuition waivers (full and partial) also available. Financial award application deadline: 4/15; financial award applicants required to submit FAFSA. *Faculty research:* Greek culture and mythology, classical sculpture, Early Imperial Roman society. *Unit head:* Dr. Matthew Roller, Chair, 410-516-5095, Fax: 410-516-4848, E-mail: mroller@jhu.edu. *Application contact:* Ginnie Miller, Admissions Coordinator, 410-516-7556, Fax: 410-516-4848, E-mail: gmiller@jhu.edu.

Kent State University, College of Arts and Sciences, Department of Modern and Classical Language Studies, Kent, OH 44242-0001. Offers French literature (MA); French, Spanish, German and Latin pedagogy (MA); German literature (MA); Spanish literature (MA); translation (MA), including French, German, Japanese, Russian, Spanish; translation studies (PhD). Part-time and evening/weekend programs available. *Faculty:* 31 full-time (15 women), 4 part-time/adjunct (2 women). *Students:* 64 full-time (45 women), 27 part-time (26 women). Average age 32. 113 applicants, 80% accepted, 42 enrolled. In 2007, 27 degrees awarded. *Degree requirements:* For master's, one foreign language, comprehensive exam (for some programs), thesis (for some programs); for doctorate, comprehensive exam, thesis/dissertation (for some programs). *Entrance requirements:* For master's, minimum GPA of 3.0, writing sample, audio tape or CD; for doctorate, 3 recommendations. Additional exam requirements/recommendations for international students: Required—TOEFL (minimum score 197 computer-based). *Application deadline:* For fall admission, 2/28 for domestic and international students. Applications are processed on a rolling basis. Application fee: $30. Electronic applications accepted. *Financial support:* In 2007–08, 31 teaching assistantships with full tuition reimbursements (averaging $8,000 per year) were awarded; research assistantships with full tuition reimbursements, career-related internships or fieldwork, Federal Work-Study, health care benefits, tuition waivers (full and partial), and unspecified assistantships also available. Support available to part-time students. Financial award application deadline: 2/1. *Faculty research:* Literature, pedagogy, applied linguistics, translation studies. *Unit head:* Dr. Gregory M Shreve, Chair, 330-672-1796, Fax: 330-672-4009, E-mail: gshreve@kent.edu. *Application contact:* Carol S. Maier, Graduate Coordinator, 330-672-1797, Fax: 330-672-4009, E-mail: cmaier@kent.edu.

Marshall University, Academic Affairs Division, College of Liberal Arts, Program in Latin, Huntington, WV 25755. Offers MA. *Faculty:* 3 full-time (2 women). *Students:* 1 full-time (0 women), 1 (woman) part-time. Average age 33. *Unit head:* Caroline Perkins, Chair, 304-696-6749, E-mail: classical-studies@marshall.edu.

McMaster University, School of Graduate Studies, Faculty of Humanities, Department of Classics, Hamilton, ON L8S 4M2, Canada. Offers MA, PhD. *Faculty:* 7 full-time. *Students:* 17 full-time. Average age 25. 25 applicants, 24% accepted. *Degree requirements:* For master's, one foreign language, thesis or alternative; for doctorate, 2 foreign languages, comprehensive exam, thesis/dissertation. *Entrance requirements:* For master's, honors degree, minimum B+ average. Additional exam requirements/recommendations for international students: Required—TOEFL (minimum score 580 paper-based; 237 computer-based). *Application deadline:* For fall admission, 2/28 priority date for domestic students. Application fee: $90. *Financial support:* In 2007–08, fellowships (averaging $5,000 per year), 16 teaching assistantships (averaging $8,440 per year) were awarded; institutionally sponsored loans and scholarships/grants also available. *Faculty research:* Ancient history, art and archaeology, Latin language and literature, Greek language and literature. Total annual research expenditures: $32,000. *Unit head:* Dr. Michele George, Chair, 905-525-9140 Ext. 23452, Fax: 905-577-6930, E-mail: georgem@mcmaster.ca. *Application contact:* Dr. Evan Haley, Graduate Adviser, 905-525-9140 Ext. 23377, Fax: 905-777-0158, E-mail: haleyev@mcmaster.ca.

Memorial University of Newfoundland, School of Graduate Studies, Department of Classics, St. John's, NL A1C 5S7, Canada. Offers MA. Part-time programs available. *Degree requirements:* For master's, one foreign language, thesis, language exam, translation exam, research essay. *Entrance requirements:* For master's, honors degree in related field, course work in Greek and Latin. Electronic applications accepted. *Faculty research:* Ancient history, historiography, literature, drama, philosophy, paleography, epigraphy, and textual criticism.

New York University, Graduate School of Arts and Science, Department of Classics, New York, NY 10012-1019. Offers classics (MA, PhD); poetics and theory (Advanced Certificate). Part-time programs available. *Faculty:* 11 full-time (3 women), 6 part-time/adjunct. *Students:* 15 full-time (5 women), 2 part-time (1 woman); includes 1 minority (Asian American or Pacific Islander), 2 international. Average age 30. 36 applicants, 28% accepted, 3 enrolled. In 2007, 1 master's, 1 doctorate awarded. *Degree requirements:* For master's, 4 foreign languages, exam or specialized project; for doctorate, 4 foreign languages, thesis/dissertation, exams. *Entrance requirements:* For master's, GRE General Test, knowledge of Greek and Latin history and literature, proficiency in Greek and Latin translation; for doctorate, GRE General Test. Additional exam requirements/recommendations for international students: Required—TOEFL. *Application deadline:* For fall admission, 1/4 priority date for domestic students. Application fee: $85. *Financial support:* Fellowships with tuition reimbursements, teaching assistantships with tuition reimbursements, Federal Work-Study, institutionally sponsored loans, scholarships/grants, health care benefits, and unspecified assistantships available. Financial award application deadline: 1/4; financial award applicants required to submit FAFSA. *Faculty research:* Greek and Latin literature, Greek and Roman history, epigraphy, Greek and Roman philosophy, classical archeology. *Unit head:* Michael Peachin, Chair, 212-998-8590, Fax: 212-995-4209, E-mail: gsas.classic@nyu.edu. *Application contact:* Michele Lawrie, Director of Graduate Studies, 212-998-8590, Fax: 212-995-4209, E-mail: gsas.classics@nyu.edu.

The Ohio State University, Graduate School, College of Humanities, Program in Classics, Columbus, OH 43210. Offers MA, PhD. *Application deadline:* Applications are processed on a rolling basis. Application fee: $40 ($50 for international students). Electronic applications accepted. *Application contact:* Graduate Admissions, 614-292-9444, Fax: 614-292-3895, E-mail: domestic.grad@osu.edu.

The Ohio State University, Graduate School, College of Humanities, Programs in Greek and Latin, Columbus, OH 43210. Offers ancient Greek (MA); Greek studies (MA, PhD); Latin studies (MA, PhD); modern Greek (MA, PhD). *Faculty:* 17. *Students:* 23 full-time (9 women), 2 part-time (both women); includes 2 minority (both Asian Americans or Pacific Islanders), 5 international. Average age 26. In 2007, 3 degrees awarded. *Degree requirements:* For master's, 2 foreign languages; for doctorate, 2 foreign languages, thesis/dissertation. *Entrance requirements:* For master's and doctorate, GRE General Test. Additional exam requirements/recommendations for international students: Required—TOEFL (minimum score 600 paper-based; 250 computer-based). *Application deadline:* For fall admission, 8/15 priority date for domestic students, 7/1 priority date for international students; for winter admission, 12/1 priority date for domestic students, 11/1 priority date for international students; for spring admission, 3/1 priority date for domestic students, 2/1 priority date for international students. Applications are processed on a rolling basis. Application fee: $40 ($50 for international students). Electronic applications accepted. *Financial support:* Fellowships, teaching assistantships, Federal Work-Study and institutionally sponsored loans available. Support available to part-time students. *Unit head:* Anthony Kaldellis, Graduate Studies Committee Chair, 614-292-2744, Fax: 614-292-7835, E-mail: kadellis.1@osu.edu. *Application contact:* 614-292-9444, Fax: 614-292-3895, E-mail: domestic.grad@osu.edu.

Princeton University, Graduate School, Department of Classics, Princeton, NJ 08544-1019. Offers ancient history (PhD); classical archaeology (PhD); classical philosophy (PhD); history, archaeology and religions of the ancient world (PhD). *Degree requirements:* For doctorate, thesis/dissertation. *Entrance requirements:* For doctorate, GRE General Test, sample of written work. Additional exam requirements/recommendations for international students: Required—TOEFL (minimum score 600 paper-based; 250 computer-based). Electronic applications accepted.

Queen's University at Kingston, School of Graduate Studies and Research, Faculty of Arts and Sciences, Department of Classics, Kingston, ON K7L 3N6, Canada. Offers classics, Greek, Latin (MA). Part-time programs available. *Degree requirements:* For master's, one foreign language, thesis (for some programs). *Entrance requirements:* For master's, 3 years of Latin, 2 years of Greek. Additional exam requirements/recommendations for international students: Required—TOEFL. Electronic applications accepted. *Faculty research:* Greek and Latin literature, Greek and Roman history, ancient philosophy, Greek archaeology.

Rutgers, The State University of New Jersey, New Brunswick, Graduate School, Department of Classics, New Brunswick, NJ 08901-1281. Offers classics (MA, MAT, PhD); interdisciplinary classical studies and ancient history (MA, PhD). Part-time and evening/weekend programs available. Terminal master's awarded for partial completion of doctoral program. *Degree requirements:* For master's, 3 foreign languages, comprehensive exam, thesis or alternative; for doctorate, 3 foreign languages, comprehensive exam, thesis/dissertation. *Entrance requirements:* For master's and doctorate, GRE General Test. *Faculty research:* Greek and Latin literature, Greek and Roman social and political history, mythology, religion, ancient philosophy.

San Francisco State University, Division of Graduate Studies, College of Humanities, Department of Classics, San Francisco, CA 94132-1722. Offers MA. Part-time programs available. *Application deadline:* Applications are processed on a rolling basis. *Unit head:* Dr. David Leitño, Chair, 415-338-2068. *Application contact:* Dr. David Smith, Graduate Coordinator, 415-338-2068, E-mail: dgsmith@sfsu.edu.

Stanford University, School of Humanities and Sciences, Department of Classics, Stanford, CA 94305-9991. Offers MA, PhD. *Degree requirements:* For master's, 2 foreign languages, thesis or alternative; for doctorate, 4 foreign languages, thesis/dissertation, general exams. *Entrance requirements:* For master's and doctorate, GRE General Test. Additional exam requirements/recommendations for international students: Required—TOEFL. Electronic applications accepted.

Texas Tech University, Graduate School, College of Arts and Sciences, Department of Classical and Modern Languages and Literatures, Program in Classics, Lubbock, TX 79409. Offers MA. *Students:* 6 full-time (1 woman); includes 1 minority (Hispanic American) Average age 24. 4 applicants, 100% accepted, 2 enrolled. In 2007, 2 degrees awarded. *Entrance requirements:* For master's, GRE General Test. Additional exam requirements/recommendations for international students: Required—TOEFL (minimum score 550 paper-based; 213 computer-based). *Application deadline:* For fall admission, 3/1 priority date for international students; for spring admission, 11/1 priority date for international students. Applications are processed on a rolling basis. Application fee: $50 ($60 for international students). Electronic applications accepted. *Expenses:* Tuition, state resident: part-time $373 per credit hour. Tuition, nonresident: part-time $651 per credit hour. Tuition and fees vary according to program. *Financial support:* Research assistantships with partial tuition reimbursements, teaching assistantships with partial tuition reimbursements available. Financial award application deadline: 4/15. *Faculty research:* Greek and Latin language; literature and criticism; art history; gender and sexuality. *Unit head:* Dr. David H.J. Larmour, Professor and Graduate Advisor, 806-742-3145 Ext. 260, Fax: 806-742-3306, E-mail: david.larmour@ttu.edu. *Application contact:* Liz Hildebrand, Senior Advisor, 806-742-4055, Fax: 806-742-3306, E-mail: liz.hildebrand@ttu.edu.

Tufts University, Graduate School of Arts and Sciences, Department of Classics, Medford, MA 02155. Offers classical archaeology (MA); classics (MA). Part-time programs available. *Faculty:* 8 full-time, 4 part-time/adjunct. *Students:* 16 (9 women); includes 1 minority (Asian American or Pacific Islander) 1 international. 26 applicants, 38% accepted, 5 enrolled. In 2007, 9 degrees awarded. *Degree requirements:* For master's, 2 foreign languages, comprehensive exam, thesis or alternative. *Entrance requirements:* For master's, GRE General Test, writing sample. Additional exam requirements/recommendations for international students: Required—TOEFL (minimum score 550 paper-based; 213 computer-based; 80 iBT). *Application deadline:* For fall admission, 2/15 for domestic students, 12/30 for international students; for spring admission, 10/15 for domestic students, 9/15 for international students. Applications are processed on a rolling basis. Application fee: $70. Electronic applications accepted. *Expenses:* Tuition: Full-time $35,052. *Financial support:* Teaching assistantships with full and partial tuition reimbursements, Federal Work-Study, scholarships/grants, and tuition waivers (partial) available. Support available to part-time students. Financial award application deadline: 2/15; financial award applicants required to submit FAFSA. *Unit head:* R. Bruce Hitchner, Chair, 617-627-3213. *Application contact:* David I. Proctor, Information Contact, 617-627-3213.

Tulane University, School of Liberal Arts, Department of Classical Studies, New Orleans, LA 70118-5669. Offers MA. *Degree requirements:* For master's, 2 foreign languages, thesis or alternative. *Entrance requirements:* For master's, GRE General Test, minimum B average in undergraduate course work. Additional exam requirements/recommendations for international students: Required—TOEFL. Electronic applications accepted.

University at Buffalo, the State University of New York, Graduate School, College of Arts and Sciences, Department of Classics, Buffalo, NY 14260. Offers MA, PhD. Terminal master's awarded for partial completion of doctoral program. *Degree requirements:* For master's, 3 foreign languages, project; for doctorate, 4 foreign languages, thesis/dissertation, general and 2 special exams. *Entrance requirements:* For master's and doctorate, GRE General Test. Additional exam requirements/recommendations for international students: Required—TOEFL. Electronic applications accepted. Expenses: Contact institution. *Faculty research:* Greek and Latin literature, historiography, and epigraphy; Greek archaeology, mythology, and ancient philosophy; ancient and Roman religion and women's studies.

University of Alberta, Faculty of Graduate Studies and Research, Department of History and Classics, Edmonton, AB T6G 2E1, Canada. Offers ancient history (PhD); classical archaeology (MA, PhD); classical literature (PhD); classics (MA); history (MA, PhD). Part-time and evening/weekend programs available. *Degree requirements:* For master's, one foreign language, thesis (for some programs); for doctorate, one foreign language, thesis/dissertation. *Entrance requirements:* For master's, minimum B+ average; for doctorate, minimum A- average. Additional exam requirements/recommendations for international students: Required—TOEFL (minimum score 580 paper-based; 237 computer-based). Electronic applications accepted. *Faculty research:* Western Canada, classical archaeology, Britain, Eastern Europe, East Asia.

The University of Arizona, Graduate College, College of Humanities, Department of Classics, Tucson, AZ 85721. Offers MA. Part-time programs available. *Faculty:* 18. *Students:* 26 full-time (16 women), 5 part-time (3 women); includes 6 minority (1 African American, 3 Asian Americans or Pacific Islanders, 2 Hispanic Americans), 1 international. Average age 27. 32 applicants, 31% accepted, 8 enrolled. In 2007, 4 degrees awarded. *Degree requirements:* For master's, one foreign language, comprehensive exam, thesis. *Entrance requirements:* For master's, GRE General Test, BA in classics, 2 letters of recommendation, letter of intent.

Classics

The University of Arizona (continued)

Additional exam requirements/recommendations for international students: Required—TOEFL (minimum score 550 paper-based). *Application deadline:* For fall admission, 2/15 for domestic students, 1/15 for international students. Applications are processed on a rolling basis. Application fee: $50. Electronic applications accepted. *Financial support:* In 2007–08, 25 students received support, including 1 fellowship with full tuition reimbursement available (averaging $5,000 per year), 18 teaching assistantships with full tuition reimbursements available (averaging $7,700 per year); research assistantships, career-related internships or fieldwork, Federal Work-Study, institutionally sponsored loans, scholarships/grants, health care benefits, tuition waivers (full), and unspecified assistantships also available. Support available to part-time students. Financial award application deadline: 4/15. *Faculty research:* Greek and Roman archaeology, ancient Greek, modern Greek, Latin, Greek and Roman religion, women in antiquity. *Unit head:* Dr. Mary Voyatzis, Head, 520-621-3446, Fax: 520-621-3678, E-mail: mev@u.arizona.edu. *Application contact:* LeeAnn Landphair, Graduate Secretary, 520-621-1396, Fax: 520-621-3678, E-mail: landphai@email.arizona.edu.

The University of British Columbia, Faculty of Arts and Faculty of Graduate Studies, Department of Classical, Near Eastern and Religious Studies, Programmes in Classics, Vancouver, BC V6T 1Z1, Canada. Offers ancient culture, religion, and ethnicity (MA); classical and near eastern archaeology (MA); classics (MA, PhD). Part-time programs available. *Faculty:* 7 full-time (4 women). *Students:* 16 full-time (7 women); includes 1 minority (Asian American or Pacific Islander) 19 applicants, 95% accepted, 7 enrolled. In 2007, 2 master's awarded. *Median time to degree:* Of those who began their doctoral program in fall 1999, 100% received their degree in 8 years or less. *Degree requirements:* For master's, 2 foreign languages, comprehensive exam, thesis, thesis or comprehensive exam; for doctorate, 2 foreign languages, comprehensive exam, thesis/dissertation. *Entrance requirements:* For master's, upper second class standing; for doctorate, MA degree. Additional exam requirements/recommendations for international students: Required—TOEFL (minimum score 600 paper-based; 250 computer-based), IELTS (minimum score 8). *Application deadline:* For fall admission, 1/31 for domestic and international students. Applications are processed on a rolling basis. Application fee: $90 Canadian dollars ($150 Canadian dollars for international students). Electronic applications accepted. *Financial support:* In 2007–08, 12 students received support, including 5 fellowships with tuition reimbursements available, 12 teaching assistantships with partial tuition reimbursements available (averaging $10,500 per year); scholarships/grants and health care benefits also available. Financial award application deadline: 1/1. *Faculty research:* Classical archaeology, ancient historians, late antiquity, ancient prose fiction, epigraphy. *Application contact:* Christine R. Dawson, Information Contact, 604-822-2515, Fax: 604-822-9431, E-mail: crdawson@interchange.ubc.ca.

University of Calgary, Faculty of Graduate Studies, Faculty of Humanities, Department of Greek and Roman Studies, Calgary, AB T2N 1N4, Canada. Offers MA, PhD. Part-time programs available. *Faculty:* 10 full-time (4 women), 1 part-time/adjunct (0 women). *Students:* 19 full-time (14 women), 1 (woman) part-time, 3 international. Average age 32. 15 applicants, 73% accepted, 4 enrolled. In 2007, 4 master's, 1 doctorate awarded. *Degree requirements:* For master's, one foreign language; for doctorate, 2 foreign languages, comprehensive exam, thesis/dissertation. *Entrance requirements:* For master's, BA in classics or related field, knowledge of Latin and/or Greek, minimum GPA of 3.7; for doctorate, MA in classics or related field, knowledge of Latin and Greek, GPA 3.7. Additional exam requirements/recommendations for international students: Required—TOEFL. *Application deadline:* For fall admission, 6/30 priority date for domestic students, 5/31 for international students. Application fee: $100 ($130 for international students). Electronic applications accepted. *Financial support:* In 2007–08, 11 students received support, including 4 teaching assistantships (averaging $9,000 per year); fellowships, research assistantships, institutionally sponsored loans, scholarships/grants, health care benefits, and unspecified assistantships also available. Financial award application deadline: 2/1. *Faculty research:* Greek literature, Latin literature, Greek history, Roman history, classical archaeology. *Unit head:* Dr. Peter Gerard Toohey, Head, 403-220-5803, Fax: 403-220-9581, E-mail: ptoohey@ucalgary.ca. *Application contact:* Eileen Corah, Department Administrator, 403-220-4831, Fax: 403-220-9581, E-mail: ecorah@ucalgary.ca.

University of California, Berkeley, Graduate Division, College of Letters and Science, Department of Classics, Berkeley, CA 94720-1500. Offers classical archaeology (MA, PhD); classics (MA, PhD); Greek (MA); Latin (MA). *Faculty:* 19 full-time, 3 part-time/adjunct. Terminal master's awarded for partial completion of doctoral program. *Degree requirements:* For master's, one foreign language, exams; for doctorate, 2 foreign languages, thesis/dissertation, qualifying exam. *Entrance requirements:* For master's and doctorate, GRE General Test, minimum GPA of 3.0, 3 letters of recommendation. Additional exam requirements/recommendations for international students: Required—TOEFL (minimum score 570 paper-based; 230 computer-based), TWE. *Application deadline:* For fall admission, 12/15 for domestic students. Application fee: $70 ($90 for international students). *Financial support:* Fellowships, research assistantships, teaching assistantships, Federal Work-Study, institutionally sponsored loans, and unspecified assistantships available. *Faculty research:* Greek and Latin literature, textual criticism, history, archaeology and philosophy. *Unit head:* Leslie Kurke, Chair, 510-642-2054, E-mail: kurke@berkeley.edu. *Application contact:* Valerie Brown, Secretary, 510-642-4218, Fax: 510-643-2959, E-mail: casmaoff@berkeley.edu.

University of California, Irvine, Office of Graduate Studies, School of Humanities, Department of Classics, Irvine, CA 92697. Offers MA, PhD. *Students:* 14 full-time (5 women); includes 3 minority (1 Asian American or Pacific Islander, 2 Hispanic Americans). 10 applicants, 50% accepted. In 2007, 1 master's awarded. Terminal master's awarded for partial completion of doctoral program. *Degree requirements:* For master's, one foreign language, thesis or alternative; for doctorate, 2 foreign languages, thesis/dissertation. *Entrance requirements:* For master's and doctorate, GRE General Test, minimum GPA of 3.0. Additional exam requirements/recommendations for international students: Required—TOEFL (minimum score 550 paper-based; 213 computer-based). *Application deadline:* For fall admission, 1/15 priority date for domestic students; for winter admission, 10/15 priority date for domestic students; for spring admission, 1/15 priority date for domestic students. Applications are processed on a rolling basis. Application fee: $60. Electronic applications accepted. *Financial support:* Fellowships, research assistantships with full tuition reimbursements, teaching assistantships, institutionally sponsored loans, traineeships, health care benefits, and unspecified assistantships available. Financial award application deadline: 3/1; financial award applicants required to submit FAFSA. *Faculty research:* Greek literature, computer application to Greek literature, Latin literature. *Unit head:* Dana Sutton, Acting Chair, 949-824-5896, Fax: 949-824-1966, E-mail: dfsutton@uci.edu. *Application contact:* DeeDee Nunez, Department Manager, 949-824-7254, Fax: 949-824-1966, E-mail: dynunez@uci.edu.

University of California, Los Angeles, Graduate Division, College of Letters and Science, Department of Classics, Los Angeles, CA 90095. Offers classics (MA, PhD); Greek (MA); Latin (MA). *Students:* 20 full-time (9 women); includes 1 minority (African American) Average age 28. 47 applicants, 28% accepted, 5 enrolled. In 2007, 5 master's, 2 doctorates awarded. *Degree requirements:* For master's, 2 foreign languages, comprehensive exam; for doctorate, 2 foreign languages, thesis/dissertation, oral and written qualifying exams. *Entrance requirements:* For master's, GRE General Test, minimum GPA of 3.0, sample of written work; for doctorate, GRE General Test, minimum undergraduate GPA of 3.0, sample of written work, MA degree in classics. *Application deadline:* For fall admission, 1/15 for domestic students. Application fee: $60 ($80 for international students). Electronic applications accepted. *Expenses:* Tuition, nonresident: full-time $5,728. Required fees: $8,966. Full-time tuition and fees vary according to program and student level. *Financial support:* In 2007–08, 32 fellowships with full and partial tuition reimbursements, 3 research assistantships with full and partial tuition reimbursements, 13 teaching assistantships with full and partial tuition reimbursements were awarded; Federal Work-Study, institutionally sponsored loans, and tuition waivers (full and partial) also available. Financial award application deadline: 3/1; financial award applicants required to submit FAFSA. *Faculty research:* Homeric studies, archaeology, ancient comedy, ancient philosophy, Augustan poetry. *Unit head:* Dr. John Papadopoulos, Chair, 310-825-3480. *Application contact:* Departmental Office, 310-825-3480, E-mail: ajaaska@humnet.ucla.edu.

University of California, Riverside, Graduate Division, Tri-Campus Program in Classics, Riverside, CA 92521-0102. Offers PhD. *Faculty:* 6 full-time (3 women). *Students:* 1 full-time (0 women). *Degree requirements:* For doctorate, 3 foreign languages, comprehensive exam, thesis/dissertation. *Entrance requirements:* For doctorate, GRE, MA in classics. Additional exam requirements/recommendations for international students: Required—TOEFL (minimum score 550 paper-based; 213 computer-based; 80 iBT). *Application deadline:* For fall admission, 1/5 for domestic students, 2/1 for international students; for winter admission, 9/1 for domestic students, 7/1 for international students; for spring admission, 12/1 for domestic students, 10/1 for international students. Applications are processed on a rolling basis. Application fee: $60 ($75 for international students). Electronic applications accepted. *Financial support:* Fellowships with tuition reimbursements, research assistantships, teaching assistantships with tuition reimbursements, scholarships/grants, health care benefits, tuition waivers (full and partial), and unspecified assistantships available. Financial award application deadline: 1/5; financial award applicants required to submit FAFSA. *Faculty research:* Rhetoric, Greek and Latin drama, Hellenistic poetry, Anglo-Latin literature, Greek and Latin prose. *Unit head:* Dr. Anthony E. Edwards, Professor of Classics, UC San Diego, 858-534-3143, Fax: 858-534-8686, E-mail: aedwards@ucsd.edu. *Application contact:* Dr. Andrew Zissos, Assistant Professor of Classics, 949-824-6584, Fax: 949-824-1966, E-mail: pzissos@ucr.edu.

University of California, Santa Barbara, Graduate Division, College of Letters and Sciences, Division of Humanities and Fine Arts, Department of Classics, Santa Barbara, CA 93106. Offers classics (MA, PhD), including ancient history, literature and theory; MA/PhD. *Faculty:* 9 full-time (4 women). *Students:* 14 full-time (9 women); includes 1 minority (Hispanic American) Average age 26. 44 applicants, 43% accepted, 6 enrolled. In 2007, 4 master's awarded. Terminal master's awarded for partial completion of doctoral program. *Median time to degree:* Of those who began their doctoral program in fall 1999, 0% received their degree in 8 years or less. *Degree requirements:* For master's, 3 foreign languages, comprehensive exam, thesis optional; for doctorate, 4 foreign languages, comprehensive exam, thesis/dissertation. *Entrance requirements:* For master's, GRE, BA in classics, minimum 2 years of college course work in Latin and Greek, writing sample; for doctorate, GRE, MA in classics. Additional exam requirements/recommendations for international students: Required—TOEFL (minimum score 550 paper-based; 213 computer-based; 80 iBT). *Application deadline:* For fall admission, 5/1 for domestic and international students; for winter admission, 11/1 for domestic and international students; for spring admission, 2/1 for domestic and international students. Applications are processed on a rolling basis. Application fee: $60. Electronic applications accepted. *Expenses:* Tuition, nonresident: full-time $14,888. Required fees: $10,108. *Financial support:* In 2007–08, 14 students received support, including 6 fellowships with full and partial tuition reimbursements available (averaging $9,900 per year), 3 research assistantships with partial tuition reimbursements available (averaging $10,900 per year), 32 teaching assistantships with partial tuition reimbursements available (averaging $16,380 per year); Federal Work-Study, institutionally sponsored loans, scholarships/grants, traineeships, health care benefits, tuition waivers (partial), unspecified assistantships, and readerships also available. Financial award application deadline: 1/2; financial award applicants required to submit FAFSA. *Faculty research:* Greek and Latin literature, ancient drama, textual criticism, ancient history, literary theory. Total annual research expenditures: $37,819. *Unit head:* Robert Morstein-Marx, Chair, 805-893-3007, Fax: 805-893-4487, E-mail: morstein@classics.ucsb.edu. *Application contact:* Anna Roberts, Graduate Program Assistant, 805-893-3556, Fax: 805-893-4487, E-mail: aroberts@classics.ucsb.edu.

University of Chicago, Division of the Humanities, Department of Classics, Chicago, IL 60637-1513. Offers ancient philosophy (AM, PhD); classical archaeology (AM, PhD); classical languages and literatures (AM, PhD). *Students:* 46. 110 applicants, 14% accepted, 5 enrolled. Terminal master's awarded for partial completion of doctoral program. *Degree requirements:* For master's, one foreign language, thesis; for doctorate, 2 foreign languages, thesis/dissertation. *Entrance requirements:* For master's and doctorate, GRE General Test. Additional exam requirements/recommendations for international students: Required—TOEFL. *Application deadline:* For fall admission, 12/15 for domestic students. Application fee: $55. *Financial support:* Fellowships, Federal Work-Study available. Financial award application deadline: 12/15; financial award applicants required to submit FAFSA. *Unit head:* Dr. Jonathan Hall, Chair, 773-702-8514.

University of Cincinnati, Graduate School, McMicken College of Arts and Sciences, Department of Classics, Cincinnati, OH 45221. Offers MA, PhD. Part-time programs available. *Faculty:* 12 full-time (4 women), 4 part-time/adjunct (all women). *Students:* 40 full-time (19 women), 15 part-time (11 women); includes 4 minority (1 African American, 1 American Indian/Alaska Native, 1 Asian American or Pacific Islander, 1 Hispanic American), 12 international. Average age 24. 75 applicants, 24% accepted, 9 enrolled. In 2007, 9 master's, 3 doctorates awarded. Terminal master's awarded for partial completion of doctoral program. *Degree requirements:* For master's, comprehensive exam (for some programs), thesis (for some programs); for doctorate, 2 foreign languages, comprehensive exam, thesis/dissertation. *Entrance requirements:* For master's and doctorate, GRE. Additional exam requirements/recommendations for international students: Required—TOEFL. *Application deadline:* For fall admission, 1/15 for domestic students. Application fee: $30. Electronic applications accepted. *Financial support:* In 2007–08, 25 fellowships with full tuition reimbursements (averaging $14,500 per year), 6 teaching assistantships with full tuition reimbursements (averaging $15,400 per year) were awarded; scholarships/grants, health care benefits, tuition waivers (partial), and unspecified assistantships also available. Financial award application deadline: 1/15. *Faculty research:* Archaeology (bronze age and classical), philosophy (Greek and Latin), ancient history (Greek and Roman). *Unit head:* Dr. William Johnson, Head, 513-556-1924, Fax: 513-556-4366, E-mail: william.johnson@uc.edu.

University of Colorado at Boulder, Graduate School, College of Arts and Sciences, Department of Classics, Boulder, CO 80309. Offers MA, PhD. Part-time programs available. *Faculty:* 11. *Students:* 29 full-time (16 women), 5 part-time (2 women); includes 2 minority (both African Americans) Average age 28. 29 applicants, 97% accepted. In 2007, 9 degrees awarded. Terminal master's awarded for partial completion of doctoral program. *Degree requirements:* For master's, one foreign language, comprehensive exam, thesis or alternative, oral exam; for doctorate, 4 foreign languages, comprehensive exam, thesis/dissertation. *Entrance requirements:* For master's, minimum undergraduate GPA of 2.75; for doctorate, master's degree in classics or related field. *Application deadline:* For fall admission, 4/10 priority date for domestic students, 4/10 for international students; for spring admission, 11/1 for domestic students, 10/1 for international students. Applications are processed on a rolling basis. Application fee: $50 ($60 for international students). *Financial support:* In 2007–08, 17 fellowships with full tuition reimbursements (averaging $6,945 per year) were awarded; Federal Work-Study, scholarships/grants, tuition waivers (full), and unspecified assistantships also available. Financial award application deadline: 2/1. *Faculty research:* Roman and Greek history, Roman and Greek art and architecture, comparative literature, Greek philosophy, textual criticism, Greek and Latin poetry, Greek and Latin prose. Total annual research expenditures: $56,000. *Unit head:* Noel Lenski, Chair, 303-492-8184, Fax: 303-492-1026, E-mail: noel.lenski@colorado.edu. *Application contact:* Graduate Director's Assistant, 303-492-6257, Fax: 303-492-1026, E-mail: classics@colorado.edu.

University of Florida, Graduate School, College of Liberal Arts and Sciences, Department of Classics, Gainesville, FL 32611. Offers classical studies (MA, PhD); Latin (MA, MAT, ML). Part-time programs available. Postbaccalaureate distance learning degree programs offered. *Faculty:* 11 full-time (4 women). *Students:* 41 (23 women) 1 international. In 2007, 10 degrees awarded. *Degree requirements:* For master's, 2 foreign languages, thesis; for doctorate, 2 foreign languages, thesis/dissertation. *Entrance requirements:* For master's, GRE General Test, minimum GPA of 3.0; for doctorate, GRE General Test, minimum GPA of 3.0, MA in classical studies. Additional exam requirements/recommendations for international students:

Required—TOEFL (minimum score 550 paper-based; 213 computer-based). *Application deadline:* For fall admission, 2/15 priority date for domestic students. Applications are processed on a rolling basis. Application fee: $30. Electronic applications accepted. *Expenses:* Tuition, state resident: full-time $7,478. Tuition, nonresident: full-time $22,603. *Financial support:* In 2007–08, 19 teaching assistantships with full tuition reimbursements (averaging $12,951 per year) were awarded; fellowships, research assistantships, unspecified assistantships also available. Financial award application deadline: 6/1. *Faculty research:* Greek, literature, epigraphy. *Unit head:* Robert Wagman, Chair, 352-392-2075 Ext. 273. *Application contact:* Dr. Tim Johnson, Coordinator, 352-392-2075, Fax: 352-846-0297, E-mail: tjohnson@classics.ufl.edu.

University of Georgia, Graduate School, College of Arts and Sciences, Department of Classics, Athens, GA 30602. Offers classical languages (MA); Greek (MA); Latin (MA). *Faculty:* 12 full-time (4 women). *Students:* 15 full-time (7 women), 3 part-time; includes 1 minority (Asian American or Pacific Islander) 28 applicants, 54% accepted, 6 enrolled. In 2007, 14 degrees awarded. *Degree requirements:* For master's, one foreign language, thesis. *Entrance requirements:* For master's, GRE General Test. *Application deadline:* For fall admission, 7/1 priority date for domestic students; for spring admission, 11/15 for domestic students. Application fee: $50. Electronic applications accepted. *Financial support:* Fellowships, research assistantships, teaching assistantships, unspecified assistantships available. *Unit head:* Dr. Charles Platter, Head, 706-542-9264, Fax: 706-542-8503, E-mail: cplatter@uga.edu. *Application contact:* Dr. Nancy Felson, Graduate Coordinator, 706-542-2153, Fax: 706-542-8503, E-mail: nfelson@uga.edu.

University of Illinois at Urbana–Champaign, Graduate College, College of Liberal Arts and Sciences, School of Literatures, Cultures and Linguistics, Department of the Classics, Champaign, IL 61820. Offers classical philosophy (PhD); classics (MA); teaching of Latin (MA). *Faculty:* 10 full-time (4 women). *Students:* 10 full-time (5 women), 6 part-time (4 women); includes 1 minority (Asian American or Pacific Islander), 3 international. 25 applicants, 16% accepted, 3 enrolled. In 2007, 3 master's, 1 doctorate awarded. *Degree requirements:* For master's, one foreign language, thesis or alternative; for doctorate, 4 foreign languages, thesis/dissertation. *Entrance requirements:* For master's, GRE, minimum GPA of 3.0. *Application deadline:* Applications are processed on a rolling basis. Application fee: $60 ($75 for international students). Electronic applications accepted. *Financial support:* In 2007–08, 6 fellowships, 1 research assistantship, 15 teaching assistantships were awarded. Financial award application deadline: 2/15. *Faculty research:* Greek and Latin language, papyrology, epigraphy, classical archaeology. *Unit head:* Gary Porton, Chair, 217-333-5572, Fax: 217-244-8430. *Application contact:* Beth Creek, Administrative Secretary, 217-333-1008, Fax: 217-244-3466, E-mail: b-creek@ucic.edu.

The University of Iowa, Graduate College, College of Liberal Arts and Sciences, Department of Classics, Iowa City, IA 52242-1316. Offers MA, PhD. *Faculty:* 9 full-time, 4 part-time/adjunct. *Students:* 8 full-time (4 women), 7 part-time (3 women); includes 1 minority (American Indian/Alaska Native). 19 applicants, 74% accepted, 4 enrolled. In 2007, 4 master's, 1 doctorate awarded. *Degree requirements:* For master's, thesis optional, exam; for doctorate, comprehensive exam, thesis/dissertation. *Entrance requirements:* For master's and doctorate, GRE General Test, minimum GPA of 3.0. Additional exam requirements/recommendations for international students: Required—TOEFL (minimum score 550 paper-based; 213 computer-based; 81 iBT). *Application deadline:* For fall admission, 2/15 for domestic and international students; for spring admission, 12/1 for domestic and international students. Application fee: $60 ($85 for international students). Electronic applications accepted. *Expenses:* Tuition, state resident: part-time $349 per hour. Tuition, nonresident: part-time $349 per hour. Tuition and fees vary according to course load and program. *Financial support:* In 2007–08, 3 fellowships, 3 research assistantships with partial tuition reimbursements, 9 teaching assistantships with partial tuition reimbursements were awarded. Financial award applicants required to submit FAFSA. *Unit head:* Carin Green, Chair, 319-335-2323, Fax: 319-335-3884.

University of Kansas, Research and Graduate Studies, College of Liberal Arts and Sciences, Department of Classics, Lawrence, KS 66045. Offers MA. Part-time programs available. *Faculty:* 8. *Students:* 10 full-time (5 women), 3 part-time (1 woman); includes 1 minority (American Indian/Alaska Native), 1 international. Average age 26. 8 applicants, 88% accepted, 3 enrolled. In 2007, 5 degrees awarded. *Degree requirements:* For master's, 3 foreign languages, comprehensive exam, thesis optional. *Entrance requirements:* For master's, GRE (recommended), 15 junior/senior hours of course work in Latin and/or Greek (recommended). Additional exam requirements/recommendations for international students: Required—TOEFL. *Application deadline:* For fall admission, 5/1 priority date for domestic students, 2/1 priority date for international students; for spring admission, 1/15 priority date for domestic students, 9/1 priority date for international students. Applications are processed on a rolling basis. Application fee: $55 ($60 for international students). Electronic applications accepted. *Expenses:* Tuition, state resident: full-time $5,838. Tuition, nonresident: full-time $13,409. Tuition and fees vary according to program. *Financial support:* Fellowships with full tuition reimbursements, teaching assistantships with full and partial tuition reimbursements, career-related internships or fieldwork, Federal Work-Study, scholarships/grants, traineeships, and unspecified assistantships available. Support available to part-time students. *Faculty research:* Greek and Roman literature, Greek cultural history, Roman cultural history, translation theory, sex and gender. *Unit head:* Pam Gordon, Chair, 785-864-3153, Fax: 785-864-5566, E-mail: pgordon@ku.edu. *Application contact:* Anthony Corbeill, Graduate Director, 785-864-2393, Fax: 785-864-5566, E-mail: corbeill@ku.edu.

University of Kentucky, Graduate School, College of Arts and Sciences, Program in Modern and Classical Languages and Literatures, Lexington, KY 40506-0032. Offers classics (MA). Part-time programs available. *Faculty:* 29 full-time (10 women), 2 part-time/adjunct (1 woman). *Students:* 12 full-time (3 women), 4 part-time. Average age 29. 27 applicants, 63% accepted, 6 enrolled. In 2007, 2 degrees awarded. *Degree requirements:* For master's, one foreign language, comprehensive exam, thesis optional. *Entrance requirements:* For master's, GRE General Test, minimum undergraduate GPA of 2.75. Additional exam requirements/recommendations for international students: Required—TOEFL (minimum score 550 paper-based; 213 computer-based). *Application deadline:* For fall admission, 7/17 priority date for domestic students, 2/1 priority date for international students; for spring admission, 12/13 priority date for domestic students, 6/15 priority date for international students. Application fee: $50 ($65 for international students). Electronic applications accepted. *Expenses:* Tuition, state resident: part-time $437 per credit hour. Tuition, nonresident: part-time $931 per credit hour. *Financial support:* In 2007–08, 7 students received support, including 2 fellowships with full tuition reimbursements available (averaging $2,486 per year), 6 teaching assistantships with full tuition reimbursements available (averaging $10,774 per year); research assistantships with full tuition reimbursements available, career-related internships or fieldwork, Federal Work-Study, institutionally sponsored loans, scholarships/grants, traineeships, health care benefits, tuition waivers (partial), and unspecified assistantships also available. Support available to part-time students. Financial award application deadline: 3/15. *Faculty research:* Erasmus, Renaissance Latin, Greek and Roman epic, Greek biography, early Christian literature, classical philosophy. *Unit head:* Dr. Milena Minkova, Director of Graduate Studies, 859-257-5710, Fax: 859-257-3743, E-mail: mmink2@uky.edu. *Application contact:* Dr. Brian Jackson, Senior Associate Dean, 859-257-4667, Fax: 859-257-4676, E-mail: brian.jackson@uky.edu.

University of Manitoba, Faculty of Graduate Studies, Faculty of Arts, Department of Classics, Winnipeg, MB R3T 2N2, Canada. Offers MA. *Degree requirements:* For master's, thesis.

University of Maryland, College Park, Graduate Studies, College of Arts and Humanities, Department of Classics, College Park, MD 20742. Offers MA. *Faculty:* 5 full-time (2 women), 3 part-time/adjunct (2 women). *Students:* 7 full-time (4 women), 3 part-time (all women). 21 applicants, 48% accepted, 2 enrolled. In 2007, 3 degrees awarded. *Degree requirements:* For master's, 2 foreign languages, thesis or alternative. *Entrance requirements:* For master's, writing sample, 3 letters of recommendation. Additional exam requirements/recommendations for international students: Required—TOEFL. *Application deadline:* For fall admission, 2/1 for domestic and international students; for spring admission, 10/1 for domestic students, 6/1 for international students. Applications are processed on a rolling basis. Application fee: $60. Electronic applications accepted. *Financial support:* In 2007–08, 6 teaching assistantships with tuition reimbursements (averaging $14,996 per year) were awarded; fellowships with full tuition reimbursements, Federal Work-Study and scholarships/grants also available. Support available to part-time students. Financial award applicants required to submit FAFSA. *Faculty research:* Latin, Greek, and Roman culture. Total annual research expenditures: $9,898. *Unit head:* Dr. Hugh Lee, Chair, 301-405-2014, Fax: 301-314-9084, E-mail: hlee@umd.edu. *Application contact:* Dean of Graduate School, 301-405-4190, Fax: 301-314-9305.

University of Massachusetts Amherst, Graduate School, College of Humanities and Fine Arts, Department of Classics, Amherst, MA 01003. Offers Latin and classical humanities (MAT). Part-time programs available. *Faculty:* 9 full-time (4 women). *Students:* 12 full-time (6 women). Average age 27. 20 applicants, 30% accepted, 6 enrolled. In 2007, 7 degrees awarded. *Degree requirements:* For master's, thesis or alternative. *Entrance requirements:* For master's, GRE General Test. Additional exam requirements/recommendations for international students: Required—TOEFL (minimum score 530 paper-based; 197 computer-based). *Application deadline:* For fall admission, 2/1 priority date for domestic and international students. Applications are processed on a rolling basis. Application fee: $50 ($65 for international students). Electronic applications accepted. *Expenses:* Tuition, state resident: full-time $2,640; part-time $110 per credit. Tuition, nonresident: full-time $9,936; part-time $414 per credit. Required fees: $7,455. One-time fee: $332. Tuition and fees vary according to course load, campus/location, program and reciprocity agreements. *Financial support:* In 2007–08, 12 teaching assistantships with full tuition reimbursements (averaging $13,376 per year) were awarded; fellowships with full tuition reimbursements, research assistantships with full tuition reimbursements, career-related internships or fieldwork, Federal Work-Study, scholarships/grants, traineeships, and unspecified assistantships also available. Support available to part-time students. Financial award application deadline: 2/1. *Unit head:* Dr. Rex Wallace, Chair, 413-545-0512, E-mail: rwallace@classics.umass.edu.

University of Michigan, Horace H. Rackham School of Graduate Studies, College of Literature, Science, and the Arts, Department of Classical Studies, Ann Arbor, MI 48109. Offers classical studies (PhD); Greek (AM); Latin (AM); teaching Latin (MAT). *Faculty:* 22 full-time (7 women), 7 part-time/adjunct (3 women). *Students:* 30 full-time (16 women); includes 2 minority (1 Asian American or Pacific Islander, 1 Hispanic American), 1 international. Average age 28. 84 applicants, 13% accepted, 7 enrolled. In 2007, 3 master's, 1 doctorate awarded. Terminal master's awarded for partial completion of doctoral program. *Median time to degree:* Of those who began their doctoral program in fall 1999, 100% received their degree in 8 years or less. *Degree requirements:* For master's, one foreign language, comprehensive exam; for doctorate, 4 foreign languages, thesis/dissertation, oral defense of dissertation, preliminary exam. *Entrance requirements:* For master's, GRE General Test; for doctorate, GRE General Test, 3 years college-level Latin; 2 years college-level Greek. Additional exam requirements/recommendations for international students: Required—TOEFL (minimum score 560 paper-based; 220 computer-based). *Application deadline:* For fall admission, 1/5 for domestic students. Application fee: $60 ($75 for international students). Electronic applications accepted. *Financial support:* In 2007–08, 30 students received support, including 6 fellowships with full tuition reimbursements available (averaging $18,000 per year), 23 teaching assistantships with full tuition reimbursements available (averaging $15,199 per year); research assistantships, career-related internships or fieldwork, Federal Work-Study, institutionally sponsored loans, scholarships/grants, traineeships, health care benefits, and unspecified assistantships also available. Financial award application deadline: 3/15. *Faculty research:* Greek and Latin literature, ancient history, papyrology, archaeology. Total annual research expenditures: $47,650. *Unit head:* Ruth Scodel, Chair, 734-764-0360, Fax: 734-763-4959, E-mail: classics@umich.edu. *Application contact:* Michelle M. Biggs, Graduate Coordinator, 734-647-2330, Fax: 734-763-4959, E-mail: mbiggs@umich.edu.

University of Michigan, Horace H. Rackham School of Graduate Studies, College of Literature, Science, and the Arts, Interdepartmental Program in Greek and Roman History, Ann Arbor, MI 48109. Offers PhD, Certificate. *Faculty:* 4 full-time (1 woman), 17 part-time/adjunct (7 women). *Students:* 9 full-time (4 women). Average age 27. 28 applicants, 7% accepted, 2 enrolled. *Degree requirements:* For doctorate, 4 foreign languages, comprehensive exam, thesis/dissertation, oral defense of dissertation, dissertation prospectus, preliminary exams. *Entrance requirements:* For doctorate, GRE, knowledge of classical Greek and Latin. Additional exam requirements/recommendations for international students: Required—TOEFL (minimum score 560 paper-based; 220 computer-based). *Application deadline:* For fall admission, 12/15 for domestic and international students. Application fee: $60 ($75 for international students). Electronic applications accepted. *Financial support:* In 2007–08, 9 students received support, including 4 fellowships with full tuition reimbursements available (averaging $15,200 per year), 7 teaching assistantships with full tuition reimbursements available (averaging $15,199 per year); career-related internships or fieldwork, Federal Work-Study, institutionally sponsored loans, scholarships/grants, traineeships, health care benefits, and unspecified assistantships also available. Financial award application deadline: 3/15. *Faculty research:* Greek history, Roman history. *Unit head:* Raymond Van Dam, Professor, 734-763-1193, E-mail: rvandam@umich.edu. *Application contact:* Michelle M. Biggs, Graduate Coordinator, 734-647-2330, Fax: 734-763-4959, E-mail: mbiggs@umich.edu.

University of Minnesota, Twin Cities Campus, Graduate School, College of Liberal Arts, Department of Classical and Near Eastern Studies, Minneapolis, MN 55455-0213. Offers ancient and medieval art and archaeology (MA, PhD); classics (MA, PhD); Greek (MA, PhD); Latin (MA, PhD); religions in antiquity (MA). Part-time programs available. *Faculty:* 12 full-time (2 women), 3 part-time/adjunct (2 women). *Students:* 24 full-time (10 women), 8 part-time (2 women); includes 1 minority (African American), 1 international. Average age 29. 37 applicants, 32% accepted, 9 enrolled. In 2007, 4 master's, 1 doctorate awarded. Terminal master's awarded for partial completion of doctoral program. *Degree requirements:* For master's, 2 foreign languages, comprehensive exam, thesis or alternative; for doctorate, variable foreign language requirement, comprehensive exam, thesis/dissertation. *Entrance requirements:* For master's and doctorate, GRE, 3 letters of recommendation, department application, writing sample, copies of transcripts, personal statement. Additional exam requirements/recommendations for international students: Required—TOEFL. *Application deadline:* For fall admission, 1/4 for domestic students. Application fee: $55 ($75 for international students). Electronic applications accepted. *Financial support:* In 2007–08, 10 fellowships with full and partial tuition reimbursements (averaging $11,165 per year), 4 research assistantships (averaging $23,166 per year), 20 teaching assistantships (averaging $23,357 per year) were awarded; career-related internships or fieldwork, Federal Work-Study, institutionally sponsored loans, and tuition waivers (full and partial) also available. Support available to part-time students. Financial award application deadline: 1/4. *Faculty research:* Greek and Latin literature, archaeology, religions in antiquity, ancient Near East. Total annual research expenditures: $14,849. *Unit head:* George A. Sheets, Chair, 612-625-3326, Fax: 612-624-4894, E-mail: gasheets@umn.edu. *Application contact:* Victoria Keller, Administrative Assistant, Fax: 612-624-4894, E-mail: kell0801@umn.edu.

University of Mississippi, Graduate School, College of Liberal Arts, Department of Classics, Oxford, University, MS 38677. Offers MA. *Faculty:* 5 full-time (2 women). *Degree requirements:* For master's, thesis. *Entrance requirements:* For master's, GRE General Test, minimum GPA of 3.0. Additional exam requirements/recommendations for international students: Required—TOEFL. *Application deadline:* For fall admission, 4/1 for domestic students; for spring admission, 10/1 for domestic students. Applications are processed on a rolling basis. Application fee: $25. Electronic applications accepted. *Expenses:* Tuition, state resident: full-time $4,932. Tuition, nonresident: full-time $11,436. *Financial support:* Scholarships/grants available. Financial award application deadline: 3/1; financial award applicants required to submit FAFSA. *Unit head:* Dr. Aileen Ajootian, Acting Chair, 662-915-1152, E-mail: ajootian@olemiss.edu.

University of Missouri–Columbia, Graduate School, College of Arts and Sciences, Department of Classical Studies, Columbia, MO 65211. Offers MA, PhD. Terminal master's awarded for

Classics

University of Missouri–Columbia (continued)
partial completion of doctoral program. *Degree requirements:* For master's, one foreign language; for doctorate, 2 foreign languages, thesis/dissertation. *Entrance requirements:* For master's and doctorate, GRE General Test, minimum GPA of 3.0. Additional exam requirements/ recommendations for international students: Required—TOEFL (minimum score 500 paper-based; 173 computer-based; 61 iBT), IELTS (minimum score 6).

University of Nebraska–Lincoln, Graduate College, College of Arts and Sciences, Department of Classics and Religious Studies, Lincoln, NE 68588. Offers MA. *Degree requirements:* For master's, thesis optional. *Entrance requirements:* For master's, GRE. Additional exam requirements/recommendations for international students: Required—TOEFL (minimum score 550 paper-based; 213 computer-based). Electronic applications accepted. *Faculty research:* Greek and Latin poetry and prose, Greek and Latin linguistics, patristics, gnosticism, religion of late antiquity.

University of New Brunswick Fredericton, School of Graduate Studies, Faculty of Arts, Department of Classics and Ancient History, Fredericton, NB E3B 5A3, Canada. Offers classics (MA). Part-time programs available. *Faculty:* 5 full-time (1 woman). *Students:* 1 (woman) full-time. 2 applicants, 100% accepted, 0 enrolled. *Degree requirements:* For master's, thesis. *Entrance requirements:* For master's, minimum GPA of 3.0, minimum of 18 credit hours or equivalent in either Greek or Latin. Additional exam requirements/ recommendations for international students: Required—TOEFL, TWE. *Application deadline:* 1/31 for domestic and international students. Applications are processed on a rolling basis. Application fee: $50 Canadian dollars. *Financial support:* Application deadline: 1/31. *Faculty research:* Roman history, silver-age Latin poetry, stamped roof tiles, Plato, early Christianity, Greek and Roman archaeology. *Unit head:* Prof. William Kerr, Director of Graduate Studies, 506-458-7507, Fax: 506-447-3072, E-mail: wkerr@unb.ca. *Application contact:* Susan Miller, Graduate Secretary, 506-453-4762, Fax: 506-447-3072, E-mail: smiller@unb.ca.

The University of North Carolina at Chapel Hill, Graduate School, College of Arts and Sciences, Department of Classics, Chapel Hill, NC 27599. Offers classical archaeology (MA, PhD); classics (MA, PhD). Terminal master's awarded for partial completion of doctoral program. *Degree requirements:* For master's, one foreign language, comprehensive exam, thesis; for doctorate, 2 foreign languages, comprehensive exam, thesis/dissertation. *Entrance requirements:* For master's and doctorate, GRE General Test, minimum GPA of 3.0. Electronic applications accepted.

The University of North Carolina at Greensboro, Graduate School, College of Arts and Sciences, Department of Classical Studies, Greensboro, NC 27412-5001. Offers Latin (M Ed). *Faculty:* 6 full-time (2 women). *Students:* 2 full-time (both women), 5 part-time (1 woman); includes 1 minority (Asian American or Pacific Islander) 4 applicants, 75% accepted. *Entrance requirements:* For master's, GRE General Test, MAT, or PRAXIS. Additional exam requirements/ recommendations for international students: Required—TOEFL. *Application deadline:* For fall admission, 6/15 priority date for domestic students; for spring admission, 3/15 priority date for domestic students. Applications are processed on a rolling basis. Application fee: $45. Electronic applications accepted. *Financial support:* In 2007–08, 1 student received support; fellowships available. *Unit head:* Dr. Susan C. Shelmerdine, Head, 336-334-5214, Fax: 336-334-5158, E-mail: shelmerd@uncg.edu. *Application contact:* Michelle Harkleroad, Director of Graduate Admissions, 336-334-4884, Fax: 336-334-4424, E-mail: mbharkle@uncg.edu.

University of Oregon, Graduate School, College of Arts and Sciences, Department of Classics, Eugene, OR 97403. Offers classical civilization (MA); classics (MA), including Greek, Latin; Greek (MA); Latin (MA). Part-time programs available. *Faculty:* 4 full-time (2 women), 1 (woman) part-time/adjunct. *Students:* 4 full-time (1 woman), 1 (woman) part-time; includes 1 minority (Hispanic American) Average age 31. 4 applicants, 100% accepted. In 2007, 1 degree awarded. *Degree requirements:* For master's, 2 foreign languages, thesis or alternative. *Entrance requirements:* For master's, GRE General Test, minimum GPA of 3.0. Additional exam requirements/recommendations for international students: Required—TOEFL. *Application deadline:* For fall admission, 7/18 for domestic students. Application fee: $50. *Financial support:* In 2007–08, 1 teaching assistantship was awarded; Federal Work-Study and institutionally sponsored loans also available. Financial award application deadline: 3/15. *Faculty research:* Roman religion, Greek philosophy, archaeology, Greek and Roman literature. *Unit head:* Malcolm Wilson, Head, 541-346-4069, Fax: 541-346-5544. *Application contact:* Carol Kleinheksel, Admissions Contact, 541-346-4069, Fax: 541-346-5544, E-mail: classics@oregon.uoregon.edu.

University of Ottawa, Faculty of Graduate and Postdoctoral Studies, Faculty of Arts, Department of Classics and Religious Studies, Ottawa, ON K1N 6N5, Canada. Offers classical studies (MA); religious studies (PhD). *Degree requirements:* For master's, comprehensive exam, thesis or alternative; for doctorate, comprehensive exam, thesis/dissertation. *Entrance requirements:* For master's, honors degree or equivalent, minimum B average; for doctorate, master's degree, minimum B+ average. Electronic applications accepted. *Faculty research:* Religions in Canada, including Amerindian and Inuit religions; religion and culture; late antiquity.

University of Pennsylvania, School of Arts and Sciences, Graduate Group in Classical Studies, Philadelphia, PA 19104. Offers AM, PhD. Terminal master's awarded for partial completion of doctoral program. *Degree requirements:* For master's, 3 foreign languages, thesis or alternative; for doctorate, 4 foreign languages, thesis/dissertation. *Entrance requirements:* For master's and doctorate, GRE General Test, undergraduate course work in classical language and history. Additional exam requirements/recommendations for international students: Required—TOEFL. Electronic applications accepted.

University of Pittsburgh, School of Arts and Sciences, Department of Classics, Pittsburgh, PA 15260. Offers MA, PhD. Part-time programs available. *Faculty:* 7 full-time (1 woman), 2 part-time/adjunct (1 woman). *Students:* 8 full-time (1 woman). Average age 29. 13 applicants, 38% accepted, 0 enrolled. In 2007, 2 master's, 1 doctorate awarded. Terminal master's awarded for partial completion of doctoral program. *Degree requirements:* For master's, one foreign language, comprehensive exam, thesis optional; for doctorate, 2 foreign languages, comprehensive exam, thesis/dissertation. *Entrance requirements:* For master's, GRE General Test, background in Greek and Latin; for doctorate, GRE General Test, knowledge of Greek and Latin. Additional exam requirements/recommendations for international students: Required—TOEFL. *Application deadline:* For fall admission, 1/16 for domestic students; for spring admission, 12/1 priority date for domestic students. Application fee: $50. Electronic applications accepted. *Financial support:* In 2007–08, fellowships with tuition reimbursements (averaging $15,070 per year), 6 teaching assistantships with tuition reimbursements (averaging $14,485 per year) were awarded; scholarships/grants also available. Financial award application deadline: 1/16. *Faculty research:* Greek and Roman poetry, Greek drama, Greek and Roman historiography, Greek philosophy, societal organization. *Unit head:* Dr. D Mark Possanza, Chairman, 412-624-4486, Fax: 412-624-4419, E-mail: possanza@pitt.edu. *Application contact:* Dr. Andrew M. Miller, Graduate Adviser, 412-624-4485, Fax: 412-624-4419, E-mail: amm2@pitt.edu.

University of South Africa, College of Human Sciences, Pretoria, South Africa. Offers adult education (M Ed); African languages (MA, PhD); African politics (MA, PhD); Afrikaans (MA, PhD); ancient history (MA, PhD); ancient Near Eastern studies (MA, PhD); anthropology (MA, PhD); applied linguistics (MA); Arabic (MA, PhD); archaeology (MA); art history (MA); Biblical archaeology (MA); Biblical studies (M Th, D Th, PhD); Christian spirituality (M Th, D Th); church history (M Th, D Th); classical studies (MA, PhD); clinical psychology (MA); communication (MA, PhD); comparative education (M Ed, Ed D); consulting psychology (D Admin, D Com, PhD); curriculum studies (M Ed, Ed D); development studies (M Admin, MA, D Admin, PhD); didactics (M Ed, Ed D); education (M Tech); education management (M Ed, Ed D); educational psychology (M Ed); English (MA); environmental education (M Ed); French (MA, PhD); German (MA, PhD); Greek (MA); guidance and counseling (M Ed); health studies (MA, PhD), including health sciences education (MA), health services management (MA), medical and surgical nursing science (critical care general) (MA), midwifery and neonatal nursing science (MA), trauma and emergency care (MA); history (MA, PhD); history of education (Ed D); inclusive education (M Ed, Ed D); information and communications technology policy and regulation (MA); information science (MA, MIS, PhD); international politics (MA, PhD); Islamic studies (MA, PhD); Italian (MA, PhD); Judaica (MA, PhD); linguistics (MA, PhD); mathematical education (M Ed); mathematics education (MA); missiology (M Th, D Th); modern Hebrew (MA, PhD); musicology (MA, MMus, D Mus, PhD); natural science education (M Ed); New Testament (M Th, D Th); Old Testament (D Th); pastoral therapy (M Th, D Th); philosophy (MA); philosophy of education (M Ed, Ed D); politics (MA, PhD); Portuguese (MA, PhD); practical theology (M Th, D Th); psychology (MA, MS, PhD); psychology of education (M Ed, Ed D); public health (MA); religious studies (MA, D Th, PhD); Romance languages (MA); Russian (MA, PhD); Semitic languages (MA, PhD); social behavior studies in HIV/AIDS (MA); social science (mental health) (MA); social science in development studies (MA); social science in psychology (MA); social science in social work (MA); social science in sociology (MA); social work (MSW, DSW, PhD); socio-education (M Ed, Ed D); sociolinguistics (MA); sociology (MA, PhD); Spanish (MA, PhD); systematic theology (M Th, D Th); TESOL (teaching English to speakers of other languages) (MA); theological ethics (M Th, D Th); theory of literature (MA, PhD); urban ministries (D Th); urban ministry (M Th).

University of Southern California, Graduate School, College of Letters, Arts and Sciences, Department of Classics, Los Angeles, CA 90089. Offers MA, PhD. *Faculty:* 12 full-time (4 women), 1 (woman) part-time/adjunct. *Students:* 20 full-time (12 women), 2 part-time (1 woman); includes 1 minority (Hispanic American), 5 international. 17 applicants, 35% accepted. In 2007, 2 master's, 2 doctorates awarded. *Degree requirements:* For doctorate, 4 foreign languages, thesis/dissertation. *Entrance requirements:* For master's and doctorate, GRE General Test. *Application deadline:* For fall admission, 12/1 priority date for domestic students. Application fee: $85. *Financial support:* In 2007–08, 20 students received support; fellowships with tuition reimbursements available, teaching assistantships with tuition reimbursements available, Federal Work-Study, institutionally sponsored loans, and scholarships/grants available. Financial award application deadline: 2/15; financial award applicants required to submit FAFSA. *Unit head:* Dr. Tom Habinek, Chairman, 213-740-2311, E-mail: classics@usc.edu. *Application contact:* Vincent Farenga, Information Contact, 213-740-2311.

The University of Texas at Austin, Graduate School, College of Liberal Arts, Department of Classics, Austin, TX 78712-1111. Offers MA, PhD. *Degree requirements:* For master's, 2 foreign languages, comprehensive exam, thesis; for doctorate, 4 foreign languages, comprehensive exam, thesis/dissertation. *Entrance requirements:* For master's, GRE General Test, proficiency in classics; for doctorate, GRE General Test, master's degree in classics. Electronic applications accepted.

University of Toronto, School of Graduate Studies, Humanities Division, Department of Classics, Toronto, ON M5S 1A1, Canada. Offers MA, PhD. Part-time programs available. *Faculty:* 12 full-time, 6 part-time/adjunct. *Students:* 50 full-time (23 women), 17 international. 55 applicants, 42% accepted. In 2007, 4 degrees awarded. *Degree requirements:* For master's, qualifying examinations, sight translation exams in Greek and Latin; for doctorate, thesis/ dissertation, qualifying examinations, sight translation exams in Greek and Latin. *Entrance requirements:* For master's, minimum B+ average in final year of an undergraduate program in classics, 3–4 years of course work in Greek and Latin; for doctorate, minimum B+ average with at least one A–; MA in classics. *Application deadline:* For fall admission, 6/1 for domestic students, 4/15 for international students. Application fee: $100 Canadian dollars. *Financial support:* Research assistantships, teaching assistantships available. *Unit head:* Prof. John Magee, Acting Chair and Acting Graduate Chair, 416-978-3179, Fax: 416-978-7307, E-mail: chair.classics@utoronto.ca. *Application contact:* Coral Gavrilovic, Graduate Assistant, 416-978-5513, Fax: 416-978-7307, E-mail: k.gavrilovic@utoronto.ca.

University of Vermont, Graduate College, College of Arts and Sciences, Department of Classics, Burlington, VT 05405. Offers Greek (MA); Greek and Latin (MAT); Latin (MA). *Students:* 8 (3 women). 6 applicants, 100% accepted, 4 enrolled. *Degree requirements:* For master's, one foreign language, thesis. *Entrance requirements:* For master's, GRE General Test. Additional exam requirements/recommendations for international students: Required—TOEFL (minimum score 550 paper-based; 213 computer-based; 80 iBT). *Application deadline:* For fall admission, 4/1 priority date for domestic students. Applications are processed on a rolling basis. Application fee: $40. Electronic applications accepted. *Financial support:* Fellowships, teaching assistantships available. Financial award application deadline: 3/1. *Faculty research:* Early Greek literature. *Unit head:* Dr. Mark Usher, Chair, 802-656-3210. *Application contact:* Jacques Bailly, Coordinator, 802-656-3210.

University of Victoria, Faculty of Graduate Studies, Faculty of Humanities, Department of Greek and Roman Studies, Victoria, BC V8W 2Y2, Canada. Offers MA, PhD. PhD offered by special arrangement. Part-time programs available. *Faculty:* 7 full-time (2 women). *Students:* 9 full-time (5 women). Average age 22. 12 applicants, 42% accepted, 4 enrolled. *Degree requirements:* For master's, 3 foreign languages, thesis. *Entrance requirements:* For master's, knowledge of Greek and Latin. Additional exam requirements/recommendations for international students: Required—TOEFL (minimum score 575 paper-based; 233 computer-based), IELTS (minimum score 7). *Application deadline:* For fall admission, 4/1 for domestic students, 12/15 priority date for international students. Applications are processed on a rolling basis. Application fee: $75 ($125 for international students). Electronic applications accepted. *Expenses:* Tuition, state resident: full-time $3,110. International tuition: $3,700 full-time. Tuition and fees vary according to program. *Financial support:* In 2007–08, 3 students received support, including 1 fellowship (averaging $13,400 per year), 1 teaching assistantship (averaging $6,000 per year); institutionally sponsored loans, scholarships/grants, and unspecified assistantships also available. Support available to part-time students. Financial award application deadline: 2/15. *Faculty research:* Roman social history, Roman archaeology and technology, Roman literature, Greek literature, Homer and tragedy, Greek historiography. *Unit head:* Cedric Littlewood, Chair, 250-721-8515, E-mail: calwood@uvic.ca. *Application contact:* Gregory D. Rowe, Graduate Adviser, 250-721-8521, Fax: 250-721-8516, E-mail: gdrowe@uvic.ca.

University of Virginia, College and Graduate School of Arts and Sciences, Department of Classics, Charlottesville, VA 22903. Offers MA, PhD. *Faculty:* 10 full-time (3 women). *Students:* 22 full-time (10 women); includes 3 minority (2 Asian Americans or Pacific Islanders, 1 Hispanic American), 3 international. Average age 29. 50 applicants, 48% accepted, 9 enrolled. In 2007, 3 master's, 3 doctorates awarded. *Degree requirements:* For master's, one foreign language, comprehensive exam, thesis, oral exam; for doctorate, 2 foreign languages, thesis/ dissertation, oral exam. *Entrance requirements:* For master's and doctorate, GRE General Test. *Application deadline:* Applications are processed on a rolling basis. Application fee: $60. Electronic applications accepted. *Financial support:* Unspecified assistantships available. Financial award applicants required to submit FAFSA. *Unit head:* John Miller, Chair, 434-924-3008, Fax: 434-924-3062, E-mail: classics@virginia.edu.

University of Washington, Graduate School, College of Arts and Sciences, Department of Classics, Seattle, WA 98195. Offers MA, PhD. Part-time programs available. *Faculty:* 10 full-time (5 women). *Students:* 21 full-time (13 women), 4 part-time (2 women); includes 3 minority (all Hispanic Americans), 2 international. Average age 29. 62 applicants, 39% accepted, 8 enrolled. In 2007, 1 master's, 4 doctorates awarded. Terminal master's awarded for partial completion of doctoral program. *Degree requirements:* For master's, one foreign language, thesis or alternative; for doctorate, 2 foreign languages, comprehensive exam, thesis/ dissertation. *Entrance requirements:* For master's, GRE, bachelor's degree in classics, Greek, or Latin; minimum GPA of 3.0; for doctorate, GRE, minimum GPA of 3.0. Additional exam requirements/recommendations for international students: Required—TOEFL. *Application deadline:* For fall admission, 1/5 for domestic students. Application fee: $50. Electronic applications accepted. *Financial support:* In 2007–08, 2 fellowships with full tuition reimbursements (averaging $13,059 per year), 1 research assistantship with full tuition reimbursement (averaging $13,059 per year), 14 teaching assistantships with full tuition reimbursements (averaging

$13,059 per year) were awarded; Federal Work-Study, institutionally sponsored loans, and tuition waivers (partial) also available. Financial award application deadline: 3/1; financial award applicants required to submit FAFSA. *Faculty research:* Greek and Latin poetry, Greek and Roman cultural institutions, Greek and Latin historiography, ancient medicine, Greek tragedy. *Unit head:* Alain M. Gowing, Chair, 206-543-2266, Fax: 206-543-2267, E-mail: alain@u.washington.edu. *Application contact:* Catherine Connors, Graduate Coordinator, 206-543-2266, Fax: 206-543-2267, E-mail: cconnors@u.washington.edu.

University of Washington, Graduate School, College of Arts and Sciences, Department of Philosophy, Seattle, WA 98195. Offers classics and philosophy (PhD); philosophy (MA, PhD). Terminal master's awarded for partial completion of doctoral program. *Degree requirements:* For master's, 3 papers; for doctorate, thesis/dissertation, general exam. *Entrance requirements:* For master's and doctorate, GRE, minimum GPA of 3.0. Additional exam requirements/recommendations for international students: Required—TOEFL. *Faculty research:* History and philosophy of science, epistemology, Aristotle's metaphysics, ethics and politics, causation in modern philosophy.

The University of Western Ontario, Faculty of Graduate Studies, Faculty of Arts and Humanities, Department of Classical Studies, London, ON N6A 5B8, Canada. Offers MA. Part-time programs available. *Faculty:* 7 full-time (1 woman), 5 part-time/adjunct (3 women). *Students:* 7 full-time (5 women). 7 applicants, 86% accepted. In 2007, 4 degrees awarded. *Degree requirements:* For master's, one foreign language. *Entrance requirements:* For master's, honors degree, minimum B+ average, statement of interest. Additional exam requirements/recommendations for international students: Required—TOEFL. *Application deadline:* For fall admission, 2/15 priority date for domestic students, 2/15 for international students. Application fee: $50. *Financial support:* In 2007–08, 7 teaching assistantships (averaging $8,632 per year) were awarded; fellowships, research assistantships also available. Financial award application deadline: 4/1. *Faculty research:* Greek literature, Roman history and law, ancient sport, Byzantine literature, Bronze Age archaeology. Total annual research expenditures: $6,800. *Unit head:* Prof. Chris G. Brown, Chair, 519-661-2111 Ext. 84519, Fax: 519-850-2388, E-mail: pindar@uwo.ca. *Application contact:* Judy Laforme, Graduate Assistant, 519-661-2111, Fax: 519-850-2388, E-mail: classics@uwo.ca.

University of Wisconsin–Madison, Graduate School, College of Letters and Science, Department of Classics, Madison, WI 53706-1380. Offers classics (MA, PhD); Greek (MA); Latin (MA). Part-time programs available. Terminal master's awarded for partial completion of doctoral program. *Degree requirements:* For master's, 3 foreign languages, oral and written exams; for doctorate, 4 foreign languages, thesis/dissertation, written exams. *Entrance requirements:* For master's, GRE; for doctorate, master's degree. Electronic applications accepted. *Faculty research:* Greek tragedy, Latin elegy, historiography, Homer, Greek lyric poetry.

University of Wisconsin–Milwaukee, Graduate School, College of Letters and Sciences, Interdepartmental Program in Foreign Language and Literature, Milwaukee, WI 53201-0413. Offers classics and Hebrew studies (MAFLL); comparative literature (MAFLL); French and Italian (MAFLL); German (MAFLL); Slavic studies (MAFLL); Spanish (MAFLL). Part-time programs available. *Faculty:* 39 full-time (17 women). *Students:* 29 full-time (21 women), 31 part-time (23 women); includes 8 minority (1 Asian American or Pacific Islander, 7 Hispanic Americans), 22 international. 54 applicants, 67% accepted, 26 enrolled. In 2007, 34 degrees awarded. *Degree requirements:* For master's, 2 foreign languages, thesis or alternative. *Application deadline:* For fall admission, 1/1 priority date for domestic students; for spring admission, 9/1 for domestic students. Applications are processed on a rolling basis. Application fee: $45 ($75 for international students). *Expenses:* Tuition, state resident: part-time $530 per credit. Tuition, nonresident: part-time $1,428 per credit. Required fees: $19 per credit. $229 per term. Tuition and fees vary according to course load and program. *Financial support:* In 2007–08, 44 teaching assistantships were awarded; fellowships, research assistantships, career-related internships or fieldwork and unspecified assistantships also available. Support available to part-time students. Financial award application deadline: 4/15. *Unit head:* Gabrielle Verdier, Representative, 414-229-3346, Fax: 414-229-2741, E-mail: verdier@uwm.edu.

Vanderbilt University, Graduate School, Department of Classical Studies, Nashville, TN 37240-1001. Offers classics (MA); Latin (MAT). *Faculty:* 13 full-time (6 women). *Students:* 4 full-time (3 women). Average age 26. 36 applicants, 14% accepted, 2 enrolled. In 2007, 3 degrees awarded. *Degree requirements:* For master's, 2 foreign languages, thesis. *Entrance requirements:* For master's, GRE General Test. *Application deadline:* For fall admission, 1/15 for domestic and international students. Application fee: $0. Electronic applications accepted. *Financial support:* Fellowships with full and partial tuition reimbursements, teaching assistantships with full and partial tuition reimbursements, Federal Work-Study, institutionally sponsored loans, and health care benefits available. Financial award application deadline: 1/15; financial award applicants required to submit CSS PROFILE or FAFSA. *Faculty research:* Greek and Latin literature and language, Greek and Roman history, classical archaeology, philosophy, religion. *Unit head:* Barbara Tsakirgis, Chair, 615-322-2516, Fax: 615-343-7261, E-mail: barbara.tsakirgis@vanderbilt.edu. *Application contact:* Kathy L. Gaca, Director of Graduate Studies, 615-322-2516, Fax: 615-343-7261, E-mail: kathy.l.gaca@vanderbilt.edu.

Villanova University, Graduate School of Liberal Arts and Sciences, Department of Classical and Modern Languages and Literature, Villanova, PA 19085-1699. Offers classics (MA); Hispanic studies (MA). Part-time and evening/weekend programs available. *Faculty:* 4 full-time (3 women), 1 part-time/adjunct (0 women). *Students:* 15 full-time (9 women), 12 part-time (11 women); includes 12 minority (1 Asian American or Pacific Islander, 11 Hispanic Americans), 7 international. Average age 33. 16 applicants, 94% accepted. In 2007, 7 degrees awarded. *Degree requirements:* For master's, one foreign language, comprehensive exam, thesis optional. *Entrance requirements:* For master's, minimum GPA of 3.0. Additional exam requirements/recommendations for international students: Required—TOEFL. *Application deadline:* For fall admission, 8/1 for domestic and international students; for spring admission, 12/1 for domestic and international students. Applications are processed on a rolling basis. Application fee: $50. Electronic applications accepted. *Financial support:* Teaching assistantships with tuition reimbursements, Federal Work-Study and scholarships/grants available. Financial award applicants required to submit FAFSA. *Unit head:* Silvia Nagy-Zekmi, Chair, 610-519-7478.

Washington University in St. Louis, Graduate School of Arts and Sciences, Department of Classics, St. Louis, MO 63130-4899. Offers MA, MAT. *Degree requirements:* For master's, thesis or alternative. *Entrance requirements:* For master's, GRE General Test. Electronic applications accepted.

Wayne State University, College of Liberal Arts and Sciences, Department of Classical and Modern Languages, Literatures, and Cultures, Program in Classics, Greek, and Latin, Detroit, MI 48202. Offers classics (MA); Latin (MA). *Students:* 3 full-time (2 women), 3 part-time. Average age 26. 3 applicants, 100% accepted, 2 enrolled. *Degree requirements:* For master's, thesis optional. *Entrance requirements:* For master's, GRE, bachelor's degree in Latin, Greek, or classics; letters of recommendation; personal statement; writing sample. Additional exam requirements/recommendations for international students: Required—TOEFL (minimum score 550 paper-based; 213 computer-based); Recommended—TWE (minimum score 6). *Application deadline:* For fall admission, 7/1 priority date for domestic students, 6/1 for international students; for winter admission, 10/1 for international students; for spring admission, 2/1 for international students. Applications are processed on a rolling basis. Application fee: $30 ($50 for international students). Electronic applications accepted. *Expenses:* Tuition, state resident: part-time $403 per credit hour. Tuition, nonresident: part-time $890 per credit hour. *Financial support:* Teaching assistantships available. *Unit head:* Kathleen McNamee, Chair, 313-577-3032, Fax: 313-577-3266, E-mail: aa2046@wayne.edu. *Application contact:* Joel Itzkowitz, Associate Professor, 313-577-6591, E-mail: jitzkowitz@wayne.edu.

West Chester University of Pennsylvania, Office of Graduate Studies and Extended Education, College of Arts and Sciences, Department of Foreign Languages, West Chester, PA 19383. Offers French (M Ed, MA); German (M Ed); Latin (M Ed); Spanish (M Ed, MA). Part-time and evening/weekend programs available. *Students:* 7 full-time (all women), 18 part-time (15 women); includes 2 minority (both Hispanic Americans) Average age 35. 10 applicants, 100% accepted, 6 enrolled. In 2007, 7 degrees awarded. *Degree requirements:* For master's, one foreign language, comprehensive exam, thesis optional. *Entrance requirements:* For master's, GRE, placement test. Additional exam requirements/recommendations for international students: Required—TOEFL (minimum score 550 paper-based; 213 computer-based; 80 iBT). *Application deadline:* For fall admission, 4/15 priority date for domestic students; for spring admission, 10/15 for domestic students. Applications are processed on a rolling basis. Application fee: $35. *Expenses:* Tuition, state resident: part-time $345 per credit. Tuition, nonresident: part-time $552 per credit. Tuition and fees vary according to course load. *Financial support:* In 2007–08, 2 research assistantships with full and partial tuition reimbursements (averaging $5,000 per year) were awarded; unspecified assistantships also available. Support available to part-time students. Financial award application deadline: 2/15; financial award applicants required to submit FAFSA. *Faculty research:* Implementation of world languages curriculum framework. *Unit head:* Dr. Jerry Williams, Chair, 610-436-2700, Fax: 610-436-3048, E-mail: jwilliams2@wcupa.edu. *Application contact:* Dr. Rebecca Pauly, Graduate Coordinator, 610-436-2382, E-mail: rpauly@wcupa.edu.

Wilfrid Laurier University, Faculty of Graduate Studies, Faculty of Arts, Department of Archaeology and Classical Studies, Waterloo, ON N2L 3C5, Canada. Offers MA. *Faculty:* 12 full-time, 6 part-time/adjunct. *Degree requirements:* For master's, thesis optional. *Entrance requirements:* For master's, minimum B+ average in last two undergraduate years (exclusive of first year level courses in those years). Additional exam requirements/recommendations for international students: Required—TOEFL. Application fee: $75. *Financial support:* Fellowships, research assistantships, teaching assistantships available. *Unit head:* Dr. Gerald Schaus, Graduate Officer, 519-884-0710 Ext. 3302, E-mail: gschaus@wlu.ca. *Application contact:* Jennifer Poppe, Student Contact, 519-884-0710 Ext. 3536, Fax: 519-884-1020, E-mail: gradstudies@wlu.ca.

Yale University, Graduate School of Arts and Sciences, Department of Classics, New Haven, CT 06520. Offers PhD. *Degree requirements:* For doctorate, 2 foreign languages, thesis/dissertation. *Entrance requirements:* For doctorate, GRE General Test.

Comparative Literature

American University, College of Arts and Sciences, Department of Literature, Program in Literature, Washington, DC 20016-8001. Offers MA. Part-time and evening/weekend programs available. *Students:* 22 full-time (18 women), 5 part-time (all women); includes 2 minority (1 American Indian/Alaska Native, 1 Asian American or Pacific Islander). Average age 24. In 2007, 12 degrees awarded. *Degree requirements:* For master's, comprehensive exam, thesis or alternative. *Entrance requirements:* For master's, GRE, writing sample. *Application deadline:* For fall admission, 2/1 for domestic students. Application fee: $50. *Expenses:* Tuition: Full-time $19,998; part-time $1,111 per credit hour. Required fees: $380. Tuition and fees vary according to program. *Financial support:* In 2007–08, 6 students received support; fellowships, research assistantships, teaching assistantships, career-related internships or fieldwork, Federal Work-Study, institutionally sponsored loans, and tuition waivers (full and partial) available. Support available to part-time students. Financial award application deadline: 2/1. *Faculty research:* British, American, African-American, and Third World literature; cinema studies; literary theory; feminist criticism.

The American University in Cairo, Graduate Studies and Research, School of Humanities and Social Sciences, Department of English and Comparative Literature, Cairo, Egypt. Offers MA. Part-time programs available. *Degree requirements:* For master's, one foreign language, thesis, proficiency in French or German. *Entrance requirements:* Additional exam requirements/recommendations for international students: Required—English entrance exam and/or TOEFL.

Antioch University McGregor, Graduate Programs, Individualized Liberal and Professional Studies Program, Yellow Springs, OH 45387-1609. Offers liberal and professional studies (MA), including counseling, creative writing, education, film studies, liberal studies, management, modern literature, psychology, theatre, visual arts. Part-time and evening/weekend programs available. Postbaccalaureate distance learning degree programs offered (minimal on-campus study). *Faculty:* 2 full-time (1 woman), 3 part-time/adjunct (2 women). *Students:* Average age 40. 35 applicants, 63% accepted, 17 enrolled. In 2007, 31 degrees awarded. *Degree requirements:* For master's, thesis or alternative. *Entrance requirements:* For master's, resumé, 2 letters of reference. *Application deadline:* For fall admission, 8/25 for domestic students; for winter admission, 12/5 for domestic students; for spring admission, 3/8 for domestic students. Applications are processed on a rolling basis. Application fee: $50. Electronic applications accepted. *Expenses:* Contact institution. *Financial support:* Federal Work-Study available. Financial award applicants required to submit FAFSA. *Unit head:* Suzanne Fest, Chair, 937-769-1876, Fax: 937-769-1807, E-mail: sfest@mcgregor.edu. *Application contact:* Seth Gordon, Assistant Director of Admissions, 937-769-1800 Ext. 1825, Fax: 937-769-1804, E-mail: sgordon@mcgregor.edu.

See Close-Up on page 443.

Arizona State University, Graduate College, College of Liberal Arts and Sciences, Division of Humanities, Department of English, Tempe, AZ 85287. Offers English (MA, PhD), including comparative literature (MA), linguistics (MA), literature (PhD), literature and language (MA), rhetoric and composition (MA), rhetoric/composition and linguistics (PhD); teaching English as a second language (MTESL). *Degree requirements:* For doctorate, thesis/dissertation. *Entrance requirements:* For master's and doctorate, GRE.

Brigham Young University, Graduate Studies, College of Humanities, Department of Humanities, Classics, and Comparative Literature, Provo, UT 84602-1001. Offers comparative literature (MA); comparative studies (MA); humanities (MA). *Faculty:* 26 full-time (4 women). *Students:* 27 full-time (14 women). Average age 27. 15 applicants, 80% accepted, 6 enrolled. In 2007, 5 degrees awarded. *Degree requirements:* For master's, 2 foreign languages, thesis. *Entrance requirements:* For master's, GRE, minimum GPA of 3.0 in last 60 hours. *Application deadline:* For fall admission, 3/1 for domestic and international students. Application fee: $50. Electronic applications accepted. *Financial support:* In 2007–08, 27 students received support, including 7 research assistantships (averaging $4,680 per year), 29 teaching assistantships (averaging $65,678 per year); fellowships, career-related internships or fieldwork, institutionally

Comparative Literature

Brigham Young University (continued)
sponsored loans, scholarships/grants, tuition waivers (full and partial), and student instructorships also available. Support available to part-time students. *Unit head:* Dr. Michael J. Call, Chair, 801-422-2550, Fax: 801-422-0305, E-mail: michael_call@byu.edu. *Application contact:* Carolyn Hone, Graduate Secretary for Humanities and Comparative Literature, 801-422-4430, Fax: 801-422-0305, E-mail: carolyn_hone@byu.edu.

Brock University, Faculty of Graduate Studies, Faculty of Humanities, Program in Studies in Comparative Literatures and Arts, St. Catharines, ON L2S 3A1, Canada. Offers MA. *Degree requirements:* For master's, thesis optional. *Entrance requirements:* For master's, honors degree. Additional exam requirements/recommendations for international students: Required—TOEFL (minimum score 550 paper-based; 213 computer-based; 80 iBT), IELTS (minimum score 7), TWE (minimum score 4). Electronic applications accepted.

Brown University, Graduate School, Department of Comparative Literature, Providence, RI 02912. Offers AM, PhD. *Degree requirements:* For master's, 2 foreign languages, thesis or alternative; for doctorate, 2 foreign languages, thesis/dissertation, preliminary exam. *Entrance requirements:* For master's and doctorate, GRE General Test, GRE Subject Test.

California State University, Fullerton, Graduate Studies, College of Humanities and Social Sciences, Department of English and Comparative Literature, Fullerton, CA 92834-9480. Offers comparative literature (MA); English (MA). Part-time programs available. *Students:* 27 full-time (22 women), 77 part-time (50 women); includes 19 minority (1 African American, 5 Asian Americans or Pacific Islanders, 13 Hispanic Americans). Average age 32. 78 applicants, 53% accepted, 29 enrolled. In 2007, 38 degrees awarded. *Degree requirements:* For master's, comprehensive exam, thesis or alternative. *Entrance requirements:* For master's, minimum GPA of 3.0 in major, 2.5 in last 60 hours. Application fee: $55. *Financial support:* Teaching assistantships, Federal Work-Study, institutionally sponsored loans, and scholarships/grants available. Support available to part-time students. Financial award application deadline: 3/1. *Unit head:* Dr. Joseph Sawicki, Chair, 714-278-3163. *Application contact:* Dr. Susan Jacobsen, Adviser, 714-278-3163.

California State University, Northridge, Graduate Studies, College of Humanities, Department of English, Northridge, CA 91330. Offers creative writing (MA); literature (MA); rhetoric and composition theory (MA). Part-time and evening/weekend programs available. *Faculty:* 37 full-time (19 women), 85 part-time/adjunct (69 women). *Students:* 40 full-time (29 women), 125 part-time (92 women); includes 38 minority (3 African Americans, 1 American Indian/Alaska Native, 13 Asian Americans or Pacific Islanders, 21 Hispanic Americans). Average age 34. 99 applicants, 75% accepted, 40 enrolled. In 2007, 38 degrees awarded. *Degree requirements:* For master's, thesis or alternative. *Entrance requirements:* For master's, writing proficiency test, GRE General Test or minimum GPA of 3.0. Additional exam requirements/recommendations for international students: Required—TOEFL. *Application deadline:* For fall admission, 11/30 for domestic students. Application fee: $55. *Financial support:* Teaching assistantships available. Financial award application deadline: 3/1. *Faculty research:* Reading improvement, professional writing, Dickens, Shaw, English as a second language. *Unit head:* Dr. George Uba, Chair, 818-677-3434, E-mail: george.uba@csun.edu. *Application contact:* Dr. Marjie Seagoe, Graduate Studies Secretary, 818-677-3433.

Carleton University, Faculty of Graduate Studies, Faculty of Arts and Social Sciences, School for Languages, Literatures, and Comparative Literary Studies, Ottawa, ON K1S 5B6, Canada. Offers cultural mediations (PhD). *Entrance requirements:* Additional exam requirements/recommendations for international students: Required—TOEFL. *Application deadline:* Applications are processed on a rolling basis. Application fee: $77. *Financial support:* Fellowships, teaching assistantships available. *Faculty research:* Literary history, theory of literature, cross-cultural studies, modernism/postmodernism, comparative Canadian literature. *Unit head:* Paul Thèberge, Director, 613-520-2600 Ext. 2177, Fax: 613-520-2564. *Application contact:* Olga Cada, School Administrator, 613-520-2600 Ext. 2177, Fax: 613-520-2564, E-mail: olga_cada@carleton.ca.

Carnegie Mellon University, College of Humanities and Social Sciences, Department of English, Pittsburgh, PA 15213-3891. Offers communication planning and design (M Des); English (MA); literary and cultural studies (MA, PhD); professional writing (MAPW), including design, professional writing, research, rhetorical theory, science writing, technical; rhetoric (MA, PhD). Part-time programs available. Terminal master's awarded for partial completion of doctoral program. *Degree requirements:* For doctorate, 2 foreign languages, comprehensive exam, thesis/dissertation. *Entrance requirements:* For master's and doctorate, GRE General Test. Additional exam requirements/recommendations for international students: Required—TOEFL, TWE. *Faculty research:* Cognitive processes in discourse with emphasis on writing, testing, and evaluation.

Case Western Reserve University, School of Graduate Studies, Department of English, Cleveland, OH 44106. Offers comparative literature (MA); English and American literature (MA, PhD). Part-time programs available. *Faculty:* 14 full-time (6 women). *Students:* 7 full-time (all women), 28 part-time (17 women), 3 international. Average age 29. 55 applicants, 27% accepted, 8 enrolled. In 2007, 3 master's, 3 doctorates awarded. *Degree requirements:* For master's, written exam; for doctorate, one foreign language, thesis/dissertation, oral and written exams. *Entrance requirements:* For master's and doctorate, GRE General Test, sample of written work. Additional exam requirements/recommendations for international students: Required—TOEFL. *Application deadline:* For fall admission, 5/30 priority date for domestic students; for spring admission, 1/2 for domestic students. Applications are processed on a rolling basis. Application fee: $50. Electronic applications accepted. *Financial support:* Research assistantships, teaching assistantships, Federal Work-Study, institutionally sponsored loans, and tuition waivers (partial) available. Financial award application deadline: 1/31. *Faculty research:* Sixteenth- to twentieth-century English literature, rhetorical and critical theory, women's studies, genre studies, Renaissance, America modernism, authorship. *Unit head:* William Siebenschuh, Chair, 216-368-4118, Fax: 216-368-4681, E-mail: william.siebenschuh@case.edu. *Application contact:* Jamie McDaniel, Admissions, 216-368-2370, Fax: 216-368-4367, E-mail: jlm25@case.edu.

Case Western Reserve University, School of Graduate Studies, Department of Modern Languages and Literatures and Department of English, Program in World Literature, Cleveland, OH 44106. Offers MA. *Faculty:* 6 full-time (4 women). *Students:* 1 full-time (0 women), 1 international. In 2007, 1 degree awarded. *Degree requirements:* For master's, 2 foreign languages, written exam. *Entrance requirements:* For master's, GRE General Test, sample of written work. Additional exam requirements/recommendations for international students: Required—TOEFL. *Application deadline:* For fall admission, 7/30 for domestic students. Applications are processed on a rolling basis. Application fee: $50. Electronic applications accepted. *Financial support:* Fellowships, career-related internships or fieldwork, institutionally sponsored loans, and tuition waivers (partial) available. Financial award application deadline: 3/1; financial award applicants required to submit FAFSA. *Faculty research:* Literary theory, literary translation, Romanticism. *Unit head:* Chair, 216-368-2217, Fax: 216-368-2216.

The Catholic University of America, School of Arts and Sciences, Program in Comparative Literature, Washington, DC 20064. Offers MA, PhD. Part-time programs available. *Students:* Average age 33. *Degree requirements:* For master's, one foreign language, comprehensive exam, thesis or alternative; for doctorate, 2 foreign languages, comprehensive exam, thesis/dissertation, oral examination. *Entrance requirements:* For master's and doctorate, GRE General Test, 3 letters of recommendation, writing sample. Additional exam requirements/recommendations for international students: Required—TOEFL (minimum score 580 paper-based; 237 computer-based). *Application deadline:* For fall admission, 2/1 priority date for domestic students; for spring admission, 11/15 priority date for domestic students. Applications are processed on a rolling basis. Application fee: $55. Electronic applications accepted. *Financial support:* Research assistantships, teaching assistantships, career-related internships or fieldwork, Federal Work-Study, scholarships/grants, tuition waivers (full and partial), and unspecified assistantships available. Support available to part-time students. Financial award application deadline: 2/1; financial award applicants required to submit FAFSA. *Faculty research:* Medieval literature, romanticism, religion and literature, modern literature, theory and criticism. *Unit head:* Dr. Joseph Sendry, Director, 202-319-5480, E-mail: sendry@cua.edu.

Claremont Graduate University, Graduate Programs, School of Arts and Humanities, Department of English, Claremont, CA 91711-6160. Offers American studies (MA, PhD); critical theory (MA, PhD); early modern studies (MA, PhD); English (M Phil, MA, PhD); literary theory (PhD); literature (MA, PhD); literature and creative writing (MA); literature and film (MA); MBA/MA; MBA/PhD. Part-time programs available. *Faculty:* 2 full-time (1 woman), 2 part-time/adjunct (0 women). *Students:* 81 full-time (49 women), 14 part-time (10 women); includes 18 minority (3 American Indian/Alaska Native, 10 Asian Americans or Pacific Islanders, 5 Hispanic Americans), 3 international. Average age 35. In 2007, 14 master's, 5 doctorates awarded. *Degree requirements:* For master's, one foreign language, comprehensive exam; for doctorate, 2 foreign languages, comprehensive exam, thesis/dissertation. *Entrance requirements:* For master's, GRE General Test; for doctorate, GRE General Test, MA in literature. *Application deadline:* For fall admission, 2/15 priority date for domestic students; for spring admission, 11/15 for domestic students. Applications are processed on a rolling basis. Electronic applications accepted. *Expenses:* Tuition: Full-time $31,640; part-time $1,376 per unit. Required fees: $145 per semester. Tuition and fees vary according to course load, degree level and program. *Financial support:* Fellowships, Federal Work-Study and institutionally sponsored loans available. Support available to part-time students. Financial award application deadline: 2/15; financial award applicants required to submit FAFSA. *Faculty research:* American, comparative, and English Renaissance literature; modernism; feminist literature and theory. *Unit head:* Wendy Martin, Chair, 909-621-8612, Fax: 909-607-1221, E-mail: wendy.martin@cgu.edu.

College of the Humanities and Sciences, Harrison Middleton University, Graduate Program, Tempe, AZ 85282. Offers education (MA, Ed D); humanities (MA); imaginative literature (MA); jurisprudence (MA); natural science (MA); philosophy and religion (MA); social science (MA). Part-time and evening/weekend programs available. Postbaccalaureate distance learning degree programs offered (no on-campus study).

Columbia University, Graduate School of Arts and Sciences, Division of Humanities, Department of English and Comparative Literature, New York, NY 10027. Offers comparative literature (M Phil, MA, PhD); English literature (M Phil, MA, PhD); literature-writing (M Phil, MA, PhD). Part-time programs available. *Faculty:* 41 full-time, 2 part-time/adjunct. *Students:* 176 full-time (104 women), 28 part-time (19 women). Average age 32. 627 applicants, 12% accepted. In 2007, 27 master's, 24 doctorates awarded. *Degree requirements:* For master's, one foreign language, comprehensive exam, seminar papers; for doctorate, thesis/dissertation. *Entrance requirements:* For master's and doctorate, GRE General Test. Additional exam requirements/recommendations for international students: Required—TOEFL. Application fee: $90. *Expenses:* Tuition: Part-time $1,452 per credit. Required fees: $152 per term. One-time fee: $75 part-time. Full-time tuition and fees vary according to course level, course load, degree level and program. *Financial support:* Fellowships, teaching assistantships, Federal Work-Study and institutionally sponsored loans available. Support available to part-time students. Financial award application deadline: 1/5; financial award applicants required to submit FAFSA. *Faculty research:* Medieval through modern literature, drama, literary criticism. *Unit head:* David Kastan, Chair, 212-854-6257, Fax: 212-854-5398, E-mail: dsk@columbia.edu.

Cornell University, Graduate School, Graduate Fields of Arts and Sciences, Field of Comparative Literature, Ithaca, NY 14853-0001. Offers PhD. *Faculty:* 38 full-time (15 women). *Students:* 31 full-time (22 women); includes 5 minority (1 African American, 1 Asian American or Pacific Islander, 3 Hispanic Americans), 10 international. Average age 29. 108 applicants, 9% accepted, 3 enrolled. In 2007, 2 doctorates awarded. *Degree requirements:* For doctorate, 2 foreign languages, comprehensive exam, thesis/dissertation, teaching experience. *Entrance requirements:* For doctorate, GRE General Test, proficiency in 2 foreign literatures, writing sample, 3 letters of recommendation. Additional exam requirements/recommendations for international students: Required—TOEFL (minimum score 550 paper-based; 213 computer-based; 77 iBT). *Application deadline:* For fall admission, 1/10 for domestic students. Application fee: $70. Electronic applications accepted. *Financial support:* In 2007–08, 27 students received support, including 13 fellowships with full tuition reimbursements available, 14 teaching assistantships with full tuition reimbursements available; research assistantships with full tuition reimbursements available, institutionally sponsored loans, health care benefits, and tuition waivers (full and partial) also available. Financial award applicants required to submit FAFSA. *Faculty research:* Critical theory, European studies, Latin American studies, Asian studies. *Unit head:* Director of Graduate Studies, 607-255-4155. *Application contact:* Graduate Field Assistant, 607-255-4155, E-mail: complit@cornell.edu.

Dartmouth College, Arts and Sciences Graduate Programs, Comparative Literature Program, Hanover, NH 03755. Offers AM. *Faculty:* 1 (woman) full-time, 2 part-time/adjunct (1 woman). *Students:* 11 full-time (6 women); includes 1 minority (Hispanic American), 5 international. Average age 25. 31 applicants, 42% accepted, 11 enrolled. In 2007, 10 degrees awarded. *Degree requirements:* For master's, final paper, oral exams. *Entrance requirements:* For master's, proficiency in 2 languages. Additional exam requirements/recommendations for international students: Required—TOEFL. *Application deadline:* For fall admission, 2/1 priority date for domestic students. Application fee: $30. Electronic applications accepted. *Financial support:* In 2007–08, 5 students received support, including fellowships with full tuition reimbursements available (averaging $13,972 per year); career-related internships or fieldwork, institutionally sponsored loans, scholarships/grants, and tuition waivers (full) also available. Support available to part-time students. Financial award applicants required to submit CSS PROFILE. *Unit head:* Dr. John Kopper, Chair, 603-646-3281. *Application contact:* Wanda Bachmann, Administrative Assistant, 603-646-2912, Fax: 603-646-2912, E-mail: wanda.bachmann@dartmouth.edu.

Duke University, Graduate School, Program in Literature, Durham, NC 27708. Offers PhD. *Faculty:* 24 full-time. *Students:* 48 full-time (24 women); includes 13 minority (4 African Americans, 4 Asian Americans or Pacific Islanders, 5 Hispanic Americans), 12 international. 161 applicants, 4% accepted, 5 enrolled. In 2007, 3 doctorates awarded. *Degree requirements:* For doctorate, 2 foreign languages, thesis/dissertation. *Entrance requirements:* For doctorate, GRE General Test. Additional exam requirements/recommendations for international students: Required—TOEFL (minimum score 550 paper-based; 213 computer-based; 83 iBT), IELTS (minimum score 7). *Application deadline:* For fall admission, 12/15 priority date for domestic and international students. Application fee: $75. *Financial support:* Fellowships, research assistantships, teaching assistantships, Federal Work-Study available. Financial award application deadline: 12/31. *Unit head:* Toril Moi, Director of Graduate Studies, 919-684-4233, Fax: 919-684-3598, E-mail: johns194@duke.edu.

Emory University, Graduate School of Arts and Sciences, Department of Comparative Literature, Atlanta, GA 30322-1100. Offers comparative literature (PhD); English (Certificate); French (Certificate); Middle Eastern studies (PhD); philosophy (Certificate); psychoanalytic studies (PhD); religion (PhD); Spanish (Certificate); women studies (Certificate). *Degree requirements:* For doctorate, 2 foreign languages, comprehensive exam, thesis/dissertation. *Entrance requirements:* For doctorate, GRE General Test, minimum GPA of 3.0. Additional exam requirements/recommendations for international students: Required—TOEFL. Electronic applications accepted. *Faculty research:* Literary theory, psychoanalysis trauma and testimony, literature and religion, literature and technology, literature and philosophy, politics and global culture, literature and aesthetics.

Emory University, Graduate School of Arts and Sciences, Department of Spanish and Portuguese, Atlanta, GA 30322-1100. Offers comparative literature (Certificate); film studies (Certificate); Spanish (PhD); women's studies (Certificate). *Degree requirements:* For doctorate, 2 foreign languages, comprehensive exam, thesis/dissertation. *Entrance requirements:* For doctorate, GRE General Test. Additional exam requirements/recommendations for international students: Required—TOEFL. Electronic applications accepted. *Faculty research:* Spanish literature, Spanish-American literature, literary theory, criticism, cultural studies.

Fairleigh Dickinson University, Metropolitan Campus, University College: Arts, Sciences, and Professional Studies, Department of English, Philosophy, and Humanities, Program in English and Literature, Teaneck, NJ 07666-1914. Offers MA. *Students:* Average age 29. 4 applicants, 100% accepted, 3 enrolled. In 2007, 1 degree awarded. Application fee: $40. *Expenses:* Tuition: Part-time $869 per credit. Tuition and fees vary according to degree level, campus/location and program. *Unit head:* Dr. Jason Scorza, Director, Department of English, Philosophy, and Humanities, 201-692-2000.

Florida Atlantic University, Dorothy F. Schmidt College of Arts and Letters, Department of Languages and Linguistics, Boca Raton, FL 33431-0991. Offers comparative literature (MA); French (MA); German (MA); Spanish (MA); teaching French (MAT); teaching German (MAT); teaching Spanish (MAT). Part-time programs available. *Degree requirements:* For master's, one foreign language, comprehensive exam, thesis optional. *Entrance requirements:* For master's, GRE General Test, minimum GPA of 3.0. *Faculty research:* Modern European studies, modern Latin America, medieval Europe.

Graduate School and University Center of the City University of New York, Graduate Studies, Program in Comparative Literature, New York, NY 10016-4039. Offers comparative literature (MA, PhD), including classics (PhD), German (PhD), Italian (PhD). *Faculty:* 16 full-time (3 women). *Students:* 98 full-time (59 women), 11 part-time (9 women); includes 7 minority (2 Asian Americans or Pacific Islanders, 5 Hispanic Americans), 26 international. Average age 36. 66 applicants, 35% accepted, 14 enrolled. In 2007, 6 master's, 5 doctorates awarded. Terminal master's awarded for partial completion of doctoral program. *Degree requirements:* For master's, 2 foreign languages, comprehensive exam, thesis; for doctorate, 3 foreign languages, comprehensive exam, thesis/dissertation. *Entrance requirements:* For master's and doctorate, GRE General Test. Additional exam requirements/recommendations for international students: Required—TOEFL. *Application deadline:* For fall admission, 4/15 for domestic students; for spring admission, 11/15 for domestic students. Application fee: $125. Electronic applications accepted. *Financial support:* In 2007–08, 63 students received support, including 53 fellowships, 5 research assistantships, 14 teaching assistantships; career-related internships or fieldwork, Federal Work-Study, institutionally sponsored loans, and tuition waivers (full and partial) also available. Financial award application deadline: 2/1; financial award applicants required to submit FAFSA. *Unit head:* Dr. Andre Aciman, Executive Officer, 212-817-8170, Fax: 212-817-1509, E-mail: aaciman@gc.cuny.edu.

Harvard University, Graduate School of Arts and Sciences, Department of Comparative Literature, Cambridge, MA 02138. Offers comparative literature (PhD); oral literature (PhD). *Degree requirements:* For doctorate, 4 foreign languages, thesis/dissertation, written and oral exams. *Entrance requirements:* For doctorate, GRE General Test, GRE Subject Test (recommended), sample of written work. Additional exam requirements/recommendations for international students: Required—TOEFL. *Expenses:* Tuition: Full-time $31,456. Full-time tuition and fees vary according to program and student level.

Hofstra University, College of Liberal Arts and Sciences, Department of Comparative Literature and Languages, Hempstead, NY 11549. Offers applied linguistics (MA). Part-time programs available. *Faculty:* 2 full-time (0 women), 3 part-time/adjunct (0 women). *Students:* 1 (woman) full-time, 3 part-time (all women), 1 international. Average age 27. 12 applicants, 75% accepted, 0 enrolled. In 2007, 10 degrees awarded. *Degree requirements:* For master's, thesis, BA, 36 credits, capstone. *Entrance requirements:* For master's, bachelor's degree in related area, interview, 2 letters of recommendation. Additional exam requirements/recommendations for international students: Required—TOEFL (minimum score 550 paper-based; 213 computer-based). *Application deadline:* Applications are processed on a rolling basis. Application fee: $60. Electronic applications accepted. *Expenses:* Tuition: Full-time $14,220; part-time $820 per credit. Required fees: $970; $165 per term. Tuition and fees vary according to program. *Financial support:* Fellowships with tuition reimbursements, research assistantships with full and partial tuition reimbursements, Federal Work-Study, institutionally sponsored loans, scholarships/grants, tuition waivers (full and partial), and unspecified assistantships available. Support available to part-time students. Financial award applicants required to submit FAFSA. *Faculty research:* Second language acquisition, second language writing. *Unit head:* Dr. Robert A. Leonard, Chairperson, 516-463-5440, E-mail: cclral@hofstra.edu. *Application contact:* Carol Drummer, Dean of Graduate Admissions, 516-463-4876, Fax: 516-463-4664, E-mail: gradstudent@hofstra.edu.

Indiana State University, School of Graduate Studies, College of Arts and Sciences, Department of English, Terre Haute, IN 47809-1401. Offers English teaching (MA); history (MA); literature (MA). Part-time and evening/weekend programs available. *Faculty:* 16 full-time (4 women), 7 part-time/adjunct (2 women). *Students:* 12 full-time (10 women), 16 part-time (11 women); includes 1 minority (African American) Average age 32. 11 applicants, 100% accepted, 6 enrolled. In 2007, 14 degrees awarded. *Degree requirements:* For master's, one foreign language, thesis optional. *Entrance requirements:* For master's, minimum GPA of 2.75 in all English courses above freshman level. Additional exam requirements/recommendations for international students: Required—TOEFL (minimum score 550 paper-based). *Application deadline:* For fall admission, 7/1 priority date for domestic students; for spring admission, 11/1 priority date for domestic students. Applications are processed on a rolling basis. Application fee: $35. Electronic applications accepted. *Expenses:* Tuition, state resident: full-time $7,056; part-time $294 per semester hour. Tuition, nonresident: full-time $14,016; part-time $584 per semester hour. Required fees: $175 per semester. *Financial support:* In 2007–08, 11 teaching assistantships with partial tuition reimbursements (averaging $3,000 per year) were awarded; career-related internships or fieldwork, Federal Work-Study, and tuition waivers (partial) also available. Support available to part-time students. Financial award application deadline: 3/1; financial award applicants required to submit FAFSA. *Unit head:* Dr. Robert Perrin, Interim Chairperson, 812-237-3160.

Indiana University Bloomington, University Graduate School, College of Arts and Sciences, Department of Comparative Literature, Bloomington, IN 47405-7000. Offers MA, MAT, PhD. Part-time programs available. *Faculty:* 6 full-time (3 women), 18 part-time/adjunct (11 women). *Students:* 39 full-time (28 women), 10 part-time (8 women); includes 5 minority (1 African American, 1 American Indian/Alaska Native, 2 Asian Americans or Pacific Islanders, 1 Hispanic American), 14 international. Average age 32. 58 applicants, 17% accepted, 4 enrolled. In 2007, 4 master's, 2 doctorates awarded. *Median time to degree:* Of those who began their doctoral program in fall 1999, 20% received their degree in 8 years or less. *Degree requirements:* For master's, 2 foreign languages, comprehensive exam (for some programs), thesis (for some programs); for doctorate, 3 foreign languages, comprehensive exam, thesis/dissertation. *Entrance requirements:* For master's, GRE, proficiency in 1 foreign language, writing sample; for doctorate, GRE, proficiency in 2 foreign languages, writing sample. Additional exam requirements/recommendations for international students: Required—TOEFL (minimum score 550 paper-based; 213 computer-based; 79 iBT). *Application deadline:* For fall admission, 1/15 for domestic students, 12/15 priority date for international students. Application fee: $50 ($60 for international students). Electronic applications accepted. *Financial support:* Fellowships with full tuition reimbursements, research assistantships with partial tuition reimbursements, teaching assistantships with full tuition reimbursements, Federal Work-Study and unspecified assistantships available. *Faculty research:* East-West literary relations, film studies, translation, medieval studies, comparative arts. *Unit head:* Eileen Julien, Head, 812-855-8422, Fax: 812-855-2688, E-mail: ejulien@indiana.edu. *Application contact:* Connie May, Graduate Secretary, 812-855-9602, Fax: 812-855-2688, E-mail: csmay@indiana.edu.

The Johns Hopkins University, Zanvyl Krieger School of Arts and Sciences, Humanities Center, Baltimore, MD 21218-2699. Offers PhD. Part-time programs available. *Faculty:* 5 full-time (2 women), 5 part-time/adjunct (1 woman). *Students:* 23 full-time (12 women), 1 part-time; includes 2 minority (both Asian Americans or Pacific Islanders), 6 international. Average age 24. 56 applicants, 5% accepted, 2 enrolled. In 2007, 2 degrees awarded. *Median time to degree:* Of those who began their doctoral program in fall 1999, 67% received their degree in 8 years or less. *Degree requirements:* For doctorate, 2 foreign languages, thesis/dissertation. *Entrance requirements:* For doctorate, GRE General Test, samples of written work. Additional exam requirements/recommendations for international students: Recommended—IELTS. *Application deadline:* For fall admission, 1/15 for domestic and international students. Application fee: $65. Electronic applications accepted. *Financial support:* In 2007–08, 20 students received support, including 4 fellowships with full tuition reimbursements available (averaging $16,000 per year), 1 research assistantship with full tuition reimbursement available (averaging $16,000 per year), 7 teaching assistantships with full tuition reimbursements available (averaging $16,000 per year); Federal Work-Study, institutionally sponsored loans, tuition waivers (full), and health insurance for full-time students also available. Financial award application deadline: 3/14; financial award applicants required to submit FAFSA. *Unit head:* Ruth Leys, Chair, 410-516-7368, Fax: 410-516-4897, E-mail: leys@jhu.edu. *Application contact:* Marva Philip, Administrator, 410-516-7619, Fax: 410-516-4897, E-mail: mphilip@jhu.edu.

Kent State University, College of Arts and Sciences, Department of English, Kent, OH 44242-0001. Offers comparative literature (MA); creative writing (MFA); English (PhD); English for teachers (MA); literature and writing (MA); rhetoric and composition (PhD); teaching English as a second language (MA). Part-time programs available. *Faculty:* 46 full-time (23 women). *Students:* 107 full-time (59 women), 15 part-time (8 women); includes 19 minority (1 African American, 17 Asian Americans or Pacific Islanders, 1 Hispanic American). Average age 33. 105 applicants, 80% accepted, 35 enrolled. In 2007, 34 master's, 1 doctorate awarded. Terminal master's awarded for partial completion of doctoral program. *Median time to degree:* Of those who began their doctoral program in fall 1999, 50% received their degree in 8 years or less. *Degree requirements:* For master's, one foreign language, thesis optional; for doctorate, one foreign language, thesis/dissertation, qualifying exams. *Entrance requirements:* For master's and doctorate, GRE General Test, writing sample, letters of recommendation. Additional exam requirements/recommendations for international students: Required—TOEFL (minimum score 600 paper-based). *Application deadline:* For fall admission, 2/1 priority date for domestic and international students. Applications are processed on a rolling basis. Application fee: $30. Electronic applications accepted. *Financial support:* In 2007–08, 2 fellowships with full tuition reimbursements (averaging $12,000 per year), 55 teaching assistantships with full tuition reimbursements (averaging $11,020 per year) were awarded; research assistantships with full tuition reimbursements, Federal Work-Study, institutionally sponsored loans, scholarships/grants, traineeships, health care benefits, and unspecified assistantships also available. Financial award application deadline: 2/1. *Faculty research:* British and American literature, textual editing, rhetoric and composition, cultural studies, linguistic and critical theories. *Unit head:* Ronald Corthell, Chair, 330-672-3211, Fax: 330-672-3152, E-mail: rcorthel@kent.edu. *Application contact:* Ray Craig, Information Contact, 330-672-1755, E-mail: rcraig2@kent.edu.

See Close-Up on page 567.

Long Island University, Brooklyn Campus, Richard L. Conolly College of Liberal Arts and Sciences, Department of English, Brooklyn, NY 11201-8423. Offers English literature (MA); professional and creative writing (MA); teaching of writing (MA). Part-time and evening/weekend programs available. *Degree requirements:* For master's, thesis or alternative. *Entrance requirements:* For master's, 2 letters of recommendation. Additional exam requirements/recommendations for international students: Required—TOEFL (minimum score 550 paper-based; 173 computer-based). Electronic applications accepted.

See Close-Up on page 569.

Louisiana State University and Agricultural and Mechanical College, Graduate School, College of Arts and Sciences, Interdepartmental Program in Comparative Literature, Baton Rouge, LA 70803. Offers MA, PhD. *Students:* 13 full-time (10 women), 5 part-time (2 women); includes 3 minority (1 Asian American or Pacific Islander, 2 Hispanic Americans), 3 international. Average age 36. 1 applicant, 300% accepted, 2 enrolled. In 2007, 1 master's, 1 doctorate awarded. Terminal master's awarded for partial completion of doctoral program. *Degree requirements:* For master's, 2 foreign languages, thesis optional; for doctorate, 2 foreign languages, thesis/dissertation. *Entrance requirements:* For master's and doctorate, GRE General Test, minimum GPA of 3.0. Additional exam requirements/recommendations for international students: Required—TOEFL (minimum score 550 paper-based; 213 computer-based; 79 iBT). *Application deadline:* For fall admission, 7/1 priority date for domestic students, 5/15 for international students; for spring admission, 10/15 for international students. Applications are processed on a rolling basis. Application fee: $25. Electronic applications accepted. *Financial support:* In 2007–08, 14 students received support, including 11 teaching assistantships with full and partial tuition reimbursements available (averaging $15,856 per year); fellowships with full tuition reimbursements available, research assistantships with full and partial tuition reimbursements available, health care benefits and unspecified assistantships also available. Financial award application deadline: 3/15; financial award applicants required to submit FAFSA. *Faculty research:* World literature, Islamic studies, Dante, Foucault. *Unit head:* Dr. Greg Stone, Director, 225-578-6627, Fax: 225-578-6628, E-mail: stone@lsu.edu.

New York University, Graduate School of Arts and Science, Department of Comparative Literature, New York, NY 10012-1019. Offers MA, PhD. Part-time programs available. *Faculty:* 15 full-time (4 women). *Students:* 41 full-time (25 women), 14 part-time (6 women); includes 7 minority (2 African Americans, 2 Asian Americans or Pacific Islanders, 3 Hispanic Americans), 21 international. Average age 31. 212 applicants, 7% accepted, 9 enrolled. In 2007, 5 master's, 9 doctorates awarded. *Degree requirements:* For master's, 2 foreign languages, thesis; for doctorate, 3 foreign languages, thesis/dissertation. *Entrance requirements:* For master's and doctorate, GRE General Test. Additional exam requirements/recommendations for international students: Required—TOEFL. *Application deadline:* For fall admission, 1/4 for domestic students. Application fee: $85. *Financial support:* Fellowships with tuition reimbursements, teaching assistantships with tuition reimbursements, Federal Work-Study, institutionally sponsored loans, scholarships/grants, health care benefits, and unspecified assistantships available. Financial award application deadline: 1/4; financial award applicants required to submit FAFSA. *Faculty research:* European and non-European literature and culture, comparative poetics, cultural studies, colonial and post-colonial literature and theory, philosophical issues and literary theory. *Unit head:* Nancy Ruttenburg, Chair, 212-998-8790, Fax: 212-995-4377, E-mail: complit.info@nyu.edu. *Application contact:* Mark J. Sanders, Director of Graduate Studies, 212-998-8790, Fax: 212-995-4377, E-mail: complit.info@nyu.edu.

Northwestern University, The Graduate School, Interdepartmental Degree Programs, Program in Literature, Evanston, IL 60208. Offers MA. Part-time programs available. *Degree requirements:* For master's, thesis. *Entrance requirements:* For master's, writing sample. Additional exam requirements/recommendations for international students: Required—TOEFL. *Faculty research:* Sociology of literature, creative writing, women writers, modernism and post-modernism.

Northwestern University, The Graduate School, Judd A. and Marjorie Weinberg College of Arts and Sciences, Department of French and Italian, Evanston, IL 60208. Offers eighteenth-century studies (Certificate); French (PhD); French and comparative literature (PhD); Italian studies (Certificate). Admissions and degrees offered through The Graduate School. *Degree requirements:* For doctorate, one foreign language, thesis/dissertation, written and oral exams. *Entrance requirements:* For doctorate, GRE, writing sample, cassette recording. Additional exam requirements/recommendations for international students: Required—TOEFL. *Faculty research:* Francophone studies, 18th century contemporary theory.

Northwestern University, The Graduate School, Judd A. and Marjorie Weinberg College of Arts and Sciences, Program in Comparative Literary Studies, Evanston, IL 60208. Offers PhD. Admissions and degrees offered through The Graduate School. Part-time programs available. *Degree requirements:* For doctorate, 2 foreign languages, thesis/dissertation, preliminary exams. *Entrance requirements:* For doctorate, GRE General Test, sample of written work. Additional exam requirements/recommendations for international students: Required—TOEFL. *Faculty*

Comparative Literature

Northwestern University (continued)
research: The novel, modernism, post-colonial literature and theory, literature and the arts, Middle Ages and Renaissance, literature and philosophy.

Oklahoma City University, Petree College of Arts and Sciences, Program in Liberal Arts, Oklahoma City, OK 73106-1402. Offers art (MLA); general studies (MLA); leadership/ management (MLA); literature (MLA); mass communications (MLA); philosophy (MLA); writing (MLA). Part-time and evening/weekend programs available. *Faculty:* 18 full-time (7 women), 14 part-time/adjunct (4 women). *Students:* 24 full-time (18 women), 23 part-time (17 women); includes 6 minority (3 African Americans, 1 American Indian/Alaska Native, 1 Asian American or Pacific Islander, 1 Hispanic American), 14 international. Average age 31. 20 applicants, 95% accepted. In 2007, 13 degrees awarded. *Degree requirements:* For master's, comprehensive exam, thesis optional. *Entrance requirements:* Additional exam requirements/ recommendations for international students: Required—TOEFL. *Application deadline:* For fall admission, 8/22 for domestic students; for spring admission, 1/15 for domestic students. Applications are processed on a rolling basis. Application fee: $30 ($70 for international students). *Expenses:* Tuition: Full-time $14,040; part-time $780 per hour. Required fees: $881; $32 per hour. *Financial support:* Fellowships with partial tuition reimbursements, career-related internships or fieldwork, Federal Work-Study, institutionally sponsored loans, and tuition waivers (partial) available. Support available to part-time students. Financial award application deadline: 8/1; financial award applicants required to submit FAFSA. *Unit head:* Dr. Regina Benuett, Director, 405-208-5178, Fax: 405-208-5451, E-mail: rebeunett@okcu.edu. *Application contact:* Leslie McKenzie, Director, Graduate Admissions, 800-633-7242, Fax: 405-208-5356, E-mail: gadmissions@okcu.edu.

Penn State University Park, Graduate School, College of the Liberal Arts, Department of Languages and Literature, State College, University Park, PA 16802-1503. Offers comparative literature (MA, PhD); Russian and comparative literature (MA). *Expenses:* Tuition, state resident: full-time $14,738; part-time $614 per credit. Tuition, nonresident: full-time $26,050; part-time $1,085 per credit. Tuition and fees vary according to course load, program and student level. *Unit head:* Dr. Caroline D. Eckhardt, Head, 814-863-0589, Fax: 814-863-8882, E-mail: e82@ psu.edu.

Princeton University, Graduate School, Department of Comparative Literature, Princeton, NJ 08544-1019. Offers PhD. *Degree requirements:* For doctorate, variable foreign language requirement, thesis/dissertation. *Entrance requirements:* For doctorate, GRE General Test, GRE Subject Test, sample of written work. Additional exam requirements/recommendations for international students: Required—TOEFL (minimum score 600 paper-based; 250 computer-based). Electronic applications accepted.

Purdue University, Graduate School, College of Liberal Arts, Program in Comparative Literature, West Lafayette, IN 47907. Offers MA, PhD. Part-time programs available. *Degree requirements:* For master's, one foreign language; for doctorate, 2 foreign languages, thesis/dissertation. *Entrance requirements:* For master's, GRE General Test, writing sample; for doctorate, GRE General Test. Additional exam requirements/recommendations for international students: Required—TOEFL. Electronic applications accepted. *Faculty research:* Theory and criticism, philosophy and aesthetics, East Asian literature, postcolonial literature, classics.

Rutgers, The State University of New Jersey, New Brunswick, Graduate School, Program in Comparative Literature, New Brunswick, NJ 08901-1281. Offers MA, PhD. Part-time programs available. Terminal master's awarded for partial completion of doctoral program. *Degree requirements:* For master's, comprehensive exam; for doctorate, 3 foreign languages, thesis/dissertation, written and oral exams. *Entrance requirements:* For doctorate, GRE General Test, GRE Subject Test (recommended). Additional exam requirements/recommendations for international students: Required—TOEFL. Electronic applications accepted. *Faculty research:* Genres and periods, modern literary theory, psychoanalytic approaches to literature, literature and gender, cultural studies.

San Francisco State University, Division of Graduate Studies, College of Humanities, Department of Comparative and World Literature, San Francisco, CA 94132-1722. Offers comparative literature (MA). Part-time programs available. *Degree requirements:* For master's, one foreign language. *Application deadline:* Applications are processed on a rolling basis. *Unit head:* Dr. David Leitño, Chair, 415-338-2068. *Application contact:* Dr. Dane Johnson, Graduate Coordinator, 415-338-2068, E-mail: danej@sfsu.edu.

San Jose State University, Graduate Studies and Research, College of Humanities and the Arts, Department of English and Comparative Literature, San Jose, CA 95192-0001. Offers creative writing (MFA); literature (MA); secondary English education (Certificate). *Students:* 37 full-time (23 women), 57 part-time (37 women); includes 22 minority (5 African Americans, 1 American Indian/Alaska Native, 11 Asian Americans or Pacific Islanders, 5 Hispanic Americans), 2 international. Average age 33. 95 applicants, 68% accepted, 42 enrolled. In 2007, 18 degrees awarded. *Degree requirements:* For master's, one foreign language, thesis or alternative. *Entrance requirements:* For master's, GRE. Additional exam requirements/ recommendations for international students: Required—TOEFL. *Application deadline:* For fall admission, 6/29 for domestic students; for spring admission, 11/30 for domestic students. Applications are processed on a rolling basis. Application fee: $59. Electronic applications accepted. *Financial support:* Applicants required to submit FAFSA. *Unit head:* John Engell, Chair, 408-924-4499, Fax: 408-924-4580, E-mail: john.engell@email.sjsu.edu. *Application contact:* Dr. Noelle Brada-Williams, Graduate Coordinator, 408-924-4439.

Stanford University, School of Humanities and Sciences, Department of Comparative Literature, Stanford, CA 94305-9991. Offers PhD. *Degree requirements:* For doctorate, 3 foreign languages, thesis/dissertation, qualification procedures. *Entrance requirements:* For doctorate, GRE General Test, GRE Subject Test. Additional exam requirements/recommendations for international students: Required—TOEFL. Electronic applications accepted.

Stanford University, School of Humanities and Sciences, Program in Modern Thought and Literature, Stanford, CA 94305-9991. Offers PhD. *Degree requirements:* For doctorate, 2 foreign languages, thesis/dissertation, qualifying paper, oral exam. *Entrance requirements:* For doctorate, GRE General Test. Additional exam requirements/recommendations for international students: Required—TOEFL. Electronic applications accepted.

State University of New York at Binghamton, Graduate School, School of Arts and Sciences, Department of Comparative Literature, Binghamton, NY 13902-6000. Offers MA, PhD. Part-time programs available. *Faculty:* 9 full-time (5 women), 2 part-time/adjunct (1 woman). *Students:* 32 full-time (18 women), 33 part-time (20 women); includes 11 minority (2 African Americans, 1 American Indian/Alaska Native, 4 Asian Americans or Pacific Islanders, 4 Hispanic Americans), 27 international. Average age 34. 43 applicants, 60% accepted, 11 enrolled. In 2007, 13 master's, 8 doctorates awarded. Terminal master's awarded for partial completion of doctoral program. *Degree requirements:* For master's, 2 foreign languages, thesis or alternative, written exam; for doctorate, 3 foreign languages, comprehensive exam, thesis/dissertation. *Entrance requirements:* For master's and doctorate, GRE General Test, GRE Subject Test. Additional exam requirements/recommendations for international students: Required—TOEFL. *Application deadline:* For fall admission, 4/15 priority date for domestic students, 1/15 priority date for international students; for spring admission, 11/1 for domestic students, 10/15 priority date for international students. Applications are processed on a rolling basis. Application fee: $60. Electronic applications accepted. *Financial support:* In 2007–08, 30 students received support, including 3 fellowships with full tuition reimbursements available (averaging $11,250 per year), 15 teaching assistantships with full tuition reimbursements available (averaging $14,500 per year); research assistantships, career-related internships or fieldwork, Federal Work-Study, institutionally sponsored loans, tuition waivers (full and partial), and unspecified assistantships also available. Support available to part-time students. Financial award application deadline: 2/15. *Unit head:* Dr. Luiza Moreira, Chairperson, 607-777-3673, E-mail: lmoreira@ binghamton.edu.

Stony Brook University, State University of New York, Graduate School, College of Arts and Sciences, Department of Comparative Literary and Cultural Studies, Stony Brook, NY 11794. Offers comparative literature (MA, PhD); cultural studies (PhD). Evening/weekend programs available. *Faculty:* 7 full-time (2 women). *Students:* 28 full-time (21 women), 9 part-time (8 women); includes 6 minority (1 African American, 5 Asian Americans or Pacific Islanders), 15 international. Average age 30. 58 applicants, 17% accepted. In 2007, 3 master's, 2 doctorates awarded. Terminal master's awarded for partial completion of doctoral program. *Degree requirements:* For master's, 2 foreign languages, exam; for doctorate, 3 foreign languages, comprehensive exam, thesis/dissertation. *Entrance requirements:* For master's and doctorate, GRE General Test, minimum GPA of 3.5 in major, 3.0 overall. Additional exam requirements/recommendations for international students: Required—TOEFL. *Application deadline:* For fall admission, 1/15 for domestic students. Application fee: $60. *Financial support:* In 2007–08, 17 teaching assistantships were awarded; fellowships, research assistantships also available. *Faculty research:* Literary theory, interdisciplinary studies, literary history. *Unit head:* Dr. Robert Harvey, Chairman, 631-632-7456.

Announcement: The Department of Comparative Literary and Cultural Studies (CLCS) at Stony Brook offers a collegial environment for graduate studies, fostering innovative approaches to comparative literary and cultural studies. Core and affiliated faculty members, as well as the diverse graduate student body, work in a broad range of cultural and linguistic traditions and disciplinary and interdisciplinary frameworks, genres, and media. With assistantship support, students become versatile teachers, and graduates have an excellent record of placement in tenure-track jobs.

See Close-Up on page 583.

Université de Montréal, Faculty of Arts and Sciences, Department of Comparative Literature, Montréal, QC H3C 3J7, Canada. Offers comparative literature (MA); literature (PhD). *Faculty:* 11 full-time (4 women), 1 (woman) part-time/adjunct. *Students:* 122 full-time (73 women), 1 (woman) part-time. 59 applicants, 34% accepted, 24 enrolled. In 2007, 16 master's, 11 doctorates awarded. *Degree requirements:* For master's, 2 foreign languages, thesis; for doctorate, 3 foreign languages, thesis/dissertation, general exam. *Entrance requirements:* For doctorate, MA with minimum B+ average. *Application deadline:* For fall admission, 2/1 priority date for domestic students; for winter admission, 11/1 priority date for domestic students; for spring admission, 2/1 priority date for domestic students. Application fee: $100. Electronic applications accepted. *Financial support:* Fellowships, research assistantships, teaching assistantships available. *Unit head:* Terry Cochran, Graduate Chairman, 514-343-7130, Fax: 514-343-2211, E-mail: terry.cochran@umontreal.ca. *Application contact:* Rodica-Livia Monnet, Chairperson, 514-343-7130, Fax: 514-343-2211, E-mail: rodica-livia.monnet@umontreal.ca.

Université de Sherbrooke, Faculty of Letters and Human Sciences, Department of Letters and Communications, Sherbrooke, QC J1K 2R1, Canada. Offers comparative Canadian literature (MA, PhD); French literature (MA, PhD); linguistics (MA); lit&erature de création (MA, PhD); theatre (MA). *Degree requirements:* For master's, thesis or alternative; for doctorate, thesis/ dissertation. *Entrance requirements:* For master's, minimum GPA of 2.8; for doctorate, minimum GPA of 3.0.

Université du Québec à Chicoutimi, Graduate Programs, Program in Literary Studies, Chicoutimi, QC G7H 2B1, Canada. Offers MA. Part-time programs available. *Degree requirements:* For master's, thesis optional. *Entrance requirements:* For master's, appropriate bachelor's degree, proficiency in French.

Université du Québec à Montréal, Graduate Programs, Program in Literary Studies, Montréal, QC H3C 3P8, Canada. Offers MA, PhD. Part-time programs available. *Degree requirements:* For master's, thesis; for doctorate, thesis/dissertation. *Entrance requirements:* For master's, appropriate bachelor's degree or equivalent, proficiency in French; for doctorate, appropriate master's degree or equivalent, proficiency in French.

Université du Québec à Montréal, Graduate Programs, Program in Semiology, Montréal, QC H3C 3P8, Canada. Offers PhD. Part-time programs available. *Degree requirements:* For doctorate, thesis/dissertation. *Entrance requirements:* For doctorate, appropriate master's degree or equivalent, proficiency in French.

Université du Québec à Rimouski, Graduate Programs, Program in Literary Studies, Rimouski, QC G5L 3A1, Canada. Offers MA, PhD. Part-time programs available. *Students:* 12 full-time, 3 part-time. *Degree requirements:* For master's, thesis or alternative. *Entrance requirements:* For master's, appropriate bachelor's degree, proficiency in French. *Application deadline:* For fall admission, 5/1 priority date for domestic students. Application fee: $50. *Financial support:* Fellowships, research assistantships, teaching assistantships available. *Unit head:* Frances Fortier, Director, 418-724-1656, Fax: 418-724-1525, E-mail: frances_fortier@uqar.ca.

Université du Québec à Trois-Rivières, Graduate Programs, Program in Literary Studies, Trois-Rivières, QC G9A 5H7, Canada. Offers MA. Part-time programs available. *Degree requirements:* For master's, thesis optional. *Entrance requirements:* For master's, appropriate bachelor's degree, proficiency in French.

Université Laval, Faculty of Letters, Department of Literature, Programs in Literary Studies, Québec, QC G1K 7P4, Canada. Offers MA, PhD. Part-time programs available. Terminal master's awarded for partial completion of doctoral program. *Degree requirements:* For master's, thesis; for doctorate, comprehensive exam, thesis/dissertation. *Entrance requirements:* For master's and doctorate, linguistics exams, knowledge of French, knowledge of a second language. Electronic applications accepted.

University at Buffalo, the State University of New York, Graduate School, College of Arts and Sciences, Department of Comparative Literature, Buffalo, NY 14260. Offers MA, PhD. Part-time programs available. Terminal master's awarded for partial completion of doctoral program. *Degree requirements:* For master's, one foreign language, exam or thesis; for doctorate, 2 foreign languages, comprehensive exam, thesis/dissertation. *Entrance requirements:* For master's and doctorate, GRE General Test, writing sample, 3 letters of recommendation. Additional exam requirements/recommendations for international students: Required—TOEFL (minimum score 550 paper-based; 213 computer-based). Electronic applications accepted. *Faculty research:* Theory; interaction between literature and philosophy; European, Francophone, African, American, and South American literature; postmodernism; postcolonialism.

University of Arkansas, Graduate School, Interdisciplinary Program in Comparative Literature and Cultural Studies, Fayetteville, AR 72701-1201. Offers classical studies (MA); comparative literature (PhD). *Students:* 7 full-time (6 women), 19 part-time (13 women); includes 4 minority (1 American Indian/Alaska Native, 3 Hispanic Americans), 12 international. In 2007, 2 master's, 1 doctorate awarded. *Degree requirements:* For master's, one foreign language, comprehensive exam, thesis optional; for doctorate, 2 foreign languages, comprehensive exam, thesis/ dissertation. *Entrance requirements:* For master's and doctorate, GRE General Test. Application fee: $40 ($50 for international students). *Financial support:* In 2007–08, 1 fellowship, 5 research assistantships, 9 teaching assistantships were awarded; Federal Work-Study and institutionally sponsored loans also available. *Faculty research:* Literary and cultural theory, cultural studies, postcolonial theory, gender studies, world literature. *Unit head:* Luis Fernando Restrepo, Director, 479-575-2951, Fax: 479-575-6795, E-mail: lrestr@uark.edu.

University of California, Berkeley, Graduate Division, College of Letters and Science, Department of Comparative Literature, Berkeley, CA 94720-1500. Offers PhD. *Degree requirements:* For doctorate, thesis/dissertation, 3 languages (department may require more for some programs), qualifying exam. *Entrance requirements:* For doctorate, GRE General Test, fluency in 1 foreign language (2 preferred), minimum GPA of 3.0, writing sample, 3 letters of recommendation. *Application deadline:* For fall admission, 12/5 for domestic students. Application fee: $70 ($90 for international students). *Financial support:* Fellowships, research assistantships, teaching assistantships, institutionally sponsored loans, tuition waivers (full and partial), and unspecified assistantships available. Financial award applicants required to submit FAFSA. *Unit head:* Eric Naiman, Chair, 510-642-6204, E-mail: naiman@berkeley.edu. *Application contact:* Erica Roberts, Student Affairs Officer, 510-642-2629, Fax: 510-642-8852, E-mail: complit@ls.berkeley.edu.

University of California, Davis, Graduate Studies, Graduate Group in Comparative Literature, Davis, CA 95616. Offers PhD. *Degree requirements:* For doctorate, 3 foreign languages, thesis/dissertation. *Entrance requirements:* For doctorate, GRE General Test, minimum GPA of 3.0. Additional exam requirements/recommendations for international students: Required—TOEFL (minimum score 550 paper-based; 213 computer-based). Electronic applications accepted. *Faculty research:* Literary criticism, literary theory, gender history and literature, genre.

University of California, Irvine, Office of Graduate Studies, School of Humanities, Department of English and Comparative Literature, Program in Comparative Literature, Irvine, CA 92697. Offers MA, PhD. *Faculty:* 9 full-time (5 women), 1 part-time/adjunct (0 women). *Students:* 54 full-time (32 women); includes 12 minority (2 American Indian/Alaska Native, 7 Asian Americans or Pacific Islanders, 3 Hispanic Americans), 2 international. Average age 31. 58 applicants, 34% accepted, 10 enrolled. In 2007, 7 master's awarded. *Degree requirements:* For master's, one foreign language; for doctorate, 2 foreign languages, thesis/dissertation. *Entrance requirements:* For doctorate, GRE General Test, minimum GPA of 3.5, sample of written work, 3 letters of recommendation. Additional exam requirements/recommendations for international students: Required—TOEFL (minimum score 550 paper-based; 213 computer-based). *Application deadline:* For fall admission, 1/15 for domestic students. Application fee: $60. Electronic applications accepted. *Financial support:* In 2007–08, fellowships with full tuition reimbursements (averaging $1,400 per year), research assistantships with full tuition reimbursements (averaging $15,000 per year), teaching assistantships with partial tuition reimbursements (averaging $14,145 per year) were awarded; institutionally sponsored loans and tuition waivers (partial) also available. Financial award application deadline: 3/2; financial award applicants required to submit FAFSA. *Faculty research:* Critical theory, feminist studies, Asian American studies. Total annual research expenditures: $99,000. *Unit head:* Director, 949-824-6718, Fax: 949-824-2916. *Application contact:* Arielle Read, Graduate Administrator, 949-824-6718, Fax: 949-824-2916, E-mail: eclgradapp@uci.edu.

University of California, Los Angeles, Graduate Division, College of Letters and Science, Department of Comparative Literature, Los Angeles, CA 90095. Offers MA, PhD. *Students:* 56 full-time (37 women); includes 13 minority (2 African Americans, 7 Asian Americans or Pacific Islanders, 4 Hispanic Americans), 5 international. Average age 29. 85 applicants, 22% accepted, 10 enrolled. In 2007, 2 master's, 6 doctorates awarded. Terminal master's awarded for partial completion of doctoral program. *Median time to degree:* Of those who began their doctoral program in fall 1999, 40% received their degree in 8 years or less. *Degree requirements:* For master's, 2 foreign languages, comprehensive exam; for doctorate, 2 foreign languages, thesis/dissertation, oral and written qualifying exams. *Entrance requirements:* For master's, GRE General Test, sample of written work, previous course work in literature, minimum GPA of 3.4 in upper-division course work, degree objective must be Ph.D. in FL literary proficiency; for doctorate, GRE General Test, sample of written work, MA in comparative literature. *Application deadline:* For fall admission, 12/15 for domestic students. Application fee: $60. Electronic applications accepted. *Expenses:* Tuition, nonresident: full-time $5,728. Required fees:$8,966. Full-time tuition and fees vary according to program and student level. *Financial support:* In 2007–08, 37 fellowships with full and partial tuition reimbursements, 12 research assistantships with full and partial tuition reimbursements, 30 teaching assistantships with full and partial tuition reimbursements were awarded; Federal Work-Study, institutionally sponsored loans, and tuition waivers (full and partial) also available. Financial award application deadline: 3/1; financial award applicants required to submit FAFSA. *Unit head:* Ali Behdad, Chair, 310-825-7650. *Application contact:* Departmental Office, 310-825-7650, E-mail: klipp@humnet.ucla.edu.

University of California, Riverside, Graduate Division, Department of Comparative Literature and Foreign Languages, Riverside, CA 92521-0102. Offers comparative literature (MA, PhD). *Faculty:* 17 full-time (9 women), 16 part-time/adjunct (13 women). *Students:* 21 full-time (17 women); includes 3 minority (all Asian Americans or Pacific Islanders), 12 international. Average age 29. 30 applicants, 23% accepted, 7 enrolled. In 2007, 8 master's awarded. Terminal master's awarded for partial completion of doctoral program. *Degree requirements:* For master's, 3 foreign languages, comprehensive exam; for doctorate, 3 foreign languages, thesis/dissertation, qualifying exams. *Entrance requirements:* For master's and doctorate, GRE General Test, minimum GPA of 3.2. Additional exam requirements/recommendations for international students: Required—TOEFL (minimum score 550 paper-based; 213 computer-based; 80 iBT). *Application deadline:* For fall admission, 1/5 for domestic students, 2/1 for international students; for winter admission, 9/1 for domestic students, 7/1 for international students; for spring admission, 12/1 for domestic students, 10/1 for international students. Applications are processed on a rolling basis. Application fee: $60 ($75 for international students). Electronic applications accepted. *Financial support:* Fellowships with partial tuition reimbursements, research assistantships, teaching assistantships with partial tuition reimbursements, career-related internships or fieldwork, Federal Work-Study, institutionally sponsored loans, and tuition waivers (full and partial) available. Financial award application deadline: 1/5; financial award applicants required to submit FAFSA. *Faculty research:* French and German Enlightenment, modern drama and theatre, contemporary critical theory, East-West comparative studies, science fiction and fantasy. *Unit head:* Dr. Thomas F. Scanlon, Chair, 951-827-1462, Fax: 951-827-2160, E-mail: thomas.scanlon@ucr.edu. *Application contact:* Dr. Marguerite Waller, Graduate Advisor, 951-827-7859, Fax: 951-827-2160, E-mail: clhsgrad@ucr.edu.

University of California, San Diego, Office of Graduate Studies, Department of Literature, Program in Comparative Literature, La Jolla, CA 92093. Offers MA, PhD. *Degree requirements:* For master's, thesis; for doctorate, thesis/dissertation. *Entrance requirements:* For master's and doctorate, GRE General Test, GRE Subject Test. Electronic applications accepted. *Faculty research:* Problems of theory and method, relationship of the humanities to the social sciences.

University of California, Santa Barbara, Graduate Division, College of Letters and Sciences, Division of Humanities and Fine Arts, Program in Comparative Literature, Santa Barbara, CA 93106. Offers comparative literature (PhD); East Asian literatures (PhD); women's studies (PhD); MA/PhD. *Faculty:* 22 full-time (18 women). *Students:* 25 full-time (19 women); includes 4 minority (2 Asian Americans or Pacific Islanders, 2 Hispanic Americans), 4 international. Average age 31. 33 applicants, 39% accepted, 8 enrolled. In 2007, 4 doctorates awarded. Terminal master's awarded for partial completion of doctoral program. *Median time to degree:* Of those who began their doctoral program in fall 1999, 25% received their degree in 8 years or less. *Degree requirements:* For doctorate, 2 foreign languages, comprehensive exam, thesis/dissertation. *Entrance requirements:* For doctorate, GRE, samples of written work, study of literature in at least 2 approved languages, demonstration of foreign language proficiency. Additional exam requirements/recommendations for international students: Required—TOEFL (minimum score 550 paper-based; 213 computer-based; 80 iBT). *Application deadline:* For fall admission, 12/15 for domestic and international students. Application fee: $60. Electronic applications accepted. *Expenses:* Tuition, nonresident: full-time $14,888. Required fees: $10,108. *Financial support:* In 2007–08, 25 students received support, including 11 fellowships with full and partial tuition reimbursements available (averaging $13,200 per year), 7 teaching assistantships with full and partial tuition reimbursements available (averaging $16,389 per year); Federal Work-Study, institutionally sponsored loans, scholarships/grants, and health care benefits also available. Financial award application deadline: 12/15; financial award applicants required to submit FAFSA. *Faculty research:* Interdisciplinary studies, literary theory, cultural studies, early-modern and modern literature, critical theory. *Unit head:* Prof. Elisabeth Weber, Chair, 805-893-2295, E-mail: weber@gss.ucsb.edu. *Application contact:* Sierra Gray, Graduate Program Assistant, 805-893-2131, Fax: 805-893-2374, E-mail: sierra@gss.ucsb.edu.

University of California, Santa Cruz, Division of Graduate Studies, Division of Humanities, Department of Literature, Santa Cruz, CA 95064. Offers MA, PhD. *Faculty:* 33 full-time (15 women). *Students:* 86. 150 applicants, 16% accepted. In 2007, 3 master's, 4 doctorates awarded. Terminal master's awarded for partial completion of doctoral program. *Degree requirements:* For master's, thesis; for doctorate, one foreign language, thesis/dissertation, qualifying exam. *Entrance requirements:* For master's, GRE General Test, writing sample, minimum GPA of 3.5; for doctorate, GRE General Test, minimum GPA of 3.5, writing sample. *Application deadline:* For fall admission, 12/1 for domestic students. Application fee: $60. Electronic applications accepted. *Expenses:* Tuition, nonresident: full-time $14,694. Required fees: $11,360. *Financial support:* Fellowships, teaching assistantships, Federal Work-Study and institutionally sponsored loans available. Financial award application deadline: 12/1. *Faculty research:* Comparative literature; German, Spanish, classical, American, and English literature. *Unit head:* Mary-Kay Gamel, Chairperson, 831-459-4129, E-mail: mkgamel@ucsc.edu. *Application contact:* Judy L. Glass, Reporting Analyst for Graduate Admissions, 831-459-5906, Fax: 831-459-4843, E-mail: jlglass@ucsc.edu.

University of Chicago, Division of the Humanities, Department of Comparative Literature, Chicago, IL 60637-1513. Offers AM, PhD. *Faculty:* 44. *Students:* 37. 88 applicants, 10% accepted, 3 enrolled.Terminal master's awarded for partial completion of doctoral program. *Degree requirements:* For master's, 2 foreign languages, thesis; for doctorate, 3 foreign languages, thesis/dissertation. *Entrance requirements:* For master's and doctorate, GRE General Test. *Application deadline:* For fall admission, 12/15 for domestic students. Application fee: $55. *Financial support:* Fellowships, Federal Work-Study and institutionally sponsored loans available. Financial award application deadline: 12/15; financial award applicants required to submit FAFSA. *Unit head:* Dr. Joshua Scodel, Head, 773-702-1234.

University of Colorado at Boulder, Graduate School, College of Arts and Sciences, Department of Comparative Literature, Boulder, CO 80309. Offers MA, PhD. *Faculty:* 3. *Students:* 19 full-time (14 women), 5 part-time (all women); includes 2 minority (1 Asian American or Pacific Islander, 1 Hispanic American), 2 international. Average age 34. 9 applicants, 78% accepted. In 2007, 5 master's, 1 doctorate awarded. Terminal master's awarded for partial completion of doctoral program. *Degree requirements:* For master's, 2 foreign languages, comprehensive exam, thesis or alternative; for doctorate, 3 foreign languages, comprehensive exam, thesis/dissertation. *Entrance requirements:* For master's, GRE General Test, minimum undergraduate GPA of 2.75; for doctorate, GRE General Test, MA in related field. *Application deadline:* For fall admission, 1/1 priority date for domestic students, 12/1 for international students. Applications are processed on a rolling basis. Application fee: $50 ($60 for international students). *Financial support:* In 2007–08, 19 fellowships (averaging $6,119 per year), 2 research assistantships (averaging $10,071 per year) were awarded; tuition waivers (full) also available. Financial award application deadline: 1/1. *Faculty research:* Enlightenment to modern literature; literary theory and history; philosophy and literature; popular culture studies; reception, translation and interpretation; gender and sexual orientation; nationalism. *Unit head:* Adeleke Adeeko, Chair, 303-492-7550, Fax: 303-492-2311, E-mail: adeleke.adeeko@colorado.edu. *Application contact:* Administrative Assistant, 303-492-7376, Fax: 303-492-2311, E-mail: complit@colorado.edu.

University of Connecticut, Graduate School, College of Liberal Arts and Sciences, Department of Modern and Classical Languages, Field of Comparative Literature and Cultural Studies, Storrs, CT 06269. Offers MA, PhD. *Faculty:* 24 full-time (11 women). *Students:* 15 full-time (8 women), 7 part-time (5 women); includes 4 minority (all Hispanic Americans), 4 international. Average age 35. 31 applicants, 19% accepted, 6 enrolled. In 2007, 2 master's, 1 doctorate awarded. Terminal master's awarded for partial completion of doctoral program. *Degree requirements:* For master's, comprehensive exam; for doctorate, thesis/dissertation. *Entrance requirements:* For master's and doctorate, GRE General Test, GRE Subject Test. Additional exam requirements/recommendations for international students: Required—TOEFL (minimum score 550 paper-based; 213 computer-based). *Application deadline:* For fall admission, 2/1 priority date for domestic and international students; for spring admission, 11/1 for domestic students, 10/1 for international students. Applications are processed on a rolling basis. Application fee: $55. Electronic applications accepted. *Expenses:* Tuition, state resident: part-time $469 per credit hour. Tuition, nonresident: part-time $1,218 per credit hour. *Financial support:* In 2007–08, 1 research assistantship, 9 teaching assistantships with full tuition reimbursements were awarded; fellowships, Federal Work-Study, scholarships/grants, health care benefits, and unspecified assistantships also available. Financial award application deadline: 2/1; financial award applicants required to submit FAFSA. *Unit head:* Lucy S. McNeece, Co-Chair, 860-486-3315, E-mail: lucy.mcneece@uconn.edu.

See Close-Up on page 587.

University of Dallas, Braniff Graduate School of Liberal Arts, Institute of Philosophic Studies, Program in Literature, Irving, TX 75062-4736. Offers PhD. *Faculty:* 1 full-time (0 women), 5 part-time/adjunct (3 women). *Students:* 20 full-time (9 women), 5 part-time (1 woman); includes 3 minority (1 American Indian/Alaska Native, 2 Hispanic Americans). Average age 29. 11 applicants, 55% accepted, 5 enrolled. In 2007, 1 degree awarded. *Degree requirements:* For doctorate, 2 foreign languages, comprehensive exam, thesis/dissertation, qualifying exams. *Entrance requirements:* For doctorate, GRE General Test. Additional exam requirements/recommendations for international students: Required—TOEFL. *Application deadline:* For fall admission, 2/15 priority date for domestic students. Application fee: $50. *Expenses:* Tuition: Part-time $600 per credit. Required fees: $15 per credit. *Financial support:* In 2007–08, 19 students received support. Scholarships/grants available. Financial award application deadline: 2/15. *Faculty research:* Medieval studies, modern literature, Renaissance, Shakespeare. *Unit head:* Dr. John Alvis, Director, 972-721-5365, Fax: 972-721-4007, E-mail: alvis@udallas.edu. *Application contact:* Graduate Coordinator, 972-721-5106, Fax: 972-721-5280, E-mail: graduate@acad.udallas.edu.

University of Georgia, Graduate School, College of Arts and Sciences, Department of Comparative Literature, Athens, GA 30602. Offers MA, PhD. *Faculty:* 19 full-time (8 women). *Students:* 26 full-time (14 women), 7 part-time (2 women); includes 1 minority (Hispanic American), 8 international. 25 applicants, 40% accepted, 4 enrolled. In 2007, 2 master's, 1 doctorate awarded. *Degree requirements:* For master's, 2 foreign languages, thesis; for doctorate, one foreign language, thesis/dissertation. *Entrance requirements:* For master's and doctorate, GRE General Test. *Application deadline:* For fall admission, 7/1 priority date for domestic students; for spring admission, 11/15 for domestic students. Application fee: $50. Electronic applications accepted. *Financial support:* Fellowships, research assistantships, teaching assistantships, unspecified assistantships available. *Unit head:* Dr. James H. McGregor, Department Co-Head, 706-542-0420, E-mail: mcgregor@uga.edu. *Application contact:* Dr. Thomas Cerbu, Graduate Advisor, 706-542-2263, Fax: 706-542-2155, E-mail: tcerbu@uga.edu.

University of Guelph, Graduate Program Services, College of Arts, School of English and Theatre Studies, Joint Program in Literary Studies/Theatre Studies in English, Guelph, ON N1G 2W1, Canada. Offers PhD. Part-time programs available. *Faculty:* 30 full-time (15 women). *Students:* 22 full-time (10 women), 1 (woman) part-time; includes 1 African American, 1 Asian American or Pacific Islander. 31 applicants, 35% accepted, 6 enrolled. In 2007, 1 degree awarded. *Degree requirements:* For doctorate, one foreign language, comprehensive exam, thesis/dissertation. *Entrance requirements:* For doctorate, MA, 3 letters of reference, writing samples, resumé, minimum A- average in graduate course work. Additional exam requirements/recommendations for international students: Required—TOEFL. *Application deadline:* For fall admission, 2/1 priority date for domestic students, 2/1 for international students. Application fee: $85. Electronic applications accepted. *Financial support:* In 2007–08, 6 students received support, including research assistantships (averaging $9,212 per year), teaching assistantships (averaging $9,212 per year); tuition waivers (full) also available. Financial award application deadline: 2/15. *Faculty research:* Canadian studies, Early Modern studies, Postcolonial studies, studies in gender and genre, 19th Century studies. Total annual

Comparative Literature

University of Guelph (continued)

research expenditures: $500,000. *Application contact:* Dr. Daniel O'Quinn, Graduate Coordinator, 519-824-4120 Ext. 53250, Fax: 519-766-0844, E-mail: doquinn@uoguelph.ca.

University of Illinois at Urbana–Champaign, Graduate College, College of Liberal Arts and Sciences, School of Literatures, Cultures and Linguistics, Program in Comparative and World Literature, Champaign, IL 61820. Offers comparative literature (MA, PhD). *Faculty:* 6 full-time (5 women), 1 (woman) part-time/adjunct. *Students:* 21 full-time (16 women), 17 part-time (14 women); includes 3 minority (1 Asian American or Pacific Islander, 2 Hispanic Americans), 19 international. 35 applicants, 40% accepted, 3 enrolled. In 2007, 9 master's awarded. *Degree requirements:* For master's, 2 foreign languages; for doctorate, 3 foreign languages, thesis/dissertation. *Entrance requirements:* For master's, minimum GPA of 3.0. *Application deadline:* For fall admission, 1/19 for domestic students; for spring admission, 1/19 for domestic students. Applications are processed on a rolling basis. Application fee: $60 ($75 for international students). Electronic applications accepted. *Financial support:* In 2007–08, 6 fellowships, 2 research assistantships, 27 teaching assistantships were awarded. Financial award application deadline: 2/15. *Unit head:* Lawrence R. Schehr, Director, 217-333-4987, Fax: 217-244-4019. *Application contact:* Lynn Stanke, Secretary, 217-244-6269, Fax: 217-244-4019, E-mail: stanke@uiuc.edu.

The University of Iowa, Graduate College, College of Liberal Arts and Sciences, Department of Cinema and Comparative Literature, Program in Comparative Literature, Iowa City, IA 52242-1316. Offers MA, PhD. *Students:* 5 full-time (3 women), 6 part-time (all women), 6 international. 16 applicants, 38% accepted, 3 enrolled. In 2007, 2 master's, 1 doctorate awarded. *Degree requirements:* For master's, thesis optional, exam; for doctorate, comprehensive exam, thesis/dissertation. *Entrance requirements:* For master's and doctorate, GRE General Test, minimum GPA of 3.0. Additional exam requirements/recommendations for international students: Required—TOEFL (minimum score 520 paper-based; 213 computer-based; 81 iBT). *Application deadline:* For fall admission, 1/11 priority date for domestic and international students. Application fee: $60 ($85 for international students). Electronic applications accepted. *Expenses:* Tuition, state resident: part-time $349 per hour. Tuition, nonresident: part-time $349 per hour. Tuition and fees vary according to course load and program. *Financial support:* In 2007–08, 4 research assistantships with partial tuition reimbursements, 6 teaching assistantships with partial tuition reimbursements were awarded; fellowships also available. Financial award applicants required to submit FAFSA. *Unit head:* Sabine Golz, Director, 319-335-2281, Fax: 319-335-3446.

The University of Iowa, Graduate College, College of Liberal Arts and Sciences, Department of Cinema and Comparative Literature, Program in Comparative Literature Translation, Iowa City, IA 52242-1316. Offers MFA. *Students:* 11 full-time (9 women), 1 (woman) part-time, 1 international. 13 applicants, 85% accepted, 8 enrolled. In 2007, 2 degrees awarded. *Degree requirements:* For master's, thesis, exam. *Entrance requirements:* For master's, GRE General Test, minimum GPA of 3.0. Additional exam requirements/recommendations for international students: Required—TOEFL (minimum score 550 paper-based; 213 computer-based; 81 iBT). *Application deadline:* For fall admission, 1/11 priority date for domestic and international students. Application fee: $60 ($85 for international students). Electronic applications accepted. *Expenses:* Tuition, state resident: part-time $349 per hour. Tuition, nonresident: part-time $349 per hour. Tuition and fees vary according to course load and program. *Financial support:* In 2007–08, 2 fellowships, 2 teaching assistantships with partial tuition reimbursements were awarded; research assistantships with partial tuition reimbursements. Financial award applicants required to submit FAFSA. *Unit head:* Maureen Robertson, Director, 319-335-2821, Fax: 319-335-3446.

University of Maryland, College Park, Graduate Studies, College of Arts and Humanities, Department of English, Program in Comparative Literature, College Park, MD 20742. Offers MA, PhD. *Students:* 8 full-time (7 women), 4 international. 19 applicants, 5% accepted, 0 enrolled. In 2007, 7 doctorates awarded. *Degree requirements:* For master's, thesis, oral defense; for doctorate, 3 foreign languages, thesis/dissertation, comprehensive exams in 4 areas. *Entrance requirements:* For master's, GRE General Test, minimum GPA of 3.0, foreign language, writing sample, 3 letters of recommendation; for doctorate, GRE General Test, minimum GPA of 3.0, foreign language, writing sample. Additional exam requirements/recommendations for international students: Required—TOEFL. *Application deadline:* For fall admission, 1/15 for domestic students, 2/1 for international students. Applications are processed on a rolling basis. Application fee: $60. Electronic applications accepted. *Financial support:* In 2007–08, 3 teaching assistantships with tuition reimbursements (averaging $15,747 per year) were awarded; fellowships with full tuition reimbursements, research assistantships, career-related internships or fieldwork, Federal Work-Study, and scholarships/grants also available. Support available to part-time students. Financial award applicants required to submit FAFSA. *Faculty research:* Renaissance studies, drama, modern literature, postcolonial studies, feminist scholarship. *Application contact:* Dean of Graduate School, 301-405-0358, Fax: 301-314-9305.

University of Massachusetts Amherst, Graduate School, College of Humanities and Fine Arts, Department of Comparative Literature, Amherst, MA 01003. Offers MA, PhD. Part-time programs available. *Faculty:* 11 full-time (4 women). *Students:* 32 full-time (18 women), 5 part-time (all women); includes 6 minority (1 African American, 1 Asian American or Pacific Islander, 4 Hispanic Americans), 15 international. Average age 31. 72 applicants, 36% accepted, 8 enrolled. In 2007, 3 master's, 9 doctorates awarded. Terminal master's awarded for partial completion of doctoral program. *Degree requirements:* For master's, 2 foreign languages, thesis or alternative; for doctorate, 2 foreign languages, thesis/dissertation. *Entrance requirements:* For master's and doctorate, GRE General Test, writing samples. Additional exam requirements/recommendations for international students: Required—TOEFL (minimum score 530 paper-based; 197 computer-based). *Application deadline:* For fall admission, 2/1 priority date for domestic and international students. Applications are processed on a rolling basis. Application fee: $50 ($65 for international students). Electronic applications accepted. *Expenses:* Tuition, state resident: full-time $2,640; part-time $110 per credit. Tuition, nonresident: full-time $9,936; part-time $414 per credit. Required fees: $7,455. One-time fee: $332. Tuition and fees vary according to course load, campus/location, program and reciprocity agreements. *Financial support:* In 2007–08, 2 research assistantships with full tuition reimbursements (averaging $6,688 per year), 18 teaching assistantships with full tuition reimbursements (averaging $12,624 per year) were awarded; fellowships with full tuition reimbursements, career-related internships or fieldwork, Federal Work-Study, scholarships/grants, traineeships, and unspecified assistantships also available. Support available to part-time students. Financial award application deadline: 2/1. *Unit head:* Dr. William Moebius, Head, 413-545-0929, Fax: 413-545-0908, E-mail: bmoebius@complit.umass.edu.

University of Michigan, Horace H. Rackham School of Graduate Studies, College of Literature, Science, and the Arts, Department of Comparative Literature, Ann Arbor, MI 48109. Offers PhD. *Faculty:* 17 full-time (10 women), 2 part-time/adjunct (1 woman). *Students:* 42 full-time (22 women); includes 1 African American, 3 Hispanic Americans, 21 international. Average age 25. 42 applicants, 14% accepted, 6 enrolled. In 2007, 3 doctorates awarded. *Median time to degree:* Of those who began their doctoral program in fall 1999, 70% received their degree in 8 years or less. *Degree requirements:* For doctorate, 2 foreign languages, thesis/dissertation, oral defense of dissertation, preliminary exam. *Entrance requirements:* For doctorate, GRE General Test. Additional exam requirements/recommendations for international students: Required—TOEFL (paper 560; computer 220; iBT 84) or Michigan English Language Assessment Battery, IELTS (6.5). *Application deadline:* For fall admission, 1/4 for domestic and international students. Application fee: $60 ($75 for international students). Electronic applications accepted. *Financial support:* In 2007–08, 32 students received support, including 5 fellowships with full tuition reimbursements available (averaging $14,000 per year), 21 teaching assistantships with full tuition reimbursements available (averaging $14,756 per year); research assistantships, career-related internships or fieldwork, Federal Work-Study, institutionally sponsored loans, scholarships/grants, health care benefits, and unspecified assistantships also available. Support available to part-time students. Financial award application deadline: 1/4. *Faculty research:* Postcolonial theory, cultural studies, ideology of aesthetics, translation studies, medieval philosophy. *Unit head:* Yopie Prins, Chair, 734-763-2351, Fax: 734-764-8503, E-mail: yprins@umich.edu. *Application contact:* Nancy E.W. Harris, Student Services Coordinator, 734-647-4894, Fax: 734-764-8503, E-mail: nwh@umich.edu.

University of Minnesota, Twin Cities Campus, Graduate School, College of Liberal Arts, Department of Cultural Studies and Comparative Literature, Program in Comparative Literature, Minneapolis, MN 55455-0213. Offers PhD. *Faculty:* 12 full-time (2 women), 6 part-time/adjunct (4 women). *Students:* 21 full-time (10 women); includes 1 minority (African American), 4 international. 26 applicants, 19% accepted, 3 enrolled. In 2007, 1 degree awarded. *Degree requirements:* For doctorate, 3 foreign languages, thesis/dissertation. *Entrance requirements:* For doctorate, GRE General Test, sample of written work. Additional exam requirements/recommendations for international students: Required—TOEFL. *Application deadline:* For fall admission, 12/10 for domestic students. Application fee: $55 ($75 for international students). *Financial support:* In 2007–08, 1 fellowship with full tuition reimbursement (averaging $16,000 per year), 1 research assistantship with full tuition reimbursement (averaging $6,232 per year), 18 teaching assistantships with full tuition reimbursements (averaging $12,665 per year) were awarded; Federal Work-Study, institutionally sponsored loans, health care benefits, and tuition waivers (full and partial) also available. Financial award application deadline: 12/10. *Faculty research:* Literary theory, emergent literatures, popular culture, postcolonial literature, gender and sexuality. *Unit head:* Liz Kotz, Director, 612-625-4571, Fax: 612-626-0228, E-mail: complit@tc.umn.edu. *Application contact:* Elizabeth Wilson, Executive Secretary, 612-624-7896, Fax: 312-626-0228, E-mail: ejwilson@umn.edu.

University of Missouri–Columbia, Graduate School, College of Arts and Sciences, Department of Romance Languages and Literature, Columbia, MO 65211. Offers French (MA, PhD); literature (MA); Spanish (MA, PhD); teaching (MA). Terminal master's awarded for partial completion of doctoral program. *Degree requirements:* For master's, one foreign language; for doctorate, 4 foreign languages, thesis/dissertation. *Entrance requirements:* For master's and doctorate, GRE General Test, minimum GPA of 3.0.

University of New Hampshire, Graduate School, College of Liberal Arts, Department of English, Durham, NH 03824. Offers English (MFA, PhD); English education (MST); language and linguistics (MA); literature (MA); writing (MA). Part-time programs available. *Faculty:* 44 full-time. *Students:* 38 full-time (21 women), 64 part-time (43 women); includes 6 minority (1 American Indian/Alaska Native, 3 Asian Americans or Pacific Islanders, 2 Hispanic Americans), 3 international. Average age 34. 251 applicants, 45% accepted, 31 enrolled. In 2007, 25 master's, 6 doctorates awarded. *Degree requirements:* For master's, one foreign language; for doctorate, 2 foreign languages, thesis/dissertation. *Entrance requirements:* For master's, GRE General Test, sample of written work; for doctorate, GRE General Test, GRE Subject Test, sample of written work. Additional exam requirements/recommendations for international students: Required—TOEFL (minimum score 550 paper-based; 213 computer-based; 80 iBT). *Application deadline:* For fall admission, 2/15 priority date for domestic students, 2/15 for international students. Applications are processed on a rolling basis. Application fee: $60. Electronic applications accepted. *Financial support:* In 2007–08, 1 fellowship, 1 research assistantship, 43 teaching assistantships were awarded; career-related internships or fieldwork, Federal Work-Study, scholarships/grants, and tuition waivers (full and partial) also available. Support available to part-time students. Financial award application deadline: 2/15. *Unit head:* Dr. Andrew Merton, Chairperson, 603-862-3977. *Application contact:* Sue Smith, Administrative Assistant, 603-862-3963, E-mail: engl.grad@unh.edu.

University of New Mexico, Graduate School, College of Arts and Sciences, Department of Foreign Languages and Literature, Albuquerque, NM 87131-2039. Offers comparative literature and cultural studies (MA); French (MA); French studies (PhD); German studies (MA). Part-time programs available. *Faculty:* 15 full-time (11 women), 8 part-time/adjunct (4 women). *Students:* 9 full-time (8 women), 4 part-time (2 women), 6 international. Average age 33. 9 applicants, 44% accepted, 3 enrolled. In 2007, 5 master's awarded. *Degree requirements:* For master's, one foreign language, thesis optional; for doctorate, 2 foreign languages, thesis/dissertation. *Application deadline:* For fall admission, 2/1 priority date for domestic students; for spring admission, 10/1 priority date for domestic students. Application fee: $50. Electronic applications accepted. *Financial support:* In 2007–08, 20 teaching assistantships with tuition reimbursements (averaging $12,023 per year) were awarded; Federal Work-Study, health care benefits, and unspecified assistantships also available. Financial award application deadline: 3/1; financial award applicants required to submit FAFSA. *Faculty research:* German, Russian, Italian, Japanese, French, Comparative Lit, culture studies, classics. Total annual research expenditures: $4,750. *Unit head:* Dr. Natasha Kolchevska, Chair, 505-277-4771, Fax: 505-277-3599, E-mail: nakol@unm.edu. *Application contact:* Dean Aragon, Application and Graduation Advisor, 505-277-4471, Fax: 505-277-3599, E-mail: peaslee@unm.edu.

The University of North Carolina at Chapel Hill, Graduate School, College of Arts and Sciences, Curriculum in Comparative Literature, Chapel Hill, NC 27599. Offers MA, PhD. Terminal master's awarded for partial completion of doctoral program. *Degree requirements:* For master's, one foreign language, thesis, exams; for doctorate, 2 foreign languages, thesis/dissertation, exams. *Entrance requirements:* For master's and doctorate, GRE General Test, minimum GPA of 3.0. Additional exam requirements/recommendations for international students: Required—TOEFL (minimum score 600 paper-based; 250 computer-based). Electronic applications accepted. *Faculty research:* Realism, literature and medicine, Proust, literary theory, Arthurian romance.

University of Notre Dame, Graduate School, College of Arts and Letters, Division of Humanities, PhD Program in Literature, Notre Dame, IN 46556. Offers PhD. *Faculty:* 17 full-time (3 women). *Students:* 26 full-time (17 women); includes 5 minority (2 Asian Americans or Pacific Islanders, 3 Hispanic Americans), 4 international. 44 applicants, 20% accepted, 6 enrolled. *Degree requirements:* For doctorate, 3 foreign languages, thesis/dissertation, candidacy exam. *Entrance requirements:* For doctorate, GRE General Test. Additional exam requirements/recommendations for international students: Required—TOEFL (minimum score 600 paper-based; 250 computer-based; 80 iBT). *Application deadline:* For fall admission, 2/1 for domestic and international students. Application fee: $50. Electronic applications accepted. *Financial support:* In 2007–08, 5 fellowships with full tuition reimbursements (averaging $22,000 per year), research assistantships with full tuition reimbursements (averaging $16,000 per year), teaching assistantships (averaging $16,000 per year) were awarded; tuition waivers (full) also available. Financial award application deadline: 2/1. *Faculty research:* Interdisciplinary study of literature from a transitional and intercultural perspective; Classics, East Asian, French, German, Irish, Italian, Iberian and Latin American (Portuguese, Spanish). *Unit head:* Dr. Joseph Buttigieg, Director of Graduate Studies, 574-631-0481, E-mail: litprog@nd.edu. *Application contact:* Dr. Jarren Gonzales, Director of Graduate Admissions, 574-631-7706, Fax: 574-631-4183.

University of Oregon, Graduate School, College of Arts and Sciences, Program in Comparative Literature, Eugene, OR 97403. Offers MA, PhD. Part-time programs available. *Faculty:* 3 full-time (0 women), 1 (woman) part-time/adjunct. *Students:* 22 full-time (14 women), 2 part-time (1 woman); includes 1 African American, 1 Asian American or Pacific Islander, 1 Hispanic American, 7 international. Average age 33. 35 applicants, 20% accepted. In 2007, 1 degree awarded. Terminal master's awarded for partial completion of doctoral program. *Degree requirements:* For master's, 2 foreign languages, field exam; for doctorate, 2 foreign languages, thesis/dissertation, field exam. *Entrance requirements:* For master's, previous course work in English and literature, proficiency in 3 foreign languages, writing sample; for doctorate, previous course work in English and literature, proficiency in 2 foreign languages, writing sample. Additional exam requirements/recommendations for international students: Required—TOEFL. *Application deadline:* For fall admission, 1/15 for domestic students. Application fee: $50. *Financial support:* In 2007–08, 27 teaching assistantships were awarded; Federal Work-Study also available. Financial award application deadline: 1/15. *Faculty research:* Critical theory, historical periods, interdisciplinary approach, Feminist studies. *Unit head:* Lisa Freinkel, Director,

541-346-0825, E-mail: complit@oregon.uoregon.edu. *Application contact:* Cynthia Stockwell, Admissions Contact, 541-346-3986, E-mail: raymong@uoregon.edu.

University of Pennsylvania, School of Arts and Sciences, Graduate Group in Comparative Literature and Literary Theory, Philadelphia, PA 19104. Offers comparative literature (AM, PhD); literary theory (AM, PhD). *Degree requirements:* For master's, one foreign language, thesis; for doctorate, variable foreign language requirement, thesis/dissertation. *Entrance requirements:* For master's, GRE General Test, proficiency in 1 foreign language; for doctorate, GRE General Test, master's degree in a literature field, proficiency in 1 foreign language. Additional exam requirements/recommendations for international students: Required—TOEFL. Electronic applications accepted.

University of Puerto Rico, Río Piedras, College of Humanities, Department of Comparative Literature, San Juan, PR 00931-3300. Offers MA. Part-time programs available. *Students:* 16 full-time (9 women), 10 part-time (8 women); includes 25 minority (all Hispanic Americans) Average age 29. In 2007, 5 degrees awarded. *Degree requirements:* For master's, comprehensive exam, thesis. *Entrance requirements:* For master's, EXADEP, interview, minimum GPA of 3.0, letter of recommendation. *Application deadline:* For fall admission, 2/1 for domestic and international students. Application fee: $17. *Expenses:* Tuition, state resident: full-time $1,808; part-time $113 per credit. Tuition, nonresident: full-time $5,248; part-time $328 per credit. Required fees: $72 per term. *Financial support:* Fellowships, research assistantships, teaching assistantships, Federal Work-Study, institutionally sponsored loans, and tuition waivers (partial) available. Financial award application deadline: 5/31. *Unit head:* Dr. Ada M. Vilar-Kerkoff, Director, 787-764-0000 Ext. 3523, Fax: 787-763-5879.

University of South Carolina, The Graduate School, College of Arts and Sciences, Department of Languages, Literatures, and Cultures, Columbia, SC 29208. Offers comparative literature (MA, PhD); foreign languages (MAT), including French, German, Spanish; French (MA); German (MA); Spanish (MA). MAT offered in cooperation with the College of Education. Part-time programs available. *Faculty:* 39 full-time (19 women). *Students:* 43 full-time (31 women), 19 part-time (12 women); includes 12 minority (3 African Americans, 1 Asian American or Pacific Islander, 8 Hispanic Americans), 15 international. Average age 29. 40 applicants, 65% accepted, 18 enrolled. In 2007, 7 master's awarded. *Degree requirements:* For master's, one foreign language, comprehensive exam, thesis optional; for doctorate, 2 foreign languages, comprehensive exam, thesis/dissertation. *Entrance requirements:* For master's and doctorate, GRE General Test, writing sample. Additional exam requirements/recommendations for international students: Required—TOEFL (minimum score 230 computer-based; 75 iBT). *Application deadline:* For fall admission, 2/1 priority date for domestic and international students. Applications are processed on a rolling basis. Application fee: $40. Electronic applications accepted. *Expenses:* Tuition, state resident: part-time $440 per hour. Tuition, nonresident: part-time $936 per hour. Required fees: $17 per hour. Tuition and fees vary according to program. *Financial support:* In 2007–08, 40 teaching assistantships with full tuition reimbursements (averaging $11,000 per year) were awarded; fellowships, research assistantships with full tuition reimbursements also available. Financial award application deadline: 2/1. *Faculty research:* Modern literature, linguistics, literature and culture, medieval literature, literary theory. Total annual research expenditures: $23,000. *Unit head:* Dr. Marja Warehime, Chair, 803-777-9734, Fax: 803-777-0454, E-mail: warehime@sc.edu. *Application contact:* Dr. Nicholas Vazsonyi, Graduate Director, 803-777-2935, Fax: 803-777-0454, E-mail: vazsonyi@sc.edu.

University of Southern California, Graduate School, College of Letters, Arts and Sciences, Department of Comparative Literature, Los Angeles, CA 90089. Offers MA, PhD. *Faculty:* 21 full-time (7 women), 1 part-time/adjunct (0 women). *Students:* 25 full-time (18 women); includes 7 minority (2 African Americans, 2 Asian Americans or Pacific Islanders, 3 Hispanic Americans), 7 international. 31 applicants, 19% accepted. In 2007, 2 master's, 2 doctorates awarded. Terminal master's awarded for partial completion of doctoral program. *Degree requirements:* For master's, 2 foreign languages; for doctorate, 2 foreign languages, thesis/dissertation. *Entrance requirements:* For master's and doctorate, GRE General Test. *Application deadline:* For fall admission, 12/1 priority date for domestic students. Application fee: $85. *Financial support:* In 2007–08, 24 students received support, including fellowships with full tuition reimbursements available (averaging $19,000 per year), teaching assistantships with full tuition reimbursements available (averaging $18,570 per year); Federal Work-Study, institutionally sponsored loans, and scholarships/grants also available. Support available to part-time students. Financial award application deadline: 2/15; financial award applicants required to submit FAFSA. *Faculty research:* Literary theory, film and literary, Asian-American literature, humanities and environment. *Unit head:* Dr. Peggy Kamuf, Chair, 213-740-2311, E-mail: complit@usc.edu. *Application contact:* Melinda Menjou, Information Contact, 213-740-2311.

The University of Texas at Austin, Graduate School, College of Liberal Arts, Program in Comparative Literature, Austin, TX 78712-1111. Offers MA, PhD. *Degree requirements:* For master's, 2 foreign languages, report or thesis; for doctorate, 3 foreign languages, thesis/dissertation. *Entrance requirements:* For master's and doctorate, GRE General Test. Electronic applications accepted.

The University of Texas at Dallas, School of Arts and Humanities, Richardson, TX 75083-0688. Offers arts and technology (MFA); humanities (MA, MAT, PhD), including aesthetic studies, arts and technology (MA), historical studies (MA), history of ideas, studies in literature. Part-time and evening/weekend programs available. *Faculty:* 49 full-time (14 women), 4 part-time/adjunct (1 woman). *Students:* 192 full-time (104 women), 217 part-time (118 women); includes 98 minority (33 African Americans, 3 American Indian/Alaska Native, 28 Asian Americans or Pacific Islanders, 34 Hispanic Americans), 29 international. Average age 37. 161 applicants, 75% accepted, 86 enrolled. In 2007, 76 master's, 13 doctorates awarded. *Degree requirements:* For master's, one foreign language, portfolio; for doctorate, one foreign language, thesis/dissertation. *Entrance requirements:* For master's and doctorate, GRE General Test, minimum GPA of 3.0 in undergraduate course work in field. Additional exam requirements/recommendations for international students: Required—TOEFL (minimum score 550 paper-based; 213 computer-based). *Application deadline:* For fall admission, 7/15 for domestic students; for spring admission, 11/15 for domestic students. Applications are processed on a rolling basis. Application fee: $50 ($100 for international students). Electronic applications accepted. *Expenses:* Tuition, state resident: full-time $7,052. Tuition, nonresident: full-time $12,632. Tuition and fees vary according to course load. *Financial support:* In 2007–08, 1 research assistantship with tuition reimbursement (averaging $11,700 per year), 73 teaching assistantships with tuition reimbursements (averaging $9,750 per year) were awarded; fellowships, Federal Work-Study, institutionally sponsored loans, scholarships/grants, and unspecified assistantships also available. Support available to part-time students. Financial award application deadline: 4/30; financial award applicants required to submit FAFSA. *Faculty research:* Translation, science and the arts and humanities, intellectual and philosophical history, cultural studies. Total annual research expenditures: $368,048. *Unit head:* Dr. Dennis M. Kratz, Dean, 972-883-2984, Fax: 972-883-2989, E-mail: dkratz@utdallas.edu. *Application contact:* Dr. W. Jackson Rushing, Associate Dean of Graduate Studies, 972-883-2226, Fax: 972-883-2989, E-mail: jackson.rushing@utdallas.edu.

University of Toronto, School of Graduate Studies, Humanities Division, Centre for Comparative Literature, Toronto, ON M5S 1A1, Canada. Offers MA, PhD. Part-time programs available. *Faculty:* 14 full-time, 41 part-time/adjunct. *Students:* 46 full-time (30 women), 14 international. 60 applicants, 45% accepted. In 2007, 7 master's, 4 doctorates awarded. *Degree requirements:* For doctorate, thesis/dissertation. *Entrance requirements:* For master's and doctorate, 2 letters of recommendation, sample of work (short essay on a literary topic preferred), resumé. *Application deadline:* For fall admission, 6/1 for domestic students. Application fee: $100 Canadian dollars. *Financial support:* In 2007–08, fellowships with tuition reimbursements (averaging $12,000 Canadian dollars per year). *Unit head:* Prof. Roland J. Le Huenen, Chair, 416-813-4042, Fax: 416-978-6867. *Application contact:* Bao Nguyen, Graduate Administrator, 416-978-6363, Fax: 416-978-6867, E-mail: complit@epas.utoronto.ca.

University of Utah, The Graduate School, College of Humanities, Department of Languages and Literature, Salt Lake City, UT 84112-1107. Offers comparative literary and cultural studies (MA, PhD); French (MA, MALP); German (MA, MALP, PhD); language pedagogy (MALP); Spanish (MA, MALP, PhD); world languages with secondary teaching licensure (MA). *Faculty:* 38 full-time (21 women). *Students:* 28 full-time (15 women), 12 part-time (10 women); includes 10 minority (all Hispanic Americans), 7 international. Average age 35. 32 applicants, 47% accepted, 10 enrolled. In 2007, 14 master's, 2 doctorates awarded. Terminal master's awarded for partial completion of doctoral program. *Median time to degree:* Of those who began their doctoral program in fall 1999, 66% received their degree in 8 years or less. *Degree requirements:* For master's, standard proficiency in 2 languages other than English, comprehensive exam or thesis; for doctorate, comprehensive exam, standard proficiency in 2 languages other than English and language of study, advanced proficiency in 1 language other than English and language of study, dissertation. *Entrance requirements:* For master's, bachelor's degree or strong undergraduate record in target languages, GPA of 3.0, literature-survey courses; for doctorate, successful completion of MA and advanced proficiency in a target language. Additional exam requirements/recommendations for international students: Required—TOEFL (minimum score 500 paper-based; 173 computer-based). *Application deadline:* For fall admission, 2/1 priority date for domestic students, 1/15 priority date for international students. Application fee: $45 ($65 for international students). Electronic applications accepted. *Financial support:* In 2007–08, 25 students received support, including 25 teaching assistantships with full tuition reimbursements available (averaging $11,000 per year); fellowships with tuition reimbursements available, health care benefits also available. Financial award application deadline: 2/1; financial award applicants required to submit FAFSA. *Faculty research:* Literary theory, stylistics, Russian and Soviet literature, existentialism, theory of criticism. Total annual research expenditures: $35,321. *Unit head:* Dr. Christine A. Jones, Director of Graduate Studies, 801-585-3002, Fax: 801-581-7581, E-mail: cjones@hum.utah.edu. *Application contact:* Corky Reeser, Executive Graduate Secretary, 801-581-7570, Fax: 801-581-7581, E-mail: c.reeser@mail.hum.utah.edu.

Announcement: Degrees offered include MA in comparative literary and cultural studies (CLCS); MA and MALP in French, German, and Spanish; MA in world languages with licensure (WLMA); PhD in CLCS, German, and Spanish. The programs train students in literary critical analysis, cultural studies, linguistics, and in recent innovations in L2 (second language) pedagogy.

University of Washington, Graduate School, College of Arts and Sciences, Department of Comparative Literature, Seattle, WA 98195. Offers MA, PhD. Part-time programs available. Terminal master's awarded for partial completion of doctoral program. *Degree requirements:* For master's, 2 foreign languages, thesis optional; for doctorate, 3 foreign languages, thesis/dissertation. *Entrance requirements:* For master's, GRE General Test, BA in comparative literature or equivalent, minimum GPA of 3.0, proficiency in 1 foreign language; for doctorate, GRE General Test, MA in comparative literature or equivalent, minimum GPA of 3.0, proficiency in 2 foreign languages. Additional exam requirements/recommendations for international students: Required—TOEFL. Electronic applications accepted. *Faculty research:* Literature and culture from classical antiquity to twentieth-century, literary theory and criticism.

The University of Western Ontario, Faculty of Graduate Studies, Faculty of Arts and Humanities, Department of Comparative Literature, London, ON N6A 5B8, Canada. Offers comparative literature (MA, PhD); Spanish (MA). Part-time programs available. *Faculty:* 28 full-time (13 women). *Students:* 34 full-time (24 women). Average age 26. 50 applicants, 56% accepted, 26 enrolled. In 2007, 8 degrees awarded. *Degree requirements:* For master's, 2 foreign languages, thesis (for some programs). *Entrance requirements:* For master's, honors degree in Spanish or equivalent, minimum B average. Additional exam requirements/recommendations for international students: Required—TOEFL, TOEFL (comparative literature). *Application deadline:* For fall admission, 2/1 priority date for domestic students. Applications are processed on a rolling basis. Application fee: $30 Canadian dollars. *Financial support:* In 2007–08, 26 teaching assistantships (averaging $8,500 Canadian dollars per year) were awarded; fellowships, scholarships/grants also available. Financial award application deadline: 4/1. *Faculty research:* Spanish golden age, Latin-American, romance, medieval, film. *Unit head:* Melitta Adamson, Chair, 519-661-2111 Ext. 85861, E-mail: melitta@uwo.ca. *Application contact:* Teresa McLauchlan, Graduate Assistant, 519-661-2111 Ext. 85846, Fax: 519-661-4093, E-mail: tmclauch@uwo.ca.

University of Wisconsin–Madison, Graduate School, College of Letters and Science, Department of Comparative Literature, Madison, WI 53706-1380. Offers MA, PhD. Part-time programs available. Terminal master's awarded for partial completion of doctoral program. *Degree requirements:* For master's, one foreign language, second-year exam; for doctorate, 3 foreign languages, thesis/dissertation, 3 preliminary exams. *Entrance requirements:* For master's, GRE General Test, writing sample; for doctorate, GRE General Test. Electronic applications accepted. *Faculty research:* Literary theory, cultural criticism, classics through early modern literature, postmodernity, gender studies.

University of Wisconsin–Milwaukee, Graduate School, College of Letters and Sciences, Department of English, Milwaukee, WI 53201-0413. Offers MA, PhD, Certificate, MLIS/MA. *Faculty:* 47 full-time (21 women). *Students:* 113 full-time (70 women), 95 part-time (59 women); includes 15 minority (8 African Americans, 1 American Indian/Alaska Native, 2 Asian Americans or Pacific Islanders, 4 Hispanic Americans), 28 international. 191 applicants, 55% accepted, 40 enrolled. In 2007, 15 master's, 12 doctorates awarded. *Degree requirements:* For master's, thesis or alternative; for doctorate, one foreign language, thesis/dissertation. *Entrance requirements:* For master's, GRE General Test, GRE Subject Test. *Application deadline:* For fall admission, 1/1 priority date for domestic students; for spring admission, 9/1 for domestic students. Applications are processed on a rolling basis. Application fee: $45 ($75 for international students). *Expenses:* Tuition, state resident: part-time $530 per credit. Tuition, nonresident: part-time $1,428 per credit. Required fees: $19 per credit. $229 per term. Tuition and fees vary according to course load and program. *Financial support:* In 2007–08, 73 teaching assistantships were awarded; fellowships, research assistantships, career-related internships or fieldwork and unspecified assistantships also available. Support available to part-time students. Financial award application deadline: 4/15. *Unit head:* George Clark, Representative, 414-229-4673, Fax: 414-229-2643.

University of Wisconsin–Milwaukee, Graduate School, College of Letters and Sciences, Interdepartmental Program in Foreign Language and Literature, Milwaukee, WI 53201-0413. Offers classics and Hebrew studies (MAFLL); comparative literature (MAFLL); French and Italian (MAFLL); German (MAFLL); Slavic studies (MAFLL); Spanish (MAFLL). Part-time programs available. *Faculty:* 39 full-time (17 women). *Students:* 29 full-time (21 women), 31 part-time (23 women); includes 8 minority (1 Asian American or Pacific Islander, 7 Hispanic Americans), 22 international. 54 applicants, 67% accepted, 26 enrolled. In 2007, 34 degrees awarded. *Degree requirements:* For master's, 2 foreign languages, thesis or alternative. *Application deadline:* For fall admission, 1/1 priority date for domestic students; for spring admission, 9/1 for domestic students. Applications are processed on a rolling basis. Application fee: $45 ($75 for international students). *Expenses:* Tuition, state resident: part-time $530 per credit. Tuition, nonresident: part-time $1,428 per credit. Required fees: $19 per credit. $229 per term. Tuition and fees vary according to course load and program. *Financial support:* In 2007–08, 44 teaching assistantships were awarded; fellowships, research assistantships, career-related internships or fieldwork and unspecified assistantships also available. Support available to part-time students. Financial award application deadline: 4/15. *Unit head:* Gabrielle Verdier, Representative, 414-229-3346, Fax: 414-229-2741, E-mail: verdier@uwm.edu.

Washington University in St. Louis, Graduate School of Arts and Sciences, Department of Asian and Near Eastern Languages and Literatures, St. Louis, MO 63130-4899. Offers Asian language (MA); Asian studies (MA); Chinese (PhD); comparative literature (MA, PhD); Japanese (PhD). Terminal master's awarded for partial completion of doctoral program. *Degree*

Comparative Literature

Washington University in St. Louis (continued)
requirements: For master's, thesis optional; for doctorate, thesis/dissertation. *Entrance requirements:* For master's and doctorate, GRE General Test. Electronic applications accepted.

Washington University in St. Louis, Graduate School of Arts and Sciences, Program in Comparative Literature, St. Louis, MO 63130-4899. Offers MA, PhD. Terminal master's awarded for partial completion of doctoral program. *Degree requirements:* For master's, thesis or alternative; for doctorate, thesis/dissertation. *Entrance requirements:* For master's and doctorate, GRE General Test. Electronic applications accepted.

Wayne State University, College of Liberal Arts and Sciences, Department of English, Program in Comparative Literature, Detroit, MI 48202. Offers MA. *Students:* 1 (woman) full-time. Average age 39. 1 applicant, 0% accepted. *Degree requirements:* For master's, one foreign language, essay or thesis. *Entrance requirements:* For master's, GRE General Test, minimum GPA of 3.25 in English, 3.0 overall. Additional exam requirements/recommendations for international students: Required—TOEFL (minimum score 550 paper-based; 213 computer-based); Recommended—TWE (minimum score 6). *Application deadline:* For fall admission, 7/1 for domestic students, 6/1 for international students; for winter admission, 10/1 for international students; for spring admission, 2/1 for international students. Application fee: $30 ($50 for international students). Electronic applications accepted. *Expenses:* Tuition, state resident: part-time $403 per credit hour. Tuition, nonresident: part-time $890 per credit hour. *Financial support:* Application deadline: 3/1. *Application contact:* Ross Pudaloff, Graduate Director, 313-577-7699, E-mail: r.pudaloff@wayne.edu.

Western Kentucky University, Graduate Studies, Potter College of Arts and Letters, Department of English, Bowling Green, KY 42101. Offers education (MA); English (MA Ed); literature (MA), including American literature, British literature, literary theory, women writers, world literature; teaching English as a second language (MA); writing (MA). Part-time and evening/weekend programs available. *Degree requirements:* For master's, comprehensive exam, thesis optional, final exam. *Entrance requirements:* For master's, GRE General Test, minimum GPA of 2.75. Additional exam requirements/recommendations for international students: Required—TOEFL (minimum score 555 paper-based; 213 computer-based; 79 iBT). *Faculty research:* Improving writing, linking teacher knowledge and performance, Victorian women writers, Kentucky women writers, Kentucky poets.

Yale University, Graduate School of Arts and Sciences, Department of Comparative Literature, New Haven, CT 06520. Offers PhD. *Degree requirements:* For doctorate, 2 foreign languages, thesis/dissertation. *Entrance requirements:* For doctorate, GRE General Test.

English

Abilene Christian University, Graduate School, College of Arts and Sciences, Department of English, Abilene, TX 79699-9100. Offers composition/rhetoric (MA); literature (MA); writing (MA). Part-time programs available. *Faculty:* 15 part-time/adjunct (5 women). *Students:* 12 full-time (7 women), 3 part-time (all women); includes 1 minority (Hispanic American), 1 international. 4 applicants, 225% accepted, 8 enrolled. In 2007, 5 degrees awarded. *Degree requirements:* For master's, one foreign language, comprehensive exam, thesis optional. *Entrance requirements:* For master's, GRE General Test. *Application deadline:* For fall admission, 4/1 priority date for domestic students; for spring admission, 11/1 for domestic students. Applications are processed on a rolling basis. Application fee: $40 ($45 for international students). Electronic applications accepted. *Expenses:* Tuition: Full-time $13,368; part-time $557 per hour. Required fees: $700; $34 per hour. $10 per semester. Tuition and fees vary according to degree level and campus/location. *Financial support:* Teaching assistantships, Federal Work-Study available. Support available to part-time students. Financial award application deadline: 4/1. *Faculty research:* Feminism, Shakespearean dimensions of new literature, poetic consciousness, deconstruction myths. *Unit head:* Dr. Bill Rankin, Graduate Adviser, 325-674-2253, Fax: 325-674-2408, E-mail: rankinw@acu.edu. *Application contact:* William Horn, Graduate Admissions Counselor, 325-674-2656, Fax: 325-674-6717, E-mail: gradinfo@acu.edu.

Acadia University, Faculty of Arts, Department of English, Wolfville, NS B4P 2R6, Canada. Offers MA. *Faculty:* 15 full-time (6 women). *Students:* 4 full-time (2 women), 1 (woman) part-time. Average age 25. 19 applicants, 68% accepted, 4 enrolled. In 2007, 5 degrees awarded. *Degree requirements:* For master's, thesis. *Entrance requirements:* For master's, honors degree in English, minimum A- average. Additional exam requirements/recommendations for international students: Required—TOEFL (minimum score 630 paper-based; 267 computer-based; 93 iBT), IELTS (minimum score 7). *Application deadline:* For fall admission, 2/1 priority date for domestic students; for spring admission, 3/30 for domestic students. Applications are processed on a rolling basis. Application fee: $50. *Financial support:* In 2007–08, 4 students received support, including 4 teaching assistantships (averaging $9,000 per year); scholarships/grants and unspecified assistantships also available. Financial award application deadline: 2/1. *Faculty research:* Renaissance, Canadian, Medieval, Victorian, and Romantic literature. *Unit head:* Dr. Patricia Rigg, Chair, 902-585-1503, Fax: 902-585-1070, E-mail: patricia.rigg@acadiau.ca. *Application contact:* Christine Reed, Secretary, 902-585-1502, Fax: 902-585-1070, E-mail: christine.reed@acadiau.ca.

The American University in Cairo, Graduate Studies and Research, School of Humanities and Social Sciences, Department of English and Comparative Literature, Cairo, Egypt. Offers MA. Part-time programs available. *Degree requirements:* For master's, one foreign language, thesis, proficiency in French or German. *Entrance requirements:* Additional exam requirements/recommendations for international students: Required—English entrance exam and/or TOEFL.

American University of Beirut, Graduate Programs, Faculty of Arts and Sciences, Beirut, Lebanon. Offers anthropology (MA); Arabic language and literature (MA); archaeology (MA); biology (MS); chemistry (MS); computer science (MS); economics (MA); education (MA); English language (MA); English literature (MA); environmental policy planning (MSES); financial economics (MAFE); geology (MS); history (MA); mathematics (MA, MS); Middle Eastern studies (MA); philosophy (MA); physics (MS); political studies (MA); psychology (MA); public administration (MA); sociology (MA); statistics (MA, MS). Part-time programs available. *Faculty:* 108 full-time (29 women), 5 part-time/adjunct (3 women). *Students:* 134 full-time (92 women), 228 part-time (167 women). Average age 25. 319 applicants, 67% accepted, 91 enrolled. In 2007, 144 degrees awarded. *Degree requirements:* For master's, one foreign language, comprehensive exam, thesis (for some programs). *Entrance requirements:* For master's, GRE, letter of recommendation. Additional exam requirements/recommendations for international students: Required—TOEFL (minimum score 600 paper-based; 250 computer-based; 100 iBT), IELTS (minimum score 8). *Application deadline:* For fall admission, 4/30 for domestic and international students; for spring admission, 11/1 for domestic and international students. Application fee: $50. *Expenses:* Tuition: Full-time $9,954; part-time $553 per credit. Tuition and fees vary according to course load and program. *Financial support:* In 2007–08, 28 students received support. Career-related internships or fieldwork, institutionally sponsored loans, scholarships/grants, health care benefits, and unspecified assistantships available. Financial award application deadline: 2/4; financial award applicants required to submit FAFSA. *Faculty research:* String theory and supergravity; computer graphics; algebra and number theory; popular Arabic literature; marine and freshwater biology; integrating science, math and technology. Total annual research expenditures: $132,270. *Unit head:* Khalil Bitar, Dean, 961-1374374 Ext. 3800, Fax: 961-1744461, E-mail: kmb@aub.edu.lb. *Application contact:* Dr. Salim Kanaan, Director, Admissions Office, 961-1350000 Ext. 2594, Fax: 961-1750775, E-mail: sk00@aub.edu.lb.

Andrews University, School of Graduate Studies, College of Arts and Sciences, Department of English, Berrien Springs, MI 49104. Offers MA, MAT. Part-time programs available. *Degree requirements:* For master's, one foreign language, thesis optional. *Entrance requirements:* For master's, GRE Subject Test. *Faculty research:* Christianity and literature, Victorian literature, social linguistics, rhetoric, American literature.

Angelo State University, College of Graduate Studies, College of Liberal and Fine Arts, Department of English, San Angelo, TX 76909. Offers MA. Part-time and evening/weekend programs available. *Faculty:* 5 full-time (2 women). *Students:* Average age 29. 4 applicants, 100% accepted, 2 enrolled. In 2007, 5 degrees awarded. *Degree requirements:* For master's, comprehensive exam, thesis optional. *Entrance requirements:* For master's, GRE General Test. Additional exam requirements/recommendations for international students: Required—TOEFL or IELTS. *Application deadline:* For fall admission, 7/15 priority date for domestic students, 6/10 for international students; for spring admission, 12/8 for domestic students, 11/1 for international students. Applications are processed on a rolling basis. Application fee: $40 ($50 for international students). Electronic applications accepted. *Financial support:* In 2007–08, 9 students received support, including 4 teaching assistantships (averaging $10,251 per year); Federal Work-Study, scholarships/grants, and unspecified assistantships also available. Support available to part-time students. Financial award application deadline: 3/1; financial award applicants required to submit FAFSA. *Unit head:* Dr. Nancy G. Allen, Department Head, 325-942-2273 Ext. 231, E-mail: nancy.allen@angelo.edu. *Application contact:* Dr. Terry Dalrymple, Graduate Advisor, 325-942-2252 Ext. 225, E-mail: terry.dalrymple@angelo.edu.

Appalachian State University, Cratis D. Williams Graduate School, Department of English, Boone, NC 28608. Offers English (MA); English education (MA). Part-time programs available. *Faculty:* 36 full-time (18 women). *Students:* 32 full-time (19 women), 13 part-time (9 women); includes 5 minority (2 African Americans, 3 Asian Americans or Pacific Islanders), 1 international. 26 applicants, 77% accepted, 11 enrolled. In 2007, 14 master's awarded. *Degree requirements:* For master's, one foreign language, comprehensive exam, thesis (for some programs). *Entrance requirements:* For master's, GRE General Test, 3 letters of recommendation. Additional exam requirements/recommendations for international students: Required—TOEFL (minimum score 570 paper-based; 230 computer-based; 79 iBT), IELTS (minimum score 7), TOEFL or IELTS. *Application deadline:* For fall admission, 7/1 priority date for domestic students, 1/1 for international students; for spring admission, 11/1 for domestic students, 6/1 for international students. Applications are processed on a rolling basis. Application fee: $50. Electronic applications accepted. *Expenses:* Tuition, state resident: part-time $127 per semester hour. Tuition, nonresident: part-time $597 per semester hour. Required fees: $18 per semester. *Financial support:* In 2007–08, 10 research assistantships (averaging $7,500 per year), 16 teaching assistantships (averaging $7,500 per year) were awarded; fellowships, career-related internships or fieldwork, Federal Work-Study, scholarships/grants, and unspecified assistantships also available. Financial award application deadline: 4/1. *Faculty research:* Contemporary Irish literature, Romantic psychology, cultural practices of everyday life, Gullah linguistics, Renaissance women's writing. Total annual research expenditures: $10,250. *Unit head:* Dr. Jeanne Dubino, Chair, 828-262-3098. *Application contact:* Dr. Bill Brewer, Graduate Adviser, 828-262-3098, E-mail: brewerwd@appstate.edu.

Arcadia University, Graduate Studies, Department of English, Glenside, PA 19038-3295. Offers MAE. Part-time and evening/weekend programs available. *Degree requirements:* For master's, thesis optional.

Arizona State University, Graduate College, College of Liberal Arts and Sciences, Division of Humanities, Department of English, Tempe, AZ 85287. Offers English (MA, PhD), including comparative literature (MA), linguistics (MA), literature (PhD), literature and language (MA), rhetoric and composition (MA), rhetoric/composition and linguistics (PhD); teaching English as a second language (MTESL). *Degree requirements:* For doctorate, thesis/dissertation. *Entrance requirements:* For master's and doctorate, GRE.

Arkansas State University, Graduate School, College of Humanities and Social Sciences, Department of English and Philosophy, Jonesboro, State University, AR 72467. Offers English (MA); English education (MSE, SCCT). Part-time programs available. *Faculty:* 14 full-time (4 women). *Students:* 5 full-time (3 women), 13 part-time (8 women); includes 5 minority (all African Americans), 2 international. Average age 30. 9 applicants, 78% accepted, 5 enrolled. In 2007, 7 degrees awarded. *Degree requirements:* For master's, one foreign language, comprehensive exam, thesis or alternative; for SCCT, comprehensive exam. *Entrance requirements:* For master's, GRE General Test or MAT, appropriate bachelor's degree, official transcript; for SCCT, GRE General Test or MAT, interview, master's degree, official transcript. Additional exam requirements/recommendations for international students: Required—TOEFL (minimum score 213 computer-based). *Application deadline:* Applications are processed on a rolling basis. Application fee: $30 ($40 for international students). Electronic applications accepted. *Expenses:* Tuition, state resident: full-time $3,528; part-time $196 per hour. Tuition, nonresident: full-time $8,928; part-time $496 per hour. Required fees: $842; $44 per hour. $25 per term. Tuition and fees vary according to course load and program. *Financial support:* Teaching assistantships, scholarships/grants and unspecified assistantships available. Financial award application deadline: 7/1; financial award applicants required to submit FAFSA. *Faculty research:* Cognitive science, critical race theory, history of English, linguistics, popular culture. *Unit head:* Dr. Charles Carr, Chair, 870-972-3043, Fax: 870-972-3045, E-mail: crcarr@astate.edu.

Arkansas Tech University, Graduate School, School of Liberal and Fine Arts, Russellville, AR 72801. Offers communication (MLA); English (M Ed, MA); fine arts (MLA); history (MA); multi-media journalism (MA); social science (MLA); social studies (M Ed); Spanish (MA, MLA); teaching English as a second language (MA, MLA). Part-time programs available. *Students:* 54 full-time (43 women), 79 part-time (54 women); includes 11 minority (3 African Americans, 1 American Indian/Alaska Native, 1 Asian American or Pacific Islander, 6 Hispanic Americans), 29 international. Average age 33. In 2007, 71 degrees awarded. *Degree requirements:* For master's, project. *Entrance requirements:* For master's, GRE General Test or MAT. Additional exam requirements/recommendations for international students: Required—TOEFL (minimum score 500 paper-based; 173 computer-based; 61 iBT). *Application deadline:* For fall admission, 3/1 priority date for domestic students, 5/1 priority date for international students; for winter admission, 10/1 priority date for international students; for spring admission, 10/1 priority date for domestic and international students. Applications are processed on a rolling basis. Application fee: $0 ($30 for international students). Electronic applications accepted. *Expenses:* Tuition, state resident: full-time $3,150; part-time $175 per hour. Tuition, nonresident: full-time $6,300; part-time $350 per hour. Required fees: $384; $8 per hour. $120 per term. Tuition and fees vary according to course load. *Financial support:* In 2007–08, teaching assistantships with full tuition reimbursements (averaging $4,000 per year); career-related internships or fieldwork, Federal Work-Study, scholarships/grants, health care benefits, and unspecified assistantships also available. Support available to part-time students. Financial award application deadline: 4/15; financial award applicants required to submit FAFSA. *Unit head:* Dr. Georgena Duncan,

Dean, 479-968-0266, Fax: 479-968-0275, E-mail: georgena.duncan@atu.edu. *Application contact:* Dr. Eldon G. Clary, Dean of Graduate School, 479-968-0398, Fax: 479-964-0542, E-mail: graduate.school@atu.edu.

Asbury College, Graduate Programs, Wilmore, KY 40390-1198. Offers biology: alternative certificate (MA Ed); chemistry: alternative certificate (MA Ed); English (Certificate); English as a second language (MA Ed); ESL (Certificate); French (Certificate); mathematics: alternative certificate (MA Ed); reading / writing (MA Ed); social studies (Certificate); Spanish (Certificate); special education (MA Ed); special education: alternative certificate (MA Ed). *Accreditation:* NCATE. Part-time programs available. *Faculty:* 8 full-time (7 women), 9 part-time/adjunct (4 women). *Students:* Average age 36. 14 applicants, 100% accepted, 14 enrolled. In 2007, 10 degrees awarded. *Degree requirements:* For master's, action research project, portfolio. *Entrance requirements:* For master's, PRAXIS/NTE, minimum GPA of 2.75, letters of recommendation. Additional exam requirements/recommendations for international students: Required—TOEFL (minimum score 550 paper-based). *Application deadline:* Applications are processed on a rolling basis. Application fee: $25. *Expenses:* Tuition: Part-time $353 per credit hour. *Financial support:* Scholarships/grants and traineeships available. Financial award applicants required to submit FAFSA. *Unit head:* Dr. Bonnie J. Banker, Director, 859-858-3511 Ext. 2221, Fax: 859-858-3921, E-mail: bonnie.banker@asbury.edu. *Application contact:* Melanie S. Kinnell, Graduate Program Assistant and Certification Specialist, 859-858-3511 Ext. 2304, Fax: 859-858-3921, E-mail: graded@asbury.edu.

Auburn University, Graduate School, College of Liberal Arts, Department of English, Auburn University, AL 36849. Offers MA, MTPC, PhD. Part-time programs available. *Faculty:* 39 full-time (13 women), 1 part-time/adjunct (0 women). *Students:* 20 full-time (14 women), 64 part-time (46 women); includes 10 minority (8 African Americans, 2 Hispanic Americans), 2 international. Average age 32. 65 applicants, 51% accepted, 20 enrolled. In 2007, 18 master's, 3 doctorates awarded. *Degree requirements:* For master's, one foreign language, thesis optional, written exam; for doctorate, 2 foreign languages, thesis/dissertation, oral and written exams. *Entrance requirements:* For master's, GRE General Test, sample of written work; for doctorate, GRE General Test, GRE Subject Test, sample of written work. *Application deadline:* For fall admission, 7/7 for domestic students; for spring admission, 11/24 for domestic students. Applications are processed on a rolling basis. Application fee: $25 ($50 for international students). Electronic applications accepted. *Financial support:* Fellowships, teaching assistantships, Federal Work-Study available. Support available to part-time students. Financial award application deadline: 3/15. *Faculty research:* English literature, American literature, linguistics, rhetoric and composition, literary theory. *Unit head:* Dr. George W. Crandell, Head, 334-844-4620. *Application contact:* Dr. Joe Pittman, Interim Dean of the Graduate School, 334-844-4700.

See Close-Up on page 559.

Austin Peay State University, College of Graduate Studies, College of Arts and Letters, Department of Languages and Literature, Clarksville, TN 37044. Offers English (MA). Part-time programs available. Postbaccalaureate distance learning degree programs offered (minimal on-campus study). *Faculty:* 14 full-time (6 women). *Students:* 14 full-time (11 women), 7 part-time (5 women); includes 2 minority (both African Americans) Average age 29. In 2007, 7 degrees awarded. *Degree requirements:* For master's, comprehensive exam, thesis optional. *Entrance requirements:* For master's, GRE General Test, 3 letters of recommendation. Additional exam requirements/recommendations for international students: Required—TOEFL (minimum score 500 paper-based; 173 computer-based). *Application deadline:* For fall admission, 7/31 priority date for domestic students; for spring admission, 12/17 priority date for domestic students. Applications are processed on a rolling basis. Application fee: $25. Electronic applications accepted. *Expenses:* Tuition, state resident: full-time $5,446; part-time $288 per credit hour. Tuition, nonresident: full-time $15,722; part-time $734 per credit hour. Required fees: $1,180. Part-time tuition and fees vary according to course load. *Financial support:* In 2007–08, research assistantships (averaging $10,368 per year); career-related internships or fieldwork, Federal Work-Study, institutionally sponsored loans, scholarships/grants, and unspecified assistantships also available. Support available to part-time students. Financial award application deadline: 3/1; financial award applicants required to submit FAFSA. *Faculty research:* English literature, creative writing, American literature, linguistics. *Unit head:* Dr. David Guest, Professor/Chair, 931-221-7891, Fax: 931-221-7219, E-mail: mcnabbw@apsu.edu.

Ball State University, Graduate School, College of Sciences and Humanities, Department of English, Muncie, IN 47306-1099. Offers English (MA, PhD), including composition, creative writing (MA), general (MA), literature; linguistics (MA, PhD), including applied linguistics (PhD); linguistics and teaching English to speakers of other languages (MA); teaching English to speakers of other languages (MA). *Faculty:* 38. *Students:* 42 full-time (27 women), 31 part-time (18 women), 20 international. Average age 27. 99 applicants, 52% accepted, 26 enrolled. In 2007, 22 master's, 6 doctorates awarded. *Degree requirements:* For doctorate, variable foreign language requirement, thesis/dissertation. *Entrance requirements:* For master's, GRE General Test, writing sample; for doctorate, GRE General Test, GRE Subject Test, minimum graduate GPA of 3.2, writing sample. Application fee: $25 ($35 for international students). *Expenses:* Tuition, state resident: full-time $6,864. Tuition, nonresident: full-time $17,932. Required fees: $1,866. *Financial support:* In 2007–08, 2 fellowships with full tuition reimbursements (averaging $15,500 per year), 48 teaching assistantships with full tuition reimbursements (averaging $15,314 per year) were awarded; research assistantships with full tuition reimbursements, career-related internships or fieldwork and unspecified assistantships also available. Financial award application deadline: 3/1. *Faculty research:* American literature; literary editing; Medieval, Renaissance, and eighteenth century British literature; rhetoric. *Unit head:* Dr. Kecia McBride, Chairperson, 765-285-8535, Fax: 765-285-3765.

Baylor University, Graduate School, College of Arts and Sciences, Department of English, Waco, TX 76798. Offers MA, PhD. Part-time programs available. *Faculty:* 19 full-time (6 women). *Students:* 27 full-time (19 women), 33 part-time (27 women); includes 2 minority (1 American Indian/Alaska Native, 1 Hispanic American), 2 international. 25 applicants, 88% accepted. In 2007, 3 master's, 4 doctorates awarded. *Degree requirements:* For master's, one foreign language, thesis; for doctorate, 2 foreign languages, thesis/dissertation. *Entrance requirements:* For master's, GRE General Test, 18 hours of upper-level course work in English; for doctorate, GRE General Test. *Application deadline:* For fall admission, 3/15 priority date for domestic students. Applications are processed on a rolling basis. Application fee: $25. Electronic applications accepted. *Financial support:* In 2007–08, 10 research assistantships, 28 teaching assistantships were awarded; fellowships, Federal Work-Study, institutionally sponsored loans, unspecified assistantships, and laboratory assistantships also available. *Faculty research:* Nineteenth century British literature, Renaissance studies, American studies, Medieval studies, rhetoric and composition. Total annual research expenditures: $48,400. *Unit head:* Dr. Robert Ray, Graduate Program Director, 254-710-1768, Fax: 254-710-3894. *Application contact:* Suzanne Keener, Administrative Assistant, 254-710-3588, Fax: 254-710-3870.

Belmont University, College of Arts and Sciences, Department of English, Nashville, TN 37212-3757. Offers literature (MA); writing (MA). Part-time and evening/weekend programs available. *Faculty:* 17 full-time (13 women). *Students:* 1 (woman) full-time, 37 part-time (30 women); includes 5 minority (4 African Americans, 1 Hispanic American). Average age 31. 15 applicants, 73% accepted, 10 enrolled. In 2007, 10 degrees awarded. *Degree requirements:* For master's, one foreign language, comprehensive exam (for some programs), thesis optional. *Entrance requirements:* For master's, GRE, letters of recommendation, writing sample. Additional exam requirements/recommendations for international students: Required—TOEFL. *Application deadline:* For fall admission, 8/1 for domestic students; for spring admission, 12/1 for domestic students. Applications are processed on a rolling basis. Application fee: $50. Electronic applications accepted. *Expenses:* Contact institution. *Financial support:* In 2007–08, 20 students received support. Federal Work-Study and scholarships/grants available. Financial award applicants required to submit FAFSA. *Faculty research:* Gender, autobiography, folklore. *Unit head:* Dr. James Wells, Director, 615-460-6239, Fax: 615-460-5720, E-mail: wellsj@mail.belmont.edu.

Bemidji State University, School of Graduate Studies, College of Arts and Letters, Department of English, Bemidji, MN 56601-2699. Offers MA, MS. Part-time programs available. *Faculty:* 13 full-time (9 women). *Students:* 2 full-time (both women), 23 part-time (15 women); includes 1 minority (American Indian/Alaska Native). 10 applicants, 100% accepted. In 2007, 8 degrees awarded. *Degree requirements:* For master's, one foreign language, thesis. *Entrance requirements:* For master's, letters of Rec. Additional exam requirements/recommendations for international students: Required—TOEFL. *Application deadline:* For fall admission, 5/1 priority date for domestic students. Applications are processed on a rolling basis. Application fee: $20. Electronic applications accepted. *Expenses:* Tuition, state resident: full-time $5,310; part-time $295 per credit. Required fees: $833; $81 per credit. $1 per term. One-time fee: $20. Tuition and fees vary according to course load, campus/location and reciprocity agreements. *Financial support:* In 2007–08, 3 research assistantships with partial tuition reimbursements (averaging $8,250 per year), 9 teaching assistantships with partial tuition reimbursements (averaging $8,250 per year) were awarded; career-related internships or fieldwork, Federal Work-Study, scholarships/grants, health care benefits, and unspecified assistantships also available. Support available to part-time students. Financial award application deadline: 5/1. *Faculty research:* Creative writing; modern languages; film; electronic writing; rhetoric and composition; literary criticism. *Unit head:* Susan Hauser, Chair, 218-755-3355, E-mail: shauser@bemidjistate.edu.

Bennington College, Graduate Programs, Program in Writing and Literature, Bennington, VT 05201. Offers creative writing (MFA). Postbaccalaureate distance learning degree programs offered (minimal on-campus study). *Faculty:* 14 full-time (8 women), 9 part-time/adjunct (4 women). *Students:* 104 full-time (75 women); includes 6 minority (1 African American, 5 Asian Americans or Pacific Islanders), 3 international. Average age 40. 157 applicants, 27% accepted, 28 enrolled. In 2007, 43 degrees awarded. *Degree requirements:* For master's, thesis, collection of essays or poems, or collection of short stories and/or a novel. *Entrance requirements:* For master's, manuscript. *Application deadline:* For fall admission, 3/1 for domestic students; for spring admission, 9/1 for domestic students. Application fee: $60. *Expenses:* Contact institution. One-time fee: $75 full-time. Tuition and fees vary according to program. *Financial support:* In 2007–08, 6 students received support. Scholarships/grants available. Financial award application deadline: 4/1; financial award applicants required to submit FAFSA. *Unit head:* Sven Birkerts, Director, Writing Seminars, 802-440-4452, Fax: 802-440-4453, E-mail: writing@bennington.edu. *Application contact:* Victoria Clausi, Associate Director of Writing Seminars, 802-440-4454, Fax: 802-440-4453, E-mail: writing@bennington.edu.

Bob Jones University, Graduate Programs, Greenville, SC 29614. Offers accountancy (MS); Bible (MA); Bible translation (MA); Biblical studies (Certificate); broadcast management (MS); business administration (MBA); church history (MA, PhD); church ministries (MA); church music (MM); cinema and video production (MA); counseling (MS); curriculum and instruction (Ed D); divinity (M Div); dramatic production (MA); educational leadership (MS, Ed D, Ed S); elementary education (M Ed, MAT); English (M Ed, MA, MAT); fine arts (MA); graphic design (MA); history (M Ed, MA); illustration (MA); interpretative speech (MA); mathematics (M Ed, MAT); medical missions (Certificate); ministry (MM, D Min); multi-categorical special education (M Ed, MAT); music (M Ed); New Testament interpretation (PhD); Old Testament interpretation (PhD); orchestral instrument performance (MM); organ performance (MM); pastoral studies (MA); personnel services (MS, Ed S); piano pedagogy (MM); piano performance (MM); platform arts (MA); radio and television broadcasting (MS); rhetoric and public address (MA); secondary education (M Ed); studio art (MA); teaching Bible (MA); theology (MA, PhD); voice performance (MM); youth ministries (MA); M Div/MM.

Boise State University, Graduate College, College of Arts and Sciences, Department of English, Program in English, Boise, ID 83725-0399. Offers MA. Part-time programs available. *Degree requirements:* For master's, thesis. *Entrance requirements:* For master's, GRE General Test, minimum GPA of 3.0. Electronic applications accepted.

Boston College, Graduate School of Arts and Sciences, Department of English, Chestnut Hill, MA 02467-3800. Offers MA, PhD. *Students:* 63 full-time (35 women), 49 part-time (31 women); includes 9 minority (1 African American, 8 Asian Americans or Pacific Islanders), 2 international. 327 applicants, 38% accepted, 53 enrolled. In 2007, 36 master's, 3 doctorates awarded. *Degree requirements:* For master's, one foreign language, thesis optional; for doctorate, 2 foreign languages, thesis/dissertation. *Entrance requirements:* For master's and doctorate, GRE General Test, GRE Subject Test. Additional exam requirements/recommendations for international students: Required—TOEFL (minimum score 590 paper-based; 250 computer-based; 91 iBT). *Application deadline:* For fall admission, 1/15 priority date for domestic students. Application fee: $70. Electronic applications accepted. *Financial support:* Fellowships, teaching assistantships, Federal Work-Study, scholarships/grants, and tuition waivers (full and partial) available. Support available to part-time students. Financial award application deadline: 3/1; financial award applicants required to submit FAFSA. *Faculty research:* English and American literature, critical theory. *Unit head:* Dr. Mary Crane, Chairperson, 617-552-3701, E-mail: mary.crane@bc.edu. *Application contact:* Dr. Robert Stanton, Graduate Program Director, 617-552-3701, E-mail: robert.stanton@bc.edu.

Boston University, Graduate School of Arts and Sciences, Department of English, Boston, MA 02215. Offers creative writing (MA); English (MA, PhD). *Students:* 51 full-time (33 women), 11 part-time (6 women), 1 international. Average age 30. 665 applicants, 14% accepted, 40 enrolled. In 2007, 16 master's, 7 doctorates awarded. Terminal master's awarded for partial completion of doctoral program. *Degree requirements:* For master's, one foreign language, thesis; for doctorate, 2 foreign languages, comprehensive exam, thesis/dissertation, qualifying/oral exam. *Entrance requirements:* For master's and doctorate, GRE General Test, GRE Subject Test, sample of written work, 2 letters of recommendation. Additional exam requirements/recommendations for international students: Required—TOEFL (minimum score 550 paper-based; 213 computer-based). *Application deadline:* For fall admission, 1/15 for domestic students, 2/15 for international students. Application fee: $70. *Expenses:* Tuition: Full-time $34,930; part-time $1,092 per credit. Tuition and fees vary according to class time, course level and program. *Financial support:* In 2007–08, 39 students received support, including 2 fellowships with full tuition reimbursements available (averaging $18,000 per year), 25 teaching assistantships with partial tuition reimbursements available (averaging $16,500 per year); Federal Work-Study, scholarships/grants, and unspecified assistantships also available. Financial award application deadline: 1/15; financial award applicants required to submit FAFSA. *Unit head:* Laurence Breiner, Interim Chairman, 617-353-2509, Fax: 617-353-3653, E-mail: lbrei@bu.edu. *Application contact:* Harriet T. Lane, Administrative Assistant, 617-353-2509, Fax: 617-353-3653, E-mail: hlane@bu.edu.

Bowie State University, Graduate Programs, Program in English, Bowie, MD 20715-9465. Offers MA. Part-time and evening/weekend programs available. *Entrance requirements:* For master's, minimum 2.5 GPA, English Degree. Electronic applications accepted.

Bowling Green State University, Graduate College, College of Arts and Sciences, Department of English, Program in English, Bowling Green, OH 43403. Offers English (MA, PhD); literature (MA); rhetoric and writing (PhD); scientific and technical communication (MA). Part-time programs available. *Students:* 49 full-time (36 women), 12 part-time (9 women); includes 1 African American, 3 Asian Americans or Pacific Islanders, 1 Hispanic American, 9 international. Average age 31. 64 applicants, 67% accepted, 21 enrolled. In 2007, 14 master's, 6 doctorates awarded. *Degree requirements:* For master's, thesis or alternative; for doctorate, comprehensive exam, thesis/dissertation, foreign language or proficiency in Old English. *Entrance requirements:* For master's and doctorate, GRE General Test. Additional exam requirements/recommendations for international students: Required—TOEFL. *Application deadline:* For fall admission, 2/15 priority date for domestic students. Applications are processed on a rolling basis. Application fee: $30. Electronic applications accepted. *Financial support:* In 2007–08, 3 fellowships with full tuition reimbursements (averaging $14,707 per year), 8 research assistantships with full tuition reimbursements (averaging $9,664 per year), 34 teaching assistantships with full tuition reimbursements (averaging $10,480 per year) were

English

Bowling Green State University (continued)

awarded; Federal Work-Study and unspecified assistantships also available. Financial award applicants required to submit FAFSA. *Faculty research:* Postmodern literary theory, rhetorical theory, ethnic American literature, literature and culture, composition pedagogy.

Bradley University, Graduate School, College of Liberal Arts and Sciences, Department of English, Peoria, IL 61625-0002. Offers MA. Part-time programs available. *Students:* 11 applicants, 45% accepted, 4 enrolled. In 2007, 5 degrees awarded. *Degree requirements:* For master's, comprehensive exam. *Entrance requirements:* For master's, writing sample, 2 letters of recommendation. Additional exam requirements/recommendations for international students: Required—TOEFL (minimum score 550 paper-based; 213 computer-based; 79 iBT). *Application deadline:* For fall admission, 5/15 priority date for domestic and international students; for spring admission, 10/15 priority date for domestic and international students. Applications are processed on a rolling basis. Application fee: $40 ($50 for international students). *Financial support:* Research assistantships with full and partial tuition reimbursements, teaching assistantships, scholarships/grants, tuition waivers (partial), and unspecified assistantships available. Support available to part-time students. Financial award application deadline: 4/1. *Unit head:* Dr. Peter Dusenberry, Chairperson, 309-677-2465. *Application contact:* Dr. Robert Prescott, Graduate Coordinator, 309-677-2468, E-mail: prescott@bradley.edu.

Brandeis University, Graduate School of Arts and Sciences, Department of English and American Literature, Waltham, MA 02454-9110. Offers English and American literature (MA, PhD); English and women's studies (MA). Part-time programs available. *Faculty:* 14 full-time (8 women). *Students:* 47 full-time (29 women), 1 (woman) part-time; includes 2 minority (1 Asian American or Pacific Islander, 1 Hispanic American), 6 international. Average age 31. 119 applicants, 20% accepted, 9 enrolled. In 2007, 6 master's, 3 doctorates awarded. *Degree requirements:* For master's, one foreign language, thesis, symposium; for doctorate, 2 foreign languages, thesis/dissertation, field exam, symposium presentation, prospectus defense. *Entrance requirements:* For master's, GRE General Test, resumé, sample of work, letters of recommendation; for doctorate, GRE General Test, GRE Subject Test, resumé, sample of work, letters of recommendation. Additional exam requirements/recommendations for international students: Required—TOEFL (minimum score 600 paper-based; 250 computer-based; 100 iBT), IELTS (minimum score 7). *Application deadline:* For fall admission, 1/5 for domestic students. Application fee: $55. Electronic applications accepted. *Financial support:* In 2007–08, 58 students received support, including 28 fellowships with full tuition reimbursements available (averaging $16,500 per year), 30 teaching assistantships with full tuition reimbursements available (averaging $4,000 per year); research assistantships with full tuition reimbursements available, scholarships/grants, health care benefits, and tuition waivers (full and partial) also available. Financial award application deadline: 4/15; financial award applicants required to submit CSS PROFILE or FAFSA. *Faculty research:* Feminist and gender theory, American literature, Anglophone literature, early modern literature, modernism. *Unit head:* Dr. Ramie Targoff, Director of Graduate Studies, 781-736-2148, Fax: 781-736-2179, E-mail: chaucer@brandeis.edu.

Bridgewater State College, School of Graduate Studies, School of Arts and Sciences, Department of English, Bridgewater, MA 02325-0001. Offers MA, MAT. Part-time and evening/weekend programs available. *Degree requirements:* For master's, one foreign language, comprehensive exam, thesis optional. *Entrance requirements:* For master's, GRE General Test. *Application deadline:* For fall admission, 4/1 priority date for domestic students; for spring admission, 10/1 priority date for domestic students. Application fee: $50. *Financial support:* Career-related internships or fieldwork, health care benefits, and unspecified assistantships available. Support available to part-time students.

Brigham Young University, Graduate Studies, College of Humanities, Department of English, Provo, UT 84602-1001. Offers MA. *Faculty:* 54 full-time (18 women). *Students:* 83 full-time (53 women), 3 part-time (1 woman). Average age 25. 71 applicants, 49% accepted, 27 enrolled. In 2007, 17 degrees awarded. *Degree requirements:* For master's, one foreign language, thesis. *Entrance requirements:* For master's, GRE General Test. Additional exam requirements/recommendations for international students: Required—TOEFL. *Application deadline:* For fall admission, 1/15 for domestic students. Application fee: $50. Electronic applications accepted. *Financial support:* In 2007–08, 75 students received support, including 13 research assistantships (averaging $2,600 per year), 62 teaching assistantships (averaging $6,000 per year); career-related internships or fieldwork, institutionally sponsored loans, scholarships/grants, and tuition waivers (partial) also available. Support available to part-time students. Financial award application deadline: 3/15. *Faculty research:* English literature, American literature, rhetoric, creative writing. *Unit head:* Prof. Ed Cutler, Head, 801-422-3581, Fax: 801-422-0221, E-mail: ed_cutler@byu.edu. *Application contact:* Lou Ann C. Crisler, Graduate Secretary, 801-422-8673, Fax: 801-422-0221, E-mail: louann_crisler@byu.edu.

Brock University, Faculty of Graduate Studies, Faculty of Humanities, Program in English, St. Catharines, ON L2S 3A1, Canada. Offers MA. Part-time programs available. *Degree requirements:* For master's, thesis optional. *Entrance requirements:* For master's, honours in English. Additional exam requirements/recommendations for international students: Required—TOEFL (minimum score 550 paper-based; 213 computer-based; 80 iBT), IELTS (minimum score 7), TWE (minimum score 4). Electronic applications accepted. *Faculty research:* Literary theory, Canadian literature, Milton and 17th century American literature, 19th century American literature, British Romantic literature and culture.

Brooklyn College of the City University of New York, Division of Graduate Studies, Department of English, Brooklyn, NY 11210-2889. Offers creative writing (MFA), including fiction, playwriting, poetry; English (MA, PhD). The department offers courses at Brooklyn College that are creditable toward the CUNY doctoral degree (with permission of the executive officer of the doctoral program). Part-time and evening/weekend programs available. *Students:* 21 full-time (11 women), 160 part-time (108 women); includes 39 minority (20 African Americans, 7 Asian Americans or Pacific Islanders, 12 Hispanic Americans), 5 international. 388 applicants, 32% accepted, 71 enrolled. In 2007, 82 degrees awarded. *Degree requirements:* For master's, one foreign language, comprehensive exam (for some programs), thesis (for some programs). *Entrance requirements:* For master's, advanced undergraduate courses in English, 2 letters of recommendation, writing sample, statement of purpose. Additional exam requirements/recommendations for international students: Required—TOEFL. *Application deadline:* For fall admission, 3/1 priority date for domestic students, 2/1 for international students; for spring admission, 11/1 for domestic students, 10/1 for international students. Applications are processed on a rolling basis. Application fee: $125. Electronic applications accepted. *Financial support:* Federal Work-Study, institutionally sponsored loans, and scholarships/grants available. Support available to part-time students. Financial award application deadline: 5/1; financial award applicants required to submit FAFSA. *Faculty research:* Cultural studies, medieval literature, Virginia Woolf. *Unit head:* Dr. Ellen Tremper, Chairperson, 718-951-5195, E-mail: etremper@brooklyn.cuny.edu. *Application contact:* Hernan Sierra, Graduate Admissions Coordinator, 718-951-4536, Fax: 718-951-4506, E-mail: grads@brooklyn.cuny.edu.

Brown University, Graduate School, Department of English, Program in English Literature and Language, Providence, RI 02912. Offers AM, PhD. *Degree requirements:* For doctorate, variable foreign language requirement, thesis/dissertation. *Entrance requirements:* For master's and doctorate, GRE General Test, GRE Subject Test.

Bucknell University, Graduate Studies, College of Arts and Sciences, Department of English, Lewisburg, PA 17837. Offers MA. Part-time programs available. *Faculty:* 22 full-time (12 women), 1 part-time/adjunct (0 women). *Students:* 10 full-time (7 women), 1 (woman) part-time; includes 3 minority (2 Asian Americans or Pacific Islanders, 1 Hispanic American). *Degree requirements:* For master's, one foreign language, thesis. *Entrance requirements:* For master's, GRE General Test, GRE Subject Test, minimum GPA of 2.8. Additional exam requirements/recommendations for international students: Required—TOEFL. *Application deadline:* For fall admission, 6/1 priority date for domestic students, 3/1 for international students; for spring admission, 12/1 priority date for domestic students. Applications are processed on a rolling basis. Application fee: $25. *Expenses:* Tuition: Full-time $16,660; part-time $1,041 per credit hour. *Financial support:* In 2007–08, 7 students received support. Unspecified assistantships available. Financial award application deadline: 3/1. *Unit head:* Dr. Harold Schweizer, Chair, 570-577-1553.

Buffalo State College, State University of New York, Graduate Studies and Research, Faculty of Arts and Humanities, Department of English, Buffalo, NY 14222-1095. Offers English (MA); secondary education (MS Ed), including English. Part-time and evening/weekend programs available. *Degree requirements:* For master's, thesis or project, 1 foreign language (MS Ed). *Entrance requirements:* For master's, minimum GPA of 2.75, 36 hours in English, New York teaching certificate (MS Ed). Additional exam requirements/recommendations for international students: Required—TOEFL (minimum score 550 paper-based; 213 computer-based).

Butler University, College of Liberal Arts and Sciences, Department of English, Indianapolis, IN 46208-3485. Offers MA. Part-time and evening/weekend programs available. *Faculty:* 1 full-time (0 women), 1 part-time/adjunct (0 women). *Students:* 2 full-time (both women), 12 part-time (8 women), 6 international. Average age 33. 9 applicants, 67% accepted, 4 enrolled. In 2007, 2 degrees awarded. *Entrance requirements:* For master's, GRE General Test, GRE Subject Test. *Application deadline:* For fall admission, 8/15 priority date for domestic students. Applications are processed on a rolling basis. Application fee: $35. Electronic applications accepted. *Expenses:* Tuition: Full-time $6,300; part-time $350 per credit. Tuition and fees vary according to program. *Financial support:* Applicants required to submit FAFSA. *Faculty research:* Modern poetry, ethnic literature, liberal education, Chaucer, ethics. *Unit head:* Dr. Hilene Flanzbaum, Head, 317-940-9860, E-mail: hflanzba@butler.edu.

California Baptist University, Program in English, Riverside, CA 92504-3206. Offers MA. Part-time programs available. *Faculty:* 4 full-time (3 women). *Students:* 6 full-time (4 women), 23 part-time (17 women); includes 6 minority (1 African American, 3 Asian Americans or Pacific Islanders, 2 Hispanic Americans), 4 international. 10 applicants, 60% accepted, 4 enrolled. In 2007, 5 degrees awarded. *Degree requirements:* For master's, thesis (for some programs). *Entrance requirements:* For master's, minimum undergraduate GPA of 2.75, 18 semester hours of course work in English beyond freshman level. Additional exam requirements/recommendations for international students: Required—TOEFL (minimum score 575 paper-based; 230 computer-based), IELTS (minimum score 7). *Application deadline:* For fall admission, 9/1 for domestic students, 7/1 priority date for international students; for spring admission, 1/3 for domestic students, 10/15 priority date for international students. Applications are processed on a rolling basis. Application fee: $45. Electronic applications accepted. *Expenses:* Tuition: Full-time $7,992; part-time $444 per semester hour. Required fees: $510; $125 per semester. *Financial support:* Federal Work-Study available. Support available to part-time students. Financial award applicants required to submit FAFSA. *Unit head:* Dr. Jennifer Newton, Director, 951-343-4276, Fax: 951-343-4661, E-mail: jnewton@calbaptist.edu. *Application contact:* Gail Ronveaux, Dean of Graduate Enrollment, 951-343-5045, Fax: 951-343-5095, E-mail: graduateadmissions@calbaptist.edu.

California Polytechnic State University, San Luis Obispo, College of Liberal Arts, Department of English, San Luis Obispo, CA 93407. Offers MA. Part-time programs available. *Faculty:* 4 full-time (3 women). *Students:* 8 full-time (6 women), 23 part-time (12 women); includes 8 minority (1 African American, 3 Asian Americans or Pacific Islanders, 4 Hispanic Americans). 19 applicants, 74% accepted, 9 enrolled. In 2007, 11 degrees awarded. *Degree requirements:* For master's, one foreign language, comprehensive exam. *Entrance requirements:* For master's, minimum GPA of 3.0 in last 90 quarter units of course work, writing sample. Additional exam requirements/recommendations for international students: Required—TOEFL (minimum score 550 paper-based; 213 computer-based), TWE (minimum score 4.5). *Application deadline:* For fall admission, 7/1 for domestic students, 11/30 for international students; for winter admission, 11/1 for domestic students, 6/30 for international students; for spring admission, 2/1 for domestic students. Applications are processed on a rolling basis. Application fee: $55. *Expenses:* Tuition, nonresident: part-time $226 per unit. Required fees: $1,777 per quarter. *Financial support:* Teaching assistantships, career-related internships or fieldwork, Federal Work-Study, institutionally sponsored loans, and tutorships, writing laboratory assistantships available. Support available to part-time students. Financial award application deadline: 3/2; financial award applicants required to submit FAFSA. *Faculty research:* Feminist literary criticism, modern British novel, literary theory, Shakespeare, Victorian literature. *Unit head:* Dr. Debora Schwartz, Graduate Coordinator, 805-756-2636, Fax: 805-756-6374, E-mail: dschwart@calpoly.edu.

California State Polytechnic University, Pomona, Academic Affairs, College of Letters, Arts, and Social Sciences, Program in English, Pomona, CA 91768-2557. Offers MA. Part-time programs available. *Students:* 27 full-time (18 women), 60 part-time (41 women); includes 28 minority (3 African Americans, 11 Asian Americans or Pacific Islanders, 14 Hispanic Americans), 5 international. Average age 34. 36 applicants, 72% accepted, 20 enrolled. In 2007, 23 degrees awarded. *Degree requirements:* For master's, one foreign language, thesis or alternative. *Application deadline:* For fall admission, 5/1 priority date for domestic students; for winter admission, 10/15 priority date for domestic students; for spring admission, 1/20 priority date for domestic students. Applications are processed on a rolling basis. Application fee: $55. Electronic applications accepted. *Expenses:* Tuition, nonresident: full-time $7,232; part-time $226 per unit. Required fees: $3,920. One-time fee: $2,486 part-time. *Financial support:* In 2007–08, 2 fellowships were awarded; Federal Work-Study and institutionally sponsored loans also available. Support available to part-time students. Financial award application deadline: 3/2; financial award applicants required to submit FAFSA. *Unit head:* Dr. Karen A. Russikoff, Coordinator, 909-869-3836.

California State University, Bakersfield, Division of Graduate Studies, School of Humanities and Social Sciences, Program in English, Bakersfield, CA 93311-1022. Offers MA. *Degree requirements:* For master's, comprehensive exam or thesis. *Entrance requirements:* For master's, GRE General Test, GRE Subject Test (literature), minimum GPA of 2.5 for last 90 quarter units. Additional exam requirements/recommendations for international students: Required—TOEFL (minimum score 550 paper-based; 213 computer-based).

California State University, Chico, Graduate School, College of Humanities and Fine Arts, Department of English, Program in English, Chico, CA 95929-0830. Offers MA. *Students:* 23 full-time (11 women), 12 part-time (all women); includes 4 minority (all Hispanic Americans) Average age 33. 14 applicants, 79% accepted, 9 enrolled. In 2007, 8 degrees awarded. *Degree requirements:* For master's, thesis. *Entrance requirements:* For master's, GRE General Test, Two letters of recommendation, Statement of Purpose, writing sample. Additional exam requirements/recommendations for international students: Required—TOEFL (minimum score 550 paper-based; 213 computer-based; 80 iBT), IELTS (minimum score 7). *Application deadline:* For fall admission, 3/1 for domestic and international students; for spring admission, 9/15 for domestic and international students. Application fee: $55. *Unit head:* Dr. Rob Davidson, Graduate Coordinator, 530-898-6457.

California State University, Dominguez Hills, College of Arts and Humanities, Department of English, Carson, CA 90747-0001. Offers English (MA); rhetoric and composition (Certificate); teaching English as a second language (Certificate). Part-time and evening/weekend programs available. *Faculty:* 15 full-time (6 women). *Students:* 28 full-time (17 women), 41 part-time (28 women); includes 29 minority (12 African Americans, 5 Asian Americans or Pacific Islanders, 12 Hispanic Americans), 5 international. Average age 36. 34 applicants, 88% accepted, 15 enrolled. In 2007, 27 degrees awarded. *Degree requirements:* For master's, comprehensive exam (for some programs), thesis or alternative. *Entrance requirements:* For master's, minimum GPA of 3.0 in last 60 units. Additional exam requirements/recommendations for international students: Required—TOEFL (minimum score 550 paper-based; 213 computer-based). *Application deadline:* Applications are processed on a rolling basis. Application fee: $55. Electronic applications accepted. *Faculty research:* Gender studies, transnationalism, discourse analysis, visual culture, Shakespeare. *Unit head:* Dr. Cyril Zoerner, Chair, 310-243-3322. *Application contact:* 310-243-3600.

California State University, East Bay, Academic Programs and Graduate Studies, College of Letters, Arts, and Social Sciences, Department of English, Hayward, CA 94542-3000. Offers MA. Part-time and evening/weekend programs available. *Faculty:* 6 full-time (5 women), 1 (woman) part-time/adjunct. *Students:* 18 full-time (12 women), 64 part-time (42 women); includes 17 minority (3 African Americans, 9 Asian Americans or Pacific Islanders, 5 Hispanic Americans), 5 international. Average age 37. 58 applicants, 50% accepted, 20 enrolled. In 2007, 41 degrees awarded. *Degree requirements:* For master's, one foreign language, comprehensive exam, thesis optional. *Entrance requirements:* For master's, minimum GPA of 3.0 in field. Additional exam requirements/recommendations for international students: Required—TOEFL (minimum score 550 paper-based; 213 computer-based). *Application deadline:* For fall admission, 5/31 for domestic students, 4/30 for international students; for winter admission, 9/30 for domestic and international students; for spring admission, 12/31 for domestic students, 11/30 for international students. Applications are processed on a rolling basis. Application fee: $55. Electronic applications accepted. *Expenses:* Required fees: $3,987; $851 per quarter. *Financial support:* Fellowships, teaching assistantships, career-related internships or fieldwork, Federal Work-Study, institutionally sponsored loans, and scholarships/grants available. Support available to part-time students. Financial award application deadline: 3/2. *Unit head:* Dr. E. J. Murphy, Chair, 510-885-3151, Fax: 510-885-4797, E-mail: james.murphy@csueastbay.edu. *Application contact:* My Huynh, Graduate Prospect Specialist, 510-885-2989, Fax: 510-885-4059, E-mail: my.huynh@csueastbay.edu.

California State University, Fresno, Division of Graduate Studies, College of Arts and Humanities, Department of English, Fresno, CA 93740-8027. Offers composition theory (MA); creative writing (MFA); literature (MA). Part-time and evening/weekend programs available. *Faculty:* 27 full-time (13 women). *Students:* 102; includes 30 minority (1 African American, 1 American Indian/Alaska Native, 4 Asian Americans or Pacific Islanders, 24 Hispanic Americans), 1 international. Average age 28. 22 applicants. In 2007, 18 degrees awarded. *Degree requirements:* For master's, one foreign language, thesis. *Entrance requirements:* For master's, GRE General Test, minimum GPA of 3.0, writing sample. Additional exam requirements/recommendations for international students: Required—TOEFL. *Application deadline:* For fall admission, 5/1 for domestic and international students; for spring admission, 10/1 for domestic and international students. Applications are processed on a rolling basis. Application fee: $55. Electronic applications accepted. *Financial support:* In 2007–08, 32 teaching assistantships were awarded; career-related internships or fieldwork, Federal Work-Study, and scholarships/grants also available. Support available to part-time students. Financial award application deadline: 3/1; financial award applicants required to submit FAFSA. *Faculty research:* American literature, Renaissance literature, foreign literature. *Unit head:* Dr. James Walton, Chair, 559-278-2553, Fax: 559-278-7143, E-mail: james_walton@csufresno.edu. *Application contact:* Dr. James Lyn Johnson, Graduate Program Coordinator, 559-278-2553, Fax: 559-278-7143, E-mail: james_johnson@csufresno.edu.

California State University, Fullerton, Graduate Studies, College of Humanities and Social Sciences, Department of English and Comparative Literature, Fullerton, CA 92834-9480. Offers comparative literature (MA); English (MA). Part-time programs available. *Students:* 27 full-time (22 women), 77 part-time (50 women); includes 19 minority (1 African American, 5 Asian Americans or Pacific Islanders, 13 Hispanic Americans). Average age 32. 78 applicants, 53% accepted, 29 enrolled. In 2007, 38 degrees awarded. *Degree requirements:* For master's, comprehensive exam, thesis or alternative. *Entrance requirements:* For master's, minimum GPA of 3.0 in major, 2.5 in last 60 hours. Application fee: $55. *Financial support:* Teaching assistantships, Federal Work-Study, institutionally sponsored loans, and scholarships/grants available. Support available to part-time students. Financial award application deadline: 3/1. *Unit head:* Dr. Joseph Sawicki, Chair, 714-278-3163. *Application contact:* Dr. Susan Jacobsen, Adviser, 714-278-3163.

California State University, Long Beach, Graduate Studies, College of Liberal Arts, Department of English, Long Beach, CA 90840. Offers creative writing (MFA); English (MA). Part-time programs available. *Faculty:* 50 full-time (24 women), 78 part-time/adjunct (45 women). *Students:* 60 full-time (42 women), 114 part-time (78 women); includes 43 minority (5 African Americans, 1 American Indian/Alaska Native, 17 Asian Americans or Pacific Islanders, 20 Hispanic Americans). Average age 34. *Degree requirements:* For master's, one foreign language, comprehensive exam or thesis. *Entrance requirements:* For master's, GRE Subject Test, minimum GPA of 3.0 in English. *Application deadline:* For fall admission, 7/1 for domestic students; for spring admission, 12/1 for domestic students. Applications are processed on a rolling basis. Application fee: $55. Electronic applications accepted. *Financial support:* Federal Work-Study, institutionally sponsored loans, and scholarships/grants available. Financial award application deadline: 3/2. *Faculty research:* English and American literature, literary theory, linguistics, rhetoric and composition. *Unit head:* Dr. Eileen S. Klink, Chair, 562-985-4223, Fax: 562-985-2369, E-mail: eklink@csulb.edu. *Application contact:* Dr. George Hart, Graduate Adviser, 562-985-4235, Fax: 562-985-2369, E-mail: ghart@csulb.edu.

California State University, Los Angeles, Graduate Studies, College of Arts and Letters, Department of English, Los Angeles, CA 90032-8530. Offers MA. Part-time and evening/weekend programs available. *Faculty:* 21 full-time (8 women). *Students:* 25 full-time (13 women), 109 part-time (68 women); includes 46 minority (7 African Americans, 1 American Indian/Alaska Native, 10 Asian Americans or Pacific Islanders, 28 Hispanic Americans), 17 international. Average age 34. In 2007, 27 degrees awarded. *Degree requirements:* For master's, comprehensive exam or thesis. *Entrance requirements:* Additional exam requirements/recommendations for international students: Required—TOEFL. *Application deadline:* For fall admission, 6/30 for domestic students; for spring admission, 2/1 for domestic students. Applications are processed on a rolling basis. Application fee: $55. *Financial support:* Federal Work-Study available. Support available to part-time students. Financial award application deadline: 3/1. *Faculty research:* English and American literature, linguistics, composition. *Unit head:* Dr. John Cleman, Acting Chair, 323-343-4140 Ext. 34298, Fax: 323-343-6470, E-mail: jcleman@calstatela.edu.

California State University, Northridge, Graduate Studies, College of Humanities, Department of English, Northridge, CA 91330. Offers creative writing (MA); literature (MA); rhetoric and composition theory (MA). Part-time and evening/weekend programs available. *Faculty:* 37 full-time (19 women), 85 part-time/adjunct (69 women). *Students:* 40 full-time (29 women), 125 part-time (92 women); includes 38 minority (3 African Americans, 1 American Indian/Alaska Native, 13 Asian Americans or Pacific Islanders, 21 Hispanic Americans). Average age 34. 99 applicants, 75% accepted, 40 enrolled. In 2007, 38 degrees awarded. *Degree requirements:* For master's, thesis or alternative. *Entrance requirements:* For master's, writing proficiency test, GRE General Test or minimum GPA of 3.0. Additional exam requirements/recommendations for international students: Required—TOEFL. *Application deadline:* For fall admission, 11/30 for domestic students. Application fee: $55. *Financial support:* Teaching assistantships available. Financial award application deadline: 3/1. *Faculty research:* Reading improvement, professional writing, Dickens, Shaw, English as a second language. *Unit head:* Dr. George Uba, Chair, 818-677-3434, E-mail: george.uba@csun.edu. *Application contact:* Dr. Marjie Seagoe, Graduate Studies Secretary, 818-677-3433.

California State University, Sacramento, Graduate Studies, College of Arts and Letters, Department of English, Sacramento, CA 95819-6048. Offers creative writing (MA); teaching English to speakers of other languages (MA). Part-time programs available. *Students:* 66 full-time (47 women), 89 part-time (57 women); includes 21 minority (3 African Americans, 2 American Indian/Alaska Native, 3 Asian Americans or Pacific Islanders, 13 Hispanic Americans), 3 international. Average age 32. 96 applicants, 74% accepted, 49 enrolled. *Degree requirements:* For master's, thesis, project, or comprehensive exam; writing proficiency exam. *Entrance requirements:* For master's, portfolio (creative writing); minimum GPA of 3.0 in English, 2.75 overall during previous 2 years. Additional exam requirements/recommendations for international students: Required—TOEFL. *Application deadline:* Applications are processed on a rolling basis. Application fee: $55. Electronic applications accepted. *Expenses:* Tuition, state resident: full-time $3,414. Tuition, nonresident: full-time $13,584; part-time $339 per unit. Required fees: $786; $393 per semester. *Financial support:* Research assistantships, teaching assistantships, career-related internships or fieldwork and Federal Work-Study available. Support available to part-time students. Financial award application deadline: 3/1. *Faculty research:* Teaching composition, remedial writing. *Unit head:* Dr. Sheree Meyer, Chairman, 916-278-6586, Fax: 916-278-4588.

California State University, San Bernardino, Graduate Studies, College of Arts and Letters, Department of English, San Bernardino, CA 92407-2397. Offers English composition (MA). Part-time and evening/weekend programs available. *Faculty:* 41 full-time, 23 part-time/adjunct. *Students:* 67 full-time (52 women), 49 part-time (34 women); includes 29 minority (8 African Americans, 1 American Indian/Alaska Native, 3 Asian Americans or Pacific Islanders, 17 Hispanic Americans), 2 international. Average age 31. 33 applicants, 61% accepted, 13 enrolled. In 2007, 31 degrees awarded. *Degree requirements:* For master's, one foreign language, thesis. *Entrance requirements:* For master's, BA in English or linguistics, minimum GPA of 3.0. *Application deadline:* For fall admission, 8/31 priority date for domestic students. Application fee: $55. *Financial support:* Research assistantships, teaching assistantships, career-related internships or fieldwork, Federal Work-Study, institutionally sponsored loans, and writing center tutorships available. Support available to part-time students. Financial award application deadline: 3/1. *Faculty research:* Composition and literary theory, theatrical theory, creative writing, relationship between evaluating writing and teaching composition. *Unit head:* Dr. Rong Chen, Chair, 909-537-5824, Fax: 909-537-7086, E-mail: rchen@csusb.edu.

California State University, San Marcos, College of Arts and Sciences, Program in Literature and Writing Studies, San Marcos, CA 92096-0001. Offers MA. Part-time and evening/weekend programs available. *Faculty:* 11 full-time (6 women), 13 part-time/adjunct (8 women). *Students:* 21 full-time (15 women), 18 part-time (13 women); includes 8 minority (1 African American, 2 Asian Americans or Pacific Islanders, 5 Hispanic Americans), 2 international. Average age 36. In 2007, 2 degrees awarded. *Degree requirements:* For master's, one foreign language, thesis. *Entrance requirements:* For master's, GRE General Test, minimum GPA of 3.0, writing sample. *Application deadline:* For fall admission, 3/15 priority date for domestic students; for spring admission, 11/15 priority date for domestic students. Applications are processed on a rolling basis. Application fee: $55. *Financial support:* Teaching assistantships with partial tuition reimbursements available. *Faculty research:* Postcolonialism, feminism rhetoric, cultural studies, creative writing, critical theory. *Unit head:* Dr. Dawn Fomo, Department Chair, 760-750-4199, Fax: 760-750-4082, E-mail: scassel@csusm.edu. *Application contact:* Anita Nix, Administrative Coordinator, 760-750-4147, E-mail: anix@csusm.edu.

California State University, Stanislaus, College of Humanities and Social Sciences, Department of English, Turlock, CA 95382. Offers English (MA); literature (MA); rhetoric and teaching of writing (MA); TESOL (MA, Certificate). Part-time programs available. *Faculty:* 21. *Students:* 11 full-time (8 women), 42 part-time (27 women); includes 11 minority (1 Asian American or Pacific Islander, 10 Hispanic Americans). Average age 32. 28 applicants, 100% accepted, 16 enrolled. In 2007, 12 degrees awarded. *Degree requirements:* For master's, one foreign language, comprehensive exam, thesis. *Entrance requirements:* For master's, GRE General Test, minimum GPA of 3.0, 2 letters of reference, personal statement; for Certificate, minimum GPA of 3.0, 2 letters of reference. Additional exam requirements/recommendations for international students: Required—TOEFL (minimum score 550 paper-based; 213 computer-based), TWE (minimum score 4). *Application deadline:* For fall admission, 7/1 for domestic and international students; for winter admission, 10/1 for domestic and international students; for spring admission, 11/1 for domestic and international students. Application fee: $55. Electronic applications accepted. *Expenses:* Tuition, nonresident: full-time $10,170; part-time $339 per unit. Required fees: $3,972; $2,538 per term. $1,165 per semester. *Financial support:* Fellowships, research assistantships, teaching assistantships, career-related internships or fieldwork and Federal Work-Study available. Financial award application deadline: 3/2; financial award applicants required to submit FAFSA. *Faculty research:* Transnational literacies, Renaissance and Medieval literature, abolition writings and slave narratives, qualitative writing. *Application contact:* Dr. Mark Thompson, Chair, 209-667-3361, Fax: 209-667-3720.

Carleton University, Faculty of Graduate Studies, Faculty of Arts and Social Sciences, Department of English Language and Literature, Ottawa, ON K1S 5B6, Canada. Offers MA, PhD. *Degree requirements:* For master's, thesis optional. *Entrance requirements:* For master's, honors degree. Additional exam requirements/recommendations for international students: Required—TOEFL. Application fee: $77. *Financial support:* Fellowships, research assistantships, teaching assistantships, institutionally sponsored loans, scholarships/grants, and unspecified assistantships available. *Faculty research:* British, Canadian, American, and Commonwealth literatures; English language and writing; literary criticism; social and historical context of literature. *Unit head:* Paul Keen, Chair, 613-520-2600 Ext. 2310, Fax: 613-520-3544, E-mail: chair_english@carleton.ca. *Application contact:* Grant Williams, Supervisor of Graduate Studies, 613-520-2600 Ext. 2310, Fax: 613-520-3544, E-mail: english@carleton.ca.

Carnegie Mellon University, College of Humanities and Social Sciences, Department of English, Pittsburgh, PA 15213-3891. Offers communication planning and design (M Des); English (MA); literary and cultural studies (MA, PhD); professional writing (MAPW), including design, professional writing, research, rhetorical theory, science writing, technical; rhetoric (MA, PhD). Part-time programs available. Terminal master's awarded for partial completion of doctoral program. *Degree requirements:* For doctorate, 2 foreign languages, comprehensive exam, thesis/dissertation. *Entrance requirements:* For master's and doctorate, GRE General Test. Additional exam requirements/recommendations for international students: Required—TOEFL, TWE. *Faculty research:* Cognitive processes in discourse with emphasis on writing, testing, and evaluation.

Case Western Reserve University, School of Graduate Studies, Department of English, Cleveland, OH 44106. Offers comparative literature (MA); English and American literature (MA, PhD). Part-time programs available. *Faculty:* 14 full-time (6 women). *Students:* 7 full-time (all women), 28 part-time (17 women), 3 international. Average age 29. 55 applicants, 27% accepted, 8 enrolled. In 2007, 3 master's, 3 doctorates awarded. *Degree requirements:* For master's, written exam; for doctorate, one foreign language, thesis/dissertation, oral and written exams. *Entrance requirements:* For master's and doctorate, GRE General Test, sample of written work. Additional exam requirements/recommendations for international students: Required—TOEFL. *Application deadline:* For fall admission, 5/30 priority date for domestic students; for spring admission, 1/2 for domestic students. Applications are processed on a rolling basis. Application fee: $50. Electronic applications accepted. *Financial support:* Research assistantships, teaching assistantships, Federal Work-Study, institutionally sponsored loans, and tuition waivers (partial) available. Financial award application deadline: 1/31. *Faculty research:* Sixteenth- to twentieth-century English literature, rhetorical and critical theory, women's studies, genre studies, Renaissance, America modernism, authorship. *Unit head:* William Siebenschuh, Chair, 216-368-4118, Fax: 216-368-4681, E-mail: william.siebenschuh@case.edu. *Application contact:* Jamie McDaniel, Admissions, 216-368-2370, Fax: 216-368-4367, E-mail: jlm25@case.edu.

The Catholic University of America, School of Arts and Sciences, Department of English Language and Literature, Washington, DC 20064. Offers English language and literature (MA, PhD); rhetoric (MA, PhD); MSLS/MA. Part-time and evening/weekend programs available. *Faculty:* 11 full-time (3 women), 4 part-time/adjunct (1 woman). *Students:* 22 full-time (11 women), 38 part-time (22 women), 1 international. Average age 29. 72 applicants, 60% accepted, 21 enrolled. In 2007, 13 master's, 1 doctorate awarded. Terminal master's awarded for partial completion of doctoral program. *Degree requirements:* For master's, one foreign language, comprehensive exam, thesis or alternative; for doctorate, 2 foreign languages, comprehensive exam, thesis/dissertation. *Entrance requirements:* For master's and doctorate,

English

The Catholic University of America (continued)
GRE General Test, 3 letters of recommendation, writing sample. Additional exam requirements/recommendations for international students: Required—TOEFL (minimum score 580 paper-based; 237 computer-based). *Application deadline:* For fall admission, 2/1 priority date for domestic students; for spring admission, 11/15 priority date for domestic students. Applications are processed on a rolling basis. Application fee: $55. Electronic applications accepted. *Financial support:* Fellowships, teaching assistantships, career-related internships or fieldwork, Federal Work-Study, scholarships/grants, tuition waivers (full and partial), and unspecified assistantships available. Support available to part-time students. Financial award application deadline: 2/1; financial award applicants required to submit FAFSA. *Faculty research:* Medieval literature, theory and history of rhetoric, modern Irish literature, religion and literature, English and American drama. *Unit head:* Dr. Ernest Suarez, Chair, 202-319-5488, Fax: 202-319-4188, E-mail: suarez@cua.edu.

Central Connecticut State University, School of Graduate Studies, School of Arts and Sciences, Department of English, Program in English, New Britain, CT 06050-4010. Offers MA, Certificate. *Students:* 28 full-time (20 women), 39 part-time (27 women); includes 5 minority (1 African American, 2 Asian Americans or Pacific Islanders, 2 Hispanic Americans). 38 applicants, 42% accepted, 12 enrolled. In 2007, 5 master's, 1 other advanced degree awarded. *Degree requirements:* For master's, comprehensive exam, thesis or alternative. *Entrance requirements:* For master's, minimum GPA of 2.7. Additional exam requirements/recommendations for international students: Required—TOEFL. *Application deadline:* For fall admission, 7/1 for domestic students; for spring admission, 12/1 for domestic students. Applications are processed on a rolling basis. Application fee: $50. Electronic applications accepted. *Expenses:* Tuition, area resident: Full-time $4,169. Tuition, state resident: full-time $6,253. Tuition, nonresident: full-time $11,614; part-time $400 per credit. Required fees: $3,322. One-time fee: $62 part-time. Tuition and fees vary according to degree level and program.

Central Michigan University, College of Graduate Studies, College of Humanities and Social and Behavioral Sciences, Department of English Language and Literature, Mount Pleasant, MI 48859. Offers composition and communication (MA); creative writing (MA); English language and literature (MA); teaching English to speakers of other languages (MA). *Degree requirements:* For master's, thesis or alternative. *Entrance requirements:* For master's, minimum GPA of 2.7, portfolio. Additional exam requirements/recommendations for international students: Required—TOEFL, Michigan English Language Assessment Battery. *Faculty research:* Composition theory, science fiction history and bibliography, medieval studies, nineteenth century American literature, applied linguistics.

See Close-Up on page 565.

Central Washington University, Graduate Studies, Research and Continuing Education, College of Arts and Humanities, Department of English, Ellensburg, WA 98926. Offers English (MA); teaching English as a second language (MA). Part-time programs available. *Faculty:* 20 full-time (11 women). *Students:* 18 full-time (6 women), 5 part-time (3 women); includes 2 minority (1 American Indian/Alaska Native, 1 Asian American or Pacific Islander). 28 applicants, 68% accepted, 19 enrolled. In 2007, 15 degrees awarded. *Degree requirements:* For master's, thesis or alternative. *Entrance requirements:* For master's, GRE General Test, minimum GPA of 3.0, writing sample. Additional exam requirements/recommendations for international students: Required—TOEFL (minimum score 550 paper-based; 213 computer-based; 79 iBT). *Application deadline:* For fall admission, 4/1 priority date for domestic students; for winter admission, 10/1 for domestic students; for spring admission, 1/1 for domestic students. Applications are processed on a rolling basis. Application fee: $50. Electronic applications accepted. *Expenses:* Tuition, state resident: full-time $2,209; part-time $221 per credit. Tuition, nonresident: full-time $4,939; part-time $442 per credit. Required fees: $207 per quarter. Tuition and fees vary according to degree level. *Financial support:* In 2007–08, 12 teaching assistantships with partial tuition reimbursements (averaging $8,100 per year) were awarded; research assistantships with partial tuition reimbursements, Federal Work-Study, health care benefits, and unspecified assistantships also available. Financial award application deadline: 3/1; financial award applicants required to submit FAFSA. *Unit head:* Dr. George Drake, Chair, 509-963-1546, Fax: 509-963-1561, E-mail: drakeg@cwu.edu. *Application contact:* Justine Eason, Admissions Program Coordinator, 509-963-3103, Fax: 509-963-1799, E-mail: masters@cwu.edu.

Chapman University, Graduate Studies, Wilkinson College of Social Sciences and Humanities, Program in English, Orange, CA 92866. Offers MA. Part-time and evening/weekend programs available. *Faculty:* 19 full-time (8 women), 19 part-time/adjunct (11 women). *Students:* 31 full-time (26 women), 28 part-time (16 women); includes 6 minority (1 Asian American or Pacific Islander, 5 Hispanic Americans), 1 international. Average age 29. 32 applicants, 84% accepted, 18 enrolled. In 2007, 27 degrees awarded. *Degree requirements:* For master's, comprehensive exam. *Entrance requirements:* For master's, GRE General Test or MAT, minimum undergraduate GPA of 3.0. Additional exam requirements/recommendations for international students: Required—TOEFL (minimum score 550 paper-based). *Application deadline:* Applications are processed on a rolling basis. Application fee: $55. Electronic applications accepted. *Expenses:* Contact institution. *Financial support:* Fellowships, Federal Work-Study and scholarships/grants available. Financial award application deadline: 6/30; financial award applicants required to submit FAFSA. *Unit head:* Dr. Richard Ruppel, Chair, 714-997-6754, E-mail: ruppel@chapman.edu. *Application contact:* Jim Blaylock, Coordinator, 714-997-6750, E-mail: blaylock@chapman.edu.

Chicago State University, School of Graduate and Professional Studies, College of Arts and Sciences, Department of English, Chicago, IL 60628. Offers creative writing (MFA); English (MA). *Degree requirements:* For master's, comprehensive exam. *Entrance requirements:* For master's, minimum GPA of 2.75.

The Citadel, The Military College of South Carolina, Citadel Graduate College, Department of English, Charleston, SC 29409. Offers MA. Part-time and evening/weekend programs available. *Students:* 1 (woman) full-time, 6 part-time (all women); includes 1 minority (African American) Average age 28. In 2007, 3 degrees awarded. *Degree requirements:* For master's, one foreign language, comprehensive exam, thesis optional. *Entrance requirements:* For master's, GRE General Test, MAT. Additional exam requirements/recommendations for international students: Required—TOEFL (minimum score 550 paper-based; 213 computer-based). *Application deadline:* For fall admission, 6/1 for domestic students; for spring admission, 11/1 for domestic students. Application fee: $30. *Expenses:* Tuition, state resident: part-time $280 per credit hour. Tuition, nonresident: part-time $503 per credit hour. *Financial support:* Research assistantships available. Support available to part-time students. Financial award application deadline: 7/1. *Faculty research:* Renaissance literature; eighteenth and nineteenth century British literature; eighteenth, nineteenth, and twentieth century American literature. *Unit head:* Dr. Jim Leonard, Head, 843-953-5068, E-mail: leonardj@citadel.edu. *Application contact:* Dr. Raymond S. Jones, Associate Dean, Citadel Graduate College, 843-953-5089, Fax: 843-953-7630, E-mail: ray.jones@citadel.edu.

City College of the City University of New York, Graduate School, College of Liberal Arts and Science, Division of the Humanities and Arts, Department of English, Program in English and American Literature, New York, NY 10031-9198. Offers MA. *Students:* 38. 31 applicants, 55% accepted, 12 enrolled. *Degree requirements:* For master's, one foreign language, comprehensive exam, thesis. *Entrance requirements:* For master's, GRE, minimum GPA of 3.0. Additional exam requirements/recommendations for international students: Required—TOEFL (minimum score 600 paper-based; 250 computer-based). *Application deadline:* For fall admission, 5/1 for domestic students; for spring admission, 11/1 for domestic students. Application fee: $125. *Unit head:* Prof. Renata Miller, Advisor, 212-650-6694, E-mail: remiller@ccny.cuny.edu.

Claremont Graduate University, Graduate Programs, School of Arts and Humanities, Department of English, Claremont, CA 91711-6160. Offers American studies (MA, PhD); critical theory (MA, PhD); early modern studies (MA, PhD); English (M Phil, MA, PhD); literary theory (PhD); literature (MA, PhD); literature and creative writing (MA); literature and film (MA); MBA/MA; MBA/PhD. Part-time programs available. *Faculty:* 2 full-time (1 woman), 2 part-time/adjunct (0 women). *Students:* 81 full-time (49 women), 14 part-time (10 women); includes 18 minority (3 American Indian/Alaska Native, 10 Asian Americans or Pacific Islanders, 5 Hispanic Americans), 3 international. Average age 35. In 2007, 14 master's, 5 doctorates awarded. *Degree requirements:* For master's, one foreign language, comprehensive exam; for doctorate, 2 foreign languages, comprehensive exam, thesis/dissertation. *Entrance requirements:* For master's, GRE General Test; for doctorate, GRE General Test, MA in literature. *Application deadline:* For fall admission, 2/15 priority date for domestic students; for spring admission, 11/15 for domestic students. Applications are processed on a rolling basis. Electronic applications accepted. *Expenses:* Tuition: Full-time $31,640; part-time $1,376 per unit. Required fees: $145 per semester. Tuition and fees vary according to course load, degree level and program. *Financial support:* Fellowships, Federal Work-Study and institutionally sponsored loans available. Support available to part-time students. Financial award application deadline: 2/15; financial award applicants required to submit FAFSA. *Faculty research:* American, comparative, and English Renaissance literature; modernism; feminist literature and theory. *Unit head:* Wendy Martin, Chair, 909-621-8612, Fax: 909-607-1221, E-mail: wendy.martin@cgu.edu.

Clarion University of Pennsylvania, Office of Research and Graduate Studies, College of Arts and Sciences, Department of English, Clarion, PA 16214. Offers MA. *Faculty:* 21 full-time (11 women). *Students:* 7 full-time (4 women), 2 part-time (both women); includes 2 minority (1 African American, 1 Asian American or Pacific Islander), 1 international. 7 applicants, 29% accepted, 2 enrolled. In 2007, 2 degrees awarded. *Degree requirements:* For master's, thesis optional. *Entrance requirements:* For master's, GRE General Test, minimum QPA of 2.75. Additional exam requirements/recommendations for international students: Required—TOEFL (minimum score 550 paper-based; 213 computer-based; 80 iBT). *Application deadline:* For fall admission, 8/1 priority date for domestic students, 4/15 priority date for international students; for spring admission, 12/1 for domestic students, 9/15 priority date for international students. Applications are processed on a rolling basis. Application fee: $30. Electronic applications accepted. *Financial support:* Research assistantships with full tuition reimbursements available. Support available to part-time students. Financial award application deadline: 3/1. *Unit head:* Elizabeth MacDaniel, Chair, 814-393-2159, Fax: 814-393-3630, E-mail: emacdaniel@clarion.edu. *Application contact:* Dr. Richard Lane, Graduate Coordinator, 814-393-2740, Fax: 814-393-3630, E-mail: rlane@clarion.edu.

Clark Atlanta University, School of Arts and Sciences, Department of English, Atlanta, GA 30314. Offers MA, DAH. Part-time programs available. *Faculty:* 1 (woman) full-time, 4 part-time/adjunct (2 women). *Students:* 4 full-time (all women), 18 part-time (16 women); all minorities (all African Americans) Average age 37. 2 applicants, 50% accepted, 1 enrolled. In 2007, 1 degree awarded. *Degree requirements:* For master's, one foreign language, thesis. *Entrance requirements:* For master's, GRE General Test, minimum GPA of 2.5. Additional exam requirements/recommendations for international students: Required—TOEFL (minimum score 500 paper-based; 173 computer-based). *Application deadline:* For fall admission, 4/1 for domestic and international students; for spring admission, 11/1 for domestic and international students. Applications are processed on a rolling basis. Application fee: $40 ($55 for international students). *Expenses:* Tuition: Full-time $11,664; part-time $648 per credit hour. Required fees: $550; $275 per semester. *Financial support:* Career-related internships or fieldwork, Federal Work-Study, scholarships/grants, and unspecified assistantships available. Support available to part-time students. Financial award application deadline: 4/30; financial award applicants required to submit FAFSA. *Unit head:* Dr. Alma Vineyard, Chairperson, 404-880-6067, E-mail: avineyard@cau.edu. *Application contact:* Michelle Clark-Davis, Graduate Program Admissions, 404-880-8709, E-mail: mdowis@cau.edu.

Clark University, Graduate School, Department of English, Worcester, MA 01610-1477. Offers MA. Part-time programs available. *Faculty:* 9 full-time (6 women), 12 part-time/adjunct (6 women). *Students:* 13 full-time (9 women), 4 part-time (3 women); includes 1 minority (African American), 5 international. Average age 25. 16 applicants, 94% accepted, 12 enrolled. In 2007, 9 degrees awarded. *Degree requirements:* For master's, thesis, oral exam. *Entrance requirements:* For master's, GRE Subject Test. Additional exam requirements/recommendations for international students: Required—TOEFL. *Application deadline:* For fall admission, 2/1 priority date for domestic students. Applications are processed on a rolling basis. Application fee: $55. *Expenses:* Tuition: Full-time $32,600; part-time $1,019 per credit. Required fees: $30. Tuition and fees vary according to program. *Financial support:* In 2007–08, fellowships with tuition reimbursements (averaging $10,300 per year), research assistantships with full and partial tuition reimbursements (averaging $10,300 per year), 4 teaching assistantships with full and partial tuition reimbursements (averaging $10,300 per year) were awarded; career-related internships or fieldwork and tuition waivers (partial) also available. Support available to part-time students. Financial award application deadline: 2/15. *Faculty research:* Writings of James Fenimore Cooper, Renaissance literature, American literature, medieval literature, Victorian literature. *Unit head:* Dr. Virginia Vaughan, Chair, 508-793-7142. *Application contact:* Terri Rutkiewicz, Academic Secretary, 508-793-7142, Fax: 508-793-8892, E-mail: engma@clarku.edu.

Clemson University, Graduate School, College of Architecture, Arts, and Humanities, Department of English, Program in English, Clemson, SC 29634. Offers MA. *Students:* 47 full-time (26 women), 7 part-time (6 women); includes 1 minority (African American), 1 international. Average age 23. 44 applicants, 39% accepted, 5 enrolled. In 2007, 19 degrees awarded. *Degree requirements:* For master's, one foreign language, thesis optional, oral exam. *Entrance requirements:* For master's, GRE General Test, minimum undergraduate GPA of 3.0. *Application deadline:* For fall admission, 6/1 priority date for domestic students, 4/15 for international students; for spring admission, 12/1 for domestic students, 9/15 for international students. Applications are processed on a rolling basis. Application fee: $55. *Financial support:* In 2007–08, 11 research assistantships were awarded. Financial award application deadline: 4/1; financial award applicants required to submit FAFSA. *Unit head:* Dr. Alma Bennett, Coordinator, 864-656-5405, Fax: 864-656-1345, E-mail: balma@clemson.edu.

Cleveland State University, College of Graduate Studies, College of Liberal Arts and Social Sciences, Department of English, Cleveland, OH 44115. Offers creative writing (MFA); English (MA). Part-time and evening/weekend programs available. *Faculty:* 17 full-time (6 women), 2 part-time/adjunct (1 woman). *Students:* 21 full-time (11 women), 63 part-time (46 women); includes 4 minority (all African Americans), 1 international. Average age 35. 56 applicants, 50% accepted, 15 enrolled. In 2007, 18 degrees awarded. *Degree requirements:* For master's, comprehensive exam, thesis. *Entrance requirements:* For master's, minimum GPA of 2.75, undergraduate concentration in English, writing sample, portfolio. Additional exam requirements/recommendations for international students: Required—TOEFL (525 paper-based; 197 computer-based) or IELTS (6 paper-based). *Application deadline:* For fall admission, 7/18 priority date for domestic students, 5/15 for international students; for spring admission, 12/15 for domestic students, 11/1 for international students. Applications are processed on a rolling basis. Application fee: $30. Electronic applications accepted. *Financial support:* In 2007–08, 20 students received support, including 1 fellowship (averaging $1,000 per year), 5 research assistantships with full and partial tuition reimbursements available (averaging $3,480 per year), 7 teaching assistantships with full and partial tuition reimbursements available (averaging $3,480 per year); Federal Work-Study, institutionally sponsored loans, tuition waivers (full and partial), and unspecified assistantships also available. Support available to part-time students. Financial award application deadline: 2/15. *Faculty research:* Literary history and criticism, linguistics, literature. Total annual research expenditures: $5,000. *Unit head:* Dr. David M. Larson, Chairperson, 216-687-3951, Fax: 216-687-6943, E-mail: d.larson@csuohio.edu. *Application contact:* Dr. Jennifer M. Jeffers, Graduate Director, 216-687-3975, Fax: 216-687-6943, E-mail: j.m.jeffers53@csuohio.edu.

The College at Brockport, State University of New York, School of Letters and Sciences, Department of English, Brockport, NY 14420-2997. Offers MA. Part-time programs available. *Students:* 10 full-time (6 women), 36 part-time (23 women); includes 2 minority (1 African

American, 1 Hispanic American). 19 applicants, 84% accepted, 16 enrolled. In 2007, 13 degrees awarded. *Degree requirements:* For master's, thesis. *Entrance requirements:* For master's, minimum GPA of 3.0, letters of recommendation, writing sample. Additional exam requirements/recommendations for international students: Required—TOEFL (minimum score 550 paper-based; 213 computer-based; 79 iBT). *Application deadline:* For fall admission, 4/15 for domestic and international students; for spring admission, 11/15 for domestic and international students. Application fee: $50. *Expenses:* Tuition, state resident: full-time $6,900; part-time $288 per credit. Tuition, nonresident: full-time $10,920; part-time $455 per credit. Required fees: $738; $31 per credit. *Financial support:* In 2007–08, 3 teaching assistantships (averaging $6,000 per year) were awarded; Federal Work-Study, scholarships/grants, and unspecified assistantships also available. Support available to part-time students. Financial award application deadline: 3/15; financial award applicants required to submit FAFSA. *Faculty research:* British and American literature, creative writing, film studies, children's literature, Ancient and Modern World Literature. *Unit head:* Dr. Janie W. Hinds, Chairperson, 585-395-2503, E-mail: jhinds@brockport.edu. *Application contact:* Dr. Miriam Burstein, Graduate Program Director, 585-395-5827, E-mail: mburstei@brockport.edu.

College of Charleston, Graduate School, School of Humanities and Social Sciences, Program in English, Charleston, SC 29424-0001. Offers MA. *Faculty:* 40 full-time (17 women). *Students:* 22 full-time (15 women), 16 part-time (9 women); includes 2 minority (1 African American, 1 American Indian/Alaska Native). Average age 29. 31 applicants, 61% accepted, 13 enrolled. In 2007, 14 degrees awarded. *Degree requirements:* For master's, one foreign language, comprehensive exam, thesis optional. *Entrance requirements:* For master's, GRE General Test or MAT, minimum GPA of 2.5, 3.0 in major; 2 letters of recommendation; writing sample. Additional exam requirements/recommendations for international students: Required—TOEFL. *Application deadline:* For fall admission, 6/1 for domestic students; for spring admission, 11/1 for domestic students. Application fee: $35. Electronic applications accepted. *Expenses:* Tuition, state resident: full-time $7,778; part-time $324 per hour. Tuition, nonresident: full-time $18,732; part-time $781 per hour. *Financial support:* In 2007–08, 5 research assistantships were awarded; fellowships also available. Financial award applicants required to submit FAFSA. *Unit head:* Dr. Julia Eichelberger, Director, 843-953-5648, Fax: 843-953-3180, E-mail: eichelbergerj@cofc.edu. *Application contact:* Susan Hallatt, Assistant Director of Graduate Admissions, 843-953-5614, Fax: 843-953-1434, E-mail: hallatts@cofc.edu.

The College of New Jersey, Graduate Division, School of Culture and Society, Department of English, Program in English, Ewing, NJ 08628. Offers MA. Part-time and evening/weekend programs available. *Students:* 11 applicants, 100% accepted. In 2007, 10 degrees awarded. *Entrance requirements:* For master's, GRE, minimum GPA of 3.0 in field or 2.75 overall. Additional exam requirements/recommendations for international students: Required—TOEFL. *Application deadline:* For fall admission, 4/15 for domestic students; for spring admission, 10/15 for domestic students. Application fee: $60. Electronic applications accepted. *Financial support:* Application deadline: 5/1; *Unit head:* Dr. Michele Tarter, Coordinator, 609-771-3115. *Application contact:* Susan L. Hydro, Office of Graduate Studies, Assistant Dean, 609-771-2300, Fax: 609-637-5105, E-mail: graduate@tcnj.edu.

The College of Saint Rose, Graduate Studies, School of Arts and Humanities, Department of English, Albany, NY 12203-1419. Offers MA. Part-time and evening/weekend programs available. *Faculty:* 17 full-time (12 women), 24 part-time/adjunct (18 women). *Students:* 14 full-time (10 women), 19 part-time (12 women); includes 1 minority (Asian American or Pacific Islander) Average age 34. 21 applicants, 86% accepted, 11 enrolled. In 2007, 6 degrees awarded. *Degree requirements:* For master's, thesis optional, advanced project. *Entrance requirements:* For master's, 24 credits in English, minimum undergraduate GPA of 3.2, writing sample. Additional exam requirements/recommendations for international students: Required—TOEFL (minimum score 550 paper-based; 213 computer-based). *Application deadline:* For fall admission, 7/15 priority date for domestic and international students; for spring admission, 11/15 priority date for domestic and international students. Applications are processed on a rolling basis. Application fee: $35. Electronic applications accepted. *Financial support:* Scholarships/grants, tuition waivers (partial), and unspecified assistantships available. Support available to part-time students. Financial award application deadline: 3/1; financial award applicants required to submit FAFSA. *Unit head:* Catherine Cavanaugh, Chair, 518-454-5221, Fax: 518-485-3920, E-mail: cavanaughc@strose.edu. *Application contact:* Susan Patterson, Assistant Vice President for Graduate Admission, 518-454-5136, Fax: 518-458-5479, E-mail: ace@strose.edu.

College of Staten Island of the City University of New York, Graduate Programs, Program in English, Staten Island, NY 10314-6600. Offers MA. Part-time and evening/weekend programs available. *Faculty:* 6 full-time (2 women). *Students:* 3 full-time (all women), 40 part-time (30 women); includes 6 minority (3 Asian Americans or Pacific Islanders, 3 Hispanic Americans), 3 international. Average age 31. 23 applicants, 96% accepted, 11 enrolled. In 2007, 15 degrees awarded. *Degree requirements:* For master's, comprehensive exam, 3 hour written exam, 2 master's papers. *Entrance requirements:* For master's, 32 undergraduate credits in English, minimum GPA of 3.0. Additional exam requirements/recommendations for international students: Required—TOEFL (minimum score 550 paper-based; 213 computer-based; 79 iBT). *Application deadline:* Applications are processed on a rolling basis. Application fee: $125. Electronic applications accepted. *Expenses:* Tuition, state resident: part-time $270 per credit. Tuition, nonresident: part-time $500 per credit. Required fees: $38 per semester. One-time fee: $15 part-time. Tuition and fees vary according to course load. *Financial support:* In 2007–08, 1 student received support. Federal Work-Study, institutionally sponsored loans, and institutional work-study in form of writing center tutors available. Financial award application deadline: 4/1; financial award applicants required to submit CSS PROFILE or FAFSA. *Faculty research:* Comparative morpho-syntax of Appalachian English; adverb placement and non-finite and imperative verbs in romance; reading and writing in 'Women and Literature". *Unit head:* Dr. Maryann Feola, Coordinator, 718-982-3666, Fax: 718-982-3643, E-mail: englishmasters@mail.csi.cuny.edu. *Application contact:* Sasha Spence, Assistant Director of Graduate Recruitment Admissions, 718-982-2699, Fax: 718-982-2500, E-mail: spence@mail.csi.cuny.edu.

Columbia University, Graduate School of Arts and Sciences, Division of Humanities, Department of English and Comparative Literature, New York, NY 10027. Offers comparative literature (M Phil, MA, PhD); English literature (M Phil, MA, PhD); literature-writing (M Phil, MA, PhD). Part-time programs available. *Faculty:* 41 full-time, 2 part-time/adjunct. *Students:* 176 full-time (104 women), 28 part-time (19 women). Average age 32. 627 applicants, 12% accepted. In 2007, 27 master's, 24 doctorates awarded. *Degree requirements:* For master's, one foreign language, comprehensive exam, seminar papers; for doctorate, thesis/dissertation. *Entrance requirements:* For master's and doctorate, GRE General Test. Additional exam requirements/recommendations for international students: Required—TOEFL. Application fee: $90. *Expenses:* Tuition: Part-time $1,452 per credit. Required fees: $152 per term. One-time fee: $75 part-time. Full-time tuition and fees vary according to course level, course load, degree level and program. *Financial support:* Fellowships, teaching assistantships, Federal Work-Study and institutionally sponsored loans available. Support available to part-time students. Financial award application deadline: 1/5; financial award applicants required to submit FAFSA. *Faculty research:* Medieval through modern literature, drama, literary criticism. *Unit head:* David Kastan, Chair, 212-854-6257, Fax: 212-854-5398, E-mail: dsk@columbia.edu.

Concordia University, School of Graduate Studies, Faculty of Arts and Science, Department of English, Program in English, Montréal, QC H3G 1M8, Canada. Offers MA. *Degree requirements:* For master's, one foreign language, thesis optional. *Entrance requirements:* For master's, honors degree in English, minimum GPA of 3.3 in English literature.

Converse College, School of Education and Graduate Studies, Program in Liberal Arts, Spartanburg, SC 29302-0006. Offers English (MLA); history (MLA); political science (MLA). *Degree requirements:* For master's, capstone paper. *Entrance requirements:* For master's, minimum GPA of 3.0, 2 recommendations.

Cornell University, Graduate School, Graduate Fields of Arts and Sciences, Field of English Language and Literature, Ithaca, NY 14853-0001. Offers African-American literature (PhD); American literature after 1865 (PhD); American literature to 1865 (PhD); American studies (PhD); colonial and postcolonial literature (PhD); creative writing (MFA); cultural studies (PhD); dramatic literature (PhD); English poetry (PhD); English Renaissance to 1660 (PhD); lesbian, bisexual, and gay literature studies (PhD); literary criticism and theory (PhD); nineteenth century (PhD); Old and Middle English (PhD); prose fiction (PhD); Restoration and eighteenth century (PhD); twentieth century (PhD); women's literature (PhD); MFA/PhD. *Faculty:* 59 full-time (28 women). *Students:* 97 full-time (53 women); includes 20 minority (7 African Americans, 3 American Indian/Alaska Native, 5 Asian Americans or Pacific Islanders, 5 Hispanic Americans), 13 international. Average age 28. 759 applicants, 7% accepted, 21 enrolled. In 2007, 29 master's, 8 doctorates awarded. Terminal master's awarded for partial completion of doctoral program. *Degree requirements:* For master's, one foreign language, thesis; for doctorate, one foreign language, comprehensive exam, thesis/dissertation, teaching experience. *Entrance requirements:* For master's, GRE General Test, 3 letters of recommendation, creative writing sample; for doctorate, GRE General Test, GRE Subject Test (English), 3 letters of recommendation, writing sample. Additional exam requirements/recommendations for international students: Required—TOEFL (minimum score 600 paper-based; 250 computer-based; 77 iBT). *Application deadline:* For fall admission, 1/10 for domestic students. Application fee: $70. Electronic applications accepted. *Financial support:* In 2007–08, 92 students received support, including 32 fellowships with full tuition reimbursements available, 60 teaching assistantships with full tuition reimbursements available; research assistantships with full tuition reimbursements available, institutionally sponsored loans, scholarships/grants, health care benefits, tuition waivers (full and partial), and unspecified assistantships also available. Financial award applicants required to submit FAFSA. *Faculty research:* English and American literature, women's writing, ethnic and post-colonial literature, critical theory, medievalism. *Unit head:* Director of Graduate Studies, 607-255-7989, Fax: 607-255-6661. *Application contact:* Graduate Field Assistant, 607-255-7989, Fax: 607-255-6661, E-mail: english_grad@cornell.edu.

Cornell University, Graduate School, Graduate Fields of Arts and Sciences, Field of Linguistics, Ithaca, NY 14853-0001. Offers applied linguistics (MA, PhD); East Asian linguistics (MA, PhD); English linguistics (MA, PhD); general linguistics (MA, PhD); Germanic linguistics (MA, PhD); Indo-European linguistics (MA, PhD); phonetics (MA, PhD); phonological theory (MA, PhD); Romance linguistics (MA, PhD); second language acquisition (MA, PhD); semantics (MA, PhD); Slavic linguistics (MA, PhD); sociolinguistics (MA, PhD); South Asian linguistics (MA, PhD); Southeast Asian linguistics (MA, PhD); syntactic theory (MA, PhD). *Faculty:* 19 full-time. *Students:* 31 full-time (16 women); includes 1 minority (Hispanic American), 19 international. Average age 28. 89 applicants, 17% accepted, 8 enrolled. In 2007, 2 master's, 1 doctorate awarded. Terminal master's awarded for partial completion of doctoral program. *Degree requirements:* For master's, one foreign language, thesis; for doctorate, one foreign language, comprehensive exam, thesis/dissertation. *Entrance requirements:* For master's and doctorate, GRE General Test, 2 letters of recommendation. Additional exam requirements/recommendations for international students: Required—TOEFL (minimum score 600 paper-based; 250 computer-based; 77 iBT). *Application deadline:* For fall admission, 1/15 for domestic students. Application fee: $70. Electronic applications accepted. *Financial support:* In 2007–08, 30 students received support, including 14 fellowships with full tuition reimbursements available, 2 research assistantships with full tuition reimbursements available, 14 teaching assistantships with full tuition reimbursements available; institutionally sponsored loans, scholarships/grants, health care benefits, tuition waivers (full and partial), and unspecified assistantships also available. Financial award applicants required to submit FAFSA. *Faculty research:* Phonology and phonetics; syntax and semantics; historical linguistics; philosophy of language; language acquisition. *Unit head:* Director of Graduate Studies, 607-255-1105. *Application contact:* Graduate Field Assistant, 607-255-1105, E-mail: lingfield@cornell.edu.

Creighton University, Graduate School, College of Arts and Sciences, Department of English, Omaha, NE 68178-0001. Offers MA. Part-time programs available. *Students:* 6 full-time (4 women), 2 part-time (1 woman). 11 applicants, 55% accepted, 4 enrolled. In 2007, 6 degrees awarded. *Degree requirements:* For master's, thesis optional. *Entrance requirements:* For master's, GRE Subject Test in English, 10-15 page writing sample, 3 letters of recommendation. Additional exam requirements/recommendations for international students: Required—TOEFL (minimum score 550 paper-based; 213 computer-based; 80 iBT). *Application deadline:* For fall admission, 3/1 priority date for domestic and international students. Applications are processed on a rolling basis. Application fee: $50. Electronic applications accepted. *Financial support:* In 2007–08, 5 fellowships with full and partial tuition reimbursements (averaging $10,075 per year) were awarded; tuition waivers (partial) also available. Financial award applicants required to submit FAFSA. *Unit head:* Dr. Greg Zacharias, Director, 402-280-2729, E-mail: gregzacharias@creighton.edu. *Application contact:* LuAnn M. Schwery, Assistant Dean, 402-280-2870, Fax: 402-280-5762, E-mail: schwery@creighton.edu.

Dalhousie University, Faculty of Arts and Social Science, Department of English, Halifax, NS B3H 4R2, Canada. Offers MA, PhD. Part-time programs available. *Faculty:* 18 full-time, 34 part-time/adjunct. *Students:* 37 full-time (22 women), 1 (woman) part-time. 65 applicants, 20% accepted. In 2007, 12 master's, 1 doctorate awarded. *Degree requirements:* For master's, one foreign language, thesis; for doctorate, one foreign language, thesis/dissertation. *Entrance requirements:* For doctorate, MA. Additional exam requirements/recommendations for international students: Required—TOEFL. *Application deadline:* For fall admission, 2/15 priority date for domestic students. Applications are processed on a rolling basis. Application fee: $60. Electronic applications accepted. *Financial support:* Fellowships available. *Faculty research:* Victorian, Canadian, Renaissance, eighteenth-century, and modern literature. *Unit head:* Dr. Melissa Furrow, Chair, 902-494-6924, Fax: 902-494-2176, E-mail: gradengl@dal.ca. *Application contact:* Dr. Rohan Maitzen, Graduate Coordinator, 902-494-6924, Fax: 902-494 Ext. 2176, E-mail: gradengl@dal.ca.

DePaul University, College of Liberal Arts and Sciences, Department of English, Chicago, IL 60604-2287. Offers English (MA); writing (MA). Part-time and evening/weekend programs available. *Faculty:* 29 full-time (12 women). *Students:* 129 full-time (96 women), 81 part-time (62 women); includes 28 minority (11 African Americans, 4 Asian Americans or Pacific Islanders, 13 Hispanic Americans). Average age 27. 95 applicants, 56% accepted. In 2007, 100 degrees awarded. *Degree requirements:* For master's, written exam. *Entrance requirements:* Additional exam requirements/recommendations for international students: Required—TOEFL. *Application deadline:* For fall admission, 7/1 priority date for domestic students; for winter admission, 10/1 priority date for domestic students; for spring admission, 2/1 priority date for domestic students. Applications are processed on a rolling basis. Application fee: $40. Electronic applications accepted. *Financial support:* In 2007–08, 2 research assistantships with full tuition reimbursements, 7 teaching assistantships with full tuition reimbursements (averaging $7,500 per year) were awarded; fellowships with partial tuition reimbursements, career-related internships or fieldwork, institutionally sponsored loans, scholarships/grants, tuition waivers (partial), and unspecified assistantships also available. Support available to part-time students. Financial award application deadline: 4/1. *Faculty research:* Rhetoric and composition, technical writing, creative writing, linguistics, literacy theory. *Unit head:* Dr. William Fahrenbach, Chairperson, 773-325-1776, E-mail: bfahrenb@depaul.edu. *Application contact:* Dr. Lesley Kordecki, Director, 773-325-1786, Fax: 773-325-8607, E-mail: lkordeck@depaul.edu.

Drew University, Caspersen School of Graduate Studies, Program in English Literature, Madison, NJ 07940-1493. Offers MA, PhD. Part-time programs available. Terminal master's awarded for partial completion of doctoral program. *Degree requirements:* For master's, one foreign language, thesis; for doctorate, 2 foreign languages, comprehensive exam, thesis/dissertation. *Entrance requirements:* For master's and doctorate, GRE General Test. *Faculty research:* British literature/American literature, Victorian literature, Shakespeare, Cather studies, postmodernity.

Drew University, Caspersen School of Graduate Studies, Program in Modern History and Literature, Madison, NJ 07940-1493. Offers MA, PhD. Part-time and evening/weekend

English

Drew University (continued)
programs available. Terminal master's awarded for partial completion of doctoral program. *Degree requirements:* For master's, one foreign language, thesis; for doctorate, 2 foreign languages, comprehensive exam, thesis/dissertation. *Entrance requirements:* For master's and doctorate, GRE General Test. *Faculty research:* History of the book, modern American history/European history, cultural and intellectual history, eighteenth- to twentieth-century history and literature, history of science.

Duke University, Graduate School, Department of English, Durham, NC 27708. Offers PhD, JD/AM. *Faculty:* 30 full-time. *Students:* 76 full-time (47 women); includes 15 minority (9 African Americans, 2 American Indian/Alaska Native, 3 Asian Americans or Pacific Islanders, 1 Hispanic American), 12 international. 388 applicants, 5% accepted, 91 enrolled. In 2007, 7 doctorates awarded. *Degree requirements:* For doctorate, 2 foreign languages, thesis/dissertation. *Entrance requirements:* For doctorate, GRE General Test. Additional exam requirements/recommendations for international students: Required—TOEFL (minimum score 550 paper-based; 213 computer-based; 83 iBT), IELTS (minimum score 7). *Application deadline:* For fall admission, 12/15 priority date for domestic and international students. Application fee: $75. Electronic applications accepted. *Financial support:* Fellowships, research assistantships, teaching assistantships, Federal Work-Study available. Financial award application deadline: 12/31. *Unit head:* Kathy Psomiades, Director of Graduate Studies, 919-684-5538, Fax: 919-684-4871, E-mail: hjocius@duke.edu.

Duquesne University, Graduate School of Liberal Arts, Program in English, Pittsburgh, PA 15282-0001. Offers MA, PhD. Part-time and evening/weekend programs available. *Faculty:* 17 full-time (10 women), 29 part-time/adjunct (17 women). *Students:* 61 full-time (44 women), 17 part-time (13 women). Average age 25. In 2007, 14 master's, 1 doctorate awarded. *Degree requirements:* For master's, one foreign language, comprehensive exam, thesis or alternative; for doctorate, 2 foreign languages, comprehensive exam, thesis/dissertation. *Entrance requirements:* For master's and doctorate, GRE General Test, bachelor's degree in English, writing sample. Additional exam requirements/recommendations for international students: Required—TOEFL. *Application deadline:* For fall admission, 2/1 priority date for domestic and international students. Applications are processed on a rolling basis. Application fee: $50. *Expenses:* Tuition: Part-time $774 per credit. Required fees: $74 per credit. Tuition and fees vary according to program. *Financial support:* In 2007–08, 1 research assistantship with full tuition reimbursement (averaging $10,000 per year), 21 teaching assistantships with full tuition reimbursements (averaging $10,000 per year) were awarded; Federal Work-Study, scholarships/grants, tuition waivers (partial), and unspecified assistantships also available. Support available to part-time students. Financial award application deadline: 5/1. *Unit head:* Dr. Macali Michael, Chair, 412-396-6440. *Application contact:* Dr. Daniel Watkins, Director of Graduate Studies in English, 412-396-6420.

East Carolina University, Graduate School, Thomas Harriot College of Arts and Sciences, Department of English, Greenville, NC 27858-4353. Offers MA. Part-time and evening/weekend programs available. *Faculty:* 44 full-time (18 women). *Students:* 48 full-time (28 women), 80 part-time (60 women); includes 21 minority (19 African Americans, 1 American Indian/Alaska Native, 1 Hispanic American), 3 international. Average age 33. 29 applicants, 41% accepted, 9 enrolled. In 2007, 51 master's awarded. *Degree requirements:* For master's, one foreign language, comprehensive exam, thesis optional. *Entrance requirements:* For master's, GRE General Test, MAT (MA Ed). Additional exam requirements/recommendations for international students: Required—TOEFL. *Application deadline:* For fall admission, 6/1 priority date for domestic students; for spring admission, 10/15 for domestic students. Applications are processed on a rolling basis. Application fee: $50. *Financial support:* Research assistantships with partial tuition reimbursements, teaching assistantships with partial tuition reimbursements, Federal Work-Study available. Support available to part-time students. Financial award application deadline: 6/1. *Unit head:* Dr. Bruce Southard, Chair, 252-328-6378, Fax: 252-328-4889, E-mail: southardo@ecu.edu. *Application contact:* Dean of Graduate School, 252-328-6012, Fax: 252-328-6071, E-mail: gradschool@ecu.edu.

Eastern Illinois University, Graduate School, College of Arts and Humanities, Department of English, Charleston, IL 61920-3099. Offers MA. Part-time programs available. *Faculty:* 40 full-time (12 women). In 2007, 12 degrees awarded. *Entrance requirements:* For master's, GRE General Test. *Application deadline:* For fall admission, 7/31 priority date for domestic students. Applications are processed on a rolling basis. Application fee: $30. *Expenses:* Tuition, state resident: part-time $218 per hour. Tuition, nonresident: part-time $654 per hour. *Financial support:* In 2007–08, research assistantships (averaging $7,200 per year), 9 teaching assistantships (averaging $7,200 per year) were awarded. *Unit head:* Dr. Dana Ringuette, Chairperson, 217-581-2428, Fax: 217-581-7209, E-mail: dringuette@eiu.edu. *Application contact:* Dr. James D. Smith, Coordinator, 217-581-6290, Fax: 217-581-7209, E-mail: jdsmith3@eiu.edu.

Eastern Kentucky University, The Graduate School, College of Arts and Sciences, Department of English and Theatre, Richmond, KY 40475-3102. Offers creative writing (MFA); English (MA). Part-time and evening/weekend programs available. *Faculty:* 13 full-time (11 women), 1 (woman) part-time/adjunct. *Students:* 19 full-time (11 women), 18 part-time (12 women). Average age 28. 45 applicants, 33% accepted, 8 enrolled. In 2007, 24 degrees awarded. *Degree requirements:* For master's, thesis optional. *Entrance requirements:* For master's, GRE General Test, minimum GPA of 2.5, minor in English with 3.0 GPA. Application fee: $35. *Financial support:* In 2007–08, 21 students received support, including 5 teaching assistantships (averaging $7,500 per year); career-related internships or fieldwork, Federal Work-Study, institutionally sponsored loans, and proctorships, writing laboratory tutorships, computer laboratory tutorships also available. Support available to part-time students. *Faculty research:* Old English, Victorian studies, women's studies, rhetoric, popular culture, novel studies. Total annual research expenditures: $35,000. *Unit head:* Dr. Jim Keller, Interim Chair, 859-622-5861, Fax: 859-622-3156, E-mail: james.keller@eku.edu. *Application contact:* Dr. Susan Krucg, MD Program Coordinator, 859-622-2282, Fax: 859-622-3156, E-mail: susan.krucg@eku.edu.

Eastern Michigan University, Graduate School, College of Arts and Sciences, Department of English Language and Literature, Program in Children's Literature, Ypsilanti, MI 48197. Offers MA. Part-time and evening/weekend programs available. Postbaccalaureate distance learning degree programs offered (minimal on-campus study). *Students:* 6 full-time (4 women), 17 part-time (14 women); includes 1 minority (American Indian/Alaska Native), 2 international. Average age 33. In 2007, 5 degrees awarded. *Entrance requirements:* Additional exam requirements/recommendations for international students: Required—TOEFL. *Application deadline:* Applications are processed on a rolling basis. Application fee: $35. *Expenses:* Tuition, state resident: full-time $8,952; part-time $373 per credit hour. Tuition, nonresident: full-time $17,634; part-time $735 per credit hour. Required fees: $896; $34 per credit hour. Tuition and fees vary according to course level, degree level and program. *Financial support:* Fellowships, research assistantships with full tuition reimbursements, teaching assistantships with full tuition reimbursements, tuition waivers (partial) available. Financial award applicants required to submit FAFSA. *Application contact:* Dr. Annette Wannamaker, Program Advisor, 734-487-0148, Fax: 734-483-9744, E-mail: awannamak@emich.edu.

Eastern Michigan University, Graduate School, College of Arts and Sciences, Department of English Language and Literature, Program in English Linguistics, Ypsilanti, MI 48197. Offers MA. Part-time and evening/weekend programs available. Postbaccalaureate distance learning degree programs offered (minimal on-campus study). *Students:* 8 full-time (5 women), 16 part-time (9 women); includes 3 minority (1 American Indian/Alaska Native, 1 Asian American or Pacific Islander, 1 Hispanic American), 7 international. Average age 29. In 2007, 6 degrees awarded. *Degree requirements:* For master's, thesis (for some programs). *Entrance requirements:* Additional exam requirements/recommendations for international students: Required—TOEFL. *Application deadline:* Applications are processed on a rolling basis. Application fee: $35. *Expenses:* Tuition, state resident: full-time $8,952; part-time $373 per credit hour. Tuition, nonresident: full-time $17,634; part-time $735 per credit hour. Required fees: $896; $34 per credit hour. Tuition and fees vary according to course level, degree level and program. *Financial support:* Fellowships with tuition reimbursements, research assistantships with full tuition reimbursements, teaching assistantships with full tuition reimbursements, career-related internships or fieldwork, Federal Work-Study, institutionally sponsored loans, scholarships/grants, tuition waivers (partial), and unspecified assistantships available. Support available to part-time students. Financial award applicants required to submit FAFSA. *Application contact:* Dr. Daniel Steely, Program Advisor, 734-487-0145, Fax: 734-483-9744, E-mail: tsteely@emich.edu.

Eastern Michigan University, Graduate School, College of Arts and Sciences, Department of English Language and Literature, Program in Literature, Ypsilanti, MI 48197. Offers MA, Graduate Certificate. Part-time and evening/weekend programs available. Postbaccalaureate distance learning degree programs offered (minimal on-campus study). *Students:* 10 full-time (5 women), 43 part-time (28 women); includes 5 minority (3 African Americans, 2 Asian Americans or Pacific Islanders), 1 international. Average age 30. In 2007, 17 degrees awarded. *Entrance requirements:* Additional exam requirements/recommendations for international students: Required—TOEFL. *Application deadline:* Applications are processed on a rolling basis. Application fee: $35. *Expenses:* Tuition, state resident: full-time $8,952; part-time $373 per credit hour. Tuition, nonresident: full-time $17,634; part-time $735 per credit hour. Required fees: $896; $34 per credit hour. Tuition and fees vary according to course level, degree level and program. *Financial support:* Fellowships, research assistantships with full tuition reimbursements, teaching assistantships with full tuition reimbursements, career-related internships or fieldwork, Federal Work-Study, institutionally sponsored loans, scholarships/grants, tuition waivers (partial), and unspecified assistantships available. Support available to part-time students. Financial award applicants required to submit FAFSA. *Application contact:* Dr. Andrea Kaston-Tange, Program Coordinator, 734-487-2296, Fax: 734-483-9744, E-mail: akastont@emich.edu.

Eastern New Mexico University, Graduate School, College of Liberal Arts and Sciences, Department of Languages and Literature, Portales, NM 88130. Offers English (MA). Part-time programs available. *Faculty:* 7 full-time (2 women), 1 (woman) part-time/adjunct. *Students:* Average age 38. 8 applicants, 100% accepted. In 2007, 4 degrees awarded. *Degree requirements:* For master's, one foreign language, thesis optional. *Entrance requirements:* For master's, minimum GPA of 2.5. *Application deadline:* For fall admission, 8/20 priority date for domestic students. Applications are processed on a rolling basis. Application fee: $0. Electronic applications accepted. *Expenses:* Tuition, state resident: full-time $2,592; part-time $108 per credit hour. Tuition, nonresident: full-time $8,136; part-time $339 per credit hour. Required fees: $3,850 per credit hour. *Financial support:* In 2007–08, 3 research assistantships (averaging $8,200 per year), 8 teaching assistantships (averaging $8,200 per year) were awarded; fellowships, Federal Work-Study also available. Support available to part-time students. Financial award application deadline: 3/1. *Unit head:* Dr. Linda Sumption, Graduate Coordinator, 575-562-2136, E-mail: linda.sumption@emnu.edu.

Eastern Washington University, Graduate Studies, College of Arts and Letters, Department of English, Cheney, WA 99004-2431. Offers MA. *Degree requirements:* For master's, comprehensive exam, thesis or alternative. *Entrance requirements:* For master's, GRE General Test, minimum GPA of 3.0.

East Tennessee State University, School of Graduate Studies, College of Arts and Sciences, Department of English, Johnson City, TN 37614. Offers MA. Part-time and evening/weekend programs available. *Degree requirements:* For master's, oral defense of thesis. *Entrance requirements:* For master's, GRE General Test or GRE Subject Test, minimum undergraduate GPA of 3.0 in English. Additional exam requirements/recommendations for international students: Required—TOEFL (minimum score 550 paper-based; 213 computer-based). *Faculty research:* Appalachian studies, women's studies, sports images in religion, British and American literature.

Elmhurst College, Graduate Programs, Program in English Studies, Elmhurst, IL 60126-3296. Offers MA. Part-time and evening/weekend programs available. *Faculty:* 2 full-time (1 woman). *Students:* Average age 27. 8 applicants, 63% accepted, 4 enrolled. In 2007, 4 degrees awarded. *Degree requirements:* For master's, thesis optional. *Entrance requirements:* For master's, 3 recommendations. Additional exam requirements/recommendations for international students: Required—TOEFL (minimum score 550 paper-based; 213 computer-based). *Application deadline:* Applications are processed on a rolling basis. Application fee: $25. Electronic applications accepted. *Financial support:* In 2007–08, 23 students received support. Federal Work-Study and scholarships/grants available. Support available to part-time students. Financial award application deadline: 6/1; financial award applicants required to submit FAFSA. *Application contact:* Elizabeth D. Kuebler, Director of Adult and Graduate Admission, 630-617-3069, Fax: 630-617-5501, E-mail: betsyk@elmhurst.edu.

Emory University, Graduate School of Arts and Sciences, Department of Comparative Literature, Atlanta, GA 30322-1100. Offers comparative literature (PhD); English (Certificate); French (Certificate); Middle Eastern studies (PhD); philosophy (Certificate); psychoanalytic studies (PhD); religion (PhD); Spanish (Certificate); women studies (Certificate). *Degree requirements:* For doctorate, 2 foreign languages, comprehensive exam, thesis/dissertation. *Entrance requirements:* For doctorate, GRE General Test, minimum GPA of 3.0. Additional exam requirements/recommendations for international students: Required—TOEFL. Electronic applications accepted. *Faculty research:* Literary theory, psychoanalysis trauma and testimony, literature and religion, literature and technology, literature and philosophy, politics and global culture, literature and aesthetics.

Emory University, Graduate School of Arts and Sciences, Department of English, Atlanta, GA 30322-1100. Offers PhD. *Degree requirements:* For doctorate, one foreign language, comprehensive exam, thesis/dissertation. *Entrance requirements:* For doctorate, GRE General Test, minimum GPA of 3.0. Additional exam requirements/recommendations for international students: Required—TOEFL. Electronic applications accepted. *Faculty research:* American literature, renaissance literature, twentieth century poetry, Irish literature, cultural studies.

Emporia State University, School of Graduate Studies, College of Liberal Arts and Sciences, Department of English, Emporia, KS 66801-5087. Offers MA. Part-time programs available. *Faculty:* 9 full-time (1 woman), 1 (woman) part-time/adjunct. *Students:* 4 full-time (all women), 13 part-time (8 women); includes 1 minority (American Indian/Alaska Native), 2 international. 6 applicants, 67% accepted, 4 enrolled. In 2007, 10 degrees awarded. *Degree requirements:* For master's, comprehensive exam or thesis. *Entrance requirements:* For master's, appropriate undergraduate degree, writing sample. Additional exam requirements/recommendations for international students: Required—TOEFL (minimum score 575 paper-based). *Application deadline:* For fall admission, 8/15 priority date for domestic students. Applications are processed on a rolling basis. Application fee: $30 ($75 for international students). Electronic applications accepted. *Expenses:* Tuition, state resident: part-time $157 per credit hour. Tuition, nonresident: part-time $475 per credit hour. Required fees: $47 per credit hour. Tuition and fees vary according to campus/location. *Financial support:* In 2007–08, 14 teaching assistantships with full tuition reimbursements (averaging $6,887 per year) were awarded; research assistantships, Federal Work-Study, institutionally sponsored loans, health care benefits, and unspecified assistantships also available. Financial award application deadline: 3/15; financial award applicants required to submit FAFSA. *Unit head:* Dr. Jim Hoy, Interim Chair, 620-341-5216, E-mail: jhoy@emporia.edu. *Application contact:* Dr. Mel Storm, Graduate Coordinator, 620-341-5563, E-mail: mstorm@emporia.edu.

Fairleigh Dickinson University, Metropolitan Campus, University College: Arts, Sciences, and Professional Studies, Department of English, Philosophy, and Humanities, Program in English and Literature, Teaneck, NJ 07666-1914. Offers MA. *Students:* Average age 29. 4 applicants, 100% accepted, 3 enrolled. In 2007, 1 degree awarded. Application fee: $40. *Expenses:* Tuition: Part-time $869 per credit. Tuition and fees vary according to degree level, campus/location and program. *Unit head:* Dr. Jason Scorza, Director, Department of English, Philosophy, and Humanities, 201-692-2000.

English

Fayetteville State University, Graduate School, Program in English, Fayetteville, NC 28301-4298. Offers MA. Part-time and evening/weekend programs available. *Faculty:* 7 full-time (2 women). *Students:* 3 full-time (all women), 6 part-time (4 women); includes 5 minority (2 African Americans, 3 Asian Americans or Pacific Islanders). Average age 28. 2 applicants, 100% accepted, 2 enrolled. In 2007, 1 degree awarded. *Degree requirements:* For master's, comprehensive exam, thesis, internship. *Entrance requirements:* For master's, GRE General Test. *Application deadline:* For fall admission, 7/1 for domestic students; for spring admission, 12/1 for domestic students. Applications are processed on a rolling basis. Application fee: $25. Electronic applications accepted. *Expenses:* Tuition, state resident: full-time $2,118; part-time $265 per credit hour. Tuition, nonresident: full-time $11,708; part-time $1,464 per credit hour. Required fees: $1,218; $152 per credit hour. *Faculty research:* Online film culture; literature and pre-Raphaelite, Symbolist, and Surrealist painting; aesthetics of African-American gospel music; power of sheltered instruction. Total annual research expenditures: $19,000. *Unit head:* Dr. Edward McShane, Chairperson, 910-672-1416, E-mail: emcshane@uncsfu.edu.

Fitchburg State College, Division of Graduate and Continuing Education, Programs in English and Teaching English (Secondary Level), Fitchburg, MA 01420-2697. Offers MA, MAT, Certificate. *Accreditation:* NCATE. Part-time and evening/weekend programs available. *Students:* 2 full-time (both women), 22 part-time (16 women); includes 1 minority (African American) Average age 31. 15 applicants, 100% accepted, 9 enrolled. In 2007, 17 degrees awarded. *Entrance requirements:* For master's, GRE General Test or MAT, letters of recommendation, resumé. Additional exam requirements/recommendations for international students: Required—TOEFL (minimum score 550 paper-based; 213 computer-based; 79 iBT). *Application deadline:* Applications are processed on a rolling basis. Application fee: $25 ($50 for international students). *Expenses:* Tuition, nonresident: part-time $150 per credit. Required fees: $109 per credit. *Financial support:* In 2007–08, research assistantships with partial tuition reimbursements (averaging $5,500 per year); Federal Work-Study, scholarships/grants, and unspecified assistantships also available. Support available to part-time students. Financial award application deadline: 3/1; financial award applicants required to submit FAFSA. *Unit head:* Dr. Chola Chisunka, Chair, 978-665-3445, Fax: 978-665-3658, E-mail: gce@fsc.edu. *Application contact:* Director of Admissions, 978-665-3144, Fax: 978-665-4540, E-mail: admissions@fsc.edu.

Florida Atlantic University, Dorothy F. Schmidt College of Arts and Letters, Department of English, Boca Raton, FL 33431-0991. Offers American literature (MA); creative writing (MFA); English literature (MA); fantasy and science fiction (MA); multicultural literature (MA). Part-time programs available. *Degree requirements:* For master's, one foreign language, thesis. *Entrance requirements:* For master's, GRE General Test, minimum GPA of 3.0, writing samples, 2 letters of recommendation. Electronic applications accepted. *Faculty research:* African-American writers, critical theory, British American, Asian American.

Florida Gulf Coast University, College of Arts and Sciences, Program in English, Fort Myers, FL 33965-6565. Offers MA. *Faculty:* 82 full-time (31 women), 103 part-time/adjunct (46 women). *Students:* 16 full-time (12 women), 12 part-time (9 women); includes 6 minority (1 Asian American or Pacific Islander, 5 Hispanic Americans). Average age 31. 22 applicants, 82% accepted, 13 enrolled. In 2007, 2 degrees awarded. *Entrance requirements:* For master's, GRE General Test, minimum GPA of 3.0. Additional exam requirements/recommendations for international students: Required—TOEFL (minimum score 550 paper-based; 213 computer-based). *Application deadline:* For fall admission, 4/1 for domestic students. Application fee: $30. *Expenses:* Tuition, state resident: full-time $4,542. Tuition, nonresident: full-time $19,449. Required fees: $1,297. *Unit head:* Joe Wisdom, Chair, 239-590-7157, E-mail: jwisdom@fgcu.edu.

Florida International University, College of Arts and Sciences, Department of English, Program in English, Miami, FL 33199. Offers MA. Part-time and evening/weekend programs available. *Students:* 15 full-time (9 women), 33 part-time (27 women); includes 53 minority (20 African Americans, 2 Asian Americans or Pacific Islanders, 31 Hispanic Americans). Average age 31. 23 applicants, 70% accepted, 9 enrolled. In 2007, 3 degrees awarded. *Degree requirements:* For master's, thesis. *Entrance requirements:* For master's, GRE General Test, writing examples, minimum GPA of 3.0, letters of recommendation. Additional exam requirements/recommendations for international students: Required—TOEFL (minimum score 550 paper-based; 213 computer-based). *Application deadline:* For fall admission, 2/15 for domestic and international students; for spring admission, 10/1 for domestic students, 9/1 for international students. Applications are processed on a rolling basis. Application fee: $30. Electronic applications accepted. *Expenses:* Tuition, state resident: full-time $6,106. Tuition, nonresident: full-time $15,528. Required fees: $284. *Financial support:* Teaching assistantships, scholarships/grants available. Financial award application deadline: 4/1. *Unit head:* Dr. Carmela Pinto McIntire, Chairperson, Department of English, 305-348-2048, Fax: 305-348-3766, E-mail: carmela.pinto_mcintire@fiu.edu.

Florida State University, Graduate Studies, College of Arts and Sciences, Department of English, Tallahassee, FL 32306. Offers creative writing (MFA, PhD); literature (MA, PhD); rhetoric and composition (MA, PhD). Part-time programs available. *Faculty:* 57 full-time (25 women), 14 part-time/adjunct (9 women). *Students:* 148 full-time (105 women), 20 part-time (10 women); includes 30 minority (13 African Americans, 1 American Indian/Alaska Native, 8 Asian Americans or Pacific Islanders, 8 Hispanic Americans). Average age 30. 427 applicants, 17% accepted, 57 enrolled. In 2007, 25 master's, 18 doctorates awarded. *Median time to degree:* Of those who began their doctoral program in fall 1999, 80% received their degree in 8 years or less. *Degree requirements:* For master's, one foreign language, thesis or alternative; for doctorate, 2 foreign languages, thesis/dissertation. *Entrance requirements:* For master's, GRE General Test, GRE Subject Test (literature), sample of written work, 3 letters of recommendation; for doctorate, GRE General Test, sample of written work, 3 letters of recommendation. *Application deadline:* For fall admission, 2/1 priority date for domestic students. Application fee: $30. Electronic applications accepted. *Expenses:* Tuition, state resident: part-time $248 per credit hour. Tuition, nonresident: part-time $880 per credit hour. Tuition and fees vary according to program. *Financial support:* In 2007–08, 155 students received support, including 5 fellowships, 150 teaching assistantships (averaging $11,375 per year); career-related internships or fieldwork, Federal Work-Study, and institutionally sponsored loans also available. Financial award application deadline: 2/1; financial award applicants required to submit FAFSA. *Faculty research:* British literature, American literature, creative writing, rhetoric, multiethnic literature. *Unit head:* Dr. Ralph Berry, Chairman, 850-644-5158, Fax: 850-644-0811, E-mail: rberry@fsu.edu. *Application contact:* Dr. Stan Gontarski, Director, 850-644-6038, Fax: 850-644-0811, E-mail: sgontarski@fsu.edu.

Fordham University, Graduate School of Arts and Sciences, Department of English Language and Literature, New York, NY 10458. Offers MA, PhD. Part-time and evening/weekend programs available. *Faculty:* 37 full-time (23 women). *Students:* 41 full-time (31 women), 72 part-time (46 women); includes 4 minority (1 American Indian/Alaska Native, 3 Hispanic Americans), 3 international. Average age 30. 201 applicants, 37% accepted, 19 enrolled. In 2007, 7 master's, 2 doctorates awarded. Terminal master's awarded for partial completion of doctoral program. *Median time to degree:* Of those who began their doctoral program in fall 1999, 0% received their degree in 8 years or less. *Degree requirements:* For master's, one foreign language, comprehensive exam, thesis optional; for doctorate, 2 foreign languages, comprehensive exam, thesis/dissertation. *Entrance requirements:* For master's, GRE General Test; for doctorate, GRE General Test, GRE Subject Test. Additional exam requirements/recommendations for international students: Required—TOEFL (minimum score 650 paper-based; 280 computer-based). *Application deadline:* For fall admission, 1/4 priority date for domestic students; for spring admission, 11/1 for domestic students. Application fee: $70. Electronic applications accepted. *Expenses:* Tuition: Full-time $23,880; part-time $995 per credit. *Financial support:* In 2007–08, 60 students received support, including 6 fellowships with tuition reimbursements available (averaging $21,891 per year), 24 research assistantships with tuition reimbursements available (averaging $17,554 per year), 30 teaching assistantships with tuition reimbursements available (averaging $12,940 per year); institutionally sponsored loans, tuition waivers (full and partial), and unspecified assistantships also available. Financial award application deadline: 1/4; financial award applicants required to submit FAFSA. *Faculty research:* 19th century British and American literature, Shakespeare and early modern drama, Aesthetic theory, Old Norse, poetics of race and gender, Anglo-Norman. Total annual research expenditures: $22,000. *Unit head:* Dr. Nicola Pitchford, Chair, 718-817-4007, Fax: 718-817-4010, E-mail: pitchford@fordham.edu. *Application contact:* Charlene Dundie, Director of Graduate Admissions, 718-817-4420, Fax: 718-817-3566, E-mail: dundie@fordham.edu.

Fort Hays State University, Graduate School, College of Arts and Sciences, Department of English, Hays, KS 67601-4099. Offers MA. *Faculty:* 10 full-time (2 women). *Students:* 4 full-time (3 women), 7 part-time (6 women); includes 1 minority (African American) Average age 42. 2 applicants, 100% accepted. In 2007, 5 degrees awarded. *Degree requirements:* For master's, comprehensive exam, thesis or alternative. *Entrance requirements:* Additional exam requirements/recommendations for international students: Required—TOEFL (minimum score 550 paper-based; 213 computer-based). *Application deadline:* For fall admission, 7/1 priority date for domestic students. Applications are processed on a rolling basis. Application fee: $35. Electronic applications accepted. *Expenses:* Tuition, state resident: part-time $155 per credit hour. Tuition, nonresident: part-time $409 per credit hour. Tuition and fees vary according to class time, course level, course load, degree level, campus/location and program. *Financial support:* In 2007–08, 1 teaching assistantship with tuition reimbursement (averaging $7,000 per year) was awarded; research assistantships, institutionally sponsored loans and tuition waivers (full and partial) also available. *Faculty research:* Eisenhower and Hansen papers, Celtic literature and culture, poetry of Robert Frost. *Unit head:* Dr. Carl Singleton, Chair, 785-628-4285, E-mail: csinglet@fhsu.edu.

Gannon University, School of Graduate Studies, College of Humanities, Business, and Education, School of Humanities, Program in English, Erie, PA 16541-0001. Offers MA. Part-time and evening/weekend programs available. *Students:* 7 full-time (5 women), 13 part-time (8 women); includes 1 minority (Asian American or Pacific Islander) Average age 28. 19 applicants, 84% accepted, 9 enrolled. In 2007, 8 degrees awarded. *Degree requirements:* For master's, comprehensive exam, thesis. *Entrance requirements:* For master's, interview. Additional exam requirements/recommendations for international students: Required—TOEFL (minimum score 500 paper-based; 173 computer-based). *Application deadline:* Applications are processed on a rolling basis. Application fee: $25. *Expenses:* Tuition: Full-time $13,050; part-time $725 per credit. Required fees: $502; $16 per credit. Tuition and fees vary according to course load, degree level, campus/location and program. *Financial support:* Teaching assistantships, career-related internships or fieldwork available. Support available to part-time students. Financial award application deadline: 7/1; financial award applicants required to submit FAFSA. *Unit head:* Michael Tkach, Chair, 814-871-5807, E-mail: tkach001@gannon.edu. *Application contact:* Debra Meszaros, Director of Graduate Recruitment, 814-871-5819, Fax: 814-871-5827, E-mail: cfal@gannon.edu.

Gardner-Webb University, Graduate School, Department of English, Boiling Springs, NC 28017. Offers English (MA); English education (MA). Part-time and evening/weekend programs available. *Faculty:* 2 full-time (both women), 1 (woman) part-time/adjunct. *Students:* 2 full-time (1 woman), 6 part-time (5 women); includes 2 minority (both African Americans) Average age 25. 2 applicants, 100% accepted, 2 enrolled. In 2007, 2 degrees awarded. *Degree requirements:* For master's, comprehensive exam. *Entrance requirements:* For master's, GRE General Test, MAT, or NTE; PRAXIS, minimum GPA of 2.5. *Application deadline:* For fall admission, 8/1 priority date for domestic students. Applications are processed on a rolling basis. Application fee: $25. Electronic applications accepted. *Expenses:* Tuition: Part-time $275 per hour. *Financial support:* Unspecified assistantships available. *Unit head:* Dr. Gayle B. Price, Chair, 704-406-4414, Fax: 704-406-3921, E-mail: gprice@gardner-webb.edu.

George Mason University, College of Humanities and Social Sciences, Department of English, Fairfax, VA 22030. Offers creative writing (MFA); English (MA); English literature (MA); linguistics (MA); professional writing and editing (MA, Certificate); teaching English as a second language (Certificate); teaching writing and literature (MA). *Faculty:* 79 full-time (45 women), 45 part-time/adjunct (26 women). *Students:* 27 full-time (20 women), 136 part-time (108 women); includes 23 minority (7 African Americans, 2 American Indian/Alaska Native, 9 Asian Americans or Pacific Islanders, 5 Hispanic Americans), 3 international. Average age 31. 337 applicants, 57% accepted, 103 enrolled. In 2007, 55 degrees awarded. *Degree requirements:* For master's, thesis (for some programs). *Entrance requirements:* For master's, minimum GPA of 3.0 in last 60 hours of course work. *Application deadline:* For fall admission, 5/1 for domestic students; for spring admission, 11/1 for domestic students. Application fee: $60 ($75 for international students). Electronic applications accepted. *Financial support:* Fellowships, research assistantships, teaching assistantships available. Support available to part-time students. Financial award application deadline: 3/1; financial award applicants required to submit FAFSA. *Faculty research:* Literature, professional writing and editing, writing of fiction or poetry. *Unit head:* Dr. Deborah Kaplan, Chair, 703-993-1170, Fax: 703-993-1161, E-mail: dkaplan@gmu.edu.

Georgetown University, Graduate School of Arts and Sciences, Department of English, Washington, DC 20057. Offers British and American literature (MA). *Degree requirements:* For master's, thesis or alternative, independent study, oral exam. *Entrance requirements:* For master's, GRE General Test. Additional exam requirements/recommendations for international students: Required—TOEFL.

The George Washington University, Columbian College of Arts and Sciences, Department of English, Washington, DC 20052. Offers MA, PhD. Part-time and evening/weekend programs available. Terminal master's awarded for partial completion of doctoral program. *Degree requirements:* For master's, one foreign language, comprehensive exam, thesis or alternative; for doctorate, 2 foreign languages, thesis/dissertation, general exam. *Entrance requirements:* For master's and doctorate, GRE General Test, GRE Subject Test, minimum GPA of 3.0, writing sample. Additional exam requirements/recommendations for international students: Required—TOEFL (minimum score 550 paper-based; 213 computer-based). Electronic applications accepted.

Georgia College & State University, Graduate School, School of Liberal Arts and Sciences, Department of English, Speech, and Journalism, Program in English, Milledgeville, GA 31061. Offers MA. *Students:* 6 full-time (3 women), 5 part-time (3 women); includes 1 minority (African American) Average age 33. 9 applicants, 56% accepted, 3 enrolled. In 2007, 3 degrees awarded. *Degree requirements:* For master's, one foreign language, comprehensive exam, thesis. *Entrance requirements:* For master's, GRE (minimum score: 550 verbal, 4.5 analytical), undergraduate major in English, minimum GPA of 3.0, letters of recommendation. *Expenses:* Tuition, state resident: full-time $3,726. Tuition, nonresident: full-time $14,868. Required fees: $858. Tuition and fees vary according to campus/location. *Financial support:* In 2007–08, 5 research assistantships (averaging $3,800 per year) were awarded.

Georgia Southern University, Jack N. Averitt College of Graduate Studies, College of Liberal Arts and Social Sciences, Department of Literature and Philosophy, Statesboro, GA 30460. Offers English (MA). Part-time programs available. *Students:* 13 full-time (9 women), 8 part-time (5 women); includes 2 minority (both African Americans) Average age 26. 10 applicants, 100% accepted, 8 enrolled. In 2007, 9 degrees awarded. *Degree requirements:* For master's, one foreign language, thesis optional, terminal exams. *Entrance requirements:* For master's, GRE General Test, minimum GPA of 3.0, letters of reference. Additional exam requirements/recommendations for international students: Required—TOEFL (minimum score 550 paper-based; 213 computer-based; 80 iBT). *Application deadline:* For fall admission, 3/1 priority date for domestic and international students; for spring admission, 10/1 priority date for domestic students, 10/1 for international students. Applications are processed on a rolling basis. Application fee: $50. Electronic applications accepted. *Expenses:* Tuition, state resident: full-time $3,516; part-time $147 per semester hour. Tuition, nonresident: full-time $14,060; part-time $586 per semester hour. Required fees: $562 per term. *Financial support:* In 2007–08, 16 students received support, including research assistantships with partial tuition reimbursements available (averaging $6,850 per year), teaching assistantships with partial tuition

English

Georgia Southern University (continued)
reimbursements available (averaging $6,850 per year); career-related internships or fieldwork, Federal Work-Study, scholarships/grants, tuition waivers (partial), and unspecified assistantships also available. Support available to part-time students. Financial award application deadline: 4/15; financial award applicants required to submit FAFSA. *Faculty research:* The fiction of Nuguib Mahfouz and Shusako Enato, a book-length collection of essays on playwright Paula Vogel, a critical edition of math, Gregory Lewis's Tales of Wonder (1800), ongoing studies in the dramatic works of English poet John Dryden, post modern childhoods, post modern poetries. *Unit head:* David Dudley, Chair, 912-478-5471, E-mail: dldudley@georgiasouthern.edu. *Application contact:* 912-478-5384, Fax: 912-478-0740, E-mail: gradadmissions@georgiasouthern.edu.

Georgia State University, College of Arts and Sciences, Department of English, Atlanta, GA 30303-3083. Offers creative writing (MA, MFA, PhD); English (MA, PhD); fiction (MFA); literary studies and composition (MA, PhD); poetry (MFA); rhetoric (MA, PhD). Part-time and evening/weekend programs available. *Faculty:* 43 full-time (21 women). *Students:* 128 full-time (96 women), 103 part-time (58 women); includes 34 minority (23 African Americans, 2 American Indian/Alaska Native, 4 Asian Americans or Pacific Islanders, 5 Hispanic Americans), 11 international. 232 applicants, 44% accepted, 54 enrolled. In 2007, 20 master's, 9 doctorates awarded. *Degree requirements:* For master's, one foreign language, thesis; for doctorate, 2 foreign languages, comprehensive exam, thesis/dissertation, exam. *Entrance requirements:* For master's and doctorate, GRE General Test. Additional exam requirements/recommendations for international students: Required—TOEFL. *Application deadline:* For fall admission, 2/15 for domestic students. Applications are processed on a rolling basis. Application fee: $50. Electronic applications accepted. *Expenses:* Tuition, state resident: part-time $221 per credit hour. *Financial support:* In 2007–08, 5 research assistantships with tuition reimbursements, 11 teaching assistantships with tuition reimbursements were awarded; Federal Work-Study, institutionally sponsored loans, and unspecified assistantships also available. Support available to part-time students. Financial award application deadline: 2/15; financial award applicants required to submit FAFSA. *Faculty research:* Literary biography, folklore, Southern literature, medieval literature. *Unit head:* Dr. Matthew Roudane, Chair, 404-413-5804, E-mail: engmcr@langate.gsu.edu. *Application contact:* Melissa McLeod, Assistant to Director of Graduate Studies, 404-413-5807, Fax: 404-413-5830, E-mail: engmkm@langate.gsu.edu.

Governors State University, College of Arts and Sciences, Program in English, University Park, IL 60466-0975. Offers MA. Part-time and evening/weekend programs available. *Students:* 8 full-time, 27 part-time. Average age 35. *Degree requirements:* For master's, thesis or alternative. *Entrance requirements:* For master's, bachelor's degree in related field. *Application deadline:* For fall admission, 7/15 priority date for domestic students; for spring admission, 11/10 for domestic students. Applications are processed on a rolling basis. Application fee: $25. *Financial support:* Research assistantships, Federal Work-Study, institutionally sponsored loans, and scholarships/grants available. Support available to part-time students. Financial award application deadline: 5/1. *Unit head:* Dr. Eric V. Martin, Dean, College of Arts and Sciences, 708-534-4101.

Graduate School and University Center of the City University of New York, Graduate Studies, Program in English, New York, NY 10016-4039. Offers PhD. *Faculty:* 51 full-time (13 women). *Students:* 272 full-time (163 women), 3 part-time (all women); includes 36 minority (14 African Americans, 1 American Indian/Alaska Native, 10 Asian Americans or Pacific Islanders, 11 Hispanic Americans), 24 international. Average age 34. 260 applicants, 27% accepted, 34 enrolled. In 2007, 28 degrees awarded. *Degree requirements:* For doctorate, 2 foreign languages, thesis/dissertation. *Entrance requirements:* For doctorate, GRE General Test, GRE Subject Test, writing sample, curriculum vitae. Additional exam requirements/recommendations for international students: Required—TOEFL. *Application deadline:* For fall admission, 1/1 for domestic students. Application fee: $125. Electronic applications accepted. *Financial support:* In 2007–08, 201 students received support, including 173 fellowships, 29 research assistantships, 27 teaching assistantships; career-related internships or fieldwork, Federal Work-Study, institutionally sponsored loans, and tuition waivers (full and partial) also available. Financial award application deadline: 2/1; financial award applicants required to submit FAFSA. *Unit head:* Dr. Steven Kruger, Executive Officer, 212-817-8352, Fax: 212-817-1518.

Grand Valley State University, College of Liberal Arts and Sciences, English Department, Allendale, MI 49401-9403. Offers MA. *Faculty:* 21 full-time (13 women). *Students:* 6 full-time (3 women), 33 part-time (24 women); includes 2 minority (1 African American, 1 Asian American or Pacific Islander). Average age 34. 14 applicants, 79% accepted, 8 enrolled. In 2007, 4 degrees awarded. *Entrance requirements:* Additional exam requirements/recommendations for international students: Required—TOEFL. Application fee: $30. *Financial support:* In 2007–08, 1 research assistantship with full and partial tuition reimbursement (averaging $8,000 per year) was awarded. *Faculty research:* Literary history, philosophy and literature, feminist issues in literature. *Unit head:* Dr. Jill VanAntwerp, Chair, 616-331-3405, E-mail: vanantwj@gvsu.edu. *Application contact:* Dr. Ben Lockerd, Information Contact, 616-331-3575, E-mail: lockerdb@gvsu.edu.

Hardin-Simmons University, Graduate School, Cynthia Ann Parker College of Liberal Arts, Department of English, Abilene, TX 79698-0001. Offers MA. Part-time programs available. *Faculty:* 5 full-time (2 women), 1 part-time/adjunct (0 women). *Students:* 2 full-time (both women), 8 part-time (7 women); includes 1 minority (Hispanic American) Average age 33. 7 applicants, 71% accepted, 2 enrolled. In 2007, 1 degree awarded. *Degree requirements:* For master's, one foreign language, comprehensive exam, thesis or alternative. *Entrance requirements:* For master's, minimum undergraduate GPA of 3.0 in English, 2.7 overall; writing sample; letters of recommendation; interview. Additional exam requirements/recommendations for international students: Required—TOEFL (minimum score 550 paper-based; 213 computer-based). *Application deadline:* For fall admission, 8/15 priority date for domestic students; for spring admission, 1/5 priority date for domestic students. Applications are processed on a rolling basis. Application fee: $50 ($100 for international students). *Expenses:* Tuition: Full-time $9,810; part-time $545 per hour. Required fees: $590; $75 per semester. One-time fee: $50 part-time. *Financial support:* In 2007–08, 7 students received support, including 4 fellowships (averaging $1,100 per year); scholarships/grants also available. Support available to part-time students. Financial award application deadline: 6/30; financial award applicants required to submit FAFSA. *Faculty research:* Milton, Tennyson, American Romantic period, Derek Walcott, woman's literature. *Unit head:* Dr. Laura Pogue, Program Director, 325-670-1366, Fax: 325-670-5859, E-mail: lpogue@hsutx.edu. *Application contact:* Dr. Gary Stanlake, Dean of Graduate Studies, 325-670-1298, Fax: 325-670-1564, E-mail: gradoff@hsutx.edu.

Harvard University, Extension School, Cambridge, MA 02138-3722. Offers applied sciences (CAS); biotechnology (ALM); educational technologies (ALM); educational technology (CET); English for graduate and professional studies (DGP); environmental management (ALM, CEM); information technology (ALM); journalism (ALM); liberal arts (ALM); management (ALM, CM); mathematics for teaching (ALM); museum studies (ALM); premedical studies (Diploma); publication and communication (CPC). Part-time and evening/weekend programs available. *Faculty:* 242 part-time/adjunct. *Students:* Average age 35. In 2007, 190 master's, 78 other advanced degrees awarded. *Degree requirements:* For master's, thesis. *Entrance requirements:* For master's, 3 completed graduate courses with grade of B or higher. Additional exam requirements/recommendations for international students: Required—TOEFL (minimum score 600 paper-based; 250 computer-based), TWE (minimum score 5). *Application deadline:* Applications are processed on a rolling basis. Application fee: $75. *Expenses:* Contact institution. Full-time tuition and fees vary according to program and student level. *Financial support:* In 2007–08, 198 students received support. Scholarships/grants available. Support available to part-time students. Financial award application deadline: 8/6; financial award applicants required to submit FAFSA. *Unit head:* Michael Shinagel, Dean, 617-495-1000. *Application contact:* Program Director, 617-495-4024, Fax: 617-495-9176.

Harvard University, Graduate School of Arts and Sciences, Department of English and American Literature and Language, Cambridge, MA 02138. Offers critical theory (PhD); eighteenth-century literature (PhD); literature: nineteenth-century to the present (PhD); medieval literature and language (PhD); modern British and American literature (PhD); Renaissance literature (PhD). Terminal master's awarded for partial completion of doctoral program. *Degree requirements:* For doctorate, 2 foreign languages, thesis/dissertation, oral exam. *Entrance requirements:* For doctorate, GRE General Test, GRE Subject Test, writing sample. Additional exam requirements/recommendations for international students: Required—TOEFL. *Expenses:* Tuition: Full-time $31,456. Full-time tuition and fees vary according to program and student level. *Faculty research:* Old and Middle English language and literature, drama, creative writing, transition to Romanticism, history and theory of criticism.

Heritage University, Graduate Programs in Education, Program in Professional Studies, Toppenish, WA 98948-9599. Offers bilingual education/ESL (M Ed); biology (M Ed); English and literature (M Ed); reading/literacy (M Ed); special education (M Ed). Part-time and evening/weekend programs available. *Degree requirements:* For master's, comprehensive exam (for some programs), thesis (for some programs).

Hofstra University, College of Liberal Arts and Sciences, Department of English, Hempstead, NY 11549. Offers English and creative writing (MA); English literature (MA). Part-time programs available. *Faculty:* 9 full-time (5 women), 2 part-time/adjunct (both women). *Students:* 17 full-time (11 women), 19 part-time (13 women); includes 4 minority (2 African Americans, 1 Asian American or Pacific Islander, 1 Hispanic American). Average age 28. 39 applicants, 67% accepted, 13 enrolled. In 2007, 7 degrees awarded. *Degree requirements:* For master's, thesis optional. *Entrance requirements:* For master's, writing sample, essay, minimum GPA of 3.0 in Literature courses. Additional exam requirements/recommendations for international students: Required—TOEFL (minimum score 550 paper-based; 213 computer-based). *Application deadline:* Applications are processed on a rolling basis. Application fee: $60. Electronic applications accepted. *Expenses:* Tuition: Full-time $14,220; part-time $820 per credit. Required fees: $970; $165 per term. Tuition and fees vary according to program. *Financial support:* In 2007–08, 18 students received support, including 1 fellowship with tuition reimbursement available (averaging $3,000 per year), 3 research assistantships with full and partial tuition reimbursements available (averaging $8,880 per year); Federal Work-Study, institutionally sponsored loans, scholarships/grants, and tuition waivers (full and partial) also available. Support available to part-time students. Financial award applicants required to submit FAFSA. *Faculty research:* Herman Melville, disability studies, Early American Literature; Queer Theory; Twentieth-Century Popular culture. *Unit head:* Dr. Joseph A. Fichtelberg, Chairperson, 516-463-6279, Fax: 516-463-6395, E-mail: engjaf@hofstra.edu. *Application contact:* Carol Drummer, Dean of Graduate Admissions, 516-463-4876, Fax: 516-463-4664, E-mail: gradstudent@hofstra.edu.

Hollins University, Graduate Programs, Program in Children's Literature, Roanoke, VA 24020-1603. Offers MA, MFA. Offered during summer only. Part-time programs available. *Faculty:* 1 (woman) full-time, 7 part-time/adjunct (4 women). *Students:* 67 full-time (61 women), 4 part-time (all women); includes 5 minority (2 African Americans, 1 Asian American or Pacific Islander, 2 Hispanic Americans), 2 international. Average age 37. 49 applicants, 100% accepted, 35 enrolled. In 2007, 9 degrees awarded. *Degree requirements:* For master's, one foreign language, comprehensive exam, thesis. *Entrance requirements:* For master's, letters of recommendation, portfolio. Additional exam requirements/recommendations for international students: Required—TOEFL (minimum score 550 paper-based; 213 computer-based). *Application deadline:* For fall admission, 2/15 for domestic and international students. Application fee: $40. Electronic applications accepted. *Expenses:* Tuition: Part-time $265 per credit hour. Tuition and fees vary according to course load and program. *Financial support:* In 2007–08, 48 students received support, including 26 fellowships (averaging $900 per year); Federal Work-Study, scholarships/grants, and unspecified assistantships also available. Support available to part-time students. Financial award application deadline: 2/15; financial award applicants required to submit FAFSA. *Faculty research:* Fantasy, children's film, gender studies, mythology and folk tales, children's poetry, young adult fiction. *Unit head:* Amanda Cockrell, Director, 540-362-6024, Fax: 540-362-6642, E-mail: acockrell@hollins.edu. *Application contact:* Cathy S. Koon, Manager of Graduate Services, 540-362-6326, Fax: 540-362-6288, E-mail: ckoon@hollins.edu.

Howard University, Graduate School, Department of English, Washington, DC 20059-0002. Offers MA, PhD. Part-time programs available. *Degree requirements:* For master's, one foreign language, comprehensive exam, thesis; for doctorate, 2 foreign languages, comprehensive exam, thesis/dissertation, qualifying exam. *Entrance requirements:* For master's, GRE General Test, minimum GPA of 3.0; for doctorate, GRE General Test. *Expenses:* Tuition: Full-time $16,175; part-time $899 per credit hour. Required fees: $805.

Humboldt State University, Graduate Studies, College of Arts, Humanities, and Social Sciences, Department of English, Arcata, CA 95521-8299. Offers MA. *Students:* 29 full-time (19 women), 7 part-time (3 women); includes 5 minority (1 African American, 1 Asian American or Pacific Islander, 3 Hispanic Americans). Average age 31. 36 applicants, 56% accepted, 12 enrolled. In 2007, 5 degrees awarded. *Degree requirements:* For master's, one foreign language, thesis or alternative, qualifying exam. *Entrance requirements:* For master's, minimum GPA of 2.5, 3 letters of recommendation. Additional exam requirements/recommendations for international students: Required—TOEFL (minimum score 500 paper-based; 173 computer-based). *Application deadline:* For fall admission, 3/1 for domestic students; for spring admission, 11/1 for domestic students. Applications are processed on a rolling basis. Application fee: $55. *Financial support:* Teaching assistantships, career-related internships or fieldwork, Federal Work-Study, and institutionally sponsored loans available. Financial award application deadline: 3/1; financial award applicants required to submit FAFSA. *Faculty research:* Teaching of writing, literature. *Unit head:* Dr. Susan G. Bennett, Chair, 707-826-3758, Fax: 707-826-5939, E-mail: sgb1@humboldt.edu. *Application contact:* Dr. Michael S. Eldridge, Graduate Coordinator, 707-826-5906, Fax: 707-826-5939, E-mail: me2@humboldt.edu.

Hunter College of the City University of New York, Graduate School, School of Arts and Sciences, Department of English, Program in British and American Literature, New York, NY 10021-5085. Offers MA. Part-time and evening/weekend programs available. *Faculty:* 24 full-time (15 women), 1 (woman) part-time/adjunct. *Students:* 1 full-time (0 women), 70 part-time (47 women); includes 3 minority (2 African Americans, 1 Hispanic American). Average age 32. 53 applicants, 51% accepted, 18 enrolled. In 2007, 12 degrees awarded. *Degree requirements:* For master's, one foreign language, comprehensive exam, thesis, essay. *Entrance requirements:* For master's, GRE General Test, minimum 18 credits of course work in English, excluding journalism and writing. Additional exam requirements/recommendations for international students: Required—TOEFL. *Application deadline:* For fall admission, 4/1 for domestic students, 2/1 for international students; for spring admission, 11/1 for domestic students, 9/1 for international students. Application fee: $125. *Expenses:* Tuition, state resident: full-time $6,400; part-time $270 per credit. Tuition, nonresident: part-time $500 per credit. One-time fee: $125 full-time. Tuition and fees vary according to program. *Financial support:* Federal Work-Study and tuition waivers (partial) available. Support available to part-time students. Financial award application deadline: 4/15. *Application contact:* David Carlson, Education Adviser, 212-772-5074, E-mail: dcarlson@hunter.cuny.edu.

Idaho State University, Office of Graduate Studies, College of Arts and Sciences, Department of English, Pocatello, ID 83209. Offers MA, DA, Post-Master's Certificate. *Faculty:* 20 full-time (7 women). *Students:* 30 full-time (16 women), 22 part-time (12 women); includes 2 minority (both Hispanic Americans), 3 international. Average age 38. In 2007, 8 master's, 1 doctorate awarded. *Degree requirements:* For master's, one foreign language, comprehensive exam, thesis optional; for doctorate, one foreign language, comprehensive exam, thesis/dissertation, 2 papers, 2 teaching internships; for Post-Master's Certificate, 6 credits of elective linguistics, practicum. *Entrance requirements:* For master's, GRE General Test, general literature exam, minimum GPA of 3.0, 3 letters of recommendation; for doctorate, GRE General Test, GRE Subject Test, minimum GPA of 3.5, writing examples, 3 letters of recommendation, master's degree in English; for Post-Master's Certificate, GRE, bachelor's degree, minimum undergraduate GPA of 3.0 in last 2 years, 3 letters of recommendation, knowledge of 2nd language. Additional exam requirements/recommendations for international students: Required—TOEFL (minimum score 550 paper-based; 213 computer-based; 80 iBT). *Application deadline:* For fall admission, 7/1 for domestic students, 6/1 for international students; for spring admission, 12/1 for domestic students, 11/1 for international students. Applications are processed on a rolling basis. Application fee: $55. Electronic applications accepted. *Expenses:* Tuition, state resident: full-time $2,882; part-time $259 per credit hour. Tuition, nonresident: full-time $11,566; part-time $379 per credit hour. Required fees: $2,278. Full-time tuition and fees vary according to program. Part-time tuition and fees vary according to course load. *Financial support:* In 2007–08, 6 fellowships with full and partial tuition reimbursements (averaging $12,772 per year), 4 research assistantships (averaging $9,128 per year), 12 teaching assistantships with full and partial tuition reimbursements (averaging $9,128 per year) were awarded; career-related internships or fieldwork, Federal Work-Study, institutionally sponsored loans, scholarships/grants, health care benefits, and unspecified assistantships also available. Support available to part-time students. Financial award application deadline: 1/1; financial award applicants required to submit FAFSA. *Faculty research:* American literature, Renaissance literature, composition and rhetoric, Intermountain West studies, ethics. *Unit head:* Dr. Terry O. Engebretsen, Chairman, 208-282-2478, Fax: 208-282-4472, E-mail: engeterr@isu.edu. *Application contact:* Ellen Combs, Graduate School Technical Records Specialist, 208-282-2150, Fax: 208-282-4847.

Illinois State University, Graduate School, College of Arts and Sciences, Department of English, Program in English, Normal, IL 61790-2200. Offers English (MA, MS); English studies (PhD). *Students:* 80 full-time (49 women), 44 part-time (23 women); includes 10 minority (5 African Americans, 1 American Indian/Alaska Native, 2 Asian Americans or Pacific Islanders, 2 Hispanic Americans), 31 international. 94 applicants, 56% accepted. In 2007, 12 master's, 12 doctorates awarded. *Degree requirements:* For doctorate, thesis/dissertation, 2 terms of residency. *Entrance requirements:* For master's, GRE General Test, minimum GPA of 3.0 in last 60 hours; for doctorate, GRE General Test. *Application deadline:* Applications are processed on a rolling basis. Application fee: $40. *Expenses:* Tuition, state resident: full-time $3,492; part-time $194 per credit hour. Tuition, nonresident: full-time $7,272; part-time $404 per credit hour. Required fees: $1,024; $57 per credit hour. *Financial support:* Tuition waivers (full) and unspecified assistantships available. Financial award application deadline: 4/1. *Unit head:* Dr. Timothy Hunt, Chairperson, Department of English, 309-438-3667.

Indiana State University, School of Graduate Studies, College of Arts and Sciences, Department of English, Terre Haute, IN 47809-1401. Offers English teaching (MA); history (MA); literature (MA). Part-time and evening/weekend programs available. *Faculty:* 16 full-time (4 women), 7 part-time/adjunct (2 women). *Students:* 12 full-time (10 women), 16 part-time (11 women); includes 1 minority (African American) Average age 32. 11 applicants, 100% accepted, 6 enrolled. In 2007, 14 degrees awarded. *Degree requirements:* For master's, one foreign language, thesis optional. *Entrance requirements:* For master's, minimum GPA of 2.75 in all English courses above freshman level. Additional exam requirements/recommendations for international students: Required—TOEFL (minimum score 550 paper-based). *Application deadline:* For fall admission, 7/1 priority date for domestic students; for spring admission, 11/1 priority date for domestic students. Applications are processed on a rolling basis. Application fee: $35. Electronic applications accepted. *Expenses:* Tuition, state resident: full-time $7,056; part-time $294 per semester hour. Tuition, nonresident: full-time $14,016; part-time $584 per semester hour. Required fees: $175 per semester. *Financial support:* In 2007–08, 11 teaching assistantships with partial tuition reimbursements (averaging $3,000 per year) were awarded; career-related internships or fieldwork, Federal Work-Study, and tuition waivers (partial) also available. Support available to part-time students. Financial award application deadline: 3/1; financial award applicants required to submit FAFSA. *Unit head:* Dr. Robert Perrin, Interim Chairperson, 812-237-3160.

Indiana University Bloomington, University Graduate School, College of Arts and Sciences, Department of English, Bloomington, IN 47405-7000. Offers composition, literacy, and culture (PhD); creative writing (MA, MFA), including fiction, poetry; language (MA); literature (MA, PhD); writing (MA). Part-time programs available. *Faculty:* 51 full-time (23 women). *Students:* 148 full-time (89 women), 52 part-time (34 women); includes 20 minority (8 African Americans, 7 Asian Americans or Pacific Islanders, 5 Hispanic Americans), 9 international. Average age 29. 560 applicants, 6% accepted, 32 enrolled. In 2007, 34 master's, 12 doctorates awarded. Terminal master's awarded for partial completion of doctoral program. *Median time to degree:* Of those who began their doctoral program in fall 1999, 30% received their degree in 8 years or less. *Degree requirements:* For master's, one foreign language, thesis (for some programs); for doctorate, 2 foreign languages, thesis/dissertation. *Entrance requirements:* For master's, GRE General Test, minimum GPA of 3.5; for doctorate, GRE General Test, minimum GPA of 3.7. Additional exam requirements/recommendations for international students: Required—TOEFL. *Application deadline:* For fall admission, 1/15 priority date for domestic students, 12/15 for international students; for spring admission, 9/1 for domestic and international students. Application fee: $50 ($60 for international students). *Financial support:* Fellowships, research assistantships, teaching assistantships, career-related internships or fieldwork available. Financial award application deadline: 2/1. *Unit head:* George Hutchinson, Chair, 812-855-8225, E-mail: gbhutchi@indiana.edu. *Application contact:* Patricia Ingham, Director of Admissions, 812-855-0521, Fax: 812-855-9535, E-mail: pingham@indiana.edu.

Indiana University of Pennsylvania, School of Graduate Studies and Research, College of Humanities and Social Sciences, Department of English, Program in Composition and Teaching English to Speakers of Other Languages, Indiana, PA 15705-1087. Offers composition and teaching English to speakers of other languages (PhD); teaching English (MAT); teaching English to speakers of other languages (MA). *Faculty:* 32 full-time (16 women). *Students:* 49 full-time (29 women), 125 part-time (75 women); includes 9 minority (3 African Americans, 1 American Indian/Alaska Native, 2 Asian Americans or Pacific Islanders, 3 Hispanic Americans), 64 international. Average age 38. 213 applicants, 42% accepted, 38 enrolled. In 2007, 17 master's, 10 doctorates awarded. *Degree requirements:* For master's, thesis optional; for doctorate, one foreign language, comprehensive exam, thesis/dissertation. *Entrance requirements:* For master's and doctorate, 2 letters of recommendation. Additional exam requirements/recommendations for international students: Required—TOEFL. *Application deadline:* For fall admission, 7/1 priority date for domestic students; for spring admission, 11/1 for domestic students. Applications are processed on a rolling basis. Application fee: $30. *Expenses:* Tuition, state resident: full-time $6,214; part-time $345 per credit. Tuition, nonresident: full-time $9,944; part-time $552 per credit. Required fees: $43 per credit. One-time fee: $140 part-time. Tuition and fees vary according to course load. *Financial support:* In 2007–08, 5 fellowships (averaging $5,000 per year), 18 research assistantships with full and partial tuition reimbursements (averaging $6,170 per year), 10 teaching assistantships with partial tuition reimbursements (averaging $17,001 per year) were awarded. Financial award application deadline: 3/15; financial award applicants required to submit FAFSA. *Unit head:* Dr. Ben Rafoth, Graduate Coordinator, 724-357-2272.

Indiana University of Pennsylvania, School of Graduate Studies and Research, College of Humanities and Social Sciences, Department of English, Program in Literature and Criticism, Indiana, PA 15705-1087. Offers generalist (MA); literature (MA); literature and criticism (PhD). *Faculty:* 32 full-time (16 women). *Students:* 28 full-time (10 women), 66 part-time (40 women); includes 9 minority (7 African Americans, 2 Hispanic Americans), 23 international. Average age 37. 65 applicants, 66% accepted, 17 enrolled. In 2007, 12 doctorates awarded. *Degree requirements:* For master's, thesis optional; for doctorate, one foreign language, comprehensive exam, thesis/dissertation. *Entrance requirements:* For master's and doctorate, 2 letters of recommendation. Additional exam requirements/recommendations for international students: Required—TOEFL. *Application deadline:* For fall admission, 7/1 priority date for domestic students; for spring admission, 11/1 for domestic students. Applications are processed on a rolling basis. Application fee: $30. *Expenses:* Tuition, state resident: full-time $6,214; part-time $345 per credit. Tuition, nonresident: full-time $9,944; part-time $552 per credit. Required fees: $43 per credit. One-time fee: $140 part-time. Tuition and fees vary according to course load. *Financial support:* In 2007–08, 4 fellowships (averaging $5,000 per year), 24 research assistantships with full and partial tuition reimbursements (averaging $6,170 per year), 10 teaching assistantships with partial tuition reimbursements (averaging $17,001 per year) were awarded. Financial award application deadline: 3/15; financial award applicants required to submit FAFSA. *Unit head:* Dr. Karen Dandurand, Graduate Coordinator, 724-357-3963, E-mail: karenddd@iup.edu.

Indiana University–Purdue University Fort Wayne, College of Arts and Sciences, Department of English and Linguistics, Fort Wayne, IN 46805-1499. Offers English (MA, MAT); TENL (teaching English as a new language) (Certificate). Part-time programs available. *Faculty:* 28 full-time (15 women). *Students:* 10 full-time (7 women), 18 part-time (11 women); includes 2 minority (1 Asian American or Pacific Islander, 1 Hispanic American). Average age 33. 11 applicants, 91% accepted, 10 enrolled. In 2007, 12 master's, 2 other advanced degrees awarded. *Degree requirements:* For master's, one foreign language, thesis (for some programs), teaching certificate (MAT). *Entrance requirements:* For master's, GRE General Test, minimum GPA of 3.0, major or minor in English, 3 letters of recommendation; for Certificate, bachelor's degree with minimum GPA of 2.5. Additional exam requirements/recommendations for international students: Required—TOEFL (minimum score 600 paper-based; 260 computer-based). *Application deadline:* For fall admission, 8/1 for domestic students; for spring admission, 10/15 for domestic students. Applications are processed on a rolling basis. Application fee: $30. *Expenses:* Tuition, state resident: full-time $4,203; part-time $234 per credit. Tuition, nonresident: full-time $9,761; part-time $542 per credit. Required fees: $466; $26 per credit. Tuition and fees vary according to course load. *Financial support:* In 2007–08, 6 teaching assistantships with partial tuition reimbursements (averaging $12,310 per year) were awarded; career-related internships or fieldwork, scholarships/grants, and unspecified assistantships also available. Support available to part-time students. Financial award application deadline: 3/1; financial award applicants required to submit FAFSA. *Faculty research:* Takiguchi Shuzo and Japanese surrealism, hypnosis of breathing, mythology of death, cross-cultural communication, Hindu-yoga and the politics of surrealism. Total annual research expenditures: $55,201. *Unit head:* Dr. Hardin Aasand, Chairperson, 260-481-6750, Fax: 260-481-6985, E-mail: aasandh@ipfw.edu. *Application contact:* Dr. Michael Stapleton, Graduate Program Director, 260-481-6770, Fax: 260-481-6985.

Indiana University–Purdue University Indianapolis, Department of English, Indianapolis, IN 46202-2896. Offers English (MA); teaching English (MA). *Faculty:* 20 full-time (8 women). *Students:* 3 full-time (all women), 38 part-time (21 women); includes 5 minority (3 African Americans, 1 Asian American or Pacific Islander, 1 Hispanic American), 2 international. Average age 32. In 2007, 10 degrees awarded. *Entrance requirements:* For master's, GRE. Application fee: $50 ($60 for international students). *Expenses:* Tuition, state resident: full-time $5,818; part-time $242 per credit hour. Tuition, nonresident: full-time $17,106; part-time $713 per credit hour. Required fees: $629. Tuition and fees vary according to course load, campus/location and program. *Financial support:* In 2007–08, 2 fellowships (averaging $10,000 per year), 12 teaching assistantships (averaging $7,103 per year) were awarded; research assistantships, career-related internships or fieldwork also available. *Unit head:* Susanmarie Harrington, Chair, 317-2788-1153.

Indiana University South Bend, College of Liberal Arts and Sciences, South Bend, IN 46634-7111. Offers applied mathematics and computer science (MS); applied psychology (MA); English (MA); liberal studies (MLS). Part-time and evening/weekend programs available. *Faculty:* 79 full-time (33 women). *Students:* 11 full-time (6 women), 71 part-time (44 women); includes 14 minority (8 African Americans, 1 American Indian/Alaska Native, 3 Asian Americans or Pacific Islanders, 2 Hispanic Americans), 8 international. Average age 37. In 2007, 24 degrees awarded. *Degree requirements:* For master's, thesis (for some programs). *Entrance requirements:* For master's, minimum GPA of 3.0. Additional exam requirements/recommendations for international students: Required—TOEFL. *Application deadline:* For fall admission, 7/31 priority date for domestic students, 7/1 priority date for international students; for spring admission, 3/31 priority date for domestic students, 11/1 priority date for international students. Applications are processed on a rolling basis. Application fee: $46 ($58 for international students). *Expenses:* Tuition, state resident: full-time $4,762; part-time $198 per credit hour. Tuition, nonresident: full-time $11,720; part-time $488 per credit hour. Required fees: $422; $422 per year. Full-time tuition and fees vary according to course load, campus/location and program. *Financial support:* In 2007–08, 5 students received support, including 5 teaching assistantships; Federal Work-Study also available. Support available to part-time students. *Faculty research:* Artificial intelligence, bioinformatics, English language and literature, creative writing, computer networks. Total annual research expenditures: $127,000. *Unit head:* Dr. Lynn R. Williams, Dean, 574-520-4322, Fax: 574-520-4528, E-mail: lwilliam@iusb.edu.

Iona College, School of Arts and Science, Department of English, New Rochelle, NY 10801-1890. Offers MA. Part-time and evening/weekend programs available. *Faculty:* 11 full-time (5 women). *Students:* 1 full-time (0 women), 11 part-time (8 women); includes 1 minority (African American) Average age 30. 6 applicants, 83% accepted, 2 enrolled. In 2007, 12 degrees awarded. *Degree requirements:* For master's, one foreign language, thesis or alternative. *Entrance requirements:* For master's, minimum GPA of 3.0. Additional exam requirements/recommendations for international students: Required—TOEFL (minimum score 550 paper-based; 213 computer-based). *Application deadline:* Applications are processed on a rolling basis. Application fee: $50. Electronic applications accepted. *Expenses:* Tuition: Part-time $712 per credit. Required fees: $150 per term. *Financial support:* Tuition waivers (partial) and unspecified assistantships available. Support available to part-time students. *Faculty research:* Victorian fiction, women's studies, nineteenth century American literature, Irish literature, Shakespeare. *Unit head:* Dr. Hugh Short, Chair, 914-637-7725, E-mail: hshort@iona.edu. *Application contact:* Veronica Jarek-Prinz, Director of Graduate Admissions, 914-633-2420, Fax: 914-633-2277, E-mail: vjarekprinz@iona.edu.

Iowa State University of Science and Technology, Graduate College, College of Liberal Arts and Sciences, Department of English, Ames, IA 50011. Offers English (MA); rhetoric and professional communication (PhD). *Faculty:* 54 full-time (30 women), 4 part-time/adjunct (2 women). *Students:* 96 full-time (57 women), 23 part-time (17 women); includes 4 minority (1 African American, 3 Hispanic Americans), 24 international. 119 applicants, 49% accepted, 37 enrolled. In 2007, 35 master's, 6 doctorates awarded. *Degree requirements:* For master's, thesis or alternative; for doctorate, thesis/dissertation. *Entrance requirements:* For master's, GRE General Test, sample of written work, resumé, portfolio in creative writing; for doctorate, GRE General Test, sample of written work, resumé. Additional exam requirements/recommendations for international students: Required—TOEFL (paper-based 600; computer-based 250; iBT 100) or IELTS (7.0). *Application deadline:* For fall admission, 1/15 priority date for domestic and international students. Application fee: $30 ($70 for international students). Electronic applications accepted. *Financial support:* In 2007–08, 4 research assistantships with partial tuition reimbursements (averaging $18,159 per year), 81 teaching assistantships with partial tuition reimbursements (averaging $18,445 per year) were awarded; fellowships, scholarships/grants, health care benefits, and unspecified assistantships also available. *Faculty research:* Creative writing, literature, rhetoric, composition and professional communication, teaching English as a second language, applied linguistics. *Unit head:* Dr. Charles Kostelnick, Chair, 515-294-2477, Fax: 515-294-2125, E-mail: englgrad@iastate.edu. *Application contact:* Dr. Helen Ewald, Director of Graduate Education, 515-294-2477, E-mail: englgrad@iastate.edu.

Jackson State University, Graduate School, School of Liberal Arts, Department of English and Modern Foreign Languages, Jackson, MS 39217. Offers English (MA); teaching English (MAT). Part-time and evening/weekend programs available. *Degree requirements:* For master's, comprehensive exam, thesis or alternative. *Entrance requirements:* For master's,

English

Jackson State University (continued)
GRE General Test. Additional exam requirements/recommendations for international students: Required—TOEFL.

Jacksonville State University, College of Graduate Studies and Continuing Education, College of Arts and Sciences, Department of English, Jacksonville, AL 36265-1602. Offers MA. *Faculty:* 12 full-time (5 women), 1 (woman) part-time/adjunct. *Students:* 5 full-time (4 women), 14 part-time (12 women); includes 1 minority (African American), 1 international. In 2007, 9 degrees awarded. *Degree requirements:* For master's, thesis optional. *Entrance requirements:* For master's, GRE General Test or MAT. *Application deadline:* Applications are processed on a rolling basis. Application fee: $20. *Financial support:* Available to part-time students. Application deadline: 4/1. *Unit head:* Dr. Robert Felgar, Head, 256-782-5413. *Application contact:* 256-782-5329, Fax: 256-782-5321, E-mail: graduate@jsu.edu.

James Madison University, The Graduate School, College of Arts and Letters, Department of English, Harrisonburg, VA 22807. Offers MA. Part-time programs available. *Faculty:* 10 full-time (6 women). *Students:* 15 full-time (7 women), 13 part-time (11 women), 1 international. Average age 27. In 2007, 5 degrees awarded. *Degree requirements:* For master's, one foreign language, thesis, reading exam in languages, formal exam based on required reading list. *Entrance requirements:* For master's, GRE General Test, GRE Subject Test, 2 letters of recommendation, writing sample, resumé (recommended). Additional exam requirements/recommendations for international students: Required—TOEFL. *Application deadline:* For fall admission, 2/10 priority date for domestic students. Applications are processed on a rolling basis. Application fee: $55. Electronic applications accepted. *Expenses:* Tuition, state resident: full-time $6,720; part-time $280 per credit hour. Tuition, nonresident: full-time $19,104; part-time $796 per credit hour. *Financial support:* In 2007–08, 8 students received support, including 6 teaching assistantships with full tuition reimbursements available (averaging $8,494 per year); Federal Work-Study, unspecified assistantships, and 2 graduate assistantships ($7,237) also available. Financial award application deadline: 3/1; financial award applicants required to submit FAFSA. *Unit head:* Dr. Robert V. Hoskins, Academic Unit Head, 540-568-6170.

John Carroll University, Graduate School, Department of English, University Heights, OH 44118-4581. Offers MA. Part-time and evening/weekend programs available. *Faculty:* 16 full-time (5 women). *Students:* 11 full-time (8 women), 9 part-time (5 women); includes 1 minority (Hispanic American) Average age 28. 36 applicants, 61% accepted, 10 enrolled. In 2007, 6 degrees awarded. *Degree requirements:* For master's, comprehensive exam, thesis (for some programs), research essay or thesis. *Entrance requirements:* For master's, GRE General Test, GRE Subject Test, minimum 3.0 GPA, writing sample. Additional exam requirements/recommendations for international students: Required—TOEFL. *Application deadline:* For fall admission, 8/15 priority date for domestic students; for spring admission, 3/15 for domestic students. Applications are processed on a rolling basis. Application fee: $25 ($35 for international students). Electronic applications accepted. *Financial support:* In 2007–08, 11 students received support, including 11 teaching assistantships with full tuition reimbursements available (averaging $8,400 per year). Financial award application deadline: 3/15; financial award applicants required to submit FAFSA. *Faculty research:* Post-colonial literature, African-American literature, Renaissance poetry, Anglo-Saxon literature, American literature. *Unit head:* Dr. Chris Roark, Chair, 216-397-4478, Fax: 216-397-1723, E-mail: croark@jcu.edu. *Application contact:* Dr. Deborah Rosenthal, Graduate Admissions Director, 216-397-4758, E-mail: drosenthal@jcu.edu.

The Johns Hopkins University, Zanvyl Krieger School of Arts and Sciences, Department of English, Baltimore, MD 21218-2699. Offers English and American literature (PhD). *Faculty:* 7 full-time (3 women). *Students:* 29 full-time (12 women), 1 (woman) part-time; includes 2 minority (1 African American, 1 Asian American or Pacific Islander), 2 international. Average age 30. 130 applicants, 12% accepted, 6 enrolled. In 2007, 4 doctorates awarded. *Median time to degree:* Of those who began their doctoral program in fall 1999, 67% received their degree in 8 years or less. *Degree requirements:* For doctorate, 2 foreign languages, comprehensive exam, thesis/dissertation, 10 seminars, 2 oral exams. *Application deadline:* For fall admission, 12/11 for domestic students. Application fee: $75. Electronic applications accepted. *Financial support:* In 2007–08, 30 students received support, including 10 fellowships with full tuition reimbursements available (averaging $16,000 per year), 3 research assistantships with full tuition reimbursements available (averaging $21,000 per year), 12 teaching assistantships with full tuition reimbursements available (averaging $16,000 per year); Federal Work-Study, institutionally sponsored loans, and unspecified assistantships also available. Financial award application deadline: 4/15; financial award applicants required to submit FAFSA. *Faculty research:* 19th century British, 18th century, Renaissance, American, cultural studies. *Unit head:* Dr. Amanda Anderson, Chair, 410-516-8033, Fax: 410-516-4757, E-mail: a.anderson@jhu.edu. *Application contact:* Nicole Goode, Admissions Coordinator, 410-516-4311, Fax: 410-516-4757, E-mail: ngoode@jhu.edu.

Kansas State University, Graduate School, College of Arts and Sciences, Department of English, Manhattan, KS 66506. Offers MA. Part-time programs available. *Faculty:* 24 full-time (13 women), 1 part-time/adjunct (0 women). *Students:* 98 full-time (59 women), 10 part-time (7 women); includes 6 minority (3 African Americans, 1 American Indian/Alaska Native, 2 Hispanic Americans), 7 international. Average age 25. 45 applicants, 93% accepted, 22 enrolled. In 2007, 27 degrees awarded. *Degree requirements:* For master's, one foreign language, thesis optional. *Entrance requirements:* For master's, GRE, minimum B average in English. Additional exam requirements/recommendations for international students: Required—TOEFL. *Application deadline:* For fall admission, 2/1 priority date for domestic and international students; for spring admission, 9/1 priority date for domestic students, 8/1 priority date for international students. Applications are processed on a rolling basis. Application fee: $30 ($55 for international students). Electronic applications accepted. *Financial support:* In 2007–08, 44 teaching assistantships with full tuition reimbursements (averaging $8,880 per year) were awarded; career-related internships or fieldwork, Federal Work-Study, institutionally sponsored loans, scholarships/grants, and tuition waivers (full) also available. Support available to part-time students. Financial award application deadline: 3/1; financial award applicants required to submit FAFSA. *Faculty research:* Cultural studies, children's literature, American literature, rhetorical and composition theory, British literature. *Unit head:* Karin Westman, Head, 785-532-2190, Fax: 785-532-2192, E-mail: westmank@ksu.edu. *Application contact:* Greg Eiselein, Director, 785-532-0386, Fax: 785-532-2192, E-mail: eiselei@ksu.edu.

Kent State University, College of Arts and Sciences, Department of English, Kent, OH 44242-0001. Offers comparative literature (MA); creative writing (MFA); English (PhD); English for teachers (MA); literature and writing (MA); rhetoric and composition (PhD); teaching English as a second language (MA). Part-time programs available. *Faculty:* 46 full-time (23 women). *Students:* 107 full-time (59 women), 15 part-time (8 women); includes 19 minority (1 African American, 17 Asian Americans or Pacific Islanders, 1 Hispanic American). Average age 33. 105 applicants, 80% accepted, 35 enrolled. In 2007, 34 master's, 1 doctorate awarded. Terminal master's awarded for partial completion of doctoral program. *Median time to degree:* Of those who began their doctoral program in fall 1999, 50% received their degree in 8 years or less. *Degree requirements:* For master's, one foreign language, thesis optional; for doctorate, one foreign language, thesis/dissertation, qualifying exams. *Entrance requirements:* For master's and doctorate, GRE General Test, writing sample, letters of recommendation. Additional exam requirements/recommendations for international students: Required—TOEFL (minimum score 600 paper-based). *Application deadline:* For fall admission, 2/1 priority date for domestic and international students. Applications are processed on a rolling basis. Application fee: $30. Electronic applications accepted. *Financial support:* In 2007–08, 2 fellowships with full tuition reimbursements (averaging $12,000 per year), 55 teaching assistantships with full tuition reimbursements (averaging $11,020 per year) were awarded; research assistantships with full tuition reimbursements, Federal Work-Study, institutionally sponsored loans, scholarships/grants, traineeships, health care benefits, and unspecified assistantships also available. Financial award application deadline: 2/1. *Faculty research:* British and American literature, textual editing, rhetoric and composition, cultural studies, linguistic and critical theories. *Unit head:* Ronald Corthell, Chair, 330-672-3211, Fax: 330-672-3152, E-mail: rcorthel@kent.edu. *Application contact:* Ray Craig, Information Contact, 330-672-1755, E-mail: rcraig2@kent.edu.

See Close-Up on page 567.

Kutztown University of Pennsylvania, College of Graduate Studies and Extended Learning, College of Liberal Arts and Sciences, Program in English, Kutztown, PA 19530-0730. Offers MA. Part-time and evening/weekend programs available. *Faculty:* 4 full-time (2 women). *Students:* 8 full-time (5 women), 15 part-time (13 women). Average age 32. 18 applicants, 56% accepted, 5 enrolled. In 2007, 4 degrees awarded. *Degree requirements:* For master's, one foreign language, comprehensive exam, thesis optional. *Entrance requirements:* For master's, GRE General Test. Additional exam requirements/recommendations for international students: Required—TOEFL. *Application deadline:* Applications are processed on a rolling basis. Application fee: $35. Electronic applications accepted. *Expenses:* Tuition, state resident: full-time $6,214; part-time $345 per credit. Tuition, nonresident: full-time $9,944; part-time $552 per credit. Required fees: $1,536; $78 per credit. $65 per semester. *Financial support:* Career-related internships or fieldwork, Federal Work-Study, scholarships/grants, and unspecified assistantships available. Financial award application deadline: 3/15; financial award applicants required to submit FAFSA. *Faculty research:* Women science fiction writers, Joyce Cary, myth and symbol, folklore, Victorian revision modes. *Unit head:* Dr. Janice Chernekoff, Chairperson, 610-683-4353, Fax: 610-683-4355, E-mail: cherneko@kutztown.edu.

Lakehead University, Graduate Studies, Faculty of Social Sciences and Humanities, Department of English, Thunder Bay, ON P7B 5E1, Canada. Offers MA. Part-time and evening/weekend programs available. *Degree requirements:* For master's, one foreign language, thesis optional. *Entrance requirements:* For master's, minimum B average. Additional exam requirements/recommendations for international students: Required—TOEFL. *Faculty research:* Rhetoric and literary studies, children's literature, nineteenth- and twentieth-century American literature, modern literature, women's studies.

Lamar University, College of Graduate Studies, College of Arts and Sciences, Department of English and Foreign Languages, Beaumont, TX 77710. Offers English (MA). Part-time and evening/weekend programs available. *Faculty:* 8 full-time (2 women). *Students:* 2 full-time (both women), 19 part-time (14 women); includes 1 minority (Hispanic American) Average age 35. 14 applicants, 64% accepted, 5 enrolled. In 2007, 6 degrees awarded. *Degree requirements:* For master's, one foreign language, thesis optional, practicum. *Entrance requirements:* For master's, GRE General Test, minimum GPA of 2.5 in last 60 hours of undergraduate course work. Additional exam requirements/recommendations for international students: Required—TOEFL. *Application deadline:* For fall admission, 8/1 for domestic students; for spring admission, 12/1 for domestic students. Applications are processed on a rolling basis. Application fee: $25 ($50 for international students). *Expenses:* Tuition, state resident: part-time $348 per semester hour. Tuition, nonresident: part-time $626 per semester hour. Tuition and fees vary according to course load. *Financial support:* In 2007–08, 6 students received support, including 4 teaching assistantships (averaging $8,000 per year); career-related internships or fieldwork, Federal Work-Study, and institutionally sponsored loans also available. Support available to part-time students. Financial award application deadline: 4/1. *Faculty research:* British, Renaissance, nineteenth century, and American literature; creative writing; modern literature; African-American literature. *Unit head:* Dr. Joe E. Nordgren, Chair, 409-880-8558, Fax: 409-880-8591, E-mail: nordgrenje@hal.lamar.edu.

La Sierra University, College of Arts and Sciences, Department of English, Riverside, CA 92515. Offers MA. Part-time programs available. *Degree requirements:* For master's, one foreign language. *Entrance requirements:* For master's, GRE General Test.

Lehigh University, College of Arts and Sciences, Department of English, Bethlehem, PA 18015-3094. Offers MA, PhD. *Faculty:* 17 full-time (7 women). *Students:* 46 full-time (30 women), 9 part-time (2 women); includes 1 minority (Asian American or Pacific Islander), 2 international. Average age 32. 56 applicants, 29% accepted, 9 enrolled. In 2007, 6 master's, 7 doctorates awarded. Terminal master's awarded for partial completion of doctoral program. *Degree requirements:* For master's, thesis; for doctorate, one foreign language, comprehensive exam, thesis/dissertation. *Entrance requirements:* For master's, GRE Subject Test (literature), GRE General Test, minimum GPA of 3.0 in undergraduate English courses; for doctorate, GRE Subject Test (literature), GRE General Test, minimum GPA of 3.5 in MA coursework. Additional exam requirements/recommendations for international students: Required—TOEFL (minimum score 620 paper-based; 260 computer-based; 96 iBT). *Application deadline:* For fall admission, 1/15 priority date for domestic and international students. Application fee: $65. Electronic applications accepted. *Financial support:* In 2007–08, 4 fellowships with full tuition reimbursements (averaging $22,000 per year), 31 teaching assistantships with full tuition reimbursements (averaging $16,400 per year) were awarded; career-related internships or fieldwork, Federal Work-Study, institutionally sponsored loans, scholarships/grants, tuition waivers (full and partial), and unspecified assistantships also available. Support available to part-time students. Financial award application deadline: 1/15. *Faculty research:* Literature and social justice, narrative theory, modernism, transatlantic study, literature and medicine. *Unit head:* Dr. Barry M. Kroll, Chairperson, 610-758-3311, Fax: 610-758-6616, E-mail: bmk3@lehigh.edu. *Application contact:* Dr. Dawn Keetley, Director of Graduate Studies, 610-758-5926, Fax: 610-758-6616, E-mail: dek7@lehigh.edu.

Lehman College of the City University of New York, Division of Arts and Humanities, Department of English, Bronx, NY 10468-1589. Offers MA. *Degree requirements:* For master's, thesis. *Entrance requirements:* For master's, GRE, 18 upper-level credits in U.S. or English literature.

Long Island University, Brooklyn Campus, Richard L. Conolly College of Liberal Arts and Sciences, Department of English, Brooklyn, NY 11201-8423. Offers English literature (MA); professional and creative writing (MA); teaching of writing (MA). Part-time and evening/weekend programs available. *Degree requirements:* For master's, thesis or alternative. *Entrance requirements:* For master's, 2 letters of recommendation. Additional exam requirements/recommendations for international students: Required—TOEFL (minimum score 550 paper-based; 173 computer-based). Electronic applications accepted.

See Close-Up on page 569.

Long Island University, C.W. Post Campus, College of Liberal Arts and Sciences, Department of English, Brookville, NY 11548-1300. Offers English (MA); English for adolescence education (MS). Part-time and evening/weekend programs available. *Faculty:* 9 full-time (4 women), 2 part-time/adjunct (1 woman). *Students:* 8 full-time (5 women), 13 part-time (9 women). Average age 31. 12 applicants, 83% accepted, 7 enrolled. In 2007, 14 degrees awarded. *Degree requirements:* For master's, comprehensive exam (for some programs), thesis (for some programs). *Entrance requirements:* For master's, minimum GPA of 3.5 in major, 3.0 overall; 21 credits of English. *Application deadline:* Applications are processed on a rolling basis. Application fee: $30. Electronic applications accepted. *Expenses:* Tuition: Part-time $825 per credit. Tuition and fees vary according to course load. *Financial support:* Teaching assistantships, Federal Work-Study, institutionally sponsored loans, and tuition waivers (full and partial) available. Support available to part-time students. Financial award application deadline: 5/15; financial award applicants required to submit CSS PROFILE or FAFSA. *Faculty research:* English Renaissance, Sinclair Lewis: The Early Years, puppetry archives, Irish-American Experiences: literature of memory, Henry James's anxiety of Poe's influence. *Unit head:* Dr. Edmund Miller, Chair, 516-299-2391, Fax: 516-299-2997, E-mail: edmund.miller@liu.edu.

Longwood University, Office of Graduate Studies, Department of English and Modern Languages, Farmville, VA 23909. Offers 6-12 initial teaching/licensure (MA); creative writing (MA); English education and writing (MA); literature (MA). Part-time programs available.

Degree requirements: For master's, comprehensive exam (for some programs), thesis (for some programs). *Entrance requirements:* For master's, minimum GPA of 2.75. Additional exam requirements/recommendations for international students: Required—TOEFL (minimum score 550 paper-based; 213 computer-based).

Louisiana State University and Agricultural and Mechanical College, Graduate School, College of Arts and Sciences, Department of English, Baton Rouge, LA 70803. Offers creative writing (MFA); English (MA, PhD). Part-time programs available. *Faculty:* 53 full-time (22 women). *Students:* 76 full-time (41 women), 6 part-time (3 women); includes 6 minority (2 African Americans, 1 American Indian/Alaska Native, 1 Asian American or Pacific Islander, 2 Hispanic Americans), 8 international. Average age 30. 138 applicants, 14% accepted, 18 enrolled. In 2007, 10 master's, 7 doctorates awarded. Terminal master's awarded for partial completion of doctoral program. *Degree requirements:* For master's, comprehensive exam; for doctorate, one foreign language, comprehensive exam, thesis/dissertation. *Entrance requirements:* For master's, GRE General Test, minimum GPA of 3.0; for doctorate, GRE General Test, GRE Subject Test, minimum GPA of 3.0. Additional exam requirements/recommendations for international students: Required—TOEFL (minimum score 550 paper-based; 213 computer-based; 79 iBT). *Application deadline:* For fall admission, 5/15 priority date for domestic students, 5/15 for international students; for spring admission, 10/15 priority date for domestic students, 10/15 for international students. Applications are processed on a rolling basis. Application fee: $25. Electronic applications accepted. *Financial support:* In 2007–08, 75 students received support, including 1 fellowship with full tuition reimbursement available (averaging $17,429 per year), 2 research assistantships with partial tuition reimbursements available (averaging $13,500 per year), 71 teaching assistantships with partial tuition reimbursements available (averaging $16,510 per year); career-related internships or fieldwork, Federal Work-Study, traineeships, and health care benefits also available. Financial award application deadline: 2/1; financial award applicants required to submit FAFSA. *Faculty research:* American literature, British literature, cultural studies, rhetoric and composition, folklore. Total annual research expenditures: $206,310. *Unit head:* Dr. Anna Nardo, Chair, 225-578-0812, Fax: 225-578-2214, E-mail: english@lsu.edu. *Application contact:* Dr. Carl Freedman, Director of Graduate Studies, 225-578-7803, Fax: 225-578-4129, E-mail: egs@lsu.edu.

Louisiana Tech University, Graduate School, College of Liberal Arts, Department of English, Ruston, LA 71272. Offers MA. Part-time programs available. *Degree requirements:* For master's, thesis or alternative. *Entrance requirements:* For master's, GRE General Test. *Application deadline:* For fall admission, 7/29 for domestic students; for spring admission, 2/3 for domestic students. Applications are processed on a rolling basis. Application fee: $20 ($30 for international students). *Financial support:* In 2007–08, 7 students received support; fellowships, research assistantships, teaching assistantships, career-related internships or fieldwork available. Financial award application deadline: 2/1. *Unit head:* Dr. Dan Kaczvinsky, Head, 318-257-2718, Fax: 318-257-2719.

Loyola Marymount University, Graduate Division, College of Liberal Arts, Department of English, Los Angeles, CA 90045-2659. Offers creative writing (MA); literature (MA), including . Part-time and evening/weekend programs available. *Faculty:* 24 full-time (10 women), 34 part-time/adjunct (23 women). *Students:* 31 full-time (18 women), 10 part-time (7 women); includes 12 minority (4 African Americans, 1 American Indian/Alaska Native, 2 Asian Americans or Pacific Islanders, 5 Hispanic Americans). Average age 29. 61 applicants, 30% accepted, 14 enrolled. In 2007, 16 degrees awarded. *Degree requirements:* For master's, comprehensive exam. *Entrance requirements:* For master's, GRE General Test, minimum GPA of 3.0. Additional exam requirements/recommendations for international students: Required—TOEFL (minimum score 600 paper-based; 250 computer-based). *Application deadline:* For fall admission, 3/15 for domestic students. Application fee: $50. Electronic applications accepted. *Financial support:* In 2007–08, 29 students received support, including 2 research assistantships (averaging $12,370 per year); scholarships/grants and unspecified assistantships also available. Support available to part-time students. Financial award application deadline: 6/1; financial award applicants required to submit FAFSA. *Unit head:* Dr. Paul Harris, Graduate Director, 310-338-4452, Fax: 310-338-7727, E-mail: pharris@lmu.edu.

Loyola University Chicago, Graduate School, Department of English, Chicago, IL 60611-2196. Offers MA, PhD. Part-time and evening/weekend programs available. *Faculty:* 21 full-time (8 women). *Students:* 56 full-time (31 women), 3 part-time (2 women); includes 7 minority (2 African Americans, 1 Asian American or Pacific Islander, 4 Hispanic Americans), 2 international. Average age 30. 131 applicants, 31% accepted, 17 enrolled. In 2007, 18 master's, 4 doctorates awarded. Terminal master's awarded for partial completion of doctoral program. *Degree requirements:* For master's, comprehensive exam, thesis or alternative; for doctorate, one foreign language, comprehensive exam, thesis/dissertation. *Entrance requirements:* For master's and doctorate, GRE General Test, GRE Subject Test. Additional exam requirements/recommendations for international students: Required—TOEFL, IELTS. *Application deadline:* For fall admission, 6/1 for domestic students. Applications are processed on a rolling basis. Application fee: $50. Electronic applications accepted. *Expenses:* Tuition: Full-time $12,780; part-time $710 per credit hour. Required fees: $55 per semester. Full-time tuition and fees vary according to program. *Financial support:* In 2007–08, 26 students received support, including 5 fellowships with full tuition reimbursements available (averaging $13,500 per year), research assistantships with full tuition reimbursements available (averaging $10,000 per year), 21 teaching assistantships with full tuition reimbursements available (averaging $10,000 per year); Federal Work-Study, institutionally sponsored loans, tuition waivers (partial), and unspecified assistantships also available. Support available to part-time students. Financial award application deadline: 1/15; financial award applicants required to submit FAFSA. *Faculty research:* Medieval and Renaissance studies, Romantic period, literary history and theory, American studies, modernism and postmodernism. *Unit head:* Dr. Pamela Caughie, Chair, 773-508-2240, Fax: 773-508-8696, E-mail: pcaughi@luc.edu. *Application contact:* Maureen Taylor, Graduate Program Secretary, 773-508-2255, Fax: 773-508-8696, E-mail: mtaylo3@luc.edu.

Marquette University, Graduate School, College of Arts and Sciences, Department of English, Milwaukee, WI 53201-1881. Offers American literature (PhD); British and American literature (MA); British literature (PhD). Part-time programs available. *Faculty:* 33 full-time (15 women), 22 part-time/adjunct (13 women). *Students:* 46 full-time (28 women), 15 part-time (10 women); includes 2 minority (both Hispanic Americans) Average age 30. 70 applicants, 69% accepted, 22 enrolled. In 2007, 9 master's, 5 doctorates awarded. Terminal master's awarded for partial completion of doctoral program. *Degree requirements:* For master's, comprehensive exam, thesis or alternative; for doctorate, one foreign language, thesis/dissertation, qualifying exam. *Entrance requirements:* For master's and doctorate, GRE General Test, GRE Subject Test. Additional exam requirements/recommendations for international students: Required—TOEFL. Application fee: $40. *Financial support:* In 2007–08, 5 research assistantships, 35 teaching assistantships were awarded; Federal Work-Study, institutionally sponsored loans, scholarships/grants, and tuition waivers (full and partial) also available. Support available to part-time students. Financial award application deadline: 2/15. *Faculty research:* Discourse analysis, cultural studies, textual criticism, literary history, literary theory. Total annual research expenditures: $1,000. *Unit head:* Dr. Tim Machan, Chair, 414-288-7179, Fax: 414-288-1578. *Application contact:* Dr. Ed Block, Director of Graduate Studies, 414-288-7260.

Marshall University, Academic Affairs Division, College of Liberal Arts, Department of English, Huntington, WV 25755. Offers MA. *Faculty:* 24 full-time (10 women), 15 part-time/adjunct (10 women). *Students:* 39 full-time (25 women), 15 part-time (12 women); includes 1 minority (Hispanic American), 6 international. Average age 29. In 2007, 16 degrees awarded. *Degree requirements:* For master's, one foreign language, thesis optional. *Entrance requirements:* For master's, GRE General Test. Application fee: $40. *Unit head:* Dr. David Hatfield, Chairperson, 304-696-6638, E-mail: hatfield@marshall.edu. *Application contact:* Information Contact, 304-746-1900, Fax: 304-746-1902, E-mail: services@marshall.edu.

Mary Baldwin College, Graduate Studies, Program in Shakespeare and Renaissance Literature in Performance, Staunton, VA 24401-3610. Offers acting (M Litt); directing (M Litt); Shakespeare and Renaissance literature in performance (MFA); teaching (M Litt). *Entrance requirements:* For master's, GRE (M Litt).

Marymount University, School of Arts and Sciences, Program in Literature and Languages, Arlington, VA 22207-4299. Offers MA. Part-time and evening/weekend programs available. *Faculty:* 3 full-time (2 women), 1 (woman) part-time/adjunct. *Students:* 3 full-time (all women), 13 part-time (10 women); includes 3 minority (2 African Americans, 1 Hispanic American), 2 international. Average age 33. 15 applicants, 93% accepted, 8 enrolled. In 2007, 4 degrees awarded. *Degree requirements:* For master's, one foreign language, thesis or alternative. *Entrance requirements:* For master's, interview, writing sample, 2 letters of recommendation. Additional exam requirements/recommendations for international students: Required—TOEFL (minimum score 600 paper-based; 250 computer-based; 100 iBT). *Application deadline:* Applications are processed on a rolling basis. Application fee: $40. Electronic applications accepted. *Expenses:* Tuition: Full-time $11,790; part-time $655 per credit. Required fees: $121; $6.7 per credit. *Financial support:* Research assistantships with full tuition reimbursements, career-related internships or fieldwork, scholarships/grants, and unspecified assistantships available. Support available to part-time students. Financial award applicants required to submit FAFSA. *Unit head:* Dr. Susan Fay, Chair, 703-284-3858, Fax: 703-284-3859, E-mail: susan.fay@marymount.edu.

McGill University, Faculty of Graduate and Postdoctoral Studies, Faculty of Arts, Department of English, Montréal, QC H3A 2T5, Canada. Offers MA, PhD. *Faculty:* 34 full-time (15 women), 14 part-time/adjunct (6 women). *Students:* 62 full-time (44 women), 5 part-time (4 women). 274 applicants, 31% accepted, 20 enrolled. In 2007, 21 master's, 6 doctorates awarded. Electronic applications accepted.

McMaster University, School of Graduate Studies, Faculty of Humanities, Department of English and Cultural Studies, Hamilton, ON L8S 4M2, Canada. Offers cultural studies and critical theory (MA); English (MA, PhD). Part-time programs available. *Faculty:* 25 full-time. *Students:* 97 full-time. 116 applicants, 20% accepted. *Degree requirements:* For master's, one foreign language, thesis; for doctorate, one foreign language, comprehensive exam, thesis/dissertation. *Entrance requirements:* For master's, honors degree, minimum B+ average in at least 6 full courses of English beyond year 1; for doctorate, MA; minimum A- average in two of three courses. Additional exam requirements/recommendations for international students: Required—TOEFL (minimum score 580 paper-based; 237 computer-based). *Application deadline:* For fall admission, 2/15 for domestic students. Applications are processed on a rolling basis. Application fee: $90. *Financial support:* In 2007–08, fellowships (averaging $7,500 per year), teaching assistantships (averaging $8,440 per year) were awarded; research assistantships, scholarships/grants also available. *Faculty research:* Literary theory, feminist theory, literature of migration, Bakhting globalization. *Unit head:* Dr. Mary O'Connor, Chair, 905-525-9140 Ext. 23731, Fax: 905-777-8316, E-mail: moconnor@mcmaster.ca. *Application contact:* Dr. Grace Kehler, Chair, Graduate Studies, 905-525-9140 Ext. 23723, Fax: 905-777-8316, E-mail: kehlerg@mcmaster.ca.

McNeese State University, Graduate School, College of Liberal Arts, Department of English and Foreign Languages, Program in English, Lake Charles, LA 70609. Offers MA. Evening/weekend programs available. *Faculty:* 14 full-time (7 women). *Students:* 6 full-time (2 women), 4 part-time (3 women); includes 2 minority (both African Americans) In 2007, 9 degrees awarded. *Degree requirements:* For master's, one foreign language, thesis or alternative. *Entrance requirements:* For master's, GRE. *Application deadline:* For fall admission, 5/15 priority date for domestic students. Applications are processed on a rolling basis. Application fee: $20 ($30 for international students). *Expenses:* Tuition, state resident: full-time $2,226; part-time $193 per hour. Required fees: $935; $110 per hour. Tuition and fees vary according to course load. *Financial support:* Teaching assistantships available. Financial award application deadline: 5/1. *Faculty research:* Textual criticism, seventeenth century literature, American women writers, Romanticism and the origins of diplomacy. *Unit head:* Dr. Joe L. Cash, Head, Department of English and Foreign Languages, 337-475-5326, Fax: 337-475-5327, E-mail: jcash@mcneese.edu.

Memorial University of Newfoundland, School of Graduate Studies, Department of English Language and Literature, St. John's, NL A1C 5S7, Canada. Offers MA, PhD. *Degree requirements:* For master's, thesis optional; for doctorate, one foreign language, comprehensive exam, thesis/dissertation, oral thesis defense, minimum 3 semesters of full-time study. *Entrance requirements:* For master's, honors degree. Electronic applications accepted. *Faculty research:* American, British, Canadian, and Anglo-Irish literature; Newfoundland literature.

Mercy College, Division of Literature, Language, and Communication, Dobbs Ferry, NY 10522-1189. Offers English literature (MA). Part-time and evening/weekend programs available. Postbaccalaureate distance learning degree programs offered (minimal on-campus study). *Students:* 6 full-time (4 women), 34 part-time (25 women); includes 8 minority (2 African Americans, 1 American Indian/Alaska Native, 1 Asian American or Pacific Islander, 4 Hispanic Americans), 1 international. Average age 39. In 2007, 10 degrees awarded. *Degree requirements:* For master's, comprehensive exam, thesis. *Entrance requirements:* For master's, resumé. Additional exam requirements/recommendations for international students: Required—TOEFL. *Application deadline:* Applications are processed on a rolling basis. Application fee: $37. *Expenses:* Tuition: Part-time $575 per credit. Required fees: $220 per semester. Tuition and fees vary according to program. *Financial support:* In 2007–08, 1 student received support, including 1 research assistantship with full tuition reimbursement available (averaging $1,200 per year). *Unit head:* Dr. Sean Dugan, Program Director, 914-674-7356, Fax: 914-962-0931, E-mail: sdugan@mercy.edu.

Miami University, Graduate School, College of Arts and Sciences, Department of English, Oxford, OH 45056. Offers composition and rhetoric (MA, PhD); creative writing (MA); criticism (PhD); English and American literature and language (PhD); English education (MAT); library theory (PhD); literature (MA, MAT, PhD); technical and scientific communication (MTSC). Part-time programs available. *Degree requirements:* For master's, final exam; for doctorate, 2 foreign languages, comprehensive exam, thesis/dissertation, final exams. *Entrance requirements:* For master's, minimum undergraduate GPA of 3.0 during previous 2 years or 2.75 overall; for doctorate, GRE General Test, GRE Subject Test, minimum GPA of 2.75 (undergraduate), 3.0 (graduate). Additional exam requirements/recommendations for international students: Required—TOEFL (minimum score 550 paper-based; 213 computer-based), TWE (minimum score 4). Electronic applications accepted.

Michigan State University, The Graduate School, College of Arts and Letters, Department of English, East Lansing, MI 48824. Offers English (PhD); literature in English (MA). *Entrance requirements:* For master's, GRE General Test, minimum GPA of 3.25, 2 years of foreign language or American Sign Language study, 3 letters of recommendation; for doctorate, GRE General Test, master's degree in English, 2 years of foreign language study, 3 letters of recommendation. Additional exam requirements/recommendations for international students: Required—TOEFL. Electronic applications accepted. *Expenses:* Tuition, state resident: part-time $379 per credit hour. Tuition, nonresident: part-time $800 per credit hour. Tuition and fees vary according to program.

Middlebury College, Bread Loaf School of English, Middlebury, VT 05753-6002. Offers M Litt, MA. Offered during summer only. *Faculty:* 55 full-time. *Students:* 488 full-time; includes 37 minority (18 African Americans, 1 American Indian/Alaska Native, 9 Asian Americans or Pacific Islanders, 9 Hispanic Americans). Average age 31. In 2007, 88 master's awarded. *Application deadline:* Applications are processed on a rolling basis. Application fee: $55. *Financial support:* In 2007–08, 201 students received support, including 41 fellowships; scholarships/grants also available. Support available to part-time students. *Unit head:* Dr. James Maddox, Director, 802-443-5418, Fax: 802-443-2060, E-mail: blse@breadnet.middlebury.edu.

Middle Tennessee State University, College of Graduate Studies, College of Liberal Arts, Department of English, Murfreesboro, TN 37132. Offers MA, PhD. Part-time and evening/

English

Middle Tennessee State University (continued)
weekend programs available. Postbaccalaureate distance learning degree programs offered. *Faculty:* 41 full-time (24 women). *Students:* Average age 32. 81 applicants, 73% accepted. In 2007, 12 master's, 6 doctorates awarded. *Degree requirements:* For master's, one foreign language, comprehensive exam, thesis optional; for doctorate, one foreign language, comprehensive exam, thesis/dissertation. *Entrance requirements:* For master's and doctorate, GRE. Additional exam requirements/recommendations for international students: Required—TOEFL (paper-based 525; computer-based 195; IBT 71) or IELTS (6.0). *Application deadline:* For fall admission, 8/1 priority date for domestic students. Applications are processed on a rolling basis. Application fee: $25. Electronic applications accepted. *Financial support:* In 2007–08, 40 students received support. Career-related internships or fieldwork and institutionally sponsored loans available. Support available to part-time students. Financial award application deadline: 5/1; financial award applicants required to submit FAFSA. *Unit head:* Dr. Tom Strawman, Chair, 615-898-2573, Fax: 615-898-5098, E-mail: strawman@mtsu.edu.

Midwestern State University, Graduate Studies, College of Humanities and Social Sciences, Department of English, Wichita Falls, TX 76308. Offers MA. Part-time and evening/weekend programs available. *Degree requirements:* For master's, one foreign language, thesis optional. *Entrance requirements:* For master's, GRE General Test, MAT or GMAT. Additional exam requirements/recommendations for international students: Required—TOEFL (minimum score 550 paper-based; 213 computer-based). Electronic applications accepted. *Faculty research:* Jung and literature, Shakespeare, Oscar Hahn, origins of language, modern American literature.

Millersville University of Pennsylvania, Graduate School, School of Humanities and Social Sciences, Department of English, Millersville, PA 17551-0302. Offers English (MA); English education (M Ed). Part-time and evening/weekend programs available. *Faculty:* 29 full-time (16 women), 9 part-time/adjunct (7 women). *Students:* 8 full-time (4 women), 23 part-time (18 women); includes 3 minority (2 African Americans, 1 Hispanic American). Average age 29. 10 applicants, 90% accepted, 7 enrolled. In 2007, 12 degrees awarded. *Degree requirements:* For master's, one foreign language, thesis optional, departmental exam. *Entrance requirements:* For master's, GRE or MAT. Additional exam requirements/recommendations for international students: Required—TOEFL (minimum score 500 paper-based; 183 computer-based). *Application deadline:* For fall admission, 2/1 priority date for domestic students; for winter admission, 10/1 priority date for domestic students; for spring admission, 10/1 priority date for domestic students. Applications are processed on a rolling basis. Application fee: $40. Electronic applications accepted. *Expenses:* Tuition, state resident: full-time $6,214; part-time $345 per credit. Tuition, nonresident: full-time $9,944; part-time $552 per credit. Required fees: $1,442. Tuition and fees vary according to course load. *Financial support:* In 2007–08, 6 students received support, including 6 research assistantships with full tuition reimbursements available (averaging $5,200 per year); institutionally sponsored loans and unspecified assistantships also available. Support available to part-time students. Financial award application deadline: 3/15; financial award applicants required to submit FAFSA. *Faculty research:* Literary criticism, rhetoric and composition studies, distance teaching, creative writing, journalism history. Total annual research expenditures: $7,500. *Unit head:* Dr. Beverly Schneller, Chair, 717-871-2342, Fax: 717-871-2446, E-mail: beverly.schneller@millersville.edu. *Application contact:* Dr. Victor S. DeSantis, Dean of Graduate Studies, 717-872-3099, Fax: 717-871-2022, E-mail: victor.desantis@millersville.edu.

Mills College, Graduate Studies, Department of English, Oakland, CA 94613-1000. Offers creative writing (MFA); English (MFA); English and American literature (MA). Part-time programs available. *Faculty:* 9 full-time (7 women), 20 part-time/adjunct (17 women). *Students:* 82 full-time (68 women), 6 part-time (all women); includes 28 minority (12 African Americans, 10 Asian Americans or Pacific Islanders, 6 Hispanic Americans). Average age 32. 137 applicants, 83% accepted, 46 enrolled. In 2007, 49 degrees awarded. *Degree requirements:* For master's, comprehensive exam, thesis. *Entrance requirements:* For master's, manuscript, writing sample. Additional exam requirements/recommendations for international students: Required—TOEFL. *Application deadline:* For fall admission, 2/1 priority date for domestic students; for spring admission, 11/1 for domestic students. Applications are processed on a rolling basis. Application fee: $50. Electronic applications accepted. *Expenses:* Tuition: Full-time $22,792; part-time $5,702 per credit. Required fees: $828. Part-time tuition and fees vary according to course load and program. *Financial support:* In 2007–08, 72 fellowships (averaging $7,517 per year), 22 teaching assistantships with partial tuition reimbursements (averaging $2,655 per year) were awarded; career-related internships or fieldwork, institutionally sponsored loans, scholarships/grants, tuition waivers (partial), and residence awards also available. Support available to part-time students. Financial award application deadline: 2/1; financial award applicants required to submit CSS PROFILE or FAFSA. *Faculty research:* Creative writing, African-American literature, Victorian women writers, theories of sexuality, Shakespeare. *Unit head:* Cynthia Scheinberg, Chair, 510-430-2213, E-mail: cyns@mills.edu. *Application contact:* Linda Guzman, Graduate Admission Specialist, 510-430-3309, Fax: 510-430-2159, E-mail: grad-studies@mills.edu.

Minnesota State University Mankato, College of Graduate Studies, College of Arts and Humanities, Department of English, Mankato, MN 56001. Offers creative writing (MFA); English (MA, MS); English literature (MA); teaching English (MS, MT); teaching English as a second language (MA); technical communication (Certificate). Part-time programs available. *Students:* 51 full-time (35 women), 78 part-time (54 women). Average age 32. In 2007, 29 degrees awarded. *Degree requirements:* For master's, one foreign language, comprehensive exam, thesis or alternative. *Entrance requirements:* For master's, minimum GPA of 3.0 during previous 2 years, writing sample (MFA). *Application deadline:* Applications are processed on a rolling basis. Application fee: $40. Electronic applications accepted. *Financial support:* Research assistantships with full tuition reimbursements, teaching assistantships with full tuition reimbursements, career-related internships or fieldwork, Federal Work-Study, and unspecified assistantships available. Financial award application deadline: 3/15; financial award applicants required to submit FAFSA. *Faculty research:* Keats and Christianity. *Unit head:* Dr. John Banschbach, Chairperson, 507-389-2117. *Application contact:* 507-389-2321, E-mail: grad@mnsu.edu.

Mississippi College, Graduate School, College of Arts and Sciences, School of Humanities and Social Sciences, Department of English, Clinton, MS 39058. Offers M Ed, MA. Part-time and evening/weekend programs available. *Faculty:* 7 full-time (4 women). *Students:* 2 full-time (0 women), 15 part-time (12 women); includes 4 minority (all African Americans) Average age 27. In 2007, 1 degree awarded. *Degree requirements:* For master's, one foreign language, comprehensive exam, thesis or alternative. *Entrance requirements:* For master's, GRE or NTE, minimum GPA of 2.5. Additional exam requirements/recommendations for international students: Recommended—IELTS. *Application deadline:* For fall admission, 4/1 for domestic students. Applications are processed on a rolling basis. Application fee: $25. Electronic applications accepted. *Expenses:* Tuition: Full-time $7,470; part-time $415 per hour. Required fees: $1,160 per term. Part-time tuition and fees vary according to course load and degree level. *Financial support:* Teaching assistantships, Federal Work-Study, tuition waivers (partial), and unspecified assistantships available. Support available to part-time students. Financial award application deadline: 4/1; financial award applicants required to submit FAFSA. *Unit head:* Dr. David Miller, Interim Chair, 601-925-3336, Fax: 601-925-3998, E-mail: dmiller@mc.edu.

Mississippi State University, College of Arts and Sciences, Department of English, Mississippi State, MS 39762. Offers MA. Part-time programs available. *Faculty:* 39 full-time (23 women), 3 part-time/adjunct (2 women). *Students:* 31 full-time (15 women), 8 part-time (5 women); includes 4 minority (all African Americans) Average age 28. 13 applicants, 85% accepted, 10 enrolled. In 2007, 11 degrees awarded. *Degree requirements:* For master's, thesis optional, comprehensive oral or written exam. *Entrance requirements:* For master's, GRE General Test, minimum GPA of 2.75. Additional exam requirements/recommendations for international students: Required—TOEFL. *Application deadline:* For fall admission, 7/1 for domestic students; for spring admission, 11/1 for domestic students. Applications are processed on a rolling basis. Application fee: $30. *Expenses:* Tuition, state resident: full-time $4,978; part-time $274 per hour. Tuition, nonresident: full-time $11,469; part-time $635 per hour. *Financial support:* In 2007–08, 19 teaching assistantships (averaging $9,337 per year) were awarded; Federal Work-Study, institutionally sponsored loans, and unspecified assistantships also available. Financial award applicants required to submit FAFSA. *Faculty research:* Literary criticism, linguistics, textual editing, editing *Mississippi Quarterly*, Southern literature. *Unit head:* Dr. Richard Raymond, Head, 662-325-3606, Fax: 662-325-3645, E-mail: rr165@msstate.edu. *Application contact:* Dr. William A. Person, Interim Associate Vice President for Academic Affairs/Interim Dean of Graduate Studies, 662-325-7400, Fax: 662-325-1967, E-mail: grad@grad.msstate.edu.

Missouri State University, Graduate College, College of Arts and Letters, Department of English, Springfield, MO 65804-0094. Offers English and writing (MA); secondary education (MS Ed), including English. Part-time and evening/weekend programs available. *Faculty:* 24 full-time (13 women). *Students:* 46 full-time (29 women), 58 part-time (38 women); includes 1 minority (Hispanic American), 9 international. Average age 30. 37 applicants, 89% accepted, 29 enrolled. In 2007, 28 degrees awarded. *Degree requirements:* For master's, one foreign language, comprehensive exam, thesis or alternative. *Entrance requirements:* For master's, GRE (MA), minimum GPA of 3.0 (MA), 9-12 teacher certification (MS Ed). Additional exam requirements/recommendations for international students: Required—TOEFL (minimum score 550 paper-based; 213 computer-based; 79 iBT). *Application deadline:* For fall admission, 7/20 for domestic students; for spring admission, 12/20 for domestic students. Applications are processed on a rolling basis. Application fee: $35. Electronic applications accepted. *Expenses:* Tuition, state resident: full-time $3,708; part-time $206 per credit hour. Tuition, nonresident: full-time $7,236; part-time $206 per credit hour. Required fees: $622. Full-time tuition and fees vary according to course level, course load, program and reciprocity agreements. *Financial support:* In 2007–08, 39 teaching assistantships with full tuition reimbursements (averaging $7,050 per year) were awarded; research assistantships with full tuition reimbursements, Federal Work-Study, institutionally sponsored loans, scholarships/grants, tuition waivers (partial), and unspecified assistantships also available. Support available to part-time students. Financial award application deadline: 3/31; financial award applicants required to submit FAFSA. *Unit head:* Dr. W. D. Blackmon, Head, 417-836-5107, Fax: 417-836-6940, E-mail: wdblackon@missouristate.edu.

Monmouth University, Graduate School, Department of English, West Long Branch, NJ 07764-1898. Offers MA. Part-time and evening/weekend programs available. *Faculty:* 10 full-time (7 women). *Students:* 5 full-time (3 women), 19 part-time (14 women). Average age 31. 21 applicants, 100% accepted, 7 enrolled. In 2007, 1 degree awarded. *Degree requirements:* For master's, comprehensive exam (for some programs), thesis (for some programs), 30 credits. *Entrance requirements:* For master's, minimum 2.75 overall GPA, at least 15 credits in literary studies. Additional exam requirements/recommendations for international students: Required—TOEFL (minimum score 550 paper-based; 213 computer-based; 79 iBT), IELTS (minimum score 5), MELAB 77, Cambridge A, B, C. *Application deadline:* For fall admission, 7/15 for domestic students; for spring admission, 11/15 for domestic students. Application fee: $50. *Financial support:* In 2007–08, 20 students received support, including 20 fellowships (averaging $1,456 per year), 1 research assistantship (averaging $4,902 per year); scholarships/grants, tuition waivers (partial), and unspecified assistantships also available. Support available to part-time students. *Faculty research:* Renaissance and medieval literature, 19th century America literature, 18th century British literature and women's studies, Old English and Middle English, African diasposa and African post colonial literature. *Unit head:* Dr. Hiede Estes, Program Director, 732-571-7547, E-mail: hestes@monmouth.edu. *Application contact:* Kevin Roane, Director, Office of Graduate Admission, 732-571-3452, Fax: 732-263-5123, E-mail: gradadm@monmouth.edu.

Montana State University, College of Graduate Studies, College of Letters and Science, Department of English, Bozeman, MT 59717. Offers MA. Part-time programs available. *Faculty:* 14 full-time (8 women), 16 part-time/adjunct (11 women). *Students:* 4 full-time (2 women), 11 part-time (8 women); includes 1 minority (Asian American or Pacific Islander) Average age 28. 10 applicants, 60% accepted, 4 enrolled. In 2007, 8 degrees awarded. *Degree requirements:* For master's, comprehensive exam. *Entrance requirements:* For master's, GRE General Test. Additional exam requirements/recommendations for international students: Required—TOEFL (minimum score 550 paper-based; 213 computer-based). *Application deadline:* For fall admission, 7/15 priority date for domestic students, 5/15 for international students; for spring admission, 12/1 priority date for domestic students, 10/1 for international students. Applications are processed on a rolling basis. Application fee: $30. Electronic applications accepted. *Expenses:* Tuition, state resident: full-time $5,176. Tuition, nonresident: full-time $13,070. *Financial support:* Application deadline: 3/1; *Faculty research:* British literature, American literature, global literacy, English pedagogy, Western literature. Total annual research expenditures: $25,407. *Unit head:* Dr. Linda Karell, Head, 406-994-3768, Fax: 406-994-2422, E-mail: lkarell@english.montana.edu.

Montclair State University, The Office of Graduate Admissions and Support Services, College of Humanities and Social Sciences, Department of English, Montclair, NJ 07043-1624. Offers MA, Certificate. Part-time and evening/weekend programs available. *Faculty:* 31 full-time (15 women), 52 part-time/adjunct (39 women). *Students:* 17 full-time (14 women), 65 part-time (47 women); includes 6 minority (1 African American, 2 Asian Americans or Pacific Islanders, 3 Hispanic Americans). 72 applicants, 53% accepted, 30 enrolled. In 2007, 17 master's, 3 other advanced degrees awarded. *Degree requirements:* For master's, thesis. *Entrance requirements:* For master's, GRE General Test, minimum GPA of 3.0, 2 letters of recommendation. Additional exam requirements/recommendations for international students: Required—TOEFL (minimum score 83 computer-based). *Application deadline:* For fall admission, 4/1 for domestic and international students; for spring admission, 11/1 for domestic and international students. Applications are processed on a rolling basis. Application fee: $60. Electronic applications accepted. *Financial support:* In 2007–08, 6 research assistantships with full tuition reimbursements (averaging $7,000 per year) were awarded; Federal Work-Study, scholarships/grants, and unspecified assistantships also available. Support available to part-time students. Financial award application deadline: 3/1; financial award applicants required to submit FAFSA. *Unit head:* Dr. Dan Bronson, Chairperson, 973-655-4274. *Application contact:* Dr. Art Simon, Adviser, 973-655-7942, E-mail: simona@mail.montclair.edu.

Morehead State University, Graduate Programs, Caudill College of Humanities, Department of English, Foreign Languages, and Philosophy, Morehead, KY 40351. Offers English (MA). Part-time and evening/weekend programs available. *Faculty:* 6 full-time (3 women). *Students:* 8 full-time (5 women), 23 part-time (18 women). Average age 35. In 2007, 8 degrees awarded. *Degree requirements:* For master's, comprehensive exam, thesis optional. *Entrance requirements:* For master's, GRE General Test, minimum GPA of 3.0 in English, 2.5 overall; undergraduate major or minor in English. Additional exam requirements/recommendations for international students: Required—TOEFL (minimum score 500 paper-based; 173 computer-based). *Application deadline:* For fall admission, 8/1 priority date for domestic and international students; for spring admission, 12/1 priority date for domestic and international students. Applications are processed on a rolling basis. Application fee: $0 ($55 for international students). *Financial support:* In 2007–08, 4 teaching assistantships (averaging $6,000 per year) were awarded; career-related internships or fieldwork, Federal Work-Study, and unspecified assistantships also available. Financial award application deadline: 4/1; financial award applicants required to submit FAFSA. *Faculty research:* Nineteenth and twentieth century American literature, linguistics, Victorian literature, modern British literature, creative writing. *Unit head:* Dr. Philip Krummich, Chair, 606-783-2185, Fax: 606-783-5346, E-mail: p.krummich@moreheadstate.edu. *Application contact:* Michelle Barber, Graduate Admissions Counselor, 606-783-2039, Fax: 606-783-5061, E-mail: m.barber@moreheadstate.edu.

Morgan State University, School of Graduate Studies, College of Liberal Arts, Department of English, Baltimore, MD 21251. Offers MA, PhD. Part-time programs available. *Faculty:* 17. *Students:* 40. *Degree requirements:* For master's, comprehensive exam, thesis; for doctorate, comprehensive exam, thesis/dissertation. *Entrance requirements:* For master's, GRE, minimum GPA of 2.5; for doctorate, GRE. Additional exam requirements/recommendations for international students: Required—TOEFL (minimum score 550 paper-based; 213 computer-based). *Application deadline:* For fall admission, 2/1 priority date for domestic students; for spring admission, 10/1 priority date for domestic students. Applications are processed on a rolling basis. Application fee: $0. *Financial support:* Fellowships, research assistantships, teaching assistantships available. Financial award application deadline: 2/1. *Faculty research:* African and African-American studies, nineteenth century American literature, rhetoric, women's studies, children's literature. *Unit head:* Dr. Dolan Hubbard, Chair, 443-885-3165, E-mail: dolan.hubbard@morgan.edu. *Application contact:* Dr. Mark Garrison, Associate Dean, 443-885-3185, Fax: 443-885-8226, E-mail: mark.garrison@morgan.edu.

Mount Mary College, Graduate Programs, Program in English, Milwaukee, WI 53222-4597. Offers MA. Evening/weekend programs available. *Faculty:* 3 full-time (all women), 2 part-time/adjunct (both women). *Students:* 12 full-time (10 women), 22 part-time (all women); includes 5 minority (4 African Americans, 1 Hispanic American). 18 applicants, 94% accepted, 16 enrolled. In 2007, 1 degree awarded. *Degree requirements:* For master's, comprehensive exam, thesis or alternative. *Entrance requirements:* For master's, GPa of 2.75. Additional exam requirements/recommendations for international students: Required—TOEFL (minimum score 500 paper-based; 173 computer-based). *Application deadline:* For fall admission, 8/1 priority date for domestic and international students; for spring admission, 12/1 priority date for domestic and international students. Applications are processed on a rolling basis. Application fee: $35 ($75 for international students). Electronic applications accepted. *Expenses:* Tuition: Part-time $545 per credit. Required fees: $60 per semester. Part-time tuition and fees vary according to program. *Financial support:* Career-related internships or fieldwork available. Financial award application deadline: 5/1; financial award applicants required to submit FAFSA. *Unit head:* Dr. Kristi Siegel, Director, 414-258-4810 Ext. 395, E-mail: siegelkr@mtmary.edu.

Murray State University, College of Humanities and Fine Arts, Department of English and Philosophy, Program in English, Murray, KY 42071. Offers MA. Part-time programs available. *Degree requirements:* For master's, comprehensive exam, thesis (for some programs).

National University, Academic Affairs, College of Letters and Sciences, Department of Art and Humanities, La Jolla, CA 92037-1011. Offers creative writing (MFA); English (MA). Part-time and evening/weekend programs available. Postbaccalaureate distance learning degree programs offered (no on-campus study). *Faculty:* 18 full-time (6 women), 219 part-time/adjunct (120 women). *Students:* 139 full-time (101 women), 353 part-time (250 women); includes 91 minority (41 African Americans, 4 American Indian/Alaska Native, 15 Asian Americans or Pacific Islanders, 31 Hispanic Americans). Average age 37. 371 applicants, 330 enrolled. In 2007, 100 degrees awarded. *Degree requirements:* For master's, thesis (for some programs). *Entrance requirements:* For master's, interview, minimum GPA of 2.5. Additional exam requirements/recommendations for international students: Required—TOEFL (minimum score 550 paper-based; 213 computer-based; 80 iBT), IELTS (minimum score 6). *Application deadline:* Applications are processed on a rolling basis. Application fee: $60 ($65 for international students). Electronic applications accepted. *Expenses:* Tuition: Full-time $8,262; part-time $306 per unit. One-time fee: $60. *Financial support:* Career-related internships or fieldwork, institutionally sponsored loans, scholarships/grants, and tuition waivers (partial) available. Support available to part-time students. Financial award application deadline: 6/30; financial award applicants required to submit FAFSA. *Unit head:* Dr. Janet Baker, Chair, 858-642-8472, Fax: 858-642-8715, E-mail: jbaker@nu.edu. *Application contact:* Dominick Giovanniello, Associate Regional Dean—San Diego, 800-NAT-UNIV, Fax: 858-642-8709, E-mail: dgiovann@nu.edu.

New Mexico Highlands University, Graduate Studies, College of Arts and Sciences, Department of Humanities, Las Vegas, NM 87701. Offers English (MA), including creative writing, language, rhetoric and composition, literature. *Faculty:* 6 full-time (3 women). *Students:* 11 full-time (5 women), 7 part-time (5 women); includes 5 minority (all Hispanic Americans) Average age 32. 17 applicants, 82% accepted, 7 enrolled. In 2007, 3 degrees awarded. *Degree requirements:* For master's, comprehensive exam, thesis. *Entrance requirements:* For master's, minimum undergraduate GPA of 3.0. Additional exam requirements/recommendations for international students: Required—TOEFL (minimum score 540 paper-based; 190 computer-based). *Application deadline:* For fall admission, 8/1 priority date for domestic students. Applications are processed on a rolling basis. Application fee: $15. *Expenses:* Tuition, state resident: full-time $2,642; part-time $110 per credit hour. Tuition, nonresident: full-time $3,964; part-time $165 per credit hour. International tuition: $5,285 full-time. One-time fee: $20 full-time. *Financial support:* In 2007–08, 8 students received support, including teaching assistantships with full and partial tuition reimbursements available (averaging $6,500 per year); career-related internships or fieldwork, Federal Work-Study, institutionally sponsored loans, scholarships/grants, tuition waivers (full and partial), and unspecified assistantships also available. Support available to part-time students. Financial award application deadline: 3/1; financial award applicants required to submit FAFSA. *Faculty research:* Motivation, self-actualization, humanistic psychology, stand up comedy, language and cognition. *Unit head:* Dr. Barbara Risch, Chair, 505-454-3451, Fax: 505-454-3389, E-mail: brisch55@yahoo.com. *Application contact:* Diane Trujillo, Administrative Assistant Graduate Studies, 505-454-3266, Fax: 505-454-3558, E-mail: dtrujillo@nmhu.edu.

New Mexico State University, Graduate School, College of Arts and Sciences, Department of English, Las Cruces, NM 88003-8001. Offers creative writing (MFA); English (MA); rhetoric and professional communication (PhD). Part-time programs available. *Faculty:* 17 full-time (9 women), 1 part-time/adjunct (0 women). *Students:* 70 full-time (37 women), 23 part-time (12 women); includes 12 minority (1 African American, 1 American Indian/Alaska Native, 10 Hispanic Americans), 6 international. Average age 33. 55 applicants, 45% accepted, 19 enrolled. In 2007, 25 master's, 5 doctorates awarded. *Median time to degree:* Of those who began their doctoral program in fall 1999, 80% received their degree in 8 years or less. *Degree requirements:* For master's, one foreign language, comprehensive exam (for some programs), thesis (for some programs); for doctorate, comprehensive exam, thesis/dissertation, internship. *Entrance requirements:* For master's and doctorate, sample of written work. *Application deadline:* For fall admission, 2/1 for domestic and international students. Application fee: $30 ($50 for international students). Electronic applications accepted. *Expenses:* Tuition, state resident: full-time $3,602; part-time $199 per credit. Tuition, nonresident: full-time $13,380; part-time $607 per credit. Required fees: $1,178. *Financial support:* In 2007–08, 3 fellowships, 3 research assistantships, 50 teaching assistantships were awarded; career-related internships or fieldwork, Federal Work-Study, institutionally sponsored loans, scholarships/grants, health care benefits, and unspecified assistantships also available. Financial award application deadline: 2/1; financial award applicants required to submit FAFSA. *Faculty research:* Composition research, history and theory of rhetoric, technical/professional communication, creative writing, English and American literature. *Unit head:* Dr. Harriet Kramer Linkin, Head, 575-646-3931, Fax: 575-646-7725. *Application contact:* Dr. Monica Torres, Director of Graduate Studies, 575-646-3931, E-mail: mftorres@nmsu.edu.

New York University, Graduate School of Arts and Science, Department of English, Program in English and American Literature, New York, NY 10012-1019. Offers MA, PhD. *Faculty:* 36 full-time (10 women), 35 part-time/adjunct. *Students:* 108 full-time (71 women), 61 part-time (37 women); includes 23 minority (4 African Americans, 2 American Indian/Alaska Native, 7 Asian Americans or Pacific Islanders, 10 Hispanic Americans), 14 international. Average age 29. 633 applicants, 23% accepted, 44 enrolled. In 2007, 46 master's, 8 doctorates awarded. *Degree requirements:* For master's, one foreign language, thesis or alternative, qualifying exams, special project; for doctorate, one foreign language, thesis/dissertation. *Entrance requirements:* For master's, GRE General Test. Additional exam requirements/recommendations for international students: Required—TOEFL. *Application deadline:* For fall admission, 12/15 for domestic students. Application fee: $85. *Financial support:* Fellowships with tuition reimbursements, teaching assistantships with tuition reimbursements, Federal Work-Study, institutionally sponsored loans, scholarships/grants, health care benefits, and unspecified assistantships available. Financial award application deadline: 12/18; financial award applicants required to submit FAFSA. *Application contact:* Cyrus Patell, Director of Graduate Studies, 212-998-8800, Fax: 212-995-4019, E-mail: gsas.english.admissions@nyu.edu.

North Carolina Agricultural and Technical State University, Graduate School, College of Arts and Sciences, Department of English, Greensboro, NC 27411. Offers English (MA); English and Afro-American literature (MA). Part-time and evening/weekend programs available. *Degree requirements:* For master's, comprehensive exam, qualifying exam. *Entrance requirements:* For master's, GRE General Test, minimum GPA of 3.0.

North Carolina Central University, Division of Academic Affairs, College of Arts and Sciences, Department of English, Durham, NC 27707-3129. Offers MA. Part-time and evening/weekend programs available. *Degree requirements:* For master's, one foreign language, comprehensive exam, thesis. *Entrance requirements:* For master's, GRE, minimum GPA of 3.0 in major, 2.5 overall. Additional exam requirements/recommendations for international students: Required—TOEFL. *Faculty research:* Victorian literature, African-American literature, women's studies, literature and film, twentieth-century literature.

North Carolina State University, Graduate School, College of Humanities and Social Sciences, Department of English, Program in English, Raleigh, NC 27695. Offers MA. *Degree requirements:* For master's, thesis. *Entrance requirements:* For master's, GRE General Test. Electronic applications accepted. *Faculty research:* Creative writing, linguistics, rhetoric and composition, rhetoric and technical communication, film studies.

North Dakota State University, College of Graduate and Interdisciplinary Studies, College of Arts, Humanities and Social Sciences, Department of English, Fargo, ND 58105. Offers MA, MS. Part-time programs available. *Faculty:* 12 full-time (6 women), 1 part-time/adjunct (0 women). *Students:* 23 full-time (16 women), 10 part-time (7 women); includes 1 minority (Asian American or Pacific Islander), 1 international. Average age 31. 33 applicants, 61% accepted, 14 enrolled. In 2007, 3 degrees awarded. *Degree requirements:* For master's, one foreign language, thesis. *Entrance requirements:* Additional exam requirements/recommendations for international students: Required—TOEFL (minimum score 600 paper-based; 250 computer-based; 100 iBT), IELTS (minimum score 7). *Application deadline:* For fall admission, 4/1 priority date for domestic students; for spring admission, 12/15 priority date for domestic students. Applications are processed on a rolling basis. Application fee: $45 ($60 for international students). Electronic applications accepted. *Expenses:* Tuition, state resident: full-time $5,376; part-time $224 per credit. Tuition, nonresident: full-time $14,354; part-time $598 per credit. Required fees: $962; $40 per credit. Part-time tuition and fees vary according to course load and reciprocity agreements. *Financial support:* In 2007–08, 3 fellowships with full tuition reimbursements (averaging $12,150 per year), 1 research assistantship (averaging $3,000 per year), 18 teaching assistantships with full tuition reimbursements (averaging $8,100 per year) were awarded; Federal Work-Study, institutionally sponsored loans, and scholarships/grants also available. Support available to part-time students. Financial award application deadline: 5/1. *Faculty research:* American and English literature, women's studies, language attitudes, composition practices, computers and composition. *Unit head:* Dr. Dale Sullivan, Head, 701-231-7143, Fax: 701-231-1047, E-mail: dale.sullivan@ndsu.edu.

Northeastern Illinois University, Graduate College, College of Arts and Sciences, Department of English, Programs in English, Chicago, IL 60625-4699. Offers composition/writing (MA); literature (MA). Part-time and evening/weekend programs available. *Faculty:* 14 full-time (4 women). *Students:* 7 full-time (6 women), 44 part-time (28 women); includes 4 minority (2 African Americans, 2 Hispanic Americans), 2 international. Average age 40. 25 applicants, 52% accepted. In 2007, 7 degrees awarded. *Degree requirements:* For master's, comprehensive exam, thesis optional, minimum GPA of 3.0. *Entrance requirements:* For master's, 30 hours of undergraduate course work in literature and composition (literature), BA in English or approval (composition/writing), minimum GPA of 2.75. Additional exam requirements/recommendations for international students: Required—TOEFL (minimum score 550 paper-based; 213 computer-based; 80 iBT). *Application deadline:* Applications are processed on a rolling basis. Application fee: $25. Electronic applications accepted. *Expenses:* Tuition, state resident: part-time $243 per credit hour. Tuition, nonresident: part-time $443 per credit hour. *Financial support:* In 2007–08, 13 students received support, including 4 research assistantships with full tuition reimbursements available (averaging $6,600 per year); career-related internships or fieldwork, Federal Work-Study, institutionally sponsored loans, scholarships/grants, tuition waivers (full and partial), and unspecified assistantships also available. Support available to part-time students. Financial award applicants required to submit FAFSA. *Faculty research:* Arthurian literature, Southern American literature, rhetoric and theories of authorship. *Unit head:* Dr. Timothy Libretti, Graduate Adviser, 773-442-5820, Fax: 773-442-5490, E-mail: t-libretti@neiu.edu. *Application contact:* Dr. Mohan K. Sood, Dean of the Graduate College, 773-442-6010, Fax: 773-442-6020, E-mail: m-sood@neiu.edu.

Northeastern State University, Graduate College, College of Liberal Arts, Department of Languages and Literature, Tahlequah, OK 74464-2399. Offers English (MA), including literature, rhetoric/composition. *Students:* 7 full-time (6 women), 45 part-time (29 women); includes 10 minority (2 African Americans, 7 American Indian/Alaska Native, 1 Hispanic American). In 2007, 14 degrees awarded. *Degree requirements:* For master's, thesis. *Entrance requirements:* For master's, GRE or MAT, minimum GPA of 2.5. Additional exam requirements/recommendations for international students: Required—TOEFL (minimum score 213 computer-based). *Application deadline:* For fall admission, 6/1 priority date for domestic students. Applications are processed on a rolling basis. Application fee: $0 ($25 for international students). Electronic applications accepted. *Financial support:* Application deadline: 3/1. *Unit head:* Dr. Jacqueline Wilcox, Chair, 918-456-5511 Ext. 3609, E-mail: wilcoxj@nsuok.edu.

Northeastern University, College of Arts and Sciences, Department of English, Boston, MA 02115-5096. Offers cinema studies (Certificate); English (MA, PhD); women's studies (Certificate). Part-time and evening/weekend programs available. *Faculty:* 21 full-time (11 women), 49 part-time/adjunct. *Students:* 50 full-time (29 women), 7 part-time (4 women). 115 applicants, 27% accepted. In 2007, 12 master's awarded. *Degree requirements:* For master's, one foreign language, comprehensive exam; for doctorate, 2 foreign languages, comprehensive exam, thesis/dissertation, qualifying exams. *Entrance requirements:* For master's and doctorate, GRE General Test, GRE Subject Test, sample of written work. Additional exam requirements/recommendations for international students: Required—TOEFL. *Application deadline:* For fall admission, 2/1 priority date for domestic students. Applications are processed on a rolling basis. Application fee: $50. *Financial support:* In 2007–08, 23 teaching assistantships with tuition reimbursements (averaging $14,035 per year) were awarded; fellowships with tuition reimbursements, research assistantships with tuition reimbursements, career-related internships or fieldwork, tuition waivers (full and partial), and unspecified assistantships also available. Financial award application deadline: 2/1; financial award applicants required to submit FAFSA. *Faculty research:* Literature, creative writing, composition studies, linguistics. *Unit head:* Dr. Timothy Donovan, Chair, 617-373-3692, Fax: 617-373-2509, E-mail: gradenglish@neu.edu. *Application contact:* Melissa Daigle, Graduate Program Assistant, 617-373-3692, Fax: 617-373-2509, E-mail: gradenglish@neu.edu.

Northern Arizona University, Graduate College, College of Arts and Letters, Department of English, Program in English, Flagstaff, AZ 86011. Offers creative writing (MA); English education (MA); general English (MA); literature (MA); rhetoric (MA). *Degree requirements:* For master's, departmental qualifying exam. *Entrance requirements:* For master's, GRE General Test, GRE Subject Test.

Northern Illinois University, Graduate School, College of Liberal Arts and Sciences, Department of English, De Kalb, IL 60115-2854. Offers MA, PhD. Part-time programs available. *Faculty:* 32 full-time (13 women), 2 part-time/adjunct (both women). *Students:* 70 full-time (41 women), 82 part-time (51 women); includes 9 minority (4 African Americans, 2 Asian Americans or Pacific Islanders, 3 Hispanic Americans), 4 international. Average age 34. 113 applicants, 42% accepted, 32 enrolled. In 2007, 21 master's, 6 doctorates awarded. Terminal master's awarded for partial completion of doctoral program. *Degree requirements:* For master's, variable foreign language requirement, comprehensive exam, thesis optional; for doctorate, variable foreign language requirement, thesis/dissertation, candidacy exam, dissertation defense. *Entrance requirements:* For master's, GRE General Test, minimum GPA of 2.75; for doctorate,

English

Northern Illinois University (continued)
GRE General Test, minimum GPA of 2.75 (undergraduate), 3.2 (graduate). Additional exam requirements/recommendations for international students: Required—TOEFL (minimum score 550 paper-based; 213 computer-based). *Application deadline:* For fall admission, 6/1 for domestic students, 5/1 for international students; for spring admission, 11/1 for domestic students, 10/1 for international students. Applications are processed on a rolling basis. Application fee: $30. Electronic applications accepted. *Expenses:* Tuition, area resident: Part-time $226 per credit hour. Tuition, state resident: full-time $5,424; part-time $225 per credit hour. Tuition, nonresident: full-time $10,848. Required fees: $2,416; $64 per credit hour. *Financial support:* In 2007–08, 1 research assistantship with full tuition reimbursement, 62 teaching assistantships with full tuition reimbursements were awarded; fellowships with full tuition reimbursements, career-related internships or fieldwork, Federal Work-Study, scholarships/grants, tuition waivers (full), and unspecified assistantships also available. Support available to part-time students. Financial award applicants required to submit FAFSA. *Faculty research:* 19th century English literature, linguistic programs, portfolio assembly, Mideast literature, old English folklore. *Unit head:* Dr. Phillip Eubanks, Chair, 815-753-0615, Fax: 815-753-0606, E-mail: eubanks@niu.edu. *Application contact:* Dr. Jeffrey Johnson, Director, Graduate Studies, 815-753-6602, E-mail: jsjohnson@niu.edu.

Northern Michigan University, College of Graduate Studies, College of Arts and Sciences, Department of English, Marquette, MI 49855-5301. Offers creative writing (MFA); literature (MA); pedagogy (MA); writing (MA). Part-time programs available. *Degree requirements:* For master's, thesis or alternative. *Entrance requirements:* For master's, minimum GPA of 2.75.

Northwestern State University of Louisiana, Graduate Studies and Research, Department of Language and Communication, Natchitoches, LA 71497. Offers English (MA). *Faculty:* 6 full-time (4 women). *Students:* 23 full-time (15 women), 14 part-time (9 women); includes 5 minority (all African Americans) Average age 29. In 2007, 9 degrees awarded. *Degree requirements:* For master's, one foreign language, comprehensive exam, thesis or alternative. *Entrance requirements:* For master's, GRE General Test, minimum undergraduate GPA of 2.5. *Application deadline:* For fall admission, 8/1 priority date for domestic students; for spring admission, 1/10 for domestic students. Applications are processed on a rolling basis. Application fee: $20 ($30 for international students). *Financial support:* Application deadline: 7/15. *Unit head:* Dr. Lisa Abney, Chairman, 318-357-6166, Fax: 318-357-5942, E-mail: abney@nsula.edu. *Application contact:* Dr. Steven G. Horton, Associate Provost/Dean, Graduate Studies, Research, and Information Systems, 318-357-5851, Fax: 318-357-5019, E-mail: grad_school@nsula.edu.

Northwestern University, The Graduate School, Judd A. and Marjorie Weinberg College of Arts and Sciences, Department of English, Evanston, IL 60208. Offers MA, PhD. Admissions and degrees offered through The Graduate School. Terminal master's awarded for partial completion of doctoral program. *Degree requirements:* For master's, thesis; for doctorate, one foreign language, thesis/dissertation, oral and written qualifying exam. *Entrance requirements:* For master's and doctorate, GRE General Test, sample of written work. Additional exam requirements/recommendations for international students: Required—TOEFL. Electronic applications accepted. *Faculty research:* Renaissance literature, theatre and drama, American literature, modern European contemporary literature, poetry, cultural history.

Announcement: Small, highly selective doctoral program oriented toward research. Departmental strengths include medieval, early modern, American, Victorian, cultural history, and critical theory. Close contact with senior faculty members; closely supervised teaching. Doctoral students are supported by fellowships and teaching assistantships for 5 academic years and 4 summers. Web site: www.english.northwestern.edu.

Northwest Missouri State University, Graduate School, College of Arts and Sciences, Department of English, Maryville, MO 64468-6001. Offers English (MA); English with speech emphasis (MA); teaching English (option 1) (MS Ed); teaching English with speech emphasis (MS Ed). Part-time programs available. *Faculty:* 12 full-time (4 women). *Students:* 8 full-time (6 women), 7 part-time (4 women); includes 1 minority (Hispanic American) 7 applicants, 100% accepted, 4 enrolled. In 2007, 3 degrees awarded. *Degree requirements:* For master's, comprehensive exam, thesis optional. *Entrance requirements:* For master's, GRE General Test, minimum undergraduate GPA of 2.5, writing sample. Additional exam requirements/recommendations for international students: Required—TOEFL (minimum score 550 paper-based; 213 computer-based). *Application deadline:* For fall admission, 7/1 for domestic and international students; for spring admission, 11/15 for domestic and international students. Applications are processed on a rolling basis. Application fee: $0 ($50 for international students). *Financial support:* In 2007–08, 3 teaching assistantships with full tuition reimbursements (averaging $6,000 per year) were awarded. Financial award application deadline: 3/1; financial award applicants required to submit FAFSA. *Unit head:* Dr. Beth Richards, Chairperson, 660-562-1745. *Application contact:* Dr. Frances Shipley, Dean of Graduate School, 660-562-1145, Fax: 660-562-1096, E-mail: gradsch@nwmissouri.edu.

Notre Dame de Namur University, Division of Academic Affairs, School of Arts and Humanities, Department of English, Belmont, CA 94002-1908. Offers English (MA); teaching English to speakers of other languages (Certificate). Part-time and evening/weekend programs available. *Faculty:* 5 full-time (2 women), 5 part-time/adjunct (3 women). *Students:* 3 full-time (all women), 15 part-time (12 women); includes 4 minority (1 Asian American or Pacific Islander, 3 Hispanic Americans), 1 international. Average age 28. 6 applicants, 100% accepted, 4 enrolled. In 2007, 7 degrees awarded. *Degree requirements:* For master's, thesis optional, exam. *Entrance requirements:* For master's, minimum GPA of 2.5, writing sample. Additional exam requirements/recommendations for international students: Required—TOEFL. *Application deadline:* For fall admission, 8/1 priority date for domestic students; for spring admission, 12/1 priority date for domestic students. Applications are processed on a rolling basis. Application fee: $50 ($500 for international students). Electronic applications accepted. *Financial support:* Career-related internships or fieldwork available. Support available to part-time students. Financial award applicants required to submit FAFSA. *Unit head:* Jacqueline Berger, Director, 650-508-3730. *Application contact:* Helen Valine, Director of Graduate Admissions, 650-508-3534, Fax: 650-508-3426, E-mail: grad.admit@ndnu.edu.

Oakland University, Graduate Study and Lifelong Learning, College of Arts and Sciences, Department of English, Rochester, MI 48309-4401. Offers MA. Part-time and evening/weekend programs available. *Faculty:* 3 full-time (1 woman). *Students:* 14 full-time (8 women), 19 part-time (14 women), 1 international. Average age 30. 11 applicants, 73% accepted, 7 enrolled. In 2007, 8 degrees awarded. *Entrance requirements:* For master's, minimum GPA of 3.0 for unconditional admission. Additional exam requirements/recommendations for international students: Required—TOEFL (minimum score 550 paper-based; 213 computer-based). *Application deadline:* For fall admission, 4/1 priority date for domestic students, 5/1 for international students; for winter admission, 11/20 priority date for domestic students, 9/1 for international students. Applications are processed on a rolling basis. Application fee: $35. Electronic applications accepted. *Expenses:* Tuition, state resident: full-time $9,936; part-time $414 per credit. Tuition, nonresident: full-time $17,202; part-time $716 per credit. *Financial support:* Federal Work-Study, institutionally sponsored loans, and tuition waivers (full) available. Financial award application deadline: 3/1; financial award applicants required to submit FAFSA. *Unit head:* Dr. Kevin Grimm, Chair, 248-370-2250, Fax: 248-370-4429, E-mail: grimm@oakland.edu. *Application contact:* Dr. Kathy Pfeifer, Coordinator, 248-370-2255, Fax: 248-370-4429, E-mail: pfeifer@oakland.edu.

The Ohio State University, Graduate School, College of Humanities, Department of English, Columbus, OH 43210. Offers MA, MFA, PhD. *Faculty:* 100. *Students:* 155 full-time (95 women), 13 part-time (11 women); includes 17 minority (5 African Americans, 8 Asian Americans or Pacific Islanders, 4 Hispanic Americans), 5 international. Average age 29. In 2007, 45 master's, 11 doctorates awarded. *Degree requirements:* For master's, one foreign language, thesis or written exam; for doctorate, one foreign language, thesis/dissertation. *Entrance requirements:* For master's and doctorate, GRE General Test. Additional exam requirements/recommendations for international students: Required—TOEFL (minimum score 600 paper-based; 250 computer-based). *Application deadline:* For fall admission, 8/15 priority date for domestic students, 7/1 priority date for international students; for winter admission, 12/1 priority date for domestic students, 11/1 priority date for international students; for spring admission, 3/1 priority date for domestic students, 2/1 priority date for international students. Applications are processed on a rolling basis. Application fee: $40 ($50 for international students). Electronic applications accepted. *Financial support:* Fellowships, research assistantships, teaching assistantships, Federal Work-Study, institutionally sponsored loans, and unspecified assistantships available. Support available to part-time students. *Unit head:* Claire Simmons, Graduate Studies Committee Chair, 614-292-6065, Fax: 614-292-7816, E-mail: simmons.9@osu.edu. *Application contact:* Graduate Admissions, 614-292-9444, Fax: 614-292-3895, E-mail: domestic.grad@osu.edu.

Ohio University, Graduate College, College of Arts and Sciences, Department of English Language and Literature, Athens, OH 45701-2979. Offers MA, PhD. Part-time programs available. *Faculty:* 36 full-time (15 women). *Students:* 63 full-time (39 women), 3 part-time; includes 4 minority (3 African Americans, 1 Hispanic American), 16 international. Average age 24. In 2007, 12 master's, 5 doctorates awarded. *Median time to degree:* Of those who began their doctoral program in fall 1999, 80% received their degree in 8 years or less. *Degree requirements:* For master's, one foreign language, thesis or alternative; for doctorate, one foreign language, comprehensive exam, thesis/dissertation, oral exam, public lecture. *Entrance requirements:* For master's, GRE General Test, minimum GPA of 3.0; for doctorate, GRE General Test, minimum GPA of 3.0, master's degree in English. Additional exam requirements/recommendations for international students: Required—TOEFL (minimum score 600 paper-based; 260 computer-based). *Application deadline:* For fall admission, 1/15 for domestic students. Application fee: $50 ($55 for international students). Electronic applications accepted. *Financial support:* In 2007–08, 2 students received support, including teaching assistantships with full tuition reimbursements available (averaging $10,500 per year); Federal Work-Study, institutionally sponsored loans, and unspecified assistantships also available. Financial award application deadline: 4/15. *Faculty research:* Environmental literature, post-colonial studies, print culture, film in popular culture, computers in pedagogy. Total annual research expenditures: $54,676. *Unit head:* Dr. Joseph McLaughlin, Head, 740-593-2838, Fax: 740-593-2818, E-mail: mclaughj@ohio.edu. *Application contact:* Dr. Andrew Escobedo, Graduate Chair, 740-593-2837, Fax: 740-593-2832, E-mail: escobedo@ohio.edu.

Oklahoma State University, College of Arts and Sciences, Department of English, Stillwater, OK 74078. Offers creative writing (MA, PhD); literature (MA, PhD); technical writing (MA, PhD). *Faculty:* 51 full-time (29 women), 8 part-time/adjunct (3 women). *Students:* 15 full-time (8 women), 115 part-time (75 women); includes 11 minority (3 African Americans, 6 American Indian/Alaska Native, 2 Hispanic Americans), 20 international. Average age 32. 123 applicants, 45% accepted, 36 enrolled. In 2007, 4 master's, 6 doctorates awarded. *Degree requirements:* For master's, one foreign language, thesis; for doctorate, thesis/dissertation. *Entrance requirements:* For master's, GRE General Test or GMAT, GRE Subject Test, minimum GPA of 3.0; for doctorate, GRE General Test or GMAT, GRE Subject Test, minimum GPA of 3.5, writing sample. Additional exam requirements/recommendations for international students: Required—TOEFL. *Application deadline:* For fall admission, 3/1 priority date for international students; for spring admission, 8/1 priority date for international students. Applications are processed on a rolling basis. Application fee: $40 ($75 for international students). Electronic applications accepted. *Expenses:* Tuition, state resident: full-time $4,993; part-time $148 per credit hour. Tuition, nonresident: full-time $14,755; part-time $555 per credit hour. Tuition and fees vary according to program. *Financial support:* In 2007–08, 8 research assistantships (averaging $4,613 per year), 75 teaching assistantships (averaging $14,116 per year) were awarded; career-related internships or fieldwork, Federal Work-Study, scholarships/grants, health care benefits, tuition waivers (partial), and unspecified assistantships also available. Support available to part-time students. Financial award application deadline: 3/1. *Faculty research:* American and British novel, poetry, and autobiography; Native American languages and literature; institutional history of American film, history, and adaptations; rhetoric and theories of human communication; learning strategies of second language learners. *Unit head:* Dr. Carol Moder, Head, 405-744-9474, Fax: 405-744-6326, E-mail: epu@okstate.edu.

Old Dominion University, College of Arts and Letters, Program in English, Norfolk, VA 23529. Offers MA, PhD. Part-time and evening/weekend programs available. Postbaccalaureate distance learning degree programs offered (minimal on-campus study). *Faculty:* 17 full-time (8 women). *Students:* 35 full-time (30 women), 55 part-time (45 women); includes 18 minority (16 African Americans, 2 Asian Americans or Pacific Islanders), 2 international. Average age 33. 56 applicants, 66% accepted, 30 enrolled. In 2007, 22 degrees awarded. *Degree requirements:* For master's, comprehensive exam, thesis optional; for doctorate, one foreign language, comprehensive exam, thesis/dissertation. *Entrance requirements:* For master's, GRE General Test, 24 hours in English, minimum B average, sample of written work; for doctorate, GRE General Test, M.A in English or related field, writing sample. Additional exam requirements/recommendations for international students: Required—TOEFL. *Application deadline:* For fall admission, 6/1 priority date for domestic students; for winter admission, 11/1 priority date for domestic students; for spring admission, 3/1 priority date for domestic students. Applications are processed on a rolling basis. Application fee: $40. Electronic applications accepted. *Expenses:* Tuition, state resident: part-time $304 per credit hour. Tuition, nonresident: part-time $761 per credit hour. *Financial support:* In 2007–08, 3 fellowships with full tuition reimbursements (averaging $15,000 per year), 3 research assistantships with partial tuition reimbursements (averaging $8,119 per year), 14 teaching assistantships with partial tuition reimbursements (averaging $12,000 per year) were awarded; career-related internships or fieldwork, scholarships/grants, and unspecified assistantships also available. Support available to part-time students. Financial award application deadline: 2/15; financial award applicants required to submit FAFSA. *Faculty research:* Literary theory, composition theory, professional writing, rhetoric, British and American literature. Total annual research expenditures: $3,451. *Unit head:* Dr. Jeffrey H. Richards, Graduate Program Director, 757-683-4032, Fax: 757-683-3241, E-mail: jhrichar@odu.edu.

See Close-Up on page 571.

Old Dominion University, Darden College of Education, Programs in Secondary Education, Norfolk, VA 23529. Offers biology (MS Ed); chemistry (MS Ed); English (MS Ed); instructional technology (MS Ed); library science (MS Ed); secondary education (MS Ed). *Accreditation:* NCATE. Part-time and evening/weekend programs available. Postbaccalaureate distance learning degree programs offered (minimal on-campus study). *Faculty:* 28 full-time (11 women). *Students:* 57 full-time (39 women), 175 part-time (118 women); includes 43 minority (28 African Americans, 6 Asian Americans or Pacific Islanders, 9 Hispanic Americans), 1 international. Average age 34. 54 applicants, 91% accepted. In 2007, 118 degrees awarded. *Degree requirements:* For master's, comprehensive exam, thesis, writing exam. *Entrance requirements:* For master's, GRE General Test or MAT, PRAXIS I (for licensure), minimum GPA of 2.8, teaching certificate. Additional exam requirements/recommendations for international students: Required—TOEFL. *Application deadline:* Applications are processed on a rolling basis. Application fee: $40. Electronic applications accepted. *Expenses:* Tuition, state resident: part-time $304 per credit hour. Tuition, nonresident: part-time $761 per credit hour. *Financial support:* In 2007–08, 58 students received support, including fellowships (averaging $15,000 per year), 2 research assistantships with tuition reimbursements available (averaging $9,000 per year), 3 teaching assistantships with tuition reimbursements available (averaging $12,500 per year); career-related internships or fieldwork, Federal Work-Study, institutionally sponsored loans, scholarships/grants, and tuition waivers (partial) also available. Support available to part-time students. Financial award application deadline: 2/15; financial award applicants required to submit FAFSA. *Faculty research:* Mathematics retraining, writing project for teachers, geography teaching, reading. *Unit head:* Dr. Robert Lucking, Graduate Program Director, 757-683-5545, Fax: 757-683-5862, E-mail: rlucking@odu.edu.

Oregon State University, Graduate School, College of Liberal Arts, Department of English, Corvallis, OR 97331. Offers MA, MAIS, MFA. *Faculty:* 26 full-time (11 women), 6 part-time/

adjunct (2 women). *Students:* 14 full-time (10 women), 3 part-time (2 women); includes 1 minority (American Indian/Alaska Native). Average age 29. In 2007, 8 degrees awarded. *Degree requirements:* For master's, one foreign language, thesis. *Entrance requirements:* For master's, minimum GPA of 3.0 in last 90 hours of course work. Additional exam requirements/recommendations for international students: Required—TOEFL. Application fee: $50. *Expenses:* Tuition, state resident: full-time $9,126; part-time $338 per credit. Tuition, nonresident: full-time $14,796; part-time $548 per credit. Required fees: $1,447. *Financial support:* Fellowships, teaching assistantships, career-related internships or fieldwork, Federal Work-Study, and institutionally sponsored loans available. Support available to part-time students. Financial award application deadline: 2/1. *Faculty research:* Composition and rhetoric, American literature theory, American renaissance, gender studies, English drama. *Unit head:* Dr. Tracy Daugherty, Chair, 541-737-1634, Fax: 541-737-3589, E-mail: tdaugherty@oregonstate.edu.

Our Lady of the Lake University of San Antonio, College of Arts and Sciences, Program in English, San Antonio, TX 78207-4689. Offers English communication arts (MA); language and literature (MA). Part-time and evening/weekend programs available. *Degree requirements:* For master's, comprehensive exam, thesis optional. *Entrance requirements:* For master's, GRE General Test or MAT, minimum GPA of 3.0 in last 60 hours, 2.5 overall. Additional exam requirements/recommendations for international students: Required—TOEFL. Electronic applications accepted. *Faculty research:* Writing theory and research, contemporary Southern literature, popular culture, poetry, literature of the Southwest.

Penn State University Park, Graduate School, College of the Liberal Arts, Department of English, State College, University Park, PA 16802-1503. Offers MA, MFA, PhD. *Expenses:* Tuition, state resident: full-time $14,738; part-time $614 per credit. Tuition, nonresident: full-time $26,050; part-time $1,085 per credit. Tuition and fees vary according to course load, program and student level. *Unit head:* Dr. Robin G. Schulze, Director of Graduate Studies, 814-863-2626, Fax: 814-863-7285. *Application contact:* Information Contact, 814-863-3069, E-mail: englgradoffice@psu.edu.

Pittsburg State University, Graduate School, College of Arts and Sciences, Department of English, Pittsburg, KS 66762. Offers MA. *Degree requirements:* For master's, thesis or alternative. *Faculty research:* American fiction, American poetry, British fiction, British poetry, composition theory.

Portland State University, Graduate Studies, College of Liberal Arts and Sciences, Department of English, Portland, OR 97207-0751. Offers MA, MA/MS. Part-time and evening/weekend programs available. *Faculty:* 39 full-time (20 women), 29 part-time/adjunct (16 women). *Students:* 103 full-time (67 women), 107 part-time (75 women); includes 10 minority (1 African American, 1 American Indian/Alaska Native, 6 Asian Americans or Pacific Islanders, 2 Hispanic Americans), 4 international. Average age 34. 198 applicants, 51% accepted, 71 enrolled. In 2007, 75 degrees awarded. *Degree requirements:* For master's, one foreign language, comprehensive exam (for some programs), thesis (for some programs), oral and written exams. *Entrance requirements:* For master's, minimum GPA of 3.25 in upper-division course work or 2.75 overall, 3 letters of recommendation, minimum 3.25 in English courses. Additional exam requirements/recommendations for international students: Required—TOEFL (minimum score 600 paper-based). *Application deadline:* For fall admission, 2/1 for domestic and international students. Application fee: $50. *Expenses:* Tuition, state resident: full-time $7,047. Tuition, nonresident: full-time $11,178. *Financial support:* In 2007–08, 17 teaching assistantships with full tuition reimbursements (averaging $5,836 per year) were awarded; research assistantships, career-related internships or fieldwork, Federal Work-Study, scholarships/grants, and unspecified assistantships also available. Support available to part-time students. Financial award application deadline: 3/1; financial award applicants required to submit FAFSA. *Faculty research:* American literature and cultural studies, Medieval and British literature, writing prose fiction and poetry, rhetoric and composition, women's literature. Total annual research expenditures: $5,000. *Unit head:* Dr. Elisabeth Ceppi, Interim Chair, 503-725-9521, Fax: 503-725-3561. *Application contact:* Nixie Stark, Program Administrator, 503-725-3521, Fax: 503-725-3561, E-mail: starkn@pdx.edu.

Prairie View A&M University, College of Arts and Sciences, Department of Languages and Communication, Prairie View, TX 77446-0519. Offers English (MA). Part-time programs available. *Faculty:* 7 part-time/adjunct (5 women). *Students:* 1 (woman) full-time, 7 part-time (all women); includes 7 minority (all African Americans) Average age 33. 2 applicants, 100% accepted, 2 enrolled. *Degree requirements:* For master's, comprehensive exam, thesis, exit exam. *Entrance requirements:* For master's, GRE General Test, bachelor's degree in English or equivalent. Additional exam requirements/recommendations for international students: Required—TOEFL. *Application deadline:* For fall admission, 7/1 for domestic students, 6/1 for international students; for winter admission, 4/1 for domestic students, 10/1 for international students; for spring admission, 3/1 for domestic students, 2/1 for international students. Application fee: $50. *Financial support:* In 2007–08, 8 fellowships with tuition reimbursements (averaging $12,000 per year), 10 research assistantships with partial tuition reimbursements (averaging $15,000 per year) were awarded; teaching assistantships with partial tuition reimbursements, career-related internships or fieldwork, Federal Work-Study, institutionally sponsored loans, and tuition waivers (full and partial) also available. Support available to part-time students. Financial award application deadline: 4/1; financial award applicants required to submit FAFSA. *Faculty research:* Composition, rhetoric, technical writing, literature, communication, pedagogy in general and literature, online teaching. *Unit head:* Dr. Dejun Liu, Head, 936-261-3731, Fax: 936-261-3209, E-mail: deliu@pvamu.edu. *Application contact:* Dr. Diljit K. Chatha, Professor, 936-261-8715, Fax: 936-261-3739, E-mail: dkchatha@pvamu.edu.

Princeton University, Graduate School, Department of English, Princeton, NJ 08544-1019. Offers PhD. *Degree requirements:* For doctorate, 2 foreign languages, thesis/dissertation. *Entrance requirements:* For doctorate, GRE General Test, GRE Subject Test, sample of written work. Additional exam requirements/recommendations for international students: Required—TOEFL (minimum score 600 paper-based; 250 computer-based). Electronic applications accepted.

Purdue University, Graduate School, College of Liberal Arts, Department of English, West Lafayette, IN 47907. Offers creative writing (MFA); literature (MA, PhD), including linguistics, literature and philosophy (PhD), rhetoric and composition, theory and cultural studies (PhD). Part-time programs available. *Degree requirements:* For master's, one foreign language; for doctorate, one foreign language, thesis/dissertation. *Entrance requirements:* For master's and doctorate, GRE General Test, sample of written work. Additional exam requirements/recommendations for international students: Required—TOEFL. Electronic applications accepted. *Faculty research:* Cultural studies, postmodern narrative, contemporary women writers, composition theory, slave narratives.

Purdue University Calumet, Graduate School, School of Liberal Arts and Sciences, Department of English and Philosophy, Hammond, IN 46323-2094. Offers MA. Part-time and evening/weekend programs available. Postbaccalaureate distance learning degree programs offered (minimal on-campus study). *Degree requirements:* For master's, comprehensive exam, thesis optional. *Entrance requirements:* Additional exam requirements/recommendations for international students: Required—TOEFL. Electronic applications accepted. *Faculty research:* English literature, American literature, critical theory, women's studies, historical philosophy.

Queens College of the City University of New York, Division of Graduate Studies, Arts and Humanities Division, Department of English, Flushing, NY 11367-1597. Offers creative writing (MA); English language and literature (MA). Part-time and evening/weekend programs available. *Faculty:* 53 full-time (25 women). *Students:* 3 full-time (1 woman), 114 part-time (80 women). 111 applicants, 81% accepted, 67 enrolled. In 2007, 43 degrees awarded. *Degree requirements:* For master's, one foreign language, thesis (for some programs), oral exam (English language and literature). *Entrance requirements:* For master's, manuscript (creative writing), minimum GPA of 3.0. Additional exam requirements/recommendations for international students: Required—TOEFL. *Application deadline:* For fall admission, 4/1 for domestic students; for spring admission, 11/1 for domestic students. Applications are processed on a rolling basis. Application fee: $125. *Financial support:* Career-related internships or fieldwork, Federal Work-Study, institutionally sponsored loans, tuition waivers (partial), and adjunct lectureships available. Support available to part-time students. Financial award application deadline: 4/1; financial award applicants required to submit FAFSA. *Unit head:* Dr. Nancy Comley, Chairperson, 718-997-4600, E-mail: nancy_comley@qc.edu. *Application contact:* Dr. Talia Schaffer, Graduate Adviser, 718-997-4600, E-mail: talia_schaffer@qc.edu.

Queen's University at Kingston, School of Graduate Studies and Research, Faculty of Arts and Sciences, Department of English Language and Literature, Kingston, ON K7L 3N6, Canada. Offers MA, PhD. *Degree requirements:* For master's, one foreign language, thesis optional; for doctorate, 2 foreign languages, comprehensive exam, thesis/dissertation. *Entrance requirements:* For master's, B.A.H. upper 2nd class standing, 10 full courses in English; for doctorate, M.A. upper 2nd class standing. Additional exam requirements/recommendations for international students: Required—TOEFL, TWE. *Faculty research:* Renaissance, 18th century, post colonial, Canadian, 19th century.

Radford University, Graduate College, College of Humanities and Behavioral Sciences, Department of English, Radford, VA 24142. Offers MA, MS. Part-time programs available. Postbaccalaureate distance learning degree programs offered (minimal on-campus study). *Faculty:* 20 full-time (9 women). *Students:* 4 full-time (3 women), 36 part-time (26 women); includes 1 American Indian/Alaska Native, 1 Hispanic American, 1 international. Average age 28. 22 applicants, 100% accepted, 14 enrolled. In 2007, 15 degrees awarded. *Degree requirements:* For master's, comprehensive exam, thesis (for some programs). *Entrance requirements:* For master's, GRE. Additional exam requirements/recommendations for international students: Required—TOEFL. *Application deadline:* For fall admission, 3/1 priority date for domestic students, 12/1 for international students; for spring admission, 10/1 for domestic students, 7/1 for international students. Applications are processed on a rolling basis. Application fee: $40. *Financial support:* In 2007–08, 19 students received support, including 6 research assistantships with partial tuition reimbursements available (averaging $8,000 per year), 12 teaching assistantships with partial tuition reimbursements available (averaging $8,700 per year); career-related internships or fieldwork, Federal Work-Study, institutionally sponsored loans, scholarships/grants, and unspecified assistantships also available. Financial award application deadline: 3/1; financial award applicants required to submit FAFSA. *Unit head:* Dr. Rosemary F. Guruswamy, Chair, 540-831-5614, Fax: 540-831-6800, E-mail: rguruswa@radford.edu.

Rhode Island College, School of Graduate Studies, Faculty of Arts and Sciences, Department of English, Providence, RI 02908-1991. Offers creative writing (MA); English (MA). Part-time and evening/weekend programs available. *Faculty:* 15 full-time (8 women). *Students:* 5 full-time (4 women), 16 part-time (11 women). Average age 36. In 2007, 4 degrees awarded. *Degree requirements:* For master's, thesis (for some programs). *Entrance requirements:* For master's, GRE General Test, 3 letters of recommendation, interview. *Application deadline:* For fall admission, 4/1 for domestic students; for spring admission, 11/1 for domestic students. Applications are processed on a rolling basis. Application fee: $50. *Expenses:* Tuition, state resident: full-time $6,240; part-time $260 per credit hour. Tuition, nonresident: full-time $13,104; part-time $546 per credit hour. Required fees: $332; $14 per credit hour. One-time fee: $66 part-time. *Financial support:* In 2007–08, 1 teaching assistantship with full tuition reimbursement (averaging $4,000 per year) was awarded; career-related internships or fieldwork, Federal Work-Study, scholarships/grants, health care benefits, and unspecified assistantships also available. Support available to part-time students. Financial award application deadline: 5/15; financial award applicants required to submit FAFSA. *Unit head:* Dr. Maureen Reddy, Chair, 401-456-8028, E-mail: mreddy@ric.edu.

Rice University, Graduate Programs, School of Humanities, Department of English, Houston, TX 77251-1892. Offers MA, PhD. Terminal master's awarded for partial completion of doctoral program. *Degree requirements:* For master's, comprehensive exam, thesis (for some programs); for doctorate, comprehensive exam, thesis/dissertation. *Entrance requirements:* For master's and doctorate, GRE General Test, minimum GPA of 3.0. Additional exam requirements/recommendations for international students: Required—TOEFL (minimum score 600 paper-based; 250 computer-based; 90 iBT). Electronic applications accepted. *Faculty research:* Traditional periods and genres (excluding Old English), literary criticism and theory, Victorian literature, feminist literature, Renaissance literature, American literature, African-American literature.

Rivier College, School of Graduate Studies, Department of English, Nashua, NH 03060. Offers English (MA, MAT); writing and literature (MA); MA/MAT. Part-time and evening/weekend programs available. *Degree requirements:* For master's, comprehensive exam (for some programs). *Entrance requirements:* For master's, GRE Subject Test.

Roosevelt University, Graduate Division, College of Arts and Sciences, Department of Literature and Languages, Program in English, Chicago, IL 60605-1394. Offers MA. Part-time and evening/weekend programs available. *Students:* 1 (woman) full-time, 6 part-time (5 women); includes 1 minority (Hispanic American) Average age 31. 19 applicants, 21% accepted, 3 enrolled. In 2007, 1 degree awarded. *Degree requirements:* For master's, one foreign language, thesis or alternative. *Application deadline:* For fall admission, 6/1 priority date for domestic students. Applications are processed on a rolling basis. Application fee: $25 ($35 for international students). *Financial support:* Research assistantships available. Financial award application deadline: 2/15. *Faculty research:* Eighteenth-century Victorian literature and culture, creative writing, eighteenth through twentieth century literature, American literature and culture. *Unit head:* Bonnie Gunzenhauser, Chair, 312-341-3670. *Application contact:* Joanne Canyon-Heller, Coordinator of Graduate Admission, 877-APPLY RU, Fax: 312-281-3356, E-mail: applyru@roosevelt.edu.

Rosemont College, Graduate School, Program in English and Publishing and English Literature, Rosemont, PA 19010-1699. Offers English and publishing (MA); English literature (MA). Part-time programs available. *Faculty:* 13 part-time/adjunct (9 women). *Students:* 21 full-time (16 women), 87 part-time (73 women); includes 8 minority (6 African Americans, 2 Hispanic Americans), 1 international. Average age 30. 39 applicants, 79% accepted, 28 enrolled. In 2007, 41 degrees awarded. *Degree requirements:* For master's, comprehensive exam (for some programs), thesis. *Entrance requirements:* For master's, Baccalaureat Degree 3.0 college GPA, statement of purpose, 3 letters of recommendation. Additional exam requirements/recommendations for international students: Required—TOEFL. *Application deadline:* Applications are processed on a rolling basis. Application fee: $50. Electronic applications accepted. *Expenses:* Tuition: Part-time $525 per credit. Tuition and fees vary according to program. *Financial support:* Institutionally sponsored loans and unspecified assistantships available. *Unit head:* Elizabeth Corcoran, Director, 610-527-0200, Fax: 610-526-2964. *Application contact:* Karen Scales, Director, Enrollment and Student Services, 610-527-0200 Ext. 2187, Fax: 610-526-2964, E-mail: gradstudies@rosemont.edu.

Rutgers, The State University of New Jersey, Camden, Graduate School of Arts and Sciences, Program in English, Camden, NJ 08102-1401. Offers MA. Part-time and evening/weekend programs available. *Degree requirements:* For master's, comprehensive exam, thesis optional. *Entrance requirements:* For master's, GRE General Test. *Faculty research:* British literature; American literature; women's studies; literary, poetic, and rhetorical theory; creative writing.

Rutgers, The State University of New Jersey, Newark, Graduate School, Program in English, Newark, NJ 07102. Offers MA. Part-time and evening/weekend programs available. *Degree requirements:* For master's, one foreign language, comprehensive exam, thesis optional. *Entrance requirements:* For master's, GRE, minimum undergraduate B average. Electronic applications accepted. *Faculty research:* British and American literature, cultural studies, literary theory, minority literatures.

English

Rutgers, The State University of New Jersey, New Brunswick, Graduate School, Program of Literatures in English, New Brunswick, NJ 08901-1281. Offers PhD. *Degree requirements:* For doctorate, one foreign language, thesis/dissertation, qualifying exam. *Entrance requirements:* For doctorate, GRE General Test, GRE Subject Test, writing sample, 3 letters of recommendation. Additional exam requirements/recommendations for international students: Required—TOEFL. Electronic applications accepted. *Faculty research:* Medieval literature; Renaissance; African American literature; 18th century British literature; feminism, gender, and sexuality; postcolonial studies.

St. Bonaventure University, School of Graduate Studies, School of Arts and Sciences, Department of English, St. Bonaventure, NY 14778-2284. Offers MA. Part-time programs available. *Degree requirements:* For master's, one foreign language, comprehensive exam, thesis optional. *Entrance requirements:* For master's, GRE Subject Test. Additional exam requirements/recommendations for international students: Required—TOEFL. *Faculty research:* Victorian, Renaissance, American, modern British, and Romantic literature.

St. Cloud State University, School of Graduate Studies, College of Fine Arts and Humanities, Department of English, St. Cloud, MN 56301-4498. Offers English (MA, MS); teaching English as a second language (MA). Part-time programs available. *Faculty:* 35 full-time (16 women). *Students:* 53 full-time (34 women), 78 part-time (59 women); includes 5 minority (2 African Americans, 3 Asian Americans or Pacific Islanders), 19 international. 18 applicants, 100% accepted. In 2007, 19 degrees awarded. *Degree requirements:* For master's, thesis or alternative. *Entrance requirements:* For master's, GRE General Test, minimum GPA of 2.75. Additional exam requirements/recommendations for international students: Required—MELAB; Recommended—TOEFL (minimum score 550 paper-based; 213 computer-based), IELTS (minimum score 7). *Application deadline:* For fall admission, 6/1 priority date for domestic students, 4/1 for international students; for spring admission, 10/1 priority date for domestic students, 8/1 for international students. Applications are processed on a rolling basis. Application fee: $35. Electronic applications accepted. *Expenses:* Tuition, state resident: part-time $267 per credit. Tuition, nonresident: part-time $418 per credit. Required fees: $28 per credit. *Financial support:* Federal Work-Study, scholarships/grants, and unspecified assistantships available. Financial award application deadline: 3/1. *Unit head:* Dr. Robert Inkster, Chairperson, 320-308-3061, Fax: 320-308-5524. *Application contact:* Linda Lou Krueger, School of Graduate Studies, 320-308-2113, Fax: 320-308-5371, E-mail: lekrueger@stcloudstate.edu.

St. John's University, St. John's College of Liberal Arts and Sciences, Department of English, Queens, NY 11439. Offers MA, DA. Part-time and evening/weekend programs available. *Faculty:* 25 full-time (12 women), 22 part-time/adjunct (14 women). *Students:* 15 full-time (10 women), 58 part-time (40 women); includes 19 minority (4 African Americans, 4 Asian Americans or Pacific Islanders, 11 Hispanic Americans). Average age 32. 41 applicants, 54% accepted, 25 enrolled. In 2007, 10 master's, 1 doctorate awarded. *Degree requirements:* For master's, thesis optional; for doctorate, one foreign language, comprehensive exam, thesis/dissertation, residency. *Entrance requirements:* For master's, GRE General Test, GRE Subject Test, minimum GPA of 3.0; for doctorate, GRE General Test, GRE Subject Test, interview; minimum GPA of 3.5 in literature, 3.0 overall; writing sample. Additional exam requirements/recommendations for international students: Required—TOEFL (minimum score 500 paper-based; 173 computer-based; 61 iBT), IELTS (minimum score 6). *Application deadline:* For fall admission, 5/1 priority date for domestic and international students; for spring admission, 11/1 priority date for domestic and international students. Applications are processed on a rolling basis. Application fee: $40. Electronic applications accepted. *Financial support:* Fellowships, research assistantships, scholarships/grants available. Support available to part-time students. Financial award application deadline: 3/1; financial award applicants required to submit FAFSA. *Faculty research:* Modern comparative drama, literary theories and criticism, nineteenth and early twentieth century American literature, Chaucer, Elizabethan drama. *Unit head:* Dr. Stephen Sicari, Chair, 718-990-6390, E-mail: sicaris@stjohns.edu. *Application contact:* Beth Evans, Associate Vice President and Executive Director, Enrollment Management, 718-990-6999, Fax: 718-990-5686, E-mail: gradhelp@stjohns.edu.

Saint Louis University, Graduate School, College of Arts and Sciences and Graduate School, Department of English, St. Louis, MO 63103-2097. Offers MA, MA-R, PhD. Part-time programs available. *Faculty:* 17 full-time (6 women). *Students:* 46 full-time (28 women), 38 part-time (23 women); includes 8 minority (4 African Americans, 2 Asian Americans or Pacific Islanders, 2 Hispanic Americans), 1 international. Average age 30. 53 applicants, 72% accepted, 15 enrolled. In 2007, 13 master's, 6 doctorates awarded. *Median time to degree:* Of those who began their doctoral program in fall 1999, 90% received their degree in 8 years or less. *Degree requirements:* For master's, one foreign language, comprehensive exam, thesis optional, comprehensive oral exam; for doctorate, 2 foreign languages, comprehensive exam, thesis/dissertation, preliminary oral and written exams. *Entrance requirements:* For master's, GRE General Test, GRE Subject Test, letters of recommendation, resumé, writing sample, interview, goal statement, transcripts; for doctorate, GRE General Test, GRE Subject Test, letters of recommendation, resumé, writing sample, interview, goal statement, writing sample. Additional exam requirements/recommendations for international students: Required—TOEFL (minimum score 550 paper-based; 213 computer-based). *Application deadline:* For fall admission, 7/1 for domestic and international students; for spring admission, 11/1 for domestic and international students. Applications are processed on a rolling basis. Application fee: $40. *Expenses:* Tuition: Part-time $845 per credit hour. Required fees: $105 per semester. *Financial support:* In 2007–08, 57 students received support, including 3 research assistantships with full tuition reimbursements available (averaging $13,333 per year), 20 teaching assistantships with full tuition reimbursements available (averaging $12,000 per year); Federal Work-Study, scholarships/grants, traineeships, health care benefits, tuition waivers, and unspecified assistantships also available. Support available to part-time students. Financial award application deadline: 2/1; financial award applicants required to submit FAFSA. *Faculty research:* English literature, American literature, post-colonial literature, composition, literary theory. Total annual research expenditures: $51,000. *Unit head:* Dr. Sara van den Berg, Chairperson, 314-977-3010, Fax: 314-977-1514, E-mail: vandens@slu.edu. *Application contact:* Gary U. Behrman, Associate Dean of Graduate School Admissions, 314-977-3827, Fax: 314-977-3943, E-mail: behrmang@slu.edu.

Saint Louis University, Madrid, Graduate Programs, Program in English, Madrid, Spain. Offers MA. Part-time programs available. *Faculty:* 6 full-time (3 women). *Students:* 11 applicants, 82% accepted, 5 enrolled. *Degree requirements:* For master's, one foreign language, comprehensive exam, thesis optional. *Entrance requirements:* For master's, GRE General Test, GRE Subject Test, 3 letters of recommendation, writing sample, curriculum vitae. *Application deadline:* For fall admission, 3/31 for domestic and international students; for winter admission, 12/1 for domestic and international students; for spring admission, 2/1 for domestic and international students. Applications are processed on a rolling basis. Application fee: $40. Electronic applications accepted. *Expenses:* Tuition: Full-time $10,440; part-time $580 per credit. *Financial support:* In 2007–08, 11 students received support; teaching assistantships with full tuition reimbursements available, institutionally sponsored loans, scholarships/grants, traineeships, tuition waivers (full and partial), and unspecified assistantships available. Support available to part-time students. Financial award application deadline: 4/30; financial award applicants required to submit FAFSA. *Faculty research:* Literature in English, linguistics. *Unit head:* Dr. Paul Anthony Vita, Chair, 34-91-554-58-58, Fax: 34-91-554-62-02, E-mail: vitap@madrid.slu.edu. *Application contact:* Phyllis Chaney, Director of Admissions, 34-91-554-58-58 Ext. 232, Fax: 34-91-554-62-02, E-mail: graduate_admissions@madrid.slu.edu.

See Close-Up on page 573.

St. Mary's University, Graduate School, Department of English and Communication Studies, Program in English Literature and Language, San Antonio, TX 78228-8507. Offers MA. *Students:* 5 full-time (4 women), 12 part-time (6 women); includes 9 minority (all Hispanic Americans) In 2007, 1 degree awarded. Application fee: $0. *Unit head:* Dr. Gwendolyn Diaz, Director, 210-436-3107, E-mail: gdiaz@stmarytx.edu.

Saint Xavier University, Graduate Studies, School of Arts and Sciences, Department of English, Chicago, IL 60655-3105. Offers English (CAS); literary studies (MA); teaching of writing (MA); writing pedagogy (CAS). Part-time and evening/weekend programs available. In 2007, 14 degrees awarded. *Entrance requirements:* For master's, MAT or GRE, minimum GPA of 3.0. *Application deadline:* For fall admission, 8/15 priority date for domestic students. Applications are processed on a rolling basis. Application fee: $35. *Financial support:* Applicants required to submit FAFSA. *Unit head:* Dr. Nelson Hathcock, Director, 773-298-3235, Fax: 773-779-9061, E-mail: hathcock@sxu.edu. *Application contact:* Beth Gierach, Managing Director of Admission, 773-298-3053, Fax: 773-298-3076, E-mail: gierach@sxu.edu.

Salem State College, Graduate School, Program in English, Salem, MA 01970-5353. Offers English (MA, MAT, MA/MAT); English as a second language (MAT); MA/MAT. Part-time and evening/weekend programs available. *Faculty:* 3 part-time/adjunct (1 woman). *Students:* 8 full-time (all women), 72 part-time (53 women); includes 6 minority (1 African American, 3 Asian Americans or Pacific Islanders, 2 Hispanic Americans), 2 international. Average age 32. In 2007, 15 degrees awarded. *Degree requirements:* For master's, one foreign language. *Entrance requirements:* For master's, GRE General Test, MAT. *Application deadline:* Applications are processed on a rolling basis. Application fee: $35. *Unit head:* Lisa Molman, Coordinator, 978-542-6321, E-mail: lmolman@salemstate.edu.

Salisbury University, Graduate Division, Program in English, Salisbury, MD 21801-6837. Offers composition, language and rhetoric (MA); literature (MA); teaching English to speakers of other languages (MA). Part-time programs available. *Faculty:* 10 full-time (5 women), 1 part-time/adjunct (0 women). *Students:* 7 full-time (5 women), 26 part-time (18 women); includes 4 minority (2 African Americans, 2 Hispanic Americans). Average age 29. 25 applicants, 72% accepted, 13 enrolled. In 2007, 22 degrees awarded. *Degree requirements:* For master's, thesis optional. *Entrance requirements:* For master's, GRE General Test, MAT or PRAXIS, minimum GPA of 3.0, 2 letters of recommendation. Additional exam requirements/recommendations for international students: Required—TOEFL (minimum score 550 paper-based; 213 computer-based). *Application deadline:* For fall admission, 8/1 for domestic students; for spring admission, 1/1 for domestic students. Applications are processed on a rolling basis. Application fee: $45. Electronic applications accepted. *Expenses:* Tuition, state resident: part-time $260 per credit hour. Tuition, nonresident: part-time $556 per credit hour. *Financial support:* Teaching assistantships with full tuition reimbursements, career-related internships or fieldwork and scholarships/grants available. Support available to part-time students. Financial award applicants required to submit FAFSA. *Faculty research:* Shakespeare, Keats, J. D. Salinger, feminist theory, film, folklore. *Unit head:* Dr. Elizabeth H. Curtin, Director, 410-548-5594, Fax: 410-548-2142, E-mail: ehcurtin@salisbury.edu.

Sam Houston State University, College of Humanities and Social Sciences, Department of English and Foreign Languages, Huntsville, TX 77341. Offers English (MA). Part-time and evening/weekend programs available. *Faculty:* 24 full-time (13 women). *Students:* 16 full-time (10 women), 29 part-time (25 women); includes 4 minority (1 African American, 1 Asian American or Pacific Islander, 2 Hispanic Americans). Average age 31. In 2007, 11 degrees awarded. *Degree requirements:* For master's, comprehensive exam, thesis optional. *Entrance requirements:* For master's, GRE General Test. Additional exam requirements/recommendations for international students: Required—TOEFL (minimum score 550 paper-based; 213 computer-based). *Application deadline:* For fall admission, 8/1 for domestic students; for spring admission, 12/31 for domestic students. Applications are processed on a rolling basis. Application fee: $20. *Expenses:* Tuition, state resident: full-time $5,026; part-time $184 per semester hour. Tuition, nonresident: full-time $10,586; part-time $462 per semester hour. Required fees: $494 per semester. *Financial support:* Teaching assistantships, Federal Work-Study and institutionally sponsored loans available. Support available to part-time students. Financial award application deadline: 5/31; financial award applicants required to submit FAFSA. *Unit head:* Dr. Bill Bridges, Chair, 936-294-1402, Fax: 936-294-1408, E-mail: eng_cwb@shsu.edu. *Application contact:* Dr. Paul Child, Advisor, 936-294-1412, E-mail: eng_pwc@shsu.edu.

San Diego State University, Graduate and Research Affairs, College of Arts and Letters, Department of English and Comparative Literature, San Diego, CA 92182. Offers creative writing (MFA); English (MA). *Students:* 86 full-time (54 women), 59 part-time (36 women); includes 35 minority (6 African Americans, 8 Asian Americans or Pacific Islanders, 21 Hispanic Americans), 2 international. 154 applicants, 62% accepted, 40 enrolled. In 2007, 38 degrees awarded. *Degree requirements:* For master's, one foreign language, comprehensive exam (for some programs), thesis (for some programs). *Entrance requirements:* For master's, GRE General Test, minimum GPA of 2.85, writing sample, 3 letters of recommendation. Additional exam requirements/recommendations for international students: Required—TOEFL. *Application deadline:* For fall admission, 4/1 for domestic and international students; for spring admission, 10/1 for domestic and international students. Applications are processed on a rolling basis. Application fee: $55. Electronic applications accepted. *Financial support:* In 2007–08, 22 teaching assistantships were awarded; fellowships, research assistantships, career-related internships or fieldwork also available. Financial award applicants required to submit FAFSA. Total annual research expenditures: $105,868. *Unit head:* Sherry Little, Chair, 619-594-5237, Fax: 619-594-4998, E-mail: slittle@mail.sdsu.edu. *Application contact:* Dr. Claire E. Colquitt, Graduate Adviser, 619-594-6219, Fax: 619-594-4998, E-mail: colquitt@mail.sdsu.edu.

San Francisco State University, Division of Graduate Studies, College of Humanities, Department of English Language and Literature, Program in Composition, San Francisco, CA 94132-1722. Offers MA, Certificate. Part-time programs available. *Degree requirements:* For master's, comprehensive exam. *Entrance requirements:* Additional exam requirements/recommendations for international students: Required—TOEFL, TWE. *Application deadline:* Applications are processed on a rolling basis. *Application contact:* Dr. Jennifer Trainor, Graduate Coordinator, 415-338-2264, E-mail: jtrainor@sfsu.edu.

San Francisco State University, Division of Graduate Studies, College of Humanities, Department of English Language and Literature, Program in Literature, San Francisco, CA 94132-1722. Offers MA. Part-time programs available. *Application deadline:* Applications are processed on a rolling basis. *Application contact:* Dr. Geoffrey Green, Graduate Coordinator, 415-338-2264, E-mail: ggreen@sfsu.edu.

San Jose State University, Graduate Studies and Research, College of Humanities and the Arts, Department of English and Comparative Literature, San Jose, CA 95192-0001. Offers creative writing (MFA); literature (MA); secondary English education (Certificate). *Students:* 37 full-time (23 women), 57 part-time (37 women); includes 22 minority (5 African Americans, 1 American Indian/Alaska Native, 11 Asian Americans or Pacific Islanders, 5 Hispanic Americans), 2 international. Average age 33. 95 applicants, 68% accepted, 42 enrolled. In 2007, 18 degrees awarded. *Degree requirements:* For master's, one foreign language, thesis or alternative. *Entrance requirements:* For master's, GRE. Additional exam requirements/recommendations for international students: Required—TOEFL. *Application deadline:* For fall admission, 6/29 for domestic students; for spring admission, 11/30 for domestic students. Applications are processed on a rolling basis. Application fee: $59. Electronic applications accepted. *Financial support:* Applicants required to submit FAFSA. *Unit head:* John Engell, Chair, 408-924-4499, Fax: 408-924-4580, E-mail: john.engell@email.sjsu.edu. *Application contact:* Dr. Noelle Brada-Williams, Graduate Coordinator, 408-924-4439.

Seton Hall University, College of Arts and Sciences, Department of English, South Orange, NJ 07079-2697. Offers MA. Part-time and evening/weekend programs available. *Degree requirements:* For master's, one foreign language, comprehensive exam, thesis optional, research seminars. Electronic applications accepted. *Faculty research:* The essay, modern poetry, the novel, medieval poetry, Renaissance drama.

See Close-Up on page 577.

Sewanee: The University of the South, Sewanee School of Letters, Sewanee, TN 37383-1000. Offers American literature and English literature (MA); creative writing (MFA). Programs offered only during the summer. Part-time programs available. *Faculty:* 7 full-time (3 women). *Students:* 41 full-time (20 women); includes 1 minority (African American) Average age 31. 43 applicants, 100% accepted, 41 enrolled. *Degree requirements:* For master's, thesis (for some programs). *Entrance requirements:* For master's, writing sample, 2 letters of recommendation. *Application deadline:* For spring admission, 2/1 priority date for domestic and international students. Applications are processed on a rolling basis. Application fee: $40. Electronic applications accepted. *Expenses: Contact institution. Financial support:* Application deadline: 4/1; *Unit head:* Dr. John M Grammer, Director, 931-598-1483, Fax: 931-598-3303, E-mail: jgrammer@sewanee.edu. *Application contact:* Margaret D Binnicker, Coordinator, 931-598-1636, Fax: 931-598-3303, E-mail: mbinnick@sewanee.edu.

See Close-Up on page 579.

Simmons College, College of Arts and Sciences Graduate Studies, Program in Children's Literature, Boston, MA 02115. Offers children's literature (MA); writing for children (MFA); MA/MFA; MAT/MA. Part-time programs available. *Faculty:* 3 full-time (all women), 5 part-time/adjunct (3 women). *Students:* 2 full-time (both women), 19 part-time (all women); includes 1 minority (Asian American or Pacific Islander), 1 international. Average age 31. 36 applicants, 61% accepted, 18 enrolled. In 2007, 8 degrees awarded. *Degree requirements:* For master's, thesis optional. *Entrance requirements:* For master's, writing portfolio (for MFA). Additional exam requirements/recommendations for international students: Required—TOEFL (minimum score 600 paper-based; 250 computer-based; 100 iBT). *Application deadline:* For fall admission, 8/1 priority date for domestic and international students; for spring admission, 12/15 priority date for domestic and international students. Applications are processed on a rolling basis. Application fee: $35. Electronic applications accepted. *Expenses: Contact institution.* Tuition and fees vary according to degree level and program. *Financial support:* In 2007–08, 31 students received support. Institutionally sponsored loans available. Financial award application deadline: 3/1; financial award applicants required to submit FAFSA. *Faculty research:* Construction of childhood and adolescence, gender and reading, narratology and young adult relation, queer theory and children's literature, bio criticism. *Unit head:* Dr. Cathryn Mercier, Associate Dean, Director—Center for the Study of Children's Literature, 617-521-2541. *Application contact:* Kristen Haack, Director, Graduate Studies Admission, 617-521-2917, Fax: 617-521-3058, E-mail: gsa@simmons.edu.

Simmons College, College of Arts and Sciences Graduate Studies, Program in English, Boston, MA 02115. Offers MA, MAT/MA. Part-time programs available. *Faculty:* 12 full-time (6 women). *Students:* 9 full-time (all women), 21 part-time (all women); includes 3 minority (2 Asian Americans or Pacific Islanders, 1 Hispanic American). Average age 28. 31 applicants, 48% accepted, 7 enrolled. In 2007, 11 degrees awarded. *Degree requirements:* For master's, one foreign language, thesis optional. *Entrance requirements:* For master's, analytical writing sample. Additional exam requirements/recommendations for international students: Required—TOEFL (minimum score 600 paper-based; 250 computer-based; 100 iBT). *Application deadline:* For fall admission, 8/1 priority date for domestic and international students; for spring admission, 12/15 priority date for domestic and international students. Applications are processed on a rolling basis. Application fee: $35. Electronic applications accepted. *Expenses: Contact institution. Financial support:* In 2007–08, 22 students received support. Scholarships/grants available. Financial award application deadline: 3/1; financial award applicants required to submit FAFSA. *Faculty research:* Postcolonial literature and theory, film studies, 19th century American women writers, creative writing, psychoanalysis and race. *Unit head:* Dr. Pamela Bromberg, Director, 617-521-2214 Ext. 2176. *Application contact:* Kristen Haack, Director, Graduate Studies Admission, 617-521-2917, Fax: 617-521-3058, E-mail: gsa@simmons.edu.

Simon Fraser University, Graduate Studies, Faculty of Arts and Social Sciences, Department of English, Burnaby, BC V5A 1S6, Canada. Offers MA, PhD. Part-time programs available. *Degree requirements:* For master's, one foreign language, thesis or alternative; for doctorate, one foreign language, thesis/dissertation, field exams. *Entrance requirements:* For master's, minimum GPA of 3.0; for doctorate, minimum GPA of 3.5. Additional exam requirements/recommendations for international students: Required—TOEFL or IELTS. *Faculty research:* Literary criticism, literature and psychoanalysis, Renaissance drama and poetry, Shakespeare, Canadian and American literature.

Slippery Rock University of Pennsylvania, Graduate Studies (Recruitment), College of Humanities, Fine and Performing Arts, Department of English, Slippery Rock, PA 16057-1383. Offers MA. Part-time and evening/weekend programs available. *Degree requirements:* For master's, comprehensive exam (for some programs), thesis (for some programs). *Entrance requirements:* For master's, GRE General Test, MAT, minimum GPA of 2.75. *Application deadline:* For fall admission, 7/1 priority date for domestic and international students; for spring admission, 11/1 priority date for domestic and international students. Applications are processed on a rolling basis. Application fee: $25. Electronic applications accepted. *Expenses:* Tuition, state resident: part-time $345 per credit hour. Tuition, nonresident: part-time $552 per credit hour. Required fees: $142 per credit hour. *Financial support:* Career-related internships or fieldwork, Federal Work-Study, scholarships/grants, and unspecified assistantships available. Support available to part-time students. Financial award application deadline: 5/1; financial award applicants required to submit FAFSA. *Unit head:* Dr. Joseph McCarren, Graduate Coordinator, 724-738-2868, Fax: 724-738-4829, E-mail: joseph.mccarren@sru.edu. *Application contact:* April Longwell, Interim Director of Graduate Studies, 724-738-2051 Ext. 2116, Fax: 724-738-2146, E-mail: graduate.studies@sru.edu.

Sonoma State University, School of Arts and Humanities, Department of English, Rohnert Park, CA 94928-3609. Offers American literature (MA); creative writing (MA); English literature (MA); world literature (MA). Part-time and evening/weekend programs available. *Students:* 19 full-time (15 women), 6 part-time (5 women); includes 2 minority (1 Asian American or Pacific Islander, 1 Hispanic American). Average age 35. 14 applicants, 93% accepted, 6 enrolled. In 2007, 14 degrees awarded. *Degree requirements:* For master's, one foreign language, thesis or alternative. *Entrance requirements:* For master's, minimum GPA of 2.5. *Application deadline:* For fall admission, 11/30 priority date for domestic students. Application fee: $55. *Financial support:* In 2007–08, 9 teaching assistantships with partial tuition reimbursements were awarded; career-related internships or fieldwork and Federal Work-Study also available. Financial award application deadline: 3/2. *Faculty research:* Women writers, international literature in English, literature of fantasy. *Unit head:* Dr. Greta Vollmer, Chair, 707-661-2140, E-mail: vollmer@sonoma.edu.

South Dakota State University, Graduate School, College of Arts and Science, Department of English, Brookings, SD 57007. Offers MA. Part-time programs available. *Degree requirements:* For master's, comprehensive exam (for some programs), thesis (for some programs), oral and written exams. *Entrance requirements:* For master's, minimum GPA of 2.75. Additional exam requirements/recommendations for international students: Required—TOEFL. *Faculty research:* English and American literature topics, regional literature (Midwestern), women's literature, Lakota literature and culture, rhetoric and writing.

Southeastern Louisiana University, College of Arts, Humanities and Social Sciences, Department of English, Hammond, LA 70402. Offers MA. Part-time and evening/weekend programs available. *Faculty:* 20 full-time (9 women), 1 part-time/adjunct (0 women). *Students:* 14 full-time (11 women), 36 part-time (24 women); includes 12 minority (all African Americans) Average age 31. 13 applicants, 100% accepted, 9 enrolled. In 2007, 6 degrees awarded. *Degree requirements:* For master's, one foreign language, comprehensive exam, thesis optional. *Entrance requirements:* For master's, GRE General Test, 24 undergraduate credit hours in English, minimum GPA of 2.5. Additional exam requirements/recommendations for international students: Required—TOEFL (minimum score 500 paper-based; 173 computer-based). *Application deadline:* For fall admission, 7/15 priority date for domestic students, 6/1 priority date for international students; for spring admission, 12/1 priority date for domestic students, 10/1 priority date for international students. Applications are processed on a rolling basis. Application fee: $20 ($30 for international students). Electronic applications accepted. *Expenses:* Tuition, state resident: full-time $2,216; part-time $123 per credit. Tuition, nonresident: full-time $6,716; part-time $373 per credit. Required fees: $1,105; $61 per credit. *Financial support:* Career-related internships or fieldwork, Federal Work-Study, institutionally sponsored loans, scholarships/grants, unspecified assistantships, and administrative assistantships available. Support available to part-time students. Financial award application deadline: 5/1; financial award applicants required to submit FAFSA. *Faculty research:* Native American, composition/rhetoric; post colonial; Chaucer; professional writing. *Unit head:* Dr. David Hanson, Department Head, 985-549-2100, Fax: 985-549-5021, E-mail: dhanson@selu.edu. *Application contact:* Sandra Meyers, Graduate Admissions Analyst, 985-549-2066, Fax: 985-549-5632, E-mail: admissions@selu.edu.

Southeast Missouri State University, School of Graduate Studies, Department of English, Cape Girardeau, MO 63701-4799. Offers English (MA); teaching English to speakers of other languages (MA). Part-time and evening/weekend programs available. *Faculty:* 17 full-time (8 women). *Students:* 25 full-time (18 women), 82 part-time (69 women); includes 6 minority (3 African Americans, 1 Asian American or Pacific Islander, 2 Hispanic Americans), 10 international. Average age 36. 47 applicants, 96% accepted. In 2007, 20 degrees awarded. *Degree requirements:* For master's, comprehensive exam (for some programs), thesis or alternative. *Entrance requirements:* For master's, minimum GPA of 2.5. Additional exam requirements/recommendations for international students: Required—TOEFL (minimum score 550 paper-based; 213 computer-based). *Application deadline:* For fall admission, 8/1 for domestic students, 6/1 for international students; for spring admission, 11/21 for domestic students, 10/1 for international students. Applications are processed on a rolling basis. Application fee: $25 ($100 for international students). Electronic applications accepted. *Expenses:* Tuition, state resident: part-time $224 per credit hour. Tuition, nonresident: part-time $395 per credit hour. Tuition and fees vary according to course load and program. *Financial support:* In 2007–08, 43 students received support, including 1 research assistantship with full tuition reimbursement available (averaging $7,600 per year), 16 teaching assistantships with full tuition reimbursements available (averaging $7,600 per year); unspecified assistantships also available. Financial award applicants required to submit FAFSA. *Faculty research:* Hawthorne, Mark Twain, Faulkner. *Unit head:* Dr. Carol Scates, Chairperson, 573-651-2156, E-mail: cscates@semo.edu. *Application contact:* Marsha L. Arant, Senior Administrative Assistant, Office of Graduate Studies, 573-651-2192, Fax: 573-651-2001, E-mail: marant@semo.edu.

Southern Connecticut State University, School of Graduate Studies, School of Arts and Sciences, Department of English, New Haven, CT 06515-1355. Offers MA, MS, MLS/MS. Part-time and evening/weekend programs available. *Faculty:* 15 full-time, 1 part-time/adjunct. *Students:* 35 full-time (21 women), 58 part-time (39 women). 46 applicants, 61% accepted, 22 enrolled. In 2007, 17 degrees awarded. *Degree requirements:* For master's, one foreign language, thesis or alternative. *Entrance requirements:* For master's, interview. *Application deadline:* For fall admission, 5/1 priority date for domestic students; for spring admission, 12/1 priority date for domestic students. Applications are processed on a rolling basis. Application fee: $50. Electronic applications accepted. *Financial support:* In 2007–08, teaching assistantships (averaging $4,800 per year). Financial award application deadline: 4/15; financial award applicants required to submit FAFSA. *Unit head:* Dr. Robert McEachern, Chairperson, 203-392-5526, Fax: 203-392-6731, E-mail: mceachernr1@southernct.edu. *Application contact:* Dr. Ken Florey, Coordinator, 203-392-6733, Fax: 203-392-6731, E-mail: floreyk1@southernct.edu.

Southern Illinois University Carbondale, Graduate School, College of Liberal Arts, Department of English, Carbondale, IL 62901-4701. Offers composition (MA, PhD), including composition, literature, rhetoric; creative writing (MFA). *Faculty:* 33 full-time (14 women), 1 (woman) part-time/adjunct. *Students:* 30 full-time (15 women), 61 part-time (41 women); includes 3 minority (1 African American, 2 Hispanic Americans), 9 international. 59 applicants, 36% accepted, 8 enrolled. In 2007, 10 master's, 4 doctorates awarded. *Degree requirements:* For master's, one foreign language, thesis; for doctorate, 2 foreign languages, thesis/dissertation. *Entrance requirements:* For master's, GRE General Test, GRE Subject Test, minimum GPA of 2.7; for doctorate, GRE General Test, GRE Subject Test, minimum GPA of 3.25. Additional exam requirements/recommendations for international students: Required—TOEFL. *Application deadline:* For fall admission, 2/15 for domestic students; for spring admission, 11/15 for domestic students. Applications are processed on a rolling basis. Application fee: $20. *Financial support:* In 2007–08, 2 fellowships with full tuition reimbursements, 5 research assistantships with full tuition reimbursements, 72 teaching assistantships with full tuition reimbursements were awarded; career-related internships or fieldwork, Federal Work-Study, institutionally sponsored loans, and tuition waivers (full) also available. Support available to part-time students. *Faculty research:* British literature, English literature, modern Continental literature, literary criticism and theory, film studies, Irish studies. *Unit head:* Dr. Michael Humphries, Chair, 618-453-6854, Fax: 618-453-3253, E-mail: mhumphri@siu.edu. *Application contact:* Donna Schumaier, Administrative Clerk, 618-453-6894, Fax: 618-453-3253, E-mail: gradengl@siu.edu.

Announcement: The department is active and vital, with strong programs in creative writing, literary and cultural studies, and rhetoric and composition. Whatever one's interest, as a student or a potential colleague, there is much to explore in Carbondale. The *Crab Orchard Review* is Carbondale's nationally recognized literary magazine.

See Close-Up on page 581.

Southern Illinois University Edwardsville, Graduate Studies and Research, College of Arts and Sciences, Department of English Language and Literature, Program in American and English Literature, Edwardsville, IL 62026-0001. Offers MA, Postbaccalaureate Certificate. Part-time programs available. *Students:* 5 full-time (3 women), 11 part-time (8 women); includes 3 minority (1 African American, 2 Hispanic Americans). Average age 33. In 2007, 7 degrees awarded. *Degree requirements:* For master's, one foreign language, thesis or alternative, written papers, oral examination. *Entrance requirements:* Additional exam requirements/recommendations for international students: Required—TOEFL. *Application deadline:* For fall admission, 7/20 for domestic students, 6/1 for international students; for spring admission, 12/14 for domestic students, 10/1 for international students. Application fee: $30. Electronic applications accepted. *Financial support:* Fellowships with full tuition reimbursements, research assistantships with full tuition reimbursements, teaching assistantships with full tuition reimbursements, Federal Work-Study, institutionally sponsored loans, and unspecified assistantships available. Support available to part-time students. Financial award application deadline: 3/1. *Unit head:* Dr. Eileen Joy, Director, 618-650-3971, E-mail: ejoy@siue.edu.

Southern Methodist University, Dedman College, Department of English, Dallas, TX 75275. Offers MA, PhD. *Faculty:* 45 full-time (26 women), 17 part-time/adjunct (12 women). *Students:* 7 full-time (4 women), 7 part-time (5 women); includes 2 minority (1 African American, 1 American Indian/Alaska Native), 1 international. Average age 26. 10 applicants, 30% accepted, 3 enrolled. In 2007, 4 degrees awarded. *Degree requirements:* For master's, one foreign language, comprehensive exam, thesis optional, oral exam; for doctorate, one foreign language, comprehensive exam, thesis/dissertation. *Entrance requirements:* For master's, GRE General Test, minimum GPA of 3.0; for doctorate, GRE General Test, GRE Subject Test, minimum GPA of 3.5, BA in English or other appropriate field. Additional exam requirements/recommendations for international students: Required—TOEFL (minimum score 550 paper-based). Electronic applications accepted. *Financial support:* In 2007–08, 6 fellowships with full tuition reimbursements (averaging $24,000 per year) were awarded; tuition waivers (full) also available. Financial award application deadline: 1/15. *Faculty research:* British/American literature, critical theory, medieval studies, gender studies, American borderlands. *Unit head:* Ezra Greenspan, Chair, 214-768-2946, Fax: 214-768-1234, E-mail: egreensp@smu.edu. *Application contact:* Steven

English

Southern Methodist University (continued)
Weisenburger, Director of Graduate Studies, 214-768-2946, Fax: 214-768-1234, E-mail: sweisenb@smu.edu.

Stanford University, School of Humanities and Sciences, Department of English, Stanford, CA 94305-9991. Offers MA, PhD. Terminal master's awarded for partial completion of doctoral program. *Degree requirements:* For master's, one foreign language, thesis (for some programs); for doctorate, 2 foreign languages, thesis/dissertation, oral exam. *Entrance requirements:* For master's and doctorate, GRE General Test, GRE Subject Test. Additional exam requirements/recommendations for international students: Required—TOEFL. Electronic applications accepted.

State University of New York at Binghamton, Graduate School, School of Arts and Sciences, Department of English, Binghamton, NY 13902-6000. Offers MA, PhD. Part-time programs available. *Faculty:* 32 full-time (16 women), 26 part-time/adjunct (14 women). *Students:* 76 full-time (42 women), 52 part-time (35 women); includes 13 minority (3 African Americans, 3 Asian Americans or Pacific Islanders, 7 Hispanic Americans), 9 international. Average age 32. 122 applicants, 56% accepted, 28 enrolled. In 2007, 27 master's, 11 doctorates awarded. Terminal master's awarded for partial completion of doctoral program. *Degree requirements:* For master's, thesis (for some programs), written exam; for doctorate, one foreign language, comprehensive exam, thesis/dissertation. *Entrance requirements:* For master's and doctorate, GRE General Test, GRE Subject Test, critical writing sample. Additional exam requirements/recommendations for international students: Required—TOEFL. *Application deadline:* For fall admission, 4/15 priority date for domestic students, 1/15 priority date for international students; for spring admission, 11/1 for domestic students, 10/1 priority date for international students. Applications are processed on a rolling basis. Application fee: $60. Electronic applications accepted. *Financial support:* In 2007–08, 66 students received support, including 8 fellowships with full tuition reimbursements available (averaging $11,000 per year), 47 teaching assistantships with full tuition reimbursements available (averaging $14,000 per year); research assistantships, career-related internships or fieldwork, Federal Work-Study, institutionally sponsored loans, tuition waivers (full and partial), and unspecified assistantships also available. Support available to part-time students. Financial award application deadline: 2/15. *Unit head:* Dr. David Bartine, Chairperson, 607-777-2169, E-mail: dbartine@binghamton.edu.

State University of New York at Fredonia, Graduate Studies, Department of English, Fredonia, NY 14063-1136. Offers MA, MS Ed. Part-time and evening/weekend programs available. *Degree requirements:* For master's, thesis optional.

State University of New York at New Paltz, Graduate School, Faculty of Liberal Arts and Sciences, Department of English, New Paltz, NY 12561. Offers MA. Part-time and evening/weekend programs available. *Faculty:* 27 full-time (11 women), 24 part-time/adjunct (15 women). *Students:* 10 full-time (7 women), 37 part-time (14 women). Average age 30. In 2007, 16 degrees awarded. *Degree requirements:* For master's, comprehensive exam, thesis (for some programs), foreign language proficiency exam. *Entrance requirements:* For master's, minimum GPA of 3.0, 10–15 page writing sample. Additional exam requirements/recommendations for international students: Required—TOEFL (minimum score 550 paper-based; 213 computer-based; 80 iBT). *Application deadline:* For fall admission, 5/15 priority date for domestic students, 5/15 for international students; for spring admission, 11/15 for domestic and international students. Application fee: $50. Electronic applications accepted. *Expenses:* Tuition, state resident: full-time $6,900; part-time $288 per credit hour. Tuition, nonresident: full-time $10,920; part-time $455 per credit hour. Required fees: $1,040; $30 per credit hour. $153 per credit hour. Tuition and fees vary according to program. *Financial support:* In 2007–08, 20 students received support, including 17 teaching assistantships with partial tuition reimbursements available (averaging $5,000 per year); career-related internships or fieldwork, Federal Work-Study, and institutionally sponsored loans also available. *Faculty research:* Twentieth Century British Literature, Hemingway and Modernism, British Modernist Fiction, Faulkner and the Southern Renaissance, Revisionary Approaches to Early Twentieth-Century Literature. *Unit head:* Dr. Thomas Olsen, Chairman, 845-257-2723, E-mail: deenm@newpaltz.edu. *Application contact:* Dr. Daniel Kempton, Graduate Coordinator, 845-257-2728.

State University of New York at Oswego, Graduate Studies, College of Arts and Sciences, Department of English, Oswego, NY 13126. Offers MA. Part-time programs available. *Faculty:* 10 full-time, 1 part-time/adjunct. *Students:* 7 full-time (5 women), 7 part-time (2 women). Average age 25. 9 applicants, 100% accepted. In 2007, 11 degrees awarded. *Degree requirements:* For master's, thesis optional. *Entrance requirements:* Additional exam requirements/recommendations for international students: Required—TOEFL (minimum score 560 paper-based; 220 computer-based). *Application deadline:* For fall admission, 4/1 for domestic students; for spring admission, 11/1 for domestic students. Applications are processed on a rolling basis. Application fee: $50. *Expenses:* Tuition, state resident: full-time $6,900; part-time $288 per credit. Tuition, nonresident: full-time $10,920; part-time $455 per credit. Required fees: $607; $32 per credit. $225 per term. Tuition and fees vary according to degree level. *Financial support:* In 2007–08, 3 students received support, including 3 teaching assistantships with partial tuition reimbursements available (averaging $3,800 per year); fellowships with full tuition reimbursements available, career-related internships or fieldwork, Federal Work-Study, institutionally sponsored loans, scholarships/grants, health care benefits, and unspecified assistantships also available. Support available to part-time students. Financial award application deadline: 4/1; financial award applicants required to submit FAFSA. *Unit head:* Dr. Bennet Schaber, Chair, 315-312-2150. *Application contact:* Dr. Thomas Loe, Graduate Program Coordinator, 315-312-2595.

State University of New York College at Cortland, Graduate Studies, School of Arts and Sciences, Department of English, Cortland, NY 13045. Offers MA, MAT, MS Ed. Part-time and evening/weekend programs available. *Degree requirements:* For master's, one foreign language, comprehensive exam, thesis (for some programs). *Entrance requirements:* For master's, GRE General Test.

State University of New York College at Potsdam, School of Arts and Sciences, Department of English, Potsdam, NY 13676. Offers English and communication (MA). Part-time and evening/weekend programs available. *Faculty:* 4 full-time (3 women), 1 (woman) part-time/adjunct. *Students:* 11 full-time (4 women), 3 part-time (all women). 5 applicants, 80% accepted, 3 enrolled. In 2007, 1 degree awarded. *Degree requirements:* For master's, one foreign language, thesis or alternative. *Entrance requirements:* For master's, minimum GPA of 3.0 in last 60 hours of undergraduate course work. Additional exam requirements/recommendations for international students: Required—TOEFL (minimum score 550 paper-based; 213 computer-based; 80 iBT), IELTS (minimum score 6). *Application deadline:* Applications are processed on a rolling basis. Application fee: $50. *Financial support:* In 2007–08, 1 student received support; teaching assistantships with full tuition reimbursements available, Federal Work-Study and unspecified assistantships available. Support available to part-time students. Financial award application deadline: 3/1; financial award applicants required to submit FAFSA. *Unit head:* Dr. Lisa Wilson, Director of Graduate Studies, English and Communication, 315-267-2004, Fax: 315-267-3256, E-mail: wilsonlm@potsdam.edu. *Application contact:* Peter Cutler, Graduate Admissions Counselor, 315-267-3154, Fax: 315-267-4802, E-mail: cutlerpj@potsdam.edu.

State University of New York College at Potsdam, School of Education, Program in Secondary Education, Potsdam, NY 13676. Offers adolescence education (grades 7-12) (MS Ed, MST); English (MST); mathematics (with grades 5-6 extension) (MST); science (MST), including biology, chemistry, earth science, physics; social studies (MS Ed, MST). *Accreditation:* NCATE. Part-time programs available. *Faculty:* 10 full-time (4 women), 3 part-time/adjunct (2 women). *Students:* 61 full-time (39 women), 12 part-time (4 women); includes 4 minority (2 African Americans, 1 Asian American or Pacific Islander, 1 Hispanic American), 9 international. In 2007, 36 degrees awarded. *Degree requirements:* For master's, thesis optional, culminating experience. *Entrance requirements:* For master's, minimum GPA of 2.75 in last 60 hours of course work, 3.0 for English program. Additional exam requirements/recommendations for international students: Required—TOEFL (minimum score 550 paper-based; 213 computer-based; 80 iBT), IELTS (minimum score 6). *Application deadline:* Applications are processed on a rolling basis. Application fee: $50. *Financial support:* Fellowships, teaching assistantships, career-related internships or fieldwork, Federal Work-Study, scholarships/grants, and unspecified assistantships available. Support available to part-time students. Financial award application deadline: 3/1; financial award applicants required to submit FAFSA. *Unit head:* Dr. Peter Brouwer, Chairperson, 315-267-3018, Fax: 315-267-4802, E-mail: brouweps@potsdam.edu. *Application contact:* Peter Cutler, Graduate Admissions Counselor, 315-267-3154, Fax: 315-267-4802, E-mail: cutlerpj@potsdam.edu.

Stephen F. Austin State University, Graduate School, College of Liberal Arts, Department of English and Philosophy, Nacogdoches, TX 75962. Offers English (MA). *Degree requirements:* For master's, comprehensive exam. *Entrance requirements:* For master's, GRE General Test. Additional exam requirements/recommendations for international students: Required—TOEFL. *Faculty research:* Creative writing, Latin American literature, modern American literature, modern British literature, literature for children.

Stetson University, College of Arts and Sciences, Division of Humanities, Department of English, DeLand, FL 32723. Offers MA. *Students:* Average age 29. In 2007, 2 degrees awarded. *Degree requirements:* For master's, thesis. *Entrance requirements:* For master's, GRE General Test. *Application deadline:* For fall admission, 3/1 priority date for domestic students; for spring admission, 11/1 for domestic students. Applications are processed on a rolling basis. Application fee: $25. *Unit head:* Dr. Joseph Witek, Director, 386-822-7720. *Application contact:* Diana Belian, Office of Graduate Studies, 386-822-7075, Fax: 386-822-7388, E-mail: dbelian@stetson.edu.

Stony Brook University, State University of New York, Graduate School, College of Arts and Sciences, Department of Comparative Literary and Cultural Studies, Stony Brook, NY 11794. Offers comparative literature (MA, PhD); cultural studies (PhD). Evening/weekend programs available. *Faculty:* 7 full-time (2 women). *Students:* 28 full-time (21 women), 9 part-time (8 women); includes 6 minority (1 African American, 5 Asian Americans or Pacific Islanders), 15 international. Average age 30. 58 applicants, 17% accepted. In 2007, 3 master's, 2 doctorates awarded. Terminal master's awarded for partial completion of doctoral program. *Degree requirements:* For master's, 2 foreign languages, exam; for doctorate, 3 foreign languages, comprehensive exam, thesis/dissertation. *Entrance requirements:* For master's and doctorate, GRE General Test, minimum GPA of 3.5 in major, 3.0 overall. Additional exam requirements/recommendations for international students: Required—TOEFL. *Application deadline:* For fall admission, 1/15 for domestic students. Application fee: $60. *Financial support:* In 2007–08, 17 teaching assistantships were awarded; fellowships, research assistantships also available. *Faculty research:* Literary theory, interdisciplinary studies, literary history. *Unit head:* Dr. Robert Harvey, Chairman, 631-632-7456.

See Close-Up on page 583.

Stony Brook University, State University of New York, Graduate School, College of Arts and Sciences, Department of English, Stony Brook, NY 11794. Offers composition studies (Certificate); English (MA, PhD); English education (MAT). MAT offered through the School of Professional Development. Evening/weekend programs available. *Faculty:* 19 full-time (8 women), 1 (woman) part-time/adjunct. *Students:* 80 full-time (51 women), 48 part-time (39 women); includes 18 minority (6 African Americans, 4 Asian Americans or Pacific Islanders, 8 Hispanic Americans), 3 international. Average age 32. 195 applicants, 39% accepted. In 2007, 16 master's, 8 doctorates, 1 other advanced degree awarded. Terminal master's awarded for partial completion of doctoral program. *Degree requirements:* For doctorate, thesis/dissertation. *Entrance requirements:* For master's and doctorate, GRE General Test. Additional exam requirements/recommendations for international students: Required—TOEFL. *Application deadline:* For fall admission, 1/15 for domestic students. Application fee: $60. *Financial support:* In 2007–08, 3 fellowships, 49 teaching assistantships were awarded; research assistantships. *Faculty research:* American literature, British literature, literary critical theory, rhetoric and composition theory, women's studies. *Unit head:* Dr. Stephen Spector, Chair, 631-632-7420, Fax: 631-632-7568. *Application contact:* Dr. Helen M. Cooper, Director, 631-632-7784, Fax: 631-632-7568, E-mail: hcooper@notes.cc.sunysb.edu.

See Close-Up on page 585.

Sul Ross State University, School of Arts and Sciences, Department of Languages and Literature, Alpine, TX 79832. Offers English (MA). Part-time and evening/weekend programs available. *Degree requirements:* For master's, thesis optional. *Entrance requirements:* For master's, GRE General Test, minimum GPA of 2.5 in last 60 hours of undergraduate work. *Faculty research:* Narrative theory, feminist literary criticism, autobiography studies, multiculturalism, biblical narrative.

Syracuse University, Graduate School, College of Arts and Sciences, Department of English, Programs in English, Syracuse, NY 13244. Offers MA, PhD. *Students:* 30 full-time (17 women); includes 3 minority (1 American Indian/Alaska Native, 1 Asian American or Pacific Islander, 1 Hispanic American), 6 international. 91 applicants, 23% accepted, 10 enrolled. In 2007, 7 master's, 4 doctorates awarded. *Entrance requirements:* For master's and doctorate, GRE General Test. Additional exam requirements/recommendations for international students: Required—TOEFL. *Application deadline:* For fall admission, 1/10 for domestic students. Application fee: $75. *Expenses:* Tuition: Full-time $18,216; part-time $1,012 per credit. Required fees: $980. Tuition and fees vary according to program. *Unit head:* Linda Shires, Director of Graduate Studies, 315-443-2174. *Application contact:* Terri Zollo, Information Contact, 315-443-2174.

Tarleton State University, College of Graduate Studies, College of Liberal and Fine Arts, Department of English and Languages, Stephenville, TX 76402. Offers English (MA). Part-time and evening/weekend programs available. *Faculty:* 6 full-time (3 women). *Students:* 7 full-time (2 women), 8 part-time (all women). Average age 33. 9 applicants, 100% accepted, 7 enrolled. In 2007, 3 degrees awarded. *Degree requirements:* For master's, comprehensive exam, thesis (for some programs). *Entrance requirements:* For master's, GRE General Test, minimum GPA of 3.0. Additional exam requirements/recommendations for international students: Required—TOEFL (minimum score 550 paper-based; 213 computer-based). *Application deadline:* For fall admission, 8/5 priority date for domestic students; for spring admission, 12/1 for domestic students. Applications are processed on a rolling basis. Application fee: $25 ($125 for international students). Electronic applications accepted. *Expenses:* Tuition, state resident: full-time $2,520; part-time $140 per credit hour. Tuition, nonresident: full-time $7,344; part-time $408 per credit hour. Required fees: $948; $39 per credit hour. *Financial support:* In 2007–08, 5 research assistantships (averaging $13,600 per year) were awarded; teaching assistantships, career-related internships or fieldwork and Federal Work-Study also available. Support available to part-time students. Financial award application deadline: 5/1; financial award applicants required to submit FAFSA. *Unit head:* Dr. Jeanelle Barrett, Head, 254-968-9039, Fax: 254-968-1931, E-mail: jbarrett@tarleton.edu.

Temple University, Graduate School, College of Liberal Arts, Department of English, Philadelphia, PA 19122-6096. Offers creative writing (MA); English (MA, PhD). Part-time programs available. *Degree requirements:* For doctorate, 2 foreign languages, thesis/dissertation. *Entrance requirements:* For master's and doctorate, GRE General Test, minimum GPA of 3.0. Additional exam requirements/recommendations for international students: Required—TOEFL (minimum score 550 paper-based; 213 computer-based; 79 iBT). Electronic applications accepted. *Faculty research:* Renaissance, Victorian, Modern British, and American literature; critical theory; composition.

Tennessee State University, The School of Graduate Studies and Research, College of Arts and Sciences, Department of Languages, Literature, and Philosophy, Nashville, TN 37209-1561. Offers English (MA). *Faculty:* 16 full-time (9 women), 3 part-time/adjunct (2 women). *Students:* 8 full-time (4 women), 14 part-time (12 women); includes 12 minority (all African

Americans) Average age 27. 17 applicants, 76% accepted, 7 enrolled. In 2007, 2 degrees awarded. *Degree requirements:* For master's, thesis optional. *Entrance requirements:* For master's, GRE General Test or MAT. Application fee: $25. *Expenses:* Tuition, state resident: full-time $6,271; part-time $490 per hour. Tuition, nonresident: full-time $16,550; part-time $936 per hour. *Faculty research:* American literature, British literature, Anglo/Saxon literature, cultural/women's studies. *Unit head:* Dr. Warren Wescott, Head, 615-963-5715, E-mail: wwescott@tnstate.edu. *Application contact:* Dr. Jo Helen Railsback, Graduate Coordinator, 615-963-5724.

Tennessee Technological University, Graduate School, College of Arts and Sciences, Department of English, Cookeville, TN 38505. Offers MA. Part-time programs available. *Faculty:* 23 full-time (8 women). *Students:* 6 full-time (3 women), 12 part-time (9 women). Average age 28. 8 applicants, 88% accepted, 6 enrolled. In 2007, 7 degrees awarded. *Degree requirements:* For master's, thesis. *Entrance requirements:* For master's, GRE General Test. Additional exam requirements/recommendations for international students: Required—TOEFL. *Application deadline:* For fall admission, 3/1 priority date for domestic students; for spring admission, 8/1 for domestic students. Application fee: $25 ($30 for international students). *Expenses:* Tuition, state resident: full-time $9,450; part-time $347 per semester hour. Tuition, nonresident: full-time $24,864; part-time $793 per semester hour. Required fees: $347 per semester hour. $3,150 per semester. *Financial support:* In 2007–08, research assistantships (averaging $4,000 per year), 9 teaching assistantships (averaging $6,750 per year) were awarded; fellowships also available. Financial award application deadline: 4/1. *Unit head:* Dr. Homer Kemp, Interim Chairperson, 931-372-3343, Fax: 931-372-6142. *Application contact:* Dr. Francis O. Otuonye, Associate Vice President for Research and Graduate Studies, 931-372-3233, Fax: 931-372-3497, E-mail: fotuonye@tntech.edu.

Texas A&M International University, Office of Graduate Studies and Research, College of Arts and Sciences, Department of Language and Literature, Laredo, TX 78041-1900. Offers English (MA); Hispanic studies (PhD); Spanish (MA). *Faculty:* 5 full-time (1 woman). *Students:* 2 full-time (1 woman), 19 part-time (13 women); includes 19 minority (all Hispanic Americans) Average age 29. 17 applicants, 76% accepted, 7 enrolled. In 2007, 1 degree awarded. *Entrance requirements:* For master's, GRE General Test. Additional exam requirements/recommendations for international students: Required—TOEFL (minimum score 550 paper-based; 213 computer-based). *Application deadline:* For fall admission, 7/15 priority date for domestic students; for spring admission, 11/12 for domestic students. Applications are processed on a rolling basis. Application fee: $25. *Financial support:* In 2007–08, 5 students received support. Application deadline: 11/1. *Unit head:* Dr. Sean Chadwell, Chair, 956-326-2471, E-mail: schadwell@tamiu.edu. *Application contact:* Rosie Espinoza-Dickinson, Director of Admissions, 956-326-2200, Fax: 956-326-2199, E-mail: enroll@tamiu.edu.

Texas A&M University, College of Liberal Arts, Department of English, College Station, TX 77843. Offers MA, PhD. *Faculty:* 35. *Students:* 105 full-time (70 women), 16 part-time (12 women); includes 10 minority (5 African Americans, 1 American Indian/Alaska Native, 2 Asian Americans or Pacific Islanders, 2 Hispanic Americans), 29 international. Average age 24. 95 applicants, 41% accepted, 23 enrolled. In 2007, 10 master's, 7 doctorates awarded. Terminal master's awarded for partial completion of doctoral program. *Median time to degree:* Of those who began their doctoral program in fall 1999, 80% received their degree in 8 years or less. *Degree requirements:* For master's, one foreign language, thesis optional; for doctorate, 2 foreign languages, thesis/dissertation. *Entrance requirements:* For master's and doctorate, GRE General Test, sample of written work. Additional exam requirements/recommendations for international students: Required—TOEFL. *Application deadline:* For fall admission, 2/1 priority date for domestic and international students; for spring admission, 10/1 priority date for domestic and international students. Applications are processed on a rolling basis. Application fee: $50 ($75 for international students). Electronic applications accepted. *Expenses:* Tuition, state resident: full-time $6,129. Tuition, nonresident: full-time $11,689. Tuition and fees vary according to course load. *Financial support:* In 2007–08, fellowships with partial tuition reimbursements (averaging $10,000 per year), research assistantships with partial tuition reimbursements (averaging $12,000 per year), teaching assistantships with partial tuition reimbursements (averaging $12,000 per year) were awarded; career-related internships or fieldwork, Federal Work-Study, institutionally sponsored loans, scholarships/grants, and unspecified assistantships also available. Financial award application deadline: 4/1. *Faculty research:* American, Renaissance, Medieval, textual studies, discourse studies. *Unit head:* Dr. Paul Parrish, Head, 979-845-9836, Fax: 979-845-2292, E-mail: info-grad@english.tamu.edu. *Application contact:* Howard Marchitello, Director of Graduate Programs, 979-845-9836, Fax: 979-862-2292, E-mail: info-grad@english.tamu.edu.

Texas A&M University–Commerce, Graduate School, College of Arts and Sciences, Department of Literature and Languages, Commerce, TX 75429-3011. Offers college teaching of English (PhD); English (MA, MS); Spanish (MA). Part-time programs available. *Faculty:* 13 full-time (8 women), 1 part-time/adjunct (0 women). *Students:* 19 full-time (15 women), 47 part-time (34 women); includes 13 minority (1 African American, 2 American Indian/Alaska Native, 3 Asian Americans or Pacific Islanders, 7 Hispanic Americans), 2 international. Average age 36. In 2007, 7 degrees awarded. Terminal master's awarded for partial completion of doctoral program. *Degree requirements:* For master's, comprehensive exam, thesis (for some programs); for doctorate, one foreign language, thesis/dissertation, departmental qualifying exam. *Entrance requirements:* For master's and doctorate, GRE General Test. *Application deadline:* For fall admission, 6/1 priority date for domestic students; for spring admission, 11/1 priority date for domestic students. Applications are processed on a rolling basis. Application fee: $0 ($25 for international students). Electronic applications accepted. *Financial support:* In 2007–08, research assistantships (averaging $7,875 per year), teaching assistantships (averaging $7,875 per year) were awarded; Federal Work-Study, institutionally sponsored loans, and scholarships/grants also available. Financial award application deadline: 5/1; financial award applicants required to submit FAFSA. *Faculty research:* Latino literature, American film studies, ethnographic research, Willa Carter. *Unit head:* Dr. Gerald Duchovnay, Head, 903-886-5260, Fax: 903-886-5980, E-mail: gerald_duchovnay@tamu-commerce.edu. *Application contact:* Tammi Thompson, Graduate Admissions Adviser, 843-886-5167, Fax: 843-886-5165, E-mail: tammi_thompson@tamu-commerce.edu.

Texas A&M University–Corpus Christi, Graduate Studies and Research, College of Liberal Arts, Program in English, Corpus Christi, TX 78412-5503. Offers MA. Part-time and evening/weekend programs available. *Students:* 2 full-time (both women), 36 part-time (25 women); includes 17 minority (all Hispanic Americans) 17 applicants, 71% accepted, 10 enrolled. In 2007, 9 degrees awarded. *Degree requirements:* For master's, comprehensive exam, thesis (for some programs). *Entrance requirements:* For master's, GRE General Test. Additional exam requirements/recommendations for international students: Required—TOEFL. *Application deadline:* For fall admission, 7/15 priority date for domestic students, 5/1 priority date for international students; for spring admission, 11/15 priority date for domestic students, 9/1 priority date for international students. Applications are processed on a rolling basis. Application fee: $30 ($50 for international students). Electronic applications accepted. *Expenses:* Tuition, state resident: part-time $63 per credit hour. Tuition, nonresident: part-time $341 per credit hour. Tuition and fees vary according to course load. *Financial support:* Research assistantships, teaching assistantships, career-related internships or fieldwork, Federal Work-Study, institutionally sponsored loans, scholarships/grants, health care benefits, and unspecified assistantships available. Support available to part-time students. Financial award application deadline: 3/15; financial award applicants required to submit FAFSA. *Unit head:* Dr. Cristina Kirklighter, Head, 361-825-2263, E-mail: cristina.kirklighter@tamucc.edu. *Application contact:* Maria Martinez, Graduate Admissions Coordinator, 361-825-2177, Fax: 361-825-2755, E-mail: gradweb@tamucc.edu.

Texas A&M University–Kingsville, College of Graduate Studies, College of Arts and Sciences, Department of Language and Literature, Kingsville, TX 78363. Offers English (MA, MS); Spanish (MA). Part-time and evening/weekend programs available. *Degree requirements:* For master's, comprehensive exam, thesis or alternative. *Entrance requirements:* For master's, GRE General Test, minimum GPA of 3.0. Additional exam requirements/recommendations for international students: Required—TOEFL. *Faculty research:* Linguistics, culture, Spanish American literature, Spanish peninsular literature, American literature.

Texas A&M University–Texarkana, Graduate Studies and Research, College of Arts and Sciences and Education, Texarkana, TX 75505-5518. Offers adult education (MS); curriculum and instruction (MS); education (MS); educational administration (M Ed); English (MA); history (MS); instructional technology (MS); interdisciplinary studies (MS); special education (M Ed, MS). Part-time and evening/weekend programs available. *Students:* 273. Average age 32. In 2007, 86 degrees awarded. *Degree requirements:* For master's, comprehensive exam (for some programs), thesis optional. *Entrance requirements:* For master's, minimum GPA of 2.5 on last 60 hours of bachelor's degree. Additional exam requirements/recommendations for international students: Required—TOEFL. *Application deadline:* For fall admission, 7/15 priority date for domestic students; for spring admission, 12/1 priority date for domestic students. Applications are processed on a rolling basis. Application fee: $0 ($25 for international students). Electronic applications accepted. *Financial support:* Career-related internships or fieldwork and scholarships/grants available. Financial award applicants required to submit FAFSA. *Application contact:* Patricia E. Black, Director of Admissions and Registrar, 903-223-3068, Fax: 903-223-3140, E-mail: pat.black@tamut.edu.

Texas Christian University, AddRan College of Humanities and Social Sciences, Department of English, Fort Worth, TX 76129-0002. Offers MA, PhD. Part-time and evening/weekend programs available. *Degree requirements:* For master's, one foreign language, thesis, candidacy exam; for doctorate, one foreign language, thesis/dissertation, diagnostic exam, qualifying exam. *Entrance requirements:* For master's and doctorate, GRE General Test. Additional exam requirements/recommendations for international students: Required—TOEFL. *Application deadline:* For fall admission, 3/1 for domestic students; for spring admission, 12/1 for domestic students. Applications are processed on a rolling basis. Application fee: $0. *Expenses:* Tuition: Part-time $865 per credit hour. Required fees: $48 per year. *Financial support:* Fellowships, teaching assistantships, unspecified assistantships available. Financial award application deadline: 3/1. *Unit head:* Dr. Dan Williams, Chairperson, 817-257-7240. *Application contact:* Dr. Mike Butler, Associate Dean, AddRan College of Humanities and Social Sciences, E-mail: m.butler@tcu.edu.

Texas Southern University, Graduate School, College of Liberal Arts and Behavioral Sciences, Department of English, Houston, TX 77004-4584. Offers MA. Part-time programs available. *Faculty:* 5 full-time (1 woman). *Students:* 2 full-time (both women), 7 part-time (6 women); includes 8 minority (all African Americans), 1 international. Average age 34. 63 applicants, 97% accepted, 3 enrolled. *Degree requirements:* For master's, one foreign language, comprehensive exam, thesis. *Entrance requirements:* For master's, GRE General Test, minimum GPA of 2.5. Additional exam requirements/recommendations for international students: Required—TOEFL. *Application deadline:* For fall admission, 7/15 priority date for domestic students. Applications are processed on a rolling basis. Application fee: $50 ($75 for international students). *Financial support:* Teaching assistantships, Federal Work-Study and institutionally sponsored loans available. Financial award application deadline: 5/1. *Faculty research:* Linguistics, teaching of English, African-American literature, African literature, developmental English. *Unit head:* Dr. Rhonda Saldivar, Interim Chair, 713-313-7536, Fax: 713-313-7538, E-mail: saldivar_rx@tsu.edu.

Texas State University–San Marcos, Graduate School, College of Liberal Arts, Department of English, Program in Literature, San Marcos, TX 78666. Offers MA. Part-time and evening/weekend programs available. *Faculty:* 14 full-time (10 women). *Students:* 28 full-time (17 women), 50 part-time (32 women); includes 14 minority (2 African Americans, 3 Asian Americans or Pacific Islanders, 9 Hispanic Americans), 1 international. Average age 30. 33 applicants, 94% accepted, 23 enrolled. In 2007, 22 degrees awarded. *Degree requirements:* For master's, comprehensive exam. *Entrance requirements:* For master's, minimum GPA of 2.75 in last 60 hours, 24 undergraduate hours of course work in English (12 advanced) with minimum GPA of 3.25, 6 hours of course work in foreign language. Additional exam requirements/recommendations for international students: Required—TOEFL (minimum score 550 paper-based; 213 computer-based). *Application deadline:* For fall admission, 6/15 priority date for domestic students, 6/1 for international students; for spring admission, 10/15 priority date for domestic students, 10/1 for international students. Applications are processed on a rolling basis. Application fee: $40 ($90 for international students). Electronic applications accepted. *Expenses:* Tuition, state resident: full-time $3,780; part-time $210 per credit hour. Tuition, nonresident: full-time $8,784; part-time $488 per credit hour. Required fees: $493 per semester. Full-time tuition and fees vary according to course load. *Financial support:* In 2007–08, 60 students received support, including 3 research assistantships (averaging $4,552 per year), 15 teaching assistantships (averaging $5,213 per year); Federal Work-Study and institutionally sponsored loans also available. Support available to part-time students. Financial award application deadline: 4/1; financial award applicants required to submit FAFSA. *Unit head:* Dr. Paul Cohen, Acting Graduate Adviser, 512-245-2163, Fax: 512-245-8546.

Texas Tech University, Graduate School, College of Arts and Sciences, Department of English, Lubbock, TX 79409. Offers English (MA, PhD); technical communication (MA); technical communication and rhetoric (PhD). Part-time programs available. *Faculty:* 38 full-time (13 women), 2 part-time/adjunct (both women). *Students:* 114 full-time (64 women), 84 part-time (56 women); includes 21 minority (4 African Americans, 3 American Indian/Alaska Native, 3 Asian Americans or Pacific Islanders, 11 Hispanic Americans), 13 international. Average age 34. 155 applicants, 49% accepted, 47 enrolled. In 2007, 18 master's, 11 doctorates awarded. *Degree requirements:* For master's, one foreign language, thesis (for some programs); for doctorate, thesis/dissertation. *Entrance requirements:* For master's and doctorate, GRE General Test. Additional exam requirements/recommendations for international students: Required—TOEFL (minimum score 550 paper-based; 213 computer-based). *Application deadline:* For fall admission, 3/1 priority date for international students; for spring admission, 11/1 priority date for international students. Applications are processed on a rolling basis. Application fee: $50 ($60 for international students). Electronic applications accepted. *Expenses:* Tuition, state resident: part-time $373 per credit hour. Tuition, nonresident: part-time $651 per credit hour. Tuition and fees vary according to program. *Financial support:* In 2007–08, 101 students received support, including 98 teaching assistantships with partial tuition reimbursements available (averaging $14,187 per year); research assistantships with partial tuition reimbursements available, Federal Work-Study and institutionally sponsored loans also available. Support available to part-time students. Financial award application deadline: 4/15; financial award applicants required to submit FAFSA. *Faculty research:* Southwestern literature and language; computers and writing; technical communication and rhetoric; creative writing; nineteenth century studies. Total annual research expenditures: $18,946. *Unit head:* Dr. Sam Dragga, Chair, 806-742-2501, Fax: 806-742-0989, E-mail: sam.dragga@ttu.edu. *Application contact:* Dr. Sean Grass, Director of Graduate Studies, 806-742-2501, Fax: 806-742-0989, E-mail: english.gradadvisor@ttu.edu.

Texas Woman's University, Graduate School, College of Arts and Sciences, Department of English, Speech, and Foreign Languages, Denton, TX 76201. Offers English (MA); rhetoric (PhD). Part-time programs available. *Students:* 9 full-time (7 women), 47 part-time (41 women); includes 10 minority (5 African Americans, 1 American Indian/Alaska Native, 1 Asian American or Pacific Islander, 3 Hispanic Americans), 1 international. Average age 38. In 2007, 7 master's, 4 doctorates awarded. *Degree requirements:* For master's, one foreign language, comprehensive exam, thesis; for doctorate, 2 foreign languages, comprehensive exam, thesis/dissertation. *Entrance requirements:* For master's, GRE General Test, writing sample, 3 letters of reference, interview, minimum GPA of 3.0; for doctorate, GRE General Test, writing sample, 3 letters of reference, interview, 3.0 GPA on previous upper division and graduate work. Additional exam requirements/recommendations for international students: Required—TOEFL (minimum score 550 paper-based; 213 computer-based; 79 iBT). *Application deadline:* For fall admission, 4/1 for international students; for spring admission, 8/1 for international students. Applications are processed on a rolling basis. Application fee: $30 ($50 for international students).

English

Texas Woman's University (continued)

Electronic applications accepted. *Expenses:* Tuition, state resident: full-time $3,294; part-time $183 per credit. Tuition, nonresident: full-time $8,298; part-time $461 per credit. Required fees: $985; $55 per credit. Tuition and fees vary according to degree level. *Financial support:* In 2007–08, 9 research assistantships (averaging $10,494 per year), 15 teaching assistantships (averaging $10,746 per year) were awarded; career-related internships or fieldwork, Federal Work-Study, institutionally sponsored loans, scholarships/grants, traineeships, health care benefits, and unspecified assistantships also available. Support available to part-time students. Financial award application deadline: 3/1; financial award applicants required to submit FAFSA. *Faculty research:* British and American literature; rhetoric: historical and applied; composition studies and technology; literary theory and criticism; women's literature and feminist rhetoric. *Unit head:* Dr. Bruce Krajewski, Chair, 940-898-2324, Fax: 940-898-2297, E-mail: bkrajewski@twu.edu. *Application contact:* Samuel Wheeler, Assistant Director of Admissions, 940-898-3188, Fax: 940-898-3081, E-mail: wheelersr@twu.edu.

Trinity College, Graduate Programs, Department of English, Hartford, CT 06106-3100. Offers MA. Part-time and evening/weekend programs available. *Degree requirements:* For master's, thesis. *Entrance requirements:* For master's, minimum GPA of 3.0.

Trinity Western University, Faculty of Graduate Studies, Program in Interdisciplinary Humanities, Langley, BC V2Y 1Y1, Canada. Offers general humanities (MAIH); specialized (MAIH), including English, history, philosophy. Part-time and evening/weekend programs available. Postbaccalaureate distance learning degree programs offered (minimal on-campus study). *Faculty:* 19 full-time (6 women), 3 part-time/adjunct (0 women). *Students:* 9 full-time (4 women), 24 part-time (13 women). Average age 30. 16 applicants, 75% accepted, 9 enrolled. In 2007, 2 degrees awarded. *Degree requirements:* For master's, 36 semester hours. *Entrance requirements:* For master's, strong undergraduate degree in Humanities or English, History or Philosophy. *Application deadline:* For fall admission, 5/15 priority date for domestic students; for winter admission, 11/1 priority date for domestic students. Application fee: $40. *Financial support:* In 2007–08, 12 students received support, including 3 fellowships (averaging $17,500 per year), 1 research assistantship (averaging $12,000 per year); career-related internships or fieldwork, scholarships/grants, and traineeships also available. Financial award application deadline: 4/1. *Faculty research:* Literary theory, gender, medieval and early modern literature, philosophy of religion, Thomas Merton's poetics. Total annual research expenditures: $145,000 Canadian dollars. *Unit head:* Dr. Bob Burkinshaw, Director, 604-888-7511 Ext. 3111, Fax: 604-513-2143, E-mail: burkinsh@twu.ca. *Application contact:* Vic Cornish, Director, Graduate Admissions, 604-888-7511 Ext. 3130, Fax: 604-513-2064, E-mail: vic.cornish@twu.edu.

Truman State University, Graduate School, College of Arts and Sciences, Program in English, Kirksville, MO 63501-4221. Offers MA. *Students:* 17 full-time (6 women), 4 part-time (3 women); includes 1 African American, 1 Asian American or Pacific Islander. 16 applicants, 100% accepted. In 2007, 6 degrees awarded. *Degree requirements:* For master's, thesis. *Entrance requirements:* For master's, GRE General Test, minimum GPA of 3.0. Additional exam requirements/recommendations for international students: Required—TOEFL (minimum score 550 paper-based; 213 computer-based). *Application deadline:* For fall admission, 6/15 priority date for domestic students, 6/15 for international students; for spring admission, 11/1 priority date for domestic students, 11/1 for international students. Applications are processed on a rolling basis. Application fee: $0. Electronic applications accepted. *Expenses:* Tuition, state resident: part-time $280 per credit hour. Tuition, nonresident: part-time $478 per credit hour. *Financial support:* In 2007–08, research assistantships with tuition reimbursements (averaging $8,000 per year), teaching assistantships with tuition reimbursements (averaging $8,000 per year) were awarded; career-related internships or fieldwork and Federal Work-Study also available. Financial award application deadline: 5/1; financial award applicants required to submit FAFSA. *Unit head:* Dr. Alanna Preussner, Program Director, 660-785-4489. *Application contact:* Doris Snyder, Graduate Office Secretary, E-mail: dsnyder@truman.edu.

Tufts University, Graduate School of Arts and Sciences, Department of English, Medford, MA 02155. Offers MA, PhD. *Faculty:* 18 full-time, 35 part-time/adjunct. *Students:* 57 (42 women); includes 4 minority (2 African Americans, 2 Hispanic Americans) 2 international. 124 applicants, 15% accepted, 9 enrolled. In 2007, 4 master's, 4 doctorates awarded. Terminal master's awarded for partial completion of doctoral program. *Degree requirements:* For master's, one foreign language, thesis; for doctorate, 2 foreign languages, thesis/dissertation. *Entrance requirements:* For master's and doctorate, GRE General Test, GRE Subject Test, writing sample. Additional exam requirements/recommendations for international students: Required—TOEFL (minimum score 550 paper-based; 213 computer-based; 80 iBT). *Application deadline:* For fall admission, 1/15 for domestic students, 12/30 for international students. Applications are processed on a rolling basis. Application fee: $70. Electronic applications accepted. *Expenses:* Tuition: Full-time $35,052. *Financial support:* Fellowships with full and partial tuition reimbursements, teaching assistantships with full and partial tuition reimbursements, Federal Work-Study, scholarships/grants, and tuition waivers (full and partial) available. Support available to part-time students. Financial award application deadline: 2/15; financial award applicants required to submit FAFSA. *Unit head:* Dr. Lee Edelman, Chair, 617-627-3459. *Application contact:* Dr. Joe Litvac, Head, 617-627-3459.

Tulane University, School of Liberal Arts, Department of English, New Orleans, LA 70118-5669. Offers MA, PhD. *Degree requirements:* For master's, one foreign language, thesis or alternative; for doctorate, 2 foreign languages, thesis/dissertation. *Entrance requirements:* For master's, GRE General Test, minimum B average in undergraduate course work; for doctorate, GRE General Test. Additional exam requirements/recommendations for international students: Required—TOEFL. Electronic applications accepted.

Universidad de las Américas–Puebla, Division of Graduate Studies, School of Humanities, Program in Literature, Puebla, Mexico. Offers MA. Part-time and evening/weekend programs available. *Degree requirements:* For master's, one foreign language, thesis. *Entrance requirements:* Additional exam requirements/recommendations for international students: Required—TOEFL. *Faculty research:* Women in literature, Mexican and Hispanic literature.

Université de Montréal, Faculty of Arts and Sciences, Department of English Studies, Montréal, QC H3C 3J7, Canada. Offers MA, PhD. *Faculty:* 10 full-time (4 women). *Students:* 61 full-time (42 women), 6 part-time (4 women). 44 applicants, 25% accepted, 10 enrolled. In 2007, 13 master's, 1 doctorate awarded. *Degree requirements:* For doctorate, thesis/dissertation, general exam. *Entrance requirements:* For master's, BA in English with minimum B+ average; for doctorate, MA in English with minimum B+ average. *Application deadline:* For fall admission, 2/1 priority date for domestic students; for winter admission, 11/1 priority date for domestic students; for spring admission, 2/1 priority date for domestic students. Application fee: $100. Electronic applications accepted. *Financial support:* Teaching assistantships available. *Faculty research:* British, Canadian, and American literature. *Unit head:* Robert Schwartzwald, Director, 514-343-7926, Fax: 514-343-6443, E-mail: robert.schwartzwald@umontreal.ca. *Application contact:* Heike Harting, Information Contact, 514-343-6192, Fax: 514-343-6443, E-mail: heike.harting@umontreal.ca.

Université Laval, Faculty of Letters, Department of Literature, Programs in Ancient Civilization, Québec, QC G1K 7P4, Canada. Offers MA, PhD. Part-time programs available. Terminal master's awarded for partial completion of doctoral program. *Degree requirements:* For master's, thesis; for doctorate, comprehensive exam, thesis/dissertation. *Entrance requirements:* For master's and doctorate, English test (comprehension of written English), knowledge of French, knowledge of an ancient language. Electronic applications accepted.

Université Laval, Faculty of Letters, Department of Literature, Programs in English Literatures, Québec, QC G1K 7P4, Canada. Offers MA, PhD. Part-time programs available. Terminal master's awarded for partial completion of doctoral program. *Degree requirements:* For master's, thesis (for some programs); for doctorate, comprehensive exam, thesis/dissertation. *Entrance requirements:* For master's, French exam, knowledge of English; for doctorate, French exam, knowledge of English, knowledge of a third language. Electronic applications accepted.

University at Albany, State University of New York, College of Arts and Sciences, Department of English, Albany, NY 12222-0001. Offers MA, PhD. *Students:* 50 full-time (18 women), 47 part-time (28 women). Average age 34. In 2007, 24 master's, 4 doctorates awarded. *Degree requirements:* For master's, one foreign language; for doctorate, one foreign language, comprehensive exam, thesis/dissertation, residency. *Entrance requirements:* For master's and doctorate, GRE General Test, GRE Subject Test. Additional exam requirements/recommendations for international students: Required—TOEFL (minimum score 550 paper-based; 213 computer-based). *Application deadline:* For fall admission, 6/15 for domestic students, 1/15 for international students; for spring admission, 11/1 for international students. Applications are processed on a rolling basis. Application fee: $75. Electronic applications accepted. *Expenses:* Tuition, state resident: part-time $576 per credit. Tuition, nonresident: part-time $910 per credit. Tuition and fees vary according to program. *Financial support:* Fellowships, career-related internships or fieldwork available. Financial award application deadline: 2/15. *Faculty research:* Women playwrights; critical literary theory; poetry and poetics; media history, writing and reporting; creative non-fiction. *Unit head:* Michael Hill, Chair, 518-442-4056.

University at Buffalo, the State University of New York, Graduate School, College of Arts and Sciences, Department of English, Buffalo, NY 14260. Offers MA, PhD. Part-time programs available. Terminal master's awarded for partial completion of doctoral program. *Degree requirements:* For master's, thesis or alternative; for doctorate, thesis/dissertation, departmental qualifying exam. *Entrance requirements:* For master's and doctorate, GRE General Test, sample of written work. Additional exam requirements/recommendations for international students: Required—TOEFL. Electronic applications accepted. *Faculty research:* Psychoanalysis, early modern British literature, poetics, 19th century American literature.

The University of Akron, Graduate School, Buchtel College of Arts and Sciences, Department of English, Akron, OH 44325. Offers composition (MA); creative writing (MFA); literature (MA). Part-time programs available. *Faculty:* 19 full-time (8 women), 1 part-time/adjunct (0 women). *Students:* 39 full-time (22 women), 32 part-time (20 women); includes 4 minority (3 African Americans, 1 Hispanic American), 1 international. Average age 35. 44 applicants, 89% accepted, 26 enrolled. In 2007, 14 master's awarded. *Degree requirements:* For master's, thesis optional. *Entrance requirements:* For master's, BA in English, minimum GPA of 2.75, writing portfolio, letters of recommendation. Additional exam requirements/recommendations for international students: Required—TOEFL (minimum score 580 paper-based; 237 computer-based; 92 iBT). *Application deadline:* For fall admission, 2/15 priority date for domestic students; for spring admission, 10/15 priority date for domestic students. Applications are processed on a rolling basis. Application fee: $30 ($40 for international students). Electronic applications accepted. *Expenses:* Tuition, state resident: full-time $6,164; part-time $342 per credit. Tuition, nonresident: full-time $10,575; part-time $588 per credit. Required fees: $806; $43 per credit. $12 per term. Tuition and fees vary according to course load, degree level and program. *Financial support:* In 2007–08, 6 research assistantships with full tuition reimbursements, 17 teaching assistantships with full tuition reimbursements were awarded; scholarships/grants and unspecified assistantships also available. *Faculty research:* British and American literary studies, literary theory, creative writing, applied linguistics. Total annual research expenditures: $29,305. *Unit head:* Dr. Diana Reep, Chair, 330-972-6873, E-mail: dreep@uakron.edu. *Application contact:* Dr. Hillary Nunn, Director of Graduate Studies, 330-972-7601, E-mail: nunn@uakron.edu.

The University of Alabama, Graduate School, College of Arts and Sciences, Department of English, Tuscaloosa, AL 35487. Offers composition and rhetoric (PhD); creative writing (MFA), including fiction, poetry; literature (MA, PhD); rhetoric and composition (MA); teaching English as a second language (MATESOL). *Faculty:* 30 full-time (12 women). *Students:* 119 full-time (66 women), 16 part-time (12 women); includes 18 minority (11 African Americans, 2 American Indian/Alaska Native, 3 Asian Americans or Pacific Islanders, 2 Hispanic Americans), 7 international. Average age 28. 252 applicants, 20% accepted, 31 enrolled. In 2007, 28 master's, 7 doctorates awarded. *Median time to degree:* Of those who began their doctoral program in fall 1999, 100% received their degree in 8 years or less. *Degree requirements:* For master's, one foreign language, comprehensive exam, thesis (for some programs); for doctorate, 2 foreign languages, comprehensive exam, thesis/dissertation. *Entrance requirements:* For master's and doctorate, GRE, minimum GPA of 3.0, critical writing sample. Additional exam requirements/recommendations for international students: Required—TOEFL. *Application deadline:* For fall admission, 1/15 priority date for domestic students, 1/15 for international students. Application fee: $30. Electronic applications accepted. *Expenses:* Tuition, state resident: full-time $5,700. Tuition, nonresident: full-time $16,518. *Financial support:* In 2007–08, 7 fellowships with full tuition reimbursements (averaging $15,000 per year), 1 research assistantship (averaging $11,708 per year), 106 teaching assistantships with full tuition reimbursements (averaging $11,708 per year) were awarded; career-related internships or fieldwork, scholarships/grants, health care benefits, and unspecified assistantships also available. Financial award application deadline: 1/15. *Faculty research:* Critical theory; modern, Renaissance, and African-American literature. *Unit head:* Dr. Catherine E. Davies, Director of Graduate Studies, 205-348-8499, E-mail: cdavies@bama.ua.edu. *Application contact:* Vernita W. James, Office Assistant II, 205-348-0766, Fax: 205-348-1388, E-mail: vwjames@bama.ua.edu.

The University of Alabama at Birmingham, School of Arts and Humanities, Department of English, Birmingham, AL 35294. Offers MA. *Students:* 17 full-time (7 women), 31 part-time (19 women). Average age 33. 18 applicants, 61% accepted. In 2007, 10 degrees awarded. *Degree requirements:* For master's, one foreign language, comprehensive exam, thesis optional. *Entrance requirements:* For master's, GRE General Test or MAT, minimum GPA of 2.75. *Application deadline:* Applications are processed on a rolling basis. Application fee: $35 ($60 for international students). Electronic applications accepted. *Financial support:* Teaching assistantships, career-related internships or fieldwork available. *Unit head:* Dr. Peter J. Bellis, Chair, 205-934-4083, Fax: 205-975-6610.

The University of Alabama in Huntsville, School of Graduate Studies, College of Liberal Arts, Department of English, Huntsville, AL 35899. Offers English (MA); teaching of English to speakers of other languages (Certificate); technical communications (Certificate). Part-time and evening/weekend programs available. *Faculty:* 17 full-time (9 women). *Students:* 25 full-time (20 women), 50 part-time (34 women); includes 12 minority (9 African Americans, 1 American Indian/Alaska Native, 2 Hispanic Americans), 1 international. Average age 33. 49 applicants, 80% accepted, 32 enrolled. In 2007, 11 master's, 9 other advanced degrees awarded. *Degree requirements:* For master's, one foreign language, comprehensive exam, thesis or alternative, oral and written exams. *Entrance requirements:* For master's, GRE General Test, minimum GPA of 3.0. Additional exam requirements/recommendations for international students: Required—TOEFL (minimum score 500 paper-based; 173 computer-based; 62 iBT). *Application deadline:* For fall admission, 7/18 for domestic students, 4/1 for international students; for spring admission, 11/30 for domestic students, 9/1 for international students. Applications are processed on a rolling basis. Application fee: $40 ($50 for international students). Electronic applications accepted. *Expenses:* Tuition, state resident: full-time $6,548; part-time $276 per credit hour. Tuition, nonresident: full-time $13,466; part-time $565 per credit hour. *Financial support:* In 2007–08, 10 students received support, including 7 teaching assistantships with full and partial tuition reimbursements available (averaging $8,357 per year); fellowships with full and partial tuition reimbursements available, research assistantships with full and partial tuition reimbursements available, career-related internships or fieldwork, Federal Work-Study, institutionally sponsored loans, scholarships/grants, health care benefits, and unspecified assistantships also available. Support available to part-time students. Financial award application deadline: 4/1; financial award applicants required to submit FAFSA. *Faculty research:* American and British literature, linguistics, technical writing, women's studies, rhetoric. *Unit head:* Dr. Rose Norman, Chair, 256-824-6320, Fax: 256-824-6949, E-mail: normanr@uah.edu.

University of Alaska Anchorage, College of Arts and Sciences, Department of English, Anchorage, AK 99508-8060. Offers MA. Part-time programs available. *Degree requirements:*

For master's, comprehensive exam, thesis or alternative. *Entrance requirements:* For master's, GRE General Test, GRE Subject Test, portfolio, minimum GPA of 3.5, writing sample. Additional exam requirements/recommendations for international students: Required—TOEFL (minimum score 550 paper-based; 213 computer-based). *Faculty research:* The rhetoric of essays, American and American Indian literature, linguistics, Shakespeare, literature of war.

University of Alaska Fairbanks, College of Liberal Arts, Department of English, Fairbanks, AK 99775-7520. Offers creative writing (MFA); English (MA). Part-time programs available. *Degree requirements:* For master's, comprehensive exam, thesis or alternative, oral exams. *Entrance requirements:* For master's, GRE General Test. Additional exam requirements/ recommendations for international students: Required—TOEFL (minimum score 550 paper-based; 213 computer-based). Electronic applications accepted. *Faculty research:* Traditional Alaskan native literature, British literature, pedagogy, American literature, rhetoric/ composition history.

University of Alberta, Faculty of Graduate Studies and Research, Department of English and Film Studies, Edmonton, AB T6G 2E1, Canada. Offers English (MA, PhD). Part-time and evening/weekend programs available. *Degree requirements:* For master's, one foreign language, thesis optional; for doctorate, 2 foreign languages, thesis/dissertation. *Entrance requirements:* For master's, honors BA or equivalent; for doctorate, honors BA and MA. Additional exam requirements/recommendations for international students: Required—TOEFL (minimum score 600 paper-based). Electronic applications accepted. *Faculty research:* Women's writing, postcolonial theory, Victorian literature, Renaissance literature, Canadian literature.

The University of Arizona, Graduate College, College of Humanities, Department of English, Tucson, AZ 85721. Offers creative writing (MFA); English (MA, PhD); rhetoric, composition and the teaching of English (MA, PhD). Part-time programs available. *Faculty:* 51 full-time, 1 part-time/adjunct. *Students:* 153 full-time (91 women), 55 part-time (35 women); includes 27 minority (4 African Americans, 4 American Indian/Alaska Native, 4 Asian Americans or Pacific Islanders, 15 Hispanic Americans), 5 international. Average age 32. 95 applicants, 62% accepted, 59 enrolled. In 2007, 51 master's, 7 doctorates awarded. Terminal master's awarded for partial completion of doctoral program. *Degree requirements:* For master's, one foreign language, comprehensive exam; for doctorate, one foreign language, comprehensive exam, thesis/dissertation, preliminary and qualifying exams. *Entrance requirements:* For master's, GRE General Test, GRE Subject Test, sample of written work, 3 letters of recommendation, minimum GPA of 3.0, statement of purpose; for doctorate, GRE General Test, GRE Subject Test (literature), sample of written work, 3 letters of recommendation, minimum GPA of 3.0, statement of purpose. Additional exam requirements/recommendations for international students: Required—TOEFL (minimum score 550 paper-based). *Application deadline:* Applications are processed on a rolling basis. Application fee: $50. Electronic applications accepted. *Financial support:* In 2007–08, 12 fellowships with partial tuition reimbursements (averaging $3,000 per year), 120 teaching assistantships with partial tuition reimbursements (averaging $27,000 per year) were awarded; research assistantships with partial tuition reimbursements, career-related internships or fieldwork, scholarships/grants, health care benefits, tuition waivers (full and partial), and unspecified assistantships also available. *Faculty research:* Literature, women's studies, Southwestern literature, feminist theory. Total annual research expenditures: $207,754. *Unit head:* Dr. Jun Lin, Head, 520-621-3287, E-mail: junliu@email.arizona.edu. *Application contact:* Marcia Marma, Graduate Secretary, 520-621-1358, E-mail: mmarma@u.arizona.edu.

University of Arkansas, Graduate School, J. William Fulbright College of Arts and Sciences, Department of English, Program in English, Fayetteville, AR 72701-1201. Offers MA, PhD. *Students:* 14 full-time (10 women), 56 part-time (31 women); includes 3 minority (2 African Americans, 1 American Indian/Alaska Native), 1 international. In 2007, 11 master's awarded. *Degree requirements:* For master's, thesis; for doctorate, thesis/dissertation. *Entrance requirements:* For master's, GRE General Test; for doctorate, GRE General Test, GRE Subject Test. Application fee: $40 ($50 for international students). *Financial support:* In 2007–08, 10 fellowships with tuition reimbursements, 1 research assistantship, 42 teaching assistantships were awarded; career-related internships or fieldwork and Federal Work-Study also available. Support available to part-time students. Financial award application deadline: 4/1; financial award applicants required to submit FAFSA. *Faculty research:* Creative writing, seventeenth century literature, twentieth century literature, American literature. *Application contact:* Dr. Keith Booker, Graduate Coordinator, 479-575-4301, Fax: 479-575-5919, E-mail: kbooker@uark.edu.

The University of British Columbia, Faculty of Arts and Faculty of Graduate Studies, Department of English, Vancouver, BC V6T 1Z1, Canada. Offers MA, PhD. *Faculty:* 51 full-time (27 women). *Students:* 103 full-time (64 women). Average age 34. 241 applicants, 24% accepted, 24 enrolled. In 2007, 19 master's, 4 doctorates awarded. *Degree requirements:* For master's, thesis or alternative, non-thesis 30 credits, with thesis 21 credits; for doctorate, one foreign language, comprehensive exam, thesis/dissertation. *Entrance requirements:* For master's, 4 year BA; for doctorate, MA. Additional exam requirements/recommendations for international students: Required—TOEFL (minimum score 615 paper-based; 258 computer-based; 104 iBT), IELTS (minimum score 8). *Application deadline:* For fall admission, 1/15 for domestic and international students. Application fee: $90 Canadian dollars ($150 Canadian dollars for international students). Electronic applications accepted. *Financial support:* In 2007–08, 86 students received support, including fellowships (averaging $16,000 per year), research assistantships (averaging $4,000 per year), 50 teaching assistantships; tuition waivers (full) also available. *Faculty research:* English, American, Canadian, and Commonwealth post-colonial literature; English language; rhetoric. *Unit head:* Dr. Dennis Danielson, Head, 604-822-3174, Fax: 604-822-6906, E-mail: danielso@interchange.ubc.ca. *Application contact:* Dr. Mark Vessey, Graduate Chair and Associate Head, 604-822-5301, Fax: 604-822-6906, E-mail: mvessey@interchange.ubc.ca.

The University of British Columbia, Faculty of Arts, School of Library, Archival and Information Studies, Children's Literature Program, Vancouver, BC V6T 1Z1, Canada. Offers MA. Part-time programs available. *Faculty:* 1 (woman) full-time, 1 (woman) part-time/adjunct. *Students:* 15 full-time (14 women), 2 part-time (both women). Average age 31. 16 applicants, 50% accepted, 6 enrolled. In 2007, 8 degrees awarded. *Degree requirements:* For master's, thesis. *Entrance requirements:* For master's, minimum GPA of 3.3 in undergraduate upper-division courses. Additional exam requirements/recommendations for international students: Required—TOEFL (minimum score 600 paper-based; 250 computer-based; 100 iBT). *Application deadline:* For fall admission, 2/1 for domestic and international students. Application fee: $90 Canadian dollars ($150 Canadian dollars for international students). Electronic applications accepted. *Financial support:* In 2007–08, 5 students received support; fellowships, research assistantships, Federal Work-Study, institutionally sponsored loans, scholarships/grants, health care benefits, tuition waivers (partial), and unspecified assistantships available. *Faculty research:* Language and literacy education; writing children's literature; teaching children's literature. *Application contact:* Graduate Admissions Secretary, 604-822-2404, Fax: 604-822-6006, E-mail: slais.admissions@ubc.ca.

University of Calgary, Faculty of Graduate Studies, Faculty of Humanities, Department of English, Calgary, AB T2N 1N4, Canada. Offers MA, PhD. Part-time programs available. *Faculty:* 34 full-time (22 women). *Students:* 64 full-time (38 women); includes 1 American Indian/Alaska Native, 8 international. Average age 27. 88 applicants, 40% accepted, 18 enrolled. In 2007, 11 master's, 3 doctorates awarded. *Degree requirements:* For master's, one foreign language, comprehensive exam (for some programs), thesis; for doctorate, one foreign language, thesis/dissertation, candidacy exam. *Entrance requirements:* Additional exam requirements/recommendations for international students: Required—TOEFL (minimum score 600 paper-based; 250 computer-based). *Application deadline:* For winter admission, 1/10 for domestic and international students. Application fee: $100 ($130 for international students). Electronic applications accepted. *Financial support:* In 2007–08, 12 fellowships (averaging $8,150 per year), 30 research assistantships (averaging $4,100 per year), 35 teaching assistantships (averaging $7,020 per year) were awarded. Financial award application deadline: 2/1. *Faculty research:* Various national and period literatures, creative writing, literary theory, gender and women's studies, postcolonial literatures. *Unit head:* Dr. Susan A. Rudy, Head, 403-220-6572, Fax: 403-289-1123, E-mail: srudy@ucalgary.ca. *Application contact:* Barb H. Howe, Graduate Program Administrator, 403-220-5484, Fax: 403-289-1123, E-mail: enggrad@ucalgary.ca.

University of California, Berkeley, Graduate Division, College of Letters and Science, Department of English, Berkeley, CA 94720-1500. Offers PhD. In 2007, 30 degrees awarded. *Degree requirements:* For doctorate, 2 foreign languages, thesis/dissertation, qualifying exam. *Entrance requirements:* For doctorate, GRE General Test, GRE Subject Test, minimum GPA of 3.0, writing sample, 3 letters of recommendation. *Application deadline:* For fall admission, 12/10 for domestic students. Application fee: $70 ($90 for international students). *Financial support:* Fellowships, research assistantships, teaching assistantships, Federal Work-Study, institutionally sponsored loans, scholarships/grants, tuition waivers (partial), and unspecified assistantships available. Financial award applicants required to submit FAFSA. *Unit head:* Ian Duncan, Chair, 510-642-3877, E-mail: iduncan@berkeley.edu. *Application contact:* Doreen L. Barton, Graduate Assistant, 510-642-4005, Fax: 510-642-8738, E-mail: dlbarton@berkeley.edu.

University of California, Davis, Graduate Studies, Program in English, Davis, CA 95616. Offers creative writing (MA); English (MA, PhD). Terminal master's awarded for partial completion of doctoral program. *Degree requirements:* For master's, one foreign language, thesis optional; for doctorate, 2 foreign languages, thesis/dissertation. *Entrance requirements:* For master's and doctorate, GRE General Test, GRE Subject Test, minimum GPA of 3.0, writing sample. Additional exam requirements/recommendations for international students: Required—TOEFL (minimum score 550 paper-based; 213 computer-based). Electronic applications accepted. *Faculty research:* Feminist theory, ethnic literature, literary theory, history of literature, literature of nature.

University of California, Irvine, Office of Graduate Studies, School of Humanities, Department of English and Comparative Literature, English Summer Program, Irvine, CA 92697. Offers MA. Offered during summer only. *Faculty:* 8 full-time (2 women). *Students:* Average age 31. 35 applicants, 57% accepted, 18 enrolled. *Degree requirements:* For master's, thesis. *Entrance requirements:* For master's, GRE General Test, GRE Subject Test, writing sample, 3 letters of recommendation. *Application deadline:* For fall admission, 3/15 priority date for domestic students. Application fee: $60. Electronic applications accepted. *Expenses:* Contact institution. *Financial support:* Institutionally sponsored loans available. Financial award application deadline: 3/2; financial award applicants required to submit FAFSA. *Faculty research:* Shakespeare, American multiculturalism, literary theory. *Unit head:* Dr. Richard Kroll, Director, 949-824-2557, Fax: 949-824-2916, E-mail: rwkroll@uci.edu. *Application contact:* Kitty Roos, Graduate Administrator, 949-824-6714, Fax: 949-824-2916, E-mail: kroos@uci.edu.

University of California, Irvine, Office of Graduate Studies, School of Humanities, Department of English and Comparative Literature, Program in English, Irvine, CA 92697. Offers English (MA); English and American literature (PhD). *Faculty:* 21 full-time (9 women), 2 part-time/ adjunct (1 woman). *Students:* 96 full-time (49 women); includes 15 minority (10 Asian Americans or Pacific Islanders, 5 Hispanic Americans), 1 international. Average age 31. 168 applicants, 20% accepted, 17 enrolled. In 2007, 33 master's, 10 doctorates awarded. Terminal master's awarded for partial completion of doctoral program. *Degree requirements:* For master's, one foreign language, comprehensive exam; for doctorate, 2 foreign languages, comprehensive exam, thesis/dissertation. *Entrance requirements:* For doctorate, GRE General Test, GRE Subject Test, minimum GPA of 3.5, sample of written work, 3 letters of recommendation. Additional exam requirements/recommendations for international students: Required—TOEFL (minimum score 550 paper-based; 213 computer-based). *Application deadline:* For fall admission, 1/15 for domestic students. Application fee: $60. Electronic applications accepted. *Financial support:* In 2007–08, 75 students received support, including 30 fellowships with full tuition reimbursements available (averaging $14,000 per year), 3 research assistantships (averaging $15,000 per year), 41 teaching assistantships with partial tuition reimbursements available (averaging $14,145 per year); institutionally sponsored loans, health care benefits, tuition waivers (full and partial), and unspecified assistantships also available. Financial award application deadline: 3/2; financial award applicants required to submit FAFSA. *Faculty research:* Critical theory, literary history, cultural studies. *Unit head:* Chair, 949-824-4857, Fax: 949-824-2916. *Application contact:* Nancy Benay, Graduate Administrator, 949-824-4857, Fax: 949-824-2916, E-mail: ndbenay@uci.edu.

University of California, Los Angeles, Graduate Division, College of Letters and Science, Department of English, Los Angeles, CA 90095. Offers MA, PhD. *Students:* 93 full-time (51 women); includes 24 minority (7 African Americans, 9 Asian Americans or Pacific Islanders, 8 Hispanic Americans), 2 international. Average age 29. 329 applicants, 11% accepted, 14 enrolled. In 2007, 10 master's, 10 doctorates awarded. Terminal master's awarded for partial completion of doctoral program. *Median time to degree:* Of those who began their doctoral program in fall 1999, 25% received their degree in 8 years or less. *Degree requirements:* For master's, comprehensive exam or thesis; for doctorate, 2 foreign languages, thesis/dissertation, oral and written qualifying exams. *Entrance requirements:* For master's, GRE General Test, GRE Subject Test (literature), minimum GPA of 3.0, sample of written work, degree objective of Ph.D; for doctorate, GRE General Test, GRE Subject Test (literature), minimum GPA of 3.5 (undergraduate), 3.7 (graduate), sample of written work. *Application deadline:* For fall admission, 12/15 for domestic students. Application fee: $60. Electronic applications accepted. *Expenses:* Tuition, nonresident: full-time $5,728. Required fees: $8,966. Full-time tuition and fees vary according to program and student level. *Financial support:* In 2007–08, 62 fellowships with full and partial tuition reimbursements, 19 research assistantships with full and partial tuition reimbursements, 64 teaching assistantships with full and partial tuition reimbursements were awarded; Federal Work-Study, institutionally sponsored loans, scholarships/grants, and tuition waivers (full and partial) also available. Financial award application deadline: 3/1; financial award applicants required to submit FAFSA. *Unit head:* Dr. Rafael Perez-Torrez, Chair, 310-825-3927. *Application contact:* Departmental Office, 310-825-3927, E-mail: graduate@english.ucla.edu.

University of California, Riverside, Graduate Division, Department of English, Riverside, CA 92521-0102. Offers MA, PhD. *Faculty:* 27 full-time (15 women). *Students:* 86 full-time (57 women); includes 20 minority (3 African Americans, 1 American Indian/Alaska Native, 10 Asian Americans or Pacific Islanders, 6 Hispanic Americans), 3 international. Average age 31. In 2007, 5 master's, 11 doctorates awarded. *Degree requirements:* For master's, one foreign language, comprehensive exam; for doctorate, 2 foreign languages, thesis/dissertation, qualifying exams. *Entrance requirements:* For master's and doctorate, GRE General Test, minimum GPA of 3.5. Additional exam requirements/recommendations for international students: Required—TOEFL (minimum score 550 paper-based; 213 computer-based; 80 iBT). *Application deadline:* For fall admission, 5/1 for domestic students, 2/1 priority date for international students. Applications are processed on a rolling basis. Application fee: $60 ($75 for international students). Electronic applications accepted. *Financial support:* In 2007–08, fellowships with full and partial tuition reimbursements (averaging $12,000 per year), teaching assistantships with partial tuition reimbursements (averaging $16,500 per year) were awarded; research assistantships with tuition reimbursements, career-related internships or fieldwork, Federal Work-Study, institutionally sponsored loans, and tuition waivers (full and partial) also available. Financial award application deadline: 12/10; financial award applicants required to submit FAFSA. *Faculty research:* Critical theory, cultural and film studies, lesbian and gay studies, minority and feminist discourses, rhetoric and composition. *Unit head:* Dr. Katherine Kinney, Chair, 951-827-1458, Fax: 951-827-3967, E-mail: katherine.kinney@ucr.edu. *Application contact:* Tina M. Feldmann, Graduate Program Assistant, 951-827-1454, Fax: 951-827-3967, E-mail: english@ucr.edu.

University of California, San Diego, Office of Graduate Studies, Department of Literature, Program in Literatures in English, La Jolla, CA 92093. Offers MA. *Degree requirements:* For

English

University of California, San Diego (continued)
master's, thesis. *Entrance requirements:* For master's, GRE General Test, GRE Subject Test. Electronic applications accepted.

University of California, Santa Barbara, Graduate Division, College of Letters and Sciences, Division of Humanities and Fine Arts, Department of English, Santa Barbara, CA 93106. Offers English literature (PhD); MA/PhD. *Faculty:* 92 full-time (52 women). *Students:* 80 full-time (46 women); includes 11 minority (2 African Americans, 1 American Indian/Alaska Native, 4 Asian Americans or Pacific Islanders, 4 Hispanic Americans), 2 international. Average age 31. 186 applicants, 17% accepted, 12 enrolled. In 2007, 5 doctorates awarded. Terminal master's awarded for partial completion of doctoral program. *Median time to degree:* Of those who began their doctoral program in fall 1999, 33% received their degree in 8 years or less. *Degree requirements:* For doctorate, one foreign language, comprehensive exam, thesis/dissertation, 24 units of graded graduate coursework. *Entrance requirements:* For doctorate, GRE General Test, GRE Subject Test, sample of written work, 3 letters of recommendation. Additional exam requirements/recommendations for international students: Required—TOEFL (minimum score 550 paper-based; 213 computer-based; 80 iBT). *Application deadline:* For fall admission, 1/1 for domestic and international students. Application fee: $60. Electronic applications accepted. *Expenses:* Tuition, nonresident: full-time $14,888. Required fees: $10,108. *Financial support:* In 2007–08, 77 students received support, including 25 fellowships with full and partial tuition reimbursements available (averaging $9,900 per year), 30 teaching assistantships with full and partial tuition reimbursements available (averaging $15,611 per year); Federal Work-Study, institutionally sponsored loans, scholarships/grants, health care benefits, tuition waivers (full and partial), and unspecified assistantships also available. Financial award application deadline: 1/1; financial award applicants required to submit FAFSA. *Faculty research:* Renaissance literature, 18th century British literature, American literature, race and ethnic studies, literature and theory of technology/media/information. *Unit head:* Prof. William Warner, Chair, 805-893-8711. *Application contact:* Susan Gosling, Graduate Program Advisor, 805-893-2639, Fax: 805-893-4622, E-mail: gosling@english.ucsb.edu.

University of California, Santa Cruz, Division of Graduate Studies, Division of Humanities, Department of Literature, Santa Cruz, CA 95064. Offers MA, PhD. *Faculty:* 33 full-time (15 women). *Students:* 86. 150 applicants, 16% accepted. In 2007, 3 master's, 4 doctorates awarded. Terminal master's awarded for partial completion of doctoral program. *Degree requirements:* For master's, thesis; for doctorate, one foreign language, thesis/dissertation, qualifying exam. *Entrance requirements:* For master's, GRE General Test, writing sample, minimum GPA of 3.5; for doctorate, GRE General Test, minimum GPA of 3.5, writing sample. *Application deadline:* For fall admission, 12/1 for domestic students. Application fee: $60. Electronic applications accepted. *Expenses:* Tuition, nonresident: full-time $14,694. Required fees: $11,360. *Financial support:* Fellowships, teaching assistantships, Federal Work-Study and institutionally sponsored loans available. Financial award application deadline: 12/1. *Faculty research:* Comparative literature; German, Spanish, classical, American, and English literature. *Unit head:* Mary-Kay Gamel, Chairperson, 831-459-4129, E-mail: mkgamel@ucsc.edu. *Application contact:* Judy L. Glass, Reporting Analyst for Graduate Admissions, 831-459-5906, Fax: 831-459-4843, E-mail: jlglass@ucsc.edu.

University of Central Arkansas, Graduate School, College of Liberal Arts, Department of English, Conway, AR 72035-0001. Offers MA. Part-time programs available. *Faculty:* 17 full-time (2 women). *Students:* 19 full-time (14 women), 7 part-time (4 women); includes 2 minority (both African Americans) 16 applicants, 88% accepted, 14 enrolled. In 2007, 6 degrees awarded. *Degree requirements:* For master's, comprehensive exam, thesis optional. *Entrance requirements:* For master's, GRE General Test, minimum GPA of 2.7. Additional exam requirements/recommendations for international students: Required—TOEFL (minimum score 550 paper-based; 213 computer-based). *Application deadline:* For fall admission, 3/1 priority date for domestic and international students; for spring admission, 10/1 priority date for domestic and international students. Applications are processed on a rolling basis. Application fee: $25 ($50 for international students). *Expenses:* Tuition, state resident: full-time $4,513; part-time $240 per credit. Tuition, nonresident: full-time $8,805; part-time $440 per credit. International tuition: $9,700 full-time. Required fees: $100 per term. *Financial support:* Federal Work-Study, scholarships/grants, and unspecified assistantships available. Financial award application deadline: 2/15; financial award applicants required to submit FAFSA. *Faculty research:* Writing project. *Unit head:* Dr. Jay Ruud, Chairperson, 501-450-5100, Fax: 501-450-5102, E-mail: jruud@uca.edu. *Application contact:* Brenda Herring, Admissions Assistant, 501-450-5065, Fax: 501-450-5678, E-mail: bherring@uca.edu.

University of Central Florida, College of Arts and Humanities, Department of English, Program in English, Orlando, FL 32816. Offers creative writing (MFA); English (MA). *Expenses:* Tuition, state resident: full-time $6,484. Tuition, nonresident: full-time $23,938. Tuition and fees vary according to program. *Financial support:* Fellowships, research assistantships, teaching assistantships available.

University of Central Missouri, The Graduate School, College of Arts, Humanities and Social Sciences, Department of English and Philosophy, Warrensburg, MO 64093. Offers English (MA); teaching English as a second language (MA). Part-time programs available. *Faculty:* 19 full-time (5 women). *Students:* 13 full-time (9 women), 27 part-time (20 women); includes 2 minority (1 Asian American or Pacific Islander, 1 Hispanic American), 5 international. Average age 31. 18 applicants, 78% accepted, 9 enrolled. In 2007, 21 degrees awarded. *Degree requirements:* For master's, comprehensive exam. *Entrance requirements:* For master's, minimum GPA of 2.75 overall and in major, 18 hours of course work in English. Additional exam requirements/recommendations for international students: Required—TOEFL (minimum score 500 paper-based; 173 computer-based). *Application deadline:* For fall admission, 6/1 priority date for domestic students, 5/1 priority date for international students; for spring admission, 10/1 priority date for domestic students, 10/1 for international students. Applications are processed on a rolling basis. Application fee: $30 ($50 for international students). *Expenses:* Tuition, state resident: full-time $6,259; part-time $256 per credit hour. Tuition, nonresident: full-time $11,915; part-time $491 per credit hour. Required fees: $604; $20 per credit hour. *Financial support:* In 2007–08, 12 students received support; teaching assistantships with full and partial tuition reimbursements available, Federal Work-Study, scholarships/grants, unspecified assistantships, and administrative and laboratory assistantships available. Support available to part-time students. Financial award application deadline: 3/1; financial award applicants required to submit FAFSA. *Unit head:* Dr. Cheryl Eason, Chair, 660-543-4425, Fax: 660-543-8544, E-mail: eason@ucmo.edu.

University of Central Oklahoma, College of Graduate Studies and Research, College of Liberal Arts, Department of English, Edmond, OK 73034-5209. Offers composition skills (MA); contemporary literature (MA); creative writing (MA); teaching English as a second language (MA); traditional studies (MA). Part-time programs available. *Faculty:* 18 full-time (9 women), 5 part-time/adjunct (2 women). *Students:* 31 full-time (16 women), 57 part-time (42 women); includes 11 minority (6 African Americans, 2 Asian Americans or Pacific Islanders, 3 Hispanic Americans), 3 international. Average age 33. 25 applicants, 100% accepted. In 2007, 17 degrees awarded. *Degree requirements:* For master's, one foreign language. *Entrance requirements:* For master's, 24 hours of course work in English language and literature. Additional exam requirements/recommendations for international students: Required—TOEFL (minimum score 550 paper-based; 213 computer-based). *Application deadline:* For fall admission, 7/1 for international students; for spring admission, 11/1 for international students. Applications are processed on a rolling basis. Application fee: $25. Electronic applications accepted. *Expenses:* Tuition, state resident: full-time $3,516; part-time $147 per hour. Tuition, nonresident: full-time $9,054; part-time $377 per hour. Required fees: $433; $18 per hour. *Financial support:* In 2007–08, 6 teaching assistantships with partial tuition reimbursements were awarded; career-related internships or fieldwork, Federal Work-Study, and unspecified assistantships also available. Financial award application deadline: 3/31; financial award applicants required to submit FAFSA. *Faculty research:* John Milton, Harriet Beecher Stowe. *Unit head:* Dr. David Macey, Chairman, 405-974-5894, Fax: 405-974-3823. *Application contact:* Dr. Kurt Hochenauer, Director, 405-974-5607 Ext. 5607, Fax: 405-974-3823.

University of Chicago, Division of the Humanities, Department of English Language and Literature, Chicago, IL 60637-1513. Offers AM, PhD. *Students:* 124. 477 applicants, 6% accepted, 14 enrolled. *Degree requirements:* For master's, one foreign language, thesis; for doctorate, 2 foreign languages, thesis/dissertation. *Entrance requirements:* For master's and doctorate, GRE General Test, GRE Subject Test (English). Additional exam requirements/recommendations for international students: Required—TOEFL. *Application deadline:* For fall admission, 12/15 for domestic students. Application fee: $55. *Financial support:* Fellowships, Federal Work-Study available. Financial award application deadline: 12/15; financial award applicants required to submit FAFSA. *Unit head:* Dr. Jay Schleusener, Chair, 773-702-8536.

University of Cincinnati, Graduate School, McMicken College of Arts and Sciences, Department of English, Cincinnati, OH 45221. Offers MA, MAT, PhD. Part-time programs available. *Faculty:* 41 full-time (14 women). *Students:* 65 full-time (41 women), 19 part-time (15 women); includes 3 minority (1 African American, 1 Asian American or Pacific Islander, 1 Hispanic American), 3 international. Average age 27. 166 applicants, 92% accepted, 37 enrolled. In 2007, 20 master's, 5 doctorates awarded. Terminal master's awarded for partial completion of doctoral program. *Median time to degree:* Of those who began their doctoral program in fall 1999, 90% received their degree in 8 years or less. *Degree requirements:* For master's, one foreign language, thesis (for some programs); for doctorate, 2 foreign languages, thesis/dissertation. *Entrance requirements:* For master's, GRE General Test, letters of recommendation (3), writing samples; for doctorate, GRE General Test, GRE Subject Test, letters of recommendation (3), writing samples. Additional exam requirements/recommendations for international students: Required—TOEFL. *Application deadline:* For fall admission, 2/1 priority date for domestic and international students. Applications are processed on a rolling basis. Application fee: $40. Electronic applications accepted. *Financial support:* In 2007–08, 59 students received support, including 4 fellowships with full tuition reimbursements available (averaging $18,000 per year), 44 teaching assistantships with full tuition reimbursements available (averaging $11,000 per year); career-related internships or fieldwork, scholarships/grants, health care benefits, tuition waivers (partial), unspecified assistantships, and editorial assistantships also available. Financial award application deadline: 2/1. *Faculty research:* Literature/theory, creative writing, composition, professional writing/editing, linguistics. Total annual research expenditures: $161,900. *Unit head:* Leland S. Person, Head, 513-556-3901, Fax: 513-556-5960, E-mail: leland.person@uc.edu. *Application contact:* Jonathan Z. Kamholtz, Graduate Program Director, 513-556-3905, Fax: 513-556-5960, E-mail: jonathan.kamholtz@uc.edu.

University of Colorado at Boulder, Graduate School, College of Arts and Sciences, Department of English, Boulder, CO 80309. Offers literature (MA, PhD), including creative writing (MA). Part-time programs available. *Faculty:* 41. *Students:* 101 full-time (62 women), 23 part-time (15 women); includes 18 minority (2 African Americans, 5 Asian Americans or Pacific Islanders, 11 Hispanic Americans), 4 international. Average age 30. 43 applicants, 81% accepted. In 2007, 20 master's, 4 doctorates awarded. *Degree requirements:* For master's, one foreign language, comprehensive exam, thesis or alternative; for doctorate, 2 foreign languages, comprehensive exam, thesis/dissertation. *Entrance requirements:* For master's, GRE General Test, GRE Subject Test, minimum undergraduate GPA of 3.0; for doctorate, GRE General Test, GRE Subject Test. *Application deadline:* For fall admission, 1/1 for domestic students, 12/1 for international students. Application fee: $50 ($60 for international students). *Financial support:* In 2007–08, 24 fellowships (averaging $5,514 per year) were awarded; Federal Work-Study and tuition waivers (full) also available. Financial award application deadline: 1/1; financial award applicants required to submit FAFSA. *Faculty research:* Creative writing (MA), language, critical theory, literature. *Unit head:* Katherine Eggert, Chair, 303-492-7382, Fax: 303-492-8904, E-mail: katherine.eggert@colorado.edu. *Application contact:* Graduate Programs Assistant, 303-492-6434, Fax: 303-492-8904, E-mail: ssengl@colorado.edu.

University of Colorado at Boulder, Graduate School, College of Arts and Sciences, Department of Spanish and Portuguese, Boulder, CO 80309. Offers Hispanic linguistics (MA); medieval/early modern Hispanic literatures (PhD); Spanish literature (MA, PhD), including 18th and 19th century peninsular literature (MA), Golden Age (MA), medieval Iberian literature (MA). Part-time programs available. *Faculty:* 14. *Students:* 28 full-time (19 women), 14 part-time (10 women); includes 12 minority (all Hispanic Americans), 18 international. Average age 32. 17 applicants, 88% accepted. In 2007, 5 master's, 4 doctorates awarded. Terminal master's awarded for partial completion of doctoral program. *Degree requirements:* For master's, one foreign language, comprehensive exam, thesis or alternative; for doctorate, 2 foreign languages, thesis/dissertation. *Entrance requirements:* For master's, minimum undergraduate GPA of 2.75. *Application deadline:* For fall admission, 12/15 priority date for domestic students, 12/15 for international students. Applications are processed on a rolling basis. Application fee: $50 ($60 for international students). *Financial support:* In 2007–08, 41 fellowships with full tuition reimbursements (averaging $1,663 per year) were awarded; tuition waivers (full) also available. Financial award application deadline: 12/15. *Faculty research:* Spanish peninsular and Spanish-American literatures; Hispanic linguistics; Medieval, Golden Age, eighteenth and nineteenth century literatures. Total annual research expenditures: $6,076. *Unit head:* Ricardo Laudiera, Chair, 303-492-5386, Fax: 303-492-3699, E-mail: laudiera@colorado.edu. *Application contact:* Graduate Program Assistant, 303-492-7308, Fax: 303-492-3699, E-mail: spanport@colorado.edu.

University of Colorado Denver, College of Liberal Arts and Sciences, Department of English, Denver, CO 80217-3364. Offers applied linguistics (MA); English studies (MA); literature (MA); teaching English to speakers of other languages (Certificate); teaching of writing (MA). Part-time and evening/weekend programs available. *Faculty:* 33 full-time (21 women). *Students:* 6 full-time (5 women), 49 part-time (28 women); includes 6 minority (3 Asian Americans or Pacific Islanders, 3 Hispanic Americans), 1 international. Average age 32. 18 applicants, 56% accepted, 5 enrolled. In 2007, 23 degrees awarded. *Degree requirements:* For master's, thesis optional. *Entrance requirements:* For master's, GRE General Test, minimum GPA of 3.0. Additional exam requirements/recommendations for international students: Required—TOEFL (minimum score 550 paper-based). *Application deadline:* For fall admission, 5/25 for domestic students; for spring admission, 10/25 for domestic students. Applications are processed on a rolling basis. Application fee: $50 ($75 for international students). Electronic applications accepted. *Financial support:* Research assistantships, teaching assistantships, Federal Work-Study available. Financial award application deadline: 4/1; financial award applicants required to submit FAFSA. *Unit head:* Prof. Nancy Ciccone, Chair, 303-556-8395, Fax: 303-556-2959, E-mail: nancy.ciccone@cudenver.edu. *Application contact:* Prof. Ian Ying, Program Advisor, 303-556-6728, Fax: 303-556-2959, E-mail: hongguang.ying@cudenver.edu.

University of Connecticut, Graduate School, College of Liberal Arts and Sciences, Department of English, Field of English, Storrs, CT 06269. Offers MA, PhD. *Faculty:* 59 full-time (30 women). *Students:* 87 full-time (53 women), 12 part-time (6 women); includes 5 minority (2 African Americans, 3 Hispanic Americans), 3 international. Average age 32. 180 applicants, 13% accepted, 24 enrolled. In 2007, 12 master's, 9 doctorates awarded. Terminal master's awarded for partial completion of doctoral program. *Degree requirements:* For master's, comprehensive exam; for doctorate, thesis/dissertation. *Entrance requirements:* For master's and doctorate, GRE General Test, GRE Subject Test. Additional exam requirements/recommendations for international students: Required—TOEFL (minimum score 550 paper-based; 213 computer-based). *Application deadline:* For fall admission, 2/1 priority date for domestic and international students; for spring admission, 11/1 for domestic students, 10/1 for international students. Applications are processed on a rolling basis. Application fee: $55. Electronic applications accepted. *Expenses:* Tuition, state resident: part-time $469 per credit hour. Tuition, nonresident: part-time $1,218 per credit hour. *Financial support:* In 2007–08, 1 research assistantship with full tuition reimbursement, 86 teaching assistantships with full tuition reimbursements were awarded; fellowships, Federal Work-Study, scholarships/grants, health care benefits, and unspecified assistantships also available. Financial award application deadline: 2/1; financial award applicants required to submit FAFSA. *Application contact:* Mary Udal, Administrative Assistant, 860-486-2329, Fax: 860-486-1530, E-mail: mary.udal@uconn.edu.

See Close-Up on page 587.

University of Dallas, Braniff Graduate School of Liberal Arts, Department of English, Irving, TX 75062-4736. Offers English literature (MA, MEL). Part-time programs available. *Faculty:* 1 full-time (0 women), 5 part-time/adjunct (3 women). *Students:* 12 full-time (4 women), 10 part-time (7 women); includes 1 minority (Asian American or Pacific Islander), 1 international. Average age 25. 14 applicants, 100% accepted, 8 enrolled. In 2007, 12 degrees awarded. *Degree requirements:* For master's, one foreign language. *Entrance requirements:* For master's, GRE General Test. *Application deadline:* For fall admission, 2/15 priority date for domestic students; for spring admission, 11/15 for domestic students. Applications are processed on a rolling basis. Application fee: $50. *Expenses:* Tuition: Part-time $600 per credit. Required fees: $15 per credit. *Financial support:* In 2007–08, 25 students received support. Scholarships/grants available. Financial award application deadline: 2/15. *Faculty research:* Modern literature, Renaissance, Shakespeare, medieval studies. *Unit head:* Dr. John Alvis, Chair, 972-721-5213, Fax: 972-721-4007, E-mail: alvis@udallas.edu. *Application contact:* Graduate Coordinator, 972-721-5106, Fax: 972-721-5280, E-mail: graduate@acad.udallas.edu.

University of Dayton, Graduate School, College of Arts and Sciences, Department of English, Dayton, OH 45469-1300. Offers MA. Part-time and evening/weekend programs available. *Faculty:* 16 full-time (9 women). *Students:* 19 full-time (15 women), 12 part-time (all women); includes 5 minority (4 African Americans, 1 Hispanic American). Average age 25. 43 applicants, 53% accepted, 15 enrolled. In 2007, 13 degrees awarded. *Degree requirements:* For master's, thesis optional. *Entrance requirements:* For master's, minimum GPA of 3.0, 24 upper level credit hours of course work in English. Additional exam requirements/recommendations for international students: Required—TOEFL (minimum score 550 paper-based; 213 computer-based; 80 iBT). *Application deadline:* For fall admission, 4/4 priority date for domestic students, 3/1 priority date for international students; for winter admission, 7/1 priority date for international students; for spring admission, 1/1 priority date for international students. Applications are processed on a rolling basis. Application fee: $0 ($50 for international students). Electronic applications accepted. *Financial support:* In 2007–08, 12 teaching assistantships with full tuition reimbursements (averaging $9,250 per year) were awarded; institutionally sponsored loans, health care benefits, and unspecified assistantships also available. Financial award applicants required to submit FAFSA. *Faculty research:* Religion and literature, rhetoric and composition, teaching literature and writing and creative writing. Total annual research expenditures: $6,000. *Unit head:* Dr. Sheila Hughes, Chair, 937-229-3434, Fax: 937-229-3563, E-mail: sheila.hughes@notes.udayton.edu. *Application contact:* Angela Jones-Glukhov, Associate Director of Graduate Admissions, 937-229-4305, Fax: 937-229-4729.

University of Delaware, College of Arts and Sciences, Department of English, Newark, DE 19716. Offers English and American literature (MA, PhD); MA/PhD. *Faculty:* 49 full-time (17 women). *Students:* 58 full-time (41 women); includes 4 minority (3 African Americans, 1 Asian American or Pacific Islander), 3 international. Average age 28. 93 applicants, 25% accepted, 13 enrolled. In 2007, 16 master's, 6 doctorates awarded. Terminal master's awarded for partial completion of doctoral program. *Degree requirements:* For master's, one foreign language, thesis optional; for doctorate, 2 foreign languages, comprehensive exam, thesis/dissertation, specialty exam. *Entrance requirements:* For master's and doctorate, GRE General Test, GRE Subject Test. Additional exam requirements/recommendations for international students: Required—TOEFL (minimum score 550 paper-based; 213 computer-based). *Application deadline:* For fall admission, 2/15 for domestic and international students. Application fee: $60. Electronic applications accepted. *Financial support:* In 2007–08, 47 students received support, including 4 fellowships with full tuition reimbursements available (averaging $13,000 per year), 7 research assistantships with full tuition reimbursements available (averaging $13,000 per year), 36 teaching assistantships with full tuition reimbursements available (averaging $13,000 per year); career-related internships or fieldwork, institutionally sponsored loans, health care benefits, and tuition waivers (full) also available. Financial award application deadline: 2/15. *Faculty research:* Significant strengths in American literature and culture, material cultural studies, Renaissance studies, archival studies. Total annual research expenditures: $100,000. *Unit head:* Dr. Matthew Kinservik, Director of Graduate Studies in English, 302-831-2363, Fax: 302-831-1586, E-mail: matthewk@udel.edu. *Application contact:* Wanda McCracken, Information Contact, 302-831-22363, E-mail: wtm@udel.edu.

Announcement: MA students receive stipends and tuition scholarship for two years; PhD students, for three years. Minimum stipend in 2008–09 is $14,600, plus full tuition. Approximately 12 new awards annually. Fellowships. Excellent range of TA assignments: writing center, instruction, research, editorial, and special collections positions. Rich teaching opportunities, including literature courses in the student's field of specialization.

University of Denver, Faculty of Arts and Humanities/Social Sciences, Department of English, Denver, CO 80208. Offers MA, PhD. Part-time programs available. *Faculty:* 21 full-time (9 women). *Students:* 29 full-time (20 women), 8 part-time (5 women), 1 international. Average age 33. In 2007, 5 master's, 13 doctorates awarded. *Degree requirements:* For master's, one foreign language, thesis; for doctorate, 2 foreign languages, thesis/dissertation. *Entrance requirements:* For master's and doctorate, GRE General Test, GRE Subject Test. Additional exam requirements/recommendations for international students: Required—TOEFL. *Application deadline:* Applications are processed on a rolling basis. Application fee: $50. Electronic applications accepted. *Financial support:* In 2007–08, 28 teaching assistantships with full and partial tuition reimbursements (averaging $12,000 per year) were awarded; Federal Work-Study, institutionally sponsored loans, and scholarships/grants also available. Support available to part-time students. Financial award application deadline: 2/1; financial award applicants required to submit FAFSA. *Faculty research:* Cultural studies, creative nonfiction, eighteenth century colonial literature, multicultural literature, Cervantes. *Unit head:* Dr. Ann Dobyns, Chair, 303-871-2266. *Application contact:* Information Contact, 303-871-2742, E-mail: engl-info@du.edu.

University of Florida, Graduate School, College of Liberal Arts and Sciences, Department of English, Gainesville, FL 32611. Offers creative writing (MFA); English (MA, PhD). *Faculty:* 54 full-time (18 women), 1 (woman) part-time/adjunct. *Students:* 173 (99 women); includes 21 minority (9 African Americans, 6 Asian Americans or Pacific Islanders, 6 Hispanic Americans) 11 international. In 2007, 31 master's, 21 doctorates awarded. *Degree requirements:* For master's, variable foreign language requirement, thesis or alternative; for doctorate, thesis/dissertation. *Entrance requirements:* For master's and doctorate, GRE General Test, minimum GPA of 3.0. Additional exam requirements/recommendations for international students: Required—TOEFL (minimum score 550 paper-based; 213 computer-based). *Application deadline:* For fall admission, 1/15 for domestic students. Application fee: $30. Electronic applications accepted. *Expenses:* Tuition, state resident: full-time $7,478. Tuition, nonresident: full-time $22,603. *Financial support:* In 2007–08, 4 research assistantships with tuition reimbursements (averaging $14,050 per year), 61 teaching assistantships with tuition reimbursements (averaging $13,833 per year) were awarded; fellowships with tuition reimbursements, unspecified assistantships also available. Financial award application deadline: 1/15. *Unit head:* John Leavey, Chair, 352-392-6650 Ext. 230, Fax: 352-392-0860, E-mail: jpl@english.ufl.edu. *Application contact:* Dr. Pamela Gilbert, Coordinator, 352-392-6650 Ext. 231, Fax: 352-392-0860, E-mail: pgilbert@english.ufl.edu.

University of Georgia, Graduate School, College of Arts and Sciences, Department of English, Athens, GA 30602. Offers creative writing (MFA, PhD); English (MA, MAT, PhD). *Faculty:* 37 full-time (16 women). *Students:* 107 full-time (64 women), 18 part-time (12 women); includes 5 minority (all African Americans) 241 applicants, 33% accepted, 23 enrolled. In 2007, 25 master's, 4 doctorates awarded. *Degree requirements:* For master's, one foreign language, thesis (MA); for doctorate, 2 foreign languages, thesis/dissertation. *Entrance requirements:* For master's and doctorate, GRE General Test. Additional exam requirements/recommendations for international students: Required—TWE. *Application deadline:* For fall admission, 7/1 priority date for domestic students; for spring admission, 11/15 for domestic students. Application fee: $50. Electronic applications accepted. *Financial support:* Fellowships, research assistantships, teaching assistantships, unspecified assistantships available. *Unit head:* Dr. Valerie Babb, Head, 706-543-0378, Fax: 706-542-2181, E-mail: vbabb@uga.edu. *Application contact:* Dr. Kris Boudreau, Graduate Coordinator, 706-542-3110, E-mail: boudreau@uga.edu.

University of Guam, Office of Graduate Studies, Liberal Arts and Social Sciences, Department of English, Mangilao, GU 96923. Offers MA. *Faculty:* 4 full-time (1 woman). *Students:* 3 full-time (2 women), 6 part-time (4 women); includes 6 Asian Americans or Pacific Islanders. Average age 33. *Entrance requirements:* For master's, GRE. Additional exam requirements/recommendations for international students: Required—TOEFL. Application fee: $49 ($74 for international students). *Unit head:* Dr. Christopher Schreiner, Program Chairperson, 671-735-2738, E-mail: csscamel@yahoo.com. *Application contact:* Charlie A. Alcantara, Program Coordinator, Graduate Studies Office, 671-735-2173, Fax: 671-734-3676, E-mail: charliea@uguam.uog.edu.

University of Guelph, Graduate Program Services, College of Arts, School of English and Theatre Studies, Program in English, Guelph, ON N1G 2W1, Canada. Offers MA. Part-time programs available. *Faculty:* 30 full-time (15 women). *Students:* 21 full-time (16 women); includes 1 minority (Asian American or Pacific Islander) Average age 25. 80 applicants, 63% accepted, 21 enrolled. In 2007, 17 degrees awarded. *Degree requirements:* For master's, thesis (for some programs). *Entrance requirements:* For master's, letters of reference, 4-year honours undergraduate degree in English or drama. Additional exam requirements/recommendations for international students: Required—TOEFL. *Application deadline:* For fall admission, 2/1 for domestic and international students. Application fee: $85. Electronic applications accepted. *Financial support:* In 2007–08, 4 research assistantships with tuition reimbursements (averaging $9,212 per year), 38 teaching assistantships with tuition reimbursements (averaging $9,212 per year) were awarded; scholarships/grants, health care benefits, tuition waivers (full), and unspecified assistantships also available. Support available to part-time students. Financial award application deadline: 2/15. *Faculty research:* Post-colonial literature, Canadian literature, children's literature, Scottish literature, American literature, cultural studies. Total annual research expenditures: $500,000. *Application contact:* Dr. Daniel O'Quinn, Graduate Coordinator, 519-824-4120 Ext. 53250, Fax: 519-766-0844, E-mail: doquinn@uoguelph.ca.

University of Hawaii at Manoa, Graduate Division, Colleges of Arts and Sciences, College of Language, Linguistics and Literature, Department of English, Honolulu, HI 96822. Offers MA, PhD. Part-time programs available. *Faculty:* 51 full-time (19 women). *Students:* 69 full-time (53 women), 35 part-time (19 women); includes 43 minority (39 Asian Americans or Pacific Islanders, 4 Hispanic Americans), 10 international. Average age 33. 125 applicants, 38% accepted, 32 enrolled. *Median time to degree:* Of those who began their doctoral program in fall 1999, 100% received their degree in 8 years or less. *Degree requirements:* For master's, 2 foreign languages, thesis optional; for doctorate, 2 foreign languages, comprehensive exam, thesis/dissertation. *Entrance requirements:* For master's, GRE General Test; for doctorate, GRE General Test, GRE Subject Test. Additional exam requirements/recommendations for international students: Required—TOEFL (minimum score 600 paper-based; 250 computer-based; 100 iBT), IELTS (minimum score 7). Application fee: $50. *Financial support:* In 2007–08, 40 teaching assistantships (averaging $14,341 per year) were awarded; research assistantships, tuition waivers (full) also available. Financial award application deadline: 3/1. *Faculty research:* British and American literature, creative writing, cultural studies, rhetoric and composition. Total annual research expenditures: $31,834. *Application contact:* Paul Lyons, Graduate Chair, 808-956-8956, Fax: 808-956-3083, E-mail: enggrad@hawaii.edu.

University of Houston, College of Liberal Arts and Social Sciences, Department of English, Houston, TX 77204. Offers applied English linguistics (MA); English and American literature (MA, PhD); literature and creative writing (MA, MFA, PhD). Postbaccalaureate distance learning degree programs offered. *Faculty:* 26 full-time (9 women), 6 part-time/adjunct (3 women). *Students:* 85 full-time (39 women), 65 part-time (51 women); includes 17 minority (3 African Americans, 6 Asian Americans or Pacific Islanders, 8 Hispanic Americans), 6 international. Average age 32. 63 applicants, 73% accepted, 29 enrolled. In 2007, 19 master's, 14 doctorates awarded. *Degree requirements:* For master's, one foreign language, thesis (for some programs); for doctorate, 2 foreign languages, comprehensive exam, thesis/dissertation. *Entrance requirements:* For master's, GRE General Test, GRE Subject Test, minimum GPA of 3.0 in last 60 hours of course work; for doctorate, GRE General Test, GRE Subject Test, writing sample. Additional exam requirements/recommendations for international students: Required—TOEFL. *Application deadline:* For fall admission, 1/1 priority date for domestic students. Applications are processed on a rolling basis. Application fee: $50. *Expenses:* Tuition, state resident: full-time $6,297; part-time $262 per credit. Tuition, nonresident: full-time $12,969; part-time $540 per credit. Required fees: $2,696. *Financial support:* In 2007–08, 2 fellowships with full tuition reimbursements (averaging $1,700 per year), 72 teaching assistantships with full tuition reimbursements (averaging $1,200 per year) were awarded; research assistantships with full tuition reimbursements, career-related internships or fieldwork, Federal Work-Study, institutionally sponsored loans, scholarships/grants, health care benefits, and unspecified assistantships also available. Support available to part-time students. Financial award application deadline: 2/1. *Unit head:* Wyman Henderson, Chairperson, 713-743-3004, Fax: 713-743-3215, E-mail: whh@uh.edu. *Application contact:* Ruby Jones, Advising Assistant, 713-743-2941, Fax: 713-743-3215, E-mail: rjones@uh.edu.

University of Houston–Clear Lake, School of Human Sciences and Humanities, Programs in Humanities and Fine Arts, Houston, TX 77058-1098. Offers history (MA); humanities (MA); literature (MA). Part-time and evening/weekend programs available. Postbaccalaureate distance learning degree programs offered (minimal on-campus study). *Degree requirements:* For master's, thesis or alternative. *Entrance requirements:* For master's, GRE General Test. Additional exam requirements/recommendations for international students: Required—TOEFL (minimum score 550 paper-based; 213 computer-based). *Faculty research:* Digital media studies, Latin American history, labor history, Chaucer evolution versus creationism debate.

University of Houston–Downtown, Graduate Programs, College of Humanities and Social Sciences, Department of English, Houston, TX 77002-1001. Offers professional writing and technical communication (MS). Part-time and evening/weekend programs available. *Faculty:* 5 full-time (4 women). *Students:* 4 full-time (3 women), 23 part-time (19 women); includes 14 minority (9 African Americans, 3 Asian Americans or Pacific Islanders, 2 Hispanic Americans). Average age 40. In 2007, 4 degrees awarded. *Degree requirements:* For master's, thesis (for some programs). *Entrance requirements:* For master's, GRE, resumé, personal statement, writing sample, 3 letters of recommendation. Additional exam requirements/recommendations for international students: Required—TOEFL (minimum score 600 paper-based; 250 computer-based; 86 iBT). *Application deadline:* For fall admission, 3/31 for domestic and international students; for spring admission, 11/30 for domestic and international students. Applications are processed on a rolling basis. Application fee: $35 ($60 for international students). Electronic applications accepted. *Expenses:* Tuition, state resident: full-time $3,060; part-time $170 per credit. Tuition, nonresident: full-time $7,434; part-time $413 per credit. Required fees: $704. *Financial support:* Application deadline: 4/1; *Unit head:* Dr. William Gilbert, Chair, 713-221-8013, Fax: 713-226-5205, E-mail: gilbertw@uhd.edu. *Application contact:* Traneshia Parker, Assistant Director of Admissions, Graduate and International Admissions, 713-221-8910, Fax: 713-223-7984, E-mail: parkert@uhd.edu.

University of Idaho, College of Graduate Studies, College of Letters, Arts and Social Sciences, Department of English, Program in English, Moscow, ID 83844-2282. Offers MA, MAT. *Students:* 19 (11 women). Average age 29. In 2007, 7 degrees awarded. *Entrance requirements:* For master's, minimum GPA of 2.8. *Application deadline:* For fall admission, 8/1 for domestic students; for spring admission, 12/15 for domestic students. Application fee: $55 ($60 for international students). *Financial support:* Research assistantships, teaching assistantships

English

University of Idaho (continued)
available. Financial award application deadline: 2/15. *Unit head:* Dr. Kurt Olsson, Chair, Department of English, 208-883-6156.

University of Illinois at Chicago, Graduate College, College of Liberal Arts and Sciences, Department of English, Chicago, IL 60607-7128. Offers English (MA, PhD), including creative writing, language, literacy and rhetoric (PhD), literature, teaching of English (MA); language, literacy, and rhetoric (PhD); linguistics (MA), including applied linguistics (teaching English as a second language). Part-time and evening/weekend programs available. *Degree requirements:* For doctorate, variable foreign language requirement, thesis/dissertation, written and oral exams. *Entrance requirements:* For master's, GRE General Test, GRE Subject Test; for doctorate, GRE General Test, GRE Subject Test, minimum GPA of 2.0. Additional exam requirements/recommendations for international students: Required—TOEFL. Electronic applications accepted. *Faculty research:* Literary history and theory.

University of Illinois at Springfield, Graduate Programs, College of Liberal Arts and Sciences, Program in English, Springfield, IL 62703-5407. Offers MA. Part-time and evening/weekend programs available. *Faculty:* 10 full-time (6 women). *Students:* 6 full-time (3 women), 29 part-time (20 women); includes 2 minority (1 African American, 1 Asian American or Pacific Islander). Average age 33. 17 applicants, 59% accepted, 8 enrolled. In 2007, 7 degrees awarded. *Degree requirements:* For master's, comprehensive exam, thesis, or project. *Entrance requirements:* For master's, GRE General Test, sample of written work, 2 letters of reference, bachelor's degree in English or related field. Additional exam requirements/recommendations for international students: Required—TOEFL (minimum score 600 paper-based). *Application deadline:* Applications are processed on a rolling basis. Application fee: $50 ($60 for international students). Electronic applications accepted. *Expenses:* Tuition, state resident: full-time $5,424; part-time $226 per credit hour. Tuition, nonresident: part-time $553 per credit hour. Required fees: $618 per term. *Financial support:* In 2007–08, research assistantships (averaging $7,988 per year), teaching assistantships (averaging $7,988 per year) were awarded; career-related internships or fieldwork, Federal Work-Study, scholarships/grants, health care benefits, and unspecified assistantships also available. Support available to part-time students. Financial award application deadline: 11/15; financial award applicants required to submit FAFSA. *Unit head:* Dr. James Ottery, Program Administrator, 217-206-7443, Fax: 217-206-6217, E-mail: ottery.james@uis.edu.

University of Illinois at Urbana–Champaign, Graduate College, College of Liberal Arts and Sciences, Department of English, Champaign, IL 61820. Offers creative writing (MFA); English (MA, PhD). *Faculty:* 60 full-time (25 women), 1 (woman) part-time/adjunct. *Students:* 84 full-time (54 women), 69 part-time (42 women); includes 14 minority (6 African Americans, 1 American Indian/Alaska Native, 5 Asian Americans or Pacific Islanders, 2 Hispanic Americans), 15 international. 323 applicants, 8% accepted, 24 enrolled. In 2007, 19 master's, 8 doctorates awarded. *Degree requirements:* For master's, one foreign language, area exams; for doctorate, one foreign language, thesis/dissertation, special field exam. *Entrance requirements:* For master's and doctorate, GRE General Test, GRE Subject Test, minimum GPA of 3.0. *Application deadline:* For fall admission, 1/5 for domestic students; for spring admission, 1/5 for domestic students. Applications are processed on a rolling basis. Application fee: $60 ($75 for international students). Electronic applications accepted. *Financial support:* In 2007–08, 65 fellowships, 9 research assistantships, 124 teaching assistantships were awarded. Financial award application deadline: 2/15. *Faculty research:* English and American literature, cultural studies and critical theory. *Unit head:* Martin Camargo, Head, 217-333-2390, Fax: 217-333-4321, E-mail: mcamargo@uiuc.edu. *Application contact:* Stephanie Shockey, Secretary, 217-244-3646, Fax: 217-333-4321, E-mail: shockey@uiuc.edu.

University of Indianapolis, Graduate Programs, College of Arts and Sciences, Department of English Language and Literature, Indianapolis, IN 46227-3697. Offers English (MA). Part-time and evening/weekend programs available. *Faculty:* 6 full-time (4 women), 2 part-time/adjunct (both women). *Students:* 2 full-time (both women), 9 part-time (8 women), 2 international. Average age 31. *Entrance requirements:* For master's, GRE Subject Test, Minimum 2.5 GPA. Additional exam requirements/recommendations for international students: Required—TOEFL (minimum score 550 paper-based; 213 computer-based). *Application deadline:* Applications are processed on a rolling basis. Application fee: $30. Electronic applications accepted. *Financial support:* Federal Work-Study available. Financial award application deadline: 5/1; financial award applicants required to submit FAFSA. *Unit head:* Dr. Toni J. Morris, Chair, 317-788-2072, Fax: 317-788-3300. *Application contact:* Dr. William R. Dynes, Professor, 317-788-2072, Fax: 317-788-3480, E-mail: dynes@uindy.edu.

The University of Iowa, Graduate College, College of Liberal Arts and Sciences, Department of English, Iowa City, IA 52242-1316. Offers English (PhD); literary criticism (PhD); literary history (PhD); literary studies (MA); nonfiction writing (MFA); rhetorical theory and stylistics (PhD); writer's workshop (MFA); JD/PhD. *Faculty:* 54 full-time, 41 part-time/adjunct. *Students:* 158 full-time (90 women), 89 part-time (53 women); includes 40 minority (16 African Americans, 3 American Indian/Alaska Native, 13 Asian Americans or Pacific Islanders, 8 Hispanic Americans), 11 international. 1,337 applicants, 9% accepted, 72 enrolled. In 2007, 72 master's, 12 doctorates awarded. *Degree requirements:* For master's, thesis (for some programs), exam; for doctorate, comprehensive exam, thesis/dissertation. *Entrance requirements:* For master's and doctorate, GRE General Test, minimum GPA of 3.0. Additional exam requirements/recommendations for international students: Required—TOEFL (minimum score 640 paper-based; 273 computer-based; 112 iBT). Application fee: $60 ($85 for international students). Electronic applications accepted. *Expenses:* Tuition, state resident: part-time $349 per hour. Tuition, nonresident: part-time $349 per hour. Tuition and fees vary according to course load and program. *Financial support:* In 2007–08, 31 fellowships, 21 research assistantships with partial tuition reimbursements, 160 teaching assistantships with partial tuition reimbursements were awarded. Financial award applicants required to submit FAFSA. *Unit head:* Jonathan Wilcox, Chair, 319-335-0454, Fax: 319-335-2535.

University of Kansas, Research and Graduate Studies, College of Liberal Arts and Sciences, Department of English, Lawrence, KS 66045. Offers creative writing (MFA); English (MA, PhD). Part-time programs available. *Faculty:* 39. *Students:* 80 full-time (55 women), 31 part-time (21 women); includes 8 minority (4 African Americans, 4 Hispanic Americans), 6 international. Average age 33. 148 applicants, 31% accepted, 27 enrolled. In 2007, 19 master's, 4 doctorates awarded. *Degree requirements:* For master's, one foreign language, comprehensive exam (for some programs), thesis or alternative; for doctorate, 2 foreign languages, comprehensive exam, thesis/dissertation. *Entrance requirements:* For master's and doctorate, GRE General Test, minimum GPA of 3.3. Additional exam requirements/recommendations for international students: Required—TOEFL. *Application deadline:* For fall admission, 1/1 priority date for domestic and international students. Applications are processed on a rolling basis. Application fee: $55 ($60 for international students). Electronic applications accepted. *Expenses:* Tuition, state resident: full-time $5,838. Tuition, nonresident: full-time $13,409. Tuition and fees vary according to program. *Financial support:* Fellowships, research assistantships, teaching assistantships with full and partial tuition reimbursements, unspecified assistantships available. Financial award application deadline: 1/1. *Faculty research:* African-American literature, 20th century American literature, renaissance literature, creative writing. *Unit head:* Dorice Elliott, Chair, 785-864-4520, E-mail: delliott@ku.edu. *Application contact:* Byron Caminero-Santangelo, Director of Graduate Studies, 785-864-2522, E-mail: bsantang@ku.edu.

University of Kentucky, Graduate School, College of Arts and Sciences, Program in English, Lexington, KY 40506-0032. Offers MA, PhD. *Faculty:* 26 full-time (13 women), 2 part-time/adjunct (0 women). *Students:* 57 full-time (40 women), 20 part-time (10 women); includes 5 minority (all African Americans), 5 international. Average age 33. 121 applicants, 23% accepted, 20 enrolled. In 2007, 7 master's, 7 doctorates awarded. *Median time to degree:* Of those who began their doctoral program in fall 1999, 62% received their degree in 8 years or less. *Degree requirements:* For master's, one foreign language, comprehensive exam, thesis optional; for doctorate, one foreign language, comprehensive exam, thesis/dissertation. *Entrance requirements:* For master's, GRE General Test, minimum undergraduate GPA of 2.75; for doctorate, GRE General Test, minimum graduate GPA of 3.0. Additional exam requirements/recommendations for international students: Required—TOEFL (minimum score 550 paper-based; 213 computer-based). *Application deadline:* For fall admission, 7/17 priority date for domestic students, 2/1 priority date for international students; for spring admission, 12/13 priority date for domestic students, 6/15 priority date for international students. Applications are processed on a rolling basis. Application fee: $50 ($65 for international students). Electronic applications accepted. *Expenses:* Tuition, state resident: part-time $437 per credit hour. Tuition, nonresident: part-time $931 per credit hour. *Financial support:* In 2007–08, 51 students received support, including 9 fellowships with full tuition reimbursements available (averaging $2,898 per year), 1 research assistantship (averaging $6,379 per year), 47 teaching assistantships with full tuition reimbursements available (averaging $12,758 per year); Federal Work-Study, scholarships/grants, traineeships, health care benefits, tuition waivers (partial), and unspecified assistantships also available. Support available to part-time students. Financial award application deadline: 3/15. *Unit head:* Dr. Michael Trask, Director of Graduate Studies, 859-257-6960, Fax: 859-258-1072. *Application contact:* Dr. Brian Jackson, Senior Associate Dean, 859-257-4667, Fax: 859-257-4676, E-mail: brian.jackson@uky.edu.

University of Lethbridge, School of Graduate Studies, Lethbridge, AB T1K 3M4, Canada. Offers accounting (MScM); addictions counseling (M Sc); agricultural biotechnology (M Sc); agricultural studies (M Sc, MA); anthropology (MA); archaeology (MA); art (MA); biochemistry (M Sc); biological sciences (M Sc); biomolecular science (PhD); biosystems and biodiversity (PhD); Canadian studies (MA); chemistry (M Sc); computer science (M Sc); computer science and geographical information science (M Sc); counseling psychology (M Ed); dramatic arts (MA); earth, space, and physical science (PhD); economics (MA); educational leadership (M Ed); English (MA); environmental science (M Sc); evolution and behavior (PhD); exercise science (M Sc); finance (MScM); French (MA); French/German (MA); French/Spanish (MA); general education (M Ed); general management (MScM); geography (M Sc, MA); German (MA); health sciences (M Sc, MA); history (MA); human resource management and labour relations (MScM); individualized multidisciplinary (M Sc, MA); information systems (MScM); international management (MScM); kinesiology (M Sc, MA); management (M Sc, MA); marketing (MScM); mathematics (M Sc); music (MA); Native American studies (MA); neuroscience (M Sc, PhD); new media (MA); nursing (M Sc); philosophy (MA); physics (M Sc); policy and strategy (MScM); political science (MA); psychology (M Sc, MA); religious studies (MA); sociology (MA); theoretical and computational science (PhD); urban and regional studies (MA). Part-time and evening/weekend programs available. *Students:* 215 full-time, 98 part-time. In 2007, 87 master's, 1 doctorate awarded. *Degree requirements:* For doctorate, comprehensive exam, thesis/dissertation. *Entrance requirements:* For master's, GMAT (M Sc in management), bachelor's degree in related field, minimum GPA of 3.0 during previous 20 graded semester courses, 2 years teaching or related experience (M Ed); for doctorate, master's degree, minimum graduate GPA of 3.5. Additional exam requirements/recommendations for international students: Required—TOEFL. Application fee: $60 Canadian dollars. *Financial support:* Fellowships, research assistantships, teaching assistantships, scholarships/grants, health care benefits, and unspecified assistantships available. *Faculty research:* Movement and brain plasticity, gibberellin physiology, photosynthesis, carbon cycling, molecular properties of main-group ring components. *Unit head:* Dr. Jo-Anne Fiske, Interim Dean, 403-329-2121, Fax: 403-329-2097. *Application contact:* Jennifer Geddes, Graduate Liaison Officer, 403-329-2762, Fax: 403-329-5159, E-mail: jennifer.geddes@uleth.ca.

University of Louisiana at Lafayette, Graduate School, College of Liberal Arts, Department of English, Lafayette, LA 70504. Offers British and American literature (MA), including creative writing, folklore, rhetoric; creative writing (PhD); literature (PhD); rhetoric (PhD). Part-time programs available. Terminal master's awarded for partial completion of doctoral program. *Degree requirements:* For master's, one foreign language, thesis or alternative; for doctorate, 2 foreign languages, comprehensive exam, thesis/dissertation. *Entrance requirements:* For master's, GRE General Test, minimum GPA of 2.75; for doctorate, GRE General Test, minimum GPA of 3.0. Additional exam requirements/recommendations for international students: Required—TOEFL (minimum score 550 paper-based; 213 computer-based). Electronic applications accepted. *Faculty research:* Composition theory, Southern literature, medieval literature.

University of Louisiana at Monroe, Graduate Studies and Research, College of Arts and Sciences, Department of English, Monroe, LA 71209-0001. Offers MA. Part-time and evening/weekend programs available. *Faculty:* 3 full-time (1 woman). *Students:* 10 full-time (9 women), 11 part-time (9 women); includes 5 minority (3 African Americans, 1 Asian American or Pacific Islander, 1 Hispanic American). Average age 26. In 2007, 1 degree awarded. *Degree requirements:* For master's, one foreign language, thesis optional. *Entrance requirements:* For master's, GRE General Test (minimum verbal and quantitative score: 900), minimum GPA of 3.0. Additional exam requirements/recommendations for international students: Required—TOEFL (minimum score 500 paper-based; 173 computer-based; 61 iBT), TOEFL or Michigan English Language Assessment Battery. *Application deadline:* For fall admission, 8/22 priority date for domestic students, 7/1 for international students; for winter admission, 12/12 priority date for domestic students; for spring admission, 1/17 for domestic students, 11/1 for international students. Applications are processed on a rolling basis. Application fee: $20 ($30 for international students). Electronic applications accepted. *Expenses:* Tuition, state resident: full-time $2,220. Tuition, nonresident: full-time $8,172. *Financial support:* In 2007–08, 1 research assistantship with full tuition reimbursement (averaging $2,600 per year), 2 teaching assistantships with full tuition reimbursements (averaging $2,600 per year) were awarded; career-related internships or fieldwork, Federal Work-Study, institutionally sponsored loans, and unspecified assistantships also available. Financial award application deadline: 4/1; financial award applicants required to submit FAFSA. *Faculty research:* Creative writing, American literature, British literature, multicultural literature, literary theory. *Unit head:* Dr. Fleming J. McClelland, Interim Head, 318-342-1485, Fax: 318-342-1491, E-mail: mcclelland@ulm.edu. *Application contact:* Dr. Julia Guernsey-Shaw, Information Contact, 318-342-1496, E-mail: shaw@ulm.edu.

University of Louisville, Graduate School, College of Arts and Sciences, Department of English, Program in English, Louisville, KY 40292-0001. Offers English literature (MA). *Students:* 35 full-time (20 women), 32 part-time (22 women); includes 6 minority (all African Americans), 2 international. Average age 32. In 2007, 22 degrees awarded. *Degree requirements:* For master's, one foreign language, culminating project or thesis. *Entrance requirements:* For master's, GRE General Test, GRE Subject Test, critical writing sample. *Application deadline:* For fall admission, 3/1 priority date for domestic students; for spring admission, 12/1 priority date for domestic students. Applications are processed on a rolling basis. Application fee: $50. Electronic applications accepted. *Financial support:* Teaching assistantships with full tuition reimbursements, unspecified assistantships available. Financial award application deadline:3/1. *Unit head:* Dr. Susan Griffin, Chair, Department of English, 502-852-6801, Fax: 502-852-4182, E-mail: smgriff01@louisville.edu.

University of Louisville, Graduate School, College of Arts and Sciences, Department of English, Program in English Rhetoric and Composition, Louisville, KY 40292-0001. Offers PhD. *Students:* 40 full-time (26 women), 2 part-time (both women); includes 5 minority (4 African Americans, 1 Hispanic American), 2 international. Average age 34. In 2007, 6 degrees awarded. *Degree requirements:* For doctorate, 2 foreign languages, thesis/dissertation. *Entrance requirements:* For doctorate, GRE General Test, writing sample. *Application deadline:* For fall admission, 3/1 for domestic students. Applications are processed on a rolling basis. Application fee: $50. *Financial support:* Fellowships with full tuition reimbursements, teaching assistantships with full tuition reimbursements available. Financial award application deadline: 3/1. *Unit head:* Dr. Susan Griffin, Chair, Department of English, 502-852-6801, Fax: 502-852-4182, E-mail: smgriff01@louisville.edu.

University of Maine, Graduate School, College of Liberal Arts and Sciences, Department of English, Orono, ME 04469. Offers MA. Part-time and evening/weekend programs available. *Faculty:* 20. *Students:* 39 full-time (22 women), 10 part-time (6 women), 2 international.

English

Average age 28. 36 applicants, 83% accepted, 19 enrolled. In 2007, 9 master's awarded. *Degree requirements:* For master's, one foreign language, thesis optional. *Entrance requirements:* For master's, GRE General Test, minimum GPA of 3.0. Additional exam requirements/recommendations for international students: Required—TOEFL. *Application deadline:* For fall admission, 2/1 priority date for domestic students. Applications are processed on a rolling basis. Application fee: $60. Electronic applications accepted. *Financial support:* In 2007–08, 21 teaching assistantships with tuition reimbursements (averaging $9,010 per year) were awarded; Federal Work-Study and tuition waivers (full and partial) also available. Financial award application deadline: 3/1. *Faculty research:* Contemporary poetics, contemporary criticism, composition theory and pedagogy, feminist approaches to literature. *Unit head:* Dr. Margaret Lukens, Chair, 207-581-3822, Fax: 207-581-1604. *Application contact:* Scott G. Delcourt, Associate Dean of the Graduate School, 207-581-3219, Fax: 207-581-3232, E-mail: graduate@maine.edu.

University of Manitoba, Faculty of Graduate Studies, Faculty of Arts, Department of English, Winnipeg, MB R3T 2N2, Canada. Offers MA, PhD. *Degree requirements:* For master's, one foreign language, thesis; for doctorate, one foreign language, thesis/dissertation.

University of Maryland, College Park, Graduate Studies, College of Arts and Humanities, Department of English, Program in English Language and Literature, College Park, MD 20742. Offers MA, PhD. *Students:* 147 full-time (106 women), 31 part-time (22 women); includes 30 minority (24 African Americans, 3 Asian Americans or Pacific Islanders, 3 Hispanic Americans), 4 international. 359 applicants, 33% accepted, 38 enrolled. In 2007, 24 master's, 15 doctorates awarded. *Median time to degree:* Of those who began their doctoral program in fall 1999, 39% received their degree in 8 years or less. *Degree requirements:* For master's, thesis optional; for doctorate, one foreign language, thesis/dissertation, oral and written exams. *Entrance requirements:* For master's, GRE General Test, minimum GPA of 3.5, writing sample, 3 letters of recommendation; for doctorate, GRE General Test, minimum GPA of 3.7, writing sample. Additional exam requirements/recommendations for international students: Required—TOEFL. *Application deadline:* For fall admission, 12/8 for domestic students, 2/1 for international students. Applications are processed on a rolling basis. Application fee: $60. Electronic applications accepted. *Financial support:* Fellowships, teaching assistantships available. Financial award applicants required to submit FAFSA. *Application contact:* Dean of Graduate School, 301-405-4190, Fax: 301-314-9305.

University of Massachusetts Amherst, Graduate School, College of Humanities and Fine Arts, Department of English, Amherst, MA 01003. Offers creative writing (MFA); English and American literature (MA, PhD). Part-time programs available. *Faculty:* 42 full-time (20 women). *Students:* 97 full-time (50 women), 94 part-time (55 women); includes 27 minority (11 African Americans, 1 American Indian/Alaska Native, 7 Asian Americans or Pacific Islanders, 8 Hispanic Americans), 8 international. Average age 30. 878 applicants, 16% accepted, 52 enrolled. In 2007, 32 master's, 12 doctorates awarded. Terminal master's awarded for partial completion of doctoral program. *Degree requirements:* For master's, one foreign language, thesis optional; for doctorate, one foreign language, thesis/dissertation. *Entrance requirements:* For master's, GRE General Test, GRE Subject Test (MA), writing sample (MFA); for doctorate, GRE General Test, GRE Subject Test. Additional exam requirements/recommendations for international students: Required—TOEFL (minimum score 530 paper-based; 197 computer-based). *Application deadline:* For fall admission, 1/15 priority date for domestic and international students. Applications are processed on a rolling basis. Application fee: $50 ($65 for international students). Electronic applications accepted. *Expenses:* Tuition, state resident: full-time $2,640; part-time $110 per credit. Tuition, nonresident: full-time $9,936; part-time $414 per credit. Required fees: $7,455. One-time fee: $332. Tuition and fees vary according to course load, campus/location, program and reciprocity agreements. *Financial support:* In 2007–08, 4 fellowships with full tuition reimbursements (averaging $5,766 per year), 7 research assistantships with full tuition reimbursements (averaging $7,803 per year), 41 teaching assistantships with full tuition reimbursements (averaging $8,477 per year) were awarded; career-related internships or fieldwork, Federal Work-Study, scholarships/grants, traineeships, and unspecified assistantships also available. Support available to part-time students. Financial award application deadline: 1/15. *Unit head:* Dr. Joseph Bartolomeo, Head, 413-545-2575, Fax: 413-545-3880. *Application contact:* 413-545-0643.

University of Massachusetts Boston, Office of Graduate Studies, College of Liberal Arts, Program in English, Boston, MA 02125-3393. Offers MA. Part-time and evening/weekend programs available. *Degree requirements:* For master's, one foreign language, final project. *Entrance requirements:* For master's, minimum GPA of 2.75. *Faculty research:* Working class literature, women writers, British fiction, composition theory, modern American literature.

University of Memphis, Graduate School, College of Arts and Sciences, Department of English, Memphis, TN 38152. Offers creative writing (MFA); English (MA); writing and language studies (PhD). Part-time programs available. *Faculty:* 33 full-time (17 women), 1 (woman) part-time/adjunct. *Students:* 46 full-time (32 women), 65 part-time (50 women); includes 24 minority (18 African Americans, 5 Asian Americans or Pacific Islanders, 1 Hispanic American), 4 international. Average age 34. 117 applicants, 74% accepted, 28 enrolled. In 2007, 28 master's, 3 doctorates awarded. Terminal master's awarded for partial completion of doctoral program. *Degree requirements:* For master's, one foreign language, comprehensive exam, thesis or alternative; for doctorate, 2 foreign languages, comprehensive exam, thesis/dissertation. *Entrance requirements:* For master's, GRE General Test or MAT, minimum GPA of 2.5; for doctorate, GRE General Test, minimum GPA of 3.0. *Application deadline:* For fall admission, 8/1 for domestic students; for spring admission, 12/1 for domestic students. Applications are processed on a rolling basis. Application fee: $35 ($60 for international students). *Expenses:* Tuition, state resident: full-time $6,990; part-time $377 per hour. Tuition, nonresident: full-time $17,818; part-time $830 per hour. Tuition and fees vary according to course load and program. *Financial support:* In 2007–08, 9 research assistantships with full tuition reimbursements (averaging $3,450 per year), 42 teaching assistantships with full tuition reimbursements (averaging $3,650 per year) were awarded. *Faculty research:* American literature, cultural studies, ESL/linguistics, composition studies/professional writing. *Unit head:* Dr. Steve E. Tabachnick, Chair, 901-678-2651, Fax: 901-678-2226, E-mail: stbchnck@memphis.edu. *Application contact:* Dr. Verner D. Mitchell, Director, Graduate Studies, 901-678-3099, Fax: 901-678-2226, E-mail: vdmtchll@memphis.edu.

University of Miami, Graduate School, College of Arts and Sciences, Department of English, Coral Gables, FL 33124. Offers creative writing (MFA); English (MA, PhD). Part-time programs available. *Faculty:* 30 full-time (14 women), 1 (woman) part-time/adjunct. *Students:* 56 full-time (38 women), 2 part-time (both women); includes 16 minority (5 African Americans, 1 Asian American or Pacific Islander, 10 Hispanic Americans), 7 international. Average age 30. 109 applicants, 26% accepted, 18 enrolled. In 2007, 17 master's, 6 doctorates awarded. Terminal master's awarded for partial completion of doctoral program. *Median time to degree:* Of those who began their doctoral program in fall 1999, 63% received their degree in 8 years or less. *Degree requirements:* For master's, one foreign language, thesis optional; for doctorate, one foreign language, thesis/dissertation. *Entrance requirements:* For master's and doctorate, GRE General Test. *Application deadline:* For fall admission, 2/1 priority date for domestic students. Applications are processed on a rolling basis. Application fee: $50. Electronic applications accepted. *Financial support:* In 2007–08, 47 students received support, including 6 fellowships with full tuition reimbursements available (averaging $20,000 per year), 41 teaching assistantships with full tuition reimbursements available (averaging $16,000 per year); institutionally sponsored loans and unspecified assistantships also available. Financial award application deadline: 2/1; financial award applicants required to submit FAFSA. *Faculty research:* Anglo-Irish literature, feminist criticism and theory, Caribbean literature, early modern literature and culture, postcolonial and ethnic studies. *Unit head:* Prof. Patrick A. McCarthy, Department Chair, 305-284-3840. *Application contact:* Prof. Mihoko Suzuki, Director of Graduate Studies, 305-284-3840, E-mail: englishgrad@miami.edu.

University of Michigan, Horace H. Rackham School of Graduate Studies, College of Literature, Science, and the Arts, Department of English Language and Literature, Ann Arbor, MI 48109. Offers creative writing (MFA); English and education (PhD); English and women's studies (PhD); English language and literature (PhD). *Faculty:* 63 full-time (35 women). *Students:* 76 full-time (44 women); includes 14 minority (4 African Americans, 9 Asian Americans or Pacific Islanders, 1 Hispanic American), 9 international. 275 applicants, 8% accepted, 13 enrolled. *Degree requirements:* For doctorate, 2 foreign languages, comprehensive exam, thesis/dissertation, oral defense of dissertation, preliminary exam. *Entrance requirements:* For doctorate, GRE General Test, GRE Subject Test, writing sample. Additional exam requirements/recommendations for international students: Required—TOEFL (minimum score 620 paper-based; 260 computer-based; 106 iBT). *Application deadline:* For fall admission, 1/1 for domestic and international students. Application fee: $60 ($75 for international students). Electronic applications accepted. *Financial support:* Fellowships with full tuition reimbursements, teaching assistantships with full tuition reimbursements, health care benefits available. *Faculty research:* Post colonialism, modernism, early modern, American, British. *Unit head:* Dr. Sara Blair, Graduate Chair, 734-647-7678. *Application contact:* Graduate Admissions Office, 734-936-2274, Fax: 734-763-3128, E-mail: grad.eng.admis@um.cc.umich.edu.

University of Michigan, Horace H. Rackham School of Graduate Studies, College of Literature, Science, and the Arts, Department of Women's Studies, Ann Arbor, MI 48109. Offers English and women's studies (PhD); history and women's studies (PhD); lesbian, gay, bisexual, transgender, queer (LGBTQ) studies (Certificate); psychology and women's studies (PhD); sociology and women's studies (PhD); women's studies (Certificate). *Faculty:* 71 full-time (68 women). *Students:* 70 full-time (69 women); includes 12 minority (4 African Americans, 5 Asian Americans or Pacific Islanders, 3 Hispanic Americans), 9 international. Average age 30. 140 applicants, 9% accepted. In 2007, 6 doctorates, 5 other advanced degrees awarded. *Degree requirements:* For doctorate, variable foreign language requirement, thesis/dissertation. *Entrance requirements:* For doctorate, GRE General Test, previous undergraduate course work in women's studies. *Application deadline:* For fall admission, 12/15 for domestic students. Application fee: $60 ($75 for international students). Electronic applications accepted. *Financial support:* In 2007–08, 23 fellowships with full tuition reimbursements (averaging $16,000 per year), 19 teaching assistantships with full and partial tuition reimbursements (averaging $15,199 per year) were awarded; career-related internships or fieldwork, institutionally sponsored loans, scholarships/grants, traineeships, health care benefits, and unspecified assistantships also available. *Faculty research:* Gender issues; LGBTQ studies; sexuality; women and science; global feminism. *Unit head:* Valerie Traub, Chair, 734-763-2047, Fax: 734-647-4943, E-mail: traubv@umich.edu. *Application contact:* Jen Sarafin, Graduate Student Services Coordinator, 734-763-2047, Fax: 734-647-4943, E-mail: jsarafin@umich.edu.

University of Michigan–Flint, College of Arts and Sciences, Program in English, Flint, MI 48502-1950. Offers MA. Part-time programs available. *Faculty:* 2 full-time (0 women). *Students:* 3 full-time (1 woman), 28 part-time (22 women); includes 2 minority (both African Americans) Average age 36. 48 applicants, 75% accepted, 31 enrolled. *Entrance requirements:* Additional exam requirements/recommendations for international students: Required—TOEFL (minimum score 550 paper-based; 220 computer-based), IELTS (minimum score 7). *Application deadline:* For fall admission, 8/1 priority date for domestic students, 3/1 priority date for international students; for winter admission, 11/15 priority date for domestic students, 7/15 priority date for international students; for spring admission, 3/15 priority date for domestic students, 11/15 priority date for international students. Application fee: $55. *Expenses:* Contact institution. Tuition and fees vary according to course load, degree level and program. *Financial support:* In 2007–08, 1 research assistantship (averaging $3,850 per year) was awarded; Federal Work-Study, scholarships/grants, and unspecified assistantships also available. Support available to part-time students. Financial award application deadline: 6/1; financial award applicants required to submit FAFSA. *Unit head:* Dr. Steve Bernstein, Chair, 810-766-6601, E-mail: englishma@umflint.edu. *Application contact:* Bradley T. Maki, Director of Graduate Admissions, 810-762-3171, Fax: 810-766-6789, E-mail: bmaki@umflint.edu.

University of Minnesota, Duluth, Graduate School, College of Liberal Arts, Department of English, Duluth, MN 55812-2496. Offers MA. Part-time programs available. *Faculty:* 20 full-time (6 women), 6 part-time/adjunct (3 women). *Students:* 14 full-time (9 women), 2 part-time (1 woman); includes 1 minority (Asian American or Pacific Islander) Average age 27. 16 applicants, 100% accepted, 11 enrolled. In 2007, 3 degrees awarded. *Degree requirements:* For master's, one foreign language, comprehensive exam, 2 extended papers or projects. *Entrance requirements:* For master's, GRE General Test, minimum GPA of 3.0. Additional exam requirements/recommendations for international students: Required—TOEFL (minimum score 213 computer-based). *Application deadline:* For fall admission, 7/15 for domestic and international students; for spring admission, 11/1 for domestic students, 11/15 for international students. Applications are processed on a rolling basis. Application fee: $55 ($75 for international students). *Expenses:* Tuition, state resident: part-time $812 per credit. Tuition, nonresident: part-time $1,403 per credit. Tuition and fees vary according to program. *Financial support:* In 2007–08, 7 students received support, including 3 fellowships with full and partial tuition reimbursements available (averaging $3,666 per year), 7 teaching assistantships with full and partial tuition reimbursements available (averaging $11,200 per year); scholarships/grants, health care benefits, tuition waivers (full and partial), and unspecified assistantships also available. Support available to part-time students. Financial award application deadline: 3/15. *Faculty research:* British cultural studies, Irish literature, American studies, linguistics, information design. *Unit head:* Dr. Krista Sue-Lo Twu, Director of Graduate Studies, 218-726-6958, Fax: 218-726-6882, E-mail: ktwu@d.umn.edu.

University of Minnesota, Twin Cities Campus, Graduate School, College of Liberal Arts, Department of English, Minneapolis, MN 55455-0213. Offers MA, MFA, PhD. Part-time programs available. *Faculty:* 37 full-time (19 women), 2 part-time/adjunct (0 women). *Students:* 116 full-time (70 women), 19 part-time (17 women); includes 15 minority (4 African Americans, 10 Asian Americans or Pacific Islanders, 1 Hispanic American), 10 international. 479 applicants, 11% accepted, 28 enrolled. In 2007, 4 master's, 16 doctorates awarded. Terminal master's awarded for partial completion of doctoral program. *Degree requirements:* For master's, one foreign language, thesis or alternative; for doctorate, 2 foreign languages, thesis/dissertation. *Entrance requirements:* For master's and doctorate, GRE General Test. Additional exam requirements/recommendations for international students: Required—TOEFL. *Application deadline:* For fall admission, 12/20 for domestic and international students. Application fee: $55 ($75 for international students). Electronic applications accepted. *Financial support:* In 2007–08, 132 students received support, including 9 fellowships with full tuition reimbursements available (averaging $16,000 per year), 1 research assistantship with full tuition reimbursement available (averaging $11,895 per year), 95 teaching assistantships with full tuition reimbursements available (averaging $11,985 per year); career-related internships or fieldwork, Federal Work-Study, institutionally sponsored loans, health care benefits, and tuition waivers (partial) also available. Support available to part-time students. Financial award application deadline: 12/20. *Faculty research:* British and American literature, postcolonial literature, feminist studies in literature, composition and creative writing, cultural studies. *Unit head:* Paula Rabinowitz, Chair, 612-625-3363, Fax: 612-626-1659, E-mail: rabin001@umn.edu. *Application contact:* Lois Cucullo, Director of Graduate Studies, 612-625-3882, Fax: 612-624-8228, E-mail: lcucullo@umn.edu.

University of Mississippi, Graduate School, College of Liberal Arts, Department of English, Oxford, University, MS 38677. Offers MA, MFA, PhD. *Faculty:* 52 full-time (19 women), 12 part-time/adjunct (7 women). *Students:* 59 full-time (35 women), 27 part-time (13 women); includes 9 minority (7 African Americans, 1 American Indian/Alaska Native, 1 Hispanic American), 4 international. In 2007, 12 master's, 4 doctorates awarded. *Degree requirements:* For master's, one foreign language, thesis; for doctorate, 2 foreign languages, thesis/dissertation. *Entrance requirements:* For master's, GRE General Test, minimum GPA of 3.0; for doctorate, GRE General Test. Additional exam requirements/recommendations for international students: Required—TOEFL. *Application deadline:* For fall admission, 2/1 for domestic students; for spring admission, 10/1 for domestic students. Applications are processed on a rolling basis. Application fee: $25. *Expenses:* Tuition, state resident: full-time $4,932. Tuition, nonresident: full-time $11,436. *Financial support:* Scholarships/grants available. Financial award application

English

University of Mississippi (continued)
deadline: 3/1; financial award applicants required to submit FAFSA. *Unit head:* Dr. Patrick Quinn, Chairman, 662-915-7439, Fax: 662-915-5787, E-mail: engl@olemiss.edu.

University of Missouri–Columbia, Graduate School, College of Arts and Sciences, Department of English, Columbia, MO 65211. Offers MA, PhD. Terminal master's awarded for partial completion of doctoral program. *Degree requirements:* For doctorate, 2 foreign languages, thesis/dissertation. *Entrance requirements:* For master's and doctorate, GRE General Test, minimum GPA of 3.0.

University of Missouri–Kansas City, College of Arts and Sciences, Department of English, Kansas City, MO 64110-2499. Offers MA, PhD. PhD offered through the School of Graduate Studies. Part-time and evening/weekend programs available. *Faculty:* 22 full-time (16 women), 19 part-time/adjunct (13 women). *Students:* 12 full-time (7 women), 36 part-time (24 women); includes 7 minority (5 African Americans, 2 Hispanic Americans), 2 international. Average age 31. 38 applicants, 45% accepted, 15 enrolled. In 2007, 15 degrees awarded. *Degree requirements:* For master's, one foreign language; for doctorate, 2 foreign languages, comprehensive exam, thesis/dissertation. *Entrance requirements:* For master's, GRE General Test, writing sample, statement of purpose, 3 letters of recommendation. Additional exam requirements/recommendations for international students: Required—TOEFL. *Application deadline:* For fall admission, 1/15 for domestic students, 1/15 priority date for international students. Applications are processed on a rolling basis. Application fee: $35 ($50 for international students). Electronic applications accepted. *Expenses:* Tuition, state resident: part-time $287 per hour. Tuition, nonresident: part-time $741 per hour. Required fees: $31 per hour. Tuition and fees vary according to program. *Financial support:* In 2007–08, 17 students received support, including 15 teaching assistantships (averaging $13,350 per year); career-related internships or fieldwork, Federal Work-Study, and institutionally sponsored loans also available. Support available to part-time students. Financial award application deadline: 3/1; financial award applicants required to submit FAFSA. *Faculty research:* Creative writing: poetry and prose, computational linguistics, rhetoric and composition, African American and British literature, print culture. Total annual research expenditures: $225,854. *Unit head:* Dr. Jeff Rydberg-Cox, Chair, 816-235-2560, Fax: 816-235-1308, E-mail: rydbergcoxj@umkc.edu. *Application contact:* Dr. Jennifer Phegley, Graduate Advisor, 816-235-2766, E-mail: phegleyj@umkc.edu.

University of Missouri–St. Louis, College of Arts and Sciences, Department of English, St. Louis, MO 63121. Offers American literature (MA); creative writing (MFA); English (MA); English literature (MA); linguistics (MA); teaching of writing (Graduate Certificate). *Faculty:* 19 full-time (12 women), 1 part-time/adjunct (0 women). *Students:* 16 full-time (12 women), 90 part-time (68 women); includes 9 minority (5 African Americans, 3 Asian Americans or Pacific Islanders, 1 Hispanic American). Average age 32. In 2007, 30 degrees awarded. *Degree requirements:* For master's, thesis optional. *Entrance requirements:* For master's, GRE General Test, writing sample. Additional exam requirements/recommendations for international students: Required—TOEFL (minimum score 550 paper-based; 213 computer-based). *Application deadline:* For fall admission, 7/15 priority date for domestic students; for spring admission, 12/15 priority date for domestic students. Applications are processed on a rolling basis. Application fee: $35 ($40 for international students). Electronic applications accepted. *Financial support:* In 2007–08, 1 research assistantship (averaging $9,000 per year), 6 teaching assistantships with full and partial tuition reimbursements (averaging $9,000 per year) were awarded. *Faculty research:* Victorian literature, Shakespeare and Renaissance literature, eighteenth century literature, composition theory. *Unit head:* Dr. Richard Cook, Director of Graduate Studies, 314-516-5516, Fax: 314-516-5415, E-mail: rcook@umsl.edu. *Application contact:* 314-516-5458, Fax: 314-516-5310, E-mail: gradadm@umsl.edu.

The University of Montana, Graduate School, College of Arts and Sciences, Department of English, Program in Literature, Missoula, MT 59812-0002. Offers MA. *Degree requirements:* For master's, thesis optional. *Entrance requirements:* For master's, GRE General Test, sample of written work. Additional exam requirements/recommendations for international students: Required—TOEFL. *Faculty research:* Literary history, cultural studies, criticism and theory, Western studies.

University of Montevallo, College of Arts and Sciences, Department of English, Montevallo, AL 35115. Offers English literature (MA). Part-time programs available. *Degree requirements:* For master's, comprehensive exam, thesis optional. *Entrance requirements:* For master's, GRE General Test, MAT, minimum undergraduate GPA of 2.75 in last 60 hours or 2.5 overall, bachelor's degree in English or equivalent. Additional exam requirements/recommendations for international students: Required—TOEFL (minimum score 550 paper-based; 213 computer-based).

University of Nebraska at Kearney, College of Graduate Study, College of Fine Arts and Humanities, Department of English, Kearney, NE 68849-0001. Offers creative writing (MA); literature (MA). Part-time and evening/weekend programs available. *Degree requirements:* For master's, thesis optional. *Entrance requirements:* For master's, GRE General Test, writing samples. Additional exam requirements/recommendations for international students: Required—TOEFL (minimum score 550 paper-based; 213 computer-based). Electronic applications accepted. *Faculty research:* Narrative theory, popular culture, western and plains literature, women's studies, media studies.

University of Nebraska at Omaha, Graduate Studies and Research, College of Arts and Sciences, Department of English, Omaha, NE 68182. Offers advanced writing (Certificate); English (MA); teaching English to speakers of other languages (Certificate); technical communication (Certificate). Part-time and evening/weekend programs available. *Faculty:* 17 full-time (9 women). *Students:* 11 full-time (8 women), 49 part-time (33 women); includes 3 minority (1 African American, 1 Asian American or Pacific Islander, 1 Hispanic American), 2 international. Average age 34. 39 applicants, 72% accepted, 20 enrolled. In 2007, 13 master's, 9 other advanced degrees awarded. *Degree requirements:* For master's, comprehensive exam, thesis (for some programs). *Entrance requirements:* For master's, minimum GPA of 3.0, statement of purpose, 3 letters of recommendation, writing sample. Additional exam requirements/recommendations for international students: Required—TOEFL (minimum score 600 paper-based; 250 computer-based; 100 iBT). *Application deadline:* For fall admission, 8/1 priority date for domestic students; for spring admission, 12/1 priority date for domestic students. Applications are processed on a rolling basis. Application fee: $45. Electronic applications accepted. *Financial support:* In 2007–08, 30 students received support; fellowships, teaching assistantships with tuition reimbursements available, Federal Work-Study, institutionally sponsored loans, scholarships/grants, tuition waivers (partial), and unspecified assistantships available. Support available to part-time students. Financial award application deadline: 3/1; financial award applicants required to submit FAFSA. *Unit head:* Dr. Susan Maher, Chairperson, 402-554-3636. *Application contact:* Dr. Joan Latchaw, Student Contact, 402-554-3636.

University of Nebraska–Lincoln, Graduate College, College of Arts and Sciences, Department of English, Lincoln, NE 68588-0333. Offers MA, PhD. *Degree requirements:* For master's, thesis optional; for doctorate, one foreign language, comprehensive exam, thesis/dissertation. *Entrance requirements:* For master's, writing sample; for doctorate, GRE General Test, writing sample. Additional exam requirements/recommendations for international students: Required—TOEFL (minimum score 600 paper-based; 250 computer-based). Electronic applications accepted. *Faculty research:* Creative writing, composition and rhetoric, women's studies, North American literature, medieval/Renaissance studies.

University of Nevada, Las Vegas, Graduate College, College of Liberal Arts, Department of English, Las Vegas, NV 89154-9900. Offers creative writing (MFA); English (PhD); language/composition theory study (MA); literature study (MA). Part-time programs available. *Faculty:* 37 full-time (12 women), 1 part-time/adjunct (0 women). *Students:* 63 full-time (29 women), 27 part-time (15 women); includes 6 minority (3 Asian Americans or Pacific Islanders, 3 Hispanic Americans), 4 international. 118 applicants, 22% accepted, 18 enrolled. In 2007, 16 master's, 5 doctorates awarded. *Degree requirements:* For master's, one foreign language, comprehensive exam, thesis (for some programs); for doctorate, 2 foreign languages, comprehensive exam, thesis/dissertation. *Entrance requirements:* For master's, GRE General Test, GRE Subject Test, minimum GPA of 3.0 during previous 2 years, 2.75 overall; for doctorate, GRE General Test, GRE Subject Test, MA in English, minimum GPA of 3.5. Additional exam requirements/recommendations for international students: Required—TOEFL (minimum score 550 paper-based; 213 computer-based; 80 iBT). *Application deadline:* For fall admission, 2/15 for domestic and international students. Application fee: $60 ($75 for international students). Electronic applications accepted. *Expenses:* Tuition, state resident: part-time $198 per credit. Tuition, nonresident: part-time $416 per credit. Required fees: $256 per semester. Tuition and fees vary according to course load and reciprocity agreements. *Financial support:* In 2007–08, 2 research assistantships with partial tuition reimbursements (averaging $10,000 per year), 52 teaching assistantships with partial tuition reimbursements (averaging $11,000 per year) were awarded; career-related internships or fieldwork, Federal Work-Study, institutionally sponsored loans, scholarships/grants, health care benefits, and unspecified assistantships also available. Support available to part-time students. Financial award application deadline: 3/1. *Unit head:* Dr. Chris Hudgins, Chair, 702-895-3533. *Application contact:* Graduate College Admissions Evaluator, 702-895-3320, Fax: 702-895-4180, E-mail: gradcollege@unlv.edu.

University of Nevada, Reno, Graduate School, College of Liberal Arts, Department of English, Reno, NV 89557. Offers MA, MATE, PhD. *Faculty:* 31. *Students:* 22 full-time (9 women), 52 part-time (35 women); includes 4 minority (2 Asian Americans or Pacific Islanders, 2 Hispanic Americans). Average age 34. 63 applicants, 38% accepted, 19 enrolled. In 2007, 15 master's, 4 doctorates awarded. Terminal master's awarded for partial completion of doctoral program. *Degree requirements:* For master's, variable foreign language requirement, thesis optional; for doctorate, variable foreign language requirement, thesis/dissertation. *Entrance requirements:* For master's, GRE General Test, minimum GPA of 2.75; for doctorate, GRE General Test, minimum GPA of 3.0. Additional exam requirements/recommendations for international students: Required—TOEFL. *Application deadline:* For fall admission, 2/1 for domestic students. Application fee: $60 ($95 for international students). *Expenses:* Tuition, state resident: full-time $2,774; part-time $154 per credit. Tuition, nonresident: full-time $13,578; part-time $330 per credit. Required fees: $49 per semester. *Financial support:* In 2007–08, 2 research assistantships, 36 teaching assistantships were awarded; Federal Work-Study, institutionally sponsored loans, and unspecified assistantships also available. Financial award application deadline: 3/1. *Faculty research:* Translating Persian/Iraqi literature, Shakespearean literature, modern American literature, composition and rhetoric. *Unit head:* Dr. Don Hardy, Graduate Program Director, 775-784-8689.

University of New Brunswick Fredericton, School of Graduate Studies, Faculty of Arts, Department of English, Fredericton, NB E3B 5A3, Canada. Offers MA, PhD. Part-time programs available. *Faculty:* 21 full-time (11 women), 1 (woman) part-time/adjunct. *Students:* 45 full-time (26 women), 4 part-time (1 woman). Average age 25. 62 applicants, 53% accepted, 15 enrolled. In 2007, 16 master's, 1 doctorate awarded. *Degree requirements:* For master's, thesis; for doctorate, comprehensive exam, thesis/dissertation. *Entrance requirements:* For master's and doctorate, minimum GPA of 3.7. Additional exam requirements/recommendations for international students: Required—TOEFL (minimum score 550 paper-based), TWE (minimum score 4). *Application deadline:* 1/31 priority date for domestic and international students. Applications are processed on a rolling basis. Application fee: $50 Canadian dollars. *Financial support:* In 2007–08, 1 fellowship (averaging $4,000 per year), 12 research assistantships, 5 teaching assistantships were awarded; health care benefits also available. Financial award application deadline: 1/31. *Faculty research:* Creative writing, Canadian literature, Post Colonial literature, Early Modern literature, scholarly editing and textual studies. *Unit head:* Dr. John Ball, Director of Graduate Studies, 506-458-7409, Fax: 506-453-5069, E-mail: jball@unb.ca. *Application contact:* Theresa Keenan, Graduate Secretary, 506-451-6809, Fax: 506-453-5069, E-mail: tkeenan@unb.ca.

University of New Hampshire, Graduate School, College of Liberal Arts, Department of English, Durham, NH 03824. Offers English (MFA, PhD); English education (MST); language and linguistics (MA); literature (MA); writing (MA). Part-time programs available. *Faculty:* 44 full-time. *Students:* 38 full-time (21 women), 64 part-time (43 women); includes 6 minority (1 American Indian/Alaska Native, 3 Asian Americans or Pacific Islanders, 2 Hispanic Americans), 3 international. Average age 34. 251 applicants, 45% accepted, 31 enrolled. In 2007, 25 master's, 6 doctorates awarded. *Degree requirements:* For master's, one foreign language; for doctorate, 2 foreign languages, thesis/dissertation. *Entrance requirements:* For master's, GRE General Test, sample of written work; for doctorate, GRE General Test, GRE Subject Test, sample of written work. Additional exam requirements/recommendations for international students: Required—TOEFL (minimum score 550 paper-based; 213 computer-based; 80 iBT). *Application deadline:* For fall admission, 2/15 priority date for domestic students, 2/15 for international students. Applications are processed on a rolling basis. Application fee: $60. Electronic applications accepted. *Financial support:* In 2007–08, 1 fellowship, 1 research assistantship, 43 teaching assistantships were awarded; career-related internships or fieldwork, Federal Work-Study, scholarships/grants, and tuition waivers (full and partial) also available. Support available to part-time students. Financial award application deadline: 2/15. *Unit head:* Dr. Andrew Merton, Chairperson, 603-862-3977. *Application contact:* Sue Smith, Administrative Assistant, 603-862-3963, E-mail: engl.grad@unh.edu.

University of New Mexico, Graduate School, College of Arts and Sciences, Department of English, Program in English, Albuquerque, NM 87131-2039. Offers MA, PhD. *Students:* 53 full-time (43 women), 19 part-time (12 women); includes 14 minority (1 African American, 2 American Indian/Alaska Native, 2 Asian Americans or Pacific Islanders, 9 Hispanic Americans), 3 international. Average age 37. 82 applicants, 40% accepted, 17 enrolled. In 2007, 14 master's, 3 doctorates awarded. *Degree requirements:* For master's, one foreign language, comprehensive exam (for some programs), thesis (for some programs), portfolio; for doctorate, 2 foreign languages, comprehensive exam, thesis/dissertation. *Entrance requirements:* For master's, GRE General Test, GRE Subject Test (literature MA); for doctorate, GRE General Test, GRE Subject Test. *Application deadline:* For fall admission, 1/15 for domestic students. Application fee: $50. *Financial support:* In 2007–08, 75 teaching assistantships with full tuition reimbursements were awarded. *Faculty research:* American literature, Native American literature, Chicano literature, British and Irish literature, rhetoric and writing. *Application contact:* N. Ezra Meier, Graduate Advisor, 505-277-4437, Fax: 505-277-0021, E-mail: english@unm.edu.

University of New Orleans, Graduate School, College of Liberal Arts, Department of English, Program in English, New Orleans, LA 70148. Offers MA. Part-time and evening/weekend programs available. *Faculty:* 12 full-time (2 women). *Students:* 35 full-time (28 women), 40 part-time (29 women); includes 7 minority (4 African Americans, 1 Asian American or Pacific Islander, 2 Hispanic Americans), 4 international. Average age 31. 35 applicants, 91% accepted, 11 enrolled. In 2007, 13 degrees awarded. *Degree requirements:* For master's, one foreign language, thesis (for some programs). *Entrance requirements:* For master's, GRE General Test. Additional exam requirements/recommendations for international students: Required—TOEFL (minimum score 550 paper-based; 213 computer-based; 79 iBT). *Application deadline:* For fall admission, 7/1 priority date for domestic students, 6/1 for international students; for spring admission, 11/15 priority date for domestic students, 10/1 for international students. Applications are processed on a rolling basis. Application fee: $20. Electronic applications accepted. *Financial support:* Research assistantships, teaching assistantships, career-related internships or fieldwork and tuition waivers (partial) available. Financial award application deadline: 5/15; financial award applicants required to submit FAFSA. *Unit head:* Dr. Carl Malmgren, Graduate Coordinator, 504-280-6975, Fax: 504-280-7334, E-mail: cmalmgre@uno.edu.

University of North Alabama, College of Arts and Sciences, Department of English, Florence, AL 35632-0001. Offers MAEN. Part-time and evening/weekend programs available. *Faculty:* 6 part-time/adjunct (3 women). *Students:* 8 full-time (6 women), 15 part-time (13 women), 1 international. Average age 32. In 2007, 8 degrees awarded. *Application deadline:* For fall admission, 7/1 priority date for domestic students; for spring admission, 12/1 for domestic students. Applications are processed on a rolling basis. Application fee: $25. Electronic applications accepted. *Expenses:* Tuition, state resident: part-time $170 per credit hour. Tuition, nonresident: part-time $340 per credit hour. *Unit head:* Dr. Ronald Smith, Chair, 256-765-4238, Fax: 256-765-4239, E-mail: resmith@una.edu. *Application contact:* Dr. Sue Wilson, Dean of Enrollment Management, 256-765-4316, Fax: 256-765-4349, E-mail: sjwilson@una.edu.

The University of North Carolina at Chapel Hill, Graduate School, College of Arts and Sciences, Department of English, Chapel Hill, NC 27599. Offers MA, PhD. *Degree requirements:* For master's, one foreign language, comprehensive exam, thesis; for doctorate, 2 foreign languages, comprehensive exam, thesis/dissertation. *Entrance requirements:* For master's and doctorate, GRE General Test, GRE Subject Test, minimum GPA of 3.0 for last 2 undergraduate years, writing sample. Additional exam requirements/recommendations for international students: Required—TOEFL. Electronic applications accepted. *Faculty research:* African American, Southern, period studies, genre studies, critical theory/culture studies.

The University of North Carolina at Charlotte, Graduate School, College of Arts and Sciences, Department of English, Charlotte, NC 28223-0001. Offers English (MA); English education (MA). Part-time and evening/weekend programs available. *Faculty:* 32 full-time (15 women). *Students:* 19 full-time (15 women), 41 part-time (29 women); includes 6 minority (5 African Americans, 1 Asian American or Pacific Islander), 1 international. Average age 32. 37 applicants, 78% accepted, 21 enrolled. In 2007, 28 degrees awarded. *Degree requirements:* For master's, comprehensive exam. *Entrance requirements:* For master's, GRE General Test, minimum undergraduate GPA of 3.0 in major, 2.75 overall. Additional exam requirements/recommendations for international students: Required—TOEFL (minimum score 557 paper-based; 220 computer-based). *Application deadline:* For fall admission, 7/15 for domestic students, 5/1 for international students; for spring admission, 11/15 for domestic students, 10/1 for international students. Applications are processed on a rolling basis. Application fee: $55. Electronic applications accepted. *Expenses:* Tuition, state resident: full-time $2,855. Tuition, nonresident: full-time $13,062. Required fees: $1,692. *Financial support:* In 2007–08, 15 teaching assistantships (averaging $7,533 per year) were awarded; fellowships, research assistantships, career-related internships or fieldwork, Federal Work-Study, institutionally sponsored loans, scholarships/grants, and unspecified assistantships also available. Support available to part-time students. Financial award application deadline: 4/1; financial award applicants required to submit FAFSA. *Faculty research:* English as a second language (ESL), composition theory and pedagogy, children's literature, technical and professional writing, English for specific purposes (ESP). Total annual research expenditures: $700,000. *Unit head:* Dr. Cyril H. Knoblauch, Chair, 704-687-2296, Fax: 704-687-3961, E-mail: chknobla@email.uncc.edu. *Application contact:* Kathy B. Giddings, Director of Graduate Admissions, 704-687-3366, Fax: 704-687-3279, E-mail: agidding@uncc.edu.

The University of North Carolina at Greensboro, Graduate School, College of Arts and Sciences, Department of English, Program in English, Greensboro, NC 27412-5001. Offers American literature (PhD); English (M Ed, MA); English literature (PhD); rhetoric and composition (PhD). *Students:* 82 full-time (56 women), 35 part-time (24 women); includes 15 minority (13 African Americans, 1 American Indian/Alaska Native, 1 Asian American or Pacific Islander). *Degree requirements:* For master's, comprehensive exam, thesis or alternative; for doctorate, variable foreign language requirement, thesis/dissertation, preliminary exam. *Entrance requirements:* For master's, GRE General Test, GRE Subject Test, minimum GPA of 3.0; for doctorate, GRE General Test, GRE Subject Test, critical writing sample, minimum GPA of 3.0. Additional exam requirements/recommendations for international students: Required—TOEFL. *Application deadline:* For fall admission, 1/20 priority date for domestic students; for spring admission, 11/1 for domestic students. Application fee: $45. Electronic applications accepted. *Financial support:* Fellowships, research assistantships, teaching assistantships available. *Unit head:* Dr. Christian Moraru, Director of Graduate Studies, 336-334-3564, E-mail: c_moraru@uncg.edu. *Application contact:* Michelle Harkleroad, Director of Graduate Admissions, 336-334-4884, Fax: 336-334-4424, E-mail: mbharkle@uncg.edu.

The University of North Carolina Wilmington, College of Arts and Sciences, Department of English, Wilmington, NC 28403-3297. Offers MA. *Students:* 26 full-time (16 women), 16 part-time (8 women); includes 2 minority (both African Americans) Average age 27. 30 applicants, 73% accepted, 14 enrolled. In 2007, 18 degrees awarded. *Degree requirements:* For master's, comprehensive exam, thesis. *Entrance requirements:* For master's, GRE General Test, minimum B average in undergraduate major. *Application deadline:* For fall admission, 3/1 for domestic students. Applications are processed on a rolling basis. Application fee: $45. *Expenses:* Tuition, state resident: full-time $2,714. Tuition, nonresident: full-time $12,579. Required fees: $1,985. *Financial support:* In 2007–08, 9 teaching assistantships were awarded; career-related internships or fieldwork and Federal Work-Study also available. Support available to part-time students. Financial award application deadline: 3/15. *Unit head:* Dr. Christopher Gould, Chair, 910-962-3268, Fax: 910-962-7186. *Application contact:* Dr. Robert D. Roer, Dean, Graduate School, 910-962-4117, Fax: 910-962-3787, E-mail: roer@uncw.edu.

University of North Dakota, Graduate School, College of Arts and Sciences, Department of English, Grand Forks, ND 58202. Offers MA, PhD. *Faculty:* 17 full-time (12 women). *Students:* 15 full-time (7 women), 42 part-time (26 women); includes 4 minority (2 American Indian/Alaska Native, 2 Hispanic Americans), 8 international. 34 applicants, 50% accepted, 17 enrolled. In 2007, 3 master's, 2 doctorates awarded. *Degree requirements:* For master's, one foreign language, comprehensive exam, thesis or alternative; for doctorate, one foreign language, comprehensive exam, thesis/dissertation. *Entrance requirements:* For master's and doctorate, GRE General Test, minimum GPA of 3.0. Additional exam requirements/recommendations for international students: Required—TOEFL (minimum score 550 paper-based; 213 computer-based; 79 iBT), IELTS (minimum score 7). *Application deadline:* For fall admission, 3/1 for domestic and international students. Electronic applications accepted. *Expenses:* Tuition, state resident: full-time $4,050; part-time $225 per credit. Tuition, nonresident: full-time $10,818; part-time $601 per credit. Required fees: $110 per semester. Tuition and fees vary according to class time, campus/location, program and reciprocity agreements. *Financial support:* In 2007–08, 1 research assistantship with full and partial tuition reimbursement (averaging $5,379 per year), 25 teaching assistantships with full tuition reimbursements (averaging $9,575 per year) were awarded; fellowships with full and partial tuition reimbursements, Federal Work-Study, institutionally sponsored loans, scholarships/grants, health care benefits, tuition waivers (full and partial), and unspecified assistantships also available. Support available to part-time students. Financial award application deadline: 3/15; financial award applicants required to submit FAFSA. *Faculty research:* Creative writing, rhetorical theory, cinema, American literature, European literature. *Unit head:* Dr. Eric Wolfe, Graduate Director, 701-777-3321, Fax: 701-777-2373. *Application contact:* Brenda Halle, Admissions Specialist, 701-777-2947, Fax: 701-777-3619, E-mail: brendahalle@mail.und.edu.

University of Northern Colorado, Graduate School, College of Humanities and Social Sciences, School of English Language and Literature, Program in English, Greeley, CO 80639. Offers MA. Part-time programs available. *Faculty:* 9 full-time (4 women). *Students:* 20 full-time (11 women), 3 part-time (2 women); includes 1 minority (African American) Average age 30. 14 applicants, 100% accepted, 7 enrolled. In 2007, 7 degrees awarded. *Degree requirements:* For master's, comprehensive exam. *Entrance requirements:* For master's, GRE General Test, 2 letters of recommendation. *Application deadline:* Applications are processed on a rolling basis. Application fee: $50 ($60 for international students). Electronic applications accepted. *Expenses:* Tuition, state resident: part-time $222 per credit. Tuition, nonresident: part-time $627 per credit. Required fees: $36 per credit. *Financial support:* In 2007–08, 7 research assistantships (averaging $4,768 per year), 10 teaching assistantships (averaging $10,700 per year) were awarded; unspecified assistantships also available. Financial award application deadline: 3/1; financial award applicants required to submit FAFSA. *Unit head:* Dr. Marcus Embry, Program Coordinator, 970-351-2971, Fax: 970-351-3378.

University of Northern Iowa, Graduate College, College of Humanities and Fine Arts, Department of English Language and Literature, Cedar Falls, IA 50614. Offers English (MA); teaching English to speakers of other languages (MA). Part-time and evening/weekend programs available. *Students:* 31 full-time (20 women), 20 part-time (16 women); includes 2 minority (both Asian Americans or Pacific Islanders), 6 international. 46 applicants, 72% accepted, 19 enrolled. In 2007, 25 degrees awarded. *Degree requirements:* For master's, one foreign language, comprehensive exam, thesis or alternative, portfolio. *Entrance requirements:* For master's, minimum GPA of 3.0. Additional exam requirements/recommendations for international students: Required—TOEFL (minimum score 600 paper-based; 250 computer-based; 100 iBT). *Application deadline:* For fall admission, 8/1 priority date for domestic students. Applications are processed on a rolling basis. Application fee: $30 ($50 for international students). Electronic applications accepted. *Expenses:* Tuition, state resident: full-time $6,246; part-time $694 per credit hour. Tuition, nonresident: full-time $14,554; part-time $694 per credit hour. Required fees: $838; $119 per semester. *Financial support:* Career-related internships or fieldwork, Federal Work-Study, scholarships/grants, and tuition waivers (full and partial) available. Support available to part-time students. Financial award application deadline: 2/1. *Unit head:* Dr. Jeffrey S. Copeland, Head, 319-273-3855, Fax: 319-273-5807, E-mail: jeffrey.copeland@uni.edu.

University of North Florida, College of Arts and Sciences, Department of English, Jacksonville, FL 32224-2645. Offers MA. Part-time and evening/weekend programs available. *Faculty:* 11 full-time (2 women). *Students:* 19 full-time (16 women), 48 part-time (37 women); includes 8 minority (5 African Americans, 3 Hispanic Americans). Average age 31. 32 applicants, 75% accepted, 19 enrolled. In 2007, 27 degrees awarded. *Degree requirements:* For master's, comprehensive exam, thesis optional. *Entrance requirements:* For master's, GRE General Test, minimum GPA of 3.0 in last 60 hours, writing sample. Additional exam requirements/recommendations for international students: Required—TOEFL (minimum score 500 paper-based; 173 computer-based). *Application deadline:* For fall admission, 7/6 priority date for domestic students, 5/1 for international students; for spring admission, 11/1 priority date for domestic students, 10/1 for international students. Applications are processed on a rolling basis. Application fee: $30. Electronic applications accepted. *Expenses:* Tuition, state resident: part-time $266 per credit hour. Tuition, nonresident: part-time $858 per credit hour. One-time fee: $35 part-time. Tuition and fees vary according to program. *Financial support:* In 2007–08, 43 students received support; research assistantships, Federal Work-Study and tuition waivers (partial) available. Support available to part-time students. Financial award application deadline: 4/1; financial award applicants required to submit FAFSA. *Faculty research:* Genre, period, and individual author studies in British, American, and world literature; literary criticism and theory—psychological, new historical and cultural, deconstructive, feminist, narrative, mythic; film and popular culture; online poetry publishing. *Unit head:* Dr. Samuel A. Kimball, Chair, 904-620-2273, Fax: 904-620-3949, E-mail: skimball@unf.edu. *Application contact:* Dr. Christopher Gabbard, Graduate Coordinator, 904-620-1254, Fax: 904-620-3940, E-mail: cgabbard@unf.edu.

University of North Texas, Robert B. Toulouse School of Graduate Studies, College of Arts and Sciences, Department of English, Denton, TX 76203. Offers creative writing (MA); English (MA, PhD); English as a second language (MA); linguistics (MA); Technical writing (MA). *Faculty:* 60 full-time (36 women). *Students:* 82 full-time (46 women), 91 part-time (65 women); includes 19 minority (4 African Americans, 1 American Indian/Alaska Native, 6 Asian Americans or Pacific Islanders, 8 Hispanic Americans), 13 international. Average age 30. 91 applicants, 47% accepted, 21 enrolled. In 2007, 38 master's, 5 doctorates awarded. Terminal master's awarded for partial completion of doctoral program. *Degree requirements:* For master's, one foreign language, comprehensive exam, thesis optional; for doctorate, one foreign language, comprehensive exam, thesis/dissertation. *Entrance requirements:* For master's, GRE General Test, 3.0 GPA, personal statement, current vita/resumè, writing sample for creative writing program; for doctorate, GRE General Test, 3.5 GPA, 3 letters of recommendation, personal statement, writing sample. Additional exam requirements/recommendations for international students: Required—proof of English language proficiency required for non-native English speakers; Recommended—TOEFL (minimum score 550 paper-based; 213 computer-based). *Application deadline:* For fall admission, 7/15 priority date for domestic students; for spring admission, 11/15 for domestic students. Application fee: $50 ($75 for international students). *Financial support:* In 2007–08, 8 students received support, including 2 fellowships with full tuition reimbursements available (averaging $20,000 per year), 42 teaching assistantships (averaging $11,000 per year); career-related internships or fieldwork, Federal Work-Study, institutionally sponsored loans, scholarships/grants, health care benefits, and unspecified assistantships also available. Financial award application deadline: 4/1. *Faculty research:* Creative writing, British and American literature, composition and rhetoric. Total annual research expenditures: $25,000. *Unit head:* Dr. David Holdeman, Chair, 940-565-2050, Fax: 940-565-4355, E-mail: holdeman@cas1.unt.edu. *Application contact:* Dr. Robert K. Upchuerch, Chair of Graduate Studies, 940-565-2114, Fax: 940-565-4355, E-mail: robertu@unt.edu.

University of Notre Dame, Graduate School, College of Arts and Letters, Division of Humanities, Department of English, Notre Dame, IN 46556. Offers creative writing (MFA); English (MA, PhD). *Faculty:* 46 full-time (21 women). *Students:* 64 full-time (39 women), 2 part-time; includes 13 minority (2 African Americans, 1 American Indian/Alaska Native, 1 Asian American or Pacific Islander, 9 Hispanic Americans), 5 international. 313 applicants, 7% accepted, 15 enrolled. In 2007, 5 master's, 10 doctorates awarded. *Median time to degree:* Of those who began their doctoral program in fall 1999, 63% received their degree in 8 years or less. *Degree requirements:* For doctorate, one foreign language, thesis/dissertation, candidacy exam. *Entrance requirements:* For master's, GRE General Test, minimum GPA of 3.0; for doctorate, GRE General Test, GRE Subject Test, minimum GPA of 3.0. Additional exam requirements/recommendations for international students: Required—TOEFL (minimum score 600 paper-based; 250 computer-based; 80 iBT). *Application deadline:* For fall admission, 1/1 priority date for domestic students, 1/1 for international students. Applications are processed on a rolling basis. Application fee: $50. Electronic applications accepted. *Financial support:* In 2007–08, 12 fellowships with full tuition reimbursements (averaging $22,000 per year), research assistantships with full tuition reimbursements (averaging $16,000 per year), 47 teaching assistantships with full tuition reimbursements (averaging $16,000 per year) were awarded; tuition waivers (full) also available. Financial award application deadline: 2/1. *Faculty research:* Early modern studies (medieval/Renaissance), modern British studies (18th-20th centuries), American Studies, literature and philosophy, Irish studies. *Unit head:* Dr. Graham Hammill, Director of Graduate Studies, 574-631-618, E-mail: english.13@nd.edu. *Application contact:* Dr. Jarren Gonzales, Director of Graduate Admissions, 574-631-7706, Fax: 574-631-4183.

University of Oklahoma, Graduate College, College of Arts and Sciences, Department of English, Norman, OK 73019-0390. Offers MA, PhD. *Faculty:* 33 full-time (13 women). *Students:* 51 full-time (30 women), 6 part-time (5 women); includes 12 minority (3 African Americans, 7 American Indian/Alaska Native, 2 Hispanic Americans), 2 international. 50 applicants, 26% accepted, 3 enrolled. In 2007, 10 master's, 2 doctorates awarded. *Degree requirements:* For master's, one foreign language, thesis or alternative, qualifying exam; for doctorate, 2 foreign languages, thesis/dissertation, qualifying exam. *Entrance requirements:* For master's, GRE General Test, minimum GPA of 3.0, BA with 27 hours of course work in English or 15 hours of upper-level courses; for doctorate, GRE General Test, GRE Subject Test (English literature), minimum graduate GPA of 3.5. Additional exam requirements/recommendations for international students: Required—TOEFL (minimum score 550 paper-based; 213 computer-based). *Application deadline:* For fall admission, 4/1 priority date for domestic students, 4/1 for international students; for spring admission, 11/1 for domestic students, 9/1 for international students. Applications are processed on a rolling basis. Application fee: $40 ($90 for international students). Electronic applications accepted. *Expenses:* Tuition, state resident: full-time $3,451; part-time $144 per credit hour. Tuition, nonresident: full-time $12,432; part-time $518 per credit hour. Required fees: $1,925; $70 per credit hour. $122 per semester. *Financial support:* In 2007–08, 27 students received support, including 2 fellowships with full tuition reimbursements available (averaging $2,500 per year), 3 research assistantships with partial

English

University of Oklahoma (continued)

tuition reimbursements available (averaging $12,515 per year), 53 teaching assistantships with partial tuition reimbursements available (averaging $11,809 per year); scholarships/grants, health care benefits, tuition waivers (full and partial), and unspecified assistantships also available. Financial award application deadline: 3/1; financial award applicants required to submit FAFSA. *Faculty research:* Native American studies, medieval/early modern studies, modern contemporary literature, literary theory. Total annual research expenditures: $52,828. *Unit head:* David Mair, Chair, 405-325-4661, Fax: 405-325-0831, E-mail: dmair@ou.edu. *Application contact:* Dr. Timothy S Murphy, Graduate Liaison, 405-325-4661, Fax: 405-325-0831, E-mail: tmurphy@ou.edu.

University of Oregon, Graduate School, College of Arts and Sciences, Department of English, Eugene, OR 97403. Offers MA, PhD. *Faculty:* 40 full-time (18 women), 5 part-time/adjunct (4 women). *Students:* 71 full-time (43 women), 8 part-time (6 women); includes 4 minority (2 African Americans, 2 Asian Americans or Pacific Islanders), 2 international. 149 applicants, 18% accepted. In 2007, 7 master's, 7 doctorates awarded. Terminal master's awarded for partial completion of doctoral program. *Degree requirements:* For master's, one foreign language; for doctorate, 2 foreign languages, thesis/dissertation. *Entrance requirements:* For master's, GRE General Test; for doctorate, GRE Subject Test (English literature), minimum GPA of 3.5. Additional exam requirements/recommendations for international students: Required—TOEFL. *Application deadline:* For fall admission, 7/1 for domestic students; for winter admission, 10/1 for domestic students; for spring admission, 1/10 for domestic students. Application fee: $50. *Financial support:* In 2007–08, 69 teaching assistantships were awarded; Federal Work-Study, institutionally sponsored loans, and unspecified assistantships also available. Financial award application deadline: 1/15. *Faculty research:* Old and Middle English, women writers, critical theory, literature and the environment, rhetoric and composition. *Unit head:* Henry Wonham, Head, 541-346-3911. *Application contact:* Michael Stamm, Admissions Contact, 541-346-1501, E-mail: mstamm@uoregon.edu.

University of Ottawa, Faculty of Graduate and Postdoctoral Studies, Faculty of Arts, Department of English, Ottawa, ON K1N 6N5, Canada. Offers MA, PhD. Part-time and evening/weekend programs available. *Degree requirements:* For master's, one foreign language, thesis optional; for doctorate, 2 foreign languages, comprehensive exam, thesis/dissertation. *Entrance requirements:* For master's, honors degree or equivalent, minimum B average; for doctorate, master's degree, minimum B+ average. Electronic applications accepted. *Faculty research:* Anglo-Saxon and medieval literature.

University of Pennsylvania, School of Arts and Sciences, Graduate Group in English, Philadelphia, PA 19104. Offers AM, PhD. Terminal master's awarded for partial completion of doctoral program. *Degree requirements:* For master's, one foreign language; for doctorate, 2 foreign languages, thesis/dissertation, oral and written qualifying exams. *Entrance requirements:* For master's, GRE General Test, GRE Subject Test, sample of written work; for doctorate, GRE General Test, GRE Subject Test. Additional exam requirements/recommendations for international students: Required—TOEFL. Electronic applications accepted. *Faculty research:* Renaissance literature and intellectual theory, feminist studies, literary theory.

University of Pittsburgh, School of Arts and Sciences, Department of English, Pittsburgh, PA 15260. Offers cultural and critical studies (PhD); English (MA); writing (MFA). Part-time programs available. *Faculty:* 55 full-time (23 women). *Students:* 197 full-time (119 women), 37 part-time (34 women); includes 33 minority (11 African Americans, 6 Asian Americans or Pacific Islanders, 16 Hispanic Americans), 4 international. 363 applicants, 29% accepted, 35 enrolled. In 2007, 31 master's, 13 doctorates awarded. *Degree requirements:* For master's, one foreign language; for doctorate, 2 foreign languages, comprehensive exam, thesis/dissertation. *Entrance requirements:* For master's and doctorate, GRE General Test, writing sample. Additional exam requirements/recommendations for international students: Required—TOEFL. *Application deadline:* For fall admission, 12/12 for domestic and international students. Application fee: $50. *Financial support:* In 2007–08, 100 students received support, including 24 fellowships with full tuition reimbursements available (averaging $17,162 per year), 6 research assistantships with full and partial tuition reimbursements available (averaging $11,830 per year), 68 teaching assistantships with full tuition reimbursements available (averaging $14,485 per year); Federal Work-Study, tuition waivers (full and partial), and unspecified assistantships also available. Financial award application deadline: 12/12. *Faculty research:* Cultural studies, literary history and theory, film, composition. *Unit head:* Dr. David Bartholomae, Chairman, 412-624-6509, Fax: 412-624-6639, E-mail: barth@pitt.edu. *Application contact:* Connie Arelt, Graduate Administrator, 412-624-6549, Fax: 412-624-6639, E-mail: car100@pitt.edu.

Announcement: Graduate programs stimulate work across literary history, critical and cultural theory, composition, film, and creative writing. MA and PhD courses articulate theoretical issues through historical investigations of discursive practices ranging from canonical British and American literature to film and student writing. Special attention to social conditions of literary and critical writing, pedagogical practices, and the interrelationships of reading and writing, film and literature, and critical theory, composition, and literary study. MFA offers specializations in poetry, fiction, and creative nonfiction; includes training in criticism and theory; final manuscript of professional quality.

University of Puerto Rico, Mayagüez Campus, Graduate Studies, College of Arts and Sciences, Department of English, Mayagüez, PR 00681-9000. Offers English education (MA). Part-time programs available. *Faculty:* 37 full-time (28 women). *Students:* 26 full-time (20 women), 46 part-time (35 women); includes 71 minority (all Hispanic Americans), 1 international. 21 applicants, 95% accepted, 15 enrolled. In 2007, 6 degrees awarded. *Degree requirements:* For master's, comprehensive exam, thesis optional. *Entrance requirements:* For master's, course work in linguistics or language, American literature, British literature, and structure/grammar or syntax. *Application deadline:* For fall admission, 2/15 for domestic and international students; for spring admission, 9/15 for domestic and international students. Applications are processed on a rolling basis. Application fee: $25. *Financial support:* In 2007–08, 20 students received support, including fellowships (averaging $12,000 per year), 1 research assistantship (averaging $15,000 per year), 19 teaching assistantships (averaging $8,500 per year); Federal Work-Study and institutionally sponsored loans also available. *Faculty research:* Teaching English as a second language, linguistics, American literature, British literature. *Unit head:* Dr. Betsy Morales, Director, 787-265-3847, Fax: 787-265-3847, E-mail: betsym@uprm.edu. *Application contact:* Prof. Gayle Griggs, Associate Director, 787-832-4040 Ext. 3064, Fax: 787-265-3847, E-mail: ggriggs@gmail.com.

University of Puerto Rico, Río Piedras, College of Humanities, Department of English, San Juan, PR 00931-3300. Offers MA, PhD. Part-time programs available. *Students:* 56 full-time (43 women), 25 part-time (20 women); includes 78 minority (all Hispanic Americans) Average age 37. In 2007, 4 master's, 4 doctorates awarded. *Degree requirements:* For master's, one foreign language, comprehensive exam, thesis; for doctorate, residency. *Entrance requirements:* For master's, PAEG or GRE, interview, minimum GPA of 3.0, 2 letters of recommendation; for doctorate, PAEG or GRE, minimum GPA of 3.0, 3 letters of recommendation, interview. *Application deadline:* For fall admission, 2/1 for domestic and international students. Application fee: $17. *Expenses:* Tuition, state resident: full-time $1,808; part-time $113 per credit. Tuition, nonresident: full-time $5,248; part-time $328 per credit. Required fees: $72 per term. *Financial support:* Fellowships, research assistantships, teaching assistantships, Federal Work-Study, institutionally sponsored loans, and tuition waivers (partial) available. Financial award application deadline: 5/31. *Unit head:* Dr. Loretta Collins, Director, 787-764-0000 Ext. 3797. *Application contact:* Information Contact, 787-764-0000, Fax: 787-763-5879.

University of Regina, Faculty of Graduate Studies and Research, Faculty of Arts, Department of English, Regina, SK S4S 0A2, Canada. Offers MA, PhD. Part-time programs available. *Faculty:* 23 full-time (10 women). *Students:* 16 full-time (8 women), 9 part-time (5 women). 19 applicants, 74% accepted. In 2007, 8 degrees awarded. *Degree requirements:* For master's, thesis optional; for doctorate, thesis/dissertation. *Entrance requirements:* For master's, writing sample. Additional exam requirements/recommendations for international students: Required—TOEFL (minimum score 580 paper-based; 237 computer-based; 88 iBT). *Application deadline:* For fall admission, 3/15 for international students. Application fee: $85 ($100 for international students). Electronic applications accepted. *Financial support:* In 2007–08, 19 students received support, including 8 fellowships (averaging $15,750 per year), 1 research assistantship (averaging $13,875 per year), 4 teaching assistantships (averaging $13,060 per year); scholarships/grants also available. Financial award application deadline: 6/15. *Faculty research:* British, American, Canadian and post-colonial literature. *Unit head:* Dr. Louis Cameron, Head, 306-585-4429, Fax: 306-585-5429, E-mail: louis.cameron@uregina.ca. *Application contact:* Dr. Ken Probert, Graduate Program Coordinator, 306-585-4432, Fax: 306-585-5429, E-mail: ken.probert@uregina.ca.

University of Rhode Island, Graduate School, College of Arts and Sciences, Department of English, Kingston, RI 02881. Offers MA, PhD. In 2007, 7 master's, 8 doctorates awarded. *Application deadline:* For fall admission, 4/15 priority date for domestic students. Applications are processed on a rolling basis. Application fee: $35. *Expenses:* Tuition, state resident: full-time $6,936; part-time $385 per credit. Tuition, nonresident: full-time $19,044; part-time $1,058 per credit. Required fees: $1,508; $48 per credit. $30 per semester. One-time fee: $80 part-time. *Unit head:* Alain-Philippe Durand, Interim Chair, 401-874-9088.

University of Rochester, The College, Arts and Sciences, Department of English, Rochester, NY 14627-0250. Offers MA, PhD. Terminal master's awarded for partial completion of doctoral program. *Degree requirements:* For doctorate, one foreign language, thesis/dissertation, qualifying exam. *Entrance requirements:* For master's and doctorate, GRE General Test. Additional exam requirements/recommendations for international students: Required—TOEFL.

University of St. Thomas, Graduate Studies, College of Arts and Sciences, Graduate Program in English, St. Paul, MN 55105-1096. Offers MA. Part-time and evening/weekend programs available. *Degree requirements:* For master's, essay. *Entrance requirements:* For master's, minimum GPA of 3.0, previous course work in literature, sample of written work. Additional exam requirements/recommendations for international students: Required—TOEFL. Expenses: Contact institution. *Faculty research:* Multicultural literature, literature and theory, regional writers.

See Close-Up on page 589.

University of Saskatchewan, College of Graduate Studies and Research, College of Arts and Sciences, Department of English, Saskatoon, SK S7N 5A2, Canada. Offers MA, PhD. *Degree requirements:* For master's, one foreign language, thesis; for doctorate, one foreign language, thesis/dissertation. *Entrance requirements:* Additional exam requirements/recommendations for international students: Required—TOEFL.

University of South Africa, College of Human Sciences, Pretoria, South Africa. Offers adult education (M Ed); African languages (MA, PhD); African politics (MA, PhD); Afrikaans (MA, PhD); ancient history (MA, PhD); ancient Near Eastern studies (MA, PhD); anthropology (MA, PhD); applied linguistics (MA); Arabic (MA, PhD); archaeology (MA); art history (MA); Biblical archaeology (MA); Biblical studies (M Th, D Th, PhD); Christian spirituality (M Th, D Th); church history (M Th, D Th); classical studies (MA, PhD); clinical psychology (MA); communication (MA, PhD); comparative education (M Ed, Ed D); consulting psychology (D Admin, D Com, PhD); curriculum studies (M Ed, Ed D); development studies (M Admin, MA, D Admin, PhD); didactics (M Ed, Ed D); education (M Tech); education management (M Ed, Ed D); educational psychology (M Ed); English (MA); environmental education (M Ed); French (MA, PhD); German (MA, PhD); Greek (MA); guidance and counseling (M Ed); health studies (MA, PhD), including health sciences education (MA), health services management (MA), medical and surgical nursing science (critical care general) (MA), midwifery and neonatal nursing science (MA), trauma and emergency care (MA); history (MA, PhD); history of education (Ed D); inclusive education (M Ed, Ed D); information and communications technology policy and regulation (MA); information science (MA, MIS, PhD); international politics (MA, PhD); Islamic studies (MA, PhD); Italian (MA, PhD); Judaica (MA, PhD); linguistics (MA, PhD); mathematical education (M Ed); mathematics education (MA); missiology (M Th, D Th); modern Hebrew (MA, PhD); musicology (MA, MMus, D Mus, PhD); natural science education (M Ed); New Testament (M Th, D Th); Old Testament (D Th); pastoral therapy (M Th, D Th); philosophy (MA); philosophy of education (M Ed, Ed D); politics (MA, PhD); Portuguese (MA, PhD); practical theology (M Th, D Th); psychology (MA, MS, PhD); psychology of education (M Ed, Ed D); public health (MA); religious studies (MA, D Th, PhD); Romance languages (MA); Russian (MA, PhD); Semitic languages (MA, PhD); social behavior studies in HIV/AIDS (MA); social science (mental health) (MA); social science in development studies (MA); social science in psychology (MA); social science in social work (MA); social science in sociology (MA); social work (MSW, DSW, PhD); socio-education (M Ed, Ed D); sociolinguistics (MA); sociology (MA, PhD); Spanish (MA, PhD); systematic theology (M Th, D Th); TESOL (teaching English to speakers of other languages) (MA); theological ethics (M Th, D Th); theory of literature (MA, PhD); urban ministries (D Th); urban ministry (M Th).

University of South Alabama, Graduate School, College of Arts and Sciences, Department of English, Mobile, AL 36688-0002. Offers MA. Part-time and evening/weekend programs available. *Faculty:* 5 full-time (4 women), 11 part-time/adjunct (4 women). *Students:* 27 full-time (21 women), 6 part-time (3 women); includes 6 minority (3 African Americans, 2 American Indian/Alaska Native, 1 Asian American or Pacific Islander). 23 applicants, 96% accepted, 15 enrolled. In 2007, 11 degrees awarded. *Degree requirements:* For master's, one foreign language, comprehensive exam, thesis optional. *Entrance requirements:* For master's, GRE General Test, BA in English or 40 hours of course work in English, minimum GPA of 3.0. *Application deadline:* For fall admission, 9/1 priority date for domestic students. Applications are processed on a rolling basis. Application fee: $25. *Expenses:* Tuition, state resident: full-time $4,224; part-time $176 per credit hour. Tuition, nonresident: full-time $8,448; part-time $352 per credit hour. Required fees: $802. Full-time tuition and fees vary according to program and student level. *Financial support:* Research assistantships available. Support available to part-time students. Financial award application deadline: 4/1. *Unit head:* Dr. Sue Walker, Chair, 251-460-6146.

University of South Carolina, The Graduate School, College of Arts and Sciences, Department of English Language and Literature, Columbia, SC 29208. Offers creative writing (MFA); English (MA, PhD); English education (MAT); MLIS/MA. MAT offered in cooperation with the College of Education. Part-time programs available. *Faculty:* 53 full-time (23 women). *Students:* 147 full-time (86 women); includes 18 minority (10 African Americans, 2 American Indian/Alaska Native, 5 Asian Americans or Pacific Islanders, 1 Hispanic American), 1 international. Average age 32. 179 applicants, 21% accepted. In 2007, 8 master's, 14 doctorates awarded. *Degree requirements:* For master's, one foreign language, comprehensive exam, thesis; for doctorate, 2 foreign languages, comprehensive exam, thesis/dissertation. *Entrance requirements:* For master's, GRE General Test (MFA), GRE Subject Test (MA, MAT), sample of written work; for doctorate, GRE General Test, GRE Subject Test, sample of written work. Additional exam requirements/recommendations for international students: Required—TOEFL. *Application deadline:* For fall admission, 1/30 priority date for domestic and international students. Applications are processed on a rolling basis. Application fee: $40. Electronic applications accepted. *Expenses:* Tuition, state resident: part-time $440 per hour. Tuition, nonresident: part-time $936 per hour. Required fees: $17 per hour. Tuition and fees vary according to program. *Financial support:* In 2007–08, 123 students received support, including 17 fellowships with full tuition reimbursements available (averaging $3,000 per year), 10 research assistantships with full tuition reimbursements available (averaging $3,000 per year), 80 teaching assistantships with full tuition reimbursements available (averaging $12,000 per year); institutionally sponsored loans, scholarships/grants, health care benefits, unspecified assistantships, and graders, tutors also available. Financial award application deadline: 1/31. *Faculty research:* American literature, British literature, composition and rhetoric, linguistics, speech communication. Total annual research expenditures: $230,000. *Unit head:* Dr. William Rivers, Interim Chair, 803-777-7120,

Fax: 803-777-9064, E-mail: riversw@gwm.sc.edu. *Application contact:* Dr. Lawrence Rhu, Director of Graduate Studies, 803-777-5063, Fax: 803-777-9064, E-mail: rhul@gwm.sc.edu.

The University of South Dakota, Graduate School, College of Arts and Sciences, Department of English, Vermillion, SD 57069-2390. Offers MA, PhD. *Faculty:* 13 full-time (4 women), 1 (woman) part-time/adjunct. *Students:* 54 (31 women). In 2007, 13 master's, 2 doctorates awarded. *Degree requirements:* For master's, comprehensive exam (for some programs), thesis (for some programs); for doctorate, comprehensive exam, thesis/dissertation. *Entrance requirements:* For master's, minimum GPA of 3.0, writing sample; for doctorate, GRE, minimum GPA of 3.0, writing sample. Additional exam requirements/recommendations for international students: Required—TOEFL (minimum score 620 paper-based; 260 computer-based; 105 iBT). *Application deadline:* For fall admission, 2/1 priority date for domestic and international students. Applications are processed on a rolling basis. Application fee: $35. Electronic applications accepted. *Financial support:* In 2007–08, research assistantships with partial tuition reimbursements (averaging $8,500 per year), teaching assistantships with partial tuition reimbursements (averaging $8,500 per year) were awarded; career-related internships or fieldwork, Federal Work-Study, and scholarships/grants also available. Financial award applicants required to submit FAFSA. *Unit head:* Dr. Emily Haddad, Chair, 605-677-5486, Fax: 605-677-5298, E-mail: english@usd.edu. *Application contact:* Dr. John Dudley, Graduate Student Adviser, 605-677-5486, Fax: 605-677-5298, E-mail: english@usd.edu.

University of Southern California, Graduate School, College of Letters, Arts and Sciences, Department of English, Los Angeles, CA 90089. Offers English and American literature (MA, PhD); English literature and creative writing (PhD). *Faculty:* 34 full-time (17 women). *Students:* 110 full-time (72 women), 2 part-time (both women); includes 25 minority (3 African Americans, 2 American Indian/Alaska Native, 9 Asian Americans or Pacific Islanders, 11 Hispanic Americans), 9 international. 236 applicants, 10% accepted. In 2007, 4 master's, 9 doctorates awarded. Terminal master's awarded for partial completion of doctoral program. *Degree requirements:* For doctorate, one foreign language, thesis/dissertation. *Entrance requirements:* For doctorate, GRE General Test, GRE Subject Test. *Application deadline:* For fall admission, 12/1 priority date for domestic students. Application fee: $85. *Financial support:* In 2007–08, 89 students received support, including fellowships with full tuition reimbursements available (averaging $19,000 per year), teaching assistantships with full tuition reimbursements available (averaging $19,532 per year); scholarships/grants also available. Support available to part-time students. Financial award application deadline: 2/15; financial award applicants required to submit FAFSA. *Faculty research:* Creative writing and literature, early modern studies, gender and sexuality, narrative studies, poetry and poetics, media, film and popular culture. *Unit head:* Dr. Bruce Smith, Chair, 213-740-2808. *Application contact:* William Handley, Information Contact, 213-740-2311.

University of Southern Mississippi, Graduate School, College of Arts and Letters, Department of English, Hattiesburg, MS 39406-0001. Offers MA, PhD. *Faculty:* 9 full-time (6 women). *Students:* 57 full-time (28 women), 33 part-time (25 women); includes 8 minority (3 African Americans, 2 American Indian/Alaska Native, 1 Asian American or Pacific Islander, 2 Hispanic Americans), 2 international. Average age 31. 65 applicants, 71% accepted, 22 enrolled. In 2007, 12 master's, 3 doctorates awarded. *Degree requirements:* For master's, one foreign language, comprehensive exam, thesis; for doctorate, 2 foreign languages, comprehensive exam, thesis/dissertation. *Entrance requirements:* For master's, GRE General Test, minimum GPA of 3.0 in field of study, 2.75 in last 2 years; for doctorate, GRE General Test, minimum GPA of 3.5. Additional exam requirements/recommendations for international students: Required—TOEFL. *Application deadline:* For fall admission, 3/15 priority date for domestic students, 3/15 for international students. Application fee: $30. Electronic applications accepted. *Financial support:* In 2007–08, 5 research assistantships with full tuition reimbursements (averaging $9,788 per year), 40 teaching assistantships with full tuition reimbursements (averaging $9,788 per year) were awarded; Federal Work-Study, institutionally sponsored loans, scholarships/grants, and unspecified assistantships also available. Financial award application deadline: 3/15. *Faculty research:* English and American literature, critical theory and cultural studies, creative writing. *Unit head:* Dr. W. Michael Mays, Chair, 601-266-4319, Fax: 601-266-5757, E-mail: michael.mays@usm.edu. *Application contact:* Dr. Jameela Lares, Graduate Coordinator, 601-266-4320, Fax: 601-266-5757.

University of South Florida, Graduate School, College of Arts and Sciences, Department of English, Tampa, FL 33620-9951. Offers MA, PhD. Part-time and evening/weekend programs available. *Faculty:* 24 full-time (16 women), 3 part-time/adjunct (2 women). *Students:* 70 full-time (51 women), 49 part-time (31 women); includes 7 minority (2 African Americans, 1 American Indian/Alaska Native, 4 Hispanic Americans), 5 international. 96 applicants, 59% accepted, 38 enrolled. In 2007, 11 master's, 10 doctorates awarded. *Degree requirements:* For master's, comprehensive exam; for doctorate, 2 foreign languages, comprehensive exam. *Entrance requirements:* For master's, GRE General Test, minimum GPA of 3.5; for doctorate, GRE General Test, minimum GPA of 3.7. *Application deadline:* For fall admission, 3/1 for domestic students; for spring admission, 10/1 for domestic students. Applications are processed on a rolling basis. Application fee: $30. Electronic applications accepted. *Financial support:* Scholarships/grants and unspecified assistantships available. Financial award application deadline: 6/30; financial award applicants required to submit FAFSA. *Faculty research:* British and American literature, rhetoric and composition. Total annual research expenditures:$64,569. *Unit head:* Philip Sipiera, Chairperson, 813-974-2421, Fax: 813-974-2270. *Application contact:* Dr. Laura Runge, Director of Graduate Studies, 813-974-9469, Fax: 813-974-2270, E-mail: runge@chuma.cas.usf.edu.

The University of Tennessee, Graduate School, College of Arts and Sciences, Department of English, Knoxville, TN 37996. Offers MA, PhD. Part-time programs available. *Degree requirements:* For master's, one foreign language, thesis or alternative; for doctorate, one foreign language, thesis/dissertation. *Entrance requirements:* For master's, GRE General Test, minimum GPA of 2.7; for doctorate, GRE General Test, GRE Subject Test, minimum GPA of 2.7. Additional exam requirements/recommendations for international students: Required—TOEFL. Electronic applications accepted.

The University of Tennessee at Chattanooga, Graduate School, College of Arts and Sciences, Department of English, Program in English, Chattanooga, TN 37403-2598. Offers MA. Part-time and evening/weekend programs available. *Faculty:* 13 full-time (7 women). *Students:* 10 full-time (7 women), 42 part-time (27 women); includes 1 minority (Hispanic American) Average age 31. 33 applicants, 85% accepted, 17 enrolled. In 2007, 14 degrees awarded. *Degree requirements:* For master's, one foreign language, comprehensive exam, thesis. *Entrance requirements:* For master's, GRE General Test or GRE Subject Test in literature, minimum GPA of 3.0 in English. Additional exam requirements/recommendations for international students: Required—TOEFL (minimum score 550 paper-based; 213 computer-based; 79 iBT); Recommended—IELTS (minimum score 6). *Application deadline:* For fall admission, 8/1 priority date for domestic students, 6/1 for international students; for spring admission, 12/1 priority date for domestic students, 10/1 for international students. Applications are processed on a rolling basis. Application fee: $30 ($35 for international students). *Expenses:* Tuition, state resident: full-time $5,854; part-time $393 per hour. Tuition, nonresident: full-time $15,816; part-time $946 per hour. Required fees: $1,090; $256 per hour. *Financial support:* In 2007–08, 5 fellowships with full and partial tuition reimbursements (averaging $3,300 per year) were awarded; career-related internships or fieldwork, Federal Work-Study, institutionally sponsored loans, scholarships/grants, tuition waivers (partial), and unspecified assistantships also available. Support available to part-time students. Financial award application deadline: 4/1. *Faculty research:* Technical writing, African-American literature, Milton, creative writing and poetry, American modernism and gender theory. Total annual research expenditures: $164,000. *Unit head:* Dr. Joyce Smith, Director of Graduate Programs, 423-425-4623, E-mail: joyce-smith@utc.edu. *Application contact:* Dr. Deborah E. Arfken, Dean of Graduate Studies, 423-425-4666, Fax: 423-425-5223, E-mail: deborah-arfken@utc.edu.

The University of Texas at Arlington, Graduate School, College of Liberal Arts, Department of English, Arlington, TX 76019. Offers English (MA); literature (PhD); rhetoric (PhD). Part-time and evening/weekend programs available. *Faculty:* 8 full-time (5 women). *Students:* 18 full-time (15 women), 88 part-time (53 women); includes 17 minority (7 African Americans, 3 Asian Americans or Pacific Islanders, 7 Hispanic Americans), 11 international. 33 applicants, 67% accepted, 19 enrolled. In 2007, 10 master's, 3 doctorates awarded. *Degree requirements:* For master's, thesis or comprehensive exam; for doctorate, one foreign language, comprehensive exam, thesis/dissertation. *Entrance requirements:* For master's, GRE General Test, minimum 5-page writing sample, minimum GPA of 3.0, 3 letters of recommendation; for doctorate, GRE General Test, minimum graduate GPA of 3.5, writing sample, 3 letters of recommendation. Additional exam requirements/recommendations for international students: Required—TOEFL (minimum score 550 paper-based; 213 computer-based). *Application deadline:* For fall admission, 6/16 for domestic students. Applications are processed on a rolling basis. Application fee: $35 ($50 for international students). *Expenses:* Tuition, state resident: full-time $5,934. Tuition, nonresident: full-time $10,938. *Financial support:* In 2007–08, 6 fellowships (averaging $1,000 per year), 2 research assistantships, 26 teaching assistantships (averaging $8,500 per year) were awarded; scholarships/grants also available. Financial award application deadline: 5/1. *Faculty research:* Rhetoric composition, American literature, British literature, cultural studies, women's studies. *Unit head:* Dr. Wendy Faris, Chair, 817-272-2692, Fax: 817-272-2718, E-mail: wbfaris@uta.edu. *Application contact:* Dr. Kevin Gustafson, Associate Chair for Graduate Studies, 817-272-2739, E-mail: gustafson@uta.edu.

The University of Texas at Austin, Graduate School, College of Liberal Arts, Department of English, Austin, TX 78712-1111. Offers MA, PhD. Part-time programs available. Terminal master's awarded for partial completion of doctoral program. *Degree requirements:* For master's, 2 foreign languages; for doctorate, variable foreign language requirement. *Entrance requirements:* For master's and doctorate, GRE General Test. Electronic applications accepted.

The University of Texas at Brownsville, Graduate Studies, College of Liberal Arts, Department of English, Brownsville, TX 78520-4991. Offers English (MA); interdisciplinary studies (MAIS). Part-time and evening/weekend programs available. *Degree requirements:* For master's, comprehensive exam or thesis. *Entrance requirements:* For master's, GRE General Test. Additional exam requirements/recommendations for international students: Required—TOEFL. *Faculty research:* Sandra Cisneros, Nathaniel Hawthorne, Rodolfo Araya, Isabel Allende, linguistics.

The University of Texas at El Paso, Graduate School, College of Liberal Arts, Department of English, El Paso, TX 79968-0001. Offers English and American literature (MA); professional writing and rhetoric (MA); teaching English (MAT). Part-time and evening/weekend programs available. *Degree requirements:* For master's, thesis optional. *Entrance requirements:* For master's, GRE General Test, minimum GPA of 3.0. Additional exam requirements/recommendations for international students: Required—TOEFL. Electronic applications accepted. *Faculty research:* Literature, creative writing, literary theory.

The University of Texas at San Antonio, College of Liberal and Fine Arts, Department of English, Classics and Philosophy, San Antonio, TX 78249-0617. Offers English (MA, PhD). Part-time and evening/weekend programs available. *Faculty:* 15 full-time (11 women), 2 part-time/adjunct (1 woman). *Students:* 38 full-time (29 women), 70 part-time (47 women); includes 37 minority (5 African Americans, 3 Asian Americans or Pacific Islanders, 29 Hispanic Americans), 4 international. Average age 33. 79 applicants, 62% accepted, 47 enrolled. In 2007, 24 degrees awarded. *Degree requirements:* For master's, comprehensive exam, thesis optional; for doctorate, comprehensive exam, thesis/dissertation. *Entrance requirements:* For master's, GRE General Test, minimum GPA of 3.3 on all upper division English courses; for doctorate, GRE General Test. Additional exam requirements/recommendations for international students: Required—TOEFL (minimum score 500 paper-based; 173 computer-based). *Application deadline:* For fall admission, 7/1 for domestic students, 4/1 for international students; for spring admission, 11/1 for domestic students, 9/1 for international students. Applications are processed on a rolling basis. Application fee: $45 ($80 for international students). Electronic applications accepted. *Financial support:* In 2007–08, 5 research assistantships (averaging $5,633 per year), 13 teaching assistantships (averaging $800 per year) were awarded; Federal Work-Study and institutionally sponsored loans also available. Support available to part-time students. *Faculty research:* English and American literature, linguistics. Total annual research expenditures: $30,913. *Unit head:* Dr. Bernadette Andrea, Chair, 210-458-5130, Fax: 210-458-5366, E-mail: bandrea@utsa.edu.

The University of Texas at Tyler, College of Arts and Sciences, Department of Literature and Languages, Tyler, TX 75799-0001. Offers English (MA); interdisciplinary studies (MAIS). Part-time and evening/weekend programs available. *Faculty:* 8 full-time (5 women). *Students:* 7 full-time (2 women), 14 part-time (11 women); includes 5 minority (2 African Americans, 1 Asian American or Pacific Islander, 2 Hispanic Americans). Average age 37. 10 applicants, 100% accepted, 7 enrolled. In 2007, 2 degrees awarded. *Degree requirements:* For master's, one foreign language, comprehensive exam, thesis optional. *Entrance requirements:* For master's, GRE General Test, minimum GPA of 3.0, four semesters—or the equivalent—of one foreign language. *Application deadline:* For fall admission, 8/21 for domestic students; for spring admission, 1/13 for domestic students. Applications are processed on a rolling basis. Application fee: $0. Electronic applications accepted. *Expenses:* Tuition, state resident: part-time $627 per semester hour. Tuition, nonresident: part-time $908 per semester hour. Required fees: $107 per semester hour. Tuition and fees vary according to course load. *Financial support:* In 2007–08, fellowships with full and partial tuition reimbursements (averaging $1,000 per year), 1 research assistantship with full and partial tuition reimbursement (averaging $6,000 per year) were awarded; teaching assistantships with full and partial tuition reimbursements, Federal Work-Study, institutionally sponsored loans, scholarships/grants, tuition waivers, unspecified assistantships, and writing center teaching staff also available. Financial award application deadline: 7/1; financial award applicants required to submit FAFSA. *Faculty research:* Medieval and Tudor drama, Shakespeare, British Romanticism, British and Irish modernism, American Realism, Greek drama, Nineteenth Century American Lit. *Unit head:* Dr. Victor I. Scherb, Chair, 903-566-7374, Fax: 903-565-5700, E-mail: vscherb@mail.uttyl.edu. *Application contact:* Pam Morrow, Assistant to Dean for Enrollment Management, 903-566-7205, Fax: 903-566-7068, E-mail: pmorrow@uttyler.edu.

The University of Texas of the Permian Basin, Office of Graduate Studies, College of Arts and Sciences, Department of Humanities and Fine Arts, Program in English, Odessa, TX 79762-0001. Offers MA. Part-time and evening/weekend programs available. *Degree requirements:* For master's, comprehensive exam (for some programs), thesis (for some programs). *Entrance requirements:* For master's, GRE General Test. Additional exam requirements/recommendations for international students: Required—TOEFL (minimum score 550 paper-based; 213 computer-based).

The University of Texas–Pan American, College of Arts and Humanities, Department of English, Edinburg, TX 78541-2999. Offers English (MA, MAIS); English as a second language (MA). Part-time and evening/weekend programs available. *Degree requirements:* For master's, comprehensive exam, thesis optional. *Entrance requirements:* For master's, GRE General Test, minimum GPA of 3.0. *Faculty research:* Oral vs. literary culture, Borderland literature, Mexican-American literature, topics in British and American literature, discourse analysis.

University of the District of Columbia, College of Arts and Sciences, Department of English, Program in English Composition and Rhetoric, Washington, DC 20008-1175. Offers MA. *Students:* 5 full-time (3 women), 8 part-time (4 women); includes 11 minority (all African Americans) Average age 29. 5 applicants, 80% accepted, 3 enrolled. *Degree requirements:* For master's, comprehensive exam. *Entrance requirements:* For master's, writing proficiency exam. *Application deadline:* For fall admission, 6/15 priority date for domestic students; for spring admission, 11/1 for domestic students. Applications are processed on a rolling basis. Application fee: $20. *Application contact:* LaVerne Hill Flannigan, Director of Admission, 202-274-6069.

English

The University of Toledo, College of Graduate Studies, College of Arts and Sciences, Department of English Language and Literature, Toledo, OH 43606-3390. Offers English as a second language (MA); literature (MA); teaching of writing (Certificate). Part-time programs available. *Faculty:* 21. *Students:* 36 full-time (27 women), 12 part-time (7 women); includes 4 minority (3 African Americans, 1 Hispanic American), 5 international. Average age 31. 34 applicants, 76% accepted, 19 enrolled. In 2007, 13 degrees awarded. *Degree requirements:* For master's, one foreign language. *Entrance requirements:* For master's, minimum GPA of 2.7. *Application deadline:* For fall admission, 1/15 priority date for domestic students. Applications are processed on a rolling basis. Application fee: $45. Electronic applications accepted. *Financial support:* In 2007–08, 36 teaching assistantships with full tuition reimbursements (averaging $8,200 per year) were awarded; research assistantships, Federal Work-Study, institutionally sponsored loans, scholarships/grants, tuition waivers (full), and unspecified assistantships also available. Support available to part-time students. Financial award application deadline: 4/1; financial award applicants required to submit FAFSA. *Faculty research:* Literary criticism, linguistics, creative writing, folklore and cultural studies. *Unit head:* Dr. Sara Lundquist, Interim Chair, 419-530-2506, Fax: 419-530-2590, E-mail: sara.lundquist@utoledo.edu.

University of Toronto, School of Graduate Studies, Humanities Division, Department of English, Toronto, ON M5S 1A1, Canada. Offers MA, PhD. Part-time programs available. *Faculty:* 66 full-time, 20 part-time/adjunct. *Students:* 229 full-time (145 women), 9 part-time, 38 international. 565 applicants, 37% accepted. In 2007, 60 master's, 5 doctorates awarded. *Degree requirements:* For master's, thesis optional; for doctorate, 2 foreign languages, thesis/dissertation. *Entrance requirements:* For master's, minimum B+ average, 2 letters of reference, portfolio (creative writing program); for doctorate, minimum A– average, 2 letters of reference, writing sample. *Application deadline:* For fall admission, 12/15 for domestic students. Application fee: $100 Canadian dollars. *Financial support:* Teaching assistantships available. *Unit head:* Prof. Brian Corman, Chair, 416-978-3197, Fax: 416-978-0472, E-mail: bcorman@chass.utoronto.ca. *Application contact:* Cecilia Martino, Graduate Secretary, 416-978-2526, Fax: 416-978-2836, E-mail: c.martino@utoronto.ca.

University of Tulsa, Graduate School, College of Arts and Sciences, Department of English Language and Literature, Tulsa, OK 74104-3189. Offers MA, MTA, PhD, JD/MA. Part-time and evening/weekend programs available. *Faculty:* 14 full-time (5 women). *Students:* 42 full-time (26 women), 9 part-time (6 women); includes 2 minority (both American Indian/Alaska Native), 3 international. Average age 29. 43 applicants, 74% accepted, 18 enrolled. In 2007, 8 master's, 1 doctorate awarded. *Degree requirements:* For master's, independent research project; for doctorate, one foreign language, comprehensive exam, thesis/dissertation. *Entrance requirements:* For master's and doctorate, GRE General Test. Additional exam requirements/recommendations for international students: Required—TOEFL (minimum score 575 paper-based; 231 computer-based; 91 iBT), IELTS (minimum score 7). *Application deadline:* For fall admission, 2/1 priority date for domestic students. Applications are processed on a rolling basis. Application fee: $40. Electronic applications accepted. *Expenses:* Tuition: Full-time $14,004; part-time $778 per credit hour. Required fees: $60; $30 per term. Tuition and fees vary according to course load. *Financial support:* In 2007–08, 36 students received support, including 6 fellowships with full and partial tuition reimbursements available (averaging $11,221 per year), 30 teaching assistantships with full and partial tuition reimbursements available (averaging $10,755 per year); research assistantships with full and partial tuition reimbursements available, Federal Work-Study, scholarships/grants, tuition waivers (full and partial), and unspecified assistantships also available. Support available to part-time students. Financial award application deadline: 2/1; financial award applicants required to submit FAFSA. *Faculty research:* Women's literature; modern British, Irish, and American literature; 19th century poetry and prose; literary theory, Renaissance literature. Total annual research expenditures: $240,082. *Unit head:* Dr. Lars Engle, Chairperson, 918-631-2807, E-mail: lars-engle@utulsa.edu. *Application contact:* Dr. Sean Latham, Advisor, 918-631-2857, Fax: 918-631-3033, E-mail: sean-latham@utulsa.edu.

University of Utah, The Graduate School, College of Humanities, Department of English, Salt Lake City, UT 84112-1107. Offers American studies (MA, PhD); British American literature (MA, PhD); creative writing (MFA, PhD); literature (PhD); rhetoric and composition (PhD). *Faculty:* 39 full-time (16 women). *Students:* 59 full-time (39 women), 23 part-time (14 women); includes 5 minority (2 African Americans, 1 American Indian/Alaska Native, 2 Asian Americans or Pacific Islanders), 1 international. Average age 33. 177 applicants, 23% accepted, 22 enrolled. In 2007, 14 master's, 7 doctorates awarded. *Median time to degree:* Of those who began their doctoral program in fall 1999, 83% received their degree in 8 years or less. *Degree requirements:* For master's, one foreign language, thesis (for some programs), written exam; for doctorate, 2 foreign languages, comprehensive exam, thesis/dissertation. *Entrance requirements:* For master's and doctorate, GRE General Test, minimum GPA of 3.2. Additional exam requirements/recommendations for international students: Required—TOEFL (minimum score 500 paper-based; 173 computer-based; 120 iBT). *Application deadline:* For fall admission, 12/15 for domestic and international students. Applications are processed on a rolling basis. Application fee: $45 ($65 for international students). Electronic applications accepted. *Financial support:* In 2007–08, 49 students received support, including 8 fellowships with full tuition reimbursements available (averaging $12,000 per year), 41 teaching assistantships with full tuition reimbursements available (averaging $12,000 per year); research assistantships, health care benefits also available. Financial award application deadline: 12/15; financial award applicants required to submit FAFSA. *Faculty research:* Poetics and modern poetry, 19th and 20th century British and American literature, the American west, environmental studies, critical theory and race and gender studies. Total annual research expenditures: $36,210. *Unit head:* Prof. Vincent P. Pecora, Chair, 801-581-6168, E-mail: v.pecora@utah.edu. *Application contact:* Prof. Matthew Potolsky, Director of Graduate Studies, 801-581-5245, E-mail: m.potolsky@utah.edu.

University of Vermont, Graduate College, College of Arts and Sciences, Department of English, Burlington, VT 05405. Offers MA. *Students:* 33 (17 women); includes 3 minority (all Asian Americans or Pacific Islanders) 1 international. 68 applicants, 79% accepted, 9 enrolled. In 2007, 9 degrees awarded. *Degree requirements:* For master's, one foreign language, thesis. *Entrance requirements:* For master's, GRE General Test. Additional exam requirements/recommendations for international students: Required—TOEFL (minimum score 550 paper-based; 213 computer-based; 80 iBT). *Application deadline:* For fall admission, 2/15 priority date for domestic students. Applications are processed on a rolling basis. Application fee: $40. Electronic applications accepted. *Financial support:* Fellowships, teaching assistantships available. Financial award application deadline: 3/1. *Unit head:* Dr. LoKangaka Losambe, Chair, 802-656-3056. *Application contact:* Dr. A. Barnaby, Coordinator, 802-656-3056.

University of Victoria, Faculty of Graduate Studies, Faculty of Humanities, Department of English, Victoria, BC V8W 2Y2, Canada. Offers MA, PhD. Part-time programs available. *Faculty:* 31 full-time (12 women), 3 part-time/adjunct (0 women). *Students:* 63, 5 international. Average age 28. 106 applicants, 53% accepted, 42 enrolled. In 2007, 7 master's, 1 doctorate awarded. *Median time to degree:* Of those who began their doctoral program in fall 1999, 40% received their degree in 8 years or less. *Degree requirements:* For master's, one foreign language, thesis (for some programs); for doctorate, 2 foreign languages, comprehensive exam, thesis/dissertation, candidacy exam. *Entrance requirements:* For master's, minimum A-average in last 2 years of undergraduate course work, writing sample, resumé; for doctorate, minimum A- average in graduate course work, writing sample, resumé. Additional exam requirements/recommendations for international students: Required—TOEFL (minimum score 630 paper-based; 267 computer-based). *Application deadline:* For fall admission, 2/15 priority date for domestic students, 1/15 priority date for international students; for spring admission, 10/31 priority date for domestic and international students. Applications are processed on a rolling basis. Application fee: $75 ($125 for international students). Electronic applications accepted. *Expenses:* Tuition, state resident: full-time $3,110. International tuition: $3,700 full-time. Tuition and fees vary according to program. *Financial support:* In 2007–08, 35 students received support, including 5 fellowships (averaging $12,900 per year), 4 research assistantships (averaging $2,275 per year), 8 teaching assistantships (averaging $7,500 per year); Federal Work-Study and scholarships/grants also available. Financial award application deadline: 2/15. *Faculty research:* Critical theory, nineteenth century literature, postcolonialism/multiculturalism, medieval and Renaissance literature, cultural theory. *Unit head:* Dr. Robert Miles, Chair, 250-721-7235, Fax: 250-721-6498, E-mail: rmiles@uvic.ca. *Application contact:* Dr. Stephen Arthur Ross, Graduate Advisor, 250-721-7237, Fax: 250-721-6498, E-mail: saross@uvic.ca.

University of Virginia, College and Graduate School of Arts and Sciences, Department of English Language and Literature, Program in English, Charlottesville, VA 22903. Offers MA, PhD. *Faculty:* 42 full-time (19 women), 1 part-time/adjunct (0 women). *Students:* 167 full-time (95 women), 6 part-time (4 women); includes 12 minority (8 African Americans, 2 Asian Americans or Pacific Islanders, 2 Hispanic Americans), 10 international. Average age 28. 480 applicants, 20% accepted, 44 enrolled. In 2007, 31 master's, 28 doctorates awarded. *Degree requirements:* For master's, one foreign language, oral exam or thesis; for doctorate, 2 foreign languages, comprehensive exam, thesis/dissertation. *Entrance requirements:* For master's and doctorate, GRE General Test, GRE Subject Test. *Application deadline:* Applications are processed on a rolling basis. Application fee: $60. Electronic applications accepted. *Financial support:* Applicants required to submit FAFSA.

University of Washington, Graduate School, College of Arts and Sciences, Department of English, Seattle, WA 98195. Offers English (MA, MAT, MFA, PhD); English as a second language (MAT). Part-time programs available. Terminal master's awarded for partial completion of doctoral program. *Degree requirements:* For master's, one foreign language, thesis (for some programs); for doctorate, one foreign language, thesis/dissertation. *Entrance requirements:* For master's, GRE General Test, GRE Subject Test (for English (MA, MAT) only), minimum GPA of 3.0; for doctorate, GRE General Test, GRE Subject Test. Additional exam requirements/recommendations for international students: Required—TOEFL. Electronic applications accepted. *Faculty research:* English and American literature, critical theory, creative writing, language theory.

University of Waterloo, Graduate Studies, Faculty of Arts, Department of English, Language and Literature, Waterloo, ON N2L 3G1, Canada. Offers English language and literature (PhD); literary studies (MA); rhetoric and communication design (MA). Part-time programs available. *Faculty:* 20 full-time (8 women), 19 part-time/adjunct (9 women). *Students:* 105. 106 applicants, 25% accepted, 26 enrolled. In 2007, 12 master's, 4 doctorates awarded. *Degree requirements:* For master's, one foreign language, thesis optional; for doctorate, 2 foreign languages, thesis/dissertation. *Entrance requirements:* For master's, honors degree, minimum B+ average; for doctorate, master's degree, minimum A- average. Additional exam requirements/recommendations for international students: Required—TOEFL, TWE. *Application deadline:* For fall admission, 2/1 for domestic students. Application fee: $75 Canadian dollars. Electronic applications accepted. *Financial support:* Teaching assistantships, career-related internships or fieldwork and scholarships/grants available. Financial award application deadline: 2/1. *Faculty research:* Shakespeare, American literature, rhetoric, Romantics, moderns. *Unit head:* Dr. M. McArthur, Chair, 519-888-4567 Ext. 33359, Fax: 519-746-5788, E-mail: mmcarthu@watarts.uwaterloo.ca. *Application contact:* Dr. V. Lamont, Graduate Officer, 519-888-4567 Ext. 33318, Fax: 519-746-5788, E-mail: vlamont@uwaterloo.ca.

The University of Western Ontario, Faculty of Graduate Studies, Faculty of Arts and Humanities, Department of English, London, ON N6A 5B8, Canada. Offers Canadian literature (MA); English (PhD); English literature (MA). *Faculty:* 41 full-time (13 women). *Students:* 77 full-time (44 women), 4 part-time (3 women). 174 applicants, 39% accepted, 32 enrolled. In 2007, 23 master's, 6 doctorates awarded. *Degree requirements:* For master's, one foreign language, thesis or alternative; for doctorate, 2 foreign languages, thesis/dissertation, qualifying exam. *Entrance requirements:* For master's, minimum A average in appropriate field; for doctorate, MA or equivalent, minimum A average. Additional exam requirements/recommendations for international students: Required—TOEFL (minimum score 630 paper-based; 267 computer-based). *Application deadline:* For fall admission, 2/1 for domestic students. Application fee: $75 Canadian dollars. *Financial support:* In 2007–08, 64 students received support, including 56 teaching assistantships (averaging $9,048 Canadian dollars per year); fellowships, research assistantships also available. Financial award application deadline: 2/1. *Faculty research:* Renaissance, nineteenth-century, modern, and postcolonial literature. *Unit head:* Dr. Russell Poole, Chair (Acting), 519-661-2111 Ext. 85782, E-mail: rpoole@uwo.ca. *Application contact:* Leanne Trask, Graduate Assistant, 519-661-2111, E-mail: ltraskro@uwo.ca.

University of West Florida, College of Arts and Sciences: Arts, Department of English and Foreign Languages, Pensacola, FL 32514-5750. Offers creative writing (MA); literature (MA). Part-time and evening/weekend programs available. *Faculty:* 6 full-time (3 women), 1 (woman) part-time/adjunct. *Students:* 2 full-time (1 woman), 23 part-time (17 women); includes 4 minority (1 African American, 1 American Indian/Alaska Native, 2 Asian Americans or Pacific Islanders). Average age 29. 14 applicants, 64% accepted, 8 enrolled. In 2007, 1 degree awarded. *Degree requirements:* For master's, thesis. *Entrance requirements:* For master's, GRE General Test, minimum GPA of 3.0. Additional exam requirements/recommendations for international students: Required—TOEFL (minimum score 550 paper-based; 213 computer-based). *Application deadline:* For fall admission, 6/1 for domestic students, 5/15 for international students; for spring admission, 11/1 for domestic students, 10/1 for international students. Applications are processed on a rolling basis. Application fee: $30. *Expenses:* Tuition, state resident: full-time $6,054; part-time $252 per credit. Tuition, nonresident: full-time $21,886; part-time $912 per credit. *Financial support:* In 2007–08, 8 research assistantships with partial tuition reimbursements (averaging $1,570 per year), 1 teaching assistantship with partial tuition reimbursement (averaging $2,826 per year) were awarded; fellowships, scholarships/grants, tuition waivers (partial), and unspecified assistantships also available. Support available to part-time students. Financial award application deadline: 4/15; financial award applicants required to submit FAFSA. *Faculty research:* Faulkner, Shakespeare, American humor, women's studies, poetry. *Unit head:* Dr. Bob Yeager, Chairperson, 850-474-2923.

University of West Georgia, Graduate School, College of Arts and Sciences, Department of English and Philosophy, Carrollton, GA 30118. Offers English (MA). Part-time and evening/weekend programs available. *Faculty:* 18 full-time (11 women). *Students:* 1 full-time (0 women), 17 part-time (13 women). Average age 31. In 2007, 3 degrees awarded. *Degree requirements:* For master's, one foreign language, comprehensive exam, thesis optional. *Entrance requirements:* For master's, GRE General Test, NTE, undergraduate degree in English, minimum GPA of 3.2. *Application deadline:* For fall admission, 7/18 priority date for domestic students; for spring admission, 11/27 for domestic students. Application fee: $30. Electronic applications accepted. *Expenses:* Tuition, state resident: full-time $2,448; part-time $136 per semester hour. Tuition, nonresident: full-time $9,774; part-time $543 per semester hour. Required fees: $26 per semester hour. $173 per semester. *Financial support:* In 2007–08, 10 research assistantships with full tuition reimbursements (averaging $4,000 per year) were awarded; career-related internships or fieldwork and unspecified assistantships also available. Support available to part-time students. Financial award applicants required to submit FAFSA. *Unit head:* Dr. Jane B. Hill, Chair, 678-839-6512, Fax: 678-839-4849, E-mail: jhill@westga.edu. *Application contact:* Dr. Charles W. Clark, Interim Dean, 678-839-6508, E-mail: cclark@westga.edu.

University of Windsor, Faculty of Graduate Studies, Faculty of Arts and Social Sciences, Department of English Language, Literature and Creative Writing, Windsor, ON N9B 3P4, Canada. Offers English: creative writing and language and literature (MA); English: language and literature (MA). Part-time programs available. *Faculty:* 14 full-time (7 women). *Students:* 29 full-time (17 women), 2 part-time (1 woman). 50 applicants, 58% accepted. In 2007, 6 degrees awarded. *Degree requirements:* For master's, thesis. *Entrance requirements:* For master's, minimum B average, portfolio. Additional exam requirements/recommendations for international students: Required—TOEFL (minimum score 600 paper-based; 250 computer-based). *Application deadline:* For fall admission, 7/1 priority date for domestic students; for winter admission, 11/1 for domestic students; for spring admission, 3/1 for domestic students. Applications are processed on a rolling basis. Application fee: $55. Electronic applications accepted. *Financial support:* In 2007–08, 19 teaching assistantships (averaging $8,901 per year) were awarded; Federal Work-Study, scholarships/grants, tuition waivers (full and partial), unspecified assistantships, and bursaries also available. Financial award application deadline: 2/15. *Faculty research:* Use of gender-related terms in popular culture; international and Aboriginal literatures: expression of cultural identity; critical analysis of authors: Pope, Munroe, Lady Morgan, Orwell, Thomas; the "feminine" voice in literature and contemporary culture. *Unit head:* Dr. Karl Jirgens, Head, 519-253-3000 Ext. 2289, Fax: 519-971-3676, E-mail: jirgens@uwindsor.ca. *Application contact:* Applicant Services, 519-253-3000 Ext. 6459, Fax: 519-971-3653, E-mail: gradadmit@uwindsor.ca.

University of Wisconsin–Eau Claire, College of Arts and Sciences, Program in English, Eau Claire, WI 54702-4004. Offers MA. *Faculty:* 26 full-time (16 women), 1 part-time/adjunct (0 women). *Students:* 5 full-time (4 women), 17 part-time (12 women); includes 1 minority (Asian American or Pacific Islander) Average age 29. 9 applicants, 89% accepted, 7 enrolled. In 2007, 4 degrees awarded. *Degree requirements:* For master's, thesis optional, written exam, written project (oral defense). *Entrance requirements:* For master's, minimum GPA of 3.25 in English, 2.75 overall. *Application deadline:* For fall admission, 7/1 for domestic students; for spring admission, 12/1 for domestic students. Applications are processed on a rolling basis. Application fee: $45. Electronic applications accepted. *Expenses:* Tuition, state resident: full-time $6,870; part-time $381 per credit. Tuition, nonresident: full-time $17,480; part-time $971 per credit. Tuition and fees vary according to reciprocity agreements. *Financial support:* In 2007–08, 15 students received support, including 4 teaching assistantships (averaging $5,800 per year); Federal Work-Study also available. Financial award application deadline: 4/15; financial award applicants required to submit FAFSA. *Unit head:* Dr. Jennifer Shaddock, Program Director, 715-836-5476, Fax: 715-836-5996, E-mail: shaddoj@uwec.edu.

University of Wisconsin–Madison, Graduate School, College of Letters and Science, Department of English, Madison, WI 53706-1380. Offers applied English linguistics (MA); composition studies (PhD); English language and linguistics (PhD); literature (MA, PhD). *Degree requirements:* For doctorate, thesis/dissertation.

University of Wisconsin–Milwaukee, Graduate School, College of Letters and Sciences, Department of English, Milwaukee, WI 53201-0413. Offers MA, PhD, Certificate, MLIS/MA. *Faculty:* 47 full-time (21 women). *Students:* 113 full-time (70 women), 95 part-time (59 women); includes 15 minority (8 African Americans, 1 American Indian/Alaska Native, 2 Asian Americans or Pacific Islanders, 4 Hispanic Americans), 28 international. 191 applicants, 55% accepted, 40 enrolled. In 2007, 15 master's, 12 doctorates awarded. *Degree requirements:* For master's, thesis or alternative; for doctorate, one foreign language, thesis/dissertation. *Entrance requirements:* For master's, GRE General Test, GRE Subject Test. *Application deadline:* For fall admission, 1/1 priority date for domestic students; for spring admission, 9/1 for domestic students. Applications are processed on a rolling basis. Application fee: $45 ($75 for international students). *Expenses:* Tuition, state resident: part-time $530 per credit. Tuition, nonresident: part-time $1,428 per credit. Required fees: $19 per credit. $229 per term. Tuition and fees vary according to course load and program. *Financial support:* In 2007–08, 73 teaching assistantships were awarded; fellowships, research assistantships, career-related internships or fieldwork and unspecified assistantships also available. Support available to part-time students. Financial award application deadline: 4/15. *Unit head:* George Clark, Representative, 414-229-4673, Fax: 414-229-2643.

University of Wisconsin–Oshkosh, The Office of Graduate Studies, College of Letters and Science, Department of English, Oshkosh, WI 54901. Offers MA. Part-time programs available. *Faculty:* 28 full-time (19 women), 7 part-time/adjunct (3 women). *Students:* 32. 6 applicants, 33% accepted. In 2007, 4 degrees awarded. *Degree requirements:* For master's, thesis or alternative. *Entrance requirements:* For master's, GRE. Additional exam requirements/recommendations for international students: Required—TOEFL (minimum score 550 paper-based; 213 computer-based; 79 iBT). *Application deadline:* For fall admission, 3/15 for domestic students; for spring admission, 9/15 for domestic students. Application fee: $45. Electronic applications accepted. *Financial support:* Fellowships, institutionally sponsored loans, scholarships/grants, tuition waivers (partial), and unspecified assistantships available. Financial award application deadline: 3/15; financial award applicants required to submit FAFSA. *Unit head:* Dr. Margaret Hostetler, Graduate Program Coordinator, 920-424-7281, E-mail: hostetle@uwosh.edu.

University of Wisconsin–Stevens Point, College of Letters and Science, Department of English, Stevens Point, WI 54481-3897. Offers MST. *Degree requirements:* For master's, thesis or alternative. *Application deadline:* For fall admission, 5/1 priority date for domestic students. Applications are processed on a rolling basis. Application fee: $45. *Expenses:* Tuition, state resident: full-time $6,161. Tuition, nonresident: full-time $16,771. Required fees: $884. Tuition and fees vary according to course load. *Financial support:* Federal Work-Study and unspecified assistantships available. Financial award application deadline: 5/1; financial award applicants required to submit FAFSA. *Unit head:* Dr. Michael Williams, Chair, 715-346-4757, Fax: 715-346-4215.

University of Wyoming, Graduate School, College of Arts and Sciences, Department of English, Laramie, WY 82070. Offers creative writing (MFA); English (MA). Part-time programs available. *Faculty:* 25 full-time (11 women). *Students:* 35 full-time (19 women), 10 part-time (8 women); includes 4 minority (1 African American, 3 Hispanic Americans), 1 international. Average age 32. 58 applicants, 34% accepted. In 2007, 15 degrees awarded. *Degree requirements:* For master's, one foreign language, thesis or alternative. *Entrance requirements:* For master's, GRE General Test, minimum GPA of 3.0. *Application deadline:* For fall admission, 3/1 priority date for domestic students; for spring admission, 12/1 for domestic students. Applications are processed on a rolling basis. Application fee: $50. Electronic applications accepted. *Financial support:* In 2007–08, 14 teaching assistantships were awarded; institutionally sponsored loans also available. Financial award application deadline: 3/1. *Faculty research:* Literature and theory, creative writing, English as a second language, ethnic and women's studies, composition. *Unit head:* Janice Harris, Chair, 307-766-6453, Fax: 307-766-3189, E-mail: jharris@uwyo.edu.

Utah State University, School of Graduate Studies, College of Humanities, Arts and Social Sciences, Department of English, Logan, UT 84322. Offers American studies (MA, MS), including folklore, western American literature and culture; English (MA, MS), including literature and writing, technical writing. Part-time and evening/weekend programs available. *Degree requirements:* For master's, thesis or alternative. *Entrance requirements:* For master's, GRE General Test or MAT, minimum GPA of 3.0, recommendation letters, writing samples. Additional exam requirements/recommendations for international students: Required—TOEFL. *Faculty research:* Scottish enlightenment, material culture, composition theory, creative nonfiction, literary criticism.

Valdosta State University, Graduate School, College of Arts and Sciences, Department of English, Valdosta, GA 31698. Offers MA. Part-time programs available. *Faculty:* 22 full-time (13 women). *Students:* 4 full-time (3 women), 14 part-time (9 women); includes 2 minority (1 Asian American or Pacific Islander, 1 Hispanic American). Average age 25. 9 applicants, 44% accepted, 4 enrolled. In 2007, 4 degrees awarded. *Degree requirements:* For master's, one foreign language, thesis, comprehensive written and/or oral exams. *Entrance requirements:* For master's, GRE General Test, minimum GPA of 3.0. Additional exam requirements/recommendations for international students: Required—TOEFL (minimum score 523 paper-based; 193 computer-based). *Application deadline:* For fall admission, 7/1 for domestic and international students; for spring admission, 11/1 for domestic and international students. Applications are processed on a rolling basis. Application fee: $40. Electronic applications accepted. *Expenses:* Tuition, state resident: part-time $147 per hour. Tuition, nonresident: part-time $586 per hour. Required fees: $520 per semester. Tuition and fees vary according to course level, course load, campus/location and program. *Financial support:* In 2007–08, 4 students received support, including 2 research assistantships with full tuition reimbursements available (averaging $2,452 per year), 2 teaching assistantships with full tuition reimbursements available (averaging $2,800 per year); institutionally sponsored loans, scholarships/grants, and unspecified assistantships also available. Support available to part-time students. Financial award application deadline: 7/1; financial award applicants required to submit FAFSA. *Faculty research:* American literature. *Unit head:* Dr. Mark Smith, Head, 229-333-5946, E-mail: marksmit@valdosta.edu.

Valparaiso University, Graduate Division, Program in Liberal Studies, Concentration in English, Valparaiso, IN 46383. Offers MALS, Post-Master's Certificate, JD/MALS. Part-time and evening/weekend programs available. *Students:* 4 full-time (2 women), 8 part-time (all women); includes 3 minority (all African Americans) Average age 31. In 2007, 5 degrees awarded. *Entrance requirements:* For master's, minimum GPA of 3.0. Additional exam requirements/recommendations for international students: Required—TOEFL (minimum score 550 paper-based; 213 computer-based). *Application deadline:* Applications are processed on a rolling basis. Application fee: $30 ($50 for international students). Electronic applications accepted. *Financial support:* Available to part-time students. Applicants required to submit FAFSA. *Application contact:* Jamie Haney, Coordinator of Recruitment Activities, 219-464-5313, Fax: 219-464-5381, E-mail: jamie.haney@valpo.edu.

Vanderbilt University, Graduate School, Department of English, Nashville, TN 37240-1001. Offers MA, MAT, PhD. *Faculty:* 46 full-time (22 women). *Students:* 33 full-time (20 women), 5 part-time (4 women); includes 8 minority (3 African Americans, 1 American Indian/Alaska Native, 3 Asian Americans or Pacific Islanders, 1 Hispanic American), 1 international. Average age 29. 332 applicants, 5% accepted, 6 enrolled. In 2007, 3 master's, 3 doctorates awarded. *Degree requirements:* For master's, one foreign language, comprehensive exam; for doctorate, 2 foreign languages, thesis/dissertation, final and qualifying exams. *Entrance requirements:* For master's and doctorate, GRE General Test, GRE Subject Test, sample of written work. *Application deadline:* For fall admission, 1/15 for domestic and international students. Application fee: $0. Electronic applications accepted. *Financial support:* Fellowships with full and partial tuition reimbursements, research assistantships with full and partial tuition reimbursements, teaching assistantships with full tuition reimbursements, Federal Work-Study, institutionally sponsored loans, and health care benefits available. Financial award application deadline: 1/15; financial award applicants required to submit CSS PROFILE or FAFSA. *Faculty research:* Literature of the South, British and American literature, Shakespeare, language, literary theory, film, cultural studies. *Unit head:* Jay Clayton, Chair, 615-322-2541, Fax: 615-343-8028. *Application contact:* Kathryn Schwarz, Director of Graduate Studies, 615-322-2541, Fax: 615-343-8028, E-mail: kathryn.schwarz@vanderbilt.edu.

Villanova University, Graduate School of Liberal Arts and Sciences, Department of English, Villanova, PA 19085-1699. Offers MA. Part-time and evening/weekend programs available. *Faculty:* 6 full-time (all women). *Students:* 26 full-time (17 women), 29 part-time (19 women); includes 5 minority (1 African American, 3 Asian Americans or Pacific Islanders, 1 Hispanic American). Average age 28. 49 applicants, 82% accepted. In 2007, 9 degrees awarded. *Degree requirements:* For master's, comprehensive exam, thesis optional. *Entrance requirements:* For master's, GRE General Test, GRE Subject Test, minimum GPA of 3.0. *Application deadline:* For fall admission, 5/1 for domestic and international students; for spring admission, 11/15 for domestic and international students. Applications are processed on a rolling basis. Application fee: $50. Electronic applications accepted. *Financial support:* Research assistantships, Federal Work-Study and scholarships/grants available. Financial award applicants required to submit FAFSA. *Unit head:* Dr. Evan Radcliffe, Chairperson, 610-519-4630.

See Close-Up on page 591.

Virginia Commonwealth University, Graduate School, College of Humanities and Sciences, Department of English, Program in English, Richmond, VA 23284-9005. Offers literature (MA); writing and rhetoric (MA). *Application deadline:* For fall admission, 2/1 for domestic students; for spring admission, 11/15 for domestic students. Applications are processed on a rolling basis. Application fee: $50. *Expenses:* Tuition, state resident: full-time $7,224; part-time $401 per credit. Tuition, nonresident: full-time $16,072; part-time $891 per credit. Required fees: $1,679; $63 per credit. Tuition and fees vary according to campus/location. *Unit head:* Katherine Bassard, Program Director, E-mail: kcbassar@vcu.edu.

See Close-Up on page 457.

Virginia Polytechnic Institute and State University, Graduate School, College of Liberal Arts and Human Sciences, Department of English, Blacksburg, VA 24061. Offers creative writing (MFA); English (MA); rhetoric and writing (PhD). *Entrance requirements:* For master's, GRE General Test, GRE Subject Test. Additional exam requirements/recommendations for international students: Required—TOEFL (minimum score 600 paper-based; 250 computer-based). Electronic applications accepted. *Faculty research:* Critical theory, feminist criticism, textual editing, literary history.

Virginia State University, School of Graduate Studies, Research, and Outreach, School of Liberal Arts and Education, Department of Languages and Literature, Petersburg, VA 23806-0001. Offers English (MA). Part-time and evening/weekend programs available. *Degree requirements:* For master's, one foreign language, thesis (for some programs). *Entrance requirements:* For master's, GRE General Test. *Faculty research:* Writing and learning instruction, high-risk students, twentieth-century literature.

Wake Forest University, Graduate School of Arts and Sciences, Department of English, Winston-Salem, NC 27109. Offers MA. Part-time programs available. *Faculty:* 22 full-time (10 women). *Students:* 22 full-time (14 women), 1 international. Average age 26. 37 applicants, 46% accepted, 9 enrolled. In 2007, 12 degrees awarded. *Degree requirements:* For master's, one foreign language, thesis. *Entrance requirements:* For master's, GRE General Test, GRE Subject Test, writing sample. Additional exam requirements/recommendations for international students: Required—TOEFL (minimum score 213 computer-based; 79 iBT). *Application deadline:* For fall admission, 1/15 for domestic and international students. Application fee: $45 ($55 for international students). Electronic applications accepted. *Financial support:* In 2007–08, 20 students received support, including 2 fellowships with full tuition reimbursements available (averaging $4,000 per year), 5 teaching assistantships with full tuition reimbursements available (averaging $8,000 per year); scholarships/grants, tuition waivers (full and partial), and unspecified assistantships also available. Support available to part-time students. Financial award application deadline: 1/15; financial award applicants required to submit FAFSA. *Faculty research:* Modern and contemporary poetry, feminist criticism and theory, Irish literature, British Commonwealth literature, medieval poetry. *Unit head:* Dr. Scott Klein, Director, 336-758-5399, Fax: 336-758-7193, E-mail: klein@wfu.edu.

Washington College, Graduate Programs, Department of English, Chestertown, MD 21620-1197. Offers MA. Part-time and evening/weekend programs available.

Washington State University, Graduate School, College of Liberal Arts, Department of English, Pullman, WA 99164. Offers composition (MA); English (MA, PhD); teaching of English (MA). *Faculty:* 34. *Students:* 56 full-time (33 women), 2 part-time (1 woman); includes 8 minority (1 African American, 2 American Indian/Alaska Native, 3 Asian Americans or Pacific Islanders, 2 Hispanic Americans), 6 international. Average age 32. 81 applicants, 25% accepted, 18 enrolled. In 2007, 9 master's, 10 doctorates awarded. *Degree requirements:* For master's, one foreign language, comprehensive exam (for some programs), thesis (for some programs), oral exam; for doctorate, 2 foreign languages, comprehensive exam, thesis/dissertation, oral exam, written exam. *Entrance requirements:* For master's and doctorate, GRE General Test, GRE Subject Test, minimum GPA of 3.0, 10 page writing sample, 3 letters of recommendation. Additional exam requirements/recommendations for international students: Required—TOEFL. *Application deadline:* For fall admission, 1/10 priority date for domestic students, 1/10 for international students. Applications are processed on a rolling basis. Application fee: $50. *Financial support:* In 2007–08, 48 students received support, including 1 fellowship (averaging $2,000 per year), 2 research assistantships with full and partial tuition reimbursements available (averaging $13,917 per year), 44 teaching assistantships with full and partial tuition reimburse-

English

Washington State University (continued)
ments available (averaging $13,056 per year); career-related internships or fieldwork, Federal Work-Study, institutionally sponsored loans, scholarships/grants, health care benefits, and tuition waivers (partial) also available. Financial award application deadline: 4/1; financial award applicants required to submit FAFSA. *Faculty research:* Nationalism and gender in the American West, slavery and exploitation in 19th century Britain, photography and the color line, D.H. Lawrence and Mexico, social movement cultures and the arts. Total annual research expenditures: $81,455. *Unit head:* Dr. George E. Kennedy, Chair, 509-335-2581, Fax: 509-335-2582, E-mail: gkennedy@wsu.edu. *Application contact:* Graduate School Admissions, 800-GRADWSU, Fax: 509-335-1949, E-mail: gradsch@wsu.edu.

Washington State University, Graduate School, College of Liberal Arts, Program in American Studies, Pullman, WA 99164. Offers ethnic studies (MA, PhD); feminist studies (MA, PhD); history (MA, PhD); literature (MA, PhD). *Faculty:* 39. *Students:* 27 full-time (19 women), 4 part-time (2 women); includes 17 minority (6 African Americans, 4 American Indian/Alaska Native, 2 Asian Americans or Pacific Islanders, 5 Hispanic Americans), 3 international. Average age 35. 78 applicants, 15% accepted, 12 enrolled. In 2007, 5 master's, 1 doctorate awarded. *Degree requirements:* For master's, one foreign language, comprehensive exam (for some programs), thesis optional, oral exam; for doctorate, one foreign language, comprehensive exam (for some programs), thesis/dissertation, oral exam. *Entrance requirements:* For master's and doctorate, GRE General Test, minimum GPA of 3.0, writing sample, 3 letters of recommendation. Additional exam requirements/recommendations for international students: Required—TOEFL. *Application deadline:* For fall admission, 2/1 priority date for domestic students, 3/1 for international students; for spring admission, 7/1 for international students. Applications are processed on a rolling basis. Application fee: $50. *Financial support:* In 2007–08, 24 students received support, including 1 fellowship (averaging $6,950 per year), 3 research assistantships with full and partial tuition reimbursements available (averaging $13,917 per year), 17 teaching assistantships with full and partial tuition reimbursements available (averaging $13,056 per year); career-related internships or fieldwork, Federal Work-Study, institutionally sponsored loans, tuition waivers (partial), and teaching associateships also available. Financial award application deadline: 3/1; financial award applicants required to submit FAFSA. *Faculty research:* The American West in multicultural perspective; nineteenth century historical, literary, and cultural studies; comparative American ethnic literatures and cultures; American cultures and the environment; American rhetoric. *Unit head:* Dr. Noel Sturgeon, Director, 509-335-1560, E-mail: reedtv@wsu.edu. *Application contact:* Graduate School Admissions, 800-GRADWSU, Fax: 509-335-1949, E-mail: gradsch@wsu.edu.

Washington University in St. Louis, Graduate School of Arts and Sciences, Department of English and American Literature, St. Louis, MO 63130-4899. Offers English and American literature (MA, PhD); writing (MFAW). Terminal master's awarded for partial completion of doctoral program. *Degree requirements:* For master's, thesis or written exam; for doctorate, 2 foreign languages, thesis/dissertation. *Entrance requirements:* For master's and doctorate, GRE General Test, sample of written work. Electronic applications accepted.

Wayne State University, College of Liberal Arts and Sciences, Department of English, Detroit, MI 48202. Offers comparative literature (MA); English (MA, PhD). *Students:* 84 full-time (55 women), 37 part-time (24 women); includes 11 minority (9 African Americans, 1 Asian American or Pacific Islander, 1 Hispanic American), 10 international. Average age 34. 73 applicants, 48% accepted, 12 enrolled. In 2007, 10 master's, 3 doctorates awarded. *Degree requirements:* For master's, one foreign language, essay or thesis; for doctorate, one foreign language, thesis/dissertation. *Entrance requirements:* For master's, GRE General Test, minimum GPA of 3.25 in English, 3.0 overall, statement of purpose; references; sample essay; for doctorate, GRE General Test, GRE Subject Test, statement of purpose, references, sample essay. Additional exam requirements/recommendations for international students: Required—TOEFL (minimum score 550 paper-based; 213 computer-based); Recommended—TWE (minimum score 6). *Application deadline:* For fall admission, 6/1 for international students; for winter admission, 10/1 for international students; for spring admission, 2/1 for international students. Applications are processed on a rolling basis. Application fee: $30 ($50 for international students). Electronic applications accepted. *Expenses:* Tuition, state resident: part-time $403 per credit hour. Tuition, nonresident: part-time $890 per credit hour. *Financial support:* In 2007–08, 40 students received support, including 2 fellowships (averaging $13,001 per year), 32 teaching assistantships (averaging $12,922 per year); research assistantships, career-related internships or fieldwork, institutionally sponsored loans, and tuition waivers (full and partial) also available. Support available to part-time students. Financial award application deadline: 3/1. *Faculty research:* English and American literature, cultural studies, composition, linguistics, film. *Unit head:* Dr. Richard Grusin, Chair, 313-577-7692, Fax: 313-577-8618, E-mail: aj4671@wayne.edu. *Application contact:* Ross Pudaloff, Graduate Director, 313-577-7699, E-mail: r.pudaloff@wayne.edu.

Weber State University, College of Arts and Humanities, Program in English, Ogden, UT 84408-1001. Offers MENG. Part-time and evening/weekend programs available. *Faculty:* 22 part-time/adjunct (11 women). *Students:* 5 full-time (2 women), 44 part-time (29 women); includes 1 minority (Asian American or Pacific Islander), 1 international. Average age 37. 20 applicants, 80% accepted, 11 enrolled. *Degree requirements:* For master's, one foreign language, additional course hours, thesis or research project. *Entrance requirements:* For master's, MAT or GRE, 3 letter of recommendation, transcript, writing sample, bachelor's degree. *Application deadline:* Applications are processed on a rolling basis. Application fee: $30. *Financial support:* Tuition waivers (partial) available. *Faculty research:* Victoria literature, Middle East women writers, Irish literature (Seamus Heanes). *Unit head:* Dr. Kathleen Marie Herndon, Chair, 801-626-6217, Fax: 801-626-7760, E-mail: kherndon@weber.edu. *Application contact:* Robin L. Scott, Secretary II/English, 801-626-6251, Fax: 801-626-7760, E-mail: robinscott@weber.edu.

West Chester University of Pennsylvania, Office of Graduate Studies and Extended Education, College of Arts and Sciences, Department of English, West Chester, PA 19383. Offers English (MA); English—non-thesis option (MA). Part-time and evening/weekend programs available. *Students:* 21 full-time (14 women), 42 part-time (31 women); includes 5 minority (all African Americans), 1 international. Average age 33. 35 applicants, 100% accepted, 19 enrolled. In 2007, 25 degrees awarded. *Degree requirements:* For master's, comprehensive exam, thesis optional. *Entrance requirements:* For master's, GRE General Test, writing sample. Additional exam requirements/recommendations for international students: Required—TOEFL (minimum score 550 paper-based; 213 computer-based; 80 iBT). *Application deadline:* For fall admission, 4/15 priority date for domestic students; for spring admission, 10/15 for domestic students. Applications are processed on a rolling basis. Application fee: $35. *Expenses:* Tuition, state resident: part-time $345 per credit. Tuition, nonresident: part-time $552 per credit. Tuition and fees vary according to course load. *Financial support:* In 2007–08, 16 research assistantships with full and partial tuition reimbursements (averaging $5,000 per year) were awarded. Support available to part-time students. Financial award application deadline: 2/15; financial award applicants required to submit FAFSA. *Faculty research:* William Smith, Sara Winnemucca Hopkins, literacy practices for students at risk. *Unit head:* Dr. Anne Herzog, Chair, 610-436-2822, E-mail: aherzog@wcupa.edu. *Application contact:* Dr. Karen Fitts, Graduate Coordinator, 610-436-2745, E-mail: kfitts@wcupa.edu.

Western Carolina University, Graduate School, College of Arts and Sciences, Department of English, Cullowhee, NC 28723. Offers English (MA); teaching English as a second language or foreign language (MA). Part-time and evening/weekend programs available. *Faculty:* 21 full-time (13 women), 2 part-time/adjunct (1 woman). *Students:* 13 full-time (8 women), 25 part-time (20 women); includes 1 minority (American Indian/Alaska Native), 1 international. Average age 33. 21 applicants, 90% accepted, 13 enrolled. In 2007, 7 degrees awarded. *Degree requirements:* For master's, one foreign language, comprehensive exam, thesis (for some programs). *Entrance requirements:* For master's, GRE General Test, appropriate undergraduate, writing sample, 3 letters of recommendation. Additional exam requirements/recommendations for international students: Required—TOEFL (minimum score 550 paper-based; 270 computer-based; 79 iBT). *Application deadline:* For fall admission, 5/1 priority date for domestic students; for spring admission, 9/1 priority date for domestic students. Applications are processed on a rolling basis. Application fee: $40. *Expenses:* Tuition, state resident: full-time $2,314. Tuition, nonresident: full-time $11,899. Required fees: $2,033. Tuition and fees vary according to course load. *Financial support:* In 2007–08, 13 students received support, including 7 research assistantships with full and partial tuition reimbursements available (averaging $7,429 per year), 5 teaching assistantships with full and partial tuition reimbursements available (averaging $7,500 per year); fellowships with full and partial tuition reimbursements available, career-related internships or fieldwork, institutionally sponsored loans, scholarships/grants, and unspecified assistantships also available. Financial award application deadline: 3/31; financial award applicants required to submit FAFSA. *Faculty research:* TESOL, language assessment, applied linguistics, poetry, folk and fairy tales, post World War II British literature, Appalachian and southern literature. *Unit head:* Dr. Elizabeth Addison, Head, 828-227-7264, Fax: 828-227-7266, E-mail: addisson@email.wcu.edu. *Application contact:* Admission Specialist for Department of English, 828-227-7398, Fax: 828-227-7480, E-mail: gradsch@email.wcu.edu.

Western Connecticut State University, Division of Graduate Studies, School of Arts and Sciences, Department of English, Danbury, CT 06810-6885. Offers English (MA); literature option (MA); TESOL option (MA); writing option (MA). Part-time and evening/weekend programs available. *Faculty:* 10 full-time (4 women). *Students:* 3 full-time (1 woman), 30 part-time (22 women); includes 2 minority (1 African American, 1 Asian American or Pacific Islander), 1 international. Average age 41. 18 applicants, 83% accepted, 11 enrolled. In 2007, 12 degrees awarded. *Degree requirements:* For master's, thesis or comprehensive exam. *Entrance requirements:* For master's, minimum GPA of 2.5, writing sample. *Application deadline:* For fall admission, 8/5 priority date for domestic students; for spring admission, 1/5 priority date for domestic students. Applications are processed on a rolling basis. Application fee: $50. *Expenses:* Tuition, state resident: full-time $4,169. Tuition, nonresident: full-time $11,614. Required fees: $3,278. *Financial support:* Teaching assistantships, career-related internships or fieldwork available. Support available to part-time students. Financial award application deadline: 5/1; financial award applicants required to submit FAFSA. *Unit head:* Dr. Oscar De Los Santos, Associate Professor, 203-837-9044. *Application contact:* Chris Shankle, Associate Director of Graduate Admissions, 203-837-8244, Fax: 203-837-8338, E-mail: shanklec@wcsu.edu.

Western Illinois University, School of Graduate Studies, College of Arts and Sciences, Department of English and Journalism, Macomb, IL 61455-1390. Offers literature and language (MA); writing (MA). Part-time programs available. *Students:* 14 full-time (10 women), 31 part-time (21 women); includes 2 minority (1 Asian American or Pacific Islander, 1 Hispanic American), 4 international. Average age 31. 21 applicants, 90% accepted. In 2007, 13 degrees awarded. *Degree requirements:* For master's, thesis or alternative. *Entrance requirements:* For master's, minimum GPA of 2.75. Additional exam requirements/recommendations for international students: Required—TOEFL (minimum score 550 paper-based; 213 computer-based; 80 iBT). *Application deadline:* Applications are processed on a rolling basis. Application fee: $30. Electronic applications accepted. *Expenses:* Tuition, state resident: part-time $217 per credit hour. Tuition, nonresident: part-time $433 per credit hour. Required fees: $54 per credit hour. *Financial support:* In 2007–08, 14 students received support, including 7 research assistantships with full tuition reimbursements available (averaging $6,800 per year), 7 teaching assistantships with full tuition reimbursements available (averaging $7,840 per year). Financial award applicants required to submit FAFSA. *Unit head:* Dr. David Boocker, Chairperson, 309-298-1103. *Application contact:* Dr. Barbara Baily, Director of Graduate Studies/Associate Provost, 309-298-1806, Fax: 309-298-2345, E-mail: grad-office@wiu.edu.

Western Kentucky University, Graduate Studies, Potter College of Arts and Letters, Department of English, Bowling Green, KY 42101. Offers education (MA); English (MA Ed); literature (MA), including American literature, British literature, literary theory, women writers, world literature; teaching English as a second language (MA); writing (MA). Part-time and evening/weekend programs available. *Degree requirements:* For master's, comprehensive exam, thesis optional, final exam. *Entrance requirements:* For master's, GRE General Test, minimum GPA of 2.75. Additional exam requirements/recommendations for international students: Required—TOEFL (minimum score 555 paper-based; 213 computer-based; 79 iBT). *Faculty research:* Improving writing, linking teacher knowledge and performance, Victorian women writers, Kentucky women writers, Kentucky poets.

Western Michigan University, Graduate College, College of Arts and Sciences, Department of English, Kalamazoo, MI 49008-5202. Offers creative writing (MFA); English (MA, PhD); English education (MA, PhD); professional writing (MA). *Degree requirements:* For master's, oral exams; for doctorate, one foreign language, thesis/dissertation, oral exam, written exams. *Entrance requirements:* For master's and doctorate, GRE General Test, GRE Subject Test.

Western Washington University, Graduate School, College of Humanities and Social Sciences, Department of English, Bellingham, WA 98225-5996. Offers MA. Part-time programs available. *Faculty:* 28. *Students:* 39 full-time (22 women). 70 applicants, 57% accepted, 12 enrolled. In 2007, 20 degrees awarded. *Degree requirements:* For master's, one foreign language, comprehensive exam, thesis (for some programs). *Entrance requirements:* For master's, GRE General Test, writing sample, minimum GPA of 3.0 in last 60 semester hours or last 90 quarter hours of course work. Additional exam requirements/recommendations for international students: Required—TOEFL (minimum score 567 paper-based; 227 computer-based). *Application deadline:* For fall admission, 3/1 priority date for domestic students; for winter admission, 10/1 for domestic students; for spring admission, 2/1 for domestic students. Application fee: $50. Electronic applications accepted. *Expenses:* Tuition, state resident: part-time $208 per credit. Tuition, nonresident: part-time $541 per credit. Required fees: $241 per quarter. One-time fee: $250 part-time. *Financial support:* In 2007–08, 28 teaching assistantships with partial tuition reimbursements (averaging $9,339 per year) were awarded; career-related internships or fieldwork, Federal Work-Study, institutionally sponsored loans, scholarships/grants, tuition waivers (partial), and unspecified assistantships also available. Support available to part-time students. Financial award application deadline: 2/15; financial award applicants required to submit FAFSA. *Faculty research:* Literature and technology, film, composition and rhetoric, technical writing, critical and cultural theory. *Unit head:* Marc Geisler, Chair, 360-650-3209. *Application contact:* Dr. Dawn Dietrich, Director of Graduate Studies, 360-650-3225.

Westfield State College, Division of Graduate and Continuing Education, Department of English, Westfield, MA 01086. Offers MA. Part-time and evening/weekend programs available. *Degree requirements:* For master's, one foreign language, thesis. *Entrance requirements:* For master's, GRE General Test, MAT, minimum undergraduate GPA of 2.7, undergraduate course work in English.

West Texas A&M University, College of Fine Arts and Humanities, Department of English and Modern Languages, Canyon, TX 79016-0001. Offers English (MA). Part-time and evening/weekend programs available. *Degree requirements:* For master's, comprehensive exam, thesis optional. *Entrance requirements:* For master's, GRE General Test. Additional exam requirements/recommendations for international students: Required—TOEFL (minimum score 550 paper-based). Electronic applications accepted. *Faculty research:* Medieval studies, composition theory, literary criticism, Evelyn Scott, transformation of literacy in computer mediated communication.

West Virginia University, Eberly College of Arts and Sciences, Department of English, Morgantown, WV 26506. Offers creative writing (MFA); English (MA, PhD); literary/cultural studies (MA, PhD); writing (MA). Part-time and evening/weekend programs available. *Faculty:* 36 full-time (16 women), 18 part-time/adjunct (14 women). *Students:* 63 full-time (42 women), 19 part-time (14 women); includes 3 minority (all Asian Americans or Pacific Islanders), 5 international. Average age 29. 141 applicants, 35% accepted, 23 enrolled. In 2007, 22 master's, 1 doctorate awarded. *Median time to degree:* Of those who began their doctoral program in fall 1999, 100% received their degree in 8 years or less. *Degree requirements:* For master's, one foreign language, thesis optional; for doctorate, one foreign language, thesis/dissertation, preliminary exam. *Entrance requirements:* For master's, GRE General Test, minimum GPA of 3.0; for doctorate, GRE General Test, GRE Subject Test, minimum GPA of 3.0. Additional exam requirements/recommendations for international students: Required—TOEFL. *Application deadline:* For fall admission, 1/15 for domestic and international students. Application fee: $50. Electronic applications accepted. *Expenses:* Tuition, state resident: full-time $5,196; part-time $292 per credit hour. Tuition, nonresident: full-time $15,064; part-time $840 per credit hour. Tuition and fees vary according to program. *Financial support:* In 2007–08, 76 students received support, including research assistantships with full tuition reimbursements available (averaging $12,000 per year), 60 teaching assistantships with full tuition reimbursements available (averaging $12,000 per year); institutionally sponsored loans, health care benefits, and tuition waivers (full and partial) also available. Financial award application deadline: 1/15; financial award applicants required to submit FAFSA. *Faculty research:* American studies, gender studies, media studies, cultural studies. Total annual research expenditures: $54,473. *Unit head:* Dr. Donald E. Hall, Chair, 304-293-3100, Fax: 304-293-5380, E-mail: donald.hall@mail.wvu.edu. *Application contact:* Amanda Riley, Graduate Secretary, 304-293-2947, Fax: 304-293-5380, E-mail: amanda.riley@mail.wvu.edu.

Wichita State University, Graduate School, Fairmount College of Liberal Arts and Sciences, Department of English, Wichita, KS 67260. Offers creative writing (MA, MFA); English (MA, MFA). Part-time and evening/weekend programs available. *Degree requirements:* For master's, comprehensive exam. *Entrance requirements:* For master's, GRE, writing sample (MFA). Additional exam requirements/recommendations for international students: Required—TOEFL. Electronic applications accepted.

Wilfrid Laurier University, Faculty of Graduate Studies, Faculty of Arts, Department of English and Film Studies, Waterloo, ON N2L 3C5, Canada. Offers MA, PhD. *Faculty:* 25 full-time. *Students:* 29 full-time, 1 part-time. 73 applicants, 42% accepted, 19 enrolled. In 2007, 12 degrees awarded. *Degree requirements:* For master's, thesis optional; for doctorate, thesis/dissertation. *Entrance requirements:* For master's, honours BA or the equivalent in English, minimum B+ in English courses above first year level; for doctorate, MA in English, minimum A- average in graduate work. Additional exam requirements/recommendations for international students: Recommended—TOEFL (minimum score 230 computer-based; 89 iBT). *Application deadline:* For fall admission, 2/1 priority date for domestic students. Application fee: $75. Electronic applications accepted. *Financial support:* Fellowships, research assistantships, teaching assistantships available. *Faculty research:* Gender and genre, Canadian studies, early modern studies, postcolonial studies, nineteenth century studies. *Unit head:* Eleanor Ty, Chairperson, 519-884-0710 Ext. 3581, E-mail: ety@wlu.ca. *Application contact:* Jennifer Poppe, Student Contact, 519-884-0710 Ext. 3536, Fax: 519-884-1020, E-mail: gradstudies@wlu.ca.

William Paterson University of New Jersey, College of the Humanities and Social Sciences, Department of English, Wayne, NJ 07470-8420. Offers MA. Part-time and evening/weekend programs available. *Students:* 7 full-time (5 women), 44 part-time (38 women); includes 2 minority (both Hispanic Americans) In 2007, 20 degrees awarded. *Degree requirements:* For master's, thesis, essay, manuscript, portfolio. *Entrance requirements:* For master's, GRE General Test, MAT, minimum GPA of 2.75. *Application deadline:* Applications are processed on a rolling basis. Application fee: $50. Electronic applications accepted. *Financial support:* Research assistantships with full tuition reimbursements, unspecified assistantships available. Support available to part-time students. Financial award application deadline: 4/1; financial award applicants required to submit FAFSA. *Faculty research:* Thornton Wilder notebooks and diaries, minimal grammar text, Senhora text, Frank O'Hara biography, Caresse Crosby biography. *Unit head:* Andrew Barnes, Program Director, 973-720-2837. *Application contact:* Danielle Liautaud, Director, 973-720-3579, Fax: 973-720-2035, E-mail: liautaudd@wpunj.edu.

Winona State University, College of Liberal Arts, Department of English, Winona, MN 55987-5838. Offers MA, MS. Part-time programs available. *Faculty:* 14 full-time (7 women). *Students:* 19 full-time (15 women), 4 part-time (3 women); includes 7 minority (all Asian Americans or Pacific Islanders) 16 applicants, 69% accepted, 11 enrolled. In 2007, 9 degrees awarded. *Degree requirements:* For master's, thesis or alternative. *Application deadline:* For fall admission, 7/26 priority date for domestic students; for spring admission, 12/8 for domestic students. Applications are processed on a rolling basis. Application fee: $20. *Expenses:* Tuition, state resident: part-time $290 per credit. Tuition, nonresident: part-time $438 per credit. Required fees: $17 per credit. *Financial support:* In 2007–08, 6 teaching assistantships with partial tuition reimbursements (averaging $6,000 per year) were awarded; career-related internships or fieldwork, Federal Work-Study, and unspecified assistantships also available. Support available to part-time students. Financial award applicants required to submit FAFSA. *Unit head:* Dr. Ruth Forsythe, Chairperson, 507-457-5429, E-mail: rforsythe@winona.edu.

Winthrop University, College of Arts and Sciences, Department of English, Rock Hill, SC 29733. Offers MA. Part-time and evening/weekend programs available. *Faculty:* 13 full-time (9 women), 1 part-time/adjunct (0 women). *Students:* 8 full-time (7 women), 8 part-time (5 women); includes 2 minority (both African Americans) Average age 23. In 2007, 5 degrees awarded. *Degree requirements:* For master's, one foreign language, thesis optional. *Entrance requirements:* For master's, GRE General Test, MAT or PRAXIS, 24 undergraduate English hours. *Application deadline:* For fall admission, 7/15 priority date for domestic students; for spring admission, 12/1 for domestic students. Applications are processed on a rolling basis. Application fee: $50. Electronic applications accepted. *Expenses:* Tuition, state resident: full-time $9,834; part-time $412 per credit hour. Tuition, nonresident: full-time $18,280; part-time $763 per credit hour. *Financial support:* In 2007–08, 4 research assistantships with full tuition reimbursements (averaging $3,600 per year) were awarded; Federal Work-Study, scholarships/grants, and unspecified assistantships also available. Support available to part-time students. Financial award application deadline: 2/1; financial award applicants required to submit FAFSA. *Unit head:* Dr. William F. Naufftus, Graduate Program Director, 803-323-4570, Fax: 803-323-4837, E-mail: naufftusn@winthrop.edu. *Application contact:* 800-411-7041, Fax: 803-323-4837, E-mail: naufftusn@winthrop.edu.

Wright State University, School of Graduate Studies, College of Liberal Arts, Department of English Language and Literatures, Dayton, OH 45435. Offers composition and rhetoric (MA); English (MA); literature (MA); teaching English to speakers of other languages (MA). *Degree requirements:* For master's, thesis optional, portfolio. *Entrance requirements:* For master's, 20 hours in upper-level English. Additional exam requirements/recommendations for international students: Required—TOEFL. *Faculty research:* American literature, world literature in English, applied linguistics, writing theory and pedagogy.

Xavier University, College of Arts and Sciences, Department of English, Cincinnati, OH 45207. Offers MA. Part-time and evening/weekend programs available. *Faculty:* 14 full-time (6 women). *Students:* 6 full-time (4 women), 15 part-time (9 women); includes 2 minority (1 African American, 1 Asian American or Pacific Islander), 1 international. Average age 31. 29 applicants, 48% accepted, 8 enrolled. In 2007, 9 degrees awarded. *Degree requirements:* For master's, one foreign language, comprehensive exam, thesis or alternative. *Entrance requirements:* For master's, GRE, minimum GPA of 3.2 in undergraduate English course work. Additional exam requirements/recommendations for international students: Required—TOEFL (minimum score 550 paper-based; 213 computer-based). *Application deadline:* For fall admission, 8/15 priority date for domestic students. Applications are processed on a rolling basis. Application fee: $35. Electronic applications accepted. *Financial support:* Scholarships/grants and unspecified assistantships available. Support available to part-time students. Financial award applicants required to submit FAFSA. *Faculty research:* Women novelists, contemporary American poetry, literature and peace studies, Victorian literature, Shakespeare and Renaissance drama. *Unit head:* Dr. Alison Russell, Chair, 513-745-3275, Fax: 513-745-3065, E-mail: russell@xavier.edu. *Application contact:* Roger Bosse, Director of Graduate Services, 513-745-3357, Fax: 513-745-1048, E-mail: xugrad@xavier.edu.

Yale University, Graduate School of Arts and Sciences, Department of English Language and Literature, New Haven, CT 06520. Offers MA, PhD. Terminal master's awarded for partial completion of doctoral program. *Degree requirements:* For master's, 2 foreign languages; for doctorate, 3 foreign languages, thesis/dissertation. *Entrance requirements:* For master's and doctorate, GRE General Test, GRE Subject Test.

York University, Faculty of Graduate Studies, Faculty of Arts, Program in English, Toronto, ON M3J 1P3, Canada. Offers MA, PhD. Part-time programs available. *Degree requirements:* For master's, thesis or alternative; for doctorate, one foreign language, comprehensive exam, thesis/dissertation. Electronic applications accepted.

Youngstown State University, Graduate School, College of Arts and Sciences, Department of English, Youngstown, OH 44555-0001. Offers MA. Part-time programs available. *Degree requirements:* For master's, portfolio. *Entrance requirements:* For master's, bachelor's degree in English, minimum GPA of 2.7. Additional exam requirements/recommendations for international students: Required—TOEFL. *Faculty research:* Technical communications, multicultural literacy, children's literature, women's literature, film study, linguistics.

French

American University, College of Arts and Sciences, Department of Language and Foreign Studies, Program in French, Washington, DC 20016-8001. Offers translation (Certificate). Part-time and evening/weekend programs available. *Students:* 2 full-time (both women). *Degree requirements:* For Certificate, minimum 15 credit hours related course work. *Entrance requirements:* For degree, Bachelor's Degree in French or evidence of French proficiency + BA in any field. *Application deadline:* For fall admission, 2/1 for domestic students; for spring admission, 10/1 for domestic students. Application fee: $50. *Expenses:* Tuition: Full-time $19,998; part-time $1,111 per credit hour. Required fees: $380. Tuition and fees vary according to program. *Financial support:* Fellowships, career-related internships or fieldwork, Federal Work-Study, and institutionally sponsored loans available. Financial award application deadline: 2/1. *Faculty research:* Literature, language, modern French politics, contemporary French society, the civilization of Quebec, business French and translation studies.

Arizona State University, Graduate College, College of Liberal Arts and Sciences, Division of Humanities, Department of Languages and Literatures, Program in French, Tempe, AZ 85287. Offers MA. *Degree requirements:* For master's, thesis or alternative. *Entrance requirements:* For master's, GRE.

Asbury College, Graduate Programs, Wilmore, KY 40390-1198. Offers biology: alternative certificate (MA Ed); chemistry: alternative certificate (MA Ed); English (Certificate); English as a second language (MA Ed); ESL (Certificate); French (Certificate); mathematics: alternative certificate (MA Ed); reading / writing (MA Ed); social studies (Certificate); Spanish (Certificate); special education (MA Ed); special education: alternative certificate (MA Ed). *Accreditation:* NCATE. Part-time programs available. *Faculty:* 8 full-time (7 women), 9 part-time/adjunct (4 women). *Students:* Average age 36. 14 applicants, 100% accepted, 14 enrolled. In 2007, 10 degrees awarded. *Degree requirements:* For master's, action research project, portfolio. *Entrance requirements:* For master's, PRAXIS/NTE, minimum GPA of 2.75, letters of recommendation. Additional exam requirements/recommendations for international students: Required—TOEFL (minimum score 550 paper-based). *Application deadline:* Applications are processed on a rolling basis. Application fee: $25. *Expenses:* Tuition: Part-time $353 per credit hour. *Financial support:* Scholarships/grants and traineeships available. Financial award applicants required to submit FAFSA. *Unit head:* Dr. Bonnie J. Banker, Director, 859-858-3511 Ext. 2221, Fax: 859-858-3921, E-mail: bonnie.banker@asbury.edu. *Application contact:* Melanie S. Kinnell, Graduate Program Assistant and Certification Specialist, 859-858-3511 Ext. 2304, Fax: 859-858-3921, E-mail: graded@asbury.edu.

Bennington College, Graduate Programs, Program in Teaching a Second Language, Bennington, VT 05201. Offers education (MATSL); foreign language education (MATSL); French (MATSL); Spanish (MATSL). Part-time programs available. *Faculty:* 2 full-time (0 women), 3 part-time/adjunct (all women). *Students:* Average age 37. 14 applicants, 93% accepted, 12 enrolled. In 2007, 6 master's awarded. *Degree requirements:* For master's, one foreign language, 2 major projects and presentations. *Entrance requirements:* For master's, oral proficiency interview (OPI). Additional exam requirements/recommendations for international students: Required—TOEFL (minimum score 577 paper-based; 233 computer-based; 91 iBT). *Application deadline:* For spring admission, 4/1 priority date for domestic and international students. Applications are processed on a rolling basis. Application fee: $60. *Expenses: Contact institution.* One-time fee: $75 full-time. Tuition and fees vary according to program. *Financial support:* In 2007–08, 3 students received support. Scholarships/grants available. Financial award application deadline: 4/1; financial award applicants required to submit FAFSA. *Faculty research:* Acquisition, evaluation, assessment, conceptual teaching and learning content-driven communication, applied linguistics. *Unit head:* Carol Meyer, Director of Isabelle Kaplan Center for Languages and Cultures/MATSL/CCT, 802-440-4375, Fax: 802-447-4269, E-mail: cmeyer@bennington.edu. *Application contact:* Nancy Pearlman, Assistant Director, MATSL/CCT, 802-440-4710, Fax: 802-447-4269, E-mail: matsl@bennington.edu.

Boston College, Graduate School of Arts and Sciences, Department of Romance Languages and Literatures, Chestnut Hill, MA 02467-3800. Offers French (MA, PhD); Italian (MA); medieval language (PhD); Spanish (MA, PhD). Part-time programs available. *Students:* 41 full-time (29 women), 9 part-time (7 women); includes 7 minority (1 American Indian/Alaska Native, 1 Asian American or Pacific Islander, 5 Hispanic Americans), 9 international. 51 applicants, 39% accepted, 10 enrolled. In 2007, 14 master's, 3 doctorates awarded. Terminal master's awarded for partial completion of doctoral program. *Degree requirements:* For master's, one foreign language; for doctorate, 2 foreign languages, thesis/dissertation. *Entrance requirements:* Additional exam requirements/recommendations for international students: Required—TOEFL (minimum score 590 paper-based; 250 computer-based; 91 iBT). *Application deadline:* For fall admission, 1/15 for domestic students. Application fee: $70. Electronic applications accepted. *Financial support:* Fellowships with full tuition reimbursements, teaching assistantships with full tuition reimbursements, Federal Work-Study and unspecified assistantships available. Support available to part-time students. Financial award application deadline: 3/1; financial award applicants required to submit FAFSA. *Faculty research:* Spanish-American literature, philology, medieval French romance and troubadour/trouvere lyrics, Golden Age Peninsular literature, secondary language acquisition and pedagogy. *Unit head:* Dr. Dwayne Carpenter, Chairperson, 617-552-3828, E-mail: dwayne.carpenter@bc.edu.

See Close-Up on page 561.

French

Boston University, Graduate School of Arts and Sciences, Department of Romance Studies, Boston, MA 02215. Offers French language and literature (MA, PhD); Hispanic language and literatures (MA, PhD). *Students:* 45 full-time (34 women), 3 part-time (2 women); includes 6 minority (all Hispanic Americans), 19 international. Average age 32. 54 applicants, 37% accepted, 9 enrolled. In 2007, 5 doctorates awarded. Terminal master's awarded for partial completion of doctoral program. *Degree requirements:* For master's, one foreign language, comprehensive exam; for doctorate, 2 foreign languages, comprehensive exam, thesis/dissertation. *Entrance requirements:* For master's and doctorate, GRE General Test, sample of written work, 3 letters of recommendation. Additional exam requirements/recommendations for international students: Required—TOEFL (minimum score 550 paper-based; 213 computer-based). *Application deadline:* For fall admission, 7/1 for domestic and international students; for spring admission, 10/15 for domestic and international students. Application fee: $70. *Expenses:* Tuition: Full-time $34,930; part-time $1,092 per credit. Tuition and fees vary according to class time, course level and program. *Financial support:* In 2007–08, 48 students received support, including 2 fellowships with full tuition reimbursements available (averaging $18,000 per year), 35 teaching assistantships with full tuition reimbursements available (averaging $16,500 per year); research assistantships, Federal Work-Study and scholarships/grants also available. Support available to part-time students. Financial award application deadline: 1/15; financial award applicants required to submit FAFSA. *Unit head:* Christopher Maurer, Chairman, 617-353-6225, Fax: 617-353-6245, E-mail: chmaurer@bu.edu. *Application contact:* Lauren Terry, Administrative Assistant, 617-353-2641, Fax: 617-353-6245, E-mail: lkterry@bu.edu.

Bowling Green State University, Graduate College, College of Arts and Sciences, Department of Romance and Classical Studies, Program in French, Bowling Green, OH 43403. Offers French (MA); French education (MAT). Part-time programs available. *Students:* 19 full-time (15 women), 1 (woman) part-time; includes 2 minority (1 African American, 1 Hispanic American), 2 international. Average age 27. 18 applicants, 67% accepted, 8 enrolled. In 2007, 12 degrees awarded. *Degree requirements:* For master's, one foreign language, thesis or alternative. *Entrance requirements:* For master's, GRE General Test. Additional exam requirements/recommendations for international students: Required—TOEFL. *Application deadline:* For fall admission, 2/28 priority date for domestic students. Application fee: $30. Electronic applications accepted. *Financial support:* In 2007–08, 5 research assistantships with full tuition reimbursements (averaging $6,387 per year), 5 teaching assistantships with full tuition reimbursements (averaging $6,387 per year) were awarded; Federal Work-Study and unspecified assistantships also available. Financial award applicants required to submit FAFSA. *Faculty research:* Francophone literature, French cinema, business French, nineteenth and twentieth century literature. *Application contact:* Dr. Deborah Shocket, Graduate Coordinator, 419-372-8632.

Brigham Young University, Graduate Studies, College of Humanities, Department of French and Italian, Provo, UT 84602-1001. Offers French studies (MA). *Faculty:* 11 full-time (1 woman). *Students:* 4 full-time (2 women), 6 part-time (5 women); includes 3 minority (1 Asian American or Pacific Islander, 2 Hispanic Americans), 1 international. Average age 28. 5 applicants, 80% accepted, 4 enrolled. In 2007, 7 degrees awarded. *Degree requirements:* For master's, one foreign language, thesis. *Entrance requirements:* For master's, GRE General Test, BA in French. Additional exam requirements/recommendations for international students: Required—TOEFL. *Application deadline:* For fall admission, 2/28 for domestic and international students; for winter admission, 9/1 for domestic students, 6/30 for international students. Application fee: $50. Electronic applications accepted. *Financial support:* In 2007–08, 7 students received support, including 1 research assistantship (averaging $3,500 per year), 6 teaching assistantships (averaging $8,480 per year); career-related internships or fieldwork, institutionally sponsored loans, scholarships/grants, and tuition waivers (full and partial) also available. Support available to part-time students. *Faculty research:* Francophone studies, Medieval literature, Provençal literature, existentialism, second language acquisition. *Unit head:* Dr. Yvon R. Lebras, Department Chair, 801-422-2288, Fax: 901-422-0260, E-mail: yvon_lebras@byu.edu. *Application contact:* Dr. Corry L. Cropper, Graduate Coordinator, 801-422-4484, Fax: 801-422-0260, E-mail: corry_cropper@byu.edu.

Brooklyn College of the City University of New York, Division of Graduate Studies, Department of Modern Languages and Literature, Brooklyn, NY 11210-2889. Offers French (MA); modern languages and literature (PhD); Spanish (MA). The department offers courses at Brooklyn College that are creditable toward the CUNY doctoral degree (with permission of the executive officer of the doctoral program). *Students:* 5 full-time (1 woman), 23 part-time (16 women); includes 22 minority (11 African Americans, 11 Hispanic Americans), 4 international. 10 applicants, 80% accepted, 6 enrolled. In 2007, 12 degrees awarded. *Degree requirements:* For master's, comprehensive exam, comprehensive exam or research paper. *Entrance requirements:* For master's, 18 credits in advanced courses in Spanish, 2 letters of recommendation. Additional exam requirements/recommendations for international students: Required—TOEFL. *Application deadline:* For fall admission, 3/1 priority date for domestic students, 2/1 priority date for international students; for spring admission, 11/1 priority date for domestic students, 10/1 priority date for international students. Applications are processed on a rolling basis. Application fee: $125. Electronic applications accepted. *Financial support:* Federal Work-Study, institutionally sponsored loans, and scholarships/grants available. Support available to part-time students. Financial award application deadline: 5/1; financial award applicants required to submit FAFSA. *Faculty research:* Latin American contemporary novel; Caribbean female contemporary literature; 19th and 20th century Spanish novel; 20th century Mexican poetry. *Unit head:* Dr. William Childers, Chairperson, 718-951-5451, E-mail: wchilders@brooklyn.cuny.edu. *Application contact:* Hernan Sierra, Graduate Admissions Coordinator, 718-951-4536, Fax: 718-951-4506, E-mail: grads@brooklyn.cuny.edu.

Brown University, Graduate School, Department of French Studies, Providence, RI 02912. Offers AM, PhD. *Degree requirements:* For master's, one foreign language, thesis or alternative; for doctorate, variable foreign language requirement, thesis/dissertation, preliminary exam.

Bryn Mawr College, Graduate School of Arts and Sciences, Department of French, Bryn Mawr, PA 19010-2899. Offers MA, PhD. Part-time programs available. *Faculty:* 3. *Students:* 3 full-time (all women), 13 part-time (11 women), 3 international. 6 applicants, 50% accepted, 1 enrolled. In 2007, 2 degrees awarded. *Degree requirements:* For master's, one foreign language, thesis. *Entrance requirements:* For master's, GRE General Test. Additional exam requirements/recommendations for international students: Required—TOEFL (minimum score 600 paper-based; 250 computer-based). *Application deadline:* For fall admission, 1/3 for domestic and international students. Application fee: $30. *Financial support:* Fellowships with full tuition reimbursements, teaching assistantships with partial tuition reimbursements, scholarships/grants, tuition waivers, and tuition awards available. Support available to part-time students. Financial award application deadline: 1/3. *Unit head:* Dr. Grace Armstrong, Chair, 610-526-5386. *Application contact:* Lea R. Miller, Secretary, 610-526-5072, Fax: 610-526-5076, E-mail: lrmiller@brynmawr.edu.

California State University, Fullerton, Graduate Studies, College of Humanities and Social Sciences, Department of Modern Languages and Literatures, Fullerton, CA 92834-9480. Offers French (MA); German (MA); Spanish (MA); teaching English to speakers of other languages (MS). Part-time programs available. *Students:* 48 full-time (41 women), 76 part-time (63 women); includes 55 minority (17 Asian Americans or Pacific Islanders, 38 Hispanic Americans), 26 international. Average age 33. 94 applicants, 68% accepted, 32 enrolled. In 2007, 34 degrees awarded. *Degree requirements:* For master's, comprehensive exam, thesis or alternative. *Entrance requirements:* For master's, minimum GPA of 2.5 in last 60 hours of course work, undergraduate major in a language. Application fee: $55. *Financial support:* Federal Work-Study, institutionally sponsored loans, and scholarships/grants available. Support available to part-time students. Financial award application deadline: 3/1. *Unit head:* Dr. Janet Eyring, Chair, 714-278-3534.

California State University, Long Beach, Graduate Studies, College of Liberal Arts, Department of Romance, German, and Russian Languages and Literature, Program in French, Long Beach, CA 90840. Offers MA. Part-time programs available. *Students:* Average age 35. *Degree requirements:* For master's, one foreign language, comprehensive exam, thesis optional. *Entrance requirements:* For master's, BA in French. *Application deadline:* For fall admission, 7/1 for domestic students; for spring admission, 12/1 for domestic students. Applications are processed on a rolling basis. Application fee: $55. Electronic applications accepted. *Financial support:* Federal Work-Study, institutionally sponsored loans, and scholarships/grants available. Financial award application deadline: 3/2. *Faculty research:* Eighteenth century encyclopedism, development of the novel, Chanson de Roland. *Unit head:* Dr. Stephen Fleck, Graduate Advisor, 562-985-4316, Fax: 562-985-2406, E-mail: sfleck@csulb.edu. *Application contact:* Information Contact, 562-985-4316, Fax: 562-985-2406.

California State University, Los Angeles, Graduate Studies, College of Arts and Letters, Department of Modern Languages and Literatures, Major in French, Los Angeles, CA 90032-8530. Offers MA. Part-time and evening/weekend programs available. *Students:* 1 (woman) full-time, 9 part-time (4 women); includes 5 minority (2 African Americans, 1 Asian American or Pacific Islander, 2 Hispanic Americans), 1 international. Average age 43. In 2007, 1 degree awarded. *Degree requirements:* For master's, comprehensive exam. *Entrance requirements:* For master's, bachelor's degree in French or related area, minimum GPA of 3.0 in French. Additional exam requirements/recommendations for international students: Required—TOEFL. *Application deadline:* For fall admission, 6/30 for domestic students; for spring admission, 2/1 for domestic students. Applications are processed on a rolling basis. Application fee: $55. *Financial support:* Federal Work-Study available. Support available to part-time students. Financial award application deadline: 3/1. *Faculty research:* Literature, language teaching and methodology. *Unit head:* Dr. Sachiko Matsunaga, Chair, Department of Modern Languages and Literatures, 323-343-4230 Ext. 34240, Fax: 323-343-4234, E-mail: smatsun@calstatela.edu.

California State University, Sacramento, Graduate Studies, College of Social Sciences and Interdisciplinary Studies, Liberal Arts Program, Sacramento, CA 95819-6048. Offers French (MA); German (MA); Spanish (MA); theater arts (MA). *Students:* 15 full-time (10 women), 24 part-time (17 women); includes 4 minority (2 African Americans, 1 American Indian/Alaska Native, 1 Asian American or Pacific Islander). Average age 37. 17 applicants, 88% accepted, 9 enrolled. *Degree requirements:* For master's, writing proficiency exam. *Entrance requirements:* Additional exam requirements/recommendations for international students: Required—TOEFL. *Application deadline:* Applications are processed on a rolling basis. Application fee: $55. Electronic applications accepted. *Expenses:* Tuition, state resident: full-time $3,414. Tuition, nonresident: full-time $13,584; part-time $339 per unit. Required fees: $786; $393 per semester. *Financial support:* Application deadline: 3/1. *Unit head:* Dr. Lindy Valdez, Coordinator, 916-278-6342.

Carleton University, Faculty of Graduate Studies, Faculty of Arts and Social Sciences, Department of French, Ottawa, ON K1S 5B6, Canada. Offers MA. *Degree requirements:* For master's, thesis optional. *Entrance requirements:* For master's, honors degree. Application fee: $77. *Financial support:* Fellowships, teaching assistantships, institutionally sponsored loans, scholarships/grants, and unspecified assistantships available. *Faculty research:* French, French Canadian and Acadian literatures and linguistics, Francophone studies, rhetorical studies. *Unit head:* Charles Doutrelepont, Chair, 613-520-2600 Ext. 2168, Fax: 613-520-2149, E-mail: chair_french@carleton.ca. *Application contact:* Mirielle Fournier, Graduate Secretary, 613-520-2600 Ext. 2168, Fax: 613-520-2149, E-mail: french@carleton.ca.

Case Western Reserve University, School of Graduate Studies, Department of Modern Languages and Literatures, Program in French, Cleveland, OH 44106. Offers MA. Part-time programs available. *Faculty:* 6 full-time (3 women). In 2007, 1 master's awarded. Terminal master's awarded for partial completion of doctoral program. *Degree requirements:* For master's, one foreign language, thesis or alternative. *Entrance requirements:* For master's, GRE General Test. Additional exam requirements/recommendations for international students: Required—TOEFL. *Application deadline:* For fall admission, 3/1 priority date for domestic students. Applications are processed on a rolling basis. Application fee: $50. Electronic applications accepted. *Financial support:* In 2007–08, 3 fellowships were awarded; tuition waivers (full) also available. Financial award application deadline: 3/1; financial award applicants required to submit FAFSA. *Faculty research:* Eighteenth- and nineteenth-century literature (novel, poetry, drama), literary theory, women's studies, cultural criticism. *Application contact:* Marie Lathers, Director, Graduate Studies (French), 216-368-3071, Fax: 216-368-2216, E-mail: mhl5@case.edu.

The Catholic University of America, School of Arts and Sciences, Department of Modern Languages and Literatures, Program in French, Washington, DC 20064. Offers MA, PhD. Part-time programs available. *Students:* Average age 34. In 2007, 1 degree awarded. *Degree requirements:* For master's, one foreign language, comprehensive exam, thesis or alternative; for doctorate, 2 foreign languages, comprehensive exam, thesis/dissertation. *Entrance requirements:* For master's and doctorate, GRE General Test, 3 letters of recommendation. Additional exam requirements/recommendations for international students: Required—TOEFL (minimum score 580 paper-based; 237 computer-based). *Application deadline:* For fall admission, 2/1 priority date for domestic students; for spring admission, 11/15 priority date for domestic students. Applications are processed on a rolling basis. Application fee: $55. Electronic applications accepted. *Financial support:* Fellowships, teaching assistantships, career-related internships or fieldwork, Federal Work-Study, scholarships/grants, tuition waivers (full and partial), and unspecified assistantships available. Support available to part-time students. Financial award application deadline: 2/1; financial award applicants required to submit FAFSA. *Faculty research:* French language and literature. *Unit head:* Dr. Joan Grimbert, Chair, Department of Modern Languages and Literatures, 202-319-5240, Fax: 202-319-6077, E-mail: grimbert@cua.edu.

Central Connecticut State University, School of Graduate Studies, School of Arts and Sciences, Department of Modern Languages, Program in Modern Language, New Britain, CT 06050-4010. Offers French (MA); Italian (Certificate); modern language (MA). Part-time and evening/weekend programs available. *Students:* 4 full-time (3 women), 16 part-time (12 women); includes 8 minority (all Hispanic Americans) 15 applicants, 40% accepted, 6 enrolled. In 2007, 12 degrees awarded. *Degree requirements:* For master's, one foreign language, comprehensive exam, thesis or alternative. *Entrance requirements:* For master's, minimum GPA of 2.7, 24 credits of course work in French. Additional exam requirements/recommendations for international students: Required—TOEFL. *Application deadline:* For fall admission, 7/1 for domestic students; for spring admission, 12/1 for domestic students. Applications are processed on a rolling basis. Application fee: $50. Electronic applications accepted. *Expenses:* Tuition, area resident: Full-time $4,169. Tuition, state resident: full-time $6,253. Tuition, nonresident: full-time $11,614; part-time $400 per credit. Required fees: $3,322. One-time fee: $62 part-time. Tuition and fees vary according to degree level and program. *Faculty research:* Twentieth century French theater, seventeenth century French literature, French Middle Ages.

Columbia University, Graduate School of Arts and Sciences, Division of Humanities, Department of French and Romance Philology, New York, NY 10027. Offers French and Romance philology (M Phil, PhD); Romance languages (MA). Part-time programs available. *Faculty:* 15 full-time. *Students:* 76 full-time (48 women), 5 part-time (4 women); includes 7 minority (3 African Americans, 4 Asian Americans or Pacific Islanders), 17 international. Average age 34. 53 applicants, 64% accepted. In 2007, 5 master's, 8 doctorates awarded. *Degree requirements:* For master's, one foreign language, thesis, written exam; for doctorate, 2 foreign languages, thesis/dissertation. *Entrance requirements:* For master's and doctorate, GRE General Test, knowledge of Latin, writing sample. Additional exam requirements/recommendations for international students: Required—TOEFL. Application fee: $90. *Expenses:* Tuition: Part-time $1,452 per credit. Required fees: $152 per term. One-time fee: $75 part-time. Full-time tuition and fees vary according to course level, course load, degree level and program. *Financial support:* Fellowships, teaching assistantships, Federal Work-Study and institutionally sponsored loans available. Support available to part-time students. Financial award application deadline: 1/5; financial award applicants required to submit FAFSA. *Faculty* *research:* Theory of literature, literary semiotics, poetics. *Unit head:* Pierre Force, Chair/Director of Graduate Studies, 212-854-5528, Fax: 212-854-2863, E-mail: pf3@columbia.edu.

Columbia University, Graduate School of Arts and Sciences, Program in French Cultural Studies, New York, NY 10027. Offers MA. Program offered in Paris, France. *Students:* 1 full-time (0 women), 9 part-time (6 women); includes 2 minority (1 African American, 1 Asian American or Pacific Islander), 3 international. Average age 24. 21 applicants, 86% accepted. In 2007, 5 degrees awarded. Application fee: $90. *Expenses: Contact institution.* One-time fee: $75 part-time. Full-time tuition and fees vary according to course level, course load, degree level and program. *Unit head:* Beatrice Terrien, Associate Dean, 212-854-5052, Fax: 212-854-2863, E-mail: bt3@columbia.edu.

Concordia University, School of Graduate Studies, Faculty of Arts and Science, Department of Études Françaises, Montréal, QC H3G 1M8, Canada. Offers écriture (Certificate); anglais-français en langue et techniques de localisation (Certificate); littératures francophones et résonances médiatiques (MA); traductologie (MA); translation (Diploma). *Degree requirements:* For other advanced degree, one foreign language.

Cornell University, Graduate School, Graduate Fields of Arts and Sciences, Field of Romance Studies, Ithaca, NY 14853-0001. Offers French linguistics (PhD); French literature (PhD); Hispanic literature (PhD); Italian linguistics (PhD); Italian literature (PhD); Romance linguistics (PhD); Spanish linguistics (PhD). *Faculty:* 32 full-time (14 women). *Students:* 50 full-time (24 women); includes 11 minority (all Hispanic Americans), 20 international. Average age 29. 114 applicants, 23% accepted, 12 enrolled. In 2007, 2 doctorates awarded. *Degree requirements:* For doctorate, 2 foreign languages, comprehensive exam, thesis/dissertation. *Entrance requirements:* For doctorate, GRE General Test, sample of written work, 3 letters of recommendation. Additional exam requirements/recommendations for international students: Required—TOEFL (minimum score 550 paper-based; 213 computer-based; 77 iBT). *Application deadline:* For fall admission, 1/15 for domestic students. Application fee: $70. Electronic applications accepted. *Financial support:* In 2007–08, 48 students received support, including 20 fellowships with full tuition reimbursements available, 28 teaching assistantships with full tuition reimbursements available; research assistantships with full tuition reimbursements available, institutionally sponsored loans, scholarships/grants, health care benefits, tuition waivers (full and partial), and unspecified assistantships also available. Financial award applicants required to submit FAFSA. *Faculty research:* Literary theory, Hispanic studies, French studies, gender studies. *Unit head:* Director of Graduate Studies, 607-255-8222. *Application contact:* Graduate Field Assistant, 607-255-4246, E-mail: romance_studies@cornell.edu.

Dalhousie University, Faculty of Arts and Social Science, Department of French, Halifax, NS B3H 4R2, Canada. Offers MA, PhD. Part-time programs available. *Faculty:* 12 full-time, 1 part-time/adjunct. *Students:* 22 full-time (12 women), 6 part-time (all women). In 2007, 6 degrees awarded. *Degree requirements:* For master's, one foreign language, thesis; for doctorate, one foreign language, thesis/dissertation. *Entrance requirements:* For doctorate, MA. Additional exam requirements/recommendations for international students: Required—TOEFL. *Application deadline:* For fall admission, 6/1 for domestic students. Applications are processed on a rolling basis. Application fee: $60. *Financial support:* Fellowships available. *Faculty research:* Literature, linguistics, French civilization, French and Francophone literature of all periods, translation and cultural studies. *Unit head:* Dr. Betty Bednarski, Chair, 902-494-2430, Fax: 902-494-1626, E-mail: french@dal.ca. *Application contact:* Dr. Jasmina Milicevic, Graduate Coordinator, 902-494-2430, Fax: 902-494-1626, E-mail: jmilicev@dal.ca.

Duke University, Graduate School, Department of Romance Studies, Durham, NC 27708. Offers French (PhD); Spanish (PhD); JD/AM. *Faculty:* 29 full-time. *Students:* 61 full-time (40 women); includes 12 minority (1 African American, 11 Hispanic Americans), 24 international. 57 applicants, 37% accepted, 9 enrolled. In 2007, 2 doctorates awarded. *Degree requirements:* For doctorate, 2 foreign languages, thesis/dissertation. *Entrance requirements:* For doctorate, GRE General Test. Additional exam requirements/recommendations for international students: Required—TOEFL (minimum score 550 paper-based; 213 computer-based; 83 iBT), IELTS (minimum score 7). *Application deadline:* For fall admission, 12/15 priority date for domestic and international students. Application fee: $75. Electronic applications accepted. *Financial support:* Fellowships, research assistantships, teaching assistantships, Federal Work-Study available. Financial award application deadline: 12/31. *Unit head:* Roberto Doinoto, Director, 919-660-3114, Fax: 919-684-4029.

Eastern Michigan University, Graduate School, College of Arts and Sciences, Department of Foreign Languages and Bilingual Studies, Program in Foreign Languages, Ypsilanti, MI 48197. Offers French (MA); German (MA); German for business (Graduate Certificate); Hispanic language and cultures (Graduate Certificate); Japanese business practices (Graduate Certificate); Spanish (MA). Part-time and evening/weekend programs available. Post-baccalaureate distance learning degree programs offered (minimal on-campus study). *Students:* 1 (woman) full-time, 18 part-time (17 women); includes 2 minority (1 Asian American or Pacific Islander, 1 Hispanic American). Average age 35. In 2007, 8 master's, 2 other advanced degrees awarded. *Degree requirements:* For master's, one foreign language, thesis optional. *Entrance requirements:* Additional exam requirements/recommendations for international students: Required—TOEFL. *Application deadline:* Applications are processed on a rolling basis. Application fee: $35. *Expenses:* Tuition, state resident: full-time $8,952; part-time $373 per credit hour. Tuition, nonresident: full-time $17,634; part-time $735 per credit hour. Required fees: $896; $34 per credit hour. Tuition and fees vary according to course level, degree level and program. *Financial support:* Fellowships, research assistantships with full tuition reimbursements, teaching assistantships with full tuition reimbursements, career-related internships or fieldwork, Federal Work-Study, institutionally sponsored loans, scholarships/grants, tuition waivers (partial), and unspecified assistantships available. Support available to part-time students. Financial award applicants required to submit FAFSA. *Application contact:* Dr. Genevieve Peden, Program Advisor, 734-487-2283, Fax: 734-487-3411, E-mail: gpeden@emich.edu.

Emory University, Graduate School of Arts and Sciences, Department of Comparative Literature, Atlanta, GA 30322-1100. Offers comparative literature (PhD); English (Certificate); French (Certificate); Middle Eastern studies (PhD); philosophy (Certificate); psychoanalytic studies (PhD); religion (PhD); Spanish (Certificate); women studies (Certificate). *Degree requirements:* For doctorate, 2 foreign languages, comprehensive exam, thesis/dissertation. *Entrance requirements:* For doctorate, GRE General Test, minimum GPA of 3.0. Additional exam requirements/recommendations for international students: Required—TOEFL. Electronic applications accepted. *Faculty research:* Literary theory, psychoanalysis trauma and testimony, literature and religion, literature and technology, literature and philosophy, politics and global culture, literature and aesthetics.

Emory University, Graduate School of Arts and Sciences, Department of French and Italian, Atlanta, GA 30322-1100. Offers French (PhD); French and educational studies (PhD). *Degree requirements:* For doctorate, one foreign language, comprehensive exam, thesis/dissertation. *Entrance requirements:* For doctorate, GRE General Test. Electronic applications accepted. *Faculty research:* French literature through multidisciplinary critical approaches, second language acquisition theory.

Florida Atlantic University, Dorothy F. Schmidt College of Arts and Letters, Department of Languages and Linguistics, Boca Raton, FL 33431-0991. Offers comparative literature (MA); French (MA); German (MA); Spanish (MA); teaching French (MAT); teaching German (MAT); teaching Spanish (MAT). Part-time programs available. *Degree requirements:* For master's, one foreign language, comprehensive exam, thesis optional. *Entrance requirements:* For master's, GRE General Test, minimum GPA of 3.0. *Faculty research:* Modern European studies, modern Latin America, medieval Europe.

Florida State University, Graduate Studies, College of Arts and Sciences, Department of Modern Languages, Program in French, Tallahassee, FL 32306. Offers MA, PhD. Part-time programs available. *Faculty:* 8 full-time (4 women). *Students:* 19 full-time (16 women); includes 2 minority (both African Americans) Average age 25. 13 applicants, 69% accepted, 5 enrolled. In 2007, 4 master's, 5 doctorates awarded. Terminal master's awarded for partial completion of doctoral program. *Degree requirements:* For master's, thesis optional; for doctorate, thesis/dissertation, reading knowledge of French and 2 other languages. *Entrance requirements:* For master's and doctorate, GRE General Test or minimum GPA of 3.0. Additional exam requirements/recommendations for international students: Required—TOEFL (minimum score 550 paper-based; 213 computer-based). *Application deadline:* For fall admission, 1/15 for domestic and international students; for spring admission, 11/22 for domestic and international students. Applications are processed on a rolling basis. Application fee: $30. Electronic applications accepted. *Expenses:* Tuition, state resident: part-time $248 per credit hour. Tuition, nonresident: part-time $880 per credit hour. Tuition and fees vary according to program. *Financial support:* In 2007–08, 1 fellowship with partial tuition reimbursement (averaging $16,500 per year), 1 research assistantship with partial tuition reimbursement (averaging $9,500 per year), 13 teaching assistantships with partial tuition reimbursements (averaging $10,200 per year) were awarded. Financial award application deadline: 1/15; financial award applicants required to submit FAFSA. *Faculty research:* Twentieth century European novel, Renaissance and Middle Ages literature, second language acquisition. *Application contact:* Wendy E. Pigott, Graduate Academic Coordinator, 850-644-8397, Fax: 850-644-0524, E-mail: wpigott@fsu.edu.

Georgia State University, College of Arts and Sciences, Department of Modern and Classical Languages, Program in French, Atlanta, GA 30303-3083. Offers MA. Part-time and evening/weekend programs available. *Faculty:* 5 full-time (1 woman). *Students:* 11 full-time, 4 part-time; includes 2 minority (1 African American, 1 Hispanic American). Average age 28. In 2007, 2 degrees awarded. *Degree requirements:* For master's, one foreign language, thesis or alternative, general exam. *Entrance requirements:* For master's, GRE General Test. Additional exam requirements/recommendations for international students: Required—TOEFL. *Application deadline:* For fall admission, 4/15 for domestic students; for spring admission, 11/15 for domestic students. Applications are processed on a rolling basis. Application fee: $50. Electronic applications accepted. *Expenses:* Tuition, state resident: part-time $221 per credit hour. *Financial support:* In 2007–08, research assistantships (averaging $3,000 per year), teaching assistantships (averaging $9,000 per year) were awarded; career-related internships or fieldwork, Federal Work-Study, and institutionally sponsored loans also available. Support available to part-time students. Financial award applicants required to submit FAFSA. *Faculty research:* French literature of the sixteenth-, eighteenth-, nineteenth-, and twentieth-centuries.

Georgia State University, College of Arts and Sciences, Department of Modern and Classical Languages, Program in Translation and Interpretation, Atlanta, GA 30303-3083. Offers French (Certificate); German (Certificate); Spanish (Certificate). *Faculty:* 3 full-time, 2 part-time/adjunct. *Students:* Average age 32. *Application deadline:* For fall admission, 4/1 for domestic students; for spring admission, 11/15 for domestic students. Applications are processed on a rolling basis. Application fee: $50. Electronic applications accepted. *Expenses:* Tuition, state resident: part-time $221 per credit hour. *Unit head:* Dr. Annette Cash, Director, E-mail: acash@gsu.edu.

Graduate School and University Center of the City University of New York, Graduate Studies, Program in French, New York, NY 10016-4039. Offers PhD. *Faculty:* 20 full-time (11 women). *Students:* 50 full-time (36 women), 1 (woman) part-time; includes 4 minority (1 African American, 1 Asian American or Pacific Islander, 2 Hispanic Americans), 5 international. Average age 38. 21 applicants, 57% accepted, 9 enrolled. In 2007, 3 degrees awarded. *Degree requirements:* For doctorate, 2 foreign languages, thesis/dissertation. *Entrance requirements:* For doctorate, GRE General Test, writing samples (1 for applicants with BA, 2 for applicants with master's). Additional exam requirements/recommendations for international students: Required—TOEFL. *Application deadline:* For fall admission, 1/15 for domestic students. Application fee: $125. Electronic applications accepted. *Financial support:* In 2007–08, 35 students received support, including 31 fellowships, 5 research assistantships, 6 teaching assistantships; career-related internships or fieldwork, Federal Work-Study, institutionally sponsored loans, and tuition waivers (full and partial) also available. Financial award application deadline: 2/1; financial award applicants required to submit FAFSA. *Unit head:* Dr. Francesca Sautman, Executive Officer, 212-817-8366, Fax: 212-817-1520, E-mail: fsautman@gc.cuny.edu.

Harvard University, Graduate School of Arts and Sciences, Department of Romance Languages and Literatures, Cambridge, MA 02138. Offers French (AM, PhD); Italian (AM, PhD); Portuguese (AM, PhD); Spanish (AM, PhD). Terminal master's awarded for partial completion of doctoral program. *Degree requirements:* For master's, 2 foreign languages; for doctorate, 2 foreign languages, thesis/dissertation. *Entrance requirements:* For master's and doctorate, GRE General Test, sample of written work. Additional exam requirements/recommendations for international students: Required—TOEFL. *Expenses:* Tuition: Full-time $31,456. Full-time tuition and fees vary according to program and student level.

Hofstra University, School of Education and Allied Human Services, Department of Curriculum and Teaching, Program in Foreign Language Education, Hempstead, NY 11549. Offers French (MA, MS Ed); German (MA, MS Ed); Russian (MA, MS Ed); Spanish (MA, MS Ed). Part-time and evening/weekend programs available. *Students:* 3 full-time (all women), 5 part-time (all women); includes 2 minority (1 African American, 1 Hispanic American). Average age 35. 9 applicants, 100% accepted, 4 enrolled. In 2007, 8 degrees awarded. *Degree requirements:* For master's, one foreign language, thesis. *Entrance requirements:* For master's, 2 letters of recommendation, teacher certification (MA), essay. Additional exam requirements/recommendations for international students: Required—TOEFL (minimum score 550 paper-based; 213 computer-based). *Application deadline:* Applications are processed on a rolling basis. Application fee: $60. Electronic applications accepted. *Expenses:* Tuition: Full-time $14,220; part-time $820 per credit. Required fees: $970; $165 per term. Tuition and fees vary according to program. *Financial support:* In 2007–08, 1 student received support; fellowships with tuition reimbursements available, research assistantships with full and partial tuition reimbursements available, Federal Work-Study, institutionally sponsored loans, scholarships/grants, and tuition waivers (full and partial) available. Support available to part-time students. Financial award applicants required to submit FAFSA. *Faculty research:* Current literature from France and Francophone world, George Sand, music and literature, colonial and postcolonial studies, contemporary Latin American poetry. *Unit head:* Dr. Lori J. Ultsch, Chairperson, 516-463-4519, Fax: 516-463-2310, E-mail: rllju@mail1.hofstra.edu. *Application contact:* Carol Drummer, Dean of Graduate Admissions, 516-463-4876, Fax: 516-463-4664, E-mail: gradstudent@hofstra.edu.

Howard University, Graduate School, Department of Modern Languages and Literatures, Washington, DC 20059-0002. Offers French (MA); Spanish (MA). Part-time programs available. *Degree requirements:* For master's, one foreign language, comprehensive exam, thesis. *Entrance requirements:* For master's, GRE General Test, writing samples in English and French or Spanish. *Expenses:* Tuition: Full-time $16,175; part-time $899 per credit hour. Required fees: $805. *Faculty research:* African literature in French, Spanish linguistics, Spanish Peninsular literature, Spanish sociolinguistics.

Hunter College of the City University of New York, Graduate School, School of Arts and Sciences, Department of Romance Languages, Program in French, New York, NY 10021-5085. Offers French (MA); French education (MA). Part-time and evening/weekend programs available. *Faculty:* 3 full-time (1 woman). *Students:* Average age 36. 1 applicant, 100% accepted, 0 enrolled. In 2007, 2 degrees awarded. *Degree requirements:* For master's, 2 foreign languages, comprehensive exam, thesis optional. *Entrance requirements:* For master's, GRE General Test, GRE Subject Test, ability to read, speak, and write French; interview. Additional exam requirements/recommendations for international students: Required—TOEFL. *Application deadline:* For fall admission, 4/1 for domestic students, 2/1 for international students;

French

Hunter College of the City University of New York (continued)
for spring admission, 11/1 for domestic students, 9/1 for international students. Application fee: $125. *Expenses:* Tuition, state resident: full-time $6,400; part-time $270 per credit. Tuition, nonresident: part-time $500 per credit. One-time fee: $125 full-time. Tuition and fees vary according to program. *Financial support:* Fellowships, Federal Work-Study, scholarships/grants, and tuition waivers (partial) available. Support available to part-time students. Financial award application deadline: 4/15. *Faculty research:* Contemporary French theater, Villiers-dell Isle-Adam, Voltaire, medieval folklore, fin-de-siécle. *Unit head:* Prof. Marlene Barloum, Graduate Advisor, 212-650-3511, E-mail: mbarloum@hunter.cuny.edu. *Application contact:* William Zlata, Director for Graduate Admissions, 212-772-4482, Fax: 212-650-3336, E-mail: admissions@hunter.cuny.edu.

Illinois State University, Graduate School, College of Arts and Sciences, Department of Foreign Languages, Literatures and Cultures, Normal, IL 61790-2200. Offers French (MA); French and German (MA); French and Spanish (MA); German (MA); German and Spanish (MA); Spanish (MA). *Faculty:* 17 full-time (7 women). *Students:* 24 full-time (12 women), 9 part-time (8 women); includes 8 minority (4 African Americans, 1 American Indian/Alaska Native, 3 Hispanic Americans), 2 international. 18 applicants, 94% accepted. In 2007, 15 degrees awarded. *Degree requirements:* For master's, variable foreign language requirement, comprehensive exam, 1 term of residency. *Entrance requirements:* For master's, GRE General Test, minimum GPA of 2.8 in last 60 hours of course work. *Application deadline:* Applications are processed on a rolling basis. Application fee: $40. *Expenses:* Tuition, state resident: full-time $3,492; part-time $194 per credit hour. Tuition, nonresident: full-time $7,272; part-time $404 per credit hour. Required fees: $1,024; $57 per credit hour. *Financial support:* In 2007–08, 3 research assistantships (averaging $4,809 per year), 18 teaching assistantships (averaging $7,500 per year) were awarded; tuition waivers (full) and unspecified assistantships also available. Financial award application deadline: 4/1. *Unit head:* Daniel Everett, Chairperson, 309-438-2111.

Indiana University Bloomington, University Graduate School, College of Arts and Sciences, Department of French and Italian, Bloomington, IN 47405-7000. Offers French (MA, PhD), including French instruction (MA), French linguistics, French literature; Italian (MA, PhD). Part-time programs available. *Faculty:* 14 full-time (3 women). *Students:* 69 full-time (43 women), 13 part-time (5 women); includes 5 minority (2 African Americans, 1 American Indian/Alaska Native, 2 Hispanic Americans), 35 international. Average age 30. 47 applicants, 74% accepted, 19 enrolled. In 2007, 15 master's, 9 doctorates awarded. *Median time to degree:* Of those who began their doctoral program in fall 1999, 25% received their degree in 8 years or less. *Degree requirements:* For master's, one foreign language; for doctorate, 2 foreign languages, thesis/dissertation. *Entrance requirements:* For master's and doctorate, GRE General Test. Additional exam requirements/recommendations for international students: Required—TOEFL. *Application deadline:* For fall admission, 1/15 priority date for domestic students, 12/15 for international students; for spring admission, 9/1 priority date for domestic students, 9/1 for international students. Applications are processed on a rolling basis. Application fee: $50 ($60 for international students). Electronic applications accepted. *Financial support:* Fellowships with partial tuition reimbursements, research assistantships with tuition reimbursements, teaching assistantships with partial tuition reimbursements, career-related internships or fieldwork, institutionally sponsored loans, and tuition waivers (full) available. Financial award application deadline: 2/15. *Faculty research:* French-Creole studies, history of rhetoric, medieval epic and romance, post seventeenth century novel and poetry, Renaissance narrative and poetry. *Unit head:* Dr. Sonya Stephens, Chairman, 812-855-5458, Fax: 812-855-8877, E-mail: sonsteph@indiana.edu. *Application contact:* Jocelyn Karlan, Secretary, 812-855-1088, Fax: 812-855-8877, E-mail: jkarlan@indiana.edu.

The Johns Hopkins University, Zanvyl Krieger School of Arts and Sciences, Department of German and Romance Languages, Baltimore, MD 21218-2699. Offers French (PhD); German (PhD); Italian (PhD); romance languages (PhD); Spanish (PhD). *Faculty:* 14 full-time (5 women), 2 part-time/adjunct (1 woman). *Students:* 69 full-time (48 women); includes 6 minority (all Hispanic Americans), 37 international. Average age 29. 42 applicants, 36% accepted, 8 enrolled. In 2007, 13 doctorates awarded. *Median time to degree:* Of those who began their doctoral program in fall 1999, 75% received their degree in 8 years or less. *Degree requirements:* For doctorate, 2 foreign languages, thesis/dissertation. *Entrance requirements:* For doctorate, GRE General Test. Additional exam requirements/recommendations for international students: Required—TOEFL (minimum score 600 paper-based; 250 computer-based). *Application deadline:* For fall admission, 1/15 for domestic and international students. Application fee: $60. Electronic applications accepted. *Financial support:* In 2007–08, 64 students received support, including 40 fellowships with full tuition reimbursements available (averaging $16,000 per year), 2 research assistantships with full tuition reimbursements available (averaging $16,000 per year), 19 teaching assistantships with full tuition reimbursements available (averaging $16,000 per year); institutionally sponsored loans and tuition waivers (full and partial) also available. Financial award application deadline: 4/15; financial award applicants required to submit FAFSA. *Unit head:* Dr. Stephen Nichols, Chair, 410-516-4736, Fax: 410-516-5358, E-mail: stephen.nichols@jhu.edu. *Application contact:* Sally Hauf, Graduate Administrative Coordinator, 410-516-7226, Fax: 410-516-5358, E-mail: shauf@jhu.edu.

Kansas State University, Graduate School, College of Arts and Sciences, Department of Modern Languages, Manhattan, KS 66506. Offers French (MA); German (MA); Spanish (MA). Part-time and evening/weekend programs available. Postbaccalaureate distance learning degree programs offered (minimal on-campus study). *Faculty:* 15 full-time (6 women). *Students:* 11 full-time (7 women), 6 part-time (5 women); includes 1 minority (Hispanic American), 4 international. 8 applicants, 75% accepted, 5 enrolled. In 2007, 9 degrees awarded. *Degree requirements:* For master's, thesis optional. *Entrance requirements:* For master's, teaching certificate. Additional exam requirements/recommendations for international students: Required—TOEFL (minimum score 560 paper-based). *Application deadline:* For fall admission, 2/1 priority date for domestic and international students; for spring admission, 10/1 for domestic students, 8/1 priority date for international students. Applications are processed on a rolling basis. Application fee: $30 ($55 for international students). *Financial support:* In 2007–08, 19 teaching assistantships with full tuition reimbursements (averaging $11,711 per year) were awarded; fellowships, Federal Work-Study, institutionally sponsored loans, and scholarships/grants also available. Support available to part-time students. Financial award application deadline: 3/1; financial award applicants required to submit FAFSA. *Faculty research:* Second language acquisitions; Chicano literature; Francophone literature; cultural studies; German, French, Spanish, and Spanish-American literature from the Middle Ages to the modern era. *Unit head:* Robert Corum, Head, 785-532-1987, Fax: 785-532-7004, E-mail: corum@ksu.edu. *Application contact:* Claire Dehon, Director, 785-532-1929, Fax: 785-532-7004, E-mail: dehoncl@ksu.edu.

Kent State University, College of Arts and Sciences, Department of Modern and Classical Language Studies, Kent, OH 44242-0001. Offers French literature (MA); French, Spanish, German and Latin pedagogy (MA); German literature (MA); Spanish literature (MA); translation (MA), including French, German, Japanese, Russian, Spanish; translation studies (PhD). Part-time and evening/weekend programs available. *Faculty:* 31 full-time (15 women), 4 part-time/adjunct (2 women). *Students:* 64 full-time (45 women), 27 part-time (26 women). Average age 32. 113 applicants, 80% accepted, 42 enrolled. In 2007, 27 degrees awarded. *Degree requirements:* For master's, one foreign language, comprehensive exam (for some programs), thesis (for some programs); for doctorate, comprehensive exam, thesis/dissertation (for some programs). *Entrance requirements:* For master's, minimum GPA of 3.0, writing sample, audio tape or CD; for doctorate, 3 recommendations. Additional exam requirements/recommendations for international students: Required—TOEFL (minimum score 197 computer-based). *Application deadline:* For fall admission, 2/28 for domestic and international students. Applications are processed on a rolling basis. Application fee: $30. Electronic applications accepted. *Financial support:* In 2007–08, 31 teaching assistantships with full tuition reimbursements (averaging $8,000 per year) were awarded; research assistantships with full tuition reimbursements, career-related internships or fieldwork, Federal Work-Study, health care benefits, tuition waivers (full and partial), and unspecified assistantships also available. Support available to part-time students. Financial award application deadline: 2/1. *Faculty research:* Literature, pedagogy, applied linguistics, translation studies. *Unit head:* Dr. Gregory M Shreve, Chair, 330-672-1796, Fax: 330-672-4009, E-mail: gshreve@kent.edu. *Application contact:* Carol S. Maier, Graduate Coordinator, 330-672-1797, Fax: 330-672-4009, E-mail: cmaier@kent.edu.

Louisiana State University and Agricultural and Mechanical College, Graduate School, College of Arts and Sciences, Department of French Studies, Baton Rouge, LA 70803. Offers French literature and linguistics (MA, PhD). *Faculty:* 15 full-time (6 women). *Students:* 19 full-time (14 women), 9 part-time (8 women); includes 2 minority (1 African American, 1 Asian American or Pacific Islander), 5 international. Average age 29. 17 applicants, 71% accepted, 7 enrolled. In 2007, 2 master's, 4 doctorates awarded. Terminal master's awarded for partial completion of doctoral program. *Degree requirements:* For master's, thesis optional; for doctorate, 2 foreign languages, thesis/dissertation. *Entrance requirements:* For master's and doctorate, GRE General Test, minimum GPA of 3.0. Additional exam requirements/recommendations for international students: Required—TOEFL (minimum score 550 paper-based; 213 computer-based; 79 iBT). *Application deadline:* For fall admission, 1/25 priority date for domestic students, 5/15 for international students; for spring admission, 10/15 for international students. Applications are processed on a rolling basis. Application fee: $25. Electronic applications accepted. *Financial support:* In 2007–08, 22 students received support, including 2 fellowships with full tuition reimbursements available (averaging $27,404 per year), 6 research assistantships with partial tuition reimbursements available (averaging $18,091 per year), 9 teaching assistantships with partial tuition reimbursements available (averaging $18,364 per year); career-related internships or fieldwork, Federal Work-Study, institutionally sponsored loans, health care benefits, tuition waivers (full), and unspecified assistantships also available. Support available to part-time students. Financial award application deadline: 7/1; financial award applicants required to submit FAFSA. *Faculty research:* French literature of all periods, modern critical theory, linguistics, cinema, Francophonia. Total annual research expenditures: $169,002. *Unit head:* Dr. Sylvie Dubois, Chair, 225-578-6632, Fax: 225-578-6628, E-mail: sdubois@lsu.edu. *Application contact:* Dr. John Protevi, Adviser, 225-578-6664, Fax: 225-578-6628, E-mail: protevi@lsu.edu.

McGill University, Faculty of Graduate and Postdoctoral Studies, Faculty of Arts, Department of French Language and Literature, Montréal, QC H3A 2T5, Canada. Offers MA, PhD. *Faculty:* 17 full-time (8 women), 9 part-time/adjunct (3 women). *Students:* 65 full-time (46 women), 3 part-time (all women). 47 applicants, 62% accepted, 19 enrolled. In 2007, 15 master's, 1 doctorate awarded.

McMaster University, School of Graduate Studies, Faculty of Humanities, Department of French, Hamilton, ON L8S 4M2, Canada. Offers MA. Part-time and evening/weekend programs available. *Faculty:* 13 full-time. *Students:* 8 full-time, 1 part-time. 42 applicants, 86% accepted. *Degree requirements:* For master's, thesis or alternative. *Entrance requirements:* For master's, honors degree in French, minimum B+ average. Additional exam requirements/recommendations for international students: Required—TOEFL (minimum score 580 paper-based; 237 computer-based). *Application deadline:* For fall admission, 2/15 priority date for domestic students. Application fee: $90. *Financial support:* In 2007–08, fellowships (averaging $2,000 per year), teaching assistantships (averaging $8,440 per year) were awarded; scholarships/grants also available. *Faculty research:* Medieval literature, eighteenth- and nineteenth-century literature, twentieth-century French and Francophone literature, linguistics. *Unit head:* Prof. Maroussia Hajdukowski-Ahmed, Chair, 905-525-9140 Ext. 23758, Fax: 905-577-6930, E-mail: ahmedm@mcmaster.ca. *Application contact:* Beatric Kansayisa, Secretary, 905-525-9140 Ext. 24470, Fax: 905-577-6930, E-mail: frendept@mcmaster.ca.

Memorial University of Newfoundland, School of Graduate Studies, Department of French and Spanish, St. John's, NL A1C 5S7, Canada. Offers French studies (MA). Part-time programs available. *Degree requirements:* For master's, one foreign language, thesis. *Entrance requirements:* For master's, honors degree (minimum 2nd class standing). Electronic applications accepted. *Faculty research:* French and French-Canadian literature, literary theory, linguistics, philosophy, translation, Francophone culture.

Miami University, Graduate School, College of Arts and Sciences, Department of French and Italian, Oxford, OH 45056. Offers French (MA). Part-time programs available. *Degree requirements:* For master's, thesis, final exam. *Entrance requirements:* For master's, GRE General Test, minimum undergraduate GPA of 3.0 during previous 2 years or 2.75 overall. Additional exam requirements/recommendations for international students: Required—TOEFL (minimum score 550 paper-based; 213 computer-based), TWE (minimum score 4). Electronic applications accepted.

Michigan State University, The Graduate School, College of Arts and Letters, Department of French, Classics, and Italian, East Lansing, MI 48824. Offers French (MA); French language and literature (PhD). *Entrance requirements:* Additional exam requirements/recommendations for international students: Required—TOEFL. Electronic applications accepted. *Expenses:* Tuition, state resident: part-time $379 per credit hour. Tuition, nonresident: part-time $800 per credit hour. Tuition and fees vary according to program.

Middlebury College, Language Schools, French School, Middlebury, VT 05753-6002. Offers MA, DML. *Faculty:* 22 full-time (9 women). *Students:* 102 full-time (83 women); includes 16 minority (8 African Americans, 2 Asian Americans or Pacific Islanders, 6 Hispanic Americans). Average age 29. 170 applicants, 71% accepted, 102 enrolled. In 2007, 44 master's, 2 doctorates awarded. *Degree requirements:* For master's, one foreign language; for doctorate, 2 foreign languages, thesis/dissertation, residence abroad, teaching experience. *Entrance requirements:* For master's, placement exam, 3 letters of recommendation, writing sample. *Application deadline:* Applications are processed on a rolling basis. Application fee: $55. Electronic applications accepted. *Financial support:* Fellowships, scholarships/grants available. *Unit head:* Dr. Aline Germain-Rutherford, Director, 802-443-5526, Fax: 802-443-2075. *Application contact:* Beverly Keim, Coordinator, 802-443-5526, Fax: 802-443-2075, E-mail: keim@middlebury.edu.

Millersville University of Pennsylvania, Graduate School, School of Humanities and Social Sciences, Department of Foreign Languages, Program in French, Millersville, PA 17551-0302. Offers M Ed, MA. Part-time programs available. *Faculty:* 9 full-time (6 women), 3 part-time/adjunct (2 women). *Students:* Average age 48. In 2007, 1 degree awarded. *Degree requirements:* For master's, one foreign language, thesis optional, departmental exam. *Entrance requirements:* For master's, GRE or MAT, minimum undergraduate GPA of 3.0, 24 undergraduate credits in French. Additional exam requirements/recommendations for international students: Required—TOEFL (minimum score 500 paper-based; 183 computer-based). *Application deadline:* For fall admission, 2/1 priority date for domestic students; for winter admission, 10/1 priority date for domestic students; for spring admission, 10/1 priority date for domestic students. Applications are processed on a rolling basis. Application fee: $40. Electronic applications accepted. *Expenses:* Tuition, state resident: full-time $6,214; part-time $345 per credit. Tuition, nonresident: full-time $9,944; part-time $552 per credit. Required fees: $1,442. Tuition and fees vary according to course load. *Financial support:* Research assistantships with tuition reimbursements, institutionally sponsored loans available. Support available to part-time students. Financial award application deadline: 3/15; financial award applicants required to submit FAFSA. *Application contact:* Dr. Victor S. DeSantis, Dean of Graduate Studies, 717-872-3099, Fax: 717-871-2022, E-mail: victor.desantis@millersville.edu.

Minnesota State University Mankato, College of Graduate Studies, College of Arts and Humanities, Department of Modern Languages, Program in French, Mankato, MN 56001. Offers MAT, MS. In 2007, 1 degree awarded. *Degree requirements:* For master's, one foreign language, comprehensive exam, thesis or alternative. *Entrance requirements:* For master's, minimum GPA of 3.0 during previous 2 years. Additional exam requirements/recommendations for international students: Required—TOEFL. *Application deadline:* For fall admission, 7/1 priority date for domestic students; for spring admission, 11/1 for domestic students. Applications are processed on a rolling basis. Application fee: $40. Electronic applications accepted. *Financial support:* Research assistantships, teaching assistantships with full tuition reimbursements, unspecified assistantships available. Financial award application deadline: 3/15; financial award applicants required to submit FAFSA. *Unit head:* Dr. John Janc, Graduate Coordinator, 507-389-1817. *Application contact:* 507-389-2321, E-mail: grad@mnsu.edu.

Mississippi State University, College of Arts and Sciences, Department of Foreign Languages, Mississippi State, MS 39762. Offers French (MA); French/German (MA); German (MA); Spanish (MA); Spanish/French (MA); Spanish/German (MA). Part-time programs available. *Faculty:* 19 full-time (11 women), 5 part-time/adjunct (all women). *Students:* 22 full-time (12 women), 1 part-time; includes 2 minority (both Hispanic Americans), 4 international. Average age 30. 7 applicants, 86% accepted, 3 enrolled. In 2007, 7 degrees awarded. *Degree requirements:* For master's, one foreign language, thesis optional, comprehensive oral or written exam. *Entrance requirements:* For master's, minimum GPA of 2.75. Additional exam requirements/recommendations for international students: Required—TOEFL (minimum score 525 paper-based). *Application deadline:* For fall admission, 7/1 for domestic students; for spring admission, 11/1 for domestic students. Applications are processed on a rolling basis. Application fee: $30. *Expenses:* Tuition, state resident: full-time $4,978; part-time $274 per hour. Tuition, nonresident: full-time $11,469; part-time $635 per hour. *Financial support:* In 2007–08, 21 teaching assistantships with full tuition reimbursements (averaging $8,766 per year) were awarded; Federal Work-Study, institutionally sponsored loans, and unspecified assistantships also available. Financial award applicants required to submit FAFSA. *Faculty research:* French, German, Spanish literature from medieval to present; gender and cultural studies in French; Spanish American literature; foreign language methodology; linguistics. *Unit head:* Dr. Jack Jordan, Interim Head, 662-325-3480, Fax: 662-325-8209, E-mail: jordan@ra.msstate.edu. *Application contact:* Dr. William A. Person, Interim Associate Vice President for Academic Affairs/Interim Dean of Graduate Studies, 662-325-7400, Fax: 662-325-1967, E-mail: grad@grad.msstate.edu.

Missouri State University, Graduate College, College of Arts and Letters, Department of Modern and Classical Languages, Springfield, MO 65804-0094. Offers secondary education (MS Ed), including French, German, Spanish. *Faculty:* 5 full-time (2 women). *Students:* 2 full-time (both women), 5 part-time (all women); includes 2 minority (both Hispanic Americans) Average age 38. In 2007, 1 degree awarded. *Entrance requirements:* For master's, grades 9–12 teaching certification. Additional exam requirements/recommendations for international students: Required—TOEFL (minimum score 550 paper-based; 213 computer-based; 79 iBT), IELTS (minimum score 6). *Application deadline:* For fall admission, 7/20 priority date for domestic students; for spring admission, 12/20 priority date for domestic students. Application fee: $35. *Expenses:* Tuition, state resident: full-time $3,708; part-time $206 per credit hour. Tuition, nonresident: full-time $7,236; part-time $206 per credit hour. Required fees: $622. Full-time tuition and fees vary according to course level, course load, program and reciprocity agreements. *Financial support:* Teaching assistantships with full tuition reimbursements available. Financial award applicants required to submit FAFSA. *Unit head:* Dr. Madeleine Kernen, Head, 417-836-7626, E-mail: mcl@missouristate.edu.

Montclair State University, The Office of Graduate Admissions and Support Services, College of Education and Human Services, Department of Curriculum and Teaching, Montclair, NJ 07043-1624. Offers education (M Ed); educational technology (M Ed); learning disabled teacher consultant (Certificate); school library media specialist (Certificate); teaching (MAT, Certificate), including art (MAT), biological science (MAT), early childhood education (P-3) (MAT), earth science (MAT), elementary education (K-8) (MAT), English (MAT), French (MAT), health and physical education (MAT), health education (MAT), home economics (MAT), mathematics (MAT), music (MAT), physical education (MAT), physical science (MAT), social studies (MAT), Spanish (MAT), teacher of ESL (MAT), teacher of students with disabilities (MAT). Part-time and evening/weekend programs available. *Faculty:* 17 full-time (13 women), 14 part-time/adjunct (10 women). *Students:* 118 full-time (86 women), 221 part-time (187 women); includes 50 minority (25 African Americans, 8 Asian Americans or Pacific Islanders, 17 Hispanic Americans), 3 international. Average age 33. 305 applicants, 52% accepted, 124 enrolled. In 2007, 178 master's, 19 other advanced degrees awarded. *Degree requirements:* For master's, comprehensive exam, field experience. *Entrance requirements:* For master's, PRAXIS II, minimum GPA of 2.67, 2 letters of recommendation. Additional exam requirements/recommendations for international students: Required—TOEFL (minimum score 83 computer-based). *Application deadline:* For fall admission, 2/15 for domestic and international students; for spring admission, 9/15 for domestic and international students. Applications are processed on a rolling basis. Application fee: $60. Electronic applications accepted. *Financial support:* In 2007–08, 7 research assistantships with full tuition reimbursements (averaging $7,000 per year) were awarded; Federal Work-Study, scholarships/grants, and unspecified assistantships also available. Support available to part-time students. Financial award application deadline: 3/1; financial award applicants required to submit FAFSA. *Unit head:* Dr. Deborah Eldridge, Chairperson, 973-655-5187.

Montclair State University, The Office of Graduate Admissions and Support Services, College of Humanities and Social Sciences, Department of French, German and Russian, Montclair, NJ 07043-1624. Offers French (MA, Certificate), including French literature (MA), French studies (MA). Part-time and evening/weekend programs available. *Faculty:* 8 full-time (5 women), 14 part-time/adjunct (11 women). *Students:* 4 full-time (1 woman), 15 part-time (10 women); includes 4 minority (3 African Americans, 1 Hispanic American), 2 international. 12 applicants, 58% accepted, 6 enrolled. In 2007, 7 master's awarded. *Degree requirements:* For master's, comprehensive exam, thesis optional. *Entrance requirements:* For master's, GRE General Test, 24 credits of undergraduate course work in French, 2 letters of recommendation. Additional exam requirements/recommendations for international students: Required—TOEFL (minimum score 83 computer-based). *Application deadline:* For fall admission, 6/1 for international students; for spring admission, 11/1 for international students. Applications are processed on a rolling basis. Application fee: $60. Electronic applications accepted. *Financial support:* In 2007–08, 1 research assistantship with full tuition reimbursement (averaging $7,000 per year) was awarded; Federal Work-Study, scholarships/grants, and unspecified assistantships also available. Support available to part-time students. Financial award application deadline: 3/1; financial award applicants required to submit FAFSA. *Unit head:* Dr. Lois Oppenheim, Chairperson, 973-655-4283.

New York University, Graduate School of Arts and Science, Center for French Civilization and Culture, Department of French, New York, NY 10012-1019. Offers French (PhD); French language and civilization (MA); French literature (MA); Romance languages and literatures (MA). Part-time programs available. *Faculty:* 18 full-time (7 women), 2 part-time/adjunct. *Students:* 70 full-time (45 women), 3 part-time; includes 8 minority (1 African American, 6 Asian Americans or Pacific Islanders, 1 Hispanic American), 23 international. Average age 30. 81 applicants, 62% accepted, 20 enrolled. In 2007, 18 master's, 4 doctorates awarded. Terminal master's awarded for partial completion of doctoral program. *Degree requirements:* For master's, one foreign language, thesis (for some programs); for doctorate, one foreign language, thesis/dissertation. *Entrance requirements:* For master's and doctorate, GRE General Test, proficiency in French. Additional exam requirements/recommendations for international students: Required—TOEFL. *Application deadline:* For fall admission, 1/4 for domestic students; for spring admission, 11/1 for domestic students. Application fee: $85. *Financial support:* Fellowships with tuition reimbursements, teaching assistantships with tuition reimbursements, Federal Work-Study, institutionally sponsored loans, scholarships/grants, traineeships, health care benefits, unspecified assistantships, and instructorships available. Financial award application deadline: 1/4; financial award applicants required to submit FAFSA. *Faculty research:* French and Francophone literature, literary theory, and history; rhetoric and poetics; cultural history; theater and cinema. *Application contact:* Brett Underhill, Graduate Secretary, 212-998-8700, Fax: 212-995-3539, E-mail: french.grad@nyu.edu.

New York University, Graduate School of Arts and Science, Center for French Civilization and Culture, Institute of French Studies, New York, NY 10012-1019. Offers French civilization (PhD); French studies (MA, PhD, Advanced Certificate); French studies and anthropology (PhD); French studies and history (PhD); French studies and journalism (MA); French studies and sociology (PhD); JD/MA; MBA/MA. Part-time programs available. *Faculty:* 4 full-time (1 woman), 4 part-time/adjunct. *Students:* 44 full-time (33 women), 2 part-time (both women); includes 4 minority (2 African Americans, 1 Asian American or Pacific Islander, 1 Hispanic American), 12 international. Average age 28. 52 applicants, 46% accepted, 13 enrolled. In 2007, 19 master's, 1 doctorate awarded. Terminal master's awarded for partial completion of doctoral program. *Degree requirements:* For master's, one foreign language, comprehensive exam; for doctorate, one foreign language, thesis/dissertation, qualifying exam. *Entrance requirements:* For master's and doctorate, GRE General Test, knowledge of French. Additional exam requirements/recommendations for international students: Required—TOEFL. *Application deadline:* For fall admission, 1/4 for domestic students. Application fee: $85. *Financial support:* Fellowships with tuition reimbursements, teaching assistantships with tuition reimbursements, Federal Work-Study, institutionally sponsored loans, scholarships/grants, health care benefits, and unspecified assistantships available. Financial award application deadline: 1/4; financial award applicants required to submit FAFSA. *Faculty research:* Contemporary French society, politics, economy, and culture; French history since 1789; French cultural studies, French colonialism and the post-colonial world; France and the European community. *Unit head:* Edward Berenson, Director, 212-988-8740, Fax: 212-995-4142, E-mail: institute.french@nyu.edu. *Application contact:* Herrick Chapman, Director of Graduate Studies, 212-988-8740, Fax: 212-995-4142, E-mail: institute.french@nyu.edu.

North Carolina State University, Graduate School, College of Humanities and Social Sciences, Department of Foreign Languages and Literatures, Program in French Language and Literature, Raleigh, NC 27695. Offers MA. *Degree requirements:* For master's, thesis optional. *Entrance requirements:* For master's, fluency in French. Electronic applications accepted. *Faculty research:* 19th-century visual culture, translation, cinema, modern theater, linguistics.

Northern Illinois University, Graduate School, College of Liberal Arts and Sciences, Department of Foreign Languages and Literatures, De Kalb, IL 60115-2854. Offers French (MA); Spanish (MA). Part-time programs available. *Faculty:* 25 full-time (11 women). *Students:* 8 full-time (5 women), 25 part-time (22 women); includes 10 minority (1 African American, 9 Hispanic Americans), 1 international. Average age 39. 10 applicants, 60% accepted, 4 enrolled. In 2007, 11 degrees awarded. *Degree requirements:* For master's, one foreign language, comprehensive exam, thesis or alternative, language proficiency exam. *Entrance requirements:* For master's, GRE General Test, interview, minimum GPA of 2.75, undergraduate major in French or Spanish. Additional exam requirements/recommendations for international students: Required—TOEFL (minimum score 550 paper-based; 213 computer-based). *Application deadline:* For fall admission, 6/1 for domestic students, 5/1 for international students; for spring admission, 11/1 for domestic students, 10/1 for international students. Applications are processed on a rolling basis. Application fee: $30. Electronic applications accepted. *Expenses:* Tuition, area resident: Part-time $226 per credit hour. Tuition, state resident: full-time $5,424; part-time $225 per credit hour. Tuition, nonresident: full-time $10,848. Required fees: $2,416; $64 per credit hour. *Financial support:* In 2007–08, 13 teaching assistantships with full tuition reimbursements were awarded; fellowships with full tuition reimbursements, research assistantships with full tuition reimbursements, career-related internships or fieldwork, Federal Work-Study, scholarships/grants, tuition waivers (full), and unspecified assistantships also available. Support available to part-time students. Financial award applicants required to submit FAFSA. *Faculty research:* Francophone women writers, prosodies of French and Italian, early Spanish drama, business German, history of Burmese literature. *Unit head:* Anne Birbeck, Acting Chair, 815-753-1259, Fax: 815-753-5989, E-mail: annie@niu.edu.

Northwestern University, The Graduate School, Judd A. and Marjorie Weinberg College of Arts and Sciences, Department of French and Italian, Evanston, IL 60208. Offers eighteenth-century studies (Certificate); French (PhD); French and comparative literature (PhD); Italian studies (Certificate). Admissions and degrees offered through The Graduate School. *Degree requirements:* For doctorate, one foreign language, thesis/dissertation, written and oral exams. *Entrance requirements:* For doctorate, GRE, writing sample, cassette recording. Additional exam requirements/recommendations for international students: Required—TOEFL. *Faculty research:* Francophone studies, 18th century contemporary theory.

The Ohio State University, Graduate School, College of Humanities, Department of French and Italian, Columbus, OH 43210. Offers French (MA, PhD); Italian (MA). *Faculty:* 20. *Students:* 30 full-time (20 women), 6 part-time (4 women); includes 2 minority (1 African American, 1 Hispanic American), 6 international. Average age 33. In 2007, 12 master's, 4 doctorates awarded. *Degree requirements:* For master's, variable foreign language requirement, thesis optional; for doctorate, variable foreign language requirement, thesis/dissertation. *Entrance requirements:* For master's and doctorate, GRE General Test. Additional exam requirements/recommendations for international students: Required—TOEFL. *Application deadline:* For fall admission, 8/15 priority date for domestic students, 7/1 priority date for international students; for winter admission, 12/1 priority date for domestic students, 11/1 priority date for international students; for spring admission, 3/1 priority date for domestic students, 2/1 priority date for international students. Applications are processed on a rolling basis. Application fee: $40 ($50 for international students). Electronic applications accepted. *Financial support:* Fellowships, research assistantships, teaching assistantships, Federal Work-Study, institutionally sponsored loans, and unspecified assistantships available. Support available to part-time students. *Faculty research:* Italian and Romance linguistics. *Unit head:* Karlis Racevskis, Graduate Studies Committee Chair, 614-292-4938, Fax: 614-292-7403, E-mail: racevskis.1@osu.edu. *Application contact:* 614-292-9444, Fax: 614-292-3895, E-mail: domestic.grad@osu.edu.

Ohio University, Graduate College, College of Arts and Sciences, Department of Modern Languages, Athens, OH 45701-2979. Offers French (MA); Spanish (MA). Part-time programs available. *Faculty:* 18 full-time (8 women), 2 part-time/adjunct (both women). *Students:* 28 full-time (23 women), 1 part-time; includes 5 minority (all Hispanic Americans), 6 international. Average age 23. In 2007, 12 degrees awarded. *Degree requirements:* For master's, 2 foreign languages, comprehensive exam, thesis optional. *Entrance requirements:* For master's, oral and written samples. Additional exam requirements/recommendations for international students: Required—TOEFL (minimum score 500 paper-based). *Application deadline:* For fall admission, 1/15 priority date for domestic and international students. Applications are processed on a rolling basis. Application fee: $50 ($55 for international students). Electronic applications accepted. *Financial support:* In 2007–08, teaching assistantships with tuition reimbursements (averaging $10,300 per year); Federal Work-Study and institutionally sponsored loans also available. Financial award application deadline: 4/15. *Faculty research:* French and Spanish language and literature. *Unit head:* Dr. Fred Toner, Chair, 740-593-2765, Fax: 740-593-0729, E-mail: toner@ohio.edu. *Application contact:* Dr. Amado Lascar, Graduate Chair, 740-597-2724, Fax: 740-593-0729, E-mail: lascar@ohio.edu.

Penn State University Park, Graduate School, College of the Liberal Arts, Department of French, State College, University Park, PA 16802-1503. Offers MA, PhD. *Expenses:* Tuition, state resident: full-time $14,738; part-time $614 per credit. Tuition, nonresident: full-time $26,050; part-time $1,085 per credit. Tuition and fees vary according to course load, program and student level. *Unit head:* Dr. Thomas A. Hale, Head, 814-865-1492, Fax: 814-863-1103, E-mail: tah@psu.edu. *Application contact:* Carol Toscano, Information Contact, 814-865-1016, E-mail: clt4@psu.edu.

Portland State University, Graduate Studies, College of Liberal Arts and Sciences, Department of Foreign Languages and Literatures, Portland, OR 97207-0751. Offers foreign literature and language (MA); French (MA); German (MA); Japanese (MA); Spanish (MA). Part-time programs available. *Faculty:* 40 full-time (24 women), 24 part-time/adjunct (15 women). *Students:* 35 full-time (20 women), 13 part-time (12 women); includes 4 minority (1 Asian American or Pacific Islander, 3 Hispanic Americans), 11 international. Average age 32. 27 applicants, 74% accepted, 15 enrolled. In 2007, 18 master's awarded. *Degree requirements:* For master's, one foreign language, thesis (for some programs). *Entrance requirements:* Additional exam

French

Portland State University (continued)
requirements/recommendations for international students: Required—TOEFL (minimum score 550 paper-based; 213 computer-based). *Application deadline:* For fall admission, 4/1 for domestic students, 3/1 for international students; for winter admission, 8/1 for domestic students, 7/1 for international students; for spring admission, 11/1 for domestic and international students. Applications are processed on a rolling basis. Application fee: $50. *Expenses:* Tuition, state resident: full-time $7,047. Tuition, nonresident: full-time $11,178. *Financial support:* In 2007–08, 5 teaching assistantships with full tuition reimbursements (averaging $7,921 per year) were awarded; research assistantships with full tuition reimbursements, Federal Work-Study, scholarships/grants, and unspecified assistantships also available. Support available to part-time students. Financial award application deadline: 3/1; financial award applicants required to submit FAFSA. *Faculty research:* Foreign language pedagogy, applied and social linguistics, literary history and criticism. Total annual research expenditures: $69,175. *Unit head:* Dr. Sandra F. Freels, Chair, 503-725-3522, Fax: 503-725-5276. *Application contact:* Karen Popp, Office Coordinator, 503-725-3522, E-mail: poppk@pdx.edu.

Princeton University, Graduate School, Department of French and Italian, Princeton, NJ 08544-1019. Offers PhD. *Degree requirements:* For doctorate, variable foreign language requirement, thesis/dissertation. *Entrance requirements:* For doctorate, GRE General Test, sample of written work. Additional exam requirements/recommendations for international students: Required—TOEFL (minimum score 600 paper-based; 250 computer-based). Electronic applications accepted.

Purdue University, Graduate School, College of Liberal Arts, Department of Foreign Languages and Literatures, West Lafayette, IN 47907. Offers French (MA, MAT, PhD), including French (MA, PhD), French education (MAT); German (MA, MAT, PhD), including German (MA, PhD), German education (MAT); Spanish (MA, MAT, PhD), including Spanish (MA, PhD), Spanish education (MAT). Terminal master's awarded for partial completion of doctoral program. *Degree requirements:* For master's, one foreign language; for doctorate, 2 foreign languages, thesis/dissertation. *Entrance requirements:* For master's and doctorate, GRE, writing sample, sample recording of English and language of study. Additional exam requirements/recommendations for international students: Required—TOEFL. Electronic applications accepted. *Faculty research:* Linguistics, semiotics, literary criticism, pedagogy.

Queens College of the City University of New York, Division of Graduate Studies, Arts and Humanities Division, Department of European Languages and Literatures, Program in French, Flushing, NY 11367-1597. Offers MA. Part-time and evening/weekend programs available. *Faculty:* 5 full-time (1 woman). *Students:* 12 applicants, 100% accepted, 6 enrolled. In 2007, 2 degrees awarded. *Degree requirements:* For master's, 2 foreign languages, comprehensive exam, thesis or alternative. *Entrance requirements:* For master's, minimum GPA of 3.0. Additional exam requirements/recommendations for international students: Required—TOEFL. *Application deadline:* For fall admission, 4/1 for domestic students; for spring admission, 11/1 for domestic students. Applications are processed on a rolling basis. Application fee: $125. *Financial support:* Career-related internships or fieldwork, Federal Work-Study, institutionally sponsored loans, and tuition waivers (partial) available. Support available to part-time students. Financial award application deadline: 4/1; financial award applicants required to submit FAFSA. *Unit head:* Dr. Joseph Sungolowsky, Graduate Adviser, 718-997-5980. *Application contact:* Mario Caruso, Director of Graduate Admissions, 718-997-5200, Fax: 718-997-5193, E-mail: graduate_admissions@qc.edu.

Queen's University at Kingston, School of Graduate Studies and Research, Faculty of Arts and Sciences, Department of French Studies, Kingston, ON K7L 3N6, Canada. Offers MA, PhD. Part-time programs available. *Degree requirements:* For master's, thesis or 4 credits and oral exam; for doctorate, one foreign language, comprehensive exam, thesis/dissertation. *Entrance requirements:* For master's, minimum B+ average; for doctorate, minimum 80% average. Additional exam requirements/recommendations for international students: Required—TOEFL (minimum score 550 paper-based; 213 computer-based). Electronic applications accepted. *Faculty research:* Reception of Quebec literature in English Canada, autobiography and postcolonialism, irony in women's writing, critical editions of renaissance authors, aspectual systems and grammatical categories.

Rice University, Graduate Programs, School of Humanities, Department of French Studies, Houston, TX 77251-1892. Offers MA, PhD. Terminal master's awarded for partial completion of doctoral program. *Degree requirements:* For master's, one foreign language, thesis, 2 advanced research papers; for doctorate, one foreign language, thesis/dissertation. *Entrance requirements:* For master's, GRE General Test, sample of written work, minimum GPA of 3.0, BA in French studies or related field; for doctorate, GRE, BA or MA in French studies or related field, sample of written work. Additional exam requirements/recommendations for international students: Required—TOEFL (minimum score 600 paper-based; 250 computer-based; 90 iBT). Electronic applications accepted. *Faculty research:* Linguistics, modern philosophy, modern history, gender and traditional studies.

Rider University, Department of Graduate Education, Leadership and Counseling, Teacher Certification Program, Lawrenceville, NJ 08648-3001. Offers business education (Certificate); elementary education (Certificate); English as a second language (Certificate); English education (Certificate); mathematics education (Certificate); preschool to grade 3 (Certificate); science education (Certificate); social studies education (Certificate); world languages (Certificate), including French, German, Spanish. Part-time programs available. *Faculty:* 5 full-time (1 woman), 4 part-time/adjunct (3 women). *Students:* 40 full-time (34 women), 103 part-time (81 women); includes 12 minority (5 African Americans, 1 Asian American or Pacific Islander, 6 Hispanic Americans), 6 international. Average age 35. 61 applicants, 69% accepted, 39 enrolled. In 2007, 111 degrees awarded. *Degree requirements:* For Certificate, internship, professional portfolio. *Entrance requirements:* For degree, PRAXIS, resumé. Additional exam requirements/recommendations for international students: Required—TOEFL (minimum score 550 paper-based; 213 computer-based). *Application deadline:* For fall admission, 5/1 priority date for domestic students, 6/1 priority date for international students; for spring admission, 11/1 priority date for domestic and international students. Applications are processed on a rolling basis. Application fee: $50. Electronic applications accepted. *Expenses:* Tuition: Full-time $25,650; part-time $472 per credit. Required fees: $22 per credit. Tuition and fees vary according to program. *Financial support:* In 2007–08, 46 students received support. Career-related internships or fieldwork, Federal Work-Study, institutionally sponsored loans, and unspecified assistantships available. Support available to part-time students. Financial award applicants required to submit FAFSA. *Faculty research:* Conceptual foundations for optimal development of creativity; creative theory, cognitive processes in mathematics learning, teacher collaboration. *Unit head:* Dr. Austin Winther, Program Coordinator, 609-895-5473, Fax: 609-896-5362. *Application contact:* Jamie L Mitchell, Director of Graduate Admissions, 609-896-5036, Fax: 609-895-5680, E-mail: jmitchell@rider.edu.

Rutgers, The State University of New Jersey, New Brunswick, Graduate School, Program in French, New Brunswick, NJ 08901-1281. Offers French (MA, PhD); French studies (MAT). Part-time and evening/weekend programs available. Terminal master's awarded for partial completion of doctoral program. *Degree requirements:* For master's, one foreign language, written and oral exams (MA); for doctorate, 3 foreign languages, thesis/dissertation, qualifying exam. *Entrance requirements:* For master's and doctorate, GRE General Test. *Faculty research:* Literatures in French, literary history and theory, rhetoric and poetics.

Saint Louis University, Graduate School, College of Arts and Sciences and Graduate School, Department of Modern and Classical Languages, St. Louis, MO 63103-2097. Offers French (MA); Spanish (MA). Part-time programs available. *Faculty:* 12 full-time (8 women). *Students:* 22 full-time (19 women), 16 part-time (14 women); includes 8 minority (all Hispanic Americans), 2 international. Average age 31. 22 applicants, 86% accepted, 18 enrolled. In 2007, 27 degrees awarded. *Degree requirements:* For master's, one foreign language, comprehensive exam, thesis/dissertation (for Spanish). *Entrance requirements:* For master's, GRE General Test or MAT, letters of recommendation, resumé, interview, transcripts, goal statement. Additional exam requirements/recommendations for international students: Required—TOEFL (minimum score 525 paper-based; 194 computer-based). *Application deadline:* For fall admission, 7/1 for domestic and international students; for spring admission, 11/1 for domestic and international students. Applications are processed on a rolling basis. Application fee: $40. Electronic applications accepted. *Expenses:* Tuition: Part-time $845 per credit hour. Required fees: $105 per semester. *Financial support:* In 2007–08, 2 research assistantships with full tuition reimbursements (averaging $12,000 per year), 6 teaching assistantships with full tuition reimbursements (averaging $12,000 per year) were awarded; Federal Work-Study, scholarships/grants, traineeships, health care benefits, tuition waivers, and unspecified assistantships also available. Support available to part-time students. Financial award application deadline: 2/1; financial award applicants required to submit FAFSA. *Faculty research:* Culture studies, literature studies, foreign language acquisition. *Unit head:* Dr. Reinhard G. Andress, Chairperson, 314-977-2448, Fax: 314-977-3649, E-mail: andressp@slu.edu. *Application contact:* Gary U. Behrman, Associate Dean of Graduate School Admissions, 314-977-3827, Fax: 314-977-3943, E-mail: behrmang@slu.edu.

San Francisco State University, Division of Graduate Studies, College of Humanities, Department of Foreign Languages and Literatures, Program in French, San Francisco, CA 94132-1722. Offers MA. *Application deadline:* Applications are processed on a rolling basis. *Unit head:* Dr. Marie-Paule Laden, Program Coordinator, 415-338-7449, E-mail: mpladen@sfsu.edu. *Application contact:* Dr. Delphine Perret, Graduate Coordinator, 415-338-6061, E-mail: dperret@sfsu.edu.

San Jose State University, Graduate Studies and Research, College of Humanities and the Arts, Department of Foreign Languages, Program in French, San Jose, CA 95192-0001. Offers MA. *Degree requirements:* For master's, 2 foreign languages, thesis or alternative, departmental qualifying exam. *Entrance requirements:* Additional exam requirements/recommendations for international students: Required—TOEFL (minimum score 580 paper-based). *Application deadline:* For fall admission, 6/29 for domestic students; for spring admission, 11/30 for domestic students. Applications are processed on a rolling basis. Application fee: $59. Electronic applications accepted. *Financial support:* Applicants required to submit FAFSA. *Unit head:* Dr. Danielle Trudeau, Graduate Advisor, 408-924-4594, E-mail: danielle.trudeau@sjsu.edu.

Simon Fraser University, Graduate Studies, Faculty of Arts and Social Sciences, Department of French, Burnaby, BC V5A 1S6, Canada. Offers MA. *Degree requirements:* For master's, one foreign language, thesis or alternative. *Entrance requirements:* For master's, minimum GPA of 3.0. Additional exam requirements/recommendations for international students: Required—TOEFL or IELTS. *Faculty research:* French linguistics, Creole linguistics, French literature of the Middle Ages and Ancient Régime, modern and contemporary French literature, French Canadian language and literature.

Smith College, Graduate Programs, Department of French Language and Literature, Northampton, MA 01063. Offers MAT. Part-time programs available. *Faculty:* 9 full-time (7 women), 1 (woman) part-time/adjunct. *Degree requirements:* For master's, one foreign language. *Entrance requirements:* For master's, GRE General Test, GRE Subject Test. Additional exam requirements/recommendations for international students: Required—TOEFL. *Application deadline:* For fall admission, 4/1 for domestic students, 1/15 for international students; for spring admission, 12/1 for domestic students. Application fee: $60. *Expenses:* Tuition: Full-time $33,940; part-time $1,060 per credit. Tuition and fees vary according to course load. *Financial support:* Institutionally sponsored loans and scholarships/grants available. Support available to part-time students. Financial award application deadline: 1/15; financial award applicants required to submit CSS PROFILE or FAFSA. *Unit head:* Martine Gantrel, Chair, 413-585-3357.

Stanford University, School of Humanities and Sciences, Department of French and Italian, Stanford, CA 94305-9991. Offers French (MA, PhD); Italian (MA, PhD). Terminal master's awarded for partial completion of doctoral program. *Degree requirements:* For master's, one foreign language, written exam; for doctorate, 2 foreign languages, thesis/dissertation, oral exam. *Entrance requirements:* For master's and doctorate, GRE General Test. Additional exam requirements/recommendations for international students: Required—TOEFL. Electronic applications accepted.

State University of New York at Binghamton, Graduate School, School of Arts and Sciences, Department of Romance Languages and Literatures, Program in French, Binghamton, NY 13902-6000. Offers MA. *Students:* Average age 35. 3 applicants, 67% accepted, 0 enrolled. In 2007, 1 master's awarded. *Degree requirements:* For master's, one foreign language, comprehensive exam, thesis or alternative. *Entrance requirements:* For master's, GRE General Test, GRE Subject Test. Additional exam requirements/recommendations for international students: Required—TOEFL. *Application deadline:* For fall admission, 4/15 priority date for domestic students, 1/15 priority date for international students; for spring admission, 11/1 for domestic students, 10/1 priority date for international students. Applications are processed on a rolling basis. Application fee: $60. Electronic applications accepted. *Financial support:* In 2007–08, 1 student received support, including 1 teaching assistantship with full tuition reimbursement available (averaging $8,100 per year); fellowships, research assistantships, career-related internships or fieldwork, Federal Work-Study, institutionally sponsored loans, and unspecified assistantships also available. Support available to part-time students. Financial award application deadline: 2/15. *Unit head:* Dr. Antonio Sobejano-Moran, Chairperson, Department of Romance Languages and Literatures, 607-777-4635, E-mail: antobianco@msn.com.

Stony Brook University, State University of New York, Graduate School, College of Arts and Sciences, Department of European Languages, Literatures, and Cultures, Program in French, Stony Brook, NY 11794. Offers Romance languages (MA). Evening/weekend programs available. *Students:* 4 full-time (all women), 5 part-time (all women); includes 1 minority (African American), 1 international. Average age 25. *Degree requirements:* For master's, one foreign language. *Entrance requirements:* For master's, GRE General Test. Additional exam requirements/recommendations for international students: Required—TOEFL. *Application deadline:* For fall admission, 1/15 for domestic students. Application fee: $60. *Unit head:* Prosper Sanou, Coordinator, 631-632-7440, E-mail: prosper.sanou@stonybrook.edu.

Syracuse University, Graduate School, College of Arts and Sciences, Department of Languages, Literatures, and Linguistics, Program in French Language, Literature and Culture, Syracuse, NY 13244. Offers MA. Part-time programs available. *Students:* 6 full-time (3 women), 2 international. 8 applicants, 88% accepted, 6 enrolled. In 2007, 3 degrees awarded. *Entrance requirements:* For master's, GRE General Test, GRE Subject Test. Additional exam requirements/recommendations for international students: Required—TOEFL. *Application deadline:* For fall admission, 1/10 priority date for domestic students. Applications are processed on a rolling basis. Application fee: $75. Electronic applications accepted. *Expenses:* Tuition: Full-time $18,216; part-time $1,012 per credit. Required fees: $980. Tuition and fees vary according to program. *Financial support:* Fellowships with full tuition reimbursements, teaching assistantships with full tuition reimbursements, Federal Work-Study and tuition waivers (partial) available. *Unit head:* Dr. Ji-Lyun Phillipa Kim, Program Coordinator, 315-443-5496. *Application contact:* Karen Ames, Information Contact, 315-443-3022, E-mail: koames@syr.edu.

Texas Tech University, Graduate School, College of Arts and Sciences, Department of Classical and Modern Languages and Literatures, Program in Romance Languages-French, Lubbock, TX 79409. Offers MA. *Students:* 20 full-time (13 women), 5 part-time (4 women); includes 11 minority (1 African American, 10 Hispanic Americans), 3 international. Average age 30. 18 applicants, 94% accepted, 10 enrolled. In 2007, 4 degrees awarded. *Entrance requirements:* For master's, GRE General Test. Additional exam requirements/recommendations for international students: Required—TOEFL (minimum score 550 paper-based; 213 computer-based). *Application deadline:* For fall admission, 3/1 priority date for international students; for spring admission, 11/1 priority date for international students. Applications are processed on a rolling basis. Application fee: $50 ($60 for international students). Electronic applications accepted. *Expenses:* Tuition, state resident: part-time $373 per credit hour. Tuition, nonresident: part-time $651 per credit hour. Tuition and fees vary according to program. *Financial support:* Application deadline: 4/15. *Faculty research:* French and Francophone literature, French cinema, French and Francophone culture, business French. *Unit head:* Dr. Diane Wood, Professor and Graduate Advisor of French, 806-742-3145 Ext. 258, Fax: 806-742-3306, E-mail: diane.wood@ttu.edu. *Application contact:* Liz Hildebrand, Senior Advisor, 806-742-4055, Fax: 806-742-3306, E-mail: liz.hildebrand@ttu.edu.

Tufts University, Graduate School of Arts and Sciences, Program in French, Medford, MA 02155. Offers MA. Part-time programs available. *Faculty:* 23 full-time, 45 part-time/adjunct. *Students:* 3 (2 women); includes 1 minority (African American) 1 international. 1 applicant, 100% accepted, 1 enrolled. *Degree requirements:* For master's, one foreign language. *Entrance requirements:* For master's, GRE General Test, writing sample. Additional exam requirements/recommendations for international students: Required—TOEFL (minimum score 550 paper-based; 213 computer-based; 80 iBT). *Application deadline:* For fall admission, 2/15 for domestic students, 12/30 for international students; for spring admission, 10/15 for domestic students, 9/15 for international students. Applications are processed on a rolling basis. Application fee: $70. Electronic applications accepted. *Expenses:* Tuition: Full-time $35,052. *Financial support:* Teaching assistantships with full and partial tuition reimbursements, Federal Work-Study, scholarships/grants, and tuition waivers (partial) available. Financial award application deadline: 2/15; financial award applicants required to submit FAFSA. *Unit head:* Jose Mazzotti, Chair, 617-627-3289. *Application contact:* Vincent Pollina, Graduate Adviser, 617-627-5289.

Tulane University, School of Liberal Arts, Department of French and Italian, New Orleans, LA 70118-5669. Offers French (MA, PhD). *Degree requirements:* For master's, one foreign language, thesis or alternative; for doctorate, 2 foreign languages, thesis/dissertation. *Entrance requirements:* For master's, GRE General Test, minimum B average in undergraduate course work; for doctorate, GRE General Test. Additional exam requirements/recommendations for international students: Required—TOEFL. Electronic applications accepted.

Université de Moncton, Faculty of Arts and Social Sciences, Department of French Studies, Moncton, NB E1A 3E9, Canada. Offers MA, PhD. Part-time programs available. Terminal master's awarded for partial completion of doctoral program. *Degree requirements:* For master's, thesis, proficiency in French; for doctorate, thesis/dissertation, proficiency in French. *Entrance requirements:* For master's, honors degree in French; for doctorate, MA in French. Electronic applications accepted. *Faculty research:* Language, linguistics, literature, ethnology, Acadian studies.

Université de Montréal, Faculty of Arts and Sciences, Department of French Literature, Montréal, QC H3C 3J7, Canada. Offers MA, PhD. *Faculty:* 31 full-time (10 women). *Students:* 171 full-time (127 women), 10 part-time (7 women). 87 applicants, 37% accepted, 29 enrolled. In 2007, 27 master's, 12 doctorates awarded. *Degree requirements:* For master's, one foreign language, thesis; for doctorate, one foreign language, thesis/dissertation, general exam. *Application deadline:* For fall admission, 2/1 priority date for domestic students; for winter admission, 11/1 priority date for domestic students; for spring admission, 2/1 priority date for domestic students. Application fee: $100. Electronic applications accepted. *Financial support:* Fellowships, research assistantships, teaching assistantships available. *Faculty research:* Literary history, literary genres, critical edition, creative writing, Quebecois literature. *Unit head:* Benoit Melançon, Director, 514-343-6213, Fax: 514-343-2256, E-mail: benoit.melancon@umontreal.ca. *Application contact:* Jean-Philippe Beaulieu, Graduate Chairman, 514-343-6559, Fax: 514-343-6559, E-mail: jean-philippe.beaulieu@umontreal.ca.

Université de Sherbrooke, Faculty of Letters and Human Sciences, Department of Letters and Communications, Sherbrooke, QC J1K 2R1, Canada. Offers comparative Canadian literature (MA, PhD); French literature (MA, PhD); linguistics (MA); lit&erature de création (MA, PhD); theatre (MA). *Degree requirements:* For master's, thesis or alternative; for doctorate, thesis/dissertation. *Entrance requirements:* For master's, minimum GPA of 2.8; for doctorate, minimum GPA of 3.0.

Université du Québec à Chicoutimi, Graduate Programs, Program in Didactics of French-Mother Tongue, Chicoutimi, QC G7H 2B1, Canada. Offers Diploma. Part-time programs available. *Entrance requirements:* For degree, appropriate bachelor's degree, proficiency in French.

Université Laval, Faculty of Letters, Department of Literature, Program in French Studies, Québec, QC G1K 7P4, Canada. Offers MA. Part-time programs available. *Entrance requirements:* For master's, knowledge of French. Electronic applications accepted.

University at Albany, State University of New York, College of Arts and Sciences, Department of Languages, Literatures, and Cultures, Program in French, Albany, NY 12222-0001. Offers MA, PhD. *Degree requirements:* For master's, one foreign language; for doctorate, thesis/dissertation. *Application deadline:* For fall admission, 8/1 for domestic students. Application fee: $75. *Expenses:* Tuition, state resident: part-time $576 per credit. Tuition, nonresident: part-time $910 per credit. Tuition and fees vary according to program. *Unit head:* HenryK Baran, Chair, Department of Languages, Literatures, and Cultures, 518-442-4222.

University at Buffalo, the State University of New York, Graduate School, College of Arts and Sciences, Department of Romance Languages and Literatures, Buffalo, NY 14260. Offers French (MA, PhD); Spanish (MA, PhD). Part-time programs available. Terminal master's awarded for partial completion of doctoral program. *Degree requirements:* For master's, one foreign language, project; for doctorate, 2 foreign languages, thesis/dissertation. *Entrance requirements:* For master's and doctorate, GRE. Additional exam requirements/recommendations for international students: Required—TOEFL (minimum score 550 paper-based; 213 computer-based; 79 iBT). Electronic applications accepted. *Faculty research:* Romance linguistics, cultural studies, literary studies, literature and philosophy.

The University of Alabama, Graduate School, College of Arts and Sciences, Department of Modern Languages and Classics, Tuscaloosa, AL 35487. Offers French (MA, PhD); French and Spanish (PhD); German (MA); Romance languages (MA, PhD); Spanish (MA, PhD). Part-time programs available. *Faculty:* 22 full-time (12 women). *Students:* 47 full-time (35 women), 14 part-time (9 women); includes 12 minority (2 African Americans, 10 Hispanic Americans), 15 international. Average age 32. 26 applicants, 69% accepted, 14 enrolled. In 2007, 12 master's, 4 doctorates awarded. *Median time to degree:* Of those who began their doctoral program in fall 1999, 40% received their degree in 8 years or less. *Degree requirements:* For master's, comprehensive exam, thesis optional; for doctorate, one foreign language, thesis/dissertation, preliminary exam. *Entrance requirements:* For master's and doctorate, minimum GPA of 3.0, writing sample. Additional exam requirements/recommendations for international students: Required—TOEFL or IELTS. *Application deadline:* For fall admission, 7/6 priority date for domestic students, 1/15 priority date for international students; for spring admission, 12/6 priority date for domestic students, 6/1 priority date for international students. Applications are processed on a rolling basis. Application fee: $30. Electronic applications accepted. *Expenses:* Tuition, state resident: full-time $5,700. Tuition, nonresident: full-time $16,518. *Financial support:* In 2007–08, 7 students received support, including 1 fellowship, research assistantships with full tuition reimbursements available (averaging $10,291 per year), 6 teaching assistantships with full tuition reimbursements available (averaging $10,291 per year); career-related internships or fieldwork, Federal Work-Study, institutionally sponsored loans, and scholarships/grants also available. Financial award application deadline: 7/14. *Faculty research:* Non-English literature, linguistics, culture, film. Total annual research expenditures: $48,751. *Unit head:* Dr. Michael Picone, Chair and Professor, 205-348-5054, Fax: 205-348-2042, E-mail: mpicone@bama.ua.edu. *Application contact:* Dr. K. Barbara Fischer, Graduate Director and Associate Professor, 205-348-8465, Fax: 205-348-2042, E-mail: bfischer@bama.ua.edu.

University of Alberta, Faculty of Graduate Studies and Research, Department of Modern Languages and Cultural Studies, Edmonton, AB T6G 2E1, Canada. Offers applied linguistics (Germanic, Romance, Slavic) (MA); French language, literatures and linguistics (PhD); French language, literatures, and linguistics (MA); Germanic languages, literatures and linguistics (PhD); Germanic languages, literatures, and linguistics (MA); Italian studies (MA); Slavic languages and literatures (Russian, Ukrainian) (MA, PhD); Slavic linguistics (Russian, Ukrainian) (MA, PhD); Spanish and Latin American studies (MA, PhD); Ukrainian folklore (MA, PhD). Part-time programs available. *Degree requirements:* For master's, one foreign language, thesis; for doctorate, 2 foreign languages, comprehensive exam, thesis/dissertation. *Entrance requirements:* For master's and doctorate, 1 language other than English. Additional exam requirements/recommendations for international students: Required—Michigan English Language Assessment Battery or TOEFL (paper score 550; computer score 213). Electronic applications accepted. *Faculty research:* Russian/Ukrainian studies; German studies; contemporary Latin American, French and Francophone studies; Italian studies.

The University of Arizona, Graduate College, College of Humanities, Department of French and Italian, Tucson, AZ 85721. Offers French (MA, PhD). Part-time programs available. *Faculty:* 18. *Students:* 6 full-time (4 women), 12 part-time (10 women), 6 international. Average age 36. 7 applicants, 71% accepted, 5 enrolled. In 2007, 2 degrees awarded. *Degree requirements:* For doctorate, one foreign language, comprehensive exam, thesis/dissertation. *Entrance requirements:* For master's and doctorate, minimum GPA of 3.5, 3 letters of reference, statement of purpose, writing sample in French, audio sample. Additional exam requirements/recommendations for international students: Required—TOEFL (minimum score 550 paper-based; 213 computer-based; 80 iBT). *Application deadline:* For fall admission, 11/1 for domestic and international students. Applications are processed on a rolling basis. Application fee: $50. Electronic applications accepted. *Financial support:* In 2007–08, 1 fellowship with partial tuition reimbursement (averaging $5,000 per year), 1 research assistantship with partial tuition reimbursement, 13 teaching assistantships with partial tuition reimbursements were awarded; Federal Work-Study, institutionally sponsored loans, scholarships/grants, and tuition waivers (partial) also available. *Faculty research:* French literature (history, criticism, and theory), Francophone literature and culture, second language acquisition and teaching. Total annual research expenditures: $785. *Unit head:* Dr. Irene d'Almeda, Department Head, 520-621-7349, Fax: 520-626-8022, E-mail: dalmedia@email.arizona.edu. *Application contact:* Darcy Roman-Felix, Graduate Secretary, 520-621-5345, Fax: 520-626-8022, E-mail: roman@email.arizona.edu.

University of Arkansas, Graduate School, J. William Fulbright College of Arts and Sciences, Department of Foreign Languages, Program in French, Fayetteville, AR 72701-1201. Offers MA. *Students:* 6 full-time (all women), 1 (woman) part-time; includes 1 minority (African American) 8 applicants, 88% accepted. In 2007, 4 degrees awarded. *Degree requirements:* For master's, variable foreign language requirement. Application fee: $40 ($50 for international students). *Financial support:* In 2007–08, 6 teaching assistantships were awarded; fellowships, research assistantships, career-related internships or fieldwork and Federal Work-Study also available. Support available to part-time students. Financial award application deadline: 4/1; financial award applicants required to submit FAFSA. *Unit head:* Nancy Arenberg, Graduate Coordinator, 479-575-2951, Fax: 479-575-6795, E-mail: arenberg@uark.edu. *Application contact:* Nancy Arenberg, Graduate Coordinator, 479-575-2951, Fax: 479-575-6795, E-mail: arenberg@uark.edu.

The University of British Columbia, Faculty of Arts and Faculty of Graduate Studies, Department of French, Hispanic and Italian Studies, Vancouver, BC V6T 1Z1, Canada. Offers French (MA, PhD); Hispanic studies (MA, PhD). Part-time programs available. *Faculty:* 20 full-time (9 women). *Students:* 45 full-time (29 women), 1 (woman) part-time. 35 applicants, 77% accepted, 18 enrolled. In 2007, 5 master's, 1 doctorate awarded. *Degree requirements:* For master's, thesis optional; for doctorate, 2 foreign languages, comprehensive exam, thesis/dissertation. *Entrance requirements:* For master's, BA degree; for doctorate, MA degree. Additional exam requirements/recommendations for international students: Required—TOEFL (minimum score 550 paper-based; 213 computer-based; 80 iBT). *Application deadline:* For fall admission, 4/1 priority date for domestic students, 3/1 priority date for international students; for winter admission, 9/1 priority date for domestic students, 8/1 priority date for international students. Applications are processed on a rolling basis. Application fee: $90 Canadian dollars ($150 Canadian dollars for international students). Electronic applications accepted. *Financial support:* In 2007–08, 5 fellowships with partial tuition reimbursements (averaging $16,000 per year), 6 research assistantships (averaging $1,328 per year), 28 teaching assistantships (averaging $10,700 per year) were awarded; Federal Work-Study and tuition waivers (partial) also available. Financial award application deadline: 2/15. *Faculty research:* Medieval and Renaissance literature, modern literature, romance philology and linguistics, cultural studies, women's literature. *Unit head:* Dr. André C. Lamontagne, Head, 604-822-5746, Fax: 604-822-6675, E-mail: andrelam@interchange.ubc.ca. *Application contact:* Dr. Christine Rouget, Graduate Advisor, 604-822-4035, Fax: 604-822-6675, E-mail: roug@interchange.ubc.ca.

University of California, Berkeley, Graduate Division, College of Letters and Science, Department of French, Berkeley, CA 94720-1500. Offers PhD. *Degree requirements:* For doctorate, one foreign language, thesis/dissertation, qualifying exam. *Entrance requirements:* For doctorate, minimum GPA of 3.0, 3 letters of recommendation. *Application deadline:* For fall admission, 12/15 for domestic students. Application fee: $70 ($90 for international students). *Financial support:* Fellowships, research assistantships, teaching assistantships, unspecified assistantships available. *Unit head:* Michael Lucey, Chair, 510-642-0277, E-mail: mlucey@berkeley.edu. *Application contact:* Dr. Susan M. Dennehy, Graduate Student Affairs Officer, 510-642-2714, Fax: 510-642-8852, E-mail: frenchga@berkeley.edu.

University of California, Berkeley, Graduate Division, Group in Romance Languages and Literature, Program in French, Berkeley, CA 94720-1500. Offers PhD. *Entrance requirements:* For doctorate, GRE General Test, 3 letters of recommendation. *Application deadline:* For fall admission, 12/15 for domestic students. Application fee: $70 ($90 for international students). *Application contact:* Dr. Susan M. Dennehy, Graduate Student Affairs Officer, 510-642-2714, Fax: 510-642-8852, E-mail: frenchga@berkeley.edu.

University of California, Davis, Graduate Studies, Program in French, Davis, CA 95616. Offers PhD. Part-time programs available. *Degree requirements:* For doctorate, thesis/dissertation. *Entrance requirements:* For doctorate, GRE General Test, minimum GPA of 3.0. Additional exam requirements/recommendations for international students: Required—TOEFL (minimum score 550 paper-based; 213 computer-based). Electronic applications accepted. *Faculty research:* Art and art criticism, Francophone literature, travel narrative, colonial and postcolonial studies and romance linguistics.

University of California, Irvine, Office of Graduate Studies, School of Humanities, Department of French and Italian, Irvine, CA 92697. Offers French (MA, PhD). *Students:* 12 full-time (6 women), 2 international. In 2007, 4 degrees awarded. *Degree requirements:* For doctorate, thesis/dissertation. *Entrance requirements:* For master's and doctorate, GRE General Test, minimum GPA of 3.0. Additional exam requirements/recommendations for international students: Required—TOEFL (minimum score 550 paper-based; 213 computer-based). *Application deadline:* For fall admission, 1/15 for domestic students; for winter admission, 10/15 for domestic students. Applications are processed on a rolling basis. Application fee: $60. Electronic applications accepted. *Financial support:* Fellowships, research assistantships with full tuition reimbursements, teaching assistantships, institutionally sponsored loans, traineeships, health care benefits, and unspecified assistantships available. Financial award application deadline: 3/1; financial award applicants required to submit FAFSA. *Faculty research:* Montaigne, psychoanalysis, feminism and the problem of repression, aesthetics of nationalism and the limits of culture. *Unit head:* David Carroll, Chair, 949-824-4940, Fax: 949-824-1031, E-mail: dcarroll@uci.edu. *Application contact:* Lin Xi, Administrative Assistant, 949-824-6407, Fax: 949-824-1031, E-mail: lxi@uci.edu.

University of California, Los Angeles, Graduate Division, College of Letters and Science, Department of French and Francophone Studies, Los Angeles, CA 90095. Offers MA, PhD. *Students:* 20 full-time (15 women); includes 4 minority (2 African Americans, 2 Hispanic Americans), 1 international. Average age 31. 16 applicants, 56% accepted, 5 enrolled. In

French

University of California, Los Angeles (continued)
2007, 4 master's, 3 doctorates awarded. Terminal master's awarded for partial completion of doctoral program. *Median time to degree:* Of those who began their doctoral program in fall 1999, 50% received their degree in 8 years or less. *Degree requirements:* For master's, one foreign language, comprehensive exam; for doctorate, 2 foreign languages, thesis/dissertation, oral and written qualifying exams. *Entrance requirements:* For master's, GRE General Test, minimum GPA of 3.0, sample of written work in French, degree objective of Ph.D; for doctorate, GRE General Test, MA in French or equivalent; minimum undergraduate GPA of 3.0; sample of written work in French. *Application deadline:* For fall admission, 12/15 for domestic students. Application fee: $60. Electronic applications accepted. *Expenses:* Tuition, nonresident: full-time $5,728. Required fees: $8,966. Full-time tuition and fees vary according to program and student level. *Financial support:* In 2007–08, 30 fellowships with full and partial tuition reimbursements, 6 research assistantships with full and partial tuition reimbursements, 7 teaching assistantships with full and partial tuition reimbursements were awarded; Federal Work-Study, institutionally sponsored loans, and tuition waivers (full and partial) also available. Financial award applicants required to submit FAFSA. *Unit head:* Dr. Dominic Thomas, Chair, 310-825-1145. *Application contact:* Departmental Office, 310-825-1145, E-mail: allen@humnet.ucla.edu.

University of California, San Diego, Office of Graduate Studies, Department of Literature, Program in French Literature, La Jolla, CA 92093. Offers MA. *Degree requirements:* For master's, thesis. *Entrance requirements:* For master's, GRE General Test, GRE Subject Test. Electronic applications accepted.

University of California, Santa Barbara, Graduate Division, College of Letters and Sciences, Division of Humanities and Fine Arts, Department of French and Italian, Santa Barbara, CA 93106. Offers French (MA, PhD); MA/PhD. French Language Institute available during summer sessions. *Faculty:* 14 full-time (7 women). *Students:* 12 full-time (7 women), 3 international. Average age 32. 14 applicants, 64% accepted, 3 enrolled. In 2007, 1 master's, 5 doctorates awarded. Terminal master's awarded for partial completion of doctoral program. *Median time to degree:* Of those who began their doctoral program in fall 1999, 33% received their degree in 8 years or less. *Degree requirements:* For master's, 2 foreign languages, comprehensive exam, 12 seminars, knowledge of 5 areas, 1 seminar in literary theory, 9 papers, 2 quarters as a teaching assistant; for doctorate, 2 foreign languages, comprehensive exam, thesis/dissertation, coverage of 6 traditional chronological periods, 2 subject areas, field exams, 3 quarters as a teaching assistant. *Entrance requirements:* For master's, GRE, sample of written work, tape of spoken French, BA or the equivalent, 3 letters of recommendation, transcripts; for doctorate, GRE, sample of written work, tape of spoken French, MA or the equivalent, 3 letters of recommendation, transcripts. Additional exam requirements/recommendations for international students: Required—TOEFL (minimum score 550 paper-based; 213 computer-based; 80 iBT). *Application deadline:* For fall admission, 5/1 for domestic and international students; for winter admission, 10/1 for domestic and international students; for spring admission, 1/15 for domestic and international students. Applications are processed on a rolling basis. Application fee: $60. Electronic applications accepted. *Expenses:* Tuition, nonresident: full-time $14,888. Required fees: $10,108. *Financial support:* In 2007–08, 12 students received support, including 1 fellowship with full and partial tuition reimbursement available (averaging $18,000 per year), 16 teaching assistantships with full and partial tuition reimbursements available (averaging $16,391 per year); career-related internships or fieldwork, Federal Work-Study, institutionally sponsored loans, scholarships/grants, traineeships, health care benefits, tuition waivers (full and partial), and unspecified assistantships also available. Support available to part-time students. Financial award application deadline: 1/10; financial award applicants required to submit FAFSA. *Faculty research:* French and Francophone studies, comparative literature, second language acquisition, applied linguistics, performance studies, feminist and gender studies. Total annual research expenditures: $2,800. *Unit head:* Prof. Catherine Nesci, Chair, 805-893-2220, Fax: 805-893-8826, E-mail: cnesci@french-ital.ucsb.edu. *Application contact:* Rosa Pinter, Graduate Staff Advisor, 805-893-3398, Fax: 805-893-8826, E-mail: pinter@french-ital.ucsb.edu.

University of Chicago, Division of the Humanities, Department of Romance Languages and Literatures, Chicago, IL 60637-1513. Offers French (AM, PhD); Italian (AM, PhD); Spanish (AM, PhD). *Students:* 75. 56 applicants, 45% accepted, 15 enrolled.Terminal master's awarded for partial completion of doctoral program. *Degree requirements:* For master's, 2 foreign languages, thesis; for doctorate, 3 foreign languages, thesis/dissertation. *Entrance requirements:* For master's and doctorate, GRE General Test, GRE Subject Test. Additional exam requirements/recommendations for international students: Required—TOEFL. *Application deadline:* For fall admission, 12/15 for domestic students. Application fee: $55. *Financial support:* Teaching assistantships, Federal Work-Study available. Financial award application deadline: 12/15; financial award applicants required to submit FAFSA. *Unit head:* Dr. Frederick de Armas, Chair, 773-702-8481.

University of Cincinnati, Graduate School, McMicken College of Arts and Sciences, Department of Romance Languages and Literature, Program in French, Cincinnati, OH 45221. Offers MA, PhD. *Students:* 6 full-time (4 women), 2 part-time (both women), 2 international. Terminal master's awarded for partial completion of doctoral program. *Degree requirements:* For master's, thesis optional; for doctorate, 2 foreign languages, thesis/dissertation. *Entrance requirements:* For master's, minimum GPA of 3.0. *Application deadline:* For fall admission, 2/1 for domestic students. Application fee: $30. Electronic applications accepted. *Financial support:* Fellowships with full tuition reimbursements, teaching assistantships with full tuition reimbursements, tuition waivers (partial) and unspecified assistantships available. Financial award application deadline: 5/1. *Application contact:* Connie Scarborough, Graduate Program Director, 513-556-1836, Fax: 513-556-2577, E-mail: connie.scarborough@uc.edu.

University of Colorado at Boulder, Graduate School, College of Arts and Sciences, Department of French and Italian, Boulder, CO 80309. Offers French (MA, PhD). *Faculty:* 12. *Students:* 17 full-time (12 women), 7 part-time (6 women); includes 2 minority (1 Asian American or Pacific Islander, 1 Hispanic American), 6 international. Average age 33. 10 applicants, 100% accepted. In 2007, 4 master's, 1 doctorate awarded. Terminal master's awarded for partial completion of doctoral program. *Degree requirements:* For master's, 2 foreign languages, comprehensive exam, thesis or alternative; for doctorate, 3 foreign languages, thesis/dissertation. *Entrance requirements:* For master's, GRE General Test, minimum undergraduate GPA of 3.0; for doctorate, GRE General Test. *Application deadline:* For fall admission, 2/1 priority date for domestic students, 1/1 for international students. Applications are processed on a rolling basis. Application fee: $50 ($60 for international students). *Financial support:* In 2007–08, 7 fellowships (averaging $7,600 per year) were awarded; tuition waivers (full) also available. Financial award application deadline: 2/1. *Faculty research:* All periods of French literature from the Middle Ages to the present (including Francophone literature, cultural studies and literary theory). *Unit head:* Andrew Cowell, Chair, 303-492-8270, Fax: 303-492-8338, E-mail: cowellj@colorado.edu. *Application contact:* Graduate Program Assistant, 303-492-1465, Fax: 303-492-8338, E-mail: frenital@spot.colorado.edu.

University of Connecticut, Graduate School, College of Liberal Arts and Sciences, Department of Modern and Classical Languages, Field of French, Storrs, CT 06269. Offers MA, PhD. *Faculty:* 7 full-time (5 women). *Students:* 12 full-time (8 women), 4 part-time (2 women); includes 2 minority (both Hispanic Americans), 6 international. Average age 32. 10 applicants, 60% accepted, 4 enrolled. In 2007, 7 master's, 1 doctorate awarded. Terminal master's awarded for partial completion of doctoral program. *Degree requirements:* For master's, comprehensive exam; for doctorate, thesis/dissertation. *Entrance requirements:* For master's and doctorate, GRE General Test, GRE Subject Test. Additional exam requirements/recommendations for international students: Required—TOEFL (minimum score 550 paper-based; 213 computer-based). *Application deadline:* For fall admission, 2/1 priority date for domestic and international students; for spring admission, 11/1 for domestic students, 10/1 for international students. Applications are processed on a rolling basis. Application fee: $55. Electronic applications accepted. *Expenses:* Tuition, state resident: part-time $469 per credit hour. Tuition, nonresident: part-time $1,218 per credit hour. *Financial support:* In 2007–08, 2 research assistantships, 9 teaching assistantships with full tuition reimbursements were awarded; fellowships, Federal Work-Study, scholarships/grants, health care benefits, and unspecified assistantships also available. Financial award application deadline: 2/1; financial award applicants required to submit FAFSA. *Unit head:* Roger Célestin, Co-Chair, 860-486-3091, E-mail: roger.celestin@uconn.edu. *Application contact:* Anne Berthelot, Graduate Advisor, 860-486-3173, E-mail: anne.berthlot@uconn.edu.

University of Delaware, College of Arts and Sciences, Department of Foreign Languages and Literatures, Newark, DE 19716. Offers foreign languages and literatures (MA), including French, German, Spanish; foreign languages pedagogy (MA), including French, German, Spanish. *Faculty:* 27 full-time (14 women). *Students:* 33 full-time (23 women), 5 part-time (all women); includes 1 minority (African American), 10 international. Average age 25. 29 applicants, 55% accepted, 11 enrolled. In 2007, 12 degrees awarded. *Degree requirements:* For master's, one foreign language, comprehensive exam, thesis optional. *Entrance requirements:* For master's, GRE General Test, letters of recommendation, writing sample. Additional exam requirements/recommendations for international students: Required—TOEFL. *Application deadline:* For fall admission, 2/1 priority date for domestic and international students; for spring admission, 11/1 for domestic and international students. Application fee: $60. Electronic applications accepted. *Financial support:* In 2007–08, fellowships with full tuition reimbursements (averaging $14,600 per year), research assistantships with full tuition reimbursements (averaging $14,600 per year), 29 teaching assistantships with full tuition reimbursements (averaging $14,600 per year) were awarded; tuition waivers (full) and unspecified assistantships also available. Financial award application deadline: 2/1. *Faculty research:* Medieval to Modern French and Spanish literature, Twentieth Century German, French, Spanish literature by women, computer-assisted instruction. Total annual research expenditures: $12,000. *Unit head:* Dr. Richard Zipser, Chair, 302-831-6882. *Application contact:* Dr. Monika Shafi, Graduate Coordinator, 302-831-2587, E-mail: mshafi@udel.edu.

University of Florida, Graduate School, College of Liberal Arts and Sciences, Department of Romance Languages and Literatures, Program in French, Gainesville, FL 32611. Offers MA, PhD. *Faculty:* 13. *Degree requirements:* For master's, thesis optional; for doctorate, one foreign language, thesis/dissertation. *Entrance requirements:* For master's and doctorate, GRE General Test, minimum GPA of 3.0. Additional exam requirements/recommendations for international students: Required—TOEFL (minimum score 550 paper-based; 213 computer-based). *Application deadline:* For fall admission, 6/1 priority date for domestic students. Applications are processed on a rolling basis. Application fee: $30. Electronic applications accepted. *Expenses:* Tuition, state resident: full-time $7,478. Tuition, nonresident: full-time $22,603. *Financial support:* Fellowships, research assistantships, teaching assistantships, associateships available. *Faculty research:* Medieval, sixteenth, seventeenth, nineteenth, and twentieth century French literature. *Unit head:* Dr. Susan Read Baker, Coordinator, 352-392-2016 Ext. 231, Fax: 352-392-5679, E-mail: srbaker@rll.ufl.edu. *Application contact:* Terry Lopez, Graduate Secretary, 352-392-2016 Ext. 224, E-mail: tlopez@rll.ufl.edu.

University of Georgia, Graduate School, College of Arts and Sciences, Department of Romance Languages, Program in French, Athens, GA 30602. Offers MA, MAT. *Students:* 5 full-time (all women), 2 part-time (1 woman). 8 applicants, 63% accepted, 3 enrolled. *Degree requirements:* For master's, one foreign language, thesis (MA). *Entrance requirements:* For master's, GRE General Test. *Application deadline:* For fall admission, 7/1 priority date for domestic students; for spring admission, 11/15 for domestic students. Application fee: $50. Electronic applications accepted. *Financial support:* Fellowships, research assistantships, teaching assistantships, unspecified assistantships available.

University of Guelph, Graduate Program Services, College of Arts, School of Languages and Literatures, Guelph, ON N1G 2W1, Canada. Offers European studies (MA); French studies (MA). *Faculty:* 8 full-time (5 women). *Students:* 3 full-time (2 women). Average age 24. 3 applicants, 100% accepted, 3 enrolled. In 2007, 2 degrees awarded. *Entrance requirements:* For master's, BA Honours or equivalent. *Application deadline:* For fall admission, 8/15 priority date for domestic and international students. Applications are processed on a rolling basis. Application fee: $86. Electronic applications accepted. *Financial support:* In 2007–08, 5 fellowships (averaging $2,000 per year), 7 teaching assistantships (averaging $5,106 per year) were awarded. Financial award application deadline: 7/31. *Faculty research:* Sociolinguistics, poetics and politics of literature, language acquisition. *Unit head:* Dr. Daniel Chouinard, Director of School of Languages and Literatures, 519-824-4120 Ext. 54891, Fax: 519-763-9572, E-mail: dchouina@uogueloh.ca. *Application contact:* Dr. Stephanie Nutting, Graduate Coordinator, French Studies, 519-824-4120 Ext. 53168, Fax: 519-763-9572, E-mail: snutting@uoguelph.ca.

University of Hawaii at Manoa, Graduate Division, Colleges of Arts and Sciences, College of Language, Linguistics and Literature, Department of Languages and Literatures of Europe and the Americas, Program in French, Honolulu, HI 96822. Offers MA. Part-time programs available. *Faculty:* 6 full-time (5 women). *Students:* 17 full-time (14 women), 1 part-time; includes 5 minority (1 African American, 4 Asian Americans or Pacific Islanders). 14 applicants, 71% accepted, 7 enrolled. *Degree requirements:* For master's, one foreign language, thesis optional. *Entrance requirements:* Additional exam requirements/recommendations for international students: Required—TOEFL (minimum score 580 paper-based; 237 computer-based; 92 iBT), IELTS (minimum score 5). *Application deadline:* For fall admission, 3/1 for domestic students, 2/1 for international students; for spring admission, 9/1 for domestic students, 8/15 for international students. Application fee: $50. *Financial support:* In 2007–08, 1 research assistantship (averaging $15,552 per year), 12 teaching assistantships (averaging $13,296 per year) were awarded. *Application contact:* Robert Ball, Information Contact, 808-956-4715, Fax: 808-956-9536, E-mail: rball@hawaii.edu.

University of Houston, College of Liberal Arts and Social Sciences, Department of Modern and Classical Languages, Houston, TX 77204. Offers French (MA); Spanish (MA, PhD); MBA/MA. Part-time and evening/weekend programs available. Postbaccalaureate distance learning degree programs offered. *Faculty:* 10 full-time (6 women), 2 part-time/adjunct (1 woman). *Students:* 26 full-time (19 women), 41 part-time (35 women); includes 41 minority (1 African American, 40 Hispanic Americans), 9 international. Average age 36. 21 applicants, 81% accepted, 12 enrolled. In 2007, 9 master's, 4 doctorates awarded. Terminal master's awarded for partial completion of doctoral program. *Degree requirements:* For master's, one foreign language, thesis optional; for doctorate, 3 foreign languages, thesis/dissertation. *Entrance requirements:* For master's and doctorate, GRE General Test. Additional exam requirements/recommendations for international students: Required—TOEFL. *Application deadline:* For fall admission, 2/28 priority date for domestic students; for spring admission, 10/30 priority date for domestic students. Application fee: $25 ($75 for international students). *Expenses:* Tuition, state resident: full-time $6,297; part-time $262 per credit. Tuition, nonresident: full-time $12,969; part-time $540 per credit. Required fees: $2,696. *Financial support:* In 2007–08, 5 research assistantships with full tuition reimbursements (averaging $10,400 per year), 15 teaching assistantships with full tuition reimbursements (averaging $10,400 per year) were awarded; fellowships with full tuition reimbursements, career-related internships or fieldwork, Federal Work-Study, institutionally sponsored loans, scholarships/grants, health care benefits, and unspecified assistantships also available. Support available to part-time students. Financial award application deadline: 2/1; financial award applicants required to submit FAFSA. *Faculty research:* Hispanic literature and language in the U.S., Golden Age, women. *Unit head:* Dr. Marc Zimmerman, Chairperson, 713-743-3007, Fax: 713-743-0935, E-mail: mzimmerm@mail.uh.edu.

University of Illinois at Chicago, Graduate College, College of Liberal Arts and Sciences, Department of Spanish and French, Program in French, Chicago, IL 60607-7128. Offers MA. Part-time programs available. *Degree requirements:* For master's, one foreign language, thesis optional, exam. *Entrance requirements:* For master's, minimum GPA of 2.75. Additional exam requirements/recommendations for international students: Required—TOEFL. Electronic applications accepted. *Faculty research:* French civilization, feminist theory, French theater, sociology of literature, narrative theory.

University of Illinois at Urbana–Champaign, Graduate College, College of Liberal Arts and Sciences, School of Literatures, Cultures and Linguistics, Department of French, Champaign, IL 61820. Offers MA, PhD. *Faculty:* 13 full-time (7 women). *Students:* 16 full-time (8 women), 13 part-time (11 women), 6 international. 30 applicants, 43% accepted, 6 enrolled. In 2007, 8 master's, 3 doctorates awarded. *Degree requirements:* For master's, one foreign language; for doctorate, variable foreign language requirement, thesis/dissertation. *Entrance requirements:* For master's, minimum GPA of 3.0, 2 writing samples in French. *Application deadline:* Applications are processed on a rolling basis. Application fee: $60 ($75 for international students). Electronic applications accepted. *Financial support:* In 2007–08, 5 fellowships, 2 research assistantships, 31 teaching assistantships were awarded; tuition waivers (full and partial) also available. Financial award application deadline: 2/15. *Unit head:* Armine Mortimer, Head, 217-333-2000, Fax: 217-244-2223, E-mail: armine@uiuc.edu. *Application contact:* Peter Golato, Director of Graduate Program, 217-333-2020, Fax: 217-244-2223, E-mail: pgolato@uiuc.edu.

The University of Iowa, Graduate College, College of Liberal Arts and Sciences, Department of French and Italian, Iowa City, IA 52242-1316. Offers French (MA, PhD). *Faculty:* 10 full-time, 6 part-time/adjunct. *Students:* 6 full-time (5 women), 10 part-time (9 women); includes 2 minority (both African Americans), 7 international. 9 applicants, 56% accepted, 1 enrolled. In 2007, 3 doctorates awarded. *Degree requirements:* For master's, thesis optional, exam; for doctorate, comprehensive exam, thesis/dissertation. *Entrance requirements:* For master's and doctorate, GRE General Test, minimum GPA of 3.0. Additional exam requirements/recommendations for international students: Required—TOEFL (minimum score 550 paper-based; 213 computer-based; 81 iBT). *Application deadline:* For fall admission, 1/15 priority date for domestic and international students. Application fee: $60 ($85 for international students). Electronic applications accepted. *Expenses:* Tuition, state resident: part-time $349 per hour. Tuition, nonresident: part-time $349 per hour. Tuition and fees vary according to course load and program. *Financial support:* In 2007–08, 1 fellowship, 2 research assistantships with partial tuition reimbursements, 10 teaching assistantships with partial tuition reimbursements were awarded. Financial award applicants required to submit FAFSA. *Unit head:* Rob Ketterer, Acting Chair, 319-335-2253, Fax: 319-335-2270.

University of Kansas, Research and Graduate Studies, College of Liberal Arts and Sciences, Department of French and Italian, Lawrence, KS 66045. Offers French (MA, PhD). Part-time programs available. *Faculty:* 10. *Students:* 23 full-time (18 women), 1 (woman) part-time, 9 international. Average age 31. 9 applicants, 100% accepted, 6 enrolled. In 2007, 4 master's, 1 doctorate awarded. *Degree requirements:* For master's, one foreign language, comprehensive exam, thesis optional; for doctorate, 2 foreign languages, comprehensive exam, thesis/dissertation. *Entrance requirements:* For master's and doctorate, GRE. Additional exam requirements/recommendations for international students: Required—TOEFL, IELTS. *Application deadline:* For fall admission, 1/15 priority date for domestic and international students. Applications are processed on a rolling basis. Application fee: $55 ($60 for international students). Electronic applications accepted. *Expenses:* Tuition, state resident: full-time $5,838. Tuition, nonresident: full-time $13,409. Tuition and fees vary according to program. *Financial support:* Fellowships, teaching assistantships with full tuition reimbursements, unspecified assistantships available. Financial award applicants required to submit FAFSA. *Faculty research:* French literature and cultural studies; Francophone literature, film. *Unit head:* Van Kelly, Chair, 785-864-4056, Fax: 785-864-5179, E-mail: vkelly@ku.edu. *Application contact:* Caroline Jewers, Associate Professor, 785-864-9076, E-mail: cjewers@ku.edu.

University of Kentucky, Graduate School, College of Arts and Sciences, Program in French, Lexington, KY 40506-0032. Offers MA. *Faculty:* 29 full-time (10 women), 2 part-time/adjunct (1 woman). *Students:* 8 full-time (4 women), 3 part-time (2 women); includes 2 minority (both African Americans), 4 international. Average age 28. 9 applicants, 67% accepted, 4 enrolled. In 2007, 2 degrees awarded. *Degree requirements:* For master's, one foreign language, comprehensive exam. *Entrance requirements:* For master's, GRE General Test, minimum undergraduate GPA of 2.75. Additional exam requirements/recommendations for international students: Required—TOEFL (minimum score 550 paper-based; 213 computer-based). *Application deadline:* For fall admission, 7/17 priority date for domestic students, 2/1 priority date for international students; for spring admission, 12/13 priority date for domestic students, 6/15 priority date for international students. Application fee: $50 ($65 for international students). Electronic applications accepted. *Expenses:* Tuition, state resident: part-time $437 per credit hour. Tuition, nonresident: part-time $931 per credit hour. *Financial support:* In 2007–08, 9 students received support, including 1 fellowship, 8 teaching assistantships with full tuition reimbursements available (averaging $10,774 per year); research assistantships, Federal Work-Study, institutionally sponsored loans, scholarships/grants, traineeships, health care benefits, tuition waivers (partial), and unspecified assistantships also available. Support available to part-time students. Financial award application deadline: 3/15; financial award applicants required to submit FAFSA. *Faculty research:* The fables of Marie DeFrance, Rabelais and reading; the family romance in eighteenth century narrative; women of Dada and surrealism; postcolonialism; postmodernism. *Unit head:* Dr. Suzanne Pucci, Director of Graduate Studies, 859-257-5787, Fax: 859-257-3743, E-mail: spucci1@uky.edu. *Application contact:* Dr. Brian Jackson, Senior Associate Dean, 859-257-4667, Fax: 859-257-4676, E-mail: brian.jackson@uky.edu.

University of Lethbridge, School of Graduate Studies, Lethbridge, AB T1K 3M4, Canada. Offers accounting (MScM); addictions counseling (M Sc); agricultural biotechnology (M Sc); agricultural studies (M Sc, MA); anthropology (MA); archaeology (MA); art (MA); biochemistry (M Sc); biological sciences (M Sc); biomolecular science (PhD); biosystems and biodiversity (PhD); Canadian studies (MA); chemistry (M Sc); computer science (M Sc); computer science and geographical information science (M Sc); counseling psychology (M Ed); dramatic arts (MA); earth, space, and physical science (PhD); economics (MA); educational leadership (M Ed); English (MA); environmental science (M Sc); evolution and behavior (PhD); exercise science (M Sc); finance (MScM); French (MA); French/German (MA); French/Spanish (MA); general education (M Ed); general management (MScM); geography (M Sc, MA); German (MA); health sciences (M Sc, MA); history (MA); human resource management and labour relations (MScM); individualized multidisciplinary (M Sc, MA); information systems (MScM); international management (MScM); kinesiology (M Sc, MA); management (M Sc, MA); marketing (MScM); mathematics (M Sc); music (MA); Native American studies (MA); neuroscience (M Sc, PhD); new media (MA); nursing (M Sc); philosophy (MA); physics (M Sc); policy and strategy (MScM); political science (MA); psychology (M Sc, MA); religious studies (MA); sociology (MA); theoretical and computational science (PhD); urban and regional studies (MA). Part-time and evening/weekend programs available. *Students:* 215 full-time, 98 part-time. In 2007, 87 master's, 1 doctorate awarded. *Degree requirements:* For doctorate, comprehensive exam, thesis/dissertation. *Entrance requirements:* For master's, GMAT (M Sc in management), bachelor's degree in related field, minimum GPA of 3.0 during previous 20 graded semester courses, 2 years teaching or related experience (M Ed); for doctorate, master's degree, minimum graduate GPA of 3.5. Additional exam requirements/recommendations for international students: Required—TOEFL. Application fee: $60 Canadian dollars. *Financial support:* Fellowships, research assistantships, teaching assistantships, scholarships/grants, health care benefits, and unspecified assistantships available. *Faculty research:* Movement and brain plasticity, gibberellin physiology, photosynthesis, carbon cycling, molecular properties of main-group ring components. *Unit head:* Dr. Jo-Anne Fiske, Interim Dean, 403-329-2121, Fax: 403-329-2097. *Application contact:* Jennifer Geddes, Graduate Liaison Officer, 403-329-2762, Fax: 403-329-5159, E-mail: jennifer.geddes@uleth.ca.

University of Louisiana at Lafayette, Graduate School, College of Liberal Arts, Department of Modern Languages, Program in Francophone Studies, Lafayette, LA 70504. Offers PhD. *Degree requirements:* For doctorate, 2 foreign languages, comprehensive exam, thesis/dissertation. *Entrance requirements:* For doctorate, GRE General Test, minimum GPA of 2.75. Additional exam requirements/recommendations for international students: Required—TOEFL (minimum score 550 paper-based; 213 computer-based). Electronic applications accepted. *Faculty research:* Louisiana folklore, eighteenth century French literature, contemporary criticism.

University of Louisiana at Lafayette, Graduate School, College of Liberal Arts, Department of Modern Languages, Program in French, Lafayette, LA 70504. Offers MA. Part-time programs available. *Degree requirements:* For master's, 2 foreign languages, thesis or alternative. *Entrance requirements:* For master's, GRE General Test, minimum GPA of 2.75. Additional exam requirements/recommendations for international students: Required—TOEFL (minimum score 550 paper-based; 213 computer-based). Electronic applications accepted. *Faculty research:* Louisiana studies, nineteenth century French literature, Francophone studies.

University of Louisville, Graduate School, College of Arts and Sciences, Department of Classical and Modern Languages, Program in French, Louisville, KY 40292-0001. Offers MA. *Students:* 9 full-time (6 women), 9 part-time (6 women); includes 3 minority (2 African Americans, 1 Asian American or Pacific Islander), 1 international. Average age 34. In 2007, 5 degrees awarded. *Degree requirements:* For master's, one foreign language, thesis optional. *Entrance requirements:* For master's, GRE General Test. *Application deadline:* Applications are processed on a rolling basis. Application fee: $50. *Unit head:* Dr. Mary Makris, Acting Chair, Department of Classical and Modern Languages, 502-852-0491, Fax: 502-852-8885, E-mail: mmakris@louisville.edu.

University of Maine, Graduate School, College of Liberal Arts and Sciences, Department of Modern Languages and Classics, Orono, ME 04469. Offers French (MA, MAT). Part-time programs available. *Faculty:* 12 full-time (6 women). *Students:* 3 full-time (2 women), 8 part-time (6 women). Average age 41. 1 applicant, 100% accepted, 0 enrolled. In 2007, 2 master's awarded. *Degree requirements:* For master's, one foreign language, thesis (for some programs). *Entrance requirements:* For master's, GRE General Test. Additional exam requirements/recommendations for international students: Required—TOEFL. *Application deadline:* For fall admission, 2/1 priority date for domestic students. Applications are processed on a rolling basis. Application fee: $60. Electronic applications accepted. *Financial support:* In 2007–08, fellowships with tuition reimbursements (averaging $14,000 per year), 3 teaching assistantships with tuition reimbursements (averaging $9,010 per year) were awarded; research assistantships with tuition reimbursements, Federal Work-Study, tuition waivers (full and partial), and instructorships also available. Financial award application deadline: 3/1. *Faculty research:* Narratology, poetics, Quebec literature, theater, women's studies. *Unit head:* Dr. Eugene DelVecchio, Chair, 207-581-2072, Fax: 207-581-1832. *Application contact:* Scott G. Delcourt, Associate Dean of the Graduate School, 207-581-3219, Fax: 207-581-3232, E-mail: graduate@maine.edu.

University of Manitoba, Faculty of Graduate Studies, Faculty of Arts, Department of French, Spanish and Italian, Winnipeg, MB R3T 2N2, Canada. Offers MA, PhD. *Degree requirements:* For master's, one foreign language, thesis; for doctorate, 2 foreign languages, thesis/dissertation.

University of Maryland, College Park, Graduate Studies, College of Arts and Humanities, School of Languages, Literature, and Cultures, Modern French Studies Program, College Park, MD 20742. Offers PhD. *Students:* 12 full-time (all women), 2 part-time (both women), 6 international. 8 applicants, 50% accepted, 3 enrolled. In 2007, 2 degrees awarded. *Entrance requirements:* Additional exam requirements/recommendations for international students: Required—TOEFL. *Application deadline:* For fall admission, 5/1 for domestic students, 2/1 for international students; for spring admission, 10/1 for domestic students, 6/1 for international students. Application fee: $60. *Financial support:* In 2007–08, 1 fellowship (averaging $7,178 per year), 8 teaching assistantships (averaging $16,943 per year) were awarded. *Application contact:* Dean of Graduate School, 301-405-0358, Fax: 301-314-9305.

University of Maryland, College Park, Graduate Studies, College of Arts and Humanities, School of Languages, Literature, and Cultures, Program in French Language and Literature, College Park, MD 20742. Offers MA. *Students:* 6 full-time (all women), 3 part-time (2 women), 3 international. 8 applicants, 50% accepted, 3 enrolled. In 2007, 2 degrees awarded. *Degree requirements:* For master's, one foreign language, comprehensive exam, thesis or alternative. *Entrance requirements:* For master's, GRE General Test, GRE Subject Test, minimum GPA of 3.0, 3 letters of recommendation. Additional exam requirements/recommendations for international students: Required—TOEFL. *Application deadline:* For fall admission, 2/1 for domestic and international students. Applications are processed on a rolling basis. Application fee: $60. Electronic applications accepted. *Financial support:* In 2007–08, 1 fellowship with full tuition reimbursement (averaging $7,540 per year), 5 teaching assistantships with tuition reimbursements (averaging $16,413 per year) were awarded; Federal Work-Study also available. Support available to part-time students. Financial award applicants required to submit FAFSA. *Unit head:* Dr. Joseph Brami, Chair, 301-405-4026, Fax: 301-314-9938, E-mail: jbrami@umd.edu. *Application contact:* Dean of Graduate School, 301-405-4190, Fax: 301-314-9305.

University of Maryland, College Park, Graduate Studies, College of Arts and Humanities, School of Languages, Literature, and Cultures, Program in Second Language Acquisition and Application, College Park, MD 20742. Offers French (MA); German (MA); Japanese (MA); Russian (MA); second language instruction (PhD); second language learning (PhD); second language measurement and assessment (PhD); second language use (PhD); Spanish (MA). *Students:* 1 (woman) full-time, 1 international. 50 applicants, 14% accepted. *Entrance requirements:* For master's, BA or BS in related field, demonstrated language competency, 3 letters of reference. *Application deadline:* For fall admission, 1/15 for domestic students, 2/1 for international students; for spring admission, 9/15 for domestic students, 6/1 for international students. Applications are processed on a rolling basis. Application fee: $60. Electronic applications accepted. *Financial support:* In 2007–08, 1 research assistantship (averaging $20,450 per year) was awarded; fellowships also available. *Faculty research:* Second language acquisition, pedagogical perspectives, technological applications, language use in professional contexts. *Unit head:* Dr. Cynthia L. Martin, Acting Chair, 301-405-4244, E-mail: cmartin@umd.edu. *Application contact:* Dean of Graduate School, 301-405-0358, Fax: 301-314-9305.

University of Massachusetts Amherst, Graduate School, College of Humanities and Fine Arts, Department of French and Italian, Amherst, MA 01003. Offers French and Francophone studies (MA, MAT, PhD); Italian studies (MAT). Part-time programs available. *Faculty:* 9 full-time (4 women). *Students:* 9 full-time (7 women), 8 part-time (6 women); includes 1 minority (African American), 3 international. Average age 32. 16 applicants, 75% accepted, 6 enrolled. In 2007, 4 degrees awarded. *Degree requirements:* For master's, thesis or alternative. *Entrance requirements:* For master's, GRE General Test. Additional exam requirements/recommendations for international students: Required—TOEFL (minimum score 530 paper-based; 197 computer-based). *Application deadline:* For fall admission, 2/1 priority date for domestic and international students; for spring admission, 10/1 for domestic and international students. Applications are processed on a rolling basis. Application fee: $50 ($65 for international students). Electronic applications accepted. *Expenses:* Tuition, state resident: full-time $2,640; part-time $110 per credit. Tuition, nonresident: full-time $9,936; part-time $414 per credit. Required fees: $7,455. One-time fee: $332. Tuition and fees vary according to course load, campus/location, program and reciprocity agreements. *Financial support:* In 2007–08, 4 fellowships with full tuition reimbursements (averaging $5,766 per year), 7 research assistantships with full tuition reimbursements (averaging $7,803 per year), 19 teaching assistantships with full tuition reimbursements (averaging $11,099 per year) were awarded; career-related internships or fieldwork, Federal Work-Study, scholarships/grants, traineeships, and unspecified assistantships also available. Support available to part-time students. Financial award application deadline: 2/1. *Unit head:* Dr. Patrick Mensah, Head, 412-545-6697, Fax: 412-545-2314.

University of Memphis, Graduate School, College of Arts and Sciences, Department of Foreign Languages and Literatures, Memphis, TN 38152. Offers French (MA); Spanish (MA). Part-time programs available. *Faculty:* 13 full-time (7 women), 2 part-time/adjunct (0 women). *Students:* 17 full-time (12 women), 16 part-time (14 women); includes 9 minority (5 African Americans, 1 American Indian/Alaska Native, 3 Hispanic Americans), 6 international. Average age 33. 24 applicants, 88% accepted, 13 enrolled. In 2007, 4 degrees awarded. *Degree requirements:* For master's, one foreign language, comprehensive exam, thesis optional. *Entrance requirements:* For master's, GRE General Test. *Application deadline:* For fall admission,

French

University of Memphis (continued)
8/1 for domestic students; for spring admission, 12/1 for domestic students. Applications are processed on a rolling basis. Application fee: $35 ($60 for international students). *Expenses:* Tuition, state resident: full-time $6,990; part-time $377 per hour. Tuition, nonresident: full-time $17,818; part-time $830 per hour. Tuition and fees vary according to course load and program. *Financial support:* In 2007–08, 8 research assistantships with full tuition reimbursements (averaging $6,800 per year), 9 teaching assistantships with full tuition reimbursements (averaging $6,225 per year) were awarded. *Faculty research:* Spanish-American short story, Latin American women writers, French women of letters, Avevedo and Cervantes, 19th and 20th century peninsular literature, Brazilian culture and literature. *Unit head:* Dr. Ralph Albanese, Chairman, 901-678-2506, Fax: 901-678-5338, E-mail: ralbanes@memphis.edu. *Application contact:* Dr. Fernando Burgos, Coordinator of Graduate Studies, 901-678-3158, Fax: 901-678-5338, E-mail: fburgos@memphis.edu.

University of Miami, Graduate School, College of Arts and Sciences, Department of Modern Languages and Literatures, Coral Gables, FL 33124. Offers romance studies (PhD), including French, Spanish. *Faculty:* 23 full-time (14 women). *Students:* 24 full-time (14 women); includes 10 minority (3 African Americans, 2 Asian Americans or Pacific Islanders, 5 Hispanic Americans), 11 international. Average age 32. 25 applicants, 24% accepted, 6 enrolled. In 2007, 4 degrees awarded. *Median time to degree:* Of those who began their doctoral program in fall 1999, 100% received their degree in 8 years or less. *Degree requirements:* For doctorate, 2 foreign languages, thesis/dissertation, area exam, qualifying exam. *Entrance requirements:* For doctorate, 1 writing sample in English and 1 writing sample in French or Spanish, minimum GPA of 3.0; oral interview; letters of recommendation. Additional exam requirements/recommendations for international students: Required—TOEFL (minimum score 550 paper-based; 213 computer-based; 59 iBT), GRE General Test (recommended). *Application deadline:* For fall admission, 1/15 priority date for domestic and international students. Application fee: $50. Electronic applications accepted. *Financial support:* In 2007–08, 21 students received support, including 1 fellowship with full tuition reimbursement available (averaging $30,000 per year), 1 research assistantship, 16 teaching assistantships with full tuition reimbursements available (averaging $20,000 per year); career-related internships or fieldwork, Federal Work-Study, institutionally sponsored loans, scholarships/grants, health care benefits, and unspecified assistantships also available. Financial award application deadline: 3/15; financial award applicants required to submit FAFSA. *Faculty research:* Transatlantic studies, Caribbean studies, comparative literature, gender theory, cultural studies. *Unit head:* Prof. Anne J. Cruz, Chair, 305-284-5585, Fax: 305-284-2068, E-mail: ajcruz@miami.edu. *Application contact:* Prof. Gema Perez-Sanchez, Director of Graduate Studies, 305-284-4858 Ext. 7313, Fax: 305-284-2068, E-mail: gema@miami.edu.

University of Michigan, Horace H. Rackham School of Graduate Studies, College of Literature, Science, and the Arts, Department of Romance Languages and Literatures, Program in French, Ann Arbor, MI 48109. Offers PhD. *Faculty:* 9 full-time (5 women). *Students:* 25 full-time (19 women). Average age 31. 35 applicants, 11% accepted. In 2007, 2 degrees awarded. *Degree requirements:* For doctorate, 2 foreign languages, thesis/dissertation, oral defense of dissertation, preliminary exams. *Entrance requirements:* For doctorate, GRE General Test. Additional exam requirements/recommendations for international students: Required—TOEFL or Michigan English Language Assessment Battery. *Application deadline:* For fall admission, 1/1 for domestic students. Application fee: $60. Electronic applications accepted. *Financial support:* In 2007–08, 4 fellowships with full tuition reimbursements (averaging $20,000 per year) were awarded; teaching assistantships with full tuition reimbursements, institutionally sponsored loans, scholarships/grants, and unspecified assistantships also available. Financial award application deadline: 1/1. *Faculty research:* Comparative Romance studies, medieval and early modern studies, postcolonial and minority literatures, culture and materiality, reflection on the nature and function of scholarship. *Application contact:* Graduate Assistant, 734-763-0408, Fax: 734-764-8163, E-mail: rll-admissions@umich.edu.

University of Minnesota, Twin Cities Campus, Graduate School, College of Liberal Arts, Department of French and Italian, Minneapolis, MN 55455-0213. Offers French (MA, PhD). Part-time programs available. *Faculty:* 13 full-time (8 women), 2 part-time/adjunct (0 women). *Students:* 29 full-time, 16 part-time; includes 4 minority (3 African Americans, 1 Hispanic American), 10 international. Average age 26. 24 applicants, 46% accepted, 9 enrolled. In 2007, 4 master's, 5 doctorates awarded. *Degree requirements:* For master's, one foreign language, comprehensive exam, thesis optional; for doctorate, one foreign language, thesis/dissertation, individualized exam on topic areas. *Entrance requirements:* For master's and doctorate, GRE, minimum GPA of 3.25 (recommended). Additional exam requirements/recommendations for international students: Required—TOEFL (minimum score 550 paper-based; 213 computer-based). *Application deadline:* For fall admission, 1/1 priority date for domestic and international students. Applications are processed on a rolling basis. Application fee: $55 ($75 for international students). Electronic applications accepted. *Financial support:* In 2007–08, 2 fellowships with full tuition reimbursements (averaging $16,000 per year), research assistantships with full tuition reimbursements (averaging $12,500 per year), 29 teaching assistantships with full tuition reimbursements (averaging $12,500 per year) were awarded; Federal Work-Study, institutionally sponsored loans, scholarships/grants, health care benefits, and unspecified assistantships also available. Support available to part-time students. Financial award application deadline: 1/15; financial award applicants required to submit FAFSA. *Faculty research:* Francophone literature, cultural studies, feminism, critical theory, medieval studies. *Unit head:* Prof. Daniel Brewer, Chair, 612-624-0565, Fax: 612-624-6021, E-mail: dbrewer@umn.edu. *Application contact:* Prof. Judith Preckshot, Director of Graduate Studies, 612-624-4308, Fax: 612-624-6021, E-mail: preck001@umn.edu.

University of Mississippi, Graduate School, College of Liberal Arts, Department of Modern Languages, Oxford, University, MS 38677. Offers French (MA); German (MA); Spanish (MA). *Faculty:* 38 full-time (26 women), 2 part-time/adjunct (both women). *Students:* 13 full-time (5 women), 4 part-time (3 women); includes 3 minority (2 African Americans, 1 American Indian/Alaska Native), 3 international. In 2007, 3 degrees awarded. *Degree requirements:* For master's, thesis (for some programs). *Entrance requirements:* For master's, GRE General Test, minimum GPA of 3.0. Additional exam requirements/recommendations for international students: Required—TOEFL. *Application deadline:* For fall admission, 2/1 for domestic students; for spring admission, 10/1 for domestic students. Applications are processed on a rolling basis. Application fee: $25. Electronic applications accepted. *Expenses:* Tuition, state resident: full-time $4,932. Tuition, nonresident: full-time $11,436. *Financial support:* Scholarships/grants available. Financial award application deadline: 3/1; financial award applicants required to submit FAFSA. *Unit head:* Dr. Donald Dyer, Chair, 662-915-7298, Fax: 662-915-1086, E-mail: mlangs@olemiss.edu.

University of Missouri–Columbia, Graduate School, College of Arts and Sciences, Department of Romance Languages and Literature, Program in French, Columbia, MO 65211. Offers MA, PhD. *Degree requirements:* For master's, one foreign language; for doctorate, 4 foreign languages, thesis/dissertation. *Entrance requirements:* For master's and doctorate, GRE General Test, minimum GPA of 3.0.

The University of Montana, Graduate School, College of Arts and Sciences, Department of Modern and Classical Languages and Literatures, Missoula, MT 59812-0002. Offers French (MA); German (MA); Spanish (MA). *Degree requirements:* For master's, one foreign language. *Entrance requirements:* For master's, GRE General Test. Additional exam requirements/recommendations for international students: Required—TOEFL.

University of Nebraska–Lincoln, Graduate College, College of Arts and Sciences, Department of Modern Languages and Literatures, Lincoln, NE 68588. Offers French (MA, PhD); German (MA, PhD); Spanish (MA, PhD). *Degree requirements:* For master's, thesis optional; for doctorate, comprehensive exam, thesis/dissertation. *Entrance requirements:* For master's and doctorate, writing sample in target language. Additional exam requirements/recommendations for international students: Required—TOEFL (minimum score 550 paper-based; 213 computer-based). Electronic applications accepted. *Faculty research:* French, German, and Spanish language, literature, and culture.

University of Nevada, Reno, Graduate School, College of Liberal Arts, Department of Foreign Languages and Literatures, Reno, NV 89557. Offers French (MA); German (MA); Spanish (MA). *Faculty:* 18. *Students:* 8 full-time (5 women), 10 part-time (9 women); includes 3 minority (all Hispanic Americans) Average age 29. 12 applicants, 67% accepted, 7 enrolled. In 2007, 5 degrees awarded. *Degree requirements:* For master's, one foreign language, thesis optional. *Entrance requirements:* For master's, GRE General Test, minimum GPA of 2.75. Additional exam requirements/recommendations for international students: Required—TOEFL. *Application deadline:* For fall admission, 3/1 priority date for domestic students; for spring admission, 11/1 for domestic students. Applications are processed on a rolling basis. Application fee: $60 ($95 for international students). *Expenses:* Tuition, state resident: full-time $2,774; part-time $154 per credit. Tuition, nonresident: full-time $13,578; part-time $330 per credit. Required fees: $49 per semester. *Financial support:* In 2007–08, 7 teaching assistantships were awarded; Federal Work-Study and institutionally sponsored loans also available. Financial award application deadline: 3/1. *Faculty research:* Thirteenth-century mysticism, contemporary Spanish and Latin American poetry and theater, French interrelation between narration and photography, exile literature and Holocaust. *Unit head:* Dr. Miriella Melara, Graduate Program Director, 775-784-6055.

University of New Mexico, Graduate School, College of Arts and Sciences, Department of Foreign Languages and Literature, Albuquerque, NM 87131-2039. Offers comparative literature and cultural studies (MA); French (MA); French studies (PhD); German studies (MA). Part-time programs available. *Faculty:* 15 full-time (11 women), 8 part-time/adjunct (4 women). *Students:* 9 full-time (8 women), 4 part-time (2 women), 6 international. Average age 33. 9 applicants, 44% accepted, 3 enrolled. In 2007, 5 master's awarded. *Degree requirements:* For master's, one foreign language, thesis optional; for doctorate, 2 foreign languages, thesis/dissertation. *Application deadline:* For fall admission, 2/1 priority date for domestic students; for spring admission, 10/1 priority date for domestic students. Application fee: $50. Electronic applications accepted. *Financial support:* In 2007–08, 20 teaching assistantships with tuition reimbursements (averaging $12,023 per year) were awarded; Federal Work-Study, health care benefits, and unspecified assistantships also available. Financial award application deadline: 3/1; financial award applicants required to submit FAFSA. *Faculty research:* German, Russian, Italian, Japanese, French, Comparative Lit, culture studies, classics. Total annual research expenditures: $4,750. *Unit head:* Dr. Natasha Kolchevska, Chair, 505-277-4771, Fax: 505-277-3599, E-mail: nakol@unm.edu. *Application contact:* Dean Aragon, Application and Graduation Advisor, 505-277-4471, Fax: 505-277-3599, E-mail: peaslee@unm.edu.

The University of North Carolina at Chapel Hill, Graduate School, College of Arts and Sciences, Department of Romance Languages, Chapel Hill, NC 27599. Offers French (MA, PhD); Italian (MA, PhD); Portuguese (MA, PhD); Romance languages (MA, PhD); Romance philology (MA, PhD); Spanish (MA, PhD). *Degree requirements:* For master's, one foreign language, comprehensive exam, thesis; for doctorate, 2 foreign languages, comprehensive exam, thesis/dissertation. *Entrance requirements:* For master's and doctorate, GRE General Test, minimum GPA of 3.0. Additional exam requirements/recommendations for international students: Required—TOEFL (minimum score 550 paper-based; 213 computer-based). Electronic applications accepted.

The University of North Carolina at Greensboro, Graduate School, College of Arts and Sciences, Department of Romance Languages, Program in French, Greensboro, NC 27412-5001. Offers MA. *Faculty:* 2 full-time (0 women). *Students:* 8 full-time (6 women); includes 1 minority (African American). *Degree requirements:* For master's, one foreign language, comprehensive exam, thesis or alternative. *Entrance requirements:* For master's, GRE General Test, 3-5 minute tape demonstrating foreign language proficiency, composition in French, sample paper in English. Additional exam requirements/recommendations for international students: Required—TOEFL. *Application deadline:* For spring admission, 11/1 for domestic students. Applications are processed on a rolling basis. Application fee: $45. Electronic applications accepted. *Financial support:* Research assistantships, teaching assistantships available. *Unit head:* Dr. Roch C Smith, Director of Graduate Studies, 336-334-5655, Fax: 336-334-5358, E-mail: roch_smith@uncg.edu. *Application contact:* Michelle Harkleroad, Director of Graduate Admissions, 336-334-4884, Fax: 336-334-4424, E-mail: mbharkle@uncg.edu.

University of Northern Iowa, Graduate College, College of Humanities and Fine Arts, Department of Modern Languages, Program in French, Cedar Falls, IA 50614. Offers French (MA); teaching English to speakers of other languages/French (MA). Part-time and evening/weekend programs available. *Students:* 5 full-time (2 women), 12 part-time (11 women), 5 international. 8 applicants, 75% accepted, 1 enrolled. In 2007, 5 degrees awarded. *Degree requirements:* For master's, one foreign language, comprehensive exam, thesis or alternative. *Entrance requirements:* For master's, minimum GPA of 3.0, hold a valid teaching license and have documentation of successful teaching experience. Additional exam requirements/recommendations for international students: Required—TOEFL (minimum score 600 paper-based; 250 computer-based; 100 iBT). *Application deadline:* For fall admission, 8/1 priority date for domestic students. Applications are processed on a rolling basis. Application fee: $30 ($50 for international students). Electronic applications accepted. *Expenses:* Tuition, state resident: full-time $6,246; part-time $694 per credit hour. Tuition, nonresident: full-time $14,554; part-time $694 per credit hour. Required fees: $838; $119 per semester. *Financial support:* Career-related internships or fieldwork, Federal Work-Study, and tuition waivers (full and partial) available. Support available to part-time students. Financial award application deadline: 2/1. *Unit head:* Dr. Anne Lair, Coordinator, 319-273-2183, Fax: 319-273-2848, E-mail: anne.lair@uni.edu.

University of North Texas, Robert B. Toulouse School of Graduate Studies, College of Arts and Sciences, Department of Foreign Languages and Literatures, Denton, TX 76203. Offers French (MA); Spanish (MA). Part-time programs available. *Faculty:* 31 full-time (22 women). *Students:* 23 full-time (17 women), 13 part-time (10 women); includes 16 minority (3 African Americans, 13 Hispanic Americans), 1 international. Average age 30. 35 applicants, 74% accepted, 16 enrolled. In 2007, 8 degrees awarded. *Degree requirements:* For master's, 2 foreign languages, comprehensive exam, thesis optional, proficiency in a second foreign language. *Entrance requirements:* For master's, GRE General Test, minimum undergraduate GPA of 3.0, curriculum vita, 250 word essay in French or Spanish, 12 advanced credita in French or Spanish. Additional exam requirements/recommendations for international students: Recommended—TOEFL (minimum score 550 paper-based; 213 computer-based). *Application deadline:* For fall admission, 7/15 for domestic students; for spring admission, 11/15 for domestic students. Application fee: $50 ($75 for international students). *Financial support:* In 2007–08, 7 fellowships (averaging $9,534 per year), 5 teaching assistantships (averaging $9,534 per year) were awarded; career-related internships or fieldwork, Federal Work-Study, and institutionally sponsored loans also available. Financial award application deadline: 4/1. *Faculty research:* Literature of Austria, France, Germany, Latin America, Spain; culture/civilization; applied linguistics. *Unit head:* Dr. Marie-Christine Koop, Chair, 940-565-2404, Fax: 940-565-2581, E-mail: koop@unt.edu.

University of Notre Dame, Graduate School, College of Arts and Letters, Division of Humanities, Department of Romance Languages and Literatures, Notre Dame, IN 46556. Offers French and Francophone studies (MA); Iberian and Latin American studies (MA); Italian studies (MA); Romance literatures (MA). Part-time programs available. *Faculty:* 25 full-time (10 women), 4 part-time/adjunct (all women). *Students:* 18 full-time (12 women); includes 4 minority (all Hispanic Americans), 3 international. 28 applicants, 61% accepted, 9 enrolled. In 2007, 12 degrees awarded. *Degree requirements:* For master's, 2 foreign languages, comprehensive exam, thesis optional. *Entrance requirements:* For master's, GRE General Test, BA in target language. Additional exam requirements/recommendations for international students: Required—TOEFL (minimum score 600 paper-based; 250 computer-based; 80 iBT). *Application deadline:* For fall admission, 2/1 priority date for domestic students, 2/1 for international students.

Application fee: $50. Electronic applications accepted. *Financial support:* In 2007–08, 1 fellowship (averaging $15,000 per year), 10 teaching assistantships with full tuition reimbursements (averaging $12,000 per year) were awarded; research assistantships, tuition waivers (full) also available. Financial award application deadline: 2/1. *Faculty research:* Literature of discovery and exploration, modern literature, literary criticism, medieval literature, feminist critical theory. *Unit head:* Dr. John Welle, Director of Graduate Studies, 574-631-6887, Fax: 574-631-3493, E-mail: al.romland.1@nd.edu. *Application contact:* Dr. Jarren Gonzales, Director of Graduate Admissions, 574-631-7706, Fax: 574-631-4183.

University of Oklahoma, Graduate College, College of Arts and Sciences, Department of Modern Languages, Program in French, Norman, OK 73019-0390. Offers MA, PhD, MBA/MA. Part-time programs available. *Students:* 10 full-time (7 women), 3 part-time (all women); includes 2 minority (1 African American, 1 Hispanic American), 5 international. 5 applicants, 80% accepted, 4 enrolled. In 2007, 1 master's awarded. Terminal master's awarded for partial completion of doctoral program. *Degree requirements:* For master's, 2 foreign languages, comprehensive exam, thesis optional, departmental qualifying exam; for doctorate, 3 foreign languages, comprehensive exam, thesis/dissertation, departmental qualifying exam. *Entrance requirements:* For master's, BA in French or equivalent, minimum GPA of 3.0 in last 60 hours, 3 letters of recommendation. Additional exam requirements/recommendations for international students: Required—TOEFL (minimum score 550 paper-based; 213 computer-based). *Application deadline:* For fall admission, 6/1 priority date for domestic students, 4/1 for international students; for spring admission, 11/1 for domestic students, 9/1 for international students. Applications are processed on a rolling basis. Application fee: $40 ($90 for international students). Electronic applications accepted. *Expenses:* Tuition, state resident: full-time $3,451; part-time $144 per credit hour. Tuition, nonresident: full-time $12,432; part-time $518 per credit hour. Required fees: $1,925; $70 per credit hour. $122 per semester. *Financial support:* Teaching assistantships with partial tuition reimbursements, scholarships/grants, health care benefits, and unspecified assistantships available. Financial award applicants required to submit FAFSA. *Faculty research:* French and Francophone literature and cultural studies; history of medicine; critical theory; food and culture; European culture and identity. *Application contact:* Dr. Michael E. Winston, Associate Professor, 405-325-5088, Fax: 405-325-0103, E-mail: mewinston@ou.edu.

University of Oregon, Graduate School, College of Arts and Sciences, Department of Romance Languages, Program in French, Eugene, OR 97403. Offers MA. Part-time programs available. *Students:* 7 applicants, 86% accepted. In 2007, 5 degrees awarded. *Degree requirements:* For master's, one foreign language. *Entrance requirements:* For master's, GRE General Test, minimum GPA of 3.0. Additional exam requirements/recommendations for international students: Required—TOEFL. Application fee: $50. *Financial support:* Teaching assistantships available. *Application contact:* Barbara VerWest, Admissions Contact, 541-346-4013, E-mail: verwest@uoregon.edu.

University of Ottawa, Faculty of Graduate and Postdoctoral Studies, Faculty of Arts, Department of Lettres Françaises, Ottawa, ON K1N 6N5, Canada. Offers MA, PhD. *Degree requirements:* For master's, thesis or alternative; for doctorate, thesis/dissertation, oral exam. *Entrance requirements:* For master's, honors degree or equivalent, minimum B average; for doctorate, master's degree, minimum B+ average. Electronic applications accepted. *Faculty research:* Littérature française, du Moyen-Âge á nos jours; littérature québécoise, des origines au XXe siećle; création littéraire.

University of Pennsylvania, School of Arts and Sciences, Graduate Group in Romance Languages, Philadelphia, PA 19104. Offers French (AM, PhD); Italian (AM, PhD); Spanish (AM, PhD). Terminal master's awarded for partial completion of doctoral program. *Degree requirements:* For master's, one foreign language, thesis or alternative; for doctorate, 2 foreign languages, thesis/dissertation. *Entrance requirements:* For master's and doctorate, GRE General Test. Additional exam requirements/recommendations for international students: Required—TOEFL. Electronic applications accepted. *Faculty research:* Literary theory and criticism, cultural studies, history of Romance literatures, gender studies.

University of Pittsburgh, School of Arts and Sciences, Department of French and Italian, Program in French, Pittsburgh, PA 15260. Offers MA, PhD. Part-time programs available. *Faculty:* 6 full-time (4 women). *Students:* 18 full-time (10 women), 4 international. Average age 32. 12 applicants, 75% accepted, 7 enrolled. In 2007, 3 master's, 3 doctorates awarded. Terminal master's awarded for partial completion of doctoral program. *Median time to degree:* Of those who began their doctoral program in fall 1999, 0% received their degree in 8 years or less. *Degree requirements:* For master's, 2 foreign languages, comprehensive exam, seminar paper; for doctorate, 3 foreign languages, comprehensive exam, thesis/dissertation, dissertation defense. *Entrance requirements:* For master's and doctorate, GRE General Test, interview, 2 writing samples, essay. Additional exam requirements/recommendations for international students: Required—TOEFL (minimum score 554 paper-based; 213 computer-based; 80 iBT). *Application deadline:* For fall admission, 1/10 priority date for domestic and international students. Application fee: $50. Electronic applications accepted. *Financial support:* In 2007–08, 15 students received support, including 2 fellowships with full tuition reimbursements available (averaging $17,081 per year), 13 teaching assistantships with full and partial tuition reimbursements available (averaging $14,845 per year); career-related internships or fieldwork, Federal Work-Study, institutionally sponsored loans, scholarships/grants, health care benefits, tuition waivers (partial), and unspecified assistantships also available. Support available to part-time students. Financial award application deadline: 1/10; financial award applicants required to submit FAFSA. *Faculty research:* Literature and politics, literature and the arts, intellectual history of European modernity, French cinema, Francophone studies. Total annual research expenditures: $26,000. *Application contact:* Dr. Todd Reeser, Graduate Director, 412-624-6224, Fax: 412-624-6263, E-mail: reeser@pitt.edu.

University of Regina, Faculty of Graduate Studies and Research, Faculty of Arts, Department of French, Regina, SK S4S 0A2, Canada. Offers MA. *Faculty:* 5 full-time (1 woman), 1 part-time/adjunct (0 women). *Students:* 2 full-time (1 woman). 2 applicants, 100% accepted, 1 enrolled. In 2007, 2 degrees awarded. *Degree requirements:* For master's, thesis, 2 seminar presentations. *Entrance requirements:* Additional exam requirements/recommendations for international students: Required—TOEFL (minimum score 580 paper-based; 237 computer-based; 88 iBT). *Application deadline:* Applications are processed on a rolling basis. Application fee: $85 ($100 for international students). Electronic applications accepted. *Financial support:* In 2007–08, fellowships (averaging $15,750 per year), research assistantships (averaging $13,875 per year), teaching assistantships (averaging $13,060 per year) were awarded; scholarships/grants also available. Financial award application deadline: 6/15. *Faculty research:* Literature of the sixteenth- through twentieth-centuries in France, French Canadian literature, literary criticism, translation, history of ideas. *Unit head:* Dr. Emmanuel Aito, Graduate Program Coordinator, 306-585-4323, Fax: 306-585-4827, E-mail: emmanuel.aito@uregina.ca.

University of Saskatchewan, College of Graduate Studies and Research, College of Arts and Sciences, Department of Languages and Linguistics, Saskatoon, SK S7N 5A2, Canada. Offers MA. *Degree requirements:* For master's, 2 foreign languages, thesis. *Entrance requirements:* Additional exam requirements/recommendations for international students: Required—TOEFL.

University of South Africa, College of Human Sciences, Pretoria, South Africa. Offers adult education (M Ed); African languages (MA, PhD); African politics (MA, PhD); Afrikaans (MA, PhD); ancient history (MA, PhD); ancient Near Eastern studies (MA, PhD); anthropology (MA, PhD); applied linguistics (MA); Arabic (MA, PhD); archaeology (MA); art history (MA); Biblical archaeology (MA); Biblical studies (M Th, D Th, PhD); Christian spirituality (M Th, D Th); church history (M Th, D Th); classical studies (MA, PhD); clinical psychology (MA); communication (MA, PhD); comparative education (M Ed, Ed D); consulting psychology (D Admin, D Com, PhD); curriculum studies (M Ed, Ed D); development studies (M Admin, MA, D Admin, PhD); didactics (M Ed, Ed D); education (M Tech); education management (M Ed, Ed D); educational psychology (M Ed); English (MA); environmental education (M Ed); French (MA, PhD); German (MA, PhD); Greek (MA); guidance and counseling (M Ed); health studies (MA, PhD), including health sciences education (MA), health services management (MA), medical and surgical nursing science (critical care general) (MA), midwifery and neonatal nursing science (MA), trauma and emergency care (MA); history (MA, PhD); history of education (Ed D); inclusive education (M Ed, Ed D); information and communications technology policy and regulation (MA); information science (MA, MIS, PhD); international politics (MA, PhD); Islamic studies (MA, PhD); Italian (MA, PhD); Judaica (MA, PhD); linguistics (MA, PhD); mathematical education (M Ed); mathematics education (MA); missiology (M Th, D Th); modern Hebrew (MA, PhD); musicology (MA, MMus, D Mus, PhD); natural science education (M Ed); New Testament (M Th, D Th); Old Testament (D Th); pastoral therapy (M Th, D Th); philosophy (MA); philosophy of education (M Ed, Ed D); politics (MA, PhD); Portuguese (MA, PhD); practical theology (M Th, D Th); psychology (MA, MS, PhD); psychology of education (M Ed, Ed D); public health (MA); religious studies (MA, D Th, PhD); Romance languages (MA); Russian (MA, PhD); Semitic languages (MA, PhD); social behavior studies in HIV/AIDS (MA); social science (mental health) (MA); social science in development studies (MA); social science in psychology (MA); social science in social work (MA); social science in sociology (MA); social work (MSW, DSW, PhD); socio-education (M Ed, Ed D); sociolinguistics (MA); sociology (MA, PhD); Spanish (MA, PhD); systematic theology (M Th, D Th); TESOL (teaching English to speakers of other languages) (MA); theological ethics (M Th, D Th); theory of literature (MA, PhD); urban ministries (D Th); urban ministry (M Th).

University of South Carolina, The Graduate School, College of Arts and Sciences, Department of Languages, Literatures, and Cultures, Columbia, SC 29208. Offers comparative literature (MA, PhD); foreign languages (MAT), including French, German, Spanish; French (MA); German (MA); Spanish (MA). MAT offered in cooperation with the College of Education. Part-time programs available. *Faculty:* 39 full-time (19 women). *Students:* 43 full-time (31 women), 19 part-time (12 women); includes 12 minority (3 African Americans, 1 Asian American or Pacific Islander, 8 Hispanic Americans), 15 international. Average age 29. 40 applicants, 65% accepted, 18 enrolled. In 2007, 7 master's awarded. *Degree requirements:* For master's, one foreign language, comprehensive exam, thesis optional; for doctorate, 2 foreign languages, comprehensive exam, thesis/dissertation. *Entrance requirements:* For master's and doctorate, GRE General Test, writing sample. Additional exam requirements/recommendations for international students: Required—TOEFL (minimum score 230 computer-based; 75 iBT). *Application deadline:* For fall admission, 2/1 priority date for domestic and international students. Applications are processed on a rolling basis. Application fee: $40. Electronic applications accepted. *Expenses:* Tuition, state resident: part-time $440 per hour. Tuition, nonresident: part-time $936 per hour. Required fees: $17 per hour. Tuition and fees vary according to program. *Financial support:* In 2007–08, 40 teaching assistantships with full tuition reimbursements (averaging $11,000 per year) were awarded; fellowships, research assistantships with full tuition reimbursements also available. Financial award application deadline: 2/1. *Faculty research:* Modern literature, linguistics, literature and culture, medieval literature, literary theory. Total annual research expenditures: $23,000. *Unit head:* Dr. Marja Warehime, Chair, 803-777-9734, Fax: 803-777-0454, E-mail: warehime@sc.edu. *Application contact:* Dr. Nicholas Vazsonyi, Graduate Director, 803-777-2935, Fax: 803-777-0454, E-mail: vazsonyi@sc.edu.

University of Southern California, Graduate School, College of Letters, Arts and Sciences, Department of French and Italian, Los Angeles, CA 90089. Offers French (MA, PhD). *Faculty:* 8 full-time (5 women). *Students:* 7 full-time (4 women), 2 part-time (both women); includes 2 minority (both Hispanic Americans), 4 international. 5 applicants, 40% accepted. In 2007, 1 degree awarded. *Degree requirements:* For doctorate, one foreign language, thesis/dissertation. *Entrance requirements:* For doctorate, GRE General Test. *Application deadline:* For fall admission, 1/1 priority date for domestic students. Application fee: $85. *Financial support:* In 2007–08, 10 students received support, including fellowships with full tuition reimbursements available (averaging $19,300 per year), teaching assistantships with full tuition reimbursements available (averaging $18,800 per year); scholarships/grants also available. Financial award application deadline: 2/15; financial award applicants required to submit FAFSA. *Faculty research:* French renaissance, French women writers autobiographical writing. *Unit head:* Dr. Panivong Norindr, Chair, 213-740-3700.

University of South Florida, Graduate School, College of Arts and Sciences, Department of World Language Education, Program in French, Tampa, FL 33620-9951. Offers MA. *Students:* 5 full-time (4 women), 3 part-time (2 women); includes 3 minority (all Hispanic Americans), 3 international. 8 applicants, 75% accepted, 4 enrolled. In 2007, 3 degrees awarded. *Entrance requirements:* For master's, 36 hours of graduate course work in French, minimum GPA of 3.0. *Application deadline:* For fall admission, 6/1 for domestic students; for spring admission, 10/15 for domestic students. Application fee: $30. *Application contact:* Roberta Tucker, Program Director, 813-974-2548, Fax: 813-974-1718, E-mail: tucker@cas.usf.edu.

The University of Tennessee, Graduate School, College of Arts and Sciences, Department of Modern Foreign Languages and Literatures, Program in French, Knoxville, TN 37996. Offers MA. *Degree requirements:* For master's, one foreign language, thesis or alternative. *Entrance requirements:* For master's, minimum GPA of 2.7. Additional exam requirements/recommendations for international students: Required—TOEFL. Electronic applications accepted.

The University of Tennessee, Graduate School, College of Arts and Sciences, Department of Modern Foreign Languages and Literatures, Program in Modern Foreign Languages, Knoxville, TN 37996. Offers applied linguistics (PhD); French (PhD); German (PhD); Italian (PhD); Portuguese (PhD); Russian (PhD); Spanish (PhD). *Degree requirements:* For doctorate, 2 foreign languages, thesis/dissertation. *Entrance requirements:* For doctorate, minimum GPA of 2.7. Additional exam requirements/recommendations for international students: Required—TOEFL. Electronic applications accepted.

The University of Texas at Arlington, Graduate School, College of Liberal Arts, Department of Modern Languages, Arlington, TX 76019. Offers French (MA); Spanish (MA). Part-time and evening/weekend programs available. *Faculty:* 5 full-time (3 women). *Students:* 7 full-time (3 women), 27 part-time (21 women); includes 12 minority (3 African Americans, 9 Hispanic Americans), 2 international. In 2007, 1 degree awarded. *Degree requirements:* For master's, 2 foreign languages, thesis optional. *Entrance requirements:* For master's, GRE General Test, minimum GPA of 3.0, 3 letters of recommendation. Additional exam requirements/recommendations for international students: Required—TOEFL (minimum score 550 paper-based; 213 computer-based). *Application deadline:* For fall admission, 6/16 for domestic students. Applications are processed on a rolling basis. Application fee: $35 ($50 for international students). *Expenses:* Tuition, state resident: full-time $5,934. Tuition, nonresident: full-time $10,938. *Financial support:* In 2007–08, teaching assistantships (averaging $6,600 per year); fellowships, research assistantships also available. Financial award application deadline: 6/1; financial award applicants required to submit FAFSA. *Unit head:* Dr. A. Raymond Elliott, Chair, 817-272-3161, Fax: 817-272-5408, E-mail: elliott@uta.edu. *Application contact:* Dr. Aimee Israel-Pelletier, Graduate Advisor, 817-272-3161, Fax: 817-272-5408, E-mail: aip@uta.edu.

The University of Texas at Austin, Graduate School, College of Liberal Arts, Department of French and Italian, Austin, TX 78712-1111. Offers French (MA, PhD); Romance linguistics (MA, PhD). Part-time programs available. *Degree requirements:* For master's, one foreign language, thesis; for doctorate, 2 foreign languages, thesis/dissertation. *Entrance requirements:* For master's, GRE General Test, minimum GPA of 3.0, bachelor's degree in French or equivalent; for doctorate, GRE General Test, minimum GPA of 3.0, master's degree in French. Additional exam requirements/recommendations for international students: Required—TOEFL. Electronic applications accepted. *Faculty research:* Nineteenth-century Italian literature, Italian Renaissance, twentieth-century French literature, Francophone literature, fifteenth-century literature and culture.

The University of Toledo, College of Graduate Studies, College of Arts and Sciences, Department of Foreign Languages, Toledo, OH 43606-3390. Offers French (MA); German (MA); Spanish (MA). Part-time programs available. *Faculty:* 8. *Students:* 1 (woman) full-time,

French

The University of Toledo (continued)
3 part-time (2 women); includes 1 minority (Hispanic American) Average age 46. 7 applicants, 100% accepted, 3 enrolled. In 2007, 4 degrees awarded. *Degree requirements:* For master's, one foreign language, comprehensive reading exam in 1 additional foreign language. *Application deadline:* For fall admission, 1/15 priority date for domestic students. Applications are processed on a rolling basis. Application fee: $45. Electronic applications accepted. *Financial support:* In 2007–08, 1 teaching assistantship with full tuition reimbursement (averaging $7,600 per year) was awarded; Federal Work-Study, institutionally sponsored loans, scholarships/grants, tuition waivers (full), and unspecified assistantships also available. Support available to part-time students. Financial award application deadline: 4/1; financial award applicants required to submit FAFSA. *Unit head:* Dr. Antonio Varela, Chair, 419-530-2657, Fax: 419-530-2657, E-mail: avarela@uoft02.utoledo.edu.

University of Toronto, School of Graduate Studies, Humanities Division, Department of French, Toronto, ON M5S 1A1, Canada. Offers French language and literature (MA, PhD). Part-time programs available. *Faculty:* 23 full-time, 39 part-time/adjunct. *Students:* 93 full-time (76 women), 2 part-time, 6 international. 70 applicants, 70% accepted. In 2007, 12 master's, 2 doctorates awarded. *Degree requirements:* For master's, research essay; for doctorate, one foreign language, thesis/dissertation, field exam. *Entrance requirements:* For master's, 2 letters of reference, writing sample, minimum B+ average overall and in French, undergraduate major in French; for doctorate, 7 courses in French language and literature, minimum A-average, writing sample. *Application deadline:* For fall admission, 1/15 priority date for domestic students. Application fee: $100 Canadian dollars. *Financial support:* Fellowships with full tuition reimbursements, teaching assistantships with full tuition reimbursements available. *Unit head:* Prof. Parth Bhatt, Chair, 416-926-2304, Fax: 416-926-2328, E-mail: french.chair@utoronto.ca. *Application contact:* Monique Lecerf, Administrative Assistant and Student Counselor, 416-926-2307, Fax: 416-926-2328, E-mail: french.graduate@utoronto.ca.

University of Utah, The Graduate School, College of Humanities, Department of Languages and Literature, Salt Lake City, UT 84112-1107. Offers comparative literary and cultural studies (MA, PhD); French (MA, MALP); German (MA, MALP, PhD); language pedagogy (MALP); Spanish (MA, MALP, PhD); world languages with secondary teaching licensure (MA). *Faculty:* 38 full-time (21 women). *Students:* 28 full-time (15 women), 12 part-time (10 women); includes 10 minority (all Hispanic Americans), 7 international. Average age 35. 32 applicants, 47% accepted, 10 enrolled. In 2007, 14 master's, 2 doctorates awarded. Terminal master's awarded for partial completion of doctoral program. *Median time to degree:* Of those who began their doctoral program in fall 1999, 66% received their degree in 8 years or less. *Degree requirements:* For master's, standard proficiency in 2 languages other than English, comprehensive exam or thesis; for doctorate, comprehensive exam, standard proficiency in 2 languages other than English and language of study, advanced proficiency in 1 language other than English and language of study, dissertation. *Entrance requirements:* For master's, bachelor's degree or strong undergraduate record in target languages, GPA of 3.0, literature-survey courses; for doctorate, successful completion of MA and advanced proficiency in a target language. Additional exam requirements/recommendations for international students: Required—TOEFL (minimum score 500 paper-based; 173 computer-based). *Application deadline:* For fall admission, 2/1 priority date for domestic students, 1/15 priority date for international students. Application fee: $45 ($65 for international students). Electronic applications accepted. *Financial support:* In 2007–08, 25 students received support, including 25 teaching assistantships with full tuition reimbursements available (averaging $11,000 per year); fellowships with tuition reimbursements available, health care benefits also available. Financial award application deadline: 2/1; financial award applicants required to submit FAFSA. *Faculty research:* Literary theory, stylistics, Russian and Soviet literature, existentialism, theory of criticism. Total annual research expenditures: $35,321. *Unit head:* Dr. Christine A. Jones, Director of Graduate Studies, 801-585-3002, Fax: 801-581-7581, E-mail: cjones@hum.utah.edu. *Application contact:* Corky Reeser, Executive Graduate Secretary, 801-581-7570, Fax: 801-581-7581, E-mail: c.reeser@mail.hum.utah.edu.

University of Vermont, Graduate College, College of Arts and Sciences, Department of Romance Languages, Burlington, VT 05405. Offers French (MA). *Students:* 4 (3 women). 1 applicant, 0% accepted. In 2007, 1 degree awarded. *Degree requirements:* For master's, one foreign language. *Entrance requirements:* For master's, GRE General Test. Additional exam requirements/recommendations for international students: Required—TOEFL (minimum score 550 paper-based; 213 computer-based; 80 iBT). *Application deadline:* For fall admission, 8/1 priority date for domestic students. Applications are processed on a rolling basis. Application fee: $40. Electronic applications accepted. *Financial support:* Fellowships, teaching assistantships available. Financial award application deadline: 3/1. *Faculty research:* French, French-Canadian, and French-African literature. *Unit head:* Dr. G. Nunley, Chairperson, 802-656-3196. *Application contact:* Dr. J. Whatley, Coordinator, 802-656-3196.

University of Victoria, Faculty of Graduate Studies, Faculty of Humanities, Department of French, Victoria, BC V8W 2Y2, Canada. Offers literature (MA); teaching emphasis (MA). Part-time and evening/weekend programs available. *Faculty:* 10 full-time (5 women). *Students:* 12. Average age 29. 11 applicants, 36% accepted, 3 enrolled. In 2007, 3 degrees awarded. *Degree requirements:* For master's, 2 foreign languages, thesis optional. *Entrance requirements:* For master's, BA in French. Additional exam requirements/recommendations for international students: Required—TOEFL (minimum score 575 paper-based; 233 computer-based), IELTS (minimum score 7). *Application deadline:* For fall admission, 2/15 priority date for domestic students, 12/15 for international students. Applications are processed on a rolling basis. Application fee: $75 ($125 for international students). Electronic applications accepted. *Expenses:* Tuition, state resident: full-time $3,110. International tuition: $3,700 full-time. Tuition and fees vary according to program. *Financial support:* In 2007–08, 5 students received support, including 2 fellowships (averaging $12,400 per year), teaching assistantships (averaging $12,000 per year); institutionally sponsored loans also available. Financial award application deadline: 2/15. *Faculty research:* French-Canadian literature, stylistics, comparative literature, Francophone literature. *Unit head:* Dr. Sada Niang, Chair, 250-721-7364, Fax: 250-721-8724, E-mail: chairtr@uvic.ca. *Application contact:* Dr. Yvonne Hsieh, Graduate Adviser, 250-721-7376, Fax: 250-721-8724, E-mail: gradfren@uvic.ca.

University of Virginia, College and Graduate School of Arts and Sciences, Department of French, Charlottesville, VA 22903. Offers MA, PhD. *Faculty:* 15 full-time (10 women), 2 part-time/adjunct (both women). *Students:* 35 full-time (24 women), 1 part-time; includes 3 minority (1 African American, 1 Asian American or Pacific Islander, 1 Hispanic American), 6 international. Average age 30. 19 applicants, 58% accepted, 4 enrolled. In 2007, 7 master's, 2 doctorates awarded. *Degree requirements:* For master's, one foreign language, comprehensive exam; for doctorate, one foreign language, comprehensive exam, thesis/dissertation. *Entrance requirements:* For master's and doctorate, GRE General Test, minimum GPA of 3.0 in major. *Application deadline:* Applications are processed on a rolling basis. Application fee: $60. Electronic applications accepted. *Financial support:* Applicants required to submit FAFSA. *Application contact:* Peter C. Brunjes, Associate Dean for Graduate Programs and Research, 434-924-7184, Fax: 434-924-6737, E-mail: grad-a-s@virginia.edu.

University of Washington, Graduate School, College of Arts and Sciences, Department of Romance Languages and Literature, Division of French and Italian Studies, Seattle, WA 98195. Offers French (MA, PhD); Italian (MA). *Faculty:* 8 full-time (4 women), 1 part-time/adjunct (0 women). *Students:* 15 full-time (12 women); includes 2 minority (both Asian Americans or Pacific Islanders), 3 international. 14 applicants, 57% accepted, 5 enrolled. In 2007, 2 master's, 1 doctorate awarded. Terminal master's awarded for partial completion of doctoral program. *Degree requirements:* For master's, 2 foreign languages, exam; for doctorate, 3 foreign languages, thesis/dissertation, exam. *Entrance requirements:* For master's and doctorate, GRE General Test, minimum GPA of 3.0. Additional exam requirements/recommendations for international students: Required—TOEFL. *Application deadline:* For fall admission, 1/15 priority date for domestic students, 11/1 priority date for international students. Application fee: $50. Electronic applications accepted. *Financial support:* In 2007–08, 1 fellowship with full tuition reimbursement (averaging $13,059 per year), 15 teaching assistantships with full tuition reimbursements (averaging $13,534 per year) were awarded; Federal Work-Study, institutionally sponsored loans, health care benefits, unspecified assistantships, and professional development stipends also available. Financial award application deadline: 1/15; financial award applicants required to submit FAFSA. *Faculty research:* Interdisciplinary studies, literary theory and criticism, film, major periods of French and Italian literature, Francophonie. *Unit head:* Prof. Albert J. Sbragia, Chair, 206-616-3708, Fax: 206-616-3302, E-mail: sbragia@u.washington.edu. *Application contact:* Prof. Geoffrey Turnowsky, Graduate Program Coordinator, 206-685-1618, Fax: 206-616-3302, E-mail: gt2@u.washington.edu.

University of Waterloo, Graduate Studies, Faculty of Arts, Department of French Studies, Waterloo, ON N2L 3G1, Canada. Offers French (MA, PhD). Part-time programs available. *Faculty:* 12 full-time (5 women), 6 part-time/adjunct (3 women). *Students:* 21. 7 applicants, 100% accepted, 4 enrolled. *Entrance requirements:* For master's, honors degree, minimum B average, course work and assignments in French, resumé. Additional exam requirements/recommendations for international students: Required—TOEFL, TWE. *Application deadline:* For fall admission, 2/1 priority date for domestic students. Applications are processed on a rolling basis. Application fee: $75 Canadian dollars. Electronic applications accepted. *Financial support:* In 2007–08, teaching assistantships (averaging $8,000 per year); fellowships, research assistantships, scholarships/grants also available. *Faculty research:* French and Quebec literature: Middle Ages through twentieth century, phonology of Acadian dialect, computerized scholarly editions of medieval and Renaissance texts. *Application contact:* Dr. Tara Collington, Graduate Officer, 519-888-4567 Ext. 36123, Fax: 519-725-0554, E-mail: tcalling@uwaterloo.ca.

The University of Western Ontario, Faculty of Graduate Studies, Faculty of Arts and Humanities, Department of French, London, ON N6A 5B8, Canada. Offers Canadian literature (MA); French (MA, PhD). MA (Canadian literature) offered in cooperation with Department of English. *Degree requirements:* For master's, thesis or alternative; for doctorate, one foreign language, thesis/dissertation. *Entrance requirements:* For master's, minimum B average, honors degree, 2 years of teaching experience (MAT); for doctorate, MA or equivalent, minimum B average in French. Additional exam requirements/recommendations for international students: Required—TOEFL. *Application deadline:* For fall admission, 2/15 priority date for domestic and international students; for winter admission, 10/15 priority date for domestic students; for spring admission, 2/15 priority date for domestic students. Applications are processed on a rolling basis. Application fee: $50. Electronic applications accepted. *Financial support:* Fellowships, research assistantships, teaching assistantships available. Financial award application deadline: 3/1. *Unit head:* Prof. Jeff Tennant, Chair, 519-661-2111 Ext. 85703, Fax: 519-661-3470, E-mail: jtennant@uwo.ca. *Application contact:* Dr. Chrisanthi Skalkos, Graduate Assistant, 519-661-2111, Fax: 519-661-3470, E-mail: skalkos@uwo.ca.

University of Wisconsin–Madison, Graduate School, College of Letters and Science, Department of French and Italian, Program in French, Madison, WI 53706-1380. Offers MA, PhD. Part-time programs available. *Degree requirements:* For master's, one foreign language; for doctorate, one foreign language, thesis/dissertation. *Entrance requirements:* For master's and doctorate, GRE. Electronic applications accepted. *Faculty research:* Francophone literature; French literature, culture, linguistics, and language pedagogy.

University of Wisconsin–Madison, Graduate School, College of Letters and Science, Department of French and Italian, Program in French Studies, Madison, WI 53706-1380. Offers MFS, Certificate. Part-time programs available. *Degree requirements:* For master's, one foreign language, thesis, internship; for Certificate, one foreign language, internship. *Entrance requirements:* For master's, GRE. Electronic applications accepted. *Faculty research:* International development, European citizenship, French and business, foreign language education, agricultural economics.

University of Wisconsin–Milwaukee, Graduate School, College of Letters and Sciences, Interdepartmental Program in Foreign Language and Literature, Milwaukee, WI 53201-0413. Offers classics and Hebrew studies (MAFLL); comparative literature (MAFLL); French and Italian (MAFLL); German (MAFLL); Slavic studies (MAFLL); Spanish (MAFLL). Part-time programs available. *Faculty:* 39 full-time (17 women). *Students:* 29 full-time (21 women), 31 part-time (23 women); includes 8 minority (1 Asian American or Pacific Islander, 7 Hispanic Americans), 22 international. 54 applicants, 67% accepted, 26 enrolled. In 2007, 34 degrees awarded. *Degree requirements:* For master's, 2 foreign languages, thesis or alternative. *Application deadline:* For fall admission, 1/1 priority date for domestic students; for spring admission, 9/1 for domestic students. Applications are processed on a rolling basis. Application fee: $45 ($75 for international students). *Expenses:* Tuition, state resident: part-time $530 per credit. Tuition, nonresident: part-time $1,428 per credit. Required fees: $19 per credit. $229 per term. Tuition and fees vary according to course load and program. *Financial support:* In 2007–08, 44 teaching assistantships were awarded; fellowships, research assistantships, career-related internships or fieldwork and unspecified assistantships also available. Support available to part-time students. Financial award application deadline: 4/15. *Unit head:* Gabrielle Verdier, Representative, 414-229-3346, Fax: 414-229-2741, E-mail: verdier@uwm.edu.

University of Wyoming, Graduate School, College of Arts and Sciences, Department of Modern and Classical Languages, Program in French, Laramie, WY 82070. Offers MA. Part-time programs available. *Faculty:* 2 full-time (0 women). *Students:* 1 (woman) full-time, 1 international. Average age 23. 2 applicants, 0% accepted. *Degree requirements:* For master's, one foreign language, thesis or alternative. *Entrance requirements:* For master's, GRE General Test, minimum GPA of 3.0. *Application deadline:* For fall admission, 4/1 priority date for domestic students. Applications are processed on a rolling basis. Application fee: $50. *Financial support:* In 2007–08, 2 teaching assistantships with full tuition reimbursements (averaging $10,696 per year) were awarded; institutionally sponsored loans also available. Financial award application deadline: 3/1. *Faculty research:* Poetry, Asian literature, medieval literature, nineteenth- and twentieth century literature. *Application contact:* Dr. Kevin S. Larsen, Graduate Adviser, 307-766-2294, Fax: 307-766-2727, E-mail: klarsen@uwyo.edu.

Vanderbilt University, Graduate School, Department of French and Italian, Nashville, TN 37240-1001. Offers French (MA, MAT, PhD). *Faculty:* 19 full-time (14 women). *Students:* 9 full-time (4 women), 1 (woman) part-time; includes 1 minority (Hispanic American), 2 international. Average age 30. 21 applicants, 24% accepted, 3 enrolled. In 2007, 4 master's, 1 doctorate awarded. *Degree requirements:* For master's, one foreign language, comprehensive exam; for doctorate, 2 foreign languages, thesis/dissertation, final and qualifying exams. *Entrance requirements:* For master's and doctorate, GRE General Test. *Application deadline:* For fall admission, 1/15 for domestic and international students. Application fee: $0. Electronic applications accepted. *Financial support:* Fellowships with full and partial tuition reimbursements, teaching assistantships with full and partial tuition reimbursements, career-related internships or fieldwork, Federal Work-Study, institutionally sponsored loans, and health care benefits available. Financial award application deadline: 1/15; financial award applicants required to submit CSS PROFILE or FAFSA. *Faculty research:* Baudelaire, Rabelais, voyage literature, postcolonial literature, medieval epic. *Unit head:* Virginia Scott, Chair, 615-322-6900, Fax: 615-343-6909, E-mail: virginia.m.scott@vanderbilt.edu. *Application contact:* Lynn Ramey, Director of Graduate Studies, 615-322-6900, Fax: 615-343-6909.

Washington University in St. Louis, Graduate School of Arts and Sciences, Department of Romance Languages and Literatures, Program in French, St. Louis, MO 63130-4899. Offers MA, PhD. *Degree requirements:* For master's, thesis or alternative; for doctorate, thesis/dissertation. *Entrance requirements:* For master's and doctorate, GRE General Test. Electronic applications accepted.

Wayne State University, College of Liberal Arts and Sciences, Department of Classical and Modern Languages, Literatures, and Cultures, Program in French, Detroit, MI 48202. Offers MA. In 2007, 5 degrees awarded. *Degree requirements:* For master's, one foreign language, thesis optional. *Entrance requirements:* For master's, GRE General Test, minimum GPA of 3.0.

Additional exam requirements/recommendations for international students: Required—TOEFL (minimum score 550 paper-based; 213 computer-based); Recommended—TWE (minimum score 6). *Application deadline:* For fall admission, 7/1 for domestic students, 6/1 for international students; for winter admission, 10/1 for international students; for spring admission, 2/1 for international students. Applications are processed on a rolling basis. Application fee: $30 ($50 for international students). Electronic applications accepted. *Expenses:* Tuition, state resident: part-time $403 per credit hour. Tuition, nonresident: part-time $890 per credit hour. *Financial support:* Fellowships, research assistantships, teaching assistantships available. *Faculty research:* Renaissance lyric, eighteenth century theatre and poetry, Quebecois literature, nineteenth century prose, twentieth century novel and criticism. *Application contact:* Dr. Michael Giordano, Graduate Director, 313-577-3051, Fax: 313-577-6243, E-mail: m.j.giordano@wayne.edu.

West Chester University of Pennsylvania, Office of Graduate Studies and Extended Education, College of Arts and Sciences, Department of Foreign Languages, West Chester, PA 19383. Offers French (M Ed, MA); German (M Ed); Latin (M Ed); Spanish (M Ed, MA). Part-time and evening/weekend programs available. *Students:* 7 full-time (all women), 18 part-time (15 women); includes 2 minority (both Hispanic Americans) Average age 35. 10 applicants, 100% accepted, 6 enrolled. In 2007, 7 degrees awarded. *Degree requirements:* For master's, one foreign language, comprehensive exam, thesis optional. *Entrance requirements:* For master's, GRE, placement test. Additional exam requirements/recommendations for international students: Required—TOEFL (minimum score 550 paper-based; 213 computer-based; 80 iBT). *Application deadline:* For fall admission, 4/15 priority date for domestic students; for spring admission, 10/15 for domestic students. Applications are processed on a rolling basis. Application fee: $35. *Expenses:* Tuition, state resident: part-time $345 per credit. Tuition, nonresident: part-time $552 per credit. Tuition and fees vary according to course load. *Financial support:* In 2007–08, 2 research assistantships with full and partial tuition reimbursements (averaging $5,000 per year) were awarded; unspecified assistantships also available. Support available to part-time students. Financial award application deadline: 2/15; financial award applicants required to submit FAFSA. *Faculty research:* Implementation of world languages curriculum framework. *Unit head:* Dr. Jerry Williams, Chair, 610-436-2700, Fax: 610-436-3048, E-mail: jwilliams2@wcupa.edu. *Application contact:* Dr. Rebecca Pauly, Graduate Coordinator, 610-436-2382, E-mail: rpauly@wcupa.edu.

West Virginia University, Eberly College of Arts and Sciences, Department of Foreign Languages, Morgantown, WV 26506. Offers French (MA); linguistics (MA); Spanish (MA); teaching English to speakers of other languages (MA). Part-time programs available. *Faculty:* 20 full-time (13 women), 27 part-time/adjunct (24 women). *Students:* 64 full-time (42 women), 8 part-time (7 women); includes 8 minority (1 African American, 3 Asian Americans or Pacific Islanders, 4 Hispanic Americans), 31 international. Average age 29. 46 applicants, 76% accepted, 26 enrolled. In 2007, 31 degrees awarded. *Degree requirements:* For master's, one foreign language, comprehensive exam (for some programs), thesis optional. *Entrance requirements:* For master's, minimum GPA of 3.0. *Application deadline:* For fall admission, 2/1 priority date for domestic and international students; for spring admission, 10/1 for domestic and international students. Applications are processed on a rolling basis. Application fee: $50. Electronic applications accepted. *Expenses:* Tuition, state resident: full-time $5,196; part-time $292 per credit hour. Tuition, nonresident: full-time $15,064; part-time $840 per credit hour. Tuition and fees vary according to program. *Financial support:* In 2007–08, 69 students received support, including 65 teaching assistantships with full tuition reimbursements available (averaging $8,864 per year); research assistantships, Federal Work-Study, institutionally sponsored loans, and tuition waivers (full and partial) also available. Financial award application deadline: 2/1; financial award applicants required to submit FAFSA. *Faculty research:* French, German, and Spanish literature; foreign language pedagogy; English as a second language; cultural studies; linguistics. Total annual research expenditures: $36,679. *Unit head:* Dr. Angel T. Tuninetti, Chair, 304-293-5121, Fax: 304-293-7655, E-mail: angel.tuninetti@mail.wvu.edu. *Application contact:* Dr. Sandra Stjepanovic, Director of Graduate Studies, 304-293-5121, Fax: 304-293-7655, E-mail: sandra.stjepanovic@mail.wvu.edu.

Yale University, Graduate School of Arts and Sciences, Department of French, New Haven, CT 06520. Offers MA, PhD. *Degree requirements:* For doctorate, 3 foreign languages, thesis/dissertation. *Entrance requirements:* For doctorate, GRE General Test.

York University, Faculty of Graduate Studies, Glendon College, Program in French Studies, Toronto, ON M3J 1P3, Canada. Offers MA. *Degree requirements:* For master's, thesis or alternative. Electronic applications accepted.

German

Arizona State University, Graduate College, College of Liberal Arts and Sciences, Division of Humanities, Department of Languages and Literatures, Program in German, Tempe, AZ 85287. Offers MA. *Degree requirements:* For master's, thesis or alternative. *Entrance requirements:* For master's, GRE.

Bowling Green State University, Graduate College, College of Arts and Sciences, Department of German, Russian, and East Asian Languages, Bowling Green, OH 43403. Offers German (MA, MAT); MA/MA. Part-time programs available. *Faculty:* 8 full-time (3 women). *Students:* 21 full-time (12 women); includes 2 African Americans, 4 international. Average age 24. 25 applicants, 80% accepted, 15 enrolled. In 2007, 14 degrees awarded. *Degree requirements:* For master's, one foreign language, thesis or alternative. *Entrance requirements:* For master's, GRE General Test. Additional exam requirements/recommendations for international students: Required—TOEFL. *Application deadline:* For fall admission, 3/1 priority date for domestic students. Application fee: $30. Electronic applications accepted. *Financial support:* In 2007–08, 15 research assistantships with full tuition reimbursements (averaging $4,453 per year), 9 teaching assistantships with full tuition reimbursements (averaging $7,620 per year) were awarded; Federal Work-Study, institutionally sponsored loans, tuition waivers (partial), and unspecified assistantships also available. Financial award applicants required to submit FAFSA. *Unit head:* Dr. Timothy Pogacar, Chair, 419-372-8028. *Application contact:* Dr. Geoffrey Howes, Graduate Coordinator, 419-372-7139.

Brigham Young University, Graduate Studies, College of Humanities, Department of Germanic and Slavic Languages, Provo, UT 84602-1001. Offers German studies (MA). *Faculty:* 8 full-time (3 women). *Students:* 3 full-time (2 women), 3 part-time (1 woman), 1 international. Average age 24. 2 applicants, 100% accepted, 2 enrolled. In 2007, 4 degrees awarded. *Degree requirements:* For master's, thesis. *Entrance requirements:* For master's, GRE General Test, bachelor's degree in German or related field. Additional exam requirements/recommendations for international students: Required—TOEFL (minimum score 213 computer-based). *Application deadline:* For fall admission, 2/1 priority date for domestic and international students. Application fee: $50. Electronic applications accepted. *Financial support:* In 2007–08, 5 students received support, including 3 teaching assistantships with full and partial tuition reimbursements available (averaging $7,380 per year); career-related internships or fieldwork, institutionally sponsored loans, scholarships/grants, tuition waivers (full and partial), and unspecified assistantships also available. Support available to part-time students. Financial award application deadline: 6/15. *Faculty research:* Second language acquisition, modern German literature, critical theory, German women authors, German dialects. Total annual research expenditures: $4,450. *Unit head:* Dr. David K. Hart, Chair, 801-422-3373, Fax: 801-422-0268, E-mail: david_hart@byu.edu. *Application contact:* AnnMarie Hamar, Secretary to the Chair, 801-422-4923, Fax: 801-422-0268, E-mail: annmarie_hamar@byu.edu.

Brown University, Graduate School, Department of German Studies, Providence, RI 02912. Offers AM, PhD. *Degree requirements:* For master's, one foreign language, thesis or alternative; for doctorate, 2 foreign languages, thesis/dissertation, preliminary exam. *Entrance requirements:* For master's and doctorate, GRE General Test.

California State University, Fullerton, Graduate Studies, College of Humanities and Social Sciences, Department of Modern Languages and Literatures, Fullerton, CA 92834-9480. Offers French (MA); German (MA); Spanish (MA); teaching English to speakers of other languages (MS). Part-time programs available. *Students:* 48 full-time (41 women), 76 part-time (63 women); includes 55 minority (17 Asian Americans or Pacific Islanders, 38 Hispanic Americans), 26 international. Average age 33. 94 applicants, 68% accepted, 32 enrolled. In 2007, 34 degrees awarded. *Degree requirements:* For master's, comprehensive exam, thesis or alternative. *Entrance requirements:* For master's, minimum GPA of 2.5 in last 60 hours of course work, undergraduate major in a language. Application fee: $55. *Financial support:* Federal Work-Study, institutionally sponsored loans, and scholarships/grants available. Support available to part-time students. Financial award application deadline: 3/1. *Unit head:* Dr. Janet Eyring, Chair, 714-278-3534.

California State University, Long Beach, Graduate Studies, College of Liberal Arts, Department of Romance, German, and Russian Languages and Literature, Program in German, Long Beach, CA 90840. Offers MA. Part-time programs available. *Students:* Average age 39. *Degree requirements:* For master's, one foreign language, comprehensive exam or thesis. *Application deadline:* For fall admission, 7/1 for domestic students; for spring admission, 12/1 for domestic students. Applications are processed on a rolling basis. Application fee: $55. Electronic applications accepted. *Financial support:* Federal Work-Study, institutionally sponsored loans, and scholarships/grants available. Financial award application deadline: 3/2. *Faculty research:* Contemporary German society, baroque, Goethe, Wagner.

California State University, Sacramento, Graduate Studies, College of Social Sciences and Interdisciplinary Studies, Liberal Arts Program, Sacramento, CA 95819-6048. Offers French (MA); German (MA); Spanish (MA); theater arts (MA). *Students:* 15 full-time (10 women), 24 part-time (17 women); includes 4 minority (2 African Americans, 1 American Indian/Alaska Native, 1 Asian American or Pacific Islander). Average age 37. 17 applicants, 88% accepted, 9 enrolled. *Degree requirements:* For master's, writing proficiency exam. *Entrance requirements:* Additional exam requirements/recommendations for international students: Required—TOEFL. *Application deadline:* Applications are processed on a rolling basis. Application fee: $55. Electronic applications accepted. *Expenses:* Tuition, state resident: full-time $3,414. Tuition, nonresident: full-time $13,584; part-time $339 per unit. Required fees: $786; $393 per semester. *Financial support:* Application deadline: 3/1. *Unit head:* Dr. Lindy Valdez, Coordinator, 916-278-6342.

Columbia University, Graduate School of Arts and Sciences, Division of Humanities, Department of Germanic Languages, New York, NY 10027. Offers M Phil, MA, PhD. Part-time programs available. *Faculty:* 8 full-time. *Students:* 25 full-time (11 women), 1 (woman) part-time, 9 international. Average age 30. 30 applicants, 40% accepted. In 2007, 4 master's, 2 doctorates awarded. *Degree requirements:* For master's, one foreign language, written exam; for doctorate, 2 foreign languages, thesis/dissertation. *Entrance requirements:* For master's and doctorate, GRE General Test, GRE Subject Test, sample of written work. Additional exam requirements/recommendations for international students: Required—TOEFL. Application fee: $90. *Expenses:* Tuition: Part-time $1,452 per credit. Required fees: $152 per term. One-time fee: $75 part-time. Full-time tuition and fees vary according to course level, course load, degree level and program. *Financial support:* Fellowships, teaching assistantships, Federal Work-Study and institutionally sponsored loans available. Support available to part-time students. Financial award application deadline: 1/5; financial award applicants required to submit FAFSA. *Faculty research:* German language and literature, comparative literature. *Unit head:* Andreas Huyssen, Chair, 212-854-5411, Fax: 212-854-5381, E-mail: ah26@columbia.edu.

Cornell University, Graduate School, Graduate Fields of Arts and Sciences, Field of Germanic Studies, Ithaca, NY 14853-0001. Offers German area studies (MA, PhD); German intellectual history (MA, PhD); Germanic linguistics (MA, PhD); Germanic literature (MA, PhD); old Norse (MA, PhD). *Faculty:* 19 full-time (9 women). *Students:* 17 full-time (6 women), 6 international. Average age 28. 26 applicants, 38% accepted, 4 enrolled. In 2007, 1 master's, 5 doctorates awarded. Terminal master's awarded for partial completion of doctoral program. *Degree requirements:* For master's, one foreign language, thesis; for doctorate, 2 foreign languages, comprehensive exam, thesis/dissertation. *Entrance requirements:* For master's and doctorate, GRE General Test, fluency in German, writing sample, 2 letters of recommendation. Additional exam requirements/recommendations for international students: Required—TOEFL (minimum score 550 paper-based; 213 computer-based; 77 iBT). *Application deadline:* For fall admission, 1/15 for domestic students. Application fee: $70. Electronic applications accepted. *Financial support:* In 2007–08, 20 students received support, including 6 fellowships with full tuition reimbursements available, 14 teaching assistantships with full tuition reimbursements available; research assistantships with full tuition reimbursements available, institutionally sponsored loans, scholarships/grants, health care benefits, tuition waivers (full and partial), and unspecified assistantships also available. Financial award applicants required to submit FAFSA. *Faculty research:* Women's studies, minority literature, literature and intellectual history, theater and film studies, continental philosophy. *Unit head:* Director of Graduate Studies, 607-255-4047. *Application contact:* Graduate Field Assistant, 607-255-4047, E-mail: germanic_studies@cornell.edu.

Cornell University, Graduate School, Graduate Fields of Arts and Sciences, Field of Linguistics, Ithaca, NY 14853-0001. Offers applied linguistics (MA, PhD); East Asian linguistics (MA, PhD); English linguistics (MA, PhD); general linguistics (MA, PhD); Germanic linguistics (MA, PhD); Indo-European linguistics (MA, PhD); phonetics (MA, PhD); phonological theory (MA, PhD); Romance linguistics (MA, PhD); second language acquisition (MA, PhD); semantics (MA, PhD); Slavic linguistics (MA, PhD); sociolinguistics (MA, PhD); South Asian linguistics (MA, PhD); Southeast Asian linguistics (MA, PhD); syntactic theory (MA, PhD). *Faculty:* 19 full-time. *Students:* 31 full-time (16 women); includes 1 minority (Hispanic American), 19 international. Average age 28. 89 applicants, 17% accepted, 8 enrolled. In 2007, 2 master's, 1 doctorate awarded. Terminal master's awarded for partial completion of doctoral program. *Degree requirements:* For master's, one foreign language, thesis; for doctorate, one foreign language, comprehensive exam, thesis/dissertation. *Entrance requirements:* For master's and doctorate, GRE General Test, 2 letters of recommendation. Additional exam requirements/recommendations for international students: Required—TOEFL (minimum score 600 paper-based; 250 computer-based; 77 iBT). *Application deadline:* For fall admission, 1/15 for domestic students. Application fee: $70. Electronic applications accepted. *Financial support:* In 2007–08, 30 students received support, including 14 fellowships with full tuition reimbursements available, 2 research assistantships with full tuition reimbursements available, 14 teaching assistantships with full tuition reimbursements available; institutionally sponsored loans, scholarships/grants, health care benefits, tuition waivers (full and partial), and unspecified assistantships also

German

Cornell University (continued)

available. Financial award applicants required to submit FAFSA. *Faculty research:* Phonology and phonetics; syntax and semantics; historical linguistics; philosophy of language; language acquisition. *Unit head:* Director of Graduate Studies, 607-255-1105. *Application contact:* Graduate Field Assistant, 607-255-1105, E-mail: lingfield@cornell.edu.

Dalhousie University, Faculty of Arts and Social Science, Department of German, Halifax, NS B3H 4R2, Canada. Offers MA. *Faculty:* 4 full-time (1 woman), 1 part-time/adjunct (0 women). *Students:* 7 full-time (6 women). Average age 25. In 2007, 6 degrees awarded. *Degree requirements:* For master's, one foreign language, thesis. *Entrance requirements:* Additional exam requirements/recommendations for international students: Required—TOEFL. *Application deadline:* For fall admission, 6/1 for domestic students. Applications are processed on a rolling basis. Application fee: $60. *Financial support:* In 2007–08, 6 students received support; fellowships, teaching assistantships, scholarships/grants available. *Faculty research:* Baroque age in Germany, literature and philosophy of German idealism, twentieth-century German culture, aesthetics, reception of the Islamic Orient, reception of Greek and Roman antiquity, realism and ornament. *Unit head:* Dr. Jane Curran, Chair, 902-494-2161, Fax: 902-494-2719, E-mail: jcurran@dal.ca. *Application contact:* Annett Gaudig, Administrative Secretary, 902-494-2161, Fax: 902-494-2719.

Duke University, Graduate School, Interdisciplinary Program in German Studies, Durham, NC 27708-0256. Offers PhD. Part-time programs available. *Faculty:* 27 full-time. *Students:* 9 full-time (7 women); includes 1 minority (African American), 4 international. 16 applicants, 25% accepted, 1 enrolled. In 2007, 1 degree awarded. *Degree requirements:* For doctorate, thesis/dissertation. *Entrance requirements:* For doctorate, GRE General Test. Additional exam requirements/recommendations for international students: Required—TOEFL (minimum score 550 paper-based; 213 computer-based; 83 iBT), IELTS (minimum score 7). *Application deadline:* For fall admission, 12/15 priority date for domestic and international students. Application fee: $75. Electronic applications accepted. *Financial support:* Fellowships, research assistantships, teaching assistantships, Federal Work-Study available. Financial award application deadline: 12/31. *Unit head:* William Donahue, Director of Graduate Studies, 919-660-3104, Fax: 919-660-3166, E-mail: mini.jolley@duke.edu.

Eastern Michigan University, Graduate School, College of Arts and Sciences, Department of Foreign Languages and Bilingual Studies, Program in Foreign Languages, Ypsilanti, MI 48197. Offers French (MA); German (MA); German for business (Graduate Certificate); Hispanic language and cultures (Graduate Certificate); Japanese business practices (Graduate Certificate); Spanish (MA). Part-time and evening/weekend programs available. Post-baccalaureate distance learning degree programs offered (minimal on-campus study). *Students:* 1 (woman) full-time, 18 part-time (17 women); includes 2 minority (1 Asian American or Pacific Islander, 1 Hispanic American). Average age 35. In 2007, 8 master's, 2 other advanced degrees awarded. *Degree requirements:* For master's, one foreign language, thesis optional. *Entrance requirements:* Additional exam requirements/recommendations for international students: Required—TOEFL. *Application deadline:* Applications are processed on a rolling basis. Application fee: $35. *Expenses:* Tuition, state resident: full-time $8,952; part-time $373 per credit hour. Tuition, nonresident: full-time $17,634; part-time $735 per credit hour. Required fees: $896; $34 per credit hour. Tuition and fees vary according to course level, degree level and program. *Financial support:* Fellowships, research assistantships with full tuition reimbursements, teaching assistantships with full tuition reimbursements, career-related internships or fieldwork, Federal Work-Study, institutionally sponsored loans, scholarships/grants, tuition waivers (partial), and unspecified assistantships available. Support available to part-time students. Financial award applicants required to submit FAFSA. *Application contact:* Dr. Genevieve Peden, Program Advisor, 734-487-2283, Fax: 734-487-3411, E-mail: gpeden@emich.edu.

Florida Atlantic University, Dorothy F. Schmidt College of Arts and Letters, Department of Languages and Linguistics, Boca Raton, FL 33431-0991. Offers comparative literature (MA); French (MA); German (MA); Spanish (MA); teaching French (MAT); teaching German (MAT); teaching Spanish (MAT). Part-time programs available. *Degree requirements:* For master's, one foreign language, comprehensive exam, thesis optional. *Entrance requirements:* For master's, GRE General Test, minimum GPA of 3.0. *Faculty research:* Modern European studies, modern Latin America, medieval Europe.

Florida State University, Graduate Studies, College of Arts and Sciences, Department of Modern Languages, Program in German, Tallahassee, FL 32306. Offers MA. *Faculty:* 3 full-time (2 women), 3 part-time/adjunct (2 women). *Students:* 4 full-time (3 women); includes 1 minority (Asian American or Pacific Islander) Average age 25. 3 applicants, 67% accepted, 1 enrolled. *Degree requirements:* For master's, thesis optional. *Entrance requirements:* For master's, GRE General Test or minimum GPA of 3.0. Additional exam requirements/recommendations for international students: Required—TOEFL (minimum score 550 paper-based; 213 computer-based). *Application deadline:* For fall admission, 2/1 for domestic students; for spring admission, 11/22 for domestic students. Applications are processed on a rolling basis. Application fee: $30. Electronic applications accepted. *Expenses:* Tuition, state resident: part-time $248 per credit hour. Tuition, nonresident: part-time $880 per credit hour. Tuition and fees vary according to program. *Financial support:* In 2007–08, 4 students received support, including research assistantships (averaging $12,000 per year), 4 teaching assistantships with partial tuition reimbursements available (averaging $10,200 per year). Financial award application deadline: 2/1; financial award applicants required to submit FAFSA. *Unit head:* Dr. Winnifred Adolph, Divisional Coordinator, 850-644-8191, Fax: 850-644-0524, E-mail: wadolph@fsu.edu. *Application contact:* Wendy E. Pigott, Graduate Academic Coordinator, 850-644-8397, Fax: 850-644-0524, E-mail: wpigott@fsu.edu.

Georgetown University, Graduate School of Arts and Sciences, BMW Center for German and European Studies, Washington, DC 20057. Offers MA, MA/JD, MA/PhD. *Degree requirements:* For master's, 2 foreign languages, comprehensive exam. *Entrance requirements:* For master's, GRE General Test. Additional exam requirements/recommendations for international students: Required—TOEFL. *Faculty research:* Trans-Atlantic relations, European Union, German and European Studies.

Georgetown University, Graduate School of Arts and Sciences, Department of German, Washington, DC 20057. Offers MS, PhD, MA/PhD. *Degree requirements:* For master's, 2 foreign languages, research project; for doctorate, 3 foreign languages, thesis/dissertation. *Entrance requirements:* For master's, GRE General Test. Additional exam requirements/recommendations for international students: Required—TOEFL.

Georgia State University, College of Arts and Sciences, Department of Modern and Classical Languages, Program in German, Atlanta, GA 30303-3083. Offers MA. Evening/weekend programs available. *Faculty:* 2 full-time (1 woman). *Students:* 2 full-time (both women). Average age 25. *Degree requirements:* For master's, one foreign language, thesis or alternative, general exam. *Entrance requirements:* For master's, GRE General Test. Additional exam requirements/recommendations for international students: Required—TOEFL. *Application deadline:* For fall admission, 4/15 for domestic students; for spring admission, 11/15 for domestic students. Applications are processed on a rolling basis. Application fee: $50. Electronic applications accepted. *Expenses:* Tuition, state resident: part-time $221 per credit hour. *Financial support:* In 2007–08, research assistantships (averaging $3,000 per year), teaching assistantships (averaging $9,000 per year) were awarded; career-related internships or fieldwork, Federal Work-Study, and institutionally sponsored loans also available. Support available to part-time students. Financial award applicants required to submit FAFSA. *Faculty research:* Medieval and twentieth-century German literature.

Georgia State University, College of Arts and Sciences, Department of Modern and Classical Languages, Program in Translation and Interpretation, Atlanta, GA 30303-3083. Offers French (Certificate); German (Certificate); Spanish (Certificate). *Faculty:* 3 full-time, 2 part-time/adjunct. *Students:* Average age 32. *Application deadline:* For fall admission, 4/1 for domestic students; for spring admission, 11/15 for domestic students. Applications are processed on a rolling basis. Application fee: $50. Electronic applications accepted. *Expenses:* Tuition, state resident: part-time $221 per credit hour. *Unit head:* Dr. Annette Cash, Director, E-mail: acash@gsu.edu.

Graduate School and University Center of the City University of New York, Graduate Studies, Program in Comparative Literature, New York, NY 10016-4039. Offers comparative literature (MA, PhD), including classics (PhD), German (PhD), Italian (PhD). *Faculty:* 16 full-time (3 women). *Students:* 98 full-time (59 women), 11 part-time (9 women); includes 7 minority (2 Asian Americans or Pacific Islanders, 5 Hispanic Americans), 26 international. Average age 36. 66 applicants, 35% accepted, 14 enrolled. In 2007, 6 master's, 5 doctorates awarded. Terminal master's awarded for partial completion of doctoral program. *Degree requirements:* For master's, 2 foreign languages, comprehensive exam, thesis; for doctorate, 3 foreign languages, comprehensive exam, thesis/dissertation. *Entrance requirements:* For master's and doctorate, GRE General Test. Additional exam requirements/recommendations for international students: Required—TOEFL. *Application deadline:* For fall admission, 4/15 for domestic students; for spring admission, 11/15 for domestic students. Application fee: $125. Electronic applications accepted. *Financial support:* In 2007–08, 63 students received support, including 53 fellowships, 5 research assistantships, 14 teaching assistantships; career-related internships or fieldwork, Federal Work-Study, institutionally sponsored loans, and tuition waivers (full and partial) also available. Financial award application deadline: 2/1; financial award applicants required to submit FAFSA. *Unit head:* Dr. Andre Aciman, Executive Officer, 212-817-8170, Fax: 212-817-1509, E-mail: aaciman@gc.cuny.edu.

Graduate School and University Center of the City University of New York, Graduate Studies, Program in Germanic Languages and Literatures, New York, NY 10016-4039. Offers MA, PhD. *Faculty:* 11 full-time (4 women). *Students:* 3 full-time (all women). Average age 42. In 2007, 1 doctorate awarded. *Degree requirements:* For master's, one foreign language, thesis; for doctorate, 2 foreign languages, thesis/dissertation. *Entrance requirements:* For master's and doctorate, GRE General Test. *Financial support:* In 2007–08, 3 students received support, including 3 fellowships; research assistantships, teaching assistantships, career-related internships or fieldwork, Federal Work-Study, institutionally sponsored loans, and tuition waivers (full and partial) also available. Financial award application deadline: 2/1; financial award applicants required to submit FAFSA. *Unit head:* Dr. Tamara Evans, Coordinator, 718-997-5790, Fax: 212-817-1509.

Harvard University, Graduate School of Arts and Sciences, Department of Germanic Languages and Literatures, Cambridge, MA 02138. Offers German (PhD); Scandinavian (PhD). Terminal master's awarded for partial completion of doctoral program. *Degree requirements:* For doctorate, 2 foreign languages, thesis/dissertation, exams. *Entrance requirements:* For doctorate, GRE General Test, German writing sample. Additional exam requirements/recommendations for international students: Required—TOEFL. *Expenses:* Tuition: Full-time $31,456. Full-time tuition and fees vary according to program and student level.

Hofstra University, School of Education and Allied Human Services, Department of Curriculum and Teaching, Program in Foreign Language Education, Hempstead, NY 11549. Offers French (MA, MS Ed); German (MA, MS Ed); Russian (MA, MS Ed); Spanish (MA, MS Ed). Part-time and evening/weekend programs available. *Students:* 3 full-time (all women), 5 part-time (all women); includes 2 minority (1 African American, 1 Hispanic American). Average age 35. 9 applicants, 100% accepted, 4 enrolled. In 2007, 8 degrees awarded. *Degree requirements:* For master's, one foreign language, thesis. *Entrance requirements:* For master's, 2 letters of recommendation, teacher certification (MA), essay. Additional exam requirements/recommendations for international students: Required—TOEFL (minimum score 550 paper-based; 213 computer-based). *Application deadline:* Applications are processed on a rolling basis. Application fee: $60. Electronic applications accepted. *Expenses:* Tuition: Full-time $14,220; part-time $820 per credit. Required fees: $970; $165 per term. Tuition and fees vary according to program. *Financial support:* In 2007–08, 1 student received support; fellowships with tuition reimbursements available, research assistantships with full and partial tuition reimbursements available, Federal Work-Study, institutionally sponsored loans, scholarships/grants, and tuition waivers (full and partial) available. Support available to part-time students. Financial award applicants required to submit FAFSA. *Faculty research:* Current literature from France and Francophone world, George Sand, music and literature, colonial and postcolonial studies, contemporary Latin American poetry. *Unit head:* Dr. Lori J. Ultsch, Chairperson, 516-463-4519, Fax: 516-463-2310, E-mail: rlllju@mail1.hofstra.edu. *Application contact:* Carol Drummer, Dean of Graduate Admissions, 516-463-4876, Fax: 516-463-4664, E-mail: gradstudent@hofstra.edu.

Illinois State University, Graduate School, College of Arts and Sciences, Department of Foreign Languages, Literatures and Cultures, Normal, IL 61790-2200. Offers French (MA); French and German (MA); French and Spanish (MA); German (MA); German and Spanish (MA); Spanish (MA). *Faculty:* 17 full-time (7 women). *Students:* 24 full-time (12 women), 9 part-time (8 women); includes 8 minority (4 African Americans, 1 American Indian/Alaska Native, 3 Hispanic Americans), 2 international. 18 applicants, 94% accepted. In 2007, 15 degrees awarded. *Degree requirements:* For master's, variable foreign language requirement, comprehensive exam, 1 term of residency. *Entrance requirements:* For master's, GRE General Test, minimum GPA of 2.8 in last 60 hours of course work. *Application deadline:* Applications are processed on a rolling basis. Application fee: $40. *Expenses:* Tuition, state resident: full-time $3,492; part-time $194 per credit hour. Tuition, nonresident: full-time $7,272; part-time $404 per credit hour. Required fees: $1,024; $57 per credit hour. *Financial support:* In 2007–08, 3 research assistantships (averaging $4,809 per year), 18 teaching assistantships (averaging $7,500 per year) were awarded; tuition waivers (full) and unspecified assistantships also available. Financial award application deadline: 4/1. *Unit head:* Daniel Everett, Chairperson, 309-438-2111.

Indiana University Bloomington, University Graduate School, College of Arts and Sciences, Department of Germanic Studies, Bloomington, IN 47405-7000. Offers German literature and studies (PhD); German studies (MA, PhD), including German and business studies (MA), German literature and culture (MA), German literature and linguistics (MA); medieval German studies (PhD); teaching German (MAT). *Faculty:* 12 full-time (3 women), 6 part-time/adjunct (2 women). *Students:* 27 full-time (15 women), 8 part-time (3 women); includes 1 minority (African American), 9 international. Average age 31. 26 applicants, 35% accepted, 9 enrolled. In 2007, 3 master's, 6 doctorates awarded. Terminal master's awarded for partial completion of doctoral program. *Median time to degree:* Of those who began their doctoral program in fall 1999, 86% received their degree in 8 years or less. *Degree requirements:* For master's, one foreign language; for doctorate, one foreign language, comprehensive exam, thesis/dissertation. *Entrance requirements:* For master's, GRE General Test, BA in German or equivalent; for doctorate, GRE General Test, MA in German or equivalent. Additional exam requirements/recommendations for international students: Required—TOEFL. *Application deadline:* For fall admission, 1/15 priority date for domestic students, 12/15 for international students; for spring admission, 9/1 priority date for domestic students, 9/1 for international students. Applications are processed on a rolling basis. Application fee: $50 ($60 for international students). *Financial support:* Fellowships with full and partial tuition reimbursements, research assistantships, teaching assistantships with full tuition reimbursements, Federal Work-Study, institutionally sponsored loans, scholarships/grants, and unspecified assistantships available. Support available to part-time students. Financial award application deadline: 1/15; financial award applicants required to submit FAFSA. *Faculty research:* German (and European) literature: medieval to modern/postmodern, German and culture studies, Germanic philology, literary theory, literature and the other arts. *Unit head:* Kari Ellen Gade, Director of Graduate Studies, 812-855-8138, Fax: 812-855-8292, E-mail: gade@indiana.edu. *Application contact:* Michelle Dunbar, Graduate Secretary, 812-855-7947, E-mail: germanic@indiana.edu.

The Johns Hopkins University, Zanvyl Krieger School of Arts and Sciences, Department of German and Romance Languages, Baltimore, MD 21218-2699. Offers French (PhD); German

(PhD); Italian (PhD); romance languages (PhD); Spanish (PhD). *Faculty:* 14 full-time (5 women), 2 part-time/adjunct (1 woman). *Students:* 69 full-time (48 women); includes 6 minority (all Hispanic Americans), 37 international. Average age 29. 42 applicants, 36% accepted, 8 enrolled. In 2007, 13 doctorates awarded. *Median time to degree:* Of those who began their doctoral program in fall 1999, 75% received their degree in 8 years or less. *Degree requirements:* For doctorate, 2 foreign languages, thesis/dissertation. *Entrance requirements:* For doctorate, GRE General Test. Additional exam requirements/recommendations for international students: Required—TOEFL (minimum score 600 paper-based; 250 computer-based). *Application deadline:* For fall admission, 1/15 for domestic and international students. Application fee: $60. Electronic applications accepted. *Financial support:* In 2007–08, 64 students received support, including 40 fellowships with full tuition reimbursements available (averaging $16,000 per year), 2 research assistantships with full tuition reimbursements available (averaging $16,000 per year), 19 teaching assistantships with full tuition reimbursements available (averaging $16,000 per year); institutionally sponsored loans and tuition waivers (full and partial) also available. Financial award application deadline: 4/15; financial award applicants required to submit FAFSA. *Unit head:* Dr. Stephen Nichols, Chair, 410-516-4736, Fax: 410-516-5358, E-mail: stephen.nichols@jhu.edu. *Application contact:* Sally Hauf, Graduate Administrative Coordinator, 410-516-7226, Fax: 410-516-5358, E-mail: shauf@jhu.edu.

Kansas State University, Graduate School, College of Arts and Sciences, Department of Modern Languages, Manhattan, KS 66506. Offers French (MA); German (MA); Spanish (MA). Part-time and evening/weekend programs available. Postbaccalaureate distance learning degree programs offered (minimal on-campus study). *Faculty:* 15 full-time (6 women). *Students:* 11 full-time (7 women), 6 part-time (5 women); includes 1 minority (Hispanic American), 4 international. 8 applicants, 75% accepted, 5 enrolled. In 2007, 9 degrees awarded. *Degree requirements:* For master's, thesis optional. *Entrance requirements:* For master's, teaching certificate. Additional exam requirements/recommendations for international students: Required—TOEFL (minimum score 560 paper-based). *Application deadline:* For fall admission, 2/1 priority date for domestic and international students; for spring admission, 10/1 for domestic students, 8/1 priority date for international students. Applications are processed on a rolling basis. Application fee: $30 ($55 for international students). *Financial support:* In 2007–08, 19 teaching assistantships with full tuition reimbursements (averaging $11,711 per year) were awarded; fellowships, Federal Work-Study, institutionally sponsored loans, and scholarships/grants also available. Support available to part-time students. Financial award application deadline: 3/1; financial award applicants required to submit FAFSA. *Faculty research:* Second language acquisitions; Chicano literature; Francophone literature; cultural studies; German, French, Spanish, and Spanish-American literature from the Middle Ages to the modern era. *Unit head:* Robert Corum, Head, 785-532-1987, Fax: 785-532-7004, E-mail: corum@ksu.edu. *Application contact:* Claire Dehon, Director, 785-532-1929, Fax: 785-532-7004, E-mail: dehoncl@ksu.edu.

Kent State University, College of Arts and Sciences, Department of Modern and Classical Language Studies, Kent, OH 44242-0001. Offers French literature (MA); French, Spanish, German and Latin pedagogy (MA); German literature (MA); Spanish literature (MA); translation (MA), including French, German, Japanese, Russian, Spanish; translation studies (PhD). Part-time and evening/weekend programs available. *Faculty:* 31 full-time (15 women), 4 part-time/adjunct (2 women). *Students:* 64 full-time (45 women), 27 part-time (26 women). Average age 32. 113 applicants, 80% accepted, 42 enrolled. In 2007, 27 degrees awarded. *Degree requirements:* For master's, one foreign language, comprehensive exam (for some programs), thesis (for some programs); for doctorate, comprehensive exam, thesis/dissertation (for some programs). *Entrance requirements:* For master's, minimum GPA of 3.0, writing sample, audio tape or CD; for doctorate, 3 recommendations. Additional exam requirements/recommendations for international students: Required—TOEFL (minimum score 197 computer-based). *Application deadline:* For fall admission, 2/28 for domestic and international students. Applications are processed on a rolling basis. Application fee: $30. Electronic applications accepted. *Financial support:* In 2007–08, 31 teaching assistantships with full tuition reimbursements (averaging $8,000 per year) were awarded; research assistantships with full tuition reimbursements, career-related internships or fieldwork, Federal Work-Study, health care benefits, tuition waivers (full and partial), and unspecified assistantships also available. Support available to part-time students. Financial award application deadline: 2/1. *Faculty research:* Literature, pedagogy, applied linguistics, translation studies. *Unit head:* Dr. Gregory M Shreve, Chair, 330-672-1796, Fax: 330-672-4009, E-mail: gshreve@kent.edu. *Application contact:* Carol S. Maier, Graduate Coordinator, 330-672-1797, Fax: 330-672-4009, E-mail: cmaier@kent.edu.

McGill University, Faculty of Graduate and Postdoctoral Studies, Faculty of Arts, Department of German Studies, Montréal, QC H3A 2T5, Canada. Offers MA, PhD. *Faculty:* 5 full-time (1 woman), 14 part-time/adjunct (8 women). *Students:* 13 full-time (8 women), 2 part-time (both women). 8 applicants, 88% accepted, 5 enrolled. In 2007, 1 master's, 1 doctorate awarded.

Memorial University of Newfoundland, School of Graduate Studies, Department of German and Russian, St. John's, NL A1C 5S7, Canada. Offers German language and literature (M Phil, MA). Part-time programs available. *Degree requirements:* For master's, one foreign language, thesis (for some programs), comprehensive exam (M Phil). *Entrance requirements:* For master's, honors degree (minimum 2nd class standing). Electronic applications accepted. *Faculty research:* German literature from the Middle Ages to the twentieth century, German studies.

Michigan State University, The Graduate School, College of Arts and Letters, Department of Linguistics and Germanic, Slavic, Asian, and African Languages, East Lansing, MI 48824. Offers German studies (MA, PhD); linguistics (MA, PhD); teaching English to speakers of other languages (MA). Part-time and evening/weekend programs available. *Entrance requirements:* For master's, GRE General Test, minimum GPA of 3.2 in last 2 undergraduate years, 2 years of college-level foreign language, 3 letters of recommendation, portfolio (German studies); for doctorate, GRE General Test, minimum graduate GPA of 3.5, 3 letters of recommendation, master's degree or sufficient graduate course work in linguistics or language of study, master's thesis or major research paper. Additional exam requirements/recommendations for international students: Required—TOEFL. Electronic applications accepted. *Expenses:* Tuition, state resident: part-time $379 per credit hour. Tuition, nonresident: part-time $800 per credit hour. Tuition and fees vary according to program.

Middlebury College, Language Schools, German School, Middlebury, VT 05753-6002. Offers MA, DML. *Faculty:* 5 full-time (3 women). *Students:* 32 full-time (19 women); includes 5 minority (2 African Americans, 2 Asian Americans or Pacific Islanders, 1 Hispanic American). Average age 29. 49 applicants, 86% accepted, 32 enrolled. In 2007, 14 degrees awarded. *Degree requirements:* For master's, one foreign language; for doctorate, 2 foreign languages, thesis/dissertation, residence abroad, teaching experience. *Entrance requirements:* For master's, placement exam, 3 letters of recommendation. *Application deadline:* Applications are processed on a rolling basis. Application fee: $55. Electronic applications accepted. *Financial support:* Fellowships, scholarships/grants available. *Unit head:* Dr. Jochen Richter, Director, 802-443-5203, Fax: 802-443-2075, E-mail: jrichter@middlebury.edu. *Application contact:* Christina Cartwright, Coordinator, 802-443-5203, Fax: 802-443-2075, E-mail: ccartwri@middlebury.edu.

Millersville University of Pennsylvania, Graduate School, School of Humanities and Social Sciences, Department of Foreign Languages, Program in German, Millersville, PA 17551-0302. Offers M Ed, MA. Part-time programs available. *Faculty:* 9 full-time (6 women), 3 part-time/adjunct (2 women). *Students:* Average age 26. In 2007, 2 degrees awarded. *Degree requirements:* For master's, one foreign language, thesis optional, departmental exam. *Entrance requirements:* For master's, GRE or MAT, minimum undergraduate GPA of 2.75, 24 undergraduate credits in German. Additional exam requirements/recommendations for international students: Required—TOEFL (minimum score 500 paper-based; 183 computer-based). *Application deadline:* For fall admission, 2/1 priority date for domestic students; for winter admission, 10/1 priority date for domestic students; for spring admission, 10/1 priority date for domestic students. Applications are processed on a rolling basis. Application fee: $40. Electronic applications accepted. *Expenses:* Tuition, state resident: full-time $6,214; part-time $345 per credit. Tuition, nonresident: full-time $9,944; part-time $552 per credit. Required fees: $1,442. Tuition and fees vary according to course load. *Financial support:* Research assistantships with tuition reimbursements, institutionally sponsored loans available. Support available to part-time students. Financial award application deadline: 3/15; financial award applicants required to submit FAFSA. *Application contact:* Dr. Victor S. DeSantis, Dean of Graduate Studies, 717-872-3099, Fax: 717-871-2022, E-mail: victor.desantis@millersville.edu.

Mississippi State University, College of Arts and Sciences, Department of Foreign Languages, Mississippi State, MS 39762. Offers French (MA); French/German (MA); German (MA); Spanish (MA); Spanish/French (MA); Spanish/German (MA). Part-time programs available. *Faculty:* 19 full-time (11 women), 5 part-time/adjunct (all women). *Students:* 22 full-time (12 women), 1 part-time; includes 2 minority (both Hispanic Americans), 4 international. Average age 30. 7 applicants, 86% accepted, 3 enrolled. In 2007, 7 degrees awarded. *Degree requirements:* For master's, one foreign language, thesis optional, comprehensive oral or written exam. *Entrance requirements:* For master's, minimum GPA of 2.75. Additional exam requirements/recommendations for international students: Required—TOEFL (minimum score 525 paper-based). *Application deadline:* For fall admission, 7/1 for domestic students; for spring admission, 11/1 for domestic students. Applications are processed on a rolling basis. Application fee: $30. *Expenses:* Tuition, state resident: full-time $4,978; part-time $274 per hour. Tuition, nonresident: full-time $11,469; part-time $635 per hour. *Financial support:* In 2007–08, 21 teaching assistantships with full tuition reimbursements (averaging $8,766 per year) were awarded; Federal Work-Study, institutionally sponsored loans, and unspecified assistantships also available. Financial award applicants required to submit FAFSA. *Faculty research:* French, German, Spanish literature from medieval to present; gender and cultural studies in French; Spanish American literature; foreign language methodology; linguistics. *Unit head:* Dr. Jack Jordan, Interim Head, 662-325-3480, Fax: 662-325-8209, E-mail: jordan@ra.msstate.edu. *Application contact:* Dr. William A. Person, Interim Associate Vice President for Academic Affairs/Interim Dean of Graduate Studies, 662-325-7400, Fax: 662-325-1967, E-mail: grad@grad.msstate.edu.

Missouri State University, Graduate College, College of Arts and Letters, Department of Modern and Classical Languages, Springfield, MO 65804-0094. Offers secondary education (MS Ed), including French, German, Spanish. *Faculty:* 5 full-time (2 women). *Students:* 2 full-time (both women), 5 part-time (all women); includes 2 minority (both Hispanic Americans) Average age 38. In 2007, 1 degree awarded. *Entrance requirements:* For master's, grades 9–12 teaching certification. Additional exam requirements/recommendations for international students: Required—TOEFL (minimum score 550 paper-based; 213 computer-based; 79 iBT), IELTS (minimum score 6). *Application deadline:* For fall admission, 7/20 priority date for domestic students; for spring admission, 12/20 priority date for domestic students. Application fee: $35. *Expenses:* Tuition, state resident: full-time $3,708; part-time $206 per credit hour. Tuition, nonresident: full-time $7,236; part-time $206 per credit hour. Required fees: $622. Full-time tuition and fees vary according to course level, course load, program and reciprocity agreements. *Financial support:* Teaching assistantships with full tuition reimbursements available. Financial award applicants required to submit FAFSA. *Unit head:* Dr. Madeleine Kernen, Head, 417-836-7626, E-mail: mcl@missouristate.edu.

New York University, Graduate School of Arts and Science, Department of German, New York, NY 10012-1019. Offers German studies and critical thought (MA, PhD). Part-time programs available. *Faculty:* 8 full-time (5 women), 5 part-time/adjunct. *Students:* 19 full-time (10 women), 7 part-time (2 women), 13 international. Average age 34. 25 applicants, 20% accepted, 4 enrolled. In 2007, 1 master's, 1 doctorate awarded. Terminal master's awarded for partial completion of doctoral program. *Degree requirements:* For master's, one foreign language, thesis; for doctorate, 2 foreign languages, thesis/dissertation. *Entrance requirements:* For master's, GRE Subject Test; for doctorate, GRE Subject Test, sample of written work. Additional exam requirements/recommendations for international students: Required—TOEFL. *Application deadline:* For fall admission, 1/4 priority date for domestic students. Application fee: $85. *Financial support:* Fellowships with tuition reimbursements, teaching assistantships with tuition reimbursements, Federal Work-Study, institutionally sponsored loans, scholarships/grants, health care benefits, and unspecified assistantships available. Financial award application deadline: 1/4; financial award applicants required to submit FAFSA. *Faculty research:* Eighteenth to twentieth century literature, culture and critical thought, film and visual culture, philosophy, critical theory. *Unit head:* Eckart Goebel, Chair, 212-998-8650, Fax: 212-995-4823, E-mail: german.dept@nyu.edu.

Northwestern University, The Graduate School, Judd A. and Marjorie Weinberg College of Arts and Sciences, Program in German Literature and Critical Thought, Evanston, IL 60208. Offers PhD. Admissions and degrees offered through The Graduate School. *Degree requirements:* For doctorate, one foreign language, thesis/dissertation. *Entrance requirements:* For doctorate, GRE General Test. Additional exam requirements/recommendations for international students: Required—TOEFL. Electronic applications accepted. *Faculty research:* Eighteenth through twentieth century German literature, comparative literature, theory, philosophy, language pedagogy.

The Ohio State University, Graduate School, College of Humanities, Department of Germanic Languages and Literatures, Columbus, OH 43210. Offers MA, PhD. *Faculty:* 16. *Students:* 24 full-time (15 women), 3 part-time (2 women); includes 1 minority (African American), 8 international. Average age 29. In 2007, 7 master's, 2 doctorates awarded. *Degree requirements:* For master's, one foreign language, thesis optional; for doctorate, 2 foreign languages, thesis/dissertation. *Entrance requirements:* For master's and doctorate, GRE General Test. Additional exam requirements/recommendations for international students: Required—TOEFL (minimum score 600 paper-based; 250 computer-based). *Application deadline:* For fall admission, 8/15 priority date for domestic students, 7/1 priority date for international students; for winter admission, 12/1 priority date for domestic students, 11/1 priority date for international students; for spring admission, 3/1 priority date for domestic students, 2/1 priority date for international students. Applications are processed on a rolling basis. Application fee: $40 ($50 for international students). Electronic applications accepted. *Financial support:* Fellowships, research assistantships, teaching assistantships, Federal Work-Study and institutionally sponsored loans available. Support available to part-time students. *Faculty research:* German literature, Germanic philology, linguistics. *Unit head:* Kai Hammermeister, Graduate Studies Committee Chair, 614-292-6985, Fax: 614-292-8510, E-mail: hammermeister.1@osu.edu. *Application contact:* 614-292-9444, Fax: 614-292-3895, E-mail: domestic.grad@osu.edu.

Penn State University Park, Graduate School, College of the Liberal Arts, Department of Germanic and Slavic Languages and Literatures, State College, University Park, PA 16802-1503. Offers German (MA, PhD). *Expenses:* Tuition, state resident: full-time $14,738; part-time $614 per credit. Tuition, nonresident: full-time $26,050; part-time $1,085 per credit. Tuition and fees vary according to course load, program and student level. *Faculty research:* Literature, literary theory, culture, language pedagogy. *Unit head:* Dr. Adrian J. Wanner, Head, 814-865-1097, Fax: 814-863-8882, E-mail: ajw3@psu.edu. *Application contact:* Irene Grassi, Information Contact, E-mail: irg1@psu.edu.

Portland State University, Graduate Studies, College of Liberal Arts and Sciences, Department of Foreign Languages and Literatures, Portland, OR 97207-0751. Offers foreign literature and language (MA); French (MA); German (MA); Japanese (MA); Spanish (MA). Part-time programs available. *Faculty:* 40 full-time (24 women), 24 part-time/adjunct (15 women). *Students:* 35 full-time (20 women), 13 part-time (12 women); includes 4 minority (1 Asian American or Pacific Islander, 3 Hispanic Americans), 11 international. Average age 32. 27 applicants, 74% accepted, 15 enrolled. In 2007, 18 master's awarded. *Degree requirements:* For master's, one foreign language, thesis (for some programs). *Entrance requirements:* Additional exam requirements/recommendations for international students: Required—TOEFL (minimum score 550 paper-based; 213 computer-based). *Application deadline:* For fall admission, 4/1 for domestic students, 3/1 for international students; for winter admission, 8/1 for domestic students, 7/1 for international students; for spring admission, 11/1 for domestic and inter-

German

Portland State University (continued)
national students. Applications are processed on a rolling basis. Application fee: $50. *Expenses:* Tuition, state resident: full-time $7,047. Tuition, nonresident: full-time $11,178. *Financial support:* In 2007–08, 5 teaching assistantships with full tuition reimbursements (averaging $7,921 per year) were awarded; research assistantships with full tuition reimbursements, Federal Work-Study, scholarships/grants, and unspecified assistantships also available. Support available to part-time students. Financial award application deadline: 3/1; financial award applicants required to submit FAFSA. *Faculty research:* Foreign language pedagogy, applied and social linguistics, literary history and criticism. Total annual research expenditures: $69,175. *Unit head:* Dr. Sandra F. Freels, Chair, 503-725-3522, Fax: 503-725-5276. *Application contact:* Karen Popp, Office Coordinator, 503-725-3522, E-mail: poppk@pdx.edu.

Princeton University, Graduate School, Department of Germanic Languages and Literatures, Princeton, NJ 08544-1019. Offers PhD. *Degree requirements:* For doctorate, 2 foreign languages, thesis/dissertation. *Entrance requirements:* For doctorate, GRE General Test. Additional exam requirements/recommendations for international students: Required—TOEFL (minimum score 600 paper-based; 250 computer-based). Electronic applications accepted.

Purdue University, Graduate School, College of Liberal Arts, Department of Foreign Languages and Literatures, West Lafayette, IN 47907. Offers French (MA, MAT, PhD), including French (MA, PhD), French education (MAT); German (MA, MAT, PhD), including German (MA, PhD), German education (MAT); Spanish (MA, MAT, PhD), including Spanish (MA, PhD), Spanish education (MAT). Terminal master's awarded for partial completion of doctoral program. *Degree requirements:* For master's, one foreign language; for doctorate, 2 foreign languages, thesis/dissertation. *Entrance requirements:* For master's and doctorate, GRE, writing sample, sample recording of English and language of study. Additional exam requirements/recommendations for international students: Required—TOEFL. Electronic applications accepted. *Faculty research:* Linguistics, semiotics, literary criticism, pedagogy.

Queen's University at Kingston, School of Graduate Studies and Research, Faculty of Arts and Sciences, Department of German Language and Literature, Kingston, ON K7L 3N6, Canada. Offers MA, PhD. Part-time programs available. *Degree requirements:* For master's, thesis optional; for doctorate, one foreign language, comprehensive exam, thesis/dissertation. *Entrance requirements:* For master's, 7 German courses, honors bachelors degree in German; for doctorate, MA or equivalent in German. Additional exam requirements/recommendations for international students: Required—TOEFL. Electronic applications accepted. *Faculty research:* Goethe and Weimar classicism, Romanticism, nineteenth- and twentieth-century German literature.

Rider University, Department of Graduate Education, Leadership and Counseling, Teacher Certification Program, Lawrenceville, NJ 08648-3001. Offers business education (Certificate); elementary education (Certificate); English as a second language (Certificate); English education (Certificate); mathematics education (Certificate); preschool to grade 3 (Certificate); science education (Certificate); social studies education (Certificate); world languages (Certificate), including French, German, Spanish. Part-time programs available. *Faculty:* 5 full-time (1 woman), 4 part-time/adjunct (3 women). *Students:* 40 full-time (34 women), 103 part-time (81 women); includes 12 minority (5 African Americans, 1 Asian American or Pacific Islander, 6 Hispanic Americans), 6 international. Average age 35. 61 applicants, 69% accepted, 39 enrolled. In 2007, 111 degrees awarded. *Degree requirements:* For Certificate, internship, professional portfolio. *Entrance requirements:* For degree, PRAXIS, resumé. Additional exam requirements/recommendations for international students: Required—TOEFL (minimum score 550 paper-based; 213 computer-based). *Application deadline:* For fall admission, 5/1 priority date for domestic students, 6/1 priority date for international students; for spring admission, 11/1 priority date for domestic and international students. Applications are processed on a rolling basis. Application fee: $50. Electronic applications accepted. *Expenses:* Tuition: Full-time $25,650; part-time $472 per credit. Required fees: $22 per credit. Tuition and fees vary according to program. *Financial support:* In 2007–08, 46 students received support. Career-related internships or fieldwork, Federal Work-Study, institutionally sponsored loans, and unspecified assistantships available. Support available to part-time students. Financial award applicants required to submit FAFSA. *Faculty research:* Conceptual foundations for optimal development of creativity; creative theory, cognitive processes in mathematics learning, teacher collaboration. *Unit head:* Dr. Austin Winther, Program Coordinator, 609-895-5473, Fax: 609-896-5362. *Application contact:* Jamie L Mitchell, Director of Graduate Admissions, 609-896-5036, Fax: 609-895-5680, E-mail: jmitchell@rider.edu.

Rutgers, The State University of New Jersey, New Brunswick, Graduate School, Program in German, New Brunswick, NJ 08901-1281. Offers German (MAT, PhD); German literature (MA, PhD). Part-time and evening/weekend programs available. Terminal master's awarded for partial completion of doctoral program. *Degree requirements:* For master's, one foreign language, comprehensive exam, thesis or alternative; for doctorate, 2 foreign languages, comprehensive exam, thesis/dissertation. *Entrance requirements:* For master's and doctorate, GRE General Test. Additional exam requirements/recommendations for international students: Required—TOEFL. *Faculty research:* Literature and ideology; early German novella; narrative structures, mythology, psychology, and realist literature; German-American cultural history; literary theory and aesthetics.

San Francisco State University, Division of Graduate Studies, College of Humanities, Department of Foreign Languages and Literatures, Program in German, San Francisco, CA 94132-1722. Offers MA. *Application deadline:* Applications are processed on a rolling basis. *Unit head:* Dr. Volker Langbehn, Program Coordinator, 415-338-7422. *Application contact:* Dr. Ilona Vandergriff, Graduate Coordinator, 415-338-7422, E-mail: vdgriff@sfsu.edu.

Stanford University, School of Humanities and Sciences, Department of German Studies, Stanford, CA 94305-9991. Offers MA, PhD. *Degree requirements:* For master's, one foreign language, oral exam; for doctorate, 2 foreign languages, thesis/dissertation, oral exam, qualifying paper and exam. *Entrance requirements:* For master's and doctorate, GRE General Test. Additional exam requirements/recommendations for international students: Required—TOEFL. Electronic applications accepted.

Texas Tech University, Graduate School, College of Arts and Sciences, Department of Classical and Modern Languages and Literatures, Program in German, Lubbock, TX 79409. Offers MA. *Students:* 5 full-time (0 women), 2 part-time (1 woman); includes 2 minority (both Asian Americans or Pacific Islanders), 1 international. Average age 32. 7 applicants, 86% accepted, 3 enrolled. In 2007, 4 degrees awarded. *Entrance requirements:* For master's, GRE General Test. Additional exam requirements/recommendations for international students: Required—TOEFL (minimum score 550 paper-based; 213 computer-based). *Application deadline:* For fall admission, 3/1 priority date for international students; for spring admission, 11/1 priority date for international students. Applications are processed on a rolling basis. Application fee: $50 ($60 for international students). Electronic applications accepted. *Expenses:* Tuition, state resident: part-time $373 per credit hour. Tuition, nonresident: part-time $651 per credit hour. Tuition and fees vary according to program. *Financial support:* Research assistantships with partial tuition reimbursements, teaching assistantships with partial tuition reimbursements available. Financial award application deadline: 4/15. *Faculty research:* German literature, Goethe, business German, German culture, German in the southwest. *Unit head:* Dr. Charles A. Grair, Graduate Advisor and Associate Professor of German, 806-742-3145 Ext. 275, Fax: 806-742-3306, E-mail: charles.grair@ttu.edu. *Application contact:* Liz Hildebrand, Senior Advisor, 806-742-4055, Fax: 806-742-3306, E-mail: liz.hildebrand@ttu.edu.

Tufts University, Graduate School of Arts and Sciences, Department of Russian and German, Medford, MA 02155. Offers German (MA). Part-time programs available. *Faculty:* 27 full-time, 11 part-time/adjunct. *Students:* 7 (6 women); includes 1 minority (African American) 1 international. 4 applicants, 100% accepted, 3 enrolled. In 2007, 2 degrees awarded. *Degree requirements:* For master's, one foreign language, oral and written exam. *Entrance requirements:* Additional exam requirements/recommendations for international students: Required—TOEFL (minimum score 550 paper-based; 213 computer-based; 80 iBT). *Application deadline:* For fall admission, 3/1 for domestic students, 12/30 for international students; for spring admission, 10/15 for domestic students, 9/15 for international students. Applications are processed on a rolling basis. Application fee: $70. Electronic applications accepted. *Expenses:* Tuition: Full-time $35,052. *Financial support:* Teaching assistantships with full and partial tuition reimbursements, Federal Work-Study, scholarships/grants, and tuition waivers (partial) available. Support available to part-time students. Financial award application deadline: 3/1; financial award applicants required to submit FAFSA. *Unit head:* Hosea Hirata, Chair, 617-627-34442, Fax: 617-627-3945. *Application contact:* Ronald Salter, Graduate Director, 617-627-3442, Fax: 617-627-3945.

Université de Montréal, Faculty of Arts and Sciences, Department of Literatures and Modern Languages, Program in German Studies, Montréal, QC H3C 3J7, Canada. Offers MA. *Students:* 18 full-time (11 women). 8 applicants, 88% accepted, 5 enrolled. In 2007, 4 degrees awarded. *Degree requirements:* For master's, 2 foreign languages, thesis. *Application deadline:* For fall admission, 2/1 priority date for domestic students; for winter admission, 11/1 priority date for domestic students; for spring admission, 2/1 priority date for domestic students. Application fee: $100. Electronic applications accepted. *Financial support:* Teaching assistantships available. *Unit head:* Nikola von Merveldt, Responsible for German Studies Program, 514-343-5905, Fax: 514-343-2255, E-mail: n.von.merveldt@umontreal.ca.

The University of Alabama, Graduate School, College of Arts and Sciences, Department of Modern Languages and Classics, Tuscaloosa, AL 35487. Offers French (MA, PhD); French and Spanish (PhD); German (MA); Romance languages (MA, PhD); Spanish (MA, PhD). Part-time programs available. *Faculty:* 22 full-time (12 women). *Students:* 47 full-time (35 women), 14 part-time (9 women); includes 12 minority (2 African Americans, 10 Hispanic Americans), 15 international. Average age 32. 26 applicants, 69% accepted, 14 enrolled. In 2007, 12 master's, 4 doctorates awarded. *Median time to degree:* Of those who began their doctoral program in fall 1999, 40% received their degree in 8 years or less. *Degree requirements:* For master's, comprehensive exam, thesis optional; for doctorate, one foreign language, thesis/dissertation, preliminary exam. *Entrance requirements:* For master's and doctorate, minimum GPA of 3.0, writing sample. Additional exam requirements/recommendations for international students: Required—TOEFL or IELTS. *Application deadline:* For fall admission, 7/6 priority date for domestic students, 1/15 priority date for international students; for spring admission, 12/6 priority date for domestic students, 6/1 priority date for international students. Applications are processed on a rolling basis. Application fee: $30. Electronic applications accepted. *Expenses:* Tuition, state resident: full-time $5,700. Tuition, nonresident: full-time $16,518. *Financial support:* In 2007–08, 7 students received support, including 1 fellowship, research assistantships with full tuition reimbursements available (averaging $10,291 per year), 6 teaching assistantships with full tuition reimbursements available (averaging $10,291 per year); career-related internships or fieldwork, Federal Work-Study, institutionally sponsored loans, and scholarships/grants also available. Financial award application deadline: 7/14. *Faculty research:* Non-English literature, linguistics, culture, film. Total annual research expenditures: $48,751. *Unit head:* Dr. Michael Picone, Chair and Professor, 205-348-5054, Fax: 205-348-2042, E-mail: mpicone@bama.ua.edu. *Application contact:* Dr. K. Barbara Fischer, Graduate Director and Associate Professor, 205-348-8465, Fax: 205-348-2042, E-mail: bfischer@bama.ua.edu.

University of Alberta, Faculty of Graduate Studies and Research, Department of Modern Languages and Cultural Studies, Edmonton, AB T6G 2E1, Canada. Offers applied linguistics (Germanic, Romance, Slavic) (MA); French language, literatures and linguistics (PhD); French language, literatures, and linguistics (MA); Germanic languages, literatures and linguistics (PhD); Germanic languages, literatures, and linguistics (MA); Italian studies (MA); Slavic languages and literatures (Russian, Ukrainian) (MA, PhD); Slavic linguistics (Russian, Ukrainian) (MA, PhD); Spanish and Latin American studies (MA, PhD); Ukrainian folklore (MA, PhD). Part-time programs available. *Degree requirements:* For master's, one foreign language, thesis; for doctorate, 2 foreign languages, comprehensive exam, thesis/dissertation. *Entrance requirements:* For master's and doctorate, 1 language other than English. Additional exam requirements/recommendations for international students: Required—Michigan English Language Assessment Battery or TOEFL (paper score 550; computer score 213). Electronic applications accepted. *Faculty research:* Russian/Ukrainian studies; German studies; contemporary Latin American, French and Francophone studies; Italian studies.

The University of Arizona, Graduate College, College of Humanities, Department of German Studies, Tucson, AZ 85721. Offers German (MA, PhD). *Faculty:* 11. *Students:* 12 full-time (9 women); includes 2 minority (1 African American, 1 Hispanic American), 2 international. Average age 27. 7 applicants, 100% accepted, 5 enrolled. In 2007, 6 degrees awarded. *Degree requirements:* For master's, one foreign language, comprehensive exam, oral exam; for doctorate, 2 foreign languages, comprehensive exam, thesis/dissertation, oral exam, oral defense. *Entrance requirements:* For master's, GRE, minimum GPA of 3.0, 3 letters of recommendation, statement of purpose, audio sample. Additional exam requirements/recommendations for international students: Required—TOEFL (minimum score 550 paper-based). *Application deadline:* For fall admission, 3/1 for domestic students, 12/1 for international students; for spring admission, 10/1 for domestic students, 6/1 for international students. Applications are processed on a rolling basis. Application fee: $50. Electronic applications accepted. *Financial support:* In 2007–08, 2 research assistantships with partial tuition reimbursements (averaging $14,285 per year), 17 teaching assistantships with partial tuition reimbursements (averaging $14,285 per year) were awarded; Federal Work-Study, institutionally sponsored loans, scholarships/grants, and tuition waivers (partial) also available. Financial award application deadline: 3/1. *Faculty research:* Literature, language, and foreign language pedagogy; computer-assisted text analysis. Total annual research expenditures: $18,191. *Unit head:* Dr. Mary Wildner-Bassett, Head, 520-621-1799, Fax: 520-626-8268, E-mail: wildnerb@u.arizona.edu. *Application contact:* Susanna Ruiz, Information Contact, 520-626-8123, Fax: 520-626-8268, E-mail: ruizs@u.arizona.edu.

University of Arkansas, Graduate School, J. William Fulbright College of Arts and Sciences, Department of Foreign Languages, Program in German, Fayetteville, AR 72701-1201. Offers MA. *Students:* 4 full-time (all women), 1 part-time, 2 international. In 2007, 2 degrees awarded. *Degree requirements:* For master's, variable foreign language requirement. Application fee: $40 ($50 for international students). *Financial support:* In 2007–08, 6 teaching assistantships were awarded; fellowships, research assistantships, career-related internships or fieldwork and Federal Work-Study also available. Support available to part-time students. Financial award application deadline: 4/1; financial award applicants required to submit FAFSA. *Unit head:* Kathleen Condray, Graduate Coordinator, 479-575-2951, Fax: 479-575-6795, E-mail: condray@uark.edu.

The University of British Columbia, Faculty of Arts and Faculty of Graduate Studies, Department of Central, Eastern and Northern European Studies, Vancouver, BC V6T 1Z1, Canada. Offers Germanic studies (MA, PhD). Part-time programs available. *Faculty:* 8 full-time (2 women). *Students:* 15 full-time (10 women). 6 applicants, 50% accepted. In 2007, 2 master's, 2 doctorates awarded. *Median time to degree:* Of those who began their doctoral program in fall 1999, 100% received their degree in 8 years or less. *Degree requirements:* For master's, one foreign language, thesis optional, exam; for doctorate, comprehensive exam, thesis/dissertation. *Entrance requirements:* For master's, BA in German; for doctorate, MA in German. Additional exam requirements/recommendations for international students: Required—TOEFL (minimum score 550 paper-based; 213 computer-based). *Application deadline:* For fall admission, 1/15 for domestic students, 2/15 for international students. Applications are processed on a rolling basis. Application fee: $90 Canadian dollars ($150 Canadian dollars for international students). Electronic applications accepted. *Financial support:* In 2007–08, 10 students received support, including 5 fellowships with partial tuition reimbursements available (averaging $3,300 per year), 4 research assistantships with partial tuition reimbursements available (averaging $5,000 per year), 10 teaching assistantships with full tuition reimbursements available (averaging $10,000 per year); career-related internships or fieldwork, Federal Work-Study, scholarships/grants, and tuition waivers (full and partial) also available. Support available to part-time students. Financial award application deadline: 1/15. *Faculty research:* Second language acquisition, media theory, performance theory, gender studies, cultural studies. *Unit head:* Dr. Thomas Salumets, Head, 604-822-6403, Fax: 604-822-9344, E-mail: german@interchange.ubc.ca. *Application contact:* Dr. Gaby Pailer, Graduate Admissions, 604-822-4042, Fax: 604-822-9344, E-mail: german@interchange.ubc.ca.

University of Calgary, Faculty of Graduate Studies, Faculty of Humanities, Department of Germanic, Slavic and East Asian Studies, Calgary, AB T2N 1N4, Canada. Offers German (MA). Part-time programs available. *Faculty:* 5 full-time (4 women). *Students:* 6 full-time (4 women). Average age 43. 2 applicants, 100% accepted, 2 enrolled. In 2007, 1 degree awarded. *Degree requirements:* For master's, one foreign language, thesis. *Entrance requirements:* Additional exam requirements/recommendations for international students: Required—TOEFL. *Application deadline:* For fall admission, 4/1 for domestic students, 2/1 for international students; for winter admission, 9/15 for domestic students, 9/1 for international students. Applications are processed on a rolling basis. Application fee: $100 ($130 for international students). Electronic applications accepted. *Financial support:* In 2007–08, 10 research assistantships (averaging $4,100 per year), 3 teaching assistantships (averaging $7,020 per year) were awarded; fellowships, scholarships/grants also available. Financial award application deadline: 2/1. *Faculty research:* German language and linguistics, second language acquisition, medieval and early modern literature and culture, twentieth century German literature. *Unit head:* Dr. X. Jie Yang, Head, 403-220-7218, Fax: 403-284-3810, E-mail: xyang@ucalgary.ca. *Application contact:* Dr. Mary O'Brien, Graduate Coordinator, 403-220-5308, Fax: 403-284-3810, E-mail: mgobriend@ucalgary.ca.

University of California, Berkeley, Graduate Division, College of Letters and Science, Department of German, Berkeley, CA 94720-1500. Offers PhD. *Degree requirements:* For doctorate, 2 foreign languages, thesis/dissertation, qualifying exam. *Entrance requirements:* For doctorate, GRE General Test, minimum GPA of 3.0, writing sample, 3 letters of recommendation. *Application deadline:* For fall admission, 12/15 for domestic students. Application fee: $70 ($90 for international students). Electronic applications accepted. *Financial support:* Fellowships, research assistantships, teaching assistantships, Federal Work-Study, tuition waivers (full and partial), and unspecified assistantships available. *Faculty research:* German literature/culture, film, Germanic linguistics, second-language acquisition. *Unit head:* Niklaus Largier, Chair, 510-643-3984, Fax: 510-643-3243, E-mail: nlargier@berkeley.edu. *Application contact:* Elisabeth Lamoureaux, Graduate Assistant for Admissions, 510-643-2004, Fax: 510-642-3243, E-mail: germanga@berkeley.edu.

University of California, Davis, Graduate Studies, Program in German, Davis, CA 95616. Offers MA, PhD. Terminal master's awarded for partial completion of doctoral program. *Degree requirements:* For master's, comprehensive exam (for some programs), thesis (for some programs); for doctorate, thesis/dissertation. *Entrance requirements:* For master's, GRE; for doctorate, GRE, master's degree or equivalent. Additional exam requirements/recommendations for international students: Required—TOEFL (minimum score 550 paper-based; 213 computer-based). Electronic applications accepted. *Faculty research:* Sixteenth to twentieth century medieval literature, critical theory, women's studies.

University of California, Irvine, Office of Graduate Studies, School of Humanities, Department of German, Irvine, CA 92697. Offers MA, PhD. *Students:* 11 full-time (7 women); includes 1 minority (Asian American or Pacific Islander), 2 international. In 2007, 1 master's, 2 doctorates awarded. *Degree requirements:* For doctorate, thesis/dissertation. *Entrance requirements:* For master's and doctorate, GRE General Test, minimum GPA of 3.0. Additional exam requirements/recommendations for international students: Required—TOEFL (minimum score 550 paper-based; 213 computer-based). *Application deadline:* For fall admission, 1/15 priority date for domestic students; for winter admission, 10/15 priority date for domestic students. Applications are processed on a rolling basis. Application fee: $60. Electronic applications accepted. *Financial support:* In 2007–08, fellowships (averaging $15,738 per year), teaching assistantships with partial tuition reimbursements (averaging $13,594 per year) were awarded; institutionally sponsored loans, traineeships, health care benefits, and unspecified assistantships also available. Financial award application deadline: 3/1; financial award applicants required to submit FAFSA. *Faculty research:* Goethe yearbook, fin de siècle theory, Thomas Mann. *Unit head:* Jens Rieckmann, Chair, 949-824-6406, Fax: 949-824-6416, E-mail: jrieckma@uci.edu. *Application contact:* Karen Lowe, Manager, 949-824-4942, Fax: 949-824-6416, E-mail: kilowe@uci.edu.

University of California, Los Angeles, Graduate Division, College of Letters and Science, Department of Germanic Languages, Program in Germanic Languages, Los Angeles, CA 90095. Offers MA, PhD. *Students:* 12 full-time (6 women); includes 1 minority (Asian American or Pacific Islander), 3 international. Average age 32. 16 applicants, 44% accepted, 2 enrolled. In 2007, 1 master's, 3 doctorates awarded. Terminal master's awarded for partial completion of doctoral program. *Degree requirements:* For master's, one foreign language, comprehensive exam or thesis; for doctorate, 2 foreign languages, oral and written qualifying exams. *Entrance requirements:* For master's, GRE General Test, BA in German with minimum GPA of 3.0, sample of written work; for doctorate, GRE General Test, minimum undergraduate GPA of 3.0, MA in German or equivalent, sample of written work. *Application deadline:* For fall admission, 12/15 for domestic students. Application fee: $60. Electronic applications accepted. *Expenses:* Tuition, nonresident: full-time $5,728. Required fees: $8,966. Full-time tuition and fees vary according to program and student level. *Financial support:* In 2007–08, 13 fellowships with full and partial tuition reimbursements, 4 research assistantships with full and partial tuition reimbursements, 10 teaching assistantships with full and partial tuition reimbursements were awarded. Financial award applicants required to submit FAFSA. *Application contact:* Departmental Office, 310-825-3955, E-mail: allen@humnet.ucla.edu.

University of California, San Diego, Office of Graduate Studies, Department of Literature, Program in German Literature, La Jolla, CA 92093. Offers MA. *Degree requirements:* For master's, thesis. *Entrance requirements:* For master's, GRE General Test, GRE Subject Test. Electronic applications accepted.

University of California, Santa Barbara, Graduate Division, College of Letters and Sciences, Division of Humanities and Fine Arts, Department of Germanic, Slavic, and Semitic Studies, Santa Barbara, CA 93106. Offers Germanic languages and literature (MA, PhD), including applied linguistics (optional emphasis) (PhD), women's studies (optional emphasis) (PhD); MA/PhD. *Faculty:* 3 full-time (2 women). *Students:* 4 full-time (2 women), 2 international. Average age 31. 5 applicants, 80% accepted, 0 enrolled. In 2007, 1 master's, 2 doctorates awarded. Terminal master's awarded for partial completion of doctoral program. *Median time to degree:* Of those who began their doctoral program in fall 1999, 100% received their degree in 8 years or less. *Degree requirements:* For master's, 2 foreign languages, comprehensive exam, thesis, 36 units graduate level coursework; for doctorate, 3 foreign languages, comprehensive exam, thesis/dissertation. *Entrance requirements:* For master's and doctorate, GRE, sample of written work, tape of spoken German and/or English, proficiency in a foreign language. Additional exam requirements/recommendations for international students: Required—TOEFL (minimum score 550 paper-based; 213 computer-based; 80 iBT). *Application deadline:* For fall admission, 12/31 for domestic students, 5/1 for international students; for winter admission, 11/1 for domestic and international students; for spring admission, 2/1 for domestic and international students. Applications are processed on a rolling basis. Application fee: $60. Electronic applications accepted. *Expenses:* Tuition, nonresident: full-time $14,888. Required fees: $10,108. *Financial support:* In 2007–08, 4 students received support, including fellowships with full and partial tuition reimbursements available (averaging $5,400 per year), teaching assistantships with full and partial tuition reimbursements available (averaging $16,389 per year); Federal Work-Study, institutionally sponsored loans, scholarships/grants, and health care benefits also available. Financial award application deadline: 12/15; financial award applicants required to submit FAFSA. *Faculty research:* Critical theory, media-technology, psychoanalysis, German romanticism, Goethe. *Unit head:* Prof. Elisabeth Weber, Chair, 805-893-2295, E-mail: weber@gss.ucsb.edu. *Application contact:* Sierra Gray, Graduate Program Assistant, 805-893-2131, Fax: 805-893-2374, E-mail: sierra@gss.ucsb.edu.

University of Chicago, Division of the Humanities, Department of Germanic Languages and Literatures, Chicago, IL 60637-1513. Offers AM, PhD. *Students:* 24. 35 applicants, 23% accepted, 5 enrolled.Terminal master's awarded for partial completion of doctoral program. *Degree requirements:* For master's, one foreign language, thesis; for doctorate, 2 foreign languages, thesis/dissertation. *Entrance requirements:* For master's and doctorate, GRE General Test. Additional exam requirements/recommendations for international students: Required—TOEFL. *Application deadline:* For fall admission, 12/15 for domestic students. Application fee: $55. *Financial support:* Fellowships, Federal Work-Study available. Financial award application deadline: 12/15; financial award applicants required to submit FAFSA. *Unit head:* Dr. Eric Santner, Chair, 773-702-8494.

University of Cincinnati, Graduate School, McMicken College of Arts and Sciences, Department of German Studies, Cincinnati, OH 45221. Offers MA, PhD. Part-time programs available. *Faculty:* 7 full-time (3 women), 3 part-time/adjunct (1 woman). *Students:* 18 full-time (10 women), 7 part-time (6 women), 10 international. Average age 29. 21 applicants, 43% accepted, 8 enrolled. In 2007, 1 master's, 2 doctorates awarded. Terminal master's awarded for partial completion of doctoral program. *Median time to degree:* Of those who began their doctoral program in fall 1999, 100% received their degree in 8 years or less. *Degree requirements:* For master's, one foreign language, thesis or alternative; for doctorate, 3 foreign languages, thesis/dissertation. *Entrance requirements:* For master's, GRE General Test; for doctorate, GRE General Test, MA in German or equivalent. Additional exam requirements/recommendations for international students: Required—TOEFL (minimum score 560 paper-based). *Application deadline:* For fall admission, 2/1 for domestic and international students; for winter admission, 1/15 priority date for domestic students, 1/15 for international students. Applications are processed on a rolling basis. Application fee: $40. Electronic applications accepted. *Financial support:* In 2007–08, 20 students received support, including 1 fellowship with full tuition reimbursement available (averaging $14,000 per year), 3 research assistantships with full tuition reimbursements available (averaging $11,200 per year), 15 teaching assistantships with full tuition reimbursements available (averaging $11,200 per year); tuition waivers (partial) and unspecified assistantships also available. Financial award application deadline: 5/1. *Faculty research:* German literary culture, language and linguistics, medieval and early modern, German-Jewish literature, 20th and 21st century German literature and film. *Unit head:* Dr. Katharina Gerstenberger, Head, 513-556-2760, Fax: 513-556-1991, E-mail: katharina.gerstenberger@uc.edu. *Application contact:* Dr. Sara Friedrichsmeyer, Graduate Program Director, 513-556-2752, Fax: 513-556-1991, E-mail: sara.friedrichsmeyer@uc.edu.

University of Colorado at Boulder, Graduate School, College of Arts and Sciences, Department of Germanic and Slavic Languages, Boulder, CO 80309. Offers German (MA). Part-time programs available. *Faculty:* 12. *Students:* 13 full-time (10 women), 2 part-time (1 woman); includes 1 minority (African American), 4 international. Average age 26. 8 applicants, 100% accepted. In 2007, 9 degrees awarded. *Degree requirements:* For master's, 2 foreign languages, comprehensive exam, thesis or alternative. *Entrance requirements:* For master's, minimum undergraduate GPA of 2.75. *Application deadline:* For fall admission, 2/1 priority date for domestic students, 12/1 for international students; for spring admission, 9/15 for domestic and international students. Application fee: $50 ($60 for international students). *Financial support:* In 2007–08, 12 fellowships (averaging $3,658 per year) were awarded; Federal Work-Study, institutionally sponsored loans, and scholarships/grants also available. Financial award application deadline: 2/1. *Faculty research:* Eighteenth-, nineteenth-, and twentieth-century literature, culture and thought; intellectual history; film; philosophy; social and political theory; German, Scandanavian, and comparative literature. *Unit head:* Artemi Romanov, Chair, 303-492-7404, Fax: 303-492-5376, E-mail: artemi.romanov@colorado.edu. *Application contact:* Graduate Program Assistant, 303-492-7404, Fax: 303-492-5376, E-mail: gsll@colorado.edu.

University of Connecticut, Graduate School, College of Liberal Arts and Sciences, Department of Modern and Classical Languages, Field of German, Storrs, CT 06269. Offers MA, PhD. *Faculty:* 5 full-time (3 women). *Students:* 12 full-time (10 women), 8 international. Average age 28. 9 applicants, 44% accepted, 4 enrolled. In 2007, 3 master's, 1 doctorate awarded. Terminal master's awarded for partial completion of doctoral program. *Degree requirements:* For master's, comprehensive exam; for doctorate, thesis/dissertation. *Entrance requirements:* For master's and doctorate, GRE General Test. Additional exam requirements/recommendations for international students: Required—TOEFL (minimum score 550 paper-based; 213 computer-based). *Application deadline:* For fall admission, 2/1 priority date for domestic and international students; for spring admission, 11/1 for domestic students, 10/1 for international students. Applications are processed on a rolling basis. Application fee: $55. Electronic applications accepted. *Expenses:* Tuition, state resident: part-time $469 per credit hour. Tuition, nonresident: part-time $1,218 per credit hour. *Financial support:* In 2007–08, 1 research assistantship, 11 teaching assistantships with full tuition reimbursements were awarded; fellowships, Federal Work-Study, scholarships/grants, health care benefits, and unspecified assistantships also available. Financial award application deadline: 2/1; financial award applicants required to submit FAFSA. *Unit head:* Friedmann Weidauer, Chair, 860-486-1533, E-mail: freidmann.weidauer@uconn.edu.

University of Delaware, College of Arts and Sciences, Department of Foreign Languages and Literatures, Newark, DE 19716. Offers foreign languages and literatures (MA), including French, German, Spanish; foreign languages pedagogy (MA), including French, German, Spanish. *Faculty:* 27 full-time (14 women). *Students:* 33 full-time (23 women), 5 part-time (all women); includes 1 minority (African American), 10 international. Average age 25. 29 applicants, 55% accepted, 11 enrolled. In 2007, 12 degrees awarded. *Degree requirements:* For master's, one foreign language, comprehensive exam, thesis optional. *Entrance requirements:* For master's, GRE General Test, letters of recommendation, writing sample. Additional exam requirements/recommendations for international students: Required—TOEFL. *Application deadline:* For fall admission, 2/1 priority date for domestic and international students; for spring admission, 11/1 for domestic and international students. Application fee: $60. Electronic applications accepted. *Financial support:* In 2007–08, fellowships with full tuition reimbursements (averaging $14,600 per year), research assistantships with full tuition reimbursements (averaging $14,600 per year), 29 teaching assistantships with full tuition reimbursements (averaging $14,600 per year) were awarded; tuition waivers (full) and unspecified assistantships also available. Financial award application deadline: 2/1. *Faculty research:* Medieval to Modern French and Spanish literature, Twentieth Century German, French, Spanish literature by women, computer-assisted instruction. Total annual research expenditures: $12,000. *Unit head:* Dr. Richard Zipser, Chair, 302-831-6882. *Application contact:* Dr. Monika Shafi, Graduate Coordinator, 302-831-2587, E-mail: mshafi@udel.edu.

University of Florida, Graduate School, College of Liberal Arts and Sciences, Department of Germanic and Slavic Studies, Gainesville, FL 32611. Offers German (MA, PhD). *Faculty:* 17 full-time (6 women). *Students:* 12 (5 women); includes 1 minority (Hispanic American) 4 international. In 2007, 1 degree awarded. *Degree requirements:* For master's, thesis or alternative; for doctorate, thesis/dissertation. *Entrance requirements:* For master's and doctorate, GRE General Test, minimum GPA of 3.0. Additional exam requirements/recommendations for international students: Required—TOEFL (minimum score 550 paper-based; 213 computer-based). *Application deadline:* For fall admission, 6/1 priority date for domestic students. Applications are processed on a rolling basis. Application fee: $30. Electronic applications accepted. *Expenses:* Tuition, state resident: full-time $7,478. Tuition, nonresident: full-time $22,603. *Financial support:* In 2007–08, 9 teaching assistantships (averaging $16,457 per year) were awarded; fellowships, research assistantships also available. *Faculty research:* Literature and language, film and media. *Unit head:* Dr. Allan F. Burns, Chair, 352-392-2101 Ext. 212, Fax: 352-392-6929, E-mail: afburns@anthro.ufl.edu. *Application contact:* Dr. Franz Futterknecht, Coordinator, 352-392-2101, Fax: 352-392-1067, E-mail: futterk@germslav.ufl.edu.

German

University of Georgia, Graduate School, College of Arts and Sciences, Department of Germanic and Slavic Studies, Athens, GA 30602. Offers German (MA, MAT). *Faculty:* 9 full-time (5 women). *Students:* 5 full-time (all women), 1 (woman) part-time, 1 international. 10 applicants, 80% accepted, 3 enrolled. In 2007, 3 degrees awarded. *Degree requirements:* For master's, one foreign language, thesis. *Entrance requirements:* For master's, GRE General Test. *Application deadline:* For fall admission, 7/1 priority date for domestic students; for spring admission, 11/15 for domestic students. Application fee: $50. Electronic applications accepted. *Financial support:* Fellowships, research assistantships, teaching assistantships, unspecified assistantships available. *Unit head:* Dr. Martin H. Kagael, Head, 706-542-2445, E-mail: mkagel@uga.edu. *Application contact:* Dr. Alexander Sager, Graduate Coordinator, 706-542-6211, Fax: 706-542-2459, E-mail: asager@uga.edu.

University of Illinois at Chicago, Graduate College, College of Liberal Arts and Sciences, Department of Germanic Studies, Chicago, IL 60607-7128. Offers MA, PhD. Part-time programs available. Terminal master's awarded for partial completion of doctoral program. *Degree requirements:* For master's, thesis optional, exam; for doctorate, 2 foreign languages, thesis/dissertation. *Entrance requirements:* For master's and doctorate, GRE General Test, minimum GPA of 2.75. Additional exam requirements/recommendations for international students: Required—TOEFL. Electronic applications accepted. *Faculty research:* German literature.

University of Illinois at Urbana–Champaign, Graduate College, College of Liberal Arts and Sciences, School of Literatures, Cultures and Linguistics, Department of Germanic Languages and Literatures, Champaign, IL 61820. Offers MA, PhD. *Faculty:* 10 full-time (7 women). *Students:* 20 full-time (13 women), 2 international. 12 applicants, 92% accepted, 5 enrolled. In 2007, 2 master's, 1 doctorate awarded. *Degree requirements:* For master's, variable foreign language requirement; for doctorate, 3 foreign languages, thesis/dissertation. *Entrance requirements:* For master's, GRE, minimum GPA of 3.0. *Application deadline:* Applications are processed on a rolling basis. Application fee: $60 ($75 for international students). Electronic applications accepted. *Financial support:* In 2007–08, 3 fellowships, 5 research assistantships, 21 teaching assistantships were awarded. Financial award application deadline: 2/15. *Unit head:* Mara Wade, Head, 217-333-9353, Fax: 217-244-2223, E-mail: mwade@uiuc.edu. *Application contact:* Lynn Stanke, Secretary, 217-333-6269, Fax: 217-244-3050, E-mail: stanke@uiuc.edu.

The University of Iowa, Graduate College, College of Liberal Arts and Sciences, Department of German, Iowa City, IA 52242-1316. Offers MA, PhD. *Faculty:* 6 full-time, 4 part-time/adjunct. *Students:* 7 full-time (all women); includes 1 minority (Hispanic American), 2 international. 5 applicants, 60% accepted, 2 enrolled. In 2007, 1 degree awarded. *Degree requirements:* For master's, thesis optional, exam; for doctorate, comprehensive exam, thesis/dissertation. *Entrance requirements:* For master's and doctorate, GRE General Test, minimum GPA of 3.0. Additional exam requirements/recommendations for international students: Required—TOEFL (minimum score 550 paper-based; 213 computer-based; 81 iBT). *Application deadline:* For fall admission, 2/1 for domestic and international students; for spring admission, 9/1 priority date for domestic and international students. Applications are processed on a rolling basis. Application fee: $60 ($85 for international students). Electronic applications accepted. *Expenses:* Tuition, state resident: part-time $349 per hour. Tuition, nonresident: part-time $349 per hour. Tuition and fees vary according to course load and program. *Financial support:* In 2007–08, 1 fellowship, 2 research assistantships with partial tuition reimbursements, 4 teaching assistantships with partial tuition reimbursements were awarded. Financial award applicants required to submit FAFSA. *Unit head:* James Pusack, Chair, 319-335-2203, Fax: 319-335-2990.

University of Kansas, Research and Graduate Studies, College of Liberal Arts and Sciences, Department of Germanic Languages and Literatures, Lawrence, KS 66045. Offers German (MA, PhD). Part-time programs available. *Faculty:* 6. *Students:* 16 full-time (10 women); includes 1 minority (Asian American or Pacific Islander), 6 international. Average age 34. 7 applicants, 57% accepted, 2 enrolled. In 2007, 2 master's, 1 doctorate awarded. *Degree requirements:* For master's, one foreign language, comprehensive exam, thesis optional, exam; for doctorate, 2 foreign languages, comprehensive exam, thesis/dissertation, exam. *Entrance requirements:* For master's, undergraduate major in German or equivalent; for doctorate, MA in German. Additional exam requirements/recommendations for international students: Required—TOEFL. *Application deadline:* For fall admission, 1/30 priority date for domestic and international students. Applications are processed on a rolling basis. Application fee: $55 ($60 for international students). Electronic applications accepted. *Expenses:* Tuition, state resident: full-time $5,838. Tuition, nonresident: full-time $13,409. Tuition and fees vary according to program. *Financial support:* Fellowships, research assistantships with full tuition reimbursements, teaching assistantships with full tuition reimbursements, Federal Work-Study, institutionally sponsored loans, and unspecified assistantships available. Support available to part-time students. Financial award application deadline: 1/30; financial award applicants required to submit FAFSA. *Faculty research:* Humanism, eighteenth to twentieth century literature, Germanic linguistics, German-American studies, applied linguistics. *Unit head:* William Keel, Chair, 785-864-4803, Fax: 785-864-4298, E-mail: wkeel@ku.edu. *Application contact:* Leonie Marx, Graduate Director, 785-864-4803, Fax: 785-864-4298, E-mail: marx@ku.edu.

University of Kentucky, Graduate School, College of Arts and Sciences, Program in German, Lexington, KY 40506-0032. Offers MA. *Faculty:* 29 full-time (10 women), 2 part-time/adjunct (1 woman). *Students:* 9 full-time (6 women), 1 (woman) part-time, 2 international. Average age 28. 10 applicants, 80% accepted, 3 enrolled. In 2007, 5 degrees awarded. *Degree requirements:* For master's, one foreign language, comprehensive exam, thesis optional. *Entrance requirements:* For master's, GRE General Test, minimum undergraduate GPA of 2.75. Additional exam requirements/recommendations for international students: Required—TOEFL (minimum score 550 paper-based; 213 computer-based). *Application deadline:* For fall admission, 7/17 priority date for domestic students, 2/1 priority date for international students; for spring admission, 12/13 priority date for domestic students, 6/15 priority date for international students. Application fee: $50 ($65 for international students). Electronic applications accepted. *Expenses:* Tuition, state resident: part-time $437 per credit hour. Tuition, nonresident: part-time $931 per credit hour. *Financial support:* In 2007–08, 8 students received support, including 3 fellowships with full tuition reimbursements available (averaging $3,591 per year), 7 teaching assistantships with full tuition reimbursements available (averaging $5,387 per year); research assistantships with full tuition reimbursements available, Federal Work-Study, institutionally sponsored loans, scholarships/grants, traineeships, health care benefits, tuition waivers (partial), and unspecified assistantships also available. Support available to part-time students. Financial award application deadline: 3/15. *Faculty research:* Medieval studies; literature from Enlightenment to present, literary theory, intellectual history, gender studies. *Unit head:* Dr. Linda Worley, Director of Graduate Studies, 859-257-1198, Fax: 859-257-3743, E-mail: linda.worley@uky.edu. *Application contact:* Dr. Brian Jackson, Senior Associate Dean, 859-257-4667, Fax: 859-257-4676, E-mail: brian.jackson@uky.edu.

University of Lethbridge, School of Graduate Studies, Lethbridge, AB T1K 3M4, Canada. Offers accounting (MScM); addictions counseling (M Sc); agricultural biotechnology (M Sc); agricultural studies (M Sc, MA); anthropology (MA); archaeology (MA); art (MA); biochemistry (M Sc); biological sciences (M Sc); biomolecular science (PhD); biosystems and biodiversity (PhD); Canadian studies (MA); chemistry (M Sc); computer science (M Sc); computer science and geographical information science (M Sc); counseling psychology (M Ed); dramatic arts (MA); earth, space, and physical science (PhD); economics (MA); educational leadership (M Ed); English (MA); environmental science (M Sc); evolution and behavior (PhD); exercise science (M Sc); finance (MScM); French (MA); French/German (MA); French/Spanish (MA); general education (M Ed); general management (MScM); geography (M Sc, MA); German (MA); health sciences (M Sc, MA); history (MA); human resource management and labour relations (MScM); individualized multidisciplinary (M Sc, MA); information systems (MScM); international management (MScM); kinesiology (M Sc, MA); management (M Sc, MA); marketing (MScM); mathematics (M Sc); music (MA); Native American studies (MA); neuroscience (M Sc, PhD); new media (MA); nursing (M Sc); philosophy (MA); physics (M Sc); policy and strategy (MScM); political science (MA); psychology (M Sc, MA); religious studies (MA); sociology (MA); theoretical and computational science (PhD); urban and regional studies (MA). Part-time and evening/weekend programs available. *Students:* 215 full-time, 98 part-time. In 2007, 87 master's, 1 doctorate awarded. *Degree requirements:* For doctorate, comprehensive exam, thesis/dissertation. *Entrance requirements:* For master's, GMAT (M Sc in management), bachelor's degree in related field, minimum GPA of 3.0 during previous 20 graded semester courses, 2 years teaching or related experience (M Ed); for doctorate, master's degree, minimum graduate GPA of 3.5. Additional exam requirements/recommendations for international students: Required—TOEFL. Application fee: $60 Canadian dollars. *Financial support:* Fellowships, research assistantships, teaching assistantships, scholarships/grants, health care benefits, and unspecified assistantships available. *Faculty research:* Movement and brain plasticity, gibberellin physiology, photosynthesis, carbon cycling, molecular properties of main-group ring components. *Unit head:* Dr. Jo-Anne Fiske, Interim Dean, 403-329-2121, Fax: 403-329-2097. *Application contact:* Jennifer Geddes, Graduate Liaison Officer, 403-329-2762, Fax: 403-329-5159, E-mail: jennifer.geddes@uleth.ca.

University of Manitoba, Faculty of Graduate Studies, Faculty of Arts, Department of German and Slavic Studies, Winnipeg, MB R3T 2N2, Canada. Offers MA. *Degree requirements:* For master's, one foreign language, thesis or alternative.

University of Maryland, College Park, Graduate Studies, College of Arts and Humanities, School of Languages, Literature, and Cultures, Department of Germanic Studies, College Park, MD 20742. Offers Germanic language and literature (MA, PhD). *Students:* 15 full-time (11 women), 4 part-time (3 women); includes 1 minority (African American), 3 international. 10 applicants, 70% accepted, 4 enrolled. In 2007, 3 master's, 1 doctorate awarded. *Degree requirements:* For master's, one foreign language, comprehensive exam, thesis optional, exams; for doctorate, 2 foreign languages, comprehensive exam, thesis/dissertation, reading exam, oral defense. *Entrance requirements:* For master's, GRE General Test, writing sample, 3 letters of recommendation; for doctorate, GRE General Test, MA in German or related discipline. Additional exam requirements/recommendations for international students: Required—TOEFL. *Application deadline:* For fall admission, 2/1 for domestic and international students; for spring admission, 10/1 for domestic students, 6/1 for international students. Applications are processed on a rolling basis. Application fee: $60. Electronic applications accepted. *Financial support:* In 2007–08, 4 fellowships with full tuition reimbursements (averaging $10,737 per year), 10 teaching assistantships with tuition reimbursements (averaging $15,662 per year) were awarded; career-related internships or fieldwork, Federal Work-Study, and scholarships/grants also available. Support available to part-time students. Financial award applicants required to submit FAFSA. *Faculty research:* Language pedagogy, Germanic philology, medieval culture. *Unit head:* Dr. Guenter G. Pfister, Chairman, 301-405-4106, Fax: 301-314-9841, E-mail: gpfister@umd.edu. *Application contact:* Dean of Graduate School, 301-405-4190, Fax: 301-314-9305.

University of Maryland, College Park, Graduate Studies, College of Arts and Humanities, School of Languages, Literature, and Cultures, Program in Second Language Acquisition and Application, College Park, MD 20742. Offers French (MA); German (MA); Japanese (MA); Russian (MA); second language instruction (PhD); second language learning (PhD); second language measurement and assessment (PhD); second language use (PhD); Spanish (MA). *Students:* 1 (woman) full-time, 1 international. 50 applicants, 14% accepted. *Entrance requirements:* For master's, BA or BS in related field, demonstrated language competency, 3 letters of reference. *Application deadline:* For fall admission, 1/15 for domestic students, 2/1 for international students; for spring admission, 9/15 for domestic students, 6/1 for international students. Applications are processed on a rolling basis. Application fee: $60. Electronic applications accepted. *Financial support:* In 2007–08, 1 research assistantship (averaging $20,450 per year) was awarded; fellowships also available. *Faculty research:* Second language acquisition, pedagogical perspectives, technological applications, language use in professional contexts. *Unit head:* Dr. Cynthia L. Martin, Acting Chair, 301-405-4244, E-mail: cmartin@umd.edu. *Application contact:* Dean of Graduate School, 301-405-0358, Fax: 301-314-9305.

University of Massachusetts Amherst, Graduate School, College of Humanities and Fine Arts, Department of Germanic Languages and Literatures, Amherst, MA 01003. Offers MA, PhD. Part-time programs available. *Faculty:* 8 full-time (3 women). *Students:* 13 full-time (8 women), 8 part-time (all women); includes 3 minority (2 Asian Americans or Pacific Islanders, 1 Hispanic American), 5 international. Average age 32. 17 applicants, 71% accepted, 3 enrolled. In 2007, 3 doctorates awarded. Terminal master's awarded for partial completion of doctoral program. *Degree requirements:* For master's, thesis or alternative; for doctorate, 2 foreign languages, thesis/dissertation. *Entrance requirements:* For master's and doctorate, writing sample in English and German. Additional exam requirements/recommendations for international students: Required—TOEFL (minimum score 530 paper-based; 197 computer-based). *Application deadline:* For fall admission, 2/1 priority date for domestic and international students; for spring admission, 10/1 for domestic and international students. Applications are processed on a rolling basis. Application fee: $50 ($65 for international students). Electronic applications accepted. *Expenses:* Tuition, state resident: full-time $2,640; part-time $110 per credit. Tuition, nonresident: full-time $9,936; part-time $414 per credit. Required fees: $7,455. One-time fee: $332. Tuition and fees vary according to course load, campus/location, program and reciprocity agreements. *Financial support:* In 2007–08, 1 fellowship with full tuition reimbursement (averaging $3,000 per year), 3 research assistantships with full tuition reimbursements (averaging $8,918 per year), 14 teaching assistantships with full tuition reimbursements (averaging $8,999 per year) were awarded; career-related internships or fieldwork, Federal Work-Study, scholarships/grants, traineeships, and unspecified assistantships also available. Support available to part-time students. Financial award application deadline: 2/1. *Unit head:* Dr. James Cathey, Head, 413-545-6686, Fax: 413-545-6695, E-mail: cathey@german.umass.edu.

University of Michigan, Horace H. Rackham School of Graduate Studies, College of Literature, Science, and the Arts, Department of Germanic Languages and Literatures, Ann Arbor, MI 48109. Offers German (AM, PhD). *Faculty:* 5 full-time (4 women), 9 part-time/adjunct (2 women). *Students:* 17 full-time (9 women); includes 1 Asian American or Pacific Islander, 3 international. Average age 27. 28 applicants, 21% accepted, 1 enrolled. In 2007, 2 doctorates awarded. *Median time to degree:* Of those who began their doctoral program in fall 1999, 100% received their degree in 8 years or less. *Degree requirements:* For doctorate, one foreign language, thesis/dissertation, oral defense of dissertation, preliminary exam. *Entrance requirements:* For master's and doctorate, GRE General Test. Additional exam requirements/recommendations for international students: Required—TOEFL (minimum score 560 paper-based; 220 computer-based). *Application deadline:* For fall and winter admission, 1/5 priority date for domestic and international students. Application fee: $60 ($75 for international students). Electronic applications accepted. *Financial support:* In 2007–08, 4 fellowships with full tuition reimbursements (averaging $14,000 per year), 14 teaching assistantships with full tuition reimbursements (averaging $15,000 per year) were awarded; research assistantships, scholarships/grants and tuition waivers (partial) also available. Financial award application deadline: 3/15. *Faculty research:* German history, German literature, literary theory, film, political and social theory. Total annual research expenditures: $20,000. *Unit head:* Dr. Julia Hell, Chair, 734-764-8018, Fax: 734-763-6557, E-mail: hell@umich.edu. *Application contact:* Marga S. Schuhwerk-Hampel, Student Services Coordinator, 734-936-0150, Fax: 734-763-6557, E-mail: mshampel@umich.edu.

University of Minnesota, Twin Cities Campus, Graduate School, College of Liberal Arts, Department of German, Scandinavian, and Dutch, Minneapolis, MN 55455-0213. Offers Germanic studies: German and Scandinavian studies track (PhD); Germanic studies: German track (MA, PhD); Germanic studies: Germanic medieval studies track (MA, PhD); Germanic studies: Scandinavian studies track (MA); Germanic studies: teaching track (MA). Part-time programs available. *Faculty:* 19 full-time (8 women). *Students:* 22 full-time (14 women), 6 part-time (4 women); includes 2 minority (1 African American, 1 Hispanic American), 10 international. 31 applicants, 61% accepted, 8 enrolled. In 2007, 1 master's, 6 doctorates awarded. Terminal master's awarded for partial completion of doctoral program. *Degree requirements:*

For doctorate, 2 foreign languages, thesis/dissertation. *Entrance requirements:* For master's, GRE General Test, BA in German, Scandinavian, or equivalent; for doctorate, GRE General Test, MA in German, Scandinavian, or equivalent. Additional exam requirements/recommendations for international students: Required—TOEFL (minimum score 550 paper-based; 213 computer-based; 79 iBT). *Application deadline:* For fall admission, 12/15 for domestic and international students. Application fee: $55 ($75 for international students). Electronic applications accepted. *Financial support:* In 2007–08, 85 fellowships with full tuition reimbursements (averaging $18,000 per year), 1 research assistantship with full tuition reimbursement (averaging $11,985 per year), 14 teaching assistantships with full tuition reimbursements (averaging $12,839 per year) were awarded; career-related internships or fieldwork, Federal Work-Study, institutionally sponsored loans, scholarships/grants, health care benefits, and unspecified assistantships also available. Support available to part-time students. Financial award application deadline: 1/10. *Faculty research:* Cultural studies, literary theory, feminist criticism, film, Germanic philology. *Unit head:* Prof. Charlotte Melin, Chair, 612-625-2080, Fax: 612-624-8297, E-mail: melin005@umn.edu. *Application contact:* Director of Graduate Studies, 612-625-9034, Fax: 612-624-8297, E-mail: gsd@umn.edu.

University of Mississippi, Graduate School, College of Liberal Arts, Department of Modern Languages, Oxford, University, MS 38677. Offers French (MA); German (MA); Spanish (MA). *Faculty:* 38 full-time (26 women), 2 part-time/adjunct (both women). *Students:* 13 full-time (5 women), 4 part-time (3 women); includes 3 minority (2 African Americans, 1 American Indian/Alaska Native), 3 international. In 2007, 3 degrees awarded. *Degree requirements:* For master's, thesis (for some programs). *Entrance requirements:* For master's, GRE General Test, minimum GPA of 3.0. Additional exam requirements/recommendations for international students: Required—TOEFL. *Application deadline:* For fall admission, 2/1 for domestic students; for spring admission, 10/1 for domestic students. Applications are processed on a rolling basis. Application fee: $25. Electronic applications accepted. *Expenses:* Tuition, state resident: full-time $4,932. Tuition, nonresident: full-time $11,436. *Financial support:* Scholarships/grants available. Financial award application deadline: 3/1; financial award applicants required to submit FAFSA. *Unit head:* Dr. Donald Dyer, Chair, 662-915-7298, Fax: 662-915-1086, E-mail: mlangs@olemiss.edu.

University of Missouri–Columbia, Graduate School, College of Arts and Sciences, Department of German and Russian Studies, Columbia, MO 65211. Offers German (MA). *Entrance requirements:* For master's, GRE General Test, minimum GPA of 3.0.

The University of Montana, Graduate School, College of Arts and Sciences, Department of Modern and Classical Languages and Literatures, Missoula, MT 59812-0002. Offers French (MA); German (MA); Spanish (MA). *Degree requirements:* For master's, one foreign language. *Entrance requirements:* For master's, GRE General Test. Additional exam requirements/recommendations for international students: Required—TOEFL.

University of Nebraska–Lincoln, Graduate College, College of Arts and Sciences, Department of Modern Languages and Literatures, Lincoln, NE 68588. Offers French (MA, PhD); German (MA, PhD); Spanish (MA, PhD). *Degree requirements:* For master's, thesis optional; for doctorate, comprehensive exam, thesis/dissertation. *Entrance requirements:* For master's and doctorate, writing sample in target language. Additional exam requirements/recommendations for international students: Required—TOEFL (minimum score 550 paper-based; 213 computer-based). Electronic applications accepted. *Faculty research:* French, German, and Spanish language, literature, and culture.

University of Nevada, Reno, Graduate School, College of Liberal Arts, Department of Foreign Languages and Literatures, Reno, NV 89557. Offers French (MA); German (MA); Spanish (MA). *Faculty:* 18. *Students:* 8 full-time (5 women), 10 part-time (9 women); includes 3 minority (all Hispanic Americans) Average age 29. 12 applicants, 67% accepted, 7 enrolled. In 2007, 5 degrees awarded. *Degree requirements:* For master's, one foreign language, thesis optional. *Entrance requirements:* For master's, GRE General Test, minimum GPA of 2.75. Additional exam requirements/recommendations for international students: Required—TOEFL. *Application deadline:* For fall admission, 3/1 priority date for domestic students; for spring admission, 11/1 for domestic students. Applications are processed on a rolling basis. Application fee: $60 ($95 for international students). *Expenses:* Tuition, state resident: full-time $2,774; part-time $154 per credit. Tuition, nonresident: full-time $13,578; part-time $330 per credit. Required fees: $49 per semester. *Financial support:* In 2007–08, 7 teaching assistantships were awarded; Federal Work-Study and institutionally sponsored loans also available. Financial award application deadline: 3/1. *Faculty research:* Thirteenth-century mysticism, contemporary Spanish and Latin American poetry and theater, French interrelation between narration and photography, exile literature and Holocaust. *Unit head:* Dr. Miriella Melara, Graduate Program Director, 775-784-6055.

University of New Mexico, Graduate School, College of Arts and Sciences, Department of Foreign Languages and Literature, Albuquerque, NM 87131-2039. Offers comparative literature and cultural studies (MA); French (MA); French studies (PhD); German studies (MA). Part-time programs available. *Faculty:* 15 full-time (11 women), 8 part-time/adjunct (4 women). *Students:* 9 full-time (8 women), 4 part-time (2 women), 6 international. Average age 33. 9 applicants, 44% accepted, 3 enrolled. In 2007, 5 master's awarded. *Degree requirements:* For master's, one foreign language, thesis optional; for doctorate, 2 foreign languages, thesis/dissertation. *Application deadline:* For fall admission, 2/1 priority date for domestic students; for spring admission, 10/1 priority date for domestic students. Application fee: $50. Electronic applications accepted. *Financial support:* In 2007–08, 20 teaching assistantships with tuition reimbursements (averaging $12,023 per year) were awarded; Federal Work-Study, health care benefits, and unspecified assistantships also available. Financial award application deadline: 3/1; financial award applicants required to submit FAFSA. *Faculty research:* German, Russian, Italian, Japanese, French, Comparative Lit, culture studies, classics. Total annual research expenditures: $4,750. *Unit head:* Dr. Natasha Kolchevska, Chair, 505-277-4771, Fax: 505-277-3599, E-mail: nakol@unm.edu. *Application contact:* Dean Aragon, Application and Graduation Advisor, 505-277-4471, Fax: 505-277-3599, E-mail: peaslee@unm.edu.

The University of North Carolina at Chapel Hill, Graduate School, College of Arts and Sciences, Department of Germanic Languages, Chapel Hill, NC 27599. Offers literature and linguistics (MA, PhD). Part-time programs available. Terminal master's awarded for partial completion of doctoral program. *Degree requirements:* For master's, comprehensive exam, thesis; for doctorate, one foreign language, comprehensive exam, thesis/dissertation. *Entrance requirements:* For master's and doctorate, GRE General Test, minimum GPA of 3.0. *Faculty research:* Gender and sexuality, literature and politics, German and Jewish culture, medieval through modern literature, Germanic linguistics.

University of Northern Iowa, Graduate College, College of Humanities and Fine Arts, Department of Modern Languages, Program in German, Cedar Falls, IA 50614. Offers German (MA); teaching English to speakers of other languages/German (MA). Part-time and evening/weekend programs available. *Students:* 5 full-time (all women), 1 part-time, 5 international. 4 applicants, 75% accepted, 3 enrolled. In 2007, 4 degrees awarded. *Degree requirements:* For master's, one foreign language, comprehensive exam, thesis or alternative. *Entrance requirements:* For master's, minimum GPA of 3.0; hold a valid teaching license and have documentation of successful teaching experience. Additional exam requirements/recommendations for international students: Required—TOEFL (minimum score 600 paper-based; 250 computer-based; 100 iBT). *Application deadline:* For fall admission, 8/1 priority date for domestic students. Applications are processed on a rolling basis. Application fee: $30 ($50 for international students). *Expenses:* Tuition, state resident: full-time $6,246; part-time $694 per credit hour. Tuition, nonresident: full-time $14,554; part-time $694 per credit hour. Required fees: $838; $119 per semester. *Financial support:* Career-related internships or fieldwork, Federal Work-Study, and tuition waivers (full and partial) available. Support available to part-time students. Financial award application deadline: 2/1.

University of Oklahoma, Graduate College, College of Arts and Sciences, Department of Modern Languages, Program in German, Norman, OK 73019-0390. Offers MA, MBA/MA. Part-time programs available. *Students:* 5 full-time (3 women), 1 international. 3 applicants, 100% accepted, 2 enrolled. In 2007, 2 degrees awarded. Terminal master's awarded for partial completion of doctoral program. *Degree requirements:* For master's, 2 foreign languages, comprehensive exam, thesis optional, departmental qualifying exam. *Entrance requirements:* For master's, BA with 25 hours in German or equivalent, minimum GPA of 3.0 in last 60 hours, 3 letters of recommendation. Additional exam requirements/recommendations for international students: Required—TOEFL (minimum score 550 paper-based; 213 computer-based). *Application deadline:* For fall admission, 6/1 priority date for domestic students, 4/1 for international students; for spring admission, 11/1 for domestic students, 9/1 for international students. Applications are processed on a rolling basis. Application fee: $40 ($90 for international students). Electronic applications accepted. *Expenses:* Tuition, state resident: full-time $3,451; part-time $144 per credit hour. Tuition, nonresident: full-time $12,432; part-time $518 per credit hour. Required fees: $1,925; $70 per credit hour. $122 per semester. *Financial support:* Teaching assistantships with partial tuition reimbursements, scholarships/grants, health care benefits, tuition waivers (partial), and unspecified assistantships available. Financial award applicants required to submit FAFSA. *Faculty research:* Film studies; German literature and culture studies; fin-de-siecle Austria; Arthurian romance; the Goethe era. *Application contact:* Dr. Michael E. Winston, Associate Professor, 405-325-5088, Fax: 405-325-0103, E-mail: mewinston@ou.edu.

University of Oregon, Graduate School, College of Arts and Sciences, Department of Germanic Languages and Literatures, Eugene, OR 97403. Offers MA, PhD. *Faculty:* 8 full-time (5 women), 1 (woman) part-time/adjunct. *Students:* 9 full-time (5 women), 1 (woman) part-time; includes 1 minority (Asian American or Pacific Islander), 4 international. 11 applicants, 64% accepted. In 2007, 1 master's, 1 doctorate awarded. *Degree requirements:* For master's, 2 foreign languages, thesis or alternative; for doctorate, 3 foreign languages, thesis/dissertation. *Entrance requirements:* For master's and doctorate, minimum GPA of 3.0. Additional exam requirements/recommendations for international students: Required—TOEFL. *Application deadline:* For fall admission, 2/15 for domestic students. Application fee: $50. *Financial support:* In 2007–08, 8 teaching assistantships were awarded. Financial award application deadline: 2/1. *Faculty research:* Medieval language and literature, eighteenth to twentieth century literature and philosophy, literary theory, feminist literature and theory, psychoanalysis and literature. *Unit head:* Susan Anderson, Head, 541-346-4051, E-mail: kgates@uoregon.edu. *Application contact:* Kenny Gates, Admissions Contact, 541-346-4084, E-mail: gates@uoregon.edu.

University of Pennsylvania, School of Arts and Sciences, Graduate Group in Germanic Languages, Philadelphia, PA 19104. Offers AM, PhD. Terminal master's awarded for partial completion of doctoral program. *Degree requirements:* For master's, one foreign language, thesis or alternative; for doctorate, one foreign language, comprehensive exam, thesis/dissertation. *Entrance requirements:* For master's and doctorate, GRE General Test.

University of Pittsburgh, School of Arts and Sciences, Department of Germanic Languages and Literatures, Pittsburgh, PA 15260. Offers MA, PhD. Part-time programs available. *Faculty:* 6 full-time (3 women), 2 part-time/adjunct (0 women). *Students:* 8 full-time (4 women), 3 part-time (2 women), 4 international. Average age 25. 9 applicants, 56% accepted, 3 enrolled. In 2007, 2 degrees awarded. Terminal master's awarded for partial completion of doctoral program. *Degree requirements:* For master's, one foreign language, comprehensive exam (for some programs), thesis (for some programs); for doctorate, one foreign language, comprehensive exam, thesis/dissertation. *Entrance requirements:* For master's, bachelor's degree in German, minimum GPA of 3.0 or equivalent. Additional exam requirements/recommendations for international students: Required—TOEFL. *Application deadline:* For spring admission, 1/15 priority date for domestic and international students. Application fee: $50. Electronic applications accepted. *Financial support:* In 2007–08, fellowships with tuition reimbursements (averaging $15,070 per year), teaching assistantships with tuition reimbursements (averaging $14,485 per year) were awarded; scholarships/grants and health care benefits also available. Financial award application deadline: 1/15. *Faculty research:* Age of Goethe, German film, postwar culture, German-Jewish culture. *Unit head:* Dr. Clark S. Muenzer, Chair, 412-624-5909, Fax: 412-624-6318, E-mail: muenzer@pitt.edu.

University of Saskatchewan, College of Graduate Studies and Research, College of Arts and Sciences, Department of Languages and Linguistics, Saskatoon, SK S7N 5A2, Canada. Offers MA. *Degree requirements:* For master's, 2 foreign languages, thesis. *Entrance requirements:* Additional exam requirements/recommendations for international students: Required—TOEFL.

University of South Africa, College of Human Sciences, Pretoria, South Africa. Offers adult education (M Ed); African languages (MA, PhD); African politics (MA, PhD); Afrikaans (MA, PhD); ancient history (MA, PhD); ancient Near Eastern studies (MA, PhD); anthropology (MA, PhD); applied linguistics (MA); Arabic (MA, PhD); archaeology (MA); art history (MA); Biblical archaeology (MA); Biblical studies (M Th, D Th, PhD); Christian spirituality (M Th, D Th); church history (M Th, D Th); classical studies (MA, PhD); clinical psychology (MA); communication (MA, PhD); comparative education (M Ed, Ed D); consulting psychology (D Admin, D Com, PhD); curriculum studies (M Ed, Ed D); development studies (M Admin, MA, D Admin, PhD); didactics (M Ed, Ed D); education (M Tech); education management (M Ed, Ed D); educational psychology (M Ed); English (MA); environmental education (M Ed); French (MA, PhD); German (MA, PhD); Greek (MA); guidance and counseling (M Ed); health studies (MA, PhD), including health sciences education (MA), health services management (MA), medical and surgical nursing science (critical care general) (MA), midwifery and neonatal nursing science (MA), trauma and emergency care (MA); history (MA, PhD); history of education (Ed D); inclusive education (M Ed, Ed D); information and communications technology policy and regulation (MA); information science (MA, MIS, PhD); international politics (MA, PhD); Islamic studies (MA, PhD); Italian (MA, PhD); Judaica (MA, PhD); linguistics (MA, PhD); mathematical education (M Ed); mathematics education (MA); missiology (M Th, D Th); modern Hebrew (MA, PhD); musicology (MA, MMus, D Mus, PhD); natural science education (M Ed); New Testament (M Th, D Th); Old Testament (D Th); pastoral therapy (M Th, D Th); philosophy (MA); philosophy of education (M Ed, Ed D); politics (MA, PhD); Portuguese (MA, PhD); practical theology (M Th, D Th); psychology (MA, MS, PhD); psychology of education (M Ed, Ed D); public health (MA); religious studies (MA, D Th, PhD); Romance languages (MA); Russian (MA, PhD); Semitic languages (MA, PhD); social behavior studies in HIV/AIDS (MA); social science (mental health) (MA); social science in development studies (MA); social science in psychology (MA); social science in social work (MA); social science in sociology (MA); social work (MSW, DSW, PhD); socio-education (M Ed, Ed D); sociolinguistics (MA); sociology (MA, PhD); Spanish (MA, PhD); systematic theology (M Th, D Th); TESOL (teaching English to speakers of other languages) (MA); theological ethics (M Th, D Th); theory of literature (MA, PhD); urban ministries (D Th); urban ministry (M Th).

University of South Carolina, The Graduate School, College of Arts and Sciences, Department of Languages, Literatures, and Cultures, Columbia, SC 29208. Offers comparative literature (MA, PhD); foreign languages (MAT), including French, German, Spanish; French (MA); German (MA); Spanish (MA). MAT offered in cooperation with the College of Education. Part-time programs available. *Faculty:* 39 full-time (19 women). *Students:* 43 full-time (31 women), 19 part-time (12 women); includes 12 minority (3 African Americans, 1 Asian American or Pacific Islander, 8 Hispanic Americans), 15 international. Average age 29. 40 applicants, 65% accepted, 18 enrolled. In 2007, 7 master's awarded. *Degree requirements:* For master's, one foreign language, comprehensive exam, thesis optional; for doctorate, 2 foreign languages, comprehensive exam, thesis/dissertation. *Entrance requirements:* For master's and doctorate, GRE General Test, writing sample. Additional exam requirements/recommendations for international students: Required—TOEFL (minimum score 230 computer-based; 75 iBT). *Application deadline:* For fall admission, 2/1 priority date for domestic and international students. Applications are processed on a rolling basis. Application fee: $40. Electronic applications accepted.

German

University of South Carolina (continued)

Expenses: Tuition, state resident: part-time $440 per hour. Tuition, nonresident: part-time $936 per hour. Required fees: $17 per hour. Tuition and fees vary according to program. *Financial support:* In 2007–08, 40 teaching assistantships with full tuition reimbursements (averaging $11,000 per year) were awarded; fellowships, research assistantships with full tuition reimbursements also available. Financial award application deadline: 2/1. *Faculty research:* Modern literature, linguistics, literature and culture, medieval literature, literary theory. Total annual research expenditures: $23,000. *Unit head:* Dr. Marja Warehime, Chair, 803-777-9734, Fax: 803-777-0454, E-mail: warehime@sc.edu. *Application contact:* Dr. Nicholas Vazsonyi, Graduate Director, 803-777-2935, Fax: 803-777-0454, E-mail: vazsonyi@sc.edu.

The University of Tennessee, Graduate School, College of Arts and Sciences, Department of Modern Foreign Languages and Literatures, Program in German, Knoxville, TN 37996. Offers MA. Part-time programs available. *Degree requirements:* For master's, one foreign language, thesis or alternative. *Entrance requirements:* For master's, minimum GPA of 2.7. Additional exam requirements/recommendations for international students: Required—TOEFL. Electronic applications accepted.

The University of Tennessee, Graduate School, College of Arts and Sciences, Department of Modern Foreign Languages and Literatures, Program in Modern Foreign Languages, Knoxville, TN 37996. Offers applied linguistics (PhD); French (PhD); German (PhD); Italian (PhD); Portuguese (PhD); Russian (PhD); Spanish (PhD). *Degree requirements:* For doctorate, 2 foreign languages, thesis/dissertation. *Entrance requirements:* For doctorate, minimum GPA of 2.7. Additional exam requirements/recommendations for international students: Required—TOEFL. Electronic applications accepted.

The University of Texas at Austin, Graduate School, College of Liberal Arts, Department of Germanic Studies, Austin, TX 78712-1111. Offers MA, PhD. *Degree requirements:* For master's, one foreign language, thesis or alternative; for doctorate, 2 foreign languages, thesis/dissertation. *Entrance requirements:* For master's and doctorate, GRE General Test. *Faculty research:* Germanic languages and culture (German, Austrian, Swiss, Dutch, Danish, Norwegian, Swedish, Yiddish), language pedagogy and linguistics.

The University of Toledo, College of Graduate Studies, College of Arts and Sciences, Department of Foreign Languages, Toledo, OH 43606-3390. Offers French (MA); German (MA); Spanish (MA). Part-time programs available. *Faculty:* 8. *Students:* 1 (woman) full-time, 3 part-time (2 women); includes 1 minority (Hispanic American) Average age 46. 7 applicants, 100% accepted, 3 enrolled. In 2007, 4 degrees awarded. *Degree requirements:* For master's, one foreign language, comprehensive reading exam in 1 additional foreign language. *Application deadline:* For fall admission, 1/15 priority date for domestic students. Applications are processed on a rolling basis. Application fee: $45. Electronic applications accepted. *Financial support:* In 2007–08, 1 teaching assistantship with full tuition reimbursement (averaging $7,600 per year) was awarded; Federal Work-Study, institutionally sponsored loans, scholarships/grants, tuition waivers (full), and unspecified assistantships also available. Support available to part-time students. Financial award application deadline: 4/1; financial award applicants required to submit FAFSA. *Unit head:* Dr. Antonio Varela, Chair, 419-530-2657, Fax: 419-530-2657, E-mail: avarela@uoft02.utoledo.edu.

University of Toronto, School of Graduate Studies, Humanities Division, Department of Germanic Languages and Literatures, Toronto, ON M5S 1A1, Canada. Offers MA, PhD. Part-time programs available. *Faculty:* 6 full-time, 3 part-time/adjunct. *Students:* 14 full-time (11 women), 1 part-time, 2 international. 14 applicants, 79% accepted. In 2007, 1 degree awarded. *Degree requirements:* For master's, thesis optional, German language competence exam; for doctorate, thesis/dissertation, qualifying exam, thesis defense. *Entrance requirements:* For master's, 7 two-semester courses in German language and literature, minimum B+ average, 3 letters of recommendation; for doctorate, MA in German, minimum A– average, 3 letters of recommendation, writing sample, resumé. *Application deadline:* For fall admission, 2/1 for domestic students. Application fee: $100 Canadian dollars. *Financial support:* In 2007–08, teaching assistantships (averaging $8,825 Canadian dollars per year). *Unit head:* Prof. John T. Zilcosky, Chair and Graduate Chair, 416-926-2323, Fax: 416-926-2329, E-mail: zilcosky@chass.utoronto.ca. *Application contact:* Monika Lang, Administrative Assistant and Graduate Secretary, 416-926-2321, Fax: 416-926-2329, E-mail: german@chass.utoronto.ca.

University of Utah, The Graduate School, College of Humanities, Department of Languages and Literature, Salt Lake City, UT 84112-1107. Offers comparative literary and cultural studies (MA, PhD); French (MA, MALP); German (MA, MALP, PhD); language pedagogy (MALP); Spanish (MA, MALP, PhD); world languages with secondary teaching licensure (MA). *Faculty:* 38 full-time (21 women). *Students:* 28 full-time (15 women), 12 part-time (10 women); includes 10 minority (all Hispanic Americans), 7 international. Average age 35. 32 applicants, 47% accepted, 10 enrolled. In 2007, 14 master's, 2 doctorates awarded. Terminal master's awarded for partial completion of doctoral program. *Median time to degree:* Of those who began their doctoral program in fall 1999, 66% received their degree in 8 years or less. *Degree requirements:* For master's, standard proficiency in 2 languages other than English, comprehensive exam or thesis; for doctorate, comprehensive exam, standard proficiency in 2 languages other than English and language of study, advanced proficiency in 1 language other than English and language of study, dissertation. *Entrance requirements:* For master's, bachelor's degree or strong undergraduate record in target languages, GPA of 3.0, literature-survey courses; for doctorate, successful completion of MA and advanced proficiency in a target language. Additional exam requirements/recommendations for international students: Required—TOEFL (minimum score 500 paper-based; 173 computer-based). *Application deadline:* For fall admission, 2/1 priority date for domestic students, 1/15 priority date for international students. Application fee: $45 ($65 for international students). Electronic applications accepted. *Financial support:* In 2007–08, 25 students received support, including 25 teaching assistantships with full tuition reimbursements available (averaging $11,000 per year); fellowships with tuition reimbursements available, health care benefits also available. Financial award application deadline: 2/1; financial award applicants required to submit FAFSA. *Faculty research:* Literary theory, stylistics, Russian and Soviet literature, existentialism, theory of criticism. Total annual research expenditures: $35,321. *Unit head:* Dr. Christine A. Jones, Director of Graduate Studies, 801-585-3002, Fax: 801-581-7581, E-mail: cjones@hum.utah.edu. *Application contact:* Corky Reeser, Executive Graduate Secretary, 801-581-7570, Fax: 801-581-7581, E-mail: c.reeser@mail.hum.utah.edu.

University of Vermont, Graduate College, College of Arts and Sciences, Department of German and Russian, Burlington, VT 05405. Offers German (MA). *Students:* 2 (both women) 3 applicants, 100% accepted, 1 enrolled. In 2007, 1 degree awarded. *Degree requirements:* For master's, one foreign language, thesis. *Entrance requirements:* For master's, GRE General Test. Additional exam requirements/recommendations for international students: Required—TOEFL (minimum score 550 paper-based; 213 computer-based; 80 iBT). *Application deadline:* For fall admission, 4/1 priority date for domestic students. Applications are processed on a rolling basis. Application fee: $40. Electronic applications accepted. *Financial support:* Fellowships, teaching assistantships available. Financial award application deadline: 3/1. *Faculty research:* Medieval and eighteenth and nineteenth century literature, folklore. *Unit head:* Dr. W. Mieder, Chairperson, 802-656-3430. *Application contact:* Dr. D. Scrase, Coordinator, 802-656-3430.

University of Victoria, Faculty of Graduate Studies, Faculty of Humanities, Department of Germanic and Slavic Studies, Victoria, BC V8W 2Y2, Canada. Offers German studies (MA). Part-time programs available. *Faculty:* 6 full-time (1 woman), 1 part-time/adjunct (0 women). *Students:* Average age 30. 4 applicants, 25% accepted, 1 enrolled. *Degree requirements:* For master's, 2 foreign languages, oral defense of thesis. *Entrance requirements:* For master's, BA in German, minimum B+ average in undergraduate course work. Additional exam requirements/recommendations for international students: Required—TOEFL (minimum score 575 paper-based; 233 computer-based), IELTS (minimum score 7). *Application deadline:* For fall admission, 3/31 for domestic students, 12/15 priority date for international students. Applications are processed on a rolling basis. Application fee: $75 ($125 for international students). Electronic applications accepted. *Expenses:* Tuition, state resident: full-time $3,110. International tuition: $3,700 full-time. Tuition and fees vary according to program. *Financial support:* Fellowships, research assistantships, teaching assistantships, institutionally sponsored loans available. Financial award application deadline: 2/15. *Faculty research:* Nineteenth and twentieth century German literature, literature and music, language acquisition, eighteenth and twentieth century drama and theater, military history. *Unit head:* Dr. Serhy Yekelchyk, Chair/Graduate Advisor, 250-721-7505, Fax: 250-721-7319, E-mail: serhy@uvic.ca.

University of Virginia, College and Graduate School of Arts and Sciences, Department of Germanic Languages and Literatures, Charlottesville, VA 22903. Offers German (MA, PhD). *Faculty:* 11 full-time (6 women). *Students:* 14 full-time (7 women), 5 international. Average age 27. 16 applicants, 81% accepted, 2 enrolled. In 2007, 3 degrees awarded. *Degree requirements:* For master's, one foreign language, comprehensive exam, thesis; for doctorate, one foreign language, comprehensive exam, thesis/dissertation. *Entrance requirements:* For master's and doctorate, GRE General Test, GRE Subject Test. *Application deadline:* Applications are processed on a rolling basis. Application fee: $60. Electronic applications accepted. *Financial support:* Applicants required to submit FAFSA. *Unit head:* Volker Kaiser, Chair, 434-924-3530, Fax: 434-924-6692, E-mail: germandepartment@virginia.edu.

University of Washington, Graduate School, College of Arts and Sciences, Department of Germanics, Seattle, WA 98195. Offers German language and literature (MA); German literature and culture (PhD). Part-time programs available. Terminal master's awarded for partial completion of doctoral program. *Degree requirements:* For master's, one foreign language, 2 research papers; for doctorate, 2 foreign languages, thesis/dissertation, 3 research papers. *Entrance requirements:* For master's and doctorate, GRE, minimum GPA of 3.0. Additional exam requirements/recommendations for international students: Required—TOEFL. Electronic applications accepted. *Faculty research:* Modern German literature, Germanic linguistics and philology, language pedagogy, literary theory, cinema studies.

University of Waterloo, Graduate Studies, Faculty of Arts, Department of Germanic and Slavic Studies, Waterloo, ON N2L 3G1, Canada. Offers German (MA, PhD); Russian (MA). Part-time and evening/weekend programs available. *Faculty:* 11 full-time (3 women), 6 part-time/adjunct (4 women). *Students:* 71. 30 applicants, 93% accepted, 18 enrolled. In 2007, 5 degrees awarded. *Degree requirements:* For master's, one foreign language, thesis optional; for doctorate, 2 foreign languages, comprehensive exam, thesis/dissertation. *Entrance requirements:* For master's, honors degree, minimum B average; for doctorate, master's degree, minimum B average. Additional exam requirements/recommendations for international students: Required—TOEFL, TWE. *Application deadline:* For fall admission, 2/1 for domestic students. Application fee: $75 Canadian dollars. Electronic applications accepted. *Financial support:* Teaching assistantships, scholarships/grants available. *Faculty research:* Medieval theatre; history and literature; German and Russian literary relations; seventeenth, eighteenth, nineteenth, and twentieth century German literature. *Unit head:* Dr. Michael Boehringer, Acting Chair, E-mail: mboehringer@uwaterloo.ca. *Application contact:* Janet Vaughan, Contact, 519-888-4567 Ext. 2428, E-mail: jvaughan@uwaterloo.ca.

University of Wisconsin–Madison, Graduate School, College of Letters and Science, Department of German, Madison, WI 53706-1380. Offers MA, PhD. Part-time programs available. Terminal master's awarded for partial completion of doctoral program. *Degree requirements:* For master's, one foreign language, comprehensive exam, thesis optional; for doctorate, 2 foreign languages, comprehensive exam, thesis/dissertation. *Entrance requirements:* For master's and doctorate, GRE. Electronic applications accepted. *Faculty research:* Literature, culture/linguistics, film, Dutch.

University of Wisconsin–Milwaukee, Graduate School, College of Letters and Sciences, Interdepartmental Program in Foreign Language and Literature, Milwaukee, WI 53201-0413. Offers classics and Hebrew studies (MAFLL); comparative literature (MAFLL); French and Italian (MAFLL); German (MAFLL); Slavic studies (MAFLL); Spanish (MAFLL). Part-time programs available. *Faculty:* 39 full-time (17 women). *Students:* 29 full-time (21 women), 31 part-time (23 women); includes 8 minority (1 Asian American or Pacific Islander, 7 Hispanic Americans), 22 international. 54 applicants, 67% accepted, 26 enrolled. In 2007, 34 degrees awarded. *Degree requirements:* For master's, 2 foreign languages, thesis or alternative. *Application deadline:* For fall admission, 1/1 priority date for domestic students; for spring admission, 9/1 for domestic students. Applications are processed on a rolling basis. Application fee: $45 ($75 for international students). *Expenses:* Tuition, state resident: part-time $530 per credit. Tuition, nonresident: part-time $1,428 per credit. Required fees: $19 per credit. $229 per term. Tuition and fees vary according to course load and program. *Financial support:* In 2007–08, 44 teaching assistantships were awarded; fellowships, research assistantships, career-related internships or fieldwork and unspecified assistantships also available. Support available to part-time students. Financial award application deadline: 4/15. *Unit head:* Gabrielle Verdier, Representative, 414-229-3346, Fax: 414-229-2741, E-mail: verdier@uwm.edu.

University of Wyoming, Graduate School, College of Arts and Sciences, Department of Modern and Classical Languages, Program in German, Laramie, WY 82070. Offers MA. Part-time programs available. *Faculty:* 3 full-time (1 woman). *Students:* 4 full-time (2 women), 2 international. Average age 25. 3 applicants, 100% accepted. *Degree requirements:* For master's, one foreign language, thesis or alternative. *Entrance requirements:* For master's, GRE General Test, minimum GPA of 3.0. *Application deadline:* For fall admission, 4/1 priority date for domestic students. Applications are processed on a rolling basis. Application fee: $50. *Financial support:* In 2007–08, 2 teaching assistantships with full tuition reimbursements (averaging $10,696 per year) were awarded; institutionally sponsored loans also available. Financial award application deadline: 3/1. *Faculty research:* East German literature, German literature, theatre, poetry. *Application contact:* Dr. Kevin S. Larsen, Graduate Adviser, 307-766-2294, Fax: 307-766-2727, E-mail: klarsen@uwyo.edu.

Vanderbilt University, Graduate School, Department of Germanic and Slavic Languages, Nashville, TN 37240-1001. Offers German (MA, MAT, PhD). *Faculty:* 8 full-time (5 women). *Students:* 14 full-time (8 women), 1 part-time; includes 1 minority (Asian American or Pacific Islander), 5 international. Average age 36. 10 applicants, 30% accepted, 2 enrolled. In 2007, 4 degrees awarded. *Degree requirements:* For master's, one foreign language, thesis or alternative; for doctorate, 2 foreign languages, comprehensive exam, thesis/dissertation, qualifying and final exams. *Entrance requirements:* For master's and doctorate, GRE General Test, sample of written work. *Application deadline:* For fall admission, 1/15 for domestic and international students. Application fee: $0. Electronic applications accepted. *Financial support:* Fellowships with full and partial tuition reimbursements, teaching assistantships with full and partial tuition reimbursements, career-related internships or fieldwork, Federal Work-Study, institutionally sponsored loans, and health care benefits available. Financial award application deadline: 1/15; financial award applicants required to submit CSS PROFILE or FAFSA. *Faculty research:* 1750 to present, Middle Ages, baroque, language pedagogy, linguistics. *Unit head:* Dieter H. O. Sevin, Chair, 615-322-2611, Fax: 615-343-7258. *Application contact:* Meike Werner, Director of Graduate Studies, 615-322-2611, Fax: 615-343-7258, E-mail: meike.werner@vanderbilt.edu.

Washington University in St. Louis, Graduate School of Arts and Sciences, Department of Germanic Languages and Literature, St. Louis, MO 63130-4899. Offers MA, PhD. Terminal master's awarded for partial completion of doctoral program. *Degree requirements:* For master's, thesis optional; for doctorate, thesis/dissertation. *Entrance requirements:* For master's and doctorate, GRE General Test, sample of written work. Electronic applications accepted.

Wayne State University, College of Liberal Arts and Sciences, Department of Classical and Modern Languages, Literatures, and Cultures, Program in German and Slavic Studies, Detroit, MI 48202. Offers German (MA); language learning (MA); modern languages (PhD); Russian (MA). *Faculty:* 15 full-time (6 women). *Students:* 5 full-time (4 women), 2 part-time (both women), 3 international. Average age 31. 2 applicants, 100% accepted, 1 enrolled. In 2007, 1 degree awarded. *Degree requirements:* For master's, one foreign language, thesis or alternative; for doctorate, 2 foreign languages, thesis/dissertation. *Entrance requirements:* For master's and doctorate, minimum GPA of 3.0. Additional exam requirements/recommendations for international students: Required—TOEFL (minimum score 550 paper-based; 213 computer-based); Recommended—TWE (minimum score 6). *Application deadline:* For fall admission, 7/1 for domestic students, 6/1 for international students; for winter admission, 10/1 for international students; for spring admission, 2/1 for international students. Applications are processed on a rolling basis. Application fee: $30 ($50 for international students). Electronic applications accepted. *Expenses:* Tuition, state resident: part-time $403 per credit hour. Tuition, nonresident: part-time $890 per credit hour. *Financial support:* In 2007–08, 3 teaching assistantships with tuition reimbursements (averaging $12,447 per year) were awarded; fellowships, research assistantships, scholarships/grants and tuition waivers (full and partial) also available. Support available to part-time students. *Faculty research:* Exile and Holocaust, minority literature, gender studies, fairytale studies, sociolinguistics.

West Chester University of Pennsylvania, Office of Graduate Studies and Extended Education, College of Arts and Sciences, Department of Foreign Languages, West Chester, PA 19383. Offers French (M Ed, MA); German (M Ed); Latin (M Ed); Spanish (M Ed, MA). Part-time and evening/weekend programs available. *Students:* 7 full-time (all women), 18 part-time (15 women); includes 2 minority (both Hispanic Americans) Average age 35. 10 applicants, 100% accepted, 6 enrolled. In 2007, 7 degrees awarded. *Degree requirements:* For master's, one foreign language, comprehensive exam, thesis optional. *Entrance requirements:* For master's, GRE, placement test. Additional exam requirements/recommendations for international students: Required—TOEFL (minimum score 550 paper-based; 213 computer-based; 80 iBT). *Application deadline:* For fall admission, 4/15 priority date for domestic students; for spring admission, 10/15 for domestic students. Applications are processed on a rolling basis. Application fee: $35. *Expenses:* Tuition, state resident: part-time $345 per credit. Tuition, nonresident: part-time $552 per credit. Tuition and fees vary according to course load. *Financial support:* In 2007–08, 2 research assistantships with full and partial tuition reimbursements (averaging $5,000 per year) were awarded; unspecified assistantships also available. Support available to part-time students. Financial award application deadline: 2/15; financial award applicants required to submit FAFSA. *Faculty research:* Implementation of world languages curriculum framework. *Unit head:* Dr. Jerry Williams, Chair, 610-436-2700, Fax: 610-436-3048, E-mail: jwilliams2@wcupa.edu. *Application contact:* Dr. Rebecca Pauly, Graduate Coordinator, 610-436-2382, E-mail: rpauly@wcupa.edu.

Yale University, Graduate School of Arts and Sciences, Department of Germanic Language and Literature, New Haven, CT 06520. Offers MA, PhD. Terminal master's awarded for partial completion of doctoral program. *Degree requirements:* For master's, 2 foreign languages; for doctorate, 3 foreign languages, thesis/dissertation. *Entrance requirements:* For doctorate, GRE General Test.

Italian

Boston College, Graduate School of Arts and Sciences, Department of Romance Languages and Literatures, Chestnut Hill, MA 02467-3800. Offers French (MA, PhD); Italian (MA); medieval language (PhD); Spanish (MA, PhD). Part-time programs available. *Students:* 41 full-time (29 women), 9 part-time (7 women); includes 7 minority (1 American Indian/Alaska Native, 1 Asian American or Pacific Islander, 5 Hispanic Americans), 9 international. 51 applicants, 39% accepted, 10 enrolled. In 2007, 14 master's, 3 doctorates awarded. Terminal master's awarded for partial completion of doctoral program. *Degree requirements:* For master's, one foreign language; for doctorate, 2 foreign languages, thesis/dissertation. *Entrance requirements:* Additional exam requirements/recommendations for international students: Required—TOEFL (minimum score 590 paper-based; 250 computer-based; 91 iBT). *Application deadline:* For fall admission, 1/15 for domestic students. Application fee: $70. Electronic applications accepted. *Financial support:* Fellowships with full tuition reimbursements, teaching assistantships with full tuition reimbursements, Federal Work-Study and unspecified assistantships available. Support available to part-time students. Financial award application deadline: 3/1; financial award applicants required to submit FAFSA. *Faculty research:* Spanish-American literature, philology, medieval French romance and troubadour/trouvere lyrics, Golden Age Peninsular literature, secondary language acquisition and pedagogy. *Unit head:* Dr. Dwayne Carpenter, Chairperson, 617-552-3828, E-mail: dwayne.carpenter@bc.edu.

See Close-Up on page 561.

Brown University, Graduate School, Department of Italian Studies, Providence, RI 02912. Offers AM, PhD. *Degree requirements:* For master's, one foreign language, thesis; for doctorate, 2 foreign languages, thesis/dissertation, preliminary exam.

The Catholic University of America, School of Arts and Sciences, Department of Modern Languages and Literatures, Washington, DC 20064. Offers French (MA, PhD); Italian (MA); Romance languages and literatures (MA, PhD); Spanish (MA, PhD). Part-time programs available. *Faculty:* 13 full-time (7 women), 13 part-time/adjunct (all women). *Students:* 8 full-time (5 women), 9 part-time (all women); includes 4 minority (all Hispanic Americans), 4 international. Average age 33. 15 applicants, 73% accepted, 5 enrolled. In 2007, 2 master's, 5 doctorates awarded. *Degree requirements:* For master's, one foreign language, comprehensive exam, thesis or alternative; for doctorate, 2 foreign languages, comprehensive exam, thesis/dissertation. *Entrance requirements:* For master's and doctorate, GRE General Test, 3 letters of recommendation. Additional exam requirements/recommendations for international students: Required—TOEFL (minimum score 580 paper-based; 237 computer-based). *Application deadline:* For fall admission, 2/1 priority date for domestic students; for spring admission, 11/15 priority date for domestic students. Applications are processed on a rolling basis. Application fee: $55. Electronic applications accepted. *Financial support:* Fellowships, teaching assistantships, career-related internships or fieldwork, Federal Work-Study, scholarships/grants, tuition waivers (full and partial), and unspecified assistantships available. Support available to part-time students. Financial award application deadline: 2/1; financial award applicants required to submit FAFSA. *Unit head:* Dr. Joan Grimbert, Chair, 202-319-5240, Fax: 202-319-6077, E-mail: grimbert@cua.edu.

Central Connecticut State University, School of Graduate Studies, School of Arts and Sciences, Department of Modern Languages, Program in Modern Language, New Britain, CT 06050-4010. Offers French (MA); Italian (Certificate); modern language (MA). Part-time and evening/weekend programs available. *Students:* 4 full-time (3 women), 16 part-time (12 women); includes 8 minority (all Hispanic Americans) 15 applicants, 40% accepted, 6 enrolled. In 2007, 12 degrees awarded. *Degree requirements:* For master's, one foreign language, comprehensive exam, thesis or alternative. *Entrance requirements:* For master's, minimum GPA of 2.7, 24 credits of course work in French. Additional exam requirements/recommendations for international students: Required—TOEFL. *Application deadline:* For fall admission, 7/1 for domestic students; for spring admission, 12/1 for domestic students. Applications are processed on a rolling basis. Application fee: $50. Electronic applications accepted. *Expenses:* Tuition, area resident: Full-time $4,169. Tuition, state resident: full-time $6,253. Tuition, nonresident: full-time $11,614; part-time $400 per credit. Required fees: $3,322. One-time fee: $62 part-time. Tuition and fees vary according to degree level and program. *Faculty research:* Twentieth century French theater, seventeenth century French literature, French Middle Ages.

Columbia University, Graduate School of Arts and Sciences, Division of Humanities, Department of Italian, New York, NY 10027. Offers M Phil, MA, PhD. Part-time programs available. *Faculty:* 4 full-time. *Students:* 27 full-time (19 women), 4 part-time (all women); includes 2 minority (1 Asian American or Pacific Islander, 1 Hispanic American), 6 international. Average age 32. 37 applicants, 73% accepted. In 2007, 1 degree awarded. *Degree requirements:* For master's, one foreign language, oral and written exams; for doctorate, 2 foreign languages, thesis/dissertation. *Entrance requirements:* For master's and doctorate, GRE General Test, writing sample. Additional exam requirements/recommendations for international students: Required—TOEFL. Application fee: $90. *Expenses:* Tuition: Part-time $1,452 per credit. Required fees: $152 per term. One-time fee: $75 part-time. Full-time tuition and fees vary according to course level, course load, degree level and program. *Financial support:* Fellowships, teaching assistantships, Federal Work-Study and institutionally sponsored loans available. Support available to part-time students. Financial award application deadline: 1/5; financial award applicants required to submit FAFSA. *Faculty research:* Medieval and Renaissance Italian literature; Italian poetry, prose, and theater; modern and contemporary Italian literature. *Unit head:* Teodolinda Barolini, Chair, 212-854-2312, Fax: 212-854-5306, E-mail: tb27@columbia.edu.

Cornell University, Graduate School, Graduate Fields of Arts and Sciences, Field of Romance Studies, Ithaca, NY 14853-0001. Offers French linguistics (PhD); French literature (PhD); Hispanic literature (PhD); Italian linguistics (PhD); Italian literature (PhD); Romance linguistics (PhD); Spanish linguistics (PhD). *Faculty:* 32 full-time (14 women). *Students:* 50 full-time (24 women); includes 11 minority (all Hispanic Americans), 20 international. Average age 29. 114 applicants, 23% accepted, 12 enrolled. In 2007, 2 doctorates awarded. *Degree requirements:* For doctorate, 2 foreign languages, comprehensive exam, thesis/dissertation. *Entrance requirements:* For doctorate, GRE General Test, sample of written work, 3 letters of recommendation. Additional exam requirements/recommendations for international students: Required—TOEFL (minimum score 550 paper-based; 213 computer-based; 77 iBT). *Application deadline:* For fall admission, 1/15 for domestic students. Application fee: $70. Electronic applications accepted. *Financial support:* In 2007–08, 48 students received support, including 20 fellowships with full tuition reimbursements available, 28 teaching assistantships with full tuition reimbursements available; research assistantships with full tuition reimbursements available, institutionally sponsored loans, scholarships/grants, health care benefits, tuition waivers (full and partial), and unspecified assistantships also available. Financial award applicants required to submit FAFSA. *Faculty research:* Literary theory, Hispanic studies, French studies, gender studies. *Unit head:* Director of Graduate Studies, 607-255-8222. *Application contact:* Graduate Field Assistant, 607-255-4246, E-mail: romance_studies@cornell.edu.

Florida State University, Graduate Studies, College of Arts and Sciences, Department of Modern Languages, Program in Italian Studies, Tallahassee, FL 32306. Offers MA. *Faculty:* 6 full-time (2 women), 3 part-time/adjunct (2 women). *Students:* 3 full-time (1 woman). Average age 24. 4 applicants, 100% accepted, 3 enrolled. In 2007, 3 degrees awarded. *Entrance requirements:* For master's, GRE General Test or minimum GPA of 3.0. Additional exam requirements/recommendations for international students: Required—TOEFL (minimum score 550 paper-based; 213 computer-based). *Application deadline:* For fall admission, 2/1 for domestic and international students; for spring admission, 11/22 for domestic and international students. Applications are processed on a rolling basis. Application fee: $30. Electronic applications accepted. *Expenses:* Tuition, state resident: part-time $248 per credit hour. Tuition, nonresident: part-time $880 per credit hour. Tuition and fees vary according to program. *Financial support:* In 2007–08, 6 students received support, including 6 teaching assistantships with partial tuition reimbursements available (averaging $10,200 per year). Financial award application deadline: 2/15. *Unit head:* Dr. Mark Pietralunga, Coordinator, 850-644-8392, Fax: 850-644-0524, E-mail: mpietral@fsu.edu. *Application contact:* Wendy E. Pigott, Graduate Academic Coordinator, 850-644-8397, Fax: 850-644-0524, E-mail: wpigott@fsu.edu.

Graduate School and University Center of the City University of New York, Graduate Studies, Program in Comparative Literature, New York, NY 10016-4039. Offers comparative literature (MA, PhD), including classics (PhD), German (PhD), Italian (PhD). *Faculty:* 16 full-time (3 women). *Students:* 98 full-time (59 women), 11 part-time (9 women); includes 7 minority (2 Asian Americans or Pacific Islanders, 5 Hispanic Americans), 26 international. Average age 36. 66 applicants, 35% accepted, 14 enrolled. In 2007, 6 master's, 5 doctorates awarded. Terminal master's awarded for partial completion of doctoral program. *Degree requirements:* For master's, 2 foreign languages, comprehensive exam, thesis; for doctorate, 3 foreign languages, comprehensive exam, thesis/dissertation. *Entrance requirements:* For master's and doctorate, GRE General Test. Additional exam requirements/recommendations for international students: Required—TOEFL. *Application deadline:* For fall admission, 4/15 for domestic students; for spring admission, 11/15 for domestic students. Application fee: $125. Electronic applications accepted. *Financial support:* In 2007–08, 63 students received support, including 53 fellowships, 5 research assistantships, 14 teaching assistantships; career-related internships or fieldwork, Federal Work-Study, institutionally sponsored loans, and tuition waivers (full and partial) also available. Financial award application deadline: 2/1; financial award applicants required to submit FAFSA. *Unit head:* Dr. Andre Aciman, Executive Officer, 212-817-8170, Fax: 212-817-1509, E-mail: aaciman@gc.cuny.edu.

Harvard University, Graduate School of Arts and Sciences, Department of Romance Languages and Literatures, Cambridge, MA 02138. Offers French (AM, PhD); Italian (AM, PhD); Portuguese (AM, PhD); Spanish (AM, PhD). Terminal master's awarded for partial completion of doctoral program. *Degree requirements:* For master's, 2 foreign languages; for doctorate, 2 foreign languages, thesis/dissertation. *Entrance requirements:* For master's and doctorate, GRE General Test, sample of written work. Additional exam requirements/recommendations for international students: Required—TOEFL. *Expenses:* Tuition: Full-time $31,456. Full-time tuition and fees vary according to program and student level.

Hunter College of the City University of New York, Graduate School, School of Arts and Sciences, Department of Romance Languages, Program in Italian, New York, NY 10021-5085. Offers Italian (MA); Italian education (MA). *Faculty:* 1 (woman) full-time. *Students:* Average age 38. 5 applicants, 60% accepted, 2 enrolled. *Degree requirements:* For master's, 2 foreign languages, comprehensive exam, thesis optional. *Entrance requirements:* For master's, GRE General Test, GRE Subject Test, ability to read, speak, and write Italian; interview. Additional exam requirements/recommendations for international students: Required—TOEFL. *Application deadline:* For fall admission, 4/1 for domestic students, 2/1 for international students; for spring admission, 11/1 for domestic students, 9/1 for international students. Application fee: $125. *Expenses:* Tuition, state resident: full-time $6,400; part-time $270 per credit. Tuition, nonresident: part-time $500 per credit. One-time fee: $125 full-time. Tuition and fees vary according to program. *Financial support:* Federal Work-Study, scholarships/grants, and tuition waivers (partial) available. Support available to part-time students. Financial award application deadline: 4/15. *Faculty research:* Dante, Middle Ages, Renaissance, contemporary Italian novel and poetry, late Renaissance and baroque. *Unit head:* Dr. Paolo Fasoli, Graduate Co-Adviser, 212-772-5129, Fax: 212-772-5094, E-mail: pfasoli@hunter.cuny.edu. *Application contact:* William Zlata, Director for Graduate Admissions, 212-772-4482, Fax: 212-650-3336, E-mail: admissions@hunter.cuny.edu.

Italian

Indiana University Bloomington, University Graduate School, College of Arts and Sciences, Department of French and Italian, Bloomington, IN 47405-7000. Offers French (MA, PhD), including French instruction (MA), French linguistics, French literature; Italian (MA, PhD). Part-time programs available. *Faculty:* 14 full-time (3 women). *Students:* 69 full-time (43 women), 13 part-time (5 women); includes 5 minority (2 African Americans, 1 American Indian/Alaska Native, 2 Hispanic Americans), 35 international. Average age 30. 47 applicants, 74% accepted, 19 enrolled. In 2007, 15 master's, 9 doctorates awarded. *Median time to degree:* Of those who began their doctoral program in fall 1999, 25% received their degree in 8 years or less. *Degree requirements:* For master's, one foreign language; for doctorate, 2 foreign languages, thesis/dissertation. *Entrance requirements:* For master's and doctorate, GRE General Test. Additional exam requirements/recommendations for international students: Required—TOEFL. *Application deadline:* For fall admission, 1/15 priority date for domestic students, 12/15 for international students; for spring admission, 9/1 priority date for domestic students, 9/1 for international students. Applications are processed on a rolling basis. Application fee: $50 ($60 for international students). Electronic applications accepted. *Financial support:* Fellowships with partial tuition reimbursements, research assistantships with tuition reimbursements, teaching assistantships with partial tuition reimbursements, career-related internships or fieldwork, institutionally sponsored loans, and tuition waivers (full) available. Financial award application deadline: 2/15. *Faculty research:* French-Creole studies, history of rhetoric, medieval epic and romance, post seventeenth century novel and poetry, Renaissance narrative and poetry. *Unit head:* Dr. Sonya Stephens, Chairman, 812-855-5458, Fax: 812-855-8877, E-mail: sonsteph@indiana.edu. *Application contact:* Jocelyn Karlan, Secretary, 812-855-1088, Fax: 812-855-8877, E-mail: jkarlan@indiana.edu.

Iona College, School of Arts and Science, Program in Foreign Languages, New Rochelle, NY 10801-1890. Offers Italian (MA); Spanish (MA). Part-time and evening/weekend programs available. *Faculty:* 5 full-time (2 women), 2 part-time/adjunct (1 woman). *Students:* Average age 29. 6 applicants, 83% accepted, 3 enrolled. In 2007, 2 degrees awarded. *Degree requirements:* For master's, thesis or alternative. *Entrance requirements:* For master's, minimum GPA of 3.0. Additional exam requirements/recommendations for international students: Required—TOEFL (minimum score 550 paper-based; 213 computer-based). *Application deadline:* Applications are processed on a rolling basis. Application fee: $50. Electronic applications accepted. *Expenses:* Tuition: Part-time $712 per credit. Required fees: $150 per term. *Financial support:* Unspecified assistantships available. Support available to part-time students. *Faculty research:* Contemporary Spanish literature, linguistics, language acquisition, female Hispanic literature, Latina authors. *Unit head:* Dr. Victoria Ketz, Chair, 914-637-2738, E-mail: vketz@iona.edu. *Application contact:* Veronica Jarek-Prinz, Director of Graduate Admissions, 914-633-2420, Fax: 914-633-2277, E-mail: vjarekprinz@iona.edu.

The Johns Hopkins University, Zanvyl Krieger School of Arts and Sciences, Department of German and Romance Languages, Baltimore, MD 21218-2699. Offers French (PhD); German (PhD); Italian (PhD); romance languages (PhD); Spanish (PhD). *Faculty:* 14 full-time (5 women), 2 part-time/adjunct (1 woman). *Students:* 69 full-time (48 women); includes 6 minority (all Hispanic Americans), 37 international. Average age 29. 42 applicants, 36% accepted, 8 enrolled. In 2007, 13 doctorates awarded. *Median time to degree:* Of those who began their doctoral program in fall 1999, 75% received their degree in 8 years or less. *Degree requirements:* For doctorate, 2 foreign languages, thesis/dissertation. *Entrance requirements:* For doctorate, GRE General Test. Additional exam requirements/recommendations for international students: Required—TOEFL (minimum score 600 paper-based; 250 computer-based). *Application deadline:* For fall admission, 1/15 for domestic and international students. Application fee: $60. Electronic applications accepted. *Financial support:* In 2007–08, 64 students received support, including 40 fellowships with full tuition reimbursements available (averaging $16,000 per year), 2 research assistantships with full tuition reimbursements available (averaging $16,000 per year), 19 teaching assistantships with full tuition reimbursements available (averaging $16,000 per year); institutionally sponsored loans and tuition waivers (full and partial) also available. Financial award application deadline: 4/15; financial award applicants required to submit FAFSA. *Unit head:* Dr. Stephen Nichols, Chair, 410-516-4736, Fax: 410-516-5358, E-mail: stephen.nichols@jhu.edu. *Application contact:* Sally Hauf, Graduate Administrative Coordinator, 410-516-7226, Fax: 410-516-5358, E-mail: shauf@jhu.edu.

McGill University, Faculty of Graduate and Postdoctoral Studies, Faculty of Arts, Department of Italian Studies, Montréal, QC H3A 2T5, Canada. Offers MA, PhD. *Faculty:* 5 full-time (3 women), 11 part-time/adjunct (9 women). *Students:* 5 full-time (all women), 1 part-time. 6 applicants, 83% accepted, 1 enrolled. In 2007, 2 master's, 1 doctorate awarded.

Middlebury College, Language Schools, Italian School, Middlebury, VT 05753-6002. Offers MA, DML. *Faculty:* 13 full-time (4 women). *Students:* 64 full-time (49 women); includes 9 minority (2 African Americans, 1 Asian American or Pacific Islander, 6 Hispanic Americans). Average age 30. 85 applicants, 87% accepted, 64 enrolled. In 2007, 18 degrees awarded. *Degree requirements:* For master's, one foreign language; for doctorate, 2 foreign languages, thesis/dissertation, residence abroad, teaching experience. *Entrance requirements:* For master's, placement exam, 3 letters of recommendation, writing sample. *Application deadline:* Applications are processed on a rolling basis. Application fee: $55. Electronic applications accepted. *Financial support:* Fellowships, scholarships/grants available. *Unit head:* Dr. Antonio Vitti, Director, 802-443-5727, Fax: 802-443-2075, E-mail: acvitti@middlebury.edu. *Application contact:* Kara Gennarelli, Coordinator, 802-443-5727, Fax: 802-443-2075, E-mail: kgennar@middlebury.edu.

Montclair State University, The Office of Graduate Admissions and Support Services, College of Humanities and Social Sciences, Department of Spanish and Italian, Montclair, NJ 07043-1624. Offers Italian (Certificate); Spanish (MA, Certificate); translating and interpreting Spanish (Certificate). Part-time and evening/weekend programs available. *Faculty:* 15 full-time (9 women), 16 part-time/adjunct (14 women). *Students:* 9 full-time (7 women), 30 part-time (23 women); includes 12 minority (1 African American, 11 Hispanic Americans), 2 international. 39 applicants, 44% accepted, 13 enrolled. In 2007, 5 master's, 3 other advanced degrees awarded. *Degree requirements:* For master's, comprehensive exam, thesis or alternative. *Entrance requirements:* For master's, GRE General Test, BA in Spanish or at least 24 undergraduate credits of Spanish, 2 letters of recommendation. Additional exam requirements/recommendations for international students: Required—TOEFL (minimum score 83 computer-based). *Application deadline:* For fall admission, 6/1 for international students; for spring admission, 11/1 for international students. Applications are processed on a rolling basis. Application fee: $60. Electronic applications accepted. *Financial support:* In 2007–08, 1 research assistantship with full tuition reimbursement (averaging $7,000 per year) was awarded; Federal Work-Study, scholarships/grants, and unspecified assistantships also available. Support available to part-time students. Financial award application deadline: 3/1; financial award applicants required to submit FAFSA. *Unit head:* Dr. Linda Levine, Chairperson, 973-655-4285. *Application contact:* Dr. Roger Zapata, Adviser, 973-655-4285, E-mail: zapatar@mail.montclair.edu.

New York University, Graduate School of Arts and Science, Department of Italian Studies, New York, NY 10012-1019. Offers Italian (MA, PhD); Italian studies (MA). Part-time programs available. *Faculty:* 6 full-time (3 women), 6 part-time/adjunct. *Students:* 29 full-time (20 women), 4 part-time (all women); includes 1 minority (Hispanic American), 15 international. Average age 33. 40 applicants, 25% accepted, 3 enrolled. In 2007, 5 master's, 5 doctorates awarded. Terminal master's awarded for partial completion of doctoral program. *Degree requirements:* For master's, one foreign language, thesis; for doctorate, 3 foreign languages, thesis/dissertation. *Entrance requirements:* For master's, GRE General Test, sample of written work; for doctorate, GRE General Test. Additional exam requirements/recommendations for international students: Required—TOEFL. *Application deadline:* For fall admission, 1/4 priority date for domestic students. Application fee: $85. *Financial support:* Fellowships with tuition reimbursements, teaching assistantships with tuition reimbursements, Federal Work-Study, institutionally sponsored loans, scholarships/grants, and unspecified assistantships available. Financial award application deadline: 1/4; financial award applicants required to submit FAFSA. *Faculty research:* Dante, early modern literature, fascism and culture, contemporary literature, feminist theory. *Unit head:* Ruth Ben-Ghiat, Chairman, 212-998-8730, Fax: 212-995-4012, E-mail: italian.dept@nyu.edu. *Application contact:* Virginia Cox, Director of Graduate Studies, 212-998-8730, Fax: 212-995-4012, E-mail: italian.dept@nyu.edu.

Northwestern University, The Graduate School, Judd A. and Marjorie Weinberg College of Arts and Sciences, Department of French and Italian, Evanston, IL 60208. Offers eighteenth-century studies (Certificate); French (PhD); French and comparative literature (PhD); Italian studies (Certificate). Admissions and degrees offered through The Graduate School. *Degree requirements:* For doctorate, one foreign language, thesis/dissertation, written and oral exams. *Entrance requirements:* For doctorate, GRE, writing sample, cassette recording. Additional exam requirements/recommendations for international students: Required—TOEFL. *Faculty research:* Francophone studies, 18th century contemporary theory.

The Ohio State University, Graduate School, College of Humanities, Department of French and Italian, Columbus, OH 43210. Offers French (MA, PhD); Italian (MA). *Faculty:* 20. *Students:* 30 full-time (20 women), 6 part-time (4 women); includes 2 minority (1 African American, 1 Hispanic American), 6 international. Average age 33. In 2007, 12 master's, 4 doctorates awarded. *Degree requirements:* For master's, variable foreign language requirement, thesis optional; for doctorate, variable foreign language requirement, thesis/dissertation. *Entrance requirements:* For master's and doctorate, GRE General Test. Additional exam requirements/recommendations for international students: Required—TOEFL. *Application deadline:* For fall admission, 8/15 priority date for domestic students, 7/1 priority date for international students; for winter admission, 12/1 priority date for domestic students, 11/1 priority date for international students; for spring admission, 3/1 priority date for domestic students, 2/1 priority date for international students. Applications are processed on a rolling basis. Application fee: $40 ($50 for international students). Electronic applications accepted. *Financial support:* Fellowships, research assistantships, teaching assistantships, Federal Work-Study, institutionally sponsored loans, and unspecified assistantships available. Support available to part-time students. *Faculty research:* Italian and Romance linguistics. *Unit head:* Karlis Racevskis, Graduate Studies Committee Chair, 614-292-4938, Fax: 614-292-7403, E-mail: racevskis.1@osu.edu. *Application contact:* 614-292-9444, Fax: 614-292-3895, E-mail: domestic.grad@osu.edu.

Princeton University, Graduate School, Department of French and Italian, Princeton, NJ 08544-1019. Offers PhD. *Degree requirements:* For doctorate, variable foreign language requirement, thesis/dissertation. *Entrance requirements:* For doctorate, GRE General Test, sample of written work. Additional exam requirements/recommendations for international students: Required—TOEFL (minimum score 600 paper-based; 250 computer-based). Electronic applications accepted.

Queens College of the City University of New York, Division of Graduate Studies, Arts and Humanities Division, Department of European Languages and Literatures, Program in Italian, Flushing, NY 11367-1597. Offers MA. Part-time and evening/weekend programs available. *Faculty:* 8 full-time (4 women). *Students:* 7 applicants, 100% accepted, 4 enrolled. *Degree requirements:* For master's, 2 foreign languages, comprehensive exam, thesis or alternative. *Entrance requirements:* For master's, minimum GPA of 3.0. Additional exam requirements/recommendations for international students: Required—TOEFL. *Application deadline:* For fall admission, 4/1 for domestic students; for spring admission, 11/1 for domestic students. Applications are processed on a rolling basis. Application fee: $125. *Financial support:* Career-related internships or fieldwork, Federal Work-Study, institutionally sponsored loans, and tuition waivers (partial) available. Support available to part-time students. Financial award application deadline: 4/1; financial award applicants required to submit FAFSA. *Application contact:* Mario Caruso, Director of Graduate Admissions, 718-997-5200, Fax: 718-997-5193, E-mail: graduate_admissions@qc.edu.

Rutgers, The State University of New Jersey, New Brunswick, Graduate School, Program in Italian, New Brunswick, NJ 08901-1281. Offers Italian (MA, PhD); Italian literature and literary criticism (MA); language, literature and culture (MAT). Part-time and evening/weekend programs available. Terminal master's awarded for partial completion of doctoral program. *Degree requirements:* For master's, one foreign language, comprehensive exam (for some programs), thesis optional; for doctorate, 2 foreign languages, thesis/dissertation, qualifying exam. *Entrance requirements:* For master's and doctorate, GRE General Test. Additional exam requirements/recommendations for international students: Required—TOEFL. *Faculty research:* Literature.

San Francisco State University, Division of Graduate Studies, College of Humanities, Department of Foreign Languages and Literatures, Program in Italian, San Francisco, CA 94132-1722. Offers MA. *Application deadline:* Applications are processed on a rolling basis.

Stanford University, School of Humanities and Sciences, Department of French and Italian, Stanford, CA 94305-9991. Offers French (MA, PhD); Italian (MA, PhD). Terminal master's awarded for partial completion of doctoral program. *Degree requirements:* For master's, one foreign language, written exam; for doctorate, 2 foreign languages, thesis/dissertation, oral exam. *Entrance requirements:* For master's and doctorate, GRE General Test. Additional exam requirements/recommendations for international students: Required—TOEFL. Electronic applications accepted.

State University of New York at Binghamton, Graduate School, School of Arts and Sciences, Department of Romance Languages and Literatures, Program in Italian, Binghamton, NY 13902-6000. Offers MA. *Students:* 1 (woman) full-time. Average age 23. 1 applicant, 100% accepted, 0 enrolled. In 2007, 1 master's awarded. *Degree requirements:* For master's, one foreign language, comprehensive exam, thesis or alternative. *Entrance requirements:* For master's, GRE General Test, GRE Subject Test. Additional exam requirements/recommendations for international students: Required—TOEFL. *Application deadline:* For fall admission, 4/15 priority date for domestic students, 1/15 priority date for international students; for spring admission, 11/1 for domestic students, 10/1 priority date for international students. Applications are processed on a rolling basis. Application fee: $60. Electronic applications accepted. *Financial support:* Fellowships, research assistantships, teaching assistantships with full tuition reimbursements, career-related internships or fieldwork, Federal Work-Study, institutionally sponsored loans, and unspecified assistantships available. Support available to part-time students. Financial award application deadline: 2/15. *Unit head:* Dr. Antonio Sobejano-Moran, Chairperson, Department of Romance Languages and Literatures, 607-777-4635, E-mail: antobianco@msn.com.

Stony Brook University, State University of New York, Graduate School, College of Arts and Sciences, Department of European Languages, Literatures, and Cultures, Program in Italian, Stony Brook, NY 11794. Offers MA. Evening/weekend programs available. *Students:* 3 full-time (2 women), 7 part-time (6 women), 1 international. Average age 25. *Degree requirements:* For master's, one foreign language. *Entrance requirements:* For master's, GRE General Test. Additional exam requirements/recommendations for international students: Required—TOEFL. *Application deadline:* For fall admission, 1/15 for domestic students. Application fee: $60. *Unit head:* Charles Franco, Coordinator, 631-632-1494, E-mail: charles.franco@stonybrook.edu.

University at Albany, State University of New York, College of Arts and Sciences, Department of Languages, Literatures, and Cultures, Program in Italian, Albany, NY 12222-0001. Offers MA. *Application deadline:* For fall admission, 8/1 for domestic students. Application fee: $75. *Expenses:* Tuition, state resident: part-time $576 per credit. Tuition, nonresident: part-time $910 per credit. Tuition and fees vary according to program. *Unit head:* HenryK Baran, Chair, Department of Languages, Literatures, and Cultures, 518-442-4222.

University of Alberta, Faculty of Graduate Studies and Research, Department of Modern Languages and Cultural Studies, Edmonton, AB T6G 2E1, Canada. Offers applied linguistics (Germanic, Romance, Slavic) (MA); French language, literatures and linguistics (PhD); French language, literatures, and linguistics (MA); Germanic languages, literatures and linguistics

(PhD); Germanic languages, literatures, and linguistics (MA); Italian studies (MA); Slavic languages and literatures (Russian, Ukrainian) (MA, PhD); Slavic linguistics (Russian, Ukrainian) (MA, PhD); Spanish and Latin American studies (MA, PhD); Ukrainian folklore (MA, PhD). Part-time programs available. *Degree requirements:* For master's, one foreign language, thesis; for doctorate, 2 foreign languages, comprehensive exam, thesis/dissertation. *Entrance requirements:* For master's and doctorate, 1 language other than English. Additional exam requirements/recommendations for international students: Required—Michigan English Language Assessment Battery or TOEFL (paper score 550; computer score 213). Electronic applications accepted. *Faculty research:* Russian/Ukrainian studies; German studies; contemporary Latin American, French and Francophone studies; Italian studies.

University of California, Berkeley, Graduate Division, College of Letters and Science, Department of Italian Studies, Berkeley, CA 94720-1500. Offers PhD. *Faculty:* 9 full-time. *Degree requirements:* For doctorate, one foreign language, thesis/dissertation, oral and written qualifying exams. *Entrance requirements:* For doctorate, GRE General Test, minimum GPA of 3.0, 3 letters of recommendation. Additional exam requirements/recommendations for international students: Required—TOEFL (minimum score 570 paper-based; 230 computer-based). *Application deadline:* For fall admission, 12/19 for domestic students. Application fee: $70 ($90 for international students). *Financial support:* Fellowships, research assistantships, teaching assistantships, scholarships/grants and unspecified assistantships available. Financial award applicants required to submit FAFSA. *Faculty research:* Literature and culture of Italy in Middle Ages and the Renaissance, literature and culture of Italy in nineteenth- and twentieth-centuries, Italian film studies, interdisciplinary cultural studies. *Unit head:* Barbara Spackman, Chair, 510-642-1653, E-mail: spackman@berkeley.edu. *Application contact:* Sandy Jones, Student Affairs Officer, 510-642-9051, Fax: 510-643-6220, E-mail: issag@berkeley.edu.

University of California, Berkeley, Graduate Division, Group in Romance Languages and Literature, Program in Italian, Berkeley, CA 94720-1500. Offers PhD. *Entrance requirements:* For doctorate, GRE General Test, 3 letters of recommendation. *Application deadline:* For fall admission, 12/15 for domestic students. Application fee: $70 ($90 for international students). *Application contact:* Sandy Jones, Student Affairs Officer, 510-642-9051, Fax: 510-643-6220, E-mail: issag@berkeley.edu.

University of California, Los Angeles, Graduate Division, College of Letters and Science, Department of Italian, Los Angeles, CA 90095. Offers MA, PhD. *Students:* 24 full-time (14 women); includes 2 minority (both Hispanic Americans), 2 international. Average age 33. 26 applicants, 38% accepted, 6 enrolled. In 2007, 4 master's, 3 doctorates awarded. Terminal master's awarded for partial completion of doctoral program. *Median time to degree:* Of those who began their doctoral program in fall 1999, 100% received their degree in 8 years or less. *Degree requirements:* For master's, one foreign language, comprehensive exam or thesis; for doctorate, 2 foreign languages, thesis/dissertation, oral and written qualifying exams. *Entrance requirements:* For master's, GRE General Test, minimum GPA of 3.0, sample of written work; statement of purpose; for doctorate, GRE General Test, minimum undergraduate GPA of 3.0, sample of written work; statement of purpose. *Application deadline:* For fall admission, 12/15 for domestic students. Application fee: $60. Electronic applications accepted. *Expenses:* Tuition, nonresident: full-time $5,728. Required fees: $8,966. Full-time tuition and fees vary according to program and student level. *Financial support:* In 2007–08, 24 fellowships with full and partial tuition reimbursements, 6 research assistantships with full and partial tuition reimbursements, 13 teaching assistantships with full and partial tuition reimbursements were awarded; Federal Work-Study, institutionally sponsored loans, and tuition waivers (full and partial) also available. Financial award application deadline: 3/1. *Unit head:* Chair, 310-825-1940. *Application contact:* Departmental Office, 310-825-1940, E-mail: allen@humnet.ucla.edu.

University of Chicago, Division of the Humanities, Department of Romance Languages and Literatures, Chicago, IL 60637-1513. Offers French (AM, PhD); Italian (AM, PhD); Spanish (AM, PhD). *Students:* 75. 56 applicants, 45% accepted, 15 enrolled.Terminal master's awarded for partial completion of doctoral program. *Degree requirements:* For master's, 2 foreign languages, thesis; for doctorate, 3 foreign languages, thesis/dissertation. *Entrance requirements:* For master's and doctorate, GRE General Test, GRE Subject Test. Additional exam requirements/recommendations for international students: Required—TOEFL. *Application deadline:* For fall admission, 12/15 for domestic students. Application fee: $55. *Financial support:* Teaching assistantships, Federal Work-Study available. Financial award application deadline: 12/15; financial award applicants required to submit FAFSA. *Unit head:* Dr. Frederick de Armas, Chair, 773-702-8481.

University of Connecticut, Graduate School, College of Liberal Arts and Sciences, Department of Modern and Classical Languages, Field of Italian, Storrs, CT 06269. Offers MA, PhD. *Faculty:* 2 full-time (1 woman). *Students:* 9 full-time (3 women), 2 part-time (1 woman), 2 international. Average age 35. 6 applicants, 50% accepted, 2 enrolled. In 2007, 3 master's, 1 doctorate awarded. Terminal master's awarded for partial completion of doctoral program. *Degree requirements:* For master's, comprehensive exam; for doctorate, thesis/dissertation. *Entrance requirements:* For master's, GRE General Test. Additional exam requirements/recommendations for international students: Required—TOEFL (minimum score 550 paper-based; 213 computer-based). *Application deadline:* For fall admission, 2/1 priority date for domestic and international students; for spring admission, 11/1 for domestic students, 10/1 for international students. Applications are processed on a rolling basis. Application fee: $55. Electronic applications accepted. *Expenses:* Tuition, state resident: part-time $469 per credit hour. Tuition, nonresident: part-time $1,218 per credit hour. *Financial support:* In 2007–08, 19 teaching assistantships with full tuition reimbursements were awarded; fellowships, Federal Work-Study, scholarships/grants, health care benefits, and unspecified assistantships also available. Financial award application deadline: 2/1; financial award applicants required to submit FAFSA. *Unit head:* Franco Masciandaro, Section Head, 860-486-3275, E-mail: franco.masciandaro@uconn.edu.

University of Illinois at Urbana–Champaign, Graduate College, College of Liberal Arts and Sciences, School of Literatures, Cultures and Linguistics, Department of Spanish, Italian and Portuguese, Champaign, IL 61820. Offers Italian (MA, PhD); Portuguese (MA, PhD); Spanish (PhD); Spanish, Italian and Portuguese (MA). *Faculty:* 17 full-time (10 women). *Students:* 55 full-time (41 women), 11 part-time (8 women); includes 7 minority (1 African American, 6 Hispanic Americans), 40 international. 77 applicants, 42% accepted, 14 enrolled. In 2007, 6 master's, 8 doctorates awarded. *Degree requirements:* For doctorate, 2 foreign languages, thesis/dissertation. *Entrance requirements:* For master's, GRE General Test, GRE Subject Test, minimum GPA of 3.0. *Application deadline:* For fall admission, 3/1 for domestic students. Applications are processed on a rolling basis. Application fee: $60 ($75 for international students). Electronic applications accepted. *Financial support:* In 2007–08, 8 fellowships, 3 research assistantships, 62 teaching assistantships were awarded; tuition waivers (full and partial) also available. Financial award application deadline: 2/15. *Unit head:* Diane Musumeci, Head, 217-244-3250, Fax: 217-244-8430, E-mail: musumeci@uiuc.edu. *Application contact:* Lynn Stanke, Secretary, 217-333-6269, Fax: 217-244-3050, E-mail: stanke@uiuc.edu.

University of Manitoba, Faculty of Graduate Studies, Faculty of Arts, Department of French, Spanish and Italian, Winnipeg, MB R3T 2N2, Canada. Offers MA, PhD. *Degree requirements:* For master's, one foreign language, thesis; for doctorate, 2 foreign languages, thesis/dissertation.

University of Massachusetts Amherst, Graduate School, College of Humanities and Fine Arts, Department of French and Italian, Amherst, MA 01003. Offers French and Francophone studies (MA, MAT, PhD); Italian studies (MAT). Part-time programs available. *Faculty:* 9 full-time (4 women). *Students:* 9 full-time (7 women), 8 part-time (6 women); includes 1 minority (African American), 3 international. Average age 32. 16 applicants, 75% accepted, 6 enrolled. In 2007, 4 degrees awarded. *Degree requirements:* For master's, thesis or alternative. *Entrance requirements:* For master's, GRE General Test. Additional exam requirements/recommendations for international students: Required—TOEFL (minimum score 530 paper-based; 197 computer-based). *Application deadline:* For fall admission, 2/1 priority date for domestic and international students; for spring admission, 10/1 for domestic and international students. Applications are processed on a rolling basis. Application fee: $50 ($65 for international students). Electronic applications accepted. *Expenses:* Tuition, state resident: full-time $2,640; part-time $110 per credit. Tuition, nonresident: full-time $9,936; part-time $414 per credit. Required fees: $7,455. One-time fee: $332. Tuition and fees vary according to course load, campus/location, program and reciprocity agreements. *Financial support:* In 2007–08, 4 fellowships with full tuition reimbursements (averaging $5,766 per year), 7 research assistantships with full tuition reimbursements (averaging $7,803 per year), 19 teaching assistantships with full tuition reimbursements (averaging $11,099 per year) were awarded; career-related internships or fieldwork, Federal Work-Study, scholarships/grants, traineeships, and unspecified assistantships also available. Support available to part-time students. Financial award application deadline: 2/1. *Unit head:* Dr. Patrick Mensah, Head, 412-545-6697, Fax: 412-545-2314.

The University of North Carolina at Chapel Hill, Graduate School, College of Arts and Sciences, Department of Romance Languages, Chapel Hill, NC 27599. Offers French (MA, PhD); Italian (MA, PhD); Portuguese (MA, PhD); Romance languages (MA, PhD); Romance philology (MA, PhD); Spanish (MA, PhD). *Degree requirements:* For master's, one foreign language, comprehensive exam, thesis; for doctorate, 2 foreign languages, comprehensive exam, thesis/dissertation. *Entrance requirements:* For master's and doctorate, GRE General Test, minimum GPA of 3.0. Additional exam requirements/recommendations for international students: Required—TOEFL (minimum score 550 paper-based; 213 computer-based). Electronic applications accepted.

University of Notre Dame, Graduate School, College of Arts and Letters, Division of Humanities, Department of Romance Languages and Literatures, Notre Dame, IN 46556. Offers French and Francophone studies (MA); Iberian and Latin American studies (MA); Italian studies (MA); Romance literatures (MA). Part-time programs available. *Faculty:* 25 full-time (10 women), 4 part-time/adjunct (all women). *Students:* 18 full-time (12 women); includes 4 minority (all Hispanic Americans), 3 international. 28 applicants, 61% accepted, 9 enrolled. In 2007, 12 degrees awarded. *Degree requirements:* For master's, 2 foreign languages, comprehensive exam, thesis optional. *Entrance requirements:* For master's, GRE General Test, BA in target language. Additional exam requirements/recommendations for international students: Required—TOEFL (minimum score 600 paper-based; 250 computer-based; 80 iBT). *Application deadline:* For fall admission, 2/1 priority date for domestic students, 2/1 for international students. Application fee: $50. Electronic applications accepted. *Financial support:* In 2007–08, 1 fellowship (averaging $15,000 per year), 10 teaching assistantships with full tuition reimbursements (averaging $12,000 per year) were awarded; research assistantships, tuition waivers (full) also available. Financial award application deadline: 2/1. *Faculty research:* Literature of discovery and exploration, modern literature, literary criticism, medieval literature, feminist critical theory. *Unit head:* Dr. John Welle, Director of Graduate Studies, 574-631-6887, Fax: 574-631-3493, E-mail: al.romland.1@nd.edu. *Application contact:* Dr. Jarren Gonzales, Director of Graduate Admissions, 574-631-7706, Fax: 574-631-4183.

University of Oregon, Graduate School, College of Arts and Sciences, Department of Romance Languages, Program in Italian, Eugene, OR 97403. Offers MA. Part-time programs available. *Students:* 5 applicants, 80% accepted. In 2007, 3 degrees awarded. *Degree requirements:* For master's, variable foreign language requirement. *Entrance requirements:* For master's, GRE General Test, minimum GPA of 3.0. Additional exam requirements/recommendations for international students: Required—TOEFL. Application fee: $50. *Financial support:* Teaching assistantships available. *Application contact:* Barbara VerWest, Admissions Contact, 541-346-4013, E-mail: verwest@uoregon.edu.

University of Pennsylvania, School of Arts and Sciences, Graduate Group in Romance Languages, Philadelphia, PA 19104. Offers French (AM, PhD); Italian (AM, PhD); Spanish (AM, PhD). Terminal master's awarded for partial completion of doctoral program. *Degree requirements:* For master's, one foreign language, thesis or alternative; for doctorate, 2 foreign languages, thesis/dissertation. *Entrance requirements:* For master's and doctorate, GRE General Test. Additional exam requirements/recommendations for international students: Required—TOEFL. Electronic applications accepted. *Faculty research:* Literary theory and criticism, cultural studies, history of Romance literatures, gender studies.

University of Pittsburgh, School of Arts and Sciences, Department of French and Italian, Program in Italian, Pittsburgh, PA 15260. Offers MA. Part-time programs available. *Faculty:* 3 full-time (2 women). *Students:* 6 full-time (3 women). Average age 27. 2 applicants, 50% accepted, 1 enrolled. *Degree requirements:* For master's, 2 foreign languages, comprehensive exam, seminar paper. *Entrance requirements:* For master's, minimum GPA of 3.0, writing sample. Additional exam requirements/recommendations for international students: Required—TOEFL (minimum score 554 paper-based; 213 computer-based; 80 iBT). *Application deadline:* For fall admission, 2/1 priority date for domestic students. Application fee: $50. *Financial support:* In 2007–08, 6 students received support, including 6 teaching assistantships with full tuition reimbursements available (averaging $14,485 per year); Federal Work-Study, institutionally sponsored loans, scholarships/grants, health care benefits, and tuition waivers (partial) also available. Support available to part-time students. Financial award application deadline: 2/1; financial award applicants required to submit FAFSA. *Faculty research:* Seventeenth and eighteenth century literature, twentieth century holocaust literature, theater, opera, Dante and his reception, humanism. Total annual research expenditures: $20,000. *Application contact:* Prof. Francesca Savoia, Graduate Director, 412-624-6265, Fax: 412-624-6263, E-mail: savoia@pitt.edu.

University of South Africa, College of Human Sciences, Pretoria, South Africa. Offers adult education (M Ed); African languages (MA, PhD); African politics (MA, PhD); Afrikaans (MA, PhD); ancient history (MA, PhD); ancient Near Eastern studies (MA, PhD); anthropology (MA, PhD); applied linguistics (MA); Arabic (MA, PhD); archaeology (MA); art history (MA); Biblical archaeology (MA); Biblical studies (M Th, D Th, PhD); Christian spirituality (M Th, D Th); church history (M Th, D Th); classical studies (MA, PhD); clinical psychology (MA); communication (MA, PhD); comparative education (M Ed, Ed D); consulting psychology (D Admin, D Com, PhD); curriculum studies (M Ed, Ed D); development studies (M Admin, MA, D Admin, PhD); didactics (M Ed, Ed D); education (M Tech); education management (M Ed, Ed D); educational psychology (M Ed); English (MA); environmental education (M Ed); French (MA, PhD); German (MA, PhD); Greek (MA); guidance and counseling (M Ed); health studies (MA, PhD), including health sciences education (MA), health services management (MA), medical and surgical nursing science (critical care general) (MA), midwifery and neonatal nursing science (MA), trauma and emergency care (MA); history (MA, PhD); history of education (Ed D); inclusive education (M Ed, Ed D); information and communications technology policy and regulation (MA); information science (MA, MIS, PhD); international politics (MA, PhD); Islamic studies (MA, PhD); Italian (MA, PhD); Judaica (MA, PhD); linguistics (MA, PhD); mathematical education (M Ed); mathematics education (MA); missiology (M Th, D Th); modern Hebrew (MA, PhD); musicology (MA, MMus, D Mus, PhD); natural science education (M Ed); New Testament (M Th, D Th); Old Testament (D Th); pastoral therapy (M Th, D Th); philosophy (MA); philosophy of education (M Ed, Ed D); politics (MA, PhD); Portuguese (MA, PhD); practical theology (M Th, D Th); psychology (MA, MS, PhD); psychology of education (M Ed, Ed D); public health (MA); religious studies (MA, D Th, PhD); Romance languages (MA); Russian (MA, PhD); Semitic languages (MA, PhD); social behavior studies in HIV/AIDS (MA); social science (mental health) (MA); social science in development studies (MA); social science in psychology (MA); social science in social work (MA); social science in sociology (MA); social work (MSW, DSW, PhD); socio-education (M Ed, Ed D); sociolinguistics (MA); sociology (MA, PhD); Spanish (MA, PhD); systematic theology (M Th, D Th); TESOL (teaching English to speakers of other languages) (MA); theological ethics (M Th, D Th); theory of literature (MA, PhD); urban ministries (D Th); urban ministry (M Th).

The University of Tennessee, Graduate School, College of Arts and Sciences, Department of Modern Foreign Languages and Literatures, Program in Modern Foreign Languages, Knoxville, TN 37996. Offers applied linguistics (PhD); French (PhD); German (PhD); Italian

Italian

The University of Tennessee (continued)

(PhD); Portuguese (PhD); Russian (PhD); Spanish (PhD). *Degree requirements:* For doctorate, 2 foreign languages, thesis/dissertation. *Entrance requirements:* For doctorate, minimum GPA of 2.7. Additional exam requirements/recommendations for international students: Required—TOEFL. Electronic applications accepted.

University of Toronto, School of Graduate Studies, Humanities Division, Department of Italian Studies, Toronto, ON M5S 1A1, Canada. Offers MA, PhD. Part-time programs available. *Faculty:* 11 full-time. *Students:* 41 full-time (34 women), 2 part-time, 9 international. 38 applicants, 66% accepted. In 2007, 1 degree awarded. *Degree requirements:* For doctorate, 2 foreign languages, comprehensive exam, thesis/dissertation, oral defense, language exam(s). *Entrance requirements:* For master's, minimum B average in last 2 years in Italian; minimum B average in final year, overall; 2 letters of recommendation; for doctorate, MA in Italian, minimum A– average. *Application deadline:* For fall admission, 2/1 priority date for domestic students. Application fee: $100 Canadian dollars. *Financial support:* Fellowships, research assistantships, teaching assistantships available. *Unit head:* Prof. Salvatore Bancheri, Acting Chair and Acting Graduate Chair, 416-926-2347, Fax: 416-926-7107, E-mail: chair.italianstudies@utoronto.ca. *Application contact:* Gloria Cernivivo, Business Officer and Graduate Administrator, 416-926-2346, Fax: 416-978-5593, E-mail: gloria.cernivivo@utoronto.ca.

University of Victoria, Faculty of Graduate Studies, Faculty of Humanities, Department of Hispanic and Italian Studies, Victoria, BC V8W 2Y2, Canada. Offers Hispanic and Italian studies (MA); Hispanic studies (MA). *Faculty:* 4 full-time (1 woman). *Students:* 6 full-time, 1 international. Average age 25. 6 applicants, 33% accepted, 2 enrolled. *Degree requirements:* For master's, one foreign language, comprehensive exam, thesis (for some programs). *Entrance requirements:* For master's, undergraduate major in Hispanic studies, minimum B+ average. Additional exam requirements/recommendations for international students: Required—TOEFL (minimum score 575 paper-based; 233 computer-based), IELTS (minimum score 7). *Application deadline:* For fall admission, 4/1 priority date for domestic students, 12/15 priority date for international students. Applications are processed on a rolling basis. Application fee: $75 ($125 for international students). Electronic applications accepted. *Expenses:* Tuition, state resident: full-time $3,110. International tuition: $3,700 full-time. Tuition and fees vary according to program. *Financial support:* In 2007–08, 3 students received support, including teaching assistantships (averaging $5,000 per year); fellowships, scholarships/grants also available. Financial award application deadline: 2/15. *Faculty research:* Medieval/Renaissance Spanish and Italian literature, Golden Age literature, Latin American literature. Total annual research expenditures: $1,000. *Unit head:* Dr. Pablo Restrepo-Gautier, Chair, 250-721-7413, Fax: 250-721-6608, E-mail: spanit@uvic.ca. *Application contact:* Donna Fleming, Graduate Secretary, 250-721-7413, Fax: 250-721-6608, E-mail: spanit@uvic.ca.

University of Virginia, College and Graduate School of Arts and Sciences, Department of Spanish, Italian and Portuguese, Program in Italian, Charlottesville, VA 22903. Offers MA. *Students:* 7 full-time (5 women), 4 international. Average age 34. 8 applicants, 88% accepted, 4 enrolled. In 2007, 3 degrees awarded. *Degree requirements:* For master's, one foreign language, comprehensive exam, thesis. *Entrance requirements:* For master's, GRE General Test, GRE Subject Test. *Application deadline:* Applications are processed on a rolling basis. Application fee: $60. Electronic applications accepted. *Financial support:* Applicants required to submit FAFSA.

University of Washington, Graduate School, College of Arts and Sciences, Department of Romance Languages and Literature, Division of French and Italian Studies, Seattle, WA 98195. Offers French (MA, PhD); Italian (MA). *Faculty:* 8 full-time (4 women), 1 part-time/adjunct (0 women). *Students:* 15 full-time (12 women); includes 2 minority (both Asian Americans or Pacific Islanders), 3 international. 14 applicants, 57% accepted, 5 enrolled. In 2007, 2 master's, 1 doctorate awarded. Terminal master's awarded for partial completion of doctoral program. *Degree requirements:* For master's, 2 foreign languages, exam; for doctorate, 3 foreign languages, thesis/dissertation, exam. *Entrance requirements:* For master's and doctorate, GRE General Test, minimum GPA of 3.0. Additional exam requirements/recommendations for international students: Required—TOEFL. *Application deadline:* For fall admission, 1/15 priority date for domestic students, 11/1 priority date for international students. Application fee: $50. Electronic applications accepted. *Financial support:* In 2007–08, 1 fellowship with full tuition reimbursement (averaging $13,059 per year), 15 teaching assistantships with full tuition reimbursements (averaging $13,534 per year) were awarded; Federal Work-Study, institutionally sponsored loans, health care benefits, unspecified assistantships, and professional development stipends also available. Financial award application deadline: 1/15; financial award applicants required to submit FAFSA. *Faculty research:* Interdisciplinary studies, literary theory and criticism, film, major periods of French and Italian literature, Francophonie. *Unit head:* Prof. Albert J. Sbragia, Chair, 206-616-3708, Fax: 206-616-3302, E-mail: sbragia@u.washington.edu. *Application contact:* Prof. Geoffrey Turnowsky, Graduate Program Coordinator, 206-685-1618, Fax: 206-616-3302, E-mail: gt2@u.washington.edu.

University of Wisconsin–Madison, Graduate School, College of Letters and Science, Department of French and Italian, Program in Italian, Madison, WI 53706-1380. Offers MA, PhD. Part-time programs available. *Degree requirements:* For master's, one foreign language; for doctorate, 2 foreign languages, thesis/dissertation. *Entrance requirements:* For master's and doctorate, GRE. Electronic applications accepted. *Faculty research:* Italian literature, culture, linguistics, cinema, and language.

University of Wisconsin–Milwaukee, Graduate School, College of Letters and Sciences, Interdepartmental Program in Foreign Language and Literature, Milwaukee, WI 53201-0413. Offers classics and Hebrew studies (MAFLL); comparative literature (MAFLL); French and Italian (MAFLL); German (MAFLL); Slavic studies (MAFLL); Spanish (MAFLL). Part-time programs available. *Faculty:* 39 full-time (17 women). *Students:* 29 full-time (21 women), 31 part-time (23 women); includes 8 minority (1 Asian American or Pacific Islander, 7 Hispanic Americans), 22 international. 54 applicants, 67% accepted, 26 enrolled. In 2007, 34 degrees awarded. *Degree requirements:* For master's, 2 foreign languages, thesis or alternative. *Application deadline:* For fall admission, 1/1 priority date for domestic students; for spring admission, 9/1 for domestic students. Applications are processed on a rolling basis. Application fee: $45 ($75 for international students). *Expenses:* Tuition, state resident: part-time $530 per credit. Tuition, nonresident: part-time $1,428 per credit. Required fees: $19 per credit. $229 per term. Tuition and fees vary according to course load and program. *Financial support:* In 2007–08, 44 teaching assistantships were awarded; fellowships, research assistantships, career-related internships or fieldwork and unspecified assistantships also available. Support available to part-time students. Financial award application deadline: 4/15. *Unit head:* Gabrielle Verdier, Representative, 414-229-3346, Fax: 414-229-2741, E-mail: verdier@uwm.edu.

Wayne State University, College of Liberal Arts and Sciences, Department of Classical and Modern Languages, Literatures, and Cultures, Program in Italian, Detroit, MI 48202. Offers MA. *Students:* 1 (woman) full-time. Average age 37. In 2007, 1 degree awarded. *Degree requirements:* For master's, one foreign language, thesis optional. *Entrance requirements:* For master's, GRE General Test, minimum GPA of 3.0. Additional exam requirements/recommendations for international students: Required—TOEFL (minimum score 550 paper-based; 213 computer-based); Recommended—TWE (minimum score 6). *Application deadline:* For fall admission, 7/1 for domestic students, 6/1 for international students; for winter admission, 10/1 for international students; for spring admission, 2/1 for international students. Applications are processed on a rolling basis. Application fee: $30 ($50 for international students). Electronic applications accepted. *Expenses:* Tuition, state resident: part-time $403 per credit hour. Tuition, nonresident: part-time $890 per credit hour. *Financial support:* Fellowships, teaching assistantships available. *Faculty research:* Renaissance lyric, modern theatre, Dante and Bocaccio, modern novel. *Application contact:* Dr. Michael Giordano, Graduate Director, 313-577-3051, Fax: 313-577-6243, E-mail: m.j.giordano@wayne.edu.

Yale University, Graduate School of Arts and Sciences, Department of Italian Language and Literature, New Haven, CT 06520. Offers PhD. *Degree requirements:* For doctorate, 3 foreign languages, thesis/dissertation. *Entrance requirements:* For doctorate, GRE General Test.

Japanese

Cornell University, Graduate School, Graduate Fields of Arts and Sciences, Field of East Asian Literature, Ithaca, NY 14853-0001. Offers Asian religions (MA, PhD); Chinese linguistics (MA, PhD); Chinese philology (MA, PhD); classical Chinese literature (MA, PhD); classical Japanese literature (MA, PhD); Japanese linguistics (MA, PhD); Korean literature (MA, PhD); modern Chinese literature (MA, PhD); modern Japanese literature (MA, PhD). *Faculty:* 12 full-time (4 women). *Students:* 20 full-time (10 women); includes 4 minority (all Asian Americans or Pacific Islanders), 11 international. Average age 32. 41 applicants, 15% accepted, 3 enrolled. In 2007, 1 master's, 4 doctorates awarded. *Degree requirements:* For master's, 2 foreign languages, thesis, teaching experience; for doctorate, 2 foreign languages, comprehensive exam, thesis/dissertation, teaching experience. *Entrance requirements:* For master's and doctorate, GRE General Test, 3 years of study in Chinese, Japanese, Korean, or Vietnamese, 3 letters of recommendation, academic writing sample. Additional exam requirements/recommendations for international students: Required—TOEFL (minimum score 600 paper-based; 250 computer-based; 77 iBT). *Application deadline:* For fall admission, 1/10 priority date for domestic students. Application fee: $70. Electronic applications accepted. *Financial support:* In 2007–08, 19 students received support, including 15 fellowships with full tuition reimbursements available, 4 teaching assistantships with full tuition reimbursements available; research assistantships with full tuition reimbursements, institutionally sponsored loans, scholarships/grants, health care benefits, tuition waivers (full and partial), and unspecified assistantships also available. Financial award applicants required to submit FAFSA. *Faculty research:* Vietnamese literature; Chinese literature, drama, and film; Japanese theater and literature; popular culture in East Asia; Korean literature; Asian linguistics. *Unit head:* Director of Graduate Studies, 607-255-9099. *Application contact:* Graduate Field Assistant, 607-255-9099, E-mail: east_asian_lit@cornell.edu.

Eastern Michigan University, Graduate School, College of Arts and Sciences, Department of Foreign Languages and Bilingual Studies, Program in Foreign Languages, Ypsilanti, MI 48197. Offers French (MA); German (MA); German for business (Graduate Certificate); Hispanic language and cultures (Graduate Certificate); Japanese business practices (Graduate Certificate); Spanish (MA). Part-time and evening/weekend programs available. Postbaccalaureate distance learning degree programs offered (minimal on-campus study). *Students:* 1 (woman) full-time, 18 part-time (17 women); includes 2 minority (1 Asian American or Pacific Islander, 1 Hispanic American). Average age 35. In 2007, 8 master's, 2 other advanced degrees awarded. *Degree requirements:* For master's, one foreign language, thesis optional. *Entrance requirements:* Additional exam requirements/recommendations for international students: Required—TOEFL. *Application deadline:* Applications are processed on a rolling basis. Application fee: $35. *Expenses:* Tuition, state resident: full-time $8,952; part-time $373 per credit hour. Tuition, nonresident: full-time $17,634; part-time $735 per credit hour. Required fees: $896; $34 per credit hour. Tuition and fees vary according to course level, degree level and program. *Financial support:* Fellowships, research assistantships with full tuition reimbursements, teaching assistantships with full tuition reimbursements, career-related internships or fieldwork, Federal Work-Study, institutionally sponsored loans, scholarships/grants, tuition waivers (partial), and unspecified assistantships available. Support available to part-time students. Financial award applicants required to submit FAFSA. *Application contact:* Dr. Genevieve Peden, Program Advisor, 734-487-2283, Fax: 734-487-3411, E-mail: gpeden@emich.edu.

Harvard University, Graduate School of Arts and Sciences, Department of East Asian Languages and Civilizations, Cambridge, MA 02138. Offers Chinese (PhD); Japanese (PhD); Korean (PhD); Mongolian (PhD); Vietnamese (PhD). Terminal master's awarded for partial completion of doctoral program. *Degree requirements:* For doctorate, 3 foreign languages, thesis/dissertation, general exams. *Entrance requirements:* For doctorate, GRE General Test. Additional exam requirements/recommendations for international students: Required—TOEFL. *Expenses:* Tuition: Full-time $31,456. Full-time tuition and fees vary according to program and student level. *Faculty research:* Central Asian literature, religion, and premodern history.

Indiana University Bloomington, University Graduate School, College of Arts and Sciences, Department of East Asian Languages and Cultures, Bloomington, IN 47405-7000. Offers Chinese (MA, PhD); East Asian languages and cultures (PhD); East Asian studies (MA); Japanese (MA, PhD); language pedagogy (MA). Part-time programs available. *Faculty:* 7 full-time (2 women). *Students:* 19 full-time (12 women), 6 part-time (3 women); includes 3 minority (1 African American, 1 Asian American or Pacific Islander, 1 Hispanic American), 6 international. Average age 32. 77 applicants, 25% accepted, 10 enrolled. In 2007, 7 master's, 1 doctorate awarded. *Degree requirements:* For master's, 2 foreign languages, thesis; for doctorate, 2 foreign languages, thesis/dissertation. *Entrance requirements:* Additional exam requirements/recommendations for international students: Required—TOEFL. *Application deadline:* For fall admission, 1/15 for domestic students, 12/15 for international students; for spring admission, 9/1 for domestic and international students. Applications are processed on a rolling basis. Application fee: $50 ($60 for international students). Electronic applications accepted. *Financial support:* Fellowships, teaching assistantships, Federal Work-Study and tuition waivers (full) available. Financial award application deadline: 3/1. *Faculty research:* Postwar/postmodern Japanese fiction, modern Chinese film and literature, classical Chinese literature and philosophy, Chinese and Japanese linguistics and pedagogy, East Asian politics. *Unit head:* Robert Eno, Chair, 812-855-0856, E-mail: eno@indiana.edu. *Application contact:* Edith Sarra, Director of Graduate Studies, 812-855-4031, Fax: 812-855-6402, E-mail: eserra@indiana.edu.

Kent State University, College of Arts and Sciences, Department of Modern and Classical Language Studies, Kent, OH 44242-0001. Offers French literature (MA); French, Spanish, German and Latin pedagogy (MA); German literature (MA); Spanish literature (MA); translation (MA), including French, German, Japanese, Russian, Spanish; translation studies (PhD). Part-time and evening/weekend programs available. *Faculty:* 31 full-time (15 women), 4 part-time/adjunct (2 women). *Students:* 64 full-time (45 women), 27 part-time (26 women). Average age 32. 113 applicants, 80% accepted, 42 enrolled. In 2007, 27 degrees awarded. *Degree requirements:* For master's, one foreign language, comprehensive exam (for some programs), thesis (for some programs); for doctorate, comprehensive exam, thesis/dissertation (for some programs). *Entrance requirements:* For master's, minimum GPA of 3.0, writing sample, audio tape or CD; for doctorate, 3 recommendations. Additional exam requirements/recommendations for international students: Required—TOEFL (minimum score 197 computer-based). *Application deadline:* For fall admission, 2/28 for domestic and international students. Applications are processed on a rolling basis. Application fee: $30. Electronic applications accepted. *Financial support:* In 2007–08, 31 teaching assistantships with full tuition reimbursements (averaging $8,000 per year) were awarded; research assistantships with full tuition reimbursements, career-related internships or fieldwork, Federal Work-Study, health care benefits, tuition waivers (full and partial), and unspecified assistantships also available. Support available to part-time students. Financial award application deadline: 2/1. *Faculty research:* Literature, pedagogy, applied linguistics, translation studies. *Unit head:* Dr. Gregory M Shreve, Chair, 330-672-1796, Fax: 330-672-4009, E-mail: gshreve@kent.edu. *Application contact:* Carol S. Maier, Graduate Coordinator, 330-672-1797, Fax: 330-672-4009, E-mail: cmaier@kent.edu.

The Ohio State University, Graduate School, College of Humanities, Department of East Asian Languages and Literatures, Program in Japanese, Columbus, OH 43210. Offers MA, PhD. *Students:* 2 full-time (0 women). Average age 23. *Application deadline:* Applications are processed on a rolling basis. Application fee: $40 ($50 for international students). Electronic applications accepted. *Unit head:* Mineharu Nakayama, Graduate Studies Committee Chair, 614-292-5816, Fax: 614-292-3225, E-mail: nakayama.1@osu.edu. *Application contact:* Graduate Admissions, 614-292-9444, Fax: 614-292-3895, E-mail: domestic.grad@osu.edu.

Portland State University, Graduate Studies, College of Liberal Arts and Sciences, Department of Foreign Languages and Literatures, Portland, OR 97207-0751. Offers foreign literature and language (MA); French (MA); German (MA); Japanese (MA); Spanish (MA). Part-time programs available. *Faculty:* 40 full-time (24 women), 24 part-time/adjunct (15 women). *Students:* 35 full-time (20 women), 13 part-time (12 women); includes 4 minority (1 Asian American or Pacific Islander, 3 Hispanic Americans), 11 international. Average age 32. 27 applicants, 74% accepted, 15 enrolled. In 2007, 18 master's awarded. *Degree requirements:* For master's, one foreign language, thesis (for some programs). *Entrance requirements:* Additional exam requirements/recommendations for international students: Required—TOEFL (minimum score 550 paper-based; 213 computer-based). *Application deadline:* For fall admission, 4/1 for domestic students, 3/1 for international students; for winter admission, 8/1 for domestic students, 7/1 for international students; for spring admission, 11/1 for domestic and international students. Applications are processed on a rolling basis. Application fee: $50. *Expenses:* Tuition, state resident: full-time $7,047. Tuition, nonresident: full-time $11,178. *Financial support:* In 2007–08, 5 teaching assistantships with full tuition reimbursements (averaging $7,921 per year) were awarded; research assistantships with full tuition reimbursements, Federal Work-Study, scholarships/grants, and unspecified assistantships also available. Support available to part-time students. Financial award application deadline: 3/1; financial award applicants required to submit FAFSA. *Faculty research:* Foreign language pedagogy, applied and social linguistics, literary history and criticism. Total annual research expenditures: $69,175. *Unit head:* Dr. Sandra F. Freels, Chair, 503-725-3522, Fax: 503-725-5276. *Application contact:* Karen Popp, Office Coordinator, 503-725-3522, E-mail: poppk@pdx.edu.

San Francisco State University, Division of Graduate Studies, College of Humanities, Department of Foreign Languages and Literatures, Program in Japanese, San Francisco, CA 94132-1722. Offers MA. *Application deadline:* Applications are processed on a rolling basis. *Unit head:* Dr. Masahiko Minami, Program Coordinator, 415-338-7451, E-mail: mminami@sfsu.edu.

Stanford University, School of Humanities and Sciences, Department of Asian Languages, Stanford, CA 94305-9991. Offers Chinese (MA, PhD); Japanese (MA, PhD). Terminal master's awarded for partial completion of doctoral program. *Degree requirements:* For master's, one foreign language, thesis or an annotated translation of a literary or historical text; for doctorate, 2 foreign languages, thesis/dissertation, field exams. *Entrance requirements:* For master's and doctorate, GRE General Test. Additional exam requirements/recommendations for international students: Required—TOEFL. Electronic applications accepted.

University at Buffalo, the State University of New York, Graduate School, Graduate School of Education, Department of Learning and Instruction, Buffalo, NY 14260. Offers adolescence education (Certificate); biology (Ed M); chemistry (Ed M); childhood education (Ed M); early childhood and childhood education with bilingual extension (Ed M); early childhood education (Ed M); earth science (Ed M); elementary education (Ed D, PhD); English (Ed M); English education (PhD); English for speakers of other languages (Ed M); foreign and second language education (PhD); French (Ed M); general education (Ed M); German (Ed M); Italian (Ed M); Japanese (Ed M); Latin (Ed M); literary specialist (Ed M); mathematics (Ed M); mathematics education (PhD); mentoring teachers (Certificate); music education (Ed M, Certificate); physics (Ed M); reading education (PhD); Russian (Ed M); school administrator and supervisor (Certificate); science education (PhD); social studies (Ed M); Spanish (Ed M); special education (PhD); teaching and leading for diversity (Certificate); teaching English to speakers of other languages (Ed M). Part-time and evening/weekend programs available. Postbaccalaureate distance learning degree programs offered (no on-campus study). Terminal master's awarded for partial completion of doctoral program. *Degree requirements:* For master's, comprehensive exam; for doctorate, thesis/dissertation, research analysis exam, research experience component. *Entrance requirements:* For doctorate, GRE General Test or MAT, interview, writing sample, letters of recommendation. Additional exam requirements/recommendations for international students: Required—TOEFL (minimum score 600 paper-based; 250 computer-based). Electronic applications accepted. *Faculty research:* Science assessment, state-level testing, early learning, literacy, second language acquisition.

University of Alberta, Faculty of Graduate Studies and Research, Department of East Asian Studies, Edmonton, AB T6G 2E1, Canada. Offers Chinese literature (MA); East Asian interdisciplinary studies (MA); Japanese literature (MA). Part-time programs available. *Degree requirements:* For master's, one foreign language, thesis. *Entrance requirements:* Additional exam requirements/recommendations for international students: Required—TOEFL. Electronic applications accepted. *Faculty research:* Classical Chinese poetry and poetics, Chinese philosophy, modern/contemporary Chinese literature, modern Japanese literature and culture, Japanese women's writing.

University of California, Berkeley, Graduate Division, College of Letters and Science, Department of East Asian Languages and Cultures, Berkeley, CA 94720-1500. Offers Chinese language (PhD); Japanese language (PhD). *Degree requirements:* For doctorate, one foreign language, thesis/dissertation, oral qualifying exam. *Entrance requirements:* For doctorate, GRE General Test, minimum GPA of 3.0, MA thesis, 3 letters of recommendation. *Application deadline:* For fall admission, 12/8 for domestic students. Application fee: $70 ($90 for international students). Electronic applications accepted. *Financial support:* Fellowships, research assistantships, teaching assistantships, Federal Work-Study, institutionally sponsored loans, and unspecified assistantships available. Financial award applicants required to submit FAFSA. *Faculty research:* Chinese and Japanese modern and classical texts, prose, and poetry; Chinese and Japanese linguistics. *Unit head:* Dr. Alan Tansman, Chair, 510-643-4311, Fax: 510-642-6031, E-mail: tansman@berkeley.edu. *Application contact:* Information Contact, 510-642-3480, E-mail: ealang@berkeley.edu.

University of California, Irvine, Office of Graduate Studies, School of Humanities, Department of East Asian Languages and Literatures, Irvine, CA 92697. Offers Chinese (MA, PhD); East Asian languages and literatures (MA, PhD); Japanese (MA, PhD). *Students:* 14 full-time (12 women); includes 1 minority (Asian American or Pacific Islander), 10 international. In 2007, 1 master's, 1 doctorate awarded. *Degree requirements:* For doctorate, thesis/dissertation. *Entrance requirements:* For master's, GRE, minimum GPA of 3.0; for doctorate, GRE General Test, minimum GPA of 3.0. Additional exam requirements/recommendations for international students: Required—TOEFL (minimum score 550 paper-based; 213 computer-based). *Application deadline:* For fall admission, 1/15 priority date for domestic students; for winter admission, 10/15 priority date for domestic students; for spring admission, 1/15 for domestic students. Application fee: $60. Electronic applications accepted. *Financial support:* Fellowships with tuition reimbursements, research assistantships with full tuition reimbursements, teaching assistantships with partial tuition reimbursements, institutionally sponsored loans, traineeships, health care benefits, and unspecified assistantships available. Financial award application deadline: 3/1; financial award applicants required to submit FAFSA. *Faculty research:* Chinese, Japanese, and Korean literature and culture; language and textual analysis; historical, social, and cultural dimensions of literary study. *Unit head:* Michael Fuller, Interim Chair, 949-824-2151. *Application contact:* Angie Agsalog, Graduate Staff Contact, 949-824-1601, Fax: 949-824-3248, E-mail: aagsalog@uci.edu.

University of Colorado at Boulder, Graduate School, College of Arts and Sciences, Department of East Asian Languages and Civilizations, Boulder, CO 80309. Offers Chinese (MA, PhD); Japanese (MA, PhD). Part-time programs available. *Faculty:* 9. *Students:* 29 full-time (15 women), 6 part-time (4 women); includes 5 minority (all Asian Americans or Pacific Islanders), 12 international. Average age 29. 25 applicants, 64% accepted. In 2007, 6 degrees awarded. *Degree requirements:* For master's, comprehensive exam. *Entrance requirements:* For master's, BA in Chinese or Japanese, minimum undergraduate GPA of 3.0. Additional exam requirements/recommendations for international students: Required—TOEFL. *Application deadline:* For fall admission, 1/1 priority date for domestic students, 12/1 for international students; for spring admission, 10/1 for domestic students, 9/1 for international students. Applications are processed on a rolling basis. Application fee: $50 ($60 for international students). *Financial support:* In 2007–08, 12 fellowships (averaging $3,372 per year), 2 research assistantships (averaging $10,564 per year) were awarded; career-related internships or fieldwork and Federal Work-Study also available. Financial award application deadline: 2/1. *Faculty research:* Chinese and Japanese modern and classical literature, religions, linguistics, language pedagogy, pre-modern and contemporary fiction, sociolinguistics. Total annual research expenditures: $1.1 million. *Unit head:* Michael Breed, Chair, 303-492-7241, Fax: 303-492-7272, E-mail: michael.breed@colorado.edu. *Application contact:* Graduate Secretary, 303-492-6639, Fax: 303-492-7272, E-mail: ealc@colorado.edu.

University of Hawaii at Manoa, Graduate Division, Colleges of Arts and Sciences, College of Language, Linguistics and Literature, Department of East Asian Languages and Literatures, Program in Japanese, Honolulu, HI 96822. Offers MA, PhD. Part-time programs available. *Faculty:* 18 full-time (9 women). *Students:* 46 full-time (34 women), 5 part-time (2 women); includes 14 minority (all Asian Americans or Pacific Islanders), 21 international. 30 applicants, 67% accepted, 11 enrolled. *Median time to degree:* Of those who began their doctoral program in fall 1999, 67% received their degree in 8 years or less. *Degree requirements:* For master's, 2 foreign languages, thesis optional; for doctorate, 2 foreign languages, comprehensive exam, thesis/dissertation. *Entrance requirements:* For master's and doctorate, GRE General Test. Additional exam requirements/recommendations for international students: Required—TOEFL (minimum score 560 paper-based; 220 computer-based; 83 iBT), IELTS (minimum score 5). *Application deadline:* For fall admission, 2/1 for domestic and international students; for spring admission, 9/1 for domestic and international students. Application fee: $50. *Financial support:* In 2007–08, 1 research assistantship (averaging $18,924 per year), 7 teaching assistantships (averaging $14,227 per year) were awarded. *Application contact:* Leon Serafim, Graduate Chair, 808-956-2069, Fax: 808-956-9515, E-mail: serafim@hawaii.edu.

University of Hawaii at Manoa, Graduate Division, School of Pacific and Asian Studies, Program in Asian Studies, Concentration in Japanese Studies, Honolulu, HI 96822. Offers Graduate Certificate. Part-time programs available. *Students:* 1 full-time (0 women), 1 part-time; includes 1 minority (Asian American or Pacific Islander) *Degree requirements:* For Graduate Certificate, one foreign language. *Entrance requirements:* For degree, GRE. Additional exam requirements/recommendations for international students: Required—TOEFL (minimum score 560 paper-based; 220 computer-based; 83 iBT), IELTS (minimum score 5). Total annual research expenditures: $545,737. *Application contact:* Robert Huey, Director, 808-956-2664, Fax: 808-956-2666, E-mail: huey@hawaii.edu.

University of Maryland, College Park, Graduate Studies, College of Arts and Humanities, School of Languages, Literature, and Cultures, Program in Second Language Acquisition and Application, College Park, MD 20742. Offers French (MA); German (MA); Japanese (MA); Russian (MA); second language instruction (PhD); second language learning (PhD); second language measurement and assessment (PhD); second language use (PhD); Spanish (MA). *Students:* 1 (woman) full-time, 1 international. 50 applicants, 14% accepted. *Entrance requirements:* For master's, BA or BS in related field, demonstrated language competency, 3 letters of reference. *Application deadline:* For fall admission, 1/15 for domestic students, 2/1 for international students; for spring admission, 9/15 for domestic students, 6/1 for international students. Applications are processed on a rolling basis. Application fee: $60. Electronic applications accepted. *Financial support:* In 2007–08, 1 research assistantship (averaging $20,450 per year) was awarded; fellowships also available. *Faculty research:* Second language acquisition, pedagogical perspectives, technological applications, language use in professional contexts. *Unit head:* Dr. Cynthia L. Martin, Acting Chair, 301-405-4244, E-mail: cmartin@umd.edu. *Application contact:* Dean of Graduate School, 301-405-0358, Fax: 301-314-9305.

University of Massachusetts Amherst, Graduate School, College of Humanities and Fine Arts, Department of Asian Languages and Literatures, Program in Japanese, Amherst, MA 01003. Offers MA. *Students:* 11 full-time (7 women), 3 part-time (all women), 5 international. Average age 28. 11 applicants, 100% accepted, 5 enrolled. In 2007, 8 degrees awarded. *Degree requirements:* For master's, thesis, general exam. *Entrance requirements:* For master's, GRE General Test, minimum GPA of 3.0. Additional exam requirements/recommendations for international students: Required—TOEFL (minimum score 530 paper-based; 197 computer-based). *Application deadline:* For fall admission, 2/1 priority date for domestic and international students. Applications are processed on a rolling basis. Application fee: $50 ($65 for international students). Electronic applications accepted. *Expenses:* Tuition, state resident: full-time $2,640; part-time $110 per credit. Tuition, nonresident: full-time $9,936; part-time $414 per credit. Required fees: $7,455. One-time fee: $332. Tuition and fees vary according to course load, campus/location, program and reciprocity agreements. *Financial support:* Fellowships with full tuition reimbursements, research assistantships with full tuition reimbursements, teaching assistantships with full tuition reimbursements also available. Support available to part-time students. Financial award application deadline: 2/1. *Unit head:* Dr. Stephen Miller, Director, 413-545-0886, Fax: 413-545-4975. *Application contact:* Information Contact, 413-545-0886, Fax: 413-545-4975.

University of Oregon, Graduate School, College of Arts and Sciences, Department of East Asian Languages and Literature, Eugene, OR 97403. Offers Chinese (MA, PhD); Japanese (MA, PhD). *Faculty:* 15 full-time (9 women), 1 part-time/adjunct (0 women). *Students:* 15 full-time (12 women), 2 part-time (1 woman); includes 1 minority (Asian American or Pacific Islander), 12 international. 29 applicants, 21% accepted. In 2007, 10 degrees awarded. *Entrance requirements:* Additional exam requirements/recommendations for international students: Required—TOEFL. *Application deadline:* For fall admission, 2/15 for domestic students. Application fee: $50. *Financial support:* In 2007–08, 20 teaching assistantships were awarded. Financial award application deadline: 3/1. *Faculty research:* Linguistics, pedagogy. *Unit head:* Stephen Durrant, Head, 541-346-4008. *Application contact:* Michael Bardossi, Admissions Contact, 541-346-4066, E-mail: bardossm@oregon.uoregon.edu.

University of Washington, Graduate School, College of Arts and Sciences, Department of Asian Languages and Literature, Seattle, WA 98195. Offers Chinese language and literature (MA, PhD); Japanese language and literature (MA, PhD); South Asian language and literature (MA, PhD). *Degree requirements:* For master's, 2 foreign languages, general exam, thesis or 2 research papers; for doctorate, 3 foreign languages, thesis/dissertation, general exam. *Entrance requirements:* For master's, GRE, minimum GPA of 3.0; for doctorate, GRE, master's degree in related field, minimum GPA of 3.0. Additional exam requirements/recommendations for international students: Required—TOEFL. Electronic applications accepted. *Faculty research:* Textual, linguistic, philological, and literary study of languages and literatures of Asia.

University of Wisconsin–Madison, Graduate School, College of Letters and Science, Department of East Asian Languages and Literature, Program in Japanese, Madison, WI 53706-

Japanese

University of Wisconsin–Madison (continued)
1380. Offers MA, PhD. Part-time programs available. Terminal master's awarded for partial completion of doctoral program. *Degree requirements:* For master's, one foreign language, seminars, written exam; for doctorate, 3 foreign languages, thesis/dissertation, seminars, preliminary exams, oral exam. *Entrance requirements:* For master's, GRE General Test, bachelor's degree or equivalent in Japanese; for doctorate, GRE General Test, master's degree or equivalent in Japanese. Electronic applications accepted. *Faculty research:* Modern and historical Japanese linguistics, modern Japanese fiction and poetry, classical Japanese literature, language pedagogy.

Washington University in St. Louis, Graduate School of Arts and Sciences, Department of Asian and Near Eastern Languages and Literatures, St. Louis, MO 63130-4899. Offers Asian language (MA); Asian studies (MA); Chinese (PhD); comparative literature (MA, PhD); Japanese (PhD). Terminal master's awarded for partial completion of doctoral program. *Degree requirements:* For master's, thesis optional; for doctorate, thesis/dissertation. *Entrance requirements:* For master's and doctorate, GRE General Test. Electronic applications accepted.

Washington University in St. Louis, Graduate School of Arts and Sciences, Program in East Asian Studies, St. Louis, MO 63130-4899. Offers art history (PhD); Chinese (MA); Chinese and comparative literature (PhD); East Asian studies (MA); history (PhD); Japanese (MA); Japanese and comparative literature (PhD); JD/MA; MBA/MA. PhD offered through specific departments. *Entrance requirements:* For master's and doctorate, GRE General Test. Electronic applications accepted.

See Close-Up on page 815.

Near and Middle Eastern Languages

The American University in Cairo, Graduate Studies and Research, School of Humanities and Social Sciences, Department of Arabic Studies, Cairo, Egypt. Offers Arab language and literature (MA); Islamic art and architecture (MA); Islamic studies (Diploma); Middle East studies (MA, Diploma); Middle Eastern history (MA). Part-time programs available. *Degree requirements:* For master's, thesis optional, proficiency in French or German. *Entrance requirements:* Additional exam requirements/recommendations for international students: Required—English entrance exam and/or TOEFL. Electronic applications accepted. *Faculty research:* History of early Islam, Ayubbid, and Mamluk periods; nineteenth- and twentieth-century Middle East Islamic jurisprudence; contemporary Arabic literary criticism.

American University of Beirut, Graduate Programs, Faculty of Arts and Sciences, Beirut, Lebanon. Offers anthropology (MA); Arabic language and literature (MA); archaeology (MA); biology (MS); chemistry (MS); computer science (MS); economics (MA); education (MA); English language (MA); English literature (MA); environmental policy planning (MSES); financial economics (MAFE); geology (MS); history (MA); mathematics (MA, MS); Middle Eastern studies (MA); philosophy (MA); physics (MS); political studies (MA); psychology (MA); public administration (MA); sociology (MA); statistics (MA, MS). Part-time programs available. *Faculty:* 108 full-time (29 women), 5 part-time/adjunct (3 women). *Students:* 134 full-time (92 women), 228 part-time (167 women). Average age 25. 319 applicants, 67% accepted, 91 enrolled. In 2007, 144 degrees awarded. *Degree requirements:* For master's, one foreign language, comprehensive exam, thesis (for some programs). *Entrance requirements:* For master's, GRE, letter of recommendation. Additional exam requirements/recommendations for international students: Required—TOEFL (minimum score 600 paper-based; 250 computer-based; 100 iBT), IELTS (minimum score 8). *Application deadline:* For fall admission, 4/30 for domestic and international students; for spring admission, 11/1 for domestic and international students. Application fee: $50. *Expenses:* Tuition: Full-time $9,954; part-time $553 per credit. Tuition and fees vary according to course load and program. *Financial support:* In 2007–08, 28 students received support. Career-related internships or fieldwork, institutionally sponsored loans, scholarships/grants, health care benefits, and unspecified assistantships available. Financial award application deadline: 2/4; financial award applicants required to submit FAFSA. *Faculty research:* String theory and supergravity; computer graphics; algebra and number theory; popular Arabic literature; marine and freshwater biology; integrating science, math and technology. Total annual research expenditures: $132,270. *Unit head:* Khalil Bitar, Dean, 961-1374374 Ext. 3800, Fax: 961-1744461, E-mail: kmb@aub.edu.lb. *Application contact:* Dr. Salim Kanaan, Director, Admissions Office, 961-1350000 Ext. 2594, Fax: 961-1750775, E-mail: sk00@aub.edu.lb.

Brandeis University, Graduate School of Arts and Sciences, Department of Near Eastern and Judaic Studies, Waltham, MA 02454-9110. Offers Near Eastern and Judaic studies (MA, PhD); Near Eastern and Judaic studies and sociology (PhD); Near Eastern and Judaic studies and women's studies (MA); teaching of Hebrew (MAT). Part-time programs available. *Faculty:* 25 full-time (11 women), 5 part-time/adjunct (3 women). *Students:* 44 full-time (21 women), 4 part-time; includes 1 minority (African American), 10 international. Average age 33. 62 applicants, 53% accepted, 15 enrolled. In 2007, 7 master's, 4 doctorates awarded. Terminal master's awarded for partial completion of doctoral program. *Degree requirements:* For master's, one foreign language, comprehensive exam, thesis or alternative; for doctorate, 3 foreign languages, comprehensive exam, thesis/dissertation. *Entrance requirements:* For master's and doctorate, GRE General Test (recommended), letters of recommendation, transcripts, statement of purpose. Additional exam requirements/recommendations for international students: Required—TOEFL (minimum score 600 paper-based; 250 computer-based; 100 iBT), IELTS (minimum score 7). *Application deadline:* For fall admission, 1/15 priority date for domestic and international students. Applications are processed on a rolling basis. Application fee: $55. Electronic applications accepted. *Financial support:* In 2007–08, 15 students received support, including 14 fellowships with full and partial tuition reimbursements available (averaging $17,000 per year), 1 teaching assistantship with partial tuition reimbursement available (averaging $3,000 per year); research assistantships with full and partial tuition reimbursements available, scholarships/grants, health care benefits, and tuition waivers (full and partial) also available. Support available to part-time students. Financial award application deadline: 4/15; financial award applicants required to submit CSS PROFILE or FAFSA. *Faculty research:* Ancient Near East and Bible, philosophy, history, modern Middle East, Islamic studies. *Unit head:* Dr. David Wright, Chair, 781-736-2954, Fax: 781-736-2070, E-mail: wright@brandeis.edu. *Application contact:* Dr. Eugene Sheppard, Graduate Advisor, 781-736-2965, Fax: 781-736-2070, E-mail: sheppard@brandeis.edu.

The Catholic University of America, School of Arts and Sciences, Department of Semitic and Egyptian Languages and Literature, Washington, DC 20064. Offers MA, PhD. *Faculty:* 1 full-time (0 women), 5 part-time/adjunct (2 women). *Students:* 5 full-time (2 women), 14 part-time (4 women); includes 2 minority (1 African American, 1 Asian American or Pacific Islander), 2 international. Average age 40. 17 applicants, 41% accepted, 1 enrolled. In 2007, 3 master's, 1 doctorate awarded. *Degree requirements:* For master's, 2 foreign languages, comprehensive exam, thesis or alternative; for doctorate, 2 foreign languages, comprehensive exam, thesis/dissertation. *Entrance requirements:* For master's and doctorate, GRE General Test, 3 letters of recommendation. Additional exam requirements/recommendations for international students: Required—TOEFL (minimum score 580 paper-based; 237 computer-based). *Application deadline:* For fall admission, 2/1 priority date for domestic students; for spring admission, 11/15 priority date for domestic students. Applications are processed on a rolling basis. Application fee: $55. Electronic applications accepted. *Financial support:* Teaching assistantships, career-related internships or fieldwork, Federal Work-Study, scholarships/grants, tuition waivers (full and partial), and unspecified assistantships available. Support available to part-time students. Financial award application deadline: 2/1; financial award applicants required to submit FAFSA. *Faculty research:* Christian history and literature of the Near East, Hebrew Bible. *Unit head:* Dr. Michael P. O'Connor, Chairman, 202-319-5083, Fax: 202-319-4735, E-mail: oconnerm@cua.edu.

Columbia University, Graduate School of Arts and Sciences, Division of Humanities, Department of Middle East Languages and Cultures, New York, NY 10027. Offers Hebrew language and literature (M Phil, MA, PhD); Middle Eastern languages and cultures (M Phil, MA, PhD); South Asian languages and cultures (M Phil, MA, PhD). Part-time programs available. *Faculty:* 22 full-time, 11 part-time/adjunct. *Students:* 52 full-time (25 women), 4 part-time (3 women); includes 4 minority (3 Asian Americans or Pacific Islanders, 1 Hispanic American), 12 international. Average age 35. 42 applicants, 48% accepted. In 2007, 2 master's, 5 doctorates awarded. *Degree requirements:* For master's, thesis, oral and written exams; for doctorate, 3 foreign languages, thesis/dissertation. *Entrance requirements:* For master's and doctorate, GRE General Test. Additional exam requirements/recommendations for international students: Required—TOEFL. Application fee: $90. *Expenses:* Tuition: Part-time $1,452 per credit. Required fees: $152 per term. One-time fee: $75 part-time. Full-time tuition and fees vary according to course level, course load, degree level and program. *Financial support:* Fellowships, teaching assistantships, Federal Work-Study and institutionally sponsored loans available. Support available to part-time students. Financial award application deadline: 1/5; financial award applicants required to submit FAFSA. *Faculty research:* Indo-Iranian, Turkish, central Asian, and Armenian studies; Arabic and ancient Semitics. *Unit head:* Sheldon Pollock, Chair, 212-854-6781, Fax: 212-854-5517, E-mail: sp2356@columbia.edu.

Georgetown University, Graduate School of Arts and Sciences, Department of Arabic Language, Literature, and Linguistics, Washington, DC 20057. Offers MS, PhD. *Degree requirements:* For master's, comprehensive exam, research project; for doctorate, one foreign language, comprehensive exam, thesis/dissertation. *Entrance requirements:* Additional exam requirements/recommendations for international students: Required—TOEFL.

Harvard University, Graduate School of Arts and Sciences, Department of Near Eastern Languages and Civilizations, Cambridge, MA 02138. Offers Akkadian and Sumerian (AM, PhD); Arabic (AM, PhD); Armenian (AM, PhD); biblical history (AM, PhD); Hebrew (AM, PhD); Indo-Muslim culture (AM, PhD); Iranian (AM, PhD); Jewish history and literature (AM, PhD); Persian (AM, PhD); Semitic philology (AM, PhD); Syro-Palestinian archaeology (AM, PhD); Turkish (AM, PhD). *Degree requirements:* For doctorate, variable foreign language requirement, thesis/dissertation, general exams. *Entrance requirements:* For master's, GRE General Test; for doctorate, GRE General Test, proficiency in a Near Eastern language. Additional exam requirements/recommendations for international students: Required—TOEFL. *Expenses:* Tuition: Full-time $31,456. Full-time tuition and fees vary according to program and student level.

Hebrew Union College–Jewish Institute of Religion, School of Graduate Studies, Program in Hebrew Letters, New York, NY 10012-1186. Offers DHL. *Degree requirements:* For doctorate, one foreign language, thesis/dissertation. *Entrance requirements:* For doctorate, GRE. Additional exam requirements/recommendations for international students: Required—TOEFL. Expenses: Contact institution. *Faculty research:* Philosophy and theology, Bible, Hebrew, pastoral care, history and Rabbinics.

Indiana University Bloomington, University Graduate School, College of Arts and Sciences, Department of Near Eastern Languages and Cultures, Bloomington, IN 47405-7000. Offers MA, PhD. Part-time programs available. *Faculty:* 5 full-time (2 women). *Students:* 42 full-time (16 women), 9 part-time (3 women); includes 3 minority (2 Asian Americans or Pacific Islanders, 1 Hispanic American), 29 international. Average age 32. 39 applicants, 46% accepted, 15 enrolled. In 2007, 10 degrees awarded. Terminal master's awarded for partial completion of doctoral program. *Degree requirements:* For master's, 2 foreign languages, thesis or alternative; for doctorate, 3 foreign languages, thesis/dissertation. *Entrance requirements:* For master's and doctorate, GRE General Test. Additional exam requirements/recommendations for international students: Required—TOEFL. *Application deadline:* For fall admission, 1/15 priority date for domestic students, 12/15 for international students; for spring admission, 9/1 priority date for domestic students, 9/1 for international students. Applications are processed on a rolling basis. Application fee: $50 ($60 for international students). *Financial support:* Fellowships with full and partial tuition reimbursements, research assistantships with full and partial tuition reimbursements, teaching assistantships with full and partial tuition reimbursements, Federal Work-Study, institutionally sponsored loans, tuition waivers (full and partial), and unspecified assistantships available. Financial award application deadline: 3/1; financial award applicants required to submit FAFSA. *Faculty research:* Classical and modern Arabic literature and linguistics, biblical and modern Hebrew studies, Persian language and literature, Islamic civilization, Iranian history and language. *Unit head:* Dr. Nazif Shahrani, Chair, 812-855-4858. *Application contact:* Elaine Wright, Administrative Secretary, 812-855-5993.

The Ohio State University, Graduate School, College of Humanities, Department of Near Eastern Languages and Cultures, Columbus, OH 43210. Offers MA, PhD. *Faculty:* 19. *Students:* 11 full-time (2 women), 5 part-time (4 women); includes 3 minority (all Asian Americans or Pacific Islanders) Average age 31. In 2007, 5 degrees awarded. *Degree requirements:* For master's, thesis optional. *Entrance requirements:* For master's and doctorate, GRE General Test. Additional exam requirements/recommendations for international students: Required—TOEFL (minimum score 600 paper-based; 250 computer-based). *Application deadline:* For fall admission, 8/15 priority date for domestic students, 7/1 priority date for international students; for winter admission, 12/1 priority date for domestic students, 11/1 priority date for international students; for spring admission, 3/1 priority date for domestic students, 2/1 priority date for international students. Applications are processed on a rolling basis. Application fee: $40 ($50 for international students). Electronic applications accepted. *Financial support:* Fellowships, research assistantships, teaching assistantships, Federal Work-Study and institutionally sponsored loans available. Support available to part-time students. *Unit head:* Michael Swartz, Graduate Studies Committee Chair, 614-292-9255, Fax: 614-292-1262, E-mail: swartz.69@osu.edu. *Application contact:* 614-292-9444, Fax: 614-292-3895, E-mail: domestic.grad@osu.edu.

Oral Roberts University, School of Theology and Missions, Tulsa, OK 74171-0001. Offers biblical literature (MA), including advanced languages, Judaic-Christian studies; Christian counseling (MA), including marriage and family therapy; Christian education (MA); divinity (M Div); missions (MA); practical theology (MA); theological/historical studies (MA); theology (D Min). *Accreditation:* ATS; NASM. Part-time programs available. Postbaccalaureate distance learning degree programs offered (minimal on-campus study). *Faculty:* 17 full-time (2 women). *Students:* 371 full-time (156 women), 110 part-time (65 women); includes 177 minority (127 African Americans, 5 American Indian/Alaska Native, 20 Asian Americans or Pacific Islanders, 25 Hispanic Americans), 82 international. Average age 36. 159 applicants, 95% accepted, 124 enrolled. In 2007, 38 first professional degrees, 52 master's, 10 doctorates awarded. *Degree requirements:* For master's, thesis (for some programs), practicum/internship; for doctorate, thesis/dissertation, applied research project; for M Div, one foreign language, field experience.

Entrance requirements: For M Div and master's, GRE General Test or MAT, minimum GPA of 2.5; for doctorate, M Div, minimum GPA of 3.0, 3 years of full-time ministry experience. Additional exam requirements/recommendations for international students: Required—TOEFL (minimum score 500 paper-based; 213 computer-based; 79 iBT). *Application deadline:* For fall admission, 7/1 priority date for domestic and international students; for spring admission, 12/1 priority date for domestic students, 10/1 priority date for international students. Applications are processed on a rolling basis. Application fee: $35. Electronic applications accepted. *Expenses:* Tuition: Part-time $450 per hour. Required fees: $125 per semester. Tuition and fees vary according to class time, degree level and program. *Financial support:* In 2007–08, teaching assistantships (averaging $3,600 per year); scholarships/grants and employment assistantships also available. Financial award application deadline: 6/1; financial award applicants required to submit FAFSA. *Unit head:* Dr. Thomson K. Mathew, Dean, 918-495-7016, Fax: 918-495-6259, E-mail: tmathew@oru.edu. *Application contact:* Debra E. Watkins, Graduate Theology Representative, 918-495-6618, Fax: 918-495-7965, E-mail: owatkins@oru.edu.

University of California, Los Angeles, Graduate Division, College of Letters and Science, Department of Near Eastern Languages and Cultures, Los Angeles, CA 90095. Offers MA, PhD. *Students:* 40 full-time (19 women); includes 6 minority (3 Asian Americans or Pacific Islanders, 3 Hispanic Americans), 1 international. Average age 28. 55 applicants, 31% accepted, 8 enrolled. In 2007, 2 master's, 5 doctorates awarded. *Median time to degree:* Of those who began their doctoral program in fall 1999, 100% received their degree in 8 years or less. *Degree requirements:* For master's, one foreign language, comprehensive exam; for doctorate, 2 foreign languages, thesis/dissertation, oral and written qualifying exams. *Entrance requirements:* For master's and doctorate, GRE General Test, minimum GPA of 3.25, sample of written work recommended. Additional exam requirements/recommendations for international students: Required—TOEFL. *Application deadline:* For fall admission, 12/30 for domestic students. Application fee: $60. Electronic applications accepted. *Expenses:* Tuition, nonresident: full-time $5,728. Required fees: $8,966. Full-time tuition and fees vary according to program and student level. *Financial support:* In 2007–08, 35 fellowships with full and partial tuition reimbursements, 13 research assistantships with full and partial tuition reimbursements, 17 teaching assistantships with full and partial tuition reimbursements were awarded; Federal Work-Study, institutionally sponsored loans, scholarships/grants, and tuition waivers (full and partial) also available. Financial award application deadline: 3/1; financial award applicants required to submit FAFSA. *Unit head:* Dr. William Schniedewind, Chair, 310-825-4165. *Application contact:* Departmental Office, 310-825-4165, E-mail: nreast@humnet.ucla.edu.

University of Chicago, Division of the Humanities, Department of Near Eastern Languages and Civilizations, Chicago, IL 60637-1513. Offers AM, PhD. *Faculty:* 52. *Students:* 149. 113 applicants, 33% accepted, 17 enrolled.Terminal master's awarded for partial completion of doctoral program. *Degree requirements:* For master's, one foreign language, comprehensive exam, thesis; for doctorate, 2 foreign languages, comprehensive exam, thesis/dissertation. *Entrance requirements:* For master's and doctorate, GRE General Test. Additional exam requirements/recommendations for international students: Required—TOEFL. *Application deadline:* For fall admission, 12/15 for domestic students. Application fee: $55. *Financial support:* Fellowships, Federal Work-Study available. Financial award application deadline: 12/15; financial award applicants required to submit FAFSA. *Unit head:* Dr. Theo van den Hout, Chair, 773-702-9512.

University of Michigan, Horace H. Rackham School of Graduate Studies, College of Literature, Science, and the Arts, Department of Near Eastern Studies, Ann Arbor, MI 48109. Offers ancient Israel/Hebrew Bible (AM, PhD); Arabic (AM, PhD); Armenian (AM, PhD); early Christian studies (AM, PhD); Egyptology (AM, PhD); Hebrew (AM, PhD); Islamic studies (AM, PhD); Mesopotamian and ancient Near Eastern studies (AM, PhD); Persian (AM, PhD); teaching of Arabic as a foreign Language (AM); Turkish (AM, PhD). Part-time programs available. *Faculty:* 22 full-time (3 women), 8 part-time/adjunct (3 women). *Students:* 45 full-time (21 women); includes 2 minority (both African Americans), 7 international. Average age 27. 88 applicants, 17% accepted, 5 enrolled. In 2007, 2 master's, 3 doctorates awarded. Terminal master's awarded for partial completion of doctoral program. *Degree requirements:* For master's, 2 foreign languages; for doctorate, 4 foreign languages, oral defense of dissertation, preliminary exam. *Entrance requirements:* For master's, GRE General Test; for doctorate, GRE General Test, master's degree. Additional exam requirements/recommendations for international students: Required—TOEFL (minimum score 560 paper-based; 220 computer-based; 84 iBT). *Application deadline:* For fall admission, 12/15 for domestic and international students. Application fee: $60 ($75 for international students). *Financial support:* In 2007–08, 25 students received support, including 14 fellowships with full tuition reimbursements available (averaging $14,400 per year), research assistantships with tuition reimbursements available (averaging $15,200 per year), 16 teaching assistantships with full tuition reimbursements available (averaging $15,200 per year); scholarships/grants, health care benefits, and unspecified assistantships also available. *Faculty research:* Middle and Near Eastern literatures, languages, cultures from ancient times to the present. *Unit head:* Prof. Gary Beckman, Chair, 734-764-0314, Fax: 734-936-2679, E-mail: sidd@umich.edu. *Application contact:* Angela Beskow, Student Services Assistant, 734-763-4539, Fax: 734-936-2679, E-mail: aradjews@umich.edu.

University of South Africa, College of Human Sciences, Pretoria, South Africa. Offers adult education (M Ed); African languages (MA, PhD); African politics (MA, PhD); Afrikaans (MA, PhD); ancient history (MA, PhD); ancient Near Eastern studies (MA, PhD); anthropology (MA, PhD); applied linguistics (MA); Arabic (MA, PhD); archaeology (MA); art history (MA); Biblical archaeology (MA); Biblical studies (M Th, D Th, PhD); Christian spirituality (M Th, D Th); church history (M Th, D Th); classical studies (MA, PhD); clinical psychology (MA); communication (MA, PhD); comparative education (M Ed, Ed D); consulting psychology (D Admin, D Com, PhD); curriculum studies (M Ed, Ed D); development studies (M Admin, MA, D Admin, PhD); didactics (M Ed, Ed D); education (M Tech); education management (M Ed, Ed D); educational psychology (M Ed); English (MA); environmental education (M Ed); French (MA, PhD); German (MA, PhD); Greek (MA); guidance and counseling (M Ed); health studies (MA, PhD), including health sciences education (MA), health services management (MA), medical and surgical nursing science (critical care general) (MA), midwifery and neonatal nursing science (MA), trauma and emergency care (MA); history (MA, PhD); history of education (Ed D); inclusive education (M Ed, Ed D); information and communications technology policy and regulation (MA); information science (MA, MIS, PhD); international politics (MA, PhD); Islamic studies (MA, PhD); Italian (MA, PhD); Judaica (MA, PhD); linguistics (MA, PhD); mathematical education (M Ed); mathematics education (MA); missiology (M Th, D Th); modern Hebrew (MA, PhD); musicology (MA, MMus, D Mus, PhD); natural science education (M Ed); New Testament (M Th, D Th); Old Testament (D Th); pastoral therapy (M Th, D Th); philosophy (MA); philosophy of education (M Ed, Ed D); politics (MA, PhD); Portuguese (MA, PhD); practical theology (M Th, D Th); psychology (MA, MS, PhD); psychology of education (M Ed, Ed D); public health (MA); religious studies (MA, D Th, PhD); Romance languages (MA); Russian (MA, PhD); Semitic languages (MA, PhD); social behavior studies in HIV/AIDS (MA); social science (mental health) (MA); social science in development studies (MA); social science in psychology (MA); social science in social work (MA); social science in sociology (MA); social work (MSW, DSW, PhD); socio-education (M Ed, Ed D); sociolinguistics (MA); sociology (MA, PhD); Spanish (MA, PhD); systematic theology (M Th, D Th); TESOL (teaching English to speakers of other languages) (MA); theological ethics (M Th, D Th); theory of literature (MA, PhD); urban ministries (D Th); urban ministry (M Th).

The University of Texas at Austin, Graduate School, College of Liberal Arts, Department of Middle Eastern Studies, Austin, TX 78712-1111. Offers Arabic studies (MA, PhD); Hebrew studies (MA, PhD); Persian studies (MA, PhD). *Degree requirements:* For master's, one foreign language, comprehensive exam, thesis; for doctorate, 2 foreign languages, comprehensive exam, thesis/dissertation. *Entrance requirements:* For master's and doctorate, GRE General Test. Additional exam requirements/recommendations for international students: Required—TOEFL. Electronic applications accepted. *Faculty research:* Islamic studies, Persian language and literature, Hebrew language, Jewish studies, Arabic literature and language.

University of Utah, The Graduate School, College of Humanities, Program in Middle East Studies, Salt Lake City, UT 84112-1107. Offers anthropology (MA); Arabic (MA, PhD); Arabic and linguistics (MA, PhD); Hebrew (MA); history (MA, PhD); Persian (MA, PhD); political science (MA, PhD); Turkish (MA). *Faculty:* 12 full-time (3 women). *Students:* 26 full-time (12 women), 10 part-time (2 women); includes 1 minority (Asian American or Pacific Islander), 10 international. Average age 36. 36 applicants, 78% accepted, 10 enrolled. In 2007, 6 master's awarded. Terminal master's awarded for partial completion of doctoral program. *Median time to degree:* Of those who began their doctoral program in fall 1999, 100% received their degree in 8 years or less. *Degree requirements:* For master's, 2 foreign languages, comprehensive exam, thesis optional; for doctorate, 3 foreign languages, comprehensive exam, thesis/dissertation. *Entrance requirements:* For master's, GRE General Test, minimum GPA of 3.2; for doctorate, GRE General Test, MA in Middle East studies or equivalent, minimum GPA of 3.2. Additional exam requirements/recommendations for international students: Required—TOEFL (minimum score 580 paper-based; 237 computer-based; 92 iBT). *Application deadline:* For fall admission, 1/15 for domestic and international students; for spring admission, 9/15 for domestic and international students. Application fee: $45 ($65 for international students). *Financial support:* In 2007–08, 17 students received support, including 14 fellowships with full tuition reimbursements available (averaging $14,000 per year), 2 teaching assistantships with full tuition reimbursements available (averaging $12,000 per year); unspecified assistantships also available. Financial award application deadline: 1/15. *Faculty research:* Arabic literature and linguistics, Islamic studies, Middle East history, political science, Judaic studies. *Unit head:* Dr. Ibrahim A. Karawan, Director, 801-581-6181, Fax: 801-581-6183, E-mail: ibrahim.karawan@poli-sci.utah.edu. *Application contact:* Peter von Sivers, Director of Graduate Studies, 801-581-8073, Fax: 801-581-6183, E-mail: peter.vonsivers@utah.edu.

University of Wisconsin–Madison, Graduate School, College of Letters and Science, Department of Hebrew and Semitic Studies, Madison, WI 53706-1380. Offers MA, PhD. Terminal master's awarded for partial completion of doctoral program. *Degree requirements:* For master's, 2 foreign languages; for doctorate, thesis/dissertation. *Entrance requirements:* For master's and doctorate, GRE. Electronic applications accepted. *Faculty research:* Biblical language and literature, Northwest Semitic languages.

Yale University, Graduate School of Arts and Sciences, Department of Near Eastern Languages and Civilizations, New Haven, CT 06520. Offers MA, PhD. *Degree requirements:* For doctorate, 2 foreign languages, thesis/dissertation. *Entrance requirements:* For doctorate, GRE General Test.

Portuguese

Brigham Young University, Graduate Studies, College of Humanities, Department of Spanish and Portuguese, Provo, UT 84602-1001. Offers Portuguese linguistics (MA); Portuguese literature (MA); Spanish linguistics (MA); Spanish teaching (MA); Spanish/Latin American Literature (MA); Spanish/Peninsular literature (MA). Part-time programs available. *Faculty:* 29 full-time (6 women). *Students:* 18 full-time (8 women), 25 part-time (20 women); includes 12 minority (all Hispanic Americans) Average age 29. 29 applicants, 59% accepted, 14 enrolled. In 2007, 18 degrees awarded. *Degree requirements:* For master's, one foreign language, comprehensive exam, thesis, 1 semester of teaching. *Entrance requirements:* For master's, minimum GPA of 3.5 in Spanish or Portuguese, 3.3 overall. Additional exam requirements/recommendations for international students: Required—TOEFL (minimum score 580 paper-based; 237 computer-based). *Application deadline:* For fall admission, 2/1 for domestic and international students. Application fee: $50. Electronic applications accepted. *Financial support:* In 2007–08, 42 students received support, including 1 research assistantship with partial tuition reimbursement available (averaging $3,800 per year), 29 teaching assistantships with partial tuition reimbursements available (averaging $6,574 per year); institutionally sponsored loans, tuition waivers (partial), and unspecified assistantships also available. Support available to part-time students. Financial award application deadline: 6/15. *Faculty research:* Mexican prose; Latin American theater, literature, phonetics, and phonology; pedagogy; classical Portuguese literature; Peninsular prose and theater. *Unit head:* Dr. Alvin F. Sherman, Chair, 801-422-3107, Fax: 801-422-0628, E-mail: alvin_sherman@byu.edu. *Application contact:* Arwen T. Wyatt, Graduate Secretary, 801-422-2196, Fax: 801-422-0628, E-mail: arwen_wyatt@byu.edu.

Emory University, Graduate School of Arts and Sciences, Department of Spanish and Portuguese, Atlanta, GA 30322-1100. Offers comparative literature (Certificate); film studies (Certificate); Spanish (PhD); women's studies (Certificate). *Degree requirements:* For doctorate, 2 foreign languages, comprehensive exam, thesis/dissertation. *Entrance requirements:* For doctorate, GRE General Test. Additional exam requirements/recommendations for international students: Required—TOEFL. Electronic applications accepted. *Faculty research:* Spanish literature, Spanish-American literature, literary theory, criticism, cultural studies.

Harvard University, Graduate School of Arts and Sciences, Department of Romance Languages and Literatures, Cambridge, MA 02138. Offers French (AM, PhD); Italian (AM, PhD); Portuguese (AM, PhD); Spanish (AM, PhD). Terminal master's awarded for partial completion of doctoral program. *Degree requirements:* For master's, 2 foreign languages; for doctorate, 2 foreign languages, thesis/dissertation. *Entrance requirements:* For master's and doctorate, GRE General Test, sample of written work. Additional exam requirements/recommendations for international students: Required—TOEFL. *Expenses:* Tuition: Full-time $31,456. Full-time tuition and fees vary according to program and student level.

Indiana University Bloomington, University Graduate School, College of Arts and Sciences, Department of Spanish and Portuguese, Bloomington, IN 47405-7000. Offers Hispanic linguistics (MA, PhD); Hispanic literature (MA); Luso-Brazilian literature (MA); Luso-Brazilian studies (PhD); Spanish literatures (PhD); teaching Spanish (MAT). *Faculty:* 18 full-time (10 women). *Students:* 67 full-time (35 women), 11 part-time (6 women); includes 17 minority (1 African American, 16 Hispanic Americans), 16 international. Average age 30. 70 applicants, 27% accepted, 19 enrolled. In 2007, 13 master's, 3 doctorates awarded. *Median time to degree:* Of those who began their doctoral program in fall 1999, 60% received their degree in 8 years or less. *Degree requirements:* For master's, one foreign language; for doctorate, 3 foreign languages, thesis/dissertation. *Entrance requirements:* For master's, GRE General Test, GRE Subject Test, bachelor's degree in Portuguese or Spanish, minimum GPA of 3.25; for doctorate, GRE General Test, GRE Subject Test, master's degree in Portuguese or Spanish, minimum GPA of 3.25. Additional exam requirements/recommendations for international students: Required—TOEFL. *Application deadline:* For fall admission, 1/15 priority date for domestic students, 12/15 for international students; for spring admission, 9/1 for domestic and international students. Application fee: $50 ($60 for international students). *Financial support:*

Portuguese

Indiana University Bloomington (continued)
Fellowships with full tuition reimbursements, research assistantships, teaching assistantships with full tuition reimbursements, Federal Work-Study available. Financial award application deadline: 1/15. *Faculty research:* Spanish American literature, Spanish peninsular literature, Luso-Brazilian studies, Catalan studies. *Unit head:* Josep Miguel Sobrer, Chair, 812-855-8498. *Application contact:* Steven Wagschal, Student Contact, 812-855-9194, E-mail: swagscha@indiana.edu.

Michigan State University, The Graduate School, College of Arts and Letters, Department of Spanish and Portuguese, East Lansing, MI 48824. Offers applied Spanish linguistics (MA); Hispanic cultural studies (PhD); Hispanic literatures (MA). *Entrance requirements:* Additional exam requirements/recommendations for international students: Required—TOEFL. Electronic applications accepted. *Expenses:* Tuition, state resident: part-time $379 per credit hour. Tuition, nonresident: part-time $800 per credit hour. Tuition and fees vary according to program.

New York University, Graduate School of Arts and Science, Department of Spanish and Portuguese Languages and Literatures, New York, NY 10012-1019. Offers Portuguese (MA, PhD); Spanish (PhD); Spanish and Latin American literatures and cultures (MA); Spanish language and translation (MA). Part-time programs available. *Faculty:* 17 full-time (10 women), 11 part-time/adjunct. *Students:* 77 full-time (49 women), 6 part-time (all women); includes 30 minority (2 African Americans, 4 Asian Americans or Pacific Islanders, 24 Hispanic Americans), 23 international. Average age 30. 194 applicants, 44% accepted, 35 enrolled. In 2007, 28 master's, 6 doctorates awarded. *Degree requirements:* For master's, 2 foreign languages, thesis; for doctorate, 2 foreign languages, thesis/dissertation. *Entrance requirements:* For master's, GRE General Test; for doctorate, GRE General Test, master's degree. Additional exam requirements/recommendations for international students: Required—TOEFL. *Application deadline:* For fall admission, 1/4 priority date for domestic students. Application fee: $85. *Financial support:* Fellowships with tuition reimbursements, teaching assistantships with tuition reimbursements, career-related internships or fieldwork, Federal Work-Study, institutionally sponsored loans, scholarships/grants, health care benefits, and unspecified assistantships available. Financial award application deadline: 1/4; financial award applicants required to submit FAFSA. *Faculty research:* Gender and sexuality, transatlantic studies, literacy and cultural theories, colonial and post colonial studies, autobiography and modern subjectivities. *Unit head:* James Fernandez, Chair, 212-998-8770, Fax: 212-995-4148, E-mail: spanish.portuguese.info@nyu.edu. *Application contact:* Gabriela Basterra, Director of Graduate Studies, 212-998-8770, Fax: 212-995-4149, E-mail: spanish.portuguese.info@nyu.edu.

The Ohio State University, Graduate School, College of Humanities, Department of Spanish and Portuguese, Columbus, OH 43210. Offers MA, PhD. *Faculty:* 22. *Students:* 56 full-time (37 women), 8 part-time (2 women); includes 12 minority (1 African American, 2 Asian Americans or Pacific Islanders, 9 Hispanic Americans), 21 international. Average age 30. In 2007, 9 master's, 7 doctorates awarded. *Degree requirements:* For master's, thesis optional; for doctorate, thesis/dissertation. *Entrance requirements:* For master's and doctorate, GRE General Test. Additional exam requirements/recommendations for international students: Required—TOEFL (minimum score 600 paper-based; 250 computer-based). *Application deadline:* For fall admission, 8/15 priority date for domestic students, 7/1 priority date for international students; for winter admission, 12/1 priority date for domestic students, 11/1 priority date for international students; for spring admission, 3/1 priority date for domestic students, 2/1 priority date for international students. Applications are processed on a rolling basis. Application fee: $40 ($50 for international students). Electronic applications accepted. *Financial support:* Fellowships, research assistantships, teaching assistantships, Federal Work-Study, institutionally sponsored loans, and unspecified assistantships available. Support available to part-time students. *Unit head:* Salvador Garcia, Graduate Studies Committee Chair, 614-292-4958, Fax: 614-292-7726, E-mail: garcia.7@osu.edu. *Application contact:* 614-292-9444, Fax: 614-292-3895, E-mail: domestic.grad@osu.edu.

Princeton University, Graduate School, Department of Spanish and Portuguese Languages and Cultures, Princeton, NJ 08544-1019. Offers PhD. *Degree requirements:* For doctorate, variable foreign language requirement, thesis/dissertation. *Entrance requirements:* For doctorate, GRE General Test, sample of written work. Additional exam requirements/recommendations for international students: Required—TOEFL (minimum score 600 paper-based; 250 computer-based). Electronic applications accepted.

Tulane University, School of Liberal Arts, Department of Spanish and Portuguese, New Orleans, LA 70118-5669. Offers Portuguese (MA); Spanish (MA); Spanish and Portuguese (PhD). *Degree requirements:* For master's, 2 foreign languages; for doctorate, 2 foreign languages, thesis/dissertation. *Entrance requirements:* For master's, GRE General Test, minimum B average in undergraduate course work; for doctorate, GRE General Test. Additional exam requirements/recommendations for international students: Required—TOEFL. Electronic applications accepted.

University of California, Los Angeles, Graduate Division, College of Letters and Science, Department of Spanish and Portuguese, Program in Portuguese, Los Angeles, CA 90095. Offers MA. *Students:* 2 full-time (both women). 1 applicant. In 2007, 1 degree awarded. *Degree requirements:* For master's, one foreign language, comprehensive exam or thesis. *Entrance requirements:* For master's, GRE General Test, minimum GPA of 3.0, sample of written work (recommended). *Application deadline:* For fall admission, 12/31 for domestic students. Application fee: $60. Electronic applications accepted. *Expenses:* Tuition, nonresident: full-time $5,728. Required fees: $8,966. Full-time tuition and fees vary according to program and student level. *Financial support:* In 2007–08, 2 fellowships with full and partial tuition reimbursements, 2 teaching assistantships with full and partial tuition reimbursements were awarded. Financial award applicants required to submit FAFSA. *Application contact:* Departmental Office, 310-825-1036, E-mail: peinado@humnet.ucla.edu.

University of California, Santa Barbara, Graduate Division, College of Letters and Sciences, Division of Humanities and Fine Arts, Department of Spanish and Portuguese, Santa Barbara, CA 93106. Offers Hispanic languages and literature (PhD); Portuguese (MA); Spanish (MA). Spanish Language Institute available during summer sessions. *Faculty:* 16 full-time (6 women). *Students:* 27 full-time (12 women); includes 6 minority (all Hispanic Americans), 8 international. Average age 31. 34 applicants, 62% accepted, 9 enrolled. In 2007, 3 master's, 4 doctorates awarded. *Median time to degree:* Of those who began their doctoral program in fall 1999, 60% received their degree in 8 years or less. *Degree requirements:* For master's, 2 foreign languages, thesis optional; for doctorate, 2 foreign languages, comprehensive exam, thesis/dissertation. *Entrance requirements:* For master's, GRE, 2 writing samples, undergraduate major in Spanish or equivalent; for doctorate, GRE, 2 writing samples, Master's degree. Additional exam requirements/recommendations for international students: Required—TOEFL (minimum score 550 paper-based; 213 computer-based; 80 iBT). *Application deadline:* For fall admission, 3/1 for domestic and international students; for winter admission, 11/1 for domestic and international students; for spring admission, 2/1 for domestic and international students. Applications are processed on a rolling basis. Application fee: $60. Electronic applications accepted. *Expenses:* Tuition, nonresident: full-time $14,888. Required fees: $10,108. *Financial support:* In 2007–08, 27 students received support, including 6 fellowships with full tuition reimbursements available (averaging $15,500 per year), 4 research assistantships, 26 teaching assistantships with full and partial tuition reimbursements available (averaging $16,390 per year); career-related internships or fieldwork, Federal Work-Study, scholarships/grants, health care benefits, tuition waivers (full and partial), and unspecified assistantships also available. Financial award application deadline: 1/7; financial award applicants required to submit FAFSA. *Faculty research:* 19th century Spanish and Portuguese literature, Spanish and Spanish American literature, 19th and 20th century Portuguese and Brazilian literatures, Mexican literature, Catalan language and culture. *Unit head:* Prof. Francisco P. Lomeli, Chair, 805-893-2798, E-mail: rap@spanport.ucsb.edu. *Application contact:* Carol Conley, Graduate Program Assistant, 805-893-3162, Fax: 805-893-8341, E-mail: cconley@spanport.ucsb.edu.

University of Illinois at Urbana–Champaign, Graduate College, College of Liberal Arts and Sciences, School of Literatures, Cultures and Linguistics, Department of Spanish, Italian and Portuguese, Champaign, IL 61820. Offers Italian (MA, PhD); Portuguese (MA, PhD); Spanish (PhD); Spanish, Italian and Portuguese (MA). *Faculty:* 17 full-time (10 women). *Students:* 55 full-time (41 women), 11 part-time (8 women); includes 7 minority (1 African American, 6 Hispanic Americans), 40 international. 77 applicants, 42% accepted, 14 enrolled. In 2007, 6 master's, 8 doctorates awarded. *Degree requirements:* For doctorate, 2 foreign languages, thesis/dissertation. *Entrance requirements:* For master's, GRE General Test, GRE Subject Test, minimum GPA of 3.0. *Application deadline:* For fall admission, 3/1 for domestic students. Applications are processed on a rolling basis. Application fee: $60 ($75 for international students). Electronic applications accepted. *Financial support:* In 2007–08, 8 fellowships, 3 research assistantships, 62 teaching assistantships were awarded; tuition waivers (full and partial) also available. Financial award application deadline: 2/15. *Unit head:* Diane Musumeci, Head, 217-244-3250, Fax: 217-244-8430, E-mail: musumeci@uiuc.edu. *Application contact:* Lynn Stanke, Secretary, 217-333-6269, Fax: 217-244-3050, E-mail: stanke@uiuc.edu.

University of Maryland, College Park, Graduate Studies, College of Arts and Humanities, School of Languages, Literature, and Cultures, Department of Spanish and Portuguese, College Park, MD 20742. Offers MA, PhD. *Students:* 32 full-time (28 women), 6 part-time (4 women); includes 15 minority (1 American Indian/Alaska Native, 1 Asian American or Pacific Islander, 13 Hispanic Americans), 12 international. 30 applicants, 40% accepted, 9 enrolled. In 2007, 3 master's, 4 doctorates awarded. *Degree requirements:* For master's, comprehensive exam, thesis optional, scholarly paper; for doctorate, 2 foreign languages, thesis/dissertation. *Entrance requirements:* For master's, minimum GPA of 3.0, interview, sample research paper, minimum of 12 credits in upper-level literature, 3 letters of recommendation; for doctorate, minimum GPA of 3.0, interview, sample research paper, minimum of 12 credits in upper-level literature. Additional exam requirements/recommendations for international students: Required—TOEFL. *Application deadline:* For fall admission, 1/7 for domestic and international students. Applications are processed on a rolling basis. Application fee: $60. Electronic applications accepted. *Financial support:* In 2007–08, 4 fellowships with full tuition reimbursements (averaging $14,225 per year), 18 teaching assistantships with tuition reimbursements (averaging $17,462 per year) were awarded; Federal Work-Study also available. Support available to part-time students. Financial award applicants required to submit FAFSA. *Unit head:* Dr. Sandra M. Cypess, Chairman, 301-405-6449, Fax: 301-314-9752, E-mail: smcypess@umd.edu. *Application contact:* Dean of Graduate School, 301-405-4190, Fax: 301-314-9305.

University of Massachusetts Dartmouth, Graduate School, College of Arts and Sciences, Department of Portuguese, North Dartmouth, MA 02747-2300. Offers Portuguese (MA); WSO-Afro-Brazilian studies (PhD). *Faculty:* 6 full-time (2 women), 1 part-time/adjunct (0 women). *Students:* 8 full-time (6 women), 11 part-time (5 women); includes 6 minority (1 African American, 1 Asian American or Pacific Islander, 4 Hispanic Americans), 3 international. Average age 35. 18 applicants, 89% accepted, 12 enrolled. In 2007, 3 degrees awarded. *Degree requirements:* For master's, comprehensive exam (for some programs). *Entrance requirements:* For master's, GRE (recommended), 10-page writing sample; for doctorate, GRE. Additional exam requirements/recommendations for international students: Required—TOEFL (minimum score 500 paper-based). *Application deadline:* For fall admission, 4/20 priority date for domestic students, 2/20 priority date for international students; for spring admission, 11/15 priority date for domestic students, 9/15 priority date for international students. Applications are processed on a rolling basis. Application fee: $40 ($60 for international students). Electronic applications accepted. *Expenses:* Tuition, state resident: full-time $2,071; part-time $86 per credit. Tuition, nonresident: full-time $8,099; part-time $337 per credit. Part-time tuition and fees vary according to course load and program. *Financial support:* In 2007–08, 2 research assistantships with full tuition reimbursements (averaging $14,875 per year), 8 teaching assistantships with full tuition reimbursements (averaging $15,000 per year) were awarded; unspecified assistantships also available. Financial award application deadline: 3/1; financial award applicants required to submit FAFSA. *Unit head:* Victor J Mendes, Director, Graduate Studies, 508-999-8338, Fax: 508-999-9272, E-mail: vmendes@umassd.edu. *Application contact:* Carol Novo, Graduate Admissions Officer, 508-999-8604, Fax: 508-999-8183, E-mail: graduate@umassd.edu.

University of Minnesota, Twin Cities Campus, Graduate School, College of Liberal Arts, Department of Spanish and Portuguese Studies, Minneapolis, MN 55455-0213. Offers Hispanic and Luso-Brazilian literatures and linguistics (PhD); Hispanic linguistics (MA); Hispanic literature (MA); Lusophone literature (MA). *Faculty:* 12 full-time (6 women), 2 part-time/adjunct (both women). *Students:* 47 full-time (31 women), 8 part-time (5 women); includes 3 African Americans, 18 Hispanic Americans, 11 international. Average age 30. 39 applicants, 33% accepted, 6 enrolled. In 2007, 5 master's, 7 doctorates awarded. *Degree requirements:* For master's, 2 foreign languages, comprehensive exam, thesis or alternative; for doctorate, 2 foreign languages, comprehensive exam, thesis/dissertation. *Entrance requirements:* For master's and doctorate, GRE General Test, samples of written work, 3 letters of recommendation, voice sample, statement of purpose. Additional exam requirements/recommendations for international students: Required—TOEFL (minimum score 550 paper-based; 213 computer-based; 79 iBT). *Application deadline:* For fall admission, 1/5 for domestic and international students. Application fee: $55 ($75 for international students). Electronic applications accepted. *Financial support:* In 2007–08, 1 research assistantship with full tuition reimbursement (averaging $12,528 per year), 51 teaching assistantships with full tuition reimbursements (averaging $12,528 per year) were awarded; fellowships, career-related internships or fieldwork and Federal Work-Study also available. *Faculty research:* Sociohistorical approaches to literature and culture, feminist studies, literary theory, ideologies and literature, pragmatics and sociolinguistics. Total annual research expenditures: $7,200. *Unit head:* Ana Paula Ferreira, Chair, 612-625-3834, Fax: 612-625-3549, E-mail: apferrei@umn.edu. *Application contact:* Sara E Sonnenberg, Executive Administrative Specialist, Graduate Program Assistant, 612-626-7809, Fax: 612-625-3549, E-mail: sonne037@tc.umn.edu.

University of New Mexico, Graduate School, College of Arts and Sciences, Department of Spanish and Portuguese, Albuquerque, NM 87131-2039. Offers Portuguese (MA); Spanish (MA); Spanish and Portuguese (PhD). Part-time programs available. *Faculty:* 13 full-time (10 women), 2 part-time/adjunct (both women). *Students:* 49 full-time (32 women), 10 part-time (7 women); includes 26 minority (2 African Americans, 24 Hispanic Americans), 17 international. Average age 36. 47 applicants, 60% accepted, 18 enrolled. In 2007, 13 master's, 2 doctorates awarded. *Degree requirements:* For master's, one foreign language, comprehensive exam, thesis optional; for doctorate, one foreign language, comprehensive exam, thesis/dissertation. *Entrance requirements:* For master's, GRE, BA in Spanish or Portuguese, letters of recommendation, letter of intent; for doctorate, GRE, 3 letters of recommendation, letter of intent, sample research paper. Additional exam requirements/recommendations for international students: Required—TOEFL (minimum score 550 paper-based; 213 computer-based), Michigan English Language Assessment Battery. *Application deadline:* For fall admission, 1/15 priority date for domestic students; for spring admission, 11/15 for domestic students. Application fee: $50. Electronic applications accepted. *Financial support:* In 2007–08, 30 students received support, including 58 teaching assistantships with full tuition reimbursements available (averaging $13,640 per year); Federal Work-Study, institutionally sponsored loans, scholarships/grants, health care benefits, tuition waivers (full), and unspecified assistantships also available. Support available to part-time students. Financial award application deadline: 3/1; financial award applicants required to submit FAFSA. *Faculty research:* Spanish literature in Spain, Latin America, and the U.S. Spanish Southwest from its inception to present day; gender and genre studies including film, linguistic variation and change, and psycholinguistics in Spanish. *Unit head:* Dr. Tey Diana Rebolledo, Chair, 505-277-2974, Fax: 505-277-3885, E-mail: dreb@unm.edu. *Application contact:* Martha Hurd, Graduate Administration Assistant, 505-277-2974, E-mail: marthah@unm.edu.

The University of North Carolina at Chapel Hill, Graduate School, College of Arts and Sciences, Department of Romance Languages, Chapel Hill, NC 27599. Offers French (MA, PhD); Italian (MA, PhD); Portuguese (MA, PhD); Romance languages (MA, PhD); Romance philology (MA, PhD); Spanish (MA, PhD). *Degree requirements:* For master's, one foreign language, comprehensive exam, thesis; for doctorate, 2 foreign languages, comprehensive exam, thesis/dissertation. *Entrance requirements:* For master's and doctorate, GRE General Test, minimum GPA of 3.0. Additional exam requirements/recommendations for international students: Required—TOEFL (minimum score 550 paper-based; 213 computer-based). Electronic applications accepted.

University of South Africa, College of Human Sciences, Pretoria, South Africa. Offers adult education (M Ed); African languages (MA, PhD); African politics (MA, PhD); Afrikaans (MA, PhD); ancient history (MA, PhD); ancient Near Eastern studies (MA, PhD); anthropology (MA, PhD); applied linguistics (MA); Arabic (MA, PhD); archaeology (MA); art history (MA); Biblical archaeology (MA); Biblical studies (M Th, D Th, PhD); Christian spirituality (M Th, D Th); church history (M Th, D Th); classical studies (MA, PhD); clinical psychology (MA); communication (MA, PhD); comparative education (M Ed, Ed D); consulting psychology (D Admin, D Com, PhD); curriculum studies (M Ed, Ed D); development studies (M Admin, MA, D Admin, PhD); didactics (M Ed, Ed D); education (M Tech); education management (M Ed, Ed D); educational psychology (M Ed); English (MA); environmental education (M Ed); French (MA, PhD); German (MA, PhD); Greek (MA); guidance and counseling (M Ed); health studies (MA, PhD), including health sciences education (MA), health services management (MA), medical and surgical nursing science (critical care general) (MA), midwifery and neonatal nursing science (MA), trauma and emergency care (MA); history (MA, PhD); history of education (Ed D); inclusive education (M Ed, Ed D); information and communications technology policy and regulation (MA); information science (MA, MIS, PhD); international politics (MA, PhD); Islamic studies (MA, PhD); Italian (MA, PhD); Judaica (MA, PhD); linguistics (MA, PhD); mathematical education (M Ed); mathematics education (MA); missiology (M Th, D Th); modern Hebrew (MA, PhD); musicology (MA, MMus, D Mus, PhD); natural science education (M Ed); New Testament (M Th, D Th); Old Testament (D Th); pastoral therapy (M Th, D Th); philosophy (MA); philosophy of education (M Ed, Ed D); politics (MA, PhD); Portuguese (MA, PhD); practical theology (M Th, D Th); psychology (MA, MS, PhD); psychology of education (M Ed, Ed D); public health (MA); religious studies (MA, D Th, PhD); Romance languages (MA); Russian (MA, PhD); Semitic languages (MA, PhD); social behavior studies in HIV/AIDS (MA); social science (mental health) (MA); social science in development studies (MA); social science in psychology (MA); social science in social work (MA); social science in sociology (MA); social work (MSW, DSW, PhD); socio-education (M Ed, Ed D); sociolinguistics (MA); sociology (MA, PhD); Spanish (MA, PhD); systematic theology (M Th, D Th); TESOL (teaching English to speakers of other languages) (MA); theological ethics (M Th, D Th); theory of literature (MA, PhD); urban ministries (D Th); urban ministry (M Th).

The University of Tennessee, Graduate School, College of Arts and Sciences, Department of Modern Foreign Languages and Literatures, Program in Modern Foreign Languages, Knoxville, TN 37996. Offers applied linguistics (PhD); French (PhD); German (PhD); Italian (PhD); Portuguese (PhD); Russian (PhD); Spanish (PhD). *Degree requirements:* For doctorate, 2 foreign languages, thesis/dissertation. *Entrance requirements:* For doctorate, minimum GPA of 2.7. Additional exam requirements/recommendations for international students: Required—TOEFL. Electronic applications accepted.

The University of Texas at Austin, Graduate School, College of Liberal Arts, Department of Spanish and Portuguese, Austin, TX 78712-1111. Offers Hispanic literature (MA, PhD); Ibero-Romance philology and linguistics (MA, PhD); Luso-Brazilian literature (MA, PhD). *Degree requirements:* For master's, 2 foreign languages, thesis or alternative; for doctorate, 3 foreign languages, thesis/dissertation. *Entrance requirements:* For master's and doctorate, GRE General Test. Electronic applications accepted.

University of Toronto, School of Graduate Studies, Humanities Division, Department of Spanish and Portuguese, Toronto, ON M5S 1A1, Canada. Offers MA, PhD. Part-time programs available. *Faculty:* 11 full-time, 2 part-time/adjunct. *Students:* 35 full-time (27 women), 3 international. 46 applicants, 46% accepted. In 2007, 5 master's, 2 doctorates awarded. *Degree requirements:* For doctorate, thesis/dissertation. *Entrance requirements:* For master's, minimum B average in final year, 2 letters of reference; for doctorate, minimum A– average, 2 letters of reference, writing sample. Additional exam requirements/recommendations for international students: Required—TOEFL, MELAB, IELTS or COPE. *Application deadline:* For fall admission, 2/1 for domestic students. Application fee: $100 Canadian dollars. *Financial support:* Fellowships, teaching assistantships, stipend available. *Unit head:* Prof. Ricardo Sternberg, Acting Chair, 416-813-4081, Fax: 416-813-4084, E-mail: sternber@chass.utoronto.ca. *Application contact:* Bianca Talesnik, Undergraduate and Graduate Administrator, 416-813-4080, Fax: 416-813-4084, E-mail: b.talesnik@utoronto.ca.

University of Washington, Graduate School, College of Arts and Sciences, Department of Romance Languages and Literature, Division of Spanish and Portuguese Studies, Seattle, WA 98195. Offers Hispanic literary and cultural studies (MA). *Faculty:* 6 full-time (3 women), 2 part-time/adjunct (1 woman). *Students:* 16 full-time (10 women); includes 3 minority (all Hispanic Americans), 6 international. 25 applicants, 52% accepted, 9 enrolled. In 2007, 4 degrees awarded. *Degree requirements:* For master's, 2 foreign languages, thesis optional, exam. *Entrance requirements:* For master's, GRE General Test, minimum GPA of 3.0. Additional exam requirements/recommendations for international students: Required—TOEFL. *Application deadline:* For fall admission, 1/15 priority date for domestic students, 11/1 priority date for international students. Application fee: $50. Electronic applications accepted. *Financial support:* In 2007–08, 1 fellowship with full tuition reimbursement (averaging $4,677 per year), 16 teaching assistantships with full tuition reimbursements (averaging $13,059 per year) were awarded; Federal Work-Study, institutionally sponsored loans, scholarships/grants, health care benefits, and unspecified assistantships also available. Financial award application deadline: 1/15; financial award applicants required to submit FAFSA. *Faculty research:* Medieval through modern Spanish literature and film, Latin American literature, poetry and essay, pan-Hispanic ballad, Hispanic cultural studies, second language acquisition and applied linguistics. *Unit head:* Prof. Anthony Geist, Chair, 206-543-2020, Fax: 206-685-7054, E-mail: tgeist@u.washington.edu. *Application contact:* Suzanna Martinez, Academic Counselor, 206-543-2075, Fax: 206-685-7054, E-mail: spsadv@u.washington.edu.

University of Wisconsin–Madison, Graduate School, College of Letters and Science, Department of Spanish and Portuguese, Program in Portuguese, Madison, WI 53706-1380. Offers MA, PhD. *Degree requirements:* For master's, one foreign language; for doctorate, 2 foreign languages, thesis/dissertation. *Entrance requirements:* For master's, GRE (recommended), minimum GPA of 3.25 in Spanish or Portuguese; for doctorate, GRE (recommended), minimum graduate GPA of 3.4. Additional exam requirements/recommendations for international students: Required—TOEFL. Electronic applications accepted. *Faculty research:* Portuguese and Brazilian literature.

Vanderbilt University, Graduate School, Department of Spanish and Portuguese, Nashville, TN 37240-1001. Offers Portuguese (MA); Spanish (MA, MAT, PhD); Spanish and Portuguese (PhD). *Faculty:* 20 full-time (11 women), 2 part-time/adjunct (1 woman). *Students:* 29 full-time (14 women); includes 2 minority (1 African American, 1 American Indian/Alaska Native), 13 international. Average age 30. 55 applicants, 11% accepted, 6 enrolled. In 2007, 6 master's, 6 doctorates awarded. *Degree requirements:* For master's, one foreign language, thesis; for doctorate, 2 foreign languages, thesis/dissertation, final and qualifying exams. *Entrance requirements:* For master's and doctorate, GRE General Test. *Application deadline:* For fall admission, 1/15 for domestic and international students. Application fee: $0. Electronic applications accepted. *Financial support:* Fellowships with full and partial tuition reimbursements, teaching assistantships with full tuition reimbursements, Federal Work-Study, institutionally sponsored loans, and health care benefits available. Financial award application deadline: 1/15; financial award applicants required to submit CSS PROFILE or FAFSA. *Faculty research:* Spanish, Portuguese, and Latin American literatures; foreign language pedagogy; Renaissance and baroque poetry; nineteenth century Spanish novel. *Unit head:* Cathy L. Jrade, Chair, 615-322-6930, Fax: 615-343-7260, E-mail: cathy.l.jrade@vanderbilt.edu. *Application contact:* Benigno Trigo, Director of Graduate Studies, 615-322-6930, Fax: 615-343-7260, E-mail: benigno.trigo@vanderbilt.edu.

Yale University, Graduate School of Arts and Sciences, Department of Spanish and Portuguese, New Haven, CT 06520. Offers MA, PhD. Terminal master's awarded for partial completion of doctoral program. *Degree requirements:* For master's, 3 foreign languages; for doctorate, 3 foreign languages, thesis/dissertation. *Entrance requirements:* For doctorate, GRE General Test.

Romance Languages

Appalachian State University, Cratis D. Williams Graduate School, Department of Foreign Languages and Literatures, Boone, NC 28608. Offers romance languages-Spanish (MA); romance languages-Spanish teaching (MA). Part-time programs available. *Faculty:* 14 full-time (7 women). *Students:* 9 full-time (7 women), 4 part-time (3 women). 4 applicants, 75% accepted, 3 enrolled. In 2007, 5 degrees awarded. *Degree requirements:* For master's, one foreign language, comprehensive exam, thesis optional. *Entrance requirements:* For master's, GRE General Test, 3 letters of recommendation. Additional exam requirements/recommendations for international students: Required—TOEFL (minimum score 570 paper-based; 230 computer-based; 79 iBT), IELTS (minimum score 7), TOEFL or IELTS. *Application deadline:* For fall admission, 7/1 for domestic students, 1/1 for international students; for spring admission, 11/1 for domestic students, 6/1 for international students. Applications are processed on a rolling basis. Application fee: $50. Electronic applications accepted. *Expenses:* Tuition, state resident: part-time $127 per semester hour. Tuition, nonresident: part-time $597 per semester hour. Required fees: $18 per semester. *Financial support:* In 2007–08, research assistantships (averaging $7,000 per year); fellowships, teaching assistantships, career-related internships or fieldwork and unspecified assistantships also available. Financial award application deadline: 4/1. *Faculty research:* Family in medieval French romance. Total annual research expenditures: $41,594. *Unit head:* Dr. Alexandra Sterling-Hellenbrand, Chairperson, 828-262-3096, Fax: 828-262-3095, E-mail: hellenbranda@appstate.edu. *Application contact:* Dr. Beverly Moser, Graduate Coordinator, 828-262-2929, E-mail: moserba@appstate.edu.

Boston University, Graduate School of Arts and Sciences, Department of Romance Studies, Boston, MA 02215. Offers French language and literature (MA, PhD); Hispanic language and literatures (MA, PhD). *Students:* 45 full-time (34 women), 3 part-time (2 women); includes 6 minority (all Hispanic Americans), 19 international. Average age 32. 54 applicants, 37% accepted, 9 enrolled. In 2007, 5 doctorates awarded. Terminal master's awarded for partial completion of doctoral program. *Degree requirements:* For master's, one foreign language, comprehensive exam; for doctorate, 2 foreign languages, comprehensive exam, thesis/dissertation. *Entrance requirements:* For master's and doctorate, GRE General Test, sample of written work, 3 letters of recommendation. Additional exam requirements/recommendations for international students: Required—TOEFL (minimum score 550 paper-based; 213 computer-based). *Application deadline:* For fall admission, 7/1 for domestic and international students; for spring admission, 10/15 for domestic and international students. Application fee: $70. *Expenses:* Tuition: Full-time $34,930; part-time $1,092 per credit. Tuition and fees vary according to class time, course level and program. *Financial support:* In 2007–08, 48 students received support, including 2 fellowships with full tuition reimbursements available (averaging $18,000 per year), 35 teaching assistantships with full tuition reimbursements available (averaging $16,500 per year); research assistantships, Federal Work-Study and scholarships/grants also available. Support available to part-time students. Financial award application deadline: 1/15; financial award applicants required to submit FAFSA. *Unit head:* Christopher Maurer, Chairman, 617-353-6225, Fax: 617-353-6245, E-mail: chmaurer@bu.edu. *Application contact:* Lauren Terry, Administrative Assistant, 617-353-2641, Fax: 617-353-6245, E-mail: lkterry@bu.edu.

The Catholic University of America, School of Arts and Sciences, Department of Modern Languages and Literatures, Program in Romance Languages and Literatures, Washington, DC 20064. Offers MA, PhD. Part-time programs available. *Students:* Average age 30. *Degree requirements:* For master's, one foreign language, comprehensive exam, thesis or alternative; for doctorate, 2 foreign languages, comprehensive exam, thesis/dissertation. *Entrance requirements:* For master's and doctorate, GRE General Test, 3 letters of recommendation. Additional exam requirements/recommendations for international students: Required—TOEFL (minimum score 580 paper-based; 237 computer-based). *Application deadline:* For fall admission, 2/1 priority date for domestic students; for spring admission, 11/15 priority date for domestic students. Applications are processed on a rolling basis. Application fee: $55. Electronic applications accepted. *Financial support:* Fellowships, teaching assistantships, career-related internships or fieldwork, Federal Work-Study, scholarships/grants, tuition waivers (full and partial), and unspecified assistantships available. Support available to part-time students. Financial award application deadline: 2/1; financial award applicants required to submit FAFSA. *Unit head:* Dr. Joan Grimbert, Chair, Department of Modern Languages and Literatures, 202-319-5240, Fax: 202-319-6077, E-mail: grimbert@cua.edu.

Clark Atlanta University, School of Arts and Sciences, Department of Foreign Languages, Atlanta, GA 30314. Offers Romance languages (MA, DAH). Part-time programs available. *Faculty:* 2 part-time/adjunct (1 woman). *Students:* Average age 39. In 2007, 1 degree awarded. *Degree requirements:* For master's, one foreign language, thesis. *Entrance requirements:* For master's, GRE General Test, minimum GPA of 2.5. Additional exam requirements/recommendations for international students: Required—TOEFL (minimum score 500 paper-based; 173 computer-based). *Application deadline:* For fall admission, 4/1 for domestic and international students; for spring admission, 11/1 for domestic and international students. Applications are processed on a rolling basis. Application fee: $40 ($55 for international students). *Expenses:* Tuition: Full-time $11,664; part-time $648 per credit hour. Required fees: $550; $275 per semester. *Financial support:* Career-related internships or fieldwork, Federal Work-Study, scholarships/grants, and unspecified assistantships available. Support available to part-time students. Financial award application deadline: 4/30; financial award applicants required to submit FAFSA. *Unit head:* Dr. Lawrent Monye, Chairperson, 404-880-8547, E-mail: lmonye@cau.edu. *Application contact:* Michelle Clark-Davis, Graduate Program Admissions, 404-880-8709, E-mail: mdowis@cau.edu.

Columbia University, Graduate School of Arts and Sciences, Division of Humanities, Department of French and Romance Philology, New York, NY 10027. Offers French and Romance philology (M Phil, PhD); Romance languages (MA). Part-time programs available. *Faculty:* 15 full-time. *Students:* 76 full-time (48 women), 5 part-time (4 women); includes 7 minority (3 African Americans, 4 Asian Americans or Pacific Islanders), 17 international. Average age 34. 53 applicants, 64% accepted. In 2007, 5 master's, 8 doctorates awarded. *Degree requirements:* For master's, one foreign language, thesis, written exam; for doctorate, 2 foreign languages, thesis/dissertation. *Entrance requirements:* For master's and doctorate, GRE General Test, knowledge of Latin, writing sample. Additional exam requirements/

Romance Languages

Columbia University (continued)

recommendations for international students: Required—TOEFL. Application fee: $90. *Expenses:* Tuition: Part-time $1,452 per credit. Required fees: $152 per term. One-time fee: $75 part-time. Full-time tuition and fees vary according to course level, course load, degree level and program. *Financial support:* Fellowships, teaching assistantships, Federal Work-Study and institutionally sponsored loans available. Support available to part-time students. Financial award application deadline: 1/5; financial award applicants required to submit FAFSA. *Faculty research:* Theory of literature, literary semiotics, poetics. *Unit head:* Pierre Force, Chair/Director of Graduate Studies, 212-854-5528, Fax: 212-854-2863, E-mail: pf3@columbia.edu.

Cornell University, Graduate School, Graduate Fields of Arts and Sciences, Field of Linguistics, Ithaca, NY 14853-0001. Offers applied linguistics (MA, PhD); East Asian linguistics (MA, PhD); English linguistics (MA, PhD); general linguistics (MA, PhD); Germanic linguistics (MA, PhD); Indo-European linguistics (MA, PhD); phonetics (MA, PhD); phonological theory (MA, PhD); Romance linguistics (MA, PhD); second language acquisition (MA, PhD); semantics (MA, PhD); Slavic linguistics (MA, PhD); sociolinguistics (MA, PhD); South Asian linguistics (MA, PhD); Southeast Asian linguistics (MA, PhD); syntactic theory (MA, PhD). *Faculty:* 19 full-time. *Students:* 31 full-time (16 women); includes 1 minority (Hispanic American), 19 international. Average age 28. 89 applicants, 17% accepted, 8 enrolled. In 2007, 2 master's, 1 doctorate awarded. Terminal master's awarded for partial completion of doctoral program. *Degree requirements:* For master's, one foreign language, thesis; for doctorate, one foreign language, comprehensive exam, thesis/dissertation. *Entrance requirements:* For master's and doctorate, GRE General Test, 2 letters of recommendation. Additional exam requirements/recommendations for international students: Required—TOEFL (minimum score 600 paper-based; 250 computer-based; 77 iBT). *Application deadline:* For fall admission, 1/15 for domestic students. Application fee: $70. Electronic applications accepted. *Financial support:* In 2007–08, 30 students received support, including 14 fellowships with full tuition reimbursements available, 2 research assistantships with full tuition reimbursements available, 14 teaching assistantships with full tuition reimbursements available; institutionally sponsored loans, scholarships/grants, health care benefits, tuition waivers (full and partial), and unspecified assistantships also available. Financial award applicants required to submit FAFSA. *Faculty research:* Phonology and phonetics; syntax and semantics; historical linguistics; philosophy of language; language acquisition. *Unit head:* Director of Graduate Studies, 607-255-1105. *Application contact:* Graduate Field Assistant, 607-255-1105, E-mail: lingfield@cornell.edu.

Cornell University, Graduate School, Graduate Fields of Arts and Sciences, Field of Romance Studies, Ithaca, NY 14853-0001. Offers French linguistics (PhD); French literature (PhD); Hispanic literature (PhD); Italian linguistics (PhD); Italian literature (PhD); Romance linguistics (PhD); Spanish linguistics (PhD). *Faculty:* 32 full-time (14 women). *Students:* 50 full-time (24 women); includes 11 minority (all Hispanic Americans), 20 international. Average age 29. 114 applicants, 23% accepted, 12 enrolled. In 2007, 2 doctorates awarded. *Degree requirements:* For doctorate, 2 foreign languages, comprehensive exam, thesis/dissertation. *Entrance requirements:* For doctorate, GRE General Test, sample of written work, 3 letters of recommendation. Additional exam requirements/recommendations for international students: Required—TOEFL (minimum score 550 paper-based; 213 computer-based; 77 iBT). *Application deadline:* For fall admission, 1/15 for domestic students. Application fee: $70. Electronic applications accepted. *Financial support:* In 2007–08, 48 students received support, including 20 fellowships with full tuition reimbursements available, 28 teaching assistantships with full tuition reimbursements available; research assistantships with full tuition reimbursements available, institutionally sponsored loans, scholarships/grants, health care benefits, tuition waivers (full and partial), and unspecified assistantships also available. Financial award applicants required to submit FAFSA. *Faculty research:* Literary theory, Hispanic studies, French studies, gender studies. *Unit head:* Director of Graduate Studies, 607-255-8222. *Application contact:* Graduate Field Assistant, 607-255-4246, E-mail: romance_studies@cornell.edu.

Hunter College of the City University of New York, Graduate School, School of Arts and Sciences, Department of Romance Languages, New York, NY 10021-5085. Offers French (MA), including French, French education; Italian (MA), including Italian, Italian education; Spanish (MA), including Spanish, Spanish education. Part-time and evening/weekend programs available. *Faculty:* 8 full-time (5 women). *Students:* 1 (woman) full-time, 24 part-time (18 women); includes 8 minority (all Hispanic Americans) Average age 36. 17 applicants, 76% accepted, 7 enrolled. In 2007, 9 degrees awarded. *Degree requirements:* For master's, 2 foreign languages, comprehensive exam, thesis optional. *Entrance requirements:* For master's, GRE General Test, GRE Subject Test, interview, proficiency in chosen language. Additional exam requirements/recommendations for international students: Required—TOEFL. *Application deadline:* For fall admission, 4/1 for domestic students, 2/1 for international students; for spring admission, 11/1 for domestic students, 9/1 for international students. Application fee: $125. *Expenses:* Tuition, state resident: full-time $6,400; part-time $270 per credit. Tuition, nonresident: part-time $500 per credit. One-time fee: $125 full-time. Tuition and fees vary according to program. *Financial support:* Fellowships, Federal Work-Study, scholarships/grants, and tuition waivers (partial) available. Support available to part-time students. Financial award application deadline: 4/15. *Unit head:* Dr. Giuseppe Carlo DiScipio, Chair, 212-772-5109, Fax: 212-772-5094, E-mail: gdiscipi@hunter.cuny.edu. *Application contact:* William Zlata, Director for Graduate Admissions, 212-772-4482, Fax: 212-650-3336, E-mail: admissions@hunter.cuny.edu.

The Johns Hopkins University, Zanvyl Krieger School of Arts and Sciences, Department of German and Romance Languages, Baltimore, MD 21218-2699. Offers French (PhD); German (PhD); Italian (PhD); romance languages (PhD); Spanish (PhD). *Faculty:* 14 full-time (5 women), 2 part-time/adjunct (1 woman). *Students:* 69 full-time (48 women); includes 6 minority (all Hispanic Americans), 37 international. Average age 29. 42 applicants, 36% accepted, 8 enrolled. In 2007, 13 doctorates awarded. *Median time to degree:* Of those who began their doctoral program in fall 1999, 75% received their degree in 8 years or less. *Degree requirements:* For doctorate, 2 foreign languages, thesis/dissertation. *Entrance requirements:* For doctorate, GRE General Test. Additional exam requirements/recommendations for international students: Required—TOEFL (minimum score 600 paper-based; 250 computer-based). *Application deadline:* For fall admission, 1/15 for domestic and international students. Application fee: $60. Electronic applications accepted. *Financial support:* In 2007–08, 64 students received support, including 40 fellowships with full tuition reimbursements available (averaging $16,000 per year), 2 research assistantships with full tuition reimbursements available (averaging $16,000 per year), 19 teaching assistantships with full tuition reimbursements available (averaging $16,000 per year); institutionally sponsored loans and tuition waivers (full and partial) also available. Financial award application deadline: 4/15; financial award applicants required to submit FAFSA. *Unit head:* Dr. Stephen Nichols, Chair, 410-516-4736, Fax: 410-516-5358, E-mail: stephen.nichols@jhu.edu. *Application contact:* Sally Hauf, Graduate Administrative Coordinator, 410-516-7226, Fax: 410-516-5358, E-mail: shauf@jhu.edu.

Michigan State University, The Graduate School, College of Arts and Letters, Department of French, Classics, and Italian, East Lansing, MI 48824. Offers French (MA); French language and literature (PhD). *Entrance requirements:* Additional exam requirements/recommendations for international students: Required—TOEFL. Electronic applications accepted. *Expenses:* Tuition, state resident: part-time $379 per credit hour. Tuition, nonresident: part-time $800 per credit hour. Tuition and fees vary according to program.

New York University, Graduate School of Arts and Science, Center for French Civilization and Culture, Department of French, New York, NY 10012-1019. Offers French (PhD); French language and civilization (MA); French literature (MA); Romance languages and literatures (MA). Part-time programs available. *Faculty:* 18 full-time (7 women), 2 part-time/adjunct. *Students:* 70 full-time (45 women), 3 part-time; includes 8 minority (1 African American, 6 Asian Americans or Pacific Islanders, 1 Hispanic American), 23 international. Average age 30. 81 applicants, 62% accepted, 20 enrolled. In 2007, 18 master's, 4 doctorates awarded. Terminal master's awarded for partial completion of doctoral program. *Degree requirements:* For master's, one foreign language, thesis (for some programs); for doctorate, one foreign language, thesis/dissertation. *Entrance requirements:* For master's and doctorate, GRE General Test, proficiency in French. Additional exam requirements/recommendations for international students: Required—TOEFL. *Application deadline:* For fall admission, 1/4 for domestic students; for spring admission, 11/1 for domestic students. Application fee: $85. *Financial support:* Fellowships with tuition reimbursements, teaching assistantships with tuition reimbursements, Federal Work-Study, institutionally sponsored loans, scholarships/grants, traineeships, health care benefits, unspecified assistantships, and instructorships available. Financial award application deadline: 1/4; financial award applicants required to submit FAFSA. *Faculty research:* French and Francophone literature, literary theory, and history; rhetoric and poetics; cultural history; theater and cinema. *Application contact:* Brett Underhill, Graduate Secretary, 212-998-8700, Fax: 212-995-3539, E-mail: french.grad@nyu.edu.

New York University, Graduate School of Arts and Science, Department of Spanish and Portuguese Languages and Literatures, New York, NY 10012-1019. Offers Portuguese (MA, PhD); Spanish (PhD); Spanish and Latin American literatures and cultures (MA); Spanish language and translation (MA). Part-time programs available. *Faculty:* 17 full-time (10 women), 11 part-time/adjunct. *Students:* 77 full-time (49 women), 6 part-time (all women); includes 30 minority (2 African Americans, 4 Asian Americans or Pacific Islanders, 24 Hispanic Americans), 23 international. Average age 30. 194 applicants, 44% accepted, 35 enrolled. In 2007, 28 master's, 6 doctorates awarded. *Degree requirements:* For master's, 2 foreign languages, thesis; for doctorate, 2 foreign languages, thesis/dissertation. *Entrance requirements:* For master's, GRE General Test; for doctorate, GRE General Test, master's degree. Additional exam requirements/recommendations for international students: Required—TOEFL. *Application deadline:* For fall admission, 1/4 priority date for domestic students. Application fee: $85. *Financial support:* Fellowships with tuition reimbursements, teaching assistantships with tuition reimbursements, career-related internships or fieldwork, Federal Work-Study, institutionally sponsored loans, scholarships/grants, health care benefits, and unspecified assistantships available. Financial award application deadline: 1/4; financial award applicants required to submit FAFSA. *Faculty research:* Gender and sexuality, transatlantic studies, literacy and cultural theories, colonial and post colonial studies, autobiography and modern subjectivities. *Unit head:* James Fernandez, Chair, 212-998-8770, Fax: 212-995-4148, E-mail: spanish.portuguese.info@nyu.edu. *Application contact:* Gabriela Basterra, Director of Graduate Studies, 212-998-8770, Fax: 212-995-4149, E-mail: spanish.portuguese.info@nyu.edu.

Northern Illinois University, Graduate School, College of Liberal Arts and Sciences, Department of Foreign Languages and Literatures, De Kalb, IL 60115-2854. Offers French (MA); Spanish (MA). Part-time programs available. *Faculty:* 25 full-time (11 women). *Students:* 8 full-time (5 women), 25 part-time (22 women); includes 10 minority (1 African American, 9 Hispanic Americans), 1 international. Average age 39. 10 applicants, 60% accepted, 4 enrolled. In 2007, 11 degrees awarded. *Degree requirements:* For master's, one foreign language, comprehensive exam, thesis or alternative, language proficiency exam. *Entrance requirements:* For master's, GRE General Test, interview, minimum GPA of 2.75, undergraduate major in French or Spanish. Additional exam requirements/recommendations for international students: Required—TOEFL (minimum score 550 paper-based; 213 computer-based). *Application deadline:* For fall admission, 6/1 for domestic students, 5/1 for international students; for spring admission, 11/1 for domestic students, 10/1 for international students. Applications are processed on a rolling basis. Application fee: $30. Electronic applications accepted. *Expenses:* Tuition, area resident: Part-time $226 per credit hour. Tuition, state resident: full-time $5,424; part-time $225 per credit hour. Tuition, nonresident: full-time $10,848. Required fees: $2,416; $64 per credit hour. *Financial support:* In 2007–08, 13 teaching assistantships with full tuition reimbursements were awarded; fellowships with full tuition reimbursements, research assistantships with full tuition reimbursements, career-related internships or fieldwork, Federal Work-Study, scholarships/grants, tuition waivers (full), and unspecified assistantships also available. Support available to part-time students. Financial award applicants required to submit FAFSA. *Faculty research:* Francophone women writers, prosodies of French and Italian, early Spanish drama, business German, history of Burmese literature. *Unit head:* Anne Birbeck, Acting Chair, 815-753-1259, Fax: 815-753-5989, E-mail: annje@niu.edu.

Queens College of the City University of New York, Division of Graduate Studies, Arts and Humanities Division, Department of European Languages and Literatures, Flushing, NY 11367-1597. Offers French (MA); Italian (MA). Part-time and evening/weekend programs available. *Faculty:* 13 full-time (5 women). *Students:* 19 applicants, 100% accepted, 10 enrolled. In 2007, 2 degrees awarded. *Degree requirements:* For master's, 2 foreign languages, comprehensive exam, thesis or alternative. *Entrance requirements:* For master's, minimum GPA of 3.0. Additional exam requirements/recommendations for international students: Required—TOEFL. *Application deadline:* For fall admission, 4/1 for domestic students; for spring admission, 11/1 for domestic students. Applications are processed on a rolling basis. Application fee: $125. *Financial support:* Career-related internships or fieldwork, Federal Work-Study, institutionally sponsored loans, and tuition waivers (partial) available. Support available to part-time students. Financial award application deadline: 4/1; financial award applicants required to submit FAFSA. *Unit head:* Dr. Royal Brown, Chairperson, 718-997-5980, E-mail: royal_brown@qc.edu. *Application contact:* Mario Caruso, Director of Graduate Admissions, 718-997-5200, Fax: 718-997-5193, E-mail: graduate_admissions@qc.edu.

San Diego State University, Graduate and Research Affairs, College of Arts and Letters, Department of European Studies, San Diego, CA 92182. Offers MA. *Students:* 2 full-time (0 women), 3 part-time (all women); includes 2 minority (1 African American, 1 Hispanic American), 1 international. Average age 29. 4 applicants, 75% accepted, 2 enrolled. In 2007, 1 degree awarded. *Degree requirements:* For master's, one foreign language. *Entrance requirements:* For master's, GRE General Test. Additional exam requirements/recommendations for international students: Required—TOEFL. *Application deadline:* For fall admission, 5/1 for domestic and international students; for spring admission, 11/1 for domestic students, 10/1 for international students. Applications are processed on a rolling basis. Application fee: $55. Electronic applications accepted. *Financial support:* Teaching assistantships, career-related internships or fieldwork available. Financial award applicants required to submit FAFSA. *Unit head:* Dr. Edith Benkov, Chair, 619-594-5111, Fax: 619-594-8006, E-mail: ebenkov@mail.sdsu.edu. *Application contact:* Dr. Anne Donadey, Graduate Adviser, 619-594-0815, Fax: 619-594-8006, E-mail: adonadey@mail.sdsu.edu.

Stony Brook University, State University of New York, Graduate School, College of Arts and Sciences, Department of European Languages, Literatures, and Cultures, Program in French, Stony Brook, NY 11794. Offers Romance languages (MA). Evening/weekend programs available. *Students:* 4 full-time (all women), 5 part-time (all women); includes 1 minority (African American), 1 international. Average age 25. *Degree requirements:* For master's, one foreign language. *Entrance requirements:* For master's, GRE General Test. Additional exam requirements/recommendations for international students: Required—TOEFL. *Application deadline:* For fall admission, 1/15 for domestic students. Application fee: $60. *Unit head:* Prosper Sanou, Coordinator, 631-632-7440, E-mail: prosper.sanou@stonybrook.edu.

Texas Tech University, Graduate School; College of Arts and Sciences, Department of Classical and Modern Languages and Literatures, Lubbock, TX 79409. Offers applied linguistics (MA); classics (MA); German (MA); Romance language (MA); Romance languages-French (MA); Romance languages-Spanish (MA, PhD). Part-time programs available. *Faculty:* 23 full-time (9 women), 1 (woman) part-time/adjunct. *Students:* 76 full-time (43 women), 24 part-time (16 women); includes 26 minority (1 African American, 2 Asian Americans or Pacific Islanders, 23 Hispanic Americans), 18 international. Average age 32. 69 applicants, 84% accepted, 27 enrolled. In 2007, 13 master's, 2 doctorates awarded. *Degree requirements:* For doctorate, thesis/dissertation. *Entrance requirements:* For master's and doctorate, GRE General Test. Additional exam requirements/recommendations for international students: Required—TOEFL (minimum score 550 paper-based; 213 computer-based). *Application deadline:* For fall admission, 3/1 priority date for international students; for spring admission, 11/1 priority date for international students. Applications are processed on a rolling basis. Application fee: $50

($60 for international students). Electronic applications accepted. *Expenses:* Tuition, state resident: part-time $373 per credit hour. Tuition, nonresident: part-time $651 per credit hour. Tuition and fees vary according to program. *Financial support:* In 2007–08, 44 students received support, including 70 teaching assistantships with partial tuition reimbursements available (averaging $11,627 per year); research assistantships with partial tuition reimbursements available, Federal Work-Study and institutionally sponsored loans also available. Support available to part-time students. Financial award application deadline: 4/15; financial award applicants required to submit FAFSA. *Faculty research:* Literature, comparative literature, linguistics, culture, pedagogy. *Unit head:* Dr. Julian Frederick Suppe, Chair and Professor, 806-742-4355, Fax: 806-742-3306, E-mail: frederick.suppe@ttu.edu. *Application contact:* Liz Hildebrand, Senior Advisor, 806-742-4055, Fax: 806-742-3306, E-mail: liz.hildebrand@ttu.edu.

University at Buffalo, the State University of New York, Graduate School, College of Arts and Sciences, Department of Romance Languages and Literatures, Buffalo, NY 14260. Offers French (MA, PhD); Spanish (MA, PhD). Part-time programs available. Terminal master's awarded for partial completion of doctoral program. *Degree requirements:* For master's, one foreign language, project; for doctorate, 2 foreign languages, thesis/dissertation. *Entrance requirements:* For master's and doctorate, GRE. Additional exam requirements/recommendations for international students: Required—TOEFL (minimum score 550 paper-based; 213 computer-based; 79 iBT). Electronic applications accepted. *Faculty research:* Romance linguistics, cultural studies, literary studies, literature and philosophy.

The University of Alabama, Graduate School, College of Arts and Sciences, Department of Modern Languages and Classics, Tuscaloosa, AL 35487. Offers French (MA, PhD); French and Spanish (PhD); German (MA); Romance languages (MA, PhD); Spanish (MA, PhD). Part-time programs available. *Faculty:* 22 full-time (12 women). *Students:* 47 full-time (35 women), 14 part-time (9 women); includes 12 minority (2 African Americans, 10 Hispanic Americans), 15 international. Average age 32. 26 applicants, 69% accepted, 14 enrolled. In 2007, 12 master's, 4 doctorates awarded. *Median time to degree:* Of those who began their doctoral program in fall 1999, 40% received their degree in 8 years or less. *Degree requirements:* For master's, comprehensive exam, thesis optional; for doctorate, one foreign language, thesis/dissertation, preliminary exam. *Entrance requirements:* For master's and doctorate, minimum GPA of 3.0, writing sample. Additional exam requirements/recommendations for international students: Required—TOEFL or IELTS. *Application deadline:* For fall admission, 7/6 priority date for domestic students, 1/15 priority date for international students; for spring admission, 12/6 priority date for domestic students, 6/1 priority date for international students. Applications are processed on a rolling basis. Application fee: $30. Electronic applications accepted. *Expenses:* Tuition, state resident: full-time $5,700. Tuition, nonresident: full-time $16,518. *Financial support:* In 2007–08, 7 students received support, including 1 fellowship, research assistantships with full tuition reimbursements available (averaging $10,291 per year), 6 teaching assistantships with full tuition reimbursements available (averaging $10,291 per year); career-related internships or fieldwork, Federal Work-Study, institutionally sponsored loans, and scholarships/grants also available. Financial award application deadline: 7/14. *Faculty research:* Non-English literature, linguistics, culture, film. Total annual research expenditures: $48,751. *Unit head:* Dr. Michael Picone, Chair and Professor, 205-348-5054, Fax: 205-348-2042, E-mail: mpicone@bama.ua.edu. *Application contact:* Dr. K. Barbara Fischer, Graduate Director and Associate Professor, 205-348-8465, Fax: 205-348-2042, E-mail: bfischer@bama.ua.edu.

University of California, Berkeley, Graduate Division, Group in Romance Languages and Literature, Berkeley, CA 94720-1500. Offers French (PhD); Italian (PhD); Spanish (PhD). *Faculty:* 16 full-time. *Degree requirements:* For doctorate, thesis/dissertation, qualifying exam. *Entrance requirements:* For doctorate, GRE General Test, minimum GPA of 3.0, 3 letters of recommendation. Additional exam requirements/recommendations for international students: Required—TOEFL (minimum score 570 paper-based; 230 computer-based). *Application deadline:* For fall admission, 12/15 for domestic students. Application fee: $70 ($90 for international students). *Financial support:* Fellowships with full tuition reimbursements, teaching assistantships with partial tuition reimbursements, health care benefits and unspecified assistantships available. Financial award applicants required to submit FAFSA. *Unit head:* Jose Rabasa, Chair, 510-642—2105, E-mail: jrabasa@berkeley.edu.

University of Chicago, Division of the Humanities, Department of Romance Languages and Literatures, Chicago, IL 60637-1513. Offers French (AM, PhD); Italian (AM, PhD); Spanish (AM, PhD). *Students:* 75. 56 applicants, 45% accepted, 15 enrolled.Terminal master's awarded for partial completion of doctoral program. *Degree requirements:* For master's, 2 foreign languages, thesis; for doctorate, 3 foreign languages, thesis/dissertation. *Entrance requirements:* For master's and doctorate, GRE General Test, GRE Subject Test. Additional exam requirements/recommendations for international students: Required—TOEFL. *Application deadline:* For fall admission, 12/15 for domestic students. Application fee: $55. *Financial support:* Teaching assistantships, Federal Work-Study available. Financial award application deadline: 12/15; financial award applicants required to submit FAFSA. *Unit head:* Dr. Frederick de Armas, Chair, 773-702-8481.

University of Cincinnati, Graduate School, McMicken College of Arts and Sciences, Department of Romance Languages and Literature, Cincinnati, OH 45221. Offers French (MA, PhD); Romance languages and literatures (PhD); Spanish (MA, PhD). *Faculty:* 12 full-time (6 women). *Students:* 30 full-time (17 women), 4 part-time (all women); includes 5 minority (1 African American, 4 Hispanic Americans), 15 international. Average age 39. 55 applicants, 18% accepted, 9 enrolled. In 2007, 3 master's, 1 doctorate awarded. Terminal master's awarded for partial completion of doctoral program. *Median time to degree:* Of those who began their doctoral program in fall 1999, 80% received their degree in 8 years or less. *Degree requirements:* For master's, 2 foreign languages, comprehensive exam, thesis optional; for doctorate, 3 foreign languages, comprehensive exam, thesis/dissertation. *Entrance requirements:* For master's, minimum GPA of 3.0; for doctorate, MA or equivalent in French or Spanish language and literature. Additional exam requirements/recommendations for international students: Required—TOEFL (minimum score 520 paper-based; 190 computer-based). *Application deadline:* For fall admission, 2/1 priority date for domestic students, 3/15 for international students. Applications are processed on a rolling basis. Application fee: $30. Electronic applications accepted. *Financial support:* In 2007–08, 26 students received support, including fellowships with full tuition reimbursements available (averaging $12,000 per year), teaching assistantships with full tuition reimbursements available (averaging $10,000 per year); scholarships/grants and unspecified assistantships also available. Financial award application deadline: 5/1. *Faculty research:* Teaching methods in Spanish, Spanish theater, Old French, Francophone studies, poetry. *Unit head:* Dr. Lowanne Jones, Head, 513-556-1828, Fax: 513-556-2577, E-mail: lowanne.jones@uc.edu. *Application contact:* Dr. Nicasio Urbina, Graduate Program Director, 513-556-1838, Fax: 513-556-2577, E-mail: urbinan@uc.edu.

University of Georgia, Graduate School, College of Arts and Sciences, Department of Romance Languages, Program in Romance Languages, Athens, GA 30602. Offers MA, MAT, PhD. *Faculty:* 29 full-time (13 women). *Students:* 34 full-time (19 women), 7 part-time (all women); includes 11 minority (2 African Americans, 9 Hispanic Americans), 11 international. 37 applicants, 41% accepted, 7 enrolled. In 2007, 8 master's, 4 doctorates awarded. *Degree requirements:* For master's, one foreign language, thesis (MA); for doctorate, one foreign language, thesis/dissertation. *Entrance requirements:* For master's and doctorate, GRE General Test. *Application deadline:* For fall admission, 7/1 priority date for domestic students; for spring admission, 11/15 for domestic students. Application fee: $50. Electronic applications accepted. *Financial support:* Fellowships, research assistantships, teaching assistantships, unspecified assistantships available.

University of Miami, Graduate School, College of Arts and Sciences, Department of Modern Languages and Literatures, Coral Gables, FL 33124. Offers romance studies (PhD), including French, Spanish. *Faculty:* 23 full-time (14 women). *Students:* 24 full-time (14 women); includes 10 minority (3 African Americans, 2 Asian Americans or Pacific Islanders, 5 Hispanic Americans), 11 international. Average age 32. 25 applicants, 24% accepted, 6 enrolled. In 2007, 4 degrees awarded. *Median time to degree:* Of those who began their doctoral program in fall 1999, 100% received their degree in 8 years or less. *Degree requirements:* For doctorate, 2 foreign languages, thesis/dissertation, area exam, qualifying exam. *Entrance requirements:* For doctorate, 1 writing sample in English and 1 writing sample in French or Spanish, minimum GPA of 3.0; oral interview; letters of recommendation. Additional exam requirements/recommendations for international students: Required—TOEFL (minimum score 550 paper-based; 213 computer-based; 59 iBT), GRE General Test (recommended). *Application deadline:* For fall admission, 1/15 priority date for domestic and international students. Application fee: $50. Electronic applications accepted. *Financial support:* In 2007–08, 21 students received support, including 1 fellowship with full tuition reimbursement available (averaging $30,000 per year), 1 research assistantship, 16 teaching assistantships with full tuition reimbursements available (averaging $20,000 per year); career-related internships or fieldwork, Federal Work-Study, institutionally sponsored loans, scholarships/grants, health care benefits, and unspecified assistantships also available. Financial award application deadline: 3/15; financial award applicants required to submit FAFSA. *Faculty research:* Transatlantic studies, Caribbean studies, comparative literature, gender theory, cultural studies. *Unit head:* Prof. Anne J. Cruz, Chair, 305-284-5585, Fax: 305-284-2068, E-mail: ajcruz@miami.edu. *Application contact:* Prof. Gema Perez-Sanchez, Director of Graduate Studies, 305-284-4858 Ext. 7313, Fax: 305-284-2068, E-mail: gema@miami.edu.

University of Michigan, Horace H. Rackham School of Graduate Studies, College of Literature, Science, and the Arts, Department of Romance Languages and Literatures, Ann Arbor, MI 48109. Offers French (PhD); Romance linguistics (PhD); Spanish (PhD). *Faculty:* 27 full-time (12 women), 2 part-time/adjunct (1 woman). *Students:* 60 full-time (44 women). Average age 30. 54 applicants, 37% accepted. In 2007, 3 degrees awarded. *Degree requirements:* For doctorate, 2 foreign languages, thesis/dissertation, oral defense of dissertation, preliminary exams. *Entrance requirements:* For doctorate, GRE General Test. Additional exam requirements/recommendations for international students: Required—TOEFL or Michigan English Language Assessment Battery. *Application deadline:* For fall admission, 1/1 for domestic students. Application fee: $60. Electronic applications accepted. *Financial support:* In 2007–08, 5 fellowships with full tuition reimbursements (averaging $20,000 per year), 1 teaching assistantship with full tuition reimbursement were awarded; research assistantships, institutionally sponsored loans, scholarships/grants, and unspecified assistantships also available. Financial award application deadline: 1/1. *Faculty research:* Comparative Romance studies, medieval and early modern studies, postcolonial and minority literatures, culture and materiality, reflection on the nature and function of scholarship. *Unit head:* Dr. Michele Hannoosh, Chair, 734-764-5344, Fax: 734-764-8163. *Application contact:* Graduate Assistant, 734-763-0408, Fax: 734-764-8163, E-mail: rll-admissions@umich.edu.

University of Missouri–Columbia, Graduate School, College of Arts and Sciences, Department of Romance Languages and Literature, Columbia, MO 65211. Offers French (MA, PhD); literature (MA); Spanish (MA, PhD); teaching (MA). Terminal master's awarded for partial completion of doctoral program. *Degree requirements:* For master's, one foreign language; for doctorate, 4 foreign languages, thesis/dissertation. *Entrance requirements:* For master's and doctorate, GRE General Test, minimum GPA of 3.0.

University of Missouri–Kansas City, College of Arts and Sciences, Department of Foreign Languages and Literatures, Kansas City, MO 64110-2499. Offers Romance languages and literatures (MA). Part-time programs available. *Faculty:* 11 full-time (4 women), 17 part-time/adjunct (12 women). *Students:* 5 full-time (4 women), 18 part-time (13 women); includes 4 minority (2 African Americans, 2 Hispanic Americans). Average age 33. 9 applicants, 89% accepted, 4 enrolled. In 2007, 6 degrees awarded. *Degree requirements:* For master's, 2 foreign languages. *Entrance requirements:* For master's, GRE General Test, minimum GPA of 2.75, 2 letters of recommendation. Additional exam requirements/recommendations for international students: Required—TOEFL. *Application deadline:* For fall admission, 4/1 priority date for domestic and international students; for spring admission, 11/1 priority date for domestic and international students. Applications are processed on a rolling basis. Application fee: $35 ($50 for international students). Electronic applications accepted. *Expenses:* Tuition, state resident: part-time $287 per hour. Tuition, nonresident: part-time $741 per hour. Required fees: $31 per hour. Tuition and fees vary according to program. *Financial support:* In 2007–08, 5 students received support, including 1 teaching assistantship with full tuition reimbursement available (averaging $20,490 per year); Federal Work-Study, institutionally sponsored loans, and tuition waivers (full and partial) also available. Support available to part-time students. Financial award application deadline: 3/1; financial award applicants required to submit FAFSA. *Faculty research:* Literary analyses; psychology and literature; narrative techniques, poetic structure, and style; literature, politics, and society (especially Latin America). *Unit head:* Dr. Alice Reckley Valuejos, Chair, 816-235-2821, Fax: 816-235-1312.

University of New Orleans, Graduate School, College of Liberal Arts, Department of Foreign Languages, New Orleans, LA 70148. Offers MA. Part-time and evening/weekend programs available. *Students:* 28 (17 women). Average age 38. In 2007, 6 degrees awarded. *Degree requirements:* For master's, one foreign language, thesis optional. *Entrance requirements:* For master's, GRE General Test, minimum B average. Additional exam requirements/recommendations for international students: Required—TOEFL (minimum score 550 paper-based; 213 computer-based; 79 iBT). *Application deadline:* For fall admission, 7/1 priority date for domestic students, 6/1 for international students; for spring admission, 11/15 priority date for domestic students, 10/1 for international students. Applications are processed on a rolling basis. Application fee: $40. Electronic applications accepted. *Financial support:* Teaching assistantships, institutionally sponsored loans and tuition waivers (full) available. Financial award application deadline: 3/15; financial award applicants required to submit FAFSA. *Faculty research:* Translation studies, Michelet, Scève, Spanish canzoniero, theories of representation. *Unit head:* Dr. Eliza Ghil, Chairperson, 504-280-6932, Fax: 504-280-6965, E-mail: eghil@uno.edu. *Application contact:* Dr. Maria Artigas, Graduate Coordinator, 504-280-6930, Fax: 504-280-6965, E-mail: martigas@uno.edu.

The University of North Carolina at Chapel Hill, Graduate School, College of Arts and Sciences, Department of Romance Languages, Chapel Hill, NC 27599. Offers French (MA, PhD); Italian (MA, PhD); Portuguese (MA, PhD); Romance languages (MA, PhD); Romance philology (MA, PhD); Spanish (MA, PhD). *Degree requirements:* For master's, one foreign language, comprehensive exam, thesis; for doctorate, 2 foreign languages, comprehensive exam, thesis/dissertation. *Entrance requirements:* For master's and doctorate, GRE General Test, minimum GPA of 3.0. Additional exam requirements/recommendations for international students: Required—TOEFL (minimum score 550 paper-based; 213 computer-based). Electronic applications accepted.

University of Notre Dame, Graduate School, College of Arts and Letters, Division of Humanities, Department of Romance Languages and Literatures, Notre Dame, IN 46556. Offers French and Francophone studies (MA); Iberian and Latin American studies (MA); Italian studies (MA); Romance literatures (MA). Part-time programs available. *Faculty:* 25 full-time (10 women), 4 part-time/adjunct (all women). *Students:* 18 full-time (12 women); includes 4 minority (all Hispanic Americans), 3 international. 28 applicants, 61% accepted, 9 enrolled. In 2007, 12 degrees awarded. *Degree requirements:* For master's, 2 foreign languages, comprehensive exam, thesis optional. *Entrance requirements:* For master's, GRE General Test, BA in target language. Additional exam requirements/recommendations for international students: Required—TOEFL (minimum score 600 paper-based; 250 computer-based; 80 iBT). *Application deadline:* For fall admission, 2/1 priority date for domestic students, 2/1 for international students. Application fee: $50. Electronic applications accepted. *Financial support:* In 2007–08, 1 fellowship (averaging $15,000 per year), 10 teaching assistantships with full tuition reimbursements (averaging $12,000 per year) were awarded; research assistantships, tuition waivers (full) also available. Financial award application deadline: 2/1. *Faculty research:* Literature of discovery and exploration, modern literature, literary criticism, medieval literature, feminist

Romance Languages

University of Notre Dame (continued)
critical theory. *Unit head:* Dr. John Welle, Director of Graduate Studies, 574-631-6887, Fax: 574-631-3493, E-mail: al.romland.1@nd.edu. *Application contact:* Dr. Jarren Gonzales, Director of Graduate Admissions, 574-631-7706, Fax: 574-631-4183.

University of Oregon, Graduate School, College of Arts and Sciences, Department of Romance Languages, Program in Romance Languages, Eugene, OR 97403. Offers MA, PhD. Part-time programs available. *Students:* 40 full-time (20 women), 2 part-time (both women); includes 1 Asian American or Pacific Islander, 7 Hispanic Americans, 16 international. 23 applicants, 35% accepted. In 2007, 1 master's, 1 doctorate awarded. *Degree requirements:* For master's, 2 foreign languages; for doctorate, 2 foreign languages, thesis/dissertation. *Entrance requirements:* For master's and doctorate, GRE General Test, minimum GPA of 3.0. Additional exam requirements/recommendations for international students: Required—TOEFL. Application fee: $50. *Financial support:* Teaching assistantships available. *Application contact:* Barbara VerWest, Admissions Contact, 541-346-4013, E-mail: verwest@uoregon.edu.

University of Pennsylvania, School of Arts and Sciences, Graduate Group in Romance Languages, Philadelphia, PA 19104. Offers French (AM, PhD); Italian (AM, PhD); Spanish (AM, PhD). Terminal master's awarded for partial completion of doctoral program. *Degree requirements:* For master's, one foreign language, thesis or alternative; for doctorate, 2 foreign languages, thesis/dissertation. *Entrance requirements:* For master's and doctorate, GRE General Test. Additional exam requirements/recommendations for international students: Required—TOEFL. Electronic applications accepted. *Faculty research:* Literary theory and criticism, cultural studies, history of Romance literatures, gender studies.

University of South Africa, College of Human Sciences, Pretoria, South Africa. Offers adult education (M Ed); African languages (MA, PhD); African politics (MA, PhD); Afrikaans (MA, PhD); ancient history (MA, PhD); ancient Near Eastern studies (MA, PhD); anthropology (MA, PhD); applied linguistics (MA); Arabic (MA, PhD); archaeology (MA); art history (MA); Biblical archaeology (MA); Biblical studies (M Th, D Th, PhD); Christian spirituality (M Th, D Th); church history (M Th, D Th); classical studies (MA, PhD); clinical psychology (MA); communication (MA, PhD); comparative education (M Ed, Ed D); consulting psychology (D Admin, D Com, PhD); curriculum studies (M Ed, Ed D); development studies (M Admin, MA, D Admin, PhD); didactics (M Ed, Ed D); education (M Tech); education management (M Ed, Ed D); educational psychology (M Ed); English (MA); environmental education (M Ed); French (MA, PhD); German (MA, PhD); Greek (MA); guidance and counseling (M Ed); health studies (MA, PhD), including health sciences education (MA), health services management (MA), medical and surgical nursing science (critical care general) (MA), midwifery and neonatal nursing science (MA), trauma and emergency care (MA); history (MA, PhD); history of education (Ed D); inclusive education (M Ed, Ed D); information and communications technology policy and regulation (MA); information science (MA, MIS, PhD); international politics (MA, PhD); Islamic studies (MA, PhD); Italian (MA, PhD); Judaica (MA, PhD); linguistics (MA, PhD); mathematical education (M Ed); mathematics education (MA); missiology (M Th, D Th); modern Hebrew (MA, PhD); musicology (MA, MMus, D Mus, PhD); natural science education (M Ed); New Testament (M Th, D Th); Old Testament (D Th); pastoral therapy (M Th, D Th); philosophy (MA); philosophy of education (M Ed, Ed D); politics (MA, PhD); Portuguese (MA, PhD); practical theology (M Th, D Th); psychology (MA, MS, PhD); psychology of education (M Ed, Ed D); public health (MA); religious studies (MA, D Th, PhD); Romance languages (MA); Russian (MA, PhD); Semitic languages (MA, PhD); social behavior studies in HIV/AIDS (MA); social science (mental health) (MA); social science in development studies (MA); social science in psychology (MA); social science in social work (MA); social science in sociology (MA); social work (MSW, DSW, PhD); socio-education (M Ed, Ed D); sociolinguistics (MA); sociology (MA, PhD); Spanish (MA, PhD); systematic theology (M Th, D Th); TESOL (teaching English to speakers of other languages) (MA); theological ethics (M Th, D Th); theory of literature (MA, PhD); urban ministries (D Th); urban ministry (M Th).

The University of Texas at Austin, Graduate School, College of Liberal Arts, Department of French and Italian, Austin, TX 78712-1111. Offers French (MA, PhD); Romance linguistics (MA, PhD). Part-time programs available. *Degree requirements:* For master's, one foreign language, thesis; for doctorate, 2 foreign languages, thesis/dissertation. *Entrance requirements:* For master's, GRE General Test, minimum GPA of 3.0, bachelor's degree in French or equivalent; for doctorate, GRE General Test, minimum GPA of 3.0, master's degree in French. Additional exam requirements/recommendations for international students: Required—TOEFL. Electronic applications accepted. *Faculty research:* Nineteenth-century Italian literature, Italian Renaissance, twentieth-century French literature, Francophone literature, fifteenth-century literature and culture.

University of Virginia, College and Graduate School of Arts and Sciences, Department of Spanish, Italian and Portuguese, Charlottesville, VA 22903. Offers Italian (MA); Spanish (MA, PhD). *Faculty:* 22 full-time (10 women). *Students:* 45 full-time (35 women), 2 part-time (1 woman); includes 3 minority (all Hispanic Americans), 9 international. Average age 28. 87 applicants, 34% accepted, 12 enrolled. In 2007, 10 master's, 7 doctorates awarded. *Degree requirements:* For master's, comprehensive exam, thesis; for doctorate, one foreign language, comprehensive exam, thesis/dissertation. *Entrance requirements:* For master's and doctorate, GRE General Test, GRE Subject Test. *Application deadline:* Applications are processed on a rolling basis. Application fee: $60. Electronic applications accepted. *Financial support:* Applicants required to submit FAFSA. *Unit head:* Randolph Pope, Chair, 434-924-7159, Fax: 434-924-7160, E-mail: rdp6g@virginia.edu.

University of Washington, Graduate School, College of Arts and Sciences, Department of Romance Languages and Literature, Seattle, WA 98195. Offers French and Italian studies (MA, PhD), including French, Italian (MA); Spanish and Portuguese (MA), including Hispanic literary and cultural studies. *Faculty:* 13 full-time (6 women), 1 part-time/adjunct (0 women). *Students:* 31 full-time (22 women); includes 5 minority (2 Asian Americans or Pacific Islanders, 3 Hispanic Americans), 9 international. 39 applicants, 54% accepted, 14 enrolled. In 2007, 6 master's, 1 doctorate awarded. Terminal master's awarded for partial completion of doctoral program. *Degree requirements:* For master's, 2 foreign languages, thesis optional, exam; for doctorate, 3 foreign languages, thesis/dissertation, exams. *Entrance requirements:* For master's and doctorate, GRE General Test, minimum GPA of 3.0. Additional exam requirements/recommendations for international students: Required—TOEFL. *Application deadline:* For fall admission, 1/15 priority date for domestic students, 11/1 priority date for international students. Applications are processed on a rolling basis. Application fee: $50. Electronic applications accepted. *Financial support:* In 2007–08, 1 fellowship with full tuition reimbursement (averaging $13,059 per year), 21 teaching assistantships with full tuition reimbursements (averaging $13,534 per year) were awarded; Federal Work-Study, institutionally sponsored loans, scholarships/grants, health care benefits, tuition waivers (full), and unspecified assistantships also available. Financial award application deadline: 1/15.

Washington University in St. Louis, Graduate School of Arts and Sciences, Department of Romance Languages and Literatures, St. Louis, MO 63130-4899. Offers French (MA, PhD); Romance languages (MA, PhD); Spanish (MA, PhD). Terminal master's awarded for partial completion of doctoral program. *Degree requirements:* For master's, thesis or alternative; for doctorate, thesis/dissertation. *Entrance requirements:* For master's and doctorate, GRE General Test. Electronic applications accepted.

Russian

American University, College of Arts and Sciences, Department of Language and Foreign Studies, Program in Russian, Washington, DC 20016-8001. Offers translation (Certificate). Part-time and evening/weekend programs available. *Students:* Average age 28. *Degree requirements:* For Certificate, 15 credit hour minimum in related course work. *Entrance requirements:* For degree, Bachelor's Degree in Russian or evidence of Russian Proficiency and a BA. *Application deadline:* For fall admission, 2/1 for domestic students; for spring admission, 10/1 for domestic students. Application fee: $50. *Expenses:* Tuition: Full-time $19,998; part-time $1,111 per credit hour. Required fees: $380. Tuition and fees vary according to program. *Financial support:* Fellowships with full and partial tuition reimbursements, career-related internships or fieldwork, Federal Work-Study, and institutionally sponsored loans available. Financial award application deadline: 2/1. *Faculty research:* Culture, literature, and area studies; technology-assisted language instruction; linguistics.

Boston College, Graduate School of Arts and Sciences, Department of Slavic and Eastern Languages, Program in Russian and Slavic Languages and Literature, Chestnut Hill, MA 02467-3800. Offers MA, MA/JD, MBA/MA. Part-time programs available. *Degree requirements:* For master's, 3 foreign languages, comprehensive exam, thesis or alternative. *Entrance requirements:* Additional exam requirements/recommendations for international students: Required—TOEFL (minimum score 550 paper-based; 213 computer-based). *Application deadline:* For fall admission, 1/15 for domestic students. Application fee: $70. Electronic applications accepted. *Financial support:* Teaching assistantships, Federal Work-Study available. Support available to part-time students. Financial award application deadline: 3/1; financial award applicants required to submit FAFSA. *Faculty research:* Structural analysis of language, poetry and semiotic systems.

Brown University, Graduate School, Department of Slavic Languages, Providence, RI 02912. Offers Russian (AM, PhD); Slavic languages (AM, PhD). *Degree requirements:* For master's, one foreign language; for doctorate, 2 foreign languages, thesis/dissertation, preliminary exam.

Bryn Mawr College, Graduate School of Arts and Sciences, Department of Russian, Bryn Mawr, PA 19010-2899. Offers MA, PhD. Part-time programs available. *Faculty:* 4. *Students:* 5 full-time (4 women), 10 part-time (7 women), 3 international. In 2007, 3 master's, 1 doctorate awarded. *Degree requirements:* For master's, one foreign language, thesis; for doctorate, 2 foreign languages, comprehensive exam, thesis/dissertation. *Entrance requirements:* For master's and doctorate, GRE General Test. Additional exam requirements/recommendations for international students: Required—TOEFL (minimum score 600 paper-based; 250 computer-based). *Application deadline:* For fall admission, 1/3 for domestic and international students. Application fee: $30. *Financial support:* Fellowships with full tuition reimbursements, teaching assistantships with partial tuition reimbursements, scholarships/grants available. Support available to part-time students. Financial award application deadline: 1/3. *Unit head:* Dr. Elizabeth Allen, Chairman, 610-526-5188, E-mail: eallen@brynmawr.edu. *Application contact:* Lea R. Miller, Secretary, 610-526-5072, Fax: 610-526-5076, E-mail: lrmiller@brynmawr.edu.

Columbia University, Graduate School of Arts and Sciences, Division of Humanities, Department of Slavic Languages, New York, NY 10027. Offers Russian literature (M Phil, MA, PhD); Slavic languages (M Phil, MA, PhD). *Faculty:* 9 full-time, 1 part-time/adjunct. *Students:* 34 full-time (23 women), 5 part-time (3 women); includes 3 minority (2 Asian Americans or Pacific Islanders, 1 Hispanic American), 6 international. Average age 34. 39 applicants, 54% accepted. In 2007, 9 master's, 2 doctorates awarded. *Degree requirements:* For master's, one foreign language, thesis; for doctorate, 2 foreign languages, thesis/dissertation. *Entrance requirements:* For master's and doctorate, GRE General Test. Additional exam requirements/recommendations for international students: Required—TOEFL. Application fee: $90. *Expenses:* Tuition: Part-time $1,452 per credit. Required fees: $152 per term. One-time fee: $75 part-time. Full-time tuition and fees vary according to course level, course load, degree level and program. *Financial support:* Fellowships, teaching assistantships, Federal Work-Study and institutionally sponsored loans available. Support available to part-time students. Financial award application deadline: 1/5; financial award applicants required to submit FAFSA. *Faculty research:* Polish, Serbo-Croatian, Czechoslovakian, medieval and modern Russian literature. *Unit head:* Cathy Popkin, Chair, 212-854-3941, Fax: 212-854-5009, E-mail: cp18@columbia.edu.

Harvard University, Graduate School of Arts and Sciences, Department of Slavic Languages and Literatures, Cambridge, MA 02138. Offers Polish (PhD); Russian (PhD); Serbo-Croatian (PhD); Slavic philology (PhD); Ukrainian (PhD). *Degree requirements:* For doctorate, 4 foreign languages, thesis/dissertation. *Entrance requirements:* For doctorate, GRE General Test, writing sample. Additional exam requirements/recommendations for international students: Required—TOEFL. *Expenses:* Tuition: Full-time $31,456. Full-time tuition and fees vary according to program and student level.

Hofstra University, School of Education and Allied Human Services, Department of Curriculum and Teaching, Program in Foreign Language Education, Hempstead, NY 11549. Offers French (MA, MS Ed); German (MA, MS Ed); Russian (MA, MS Ed); Spanish (MA, MS Ed). Part-time and evening/weekend programs available. *Students:* 3 full-time (all women), 5 part-time (all women); includes 2 minority (1 African American, 1 Hispanic American). Average age 35. 9 applicants, 100% accepted, 4 enrolled. In 2007, 8 degrees awarded. *Degree requirements:* For master's, one foreign language, thesis. *Entrance requirements:* For master's, 2 letters of recommendation, teacher certification (MA), essay. Additional exam requirements/recommendations for international students: Required—TOEFL (minimum score 550 paper-based; 213 computer-based). *Application deadline:* Applications are processed on a rolling basis. Application fee: $60. Electronic applications accepted. *Expenses:* Tuition: Full-time $14,220; part-time $820 per credit. Required fees: $970; $165 per term. Tuition and fees vary according to program. *Financial support:* In 2007–08, 1 student received support; fellowships with tuition reimbursements available, research assistantships with full and partial tuition reimbursements available, Federal Work-Study, institutionally sponsored loans, scholarships/grants, and tuition waivers (full and partial) available. Support available to part-time students. Financial award applicants required to submit FAFSA. *Faculty research:* Current literature from France and Francophone world, George Sand, music and literature, colonial and postcolonial studies, contemporary Latin American poetry. *Unit head:* Dr. Lori J. Ultsch, Chairperson, 516-463-4519, Fax: 516-463-2310, E-mail: rllju@mail1.hofstra.edu. *Application contact:* Carol Drummer, Dean of Graduate Admissions, 516-463-4876, Fax: 516-463-4664, E-mail: gradstudent@hofstra.edu.

Kent State University, College of Arts and Sciences, Department of Modern and Classical Language Studies, Kent, OH 44242-0001. Offers French literature (MA); French, Spanish, German and Latin pedagogy (MA); German literature (MA); Spanish literature (MA); translation (MA), including French, German, Japanese, Russian, Spanish; translation studies (PhD). Part-time and evening/weekend programs available. *Faculty:* 31 full-time (15 women), 4 part-time/adjunct (2 women). *Students:* 64 full-time (45 women), 27 part-time (26 women). Average age 32. 113 applicants, 80% accepted, 42 enrolled. In 2007, 27 degrees awarded. *Degree requirements:* For master's, one foreign language, comprehensive exam (for some programs), thesis (for some programs); for doctorate, comprehensive exam, thesis/dissertation (for some programs). *Entrance requirements:* For master's, minimum GPA of 3.0, writing sample, audio tape or CD; for doctorate, 3 recommendations. Additional exam requirements/recommendations for international students: Required—TOEFL (minimum score 197 computer-based). *Application deadline:* For fall admission, 2/28 for domestic and international students. Applications are processed on a rolling basis. Application fee: $30. Electronic applications accepted. *Financial support:* In 2007–08, 31 teaching assistantships with full tuition reimbursements (averaging $8,000 per year) were awarded; research assistantships with full tuition reimbursements, career-related internships or fieldwork, Federal Work-Study, health care benefits, tuition waivers (full and partial), and unspecified assistantships also available. Support available to part-time students. Financial award application deadline: 2/1. *Faculty research:* Literature, pedagogy, applied linguistics, translation studies. *Unit head:* Dr. Gregory M Shreve, Chair, 330-672-1796, Fax: 330-672-4009, E-mail: gshreve@kent.edu. *Application contact:* Carol S. Maier, Graduate Coordinator, 330-672-1797, Fax: 330-672-4009, E-mail: cmaier@kent.edu.

McGill University, Faculty of Graduate and Postdoctoral Studies, Faculty of Arts, Department of Russian and Slavic Studies, Montréal, QC H3A 2T5, Canada. Offers Russian literature (MA, PhD). *Faculty:* 3 full-time (2 women), 5 part-time/adjunct (4 women). *Students:* 4 full-time (3 women). 5 applicants, 60% accepted, 1 enrolled. In 2007, 2 degrees awarded.

Middlebury College, Language Schools, Russian School, Middlebury, VT 05753-6002. Offers MA, DML. *Faculty:* 6 full-time (3 women). *Students:* 35 full-time (21 women); includes 4 minority (all Asian Americans or Pacific Islanders) Average age 30. 66 applicants, 56% accepted, 35 enrolled. In 2007, 8 degrees awarded. *Degree requirements:* For master's, one foreign language; for doctorate, 2 foreign languages, thesis/dissertation. *Entrance requirements:* For master's, placement exam, 3 letters of recommendation, writing sample. *Application deadline:* Applications are processed on a rolling basis. Application fee: $55. Electronic applications accepted. *Financial support:* Scholarships/grants available. *Unit head:* Dr. Karen Evans-Romaine, Director, 802-443-5230, Fax: 802-443-2075, E-mail: kevansroe@middlebury.edu. *Application contact:* John Stokes, Coordinator, 802-443-5230, Fax: 802-443-2075, E-mail: jstokes@middlebury.edu.

New York University, Graduate School of Arts and Science, Department of Russian and Slavic Studies, New York, NY 10012-1019. Offers Russian literature (MA); Slavic literature (MA). Part-time programs available. *Faculty:* 8 full-time (3 women). *Students:* 1 full-time (0 women), 3 part-time (1 woman). Average age 28. 10 applicants, 90% accepted, 1 enrolled. In 2007, 3 degrees awarded. *Degree requirements:* For master's, one foreign language, comprehensive exam, thesis. *Entrance requirements:* For master's, GRE General Test, minimum 3 years of undergraduate Russian or equivalent. Additional exam requirements/recommendations for international students: Required—TOEFL. *Application deadline:* For fall admission, 4/15 for domestic students; for spring admission, 11/1 for domestic students. Application fee: $85. *Financial support:* Career-related internships or fieldwork, Federal Work-Study, and institutionally sponsored loans available. Financial award application deadline: 4/15; financial award applicants required to submit FAFSA. *Faculty research:* Modern Russian literature and art, contemporary Russian and East European literature, literary theory, Slavic linguistics, Russian journalism. *Unit head:* Eliot Borenstein, Chair, 212-998-8670, Fax: 212-995-4606, E-mail: gsas.russian.and.slavic@nyu.edu. *Application contact:* Yanni Katsanis, Director of Graduate Studies, 212-998-8670, Fax: 212-995-4604, E-mail: gsas.russian.and.slavic@nyu.edu.

Penn State University Park, Graduate School, College of the Liberal Arts, Department of Languages and Literature, State College, University Park, PA 16802-1503. Offers comparative literature (MA, PhD); Russian and comparative literature (MA). *Expenses:* Tuition, state resident: full-time $14,738; part-time $614 per credit. Tuition, nonresident: full-time $26,050; part-time $1,085 per credit. Tuition and fees vary according to course load, program and student level. *Unit head:* Dr. Caroline D. Eckhardt, Head, 814-863-0589, Fax: 814-863-8882, E-mail: e82@psu.edu.

Stanford University, School of Humanities and Sciences, Department of Slavic Languages and Literatures, Stanford, CA 94305-9991. Offers Russian (MA); Slavic languages and literatures (PhD). Terminal master's awarded for partial completion of doctoral program. *Degree requirements:* For master's, one foreign language, thesis or alternative; for doctorate, 3 foreign languages, thesis/dissertation. *Entrance requirements:* For master's and doctorate, GRE General Test. Additional exam requirements/recommendations for international students: Required—TOEFL. Electronic applications accepted.

University at Albany, State University of New York, College of Arts and Sciences, Department of Languages, Literatures, and Cultures, Program in Russian, Albany, NY 12222-0001. Offers Russian (MA); Russian translation (Certificate). *Application deadline:* For fall admission, 4/1 priority date for domestic students. Application fee: $75. *Expenses:* Tuition, state resident: part-time $576 per credit. Tuition, nonresident: part-time $910 per credit. Tuition and fees vary according to program. *Faculty research:* Translation, phonology and morphology of modern Russian. *Unit head:* HenryK Baran, Chair, Department of Languages, Literatures, and Cultures, 518-442-4222.

The University of Arizona, Graduate College, College of Humanities, Department of Russian and Slavic Studies, Tucson, AZ 85721. Offers Russian (M Ed, MA). Part-time programs available. *Faculty:* 10. *Students:* 15 full-time (11 women), 3 part-time (2 women); includes 1 minority (Hispanic American), 3 international. Average age 30. 10 applicants, 70% accepted, 6 enrolled. In 2007, 3 degrees awarded. *Degree requirements:* For master's, one foreign language, comprehensive exam (for some programs), thesis (for some programs). *Entrance requirements:* For master's, department language proficiency exam, minimum GPA of 3.0, statement of purpose, 3 letters of recommendation, audio sample. Additional exam requirements/recommendations for international students: Required—TOEFL (minimum score 550 paper-based). *Application deadline:* For fall admission, 4/1 for domestic students, 12/1 for international students; for spring admission, 10/1 for domestic students, 6/1 for international students. Applications are processed on a rolling basis. Application fee: $50. Electronic applications accepted. *Financial support:* In 2007–08, 16 students received support, including 7 teaching assistantships with full tuition reimbursements available (averaging $13,500 per year); fellowships, Federal Work-Study, scholarships/grants, and tuition waivers (full) also available. *Faculty research:* Russian literature, language/pedagogy, linguistics, Russian culture. *Unit head:* Dr. Teresa Polowy, Head, 520-621-7341, Fax: 520-626-4007, E-mail: tpolowy@email.arizona.edu. *Application contact:* Judi Greil, Coordinator, 520-621-3702, Fax: 520-626-4007, E-mail: greilj@u.arizona.edu.

University of California, Berkeley, Graduate Division, College of Letters and Science, Department of Slavic Languages and Literatures, Berkeley, CA 94720-1500. Offers Czech (PhD), including Czech linguistics, Czech literature; Polish (PhD), including Polish linguistics, Polish literature; Russian (PhD), including Russian linguistics, Russian literature; Serbo-Croatian (PhD), including Serbo-Croatian linguistics, Serbo-Croatian literature. *Faculty:* 15 full-time. Terminal master's awarded for partial completion of doctoral program. *Degree requirements:* For doctorate, thesis/dissertation, oral and written exams. *Entrance requirements:* For doctorate, GRE General Test, minimum GPA of 3.0, 3 letters of recommendation. Additional exam requirements/recommendations for international students: Required—TOEFL (minimum score 570 paper-based; 230 computer-based). *Application deadline:* For fall admission, 12/15 for domestic students. Application fee: $70 ($90 for international students). Electronic applications accepted. *Financial support:* Fellowships, research assistantships, teaching assistantships, unspecified assistantships available. Financial award applicants required to submit FAFSA. *Unit head:* David Frick, Chair, 510-642-8623, E-mail: frick@berkeley.edu. *Application contact:* Sandy Jones, Student Affairs Officer, 510-642-9051, Fax: 510-643-6220, E-mail: issag@berkeley.edu.

University of Michigan, Horace H. Rackham School of Graduate Studies, College of Literature, Science, and the Arts, Department of Slavic Languages and Literatures, Ann Arbor, MI 48109. Offers Russian (AM); Slavic languages and literatures (PhD). *Faculty:* 9 full-time (2 women), 10 part-time/adjunct (8 women). *Students:* 7 full-time (4 women), 3 international. 13 applicants, 46% accepted, 4 enrolled. In 2007, 1 degree awarded. *Degree requirements:* For master's, 2 foreign languages, comprehensive exam; for doctorate, 3 foreign languages, comprehensive exam, thesis/dissertation, oral defense of dissertation, preliminary exam. *Entrance requirements:* For master's, GRE General Test, 3rd year foreign language proficiency; for doctorate, GRE General Test, master's degree. Additional exam requirements/recommendations for international students: Required—TOEFL (minimum score 560 paper-based; 220 computer-based). *Application deadline:* For fall admission, 1/15 priority date for domestic and international students. Applications are processed on a rolling basis. Application fee: $60 ($75 for international students). Electronic applications accepted. *Financial support:* In 2007–08, 7 students received support, including 4 fellowships with full tuition reimbursements available (averaging $15,000 per year), 7 teaching assistantships with full tuition reimbursements available (averaging $15,199 per year); Federal Work-Study, institutionally sponsored loans, scholarships/grants, health care benefits, and unspecified assistantships also available. Financial award application deadline: 1/15; financial award applicants required to submit FAFSA. *Faculty research:* Russian literature (all periods), Polish literature, Slavic linguistics, Czech literature, Ukrainian literature. *Unit head:* Dr. Herbert J. Eagle, Chair, 734-764-5355, Fax: 734-647-2127, E-mail: hjeagle@umich.edu. *Application contact:* Amanda Apostol, Student Services Assistant, 734-764-5355, Fax: 734-647-2127, E-mail: slavic@umich.edu.

The University of North Carolina at Chapel Hill, Graduate School, College of Arts and Sciences, Department of Slavic Languages and Literatures, Chapel Hill, NC 27599. Offers Polish literature (PhD); Russian literature (MA, PhD); Serbo-Croatian literature (PhD); Slavic linguistics (MA, PhD). Part-time programs available. Terminal master's awarded for partial completion of doctoral program. *Degree requirements:* For master's, 2 foreign languages, comprehensive exam, thesis; for doctorate, 4 foreign languages, comprehensive exam, thesis/dissertation. *Entrance requirements:* For master's and doctorate, GRE General Test, minimum GPA of 3.0. Electronic applications accepted. *Faculty research:* Russian cultural studies, literary translation, sociolinguistics, cognitive linguistics, émigré literature.

University of Oregon, Graduate School, College of Arts and Sciences, Program in Russian and East European Studies, Eugene, OR 97403. Offers MA. Part-time programs available. *Faculty:* 3 full-time (2 women), 1 part-time/adjunct (0 women). *Students:* 4 full-time (3 women), 1 (woman) part-time, 2 international. 11 applicants, 55% accepted. In 2007, 2 degrees awarded. *Degree requirements:* For master's, 2 foreign languages, thesis. *Entrance requirements:* For master's, GRE General Test (recommended), minimum GPA of 3.0. Additional exam requirements/recommendations for international students: Required—TOEFL. *Application deadline:* For fall admission, 1/15 for domestic students. Application fee: $50. *Financial support:* In 2007–08, 3 teaching assistantships were awarded; Federal Work-Study also available. Financial award application deadline: 3/15. *Faculty research:* L. N. Tolstoy's middle years, Russian folklore in eighteenth century contexts, Bulgarian syntax, medieval Bulgarian texts, contemporary Russian culture film. *Unit head:* Julie Hessler, Head, 541-346-4001, Fax: 541-346-1327. *Application contact:* Daniel Gorman, Coordinator, 541-346-2850, Fax: 541-346-0802, E-mail: dqgorman@uoregon.edu.

University of South Africa, College of Human Sciences, Pretoria, South Africa. Offers adult education (M Ed); African languages (MA, PhD); African politics (MA, PhD); Afrikaans (MA, PhD); ancient history (MA, PhD); ancient Near Eastern studies (MA, PhD); anthropology (MA, PhD); applied linguistics (MA); Arabic (MA, PhD); archaeology (MA); art history (MA); Biblical archaeology (MA); Biblical studies (M Th, D Th, PhD); Christian spirituality (M Th, D Th); church history (M Th, D Th); classical studies (MA, PhD); clinical psychology (MA); communication (MA, PhD); comparative education (M Ed, Ed D); consulting psychology (D Admin, D Com, PhD); curriculum studies (M Ed, Ed D); development studies (M Admin, MA, D Admin, PhD); didactics (M Ed, Ed D); education (M Tech); education management (M Ed, Ed D); educational psychology (M Ed); English (MA); environmental education (M Ed); French (MA, PhD); German (MA, PhD); Greek (MA); guidance and counseling (M Ed); health studies (MA, PhD), including health sciences education (MA), health services management (MA), medical and surgical nursing science (critical care general) (MA), midwifery and neonatal nursing science (MA), trauma and emergency care (MA); history (MA, PhD); history of education (Ed D); inclusive education (M Ed, Ed D); information and communications technology policy and regulation (MA); information science (MA, MIS, PhD); international politics (MA, PhD); Islamic studies (MA, PhD); Italian (MA, PhD); Judaica (MA, PhD); linguistics (MA, PhD); mathematical education (M Ed); mathematics education (MA); missiology (M Th, D Th); modern Hebrew (MA, PhD); musicology (MA, MMus, D Mus, PhD); natural science education (M Ed); New Testament (M Th, D Th); Old Testament (D Th); pastoral therapy (M Th, D Th); philosophy (MA); philosophy of education (M Ed, Ed D); politics (MA, PhD); Portuguese (MA, PhD); practical theology (M Th, D Th); psychology (MA, MS, PhD); psychology of education (M Ed, Ed D); public health (MA); religious studies (MA, D Th, PhD); Romance languages (MA); Russian (MA, PhD); Semitic languages (MA, PhD); social behavior studies in HIV/AIDS (MA); social science (mental health) (MA); social science in development studies (MA); social science in psychology (MA); social science in social work (MA); social science in sociology (MA); social work (MSW, DSW, PhD); socio-education (M Ed, Ed D); sociolinguistics (MA); sociology (MA, PhD); Spanish (MA, PhD); systematic theology (M Th, D Th); TESOL (teaching English to speakers of other languages) (MA); theological ethics (M Th, D Th); theory of literature (MA, PhD); urban ministries (D Th); urban ministry (M Th).

The University of Tennessee, Graduate School, College of Arts and Sciences, Department of Modern Foreign Languages and Literatures, Program in Modern Foreign Languages, Knoxville, TN 37996. Offers applied linguistics (PhD); French (PhD); German (PhD); Italian (PhD); Portuguese (PhD); Russian (PhD); Spanish (PhD). *Degree requirements:* For doctorate, 2 foreign languages, thesis/dissertation. *Entrance requirements:* For doctorate, minimum GPA of 2.7. Additional exam requirements/recommendations for international students: Required—TOEFL. Electronic applications accepted.

University of Washington, Graduate School, College of Arts and Sciences, Department of Slavic Languages and Literature, Seattle, WA 98195. Offers Russian literature (MA, PhD); Slavic linguistics (MA, PhD). *Degree requirements:* For master's, 2 foreign languages, thesis optional; for doctorate, 3 foreign languages, thesis/dissertation. *Entrance requirements:* For master's and doctorate, GRE General Test, minimum GPA of 3.0. Additional exam requirements/recommendations for international students: Required—TOEFL. Electronic applications accepted. *Faculty research:* Modern and medieval East European languages and literatures, comparative literature, Russian folk literature, Slavic literary theory and criticism, computerized morphology of Russian.

University of Waterloo, Graduate Studies, Faculty of Arts, Department of Germanic and Slavic Studies, Waterloo, ON N2L 3G1, Canada. Offers German (MA, PhD); Russian (MA). Part-time and evening/weekend programs available. *Faculty:* 11 full-time (3 women), 6 part-time/adjunct (4 women). *Students:* 71. 30 applicants, 93% accepted, 18 enrolled. In 2007, 5 degrees awarded. *Degree requirements:* For master's, one foreign language, thesis optional; for doctorate, 2 foreign languages, comprehensive exam, thesis/dissertation. *Entrance requirements:* For master's, honors degree, minimum B average; for doctorate, master's degree, minimum B average. Additional exam requirements/recommendations for international students: Required—TOEFL, TWE. *Application deadline:* For fall admission, 2/1 for domestic students. Application fee: $75 Canadian dollars. Electronic applications accepted. *Financial support:* Teaching assistantships, scholarships/grants available. *Faculty research:* Medieval theatre; history and literature; German and Russian literary relations; seventeenth, eighteenth, nineteenth, and twentieth century German literature. *Unit head:* Dr. Michael Boehringer, Acting Chair, E-mail: mboehringer@uwaterloo.ca. *Application contact:* Janet Vaughan, Contact, 519-888-4567 Ext. 2428, E-mail: jvaughan@uwaterloo.ca.

Wayne State University, College of Liberal Arts and Sciences, Department of Classical and Modern Languages, Literatures, and Cultures, Program in German and Slavic Studies, Detroit, MI

Russian

Wayne State University (continued)
48202. Offers German (MA); language learning (MA); modern languages (PhD); Russian (MA). *Faculty:* 15 full-time (6 women). *Students:* 5 full-time (4 women), 2 part-time (both women), 3 international. Average age 31. 2 applicants, 100% accepted, 1 enrolled. In 2007, 1 degree awarded. *Degree requirements:* For master's, one foreign language, thesis or alternative; for doctorate, 2 foreign languages, thesis/dissertation. *Entrance requirements:* For master's and doctorate, minimum GPA of 3.0. Additional exam requirements/recommendations for international students: Required—TOEFL (minimum score 550 paper-based; 213 computer-based); Recommended—TWE (minimum score 6). *Application deadline:* For fall admission, 7/1 for domestic students, 6/1 for international students; for winter admission, 10/1 for international students; for spring admission, 2/1 for international students. Applications are processed on a rolling basis. Application fee: $30 ($50 for international students). Electronic applications accepted. *Expenses:* Tuition, state resident: part-time $403 per credit hour. Tuition, nonresident: part-time $890 per credit hour. *Financial support:* In 2007–08, 3 teaching assistantships with tuition reimbursements (averaging $12,447 per year) were awarded; fellowships, research assistantships, scholarships/grants and tuition waivers (full and partial) also available. Support available to part-time students. *Faculty research:* Exile and Holocaust, minority literature, gender studies, fairytale studies, sociolinguistics.

Scandinavian Languages

Cornell University, Graduate School, Graduate Fields of Arts and Sciences, Field of Germanic Studies, Ithaca, NY 14853-0001. Offers German area studies (MA, PhD); German intellectual history (MA, PhD); Germanic linguistics (MA, PhD); Germanic literature (MA, PhD); old Norse (MA, PhD). *Faculty:* 19 full-time (9 women). *Students:* 17 full-time (6 women), 6 international. Average age 28. 26 applicants, 38% accepted, 4 enrolled. In 2007, 1 master's, 5 doctorates awarded. Terminal master's awarded for partial completion of doctoral program. *Degree requirements:* For master's, one foreign language, thesis; for doctorate, 2 foreign languages, comprehensive exam, thesis/dissertation. *Entrance requirements:* For master's and doctorate, GRE General Test, fluency in German, writing sample, 2 letters of recommendation. Additional exam requirements/recommendations for international students: Required—TOEFL (minimum score 550 paper-based; 213 computer-based; 77 iBT). *Application deadline:* For fall admission, 1/15 for domestic students. Application fee: $70. Electronic applications accepted. *Financial support:* In 2007–08, 20 students received support, including 6 fellowships with full tuition reimbursements available, 14 teaching assistantships with full tuition reimbursements available; research assistantships with full tuition reimbursements available, institutionally sponsored loans, scholarships/grants, health care benefits, tuition waivers (full and partial), and unspecified assistantships also available. Financial award applicants required to submit FAFSA. *Faculty research:* Women's studies, minority literature, literature and intellectual history, theater and film studies, continental philosophy. *Unit head:* Director of Graduate Studies, 607-255-4047. *Application contact:* Graduate Field Assistant, 607-255-4047, E-mail: germanic_studies@cornell.edu.

Harvard University, Graduate School of Arts and Sciences, Department of Germanic Languages and Literatures, Cambridge, MA 02138. Offers German (PhD); Scandinavian (PhD). Terminal master's awarded for partial completion of doctoral program. *Degree requirements:* For doctorate, 2 foreign languages, thesis/dissertation, exams. *Entrance requirements:* For doctorate, GRE General Test, German writing sample. Additional exam requirements/recommendations for international students: Required—TOEFL. *Expenses:* Tuition: Full-time $31,456. Full-time tuition and fees vary according to program and student level.

University of California, Berkeley, Graduate Division, College of Letters and Science, Department of Scandinavian Languages and Literatures, Berkeley, CA 94720-1500. Offers PhD. *Faculty:* 6 full-time. *Degree requirements:* For doctorate, 2 foreign languages, thesis/dissertation, 3 field papers, qualifying exam. *Entrance requirements:* For doctorate, GRE General Test, minimum GPA of 3.0, MA in Scandinavian language or equivalent, 3 letters of recommendation. Additional exam requirements/recommendations for international students: Required—TOEFL (minimum score 570 paper-based; 230 computer-based). *Application deadline:* For fall admission, 12/15 for domestic students. Application fee: $70 ($90 for international students). *Financial support:* Fellowships, teaching assistantships, unspecified assistantships available. *Faculty research:* Modern literatures, old Norse language and literatures, folklore, film, interdisciplinary. *Application contact:* Sandy Jones, Student Affairs Officer, 510-642-9051, Fax: 510-643-6220, E-mail: issag@berkeley.edu.

University of California, Los Angeles, Graduate Division, College of Letters and Science, Department of Germanic Languages, Program in Scandinavian, Los Angeles, CA 90095. Offers MA. *Degree requirements:* For master's, one foreign language, comprehensive exam. *Entrance requirements:* For master's, GRE General Test, sample of written work. *Application deadline:* For fall admission, 12/15 for domestic students. Application fee: $60. Electronic applications accepted. *Expenses:* Tuition, nonresident: full-time $5,728. Required fees:$8,966. Full-time tuition and fees vary according to program and student level. *Financial support:* In 2007–08, 1 fellowship with full and partial tuition reimbursement, 1 teaching assistantship with full and partial tuition reimbursement were awarded; research assistantships with full and partial tuition reimbursements, Federal Work-Study and institutionally sponsored loans also available. Financial award application deadline: 3/1; financial award applicants required to submit FAFSA. *Unit head:* Jim Massengale, Vice Chair, 310-825-6828. *Application contact:* Departmental Office, 310-825-6828, E-mail: allen@humnet.ucla.edu.

University of Minnesota, Twin Cities Campus, Graduate School, College of Liberal Arts, Department of German, Scandinavian, and Dutch, Minneapolis, MN 55455-0213. Offers Germanic studies: German and Scandinavian studies track (PhD); Germanic studies: German track (MA, PhD); Germanic studies: Germanic medieval studies track (MA, PhD); Germanic studies: Scandinavian studies track (MA); Germanic studies: teaching track (MA). Part-time programs available. *Faculty:* 19 full-time (8 women). *Students:* 22 full-time (14 women), 6 part-time (4 women); includes 2 minority (1 African American, 1 Hispanic American), 10 international. 31 applicants, 61% accepted, 8 enrolled. In 2007, 1 master's, 6 doctorates awarded. Terminal master's awarded for partial completion of doctoral program. *Degree requirements:* For doctorate, 2 foreign languages, thesis/dissertation. *Entrance requirements:* For master's, GRE General Test, BA in German, Scandinavian, or equivalent; for doctorate, GRE General Test, MA in German, Scandinavian, or equivalent. Additional exam requirements/recommendations for international students: Required—TOEFL (minimum score 550 paper-based; 213 computer-based; 79 iBT). *Application deadline:* For fall admission, 12/15 for domestic and international students. Application fee: $55 ($75 for international students). Electronic applications accepted. *Financial support:* In 2007–08, 85 fellowships with full tuition reimbursements (averaging $18,000 per year), 1 research assistantship with full tuition reimbursement (averaging $11,985 per year), 14 teaching assistantships with full tuition reimbursements (averaging $12,839 per year) were awarded; career-related internships or fieldwork, Federal Work-Study, institutionally sponsored loans, scholarships/grants, health care benefits, and unspecified assistantships also available. Support available to part-time students. Financial award application deadline: 1/10. *Faculty research:* Cultural studies, literary theory, feminist criticism, film, Germanic philology. *Unit head:* Prof. Charlotte Melin, Chair, 612-625-2080, Fax: 612-624-8297, E-mail: melin005@umn.edu. *Application contact:* Director of Graduate Studies, 612-625-9034, Fax: 612-624-8297, E-mail: gsd@umn.edu.

University of Washington, Graduate School, College of Arts and Sciences, Department of Scandinavian Studies, Seattle, WA 98195. Offers MA, PhD. *Degree requirements:* For master's, one foreign language, comprehensive exam, thesis optional; for doctorate, 2 foreign languages, comprehensive exam, thesis/dissertation. *Entrance requirements:* For master's, GRE, BA in Scandinavian or equivalent, minimum GPA of 3.0; for doctorate, GRE, master's degree, minimum GPA of 3.0. Additional exam requirements/recommendations for international students: Required—TOEFL. *Faculty research:* Scandinavian folklore, history, and politics; medieval to modern Scandinavian literature; Scandinavian fiction, poetry, drama, literary history, and theory.

University of Wisconsin–Madison, Graduate School, College of Letters and Science, Department of Scandinavian Studies, Madison, WI 53706-1380. Offers MA, PhD. Part-time programs available. *Degree requirements:* For master's, 2 foreign languages, exam; for doctorate, thesis/dissertation, exam. *Entrance requirements:* For master's, minimum GPA of 3.25; for doctorate, minimum GPA of 3.5. Electronic applications accepted. *Faculty research:* Historical fiction, Icelandic poetry, nineteenth-century literature, theater, gender studies, folklore.

Slavic Languages

Boston College, Graduate School of Arts and Sciences, Department of Slavic and Eastern Languages, Program in Russian and Slavic Languages and Literature, Chestnut Hill, MA 02467-3800. Offers MA, MA/JD, MBA/MA. Part-time programs available. *Degree requirements:* For master's, 3 foreign languages, comprehensive exam, thesis or alternative. *Entrance requirements:* Additional exam requirements/recommendations for international students: Required—TOEFL (minimum score 550 paper-based; 213 computer-based). *Application deadline:* For fall admission, 1/15 for domestic students. Application fee: $70. Electronic applications accepted. *Financial support:* Teaching assistantships, Federal Work-Study available. Support available to part-time students. Financial award application deadline: 3/1; financial award applicants required to submit FAFSA. *Faculty research:* Structural analysis of language, poetry and semiotic systems.

Brown University, Graduate School, Department of Slavic Languages, Providence, RI 02912. Offers Russian (AM, PhD); Slavic languages (AM, PhD). *Degree requirements:* For master's, one foreign language; for doctorate, 2 foreign languages, thesis/dissertation, preliminary exam.

Columbia University, Graduate School of Arts and Sciences, Division of Humanities, Department of Slavic Languages, New York, NY 10027. Offers Russian literature (M Phil, MA, PhD); Slavic languages (M Phil, MA, PhD). *Faculty:* 9 full-time, 1 part-time/adjunct. *Students:* 34 full-time (23 women), 5 part-time (3 women); includes 3 minority (2 Asian Americans or Pacific Islanders, 1 Hispanic American), 6 international. Average age 34. 39 applicants, 54% accepted. In 2007, 9 master's, 2 doctorates awarded. *Degree requirements:* For master's, one foreign language, thesis; for doctorate, 2 foreign languages, thesis/dissertation. *Entrance requirements:* For master's and doctorate, GRE General Test. Additional exam requirements/recommendations for international students: Required—TOEFL. Application fee: $90. *Expenses:* Tuition: Part-time $1,452 per credit. Required fees: $152 per term. One-time fee: $75 part-time. Full-time tuition and fees vary according to course level, course load, degree level and program. *Financial support:* Fellowships, teaching assistantships, Federal Work-Study and institutionally sponsored loans available. Support available to part-time students. Financial award application deadline: 1/5; financial award applicants required to submit FAFSA. *Faculty research:* Polish, Serbo-Croatian, Czechoslovakian, medieval and modern Russian literature. *Unit head:* Cathy Popkin, Chair, 212-854-3941, Fax: 212-854-5009, E-mail: cp18@columbia.edu.

Cornell University, Graduate School, Graduate Fields of Arts and Sciences, Field of Linguistics, Ithaca, NY 14853-0001. Offers applied linguistics (MA, PhD); East Asian linguistics (MA, PhD); English linguistics (MA, PhD); general linguistics (MA, PhD); Germanic linguistics (MA, PhD); Indo-European linguistics (MA, PhD); phonetics (MA, PhD); phonological theory (MA, PhD); Romance linguistics (MA, PhD); second language acquisition (MA, PhD); semantics (MA, PhD); Slavic linguistics (MA, PhD); sociolinguistics (MA, PhD); South Asian linguistics (MA, PhD); Southeast Asian linguistics (MA, PhD); syntactic theory (MA, PhD). *Faculty:* 19 full-time. *Students:* 31 full-time (16 women); includes 1 minority (Hispanic American), 19 international. Average age 28. 89 applicants, 17% accepted, 8 enrolled. In 2007, 2 master's, 1 doctorate awarded. Terminal master's awarded for partial completion of doctoral program. *Degree requirements:* For master's, one foreign language, thesis; for doctorate, one foreign language, comprehensive exam, thesis/dissertation. *Entrance requirements:* For master's and doctorate, GRE General Test, 2 letters of recommendation. Additional exam requirements/recommendations for international students: Required—TOEFL (minimum score 600 paper-based; 250 computer-based; 77 iBT). *Application deadline:* For fall admission, 1/15 for domestic students. Application fee: $70. Electronic applications accepted. *Financial support:* In 2007–08, 30 students received support, including 14 fellowships with full tuition reimbursements available, 2 research assistantships with full tuition reimbursements available, 14 teaching assistantships with full tuition reimbursements available; institutionally sponsored loans, scholarships/grants, health care benefits, tuition waivers (full and partial), and unspecified assistantships also available. Financial award applicants required to submit FAFSA. *Faculty research:* Phonology and phonetics; syntax and semantics; historical linguistics; philosophy of language; language acquisition. *Unit head:* Director of Graduate Studies, 607-255-1105. *Application contact:* Graduate Field Assistant, 607-255-1105, E-mail: lingfield@cornell.edu.

Duke University, Graduate School, Department of Slavic Languages and Literatures, Durham, NC 27708. Offers AM. Part-time programs available. *Faculty:* 7 full-time. *Students:* 1 (woman) full-time. *Entrance requirements:* For master's, GRE General Test. Additional exam requirements/recommendations for international students: Required—TOEFL (minimum score 550 paper-based; 213 computer-based; 83 iBT), IELTS (minimum score 7). *Application deadline:* For fall admission, 12/15 priority date for domestic and international students. Application fee: $75. Electronic applications accepted. *Financial support:* Application deadline: 12/31. *Unit* *head:* JoAnne VanTuyl, Director of Graduate Studies, 919-660-3140, Fax: 919-660-3141, E-mail: bhayes@duke.edu.

Florida State University, Graduate Studies, College of Arts and Sciences, Department of Modern Languages, Program in Slavic Languages/Russian, Tallahassee, FL 32306. Offers Slavic languages and literatures (MA). *Faculty:* 3 full-time (2 women). *Students:* 4 full-time (1 woman). Average age 24. 2 applicants, 100% accepted, 2 enrolled. In 2007, 2 degrees awarded. *Degree requirements:* For master's, thesis optional. *Entrance requirements:* For master's, GRE General Test or minimum GPA of 3.0. Additional exam requirements/recommendations for international students: Required—TOEFL (minimum score 550 paper-based; 213 computer-based). *Application deadline:* For fall admission, 2/1 for domestic and international students; for spring admission, 11/22 for domestic and international students. Applications are processed on a rolling basis. Application fee: $30. Electronic applications accepted. *Expenses:* Tuition, state resident: part-time $248 per credit hour. Tuition, nonresident: part-time $880 per credit hour. Tuition and fees vary according to program. *Financial support:* In 2007–08, 3 students received support, including 3 teaching assistantships with partial tuition reimbursements available (averaging $10,200 per year); fellowships, institutionally sponsored loans also available. Financial award application deadline: 2/1; financial award applicants required to submit FAFSA. *Faculty research:* Contemporary literature, emigré literature, Old Russian word formation, political rhetoric, structure of modern Russian. Total annual research expenditures: $4,500. *Unit head:* Dr. Robert Romanchuk, Divisional Coordinator, 850-644-8198, Fax: 850-644-0524, E-mail: rromanch@fsu.edu. *Application contact:* Wendy E. Pigott, Graduate Academic Coordinator, 850-644-8397, Fax: 850-644-0524, E-mail: wpigott@fsu.edu.

Harvard University, Graduate School of Arts and Sciences, Department of Slavic Languages and Literatures, Cambridge, MA 02138. Offers Polish (PhD); Russian (PhD); Serbo-Croatian (PhD); Slavic philology (PhD); Ukrainian (PhD). *Degree requirements:* For doctorate, 4 foreign languages, thesis/dissertation. *Entrance requirements:* For doctorate, GRE General Test, writing sample. Additional exam requirements/recommendations for international students: Required—TOEFL. *Expenses:* Tuition: Full-time $31,456. Full-time tuition and fees vary according to program and student level.

Indiana University Bloomington, University Graduate School, College of Arts and Sciences, Department of Slavic Languages and Literatures, Bloomington, IN 47405-7000. Offers MA, MAT, PhD. Part-time programs available. *Faculty:* 8 full-time (3 women). *Students:* 8 full-time (all women), 4 part-time (2 women), 4 international. Average age 33. 15 applicants, 60% accepted, 1 enrolled. In 2007, 1 master's, 1 doctorate awarded. Terminal master's awarded for partial completion of doctoral program. *Degree requirements:* For master's, variable foreign language requirement; for doctorate, variable foreign language requirement, comprehensive exam, thesis/dissertation. *Entrance requirements:* For master's, GRE General Test; for doctorate, admissions exam (can be waived). *Application deadline:* Applications are processed on a rolling basis. Application fee: $50 ($60 for international students). *Financial support:* Fellowships with full tuition reimbursements, research assistantships with full tuition reimbursements, teaching assistantships with full tuition reimbursements available. Financial award application deadline: 2/1. *Faculty research:* Russian stress, Slavic accentology and morphophonemics, Eastern European literature, Bible translation. *Unit head:* Dr. Ronald F. Feldstein, Chair, 812-855-2608, E-mail: feldstei@indiana.edu. *Application contact:* Tricia Wall, Summer Program and Student Services Assistant, 812-855-2608, Fax: 812-855-2107.

New York University, Graduate School of Arts and Science, Department of Russian and Slavic Studies, New York, NY 10012-1019. Offers Russian literature (MA); Slavic literature (MA). Part-time programs available. *Faculty:* 8 full-time (3 women). *Students:* 1 full-time (0 women), 3 part-time (1 woman). Average age 28. 10 applicants, 90% accepted, 1 enrolled. In 2007, 3 degrees awarded. *Degree requirements:* For master's, one foreign language, comprehensive exam, thesis. *Entrance requirements:* For master's, GRE General Test, minimum 3 years of undergraduate Russian or equivalent. Additional exam requirements/recommendations for international students: Required—TOEFL. *Application deadline:* For fall admission, 4/15 for domestic students; for spring admission, 11/1 for domestic students. Application fee: $85. *Financial support:* Career-related internships or fieldwork, Federal Work-Study, and institutionally sponsored loans available. Financial award application deadline: 4/15; financial award applicants required to submit FAFSA. *Faculty research:* Modern Russian literature and art, contemporary Russian and East European literature, literary theory, Slavic linguistics, Russian journalism. *Unit head:* Eliot Borenstein, Chair, 212-998-8670, Fax: 212-995-4606, E-mail: gsas.russian.and.slavic@nyu.edu. *Application contact:* Yanni Katsanis, Director of Graduate Studies, 212-998-8670, Fax: 212-995-4604, E-mail: gsas.russian.and.slavic@nyu.edu.

Northwestern University, The Graduate School, Judd A. and Marjorie Weinberg College of Arts and Sciences, Department of Slavic Languages and Literature, Evanston, IL 60208. Offers PhD. Admissions and degrees offered through The Graduate School. Part-time programs available. *Degree requirements:* For doctorate, 3 foreign languages, thesis/dissertation. *Entrance requirements:* For doctorate, GRE General Test. Additional exam requirements/recommendations for international students: Required—TOEFL. *Faculty research:* Russian poetry and prose, nineteenth- through twentieth-centuries, translation and Russian culture, Russian intellectual history, Slavic literature and nationalism, Polish poetry.

The Ohio State University, Graduate School, College of Humanities, Department of Slavic and East European Languages and Literatures, Columbus, OH 43210. Offers Slavic and East European studies (MA); Slavic languages and literatures (MA, PhD). *Faculty:* 13. *Students:* 26 full-time (16 women), 8 international. Average age 30. In 2007, 7 master's, 2 doctorates awarded. *Degree requirements:* For master's, variable foreign language requirement, thesis optional; for doctorate, variable foreign language requirement, thesis/dissertation. *Entrance requirements:* For master's and doctorate, GRE General Test. Additional exam requirements/recommendations for international students: Required—TOEFL (minimum score 600 paper-based; 250 computer-based). *Application deadline:* For fall admission, 8/15 priority date for domestic students, 7/1 priority date for international students; for winter admission, 12/1 priority date for domestic students, 11/1 priority date for international students; for spring admission, 3/1 priority date for domestic students, 2/1 priority date for international students. Applications are processed on a rolling basis. Application fee: $40 ($50 for international students). Electronic applications accepted. *Financial support:* Fellowships, research assistantships, teaching assistantships, Federal Work-Study and institutionally sponsored loans available. Support available to part-time students. *Faculty research:* Polish literature. *Unit head:* Charles E. Gribble, Graduate Studies Committee Chair, 614-292-6733, Fax: 614-688-3107, E-mail: gribble.3@osu.edu. *Application contact:* 614-292-9444, Fax: 614-292-3895, E-mail: domestic.grad@osu.edu.

Princeton University, Graduate School, Department of Slavic Languages and Literatures, Princeton, NJ 08544-1019. Offers PhD. *Degree requirements:* For doctorate, variable foreign language requirement, thesis/dissertation. *Entrance requirements:* For doctorate, GRE General Test. Additional exam requirements/recommendations for international students: Required—TOEFL (minimum score 600 paper-based; 250 computer-based). Electronic applications accepted.

Stanford University, School of Humanities and Sciences, Department of Slavic Languages and Literatures, Stanford, CA 94305-9991. Offers Russian (MA); Slavic languages and literatures (PhD). Terminal master's awarded for partial completion of doctoral program. *Degree requirements:* For master's, one foreign language, thesis or alternative; for doctorate, 3 foreign languages, thesis/dissertation. *Entrance requirements:* For master's and doctorate, GRE General Test. Additional exam requirements/recommendations for international students: Required—TOEFL. Electronic applications accepted.

University of Alberta, Faculty of Graduate Studies and Research, Department of Modern Languages and Cultural Studies, Edmonton, AB T6G 2E1, Canada. Offers applied linguistics (Germanic, Romance, Slavic) (MA); French language, literatures and linguistics (PhD); French language, literatures, and linguistics (MA); Germanic languages, literatures and linguistics (PhD); Germanic languages, literatures, and linguistics (MA); Italian studies (MA); Slavic languages and literatures (Russian, Ukrainian) (MA, PhD); Slavic linguistics (Russian, Ukrainian) (MA, PhD); Spanish and Latin American studies (MA, PhD); Ukrainian folklore (MA, PhD). Part-time programs available. *Degree requirements:* For master's, one foreign language, thesis; for doctorate, 2 foreign languages, comprehensive exam, thesis/dissertation. *Entrance requirements:* For master's and doctorate, 1 language other than English. Additional exam requirements/recommendations for international students: Required—Michigan English Language Assessment Battery or TOEFL (paper score 550; computer score 213). Electronic applications accepted. *Faculty research:* Russian/Ukrainian studies; German studies; contemporary Latin American, French and Francophone studies; Italian studies.

University of California, Berkeley, Graduate Division, College of Letters and Science, Department of Slavic Languages and Literatures, Berkeley, CA 94720-1500. Offers Czech (PhD), including Czech linguistics, Czech literature; Polish (PhD), including Polish linguistics, Polish literature; Russian (PhD), including Russian linguistics, Russian literature; Serbo-Croatian (PhD), including Serbo-Croatian linguistics, Serbo-Croatian literature. *Faculty:* 15 full-time. Terminal master's awarded for partial completion of doctoral program. *Degree requirements:* For doctorate, thesis/dissertation, oral and written exams. *Entrance requirements:* For doctorate, GRE General Test, minimum GPA of 3.0, 3 letters of recommendation. Additional exam requirements/recommendations for international students: Required—TOEFL (minimum score 570 paper-based; 230 computer-based). *Application deadline:* For fall admission, 12/15 for domestic students. Application fee: $70 ($90 for international students). Electronic applications accepted. *Financial support:* Fellowships, research assistantships, teaching assistantships, unspecified assistantships available. Financial award applicants required to submit FAFSA. *Unit head:* David Frick, Chair, 510-642-8623, E-mail: frick@berkeley.edu. *Application contact:* Sandy Jones, Student Affairs Officer, 510-642-9051, Fax: 510-643-6220, E-mail: issag@berkeley.edu.

University of California, Los Angeles, Graduate Division, College of Letters and Science, Department of Slavic Languages and Literatures, Los Angeles, CA 90095. Offers MA, PhD. *Students:* 13 full-time (10 women); includes 2 minority (1 American Indian/Alaska Native, 1 Hispanic American), 1 international. Average age 29. 18 applicants, 44% accepted, 4 enrolled. In 2007, 3 master's, 1 doctorate awarded. Terminal master's awarded for partial completion of doctoral program. *Degree requirements:* For master's, 2 foreign languages, comprehensive exam; for doctorate, 2 foreign languages, thesis/dissertation, oral and written qualifying exams. *Entrance requirements:* For master's, GRE General Test, minimum GPA of 3.0, sample of written work; for doctorate, GRE General Test, minimum undergraduate GPA of 3.0, proficiency in French and German, sample of written work. *Application deadline:* For fall admission, 12/31 for domestic students. Application fee: $60. Electronic applications accepted. *Expenses:* Tuition, nonresident: full-time $5,728. Required fees: $8,966. Full-time tuition and fees vary according to program and student level. *Financial support:* In 2007–08, 10 fellowships with full and partial tuition reimbursements, 3 research assistantships with full and partial tuition reimbursements, 6 teaching assistantships with full and partial tuition reimbursements were awarded; Federal Work-Study, institutionally sponsored loans, scholarships/grants, and tuition waivers (full and partial) also available. Financial award application deadline: 3/1; financial award applicants required to submit FAFSA. *Unit head:* Dr. David MacFadyen, Chair, 310-825-8724. *Application contact:* Departmental Office, 310-825-2676, E-mail: slavic@humnet.ucla.edu.

University of Chicago, Division of the Humanities, Department of Slavic Languages and Literatures, Chicago, IL 60637-1513. Offers AM, PhD. *Students:* 27. 22 applicants, 36% accepted, 6 enrolled.Terminal master's awarded for partial completion of doctoral program. *Degree requirements:* For master's, one foreign language; for doctorate, 2 foreign languages, thesis/dissertation. *Entrance requirements:* For master's and doctorate, GRE General Test. Additional exam requirements/recommendations for international students: Required—TOEFL. *Application deadline:* For fall admission, 12/15 for domestic students. Application fee: $55. *Financial support:* Fellowships, Federal Work-Study available. Financial award application deadline: 12/15; financial award applicants required to submit FAFSA. *Unit head:* Dr. Robert Bird, Chair, 773-702-8033.

University of Illinois at Chicago, Graduate College, College of Liberal Arts and Sciences, Department of Slavic and Baltic Languages and Literatures, Chicago, IL 60607-7128. Offers Slavic languages and literatures (PhD); Slavic studies (MA). Evening/weekend programs available. Terminal master's awarded for partial completion of doctoral program. *Degree requirements:* For doctorate, one foreign language, thesis/dissertation. *Entrance requirements:* For master's and doctorate, GRE General Test, minimum GPA of 3.0. Additional exam requirements/recommendations for international students: Required—TOEFL. Electronic applications accepted.

University of Illinois at Urbana–Champaign, Graduate College, College of Liberal Arts and Sciences, School of Literatures, Cultures and Linguistics, Department of Slavic Languages and Literatures, Champaign, IL 61820. Offers MA, PhD. *Faculty:* 6 full-time (1 woman). *Students:* 6 full-time (3 women), 3 part-time (2 women), 5 international. 11 applicants, 45% accepted, 1 enrolled. *Degree requirements:* For master's, one foreign language; for doctorate, 3 foreign languages, thesis/dissertation. *Entrance requirements:* For master's, GRE, minimum GPA of 3.0. *Application deadline:* For fall admission, 1/16 for domestic students. Applications are processed on a rolling basis. Application fee: $60 ($75 for international students). Electronic applications accepted. *Financial support:* In 2007–08, 3 fellowships, 2 research assistantships, 7 teaching assistantships were awarded; tuition waivers (full and partial) also available. Financial award application deadline: 2/15. *Unit head:* Harriet Murav, Head, 217-344-3066, Fax: 217-333-7310, E-mail: hlmurav@uiuc.edu. *Application contact:* Lynn Stanke, Secretary, 217-333-6269, Fax: 217-244-3050, E-mail: stanke@uiuc.edu.

University of Kansas, Research and Graduate Studies, College of Liberal Arts and Sciences, Department of Slavic Languages and Literatures, Lawrence, KS 66045. Offers MA, PhD. Part-time programs available. *Faculty:* 9. *Students:* 12 full-time (8 women), 1 international. Average age 30. 5 applicants, 80% accepted, 1 enrolled. In 2007, 1 master's awarded. Terminal master's awarded for partial completion of doctoral program. *Degree requirements:* For master's, one foreign language, comprehensive exam, thesis or alternative; for doctorate, 3 foreign languages, comprehensive exam, thesis/dissertation, 2nd Slavic language. *Entrance requirements:* For master's, GRE, BA in Slavic languages and literatures or the equivalent; for doctorate, GRE, MA in Slavic languages and literatures. Additional exam requirements/recommendations for international students: Required—TOEFL. *Application deadline:* For winter admission, 1/31 priority date for domestic and international students. Applications are processed on a rolling basis. Application fee: $55 ($60 for international students). Electronic applications accepted. *Expenses:* Tuition, state resident: full-time $5,838. Tuition, nonresident: full-time $13,409. Tuition and fees vary according to program. *Financial support:* Fellowships with tuition reimbursements, teaching assistantships with full and partial tuition reimbursements, Federal Work-Study, institutionally sponsored loans, scholarships/grants, and unspecified assistantships available. Financial award application deadline: 1/31. *Faculty research:* Russian and South Slavic linguistics, Polish and Russian literature, folklore, Russian intellectual history. *Unit head:* Prof. Marc L. Greenberg, Chair, 785-864-3313, Fax: 785-864-4298, E-mail: mlg@ku.edu. *Application contact:* Prof. Edith W. Clowes, Graduate Director, 785-864-3313, Fax: 785-864-4298, E-mail: eclowes@ku.edu.

University of Manitoba, Faculty of Graduate Studies, Faculty of Arts, Department of German and Slavic Studies, Winnipeg, MB R3T 2N2, Canada. Offers MA. *Degree requirements:* For master's, one foreign language, thesis or alternative.

University of Michigan, Horace H. Rackham School of Graduate Studies, College of Literature, Science, and the Arts, Department of Slavic Languages and Literatures, Ann Arbor, MI 48109. Offers Russian (AM); Slavic languages and literatures (PhD). *Faculty:* 9 full-time (2 women), 10 part-time/adjunct (8 women). *Students:* 7 full-time (4 women), 3 international. 13 applicants, 46% accepted, 4 enrolled. In 2007, 1 degree awarded. *Degree requirements:* For master's, 2 foreign languages, comprehensive exam; for doctorate, 3 foreign languages, comprehensive exam, thesis/dissertation, oral defense of dissertation, preliminary exam. *Entrance requirements:* For master's, GRE General Test, 3rd year foreign language proficiency; for doctorate, GRE

Slavic Languages

University of Michigan (continued)

General Test, master's degree. Additional exam requirements/recommendations for international students: Required—TOEFL (minimum score 560 paper-based; 220 computer-based). *Application deadline:* For fall admission, 1/15 priority date for domestic and international students. Applications are processed on a rolling basis. Application fee: $60 ($75 for international students). Electronic applications accepted. *Financial support:* In 2007–08, 7 students received support, including 4 fellowships with full tuition reimbursements available (averaging $15,000 per year), 7 teaching assistantships with full tuition reimbursements available (averaging $15,199 per year); Federal Work-Study, institutionally sponsored loans, scholarships/grants, health care benefits, and unspecified assistantships also available. Financial award application deadline: 1/15; financial award applicants required to submit FAFSA. *Faculty research:* Russian literature (all periods), Polish literature, Slavic linguistics, Czech literature, Ukrainian literature. *Unit head:* Dr. Herbert J. Eagle, Chair, 734-764-5355, Fax: 734-647-2127, E-mail: hjeagle@umich.edu. *Application contact:* Amanda Apostol, Student Services Assistant, 734-764-5355, Fax: 734-647-2127, E-mail: slavic@umich.edu.

The University of North Carolina at Chapel Hill, Graduate School, College of Arts and Sciences, Department of Slavic Languages and Literatures, Chapel Hill, NC 27599. Offers Polish literature (PhD); Russian literature (MA, PhD); Serbo-Croatian literature (PhD); Slavic linguistics (MA, PhD). Part-time programs available. Terminal master's awarded for partial completion of doctoral program. *Degree requirements:* For master's, 2 foreign languages, comprehensive exam, thesis; for doctorate, 4 foreign languages, comprehensive exam, thesis/dissertation. *Entrance requirements:* For master's and doctorate, GRE General Test, minimum GPA of 3.0. Electronic applications accepted. *Faculty research:* Russian cultural studies, literary translation, sociolinguistics, cognitive linguistics, émigré literature.

University of Pittsburgh, School of Arts and Sciences, Department of Slavic Languages and Literatures, Pittsburgh, PA 15260. Offers MA, PhD. Part-time programs available. *Faculty:* 7 full-time (3 women), 1 part-time/adjunct (0 women). *Students:* 11 full-time (10 women). Average age 30. 9 applicants, 33% accepted, 0 enrolled. In 2007, 2 master's, 2 doctorates awarded. Terminal master's awarded for partial completion of doctoral program. *Median time to degree:* Of those who began their doctoral program in fall 1999, 65% received their degree in 8 years or less. *Degree requirements:* For master's, one foreign language, comprehensive exam; for doctorate, 2 foreign languages, comprehensive exam, thesis/dissertation. *Entrance requirements:* For master's and doctorate, GRE General Test. Additional exam requirements/recommendations for international students: Required—TOEFL. *Application deadline:* For fall admission, 1/15 priority date for domestic and international students. Application fee: $40. *Financial support:* In 2007–08, fellowships with tuition reimbursements (averaging $15,000 per year), teaching assistantships with tuition reimbursements (averaging $14,484 per year) were awarded; Federal Work-Study, scholarships/grants, and traineeships also available. Support available to part-time students. Financial award application deadline: 1/15. *Faculty research:* Contemporary Russian literature and culture, Russian cinema. *Unit head:* Prof. David J. Birnbaum, Chair, 412-624-5906, Fax: 412-624-9714, E-mail: djbpitt@pitt.edu. *Application contact:* Christine Metil, Administrator, 412-624-5906, Fax: 412-624-9714, E-mail: metil+@pitt.edu.

University of Southern California, Graduate School, College of Letters, Arts and Sciences, Department of Slavic Languages and Literatures, Los Angeles, CA 90089. Offers MA, PhD. *Faculty:* 7 full-time (2 women). *Students:* 18 full-time (12 women), 10 international. 11 applicants, 55% accepted. In 2007, 2 master's, 1 doctorate awarded. *Degree requirements:* For master's, one foreign language; for doctorate, 3 foreign languages, thesis/dissertation. *Entrance requirements:* For doctorate, GRE General Test. *Application deadline:* For fall admission, 12/1 priority date for domestic students. Applications are processed on a rolling basis. Application fee: $85. *Financial support:* In 2007–08, 16 students received support, including fellowships with full tuition reimbursements available (averaging $19,000 per year), research assistantships with full tuition reimbursements available (averaging $18,570 per year), teaching assistantships with full tuition reimbursements available (averaging $19,300 per year); career-related internships or fieldwork and scholarships/grants also available. Financial award application deadline: 2/15; financial award applicants required to submit FAFSA. *Faculty research:* Russian avant-garde art, Russian poetry, literary criticism, Slavic linguistics, symbolism. *Unit head:* Dr. Thomas Seifrid, Chair, 213-740-2311, E-mail: slavic@usc.edu. *Application contact:* Susan Kechekian, Information Contact, 213-740-2735, Fax: 213-740-8550, E-mail: susan@usc.edu.

The University of Texas at Austin, Graduate School, College of Liberal Arts, Department of Slavic Languages and Literatures, Austin, TX 78712-1111. Offers MA, PhD. *Degree requirements:* For master's, 2 foreign languages, thesis; for doctorate, 3 foreign languages, thesis/dissertation. *Entrance requirements:* For master's and doctorate, GRE General Test. Electronic applications accepted. *Faculty research:* Slavic linguistics; applied linguistics; Russian, Czech, and Slavic literature and culture.

University of Toronto, School of Graduate Studies, Humanities Division, Department of Slavic Languages and Literatures, Toronto, ON M5S 1A1, Canada. Offers MA, PhD. Part-time programs available. *Faculty:* 12 full-time, 1 part-time/adjunct. *Students:* 19 full-time (12 women), 9 international. 23 applicants, 57% accepted. In 2007, 3 master's, 1 doctorate awarded. *Degree requirements:* For doctorate, comprehensive exam, thesis/dissertation. *Entrance requirements:* For master's, BA in related area; minimum A– average in Slavic courses taken in final year, writing sample, 2 letters of recommendation; for doctorate, MA in Slavic languages and literatures, minimum A– average, writing sample, 2 letters of recommendation. Application fee: $100 Canadian dollars. *Financial support:* Research assistantships, teaching assistantships available. *Unit head:* Prof. Börje Vähämäki, Acting Chair and Acting Graduate Chair, 416-926-1300 Ext. 3143, Fax: 416-978-1387. *Application contact:* 416-926-2075, Fax: 416-926-2076, E-mail: slavic@chass.utoronto.ca.

University of Virginia, College and Graduate School of Arts and Sciences, Department of Slavic Languages and Literatures, Charlottesville, VA 22903. Offers MA, PhD. *Faculty:* 6 full-time (2 women). *Students:* 15 full-time (10 women), 1 international. Average age 27. 11 applicants, 82% accepted, 7 enrolled. In 2007, 4 master's, 1 doctorate awarded. *Degree requirements:* For master's, 2 foreign languages, comprehensive exam, thesis (for some programs); for doctorate, 2 foreign languages, comprehensive exam, thesis/dissertation. *Entrance requirements:* For master's and doctorate, GRE General Test, GRE Subject Test. *Application deadline:* Applications are processed on a rolling basis. Application fee: $60. Electronic applications accepted. *Financial support:* Applicants required to submit FAFSA. *Unit head:* Julian W. Connolly, Chair, 434-924-3548, Fax: 434-982-2744, E-mail: slavic@virginia.edu.

University of Washington, Graduate School, College of Arts and Sciences, Department of Slavic Languages and Literature, Seattle, WA 98195. Offers Russian literature (MA, PhD); Slavic linguistics (MA, PhD). *Degree requirements:* For master's, 2 foreign languages, thesis optional; for doctorate, 3 foreign languages, thesis/dissertation. *Entrance requirements:* For master's and doctorate, GRE General Test, minimum GPA of 3.0. Additional exam requirements/recommendations for international students: Required—TOEFL. Electronic applications accepted. *Faculty research:* Modern and medieval East European languages and literatures, comparative literature, Russian folk literature, Slavic literary theory and criticism, computerized morphology of Russian.

University of Wisconsin–Madison, Graduate School, College of Letters and Science, Department of Slavic Languages and Literature, Madison, WI 53706-1380. Offers MA, PhD. Part-time programs available. Terminal master's awarded for partial completion of doctoral program. *Degree requirements:* For doctorate, thesis/dissertation. *Entrance requirements:* For master's and doctorate, GRE General Test. Additional exam requirements/recommendations for international students: Required—TOEFL. Electronic applications accepted. *Faculty research:* Polish literature, linguistics, South Slavic literature, second language acquisition, nineteenth and twentieth-century Russian literature.

University of Wisconsin–Milwaukee, Graduate School, College of Letters and Sciences, Interdepartmental Program in Foreign Language and Literature, Milwaukee, WI 53201-0413. Offers classics and Hebrew studies (MAFLL); comparative literature (MAFLL); French and Italian (MAFLL); German (MAFLL); Slavic studies (MAFLL); Spanish (MAFLL). Part-time programs available. *Faculty:* 39 full-time (17 women). *Students:* 29 full-time (21 women), 31 part-time (23 women); includes 8 minority (1 Asian American or Pacific Islander, 7 Hispanic Americans), 22 international. 54 applicants, 67% accepted, 26 enrolled. In 2007, 34 degrees awarded. *Degree requirements:* For master's, 2 foreign languages, thesis or alternative. *Application deadline:* For fall admission, 1/1 priority date for domestic students; for spring admission, 9/1 for domestic students. Applications are processed on a rolling basis. Application fee: $45 ($75 for international students). *Expenses:* Tuition, state resident: part-time $530 per credit. Tuition, nonresident: part-time $1,428 per credit. Required fees: $19 per credit. $229 per term. Tuition and fees vary according to course load and program. *Financial support:* In 2007–08, 44 teaching assistantships were awarded; fellowships, research assistantships, career-related internships or fieldwork and unspecified assistantships also available. Support available to part-time students. Financial award application deadline: 4/15. *Unit head:* Gabrielle Verdier, Representative, 414-229-3346, Fax: 414-229-2741, E-mail: verdier@uwm.edu.

Yale University, Graduate School of Arts and Sciences, Department of Slavic Languages and Literatures, New Haven, CT 06520. Offers PhD. *Degree requirements:* For doctorate, 3 foreign languages, thesis/dissertation. *Entrance requirements:* For doctorate, GRE General Test.

Spanish

American University, College of Arts and Sciences, Department of Language and Foreign Studies, Program in Spanish: Latin American Studies, Washington, DC 20016-8001. Offers Spanish: Latin American studies (MA); translation (Certificate). Part-time and evening/weekend programs available. *Students:* 17 full-time (14 women), 13 part-time (9 women); includes 8 minority (3 African Americans, 1 Asian American or Pacific Islander, 4 Hispanic Americans), 1 international. Average age 28. In 2007, 8 master's, 14 other advanced degrees awarded. *Degree requirements:* For master's, one foreign language, comprehensive exam, thesis or alternative, research requirement. *Entrance requirements:* For master's, GRE, bachelor's degree in language or equivalent, essay in Spanish; 3.2 GPA; statement of purpose; for Certificate, Bachelor's degree in Spanish or BA any field and Spanish proficiency. *Application deadline:* For fall admission, 2/1 for domestic students; for spring admission, 10/1 for domestic students. Application fee: $50. *Expenses:* Tuition: Full-time $19,998; part-time $1,111 per credit hour. Required fees: $380. Tuition and fees vary according to program. *Financial support:* Fellowships with full and partial tuition reimbursements, career-related internships or fieldwork, Federal Work-Study, and institutionally sponsored loans available. Financial award application deadline: 2/1. *Faculty research:* Latin American culture, literature, and history; computer-aided instruction.

Appalachian State University, Cratis D. Williams Graduate School, Department of Foreign Languages and Literatures, Boone, NC 28608. Offers romance languages-Spanish (MA); romance languages-Spanish teaching (MA). Part-time programs available. *Faculty:* 14 full-time (7 women). *Students:* 9 full-time (7 women), 4 part-time (3 women). 4 applicants, 75% accepted, 3 enrolled. In 2007, 5 degrees awarded. *Degree requirements:* For master's, one foreign language, comprehensive exam, thesis optional. *Entrance requirements:* For master's, GRE General Test, 3 letters of recommendation. Additional exam requirements/recommendations for international students: Required—TOEFL (minimum score 570 paper-based; 230 computer-based; 79 iBT), IELTS (minimum score 7), TOEFL or IELTS. *Application deadline:* For fall admission, 7/1 for domestic students, 1/1 for international students; for spring admission, 11/1 for domestic students, 6/1 for international students. Applications are processed on a rolling basis. Application fee: $50. Electronic applications accepted. *Expenses:* Tuition, state resident: part-time $127 per semester hour. Tuition, nonresident: part-time $597 per semester hour. Required fees: $18 per semester. *Financial support:* In 2007–08, research assistantships (averaging $7,000 per year); fellowships, teaching assistantships, career-related internships or fieldwork and unspecified assistantships also available. Financial award application deadline: 4/1. *Faculty research:* Family in medieval French romance. Total annual research expenditures: $41,594. *Unit head:* Dr. Alexandra Sterling-Hellenbrand, Chairperson, 828-262-3096, Fax: 828-262-3095, E-mail: hellenbranda@appstate.edu. *Application contact:* Dr. Beverly Moser, Graduate Coordinator, 828-262-2929, E-mail: moserba@appstate.edu.

Arizona State University, Graduate College, College of Liberal Arts and Sciences, Division of Humanities, Department of Languages and Literatures, Program in Spanish, Tempe, AZ 85287. Offers MA, PhD. *Degree requirements:* For master's, thesis or alternative; for doctorate, thesis/dissertation. *Entrance requirements:* For master's and doctorate, GRE.

Arkansas Tech University, Graduate School, School of Liberal and Fine Arts, Russellville, AR 72801. Offers communication (MLA); English (M Ed, MA); fine arts (MLA); history (MA); multi-media journalism (MA); social science (MLA); social studies (M Ed); Spanish (MA, MLA); teaching English as a second language (MA, MLA). Part-time programs available. *Students:* 54 full-time (43 women), 79 part-time (54 women); includes 11 minority (3 African Americans, 1 American Indian/Alaska Native, 1 Asian American or Pacific Islander, 6 Hispanic Americans), 29 international. Average age 33. In 2007, 71 degrees awarded. *Degree requirements:* For master's, project. *Entrance requirements:* For master's, GRE General Test or MAT. Additional exam requirements/recommendations for international students: Required—TOEFL (minimum score 500 paper-based; 173 computer-based; 61 iBT). *Application deadline:* For fall admission, 3/1 priority date for domestic students, 5/1 priority date for international students; for winter admission, 10/1 priority date for international students; for spring admission, 10/1 priority date for domestic and international students. Applications are processed on a rolling basis. Application fee: $0 ($30 for international students). Electronic applications accepted. *Expenses:* Tuition, state resident: full-time $3,150; part-time $175 per hour. Tuition, nonresident: full-time $6,300; part-time $350 per hour. Required fees: $384; $8 per hour. $120 per term. Tuition and fees vary according to course load. *Financial support:* In 2007–08, teaching assistantships with full tuition reimbursements (averaging $4,000 per year); career-related internships or fieldwork, Federal Work-Study, scholarships/grants, health care benefits, and unspecified assistantships also available. Support available to part-time students. Financial award application deadline: 4/15; financial award applicants required to submit FAFSA. *Unit head:* Dr. Georgena Duncan, Dean, 479-968-0266, Fax: 479-968-0275, E-mail: georgena.duncan@atu.edu. *Application contact:* Dr. Eldon G. Clary, Dean of Graduate School, 479-968-0398, Fax: 479-964-0542, E-mail: graduate.school@atu.edu.

Asbury College, Graduate Programs, Wilmore, KY 40390-1198. Offers biology: alternative certificate (MA Ed); chemistry: alternative certificate (MA Ed); English (Certificate); English as a second language (MA Ed); ESL (Certificate); French (Certificate); mathematics: alternative certificate (MA Ed); reading / writing (MA Ed); social studies (Certificate); Spanish (Certificate); special education (MA Ed); special education: alternative certificate (MA Ed). *Accreditation:* NCATE. Part-time programs available. *Faculty:* 8 full-time (7 women), 9 part-time/adjunct (4 women). *Students:* Average age 36. 14 applicants, 100% accepted, 14 enrolled. In 2007, 10 degrees awarded. *Degree requirements:* For master's, action research project, portfolio. *Entrance requirements:* For master's, PRAXIS/NTE, minimum GPA of 2.75, letters of recommendation. Additional exam requirements/recommendations for international students: Required—TOEFL (minimum score 550 paper-based). *Application deadline:* Applications are processed on a rolling basis. Application fee: $25. *Expenses:* Tuition: Part-time $353 per credit hour. *Financial support:* Scholarships/grants and traineeships available. Financial award applicants required to submit FAFSA. *Unit head:* Dr. Bonnie J. Banker, Director, 859-858-3511 Ext. 2221, Fax: 859-858-3921, E-mail: bonnie.banker@asbury.edu. *Application contact:* Melanie S. Kinnell, Graduate Program Assistant and Certification Specialist, 859-858-3511 Ext. 2304, Fax: 859-858-3921, E-mail: graded@asbury.edu.

Auburn University, Graduate School, College of Liberal Arts, Department of Foreign Languages and Literatures, Auburn University, AL 36849. Offers Spanish (MA, MHS). Part-time programs available. *Faculty:* 21 full-time (8 women). *Students:* 26 full-time (17 women), 5 part-time (4 women); includes 7 minority (1 African American, 6 Hispanic Americans), 6 international. Average age 27. 23 applicants, 87% accepted, 14 enrolled. In 2007, 18 degrees awarded. *Degree requirements:* For master's, one foreign language, comprehensive exam, thesis (for some programs). *Entrance requirements:* For master's, GRE General Test. *Application deadline:* For fall admission, 7/7 for domestic students; for spring admission, 11/24 for domestic students. Applications are processed on a rolling basis. Application fee: $25 ($50 for international students). Electronic applications accepted. *Financial support:* Fellowships, teaching assistantships, Federal Work-Study available. Support available to part-time students. Financial award application deadline: 3/15. *Unit head:* Dr. Robert G. Weigel, Chair, 334-844-4345, Fax: 334-844-6378. *Application contact:* Dr. Joe Pittman, Interim Dean of the Graduate School, 334-844-4700.

Baylor University, Graduate School, College of Arts and Sciences, Department of Modern Foreign Languages, Waco, TX 76798. Offers Spanish (MA). *Students:* 6 full-time (5 women); includes 1 minority (Hispanic American) In 2007, 3 degrees awarded. *Entrance requirements:* For master's, GRE General Test. *Application deadline:* Applications are processed on a rolling basis. Application fee: $25. *Unit head:* Dr. Baudelio Garza, Graduate Program Director, 254-710-3711, Fax: 254-710-3799, E-mail: baudelio_garza@baylor.edu. *Application contact:* Suzanne Keener, Administrative Assistant, 254-710-3588, Fax: 254-710-3870.

Bennington College, Graduate Programs, Program in Teaching a Second Language, Bennington, VT 05201. Offers education (MATSL); foreign language education (MATSL); French (MATSL); Spanish (MATSL). Part-time programs available. *Faculty:* 2 full-time (0 women), 3 part-time/adjunct (all women). *Students:* Average age 37. 14 applicants, 93% accepted, 12 enrolled. In 2007, 6 master's awarded. *Degree requirements:* For master's, one foreign language, 2 major projects and presentations. *Entrance requirements:* For master's, oral proficiency interview (OPI). Additional exam requirements/recommendations for international students: Required—TOEFL (minimum score 577 paper-based; 233 computer-based; 91 iBT). *Application deadline:* For spring admission, 4/1 priority date for domestic and international students. Applications are processed on a rolling basis. Application fee: $60. *Expenses: Contact institution.* One-time fee: $75 full-time. Tuition and fees vary according to program. *Financial support:* In 2007–08, 3 students received support. Scholarships/grants available. Financial award application deadline: 4/1; financial award applicants required to submit FAFSA. *Faculty research:* Acquisition, evaluation, assessment, conceptual teaching and learning content-driven communication, applied linguistics. *Unit head:* Carol Meyer, Director of Isabelle Kaplan Center for Languages and Cultures/MATSL/CCT, 802-440-4375, Fax: 802-447-4269, E-mail: cmeyer@bennington.edu. *Application contact:* Nancy Pearlman, Assistant Director, MATSL/CCT, 802-440-4710, Fax: 802-447-4269, E-mail: matsl@bennington.edu.

Boston College, Graduate School of Arts and Sciences, Department of Romance Languages and Literatures, Chestnut Hill, MA 02467-3800. Offers French (MA, PhD); Italian (MA); medieval language (PhD); Spanish (MA, PhD). Part-time programs available. *Students:* 41 full-time (29 women), 9 part-time (7 women); includes 7 minority (1 American Indian/Alaska Native, 1 Asian American or Pacific Islander, 5 Hispanic Americans), 9 international. 51 applicants, 39% accepted, 10 enrolled. In 2007, 14 master's, 3 doctorates awarded. Terminal master's awarded for partial completion of doctoral program. *Degree requirements:* For master's, one foreign language; for doctorate, 2 foreign languages, thesis/dissertation. *Entrance requirements:* Additional exam requirements/recommendations for international students: Required—TOEFL (minimum score 590 paper-based; 250 computer-based; 91 iBT). *Application deadline:* For fall admission, 1/15 for domestic students. Application fee: $70. Electronic applications accepted. *Financial support:* Fellowships with full tuition reimbursements, teaching assistantships with full tuition reimbursements, Federal Work-Study and unspecified assistantships available. Support available to part-time students. Financial award application deadline: 3/1; financial award applicants required to submit FAFSA. *Faculty research:* Spanish-American literature, philology, medieval French romance and troubadour/trouvere lyrics, Golden Age Peninsular literature, secondary language acquisition and pedagogy. *Unit head:* Dr. Dwayne Carpenter, Chairperson, 617-552-3828, E-mail: dwayne.carpenter@bc.edu.

See Close-Up on page 561.

Boston University, Graduate School of Arts and Sciences, Department of Romance Studies, Boston, MA 02215. Offers French language and literature (MA, PhD); Hispanic language and literatures (MA, PhD). *Students:* 45 full-time (34 women), 3 part-time (2 women); includes 6 minority (all Hispanic Americans), 19 international. Average age 32. 54 applicants, 37% accepted, 9 enrolled. In 2007, 5 doctorates awarded. Terminal master's awarded for partial completion of doctoral program. *Degree requirements:* For master's, one foreign language, comprehensive exam; for doctorate, 2 foreign languages, comprehensive exam, thesis/dissertation. *Entrance requirements:* For master's and doctorate, GRE General Test, sample of written work, 3 letters of recommendation. Additional exam requirements/recommendations for international students: Required—TOEFL (minimum score 550 paper-based; 213 computer-based). *Application deadline:* For fall admission, 7/1 for domestic and international students; for spring admission, 10/15 for domestic and international students. Application fee: $70. *Expenses:* Tuition: Full-time $34,930; part-time $1,092 per credit. Tuition and fees vary according to class time, course level and program. *Financial support:* In 2007–08, 48 students received support, including 2 fellowships with full tuition reimbursements available (averaging $18,000 per year), 35 teaching assistantships with full tuition reimbursements available (averaging $16,500 per year); research assistantships, Federal Work-Study and scholarships/grants also available. Support available to part-time students. Financial award application deadline: 1/15; financial award applicants required to submit FAFSA. *Unit head:* Christopher Maurer, Chairman, 617-353-6225, Fax: 617-353-6245, E-mail: chmaurer@bu.edu. *Application contact:* Lauren Terry, Administrative Assistant, 617-353-2641, Fax: 617-353-6245, E-mail: lkterry@bu.edu.

Bowling Green State University, Graduate College, College of Arts and Sciences, Department of Romance and Classical Studies, Program in Spanish, Bowling Green, OH 43403. Offers Spanish (MA); Spanish education (MAT). Part-time programs available. *Students:* 30 full-time (23 women), 3 part-time (all women); includes 5 minority (3 African Americans, 2 Hispanic Americans), 2 international. Average age 26. 19 applicants, 68% accepted, 11 enrolled. In 2007, 16 degrees awarded. *Degree requirements:* For master's, one foreign language, thesis or alternative. *Entrance requirements:* For master's, GRE General Test. Additional exam requirements/recommendations for international students: Required—TOEFL. *Application deadline:* For fall admission, 2/15 priority date for domestic students. Application fee: $30. Electronic applications accepted. *Financial support:* In 2007–08, 3 research assistantships with full tuition reimbursements (averaging $3,700 per year), 28 teaching assistantships with full tuition reimbursements (averaging $5,680 per year) were awarded; Federal Work-Study and unspecified assistantships also available. Financial award applicants required to submit FAFSA. *Faculty research:* U.S. Latino literature and culture, Latin American film and popular culture, applied linguistics, Spanish popular culture. *Application contact:* Dr. Ernesto Delgado, Graduate Coordinator, 419-372-7150.

Brigham Young University, Graduate Studies, College of Humanities, Department of Spanish and Portuguese, Provo, UT 84602-1001. Offers Portuguese linguistics (MA); Portuguese literature (MA); Spanish linguistics (MA); Spanish teaching (MA); Spanish/Latin American Literature (MA); Spanish/Peninsular literature (MA). Part-time programs available. *Faculty:* 29 full-time (6 women). *Students:* 18 full-time (8 women), 25 part-time (20 women); includes 12 minority (all Hispanic Americans) Average age 29. 29 applicants, 59% accepted, 14 enrolled. In 2007, 18 degrees awarded. *Degree requirements:* For master's, one foreign language, comprehensive exam, thesis, 1 semester of teaching. *Entrance requirements:* For master's, minimum GPA of 3.5 in Spanish or Portuguese, 3.3 overall. Additional exam requirements/recommendations for international students: Required—TOEFL (minimum score 580 paper-based; 237 computer-based). *Application deadline:* For fall admission, 2/1 for domestic and international students. Application fee: $50. Electronic applications accepted. *Financial support:* In 2007–08, 42 students received support, including 1 research assistantship with partial tuition reimbursement available (averaging $3,800 per year), 29 teaching assistantships with partial tuition reimbursements available (averaging $6,574 per year); institutionally sponsored loans, tuition waivers (partial), and unspecified assistantships also available. Support available to part-time students. Financial award application deadline: 6/15. *Faculty research:* Mexican prose; Latin American theater, literature, phonetics, and phonology; pedagogy; classical Portuguese literature; Peninsular prose and theater. *Unit head:* Dr. Alvin F. Sherman, Chair, 801-422-3107, Fax: 801-422-0628, E-mail: alvin_sherman@byu.edu. *Application contact:* Arwen T. Wyatt, Graduate Secretary, 801-422-2196, Fax: 801-422-0628, E-mail: arwen_wyatt@byu.edu.

Brooklyn College of the City University of New York, Division of Graduate Studies, Department of Modern Languages and Literature, Brooklyn, NY 11210-2889. Offers French (MA); modern languages and literature (PhD); Spanish (MA). The department offers courses at Brooklyn College that are creditable toward the CUNY doctoral degree (with permission of the executive officer of the doctoral program). *Students:* 5 full-time (1 woman), 23 part-time (16 women); includes 22 minority (11 African Americans, 11 Hispanic Americans), 4 international. 10 applicants, 80% accepted, 6 enrolled. In 2007, 12 degrees awarded. *Degree requirements:* For master's, comprehensive exam, comprehensive exam or research paper. *Entrance requirements:* For master's, 18 credits in advanced courses in Spanish, 2 letters of recommendation. Additional exam requirements/recommendations for international students: Required—TOEFL. *Application deadline:* For fall admission, 3/1 priority date for domestic students, 2/1 priority date for international students; for spring admission, 11/1 priority date for domestic students, 10/1 priority date for international students. Applications are processed on a rolling basis. Application fee: $125. Electronic applications accepted. *Financial support:* Federal Work-Study, institutionally sponsored loans, and scholarships/grants available. Support available to part-time students. Financial award application deadline: 5/1; financial award applicants required to submit FAFSA. *Faculty research:* Latin American contemporary novel; Caribbean female contemporary literature; 19th and 20th century Spanish novel; 20th century Mexican poetry. *Unit head:* Dr. William Childers, Chairperson, 718-951-5451, E-mail: wchilders@brooklyn.cuny.edu. *Application contact:* Hernan Sierra, Graduate Admissions Coordinator, 718-951-4536, Fax: 718-951-4506, E-mail: grads@brooklyn.cuny.edu.

California State University, Bakersfield, Division of Graduate Studies, School of Humanities and Social Sciences, Program in Spanish, Bakersfield, CA 93311-1022. Offers MA. *Degree requirements:* For master's, capstone course.

California State University, Fresno, Division of Graduate Studies, College of Arts and Humanities, Department of Modern and Classical Languages and Literatures, Fresno, CA 93740-8027. Offers Spanish (MA). Part-time programs available. *Faculty:* 5 full-time (2 women). *Students:* 50; includes 44 minority (all Hispanic Americans) Average age 28. In 2007, 4 degrees awarded. *Degree requirements:* For master's, one foreign language, thesis or alternative. *Entrance requirements:* For master's, GRE General Test, BA in Spanish, minimum GPA of 3.0. Additional exam requirements/recommendations for international students: Required—TOEFL. *Application deadline:* For fall admission, 5/1 for domestic and international students; for spring admission, 10/1 for domestic and international students. Applications are processed on a rolling basis. Application fee: $55. Electronic applications accepted. *Financial support:* Teaching assistantships, career-related internships or fieldwork, Federal Work-Study, and scholarships/grants available. Support available to part-time students. Financial award application deadline: 3/1; financial award applicants required to submit FAFSA. *Unit head:* Dr. Barbara Birch, Chair, 559-278-2386, Fax: 559-278-7878, E-mail: barbara_birch@csufresno.edu. *Application contact:* Dr. Saul Jimenez-Sandoval, Coordinator, 559-278-2386, Fax: 559-278-7878, E-mail: sjimenez@csufresno.edu.

California State University, Fullerton, Graduate Studies, College of Humanities and Social Sciences, Department of Modern Languages and Literatures, Fullerton, CA 92834-9480. Offers French (MA); German (MA); Spanish (MA); teaching English to speakers of other languages (MS). Part-time programs available. *Students:* 48 full-time (41 women), 76 part-time (63 women); includes 55 minority (17 Asian Americans or Pacific Islanders, 38 Hispanic Americans), 26 international. Average age 33. 94 applicants, 68% accepted, 32 enrolled. In 2007, 34 degrees awarded. *Degree requirements:* For master's, comprehensive exam, thesis or alternative. *Entrance requirements:* For master's, minimum GPA of 2.5 in last 60 hours of course work, undergraduate major in a language. Application fee: $55. *Financial support:* Federal Work-Study, institutionally sponsored loans, and scholarships/grants available. Support available to part-time students. Financial award application deadline: 3/1. *Unit head:* Dr. Janet Eyring, Chair, 714-278-3534.

California State University, Long Beach, Graduate Studies, College of Liberal Arts, Department of Romance, German, and Russian Languages and Literature, Program in Spanish, Long Beach, CA 90840. Offers MA. Part-time programs available. *Students:* Average age 32. *Degree requirements:* For master's, one foreign language, thesis or alternative, research paper. *Entrance requirements:* For master's, BA in Spanish. *Application deadline:* For fall admission, 7/1 for domestic students; for spring admission, 12/1 for domestic students. Applications are processed on a rolling basis. Application fee: $55. Electronic applications accepted. *Financial support:* Federal Work-Study, institutionally sponsored loans, and scholarships/grants available. Financial award application deadline: 3/2. *Faculty research:* Literary translation, literature and politics, women writers, Latin American poetry, Latin American theatre. *Unit head:* Dr. Claire Martin, Director, 562-985-4318, Fax: 562-985-2406.

California State University, Los Angeles, Graduate Studies, College of Arts and Letters, Department of Modern Languages and Literatures, Major in Spanish, Los Angeles, CA 90032-8530. Offers MA. Part-time and evening/weekend programs available. *Students:* 25 full-time (23 women), 33 part-time (28 women); includes 30 minority (all Hispanic Americans), 23 international. Average age 35. In 2007, 7 degrees awarded. *Degree requirements:* For master's, comprehensive exam. *Entrance requirements:* For master's, GRE Subject Test, bachelor's degree in Spanish or related area, minimum GPA of 3.0 in Spanish, minimum GPA of 2.75 in last 90 units of course work. Additional exam requirements/recommendations for international students: Required—TOEFL. *Application deadline:* For fall admission, 6/30 for domestic students; for spring admission, 2/1 for domestic students. Applications are processed on a rolling basis. Application fee: $55. *Financial support:* Federal Work-Study available. Support available to part-time students. Financial award application deadline: 3/1. *Faculty research:* Spanish-American fiction, Spanish poetry. *Unit head:* Dr. Sachiko Matsunaga, Chair, Department of Modern Languages and Literatures, 323-343-4230 Ext. 34240, Fax: 323-343-4234, E-mail: smatsun@calstatela.edu.

California State University, Northridge, Graduate Studies, College of Humanities, Department of Modern and Classical Languages and Literatures, Northridge, CA 91330. Offers Spanish (MA).

Spanish

California State University, Northridge (continued)
Part-time and evening/weekend programs available. *Faculty:* 14 full-time (6 women), 24 part-time/adjunct (17 women). *Students:* 16 full-time (8 women), 9 part-time (7 women); includes 20 minority (1 African American, 19 Hispanic Americans). Average age 36. 17 applicants, 88% accepted, 10 enrolled. In 2007, 7 degrees awarded. *Degree requirements:* For master's, one foreign language. *Entrance requirements:* For master's, GRE General Test or minimum GPA of 3.0. Additional exam requirements/recommendations for international students: Required—TOEFL. *Application deadline:* For fall admission, 11/30 for domestic students. Application fee: $55. *Financial support:* Application deadline: 3/1. *Unit head:* Dr. Brian Castronovo, Chair, 818-677-3467, E-mail: brian.castronovo@csun.edu.

California State University, Sacramento, Graduate Studies, College of Social Sciences and Interdisciplinary Studies, Liberal Arts Program, Sacramento, CA 95819-6048. Offers French (MA); German (MA); Spanish (MA); theater arts (MA). *Students:* 15 full-time (10 women), 24 part-time (17 women); includes 4 minority (2 African Americans, 1 American Indian/Alaska Native, 1 Asian American or Pacific Islander). Average age 37. 17 applicants, 88% accepted, 9 enrolled. *Degree requirements:* For master's, writing proficiency exam. *Entrance requirements:* Additional exam requirements/recommendations for international students: Required—TOEFL. *Application deadline:* Applications are processed on a rolling basis. Application fee: $55. Electronic applications accepted. *Expenses:* Tuition, state resident: full-time $3,414. Tuition, nonresident: full-time $13,584; part-time $339 per unit. Required fees: $786; $393 per semester. *Financial support:* Application deadline: 3/1. *Unit head:* Dr. Lindy Valdez, Coordinator, 916-278-6342.

California State University, San Bernardino, Graduate Studies, College of Arts and Letters, Department of World Languages and Literatures, San Bernardino, CA 92407-2397. Offers Spanish (MA). Part-time and evening/weekend programs available. *Faculty:* 12 full-time, 18 part-time/adjunct. *Students:* 6 full-time (5 women), 26 part-time (18 women); includes 21 minority (1 African American, 20 Hispanic Americans), 6 international. Average age 29. 18 applicants, 67% accepted, 10 enrolled. In 2007, 10 degrees awarded. *Application deadline:* Applications are processed on a rolling basis. Application fee: $55. *Financial support:* Career-related internships or fieldwork, Federal Work-Study, and institutionally sponsored loans available. Support available to part-time students. *Unit head:* Dr. Margaret Perry, Chair, 909-537-5849, Fax: 909-537-7091, E-mail: mperry@csusb.edu.

California State University, San Marcos, College of Arts and Sciences, Program in World Languages, San Marcos, CA 92096-0001. Offers Spanish (MA). Part-time and evening/weekend programs available. *Faculty:* 9 full-time (5 women), 10 part-time/adjunct (4 women). *Students:* 10 full-time (4 women), 5 part-time (4 women); includes 10 minority (all Hispanic Americans), 2 international. Average age 34. *Degree requirements:* For master's, 2 foreign languages, exam. *Entrance requirements:* For master's, GRE General Test, minimum GPA of 2.5, minimum GPA of 3.0 in upper division Spanish courses. *Application deadline:* For fall admission, 3/15 priority date for domestic students. Applications are processed on a rolling basis. Application fee: $55. Electronic applications accepted. *Financial support:* Teaching assistantships available. *Faculty research:* Applied linguistics, golden age Spanish literature, Latin American literature, poetry, Chicano studies. *Unit head:* Dr. Veronica Anover, Department Chair, 760-750-4143. *Application contact:* Oneita Billings, Administrative Coordinator, 760-750-4208, E-mail: obilling@csusm.edu.

The Catholic University of America, School of Arts and Sciences, Department of Modern Languages and Literatures, Program in Spanish, Washington, DC 20064. Offers MA, PhD. Part-time programs available. *Students:* 8 full-time (5 women), 7 part-time (all women); includes 3 minority (all Hispanic Americans), 4 international. Average age 34. 15 applicants, 73% accepted, 5 enrolled. In 2007, 2 master's, 4 doctorates awarded. *Degree requirements:* For master's, one foreign language, comprehensive exam, thesis or alternative; for doctorate, 2 foreign languages, comprehensive exam, thesis/dissertation. *Entrance requirements:* For master's and doctorate, GRE General Test, 3 letters of recommendation. Additional exam requirements/recommendations for international students: Required—TOEFL (minimum score 580 paper-based; 237 computer-based). *Application deadline:* For fall admission, 2/1 priority date for domestic students; for spring admission, 11/15 priority date for domestic students. Applications are processed on a rolling basis. Application fee: $55. Electronic applications accepted. *Financial support:* Fellowships, teaching assistantships, career-related internships or fieldwork, Federal Work-Study, scholarships/grants, tuition waivers (full and partial), and unspecified assistantships available. Support available to part-time students. Financial award application deadline: 2/1; financial award applicants required to submit FAFSA. *Faculty research:* Latin American theatre, Medieval and Golden Age literature, colonial literature, nineteenth century Spanish literature. *Unit head:* Dr. Joan Grimbert, Chair, Department of Modern Languages and Literatures, 202-319-5240, Fax: 202-319-6077, E-mail: grimbert@cua.edu.

Central Connecticut State University, School of Graduate Studies, School of Arts and Sciences, Department of Modern Languages, Program in Spanish, New Britain, CT 06050-4010. Offers Spanish (MS, Certificate); Spanish language and Hispanic culture (MA). Specialization in Spanish language and Hispanic cultures offered jointly with the University of Salamanca, Spain. Part-time and evening/weekend programs available. *Students:* 2 full-time (both women), 5 part-time (all women); includes 1 minority (Hispanic American) 5 applicants, 60% accepted, 0 enrolled. In 2007, 2 master's, 2 other advanced degrees awarded. *Degree requirements:* For master's, one foreign language, comprehensive exam, thesis or alternative. *Entrance requirements:* For master's, 24 credits in Spanish, minimum GPA of 2.7. Additional exam requirements/recommendations for international students: Required—TOEFL. *Application deadline:* For fall admission, 7/1 for domestic students; for spring admission, 12/1 for domestic students. Applications are processed on a rolling basis. Application fee: $50. Electronic applications accepted. *Expenses:* Tuition, area resident: Full-time $4,169. Tuition, state resident: full-time $6,253. Tuition, nonresident: full-time $11,614; part-time $400 per credit. Required fees: $3,322. One-time fee: $62 part-time. Tuition and fees vary according to degree level and program. *Faculty research:* Linguistics, nineteenth to twentieth century Spanish literature, Spanish Golden Age prose/drama. *Unit head:* Dr. Lilian Uribe, Chair, Department of Modern Languages, 860-832-2875.

Central Michigan University, College of Graduate Studies, College of Humanities and Social and Behavioral Sciences, Department of Foreign Languages, Literatures, and Cultures, Mount Pleasant, MI 48859. Offers Spanish (MA). Evening/weekend programs available. *Degree requirements:* For master's, thesis or alternative. *Entrance requirements:* For master's, minimum GPA of 3.0 in Spanish, 2.7 overall.

Cheyney University of Pennsylvania, School of Education, Program in Spanish, Cheyney, PA 19319-0200. Offers Certificate. *Faculty:* 8 full-time (1 woman), 5 part-time/adjunct (3 women). *Students:* Average age 37. *Expenses:* Tuition, state resident: full-time $6,214; part-time $345 per credit. Tuition, nonresident: full-time $9,944; part-time $552 per credit. Required fees: $645; $161 per semester. *Unit head:* Dr. O. Denis Ekwerike, Chair, 215-560-3891, Fax: 215-560-3893. *Application contact:* Dr. John Williams, Executive Dean of Graduate Studies, 215-560-7034, Fax: 215-560-3893, E-mail: jwilliams@cheyney.edu.

City College of the City University of New York, Graduate School, College of Liberal Arts and Science, Division of the Humanities and Arts, Department of Foreign Languages, New York, NY 10031-9198. Offers Spanish (MA). *Students:* 1 full-time (0 women), 58 part-time (45 women); includes 52 minority (4 African Americans, 5 Asian Americans or Pacific Islanders, 43 Hispanic Americans). 13 applicants, 15% accepted, 7 enrolled. In 2007, 9 degrees awarded. *Degree requirements:* For master's, one foreign language, comprehensive exam, thesis or alternative. *Entrance requirements:* For master's, minimum GPA of 3.0. Additional exam requirements/recommendations for international students: Required—TOEFL (minimum score 500 paper-based; 173 computer-based). *Application deadline:* For fall admission, 5/1 for domestic students; for spring admission, 11/1 for domestic students. Application fee: $125. *Financial support:* Fellowships, Federal Work-Study available. Support available to part-time students. Financial award application deadline: 5/1. *Unit head:* Richard Calichman, Chairman, 212-650-6731. *Application contact:* Angel Esterez, Graduate Adviser, 212-650-6377.

Cleveland State University, College of Graduate Studies, College of Liberal Arts and Social Sciences, Department of Modern Languages, Cleveland, OH 44115. Offers Spanish (MA). Part-time and evening/weekend programs available. *Faculty:* 11 full-time (7 women), 2 part-time/adjunct (both women). *Students:* 6 full-time (5 women), 13 part-time (8 women); includes 8 minority (1 African American, 7 Hispanic Americans), 2 international. Average age 33. 11 applicants, 100% accepted, 8 enrolled. In 2007, 5 degrees awarded. *Degree requirements:* For master's, one foreign language, comprehensive exam, thesis optional, study abroad, ACTFLOPI rating of advanced low (or above). *Entrance requirements:* For master's, undergraduate major in Spanish or equivalent, essay in Spanish, writing sample. Additional exam requirements/recommendations for international students: Required—TOEFL (minimum score 525 paper-based; 197 computer-based). *Application deadline:* For fall admission, 7/25 for domestic students; for spring admission, 12/15 for domestic students. Applications are processed on a rolling basis. Application fee: $30. Electronic applications accepted. *Financial support:* In 2007–08, 5 students received support, including 5 teaching assistantships with full and partial tuition reimbursements available (averaging $4,760 per year); Federal Work-Study, tuition waivers (full), and unspecified assistantships also available. *Faculty research:* Second language acquisition, sociolinguistics, contemporary Spanish novel, Arabic diaspora in Latin America, border literature. *Unit head:* Tama L. Engelking, Chairperson, 216-523-7175, Fax: 216-687-4650, E-mail: t.engelking@csuohio.edu. *Application contact:* Dr. Antonio Medina-Rivera, Director, 216-523-7168, Fax: 216-687-4650, E-mail: a.medinarivera@csuohio.edu.

The College of New Jersey, Graduate Division, School of Culture and Society, Department of Modern Language, Ewing, NJ 08628. Offers applied Spanish studies (MA). In 2007, 3 degrees awarded. *Entrance requirements:* For master's, GRE, minimum GPA of 3.0 in field or 2.75 overall. Additional exam requirements/recommendations for international students: Required—TOEFL. *Application deadline:* For fall admission, 4/15 for domestic students; for spring admission, 10/15 for domestic students. Application fee: $60. Electronic applications accepted. *Financial support:* Application deadline: 5/1; *Unit head:* Deborah Compte, Coordinator, 609-771-2392, E-mail: dcompte@tcnj.edu. *Application contact:* Susan L. Hydro, Office of Graduate Studies, Assistant Dean, 609-771-2300, Fax: 609-637-5105, E-mail: graduate@tcnj.edu.

Columbia University, Graduate School of Arts and Sciences, Division of Humanities, Department of Spanish and Portuguese, New York, NY 10027. Offers M Phil, MA, PhD. Part-time programs available. *Faculty:* 12 full-time, 1 part-time/adjunct. *Students:* 45 full-time (32 women), 5 part-time (2 women); includes 17 minority (2 African Americans, 15 Hispanic Americans), 12 international. Average age 31. 80 applicants, 51% accepted. In 2007, 7 master's, 4 doctorates awarded. *Degree requirements:* For master's, one foreign language, written exam; for doctorate, 3 foreign languages, thesis/dissertation. *Entrance requirements:* For master's and doctorate, GRE General Test, GRE Subject Test, sample of written work. Additional exam requirements/recommendations for international students: Required—TOEFL. Application fee: $90. *Expenses:* Tuition: Part-time $1,452 per credit. Required fees: $152 per term. One-time fee: $75 part-time. Full-time tuition and fees vary according to course level, course load, degree level and program. *Financial support:* Fellowships, teaching assistantships, Federal Work-Study and institutionally sponsored loans available. Support available to part-time students. Financial award application deadline: 1/5; financial award applicants required to submit FAFSA. *Faculty research:* Literary theory and criticism, Spain's Golden Age: sixteenth- and seventeenth-centuries, contemporary Spanish American literature. *Unit head:* Carlos Alonso, Chair, 212-854-5177, Fax: 212-854-5322, E-mail: calonso@columbia.edu.

Cornell University, Graduate School, Graduate Fields of Arts and Sciences, Field of Romance Studies, Ithaca, NY 14853-0001. Offers French linguistics (PhD); French literature (PhD); Hispanic literature (PhD); Italian linguistics (PhD); Italian literature (PhD); Romance linguistics (PhD); Spanish linguistics (PhD). *Faculty:* 32 full-time (14 women). *Students:* 50 full-time (24 women); includes 11 minority (all Hispanic Americans), 20 international. Average age 29. 114 applicants, 23% accepted, 12 enrolled. In 2007, 2 doctorates awarded. *Degree requirements:* For doctorate, 2 foreign languages, comprehensive exam, thesis/dissertation. *Entrance requirements:* For doctorate, GRE General Test, sample of written work, 3 letters of recommendation. Additional exam requirements/recommendations for international students: Required—TOEFL (minimum score 550 paper-based; 213 computer-based; 77 iBT). *Application deadline:* For fall admission, 1/15 for domestic students. Application fee: $70. Electronic applications accepted. *Financial support:* In 2007–08, 48 students received support, including 20 fellowships with full tuition reimbursements available, 28 teaching assistantships with full tuition reimbursements available; research assistantships with full tuition reimbursements available, institutionally sponsored loans, scholarships/grants, health care benefits, tuition waivers (full and partial), and unspecified assistantships also available. Financial award applicants required to submit FAFSA. *Faculty research:* Literary theory, Hispanic studies, French studies, gender studies. *Unit head:* Director of Graduate Studies, 607-255-8222. *Application contact:* Graduate Field Assistant, 607-255-4246, E-mail: romance_studies@cornell.edu.

Duke University, Graduate School, Department of Romance Studies, Durham, NC 27708. Offers French (PhD); Spanish (PhD); JD/AM. *Faculty:* 29 full-time. *Students:* 61 full-time (40 women); includes 12 minority (1 African American, 11 Hispanic Americans), 24 international. 57 applicants, 37% accepted, 9 enrolled. In 2007, 2 doctorates awarded. *Degree requirements:* For doctorate, 2 foreign languages, thesis/dissertation. *Entrance requirements:* For doctorate, GRE General Test. Additional exam requirements/recommendations for international students: Required—TOEFL (minimum score 550 paper-based; 213 computer-based; 83 iBT), IELTS (minimum score 7). *Application deadline:* For fall admission, 12/15 priority date for domestic and international students. Application fee: $75. Electronic applications accepted. *Financial support:* Fellowships, research assistantships, teaching assistantships, Federal Work-Study available. Financial award application deadline: 12/31. *Unit head:* Roberto Doinoto, Director, 919-660-3114, Fax: 919-684-4029.

Eastern Michigan University, Graduate School, College of Arts and Sciences, Department of Foreign Languages and Bilingual Studies, Program in Foreign Languages, Ypsilanti, MI 48197. Offers French (MA); German (MA); German for business (Graduate Certificate); Hispanic language and cultures (Graduate Certificate); Japanese business practices (Graduate Certificate); Spanish (MA). Part-time and evening/weekend programs available. Post-baccalaureate distance learning degree programs offered (minimal on-campus study). *Students:* 1 (woman) full-time, 18 part-time (17 women); includes 2 minority (1 Asian American or Pacific Islander, 1 Hispanic American). Average age 35. In 2007, 8 master's, 2 other advanced degrees awarded. *Degree requirements:* For master's, one foreign language, thesis optional. *Entrance requirements:* Additional exam requirements/recommendations for international students: Required—TOEFL. *Application deadline:* Applications are processed on a rolling basis. Application fee: $35. *Expenses:* Tuition, state resident: full-time $8,952; part-time $373 per credit hour. Tuition, nonresident: full-time $17,634; part-time $735 per credit hour. Required fees: $896; $34 per credit hour. Tuition and fees vary according to course level, degree level and program. *Financial support:* Fellowships, research assistantships with full tuition reimbursements, teaching assistantships with full tuition reimbursements, career-related internships or fieldwork, Federal Work-Study, institutionally sponsored loans, scholarships/grants, tuition waivers (partial), and unspecified assistantships available. Support available to part-time students. Financial award applicants required to submit FAFSA. *Application contact:* Dr. Genevieve Peden, Program Advisor, 734-487-2283, Fax: 734-487-3411, E-mail: gpeden@emich.edu.

Emory University, Graduate School of Arts and Sciences, Department of Comparative Literature, Atlanta, GA 30322-1100. Offers comparative literature (PhD); English (Certificate); French (Certificate); Middle Eastern studies (PhD); philosophy (Certificate); psychoanalytic

Spanish

studies (PhD); religion (PhD); Spanish (Certificate); women studies (Certificate). *Degree requirements:* For doctorate, 2 foreign languages, comprehensive exam, thesis/dissertation. *Entrance requirements:* For doctorate, GRE General Test, minimum GPA of 3.0. Additional exam requirements/recommendations for international students: Required—TOEFL. Electronic applications accepted. *Faculty research:* Literary theory, psychoanalysis trauma and testimony, literature and religion, literature and technology, literature and philosophy, politics and global culture, literature and aesthetics.

Emory University, Graduate School of Arts and Sciences, Department of Spanish and Portuguese, Atlanta, GA 30322-1100. Offers comparative literature (Certificate); film studies (Certificate); Spanish (PhD); women's studies (Certificate). *Degree requirements:* For doctorate, 2 foreign languages, comprehensive exam, thesis/dissertation. *Entrance requirements:* For doctorate, GRE General Test. Additional exam requirements/recommendations for international students: Required—TOEFL. Electronic applications accepted. *Faculty research:* Spanish literature, Spanish-American literature, literary theory, criticism, cultural studies.

Florida Atlantic University, Dorothy F. Schmidt College of Arts and Letters, Department of Languages and Linguistics, Boca Raton, FL 33431-0991. Offers comparative literature (MA); French (MA); German (MA); Spanish (MA); teaching French (MAT); teaching German (MAT); teaching Spanish (MAT). Part-time programs available. *Degree requirements:* For master's, one foreign language, comprehensive exam, thesis optional. *Entrance requirements:* For master's, GRE General Test, minimum GPA of 3.0. *Faculty research:* Modern European studies, modern Latin America, medieval Europe.

Florida International University, College of Arts and Sciences, Department of Modern Languages, Miami, FL 33199. Offers Spanish (MA, PhD). Part-time and evening/weekend programs available. *Faculty:* 22 full-time (13 women). *Students:* 18 full-time (15 women), 27 part-time (19 women); includes 43 minority (2 African Americans, 1 Asian American or Pacific Islander, 40 Hispanic Americans), 2 international. Average age 43. 18 applicants, 56% accepted, 4 enrolled. In 2007, 6 master's, 3 doctorates awarded. *Degree requirements:* For master's, 2 foreign languages, thesis or alternative; for doctorate, 3 foreign languages, comprehensive exam, thesis/dissertation. *Entrance requirements:* For master's, 2 letters of recommendation, minimum GPA of 3.0; for doctorate, GRE General Test or EXADEP, minimum GPA of 3.0, writing example. Additional exam requirements/recommendations for international students: Required—TOEFL (minimum score 550 paper-based; 213 computer-based). *Application deadline:* For fall admission, 2/15 for domestic and international students; for spring admission, 10/1 for domestic students, 9/1 for international students. Applications are processed on a rolling basis. Application fee: $30. Electronic applications accepted. *Expenses:* Tuition, state resident: full-time $6,106. Tuition, nonresident: full-time $15,528. Required fees: $284. *Financial support:* Teaching assistantships, institutionally sponsored loans and scholarships/grants available. Support available to part-time students. *Faculty research:* Contemporary Spanish/Spanish-American literature, Spanish/Spanish-American linguistics, traductology. *Unit head:* Dr. Pascale Becel, Chairperson, 305-348-2851, Fax: 305-348-1085, E-mail: pascale.becel@fiu.edu.

Florida State University, Graduate Studies, College of Arts and Sciences, Department of Modern Languages, Program in Spanish, Tallahassee, FL 32306. Offers MA, PhD. *Faculty:* 14 full-time (8 women), 4 part-time/adjunct (2 women). *Students:* 28 full-time (22 women), 10 part-time (4 women); includes 2 African Americans, 12 Hispanic Americans. Average age 25. 30 applicants, 70% accepted, 13 enrolled. In 2007, 7 master's, 3 doctorates awarded. Terminal master's awarded for partial completion of doctoral program. *Degree requirements:* For master's, thesis optional; for doctorate, 2 foreign languages, thesis/dissertation. *Entrance requirements:* For master's and doctorate, GRE General Test or minimum GPA of 3.0. Additional exam requirements/recommendations for international students: Required—TOEFL (minimum score 550 paper-based; 213 computer-based). *Application deadline:* For fall admission, 1/15 for domestic and international students; for spring admission, 11/22 for domestic and international students. Applications are processed on a rolling basis. Application fee: $30. Electronic applications accepted. *Expenses:* Tuition, state resident: part-time $248 per credit hour. Tuition, nonresident: part-time $880 per credit hour. Tuition and fees vary according to program. *Financial support:* In 2007–08, 1 fellowship with partial tuition reimbursement (averaging $14,000 per year), 1 research assistantship with partial tuition reimbursement (averaging $12,000 per year), 39 teaching assistantships with partial tuition reimbursements (averaging $11,200 per year) were awarded. Financial award application deadline: 2/1; financial award applicants required to submit FAFSA. *Faculty research:* Latin American theater, Hispanic literature of the United States, twentieth century Latin American poetry, Spanish American colonial. *Unit head:* Dr. Delia Poey, Divisional Coordinator and Professor, 850-644-8394, Fax: 850-644-0524, E-mail: dpoey@fsu.edu. *Application contact:* Wendy E. Pigott, Graduate Academic Coordinator, 850-644-8397, Fax: 850-644-0524, E-mail: wpigott@fsu.edu.

Framingham State College, Division of Graduate and Continuing Education, Program in Spanish, Framingham, MA 01701-9101. Offers M Ed. *Students:* 19. In 2007, 7 degrees awarded. *Unit head:* Dr. Michael Wong-Russell, Coordinator, 508-626-4550, Fax: 508-626-4030, E-mail: mwongru@frc.mass.edu. *Application contact:* 508-626-4550, Fax: 508-626-4030, E-mail: dgce@frc.mass.edu.

Georgetown University, Graduate School of Arts and Sciences, Department of Spanish and Portuguese, Washington, DC 20057. Offers Spanish (MS, PhD), including Hispanic literature, Spanish linguistics, Spanish literature; MS/PhD. *Degree requirements:* For master's, one foreign language, research project; for doctorate, 3 foreign languages, thesis/dissertation. *Entrance requirements:* Additional exam requirements/recommendations for international students: Required—TOEFL.

Georgia Southern University, Jack N. Averitt College of Graduate Studies, College of Liberal Arts and Social Sciences, Department of Foreign Languages, Statesboro, GA 30460. Offers Spanish (MA). Part-time and evening/weekend programs available. *Students:* 5 full-time (all women), 6 part-time (5 women); includes 4 minority (all Hispanic Americans) Average age 34. 1 applicant, 100% accepted, 1 enrolled. *Degree requirements:* For master's, one foreign language, thesis optional. *Entrance requirements:* For master's, GRE, minimum GPA of 3.0. Additional exam requirements/recommendations for international students: Required—TOEFL (minimum score 550 paper-based; 213 computer-based; 80 iBT). *Application deadline:* For fall admission, 3/1 priority date for domestic and international students; for spring admission, 10/1 priority date for domestic students, 10/1 for international students. Applications are processed on a rolling basis. Application fee: $50. Electronic applications accepted. *Expenses:* Tuition, state resident: full-time $3,516; part-time $147 per semester hour. Tuition, nonresident: full-time $14,060; part-time $586 per semester hour. Required fees: $562 per term. *Financial support:* In 2007–08, 3 students received support, including research assistantships with partial tuition reimbursements available (averaging $6,850 per year), teaching assistantships with partial tuition reimbursements available (averaging $6,850 per year); career-related internships or fieldwork, Federal Work-Study, scholarships/grants, tuition waivers (partial), and unspecified assistantships also available. Support available to part-time students. Financial award application deadline: 4/15. *Unit head:* Dr. Donnie Richards, Chair, 912-478-5282, Fax: 912-478-0652, E-mail: forlangs@georgiasouthern.edu. *Application contact:* 912-478-5384, Fax: 912-478-0740, E-mail: gradadmissions@georgiasouthern.edu.

Georgia State University, College of Arts and Sciences, Department of Modern and Classical Languages, Program in Spanish, Atlanta, GA 30303-3083. Offers MA. Evening/weekend programs available. *Faculty:* 10 full-time (3 women), 3 part-time/adjunct. *Students:* 20 full-time, 8 part-time; includes 9 minority (4 African Americans, 1 Asian American or Pacific Islander, 4 Hispanic Americans). Average age 28. In 2007, 9 degrees awarded. *Degree requirements:* For master's, one foreign language, thesis or alternative, general exam. *Entrance requirements:* For master's, GRE General Test. Additional exam requirements/recommendations for international students: Required—TOEFL. *Application deadline:* For fall admission, 8/1 for domestic students; for spring admission, 12/1 for domestic students. Applications are processed on a rolling basis. Application fee: $50. Electronic applications accepted. *Expenses:* Tuition, state resident: part-time $221 per credit hour. *Financial support:* In 2007–08, research assistantships (averaging $3,000 per year), teaching assistantships (averaging $9,000 per year) were awarded; career-related internships or fieldwork, Federal Work-Study, and institutionally sponsored loans also available. Support available to part-time students. Financial award applicants required to submit FAFSA. *Faculty research:* Spanish and Latin-American literature. Total annual research expenditures: $15,000. *Application contact:* Dr. Elena del Rio Parra, Director of Graduate Studies, 404-413-6592, Fax: 404-413-5982, E-mail: mcledd@langate.gsu.edu.

Georgia State University, College of Arts and Sciences, Department of Modern and Classical Languages, Program in Translation and Interpretation, Atlanta, GA 30303-3083. Offers French (Certificate); German (Certificate); Spanish (Certificate). *Faculty:* 3 full-time, 2 part-time/adjunct. *Students:* Average age 32. *Application deadline:* For fall admission, 4/1 for domestic students; for spring admission, 11/15 for domestic students. Applications are processed on a rolling basis. Application fee: $50. Electronic applications accepted. *Expenses:* Tuition, state resident: part-time $221 per credit hour. *Unit head:* Dr. Annette Cash, Director, E-mail: acash@gsu.edu.

Graduate School and University Center of the City University of New York, Graduate Studies, Program in Hispanic and Luso-Brazilian Literatures and Languages, New York, NY 10016-4039. Offers PhD. *Faculty:* 23 full-time (8 women). *Students:* 105 full-time (66 women), 6 part-time (5 women); includes 57 minority (2 Asian Americans or Pacific Islanders, 55 Hispanic Americans), 36 international. Average age 41. 43 applicants, 67% accepted, 17 enrolled. In 2007, 5 degrees awarded. *Degree requirements:* For doctorate, 2 foreign languages, thesis/dissertation. *Entrance requirements:* For doctorate, GRE General Test. Additional exam requirements/recommendations for international students: Required—TOEFL. *Application deadline:* For fall admission, 1/15 for domestic students; for spring admission, 11/15 for domestic students. Application fee: $125. Electronic applications accepted. *Financial support:* In 2007–08, 68 students received support, including 58 fellowships, 2 research assistantships, 9 teaching assistantships; career-related internships or fieldwork, Federal Work-Study, institutionally sponsored loans, and tuition waivers (full and partial) also available. Financial award application deadline: 2/1; financial award applicants required to submit FAFSA. *Unit head:* Dr. Lia Schwartz, Executive Officer, 212-817-8411, Fax: 212-817-1522, E-mail: lschwartz@gc.cuny.edu.

Harvard University, Graduate School of Arts and Sciences, Department of Romance Languages and Literatures, Cambridge, MA 02138. Offers French (AM, PhD); Italian (AM, PhD); Portuguese (AM, PhD); Spanish (AM, PhD). Terminal master's awarded for partial completion of doctoral program. *Degree requirements:* For master's, 2 foreign languages; for doctorate, 2 foreign languages, thesis/dissertation. *Entrance requirements:* For master's and doctorate, GRE General Test, sample of written work. Additional exam requirements/recommendations for international students: Required—TOEFL. *Expenses:* Tuition: Full-time $31,456. Full-time tuition and fees vary according to program and student level.

Hofstra University, College of Liberal Arts and Sciences, Department of Romance Languages and Literatures, Hempstead, NY 11549. Offers Spanish (MA). *Accreditation:* NCATE. Part-time and evening/weekend programs available. *Faculty:* 5 full-time (3 women), 2 part-time/adjunct (1 woman). *Students:* 4 full-time (3 women), 8 part-time (6 women); includes 7 minority (1 Asian American or Pacific Islander, 6 Hispanic Americans), 1 international. Average age 34. 6 applicants, 83% accepted, 2 enrolled. In 2007, 2 degrees awarded. *Degree requirements:* For master's, one foreign language, thesis. *Entrance requirements:* For master's, essay. Additional exam requirements/recommendations for international students: Required—TOEFL (minimum score 550 paper-based; 213 computer-based). *Application deadline:* Applications are processed on a rolling basis. Application fee: $60. Electronic applications accepted. *Expenses:* Tuition: Full-time $14,220; part-time $820 per credit. Required fees: $970; $165 per term. Tuition and fees vary according to program. *Financial support:* In 2007–08, 10 students received support, including 1 fellowship with tuition reimbursement available (averaging $3,000 per year); research assistantships with full and partial tuition reimbursements available, Federal Work-Study, institutionally sponsored loans, scholarships/grants, and tuition waivers (full and partial) also available. Support available to part-time students. Financial award applicants required to submit FAFSA. *Faculty research:* Latin American poetry; Spanish cultural studies; Latin American cultural studies; politics of language; colonial and postcolonial studies; theatre. *Unit head:* Dr. Benita Sampedro, Chairperson, 516-463-4521, Fax: 516-463-2310, E-mail: benita.sampedro@hofstra.edu. *Application contact:* Carol Drummer, Dean of Graduate Admissions, 516-463-4876, Fax: 516-463-4664, E-mail: gradstudent@hofstra.edu.

Hofstra University, School of Education and Allied Human Services, Department of Curriculum and Teaching, Program in Foreign Language Education, Hempstead, NY 11549. Offers French (MA, MS Ed); German (MA, MS Ed); Russian (MA, MS Ed); Spanish (MA, MS Ed). Part-time and evening/weekend programs available. *Students:* 3 full-time (all women), 5 part-time (all women); includes 2 minority (1 African American, 1 Hispanic American). Average age 35. 9 applicants, 100% accepted, 4 enrolled. In 2007, 8 degrees awarded. *Degree requirements:* For master's, one foreign language, thesis. *Entrance requirements:* For master's, 2 letters of recommendation, teacher certification (MA), essay. Additional exam requirements/recommendations for international students: Required—TOEFL (minimum score 550 paper-based; 213 computer-based). *Application deadline:* Applications are processed on a rolling basis. Application fee: $60. Electronic applications accepted. *Expenses:* Tuition: Full-time $14,220; part-time $820 per credit. Required fees: $970; $165 per term. Tuition and fees vary according to program. *Financial support:* In 2007–08, 1 student received support; fellowships with tuition reimbursements available, research assistantships with full and partial tuition reimbursements available, Federal Work-Study, institutionally sponsored loans, scholarships/grants, and tuition waivers (full and partial) available. Support available to part-time students. Financial award applicants required to submit FAFSA. *Faculty research:* Current literature from France and Francophone world, George Sand, music and literature, colonial and postcolonial studies, contemporary Latin American poetry. *Unit head:* Dr. Lori J. Ultsch, Chairperson, 516-463-4519, Fax: 516-463-2310, E-mail: rllju@mail1.hofstra.edu. *Application contact:* Carol Drummer, Dean of Graduate Admissions, 516-463-4876, Fax: 516-463-4664, E-mail: gradstudent@hofstra.edu.

Howard University, Graduate School, Department of Modern Languages and Literatures, Washington, DC 20059-0002. Offers French (MA); Spanish (MA). Part-time programs available. *Degree requirements:* For master's, one foreign language, comprehensive exam, thesis. *Entrance requirements:* For master's, GRE General Test, writing samples in English and French or Spanish. *Expenses:* Tuition: Full-time $16,175; part-time $899 per credit hour. Required fees: $805. *Faculty research:* African literature in French, Spanish linguistics, Spanish Peninsular literature, Spanish sociolinguistics.

Hunter College of the City University of New York, Graduate School, School of Arts and Sciences, Department of Romance Languages, Program in Spanish, New York, NY 10021-5085. Offers Spanish (MA); Spanish education (MA). Part-time and evening/weekend programs available. *Faculty:* 4 full-time (3 women). *Students:* 1 (woman) full-time, 12 part-time (10 women); includes 8 minority (all Hispanic Americans) Average age 33. 11 applicants, 82% accepted, 5 enrolled. In 2007, 7 degrees awarded. *Degree requirements:* For master's, 2 foreign languages, comprehensive exam, thesis optional. *Entrance requirements:* For master's, GRE General Test, GRE Subject Test, ability to read, speak, and write Spanish; interview. Additional exam requirements/recommendations for international students: Required—TOEFL. *Application deadline:* For fall admission, 4/1 for domestic students, 2/1 for international students; for spring admission, 11/1 for domestic students, 9/1 for international students. Application fee: $125. *Expenses:* Tuition, state resident: full-time $6,400; part-time $270 per credit. Tuition, nonresident: part-time $500 per credit. One-time fee: $125 full-time. Tuition and fees vary according to program. *Financial support:* Federal Work-Study and tuition waivers (partial) available. Support available to part-time students. Financial award application deadline: 4/15. *Faculty research:* Galician studies, contemporary Spanish poetry, Lope de Vega, comparative

Spanish

Hunter College of the City University of New York (continued)
Hispanic literatures, contemporary Hispanic poetry. *Unit head:* Dr. James O. Pellier, Graduate Advisor, 212-772-5625, E-mail: jpellice@hunter.cuny.edu. *Application contact:* William Zlata, Director for Graduate Admissions, 212-772-4482, Fax: 212-650-3336, E-mail: admissions@hunter.cuny.edu.

Illinois State University, Graduate School, College of Arts and Sciences, Department of Foreign Languages, Literatures and Cultures, Normal, IL 61790-2200. Offers French (MA); French and German (MA); French and Spanish (MA); German (MA); German and Spanish (MA); Spanish (MA). *Faculty:* 17 full-time (7 women). *Students:* 24 full-time (12 women), 9 part-time (8 women); includes 8 minority (4 African Americans, 1 American Indian/Alaska Native, 3 Hispanic Americans), 2 international. 18 applicants, 94% accepted. In 2007, 15 degrees awarded. *Degree requirements:* For master's, variable foreign language requirement, comprehensive exam, 1 term of residency. *Entrance requirements:* For master's, GRE General Test, minimum GPA of 2.8 in last 60 hours of course work. *Application deadline:* Applications are processed on a rolling basis. Application fee: $40. *Expenses:* Tuition, state resident: full-time $3,492; part-time $194 per credit hour. Tuition, nonresident: full-time $7,272; part-time $404 per credit hour. Required fees: $1,024; $57 per credit hour. *Financial support:* In 2007–08, 3 research assistantships (averaging $4,809 per year), 18 teaching assistantships (averaging $7,500 per year) were awarded; tuition waivers (full) and unspecified assistantships also available. Financial award application deadline: 4/1. *Unit head:* Daniel Everett, Chairperson, 309-438-2111.

Indiana University Bloomington, University Graduate School, College of Arts and Sciences, Department of Spanish and Portuguese, Bloomington, IN 47405-7000. Offers Hispanic linguistics (MA, PhD); Hispanic literature (MA); Luso-Brazilian literature (MA); Luso-Brazilian studies (PhD); Spanish literatures (PhD); teaching Spanish (MAT). *Faculty:* 18 full-time (10 women). *Students:* 67 full-time (35 women), 11 part-time (6 women); includes 17 minority (1 African American, 16 Hispanic Americans), 16 international. Average age 30. 70 applicants, 27% accepted, 19 enrolled. In 2007, 13 master's, 3 doctorates awarded. *Median time to degree:* Of those who began their doctoral program in fall 1999, 60% received their degree in 8 years or less. *Degree requirements:* For master's, one foreign language; for doctorate, 3 foreign languages, thesis/dissertation. *Entrance requirements:* For master's, GRE General Test, GRE Subject Test, bachelor's degree in Portuguese or Spanish, minimum GPA of 3.25; for doctorate, GRE General Test, GRE Subject Test, master's degree in Portuguese or Spanish, minimum GPA of 3.25. Additional exam requirements/recommendations for international students: Required—TOEFL. *Application deadline:* For fall admission, 1/15 priority date for domestic students, 12/15 for international students; for spring admission, 9/1 for domestic and international students. Application fee: $50 ($60 for international students). *Financial support:* Fellowships with full tuition reimbursements, research assistantships, teaching assistantships with full tuition reimbursements, Federal Work-Study available. Financial award application deadline: 1/15. *Faculty research:* Spanish American literature, Spanish peninsular literature, Luso-Brazilian studies, Catalan studies. *Unit head:* Josep Miguel Sobrer, Chair, 812-855-8498. *Application contact:* Steven Wagschal, Student Contact, 812-855-9194, E-mail: swagscha@indiana.edu.

Inter American University of Puerto Rico, Metropolitan Campus, Faculty of Liberal Arts, Program in Spanish, San Juan, PR 00919-1293. Offers MA. Part-time and evening/weekend programs available. *Degree requirements:* For master's, one foreign language, comprehensive exam. *Entrance requirements:* For master's, GRE or EXADEP, interview, minimum GPA of 2.5, 6 credits each of Spanish literature and Hispanic-American literature. Electronic applications accepted.

Inter American University of Puerto Rico, Ponce Campus, Graduate School, Mercedita, PR 00715-1602. Offers accounting (MBA); biology (M Ed); chemistry (M Ed); criminal justice (MA); elementary education (M Ed); English as a Second Language (M Ed); finance (MBA); history (M Ed); human resources (MBA); marketing (MBA); mathematics (M Ed); Spanish (M Ed). *Entrance requirements:* For master's, minimum GPA of 2.5.

Iona College, School of Arts and Science, Program in Foreign Languages, New Rochelle, NY 10801-1890. Offers Italian (MA); Spanish (MA). Part-time and evening/weekend programs available. *Faculty:* 5 full-time (2 women), 2 part-time/adjunct (1 woman). *Students:* Average age 29. 6 applicants, 83% accepted, 3 enrolled. In 2007, 2 degrees awarded. *Degree requirements:* For master's, thesis or alternative. *Entrance requirements:* For master's, minimum GPA of 3.0. Additional exam requirements/recommendations for international students: Required—TOEFL (minimum score 550 paper-based; 213 computer-based). *Application deadline:* Applications are processed on a rolling basis. Application fee: $50. Electronic applications accepted. *Expenses:* Tuition: Part-time $712 per credit. Required fees: $150 per term. *Financial support:* Unspecified assistantships available. Support available to part-time students. *Faculty research:* Contemporary Spanish literature, linguistics, language acquisition, female Hispanic literature, Latina authors. *Unit head:* Dr. Victoria Ketz, Chair, 914-637-2738, E-mail: vketz@iona.edu. *Application contact:* Veronica Jarek-Prinz, Director of Graduate Admissions, 914-633-2420, Fax: 914-633-2277, E-mail: vjarekprinz@iona.edu.

The Johns Hopkins University, Zanvyl Krieger School of Arts and Sciences, Department of German and Romance Languages, Baltimore, MD 21218-2699. Offers French (PhD); German (PhD); Italian (PhD); romance languages (PhD); Spanish (PhD). *Faculty:* 14 full-time (5 women), 2 part-time/adjunct (1 woman). *Students:* 69 full-time (48 women); includes 6 minority (all Hispanic Americans), 37 international. Average age 29. 42 applicants, 36% accepted, 8 enrolled. In 2007, 13 doctorates awarded. *Median time to degree:* Of those who began their doctoral program in fall 1999, 75% received their degree in 8 years or less. *Degree requirements:* For doctorate, 2 foreign languages, thesis/dissertation. *Entrance requirements:* For doctorate, GRE General Test. Additional exam requirements/recommendations for international students: Required—TOEFL (minimum score 600 paper-based; 250 computer-based). *Application deadline:* For fall admission, 1/15 for domestic and international students. Application fee: $60. Electronic applications accepted. *Financial support:* In 2007–08, 64 students received support, including 40 fellowships with full tuition reimbursements available (averaging $16,000 per year), 2 research assistantships with full tuition reimbursements available (averaging $16,000 per year), 19 teaching assistantships with full tuition reimbursements available (averaging $16,000 per year); institutionally sponsored loans and tuition waivers (full and partial) also available. Financial award application deadline: 4/15; financial award applicants required to submit FAFSA. *Unit head:* Dr. Stephen Nichols, Chair, 410-516-4736, Fax: 410-516-5358, E-mail: stephen.nichols@jhu.edu. *Application contact:* Sally Hauf, Graduate Administrative Coordinator, 410-516-7226, Fax: 410-516-5358, E-mail: shauf@jhu.edu.

Kansas State University, Graduate School, College of Arts and Sciences, Department of Modern Languages, Manhattan, KS 66506. Offers French (MA); German (MA); Spanish (MA). Part-time and evening/weekend programs available. Postbaccalaureate distance learning degree programs offered (minimal on-campus study). *Faculty:* 15 full-time (6 women). *Students:* 11 full-time (7 women), 6 part-time (5 women); includes 1 minority (Hispanic American), 4 international. 8 applicants, 75% accepted, 5 enrolled. In 2007, 9 degrees awarded. *Degree requirements:* For master's, thesis optional. *Entrance requirements:* For master's, teaching certificate. Additional exam requirements/recommendations for international students: Required—TOEFL (minimum score 560 paper-based). *Application deadline:* For fall admission, 2/1 priority date for domestic and international students; for spring admission, 10/1 for domestic students, 8/1 priority date for international students. Applications are processed on a rolling basis. Application fee: $30 ($55 for international students). *Financial support:* In 2007–08, 19 teaching assistantships with full tuition reimbursements (averaging $11,711 per year) were awarded; fellowships, Federal Work-Study, institutionally sponsored loans, and scholarships/grants also available. Support available to part-time students. Financial award application deadline: 3/1; financial award applicants required to submit FAFSA. *Faculty research:* Second language acquisitions; Chicano literature; Francophone literature; cultural studies; German, French, Spanish, and Spanish-American literature from the Middle Ages to the modern era. *Unit head:* Robert Corum, Head, 785-532-1987, Fax: 785-532-7004, E-mail: corum@ksu.edu. *Application contact:* Claire Dehon, Director, 785-532-1929, Fax: 785-532-7004, E-mail: dehoncl@ksu.edu.

Kean University, College of Education, Program in Classroom Instruction and Curriculum, Union, NJ 07083. Offers bilingual classroom instruction (MA); bilingual/bicultural education (MA); classroom instruction (MA); earth science (MA); educational technology (MA); mathematics/science/computer education (MA); teaching (MA); teaching English as a second language (MA); world languages (Spanish) (MA). *Accreditation:* NCATE. Part-time and evening/weekend programs available. *Faculty:* 19 full-time (8 women). *Students:* 37 full-time (27 women), 156 part-time (124 women); includes 10 African Americans, 6 Asian Americans or Pacific Islanders, 55 Hispanic Americans, 4 international. Average age 34. 74 applicants, 85% accepted, 50 enrolled. In 2007, 49 degrees awarded. *Degree requirements:* For master's, 2 foreign languages, comprehensive exam, thesis, language proficiency. *Entrance requirements:* For master's, GRE General Test or MAT, PRAXIS, minimum GPA of 2.75, 2 letters of recommendation, interview, teaching certification (for some programs). *Application deadline:* For fall admission, 5/1 for domestic students; for spring admission, 11/1 for domestic students. Application fee: $60 ($150 for international students). Electronic applications accepted. *Expenses:* Tuition, state resident: full-time $9,384; part-time $391 per credit. Tuition, nonresident: full-time $12,720; part-time $530 per credit. Required fees: $2,382; $99 per credit. Part-time tuition and fees vary according to course load. *Financial support:* In 2007–08, 3 research assistantships with full tuition reimbursements (averaging $3,217 per year) were awarded; unspecified assistantships also available. *Unit head:* Dr. Thomas Walsh, Program Coordinator, 908-737-4296, E-mail: twalsh@kean.edu. *Application contact:* Joanne Morris, Director of Graduate Admissions, 908-737-3355, Fax: 908-737-3354, E-mail: grad-adm@kean.edu.

Kent State University, College of Arts and Sciences, Department of Modern and Classical Language Studies, Kent, OH 44242-0001. Offers French literature (MA); French, Spanish, German and Latin pedagogy (MA); German literature (MA); Spanish literature (MA); translation (MA), including French, German, Japanese, Russian, Spanish; translation studies (PhD). Part-time and evening/weekend programs available. *Faculty:* 31 full-time (15 women), 4 part-time/adjunct (2 women). *Students:* 64 full-time (45 women), 27 part-time (26 women). Average age 32. 113 applicants, 80% accepted, 42 enrolled. In 2007, 27 degrees awarded. *Degree requirements:* For master's, one foreign language, comprehensive exam (for some programs), thesis (for some programs); for doctorate, comprehensive exam, thesis/dissertation (for some programs). *Entrance requirements:* For master's, minimum GPA of 3.0, writing sample, audio tape or CD; for doctorate, 3 recommendations. Additional exam requirements/recommendations for international students: Required—TOEFL (minimum score 197 computer-based). *Application deadline:* For fall admission, 2/28 for domestic and international students. Applications are processed on a rolling basis. Application fee: $30. Electronic applications accepted. *Financial support:* In 2007–08, 31 teaching assistantships with full tuition reimbursements (averaging $8,000 per year) were awarded; research assistantships with full tuition reimbursements, career-related internships or fieldwork, Federal Work-Study, health care benefits, tuition waivers (full and partial), and unspecified assistantships also available. Support available to part-time students. Financial award application deadline: 2/1. *Faculty research:* Literature, pedagogy, applied linguistics, translation studies. *Unit head:* Dr. Gregory M Shreve, Chair, 330-672-1796, Fax: 330-672-4009, E-mail: gshreve@kent.edu. *Application contact:* Carol S. Maier, Graduate Coordinator, 330-672-1797, Fax: 330-672-4009, E-mail: cmaier@kent.edu.

Lehman College of the City University of New York, Division of Arts and Humanities, Department of Languages and Literatures, Bronx, NY 10468-1589. Offers Spanish (MA). Part-time and evening/weekend programs available. *Degree requirements:* For master's, one foreign language.

Long Island University, C.W. Post Campus, College of Liberal Arts and Sciences, Department of Foreign Languages, Brookville, NY 11548-1300. Offers Spanish (MA); Spanish education (MS). Part-time programs available. *Degree requirements:* For master's, 2 foreign languages, comprehensive exam, thesis or alternative. *Entrance requirements:* For master's, 24 credits of undergraduate Spanish. Electronic applications accepted. *Expenses:* Tuition: Part-time $825 per credit. Tuition and fees vary according to course load. *Faculty research:* Making of superhero, dialogue in the 19th century novel, nicknames, Menendez Pidal and Spanish School of Philology, women writers of Latin America.

Loyola University Chicago, Graduate School, Department of Modern Languages and Literatures, Chicago, IL 60611-2196. Offers Spanish (MA). Part-time and evening/weekend programs available. *Faculty:* 6 full-time (4 women), 1 part-time/adjunct (0 women). *Students:* 12 full-time (7 women), 17 part-time (12 women); includes 13 minority (1 African American, 1 Asian American or Pacific Islander, 11 Hispanic Americans), 2 international. Average age 30. 16 applicants, 100% accepted, 11 enrolled. In 2007, 8 master's awarded. *Degree requirements:* For master's, 2 foreign languages, comprehensive exam, thesis or alternative. *Entrance requirements:* Additional exam requirements/recommendations for international students: Required—TOEFL. Application fee: $50. *Expenses:* Tuition: Full-time $12,780; part-time $710 per credit hour. Required fees: $55 per semester. Full-time tuition and fees vary according to program. *Financial support:* In 2007–08, 6 students received support, including 3 teaching assistantships with full tuition reimbursements available (averaging $10,000 per year); scholarships/grants also available. Financial award applicants required to submit FAFSA. *Faculty research:* Linguistics, Latin American contemporary narrative, Latin American culture and civilization, Hispanic women's studies, twentieth century peninsular writing, Golden Age, Don Quixote. *Unit head:* Dr. Olympia Gonzalez, Chair, 773-508-2872, Fax: 773-508-3514, E-mail: ogonzal@luc.edu.

Marquette University, Graduate School, College of Arts and Sciences, Department of Foreign Languages and Literatures, Milwaukee, WI 53201-1881. Offers Spanish (MA, MAT). Part-time programs available. *Faculty:* 33 full-time (22 women), 4 part-time/adjunct (3 women). *Students:* 8 full-time (3 women), 3 part-time (all women); includes 4 minority (1 Asian American or Pacific Islander, 3 Hispanic Americans), 1 international. Average age 26. 11 applicants, 100% accepted, 5 enrolled. In 2007, 3 degrees awarded. *Degree requirements:* For master's, one foreign language, comprehensive exam or thesis. *Entrance requirements:* Additional exam requirements/recommendations for international students: Required—TOEFL. Application fee: $40. *Financial support:* In 2007–08, 5 research assistantships were awarded; teaching assistantships, Federal Work-Study, institutionally sponsored loans, scholarships/grants, and tuition waivers (full and partial) also available. Support available to part-time students. Financial award application deadline: 2/15. *Faculty research:* Magic realism, African-Hispanic literature, women studies, Hispanic linguistics. *Unit head:* Dr. Belén Castaneda, Chair, 414-288-7063, Fax: 414-288-1578. *Application contact:* Dr. Armando Gonzáles-Percz, Director of Graduate Studies, 414-288-7268, Fax: 414-288-1578.

Miami University, Graduate School, College of Arts and Sciences, Department of Spanish and Portuguese, Oxford, OH 45056. Offers Spanish (MA). Part-time programs available. *Degree requirements:* For master's, thesis (for some programs), final exam. *Entrance requirements:* For master's, minimum undergraduate GPA of 3.0 during previous 2 years or 2.75 overall. Additional exam requirements/recommendations for international students: Required—TOEFL (minimum score 550 paper-based; 213 computer-based), TWE (minimum score 4). Electronic applications accepted.

Michigan State University, The Graduate School, College of Arts and Letters, Department of Spanish and Portuguese, East Lansing, MI 48824. Offers applied Spanish linguistics (MA); Hispanic cultural studies (PhD); Hispanic literatures (MA). *Entrance requirements:* Additional exam requirements/recommendations for international students: Required—TOEFL. Electronic applications accepted. *Expenses:* Tuition, state resident: part-time $379 per credit hour. Tuition, nonresident: part-time $800 per credit hour. Tuition and fees vary according to program.

Middlebury College, Language Schools, Spanish School, Middlebury, VT 05753-6002. Offers MA, DML. *Faculty:* 23 full-time (10 women). *Students:* 196 full-time (140 women);

includes 35 minority (4 African Americans, 1 Asian American or Pacific Islander, 30 Hispanic Americans). Average age 30. 370 applicants, 70% accepted, 196 enrolled. In 2007, 87 master's, 1 doctorate awarded. *Degree requirements:* For master's, one foreign language; for doctorate, 2 foreign languages, thesis/dissertation, residence abroad, teaching experience. *Entrance requirements:* For master's, placement exam, 3 letters of recommendation, writing sample. Application fee: $55. Electronic applications accepted. *Financial support:* Fellowships, scholarships/grants available. *Unit head:* Dr. Susan Carvalho, Director, 802-443-5539. *Application contact:* Audrey LaRock, Coordinator, 802-443-5539, Fax: 802-443-2075.

Millersville University of Pennsylvania, Graduate School, School of Humanities and Social Sciences, Department of Foreign Languages, Program in Spanish, Millersville, PA 17551-0302. Offers M Ed, MA. Part-time programs available. *Faculty:* 9 full-time (6 women), 3 part-time/adjunct (2 women). *Students:* 1 (woman) full-time, 2 part-time (1 woman); includes 1 minority (Hispanic American) Average age 30. 2 applicants, 50% accepted, 1 enrolled. In 2007, 4 degrees awarded. *Degree requirements:* For master's, one foreign language, thesis optional, departmental exam. *Entrance requirements:* For master's, GRE or MAT, 24 undergraduate credits in Spanish, minimum undergraduate GPA of 3.0. Additional exam requirements/recommendations for international students: Required—TOEFL (minimum score 500 paper-based; 183 computer-based). *Application deadline:* For fall admission, 2/1 priority date for domestic students; for winter admission, 10/1 priority date for domestic students; for spring admission, 10/1 priority date for domestic students. Applications are processed on a rolling basis. Application fee: $40. Electronic applications accepted. *Expenses:* Tuition, state resident: full-time $6,214; part-time $345 per credit. Tuition, nonresident: full-time $9,944; part-time $552 per credit. Required fees: $1,442. Tuition and fees vary according to course load. *Financial support:* Research assistantships with tuition reimbursements, institutionally sponsored loans available. Support available to part-time students. Financial award application deadline: 3/15; financial award applicants required to submit FAFSA. *Application contact:* Dr. Victor S. DeSantis, Dean of Graduate Studies, 717-872-3099, Fax: 717-871-2022, E-mail: victor.desantis@millersville.edu.

Minnesota State University Mankato, College of Graduate Studies, College of Arts and Humanities, Department of Modern Languages, Program in Spanish, Mankato, MN 56001. Offers MAT, MS. *Students:* 5 full-time (4 women), 12 part-time (9 women). Average age 31. In 2007, 3 degrees awarded. *Degree requirements:* For master's, one foreign language, comprehensive exam, thesis. *Entrance requirements:* For master's, minimum GPA of 3.0 during previous 2 years. *Application deadline:* For fall admission, 7/1 priority date for domestic students; for spring admission, 11/1 for domestic students. Applications are processed on a rolling basis. Application fee: $40. Electronic applications accepted. *Financial support:* Research assistantships with full tuition reimbursements, teaching assistantships with full tuition reimbursements, career-related internships or fieldwork, Federal Work-Study, institutionally sponsored loans, and unspecified assistantships available. Support available to part-time students. Financial award application deadline: 3/15. *Unit head:* Dr. Kimberly Contag, Graduate Coordinator, 507-389-5358. *Application contact:* 507-389-2321, E-mail: grad@mnsu.edu.

Mississippi State University, College of Arts and Sciences, Department of Foreign Languages, Mississippi State, MS 39762. Offers French (MA); French/German (MA); German (MA); Spanish (MA); Spanish/French (MA); Spanish/German (MA). Part-time programs available. *Faculty:* 19 full-time (11 women), 5 part-time/adjunct (all women). *Students:* 22 full-time (12 women), 1 part-time; includes 2 minority (both Hispanic Americans), 4 international. Average age 30. 7 applicants, 86% accepted, 3 enrolled. In 2007, 7 degrees awarded. *Degree requirements:* For master's, one foreign language, thesis optional, comprehensive oral or written exam. *Entrance requirements:* For master's, minimum GPA of 2.75. Additional exam requirements/recommendations for international students: Required—TOEFL (minimum score 525 paper-based). *Application deadline:* For fall admission, 7/1 for domestic students; for spring admission, 11/1 for domestic students. Applications are processed on a rolling basis. Application fee: $30. *Expenses:* Tuition, state resident: full-time $4,978; part-time $274 per hour. Tuition, nonresident: full-time $11,469; part-time $635 per hour. *Financial support:* In 2007–08, 21 teaching assistantships with full tuition reimbursements (averaging $8,766 per year) were awarded; Federal Work-Study, institutionally sponsored loans, and unspecified assistantships also available. Financial award applicants required to submit FAFSA. *Faculty research:* French, German, Spanish literature from medieval to present; gender and cultural studies in French; Spanish American literature; foreign language methodology; linguistics. *Unit head:* Dr. Jack Jordan, Interim Head, 662-325-3480, Fax: 662-325-8209, E-mail: jordan@ra.msstate.edu. *Application contact:* Dr. William A. Person, Interim Associate Vice President for Academic Affairs/Interim Dean of Graduate Studies, 662-325-7400, Fax: 662-325-1967, E-mail: grad@grad.msstate.edu.

Missouri State University, Graduate College, College of Arts and Letters, Department of Modern and Classical Languages, Springfield, MO 65804-0094. Offers secondary education (MS Ed), including French, German, Spanish. *Faculty:* 5 full-time (2 women). *Students:* 2 full-time (both women), 5 part-time (all women); includes 2 minority (both Hispanic Americans) Average age 38. In 2007, 1 degree awarded. *Entrance requirements:* For master's, grades 9–12 teaching certification. Additional exam requirements/recommendations for international students: Required—TOEFL (minimum score 550 paper-based; 213 computer-based; 79 iBT), IELTS (minimum score 6). *Application deadline:* For fall admission, 7/20 priority date for domestic students; for spring admission, 12/20 priority date for domestic students. Application fee: $35. *Expenses:* Tuition, state resident: full-time $3,708; part-time $206 per credit hour. Tuition, nonresident: full-time $7,236; part-time $206 per credit hour. Required fees: $622. Full-time tuition and fees vary according to course level, course load, program and reciprocity agreements. *Financial support:* Teaching assistantships with full tuition reimbursements available. Financial award applicants required to submit FAFSA. *Unit head:* Dr. Madeleine Kernen, Head, 417-836-7626, E-mail: mcl@missouristate.edu.

Montclair State University, The Office of Graduate Admissions and Support Services, College of Education and Human Services, Department of Curriculum and Teaching, Montclair, NJ 07043-1624. Offers education (M Ed); educational technology (M Ed); learning disabled teacher consultant (Certificate); school library media specialist (Certificate); teaching (MAT, Certificate), including art (MAT), biological science (MAT), early childhood education (P-3) (MAT), earth science (MAT), elementary education (K-8) (MAT), English (MAT), French (MAT), health and physical education (MAT), health education (MAT), home economics (MAT), mathematics (MAT), music (MAT), physical education (MAT), physical science (MAT), social studies (MAT), Spanish (MAT), teacher of ESL (MAT), teacher of students with disabilities (MAT). Part-time and evening/weekend programs available. *Faculty:* 17 full-time (13 women), 14 part-time/adjunct (10 women). *Students:* 118 full-time (86 women), 221 part-time (187 women); includes 50 minority (25 African Americans, 8 Asian Americans or Pacific Islanders, 17 Hispanic Americans), 3 international. Average age 33. 305 applicants, 52% accepted, 124 enrolled. In 2007, 178 master's, 19 other advanced degrees awarded. *Degree requirements:* For master's, comprehensive exam, field experience. *Entrance requirements:* For master's, PRAXIS II, minimum GPA of 2.67, 2 letters of recommendation. Additional exam requirements/recommendations for international students: Required—TOEFL (minimum score 83 computer-based). *Application deadline:* For fall admission, 2/15 for domestic and international students; for spring admission, 9/15 for domestic and international students. Applications are processed on a rolling basis. Application fee: $60. Electronic applications accepted. *Financial support:* In 2007–08, 7 research assistantships with full tuition reimbursements (averaging $7,000 per year) were awarded; Federal Work-Study, scholarships/grants, and unspecified assistantships also available. Support available to part-time students. Financial award application deadline: 3/1; financial award applicants required to submit FAFSA. *Unit head:* Dr. Deborah Eldridge, Chairperson, 973-655-5187.

Montclair State University, The Office of Graduate Admissions and Support Services, College of Humanities and Social Sciences, Department of Spanish and Italian, Montclair, NJ 07043-1624. Offers Italian (Certificate); Spanish (MA, Certificate); translating and interpreting Spanish (Certificate). Part-time and evening/weekend programs available. *Faculty:* 15 full-time (9 women), 16 part-time/adjunct (14 women). *Students:* 9 full-time (7 women), 30 part-time (23 women); includes 12 minority (1 African American, 11 Hispanic Americans), 2 international. 39 applicants, 44% accepted, 13 enrolled. In 2007, 5 master's, 3 other advanced degrees awarded. *Degree requirements:* For master's, comprehensive exam, thesis or alternative. *Entrance requirements:* For master's, GRE General Test, BA in Spanish or at least 24 undergraduate credits of Spanish, 2 letters of recommendation. Additional exam requirements/recommendations for international students: Required—TOEFL (minimum score 83 computer-based). *Application deadline:* For fall admission, 6/1 for international students; for spring admission, 11/1 for international students. Applications are processed on a rolling basis. Application fee: $60. Electronic applications accepted. *Financial support:* In 2007–08, 1 research assistantship with full tuition reimbursement (averaging $7,000 per year) was awarded; Federal Work-Study, scholarships/grants, and unspecified assistantships also available. Support available to part-time students. Financial award application deadline: 3/1; financial award applicants required to submit FAFSA. *Unit head:* Dr. Linda Levine, Chairperson, 973-655-4285. *Application contact:* Dr. Roger Zapata, Adviser, 973-655-4285, E-mail: zapatar@mail.montclair.edu.

New Mexico State University, Graduate School, College of Arts and Sciences, Department of Languages and Linguistics, Las Cruces, NM 88003-8001. Offers Spanish (MA). Part-time programs available. *Faculty:* 10 full-time (3 women). *Students:* 22 full-time (10 women), 6 part-time (4 women); includes 5 minority (all Hispanic Americans) Average age 32. 10 applicants, 80% accepted, 5 enrolled. In 2007, 13 degrees awarded. *Degree requirements:* For master's, one foreign language, comprehensive exam, thesis optional, oral and written exams. *Entrance requirements:* For master's, sample of written work in Spanish, cassette tape in Spanish, 3 letters of reference. *Application deadline:* For fall admission, 2/15 for domestic students; for spring admission, 10/12 for domestic students. Applications are processed on a rolling basis. Application fee: $30 ($50 for international students). Electronic applications accepted. *Expenses:* Tuition, state resident: full-time $3,602; part-time $199 per credit. Tuition, nonresident: full-time $13,380; part-time $607 per credit. Required fees: $1,178. *Financial support:* In 2007–08, 15 teaching assistantships were awarded; Federal Work-Study, institutionally sponsored loans, scholarships/grants, health care benefits, and unspecified assistantships also available. Support available to part-time students. Financial award application deadline: 3/1. *Faculty research:* Spanish-American literature, U.S. Hispanic and Chicano literature and border culture, Hispanic linguistics, French and German literature and linguistics. *Unit head:* Dr. Richard Rundell, Head, 575-646-3408, Fax: 575-646-7876, E-mail: rrundell@nmsu.edu.

New York University, Graduate School of Arts and Science, Department of Spanish and Portuguese Languages and Literatures, New York, NY 10012-1019. Offers Portuguese (MA, PhD); Spanish (PhD); Spanish and Latin American literatures and cultures (MA); Spanish language and translation (MA). Part-time programs available. *Faculty:* 17 full-time (10 women), 11 part-time/adjunct. *Students:* 77 full-time (49 women), 6 part-time (all women); includes 30 minority (2 African Americans, 4 Asian Americans or Pacific Islanders, 24 Hispanic Americans), 23 international. Average age 30. 194 applicants, 44% accepted, 35 enrolled. In 2007, 28 master's, 6 doctorates awarded. *Degree requirements:* For master's, 2 foreign languages, thesis; for doctorate, 2 foreign languages, thesis/dissertation. *Entrance requirements:* For master's, GRE General Test; for doctorate, GRE General Test, master's degree. Additional exam requirements/recommendations for international students: Required—TOEFL. *Application deadline:* For fall admission, 1/4 priority date for domestic students. Application fee: $85. *Financial support:* Fellowships with tuition reimbursements, teaching assistantships with tuition reimbursements, career-related internships or fieldwork, Federal Work-Study, institutionally sponsored loans, scholarships/grants, health care benefits, and unspecified assistantships available. Financial award application deadline: 1/4; financial award applicants required to submit FAFSA. *Faculty research:* Gender and sexuality, transatlantic studies, literacy and cultural theories, colonial and post colonial studies, autobiography and modern subjectivities. *Unit head:* James Fernandez, Chair, 212-998-8770, Fax: 212-995-4148, E-mail: spanish.portuguese.info@nyu.edu. *Application contact:* Gabriela Basterra, Director of Graduate Studies, 212-998-8770, Fax: 212-995-4149, E-mail: spanish.portuguese.info@nyu.edu.

North Carolina State University, Graduate School, College of Humanities and Social Sciences, Department of Foreign Languages and Literatures, Program in Spanish Language and Literature, Raleigh, NC 27695. Offers MA. *Degree requirements:* For master's, thesis optional. *Entrance requirements:* For master's, fluency in Spanish. Electronic applications accepted. *Faculty research:* Applied linguistics, technology-assisted language instruction, Latin-American literature and culture, 20th and 21st Century Spanish narrative and film, children's literature.

Northern Illinois University, Graduate School, College of Liberal Arts and Sciences, Department of Foreign Languages and Literatures, De Kalb, IL 60115-2854. Offers French (MA); Spanish (MA). Part-time programs available. *Faculty:* 25 full-time (11 women). *Students:* 8 full-time (5 women), 25 part-time (22 women); includes 10 minority (1 African American, 9 Hispanic Americans), 1 international. Average age 39. 10 applicants, 60% accepted, 4 enrolled. In 2007, 11 degrees awarded. *Degree requirements:* For master's, one foreign language, comprehensive exam, thesis or alternative, language proficiency exam. *Entrance requirements:* For master's, GRE General Test, interview, minimum GPA of 2.75, undergraduate major in French or Spanish. Additional exam requirements/recommendations for international students: Required—TOEFL (minimum score 550 paper-based; 213 computer-based). *Application deadline:* For fall admission, 6/1 for domestic students, 5/1 for international students; for spring admission, 11/1 for domestic students, 10/1 for international students. Applications are processed on a rolling basis. Application fee: $30. Electronic applications accepted. *Expenses:* Tuition, area resident: Part-time $226 per credit hour. Tuition, state resident: full-time $5,424; part-time $225 per credit hour. Tuition, nonresident: full-time $10,848. Required fees: $2,416; $64 per credit hour. *Financial support:* In 2007–08, 13 teaching assistantships with full tuition reimbursements were awarded; fellowships with full tuition reimbursements, research assistantships with full tuition reimbursements, career-related internships or fieldwork, Federal Work-Study, scholarships/grants, tuition waivers (full), and unspecified assistantships also available. Support available to part-time students. Financial award applicants required to submit FAFSA. *Faculty research:* Francophone women writers, prosodies of French and Italian, early Spanish drama, business German, history of Burmese literature. *Unit head:* Anne Birbeck, Acting Chair, 815-753-1259, Fax: 815-753-5989, E-mail: annie@niu.edu.

Nova Southeastern University, Fischler School of Education and Human Services, Graduate Teacher Education Program, Fort Lauderdale, FL 33314-7796. Offers athletic administration (MS); brain research (MS, Ed S); charter school education/leadership (MS); cognitive and behavioral disabilities (MS); computer science education (Ed S); computer science education (K-12) (MS); curriculum and teaching (Ed S); curriculum, instruction and technology (MS); curriculum, instruction, management and administration (Ed S); early childhood education (MS); early literacy and reading (Ed S); early literacy education (MS); education technology (MS); educational leadership (administration K–12) (MS, Ed S); educational media (Ed S); educational media (K-12) (MS); elementary education (MS, Ed S), including ESOL endorsement (MS); English education (MS, Ed S); environmental education (MS); exceptional student education (MS), including ESOL endorsement; exceptional student education and reading (MS); gifted education (MS, Ed S); interdisciplinary arts education (MS); management and administration of educational programs (MS); mathematics (MS); mathematics education (Ed S); multicultural early intervention (MS); pre-kindergarten/primary (MS); preschool education (MS); reading (MS); reading and TESOL (MS); reading education (Ed S); science (MS); science education (Ed S); secondary education (MS); social studies (MS, Ed S); Spanish language (MS); teaching and learning (MA, MS), including curriculum and instruction (MA), elementary mathematics (MA), elementary reading (MA), K-12 technology integration (MA); teaching English to speakers of other languages (MS, Ed S); technology management and administration (Ed S); urban studies education (MS). Part-time and evening/weekend programs available. Postbaccalaureate distance learning degree programs offered (minimal on-campus study). *Faculty:* 32 full-time (18 women), 334 part-time/adjunct (224 women). *Students:* 1,404 full-time (1,124 women), 3,678 part-time (3,097 women); includes 2,562 minority (1,800 African Americans, 11 American Indian/Alaska Native, 39 Asian Americans or Pacific Islanders, 712 Hispanic Americans), 89 international. Average age 38. 1,771 applicants, 80% accepted, 1419 enrolled. In 2007, 2,171 master's, 639 other advanced degrees awarded. *Degree requirements:*

Spanish

Nova Southeastern University (continued)

For master's and Ed S, thesis, practicum, internship. *Entrance requirements:* For master's, MAT, GRE, CLAST, CBEST, PRAXIS I, GKT, minimum GPA of 2.5; for Ed S, MAT or GRE, master's degree, teaching certificate, minimum GPA of 3.0. Additional exam requirements/recommendations for international students: Required—TSE recommended 50; Recommended—TOEFL (minimum score 550 paper-based; 213 computer-based; 80 iBT), IELTS (minimum score 6). *Application deadline:* For fall admission, 8/11 priority date for domestic and international students; for winter admission, 12/28 priority date for domestic and international students; for spring admission, 4/22 priority date for domestic and international students. Applications are processed on a rolling basis. Application fee: $50. Electronic applications accepted. *Financial support:* Federal Work-Study available. Support available to part-time students. Financial award application deadline: 1/7. *Faculty research:* School effectiveness, critical thinking, leadership skills acquisition, child education, multicultural education. *Unit head:* Dr. Dana Mills, Executive Dean, 954-262-8500 Ext. 7818, Fax: 954-262-3912, E-mail: dmills@nova.edu. *Application contact:* Dr. Jennifer Quiñones Nottingham, Dean of Student Affairs, 800-986-3223 Ext. 8624, Fax: 954-262-3883, E-mail: jlquinon@nova.edu.

The Ohio State University, Graduate School, College of Humanities, Department of Spanish and Portuguese, Columbus, OH 43210. Offers MA, PhD. *Faculty:* 22. *Students:* 56 full-time (37 women), 8 part-time (2 women); includes 12 minority (1 African American, 2 Asian Americans or Pacific Islanders, 9 Hispanic Americans), 21 international. Average age 30. In 2007, 9 master's, 7 doctorates awarded. *Degree requirements:* For master's, thesis optional; for doctorate, thesis/dissertation. *Entrance requirements:* For master's and doctorate, GRE General Test. Additional exam requirements/recommendations for international students: Required—TOEFL (minimum score 600 paper-based; 250 computer-based). *Application deadline:* For fall admission, 8/15 priority date for domestic students, 7/1 priority date for international students; for winter admission, 12/1 priority date for domestic students, 11/1 priority date for international students; for spring admission, 3/1 priority date for domestic students, 2/1 priority date for international students. Applications are processed on a rolling basis. Application fee: $40 ($50 for international students). Electronic applications accepted. *Financial support:* Fellowships, research assistantships, teaching assistantships, Federal Work-Study, institutionally sponsored loans, and unspecified assistantships available. Support available to part-time students. *Unit head:* Salvador Garcia, Graduate Studies Committee Chair, 614-292-4958, Fax: 614-292-7726, E-mail: garcia.7@osu.edu. *Application contact:* 614-292-9444, Fax: 614-292-3895, E-mail: domestic.grad@osu.edu.

Ohio University, Graduate College, College of Arts and Sciences, Department of Modern Languages, Athens, OH 45701-2979. Offers French (MA); Spanish (MA). Part-time programs available. *Faculty:* 18 full-time (8 women), 2 part-time/adjunct (both women). *Students:* 28 full-time (23 women), 1 part-time; includes 5 minority (all Hispanic Americans), 6 international. Average age 23. In 2007, 12 degrees awarded. *Degree requirements:* For master's, 2 foreign languages, comprehensive exam, thesis optional. *Entrance requirements:* For master's, oral and written samples. Additional exam requirements/recommendations for international students: Required—TOEFL (minimum score 500 paper-based). *Application deadline:* For fall admission, 1/15 priority date for domestic and international students. Applications are processed on a rolling basis. Application fee: $50 ($55 for international students). Electronic applications accepted. *Financial support:* In 2007–08, teaching assistantships with tuition reimbursements (averaging $10,300 per year); Federal Work-Study and institutionally sponsored loans also available. Financial award application deadline: 4/15. *Faculty research:* French and Spanish language and literature. *Unit head:* Dr. Fred Toner, Chair, 740-593-2765, Fax: 740-593-0729, E-mail: toner@ohio.edu. *Application contact:* Dr. Amado Lascar, Graduate Chair, 740-597-2724, Fax: 740-593-0729, E-mail: lascar@ohio.edu.

Penn State University Park, Graduate School, College of the Liberal Arts, Department of Spanish, Italian, and Portuguese, State College, University Park, PA 16802-1503. Offers Spanish (MA, PhD). *Expenses:* Tuition, state resident: full-time $14,738; part-time $614 per credit. Tuition, nonresident: full-time $26,050; part-time $1,085 per credit. Tuition and fees vary according to course load, program and student level. *Unit head:* Dr. William R. Blue, Interim Head, 814-865-4252, Fax: 814-863-7944, E-mail: wrb10@psu.edu. *Application contact:* Carol Toscano, Information Contact, 814-865-1016, E-mail: clt4@psu.edu.

Pontifical Catholic University of Puerto Rico, College of Arts and Humanities, Department of Hispanic Studies, Ponce, PR 00717-0777. Offers grammar and writing (Professional Certificate); Hispanic studies (MA). Part-time and evening/weekend programs available. *Degree requirements:* For master's, variable foreign language requirement, comprehensive exam, thesis or alternative. *Entrance requirements:* For master's, GRE General Test, 2 letters of recommendation, interview, minimum GPA of 2.75. Electronic applications accepted.

Portland State University, Graduate Studies, College of Liberal Arts and Sciences, Department of Foreign Languages and Literatures, Portland, OR 97207-0751. Offers foreign literature and language (MA); French (MA); German (MA); Japanese (MA); Spanish (MA). Part-time programs available. *Faculty:* 40 full-time (24 women), 24 part-time/adjunct (15 women). *Students:* 35 full-time (20 women), 13 part-time (12 women); includes 4 minority (1 Asian American or Pacific Islander, 3 Hispanic Americans), 11 international. Average age 32. 27 applicants, 74% accepted, 15 enrolled. In 2007, 18 master's awarded. *Degree requirements:* For master's, one foreign language, thesis (for some programs). *Entrance requirements:* Additional exam requirements/recommendations for international students: Required—TOEFL (minimum score 550 paper-based; 213 computer-based). *Application deadline:* For fall admission, 4/1 for domestic students, 3/1 for international students; for winter admission, 8/1 for domestic students, 7/1 for international students; for spring admission, 11/1 for domestic and international students. Applications are processed on a rolling basis. Application fee: $50. *Expenses:* Tuition, state resident: full-time $7,047. Tuition, nonresident: full-time $11,178. *Financial support:* In 2007–08, 5 teaching assistantships with full tuition reimbursements (averaging $7,921 per year) were awarded; research assistantships with full tuition reimbursements, Federal Work-Study, scholarships/grants, and unspecified assistantships also available. Support available to part-time students. Financial award application deadline: 3/1; financial award applicants required to submit FAFSA. *Faculty research:* Foreign language pedagogy, applied and social linguistics, literary history and criticism. Total annual research expenditures: $69,175. *Unit head:* Dr. Sandra F. Freels, Chair, 503-725-3522, Fax: 503-725-5276. *Application contact:* Karen Popp, Office Coordinator, 503-725-3522, E-mail: poppk@pdx.edu.

Princeton University, Graduate School, Department of Spanish and Portuguese Languages and Cultures, Princeton, NJ 08544-1019. Offers PhD. *Degree requirements:* For doctorate, variable foreign language requirement, thesis/dissertation. *Entrance requirements:* For doctorate, GRE General Test, sample of written work. Additional exam requirements/recommendations for international students: Required—TOEFL (minimum score 600 paper-based; 250 computer-based). Electronic applications accepted.

Purdue University, Graduate School, College of Liberal Arts, Department of Foreign Languages and Literatures, West Lafayette, IN 47907. Offers French (MA, MAT, PhD), including French (MA, PhD), French education (MAT); German (MA, MAT, PhD), including German (MA, PhD), German education (MAT); Spanish (MA, MAT, PhD), including Spanish (MA, PhD), Spanish education (MAT). Terminal master's awarded for partial completion of doctoral program. *Degree requirements:* For master's, one foreign language; for doctorate, 2 foreign languages, thesis/dissertation. *Entrance requirements:* For master's and doctorate, GRE, writing sample, sample recording of English and language of study. Additional exam requirements/recommendations for international students: Required—TOEFL. Electronic applications accepted. *Faculty research:* Linguistics, semiotics, literary criticism, pedagogy.

Queens College of the City University of New York, Division of Graduate Studies, Arts and Humanities Division, Department of Hispanic Languages and Literatures, Program in Spanish, Flushing, NY 11367-1597. Offers MA. Part-time and evening/weekend programs available. *Faculty:* 10 full-time (6 women). *Students:* 2 full-time (both women), 19 part-time (14 women). 33 applicants, 91% accepted. In 2007, 7 degrees awarded. *Degree requirements:* For master's, 2 foreign languages, comprehensive exam, thesis or alternative. *Entrance requirements:* For master's, minimum GPA of 3.0. Additional exam requirements/recommendations for international students: Required—TOEFL. *Application deadline:* For fall admission, 4/1 for domestic students; for spring admission, 11/1 for domestic students. Applications are processed on a rolling basis. Application fee: $125. *Financial support:* Career-related internships or fieldwork, Federal Work-Study, institutionally sponsored loans, tuition waivers (partial), and adjunct lectureships available. Support available to part-time students. Financial award application deadline: 4/1; financial award applicants required to submit FAFSA. *Unit head:* Dr. Irma Llorens, Graduate Adviser, 718-997-5649. *Application contact:* Mario Caruso, Director of Graduate Admissions, 718-997-5200, Fax: 718-997-5193, E-mail: graduate_admissions@qc.edu.

Queen's University at Kingston, School of Graduate Studies and Research, Faculty of Arts and Sciences, Department of Spanish, Kingston, ON K7L 3N6, Canada. Offers MA. Part-time programs available. *Degree requirements:* For master's, one foreign language, thesis. *Entrance requirements:* Additional exam requirements/recommendations for international students: Required—TOEFL. Electronic applications accepted. *Faculty research:* Golden Age, nineteenth- and twentieth-century Peninsular novel, literary theory, colonial Latin America, nineteenth-and-twentieth century Latin America.

Rice University, Graduate Programs, School of Humanities, Department of Hispanic Studies, Houston, TX 77251-1892. Offers Spanish (MA). Part-time programs available. *Degree requirements:* For master's, one foreign language, thesis. *Entrance requirements:* For master's, GRE General Test, minimum GPA of 3.0. Additional exam requirements/recommendations for international students: Required—TOEFL (minimum score 600 paper-based; 250 computer-based; 90 iBT). Electronic applications accepted. *Faculty research:* Golden Age Spanish literature, Modern Spanish literature, modern Latin American literature, linguistics and Hispanic cultural studies.

Rider University, Department of Graduate Education, Leadership and Counseling, Teacher Certification Program, Lawrenceville, NJ 08648-3001. Offers business education (Certificate); elementary education (Certificate); English as a second language (Certificate); English education (Certificate); mathematics education (Certificate); preschool to grade 3 (Certificate); science education (Certificate); social studies education (Certificate); world languages (Certificate), including French, German, Spanish. Part-time programs available. *Faculty:* 5 full-time (1 woman), 4 part-time/adjunct (3 women). *Students:* 40 full-time (34 women), 103 part-time (81 women); includes 12 minority (5 African Americans, 1 Asian American or Pacific Islander, 6 Hispanic Americans), 6 international. Average age 35. 61 applicants, 69% accepted, 39 enrolled. In 2007, 111 degrees awarded. *Degree requirements:* For Certificate, internship, professional portfolio. *Entrance requirements:* For degree, PRAXIS, resumé. Additional exam requirements/recommendations for international students: Required—TOEFL (minimum score 550 paper-based; 213 computer-based). *Application deadline:* For fall admission, 5/1 priority date for domestic students, 6/1 priority date for international students; for spring admission, 11/1 priority date for domestic and international students. Applications are processed on a rolling basis. Application fee: $50. Electronic applications accepted. *Expenses:* Tuition: Full-time $25,650; part-time $472 per credit. Required fees: $22 per credit. Tuition and fees vary according to program. *Financial support:* In 2007–08, 46 students received support. Career-related internships or fieldwork, Federal Work-Study, institutionally sponsored loans, and unspecified assistantships available. Support available to part-time students. Financial award applicants required to submit FAFSA. *Faculty research:* Conceptual foundations for optimal development of creativity; creative theory, cognitive processes in mathematics learning, teacher collaboration. *Unit head:* Dr. Austin Winther, Program Coordinator, 609-895-5473, Fax: 609-896-5362. *Application contact:* Jamie L Mitchell, Director of Graduate Admissions, 609-896-5036, Fax: 609-895-5680, E-mail: jmitchell@rider.edu.

Roosevelt University, Graduate Division, College of Arts and Sciences, Department of Literature and Languages, Program in Spanish, Chicago, IL 60605-1394. Offers MA. Part-time and evening/weekend programs available. *Students:* 1 (woman) full-time, 12 part-time (10 women); includes 6 minority (1 African American, 5 Hispanic Americans). Average age 36. 15 applicants, 60% accepted, 8 enrolled. In 2007, 10 degrees awarded. *Degree requirements:* For master's, variable foreign language requirement, thesis or alternative. *Entrance requirements:* For master's, BA in Spanish or the equivalent. *Application deadline:* For fall admission, 6/1 priority date for domestic students. Applications are processed on a rolling basis. Application fee: $25 ($35 for international students). *Financial support:* Scholarships/grants available. Financial award application deadline: 2/15. *Faculty research:* Latin American narrative, feminism, Hispanic cultures, twentieth century Hispanic literature, Latino studies. *Unit head:* Priscilla Archibald, Chair, 312-341-3670. *Application contact:* Joanne Canyon-Heller, Coordinator of Graduate Admission, 877-APPLY RU, Fax: 312-281-3356, E-mail: applyru@roosevelt.edu.

Rutgers, The State University of New Jersey, New Brunswick, Graduate School, Program in Spanish, New Brunswick, NJ 08901-1281. Offers bilingualism and second language acquisition (MA, PhD); Spanish (MA, MAT, PhD); Spanish literature (MA, PhD); translation (MA). Part-time programs available. *Degree requirements:* For master's, comprehensive exam (for some programs), thesis (for some programs); for doctorate, 2 foreign languages, comprehensive exam, thesis/dissertation. *Entrance requirements:* For master's and doctorate, GRE General Test. Additional exam requirements/recommendations for international students: Required—TOEFL. Electronic applications accepted. *Faculty research:* Hispanic literature, Luso-Brazilian literature, Spanish linguistics.

St. John's University, St. John's College of Liberal Arts and Sciences, Department of Languages and Literatures, Queens, NY 11439. Offers languages and literatures (Adv C); Spanish (MA). Part-time and evening/weekend programs available. *Faculty:* 16 full-time (10 women), 48 part-time/adjunct (25 women). *Students:* 5 full-time (4 women), 11 part-time (10 women); includes 10 minority (all Hispanic Americans), 1 international. Average age 33. 9 applicants, 78% accepted, 4 enrolled. In 2007, 12 master's, 2 other advanced degrees awarded. *Degree requirements:* For master's, thesis optional. *Entrance requirements:* For master's, 24 credits of undergraduate course work in languages with 18 credits in Spanish, minimum GPA of 3.0. Additional exam requirements/recommendations for international students: Required—TOEFL (minimum score 500 paper-based; 173 computer-based; 61 iBT), IELTS (minimum score 6). *Application deadline:* For fall admission, 5/1 priority date for domestic and international students; for spring admission, 11/1 priority date for domestic and international students. Applications are processed on a rolling basis. Application fee: $40. Electronic applications accepted. *Financial support:* Research assistantships, scholarships/grants available. Support available to part-time students. Financial award application deadline: 3/1; financial award applicants required to submit FAFSA. *Unit head:* Dr. Nicholas J. Toscano, Chair, 718-990-5250, E-mail: toscanon@stjohns.edu. *Application contact:* Beth Evans, Associate Vice President and Executive Director, Enrollment Management, 718-990-6999, Fax: 718-990-5686, E-mail: gradhelp@stjohns.edu.

Saint Louis University, Graduate School, College of Arts and Sciences and Graduate School, Department of Modern and Classical Languages, St. Louis, MO 63103-2097. Offers French (MA); Spanish (MA). Part-time programs available. *Faculty:* 12 full-time (8 women). *Students:* 22 full-time (19 women), 16 part-time (14 women); includes 8 minority (all Hispanic Americans), 2 international. Average age 31. 22 applicants, 86% accepted, 18 enrolled. In 2007, 27 degrees awarded. *Degree requirements:* For master's, one foreign language, comprehensive exam, thesis/dissertation (for Spanish). *Entrance requirements:* For master's, GRE General Test or MAT, letters of recommendation, resumé, interview, transcripts, goal statement. Additional exam requirements/recommendations for international students: Required—TOEFL (minimum score 525 paper-based; 194 computer-based). *Application deadline:* For fall admission, 7/1 for domestic and international students; for spring admission, 11/1 for domestic and international students. Applications are processed on a rolling basis. Application fee: $40. Electronic applications accepted. *Expenses:* Tuition: Part-time $845 per credit hour. Required fees: $105 per semester. *Financial support:* In 2007–08, 2 research assistantships with full tuition reimbursements (averaging $12,000 per year), 6 teaching assistantships with full tuition reimbursements (averaging $12,000 per year) were awarded; Federal Work-Study, scholarships/grants, traineeships, health care benefits, tuition waivers, and unspecified assistantships also available. Support available to part-time students. Financial award application deadline: 2/1; financial award applicants required to submit FAFSA. *Faculty research:* Culture studies, literature studies, foreign language acquisition. *Unit head:* Dr. Reinhard G. Andress, Chairperson, 314-977-2448, Fax: 314-977-3649, E-mail: andressp@slu.edu. *Application contact:* Gary U. Behrman, Associate Dean of Graduate School Admissions, 314-977-3827, Fax: 314-977-3943, E-mail: behrmang@slu.edu.

Saint Louis University, Madrid, Graduate Programs, Program in Spanish Language and Literature, Madrid, Spain. Offers MA. Part-time programs available. *Faculty:* 7 full-time (4 women). *Students:* 22 applicants, 82% accepted, 16 enrolled. In 2007, 10 degrees awarded. *Degree requirements:* For master's, one foreign language, comprehensive exam, thesis optional. *Entrance requirements:* For master's, GRE General Test or MAT, 3 letters of recommendation, curriculum vitae. *Application deadline:* For fall admission, 5/30 for domestic students; for spring admission, 10/30 for domestic students. Applications are processed on a rolling basis. Application fee: $40. *Expenses:* Tuition: Full-time $10,440; part-time $580 per credit. *Financial support:* In 2007–08, 4 students received support, including 2 research assistantships with partial tuition reimbursements available (averaging $2,000 per year); teaching assistantships, career-related internships or fieldwork, institutionally sponsored loans, and scholarships/grants also available. Financial award application deadline: 4/1; financial award applicants required to submit FAFSA. *Faculty research:* Linguistics, cultural studies. *Unit head:* Dr. Angeles Encinar, Chair, 34-91-554-58-58 Ext. 219, Fax: 34-91-554-62-02, E-mail: encinara@madrid.sluiberica.slu.edu. *Application contact:* Phyllis Chaney, Director of Admissions, 34-91-554-58-58 Ext. 232, Fax: 34-91-554-62-02, E-mail: graduate_admissions@madrid.slu.edu.

See Close-Up on page 575.

Salem State College, Graduate School, Program in Spanish, Salem, MA 01970-5353. Offers MAT. Part-time and evening/weekend programs available. *Students:* 1 full-time (0 women), 25 part-time (24 women); includes 1 Hispanic American. Average age 33. In 2007, 2 degrees awarded. Application fee: $35. *Unit head:* Dr. Nicole Sherf, Coordinator, 978-542-6468, E-mail: nsherf@salemstate.edu.

San Diego State University, Graduate and Research Affairs, College of Arts and Letters, Department of Spanish and Portuguese Languages and Literatures, San Diego, CA 92182. Offers Spanish (MA). *Students:* 17 full-time (12 women), 32 part-time (20 women); includes 30 minority (1 African American, 29 Hispanic Americans), 7 international. Average age 29. 26 applicants, 69% accepted, 15 enrolled. In 2007, 17 degrees awarded. *Degree requirements:* For master's, one foreign language. *Entrance requirements:* For master's, GRE General Test, 3 letters of reference. Additional exam requirements/recommendations for international students: Required—TOEFL. *Application deadline:* For fall admission, 5/1 for domestic and international students; for spring admission, 11/1 for domestic students, 10/1 for international students. Applications are processed on a rolling basis. Application fee: $55. Electronic applications accepted. *Financial support:* In 2007–08, 34 teaching assistantships were awarded; fellowships also available. Financial award applicants required to submit FAFSA. *Faculty research:* New strategies for teaching foreign languages. Total annual research expenditures: $65,000. *Unit head:* Dr. Roger Frantz, Interim Chair, 619-594-6588, Fax: 619-594-5293, E-mail: rfrantz@mail.sdsu.edu. *Application contact:* Juan M. Godoy, Graduate Advisor, 619-594-6387, Fax: 619-594-5293, E-mail: jgodoy@mail.sdsu.edu.

San Francisco State University, Division of Graduate Studies, College of Humanities, Department of Foreign Languages and Literatures, Program in Spanish, San Francisco, CA 94132-1722. Offers MA. Part-time programs available. *Application deadline:* Applications are processed on a rolling basis. Electronic applications accepted. *Financial support:* Unspecified assistantships available. *Unit head:* Dr. Gustavo Adolfo Calderón, Program Coordinator, 415-338-7426, E-mail: gusto@sfsu.edu. *Application contact:* Dr. Paola Cortes-Rocca, Graduate Coordinator, 415-338-1421, E-mail: pcortes@sfsu.edu.

San Jose State University, Graduate Studies and Research, College of Humanities and the Arts, Department of Foreign Languages, Program in Spanish, San Jose, CA 95192-0001. Offers MA. *Degree requirements:* For master's, 2 foreign languages, thesis or alternative. *Application deadline:* For fall admission, 6/29 for domestic students; for spring admission, 11/30 for domestic students. Applications are processed on a rolling basis. Application fee: $59. Electronic applications accepted. *Financial support:* Applicants required to submit FAFSA. *Unit head:* Eleanor Marsh, Graduate Advisor, 408-924-4614, E-mail: eleanor.marsh@sjsu.edu.

Simmons College, College of Arts and Sciences Graduate Studies, Program in Spanish, Boston, MA 02115. Offers MA, MAT/MA. Part-time programs available. *Faculty:* 4 full-time (all women). *Students:* 3 full-time (2 women), 6 part-time (3 women); includes 3 minority (1 Asian American or Pacific Islander, 2 Hispanic Americans). Average age 23. 10 applicants, 60% accepted, 5 enrolled. In 2007, 3 degrees awarded. *Degree requirements:* For master's, one foreign language. *Entrance requirements:* For master's, analytical writing samples in Spanish. Additional exam requirements/recommendations for international students: Required—TOEFL (minimum score 600 paper-based; 250 computer-based; 100 iBT). *Application deadline:* For fall admission, 8/1 priority date for domestic and international students; for spring admission, 12/15 priority date for domestic and international students. Applications are processed on a rolling basis. Application fee: $35. Electronic applications accepted. *Expenses:* Tuition: Full-time $8,500. Tuition and fees vary according to degree level and program. *Financial support:* In 2007–08, 1 student received support. Scholarships/grants available. Financial award application deadline: 3/1; financial award applicants required to submit FAFSA. *Faculty research:* Latin American contemporary fiction, women writers, medieval Spanish literature, Golden Age Spanish literature, contemporary Spanish literature. *Unit head:* Dr. Raquel María Halty, Director, 617-521-2182, Fax: 617-521-3090, E-mail: raquel.halty@simmons.edu. *Application contact:* Kristen Haack, Director, Graduate Studies Admission, 617-521-2917, Fax: 617-521-3058, E-mail: gsa@simmons.edu.

Stanford University, School of Humanities and Sciences, Department of Spanish and Portuguese, Stanford, CA 94305-9991. Offers Spanish (MA, PhD). Terminal master's awarded for partial completion of doctoral program. *Degree requirements:* For master's, 2 foreign languages; for doctorate, 3 foreign languages, thesis/dissertation, oral exam. *Entrance requirements:* For master's and doctorate, GRE General Test. Additional exam requirements/recommendations for international students: Required—TOEFL. Electronic applications accepted.

State University of New York at Binghamton, Graduate School, School of Arts and Sciences, Department of Romance Languages and Literatures, Program in Spanish, Binghamton, NY 13902-6000. Offers Spanish (MA); translation (Certificate). *Students:* 5 full-time (2 women); includes 1 minority (Hispanic American), 1 international. Average age 24. 6 applicants, 100% accepted, 3 enrolled. In 2007, 4 master's awarded. *Degree requirements:* For master's, one foreign language, comprehensive exam, thesis or alternative. *Entrance requirements:* For master's, GRE General Test, GRE Subject Test. Additional exam requirements/recommendations for international students: Required—TOEFL. *Application deadline:* For fall admission, 4/15 priority date for domestic students, 1/15 priority date for international students; for spring admission, 11/1 for domestic students, 10/1 priority date for international students. Applications are processed on a rolling basis. Application fee: $60. Electronic applications accepted. *Financial support:* In 2007–08, 5 students received support, including 2 teaching assistantships with full tuition reimbursements available (averaging $8,328 per year); fellowships, research assistantships, career-related internships or fieldwork, Federal Work-Study, institutionally sponsored loans, and unspecified assistantships also available. Support available to part-time students. Financial award application deadline: 2/15. *Unit head:* Dr. Antonio Sobejano-Moran, Chairperson, Department of Romance Languages and Literatures, 607-777-4635, E-mail: antobianco@msn.com.

Syracuse University, Graduate School, College of Arts and Sciences, Department of Languages, Literatures, and Linguistics, Program in Spanish Language, Literature and Culture, Syracuse, NY 13244. Offers MA. Part-time programs available. *Students:* 10 full-time (8 women), 2 part-time (1 woman); includes 3 minority (1 African American, 2 Hispanic Americans), 2 international. 6 applicants, 67% accepted, 4 enrolled. In 2007, 2 degrees awarded. *Entrance requirements:* For master's, GRE General Test. Additional exam requirements/recommendations for international students: Required—TOEFL. *Application deadline:* For fall admission, 1/10 for domestic students. Applications are processed on a rolling basis. Application fee: $75. Electronic applications accepted. *Expenses:* Tuition: Full-time $18,216; part-time $1,012 per credit. Required fees: $980. Tuition and fees vary according to program. *Financial support:* Fellowships with full tuition reimbursements, teaching assistantships with full tuition reimbursements, tuition waivers (partial) available. *Unit head:* Dr. Gail Bulman, Program Coordinator, 315-443-5385, Fax: 315-443-5376. *Application contact:* Karen Ames, Information Contact, 315-443-3022, E-mail: koames@syr.edu.

Temple University, Graduate School, College of Liberal Arts, Department of Spanish and Portuguese, Philadelphia, PA 19122-6096. Offers Spanish (MA, PhD). Part-time and evening/weekend programs available. Terminal master's awarded for partial completion of doctoral program. *Degree requirements:* For master's, one foreign language; for doctorate, 2 foreign languages, thesis/dissertation. *Entrance requirements:* For master's and doctorate, GRE General Test, minimum GPA of 3.0. Additional exam requirements/recommendations for international students: Required—TOEFL (minimum score 550 paper-based; 213 computer-based; 79 iBT). Electronic applications accepted. *Faculty research:* Spanish American literature, Spanish Peninsular literature, Hispanic linguistics.

Texas A&M International University, Office of Graduate Studies and Research, College of Arts and Sciences, Department of Language and Literature, Laredo, TX 78041-1900. Offers English (MA); Hispanic studies (PhD); Spanish (MA). *Faculty:* 5 full-time (1 woman). *Students:* 2 full-time (1 woman), 19 part-time (13 women); includes 19 minority (all Hispanic Americans) Average age 29. 17 applicants, 76% accepted, 7 enrolled. In 2007, 1 degree awarded. *Entrance requirements:* For master's, GRE General Test. Additional exam requirements/recommendations for international students: Required—TOEFL (minimum score 550 paper-based; 213 computer-based). *Application deadline:* For fall admission, 7/15 priority date for domestic students; for spring admission, 11/12 for domestic students. Applications are processed on a rolling basis. Application fee: $25. *Financial support:* In 2007–08, 5 students received support. Application deadline: 11/1. *Unit head:* Dr. Sean Chadwell, Chair, 956-326-2471, E-mail: schadwell@tamiu.edu. *Application contact:* Rosie Espinoza-Dickinson, Director of Admissions, 956-326-2200, Fax: 956-326-2199, E-mail: enroll@tamiu.edu.

Texas A&M University, College of Liberal Arts, Department of Hispanic Studies, College Station, TX 77843. Offers MA, PhD. *Faculty:* 6. *Students:* 16 full-time (11 women), 17 part-time (11 women); includes 17 minority (1 Asian American or Pacific Islander, 16 Hispanic Americans), 3 international. 18 applicants, 83% accepted, 11 enrolled. In 2007, 2 degrees awarded. *Expenses:* Tuition, state resident: full-time $6,129. Tuition, nonresident: full-time $11,689. Tuition and fees vary according to course load. *Unit head:* Victor Arizpe, Head, 979-845-2125.

Texas A&M University–Commerce, Graduate School, College of Arts and Sciences, Department of Literature and Languages, Commerce, TX 75429-3011. Offers college teaching of English (PhD); English (MA, MS); Spanish (MA). Part-time programs available. *Faculty:* 13 full-time (8 women), 1 part-time/adjunct (0 women). *Students:* 19 full-time (15 women), 47 part-time (34 women); includes 13 minority (1 African American, 2 American Indian/Alaska Native, 3 Asian Americans or Pacific Islanders, 7 Hispanic Americans), 2 international. Average age 36. In 2007, 7 degrees awarded. Terminal master's awarded for partial completion of doctoral program. *Degree requirements:* For master's, comprehensive exam, thesis (for some programs); for doctorate, one foreign language, thesis/dissertation, departmental qualifying exam. *Entrance requirements:* For master's and doctorate, GRE General Test. *Application deadline:* For fall admission, 6/1 priority date for domestic students; for spring admission, 11/1 priority date for domestic students. Applications are processed on a rolling basis. Application fee: $0 ($25 for international students). Electronic applications accepted. *Financial support:* In 2007–08, research assistantships (averaging $7,875 per year), teaching assistantships (averaging $7,875 per year) were awarded; Federal Work-Study, institutionally sponsored loans, and scholarships/grants also available. Financial award application deadline: 5/1; financial award applicants required to submit FAFSA. *Faculty research:* Latino literature, American film studies, ethnographic research, Willa Carter. *Unit head:* Dr. Gerald Duchovnay, Head, 903-886-5260, Fax: 903-886-5980, E-mail: gerald_duchovnay@tamu-commerce.edu. *Application contact:* Tammi Thompson, Graduate Admissions Adviser, 843-886-5167, Fax: 843-886-5165, E-mail: tammi_thompson@tamu-commerce.edu.

Texas A&M University–Kingsville, College of Graduate Studies, College of Arts and Sciences, Department of Language and Literature, Kingsville, TX 78363. Offers English (MA, MS); Spanish (MA). Part-time and evening/weekend programs available. *Degree requirements:* For master's, comprehensive exam, thesis or alternative. *Entrance requirements:* For master's, GRE General Test, minimum GPA of 3.0. Additional exam requirements/recommendations for international students: Required—TOEFL. *Faculty research:* Linguistics, culture, Spanish American literature, Spanish peninsular literature, American literature.

Texas State University–San Marcos, Graduate School, College of Liberal Arts, Department of Modern Languages, Program in Spanish, San Marcos, TX 78666. Offers MA. Part-time and evening/weekend programs available. *Faculty:* 5 full-time (3 women). *Students:* 12 full-time (8 women), 8 part-time (5 women); includes 14 minority (1 Asian American or Pacific Islander, 13 Hispanic Americans), 1 international. Average age 33. 9 applicants, 100% accepted, 9 enrolled. In 2007, 3 degrees awarded. *Degree requirements:* For master's, one foreign language, comprehensive exam, internship (MAT), thesis (MA). *Entrance requirements:* For master's, minimum GPA of 3.0 in last 12 undergraduate hours of advanced Spanish with 6 hours in literature. Additional exam requirements/recommendations for international students: Required—TOEFL (minimum score 550 paper-based; 213 computer-based). *Application deadline:* For fall admission, 6/15 priority date for domestic students, 6/1 for international students; for spring admission, 10/15 priority date for domestic students, 10/1 for international students. Applications are processed on a rolling basis. Application fee: $40 ($90 for international students). Electronic applications accepted. *Expenses:* Tuition, state resident: full-time $3,780; part-time $210 per credit hour. Tuition, nonresident: full-time $8,784; part-time $488 per credit hour. Required fees: $493 per semester. Full-time tuition and fees vary according to course load. *Financial support:* In 2007–08, 11 students received support, including 1 research assistantship (averaging $5,339 per year), 4 teaching assistantships (averaging $5,751 per year); career-related internships or fieldwork, Federal Work-Study, and institutionally sponsored loans also available. Support available to part-time students. Financial award application deadline: 4/1; financial award applicants required to submit FAFSA. *Faculty research:* Hispanic literature, linguistics, literary theory, computer-assisted language instruction, Hispanic philology. *Unit head:* Dr. Catherine Jaffe, Advisor, 512-245-2360, Fax: 512-245-8298, E-mail: cj10@txstate.edu.

Texas Tech University, Graduate School, College of Arts and Sciences, Department of Classical and Modern Languages and Literatures, Program in Romance Languages-Spanish, Lubbock, TX 79409. Offers MA, PhD. Part-time programs available. *Students:* 19 full-time (13 women), 11 part-time (6 women); includes 10 minority (all Hispanic Americans), 10 international. Average age 39. 16 applicants, 56% accepted, 2 enrolled. In 2007, 2 doctorates awarded. *Degree requirements:* For master's, one foreign language, thesis optional; for doctorate, one foreign language, comprehensive exam, thesis/dissertation. *Entrance requirements:* For master's and doctorate, GRE General Test. Additional exam requirements/recommendations for international students: Required—TOEFL (minimum score 550 paper-based; 213 computer-based). *Application deadline:* For fall admission, 3/1 priority date for international students; for spring admission, 11/1 priority date for international students. Applications are processed on a rolling basis. Application fee: $50 ($60 for international students). Electronic applications accepted. *Expenses:* Tuition, state resident: part-time $373 per credit hour. Tuition,

Spanish

Texas Tech University (continued)
nonresident: part-time $651 per credit hour. Tuition and fees vary according to program. *Financial support:* Research assistantships with partial tuition reimbursements, teaching assistantships with partial tuition reimbursements available. Financial award application deadline: 4/15. *Faculty research:* Peninsular literature, Latin-American literature, Portuguese language and literature, Spanish linguistics. *Unit head:* Dr. Genaro Perez, Professor and Graduate Advisor of Spanish, 806-742-3145 Ext. 281, Fax: 806-742-3306, E-mail: genaro.perez@ttu.edu.

Tulane University, School of Liberal Arts, Department of Spanish and Portuguese, New Orleans, LA 70118-5669. Offers Portuguese (MA); Spanish (MA); Spanish and Portuguese (PhD). *Degree requirements:* For master's, 2 foreign languages; for doctorate, 2 foreign languages, thesis/dissertation. *Entrance requirements:* For master's, GRE General Test, minimum B average in undergraduate course work; for doctorate, GRE General Test. Additional exam requirements/recommendations for international students: Required—TOEFL. Electronic applications accepted.

Universidad Adventista de las Antillas, EGECED Department, Mayagüez, PR 00681-0118. Offers curriculum and instruction (MA), including elementary, secondary biology, secondary history, secondary Spanish; education (MA), including ESL (elementary school level), ESL (high school level), school administration and supervision. *Faculty:* 10 part-time/adjunct (5 women). *Students:* 12 full-time (11 women), 29 part-time (24 women); all minorities (all Hispanic Americans) Average age 30. 60 applicants, 88% accepted, 28 enrolled. In 2007, 5 degrees awarded. *Degree requirements:* For master's, comprehensive exam (for some programs), thesis (for some programs). *Entrance requirements:* For master's, EXADEP or GRE, recommendations, transcripts (original). Application fee: $175. Electronic applications accepted. *Expenses:* Tuition: Part-time $175 per credit. *Financial support:* Fellowships, Federal Work-Study available. *Unit head:* Dr. Zilma Sepulveda, Director, 787-834-9595 Ext. 2282, Fax: 787-834-9595, E-mail: zsantiago@uaa.edu. *Application contact:* Prof. Evelyn del Valle, Admissions Department Director, 787-834-9595 Ext. 2261, Fax: 787-834-9597, E-mail: admissions@uaa.edu.

Université de Montréal, Faculty of Arts and Sciences, Department of Literatures and Modern Languages, Program in Hispanic Studies, Montréal, QC H3C 3J7, Canada. Offers MA. *Students:* 26 full-time (19 women), 5 part-time (4 women). 11 applicants, 73% accepted, 7 enrolled. In 2007, 7 degrees awarded. *Degree requirements:* For master's, 2 foreign languages, thesis. *Application deadline:* For fall admission, 2/1 priority date for domestic students; for winter admission, 11/1 priority date for domestic students; for spring admission, 2/1 priority date for domestic students. Application fee: $100. Electronic applications accepted. *Financial support:* Research assistantships, teaching assistantships, scholarships/grants available. *Faculty research:* Spanish literature and culture, Latin American literature and culture. *Unit head:* Javier Rubiera, Responsible, 514-343-5892, Fax: 514-343-2255, E-mail: javier.rubiera@umontreal.ca.

Université Laval, Faculty of Letters, Department of Literature, Programs in Spanish Literatures, Québec, QC G1K 7P4, Canada. Offers MA, PhD. Part-time programs available. Terminal master's awarded for partial completion of doctoral program. *Degree requirements:* For master's, thesis; for doctorate, comprehensive exam, thesis/dissertation. *Entrance requirements:* For master's and doctorate, linguistics exams, knowledge of French and Spanish. Electronic applications accepted.

University at Albany, State University of New York, College of Arts and Sciences, Department of Languages, Literatures, and Cultures, Program in Spanish, Albany, NY 12222-0001. Offers MA, PhD. *Degree requirements:* For doctorate, thesis/dissertation. *Entrance requirements:* For doctorate, GRE General Test. *Application deadline:* For fall admission, 4/1 priority date for domestic students. Application fee: $75. *Expenses:* Tuition, state resident: part-time $576 per credit. Tuition, nonresident: part-time $910 per credit. Tuition and fees vary according to program. *Unit head:* HenryK Baran, Chair, Department of Languages, Literatures, and Cultures, 518-442-4222.

University at Buffalo, the State University of New York, Graduate School, College of Arts and Sciences, Department of Romance Languages and Literatures, Buffalo, NY 14260. Offers French (MA, PhD); Spanish (MA, PhD). Part-time programs available. Terminal master's awarded for partial completion of doctoral program. *Degree requirements:* For master's, one foreign language, project; for doctorate, 2 foreign languages, thesis/dissertation. *Entrance requirements:* For master's and doctorate, GRE. Additional exam requirements/recommendations for international students: Required—TOEFL (minimum score 550 paper-based; 213 computer-based; 79 iBT). Electronic applications accepted. *Faculty research:* Romance linguistics, cultural studies, literary studies, literature and philosophy.

The University of Akron, Graduate School, Buchtel College of Arts and Sciences, Department of Modern Languages, Program in Spanish, Akron, OH 44325. Offers MA. Part-time and evening/weekend programs available. *Faculty:* 6 full-time (3 women). *Students:* 8 full-time (7 women); includes 2 minority (both Hispanic Americans) Average age 25. 7 applicants, 71% accepted, 1 enrolled. In 2007, 8 degrees awarded. *Degree requirements:* For master's, one foreign language, comprehensive exam, thesis optional, oral exam, essay, research paper. *Entrance requirements:* For master's, interview, minimum GPA of 3.0, proficiency in Spanish, letters of recommendation. Additional exam requirements/recommendations for international students: Required—TOEFL (minimum score 550 paper-based; 213 computer-based; 79 iBT). *Application deadline:* Applications are processed on a rolling basis. Application fee: $30 ($40 for international students). Electronic applications accepted. *Expenses:* Tuition, state resident: full-time $6,164; part-time $342 per credit. Tuition, nonresident: full-time $10,575; part-time $588 per credit. Required fees: $806; $43 per credit. $12 per term. Tuition and fees vary according to course load, degree level and program. *Financial support:* Research assistantships with full tuition reimbursements, teaching assistantships with full tuition reimbursements, institutionally sponsored loans and tuition waivers (full) available. *Unit head:* Dr. Parizad Dejbord-Sawan, Director of Graduate Studies, 330-972-7824, E-mail: parizad@uakron.edu.

The University of Alabama, Graduate School, College of Arts and Sciences, Department of Modern Languages and Classics, Tuscaloosa, AL 35487. Offers French (MA, PhD); French and Spanish (PhD); German (MA); Romance languages (MA, PhD); Spanish (MA, PhD). Part-time programs available. *Faculty:* 22 full-time (12 women). *Students:* 47 full-time (35 women), 14 part-time (9 women); includes 12 minority (2 African Americans, 10 Hispanic Americans), 15 international. Average age 32. 26 applicants, 69% accepted, 14 enrolled. In 2007, 12 master's, 4 doctorates awarded. *Median time to degree:* Of those who began their doctoral program in fall 1999, 40% received their degree in 8 years or less. *Degree requirements:* For master's, comprehensive exam, thesis optional; for doctorate, one foreign language, thesis/dissertation, preliminary exam. *Entrance requirements:* For master's and doctorate, minimum GPA of 3.0, writing sample. Additional exam requirements/recommendations for international students: Required—TOEFL or IELTS. *Application deadline:* For fall admission, 7/6 priority date for domestic students, 1/15 priority date for international students; for spring admission, 12/6 priority date for domestic students, 6/1 priority date for international students. Applications are processed on a rolling basis. Application fee: $30. Electronic applications accepted. *Expenses:* Tuition, state resident: full-time $5,700. Tuition, nonresident: full-time $16,518. *Financial support:* In 2007–08, 7 students received support, including 1 fellowship, research assistantships with full tuition reimbursements available (averaging $10,291 per year), 6 teaching assistantships with full tuition reimbursements available (averaging $10,291 per year); career-related internships or fieldwork, Federal Work-Study, institutionally sponsored loans, and scholarships/grants also available. Financial award application deadline: 7/14. *Faculty research:* Non-English literature, linguistics, culture, film. Total annual research expenditures: $48,751. *Unit head:* Dr. Michael Picone, Chair and Professor, 205-348-5054, Fax: 205-348-2042, E-mail: mpicone@bama.ua.edu. *Application contact:* Dr. K. Barbara Fischer, Graduate Director and Associate Professor, 205-348-8465, Fax: 205-348-2042, E-mail: bfischer@bama.ua.edu.

The University of Arizona, Graduate College, College of Humanities, Department of Spanish and Portuguese, Tucson, AZ 85721. Offers Spanish (M Ed, MA, PhD). *Faculty:* 25. *Students:* 59 full-time (33 women), 27 part-time (20 women); includes 35 minority (1 American Indian/Alaska Native, 1 Asian American or Pacific Islander, 33 Hispanic Americans), 21 international. Average age 35. 70 applicants, 24% accepted, 14 enrolled. In 2007, 11 master's, 3 doctorates awarded. Terminal master's awarded for partial completion of doctoral program. *Median time to degree:* Of those who began their doctoral program in fall 1999, 50% received their degree in 8 years or less. *Degree requirements:* For master's, one foreign language, comprehensive exam, thesis optional; for doctorate, 3 foreign languages, comprehensive exam, thesis/dissertation. *Entrance requirements:* For master's, GRE General Test, BA in Spanish, minimum GPA of 3.3, writing sample, 3 letters of recommendation, statement of purpose; for doctorate, GRE General Test, BA in Spanish, writing sample, minimum GPA of 3.4, 3 letters of recommendation, statement of purpose. Additional exam requirements/recommendations for international students: Required—TOEFL (minimum score 550 paper-based; 213 computer-based). Application fee: $50. *Financial support:* In 2007–08, 7 fellowships with full tuition reimbursements (averaging $2,888 per year), 85 teaching assistantships with partial tuition reimbursements (averaging $12,597 per year) were awarded; institutionally sponsored loans, scholarships/grants, health care benefits, and tuition waivers (full) also available. Financial award application deadline: 2/15. *Faculty research:* Spanish and Latin American literature and linguistics, literary theory. Total annual research expenditures:$13,355. *Unit head:* Dr. Malcolm A. Compitello, Head, 520-621-3123, E-mail: compitel@email.arizona.edu. *Application contact:* Isela Gonzales, Administrative Assistant, 520-621-3125, Fax: 520-621-6104, E-mail: iselag@email.arizona.edu.

University of Arkansas, Graduate School, J. William Fulbright College of Arts and Sciences, Department of Foreign Languages, Program in Spanish, Fayetteville, AR 72701-1201. Offers MA. *Faculty:* 6 full-time (4 women). *Students:* 9 full-time (5 women), 5 part-time (4 women); includes 1 minority (Hispanic American), 5 international. In 2007, 11 degrees awarded. *Degree requirements:* For master's, one foreign language, comprehensive exam, thesis optional. *Entrance requirements:* Additional exam requirements/recommendations for international students: Required—TOEFL (minimum score 550 paper-based; 213 computer-based), IELTS (minimum score 7). *Application deadline:* For fall admission, 1/15 priority date for domestic students; for spring admission, 9/15 priority date for domestic students. Application fee: $40 ($50 for international students). Electronic applications accepted. *Financial support:* In 2007–08, fellowships with tuition reimbursements (averaging $2,178 per year), 10 teaching assistantships (averaging $8,200 per year) were awarded; research assistantships, career-related internships or fieldwork and Federal Work-Study also available. Support available to part-time students. Financial award application deadline: 1/15; financial award applicants required to submit FAFSA. *Faculty research:* Medieval and Golden Age poetry, colonial Latin America, contemporary Latin America. *Unit head:* Reoma Ruiz, Graduate Coordinator, 479-575-2951, Fax: 479-575-6795, E-mail: rruiz@uark.edu.

University of California, Berkeley, Graduate Division, College of Letters and Science, Department of Hispanic Languages and Literature, Berkeley, CA 94720-1500. Offers PhD. *Faculty:* 16 full-time (6 women). *Degree requirements:* For doctorate, thesis/dissertation, qualifying exam. *Entrance requirements:* For doctorate, GRE General Test, minimum GPA of 3.0, 3 letters of recommendation. Additional exam requirements/recommendations for international students: Required—TOEFL (minimum score 570 paper-based; 230 computer-based). *Application deadline:* For fall admission, 12/15 for domestic students. Application fee: $70 ($90 for international students). *Financial support:* Fellowships with full tuition reimbursements, research assistantships, teaching assistantships with partial tuition reimbursements, unspecified assistantships available. Financial award applicants required to submit FAFSA. *Unit head:* Jose Rabasa, Chair, 510-642—2105, E-mail: jrabasa@berkeley.edu. *Application contact:* Veronica Lopez, Student Affairs Officer, 510-642-8037, Fax: 510-8037, E-mail: spanga@berkeley.edu.

University of California, Berkeley, Graduate Division, Group in Romance Languages and Literature, Program in Spanish, Berkeley, CA 94720-1500. Offers PhD. *Entrance requirements:* For doctorate, GRE General Test, 3 letters of recommendation. *Application deadline:* For fall admission, 12/15 for domestic students. Application fee: $70 ($90 for international students). *Application contact:* Veronica Lopez, Student Affairs Officer, 510-642-8037, Fax: 510-8037, E-mail: spanga@berkeley.edu.

University of California, Davis, Graduate Studies, Program in Spanish, Davis, CA 95616. Offers MA, PhD. Terminal master's awarded for partial completion of doctoral program. *Degree requirements:* For master's, comprehensive exam (for some programs), thesis (for some programs); for doctorate, 2 foreign languages, thesis/dissertation. *Entrance requirements:* For master's, GRE General Test, minimum GPA of 3.0; for doctorate, GRE General Test, master's degree, minimum GPA of 3.0. Additional exam requirements/recommendations for international students: Required—TOEFL (minimum score 550 paper-based; 213 computer-based). *Faculty research:* Medieval Spanish language and literature, Spanish linguistics, Latin American literature, nineteenth century Peninsular literature.

University of California, Irvine, Office of Graduate Studies, School of Humanities, Department of Spanish and Portuguese, Irvine, CA 92697. Offers Spanish (MA, MAT, PhD). *Students:* 45 full-time (27 women); includes 26 minority (1 Asian American or Pacific Islander, 25 Hispanic Americans), 2 international. In 2007, 4 doctorates awarded. *Degree requirements:* For doctorate, thesis/dissertation. *Entrance requirements:* For master's and doctorate, GRE General Test, minimum GPA of 3.0. Additional exam requirements/recommendations for international students: Required—TOEFL (minimum score 550 paper-based; 213 computer-based). *Application deadline:* For fall admission, 1/15 priority date for domestic students; for winter admission, 10/15 priority date for domestic students. Applications are processed on a rolling basis. Application fee: $60. Electronic applications accepted. *Financial support:* Fellowships, teaching assistantships, institutionally sponsored loans, traineeships, health care benefits, and unspecified assistantships available. Financial award application deadline: 3/1; financial award applicants required to submit FAFSA. *Faculty research:* Latin American literature, Spanish literature, Spanish linguistics in Creole studies, Hispanic literature in the U.S., Luso-Brazilian literature. *Unit head:* Ana Paula Ferreira, Chair, 949-824-7265, Fax: 949-824-2803, E-mail: apferrei@uci.edu. *Application contact:* Linda T. Le, Graduate Coordinator, 949-824-8793, Fax: 949-824-2803, E-mail: ttle@uci.edu.

University of California, Los Angeles, Graduate Division, College of Letters and Science, Department of Spanish and Portuguese, Program in Spanish, Los Angeles, CA 90095. Offers MA. *Students:* 2. 25 applicants, 0% accepted. In 2007, 8 degrees awarded. Terminal master's awarded for partial completion of doctoral program. *Degree requirements:* For master's, one foreign language, comprehensive exam or thesis. *Entrance requirements:* For master's, GRE General Test, minimum GPA of 3.0, sample of written work (recommended). *Application deadline:* For fall admission, 12/31 for domestic students. Application fee: $60. Electronic applications accepted. *Expenses:* Tuition, nonresident: full-time $5,728. Required fees:$8,966. Full-time tuition and fees vary according to program and student level. *Financial support:* In 2007–08, 6 fellowships with full and partial tuition reimbursements, 4 teaching assistantships with full and partial tuition reimbursements were awarded; research assistantships with full and partial tuition reimbursements, scholarships/grants and tuition waivers (full and partial) also available. Financial award applicants required to submit FAFSA. *Application contact:* Departmental Office, 310-825-1036, E-mail: peinado@humnet.ucla.edu.

University of California, Riverside, Graduate Division, Department of Hispanic Studies, Riverside, CA 92521-0102. Offers Spanish (MA, PhD). *Faculty:* 8 full-time (3 women). *Students:* 22 full-time (14 women), 1 part-time; includes 16 minority (all Hispanic Americans), 2 international. Average age 34. 14 applicants, 21% accepted, 3 enrolled. In 2007, 6 master's, 1 doctorate awarded. Terminal master's awarded for partial completion of doctoral program.

Degree requirements: For master's, one foreign language, comprehensive exam; for doctorate, one foreign language, thesis/dissertation, qualifying exams, 1 quarter of teaching experience. *Entrance requirements:* For master's and doctorate, GRE General Test, minimum GPA of 3.2. Additional exam requirements/recommendations for international students: Required—TOEFL (minimum score 550 paper-based; 213 computer-based; 80 iBT). *Application deadline:* For fall admission, 1/5 for domestic students, 2/1 for international students; for winter admission, 9/1 for domestic students, 7/1 for international students; for spring admission, 12/1 for domestic students, 10/1 for international students. Applications are processed on a rolling basis. Application fee: $60 ($75 for international students). Electronic applications accepted. *Financial support:* In 2007–08, fellowships with tuition reimbursements (averaging $12,000 per year), teaching assistantships with tuition reimbursements (averaging $16,500 per year) were awarded; career-related internships or fieldwork, Federal Work-Study, institutionally sponsored loans, scholarships/grants, health care benefits, and tuition waivers (full and partial) also available. Financial award application deadline: 1/5; financial award applicants required to submit FAFSA. *Faculty research:* Spanish literature of sixteenth, seventeenth and twentieth century; pre-Columbian and colonial Latin American literature; nineteenth and twentieth century Latin American literature. *Unit head:* Dr. David E. Hevzberger, Chair, 951-827-5007 Ext. 11462, Fax: 951-827-2160, E-mail: david.herzberger@ucr.edu. *Application contact:* Dr. Susan Antebi, Graduate Advisor, 951-827-1969, Fax: 951-827-2294, E-mail: clhsgrad@ucr.edu.

University of California, San Diego, Office of Graduate Studies, Department of Literature, Program in Spanish Literature, La Jolla, CA 92093. Offers MA. *Degree requirements:* For master's, thesis. *Entrance requirements:* For master's, GRE General Test, GRE Subject Test. Electronic applications accepted.

University of California, Santa Barbara, Graduate Division, College of Letters and Sciences, Division of Humanities and Fine Arts, Department of Spanish and Portuguese, Santa Barbara, CA 93106. Offers Hispanic languages and literature (PhD); Portuguese (MA); Spanish (MA). Spanish Language Institute available during summer sessions. *Faculty:* 16 full-time (6 women). *Students:* 27 full-time (12 women); includes 6 minority (all Hispanic Americans), 8 international. Average age 31. 34 applicants, 62% accepted, 9 enrolled. In 2007, 3 master's, 4 doctorates awarded. *Median time to degree:* Of those who began their doctoral program in fall 1999, 60% received their degree in 8 years or less. *Degree requirements:* For master's, 2 foreign languages, thesis optional; for doctorate, 2 foreign languages, comprehensive exam, thesis/dissertation. *Entrance requirements:* For master's, GRE, 2 writing samples, undergraduate major in Spanish or equivalent; for doctorate, GRE, 2 writing samples, Master's degree. Additional exam requirements/recommendations for international students: Required—TOEFL (minimum score 550 paper-based; 213 computer-based; 80 iBT). *Application deadline:* For fall admission, 3/1 for domestic and international students; for winter admission, 11/1 for domestic and international students; for spring admission, 2/1 for domestic and international students. Applications are processed on a rolling basis. Application fee: $60. Electronic applications accepted. *Expenses:* Tuition, nonresident: full-time $14,888. Required fees: $10,108. *Financial support:* In 2007–08, 27 students received support, including 6 fellowships with full tuition reimbursements available (averaging $15,500 per year), 4 research assistantships, 26 teaching assistantships with full and partial tuition reimbursements available (averaging $16,390 per year); career-related internships or fieldwork, Federal Work-Study, scholarships/grants, health care benefits, tuition waivers (full and partial), and unspecified assistantships also available. Financial award application deadline: 1/7; financial award applicants required to submit FAFSA. *Faculty research:* 19th century Spanish and Portuguese literature, Spanish and Spanish American literature, 19th and 20th century Portuguese and Brazilian literatures, Mexican literature, Catalan language and culture. *Unit head:* Prof. Francisco P. Lomeli, Chair, 805-893-2798, E-mail: rap@spanport.ucsb.edu. *Application contact:* Carol Conley, Graduate Program Assistant, 805-893-3162, Fax: 805-893-8341, E-mail: cconley@spanport.ucsb.edu.

University of Central Florida, College of Arts and Humanities, Department of Modern Languages and Literatures, Program in Spanish, Orlando, FL 32816. Offers MA. Part-time and evening/weekend programs available. *Students:* Average age 37. *Degree requirements:* For master's, one foreign language, comprehensive exam, thesis or alternative. *Entrance requirements:* For master's, GRE General Test, minimum GPA of 3.0 in last 60 hours. Additional exam requirements/recommendations for international students: Required—TOEFL. *Application deadline:* For fall admission, 6/1 for domestic students; for spring admission, 12/1 for domestic students. Application fee: $30. Electronic applications accepted. *Expenses:* Tuition, state resident: full-time $6,484. Tuition, nonresident: full-time $23,938. Tuition and fees vary according to program. *Financial support:* Fellowships with partial tuition reimbursements, research assistantships with partial tuition reimbursements, teaching assistantships with partial tuition reimbursements, career-related internships or fieldwork, Federal Work-Study, institutionally sponsored loans, tuition waivers (partial), and unspecified assistantships available. Financial award application deadline: 3/1; financial award applicants required to submit FAFSA. *Unit head:* Dr. Celestino A. Villanueva, Coordinator, 407-823-5935, E-mail: cvillanv@mail.ucf.edu.

University of Chicago, Division of the Humanities, Department of Romance Languages and Literatures, Chicago, IL 60637-1513. Offers French (AM, PhD); Italian (AM, PhD); Spanish (AM, PhD). *Students:* 75. 56 applicants, 45% accepted, 15 enrolled.Terminal master's awarded for partial completion of doctoral program. *Degree requirements:* For master's, 2 foreign languages, thesis; for doctorate, 3 foreign languages, thesis/dissertation. *Entrance requirements:* For master's and doctorate, GRE General Test, GRE Subject Test. Additional exam requirements/recommendations for international students: Required—TOEFL. *Application deadline:* For fall admission, 12/15 for domestic students. Application fee: $55. *Financial support:* Teaching assistantships, Federal Work-Study available. Financial award application deadline: 12/15; financial award applicants required to submit FAFSA. *Unit head:* Dr. Frederick de Armas, Chair, 773-702-8481.

University of Cincinnati, Graduate School, McMicken College of Arts and Sciences, Department of Romance Languages and Literature, Program in Spanish, Cincinnati, OH 45221. Offers MA, PhD. *Students:* 8 full-time (7 women); includes 3 minority (1 African American, 2 Hispanic Americans), 2 international. Terminal master's awarded for partial completion of doctoral program. *Degree requirements:* For master's, thesis optional; for doctorate, 2 foreign languages, thesis/dissertation. *Entrance requirements:* For master's, minimum GPA of 3.0. *Application deadline:* For fall admission, 2/1 for domestic students. Application fee: $30. Electronic applications accepted. *Financial support:* Fellowships with full tuition reimbursements, teaching assistantships with full tuition reimbursements, tuition waivers (partial) and unspecified assistantships available. Financial award application deadline: 5/1. *Faculty research:* Applied linguistics, Spanish essay, Latin American culture, women's studies, poetry. *Application contact:* Connie Scarborough, Graduate Program Director, 513-556-1836, Fax: 513-556-2577, E-mail: connie.scarborough@uc.edu.

University of Colorado at Boulder, Graduate School, College of Arts and Sciences, Department of Spanish and Portuguese, Boulder, CO 80309. Offers Hispanic linguistics (MA); medieval/early modern Hispanic literatures (PhD); Spanish literature (MA, PhD), including 18th and 19th century peninsular literature (MA), Golden Age (MA), medieval Iberian literature (MA). Part-time programs available. *Faculty:* 14. *Students:* 28 full-time (19 women), 14 part-time (10 women); includes 12 minority (all Hispanic Americans), 18 international. Average age 32. 17 applicants, 88% accepted. In 2007, 5 master's, 4 doctorates awarded. Terminal master's awarded for partial completion of doctoral program. *Degree requirements:* For master's, one foreign language, comprehensive exam, thesis or alternative; for doctorate, 2 foreign languages, thesis/dissertation. *Entrance requirements:* For master's, minimum undergraduate GPA of 2.75. *Application deadline:* For fall admission, 12/15 priority date for domestic students, 12/15 for international students. Applications are processed on a rolling basis. Application fee: $50 ($60 for international students). *Financial support:* In 2007–08, 41 fellowships with full tuition reimbursements (averaging $1,663 per year) were awarded; tuition waivers (full) also available. Financial award application deadline: 12/15. *Faculty research:* Spanish peninsular and Spanish-American literatures; Hispanic linguistics; Medieval, Golden Age, eighteenth and nineteenth century literatures. Total annual research expenditures: $6,076. *Unit head:* Ricardo Laudiera, Chair, 303-492-5386, Fax: 303-492-3699, E-mail: laudiera@colorado.edu. *Application contact:* Graduate Program Assistant, 303-492-7308, Fax: 303-492-3699, E-mail: spanport@colorado.edu.

University of Colorado Denver, College of Liberal Arts and Sciences, Department of Modern Languages, Denver, CO 80217-3364. Offers Spanish (MA). *Faculty:* 2 full-time (1 woman). *Students:* 5 full-time (4 women), 21 part-time (16 women); includes 12 minority (all Hispanic Americans) 12 applicants, 100% accepted, 9 enrolled. *Entrance requirements:* For master's, GRE, minimum undergraduate GPA of 2.5, 3.0 in all Spanish courses. Additional exam requirements/recommendations for international students: Required—TOEFL. Application fee: $50. *Unit head:* Dr. Kathleen Bolland, Chair, 303-556-2572, E-mail: kathleen.bolland@cudenver.edu.

University of Connecticut, Graduate School, College of Liberal Arts and Sciences, Department of Modern and Classical Languages, Field of Spanish, Storrs, CT 06269. Offers MA, PhD. *Faculty:* 10 full-time (4 women). *Students:* 18 full-time (9 women), 6 part-time (2 women); includes 3 minority (all Hispanic Americans), 13 international. Average age 34. 25 applicants, 20% accepted, 5 enrolled. In 2007, 2 master's, 1 doctorate awarded. Terminal master's awarded for partial completion of doctoral program. *Degree requirements:* For master's, one foreign language, comprehensive exam; for doctorate, 2 foreign languages, thesis/dissertation. *Entrance requirements:* For master's and doctorate, GRE General Test, GRE Subject Test. Additional exam requirements/recommendations for international students: Required—TOEFL (minimum score 550 paper-based; 213 computer-based). *Application deadline:* For fall admission, 2/1 priority date for domestic and international students; for spring admission, 11/1 for domestic students, 10/1 for international students. Applications are processed on a rolling basis. Application fee: $55. Electronic applications accepted. *Expenses:* Tuition, state resident: part-time $469 per credit hour. Tuition, nonresident: part-time $1,218 per credit hour. *Financial support:* In 2007–08, 18 teaching assistantships with full tuition reimbursements were awarded; fellowships, research assistantships, Federal Work-Study, scholarships/grants, health care benefits, and unspecified assistantships also available. Financial award application deadline: 2/1; financial award applicants required to submit FAFSA. *Unit head:* Miguel Gomes, Professor, 860-486-3288, E-mail: miguel.gomes@uconn.edu.

University of Delaware, College of Arts and Sciences, Department of Foreign Languages and Literatures, Newark, DE 19716. Offers foreign languages and literatures (MA), including French, German, Spanish; foreign languages pedagogy (MA), including French, German, Spanish. *Faculty:* 27 full-time (14 women). *Students:* 33 full-time (23 women), 5 part-time (all women); includes 1 minority (African American), 10 international. Average age 25. 29 applicants, 55% accepted, 11 enrolled. In 2007, 12 degrees awarded. *Degree requirements:* For master's, one foreign language, comprehensive exam, thesis optional. *Entrance requirements:* For master's, GRE General Test, letters of recommendation, writing sample. Additional exam requirements/recommendations for international students: Required—TOEFL. *Application deadline:* For fall admission, 2/1 priority date for domestic and international students; for spring admission, 11/1 for domestic and international students. Application fee: $60. Electronic applications accepted. *Financial support:* In 2007–08, fellowships with full tuition reimbursements (averaging $14,600 per year), research assistantships with full tuition reimbursements (averaging $14,600 per year), 29 teaching assistantships with full tuition reimbursements (averaging $14,600 per year) were awarded; tuition waivers (full) and unspecified assistantships also available. Financial award application deadline: 2/1. *Faculty research:* Medieval to Modern French and Spanish literature, Twentieth Century German, French, Spanish literature by women, computer-assisted instruction. Total annual research expenditures: $12,000. *Unit head:* Dr. Richard Zipser, Chair, 302-831-6882. *Application contact:* Dr. Monika Shafi, Graduate Coordinator, 302-831-2587, E-mail: mshafi@udel.edu.

University of Florida, Graduate School, College of Liberal Arts and Sciences, Department of Romance Languages and Literatures, Program in Spanish, Gainesville, FL 32611. Offers MA, PhD. *Faculty:* 12. *Degree requirements:* For master's, one foreign language, thesis optional; for doctorate, one foreign language, thesis/dissertation. *Entrance requirements:* For master's and doctorate, GRE General Test, minimum GPA of 3.0. Additional exam requirements/recommendations for international students: Required—TOEFL (minimum score 550 paper-based; 213 computer-based). *Application deadline:* For fall admission, 4/1 priority date for domestic students. Applications are processed on a rolling basis. Application fee: $30. Electronic applications accepted. *Expenses:* Tuition, state resident: full-time $7,478. Tuition, nonresident: full-time $22,603. *Financial support:* In 2007–08, 15 students received support, including fellowships with full tuition reimbursements available (averaging $15,000 per year), research assistantships with full tuition reimbursements available (averaging $15,000 per year), teaching assistantships with full tuition reimbursements available (averaging $12,700 per year). *Faculty research:* Peninsular literature, Latin American literature, Hispanic linguistics. *Unit head:* Dr. Reynaldo L. Jiménez, Coordinator, 352-392-2016 Ext. 242, E-mail: jimenez@rll.ufl.edu. *Application contact:* Terry Lopez, Graduate Secretary, 352-392-2016 Ext. 224, E-mail: tlopez@rll.ufl.edu.

University of Georgia, Graduate School, College of Arts and Sciences, Department of Romance Languages, Program in Spanish, Athens, GA 30602. Offers MA, MAT. *Students:* 12 full-time (7 women), 2 part-time (both women); includes 2 Hispanic Americans, 1 international. 26 applicants, 38% accepted, 4 enrolled. In 2007, 8 degrees awarded. *Degree requirements:* For master's, one foreign language, thesis (MA). *Entrance requirements:* For master's, GRE General Test. *Application deadline:* For fall admission, 7/1 priority date for domestic students; for spring admission, 11/15 for domestic students. Application fee: $50. Electronic applications accepted. *Financial support:* Fellowships, research assistantships, teaching assistantships, unspecified assistantships available.

University of Hawaii at Manoa, Graduate Division, Colleges of Arts and Sciences, College of Language, Linguistics and Literature, Department of Languages and Literatures of Europe and the Americas, Program in Spanish, Honolulu, HI 96822. Offers MA. Part-time programs available. *Faculty:* 6 full-time (2 women). *Students:* 13 full-time (6 women), 2 part-time (both women); includes 3 minority (all Hispanic Americans), 4 international. 10 applicants, 80% accepted, 7 enrolled. *Degree requirements:* For master's, one foreign language, thesis optional. *Entrance requirements:* For master's, GRE General Test. Additional exam requirements/recommendations for international students: Required—TOEFL (minimum score 580 paper-based; 237 computer-based; 92 iBT), IELTS (minimum score 5). *Application deadline:* For fall admission, 3/1 for domestic students, 2/1 for international students; for spring admission, 9/1 for domestic students, 8/15 for international students. Application fee: $50. *Financial support:* In 2007–08, 1 research assistantship (averaging $16,176 per year), 11 teaching assistantships (averaging $13,296 per year) were awarded. *Application contact:* Robert Ball, Information Contact, 808-956-4715, Fax: 808-956-9536, E-mail: rball@hawaii.edu.

University of Houston, College of Liberal Arts and Social Sciences, Department of Modern and Classical Languages, Houston, TX 77204. Offers French (MA); Spanish (MA, PhD); MBA/MA. Part-time and evening/weekend programs available. Postbaccalaureate distance learning degree programs offered. *Faculty:* 10 full-time (6 women), 2 part-time/adjunct (1 woman). *Students:* 26 full-time (19 women), 41 part-time (35 women); includes 41 minority (1 African American, 40 Hispanic Americans), 9 international. Average age 36. 21 applicants, 81% accepted, 12 enrolled. In 2007, 9 master's, 4 doctorates awarded. Terminal master's awarded for partial completion of doctoral program. *Degree requirements:* For master's, one foreign language, thesis optional; for doctorate, 3 foreign languages, thesis/dissertation. *Entrance requirements:* For master's and doctorate, GRE General Test. Additional exam requirements/recommendations for international students: Required—TOEFL. *Application deadline:* For fall admission, 2/28 priority date for domestic students; for spring admission, 10/30 priority date for domestic students. Application fee: $25 ($75 for international students). *Expenses:* Tuition, state resident: full-time $6,297; part-time $262 per credit. Tuition, nonresident: full-time $12,969; part-time $540 per credit. Required fees: $2,696. *Financial support:* In 2007–08, 5 research assistantships with full tuition reimbursements (averaging $10,400 per year), 15 teaching assistantships

Spanish

University of Houston (continued)
with full tuition reimbursements (averaging $10,400 per year) were awarded; fellowships with full tuition reimbursements, career-related internships or fieldwork, Federal Work-Study, institutionally sponsored loans, scholarships/grants, health care benefits, and unspecified assistantships also available. Support available to part-time students. Financial award application deadline: 2/1; financial award applicants required to submit FAFSA. *Faculty research:* Hispanic literature and language in the U.S., Golden Age, women. *Unit head:* Dr. Marc Zimmerman, Chairperson, 713-743-3007, Fax: 713-743-0935, E-mail: mzimmerm@mail.uh.edu.

University of Illinois at Urbana–Champaign, Graduate College, College of Liberal Arts and Sciences, School of Literatures, Cultures and Linguistics, Department of Spanish, Italian and Portuguese, Champaign, IL 61820. Offers Italian (MA, PhD); Portuguese (MA, PhD); Spanish (PhD); Spanish, Italian and Portuguese (MA). *Faculty:* 17 full-time (10 women). *Students:* 55 full-time (41 women), 11 part-time (8 women); includes 7 minority (1 African American, 6 Hispanic Americans), 40 international. 77 applicants, 42% accepted, 14 enrolled. In 2007, 6 master's, 8 doctorates awarded. *Degree requirements:* For doctorate, 2 foreign languages, thesis/dissertation. *Entrance requirements:* For master's, GRE General Test, GRE Subject Test, minimum GPA of 3.0. *Application deadline:* For fall admission, 3/1 for domestic students. Applications are processed on a rolling basis. Application fee: $60 ($75 for international students). Electronic applications accepted. *Financial support:* In 2007–08, 8 fellowships, 3 research assistantships, 62 teaching assistantships were awarded; tuition waivers (full and partial) also available. Financial award application deadline: 2/15. *Unit head:* Diane Musumeci, Head, 217-244-3250, Fax: 217-244-8430, E-mail: musumeci@uiuc.edu. *Application contact:* Lynn Stanke, Secretary, 217-333-6269, Fax: 217-244-3050, E-mail: stanke@uiuc.edu.

The University of Iowa, Graduate College, College of Liberal Arts and Sciences, Department of Spanish and Portuguese, Iowa City, IA 52242-1316. Offers Spanish (MA, PhD). *Faculty:* 17 full-time, 19 part-time/adjunct. *Students:* 28 full-time (13 women), 14 part-time (7 women); includes 5 minority (all Hispanic Americans), 16 international. 33 applicants, 67% accepted, 13 enrolled. In 2007, 2 master's, 4 doctorates awarded. *Degree requirements:* For master's, thesis optional, exam; for doctorate, comprehensive exam, thesis/dissertation. *Entrance requirements:* For master's and doctorate, minimum GPA of 3.0. Additional exam requirements/recommendations for international students: Required—TOEFL (minimum score 600 paper-based; 250 computer-based; 100 iBT). *Application deadline:* For fall admission, 2/1 priority date for domestic and international students; for spring admission, 8/15 priority date for domestic and international students. Applications are processed on a rolling basis. Application fee: $60 ($85 for international students). Electronic applications accepted. *Expenses:* Tuition, state resident: part-time $349 per hour. Tuition, nonresident: part-time $349 per hour. Tuition and fees vary according to course load and program. *Financial support:* In 2007–08, 3 research assistantships with partial tuition reimbursements, 23 teaching assistantships with partial tuition reimbursements were awarded; fellowships also available. Financial award applicants required to submit FAFSA. *Unit head:* Thomas E. Lewis, Chair, 319-335-2244, Fax: 319-335-2990.

University of Kansas, Research and Graduate Studies, College of Liberal Arts and Sciences, Department of Spanish and Portuguese, Lawrence, KS 66045. Offers Spanish (MA, PhD). *Faculty:* 15. *Students:* 40 full-time (24 women), 3 part-time (1 woman); includes 4 minority (all Hispanic Americans), 12 international. Average age 30. 29 applicants, 62% accepted, 9 enrolled. In 2007, 6 master's, 3 doctorates awarded. *Degree requirements:* For master's, 2 foreign languages; for doctorate, 3 foreign languages, thesis/dissertation. *Entrance requirements:* For master's and doctorate, GRE. Additional exam requirements/recommendations for international students: Required—TOEFL. *Application deadline:* For fall admission, 5/15 priority date for domestic students, 12/15 priority date for international students; for spring admission, 10/15 priority date for domestic students, 5/15 priority date for international students. Applications are processed on a rolling basis. Application fee: $55 ($60 for international students). *Expenses:* Tuition, state resident: full-time $5,838. Tuition, nonresident: full-time $13,409. Tuition and fees vary according to program. *Financial support:* Fellowships with tuition reimbursements, research assistantships, teaching assistantships with full and partial tuition reimbursements, unspecified assistantships available. Financial award application deadline: 1/15. *Faculty research:* Latin American literary and cultural studies; medieval, early modern and contemporary Spanish literary and cultural studies. *Unit head:* Vicky Unruh, Chair, 785-864-3851, Fax: 785-864-4298, E-mail: spanport@ku.edu. *Application contact:* Rhonda Cook, Office Manager, 785-864-3851, Fax: 785-864-4298, E-mail: rcook@ku.edu.

University of Lethbridge, School of Graduate Studies, Lethbridge, AB T1K 3M4, Canada. Offers accounting (MScM); addictions counseling (M Sc); agricultural biotechnology (M Sc); agricultural studies (M Sc, MA); anthropology (MA); archaeology (MA); art (MA); biochemistry (M Sc); biological sciences (M Sc); biomolecular science (PhD); biosystems and biodiversity (PhD); Canadian studies (MA); chemistry (M Sc); computer science (M Sc); computer science and geographical information science (M Sc); counseling psychology (M Ed); dramatic arts (MA); earth, space, and physical science (PhD); economics (MA); educational leadership (M Ed); English (MA); environmental science (M Sc); evolution and behavior (PhD); exercise science (M Sc); finance (MScM); French (MA); French/German (MA); French/Spanish (MA); general education (M Ed); general management (MScM); geography (M Sc, MA); German (MA); health sciences (M Sc, MA); history (MA); human resource management and labour relations (MScM); individualized multidisciplinary (M Sc, MA); information systems (MScM); international management (MScM); kinesiology (M Sc, MA); management (M Sc, MA); marketing (MScM); mathematics (M Sc); music (MA); Native American studies (MA); neuroscience (M Sc, PhD); new media (MA); nursing (M Sc); philosophy (MA); physics (M Sc); policy and strategy (MScM); political science (MA); psychology (M Sc, MA); religious studies (MA); sociology (MA); theoretical and computational science (PhD); urban and regional studies (MA). Part-time and evening/weekend programs available. *Students:* 215 full-time, 98 part-time. In 2007, 87 master's, 1 doctorate awarded. *Degree requirements:* For doctorate, comprehensive exam, thesis/dissertation. *Entrance requirements:* For master's, GMAT (M Sc in management), bachelor's degree in related field, minimum GPA of 3.0 during previous 20 graded semester courses, 2 years teaching or related experience (M Ed); for doctorate, master's degree, minimum graduate GPA of 3.5. Additional exam requirements/recommendations for international students: Required—TOEFL. Application fee: $60 Canadian dollars. *Financial support:* Fellowships, research assistantships, teaching assistantships, scholarships/grants, health care benefits, and unspecified assistantships available. *Faculty research:* Movement and brain plasticity, gibberellin physiology, photosynthesis, carbon cycling, molecular properties of main-group ring components. *Unit head:* Dr. Jo-Anne Fiske, Interim Dean, 403-329-2121, Fax: 403-329-2097. *Application contact:* Jennifer Geddes, Graduate Liaison Officer, 403-329-2762, Fax: 403-329-5159, E-mail: jennifer.geddes@uleth.ca.

University of Louisville, Graduate School, College of Arts and Sciences, Department of Classical and Modern Languages, Program in Spanish, Louisville, KY 40292-0001. Offers MA. *Students:* 17 full-time (13 women), 9 part-time (7 women); includes 11 minority (1 African American, 1 Asian American or Pacific Islander, 9 Hispanic Americans), 1 international. Average age 36. In 2007, 8 degrees awarded. *Degree requirements:* For master's, one foreign language, thesis optional. *Entrance requirements:* For master's, GRE General Test. *Application deadline:* Applications are processed on a rolling basis. Application fee: $50. *Unit head:* Dr. Mary Makris, Acting Chair, Department of Classical and Modern Languages, 502-852-0491, Fax: 502-852-8885, E-mail: mmakris@louisville.edu.

University of Manitoba, Faculty of Graduate Studies, Faculty of Arts, Department of French, Spanish and Italian, Winnipeg, MB R3T 2N2, Canada. Offers MA, PhD. *Degree requirements:* For master's, one foreign language, thesis; for doctorate, 2 foreign languages, thesis/dissertation.

University of Maryland, College Park, Graduate Studies, College of Arts and Humanities, School of Languages, Literature, and Cultures, Department of Spanish and Portuguese, College Park, MD 20742. Offers MA, PhD. *Students:* 32 full-time (28 women), 6 part-time (4 women); includes 15 minority (1 American Indian/Alaska Native, 1 Asian American or Pacific Islander, 13 Hispanic Americans), 12 international. 30 applicants, 40% accepted, 9 enrolled. In 2007, 3 master's, 4 doctorates awarded. *Degree requirements:* For master's, comprehensive exam, thesis optional, scholarly paper; for doctorate, 2 foreign languages, thesis/dissertation. *Entrance requirements:* For master's, minimum GPA of 3.0, interview, sample research paper, minimum of 12 credits in upper-level literature, 3 letters of recommendation; for doctorate, minimum GPA of 3.0, interview, sample research paper, minimum of 12 credits in upper-level literature. Additional exam requirements/recommendations for international students: Required—TOEFL. *Application deadline:* For fall admission, 1/7 for domestic and international students. Applications are processed on a rolling basis. Application fee: $60. Electronic applications accepted. *Financial support:* In 2007–08, 4 fellowships with full tuition reimbursements (averaging $14,225 per year), 18 teaching assistantships with tuition reimbursements (averaging $17,462 per year) were awarded; Federal Work-Study also available. Support available to part-time students. Financial award applicants required to submit FAFSA. *Unit head:* Dr. Sandra M. Cypess, Chairman, 301-405-6449, Fax: 301-314-9752, E-mail: smcypess@umd.edu. *Application contact:* Dean of Graduate School, 301-405-4190, Fax: 301-314-9305.

University of Maryland, College Park, Graduate Studies, College of Arts and Humanities, School of Languages, Literature, and Cultures, Program in Second Language Acquisition and Application, College Park, MD 20742. Offers French (MA); German (MA); Japanese (MA); Russian (MA); second language instruction (PhD); second language learning (PhD); second language measurement and assessment (PhD); second language use (PhD); Spanish (MA). *Students:* 1 (woman) full-time, 1 international. 50 applicants, 14% accepted. *Entrance requirements:* For master's, BA or BS in related field, demonstrated language competency, 3 letters of reference. *Application deadline:* For fall admission, 1/15 for domestic students, 2/1 for international students; for spring admission, 9/15 for domestic students, 6/1 for international students. Applications are processed on a rolling basis. Application fee: $60. Electronic applications accepted. *Financial support:* In 2007–08, 1 research assistantship (averaging $20,450 per year) was awarded; fellowships also available. *Faculty research:* Second language acquisition, pedagogical perspectives, technological applications, language use in professional contexts. *Unit head:* Dr. Cynthia L. Martin, Acting Chair, 301-405-4244, E-mail: cmartin@umd.edu. *Application contact:* Dean of Graduate School, 301-405-0358, Fax: 301-314-9305.

University of Massachusetts Amherst, Graduate School, College of Humanities and Fine Arts, Department of Spanish and Portuguese, Amherst, MA 01003. Offers Hispanic literatures and linguistics (MA, PhD); teaching Spanish (MAT). Part-time programs available. *Faculty:* 9 full-time (4 women). *Students:* 30 full-time (21 women), 20 part-time (11 women); includes 16 minority (1 Asian American or Pacific Islander, 15 Hispanic Americans), 20 international. Average age 33. 47 applicants, 49% accepted, 9 enrolled. In 2007, 8 master's, 4 doctorates awarded. Terminal master's awarded for partial completion of doctoral program. *Degree requirements:* For master's, one foreign language, thesis or alternative; for doctorate, 2 foreign languages. *Entrance requirements:* For master's and doctorate, GRE General Test, sample term paper. Additional exam requirements/recommendations for international students: Required—TOEFL (minimum score 530 paper-based; 197 computer-based). *Application deadline:* For fall admission, 2/1 priority date for domestic and international students. Applications are processed on a rolling basis. Application fee: $50 ($65 for international students). *Expenses:* Tuition, state resident: full-time $2,640; part-time $110 per credit. Tuition, nonresident: full-time $9,936; part-time $414 per credit. Required fees: $7,455. One-time fee: $332. Tuition and fees vary according to course load, campus/location, program and reciprocity agreements. *Financial support:* In 2007–08, 40 teaching assistantships with full tuition reimbursements (averaging $13,191 per year) were awarded; fellowships with full tuition reimbursements, research assistantships with full tuition reimbursements, career-related internships or fieldwork, Federal Work-Study, scholarships/grants, traineeships, and unspecified assistantships also available. Support available to part-time students. Financial award application deadline: 2/1. *Unit head:* Dr. Jose Ornelas, Head, 413-545-4912, Fax: 413-545-3178, E-mail: ornelas@spanport.umass.edu.

University of Memphis, Graduate School, College of Arts and Sciences, Department of Foreign Languages and Literatures, Memphis, TN 38152. Offers French (MA); Spanish (MA). Part-time programs available. *Faculty:* 13 full-time (7 women), 2 part-time/adjunct (0 women). *Students:* 17 full-time (12 women), 16 part-time (14 women); includes 9 minority (5 African Americans, 1 American Indian/Alaska Native, 3 Hispanic Americans), 6 international. Average age 33. 24 applicants, 88% accepted, 13 enrolled. In 2007, 4 degrees awarded. *Degree requirements:* For master's, one foreign language, comprehensive exam, thesis optional. *Entrance requirements:* For master's, GRE General Test. *Application deadline:* For fall admission, 8/1 for domestic students; for spring admission, 12/1 for domestic students. Applications are processed on a rolling basis. Application fee: $35 ($60 for international students). *Expenses:* Tuition, state resident: full-time $6,990; part-time $377 per hour. Tuition, nonresident: full-time $17,818; part-time $830 per hour. Tuition and fees vary according to course load and program. *Financial support:* In 2007–08, 8 research assistantships with full tuition reimbursements (averaging $6,800 per year), 9 teaching assistantships with full tuition reimbursements (averaging $6,225 per year) were awarded. *Faculty research:* Spanish-American short story, Latin American women writers, French women of letters, Avevedo and Cervantes, 19th and 20th century peninsular literature, Brazilian culture and literature. *Unit head:* Dr. Ralph Albanese, Chairman, 901-678-2506, Fax: 901-678-5338, E-mail: ralbanes@memphis.edu. *Application contact:* Dr. Fernando Burgos, Coordinator of Graduate Studies, 901-678-3158, Fax: 901-678-5338, E-mail: fburgos@memphis.edu.

University of Miami, Graduate School, College of Arts and Sciences, Department of Modern Languages and Literatures, Coral Gables, FL 33124. Offers romance studies (PhD), including French, Spanish. *Faculty:* 23 full-time (14 women). *Students:* 24 full-time (14 women); includes 10 minority (3 African Americans, 2 Asian Americans or Pacific Islanders, 5 Hispanic Americans), 11 international. Average age 32. 25 applicants, 24% accepted, 6 enrolled. In 2007, 4 degrees awarded. *Median time to degree:* Of those who began their doctoral program in fall 1999, 100% received their degree in 8 years or less. *Degree requirements:* For doctorate, 2 foreign languages, thesis/dissertation, area exam, qualifying exam. *Entrance requirements:* For doctorate, 1 writing sample in English and 1 writing sample in French or Spanish, minimum GPA of 3.0; oral interview; letters of recommendation. Additional exam requirements/recommendations for international students: Required—TOEFL (minimum score 550 paper-based; 213 computer-based; 59 iBT), GRE General Test (recommended). *Application deadline:* For fall admission, 1/15 priority date for domestic and international students. Application fee: $50. Electronic applications accepted. *Financial support:* In 2007–08, 21 students received support, including 1 fellowship with full tuition reimbursement available (averaging $30,000 per year), 1 research assistantship, 16 teaching assistantships with full tuition reimbursements available (averaging $20,000 per year); career-related internships or fieldwork, Federal Work-Study, institutionally sponsored loans, scholarships/grants, health care benefits, and unspecified assistantships also available. Financial award application deadline: 3/15; financial award applicants required to submit FAFSA. *Faculty research:* Transatlantic studies, Caribbean studies, comparative literature, gender theory, cultural studies. *Unit head:* Prof. Anne J. Cruz, Chair, 305-284-5585, Fax: 305-284-2068, E-mail: ajcruz@miami.edu. *Application contact:* Prof. Gema Perez-Sanchez, Director of Graduate Studies, 305-284-4858 Ext. 7313, Fax: 305-284-2068, E-mail: gema@miami.edu.

University of Miami, Graduate School, School of Communication, Coral Gables, FL 33124. Offers communication (PhD); communication studies (MA); film studies (MA, PhD); motion pictures (MFA), including production, producing, and screenwriting; print journalism (MA); public relations (MA); Spanish language journalism (MA); television broadcast journalism (MA). *Accreditation:* ACEJMC. Part-time programs available. *Faculty:* 39 full-time (12 women). *Students:* 113 full-time (61 women), 16 part-time (5 women); includes 28 minority (8 African Americans, 1 Asian American or Pacific Islander, 19 Hispanic Americans), 14 international. Average age 27. 374 applicants, 56% accepted, 64 enrolled. In 2007, 48 master's, 2 doctorates awarded. *Degree requirements:* For master's, comprehensive exam (for some programs), thesis (for some programs); for doctorate, comprehensive exam, thesis/dissertation.

Entrance requirements: For master's, GRE General Test; for doctorate, GRE General Test, master's thesis or scholarly research. Additional exam requirements/recommendations for international students: Required—TOEFL (minimum score 600 paper-based; 250 computer-based; 100 iBT). *Application deadline:* For fall admission, 12/15 priority date for domestic and international students. Applications are processed on a rolling basis. Application fee: $50. Electronic applications accepted. *Financial support:* In 2007–08, 68 students received support, including 10 teaching assistantships with full tuition reimbursements available; fellowships with full tuition reimbursements available, Federal Work-Study, institutionally sponsored loans, scholarships/grants, tuition waivers (partial), and unspecified assistantships also available. Financial award application deadline: 3/1; financial award applicants required to submit FAFSA. *Faculty research:* Communication studies, mass communication, international/interpersonal communication, film studies, journalism. *Unit head:* Dr. Sam L. Grogg, Dean, 305-284-3420, Fax: 305-284-2454, E-mail: sgrogg@miami.edu. *Application contact:* Dr. Leonardo C. Ferreira, Director of Graduate Studies, 305-284-3180, Fax: 305-284-8701, E-mail: lferreira@miami.edu.

See Close-Up on page 943.

University of Michigan, Horace H. Rackham School of Graduate Studies, College of Literature, Science, and the Arts, Department of Romance Languages and Literatures, Program in Spanish, Ann Arbor, MI 48109. Offers PhD. *Faculty:* 19 full-time (7 women). *Students:* 40 full-time (28 women). Average age 30. 46 applicants, 11% accepted. In 2007, 1 degree awarded. *Degree requirements:* For doctorate, 2 foreign languages, thesis/dissertation, oral defense of dissertation, preliminary exams. *Entrance requirements:* For doctorate, GRE General Test. Additional exam requirements/recommendations for international students: Required—TOEFL or Michigan English Language Assessment Battery. *Application deadline:* For fall admission, 1/1 for domestic students. Application fee: $60. Electronic applications accepted. *Financial support:* In 2007–08, 5 fellowships with full tuition reimbursements (averaging $20,000 per year) were awarded; teaching assistantships with full tuition reimbursements, institutionally sponsored loans, scholarships/grants, and unspecified assistantships also available. Financial award application deadline: 1/1. *Faculty research:* Comparative Romance studies, medieval and early modern studies, postcolonial and minority literatures, culture and materiality, reflection in the nature and function of scholarship. *Application contact:* Graduate Assistant, 734-763-0408, Fax: 734-764-8163, E-mail: rll-admissions@umich.edu.

University of Minnesota, Twin Cities Campus, Graduate School, College of Liberal Arts, Department of Spanish and Portuguese Studies, Minneapolis, MN 55455-0213. Offers Hispanic and Luso-Brazilian literatures and linguistics (PhD); Hispanic linguistics (MA); Hispanic literature (MA); Lusophone literature (MA). *Faculty:* 12 full-time (6 women), 2 part-time/adjunct (both women). *Students:* 47 full-time (31 women), 8 part-time (5 women); includes 3 African Americans, 18 Hispanic Americans, 11 international. Average age 30. 39 applicants, 33% accepted, 6 enrolled. In 2007, 5 master's, 7 doctorates awarded. *Degree requirements:* For master's, 2 foreign languages, comprehensive exam, thesis or alternative; for doctorate, 2 foreign languages, comprehensive exam, thesis/dissertation. *Entrance requirements:* For master's and doctorate, GRE General Test, samples of written work, 3 letters of recommendation, voice sample, statement of purpose. Additional exam requirements/recommendations for international students: Required—TOEFL (minimum score 550 paper-based; 213 computer-based; 79 iBT). *Application deadline:* For fall admission, 1/5 for domestic and international students. Application fee: $55 ($75 for international students). Electronic applications accepted. *Financial support:* In 2007–08, 1 research assistantship with full tuition reimbursement (averaging $12,528 per year), 51 teaching assistantships with full tuition reimbursements (averaging $12,528 per year) were awarded; fellowships, career-related internships or fieldwork and Federal Work-Study also available. *Faculty research:* Sociohistorical approaches to literature and culture, feminist studies, literary theory, ideologies and literature, pragmatics and sociolinguistics. Total annual research expenditures: $7,200. *Unit head:* Ana Paula Ferreira, Chair, 612-625-3834, Fax: 612-625-3549, E-mail: apferrei@umn.edu. *Application contact:* Sara E Sonnenberg, Executive Administrative Specialist, Graduate Program Assistant, 612-626-7809, Fax: 612-625-3549, E-mail: sonne037@tc.umn.edu.

University of Mississippi, Graduate School, College of Liberal Arts, Department of Modern Languages, Oxford, University, MS 38677. Offers French (MA); German (MA); Spanish (MA). *Faculty:* 38 full-time (26 women), 2 part-time/adjunct (both women). *Students:* 13 full-time (5 women), 4 part-time (3 women); includes 3 minority (2 African Americans, 1 American Indian/Alaska Native), 3 international. In 2007, 3 degrees awarded. *Degree requirements:* For master's, thesis (for some programs). *Entrance requirements:* For master's, GRE General Test, minimum GPA of 3.0. Additional exam requirements/recommendations for international students: Required—TOEFL. *Application deadline:* For fall admission, 2/1 for domestic students; for spring admission, 10/1 for domestic students. Applications are processed on a rolling basis. Application fee: $25. Electronic applications accepted. *Expenses:* Tuition, state resident: full-time $4,932. Tuition, nonresident: full-time $11,436. *Financial support:* Scholarships/grants available. Financial award application deadline: 3/1; financial award applicants required to submit FAFSA. *Unit head:* Dr. Donald Dyer, Chair, 662-915-7298, Fax: 662-915-1086, E-mail: mlangs@olemiss.edu.

University of Missouri–Columbia, Graduate School, College of Arts and Sciences, Department of Romance Languages and Literature, Program in Spanish, Columbia, MO 65211. Offers MA, PhD. *Degree requirements:* For master's, one foreign language; for doctorate, 4 foreign languages, thesis/dissertation. *Entrance requirements:* For master's and doctorate, GRE General Test, minimum GPA of 3.0.

The University of Montana, Graduate School, College of Arts and Sciences, Department of Modern and Classical Languages and Literatures, Missoula, MT 59812-0002. Offers French (MA); German (MA); Spanish (MA). *Degree requirements:* For master's, one foreign language. *Entrance requirements:* For master's, GRE General Test. Additional exam requirements/recommendations for international students: Required—TOEFL.

University of Nebraska–Lincoln, Graduate College, College of Arts and Sciences, Department of Modern Languages and Literatures, Lincoln, NE 68588. Offers French (MA, PhD); German (MA, PhD); Spanish (MA, PhD). *Degree requirements:* For master's, thesis optional; for doctorate, comprehensive exam, thesis/dissertation. *Entrance requirements:* For master's and doctorate, writing sample in target language. Additional exam requirements/recommendations for international students: Required—TOEFL (minimum score 550 paper-based; 213 computer-based). Electronic applications accepted. *Faculty research:* French, German, and Spanish language, literature, and culture.

University of Nevada, Las Vegas, Graduate College, College of Liberal Arts, Department of Foreign Languages, Las Vegas, NV 89154-9900. Offers Spanish language, culture and technology (MA). Part-time programs available. *Faculty:* 10 full-time (5 women). *Students:* 2 full-time (both women), 11 part-time (6 women); includes 6 minority (1 Asian American or Pacific Islander, 5 Hispanic Americans). 9 applicants, 0% accepted. In 2007, 1 master's awarded. *Degree requirements:* For master's, one foreign language, comprehensive exam. *Entrance requirements:* For master's, minimum GPA of 3.0 during previous 2 years, 2.75 overall. Additional exam requirements/recommendations for international students: Required—TOEFL (minimum score 550 paper-based; 213 computer-based; 80 iBT). *Application deadline:* For fall admission, 6/15 for domestic students, 5/1 for international students; for spring admission, 11/15 for domestic students, 10/1 for international students. Application fee: $60 ($75 for international students). Electronic applications accepted. *Expenses:* Tuition, state resident: part-time $198 per credit. Tuition, nonresident: part-time $416 per credit. Required fees: $256 per semester. Tuition and fees vary according to course load and reciprocity agreements. *Financial support:* Teaching assistantships with partial tuition reimbursements, career-related internships or fieldwork, Federal Work-Study, institutionally sponsored loans, scholarships/grants, health care benefits, and unspecified assistantships available. Support available to part-time students. Financial award application deadline: 3/1. *Unit head:* Dr. Margaret Harp, Chair, 702-895-3431. *Application contact:* Graduate College Admissions Evaluator, 702-895-3320, Fax: 702-895-4180, E-mail: gradcollege@unlv.edu.

University of Nevada, Reno, Graduate School, College of Liberal Arts, Department of Foreign Languages and Literatures, Reno, NV 89557. Offers French (MA); German (MA); Spanish (MA). *Faculty:* 18. *Students:* 8 full-time (5 women), 10 part-time (9 women); includes 3 minority (all Hispanic Americans) Average age 29. 12 applicants, 67% accepted, 7 enrolled. In 2007, 5 degrees awarded. *Degree requirements:* For master's, one foreign language, thesis optional. *Entrance requirements:* For master's, GRE General Test, minimum GPA of 2.75. Additional exam requirements/recommendations for international students: Required—TOEFL. *Application deadline:* For fall admission, 3/1 priority date for domestic students; for spring admission, 11/1 for domestic students. Applications are processed on a rolling basis. Application fee: $60 ($95 for international students). *Expenses:* Tuition, state resident: full-time $2,774; part-time $154 per credit. Tuition, nonresident: full-time $13,578; part-time $330 per credit. Required fees: $49 per semester. *Financial support:* In 2007–08, 7 teaching assistantships were awarded; Federal Work-Study and institutionally sponsored loans also available. Financial award application deadline: 3/1. *Faculty research:* Thirteenth-century mysticism, contemporary Spanish and Latin American poetry and theater, French interrelation between narration and photography, exile literature and Holocaust. *Unit head:* Dr. Miriella Melara, Graduate Program Director, 775-784-6055.

University of New Hampshire, Graduate School, College of Liberal Arts, Department of Spanish, Durham, NH 03824. Offers MA. *Faculty:* 9 full-time. *Students:* 8 full-time (6 women), 6 part-time (4 women); includes 5 minority (1 African American, 4 Hispanic Americans), 1 international. Average age 36. 8 applicants, 100% accepted, 3 enrolled. In 2007, 3 degrees awarded. *Degree requirements:* For master's, one foreign language, thesis or alternative. *Entrance requirements:* Additional exam requirements/recommendations for international students: Required—TOEFL (minimum score 550 paper-based; 213 computer-based; 80 iBT). *Application deadline:* For fall admission, 4/1 priority date for domestic students, 4/1 for international students; for winter admission, 12/1 for domestic students; for spring admission, 12/1 priority date for domestic students. Applications are processed on a rolling basis. Application fee: $60. Electronic applications accepted. *Financial support:* In 2007–08, 5 teaching assistantships were awarded; fellowships, research assistantships, career-related internships or fieldwork, Federal Work-Study, scholarships/grants, and tuition waivers (full and partial) also available. Support available to part-time students. Financial award application deadline: 2/15. *Unit head:* Dr. Edward Larkin, Chairperson, 603-862-3549. *Application contact:* Holly Harris, Administrative Assistant, 603-862-3121, E-mail: spanish.master@unh.edu.

University of New Mexico, Graduate School, College of Arts and Sciences, Department of Spanish and Portuguese, Albuquerque, NM 87131-2039. Offers Portuguese (MA); Spanish (MA); Spanish and Portuguese (PhD). Part-time programs available. *Faculty:* 13 full-time (10 women), 2 part-time/adjunct (both women). *Students:* 49 full-time (32 women), 10 part-time (7 women); includes 26 minority (2 African Americans, 24 Hispanic Americans), 17 international. Average age 36. 47 applicants, 60% accepted, 18 enrolled. In 2007, 13 master's, 2 doctorates awarded. *Degree requirements:* For master's, one foreign language, comprehensive exam, thesis optional; for doctorate, one foreign language, comprehensive exam, thesis/dissertation. *Entrance requirements:* For master's, GRE, BA in Spanish or Portuguese, letters of recommendation, letter of intent; for doctorate, GRE, 3 letters of recommendation, letter of intent, sample research paper. Additional exam requirements/recommendations for international students: Required—TOEFL (minimum score 550 paper-based; 213 computer-based), Michigan English Language Assessment Battery. *Application deadline:* For fall admission, 1/15 priority date for domestic students; for spring admission, 11/15 for domestic students. Application fee: $50. Electronic applications accepted. *Financial support:* In 2007–08, 30 students received support, including 58 teaching assistantships with full tuition reimbursements available (averaging $13,640 per year); Federal Work-Study, institutionally sponsored loans, scholarships/grants, health care benefits, tuition waivers (full), and unspecified assistantships also available. Support available to part-time students. Financial award application deadline: 3/1; financial award applicants required to submit FAFSA. *Faculty research:* Spanish literature in Spain, Latin America, and the U.S. Spanish Southwest from its inception to present day; gender and genre studies including film, linguistic variation and change, and psycholinguistics in Spanish. *Unit head:* Dr. Tey Diana Rebolledo, Chair, 505-277-2974, Fax: 505-277-3885, E-mail: dreb@unm.edu. *Application contact:* Martha Hurd, Graduate Administration Assistant, 505-277-2974, E-mail: marthah@unm.edu.

The University of North Carolina at Chapel Hill, Graduate School, College of Arts and Sciences, Department of Romance Languages, Chapel Hill, NC 27599. Offers French (MA, PhD); Italian (MA, PhD); Portuguese (MA, PhD); Romance languages (MA, PhD); Romance philology (MA, PhD); Spanish (MA, PhD). *Degree requirements:* For master's, one foreign language, comprehensive exam, thesis; for doctorate, 2 foreign languages, comprehensive exam, thesis/dissertation. *Entrance requirements:* For master's and doctorate, GRE General Test, minimum GPA of 3.0. Additional exam requirements/recommendations for international students: Required—TOEFL (minimum score 550 paper-based; 213 computer-based). Electronic applications accepted.

The University of North Carolina at Charlotte, Graduate School, College of Arts and Sciences, Department of Languages and Culture Studies, Charlotte, NC 28223-0001. Offers Spanish (MA). Part-time and evening/weekend programs available. *Faculty:* 19 full-time (10 women), 1 part-time/adjunct (0 women). *Students:* 6 full-time (all women), 15 part-time (8 women); includes 7 minority (3 African Americans, 4 Hispanic Americans), 1 international. Average age 30. 8 applicants, 75% accepted, 4 enrolled. In 2007, 12 degrees awarded. *Degree requirements:* For master's, thesis optional. *Entrance requirements:* For master's, GRE, 3 letters of reference, minimum GPA of 2.75. Additional exam requirements/recommendations for international students: Required—TOEFL (minimum score 557 paper-based; 220 computer-based). *Application deadline:* For fall admission, 7/15 for domestic students, 5/1 for international students; for spring admission, 11/15 for domestic students, 10/1 for international students. Applications are processed on a rolling basis. Application fee: $55. Electronic applications accepted. *Expenses:* Tuition, state resident: full-time $2,855. Tuition, nonresident: full-time $13,062. Required fees: $1,692. *Financial support:* In 2007–08, 4 teaching assistantships (averaging $6,750 per year) were awarded; fellowships, research assistantships, career-related internships or fieldwork, Federal Work-Study, institutionally sponsored loans, scholarships/grants, and unspecified assistantships also available. Support available to part-time students. Financial award application deadline: 4/1; financial award applicants required to submit FAFSA. *Faculty research:* Twentieth and twenty-first century Spanish literature, Central American literature, Caribbean literature, Mexican literature, literature of the Southern Cone. *Unit head:* Robert L. Reimer, Chair, 704-687-8767, Fax: 704-687-3496. *Application contact:* Kathy B. Giddings, Director of Graduate Admissions, 704-687-3366, Fax: 704-687-3279, E-mail: gidding@uncc.edu.

The University of North Carolina at Greensboro, Graduate School, College of Arts and Sciences, Department of Romance Languages, Program in Spanish, Greensboro, NC 27412-5001. Offers advanced Spanish language and Hispanic cultural studies (Certificate); Spanish (MA). *Faculty:* 10 full-time (7 women), 1 part-time/adjunct (0 women). *Students:* 2 full-time (1 woman), 3 part-time (all women). *Degree requirements:* For master's, one foreign language, comprehensive exam, thesis or alternative. *Entrance requirements:* For master's, GRE General Test, 3-5 minute tape demonstrating foreign language proficiency, composition in Spanish, sample paper in English. Additional exam requirements/recommendations for international students: Required—TOEFL. *Application deadline:* For spring admission, 11/1 for domestic students. Applications are processed on a rolling basis. Application fee: $45. Electronic applications accepted. *Financial support:* Research assistantships, teaching assistantships, unspecified assistantships available. *Application contact:* Michelle Harkleroad, Director of Graduate Admissions, 336-334-4884, Fax: 336-334-4424, E-mail: mbharkle@uncg.edu.

University of Northern Colorado, Graduate School, College of Humanities and Social Sciences, School of Modern Languages and Cultural Studies, Program in Foreign Languages, Greeley, CO 80639. Offers Spanish/teaching (MA). Part-time programs available. *Faculty:* 12 full-time (6 women). *Students:* 1 (woman) full-time, 3 part-time (all women); includes 3 minority (all

Spanish

University of Northern Colorado (continued)

Hispanic Americans) Average age 41. 1 applicant, 100% accepted, 0 enrolled. In 2007, 7 degrees awarded. *Degree requirements:* For master's, comprehensive exam, thesis or alternative. *Entrance requirements:* For master's, minimum undergraduate GPA of 3.0, BA in Spanish, 1 year of secondary teaching. *Application deadline:* Applications are processed on a rolling basis. Application fee: $50 ($60 for international students). Electronic applications accepted. *Expenses:* Tuition, state resident: part-time $222 per credit. Tuition, nonresident: part-time $627 per credit. Required fees: $36 per credit. *Financial support:* Fellowships, research assistantships, teaching assistantships, unspecified assistantships available. Financial award application deadline: 3/1; financial award applicants required to submit FAFSA. *Unit head:* Dr. Joy Landeira, Program Coordinator, 970-351-2221, Fax: 970-351-1571.

University of Northern Iowa, Graduate College, College of Humanities and Fine Arts, Department of Modern Languages, Program in Spanish, Cedar Falls, IA 50614. Offers Spanish (MA); teaching English to speakers of other languages/Spanish (MA). Part-time and evening/weekend programs available. *Students:* 8 full-time (6 women), 3 part-time (all women), 2 international. 9 applicants, 78% accepted, 5 enrolled. In 2007, 30 degrees awarded. *Degree requirements:* For master's, one foreign language, comprehensive exam, thesis or alternative. *Entrance requirements:* For master's, minimum GPA 3.0; hold a valid teaching license and have documentation of successful teaching experience. Additional exam requirements/recommendations for international students: Required—TOEFL (minimum score 600 paper-based; 250 computer-based; 100 iBT). *Application deadline:* For fall admission, 8/1 priority date for domestic students. Applications are processed on a rolling basis. Application fee: $30 ($50 for international students). Electronic applications accepted. *Expenses:* Tuition, state resident: full-time $6,246; part-time $694 per credit hour. Tuition, nonresident: full-time $14,554; part-time $694 per credit hour. Required fees: $838; $119 per semester. *Financial support:* Career-related internships or fieldwork, Federal Work-Study, and tuition waivers (full and partial) available. Support available to part-time students. Financial award application deadline: 2/1. *Unit head:* Dr. Juan Carlos, Coordinator, 319-273-2200, Fax: 319-273-2848.

University of North Texas, Robert B. Toulouse School of Graduate Studies, College of Arts and Sciences, Department of Foreign Languages and Literatures, Denton, TX 76203. Offers French (MA); Spanish (MA). Part-time programs available. *Faculty:* 31 full-time (22 women). *Students:* 23 full-time (17 women), 13 part-time (10 women); includes 16 minority (3 African Americans, 13 Hispanic Americans), 1 international. Average age 30. 35 applicants, 74% accepted, 16 enrolled. In 2007, 8 degrees awarded. *Degree requirements:* For master's, 2 foreign languages, comprehensive exam, thesis optional, proficiency in a second foreign language. *Entrance requirements:* For master's, GRE General Test, minimum undergraduate GPA of 3.0, curriculum vita, 250 word essay in French or Spanish, 12 advanced credita in French or Spanish. Additional exam requirements/recommendations for international students: Recommended—TOEFL (minimum score 550 paper-based; 213 computer-based). *Application deadline:* For fall admission, 7/15 for domestic students; for spring admission, 11/15 for domestic students. Application fee: $50 ($75 for international students). *Financial support:* In 2007–08, 7 fellowships (averaging $9,534 per year), 5 teaching assistantships (averaging $9,534 per year) were awarded; career-related internships or fieldwork, Federal Work-Study, and institutionally sponsored loans also available. Financial award application deadline: 4/1. *Faculty research:* Literature of Austria, France, Germany, Latin America, Spain; culture/civilization; applied linguistics. *Unit head:* Dr. Marie-Christine Koop, Chair, 940-565-2404, Fax: 940-565-2581, E-mail: koop@unt.edu.

University of Notre Dame, Graduate School, College of Arts and Letters, Division of Humanities, Department of Romance Languages and Literatures, Notre Dame, IN 46556. Offers French and Francophone studies (MA); Iberian and Latin American studies (MA); Italian studies (MA); Romance literatures (MA). Part-time programs available. *Faculty:* 25 full-time (10 women), 4 part-time/adjunct (all women). *Students:* 18 full-time (12 women); includes 4 minority (all Hispanic Americans), 3 international. 28 applicants, 61% accepted, 9 enrolled. In 2007, 12 degrees awarded. *Degree requirements:* For master's, 2 foreign languages, comprehensive exam, thesis optional. *Entrance requirements:* For master's, GRE General Test, BA in target language. Additional exam requirements/recommendations for international students: Required—TOEFL (minimum score 600 paper-based; 250 computer-based; 80 iBT). *Application deadline:* For fall admission, 2/1 priority date for domestic students, 2/1 for international students. Application fee: $50. Electronic applications accepted. *Financial support:* In 2007–08, 1 fellowship (averaging $15,000 per year), 10 teaching assistantships with full tuition reimbursements (averaging $12,000 per year) were awarded; research assistantships, tuition waivers (full) also available. Financial award application deadline: 2/1. *Faculty research:* Literature of discovery and exploration, modern literature, literary criticism, medieval literature, feminist critical theory. *Unit head:* Dr. John Welle, Director of Graduate Studies, 574-631-6887, Fax: 574-631-3493, E-mail: al.romland.1@nd.edu. *Application contact:* Dr. Jarren Gonzales, Director of Graduate Admissions, 574-631-7706, Fax: 574-631-4183.

University of Oklahoma, Graduate College, College of Arts and Sciences, Department of Modern Languages, Program in Spanish, Norman, OK 73019-0390. Offers MA, PhD, MBA/MA. Part-time programs available. *Students:* 16 full-time (9 women), 4 part-time (all women); includes 6 minority (all Hispanic Americans), 3 international. 8 applicants, 75% accepted, 4 enrolled. In 2007, 2 master's awarded. Terminal master's awarded for partial completion of doctoral program. *Degree requirements:* For master's, one foreign language, comprehensive exam, thesis optional, departmental qualifying exam; for doctorate, 2 foreign languages, comprehensive exam, thesis/dissertation, departmental qualifying exam. *Entrance requirements:* For master's, BA in Spanish literature, minimum GPA of 3.0 in last 60 hours, 3 letters of recommendation; for doctorate, MA in Spanish, 3 letters of recommendation, minimum graduate GPA of 3.5. Additional exam requirements/recommendations for international students: Required—TOEFL (minimum score 550 paper-based; 213 computer-based). *Application deadline:* For fall admission, 4/1 for domestic and international students; for spring admission, 10/1 for domestic students, 9/1 for international students. Application fee: $40 ($90 for international students). Electronic applications accepted. *Expenses:* Tuition, state resident: full-time $3,451; part-time $144 per credit hour. Tuition, nonresident: full-time $12,432; part-time $518 per credit hour. Required fees: $1,925; $70 per credit hour. $122 per semester. *Financial support:* Teaching assistantships with partial tuition reimbursements, scholarships/grants, health care benefits, tuition waivers (partial), and unspecified assistantships available. Financial award applicants required to submit FAFSA. *Faculty research:* Spanish and Latin American literatures, 20th century literature of Latin American social issues; women writers; Medieval and Early modern Intellectual history; Golden Age Drama. *Application contact:* Dr. Michael E. Winston, Associate Professor, 405-325-5088, Fax: 405-325-0103, E-mail: mewinston@ou.edu.

University of Oregon, Graduate School, College of Arts and Sciences, Department of Romance Languages, Program in Spanish, Eugene, OR 97403. Offers MA. Part-time programs available. *Students:* 4 applicants, 50% accepted. In 2007, 5 degrees awarded. *Degree requirements:* For master's, one foreign language. *Entrance requirements:* For master's, GRE General Test, minimum GPA of 3.0. Additional exam requirements/recommendations for international students: Required—TOEFL. Application fee: $50. *Financial support:* Teaching assistantships available. *Application contact:* Barbara VerWest, Admissions Contact, 541-346-4013, E-mail: verwest@uoregon.edu.

University of Ottawa, Faculty of Graduate and Postdoctoral Studies, Faculty of Arts, Department of Modern Languages and Literatures, Ottawa, ON K1N 6N5, Canada. Offers Spanish (MA, PhD). Part-time and evening/weekend programs available. *Degree requirements:* For master's, one foreign language, thesis or alternative; for doctorate, one foreign language, comprehensive exam, thesis/dissertation. *Entrance requirements:* For master's, BA with honors in Spanish, minimum B average; for doctorate, MA in Spanish or equivalent, minimum B average. Electronic applications accepted. *Faculty research:* Spanish American literature, Mexican literature and film studies, Spanish golden age literature, twentieth century Spanish literature, Hispanic linguistics with special emphasis on linguistic theory.

University of Pennsylvania, School of Arts and Sciences, Graduate Group in Romance Languages, Philadelphia, PA 19104. Offers French (AM, PhD); Italian (AM, PhD); Spanish (AM, PhD). Terminal master's awarded for partial completion of doctoral program. *Degree requirements:* For master's, one foreign language, thesis or alternative; for doctorate, 2 foreign languages, thesis/dissertation. *Entrance requirements:* For master's and doctorate, GRE General Test. Additional exam requirements/recommendations for international students: Required—TOEFL. Electronic applications accepted. *Faculty research:* Literary theory and criticism, cultural studies, history of Romance literatures, gender studies.

University of Pittsburgh, School of Arts and Sciences, Department of Hispanic Languages and Literatures, Pittsburgh, PA 15260. Offers MA, PhD. Part-time programs available. *Faculty:* 9 full-time (2 women). *Students:* 44 full-time (29 women); includes 13 minority (2 African Americans, 2 Asian Americans or Pacific Islanders, 9 Hispanic Americans), 27 international. Average age 30. 41 applicants, 54% accepted, 11 enrolled. In 2007, 8 master's, 5 doctorates awarded. Terminal master's awarded for partial completion of doctoral program. *Median time to degree:* Of those who began their doctoral program in fall 1999, 57% received their degree in 8 years or less. *Degree requirements:* For master's, one foreign language, comprehensive exam (for some programs), thesis or alternative, research paper; for doctorate, 2 foreign languages, comprehensive exam, thesis/dissertation. *Entrance requirements:* Additional exam requirements/recommendations for international students: Required—TOEFL (minimum score 550 paper-based; 213 computer-based; 80 iBT). *Application deadline:* For fall admission, 1/15 priority date for domestic and international students. Application fee: $50. Electronic applications accepted. *Financial support:* In 2007–08, 32 students received support, including 7 fellowships with full tuition reimbursements available (averaging $15,500 per year), 24 teaching assistantships with full tuition reimbursements available (averaging $14,500 per year); scholarships/grants, health care benefits, and tuition waivers (partial) also available. Financial award application deadline: 1/15. *Faculty research:* Latin American, Luso-Brazilian, and peninsular literature; cultural theory; cultural studies; race, ethnicity, and post-colonial studies. *Unit head:* Dr. Elizabeth Monasterios, Chair, 412-624-5226, Fax: 412-624-8505, E-mail: elm15@pitt.edu. *Application contact:* Dr. Juan Duchesne-Winter, Director of Graduate Studies, 412-624-0141, Fax: 412-624-8505, E-mail: duchesne@pitt.edu.

University of Pittsburgh, School of Arts and Sciences, Department of Linguistics, Program in Hispanic Linguistics, Pittsburgh, PA 15260. Offers MA, PhD. *Faculty:* 3 full-time (2 women). *Students:* 5 full-time (3 women), 1 international. Average age 30. 16 applicants, 63% accepted, 3 enrolled. In 2007, 2 degrees awarded. *Degree requirements:* For master's, one foreign language, thesis; for doctorate, 2 foreign languages, comprehensive exam, thesis/dissertation. *Entrance requirements:* For master's, GRE General Test; for doctorate, GRE General Test, MA in Linguistics. Additional exam requirements/recommendations for international students: Required—TOEFL (minimum score 600 paper-based; 250 computer-based). *Application deadline:* For fall admission, 12/15 for domestic and international students. Applications are processed on a rolling basis. Application fee: $50. Electronic applications accepted. *Financial support:* In 2007–08, 5 students received support, including 4 teaching assistantships with tuition reimbursements available (averaging $14,485 per year); Federal Work-Study, scholarships/grants, health care benefits, and unspecified assistantships also available. Support available to part-time students. Financial award application deadline: 12/15. *Faculty research:* Hispanic Linguistics. *Application contact:* Patricia C Cochran, Graduate Secretary, 412-624-5900, Fax: 412-624-6130, E-mail: lingpitt@pitt.edu.

University of Rhode Island, Graduate School, College of Arts and Sciences, Department of Modern and Classical Languages and Literatures, Kingston, RI 02881. Offers Spanish (MA). *Degree requirements:* For master's, one foreign language. *Application deadline:* For fall admission, 4/15 priority date for domestic students. Applications are processed on a rolling basis. Application fee: $35. *Expenses:* Tuition, state resident: full-time $6,936; part-time $385 per credit. Tuition, nonresident: full-time $19,044; part-time $1,058 per credit. Required fees: $1,508; $48 per credit. $30 per semester. One-time fee: $80 part-time. *Unit head:* Dr. Joseph Morello, Head, 401-874-5911.

University of South Africa, College of Human Sciences, Pretoria, South Africa. Offers adult education (M Ed); African languages (MA, PhD); African politics (MA, PhD); Afrikaans (MA, PhD); ancient history (MA, PhD); ancient Near Eastern studies (MA, PhD); anthropology (MA, PhD); applied linguistics (MA); Arabic (MA, PhD); archaeology (MA); art history (MA); Biblical archaeology (MA); Biblical studies (M Th, D Th, PhD); Christian spirituality (M Th, D Th); church history (M Th, D Th); classical studies (MA, PhD); clinical psychology (MA); communication (MA, PhD); comparative education (M Ed, Ed D); consulting psychology (D Admin, D Com, PhD); curriculum studies (M Ed, Ed D); development studies (M Admin, MA, D Admin, PhD); didactics (M Ed, Ed D); education (M Tech); education management (M Ed, Ed D); educational psychology (M Ed); English (MA); environmental education (M Ed); French (MA, PhD); German (MA, PhD); Greek (MA); guidance and counseling (M Ed); health studies (MA, PhD), including health sciences education (MA), health services management (MA), medical and surgical nursing science (critical care general) (MA), midwifery and neonatal nursing science (MA), trauma and emergency care (MA); history (MA, PhD); history of education (Ed D); inclusive education (M Ed, Ed D); information and communications technology policy and regulation (MA); information science (MA, MIS, PhD); international politics (MA, PhD); Islamic studies (MA, PhD); Italian (MA, PhD); Judaica (MA, PhD); linguistics (MA, PhD); mathematical education (M Ed); mathematics education (MA); missiology (M Th, D Th); modern Hebrew (MA, PhD); musicology (MA, MMus, D Mus, PhD); natural science education (M Ed); New Testament (M Th, D Th); Old Testament (D Th); pastoral therapy (M Th, D Th); philosophy (MA); philosophy of education (M Ed, Ed D); politics (MA, PhD); Portuguese (MA, PhD); practical theology (M Th, D Th); psychology (MA, MS, PhD); psychology of education (M Ed, Ed D); public health (MA); religious studies (MA, D Th, PhD); Romance languages (MA); Russian (MA, PhD); Semitic languages (MA, PhD); social behavior studies in HIV/AIDS (MA); social science (mental health) (MA); social science in development studies (MA); social science in psychology (MA); social science in social work (MA); social science in sociology (MA); social work (MSW, DSW, PhD); socio-education (M Ed, Ed D); sociolinguistics (MA); sociology (MA, PhD); Spanish (MA, PhD); systematic theology (M Th, D Th); TESOL (teaching English to speakers of other languages) (MA); theological ethics (M Th, D Th); theory of literature (MA, PhD); urban ministries (D Th); urban ministry (M Th).

University of South Carolina, The Graduate School, College of Arts and Sciences, Department of Languages, Literatures, and Cultures, Columbia, SC 29208. Offers comparative literature (MA, PhD); foreign languages (MAT), including French, German, Spanish; French (MA); German (MA); Spanish (MA). MAT offered in cooperation with the College of Education. Part-time programs available. *Faculty:* 39 full-time (19 women). *Students:* 43 full-time (31 women), 19 part-time (12 women); includes 12 minority (3 African Americans, 1 Asian American or Pacific Islander, 8 Hispanic Americans), 15 international. Average age 29. 40 applicants, 65% accepted, 18 enrolled. In 2007, 7 master's awarded. *Degree requirements:* For master's, one foreign language, comprehensive exam, thesis optional; for doctorate, 2 foreign languages, comprehensive exam, thesis/dissertation. *Entrance requirements:* For master's and doctorate, GRE General Test, writing sample. Additional exam requirements/recommendations for international students: Required—TOEFL (minimum score 230 computer-based; 75 iBT). *Application deadline:* For fall admission, 2/1 priority date for domestic and international students. Applications are processed on a rolling basis. Application fee: $40. Electronic applications accepted. *Expenses:* Tuition, state resident: part-time $440 per hour. Tuition, nonresident: part-time $936 per hour. Required fees: $17 per hour. Tuition and fees vary according to program. *Financial support:* In 2007–08, 40 teaching assistantships with full tuition reimbursements (averaging $11,000 per year) were awarded; fellowships, research assistantships with full tuition reimbursements also available. Financial award application deadline: 2/1. *Faculty research:* Modern literature, linguistics, literature and culture, medieval literature, literary theory. Total annual research expenditures: $23,000. *Unit head:* Dr. Marja Warehime, Chair, 803-777-

9734, Fax: 803-777-0454, E-mail: warehime@sc.edu. *Application contact:* Dr. Nicholas Vazsonyi, Graduate Director, 803-777-2935, Fax: 803-777-0454, E-mail: vazsonyi@sc.edu.

University of South Florida, Graduate School, College of Arts and Sciences, Department of World Language Education, Program in Spanish, Tampa, FL 33620-9951. Offers MA. *Students:* 10 full-time (6 women), 9 part-time (5 women); includes 11 minority (all Hispanic Americans), 3 international. 14 applicants, 93% accepted, 5 enrolled. In 2007, 4 degrees awarded. *Entrance requirements:* For master's, minimum GPA of 3.0, 36 hours of graduate course work in French. *Application deadline:* For fall admission, 6/1 for domestic students; for spring admission, 10/15 for domestic students. Application fee: $30. *Application contact:* Maria Esformes, Program Director, 813-974-2548, Fax: 813-974-1718, E-mail: esformes@chuma1.cas.usf.edu.

The University of Tennessee, Graduate School, College of Arts and Sciences, Department of Modern Foreign Languages and Literatures, Program in Modern Foreign Languages, Knoxville, TN 37996. Offers applied linguistics (PhD); French (PhD); German (PhD); Italian (PhD); Portuguese (PhD); Russian (PhD); Spanish (PhD). *Degree requirements:* For doctorate, 2 foreign languages, thesis/dissertation. *Entrance requirements:* For doctorate, minimum GPA of 2.7. Additional exam requirements/recommendations for international students: Required—TOEFL. Electronic applications accepted.

The University of Tennessee, Graduate School, College of Arts and Sciences, Department of Modern Foreign Languages and Literatures, Program in Spanish, Knoxville, TN 37996. Offers MA. *Degree requirements:* For master's, one foreign language, thesis or alternative. *Entrance requirements:* For master's, minimum GPA of 2.7. Additional exam requirements/recommendations for international students: Required—TOEFL. Electronic applications accepted.

The University of Texas at Arlington, Graduate School, College of Liberal Arts, Department of Modern Languages, Arlington, TX 76019. Offers French (MA); Spanish (MA). Part-time and evening/weekend programs available. *Faculty:* 5 full-time (3 women). *Students:* 7 full-time (3 women), 27 part-time (21 women); includes 12 minority (3 African Americans, 9 Hispanic Americans), 2 international. In 2007, 1 degree awarded. *Degree requirements:* For master's, 2 foreign languages, thesis optional. *Entrance requirements:* For master's, GRE General Test, minimum GPA of 3.0, 3 letters of recommendation. Additional exam requirements/recommendations for international students: Required—TOEFL (minimum score 550 paper-based; 213 computer-based). *Application deadline:* For fall admission, 6/16 for domestic students. Applications are processed on a rolling basis. Application fee: $35 ($50 for international students). *Expenses:* Tuition, state resident: full-time $5,934. Tuition, nonresident: full-time $10,938. *Financial support:* In 2007–08, teaching assistantships (averaging $6,600 per year); fellowships, research assistantships also available. Financial award application deadline: 6/1; financial award applicants required to submit FAFSA. *Unit head:* Dr. A. Raymond Elliott, Chair, 817-272-3161, Fax: 817-272-5408, E-mail: elliott@uta.edu. *Application contact:* Dr. Aimee Israel-Pelletier, Graduate Advisor, 817-272-3161, Fax: 817-272-5408, E-mail: aip@uta.edu.

The University of Texas at Austin, Graduate School, College of Liberal Arts, Department of Spanish and Portuguese, Austin, TX 78712-1111. Offers Hispanic literature (MA, PhD); Ibero-Romance philology and linguistics (MA, PhD); Luso-Brazilian literature (MA, PhD). *Degree requirements:* For master's, 2 foreign languages, thesis or alternative; for doctorate, 3 foreign languages, thesis/dissertation. *Entrance requirements:* For master's and doctorate, GRE General Test. Electronic applications accepted.

The University of Texas at Brownsville, Graduate Studies, College of Liberal Arts, Department of Modern Languages, Brownsville, TX 78520-4991. Offers interdisciplinary studies (MAIS); Spanish (MA). Part-time and evening/weekend programs available. *Degree requirements:* For master's, comprehensive exam, thesis optional. *Entrance requirements:* For master's, GRE General Test, letters of recommendation, interview. Additional exam requirements/recommendations for international students: Required—TOEFL. *Faculty research:* Children's literature, Hispanic folklore, translation.

The University of Texas at El Paso, Graduate School, College of Liberal Arts, Department of Languages and Linguistics, El Paso, TX 79968-0001. Offers linguistics (MA); Spanish (MA). Part-time and evening/weekend programs available. *Degree requirements:* For master's, thesis optional. *Entrance requirements:* For master's, departmental exam, GRE General Test, sample of written work, minimum GPA of 3.0. Additional exam requirements/recommendations for international students: Required—TOEFL. Electronic applications accepted.

The University of Texas at El Paso, Graduate School, College of Liberal Arts, Interdisciplinary Program in Creative Writing, El Paso, TX 79968-0001. Offers creative writing in English (MFA); creative writing in Spanish (MFA). Part-time and evening/weekend programs available. *Degree requirements:* For master's, thesis. *Entrance requirements:* For master's, departmental exam (creative writing in Spanish), minimum GPA of 3.0. Additional exam requirements/recommendations for international students: Required—TOEFL. Electronic applications accepted.

The University of Texas at San Antonio, College of Liberal and Fine Arts, Department of Modern Languages and Literatures, San Antonio, TX 78249-0617. Offers Hispanic culture (MA); Spanish (MA). Part-time and evening/weekend programs available. *Faculty:* 5 full-time (3 women), 1 (woman) part-time/adjunct. *Students:* 5 full-time (4 women), 26 part-time (20 women); includes 28 minority (1 Asian American or Pacific Islander, 27 Hispanic Americans), 1 international. Average age 38. 17 applicants, 88% accepted, 14 enrolled. In 2007, 10 degrees awarded. *Degree requirements:* For master's, one foreign language, comprehensive exam, thesis optional. *Entrance requirements:* For master's, GRE, minimum GPA of 3.0, sample of written and spoken work. Additional exam requirements/recommendations for international students: Required—TOEFL (minimum score 500 paper-based; 173 computer-based). *Application deadline:* For fall admission, 7/1 for domestic students, 4/1 for international students; for spring admission, 11/1 for domestic students, 9/1 for international students. Applications are processed on a rolling basis. Application fee: $45 ($80 for international students). Electronic applications accepted. *Financial support:* In 2007–08, 1 teaching assistantship (averaging $7,676 per year) was awarded; career-related internships or fieldwork, Federal Work-Study, and institutionally sponsored loans also available. Support available to part-time students. Total annual research expenditures: $18,771. *Unit head:* Dr. Ritva M. Nummikoski, Chair, 210-458-4373, Fax: 210-458-5672, E-mail: mnummikoski@utsa.edu. *Application contact:* Dr. Jack Himelblau, Graduate Advisor, 210-458-5218, E-mail: jhimelblau@utsa.edu.

The University of Texas–Pan American, College of Arts and Humanities, Department of Modern Languages and Literatures, Edinburg, TX 78541-2999. Offers Spanish (MA). Part-time programs available. *Degree requirements:* For master's, comprehensive exam, thesis or alternative. *Entrance requirements:* For master's, GRE General Test, minimum GPA of 3.0. *Faculty research:* Latin American literature, women's literature, Caribbean literature, Latina/o studies, sociolinguistics, applied linguistics, creative writing.

The University of Toledo, College of Graduate Studies, College of Arts and Sciences, Department of Foreign Languages, Toledo, OH 43606-3390. Offers French (MA); German (MA); Spanish (MA). Part-time programs available. *Faculty:* 8. *Students:* 1 (woman) full-time, 3 part-time (2 women); includes 1 minority (Hispanic American) Average age 46. 7 applicants, 100% accepted, 3 enrolled. In 2007, 4 degrees awarded. *Degree requirements:* For master's, one foreign language, comprehensive reading exam in 1 additional foreign language. *Application deadline:* For fall admission, 1/15 priority date for domestic students. Applications are processed on a rolling basis. Application fee: $45. Electronic applications accepted. *Financial support:* In 2007–08, 1 teaching assistantship with full tuition reimbursement (averaging $7,600 per year) was awarded; Federal Work-Study, institutionally sponsored loans, scholarships/grants, tuition waivers (full), and unspecified assistantships also available. Support available to part-time students. Financial award application deadline: 4/1; financial award applicants required to submit FAFSA. *Unit head:* Dr. Antonio Varela, Chair, 419-530-2657, Fax: 419-530-2657, E-mail: avarela@uoft02.utoledo.edu.

University of Toronto, School of Graduate Studies, Humanities Division, Department of Spanish and Portuguese, Toronto, ON M5S 1A1, Canada. Offers MA, PhD. Part-time programs available. *Faculty:* 11 full-time, 2 part-time/adjunct. *Students:* 35 full-time (27 women), 3 international. 46 applicants, 46% accepted. In 2007, 5 master's, 2 doctorates awarded. *Degree requirements:* For doctorate, thesis/dissertation. *Entrance requirements:* For master's, minimum B average in final year, 2 letters of reference; for doctorate, minimum A– average, 2 letters of reference, writing sample. Additional exam requirements/recommendations for international students: Required—TOEFL, MELAB, IELTS or COPE. *Application deadline:* For fall admission, 2/1 for domestic students. Application fee: $100 Canadian dollars. *Financial support:* Fellowships, teaching assistantships, stipend available. *Unit head:* Prof. Ricardo Sternberg, Acting Chair, 416-813-4081, Fax: 416-813-4084, E-mail: sternber@chass.utoronto.ca. *Application contact:* Bianca Talesnik, Undergraduate and Graduate Administrator, 416-813-4080, Fax: 416-813-4084, E-mail: b.talesnik@utoronto.ca.

University of Utah, The Graduate School, College of Humanities, Department of Languages and Literature, Salt Lake City, UT 84112-1107. Offers comparative literary and cultural studies (MA, PhD); French (MA, MALP); German (MA, MALP, PhD); language pedagogy (MALP); Spanish (MA, MALP, PhD); world languages with secondary teaching licensure (MA). *Faculty:* 38 full-time (21 women). *Students:* 28 full-time (15 women), 12 part-time (10 women); includes 10 minority (all Hispanic Americans), 7 international. Average age 35. 32 applicants, 47% accepted, 10 enrolled. In 2007, 14 master's, 2 doctorates awarded. Terminal master's awarded for partial completion of doctoral program. *Median time to degree:* Of those who began their doctoral program in fall 1999, 66% received their degree in 8 years or less. *Degree requirements:* For master's, standard proficiency in 2 languages other than English, comprehensive exam or thesis; for doctorate, comprehensive exam, standard proficiency in 2 languages other than English and language of study, advanced proficiency in 1 language other than English and language of study, dissertation. *Entrance requirements:* For master's, bachelor's degree or strong undergraduate record in target languages, GPA of 3.0, literature-survey courses; for doctorate, successful completion of MA and advanced proficiency in a target language. Additional exam requirements/recommendations for international students: Required—TOEFL (minimum score 500 paper-based; 173 computer-based). *Application deadline:* For fall admission, 2/1 priority date for domestic students, 1/15 priority date for international students. Application fee: $45 ($65 for international students). Electronic applications accepted. *Financial support:* In 2007–08, 25 students received support, including 25 teaching assistantships with full tuition reimbursements available (averaging $11,000 per year); fellowships with tuition reimbursements available, health care benefits also available. Financial award application deadline: 2/1; financial award applicants required to submit FAFSA. *Faculty research:* Literary theory, stylistics, Russian and Soviet literature, existentialism, theory of criticism. Total annual research expenditures: $35,321. *Unit head:* Dr. Christine A. Jones, Director of Graduate Studies, 801-585-3002, Fax: 801-581-7581, E-mail: cjones@hum.utah.edu. *Application contact:* Corky Reeser, Executive Graduate Secretary, 801-581-7570, Fax: 801-581-7581, E-mail: c.reeser@mail.hum.utah.edu.

University of Virginia, College and Graduate School of Arts and Sciences, Department of Spanish, Italian and Portuguese, Program in Spanish, Charlottesville, VA 22903. Offers MA, PhD. *Students:* 38 full-time (30 women), 2 part-time (1 woman); includes 3 minority (all Hispanic Americans), 5 international. Average age 27. 79 applicants, 29% accepted, 8 enrolled. In 2007, 7 master's, 7 doctorates awarded. *Degree requirements:* For master's, one foreign language, comprehensive exam, thesis; for doctorate, 2 foreign languages, comprehensive exam, thesis/dissertation. *Entrance requirements:* For master's and doctorate, GRE General Test, GRE Subject Test. *Application deadline:* Applications are processed on a rolling basis. Application fee: $60. Electronic applications accepted. *Financial support:* Applicants required to submit FAFSA.

University of Washington, Graduate School, College of Arts and Sciences, Department of Romance Languages and Literature, Division of Spanish and Portuguese Studies, Seattle, WA 98195. Offers Hispanic literary and cultural studies (MA). *Faculty:* 6 full-time (3 women), 2 part-time/adjunct (1 woman). *Students:* 16 full-time (10 women); includes 3 minority (all Hispanic Americans), 6 international. 25 applicants, 52% accepted, 9 enrolled. In 2007, 4 degrees awarded. *Degree requirements:* For master's, 2 foreign languages, thesis optional, exam. *Entrance requirements:* For master's, GRE General Test, minimum GPA of 3.0. Additional exam requirements/recommendations for international students: Required—TOEFL. *Application deadline:* For fall admission, 1/15 priority date for domestic students, 11/1 priority date for international students. Application fee: $50. Electronic applications accepted. *Financial support:* In 2007–08, 1 fellowship with full tuition reimbursement (averaging $4,677 per year), 16 teaching assistantships with full tuition reimbursements (averaging $13,059 per year) were awarded; Federal Work-Study, institutionally sponsored loans, scholarships/grants, health care benefits, and unspecified assistantships also available. Financial award application deadline: 1/15; financial award applicants required to submit FAFSA. *Faculty research:* Medieval through modern Spanish literature and film, Latin American literature, poetry and essay, pan-Hispanic ballad, Hispanic cultural studies, second language acquisition and applied linguistics. *Unit head:* Prof. Anthony Geist, Chair, 206-543-2020, Fax: 206-685-7054, E-mail: tgeist@u.washington.edu. *Application contact:* Suzanna Martinez, Academic Counselor, 206-543-2075, Fax: 206-685-7054, E-mail: spsadv@u.washington.edu.

The University of Western Ontario, Faculty of Graduate Studies, Faculty of Arts and Humanities, Department of Comparative Literature, London, ON N6A 5B8, Canada. Offers comparative literature (MA, PhD); Spanish (MA). Part-time programs available. *Faculty:* 28 full-time (13 women). *Students:* 34 full-time (24 women). Average age 26. 50 applicants, 56% accepted, 26 enrolled. In 2007, 8 degrees awarded. *Degree requirements:* For master's, 2 foreign languages, thesis (for some programs). *Entrance requirements:* For master's, honors degree in Spanish or equivalent, minimum B average. Additional exam requirements/recommendations for international students: Required—TOEFL, TOEFL (comparative literature). *Application deadline:* For fall admission, 2/1 priority date for domestic students. Applications are processed on a rolling basis. Application fee: $30 Canadian dollars. *Financial support:* In 2007–08, 26 teaching assistantships (averaging $8,500 Canadian dollars per year) were awarded; fellowships, scholarships/grants also available. Financial award application deadline: 4/1. *Faculty research:* Spanish golden age, Latin-American, romance, medieval, film. *Unit head:* Melitta Adamson, Chair, 519-661-2111 Ext. 85861, E-mail: melitta@uwo.ca. *Application contact:* Teresa McLauchlan, Graduate Assistant, 519-661-2111 Ext. 85846, Fax: 519-661-4093, E-mail: tmclauch@uwo.ca.

University of Wisconsin–Madison, Graduate School, College of Letters and Science, Department of Spanish and Portuguese, Program in Spanish, Madison, WI 53706-1380. Offers MA, PhD. *Degree requirements:* For master's, one foreign language; for doctorate, 2 foreign languages, thesis/dissertation. *Entrance requirements:* For master's, GRE (recommended), minimum GPA of 3.25 in Spanish or Portuguese; for doctorate, GRE (recommended), minimum graduate GPA of 3.4, writing sample. Additional exam requirements/recommendations for international students: Required—TOEFL. Electronic applications accepted. *Faculty research:* Hispanic linguistics, Spanish and Spanish-American literature.

University of Wisconsin–Milwaukee, Graduate School, College of Letters and Sciences, Interdepartmental Program in Foreign Language and Literature, Milwaukee, WI 53201-0413. Offers classics and Hebrew studies (MAFLL); comparative literature (MAFLL); French and Italian (MAFLL); German (MAFLL); Slavic studies (MAFLL); Spanish (MAFLL). Part-time programs available. *Faculty:* 39 full-time (17 women). *Students:* 29 full-time (21 women), 31 part-time (23 women); includes 8 minority (1 Asian American or Pacific Islander, 7 Hispanic Americans), 22 international. 54 applicants, 67% accepted, 26 enrolled. In 2007, 34 degrees awarded. *Degree requirements:* For master's, 2 foreign languages, thesis or alternative. *Application deadline:* For fall admission, 1/1 priority date for domestic students; for spring admission, 9/1 for domestic students. Applications are processed on a rolling basis. Application fee: $45 ($75 for international students). *Expenses:* Tuition, state resident: part-time $530 per credit. Tuition, nonresident: part-time $1,428 per credit. Required fees: $19 per credit. $229 per

Spanish

University of Wisconsin–Milwaukee (continued)
term. Tuition and fees vary according to course load and program. *Financial support:* In 2007–08, 44 teaching assistantships were awarded; fellowships, research assistantships, career-related internships or fieldwork and unspecified assistantships also available. Support available to part-time students. Financial award application deadline: 4/15. *Unit head:* Gabrielle Verdier, Representative, 414-229-3346, Fax: 414-229-2741, E-mail: verdier@uwm.edu.

University of Wyoming, Graduate School, College of Arts and Sciences, Department of Modern and Classical Languages, Program in Spanish, Laramie, WY 82070. Offers MA. Part-time programs available. *Faculty:* 5 full-time (1 woman). *Students:* 7 full-time (5 women), 5 part-time (2 women); includes 2 minority (both Hispanic Americans) Average age 33. 8 applicants, 100% accepted. In 2007, 5 degrees awarded. *Degree requirements:* For master's, one foreign language, thesis or alternative. *Entrance requirements:* For master's, GRE General Test, minimum GPA of 3.0. *Application deadline:* For fall admission, 4/1 priority date for domestic students. Applications are processed on a rolling basis. Application fee: $50. *Financial support:* In 2007–08, 4 students received support, including teaching assistantships with full tuition reimbursements available (averaging $10,696 per year); institutionally sponsored loans also available. Financial award application deadline: 3/1. *Faculty research:* Peninsular literature, Latin American literature, theatre, science and literature, linguistics. *Application contact:* Dr. Kevin S. Larsen, Graduate Adviser, 307-766-2294, Fax: 307-766-2727, E-mail: klarsen@uwyo.edu.

Vanderbilt University, Graduate School, Department of Spanish and Portuguese, Nashville, TN 37240-1001. Offers Portuguese (MA); Spanish (MA, MAT, PhD); Spanish and Portuguese (PhD). *Faculty:* 20 full-time (11 women), 2 part-time/adjunct (1 woman). *Students:* 29 full-time (14 women); includes 2 minority (1 African American, 1 American Indian/Alaska Native), 13 international. Average age 30. 55 applicants, 11% accepted, 6 enrolled. In 2007, 6 master's, 6 doctorates awarded. *Degree requirements:* For master's, one foreign language, thesis; for doctorate, 2 foreign languages, thesis/dissertation, final and qualifying exams. *Entrance requirements:* For master's and doctorate, GRE General Test. *Application deadline:* For fall admission, 1/15 for domestic and international students. Application fee: $0. Electronic applications accepted. *Financial support:* Fellowships with full and partial tuition reimbursements, teaching assistantships with full tuition reimbursements, Federal Work-Study, institutionally sponsored loans, and health care benefits available. Financial award application deadline: 1/15; financial award applicants required to submit CSS PROFILE or FAFSA. *Faculty research:* Spanish, Portuguese, and Latin American literatures; foreign language pedagogy; Renaissance and baroque poetry; nineteenth century Spanish novel. *Unit head:* Cathy L. Jrade, Chair, 615-322-6930, Fax: 615-343-7260, E-mail: cathy.l.jrade@vanderbilt.edu. *Application contact:* Benigno Trigo, Director of Graduate Studies, 615-322-6930, Fax: 615-343-7260, E-mail: benigno.trigo@vanderbilt.edu.

Washington State University, Graduate School, College of Liberal Arts, Department of Foreign Languages and Cultures, Pullman, WA 99164. Offers foreign languages with emphasis in Spanish (MA). *Faculty:* 20. *Students:* 12 full-time (7 women); includes 5 minority (1 Asian American or Pacific Islander, 4 Hispanic Americans), 5 international. Average age 28. 14 applicants, 86% accepted, 8 enrolled. In 2007, 6 degrees awarded. *Degree requirements:* For master's, comprehensive exam (for some programs), thesis (for some programs), 4 written exams, oral exam, master's paper. *Entrance requirements:* For master's, minimum GPA of 3.0, speech tapes, writing sample, 3 letters of recommendation. Additional exam requirements/recommendations for international students: Required—TOEFL (minimum score 550 paper-based). *Application deadline:* For fall admission, 2/1 priority date for domestic and international students; for spring admission, 10/1 priority date for domestic students. Application fee: $50. Electronic applications accepted. *Financial support:* In 2007–08, fellowships (averaging $2,200 per year), teaching assistantships with full and partial tuition reimbursements (averaging $13,056 per year) were awarded; career-related internships or fieldwork, Federal Work-Study, institutionally sponsored loans, scholarships/grants, and health care benefits also available. Financial award application deadline: 4/1; financial award applicants required to submit FAFSA. *Faculty research:* Spanish and Latin American literature, film, and culture; pedagogy; computer-aided instruction. *Unit head:* Dr. Eloy Gonzalez, Chair, 509-335-2756, Fax: 509-335-3708, E-mail: eloygonz@wsunix.wsu.edu. *Application contact:* Graduate School Admissions, 800-GRADWSU, Fax: 509-335-1949, E-mail: gradsch@wsu.edu.

Washington University in St. Louis, Graduate School of Arts and Sciences, Department of Romance Languages and Literatures, Program in Spanish, St. Louis, MO 63130-4899. Offers MA, PhD. *Degree requirements:* For master's, thesis or alternative; for doctorate, thesis/dissertation. *Entrance requirements:* For master's and doctorate, GRE General Test. Electronic applications accepted.

Wayne State University, College of Liberal Arts and Sciences, Department of Classical and Modern Languages, Literatures, and Cultures, Program in Spanish, Detroit, MI 48202. Offers MA. *Students:* 1 full-time (0 women), 2 part-time (both women); includes 5 minority (1 African American, 4 Hispanic Americans). Average age 32. 10 applicants, 30% accepted, 3 enrolled. In 2007, 1 degree awarded. *Degree requirements:* For master's, one foreign language, thesis optional. *Entrance requirements:* For master's, GRE General Test, minimum GPA of 3.0. Additional exam requirements/recommendations for international students: Required—TOEFL (minimum score 550 paper-based; 213 computer-based); Recommended—TWE (minimum score 6). *Application deadline:* For fall admission, 7/1 for domestic students, 6/1 for international students; for winter admission, 10/1 for international students; for spring admission, 2/1 for international students. Applications are processed on a rolling basis. Application fee: $30 ($50 for international students). Electronic applications accepted. *Expenses:* Tuition, state resident: part-time $403 per credit hour. Tuition, nonresident: part-time $890 per credit hour. *Financial support:* Fellowships, research assistantships, teaching assistantships available. *Faculty research:* Drama of the Golden Age, eighteenth century humanism, Romanticism, twentieth century essay. *Application contact:* Dr. Michael Giordano, Graduate Director, 313-577-3051, Fax: 313-577-6243, E-mail: m.j.giordano@wayne.edu.

West Chester University of Pennsylvania, Office of Graduate Studies and Extended Education, College of Arts and Sciences, Department of Foreign Languages, West Chester, PA 19383. Offers French (M Ed, MA); German (M Ed); Latin (M Ed); Spanish (M Ed, MA). Part-time and evening/weekend programs available. *Students:* 7 full-time (all women), 18 part-time (15 women); includes 2 minority (both Hispanic Americans) Average age 35. 10 applicants, 100% accepted, 6 enrolled. In 2007, 7 degrees awarded. *Degree requirements:* For master's, one foreign language, comprehensive exam, thesis optional. *Entrance requirements:* For master's, GRE, placement test. Additional exam requirements/recommendations for international students: Required—TOEFL (minimum score 550 paper-based; 213 computer-based; 80 iBT). *Application deadline:* For fall admission, 4/15 priority date for domestic students; for spring admission, 10/15 for domestic students. Applications are processed on a rolling basis. Application fee: $35. *Expenses:* Tuition, state resident: part-time $345 per credit. Tuition, nonresident: part-time $552 per credit. Tuition and fees vary according to course load. *Financial support:* In 2007–08, 2 research assistantships with full and partial tuition reimbursements (averaging $5,000 per year) were awarded; unspecified assistantships also available. Support available to part-time students. Financial award application deadline: 2/15; financial award applicants required to submit FAFSA. *Faculty research:* Implementation of world languages curriculum framework. *Unit head:* Dr. Jerry Williams, Chair, 610-436-2700, Fax: 610-436-3048, E-mail: jwilliams2@wcupa.edu. *Application contact:* Dr. Rebecca Pauly, Graduate Coordinator, 610-436-2382, E-mail: rpauly@wcupa.edu.

Western Michigan University, Graduate College, College of Arts and Sciences, Department of Foreign Languages and Literatures, Kalamazoo, MI 49008-5202. Offers Spanish (MA). *Degree requirements:* For master's, oral exam.

West Virginia University, Eberly College of Arts and Sciences, Department of Foreign Languages, Morgantown, WV 26506. Offers French (MA); linguistics (MA); Spanish (MA); teaching English to speakers of other languages (MA). Part-time programs available. *Faculty:* 20 full-time (13 women), 27 part-time/adjunct (24 women). *Students:* 64 full-time (42 women), 8 part-time (7 women); includes 8 minority (1 African American, 3 Asian Americans or Pacific Islanders, 4 Hispanic Americans), 31 international. Average age 29. 46 applicants, 76% accepted, 26 enrolled. In 2007, 31 degrees awarded. *Degree requirements:* For master's, one foreign language, comprehensive exam (for some programs), thesis optional. *Entrance requirements:* For master's, minimum GPA of 3.0. *Application deadline:* For fall admission, 2/1 priority date for domestic and international students; for spring admission, 10/1 for domestic and international students. Applications are processed on a rolling basis. Application fee: $50. Electronic applications accepted. *Expenses:* Tuition, state resident: full-time $5,196; part-time $292 per credit hour. Tuition, nonresident: full-time $15,064; part-time $840 per credit hour. Tuition and fees vary according to program. *Financial support:* In 2007–08, 69 students received support, including 65 teaching assistantships with full tuition reimbursements available (averaging $8,864 per year); research assistantships, Federal Work-Study, institutionally sponsored loans, and tuition waivers (full and partial) also available. Financial award application deadline: 2/1; financial award applicants required to submit FAFSA. *Faculty research:* French, German, and Spanish literature; foreign language pedagogy; English as a second language; cultural studies; linguistics. Total annual research expenditures: $36,679. *Unit head:* Dr. Angel T. Tuninetti, Chair, 304-293-5121, Fax: 304-293-7655, E-mail: angel.tuninetti@mail.wvu.edu. *Application contact:* Dr. Sandra Stjepanovic, Director of Graduate Studies, 304-293-5121, Fax: 304-293-7655, E-mail: sandra.stjepanovic@mail.wvu.edu.

Wichita State University, Graduate School, Fairmount College of Liberal Arts and Sciences, Department of Modern and Classical Languages and Literatures, Wichita, KS 67260. Offers Spanish (MA). Part-time programs available. *Degree requirements:* For master's, one foreign language, comprehensive exam. *Entrance requirements:* For master's, GRE. Additional exam requirements/recommendations for international students: Required—TOEFL. Electronic applications accepted.

Winthrop University, College of Arts and Sciences, Program in Spanish, Rock Hill, SC 29733. Offers MA. Part-time programs available. *Faculty:* 2 full-time (1 woman), 2 part-time/adjunct (1 woman). *Students:* Average age 42. In 2007, 4 degrees awarded. *Entrance requirements:* For master's, GRE General Test and PRAXIS, minimum GPA of 3.0, 24 hours of undergraduate Spanish, or interview. *Application deadline:* For fall admission, 4/15 priority date for domestic students; for spring admission, 10/15 for domestic students. Applications are processed on a rolling basis. Application fee: $50. Electronic applications accepted. *Expenses:* Tuition, state resident: full-time $9,834; part-time $412 per credit hour. Tuition, nonresident: full-time $18,280; part-time $763 per credit hour. *Financial support:* In 2007–08, 1 research assistantship with full tuition reimbursement (averaging $3,600 per year) was awarded; Federal Work-Study, scholarships/grants, and unspecified assistantships also available. Support available to part-time students. Financial award application deadline: 2/1; financial award applicants required to submit FAFSA. *Unit head:* Dr. Barbara Equival-Heinemann, Graduate Program Director, 803-323-2612, Fax: 803-323-4043, E-mail: heinemannb@winthrop.edu. *Application contact:* 800-411-7041, Fax: 80-323-2292, E-mail: graduatestu@winthrop.edu.

Yale University, Graduate School of Arts and Sciences, Department of Spanish and Portuguese, New Haven, CT 06520. Offers MA, PhD. Terminal master's awarded for partial completion of doctoral program. *Degree requirements:* For master's, 3 foreign languages; for doctorate, 3 foreign languages, thesis/dissertation. *Entrance requirements:* For doctorate, GRE General Test.

AUBURN UNIVERSITY

College of Liberal Arts
Department of English

Programs of Study Auburn University offers programs of study leading to the Master of Arts (M.A.), the Master of Technical and Professional Communication (M.T.P.C.), and the Doctorate (Ph.D.) degrees. The Department offers a wide range of courses in American, British, and comparative literatures; literary theory; creative writing; linguistics; rhetoric and composition; and technical and professional communication.

Functioning as a terminal degree as well as preparation for doctoral study, Auburn University's M.A. is a flexible degree that enhances students' previous training. Minimum requirements are eight courses and a thesis (thesis option) or ten courses (nonthesis option). Students must also demonstrate reading ability in a foreign language. Students can focus course work in any of the above listed areas or combine courses from several areas to create an individualized program of study. Two courses from another department may be approved as a minor within this degree program. In addition to course work, students take written examinations based on reading lists in three (thesis option) or four (nonthesis option) areas.

The M.T.P.C. prepares students for careers as editors, professional writers, technical communicators, and teachers of technical and professional communication, as well as for doctoral work in the field. Students take four required courses, three electives in English, and three courses in a coordinated minor field. Students must also pass a comprehensive exam and submit a portfolio of work.

The Ph.D. prepares students to become scholars and to teach in higher education. The Ph.D. program requires a minimum of sixteen courses beyond the B.A. or seven courses beyond the M.A. Working in consultation with their advisory committees, doctoral students balance broad preparation with the development of three specialized areas for their written and oral examinations. These areas include topics in literature (e.g. major authors, literary genres and periods, critical theory) and language (e.g. composition, linguistics, stylistics, rhetoric). Doctoral students must demonstrate a reading knowledge of two foreign languages or extensive knowledge of one foreign language. The Ph.D. program requires candidates to write and defend a dissertation.

Research Facilities The University and the English Department offer graduate students ready access to current technologies.

Draughon Library, a member of the Association of Research Libraries, is a leader in computer-assisted research tools and facilities. It houses more than 2.7 million volumes and has nearly 3 million items on microform, including full and current collections in English studies. Additionally, the library receives more than 35,000 current periodicals, many of which are available online, and provides access to more than 200 databases.

Financial Aid Most students admitted to graduate programs in English receive financial aid in the form of a renewable graduate teaching assistantship. Typically, graduate assistants teach three sections of introductory composition each year. Entering master's-level graduate assistants co-teach two sections over the year with experienced instructors. Doctoral-level graduate assistants may also teach world literature. The 2007–08 stipend was $13,528 for M.A. and M.T.P.C. students and $14,212 for Ph.D. students. Each year, 5 first-year students receive financial aid packages composed of a fellowship and an assistantship. Minority doctoral students are eligible for a renewable financial aid package of approximately $20,000 per year. The Department usually offers some support for professional travel.

Cost of Study In 2007–08, full-time tuition for Alabama residents was $2625 per semester. Out-of-state students paid $7875 per semester. However, the University pays tuition for graduate teaching assistants, who pay a small matriculation fee each semester. The 2007–08 fee was $248. Thesis and graduation expenses usually amount to $100 for M.A. students and $200 for Ph.D. students.

Living and Housing Costs Room and board cost approximately $7500 annually. Married students or those with dependents typically spend more. Graduate students have a wide variety of affordable housing from which to choose, including rental apartments, duplexes, and town houses.

Student Group The Department seeks to enroll 6–8 new Ph.D. students and 12–15 new master's-level students each year. More than 70 graduate students are currently enrolled in graduate programs; about half of them are Ph.D. students. There are slightly more women than men enrolled in the Ph.D. program.

Student Outcomes Recent graduates of the M.A. program have advanced to doctoral or other professional programs at Auburn and other universities, including Cornell, Emory, Florida, North Carolina, Pittsburgh, South Carolina, Texas, Tufts, and Wisconsin; others have begun careers in teaching, editing, and professional and technical writing. Recent graduates of the Ph.D. program have found tenure-track positions at Coastal Carolina University, Gonzaga University, Huntington College, Saint Louis University, Oregon State University, the Savannah College of Art and Design, Stephen F. Austin State University, and Tuskegee University. A few Ph.D. graduates have also established successful careers in software development, editing, and humanities administration.

Location The University is located in Auburn, Alabama, 60 miles from Montgomery, home of the Alabama Shakespeare Festival and the Civil Rights Memorial, and 120 miles from both Birmingham and Atlanta. All three cities are easily accessible by interstate highways. Gulf Coast beaches are about 4 hours away by car. Although the area has a population of more than 100,000, Auburn affords the security, seclusion, and clean air of a small town in rural surroundings. There are many recreational opportunities.

The University and The Department Chartered in 1856 as a private college, Auburn University is now Alabama's public land-grant institution and the largest university in the state, enrolling almost 24,000 students, including more than 3,000 graduate students. Auburn operates on the semester system. It is traditionally known for its applied programs in science, agriculture, and veterinary medicine. English is the largest single department in the University. Among its 32 members of the graduate faculty are 5 named chairs. Additionally, the Department plays a vital role in the University's core curriculum, teaching writing and world literature courses to every Auburn student. The Department sponsors lectures, readings, and discussion groups and is home to the *Southern Humanities Review.*

Applying Students matriculate in the fall semester, when graduate assistantship appointments begin. Review of applications begins January 15; initial offers of admission with aid are generally made in March. Successful applicants present strong undergraduate preparation and competitive GRE scores with cogent writing samples and statements of purpose. Applications and information requests can be processed online through the Department's Web site.

Correspondence and Information

Coordinator of Graduate Studies
Department of English
9030 Haley Center
Auburn University
Auburn, Alabama 36849-5203

Phone: 334-844-4620
Fax: 334-844-9027
E-mail: gradenglish@auburn.edu
Web site: http://www.auburn.edu/english/gs/

Auburn University

THE FACULTY AND THEIR RESEARCH

Paula R. Backscheider, Professor and West Point Stevens–H. M. Philpott Eminent Scholar in English; Ph.D., Purdue, 1972. Restoration and eighteenth-century literature, the novel and novel theory, feminist criticism and theory.
Craig Bertolet, Associate Professor; Ph.D., Penn State, 1995. Medieval literature.
Jon Bolton, Associate Professor; Ph.D., Maryland, 1996. Twentieth-century British literature.
Alicia Carroll, Associate Professor; Ph.D., CUNY Graduate Center, 1995. Nineteenth-century British fiction.
Miriam Marty Clark, Associate Professor; Ph.D., North Carolina at Chapel Hill, 1986. Twentieth-century literature, the short story, poetry.
George W. Crandell, Professor; Ph.D., Texas, 1985. Twentieth-century American literature, bibliography, textual criticism, Tennessee Williams.
Jeremy M. Downes, Associate Professor; Ph.D., Wisconsin, 1991. Poetry, poetics, poetry writing, the epic.
R. James Goldstein, Professor; Ph.D., Virginia, 1987. Medieval literature, critical theory.
Bert Hitchcock, Hargis Professor of American Literature; Ph.D., Duke, 1971. Nineteenth-century American literature, Southern literature.
Christopher Keirstead, Assistant Professor; Ph.D., Delaware, 1999. Nineteenth-century British poetry, travel literature.
Virginia M. Kouidis, Associate Professor; Ph.D., Iowa, 1972. American literature, twentieth-century English and American literature, modern poetry, women's literature, feminist criticism.
Dan Latimer, Professor; Ph.D., Michigan, 1972. Criticism, comparative literature, modernism, symbolism.
Trimiko Melancon, Assistant Professor; Ph.D., Massachusetts Amherst, 2006. African American literature.
Susanna Morris, Assistant Professor; Ph.D., Emory, 2007. African American literature.
Thomas E. Nunnally, Associate Professor; Ph.D., Georgia, 1985. Historical English linguistics, Old English language and literature, grammatical theories, usage study.
Tiffany Portewig, Assistant Professor; Ph.D., Texas Tech, 2006. Technical and professional communication.
Constance C. Relihan, Hargis Professor; Ph.D., Minnesota, 1989. Renaissance literature, prose fiction before 1700, Shakespeare, early women writers.
Anya Riehl, Assistant Professor; Ph.D., Illinois at Chicago, 2007. Early modern British literature.
Kevin Roozen, Assistant Professor; Ph.D., Illinois at Urbana-Champaign, 2005. Composition and rhetoric.
Joyce Rothschild, Assistant Professor; Ph.D., Maryland, 1983. Technical communication, professional editing.
James Emmett Ryan, Associate Professor; Ph.D., North Carolina at Chapel Hill, 1999. Nineteenth-century American literature, religion and literature.
Robin Sabino, Associate Professor; Ph.D., Pennsylvania, 1990. Sociolinguistics, ESL, phonetics/phonology, grammatical theory.
Michelle A. Sidler, Assistant Professor; Ph.D., Purdue, 1998. Composition and rhetoric, literary theory.
Marc Silverstein, Hollifield Associate Professor of English Literature; Ph.D., Brown, 1989. Contemporary drama, critical theory, drama as a genre, postmodernism.
Sunny Stalter, Assistant Professor; Ph.D., Rutgers, 2007. Twentieth-century American literature, modernism, American studies.
Isabelle Thompson, Professor; Ed.D., Duke, 1982. Composition and rhetoric, technical communication.
Joanne Tong, Assistant Professor; Ph.D., UCLA, 2005. British Romanticism.
Judy Troy, Professor and Alumni Writer in Residence; M.A., Indiana, 1981. Fiction writing, the short story, twentieth-century American fiction.
Donald R. Wehrs, Associate Professor; Ph.D., Virginia, 1986. The novel, eighteenth-century British literature, critical theory.
Hilary E. Wyss, Associate Professor; Ph.D., North Carolina at Chapel Hill, 1998. Early American literature, Native American literature, American studies.
Dave Yeats, Assistant Professor; Ph.D., Texas Tech, 2005. Technical and professional communication.
Matt Zarnowiecki, Assistant Professor; Ph.D., Columbia, 2007. Early modern British literature.

BOSTON COLLEGE

Graduate School of Arts and Sciences
Department of Romance Languages and Literatures

Programs of Study The Department of Romance Languages and Literatures at Boston College offers an extensive program of language, literature, and cultural study in French, Italian, and Spanish on the Chestnut Hill, Massachusetts, campus and in many countries overseas through a variety of international partnerships. The Department offers Master of Arts (M.A.) degrees in French, Hispanic, and Italian literature and culture and Master of Arts in Teaching (M.A.T.) degrees in French and Hispanic studies. Ph.D. degrees are available in French, Hispanic, and Italian literature and in French, Hispanic, and Italian studies.

The master's program in French, Hispanic, or Italian literature and culture requires 30 credits (10 courses) in Romance languages and literatures. M.A. candidates may receive a maximum of 9 credits for courses taken in languages/literatures other than the primary language/literature of study, including courses on literary theory, pedagogy, and linguistics. Included in this limit, and with the approval of the Graduate Studies Committee, up to 6 credits may be earned from courses in related areas of study.

The Master of Arts in Teaching program is administered through the Lynch Graduate School of Education in cooperation with the Department of Romance Languages and Literatures. Applicants to the M.A.T. program should apply directly to the Lynch Graduate School of Education. The program provides certification and continued professional development for primary and secondary school teachers of French and Hispanic studies. Students must complete a minimum of 30 credits, with an average of B or better. A minimum of 15 credits must be completed in the School of Education.

The program of doctoral study in French, Hispanic, or Italian studies is designed to build on each candidate's strengths and develop individual interests that culminate in fields of specialization—the springboards for a professional academic career. Students enroll in Plan I or Plan II of the Ph.D. program. Plan I involves in-depth work in one literature and culture. In Plan II, students work concurrently in two languages and literatures. One of the most frequently pursued fields in the Plan II doctoral program is the exceptional Medieval Studies program. Students choose two of the following literatures: medieval Catalan, French, Italian, Spanish, or Provençal. Boston College offers a rich array of courses in medieval studies in such departments as Theology, History, Philosophy, Fine Arts, and Political Science. Students entering with an M.A. who are accepted for the doctoral program are granted transfer credit for the M.A. degree or its equivalent of 30 credits. The M.A. equivalency of foreign degrees is determined, whenever appropriate, through communication with the Bureau of Comparative Education of the Division of the International Education in Washington, D.C. Students with a bachelor's degree entering the Ph.D. program must take a course of study equivalent to that required for the M.A. in French or Hispanic literatures. After earning 30 credits, students are evaluated as potential Ph.D. candidates.

The Graduate School of Arts and Sciences stipulates that a student must complete all requirements for the M.A. degree within five consecutive years from the date of acceptance into the program. Despite the University's five-year time limit for finishing the M.A. degree, the Department fully expects students to complete all requirements within two years of entering the program.

Research Facilities Boston College provides its students with state-of-the-art facilities for learning, including a full range of computer services, online access to databases, and a library system with more than 1.9 million books, periodicals, and government documents and 3.4 million microform units. The library's membership in the Boston Library Consortium provides access to ten major research libraries in the Boston area, and an interlibrary loan system provides further resources.

The Language Laboratory serves the language learning and teaching needs of Boston College's language departments, students of English as a foreign language, and the community at large from its center in Lyons Hall. The facility provides access to installed and portable equipment for use with audio, video, cable television, Internet, and multimedia language-learning tools. The lab has an extensive catalog of resources in seventeen languages to facilitate language learning and teaching and to promote cultural awareness.

Financial Aid The following forms of financial assistance are available to students in the Department: teaching fellowships, graduate assistantships, and two Fellow-in-Residence positions. Appointments and awards are competitive and are based on the candidate's academic background and experience. For those seeking teaching fellowships, an interview in French, Italian, or Spanish is required. For more information about Boston College's financial assistance or government grants, students should contact the Office of Student Services.

Cost of Study The tuition rate for the Graduate School of Arts and Sciences was $1092 per credit for the 2007–08 year. The student activities fee ranges from $25 to $50 per semester, depending on the number of credits taken. The cost of books varies by semester. Additional fees may apply.

Living and Housing Costs Rental housing is plentiful in the surrounding cities and towns. Many different types of housing are available, ranging from one-room rentals in large Victorian homes to triple-decker brownstones and apartment high-rises. Allston-Brighton and Jamaica Plain are among the nearby Boston neighborhoods that attract students from many colleges and universities because of their diverse communities and relative affordability. Graduate students also have found Newton, Brookline, Waltham, Watertown, and Boston's West Roxbury neighborhood attractive places to live. Boston College's Off-Campus Housing Office is available to assist in the housing search. The Off-Campus Housing Office maintains an extensive database of available rental listings, roommates, and helpful local realtors.

Student Group In 2007–08, there were more than 60 students enrolled in the Department's various degree programs.

Location The Graduate School of Arts and Sciences is located on the Chestnut Hill campus of Boston College, approximately 6 miles west of the city of Boston, Massachusetts. Boston offers students the opportunity to experience one of the oldest cities in the U.S., with museums, a symphony orchestra, and world championship professional basketball, baseball, ice hockey, and football teams. The city of Boston also offers a wide variety of shopping, dining, and cultural experiences—all located on the beautiful Boston Harbor and Charles River.

The College and The School Founded in 1863, Boston College is one of the oldest Jesuit-sponsored universities in the United States. It has professional and graduate schools, doctoral programs, research institutes, community service programs, an excellent faculty, and rich resources of libraries, research equipment, computers, and other facilities. A coeducational university, it has an enrollment of approximately 9,000 undergraduate and 4,700 graduate and professional students representing every state and nearly 100 countries. Boston College confers degrees in more than fifty fields of study through its eleven schools and colleges. It has more than 600 full-time faculty members committed to both teaching and research.

The Graduate School of Arts and Sciences is the oldest of the seven graduate and professional schools at Boston College. The Graduate School offers programs of study in the humanities, social sciences, and natural sciences, leading to the degrees of Doctor of Philosophy (Ph.D.), Master of Arts (M.A.), and Master of Science (M.S.). In addition, the Graduate School offers numerous dual-degree options in cooperation with the Graduate School of Social Work, the Lynch School of Education, the Carroll School of Management, and the Boston College Law School. Non-degree-seeking students may be admitted into the Graduate School as Special Students. The Graduate School of Arts and Sciences operates on a semester calendar, with the fall semester running from late August until mid-December and the spring semester running from late January until late May.

Applying Students are generally admitted only in the fall semester. The deadline for applying for the fall semester is January 15. Candidates for all Master of Arts programs should have an undergraduate major or its equivalent in the appropriate field, including advanced composition and surveys of the pertinent literatures. Because all courses in the Department are conducted in French, Italian, or Spanish, students are expected to enter the program with sufficiently advanced oral and written proficiency to perform with ease in the linguistic environment. Applicants must submit a completed application directly to the Graduate School of Arts and Sciences. Along with the application, students must submit official transcripts of all undergraduate study, three letters of recommendation, a statement of purpose, a writing sample in the selected Romance language, and a $70 nonrefundable application fee.

Correspondence and Information

Department of Romance Languages and Literatures
Lyons Hall, Room 304
Boston College
140 Commonwealth Avenue
Chestnut Hill, Massachusetts 02467-3804

Phone: 617-552-3820
Fax: 617-552-2064
E-mail: rll@bc.edu
Web site: http://www.bc.edu/schools/cas/romlang

Boston College

THE FACULTY AND THEIR RESEARCH

Norman Araujo, Associate Professor of French; Ph.D., Harvard. Nineteenth-century French literature, with emphasis on the novel.

Sarah H. Beckjord, Assistant Professor of Spanish; Ph.D., Columbia. Colonial Spanish-American literature, with an emphasis on historiography; nineteenth-century Spanish-American literature.

Stephen C. Bold, Associate Professor of French; Ph.D., NYU. Seventeenth-century French literature, especially philosophical literature, theater, and literature and the arts; linguistics.

Joseph Breines, Adjunct Assistant Professor of French; Ph.D., Yale. Post-Romantic French literature, narrative and theory.

Matilda Tomaryn Bruckner, Professor of French; Ph.D., Yale. Medieval French literature, especially twelfth- and thirteenth-century Romance, verse and prose narrative, troubadour and trouvère lyric.

Dwayne E. Carpenter, Professor of Spanish; Ph.D., Berkeley; Ph.D., Graduate Theological Union. Medieval Spanish literature and history, textual criticism, Jewish-Muslim-Christian relations.

Jeff Flagg, Adjunct Associate Professor of French; Ph.D., Boston University. Reformation, eighteenth-century French literature, Huguenots, French perspectives on America.

Rena A. Lamparska, Associate Professor of Italian; Ph.D., Harvard. Modern Italian literature, with emphasis on the late seventeenth- and eighteenth-century literary theories; Gregorio Caloprese, Giacomo Leopardi, Luigi Pirandello, Italo Calvino.

Catherine Wood Lange, Adjunct Senior Lecturer of Spanish; Ph.D., Stony Brook, SUNY. Contemporary Latin American and peninsular literature/film/cultural studies, language/technology pedagogy, translation, Spanish for business/health care.

Kathy Lee, Adjunct Assistant Professor of Spanish; Ph.D., Yale. Nineteenth- and twentieth-century Peninsular literature.

Ernesto Livón-Grosman, Assistant Professor of Hispanic Studies; Ph.D., NYU. Latin-American poetry, autobiography, literary theory.

Irene Mizrahi, Associate Professor of Spanish; Ph.D., Connecticut. Nineteenth- and twentieth-century Spanish literature, Spanish Romanticism (Gustavo Adolfo Bécquer), generation of 1914 (José Ortega y Gasset), contemporary theater (Buero Vallejo), current critical theory.

Franco Mormando, Associate Professor of Italian; Ph.D., Harvard. Popular and Ecclesiastical literature and preaching, fifteenth to seventeenth centuries, social context of Renaissance and Baroque art.

Ourida Mostefai, Associate Professor of French; Ph.D., NYU. Eighteenth-century French literature, Rousseau, polemical literature.

Kevin Newmark, Associate Professor of French; Ph.D., Yale. Nineteenth- and twentieth-century French literature, literary theory.

Elizabeth Rhodes, Associate Professor of Spanish; Ph.D., Bryn Mawr. Early modern Spanish literature, theology and religious culture, women's studies and feminist theory, needle arts.

Harry L. Rosser, Associate Professor of Spanish; Ph.D., North Carolina at Chapel Hill. Latin-American novel, short prose fiction, essay, Latin-American studies, applied linguistics.

Laurie Shepard, Associate Professor of Italian; Ph.D., Boston College. Status of opinion in medieval and Renaissance public discourse, Boccaccio's readers in the fourteenth and fifteenth centuries, coblas esparsa and the decline of the troubadour tradition.

Christopher R. Wood, Adjunct Assistant Professor of Spanish; Ph.D., Yale. Twentieth-century Spanish literature, medieval Spanish and medievalism.

BRYN MAWR COLLEGE

Graduate School of Arts and Sciences
Department of Greek, Latin, and Classical Studies

Programs of Study

The Department of Greek, Latin, and Classical Studies at Bryn Mawr College offers M.A. and Ph.D. degrees in Greek, Latin, and classical languages. In cooperation with the Department of Classical and Near Eastern Archaeology, it also offers the M.A. and Ph.D. in classical studies. It is one of three independent departments that comprise the Graduate Group in Archaeology, Classics, and History of Art.

The focus of the Department has always been on the precise study of ancient texts. Rigorous training in philology and literary analysis is its hallmark. Seminars in Greek tragedy, poetry, history, religion, and magic; Latin poetry, rhetoric, and history; and late antique and early Christian writers are offered regularly. Students are also encouraged to explore the reception of classical texts and the relationship between texts and material culture through interdisciplinary seminars and internships in Philadelphia-area museums and libraries, under the auspices of the Graduate Group. Course work and the M.A. thesis can normally be completed within three years. Ph.D. preliminary examinations should be taken in the fourth or fifth year, followed by the dissertation. For the Ph.D., the median time-to-degree of recent graduates is 8.5 years.

Students are encouraged to develop their own research projects in consultation with a faculty adviser. Recent dissertation projects include Vergilian imitation in Silius Italicus' Punica, Sedulius and Vergil, Female Friendship in Antiquity, Ovid's Remedia Amoris and the Heroides, and Rome's Appropriation of Egypt.

Seventy percent of Ph.D. graduates of the past ten years hold college or university positions teaching classics. M.A. graduates typically teach in public and private secondary schools.

Research Facilities

The reference collection for classics is housed in the award-winning Rhys Carpenter Library, inaugurated in 1997, which is also a specialized library for archaeology and the history of art. Fully wired carrels are available to all students in the Graduate Group in Archaeology, Classics, and History of Art. In addition to the more than 135,000 volumes in Carpenter Library, the tri-college library consortium of Bryn Mawr, Haverford, and Swarthmore Colleges contains over 2 million volumes. Bryn Mawr currently subscribes to more than 300 periodicals and serials in classics and in archaeology. Online reference sources include the TLG, Dyabola, Library of Latin Texts, and *l'Année philologique.* The special collections in the Mariam Coffin Canaday Library include significant resources for classics, including one of the largest collections of incunables in the United States.

Financial Aid

Bryn Mawr offers a number of fellowships for full-time study, as well as grants, tuition awards, and summer stipends. Fellowship stipends begin at $17,500, including a summer stipend, and can be guaranteed for multiple years. Special awards include Areté (Excellence) Fellowships with a package of $18,500 plus health insurance. Each year, the Department offers two part-time teaching assistantships with stipends ranging from $7880 to $9575 including health insurance; assistantship stipends can be supplemented by grants to a maximum of $16,575. Opportunities reserved for students in the Graduate Group in Archaeology, Classics, and History of Art are fellowships for multidisciplinary study, with twelve-month stipends of $19,000, and curatorial internships. Currently, 67 percent of the students enrolled in the program in Greek, Latin, and Classical Studies receive some form of financial aid.

Cost of Study

Full-time tuition, consisting of six courses per year, is $30,140; part-time tuition is $5090 per course. Units of supervised work cost $815, and the fee for maintaining matriculation (continuing enrollment) is $415 per semester.

Living and Housing Costs

Students live locally or in Philadelphia. Shared apartments can be rented for $600 to $900 per month, studio apartments begin at $700 per month, and food costs are about $200 per month. Other expenses include transportation (about $150 per month if commuting from Philadelphia) and health insurance ($1590 to $5150 per year, depending on age, for domestic students; $1432 for international students).

Student Group

In 2008–09, there are 19 students enrolled in classics: 12 women and 7 men. Five students have progressed to Ph.D. candidacy, 7 are candidates for the M.A., and the rest are in course work.

Student Outcomes

Ph.D. graduates of the past ten years are currently teaching at Carleton University; Christopher Newport University; Fresno Pacific University; Kent State University; Lewis and Clark College; Rutgers University, Newark; and Yale University.

Location

Bryn Mawr is a suburb of Philadelphia, the fifth-largest city in the U.S. It is well served by rail lines and by bus. Philadelphia is renowned for music, museums, and sports, and it is also a culinary mecca, with restaurants serving many cuisines. The metropolitan area has more than 100 museums and fifty colleges and universities, with a total population of 220,000 students.

The College and The Department

Bryn Mawr is a liberal arts college for women, founded in 1885. It was the first women's college to offer graduate education through the Ph.D. and the first U.S. institution to offer fellowships to women for graduate study. Throughout its history, the College has been committed first and foremost to providing the most rigorous and challenging education to women and, in the Graduate School of Arts and Sciences, also to men. The current enrollment is 1,405 undergraduate students, 164 graduate students in the Graduate School of Arts and Sciences, and about 250 students in the Graduate School of Social Work and Social Research.

Classics has always been a preeminent field of instruction at Bryn Mawr; even the College hymn is in Greek. The Department's tradition of outstanding scholarship and teaching was established by such faculty members as Lily Ross Taylor (1927–1952), Agnes Kirsopp Michaels (1934–1975), Richmond Lattimore (1935–1971), and Mabel Lang (1945–1988). The Department is known worldwide as the home of *The Bryn Mawr Classical Review,* edited by Professor Richard Hamilton, and the *Bryn Mawr Commentaries.*

Applying

Application for admission and financial aid should be made on the form available from the Graduate School of Arts and Sciences. Applicants can also download this form from the Graduate School's Web site at http://www.brynmawr.edu/gsas/. The deadline for admission with financial aid is January 2, 2009. Applications for admission without financial aid are accepted until June 30, 2009.

Students admitted to graduate work in classics typically have demonstrated exceptional aptitude in at least one classical language, excellent command of written English, and a predilection for independent thinking and research. Applicants must submit GRE scores; TOEFL scores, if not native speakers of English; a statement of interest; and a recent research paper or critical essay. Prerequisites include at least three years at the undergraduate level of Greek or Latin. For a degree in classical languages, three years of Greek and Latin are prerequisites.

Students are encouraged to contact the Department and to visit. The Department Web site is http://www.brynmawr.edu/gradgroup/classics/index.htm.

Correspondence and Information

Lea Miller, Secretary
Graduate School of Arts and Sciences
Bryn Mawr College
101 North Merion Avenue
Bryn Mawr, Pennsylvania 19010

Phone: 610-526-5072
Fax: 610-526-5076
E-mail: gsas@brynmawr.edu
Web site: http://www.brynmawr.edu/gsas/

Bryn Mawr College

THE FACULTY AND THEIR RESEARCH

Annette Baertschi, Assistant Professor; Ph.D., Humboldt, 2006. Post-Augustan poetry, ancient magic, Latin meter, reception.
Catherine Conybeare, Associate Professor; Ph.D., Toronto, 1997. Late antique and early medieval Latin prose, cultural history, critical theory.
Radcliffe G. Edmonds III, Associate Professor; Ph.D., Chicago, 1999. Greek myth, Greco-Roman religion and magic, Greek philosophy.
Richard Hamilton, Paul Shorey Professor of Greek; Ph.D., Michigan, 1971. Greek lyric poetry, Greek drama, Greek religion.
Russell T. Scott, Doreen C. Spitzer Professor of Latin and Classical Studies; Ph.D., Yale, 1964. Roman history and historiography, Latin literature, Roman archaeology.

Affiliated Faculty

Mehmet-Ali Ataç, Assistant Professor, Department of Classical and Near Eastern Archaeology; Ph.D., Harvard, 2003. Visual and intellectual traditions of the ancient Near East; Neo-Assyrian art and architecture, ancient Near Eastern and Egyptian kingship.
A. A. Donohue, Professor, Department of Classical and Near Eastern Archaeology; Ph.D., NYU, 1984. History and historiography of classical art.
Robert Germany, Assistant Professor, Haverford College; Ph.D., Chicago, 2008. Roman comedy, the ancient novel, the Homeric hymns, magic in Latin literature, seventeenth- and eighteenth-century German reception of classics.
Peter Magee, Associate Professor, Department of Classical and Near Eastern Archaeology; Ph.D., Sydney, 1996. Archaeology of South Asia, Iran, and Arabia; ancient imperialism; field methods; materials analysis.
Bret Mulligan, Assistant Professor, Haverford College; Ph.D., Brown. Greek and Latin epic and epistolography, late antique Greek and Latin literature, the classical tradition.
Deborah H. Roberts, Professor, Haverford College; Ph.D., Yale. Greek tragedy, Latin poetry, reception and translation of classical literature, literary theory.
James C. Wright, Professor, Department of Classical and Near Eastern Archaeology; Ph.D., Bryn Mawr, 1978. Prehistory of the Aegean basin, settlement forms and architecture of classical Greece, theory and method in archaeology.

CENTRAL MICHIGAN UNIVERSITY

Department of English Language and Literature

Programs of Study

At the graduate level, the Department offers Master of Arts degrees in three specializations—English language and literature, which includes an option in creative writing; English composition and communication; and teaching English to speakers of other languages (TESOL). Faculty members in the Department are active in a number of areas, producing literary works as well as doing research in literature, linguistics, and pedagogical theory. Graduate classes are small and provide the student with ample opportunity for interaction with professors and other graduate students. Because so many graduate students are working adults, graduate-level classes are offered in the late afternoon and evening.

The M.A. in English language and literature is designed to meet the needs of students seeking preparation for advanced study at the doctoral level at another university, students who wish to teach English at a community college, or students teaching English at the secondary level who wish to pursue more study in the discipline. Students must either complete a thesis or enroll in an additional 15 semester hours of course work and complete a scholarly paper. Students interested in the creative writing option must submit a portfolio of original poetry or fiction for approval.

The M.A. in English composition and communication is a program of courses centering on theory and practice in nonfiction forms of writing. It prepares graduate students to be career writers composing in disciplines other than English, professional writers composing within their own disciplines, creative writers composing in nonfiction forms, or teachers specializing in nonfiction forms. It allows for breadth of background and experience in composition as well as concentration in a selected area of interest. Required courses in this master's degree ground students in writing, editing, and rhetorical analysis, while elective courses give the opportunity to focus on creative, professional, and pedagogical development.

The M.A. in TESOL is designed to prepare teachers for careers in teaching English as a second or foreign language in the United States or abroad. Students study the formal aspects of language and its acquisition and use, and they gain knowledge and experience in current theories, approaches, and methods of language teaching and language assessment.

Research Facilities

The University's library system includes off-campus library services, the Clarke Historical Library, and the main library, with numerous books and publications, electronic and paper journals, and access to several databases. There are three large public computer labs on campus that contain 400 PC and Mac workstations, and the library offers more than 300 public workstations that are distributed throughout the facility. A large selection of general software is available, including Adobe Photoshop, Microsoft Office, SPSS, SAS, and Minitab.

Financial Aid

All admitted students can be considered for any assistantship. Currently, the stipend is at least $9000 for the first year, and the position is renewable for the second year. Students also get a tuition credit of 20 semester hours per year. To learn more about the teaching assistantship, students should contact Daniel Patterson, Coordinator of Graduate Studies in English.

Cost of Study

For the 2007–08 academic year, tuition was $388 per credit for Michigan residents and $719 per credit for out-of-state students.

Living and Housing Costs

Single-student and one- to three-bedroom family apartments are available in apartment complexes on campus. Rent includes electricity, gas, water, heat, telephone, cable TV, and other such services as the University deems appropriate. Off-campus housing is available from $250 per month, depending on the neighborhood, number of roommates, and size of apartment.

Student Group

There are 47 students; 14 are full-time, 33 are part-time students, and 32 are women. The average age is 31.

Location

Mount Pleasant is located in Michigan's Lower Peninsula. The downtown district features specialty stores and boutiques of all types within walking distance of the campus. Thirteen golf courses are located within a 30-minute drive, and surrounding state preserves are frequented by local hunters. Eleven parks covering 300 acres—plus another 900 acres in Isabella County—offer venues for swimming, canoeing, hiking, camping, and cross-country skiing.

The University

Central Michigan University opened its doors in 1892 to formally train teachers in the state. Bachelor's degrees were first awarded in 1918, and graduate courses were first offered in 1938. Today the University enrolls more than 28,000 students in more than 200 programs leading to twenty-seven degrees at the bachelor's, master's, specialist, and doctoral levels. The University's $50-million New Vision of Excellence Campaign is a broadly focused initiative to raise academic standards, strengthen discovery and creative activity, and enhance learning-environment facilities and technology.

Applying

Applicants should have an undergraduate major or minor in English with a GPA of at least 3.0 on a 4.0 scale and a cumulative grade point average of at least 2.7. Specific requirements vary by program; students should contact the Department for details. In general, students must submit the completed application, the nonrefundable application fee ($35 for U.S. citizens and resident aliens, $45 for international applicants), and official transcripts from each college or university attended. For applicants whose native language is not English, a TOEFL score of at least 550 (213 CBT) and a TWE score of at least 5 or a MELAB score of 85 are required for admission.

Correspondence and Information

Daniel Patterson
Coordinator, Graduate Studies in English
Dept. of English Language and Literature
215 Anspach Hall
Central Michigan University
Mount Pleasant, Michigan 48859
Phone: 989-774-3171
Fax: 989-774-7106
E-mail: patte2dj@cmich.edu
Web site: http://www.chsbs.cmich.edu/English

Central Michigan University

THE FACULTY AND THEIR RESEARCH

Marcy Taylor, Professor and Chair; Ph.D., Washington (Seattle), 1996. Graduate assistant training, pedagogy, postprocess theory, ethnographic research methods. Editors' introduction in *Pedagogy: Critical Approaches Teaching Literature, Language, Composition, Culture* 7(1), 2007.
Daniel Patterson, Associate Professor and Coordinator of Graduate Studies; Ph.D., Kent State, 1985. American literature, environmental and nature literature. *American Nature Writers Before 1900: Prose.* Gale Group, 2007.

Anne Alton, Professor; Ph.D., Toronto, 1995. Children's literature, British literature. *Arousing Delight: Arthur Rackham, Artist and Illustrator.* Central Michigan University, 2006.
Ronnie Apter, Professor; Ph.D., Fordham, 1980. Translation theory and practice, translation of opera libretti, translation of poetry, troubadour lyrics, interrelation of words and music.
Semiotic clash in Maria Stuarda: Music and libretto versus the Protestant version of British history. In *Song and Significance: Virtues and Vices of Vocal Translation,* pp. 163–84, ed. D. Gorlée. New York: Rodopi, 2005.
Ari Berk, Professor; Ph.D., Arizona, 1998. Folklore belief and custom in rural Britain, Celtic mythology, uses and development of historiography and ethnography in early modern intercultural encounters, texts and contexts, American Indian ethnography, oral tradition and literature.
Lady Cottington's Pressed Fairy Letters. New York: Harry N. Abrams Books, 2005.
William Brevda, Professor; Ph.D., Connecticut, 1980. Twentieth-century American literature, late nineteenth- and early twentieth–century American literature.
Neon lights around everything: West's "west," Hitler's "empire," Postmodernism's "reality." *Soundings Interdiscipl. J.* 85(3–4):381–422, 2002.
Elizabeth Brockman, Ph.D. English education, composition.
Kim Chinquee, M.F.A. Creative writing, fiction.
Mary Ann Crawford, Associate Professor and Director of Basic Writing and the Writing Center; Ph.D., Michigan State, 1997. Discourse (academic, disciplinary, and community) theory and applications, writing center theory and pedagogy, gender language and discourse issues, basic writing and English as second language pedagogy.
A group of our own: Women and writing groups, a re-consideration. In *By Any Other Name: Writing Groups Inside and Outside the Classroom*, eds. B. Moss, M. Dunbar, and N. Highberg. National Writing Centers Association Press, 2001.
John Dinan, Professor; Ph.D., Massachusetts, 1976. Composition/rhetoric.
Mark Freed, Associate Professor; Ph.D., Michigan State, 1996. Cultural theory, literature and philosophy, literature and science, Frankfurt critical theory, French poststructuralism, Austrian modernism.
Latour, Lyotard, and the problematics of legitimation. *Angelaki: J. Theor. Humanit.*, winter 2005.
Pamela Gates, Ph.D. Children's literature, English education.
Susan Griffith, Assistant Professor; Ph.D., Lesley, 2001. Creative response to literature, social justice theories in children's literature, role of reflection in teaching, writing in the elementary and middle school.
Bringing what is hidden to light: Jane Addams and the 2006 Jane Addams Children's Book Award. *Looking Glass: New Perspectives Children's Literature* 10(3), 2006.
Desmond Harding, Assistant Professor; Ph.D., USC, 1999. Trans-Atlantic modernism, literature and the urban experience, British and Irish literature and culture, American Studies, social and cultural theory.
Bearing witness: *Heartbreak House* and the poetics of trauma. *SHAW Annual (The Annual of Bernard Shaw Studies)* 26:6–26, 2006.
Rochelle Harris, Ph.D. Composition, creative nonfiction.
Janice Hartwick-Dressel, Ph.D. Children's literature, English education.
Troy Hicks, Ph.D. English education.
Cathy Hicks-Kennard, Ph.D. Linguistics.
Heidi Holder, Assistant Professor; Ph.D. British literature, British drama.
Stephen C. Holder, Associate Professor; Ph.D., Michigan State, 1972. American popular culture, American studies, American literature.
The best of both worlds: The problem of John P. Marquand. *J. Popular Cult.* 38, November 2004.
Peter T. Koper, Professor; Ph.D., Texas Christian, 1973. Classical rhetoric, anthropological studies of literacy and the classics following the work of René Girard, the American tradition of writing about nature.
Melinda Kreth, Associate Professor; Ph.D., Louisville, 1998. Business, technical, and scientific communication; ethical issues in professional communication; experiential learning; feminist theory and discourse; rhetoric of inquiry; rhetoric of science and technology; writing across the curriculum; writing in the disciplines.
From wordsmith to communication strategist: Heresthetic and political maneuvering in technical communication. *Tech. Comm. Q.* 52(3):302–22, 2005. With Moore.
Susan Larkin, Assistant Professor; Ph.D., Illinois State, 2005. Intersections of life writing and children's literature, conceptions of the female hero, transformations of the Bildungsroman, multicultural perspectives of girlhood in America.
Do you believe in magic?: Considering power, agency, and wizardry in the Harry Potter novels. Midwest Modern Language Association Conference, Chicago, Illinois, November 2006.
Kristen McDermott, Assistant Professor; Ph.D., UCLA, 1995. Ben Jonson, early modern drama, Shakespeare studies and Shakespeare pedagogy, early music and vocal performance.
The Tempest at the New Globe, summer 2000 season. *Theat. J.* 52:553–4, 2000.
Gretchen Papazian, Ph.D. Children's literature, American literature.
John R. Pfeiffer, Professor; Ph.D., Kentucky. Bibliography, English literature.
A continuing checklist of Shaviana. *SHAW Annual (The Annual of Bernard Shaw Studies)* 25:260–87, 2005.
Ronald Primeau, Professor; Ph.D., Illinois at Urbana-Champaign, 1971. American road literature, Edgar Lee Masters, popular culture, Herbert W. Martin.
Herbert Woodward Martin and the African American Tradition in Poetry. Kent, Ohio: Kent State University Press, 2004.
Laura Renzi-Keener, Ph.D. English education.
Matthew Roberson, Ph.D. Creative writing, fiction.
Beth Samuelson, Assistant Professor; Ph.D., Berkeley, 2004. Second-language writing assessment, human rights education, discourse analysis.
I used to go to school, now I learn: The discourse of unschoolers. In *What They Don't Learn in School: Literacy in the Lives of Urban Youth,* ed. Jabari Mahiri. New York: Peter Lang, 2004.
Susan Schiller, Professor; Ph.D., Wayne State, 1991. Spirituality and contemplation in writing and literature, teacher education and pedagogy holistic education, studies in Willa Cather.
Uniting creativity and research: A holistic approach to learning. *J. Assemb. Expand. Perspectiv. Learn.* January, 2007.
William Spruiell, Assistant Professor; Ph.D., Rice, 1990. Functions of complex derived nominal elements in grammar and discourse, typology of derivational morphology, theory and historical views of fundamental grammatical categories, cognitive psychological studies of lexical organization and storage, language development (specifically, development of grammatical categories), history and structure of English.
Susan Stan, Associate Professor; Ph.D., Minnesota, 1997. Cultural identity in children's books, trends in the international young adult novel.
Rose Blanche in translation. *Child. Lit. Educ.* 35(1):21–33, 2004.
Susan Steffel, Professor; Ph.D., Michigan State, 1993. Young adult literature, secondary literature instruction, use of technology in the literature classroom, professional mentoring, the use of read-alouds in the upper grades.
Connections Really Do Make a World of Difference. *Mich. Engl. Teach.* 54(3):1–2, 2004.
Sharon Stevenson, Associate Professor; Ph.D., Florida, 1971. Renaissance of the twelfth century, tales of power in the medieval world, medieval romance.
The Nature of Outsider Dystopias: Atwood, Starhawk, and Abbey. Dystopias, ed. M. Bartter. London: Praeger, 2004.
Griselda Thomas, Assistant Professor; Ph.D. African studies.
Eric Torgersen, M.F.A. Creative writing, poetry.
William Wandless, Ph.D. British literature.
Jeffrey Weinstock, Associate Professor; Ph.D., George Washington, 1999. Nineteenth- and early twentieth–century American literature, literature of the fantastic, literary and critical theory, approaches to popular culture.
Scare Tactics: Supernatural Fiction by American Women as a Form of Social Protest, 1849–1931. New York: Fordham University Press, 2008.
Stephenie Young, Ph.D., Assistant Professor; Ph.D., SUNY at Binghamton, 2006. Non-Western literature
Review of Adam Lowenstein's shocking representation: Historical trauma, national cinema, and the modern horror film. *Journal of the Fantastic in the Arts* 85–89, spring 2006.

KENT STATE UNIVERSITY

College of Arts and Sciences
Department of English

Programs of Study The Department of English at Kent State University (KSU) offers the Master of Arts (M.A.) in four areas: English literature and writing, English for teachers, teaching English as a second language (TESL), and rhetoric and composition. The master's program offers a broad range of courses and allows intensive study of special interests through electives. Students benefit from small classes and close interaction with faculty members. The Department offers two doctoral degrees: a Ph.D. in rhetoric and composition and a Ph.D. in English. The Department also offers an M.F.A. in creative writing through a consortium of Kent State and three other Ohio universities. The Department has particular strengths in composition and rhetoric, psychoanalysis and literature, and nineteenth- and twentieth-century British and American literature.

Research Facilities The doctoral program in literacy, rhetoric, and social practice (rhetoric and composition) foregrounds basic, applied, and theoretical research. Faculty members involve students in the program's ongoing studies of writing programs, print literacy, civic centers, digital and rhetorical environments, and workplace settings for business, industry, and nonprofit agencies.

The Institute for Bibliography and Editing (IBE) has goals of fostering basic research in the humanities and related areas that contribute to knowledge and understanding of America's political, social, and cultural heritage and exploring and leading the way in adapting computer technology to text processing and production. Kent State's IBE is one of the most advanced research centers in the nation in computerizing the editorial process from beginning to end.

The Center for Literature and Psychoanalysis was founded through an Academic Challenge Grant in 1986 for the purposes of promoting faculty development, enhancing the training of graduate students, and enhancing the research profile of the English Department and the University. The center also develops other initiatives that might benefit the University, the local and regional communities, and the people of the state of Ohio.

Financial Aid Graduate students receive financial aid in the form of graduate assistantships, research assistantships, and teaching fellowships. Graduate assistantships currently provide nine-month stipends of $8200 for M.A.-level students and $12,000 for Ph.D. students, with an exemption from all instructional and out-of-state fees. Applications for financial aid must be received by February 1 for September admission.

Cost of Study For the fall 2008 semester, the graduate tuition per credit is $408 for an Ohio resident and $728 for a nonresident.

Living and Housing Costs Rooms in the graduate residence hall are $2290 to $2515 per semester; married students' apartments may be rented for $669 to $699 per month (all utilities included). Information concerning off-campus housing may be obtained from the University Housing Office. Costs vary widely, but apartments typically rent for $450 to $550 per month.

Student Group More than 22,500 Kent State University students are enrolled at the Kent Campus, the largest residential campus in northeast Ohio. Of those students, 17,671 (79 percent) are undergraduates and 4,829 (21 percent) are graduate students.

Location Kent, a city of about 30,000, is located 35 miles southeast of Cleveland and 12 miles east of Akron. Kent offers the cultural advantages of a major metropolitan complex as well as a mix of rural-residential, suburban, and small-town living. There are a number of theater and art groups at the University and in the community. Blossom Music Center, the summer home of the Cleveland Orchestra and the site of Kent State's cooperative programs in art, music, and theater, is only 15 miles from the main campus. The Akron and Cleveland art museums are also within easy reach of the campus. There are a wide variety of recreational facilities available on the campus and within the local area, including West Branch State Park and the Cuyahoga Valley National Recreation Area. Opportunities for outdoor activities such as summer sports, ice skating, swimming, and downhill and cross-country skiing abound.

The University Established in 1910, Kent State University is one of Ohio's largest state universities. The campus is situated on 866 acres and includes an airport and an eighteen-hole golf course. There are approximately 100 buildings on the main campus. Bachelor's, master's, and doctoral degrees are offered in more than thirty subject areas. The faculty numbers approximately 800 members.

Applying Applicants are usually expected to have a minimum 3.0 GPA in at least 16 hours of undergraduate work in English or related subjects beyond the freshman level. Applicants are required to present transcripts of previous degree work; GRE scores (General Test only) or comparable evidence of aptitude for graduate study, such as successful postbaccalaureate academic work, appropriate publications, and conference presentations; three letters of recommendation; and a brief (one- to two-page) statement of purpose. A writing sample (ten to fifteen pages of scholarly work) is required for both the Ph.D. and M.A. program applications.

Correspondence and Information

Dr. Raymond A. Craig
Graduate Studies Coordinator
Department of English
Kent State University
Kent, Ohio 44242
Phone: 330-672-1741
E-mail: raymond.craig@kent.edu
Web site: http://www.kent.edu/english/

Kent State University

THE FACULTY AND THEIR RESEARCH

Maggie Anderson, Professor and Wick Poetry Program Coordinator; M.A. (English–creative writing), West Virginia. Creative writing (poetry), Appalachian literature.
Mark Bracher, Professor and Director, Center for Literature and Psychoanalysis; Ph.D. (English), Vanderbilt. Psychoanalytic cultural criticism, literary theory, literature and ethics, pedagogy.
Vera J. Camden, Associate Professor; Ph.D. (English), Virginia. Seventeenth- and eighteenth-century literature, critical theory, psychoanalysis.
Gary M. Ciuba, Associate Professor and Campus Coordinator; Ph.D., Fordham.
Tammy Clewell, Assistant Professor; Ph.D. (English), Florida State. Twentieth-century British literature, modernism and postmodernism, contemporary critical theory.
Ronald J. Corthell, Professor and Chair; Ph.D. (English), Cornell. Seventeenth-century literature, critical theory.
Raymond A. Craig, Associate Professor; Ph.D. (English), California, Davis. Early American literature, American poetry to 1900, writing technologies, sign systems, rhetoric.
Roger J. Craik, Associate Professor and Campus Coordinator; Ph.D., Southampton (England).
Claire A. Culleton, Professor; Ph.D., Miami (Florida). Modernism, British and Irish twentieth-century literature, cultural studies, working-class culture, teaching with technology.
Florence W. Dore, Assistant Professor; Ph.D. (English), Berkeley. Feminist theory, twentieth-century American literature.
Don-John Dugas, Assistant Professor; Ph.D. (English), Penn State. Shakespeare; English professional drama, 1567–1737; print culture; theater history.
Patricia L. Dunmire, Associate Professor; Ph.D. (rhetoric), Carnegie Mellon. Rhetorical theory and criticism, critical discourse analysis.
Zelma I. Edgell, Associate Professor; B.A. equivalent (journalism), Central London Polytechnic. Creative writing (fiction) literature of the Caribbean.
Susanna G. Fein, Professor and Coordinator of Ancient, Medieval, and Renaissance Studies; Ph.D. (English and American literature and language), Harvard. Medieval literature, Chaucer, Middle English manuscripts and editing, vernacular literacy.
Kristen M. Figg, Professor; Ph.D., Kent State. Medieval literature and culture, history of the English language, genre studies, composition studies.
Kevin Floyd, Assistant Professor; Ph.D. (English), Iowa. Twentieth-century American literature and culture, Marxism, gender studies, queer studies.
Lewis Fried, Professor; Ph.D. (American literature), Massachusetts. Twentieth-century literature of the U.S., American realism, American social novel, Jewish American fiction.
Paul L. Gaston, Professor and Provost; Ph.D. (English), Virginia. Twentieth-century fiction, poetry (seventeenth century through modern), higher education administration.
Klaus Gommlich, Associate Professor and ESL Director; Ph.D. (English semantics), Ph.D. (translation studies), Leipzig (Germany). Linguistics, translation studies, second-language acquisition, ESL pedagogy.
Christina Haas, Associate Professor; Ph.D. (rhetoric), Carnegie Mellon. Literacy, technology studies, process research, writing theory.
Yoshinobu Hakutani, Professor; Ph.D. (English), Penn State. Modern American literature, African-American literature, cross-culturalism.
Donald M. Hassler, Professor; Ph.D. (English), Columbia. Eighteenth-century British literature, British and American science fiction.
Brian Huot, Professor and Writing Program Coordinator; Ph.D., Indiana of Pennsylvania. Rhetoric and composition, writing assessment, computers and writing.
Pam Lieske, Assistant Professor; Ph.D., Massachusetts. Eighteenth-century British literature and culture, women's literature.
Michael F. Lynch, Associate Professor; Ph.D., Kent State. African-American literature.
Babacar M'Baye, Assistant Professor; Ph.D., Bowling Green State. African and African-American literature and culture.
Sara Newman, Assistant Professor; Ph.D. (rhetoric), Minnesota. Classical rhetorical theory, history of rhetoric, style.
Varley O'Connor, Assistant Professor; M.F.A., California, Irvine. Creative writing, creative nonfiction.
Craig F. Paulenich, Associate Professor and Campus Coordinator; Ph.D., Bowling Green State. Creative writing.
Kristin Precht, Assistant Professor; Ph.D. (applied linguistics), Northern Arizona. Corpus linguistics, register studies, sociolinguistics.
Masood Raja, Assistant Professor; Ph.D., Florida State. Postcolonial literature and theory.
Sarah Rilling, Assistant Professor and TESL Coordinator; Ph.D. (applied linguistics), Northern Arizona. English as a second language pedagogy, applied linguistics.
Margaret L. Shaw, Associate Professor; Ph.D. (critical and cultural studies), Pittsburgh. Victorian literature, composition theory and pedagogy, literacy studies.
Gregory M. Shreve, Professor and Director, Institute for Applied Linguistics; Ph.D. (linguistics), Ohio State. Applied linguistics, translation.
Lawrence J. Starzyk, Professor; Ph.D. (English), Chicago. Victorian literature and aesthetics.
Pamela Takayoshi, Associate Professor; Ph.D., Purdue. Rhetoric and composition, writing and computers, gender and writing technologies.
Robert Trogdon, Assistant Professor; Ph.D. (English), South Carolina. Twentieth-century American literature, textual editing and descriptive bibliography, history of the book and profession of authorship.
Karl Uhrig, Assistant Professor; Ph.D., Indiana. Teaching English as a second language.

LONG ISLAND UNIVERSITY, BROOKLYN CAMPUS

Department of English
Graduate Programs in English

Programs of Study

The Brooklyn Campus Department of English at Long Island University (LIU) offers two master's programs: the Master of Fine Arts in Creative Writing and the Master of Arts in English, which has concentrations in professional writing, literature, and writing and rhetoric.

The M.F.A. in Creative Writing program offers writers the opportunity to work in poetry, fiction, and cross-genre projects ranging from the contemplative to the experimental and avant-garde. Elective courses are also offered in playwriting, screenwriting, translation, creative nonfiction, and autobiography. The poetics of the program places an emphasis on explorative work that takes risks while moving in the context of multiple traditions, as opposed to that of a conventional and commercial orientation. The links between writing and theory are examined, as are the interconnections between writing, reading, music, and painting. The program setting is small and intimate, enabling easy access to faculty and strong mentoring and careful attention to the interests and concerns of individual students. The requirements for the degree are a course in methods of research and criticism, three process and techniques courses, five writing workshops, three literature electives, and a thesis, for a total of 39 credits.

The M.A. in English with a concentration in literature is designed for teachers, future doctoral students, or individuals who are interested in expanding their knowledge of literature. It is a program based predominantly on courses in American, British, and comparative literatures. Faculty members bring a variety of critical approaches, helping students develop to become knowledgeable critics of literature. Thirty-three credits are required, including 3 credits for a thesis and 21 credits in literature.

The M.A. in English with a concentration in professional writing is designed for students interested primarily in writing-related careers associated with the professions, businesses, nonprofit organizations, science and technology, and new electronic media. The concentration is designed to provide students with both individual attention and professional guidance in writing workshops and independent studies. The goal is to expand the student's knowledge and practice of nonfiction professional writing genres with attention also to history, theory, research, and professional practices. Thirty-three credits are required.

The M.A. in English with a concentration in writing and rhetoric is designed to deepen students' knowledge and practice of writing, to familiarize them with the history and theory of rhetoric, and to develop their expertise in the teaching of writing. It supports the development of nonfiction, academic, and workplace writing; helps prepare teachers of writing in secondary and postsecondary education; and can lead to advanced work in rhetoric and related fields. Students receive extensive feedback on their own writing, in-depth instruction in rhetorical theory and research methods, and training in the teaching of writing from diagnostics to evaluation, including a practicum in which students teach composition under the guidance of experienced instructors. The program addresses writing problems—from pedagogical and theoretical perspectives—encountered at all levels of writing, from very basic to advanced composition. Thirty three credits are required.

Research Facilities

The Salena Library Learning Center houses 266,000 volumes, 2,000 periodical titles, more than 6,000 videos, and other media, such as audiocassettes, compact discs, and computer software on diskette. There are several other approaches to obtaining material: interlibrary loan (ILL), Academic Libraries of Brooklyn card (ALB), and the METRO card. In addition, three of the more than fifty Brooklyn Public Library branches are in proximity to Long Island University.

Financial Aid

Scholarships (on a limited basis) are available to M.F.A. students. Both M.A. and M.F.A. students may apply for graduate assistantships, teaching fellowships, and research fellowships. Some tuition remission and stipends are available with these positions.

Cost of Study

Graduate tuition and fees for spring 2008 were $835 per credit.

Living and Housing Costs

Living and housing costs change each year. For up-to-date costs, students should visit the LIU Web site at http://www.brooklyn.liunet.edu.

Student Group

Graduate students in the Department of English form an ethnically and racially diverse group of individuals. Many of the students work full-time and attend on a part-time basis; the average length of study is three years. The multicultural backgrounds of the graduates, along with the expertise of the full-time faculty members and small classes, combine for a vibrant, personalized learning community.

Location

The Long Island University, Brooklyn Campus is located just over the Manhattan Bridge in Brooklyn, New York, near the Metrotech complex, Fulton Mall, and Brooklyn Academy of Music. Visitors should take the B, Q, M, or R subway train to DeKalb Avenue or the No. 2, 3, 4, or 5 IRT train to Nevins Street. The main entrance to the campus is located just north of the corner of DeKalb Avenue and Flatbush Extension. This convenient location allows for exploration of the fastest-developing part of Brooklyn and allows easy access to Manhattan.

The University and The Department

Long Island University was chartered by the New York State Education Department in 1926 in Brooklyn, New York, as a nonsectarian, coeducational, private university to provide excellent higher education to people from all walks of life. Admission to the University from its beginning has been based solely on merit and promise and has been offered to large numbers of immigrants and children of immigrants seeking to achieve the American dream. In keeping with this philosophy, the Department of English extends its welcome to a wide variety of students with diverse backgrounds and experiences.

Applying

Potential graduate students should complete an application form online and also submit to the Admissions Office an official transcript of their undergraduate studies, a writing sample commensurate with their area of study, two letters of recommendation, and a letter of intent. There is a nonrefundable application fee. There is no specific deadline for applications. However, students should be sure to submit their application at least three months prior to the semester in which they hope to begin their studies. Students may go to the Department of English Web site for more information.

Correspondence and Information

Marilyn Boutwell, Graduate Student Advisement
Department of English
Long Island University, Brooklyn Campus
1 University Plaza
Brooklyn, New York 11201-8423
Phone: 718-246-6336
Fax: 718-246-6302
E-mail: marilyn.boutwell@liu.edu
Web site: http://www.brooklyn.liu.edu/depts/english/graduate.htm

Long Island University, Brooklyn Campus

THE FACULTY AND THEIR RESEARCH

Carol Allen, Associate Professor; Ph.D., Rutgers. American literature, African Diaspora, women's studies.
Michael Bennett, Associate Professor; Ph.D., Virginia. American literature, African American studies, ecocriticism, sexuality and gender studies.
Michael J. K. Bokor, Assistant Professor; Ph.D., Illinois State. Technical and professional writing, world Englishes in composition studies, globalization studies, non-Western rhetoric.
Leah Dilworth, Professor; Ph.D., Yale. American literature and literary history, cultural studies, regionalism, tourism, collecting.
Sealy Gilles, Associate Professor and Department Chairperson; Ph.D., CUNY Graduate Center. Medieval British literature, Old English language and literature, Chaucer.
Jessica Hagedorn, Parsons Family Professor of Creative Writing. Fictionista/fashionista, poetry, playwriting, screenwriting, postcolonial literature, Asian American and Philippine literature.
Jonathan Haynes, Associate Professor; Ph.D., Yale. African film and literature, English Renaissance literature, third-world film and literature.
John High, Assistant Professor; M.A., San Francisco State. Fiction, poetry translation, cross-genre writing.
Patrick Horrigan, Associate Professor; Ph.D., Columbia. Nineteenth- and twentieth-century American literature, cultural studies, lesbian and gay culture, literary theory, modernism, film, autobiography.
Robert Hullot-Kentor, Associate Professor; Ph.D., Massachusetts. American and European literature, aesthetics, continental philosophy and social criticism, twentieth-century painting and music.
John Killoran, Assistant Professor; Ph.D., Waterloo. Professional writing, technical communication, Web communication, genre theory.
Xiao-Ming Li, Associate Professor; Ph.D., New Hampshire. ESL writing, applied linguistics, Asian American and Asian literature.
Harriet Malinowitz, Professor; Ph.D., NYU. Women's studies, personal writing, lesbian and gay studies, rhetoric and composition.
Donald McCrary, Associate Professor; Ph.D., NYU. Sociolinguistics, theory and philosophy of composition and rhetoric, womanist theology, advanced composition, developmental writing.
Maria McGarrity, Assistant Professor; Ph.D., Miami (Florida). Joyce; Irish, Caribbean, world, and postcolonial literature and theory; the twentieth century and transatlantic studies.
Deborah Mutnick, Professor; Ph.D., NYU. Rhetoric and composition, autobiography and memoir literature, creative nonfiction and oral history.
Louis Parascandola, Associate Professor; Ph.D., CUNY Graduate Center. Nineteenth-century British literature, Black literature.
Robert Pattison, Professor; Ph.D., Columbia. Nineteenth-century British literature, classical literature in translation, history of the English language, religion and literary studies.
Bernard Schweizer, Assistant Professor; Ph.D., Duke. Twentieth-century British literature, travel writing, Rebecca West.
Patricia Stephens, Associate Professor and Director, Writing Center; Ph.D., NYU. Theories of writing and writing pedagogy; writing program administration and history; feminist theories; queer theories, gender, race, class, and sexuality in education and the workplace.
Srividhya Swaminathan, Assistant Professor; Ph.D., Penn State. Restoration and eighteenth-century novel and drama; gender and the eighteenth century; rhetoric of social movement, race, and the eighteenth century.
Lewis Warsh, Assistant Professor; M.F.A., CUNY City College. Fiction, poetry, modernism, the English Romantic poets, the new French novel and fiction (c. 1955–1970), twentieth-century painting and poetry.

OLD DOMINION UNIVERSITY

Department of English
M.A., Ph.D. in English

Programs of Study
The Department of English is the largest department within the College of Arts and Letters at Old Dominion University (ODU). The 30-credit-hour Master of Arts program in English develops professional competency in literary analysis and in writing. The program offers courses of study in literature, professional writing, rhetoric and composition, and the teaching of English. The program prepares students for further graduate study in English; professional writing and editing; teaching in secondary schools and colleges; further study in such fields as anthropology, law, psychology, and philosophy; careers in government and industry; and other professions requiring analytical, literary, linguistic, or writing skills. Students can pursue the thesis or the nonthesis option. Writing a thesis may be of particular benefit to those who contemplate further graduate work or who have a strong desire to pursue a single topic in great depth. Nonthesis students must pass an oral comprehensive exam, which covers each student's particular program of study. Professional writing concentration students may use a portfolio to fulfill part of the M.A. examination requirement.

The Ph.D. in English integrates writing, rhetoric, discourse, technology, and textual studies. Offering opportunities for creative reinterpretation of these fields within the discipline of English, ODU emphasizes research that examines texts in a variety of overlapping and sometimes competing language-based worlds. The program focuses on how the creation and reception of texts and media are affected by form, purpose, technology of composition, audience, cultural location, and communities of discourse. Students may pursue full- or part-time study through on-campus course offerings or part-time study through distance learning. Students begin their studies with a cluster of core courses that focus on texts, technology, research methods, instructional design, cross-cultural communication, and major debates in English; then they complete a field concentration that allows for intensive specialization in one of two tracks—rhetoric and textual studies or professional writing and new media. In addition, students are encouraged to use their electives to enhance their interdisciplinary knowledge of a field concentration and to enhance their understanding of theoretical modeling, quantitative/qualitative research methods, or history and culture. All Ph.D. students must write and defend a thesis.

Research Facilities
The University provides a rich array of resources to support research and creative work. The Perry library provides a full complement of state-of-the-art services, with more than 2.8 million items.

Financial Aid
Financial aid is available in the form of fellowships, research and teaching assistantships, and scholarships. The Department awards three teaching assistantships per academic year to Ph.D. students. Low-interest, deferred-repayment graduate loans are also available to U.S. citizens who can demonstrate need.

Cost of Study
In-state tuition for 2007–08 was $304 per credit hour. Out-of-state tuition was $761 per credit hour. Other fees amounted to approximately $100 per semester.

Living and Housing Costs
There are a wide range of affordable living and housing options on campus, close to campus, and in the Hampton Roads area. Campus residence halls with meal plans are also available.

Student Group
There are 31 full-time and 51 part-time students. This includes 68 women, 1 international student, and 18 students who are members of minority groups. The average age is 32.

Location
Old Dominion University's main campus is located in Norfolk, Virginia, one of seven major cities that make up Hampton Roads, an area with a population of 1.4 million. The campus is approximately 200 miles south of Washington, D.C., within minutes of the world's largest naval base and the largest East Coast seaport and 30 minutes from the Virginia Beach oceanfront. ODU also operates Higher Education Centers in northern Virginia, Virginia Beach, Hampton, and the tri-cities of Portsmouth, Chesapeake, and Suffolk. Old Dominion sponsors fifty distance learning sites in Virginia, the District of Columbia, North Carolina, Georgia, Arizona, and Washington and delivers programs to Navy ships worldwide.

The College
Old Dominion University is a cutting-edge research university and an innovative educational institution that is home to more than 22,000 students. The University's 6,500 graduate students have the opportunity to take their education to the next level by working with world-class scholars who are pushing the boundaries of their disciplines. As Virginia's international university, top students from all fifty states and 108 countries have dynamic exchanges in seminars, laboratories, and studios.

Old Dominion University has been designated an RU/H: Research University (high research activity) by the Carnegie Foundation. This designation reflects the strong commitment to graduate studies and research in all six of its colleges: the College of Arts and Letters, the College of Business and Public Administration, the Darden College of Education, the Frank Batten College of Engineering and Technology, the College of Health Sciences, and the College of Sciences. Graduate students at Old Dominion can choose their academic and professional interests from among sixty-five master's degree programs, two education specialist programs, twenty-three doctoral programs, and numerous opportunities for internships.

Applying
For regular admission to the M.A. program, students must generally have completed at least 24 undergraduate hours in English or a closely related field with a grade point average of 3.0 or better. However, students applying to the professional writing concentration may have little or no undergraduate course work relating to English, provided they have an average of 3.0 or better in their undergraduate major. Applicants must submit the completed application, the application fee, official transcripts, letters of recommendation, and GRE General Test scores. Students applying to the professional writing concentration must also provide a writing sample, preferably of previous professional work, that demonstrates their preparation for graduate-level writing. International students must submit scores from the TOEFL, a sample of scholarly writing, and three letters of recommendation, at least one of which evaluates ability in English. For regular admission, students must have a minimum score of 230 on the computer-based TOEFL (the equivalent of 570 on the older, paper-based score scale).

Ph.D. applicants must have a completed master's degree (or its equivalent) in English or in an appropriate field (such as rhetoric, composition, English education, communication, or computer science) from a regionally accredited institution of higher education, with a minimum grade point average of 3.5 overall for the master's degree. Students must submit the completed application, the application fee, official transcripts, scores from the GRE General Test, three letters of recommendation, a 1,000-word statement of the applicant's academic and professional goals and a discussion of how the Ph.D. in English will help achieve them, and a writing sample of at least 20 double-spaced pages on a topic related to the applicant's expertise. If the applicant's native language is not English, a current TOEFL score of at least 600 (paper-based test) and/or an interview to assess the applicant's comprehension and fluency in English is required. Applicants requesting financial aid are encouraged to submit all required credentials by February 15.

Correspondence and Information
Edward Jacobs
Acting Graduate Program Director
Department of English
College of Arts and Letters
Old Dominion University
Norfolk, Virginia 23529

Phone: 757-683-4028
Fax: 757-683-3241
E-mail: ejacobs@odu.edu
Web site: http://al.odu.edu/english/

Old Dominion University

THE FACULTY AND THEIR RESEARCH

Akeel Al-Khakani, Assistant Professor; Ph.D., Purdue. Postcolonial literature.
Bridget Anderson, Assistant Professor; Ph.D., Michigan. Sociophonetics, language ideology, Appalachian English, Southern English, African American English, American English, voice recognition (with emphasis on vernacular features).
Sarah Appleton, Visiting Lecturer; Ph.D., Connecticut. Contemporary and women's literatures, American literature, rhetoric and composition.
Catie Berkenfield, Lecturer; M.A., New Mexico. Discourses of gender and race, language in society, metaphor theory, feminist linguistic theory and practice.
Janet Bing, Professor; Ph.D., Massachusetts Amherst. Phonology (syllable, tone, stress, intonation) and coronals, phonetics (intonation), language and gender, frame analysis, humor.
Michael Blumenthal, Visiting Professor and Mina Hohenberg Darden Chair in Creative Writing; J.D., Cornell. Poetry, creative nonfiction.
Tim Bostic, Visiting Assistant Professor; Ph.D., Virginia Commonwealth. Educational policy, instructional and motivational strategies, Virginia standards of learning.
Joe Cosco, Associate Professor; Ph.D., William and Mary. Journalism/periodicals history, nineteenth- and early twentieth-century American literature, travel narratives, American cultural history, immigration/ethnicity/race.
Kevin DePew, Assistant Professor and Director of Writing Tutorial Services; Ph.D., Purdue. Computer-mediated communication, second-language writing, teaching writing with technology.
Kathy Fowler, Lecturer; M.F.A., Old Dominion. American literature.
Kathie Gossett, Assistant Professor; Ph.D., Illinois at Urbana-Champaign. Composition theory and pedagogy, computers and writing, new media, memory, multimodal composition, rhetorics (classical, medieval, digital).
Imtiaz Habib, Associate Professor; Ph.D., Indiana. Shakespeare, English Renaissance drama, postcolonial literature and theory, history of English drama, modern drama.
Lenore Hart, Visiting Assistant Professor; M.F.A., Old Dominion; M.L.S., Florida State.
Dana Heller, Professor and Director of the Humanities Institute; Ph.D., CUNY. American studies, popular culture(s), gay and lesbian studies, comparative cultural studies.
Joyce Hoffmann, Associate Professor; Ph.D., NYU. Theodore H. White and journalism as illusion, Vietnam and the press.
Luisa A. Igloria, Associate Professor; Ph.D., Illinois at Chicago. Modern and contemporary American poetry, Filipino American and Philippine literature, Asian American literature, postcolonial and diasporic literature, women writers, short story.
Katherine Jackson, Instructor; M.F.A., Old Dominion. Fiction, public relations.
Edward Jacobs, Associate Professor and Acting Graduate Program Director; Ph.D., Illinois at Urbana-Champaign. British literature 1640–1848, history of the book, British circulating libraries.
Miranda Johnson-Parries, Instructor; M.A., Old Dominion. Composition studies.
Julie Manthey, Instructor; M.A., Wright State. Writing, student conferencing.
Guy McCormick, Senior Lecturer; Ph.D., Indiana of Pennsylvania. Business writing, composition, academic skills.
Denise McNelly, Instructor; M.F.A., Old Dominion. Writing.
Tracey Mershon, Lecturer; M.F.A., CUNY, Brooklyn. Writing, ESL.
David Metzger, Professor; Ph.D., Missouri. History of rhetoric (biblical, classical, modern), Bible as literature, Jewish studies, composition and pedagogy, psychoanalytic theory, medieval literature.
Manuela Mourão, Associate Professor; Ph.D., Illinois at Urbana-Champaign. Gender in fiction, fiction, Victorian literature, critical theory, comparative literature.
Joyce Neff, Associate Professor; Ph.D., Pennsylvania. Grounded theory, distance education, writing across the curriculum, representations of students as writers, writing in government agencies, hypertext and writing, writing centers.
Ebony Nelson, Visiting Lecturer.
Matt Oliver, Lecturer; M.F.A., Old Dominion. Distance learning, memoir, creative nonfiction, writing in the discipline.
David Pagano, Lecturer; Ph.D., California, Irvine. Interdisciplinary study of time; horror, gothic, and apocalyptic narrative; critical and rhetorical theory; film and film theory; American literature.
Michael Pearson, Professor; Ph.D., Penn State. American literature, literary nonfiction, memoirs.
Janet Peery, Associate Professor; M.F.A., Wichita State. Creative writing (fiction), narrative form and theory.
Princess Perry, Lecturer; M.F.A., Old Dominion. American literature.
Kya Reaves-Ellis, Visiting Assistant Professor.
Sheri Reynolds, Associate Professor, Director of Creative Writing, and Ruth and Perry Morgan Chair of Southern Literature; M.F.A., Virginia Commonwealth. Women writers, form and theory of narrative, Southern literature.
Jeffrey Richards, Professor; Ph.D., North Carolina at Chapel Hill. Calvinism in the Colonial South, early and nineteenth-century American literature, American drama.
Katherine Rocca, Instructor; M.A., Louisville. Writing.
Julia Romberger, Assistant Professor; Ph.D., Purdue. Digital rhetoric, usability research, professional/technical writing, teaching writing with technology, visual rhetoric.
Joanne Scheibman, Associate Professor; Ph.D., New Mexico. Analysis of English conversation, linguistic subjectivity, discourse and grammar.
Timothy Seibles, Associate Professor; M.F.A., Norwich. Literature.
Jennifer Sloggie, Instructor; M.A., Old Dominion. Composition, Web site design, writing about film, distance learning.
Janis Smith, Lecturer; M.A., Wake Forest. Writing.
Craig Stewart, Assistant Professor; Ph.D., Carnegie Mellon. Rhetoric of science, critical discourse studies, argumentation and persuasion, qualitative and quantitative research methods.
Virginia Tucker, Lecturer; M.A., Old Dominion. Composition, Web development, electronic portfolios.
Walter Unterreiner, Instructor; M.A., Old Dominion. Writing.
Alfredo Urzua, Assistant Professor; Ph.D., Northern Arizona. Reflective discourse, teachers' professional development, discourse in the professions, academic language.
Charles Wilson, Professor; Ph.D., Georgia. Black manhood; race, class, and gender in Southern fiction; intersection of past and present in the South.

SAINT LOUIS UNIVERSITY, MADRID

Double-Degree Master's Program in English

Program of Study

The Master's Program in English is offered as a combined effort of the English departments of the St. Louis, Missouri, and Madrid, Spain, campuses of Saint Louis University (SLU) and of the Universidad Autónoma de Madrid (UAM).

Saint Louis University and the Universidad Autónoma de Madrid offer the first master's degree in English recognized by both an American and a Spanish university. Students completing the two-year program (30 credit hours in the American system, 70 in the European (ECTS)) earn a Master of Arts in English from Saint Louis University and a *Master en Estudios Culturales y Anglo-norteamericanos* from the Universidad Autónoma de Madrid. The program is designed for holders of a B.A. or Licenciatura in English or a related field, high school teachers, literary scholars and translators, and others who want to explore the masterpieces of literature in English.

All classes take place at Saint Louis University, Madrid on a trimester basis (October–December, January–March, April–June). Students also take two seminars during a six-week summer session at Saint Louis University's Frost campus in St. Louis, Missouri. At the conclusion of their course work, students take a 1-hour oral examination on a reading list, which they have a hand in shaping. The program is accredited by the North Central Association of Schools and Colleges (NCA). Credits earned are also recognized as *Formación Permanente del Profesorado* (8° Apartado de la Resolución de 27 Abril de 1997, B.O.E. de 25 de Mayo).

The master's seminars are taught by American and European Ph.D. faculty members from both SLU and UAM, providing a unique, international perspective on British, North American, and Anglophone literature. The individualized course of study allows students to select ten graduate seminars from such areas as the traditional periods and genres of literature in English, literary theory, linguistics, the teaching of writing, and translation. Since enrollment is limited to 20, students receive specialized attention in their study and research. They also participate in an international community of writers and scholars who are invited to campus each year.

Research Facilities

The resources of the Madrid Campus Library are bilingual in nature and designed primarily to meet the needs of the students studying at this campus. The 9,000 books and 60 journals that compose its collection respond to specific bibliographies that supplement courses offered. Furthermore, the Madrid Campus Library offers students and faculty members access to all electronic resources available at the University's main campus in St. Louis, Missouri, via the SLU proxy server and to other electronic research aids via the library Web page at http://spain.slu.edu/library_itresources/lib_library.html.

The libraries of the Universidad Autónoma de Madrid contain more than 500,000 books and 4,500 periodical subscriptions. The UAM's online services provide direct links to databases, information resources, electronic journals, and catalogs of other university libraries in Madrid and around the world. The UAM libraries support both a B.A. and a doctorate program in English language and literature.

Students are granted reading privileges at nearly all libraries in Madrid and Europe, including Spain's National Library (*Biblioteca Nacional*), the country's foremost research library; the Center of North American Studies Library; the British Studies Information Center; and the British Council Library. A directory of all libraries in Madrid is available from the reference desk at the Saint Louis University Madrid Campus Library and on the SLU library Web page. Interlibrary loan facilities are also available, with exceptionally fast access to current periodicals via the British Library (UK) Document Supply Service as well as several Spanish research libraries.

Students have access to holdings of the Saint Louis University libraries, which total more than 1.4 million volumes, 12,800 serial subscriptions, 1.1 million microfilms, and more than 200,000 government documents.

Financial Aid

U.S. citizens may be eligible for financial aid through traditional U.S. financial aid programs. All students are eligible to apply for financial aid, including work-study grants and tuition discounts. Awards are made only after a student gains full admission to the program.

Cost of Study

Costs for the 2007–08 academic year are €445 per credit hour for international students and $580 per credit hour for U.S. students. (Price per credit refers to the American credit system.) Students may enroll full-time (6 credits per trimester) or part-time (3 credits per trimester).

Living and Housing Costs

Most graduate students choose to rent apartments near the campus. While prices vary according to apartment size and neighborhood, two-bedroom apartments usually start at €1000 per month in Madrid.

Students may also take part in the Madrid campus residential housing program, which allows them to live in a Spanish household. Costs range from €575 to €850 per month, depending on board plan, kitchen privileges, and other factors.

Student Group

Enrollment in the master's program at the Madrid campus is limited to 20 students.

Location

The Madrid campus of Saint Louis University is located in the city's residential northwest corner alongside other private and public universities and private homes, only a few metro stops from Puerta del Sol, the geographical center of the Iberian peninsula. The Frost campus of Saint Louis University is an architecturally rich urban campus centrally located in St. Louis, Missouri. The Universidad Autónoma de Madrid's spacious campus, located in Cantoblanco, is a few kilometers north of Madrid and is easily accessible via public transportation.

The University

Saint Louis University is a Catholic Jesuit university and leading research institution. Founded in 1818, the University strives to foster the intellectual and spiritual growth of its students through a broad array of undergraduate, graduate, and professional-degree programs on campuses in St. Louis, Missouri, and Madrid, Spain.

Applying

Applications for admission to the Master's Program in English are reviewed by faculty members from both Saint Louis University and the Universidad Autónoma de Madrid. Candidates are evaluated for evidence of preparation for advanced study of literature and the likelihood of academic success.

Applicants should hold a B.A. or Licenciatura in English or equivalent with an excellent academic record. Saint Louis University's Graduate School of Arts and Sciences also requires evidence of competence or successful study of a classical or modern foreign language. Native speakers of a language other than English fulfill this requirement automatically. Candidates must submit an application, undergraduate academic transcripts, three letters of recommendation, Graduate Record Examinations (GRE) scores (both general and subject tests), a current CV, a 500-word statement of purpose, a writing sample, and a $40 application fee.

To be considered for October admission, candidates must submit materials by March 1; for January, by December 1; and for April, by February 1.

Correspondence and Information

Graduate Admissions
The Master's Program in English
Saint Louis University, Madrid
Avenida del Valle, 34
28003 Madrid, España

Phone: 34-91-554-5858 (main office)
E-mail: graduate_admissions@madrid.slu.edu
Web site: http://spain.slu.edu

Saint Louis University, Madrid

THE FACULTY AND THEIR RESEARCH

Students pursuing the dual master's in English work within the combined English department faculties of the Universidad Autónoma de Madrid; Saint Louis University, Madrid; and Saint Louis University's Frost campus.

Sara van den Berg, Chair, Department of English; Ph.D., Yale. Ben Jonson, Milton, seventeenth-century literature, psychoanalytic theory, medicine and the humanities.
Paul Vita, Chair, Department of English (Madrid campus); Ph.D., Columbia. Nineteenth-century British literature, narrative theory, literature and the arts.
María Lozano, Program Director; Ph.D., Universidad de Zaragoza (Spain). Twentieth-century American literature.
Stephen Casmier, Ph.D., Université de Nice-Sophia Antipolis (France). African-American literature, theory and expressive culture, African literature, twentieth-century American literature.
Anne Day Dewey, Ph.D., Stanford. American poetry, twentieth-century American literature, women's poetry.
Antony Hasler, Ph.D., Cambridge. Chaucer, medieval literature, late medieval/early modern British literature, drama.
Elizabeth Heard, Ph.D., Penn State. Restoration and eighteenth-century British literature, drama, African American literature.
Georgia Johnston, Ph.D., Rutgers. Twentieth-century British literature, autobiography, creative writing (poetry).
Matthew Kineen, Ph.D., Wisconsin. Theory of genres, comparative literature.
Anne McCabe, Ph.D., Aston (England). Systemic functional linguistics, contrastive rhetoric, text linguistics/analysis, teaching writing, English for academic purposes, teacher development.
Janice McIntire-Strasburg, Ph.D., Nevada. Computers and writing, Mark Twain, American literature, Native American literature.
Eulalia Piñero, Ph.D., Universidad Complutense de Madrid (Spain). Ethnic American literatures.
Esteban Pujals, Ph.D., Universidad Complutense de Madrid (Spain). Twentieth-century American poetry.
Julia Salmerón, Ph.D., Hull (England). Gender studies, twentieth-century British literature.
Pilar Somacarrera, Ph.D., Universidad de Salamanca (Spain). Canadian literature, postcolonial literatures.
Maura Tarnoff, Ph.D., Virginia. Renaissance literature.

SAINT LOUIS UNIVERSITY, MADRID

Master's Program in Spanish Language and Literature

Programs of Study

Two programs of study are offered—the master's degree in Spanish and special *Cursos de Perfeccionamiento.*

The Master of Arts degree program in Spanish is specifically designed for students interested in pursuing concentrated studies in a combination of Spanish language and Hispanic cultures and literature. The curriculum is suited to those individuals planning, or already engaged in, professional careers such as teaching or international affairs. The program also prepares students who wish to continue study in a Ph.D. degree program in Spanish or a related field.

Students who choose to enroll in the program at the Madrid campus have the opportunity to immerse themselves in Spanish culture, taking with them not only a graduate degree and a stronger knowledge of Spanish language and literature, but also the experience of studying a language in its native country. Participants perfect their oral and written Spanish communication skills and broaden their knowledge of the rich Spanish literature and culture as they study with Ph.D. faculty members, all of whom are native Spaniards.

The master's program may be completed during a series of five-week summer sessions (usually three or four, but up to five summers). It may also be completed through attending classes during the traditional academic year, complemented by a summer or two. If students choose to spend three summers in Madrid, each summer they take two M.A. courses, each worth 3 credits, and two *Cursos de Perfeccionamiento* or optional M.A. courses, each worth 2 credits. Throughout their program, a full-time faculty member serves as their adviser. During their last session, students take the final written and oral exams.

Cursos de Perfeccionamiento, designed for secondary school teachers of Spanish, are in-service language and literature classes that allow students to earn from 2 to 8 credits by taking from one to four enrichment courses.

Both programs are accredited by the North Central Association of Schools and Colleges (NCA).

Research Facilities

The resources of the Madrid Campus Library are bilingual in nature and designed primarily to meet the needs of the students studying at this campus. The 9,000 books and 60 journals that compose its collection respond to specific bibliographies that supplement courses offered. Furthermore, the Madrid Campus Library offers students and faculty members access to all electronic resources available at the University's main campus in St. Louis, Missouri, via the SLU proxy server and to other electronic research aids via the library Web page at http://spain.slu.edu/library_itresources/lib_library.html. The Madrid Campus Library also has agreements with all of Madrid's public libraries and the prestigious *Biblioteca Nacional.*

Financial Aid

U.S. citizens may be eligible for financial aid through traditional U.S. financial aid programs. All students are eligible to apply for financial aid, including work-study grants. Awards are made only after a student gains full admission to the program.

Cost of Study

Costs for the 2007–08 academic year are €445 per credit hour for international students and $580 per credit hour for U.S. students. Students may enroll on a full-time or part-time basis. Costs for *Cursos de Perfeccionamiento* are €360 per credit.

Living and Housing Costs

During the summer, housing is available for individuals in University residencias (half room and board costs €1100). For couples and families, arrangements can be made to live in private apartments can be made.

During the traditional academic year, most graduate students choose to rent apartments near campus. While prices vary according to apartment size and neighborhood, two-bedroom apartments usually start at €1000 per month in Madrid. Students may also take part in the Madrid campus residential housing program, which allows them to live in a Spanish household. Costs range from €550 to €740 per month, depending on board plan and kitchen privileges, and other factors.

Student Group

This course is designed for students who have a strong knowledge of the Spanish language and its literature and are interested in increasing this knowledge through the experience of studying and living in Spain. Class sizes are limited.

Location

Madrid has been the capital of Spain since 1562. Located in the geographic center of the Iberian Peninsula, the climate of Madrid is characterized by warm, dry summers and cool winters. Madrid is a city of monuments. Among the highlights are the medieval center, dating back to the Habsburg Empire, and the Prado Museum. Madrid offers its visitors and natives a unique cultural destination with many options for entertainment, including pubs, cafés, and nightclubs open late into the evening.

The Madrid campus of Saint Louis University is located in the city's residential northwest corner, alongside other private and public universities and private homes, only a few metro stops from *Puerta del Sol.*

The University

Saint Louis University is a Catholic Jesuit university and leading research institution. Founded in 1818, the University strives to foster the intellectual and spiritual growth of its students through a broad array of undergraduate, graduate, and professional degree programs on campuses in St. Louis, Missouri, and Madrid, Spain.

Applying

Applications are evaluated for evidence of preparation for advanced study of language and literature and the likelihood of academic success.

M.A. program applicants need to submit a classified (degree-seeking) application (which is included in the application packet and is available online), an application fee of US$40, Graduate Record Examinations (GRE) General Test or Miller Analogies Test scores, official transcripts of all academic work completed in undergraduate, graduate and/or professional schools, three letters of recommendation (forms are included in the application packet and are available online), a biographical goal statement of 500 words that addresses the applicant's intellectual and professional goals, a writing sample, and a curriculum vitae.

Students should make arrangements to take the Graduate Record Examinations (GRE) or Miller Analogies Test as soon as possible and have the score reports sent directly to Saint Louis University. All other materials should be sent directly to the Madrid campus.

To be considered for summer admission, candidates should submit all documents to Saint Louis University, Madrid, by April 1. The deadline for fall admission is May 30. For spring admission, the deadline is October 15.

Cursos candidates must submit an online application as a visiting U.S. student for the second summer session, an application fee of $45 (payable online), and official transcripts of all academic work completed. Though not required, it is highly recommended that students submit at least one letter of recommendation from their department chair, principal, or other professional contact. To be considered for summer admission, all documents must be received by Saint Louis University, Madrid, by April 30.

Correspondence and Information

Graduate Admissions
Saint Louis University, Madrid
Avenida del Valle, 34
28003 Madrid, España

Phone: 34-91-554-5858
Fax: 34-91-554-6202
E-mail: graduate_admissions@madrid.slu.edu
Web site: http://spain.slu.edu

Saint Louis University, Madrid

THE FACULTY AND THEIR RESEARCH

All faculty members for the Master of Arts and *cursos* programs hold Ph.D.'s and are approved members of the graduate faculty of Saint Louis University. Each summer, one member of Saint Louis University's Spanish department joins the faculty in Madrid to teach a course and assist with exams.

Aitor Bikandi, Ph.D., Cincinnati. Nineteenth- and twentieth-century peninsular narrative, cultural studies, peninsular film.
Xelo Candel, Ph.D., Universidad de Valencia. Twentieth-century Latin American and peninsular poetry, golden age poetry, cultural studies.
Angeles Encinar, Ph.D., Washington (St. Louis). Nineteenth- and twentieth-century peninsular narrative, twentieth-century Latin American narrative, women's narrative.
Cristina Matute, Ph.D., Universidad Autónoma de Madrid. History of Spanish grammar, Spanish phonetics and phonology, linguistics.
Alicia Ramos, Ph.D., Northwestern. Twentieth-century peninsular narrative, twentieth-century peninsular thought, medieval literature, survey of Hispanic narrative and film.
Rafael Reig, Ph.D., SUNY at Stony Brook. Nineteenth- and twentieth-century peninsular narrative, creative writing.
Maria Teresa Rodriguez, Ph.D., Universidad Autónoma de Madrid. History of Spanish grammar, Spanish phonetics and phonology, linguistics.

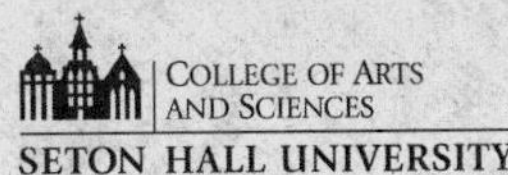

SETON HALL UNIVERSITY

Department of English
English Literature and Writing

Programs of Study

The Department of English at Seton Hall University offers a Master of Arts degree program with two options: one in literature and one in writing. The program requires 30 credits, with at least 6 at the 7000 level. All students are required to take the 12 credit "hub," which includes English 6010: Introduction to Literary Research; two literature electives (one American, one British); and English 7011: Studies in Criticism. Students then follow a "spoke" of 18 credits (either in literature or writing); students in the literature spoke generally write a thesis.

Recent courses include the African-American Literary Experience, Studies in Medieval Literature, the English Novel, American Literature 1900–1945, Shakespeare, Studies in Victorian Literature, Modern Rhetoric and Writing, Art and Craft of Writing, Modern British Drama, the American Renaissance, Renaissance Literature, and Composition Workshop.

The master's program requires all students to pass a foreign language translation exam (demonstrating reading knowledge) and a comprehensive exam, generally taken in the student's last semester.

The literature spoke provides a good basis for students interested in continuing in a doctoral program. Students have recently gone on to Ph.D. programs at the University of Tulsa; the University of California, Riverside; Temple; Michigan State; Fordham; Drew; Lehigh; and the University of Edinburgh. The literature spoke is also well suited to secondary-school English teachers.

The writing option is particularly attractive to secondary school teachers and students who are interested in teaching at two-year colleges; many students who seek careers in editing and publishing, and students planning to continue on to receive an M.F.A., also select this option. Students pursuing this spoke have gone on to careers in medical editing, public relations, educational publishing, and teaching.

Further information is available online at http://www.shu.edu/academics/artsci/ma-english/index.cfm.

Research Facilities

Students have access to the Seton Hall Library as well as libraries at area colleges and the many important research facilities in New York City. Seton Hall's Walsh Library is a pioneer in electronic research facilities, making numerous online databases and resources available both on and off campus.

The Language Resource Center (LRC) in the College of Arts and Sciences houses the theater-style Screening Room and a state-of-the-art computer workstation area. All computers have keyboards installed in a number of languages, including Arabic, Chinese, and Japanese, and have Internet access, video recording and editing software, and connections to a VCR/DVD combo for viewing. The LRC provides DVDs, videos, and other media in Arabic, Chinese, English, French, German, Italian, Japanese, Spanish, Russian, and other languages and offers self-paced language learning materials for Seton Hall community members who wish to study a language on their own.

Financial Aid

The teaching assistantship program allows Master of Arts students to teach freshman English courses. Teaching assistants receive extensive training during the summer. They then teach two sections of freshman English each semester. The teaching assistantships cover tuition (but not fees) and provide an additional stipend of $8500 for the academic year. Teaching assistants are also given an IBM laptop computer and participate in Seton Hall's Mobile Computing program, which brings information technology into the classroom. Students should contact the Department for information about applying for one of these positions.

Graduate assistantships are also available through the Office of Graduate Programs (http://www.shu.edu/applying/graduate/grad-finaid.cfm). Graduate assistants work in a variety of campus positions and receive tuition remission and a stipend.

Cost of Study

In 2008–09, tuition is $875 per credit. Full-time students pay $305 per semester in University and technology fees; part-time students pay $185.

Living and Housing Costs

Housing and living costs in South Orange and surrounding towns are comparable to most suburban cities, with studio and one-bedroom apartments renting for $750 to $1000 per month.

Student Group

The master's program enrolls approximately 30 students. Eight students receive teaching assistantships, which cover tuition and provide a stipend of $8500 per year. About half of the program's students are enrolled part-time. Entering classes consist of 12 to 18 students.

Location

Seton Hall University is located in the Village of South Orange, New Jersey, only 14 miles (or a 30-minute direct train ride) from New York City. The University's proximity to New York City allows students to take advantage of all the city has to offer while living in a charming suburban area.

The University and The Department

Seton Hall is New Jersey's only Catholic university. The University's diverse academic program is characterized by a strong teaching faculty and a wide range of academic choices. Students benefit from the personal attention generated by small classes and a low student-faculty ratio. At Seton Hall, students find people who are willing to listen, offer support, and help them get the most out of their education.

The Department of English's faculty members are distinguished by their scholarship and their love of teaching. Senior faculty members contribute their years of commitment to excellent teaching, while the junior faculty members—a growing number from eminent graduate programs across the country—bring energy, enthusiasm, and new areas of expertise to their classes. Faculty members regularly publish articles and books and take part in local, regional, and international conferences. Students are encouraged to join faculty members at conferences and to participate in them, as well. The Department is active in its graduate students' professional development, sponsoring seminars for students who are interested in continuing their study in doctoral programs; publishing their work, both creative and scholarly; or exploring the academic job market.

Applying

Students who have completed 18 credits or more of undergraduate study in English (at least six semester-long courses) are eligible to apply to this program, which seeks to provide them with a comprehensive background in English and literature. For applications, students should visit http://www.shu.edu/academics/artsci/apply-graduate.cfm.

Students must submit the general Seton Hall University Graduate Application, which includes three letters of recommendation, a resume, and a personal statement. All applicants must take the GRE General Test before an admissions decision can be made. Candidates applying for a teaching assistantship should also submit the TA application, a statement of interest in the position, and a writing sample by March 15 of their application year. The Graduate Application should be returned to the Office of Graduate Programs or submitted online; however, the TA application should be sent directly to the Director of Graduate Studies, Department of English, Seton Hall University, South Orange, New Jersey 07079.

Correspondence and Information

Dr. Angela Weisl, Director of Graduate Studies
Department of English
College of Arts and Sciences
Fahy Hall, Room 362
Seton Hall University
400 South Orange Avenue
South Orange, New Jersey 07042

Phone: 973-275-5889
Fax: 973-761-9453
E-mail: weislang@shu.edu
Web site: http://www.shu.edu/academics/artsci/ma-english/index.cfm

Seton Hall University

THE GRADUATE FACULTY AND THEIR RESEARCH

Mary MacAleer Balkun, Ph.D., NYU. Early American literature, African American literature, women's studies.
Martha C. Carpentier, Ph.D., Fordham. Modern British literature, feminist theory.
Karen Bloom Gevirtz, Ph.D., Emory. Eighteenth-century literature, women's studies, the rise of the novel.
Jeffrey Gray, Ph.D., California, Riverside. Modern and contemporary poetry, post-colonial literature, literary theory.
Chrysanthy M. Grieco, Ph.D., Drew. Shakespeare, drama, nineteenth-century literature.
Edmund Jones, Ph.D., NYU. Composition theory.
James R. Lindroth, Ph.D., NYU. American literature, 1900–present; film studies.
Kelly Shea, Ph.D., Pennsylvania. Creative nonfiction, composition theory.
John Wargacki, Ph.D., NYU. Hart Crane, American poetry and literature in spirituality.
Angela Jane Weisl, Ph.D., Columbia. Chaucer, medieval literature, women's studies.
Leigh Winser, Ph.D., Columbia. Milton, Renaissance nondramatic literature, Shakespeare.

SEWANEE: THE UNIVERSITY OF THE SOUTH

Sewanee School of Letters

Programs of Study

Sharing quarters with *The Sewanee Review,* the nation's oldest continuously published literary quarterly, and the Sewanee Writers' Conference, perhaps its premiere summer literary gathering, the Sewanee School of Letters allows students to earn an M.A. in English and American literature or an M.F.A. in creative writing through summer study. The degrees can be completed in five summers (four if the thesis is written elsewhere), with classes taken in June and July. With a distinguished faculty from Sewanee and other universities, these master's programs offer small class sizes in a friendly and intimate atmosphere.

Completion of the M.F.A. requires 10 course credits. Four of these are earned in writing workshops and four in classes on literary criticism and history, which should come from both the British and American sides and cover several literary periods. Students earn their final 2 credits by submitting a thesis—a manuscript of poetry, fiction, or creative nonfiction. Students at the thesis level may do their work at home, corresponding with their thesis advisers. M.A. students must complete 10 course credits, including courses in both English literature (one course must be Shakespeare) and American literature (one course must cover literature written before 1900). In addition, students are expected to take one class in non-English literature in translation. They can earn their final 2 credits either with a thesis or with additional course work.

Courses offered in the program to date include Classical Literature in Translation, Bible as Literature, Spenser, Shakespeare, Seventeenth Century English Poetry, British Romanticism, The American Renaissance, Modern British Poetry, Modern American Poetry, American Poetry and the Environment, Faulkner, Literature of the American South, African American Literature, American Environmental Literature and Ecocriticism, Contemporary American Poetry, Workshop in Poetry Writing, Workshop in Fiction Writing, and Workshop in Creative Nonfiction.

Research Facilities

The Jessie Ball duPont Library serves as the hub for access to an enormous array of information resources. The building houses the University's collection of 676,000 print volumes; 293,000 microforms; 6,900 records, tapes, and CDs; and more than 8,000 videocassettes and DVDs. As the oldest federal document depository in the state, beginning in 1873, the library contains 350,000 government publications. In addition to more than 2,500 print periodical subscriptions, the library also provides access to 261 online research databases and more than 18,000 electronic journals. Reference librarians provide all levels of assistance, from brief reference questions to in-depth research guidance.

Academic Technology Services is also located in the library building. There are more than fifty networked computers, many with advanced multimedia capabilities, available for student use. Other Academic Technology Services facilities housed in the library include three computer classrooms, a screening room for video, and a digital video-editing lab. With a renovation completed in 2005, the Gailor Center for Literature and Languages is home to Sewanee Writers' Conference, the Sewanee Young Writers' Conference, and *The Sewanee Review.*

Financial Aid

Summer 2009 prospective graduate students applying for need-based assistance must complete the 2008–09 version of the Free Application for Federal Student Aid (FAFSA), which initiates the process to determine whether a student is eligible for the federally funded Stafford Student Loan Program.

Cost of Study

For summer 2008, tuition and fees were $4185.

Living and Housing Costs

Students who request campus housing stay in Humphreys Hall, the newest and nicest of Sewanee's dorms. Completed in 2003, it consists of comfortable, air-conditioned suites. Students take their meals in McClurg Dining Hall, completed in 2000. Room and board total $1605.

Student Group

Students in the program include teachers, lawyers, doctors, journalists, clerics, business people, and college professors. They hail from all sections of the United States and range in age from their twenties to their seventies. The program maintains a total enrollment of fewer than 100 students, with a 1:5 teacher-student ratio.

Location

The University sits atop the Cumberland Plateau in Tennessee. Sewanee's physical environment, which includes a 10,000-acre campus (known as the Domain), provides an unparalleled place in which to study and reflect and has, over its history, become a meeting place for some of America's most respected literary figures. The Domain offers excellent hiking, biking, caving, and other recreational activities. Several sports camps and clinics for children and adults, run by the University's athletic department, also operate in the summer. The University is located near I-24, 50 miles northwest of Chattanooga and 90 miles southeast of Nashville.

The University

Known simply as "Sewanee," the University offers an unmatched educational experience that is characterized by serious intellectual engagement between its teachers and students. Sewanee graduates have enjoyed a large measure of success. The current editors of both *Newsweek* and *Harper's,* 25 Rhodes scholars, and numerous professionals in business, medicine, law, and politics all trace their formative years back to Sewanee. Sewanee: The University of the South is accredited by the Southern Association of Colleges and Schools.

Applying

Prospective students should submit the completed application form; a writing sample, which should include eight to ten pages of poems or 15 to 25 pages of fiction or creative nonfiction for M.F.A. candidates or 15 to 25 pages of critical prose from one or more essays for M.A. students; the $40 nonrefundable application fee; two letters of recommendation; and official transcripts from all colleges and graduate schools previously attended. Applications should be submitted by the end of January but are accepted until the entering class fills.

Correspondence and Information

Meg Binnicker, Coordinator
Sewanee School of Letters
Sewanee: The University of the South
735 University Avenue
Sewanee, Tennessee 37383

Phone: 931-598-1636
Fax: 931-598-3303
E-mail: sletters@sewanee.edu
Web site: http://www.sewanee.edu/SL/SLHome.htm

Sewanee: The University of the South

THE FACULTY

A distinguished faculty, from Sewanee and other institutions, is assembled each summer for this program. Faculty who have taught in the program include these scholars and writers:

Writing Faculty
Michael Griffith, University of Cincinnati.
Andrew Hudgins, Ohio State University.
Charles Martin, Syracuse University.
Erin McGraw, Ohio State University.
Ellen Slezak.
John Jeremiah Sullivan, University of North Carolina, Wilmington.

Literature Faculty
Ann Jennalie Cook, Vanderbilt University.
John Ernest, West Virginia University.
Angus Fletcher, City University of New York.
John Gatta, University of the South.
Anne Goodwyn Jones, University of Mississippi.
Jennifer Lewin, Boston University.
Lawrence Lipking, Northwestern University.
Kelly Malone, University of the South.
Christopher McDonough, University of the South.

SOUTHERN ILLINOIS UNIVERSITY CARBONDALE

Department of English
Ph.D. in English

Programs of Study

The Doctor of Philosophy degree (Ph.D.) in English at Southern Illinois University Carbondale (SIUC) prepares graduates for careers in the field of higher education as scholars and educators, with course work, qualifying examinations, and dissertations in the full range of literary areas, including critical theory, cultural studies, and rhetoric and composition.

Students benefit from a wide range of specializations, including medieval and Renaissance literature, British literature (eighteenth, nineteenth, and twentieth centuries), American literature (nineteenth century and modern), literary theory, cultural studies, gender studies, writing studies, and popular culture.

The Department of English also maintains a highly regarded Irish and Irish immigration studies program that is complemented by Morris Library's special collections of internationally recognized manuscript and archival holdings and that affords graduate students the opportunity for study abroad at the University College, Galway.

The Ph.D. program is designed as a four- to five-year program for full-time students. Its residency requirement is satisfied by completion of 24 semester hours of graduate credit before the qualifying examinations followed by 24 semester hours of dissertation credit. The doctoral program maintains a research-tool requirement consisting of two foreign languages or one foreign language and course work in a field of study directly related to the dissertation. The doctoral student's course work is developed in consultation with an advisory committee to suit his or her particular needs. Qualifying examinations cover one major and two minor areas of study as chosen by the student in consultation with the committee. Upon successful completion of the examinations, the student is advanced to candidacy and proceeds directly to the dissertation prospectus and writing the dissertation. Once the dissertation is completed, the student presents an oral defense of the dissertation before the committee, including any designated outside readers. A successful defense means that the student has completed all requirements for the Ph.D. degree.

Research Facilities

SIUC's Morris Library contains more than 2.5 million volumes, 3 million microfilms, and more than 12,000 current serial subscriptions. Library users have electronic access to a statewide automated catalog system and nearly 600 electronic data files and CD-ROM products via workstations located throughout the building. The library's special collections are extensive in areas pertinent to graduate students and research and include papers, manuscripts, letters, and research materials in American and British expatriate literature; twentieth-century philosophy, especially John Dewey and the Open Court press; the Irish literary renaissance; literary modernism, with an especially strong collection of James Joyce materials; and proletariat theater. The Humanities Library is particularly rich in both traditional and contemporary monographs and periodicals.

Financial Aid

SIUC offers a number of competitive fellowships to full-time graduate students. Awards are made by the Graduate School on the recommendation of the Graduate Studies Committee. For further information, students should contact the Graduate School. The deadline for applicants for fellowships is usually one month earlier than the deadline for graduate assistantships. Almost all M.F.A. students hold graduate assistantships that provide stipends for the academic year and full remission of tuition. The application deadline for admission with assistantship support is early February, with student notification before April 1.

Cost of Study

In-state graduate tuition is $313.90 per credit hour in 2008–09. Out-of-state tuition is 2.5 times the in-state tuition rate ($784.75 per credit hour). Graduate students with at least a 25 percent appointment as a graduate assistant receive a tuition scholarship. Fees vary from $511.26 (1 credit hour) to $1416.05 (12 credit hours). Students with a graduate assistantship receive a 25 percent reduction in the Primary Care Medical Fee.

Living and Housing Costs

For married couples, students with families, and single graduate students, the University has 690 efficiency and one-, two-, three-, and four-bedroom apartments that rent for $484 to $686 per month in 2008–09. Residence halls for single graduate students are also available, as are accessible residence hall rooms and apartments for students with disabilities.

Student Group

The University's total enrollment exceeds 21,000, including more than 4,000 graduate students. Men and women come from all 50 states and more than 100 other countries. About 53 percent of the graduate students are women, 23 percent are international, and 13 percent are members of American minority groups.

Location

SIUC is 350 miles south of Chicago and 100 miles southeast of St. Louis. Nestled in rolling hills bordered by the Ohio and Mississippi Rivers and enhanced by a mild climate, the area has state parks, national forests and wildlife refuges, and large lakes for outdoor recreation. Cultural offerings include theater, opera, concerts, art exhibits, and cinema. Educational facilities for the families of students are excellent.

The University

Southern Illinois University Carbondale is a comprehensive public university with a variety of general and professional education programs. The University offers bachelor's, associate, master's, and doctoral degrees; the J.D. degree; and the M.D. degree. The University is fully accredited by the North Central Association of Colleges and Schools. The Graduate School has an essential role in the development and coordination of graduate instruction and research programs. The Graduate Council has academic responsibility for determining graduate standards, recommending new graduate programs and research centers, and establishing policies to facilitate the research effort. Southern Illinois University Carbondale is a state-funded university founded in 1869.

Applying

Applicants to the Ph.D. program must complete all forms in the application package, including a separate application for admission to the Graduate School, a nonrefundable processing fee of $40, three letters of recommendation, a statement of purpose, and a writing sample. International students must submit TOEFL scores and a statement showing sufficient financial support at the time of application. The minimum GPA required for admission to SIUC's Graduate School is 2.7, out of 4.0.

Application materials for admission, including graduate assistantship support, are available from the Department of English. Application material is also available online at the Departmental Web site. Separate application forms for fellowships are available from the Graduate School.

Correspondence and Information

Michael R. Molino, Director of Graduate Studies
Graduate Studies in English
Department of English
Southern Illinois University Carbondale
Carbondale, Illinois 62901-4503

Phone: 618-453-6894
E-mail: gradengl@siu.edu
Web site: http://www.siu.edu/departments/english

Southern Illinois University Carbondale

THE FACULTY AND THEIR RESEARCH

Michael L. Humphries, Associate Professor and Chair; Ph.D., Claremont, 1990. Classical literature, mythology and folklore, biblical literature.
Mark Addison Amos, Associate Professor; Ph.D., Duke, 1994. Middle English literature and culture, continental medieval literature, issues of representation, gender studies.
David J. Anthony, Associate Professor; Ph.D., Michigan, 1998. Nineteenth-century American literature; studies of emotion, race, and mass culture.
Mary L. Bogumil, Assistant Professor; Ph.D., South Florida, 1988. Modern and contemporary British and American drama and fiction, multiculturalism.
George Boulukos, Assistant Professor; Ph.D., Texas at Austin, 1998. Eighteenth-century British literature.
Edward J. Brunner, Professor; Ph.D., Iowa, 1974. Modern American literature, twentieth-century poetry.
Anne Chandler, Associate Professor; Ph.D., Duke, 1995. Eighteenth-century English literature, the novel.
Jane N. Cogie, Associate Professor and Director, Writing Center; Ph.D., Iowa, 1984. Rhetoric and composition.
K. K. Collins, Associate Professor; Ph.D., Vanderbilt, 1976. Nineteenth-century English literature.
Kevin J. H. Dettmar, Professor; Ph.D., UCLA, 1990. Twentieth-century English literature.
Ronda L. Dively, Associate Professor and Director, Undergraduate Studies; D.A., Illinois State, 1994. Rhetoric and composition, English education.
Jane Dougherty, Assistant Professor; Ph.D., Tufts, 2001. Irish studies.
Charles F. Fanning, Professor and Director, Irish and Irish Immigration Studies; Ph.D., Pennsylvania, 1972. Twentieth-century poetry, Irish literature, immigration and ethnicity studies.
Robert Elliott Fox, Professor; Ph.D., SUNY at Buffalo, 1976. American literature, African and African American literature, science fiction.
Rodney Jones, Professor; M.F.A., North Carolina at Greensboro, 1973. Poetry writing.
Judy Jordan, Assistant Professor; M.F.A., Utah, 2000; M.F.A., Virginia, 1995. Creative writing, poetry.
Allison E. Joseph, Associate Professor; M.F.A., Indiana, 1992. Poetry writing.
Elizabeth Klaver, Professor; Ph.D., California, Riverside, 1990. Modern American literature, postmodernism, drama, literary theory.
Mary E. Lamb, Professor; Ph.D., Columbia, 1975. Renaissance literature, feminist and gender studies.
E. Beth Lordan, Professor and Assistant to the Chair; M.F.A., Cornell, 1987. Fiction writing.
Michael Magnuson, Associate Professor and Director, Creative Writing; M.F.A., Florida, 1997. Fiction writing.
Lisa J. McClure, Associate Professor; D.A., Michigan, 1988. Rhetoric and composition.
Scott J. McEathron, Associate Professor; Ph.D., Duke, 1993. Nineteenth-century English literature.
Michael R. Molino, Associate Professor and Director, Graduate Studies; Ph.D., 1986. Twentieth-century British and Irish literature.
R. Gerald Nelms, Associate Professor; Ph.D., Ohio State, 1990. Rhetoric and composition, linguistics, oral history.
Ryan Netzley, Assistant Professor; Ph.D., Penn State, 2002. Milton, seventeenth-century British literature.
Anita R. Riedlinger, Associate Professor; Ph.D., NYU, 1985. Old and middle English literature.
Jeremy Wells, Assistant Professor; Ph.D., Michigan, 2000. Nineteenth-century American literature, Southern literature.
Clarisse Zimra, Associate Professor; Ph.D., Washington (Seattle), 1974. Literary theory, continental and Caribbean literature.

STONY BROOK UNIVERSITY, STATE UNIVERSITY OF NEW YORK

Department of Comparative Literary and Cultural Studies
M.A. and Ph.D.

Programs of Study

The Department of Comparative Literary and Cultural Studies (CLCS) offers an M.A. and a Ph.D. in Comparative Literature and a Ph.D. in Cultural Studies. The two programs are distinct, with different requirements. Applicants must specify which program they are applying to, but students in one program may include the other as a primary field of study. Complete information about faculty members, current students, requirements, and courses is available on the Department's Web site.

The Department supports innovative work in comparative literature, literary and cultural theory, and cultural studies. The Department prides itself on the linguistic, cultural, and scholarly range of its faculty and student cohort.

Ph.D. students take an array of courses in cultural studies and comparative literature as well as electives in literature, film, theory, and other comparative fields across a range of departments in the humanities and the social sciences. In certain cases, students may also take seminars at Columbia, CUNY Graduate Center, Fordham, The New School, NYU, Princeton, and Rutgers. This consortium exists to enable advanced doctoral students in the arts and sciences to take courses unavailable at their home institutions. Stony Brook students participating in IUDC pay tuition only to Stony Brook University.

Advanced students have the opportunity to present their work in the Interdepartmental Student/Faculty Colloquium Series, which was established by graduate students in the Department, and at Stony Brook's yearly Graduate Student Conference. Doctoral candidates also present their work at major conferences and have published an impressive array of articles in professional journals. The Department also welcomes visiting scholars from research centers around the world.

The Master's Program in Comparative Literature is designed for students who seek only an M.A. degree. Master's students take a total of 30 credits of graduate courses, including the history of literary theory, comparative literature methodology, and three electives, in addition to work in foreign languages.

Research Facilities

The Graduate Program in Comparative Literature works in close collaboration with Humanities Institute at Stony Brook (HISB), an internationally known center for interdisciplinary humanities and social science research. HISB sponsors Visiting Fellows, who offer public lectures as well as seminars that allow students to engage the fellows in a more sustained fashion. Recent visiting fellows include Dipesh Chakrabarty, Paul Gilroy, Judith Halberstam, Michael Hardt, and N. Katherine Hayles. In addition, HISB designs graduate seminars and cosponsors events with local community organizations.

The Frank Melville, Jr. Memorial Library, a member of the Association of Research Libraries, is a center for research and study with over 2.1 million books, 4 million publications in microformat, and more than 6000 VHS video titles and DVDs. It provides access to hundreds of databases and over 10,000 electronic journals.

Financial Aid

CLCS is committed to supporting admitted students with teaching assistantships. Stony Brook's Graduate School supports teaching assistants for a full four years, and the Department systematically arranges opportunities for continued support beyond the fourth year in the form of adjunct teaching. Typically, advanced students teach free-standing sections of undergraduate courses, enhancing their teaching experience before entering the job market. There are also several nonteaching Graduate Assistantships available to advanced students. The Graduate School also provides two competitive fellowships for U.S. citizens and permanent residents. Graduate Council fellowships are for outstanding doctoral candidates studying in any discipline, and W. Burghardt Turner Fellowships target outstanding African-American, Hispanic American, and Native American students entering either a doctoral or master's degree program. For doctoral students, both fellowships provide an annual stipend of at least $18,572 for up to five years, as well as a full-tuition scholarship. For master's students, the Turner Fellowship provides an annual stipend of $10,000 for up to two years, along with a full tuition scholarship. Health insurance subsidies are also provided within a scale, depending on the size of the fellow's dependent family.

Cost of Study

In 2008–09, full-time tuition at 12 credits for entering in-state residents is $3450 per semester, while out-of-state residents and international students pay $5460. Additional fees for each semester, including (but not limited to) the infirmary, activity, technology, and transportation fees, total about $875. International students also pay a service fee of approximately $35 per semester and an orientation fee of $50. Fees for the mandatory Student Health Insurance Plan vary depending on citizenship and employment status.

Living and Housing Costs

For 2008–09, Stony Brook calculates the cost of education excluding tuition, fees, and insurance at $14,228 per year. On-campus apartments range in cost from approximately $336 per month to approximately $1456 per month, depending on the size of the unit and the number of students sharing the space. Off-campus housing options include rooms, houses, and apartments that can be rented from approximately $350 to $2500 per month. Costs including books, food, and transportation may vary depending on academic program and/or personal circumstances.

Student Outcomes

Over the past ten years, graduates of Stony Brook's programs in comparative literature and cultural studies have been very successful in securing tenure-track appointments at major colleges and universities. Teacher training and experience, coupled with the highest research standards and a supportive and collegial departmental culture, contribute to the students' success.

Location

Stony Brook's campus is approximately 50 miles east of Manhattan on the North Shore of Long Island. The cultural offerings of New York City and Suffolk County's countryside and seashore are conveniently located nearby.

The University

The University, established in 1957, achieved national and international stature within a generation. Founded in Oyster Bay, Long Island, the school moved to its present location in 1962. Stony Brook has grown to encompass more than 110 buildings on 1,100 acres. There are more than 1,568 faculty members, and the annual budget is more than $805 million. The Graduate Student Organization oversees the spending of the student activity fee for graduate student campus events. International students find the additional four-week Summer Institute in American Living to be very helpful. The Intensive English Center offers classes in English as a second language. The Career Development Office assists with career planning and has information on permanent full-time employment. Disabled Student Services has a resource center that offers placement testing, tutoring, vocational assessment, and psychological counseling. The Counseling Center provides individual, group, family, and marital counseling and psychotherapy. Day-care services are provided in four on-campus facilities. The Writing Center offers tutoring in all phases of writing.

Applying

Applicants must hold a Bachelor of Arts (B.A.) or equivalent degree from an accredited college or university, with a good overall GPA and a high average in a major field. Applicants should also have a good command of at least one foreign language. Graduate application can be completed online at http://www.grad.sunysb.edu/prospective/applying/index.shtml and must be accompanied by three letters of academic recommendation, Graduate Record Examinations (GRE) scores, two term or research papers, an application fee of $60, and two official copies of all previous college transcripts. Transcripts of both undergraduate and graduate work must be submitted; if a student attended a junior college whose credits and grades are not listed on the senior college transcript, a separate junior college transcript is required. International students must submit certified English translations of transcripts. In addition, international students must demonstrate proficiency in English with a score of 550 or better on the Test of English as a Foreign Language (TOEFL), submit a cassette demonstrating their ability to speak English, and submit an international student financial affidavit.

Correspondence and Information

Robert Harvey
Department of Comparative Literary and Cultural Studies
Stony Brook University
Stony Brook, New York 11794-5355

Phone: 631-632-7460
Fax: 631-632-5707
Web site: http://www.stonybrook.edu/complit/new/index.html

Stony Brook University, State University of New York

THE FACULTY AND THEIR RESEARCH

Ruth B. Bottigheimer, Adjunct Professor; D.A., SUNY at Stony Brook, 1981. Tale collections, children's literature, fairy tales, sociocultural analysis of literature.
Lou Charnon-Deutsch, Professor of Hispanic Languages and Literatures; Ph.D., Chicago, 1978. Eighteenth- and nineteenth-century Spanish Peninsular literature, feminist theory.
William C. Chittick, Professor of Asian and Asian American Studies and Comparative Literary and Cultural Studies; Ph.D., Tehran, 1973. Sufism, Islamic thought, Persian literature, Arabic literature, Islam in India, comparative mysticism.
Themis Chronopoulos, Assistant Professor of History; Ph.D., Brown, 2004. Urban history, race and ethnicity, popular culture, public policy.
Helen Cooper, Associate Professor of English; Ph.D., Rutgers, 1982. Nineteenth-century British Colonial studies, postcolonial theory and literatures.
Lisa Diedrich, Associate Professor of Women's Studies; Ph.D., Emory, 2001. Feminist cultural studies of health and illness, disability studies, global feminisms, feminist theories and methodologies.
Christa Erickson, Associate Professor of Art; M.F.A., California, San Diego, 1995. Electronic installation, digital media, video art.
Krin Gabbard, Professor of Comparative Literary and Cultural Studies; Ph.D., Indiana, 1979. Film theory and history; jazz; interrelations of literature, art, music, and film; psychoanalytic approaches to the arts; ancient Greek literature.
Raiford Guins, Assistant Professor; Ph.D., Leeds (England), 2000. Popular culture and subculture, video games, technoculture and ethnicity, governmentality and control, media regulation, horror and exploitation films, cinema exhibition, visual culture, material culture.
Robert Harvey, Professor of French, Philosophy, and Comparative Literary and Cultural Studies and Chair of CLCS; Ph.D., Berkeley, 1988. Twentieth-century and contemporary literature in French and English, critical theory, film, relations between philosophy and literature.
Victoria Hesford, Lecturer in Women's Studies; Ph.D., Emory, 2001. Feminist cultural studies, American feminist histories and theory, queer histories and theory, media studies, post-1945 English and American literatures.
Young-Sun Hong, Associate Professor of History; Ph.D., Michigan, 1989. Social and cultural history of modern Germany and Europe; transnational and postcolonial studies; race and gender; medicine and the body; citizenship, state formation, and civil society.
Don Ihde, Professor of Philosophy; Ph.D., Boston University, 1964. Phenomenology and hermeneutics, philosophy of science, philosophy of technology, science studies.
Izabela Kalinowska-Blackwood, Assistant Professor of Slavic Languages and Literatures; Ph.D., Yale, 1995. Russian and Polish literature, culture, and film.
E. Ann Kaplan, Professor of English and Comparative Literary and Cultural Studies and Director of the Humanities Institute; Ph.D., Rutgers, 1970. Contemporary theory regarding film, literature, and popular culture; psychoanalysis and postmodernism; gender and cultural studies.
Shirley Jennifer Lim, Assistant Professor of History; Ph.D., UCLA, 1998. U.S. racial minority women's cultural history.
John Lutterbie, Associate Professor of Theatre Arts; Ph.D., Washington (Seattle), 1983. Performance theory, history and theory of theater.
Iona Man-Cheong, Associate Professor of History, Ph.D., Yale, 1991. Chinese history, culture, and society, particularly Qing Dynasty; women, gender, and sexuality in China.
Peter Manning, Professor of English, Ph.D., Yale, 1968. British Romanticism, psychoanalytic criticism, material histories of the book.
Celia Marshik, Associate Professor of English; Ph.D., Northwestern, 1999. Twentieth-century British literature, modernism, cultural studies, feminist studies.
Eduardo Mendieta, Associate Professor of Philosophy; Ph.D., New School for Social Research, 1996. Global ethics, modernity, postmodernity, post colonialism, Latin American philosophy, biophilosophy, race theory.
Clyde Lee Miller, Professor of Philosophy; Ph.D., Yale, 1974. Ancient and medieval philosophy, Nicholas of Cusa, ethics.
Adrienne Munich, Professor of Women's Studies and English; Ph.D., CUNY, 1976. Victorian cultural studies, feminist theory, popular culture.
Sachiko Murata, Associate Professor of Asian and Asian American Studies and Comparative Literary and Cultural Studies; Ph.D.; Tehran, 1971. Islamic law, Persian literature, feminine spirituality, Islamic thought, Japanese religions, Confucianism and Taoism.
Patrice Nganang, Assistant Professor of Comparative Literary and Cultural Studies; Ph.D., Johann Wolfgang Goethe (Germany), 1998. Postcolonial theory, media theory, cinema and colonialism, German literature and philosophy, African literature.
Adrian Pérez-Melgosa, Visiting Assistant Professor of Hispanic Languages and Literatures and Comparative Literary and Cultural Studies; Ph.D., Rochester, 1995. Cinema and the novel in the Americas; cultural studies.
Sandy Petrey, Professor of French and Comparative Literary and Cultural Studies; Ph.D., Yale, 1966. Nineteenth-century fiction, theories of the novel, contemporary criticism.
Ilona N. Rashkow, Associate Professor Emerita of Comparative Literary and Cultural Studies, Judaic Studies, and Women's Studies; Ph.D., Maryland, 1988. Literature and politics, modern theoretical approaches to the Hebrew Bible, Renaissance literature.
Mary C. Rawlinson, Associate Professor of Philosophy; Ph.D., Northwestern, 1978. Nineteenth-century philosophy, especially Hegel; aesthetics and philosophy of literature; philosophy of medicine.
Jacqueline Reich, Associate Professor of Italian; Ph.D., Berkeley, 1994. European languages, literatures and cultures; film theory and history; gender studies.
Nicholas Rzhevsky, Professor of Slavic Languages and Literatures; Ph.D., Princeton, 1972. Nineteenth- and twentieth-century Russian literature, Russian literature and ideology, Russian literature and theater, ideology, critical theory, history of the novel.
Susan Scheckel, Associate Professor of English; Ph.D., Berkeley, 1992. American literature.
Hugh J. Silverman, Professor of Philosophy; Ph.D., Stanford, 1973. Contemporary literary/art/film/cultural theory, Continental philosophy, and criticism; interdisciplinary studies in philosophy, literature, and culture; history of literary and aesthetic theory; the philosophical essay.
E. K. Tan, Assistant Professor of Comparative Literary and Cultural Studies; Ph.D., Illinois at Urbana-Champaign, 2007. Chinese literature and film, Asian diaspora studies, psychoanalysis, cultural translation, film and critical theory.
Andrew V. Uroskie, Assistant Professor of Art History and Criticism; Ph.D., Berkeley, 2005. Late modern and contemporary art, experimental film and video, theories of photography, psychoanalysis, continental aesthetics.
Louise O. Vásvari, Professor Emerita of Comparative Literary and Cultural Studies; Ph.D., Berkeley, 1969. Medieval literature, literature and folklore, literature and linguistics, translation theory, Romance philology, semiology, art and literature, sexuality and literature.
Kathleen Vernon, Associate Professor of Hispanic Languages; Ph.D., Chicago, 1982. Spanish and Latin American cinema, Hispanic literature and popular culture.
Milind Wakankar, Assistant Professor of English; Ph.D., Columbia, 2002. Derrida and Spivak on ethics, South Asian interpretive traditions in the Indo-Islamic millennium, Levinas on language, the political thought of Partha Chatterjee, Weimer cultural critique.
Tracey Walters, Assistant Professor of Africana Studies and English; Ph.D., Howard, 1999. African-American literature; Black-British literature and culture.
Kathleen Wilson, Professor of History; Ph.D., Yale, 1985. Eighteenth- and nineteenth-century British cultural history.

STONY BROOK UNIVERSITY, STATE UNIVERSITY OF NEW YORK

Department of English
Master of Arts and Ph.D. in English

Programs of Study

The Master of Arts (M.A.) program offers courses in historical periods, literary genres, and various single authors. The program leads to a Master of Arts degree and requires 30 credits for completion. Students enrolled in the Ph.D. program pursue a course of study that is designed, in large part, around individual interests that move from a broad-based survey to a more narrowly focused specialization. Eleven courses are required of each student, including the Discipline of Literary Studies, which must be taken during the first fall semester of study. Students select their remaining courses in consultation with faculty advisers. These courses are intended to strengthen the student's literary background and theoretical knowledge, and further define chosen areas of inquiry. To accommodate the latter goal, students may take courses in different departments. An M.A.T. in English 7–12 is available through the School of Professional Development. Certificates in women's studies, composition studies, and cultural studies are also available.

Research Facilities

Research support is provided by the Frank Melville, Jr. Memorial Library, which holds more than 2 million volumes, 3 million publications in microformat, and numerous full-text databases. Computers in the library, the Division of Information Technology, and in other academic departments are available for general research use. E-mail and Internet accounts are provided to all full-time students.

Financial Aid

Because Stony Brook is committed to attracting high-quality students, the Graduate School provides two competitive fellowships for U.S. citizens and permanent residents. Graduate Council Fellowships are for outstanding doctoral candidates studying in any discipline, and the W. Burghardt Turner Fellowships target outstanding African-American, Hispanic American, and Native American students entering either a doctoral or master's degree program. For doctoral students, both fellowships provide an annual stipend of at least $16,138 for up to five years, as well as a full tuition scholarship. For master's students, the Turner Fellowship provides an annual stipend of $10,000 for up to two years, along with a full tuition scholarship. Health insurance subsidies are also provided within a scale, depending on the size of the fellow's dependent family. Departments and degree programs award approximately 900 teaching and graduate assistantships and approximately 600 research assistantships on an annual basis. Full assistantships carry a stipend of $12,276 for teaching assistants in the Department of English.

Cost of Study

In 2008–09, full-time tuition at 12 credits for entering in-state residents is $3450 per semester, while out-of-state residents and international students pay $5460. Additional fees for each semester, including (but not limited to) the infirmary, activity, technology, and transportation fees, total about $875. International students also pay a service fee of approximately $35 per semester and an orientation fee of $50. Fees for the mandatory Student Health Insurance Plan vary depending on citizenship and employment status. The Department of English fully supports students admitted to the Ph.D. program unless there is a specific request by a student who meets the high admission standards and has sufficient funds to pay for the program.

Living and Housing Costs

For 2008–09, Stony Brook calculates the cost of education excluding tuition, fees, and insurance at $14,228 per year. On-campus apartments range in cost from approximately $336 per month to approximately $1456 per month, depending on the size of the unit and the number of students sharing the space. Off-campus housing options include rooms, houses, and apartments that can be rented from approximately $350 to $2500 per month. Costs including books, food, and transportation may vary depending on academic program and/or personal circumstances.

Location

Stony Brook's campus is approximately 50 miles east of Manhattan on the North Shore of Long Island. The cultural offerings of New York City and Suffolk County's countryside and seashore are conveniently located nearby. Cold Spring Harbor Laboratories and Brookhaven National Laboratories are easily accessible from, and have close relationships with, the University.

The University

The University, established in 1957, achieved national stature within a generation. Founded in Oyster Bay, Long Island, the school moved to its present location in 1962. Stony Brook has grown to encompass more than 110 buildings on 1,100 acres. There are more than 1,568 faculty members. The Graduate Student Organization oversees the spending of the student activity fee for graduate student campus events. The Intensive English Center offers classes in English as a second language. The Career Development Office assists with career planning and has information on permanent full-time employment. Disabled Student Services has a Resource Center that offers placement testing, tutoring, vocational assessment, and psychological counseling. The Counseling Center provides individual, group, family, and marital counseling and psychotherapy. Day-care services are provided in four on-campus facilities. The Writing Center offers tutoring in all phases of writing.

Applying

Applicants for admission to all graduate programs in English should submit all materials by January 15 for fall semester admission. In all cases, admission is determined by the graduate admissions department under the guidelines established by the Graduate School. Applicants are admitted on the basis of their total records, including scores on the Graduate Record Examinations, and there are no predetermined quantitative criteria that by themselves ensure a positive or negative decision. There is spring semester admission to the M.A. program, but not the Ph.D. program. Applicants for spring admission to the M.A. program in English should submit all materials by October 1. For the M.A. program, an applicant must have a bachelor's degree from an accredited institution and an average of at least B for the final two years of undergraduate work and submit a sample of scholarly writing, an official undergraduate transcript, and three letters of recommendation from instructors. A Ph.D. applicant, in addition, must show proficiency in a foreign language equivalent to two years of college work.

Correspondence and Information

Joaquin Martinez-Pizarro
Department of English
Stony Brook University, State University of New York
Stony Brook, New York 11794-4433

Phone: 631-632-7373
Fax: 631-632-1303
E-mail: Joaquin.Martinez-Pizarro@stonybrook.edu
Web site: http://naples.cc.sunysb.edu/CAS/englishweb.nsf/pages/grad

Stony Brook University, State University of New York

THE FACULTY AND THEIR RESEARCH

Bruce Bashford, Associate Professor; Ph.D., Northwestern, 1970. History and theory of criticism, rhetoric and the teaching of writing, the logic of interpretation and critical argument, humanism, Oscar Wilde.
Pat Belanoff, Professor; Ph.D., NYU, 1982. Composition and rhetoric, medieval literature, history of the language.
Helen M. Cooper, Associate Professor; Ph.D., Rutgers, 1982. Nineteenth-century British and colonial studies, twentieth-century Black British literature, Caribbean literature, feminist and postcolonial theory, cultural studies.
Paul J. Dolan, Associate Professor Emeritus; Ph.D., NYU, 1966. Modern British and Irish literature, American poetry.
Patricia A. Dunn, Associate Professor; Doctor of Arts, SUNY at Albany. Rhetoric and composition, English education.
Homer Goldberg, Distinguished Teaching Professor Emeritus; Ph.D., Chicago. Formal analysis of fiction, pedagogy, Restoration and eighteenth-century literature.
Eric Haralson, Associate Professor; Ph.D., Columbia, 1993. Nineteenth- and twentieth-century American literatures, Victorian and modern gender studies, queer theory, poetry, Henry James.
Clifford Huffman, Professor; Ph.D., Columbia, 1969. The Renaissance, Shakespeare.
Heidi Hutner, Associate Professor; Ph.D., Washington (Seattle), 1993. Restoration and eighteenth-century studies, drama, the novel, women writers, feminist theory and criticism, eco-criticism, race studies.
E. Ann Kaplan, Distinguished University Professor and Director of the Humanities Institute; Ph.D., Rutgers, 1970. Nineteenth- and twentieth-century American literature, feminist theory (psychoanalysis and postmodernism), trauma theory, women in film, cultural studies (multiculturalism, popular culture).
Shirley Strum Kenny, Professor and President of the University; Ph.D., Chicago, 1964. Restoration and eighteenth-century British drama.
Jonathan Levy, Distinguished Teaching Professor; Ph.D., Columbia, 1966. Playwriting, translation and adaptation for the stage, theater for children.
Kenneth Lindblom, Associate Professor and Director of English Education; Ph.D., Syracuse. Rhetoric and composition, English education.
Peter J. Manning, Professor; Ph.D., Yale. English Romantic literature, literary theory.
Celia Marshik, Assistant Professor; Ph.D., Northwestern, 1999. Modernism, feminist studies.
Adrienne Munich, Professor; Ph.D., CUNY, 1976. Victorian literature, art, and culture; feminist theory and women's studies.
Stacey Olster, Associate Professor; Ph.D., Michigan. Twentieth-century British and American literature, the novel, popular culture, film.
Rowan Ricardo Phillips, Assistant Professor; Ph.D., Brown, 2002. African-American and Caribbean literature, poetry, poetics.
Joaquín Martínez Pizarro, Professor; Ph.D., Harvard, 1976. Old English and Old Norse, medieval Latin, early medieval narrative, historiography as literature.
Robert Reeves, Professor and Director of Creative Writing; M.A., Harvard, 1977. Creative writing.
Benedict Robinson, Assistant Professor; Ph.D., Columbia, 2001. Renaissance poetry and drama, literature, print culture, and politics; representations of Islam.
Carol Rosen, Professor; Ph.D., Columbia. Dramatic theory and criticism, dramaturgy, comparative modern drama, Tudor and Stuart drama.
Roger Rosenblatt, Professor; Ph.D., Harvard. Creative writing (essays, drama, fiction).
Susan Scheckel, Associate Professor; Ph.D., Berkeley, 1992. Nineteenth-century American literature and culture.
David Sheehan, Associate Professor Emeritus; Ph.D., Wisconsin–Madison, 1974. Late seventeenth-century and eighteenth-century British literature, contemporary Native American literature.
Stephen Spector, Professor and Chair; Ph.D., Yale, 1973. Old and Middle English literature, history of the English language, the Bible, intolerance in medieval literature, Christianity and Judaism, manuscript study and bibliography.
Bente A. Videbaek, Lecturer; Ph.D., Northwestern, 1992. Shakespeare, Renaissance literature.
Milind Wakankar, Assistant Professor; Ph.D., Columbia, 2002. English and comparative literature, postcolonial theory.
Kathleen E. Welch, Professor and Director of the Writing Program; Ph.D., Iowa, 1982. Composition and rhetoric, literacy studies, computers and writing, women's writing and pedagogy.

UNIVERSITY OF CONNECTICUT

Programs in English and Medieval Studies

Programs of Study

The Department of English offers graduate programs in critical theory, criticism, English language and composition theory, and literature leading to the M.A. and Ph.D. degrees. Courses at the 300-level normally involve a broad study of literary schools and topics and are limited to 10 students per course; 400-level seminars are more specialized and are restricted to 8 students per course. Courses of study in comparative literature, medieval studies, American studies, and linguistics are available in cooperation with other departments. In the M.A. program, students complete 15 credits of course work and a thesis (Plan A) or 30 credits and a competency exam based on a specified reading list (Plan B). A 300-level course is provided for instruction in research and up-to-date computerized bibliographic research. Before writing a dissertation, Ph.D. students ordinarily complete 24 credits of full-time course work beyond the M.A. and take a series of preliminary exams in selected literary fields, topics, and authors. The Medieval Studies Program offers course work leading to interdisciplinary M.A. and Ph.D. degrees. Students normally take courses in three cooperating departments—chosen from art, dramatic arts, English, history, modern and classical languages, and philosophy—but select a major emphasis in one. Each year, a visiting professorship gives students access to eminent medievalists, and the Medieval Studies Consortium hosts a conference where students present their research papers.

Research Facilities

The spacious Homer Babbidge Library, with holdings of nearly 2 million volumes, includes a Special Collections Department with notable gatherings of little magazines, early Americana, and contemporary poetry. The Charles Olson archives, the Charles A. Owen Jr. Collection, and the Elizabeth Salter Memorial Collection of visual materials related to medieval studies are also open to researchers. The library currently subscribes to more than 12,000 serial publications and is well supplied with microform materials, including the Early American Imprint series. Advanced graduate students may apply for individual carrels. Among the computer research facilities available in the library is CD-ROM access to the MLA bibliography; the eighteenth-century collections online (ECCO), which provides access to more than 150,000 titles; and new archives in the Thomas J. Dodd Research Center.

Financial Aid

The English Department ordinarily provides four semesters of financial support to students in the M.A. program and ten semesters to those in the Ph.D. program. Financial aid comes in the form of teaching assistantships. Assistantships carry a stipend, which in 2008–09 is $19,098.89 at entry level for nine months, as well as a tuition waiver and medical coverage. Also available are predoctoral fellowships, dissertation fellowships, summer fellowships, work-study funds, need-based awards of tuition remission, and low-interest loans.

Cost of Study

In 2008–09, the estimated cost of registering for 6 credits plus general University fees is $5345 per semester for Connecticut residents and $8274 per semester for out-of-state residents. Tuition is not paid by teaching assistants; however, they pay the full-time University fee of $842.

Living and Housing Costs

During 2008–09, the cost of room and board for students living in a graduate residence hall on campus is $3800 per semester; meal plans are separate. Yearly expenses, including books and travel, for a single student living off campus are about $18,000.

Student Group

The English Department graduate community is made up of students from throughout the United States and abroad, with strong representation from England, Ireland, and India. Currently, more than 30 M.A. students and almost 70 doctoral students are actively enrolled. Of the 21 students who entered in 2008–09, 14 are women. In addition to maintaining their own Student Association, English graduate students are involved in larger departmental affairs as a group and through their representatives on some departmental committees.

Location

The University's main campus at Storrs is pleasantly situated in rural northeastern Connecticut, about 40 minutes from Hartford and within easy reach of Boston, New York, and New Haven. The University sponsors a rich program of cultural events at the Jorgensen Auditorium and the von der Mehden Recital Hall. Located in a picturesque New England region graced with stone walls, forests, and hiking trails, Storrs is nonetheless connected with the greater northeast metropolitan area, including New York, Hartford, and Boston, with their libraries, museums, and cultural facilities.

The University

Connecticut's largest public institution of higher learning was established in 1881 by the state General Assembly and was formally designated the University of Connecticut in 1936. Today the University has a faculty of 1,500 and is the only state-supported institution in Connecticut that awards the Ph.D. The University sponsors graduate work in eighty-three fields. Through its Research Foundation, the Graduate School supports research, travel, colloquia, and fellowships.

Applying

For fall admissions, all applications must be received by January 15. Scores from the verbal portion of the GRE General Test and the Subject Test in literature are required. Candidates are rarely admitted with a GPA below 3.2, or 3.4 in the major field. TOEFL scores are required for international applicants.

Correspondence and Information

Prospective students may request application forms and the Graduate School catalog from the Graduate Admissions Office, Box U-1006, University of Connecticut, Storrs, Connecticut 06269-1006. Applications can also be obtained online at http://www.grad.uconn.edu.

English Department inquiries:
Professor Greg Semenza, Director
Department of English, U-4025
University of Connecticut
215 Glenbrook Road
Storrs, Connecticut 06269-4025
Phone: 860-486-2329
Web site: http://english.uconn.edu/

Medieval Studies inquiries:
Professor Thomas Jambeck, Director
Professor Robert Hasenfratz, Director
Department of English, U-4025
University of Connecticut
215 Glenbrook Road
Storrs, Connecticut 06269-4025
Phone: 860-486-1525
Web site: http://www.medievalstudies.uconn.edu/

University of Connecticut

THE FACULTY AND THEIR RESEARCH

Raymond Anselment, Ph.D., Rochester. Seventeenth-century literature.
Amanda Bailey, Ph.D., Brown. Renaissance, classical, and medieval literature.
Regina Barreca, Ph.D., CUNY Graduate Center. Modern literature, women's literature, comedy.
C. David Benson, Ph.D., Berkeley. Medieval literature: Chaucer.
Frederick Biggs, Ph.D., Cornell. Medieval literature: Old English.
Lynn Bloom, Aetna Professor of Writing; Ph.D., Michigan. Writing and rhetoric, biography and autobiography.
Margaret Breen, Ph.D., Rutgers. Gay and lesbian literature, eighteenth- and nineteenth-century British literature.
Mary Burke, Ph.D., Queen's (Belfast). Irish literature and language.
Kerry Bystrom, Ph.D., Princeton. Postcolonial, world literature in English, literary/critical theory, drama.
Ellen Carillo, Ph.D., Pittsburgh. Pedagogy, composition and rhetoric, literary modernism and criticism, cultural studies.
Ann Charters, Ph.D., Columbia. Twentieth-century American literature: the Beats; short story.
Eleni Coundouriotis, Ph.D., Harvard. Postcolonial literature, African literature.
Martha Cutter, Ph.D., Brown. Ethnic literature, African American studies, women's literature.
Tom Deans, Ph.D., Massachusetts Amherst. Rhetoric, writing, and composition; Renaissance literature.
A. Harris Fairbanks, Ph.D., Berkeley. Nineteenth-century literature: Romantics; autobiography.
Wayne Franklin, Ph.D., Pittsburgh. Early- to nineteenth-century American literature, James Fenimore Cooper.
Sharon Harris, Ph.D., Washington (Seattle). Nineteenth-century U.S. literature, women writers.
F. Elizabeth Hart, Ph.D., Vanderbilt. Renaissance literature: Shakespeare; cognitive theory.
Robert Hasenfratz, Ph.D., Penn State. Medieval literature, English language.
Margaret Higonnet, Ph.D., Yale. Modern and comparative literature, feminist criticism.
Patrick Hogan, Ph.D., SUNY at Buffalo. Critical theory, modern British literature.
Donna Hollenberg, Ph.D., Tufts. Modern poetry, women writers.
Jonathan Hufstader, Ph.D., Columbia. Modern British literature, modern poetry.
Thomas J. Jambeck, Ph.D., Colorado. Medieval literature: drama, Old English; the Bible and literature.
Clare King'oo, Ph.D., Pennsylvania. Late medieval and Renaissance literature, history of material texts.
Kathy Knapp, Ph.D., Fordham. Twentieth-century literature, cultural studies, immigrant literature.
Ellen Litman, M.F.A., Syracuse. Ethnic American literature, the novel, creative writing.
Charles Mahoney, Ph.D., Cornell. Nineteenth-century literature; romanticism and politics.
Veronica Makowsky, Ph.D., Princeton. American literature, Southern literature, and women's literature.
John Manning, Ph.D., Michigan. Renaissance literature: Shakespeare.
Jean Marsden, Ph.D., Harvard. Eighteenth-century literature, drama, women's literature.
Michael Meyer, Ph.D., Connecticut. American literature: Thoreau.
Ross Miller, Ph.D., Cornell. American and comparative literature, architecture.
Brenda Murphy, Ph.D., Brown. American literature, drama.
Marilyn Nelson, Ph.D., Minnesota. Poetry.
Penelope Pelizzon, Ph.D., Missouri. Poetics, creative writing, nineteenth- and twentieth-century visual culture, film studies.
Richard S. Peterson, Ph.D., Berkeley. Renaissance literature: Spenser, Jonson; literature and the arts.
Jerry Phillips, Ph.D., Essex (England). African American literature, African-Caribbean literature.
Samuel Pickering, Ph.D., Princeton. Familiar essay, eighteenth-century literature, children's literature.
Thomas Recchio, Ph.D., Rutgers. Writing and rhetoric.
Shawn Salvant, Ph.D., Berkeley. Nineteenth-century African American literature, nineteenth-century American literature, racial science, literature and science.
Lisa Sanchez Gonzalez, Ph.D., UCLA. American and ethnic literature, women's literature.
Cathy Schlund-Vials, Ph.D., Massachusetts Amherst. Asian American literature, ethnic American literature.
Gregory M. Colón Semenza, Ph.D., Penn State. Renaissance literature: Shakespeare, Milton; cultural history.
Katharine C. Smith, Ph.D., Connecticut. Children's literature, African American literature.
David Sonstroem, Ph.D., Harvard. Nineteenth-century literature: Rossetti, Dickens; the novel.
Robert Tilton, Ph.D., Stanford. American Indian literature, colonial and early national literature, American Romanticism.
Kathleen Tonry, Ph.D., Notre Dame. Rhetoric, late medieval literature, William Caxton, history of the English language.
Roger Wilkenfeld, Ph.D., Rochester. Nineteenth-century literature: Arnold, Milton.
Sarah Winter, Ph.D., Yale. Rhetoric, nineteenth-century literature: Freud, Dickens.

Journals Based in the Department of English
LIT (Literature/Interpretation/Theory). Editor: Regina Barreca.
MELUS (Multi-Ethnic Literature of the United States). Editor: Martha Cutter.
Mystics Quarterly. Editor: Robert Hasenfratz.

UNIVERSITY OF ST. THOMAS

Department of English
Master of Arts Program

Program of Study The Department offers a general Master of Arts program that allows for great flexibility. Students may take courses in English and American literature, multicultural literature, critical theory, women's literature, rhetoric, and writing pedagogy. The program requires 30 semester credits: 12 credits of required courses, 15 credits of electives, and 3 credits for a master's essay.

Research Facilities The University has four libraries that contain more than 815,000 volumes and provide access to 88,000 electronic book titles. The libraries also have over 2,500 current subscriptions to periodicals and allow access to 32,000 electronic titles. In addition to reference and general collections, the O'Shaughnessy-Frey Library Center houses a robust media collection, the Luxembourg Collection, the Celtic Collection (one of the most outstanding of its kind in the country), and a notable Chesterton-Belloc Collection. The Archbishop Ireland Memorial Library, the theology library, is strong in areas ancillary to the study of language and literature. Through Cooperating Libraries in Consortium (CLIC), the University has access to seven other local academic libraries giving access to over 2,000,000 volumes. The CLIC libraries jointly maintain an electronic catalog that can be accessed off campus. CLIC can also access the libraries in four Midwestern states through Minitex. The University also participates in international interlibrary loan systems.

Financial Aid Three full-time and eight part-time fellowships are available for students of exceptional academic promise. The three full-time fellowships, renewable until completion of the degree, provide a tuition waiver and a stipend of $5000 per semester. Students holding full-time fellowships must ordinarily take three courses each semester and maintain a minimum 3.5 GPA. The eight part-time scholarships offer a tuition waiver for one course per semester until completion of the degree. The University of St. Thomas also administers two federal loan programs (Stafford subsidized and unsubsidized loans) and one Minnesota program (SELF). SELF is non-need based. These loan programs are open to full- and part-time students.

Cost of Study Tuition for 2008–09 is $647 per credit for both in-state and out-of-state students. A health-care center provides services for minor illnesses free of charge. Students may purchase medical insurance through the University. Students with a valid ID may use all athletic and other facilities.

Living and Housing Costs Off-campus housing is available within convenient walking distance of the campus.

Student Group The Department enrolls 65 to 70 master's degree students (full-time and part-time) each semester; the student body profile includes a wide range of ages, careers, and goals. Class enrollments are kept low to allow for close faculty-student interaction. Students are invited to participate fully in the intellectual and social life of the Department, which includes a colloquium series, academic conference presentations, and off-campus graduate events. Master's students also have representation on the Graduate Committee.

Location The metropolitan area of St. Paul and Minneapolis regularly ranks at or near the top of the lists of the most desirable cities in the country. The Twin Cities are the home of the renowned Guthrie Theater, two world-class orchestras, The Loft (one of the largest literary centers in the country), several museums, galleries, and more than 100 small, live theaters. Numerous lakes, parks, and recreational areas are within minutes of both downtowns.

The University and The Department Founded in 1885, the University of St. Thomas is a comprehensive, coeducational, Catholic university. Inspired by Catholic intellectual tradition, the University of St. Thomas educates students to be morally responsible leaders who think critically, act wisely, and work skillfully for the common good. More than 10,500 students attend St. Thomas, with slightly more than half at the graduate level. Graduate programs emphasize the integration of theory with practice, enhance the professional competence and ethical judgments of their students, and foster both personal growth and an appreciation of lifelong learning.

The Department of English has 26 full-time faculty members. Two academic journals are edited by the English faculty members and published by the University of St. Thomas: *LOGOS: A Journal of Catholic Thought and Culture* and *New Hibernia Review*.

Applying Requirements for admission are a bachelor's degree, a minimum undergraduate GPA of 3.0, at least five courses beyond the first year or introductory level in language or literature (earning a grade of B or better), three letters of recommendation (at least one must be from a former professor), and a writing sample that demonstrates critical or analytical skills. The application fee is $50. Application deadlines are March 1 for the summer and fall and October 1 for the spring.

Correspondence and Information

Dr. Catherine Craft-Fairchild
Director of Graduate Studies in English
Department of English
University of St. Thomas
Mail #JRC 333
2115 Summit Avenue
St. Paul, Minnesota 55105

Phone: 651-962-5628
800-328-6819 Ext. 2-5628 (toll-free)
Fax: 651-962-5623
E-mail: gradenglish@stthomas.edu
Web site: http://www.stthomas.edu/gradenglish

University of St. Thomas

THE FACULTY

Young-Ok An, Ph.D., USC. Romanticism, eighteenth- and nineteenth-century British literature, literary theory, postcolonialism and cultural critique.

Matthew Batt, Ph.D., Utah. Creative nonfiction, prose writing.

Heather Bouwman, Ph.D., Illinois at Urbana–Champaign. Colonial and early American literature, Native American literature, poetry as genre, American poetry.

Susan Callaway, Ph.D., Wisconsin–Milwaukee; Director, The Center for Writing. Composition theory and pedagogy, writing center theory and administration, writing across the curriculum.

Kanishka Chowdhury, Ph.D., Purdue. Postcolonial literature and theory, world literature, cultural theory.

Catherine Craft-Fairchild, Ph.D., Rochester. Restoration and eighteenth-century British literature, feminist theory, psychoanalysis and film theory, history of the novel.

Alexis Easley, Ph.D., Oregon. Victorian studies, British literature, the novel, literary geography, new historicism, gender studies, media history, multicultural literatures, creative writing, composition theory/pedagogy.

Carmela Garritano, Ph.D., Michigan State. Feminist and postcolonial theory, African and Third World literature and film.

(John) Chris Hallman, M.F.A., Iowa; M.A., Johns Hopkins. Creative nonfiction, prose writing.

Michael C. Jordan, Ph.D., North Carolina at Chapel Hill. Comparative literature, literary theory, Classical Greek literature, philosophical anthropology, history and theory of liberal education.

Paul Lai, M.A., North Carolina at Chapel Hill. Asian American literature, transnational feminist studies, cultural studies.

Kelli Larson, Ph.D., Michigan State. Eighteenth- and nineteenth-century and modern American literature.

(David) Todd Lawrence, Ph.D., Missouri–Columbia. African-American literature and culture, African diasporic studies, folklore and folkloristics, the Black Arts Movement.

Juan Li, Ph.D., Washington (Seattle). Discourse theory and analysis, linguistics and English language study, language and ideology, rhetoric and stylistics.

Raymond MacKenzie, Ph.D., Kansas State. Milton, Nineteenth- and twentieth-century British literature, literary criticism.

Michael Mikolajczak, Ph.D., Wisconsin–Milwaukee. Sixteenth- and seventeenth-century British literature, Shakespeare, Milton, religion and literature, rhetoric.

Leslie Adrienne Miller, Ph.D., Texas at Houston. Contemporary American poetry, rhetorical theory and criticism, British romanticism, medieval literature.

Amy Muse, Ph.D., Auburn. Drama, theater and revolutionary movements, Romanticism, eighteenth- and nineteenth-century literature and theater culture, writing and civic education.

Lon Otto, Ph.D., Indiana. Creative writing, novel since World War II, modern poetry, short story, travel writing, Faulkner.

Joan Piorkowski, Ph.D., Temple. Eighteenth-century British and Gothic literature, basic writing.

Brenda J. Powell, Ph.D., North Carolina at Chapel Hill. Literature by women, mythology, classical literature, multicultural literature.

Thomas Dillon Redshaw, Ph.D., NYU; Senior Fellow, Institute of Irish Studies, Queen's University (Belfast). Modern and contemporary Irish literature, British literature between the wars, seventeenth-century British literature.

Andrew Scheiber, Ph.D., Michigan State; Department Chair. Nineteenth- and twentieth-century American literature, literary criticism, literature and linguistics, women's studies, history of the novel, African-American literature.

Erika Scheurer, Ph.D., Massachusetts Amherst. Composition theory and pedagogy, Dickinson.

Martin Warren, Ph.D., Minnesota. Medieval literature, religion and literature, linguistics, hypertext and literacy.

VILLANOVA UNIVERSITY

Graduate Program in English Language and Literature

Program of Study

Villanova has been granting its master's degree in English language and literature for more than half a century. Villanova weds this sense of history with a keen awareness of the contemporary, interdisciplinary spirit of literary study. The curriculum balances a traditional, historical understanding of literary periods with newer, theoretically based considerations of writing and reading. This range of approaches provides students with expertise in much of the literature written in English, highly refined interpretive skills, and familiarity with the major intellectual currents shaping the discipline of literary study today.

All courses are conducted as small seminars, with a maximum enrollment of 15 students. Course work provides a broad range of study in a variety of areas, and the thesis or field exam provides focus within a particular field. The thesis offers an opportunity for sustained critical examination of a work, author, or topic, while the field examination is taken on a list of works compiled in consultation with the student's adviser within a field of the student's choosing.

To satisfy the requirements for the master's degree, students must complete a minimum of 30 credits, including successful completion of a thesis or an oral/written field examination. Students are expected to take at least one course in British literature before 1800 and another in American literature before 1900. An average grade of at least a B must be maintained to remain in the program. Students usually complete the curriculum in two years, taking two or three courses each semester, but may pursue their studies on a part-time basis, in which case they are allowed a period of six years to earn the degree.

At all stages, the program is deeply committed to the individual student's development and maturation as a literary scholar. Upon matriculation, each student is assigned an adviser, who assists in planning the individual course of study. After successful completion of 9 credits, the student may request an adviser with particular expertise in the student's area of interest.

Research Facilities

The Falvey Memorial Library at Villanova University houses more than 600,000 volumes and 3,000 periodicals. An interlibrary loan system operates with the efficiency of e-mail. Special holdings include the McGarrity and Worthington collections, major resources of literature and periodicals about Irish history, Irish-American relations, and writings by and about James Joyce. The library is located in the middle of the campus and includes numerous public-use computer stations that are equipped with sophisticated search engines and data-retrieval mechanisms.

Financial Aid

Applicants may compete for full financial awards, including tuition remission and a yearly stipend of approximately $13,000, which are renewable for a second year. Tuition scholarships (tuition remission without a stipend) are also offered and are renewable for the second year. The work these awards require ranges from helping individual faculty members with research materials to assisting in the University Writing and Learning Center.

Since classes in the master's program meet in the evenings, students without financial aid are often able to support their graduate study through daytime employment outside the University.

Cost of Study

Fees and expenses for graduate students in 2007–08 were $50 for the application fee, $585 per credit for tuition, and $30 per semester for general University fees.

Living and Housing Costs

A variety of affordable housing possibilities are available near the Villanova University campus. Housing costs vary in accordance with the option chosen. Villanova University does not provide on-campus housing for graduate students.

Student Group

There are usually about 50 students matriculated in the program, and the ratio of men to women is approximately 2:3. While some graduate students are dedicated to becoming professors of English, others are seeking the master's because they want to learn more about the discipline in order to decide whether a Ph.D. is right for them, they wish to advance their careers as teachers of secondary school, or they simply love literature and want to immerse themselves in it. Some students come directly from undergraduate programs, while others have pursued other careers and are returning to school to pursue a lifelong ambition.

Student Outcomes

In recent years, recipients of the master's degree in English from Villanova have been admitted to highly competitive Ph.D. programs, including Harvard, Ohio State, Penn State, Princeton, Rutgers, UCLA, and the Universities of Kansas, Maryland, North Carolina, and Pennsylvania. Others have elected to use the degree to pursue teaching positions at the excellent secondary schools adjacent to the University. Still others have chosen to pursue careers in publishing and other fields, including business and law, which demand the verbal acumen and analytical rigor Villanova's program cultivates.

Location

Villanova is situated on the historic Main Line, in a beautiful western suburb of Philadelphia. Philadelphia offers a wide variety of museums, libraries, concerts, and other cultural opportunities. Home to the greatest variety of eighteenth-century buildings in America, the city is also enjoying a renaissance in modern architecture, restaurants, and the performing arts. By car or train, the campus is only 30 minutes from downtown. It is 2 minutes from the Blue Route (Route 476) and 5 minutes from the Pennsylvania Turnpike, the Schuylkill Expressway, and Route 202. With ample parking and mass transit stops right on campus grounds, students can travel easily to and from the campus by car, bus, or train.

The University and The Department

Founded in 1842 by the friars of the Order of St. Augustine, Villanova is a comprehensive Roman Catholic institution that welcomes students of all faiths. Roughly 10,000 students attend the University, including 6,000 undergraduates and 4,000 graduate students. The Department of English at Villanova includes a number of distinguished critics, whose scholarship has earned them national and international recognition. They are well acquainted with the methods and values of current scholarship in English literature, and they seek equally to deepen the student's acquaintance with these critical discourses and develop each student's individual critical sensibility.

Applying

Villanova typically requires that applicants have at least 18 undergraduate credits and a 3.0 average in English. However, the University occasionally accepts applications from candidates who majored in related fields.

Applicants should send the three letters of recommendation (at least two of which should be from former professors), a writing sample of approximately ten pages, and a one-page personal statement to the Graduate English Program, Department of English, Villanova University, 800 Lancaster Avenue, Villanova, Pennsylvania 19085-1699; they should send the application for admission, the nonrefundable application fee, all official postsecondary transcripts, and the GRE scores from both the General Test and the English Subject Test to the Graduate Studies Office, College of Liberal Arts and Sciences, Villanova University, 800 Lancaster Avenue, Villanova, Pennsylvania 19085-1699. Application forms are available online at Villanova's Graduate School Web site. The deadline for receipt of applications for the fall semester is March 1 and for the spring semester, November 15.

Correspondence and Information

Director of Graduate Studies
Department of English
Villanova University
Villanova, Pennsylvania 19085

Phone: 610-519-7826
Fax: 610-519-6913
E-mail: gradinfo@email.villanova.edu
Web site: http://English.villanova.edu/graduate/index.html

Villanova University

THE FACULTY AND THEIR RESEARCH

Chiji Akoma, Associate Professor; Ph.D., SUNY at Binghamton. Postcolonial literature.
Michael Berthold, Associate Professor; Ph.D., Harvard. Nineteenth-century American literature, slave narrative, American Gothic.
Cristina Maria Cervone, Assistant Professor; Ph.D., Virginia. Medieval studies, poetics, history of the English language.
Charles L. Cherry, Professor; Ph.D., North Carolina. British Romanticism, madness and imagination, history of ideas.
Alice A. Dailey, Assistant Professor; Ph.D., UCLA. Renaissance literature.
Heather Hicks, Associate Professor; Ph.D., Duke. Post–World War II American fiction, postmodern theory, contemporary cultural studies.
Karyn L. Hollis, Associate Professor; Ph.D., USC. Composition studies.
Crystal J. Lucky, Associate Professor; Ph.D., Pennsylvania. African American literature, nineteenth-century African American church history, literary pedagogy.
Jean Lutes, Assistant Professor; Ph.D., Wisconsin–Madison. Modern American fiction.
Lucy McDiarmid, Professor; Ph.D., Harvard. Modern British literature, Irish cultural studies, British and Irish women's writing.
Hugh Ormsby-Lennon, Associate Professor; Ph.D., Pennsylvania. Augustan literature, eighteenth-century cultural studies, eighteenth-century Anglo-Irish literature, literary theory.
Megan Quigley, Assistant Professor; Ph.D., Yale. British and Irish Modernism.
Evan Radcliffe, Associate Professor; Ph.D., Cornell. British Romanticism, the French Revolution controversy, historicism.
Jill Rappaport, Assistant Professor; Ph.D., Virginia. Victorian literature and cultural history.
Lisa Sewell, Associate Professor; Ph.D., Tufts. Contemporary American poetry, poetics.
Lauren E. Shohet, Associate Professor; Ph.D., Brown. Renaissance and seventeenth-century literature, cultural studies, literary theory, gender studies.
Deborah A. Thomas, Professor; Ph.D., Rochester. Victorian literature and culture, Dickens, Thackeray, nineteenth-century British women's writing.

Section 10
Linguistic Studies

This section contains a directory of institutions offering graduate work in linguistic studies, followed by in-depth entries submitted by institutions that chose to prepare detailed program descriptions. Additional information about programs listed in the directory but not augmented by an in-depth entry may be obtained by writing directly to the dean of a graduate school or chair of a department at the address given in the directory.

For programs offering related work, see also in this book *Area and Cultural Studies, Language and Literature,* and *Sociology, Anthropology, and Archaeology.*

CONTENTS

Program Directories

Announcement

Close-Ups

See also:

Linguistics

Arizona State University, Graduate College, College of Liberal Arts and Sciences, Division of Humanities, Department of English, Tempe, AZ 85287. Offers English (MA, PhD), including comparative literature (MA), linguistics (MA), literature (PhD), literature and language (MA), rhetoric and composition (MA), rhetoric/composition and linguistics (PhD); teaching English as a second language (MTESL). *Degree requirements:* For doctorate, thesis/dissertation. *Entrance requirements:* For master's and doctorate, GRE.

Ball State University, Graduate School, College of Sciences and Humanities, Department of English, Program in Linguistics, Muncie, IN 47306-1099. Offers applied linguistics (PhD). *Students:* 16 full-time (10 women), 7 part-time (5 women); includes 1 minority (Asian American or Pacific Islander), 16 international. Average age 24. 14 applicants, 57% accepted, 5 enrolled. Application fee: $25 ($35 for international students). *Expenses:* Tuition, state resident: full-time $6,864. Tuition, nonresident: full-time $17,932. Required fees: $1,866. *Financial support:* Career-related internships or fieldwork and unspecified assistantships available. Financial award application deadline: 3/1. *Faculty research:* Descriptive and theoretical linguistics. *Unit head:* Dr. Deborah Mix, Director of Graduate Programs in English, 765-285-8415, Fax: 765-285-3765.

Biola University, School of Intercultural Studies, La Mirada, CA 90639-0001. Offers applied linguistics (MA); intercultural education (PhD); intercultural studies (MAICS); missiology (D Miss); missions (MA); teaching English to speakers of other languages (MA, Certificate). Part-time and evening/weekend programs available. Terminal master's awarded for partial completion of doctoral program. *Degree requirements:* For master's, one foreign language, comprehensive exam; for doctorate, one foreign language, comprehensive exam, thesis/dissertation. *Entrance requirements:* For master's, minimum undergraduate GPA of 3.0; for doctorate, MA, 3 years of ministry experience, minimum graduate GPA of 3.3. Additional exam requirements/recommendations for international students: Required—TOEFL (minimum score 550 paper-based; 213 computer-based). Electronic applications accepted.

Boston College, Graduate School of Arts and Sciences, Department of Slavic and Eastern Languages, Program in Linguistics, Chestnut Hill, MA 02467-3800. Offers MA, MA/JD, MBA/MA. Part-time programs available. *Degree requirements:* For master's, 3 foreign languages, comprehensive exam, thesis or alternative. *Application deadline:* For fall admission, 1/15 for domestic students. Application fee: $70. Electronic applications accepted. *Financial support:* Application deadline: 3/1.

Boston University, Graduate School of Arts and Sciences, Program in Applied Linguistics, Boston, MA 02215. Offers MA, PhD. Part-time programs available. *Faculty:* 17 full-time (9 women). *Students:* 21 full-time (15 women), 16 part-time (14 women); includes 2 minority (1 African American, 1 Asian American or Pacific Islander), 10 international. Average age 36. 50 applicants, 38% accepted, 8 enrolled. In 2007, 7 master's, 3 doctorates awarded. Terminal master's awarded for partial completion of doctoral program. *Degree requirements:* For master's, one foreign language, project; for doctorate, 2 foreign languages, thesis/dissertation, 1 book review, 2 research papers, oral exam. *Entrance requirements:* For master's and doctorate, GRE General Test. Additional exam requirements/recommendations for international students: Required—TOEFL. *Application deadline:* For fall admission, 1/15 priority date for domestic and international students. Applications are processed on a rolling basis. Application fee: $60. Electronic applications accepted. *Expenses:* Tuition: Full-time $34,930; part-time $1,092 per credit. Tuition and fees vary according to class time, course level and program. *Financial support:* In 2007–08, 16 students received support, including 2 teaching assistantships with full tuition reimbursements available (averaging $16,500 per year); Federal Work-Study, scholarships/grants, and unspecified assistantships also available. Financial award applicants required to submit FAFSA. *Faculty research:* Psycholinguistics, sociolinguistics, neurolinguistics, language acquisition, American Sign Language. Total annual research expenditures: $900,000. *Unit head:* M. Catherine O'Connor, Director, 617-353-3318, Fax: 617-358-2353, E-mail: mco@bu.edu. *Application contact:* Heather Jacob, Program Assistant, 617-353-6197, Fax: 617-353-2353, E-mail: linguist@bu.edu.

Brandeis University, Graduate School of Arts and Sciences, Program in Computational Linguistics, Waltham, MA 02454-9110. Offers MA. *Application contact:* David F. Cotter, Graduate School of Arts and Sciences, 781-736-3406, Fax: 781-736-3412, E-mail: cotter@brandeis.edu.

Brigham Young University, Graduate Studies, College of Humanities, Department of Linguistics and English Language, Provo, UT 84602. Offers general linguistics (MA); teaching English as a second language (MA, Certificate). Part-time programs available. *Faculty:* 18 full-time (3 women). *Students:* 78 full-time (54 women), 27 international. Average age 29. 75 applicants, 60% accepted, 32 enrolled. In 2007, 14 master's, 19 other advanced degrees awarded. *Degree requirements:* For master's, one foreign language, thesis. *Entrance requirements:* For master's, GRE General Test, minimum GPA of 3.6 in last 60 hours of course work. Additional exam requirements/recommendations for international students: Required—TOEFL (minimum score 580 paper-based; 237 computer-based; 90 iBT), TWE. *Application deadline:* 1/15 for domestic and international students. Application fee: $50. Electronic applications accepted. *Financial support:* In 2007–08, 51 students received support, including 1 fellowship with partial tuition reimbursement available (averaging $8,000 per year), 17 research assistantships with partial tuition reimbursements available (averaging $2,286 per year), 11 teaching assistantships with partial tuition reimbursements available (averaging $2,257 per year); career-related internships or fieldwork, institutionally sponsored loans, scholarships/grants, tuition waivers (partial), unspecified assistantships, and student instructorships also available. Support available to part-time students. Financial award application deadline: 3/28. *Faculty research:* Mayan languages, second language acquisition, computational linguistics, semiotics and semantics, computer-assisted language instruction. Total annual research expenditures: $2,500. *Unit head:* Dr. William G. Eggington, Chair, 801-422-2937, Fax: 801-422-0906, E-mail: bill_eggington@byu.edu. *Application contact:* Phyllis Ann Daniel, Secretary, 801-422-2937, Fax: 801-422-0906, E-mail: phyllis_daniel@byu.edu.

Brown University, Graduate School, Department of Cognitive and Linguistic Sciences, Providence, RI 02912. Offers cognitive science (Sc M, PhD); linguistics (AM, PhD). *Degree requirements:* For master's, one foreign language, thesis or alternative; for doctorate, 2 foreign languages, thesis/dissertation.

California State University, Fresno, Division of Graduate Studies, College of Arts and Humanities, Department of Linguistics, Fresno, CA 93740-8027. Offers linguistics (MA), including Teaching English as a second language. Part-time and evening/weekend programs available. *Faculty:* 8 full-time (5 women). *Students:* 31; includes 9 minority (3 Asian Americans or Pacific Islanders, 6 Hispanic Americans), 9 international. Average age 28. In 2007, 10 degrees awarded. *Degree requirements:* For master's, comprehensive exam. *Entrance requirements:* For master's, GRE General Test, minimum GPA of 3.0. Additional exam requirements/recommendations for international students: Required—TOEFL. *Application deadline:* For fall admission, 5/1 for domestic and international students; for spring admission, 10/1 for domestic and international students. Applications are processed on a rolling basis. Application fee: $55. Electronic applications accepted. *Financial support:* Career-related internships or fieldwork, Federal Work-Study, and scholarships/grants available. Support available to part-time students. Financial award application deadline: 3/1; financial award applicants required to submit FAFSA. *Faculty research:* Communication systems, bilingual education, animal communication, conflict resolution, literacy programs. *Unit head:* Dr. Ellen Lipp, Chair, 559-278-2441, Fax: 559-278-7299, E-mail: ellen_lipp@csufresno.edu. *Application contact:* Dr. Brian Agbayani, Graduate Program Coordinator, 559-278-2441, Fax: 559-278-7299, E-mail: bagbayan@csufresno.edu.

California State University, Fullerton, Graduate Studies, College of Humanities and Social Sciences, Program in Linguistics, Fullerton, CA 92834-9480. Offers analysis of specific language structures (MA); anthropological linguistics (MA); applied linguistics (MA); communication and semantics (MA); disorders of communication (MA); experimental phonetics (MA). Part-time programs available. *Students:* 10 full-time (7 women), 12 part-time (9 women); includes 6 minority (2 Asian Americans or Pacific Islanders, 4 Hispanic Americans), 5 international. Average age 33. 21 applicants, 52% accepted, 6 enrolled. In 2007, 8 degrees awarded. *Degree requirements:* For master's, one foreign language, thesis or alternative, project. *Entrance requirements:* For master's, minimum GPA of 3.0, undergraduate major in linguistics or related field. Application fee: $55. *Financial support:* Career-related internships or fieldwork, Federal Work-Study, institutionally sponsored loans, and scholarships/grants available. Support available to part-time students. Financial award application deadline: 3/1. *Unit head:* Dr. Franz Muller-Gotama, Adviser, 714-278-2441.

California State University, Long Beach, Graduate Studies, College of Liberal Arts, Department of Linguistics, Long Beach, CA 90840. Offers MA. Part-time and evening/weekend programs available. *Faculty:* 8 full-time (5 women), 5 part-time/adjunct (2 women). *Students:* 49 full-time (42 women), 38 part-time (27 women); includes 54 minority (3 African Americans, 44 Asian Americans or Pacific Islanders, 7 Hispanic Americans). Average age 34. *Degree requirements:* For master's, one foreign language, comprehensive exam, thesis optional. *Application deadline:* For fall admission, 7/1 for domestic students; for spring admission, 12/1 for domestic students. Applications are processed on a rolling basis. Application fee: $55. Electronic applications accepted. *Financial support:* Teaching assistantships, career-related internships or fieldwork, Federal Work-Study, institutionally sponsored loans, and scholarships/grants available. Financial award application deadline: 3/2. *Faculty research:* Pedagogy of language instruction, role of language in society, Khmer language instruction. *Unit head:* Dr. John J Attinasi, Chair, 562-985-5792, Fax: 562-985-2593, E-mail: jattinas@csulb.edu. *Application contact:* Dr. Malcolm Finney, Graduate Advisor, 562-985-5037, Fax: 562-985-2593, E-mail: mfinney@csulb.edu.

California State University, Northridge, Graduate Studies, College of Humanities, Linguistics Program, Northridge, CA 91330. Offers MA. Part-time and evening/weekend programs available. *Faculty:* 3 part-time/adjunct (all women). *Students:* 20 full-time (18 women), 19 part-time (15 women); includes 7 minority (2 Asian Americans or Pacific Islanders, 5 Hispanic Americans), 8 international. Average age 34. 32 applicants, 63% accepted, 11 enrolled. In 2007, 17 degrees awarded. *Degree requirements:* For master's, one foreign language, comprehensive exam, thesis, or project. *Entrance requirements:* For master's, GRE General Test or minimum GPA of 3.0. Additional exam requirements/recommendations for international students: Required—TOEFL (minimum score 563 paper-based; 223 computer-based; 85 iBT). *Application deadline:* For fall admission, 11/30 for domestic students. Application fee: $55. *Financial support:* Application deadline: 3/1. *Faculty research:* Ethnography of communication, stylistics, natural language processing, linguistics and humor, Otomanguean phonology and reconstruction. *Unit head:* Dr. Sabrina Peck, Coordinator, 818-677-3453, E-mail: sabrina.peck@csun.edu.

Carleton University, Faculty of Graduate Studies, Faculty of Arts and Social Sciences, School of Linguistics and Applied Language Studies, Ottawa, ON K1S 5B6, Canada. Offers applied language studies (MA). *Degree requirements:* For master's, thesis optional. *Entrance requirements:* For master's, honors degree. Additional exam requirements/recommendations for international students: Required—TOEFL or CAEL. *Application deadline:* Applications are processed on a rolling basis. Application fee: $77. *Financial support:* Fellowships, research assistantships, teaching assistantships, institutionally sponsored loans, scholarships/grants, and unspecified assistantships available. *Faculty research:* Language learning, acquisition and use of first and/or second languages in a variety of professional and academic contexts. *Unit head:* Randall Gess, Director, 613-520-2600 Ext. 2802, Fax: 613-520-6641, E-mail: linguistics@carleton.ca. *Application contact:* Devon Woods, Supervisor of Graduate Studies, 613-520-2600 Ext. 2802, Fax: 613-520-6641, E-mail: linguistics@carleton.ca.

Carnegie Mellon University, College of Humanities and Social Sciences, Department of Modern Languages, Pittsburgh, PA 15213-3891. Offers computer-assisted language learning (MCALL); second language acquisition (PhD). *Degree requirements:* For doctorate, one foreign language, comprehensive exam, thesis/dissertation. *Entrance requirements:* For doctorate, GRE General Test. Additional exam requirements/recommendations for international students: Required—TOEFL.

Case Western Reserve University, School of Graduate Studies, Department of Cognitive Science, Cleveland, OH 44106. Offers cognitive linguistics (MA). Part-time programs available. *Faculty:* 5 full-time (2 women), 2 part-time/adjunct (1 woman). *Degree requirements:* For master's, thesis. *Entrance requirements:* For master's, GRE, writing sample, recommendations. Additional exam requirements/recommendations for international students: Required—TOEFL. *Application deadline:* For fall admission, 3/1 priority date for domestic students. Application fee: $50. Electronic applications accepted. *Faculty research:* Application of metaphor and conceptual integration theories to a wide range of non-linguistic phenomena. *Unit head:* Dr. Mark Turner, Chair, 216-368-4753, E-mail: cogsci@case.edu. *Application contact:* Dr. Todd Oakley, Co-Director of Admission, 216-368-4753, E-mail: coglingadmission@case.edu.

Concordia University, School of Graduate Studies, Faculty of Arts and Science, Department of Education, Program in Applied Linguistics, Montréal, QC H3G 1M8, Canada. Offers applied linguistics (MA); teaching English as a second language (Certificate).

Cornell University, Graduate School, Graduate Fields of Arts and Sciences, Field of Asian Studies, Ithaca, NY 14853-0001. Offers East Asian linguistics (MA); East Asian studies (MA); South Asian linguistics (MA); South Asian studies (MA); Southeast Asian linguistics (MA); Southeast Asian studies (MA). *Faculty:* 52 full-time (17 women). *Students:* 18 full-time (0 women); includes 5 minority (3 African Americans, 1 Asian American or Pacific Islander, 1 Hispanic American), 2 international. Average age 26. 64 applicants, 61% accepted, 13 enrolled. In 2007, 10 degrees awarded. *Degree requirements:* For master's, one foreign language, thesis. *Entrance requirements:* For master's, GRE General Test, 3 letters of recommendation. Additional exam requirements/recommendations for international students: Required—TOEFL (minimum score 550 paper-based; 213 computer-based; 77 iBT). *Application deadline:* Applications are processed on a rolling basis. Application fee: $70. Electronic applications accepted. *Financial support:* In 2007–08, 4 students received support, including 4 fellowships with full tuition reimbursements available; research assistantships with full tuition reimbursements available, teaching assistantships with full tuition reimbursements available, institutionally sponsored loans, scholarships/grants, health care benefits, tuition waivers (full and partial), and unspecified assistantships also available. Financial award applicants required to submit FAFSA. *Faculty research:* East Asian studies, South Asian studies, Southeast Asian studies. *Unit head:* Director of Graduate Studies, 607-255-9099, Fax: 607-255-1345. *Application contact:* Graduate Field Assistant, 607-255-9099, Fax: 607-255-1345, E-mail: asian@cornell.edu.

Cornell University, Graduate School, Graduate Fields of Arts and Sciences, Field of Linguistics, Ithaca, NY 14853-0001. Offers applied linguistics (MA, PhD); East Asian linguistics (MA, PhD); English linguistics (MA, PhD); general linguistics (MA, PhD); Germanic linguistics (MA, PhD); Indo-European linguistics (MA, PhD); phonetics (MA, PhD); phonological theory (MA, PhD); Romance linguistics (MA, PhD); second language acquisition (MA, PhD); semantics (MA, PhD); Slavic linguistics (MA, PhD); sociolinguistics (MA, PhD); South Asian linguistics (MA, PhD); Southeast Asian linguistics (MA, PhD); syntactic theory (MA, PhD). *Faculty:* 19 full-time. *Students:* 31 full-time (16 women); includes 1 minority (Hispanic American), 19 international. Average age 28. 89 applicants, 17% accepted, 8 enrolled. In 2007, 2 master's, 1 doctorate awarded. Terminal master's awarded for partial completion of doctoral program. *Degree requirements:* For master's, one foreign language, thesis; for doctorate, one foreign language, comprehensive exam, thesis/dissertation. *Entrance requirements:* For master's and doctorate, GRE General Test, 2 letters of recommendation. Additional exam requirements/recommendations for international students: Required—TOEFL (minimum score 600 paper-based; 250 computer-based; 77 iBT). *Application deadline:* For fall admission, 1/15 for domestic students. Application fee: $70. Electronic applications accepted. *Financial support:* In 2007–08, 30 students received support, including 14 fellowships with full tuition reimbursements available, 2 research assistantships with full tuition reimbursements available, 14 teaching assistantships with full tuition reimbursements available; institutionally sponsored loans, scholarships/grants, health care benefits, tuition waivers (full and partial), and unspecified assistantships also available. Financial award applicants required to submit FAFSA. *Faculty research:* Phonology and phonetics; syntax and semantics; historical linguistics; philosophy of language; language acquisition. *Unit head:* Director of Graduate Studies, 607-255-1105. *Application contact:* Graduate Field Assistant, 607-255-1105, E-mail: lingfield@cornell.edu.

Eastern Michigan University, Graduate School, College of Arts and Sciences, Department of English Language and Literature, Program in English Linguistics, Ypsilanti, MI 48197. Offers MA. Part-time and evening/weekend programs available. Postbaccalaureate distance learning degree programs offered (minimal on-campus study). *Students:* 8 full-time (5 women), 16 part-time (9 women); includes 3 minority (1 American Indian/Alaska Native, 1 Asian American or Pacific Islander, 1 Hispanic American), 7 international. Average age 29. In 2007, 6 degrees awarded. *Degree requirements:* For master's, thesis (for some programs). *Entrance requirements:* Additional exam requirements/recommendations for international students: Required—TOEFL. *Application deadline:* Applications are processed on a rolling basis. Application fee: $35. *Expenses:* Tuition, state resident: full-time $8,952; part-time $373 per credit hour. Tuition, nonresident: full-time $17,634; part-time $735 per credit hour. Required fees: $896; $34 per credit hour. Tuition and fees vary according to course level, degree level and program. *Financial support:* Fellowships with tuition reimbursements, research assistantships with full tuition reimbursements, teaching assistantships with full tuition reimbursements, career-related internships or fieldwork, Federal Work-Study, institutionally sponsored loans, scholarships/grants, tuition waivers (partial), and unspecified assistantships available. Support available to part-time students. Financial award applicants required to submit FAFSA. *Application contact:* Dr. Daniel Steely, Program Advisor, 734-487-0145, Fax: 734-483-9744, E-mail: tsteely@emich.edu.

Florida International University, College of Arts and Sciences, Department of English, Program in Linguistics, Miami, FL 33199. Offers MA. Part-time and evening/weekend programs available. *Students:* 10 full-time (5 women), 7 part-time (5 women); includes 10 minority (all Hispanic Americans), 1 international. Average age 32. 10 applicants, 90% accepted, 7 enrolled. In 2007, 8 degrees awarded. *Degree requirements:* For master's, thesis or alternative. *Entrance requirements:* For master's, GRE General Test (for students receiving an assistantship), minimum GPA of 3.0. Additional exam requirements/recommendations for international students: Required—TOEFL (minimum score 550 paper-based; 213 computer-based). *Application deadline:* For fall admission, 3/1 for domestic and international students; for spring admission, 10/1 for domestic students, 9/1 for international students. Applications are processed on a rolling basis. Application fee: $30. Electronic applications accepted. *Expenses:* Tuition, state resident: full-time $6,106. Tuition, nonresident: full-time $15,528. Required fees: $284. *Financial support:* Teaching assistantships available. *Unit head:* Dr. Feryal Yavas, Director, 305-348-3935, Fax: 305-348-3878.

Gallaudet University, The Graduate School, Department of Linguistics, Washington, DC 20002-3625. Offers MA, PhD. Part-time programs available. *Degree requirements:* For master's, thesis optional. *Entrance requirements:* For master's, GRE General Test or MAT. *Application deadline:* For fall admission, 2/15 priority date for domestic students. Applications are processed on a rolling basis. Application fee: $50. Electronic applications accepted. *Expenses:* Tuition: Full-time $5,790. Required fees: $1,886. *Financial support:* Application deadline: 8/1. *Unit head:* Dr. Ceil Lucas, Chair, 202-651-5450. *Application contact:* Wednesday Luria, Coordinator of Prospective Graduate Student Services, 202-651-5647, Fax: 202-651-5295, E-mail: wednesday.luria@gallaudet.edu.

George Mason University, College of Humanities and Social Sciences, Department of English, Fairfax, VA 22030. Offers creative writing (MFA); English (MA); English literature (MA); linguistics (MA); professional writing and editing (MA, Certificate); teaching English as a second language (Certificate); teaching writing and literature (MA). *Faculty:* 79 full-time (45 women), 45 part-time/adjunct (26 women). *Students:* 27 full-time (20 women), 136 part-time (108 women); includes 23 minority (7 African Americans, 2 American Indian/Alaska Native, 9 Asian Americans or Pacific Islanders, 5 Hispanic Americans), 3 international. Average age 31. 337 applicants, 57% accepted, 103 enrolled. In 2007, 55 degrees awarded. *Degree requirements:* For master's, thesis (for some programs). *Entrance requirements:* For master's, minimum GPA of 3.0 in last 60 hours of course work. *Application deadline:* For fall admission, 5/1 for domestic students; for spring admission, 11/1 for domestic students. Application fee: $60 ($75 for international students). Electronic applications accepted. *Financial support:* Fellowships, research assistantships, teaching assistantships available. Support available to part-time students. Financial award application deadline: 3/1; financial award applicants required to submit FAFSA. *Faculty research:* Literature, professional writing and editing, writing of fiction or poetry. *Unit head:* Dr. Deborah Kaplan, Chair, 703-993-1170, Fax: 703-993-1161, E-mail: dkaplan@gmu.edu.

Georgetown University, Graduate School of Arts and Sciences, Department of Linguistics, Washington, DC 20057. Offers bilingual education (Certificate); linguistics (MS, PhD); teaching English as a second language (MAT, Certificate); teaching English as a second language and bilingual education (MAT). Terminal master's awarded for partial completion of doctoral program. *Degree requirements:* For master's, one foreign language, comprehensive exam, optional research project; for doctorate, 2 foreign languages, comprehensive exam, thesis/dissertation. *Entrance requirements:* For master's and doctorate, 18 undergraduate credits in a foreign language. Additional exam requirements/recommendations for international students: Required—TOEFL.

Georgia State University, College of Arts and Sciences, Department of Applied Linguistics and English as a Second Language, Atlanta, GA 30303-3083. Offers applied linguistics (MA, PhD). Part-time programs available. *Faculty:* 7 full-time (5 women), 2 part-time/adjunct (both women). *Students:* 61 full-time (49 women), 22 part-time (15 women); includes 19 minority (17 Asian Americans or Pacific Islanders, 2 Hispanic Americans). 81 applicants, 31% accepted, 17 enrolled. In 2007, 25 degrees awarded. *Degree requirements:* For master's, one foreign language, portfolio; for doctorate, one foreign language, comprehensive exam, thesis/dissertation, qualifying paper. *Entrance requirements:* For master's, GRE General Test; for doctorate, GRE. Additional exam requirements/recommendations for international students: Required—TOEFL (minimum score 600 paper-based; 250 computer-based; 97 iBT), TWE (minimum score 5). *Application deadline:* For fall admission, 8/1 for domestic students, 3/15 for international students; for spring admission, 10/15 for domestic students, 9/15 for international students. Applications are processed on a rolling basis. Application fee: $50. Electronic applications accepted. *Expenses:* Tuition, state resident: part-time $221 per credit hour. *Financial support:* In 2007–08, 30 students received support, including research assistantships with full tuition reimbursements available (averaging $3,600 per year), teaching assistantships with full tuition reimbursements available (averaging $3,600 per year); institutionally sponsored loans and scholarships/grants also available. Support available to part-time students. Financial award applicants required to submit FAFSA. *Faculty research:* Native language and second language, second language literacy, intercultural communication, classroom-centered research, learning styles/strategies. *Unit head:* Dr. Sara C. Weigle, Chair, 404-413-5192, Fax: 404-413-5201, E-mail: sweigle@langate.gsu.edu. *Application contact:* Dr. Diane D. Belcher, Director of Graduate Studies, 404-413-5194, Fax: 404-413-5201, E-mail: dbelcher1@gsu.edu.

Graduate Institute of Applied Linguistics, Graduate Programs, Dallas, TX 75236. Offers applied linguistics (MA, Certificate); language development (MA). Part-time programs available. *Faculty:* 9 full-time (2 women), 22 part-time/adjunct (5 women). *Students:* 55 full-time (25 women), 64 part-time (31 women); includes 10 minority (1 African American, 6 Asian Americans or Pacific Islanders, 3 Hispanic Americans), 6 international. Average age 31. 78 applicants, 90% accepted, 59 enrolled. In 2007, 22 degrees awarded. *Degree requirements:* For master's, one foreign language, comprehensive exam (for some programs), thesis (for some programs). *Entrance requirements:* For master's, GRE. Additional exam requirements/recommendations for international students: Required—TOEFL (minimum score 577 paper-based; 233 computer-based; 90 iBT). *Application deadline:* For fall admission, 6/5 priority date for domestic students, 1/10 priority date for international students; for spring admission, 11/20 priority date for domestic students, 7/1 priority date for international students. Applications are processed on a rolling basis. Application fee: $25 ($45 for international students). Electronic applications accepted. *Financial support:* In 2007–08, 71 students received support, including 9 teaching assistantships with partial tuition reimbursements available; scholarships/grants and tuition waivers (partial) also available. Financial award application deadline: 11/20. *Faculty research:* Minority languages, endangered languages, language documentation. *Application contact:* Heidi R. Anderson, Admissions Officer, 972-708-7343, Fax: 972-708-7396, E-mail: admissions@gial.edu.

Graduate School and University Center of the City University of New York, Graduate Studies, Program in Anthropology, New York, NY 10016-4039. Offers anthropological linguistics (PhD); archaeology (PhD); cultural anthropology (PhD); physical anthropology (PhD). *Faculty:* 39 full-time (14 women). *Students:* 158 full-time (96 women), 3 part-time (all women); includes 34 minority (11 African Americans, 8 Asian Americans or Pacific Islanders, 15 Hispanic Americans), 27 international. Average age 34. 165 applicants, 25% accepted, 21 enrolled. In 2007, 10 degrees awarded. *Degree requirements:* For doctorate, one foreign language, thesis/dissertation. *Entrance requirements:* For doctorate, GRE General Test. Additional exam requirements/recommendations for international students: Required—TOEFL. *Application deadline:* For fall admission, 1/8 priority date for domestic students. Application fee: $125. Electronic applications accepted. *Financial support:* In 2007–08, 111 students received support, including 85 fellowships, 16 research assistantships, 10 teaching assistantships; career-related internships or fieldwork, Federal Work-Study, institutionally sponsored loans, and tuition waivers (full and partial) also available. Financial award application deadline: 2/1; financial award applicants required to submit FAFSA. *Unit head:* Dr. Louise Lennihan, Executive Officer, 212-817-8006, Fax: 212-817-1501, E-mail: anthro@gc.cuny.edu. *Application contact:* Information Contact, 212-817-8005, Fax: 212-817-1501, E-mail: anthro@gc.cuny.edu.

Graduate School and University Center of the City University of New York, Graduate Studies, Program in Linguistics, New York, NY 10016-4039. Offers MA, PhD. *Faculty:* 20 full-time (5 women). *Students:* 66 full-time (56 women), 28 part-time (17 women); includes 7 minority (1 African American, 3 Asian Americans or Pacific Islanders, 3 Hispanic Americans), 26 international. Average age 36. 64 applicants, 56% accepted, 10 enrolled. In 2007, 2 master's, 5 doctorates awarded. Terminal master's awarded for partial completion of doctoral program. *Degree requirements:* For master's, one foreign language, thesis; for doctorate, 2 foreign languages, thesis/dissertation. *Entrance requirements:* For master's and doctorate, GRE General Test. Additional exam requirements/recommendations for international students: Required—TOEFL. *Application deadline:* For fall admission, 1/15 for domestic students. Application fee: $125. Electronic applications accepted. *Financial support:* In 2007–08, 43 students received support, including 33 fellowships, 2 research assistantships; teaching assistantships, career-related internships or fieldwork, Federal Work-Study, institutionally sponsored loans, and tuition waivers (full and partial) also available. Financial award application deadline: 2/1; financial award applicants required to submit FAFSA. *Unit head:* Dr. Gita Martohardjono, Executive Officer, 212-817-8501, Fax: 212-817-1526.

Harvard University, Graduate School of Arts and Sciences, Department of Linguistics, Cambridge, MA 02138. Offers descriptive linguistics (PhD); historical linguistics (PhD); theoretical linguistics (PhD). *Degree requirements:* For doctorate, 4 foreign languages, thesis/dissertation, field exam, Indo-European language exam, research paper. *Entrance requirements:* For doctorate, GRE General Test. Additional exam requirements/recommendations for international students: Required—TOEFL. *Expenses:* Tuition: Full-time $31,456. Full-time tuition and fees vary according to program and student level.

Hofstra University, College of Liberal Arts and Sciences, Department of Comparative Literature and Languages, Hempstead, NY 11549. Offers applied linguistics (MA). Part-time programs available. *Faculty:* 2 full-time (0 women), 3 part-time/adjunct (0 women). *Students:* 1 (woman) full-time, 3 part-time (all women), 1 international. Average age 27. 12 applicants, 75% accepted, 0 enrolled. In 2007, 10 degrees awarded. *Degree requirements:* For master's, thesis, BA, 36 credits, capstone. *Entrance requirements:* For master's, bachelor's degree in related area, interview, 2 letters of recommendation. Additional exam requirements/recommendations for international students: Required—TOEFL (minimum score 550 paper-based; 213 computer-based). *Application deadline:* Applications are processed on a rolling basis. Application fee: $60. Electronic applications accepted. *Expenses:* Tuition: Full-time $14,220; part-time $820 per credit. Required fees: $970; $165 per term. Tuition and fees vary according to program. *Financial support:* Fellowships with tuition reimbursements, research assistantships with full and partial tuition reimbursements, Federal Work-Study, institutionally sponsored loans, scholarships/grants, tuition waivers (full and partial), and unspecified assistantships available. Support available to part-time students. Financial award applicants required to submit FAFSA. *Faculty research:* Second language acquisition, second language writing. *Unit head:* Dr. Robert A. Leonard, Chairperson, 516-463-5440, E-mail: cclral@hofstra.edu. *Application contact:* Carol Drummer, Dean of Graduate Admissions, 516-463-4876, Fax: 516-463-4664, E-mail: gradstudent@hofstra.edu.

Indiana State University, School of Graduate Studies, College of Arts and Sciences, Department of Languages, Literatures, and Linguistics, Terre Haute, IN 47809-1401. Offers linguistics/teaching English as a second language (MA); TESL/TEFL (CAS). *Faculty:* 7 full-time (4 women), 2 part-time/adjunct (1 woman). *Students:* 26 full-time (20 women), 8 part-time (7 women); includes 6 minority (2 Asian Americans or Pacific Islanders, 4 Hispanic Americans), 19 international. Average age 32. 26 applicants, 92% accepted, 8 enrolled. In 2007, 20 degrees awarded. *Degree requirements:* For master's, comprehensive exam. *Application deadline:* For fall admission, 7/1 priority date for domestic students; for spring admission, 11/1 priority date for domestic students. Applications are processed on a rolling basis. Application fee: $35. Electronic applications accepted. *Expenses:* Tuition, state resident: full-time $7,056; part-time $294 per semester hour. Tuition, nonresident: full-time $14,016; part-time $584 per semester hour. Required fees: $175 per semester. *Financial support:* In 2007–08, 8 teaching assistantships (averaging $7,000 per year) were awarded; research assistantships with partial tuition reimbursements, tuition waivers (partial) also available. Financial award application deadline: 3/1; financial award applicants required to submit FAFSA. *Unit head:* Dr. Ronald W. Dunbar, Chairperson, 812-237-2368. *Application contact:* Information Contact, 812-237-2366.

Indiana University Bloomington, University Graduate School, College of Arts and Sciences, Department of French and Italian, Bloomington, IN 47405-7000. Offers French (MA, PhD), including French instruction (MA), French linguistics, French literature; Italian (MA, PhD). Part-time programs available. *Faculty:* 14 full-time (3 women). *Students:* 69 full-time (43 women), 13 part-time (5 women); includes 5 minority (2 African Americans, 1 American Indian/Alaska Native, 2 Hispanic Americans), 35 international. Average age 30. 47 applicants, 74% accepted, 19 enrolled. In 2007, 15 master's, 9 doctorates awarded. *Median time to degree:* Of those who began their doctoral program in fall 1999, 25% received their degree in 8 years or less. *Degree requirements:* For master's, one foreign language; for doctorate, 2 foreign languages, thesis/dissertation. *Entrance requirements:* For master's and doctorate, GRE General Test. Additional exam requirements/recommendations for international students: Required—TOEFL. *Application deadline:* For fall admission, 1/15 priority date for domestic students, 12/15 for international students; for spring admission, 9/1 priority date for domestic students, 9/1 for international students. Applications are processed on a rolling basis. Application fee: $50 ($60 for international students). Electronic applications accepted. *Financial support:* Fellowships with partial tuition reimbursements, research assistantships with tuition reimbursements, teaching assistantships with partial tuition reimbursements, career-related internships or fieldwork, institutionally sponsored loans, and tuition waivers (full) available. Financial award application deadline: 2/15. *Faculty research:* French-Creole studies, history of rhetoric,

Linguistics

Indiana University Bloomington (continued)
medieval epic and romance, post seventeenth century novel and poetry, Renaissance narrative and poetry. *Unit head:* Dr. Sonya Stephens, Chairman, 812-855-5458, Fax: 812-855-8877, E-mail: sonsteph@indiana.edu. *Application contact:* Jocelyn Karlan, Secretary, 812-855-1088, Fax: 812-855-8877, E-mail: jkarlan@indiana.edu.

Indiana University Bloomington, University Graduate School, College of Arts and Sciences, Department of Germanic Studies, Bloomington, IN 47405-7000. Offers German literature and studies (PhD); German studies (MA, PhD), including German and business studies (MA), German literature and culture (MA), German literature and linguistics (MA); medieval German studies (PhD); teaching German (MAT). *Faculty:* 12 full-time (3 women), 6 part-time/adjunct (2 women). *Students:* 27 full-time (15 women), 8 part-time (3 women); includes 1 minority (African American), 9 international. Average age 31. 26 applicants, 35% accepted, 9 enrolled. In 2007, 3 master's, 6 doctorates awarded. Terminal master's awarded for partial completion of doctoral program. *Median time to degree:* Of those who began their doctoral program in fall 1999, 86% received their degree in 8 years or less. *Degree requirements:* For master's, one foreign language; for doctorate, one foreign language, comprehensive exam, thesis/dissertation. *Entrance requirements:* For master's, GRE General Test, BA in German or equivalent; for doctorate, GRE General Test, MA in German or equivalent. Additional exam requirements/recommendations for international students: Required—TOEFL. *Application deadline:* For fall admission, 1/15 priority date for domestic students, 12/15 for international students; for spring admission, 9/1 priority date for domestic students, 9/1 for international students. Applications are processed on a rolling basis. Application fee: $50 ($60 for international students). *Financial support:* Fellowships with full and partial tuition reimbursements, research assistantships, teaching assistantships with full tuition reimbursements, Federal Work-Study, institutionally sponsored loans, scholarships/grants, and unspecified assistantships available. Support available to part-time students. Financial award application deadline: 1/15; financial award applicants required to submit FAFSA. *Faculty research:* German (and European) literature: medieval to modern/postmodern, German and culture studies, Germanic philology, literary theory, literature and the other arts. *Unit head:* Kari Ellen Gade, Director of Graduate Studies, 812-855-8138, Fax: 812-855-8292, E-mail: gade@indiana.edu. *Application contact:* Michelle Dunbar, Graduate Secretary, 812-855-7947, E-mail: germanic@indiana.edu.

Indiana University Bloomington, University Graduate School, College of Arts and Sciences, Department of Linguistics, Bloomington, IN 47405-7000. Offers African languages and linguistics (PhD); computational linguistics (MA); linguistics (PhD). *Faculty:* 10 full-time (1 woman), 14 part-time/adjunct (4 women). *Students:* 80 full-time (41 women), 3 part-time (1 woman); includes 6 minority (4 African Americans, 1 Asian American or Pacific Islander, 1 Hispanic American), 36 international. Average age 32. 93 applicants, 40% accepted, 17 enrolled. In 2007, 9 master's, 4 doctorates awarded. Terminal master's awarded for partial completion of doctoral program. *Median time to degree:* Of those who began their doctoral program in fall 1999, 38% received their degree in 8 years or less. *Degree requirements:* For master's, one foreign language, thesis optional; for doctorate, 2 foreign languages, comprehensive exam, thesis/dissertation. *Entrance requirements:* For master's and doctorate, GRE General Test. Additional exam requirements/recommendations for international students: Required—TOEFL (minimum score 580 paper-based; 237 computer-based). *Application deadline:* For fall admission, 1/15 priority date for domestic students, 12/1 priority date for international students. Applications are processed on a rolling basis. Application fee: $50 ($60 for international students). *Financial support:* In 2007–08, 25 students received support; fellowships with full tuition reimbursements available, research assistantships with full tuition reimbursements available, teaching assistantships with full tuition reimbursements available, assistantships available. *Faculty research:* African linguistics and language, semantics, phonology, syntactic theory, historical linguistics, phonetics-phonology, syntax, sociolinguistics, computational linguistics. Total annual research expenditures: $75,000. *Unit head:* Dr. Stuart Davis, Chair, 812-855-6459, Fax: 812-855-5363, E-mail: davis@indiana.edu. *Application contact:* Marilyn Estep, Secretary, 812-855-6456, Fax: 812-855-5363, E-mail: estepm@indiana.edu.

Indiana University of Pennsylvania, School of Graduate Studies and Research, College of Humanities and Social Sciences, Department of English, Indiana, PA 15705-1087. Offers composition and teaching English to speakers of other languages (MA, MAT, PhD), including composition and teaching English to speakers of other languages (PhD), teaching English (MAT), teaching English to speakers of other languages (MA); literature and criticism (MA, PhD), including generalist (MA), literature (MA), literature and criticism (PhD); rhetoric and linguistics (PhD). Part-time programs available. *Faculty:* 32 full-time (16 women). *Students:* 122 full-time (62 women), 211 part-time (136 women); includes 20 minority (11 African Americans, 1 American Indian/Alaska Native, 2 Asian Americans or Pacific Islanders, 6 Hispanic Americans), 93 international. Average age 35. 345 applicants, 48% accepted, 73 enrolled. In 2007, 48 master's, 35 doctorates awarded. *Degree requirements:* For master's, thesis optional; for doctorate, one foreign language, comprehensive exam, thesis/dissertation. *Entrance requirements:* For master's and doctorate, 2 letters of recommendation. Additional exam requirements/recommendations for international students: Required—TOEFL. *Application deadline:* For fall admission, 7/1 priority date for domestic students; for spring admission, 11/1 for domestic students. Applications are processed on a rolling basis. Application fee: $30. *Expenses:* Tuition, state resident: full-time $6,214; part-time $345 per credit. Tuition, nonresident: full-time $9,944; part-time $552 per credit. Required fees: $43 per credit. One-time fee: $140 part-time. Tuition and fees vary according to course load. *Financial support:* In 2007–08, 9 fellowships (averaging $1,200 per year), 42 research assistantships with full and partial tuition reimbursements (averaging $6,180 per year), 20 teaching assistantships with partial tuition reimbursements (averaging $17,001 per year) were awarded. Financial award application deadline: 3/15; financial award applicants required to submit FAFSA. *Unit head:* Dr. Gail I. Berlin, Chairperson, 724-357-2261, E-mail: ivy@iup.edu.

Instituto Tecnologico de Santo Domingo, Graduate School, Santo Domingo, Dominican Republic. Offers applied linguistics (MA); corporate finance (M Mgmt); education (M Ed); engineering (M Eng), including data telecommunications, industrial engineering, sanitary and environmental engineering, structural engineering; environmental science (M En S), including environmental education, environmental management, marine and coastal ecosystems, natural resources management; human resources administration (M Mgmt); management (M Mgmt); psychology (MA); social science (M Ed). *Entrance requirements:* For master's, birth certificate, minimum GPA of 2.0.

Louisiana State University and Agricultural and Mechanical College, Graduate School, College of Arts and Sciences, Interdepartmental Program in Linguistics, Baton Rouge, LA 70803. Offers MA, PhD. *Students:* 18 full-time (10 women), 3 part-time (all women); includes 1 African American, 1 Hispanic American, 5 international. Average age 32. 12 applicants, 33% accepted, 3 enrolled. In 2007, 2 degrees awarded. Terminal master's awarded for partial completion of doctoral program. *Degree requirements:* For master's, one foreign language, thesis or alternative; for doctorate, one foreign language, thesis/dissertation. *Entrance requirements:* For master's, GRE General Test, minimum GPA of 3.0; for doctorate, GRE General Test. Additional exam requirements/recommendations for international students: Required—TOEFL (minimum score 550 paper-based; 213 computer-based; 79 iBT). *Application deadline:* For fall admission, 1/25 priority date for domestic students, 5/15 for international students; for spring admission, 10/15 for international students. Applications are processed on a rolling basis. Application fee: $25. Electronic applications accepted. *Financial support:* In 2007–08, 16 students received support, including 1 fellowship with full and partial tuition reimbursement available (averaging $29,054 per year), 1 research assistantship with partial tuition reimbursement available (averaging $25,000 per year), 7 teaching assistantships with partial tuition reimbursements available (averaging $9,753 per year); health care benefits also available. Financial award application deadline: 5/1; financial award applicants required to submit FAFSA. *Faculty research:* Neurolinguistics, speech science, ESL, Hispanic linguistics, anthropological linguistics. *Unit head:* Dr. Michael Hegarty, Associate Professor of English and Linguistics, 225-578-3021, Fax: 225-578-4129, E-mail: mhegar1@lsu.edu.

Massachusetts Institute of Technology, School of Humanities, Arts, and Social Sciences, Department of Linguistics and Philosophy, Linguistics Section, Cambridge, MA 02139-4307. Offers PhD. *Faculty:* 12 full-time (4 women). *Students:* 40 full-time (17 women); includes 1 minority (American Indian/Alaska Native), 19 international. Average age 27. 144 applicants, 10% accepted, 10 enrolled. In 2007, 6 doctorates awarded. *Degree requirements:* For doctorate, one foreign language, comprehensive exam, thesis/dissertation. *Entrance requirements:* Additional exam requirements/recommendations for international students: Required—TOEFL (minimum score 577 paper-based; 233 computer-based). *Application deadline:* For fall admission, 1/2 for domestic and international students. Application fee: $70. Electronic applications accepted. *Expenses:* Tuition: Full-time $34,760; part-time $545 per unit. Required fees: $236. *Financial support:* In 2007–08, 21 fellowships with tuition reimbursements (averaging $25,196 per year), 13 research assistantships with tuition reimbursements (averaging $26,667 per year) were awarded; teaching assistantships with tuition reimbursements, Federal Work-Study, institutionally sponsored loans, scholarships/grants, health care benefits, and unspecified assistantships also available. Total annual research expenditures: $1,000. *Unit head:* Prof. Irene Heim, Chair, 617-253-4141, Fax: 617-253-5017. *Application contact:* Graduate Admissions, 617-253-4141, Fax: 617-253-5017, E-mail: lp-admissions@mit.edu.

McGill University, Faculty of Graduate and Postdoctoral Studies, Faculty of Arts, Department of Linguistics, Montréal, QC H3A 2T5, Canada. Offers language acquisition (PhD); linguistics (MA, PhD). *Faculty:* 13 full-time (6 women), 6 part-time/adjunct (1 woman). *Students:* 23 full-time (14 women). 82 applicants, 21% accepted, 9 enrolled. In 2007, 2 master's, 2 doctorates awarded.

Memorial University of Newfoundland, School of Graduate Studies, Department of Linguistics, St. John's, NL A1C 5S7, Canada. Offers MA, PhD. *Degree requirements:* For master's, one foreign language, thesis optional, comprehensive exam or thesis; for doctorate, 2 foreign languages, comprehensive exam, thesis/dissertation, oral defense of thesis. *Entrance requirements:* For master's, BA in linguistics; for doctorate, master's degree in linguistics. Electronic applications accepted. *Faculty research:* Aboriginal languages of eastern North America, historical/comparative linguistics, languages and dialects of Newfoundland and Labrador.

Michigan State University, The Graduate School, College of Arts and Letters, Department of Linguistics and Germanic, Slavic, Asian, and African Languages, East Lansing, MI 48824. Offers German studies (MA, PhD); linguistics (MA, PhD); teaching English to speakers of other languages (MA). Part-time and evening/weekend programs available. *Entrance requirements:* For master's, GRE General Test, minimum GPA of 3.2 in last 2 undergraduate years, 2 years of college-level foreign language, 3 letters of recommendation, portfolio (German studies); for doctorate, GRE General Test, minimum graduate GPA of 3.5, 3 letters of recommendation, master's degree or sufficient graduate course work in linguistics or language of study, master's thesis or major research paper. Additional exam requirements/recommendations for international students: Required—TOEFL. Electronic applications accepted. *Expenses:* Tuition, state resident: part-time $379 per credit hour. Tuition, nonresident: part-time $800 per credit hour. Tuition and fees vary according to program.

Michigan State University, The Graduate School, College of Arts and Letters, Department of Spanish and Portuguese, East Lansing, MI 48824. Offers applied Spanish linguistics (MA); Hispanic cultural studies (PhD); Hispanic literatures (MA). *Entrance requirements:* Additional exam requirements/recommendations for international students: Required—TOEFL. Electronic applications accepted. *Expenses:* Tuition, state resident: part-time $379 per credit hour. Tuition, nonresident: part-time $800 per credit hour. Tuition and fees vary according to program.

Montclair State University, The Office of Graduate Admissions and Support Services, College of Humanities and Social Sciences, Department of Linguistics, Montclair, NJ 07043-1624. Offers applied linguistics (MA); teacher of English as a second language (Certificate). Part-time and evening/weekend programs available. *Faculty:* 6 full-time (5 women), 1 (woman) part-time/adjunct. *Students:* 6 full-time (5 women), 32 part-time (27 women); includes 4 minority (2 African Americans, 1 Asian American or Pacific Islander, 1 Hispanic American), 4 international. 34 applicants, 32% accepted, 8 enrolled. In 2007, 8 master's, 9 other advanced degrees awarded. *Degree requirements:* For master's, comprehensive exam. *Entrance requirements:* For master's, GRE General Test, 2 letters of recommendation. Additional exam requirements/recommendations for international students: Required—TOEFL (minimum score 83 computer-based). *Application deadline:* For fall admission, 6/1 for international students; for spring admission, 10/1 for international students. Applications are processed on a rolling basis. Application fee: $60. Electronic applications accepted. *Financial support:* In 2007–08, 1 research assistantship with full tuition reimbursement (averaging $7,000 per year) was awarded; Federal Work-Study, scholarships/grants, and unspecified assistantships also available. Support available to part-time students. Financial award application deadline: 3/1; financial award applicants required to submit FAFSA. *Unit head:* Dr. Eileen Fitzpatrick, Chairperson, 973-655-4480. *Application contact:* Dr. Steve Seegmiller, Adviser, 973-655-7500, E-mail: seegmillerm@mail.montclair.edu.

New York University, Graduate School of Arts and Science, Department of Linguistics, New York, NY 10012-1019. Offers MA, PhD. Part-time programs available. *Faculty:* 8 full-time (2 women), 3 part-time/adjunct. *Students:* 31 full-time (15 women), 8 part-time (4 women); includes 3 minority (1 African American, 1 Asian American or Pacific Islander, 1 Hispanic American), 17 international. Average age 31. 109 applicants, 12% accepted, 3 enrolled. In 2007, 3 master's, 5 doctorates awarded. Terminal master's awarded for partial completion of doctoral program. *Degree requirements:* For master's, one foreign language, comprehensive exam, thesis optional; for doctorate, one foreign language, thesis/dissertation, 2 publishable papers. *Entrance requirements:* For master's and doctorate, GRE General Test. Additional exam requirements/recommendations for international students: Required—TOEFL. *Application deadline:* For fall admission, 1/4 priority date for domestic students. Application fee: $85. *Financial support:* Fellowships with tuition reimbursements, teaching assistantships with tuition reimbursements, Federal Work-Study, institutionally sponsored loans, scholarships/grants, health care benefits, and unspecified assistantships available. Financial award application deadline: 1/4; financial award applicants required to submit FAFSA. *Faculty research:* Phonology, syntax, sociolinguistics, cognitive science. *Unit head:* Richard Kayne, Chairman, 212-998-7950, Fax: 212-995-4707, E-mail: linguistics@nyu.edu. *Application contact:* Gregory Guy, Director of Graduate Studies, 212-998-7950, Fax: 212-995-4707, E-mail: linguistics@nyu.edu.

Northeastern Illinois University, Graduate College, College of Arts and Sciences, Department of Linguistics, Program in Linguistics, Chicago, IL 60625-4699. Offers MA. Part-time and evening/weekend programs available. *Faculty:* 7 full-time (5 women), 3 part-time/adjunct (2 women). *Students:* 17 full-time (14 women), 53 part-time (47 women); includes 12 minority (3 African Americans, 5 Asian Americans or Pacific Islanders, 4 Hispanic Americans), 4 international. Average age 32. 45 applicants, 89% accepted, 37 enrolled. In 2007, 34 degrees awarded. *Degree requirements:* For master's, one foreign language, comprehensive exam, thesis optional, minimum GPA of 3.0. *Entrance requirements:* For master's, 9 undergraduate hours in a foreign language or equivalent, minimum GPA of 2.75. Additional exam requirements/recommendations for international students: Required—TOEFL (minimum score 550 paper-based; 213 computer-based; 80 iBT). *Application deadline:* Applications are processed on a rolling basis. Application fee: $25. Electronic applications accepted. *Expenses:* Tuition, state resident: part-time $243 per credit hour. Tuition, nonresident: part-time $443 per credit hour. *Financial support:* In 2007–08, 41 students received support, including 8 research assistantships with full tuition reimbursements available (averaging $6,600 per year); career-related internships or fieldwork, Federal Work-Study, institutionally sponsored loans, scholarships/grants, tuition waivers (full and partial), and unspecified assistantships also available. Support available to part-time students. Financial award applicants required to submit FAFSA. *Faculty research:* Acquisition of literacy, Mayan language, Rotuman language, English as a second language methodology, Farsi language.

Northern Arizona University, Graduate College, College of Arts and Letters, Department of English, Program in Teaching English as a Second Language/Applied Linguistics, Flagstaff, AZ 86011. Offers applied linguistics (PhD); teaching English as a second language (MA); teaching

English as a second language/English as a second language (Certificate). *Degree requirements:* For master's, departmental qualifying exam; for doctorate, thesis/dissertation. *Entrance requirements:* For master's and doctorate, GRE General Test.

Northwestern University, The Graduate School, Judd A. and Marjorie Weinberg College of Arts and Sciences, Department of Linguistics, Evanston, IL 60208. Offers MA, PhD, JD/PhD. Admissions and degrees offered through The Graduate School. Part-time programs available. Terminal master's awarded for partial completion of doctoral program. *Degree requirements:* For master's, one foreign language, thesis; for doctorate, 2 foreign languages, thesis/dissertation, 2 qualifying papers. *Entrance requirements:* For master's and doctorate, GRE General Test. Additional exam requirements/recommendations for international students: Required—TOEFL. Electronic applications accepted. *Faculty research:* Theoretical linguistics, empirical approaches to the study of language, language and cognition.

Oakland University, Graduate Study and Lifelong Learning, College of Arts and Sciences, Department of Linguistics, Rochester, MI 48309-4401. Offers linguistics (MA); teaching English as a second language (Certificate). Part-time and evening/weekend programs available. *Faculty:* 6 full-time (3 women), 1 (woman) part-time/adjunct. *Students:* 5 full-time (4 women), 10 part-time (9 women); includes 1 minority (Asian American or Pacific Islander) Average age 35. 36 applicants, 83% accepted, 20 enrolled. In 2007, 4 master's awarded. *Entrance requirements:* For master's, minimum GPA of 3.0 for unconditional admission. Additional exam requirements/recommendations for international students: Required—TOEFL (minimum score 550 paper-based; 213 computer-based). *Application deadline:* For fall admission, 7/15 priority date for domestic students, 5/1 for international students; for winter admission, 12/1 priority date for domestic students, 9/1 for international students; for spring admission, 3/15 priority date for domestic students. Application fee: $35. *Expenses:* Tuition, state resident: full-time $9,936; part-time $414 per credit. Tuition, nonresident: full-time $17,202; part-time $716 per credit. *Financial support:* Federal Work-Study, institutionally sponsored loans, and tuition waivers (full) available. Financial award application deadline: 3/1; financial award applicants required to submit FAFSA. *Unit head:* Dr. Peter J. Binkert, Chair, 248-370-2175, Fax: 248-370-3144.

The Ohio State University, Graduate School, College of Humanities, Department of Linguistics, Columbus, OH 43210. Offers MA, PhD. *Faculty:* 16. *Students:* 38 full-time (25 women), 11 part-time (4 women); includes 4 minority (1 African American, 2 Asian Americans or Pacific Islanders, 1 Hispanic American), 14 international. Average age 28. In 2007, 4 master's, 6 doctorates awarded. *Degree requirements:* For master's, one foreign language, exam or thesis; for doctorate, 2 foreign languages, thesis/dissertation, exam. *Entrance requirements:* For master's and doctorate, GRE General Test. Additional exam requirements/recommendations for international students: Required—TOEFL (minimum score 600 paper-based; 250 computer-based). *Application deadline:* For fall admission, 8/15 priority date for domestic students, 7/1 priority date for international students; for winter admission, 12/1 priority date for domestic students, 11/1 priority date for international students; for spring admission, 3/1 priority date for domestic students, 2/1 priority date for international students. Applications are processed on a rolling basis. Application fee: $40 ($50 for international students). Electronic applications accepted. *Financial support:* Fellowships, research assistantships, teaching assistantships, Federal Work-Study and institutionally sponsored loans available. Support available to part-time students. *Faculty research:* Experimental phonetics, nonlinear phonology, process morphology (synchronically and diachronically), syntactic theory (GB, GPSG, HPSG, Categorical Grammar, Relational Grammar), Montague semantics. *Unit head:* Peter Culicover, Graduate Studies Committee Chair, 614-292-4052, Fax: 614-292-4273, E-mail: culicover.1@osu.edu. *Application contact:* 614-292-9444, Fax: 614-292-3895, E-mail: domestic.grad@osu.edu.

Ohio University, Graduate College, College of Arts and Sciences, Department of Linguistics, Athens, OH 45701-2979. Offers applied linguistics/TESOL (MA). Part-time programs available. *Faculty:* 9 full-time (3 women), 5 part-time/adjunct (3 women). *Students:* 32 full-time (24 women), 22 international. Average age 26. 42 applicants, 67% accepted, 15 enrolled. In 2007, 22 degrees awarded. *Degree requirements:* For master's, one foreign language, thesis or alternative. *Entrance requirements:* For master's, minimum GPA of 3.0. Additional exam requirements/recommendations for international students: Required—TOEFL (minimum score 600 paper-based; 250 computer-based); Recommended—TWE (minimum score 5). *Application deadline:* For fall admission, 2/15 priority date for domestic and international students. Applications are processed on a rolling basis. Application fee: $50 ($55 for international students). Electronic applications accepted. *Financial support:* In 2007–08, 2 fellowships with tuition reimbursements, 5 research assistantships with tuition reimbursements (averaging $7,000 per year), 24 teaching assistantships with tuition reimbursements (averaging $10,000 per year) were awarded; institutionally sponsored loans, tuition waivers (full and partial), and unspecified assistantships also available. Financial award application deadline: 3/15. *Faculty research:* Syntax, language learning, language teaching, computers for teaching, sociolinguistics. *Unit head:* Dr. Scott Jarvis, Chair, 740-593-4564, Fax: 740-593-2967, E-mail: jarvis@ohio.edu. *Application contact:* Dr. Hiroyuki Oshita, Graduate Chair, 740-593-4570, Fax: 740-593-2967, E-mail: oshita@ohio.edu.

Old Dominion University, College of Arts and Letters, Program in Applied Linguistics, Norfolk, VA 23529. Offers MA. Part-time and evening/weekend programs available. *Faculty:* 4 full-time (3 women). *Students:* 17 full-time (14 women), 9 part-time (8 women); includes 5 minority (3 African Americans, 1 Asian American or Pacific Islander, 1 Hispanic American), 2 international. Average age 25. 14 applicants, 93% accepted, 9 enrolled. In 2007, 18 degrees awarded. *Degree requirements:* For master's, one foreign language, comprehensive exam, thesis optional. *Entrance requirements:* For master's, GRE General Test, sample of written work, 12 hours in English, minimum B average. Additional exam requirements/recommendations for international students: Required—TOEFL (minimum score 570 paper-based; 213 computer-based; 80 iBT). *Application deadline:* For fall admission, 6/1 priority date for domestic and international students; for spring admission, 11/1 priority date for domestic and international students. Applications are processed on a rolling basis. Application fee: $40. Electronic applications accepted. *Expenses:* Tuition, state resident: part-time $304 per credit hour. Tuition, nonresident: part-time $761 per credit hour. *Financial support:* In 2007–08, 14 students received support, including 1 research assistantship with partial tuition reimbursement available (averaging $8,000 per year), 3 teaching assistantships with partial tuition reimbursements available (averaging $8,000 per year); career-related internships or fieldwork, institutionally sponsored loans, and unspecified assistantships also available. Financial award application deadline: 2/15. *Faculty research:* Discourse analysis, phonology, syntax, first and second language acquisition, gender, social linguistics. *Unit head:* Dr. Janet Bing, Graduate Program Director, 757-683-4030, Fax: 757-683-3241, E-mail: lingpd@odu.edu.

Purdue University, Graduate School, College of Liberal Arts, Department of English, West Lafayette, IN 47907. Offers creative writing (MFA); literature (MA, PhD), including linguistics, literature and philosophy (PhD), rhetoric and composition, theory and cultural studies (PhD). Part-time programs available. *Degree requirements:* For master's, one foreign language; for doctorate, one foreign language, thesis/dissertation. *Entrance requirements:* For master's and doctorate, GRE General Test, sample of written work. Additional exam requirements/recommendations for international students: Required—TOEFL. Electronic applications accepted. *Faculty research:* Cultural studies, postmodern narrative, contemporary women writers, composition theory, slave narratives.

Purdue University, Graduate School, College of Liberal Arts, Department of Speech, Language, and Hearing Sciences, West Lafayette, IN 47907. Offers audiology (MS, Au D, PhD); linguistics (MS, PhD); speech and hearing science (MS, PhD); speech-language pathology (MS, PhD). *Accreditation:* ASHA. *Degree requirements:* For master's, thesis optional; for doctorate, thesis/dissertation. *Entrance requirements:* For master's and doctorate, GRE. Additional exam requirements/recommendations for international students: Required—TOEFL. Electronic applications accepted. *Faculty research:* Psychoacoustics, speech perception, speech physiology, stuttering, child language.

Purdue University, Graduate School, College of Liberal Arts, Program in Linguistics, West Lafayette, IN 47907. Offers MS, PhD. *Entrance requirements:* For master's and doctorate, GRE, minimum GPA of 3.4. Additional exam requirements/recommendations for international students: Required—TOEFL. Electronic applications accepted. *Faculty research:* Sign languages, sociolinguistics and African American English, computational linguistics, indigenous languages, theoretical linguistics.

Queens College of the City University of New York, Division of Graduate Studies, Arts and Humanities Division, Department of Linguistics and Communication Disorders, Program in Applied Linguistics, Flushing, NY 11367-1597. Offers MA. Part-time and evening/weekend programs available. *Faculty:* 8 full-time (5 women). *Students:* 1 (woman) full-time, 9 part-time (6 women). 17 applicants, 71% accepted. In 2007, 1 degree awarded. *Degree requirements:* For master's, thesis optional. *Entrance requirements:* For master's, minimum GPA of 3.0. Additional exam requirements/recommendations for international students: Required—TOEFL. *Application deadline:* For fall admission, 4/1 for domestic students; for spring admission, 11/1 for domestic students. Applications are processed on a rolling basis. Application fee: $125. *Financial support:* Career-related internships or fieldwork, Federal Work-Study, institutionally sponsored loans, and tuition waivers (partial) available. Support available to part-time students. Financial award application deadline: 4/1; financial award applicants required to submit FAFSA. *Application contact:* Mario Caruso, Director of Graduate Admissions, 718-997-5200, Fax: 718-997-5193, E-mail: graduate_admissions@qc.edu.

Rice University, Graduate Programs, School of Humanities, Department of Linguistics, Houston, TX 77251-1892. Offers MA, PhD. Terminal master's awarded for partial completion of doctoral program. *Degree requirements:* For master's, one foreign language, thesis; for doctorate, 2 foreign languages, thesis/dissertation, 3 research papers. *Entrance requirements:* For master's and doctorate, GRE General Test, minimum GPA of 3.0. Additional exam requirements/recommendations for international students: Required—TOEFL (minimum score 600 paper-based; 250 computer-based; 90 iBT). Electronic applications accepted. *Faculty research:* Typology, fieldwork and language description, cognitive grammar, historical linguistics, corpus linguistics.

Rutgers, The State University of New Jersey, New Brunswick, Graduate School, Program in Linguistics, New Brunswick, NJ 08901-1281. Offers PhD. *Degree requirements:* For doctorate, comprehensive exam, thesis/dissertation. *Entrance requirements:* For doctorate, GRE General Test. Additional exam requirements/recommendations for international students: Required—TOEFL. *Faculty research:* Theoretical linguistics, syntax, semantics, phonology, computational linguistics, linguistics theory.

San Diego State University, Graduate and Research Affairs, College of Arts and Letters, Department of Linguistics and Oriental Languages, San Diego, CA 92182. Offers applied linguistics and English as a second language (CAL); computational linguistics (MA); English as a second language/applied linguistics (MA); general linguistics (MA). *Students:* 17 full-time (10 women), 23 part-time (19 women); includes 6 minority (3 Asian Americans or Pacific Islanders, 3 Hispanic Americans), 10 international. Average age 30. 39 applicants, 54% accepted, 14 enrolled. In 2007, 16 degrees awarded. *Degree requirements:* For master's, one foreign language, comprehensive exam, thesis optional. *Entrance requirements:* For master's, GRE General Test, 2 letters of recommendation. Additional exam requirements/recommendations for international students: Required—TOEFL (minimum score 570 paper-based). *Application deadline:* For fall admission, 5/1 for domestic and international students; for spring admission, 11/1 for domestic students, 10/1 for international students. Applications are processed on a rolling basis. Application fee: $55. Electronic applications accepted. *Financial support:* In 2007–08, 16 teaching assistantships were awarded; fellowships, career-related internships or fieldwork also available. Financial award applicants required to submit FAFSA. *Faculty research:* Cross-cultural linguistic studies of semantics. Total annual research expenditures: $256,582. *Unit head:* Jeffrey Kaplan, Chair, 619-594-5268, Fax: 619-594-4877, E-mail: jkaplan@mail.sdsu.edu. *Application contact:* Dr. Soonja Choi, Adviser, 619-594-5885, E-mail: schoi@mail.sdsu.edu.

San Francisco State University, Division of Graduate Studies, College of Humanities, Department of English Language and Literature, Program in Linguistics, San Francisco, CA 94132-1722. Offers MA. Part-time programs available. *Degree requirements:* For master's, 2 foreign languages, thesis (for some programs). *Application deadline:* Applications are processed on a rolling basis. *Faculty research:* Mental lexicon, endangered languages, language and gender, linguistics, discourse analysis. *Unit head:* Dr. Rachelle Waksler, Graduate Coordinator, 415-338-2264, E-mail: rwaksler@sfsu.edu.

San Jose State University, Graduate Studies and Research, College of Humanities and the Arts, Department of Linguistics and Language Development, San Jose, CA 95192-0001. Offers computational linguistics (Certificate); linguistics (MA, Certificate); teaching English to speakers of other languages (MA, Certificate). *Students:* 51 full-time (42 women), 48 part-time (40 women); includes 25 minority (18 Asian Americans or Pacific Islanders, 7 Hispanic Americans), 26 international. Average age 35. 88 applicants, 69% accepted, 27 enrolled. In 2007, 35 degrees awarded. *Entrance requirements:* Additional exam requirements/recommendations for international students: Required—TOEFL (minimum score 570 paper-based; 230 computer-based). *Application deadline:* For fall admission, 6/29 for domestic students; for spring admission, 11/30 for domestic students. Applications are processed on a rolling basis. Application fee: $59. Electronic applications accepted. *Financial support:* Applicants required to submit FAFSA. *Unit head:* Dr. Manjari Ohala, Chair, 408-924-3742, Fax: 408-924-4703.

Simon Fraser University, Graduate Studies, Faculty of Arts and Social Sciences, Department of Linguistics, Burnaby, BC V5A 1S6, Canada. Offers MA, PhD. *Degree requirements:* For master's, one foreign language, thesis; for doctorate, 2 foreign languages, thesis/dissertation. *Entrance requirements:* For master's, minimum GPA of 3.0; for doctorate, minimum GPA of 3.5. Additional exam requirements/recommendations for international students: Required—TOEFL or IELTS. *Faculty research:* History of linguistics, syntactic theory, relational grammar, experimental phonetics, pragmatics.

Southern Illinois University Carbondale, Graduate School, College of Liberal Arts, Department of Applied Linguistics, Carbondale, IL 62901-4701. Offers applied linguistics (MA); teaching English to speakers of other languages (MA). *Faculty:* 9 full-time (6 women), 1 part-time/adjunct (0 women). *Students:* 10 full-time (7 women), 8 part-time (5 women); includes 2 minority (1 African American, 1 Hispanic American), 6 international. Average age 27. 9 applicants, 56% accepted, 2 enrolled. In 2007, 3 degrees awarded. *Degree requirements:* For master's, one foreign language, thesis. *Entrance requirements:* For master's, minimum GPA of 3.0. Additional exam requirements/recommendations for international students: Required—TOEFL. *Application deadline:* For fall admission, 4/1 priority date for domestic students. Applications are processed on a rolling basis. Application fee: $20. *Financial support:* Fellowships with full tuition reimbursements, research assistantships with full tuition reimbursements, teaching assistantships with full tuition reimbursements, career-related internships or fieldwork, Federal Work-Study, institutionally sponsored loans, and tuition waivers (full) available. Support available to part-time students. Financial award application deadline: 4/1. *Faculty research:* Theory and methods, second language acquisition, pidgin and Creole languages, cognitive grammar. *Application contact:* Diane Korando, Departmental Secretary, 618-536-3385, Fax: 618-453-6527, E-mail: ling@siu.edu.

Stanford University, School of Humanities and Sciences, Department of Linguistics, Stanford, CA 94305-9991. Offers MA, PhD. *Degree requirements:* For master's, one foreign language, thesis; for doctorate, 2 foreign languages, thesis/dissertation, oral exam, qualifying papers. *Entrance requirements:* For master's and doctorate, GRE General Test. Additional exam requirements/recommendations for international students: Required—TOEFL. Electronic applications accepted.

Linguistics

Stony Brook University, State University of New York, Graduate School, College of Arts and Sciences, Department of Linguistics, Program in Linguistics, Stony Brook, NY 11794. Offers MA, PhD. *Students:* 27 full-time (20 women); includes 1 Hispanic American, 18 international. Average age 31. 41 applicants, 22% accepted. In 2007, 4 master's, 5 doctorates awarded. *Application deadline:* For fall admission, 1/15 for domestic students. Application fee: $60. *Financial support:* Fellowships, research assistantships, teaching assistantships available. *Application contact:* Dr. Frank Anshen, Director, 631-632-7776, Fax: 631-632-9789, E-mail: frank.anshen@stonybrook.edu.

Announcement: In 2008, department faculty members received four new externally funded grants for projects including the study of an emerging sign language, agreement universals, perception of foreign language sound sequences, and on-site Russian language training. Exciting ongoing collaborations include research with colleagues in psychology and computer science, and language, mind, brain courses.

See Close-Up on page 609.

Syracuse University, Graduate School, College of Arts and Sciences, Department of Languages, Literatures, and Linguistics, Program in Linguistic Studies, Syracuse, NY 13244. Offers MA. Part-time programs available. *Students:* 15 full-time (12 women), 2 part-time (both women), 9 international. 31 applicants, 65% accepted, 12 enrolled. In 2007, 5 degrees awarded. *Entrance requirements:* For master's, GRE General Test. Additional exam requirements/recommendations for international students: Required—TOEFL. *Application deadline:* For fall admission, 1/10 priority date for domestic students. Applications are processed on a rolling basis. Application fee: $75. Electronic applications accepted. *Expenses:* Tuition: Full-time $18,216; part-time $1,012 per credit. Required fees: $980. Tuition and fees vary according to program. *Financial support:* Fellowships with full tuition reimbursements, teaching assistantships with full tuition reimbursements, tuition waivers (partial) available. *Unit head:* Dr. William Ritchie, Program Coordinator, 315-443-5905, Fax: 315-443-5376. *Application contact:* Barbara Moon, Recruiting Contact, 315-443-5906, E-mail: bamoon@syr.edu.

Teachers College, Columbia University, Graduate Faculty of Education, Department of Arts and Humanities, Program in Applied Linguistics, New York, NY 10027-6696. Offers Ed M, MA, Ed D. Part-time and evening/weekend programs available. *Faculty:* 4 full-time (3 women), 5 part-time/adjunct. *Students:* 19 full-time (18 women), 47 part-time (40 women); includes 16 minority (1 American Indian/Alaska Native, 14 Asian Americans or Pacific Islanders, 1 Hispanic American), 18 international. Average age 34. 52 applicants, 31% accepted, 8 enrolled. In 2007, 12 master's, 7 doctorates awarded. Terminal master's awarded for partial completion of doctoral program. *Degree requirements:* For doctorate, variable foreign language requirement, thesis/dissertation. *Application deadline:* For fall admission, 5/15 for domestic students; for spring admission, 12/1 for domestic students. Application fee: $70. *Financial support:* Fellowships, research assistantships, teaching assistantships, career-related internships or fieldwork, Federal Work-Study, institutionally sponsored loans, and tuition waivers (full and partial) available. Support available to part-time students. Financial award application deadline: 2/1. *Faculty research:* Linguistics applied to education and other professions, sociolinguistics and second language acquisition, rude speech and social rules of speaking. *Application contact:* Mark E. Stearns, Associate Director of Admission, 212-678-3710, Fax: 212-678-4171.

See Close-Up on page 267.

Temple University, Health Sciences Center and Graduate School, College of Health Professions, Department of Communication Sciences, Program in Linguistics, Philadelphia, PA 19122-6096. Offers MA. Part-time and evening/weekend programs available. *Degree requirements:* For master's, comprehensive exam. *Entrance requirements:* For master's, GRE General Test, minimum GPA of 3.0. Additional exam requirements/recommendations for international students: Required—TOEFL (minimum score 550 paper-based; 213 computer-based; 79 iBT). Electronic applications accepted. *Faculty research:* Generative syntax, generative phonology, formal semantics, sociolinguistics.

Texas Tech University, Graduate School, College of Arts and Sciences, Department of Classical and Modern Languages and Literatures, Program in Applied Linguistics, Lubbock, TX 79409. Offers MA. *Students:* 26 full-time (16 women), 6 part-time (5 women); includes 2 minority (both Hispanic Americans), 4 international. Average age 29. 24 applicants, 92% accepted, 10 enrolled. In 2007, 3 degrees awarded. *Entrance requirements:* Additional exam requirements/recommendations for international students: Required—TOEFL (minimum score 550 paper-based; 213 computer-based). *Application deadline:* For fall admission, 3/1 priority date for international students; for spring admission, 11/1 priority date for international students. Application fee: $50 ($60 for international students). *Expenses:* Tuition, state resident: part-time $373 per credit hour. Tuition, nonresident: part-time $651 per credit hour. Tuition and fees vary according to program. *Financial support:* Research assistantships available. *Faculty research:* Second language acquisition; second language instruction; language processing; assessment; general linguistics. *Unit head:* Dr. Bill VanPatton, Director and Professor, 860-742-3145 Ext. 232, Fax: 860-742-3306, E-mail: bill.vanpatton@ttu.edu. *Application contact:* Liz Hildebrand, Senior Advisor, 806-742-4055, Fax: 806-742-3306, E-mail: liz.hildebrand@ttu.edu.

Trinity Western University, Faculty of Graduate Studies, Program in Linguistics, Langley, BC V2Y 1Y1, Canada. Offers MA. *Faculty:* 4 full-time (2 women), 2 part-time/adjunct (0 women). *Students:* 14 full-time (6 women), 4 part-time (2 women). Average age 30. 12 applicants, 83% accepted, 10 enrolled. In 2007, 3 degrees awarded. *Degree requirements:* For master's, 39 seminar hours; essay (for non-thesis students). *Entrance requirements:* For master's, BA; minimum GPA of 2.7, 3.0 in last two years; 12 seminar hours; linguistic prerequisites; 1 foreign language. Additional exam requirements/recommendations for international students: Required—TOEFL (minimum score 600 paper-based; 250 computer-based). *Application deadline:* For fall admission, 4/30 priority date for domestic and international students. Applications are processed on a rolling basis. Application fee: $40. Electronic applications accepted. *Expenses: Contact institution. Financial support:* In 2007–08, 11 fellowships (averaging $2,680 Canadian dollars per year), 4 teaching assistantships (averaging $1,935 Canadian dollars per year) were awarded. Financial award application deadline: 4/30. *Faculty research:* Syntax, phonology, tone, historical and comparative, discourse analysis. *Unit head:* Dr. Keith Snider, Director, MA in Linguistics Program, 604-513-2129 Ext. 3958, Fax: 604-513-2128, E-mail: keith.snider@twu.ca. *Application contact:* Vic Cornish, Director, Graduate Admissions, 604-888-7511 Ext. 3130, Fax: 604-513-2064, E-mail: vic.cornish@twu.edu.

Universidad de las Américas–Puebla, Division of Graduate Studies, School of Humanities, Program in Applied Linguistics, Puebla, Mexico. Offers linguistics (MA). Part-time and evening/weekend programs available. *Degree requirements:* For master's, one foreign language, thesis. *Entrance requirements:* Additional exam requirements/recommendations for international students: Required—TOEFL. *Faculty research:* English linguistics, teaching English to speakers of other languages.

Université de Montréal, Faculty of Arts and Sciences, Department of Linguistics and Translation, Montréal, QC H3C 3J7, Canada. Offers linguistics and translation (MA, PhD, DESS); localization (Certificate). *Faculty:* 33 full-time (14 women), 1 (woman) part-time/adjunct. *Students:* 132 full-time (101 women), 40 part-time (31 women). 199 applicants, 38% accepted, 62 enrolled. In 2007, 38 master's, 4 doctorates, 25 other advanced degrees awarded. *Degree requirements:* For master's, thesis, general exam; for doctorate, thesis/dissertation, general exam. *Application deadline:* For fall admission, 2/1 priority date for domestic students; for winter admission, 11/1 priority date for domestic students; for spring admission, 2/1 priority date for domestic students. Application fee: $100. Electronic applications accepted. *Unit head:* Richard Patry, Chairman, 514-343-6675, Fax: 514-343-2284, E-mail: richard.patry@umontreal.ca. *Application contact:* Gilles Belanger, Conseillor (Traduction), 514-343-6024, Fax: 514-343-2284, E-mail: gilles.belanger@umontreal.ca.

Université de Sherbrooke, Faculty of Letters and Human Sciences, Department of Letters and Communications, Sherbrooke, QC J1K 2R1, Canada. Offers comparative Canadian literature (MA, PhD); French literature (MA, PhD); linguistics (MA); lit&erature de crèation (MA, PhD); theatre (MA). *Degree requirements:* For master's, thesis or alternative; for doctorate, thesis/dissertation. *Entrance requirements:* For master's, minimum GPA of 2.8; for doctorate, minimum GPA of 3.0.

Université du Québec à Chicoutimi, Graduate Programs, Program in Linguistics, Chicoutimi, QC G7H 2B1, Canada. Offers MA. Part-time programs available. *Degree requirements:* For master's, thesis. *Entrance requirements:* For master's, appropriate bachelor's degree, proficiency in French.

Université du Québec à Montréal, Graduate Programs, Program in Linguistics, Montréal, QC H3C 3P8, Canada. Offers MA, PhD. Part-time programs available. *Degree requirements:* For master's, thesis optional; for doctorate, thesis/dissertation. *Entrance requirements:* For master's, appropriate bachelor's degree or equivalent, proficiency in French; for doctorate, appropriate master's degree or equivalent, proficiency in French.

Université Laval, Faculty of Letters, Department of Languages, Linguistics and Translations, Programs in Linguistics, Québec, QC G1K 7P4, Canada. Offers MA, PhD. Terminal master's awarded for partial completion of doctoral program. *Degree requirements:* For master's, thesis (for some programs); for doctorate, comprehensive exam, thesis/dissertation. *Entrance requirements:* For master's, English test (comprehension of written English), knowledge of French; for doctorate, English exam (comprehension of written English), knowledge of French. Electronic applications accepted.

University at Buffalo, the State University of New York, Graduate School, College of Arts and Sciences, Department of Linguistics, Buffalo, NY 14260. Offers MA, PhD. Terminal master's awarded for partial completion of doctoral program. *Degree requirements:* For master's, exam, project, or thesis; for doctorate, one foreign language, thesis/dissertation, qualifying paper. *Entrance requirements:* For master's and doctorate, GRE General Test. Additional exam requirements/recommendations for international students: Required—TOEFL (minimum score 600 paper-based; 250 computer-based). Electronic applications accepted. *Faculty research:* Cognitive linguistics, cross-linguistic studies, psycholinguistics, syntax, semantics.

University of Alaska Fairbanks, College of Liberal Arts, Program in Linguistics, Fairbanks, AK 99775-7520. Offers applied linguistics (MA). *Degree requirements:* For master's, comprehensive exam, thesis or alternative. *Entrance requirements:* For master's, GRE General Test. Additional exam requirements/recommendations for international students: Required—TOEFL (minimum score 550 paper-based; 213 computer-based). *Faculty research:* Second language acquisition/teaching; INUPIAQ, Athabaskan languages; language maintenance and shift; phonology, morphology.

University of Alberta, Faculty of Graduate Studies and Research, Department of Linguistics, Edmonton, AB T6G 2E1, Canada. Offers experimental linguistics (M Sc, PhD). *Degree requirements:* For master's, thesis (for some programs); for doctorate, thesis/dissertation. *Entrance requirements:* For master's, BA in linguistics; for doctorate, M Sc or MA in linguistics. Additional exam requirements/recommendations for international students: Required—TOEFL. *Faculty research:* Experimental phonetics, psycholinguistics, phonology, endangered languages, language acquisition.

University of Alberta, Faculty of Graduate Studies and Research, Department of Modern Languages and Cultural Studies, Edmonton, AB T6G 2E1, Canada. Offers applied linguistics (Germanic, Romance, Slavic) (MA); French language, literatures and linguistics (PhD); French language, literatures, and linguistics (MA); Germanic languages, literatures and linguistics (PhD); Germanic languages, literatures, and linguistics (MA); Italian studies (MA); Slavic languages and literatures (Russian, Ukrainian) (MA, PhD); Slavic linguistics (Russian, Ukrainian) (MA, PhD); Spanish and Latin American studies (MA, PhD); Ukrainian folklore (MA, PhD). Part-time programs available. *Degree requirements:* For master's, one foreign language, thesis; for doctorate, 2 foreign languages, comprehensive exam, thesis/dissertation. *Entrance requirements:* For master's and doctorate, 1 language other than English. Additional exam requirements/recommendations for international students: Required—Michigan English Language Assessment Battery or TOEFL (paper score 550; computer score 213). Electronic applications accepted. *Faculty research:* Russian/Ukrainian studies; German studies; contemporary Latin American, French and Francophone studies; Italian studies.

The University of Arizona, Graduate College, College of Social and Behavioral Sciences, Department of Linguistics, Tucson, AZ 85721. Offers human language technology (MS); linguistics and anthropology (PhD); Native American linguistics (MA); theoretical linguistics (PhD). PhD in linguistics and anthropology offered jointly with Department of Anthropology. *Faculty:* 21. *Students:* 40 full-time (20 women), 9 part-time (7 women); includes 6 minority (1 African American, 5 American Indian/Alaska Native), 11 international. Average age 33. 66 applicants, 30% accepted, 11 enrolled. In 2007, 5 master's, 9 doctorates awarded. Terminal master's awarded for partial completion of doctoral program. *Median time to degree:* Of those who began their doctoral program in fall 1999, 50% received their degree in 8 years or less. *Degree requirements:* For master's, one foreign language, thesis; for doctorate, one foreign language, comprehensive exam, thesis/dissertation. *Entrance requirements:* For master's, GRE General Test (MS), writing sample, statement of purpose, 3 letters of recommendation, departmental application, minimum GPA of 3.0; for doctorate, GRE General Test, writing sample, statement of purpose, 3 letters of recommendation, departmental application, minimum GPA of 3.0. Additional exam requirements/recommendations for international students: Required—TOEFL (minimum score 550 paper-based; 213 computer-based). *Application deadline:* For fall admission, 1/15 for domestic students, 12/1 for international students. Applications are processed on a rolling basis. Application fee: $50. Electronic applications accepted. *Financial support:* In 2007–08, 8 fellowships with full tuition reimbursements (averaging $5,000 per year), 58 research assistantships with full tuition reimbursements (averaging $15,300 per year), 33 teaching assistantships with full tuition reimbursements (averaging $15,300 per year) were awarded; career-related internships or fieldwork, institutionally sponsored loans, scholarships/grants, health care benefits, tuition waivers (full and partial), and unspecified assistantships also available. Support available to part-time students. Financial award application deadline: 4/15. *Faculty research:* Semantic, syntactic, morphological, and phonological theories of natural languages; native languages of the American Southwest, psycholinguistics and computational linguistics. Total annual research expenditures: $220,112. *Unit head:* Dr. Michael Hammond, Head, 520-621-5759, Fax: 520-626-9014, E-mail: hammond@u.arizona.edu. *Application contact:* Jennifer Columbus, Information Contact, 520-621-2113, Fax: 520-626-9014, E-mail: jennife2@email.arizona.edu.

The University of British Columbia, Faculty of Arts and Faculty of Graduate Studies, Department of Linguistics, Vancouver, BC V6T 1Z1, Canada. Offers MA, PhD. Part-time programs available. *Faculty:* 12 full-time (4 women), 4 part-time/adjunct (3 women). *Students:* 38 full-time (19 women). Average age 30. 42 applicants, 24% accepted, 7 enrolled. In 2007, 1 master's, 1 doctorate awarded. *Median time to degree:* Of those who began their doctoral program in fall 1999, 100% received their degree in 8 years or less. *Degree requirements:* For master's, one foreign language, thesis optional; for doctorate, 2 foreign languages, thesis/dissertation, 2 qualifying papers. *Entrance requirements:* Additional exam requirements/recommendations for international students: Required—TOEFL (minimum score 550 paper-based; 213 computer-based). *Application deadline:* For fall admission, 1/20 for domestic and international students. Application fee: $90 Canadian dollars ($150 Canadian dollars for international students). Electronic applications accepted. *Financial support:* In 2007–08, 35 students received support, including 11 fellowships with full tuition reimbursements available (averaging $11,727 per year), 28 research assistantships with full tuition reimbursements available (averaging $6,913 per year), 30 teaching assistantships with full tuition reimbursements available (averaging $5,344 per year); institutionally sponsored loans and tuition waivers (full) also available. Financial award application deadline: 10/15. *Faculty research:* Linguistic theory (phonology, syntax, semantics), Native American languages, African languages, first language acquisition, experimental phonetics. Total annual research expenditures: $550,000. *Unit head:*

Dr. Joseph P. Stemberger, Head, 604-822-4256, Fax: 604-822-9687, E-mail: stemberg@interchange.ubc.ca. *Application contact:* Dr. Hotze Rullmann, Graduate Admissions Officer, 604-822-4256, Fax: 604-822-9687, E-mail: rullmann@interchange.ubc.ca.

University of Calgary, Faculty of Graduate Studies, Faculty of Social Sciences, Department of Linguistics, Calgary, AB T2N 1N4, Canada. Offers MA, PhD. *Degree requirements:* For master's, one foreign language, thesis; for doctorate, one foreign language, comprehensive exam, thesis/dissertation. *Entrance requirements:* For doctorate, MA. Additional exam requirements/recommendations for international students: Required—TOEFL (minimum score 560 paper-based; 220 computer-based). Electronic applications accepted. *Faculty research:* Theoretical linguistics, historical linguistics, language acquisition, Amerindian.

University of California, Berkeley, Graduate Division, College of Letters and Science, Department of Linguistics, Berkeley, CA 94720-1500. Offers PhD. *Degree requirements:* For doctorate, thesis/dissertation, qualifying exam. *Entrance requirements:* For doctorate, GRE General Test, minimum GPA of 3.0, 3 letters of recommendation. *Application deadline:* For fall admission, 12/15 for domestic students. Application fee: $70 ($90 for international students). *Financial support:* Fellowships, teaching assistantships, unspecified assistantships available. *Unit head:* Sharon Inkelas, Chair, 510-643-7615, E-mail: inkelas@berkeley.edu. *Application contact:* Belen Flores, Student Affairs Officer, 510-643-7224, Fax: 510-643-5688, E-mail: linginfo@berkeley.edu.

University of California, Davis, Graduate Studies, Graduate Group in Linguistics, Davis, CA 95616. Offers applied linguistics (MA, PhD); linguistics (MA). *Degree requirements:* For master's, one foreign language, comprehensive exam (for some programs), thesis (for some programs); for doctorate, thesis/dissertation. *Entrance requirements:* For master's and doctorate, GRE General Test, minimum GPA of 3.0. Additional exam requirements/recommendations for international students: Required—TOEFL (minimum score 550 paper-based; 213 computer-based). Electronic applications accepted. *Faculty research:* Grammatical analysis and theory, sociolinguistics, historical linguistics, Romance linguistics, neurolinguistics.

University of California, Los Angeles, Graduate Division, College of Letters and Science, Department of Applied Linguistics and Teaching English as a Second Language, Program in Applied Linguistics, Los Angeles, CA 90095. Offers PhD. *Students:* 40 full-time (30 women); includes 5 minority (3 Asian Americans or Pacific Islanders, 2 Hispanic Americans), 20 international. Average age 33. 37 applicants, 24% accepted, 4 enrolled. In 2007, 9 degrees awarded. *Median time to degree:* Of those who began their doctoral program in fall 1999, 60% received their degree in 8 years or less. *Degree requirements:* For doctorate, one foreign language, thesis/dissertation, oral and written qualifying exams. *Entrance requirements:* For doctorate, GRE General Test, MA in relevant field, thesis or related research paper. *Application deadline:* For fall admission, 12/15 for domestic students. Application fee: $60. Electronic applications accepted. *Expenses:* Tuition, nonresident: full-time $5,728. Required fees: $8,966. Full-time tuition and fees vary according to program and student level. *Financial support:* In 2007–08, 33 fellowships with full and partial tuition reimbursements, 13 research assistantships with full and partial tuition reimbursements, 20 teaching assistantships with full and partial tuition reimbursements were awarded; Federal Work-Study, institutionally sponsored loans, scholarships/grants, and tuition waivers (full and partial) also available. Financial award application deadline: 3/1; financial award applicants required to submit FAFSA. *Unit head:* Dr. Lyle F. Bachman, Chair, 310-825-4631. *Application contact:* Departmental Office, 310-825-4631, Fax: 310-206-4118, E-mail: lyn@humnet.ucla.edu.

University of California, Los Angeles, Graduate Division, College of Letters and Science, Department of Linguistics, Los Angeles, CA 90095. Offers MA, PhD. *Students:* 41 full-time (22 women); includes 4 minority (3 Asian Americans or Pacific Islanders, 1 Hispanic American), 15 international. Average age 28. 110 applicants, 17% accepted, 9 enrolled. In 2007, 7 doctorates awarded. Terminal master's awarded for partial completion of doctoral program. *Median time to degree:* Of those who began their doctoral program in fall 1999, 71% received their degree in 8 years or less. *Degree requirements:* For master's, one foreign language, comprehensive exam or thesis; for doctorate, thesis/dissertation, oral and written qualifying exams. *Entrance requirements:* For master's, GRE General Test, minimum GPA of 3.0, sample of written work; statement of purpose; degree objective of Ph.D; for doctorate, GRE General Test, minimum undergraduate GPA of 3.0, sample of written work; statement of purpose. *Application deadline:* For fall admission, 12/15 for domestic students. Application fee: $60. Electronic applications accepted. *Expenses:* Tuition, nonresident: full-time $5,728. Required fees: $8,966. Full-time tuition and fees vary according to program and student level. *Financial support:* In 2007–08, 34 fellowships with full and partial tuition reimbursements, 17 research assistantships with full and partial tuition reimbursements, 24 teaching assistantships with full and partial tuition reimbursements were awarded; Federal Work-Study, institutionally sponsored loans, scholarships/grants, and tuition waivers (full and partial) also available. Financial award application deadline: 3/1; financial award applicants required to submit FAFSA. *Faculty research:* Phonetics, nonlinear phonology, formal syntax, formal semantics, natural language processing. *Unit head:* Dr. Anoop Mahajan, Chair, 310-825-5060. *Application contact:* Departmental Office, 310-825-0634, E-mail: linquist@humnet.ucla.edu.

University of California, San Diego, Office of Graduate Studies, Department of Linguistics, La Jolla, CA 92093. Offers PhD. *Degree requirements:* For doctorate, thesis/dissertation. *Entrance requirements:* For doctorate, GRE General Test. Electronic applications accepted.

University of California, San Diego, Office of Graduate Studies, Interdisciplinary Program in Cognitive Science, La Jolla, CA 92093. Offers cognitive science/anthropology (PhD); cognitive science/communication (PhD); cognitive science/computer science and engineering (PhD); cognitive science/linguistics (PhD); cognitive science/neuroscience (PhD); cognitive science/philosophy (PhD); cognitive science/psychology (PhD); cognitive science/sociology (PhD). Admissions offered through affiliated departments. *Faculty:* 65 full-time (14 women). *Students:* 7 full-time (3 women). Average age 26. 2 applicants, 100% accepted, 2 enrolled. In 2007, 1 degree awarded. *Degree requirements:* For doctorate, thesis/dissertation. *Entrance requirements:* For doctorate, GRE General Test, acceptance into one of the 8 participating departments. *Application deadline:* Applications are processed on a rolling basis. Application fee: $0. *Faculty research:* Language and cognition, philosophy of mind, visual perception, biological anthropology, sociolinguistics. *Unit head:* Gary Cottrell, Director, 858-534-7141, Fax: 858-534-1128, E-mail: gcottrell@ucsd.edu. *Application contact:* Beverley Walton, Coordinator, 858-534-4387, E-mail: bwalton@ucsd.edu.

University of California, Santa Barbara, Graduate Division, College of Letters and Sciences, Division of Humanities and Fine Arts, Department of Germanic, Slavic, and Semitic Studies, Santa Barbara, CA 93106. Offers Germanic languages and literature (MA, PhD), including applied linguistics (optional emphasis) (PhD), women's studies (optional emphasis) (PhD); MA/PhD. *Faculty:* 3 full-time (2 women). *Students:* 4 full-time (2 women), 2 international. Average age 31. 5 applicants, 80% accepted, 0 enrolled. In 2007, 1 master's, 2 doctorates awarded. Terminal master's awarded for partial completion of doctoral program. *Median time to degree:* Of those who began their doctoral program in fall 1999, 100% received their degree in 8 years or less. *Degree requirements:* For master's, 2 foreign languages, comprehensive exam, thesis, 36 units graduate level coursework; for doctorate, 3 foreign languages, comprehensive exam, thesis/dissertation. *Entrance requirements:* For master's and doctorate, GRE, sample of written work, tape of spoken German and/or English, proficiency in a foreign language. Additional exam requirements/recommendations for international students: Required—TOEFL (minimum score 550 paper-based; 213 computer-based; 80 iBT). *Application deadline:* For fall admission, 12/31 for domestic students, 5/1 for international students; for winter admission, 11/1 for domestic and international students; for spring admission, 2/1 for domestic and international students. Applications are processed on a rolling basis. Application fee: $60. Electronic applications accepted. *Expenses:* Tuition, nonresident: full-time $14,888. Required fees: $10,108. *Financial support:* In 2007–08, 4 students received support, including fellowships with full and partial tuition reimbursements available (averaging $5,400 per year), teaching assistantships with full and partial tuition reimbursements available (averaging $16,389 per year); Federal Work-Study, institutionally sponsored loans, scholarships/grants, and health care benefits also available. Financial award application deadline: 12/15; financial award applicants required to submit FAFSA. *Faculty research:* Critical theory, media-technology, psychoanalysis, German romanticism, Goethe. *Unit head:* Prof. Elisabeth Weber, Chair, 805-893-2295, E-mail: weber@gss.ucsb.edu. *Application contact:* Sierra Gray, Graduate Program Assistant, 805-893-2131, Fax: 805-893-2374, E-mail: sierra@gss.ucsb.edu.

University of California, Santa Barbara, Graduate Division, College of Letters and Sciences, Division of Humanities and Fine Arts, Department of Linguistics, Santa Barbara, CA 93106. Offers linguistics (PhD), including applied linguistics, cognitive science, human development, language interaction, social organizations; MA/PhD. *Faculty:* 27 full-time (20 women). *Students:* 27 full-time (20 women); includes 3 minority (2 Asian Americans or Pacific Islanders, 1 Hispanic American), 3 international. Average age 32. 46 applicants, 22% accepted, 4 enrolled. In 2007, 3 doctorates awarded. *Median time to degree:* Of those who began their doctoral program in fall 1999, 40% received their degree in 8 years or less. *Degree requirements:* For doctorate, one foreign language, thesis/dissertation, 48 units of coursework, minimum GPA of 3.7. *Entrance requirements:* For doctorate, GRE. Additional exam requirements/recommendations for international students: Required—TOEFL (minimum score 550 paper-based; 213 computer-based; 80 iBT). *Application deadline:* For fall admission, 12/1 for domestic and international students. Application fee: $60. Electronic applications accepted. *Expenses:* Tuition, nonresident: full-time $14,888. Required fees: $10,108. *Financial support:* In 2007–08, 27 students received support, including 18 fellowships with full tuition reimbursements available (averaging $10,500 per year), 4 research assistantships with full tuition reimbursements available (averaging $15,000 per year), 22 teaching assistantships (averaging $10,310 per year); Federal Work-Study, institutionally sponsored loans, scholarships/grants, health care benefits, and unspecified assistantships also available. Financial award application deadline: 12/1; financial award applicants required to submit FAFSA. *Faculty research:* Syntax, sociolinguistics, discourse and grammar, phonetics and phonology, corpus linguistics. *Unit head:* Prof. Patricia M. Clancy, Chair, 805-893-8658, E-mail: pclancy@linguistics.ucsb.edu. *Application contact:* Prof. Matthew K. Gordon, Information Contact, 805-893-5954, Fax: 805-893-7769, E-mail: mgordon@linguistics.ucsb.edu.

University of California, Santa Cruz, Division of Graduate Studies, Division of Humanities, Linguistics Research Center, Santa Cruz, CA 95064. Offers MA, PhD. *Faculty:* 15 full-time (5 women). *Students:* 25 full-time (11 women). 77 applicants, 26% accepted, 11 enrolled. In 2007, 6 master's, 2 doctorates awarded. Terminal master's awarded for partial completion of doctoral program. *Degree requirements:* For master's, one foreign language, research paper; for doctorate, one foreign language, thesis/dissertation, qualifying exam. *Entrance requirements:* For master's and doctorate, GRE General Test. *Application deadline:* For fall admission, 12/15 for domestic students. Application fee: $60. *Expenses:* Tuition, nonresident: full-time $14,694. Required fees: $11,360. *Financial support:* Fellowships, research assistantships, teaching assistantships, career-related internships or fieldwork, Federal Work-Study, and institutionally sponsored loans available. Financial award application deadline: 1/15. *Faculty research:* Phonological, morphological, syntactic, and semantic theory; computational linguistics. *Unit head:* Junko Ito, Director, 831-459-3340, E-mail: ito@ucsc.edu. *Application contact:* Judy L. Glass, Reporting Analyst for Graduate Admissions, 831-459-5906, Fax: 831-459-4843, E-mail: jlglass@ucsc.edu.

University of Chicago, Division of the Humanities, Department of Linguistics, Chicago, IL 60637-1513. Offers anthropology and linguistics (PhD); linguistics (AM, PhD). *Students:* 48. 57 applicants, 21% accepted, 6 enrolled.Terminal master's awarded for partial completion of doctoral program. *Degree requirements:* For master's, one foreign language, thesis; for doctorate, 2 foreign languages, thesis/dissertation. *Entrance requirements:* For master's and doctorate, GRE General Test. Additional exam requirements/recommendations for international students: Required—TOEFL. *Application deadline:* For fall admission, 12/15 for domestic students. Application fee: $55. *Financial support:* Fellowships, Federal Work-Study available. Financial award application deadline: 12/15; financial award applicants required to submit FAFSA. *Unit head:* Dr. Chris Kennedy, Chair, 773-702-8522.

University of Colorado at Boulder, Graduate School, College of Arts and Sciences, Department of Linguistics, Boulder, CO 80309. Offers MA, PhD. Part-time programs available. *Faculty:* 8. *Students:* 69 full-time (40 women), 7 part-time (3 women); includes 13 minority (5 American Indian/Alaska Native, 7 Asian Americans or Pacific Islanders, 1 Hispanic American), 14 international. Average age 34. 65 applicants, 78% accepted. In 2007, 11 master's, 1 doctorate awarded. Terminal master's awarded for partial completion of doctoral program. *Degree requirements:* For master's, comprehensive exam, thesis optional; for doctorate, one foreign language, thesis/dissertation. *Entrance requirements:* For master's, GRE General Test, minimum undergraduate GPA of 2.75; for doctorate, GRE General Test. *Application deadline:* For fall admission, 1/15 priority date for domestic students, 12/1 for international students. Applications are processed on a rolling basis. Application fee: $50 ($60 for international students). *Financial support:* In 2007–08, 8 fellowships (averaging $7,198 per year), 10 research assistantships (averaging $12,412 per year) were awarded; Federal Work-Study and tuition waivers (full) also available. Financial award application deadline: 1/15. *Faculty research:* Synchronic linguistics, discourse analysis, language acquisition, diachronic linguistics, lexicography, American Indian linguistics, psycholinguistics, African linguistics. Total annual research expenditures: $743,702. *Unit head:* Barbara Fox, Chair, 303-492-1609, Fax: 303-492-4416, E-mail: barbara.fox@colorado.edu. *Application contact:* Graduate Program Assistant, 303-492-8456, Fax: 303-492-4416, E-mail: linguist@colorado.edu.

University of Colorado Denver, College of Liberal Arts and Sciences, Department of English, Denver, CO 80217-3364. Offers applied linguistics (MA); English studies (MA); literature (MA); teaching English to speakers of other languages (Certificate); teaching of writing (MA). Part-time and evening/weekend programs available. *Faculty:* 33 full-time (21 women). *Students:* 6 full-time (5 women), 49 part-time (28 women); includes 6 minority (3 Asian Americans or Pacific Islanders, 3 Hispanic Americans), 1 international. Average age 32. 18 applicants, 56% accepted, 5 enrolled. In 2007, 23 degrees awarded. *Degree requirements:* For master's, thesis optional. *Entrance requirements:* For master's, GRE General Test, minimum GPA of 3.0. Additional exam requirements/recommendations for international students: Required—TOEFL (minimum score 550 paper-based). *Application deadline:* For fall admission, 5/25 for domestic students; for spring admission, 10/25 for domestic students. Applications are processed on a rolling basis. Application fee: $50 ($75 for international students). Electronic applications accepted. *Financial support:* Research assistantships, teaching assistantships, Federal Work-Study available. Financial award application deadline: 4/1; financial award applicants required to submit FAFSA. *Unit head:* Prof. Nancy Ciccone, Chair, 303-556-8395, Fax: 303-556-2959, E-mail: nancy.ciccone@cudenver.edu. *Application contact:* Prof. Ian Ying, Program Advisor, 303-556-6728, Fax: 303-556-2959, E-mail: hongguang.ying@cudenver.edu.

University of Connecticut, Graduate School, College of Liberal Arts and Sciences, Department of Linguistics, Field of Linguistics, Storrs, CT 06269. Offers MA, PhD. *Faculty:* 9 full-time (3 women). *Students:* 28 full-time (14 women), 3 part-time (1 woman), 24 international. Average age 32. 57 applicants, 9% accepted, 5 enrolled. In 2007, 3 master's, 4 doctorates awarded. *Degree requirements:* For doctorate, thesis/dissertation. *Entrance requirements:* For doctorate, GRE General Test. Additional exam requirements/recommendations for international students: Required—TOEFL (minimum score 550 paper-based; 213 computer-based). *Application deadline:* For fall admission, 2/1 priority date for domestic and international students; for spring admission, 11/1 for domestic students, 10/1 for international students. Applications are processed on a rolling basis. Application fee: $55. Electronic applications accepted. *Expenses:* Tuition, state resident: part-time $469 per credit hour. Tuition, nonresident: part-time $1,218 per credit hour. *Financial support:* In 2007–08, 13 research assistantships with full tuition reimbursements, 13 teaching assistantships with full tuition reimbursements were awarded; fellowships, Federal Work-Study, scholarships/grants, health care benefits, and unspecified assistantships also available. Financial award application deadline: 2/1; financial award applicants required to

Linguistics

University of Connecticut (continued)

submit FAFSA. *Application contact:* Catalina Ritton, Administrative Assistant, 860-486-4229, Fax: 860-486-0197, E-mail: catalina.ritton@uconn.edu.

University of Delaware, College of Arts and Sciences, Department of Linguistics, Newark, DE 19716. Offers MA, PhD. *Faculty:* 8 full-time (5 women), 1 part-time/adjunct (0 women). *Students:* 30 full-time (18 women); includes 2 minority (both Asian Americans or Pacific Islanders), 15 international. Average age 33. 47 applicants, 34% accepted, 3 enrolled. In 2007, 5 degrees awarded. *Degree requirements:* For doctorate, one foreign language, comprehensive exam, thesis/dissertation, publishable research papers. *Entrance requirements:* For master's, GRE General Test; for doctorate, GRE General Test, writing sample. Additional exam requirements/recommendations for international students: Required—TOEFL (minimum score 600 paper-based; 250 computer-based). *Application deadline:* For fall admission, 7/1 for domestic and international students; for spring admission, 12/1 for domestic and international students. Applications are processed on a rolling basis. Application fee: $60. Electronic applications accepted. *Financial support:* In 2007–08, 17 students received support, including 3 fellowships with full tuition reimbursements available (averaging $13,000 per year), 13 teaching assistantships with full tuition reimbursements available (averaging $13,000 per year); research assistantships with full tuition reimbursements available, traineeships, health care benefits, tuition waivers (full), and unspecified assistantships also available. Financial award application deadline: 3/1. *Faculty research:* East Asian, Austronesian and Romance languages, phonology, phonetics, syntax, cognitive science, semantics, psycholinguistics, language acquisition, endangered languages. Total annual research expenditures: $174,726. *Unit head:* Dr. Frederick R. Adams, Chair, 302-831-6806, Fax: 302-831-6896, E-mail: linguistics@udel.edu. *Application contact:* Dr. Benjamin Bruening, Director of Graduate Studies, 302-831-6837, Fax: 302-831-6896.

University of Florida, Graduate School, College of Liberal Arts and Sciences, Program in Linguistics, Gainesville, FL 32611. Offers linguistics (MA, PhD); teaching English as a second language (Certificate). *Faculty:* 11 full-time (8 women). *Students:* 42 (28 women); includes 1 minority (Hispanic American) 21 international. In 2007, 7 master's, 3 doctorates awarded. *Degree requirements:* For master's, one foreign language, comprehensive exam, thesis optional; for doctorate, 2 foreign languages, thesis/dissertation, qualifying exam. *Entrance requirements:* For master's and doctorate, GRE General Test, minimum GPA of 3.0. Additional exam requirements/recommendations for international students: Required—TOEFL (minimum score 550 paper-based; 213 computer-based). *Application deadline:* For fall admission, 6/1 priority date for domestic students. Applications are processed on a rolling basis. Application fee: $30. Electronic applications accepted. *Expenses:* Tuition, state resident: full-time $7,478. Tuition, nonresident: full-time $22,603. *Financial support:* In 2007–08, 1 research assistantship (averaging $15,999 per year), 7 teaching assistantships with tuition reimbursements (averaging $12,386 per year) were awarded; fellowships with tuition reimbursements, institutionally sponsored loans and unspecified assistantships also available. Financial award application deadline: 1/7. *Faculty research:* Theoretical, applied, and descriptive linguistics. *Unit head:* Dr. Caroline Wiltshire, Interim Director, 352-392-0639 Ext. 224, Fax: 352-392-8480, E-mail: wiltshir@lin.ufl.edu. *Application contact:* Dr. Caroline Wiltshire, Interim Director, 352-392-0639 Ext. 224, Fax: 352-392-8480, E-mail: wiltshir@lin.ufl.edu.

University of Georgia, Graduate School, College of Arts and Sciences, Program in Linguistics, Athens, GA 30602. Offers MA, PhD. *Students:* 32 full-time (19 women), 13 part-time (7 women); includes 8 minority (4 African Americans, 3 Asian Americans or Pacific Islanders, 1 Hispanic American), 6 international. 36 applicants, 67% accepted, 10 enrolled. In 2007, 4 master's, 3 doctorates awarded. *Degree requirements:* For master's, one foreign language, thesis; for doctorate, 2 foreign languages, comprehensive exam, thesis/dissertation. *Entrance requirements:* For master's and doctorate, GRE General Test. *Application deadline:* For fall admission, 7/1 priority date for domestic students; for spring admission, 11/15 for domestic students. Application fee: $50. Electronic applications accepted. *Expenses:* Contact institution. *Financial support:* In 2007–08, 3 fellowships, 7 research assistantships, 8 teaching assistantships were awarded; Federal Work-Study and institutionally sponsored loans also available. Financial award application deadline: 2/15. *Faculty research:* Applied linguistics, English linguistics, dialectology, lexicography, discourse analysis. *Unit head:* Dr. Jared Stephen Klein, Director, 706-542-9261, Fax: 706-542-2897, E-mail: jklein@uga.edu. *Application contact:* Dr. Don R. McCreary, Graduate Coordinator, 706-542-2238, E-mail: mccreary@uga.edu.

University of Hawaii at Manoa, Graduate Division, Colleges of Arts and Sciences, College of Language, Linguistics and Literature, Department of Linguistics, Honolulu, HI 96822. Offers MA, PhD. Part-time programs available. *Faculty:* 40 full-time (16 women), 3 part-time/adjunct (1 woman). *Students:* 60 full-time (45 women), 7 part-time (3 women); includes 13 minority (11 Asian Americans or Pacific Islanders, 2 Hispanic Americans), 33 international. Average age 34. 54 applicants, 43% accepted, 11 enrolled.Terminal master's awarded for partial completion of doctoral program. *Median time to degree:* Of those who began their doctoral program in fall 1999, 67% received their degree in 8 years or less. *Degree requirements:* For master's, 2 foreign languages, thesis optional; for doctorate, 2 foreign languages, comprehensive exam, thesis/dissertation. *Entrance requirements:* For master's and doctorate, GRE General Test. Additional exam requirements/recommendations for international students: Required—TOEFL (minimum score 600 paper-based; 250 computer-based; 100 iBT), IELTS (minimum score 7). *Application deadline:* For fall admission, 1/10 for domestic and international students; for spring admission, 9/1 for domestic and international students. Applications are processed on a rolling basis. Application fee: $50. *Financial support:* In 2007–08, 41 students received support, including 4 research assistantships (averaging $16,662 per year), 31 teaching assistantships (averaging $13,664 per year); career-related internships or fieldwork, Federal Work-Study, scholarships/grants, and tuition waivers (full and partial) also available. Support available to part-time students. Financial award application deadline: 3/1. *Faculty research:* Languages of the Pacific and Asia. *Application contact:* Patricia Donegan, Graduate Chair, 808-956-8602, Fax: 808-956-9166, E-mail: donegan@hawaii.edu.

University of Houston, College of Liberal Arts and Social Sciences, Department of English, Houston, TX 77204. Offers applied English linguistics (MA); English and American literature (MA, PhD); literature and creative writing (MA, MFA, PhD). Postbaccalaureate distance learning degree programs offered. *Faculty:* 26 full-time (9 women), 6 part-time/adjunct (3 women). *Students:* 85 full-time (39 women), 65 part-time (51 women); includes 17 minority (3 African Americans, 6 Asian Americans or Pacific Islanders, 8 Hispanic Americans), 6 international. Average age 32. 63 applicants, 73% accepted, 29 enrolled. In 2007, 19 master's, 14 doctorates awarded. *Degree requirements:* For master's, one foreign language, thesis (for some programs); for doctorate, 2 foreign languages, comprehensive exam, thesis/dissertation. *Entrance requirements:* For master's, GRE General Test, GRE Subject Test, minimum GPA of 3.0 in last 60 hours of course work; for doctorate, GRE General Test, GRE Subject Test, writing sample. Additional exam requirements/recommendations for international students: Required—TOEFL. *Application deadline:* For fall admission, 1/1 priority date for domestic students. Applications are processed on a rolling basis. Application fee: $50. *Expenses:* Tuition, state resident: full-time $6,297; part-time $262 per credit. Tuition, nonresident: full-time $12,969; part-time $540 per credit. Required fees: $2,696. *Financial support:* In 2007–08, 2 fellowships with full tuition reimbursements (averaging $1,700 per year), 72 teaching assistantships with full tuition reimbursements (averaging $1,200 per year) were awarded; research assistantships with full tuition reimbursements, career-related internships or fieldwork, Federal Work-Study, institutionally sponsored loans, scholarships/grants, health care benefits, and unspecified assistantships also available. Support available to part-time students. Financial award application deadline: 2/1. *Unit head:* Wyman Henderson, Chairperson, 713-743-3004, Fax: 713-743-3215, E-mail: whh@uh.edu. *Application contact:* Ruby Jones, Advising Assistant, 713-743-2941, Fax: 713-743-3215, E-mail: rjones@uh.edu.

University of Illinois at Chicago, Graduate College, College of Liberal Arts and Sciences, Department of English, Program in Linguistics, Chicago, IL 60607-7128. Offers applied linguistics (teaching English as a second language) (MA). Part-time programs available. *Degree requirements:* For master's, one foreign language, comprehensive exam, thesis (for some programs). *Entrance requirements:* For master's, minimum GPA of 3.0. Additional exam requirements/recommendations for international students: Required—TOEFL. Electronic applications accepted. *Faculty research:* Second language acquisition, methodology of second language teaching, lexicography, language, sex and gender.

University of Illinois at Urbana–Champaign, Graduate College, College of Liberal Arts and Sciences, School of Literatures, Cultures and Linguistics, Department of Linguistics, Champaign, IL 61820. Offers linguistics (MA, PhD); teaching of English as a second language (MA). *Faculty:* 14 full-time (5 women). *Students:* 73 full-time (51 women), 42 part-time (34 women); includes 10 minority (2 African Americans, 8 Asian Americans or Pacific Islanders), 58 international. 234 applicants, 27% accepted, 34 enrolled. In 2007, 36 master's, 8 doctorates awarded. *Degree requirements:* For doctorate, one foreign language, thesis/dissertation. *Entrance requirements:* For master's, minimum GPA of 3.0; for doctorate, minimum GPA of 3.5. *Application deadline:* For fall admission, 1/21 for domestic students. Applications are processed on a rolling basis. Application fee: $60 ($75 for international students). Electronic applications accepted. *Financial support:* In 2007–08, 24 fellowships, 24 research assistantships, 65 teaching assistantships were awarded. Financial award application deadline: 2/15. *Unit head:* Hye Suk J. Yoon, Head, 217-333-5572, Fax: 217-333-3466, E-mail: jyoon@uiuc.edu. *Application contact:* Beth Creek, Administrative Secretary, 217-333-1008, Fax: 217-244-3466, E-mail: b-creek@ucic.edu.

The University of Iowa, Graduate College, College of Liberal Arts and Sciences, Department of Linguistics, Iowa City, IA 52242-1316. Offers linguistics (MA, PhD); linguistics with TESL (MA). Linguistics with TESL option offered as part of dual degree that begins at undergraduate level. *Faculty:* 6 full-time, 12 part-time/adjunct. *Students:* 16 full-time (9 women), 7 part-time (4 women), 11 international. 28 applicants, 32% accepted, 6 enrolled. In 2007, 7 master's, 2 doctorates awarded. *Degree requirements:* For master's, thesis optional, exam; for doctorate, comprehensive exam, thesis/dissertation. *Entrance requirements:* For master's and doctorate, GRE General Test, minimum GPA of 3.0. Additional exam requirements/recommendations for international students: Required—TOEFL (minimum score 600 paper-based; 250 computer-based; 100 iBT). *Application deadline:* Applications are processed on a rolling basis. Application fee: $60 ($85 for international students). Electronic applications accepted. *Expenses:* Tuition, state resident: part-time $349 per hour. Tuition, nonresident: part-time $349 per hour. Tuition and fees vary according to course load and program. *Financial support:* In 2007–08, 4 research assistantships with partial tuition reimbursements, 15 teaching assistantships with partial tuition reimbursements were awarded; fellowships also available. Financial award applicants required to submit FAFSA. *Unit head:* Catherine Ringen, Chair, 319-335-0212, Fax: 319-335-3971.

University of Kansas, Research and Graduate Studies, College of Liberal Arts and Sciences, Department of Linguistics, Lawrence, KS 66045. Offers MA, PhD. Part-time programs available. *Faculty:* 8. *Students:* 27 full-time (9 women), 7 part-time (2 women); includes 1 minority (Asian American or Pacific Islander), 20 international. Average age 35. 20 applicants, 55% accepted, 5 enrolled. In 2007, 4 master's, 4 doctorates awarded. Terminal master's awarded for partial completion of doctoral program. *Degree requirements:* For master's, one foreign language, thesis or alternative; for doctorate, one foreign language, thesis/dissertation. *Entrance requirements:* For master's and doctorate, GRE General Test. Additional exam requirements/recommendations for international students: Required—TOEFL. *Application deadline:* For fall admission, 1/1 priority date for domestic students, 1/1 for international students. Application fee; $55 ($60 for international students). Electronic applications accepted. *Expenses:* Tuition, state resident: full-time $5,838. Tuition, nonresident: full-time $13,409. Tuition and fees vary according to program. *Financial support:* Fellowships with full and partial tuition reimbursements, research assistantships with full and partial tuition reimbursements, teaching assistantships with full and partial tuition reimbursements, unspecified assistantships available. Financial award application deadline: 1/1. *Faculty research:* Phonetics and phonology, syntax, psycholinguistics, neurolinguistics, language acquisition. *Unit head:* Dr. Allard Jongman, Chair, 785-864-3450, Fax: 785-864-5724, E-mail: liguistics@ku.edu. *Application contact:* Corinna Johnson, Department Secretary, 785-864-3450, Fax: 785-864-5724, E-mail: linguistics@ku.edu.

University of Manitoba, Faculty of Graduate Studies, Faculty of Arts, Department of Linguistics, Winnipeg, MB R3T 2N2, Canada. Offers MA, PhD.

University of Maryland, Baltimore County, Graduate School, College of Arts, Humanities and Social Sciences, Department of Modern Languages and Linguistics, Program in Intercultural Communication, Baltimore, MD 21250. Offers MA. Part-time and evening/weekend programs available. *Faculty:* 10 full-time (3 women), 3 part-time/adjunct (2 women). *Students:* 23 full-time (20 women), 14 part-time (10 women); includes 6 minority (1 African American, 2 Asian Americans or Pacific Islanders, 3 Hispanic Americans), 13 international. 29 applicants, 72% accepted, 15 enrolled. In 2007, 17 degrees awarded. *Degree requirements:* For master's, one foreign language, comprehensive exam, thesis. *Entrance requirements:* For master's, GRE General Test, minimum GPA of 3.0, 3 letters of recommendation, self-evaluation and statement of support, resumé. Additional exam requirements/recommendations for international students: Required—TOEFL. *Application deadline:* For fall admission, 1/31 for domestic and international students. Applications are processed on a rolling basis. Application fee: $45. Electronic applications accepted. *Financial support:* In 2007–08, 8 students received support, including 4 teaching assistantships with full tuition reimbursements available (averaging $11,324 per year). Financial award applicants required to submit FAFSA. *Faculty research:* Comparative television research-cross-cultural; cultural studies; social developments in Latin America; intercultural communication; French civilization and cultural studies; language, gender and sexuality; sociolinguistics; African linguistics; immigrants in U. S. and Latin American societies. *Unit head:* Dr. Edward Larkey, Director, 410-455-2104, Fax: 410-455-1025, E-mail: larkey@umbc.edu.

University of Maryland, College Park, Graduate Studies, College of Arts and Humanities, Department of Linguistics, College Park, MD 20742. Offers MA, PhD. *Faculty:* 20 full-time (10 women). *Students:* 32 full-time (16 women), 2 part-time (1 woman); includes 3 minority (1 African American, 1 Asian American or Pacific Islander, 1 Hispanic American), 15 international. 114 applicants, 8% accepted, 6 enrolled. In 2007, 10 degrees awarded. *Median time to degree:* Of those who began their doctoral program in fall 1999, 33% received their degree in 8 years or less. *Degree requirements:* For master's, thesis or alternative; for doctorate, thesis/dissertation. *Entrance requirements:* For master's, GRE General Test, minimum GPA of 3.0, sample of work, 3 letters of recommendation; for doctorate, GRE General Test, minimum GPA of 3.0, sample of work. Additional exam requirements/recommendations for international students: Required—TOEFL. *Application deadline:* For fall admission, 5/15 for domestic students, 2/1 for international students. Applications are processed on a rolling basis. Application fee: $60. Electronic applications accepted. *Financial support:* In 2007–08, 16 fellowships with full tuition reimbursements (averaging $10,586 per year), 4 research assistantships with tuition reimbursements (averaging $18,101 per year), 22 teaching assistantships with tuition reimbursements (averaging $15,579 per year) were awarded; Federal Work-Study and scholarships/grants also available. Support available to part-time students. Financial award applicants required to submit FAFSA. *Faculty research:* Psycholinguistics, computational linguistics. Total annual research expenditures: $712,730. *Unit head:* Dr. Norbert Hornstein, Chairman, 301-405-7002, Fax: 301-314-7104, E-mail: nhorste@umd.edu. *Application contact:* Dean of Graduate School, 301-405-4190, Fax: 301-314-9305.

University of Massachusetts Amherst, Graduate School, College of Humanities and Fine Arts, Department of Linguistics, Amherst, MA 01003. Offers MA, PhD. Part-time programs available. *Faculty:* 14 full-time (6 women). *Students:* 32 full-time (19 women), 7 part-time (1 woman); includes 4 minority (2 African Americans, 1 American Indian/Alaska Native, 1 Asian American or Pacific Islander), 19 international. Average age 29. 113 applicants, 15% accepted, 5 enrolled. In 2007, 1 master's, 3 doctorates awarded. Terminal master's awarded for partial completion of doctoral program. *Degree requirements:* For master's, thesis or alternative; for doctorate, thesis/dissertation. *Entrance requirements:* For master's and doctorate, GRE General Test. Additional exam requirements/recommendations for international students: Required—TOEFL (minimum score 530 paper-based; 197 computer-based). *Application deadline:* For fall admission, 1/15 priority date for domestic and international students. Applications are processed on a rolling basis. Application fee: $50 ($65 for international students). Electronic applications accepted. *Expenses:* Tuition, state resident: full-time $2,640; part-time $110 per credit. Tuition, nonresident: full-time $9,936; part-time $414 per credit. Required fees: $7,455. One-time fee: $332. Tuition and fees vary according to course load, campus/location, program and reciprocity agreements. *Financial support:* In 2007–08, 1 fellowship with full tuition reimbursement (averaging $6,875 per year), 11 research assistantships with full tuition reimbursements (averaging $10,597 per year), 29 teaching assistantships with full tuition reimbursements (averaging $13,962 per year) were awarded; career-related internships or fieldwork, Federal Work-Study, scholarships/grants, traineeships, and unspecified assistantships also available. Support available to part-time students. Financial award application deadline: 2/1. *Unit head:* Dr. Elizabeth O. Selkirk, Head, 413-545-0889, Fax: 413-545-2792, E-mail: selkirk@cs.umass.edu.

University of Massachusetts Boston, Office of Graduate Studies, College of Liberal Arts, Program in Applied Linguistics, Boston, MA 02125-3393. Offers bilingual education (MA); English as a second language (MA); foreign language pedagogy (MA). Part-time and evening/weekend programs available. *Degree requirements:* For master's, one foreign language, comprehensive exam. *Entrance requirements:* For master's, minimum GPA of 2.75. *Faculty research:* Multicultural theory and curriculum development, foreign language pedagogy, language and culture, applied psycholinguistics, bilingual education.

University of Michigan, Horace H. Rackham School of Graduate Studies, College of Literature, Science, and the Arts, Department of Linguistics, Ann Arbor, MI 48109. Offers general linguistics (PhD); linguistics and Germanic languages and literatures (PhD). *Degree requirements:* For doctorate, 2 foreign languages, thesis/dissertation, oral defense of dissertation. *Entrance requirements:* For doctorate, GRE General Test. Additional exam requirements/recommendations for international students: Required—TOEFL (minimum score 620 paper-based; 260 computer-based), TOEFL or Michigan English Language Assessment Battery. Electronic applications accepted. *Faculty research:* Broad-based approach to linguistics as a cognitive and social science including theoretical, experimental and computational approaches.

University of Michigan, Horace H. Rackham School of Graduate Studies, College of Literature, Science, and the Arts, Department of Romance Languages and Literatures, Ann Arbor, MI 48109. Offers French (PhD); Romance linguistics (PhD); Spanish (PhD). *Faculty:* 27 full-time (12 women), 2 part-time/adjunct (1 woman). *Students:* 60 full-time (44 women). Average age 30. 54 applicants, 37% accepted. In 2007, 3 degrees awarded. *Degree requirements:* For doctorate, 2 foreign languages, thesis/dissertation, oral defense of dissertation, preliminary exams. *Entrance requirements:* For doctorate, GRE General Test. Additional exam requirements/recommendations for international students: Required—TOEFL or Michigan English Language Assessment Battery. *Application deadline:* For fall admission, 1/1 for domestic students. Application fee: $60. Electronic applications accepted. *Financial support:* In 2007–08, 5 fellowships with full tuition reimbursements (averaging $20,000 per year), 1 teaching assistantship with full tuition reimbursement were awarded; research assistantships, institutionally sponsored loans, scholarships/grants, and unspecified assistantships also available. Financial award application deadline: 1/1. *Faculty research:* Comparative Romance studies, medieval and early modern studies, postcolonial and minority literatures, culture and materiality, reflection on the nature and function of scholarship. *Unit head:* Dr. Michele Hannoosh, Chair, 734-764-5344, Fax: 734-764-8163. *Application contact:* Graduate Assistant, 734-763-0408, Fax: 734-764-8163, E-mail: rll-admissions@umich.edu.

University of Minnesota, Twin Cities Campus, Graduate School, College of Liberal Arts, Institute of Linguistics, English as a Second Language, and Slavic Languages and Literatures (ILES), Program in Linguistics, Minneapolis, MN 55455-0213. Offers MA, PhD. *Faculty:* 4 full-time (3 women), 15 part-time/adjunct (7 women). *Students:* 41 full-time (17 women); includes 4 minority (3 American Indian/Alaska Native, 1 Asian American or Pacific Islander), 3 international. Average age 33. 29 applicants, 34% accepted, 6 enrolled. In 2007, 8 master's, 1 doctorate awarded. Terminal master's awarded for partial completion of doctoral program. *Degree requirements:* For master's, one foreign language, comprehensive exam, thesis; for doctorate, 2 foreign languages, comprehensive exam, thesis/dissertation. *Entrance requirements:* For master's and doctorate, GRE General Test, 3 letters of recommendation, unit questionnaire. Additional exam requirements/recommendations for international students: Required—TOEFL (minimum score 550 paper-based; 213 computer-based). *Application deadline:* For fall admission, 3/15 priority date for domestic and international students. Applications are processed on a rolling basis. Application fee: $55 ($75 for international students). Electronic applications accepted. *Financial support:* In 2007–08, 26 students received support, including 5 fellowships with full tuition reimbursements available (averaging $22,000 per year), 6 research assistantships with partial tuition reimbursements available (averaging $6,200 per year), 15 teaching assistantships (averaging $12,400 per year); Federal Work-Study, traineeships, and unspecified assistantships also available. Financial award application deadline: 1/15; financial award applicants required to submit FAFSA. *Faculty research:* Pragmatics and language processing, syntactic theory, language policy and planning, contact linguistics, language and cognition. *Unit head:* Dr. Jeanette Gundel, Professor and Head, 612-624-7564, Fax: 612-624-4579, E-mail: gunde003@umn.edu.

University of Missouri–St. Louis, College of Arts and Sciences, Department of English, St. Louis, MO 63121. Offers American literature (MA); creative writing (MFA); English (MA); English literature (MA); linguistics (MA); teaching of writing (Graduate Certificate). *Faculty:* 19 full-time (12 women), 1 part-time/adjunct (0 women). *Students:* 16 full-time (12 women), 90 part-time (68 women); includes 9 minority (5 African Americans, 3 Asian Americans or Pacific Islanders, 1 Hispanic American). Average age 32. In 2007, 30 degrees awarded. *Degree requirements:* For master's, thesis optional. *Entrance requirements:* For master's, GRE General Test, writing sample. Additional exam requirements/recommendations for international students: Required—TOEFL (minimum score 550 paper-based; 213 computer-based). *Application deadline:* For fall admission, 7/15 priority date for domestic students; for spring admission, 12/15 priority date for domestic students. Applications are processed on a rolling basis. Application fee: $35 ($40 for international students). Electronic applications accepted. *Financial support:* In 2007–08, 1 research assistantship (averaging $9,000 per year), 6 teaching assistantships with full and partial tuition reimbursements (averaging $9,000 per year) were awarded. *Faculty research:* Victorian literature, Shakespeare and Renaissance literature, eighteenth century literature, composition theory. *Unit head:* Dr. Richard Cook, Director of Graduate Studies, 314-516-5516, Fax: 314-516-5415, E-mail: rcook@umsl.edu. *Application contact:* 314-516-5458, Fax: 314-516-5310, E-mail: gradadm@umsl.edu.

The University of Montana, Graduate School, College of Arts and Sciences, Department of Anthropology, Missoula, MT 59812-0002. Offers anthropology (MA); cultural heritage (MA); cultural heritage studies (PhD); forensic anthropology (MA); historical anthropology (PhD); linguistics (MA). *Degree requirements:* For master's, thesis (for some programs). *Entrance requirements:* For master's, GRE General Test. Additional exam requirements/recommendations for international students: Required—TOEFL. *Faculty research:* Historical preservation, plateau-plains archaeology and ethnohistory.

The University of Montana, Graduate School, College of Arts and Sciences, Program in Linguistics, Missoula, MT 59812-0002. Offers MA. *Entrance requirements:* For master's, GRE General Test. Additional exam requirements/recommendations for international students: Required—TOEFL.

University of New Hampshire, Graduate School, College of Liberal Arts, Department of English, Durham, NH 03824. Offers English (MFA, PhD); English education (MST); language and linguistics (MA); literature (MA); writing (MA). Part-time programs available. *Faculty:* 44 full-time. *Students:* 38 full-time (21 women), 64 part-time (43 women); includes 6 minority (1 American Indian/Alaska Native, 3 Asian Americans or Pacific Islanders, 2 Hispanic Americans), 3 international. Average age 34. 251 applicants, 45% accepted, 31 enrolled. In 2007, 25 master's, 6 doctorates awarded. *Degree requirements:* For master's, one foreign language; for doctorate, 2 foreign languages, thesis/dissertation. *Entrance requirements:* For master's, GRE General Test, sample of written work; for doctorate, GRE General Test, GRE Subject Test, sample of written work. Additional exam requirements/recommendations for international students: Required—TOEFL (minimum score 550 paper-based; 213 computer-based; 80 iBT). *Application deadline:* For fall admission, 2/15 priority date for domestic students, 2/15 for international students. Applications are processed on a rolling basis. Application fee: $60. Electronic applications accepted. *Financial support:* In 2007–08, 1 fellowship, 1 research assistantship, 43 teaching assistantships were awarded; career-related internships or fieldwork, Federal Work-Study, scholarships/grants, and tuition waivers (full and partial) also available. Support available to part-time students. Financial award application deadline: 2/15. *Unit head:* Dr. Andrew Merton, Chairperson, 603-862-3977. *Application contact:* Sue Smith, Administrative Assistant, 603-862-3963, E-mail: engl.grad@unh.edu.

University of New Mexico, Graduate School, College of Arts and Sciences, Department of Linguistics, Albuquerque, NM 87131-2039. Offers MA, PhD. Part-time programs available. *Faculty:* 12 full-time (10 women), 4 part-time/adjunct (3 women). *Students:* 30 full-time (15 women), 10 part-time (4 women); includes 5 minority (3 American Indian/Alaska Native, 2 Hispanic Americans), 12 international. Average age 35. 43 applicants, 47% accepted, 7 enrolled. In 2007, 4 master's, 2 doctorates awarded. Terminal master's awarded for partial completion of doctoral program. *Degree requirements:* For master's, comprehensive exam, thesis optional; for doctorate, 2 foreign languages, comprehensive exam, thesis/dissertation. *Entrance requirements:* For master's, minimum GPA of 3.0, letters of recommendation, letter of intent; for doctorate, MA in linguistics or equivalent, paper of publishable quality, 3 letters of recommendation, letter of intent. *Application deadline:* For fall admission, 1/15 for domestic students; for spring admission, 10/31 for domestic students. Application fee: $50. Electronic applications accepted. *Financial support:* In 2007–08, 11 students received support, including teaching assistantships with full and partial tuition reimbursements available (averaging $6,860 per year); research assistantships, Federal Work-Study and tuition waivers (full and partial) also available. Financial award application deadline: 1/15; financial award applicants required to submit FAFSA. *Faculty research:* Functional/cognitive linguistics, sociolinguistics, Spanish linguistics, Native American linguistics, signed language linguistics. Total annual research expenditures: $37,817. *Unit head:* Dr. Sherman Wilcox, Chair, 505-277-6353, Fax: 505-277-6355, E-mail: wilcox@unm.edu. *Application contact:* Jessica Slocum, Administrative Assistant III, 505-277-6353, Fax: 505-277-6355, E-mail: jslocum@unm.edu.

University of New Mexico, Graduate School, College of Education, Department of Language, Literacy and Sociocultural Studies, Program in Educational Linguistics, Albuquerque, NM 87131-2039. Offers Ed D, PhD. Part-time programs available. *Students:* 7 full-time (6 women), 9 part-time (6 women); includes 3 minority (1 Asian American or Pacific Islander, 2 Hispanic Americans), 6 international. Average age 45. 8 applicants, 25% accepted, 1 enrolled. In 2007, 2 degrees awarded. *Degree requirements:* For doctorate, comprehensive exam, thesis/dissertation. *Entrance requirements:* For doctorate, masters in linguistics, or complementary field, recommended. Additional exam requirements/recommendations for international students: Required—TOEFL. *Application deadline:* For fall admission, 12/1 for domestic students. Application fee: $50. Electronic applications accepted. *Financial support:* In 2007–08, 3 students received support, including 3 teaching assistantships with tuition reimbursements available (averaging $5,074 per year); fellowships with tuition reimbursements available, career-related internships or fieldwork, institutionally sponsored loans, scholarships/grants, and unspecified assistantships also available. Support available to part-time students. Financial award application deadline: 3/1; financial award applicants required to submit FAFSA. *Faculty research:* Bilingualism, language maintenance and loss, bilingual deaf education, Spanish dialectical studies, English as a second language writing/composition, Native American language issues, language and thought, creativity and collaboration. *Unit head:* Dr. Julia Scherba, Graduate Director, 505-277-1406, Fax: 505-277-8362, E-mail: devalenz@unm.edu. *Application contact:* Mary Gurule Vernon, Information Contact, 505-277-5282, Fax: 505-277-8362, E-mail: mgurule2@unm.edu.

The University of North Carolina at Chapel Hill, Graduate School, College of Arts and Sciences, Department of Germanic Languages, Chapel Hill, NC 27599. Offers literature and linguistics (MA, PhD). Part-time programs available. Terminal master's awarded for partial completion of doctoral program. *Degree requirements:* For master's, comprehensive exam, thesis; for doctorate, one foreign language, comprehensive exam, thesis/dissertation. *Entrance requirements:* For master's and doctorate, GRE General Test, minimum GPA of 3.0. *Faculty research:* Gender and sexuality, literature and politics, German and Jewish culture, medieval through modern literature, Germanic linguistics.

The University of North Carolina at Chapel Hill, Graduate School, College of Arts and Sciences, Department of Linguistics, Chapel Hill, NC 27599. Offers MA, PhD. Terminal master's awarded for partial completion of doctoral program. *Degree requirements:* For master's, one foreign language, comprehensive exam, thesis; for doctorate, 2 foreign languages, comprehensive exam, thesis/dissertation. *Entrance requirements:* For master's and doctorate, GRE General Test, minimum GPA of 3.0. Additional exam requirements/recommendations for international students: Required—TOEFL (minimum score 550 paper-based; 213 computer-based). Electronic applications accepted. *Faculty research:* Phonetics, phonology, syntax, historical linguistics, Indo-European.

University of North Dakota, Graduate School, College of Arts and Sciences, Program in Linguistics, Grand Forks, ND 58202. Offers MA. *Faculty:* 5 full-time (2 women). *Students:* 2 full-time (1 woman), 5 part-time (4 women), 2 international. 1 applicant, 0% accepted. In 2007, 3 degrees awarded. *Degree requirements:* For master's, one foreign language, thesis, final examination. *Entrance requirements:* For master's, minimum GPA of 3.0. Additional exam requirements/recommendations for international students: Required—TOEFL (minimum score 550 paper-based; 213 computer-based; 79 iBT), IELTS (minimum score 7). *Application deadline:* For fall admission, 2/15 priority date for domestic and international students; for spring admission, 10/15 priority date for domestic and international students. Applications are processed on a rolling basis. Application fee: $35. Electronic applications accepted. *Expenses:* Tuition, state resident: full-time $4,050; part-time $225 per credit. Tuition, nonresident: full-time $10,818; part-time $601 per credit. Required fees: $110 per semester. Tuition and fees vary according to class time, campus/location, program and reciprocity agreements. *Financial support:* Fellowships with full and partial tuition reimbursements, research assistantships with full and partial tuition reimbursements, teaching assistantships with full and partial tuition reimbursements, Federal Work-Study, institutionally sponsored loans, tuition waivers (full and partial), and unspecified assistantships available. Support available to part-time students. Financial award application deadline: 3/15; financial award applicants required to submit FAFSA. *Faculty research:* Practice-based field studies. *Unit head:* Dr. John Clifton, Graduate Director, 701-777-2011. *Application contact:* Staci Wells, Admissions Associate, 701-777-2945, Fax: 701-777-3619, E-mail: gradschool@mail.und.nodak.edu.

University of North Texas, Robert B. Toulouse School of Graduate Studies, College of Arts and Sciences, Department of English, Denton, TX 76203. Offers creative writing (MA); English (MA, PhD); English as a second language (MA); linguistics (MA); Technical writing (MA). *Faculty:* 60 full-time (36 women). *Students:* 82 full-time (46 women), 91 part-time (65 women); includes 19 minority (4 African Americans, 1 American Indian/Alaska Native, 6 Asian Americans or Pacific Islanders, 8 Hispanic Americans), 13 international. Average age 30. 91 applicants, 47% accepted, 21 enrolled. In 2007, 38 master's, 5 doctorates awarded. Terminal master's awarded for partial completion of doctoral program. *Degree requirements:* For master's, one foreign language, comprehensive exam, thesis optional; for doctorate, one foreign language, comprehensive exam, thesis/dissertation. *Entrance requirements:* For master's, GRE General Test, 3.0 GPA, personal statement, current vita/resumé, writing sample for creative writing

Linguistics

University of North Texas (continued)

program; for doctorate, GRE General Test, 3.5 GPA, 3 letters of recommendation, personal statement, writing sample. Additional exam requirements/recommendations for international students: Required—proof of English language proficiency required for non-native English speakers; Recommended—TOEFL (minimum score 550 paper-based; 213 computer-based). *Application deadline:* For fall admission, 7/15 priority date for domestic students; for spring admission, 11/15 for domestic students. Application fee: $50 ($75 for international students). *Financial support:* In 2007–08, 8 students received support, including 2 fellowships with full tuition reimbursements available (averaging $20,000 per year), 42 teaching assistantships (averaging $11,000 per year); career-related internships or fieldwork, Federal Work-Study, institutionally sponsored loans, scholarships/grants, health care benefits, and unspecified assistantships also available. Financial award application deadline: 4/1. *Faculty research:* Creative writing, British and American literature, composition and rhetoric. Total annual research expenditures: $25,000. *Unit head:* Dr. David Holdeman, Chair, 940-565-2050, Fax: 940-565-4355, E-mail: holdeman@cas1.unt.edu. *Application contact:* Dr. Robert K. Upchuerch, Chair of Graduate Studies, 940-565-2114, Fax: 940-565-4355, E-mail: robertu@unt.edu.

University of Oregon, Graduate School, College of Arts and Sciences, Department of Linguistics, Eugene, OR 97403. Offers MA, PhD. *Faculty:* 9 full-time (4 women). *Students:* 49 full-time (33 women), 9 part-time (6 women); includes 5 minority (1 American Indian/Alaska Native, 1 Asian American or Pacific Islander, 3 Hispanic Americans), 33 international. 68 applicants, 49% accepted. In 2007, 5 master's, 3 doctorates awarded. Terminal master's awarded for partial completion of doctoral program. *Degree requirements:* For master's, 2 foreign languages; for doctorate, thesis/dissertation. *Entrance requirements:* For master's and doctorate, GRE General Test, minimum GPA of 3.0. Additional exam requirements/ recommendations for international students: Required—TOEFL. *Application deadline:* For fall admission, 2/1 for domestic students. Application fee: $50. *Financial support:* In 2007–08, 18 teaching assistantships were awarded; career-related internships or fieldwork also available. *Faculty research:* Functional syntax, discourse, empirical methods. *Unit head:* Eric Pederson, Head, 541-346-3900. *Application contact:* Anitra Ingham, Admissions Contact, 541-346-3613.

University of Ottawa, Faculty of Graduate and Postdoctoral Studies, Faculty of Arts, Department of Linguistics, Ottawa, ON K1N 6N5, Canada. Offers MA, PhD. *Degree requirements:* For master's, one foreign language, thesis or alternative; for doctorate, 2 foreign languages, comprehensive exam, thesis/dissertation. *Entrance requirements:* For master's, honors degree or equivalent, minimum B average; for doctorate, master's degree, minimum B+ average. Electronic applications accepted. *Faculty research:* Empirical linguistics, formal linguistics.

University of Pennsylvania, Graduate School of Education, Division of Language in Education, Programs in Teaching English to Speakers of Other Languages and Intercultural Communication, Philadelphia, PA 19104. Offers educational linguistics (PhD); intercultural communication (MS Ed); teaching English to speakers of other languages (MS Ed). Part-time programs available. Postbaccalaureate distance learning degree programs offered (minimal on-campus study). Terminal master's awarded for partial completion of doctoral program. *Degree requirements:* For master's, comprehensive exam, thesis (for some programs); for doctorate, one foreign language, thesis/dissertation, preliminary exam. *Entrance requirements:* For master's and doctorate, GRE General Test or MAT. Additional exam requirements/ recommendations for international students: Required—TOEFL. Electronic applications accepted. Expenses: Contact institution. *Faculty research:* Second language acquisition, social linguistics, English as a second language.

University of Pennsylvania, School of Arts and Sciences, Graduate Group in Linguistics, Philadelphia, PA 19104. Offers AM, PhD. Terminal master's awarded for partial completion of doctoral program. *Degree requirements:* For master's, thesis; for doctorate, 2 foreign languages, thesis/dissertation. *Entrance requirements:* For master's and doctorate, GRE General Test. Additional exam requirements/recommendations for international students: Required—TOEFL. Electronic applications accepted.

University of Pittsburgh, School of Arts and Sciences, Department of Linguistics, Pittsburgh, PA 15260. Offers applied linguistics (PhD); Hispanic linguistics (MA, PhD); linguistics (MA); sociolinguistics (PhD). Part-time programs available. *Faculty:* 11 full-time (4 women). *Students:* 35 full-time (23 women); includes 4 minority (3 African Americans, 1 Hispanic American), 4 international. Average age 30. 63 applicants, 56% accepted, 14 enrolled. In 2007, 2 master's, 1 doctorate awarded. Terminal master's awarded for partial completion of doctoral program. *Degree requirements:* For master's, one foreign language, thesis; for doctorate, 2 foreign languages, comprehensive exam, thesis/dissertation. *Entrance requirements:* For master's, GRE General Test; for doctorate, GRE General Test, MA in linguistics. Additional exam requirements/recommendations for international students: Required—TOEFL (minimum score 600 paper-based; 250 computer-based). *Application deadline:* For fall admission, 12/15 priority date for domestic and international students. Applications are processed on a rolling basis. Application fee: $50. Electronic applications accepted. *Financial support:* In 2007–08, 13 teaching assistantships with full and partial tuition reimbursements (averaging $14,485 per year) were awarded; fellowships, research assistantships, Federal Work-Study, scholarships/ grants, health care benefits, and unspecified assistantships also available. Support available to part-time students. Financial award application deadline: 12/15. *Faculty research:* Second language acquisition, applied linguistics, sociolinguistics, language contact. Total annual research expenditures: $301,051. *Unit head:* Dr. Scott Kiesling, Chair, 412-624-5900, Fax: 412-624-6130, E-mail: kiesling@pitt.edu. *Application contact:* Patricia C Cochran, Graduate Secretary, 412-624-5900, Fax: 412-624-6130, E-mail: lingpitt@pitt.edu.

University of Puerto Rico, Río Piedras, College of Humanities, Department of Linguistics, San Juan, PR 00931-3300. Offers MA. Part-time programs available. *Students:* 18 full-time (11 women), 11 part-time (9 women). Average age 29. In 2007, 2 degrees awarded. *Degree requirements:* For master's, one foreign language, comprehensive exam, thesis. *Entrance requirements:* For master's, PAEG or GRE, interview, minimum GPA of 3.0, letter of recommendation (2). *Application deadline:* For fall admission, 2/1 for domestic and international students. Application fee: $17. *Expenses:* Tuition, state resident: full-time $1,808; part-time $113 per credit. Tuition, nonresident: full-time $5,248; part-time $328 per credit. Required fees: $72 per term. *Financial support:* Fellowships, research assistantships, teaching assistantships, Federal Work-Study, institutionally sponsored loans, and tuition waivers (partial) available. Financial award application deadline: 5/31. *Unit head:* Prof. Patrick Andre Mather, Director, 787-764-0000 Ext. 3389.

University of Regina, Faculty of Graduate Studies and Research, Faculty of Arts, Program in Linguistics, Regina, SK S4S 0A2, Canada. Offers MA. Offered as special case program. Part-time programs available. *Faculty:* 4 full-time (0 women). *Degree requirements:* For master's, thesis. *Entrance requirements:* Additional exam requirements/recommendations for international students: Required—TOEFL (minimum score 580 paper-based; 237 computer-based). *Application deadline:* Applications are processed on a rolling basis. Application fee: $85 ($100 for international students). Electronic applications accepted. *Financial support:* In 2007–08, fellowships (averaging $15,750 per year), research assistantships (averaging $13,875 per year), teaching assistantships (averaging $13,060 per year) were awarded; scholarships/ grants also available. Financial award application deadline: 6/15. *Faculty research:* Phonology, morphology, syntax, semantics, Amerindian linguistics. *Unit head:* Dr. Arok Wolvengrey, Program Coordinator, 790-790-5950 Ext. 3310, E-mail: awolvengrey@firstnations.university.ca.

University of South Africa, College of Human Sciences, Pretoria, South Africa. Offers adult education (M Ed); African languages (MA, PhD); African politics (MA, PhD); Afrikaans (MA, PhD); ancient history (MA, PhD); ancient Near Eastern studies (MA, PhD); anthropology (MA, PhD); applied linguistics (MA); Arabic (MA, PhD); archaeology (MA); art history (MA); Biblical archaeology (MA); Biblical studies (M Th, D Th, PhD); Christian spirituality (M Th, D Th); church history (M Th, D Th); classical studies (MA, PhD); clinical psychology (MA); communication (MA, PhD); comparative education (M Ed, Ed D); consulting psychology (D Admin, D Com, PhD); curriculum studies (M Ed, Ed D); development studies (M Admin, MA, D Admin, PhD); didactics (M Ed, Ed D); education (M Tech); education management (M Ed, Ed D); educational psychology (M Ed); English (MA); environmental education (M Ed); French (MA, PhD); German (MA, PhD); Greek (MA); guidance and counseling (M Ed); health studies (MA, PhD), including health sciences education (MA), health services management (MA), medical and surgical nursing science (critical care general) (MA), midwifery and neonatal nursing science (MA), trauma and emergency care (MA); history (MA, PhD); history of education (Ed D); inclusive education (M Ed, Ed D); information and communications technology policy and regulation (MA); information science (MA, MIS, PhD); international politics (MA, PhD); Islamic studies (MA, PhD); Italian (MA, PhD); Judaica (MA, PhD); linguistics (MA, PhD); mathematical education (M Ed); mathematics education (MA); missiology (M Th, D Th); modern Hebrew (MA, PhD); musicology (MA, MMus, D Mus, PhD); natural science education (M Ed); New Testament (M Th, D Th); Old Testament (D Th); pastoral therapy (M Th, D Th); philosophy (MA); philosophy of education (M Ed, Ed D); politics (MA, PhD); Portuguese (MA, PhD); practical theology (M Th, D Th); psychology (MA, MS, PhD); psychology of education (M Ed, Ed D); public health (MA); religious studies (MA, D Th, PhD); Romance languages (MA); Russian (MA, PhD); Semitic languages (MA, PhD); social behavior studies in HIV/AIDS (MA); social science (mental health) (MA); social science in development studies (MA); social science in psychology (MA); social science in social work (MA); social science in sociology (MA); social work (MSW, DSW, PhD); socio-education (M Ed, Ed D); sociolinguistics (MA); sociology (MA, PhD); Spanish (MA, PhD); systematic theology (M Th, D Th); TESOL (teaching English to speakers of other languages) (MA); theological ethics (M Th, D Th); theory of literature (MA, PhD); urban ministries (D Th); urban ministry (M Th).

University of South Carolina, The Graduate School, College of Arts and Sciences, Linguistics Program, Columbia, SC 29208. Offers linguistics (MA, PhD); teaching English to speakers of other languages (Certificate). Part-time programs available. *Faculty:* 12 full-time (7 women), 11 part-time/adjunct (5 women). *Students:* 22 full-time (14 women), 6 part-time (4 women); includes 2 minority (1 African American, 1 Asian American or Pacific Islander), 12 international. Average age 31. 65 applicants, 57% accepted. In 2007, 12 master's, 2 doctorates awarded. Terminal master's awarded for partial completion of doctoral program. *Degree requirements:* For master's, one foreign language, comprehensive exam, thesis optional; for doctorate, 3 foreign languages, comprehensive exam, thesis/dissertation. *Entrance requirements:* For master's and Certificate, GRE General Test, minimum GPA of 3.0; for doctorate, GRE General Test, minimum GPA of 3.5. Additional exam requirements/recommendations for international students: Required—TOEFL. *Application deadline:* For fall admission, 1/15 priority date for domestic students. Applications are processed on a rolling basis. Application fee: $35. Electronic applications accepted. *Expenses:* Tuition, state resident: part-time $440 per hour. Tuition, nonresident: part-time $936 per hour. Required fees: $17 per hour. Tuition and fees vary according to program. *Financial support:* In 2007–08, 22 students received support, including 4 fellowships with partial tuition reimbursements available, 4 research assistantships with partial tuition reimbursements available (averaging $10,000 per year), 8 teaching assistantships with partial tuition reimbursements available (averaging $12,000 per year); career-related internships or fieldwork and graders also available. Financial award application deadline: 1/15. *Faculty research:* Second language acquisition, sociolinguistics, syntax, historical linguistics and phonology. Total annual research expenditures: $60,000. *Unit head:* Dr. Kurt Goblirsch, Graduate Director, 803-777-2063, Fax: 803-777-7514, E-mail: linguistics@sc.edu. *Application contact:* Dr. Eric Holt, Graduate Director, 803-777-2063, Fax: 803-777-7514, E-mail: linguistics@sc.edu.

University of Southern California, Graduate School, College of Letters, Arts and Sciences, Department of Linguistics, Los Angeles, CA 90089. Offers East Asian linguistics (PhD); Hispanic linguistics (PhD); linguistics (PhD). *Faculty:* 18 full-time (11 women). *Students:* 40 full-time (23 women), 4 part-time (3 women); includes 7 minority (4 Asian Americans or Pacific Islanders, 3 Hispanic Americans), 20 international. 62 applicants, 31% accepted. In 2007, 10 doctorates awarded. *Degree requirements:* For doctorate, 2 foreign languages, thesis/ dissertation. *Entrance requirements:* For doctorate, GRE General Test. *Application deadline:* For fall admission, 12/1 priority date for domestic students. Application fee: $85. *Financial support:* In 2007–08, fellowships with full tuition reimbursements (averaging $19,000 per year), research assistantships with full tuition reimbursements (averaging $19,000 per year), teaching assistantships with full tuition reimbursements (averaging $19,000 per year) were awarded. Financial award application deadline: 2/15; financial award applicants required to submit FAFSA. *Faculty research:* Syntax, phonology, phonetics, semantics, sociolinguistics, psycholinguistics. *Unit head:* Dr. James Higginbotham, Chair, 213-740-2986, E-mail: lingdept@usc.edu. *Application contact:* Joyce Perez, Information Contact, 213-740-2311.

University of South Florida, Graduate School, College of Arts and Sciences, Department of World Language Education, Program in Applied Linguistics, Tampa, FL 33620-9951. Offers MA. *Students:* 3 full-time (2 women), 2 part-time (both women); includes 1 minority (Hispanic American) 1 applicant, 100% accepted, 1 enrolled. In 2007, 5 degrees awarded. *Degree requirements:* For master's, one foreign language, thesis optional. *Entrance requirements:* For master's, GRE (minimum score: 430 verbal reasoning, 4.5 analytical writing), GPA of 3.0 or higher in upper level of undergraduate studies. Additional exam requirements/recommendations for international students: Required—TOEFL (minimum score 250 computer-based; 100 iBT). *Application deadline:* For fall admission, 6/1 for domestic students, 1/2 for international students; for spring admission, 10/15 for domestic students, 7/1 for international students. Application fee: $30. Electronic applications accepted. *Financial support:* In 2007–08, 15 teaching assistantships (averaging $2,250 per year) were awarded. *Unit head:* Dr. Wei Zhu, Associate Professor of Linguistics, 813-974-3805, Fax: 813-974-1718, E-mail: wzhu@cas.usf.edu.

The University of Tennessee, Graduate School, College of Arts and Sciences, Department of Modern Foreign Languages and Literatures, Program in Modern Foreign Languages, Knoxville, TN 37996. Offers applied linguistics (PhD); French (PhD); German (PhD); Italian (PhD); Portuguese (PhD); Russian (PhD); Spanish (PhD). *Degree requirements:* For doctorate, 2 foreign languages, thesis/dissertation. *Entrance requirements:* For doctorate, minimum GPA of 2.7. Additional exam requirements/recommendations for international students: Required—TOEFL. Electronic applications accepted.

The University of Texas at Arlington, Graduate School, College of Liberal Arts, Department of Linguistics and TESOL, Program in Linguistics, Arlington, TX 76019. Offers MA, PhD. Part-time and evening/weekend programs available. *Faculty:* 7 full-time (2 women). *Students:* 28 full-time (20 women), 40 part-time (24 women); includes 6 minority (3 Asian Americans or Pacific Islanders, 3 Hispanic Americans), 24 international. 4 applicants, 100% accepted, 1 enrolled. In 2007, 2 master's, 2 doctorates awarded. Terminal master's awarded for partial completion of doctoral program. *Degree requirements:* For master's, one foreign language, comprehensive exam (for some programs), thesis optional; for doctorate, 2 foreign languages, comprehensive exam, thesis/dissertation, qualifying exam, dissertation proposal defense, professional development. *Entrance requirements:* For master's, GRE General Test, minimum undergraduate GPA of 3.0, 9 credits of undergraduate foundation courses; for doctorate, GRE General Test, 30 hours of graduate work in linguistics or a related discipline, minimum GPA of 3.5. Additional exam requirements/recommendations for international students: Required—TOEFL (minimum score 550 paper-based; 213 computer-based). *Application deadline:* For fall admission, 6/16 for domestic students. Applications are processed on a rolling basis. Application fee: $35 ($50 for international students). *Expenses:* Tuition, state resident: full-time $5,934. Tuition, nonresident: full-time $10,938. *Financial support:* In 2007–08, 52 students received support, including 10 fellowships (averaging $1,000 per year), 1 research assistantship, 4 teaching assistantships; career-related internships or fieldwork and institutionally sponsored loans also available. Financial award application deadline: 3/1; financial award applicants required to submit FAFSA. *Faculty research:* Field linguistics, discourse analysis, text linguistics, phonology, teaching English as a second language. *Application contact:* Dr. Laurel Stvan, Graduate Advisor, 817-272-3133, Fax: 817-272-2731.

The University of Texas at Austin, Graduate School, College of Liberal Arts, Department of French and Italian, Austin, TX 78712-1111. Offers French (MA, PhD); Romance linguistics (MA,

PhD). Part-time programs available. *Degree requirements:* For master's, one foreign language, thesis; for doctorate, 2 foreign languages, thesis/dissertation. *Entrance requirements:* For master's, GRE General Test, minimum GPA of 3.0, bachelor's degree in French or equivalent; for doctorate, GRE General Test, minimum GPA of 3.0, master's degree in French. Additional exam requirements/recommendations for international students: Required—TOEFL. Electronic applications accepted. *Faculty research:* Nineteenth-century Italian literature, Italian Renaissance, twentieth-century French literature, Francophone literature, fifteenth-century literature and culture.

The University of Texas at Austin, Graduate School, College of Liberal Arts, Department of Linguistics, Austin, TX 78712-1111. Offers MA, PhD. *Degree requirements:* For master's, one foreign language, thesis; for doctorate, 2 foreign languages, thesis/dissertation. *Entrance requirements:* For master's and doctorate, GRE General Test. Electronic applications accepted. *Faculty research:* Theoretical linguistics, sociolinguistics, documentary and descriptive linguistics, computational linguistics.

The University of Texas at El Paso, Graduate School, College of Liberal Arts, Department of Languages and Linguistics, El Paso, TX 79968-0001. Offers linguistics (MA); Spanish (MA). Part-time and evening/weekend programs available. *Degree requirements:* For master's, thesis optional. *Entrance requirements:* For master's, departmental exam, GRE General Test, sample of written work, minimum GPA of 3.0. Additional exam requirements/recommendations for international students: Required—TOEFL. Electronic applications accepted.

University of Toronto, School of Graduate Studies, Humanities Division, Department of Linguistics, Toronto, ON M5S 1A1, Canada. Offers MA, PhD. Part-time programs available. *Faculty:* 19 full-time, 4 part-time/adjunct. *Students:* 51 full-time (40 women), 1 part-time, 11 international. 74 applicants, 38% accepted. In 2007, 5 master's, 2 doctorates awarded. *Degree requirements:* For master's, 2 foreign languages; for doctorate, thesis/dissertation, oral thesis proposal. *Entrance requirements:* For master's, BA in linguistics; for doctorate, MA in linguistics. *Application deadline:* For fall admission, 1/15 for domestic students. Application fee: $100 Canadian dollars. *Unit head:* Prof. Diane Massam, Chair and Graduate Chair, 416-978-4029, Fax: 416-978-2688, E-mail: dmassam@chass.utoronto.ca. *Application contact:* Mary Hsu, Departmental Officer, 416-978-0556, Fax: 416-971-2688, E-mail: mhsu@chass.utoronto.ca.

University of Utah, The Graduate School, College of Humanities, Department of Linguistics, Salt Lake City, UT 84112-1107. Offers applied linguistics (MA, PhD); linguistics (MA, PhD). Part-time programs available. Postbaccalaureate distance learning degree programs offered (minimal on-campus study). *Faculty:* 11 full-time (4 women), 2 part-time/adjunct (0 women). *Students:* 33 full-time (27 women), 15 part-time (9 women); includes 7 minority (4 Asian Americans or Pacific Islanders, 3 Hispanic Americans), 10 international. Average age 33. 24 applicants, 79% accepted, 15 enrolled. In 2007, 5 degrees awarded. *Degree requirements:* For master's and doctorate, 2 foreign languages, comprehensive exam. *Entrance requirements:* For master's and doctorate, GRE General Test, minimum undergraduate GPA of 3.0. Additional exam requirements/recommendations for international students: Required—TOEFL (minimum score 600 paper-based; 250 computer-based). *Application deadline:* For fall admission, 12/14 for domestic students, 11/15 for international students. Application fee: $45 ($65 for international students). Electronic applications accepted. *Financial support:* In 2007–08, 2 students received support, including 2 fellowships with tuition reimbursements available (averaging $5,000 per year), 8 research assistantships with tuition reimbursements available (averaging $10,000 per year), 17 teaching assistantships with partial tuition reimbursements available (averaging $10,000 per year); scholarships/grants and tuition waivers (partial) also available. Financial award application deadline: 2/1; financial award applicants required to submit FAFSA. *Faculty research:* American Indian languages, applied linguistics phonology, sociolinguistics, syntax. Total annual research expenditures: $67,330. *Unit head:* Dr. Edward Rubin, Chair, 801-581-8047, Fax: 801-585-7351, E-mail: erubin@linguistics.utah.edu. *Application contact:* Kate Lythgoe, Executive Secretary, 801-581-8047, Fax: 801-585-7351, E-mail: kate.lythgoe@linguistics.utah.edu.

University of Utah, The Graduate School, College of Humanities, Program in Middle East Studies, Salt Lake City, UT 84112-1107. Offers anthropology (MA); Arabic (MA, PhD); Arabic and linguistics (MA, PhD); Hebrew (MA); history (MA, PhD); Persian (MA, PhD); political science (MA, PhD); Turkish (MA). *Faculty:* 12 full-time (3 women). *Students:* 26 full-time (12 women), 10 part-time (2 women); includes 1 minority (Asian American or Pacific Islander), 10 international. Average age 36. 36 applicants, 78% accepted, 10 enrolled. In 2007, 6 master's awarded. Terminal master's awarded for partial completion of doctoral program. *Median time to degree:* Of those who began their doctoral program in fall 1999, 100% received their degree in 8 years or less. *Degree requirements:* For master's, 2 foreign languages, comprehensive exam, thesis optional; for doctorate, 3 foreign languages, comprehensive exam, thesis/dissertation. *Entrance requirements:* For master's, GRE General Test, minimum GPA of 3.2; for doctorate, GRE General Test, MA in Middle East studies or equivalent, minimum GPA of 3.2. Additional exam requirements/recommendations for international students: Required—TOEFL (minimum score 580 paper-based; 237 computer-based; 92 iBT). *Application deadline:* For fall admission, 1/15 for domestic and international students; for spring admission, 9/15 for domestic and international students. Application fee: $45 ($65 for international students). *Financial support:* In 2007–08, 17 students received support, including 14 fellowships with full tuition reimbursements available (averaging $14,000 per year), 2 teaching assistantships with full tuition reimbursements available (averaging $12,000 per year); unspecified assistantships also available. Financial award application deadline: 1/15. *Faculty research:* Arabic literature and linguistics, Islamic studies, Middle East history, political science, Judaic studies. *Unit head:* Dr. Ibrahim A. Karawan, Director, 801-581-6181, Fax: 801-581-6183, E-mail: ibrahim.karawan@poli-sci.utah.edu. *Application contact:* Peter von Sivers, Director of Graduate Studies, 801-581-8073, Fax: 801-581-6183, E-mail: peter.vonsivers@utah.edu.

University of Victoria, Faculty of Graduate Studies, Faculty of Humanities, Department of Linguistics, Victoria, BC V8W 2Y2, Canada. Offers applied linguistics (MA); linguistics (MA, PhD). Part-time programs available. *Faculty:* 10 full-time (5 women), 1 (woman) part-time/adjunct. *Students:* 16 full-time, 7 international. Average age 30. 28 applicants, 25% accepted, 4 enrolled. In 2007, 3 degrees awarded. *Degree requirements:* For master's, one foreign language, thesis, colloquium; for doctorate, 2 foreign languages, comprehensive exam, thesis/dissertation, candidacy exam. *Entrance requirements:* For master's, GRE; for doctorate, GRE, sample of written work. Additional exam requirements/recommendations for international students: Required—TOEFL. *Application deadline:* For fall admission, 1/15 priority date for domestic students, 12/15 priority date for international students. Applications are processed on a rolling basis. Application fee: $75 ($125 for international students). Electronic applications accepted. *Expenses:* Tuition, state resident: full-time $3,110. International tuition: $3,700 full-time. Tuition and fees vary according to program. *Financial support:* In 2007–08, 16 students received support, including 2 fellowships (averaging $13,000 per year), 2 research assistantships (averaging $8,000 per year), teaching assistantships (averaging $6,000 per year); institutionally sponsored loans also available. Financial award application deadline: 2/15. *Faculty research:* Grammatical theory, syntactic analysis, morphology, Western Amerindian languages, Salishan, applied linguistics. *Unit head:* Dr. Leslie Saxon, Chair, 250-721-7424, Fax: 250-721-7423, E-mail: saxon@uvic.ca. *Application contact:* Dr. Hua Lin, Graduate Advisor, 250-721-7424, E-mail: luahin@uvic.ca.

University of Virginia, College and Graduate School of Arts and Sciences, Program in Linguistics, Charlottesville, VA 22903. Offers MA. *Students:* 10 full-time (5 women), 1 international. Average age 25. 17 applicants, 59% accepted, 7 enrolled. In 2007, 1 degree awarded. *Degree requirements:* For master's, one foreign language, comprehensive exam, thesis optional. *Entrance requirements:* For master's, GRE General Test, GRE Subject Test. *Application deadline:* Applications are processed on a rolling basis. Application fee: $60. Electronic applications accepted. *Financial support:* Applicants required to submit FAFSA. *Unit head:* Emily Scida, Director, 434-924-0646, E-mail: ees2n@virginia.edu.

University of Washington, Graduate School, College of Arts and Sciences, Department of Linguistics, Seattle, WA 98195. Offers linguistics (MA, PhD); Romance linguistics (MA, PhD). Part-time programs available. Terminal master's awarded for partial completion of doctoral program. *Degree requirements:* For master's, one foreign language, thesis; for doctorate, 2 foreign languages, thesis/dissertation. *Entrance requirements:* For master's, GRE General Test, minimum GPA of 3.0; for doctorate, GRE, minimum GPA of 3.0. Additional exam requirements/recommendations for international students: Required—TOEFL. Electronic applications accepted. *Faculty research:* Syntax, phonology, semantics, phonetics, sociolinguistics.

University of Washington, Graduate School, College of Arts and Sciences, Department of Slavic Languages and Literature, Seattle, WA 98195. Offers Russian literature (MA, PhD); Slavic linguistics (MA, PhD). *Degree requirements:* For master's, 2 foreign languages, thesis optional; for doctorate, 3 foreign languages, thesis/dissertation. *Entrance requirements:* For master's and doctorate, GRE General Test, minimum GPA of 3.0. Additional exam requirements/recommendations for international students: Required—TOEFL. Electronic applications accepted. *Faculty research:* Modern and medieval East European languages and literatures, comparative literature, Russian folk literature, Slavic literary theory and criticism, computerized morphology of Russian.

University of Wisconsin–Madison, Graduate School, College of Letters and Science, Department of English, Madison, WI 53706-1380. Offers applied English linguistics (MA); composition studies (PhD); English language and linguistics (PhD); literature (MA, PhD). *Degree requirements:* For doctorate, thesis/dissertation.

University of Wisconsin–Madison, Graduate School, College of Letters and Science, Department of Linguistics, Madison, WI 53706-1380. Offers MA, PhD. Part-time programs available. Terminal master's awarded for partial completion of doctoral program. *Degree requirements:* For master's, 2 foreign languages; for doctorate, 3 foreign languages, thesis/dissertation. Electronic applications accepted. *Faculty research:* Formal linguistics, acoustic phonetics, American studies, Indo-European linguistics.

Wayne State University, College of Liberal Arts and Sciences, Interdisciplinary Program in Linguistics, Detroit, MI 48202. Offers MA. *Students:* 10 full-time (9 women), 7 part-time (6 women); includes 2 minority (both African Americans), 4 international. Average age 29. 12 applicants, 58% accepted, 0 enrolled. In 2007, 4 degrees awarded. *Degree requirements:* For master's, one foreign language, thesis. *Entrance requirements:* Additional exam requirements/recommendations for international students: Required—TOEFL (minimum score 550 paper-based; 213 computer-based); Recommended—TWE (minimum score 6). *Application deadline:* For fall admission, 7/1 for domestic students, 6/1 for international students; for winter admission, 10/1 for international students; for spring admission, 2/1 for international students. Application fee: $30 ($50 for international students). Electronic applications accepted. *Expenses:* Tuition, state resident: part-time $403 per credit hour. Tuition, nonresident: part-time $890 per credit hour. *Faculty research:* Formal linguistics, psycholinguistics, sociolinguistics, historical linguistics, language acquisition. *Unit head:* Patricia Siple, Director, 313-577-8642.

West Virginia University, Eberly College of Arts and Sciences, Department of Foreign Languages, Morgantown, WV 26506. Offers French (MA); linguistics (MA); Spanish (MA); teaching English to speakers of other languages (MA). Part-time programs available. *Faculty:* 20 full-time (13 women), 27 part-time/adjunct (24 women). *Students:* 64 full-time (42 women), 8 part-time (7 women); includes 8 minority (1 African American, 3 Asian Americans or Pacific Islanders, 4 Hispanic Americans), 31 international. Average age 29. 46 applicants, 76% accepted, 26 enrolled. In 2007, 31 degrees awarded. *Degree requirements:* For master's, one foreign language, comprehensive exam (for some programs), thesis optional. *Entrance requirements:* For master's, minimum GPA of 3.0. *Application deadline:* For fall admission, 2/1 priority date for domestic and international students; for spring admission, 10/1 for domestic and international students. Applications are processed on a rolling basis. Application fee: $50. Electronic applications accepted. *Expenses:* Tuition, state resident: full-time $5,196; part-time $292 per credit hour. Tuition, nonresident: full-time $15,064; part-time $840 per credit hour. Tuition and fees vary according to program. *Financial support:* In 2007–08, 69 students received support, including 65 teaching assistantships with full tuition reimbursements available (averaging $8,864 per year); research assistantships, Federal Work-Study, institutionally sponsored loans, and tuition waivers (full and partial) also available. Financial award application deadline: 2/1; financial award applicants required to submit FAFSA. *Faculty research:* French, German, and Spanish literature; foreign language pedagogy; English as a second language; cultural studies; linguistics. Total annual research expenditures: $36,679. *Unit head:* Dr. Angel T. Tuninetti, Chair, 304-293-5121, Fax: 304-293-7655, E-mail: angel.tuninetti@mail.wvu.edu. *Application contact:* Dr. Sandra Stjepanovic, Director of Graduate Studies, 304-293-5121, Fax: 304-293-7655, E-mail: sandra.stjepanovic@mail.wvu.edu.

Yale University, Graduate School of Arts and Sciences, Department of Linguistics, New Haven, CT 06520. Offers PhD. *Degree requirements:* For doctorate, 2 foreign languages, thesis/dissertation. *Entrance requirements:* For doctorate, GRE General Test.

York University, Faculty of Graduate Studies, Faculty of Arts, Program in Theoretical and Applied Linguistics, Toronto, ON M3J 1P3, Canada. Offers MA, PhD. *Degree requirements:* For master's, thesis.

Translation and Interpretation

American University, College of Arts and Sciences, Department of Language and Foreign Studies, Program in French, Washington, DC 20016-8001. Offers translation (Certificate). Part-time and evening/weekend programs available. *Students:* 2 full-time (both women). *Degree requirements:* For Certificate, minimum 15 credit hours related course work. *Entrance requirements:* For degree, Bachelor's Degree in French or evidence of French proficiency + BA in any field. *Application deadline:* For fall admission, 2/1 for domestic students; for spring admission, 10/1 for domestic students. Application fee: $50. *Expenses:* Tuition: Full-time $19,998; part-time $1,111 per credit hour. Required fees: $380. Tuition and fees vary according to program. *Financial support:* Fellowships, career-related internships or fieldwork, Federal Work-Study, and institutionally sponsored loans available. Financial award application deadline: 2/1. *Faculty research:* Literature, language, modern French politics, contemporary French society, the civilization of Quebec, business French and translation studies.

American University, College of Arts and Sciences, Department of Language and Foreign Studies, Program in Russian, Washington, DC 20016-8001. Offers translation (Certificate). Part-time and evening/weekend programs available. *Students:* Average age 28. *Degree*

Translation and Interpretation

American University (continued)

requirements: For Certificate, 15 credit hour minimum in related course work. *Entrance requirements:* For degree, Bachelor's Degree in Russian or evidence of Russian Proficiency and a BA. *Application deadline:* For fall admission, 2/1 for domestic students; for spring admission, 10/1 for domestic students. Application fee: $50. *Expenses:* Tuition: Full-time $19,998; part-time $1,111 per credit hour. Required fees: $380. Tuition and fees vary according to program. *Financial support:* Fellowships with full and partial tuition reimbursements, career-related internships or fieldwork, Federal Work-Study, and institutionally sponsored loans available. Financial award application deadline: 2/1. *Faculty research:* Culture, literature, and area studies; technology-assisted language instruction; linguistics.

American University, College of Arts and Sciences, Department of Language and Foreign Studies, Program in Spanish: Latin American Studies, Washington, DC 20016-8001. Offers Spanish: Latin American studies (MA); translation (Certificate). Part-time and evening/weekend programs available. *Students:* 17 full-time (14 women), 13 part-time (9 women); includes 8 minority (3 African Americans, 1 Asian American or Pacific Islander, 4 Hispanic Americans), 1 international. Average age 28. In 2007, 8 master's, 14 other advanced degrees awarded. *Degree requirements:* For master's, one foreign language, comprehensive exam, thesis or alternative, research requirement. *Entrance requirements:* For master's, GRE, bachelor's degree in language or equivalent, essay in Spanish; 3.2 GPA; statement of purpose; for Certificate, Bachelor's degree in Spanish or BA any field and Spanish proficiency. *Application deadline:* For fall admission, 2/1 for domestic students; for spring admission, 10/1 for domestic students. Application fee: $50. *Expenses:* Tuition: Full-time $19,998; part-time $1,111 per credit hour. Required fees: $380. Tuition and fees vary according to program. *Financial support:* Fellowships with full and partial tuition reimbursements, career-related internships or fieldwork, Federal Work-Study, and institutionally sponsored loans available. Financial award application deadline: 2/1. *Faculty research:* Latin American culture, literature, and history; computer-aided instruction.

Babel University School of Translation, Program in Translation, Honolulu, HI 96815-1302. Offers MS. Part-time and evening/weekend programs available. Postbaccalaureate distance learning degree programs offered (no on-campus study). *Faculty:* 3 full-time (1 woman), 24 part-time/adjunct (11 women). *Students:* Average age 32. 42 applicants, 8 enrolled. In 2007, 16 degrees awarded. *Degree requirements:* For master's, comprehensive exam, thesis. *Entrance requirements:* For master's, translation exam. Additional exam requirements/recommendations for international students: Recommended—TOEFL (minimum score 550 paper-based). *Application deadline:* For fall admission, 9/1 priority date for domestic and international students; for winter admission, 12/1 priority date for domestic and international students; for spring admission, 3/1 priority date for domestic and international students. Applications are processed on a rolling basis. Application fee: $1,000. *Financial support:* Institutionally sponsored loans and scholarships/grants available. *Unit head:* Miyoko Yuasa, Chancellor, 808-946-3773. *Application contact:* Tomoko Jones, Administration Supervisor, 808-946-3773, Fax: 808-946-3993, E-mail: pst@babel.edu.

College of Charleston, Graduate School, School of Languages, Cultures, and World Affairs, Program in Medical Interpreting, Charleston, SC 29424-0001. Offers Certificate. *Faculty:* 7 full-time (6 women). *Entrance requirements:* For degree, language exam, minimum GPA of 3.0. *Application deadline:* For fall admission, 6/15 for domestic students. Application fee: $50. *Expenses: Contact institution. Unit head:* Dr. Elizabeth A. Martinez-Gibson, Director, 843-953-8066.

Concordia University, School of Graduate Studies, Faculty of Arts and Science, Department of Études Françaises, Montréal, QC H3G 1M8, Canada. Offers écriture (Certificate); anglais-français en langue et techniques de localisation (Certificate); littératures francophones et résonances médiatiques (MA); traductologie (MA); translation (Diploma). *Degree requirements:* For other advanced degree, one foreign language.

Georgia State University, College of Arts and Sciences, Department of Modern and Classical Languages, Program in Translation and Interpretation, Atlanta, GA 30303-3083. Offers French (Certificate); German (Certificate); Spanish (Certificate). *Faculty:* 3 full-time, 2 part-time/adjunct. *Students:* Average age 32. *Application deadline:* For fall admission, 4/1 for domestic students; for spring admission, 11/15 for domestic students. Applications are processed on a rolling basis. Application fee: $50. Electronic applications accepted. *Expenses:* Tuition, state resident: part-time $221 per credit hour. *Unit head:* Dr. Annette Cash, Director, E-mail: acash@gsu.edu.

Kent State University, College of Arts and Sciences, Department of Modern and Classical Language Studies, Kent, OH 44242-0001. Offers French literature (MA); French, Spanish, German and Latin pedagogy (MA); German literature (MA); Spanish literature (MA); translation (MA), including French, German, Japanese, Russian, Spanish; translation studies (PhD). Part-time and evening/weekend programs available. *Faculty:* 31 full-time (15 women), 4 part-time/adjunct (2 women). *Students:* 64 full-time (45 women), 27 part-time (26 women). Average age 32. 113 applicants, 80% accepted, 42 enrolled. In 2007, 27 degrees awarded. *Degree requirements:* For master's, one foreign language, comprehensive exam (for some programs), thesis (for some programs); for doctorate, comprehensive exam, thesis/dissertation (for some programs). *Entrance requirements:* For master's, minimum GPA of 3.0, writing sample, audio tape or CD; for doctorate, 3 recommendations. Additional exam requirements/recommendations for international students: Required—TOEFL (minimum score 197 computer-based). *Application deadline:* For fall admission, 2/28 for domestic and international students. Applications are processed on a rolling basis. Application fee: $30. Electronic applications accepted. *Financial support:* In 2007–08, 31 teaching assistantships with full tuition reimbursements (averaging $8,000 per year) were awarded; research assistantships with full tuition reimbursements, career-related internships or fieldwork, Federal Work-Study, health care benefits, tuition waivers (full and partial), and unspecified assistantships also available. Support available to part-time students. Financial award application deadline: 2/1. *Faculty research:* Literature, pedagogy, applied linguistics, translation studies. *Unit head:* Dr. Gregory M Shreve, Chair, 330-672-1796, Fax: 330-672-4009, E-mail: gshreve@kent.edu. *Application contact:* Carol S. Maier, Graduate Coordinator, 330-672-1797, Fax: 330-672-4009, E-mail: cmaier@kent.edu.

Marygrove College, Graduate Division, Program in Modern Language Translation, Detroit, MI 48221-2599. Offers MA.

Montclair State University, The Office of Graduate Admissions and Support Services, College of Humanities and Social Sciences, Department of Spanish and Italian, Montclair, NJ 07043-1624. Offers Italian (Certificate); Spanish (MA, Certificate); translating and interpreting Spanish (Certificate). Part-time and evening/weekend programs available. *Faculty:* 15 full-time (9 women), 16 part-time/adjunct (14 women). *Students:* 9 full-time (7 women), 30 part-time (23 women); includes 12 minority (1 African American, 11 Hispanic Americans), 2 international. 39 applicants, 44% accepted, 13 enrolled. In 2007, 5 master's, 3 other advanced degrees awarded. *Degree requirements:* For master's, comprehensive exam, thesis or alternative. *Entrance requirements:* For master's, GRE General Test, BA in Spanish or at least 24 undergraduate credits of Spanish, 2 letters of recommendation. Additional exam requirements/recommendations for international students: Required—TOEFL (minimum score 83 computer-based). *Application deadline:* For fall admission, 6/1 for international students; for spring admission, 11/1 for international students. Applications are processed on a rolling basis. Application fee: $60. Electronic applications accepted. *Financial support:* In 2007–08, 1 research assistantship with full tuition reimbursement (averaging $7,000 per year) was awarded; Federal Work-Study, scholarships/grants, and unspecified assistantships also available. Support available to part-time students. Financial award application deadline: 3/1; financial award applicants required to submit FAFSA. *Unit head:* Dr. Linda Levine, Chairperson, 973-655-4285. *Application contact:* Dr. Roger Zapata, Adviser, 973-655-4285, E-mail: zapatar@mail.montclair.edu.

Monterey Institute of International Studies, Graduate School of Translation and Interpretation, Monterey, CA 93940-2691. Offers conference interpretation (MA); translation (MA); translation and interpretation (MA); translation and localization management (MA). *Faculty:* 17 full-time (11 women), 23 part-time/adjunct (15 women). *Students:* 165 full-time (134 women); includes 20 minority (1 African American, 1 American Indian/Alaska Native, 11 Asian Americans or Pacific Islanders, 7 Hispanic Americans), 95 international. Average age 28. 229 applicants, 62% accepted, 87 enrolled. In 2007, 87 degrees awarded. *Degree requirements:* For master's, one foreign language, thesis or alternative, exams. *Entrance requirements:* For master's, minimum GPA of 3.0, proficiency in a foreign language. Additional exam requirements/recommendations for international students: Required—TOEFL (minimum score 600 paper-based; 250 computer-based; 100 iBT). *Application deadline:* For fall admission, 3/15 priority date for domestic students; for spring admission, 10/1 priority date for domestic students. Applications are processed on a rolling basis. Application fee: $50. Electronic applications accepted. *Expenses:* Tuition: Full-time $27,750; part-time $1,250 per credit. Required fees: $200. *Financial support:* In 2007–08, 16 research assistantships with partial tuition reimbursements (averaging $4,000 per year) were awarded; career-related internships or fieldwork, Federal Work-Study, institutionally sponsored loans, scholarships/grants, tuition waivers (partial), and unspecified assistantships also available. Support available to part-time students. Financial award application deadline: 3/15; financial award applicants required to submit FAFSA. *Faculty research:* Assessment and testing in translation and interpretation, translation and interpretation pedagogy and curricula, integration of translation technology, language policy and planning. *Unit head:* Dr. Chuanyun Bao, Dean, 831-647-4170, Fax: 831-647-3560, E-mail: gsti@miis.edu. *Application contact:* 831-647-4123, Fax: 831-647-6405, E-mail: admit@miis.edu.

See Close-Up on page 607.

Rutgers, The State University of New Jersey, New Brunswick, Graduate School, Program in Spanish, New Brunswick, NJ 08901-1281. Offers bilingualism and second language acquisition (MA, PhD); Spanish (MA, MAT, PhD); Spanish literature (MA, PhD); translation (MA). Part-time programs available. *Degree requirements:* For master's, comprehensive exam (for some programs), thesis (for some programs); for doctorate, 2 foreign languages, comprehensive exam, thesis/dissertation. *Entrance requirements:* For master's and doctorate, GRE General Test. Additional exam requirements/recommendations for international students: Required—TOEFL. Electronic applications accepted. *Faculty research:* Hispanic literature, Luso-Brazilian literature, Spanish linguistics.

State University of New York at Binghamton, Graduate School, School of Arts and Sciences, Department of Romance Languages and Literatures, Program in Spanish, Binghamton, NY 13902-6000. Offers Spanish (MA); translation (Certificate). *Students:* 5 full-time (2 women); includes 1 minority (Hispanic American), 1 international. Average age 24. 6 applicants, 100% accepted, 3 enrolled. In 2007, 4 master's awarded. *Degree requirements:* For master's, one foreign language, comprehensive exam, thesis or alternative. *Entrance requirements:* For master's, GRE General Test, GRE Subject Test. Additional exam requirements/recommendations for international students: Required—TOEFL. *Application deadline:* For fall admission, 4/15 priority date for domestic students, 1/15 priority date for international students; for spring admission, 11/1 for domestic students, 10/1 priority date for international students. Applications are processed on a rolling basis. Application fee: $60. Electronic applications accepted. *Financial support:* In 2007–08, 5 students received support, including 2 teaching assistantships with full tuition reimbursements available (averaging $8,328 per year); fellowships, research assistantships, career-related internships or fieldwork, Federal Work-Study, institutionally sponsored loans, and unspecified assistantships also available. Support available to part-time students. Financial award application deadline: 2/15. *Unit head:* Dr. Antonio Sobejano-Moran, Chairperson, Department of Romance Languages and Literatures, 607-777-4635, E-mail: antobianco@msn.com.

State University of New York at Binghamton, Graduate School, School of Arts and Sciences, Translation Research and Instruction Program, Binghamton, NY 13902-6000. Offers Certificate. Part-time programs available. *Faculty:* 1 (woman) part-time/adjunct. *Students:* 10 full-time (7 women), 5 part-time (4 women); includes 4 minority (2 African Americans, 2 Hispanic Americans), 4 international. Average age 32. 9 applicants, 67% accepted, 2 enrolled. In 2007, 1 Certificate awarded. *Entrance requirements:* For degree, GRE General Test. *Application deadline:* For fall admission, 4/15 priority date for domestic students, 1/15 priority date for international students; for spring admission, 11/1 for domestic students, 10/1 priority date for international students. Applications are processed on a rolling basis. Application fee: $60. Electronic applications accepted. *Financial support:* In 2007–08, 1 student received support, including 1 research assistantship (averaging $7,055 per year); teaching assistantships with full tuition reimbursements available. Financial award application deadline: 2/15. *Unit head:* Rosemary Arrojo, Director, 607-777-6555, E-mail: rarrojo@binghamton.edu.

Université Laval, Faculty of Letters, Department of Languages, Linguistics and Translations, Programs in Terminology and Translation, Québec, QC G1K 7P4, Canada. Offers MA, Diploma. Part-time programs available. *Degree requirements:* For master's, thesis (for some programs). *Entrance requirements:* For master's and Diploma, knowledge of French and English. Electronic applications accepted.

University at Albany, State University of New York, College of Arts and Sciences, Department of Languages, Literatures, and Cultures, Program in Russian, Albany, NY 12222-0001. Offers Russian (MA); Russian translation (Certificate). *Application deadline:* For fall admission, 4/1 priority date for domestic students. Application fee: $75. *Expenses:* Tuition, state resident: part-time $576 per credit. Tuition, nonresident: part-time $910 per credit. Tuition and fees vary according to program. *Faculty research:* Translation, phonology and morphology of modern Russian. *Unit head:* HenryK Baran, Chair, Department of Languages, Literatures, and Cultures, 518-442-4222.

University of Arkansas, Graduate School, J. William Fulbright College of Arts and Sciences, Department of English, Program in Translation, Fayetteville, AR 72701-1201. Offers MFA. *Students:* 1 full-time (0 women), 3 part-time, 1 international. *Degree requirements:* For master's, thesis. Application fee: $40 ($50 for international students). *Financial support:* In 2007–08, 3 fellowships, 2 teaching assistantships were awarded; research assistantships, career-related internships or fieldwork and Federal Work-Study also available. Support available to part-time students. Financial award application deadline: 4/1; financial award applicants required to submit FAFSA. *Unit head:* Dr. John Du Val, Director, 479-575-4301, Fax: 479-575-5919, E-mail: jduval@uark.edu.

University of Denver, University College, Denver, CO 80208. Offers applied communication (MAS, MPS, Certificate); computer information systems (MAS, Certificate); environmental policy and management (MAS, Certificate); geographic information systems (MAS, Certificate); human resource administration (MPS, Certificate); knowledge and information technologies (MAS); liberal studies (MLS, Certificate); modern languages (MLS, Certificate); organizational leadership (MPS, Certificate); security management (Certificate); technology management (MAS, Certificate), including 21st century strategic management (MAS), international markets (MAS), project management (MAS), research and development management (MAS); telecommunications (MAS, Certificate), including broadband (MAS), telecommunications management and policy (MAS), telecommunications technology (MAS), wireless networks (MAS). Part-time and evening/weekend programs available. Postbaccalaureate distance learning degree programs offered (no on-campus study). *Students:* 29 full-time (15 women), 524 part-time (304 women); includes 92 minority (37 African Americans, 3 American Indian/Alaska Native, 17 Asian Americans or Pacific Islanders, 35 Hispanic Americans), 53 international. Average age 36. 625 applicants, 97% accepted, 359 enrolled. In 2007, 151 master's, 2 Certificates awarded. *Entrance requirements:* Additional exam requirements/recommendations for international students: Required—TOEFL (minimum score 550 paper-based; 213 computer-based). *Application deadline:* Applications are processed on a rolling basis. Application fee: $75. Electronic applications accepted. *Expenses: Contact institution. Financial support:* Applicants required to submit FAFSA. *Unit head:* Dr. James Davis, Dean, 303-871-2291, Fax: 303-871-4047, E-mail: jdavis@du.edu. *Application contact:* Information Contact, 303-871-3069.

The University of Iowa, Graduate College, College of Liberal Arts and Sciences, Department of Cinema and Comparative Literature, Program in Comparative Literature Translation, Iowa City, IA 52242-1316. Offers MFA. *Students:* 11 full-time (9 women), 1 (woman) part-time, 1 international. 13 applicants, 85% accepted, 8 enrolled. In 2007, 2 degrees awarded. *Degree requirements:* For master's, thesis, exam. *Entrance requirements:* For master's, GRE General Test, minimum GPA of 3.0. Additional exam requirements/recommendations for international students: Required—TOEFL (minimum score 550 paper-based; 213 computer-based; 81 iBT). *Application deadline:* For fall admission, 1/11 priority date for domestic and international students. Application fee: $60 ($85 for international students). Electronic applications accepted. *Expenses:* Tuition, state resident: part-time $349 per hour. Tuition, nonresident: part-time $349 per hour. Tuition and fees vary according to course load and program. *Financial support:* In 2007–08, 2 fellowships, 2 teaching assistantships with partial tuition reimbursements were awarded; research assistantships with partial tuition reimbursements. Financial award applicants required to submit FAFSA. *Unit head:* Maureen Robertson, Director, 319-335-2821, Fax: 319-335-3446.

University of Ottawa, Faculty of Graduate and Postdoctoral Studies, Faculty of Arts, Institute of Canadian Studies, Ottawa, ON K1N 6N5, Canada. Offers economics (PhD); English (PhD); geography (PhD); history (PhD); lettres Françaises (PhD); linguistics (PhD); philosophy (PhD); political science (PhD); psychology (PhD); religious studies (PhD); translation studies (PhD). *Degree requirements:* For doctorate, comprehensive exam, thesis/dissertation.

University of Ottawa, Faculty of Graduate and Postdoctoral Studies, Faculty of Arts, School of Translation and Interpretation, Ottawa, ON K1N 6N5, Canada. Offers interpreting (MA); Spanish translation (MA); translation (MA); translation studies (PhD). *Degree requirements:* For master's, one foreign language, thesis or alternative, research paper; for doctorate, thesis/dissertation, doctoral exam. *Entrance requirements:* For master's, school-administered exam, honors degree or equivalent, minimum B average; for doctorate, master's degree, minimum B+ average. Electronic applications accepted. *Faculty research:* Theory of translation, Spanish translation, conference interpreting, legal translation, translation-oriented lexicology and terminology.

University of Puerto Rico, Río Piedras, College of Humanities, Program in Translation, San Juan, PR 00931-3300. Offers MA, Certificate. Part-time and evening/weekend programs available. *Students:* 72 full-time (65 women), 35 part-time (30 women); includes 1 minority (African American) Average age 33. In 2007, 17 degrees awarded. *Degree requirements:* For master's, 2 foreign languages, comprehensive exam, thesis. *Entrance requirements:* For master's, PAEG, minimum GPA of 3.0, graduate-level knowledge of 2 languages (English, French, or Spanish), letter of recommendation. *Application deadline:* For fall admission, 2/1 for domestic students. Application fee: $17. *Expenses:* Tuition, state resident: full-time $1,808; part-time $113 per credit. Tuition, nonresident: full-time $5,248; part-time $328 per credit. Required fees: $72 per term. *Financial support:* Fellowships, research assistantships, teaching assistantships, Federal Work-Study, institutionally sponsored loans, and tuition waivers (partial) available. Financial award application deadline: 5/31. *Unit head:* Prof. Ivette Torres, Director, 787-764-0000 Ext. 12047, Fax: 787-764-4065, E-mail: pgtraduc@rrpac.upr.clu.edu.

York University, Faculty of Graduate Studies, Glendon College, Program in Translation, Toronto, ON M3J 1P3, Canada. Offers MA. *Degree requirements:* For master's, thesis or alternative. *Entrance requirements:* For master's, professional translating experience. Electronic applications accepted.

MONTEREY INSTITUTE OF INTERNATIONAL STUDIES

Graduate School of Translation and Interpretation

Programs of Study

The Graduate School of Translation and Interpretation (GSTI) offers Master of Arts degrees in four professional fields: translation and interpretation (M.A.T.I.), conference interpretation (M.A.C.I.), translation (M.A.T.), and translation and localization management (M.A.T.L.M.), each designed to be four-semester, 60-credit programs. Students must demonstrate fluency in English and one or more of the following languages: Arabic, Chinese, French, German, Japanese, Korean, Russian, or Spanish. Requirements for the advanced-entry, one-year Master of Arts degree programs are significant work experience or a degree in translation and interpretation. Nondegree certificates are offered in court or medical interpreting (Spanish only) and in the teaching of translation and interpretation.

In the first semester, all students take the same required courses: Basic Translation and Introduction to Interpretation. All students then specialize, based on their degree program and career interests. M.A.T.L.M. students may take interpretation as an elective and take accounting and computer-assisted translation courses during the first semester.

The M.A.T.I. program is a balanced mix of translation and interpretation courses, while the M.A.T. program concentrates on written, sight, and computer-assisted translation. The M.A.C.I. program focuses on simultaneous and consecutive interpretation, while the M.A.T.L.M. program incorporates business courses offered through the Institute's M.B.A. program in addition to translation technology courses. The Monterey Institute offers a variety of practicum and other courses that provide unique opportunities for interpreters-in-training to hone their skills. Translation students gain valuable training in project management, software localization, and specialized terminology in other courses.

GSTI is a member of the Conférence Internationale Permanente d'Instituts Universitaires de Traducteurs et Interprètes (CIUTI) and participates in exchanges with CIUTI schools worldwide. Students may opt for a year of overseas study to consolidate their languages. GSTI's faculty members—experienced translators, interpreters, and educators—are dedicated to excellence and outstanding performance as both professors and working professionals. They are committed to helping students develop the analytical skills, cultural literacy, conduct, competence, and professional integrity needed to become superior professionals.

Research Facilities

Innovative and challenging curricula at the Institute require appropriate facilities and cutting-edge technology. Classrooms vary in size from large halls where plenary sessions with simultaneous interpretation can be held to smaller classrooms and labs befitting seminar-style classes for 5 to 15 students.

State-of-the-art multimedia and interpreting labs simulate professional environments. Interpretation students have access to three facilities that are equipped for simultaneous interpretation: a conference room with eight booths that conform to ISO specifications and two labs with twelve booths each. The Irvine Auditorium, site of international conferences, multilingual courses, and guest presentations, has four simultaneous interpreting booths and a seating capacity of 275.

Brahler and Gentner portable interpreting equipment transforms any classroom into a multilingual seminar, giving students further opportunities to provide and practice interpretation for Institute classes and events. To keep pace with the dynamic localization industry, GSTI teaches computer-assisted translation and develops partnerships with high-technology firms. GSTI students also work in a multimedia, computer-assisted translation and interpretation laboratory where video is distributed from cable, satellite broadcasts, or the Internet, and localized versions of software and translation tools are available. A unique speech bank makes speeches in all GSTI languages available for student practice via the Internet.

The Max Kade Language and Technology Center is a fully equipped language-learning center. It provides multimedia classrooms and conference rooms with state-of-the-art technology, including a multimedia resource center and the campus Teaching and Learning Collaborative.

In addition to numerous computer labs, the campus is fully networked using the latest wireless standards. Every student is encouraged, for flexibility, to have a personal laptop computer adapted for wireless connectivity.

The William Tell Coleman Library includes 95,000 volumes, more than 500 print periodicals, over 50 online databases, more than 400 academic journals, about thirty-five newspapers, and approximately 15,000 electronic books. One third of the collection is in languages other than English.

Financial Aid

Candidates with a minimum grade point average of 3.3 on a 4.0 scale (or equivalent) are invited to compete for merit scholarships; amounts range from $4000 to $14,000 per year. Scholarships are renewable for a second year depending on the recipient's program and academic performance.

Under the Federal Stafford Loan program, students may borrow up to $8500 in subsidized loans or $18,500 in unsubsidized loans. Graduate PLUS Loans cover the cost of college minus other financial aid resources. The Federal Work-Study Program allows students to work up to 20 hours per week for up to $4000 per year.

Many faculty members employ research assistants, and numerous part-time jobs are available on campus. Some of these opportunities are awarded with scholarships and others are available when students enroll. U.S. citizens and permanent residents may apply for need-based financial aid programs, including low-interest loans.

Cost of Study

Tuition and fees for 2008–09 are $29,300.

Living and Housing Costs

The estimated variable expense for books, supplies, housing, food, local transportation, personal expenses, and health insurance is $16,160.

Student Group

Institute enrollment is approximately 800. About one third of the students are from outside the United States, representing more than sixty countries. More than 90 percent of students from the U.S. have worked or studied abroad. More than fifty languages are spoken by students on campus. Language classes are regularly offered in English, Spanish, Arabic, French, Russian, Japanese; Chinese (Mandarin), and German. Other languages are offered by request.

Student Outcomes

GSTI is one of the few translation and interpretation schools in the world to have a resident director of career management. Each year, over sixty employers participate in the GSTI Job/Internship Fair, and ten to fifteen more recruit on campus outside the fair. About 100 employers post jobs with the GSTI career manager each year on a continuous basis. International and U.S. employers are in business, educational, government, nonprofit, and translation and interpretation agency sectors. About one third of all 1,520 GSTI alumni are freelancers seeking contracts from all work sectors.

Of those seeking employment in the class of 2007, 90 percent found translation, interpretation, project management, and translation and interpretation teaching jobs with employers or launched independent contracting businesses within six months of graduation. More than 75 percent of the last three graduating classes had translation- and/or interpretation-related internships or summer jobs while students; most were paid. Selected employers in the last three years include Apple Computer; Bank for International Settlements (Switzerland); Bank of Korea; Bureau of International Recycling (Belgium); Chinese Times (San Francisco); Citigroup Asset Management (Japan); Daiwa Institute of Research (Japan); Eriksen, Inc. (Brooklyn, New York); the Open Source Center (Washington, D.C.); Honda Kaihatsu Kogyo (U.S.); Inter-American Investment Corporation (Washington, D.C.); International Criminal Court (the Netherlands); Korean Ministry of Forestry and Agriculture; Lionbridge Technologies (U.S.); Lucile Packard Children's Hospital (Stanford, California); Microsoft Asia (Japan); Monterey County Office of Education; Nikon Research (U.S.); Samsung Electronics; SAP (Germany); Sun Microsystems (San Jose, California); Toyota (Japan); and the Yuda Institute of Business Technology (China).

Many of the School's alumni provide freelance and staff translation and interpretation for international organizations, including the United Nations Secretariat, UN Criminal Tribunals, Free Trade Area of the Americas, International Civil Aviation Organization, and the World Intellectual Property Organization, in addition to governments worldwide. More information can be found at http://translate.miis.edu/careers/.

Location

The Monterey Institute is situated in one of the most spectacular natural environments in the world. The Monterey Peninsula is 130 miles south of San Francisco on California's central coast, surrounded by ocean and mountains. Silicon Valley is only a short drive away. With a population of 100,000, the area combines a variety of rich cultural resources and agricultural activities.

The Institute

Established in 1955 with summer classes in language and culture, the Monterey Institute of Foreign Studies was the first institute dedicated to the then-revolutionary concept that a living language should be taught as such: French in French, German in German, etc. Year-round degree programs began in 1961. By 1979, the Institute had grown to international distinction and was renamed the Monterey Institute of International Studies.

The Monterey Institute is an affiliate of Middlebury College. Founded in 1800, Middlebury is one the country's top liberal arts colleges. It offers students a broad curriculum embracing the arts, humanities, literature, foreign languages, social sciences, and natural sciences. The affiliation further enriches its curriculum, creates a bicoastal presence, and offers valuable connections to build greater global connection

Applying

Each of the Institute's four graduate schools has its own admission requirements; Students should check the Web site for full details. Applications for admission are accepted on a rolling basis. There are deadlines for priority scholarship consideration. For fall semester, there are three rounds: December 1, February 1, and March 15. For spring, the priority scholarship deadline is October 1. Applicants may apply online at http://www.miis.edu.

Correspondence and Information

Admissions Office
Monterey Institute of International Studies
460 Pierce Street
Monterey, California 93940

Phone: 831-647-4123
800-824-7235 (toll-free within the U.S.)
Fax: 831-647-6405
E-mail: admit@miis.edu
Web site: http://www.miis.edu

Monterey Institute of International Studies

THE FACULTY AND THEIR RESEARCH

Chuanyun Bao, Associate Professor and Dean of the Graduate School of Translation and Interpretation; Diploma, United Nations Translators and Interpreters Program, Beijing Foreign Studies University. Simultaneous and consecutive interpretation and translation of Chinese and English.

Program Heads

John Balcom, Associate Professor and Chinese Program Head; Ph.D., Washington (St. Louis). Translation of English and Chinese.
Marcos Celesia, Associate Professor and Spanish Program Head; Licentiate in Simultaneous Conference Interpretation and Certified Public Translator, Universidad del Salvador (Argentina). Simultaneous and consecutive interpretation and translation of Spanish and English.
Jacolyn Harmer, Professor and German Program Head; M.A., Monterey Institute; Commission of the European Union Stage (Brussels); DEA (Diplome d'Etudes Approfondies) Candidate, Geneva (ETI). Simultaneous and consecutive interpretation and translation of English, German, French, and Spanish.
Julie Johnson, Associate Professor and French Program Head; M.A., Monterey Institute. Simultaneous and consecutive interpretation and translation of English and French.
Rosa Kavenoki, Associate Professor and Russian Program Head; Ph.D., Saint Petersburg State Pedagogical University. Simultaneous and consecutive interpretation and translation of Russian and English.
Yun-Hyang Lee, Associate Professor; M.A., Hankuk University of Foreign Studies (Korea); Ph.D. candidate. Simultaneous and consecutive interpretation and translation of Korean and English.
Miryoung Sohn, Assistant Professor and Korean Program Head, Interpreting and Translations; M.A., Hankuk University of Foreign Studies (Korea). Simultaneous and consecutive interpretation and translation of Korean and English.
Kayoko Takeda, Assistant Professor and Japanese Program Head; Ph.D., Universitat Rovira i Virgili, (Spain). Simultaneous and consecutive interpretation and translation of Japanese and English.

Professors

Diane de Terra, Ph.D., London. Simultaneous and consecutive interpretation of English, French, and Spanish; cross-cultural communication; international development; applied anthropology.
Lydia Longstreth Hunt, Professor Emerita; Ph.D., NYU. Simultaneous and consecutive interpretation and translation of Spanish and English.
Ryoko Yamazaki Winter, Professor Emerita; Ed.D., San Francisco. Simultaneous and consecutive interpretation of Japanese and English.

Associate Professors

Laura Burian, M.A., Monterey Institute. Simultaneous and consecutive interpretation and translation of English and Chinese.
Carl Fehlandt, M.A., Translation Certificate, Monterey Institute. International studies, Spanish language and literature, translation of English and Spanish.
Mike Gillen, M.B.A., Monterey Institute. Translation of English and Russian.
Holly Mikkelson, M.A., Monterey Institute. Court interpreting, medical interpreting, translation and interpretation of English and Spanish.
Andrea Hoffman Miller, M.A., Monterey Institute. M.A., Regensburg (Germany). Simultaneous and consecutive interpretation and translation of German and English.
Lynette Xiaojing Shi, M.A., Hawaii; Diploma, Beijing Foreign Studies University. Simultaneous and consecutive interpretation and translation of Chinese and English.
Zinan Ye, M.A., University of the Pacific. Translation of Chinese and English.

Assistant Professors

Yoonji Choi, M.A., Monterey Institute. Translation, software localization, simultaneous and consecutive interpretation of Korean and English.
Antonio Canizales Gonzales, M.A., Ottawa. Translation and interpretation of Spanish and English.
Masaru Kawase, M.A., Keio (Tokyo). Simultaneous and consecutive interpretation of Japanese and English.
Barry Olsen, M.A., Monterey Institute. Simultaneous and consecutive interpretation and conference interpretation.
Tanya Pound, M.A., Toronto. Translation of English and Japanese.

STONY BROOK UNIVERSITY, STATE UNIVERSITY OF NEW YORK

Department of Linguistics

Programs of Study

The Department of Linguistics offers a Ph.D. in linguistics and an M.A. in teaching English to speakers of other languages (TESOL). The Ph.D. program is designed to prepare students for advanced research in all aspects of linguistic theory. Students receive a thorough grounding in the fundamentals of grammatical theory through courses such as syntax, semantics, phonology, phonetics, and morphology. Research interests are further developed through advanced seminars in linguistics as well as courses in psychology, computer science, philosophy, and the interdisciplinary Language, Mind, and Brain Seminar series. Students are encouraged to develop an area of concentration beyond their primary specialization by focusing a number of their electives in a specific direction. Professional skills, such as abstract writing and presentation of conference papers, are fostered through classes, workshops, and informal meetings of students and faculty members. All students gain teaching experience, and many do extensive teaching. Graduates have gone on to careers in both academia and industry.

The M.A. in TESOL is designed to equip students to become qualified teachers, teacher trainers, and curriculum specialists. Graduates of the M.A. in TESOL program generally go on to teach English as a foreign language abroad or in schools, colleges, and universities in the United States. The requirements of the M.A. satisfy a substantial portion of the requirements for New York State certification in TESOL, and students may arrange to complete the requirements for state certification in conjunction with their pursuit of the M.A. degree.

Research Facilities

The Semantics Lab contains six Macintosh computers devoted to research and instructional projects in semantics and natural language computations. The lab runs the award-winning SBU-developed applications SYNTACTICA and SEMANTICA for syntactic and semantic analysis. The Phonetics Laboratory suite includes a sound-treated room, a teaching lab, and a research lab. CSL and Praat speech-analysis platforms are available. Speech synthesis may be done with HLSyn.

In addition to the computer resources available in the labs, all student, faculty, and staff offices have high-speed Internet access. The graduate computing lab also provides Internet, word processing, scanning, and printing facilities for linguistics graduate students. Computers for Internet research, word processing, and statistical analysis are also available in a University lab in the building.

Financial Aid

Graduate traineeships (teaching assistantships and graduate assistantships) are awarded to Ph.D. students on a competitive basis by the Graduate School on the recommendation of the program for one year and may be renewed for up to four additional years. The University offers several fellowships that are awarded on the basis of merit. Among these are Graduate Council Fellowships, which are awarded to exceptional entering students who are U.S. citizens, and W. Burghardt Turner Fellowships, which are awarded to outstanding underrepresented graduate students. The duration of support from these fellowships depends on the level of study. The majority of doctoral students are supported on assistantships.

Cost of Study

In 2008–09, full-time tuition at 12 credits for entering in-state residents is $3450 per semester, while out-of-state residents and international students pay $5460. Additional fees for each semester, including (but not limited to) the infirmary, activity, technology, and transportation fees, total about $875. International students also pay a service fee of approximately $35 per semester and an orientation fee of $50. Fees for the mandatory Student Health Insurance Plan vary depending on citizenship and employment status.

Living and Housing Costs

For 2008–09, Stony Brook calculates the cost of education excluding tuition, fees, and insurance at $14,228 per year. On-campus apartments range in cost from approximately $336 per month to approximately $1456 per month, depending on the size of the unit and the number of students sharing the space. Off-campus housing options include rooms, houses, and apartments that can be rented from approximately $350 to $2500 per month. Costs including books, food, and transportation may vary depending on academic program and/or personal circumstances.

Student Group

Enrollment is approximately 50 students. The majority of the students attend full-time. About half of the students are international students, and many of the American students have traveled abroad extensively.

Admission for both programs is competitive. In particular, the Department looks for evidence that the applicant has an inquiring mind and the potential to work independently in new areas.

Student Outcomes

Graduates of the M.A. in TESOL program have been highly successful in obtaining teaching positions here and abroad at primary and secondary levels.

Recent graduates of the Ph.D. program have obtained positions in academia and industry. Placements include a language technology expert for a German translation technology firm; academic positions in Slovenia, Korea, Japan, Singapore, and China; and tenured and tenure-track positions in linguistics at colleges and universities in the United States.

Location

The University is located in one of the East Coast's most desirable spots—the North Shore of Long Island, about 60 miles east of New York City. The area surrounding the University provides excellent recreational and cultural opportunities.

The University

Stony Brook is one of the nation's finest public universities, with a high volume of federally sponsored research, a high percentage of doctoral students, and an emphasis on scholarship.

Applying

An online application is available on the Graduate School Web page at http://www.grad.sunysb.edu. In addition to the University admission requirements, applicants for the M.A. or Ph.D. program must submit two official transcripts of all undergraduate and graduate course work; official Graduate Record Examinations (GRE) scores; an acceptable score in English (the equivalent of 600 minimum on the paper-based TOEFL) for international students; three letters of recommendation; a resume/curriculum vitae; a writing sample; and a nonrefundable $60 fee.

Correspondence and Information

Graduate Program Coordinator
Department of Linguistics
Stony Brook University, State University of New York
Stony Brook, New York 11794-4376

Phone: 631-632-7774
Fax: 631-632-9789
E-mail: linguistics@notes.cc.sunysb.edu
Web site: http://www.linguistics.stonybrook.edu/

Stony Brook University, State University of New York

THE FACULTY AND THEIR RESEARCH

Professors

Mark Aronoff, Ph.D., MIT, 1974. Morphology, orthography.
Christina Y. Bethin, Ph.D., Illinois, 1978. Slavic linguistics, phonology.
Ellen Broselow, Ph.D., Massachusetts Amherst, 1976. Phonology, phonetics, second language acquisition.
Daniel L. Finer, Ph.D., Massachusetts Amherst, 1984. Syntax, semantics, language acquisition.
Alice C. Harris, Ph.D., Harvard, 1976. Historical linguistics, morphology, languages of the Caucasus.
Robert Hoberman, Ph.D., Chicago, 1983. Semitic linguistics.
Dorit Kaufman, Ph.D., SUNY at Stony Brook, 1991. Language acquisition and attrition, language education.
Richard K. Larson, Ph.D., Wisconsin, 1983. Semantics, syntax.

Associate Professors

Frank Anshen, Ph.D., NYU, 1968. Sociolinguistics, morphology.
John F. Bailyn, Ph.D., Cornell, 1995. Syntax, Russian syntax, Slavic linguistics.
Marie K. Huffman, Ph.D., UCLA, 1989. Phonetics, phonology.
Lori Repetti, Ph.D., UCLA, 1989. Italian linguistics, Romance phonology, Italian dialectology.

Section 11
Philosophy and Ethics

This section contains a directory of institutions offering graduate work in philosophy and ethics, followed by in-depth entries submitted by institutions that chose to prepare detailed program descriptions. Additional information about programs listed in the directory but not augmented by an in-depth entry may be obtained by writing directly to the dean of a graduate school or chair of a department at the address given in the directory.

For programs offering related work, see also in this book *Area and Cultural Studies, History, Humanities, Religious Studies,* and *Social Sciences.*

CONTENTS

Program Directories

Announcements

Close-Ups

See also:

Ethics

American University, College of Arts and Sciences, Department of Philosophy and Religion, Washington, DC 20016-8001. Offers ethics, peace, and global affairs (MA); history of philosophy (MA); philosophy and social policy (MA). Part-time and evening/weekend programs available. *Faculty:* 10 full-time (5 women), 5 part-time/adjunct (2 women). *Students:* 12 full-time (4 women), 4 part-time (1 woman); includes 3 minority (1 African American, 1 Asian American or Pacific Islander, 1 Hispanic American). Average age 24. 36 applicants, 58% accepted, 8 enrolled. In 2007, 11 degrees awarded. *Degree requirements:* For master's, one foreign language, comprehensive exam, thesis (for some programs). *Entrance requirements:* For master's, GRE, writing sample. Additional exam requirements/recommendations for international students: Required—TOEFL (minimum score 550 paper-based; 213 computer-based). *Application deadline:* For fall admission, 2/1 for domestic students; for spring admission, 10/1 for domestic students. Application fee: $50. *Expenses:* Tuition: Full-time $19,998; part-time $1,111 per credit hour. Required fees: $380. Tuition and fees vary according to program. *Financial support:* Fellowships, teaching assistantships, Federal Work-Study and institutionally sponsored loans available. Support available to part-time students. Financial award application deadline: 2/1. *Faculty research:* Oriental religion, classical and medieval philosophy, philosophy of law and ethics, comparative religion, philosophy of science. *Unit head:* Dr. Amy Oliver, Chair, 202-885-2140.

American University, School of International Service, Washington, DC 20016-8001. Offers comparative and regional studies (MA); cross-cultural communication (Certificate); development management (MS); environmental policy (MA); ethics, peace, and global affairs (MA); global environmental policy (MA); international communication (MA); international development (MA); international development management (Certificate); international economic policy (MA); international economic relations (Certificate); international peace and conflict resolution (MA); international politics (MA); international relations (PhD); international service (MIS); the Americas (Certificate); U.S. foreign policy (MA); JD/MA; MBA/MA. Part-time and evening/weekend programs available. *Faculty:* 73 full-time (27 women), 34 part-time/adjunct (15 women). *Students:* 528 full-time (339 women), 355 part-time (218 women); includes 137 minority (39 African Americans, 2 American Indian/Alaska Native, 45 Asian Americans or Pacific Islanders, 51 Hispanic Americans), 119 international. Average age 27. 1,840 applicants, 66% accepted, 321 enrolled. In 2007, 347 master's, 5 doctorates, 12 other advanced degrees awarded. Terminal master's awarded for partial completion of doctoral program. *Degree requirements:* For master's, one foreign language, comprehensive exam, thesis or alternative; for doctorate, one foreign language, comprehensive exam, thesis/dissertation, research practicum; for Certificate, minimum 15 credit hours related course work. *Entrance requirements:* For master's, GRE General Test, 24 credits of course work in related social sciences, minimum GPA of 3.5, 2 letters of recommendation, bachelor's Degree, resumé, statement of purpose; for doctorate, GRE General Test, 2 letters of recommendation, 24 credits in related social sciences. Additional exam requirements/recommendations for international students: Required—TOEFL (minimum score 550 paper-based; 213 computer-based). *Application deadline:* For fall admission, 1/15 priority date for domestic students; for spring admission, 10/1 priority date for domestic students. Applications are processed on a rolling basis. Application fee: $50. *Expenses:* Tuition: Full-time $19,998; part-time $1,111 per credit hour. Required fees: $380. Tuition and fees vary according to program. *Financial support:* Career-related internships or fieldwork, Federal Work-Study, and institutionally sponsored loans available. Financial award application deadline: 1/15. *Faculty research:* International intellectual property, international environmental issues, international law and legal order, international telecommunications/technology, international sustainable development. *Unit head:* Dr. Louis W. Goodman, Dean, 202-885-1600, Fax: 202-885-2494. *Application contact:* Amanda Taylor, Director of Graduate Admissions and Financial Aid, 202-885-1599, Fax: 202-885-2494.

See Close-Up on page 1139.

Azusa Pacific University, Haggard School of Theology, Program in Religion: Theology and Ethics, Azusa, CA 91702-7000. Offers MAR.

Biola University, Talbot School of Theology, La Mirada, CA 90639-0001. Offers Bible exposition (MA); biblical and theological studies (MA); Christian education (MACE); Christian ministry and leadership (MA); divinity (M Div); education (PhD); ministry (MA Min); New Testament (MA); Old Testament (MA); philosophy of religion and ethics (MA); spiritual formation (MA); spiritual formation and soul care (MA); theology (MA, Th M, D Min). *Accreditation:* ATS. Part-time and evening/weekend programs available. *Degree requirements:* For master's, variable foreign language requirement, thesis or alternative; for doctorate, variable foreign language requirement, thesis/dissertation; for M Div, thesis/dissertation or alternative. *Entrance requirements:* For M Div, minimum GPA of 2.6; for master's, minimum undergraduate GPA of 3.0; for doctorate, minimum GPA of 3.25. Additional exam requirements/recommendations for international students: Required—TOEFL (minimum score 550 paper-based; 213 computer-based). *Faculty research:* Moral development; biological, medical, and social ethics; ancient Near Eastern historical philosophy.

Claremont Graduate University, Graduate Programs, School of Religion, Claremont, CA 91711-6160. Offers Hebrew Bible (MA, PhD); history of Christianity and religions of North America (MA, PhD); New Testament (MA, PhD); philosophy of religion and theology (MA, PhD); theology, ethics and culture (MA, PhD); women's studies in religion (MA, PhD); MA/PhD; MBA/PhD. Part-time programs available. *Faculty:* 6 full-time (2 women), 9 part-time/adjunct (5 women). *Students:* 221 full-time (89 women), 7 part-time (2 women); includes 36 minority (15 African Americans, 12 Asian Americans or Pacific Islanders, 9 Hispanic Americans), 33 international. Average age 37. In 2007, 13 master's, 18 doctorates awarded. Terminal master's awarded for partial completion of doctoral program. *Degree requirements:* For master's, one foreign language, comprehensive exam (for some programs), thesis; for doctorate, 2 foreign languages, comprehensive exam, thesis/dissertation. *Entrance requirements:* For master's and doctorate, GRE General Test. *Application deadline:* For fall admission, 2/15 priority date for domestic students. Applications are processed on a rolling basis. Electronic applications accepted. *Expenses:* Tuition: Full-time $31,640; part-time $1,376 per unit. Required fees: $145 per semester. Tuition and fees vary according to course load, degree level and program. *Financial support:* Fellowships, research assistantships, teaching assistantships, Federal Work-Study and institutionally sponsored loans available. Support available to part-time students. Financial award application deadline: 2/15; financial award applicants required to submit FAFSA. *Unit head:* Karen Torjesen, Dean, 909-607-3214, Fax: 909-621-9587, E-mail: karen.torjesen@cgu.edu. *Application contact:* Patrick Horn, Associate Dean, 909-607-8411, Fax: 909-607-9587, E-mail: patrick.horn@cgu.edu.

Drew University, Caspersen School of Graduate Studies, Program in Religion and Society, Madison, NJ 07940-1493. Offers anthropology of religion (MA, PhD); Christian social ethics (MA, PhD); psychology and religion (MA, PhD); sociology of religion (MA, PhD). Part-time programs available. Terminal master's awarded for partial completion of doctoral program. *Degree requirements:* For master's, one foreign language, thesis; for doctorate, 2 foreign languages, comprehensive exam, thesis/dissertation. *Entrance requirements:* For master's and doctorate, GRE General Test. *Faculty research:* Liberation theory, feminist critique, social science critique of religion.

Drew University, Caspersen School of Graduate Studies, Program in Theological and Religious Studies, Madison, NJ 07940-1493. Offers historical studies (MA, PhD); Methodist studies (PhD); philosophy of religion (MA, PhD); systematic theology (MA, PhD); theological ethics (MA, PhD). *Accreditation:* ATS. Part-time programs available. Terminal master's awarded for partial completion of doctoral program. *Degree requirements:* For master's, one foreign language, thesis; for doctorate, 2 foreign languages, comprehensive exam, thesis/dissertation. *Entrance requirements:* For master's and doctorate, GRE General Test. *Faculty research:* History and theology of religion, postmodern theologies, patristics.

Duquesne University, School of Leadership and Professional Advancement, Pittsburgh, PA 15282-0001. Offers community leadership (MS); leadership and business ethics (MS); leadership and information technology (MS); leadership and liberal studies (MA); sports leadership (MS). Postbaccalaureate distance learning degree programs offered. *Expenses:* Tuition: Part-time $774 per credit. Required fees: $74 per credit. Tuition and fees vary according to program. *Unit head:* Shawn Gearing, Senior Academic Advisor, 412-396-5558, E-mail: gearing@duq.edu.

Fordham University, Graduate School of Arts and Sciences, Center for Ethics Education Program, New York, NY 10458. Offers health care ethics (Certificate). Part-time programs available. *Students:* 1 full-time (0 women). *Entrance requirements:* Additional exam requirements/recommendations for international students: Required—TOEFL. *Application deadline:* For fall admission, 1/4 priority date for domestic students; for spring admission, 10/31 for domestic students. Application fee: $65. Electronic applications accepted. *Expenses:* Tuition: Full-time $23,880; part-time $995 per credit. *Financial support:* In 2007–08, 1 student received support. Federal Work-Study, institutionally sponsored loans, scholarships/grants, tuition waivers (partial), and unspecified assistantships available. Financial award application deadline: 1/4. Total annual research expenditures: $49,033. *Unit head:* Dr. Celia Fisher, Director, 718-817-3793, Fax: 212-759-2009, E-mail: fisher@fordham.edu. *Application contact:* Charlene Dundie, Director of Graduate Admissions, 718-817-4420, Fax: 718-817-3566, E-mail: dundie@fordham.edu.

Graduate Theological Union, Graduate Programs, Berkeley, CA 94709-1212. Offers art and religion (MA, PhD); biblical languages (MA); biblical studies (Old and New Testament) (MA, PhD, Th D); Buddhist studies (MA); Christian spirituality (MA, PhD); cultural and historical studies of religions (MA, PhD); ethics and social theory (PhD); history (MA, PhD, Th D); homiletics (MA, PhD, Th D); interdisciplinary studies (PhD, Th D); Jewish studies (MA, PhD, Certificate); liturgical studies (MA, PhD, Th D); Near Eastern religions (PhD); Orthodox Christian studies (MA); Orthodox studies (Certificate); religion and psychology (MA, PhD); religion and society/ethics and social theory (MA); systematic and philosophical theology (MA, PhD, Th D); women's studies in religion (Certificate); MA/M Div. *Accreditation:* ATS. *Faculty:* 119 full-time (44 women), 34 part-time/adjunct (9 women). *Students:* 317 full-time (152 women), 35 part-time (19 women); includes 49 minority (15 African Americans, 2 American Indian/Alaska Native, 21 Asian Americans or Pacific Islanders, 11 Hispanic Americans), 74 international. Average age 38. 257 applicants, 59% accepted, 79 enrolled. In 2007, 45 master's, 22 doctorates awarded. Terminal master's awarded for partial completion of doctoral program. *Median time to degree:* Of those who began their doctoral program in fall 1999, 52% received their degree in 8 years or less. *Degree requirements:* For master's, one foreign language, thesis; for doctorate, one foreign language, comprehensive exam, thesis/dissertation. *Entrance requirements:* For master's, GRE General Test; for doctorate, GRE General Test, MA or M Div. Additional exam requirements/recommendations for international students: Required—TOEFL. *Application deadline:* For fall admission, 12/15 for domestic and international students; for winter admission, 2/15 for domestic and international students; for spring admission, 9/30 for domestic and international students. Application fee: $40. Electronic applications accepted. *Expenses:* Tuition: Full-time $13,310. Tuition and fees vary according to degree level and program. *Financial support:* In 2007–08, 122 students received support, including 109 fellowships (averaging $11,581 per year), 1 research assistantship (averaging $3,000 per year), 22 teaching assistantships (averaging $3,500 per year); Federal Work-Study, scholarships/grants, and tuition waivers (partial) also available. Support available to part-time students. Financial award application deadline: 2/1; financial award applicants required to submit FAFSA. *Unit head:* Dr. Arthur G. Holder, Dean, 510-649-2440, Fax: 510-649-1417, E-mail: aholder@gtu.edu. *Application contact:* Dr. Kathleen Kook, Assistant Dean for Admissions, 800-826-4488, Fax: 510-649-1730, E-mail: gtuadm@gtu.edu.

Marquette University, Graduate School, College of Arts and Sciences, Department of Philosophy, Milwaukee, WI 53201-1881. Offers ancient philosophy (MA, PhD); British empiricism and analytic philosophy (MA, PhD); Christian philosophy (MA, PhD); early modern European philosophy (MA, PhD); ethics (MA, PhD); German philosophy (MA, PhD); medieval philosophy (MA, PhD); phenomenology and existentialism (MA, PhD); philosophy of religion (MA, PhD); social and applied philosophy (MA). Part-time programs available. *Faculty:* 28 full-time (5 women), 12 part-time/adjunct (1 woman). *Students:* 48 full-time (14 women), 9 part-time (3 women); includes 1 minority (Asian American or Pacific Islander), 7 international. Average age 30. 88 applicants, 88% accepted, 19 enrolled. In 2007, 5 master's, 5 doctorates awarded. Terminal master's awarded for partial completion of doctoral program. *Degree requirements:* For master's, one foreign language, comprehensive exam, thesis; for doctorate, 2 foreign languages, thesis/dissertation, qualifying exams. *Entrance requirements:* For master's and doctorate, GRE General Test. Additional exam requirements/recommendations for international students: Required—TOEFL. Application fee: $40. *Financial support:* In 2007–08, 10 research assistantships, 12 teaching assistantships were awarded; Federal Work-Study, institutionally sponsored loans, scholarships/grants, and tuition waivers (full and partial) also available. Support available to part-time students. Financial award application deadline: 2/15. *Faculty research:* Aristotle, Augustine, Descartes, Hegel, Heidegger. Total annual research expenditures: $130,800. *Unit head:* Dr. John Jones, Chair, 414-288-6857, Fax: 414-288-1578. *Application contact:* Dr. Owen Goldin, Director of Graduate Studies, 414-288-5949, Fax: 414-288-1578.

Marquette University, Graduate School, College of Arts and Sciences, Department of Theology, Milwaukee, WI 53201-1881. Offers ethics (PhD); historical theology (MA, PhD); religious studies (PhD), including scriptural theology (MA, PhD); systematic theology (MA, PhD); theology (MA), including scriptural theology (MA, PhD); theology and society (PhD). Part-time programs available. *Faculty:* 32 full-time (7 women), 18 part-time/adjunct (2 women). *Students:* 83 full-time (21 women), 52 part-time (17 women); includes 7 minority (3 African Americans, 2 Asian Americans or Pacific Islanders, 2 Hispanic Americans), 11 international. Average age 36. 156 applicants, 38% accepted, 21 enrolled. In 2007, 3 master's, 7 doctorates awarded. Terminal master's awarded for partial completion of doctoral program. *Degree requirements:* For master's, one foreign language, comprehensive exam, thesis or alternative; for doctorate, 2 foreign languages, thesis/dissertation, qualifying exam. *Entrance requirements:* For master's and doctorate, GRE General Test. Additional exam requirements/recommendations for international students: Required—TOEFL. Application fee: $40. *Financial support:* In 2007–08, 5 fellowships, 5 research assistantships, 14 teaching assistantships were awarded; Federal Work-Study, institutionally sponsored loans, scholarships/grants, and tuition waivers (full and partial) also available. Support available to part-time students. Financial award application deadline: 2/15. *Faculty research:* Old Testament theology, New Testament theology, church history, Christian ethics. Total annual research expenditures: $81,775. *Unit head:* Rev. John Laurance, Acting Chair, 414-288-7170, Fax: 414-288-5548. *Application contact:* Dr. Christine Hinze, Director of Graduate Studies, 414-288-6802.

Northern Baptist Theological Seminary, Graduate and Professional Programs, Lombard, IL 60148-5698. Offers Bible (MA); Christian ministries (MACM); divinity (M Div); ethics (MA); history (MA); ministry (D Min); theology (MA); worship/spirituality (MAWS); youth ministry (MAYM). *Accreditation:* ATS. Part-time programs available. *Faculty:* 6 full-time (1 woman), 29 part-time/adjunct (6 women). *Students:* 98 full-time (22 women), 91 part-time (32 women); includes 67 minority (51 African Americans, 12 Asian Americans or Pacific Islanders, 4 Hispanic Americans), 3 international. Average age 40. 71 applicants, 90% accepted. In 2007, 21 first professional degrees, 10 master's, 13 doctorates awarded. *Degree requirements:* For doctorate, thesis/dissertation; for M Div, field experience. *Entrance requirements:* For doctorate, 3 years in the ministry post-M Div. Additional exam requirements/recommendations for international students: Required—TOEFL. *Application deadline:* For fall admission, 9/1 priority date for domestic students, 2/1 priority date for international students; for winter admission, 12/1 priority date for domestic students; for spring admission, 3/1 priority date for domestic students. Applications are processed on a rolling basis. Application fee: $35. Electronic applications accepted.

Expenses: Tuition: Full-time $11,340; part-time $420 per hour. Required fees: $300. Tuition and fees vary according to degree level. *Financial support:* In 2007–08, 68 students received support. Career-related internships or fieldwork and scholarships/grants available. Support available to part-time students. Financial award application deadline: 9/1. *Faculty research:* Theology, worship studies, church history, evangelism, Bible. *Unit head:* Dr. Charles Hambrick-Stowe, Dean, 630-620-2103, Fax: 630-620-2190. *Application contact:* Greg Henson, Director of Enrollment Management, 630-620-2191, Fax: 630-620-2190, E-mail: admissions@seminary.edu.

Phillips Theological Seminary, Programs in Theology, Tulsa, OK 74116. Offers administration of church agencies (M Div); campus ministry (M Div); church-related social work (M Div); college and seminary teaching (M Div); global mission work (M Div); institutional chaplaincy (M Div); ministerial vocations in Christian education (M Div); ministry (D Min), including parish ministry, pastoral counseling, practices of ministry; ministry and culture (MAMC), including Christian education, congregational leadership, history and practice of Christian spirituality, theology, ethics, and culture; ministry of music (M Div); pastoral care and counseling (M Div); pastoral ministry (M Div); theological studies (MTS). *Accreditation:* ATS. Part-time programs available. Postbaccalaureate distance learning degree programs offered (minimal on-campus study). *Degree requirements:* For master's, thesis (for some programs); for doctorate, thesis/dissertation. *Entrance requirements:* For master's, minimum GPA of 2.5; for doctorate, M Div, minimum GPA of 3.0. *Faculty research:* Biblical studies, historical studies, theology and culture, practical theology, theology and film.

St. Edward's University, School of Management and Business, Program in Organizational Leadership and Ethics, Austin, TX 78704. Offers MS. Part-time and evening/weekend programs available. *Faculty:* 2 full-time (0 women), 5 part-time/adjunct (2 women). *Students:* 1 full-time (0 women), 59 part-time (34 women); includes 15 minority (9 African Americans, 1 American Indian/Alaska Native, 5 Hispanic Americans). Average age 38. 23 applicants, 91% accepted, 19 enrolled. In 2007, 22 degrees awarded. *Degree requirements:* For master's, minimum 24 hours in residence. *Entrance requirements:* For master's, GMAT or GRE General Test, minimum GPA of 2.75 in last 60 hours of course work. Additional exam requirements/recommendations for international students: Required—TOEFL (minimum score 550 paper-based; 213 computer-based; 79 iBT). *Application deadline:* For fall admission, 8/1 for domestic students, 7/1 for international students; for spring admission, 12/1 for domestic students, 11/1 for international students. Applications are processed on a rolling basis. Application fee: $45 ($50 for international students). Electronic applications accepted. *Expenses:* Tuition: Full-time $12,672; part-time $704 per credit hour. Full-time tuition and fees vary according to program. Part-time tuition and fees vary according to course load. *Financial support:* In 2007–08, 1 student received support. Scholarships/grants available. *Faculty research:* Business ethics. *Unit head:* Dr. Tom Sechrest, Director, 512-637-1954, Fax: 512-448-8492, E-mail: thomasl@stedwards.edu. *Application contact:* Benjamin Jimenez, Recruiting Coordinator, 512-233-1694, Fax: 512-428-1032, E-mail: benjij@stedwards.edu.

Southeastern Baptist Theological Seminary, Graduate and Professional Programs, Wake Forest, NC 27588-1889. Offers advanced biblical studies (M Div); Christian education (M Div, MACE); Christian ethics (PhD); Christian ministry (M Div); Christian planting (M Div); church music (MACM); counseling (MACO); evangelism (PhD); language (M Div); ministry (D Min); New Testament (PhD); Old Testament (PhD); philosophy (PhD); theology (Th M, PhD); women's studies (M Div). *Accreditation:* ACIPE; ATS (one or more programs are accredited). *Degree requirements:* For master's, thesis (for some programs), oral exam; for doctorate, thesis/dissertation, fieldwork; for M Div, supervised ministry. *Entrance requirements:* For master's, Cooperative English Test, minimum GPA of 2.0, M Div or equivalent (Th M); for doctorate, GRE General Test or MAT, Cooperative English Test, M Div or equivalent, 3 years of professional experience.

Université de Sherbrooke, Faculty of Theology, Ethics and Philosophy, Sherbrooke, QC J1K 2R1, Canada. Offers applied ethics (Diploma); human science of religions (MA); intercultural training (Diploma); philosophy (MA, PhD); spiritual anthropology (Diploma); theology (MA, PhD, Diploma). Part-time and evening/weekend programs available. Postbaccalaureate distance learning degree programs offered. Terminal master's awarded for partial completion of doctoral program. *Entrance requirements:* For master's, bachelor's degree in related discipline; for doctorate, master's degree in related discipline. *Faculty research:* Faith and culture interrelation.

Université du Québec à Chicoutimi, Graduate Programs, Program in Ethics, Chicoutimi, QC G7H 2B1, Canada. Offers Diploma. *Entrance requirements:* For degree, appropriate bachelor's degree, proficiency in French.

Université du Québec à Rimouski, Graduate Programs, Program in Ethics, Rimouski, QC G5L 3A1, Canada. Offers MA, Diploma. Part-time programs available. *Students:* 10 full-time, 29 part-time. In 2007, 10 degrees awarded. *Degree requirements:* For master's, thesis. *Entrance requirements:* For master's, appropriate bachelor's degree, proficiency in French. *Application deadline:* For fall admission, 5/1 priority date for domestic students. Application fee: $50. *Financial support:* Fellowships, research assistantships, teaching assistantships available. *Unit head:* Dany Rondeau, Director, 418-724-1552, Fax: 418-724-1525, E-mail: dany_rondeau@uqar.ca.

Université Laval, Faculty of Theology and Religious Sciences, Program in Applied Ethics, Québec, QC G1K 7P4, Canada. Offers Diploma. Part-time programs available. *Entrance requirements:* For degree, knowledge of French. Electronic applications accepted.

University of Baltimore, Graduate School, The Yale Gordon College of Liberal Arts, Division of Legal, Ethical and Historical Studies, Program in Legal and Ethical Studies, Baltimore, MD 21201-5779. Offers MA. Part-time and evening/weekend programs available. *Faculty:* 14 full-time (7 women), 12 part-time/adjunct (4 women). *Students:* 22 full-time (11 women), 54 part-time (37 women); includes 40 minority (38 African Americans, 1 American Indian/Alaska Native, 1 Hispanic American), 2 international. Average age 34. 30 applicants, 83% accepted, 19 enrolled. In 2007, 34 degrees awarded. *Degree requirements:* For master's, thesis optional. *Entrance requirements:* For master's, minimum GPA of 3.0. Additional exam requirements/recommendations for international students: Required—TOEFL (minimum score 550 paper-based; 213 computer-based). *Application deadline:* For fall admission, 8/1 for domestic students, 6/1 for international students; for spring admission, 12/1 for domestic students, 11/1 for international students. Applications are processed on a rolling basis. Application fee: $45. Electronic applications accepted. *Expenses:* Tuition, state resident: part-time $518 per credit. Tuition, nonresident: part-time $751 per credit. Tuition and fees vary according to program. *Financial support:* In 2007–08, 3 research assistantships were awarded; fellowships, career-related internships or fieldwork and Federal Work-Study also available. Support available to part-time students. Financial award application deadline: 4/1; financial award applicants required to submit FAFSA. *Faculty research:* Morality in law and economics, religion in lawmaking, comparative legal history, law and social change, critical issues in constitutional law, theories of justice. Total annual research expenditures: $24,077. *Unit head:* Dr. Jeffrey Sawyer, Director, Program in Legal Studies, 410-837-5320, E-mail: jsawyer@ubalt.edu. *Application contact:* Wendy Bolyard.

University of Nevada, Las Vegas, Graduate College, College of Liberal Arts, Department of Political Science, Program in Ethics and Policy Studies, Las Vegas, NV 89154-9900. Offers MA. Part-time programs available. In 2007, 1 degree awarded. *Degree requirements:* For master's, thesis. *Entrance requirements:* For master's, MAT, minimum GPA of 2.75. Additional exam requirements/recommendations for international students: Required—TOEFL (minimum score 550 paper-based; 213 computer-based; 80 iBT). *Application deadline:* For fall admission, 3/1 for domestic and international students; for spring admission, 11/1 for domestic students, 10/1 for international students. Application fee: $60 ($75 for international students). Electronic applications accepted. *Expenses:* Tuition, state resident: part-time $198 per credit. Tuition, nonresident: part-time $416 per credit. Required fees: $256 per semester. Tuition and fees vary according to course load and reciprocity agreements. *Financial support:* Research assistantships with partial tuition reimbursements, career-related internships or fieldwork, Federal Work-Study, institutionally sponsored loans, scholarships/grants, health care benefits, and unspecified assistantships available. Support available to part-time students. Financial award application deadline: 3/1. *Application contact:* Graduate College Admissions Evaluator, 702-895-3320, Fax: 702-895-4180, E-mail: gradcollege@unlv.edu.

University of North Florida, College of Arts and Sciences, Department of Philosophy, Jacksonville, FL 32224-2645. Offers applied ethics (Graduate Certificate); practical philosophy and applied ethics (MA). Part-time and evening/weekend programs available. *Faculty:* 11 full-time (4 women). *Students:* 8 full-time (4 women), 7 part-time (3 women); includes 2 minority (both Hispanic Americans) Average age 36. 12 applicants, 67% accepted, 5 enrolled. In 2007, 3 degrees awarded. *Entrance requirements:* For master's, GRE General Test, minimum GPA of 3.0 in last 60 hours, 3 letters of recommendation, writing sample. Additional exam requirements/recommendations for international students: Required—TOEFL (minimum score 500 paper-based). *Application deadline:* For fall admission, 3/1 priority date for domestic students, 3/1 for international students. Applications are processed on a rolling basis. Application fee: $30. Electronic applications accepted. *Expenses:* Tuition, state resident: part-time $266 per credit hour. Tuition, nonresident: part-time $858 per credit hour. One-time fee: $35 part-time. Tuition and fees vary according to program. *Financial support:* In 2007–08, 10 students received support, including 6 teaching assistantships (averaging $6,357 per year). Financial award application deadline: 4/1; financial award applicants required to submit FAFSA. *Faculty research:* Late modern philosophy, pragmatism, religion and American culture, hermeneutics, philosophy of mind. Total annual research expenditures: $13,485. *Unit head:* Dr. Hans Herbert Köegler, Graduate Coordinator, 904-620-1330, Fax: 904-620-1840, E-mail: hkoegler@unf.edu. *Application contact:* Dr. Hans Herbert Köegler, Graduate Coordinator, 904-620-1330, Fax: 904-620-1840, E-mail: hkoegler@unf.edu.

University of South Africa, College of Human Sciences, Pretoria, South Africa. Offers adult education (M Ed); African languages (MA, PhD); African politics (MA, PhD); Afrikaans (MA, PhD); ancient history (MA, PhD); ancient Near Eastern studies (MA, PhD); anthropology (MA, PhD); applied linguistics (MA); Arabic (MA, PhD); archaeology (MA); art history (MA); Biblical archaeology (MA); Biblical studies (M Th, D Th, PhD); Christian spirituality (M Th, D Th); church history (M Th, D Th); classical studies (MA, PhD); clinical psychology (MA); communication (MA, PhD); comparative education (M Ed, Ed D); consulting psychology (D Admin, D Com, PhD); curriculum studies (M Ed, Ed D); development studies (M Admin, MA, D Admin, PhD); didactics (M Ed, Ed D); education (M Tech); education management (M Ed, Ed D); educational psychology (M Ed); English (MA); environmental education (M Ed); French (MA, PhD); German (MA, PhD); Greek (MA); guidance and counseling (M Ed); health studies (MA, PhD), including health sciences education (MA), health services management (MA), medical and surgical nursing science (critical care general) (MA), midwifery and neonatal nursing science (MA), trauma and emergency care (MA); history (MA, PhD); history of education (Ed D); inclusive education (M Ed, Ed D); information and communications technology policy and regulation (MA); information science (MA, MIS, PhD); international politics (MA, PhD); Islamic studies (MA, PhD); Italian (MA, PhD); Judaica (MA, PhD); linguistics (MA, PhD); mathematical education (M Ed); mathematics education (MA); missiology (M Th, D Th); modern Hebrew (MA, PhD); musicology (MA, MMus, D Mus, PhD); natural science education (M Ed); New Testament (M Th, D Th); Old Testament (D Th); pastoral therapy (M Th, D Th); philosophy (MA); philosophy of education (M Ed, Ed D); politics (MA, PhD); Portuguese (MA, PhD); practical theology (M Th, D Th); psychology (MA, MS, PhD); psychology of education (M Ed, Ed D); public health (MA); religious studies (MA, D Th, PhD); Romance languages (MA); Russian (MA, PhD); Semitic languages (MA, PhD); social behavior studies in HIV/AIDS (MA); social science (mental health) (MA); social science in development studies (MA); social science in psychology (MA); social science in social work (MA); social science in sociology (MA); social work (MSW, DSW, PhD); socio-education (M Ed, Ed D); sociolinguistics (MA); sociology (MA, PhD); Spanish (MA, PhD); systematic theology (M Th, D Th); TESOL (teaching English to speakers of other languages) (MA); theological ethics (M Th, D Th); theory of literature (MA, PhD); urban ministries (D Th); urban ministry (M Th).

Valparaiso University, Graduate Division, Program in Liberal Studies, Concentration in Ethics and Values, Valparaiso, IN 46383. Offers MALS, Post-Master's Certificate, JD/MALS. Part-time and evening/weekend programs available. *Students:* 1 full-time (0 women), 2 part-time (both women). Average age 43. In 2007, 3 degrees awarded. *Entrance requirements:* For master's, minimum GPA of 3.0. Additional exam requirements/recommendations for international students: Required—TOEFL (minimum score 550 paper-based; 213 computer-based). *Application deadline:* Applications are processed on a rolling basis. Application fee: $30 ($50 for international students). Electronic applications accepted. *Financial support:* Available to part-time students. Applicants required to submit FAFSA. *Application contact:* Jamie Haney, Coordinator of Recruitment Activities, 219-464-5313, Fax: 219-464-5381, E-mail: jamie.haney@valpo.edu.

Warner Pacific College, Graduate Programs, Portland, OR 97215-4099. Offers biblical and theological studies (MA); biblical studies (M Rel); education (M Ed); management/organizational leadership (MS); pastoral ministries (M Rel); religion and ethics (M Rel); teaching (MA); theology (M Rel). Part-time programs available. *Faculty:* 20 part-time/adjunct (6 women). *Students:* 57 full-time (26 women), 4 part-time (2 women); includes 5 minority (4 African Americans, 1 Asian American or Pacific Islander). *Degree requirements:* For master's, thesis or alternative, Presentation of Defense. *Entrance requirements:* For master's, interview, minimum GPA of 2.5, letters of recommendation. *Application deadline:* Applications are processed on a rolling basis. *Expenses:* Tuition: Full-time $15,642. Required fees: $150. *Financial support:* Career-related internships or fieldwork and Federal Work-Study available. Financial award application deadline: 7/1; financial award applicants required to submit FAFSA. *Faculty research:* New Testament studies, nineteenth-century Wesleyan theology, preaching and church growth, Christian ethics. *Unit head:* Director, 503-517-1045, Fax: 503-517-1350, E-mail: kazio@warnerpacific.edu.

West Chester University of Pennsylvania, Office of Graduate Studies and Extended Education, College of Arts and Sciences, Department of Philosophy, West Chester, PA 19383. Offers business ethics (Certificate); healthcare ethics (Certificate); philosophy (MA). Part-time and evening/weekend programs available. *Students:* 10 full-time (4 women), 11 part-time (3 women); includes 1 minority (African American), 1 international. Average age 28. 16 applicants, 88% accepted, 10 enrolled. In 2007, 5 degrees awarded. *Degree requirements:* For master's, one foreign language, comprehensive exam, thesis optional. *Entrance requirements:* For master's, GRE or MAT. Additional exam requirements/recommendations for international students: Required—TOEFL (minimum score 550 paper-based; 213 computer-based; 80 iBT). *Application deadline:* For fall admission, 4/15 priority date for domestic students; for spring admission, 10/15 for domestic students. Applications are processed on a rolling basis. Application fee: $35. *Expenses:* Tuition, state resident: part-time $345 per credit. Tuition, nonresident: part-time $552 per credit. Tuition and fees vary according to course load. *Financial support:* In 2007–08, 3 research assistantships with full and partial tuition reimbursements (averaging $5,000 per year) were awarded; unspecified assistantships also available. Support available to part-time students. Financial award application deadline: 2/15; financial award applicants required to submit FAFSA. *Faculty research:* International studies. *Unit head:* Dr. Fred Strukmeyer, Chair and Graduate Coordinator, 610-436-2841, E-mail: tstrukmeyer@wcupa.edu. *Application contact:* Dr. Joan Woolfrey, Graduate Coordinator, 610-436-2857, E-mail: jwoolfrey@wcupa.edu.

Wilfrid Laurier University, Waterloo Lutheran Seminary, Waterloo, ON N2L 3C5, Canada. Offers Christian ethics (M Th); divinity (M Div); homiletics (M Th); ministry (D Min); pastoral counseling (M Th); spirituality in a health care setting (Diploma); theological studies (MTS); theology (Diploma); M Div/MTS/MSW. *Accreditation:* ATS. Part-time programs available. *Faculty:* 8 full-time (2 women), 6 part-time/adjunct (2 women). *Students:* 51 full-time (33 women), 57 part-time (33 women); includes 10 minority (3 African Americans, 1 American Indian/Alaska Native, 6 Asian Americans or Pacific Islanders). Average age 42. 23 applicants, 100% accepted,

Ethics

Wilfrid Laurier University (continued)
20 enrolled. In 2007, 1 first professional degree, 8 master's awarded. *Degree requirements:* For master's, one foreign language, thesis (for some programs); for doctorate, thesis/dissertation; for M Div, one foreign language, thesis/dissertation. *Entrance requirements:* For M Div, denominational endorsement; for master's, M Div, 2 units of clinical pastoral education (M Th); for doctorate, M Div, 3 years of ministry experience, proficiency in a foreign language, basic training in clinical pastoral education. Additional exam requirements/recommendations for international students: Required—TOEFL (minimum score 573 paper-based; 230 computer-based; 89 iBT), IELTS (minimum score 7). *Application deadline:* For fall admission, 7/1 priority date for domestic students, 3/1 priority date for international students; for winter admission, 11/1 priority date for domestic students, 6/1 priority date for international students; for spring admission, 3/1 priority date for domestic students, 11/1 priority date for international students. Applications are processed on a rolling basis. Application fee: $50. Electronic applications accepted. *Expenses:* Contact institution. *Financial support:* In 2007–08, 51 students received support. Career-related internships or fieldwork, institutionally sponsored loans, and scholarships/grants available. Financial award application deadline: 10/1. *Faculty research:* Biblical study, church history, systematic theology. *Unit head:* Dr. David Pfrimmer, Principal/Dean, 519-884-0710, E-mail: dpfrimme@wlu.ca. *Application contact:* Sarina Wheeler, Student Advisor and Admissions Coordinator, 519-884-0710 Ext. 3498, Fax: 519-725-2434, E-mail: swheeler@wlu.ca.

Philosophy

American University, College of Arts and Sciences, Department of Philosophy and Religion, Washington, DC 20016-8001. Offers ethics, peace, and global affairs (MA); history of philosophy (MA); philosophy and social policy (MA). Part-time and evening/weekend programs available. *Faculty:* 10 full-time (5 women), 5 part-time/adjunct (2 women). *Students:* 12 full-time (4 women), 4 part-time (1 woman); includes 3 minority (1 African American, 1 Asian American or Pacific Islander, 1 Hispanic American). Average age 24. 36 applicants, 58% accepted, 8 enrolled. In 2007, 11 degrees awarded. *Degree requirements:* For master's, one foreign language, comprehensive exam, thesis (for some programs). *Entrance requirements:* For master's, GRE, writing sample. Additional exam requirements/recommendations for international students: Required—TOEFL (minimum score 550 paper-based; 213 computer-based). *Application deadline:* For fall admission, 2/1 for domestic students; for spring admission, 10/1 for domestic students. Application fee: $50. *Expenses:* Tuition: Full-time $19,998; part-time $1,111 per credit hour. Required fees: $380. Tuition and fees vary according to program. *Financial support:* Fellowships, teaching assistantships, Federal Work-Study and institutionally sponsored loans available. Support available to part-time students. Financial award application deadline: 2/1. *Faculty research:* Oriental religion, classical and medieval philosophy, philosophy of law and ethics, comparative religion, philosophy of science. *Unit head:* Dr. Amy Oliver, Chair, 202-885-2140.

American University of Beirut, Graduate Programs, Faculty of Arts and Sciences, Beirut, Lebanon. Offers anthropology (MA); Arabic language and literature (MA); archaeology (MA); biology (MS); chemistry (MS); computer science (MS); economics (MA); education (MA); English language (MA); English literature (MA); environmental policy planning (MSES); financial economics (MAFE); geology (MS); history (MA); mathematics (MA, MS); Middle Eastern studies (MA); philosophy (MA); physics (MS); political studies (MA); psychology (MA); public administration (MA); sociology (MA); statistics (MA, MS). Part-time programs available. *Faculty:* 108 full-time (29 women), 5 part-time/adjunct (3 women). *Students:* 134 full-time (92 women), 228 part-time (167 women). Average age 25. 319 applicants, 67% accepted, 91 enrolled. In 2007, 144 degrees awarded. *Degree requirements:* For master's, one foreign language, comprehensive exam, thesis (for some programs). *Entrance requirements:* For master's, GRE, letter of recommendation. Additional exam requirements/recommendations for international students: Required—TOEFL (minimum score 600 paper-based; 250 computer-based; 100 iBT), IELTS (minimum score 8). *Application deadline:* For fall admission, 4/30 for domestic and international students; for spring admission, 11/1 for domestic and international students. Application fee: $50. *Expenses:* Tuition: Full-time $9,954; part-time $553 per credit. Tuition and fees vary according to course load and program. *Financial support:* In 2007–08, 28 students received support. Career-related internships or fieldwork, institutionally sponsored loans, scholarships/grants, health care benefits, and unspecified assistantships available. Financial award application deadline: 2/4; financial award applicants required to submit FAFSA. *Faculty research:* String theory and supergravity; computer graphics; algebra and number theory; popular Arabic literature; marine and freshwater biology; integrating science, math and technology. Total annual research expenditures: $132,270. *Unit head:* Khalil Bitar, Dean, 961-1374374 Ext. 3800, Fax: 961-1744461, E-mail: kmb@aub.edu.lb. *Application contact:* Dr. Salim Kanaan, Director, Admissions Office, 961-1350000 Ext. 2594, Fax: 961-1750775, E-mail: sk00@aub.edu.lb.

Arizona State University, Graduate College, College of Liberal Arts and Sciences, Division of Humanities, Department of Philosophy, Tempe, AZ 85287. Offers MA, PhD. *Degree requirements:* For master's, thesis. *Entrance requirements:* For master's, GRE.

Baylor University, Graduate School, College of Arts and Sciences, Department of Philosophy, Waco, TX 76798. Offers MA, PhD. *Students:* 29 full-time (5 women), 2 part-time (1 woman); includes 1 minority (Asian American or Pacific Islander), 2 international. In 2007, 4 master's, 1 doctorate awarded. *Degree requirements:* For master's, one foreign language, thesis or alternative. *Entrance requirements:* For master's, GRE General Test. Additional exam requirements/recommendations for international students: Required—TOEFL. *Application deadline:* Applications are processed on a rolling basis. Application fee: $25. *Financial support:* Teaching assistantships, Federal Work-Study, institutionally sponsored loans, and unspecified assistantships available. *Unit head:* Dr. Stuart Rosenbaum, Graduate Program Director, 254-710-3368, Fax: 254-710-3838, E-mail: stuart_rosenbaum@baylor.edu. *Application contact:* Suzanne Keener, Administrative Assistant, 254-710-3588, Fax: 254-710-3870.

Boston College, Graduate School of Arts and Sciences, Department of Philosophy, Chestnut Hill, MA 02467-3800. Offers MA, PhD. *Students:* 81 full-time (17 women), 44 part-time (12 women); includes 10 minority (5 Asian Americans or Pacific Islanders, 5 Hispanic Americans), 23 international. 277 applicants, 49% accepted, 47 enrolled. In 2007, 21 master's, 5 doctorates awarded. Terminal master's awarded for partial completion of doctoral program. *Degree requirements:* For master's, one foreign language, thesis optional; for doctorate, 2 foreign languages, thesis/dissertation. *Entrance requirements:* For master's and doctorate, GRE General Test. Additional exam requirements/recommendations for international students: Required—TOEFL (minimum score 590 paper-based; 250 computer-based; 91 iBT). *Application deadline:* For fall admission, 1/15 for domestic students. Application fee: $70. *Financial support:* Fellowships with full tuition reimbursements, teaching assistantships with full tuition reimbursements, Federal Work-Study and scholarships/grants available. Support available to part-time students. Financial award application deadline: 3/1; financial award applicants required to submit FAFSA. *Faculty research:* History of philosophy, metaphysics, ethics. *Unit head:* Dr. Patrick Byrne, Chairperson, 617-552-3856, E-mail: patrick.byrne@bc.edu. *Application contact:* Dr. Gary Gurtler, Graduate Program Director, 617-552-3872, E-mail: gary.gurtler@bc.edu.

Boston University, Graduate School of Arts and Sciences, Department of Philosophy, Boston, MA 02215. Offers MA, PhD, JD/MA. *Students:* 50 full-time (21 women), 10 part-time (2 women); includes 2 minority (1 Asian American or Pacific Islander, 1 Hispanic American), 22 international. Average age 32. 225 applicants, 24% accepted, 17 enrolled. In 2007, 22 master's, 13 doctorates awarded. Terminal master's awarded for partial completion of doctoral program. *Degree requirements:* For master's, one foreign language, thesis; for doctorate, one foreign language, comprehensive exam, thesis/dissertation. *Entrance requirements:* For master's and doctorate, GRE General Test, sample of written work, 3 letters of recommendation. Additional exam requirements/recommendations for international students: Required—TOEFL (minimum score 600 paper-based; 250 computer-based). *Application deadline:* For fall admission, 1/15 for domestic and international students. Application fee: $70. *Expenses:* Tuition: Full-time $34,930; part-time $1,092 per credit. Tuition and fees vary according to class time, course level and program. *Financial support:* In 2007–08, 43 students received support, including 4 fellowships with full tuition reimbursements available (averaging $18,000 per year), 2 research assistantships (averaging $16,500 per year), 25 teaching assistantships with full tuition reimbursements available (averaging $16,500 per year); Federal Work-Study and scholarships/grants also available. Financial award application deadline: 1/15; financial award applicants required to submit FAFSA. *Unit head:* Dr. Daniel Dahlstrom, Chairman, 617-353-4583, Fax: 617-353-6805, E-mail: dahlstro@bu.edu. *Application contact:* Kerri French, Senior Program Coordinator, 617-353-2571, Fax: 617-353-6805, E-mail: casphilo@bu.edu.

Bowling Green State University, Graduate College, College of Arts and Sciences, Department of Philosophy, Bowling Green, OH 43403. Offers applied philosophy (PhD); institutional theory and history (PhD); philosophy (MA). Part-time programs available. *Faculty:* 11 full-time (1 woman), 8 part-time/adjunct (0 women). *Students:* 30 full-time (7 women), 5 part-time (3 women); includes 2 Asian Americans or Pacific Islanders, 2 Hispanic Americans, 6 international. Average age 30. 59 applicants, 29% accepted, 5 enrolled. In 2007, 6 master's, 6 doctorates awarded. Terminal master's awarded for partial completion of doctoral program. *Degree requirements:* For master's, thesis or alternative; for doctorate, comprehensive exam, thesis/dissertation, foreign language or research tool. *Entrance requirements:* For master's and doctorate, GRE General Test. Additional exam requirements/recommendations for international students: Required—TOEFL. *Application deadline:* For fall admission, 2/1 priority date for domestic students. Application fee: $30. Electronic applications accepted. *Financial support:* In 2007–08, 1 fellowship with full tuition reimbursement (averaging $14,707 per year), 2 research assistantships with full tuition reimbursements (averaging $11,765 per year), 23 teaching assistantships with full tuition reimbursements (averaging $11,993 per year) were awarded; Federal Work-Study and unspecified assistantships also available. Financial award applicants required to submit FAFSA. *Faculty research:* Moral philosophy and ethics, political and social philosophy, decision theory, applied ethics, public policy. *Unit head:* Dr. David Shoemaker, Chair, 419-372-6983. *Application contact:* Dr. Dan Jacobson, Graduate Coordinator, 419-372-7218.

Brock University, Faculty of Graduate Studies, Faculty of Humanities, Program in Philosophy, St. Catharines, ON L2S 3A1, Canada. Offers MA. Part-time programs available. *Degree requirements:* For master's, thesis optional. *Entrance requirements:* For master's, honors BA in philosophy. Additional exam requirements/recommendations for international students: Required—TOEFL (minimum score 550 paper-based; 213 computer-based; 80 iBT), IELTS (minimum score 7), TWE (minimum score 4). Electronic applications accepted. *Faculty research:* Contemporary continental philosophy, Chinese and comparative philosophy, Indian philosophy, ethics.

Brown University, Graduate School, Department of Philosophy, Providence, RI 02912. Offers AM, PhD. *Degree requirements:* For master's, thesis or alternative; for doctorate, variable foreign language requirement, thesis/dissertation. *Entrance requirements:* For master's and doctorate, GRE General Test.

California Institute of Integral Studies, Graduate Programs, School of Consciousness and Transformation, San Francisco, CA 94103. Offers cultural anthropology and social transformation (MA); East-West psychology (MA, PhD); integrative health studies (MA); philosophy and religion (MA, PhD), including Asian and comparative studies, philosophy, cosmology, and consciousness, social and cultural anthropology (PhD), transformative leadership (MA), transformative studies (PhD), women's spirituality, women's spirituality flex format; social and cultural anthropology (PhD); transformative leadership (MA); transformative studies (PhD). Part-time and evening/weekend programs available. Postbaccalaureate distance learning degree programs offered (minimal on-campus study). *Faculty:* 30 full-time, 28 part-time/adjunct. *Students:* 456; includes 92 minority (32 African Americans, 3 American Indian/Alaska Native, 40 Asian Americans or Pacific Islanders, 17 Hispanic Americans), 1 international. Average age 37. 206 applicants, 93% accepted, 114 enrolled. In 2007, 26 degrees awarded. Terminal master's awarded for partial completion of doctoral program. *Degree requirements:* For master's, comprehensive exam (for some programs), thesis optional; for doctorate, comprehensive exam, thesis/dissertation. *Entrance requirements:* For master's, minimum GPA of 3.0, letters of recommendation, writing sample; for doctorate, master's degree, minimum GPA of 3.0, letters of recommendation, writing sample. Additional exam requirements/recommendations for international students: Required—TOEFL. *Application deadline:* For fall admission, 2/15 priority date for domestic and international students; for spring admission, 10/15 priority date for domestic and international students. Applications are processed on a rolling basis. Application fee: $65. Electronic applications accepted. *Expenses:* Tuition: Full-time $16,930; part-time $780 per unit. Tuition and fees vary according to course load and program. *Financial support:* In 2007–08, 292 students received support; research assistantships, teaching assistantships, career-related internships or fieldwork, Federal Work-Study, institutionally sponsored loans, scholarships/grants, and tuition waivers (partial) available. Support available to part-time students. Financial award application deadline: 3/15; financial award applicants required to submit FAFSA. *Faculty research:* Altered states of consciousness, dreams, cosmology, postcolonial studies, integrative health studies. *Application contact:* Allyson Werner, Senior Admissions Counselor, 415-575-6155, Fax: 415-575-1268.

See Close-Up on page 445.

California State University, Long Beach, Graduate Studies, College of Liberal Arts, Department of Philosophy, Long Beach, CA 90840. Offers MA. Part-time programs available. *Faculty:* 12 full-time (3 women), 17 part-time/adjunct (8 women). *Students:* 12 full-time (4 women), 19 part-time (4 women); includes 10 minority (1 African American, 4 Asian Americans or Pacific Islanders, 5 Hispanic Americans). Average age 38. *Degree requirements:* For master's, comprehensive exam or thesis. *Application deadline:* For fall admission, 7/1 for domestic students; for spring admission, 12/1 for domestic students. Applications are processed on a rolling basis. Application fee: $55. Electronic applications accepted. *Financial support:* Federal Work-Study, institutionally sponsored loans, and scholarships/grants available. Financial award application deadline: 3/2. *Faculty research:* Philosophy of science, ethics. *Unit head:* Dr. Lawrence Nolan, Chair, 562-985-4331, Fax: 562-985-7135. *Application contact:* Dr. Ravi K Sharma, Graduate Advisor, 562-985-5344, Fax: 562-985-7135, E-mail: rsharma@csulb.edu.

California State University, Los Angeles, Graduate Studies, College of Arts and Letters, Department of Philosophy, Los Angeles, CA 90032-8530. Offers MA. Part-time and evening/weekend programs available. *Faculty:* 3 full-time (2 women). *Students:* 12 full-time (4 women),

36 part-time (16 women); includes 15 minority (1 African American, 5 Asian Americans or Pacific Islanders, 9 Hispanic Americans), 2 international. Average age 33. In 2007, 15 degrees awarded. *Degree requirements:* For master's, comprehensive exam. *Entrance requirements:* Additional exam requirements/recommendations for international students: Required—TOEFL. *Application deadline:* For fall admission, 6/30 for domestic students; for spring admission, 2/1 for domestic students. Applications are processed on a rolling basis. Application fee: $55. *Financial support:* Career-related internships or fieldwork and Federal Work-Study available. Support available to part-time students. Financial award application deadline: 3/1. *Faculty research:* Aesthetics, philosophy of language, ethics, philosophy of science, history of philosophy. *Unit head:* Dr. Mark Balaguer, Chair, 323-343-4180 Ext. 4189, Fax: 323-343-4193, E-mail: mbalago@calstatela.edu.

Carleton University, Faculty of Graduate Studies, Faculty of Arts and Social Sciences, Department of Philosophy, Ottawa, ON K1S 5B6, Canada. Offers MA. *Degree requirements:* For master's, thesis optional. *Entrance requirements:* For master's, honors degree. Additional exam requirements/recommendations for international students: Required—TOEFL. *Application deadline:* Applications are processed on a rolling basis. Application fee: $77. *Financial support:* Fellowships, research assistantships, teaching assistantships, institutionally sponsored loans, scholarships/grants, and unspecified assistantships available. *Faculty research:* Application of philosophical theory to issues of current concern, history of philosophy, contemporary philosophy in North America and Europe. *Unit head:* Jay Drydyk, Chair, 613-520-2600 Ext. 2110, Fax: 613-520-3962, E-mail: chair_philosophy@carleton.ca. *Application contact:* Christine Koggel, Supervisor of Graduate Studies, 613-520-2600 Ext. 2110, Fax: 613-520-3962, E-mail: philosophy@carleton.ca.

Carnegie Mellon University, College of Humanities and Social Sciences, Department of Philosophy, Pittsburgh, PA 15213-3891. Offers logic and computation (MS); logic, computation and methodology (PhD); philosophy (MA). Part-time programs available. *Faculty:* 18 full-time (3 women), 4 part-time/adjunct (3 women). *Students:* 27 full-time (1 woman), 1 part-time, 8 international. Average age 25. 67 applicants, 24% accepted, 11 enrolled. In 2007, 6 master's, 4 doctorates awarded. *Median time to degree:* Of those who began their doctoral program in fall 1999, 80% received their degree in 8 years or less. *Degree requirements:* For master's, thesis; for doctorate, comprehensive exam, thesis/dissertation. *Entrance requirements:* For master's and doctorate, GRE General Test. Additional exam requirements/recommendations for international students: Required—TOEFL. *Application deadline:* For fall admission, 1/15 priority date for domestic and international students. Applications are processed on a rolling basis. Application fee: $30. Electronic applications accepted. *Financial support:* In 2007–08, 27 students received support, including 3 research assistantships with full tuition reimbursements available (averaging $15,000 per year); fellowships, teaching assistantships, career-related internships or fieldwork, Federal Work-Study, institutionally sponsored loans, scholarships/grants, and health care benefits also available. Support available to part-time students. Financial award application deadline: 2/1; financial award applicants required to submit FAFSA. *Faculty research:* Philosophy of science, artificial intelligence. *Unit head:* Jeremy Avigad, Director of Graduate Studies, 412-268-2209, Fax: 412-268-1440, E-mail: avigad@andrew.cmu.edu. *Application contact:* Jan Mary Puhl, Academic Coordinator, 412-268-8569, Fax: 412-268-1440, E-mail: jp10@andrew.cmu.edu.

The Catholic University of America, School of Philosophy, Washington, DC 20064. Offers MA, PhD, Ph L, JD/MA. Part-time programs available. *Faculty:* 16 full-time (3 women), 2 part-time/adjunct (0 women). *Students:* 43 full-time (4 women), 76 part-time (18 women); includes 3 minority (2 Asian Americans or Pacific Islanders, 1 Hispanic American), 17 international. Average age 32. 120 applicants, 49% accepted, 35 enrolled. In 2007, 20 master's, 6 doctorates awarded. *Degree requirements:* For master's, one foreign language, thesis, oral exam; for doctorate, 2 foreign languages, comprehensive exam, thesis/dissertation, oral exam. *Entrance requirements:* For master's and doctorate, GRE General Test, previous course work in symbolic logic, 3 letters of recommendation, minimum GPA of 3.0, interview. Additional exam requirements/recommendations for international students: Required—TOEFL (minimum score 580 paper-based; 237 computer-based). *Application deadline:* For fall admission, 2/1 priority date for domestic students; for spring admission, 11/15 priority date for domestic students. Applications are processed on a rolling basis. Application fee: $55. Electronic applications accepted. *Financial support:* Fellowships, career-related internships or fieldwork, Federal Work-Study, scholarships/grants, tuition waivers (full and partial), and unspecified assistantships available. Support available to part-time students. Financial award application deadline: 2/1; financial award applicants required to submit FAFSA. *Faculty research:* Metaphysics; history of ancient, medieval, and modern philosophy; twentieth century Continental philosophy, especially Husserl and Heidegger. *Unit head:* Rev. Kurt Pritzl, OP, Dean, 202-319-5259, Fax: 202-319-4731, E-mail: pritzl@cua.edu.

Central European University, Graduate Studies, School of Social Sciences and Humanities, Budapest, Hungary. Offers economics (MA, PhD); gender studies (MA, PhD); international relations and European studies (MA, PhD); mathematics and its applications (MS, PhD); medieval studies (MA, PhD); nationalism studies (MA, PhD); philosophy (MA, PhD); political science (MA, PhD); public policy (MA, PhD); sociology and social anthropology (MA, PhD). *Faculty:* 75 full-time (25 women), 46 part-time/adjunct (10 women). *Students:* 625 full-time (355 women). Average age 26. 2,500 applicants, 31% accepted, 540 enrolled. In 2007, 325 master's, 20 doctorates awarded. Terminal master's awarded for partial completion of doctoral program. *Degree requirements:* For master's, one foreign language, thesis; for doctorate, one foreign language, comprehensive exam, thesis/dissertation. *Entrance requirements:* For master's, CEU subject tests, interview; for doctorate, GRE, CEU subject test, interview. Additional exam requirements/recommendations for international students: Required—TOEFL (minimum score 570 paper-based; 230 computer-based). *Application deadline:* For fall admission, 1/15 priority date for domestic and international students. Application fee: $0. Electronic applications accepted. Tuition charges are reported in euros. *Expenses:* Tuition: Full-time 10,000 euros; part-time 315 euros per credit. *Financial support:* In 2007–08, 402 students received support, including 350 fellowships with full and partial tuition reimbursements available (averaging $5,000 per year); career-related internships or fieldwork, institutionally sponsored loans, and scholarships/grants also available. Financial award application deadline: 1/5. *Faculty research:* Civil society, fiscal decentralization, party politics, political philosophy (especially Liberalism, theory of Democracy). Total annual research expenditures: $35,000. *Unit head:* Dr. Howard Michael Robinson, Provost, 361-327-3003, Fax: 361-327-3211, E-mail: robinson@ceu.hu. *Application contact:* Zsuzsanna Jaszberenyi, Admissions Officer, 361-327-3009, Fax: 361-327-3211, E-mail: admissions@ceu.hu.

See Close-Up on page 447.

Claremont Graduate University, Graduate Programs, School of Arts and Humanities, Department of Philosophy, Claremont, CA 91711-6160. Offers MA, PhD, MA/PhD, MBA/MA, MBA/PhD. Part-time programs available. *Faculty:* 3 full-time (1 woman), 1 part-time/adjunct (0 women). *Students:* 32 full-time (9 women), 2 part-time; includes 10 minority (1 American Indian/Alaska Native, 3 Asian Americans or Pacific Islanders, 6 Hispanic Americans). Average age 39. In 2007, 5 degrees awarded. *Degree requirements:* For master's, one foreign language, thesis; for doctorate, 2 foreign languages, thesis/dissertation, research folio. *Entrance requirements:* For master's and doctorate, GRE General Test. *Application deadline:* For fall admission, 2/15 priority date for domestic students. Applications are processed on a rolling basis. Electronic applications accepted. *Expenses:* Tuition: Full-time $31,640; part-time $1,376 per unit. Required fees: $145 per semester. Tuition and fees vary according to course load, degree level and program. *Financial support:* Fellowships, research assistantships, Federal Work-Study and institutionally sponsored loans available. Financial award application deadline: 2/15; financial award applicants required to submit FAFSA. *Faculty research:* Ancient philosophy, philosophy of science, probability theory, philosophical logic, philosophy of logic. *Unit head:* Charles Young, Chair, 909-607-3926, Fax: 909-607-1221, E-mail: charles.young@cgu.edu.

Cleveland State University, College of Graduate Studies, College of Liberal Arts and Social Sciences, Department of Philosophy, Cleveland, OH 44115. Offers bioethics (MA, Certificate); philosophy (MA). Part-time and evening/weekend programs available. *Faculty:* 9 full-time (4 women). *Students:* 8 full-time (5 women), 8 part-time (3 women); includes 3 minority (all African Americans), 1 international. Average age 29. 9 applicants, 44% accepted, 3 enrolled. In 2007, 3 degrees awarded. *Degree requirements:* For master's, comprehensive exam, thesis optional. *Entrance requirements:* For master's, minimum GPA of 2.75. Additional exam requirements/recommendations for international students: Required—TOEFL (minimum score 525 paper-based; 197 computer-based). *Application deadline:* For fall admission, 5/1 priority date for domestic and international students. Applications are processed on a rolling basis. Application fee: $30. *Financial support:* In 2007–08, 9 teaching assistantships with full tuition reimbursements (averaging $1,740 per year) were awarded; research assistantships with full tuition reimbursements, tuition waivers (full) and unspecified assistantships also available. *Faculty research:* Ethics, history of philosophy, bioethics, social and political philosophy. *Unit head:* Dr. Diane Steinberg, Chairperson, 216-687-3900, Fax: 216-523-7482, E-mail: d.steinberg@csuohio.edu.

Collège Dominicain de Philosophie et de Théologie, Graduate Programs, Program in Philosophy, Ottawa, ON K1R 7G3, Canada. Offers MA Ph, PhD. Part-time and evening/weekend programs available. *Faculty:* 8 full-time (0 women), 4 part-time/adjunct (0 women). *Students:* 33 full-time (6 women); includes 5 minority (all African Americans) Average age 37. 17 applicants, 47% accepted, 5 enrolled. In 2007, 1 master's, 3 doctorates awarded. *Degree requirements:* For master's, thesis; for doctorate, 3 foreign languages, thesis/dissertation, candidacy exam. *Entrance requirements:* For master's, honors degree in philosophy, minimum B average in undergraduate course work; for doctorate, master's degree in philosophy, minimum A average in graduate course work. *Application deadline:* For fall admission, 6/1 priority date for domestic students, 3/1 priority date for international students; for winter admission, 11/18 priority date for domestic students, 10/14 priority date for international students; for spring admission, 4/1 priority date for domestic students. Applications are processed on a rolling basis. Application fee: $40. *Expenses:* Tuition: Full-time $3,300; part-time $130 per credit. Required fees: $125. One-time fee: $105 part-time. Tuition and fees vary according to reciprocity agreements. *Financial support:* In 2007–08, 3 fellowships (averaging $1,270 per year) were awarded. *Unit head:* Jean-François Méthot, Director, 613-233-5696, Fax: 613-233-6064. *Application contact:* Francis Peddle, Master of Studies, 613-233-3696 Ext. 325, Fax: 613-233-6064, E-mail: francis.peddle@collegedominicain.ca.

College of the Humanities and Sciences, Harrison Middleton University, Graduate Program, Tempe, AZ 85282. Offers education (MA, Ed D); humanities (MA); imaginative literature (MA); jurisprudence (MA); natural science (MA); philosophy and religion (MA); social science (MA). Part-time and evening/weekend programs available. Postbaccalaureate distance learning degree programs offered (no on-campus study).

Colorado State University, Graduate School, College of Liberal Arts, Department of Philosophy, Fort Collins, CO 80523-0015. Offers MA. Part-time programs available. *Faculty:* 14 full-time (2 women), 1 part-time/adjunct (0 women). *Students:* 15 full-time (1 woman), 8 part-time (2 women); includes 1 minority (Hispanic American), 1 international. Average age 32. 25 applicants, 48% accepted, 10 enrolled. In 2007, 6 degrees awarded. *Degree requirements:* For master's, thesis or alternative. *Entrance requirements:* For master's, GRE General Test, minimum GPA of 3.25, 3 letters of recommendation, writing sample. Additional exam requirements/recommendations for international students: Required—TOEFL. *Application deadline:* For fall admission, 2/15 priority date for domestic and international students; for spring admission, 8/1 priority date for domestic and international students. Applications are processed on a rolling basis. Application fee: $50. Electronic applications accepted. *Expenses:* Tuition, state resident: full-time $4,887; part-time $272 per credit. Tuition, nonresident: full-time $16,425; part-time $913 per credit. Required fees: $1,379; $75 per credit. *Financial support:* In 2007–08, 13 teaching assistantships with full tuition reimbursements (averaging $11,293 per year) were awarded; fellowships, research assistantships, career-related internships or fieldwork, Federal Work-Study, institutionally sponsored loans, scholarships/grants, traineeships, and unspecified assistantships also available. Support available to part-time students. Financial award application deadline: 3/1; financial award applicants required to submit FAFSA. *Faculty research:* Animal ethics, environmental ethics, history of philosophy, comparative philosophy, epistemology. *Unit head:* Dr. Jane E. Kneller, Chair, 970-491-6887, Fax: 970-491-4900. *Application contact:* Dr. Michael Losonsky, Graduate Studies Coordinator, 970-491-6734, Fax: 970-491-4900, E-mail: losonsky@lamar.colostate.edu.

Columbia University, Graduate School of Arts and Sciences, Division of Humanities, Department of Philosophy, New York, NY 10027. Offers M Phil, MA, PhD, JD/MA, JD/PhD. Part-time programs available. *Faculty:* 20 full-time. *Students:* 76 full-time (19 women), 8 part-time (2 women). Average age 33. 222 applicants, 21% accepted. In 2007, 10 master's, 3 doctorates awarded. *Degree requirements:* For master's, one foreign language; for doctorate, 2 foreign languages, thesis/dissertation. *Entrance requirements:* For master's and doctorate, GRE General Test, writing sample. Additional exam requirements/recommendations for international students: Required—TOEFL. Application fee: $90. *Expenses:* Tuition: Part-time $1,452 per credit. Required fees: $152 per term. One-time fee: $75 part-time. Full-time tuition and fees vary according to course level, course load, degree level and program. *Financial support:* Fellowships, teaching assistantships, Federal Work-Study and institutionally sponsored loans available. Support available to part-time students. Financial award application deadline: 1/5; financial award applicants required to submit FAFSA. *Unit head:* Carol Rovane, Chair, 212-854-8618, Fax: 212-854-4986, E-mail: cr260@columbia.edu.

Columbia University, Graduate School of Arts and Sciences, Division of Natural Sciences, Department of Physics, Program in Philosophical Foundations of Physics, New York, NY 10027. Offers MA. Application fee: $90. *Expenses:* Tuition: Part-time $1,452 per credit. Required fees: $152 per term. One-time fee: $75 part-time. Full-time tuition and fees vary according to course level, course load, degree level and program. *Unit head:* David Albert, Program Director, 212-854-3519, Fax: 212-854-3196, E-mail: das@columbia.edu.

Concordia University, School of Graduate Studies, Faculty of Arts and Science, Department of Philosophy, Montréal, QC H3G 1M8, Canada. Offers MA. *Degree requirements:* For master's, comprehensive exam, thesis or alternative. *Entrance requirements:* For master's, honors degree in philosophy or equivalent. *Faculty research:* Anglo-American analytic thought, Continental thought, pragmatic thought.

Cornell University, Graduate School, Graduate Fields of Arts and Sciences, Field of Philosophy, Ithaca, NY 14853-0001. Offers PhD. *Faculty:* 18 full-time (4 women). *Students:* 41 full-time (12 women); includes 4 minority (2 African Americans, 2 Hispanic Americans), 16 international. Average age 29. 223 applicants, 9% accepted, 7 enrolled. In 2007, 4 doctorates awarded. *Degree requirements:* For doctorate, comprehensive exam, thesis/dissertation, teaching experience. *Entrance requirements:* For doctorate, sample of written work in philosophy, 2 letters of recommendation. Additional exam requirements/recommendations for international students: Required—TOEFL (minimum score 550 paper-based; 213 computer-based; 77 iBT). *Application deadline:* For fall admission, 1/15 for domestic students. Application fee: $70. Electronic applications accepted. *Financial support:* In 2007–08, 34 students received support, including 18 fellowships with full tuition reimbursements available, 16 teaching assistantships with full tuition reimbursements available; research assistantships with full tuition reimbursements available, institutionally sponsored loans, scholarships/grants, health care benefits, tuition waivers (full and partial), and unspecified assistantships also available. Financial award applicants required to submit FAFSA. *Unit head:* Director of Graduate Studies, 607-255-3687, Fax: 607-255-8177. *Application contact:* Graduate Field Assistant, 607-255-3687, Fax: 607-255-8177, E-mail: philosophy@cornell.edu.

Dalhousie University, Faculty of Arts and Social Science, Department of Philosophy, Halifax, NS B3H 4R2, Canada. Offers MA, PhD. Part-time programs available. *Faculty:* 11 full-time (2 women), 5 part-time/adjunct (1 woman). *Students:* 13 full-time (9 women), 1 (woman) part-

Philosophy

Dalhousie University (continued)

time. 41 applicants, 22% accepted. In 2007, 4 master's, 1 doctorate awarded. *Degree requirements:* For master's, thesis; for doctorate, one foreign language, comprehensive exam, thesis/dissertation. *Entrance requirements:* For doctorate, MA in philosophy. Additional exam requirements/recommendations for international students: Required—TOEFL. *Application deadline:* For fall admission, 1/31 priority date for domestic students. Applications are processed on a rolling basis. Application fee: $60. *Financial support:* In 2007–08, 7 fellowships with tuition reimbursements (averaging $6,000 per year), 7 teaching assistantships (averaging $2,700 per year) were awarded. Financial award application deadline: 1/31. *Faculty research:* Ethical and political philosophy; epistemology; philosophy of language, history, and logic; bioethics; feminist theory. *Unit head:* Dr. Tom Vinci, Chair, 902-494-3810, Fax: 902-494-3518, E-mail: dalphil@dal.ca. *Application contact:* Dr. Michael Uymers, Graduate Coordinator, 902-494-3810, Fax: 902-494-3518, E-mail: dalphil@dal.ca.

DePaul University, College of Liberal Arts and Sciences, Department of Philosophy, Chicago, IL 60604-2287. Offers MA, PhD. Part-time and evening/weekend programs available. *Faculty:* 22 full-time (8 women). *Students:* 22 full-time (8 women), 22 part-time (11 women); includes 3 minority (2 African Americans, 1 Hispanic American), 6 international. Average age 28. 160 applicants, 8% accepted, 7 enrolled. In 2007, 7 master's, 6 doctorates awarded. Terminal master's awarded for partial completion of doctoral program. *Degree requirements:* For master's, one foreign language, thesis optional; for doctorate, 2 foreign languages, thesis/dissertation, oral exam. *Entrance requirements:* For master's, GRE General Test, sample of written work; for doctorate, GRE General Test, MA in philosophy, sample of written work. *Application deadline:* For fall admission, 1/9 for domestic students; for winter admission, 1/9 for domestic students. Applications are processed on a rolling basis. Application fee: $25. Electronic applications accepted. *Financial support:* In 2007–08, 12 fellowships with full tuition reimbursements (averaging $15,500 per year), 24 teaching assistantships with full tuition reimbursements (averaging $15,500 per year) were awarded; tuition waivers (partial) also available. Financial award application deadline: 1/9. *Faculty research:* German idealism, contemporary Continental philosophy, social and political philosophy, critical race theory, Renaissance and early modern philosophy. *Unit head:* Richard A. Lee, Chair, 773-325-4502, Fax: 773-325-7268, E-mail: rlee17@depaul.edu. *Application contact:* Tina Chanter, Director of Recruitment, 773-325-1151, Fax: 773-325-7268, E-mail: tchanter@depaul.edu.

Dominican School of Philosophy and Theology, Graduate Programs, Department of Philosophy, Berkeley, CA 94708. Offers MA, MA/MA. Part-time programs available. *Students:* 3 full-time (1 woman), 5 part-time; includes 4 minority (1 American Indian/Alaska Native, 3 Asian Americans or Pacific Islanders). Average age 36. 4 applicants, 75% accepted, 3 enrolled. In 2007, 6 degrees awarded. *Degree requirements:* For master's, one foreign language, thesis. *Entrance requirements:* For master's, GRE General Test, minimum GPA of 3.0. Additional exam requirements/recommendations for international students: Required—TOEFL (minimum score 550 paper-based; 68 computer-based). *Application deadline:* For fall admission, 3/15 priority date for domestic and international students; for spring admission, 10/15 priority date for domestic and international students. Applications are processed on a rolling basis. Application fee: $40. *Expenses:* Tuition: Full-time $11,880; part-time $495 per unit. Required fees: $100. *Financial support:* In 2007–08, 4 students received support. Institutionally sponsored loans, scholarships/grants, and tuition waivers (partial) available. Financial award application deadline: 4/1; financial award applicants required to submit FAFSA. *Faculty research:* Pre-modernism philosophy, philosophy and science, human suffering, philosophy of language, classical philosophy. *Unit head:* Dr. Anselm Ramelow, Chair, 510-883-2074, Fax: 510-849-1372, E-mail: aramelow@dspt.edu. *Application contact:* John D. Knutsen, Director of Admissions, 510-883-2083, Fax: 510-849-1372, E-mail: admissions@dspt.edu.

Duke University, Graduate School, Department of Philosophy, Durham, NC 27708. Offers AM, PhD, JD/AM. *Faculty:* 14 full-time. *Students:* 34 full-time (12 women); includes 8 minority (1 African American, 1 American Indian/Alaska Native, 3 Asian Americans or Pacific Islanders, 3 Hispanic Americans), 5 international. 107 applicants, 9% accepted, 2 enrolled. In 2007, 2 master's, 5 doctorates awarded. *Degree requirements:* For doctorate, one foreign language, thesis/dissertation. *Entrance requirements:* For doctorate, GRE General Test. Additional exam requirements/recommendations for international students: Required—TOEFL (minimum score 550 paper-based; 213 computer-based; 83 iBT), IELTS (minimum score 7). *Application deadline:* For fall admission, 12/15 priority date for domestic and international students. Application fee: $75. Electronic applications accepted. *Financial support:* Fellowships, research assistantships, teaching assistantships, Federal Work-Study available. Financial award application deadline: 12/31. *Unit head:* Kevin Neauder, Director of Graduate Studies, 919-660-3048, Fax: 919-660-3060, E-mail: rjjc77@duke.edu.

Duquesne University, Graduate School of Liberal Arts, Department of Philosophy, Pittsburgh, PA 15282-0001. Offers MA, PhD. Part-time and evening/weekend programs available. *Faculty:* 10 full-time (3 women), 4 part-time/adjunct (2 women). *Students:* 74 full-time (11 women), 20 part-time (7 women). Average age 32. In 2007, 8 master's, 3 doctorates awarded. Terminal master's awarded for partial completion of doctoral program. *Degree requirements:* For master's, one foreign language; for doctorate, 2 foreign languages, comprehensive exam, thesis/dissertation. *Entrance requirements:* For master's, GRE General Test, bachelor's degree in philosophy, minimum GPA of 3.5; for doctorate, GRE General Test, master's degree in philosophy, minimum GPA of 3.75. Additional exam requirements/recommendations for international students: Required—TOEFL. *Application deadline:* For fall admission, 2/15 for domestic and international students. Application fee: $50. *Expenses:* Tuition: Part-time $774 per credit. Required fees: $74 per credit. Tuition and fees vary according to program. *Financial support:* In 2007–08, 3 research assistantships with full tuition reimbursements (averaging $5,000 per year), 12 teaching assistantships with full tuition reimbursements (averaging $9,700 per year) were awarded; Federal Work-Study, scholarships/grants, tuition waivers (partial), and unspecified assistantships also available. Financial award application deadline: 5/1. *Faculty research:* Phenomenology, twentieth century Continental philosophy, history of philosophy. *Unit head:* Dr. James Swindal, Chair, 412-396-6572.

Emory University, Graduate School of Arts and Sciences, Department of Comparative Literature, Atlanta, GA 30322-1100. Offers comparative literature (PhD); English (Certificate); French (Certificate); Middle Eastern studies (PhD); philosophy (Certificate); psychoanalytic studies (PhD); religion (PhD); Spanish (Certificate); women studies (Certificate). *Degree requirements:* For doctorate, 2 foreign languages, comprehensive exam, thesis/dissertation. *Entrance requirements:* For doctorate, GRE General Test, minimum GPA of 3.0. Additional exam requirements/recommendations for international students: Required—TOEFL. Electronic applications accepted. *Faculty research:* Literary theory, psychoanalysis trauma and testimony, literature and religion, literature and technology, literature and philosophy, politics and global culture, literature and aesthetics.

Emory University, Graduate School of Arts and Sciences, Department of Philosophy, Atlanta, GA 30322-1100. Offers PhD. *Degree requirements:* For doctorate, 2 foreign languages, comprehensive exam, thesis/dissertation. *Entrance requirements:* For doctorate, GRE General Test, minimum GPA of 3.0. Additional exam requirements/recommendations for international students: Required—TOEFL. Electronic applications accepted. *Faculty research:* History of philosophy, German idealism, twentieth century Continental philosophy, ethics, social theory.

Florida State University, Graduate Studies, College of Arts and Sciences, Department of Philosophy, Tallahassee, FL 32306. Offers history and philosophy of science (MA); philosophy (MA, PhD). *Faculty:* 15 full-time (3 women). *Students:* 37 full-time (11 women), 1 part-time; includes 1 minority (Asian American or Pacific Islander), 1 international. Average age 24. 60 applicants, 32% accepted, 8 enrolled. In 2007, 3 master's, 3 doctorates awarded. Terminal master's awarded for partial completion of doctoral program. *Median time to degree:* Of those who began their doctoral program in fall 1999, 100% received their degree in 8 years or less. *Degree requirements:* For master's, one foreign language, comprehensive exam (for some programs), thesis (for some programs); for doctorate, one foreign language, thesis/dissertation. *Entrance requirements:* For master's and doctorate, GRE General Test. Additional exam requirements/recommendations for international students: Required—TOEFL (minimum score 550 paper-based; 213 computer-based; 80 iBT). *Application deadline:* For fall admission, 1/3 priority date for domestic and international students. Applications are processed on a rolling basis. Application fee: $30. Electronic applications accepted. *Expenses:* Tuition, state resident: part-time $248 per credit hour. Tuition, nonresident: part-time $880 per credit hour. Tuition and fees vary according to program. *Financial support:* In 2007–08, fellowships with partial tuition reimbursements (averaging $20,000 per year), 3 research assistantships with partial tuition reimbursements (averaging $5,000 per year), 34 teaching assistantships with partial tuition reimbursements (averaging $12,000 per year) were awarded; Federal Work-Study also available. Financial award application deadline: 1/3; financial award applicants required to submit FAFSA. *Faculty research:* Philosophy of biology, Greek philosophy, ethics, action theory, philosophy of mind. *Unit head:* Dr. John Piers Rawling, Chairman, 850-644-1483, Fax: 850-644-3832, E-mail: prawling@fsu.edu. *Application contact:* Jeremy J. Johnson, Academic Support Assistant, 850-644-1483, Fax: 850-644-3832, E-mail: jjjohnson@fsu.edu.

Fordham University, Graduate School of Arts and Sciences, Department of Philosophy, New York, NY 10458. Offers philosophical resources (MA); philosophy (MA, PhD). Part-time and evening/weekend programs available. *Faculty:* 31 full-time (10 women). *Students:* 36 full-time (8 women), 56 part-time (8 women); includes 5 minority (2 African Americans, 2 Asian Americans or Pacific Islanders, 1 Hispanic American), 8 international. Average age 30. 160 applicants, 21% accepted, 11 enrolled. In 2007, 23 master's, 5 doctorates awarded. Terminal master's awarded for partial completion of doctoral program. *Median time to degree:* Of those who began their doctoral program in fall 1999, 50% received their degree in 8 years or less. *Degree requirements:* For master's, one foreign language, comprehensive exam; for doctorate, 2 foreign languages, comprehensive exam, thesis/dissertation. *Entrance requirements:* For master's and doctorate, GRE General Test. Additional exam requirements/recommendations for international students: Required—TOEFL (minimum score 650 paper-based; 280 computer-based). *Application deadline:* For fall admission, 1/4 priority date for domestic students; for spring admission, 11/1 for domestic students. Application fee: $70. Electronic applications accepted. *Expenses:* Tuition: Full-time $23,880; part-time $995 per credit. *Financial support:* In 2007–08, 45 students received support, including 2 fellowships with tuition reimbursements available (averaging $21,175 per year), 20 research assistantships with tuition reimbursements available (averaging $17,782 per year), 23 teaching assistantships with tuition reimbursements available (averaging $15,293 per year); institutionally sponsored loans, tuition waivers (full and partial), and unspecified assistantships also available. Support available to part-time students. Financial award application deadline: 1/4. *Faculty research:* Contemporary continental philosophy (including German idealism), philosophy of religion, medieval philosophy, ethics, epistemology. *Unit head:* Dr. John Drummond, S.J., Chair, 718-817-3270, Fax: 718-817-3300, E-mail: drummond@fordham.edu. *Application contact:* Charlene Dundie, Director of Graduate Admissions, 718-817-4420, Fax: 718-817-3566, E-mail: dundie@fordham.edu.

Franciscan University of Steubenville, Graduate Programs, Department of Philosophy, Steubenville, OH 43952-1763. Offers MA. Part-time programs available. *Degree requirements:* For master's, one foreign language, thesis. *Entrance requirements:* For master's, minimum undergraduate GPA of 3.0.

Georgetown University, Graduate School of Arts and Sciences, Department of Philosophy, Washington, DC 20057. Offers MA, PhD, JD/MA, JD/PhD, MD/PhD. *Degree requirements:* For master's, thesis or alternative; for doctorate, 2 foreign languages, comprehensive exam, thesis/dissertation. *Entrance requirements:* For master's and doctorate, GRE General Test. Additional exam requirements/recommendations for international students: Required—TOEFL.

The George Washington University, Columbian College of Arts and Sciences, School of Public Policy and Public Administration, Washington, DC 20052. Offers public policy (MA, MPP), including environmental and resource policy (MA), philosophy and social policy (MA), women's studies (MA); public policy and administration (PhD); public policy and public administration (MPA), including budget and public finance, federal policy, politics, and management, international development management, managing public organizations, managing state and local governments and urban policy, nonprofit management, policy analysis and evaluation, public administration; JD/MPP; MPA/JD; PhD/MPP. Part-time and evening/weekend programs available. *Degree requirements:* For doctorate, thesis/dissertation, general exam. *Entrance requirements:* For master's, GRE General Test, minimum GPA of 3.0; for doctorate, GRE General Test, interview, minimum GPA of 3.0. Additional exam requirements/recommendations for international students: Required—TOEFL (minimum score 550 paper-based; 213 computer-based). Electronic applications accepted.

The George Washington University, Columbian College of Arts and Sciences, School of Public Policy and Public Administration, Interdisciplinary Programs in Public Policy, Program in Philosophy and Social Policy, Washington, DC 20052. Offers MA. *Degree requirements:* For master's, comprehensive exam, thesis or alternative. *Entrance requirements:* For master's, GRE General Test, interview, minimum GPA of 3.0. Additional exam requirements/recommendations for international students: Required—TOEFL (minimum score 550 paper-based; 213 computer-based). Electronic applications accepted.

Georgia State University, College of Arts and Sciences, Department of Philosophy, Atlanta, GA 30302-4089. Offers MA, MA/JD. Part-time programs available. *Faculty:* 13 full-time (4 women). *Students:* 47 full-time (11 women), 7 part-time (1 woman); includes 8 minority (3 African Americans, 2 Asian Americans or Pacific Islanders, 3 Hispanic Americans), 1 international. Average age 26. 73 applicants, 64% accepted, 24 enrolled. In 2007, 11 degrees awarded. *Degree requirements:* For master's, thesis. *Entrance requirements:* For master's, GRE General Test, sample of written work. Additional exam requirements/recommendations for international students: Required—TOEFL. *Application deadline:* For fall admission, 4/15 for domestic and international students. Applications are processed on a rolling basis. Application fee: $50. Electronic applications accepted. *Expenses:* Tuition, state resident: part-time $221 per credit hour. *Financial support:* In 2007–08, 2 fellowships with full tuition reimbursements (averaging $15,000 per year), 10 research assistantships with full tuition reimbursements (averaging $6,000 per year), 12 teaching assistantships with full tuition reimbursements (averaging $10,000 per year) were awarded; career-related internships or fieldwork, Federal Work-Study, institutionally sponsored loans, and tuition waivers (partial) also available. Support available to part-time students. Financial award application deadline: 8/1; financial award applicants required to submit FAFSA. *Faculty research:* Ethics, ancient philosophy, Kant, philosophy of mind, epistemology. *Unit head:* Dr. George Rainbolt, Chair, 404-413-6109, E-mail: grainbolt@gsu.edu. *Application contact:* Dr. Tim O'Keefe, Director of Graduate Studies, 404-413-6108.

Gonzaga University, College of Arts and Sciences, Program in Philosophy, Spokane, WA 99258. Offers MA. Part-time programs available. *Faculty:* 6 full-time (1 woman), 1 part-time/adjunct (0 women). *Students:* 2 full-time (1 woman), 12 part-time (3 women); includes 1 minority (Hispanic American) Average age 33. 21 applicants, 62% accepted. In 2007, 1 degree awarded. *Degree requirements:* For master's, comprehensive exam. *Entrance requirements:* For master's, GRE General Test or MAT, minimum GPA of 3.0. Additional exam requirements/recommendations for international students: Required—TOEFL. *Application deadline:* For fall admission, 7/20 priority date for domestic students; for spring admission, 11/1 for domestic students. Applications are processed on a rolling basis. Application fee: $40. *Financial support:* Application deadline: 3/1. *Unit head:* Dr. Rosemary Volbrecht, Chairperson, 509-328-4220, E-mail: volbrecht@calvin.gonzaga.edu. *Application contact:* Dr. Theodore DiMaria, Director of Graduate Studies in Philosophy, 509-323-6762, E-mail: dimaria@gonzaga.edu.

Graduate School and University Center of the City University of New York, Graduate Studies, Program in Philosophy, New York, NY 10016-4039. Offers MA, PhD. *Faculty:* 30 full-time (8 women). *Students:* 126 full-time (34 women), 6 part-time (1 woman); includes 5 minority (1 African American, 1 Asian American or Pacific Islander, 3 Hispanic Americans), 33 international. Average age 34. 148 applicants, 26% accepted, 15 enrolled. In 2007, 7 master's,

10 doctorates awarded. Terminal master's awarded for partial completion of doctoral program. *Degree requirements:* For master's, thesis; for doctorate, one foreign language, comprehensive exam, thesis/dissertation. *Entrance requirements:* For master's, GRE General Test; for doctorate, GRE General Test, 3 letters of recommendation, writing sample. Additional exam requirements/recommendations for international students: Required—TOEFL. *Application deadline:* For fall admission, 2/1 for domestic students. Application fee: $125. Electronic applications accepted. *Financial support:* In 2007–08, 81 students received support, including 72 fellowships, 5 research assistantships, 9 teaching assistantships; career-related internships or fieldwork, Federal Work-Study, institutionally sponsored loans, and tuition waivers (full and partial) also available. Financial award application deadline: 2/1. *Unit head:* Dr. Iakovos Vasiliou, Executive Officer, 212-817-8616, Fax: 212-817-1530.

Harvard University, Graduate School of Arts and Sciences, Department of Philosophy, Cambridge, MA 02138. Offers classical philosophy (PhD); philosophy (PhD). *Degree requirements:* For doctorate, 2 foreign languages, thesis/dissertation, final exams. *Entrance requirements:* For doctorate, GRE General Test. Additional exam requirements/recommendations for international students: Required—TOEFL. *Expenses:* Tuition: Full-time $31,456. Full-time tuition and fees vary according to program and student level.

Harvard University, Graduate School of Arts and Sciences, Department of Sanskrit and Indian Studies, Cambridge, MA 02138. Offers Indian philosophy (AM, PhD); Pali (AM, PhD); Sanskrit (AM, PhD); Tibetan (AM, PhD); Urdu (AM, PhD). Terminal master's awarded for partial completion of doctoral program. *Degree requirements:* For master's, 3 foreign languages; for doctorate, 3 foreign languages, thesis/dissertation. *Entrance requirements:* For master's, GRE General Test; for doctorate, GRE General Test, proficiency in French and German. Additional exam requirements/recommendations for international students: Required—TOEFL. *Expenses:* Tuition: Full-time $31,456. Full-time tuition and fees vary according to program and student level.

Harvard University, Graduate School of Arts and Sciences, Department of the Classics, Cambridge, MA 02138. Offers Byzantine Greek (PhD); classical archaeology (PhD); classical philology (PhD); classical philosophy (PhD); medieval Latin (PhD). *Degree requirements:* For doctorate, 4 foreign languages, thesis/dissertation, preliminary and special exams. *Entrance requirements:* For doctorate, GRE General Test. Additional exam requirements/recommendations for international students: Required—TOEFL. *Expenses:* Tuition: Full-time $31,456. Full-time tuition and fees vary according to program and student level.

Howard University, Graduate School, Department of Philosophy, Washington, DC 20059-0002. Offers MA. Part-time programs available. *Degree requirements:* For master's, one foreign language, comprehensive exam, thesis. *Entrance requirements:* For master's, GRE General Test. Additional exam requirements/recommendations for international students: Required—TOEFL. *Expenses:* Tuition: Full-time $16,175; part-time $899 per credit hour. Required fees: $805. *Faculty research:* African and African-American philosophy, social and political philosophy, ethics, philosophy of culture, applied philosophy.

Indiana University Bloomington, University Graduate School, College of Arts and Sciences, Department of Philosophy, Bloomington, IN 47405-7000. Offers MA, PhD. *Faculty:* 17 full-time (5 women). *Students:* 30 full-time (10 women), 17 part-time (3 women); includes 4 minority (1 African American, 1 Asian American or Pacific Islander, 2 Hispanic Americans), 7 international. Average age 30. 82 applicants, 15% accepted, 9 enrolled. In 2007, 5 master's, 5 doctorates awarded. Terminal master's awarded for partial completion of doctoral program. *Median time to degree:* Of those who began their doctoral program in fall 1999, 63% received their degree in 8 years or less. *Degree requirements:* For master's, thesis, distribution 30 hours; for doctorate, comprehensive exam, thesis/dissertation, qualifying paper, minor, distribution 90 hours. *Entrance requirements:* For master's and doctorate, GRE General Test, writing sample. Additional exam requirements/recommendations for international students: Required—TOEFL. *Application deadline:* For fall admission, 1/15 priority date for domestic students, 12/15 for international students; for spring admission, 9/1 priority date for domestic students, 9/1 for international students. Applications are processed on a rolling basis. Application fee: $50 ($60 for international students). Electronic applications accepted. *Financial support:* In 2007–08, 32 students received support; fellowships with full tuition reimbursements available, research assistantships, teaching assistantships with full tuition reimbursements available available. Financial award application deadline: 4/15. *Faculty research:* Algebraic logic, cognitive science, history of modern philosophy, ancient and Jewish philosophy, Medieval logic and semantics, epistomology, ethics, history, philosophy of mind, philosophy of language. *Unit head:* Timothy W. O'Connor, Chair and Professor, 812-855-1093, Fax: 812-855-3777, E-mail: toconnor@indiana.edu. *Application contact:* Linda J. Harl, Department Secretary, 812-855-9503, Fax: 812-855-3777, E-mail: lharl@indiana.edu.

Indiana University–Purdue University Indianapolis, School of Liberal Arts, Department of Philosophy, Indianapolis, IN 46202-2896. Offers American philosophy (Certificate); bioethics (Certificate); philosophy (MA); JD/MA; MD/MA. Part-time programs available. *Faculty:* 13 full-time (2 women), 1 part-time/adjunct (0 women). *Students:* 3 full-time (0 women), 19 part-time (8 women); includes 1 minority (African American) Average age 32. 12 applicants, 75% accepted, 7 enrolled. *Degree requirements:* For master's, thesis optional. *Entrance requirements:* For master's, GRE. Additional exam requirements/recommendations for international students: Required—TOEFL. *Application deadline:* For fall admission, 3/1 priority date for domestic and international students; for spring admission, 11/15 for domestic and international students. Applications are processed on a rolling basis. Application fee: $50 ($60 for international students). Electronic applications accepted. *Expenses:* Tuition, state resident: full-time $5,818; part-time $242 per credit hour. Tuition, nonresident: full-time $17,106; part-time $713 per credit hour. Required fees: $629. Tuition and fees vary according to course load, campus/location and program. *Financial support:* In 2007–08, 6 students received support, including 1 fellowship (averaging $1,000 per year), 4 teaching assistantships (averaging $4,330 per year); research assistantships with full tuition reimbursements available. Financial award application deadline: 1/15; financial award applicants required to submit FAFSA. *Faculty research:* American philosophy, Peirce bioethics, metaphysics, ethical theory. *Unit head:* Dr. John Tilley, Associate Professor and Chair, 317-274-4690, Fax: 317-278-4579, E-mail: jtilley@iupui.edu. *Application contact:* Dr. Jason Thomas Eberl, Assistant Professor and Graduate Co-Director, 317-278-9239, Fax: 317-278-4579, E-mail: jeberl@iupui.edu.

Institute for Christian Studies, Graduate Programs, Toronto, ON M5T 1R4, Canada. Offers education (M Phil F, PhD); history of philosophy (M Phil F, PhD); philosophical aesthetics (M Phil F, PhD); philosophy of religion (M Phil F, PhD); political theory (M Phil F, PhD); systematic philosophy (M Phil F, PhD); theology (M Phil F, PhD); worldview studies (MWS). Part-time programs available. Postbaccalaureate distance learning degree programs offered (minimal on-campus study). *Degree requirements:* For master's, one foreign language, thesis; for doctorate, 2 foreign languages, thesis/dissertation. *Entrance requirements:* For master's and doctorate, philosophy background. Additional exam requirements/recommendations for international students: Required—TOEFL (minimum score 600 paper-based; 250 computer-based). *Faculty research:* Human rights, anthropology of self, medieval discourse, gender and body, post-modern thought; biblical hermeneutics, creational aesthetics, ecumenism, epistemology, political theory and public policy, relational psychotherapy.

The Johns Hopkins University, Zanvyl Krieger School of Arts and Sciences, Department of Philosophy, Baltimore, MD 21218-2699. Offers MA, PhD. *Faculty:* 10 full-time (2 women). *Students:* 36 full-time (8 women); includes 2 minority (1 Asian American or Pacific Islander, 1 Hispanic American), 8 international. Average age 32. 91 applicants, 23% accepted, 75 enrolled. In 2007, 3 master's, 2 doctorates awarded. *Median time to degree:* Of those who began their doctoral program in fall 1999, 33% received their degree in 8 years or less. *Degree requirements:* For doctorate, thesis/dissertation. *Entrance requirements:* For master's and doctorate, GRE General Test. Additional exam requirements/recommendations for international students: Required—TOEFL. *Application deadline:* For fall admission, 1/15 for domestic students. Application fee: $65. Electronic applications accepted. *Financial support:* In 2007–08, 2 students received support, including 9 fellowships with partial tuition reimbursements available (averaging $16,000 per year), research assistantships with partial tuition reimbursements available (averaging $500 per year), 13 teaching assistantships with tuition reimbursements available (averaging $16,600 per year); Federal Work-Study also available. Financial award application deadline: 4/15; financial award applicants required to submit FAFSA. *Faculty research:* Historical and analytical research on range of philosophical topics. Total annual research expenditures: $3,390. *Unit head:* Dr. Michael Williams, Chair, 410-516-7525, Fax: 410-516-6848, E-mail: mwilli22@jnem.jhu.edu. *Application contact:* Clarissa Costley, Academic Program Coordinator, 410-516-7524, Fax: 410-516-6848, E-mail: cc1@jhu.edu.

Kent State University, College of Arts and Sciences, Department of Philosophy, Kent, OH 44242-0001. Offers MA. Part-time programs available. *Faculty:* 13 full-time (4 women). *Students:* 7 full-time (3 women), 3 part-time. 15 applicants, 100% accepted, 6 enrolled. In 2007, 1 degree awarded. *Degree requirements:* For master's, thesis optional. *Entrance requirements:* For master's, GRE, minimum GPA of 3.0. *Application deadline:* For fall admission, 7/12 for domestic students; for spring admission, 11/29 for domestic students. Applications are processed on a rolling basis. Application fee: $30. Electronic applications accepted. *Financial support:* In 2007–08, 5 students received support, including 5 teaching assistantships with full tuition reimbursements available (averaging $6,950 per year); Federal Work-Study, institutionally sponsored loans, and tuition waivers (full) also available. Financial award application deadline: 3/15; financial award applicants required to submit FAFSA. *Unit head:* Dr. David W. Odell-Scott, Chair, 330-672-2315, Fax: 330-672-4867, E-mail: dodellsc@kent.edu. *Application contact:* Frank X. Ryan, Coordinator of Graduate Studies, 330-672-2315, Fax: 330-672-4867, E-mail: fryan@kent.edu.

Lakehead University, Graduate Studies, Department of Philosophy, Thunder Bay, ON P7B 5E1, Canada. Offers native Canadian philosophy (MA). Part-time and evening/weekend programs available. *Degree requirements:* For master's, thesis. *Entrance requirements:* For master's, bachelor's degree in philosophy, minimum B average. Additional exam requirements/recommendations for international students: Required—TOEFL. *Faculty research:* North American native world views.

Louisiana State University and Agricultural and Mechanical College, Graduate School, College of Arts and Sciences, Department of Philosophy and Religious Studies, Baton Rouge, LA 70803. Offers philosophy (MA). Part-time programs available. *Faculty:* 16 full-time (4 women). *Students:* 11 full-time (3 women), 3 part-time. Average age 29. 11 applicants, 91% accepted, 8 enrolled. In 2007, 2 degrees awarded. *Degree requirements:* For master's, one foreign language, thesis (for some programs). *Entrance requirements:* For master's, GRE General Test, minimum GPA of 3.0. Additional exam requirements/recommendations for international students: Required—TOEFL (minimum score 550 paper-based; 213 computer-based; 79 iBT). *Application deadline:* For fall admission, 4/25 priority date for domestic students, 5/15 for international students; for spring admission, 10/15 for international students. Applications are processed on a rolling basis. Application fee: $25. Electronic applications accepted. *Financial support:* In 2007–08, 12 students received support, including 1 research assistantship with partial tuition reimbursement available (averaging $18,000 per year), 5 teaching assistantships with partial tuition reimbursements available (averaging $10,500 per year); fellowships, Federal Work-Study, institutionally sponsored loans, scholarships/grants, health care benefits, and unspecified assistantships also available. Support available to part-time students. Financial award applicants required to submit FAFSA. *Faculty research:* Analytic philosophy, continental philosophy, history of philosophy, philosophy and religion, existential value theory. Total annual research expenditures: $82,228. *Unit head:* Dr. Mary Sirridge, Chair, 225-578-2278, Fax: 225-578-4897, E-mail: pisirr@lsu.edu. *Application contact:* Dr. Greg Schufrieder, Professor, 225-578-2276, Fax: 225-578-4897, E-mail: gschufr@lsu.edu.

Loyola Marymount University, Graduate Division, College of Liberal Arts, Program in Philosophy, Los Angeles, CA 90045-2659. Offers MA. *Faculty:* 19 full-time (4 women), 20 part-time/adjunct (4 women). *Students:* 19 full-time (3 women), 1 part-time; includes 3 minority (1 African American, 1 Asian American or Pacific Islander, 1 Hispanic American), 3 international. Average age 28. 25 applicants, 36% accepted, 9 enrolled. In 2007, 11 degrees awarded. *Entrance requirements:* For master's, GRE General Test. Additional exam requirements/recommendations for international students: Required—TOEFL (minimum score 600 paper-based). *Application deadline:* For fall admission, 3/15 for domestic students; for spring admission, 11/1 for domestic students. Application fee: $50. *Financial support:* In 2007–08, 3 research assistantships (averaging $12,370 per year) were awarded. Financial award application deadline: 6/1; financial award applicants required to submit FAFSA. *Unit head:* Dr. Mark Morelli, Director, 310-338-7547, Fax: 310-338-5997, E-mail: mmorelli@lmu.edu.

Loyola University Chicago, Graduate School, Department of Philosophy, Chicago, IL 60611-2196. Offers MA, PhD. Part-time and evening/weekend programs available. *Faculty:* 27 full-time (7 women), 3 part-time/adjunct (0 women). *Students:* 97 full-time (24 women), 20 part-time (5 women); includes 8 minority (3 African Americans, 4 Asian Americans or Pacific Islanders, 1 Hispanic American), 15 international. Average age 34. 171 applicants, 23% accepted, 26 enrolled. In 2007, 18 master's, 4 doctorates awarded. Terminal master's awarded for partial completion of doctoral program. *Degree requirements:* For master's, oral exam; for doctorate, one foreign language, thesis/dissertation, oral exam. *Entrance requirements:* For master's and doctorate, GRE General Test. Additional exam requirements/recommendations for international students: Required—TOEFL. *Application deadline:* For fall admission, 1/15 priority date for domestic students. Application fee: $50. Electronic applications accepted. *Expenses:* Tuition: Full-time $12,780; part-time $710 per credit hour. Required fees: $55 per semester. Full-time tuition and fees vary according to program. *Financial support:* In 2007–08, 22 students received support, including 1 fellowship with full tuition reimbursement available (averaging $20,000 per year), 5 research assistantships with full tuition reimbursements available (averaging $15,000 per year), 13 teaching assistantships with full tuition reimbursements available (averaging $15,000 per year); institutionally sponsored loans also available. Financial award application deadline: 1/15; financial award applicants required to submit FAFSA. *Faculty research:* Social philosophy, ethics, medical ethics, analytic philosophy, contemporary Continental philosophy. *Unit head:* Dr. Paul Moser, Chair, 773-508-8481, Fax: 773-508-3292, E-mail: acutrof@luc.edu. *Application contact:* Dr. Andrew Cutrofello, Graduate Program Director, 773-508-8481, Fax: 773-508-2292, E-mail: acutrof@luc.edu.

Marquette University, Graduate School, College of Arts and Sciences, Department of Philosophy, Milwaukee, WI 53201-1881. Offers ancient philosophy (MA, PhD); British empiricism and analytic philosophy (MA, PhD); Christian philosophy (MA, PhD); early modern European philosophy (MA, PhD); ethics (MA, PhD); German philosophy (MA, PhD); medieval philosophy (MA, PhD); phenomenology and existentialism (MA, PhD); philosophy of religion (MA, PhD); social and applied philosophy (MA). Part-time programs available. *Faculty:* 28 full-time (5 women), 12 part-time/adjunct (1 woman). *Students:* 48 full-time (14 women), 9 part-time (3 women); includes 1 minority (Asian American or Pacific Islander), 7 international. Average age 30. 88 applicants, 88% accepted, 19 enrolled. In 2007, 5 master's, 5 doctorates awarded. Terminal master's awarded for partial completion of doctoral program. *Degree requirements:* For master's, one foreign language, comprehensive exam, thesis; for doctorate, 2 foreign languages, thesis/dissertation, qualifying exams. *Entrance requirements:* For master's and doctorate, GRE General Test. Additional exam requirements/recommendations for international students: Required—TOEFL. Application fee: $40. *Financial support:* In 2007–08, 10 research assistantships, 12 teaching assistantships were awarded; Federal Work-Study, institutionally sponsored loans, scholarships/grants, and tuition waivers (full and partial) also available. Support available to part-time students. Financial award application deadline: 2/15. *Faculty research:* Aristotle, Augustine, Descartes, Hegel, Heidegger. Total annual research expenditures: $130,800. *Unit head:* Dr. John Jones, Chair, 414-288-6857, Fax: 414-288-1578. *Application contact:* Dr. Owen Goldin, Director of Graduate Studies, 414-288-5949, Fax: 414-288-1578.

Massachusetts Institute of Technology, School of Humanities, Arts, and Social Sciences, Department of Linguistics and Philosophy, Philosophy Section, Cambridge, MA 02139-4307.

Philosophy

Massachusetts Institute of Technology (continued)
Offers PhD. *Faculty:* 12 full-time (2 women). *Students:* 33 full-time (14 women), 14 international. Average age 27. 205 applicants, 3% accepted, 5 enrolled. In 2007, 4 degrees awarded. *Degree requirements:* For doctorate, comprehensive exam, thesis/dissertation. *Entrance requirements:* Additional exam requirements/recommendations for international students: Required—TOEFL (minimum score 577 paper-based; 233 computer-based). *Application deadline:* For fall admission, 1/2 for domestic and international students. Application fee: $70. Electronic applications accepted. *Expenses:* Tuition: Full-time $34,760; part-time $545 per unit. Required fees: $236. *Financial support:* In 2007–08, 19 fellowships with tuition reimbursements (averaging $27,115 per year), 10 teaching assistantships with tuition reimbursements (averaging $25,729 per year) were awarded; research assistantships with tuition reimbursements, Federal Work-Study, institutionally sponsored loans, scholarships/grants, health care benefits, and unspecified assistantships also available. *Faculty research:* Metaphysics; philosophy of mind; philosophy of language; ethics; political philosophy. *Application contact:* Student Contact, 617-253-4141, Fax: 617-253-5017, E-mail: lp-admissions@mit.edu.

McGill University, Faculty of Graduate and Postdoctoral Studies, Faculty of Arts, Department of Philosophy, Montréal, QC H3A 2T5, Canada. Offers bioethics (MA); philosophy (PhD). *Faculty:* 22 full-time (8 women), 9 part-time/adjunct (2 women). *Students:* 26 full-time (11 women), 1 (woman) part-time. 125 applicants, 8% accepted, 5 enrolled. In 2007, 4 master's, 2 doctorates awarded. *Median time to degree:* Of those who began their doctoral program in fall 1999, 100% received their degree in 8 years or less. *Financial support:* In 2007–08, 22 students received support.

McMaster University, School of Graduate Studies, Faculty of Humanities, Department of Philosophy, Hamilton, ON L8S 4M2, Canada. Offers MA, PhD. Part-time programs available. *Faculty:* 13 full-time, 1 part-time/adjunct. *Students:* 38 full-time, 1 part-time. 61 applicants, 13% accepted. *Degree requirements:* For master's, thesis; for doctorate, one foreign language, thesis/dissertation. *Entrance requirements:* For master's, honors degree in philosophy; minimum average B+; for doctorate, master's degree in philosophy. Additional exam requirements/recommendations for international students: Required—TOEFL (minimum score 580 paper-based; 237 computer-based). *Application deadline:* For fall admission, 2/15 priority date for domestic students. Applications are processed on a rolling basis. Application fee: $90. *Financial support:* In 2007–08, 12 fellowships (averaging $7,500 per year), 25 teaching assistantships (averaging $8,440 per year) were awarded; career-related internships or fieldwork and scholarships/grants also available. *Faculty research:* Twentieth-century European philosophy, twentieth-century Anglo-American philosophy, political philosophy, ethics, argumentation. *Unit head:* Dr. Elisabeth Gedge, Chair, 905-525-9140 Ext. 23470, Fax: 905-577-0385, E-mail: chair.philosophy@mcmaster.ca. *Application contact:* Cheryl Walker, Graduate Secretary, 905-525-9140 Ext. 24312, Fax: 905-577-0385, E-mail: walkerca@mcmaster.ca.

Memorial University of Newfoundland, School of Graduate Studies, Department of Philosophy, St. John's, NL A1C 5S7, Canada. Offers MA. Part-time programs available. *Degree requirements:* For master's, thesis. *Entrance requirements:* For master's, first-class undergraduate degree in philosophy. Electronic applications accepted. *Faculty research:* History of philosophy, philosophy of science, phenomenology and existentialism, contemporary metaphysics.

Miami University, Graduate School, College of Arts and Sciences, Department of Philosophy, Oxford, OH 45056. Offers MA. *Degree requirements:* For master's, thesis, final exam. *Entrance requirements:* For master's, minimum undergraduate GPA of 3.0 during previous 2 years or 2.75 overall. Additional exam requirements/recommendations for international students: Required—TOEFL (minimum score 550 paper-based; 213 computer-based), TWE (minimum score 4). Electronic applications accepted.

Michigan State University, The Graduate School, College of Arts and Letters, Department of Philosophy, East Lansing, MI 48824. Offers MA, PhD. *Entrance requirements:* Additional exam requirements/recommendations for international students: Required—TOEFL. Electronic applications accepted. *Expenses:* Tuition, state resident: part-time $379 per credit hour. Tuition, nonresident: part-time $800 per credit hour. Tuition and fees vary according to program.

Montclair State University, The Office of Graduate Admissions and Support Services, College of Education and Human Services, Center of Pedagogy, Montclair, NJ 07043-1624. Offers mathematics education (Ed D); philosophy for children (Ed D). Part-time programs available. *Faculty:* 18 part-time/adjunct (14 women). *Students:* 7 full-time (3 women), 13 part-time (8 women); includes 2 African Americans, 1 Asian American or Pacific Islander, 5 international. 13 applicants, 15% accepted, 1 enrolled. In 2007, 1 degree awarded. *Degree requirements:* For doctorate, thesis/dissertation. *Entrance requirements:* For doctorate, GRE, 3 letters of recommendation. Additional exam requirements/recommendations for international students: Required—TOEFL (minimum score 117 computer-based). *Application deadline:* For fall admission, 2/1 for domestic students, 11/15 for international students. Application fee: $60. Electronic applications accepted. *Financial support:* In 2007–08, 1 research assistantship with full tuition reimbursement (averaging $7,000 per year) was awarded; institutionally sponsored loans and scholarships/grants also available. Financial award application deadline: 3/1; financial award applicants required to submit FAFSA. *Unit head:* Jennifer Robinson, Director, 973-655-4262.

Montclair State University, The Office of Graduate Admissions and Support Services, College of Education and Human Services, Department of Educational Foundations, Montclair, NJ 07043-1624. Offers critical thinking (M Ed); mathematics education (Ed D); philosophy for children (M Ed, Ed D, Certificate). Part-time and evening/weekend programs available. *Faculty:* 8 full-time (3 women), 3 part-time/adjunct (0 women). *Students:* 3 full-time (2 women), 43 part-time (40 women); includes 8 minority (2 African Americans, 6 Hispanic Americans). Average age 33. 5 applicants, 0% accepted. In 2007, 7 master's, 1 Certificate awarded. *Degree requirements:* For master's, comprehensive exam, field experience; for doctorate, comprehensive exam, thesis/dissertation. *Entrance requirements:* For master's, GRE or MAT, minimum GPA of 2.67, 2 letters of recommendation, teaching certificate; for doctorate, GRE General Test, 3 years of classroom teaching experience, interview, writing sample. Additional exam requirements/recommendations for international students: Required—TOEFL (minimum score 117 computer-based). *Application deadline:* For fall admission, 2/1 for domestic students, 2/15 for international students; for spring admission, 10/15 for domestic and international students. Applications are processed on a rolling basis. Application fee: $60. Electronic applications accepted. *Financial support:* In 2007–08, 2 research assistantships with full tuition reimbursements (averaging $7,000 per year) were awarded; Federal Work-Study and scholarships/grants also available. Support available to part-time students. Financial award application deadline: 3/1; financial award applicants required to submit FAFSA. *Unit head:* Dr. Jeremy Price, Chairperson, 973-655-7039.

The New School: A University, The New School for Social Research, Department of Philosophy, New York, NY 10011. Offers MA, DS Sc, PhD. Part-time and evening/weekend programs available. *Faculty:* 11 full-time (3 women), 3 part-time/adjunct (0 women). *Students:* 146 full-time (47 women), 33 part-time (7 women); includes 17 minority (6 African Americans, 4 Asian Americans or Pacific Islanders, 7 Hispanic Americans), 44 international. Average age 31. In 2007, 23 master's, 15 doctorates awarded. Terminal master's awarded for partial completion of doctoral program. *Degree requirements:* For master's, one foreign language, exam or thesis; for doctorate, 2 foreign languages, thesis/dissertation, qualifying exam. *Entrance requirements:* For master's, GRE General Test; for doctorate, GRE General Test, MA. Additional exam requirements/recommendations for international students: Required—TOEFL (minimum score 600 paper-based; 250 computer-based). *Application deadline:* For fall admission, 1/15 priority date for domestic students. Applications are processed on a rolling basis. Application fee: $50. *Financial support:* Fellowships, research assistantships, teaching assistantships, career-related internships or fieldwork, Federal Work-Study, scholarships/grants, and tuition waivers (full and partial) available. Financial award application deadline: 3/1; financial award applicants required to submit FAFSA. *Faculty research:* Continental philosophy, history of philosophy, political philosophy, aesthetics. *Unit head:* Dr. Jay Bernstein, Chair, 212-229-5707 Ext. 3072, E-mail: bernsteinj@newschool.edu. *Application contact:* Robert MacDonald, Director of Admissions, 800-523-5710 Ext. 3007, Fax: 212-989-7102, E-mail: macdonar@newschool.edu.

See Close-Up on page 1653.

New York University, Graduate School of Arts and Science, Department of Philosophy, New York, NY 10012-1019. Offers MA, PhD, JD/MA, JD/PhD, MD/MA. Part-time programs available. *Faculty:* 16 full-time (1 woman), 9 part-time/adjunct. *Students:* 42 full-time (14 women), 6 part-time (2 women); includes 3 minority (1 African American, 2 Asian Americans or Pacific Islanders), 14 international. Average age 28. 326 applicants, 6% accepted, 10 enrolled. In 2007, 3 master's, 2 doctorates awarded. *Degree requirements:* For master's, thesis or alternative; for doctorate, one foreign language, thesis/dissertation. *Entrance requirements:* For master's and doctorate, GRE General Test, sample of written work. Additional exam requirements/recommendations for international students: Required—TOEFL. *Application deadline:* For fall admission, 1/4 for domestic students. Application fee: $85. *Financial support:* Fellowships with tuition reimbursements, teaching assistantships with tuition reimbursements, Federal Work-Study, institutionally sponsored loans, scholarships/grants, health care benefits, and unspecified assistantships available. Financial award application deadline: 1/4; financial award applicants required to submit FAFSA. *Faculty research:* Philosophy of mind and language, metaphysics, ethics and political philosophy. *Unit head:* Stephen Schiffer, Chair, 212-998-8320, Fax: 212-995-4179, E-mail: philosophy@nyu.edu. *Application contact:* Michael Strevens, Director of Graduate Studies, 212-998-8320, Fax: 212-995-4179, E-mail: philosophy@nyu.edu.

Northern Illinois University, Graduate School, College of Liberal Arts and Sciences, Department of Philosophy, De Kalb, IL 60115-2854. Offers MA. Part-time programs available. *Faculty:* 12 full-time (2 women), 1 part-time/adjunct (0 women). *Students:* 23 full-time (4 women), 14 part-time (4 women); includes 3 minority (1 African American, 1 American Indian/Alaska Native, 1 Asian American or Pacific Islander). Average age 26. 125 applicants, 30% accepted, 14 enrolled. In 2007, 9 degrees awarded. *Degree requirements:* For master's, comprehensive exam, thesis optional. *Entrance requirements:* For master's, GRE General Test, minimum GPA of 2.75, writing sample, major or minor in philosophy. Additional exam requirements/recommendations for international students: Required—TOEFL (minimum score 550 paper-based; 213 computer-based). *Application deadline:* For fall admission, 3/1 priority date for domestic students, 5/1 for international students; for spring admission, 11/1 for domestic students, 10/1 for international students. Applications are processed on a rolling basis. Application fee: $30. Electronic applications accepted. *Expenses:* Tuition, area resident: Part-time $226 per credit hour. Tuition, state resident: full-time $5,424; part-time $225 per credit hour. Tuition, nonresident: full-time $10,848. Required fees: $2,416; $64 per credit hour. *Financial support:* In 2007–08, 13 teaching assistantships with full tuition reimbursements were awarded; fellowships with full tuition reimbursements, research assistantships with full tuition reimbursements, Federal Work-Study, scholarships/grants, tuition waivers (full), and unspecified assistantships also available. Support available to part-time students. Financial award applicants required to submit FAFSA. *Faculty research:* Epistemology, philosophy of biology, animal rights, philosophy of war, international ethics. *Unit head:* Dr. Thomas Kapitan, Chair, 815-753-6299, Fax: 815-753-6302, E-mail: kapitan@niu.edu. *Application contact:* Dr. Mylan Engel, Graduate Director, 815-753-6411, E-mail: mylan-engel@niu.edu.

Northwestern University, The Graduate School, Judd A. and Marjorie Weinberg College of Arts and Sciences, Department of Philosophy, Evanston, IL 60208. Offers PhD. Admissions and degrees offered through The Graduate School. *Degree requirements:* For doctorate, 2 foreign languages, thesis/dissertation. *Entrance requirements:* For doctorate, GRE General Test, sample of written work. Additional exam requirements/recommendations for international students: Required—TOEFL. Electronic applications accepted. *Faculty research:* Phenomenology, philosophy of science, history of philosophy, ethics, social and political philosophy, epistemology.

The Ohio State University, Graduate School, College of Humanities, Department of Philosophy, Columbus, OH 43210. Offers MA, PhD. *Faculty:* 26. *Students:* 29 full-time (5 women), 2 part-time; includes 1 minority (Asian American or Pacific Islander), 4 international. Average age 28. In 2007, 2 master's, 4 doctorates awarded. *Degree requirements:* For master's, thesis optional; for doctorate, thesis/dissertation. *Entrance requirements:* For master's and doctorate, GRE General Test. Additional exam requirements/recommendations for international students: Required—TOEFL (minimum score 600 paper-based; 250 computer-based). *Application deadline:* For fall admission, 8/15 priority date for domestic students, 7/1 priority date for international students; for winter admission, 12/1 priority date for domestic students, 11/1 priority date for international students; for spring admission, 3/1 priority date for domestic students, 2/1 priority date for international students. Applications are processed on a rolling basis. Application fee: $40 ($50 for international students). Electronic applications accepted. *Financial support:* Fellowships, research assistantships, teaching assistantships, Federal Work-Study, institutionally sponsored loans, and unspecified assistantships available. Support available to part-time students. *Unit head:* Ben Caplan, Graduate Studies Committee Chair, 614-292-7914, Fax: 614-292-7502, E-mail: caplan.16@osu.edu. *Application contact:* 614-292-9444, Fax: 614-292-3895, E-mail: domestic.grad@osu.edu.

Ohio University, Graduate College, College of Arts and Sciences, Department of Philosophy, Athens, OH 45701-2979. Offers MA. Part-time programs available. *Faculty:* 8 full-time (2 women), 2 part-time/adjunct (1 woman). *Students:* 17 full-time (2 women); includes 1 minority (Asian American or Pacific Islander) Average age 24. 17 applicants, 88% accepted, 7 enrolled. In 2007, 2 degrees awarded. *Degree requirements:* For master's, thesis. *Entrance requirements:* For master's, GRE, 28 hours. in philosophy including logic, ancient and modern; minimum GPA of 3.0. Additional exam requirements/recommendations for international students: Required—TOEFL. *Application deadline:* For fall admission, 3/1 priority date for domestic students. Applications are processed on a rolling basis. Application fee: $50 ($55 for international students). *Financial support:* In 2007–08, 9 teaching assistantships with tuition reimbursements (averaging $10,800 per year) were awarded; Federal Work-Study, institutionally sponsored loans, and tuition waivers (full) also available. Financial award application deadline: 3/1. *Faculty research:* Ethics, phenomenology, applied ethics, Aristotle, Kant, epistemology. *Unit head:* Dr. Arthur Zucker, Chair, 740-593-4588, E-mail: philosophy.department@ohio.edu. *Application contact:* Dr. John W. Bender, Graduate Chair, 740-593-4599, Fax: 740-593-4597, E-mail: bender@ohio.edu.

Oklahoma City University, Petree College of Arts and Sciences, Program in Liberal Arts, Oklahoma City, OK 73106-1402. Offers art (MLA); general studies (MLA); leadership/management (MLA); literature (MLA); mass communications (MLA); philosophy (MLA); writing (MLA). Part-time and evening/weekend programs available. *Faculty:* 18 full-time (7 women), 14 part-time/adjunct (4 women). *Students:* 24 full-time (18 women), 23 part-time (17 women); includes 6 minority (3 African Americans, 1 American Indian/Alaska Native, 1 Asian American or Pacific Islander, 1 Hispanic American), 14 international. Average age 31. 20 applicants, 95% accepted. In 2007, 13 degrees awarded. *Degree requirements:* For master's, comprehensive exam, thesis optional. *Entrance requirements:* Additional exam requirements/recommendations for international students: Required—TOEFL. *Application deadline:* For fall admission, 8/22 for domestic students; for spring admission, 1/15 for domestic students. Applications are processed on a rolling basis. Application fee: $30 ($70 for international students). *Expenses:* Tuition: Full-time $14,040; part-time $780 per hour. Required fees: $881; $32 per hour. *Financial support:* Fellowships with partial tuition reimbursements, career-related internships or fieldwork, Federal Work-Study, institutionally sponsored loans, and tuition waivers (partial) available. Support available to part-time students. Financial award application deadline: 8/1; financial award applicants required to submit FAFSA. *Unit head:* Dr. Regina Benuett, Director, 405-208-5178, Fax: 405-208-5451, E-mail: rebeunett@okcu.edu. *Application contact:* Leslie McKenzie, Director, Graduate Admissions, 800-633-7242, Fax: 405-208-5356, E-mail: gadmissions@okcu.edu.

Oklahoma State University, College of Arts and Sciences, Department of Philosophy, Stillwater, OK 74078. Offers MA. *Faculty:* 13 full-time (4 women), 3 part-time/adjunct (1 woman). *Students:* 9 full-time (2 women), 9 part-time (1 woman); includes 3 minority (1 African American, 2 American Indian/Alaska Native). Average age 30. 14 applicants, 64% accepted, 9 enrolled. *Degree requirements:* For master's, comprehensive exam, thesis. *Entrance requirements:* For master's, GRE or GMAT. Additional exam requirements/recommendations for international students: Required—TOEFL. *Application deadline:* For fall admission, 3/1 priority date for international students; for spring admission, 8/1 priority date for international students. Applications are processed on a rolling basis. Application fee: $40 ($75 for international students). Electronic applications accepted. *Expenses:* Tuition, state resident: full-time $4,993; part-time $148 per credit hour. Tuition, nonresident: full-time $14,755; part-time $555 per credit hour. Tuition and fees vary according to program. *Financial support:* In 2007–08, 9 teaching assistantships (averaging $12,234 per year) were awarded; career-related internships or fieldwork, Federal Work-Study, scholarships/grants, health care benefits, tuition waivers (partial), and unspecified assistantships also available. Support available to part-time students. Financial award application deadline: 3/1. *Faculty research:* Theoretical and applied ethics, history and philosophy of science, east/west comparative philosophy, social/political/legal philosophy, truth and theory of knowledge. *Unit head:* Dr. Doren Recker, Head, 405-744-0487, Fax: 405-744-4635, E-mail: drecker@okstate.edu.

Penn State University Park, Graduate School, College of the Liberal Arts, Department of Philosophy, State College, University Park, PA 16802-1503. Offers classical American philosophy (MA, PhD); contemporary European philosophy (MA, PhD); history of philosophy (MA, PhD). *Expenses:* Tuition, state resident: full-time $14,738; part-time $614 per credit. Tuition, nonresident: full-time $26,050; part-time $1,085 per credit. Tuition and fees vary according to course load, program and student level. *Unit head:* Dr. Shannon W. Sullivan, Head, 814-865-1618, Fax: 814-865-0119, E-mail: sws10@psu.edu.

Princeton University, Graduate School, Department of Classics, Princeton, NJ 08544-1019. Offers ancient history (PhD); classical archaeology (PhD); classical philosophy (PhD); history, archaeology and religions of the ancient world (PhD). *Degree requirements:* For doctorate, thesis/dissertation. *Entrance requirements:* For doctorate, GRE General Test, sample of written work. Additional exam requirements/recommendations for international students: Required—TOEFL (minimum score 600 paper-based; 250 computer-based). Electronic applications accepted.

Princeton University, Graduate School, Department of Philosophy, Princeton, NJ 08544-1019. Offers classical philosophy (PhD); philosophy (PhD). *Degree requirements:* For doctorate, variable foreign language requirement, thesis/dissertation. *Entrance requirements:* For doctorate, GRE General Test, sample of written work in philosophy. Additional exam requirements/recommendations for international students: Required—TOEFL (minimum score 600 paper-based; 250 computer-based). Electronic applications accepted.

Princeton University, Graduate School, Department of Politics, Princeton, NJ 08544-1019. Offers political philosophy (PhD); politics (PhD). *Degree requirements:* For doctorate, comprehensive exam, thesis/dissertation, teaching experience. *Entrance requirements:* For doctorate, GRE General Test, sample of written work, letters of recommendation. Additional exam requirements/recommendations for international students: Required—TOEFL (minimum score 600 paper-based; 250 computer-based). Electronic applications accepted. *Faculty research:* American politics, comparative politics, formal and quantitative methods, international relations, public law, political theory.

Purdue University, Graduate School, College of Liberal Arts, Department of Philosophy, West Lafayette, IN 47907. Offers MA, PhD. Part-time programs available. Terminal master's awarded for partial completion of doctoral program. *Degree requirements:* For master's, thesis optional; for doctorate, one foreign language, thesis/dissertation. *Entrance requirements:* For master's and doctorate, GRE General Test. Additional exam requirements/recommendations for international students: Required—TOEFL. Electronic applications accepted. *Faculty research:* Continental philosophy, ethics and social philosophy, analytic philosophy, history of philosophy, logic.

Purdue University Calumet, Graduate School, School of Liberal Arts and Sciences, Department of English and Philosophy, Hammond, IN 46323-2094. Offers MA. Part-time and evening/weekend programs available. Postbaccalaureate distance learning degree programs offered (minimal on-campus study). *Degree requirements:* For master's, comprehensive exam, thesis optional. *Entrance requirements:* Additional exam requirements/recommendations for international students: Required—TOEFL. Electronic applications accepted. *Faculty research:* English literature, American literature, critical theory, women's studies, historical philosophy.

Queen's University at Kingston, School of Graduate Studies and Research, Faculty of Arts and Sciences, Department of Philosophy, Kingston, ON K7L 3N6, Canada. Offers MA, PhD. Part-time programs available. *Degree requirements:* For master's, thesis; for doctorate, comprehensive exam, thesis/dissertation. *Entrance requirements:* Additional exam requirements/recommendations for international students: Required—TOEFL. Electronic applications accepted. *Faculty research:* Ethics, social and political philosophy, philosophy of language, epistemology, metaphysics.

Rice University, Graduate Programs, School of Humanities, Department of Philosophy, Houston, TX 77251-1892. Offers MA, PhD. *Degree requirements:* For master's, one foreign language, thesis; for doctorate, one foreign language, thesis/dissertation. *Entrance requirements:* For master's and doctorate, GRE General Test, minimum GPA of 3.0. Additional exam requirements/recommendations for international students: Required—TOEFL (minimum score 600 paper-based; 250 computer-based; 90 iBT). Electronic applications accepted. *Faculty research:* Metaphysics, philosophy of law, philosophy of science, medical ethics, philosophy of language.

Rutgers, The State University of New Jersey, New Brunswick, Graduate School, Program in Philosophy, New Brunswick, NJ 08901-1281. Offers PhD. *Degree requirements:* For doctorate, comprehensive exam, thesis/dissertation. *Entrance requirements:* For doctorate, GRE General Test, writing sample. Electronic applications accepted. *Faculty research:* Philosophy of mind, epistemology, philosophy of language, philosophy of science, metaphysics.

St. John's University, St. John's College of Liberal Arts and Sciences, Department of Philosophy, Queens, NY 11439. Offers MA. Part-time and evening/weekend programs available. *Faculty:* 22 full-time (4 women), 26 part-time/adjunct (4 women). *Students:* 1 (woman) full-time, 59 part-time (33 women); includes 11 minority (4 African Americans, 1 American Indian/Alaska Native, 3 Asian Americans or Pacific Islanders, 3 Hispanic Americans), 3 international. Average age 35. 51 applicants, 78% accepted, 31 enrolled. In 2007, 2 degrees awarded. *Entrance requirements:* Additional exam requirements/recommendations for international students: Required—TOEFL (minimum score 500 paper-based; 173 computer-based; 61 iBT), IELTS (minimum score 6). *Application deadline:* For fall admission, 5/1 priority date for domestic and international students; for spring admission, 11/1 priority date for domestic and international students. *Financial support:* Career-related internships or fieldwork and scholarships/grants available. Support available to part-time students. *Unit head:* Dr. Paul Gaffney, Chair, 718-990-5256. *Application contact:* Beth Evans, Associate Vice President and Executive Director, Enrollment Management, 718-990-6999, Fax: 718-990-5686, E-mail: gradhelp@stjohns.edu.

Saint Louis University, Graduate School, College of Arts and Sciences and Graduate School, Department of Philosophy, St. Louis, MO 63103-2097. Offers MA, MA-R, PhD. Part-time programs available. *Faculty:* 16 full-time (3 women). *Students:* 28 full-time (6 women), 8 part-time (2 women); includes 2 minority (1 African American, 1 Hispanic American), 8 international. Average age 30. 69 applicants, 29% accepted, 8 enrolled. In 2007, 3 master's, 3 doctorates awarded. *Degree requirements:* For master's, one foreign language, thesis, comprehensive oral and written exams; for doctorate, 2 foreign languages, thesis/dissertation, preliminary exams, comprehensive oral and written exams. *Entrance requirements:* For master's and doctorate, GRE General Test, letters of recommendation, resumé, writing sample, interview, goal statement, transcripts. Additional exam requirements/recommendations for international students: Required—TOEFL (minimum score 550 paper-based; 213 computer-based). *Application deadline:* For fall admission, 2/1 for domestic and international students. Applications are processed on a rolling basis. Application fee: $40. Electronic applications accepted. *Expenses:* Tuition: Part-time $845 per credit hour. Required fees: $105 per semester. *Financial support:* In 2007–08, 34 students received support, including 5 research assistantships with full tuition reimbursements available (averaging $13,200 per year), 18 teaching assistantships with full tuition reimbursements available (averaging $12,000 per year); Federal Work-Study, scholarships/grants, traineeships, health care benefits, tuition waivers, and unspecified assistantships also available. Support available to part-time students. Financial award application deadline: 2/1; financial award applicants required to submit FAFSA. *Faculty research:* Medieval philosophy, philosophy of religion, political philosophy, ethics, epistemology. Total annual research expenditures: $10,000. *Unit head:* Rev. Theodore Vitali, Chairperson, 314-977-3149, Fax: 314-977-7211, E-mail: vitalit@slu.edu. *Application contact:* Gary U. Behrman, Associate Dean of Graduate School Admissions, 314-977-3827, Fax: 314-977-3943, E-mail: behrmang@slu.edu.

Saint Mary's University, Faculty of Arts, Department of Philosophy, Halifax, NS B3H 3C3, Canada. Offers MA. *Degree requirements:* For master's, thesis. *Entrance requirements:* For master's, GRE, honors degree, minimum B+ average. Additional exam requirements/recommendations for international students: Required—TOEFL. *Faculty research:* History of philosophy, analytic philosophy, ethics, social philosophy, logic.

San Diego State University, Graduate and Research Affairs, College of Arts and Letters, Department of Philosophy, San Diego, CA 92182. Offers MA. Part-time programs available. *Faculty:* 47 full-time (20 women). *Students:* 18 full-time (2 women), 16 part-time (3 women); includes 9 minority (1 American Indian/Alaska Native, 2 Asian Americans or Pacific Islanders, 6 Hispanic Americans). Average age 29. 26 applicants, 85% accepted, 15 enrolled. In 2007, 6 degrees awarded. *Entrance requirements:* For master's, GRE General Test. Additional exam requirements/recommendations for international students: Required—TOEFL. *Application deadline:* For fall admission, 5/1 for domestic and international students; for spring admission, 11/1 for domestic students, 10/1 for international students. Applications are processed on a rolling basis. Application fee: $55. Electronic applications accepted. *Financial support:* In 2007–08, 3 teaching assistantships were awarded; tuition waivers (partial) also available. Financial award applicants required to submit FAFSA. *Faculty research:* Ancient philosophy, modern philosophy, philosophy of technology, logic, philosophy of mind. *Unit head:* Steven Barbone, Chair, 619-594-5263, Fax: 619-594-1199, E-mail: barbone@mail.sdsu.edu.

San Francisco State University, Division of Graduate Studies, College of Humanities, Department of Philosophy, San Francisco, CA 94132-1722. Offers philosophy (MA); teaching critical thinking (Certificate). Part-time programs available. *Application deadline:* Applications are processed on a rolling basis. *Unit head:* Dr. Anita Silvers, Chair, 415-338-1596. *Application contact:* Dr. Alice Sowaal, Graduate Coordinator, 415-338-1596, E-mail: asowaal@sfsu.edu.

San Jose State University, Graduate Studies and Research, College of Humanities and the Arts, Department of Philosophy, San Jose, CA 95192-0001. Offers MA, Certificate. *Students:* 20 full-time (3 women), 19 part-time (6 women); includes 7 minority (1 American Indian/Alaska Native, 3 Asian Americans or Pacific Islanders, 3 Hispanic Americans), 2 international. Average age 32. 27 applicants, 67% accepted, 13 enrolled. In 2007, 5 degrees awarded. *Degree requirements:* For master's, one foreign language, thesis or alternative. *Application deadline:* For fall admission, 6/29 for domestic students; for spring admission, 11/30 for domestic students. Applications are processed on a rolling basis. Application fee: $59. Electronic applications accepted. *Financial support:* Applicants required to submit FAFSA. *Unit head:* Dr. Rita C. Manning, Chair, 408-924-4468, Fax: 408-924-4527.

Simon Fraser University, Graduate Studies, Faculty of Arts and Social Sciences, Department of Philosophy, Burnaby, BC V5A 1S6, Canada. Offers MA, PhD. Terminal master's awarded for partial completion of doctoral program. *Degree requirements:* For master's, thesis or alternative; for doctorate, thesis/dissertation. *Entrance requirements:* For master's, minimum GPA of 3.33; for doctorate, minimum GPA of 3.67. Additional exam requirements/recommendations for international students: Required—TOEFL or IELTS. Electronic applications accepted. *Faculty research:* Epistemology, philosophy of mind, philosophy of science, value theory, logic.

Southeastern Baptist Theological Seminary, Graduate and Professional Programs, Wake Forest, NC 27588-1889. Offers advanced biblical studies (M Div); Christian education (M Div, MACE); Christian ethics (PhD); Christian ministry (M Div); Christian planting (M Div); church music (MACM); counseling (MACO); evangelism (PhD); language (M Div); ministry (D Min); New Testament (PhD); Old Testament (PhD); philosophy (PhD); theology (Th M, PhD); women's studies (M Div). *Accreditation:* ACIPE; ATS (one or more programs are accredited). *Degree requirements:* For master's, thesis (for some programs), oral exam; for doctorate, thesis/dissertation, fieldwork; for M Div, supervised ministry. *Entrance requirements:* For master's, Cooperative English Test, minimum GPA of 2.0, M Div or equivalent (Th M); for doctorate, GRE General Test or MAT, Cooperative English Test, M Div or equivalent, 3 years of professional experience.

Southern Evangelical Seminary, Veritas Graduate School of Apologetics and Counter-Cult Ministry, Matthews, NC 28105. Offers apologetics (MA, D Min, PhD, Certificate); Islamic studies (MA); Jewish studies (MA); philosophy (MA); religion (MA). *Accreditation:* ATS. Part-time and evening/weekend programs available. Postbaccalaureate distance learning degree programs offered (minimal on-campus study). In 2007, 18 master's, 2 doctorates awarded. *Degree requirements:* For master's, thesis optional; for doctorate, comprehensive exam (for some programs), thesis/dissertation. *Entrance requirements:* Additional exam requirements/recommendations for international students: Required—TOEFL (minimum score 600 paper-based; 250 computer-based). *Application deadline:* For fall admission, 8/5 priority date for domestic and international students; for winter admission, 12/15 priority date for domestic and international students; for spring admission, 1/15 priority date for domestic and international students. Applications are processed on a rolling basis. Application fee: $25. *Financial support:* Scholarships/grants available. *Unit head:* Dr. Thomas A. Howe, Director, Apologetics Program, 704-847-5600 Ext. 209, Fax: 704-845-1747, E-mail: thowe@ses.edu.

Southern Illinois University Carbondale, Graduate School, College of Liberal Arts, Department of Philosophy, Carbondale, IL 62901-4701. Offers MA, PhD. *Faculty:* 11 full-time (2 women). *Students:* 28 full-time (5 women), 44 part-time (11 women); includes 5 minority (1 African American, 2 Asian Americans or Pacific Islanders, 2 Hispanic Americans), 9 international. Average age 25. 67 applicants, 61% accepted, 4 enrolled. In 2007, 5 master's, 10 doctorates awarded. *Degree requirements:* For master's, one foreign language, thesis; for doctorate, 2 foreign languages, thesis/dissertation. *Entrance requirements:* For master's, GRE General Test, minimum GPA of 2.7; for doctorate, GRE General Test, minimum GPA of 3.25. Additional exam requirements/recommendations for international students: Required—TOEFL. *Application deadline:* For fall admission, 2/1 for domestic students. Applications are processed on a rolling basis. Application fee: $20. *Financial support:* In 2007–08, 39 students received support, including 5 fellowships with full tuition reimbursements available, 10 research assistantships with full tuition reimbursements available, 12 teaching assistantships with full tuition reimbursements available; Federal Work-Study, institutionally sponsored loans, and tuition waivers (full) also available. Support available to part-time students. *Faculty research:* Continental philosophy, American philosophy, philosophy of mind, Asian philosophy. *Unit head:* George Schedler, Director of Graduate Studies, 618-536-6641, E-mail: geosched@siu.edu. *Application contact:* Rich Black, Administrative Assistant, 618-453-7429, E-mail: phildept@siu.edu.

Announcement: Professor Larry Hickman, the Director of the Center for Dewey Studies, was named SIUC's Outstanding Scholar in 2002. Professor Anthony Steinbock was named the College of Liberal Arts Outstanding Scholar in 2008. In addition, Professors Thomas Alexander,

Philosophy

Southern Illinois University Carbondale (continued)
Robert Hahn, Anthony Steinbock, and Pat Manfredi have all received outstanding teaching awards.

See Close-Up on page 629.

Stanford University, School of Humanities and Sciences, Department of Philosophy, Stanford, CA 94305-9991. Offers MA, PhD. Terminal master's awarded for partial completion of doctoral program. *Degree requirements:* For master's, oral exam; for doctorate, thesis/dissertation, oral exam. *Entrance requirements:* For master's and doctorate, GRE General Test. Additional exam requirements/recommendations for international students: Required—TOEFL. Electronic applications accepted.

State University of New York at Binghamton, Graduate School, School of Arts and Sciences, Department of Philosophy, Binghamton, NY 13902-6000. Offers MA, PhD. *Faculty:* 14 full-time (4 women), 4 part-time/adjunct (0 women). *Students:* 21 full-time (7 women), 13 part-time (4 women); includes 8 minority (2 African Americans, 1 American Indian/Alaska Native, 3 Asian Americans or Pacific Islanders, 2 Hispanic Americans), 7 international. Average age 28. 43 applicants, 37% accepted, 10 enrolled. In 2007, 4 master's, 1 doctorate awarded. *Degree requirements:* For master's, 2 foreign languages, thesis or alternative; for doctorate, thesis/dissertation. *Entrance requirements:* For master's and doctorate, GRE General Test, GRE Subject Test. Additional exam requirements/recommendations for international students: Required—TOEFL. *Application deadline:* For fall admission, 4/15 priority date for domestic students, 1/15 priority date for international students; for spring admission, 11/1 for domestic students, 10/1 priority date for international students. Applications are processed on a rolling basis. Application fee: $60. Electronic applications accepted. *Financial support:* In 2007–08, 41 students received support, including 11 fellowships with full tuition reimbursements available (averaging $10,000 per year), 20 teaching assistantships with full tuition reimbursements available (averaging $14,000 per year); research assistantships, career-related internships or fieldwork, Federal Work-Study, institutionally sponsored loans, tuition waivers (full and partial), and unspecified assistantships also available. Support available to part-time students. Financial award application deadline: 2/15. *Unit head:* Dr. Bat-Ami Bar-On, Chairperson, 607-777-6198, E-mail: ami@binghamton.edu.

State University of New York at Binghamton, Graduate School, School of Arts and Sciences, Philosophy, Interpretation and Culture Program, Binghamton, NY 13902-6000. Offers MA, PhD. *Students:* 22 full-time (13 women), 30 part-time (10 women); includes 12 minority (6 African Americans, 3 Asian Americans or Pacific Islanders, 3 Hispanic Americans), 21 international. Average age 35. 32 applicants, 34% accepted, 4 enrolled. In 2007, 5 master's, 11 doctorates awarded. *Unit head:* Dr. William Haver, Director, 607-777-3827.

State University of New York at Binghamton, Graduate School, School of Arts and Sciences, Social, Political, Ethical and Legal Philosophy, Binghamton, NY 13902-6000. Offers MA, PhD. *Students:* 18 full-time (7 women), 12 part-time (4 women); includes 6 minority (1 African American, 1 American Indian/Alaska Native, 2 Asian Americans or Pacific Islanders, 2 Hispanic Americans), 7 international. Average age 29. 40 applicants, 33% accepted, 7 enrolled. In 2007, 4 master's, 1 doctorate awarded. Application fee: $60. *Unit head:* Dr. Bat-Ami Bar-On, Chairperson, 607-777-6198, E-mail: ami@binghamton.edu.

Stony Brook University, State University of New York, Graduate School, College of Arts and Sciences, Department of Philosophy, Stony Brook, NY 11794. Offers MA, PhD. Evening/weekend programs available. *Faculty:* 20 full-time (3 women), 1 (woman) part-time/adjunct. *Students:* 95 full-time (30 women), 15 part-time (4 women); includes 14 minority (1 African American, 1 American Indian/Alaska Native, 4 Asian Americans or Pacific Islanders, 8 Hispanic Americans), 15 international. Average age 29. 103 applicants, 64% accepted. In 2007, 9 master's, 2 doctorates awarded. *Degree requirements:* For doctorate, one foreign language, thesis/dissertation. *Entrance requirements:* For master's and doctorate, GRE General Test. Additional exam requirements/recommendations for international students: Required—TOEFL. *Application deadline:* For fall admission, 1/15 for domestic students. Application fee: $60. *Financial support:* In 2007–08, 3 fellowships, 1 research assistantship, 37 teaching assistantships were awarded. *Faculty research:* Philosophy of science, philosophy of language, analytical philosophy, phenomenology, structuralism. *Unit head:* Dr. Robert Crease, Chair, 631-632-7590, Fax: 631-632-7522. *Application contact:* Harvey Cormier, Director of Graduate Studies, 631-632-7572, Fax: 631-632-7522, E-mail: hcormier@notes.cc.sunysb.edu.

Announcement: The Doctoral Program in Philosophy at Stony Brook prepares students to do original and innovative research on the frontiers of contemporary philosophy and to teach at all levels of higher education. Extensive offerings in contemporary European philosophy are a special focus of the program, together with central topics in Anglo-American philosophy, a major historical component, and far-reaching interdisciplinary philosophical opportunities. The MA with a focus in philosophy and the arts explores philosophical aspects of the arts per se and the art world at large.

See Close-Up on page 631.

Syracuse University, Graduate School, College of Arts and Sciences, Department of Philosophy, Syracuse, NY 13244. Offers MA, PhD. Part-time and evening/weekend programs available. *Students:* 35 full-time (8 women), 6 part-time; includes 5 minority (3 Asian Americans or Pacific Islanders, 2 Hispanic Americans), 5 international. 149 applicants, 21% accepted, 13 enrolled. In 2007, 6 degrees awarded. Terminal master's awarded for partial completion of doctoral program. *Degree requirements:* For master's, thesis or alternative; for doctorate, thesis/dissertation. *Entrance requirements:* For master's and doctorate, GRE Writing Test, writing sample. Additional exam requirements/recommendations for international students: Required—TOEFL. *Application deadline:* For fall admission, 1/15 priority date for domestic students. Applications are processed on a rolling basis. Application fee: $75. Electronic applications accepted. *Expenses:* Tuition: Full-time $18,216; part-time $1,012 per credit. Required fees: $980. Tuition and fees vary according to program. *Financial support:* In 2007–08, 25 students received support; fellowships with full and partial tuition reimbursements available, research assistantships, teaching assistantships with full tuition reimbursements available, tuition waivers (partial) available. Financial award application deadline: 1/15. *Faculty research:* Ethics, metaphysics, epistemology, philosophy of language. *Unit head:* Dr. Robert Von Gulick, Chair, 315-443-4501, Fax: 315-443-5675. *Application contact:* Lisa Farnsworth, Information Contact, 315-443-2245, E-mail: lfarmswo@syr.edu.

Temple University, Graduate School, College of Liberal Arts, Department of Philosophy, Philadelphia, PA 19122-6096. Offers MA, PhD. Part-time programs available. Terminal master's awarded for partial completion of doctoral program. *Degree requirements:* For master's, thesis or alternative; for doctorate, one foreign language, thesis/dissertation. *Entrance requirements:* For master's and doctorate, GRE General Test. Additional exam requirements/recommendations for international students: Required—TOEFL (minimum score 550 paper-based; 213 computer-based; 79 iBT). Electronic applications accepted. *Faculty research:* Philosophy of mind, aesthetics, philosophy of science, nineteenth century German philosophy, phenomenology.

Texas A&M University, College of Liberal Arts, Department of Philosophy and Humanities, College Station, TX 77843. Offers philosophy (MA, PhD). Part-time programs available. *Faculty:* 13. *Students:* 21 full-time (2 women), 7 part-time (1 woman); includes 5 minority (1 American Indian/Alaska Native, 2 Asian Americans or Pacific Islanders, 2 Hispanic Americans), 2 international. Average age 27. 54 applicants, 15% accepted, 7 enrolled. In 2007, 1 master's, 2 doctorates awarded. Terminal master's awarded for partial completion of doctoral program. *Degree requirements:* For master's, thesis optional; for doctorate, comprehensive exam, thesis/dissertation, supporting MA degree in another field. *Entrance requirements:* For master's, GRE General Test, letter of recommendation, resumé, writing sample; for doctorate, GRE General Test, letters of recommendation, resumé, writing sample. *Application deadline:* For fall admission, 1/15 for domestic students, 3/1 for international students; for winter admission, 8/1 for international students; for spring admission, 10/15 priority date for domestic students. Application fee: $50 ($75 for international students). Electronic applications accepted. *Expenses:* Tuition, state resident: full-time $6,129. Tuition, nonresident: full-time $11,689. Tuition and fees vary according to course load. *Financial support:* In 2007–08, fellowships with partial tuition reimbursements (averaging $16,000 per year), research assistantships with partial tuition reimbursements (averaging $15,000 per year), teaching assistantships with partial tuition reimbursements (averaging $9,000 per year) were awarded; career-related internships or fieldwork, institutionally sponsored loans, scholarships/grants, and unspecified assistantships also available. Financial award application deadline: 1/15; financial award applicants required to submit FAFSA. *Faculty research:* American philosophy, applied ethics, philosophy of mind, philosophy of religion, history and philosophy of logic. *Unit head:* Dr. Robin Smith, Head, 979-845-5660, Fax: 979-845-0458. *Application contact:* Dr. Hugh J. McCann, Graduate Advisor, 979-845-7133, E-mail: philstaff@www-phil.tamu.edu.

Texas Tech University, Graduate School, College of Arts and Sciences, Department of Philosophy, Lubbock, TX 79409. Offers MA. Part-time programs available. *Faculty:* 7 full-time (2 women), 1 part-time/adjunct (0 women). *Students:* 17 full-time (1 woman), 2 part-time (1 woman); includes 5 minority (1 African American, 1 Asian American or Pacific Islander, 3 Hispanic Americans), 2 international. Average age 26. 28 applicants, 71% accepted, 8 enrolled. In 2007, 9 degrees awarded. *Degree requirements:* For master's, thesis or alternative. *Entrance requirements:* For master's, GRE General Test. Additional exam requirements/recommendations for international students: Required—TOEFL (minimum score 550 paper-based; 213 computer-based). *Application deadline:* For fall admission, 3/1 priority date for international students; for spring admission, 11/1 priority date for international students. Applications are processed on a rolling basis. Application fee: $50 ($60 for international students). Electronic applications accepted. *Expenses:* Tuition, state resident: part-time $373 per credit hour. Tuition, nonresident: part-time $651 per credit hour. Tuition and fees vary according to program. *Financial support:* In 2007–08, 16 students received support, including 15 teaching assistantships with partial tuition reimbursements available (averaging $11,130 per year); research assistantships with partial tuition reimbursements available, Federal Work-Study and institutionally sponsored loans also available. Support available to part-time students. Financial award application deadline: 4/15; financial award applicants required to submit FAFSA. *Faculty research:* Aesthetics, ethics, history of philosophy, philosophy of mind, philosophy of science. Total annual research expenditures: $113,122. *Unit head:* Dr. Peder G. Christiansen, Chair, 806-742-3275 Ext. 323, Fax: 806-742-0730, E-mail: peder.christiansen@ttu.edu. *Application contact:* Dr. Daniel O. Nathan, Director of Graduate Studies, 806-742-0373 Ext. 340, Fax: 806-742-0730, E-mail: daniel.nathan@ttu.edu.

Trinity Western University, Faculty of Graduate Studies, Program in Interdisciplinary Humanities, Langley, BC V2Y 1Y1, Canada. Offers general humanities (MAIH); specialized (MAIH), including English, history, philosophy. Part-time and evening/weekend programs available. Postbaccalaureate distance learning degree programs offered (minimal on-campus study). *Faculty:* 19 full-time (6 women), 3 part-time/adjunct (0 women). *Students:* 9 full-time (4 women), 24 part-time (13 women). Average age 30. 16 applicants, 75% accepted, 9 enrolled. In 2007, 2 degrees awarded. *Degree requirements:* For master's, 36 semester hours. *Entrance requirements:* For master's, strong undergraduate degree in Humanities or English, History or Philosophy. *Application deadline:* For fall admission, 5/15 priority date for domestic students; for winter admission, 11/1 priority date for domestic students. Application fee: $40. *Financial support:* In 2007–08, 12 students received support, including 3 fellowships (averaging $17,500 per year), 1 research assistantship (averaging $12,000 per year); career-related internships or fieldwork, scholarships/grants, and traineeships also available. Financial award application deadline: 4/1. *Faculty research:* Literary theory, gender, medieval and early modern literature, philosophy of religion, Thomas Merton's poetics. Total annual research expenditures: $145,000 Canadian dollars. *Unit head:* Dr. Bob Burkinshaw, Director, 604-888-7511 Ext. 3111, Fax: 604-513-2143, E-mail: burkinsh@twu.ca. *Application contact:* Vic Cornish, Director, Graduate Admissions, 604-888-7511 Ext. 3130, Fax: 604-513-2064, E-mail: vic.cornish@twu.edu.

Tufts University, Graduate School of Arts and Sciences, Department of Philosophy, Medford, MA 02155. Offers MA. *Faculty:* 13 full-time, 6 part-time/adjunct. *Students:* 26 (6 women); includes 3 minority (2 Asian Americans or Pacific Islanders, 1 Hispanic American) 2 international. 181 applicants, 13% accepted, 11 enrolled. In 2007, 2 degrees awarded. *Degree requirements:* For master's, one foreign language, comprehensive exam, departmental qualifying exam. *Entrance requirements:* For master's, GRE General Test, writing sample. Additional exam requirements/recommendations for international students: Required—TOEFL (minimum score 550 paper-based; 213 computer-based; 80 iBT). *Application deadline:* For fall admission, 1/15 for domestic students, 12/30 for international students; for spring admission, 9/15 for domestic and international students. Applications are processed on a rolling basis. Application fee: $70. Electronic applications accepted. *Expenses:* Tuition: Full-time $35,052. *Financial support:* Teaching assistantships with full and partial tuition reimbursements, Federal Work-Study, scholarships/grants, and tuition waivers (partial) available. Support available to part-time students. Financial award application deadline: 1/15; financial award applicants required to submit FAFSA. *Unit head:* Mark Richard, Chair, 617-627-3230, Fax: 617-627-3899. *Application contact:* Nancy Bauer, Admissions Head, 617-627-3230.

Tulane University, School of Liberal Arts, Department of Philosophy, New Orleans, LA 70118-5669. Offers MA, PhD. *Degree requirements:* For master's, thesis or alternative; for doctorate, one foreign language, thesis/dissertation. *Entrance requirements:* For master's, GRE General Test, minimum B average in undergraduate course work; for doctorate, GRE General Test. Additional exam requirements/recommendations for international students: Required—TOEFL. Electronic applications accepted.

Universidad Autonoma de Guadalajara, Graduate Programs, Guadalajara, Mexico. Offers advertising and corporate communications (MA); architecture (M Arch); business (MBA); computational science (MCC); education (Ed M, Ed D); international business (MIB); international corporate law (LL M); manufacturing systems (MMS); philosophy (MA, PhD); prosecution law (LL M); quality systems (MQS); renewable energy (MS); teaching mathematics (MA).

Université de Montréal, Faculty of Arts and Sciences, Department of Philosophy, Montréal, QC H3C 3J7, Canada. Offers MA, PhD. *Faculty:* 28 full-time (4 women), 5 part-time/adjunct (1 woman). *Students:* 183 full-time (51 women), 2 part-time (1 woman). 70 applicants, 57% accepted, 36 enrolled. In 2007, 18 master's, 5 doctorates awarded. *Degree requirements:* For master's, 2 foreign languages, thesis; for doctorate, thesis/dissertation, general exam. *Application deadline:* For fall admission, 2/1 priority date for domestic students; for winter admission, 11/1 priority date for domestic students; for spring admission, 2/1 priority date for domestic students. Application fee: $100. Electronic applications accepted. *Financial support:* Fellowships, teaching assistantships available. Support available to part-time students. *Faculty research:* Ancient and modern philosophy; logic and philosophy of language, ethics, and politics; contemporary Continental philosophy. *Unit head:* Daniel Dumouchel, Director, 514-343-7693, Fax: 514-343-7899. *Application contact:* Frédéric Bouchard, Responsible, 514-343-6848, E-mail: f.bouchard@umontreal.ca.

Université de Sherbrooke, Faculty of Letters and Human Sciences, Department of Human Sciences, Sherbrooke, QC J1K 2R1, Canada. Offers history (MA); philosophy (MA). *Degree requirements:* For master's, thesis. *Entrance requirements:* For master's, minimum GPA of 2.75. *Faculty research:* Political, social, and urban history; history of women.

Université de Sherbrooke, Faculty of Theology, Ethics and Philosophy, Sherbrooke, QC J1K 2R1, Canada. Offers applied ethics (Diploma); human science of religions (MA); intercultural training (Diploma); philosophy (MA, PhD); spiritual anthropology (Diploma); theology (MA, PhD, Diploma). Part-time and evening/weekend programs available. Postbaccalaureate distance learning degree programs offered. Terminal master's awarded for partial completion of doctoral program. *Entrance requirements:* For master's, bachelor's degree in related discipline; for doctorate, master's degree in related discipline. *Faculty research:* Faith and culture interrelation.

Université du Québec à Montréal, Graduate Programs, Program in Philosophy, Montréal, QC H3C 3P8, Canada. Offers MA, PhD. Part-time programs available. *Degree requirements:* For master's, thesis; for doctorate, thesis/dissertation. *Entrance requirements:* For master's, appropriate bachelor's degree or equivalent, proficiency in French; for doctorate, appropriate master's degree or equivalent, proficiency in French.

Université du Québec à Trois-Rivières, Graduate Programs, Program in Philosophy, Trois-Rivières, QC G9A 5H7, Canada. Offers MA, PhD. Part-time programs available. *Degree requirements:* For master's, thesis; for doctorate, thesis/dissertation. *Entrance requirements:* For master's, appropriate bachelor's degree, proficiency in French; for doctorate, appropriate master's degree, proficiency in French.

Université Laval, Faculty of Philosophy, Programs in Philosophy, Québec, QC G1K 7P4, Canada. Offers MA, PhD. Terminal master's awarded for partial completion of doctoral program. *Degree requirements:* For master's, thesis; for doctorate, comprehensive exam, thesis/dissertation. *Entrance requirements:* For master's and doctorate, French exam. Electronic applications accepted.

University at Albany, State University of New York, College of Arts and Sciences, Department of Philosophy, Albany, NY 12222-0001. Offers MA, PhD. *Students:* 23 full-time (5 women), 22 part-time (6 women). Average age 36. In 2007, 4 master's, 1 doctorate awarded. *Degree requirements:* For master's, one foreign language, thesis; for doctorate, thesis/dissertation. *Entrance requirements:* For master's and doctorate, GRE General Test. Additional exam requirements/recommendations for international students: Required—TOEFL (minimum score 550 paper-based; 213 computer-based). *Application deadline:* For fall admission, 2/15 for domestic students, 5/1 for international students; for spring admission, 11/1 for international students. Applications are processed on a rolling basis. Application fee: $75. Electronic applications accepted. *Expenses:* Tuition, state resident: part-time $576 per credit. Tuition, nonresident: part-time $910 per credit. Tuition and fees vary according to program. *Financial support:* Fellowships available. Financial award application deadline: 3/15. *Faculty research:* Philosophical logic, ethics, ancient philosophy/metaphysics, aesthetics, biomedical ethics. *Unit head:* Jonathan Mandle, Chair, 508-442-4250.

University at Buffalo, the State University of New York, Graduate School, College of Arts and Sciences, Department of Philosophy, Buffalo, NY 14260. Offers MA, PhD. Terminal master's awarded for partial completion of doctoral program. *Degree requirements:* For master's, variable foreign language requirement, thesis or alternative; for doctorate, variable foreign language requirement, comprehensive exam, thesis/dissertation. *Entrance requirements:* For master's, GRE General Test, minimum GPA of 2.67; for doctorate, GRE General Test, minimum GPA of 3.0. Additional exam requirements/recommendations for international students: Required—TOEFL (minimum score 550 paper-based; 213 computer-based). Electronic applications accepted. *Faculty research:* Logic, metaphysics (historical and contemporary), aesthetics, epistemology, ethics (historical and contemporary), ontology.

University of Alberta, Faculty of Graduate Studies and Research, Department of Philosophy, Edmonton, AB T6G 2E1, Canada. Offers MA, PhD. Part-time programs available. *Degree requirements:* For master's, thesis; for doctorate, thesis/dissertation. *Entrance requirements:* Additional exam requirements/recommendations for international students: Required—TOEFL (minimum score 550 paper-based; 213 computer-based). Electronic applications accepted. *Faculty research:* Philosophy of science, cognitive science, social and political philosophy, philosophy of language and logic, environmental aesthetics.

The University of Arizona, Graduate College, College of Social and Behavioral Sciences, Department of Philosophy, Tucson, AZ 85721. Offers MA, PhD, JD/PhD. Part-time programs available. *Faculty:* 21. *Students:* 42 full-time (9 women), 7 part-time (2 women); includes 2 minority (both Hispanic Americans), 11 international. Average age 30. 200 applicants, 4% accepted, 8 enrolled. In 2007, 2 master's, 3 doctorates awarded. Terminal master's awarded for partial completion of doctoral program. *Degree requirements:* For master's, exams, qualifying paper; for doctorate, thesis/dissertation, preliminary exams. *Entrance requirements:* For master's and doctorate, GRE General Test, 3 letters of recommendation, statement of purpose, writing sample. Additional exam requirements/recommendations for international students: Required—TOEFL (minimum score 550 paper-based). *Application deadline:* For fall admission, 1/2 for domestic students, 1/1 for international students. Applications are processed on a rolling basis. Application fee: $50. Electronic applications accepted. *Financial support:* In 2007–08, 4 fellowships with tuition reimbursements (averaging $5,000 per year), 4 research assistantships (averaging $13,056 per year), 24 teaching assistantships (averaging $13,056 per year) were awarded; scholarships/grants and tuition waivers (full) also available. Financial award application deadline: 1/15. *Faculty research:* Law, social, and political philosophy; epistemology; philosophy of mind; cognitive science. Total annual research expenditures: $143,189. *Unit head:* Dr. J. Christopher Maloney, Head, 520-621-3120. *Application contact:* Debbie Jackson, Program Coordinator, 520-621-5045, Fax: 520-621-9559, E-mail: debbiej@email.arizona.edu.

University of Arkansas, Graduate School, J. William Fulbright College of Arts and Sciences, Department of Philosophy, Fayetteville, AR 72701-1201. Offers MA, PhD. Part-time programs available. *Students:* 7 full-time (0 women), 18 part-time (1 woman); includes 1 minority (Hispanic American) In 2007, 3 master's, 1 doctorate awarded. *Degree requirements:* For master's, thesis; for doctorate, 2 foreign languages, thesis/dissertation. Application fee: $40 ($50 for international students). *Financial support:* In 2007–08, 11 teaching assistantships were awarded; fellowships with tuition reimbursements, research assistantships, career-related internships or fieldwork and Federal Work-Study also available. Support available to part-time students. Financial award application deadline: 4/1; financial award applicants required to submit FAFSA. *Unit head:* Thomas Senor, Departmental Chairperson, 479-575-3551, Fax: 479-575-2642, E-mail: senor@uark.edu.

The University of British Columbia, Faculty of Arts and Faculty of Graduate Studies, Department of Philosophy, Vancouver, BC V6T 1Z1, Canada. Offers MA, PhD. *Accreditation:* NCATE. Part-time programs available. *Faculty:* 18 full-time (4 women). *Students:* 37 full-time (11 women); includes 7 minority (4 Asian Americans or Pacific Islanders, 3 Hispanic Americans). Average age 28. 110 applicants, 7% accepted, 8 enrolled. In 2007, 2 master's, 2 doctorates awarded. *Degree requirements:* For master's, thesis (for some programs); for doctorate, comprehensive exam, thesis/dissertation. *Entrance requirements:* For master's, honors BA or BA/BS with upper second class standing, minimum GPA of 3.3; for doctorate, MA or honors BA with first class standing, MA or BA with first class standing in philosophy. Additional exam requirements/recommendations for international students: Required—TOEFL (minimum score 550 paper-based; 213 computer-based; 80 iBT). *Application deadline:* For fall admission, 1/15 for domestic and international students. Application fee: $90 Canadian dollars ($150 Canadian dollars for international students). Electronic applications accepted. *Financial support:* In 2007–08, 3 students received support, including fellowships with tuition reimbursements available (averaging $16,000 per year), research assistantships with tuition reimbursements available (averaging $5,000 per year), teaching assistantships with tuition reimbursements available (averaging $10,323 per year); Federal Work-Study and tuition waivers (full) also available. Financial award application deadline: 1/1. *Faculty research:* Ethics and applied ethics, metaphysics and epistemology, history of philosophy, philosophy of science, philosophy of biology. *Unit head:* Dr. Margaret Schabas, Head, 604-822-2820, Fax: 604-822-8782, E-mail: schabas@interchange.ubc.ca. *Application contact:* Nissa Bell, Information Contact, 604-822-8837, Fax: 604-822-8782, E-mail: gradadmn@interchange.ubc.ca.

University of Calgary, Faculty of Graduate Studies, Faculty of Humanities, Department of Philosophy, Calgary, AB T2N 1N4, Canada. Offers MA, PhD. Part-time programs available. *Faculty:* 20 full-time (6 women), 8 part-time/adjunct (1 woman). *Students:* 21 full-time (7 women). Average age 30. 52 applicants, 29% accepted, 5 enrolled. In 2007, 1 master's, 2 doctorates awarded. *Degree requirements:* For master's, comprehensive exam (for some programs), thesis (for some programs); for doctorate, thesis/dissertation, candidacy exam. *Entrance requirements:* Additional exam requirements/recommendations for international students: Required—TOEFL (minimum score 550 paper-based; 213 computer-based). *Application deadline:* For fall and winter admission, 1/15 priority date for domestic and international students. Application fee: $100 ($130 for international students). Electronic applications accepted. *Financial support:* In 2007–08, 19 students received support, including 6 fellowships (averaging $3,000 per year), 16 research assistantships (averaging $4,100 per year), 23 teaching assistantships (averaging $7,020 per year); scholarships/grants also available. Financial award application deadline: 2/1. *Faculty research:* Ethics and political philosophy, metaphysics, philosophy of mind, philosophy of language. *Unit head:* Dr. Ish Haji, Graduate Director, 403-220-3165, Fax: 403-289-5698, E-mail: ihaji@ucalgary.ca. *Application contact:* Renilda Van Aerden, Graduate Program Administrator, 403-220-5533, Fax: 403-289-5698, E-mail: rvanaerd@ucalgary.ca.

University of California, Berkeley, Graduate Division, College of Letters and Science, Department of Philosophy, Berkeley, CA 94720-1500. Offers PhD. *Degree requirements:* For doctorate, thesis/dissertation, qualifying exam. *Entrance requirements:* For doctorate, GRE General Test, minimum GPA of 3.0, writing sample, 3 letters of recommendation. *Application deadline:* For fall admission, 1/6 for domestic students. Application fee: $70 ($90 for international students). *Financial support:* Fellowships, research assistantships, teaching assistantships, unspecified assistantships available. *Unit head:* R. Jay Wallace, Chair, 510-642-2730, E-mail: rjw@berkeley.edu. *Application contact:* Information Contact, 510-642-2722, E-mail: phildept@berkeley.edu.

University of California, Davis, Graduate Studies, Program in Philosophy, Davis, CA 95616. Offers MA, PhD. Terminal master's awarded for partial completion of doctoral program. *Degree requirements:* For doctorate, thesis/dissertation. *Entrance requirements:* For master's and doctorate, GRE General Test, minimum GPA of 3.0. Additional exam requirements/recommendations for international students: Required—TOEFL (minimum score 550 paper-based; 213 computer-based). Electronic applications accepted. *Faculty research:* Moral and political philosophy, philosophy of language, metaphysics, philosophy of science, history of philosophy.

University of California, Irvine, Office of Graduate Studies, School of Humanities, Department of Philosophy, Irvine, CA 92697. Offers MA, PhD. *Students:* 35 full-time (8 women); includes 5 minority (2 Asian Americans or Pacific Islanders, 3 Hispanic Americans), 3 international. In 2007, 4 master's, 4 doctorates awarded. *Degree requirements:* For master's, thesis; for doctorate, thesis/dissertation. *Entrance requirements:* For master's and doctorate, GRE General Test, minimum GPA of 3.0. Additional exam requirements/recommendations for international students: Required—TOEFL (minimum score 550 paper-based; 213 computer-based). *Application deadline:* For fall admission, 1/15 priority date for domestic students; for winter admission, 10/15 priority date for domestic students. Applications are processed on a rolling basis. Application fee: $60. Electronic applications accepted. *Financial support:* In 2007–08, teaching assistantships with partial tuition reimbursements (averaging $13,595 per year); fellowships with tuition reimbursements, institutionally sponsored loans, traineeships, health care benefits, and unspecified assistantships also available. Financial award application deadline: 3/1; financial award applicants required to submit FAFSA. *Faculty research:* Philosophy of action and decision theory, philosophy of language, philosophy of mathematics, virtue ethics, modern and contemporary Continental philosophy. *Unit head:* Nicholas White, Chair, 949-824-3289, Fax: 949-824-6520, E-mail: npwhite@uci.edu. *Application contact:* Astrid Doolaege, Graduate Coordinator, 949-824-6526, Fax: 949-824-6520, E-mail: amboetel@uci.edu.

University of California, Irvine, Office of Graduate Studies, School of Social Sciences, Department of Logic and Philosophy of Science, Irvine, CA 92697. Offers philosophy (PhD). *Students:* 20 full-time (4 women); includes 1 minority (Hispanic American), 1 international. 35 applicants, 40% accepted. In 2007, 2 doctorates awarded. *Entrance requirements:* For doctorate, GRE, minimum GPA of 3.0. Additional exam requirements/recommendations for international students: Required—TOEFL (minimum score 550 paper-based; 213 computer-based). *Application deadline:* For fall admission, 1/15 for domestic students; for winter admission, 10/15 for domestic students; for spring admission, 1/15 for domestic students. *Financial support:* Fellowships, research assistantships with full tuition reimbursements, teaching assistantships, institutionally sponsored loans, traineeships, health care benefits, and unspecified assistantships available. Financial award application deadline: 3/1. *Unit head:* Dr. Jeffrey Barrett, Chair, 949-824-6491, E-mail: jabarret@uci.edu. *Application contact:* Diane Enriquez, Graduate Counselor, 949-824-5924, Fax: 949-824-3548, E-mail: dmvargas@uci.edu.

University of California, Los Angeles, Graduate Division, College of Letters and Science, Department of Philosophy, Los Angeles, CA 90095. Offers MA, PhD. *Students:* 52 full-time (16 women); includes 7 minority (3 Asian Americans or Pacific Islanders, 4 Hispanic Americans), 5 international. Average age 29. 164 applicants, 10% accepted, 8 enrolled. In 2007, 4 master's, 3 doctorates awarded. Terminal master's awarded for partial completion of doctoral program. *Degree requirements:* For master's, one foreign language, comprehensive exam; for doctorate, one foreign language, thesis/dissertation, oral and written qualifying exams, teaching. *Entrance requirements:* For master's, GRE General Test, minimum GPA of 3.0, sample of written work, degree objective of Ph.D; for doctorate, GRE General Test, minimum undergraduate GPA of 3.0, sample of written work. Additional exam requirements/recommendations for international students: Required—TOEFL. *Application deadline:* For fall admission, 1/10 for domestic students. Application fee: $60. Electronic applications accepted. *Expenses:* Tuition, nonresident: full-time $5,728. Required fees: $8,966. Full-time tuition and fees vary according to program and student level. *Financial support:* In 2007–08, 38 fellowships with full and partial tuition reimbursements, 5 research assistantships with full and partial tuition reimbursements, 34 teaching assistantships with full and partial tuition reimbursements were awarded; Federal Work-Study, institutionally sponsored loans, scholarships/grants, and tuition waivers (full and partial) also available. Financial award application deadline: 3/1. *Unit head:* Dr. Donald Martin, Chair, 310-206-2291. *Application contact:* Departmental Office, 310-206-1356, E-mail: alaven@humnet.ucla.edu.

University of California, Riverside, Graduate Division, Department of Philosophy, Riverside, CA 92521-0102. Offers MA, PhD. *Faculty:* 18 full-time (3 women). *Students:* 34 full-time (7 women), 1 part-time; includes 4 minority (3 Asian Americans or Pacific Islanders, 1 Hispanic American), 1 international. Average age 29. In 2007, 6 master's, 6 doctorates awarded. Terminal master's awarded for partial completion of doctoral program. *Degree requirements:* For master's, logic exam, professional paper; for doctorate, one foreign language, thesis/dissertation, logic exam, proposition papers, qualifying exams. *Entrance requirements:* For master's, GRE General Test, minimum GPA of 3.2; for doctorate, GRE General Test, master's degree in philosophy, minimum GPA of 3.2. Additional exam requirements/recommendations for international students: Required—TOEFL (minimum score 550 paper-based; 213 computer-based; 80 iBT). *Application deadline:* For fall admission, 5/1 for domestic students, 2/1 for international students; for winter admission, 9/1 for domestic students, 7/1 for international students; for spring admission, 12/1 for domestic students, 10/1 for international students. Applications are processed on a rolling basis. Application fee: $60 ($75 for international students). Electronic applications accepted. *Financial support:* In 2007–08, fellowships with partial tuition reimbursements (averaging $12,000 per year), teaching assistantships with tuition reimbursements (averaging $16,500 per year) were awarded; research assistantships, career-related internships or fieldwork, Federal Work-Study, institutionally sponsored loans, health care benefits, and tuition waivers (full and partial) also available. Financial award application deadline: 1/1; financial award applicants required to submit FAFSA. *Faculty research:* Moral philosophy, philosophy of science, history of philosophy, philosophy of language, Continental philosophy. *Unit head:* Dr. John Fischer, Graduate Advisor, Fax: 951-827-7288, E-mail: john.fischer@ucr.edu. *Application contact:* Kathy Saylor, Graduate Program Assistant, 951-827-6343, Fax: 951-827-5298, E-mail: thinkers@ucr.edu.

University of California, San Diego, Office of Graduate Studies, Department of Philosophy, La Jolla, CA 92093. Offers philosophy (PhD); science studies (PhD). *Degree requirements:*

Philosophy

University of California, San Diego (continued)

For doctorate, thesis/dissertation. *Entrance requirements:* For doctorate, GRE General Test, GRE Subject Test. Electronic applications accepted.

University of California, San Diego, Office of Graduate Studies, Interdisciplinary Program in Cognitive Science, La Jolla, CA 92093. Offers cognitive science/anthropology (PhD); cognitive science/communication (PhD); cognitive science/computer science and engineering (PhD); cognitive science/linguistics (PhD); cognitive science/neuroscience (PhD); cognitive science/philosophy (PhD); cognitive science/psychology (PhD); cognitive science/sociology (PhD). Admissions offered through affiliated departments. *Faculty:* 65 full-time (14 women). *Students:* 7 full-time (3 women). Average age 26. 2 applicants, 100% accepted, 2 enrolled. In 2007, 1 degree awarded. *Degree requirements:* For doctorate, thesis/dissertation. *Entrance requirements:* For doctorate, GRE General Test, acceptance into one of the 8 participating departments. *Application deadline:* Applications are processed on a rolling basis. Application fee: $0. *Faculty research:* Language and cognition, philosophy of mind, visual perception, biological anthropology, sociolinguistics. *Unit head:* Gary Cottrell, Director, 858-534-7141, Fax: 858-534-1128, E-mail: gcottrell@ucsd.edu. *Application contact:* Beverley Walton, Coordinator, 858-534-4387, E-mail: bwalton@ucsd.edu.

University of California, Santa Barbara, Graduate Division, College of Letters and Sciences, Division of Humanities and Fine Arts, Department of Philosophy, Santa Barbara, CA 93106. Offers PhD, MA/PhD. *Faculty:* 11 full-time (1 woman), 1 part-time/adjunct (0 women). *Students:* 36 full-time (5 women); includes 3 minority (all Asian Americans or Pacific Islanders), 4 international. Average age 30. 70 applicants, 30% accepted, 6 enrolled. In 2007, 3 doctorates awarded. Terminal master's awarded for partial completion of doctoral program. *Median time to degree:* Of those who began their doctoral program in fall 1999, 50% received their degree in 8 years or less. *Degree requirements:* For doctorate, comprehensive exam (for some programs), thesis/dissertation, department courses and qualifying paper. *Entrance requirements:* For doctorate, GRE, 3 letters of recommendation, writing sample. Additional exam requirements/recommendations for international students: Required—TOEFL (minimum score 550 paper-based; 213 computer-based; 80 iBT). *Application deadline:* For fall admission, 5/1 for domestic and international students; for winter admission, 11/1 for domestic and international students; for spring admission, 2/1 for domestic and international students. Applications are processed on a rolling basis. Application fee: $60. Electronic applications accepted. *Expenses:* Tuition, nonresident: full-time $14,888. Required fees: $10,108. *Financial support:* In 2007–08, 36 students received support, including 6 fellowships with full and partial tuition reimbursements available (averaging $14,900 per year), 25 teaching assistantships with full and partial tuition reimbursements available (averaging $14,500 per year); Federal Work-Study, institutionally sponsored loans, scholarships/grants, health care benefits, tuition waivers (full and partial), and unspecified assistantships also available. Financial award application deadline: 1/15; financial award applicants required to submit FAFSA. *Faculty research:* Epistemology, philosophy of language, philosophy of mind, philosophy of logic, ethics. *Unit head:* Prof. Voula Tsouna, Chair, 805-893-3122, E-mail: vtsouna@philosophy.ucsb.edu. *Application contact:* Marsha Bonney, Graduate Program Assistant, 805-893-3122, Fax: 805-893-8221, E-mail: gd-phil@philosophy.ucsb.edu.

University of California, Santa Cruz, Division of Graduate Studies, Division of Humanities, Department of Philosophy, Santa Cruz, CA 95064. Offers MA, PhD. *Faculty:* 12 full-time (2 women). *Students:* 23. 45 applicants, 22% accepted, 6 enrolled. In 2007, 3 degrees awarded. *Degree requirements:* For doctorate, thesis/dissertation, qualifying exam. *Entrance requirements:* For master's and doctorate, GRE, official transcripts, 3 letters of recommendation. Additional exam requirements/recommendations for international students: Required—TOEFL. *Application deadline:* For fall admission, 1/15 for domestic students. Application fee: $60. *Expenses:* Tuition, nonresident: full-time $14,694. Required fees: $11,360. *Financial support:* In 2007–08, fellowships (averaging $16,218 per year), teaching assistantships (averaging $14,574 per year) were awarded. *Unit head:* Dr. Paul Roth, Chair, 831-459-2191, Fax: 831-459-4880, E-mail: paroth@ucsc.edu. *Application contact:* Elizabeth Lynn Galiste, Department Manager, 831-459-4578, E-mail: elizg@ucsc.edu.

University of Chicago, Division of the Humanities, Department of Philosophy, Chicago, IL 60637-1513. Offers ancient philosophy (AM, PhD); philosophy (AM, PhD). *Students:* 71. 183 applicants, 7% accepted, 9 enrolled. Terminal master's awarded for partial completion of doctoral program. *Degree requirements:* For master's, thesis; for doctorate, one foreign language, thesis/dissertation. *Entrance requirements:* For master's and doctorate, GRE General Test. Additional exam requirements/recommendations for international students: Required—TOEFL. *Application deadline:* For fall admission, 12/15 for domestic students. Application fee: $55. *Financial support:* Fellowships, Federal Work-Study available. Financial award application deadline: 12/15; financial award applicants required to submit FAFSA. *Unit head:* Dr. Josef Stern, Chair, 773-702-8513.

University of Cincinnati, Graduate School, McMicken College of Arts and Sciences, Department of Philosophy, Cincinnati, OH 45221. Offers MA, PhD. *Faculty:* 13 full-time (2 women). *Students:* 15 full-time (5 women), 8 part-time; includes 2 minority (1 African American, 1 Asian American or Pacific Islander), 5 international. 21 applicants, 19% accepted. In 2007, 5 master's, 1 doctorate awarded. Terminal master's awarded for partial completion of doctoral program. *Degree requirements:* For master's, thesis; for doctorate, one foreign language, comprehensive exam, thesis/dissertation. *Entrance requirements:* For master's and doctorate, GRE General Test, BA in philosophy or equivalent experience. Additional exam requirements/recommendations for international students: Required—TOEFL (minimum score 240 computer-based). *Application deadline:* For fall admission, 2/1 for domestic and international students. Application fee: $40. Electronic applications accepted. *Financial support:* In 2007–08, 16 students received support, including 3 fellowships with full tuition reimbursements available (averaging $14,500 per year), 12 teaching assistantships with full tuition reimbursements available (averaging $14,000 per year); research assistantships with full tuition reimbursements available, tuition waivers (partial) and unspecified assistantships also available. Financial award application deadline: 5/1. *Unit head:* Dr. John Bickle, Head, 513-556-6336, Fax: 513-556-2939, E-mail: bicklejw@email.uc.edu. *Application contact:* Dr. Robert Skipper, Graduate Program Director, 513-556-6340, E-mail: robert.skipper@uc.edu.

University of Colorado at Boulder, Graduate School, College of Arts and Sciences, Department of Philosophy, Boulder, CO 80309. Offers MA, PhD. *Faculty:* 20. *Students:* 54 full-time (13 women), 5 part-time (4 women); includes 5 minority (1 Asian American or Pacific Islander, 4 Hispanic Americans). Average age 31. 24 applicants, 58% accepted. In 2007, 5 master's, 3 doctorates awarded. Terminal master's awarded for partial completion of doctoral program. *Degree requirements:* For master's, comprehensive exam, thesis; for doctorate, one foreign language, thesis/dissertation, logic and qualifying papers, oral exam. *Entrance requirements:* For master's, GRE General Test, writing sample, minimum undergraduate GPA of 2.75; for doctorate, GRE General Test, writing sample. *Application deadline:* For fall admission, 1/15 priority date for domestic students, 12/1 for international students. Applications are processed on a rolling basis. Application fee: $50 ($60 for international students). *Financial support:* In 2007–08, 9 fellowships (averaging $9,617 per year) were awarded; Federal Work-Study, institutionally sponsored loans, and tuition waivers (full) also available. Financial award application deadline: 1/17. *Faculty research:* Metaphysics and epistemology, classical philosophy, moral and political philosophy, philosophy of science. *Unit head:* Robert Pasnau, Chair, 303-492-6132, Fax: 303-492-8386, E-mail: pasnau@colorado.edu. *Application contact:* Graduate Program Assistant, 303-492-3172, Fax: 303-492-8386, E-mail: phildept@colorado.edu.

University of Connecticut, Graduate School, College of Liberal Arts and Sciences, Department of Philosophy, Field of Philosophy, Storrs, CT 06269. Offers MA, PhD. *Faculty:* 15 full-time (4 women). *Students:* 26 full-time (5 women), 3 part-time (1 woman); includes 5 minority (1 African American, 3 Asian Americans or Pacific Islanders, 1 Hispanic American), 6 international. Average age 30. 66 applicants, 9% accepted, 6 enrolled. In 2007, 3 degrees awarded. Terminal master's awarded for partial completion of doctoral program. *Degree requirements:* For master's, comprehensive exam; for doctorate, 2 foreign languages, thesis/dissertation. *Entrance requirements:* For master's and doctorate, GRE General Test. Additional exam requirements/recommendations for international students: Required—TOEFL (minimum score 550 paper-based; 213 computer-based). *Application deadline:* For fall admission, 2/1 priority date for domestic and international students; for spring admission, 11/1 for domestic students, 10/1 for international students. Applications are processed on a rolling basis. Application fee: $55. Electronic applications accepted. *Expenses:* Tuition, state resident: part-time $469 per credit hour. Tuition, nonresident: part-time $1,218 per credit hour. *Financial support:* In 2007–08, 2 research assistantships with full tuition reimbursements, 24 teaching assistantships with full tuition reimbursements were awarded; fellowships, Federal Work-Study, scholarships/grants, health care benefits, and unspecified assistantships also available. Financial award application deadline: 2/1; financial award applicants required to submit FAFSA. *Application contact:* Shelly Burelle, Administrative Assistant, 860-486-4416, Fax: 860-486-0387, E-mail: shelly.burelle@uconn.edu.

University of Dallas, Braniff Graduate School of Liberal Arts, Institute of Philosophic Studies, Doctoral Program in Philosophy, Irving, TX 75062-4736. Offers PhD. *Faculty:* 7 part-time/adjunct (0 women). *Students:* 15 full-time (5 women), 7 part-time (1 woman), 1 international. Average age 31. 15 applicants, 40% accepted, 4 enrolled. *Degree requirements:* For doctorate, 2 foreign languages, comprehensive exam, thesis/dissertation, qualifying exams. *Entrance requirements:* For doctorate, GRE General Test. *Application deadline:* For fall admission, 2/15 priority date for domestic students. Application fee: $50. *Expenses:* Tuition: Part-time $600 per credit. Required fees: $15 per credit. *Financial support:* In 2007–08, 16 students received support. Scholarships/grants available. Financial award application deadline: 2/15. *Faculty research:* Aesthetics, postmodernism, Hegel, ethics, Aristotle. *Unit head:* Dr. Lance Simmons, Chair, 972-721-5274, Fax: 972-721-4005, E-mail: simmons@udallas.edu. *Application contact:* Graduate Coordinator, 972-721-5106, Fax: 972-721-5280, E-mail: graduate@acad.udallas.edu.

University of Dallas, Braniff Graduate School of Liberal Arts, Master's Program in Philosophy, Irving, TX 75062-4736. Offers MA. *Faculty:* 4 part-time/adjunct (0 women). *Students:* 7 full-time (1 woman), 5 part-time; includes 3 minority (1 African American, 2 Hispanic Americans), 1 international. Average age 26. 9 applicants, 89% accepted, 6 enrolled. In 2007, 8 degrees awarded. *Degree requirements:* For master's, one foreign language, comprehensive exam, thesis. *Entrance requirements:* For master's, GRE General Test. Additional exam requirements/recommendations for international students: Required—TOEFL. *Application deadline:* For fall admission, 2/15 priority date for domestic students; for spring admission, 11/15 for domestic students. Applications are processed on a rolling basis. Application fee: $50. *Expenses:* Tuition: Part-time $600 per credit. Required fees: $15 per credit. *Financial support:* Scholarships/grants and tuition waivers available. Financial award application deadline: 2/15. *Faculty research:* Aesthetics, postmodernism, Hegel, ethics, Aristotle. *Unit head:* Dr. Lance Simmons, Chair, 972-721-5274, Fax: 972-721-4005, E-mail: simmons@udallas.edu. *Application contact:* Graduate Coordinator, 972-721-5106, Fax: 972-721-5280, E-mail: graduate@acad.udallas.edu.

University of Florida, Graduate School, College of Liberal Arts and Sciences, Department of Philosophy, Gainesville, FL 32611. Offers MA, PhD. *Faculty:* 14 full-time (1 woman), 1 part-time/adjunct (0 women). *Students:* 32 (8 women); includes 4 minority (1 African American, 1 Asian American or Pacific Islander, 2 Hispanic Americans) 9 international. In 2007, 6 degrees awarded. *Degree requirements:* For master's, thesis or alternative; for doctorate, thesis/dissertation. *Entrance requirements:* For master's and doctorate, GRE General Test, minimum GPA of 3.0. Additional exam requirements/recommendations for international students: Required—TOEFL (minimum score 550 paper-based; 213 computer-based). *Application deadline:* For fall admission, 6/1 priority date for domestic students. Applications are processed on a rolling basis. Application fee: $30. Electronic applications accepted. *Expenses:* Tuition, state resident: full-time $7,478. Tuition, nonresident: full-time $22,603. *Financial support:* In 2007–08, 20 teaching assistantships with tuition reimbursements (averaging $16,531 per year) were awarded; fellowships with tuition reimbursements, research assistantships, unspecified assistantships also available. *Faculty research:* History of philosophy, ethics, philosophy of the mind, philosophy of science, philosophy of language. *Unit head:* Robert D'Amico, Chair, 352-392-2084 Ext. 330, Fax: 352-392-5577, E-mail: rdamico@phil.ufl.edu. *Application contact:* Dr. Kirk Ludwig, Coordinator, 352-392-2084 Ext. 303, Fax: 352-392-5577, E-mail: kludwig@phil.ufl.edu.

University of Georgia, Graduate School, College of Arts and Sciences, Department of Philosophy, Athens, GA 30602. Offers MA, PhD. Part-time programs available. *Faculty:* 11 full-time (5 women). *Students:* 17 full-time (0 women), 9 part-time; includes 2 minority (both Hispanic Americans), 1 international. 25 applicants, 48% accepted, 2 enrolled. In 2007, 1 master's, 4 doctorates awarded. *Degree requirements:* For master's, one foreign language, thesis; for doctorate, one foreign language, thesis/dissertation. *Entrance requirements:* For master's and doctorate, GRE General Test. Additional exam requirements/recommendations for international students: Required—TOEFL. *Application deadline:* For fall admission, 1/1 priority date for domestic and international students; for spring admission, 11/15 for domestic students. Application fee: $50. Electronic applications accepted. *Financial support:* In 2007–08, 19 students received support, including 4 teaching assistantships with partial tuition reimbursements available (averaging $13,342 per year); unspecified assistantships also available. Financial award application deadline: 1/1. *Unit head:* Dr. Victoria M. Davion, Head, 706-542-2823, E-mail: vdavion@uga.edu. *Application contact:* Dr. Elizabeth Brient, Graduate Coordinator, 706-583-0668, Fax: 706-542-2839, E-mail: ebrient@uga.edu.

University of Guelph, Graduate Program Services, College of Arts, Department of Philosophy, Guelph, ON N1G 2W1, Canada. Offers MA, PhD. Part-time programs available. *Faculty:* 19 full-time (6 women), 1 part-time/adjunct (0 women). *Students:* 48 full-time (15 women). 90 applicants, 21% accepted, 19 enrolled. In 2007, 12 master's, 8 doctorates awarded. *Median time to degree:* Of those who began their doctoral program in fall 1999, 100% received their degree in 8 years or less. *Degree requirements:* For master's, thesis (for some programs); for doctorate, one foreign language, thesis/dissertation. *Entrance requirements:* For master's, minimum B- average during previous 2 years of course work; for doctorate, minimum B average. Additional exam requirements/recommendations for international students: Required—TOEFL (minimum score 550 paper-based; 213 computer-based). *Application deadline:* For fall admission, 1/29 for domestic and international students. Application fee: $75. Electronic applications accepted. *Financial support:* In 2007–08, 8 students received support, including research assistantships (averaging $5,106 per year), teaching assistantships with partial tuition reimbursements available (averaging $5,106 per year); scholarships/grants also available. *Faculty research:* Philosophy of science, ethics, modern philosophy, social philosophy, Continental philosophy. *Unit head:* Dr. Andrew Bailey, Chair, 519-824-4120 Ext. 56389, Fax: 519-837-8364, E-mail: abailey@uoguelph.ca. *Application contact:* Dr. Omid A. Payrow-Shabani, Graduate Studies Coordinator, 519-824-4120 Ext. 53201, Fax: 519-837-8634, E-mail: oshabani@uoguelph.ca.

University of Hawaii at Manoa, Graduate Division, Colleges of Arts and Sciences, College of Arts and Humanities, Department of Philosophy, Honolulu, HI 96822. Offers MA, PhD. Part-time programs available. *Faculty:* 15 full-time (3 women). *Students:* 39 full-time (12 women), 10 part-time (1 woman); includes 10 minority (1 American Indian/Alaska Native, 9 Asian Americans or Pacific Islanders), 6 international. Average age 31. 58 applicants, 38% accepted, 10 enrolled. *Median time to degree:* Of those who began their doctoral program in fall 1999, 71% received their degree in 8 years or less. *Degree requirements:* For master's, variable foreign language requirement, thesis optional, culminating exam; for doctorate, variable foreign language requirement, comprehensive exam, thesis/dissertation, final oral presentation. *Entrance requirements:* For master's and doctorate, GRE General Test. Additional exam requirements/recommendations for international students: Required—TOEFL (minimum score 600 paper-based; 250 computer-based; 100 iBT), IELTS (minimum score 7). *Application deadline:* For fall admission, 2/1 for domestic students, 1/15 for international students; for spring admission, 9/1 for domestic students, 8/1 for international students. Applications are processed on a rolling basis. Application fee: $50. *Financial support:* In 2007–08, 24 students received support, including 1 research assistantship (averaging $23,946 per year), 9 teaching assistantships (averaging $14,397 per year); fellowships, Federal Work-Study and tuition waivers (full and partial) also available. Financial award application deadline: 3/1. *Faculty research:* Renaissance philosophy, Indian philosophy, logic, ethics, philosophy of science, philosophy of mathematics, Chinese philosophy. Total annual research expenditures: $27,300. *Application contact:* Ron Bontekoe, Graduate Chair, 808-956-8410, Fax: 808-956-9228, E-mail: bontekoe@hawaii.edu.

University of Houston, College of Liberal Arts and Social Sciences, Department of Philosophy, Houston, TX 77204. Offers MA. Part-time programs available. *Faculty:* 10 full-time (3 women). *Students:* 26 full-time (3 women), 10 part-time (2 women); includes 8 minority (2 Asian Americans or Pacific Islanders, 6 Hispanic Americans), 5 international. Average age 29. 42 applicants, 88% accepted, 16 enrolled. In 2007, 13 degrees awarded. *Degree requirements:* For master's, one foreign language, thesis optional. *Entrance requirements:* For master's, GRE General Test, minimum of 18 hours of course work in philosophy. *Application deadline:* For fall admission, 7/15 for domestic students. Applications are processed on a rolling basis. Application fee: $15. *Expenses:* Tuition, state resident: full-time $6,297; part-time $262 per credit. Tuition, nonresident: full-time $12,969; part-time $540 per credit. Required fees: $2,696. *Financial support:* In 2007–08, 9 teaching assistantships with full tuition reimbursements (averaging $10,400 per year) were awarded; fellowships with full tuition reimbursements, research assistantships with full tuition reimbursements, career-related internships or fieldwork, Federal Work-Study, institutionally sponsored loans, scholarships/grants, health care benefits, and unspecified assistantships also available. Support available to part-time students. Financial award application deadline: 3/10. *Faculty research:* Skepticism, nominalism, liberalism, history of philosophy, cognitive science. *Unit head:* Dr. Cynthia Freeland, Chairperson, 713-743-3010, Fax: 713-743-5162, E-mail: cfreeland@uh.edu. *Application contact:* Gregory Brown, Director of Graduate Studies, 713-743-3202, Fax: 713-743-2990, E-mail: gbrown@jetson.uh.edu.

University of Illinois at Chicago, Graduate College, College of Liberal Arts and Sciences, Department of Philosophy, Chicago, IL 60607-7128. Offers MA, PhD. Terminal master's awarded for partial completion of doctoral program. *Degree requirements:* For doctorate, thesis/dissertation, preliminary exams. *Entrance requirements:* For master's and doctorate, minimum GPA of 2.75. Additional exam requirements/recommendations for international students: Required—TOEFL. Electronic applications accepted. *Faculty research:* Philosophy of science, philosophy of language, epistemology and metaphysics, ethics, aesthetics.

University of Illinois at Urbana–Champaign, Graduate College, College of Liberal Arts and Sciences, Department of Philosophy, Champaign, IL 61820. Offers MA, PhD. *Faculty:* 12 full-time (1 woman), 2 part-time/adjunct (1 woman). *Students:* 37 full-time (8 women), 2 part-time, 3 international. Average age 26. 57 applicants, 12% accepted, 6 enrolled. In 2007, 8 master's, 6 doctorates awarded. *Degree requirements:* For doctorate, 2 foreign languages, thesis/dissertation. *Entrance requirements:* For master's, GRE, minimum GPA of 3.0; for doctorate, GRE. *Application deadline:* For fall admission, 2/16 for domestic students. Applications are processed on a rolling basis. Application fee: $60 ($75 for international students). Electronic applications accepted. *Financial support:* In 2007–08, 9 fellowships, 2 research assistantships, 41 teaching assistantships were awarded; tuition waivers (full and partial) also available. Financial award application deadline: 2/15. *Unit head:* Robert C. Cummins, Chair, 217-333-2889, Fax: 217-244-8355, E-mail: rcummins@uiuc.edu. *Application contact:* Scott E. Bartlett, Admissions and Records Officer, 217-333-2889, Fax: 217-244-8355, E-mail: sbartlet@uiuc.edu.

University of Illinois at Urbana–Champaign, Graduate College, College of Liberal Arts and Sciences, School of Literatures, Cultures and Linguistics, Department of the Classics, Champaign, IL 61820. Offers classical philosophy (PhD); classics (MA); teaching of Latin (MA). *Faculty:* 10 full-time (4 women). *Students:* 10 full-time (5 women), 6 part-time (4 women); includes 1 minority (Asian American or Pacific Islander), 3 international. 25 applicants, 16% accepted, 3 enrolled. In 2007, 3 master's, 1 doctorate awarded. *Degree requirements:* For master's, one foreign language, thesis or alternative; for doctorate, 4 foreign languages, thesis/dissertation. *Entrance requirements:* For master's, GRE, minimum GPA of 3.0. *Application deadline:* Applications are processed on a rolling basis. Application fee: $60 ($75 for international students). Electronic applications accepted. *Financial support:* In 2007–08, 6 fellowships, 1 research assistantship, 15 teaching assistantships were awarded. Financial award application deadline: 2/15. *Faculty research:* Greek and Latin language, papyrology, epigraphy, classical archaeology. *Unit head:* Gary Porton, Chair, 217-333-5572, Fax: 217-244-8430. *Application contact:* Beth Creek, Administrative Secretary, 217-333-1008, Fax: 217-244-3466, E-mail: b-creek@ucic.edu.

The University of Iowa, Graduate College, College of Liberal Arts and Sciences, Department of Philosophy, Iowa City, IA 52242-1316. Offers MA, PhD, JD/MA. *Faculty:* 7 full-time, 6 part-time/adjunct. *Students:* 11 full-time (0 women), 19 part-time (4 women); includes 3 minority (1 American Indian/Alaska Native, 1 Asian American or Pacific Islander, 1 Hispanic American). 44 applicants, 34% accepted, 6 enrolled. In 2007, 4 doctorates awarded. *Degree requirements:* For master's, thesis optional, exam; for doctorate, comprehensive exam, thesis/dissertation. *Entrance requirements:* For master's, GRE General Test or LSAT, minimum GPA of 3.0; for doctorate, GRE General Test, minimum GPA of 3.0. Additional exam requirements/recommendations for international students: Required—TOEFL (minimum score 550 paper-based; 213 computer-based; 81 iBT). *Application deadline:* For fall admission, 2/1 priority date for domestic and international students. Application fee: $60 ($85 for international students). Electronic applications accepted. *Expenses:* Tuition, state resident: part-time $349 per hour. Tuition, nonresident: part-time $349 per hour. Tuition and fees vary according to course load and program. *Financial support:* In 2007–08, 2 fellowships, 1 research assistantship with partial tuition reimbursement, 16 teaching assistantships with partial tuition reimbursements were awarded. Financial award applicants required to submit FAFSA. *Unit head:* David Stern, Chair, 319-335-0029, Fax: 319-353-2322.

University of Kansas, Research and Graduate Studies, College of Liberal Arts and Sciences, Department of Philosophy, Lawrence, KS 66045. Offers MA, PhD, JD/MA. *Faculty:* 13. *Students:* 37 full-time (10 women), 4 part-time (1 woman); includes 4 minority (3 Asian Americans or Pacific Islanders, 1 Hispanic American), 3 international. Average age 33. 21 applicants, 67% accepted, 6 enrolled. In 2007, 5 master's, 1 doctorate awarded. Terminal master's awarded for partial completion of doctoral program. *Degree requirements:* For master's, comprehensive exam, thesis or alternative; for doctorate, one foreign language, comprehensive exam, thesis/dissertation. *Entrance requirements:* For master's and doctorate, GRE. Additional exam requirements/recommendations for international students: Required—TOEFL. *Application deadline:* For fall admission, 2/1 priority date for domestic students, 6/15 for international students. Applications are processed on a rolling basis. Application fee: $55 ($60 for international students). Electronic applications accepted. *Expenses:* Tuition, state resident: full-time $5,838. Tuition, nonresident: full-time $13,409. Tuition and fees vary according to program. *Financial support:* Fellowships with full and partial tuition reimbursements, research assistantships with full and partial tuition reimbursements, teaching assistantships with full and partial tuition reimbursements available. Financial award application deadline: 1/5. *Faculty research:* Theoretical and applied ethics, social and political philosophy, history of philosophy, analytic philosophy, philosophy of mind and language. *Unit head:* Thomas M. Tuozzo, Chair, 785-864-3976, E-mail: ttuozzo@ku.edu. *Application contact:* Ben Eggleston, Graduate Director, 785-864-3976, E-mail: eggleston@ku.edu.

University of Kentucky, Graduate School, College of Arts and Sciences, Program in Philosophy, Lexington, KY 40506-0032. Offers MA, PhD. *Faculty:* 13 full-time (2 women), 1 part-time/adjunct (0 women). *Students:* 32 full-time (9 women), 4 part-time (3 women); includes 1 minority (African American), 3 international. Average age 31. 42 applicants, 33% accepted, 7 enrolled. In 2007, 3 master's, 2 doctorates awarded. *Median time to degree:* Of those who began their doctoral program in fall 1999, 61% received their degree in 8 years or less. *Degree requirements:* For master's, one foreign language, comprehensive exam, thesis; for doctorate, one foreign language, comprehensive exam, thesis/dissertation. *Entrance requirements:* For master's, GRE General Test, minimum undergraduate GPA of 2.75; for doctorate, GRE General Test, minimum graduate GPA of 3.0. Additional exam requirements/recommendations for international students: Required—TOEFL (minimum score 550 paper-based; 213 computer-based). *Application deadline:* For fall admission, 7/17 priority date for domestic students, 2/1 priority date for international students; for spring admission, 12/13 priority date for domestic students, 6/15 priority date for international students. Application fee: $50 ($65 for international students). Electronic applications accepted. *Expenses:* Tuition, state resident: part-time $437 per credit hour. Tuition, nonresident: part-time $931 per credit hour. *Financial support:* In 2007–08, 28 students received support, including 6 fellowships with full tuition reimbursements available (averaging $3,926 per year), 24 teaching assistantships with full tuition reimbursements available (averaging $10,802 per year); research assistantships, Federal Work-Study, institutionally sponsored loans, scholarships/grants, traineeships, health care benefits, tuition waivers (partial), and unspecified assistantships also available. Support available to part-time students. Financial award application deadline: 3/15. *Faculty research:* History of philosophy, history and philosophy of science, ethics, social and political philosophy. Total annual research expenditures: $140,000. *Unit head:* Dr. Brandon Look, Director of Graduate Studies, 859-257-3071, Fax: 859-257-3286, E-mail: look@uky.edu. *Application contact:* Dr. Brian Jackson, Senior Associate Dean, 859-257-4667, Fax: 859-257-4676, E-mail: brian.jackson@uky.edu.

University of Lethbridge, School of Graduate Studies, Lethbridge, AB T1K 3M4, Canada. Offers accounting (MScM); addictions counseling (M Sc); agricultural biotechnology (M Sc); agricultural studies (M Sc, MA); anthropology (MA); archaeology (MA); art (MA); biochemistry (M Sc); biological sciences (M Sc); biomolecular science (PhD); biosystems and biodiversity (PhD); Canadian studies (MA); chemistry (M Sc); computer science (M Sc); computer science and geographical information science (M Sc); counseling psychology (M Ed); dramatic arts (MA); earth, space, and physical science (PhD); economics (MA); educational leadership (M Ed); English (MA); environmental science (M Sc); evolution and behavior (PhD); exercise science (M Sc); finance (MScM); French (MA); French/German (MA); French/Spanish (MA); general education (M Ed); general management (MScM); geography (M Sc, MA); German (MA); health sciences (M Sc, MA); history (MA); human resource management and labour relations (MScM); individualized multidisciplinary (M Sc, MA); information systems (MScM); international management (MScM); kinesiology (M Sc, MA); management (M Sc, MA); marketing (MScM); mathematics (M Sc); music (MA); Native American studies (MA); neuroscience (M Sc, PhD); new media (MA); nursing (M Sc); philosophy (MA); physics (M Sc); policy and strategy (MScM); political science (MA); psychology (M Sc, MA); religious studies (MA); sociology (MA); theoretical and computational science (PhD); urban and regional studies (MA). Part-time and evening/weekend programs available. *Students:* 215 full-time, 98 part-time. In 2007, 87 master's, 1 doctorate awarded. *Degree requirements:* For doctorate, comprehensive exam, thesis/dissertation. *Entrance requirements:* For master's, GMAT (M Sc in management), bachelor's degree in related field, minimum GPA of 3.0 during previous 20 graded semester courses, 2 years teaching or related experience (M Ed); for doctorate, master's degree, minimum graduate GPA of 3.5. Additional exam requirements/recommendations for international students: Required—TOEFL. Application fee: $60 Canadian dollars. *Financial support:* Fellowships, research assistantships, teaching assistantships, scholarships/grants, health care benefits, and unspecified assistantships available. *Faculty research:* Movement and brain plasticity, gibberellin physiology, photosynthesis, carbon cycling, molecular properties of main-group ring components. *Unit head:* Dr. Jo-Anne Fiske, Interim Dean, 403-329-2121, Fax: 403-329-2097. *Application contact:* Jennifer Geddes, Graduate Liaison Officer, 403-329-2762, Fax: 403-329-5159, E-mail: jennifer.geddes@uleth.ca.

University of Louisville, Graduate School, College of Arts and Sciences, Department of Philosophy, Louisville, KY 40292-0001. Offers MA. *Students:* Average age 56. *Degree requirements:* For master's, one foreign language, thesis or alternative. *Entrance requirements:* For master's, GRE General Test. *Application deadline:* Applications are processed on a rolling basis. Application fee: $50. *Unit head:* Dr. Robert Kimball, Chair, 502-852-0488, Fax: 502-852-0459, E-mail: robert.kimball@louisville.edu.

University of Manitoba, Faculty of Graduate Studies, Faculty of Arts, Department of Philosophy, Winnipeg, MB R3T 2N2, Canada. Offers MA. *Degree requirements:* For master's, variable foreign language requirement, thesis or alternative.

University of Maryland, College Park, Graduate Studies, College of Arts and Humanities, Department of Philosophy, College Park, MD 20742. Offers MA, PhD. *Faculty:* 23 full-time (4 women), 7 part-time/adjunct (1 woman). *Students:* 46 full-time (24 women), 4 part-time; includes 4 minority (2 Asian Americans or Pacific Islanders, 2 Hispanic Americans), 12 international. 139 applicants, 9% accepted, 7 enrolled. In 2007, 4 master's, 4 doctorates awarded. *Degree requirements:* For master's, thesis optional; for doctorate, thesis/dissertation, 2 semesters of undergraduate teaching, qualification in symbolic logic. *Entrance requirements:* For master's, GRE General Test, minimum GPA of 3.0, philosophy paper, writing sample, 3 letters of recommendation; for doctorate, GRE General Test, minimum GPA of 3.0, philosophy paper, writing sample. *Application deadline:* For fall admission, 1/5 for domestic students, 2/1 for international students. Applications are processed on a rolling basis. Application fee: $60. Electronic applications accepted. *Financial support:* In 2007–08, 2 fellowships with full tuition reimbursements (averaging $10,800 per year), 32 teaching assistantships with tuition reimbursements (averaging $15,253 per year) were awarded; research assistantships with tuition reimbursements, Federal Work-Study and scholarships/grants also available. Support available to part-time students. Financial award applicants required to submit FAFSA. *Faculty research:* Contemporary British and American philosophy, the relationship between philosophy and other disciplines, ethical and conceptual issues in public policy. Total annual research expenditures: $61,776. *Unit head:* Dr. Peter M. Carruthers, Chairman, 301-405-5689, Fax: 301-405-5690, E-mail: pcarruth@umd.edu. *Application contact:* Dean of Graduate School, 301-405-0358, Fax: 301-314-9305.

University of Massachusetts Amherst, Graduate School, College of Humanities and Fine Arts, Department of Philosophy, Amherst, MA 01003. Offers MA, PhD. Part-time programs available. *Faculty:* 15 full-time (3 women). *Students:* 30 full-time (5 women), 10 part-time (2 women), 11 international. Average age 31. 120 applicants, 23% accepted, 7 enrolled. In 2007, 2 master's, 2 doctorates awarded. Terminal master's awarded for partial completion of doctoral program. *Degree requirements:* For master's, thesis optional; for doctorate, thesis/dissertation. *Entrance requirements:* For master's and doctorate, GRE General Test, writing sample. Additional exam requirements/recommendations for international students: Required—TOEFL (minimum score 530 paper-based; 197 computer-based). *Application deadline:* For fall admission, 2/1 priority date for domestic and international students. Applications are processed on a rolling basis. Application fee: $50 ($65 for international students). Electronic applications accepted. *Expenses:* Tuition, state resident: full-time $2,640; part-time $110 per credit. Tuition, nonresident: full-time $9,936; part-time $414 per credit. Required fees: $7,455. One-time fee: $332. Tuition and fees vary according to course load, campus/location, program and reciprocity agreements. *Financial support:* In 2007–08, 6 fellowships with full tuition reimbursements (averaging $9,356 per year), 23 teaching assistantships with full tuition reimbursements (averaging $10,694 per year) were awarded; research assistantships with full tuition reimbursements, career-related internships or fieldwork, Federal Work-Study, scholarships/grants, traineeships, and unspecified assistantships also available. Support available to part-time students. Financial award application deadline: 2/1. *Unit head:* Dr. Phillip Bricker, Head, 413-545-2330.

University of Memphis, Graduate School, College of Arts and Sciences, Department of Philosophy, Memphis, TN 38152. Offers MA, PhD. Part-time programs available. *Faculty:* 12 full-time (3 women). *Students:* 31 full-time (18 women), 6 part-time (4 women); includes 13 minority (10 African Americans, 3 Asian Americans or Pacific Islanders), 3 international. Average age 29. 112 applicants, 28% accepted, 11 enrolled. In 2007, 9 master's, 4 doctorates awarded. Terminal master's awarded for partial completion of doctoral program. *Degree requirements:* For master's, thesis optional, 2 written comprehensive exams; for

Philosophy

University of Memphis (continued)

doctorate, 2 foreign languages, thesis/dissertation, area and qualifying exams. *Entrance requirements:* For master's, GRE General Test, minimum GPA of 2.5, 18 hours of undergraduate course work in philosophy; for doctorate, GRE General Test, minimum GPA of 3.0, bachelor's degree in philosophy. *Application deadline:* For fall admission, 2/1 for domestic students. Application fee: $35 ($60 for international students). Electronic applications accepted. *Expenses:* Tuition, state resident: full-time $6,990; part-time $377 per hour. Tuition, nonresident: full-time $17,818; part-time $830 per hour. Tuition and fees vary according to course load and program. *Financial support:* In 2007–08, 18 research assistantships with full tuition reimbursements (averaging $10,000 per year), 9 teaching assistantships with full tuition reimbursements (averaging $10,500 per year) were awarded; fellowships with full tuition reimbursements, tuition waivers (full) also available. *Faculty research:* Continental philosophy, ethics, analytic philosophy, feminist theory, Africana philosophy. *Unit head:* Dr. Nancy Simco, Chair, 901-678-2535, Fax: 901-678-4365, E-mail: nsimco@memphis.edu. *Application contact:* Dr. Mary Beth Mader, Director of Graduation Admissions, 901-678-4526.

University of Miami, Graduate School, College of Arts and Sciences, Department of Philosophy, Coral Gables, FL 33124. Offers MA, PhD. Part-time programs available. *Faculty:* 8 full-time (2 women), 1 part-time/adjunct (0 women). *Students:* 28 full-time (6 women), 2 part-time; includes 2 minority (1 African American, 1 Hispanic American), 5 international. Average age 33. 42 applicants, 29% accepted, 6 enrolled. In 2007, 6 master's, 1 doctorate awarded. Terminal master's awarded for partial completion of doctoral program. *Degree requirements:* For master's, thesis or alternative; for doctorate, comprehensive exam, thesis/dissertation. *Entrance requirements:* For master's, GRE General Test; for doctorate, GRE General Test, minimum GPA of 3.0, 3 letters of recommendation, writing sample. Additional exam requirements/recommendations for international students: Required—TOEFL. *Application deadline:* For fall admission, 1/10 for domestic and international students. Application fee: $50. Electronic applications accepted. *Financial support:* In 2007–08, 21 students received support, including 2 fellowships with full tuition reimbursements available (averaging $30,000 per year), 16 teaching assistantships with full tuition reimbursements available (averaging $20,000 per year); Federal Work-Study and tuition waivers (partial) also available. Support available to part-time students. Financial award application deadline: 1/15; financial award applicants required to submit FAFSA. *Faculty research:* Ethics, epistemology, pragmatism, philosophy of science, metaphysics. *Unit head:* Prof. Harvey Siegel, Chairman, 305-284-5411, Fax: 305-284-5594, E-mail: hsiegel@miami.edu. *Application contact:* Prof. Otavio Bueno, Director, Graduate Studies, 305-284-9218, Fax: 305-284-5594, E-mail: otaviobueno@mac.com.

University of Michigan, Horace H. Rackham School of Graduate Studies, College of Literature, Science, and the Arts, Department of Philosophy, Ann Arbor, MI 48109. Offers AM, PhD. *Faculty:* 21 full-time (2 women). *Students:* 40 full-time (10 women); includes 1 American Indian/Alaska Native, 4 Asian Americans or Pacific Islanders, 1 Hispanic American, 9 international. Average age 29. 207 applicants, 12% accepted, 4 enrolled. In 2007, 4 master's, 5 doctorates awarded. Terminal master's awarded for partial completion of doctoral program. *Median time to degree:* Of those who began their doctoral program in fall 1999, 75% received their degree in 8 years or less. *Degree requirements:* For doctorate, one foreign language, thesis/dissertation, oral defense of dissertation. *Entrance requirements:* For master's and doctorate, GRE General Test, 3 letters of recommendation, writing sample. Additional exam requirements/recommendations for international students: Required—TOEFL. *Application deadline:* For fall admission, 1/15 for domestic students, 1/1 for international students. Application fee: $60 ($75 for international students). Electronic applications accepted. *Financial support:* In 2007–08, 40 students received support, including fellowships with full tuition reimbursements available (averaging $14,500 per year), teaching assistantships with full tuition reimbursements available (averaging $15,300 per year); health care benefits also available. Financial award application deadline: 1/15. *Faculty research:* Ethics, metaphysics, philosophy of language and mind, political and social philosophy, philosophy of science. *Unit head:* James M. Joyce, Chair, 734-764-6285, Fax: 734-763-8071, E-mail: jjoyce@umich.edu. *Application contact:* Linda Shultes, Admissions Secretary, 734-764-6285, Fax: 734-763-8071, E-mail: phil-admissions@umich.edu.

University of Minnesota, Twin Cities Campus, Graduate School, College of Liberal Arts, Department of Philosophy, Minneapolis, MN 55455-0213. Offers MA, PhD. Part-time programs available. *Faculty:* 18 full-time (6 women), 4 part-time/adjunct (1 woman). *Students:* 30 full-time (14 women), 5 part-time (3 women); includes 5 minority (2 Asian Americans or Pacific Islanders, 3 Hispanic Americans), 6 international. 91 applicants, 9% accepted, 5 enrolled. In 2007, 10 master's, 2 doctorates awarded. Terminal master's awarded for partial completion of doctoral program. *Degree requirements:* For master's, thesis (for some programs); for doctorate, thesis/dissertation. *Entrance requirements:* For master's and doctorate, GRE, references, writing sample. Additional exam requirements/recommendations for international students: Required—TOEFL (paper-based 550; computer-based 213), IELTS (score 6.5), or Michigan English Language Assessment Battery (score 80). *Application deadline:* For fall admission, 1/7 for domestic and international students. Application fee: $55 ($75 for international students). Electronic applications accepted. *Financial support:* In 2007–08, 15 fellowships with full tuition reimbursements (averaging $2,960 per year), 28 teaching assistantships with full tuition reimbursements (averaging $12,000 per year) were awarded; research assistantships with full tuition reimbursements, Federal Work-Study, institutionally sponsored loans, scholarships/grants, health care benefits, and unspecified assistantships also available. Support available to part-time students. Financial award application deadline: 1/7. *Faculty research:* Philosophy of science; ethics and social/political philosophy; logic, language, and mind. *Unit head:* Prof. Geoffrey Hellman, Chair, 612-625-7573, Fax: 612-626-8380. *Application contact:* Prof. John Wallace, Professor, 612-624-5210, Fax: 612-626-8380, E-mail: walla003@umn.edu.

University of Mississippi, Graduate School, College of Liberal Arts, Department of Philosophy and Religions, Oxford, University, MS 38677. Offers philosophy (MA). *Faculty:* 8 full-time (3 women), 4 part-time/adjunct (2 women). *Students:* 8 full-time (1 woman), 3 part-time; includes 2 minority (1 African American, 1 American Indian/Alaska Native). In 2007, 3 degrees awarded. *Degree requirements:* For master's, thesis. *Entrance requirements:* For master's, GRE General Test, minimum GPA of 3.0. Additional exam requirements/recommendations for international students: Required—TOEFL. *Application deadline:* For fall admission, 4/1 for domestic students; for spring admission, 10/1 for domestic students. Applications are processed on a rolling basis. Application fee: $25. Electronic applications accepted. *Expenses:* Tuition, state resident: full-time $4,932. Tuition, nonresident: full-time $11,436. *Financial support:* Scholarships/grants available. Financial award application deadline: 3/1; financial award applicants required to submit FAFSA. *Unit head:* Dr. William Lawhead, Chair, 662-915-7345, Fax: 662-915-5654.

University of Missouri–Columbia, Graduate School, College of Arts and Sciences, Department of Philosophy, Columbia, MO 65211. Offers MA, PhD. Terminal master's awarded for partial completion of doctoral program. *Degree requirements:* For doctorate, one foreign language, thesis/dissertation. *Entrance requirements:* For master's and doctorate, GRE General Test, minimum GPA of 3.0.

University of Missouri–St. Louis, College of Arts and Sciences, Department of Philosophy, St. Louis, MO 63121. Offers MA. *Faculty:* 10 full-time (3 women). *Students:* 16 full-time (3 women), 15 part-time; includes 4 minority (1 African American, 1 American Indian/Alaska Native, 1 Asian American or Pacific Islander, 1 Hispanic American), 2 international. Average age 29. 5 applicants. In 2007, 9 degrees awarded. *Entrance requirements:* For master's, writing sample, 3 letters of recommendation. Additional exam requirements/recommendations for international students: Required—TOEFL (minimum score 550 paper-based; 213 computer-based). *Application deadline:* For fall admission, 7/15 priority date for domestic students; for spring admission, 12/15 priority date for domestic students. Applications are processed on a rolling basis. Application fee: $35 ($40 for international students). Electronic applications accepted. *Financial support:* In 2007–08, 2 research assistantships (averaging $5,850 per year), 14 teaching assistantships with full tuition reimbursements (averaging $5,000 per year) were awarded. *Faculty research:* Ethics, philosophy and history of science, philosophical social science, aesthetics. *Unit head:* Dr. Stephanie Ross, Graduate Program Director, 314-516-5631, Fax: 314-516-5816, E-mail: sross@umsl.edu. *Application contact:* 314-516-5458, Fax: 314-516-6996, E-mail: gradadm@umsl.edu.

The University of Montana, Graduate School, College of Arts and Sciences, Department of Philosophy, Missoula, MT 59812-0002. Offers MA. *Degree requirements:* For master's, thesis or additional course work/professional paper. *Entrance requirements:* For master's, GRE General Test. Additional exam requirements/recommendations for international students: Required—TOEFL (minimum score 525 paper-based; 197 computer-based). *Faculty research:* Philosophy of law, natural science, feminism, and technology; environmental, business, and medical ethics.

University of Nebraska–Lincoln, Graduate College, College of Arts and Sciences, Department of Philosophy, Lincoln, NE 68588. Offers MA, PhD. *Degree requirements:* For master's, thesis optional; for doctorate, comprehensive exam, thesis/dissertation. *Entrance requirements:* For master's and doctorate, GRE General Test, writing sample. Additional exam requirements/recommendations for international students: Required—TOEFL (minimum score 600 paper-based; 250 computer-based). Electronic applications accepted. *Faculty research:* Ethics, epistemology, metaphysics, cognitive science, history of philosophy.

University of Nevada, Reno, Graduate School, College of Liberal Arts, Department of Philosophy, Reno, NV 89557. Offers MA. *Faculty:* 11. *Students:* 2 full-time (0 women), 3 part-time. Average age 37. 4 applicants, 100% accepted, 4 enrolled. In 2007, 5 degrees awarded. *Degree requirements:* For master's, thesis optional. *Entrance requirements:* For master's, GRE General Test, minimum GPA of 2.75. Additional exam requirements/recommendations for international students: Required—TOEFL. *Application deadline:* For fall admission, 3/1 priority date for domestic students; for spring admission, 11/1 for domestic students. Applications are processed on a rolling basis. Application fee: $60 ($95 for international students). *Expenses:* Tuition, state resident: full-time $2,774; part-time $154 per credit. Tuition, nonresident: full-time $13,578; part-time $330 per credit. Required fees: $49 per semester. *Financial support:* In 2007–08, 1 teaching assistantship was awarded; Federal Work-Study and institutionally sponsored loans also available. Financial award application deadline: 3/1. *Faculty research:* Ancient philosophy (Aristotle), ethics, political theory, violence, Continental philosophy. *Unit head:* Dr. Kenneth Lucey, Graduate Program Director, 775-784-6846.

University of New Brunswick Fredericton, School of Graduate Studies, Policy Studies Program, Fredericton, NB E3B 5A3, Canada. Offers people, property and alternative dispute resolution (M Phil); philosophy politics and economics (M Phil); sustainable development (M Phil). *Faculty:* 6 full-time (2 women), 13 part-time/adjunct (2 women). *Students:* 13 full-time (8 women), 3 part-time (2 women). In 2007, 6 degrees awarded. *Entrance requirements:* For master's, minimum GPA of 3.5, BA. Additional exam requirements/recommendations for international students: Required—TOEFL (minimum score 600 paper-based), TWE (minimum score 5). Application fee: $50 Canadian dollars. *Financial support:* In 2007–08, 5 research assistantships, 2 teaching assistantships (averaging $4,400 per year) were awarded. *Unit head:* Dr. Gwen Davies, Dean of Graduate Studies, 506-458-7150, Fax: 506-453-4817, E-mail: daviesg@unb.ca. *Application contact:* Janet Amurault, Graduate Secretary, 506-458-7558, Fax: 506-453-4817, E-mail: jamiraul@unb.ca.

University of New Mexico, Graduate School, College of Arts and Sciences, Department of Philosophy, Albuquerque, NM 87131-2039. Offers MA, PhD. Part-time programs available. *Faculty:* 11 full-time (2 women), 4 part-time/adjunct (3 women). *Students:* 16 full-time (5 women), 7 part-time (4 women); includes 3 minority (1 Asian American or Pacific Islander, 2 Hispanic Americans), 2 international. Average age 35. 58 applicants, 24% accepted, 5 enrolled. In 2007, 5 master's, 1 doctorate awarded. Terminal master's awarded for partial completion of doctoral program. *Degree requirements:* For master's, thesis (for some programs); for doctorate, one foreign language, comprehensive exam, thesis/dissertation. *Entrance requirements:* For master's and doctorate, GRE. Additional exam requirements/recommendations for international students: Required—TOEFL. *Application deadline:* For fall admission, 1/31 for domestic students; for spring admission, 11/1 for domestic students. Application fee: $50. Electronic applications accepted. *Financial support:* In 2007–08, 1 fellowship with tuition reimbursement (averaging $13,000 per year), 13 teaching assistantships with tuition reimbursements (averaging $13,000 per year) were awarded. Financial award application deadline: 1/31; financial award applicants required to submit FAFSA. *Faculty research:* History of philosophy, ethics, philosophy of art and literature, Asian philosophy, continental philosophy, philosophy of language. Total annual research expenditures: $10,103. *Unit head:* Dr. John Taber, Chair, 505-277-4019, Fax: 505-277-6362, E-mail: jataber@unm.edu. *Application contact:* Rikk Murphy, Graduate Student Liaison, 505-277-2405, Fax: 505-277-6362, E-mail: thinker@unm.edu.

The University of North Carolina at Chapel Hill, Graduate School, College of Arts and Sciences, Department of Philosophy, Chapel Hill, NC 27599. Offers MA, PhD. *Degree requirements:* For master's, comprehensive exam, thesis; for doctorate, comprehensive exam, thesis/dissertation. *Entrance requirements:* For master's and doctorate, GRE General Test, minimum GPA of 3.0.

University of North Florida, College of Arts and Sciences, Department of Philosophy, Jacksonville, FL 32224-2645. Offers applied ethics (Graduate Certificate); practical philosophy and applied ethics (MA). Part-time and evening/weekend programs available. *Faculty:* 11 full-time (4 women). *Students:* 8 full-time (4 women), 7 part-time (3 women); includes 2 minority (both Hispanic Americans) Average age 36. 12 applicants, 67% accepted, 5 enrolled. In 2007, 3 degrees awarded. *Entrance requirements:* For master's, GRE General Test, minimum GPA of 3.0 in last 60 hours, 3 letters of recommendation, writing sample. Additional exam requirements/recommendations for international students: Required—TOEFL (minimum score 500 paper-based). *Application deadline:* For fall admission, 3/1 priority date for domestic students, 3/1 for international students. Applications are processed on a rolling basis. Application fee: $30. Electronic applications accepted. *Expenses:* Tuition, state resident: part-time $266 per credit hour. Tuition, nonresident: part-time $858 per credit hour. One-time fee: $35 part-time. Tuition and fees vary according to program. *Financial support:* In 2007–08, 10 students received support, including 6 teaching assistantships (averaging $6,357 per year). Financial award application deadline: 4/1; financial award applicants required to submit FAFSA. *Faculty research:* Late modern philosophy, pragmatism, religion and American culture, hermeneutics, philosophy of mind. Total annual research expenditures: $13,485. *Unit head:* Dr. Hans Herbert Köegler, Graduate Coordinator, 904-620-1330, Fax: 904-620-1840, E-mail: hkoegler@unf.edu. *Application contact:* Dr. Hans Herbert Köegler, Graduate Coordinator, 904-620-1330, Fax: 904-620-1840, E-mail: hkoegler@unf.edu.

University of North Texas, Robert B. Toulouse School of Graduate Studies, College of Arts and Sciences, Department of Philosophy and Religion Studies, Denton, TX 76203. Offers philosophy (MA, PhD). *Faculty:* 11 full-time (1 woman). *Students:* 15 full-time (8 women), 18 part-time (6 women); includes 4 minority (1 African American, 2 Asian Americans or Pacific Islanders, 1 Hispanic American), 3 international. Average age 31. 27 applicants, 37% accepted, 8 enrolled. In 2007, 5 degrees awarded. *Degree requirements:* For master's, one foreign language, thesis or alternative. *Entrance requirements:* For master's, GRE General Test. Additional exam requirements/recommendations for international students: Required—proof of English language proficiency required for non-native English speakers; Recommended—TOEFL (minimum score 550 paper-based; 213 computer-based). *Application deadline:* For fall admission, 7/15 for domestic students; for spring admission, 11/15 for domestic students. Application fee: $50 ($75 for international students). *Unit head:* Dr. Robert Frodeman, Chair, 940-565-2266, Fax: 940-565-4448, E-mail: frodeman@unt.edu.

University of Notre Dame, Graduate School, College of Arts and Letters, Division of Humanities, Department of Philosophy, Notre Dame, IN 46556. Offers PhD. *Faculty:* 43 full-time (4 women), 4 part-time/adjunct (0 women). *Students:* 64 full-time (18 women); includes 6 minority (1

American Indian/Alaska Native, 3 Asian Americans or Pacific Islanders, 2 Hispanic Americans), 7 international. 321 applicants, 6% accepted, 8 enrolled. In 2007, 2 doctorates awarded. *Median time to degree:* Of those who began their doctoral program in fall 1999, 62% received their degree in 8 years or less. *Degree requirements:* For doctorate, 2 foreign languages, thesis/dissertation, candidacy exam. *Entrance requirements:* For doctorate, GRE General Test. Additional exam requirements/recommendations for international students: Required—TOEFL (minimum score 600 paper-based; 250 computer-based; 80 iBT). *Application deadline:* For fall admission, 1/15 for domestic and international students. Application fee: $50. Electronic applications accepted. *Financial support:* In 2007–08, 8 fellowships with full tuition reimbursements (averaging $22,000 per year), 1 research assistantship with full tuition reimbursement (averaging $16,000 per year), 37 teaching assistantships with full tuition reimbursements (averaging $16,000 per year) were awarded; tuition waivers (full) also available. Financial award application deadline: 2/1. *Faculty research:* History of philosophy, ethics, philosophy of science and logic, philosophy of religion, Continental philosophy, metaphysics. *Unit head:* Dr. Leopold Stubenberg, Director of Graduate Studies, 574-631-4278, Fax: 574-631-4268, E-mail: ndphilo.1@nd.edu. *Application contact:* Dr. Jarren Gonzales, Director of Graduate Admissions, 574-631-7706, Fax: 574-631-4183.

University of Oklahoma, Graduate College, College of Arts and Sciences, Department of Philosophy, Norman, OK 73019-0390. Offers MA, PhD. Part-time programs available. *Faculty:* 14 full-time (4 women). *Students:* 25 full-time (4 women), 10 part-time (3 women); includes 5 minority (3 American Indian/Alaska Native, 2 Asian Americans or Pacific Islanders), 1 international. 30 applicants, 57% accepted, 10 enrolled. In 2007, 3 master's, 2 doctorates awarded. Terminal master's awarded for partial completion of doctoral program. *Degree requirements:* For master's, thesis optional; for doctorate, thesis/dissertation, oral and written exams. *Entrance requirements:* For master's and doctorate, GRE General Test, 3 letters of recommendation, writing sample. Additional exam requirements/recommendations for international students: Required—TOEFL (minimum score 550 paper-based; 213 computer-based). *Application deadline:* For fall admission, 2/1 priority date for domestic and international students; for spring admission, 11/1 for domestic students, 9/1 for international students. Applications are processed on a rolling basis. Application fee: $40 ($90 for international students). Electronic applications accepted. *Expenses:* Tuition, state resident: full-time $3,451; part-time $144 per credit hour. Tuition, nonresident: full-time $12,432; part-time $518 per credit hour. Required fees: $1,925; $70 per credit hour. $122 per semester. *Financial support:* In 2007–08, 16 students received support, including fellowships (averaging $3,750 per year), research assistantships with partial tuition reimbursements available (averaging $14,485 per year), teaching assistantships with partial tuition reimbursements available (averaging $12,488 per year); scholarships/grants, health care benefits, and unspecified assistantships also available. Financial award application deadline: 2/28; financial award applicants required to submit FAFSA. *Unit head:* Dr. Hugh Benson, Chair, 405-325-6324, Fax: 405-325-2660, E-mail: hbenson@ou.edu. *Application contact:* Wayne Riggs, Director of Graduate Studies/Associate Professor, 405-325-6324, Fax: 405-325-2660, E-mail: wriggs@ou.edu.

University of Oregon, Graduate School, College of Arts and Sciences, Department of Philosophy, Eugene, OR 97403. Offers MA, PhD. *Faculty:* 9 full-time (2 women). *Students:* 29 full-time (18 women), 5 part-time (3 women); includes 6 minority (1 African American, 1 American Indian/Alaska Native, 1 Asian American or Pacific Islander, 3 Hispanic Americans), 2 international. Average age 33. 127 applicants, 9% accepted. In 2007, 1 master's, 3 doctorates awarded. Terminal master's awarded for partial completion of doctoral program. *Degree requirements:* For master's, one foreign language, thesis or alternative; for doctorate, one foreign language, thesis/dissertation. *Entrance requirements:* For master's and doctorate, GRE General Test. Additional exam requirements/recommendations for international students: Required—TOEFL. *Application deadline:* For fall admission, 3/15 for domestic students. Application fee: $50. *Financial support:* In 2007–08, 20 teaching assistantships were awarded; Federal Work-Study and institutionally sponsored loans also available. Support available to part-time students. Financial award applicants required to submit FAFSA. *Faculty research:* Social and political philosophy, feminist philosophy, American philosophy, aesthetics, philosophy of mind. *Unit head:* John Lysaker, Head, 541-346-5549, Fax: 541-346-5544. *Application contact:* T.K. McDonald, Admissions Contact, 541-346-5547, Fax: 541-346-5544, E-mail: tkonal@uoregon.edu.

University of Ottawa, Faculty of Graduate and Postdoctoral Studies, Faculty of Arts, Department of Philosophy, Ottawa, ON K1N 6N5, Canada. Offers MA, PhD. *Degree requirements:* For master's, thesis or alternative; for doctorate, comprehensive exam, thesis/dissertation. *Entrance requirements:* For master's, honors degree or equivalent, minimum B average; for doctorate, master's degree, minimum B+ average. Electronic applications accepted. *Faculty research:* History of philosophy (ancient, medieval, modern and contemporary); metaphysics/epistemology; value theory: political philosophy, ethics.

University of Pennsylvania, School of Arts and Sciences, Graduate Group in Philosophy, Philadelphia, PA 19104. Offers AM, PhD, JD/PhD. Terminal master's awarded for partial completion of doctoral program. *Degree requirements:* For master's, thesis; for doctorate, thesis/dissertation, 1 year of teaching experience. Electronic applications accepted.

University of Pittsburgh, School of Arts and Sciences, Department of History and Philosophy of Science, Pittsburgh, PA 15260. Offers MA, PhD. *Faculty:* 8 full-time (1 woman), 2 part-time/adjunct (0 women). *Students:* 23 full-time (4 women); includes 1 minority (Asian American or Pacific Islander), 4 international. Average age 29. 52 applicants, 19% accepted, 5 enrolled. In 2007, 4 degrees awarded. Terminal master's awarded for partial completion of doctoral program. *Median time to degree:* Of those who began their doctoral program in fall 1999, 83% received their degree in 8 years or less. *Degree requirements:* For master's, one foreign language, comprehensive exam; for doctorate, 2 foreign languages, comprehensive exam, thesis/dissertation. *Entrance requirements:* For master's and doctorate, GRE General Test. Additional exam requirements/recommendations for international students: Required—TOEFL (minimum score 550 paper-based; 213 computer-based). *Application deadline:* For fall admission, 1/10 for domestic and international students. Application fee: $50. Electronic applications accepted. *Financial support:* In 2007–08, 25 students received support, including 10 fellowships with full tuition reimbursements available (averaging $20,304 per year), 11 teaching assistantships with full tuition reimbursements available (averaging $15,070 per year); health care benefits also available. Financial award application deadline: 1/10. *Faculty research:* History and philosophy of biology, psychology, neuroscience; history and philosophy of physics; early modern science; rhetoric of science; philosophy of social science. *Unit head:* Dr. Sandra Mitchell, Chairman, 412-624-5896, Fax: 412-624-6825, E-mail: smitchel@pitt.edu. *Application contact:* Joann McIntyre, Graduate Admissions Secretary, 412-624-5896, Fax: 412-624-6825, E-mail: vanna@pitt.edu.

University of Pittsburgh, School of Arts and Sciences, Department of Philosophy, Pittsburgh, PA 15260. Offers MA, PhD. *Faculty:* 17 full-time (3 women). *Students:* 66 full-time (14 women); includes 6 minority (2 African Americans, 4 Asian Americans or Pacific Islanders), 23 international. 196 applicants, 12% accepted, 4 enrolled. In 2007, 1 master's, 3 doctorates awarded. Terminal master's awarded for partial completion of doctoral program. *Median time to degree:* Of those who began their doctoral program in fall 1999, 0% received their degree in 8 years or less. *Degree requirements:* For master's, one foreign language; for doctorate, one foreign language, thesis/dissertation. *Entrance requirements:* For master's and doctorate, GRE General Test. Additional exam requirements/recommendations for international students: Required—TOEFL (minimum score 550 paper-based; 213 computer-based; 79 iBT), IELTS (minimum score 7). *Application deadline:* For fall admission, 1/10 for domestic and international students. Application fee: $50. Electronic applications accepted. *Financial support:* In 2007–08, 54 students received support, including 27 fellowships with full tuition reimbursements available (averaging $19,000 per year), 2 research assistantships with full tuition reimbursements available (averaging $15,070 per year), 27 teaching assistantships with full tuition reimbursements available (averaging $15,070 per year); Federal Work-Study, institutionally sponsored loans, scholarships/grants, health care benefits, and tuition waivers (full and partial) also available. Financial award application deadline: 1/10. *Faculty research:* Metaphysics and epistemology, ethics, philosophy of science, history of philosophy. *Unit head:* Dr. Thomas Ricketts, Chairman, 412-624-5768, Fax: 412-624-5377.

University of Puerto Rico, Río Piedras, College of Humanities, Department of Philosophy, San Juan, PR 00931-3300. Offers MA. Part-time programs available. *Students:* 6 full-time (2 women), 5 part-time (1 woman); all minorities (all Hispanic Americans) Average age 28. In 2007, 2 degrees awarded. *Degree requirements:* For master's, one foreign language, comprehensive exam, thesis. *Entrance requirements:* For master's, PAEG or GRE, interview, minimum GPA of 3.0, letter of recommendation (2). *Application deadline:* For fall admission, 2/1 for domestic and international students. Application fee: $17. *Expenses:* Tuition, state resident: full-time $1,808; part-time $113 per credit. Tuition, nonresident: full-time $5,248; part-time $328 per credit. Required fees: $72 per term. *Financial support:* Fellowships, research assistantships, teaching assistantships, Federal Work-Study, institutionally sponsored loans, and tuition waivers (partial) available. Financial award application deadline: 5/31. *Unit head:* Dr. Eliseo Cruz-Vergara, Director, 787-764-0000, Fax: 787-763-5879.

University of Regina, Faculty of Graduate Studies and Research, Faculty of Arts, Department of Philosophy, Regina, SK S4S 0A2, Canada. Offers philosophy (MA); social and political thought (MA). *Faculty:* 9 full-time (3 women). *Students:* 1 (woman) full-time. *Degree requirements:* For master's, thesis. *Entrance requirements:* Additional exam requirements/recommendations for international students: Required—TOEFL (minimum score 580 paper-based; 237 computer-based; 88 iBT). *Application deadline:* Applications are processed on a rolling basis. Application fee: $85 ($100 for international students). Electronic applications accepted. *Financial support:* In 2007–08, fellowships (averaging $15,750 per year), research assistantships (averaging $13,875 per year), teaching assistantships (averaging $13,060 per year) were awarded; scholarships/grants also available. Financial award application deadline: 6/15. *Faculty research:* History of philosophy, ethics, aesthetics, metaphysics, epistemology. *Unit head:* Dr. Eldon Soifer, Head, 306-585-4301, Fax: 306-585-4827, E-mail: eldon.soifer@uregina.ca.

University of Regina, Faculty of Graduate Studies and Research, Faculty of Arts, Program in Social and Political Thought, Regina, SK S4S 0A2, Canada. Offers MA. *Faculty:* 9 full-time (3 women). *Students:* 5 full-time (1 woman), 1 part-time. 7 applicants, 71% accepted, 4 enrolled. *Degree requirements:* For master's, thesis. *Entrance requirements:* Additional exam requirements/recommendations for international students: Required—TOEFL (minimum score 580 paper-based; 237 computer-based; 88 iBT). *Application deadline:* For fall admission, 3/15 for domestic students. Application fee: $85 ($100 for international students). Electronic applications accepted. *Financial support:* In 2007–08, 1 fellowship (averaging $15,750 per year), 1 research assistantship (averaging $13,875 per year), teaching assistantships (averaging $13,060 per year) were awarded. *Unit head:* Dr. Shadia Drury, Program Coordinator, 306-585-4073, E-mail: shadia.drury@uregina.ca.

University of Rochester, The College, Arts and Sciences, Department of Philosophy, Rochester, NY 14627-0250. Offers MA, PhD. Terminal master's awarded for partial completion of doctoral program. *Degree requirements:* For doctorate, thesis/dissertation, qualifying exam. *Entrance requirements:* For master's, GRE General Test; for doctorate, GRE General Test, sample of written work. Additional exam requirements/recommendations for international students: Required—TOEFL.

University of St. Thomas, Center for Thomistic Studies, Houston, TX 77006-4696. Offers philosophy (MA, PhD). Part-time programs available. *Faculty:* 4 full-time (1 woman), 1 (woman) part-time/adjunct. *Students:* 10 full-time (1 woman), 14 part-time (1 woman); includes 5 minority (2 Asian Americans or Pacific Islanders, 3 Hispanic Americans), 3 international. Average age 33. 16 applicants, 100% accepted, 10 enrolled. In 2007, 1 master's, 2 doctorates awarded. Terminal master's awarded for partial completion of doctoral program. *Degree requirements:* For master's, one foreign language, comprehensive exam, thesis (for some programs); for doctorate, 2 foreign languages, comprehensive exam, thesis/dissertation, MA level Latin exam (completed prior to 3rd semester of study). *Entrance requirements:* For master's, GRE General Test, minimum GPA of 3.0, minimum 18 hours of undergraduate course work in philosophy; for doctorate, GRE General Test, master's degree in philosophy. *Application deadline:* For fall admission, 2/1 priority date for domestic students. Applications are processed on a rolling basis. Application fee: $35. *Financial support:* In 2007–08, 13 students received support. Federal Work-Study, scholarships/grants, and unspecified assistantships available. Support available to part-time students. Financial award application deadline: 3/1; financial award applicants required to submit FAFSA. *Unit head:* Dr. Mary Catherine Sommers, Director, 713-525-3591, Fax: 713-942-3464, E-mail: sommers@stthom.edu.

University of Saskatchewan, College of Graduate Studies and Research, College of Arts and Sciences, Department of Philosophy, Saskatoon, SK S7N 5A2, Canada. Offers MA. *Degree requirements:* For master's, thesis. *Entrance requirements:* Additional exam requirements/recommendations for international students: Required—TOEFL.

University of South Africa, College of Human Sciences, Pretoria, South Africa. Offers adult education (M Ed); African languages (MA, PhD); African politics (MA, PhD); Afrikaans (MA, PhD); ancient history (MA, PhD); ancient Near Eastern studies (MA, PhD); anthropology (MA, PhD); applied linguistics (MA); Arabic (MA, PhD); archaeology (MA); art history (MA); Biblical archaeology (MA); Biblical studies (M Th, D Th, PhD); Christian spirituality (M Th, D Th); church history (M Th, D Th); classical studies (MA, PhD); clinical psychology (MA); communication (MA, PhD); comparative education (M Ed, Ed D); consulting psychology (D Admin, D Com, PhD); curriculum studies (M Ed, Ed D); development studies (M Admin, MA, D Admin, PhD); didactics (M Ed, Ed D); education (M Tech); education management (M Ed, Ed D); educational psychology (M Ed); English (MA); environmental education (M Ed); French (MA, PhD); German (MA, PhD); Greek (MA); guidance and counseling (M Ed); health studies (MA, PhD), including health sciences education (MA), health services management (MA), medical and surgical nursing science (critical care general) (MA), midwifery and neonatal nursing science (MA), trauma and emergency care (MA); history (MA, PhD); history of education (Ed D); inclusive education (M Ed, Ed D); information and communications technology policy and regulation (MA); information science (MA, MIS, PhD); international politics (MA, PhD); Islamic studies (MA, PhD); Italian (MA, PhD); Judaica (MA, PhD); linguistics (MA, PhD); mathematical education (M Ed); mathematics education (MA); missiology (M Th, D Th); modern Hebrew (MA, PhD); musicology (MA, MMus, D Mus, PhD); natural science education (M Ed); New Testament (M Th, D Th); Old Testament (D Th); pastoral therapy (M Th, D Th); philosophy (MA); philosophy of education (M Ed, Ed D); politics (MA, PhD); Portuguese (MA, PhD); practical theology (M Th, D Th); psychology (MA, MS, PhD); psychology of education (M Ed, Ed D); public health (MA); religious studies (MA, D Th, PhD); Romance languages (MA); Russian (MA, PhD); Semitic languages (MA, PhD); social behavior studies in HIV/AIDS (MA); social science (mental health) (MA); social science in development studies (MA); social science in psychology (MA); social science in social work (MA); social science in sociology (MA); social work (MSW, DSW, PhD); socio-education (M Ed, Ed D); sociolinguistics (MA); sociology (MA, PhD); Spanish (MA, PhD); systematic theology (M Th, D Th); TESOL (teaching English to speakers of other languages) (MA); theological ethics (M Th, D Th); theory of literature (MA, PhD); urban ministries (D Th); urban ministry (M Th).

University of South Carolina, The Graduate School, College of Arts and Sciences, Department of Philosophy, Columbia, SC 29208. Offers MA, PhD. Part-time programs available. *Faculty:* 17 full-time (4 women), 6 part-time/adjunct (1 woman). *Students:* 23 full-time (6 women), 1 part-time; includes 5 minority (1 African American, 4 Asian Americans or Pacific Islanders). Average age 29. 37 applicants, 49% accepted, 6 enrolled. In 2007, 1 master's, 1 doctorate awarded. *Median time to degree:* Of those who began their doctoral program in fall 1999, 50% received their degree in 8 years or less. *Degree requirements:* For master's, one foreign language, comprehensive exam, thesis optional; for doctorate, one foreign language, comprehensive exam, thesis/dissertation, candidacy exam. *Entrance requirements:* For master's and doctorate, GRE General Test, 18 hours in philosophy, 3 letters of recommendation, writing sample. Additional exam requirements/recommendations for international students: Required—

Philosophy

University of South Carolina (continued)
TOEFL (minimum score 590 paper-based; 243 computer-based). *Application deadline:* For fall admission, 1/15 priority date for domestic and international students; for spring admission, 11/15 for domestic students, 12/1 for international students. Applications are processed on a rolling basis. Application fee: $40. Electronic applications accepted. *Expenses:* Tuition, state resident: part-time $440 per hour. Tuition, nonresident: part-time $936 per hour. Required fees: $17 per hour. Tuition and fees vary according to program. *Financial support:* In 2007–08, 23 students received support, including 4 fellowships with full tuition reimbursements available (averaging $16,000 per year), 2 research assistantships with full tuition reimbursements available (averaging $17,600 per year), 17 teaching assistantships with full tuition reimbursements available (averaging $14,000 per year); health care benefits also available. Financial award application deadline: 1/15. *Faculty research:* History of philosophy, ethics, philosophy of science, social philosophy. Total annual research expenditures: $210,000. *Unit head:* Jeremiah Hackett, Chair, 803-777-4166, Fax: 803-777-9178, E-mail: hackettj@gwm.sc.edu. *Application contact:* Dr. Thomas Burke, Graduate Director, 803-777-3733, Fax: 803-777-9178, E-mail: burke@sc.edu.

University of Southern California, Graduate School, College of Letters, Arts and Sciences, School of Philosophy, Los Angeles, CA 90089. Offers MA, PhD. *Faculty:* 19 full-time (3 women). *Students:* 33 full-time (10 women); includes 4 minority (3 Asian Americans or Pacific Islanders, 1 Hispanic American), 10 international. 105 applicants, 17% accepted. In 2007, 1 master's, 4 doctorates awarded. Terminal master's awarded for partial completion of doctoral program. *Degree requirements:* For master's, one foreign language, thesis or alternative; for doctorate, one foreign language, thesis/dissertation. *Entrance requirements:* For master's, GRE; for doctorate, GRE General Test. *Application deadline:* For fall admission, 12/15 for domestic students. Application fee: $85. *Financial support:* In 2007–08, 25 students received support, including fellowships with tuition reimbursements available (averaging $19,000 per year), teaching assistantships with tuition reimbursements available (averaging $18,800 per year); research assistantships. Financial award application deadline: 2/15; financial award applicants required to submit FAFSA. *Faculty research:* History of modern philosophy, philosophy of mind and language, moral and political philosophy, epistomology, meta physics. *Unit head:* Scott Soames, Head, 213-740-2311, E-mail: philos@usc.edu.

University of Southern Mississippi, Graduate School, College of Arts and Letters, Department of Philosophy and Religion, Hattiesburg, MS 39406-0001. Offers philosophy (MA). Part-time programs available. *Faculty:* 9 full-time (2 women). *Students:* 5 full-time (1 woman), 5 part-time (1 woman); includes 2 minority (1 African American, 1 Hispanic American). Average age 33. 3 applicants, 100% accepted, 1 enrolled. In 2007, 2 master's awarded. *Degree requirements:* For master's, one foreign language, comprehensive exam, thesis. *Entrance requirements:* For master's, GRE General Test, minimum GPA of 3.0 in philosophy, 2.75 last 60 hours. Additional exam requirements/recommendations for international students: Required—TOEFL. *Application deadline:* For fall admission, 3/1 for domestic and international students. Applications are processed on a rolling basis. Application fee: $30. *Financial support:* In 2007–08, 4 teaching assistantships with full tuition reimbursements (averaging $6,000 per year) were awarded; research assistantships, Federal Work-Study, scholarships/grants, and unspecified assistantships also available. Financial award application deadline: 3/15. *Faculty research:* Philosophy of religion, American philosophy, Oriental philosophy, philosophy of medicine. *Unit head:* Dr. David Holley, Chair, 601-266-4518, Fax: 601-266-5800. *Application contact:* Dr. Paula Smithka, Graduate Coordinator, 601-266-4518, Fax: 601-266-5800.

University of South Florida, Graduate School, College of Arts and Sciences, Department of Philosophy, Tampa, FL 33620-9951. Offers MA, PhD. Part-time and evening/weekend programs available. *Faculty:* 10 full-time (2 women). *Students:* 45 full-time (12 women), 21 part-time (5 women); includes 9 minority (2 African Americans, 7 Hispanic Americans). 35 applicants, 69% accepted, 13 enrolled. In 2007, 6 master's, 1 doctorate awarded. Terminal master's awarded for partial completion of doctoral program. *Degree requirements:* For master's, one foreign language, thesis or alternative; for doctorate, 2 foreign languages, comprehensive exam, thesis/dissertation. *Entrance requirements:* For master's, GRE General Test, minimum GPA of 3.0 in last 60 hours, writing sample, statement of purpose, references; for doctorate, GRE General Test, writing sample, statement of purpose, references. Additional exam requirements/recommendations for international students: Required—TOEFL (minimum score 550 paper-based; 213 computer-based). *Application deadline:* For fall admission, 1/2 for domestic and international students; for spring admission, 10/15 for domestic students, 8/1 for international students. Application fee: $30. Electronic applications accepted. *Financial support:* In 2007–08, 34 students received support, including 1 fellowship with partial tuition reimbursement available (averaging $11,000 per year), 26 teaching assistantships with partial tuition reimbursements available (averaging $10,500 per year); health care benefits and unspecified assistantships also available. Financial award application deadline: 1/2. *Faculty research:* Ancient philosophy, social philosophy, ethics, continental philosophy, philosophy of science. Total annual research expenditures: $10,194. *Unit head:* Dr. Roger Ariew, Chairperson, 813-974-2447, Fax: 813-974-5914, E-mail: rariew@cas.usf.edu. *Application contact:* Darlene Corcoran, Academic Program Specialist, 813-974-5955, Fax: 813-974-5914, E-mail: dcorcoran@chuma1.cas.usf.edu.

The University of Tennessee, Graduate School, College of Arts and Sciences, Department of Philosophy, Knoxville, TN 37996. Offers medical ethics (MA, PhD); philosophy (MA, PhD); religious studies (MA). Part-time programs available. *Degree requirements:* For master's, thesis or alternative; for doctorate, one foreign language, thesis/dissertation. *Entrance requirements:* For master's and doctorate, GRE General Test, minimum GPA of 2.7. Additional exam requirements/recommendations for international students: Required—TOEFL. Electronic applications accepted.

The University of Texas at Austin, Graduate School, College of Liberal Arts, Department of Philosophy, Austin, TX 78712-1111. Offers MA, PhD. Part-time programs available. Terminal master's awarded for partial completion of doctoral program. *Degree requirements:* For master's, thesis; for doctorate, one foreign language, thesis/dissertation. *Entrance requirements:* For master's and doctorate, GRE General Test. Electronic applications accepted. *Faculty research:* Ancient philosophy, cognitive science, continental philosophy, history and philosophy of science.

The University of Toledo, College of Graduate Studies, College of Arts and Sciences, Department of Philosophy, Toledo, OH 43606-3390. Offers MA. Part-time programs available. *Faculty:* 10. *Students:* 13 full-time (6 women), 4 part-time (3 women); includes 1 minority (African American), 1 international. Average age 28. 27 applicants, 81% accepted, 8 enrolled. In 2007, 2 degrees awarded. *Degree requirements:* For master's, exam. *Application deadline:* For fall admission, 1/15 priority date for domestic students. Application fee: $45. Electronic applications accepted. *Financial support:* In 2007–08, 14 teaching assistantships (averaging $8,200 per year) were awarded; research assistantships, Federal Work-Study, institutionally sponsored loans, scholarships/grants, tuition waivers (full), and unspecified assistantships also available. Support available to part-time students. Financial award application deadline: 4/1. *Faculty research:* History of philosophy, ethics, social/political philosophy, philosophy of science, European philosophy. *Unit head:* Dr. Benjamin Pryor, Chair, 419-530-6186, Fax: 419-530-6189, E-mail: benjamin.pryor@utnet.utoledo.edu.

University of Toronto, School of Graduate Studies, Humanities Division, Department of Philosophy, Toronto, ON M5S 1A1, Canada. Offers MA, PhD. Part-time programs available. *Faculty:* 47 full-time, 10 part-time/adjunct. *Students:* 95 full-time (28 women), 1 part-time, 27 international. 320 applicants, 16% accepted. In 2007, 9 degrees awarded. *Degree requirements:* For doctorate, one foreign language, thesis/dissertation. *Entrance requirements:* For master's, GRE, 6 courses in philosophy; minimum A– average in philosophy courses; B overall, 2 letters of reference, writing sample; for doctorate, GRE, MA in philosophy, minimum A– average, 2 letters of reference, writing sample. Additional exam requirements/recommendations for international students: Required—TOEFL (minimum score 600 paper-based), TWE (minimum score 5). *Application deadline:* For fall admission, 1/7 for domestic students. Application fee: $100 Canadian dollars. *Financial support:* Fellowships, teaching assistantships available. *Unit head:* Prof. Donald Ainslie, Chair, 416-978-3312, Fax: 416-978-8703, E-mail: chair.philosophy@utoronto.ca. *Application contact:* Margaret Opoku-Pare, Graduate Administrator, 416-978-3312, Fax: 416-978-8703, E-mail: m.opoku.pare@utoronto.ca.

University of Utah, The Graduate School, College of Humanities, Department of Philosophy, Salt Lake City, UT 84112-1107. Offers MA, MS, PhD. Part-time programs available. *Faculty:* 20 full-time (7 women), 1 part-time/adjunct (0 women). *Students:* 27 full-time (7 women), 9 part-time (4 women); includes 1 minority (Asian American or Pacific Islander), 3 international. Average age 33. 27 applicants, 67% accepted, 8 enrolled. In 2007, 2 master's, 1 doctorate awarded. *Degree requirements:* For master's, comprehensive exam, thesis or alternative; for doctorate, thesis/dissertation, qualifying oral exam. *Entrance requirements:* For master's, GRE General Test, minimum undergraduate GPA of 3.0; for doctorate, GRE General Test. Additional exam requirements/recommendations for international students: Required—TOEFL (minimum score 500 paper-based; 173 computer-based). *Application deadline:* For fall admission, 1/31 for domestic and international students. Application fee: $45 ($65 for international students). *Financial support:* In 2007–08, 1 fellowship with full tuition reimbursement (averaging $10,500 per year), 14 teaching assistantships with full tuition reimbursements (averaging $10,500 per year) were awarded; research assistantships, Federal Work-Study, institutionally sponsored loans, and scholarships/grants also available. Financial award application deadline: 2/15; financial award applicants required to submit FAFSA. *Faculty research:* Social philosophy, ethics, metaphysics, political philosophy, logic. Total annual research expenditures: $1,842. *Unit head:* Dr. Leslie Francis, Chair, 801-581-3489, Fax: 801-585-5195, E-mail: francisl@law.utah.edu. *Application contact:* Ron Mallon, Director of Graduate Studies, 801-581-8161, Fax: 801-585-5195, E-mail: rmallon@hum.utah.edu.

University of Victoria, Faculty of Graduate Studies, Faculty of Humanities, Department of Philosophy, Victoria, BC V8W 2Y2, Canada. Offers MA. Part-time and evening/weekend programs available. *Faculty:* 11 full-time (3 women). *Students:* Average age 26. 28 applicants, 14% accepted, 4 enrolled. In 2007, 2 degrees awarded. *Degree requirements:* For master's, thesis. *Entrance requirements:* For master's, writing sample. Additional exam requirements/recommendations for international students: Required—TOEFL (minimum score 575 paper-based; 233 computer-based), IELTS (minimum score 7). *Application deadline:* For fall admission, 2/1 priority date for domestic and international students. Application fee: $75 ($125 for international students). *Expenses:* Tuition, state resident: full-time $3,110. International tuition: $3,700 full-time. Tuition and fees vary according to program. *Financial support:* In 2007–08, 1 fellowship (averaging $13,500 per year), 3 teaching assistantships (averaging $8,000 per year) were awarded. Financial award application deadline: 2/15. *Faculty research:* Ethics, metaphysics, philosophy of mind, history of philosophy, political philosophy. *Unit head:* Dr. James O. Young, Chair, 250-721-7509, Fax: 250-721-7511, E-mail: joy@uvic.ca. *Application contact:* Dr. Jeffrey E. Foss, Graduate Advisor, 250-721-7513, Fax: 250-721-7511, E-mail: jefffoss@uvic.ca.

University of Virginia, College and Graduate School of Arts and Sciences, Department of Philosophy, Charlottesville, VA 22903. Offers MA, PhD, JD/MA. *Faculty:* 13 full-time (3 women). *Students:* 32 full-time (13 women), 7 international. Average age 30. 135 applicants, 6% accepted, 5 enrolled. In 2007, 2 master's, 6 doctorates awarded. *Degree requirements:* For master's, 2 papers; for doctorate, thesis/dissertation, 2 papers. *Entrance requirements:* For master's and doctorate, GRE General Test, GRE Subject Test. *Application deadline:* Applications are processed on a rolling basis. Application fee: $60. Electronic applications accepted. *Financial support:* Applicants required to submit FAFSA. *Unit head:* Jorge Secada, Chair, 434-924-7701, Fax: 434-924-6927, E-mail: jes2f@virginia.edu.

University of Washington, Graduate School, College of Arts and Sciences, Department of Philosophy, Seattle, WA 98195. Offers classics and philosophy (PhD); philosophy (MA, PhD). Terminal master's awarded for partial completion of doctoral program. *Degree requirements:* For master's, 3 papers; for doctorate, thesis/dissertation, general exam. *Entrance requirements:* For master's and doctorate, GRE, minimum GPA of 3.0. Additional exam requirements/recommendations for international students: Required—TOEFL. *Faculty research:* History and philosophy of science, epistemology, Aristotle's metaphysics, ethics and politics, causation in modern philosophy.

University of Waterloo, Graduate Studies, Faculty of Arts, Department of Philosophy, Waterloo, ON N2L 3G1, Canada. Offers MA, PhD. *Faculty:* 12 full-time (1 woman), 10 part-time/adjunct (3 women). *Students:* 50. 28 applicants, 43% accepted, 8 enrolled. In 2007, 3 master's, 2 doctorates awarded. *Degree requirements:* For master's, thesis or alternative; for doctorate, one foreign language, thesis/dissertation. *Entrance requirements:* For master's, honors degree, minimum B+ average, writing sample, resumé; for doctorate, master's degree, minimum A- average, resumé. Additional exam requirements/recommendations for international students: Required—TOEFL, TWE. *Application deadline:* For fall admission, 2/1 priority date for domestic students; for winter admission, 11/1 priority date for domestic students. Application fee: $75 Canadian dollars. Electronic applications accepted. *Financial support:* Research assistantships, teaching assistantships, scholarships/grants available. Financial award application deadline: 2/15. *Faculty research:* Logic, ethics, social/political, cognitive science, philosophy of science. *Application contact:* Dr. D. DeVidi, Graduate Officer, 519-888-4567 Ext. 5701, Fax: 519-746-3097, E-mail: ddevidi@uwaterloo.ca.

The University of Western Ontario, Faculty of Graduate Studies, Faculty of Arts and Humanities, Department of Philosophy, London, ON N6A 5B8, Canada. Offers MA, PhD. *Faculty:* 25 full-time (6 women). *Students:* 52 full-time (13 women), 3 part-time. 74 applicants, 42% accepted, 17 enrolled. In 2007, 8 master's, 3 doctorates awarded. *Degree requirements:* For master's, 1 competency exam; for doctorate, comprehensive exam, thesis/dissertation, 2 competency exams. *Entrance requirements:* For master's, honors degree, statement of philosophical interests. Additional exam requirements/recommendations for international students: Required—TOEFL (minimum score 600 paper-based; 250 computer-based). *Application deadline:* For fall admission, 2/1 priority date for domestic students. Applications are processed on a rolling basis. Application fee: $50 Canadian dollars. Electronic applications accepted. *Financial support:* In 2007–08, 36 students received support, including 36 teaching assistantships (averaging $10,134 Canadian dollars per year); scholarships/grants also available. Financial award application deadline: 2/1. *Faculty research:* Philosophy of science, history of philosophy, philosophy of law, ethics, epistemology. *Unit head:* Dr. John Thorp, Acting Chair, 519-661-2111 Ext. 85767, Fax: 519-661-2111, E-mail: jthorp@uwo.ca. *Application contact:* Meghan Talbot, Graduate Assistant, 519-661-2111 Ext. 85744, Fax: 519-661-3922, E-mail: mtalbot3@uwo.ca.

University of Windsor, Faculty of Graduate Studies, Faculty of Arts and Social Sciences, Department of Philosophy, Windsor, ON N9B 3P4, Canada. Offers MA. Part-time programs available. *Faculty:* 10 full-time (2 women). *Students:* 10 full-time (4 women), 2 part-time (1 woman). 15 applicants, 73% accepted. In 2007, 7 degrees awarded. *Degree requirements:* For master's, thesis. *Entrance requirements:* For master's, minimum B average. Additional exam requirements/recommendations for international students: Required—TOEFL (minimum score 600 paper-based; 250 computer-based). *Application deadline:* For fall admission, 7/1 priority date for domestic students. Applications are processed on a rolling basis. Application fee: $55. Electronic applications accepted. *Financial support:* In 2007–08, 7 teaching assistantships (averaging $8,901 per year) were awarded; fellowships, Federal Work-Study, tuition waivers (full and partial), unspecified assistantships, and bursary also available. Financial award application deadline: 2/15. *Faculty research:* Informal logic, contemporary Continental philosophy, epistemology. *Unit head:* Deborah Cook, Acting Head, 519-253-3000 Ext. 2317, Fax: 519-973-3653, E-mail: dcook@uwindsor.ca. *Application contact:* Applicant Services, 519-253-3000 Ext. 6459, Fax: 519-971-3653, E-mail: gradadmit@uwindsor.ca.

University of Wisconsin–Madison, Graduate School, College of Letters and Science, Department of Philosophy, Madison, WI 53706-1380. Offers MA, PhD. Part-time programs available. Terminal master's awarded for partial completion of doctoral program. *Degree requirements:*

For master's, thesis, preliminary exams; for doctorate, thesis/dissertation, preliminary exams. *Entrance requirements:* For doctorate, GRE, BA in philosophy or related area. Additional exam requirements/recommendations for international students: Required—TOEFL. Electronic applications accepted. *Faculty research:* History of philosophy, logic, philosophy of science, philosophy of mind, metaphysics.

University of Wisconsin–Milwaukee, Graduate School, College of Letters and Sciences, Department of Philosophy, Milwaukee, WI 53201-0413. Offers MA. Part-time programs available. *Faculty:* 13 full-time (2 women). *Students:* 22 full-time (2 women), 1 (woman) part-time; includes 3 minority (2 Asian Americans or Pacific Islanders, 1 Hispanic American). 146 applicants, 18% accepted, 11 enrolled. In 2007, 8 degrees awarded. *Degree requirements:* For master's, thesis or alternative. *Entrance requirements:* For master's, GRE General Test. *Application deadline:* For fall admission, 1/1 priority date for domestic students; for spring admission, 9/1 for domestic students. Applications are processed on a rolling basis. Application fee: $45 ($75 for international students). *Expenses:* Tuition, state resident: part-time $530 per credit. Tuition, nonresident: part-time $1,428 per credit. Required fees: $19 per credit. $229 per term. Tuition and fees vary according to course load and program. *Financial support:* In 2007–08, 19 teaching assistantships were awarded; fellowships, research assistantships, career-related internships or fieldwork and unspecified assistantships also available. Support available to part-time students. Financial award application deadline: 4/15. *Unit head:* Robert Schwartz, Representative, 414-229-5216, Fax: 414-229-5022, E-mail: schwartz@uwm.edu.

University of Wyoming, Graduate School, College of Arts and Sciences, Department of Philosophy, Laramie, WY 82070. Offers MA. Part-time programs available. *Faculty:* 5 full-time (1 woman), 1 part-time/adjunct (0 women). *Students:* 5 full-time (1 woman), 1 (woman) part-time. Average age 30. 9 applicants, 33% accepted, 2 enrolled. In 2007, 3 master's awarded. *Degree requirements:* For master's, thesis, logic proficiency, first-year paper. *Entrance requirements:* For master's, GRE General Test, minimum GPA of 3.0. Additional exam requirements/recommendations for international students: Required—TOEFL (minimum score 525 paper-based; 197 computer-based). *Application deadline:* For spring admission, 2/1 priority date for domestic students, 2/1 for international students. Applications are processed on a rolling basis. Application fee: $50. Electronic applications accepted. *Financial support:* In 2007–08, 2 teaching assistantships with full tuition reimbursements (averaging $10,696 per year) were awarded; health care benefits also available. Financial award application deadline: 2/1. *Faculty research:* Philosophy of science, political and ethical theory, philosophy of language, epistemology, philosophy of mind, early modern philosophy. *Unit head:* Dr. Ed Sherline, Head, 307-766-3204, E-mail: sherline@uwyo.edu. *Application contact:* Dr. Franz-Peter Griesmaier, Graduate Advisor, 307-766-3231, E-mail: fpg@uwyo.edu.

Vanderbilt University, Graduate School, Department of Philosophy, Nashville, TN 37240-1001. Offers MA, PhD. *Faculty:* 33 full-time (9 women). *Students:* 51 full-time (18 women); includes 3 minority (1 African American, 1 American Indian/Alaska Native, 1 Hispanic American), 2 international. Average age 32. 143 applicants, 6% accepted, 6 enrolled. In 2007, 5 degrees awarded. *Degree requirements:* For master's, one foreign language, thesis; for doctorate, one foreign language, comprehensive exam, thesis/dissertation, final and qualifying exams. *Entrance requirements:* For master's and doctorate, GRE General Test, knowledge of a foreign language, writing sample. *Application deadline:* For fall admission, 1/15 for domestic and international students. Application fee: $0. Electronic applications accepted. *Financial support:* Fellowships with full tuition reimbursements, teaching assistantships with full tuition reimbursements, Federal Work-Study, institutionally sponsored loans, and health care benefits available. Financial award application deadline: 1/15; financial award applicants required to submit CSS PROFILE or FAFSA. *Faculty research:* Ancient, medieval, and modern philosophy; philosophy of science; ethics; philosophy of language; philosophy of religion. *Unit head:* Jeffrey Tlumak, Chair, 615-322-2637, Fax: 615-343-7259, E-mail: jeffrey.tlumak@vanderbilt.edu. *Application contact:* Gregg M. Horowitz, Director of Graduate Studies, 615-322-2637, Fax: 615-343-7259, E-mail: gregg.horowitz@vanderbilt.edu.

Villanova University, Graduate School of Liberal Arts and Sciences, Department of Philosophy, Villanova, PA 19085-1699. Offers PhD. Part-time and evening/weekend programs available. *Faculty:* 7 full-time (2 women). *Students:* 47 full-time (15 women); includes 2 minority (1 Asian American or Pacific Islander, 1 Hispanic American), 4 international. Average age 27. 146 applicants, 8% accepted. In 2007, 2 doctorates awarded. *Degree requirements:* For doctorate, 2 foreign languages, comprehensive exam, thesis/dissertation. *Entrance requirements:* For doctorate, GRE General Test, GRE Subject Test, minimum GPA of 3.50. *Application deadline:* For fall admission, 2/1 for domestic and international students. Applications are processed on a rolling basis. Application fee: $50. Electronic applications accepted. *Financial support:* Research assistantships, teaching assistantships, Federal Work-Study available. Financial award applicants required to submit FAFSA. *Unit head:* Dr. Walter Brogan, Chairman, 610-519-4690.

Virginia Polytechnic Institute and State University, Graduate School, College of Liberal Arts and Human Sciences, Department of Philosophy, Blacksburg, VA 24061. Offers MA. *Entrance requirements:* For master's, GRE General Test. Additional exam requirements/recommendations for international students: Required—TOEFL (minimum score 550 paper-based; 213 computer-based). Electronic applications accepted. *Faculty research:* History of philosophy, ethics, history and philosophy of science and philosophy.

Washington State University, Graduate School, College of Liberal Arts, Department of Philosophy, Pullman, WA 99164. Offers MA. *Faculty:* 8. *Students:* 10 full-time (3 women); includes 1 minority (American Indian/Alaska Native). 14 applicants, 71% accepted, 6 enrolled. In 2007, 2 degrees awarded. *Degree requirements:* For master's, comprehensive exam (for some programs), thesis (for some programs). *Entrance requirements:* For master's, GRE, minimum GPA of 3.0, 3 letters of recommendation, writing sample. Additional exam requirements/recommendations for international students: Required—TOEFL. *Application deadline:* For fall admission, 3/1 for domestic and international students; for spring admission, 8/1 for domestic students, 7/1 for international students. Application fee: $50. *Financial support:* In 2007–08, 7 teaching assistantships with tuition reimbursements (averaging $13,056 per year) were awarded. *Faculty research:* Philosophy of language and mind, philosophy of race and ethnicity, social and political philosophy. *Unit head:* Dr. David L. Shier, Chair, 509-335-1415, E-mail: shier@wsu.edu. *Application contact:* Graduate School Admissions, 800-GRADWSU, Fax: 509-335-1949, E-mail: gradsch@wsu.edu.

Washington University in St. Louis, Graduate School of Arts and Sciences, Department of Philosophy, St. Louis, MO 63130-4899. Offers philosophy (MA, PhD); philosophy/neuroscience/psychology (PhD). Terminal master's awarded for partial completion of doctoral program. *Degree requirements:* For master's, thesis optional; for doctorate, thesis/dissertation. *Entrance requirements:* For master's and doctorate, GRE General Test, sample of written work. Electronic applications accepted.

Wayne State University, College of Liberal Arts and Sciences, Department of Philosophy, Detroit, MI 48202. Offers MA, PhD. *Students:* 15 full-time (1 woman), 1 part-time; includes 2 minority (both African Americans), 1 international. Average age 32. 19 applicants, 58% accepted, 3 enrolled. In 2007, 3 degrees awarded. Terminal master's awarded for partial completion of doctoral program. *Degree requirements:* For master's, thesis; for doctorate, one foreign language, thesis/dissertation. *Entrance requirements:* For master's, GRE General Test or minimum GPA of 3.0; for doctorate, undergraduate GPA of at least 3.0. Additional exam requirements/recommendations for international students: Required—TOEFL (minimum score 550 paper-based; 213 computer-based); Recommended—TWE (minimum score 6). *Application deadline:* For fall admission, 7/1 priority date for domestic students, 6/1 for international students; for winter admission, 10/1 for international students; for spring admission, 2/1 for international students. Applications are processed on a rolling basis. Application fee: $30 ($50 for international students). Electronic applications accepted. *Expenses:* Tuition, state resident: part-time $403 per credit hour. Tuition, nonresident: part-time $890 per credit hour. *Financial support:* In 2007–08, 1 fellowship with tuition reimbursement (averaging $13,001 per year), 10 teaching assistantships with tuition reimbursements (averaging $12,922 per year) were awarded. Financial award application deadline: 4/1. *Faculty research:* Metaphysics; ancient philosophy; philosophy of art; ethics; philosophy of science. *Unit head:* Robert Yanal, Chair, 313-577-6099, E-mail: r.yanal@wayne.edu.

West Chester University of Pennsylvania, Office of Graduate Studies and Extended Education, College of Arts and Sciences, Department of Philosophy, West Chester, PA 19383. Offers business ethics (Certificate); healthcare ethics (Certificate); philosophy (MA). Part-time and evening/weekend programs available. *Students:* 10 full-time (4 women), 11 part-time (3 women); includes 1 minority (African American), 1 international. Average age 28. 16 applicants, 88% accepted, 10 enrolled. In 2007, 5 degrees awarded. *Degree requirements:* For master's, one foreign language, comprehensive exam, thesis optional. *Entrance requirements:* For master's, GRE or MAT. Additional exam requirements/recommendations for international students: Required—TOEFL (minimum score 550 paper-based; 213 computer-based; 80 iBT). *Application deadline:* For fall admission, 4/15 priority date for domestic students; for spring admission, 10/15 for domestic students. Applications are processed on a rolling basis. Application fee: $35. *Expenses:* Tuition, state resident: part-time $345 per credit. Tuition, nonresident: part-time $552 per credit. Tuition and fees vary according to course load. *Financial support:* In 2007–08, 3 research assistantships with full and partial tuition reimbursements (averaging $5,000 per year) were awarded; unspecified assistantships also available. Support available to part-time students. Financial award application deadline: 2/15; financial award applicants required to submit FAFSA. *Faculty research:* International studies. *Unit head:* Dr. Fred Strukmeyer, Chair and Graduate Coordinator, 610-436-2841, E-mail: tstrukmeyer@wcupa.edu. *Application contact:* Dr. Joan Woolfrey, Graduate Coordinator, 610-436-2857, E-mail: jwoolfrey@wcupa.edu.

Western Michigan University, Graduate College, College of Arts and Sciences, Department of Philosophy, Kalamazoo, MI 49008-5202. Offers MA. *Degree requirements:* For master's, thesis optional.

Wilfrid Laurier University, Faculty of Graduate Studies, Faculty of Arts, Department of Philosophy, Waterloo, ON N2L 3C5, Canada. Offers MA. *Faculty:* 14 full-time. *Students:* 6 full-time. 23 applicants, 61% accepted, 6 enrolled. *Entrance requirements:* For master's, Honours BA in philosophy or equivalent with a minimum B+ in philosophy and in final year. Additional exam requirements/recommendations for international students: Required—TOEFL (minimum score 230 computer-based; 89 iBT). *Application deadline:* For fall admission, 2/1 priority date for domestic students. Application fee: $75. Electronic applications accepted. *Financial support:* Fellowships, research assistantships, teaching assistantships available. *Faculty research:* Self, agency, community. *Unit head:* Dr. Byron Williston, Chairperson, 519-884-0710 Ext. 3113, Fax: 519-883-0991. *Application contact:* Jennifer Poppe, Student Contact, 519-884-0710 Ext. 3536, Fax: 519-884-1020, E-mail: gradstudies@wlu.ca.

Yale University, Graduate School of Arts and Sciences, Department of Philosophy, New Haven, CT 06520. Offers PhD. *Degree requirements:* For doctorate, 2 foreign languages, thesis/dissertation. *Entrance requirements:* For doctorate, GRE General Test.

York University, Faculty of Graduate Studies, Faculty of Arts, Program in Philosophy, Toronto, ON M3J 1P3, Canada. Offers MA, PhD. Part-time programs available. *Degree requirements:* For master's, thesis or alternative; for doctorate, one foreign language, thesis/dissertation. Electronic applications accepted.

SOUTHERN ILLINOIS UNIVERSITY CARBONDALE

Department of Philosophy Ph.D. Program

Programs of Study

The Department of Philosophy at Southern Illinois University Carbondale (SIUC) offers the Ph.D. degree, centered on a diverse, pluralistic curriculum in several contemporary philosophical traditions and in the history of philosophy. It is internationally recognized for its strength, especially in American philosophy, including pragmatism, idealism, and process philosophy. It also offers strengths in nineteenth- and twentieth-century Continental philosophy, value studies (ethics, social and political philosophy, aesthetics), and philosophy of religion. In addition, the Department regularly offers courses in the history of ancient, medieval, and modern philosophy; Asian philosophy (Indian philosophy, Chinese philosophy, Buddhism, Islamic philosophy); metaphysics; philosophy of mind; epistemology; feminist philosophy; and philosophy of science and technology. The 15 faculty members of the Department are all committed teachers and active scholars, both nationally and internationally.

The program is designed for students looking to teach philosophy at the college level. Students pursuing the Ph.D. must complete a rigorous schedule of 30 semester hours of course work beyond the M.A. All students must demonstrate competence in formal logic during the first year of residence, as required for the M.A. degree, and also demonstrate a background in the history of philosophy by passing the Department's M.A. comprehensive examination on the history of philosophy. Incoming doctoral students are expected to take this examination within the first year after entering the Ph.D. program. Students must fulfill a research tool requirement by showing an extensive knowledge and usage of one foreign language and completing a seminar in the history of the analytic movement. All candidates must pass a written preliminary examination on the following three areas: metaphysics, epistemology, and value fields (ethics, social philosophy, and aesthetics). These examinations are normally taken only after the student has accumulated at least 24 hours of credit beyond the M.A. degree. Upon completion of 30 hours course work, students must complete a dissertation to satisfy all degree requirements.

Opportunities to enhance studies are offered through lecture series and opportunities to study abroad in countries such as Greece, Egypt, Germany, France, Japan, and Iran.

Research Facilities

The Center for Dewey Studies is widely recognized internationally as one of the leading research centers for the study of American philosophy. SIUC's Morris Library also provides excellent research facilities, with more than 2 million volumes, an extensive collection of philosophical journals, and important archives in American philosophy, including the Open Court papers of Paul Carus as well as the papers of John Dewey, J. H. Tufts, Stephen Pepper, Edward Scribner Ames, and Henry Weiman.

Financial Aid

In addition to various scholarships awarded through the Graduate School, the Department of Philosophy offers approximately thirty graduate assistantship appointments of 25 to 50 percent, which currently pay $5301 to $11,898 plus a tuition waiver.

Cost of Study

In-state graduate tuition is $313.90 per credit hour in 2008–09. Out-of-state tuition is 2.5 times the in-state tuition rate ($784.75 per credit hour). Graduate students with at least a 25 percent appointment as a graduate assistant receive a tuition scholarship. Fees vary from $511.26 (1 credit hour) to $1416.05 (12 credit hours). Students with a graduate assistantship receive a 25 percent reduction in the Primary Care Medical Fee.

Living and Housing Costs

For married couples, students with families, and single graduate students, the University has 690 efficiency and one-, two-, three-, and four-bedroom apartments that rent for $484 to $686 per month in 2008–09. Residence halls for single graduate students are also available, as are accessible residence hall rooms and apartments for students with disabilities.

Student Group

The more than 60 graduate students are encouraged to take an active role in the Department. They have their own Graduate Philosophy Union; host their own weekly colloquium, Agora; publish *Kinesis*, one of the oldest and most respected graduate journals; and annually host their own conference, Building Bridges, which aims to promote dialogue across disciplines and philosophical traditions.

Location

SIUC is 350 miles south of Chicago and 100 miles southeast of St. Louis. Nestled in rolling hills bordered by the Ohio and Mississippi Rivers and enhanced by a mild climate, the area has state parks, national forests and wildlife refuges, and large lakes for outdoor recreation, including the 240,000 acres of the Shawnee National Forest. Cultural offerings include theater, opera, concerts, art exhibits, and cinema. Educational facilities for the families of students are excellent.

The University and The Department

Southern Illinois University Carbondale is a comprehensive public university with a variety of general and professional education programs. The University offers bachelor's and associate degrees, master's and doctoral degrees, the J.D. degree, and the M.D. degree. The University is fully accredited by the North Central Association of Colleges and Schools. The Graduate School has an essential role in the development and coordination of graduate instruction and research programs. The Graduate Council has academic responsibility for determining graduate standards, recommending new graduate programs and research centers, and establishing policies to facilitate the research effort. Southern Illinois University Carbondale is a state-funded university founded in 1869. The Department of Philosophy is part of the College of Liberal Arts.

Applying

Interested students should apply online at https://www.gradapp.siu.edu/. A completed application includes a completed application form with a $45 nonrefundable application fee, an official transcript from each college attended, a sample of the applicant's written work, three letters of recommendation from individuals who are familiar with the applicant's academic work (to be sent directly to the Academic Secretary), a personal statement, and Graduate Record Examination scores (required for fellowship applications and assistantships but not for admission to the program). International students are also required to submit TOEFL scores of at least 550 (paper-based test) or 220 (computer-based test) and a copy of their passport.

For students to be properly considered for financial assistance, applications should be completed by the end of December.

Correspondence and Information

Rich Black
Academic Secretary
Department of Philosophy
980 Faner Drive, Mailcode 4505
Southern Illinois University
Carbondale, Illinois 62901

Phone: 618-453-7429
Fax: 618-453-7428
E-mail: phildept@siu.edu
Web site: http://www.siu.edu/~philos/

Southern Illinois University Carbondale

THE FACULTY AND THEIR RESEARCH

Thomas Alexander, Professor; Ph.D., Emory, 1984. American philosophy, aesthetics, classical philosophy, Dewey.

Douglas Anderson, Professor; Ph.D., Penn State, 1984. History of philosophy and American philosophy, philosophy's relationship to other dimensions of culture, Charles Peirce and the history of pragmatism.

Randall E. Auxier, Professor; Ph.D., Emory, 1992. American philosophy, post-Kantian Continental philosophy, process and systematic philosophy/theology, history of philosophy, metaphysics, moral philosophy and theology, political theory, philosophy of education.

Sara Beardsworth, Associate Professor; Ph.D., Warwick (England), 1994. Nineteenth- and twentieth-century European philosophy.

Douglas L. Berger, Assistant Professor; Ph.D., Temple, 2000. Classical and contemporary Brahminical and Indian Buddhist philosophies, classical Chinese philosophy, cross-cultural philosophical hermeneutics.

David S. Clarke Jr., Professor Emeritus; Ph.D., Emory, 1964.

Gerard Delahoussaye, Assistant Professor; Ph.D., Ottawa, 2004. Medieval philosophy, John Duns Scotus.

Elizabeth R. Eames, Professor Emerita; Ph.D., Bryn Mawr, 1951.

Eugenia Gatens-Robinson, Associate Professor Emerita; Ph.D., Southern Illinois at Carbondale, 1983.

Garth J. Gillan, Professor Emeritus; Ph.D., Duquesne, 1966.

Robert Hahn, Professor; Ph.D., Yale, 1976. Greek philosophy, Aristotle, Kant, history of philosophy.

Larry Hickman, Professor; Ph.D., Texas at Austin, 1971. Classical American philosophy (Peirce, Mead, James, Dewey), philosophy of technology, philosophy of culture.

John Howie, Professor Emeritus; Ph.D., Boston University, 1965.

Matthew J. Kelly, Associate Professor Emeritus; Ph.D., Notre Dame, 1963.

Pat Manfredi, Associate Professor; Ph.D., Notre Dame. Metaphysics, philosophy of mind, epistemology, recent analytic philosophy.

George Kimball Plochmann, Professor Emeritus; Ph.D., Chicago, 1950.

George Schedler, Professor and Chair; Ph.D., California, San Diego, 1973; J.D., Southern Illinois, 1987. Philosophy of law, social philosophy, ethics.

Anthony Steinbock, Professor; Ph.D., SUNY at Stony Brook, 1993. Contemporary French and German philosophy, phenomenology, social ontology, aesthetics.

Kenneth W. Stikkers, Professor; Ph.D., DePaul, 1982. American philosophy, Continental philosophy, ethics, Scheler, James.

Stephen Tyman, Associate Professor; Ph.D., Toronto, 1980. Eighteenth- and nineteenth-century European philosophy, phenomenology, and existentialism.

Andrew Youpa, Assistant Professor; Ph.D., California, Irvine, 2002. Modern philosophy, modern moral philosophy, contemporary moral philosophy.

STONY BROOK UNIVERSITY, STATE UNIVERSITY OF NEW YORK

Department of Philosophy

Programs of Study

The Department of Philosophy offers programs of study leading to the Master of Arts (M.A.) and to the Doctor of Philosophy (Ph.D.) degrees. Extensive offerings in contemporary European philosophy are a special focus of the doctoral program, together with central topics in Anglo-American philosophy and a major historical component. The graduate program is highly innovative, incorporating interdisciplinary research as well as skills necessary to work with texts in foreign languages into its structure. New directions in the study of philosophy initiated by the Department at Stony Brook include the establishment of graduate certificates attesting to a student's intensive course work and qualifying the student to teach at the interface of a related discipline. Currently, doctoral students can be awarded graduate certificates in art and philosophy, cultural studies, women's studies, and advanced study in literature and philosophy. The Department also offers a terminal M.A. program with a special concentration in philosophy and the arts. For the most part, M.A. seminars in this area of concentration take place at Stony Brook Manhattan.

The purpose of the doctoral program is to prepare students for independent research and scholarship in the field and to help them develop the necessary intellectual and pedagogical skills for teaching philosophy. The doctoral program's curriculum is designed so that all seminar requirements and most nonseminar work are completed by the end of the third year, leaving the fourth and fifth years for dissertation research and writing. The Department emphasizes pedagogical training in combination with courses taught by graduate students, which form an integral part of the undergraduate curriculum of the College of Arts and Sciences. A significant number of graduate students participate in conferences and publish articles in philosophy journals prior to the completion of their doctoral degrees. Students have inaugurated their own journals. They have also organized many graduate student conferences. Such conferences address questions from a broad range of philosophical perspectives and are intended to bridge the apparent divides between Anglo-American and Continental philosophy.

Advanced doctoral students have opportunities to undertake extensive study abroad programs, including, most recently, the Collegium Philosophiae Transatlanticum (in cooperation with the Universities of Wuppertal and Cologne), as well as long-standing exchanges with the University of Tübingen and universities in Paris. Distinguished international scholars frequently offer intensive seminars at Stony Brook or team-teach with the Department's faculty members. A recent initiative brings acclaimed scholars to the Department as distinguished visiting faculty members on a revolving basis. As the result of this initiative, Noam Chomsky, Jacques Derrida, and Angela Davis have given full-credit seminars at Stony Brook.

The graduate program affords advanced Stony Brook doctoral students the opportunity to take seminars for credit at universities participating in the New York–area Inter-University Doctoral Consortium. Consortium member universities are Columbia, City University of New York, Fordham, New School University, New York University, Princeton, Rutgers, and Stony Brook.

The Department offers a master's degree in philosophy with a focus on philosophy and the arts. While the majority of the courses for this M.A. are offered in Manhattan, at the Stony Brook Manhattan satellite campus on 28th Street and Park Avenue South, students are also required to take at least one graduate course at the Stony Brook campus. The core faculty is the same as the faculty of the Ph.D. program with the regular participation of artists, lecturers, and faculty members from local universities and philosophy programs. The program takes advantage of the incomparably rich museum offerings and cultural life of New York City. Stony Brook's M.A. in philosophy is designed to enable students to acquire the skills and philosophical background necessary for admission to Ph.D. programs. Advising and placement are central concerns of Stony Brook's overall graduate program.

Research Facilities

The philosophy collection is housed in Stony Brook's Melville Library stacks. In addition to the Melville Library holdings, the Department of Philosophy supports its own research library in Harriman Hall, the Jonathan Solzberg Library, which is funded by private donations, and the Stony Brook Foundation. The Department's Logic Lab, also located in Harriman Hall, is used for research as well as for teaching philosophy courses.

Financial Aid

Students admitted to the doctoral program typically receive full-tuition scholarships and graduate assistantships (currently $15,145 per year for four years) to cover living expenses. Graduate Council Fellowships and Turner Fellowships, which provide tuition scholarships plus at least $17,583 per year for five years, are available to qualifying students. Many students are awarded Graduate School Fellowships ($2000 per year for four years) to supplement the standard financial aid package. Federal Work-Study Program grants (standardly $3000–$4000 per year) are also available.

Cost of Study

In 2008–09, full-time tuition at 12 credits for entering in-state residents is $3450 per semester, while out-of-state residents and international students pay $5460. Additional fees for each semester, including (but not limited to) the infirmary, activity, technology, and transportation fees, total about $875. International students also pay a service fee of approximately $35 per semester and an orientation fee of $50. Fees for the mandatory Student Health Insurance Plan vary depending on citizenship and employment status.

Living and Housing Costs

For 2008–09, Stony Brook calculates the cost of education excluding tuition, fees, and insurance at $14,228 per year. On-campus apartments range in cost from approximately $336 per month to approximately $1456 per month, depending on the size of the unit and the number of students sharing the space. Off-campus housing options include rooms, houses, and apartments that can be rented from approximately $350 to $2500 per month. Costs including books, food, and transportation may vary depending on academic program and/or personal circumstances.

Student Group

Eighty-one students (39 percent women, 61 percent men) are enrolled in the doctoral program. Seventeen percent are from countries outside the United States. One hundred percent receive financial support. Students offered admission to the graduate program come from a wide variety of universities and liberal arts colleges in the United States and other countries.

Forty-five students (36 percent women, 64 percent men) are enrolled in the program of M.A. studies. Nine percent are currently from outside the United States. Stony Brook actively seeks international master's students supported by government grants that may be linked to Stony Brook tuition scholarships.

Student Outcomes

Graduates of Stony Brook's doctoral program in philosophy have a long record of doing exceptionally well in job placement. Since 2000, graduates have been appointed to positions at Brooklyn College, California State University at Fullerton, California State University at Los Angeles, Colby-Sawyer College, Dalhousie University, DePaul University, Dickinson College, Duquesne University, Emory University, Emporia State University, Florida International University, Georgetown University, Grinnell College, Hofstra University, Illinois Western University, Kent State University, Long Island University, Lyndon State College, Marian College, Miami University, Michigan State University, Muskingum College, Northern Arizona University, Ohio Wesleyan University, Rochester Institute of Technology, Saint Xavier University, Temple University, University College (Cork, Ireland), the University of Colorado at Boulder, the University of Colorado at Denver, the University of Guelph (Ontario), the University of Memphis, the University of New Mexico, the University of Oregon, the University of Pennsylvania, the University of Redlands, the University of Tennessee, and Wheaton College.

Since 2005, graduates of Stony Brook University's Masters Program in Philosophy and the Arts have been accepted into doctoral programs in philosophy and related disciplines at Boston College, New School University, Queen's College Belfast (Ireland), the University of Guelph (Ontario), the University of Memphis, the University of Oregon, the University of Pennsylvania, the University of Southern Florida, the State University of New York at Binghamton, the State University of New York at Buffalo, the State University of New York at Stony Brook, and Villanova University.

Location

The University at Stony Brook is located on the north shore of Long Island, about 60 miles east of New York City (midway between Montauk and Manhattan). The waters of Long Island Sound are minutes from the campus, and the beaches of the Atlantic Ocean are a short drive to the south. North of the University, within easy bicycling distance, lies the historic village of Stony Brook.

The University and The Department

The University of Stony Brook is one of North America's premier public research universities. The Department of Philosophy is integral and essential to the University's teaching and research missions, especially in interdisciplinary areas. The Department is strongly represented in University administration.

Applying

Students seeking admission should have a strong background in philosophy and a solid record of demonstrated excellence at the undergraduate and (if applicable) graduate levels. Graduate Record Examinations (GRE) scores, samples of written work, and letters of recommendation are important factors in the assessment of applicants' admission files.

Applications should be initiated electronically through the admissions link found at the Graduate School Web site (http://www.grad.sunysb.edu/prosp.shtml). Applicants must complete the electronic application form and arrange to provide two official transcripts of all undergraduate and (if applicable) graduate course work, official GRE scores, three letters of recommendation, a sample of written work, and a nonrefundable application fee payment. To be considered for admission, applicants whose first or primary language is not English must present passing scores for either the TOEFL or IELTS tests. Supporting documents that are not part of the electronic submission should be sent directly to the Department of Philosophy. The deadline for the receipt of applications and all supporting materials is January 15.

Correspondence and Information

Graduate Coordinator
Department of Philosophy
Stony Brook University
Stony Brook, New York 11794-3750

Web site: http://www.stonybrook.edu/philosophy

Stony Brook University, State University of New York

FACULTY

Detailed information about all aspects of the Graduate Program in Philosophy (including the e-mail addresses of faculty and staff members) can be found at the Department's Web site (http://www.stonybrook.edu/philosophy).

Professors

David B. Allison, Ph.D., Penn State. Recent French thought, existentialism, Nietzsche. *Reading the New Nietzsche.* Rowman & Littlefield, 2000. *Disordered Mother or Disordered Diagnosis?* Analytic, 1998 (with Roberts).
Edward S. Casey, Ph.D., Northwestern. Phenomenology, philosophical psychology, aesthetics, theory of psychoanalysis. *Earth-mapping: Artists Reshaping Landscape.* Minnesota, 2005. *Representing Place: Landscape Painting and Maps.* Minnesota, 2005. *The Fate of Place.* California, 1997.
Robert P. Crease, Ph.D., Columbia. History and philosophy of science, philosophy of the arts, modern philosophy. *The Prism and the Pendulum.* Random House, 2003. *Making Physics.* Chicago, 1999. *The Play of Nature.* Indiana, 1993.
David Dilworth, Ph.D., Fordham; Ph.D., Columbia. History of philosophy, comparative philosophy, systematic metaphysics. *Philosophy in World Perspective.* Yale, 1989.
Patrick Grim, Ph.D., Boston University. Logic, metaphysics, ethics. *The Philosophical Computer.* MIT, 1998 (with Mar and St. Denis). *The Incomplete Universe: Totality, Knowledge, and Truth.* MIT, 1991.
Dick Howard, Ph.D., Texas at Austin. American, German, and French political theory. *The Specter of Democracy.* Columbia, 2006. *From Marx to Kant.* St. Martins, 1993. *The Politics of Critique.* Minnesota, 1989.
Don Ihde, Distinguished Professor; Ph.D., Boston University. Philosophy of science and technology, hermeneutics, phenomenology. *Bodies in Technology.* Minnesota, 2002. *Expanding Hermeneutics.* Northwestern, 1998. *Postphenomenology,* 1993. *Technology and the Lifeworld.* Indiana, 1990.
Eva Feder Kittay, Ph.D., CUNY Graduate Center. Philosophy of language, feminism, ethics. *Blackwell Guide to Feminist Philosophy* (with Linda Alcoff). Blackwell, 2006. *Love's Labor: Essays on Women, Equality and Dependency.* Routledge, 1998. *Metaphor: Its Cognitive Force and Linguistic Structure.* Oxford, 1987.
Clyde Lee Miller, Ph.D., Yale. Ancient and medieval philosophy, Nicholas of Cusa, ethics. *Reading Cusanus.* Catholic University Press, 2001. Translation of Jean Gerson, *The Consolation of Theology.* Abaris, 1998. Translation of Nicholas de Cusa, *The Layman: About Mind.* Abaris, 1979.
Rita Nolan, Ph.D., Pennsylvania. Philosophy of mind, foundations of cognitive science, social epistemology, Wittgenstein. *Cognitive Practices.* Blackwell, 1994. *Foundations for an Adequate Criterion of Paraphrase.* Mouton, 1970.
Hugh J. Silverman, Ph.D., Stanford. Joint appointment, Comparative Literature. Continental philosophy and literary theory, philosophy and the arts, history of ideas. *Textualities: Between Hermeneutics and Deconstruction.* Routledge, 1994. *Inscriptions: After Phenomenology and Structuralism.* Northwestern, 1987.
Lorenzo Simpson, Ph.D., Yale. Contemporary Continental philosophy (hermeneutics and critical theory), philosophy of the social sciences, philosophy of science and technology, neopragmatism and postanalytic philosophy, philosophy and race. *The Unfinished Project: Towards a Postmetaphysical Humanism.* Routledge, 2000. *Technology, Time, and the Conversations of Modernity.* Routledge, 1995.
Marshall Spector, Ph.D., Johns Hopkins. Philosophy of science and technology, environmental issues. *Concepts of Reduction in Physical Science.* Temple, 1978. *Methodological Foundations of Relativistic Mechanics.* Notre Dame, 1972.
Donn Welton, Ph.D., Southern Illinois. Phenomenology, epistemology, philosophical psychology, theory of the person, Husserl studies. *Edmund Husserl: Critical Assessments,* 5 vols. Routledge, 2005 (edited with Bernet and Zavota). *The Other Husserl.* Indiana, 2000. *Body and Flesh: A Philosophical Reader.* Blackwell, 1998 (edited). *The Origins of Meaning.* Nijhoff, 1983.
Peter Williams, Ph.D., J.D., Harvard. Joint appointment, Preventive Medicine. Philosophy of law, philosophy of medicine, ethics.

Associate Professors

Harvey Cormier, Ph.D., Harvard. American philosophy, William James and pragmatism, philosophy and culture. *The Truth Is What Works: William James, Pragmatism and the Seed of Death.* Rowman & Littlefield, 2000.
Allegra De Laurentiis, Ph.D., Frankfurt (Germany). Nineteenth-century philosophy, especially Hegel; ancient philosophy, especially Aristotle. *Subjects in the Ancient and Modern World.* Palgrave-MacMillan, 2005.
Jeffrey Edwards, Ph.D., Marburg (Germany). History of modern philosophy, Kant. *Substance, Force and the Possibility of Knowledge: On Kant's Philosophy of Material Nature.* California, 2000.
Peter B. Manchester, Ph.D., Graduate Theological Union. Ancient and Hellenistic philosophy, phenomenology, philosophical theology. *The Syntax of Time: The Phenomenology of Time in Greek Physics and Speculative Logic.* Brill, 2005.
Gary R. Mar, Ph.D., UCLA. Logic, philosophy of mathematics, philosophy of language, metaphysics, philosophy of religion, philosophy of science. *Logic: Techniques of Formal Reasoning* (with Kalish and Montague). Oxford, 2000. *The Philosophical Computer* (with Grim and Kalish). MIT, 1998.
Eduardo Mendieta, Ph.D., New School. Moral theory, contemporary German philosophy, race and postcolonial theory. *Global Fragments: Critical Theory, Latin America and Globalizations.* SUNY, 2007. *The Adventures of Transcendental Philosophy.* Rowman & Littlefield, 2002. *Latin American Philosophy: Issues, Currents, Debates.* Indiana, 2002.
Mary C. Rawlinson, Ph.D., Northwestern. Joint appointment, Comparative Literature. Recent French philosophy, philosophy of literature, aesthetics, French feminism, nineteenth-century philosophy, philosophy of medicine. *Feminism and Derrida.* Routledge, 1997 (with Zakin and Feder). *Philosophical Problems in Psychiatric Nosology.* Reidel, 1992 (edited).

Assistant Professors

Megan Craig, Ph.D., New School. Philosophy of Art, nineteenth- and twentieth-century continental.
Ann O'Byrne, Ph.D., Vanderbilt. Twentieth-century European philosophy, continental feminism.

Section 12
Religious Studies

This section contains a directory of institutions offering graduate work in religious studies, followed by in-depth entries submitted by institutions that chose to prepare detailed program descriptions. Additional information about programs listed in the directory but not augmented by an in-depth entry may be obtained by writing directly to the dean of a graduate school or chair of a department at the address given in the directory.

For programs offering related work, see also in this book *Area and Cultural Studies, History, Humanities,* and *Philosophy.* In another guide in this series:

Graduate Programs in Business, Education, Health, Information Studies, Law & Social Work

See *Subject Areas (Religious Education)*

CONTENTS

Program Directories

Announcement

Close-Ups

See also:

Missions and Missiology

Abilene Christian University, Graduate School, College of Biblical Studies, Graduate School of Theology, Program in Missions, Abilene, TX 79699-9100. Offers MA. Part-time programs available. *Students:* 4 full-time (2 women), 1 part-time; includes 1 minority (Hispanic American) 2 applicants, 50% accepted, 1 enrolled. In 2007, 7 degrees awarded. *Entrance requirements:* For master's, GRE, MAT. *Application deadline:* For fall admission, 4/1 priority date for domestic students; for spring admission, 11/1 for domestic students. Applications are processed on a rolling basis. Application fee: $40 ($45 for international students). Electronic applications accepted. *Expenses:* Tuition: Full-time $13,368; part-time $557 per hour. Required fees: $700; $34 per hour. $10 per semester. Tuition and fees vary according to degree level and campus/location. *Financial support:* Teaching assistantships, career-related internships or fieldwork available. Financial award application deadline: 4/1. *Faculty research:* Animism, contextualization, missions education. *Unit head:* Dr. Chris Flanders, Graduate Adviser, 325-674-3742, Fax: 325-674-6180, E-mail: clf03c@acu.edu. *Application contact:* William Horn, Graduate Admissions Counselor, 325-674-2656, Fax: 325-674-6717, E-mail: gradinfo@acu.edu.

Alliance Theological Seminary, Graduate and Professional Programs, Nyack, NY 10960. Offers Christian ministry (MPS); counseling (MA); intercultural studies (MA); missions (MPS); New Testament (MA); Old Testament (MA); theology (M Div); urban ministry (MPS). *Accreditation:* ATS. Part-time programs available. *Faculty:* 19 full-time (3 women), 9 part-time/adjunct (1 woman). *Students:* 195 full-time (66 women), 452 part-time (207 women); includes 505 minority (239 African Americans, 1 American Indian/Alaska Native, 113 Asian Americans or Pacific Islanders, 152 Hispanic Americans), 35 international. Average age 39. 224 applicants, 98% accepted, 200 enrolled. In 2007, 63 first professional degrees, 46 master's awarded. *Degree requirements:* For master's, comprehensive exam (for some programs), thesis optional, internships; for M Div, 2 foreign languages, internship. *Entrance requirements:* Proficiency in New Testament Greek, minimum GPA of 2.5 (undergraduate). Additional exam requirements/recommendations for international students: Required—TOEFL (minimum score 550 paper-based; 213 computer-based). *Application deadline:* For fall admission, 6/1 priority date for international students; for spring admission, 11/1 priority date for international students. Applications are processed on a rolling basis. *Expenses:* Tuition: Part-time $450 per credit. Required fees: $20 per term. Tuition and fees vary according to course load. *Financial support:* Research assistantships, career-related internships or fieldwork, Federal Work-Study, and scholarships/grants available. Financial award applicants required to submit FAFSA. *Unit head:* Bennett Schepens, Assistant Vice President and Academic Dean, 845-353-2020, Fax: 845-358-2651. *Application contact:* Karen Shaffstall, Director of Admissions, 845-353-2020, Fax: 845-348-3912, E-mail: admissions.ats@nyack.edu.

Ambrose University College, Ambrose Seminary, Calgary, AB T2P 3T5, Canada. Offers biblical/theological studies (MA); Chinese ministries (Certificate); Christian studies (Diploma); church education (M Div); intercultural ministries (M Div, MA, Certificate, Diploma); leadership and ministry (MA, Certificate, Diploma); pastoral ministries (M Div). *Accreditation:* ATS (one or more programs are accredited). Part-time programs available. *Faculty:* 6 full-time (0 women), 28 part-time/adjunct (4 women). *Students:* 44 full-time (13 women), 118 part-time (45 women); includes 59 minority (2 African Americans, 2 American Indian/Alaska Native, 54 Asian Americans or Pacific Islanders, 1 Hispanic American). Average age 41. 45 applicants, 82% accepted, 37 enrolled. In 2007, 7 first professional degrees, 17 master's, 2 other advanced degrees awarded. *Degree requirements:* For master's, 2 foreign languages, internship; for M Div, one foreign language, internship. *Entrance requirements:* For master's, bachelor degree. Additional exam requirements/recommendations for international students: Required—TOEFL or IELTS. *Application deadline:* For fall admission, 7/31 priority date for domestic students, 3/1 priority date for international students; for winter admission, 11/30 priority date for domestic students, 6/1 priority date for international students. Applications are processed on a rolling basis. Application fee: $50. Electronic applications accepted. Tuition and fees charges are reported in Canadian dollars. *Expenses:* Tuition: Part-time $281 Canadian dollars per credit hour. Required fees: $16 Canadian dollars per credit hour. *Financial support:* In 2007–08, 40 students received support. Career-related internships or fieldwork and scholarships/grants available. Support available to part-time students. Financial award application deadline: 3/30. *Faculty research:* Evangelicalism and sociology, missiological trends, chaplaincy, intertestamental studies, postmodernism. *Unit head:* Dr. Paul Spilsbury, Academic Dean, 403-410-2000 Ext. 6905, Fax: 403-571-2556, E-mail: pspilsbu@ambrose.edu.

Anderson University, School of Theology, Anderson, IN 46012-3495. Offers missions (MA); theology (M Div, MTS, D Min). *Accreditation:* ACIPE; ATS. Part-time programs available. *Degree requirements:* For master's, one foreign language, thesis, integrative senior seminar; for doctorate, thesis/dissertation; for M Div, thesis/dissertation (for some programs). *Faculty research:* Small-church/bivocational ministry, women in ministry.

Asbury Theological Seminary, Graduate and Professional Programs, E. Stanley Jones School of World Mission and Evangelism, Wilmore, KY 40390-1199. Offers intercultural studies (MA); world mission and evangelism (MA). *Accreditation:* ATS. *Faculty:* 9 full-time (1 woman), 8 part-time/adjunct (1 woman). *Entrance requirements:* Additional exam requirements/recommendations for international students: Required—TOEFL (minimum score 550 paper-based; 79 iBT), IELTS (minimum score 7). *Application deadline:* For fall admission, 7/1 priority date for domestic students, 1/31 priority date for international students; for spring admission, 12/1 priority date for domestic students, 3/31 priority date for international students. Applications are processed on a rolling basis. Application fee: $50. Electronic applications accepted. *Expenses:* Contact institution. One-time fee: $100 part-time. *Faculty research:* Missiology, anthropology, evangelization, contextual theology, religious studies. *Unit head:* Dr. Ronald K. Crandall, Dean, 859-858-2252, Fax: 859-858-2375, E-mail: ron_crandall@asburyseminary.edu. *Application contact:* Janelle Vernon, Admissions Director, 859-858-2211, Fax: 859-858-2287, E-mail: admissions_office@asburyseminary.edu.

Assemblies of God Theological Seminary, Graduate and Professional Programs, Springfield, MO 65802. Offers Christian ministries (MA); counseling (MA); divinity (M Div); intercultural ministries (MA); intercultural studies (D Miss); relief and development (D Miss); theological studies (MA); vocational ministry (D Min). *Accreditation:* ATS. Part-time and evening/weekend programs available. Postbaccalaureate distance learning degree programs offered (minimal on-campus study). *Faculty:* 16 full-time (3 women), 21 part-time/adjunct (4 women). *Students:* 212 full-time (59 women), 236 part-time (51 women); includes 49 minority (11 African Americans, 5 American Indian/Alaska Native, 11 Asian Americans or Pacific Islanders, 22 Hispanic Americans), 7 international. Average age 36. 181 applicants, 72% accepted, 91 enrolled. In 2007, 28 first professional degrees, 66 master's, 13 doctorates awarded. *Degree requirements:* For master's, analytical reflection paper or comprehensive exam; for doctorate, thesis/dissertation; for M Div, one foreign language, analytical reflection paper. *Entrance requirements:* For M Div, minimum GPA of 2.0; for master's, minimum GPA of 2.5; for doctorate, minimum GPA of 3.0. Additional exam requirements/recommendations for international students: Required—TOEFL (minimum score 550 paper-based; 213 computer-based; 80 iBT). *Application deadline:* For fall admission, 7/1 priority date for domestic students, 6/1 priority date for international students; for spring admission, 12/1 priority date for domestic students, 11/1 priority date for international students. Applications are processed on a rolling basis. Application fee: $35. Electronic applications accepted. *Expenses:* Tuition: Part-time $465 per credit hour. *Financial support:* Career-related internships or fieldwork, Federal Work-Study, and scholarships/grants available. Support available to part-time students. Financial award application deadline: 7/15; financial award applicants required to submit FAFSA. *Unit head:* Stephen Lim, Academic Dean, 417-268-1000, Fax: 417-268-1001, E-mail: slim@agts.edu.

Associated Mennonite Biblical Seminary, Graduate and Professional Programs, Elkhart, IN 46517-1999. Offers Christian formation (MA); divinity (M Div); mission and evangelism (MA); peace studies (MA); theological studies (MA, Certificate). *Accreditation:* ACIPE; ATS. Part-time programs available. *Degree requirements:* For master's, comprehensive exam, thesis optional; for M Div, integration paper. *Entrance requirements:* For M Div, master's, and Certificate, 3 letters of reference. Additional exam requirements/recommendations for international students: Required—TOEFL (minimum score 550 paper-based; 213 computer-based). Electronic applications accepted. *Faculty research:* Biblical studies, theology, church history, church leadership.

Baptist Bible College of Pennsylvania, Baptist Bible Seminary, Clarks Summit, PA 18411-1297. Offers biblical studies (PhD); church planting (M Div); global missions (M Div); military chaplaincy (M Div); ministry (M Min, D Min); pastor of church education (M Div); pastor of outreach (M Div); pastoral counseling (M Div); pastoral leadership (M Div); theology (M Div, Th M); youth pastor (M Div). Part-time and evening/weekend programs available. Postbaccalaureate distance learning degree programs offered (minimal on-campus study). *Faculty:* 10 full-time (0 women). *Students:* 102 full-time (0 women), 104 part-time; includes 14 minority (6 African Americans, 4 Asian Americans or Pacific Islanders, 4 Hispanic Americans), 2 international. Average age 38. Terminal master's awarded for partial completion of doctoral program. *Degree requirements:* For master's, 2 foreign languages, thesis; for doctorate, 2 foreign languages, comprehensive exam (for some programs), thesis/dissertation, oral exam; for M Div, 2 foreign languages, thesis/dissertation, oral exam. *Entrance requirements:* For doctorate, Greek and Hebrew entrance exams (PhD). *Application deadline:* Applications are processed on a rolling basis. Application fee: $30. Electronic applications accepted. *Expenses:* Tuition: Full-time $6,516; part-time $362 per credit. Required fees: $468; $232 per semester. *Financial support:* Career-related internships or fieldwork and scholarships/grants available. Support available to part-time students. *Unit head:* Dr. Michael Stallard, Seminary Academic Dean, 570-585-9348, Fax: 570-585-4057, E-mail: mstallard@bbc.edu. *Application contact:* Paul Golden, Director of Seminary Admissions, 570-586-9396, E-mail: pgolden@bbc.edu.

Bethel Seminary, Graduate and Professional Programs, St. Paul, MN 55112-6998. Offers adult developments and generativity (Certificate); biblical studies (MATS, Certificate); children's and family ministry (MACFM); Christian education (MACE); Christian thought (M Div, MACT); church leadership (D Min); congregation and family care (D Min); global and contextual studies (MA); global missions (Certificate); lay ministry (Certificate); marriage and family studies (M Div); marriage and family therapy (MAMFT); missions (MATS); pastoral counseling (Certificate); pastoral ministries (M Div); spiritual formation (Certificate); theological studies (MATS, Certificate); transformational leadership (MATL); youth ministries (MACE). *Accreditation:* ACIPE; ATS (one or more programs are accredited). Part-time and evening/weekend programs available. Postbaccalaureate distance learning degree programs offered (minimal on-campus study). *Faculty:* 26 full-time (3 women), 73 part-time/adjunct (21 women). *Students:* 374 full-time (115 women), 669 part-time (268 women); includes 183 minority (90 African Americans, 2 American Indian/Alaska Native, 65 Asian Americans or Pacific Islanders, 26 Hispanic Americans). Average age 36. 417 applicants, 86% accepted, 223 enrolled. In 2007, 62 first professional degrees, 102 master's, 14 doctorates awarded. *Degree requirements:* For master's, variable foreign language requirement, thesis (for some programs); for doctorate, thesis/dissertation; for M Div, one foreign language. *Entrance requirements:* For M Div, letters of reference; for master's, letters of reference, transcripts, personal statement; for doctorate, M Div, letters of reference, essays, organizational support. Additional exam requirements/recommendations for international students: Required—TOEFL (minimum score 550 paper-based; 213 computer-based). *Application deadline:* For fall admission, 8/1 priority date for domestic students, 3/1 for international students; for winter admission, 12/1 priority date for domestic students; for spring admission, 3/1 priority date for domestic students. Applications are processed on a rolling basis. Application fee: $20. Electronic applications accepted. *Expenses:* Tuition: Part-time $325 per credit. Required fees: $10 per quarter. *Financial support:* In 2007–08, 661 students received support, including 20 teaching assistantships; career-related internships or fieldwork, Federal Work-Study, scholarships/grants, and tuition waivers (full) also available. Financial award application deadline: 7/15; financial award applicants required to submit FAFSA. *Faculty research:* Nature of theology, ethics, biblical commentaries, nature of God, science and theology. *Unit head:* Dr. Leland Eliason, Executive Vice President and Provost, 651-638-6182. *Application contact:* Joseph V. Dworak, Director of Admissions, 651-638-6288, Fax: 651-638-6002, E-mail: j-dworak@bethel.edu.

Biola University, School of Intercultural Studies, La Mirada, CA 90639-0001. Offers applied linguistics (MA); intercultural education (PhD); intercultural studies (MAICS); missiology (D Miss); missions (MA); teaching English to speakers of other languages (MA, Certificate). Part-time and evening/weekend programs available. Terminal master's awarded for partial completion of doctoral program. *Degree requirements:* For master's, one foreign language, comprehensive exam; for doctorate, one foreign language, comprehensive exam, thesis/dissertation. *Entrance requirements:* For master's, minimum undergraduate GPA of 3.0; for doctorate, MA, 3 years of ministry experience, minimum graduate GPA of 3.3. Additional exam requirements/recommendations for international students: Required—TOEFL (minimum score 550 paper-based; 213 computer-based). Electronic applications accepted.

Briercrest Seminary, Graduate Programs, Program in Christian Ministries, Caronport, SK S0H 0S0, Canada. Offers leadership (MA); marriage and family counseling (MA); missions (MA); pastoral counseling (MA); worship (MA); youth and family ministry (MA). Part-time programs available. *Degree requirements:* For master's, comprehensive exam, thesis optional. *Entrance requirements:* Additional exam requirements/recommendations for international students: Required—TOEFL (minimum score 550 paper-based; 213 computer-based).

Calvin Theological Seminary, Graduate and Professional Programs, Grand Rapids, MI 49546-4387. Offers divinity (M Div); educational ministry (MA); historical theology (PhD); missions: church growth (MA); philosophical and moral theology (PhD); systematic theology (PhD); theological studies (MTS); theology (Th M). *Accreditation:* ACIPE; ATS. Part-time programs available. *Students:* 235 full-time (35 women), 70 part-time (14 women); includes 39 minority (11 African Americans, 1 American Indian/Alaska Native, 19 Asian Americans or Pacific Islanders, 8 Hispanic Americans), 93 international. Average age 31. 159 applicants, 77% accepted, 96 enrolled. In 2007, 21 first professional degrees, 43 master's, 1 doctorate awarded. *Median time to degree:* Of those who began their doctoral program in fall 1999, 80% received their degree in 8 years or less. *Degree requirements:* For master's, thesis (for some programs); for doctorate, 4 foreign languages, comprehensive exam, thesis/dissertation; for M Div, 2 foreign languages. *Entrance requirements:* For doctorate, GRE General Test, Hebrew, Greek, and a modern foreign language. Additional exam requirements/recommendations for international students: Required—TOEFL (minimum score 550 paper-based; 213 computer-based), TWE (minimum score 4). *Application deadline:* For fall admission, 3/1 priority date for domestic and international students. Applications are processed on a rolling basis. Application fee: $25. Electronic applications accepted. *Expenses:* Tuition: Full-time $9,875; part-time $250 per credit hour. *Financial support:* In 2007–08, 187 students received support, including 4 fellowships with full tuition reimbursements available (averaging $8,405 per year), 4 teaching assistantships with full tuition reimbursements available (averaging $5,760 per year); career-related internships or fieldwork, institutionally sponsored loans, scholarships/grants, and tuition waivers (full) also available. Support available to part-time students. Financial award application deadline: 3/1; financial award applicants required to submit FAFSA. *Faculty research:* Recent Trinity theory, Christian anthropology, Proverbs, reformed confessions, Paul's view of law. *Unit head:* Dr. Cornelius Plantinga, Head, 616-957-6024, Fax: 616-957-6536, E-mail: sempres@calvinseminary.edu. *Application contact:* Rev. Gregory Janke, Director of Admissions, 616-957-7035, Fax: 616-957-8621, E-mail: gjanke@calvinseminary.edu.

Catholic Theological Union at Chicago, Graduate and Professional Programs, Chicago, IL 60615-5698. Offers biblical spirituality (Certificate); cross-cultural ministries (D Min); cross-cultural missions (Certificate); divinity (M Div); liturgical studies (Certificate); liturgy (D Min); pastoral studies (MAPS, Certificate); spiritual formation (Certificate); spirituality (D Min); theology (MA); M Div/MA; M Div/MSW; M Div/PhD. *Accreditation:* ACIPE; ATS (one or more programs are accredited). Part-time and evening/weekend programs available. *Degree requirements:* For master's, one foreign language, comprehensive exam (for some programs), thesis (for some programs); for doctorate, thesis/dissertation. *Entrance requirements:* For doctorate, master's degree, 5 years of active ministry. *Faculty research:* Doctrine, sacraments, ethics, Bible.

Central Baptist Theological Seminary, Graduate and Professional Programs, Shawnee, KS 66226. Offers missional church studies (MA); theological studies (MA); theology (M Div, Diploma). *Accreditation:* ACIPE; ATS (one or more programs are accredited). Part-time programs available. *Faculty:* 3 full-time (0 women), 13 part-time/adjunct (5 women). *Students:* 33 full-time (13 women), 69 part-time (34 women); includes 28 minority (25 African Americans, 2 American Indian/Alaska Native, 1 Hispanic American), 2 international. Average age 44. 46 applicants, 48% accepted, 21 enrolled. In 2007, 11 first professional degrees, 2 master's awarded. *Degree requirements:* For master's, thesis optional, MMPI, Myers-Briggs, Enneagram; for M Div, thesis/dissertation optional. *Entrance requirements:* For master's, accredited bachelor's degree with minimum GPA of 2.3. Additional exam requirements/recommendations for international students: Required—TOEFL (minimum score 547 paper-based; 210 computer-based; 77 iBT). *Application deadline:* For fall admission, 8/1 priority date for domestic students; for winter admission, 12/5 priority date for domestic students; for spring admission, 1/2 priority date for domestic students. Applications are processed on a rolling basis. Application fee: $0. Electronic applications accepted. *Expenses:* Tuition: Part-time $330 per credit hour. *Financial support:* In 2007–08, 42 students received support. Career-related internships or fieldwork, scholarships/grants, and tuition waivers (full and partial) available. Support available to part-time students. Financial award application deadline: 6/21; financial award applicants required to submit FAFSA. *Unit head:* Dr. Paul W. Stevens, Interim Academic Dean, 913-667-5704, Fax: 913-371-8110, E-mail: pwstevens@cbts.edu. *Application contact:* Steve Guinn, Director of Enrollment Services, 913-667-5707, Fax: 913-371-8110, E-mail: sguinn@cbts.edu.

Church of God Theological Seminary, Graduate and Professional Programs, Cleveland, TN 37320-3330. Offers church ministries (MA), including counseling, discipleship and Christian formations, missions, pastoral ministry; discipleship and Christian formations (MA); theology (M Div). *Accreditation:* ACIPE; ATS. Part-time programs available. *Degree requirements:* For M Div, 2 foreign languages, thesis/dissertation, internship. *Faculty research:* Biblical exegesis.

Columbia International University, Columbia Biblical Seminary and School of Missions, Columbia, SC 29230-3122. Offers academic ministries (M Div); bible exposition (M Div, MABE); biblical studies (Certificate); counseling ministries (Certificate); divinity (M Div); educational ministries (M Div, MAEM, Certificate); intercultural studies (M Div, MAIS, Certificate); leadership (D Min); leadership for evangelism/mobilization (MALM); member care (D Min); ministry (Certificate); missions (D Min); pastoral counseling and spiritual formation (M Div, MAPS); preaching (D Min); theology (MA). *Accreditation:* ATS (one or more programs are accredited). Part-time and evening/weekend programs available. *Degree requirements:* For master's, integrative seminar; for doctorate, comprehensive exam, thesis/dissertation; for M Div, internship. *Entrance requirements:* For master's, minimum GPA of 2.7; for doctorate, 3 years of ministerial experience, M Div. Additional exam requirements/recommendations for international students: Required—TOEFL. Electronic applications accepted.

Dallas Baptist University, College of Adult Education, Liberal Arts Program, Dallas, TX 75211-9299. Offers arts (MLA); Christian ministry (MLA); English (MLA); English as a second language (MLA); fine arts (MLA); history (MLA); missions (MLA); political science (MLA). Part-time and evening/weekend programs available. *Faculty:* 55 full-time (22 women), 114 part-time/adjunct (44 women). *Students:* 2 full-time, 41 part-time. 16 applicants, 56% accepted, 7 enrolled. In 2007, 17 degrees awarded. *Entrance requirements:* For master's, minimum GPA of 3.0. Additional exam requirements/recommendations for international students: Required—TOEFL. *Application deadline:* Applications are processed on a rolling basis. Application fee: $25. Electronic applications accepted. *Expenses:* Tuition: Full-time $9,144; part-time $508 per credit hour. *Financial support:* Federal Work-Study, institutionally sponsored loans, scholarships/grants, and tuition waivers (full and partial) available. Support available to part-time students. Financial award applicants required to submit FAFSA. *Faculty research:* Milton and seventeenth century Puritans, inter-Biblical years, nineteenth century literature, Latin American and Texas history. *Unit head:* Dr. David Stricklin, Acting Director, 214-333-5496, Fax: 214-333-5558, E-mail: graduate@dbu.edu. *Application contact:* Kit P. Montgomery, Director of Graduate Programs, 214-333-5242, Fax: 214-333-5579, E-mail: graduate@dbu.edu.

Dallas Baptist University, College of Adult Education, Professional Development Program, Dallas, TX 75211-9299. Offers accounting (MA); business (MA); church leadership (MA); corporate management (MA); counseling (MA); criminal justice (MA); English as a second language (MA); finance (MA); higher education (MA); leadership studies (MA); management (MA); management information systems (MA); marketing (MA); missions (MA). Part-time and evening/weekend programs available. *Faculty:* 55 full-time (22 women), 114 part-time/adjunct (44 women). *Students:* 19 full-time, 72 part-time. 35 applicants, 46% accepted, 12 enrolled. In 2007, 37 degrees awarded. *Entrance requirements:* For master's, minimum GPA of 3.0. Additional exam requirements/recommendations for international students: Required—TOEFL, IELTS. Application fee: $25. *Expenses:* Tuition: Full-time $9,144; part-time $508 per credit hour. *Financial support:* Federal Work-Study, institutionally sponsored loans, scholarships/grants, and tuition waivers (full and partial) available. Support available to part-time students. Financial award applicants required to submit FAFSA. *Unit head:* Dr. David Stricklin, Acting Director, 214-333-5496, Fax: 214-333-5558, E-mail: graduate@dbu.edu. *Application contact:* Kit P. Montgomery, Director of Graduate Programs, 214-333-5242, Fax: 214-333-5579, E-mail: graduate@dbu.edu.

Dallas Baptist University, Gary Cook School of Leadership and Christian Education, Program in Christian Education, Dallas, TX 75211-9299. Offers adult ministry (MA); business ministry (MA); childhood ministry (MA); collegiate ministry (MA); communication ministry (MA); counseling ministry (MA); education ministry (MA); general ministry (MA); missions ministry (MA); student ministry (MA); worship ministry (MA). Part-time and evening/weekend programs available. *Faculty:* 55 full-time (22 women), 114 part-time/adjunct (44 women). *Students:* 20 full-time, 52 part-time. 29 applicants, 52% accepted, 13 enrolled. In 2007, 34 degrees awarded. *Entrance requirements:* For master's, minimum GPA of 3.0. Additional exam requirements/recommendations for international students: Required—TOEFL. *Application deadline:* Applications are processed on a rolling basis. Application fee: $25. Electronic applications accepted. *Expenses:* Tuition: Full-time $9,144; part-time $508 per credit hour. *Financial support:* Federal Work-Study, institutionally sponsored loans, scholarships/grants, and tuition waivers (full and partial) available. Support available to part-time students. Financial award applicants required to submit FAFSA. *Unit head:* Dr. Judy Morris, Director, 214-333-5246, Fax: 214-333-5115, E-mail: graduate@dbu.edu. *Application contact:* Kit P. Montgomery, Director of Graduate Programs, 214-333-5242, Fax: 214-333-5579, E-mail: graduate@dbu.edu.

Dallas Baptist University, Gary Cook School of Leadership and Christian Education, Program in Global Leadership, Dallas, TX 75211-9299. Offers business communication (MA); Christian education/missions (MA); ESL (MA); general studies (MA); global studies (MA); international business (MA); missions (MA); worship/missions (MA). Part-time and evening/weekend programs available. *Faculty:* 55 full-time (22 women), 114 part-time/adjunct (44 women). *Students:* 2 full-time, 21 part-time. 20 applicants, 65% accepted, 13 enrolled. *Entrance requirements:* For master's, minimum GPA 3.0. Additional exam requirements/recommendations for international students: Required—TOEFL, IELTS. Application fee: $25. *Expenses:* Tuition: Full-time $9,144; part-time $508 per credit hour. *Financial support:* Federal Work-Study, institutionally sponsored loans, scholarships/grants, and tuition waivers (full and partial) available. Support available to part-time students. Financial award applicants required to submit FAFSA. *Unit head:* Dr. Jim Lemons, Director, 214-333-5506, Fax: 214-333-6955, E-mail: graduate@dbu.edu. *Application contact:* Kit P. Montgomery, Director of Graduate Programs, 214-333-5242, Fax: 214-333-5579, E-mail: graduate@dbu.edu.

Dallas Theological Seminary, Graduate Programs, Dallas, TX 75204-6499. Offers academic ministries (Th M); Bible translation (Th M); biblical and theological studies (CGS); biblical counseling (MA, Th M); biblical exegesis and linguistics (MA); biblical exposition (PhD); biblical studies (MA); Christian education (MA, D Min); cross-cultural ministries (MA, Th M); educational leadership (Th M); evangelism and discipleship (Th M); interdisciplinary studies (Th M); media and communication (MA); media arts in ministry (Th M); ministry (D Min); New Testament studies (Th M, PhD); Old Testament studies (PhD); parachurch ministries (Th M); pastoral ministries (Th M); sacred theology (STM); theological studies (PhD); women's ministry (Th M). *Accreditation:* ATS (one or more programs are accredited). Part-time and evening/weekend programs available. *Degree requirements:* For master's, variable foreign language requirement, thesis (for some programs); for doctorate, 2 foreign languages, thesis/dissertation. *Entrance requirements:* Additional exam requirements/recommendations for international students: Required—TOEFL, TWE. *Application deadline:* For fall admission, 7/1 priority date for domestic students; for winter admission, 11/1 priority date for domestic students; for spring admission, 11/15 priority date for domestic students. Applications are processed on a rolling basis. Application fee: $30. Electronic applications accepted. *Financial support:* Career-related internships or fieldwork, institutionally sponsored loans, scholarships/grants, and tuition waivers (full and partial) available. Financial award application deadline: 2/28. *Unit head:* Dr. Mark L. Bailey, President, 214-841-3676, Fax: 214-841-3565. *Application contact:* Josh Bleeker, Director of Admissions, 214-841-3661, Fax: 214-841-3664, E-mail: admissions@dts.edu.

Eastern University, Palmer Theological Seminary, Program in Renewal of the Church for Mission, St. Davids, PA 19087-3696. Offers D Min. *Degree requirements:* For doctorate, thesis/dissertation.

Fuller Theological Seminary, Graduate School of World Mission, Program in Global Ministries, Pasadena, CA 91182. Offers D Min. *Degree requirements:* For doctorate, one foreign language, thesis/dissertation. *Entrance requirements:* For doctorate, qualifying exam.

Fuller Theological Seminary, Graduate School of World Mission, Program in Intercultural Studies, Pasadena, CA 91182. Offers MA, Th M, PhD. *Degree requirements:* For master's, one foreign language, thesis optional; for doctorate, one foreign language, thesis/dissertation. *Entrance requirements:* For doctorate, qualifying exam, minimum GPA of 3.7, Th M and MA degrees from Graduate School of World Mission. Additional exam requirements/recommendations for international students: Required—TOEFL.

Fuller Theological Seminary, Graduate School of World Mission, Program in Missiology, Pasadena, CA 91182. Offers D Miss, PhD. *Degree requirements:* For doctorate, one foreign language, thesis/dissertation. *Entrance requirements:* For doctorate, qualifying exam, minimum GPA of 3.4 (D Miss), 3.7 (PhD), Th M and MA degrees from Graduate School of World Mission. Additional exam requirements/recommendations for international students: Required—TOEFL.

Gardner-Webb University, M. Christopher White School of Divinity, Boiling Springs, NC 28017. Offers Christian education (M Div); ministry (D Min); missiology (M Div); pastoral care and counseling (M Div); pastoral ministry (M Div); M Div/MA. *Accreditation:* ACIPE; ATS. Part-time programs available. *Degree requirements:* For M Div, 2 foreign languages. *Entrance requirements:* For M Div, minimum GPA of 2.0; for doctorate, minimum GPA of 2.75. Expenses: Contact institution. *Faculty research:* Jewish Christian dialogue, Islam.

Global University, Graduate School of Theology, Springfield, MO 65804. Offers biblical studies (MA); divinity (M Div); ministerial studies (MA), including education, leadership, missions, New Testament, Old Testament. Part-time and evening/weekend programs available. Postbaccalaureate distance learning degree programs offered (no on-campus study). *Faculty:* 10 full-time (1 woman), 83 part-time/adjunct (10 women). *Students:* 255 full-time (42 women), 297 part-time (55 women). Average age 41. 148 applicants, 94% accepted, 139 enrolled. In 2007, 28 degrees awarded. *Degree requirements:* For master's, thesis (for some programs). *Entrance requirements:* For M Div, minimum undergraduate GPA of 3.0; for master's, minimum undergraduate GPA of 3.0, 15 undergraduate credit hours of course work in Bible or theology. *Application deadline:* Applications are processed on a rolling basis. Application fee: $50. Electronic applications accepted. *Faculty research:* Higher education, cross-cultural missions. *Unit head:* Dr. Carl Chrisner, Dean, 417-862-9533 Ext. 2237, Fax: 417-869-5623, E-mail: cchrisner@globaluniversity.edu. *Application contact:* Jody Patterson, Graduate Student Enrollment Representative, 417-862-9533 Ext. 2347, Fax: 417-862-0863, E-mail: gradenroll@globaluniversity.edu.

Gordon-Conwell Theological Seminary, Graduate and Professional Programs, South Hamilton, MA 01982. Offers Christian education (MACE); church history (MACH); counseling (MACO); ministry (D Min); missions/evangelism (MAME); New Testament (MANT); Old Testament (MAOT); religion (MAR); theology (M Div, MATH, Th M). *Accreditation:* ACIPE; ATS (one or more programs are accredited). Part-time and evening/weekend programs available. *Degree requirements:* For master's, one foreign language, thesis optional; for doctorate, 2 foreign languages, thesis/dissertation; for M Div, 2 foreign languages. *Entrance requirements:* For M Div and master's, minimum GPA of 2.5; for doctorate, minimum GPA of 3.0.

Grace Theological Seminary, Graduate and Professional Programs, Winona Lake, IN 46590-9907. Offers biblical studies (Certificate, Diploma); counseling (M Div); ministry (MA); missions (M Div, MA); theology (M Div, MA, D Min). *Accreditation:* ATS. Part-time programs available. Postbaccalaureate distance learning degree programs offered (no on-campus study). *Degree requirements:* For master's, thesis optional; for doctorate, 2 foreign languages, thesis/dissertation; for M Div, 2 foreign languages, thesis/dissertation optional. *Entrance requirements:* For M Div and master's, MAT, minimum GPA of 2.5. Electronic applications accepted. *Faculty research:* Biblical theology, language, and church ministries.

Grand Rapids Theological Seminary of Cornerstone University, Graduate Programs, Grand Rapids, MI 49525-5897. Offers biblical counseling (MA); Biblical counseling (M Div); chaplaincy (M Div); Christian education (M Div, MA); intercultural studies (M Div, MA); New Testament (MA, Th M); Old Testament (MA, Th M); pastoral studies (M Div); systematic theology (MA); theology (Th M). *Accreditation:* ATS. Part-time programs available. Postbaccalaureate distance learning degree programs offered (minimal on-campus study). *Faculty:* 9 full-time (1 woman), 10 part-time/adjunct (1 woman). *Students:* 102 full-time (35 women), 126 part-time (42 women); includes 36 minority (28 African Americans, 2 American Indian/Alaska Native, 3 Asian Americans or Pacific Islanders, 3 Hispanic Americans), 7 international. Average age 35. 160 applicants, 91% accepted, 107 enrolled. *Entrance requirements:* Additional exam requirements/recommendations for international students: Required—TOEFL (minimum score 577 paper-based; 233 computer-based; 90 iBT). *Application deadline:* For fall admission, 8/15 for domestic students; for spring admission, 1/10 for domestic students. Applications are processed on a rolling basis. Electronic applications accepted. *Expenses:* Tuition: Full-time $6,930; part-time $385 per credit hour. Required fees: $520; $10 per credit hour. $170 per semester. Tuition and fees vary according to course load and degree level. *Financial support:* Career-related internships or fieldwork, scholarships/grants, and health care benefits available. Support available to part-time students. Financial award application deadline: 8/15; financial award applicants required to submit FAFSA. *Unit head:* Dr. Douglas L. Fagerstrom, President, 616-222-1422, Fax: 616-222-1502, E-mail: douglas_fagerstrom@cornerstone.edu. *Application contact:* Tara Danielle Kram, 800-697-1133, Fax: 616-254-1623, E-mail: tara_kram@cornerstone.edu.

Hope International University, School of Graduate Studies, Programs in Ministry, Fullerton, CA 92831-3138. Offers Christian leadership (MCM); church music (MA); church music (Korean track) (MCM); church planting (MCM); intercultural studies (MCM); worship (MCM). Part-time and evening/weekend programs available. Postbaccalaureate distance learning degree programs offered (minimal on-campus study). *Faculty:* 25. *Students:* 12 full-time (2 women), 42 part-time (15 women); includes 11 minority (2 African Americans, 7 Asian Americans or Pacific Islanders, 2 Hispanic Americans), 9 international. Average age 38. 16 applicants, 94% accepted, 14 enrolled. In 2007, 28 degrees awarded. *Degree requirements:* For master's, thesis (for some programs), project. *Entrance requirements:* For master's, minimum GPA of 3.0, MCM program

Missions and Missiology

Hope International University (continued)

requires an undergraduate degree in music, application, official transcripts, 2 references, statement of purpose. Additional exam requirements/recommendations for international students: Required—TOEFL (minimum score 550 paper-based; 213 computer-based; 86 iBT); Recommended—IELTS (minimum score 7). *Application deadline:* For fall admission, 8/3 priority date for domestic and international students; for winter admission, 12/14 priority date for domestic and international students; for spring admission, 1/4 priority date for domestic and international students. Applications are processed on a rolling basis. Application fee: $75. Electronic applications accepted. *Expenses: Contact institution. Financial support:* Scholarships/grants, health care benefits, and tuition waivers (partial) available. Support available to part-time students. Financial award applicants required to submit FAFSA. *Faculty research:* Church dynamics, growth methodologies. *Unit head:* Dr. David Timms, Chair, 714-879-3401 Ext. 2720, Fax: 714-681-7450, E-mail: djtimms@hiu.edu. *Application contact:* Ed Bort, Assistant Director of Admissions, 800-762-1294 Ext. 2322, Fax: 714-681-7450, E-mail: ebort@hiu.edu.

Knox Theological Seminary, Graduate Programs, Program in Evangelism, Fort Lauderdale, FL 33308. Offers ME. Part-time and evening/weekend programs available. *Faculty:* 5 full-time (0 women), 2 part-time/adjunct (0 women). *Students:* 1 full-time (0 women), 3 part-time (all women); includes 1 African American, 1 Asian American or Pacific Islander. Average age 38. *Entrance requirements:* Additional exam requirements/recommendations for international students: Required—TOEFL, TWE (minimum score 5). *Application deadline:* For fall admission, 6/1 priority date for domestic and international students; for winter admission, 12/1 priority date for domestic and international students; for spring admission, 1/1 priority date for domestic and international students. Applications are processed on a rolling basis. Application fee: $50. *Financial support:* In 2007–08, 3 students received support. Scholarships/grants available. Support available to part-time students. Financial award application deadline: 6/1. *Application contact:* Jim Dietz, Director of Student Services, 800-344-5669, Fax: 954-351-3343, E-mail: jdietz@knoxseminary.edu.

Luther Rice University, Graduate Programs, Lithonia, GA 30038-2454. Offers Bible/theology (M Div); Christian education (M Div); Christian studies (MA); church ministry (D Min); counseling (M Div); discipleship counseling (MA); ministry (M Div, MA); missions/evangelism (M Div). Part-time programs available. Postbaccalaureate distance learning degree programs offered (no on-campus study). *Degree requirements:* For doctorate, thesis/dissertation. *Entrance requirements:* Additional exam requirements/recommendations for international students: Required—TOEFL (minimum score 500 paper-based; 173 computer-based).

Mennonite Brethren Biblical Seminary, School of Theology, Program in Intercultural Mission, Fresno, CA 93727-5097. Offers MA. *Students:* Average age 30. 13 applicants, 92% accepted, 10 enrolled.Application fee: $35. *Unit head:* Mark Baker, Head, 559-452-1768. *Application contact:* Andy Johnson, Director of Recruitment, 559-452-1714, Fax: 559-251-7212, E-mail: ajohnson@mbseminary.edu.

Nazarene Theological Seminary, Graduate and Professional Programs, Kansas City, MO 64131-1263. Offers Christian education (MA); intercultural studies (MA); theological studies (MA); theology (M Div, D Min). *Accreditation:* ACIPE; ATS. Part-time programs available. *Faculty:* 19 full-time (3 women), 12 part-time/adjunct (2 women). *Students:* 154 full-time (43 women), 156 part-time (38 women); includes 21 minority (5 African Americans, 3 American Indian/Alaska Native, 5 Asian Americans or Pacific Islanders, 8 Hispanic Americans), 16 international. Average age 31. 129 applicants, 77% accepted, 71 enrolled. In 2007, 40 first professional degrees, 22 master's, 2 doctorates awarded. *Degree requirements:* For master's, comprehensive exam (for some programs), thesis (for some programs); for doctorate, thesis/dissertation. *Entrance requirements:* Additional exam requirements/recommendations for international students: Required—TOEFL. *Application deadline:* For fall admission, 8/1 priority date for domestic students; for spring admission, 12/1 for domestic students. Applications are processed on a rolling basis. Application fee: $25 ($200 for international students). Electronic applications accepted. *Expenses:* Tuition: Full-time $8,544; part-time $356 per credit. Required fees: $75 per semester. *Financial support:* In 2007–08, 235 students received support, including 15 teaching assistantships (averaging $1,400 per year); institutionally sponsored loans and scholarships/grants also available. Support available to part-time students. Financial award application deadline: 3/1; financial award applicants required to submit FAFSA. *Unit head:* Dr. Roger L. Hahn, Dean of the Faculty, 816-268-5412, Fax: 816-268-5500, E-mail: rlhahn@nts.edu. *Application contact:* Jay A. Sandbloom, Director of Admissions, 816-268-5451, Fax: 816-268-5500, E-mail: jasandbloom@nts.edu.

Northwest Nazarene University, Graduate Studies, Program in Religion, Nampa, ID 83686-5897. Offers Christian education (MA); missional leadership (MA); pastoral ministry (MA); religion (M Div); spiritual formation (MA). Part-time and evening/weekend programs available. Postbaccalaureate distance learning degree programs offered (no on-campus study). *Faculty:* 9 full-time (3 women), 15 part-time/adjunct (3 women). *Students:* 131 full-time (35 women), 12 part-time (5 women); includes 9 minority (1 African American, 1 American Indian/Alaska Native, 5 Asian Americans or Pacific Islanders, 2 Hispanic Americans), 3 international. In 2007, 29 degrees awarded. *Application deadline:* Applications are processed on a rolling basis. Application fee: $50. Electronic applications accepted. *Unit head:* Dr. Jay Akkerman, Director, Graduate Studies, 208-467-8437, Fax: 208-467-8252.

Oral Roberts University, School of Theology and Missions, Tulsa, OK 74171-0001. Offers biblical literature (MA), including advanced languages, Judaic-Christian studies; Christian counseling (MA), including marriage and family therapy; Christian education (MA); divinity (M Div); missions (MA); practical theology (MA); theological/historical studies (MA); theology (D Min). *Accreditation:* ATS; NASM. Part-time programs available. Postbaccalaureate distance learning degree programs offered (minimal on-campus study). *Faculty:* 17 full-time (2 women). *Students:* 371 full-time (156 women), 110 part-time (65 women); includes 177 minority (127 African Americans, 5 American Indian/Alaska Native, 20 Asian Americans or Pacific Islanders, 25 Hispanic Americans), 82 international. Average age 36. 159 applicants, 95% accepted, 124 enrolled. In 2007, 38 first professional degrees, 52 master's, 10 doctorates awarded. *Degree requirements:* For master's, thesis (for some programs), practicum/internship; for doctorate, thesis/dissertation, applied research project; for M Div, one foreign language, field experience. *Entrance requirements:* For M Div and master's, GRE General Test or MAT, minimum GPA of 2.5; for doctorate, M Div, minimum GPA of 3.0, 3 years of full-time ministry experience. Additional exam requirements/recommendations for international students: Required—TOEFL (minimum score 500 paper-based; 213 computer-based; 79 iBT). *Application deadline:* For fall admission, 7/1 priority date for domestic and international students; for spring admission, 12/1 priority date for domestic students, 10/1 priority date for international students. Applications are processed on a rolling basis. Application fee: $35. Electronic applications accepted. *Expenses:* Tuition: Part-time $450 per hour. Required fees: $125 per semester. Tuition and fees vary according to class time, degree level and program. *Financial support:* In 2007–08, teaching assistantships (averaging $3,600 per year); scholarships/grants and employment assistantships also available. Financial award application deadline: 6/1; financial award applicants required to submit FAFSA. *Unit head:* Dr. Thomson K. Mathew, Dean, 918-495-7016, Fax: 918-495-6259, E-mail: tmathew@oru.edu. *Application contact:* Debra E. Watkins, Graduate Theology Representative, 918-495-6618, Fax: 918-495-7965, E-mail: owatkins@oru.edu.

Phillips Theological Seminary, Programs in Theology, Tulsa, OK 74116. Offers administration of church agencies (M Div); campus ministry (M Div); church-related social work (M Div); college and seminary teaching (M Div); global mission work (M Div); institutional chaplaincy (M Div); ministerial vocations in Christian education (M Div); ministry (D Min), including parish ministry, pastoral counseling, practices of ministry; ministry and culture (MAMC), including Christian education, congregational leadership, history and practice of Christian spirituality, theology, ethics, and culture; ministry of music (M Div); pastoral care and counseling (M Div); pastoral ministry (M Div); theological studies (MTS). *Accreditation:* ATS. Part-time programs available. Postbaccalaureate distance learning degree programs offered (minimal on-campus study). *Degree requirements:* For master's, thesis (for some programs); for doctorate, thesis/dissertation. *Entrance requirements:* For master's, minimum GPA of 2.5; for doctorate, M Div, minimum GPA of 3.0. *Faculty research:* Biblical studies, historical studies, theology and culture, practical theology, theology and film.

Providence College and Theological Seminary, Theological Seminary, Otterburne, MB R0A 1G0, Canada. Offers children's ministry (Certificate); Christian studies (MA, Certificate); counseling (MA); cross-cultural discipleship (Certificate); divinity (M Div); educational studies (MA), including counseling psychology, educational ministries, student development, teaching English to speakers of other languages, training teachers of English to speakers of other languages; global studies (MA); lay counseling (Diploma); ministry (D Min); teaching English to speakers of other languages (Certificate); theological studies (MA); training teacher of English to speakers of other languages (Certificate); youth ministry (Certificate). *Accreditation:* ATS. Part-time programs available. *Degree requirements:* For master's, variable foreign language requirement, thesis (for some programs); for doctorate, thesis/dissertation; for M Div, 2 foreign languages, comprehensive exam, thesis/dissertation (for some programs). *Entrance requirements:* Additional exam requirements/recommendations for international students: Recommended—TOEFL (minimum score 550 paper-based; 213 computer-based). *Faculty research:* Studies in Isaiah, theology of sin.

Reformed Theological Seminary–Jackson Campus, Graduate and Professional Programs, Jackson, MS 39209-3099. Offers Bible, theology, and missions (Certificate); biblical studies (MA); Christian education (M Div, MA); counseling (M Div); divinity (M Div, Diploma); marriage and family therapy (MA); ministry (D Min); missions (M Div, MA, D Min); New Testament (Th M); Old Testament (Th M); theological studies (MA); theology (Th M); M Div/MA. *Accreditation:* AAMFT/COAMFTE (one or more programs are accredited); ATS (one or more programs are accredited). *Degree requirements:* For master's, thesis (for some programs), fieldwork; for doctorate, 2 foreign languages, thesis/dissertation; for M Div, 2 foreign languages, thesis/dissertation (for some programs). *Entrance requirements:* For M Div and master's, minimum GPA of 2.6; for doctorate, minimum GPA of 3.0. Additional exam requirements/recommendations for international students: Required—TOEFL.

Regent University, Graduate School, School of Divinity, Virginia Beach, VA 23464-9800. Offers biblical studies (MA); leadership and renewal (D Min); missiology (M Div, MA); practical theology (M Div, MA); renewal studies (PhD); M Div/M Ed; M Div/MA; M Div/MBA; M Ed/MA; MBA/MA. *Accreditation:* ACIPE; ATS. Part-time programs available. Postbaccalaureate distance learning degree programs offered (minimal on-campus study). *Faculty:* 18 full-time (4 women), 22 part-time/adjunct (7 women). *Students:* 186 full-time (76 women), 437 part-time (163 women); includes 249 minority (212 African Americans, 2 American Indian/Alaska Native, 13 Asian Americans or Pacific Islanders, 22 Hispanic Americans), 61 international. Average age 38. 302 applicants, 70% accepted, 114 enrolled. In 2007, 56 first professional degrees, 16 master's, 62 doctorates awarded. *Degree requirements:* For master's, comprehensive exam, thesis or alternative, internship; for doctorate, thesis/dissertation or alternative; for M Div, internship. *Entrance requirements:* For M Div, GRE General Test or MAT, minimum undergraduate GPA of 3.0, minimum 3 years of ministry experience, transcripts, recommendations; for master's, GRE General Test or MAT, minimum undergraduate GPA of 2.75, writing sample, clergy recommendation, transcripts ; for doctorate, M Div or theological master's degree, minimum graduate GPA of 3.5 (PhD), 3.0 (D Min), recommendations, writing sample, transcripts . Additional exam requirements/recommendations for international students: Required—TOEFL (minimum score 577 paper-based; 233 computer-based). *Application deadline:* For fall admission, 5/1 priority date for domestic students. Applications are processed on a rolling basis. Application fee: $50. Electronic applications accepted. *Expenses: Contact institution. Financial support:* In 2007–08, 500 students received support; fellowships with full and partial tuition reimbursements available, career-related internships or fieldwork, scholarships/grants, tuition waivers (full and partial), and unspecified assistantships available. Support available to part-time students. Financial award application deadline: 9/1; financial award applicants required to submit FAFSA. *Faculty research:* Greek and Hebrew etymology. *Unit head:* Dr. Michael Palmer, Dean, 757-226-4406, Fax: 757-226-4597, E-mail: mpalmer@regent.edu. *Application contact:* Althea Bishard, Registrar and Executive Director of Enrollment and Academic Services, 800-373-5504, Fax: 757-226-4381, E-mail: admissions@regent.edu.

Saint Paul University, Faculty of Human Sciences, Program in Mission and Interreligious Studies, Ottawa, ON K1S 1C4, Canada. Offers MA. *Faculty:* 3 full-time (0 women), 9 part-time/adjunct (0 women). *Students:* 24 full-time (14 women), 6 part-time (all women); includes 7 minority (5 African Americans, 1 Asian American or Pacific Islander, 1 Hispanic American). Average age 43. 10 applicants, 70% accepted, 5 enrolled. In 2007, 3 degrees awarded. *Degree requirements:* For master's, one foreign language, thesis. *Entrance requirements:* For master's, honors BA in mission, minimum B average. *Application deadline:* For fall admission, 9/15 priority date for domestic students. Applications are processed on a rolling basis. Application fee: $60. *Financial support:* In 2007–08, 6 students received support. Application deadline: 5/1. *Faculty research:* Theology of mission; mission and sociology; history of mission; faith, religion, and culture; world religions; practice of mission; religious anthropology; sociocultural anthropology. *Unit head:* Peter Pandimakil, Head, 613-236-1393, E-mail: ppandimakil@ustpaul.ca. *Application contact:* Diane Boudroault, Head, 613-236-1393 Ext. 2292, E-mail: dboudreault@ustpaul.ca.

Simpson University, A.W. Tozer Theological Seminary, Redding, CA 96003-8606. Offers Christian leadership (MA); Christian studies (MA); intercultural studies (MA); ministry (M Div). Part-time and evening/weekend programs available. Postbaccalaureate distance learning degree programs offered (minimal on-campus study). *Faculty:* 6 part-time/adjunct (0 women). *Students:* 6 full-time (0 women), 49 part-time (13 women); includes 7 minority (3 African Americans, 2 Asian Americans or Pacific Islanders, 2 Hispanic Americans), 1 international. Average age 38. 22 applicants, 73% accepted, 16 enrolled. In 2007, 5 degrees awarded. *Degree requirements:* For master's, student portfolio. *Entrance requirements:* For master's, GRE General Test (if undergraduate GPA is below 2.5), 2 letters of reference, Christian Experience statement. Additional exam requirements/recommendations for international students: Required—TOEFL. *Application deadline:* For fall admission, 9/4 priority date for domestic students, 9/4 for international students; for spring admission, 1/8 priority date for domestic students, 1/8 for international students. Applications are processed on a rolling basis. Application fee: $20. Electronic applications accepted. *Expenses: Contact institution. Financial support:* Scholarships/grants available. Support available to part-time students. Financial award application deadline: 3/20; financial award applicants required to submit FAFSA. *Unit head:* Dr. Robert Redman, Dean, 530-226-4144, Fax: 530-326-4871, E-mail: rredman@simpsonuniversity.edu. *Application contact:* Jeff Williams, Director of Enrollment Development, 530-226-4611, Fax: 530-226-4861, E-mail: jwilliams@simpsonuniversity.edu.

Southeastern Baptist Theological Seminary, Graduate and Professional Programs, Wake Forest, NC 27588-1889. Offers advanced biblical studies (M Div); Christian education (M Div, MACE); Christian ethics (PhD); Christian ministry (M Div); Christian planting (M Div); church music (MACM); counseling (MACO); evangelism (PhD); language (M Div); ministry (D Min); New Testament (PhD); Old Testament (PhD); philosophy (PhD); theology (Th M, PhD); women's studies (M Div). *Accreditation:* ACIPE; ATS (one or more programs are accredited). *Degree requirements:* For master's, thesis (for some programs), oral exam; for doctorate, thesis/dissertation, fieldwork; for M Div, supervised ministry. *Entrance requirements:* For master's, Cooperative English Test, minimum GPA of 2.0, M Div or equivalent (Th M); for doctorate, GRE General Test or MAT, Cooperative English Test, M Div or equivalent, 3 years of professional experience.

Southern Adventist University, School of Religion, Collegedale, TN 37315-0370. Offers Biblical and theological studies (MA); church leadership and management (MA); church ministry and homiletics (MA); evangelism and world mission (MA); religious studies (MA). Summer program only. Part-time programs available. *Faculty:* 5 full-time (0 women). *Students:* 2 full-time (0 women), 1 part-time; includes 1 minority (Asian American or Pacific Islander) Average age 36. 9 applicants, 100% accepted. In 2007, 6 degrees awarded. *Degree* *requirements:* For master's, comprehensive exam, thesis (for some programs). *Entrance requirements:* For master's, GRE. Additional exam requirements/recommendations for international students: Required—TOEFL (minimum score 550 paper-based). *Application deadline:* For spring admission, 4/30 priority date for domestic students, 12/30 for international students. Applications are processed on a rolling basis. Application fee: $25. *Financial support:* In 2007–08, 4 students received support. Tuition waivers (full) available. Support available to part-time students. Financial award application deadline: 4/1; financial award applicants required to submit FAFSA. *Faculty research:* Biblical archaeology. *Unit head:* Dr. Greg A. King, Dean, 423-236-2975, Fax: 423-236-1976, E-mail: gking@southern.edu. *Application contact:* Susan L. Brown, Administrative Assistant, 423-236-2977, Fax: 423-236-1977, E-mail: sbrown@southern.edu.

Southern Baptist Theological Seminary, Billy Graham School of Missions, Evangelism, and Church Growth, Louisville, KY 40280-0004. Offers Christian mission/world religion (PhD); evangelism/church growth (PhD); ministry (D Min); missiology (MA, D Miss); missions, evangelism, and church growth (M Div); theology (Th M). *Accreditation:* ATS. Part-time and evening/weekend programs available. Postbaccalaureate distance learning degree programs offered (minimal on-campus study). *Degree requirements:* For master's and M Div, 2 foreign languages; for doctorate, 4 foreign languages, thesis/dissertation. *Entrance requirements:* For doctorate, GRE General Test, MAT, field essay, M Div. Additional exam requirements/recommendations for international students: Required—TOEFL, TWE. *Faculty research:* Assimilation of church congregants, effective methodologies of evangelism, expectations of church members, spiritual warfare literature, formative church discipline.

Southern Evangelical Seminary, Graduate School of Ministry and Missions, Matthews, NC 28105. Offers apologetics (Certificate); Christian education (MA); church ministry (MA, Certificate); divinity (Certificate), including apologetics (M Div, Certificate); Islamic studies (Certificate); theology (M Div), including apologetics (M Div, Certificate), Biblical studies; youth ministry (MA). Part-time and evening/weekend programs available. Postbaccalaureate distance learning degree programs offered. In 2007, 3 degrees awarded. *Degree requirements:* For master's, thesis (for some programs); for M Div, one foreign language. *Entrance requirements:* Additional exam requirements/recommendations for international students: Required—TOEFL (minimum score 600 paper-based; 250 computer-based). *Application deadline:* For fall admission, 8/15 priority date for domestic students, 8/5 priority date for international students; for winter admission, 12/15 priority date for domestic and international students; for spring admission, 1/15 priority date for domestic and international students. Applications are processed on a rolling basis. Application fee: $25. *Financial support:* Scholarships/grants available. *Unit head:* Dr. Barry R. Leventhal, Dean, 704-847-5600 Ext. 204, Fax: 704-845-1747, E-mail: dean@ses.edu.

Taylor University College and Seminary, Graduate and Professional Programs, Edmonton, AB T6J 4T3, Canada. Offers Christian studies (Diploma); intercultural studies (MA, Diploma); theology (M Div, MTS). *Accreditation:* ATS. Part-time programs available. *Degree requirements:* For master's, comprehensive exam, thesis optional. *Entrance requirements:* Additional exam requirements/recommendations for international students: Required—TOEFL (minimum score 550 paper-based; 213 computer-based), IELTS (minimum score 7). *Faculty research:* Biblical studies, administration and organization, world religions.

Trinity Episcopal School for Ministry, Graduate Programs, Ambridge, PA 15003-2397. Offers Anglican studies (Diploma); basic Christian studies (Diploma); divinity (M Div); ministry (D Min); mission and evangelism (MAME, Diploma); religion (MAR); youth ministry (Diploma). *Accreditation:* ATS (one or more programs are accredited). Part-time programs available. *Degree requirements:* For master's, thesis optional; for doctorate, thesis/dissertation; for M Div, thesis/dissertation optional, Greek and Hebrew. *Entrance requirements:* Additional exam requirements/recommendations for international students: Required—TOEFL. *Faculty research:* Pauline Epistles, contemporary theology, history of Anglican liturgy, book of Ruth, biblical theology.

Trinity International University, Trinity Evangelical Divinity School, Deerfield, IL 60015-1284. Offers Biblical and Near Eastern archaeology and languages (MA); Christian studies (MA, Certificate); Christian thought (MA); church history (MA, Th M); congregational ministry: pastor-teacher (M Div); congregational ministry: team ministry (M Div); counseling ministries (MA); counseling psychology (MA); cross-cultural ministry (M Div); educational studies (PhD); evangelism (MA); history of Christianity in America (MA); intercultural studies (MA, PhD); leadership and ministry management (D Min); military chaplaincy (D Min); ministry (MA); mission and evangelism (Th M); missions and evangelism (D Min); New Testament (MA, Th M); Old Testament (Th M); Old Testament and Semitic languages (MA); pastoral care (M Div); pastoral care and counseling (D Min); pastoral counseling and psychology (Th M); pastoral theology (Th M); philosophy of religion (MA); preaching (D Min); religion (MA); research ministry (M Div); systematic theology (Th M); theological studies (PhD); urban ministry (MA). *Accreditation:* ATS (one or more programs are accredited). Part-time programs available. Postbaccalaureate distance learning degree programs offered (minimal on-campus study). *Faculty:* 41 full-time (4 women), 77 part-time/adjunct (17 women). *Students:* 578 full-time (141 women), 711 part-time (202 women). In 2007, 92 first professional degrees, 78 master's, 47 doctorates, 23 other advanced degrees awarded. *Degree requirements:* For master's, comprehensive exam, thesis, fieldwork; for doctorate, comprehensive exam (for some programs), thesis/dissertation; for M Div, 2 foreign languages, fieldwork; for Certificate, comprehensive exam, integrative papers. *Entrance requirements:* For M Div, GRE, MAT; for master's, GRE, MAT, minimum cumulative undergraduate GPA of 3.0; for doctorate, GRE, minimum cumulative graduate GPA of 3.2; for Certificate, GRE, MAT, minimum undergraduate GPA of 2.5. Additional exam requirements/recommendations for international students: Required—TOEFL (minimum score 580 paper-based; 237 computer-based), TWE (minimum score 4). *Application deadline:* For fall admission, 7/15 priority date for domestic and international students. Applications are processed on a rolling basis. Application fee: $25. Electronic applications accepted. *Expenses:* Tuition: Full-time $13,200; part-time $630 per credit. Required fees: $170. *Financial support:* In 2007–08, 770 students received support, including 10 fellowships with partial tuition reimbursements available (averaging $6,920 per year); teaching assistantships with partial tuition reimbursements available, career-related internships or fieldwork, Federal Work-Study, scholarships/grants, and tuition waivers (partial) also available. Financial award application deadline: 4/1; financial award applicants required to submit FAFSA. *Unit head:* Dr. Tite Tiénou, Academic Dean, 847-317-8086, Fax: 847-317-8014, E-mail: ttienou@teds.edu. *Application contact:* Ron Campbell, Director of Admissions, 800-345-8337, Fax: 847-317-8097, E-mail: rcampbel@tiu.edu.

Tyndale University College & Seminary, Graduate Programs, Toronto, ON M2M 4B3, Canada. Offers Biblical studies (M Div); Christian foundations (MTS); Christian studies (Diploma); counseling (M Div); educational ministry (M Div); missions (M Div, Diploma); pastoral and Chinese ministry (M Div); pastoral ministry (M Div); Pentecostal studies (MTS); spiritual formation (M Div, Diploma); theological studies (M Div); theology (Th M); worship and liturgy (M Div, MTS); youth and family ministry (M Div). *Accreditation:* ATS. Part-time programs available. Postbaccalaureate distance learning degree programs offered (no on-campus study). *Degree requirements:* For M Div, one foreign language, thesis/dissertation optional. *Entrance requirements:* For M Div, master's, and Diploma, minimum C+ average in undergraduate course work. Additional exam requirements/recommendations for international students: Required—TOEFL (minimum score 570 paper-based; 230 computer-based), TWE (minimum score 5). Electronic applications accepted. *Faculty research:* Canadian church history, Chinese church history, Old Testament, counseling ministries (narrative therapy), world religions.

University of South Africa, College of Human Sciences, Pretoria, South Africa. Offers adult education (M Ed); African languages (MA, PhD); African politics (MA, PhD); Afrikaans (MA, PhD); ancient history (MA, PhD); ancient Near Eastern studies (MA, PhD); anthropology (MA, PhD); applied linguistics (MA); Arabic (MA, PhD); archaeology (MA); art history (MA); Biblical archaeology (MA); Biblical studies (M Th, D Th, PhD); Christian spirituality (M Th, D Th); church history (M Th, D Th); classical studies (MA, PhD); clinical psychology (MA); communication (MA, PhD); comparative education (M Ed, Ed D); consulting psychology (D Admin, D Com, PhD); curriculum studies (M Ed, Ed D); development studies (M Admin, MA, D Admin, PhD); didactics (M Ed, Ed D); education (M Tech); education management (M Ed, Ed D); educational psychology (M Ed); English (MA); environmental education (M Ed); French (MA, PhD); German (MA, PhD); Greek (MA); guidance and counseling (M Ed); health studies (MA, PhD), including health sciences education (MA), health services management (MA), medical and surgical nursing science (critical care general) (MA), midwifery and neonatal nursing science (MA), trauma and emergency care (MA); history (MA, PhD); history of education (Ed D); inclusive education (M Ed, Ed D); information and communications technology policy and regulation (MA); information science (MA, MIS, PhD); international politics (MA, PhD); Islamic studies (MA, PhD); Italian (MA, PhD); Judaica (MA, PhD); linguistics (MA, PhD); mathematical education (M Ed); mathematics education (MA); missiology (M Th, D Th); modern Hebrew (MA, PhD); musicology (MA, MMus, D Mus, PhD); natural science education (M Ed); New Testament (M Th, D Th); Old Testament (D Th); pastoral therapy (M Th, D Th); philosophy (MA); philosophy of education (M Ed, Ed D); politics (MA, PhD); Portuguese (MA, PhD); practical theology (M Th, D Th); psychology (MA, MS, PhD); psychology of education (M Ed, Ed D); public health (MA); religious studies (MA, D Th, PhD); Romance languages (MA); Russian (MA, PhD); Semitic languages (MA, PhD); social behavior studies in HIV/AIDS (MA); social science (mental health) (MA); social science in development studies (MA); social science in psychology (MA); social science in social work (MA); social science in sociology (MA); social work (MSW, DSW, PhD); socio-education (M Ed, Ed D); sociolinguistics (MA); sociology (MA, PhD); Spanish (MA, PhD); systematic theology (M Th, D Th); TESOL (teaching English to speakers of other languages) (MA); theological ethics (M Th, D Th); theory of literature (MA, PhD); urban ministries (D Th); urban ministry (M Th).

Wesley Biblical Seminary, Graduate Programs, Jackson, MS 39206. Offers Biblical literature (MA); Christian studies (MA); evangelism (M Div); family life ministry (M Div); honors research (M Div); missions (M Div); pastoral ministry (M Div); teaching (M Div); theology (MA). *Accreditation:* ATS. Part-time programs available. *Degree requirements:* For master's, thesis. *Entrance requirements:* Additional exam requirements/recommendations for international students: Required—TOEFL. *Application deadline:* For fall admission, 7/1 priority date for domestic students; for spring admission, 12/1 priority date for domestic students. Applications are processed on a rolling basis. Application fee: $25. Electronic applications accepted. *Financial support:* Scholarships/grants available. Support available to part-time students. *Faculty research:* Patristics, missiology, culture, hermeneutics. *Unit head:* Dr. Ray R. Easley, Vice President for Academic Affairs, 601-366-8880 Ext. 112, Fax: 601-366-8832. *Application contact:* Megan Tirrill, Assistant to the Vice President for Student Development, 800-366-8880 Ext. 110, Fax: 601-366-8832, E-mail: mtirrill@wbs.edu.

Westminster Theological Seminary, Graduate and Professional Programs, Philadelphia, PA 19118. Offers apologetics (Th M); Biblical and urban studies (Certificate); Biblical counseling (MA); biblical studies (MAR); Christian studies (Certificate); church history (Th M); counseling (M Div); general studies (M Div, MAR); hermeneutics and Bible interpretations (PhD); historical and theological studies (PhD); historical theology (Th M); New Testament (Th M); Old Testament (Th M); pastoral counseling (D Min); pastoral ministry (M Div, D Min); systematic theology (Th M); theological studies (MAR); urban missions (M Div, MA, MAR, D Min). *Accreditation:* ATS. Part-time programs available. Terminal master's awarded for partial completion of doctoral program. *Degree requirements:* For master's, thesis (for some programs); for doctorate, 4 foreign languages, comprehensive exam (for some programs), thesis/dissertation; for M Div, 2 foreign languages. *Entrance requirements:* For doctorate, GRE General Test. Additional exam requirements/recommendations for international students: Required—TOEFL, TWE.

Wheaton College, Graduate School, Department of Intercultural Studies, Wheaton, IL 60187-5593. Offers evangelism (MA); intercultural studies (MA); intercultural studies/teaching English as a second language (MA); missions (MA); teaching English as a second language (Certificate). Part-time programs available. *Faculty:* 5 full-time (2 women), 4 part-time/adjunct (2 women). *Students:* 76. 69 applicants, 75% accepted, 33 enrolled. In 2007, 29 degrees awarded. *Degree requirements:* For master's, thesis or alternative. *Entrance requirements:* For master's, GRE General Test, MAT. *Application deadline:* For fall admission, 3/1 priority date for domestic students; for spring admission, 11/1 for domestic students. Applications are processed on a rolling basis. Application fee: $30. Electronic applications accepted. *Financial support:* Career-related internships or fieldwork, scholarships/grants, and unspecified assistantships available. Financial award application deadline: 3/1; financial award applicants required to submit FAFSA. *Unit head:* Dr. Evvy Campbell, Chair, 630-752-5258. *Application contact:* Julie A. Huebner, Director of Graduate Admissions, 630-752-5195, Fax: 630-752-5935, E-mail: gradadm@wheaton.edu.

Pastoral Ministry and Counseling

Abilene Christian University, Graduate School, College of Biblical Studies, Graduate School of Theology, Program in Ministry, Abilene, TX 79699-9100. Offers D Min. Part-time programs available. *Students:* 7 applicants, 86% accepted, 5 enrolled. In 2007, 7 degrees awarded. *Degree requirements:* For doctorate, one foreign language, thesis/dissertation. *Entrance requirements:* For doctorate, GRE, MAT. *Application deadline:* For fall admission, 4/1 priority date for domestic students; for spring admission, 11/1 for domestic students. Applications are processed on a rolling basis. Application fee: $40 ($45 for international students). *Expenses:* Tuition: Full-time $13,368; part-time $557 per hour. Required fees: $700; $34 per hour. $10 per semester. Tuition and fees vary according to degree level and campus/location. *Financial support:* Application deadline: 4/1. *Faculty research:* Church growth, ministry evaluation, leadership. *Unit head:* Dr. Charles Siburt, Graduate Adviser, 325-674-3732, Fax: 325-674-6180, E-mail: siburt@bible.acu.edu. *Application contact:* William Horn, Graduate Admissions Counselor, 325-674-2656, Fax: 325-674-6717, E-mail: gradinfo@acu.edu.

Abilene Christian University, Graduate School, College of Biblical Studies, Graduate School of Theology, Programs in Christian Ministry, Abilene, TX 79699-9100. Offers MACM. Part-time programs available. *Students:* 21 full-time (6 women), 36 part-time (8 women); includes 2 minority (1 American Indian/Alaska Native, 1 Hispanic American), 8 international. 17 applicants, 65% accepted, 13 enrolled. In 2007, 11 degrees awarded. *Degree requirements:* For master's, comprehensive exam. *Entrance requirements:* For master's, GRE General Test or MAT. *Application deadline:* For fall admission, 4/1 priority date for domestic students; for spring admission, 11/1 for domestic students. Applications are processed on a rolling basis. Application fee: $40 ($45 for international students). Electronic applications accepted. *Expenses:* Tuition: Full-time $13,368; part-time $557 per hour. Required fees: $700; $34 per hour. $10 per semester.

Pastoral Ministry and Counseling

Abilene Christian University (continued)
Tuition and fees vary according to degree level and campus/location. *Financial support:* Application deadline: 4/1. *Faculty research:* Program innovation, instruments for educational evaluation. *Unit head:* Dr. B.J. McMichael, Graduate Advisor, 325-674-3735, Fax: 325-674-6108, E-mail: mcmichael@bible.acu.edu. *Application contact:* William Horn, Graduate Admissions Counselor, 325-674-2656, Fax: 325-674-6717, E-mail: gradinfo@acu.edu.

Alliance Theological Seminary, Graduate and Professional Programs, Nyack, NY 10960. Offers Christian ministry (MPS); counseling (MA); intercultural studies (MA); missions (MPS); New Testament (MA); Old Testament (MA); theology (M Div); urban ministry (MPS). *Accreditation:* ATS. Part-time programs available. *Faculty:* 19 full-time (3 women), 9 part-time/adjunct (1 woman). *Students:* 195 full-time (66 women), 452 part-time (207 women); includes 505 minority (239 African Americans, 1 American Indian/Alaska Native, 113 Asian Americans or Pacific Islanders, 152 Hispanic Americans), 35 international. Average age 39. 224 applicants, 98% accepted, 200 enrolled. In 2007, 63 first professional degrees, 46 master's awarded. *Degree requirements:* For master's, comprehensive exam (for some programs), thesis optional, internships; for M Div, 2 foreign languages, internship. *Entrance requirements:* Proficiency in New Testament Greek, minimum GPA of 2.5 (undergraduate). Additional exam requirements/recommendations for international students: Required—TOEFL (minimum score 550 paper-based; 213 computer-based). *Application deadline:* For fall admission, 6/1 priority date for international students; for spring admission, 11/1 priority date for international students. Applications are processed on a rolling basis. *Expenses:* Tuition: Part-time $450 per credit. Required fees: $20 per term. Tuition and fees vary according to course load. *Financial support:* Research assistantships, career-related internships or fieldwork, Federal Work-Study, and scholarships/grants available. Financial award applicants required to submit FAFSA. *Unit head:* Bennett Schepens, Assistant Vice President and Academic Dean, 845-353-2020, Fax: 845-358-2651. *Application contact:* Karen Shaffstall, Director of Admissions, 845-353-2020, Fax: 845-348-3912, E-mail: admissions.ats@nyack.edu.

Ambrose University College, Ambrose Seminary, Calgary, AB T2P 3T5, Canada. Offers biblical/theological studies (MA); Chinese ministries (Certificate); Christian studies (Diploma); church education (M Div); intercultural ministries (M Div, MA, Certificate, Diploma); leadership and ministry (MA, Certificate, Diploma); pastoral ministries (M Div). *Accreditation:* ATS (one or more programs are accredited). Part-time programs available. *Faculty:* 6 full-time (0 women), 28 part-time/adjunct (4 women). *Students:* 44 full-time (13 women), 118 part-time (45 women); includes 59 minority (2 African Americans, 2 American Indian/Alaska Native, 54 Asian Americans or Pacific Islanders, 1 Hispanic American). Average age 41. 45 applicants, 82% accepted, 37 enrolled. In 2007, 7 first professional degrees, 17 master's, 2 other advanced degrees awarded. *Degree requirements:* For master's, 2 foreign languages, internship; for M Div, one foreign language, internship. *Entrance requirements:* For master's, bachelor degree. Additional exam requirements/recommendations for international students: Required—TOEFL or IELTS. *Application deadline:* For fall admission, 7/31 priority date for domestic students, 3/1 priority date for international students; for winter admission, 11/30 priority date for domestic students, 6/1 priority date for international students. Applications are processed on a rolling basis. Application fee: $50. Electronic applications accepted. Tuition and fees charges are reported in Canadian dollars. *Expenses:* Tuition: Part-time $281 Canadian dollars per credit hour. Required fees: $16 Canadian dollars per credit hour. *Financial support:* In 2007–08, 40 students received support. Career-related internships or fieldwork and scholarships/grants available. Support available to part-time students. Financial award application deadline: 3/30. *Faculty research:* Evangelicalism and sociology, missiological trends, chaplaincy, intertestamental studies, postmodernism. *Unit head:* Dr. Paul Spilsbury, Academic Dean, 403-410-2000 Ext. 6905, Fax: 403-571-2556, E-mail: pspilsbu@ambrose.edu.

American Baptist Seminary of the West, Graduate and Professional Programs, Berkeley, CA 94704-3029. Offers community leadership (MA); theology (M Div, MA). *Accreditation:* ACIPE; ATS (one or more programs are accredited). Part-time and evening/weekend programs available. *Faculty:* 4 full-time (all women), 8 part-time/adjunct (2 women). *Students:* 58 (32 women); includes 50 minority (44 African Americans, 6 Asian Americans or Pacific Islanders). In 2007, 15 degrees awarded. *Entrance requirements:* For M Div, minimum GPA of 2.5; for master's, minimum GPA of 3.0. Additional exam requirements/recommendations for international students: Required—TOEFL (minimum score 550 paper-based; 250 computer-based). *Application deadline:* For fall admission, 4/15 priority date for domestic students, 4/15 for international students; for spring admission, 11/1 for international students. Applications are processed on a rolling basis. Application fee: $25. Electronic applications accepted. *Expenses:* Tuition: Full-time $13,000; part-time $500 per unit. Required fees: $240 per semester. One-time fee: $250. *Financial support:* In 2007–08, 38 students received support. Career-related internships or fieldwork, institutionally sponsored loans, scholarships/grants, tuition waivers (partial), and tuition discount available. Support available to part-time students. Financial award application deadline: 4/15; financial award applicants required to submit FAFSA. *Unit head:* Dr. Paul M. Martin, President for the Interim, 510-841-1905 Ext. 224, Fax: 510-841-2446, E-mail: pmartin@absw.edu. *Application contact:* Rev. Michelle M. Holmes, Vice President, 510-841-1905 Ext. 225, Fax: 510-841-2446, E-mail: mmholmes@absw.edu.

Amridge University, Graduate and Professional Programs, Montgomery, AL 36117. Offers behavioral leadership and management (MA); biblical studies (MA, D Min, PhD); Christian ministry (M Div); family therapy (D Min, PhD), including marriage and family therapy (PhD), professional counseling (PhD); leadership and management (MS); marriage and family therapy (M Div, MA); ministerial leadership (M Div, MS); pastoral counseling (M Div, MS); practical theology (MA); professional counseling (M Div, MA). *Accreditation:* ATS. Part-time and evening/weekend programs available. Postbaccalaureate distance learning degree programs offered (no on-campus study). *Faculty:* 50 full-time (12 women), 36 part-time/adjunct (10 women). *Students:* 165 full-time (85 women), 212 part-time (111 women); includes 174 minority (164 African Americans, 1 American Indian/Alaska Native, 1 Asian American or Pacific Islander, 8 Hispanic Americans). Average age 35. In 2007, 8 first professional degrees, 35 master's, 5 doctorates awarded. *Degree requirements:* For master's, one foreign language, comprehensive exam (for some programs), thesis (for some programs); for doctorate, comprehensive exam (for some programs), thesis/dissertation; for M Div, comprehensive exam (for some programs). *Entrance requirements:* For M Div, master's, and doctorate, GRE General Test or MAT. Additional exam requirements/recommendations for international students: Required—TOEFL. *Application deadline:* For fall admission, 9/1 priority date for domestic students; for spring admission, 1/1 priority date for domestic students. Applications are processed on a rolling basis. Application fee: $50. Electronic applications accepted. *Expenses:* Tuition: Full-time $9,180; part-time $510 per semester hour. Required fees: $400 per term. Tuition and fees vary according to course load and degree level. *Financial support:* Federal Work-Study and scholarships/grants available. Support available to part-time students. Financial award applicants required to submit FAFSA. *Faculty research:* Homiletics, hermeneutics, ancient Near Eastern history. *Unit head:* Rick Johnson, Director of Enrollment Management, 800-351-4040 Ext. 7513, Fax: 334-387-3878, E-mail: rickjohnson@amridgeuniversity.edu. *Application contact:* Ora Davis, Admissions Officer, 334-387-3877 Ext. 7524, Fax: 334-387-3878, E-mail: oradavis@amridgeuniversity.edu.

Andrews University, School of Graduate Studies, Seventh-day Adventist Theological Seminary, Berrien Springs, MI 49104. Offers ministry (M Div, D Min); pastoral ministry (MA); religious education (MA, Ed D, PhD, Ed S); theology (M Th, Th D). *Accreditation:* ATS. *Degree requirements:* For master's, thesis optional; for doctorate, variable foreign language requirement, thesis/dissertation; for M Div, one foreign language, thesis/dissertation optional. *Entrance requirements:* For master's, GRE Subject Test, minimum GPA of 2.0.

Anna Maria College, Graduate Division, Program in Pastoral Ministry, Paxton, MA 01612. Offers MA. Part-time and evening/weekend programs available. *Faculty:* 1 full-time (0 women), 2 part-time/adjunct (0 women). *Students:* Average age 46. In 2007, 4 degrees awarded. *Degree requirements:* For master's, pastoral project. *Entrance requirements:* For master's, interview. Additional exam requirements/recommendations for international students: Required—TOEFL (minimum score 500 paper-based). *Application deadline:* For fall admission, 3/1 priority date for domestic and international students; for spring admission, 11/1 priority date for domestic and international students. Applications are processed on a rolling basis. Application fee: $40. Electronic applications accepted. *Expenses:* Tuition: Part-time $1,272 per course. *Financial support:* Applicants required to submit FAFSA. *Unit head:* Dr. Michael Boover, Director, 508-849-3431, Fax: 508-849-3343, E-mail: mboover@annamaria.edu. *Application contact:* Dennis Braun, Director, Graduate and Continuing Education Recruitment, 508-849-3293, Fax: 508-819-3362, E-mail: dbraun@annamaria.edu.

Aquinas Institute of Theology, Graduate and Professional Programs, St. Louis, MO 63108. Offers biblical studies (Certificate); health care mission (MAHCM); ministry (M Div); pastoral care (Certificate); pastoral ministry (MAPM); pastoral studies (MAPS); preaching (D Min); spiritual direction (Certificate); theology (M Div, MA); Thomistic studies (Certificate); M Div/MA; MAPS/MSW. *Accreditation:* ATS (one or more programs are accredited). Part-time and evening/weekend programs available. Postbaccalaureate distance learning degree programs offered (minimal on-campus study). *Faculty:* 15 full-time (8 women), 4 part-time/adjunct (2 women). *Students:* 55 full-time (22 women), 190 part-time (117 women); includes 31 minority (14 African Americans, 1 American Indian/Alaska Native, 5 Asian Americans or Pacific Islanders, 11 Hispanic Americans), 10 international. Average age 41. 39 applicants, 92% accepted, 32 enrolled. In 2007, 18 first professional degrees, 14 master's, 4 doctorates, 7 other advanced degrees awarded. *Degree requirements:* For master's, one foreign language, comprehensive exam, thesis or major paper; for doctorate, thesis/dissertation. *Entrance requirements:* For M Div and master's, MAT; for doctorate, 3 years of ministerial experience, 6 hours of graduate course work in homiletics, M Div or the equivalent, minimum GPA of 3.0. Additional exam requirements/recommendations for international students: Required—TOEFL. *Application deadline:* For fall admission, 3/15 priority date for domestic and international students; for spring admission, 11/15 priority date for domestic and international students. Applications are processed on a rolling basis. Application fee: $50. *Expenses:* Tuition: Full-time $14,208; part-time $3,552 per term. Required fees: $195 per term. Tuition and fees vary according to course load. *Financial support:* In 2007–08, 4 research assistantships with full tuition reimbursements (averaging $3,000 per year) were awarded; career-related internships or fieldwork, scholarships/grants, health care benefits, and tuition waivers (partial) also available. Support available to part-time students. Financial award application deadline: 3/15; financial award applicants required to submit CSS PROFILE or FAFSA. *Faculty research:* Theology of preaching, hermeneutics, lay ecclesiastical ministry, pastoral and practical theology. *Unit head:* Fr. Gregory Heille, Academic Dean, 314-256-8800, Fax: 314-256-8888, E-mail: heille@ai.edu. *Application contact:* David Werthmann, Director of Admissions, 314-256-8806, Fax: 314-256-8888, E-mail: admissions@ai.edu.

Argosy University, Sarasota, College of Psychology and Behavioral Sciences, Sarasota, FL 34235. Offers community counseling (MA); counseling psychology (Ed D); counselor education and supervision (Ed D); forensic psychology (MA); marriage and family therapy (MA); mental health counseling (MA); organizational leadership (Ed D); pastoral community counseling (Ed D); school counseling (MA, Ed S); school psychology (MA).

See Close-Up on page 1403.

Asbury Theological Seminary, Graduate and Professional Programs, School of Practical Theology, Wilmore, KY 40390-1199. Offers Christian education (MACE); Christian leadership (MACL); Christian ministries (MAXM); Christian studies (Certificate); counseling (MAC); pastoral counseling (MAPC); youth ministry (MAYM). *Accreditation:* ACIPE; ATS. *Entrance requirements:* Additional exam requirements/recommendations for international students: Required—TOEFL (minimum score 550 paper-based; 79 iBT), IELTS (minimum score 7). *Application deadline:* For fall admission, 1/31 priority date for international students; for spring admission, 3/31 priority date for international students. Applications are processed on a rolling basis. Application fee: $50. Electronic applications accepted. *Expenses:* Tuition: Part-time $444 per hour. One-time fee: $100 part-time. *Unit head:* Dr. Catherine Stonehouse, Dean, 859-858-3581. *Application contact:* Janelle Vernon, Admissions Director, 859-858-2211, Fax: 859-858-2287, E-mail: admissions_office@asburyseminary.edu.

Ashland Theological Seminary, Graduate Programs, Ashland, OH 44805. Offers biblical and theological studies (MA, MAR), including New Testament (MA), Old Testament (MA); Christian ministry (MAPT); Christian studies (Diploma); clinical pastoral counseling (MACPC); historical studies (MA); ministry (D Min); pastoral counseling (MAPC); pastoral ministry (M Div); theological studies (MA). *Accreditation:* ATS. Part-time programs available. *Degree requirements:* For master's, comprehensive exam (for some programs), thesis (for some programs); for doctorate, thesis/dissertation; for M Div, 2 foreign languages. *Entrance requirements:* For M Div, minimum GPA of 2.75; for master's, minimum undergraduate GPA of 2.75; for doctorate, M Div, minimum undergraduate GPA of 3.0. Additional exam requirements/recommendations for international students: Required—TOEFL (minimum score 550 paper-based). Electronic applications accepted. *Faculty research:* Semitic languages and linguistics, rhetorical and social-scientific criticism, Anabaptist studies, inner spiritual healing, African-American clergy in film and literature.

Assemblies of God Theological Seminary, Graduate and Professional Programs, Springfield, MO 65802. Offers Christian ministries (MA); counseling (MA); divinity (M Div); intercultural ministries (MA); intercultural studies (D Miss); relief and development (D Miss); theological studies (MA); vocational ministry (D Min). *Accreditation:* ATS. Part-time and evening/weekend programs available. Postbaccalaureate distance learning degree programs offered (minimal on-campus study). *Faculty:* 16 full-time (3 women), 21 part-time/adjunct (4 women). *Students:* 212 full-time (59 women), 236 part-time (51 women); includes 49 minority (11 African Americans, 5 American Indian/Alaska Native, 11 Asian Americans or Pacific Islanders, 22 Hispanic Americans), 7 international. Average age 36. 181 applicants, 72% accepted, 91 enrolled. In 2007, 28 first professional degrees, 66 master's, 13 doctorates awarded. *Degree requirements:* For master's, analytical reflection paper or comprehensive exam; for doctorate, thesis/dissertation; for M Div, one foreign language, analytical reflection paper. *Entrance requirements:* For M Div, minimum GPA of 2.0; for master's, minimum GPA of 2.5; for doctorate, minimum GPA of 3.0. Additional exam requirements/recommendations for international students: Required—TOEFL (minimum score 550 paper-based; 213 computer-based; 80 iBT). *Application deadline:* For fall admission, 7/1 priority date for domestic students, 6/1 priority date for international students; for spring admission, 12/1 priority date for domestic students, 11/1 priority date for international students. Applications are processed on a rolling basis. Application fee: $35. Electronic applications accepted. *Expenses:* Tuition: Part-time $465 per credit hour. *Financial support:* Career-related internships or fieldwork, Federal Work-Study, and scholarships/grants available. Support available to part-time students. Financial award application deadline: 7/15; financial award applicants required to submit FAFSA. *Unit head:* Stephen Lim, Academic Dean, 417-268-1000, Fax: 417-268-1001, E-mail: slim@agts.edu.

The Athenaeum of Ohio, Graduate Programs, Cincinnati, OH 45230-5900. Offers biblical studies (MABS); divinity (M Div); pastoral counseling (MAPC); religion (MAR); theology (MA Th); M Div/MA Th; M Div/MABS; M Div/MAPC. *Accreditation:* ATS (one or more programs are accredited). Part-time and evening/weekend programs available. *Degree requirements:* For master's, one foreign language, comprehensive exam (for some programs), thesis optional; for M Div, comprehensive exam.

Austin Presbyterian Theological Seminary, Graduate and Professional Programs, Austin, TX 78705-5797. Offers divinity (M Div); ministry (D Min); theological studies (MA); M Div/MATS; M Div/MSSW. *Accreditation:* ACIPE; ATS. Part-time programs available. *Faculty:* 20 full-time (6 women), 3 part-time/adjunct (0 women). *Students:* 123 full-time (60 women), 97 part-time (36 women); includes 27 minority (15 African Americans, 1 American Indian/Alaska Native, 5 Asian Americans or Pacific Islanders, 6 Hispanic Americans), 6 international. Average age 41. 89 applicants, 61% accepted, 41 enrolled. In 2007, 52 first professional degrees, 10 master's, 5 doctorates awarded. *Degree requirements:* For doctorate, thesis/dissertation; for M Div, Greek, Hebrew. *Entrance requirements:* References. Additional exam requirements/

recommendations for international students: Required—TOEFL (minimum score 550 paper-based; 213 computer-based; 79 iBT). *Application deadline:* For fall admission, 5/15 priority date for domestic students; for spring admission, 11/15 for domestic students. Applications are processed on a rolling basis. Application fee: $65. *Financial support:* In 2007–08, 130 students received support, including 6 research assistantships (averaging $1,040 per year), 6 teaching assistantships (averaging $1,040 per year); career-related internships or fieldwork, institutionally sponsored loans, scholarships/grants, and tutorships also available. Support available to part-time students. Financial award application deadline: 6/1; financial award applicants required to submit FAFSA. *Faculty research:* Mystical theology, religious pluralism, narrative preaching, social ethics, pastoral care and healing. *Unit head:* Rev. Dr. Michael Jinkins, Academic Dean, 512-404-4821, Fax: 512-479-0738, E-mail: mjinkins@austinseminary.edu. *Application contact:* Jack Barden, Director of Admissions, 512-404-4827, Fax: 512-479-0738, E-mail: jbarden@austinseminary.edu.

Ave Maria University, Graduate Programs, Ave Maria, FL 34142. Offers pastoral theology (MTS); theology (MA, PhD). Terminal master's awarded for partial completion of doctoral program. *Degree requirements:* For master's, one foreign language, thesis; for doctorate, 3 foreign languages, comprehensive exam, thesis/dissertation. *Entrance requirements:* For master's, GRE; for doctorate, GRE, M Div or equivalent; MA or MTS in religion, theology, or philosophy; bachelor's degree with strong background in religion, theology, and/or philosophy.

Ave Maria University, Institute for Pastoral Theology, Ave Maria, FL 34142. Offers MTS. Part-time and evening/weekend programs available.

Azusa Pacific University, Haggard School of Theology, Program in Divinity, Azusa, CA 91702-7000. Offers M Div.

Azusa Pacific University, Haggard School of Theology, Program in Ministry Management, Azusa, CA 91702-7000. Offers MAMM.

Azusa Pacific University, Haggard School of Theology, Program in Pastoral Studies, Azusa, CA 91702-7000. Offers MAPS.

Azusa Pacific University, Haggard School of Theology, Program in Worship Leadership, Azusa, CA 91702-7000. Offers MAWL.

Bakke Graduate University, Program in Pastoral Ministry, Seattle, WA 98104. Offers MTS, D Min. Part-time programs available. Postbaccalaureate distance learning degree programs offered (minimal on-campus study). *Faculty:* 3 full-time (1 woman), 29 part-time/adjunct (2 women). *Students:* 56 full-time (12 women), 149 part-time (31 women); includes 87 minority (50 African Americans, 1 American Indian/Alaska Native, 28 Asian Americans or Pacific Islanders, 8 Hispanic Americans). Average age 36. In 2007, 8 master's, 19 doctorates awarded. *Median time to degree:* Of those who began their doctoral program in fall 1999, 33% received their degree in 8 years or less. *Degree requirements:* For master's, thesis; for doctorate, thesis/dissertation. *Entrance requirements:* For master's, 2 years of ministry experience, BA in biblical studies or theology; for doctorate, 3 years of ministry experience, M Div. *Application deadline:* For fall admission, 7/1 priority date for domestic students; for winter admission, 12/1 for domestic students; for spring admission, 3/15 for domestic students. Applications are processed on a rolling basis. Application fee: $75. Electronic applications accepted. *Expenses:* Tuition: Part-time $425 per credit. Required fees: $25 per course. *Financial support:* In 2007–08, 46 students received support. Scholarships/grants and tuition waivers (partial) available. Financial award applicants required to submit CSS PROFILE. *Faculty research:* Theological systems, church management, worship. *Unit head:* Dr. Grace Barnes, Academic Dean, 206-264-9100 Ext. 19, Fax: 206-624-8828, E-mail: graceb@bgu.edu. *Application contact:* Judith A. Melton, Registrar, 206-246-9100, Fax: 206-246-8828, E-mail: judim@bgu.edu.

Baptist Bible College, Graduate School of Theology, Springfield, MO 65803-3498. Offers biblical counseling (MA); biblical studies (MA); church ministries (MA); intercultural studies (MA); theology (M Div). Part-time programs available. *Degree requirements:* For master's, 2 foreign languages, thesis (for some programs); for M Div, 2 foreign languages, thesis/dissertation (for some programs). *Entrance requirements:* For master's, outcomes test. Electronic applications accepted.

Baptist Bible College of Pennsylvania, Baptist Bible Seminary, Clarks Summit, PA 18411-1297. Offers biblical studies (PhD); church planting (M Div); global missions (M Div); military chaplaincy (M Div); ministry (M Min, D Min); pastor of church education (M Div); pastor of outreach (M Div); pastoral counseling (M Div); pastoral leadership (M Div); theology (M Div, Th M); youth pastor (M Div). Part-time and evening/weekend programs available. Postbaccalaureate distance learning degree programs offered (minimal on-campus study). *Faculty:* 10 full-time (0 women). *Students:* 102 full-time (0 women), 104 part-time; includes 14 minority (6 African Americans, 4 Asian Americans or Pacific Islanders, 4 Hispanic Americans), 2 international. Average age 38.Terminal master's awarded for partial completion of doctoral program. *Degree requirements:* For master's, 2 foreign languages, thesis; for doctorate, 2 foreign languages, comprehensive exam (for some programs), thesis/dissertation, oral exam; for M Div, 2 foreign languages, thesis/dissertation, oral exam. *Entrance requirements:* For doctorate, Greek and Hebrew entrance exams (PhD). *Application deadline:* Applications are processed on a rolling basis. Application fee: $30. Electronic applications accepted. *Expenses:* Tuition: Full-time $6,516; part-time $362 per credit. Required fees: $468; $232 per semester. *Financial support:* Career-related internships or fieldwork and scholarships/grants available. Support available to part-time students. *Unit head:* Dr. Michael Stallard, Seminary Academic Dean, 570-585-9348, Fax: 570-585-4057, E-mail: mstallard@bbc.edu. *Application contact:* Paul Golden, Director of Seminary Admissions, 570-586-9396, E-mail: pgolden@bbc.edu.

Baptist Bible College of Pennsylvania, Graduate School, Clarks Summit, PA 18411-1297. Offers biblical ministries (MS); Christian school education (MS); counseling (MS). Part-time and evening/weekend programs available. Postbaccalaureate distance learning degree programs offered (no on-campus study). *Faculty:* 2 full-time (0 women), 1 part-time/adjunct (0 women). *Students:* 12 full-time (7 women), 61 part-time (40 women); includes 3 minority (all African Americans), 1 international. Average age 31. In 2007, 13 degrees awarded. *Entrance requirements:* Additional exam requirements/recommendations for international students: Required—TOEFL. *Application deadline:* Applications are processed on a rolling basis. Application fee: $30. *Expenses:* Tuition: Full-time $6,516; part-time $362 per credit. Required fees: $468; $232 per semester. *Financial support:* In 2007–08, 43 students received support. Institutionally sponsored loans and scholarships/grants available. *Unit head:* Dr. James Lythe, Provost, 570-586-2400 Ext. 9222, Fax: 570-586-1753. *Application contact:* James May, Director of Admissions, 570-510-1659, Fax: 570-585-9299, E-mail: gradadmissions@bbc.edu.

Baptist Theological Seminary at Richmond, Graduate and Professional Program, Richmond, VA 23227. Offers children and family ministry (M Div); Christian education (M Div); church music (M Div); theology (D Min); youth and student ministry (M Div); M Div/MS; M Div/MSW. *Accreditation:* ATS. Part-time programs available. Postbaccalaureate distance learning degree programs offered (minimal on-campus study). *Faculty:* 14 full-time (6 women), 8 part-time/adjunct (1 woman). *Students:* 117 full-time (64 women), 17 part-time (7 women); includes 10 minority (6 African Americans, 1 Asian American or Pacific Islander, 3 Hispanic Americans), 1 international. Average age 46. In 2007, 37 first professional degrees, 6 doctorates awarded. *Median time to degree:* Of those who began their doctoral program in fall 1999, 92% received their degree in 8 years or less. *Degree requirements:* For doctorate, one foreign language, comprehensive exam, thesis/dissertation, field study, independent study; for M Div, one foreign language, comprehensive exam (for some programs), thesis/dissertation optional, mission immersion experience, internship. *Entrance requirements:* For doctorate, MAT, M Div, 3 years of full-time ministry experience. Additional exam requirements/recommendations for international students: Required—TOEFL (minimum score 481 paper-based; 213 computer-based). *Application deadline:* For fall admission, 8/1 priority date for domestic students, 5/1 priority date for international students; for winter admission, 12/1 priority date for domestic students, 9/1 priority date for international students; for spring admission, 1/1 priority date for domestic students, 10/1 priority date for international students. Applications are processed on a rolling basis. Application fee: $35. *Expenses:* Tuition: Full-time $7,500; part-time $750 per credit. Required fees: $45 per term. Full-time tuition and fees vary according to degree level. *Financial support:* In 2007–08, 98 students received support, including 16 teaching assistantships (averaging $1,300 per year); scholarships/grants and tuition waivers (partial) also available. Financial award application deadline: 2/1. *Faculty research:* New Testament studies, Old Testament studies, pastoral care, church history, theology. *Unit head:* Dr. Ronald W. Crawford, President, 804-355-8135, Fax: 804-355-8182. *Application contact:* Director of Admissions, 804-355-8135, Fax: 804-355-8182.

Barry University, School of Arts and Sciences, Department of Theology and Philosophy, Miami Shores, FL 33161-6695. Offers ministry (D Min); pastoral ministry for Hispanics (MA); pastoral theology (MA); practical theology (MA). *Accreditation:* ATS. Part-time and evening/weekend programs available. *Degree requirements:* For master's, comprehensive exam, thesis optional; for doctorate, thesis/dissertation. *Entrance requirements:* For master's, GRE General Test or MAT, minimum GPA of 3.0. *Application deadline:* Applications are processed on a rolling basis. Application fee: $30. Electronic applications accepted. *Financial support:* Research assistantships, career-related internships or fieldwork, institutionally sponsored loans, and tuition waivers (partial) available. Support available to part-time students. Financial award application deadline: 5/1; financial award applicants required to submit FAFSA. *Faculty research:* Fundamental morals, bioethics, social ethics, liturgical and sacramental theology, biblical studies. *Unit head:* Fr. Mark Wedig, Chair, 305-899-3378, Fax: 305-899-3385, E-mail: mwedig@mail.barry.edu. *Application contact:* Dave Fletcher, Director of Graduate Admissions, 305-899-3113, Fax: 305-899-2971, E-mail: dfletcher@mail.barry.edu.

Bayamón Central University, Graduate Programs, Program in Theology, Bayamón, PR 00960-1725. Offers biblical studies (MA); divinity (M Div); pastoral theology (MA); theological studies (MA); theology (MA). Part-time and evening/weekend programs available. *Entrance requirements:* For master's, EXADEP, bachelor's degree in theology or related field.

Beacon University, Graduate Programs, Columbus, GA 31909. Offers cell church development (MAPM); counseling ministry (MAPM); military chaplaincy (MAPM); organizational leadership (MAPM); pastoral ministry (MAPM); theology (M Div, MABS). Part-time and evening/weekend programs available. Postbaccalaureate distance learning degree programs offered (minimal on-campus study). *Faculty:* 35 part-time/adjunct (5 women). *Students:* 57 full-time (34 women), 37 part-time (21 women); includes 56 minority (47 African Americans, 1 Asian American or Pacific Islander, 8 Hispanic Americans), 4 international. 30 applicants, 90% accepted, 19 enrolled. In 2007, 3 first professional degrees, 28 master's awarded. *Degree requirements:* For master's and M Div, comprehensive exam. *Entrance requirements:* For M Div, MAT or GRE or GMAT or MTE, official undergrad and/or transf.; for master's, MAT or GRE or NTE or GMAT, official undergrad and/or trsfr. Additional exam requirements/recommendations for international students: Required—TOEFL (minimum score 500 paper-based; 173 computer-based; 61 iBT); Recommended—IELTS (minimum score 6). Application fee: $90. *Expenses:* Tuition: Full-time $4,608; part-time $256 per credit hour. Required fees: $105 per term. *Financial support:* In 2007–08, 69 students received support. Scholarships/grants available. Financial award application deadline: 7/1. *Unit head:* Dr. Ian A.H. Bond, President, 706-323-5364, E-mail: ian.bond@beacon.edu. *Application contact:* Cindy G. Winkles, Admissions Officer, 706-323-5364 Ext. 258, Fax: 706-323-5891, E-mail: cindy.winkles@beacon.edu.

Bethany Theological Seminary, Graduate and Professional Programs, Richmond, IN 47374-4019. Offers biblical studies (MA Th); ministry studies (M Div); peace studies (M Div, MA Th); theological studies (MA Th, CATS); youth ministry (M Div). *Accreditation:* ACIPE; ATS. Part-time programs available. Postbaccalaureate distance learning degree programs offered (minimal on-campus study). *Degree requirements:* For master's, thesis. *Entrance requirements:* For M Div, letters of reference, minimum GPA of 2.75; for master's, letters of reference, minimum GPA of 3.0. Additional exam requirements/recommendations for international students: Required—TOEFL (minimum score 550 paper-based; 218 computer-based).

Bethel College, Division of Graduate Studies, Program in Christian Ministries, Mishawaka, IN 46545-5591. Offers M Min. Part-time programs available. *Faculty:* 5 part-time/adjunct (0 women). *Students:* 13 full-time (5 women), 44 part-time (11 women); includes 8 minority (6 African Americans, 1 Asian American or Pacific Islander, 1 Hispanic American), 2 international. 35 applicants, 86% accepted, 30 enrolled. In 2007, 9 degrees awarded. *Degree requirements:* For master's, thesis or alternative. *Entrance requirements:* Additional exam requirements/recommendations for international students: Required—TOEFL (minimum score 540 paper-based; 207 computer-based). *Application deadline:* For fall admission, 5/1 for international students; for spring admission, 10/1 for international students. Applications are processed on a rolling basis. Application fee: $25. Electronic applications accepted. *Expenses:* Tuition: Full-time $5,940; part-time $330 per credit. Tuition and fees vary according to program. *Financial support:* Career-related internships or fieldwork available. Financial award applicants required to submit FAFSA. *Unit head:* Dr. Gene Carpenter, Director, 574-257-3332, E-mail: carpeng@bethelcollege.edu. *Application contact:* Dr. Robert Morris, Advisor, 574-257-2667.

Bethel Seminary, Graduate and Professional Programs, St. Paul, MN 55112-6998. Offers adult developments and generativity (Certificate); biblical studies (MATS, Certificate); children's and family ministry (MACFM); Christian education (MACE); Christian thought (M Div, MACT); church leadership (D Min); congregation and family care (D Min); global and contextual studies (MA); global missions (Certificate); lay ministry (Certificate); marriage and family studies (M Div); marriage and family therapy (MAMFT); missions (MATS); pastoral counseling (Certificate); pastoral ministries (M Div); spiritual formation (Certificate); theological studies (MATS, Certificate); transformational leadership (MATL); youth ministries (MACE). *Accreditation:* ACIPE; ATS (one or more programs are accredited). Part-time and evening/weekend programs available. Postbaccalaureate distance learning degree programs offered (minimal on-campus study). *Faculty:* 26 full-time (3 women), 73 part-time/adjunct (21 women). *Students:* 374 full-time (115 women), 669 part-time (268 women); includes 183 minority (90 African Americans, 2 American Indian/Alaska Native, 65 Asian Americans or Pacific Islanders, 26 Hispanic Americans). Average age 36. 417 applicants, 86% accepted, 223 enrolled. In 2007, 62 first professional degrees, 102 master's, 14 doctorates awarded. *Degree requirements:* For master's, variable foreign language requirement, thesis (for some programs); for doctorate, thesis/dissertation; for M Div, one foreign language. *Entrance requirements:* For M Div, letters of reference; for master's, letters of reference, transcripts, personal statement; for doctorate, M Div, letters of reference, essays, organizational support. Additional exam requirements/recommendations for international students: Required—TOEFL (minimum score 550 paper-based; 213 computer-based). *Application deadline:* For fall admission, 8/1 priority date for domestic students, 3/1 for international students; for winter admission, 12/1 priority date for domestic students; for spring admission, 3/1 priority date for domestic students. Applications are processed on a rolling basis. Application fee: $20. Electronic applications accepted. *Expenses:* Tuition: Part-time $325 per credit. Required fees: $10 per quarter. *Financial support:* In 2007–08, 661 students received support, including 20 teaching assistantships; career-related internships or fieldwork, Federal Work-Study, scholarships/grants, and tuition waivers (full) also available. Financial award application deadline: 7/15; financial award applicants required to submit FAFSA. *Faculty research:* Nature of theology, ethics, biblical commentaries, nature of God, science and theology. *Unit head:* Dr. Leland Eliason, Executive Vice President and Provost, 651-638-6182. *Application contact:* Joseph V. Dworak, Director of Admissions, 651-638-6288, Fax: 651-638-6002, E-mail: j-dworak@bethel.edu.

Biblical Theological Seminary, Graduate and Professional Programs, Hatfield, PA 19440-2499. Offers counseling (MA); ministry (MA); theology (M Div, D Min). *Accreditation:* ATS.Part-time programs available. *Degree requirements:* For M Div, thesis/dissertation. *Entrance requirements:* Additional exam requirements/recommendations for international students: Required—TOEFL (minimum score 550 paper-based; 213 computer-based). *Faculty research:* Old Testament narrative, Old Testament historiography, Hebrew syntax, parables, addictions.

Pastoral Ministry and Counseling

Bob Jones University, Graduate Programs, Greenville, SC 29614. Offers accountancy (MS); Bible (MA); Bible translation (MA); Biblical studies (Certificate); broadcast management (MS); business administration (MBA); church history (MA, PhD); church ministries (MA); church music (MM); cinema and video production (MA); counseling (MS); curriculum and instruction (Ed D); divinity (M Div); dramatic production (MA); educational leadership (MS, Ed D, Ed S); elementary education (M Ed, MAT); English (M Ed, MA, MAT); fine arts (MA); graphic design (MA); history (M Ed, MA); illustration (MA); interpretative speech (MA); mathematics (M Ed, MAT); medical missions (Certificate); ministry (MM, D Min); multi-categorical special education (M Ed, MAT); music (M Ed); New Testament interpretation (PhD); Old Testament interpretation (PhD); orchestral instrument performance (MM); organ performance (MM); pastoral studies (MA); personnel services (MS, Ed S); piano pedagogy (MM); piano performance (MM); platform arts (MA); radio and television broadcasting (MS); rhetoric and public address (MA); secondary education (M Ed); studio art (MA); teaching Bible (MA); theology (MA, PhD); voice performance (MM); youth ministries (MA); M Div/MM.

Boston College, Graduate School of Arts and Sciences, School of Theology and Ministry, Chestnut Hill, MA 02467-3800. Offers church leadership (MA); divinity (M Div); pastoral ministry (MA), including Hispanic ministry, liturgy and worship, pastoral care and counseling, spirituality; religious education (MA, PhD); sacred theology (STD, STL); social justice/social ministry (MA); spiritual direction (MA); theological studies (MTS); theology (Th M, PhD); youth ministry (MA); MA/MA; MS/MA; MSW/MA. Part-time programs available. *Students:* 103 applicants, 54% accepted, 46 enrolled. In 2007, 37 master's, 4 doctorates awarded. *Degree requirements:* For doctorate, one foreign language, thesis/dissertation. *Entrance requirements:* For doctorate, GRE. Additional exam requirements/recommendations for international students: Required—TOEFL (minimum score 550 paper-based; 213 computer-based). *Application deadline:* For fall admission, 3/1 priority date for domestic students. Application fee: $70. Electronic applications accepted. *Financial support:* Fellowships with tuition reimbursements, career-related internships or fieldwork, Federal Work-Study, and tuition waivers (full and partial) available. Support available to part-time students. Financial award application deadline: 3/1; financial award applicants required to submit FAFSA. *Faculty research:* Philosophy and practice of religious education, pastoral psychology, liturgical and spiritual theology, spiritual formation for the practice of ministry. *Unit head:* Dr. Thomas Groome, Chairperson, 617-552-8449, Fax: 617-552-0811. *Application contact:* Dr. Jennifer Bader, Assistant Director, Academic Affairs, 617-552-4478, Fax: 617-552-0811, E-mail: jennifer.bader@bc.edu.

Briercrest Seminary, Graduate Programs, Program in Christian Ministries, Caronport, SK S0H 0S0, Canada. Offers leadership (MA); marriage and family counseling (MA); missions (MA); pastoral counseling (MA); worship (MA); youth and family ministry (MA). Part-time programs available. *Degree requirements:* For master's, comprehensive exam, thesis optional. *Entrance requirements:* Additional exam requirements/recommendations for international students: Required—TOEFL (minimum score 550 paper-based; 213 computer-based).

Briercrest Seminary, Graduate Programs, Program in Theology, Caronport, SK S0H 0S0, Canada. Offers Biblical studies (M Div); leadership and management (M Div); New Testament (MATS); Old Testament (MATS); pastoral counseling (M Div); pastoral ministry (M Div); theological studies (M Div); theology (MATS); worship (M Div); youth and family ministry (M Div). *Accreditation:* ATS. Part-time programs available. *Degree requirements:* For master's, comprehensive exam, thesis optional. *Entrance requirements:* Additional exam requirements/recommendations for international students: Required—TOEFL (minimum score 550 paper-based; 213 computer-based).

Caldwell College, Graduate Studies, Program in Pastoral Ministry, Caldwell, NJ 07006-6195. Offers MA. Part-time and evening/weekend programs available. *Degree requirements:* For master's, thesis. *Entrance requirements:* For master's, minimum GPA of 3.0, 2 years of ministry experience. Additional exam requirements/recommendations for international students: Required—TOEFL (minimum score 580 paper-based; 237 computer-based). Electronic applications accepted.

California Baptist University, Program in Counseling Ministry, Riverside, CA 92504-3206. Offers MA. Part-time programs available. *Faculty:* 2 full-time (0 women). *Students:* 5 full-time (all women), 3 part-time (2 women); includes 1 minority (African American) 7 applicants, 43% accepted, 2 enrolled. In 2007, 1 degree awarded. *Degree requirements:* For master's, thesis or alternative. *Entrance requirements:* For master's, minimum undergraduate GPA of 2.75. Additional exam requirements/recommendations for international students: Required—TOEFL (minimum score 575 paper-based; 230 computer-based), IELTS (minimum score 7). *Application deadline:* For fall admission, 9/1 for domestic students, 7/1 priority date for international students; for spring admission, 1/3 for domestic students, 10/15 priority date for international students. Applications are processed on a rolling basis. Application fee: $45. Electronic applications accepted. *Expenses: Contact institution. Financial support:* Federal Work-Study available. Support available to part-time students. Financial award applicants required to submit FAFSA. *Unit head:* Dr. Nathan Lewis, Director, 951-343-4348, Fax: 951-343-4569, E-mail: nlewis@calbaptist.edu. *Application contact:* Gail Ronveaux, Dean of Graduate Enrollment, 951-343-5045, Fax: 951-343-5095, E-mail: graduateadmissions@calbaptist.edu.

Calvary Bible College and Theological Seminary, Calvary Theological Seminary, Kansas City, MO 64147-1341. Offers Bible and theology (MS); biblical counseling (MA); biblical studies (MA); Christian ministry (MA); Christian studies (MS); Christian theology (MA); New Testament (MA); Old Testament (MA); pastoral studies (M Div). Part-time and evening/weekend programs available. *Faculty:* 3 full-time (0 women), 2 part-time/adjunct (0 women). *Students:* 19 full-time (7 women), 36 part-time (11 women); includes 12 minority (9 African Americans, 1 Asian American or Pacific Islander, 2 Hispanic Americans), 2 international. Average age 37. In 2007, 3 first professional degrees, 15 master's awarded. *Degree requirements:* For master's, one foreign language, comprehensive exam, thesis; for M Div, 2 foreign languages, comprehensive exam, thesis/dissertation. *Entrance requirements:* For M Div and master's, GRE, minimum GPA of 2.5, 50 semester hours of course work in liberal arts, BA or BS degree, doctrine agreement. Additional exam requirements/recommendations for international students: Required—TOEFL (minimum score 550 paper-based; 213 computer-based). *Application deadline:* For fall admission, 7/15 priority date for domestic and international students; for spring admission, 12/1 priority date for domestic and international students. Application fee: $25. *Financial support:* In 2007–08, 13 students received support. Scholarships/grants available. Financial award application deadline: 11/5. *Unit head:* Dr. Thomas Baurain, Academic Dean, 816-322-0110 Ext. 1504, Fax: 816-331-4474. *Application contact:* Damon Horton, Director of Admissions, 800-326-3960 Ext. 1320, Fax: 816-331-4474.

Capital Bible Seminary, Graduate and Professional Programs, Lanham, MD 20706-3599. Offers biblical studies (MA, Certificate); Christian counseling (MA); Christian counseling and discipleship (Certificate); ministry leadership (MA); theology (M Div, Th M). *Accreditation:* ATS (one or more programs are accredited). Part-time and evening/weekend programs available. *Degree requirements:* For master's, 2 foreign languages, comprehensive exam, thesis (for some programs); for M Div, 2 foreign languages, comprehensive exam. *Entrance requirements:* For M Div and master's, GRE General Test, Greek exam for those with 2 years of Greek, proficiency exam in theology, previous course work in Biblical studies. Additional exam requirements/recommendations for international students: Required—TOEFL (minimum score 550 paper-based; 213 computer-based). *Faculty research:* Dead Sea Scrolls, spiritual gifts, hermeneutics.

Cardinal Stritch University, College of Arts and Sciences, Department of Religious Studies, Milwaukee, WI 53217-3985. Offers lay ministries (MA); ministry (MA); religious studies (MA). Part-time and evening/weekend programs available. *Degree requirements:* For master's, comprehensive exam, thesis, faculty recommendation, research project. *Entrance requirements:* For master's, interview, minimum GPA of 2.75.

Catholic Theological Union at Chicago, Graduate and Professional Programs, Chicago, IL 60615-5698. Offers biblical spirituality (Certificate); cross-cultural ministries (D Min); cross-cultural missions (Certificate); divinity (M Div); liturgical studies (Certificate); liturgy (D Min); pastoral studies (MAPS, Certificate); spiritual formation (Certificate); spirituality (D Min); theology (MA); M Div/MA; M Div/MSW; M Div/PhD. *Accreditation:* ACIPE; ATS (one or more programs are accredited). Part-time and evening/weekend programs available. *Degree requirements:* For master's, one foreign language, comprehensive exam (for some programs), thesis (for some programs); for doctorate, thesis/dissertation. *Entrance requirements:* For doctorate, master's degree, 5 years of active ministry. *Faculty research:* Doctrine, sacraments, ethics, Bible.

Chaminade University of Honolulu, Graduate Services, Program in Pastoral Leadership, Honolulu, HI 96816-1578. Offers MAPL. Part-time and evening/weekend programs available. Postbaccalaureate distance learning degree programs offered (minimal on-campus study). *Faculty:* 3 full-time (1 woman), 2 part-time/adjunct (1 woman). *Students:* 2 full-time (0 women), 13 part-time (7 women); includes 3 minority (all Asian Americans or Pacific Islanders) Average age 48. 7 applicants, 71% accepted, 4 enrolled. In 2007, 2 degrees awarded. *Degree requirements:* For master's, internship or thesis. *Entrance requirements:* For master's, 2 letters of recommendation. Additional exam requirements/recommendations for international students: Required—TOEFL (minimum score 550 paper-based). *Application deadline:* For fall admission, 9/15 for domestic students; for winter admission, 12/15 for domestic students; for spring admission, 3/15 for domestic students. Applications are processed on a rolling basis. Application fee: $50. Electronic applications accepted. *Expenses:* Tuition: Part-time $490 per credit hour. *Financial support:* In 2007–08, 2 students received support. *Unit head:* Regina Pfeiffer, Director, 808-735-4700, Fax: 808-739-8328, E-mail: rpfeiffer@chaminade.edu. *Application contact:* Regina Pfeiffer, Director, 808-735-4700, E-mail: mapl@chaminade.edu.

Chaminade University of Honolulu, Graduate Services, Program in Pastoral Theology, Honolulu, HI 96816-1578. Offers MPT. Part-time and evening/weekend programs available. Postbaccalaureate distance learning degree programs offered. *Faculty:* 3 full-time (1 woman), 2 part-time/adjunct (1 woman). *Students:* 2 full-time (0 women), 13 part-time (7 women); includes 9 minority (8 Asian Americans or Pacific Islanders, 1 Hispanic American), 1 international. 7 applicants, 71% accepted, 4 enrolled. In 2007, 5 degrees awarded. *Degree requirements:* For master's, capstone course. *Entrance requirements:* For master's, 2 letters of recommendation. Additional exam requirements/recommendations for international students: Required—TOEFL (minimum score 550 paper-based). *Application deadline:* For fall admission, 9/15 for domestic students; for winter admission, 12/15 for domestic students; for spring admission, 3/15 for domestic students. Applications are processed on a rolling basis. Application fee: $50. Electronic applications accepted. *Expenses:* Tuition: Part-time $490 per credit hour. *Unit head:* Regina Pfeiffer, Assistant Director, 808-735-4700, E-mail: rpfeiffe@chaminade.edu. *Application contact:* Regina Pfeiffer, Director, 808-735-4700, Fax: 808-739-8328, E-mail: mpt@chaminade.edu.

Chicago Theological Seminary, Graduate and Professional Programs, Chicago, IL 60637-1507. Offers clinical pastoral education (D Min); Jewish-Christian studies (PhD); pastoral counseling (D Min); preaching (D Min); religious studies (MA); spiritual leadership (D Min); theology (M Div); theology and the human sciences (PhD), including theology and society, theology and the personality sciences; M Div/MSW. *Accreditation:* ACIPE; ATS. Part-time programs available. *Faculty:* 13 full-time (5 women). *Students:* 83 full-time (40 women), 135 part-time (66 women); includes 54 minority (45 African Americans, 6 Asian Americans or Pacific Islanders, 3 Hispanic Americans), 33 international. 78 applicants, 94% accepted, 50 enrolled. In 2007, 15 first professional degrees, 8 master's, 22 doctorates awarded. *Degree requirements:* For master's, thesis; for doctorate, 2 foreign languages, comprehensive exam, thesis/dissertation; for M Div, thesis/dissertation. *Entrance requirements:* For doctorate, GRE General Test. Additional exam requirements/recommendations for international students: Required—TOEFL (minimum score 217 computer-based). *Application deadline:* For fall admission, 2/15 priority date for domestic and international students; for spring admission, 11/1 for domestic and international students. Application fee: $50. *Financial support:* In 2007–08, 103 students received support, including 12 fellowships (averaging $10,000 per year); institutionally sponsored loans, scholarships/grants, and tuition waivers (partial) also available. Support available to part-time students. Financial award application deadline: 3/1; financial award applicants required to submit FAFSA. *Faculty research:* Bible, culture and hermeneutics/theology, gender & sexuality/black faith and life/spirituality and psychology/practical theology. Total annual research expenditures: $150,000. *Unit head:* Dr. Theodore W. Jennings, Acting Dean, 773-752-5757, Fax: 773-752-1903, E-mail: tjennings@ctschicago.edu. *Application contact:* Rev. Lin Sanford Keppert, Director of Admissions, Recruitment and Financial Aid, E-mail: lkeppert@ctschicago.edu.

Christian Theological Seminary, Graduate and Professional Programs, Indianapolis, IN 46208-3301. Offers marriage and family (MA); pastoral care and counseling (D Min); practical theology (D Min); psychotherapy and faith (MA); sacred theology (STM); specialized ministries (MA); theological studies (MTS); theology (M Div). *Accreditation:* AAMFT/COAMFTE (one or more programs are accredited); ACIPE; ATS. Part-time programs available. Terminal master's awarded for partial completion of doctoral program. *Degree requirements:* For master's, comprehensive exam (for some programs), thesis (for some programs); for doctorate, comprehensive exam, thesis/dissertation; for M Div, comprehensive exam, thesis/dissertation (for some programs), missionary and cross-cultural experience. *Entrance requirements:* For master's, GRE General Test, MAT; for doctorate, M Div or BD. Electronic applications accepted. *Faculty research:* Faith formation, peer learning post graduation.

Christ the King Seminary, Graduate and Professional Programs, East Aurora, NY 14052. Offers divinity (M Div); pastoral ministry (MA); pastoral studies (Certificate); theology (MA). *Accreditation:* ATS. Part-time and evening/weekend programs available. *Degree requirements:* For master's, comprehensive exam, thesis; for M Div, comprehensive exam. *Entrance requirements:* For M Div and master's, previous course work in philosophy and religious studies.

Church of God Theological Seminary, Graduate and Professional Programs, Cleveland, TN 37320-3330. Offers church ministries (MA), including counseling, discipleship and Christian formations, missions, pastoral ministry; discipleship and Christian formations (MA); theology (M Div). *Accreditation:* ACIPE; ATS. Part-time programs available. *Degree requirements:* For M Div, 2 foreign languages, thesis/dissertation, internship. *Faculty research:* Biblical exegesis.

Cincinnati Christian University, Graduate School, Program in Counseling, Cincinnati, OH 45204-3200. Offers MAC. *Degree requirements:* For master's, thesis or alternative, integration paper. *Entrance requirements:* For master's, GRE General Test, interview, minimum undergraduate GPA of 3.0. Additional exam requirements/recommendations for international students: Required—TOEFL. Electronic applications accepted. Expenses: Contact institution.

Claremont School of Theology, Graduate and Professional Programs, Program in Ministry, Claremont, CA 91711-3199. Offers D Min. *Accreditation:* ACIPE. *Degree requirements:* For doctorate, thesis/dissertation. *Entrance requirements:* For doctorate, GRE General Test. Additional exam requirements/recommendations for international students: Required—TOEFL (minimum score 230 computer-based). Electronic applications accepted.

Collège Dominicain de Philosophie et de Théologie, Graduate Programs, Program in Pastoral Theology, Ottawa, ON K1R 7G3, Canada. Offers M Prof Past, M Th Past. Part-time and evening/weekend programs available. *Faculty:* 6 part-time/adjunct (1 woman). *Students:* 5 full-time (1 woman); includes 1 minority (Hispanic American), 2 international. Average age 38. 5 applicants, 100% accepted, 5 enrolled. *Degree requirements:* For master's, thesis. *Entrance requirements:* For master's, bachelor in theology. *Application deadline:* For fall admission, 9/7 priority date for domestic students. Applications are processed on a rolling basis. Application fee: $50. *Expenses:* Tuition: Full-time $3,300; part-time $130 per credit. Required fees: $125. One-time fee: $105 part-time. Tuition and fees vary according to reciprocity agreements. *Financial support:* In 2007–08, 5 fellowships (averaging $2,000 per year) were awarded. *Faculty research:* Pastoral theology. *Unit head:* Fr. Daniel Cadrin, OP, Director, 514-739-3223.

College of Mount St. Joseph, Graduate Program in Religious Studies, Cincinnati, OH 45233-1670. Offers spiritual and pastoral care (MA). Part-time and evening/weekend programs available.

Faculty: 3 full-time (1 woman), 3 part-time/adjunct (2 women). *Students:* 1 (woman) full-time, 27 part-time (25 women); includes 1 minority (African American) Average age 47. 18 applicants, 100% accepted, 11 enrolled. In 2007, 13 degrees awarded. *Degree requirements:* For master's, comprehensive exam, integrating project. *Entrance requirements:* For master's, 3 letters of recommendation, interview, essay, minimum GPA of 2.7. Additional exam requirements/recommendations for international students: Required—TOEFL (minimum score 560 paper-based; 220 computer-based). *Application deadline:* Applications are processed on a rolling basis. Application fee: $50. Electronic applications accepted. *Expenses: Contact institution. Financial support:* In 2007–08, 21 students received support. Career-related internships or fieldwork and scholarships/grants available. Support available to part-time students. Financial award application deadline: 6/1; financial award applicants required to submit FAFSA. *Faculty research:* Contextual/cultural/systematic theology, historical/spiritual theology, business/economics ethics, social justice, Biblical/cultural/pastoral theology. *Unit head:* Dr. John Trokan, Chair, 513-244-4272, Fax: 513-244-4222, E-mail: john_trokan@mail.msj.edu. *Application contact:* Marilyn Hoskins, Assistant Director of Admissions for Graduate Recruitment, 513-244-4723, Fax: 513-244-4629, E-mail: marilyn_hoskins@mail.msj.edu.

Columbia International University, Columbia Biblical Seminary and School of Missions, Columbia, SC 29230-3122. Offers academic ministries (M Div); bible exposition (M Div, MABE); biblical studies (Certificate); counseling ministries (Certificate); divinity (M Div); educational ministries (M Div, MAEM, Certificate); intercultural studies (M Div, MAIS, Certificate); leadership (D Min); leadership for evangelism/mobilization (MALM); member care (D Min); ministry (Certificate); missions (D Min); pastoral counseling and spiritual formation (M Div, MAPS); preaching (D Min); theology (MA). *Accreditation:* ATS (one or more programs are accredited). Part-time and evening/weekend programs available. *Degree requirements:* For master's, integrative seminar; for doctorate, comprehensive exam, thesis/dissertation; for M Div, internship. *Entrance requirements:* For master's, minimum GPA of 2.7; for doctorate, 3 years of ministerial experience, M Div. Additional exam requirements/recommendations for international students: Required—TOEFL. Electronic applications accepted.

Concordia University, Nebraska, Graduate Programs in Education, Program in Family Life Ministry, Seward, NE 68434-1599. Offers MS. Part-time and evening/weekend programs available. *Degree requirements:* For master's, thesis or alternative. *Entrance requirements:* For master's, GRE, MAT, or NTE, minimum GPA of 3.0, BS in education or equivalent.

Concordia University, St. Paul, College of Vocation and Ministry, St. Paul, MN 55104-5494. Offers Christian education (Certificate); Christian outreach (MA). Part-time and evening/weekend programs available. Postbaccalaureate distance learning degree programs offered (minimal on-campus study). *Faculty:* 3 full-time (0 women), 5 part-time/adjunct (3 women). *Students:* 6 full-time (5 women), 13 part-time (9 women), 1 international. Average age 35. In 2007, 7 other advanced degrees awarded. *Entrance requirements:* Additional exam requirements/recommendations for international students: Required—TOEFL. *Application deadline:* Applications are processed on a rolling basis. Application fee: $50. Electronic applications accepted. *Financial support:* Federal Work-Study and scholarships/grants available. Financial award applicants required to submit FAFSA. *Application contact:* Kimberly Craig, Director of Graduate and Cohort Admission, 651-603-6223, Fax: 651-603-6320, E-mail: craig@csp.edu.

The Criswell College, Graduate School of the Bible, Dallas, TX 75246-1537. Offers biblical studies (M Div, MA); Christian leadership (MA); ministry (MA); New Testament (MA); Old Testament (MA); theological studies (MA); theology (MA). Part-time programs available. *Degree requirements:* For master's, 2 foreign languages, thesis optional; for M Div, 2 foreign languages, thesis/dissertation optional. *Entrance requirements:* For M Div and master's, GRE General Test, minimum GPA of 2.5. Electronic applications accepted. *Faculty research:* Emphasis on biblical languages (Hebrew and Greek), expository preaching and evangelism in the local church.

Dallas Baptist University, College of Adult Education, Professional Development Program, Dallas, TX 75211-9299. Offers accounting (MA); business (MA); church leadership (MA); corporate management (MA); counseling (MA); criminal justice (MA); English as a second language (MA); finance (MA); higher education (MA); leadership studies (MA); management (MA); management information systems (MA); marketing (MA); missions (MA). Part-time and evening/weekend programs available. *Faculty:* 55 full-time (22 women), 114 part-time/adjunct (44 women). *Students:* 19 full-time, 72 part-time. 35 applicants, 46% accepted, 12 enrolled. In 2007, 37 degrees awarded. *Entrance requirements:* For master's, minimum GPA of 3.0. Additional exam requirements/recommendations for international students: Required—TOEFL, IELTS. Application fee: $25. *Expenses:* Tuition: Full-time $9,144; part-time $508 per credit hour. *Financial support:* Federal Work-Study, institutionally sponsored loans, scholarships/grants, and tuition waivers (full and partial) available. Support available to part-time students. Financial award applicants required to submit FAFSA. *Unit head:* Dr. David Stricklin, Acting Director, 214-333-5496, Fax: 214-333-5558, E-mail: graduate@dbu.edu. *Application contact:* Kit P. Montgomery, Director of Graduate Programs, 214-333-5242, Fax: 214-333-5579, E-mail: graduate@dbu.edu.

Dallas Baptist University, Gary Cook School of Leadership and Christian Education, Program in Christian Education, Dallas, TX 75211-9299. Offers adult ministry (MA); business ministry (MA); childhood ministry (MA); collegiate ministry (MA); communication ministry (MA); counseling ministry (MA); education ministry (MA); general ministry (MA); missions ministry (MA); student ministry (MA); worship ministry (MA). Part-time and evening/weekend programs available. *Faculty:* 55 full-time (22 women), 114 part-time/adjunct (44 women). *Students:* 20 full-time, 52 part-time. 29 applicants, 52% accepted, 13 enrolled. In 2007, 34 degrees awarded. *Entrance requirements:* For master's, minimum GPA of 3.0. Additional exam requirements/recommendations for international students: Required—TOEFL. *Application deadline:* Applications are processed on a rolling basis. Application fee: $25. Electronic applications accepted. *Expenses:* Tuition: Full-time $9,144; part-time $508 per credit hour. *Financial support:* Federal Work-Study, institutionally sponsored loans, scholarships/grants, and tuition waivers (full and partial) available. Support available to part-time students. Financial award applicants required to submit FAFSA. *Unit head:* Dr. Judy Morris, Director, 214-333-5246, Fax: 214-333-5115, E-mail: graduate@dbu.edu. *Application contact:* Kit P. Montgomery, Director of Graduate Programs, 214-333-5242, Fax: 214-333-5579, E-mail: graduate@dbu.edu.

Dallas Baptist University, Gary Cook School of Leadership and Christian Education, Program in Christian Education: Childhood Ministry, Dallas, TX 75211-9299. Offers MA. Part-time and evening/weekend programs available. *Faculty:* 55 full-time (22 women), 114 part-time/adjunct (44 women). *Students:* 3 full-time, 19 part-time. 15 applicants, 73% accepted, 11 enrolled. *Entrance requirements:* For master's, Minimum GPA of 3.0. Additional exam requirements/recommendations for international students: Required—TOEFL, IELTS. Application fee: $25. *Expenses:* Tuition: Full-time $9,144; part-time $508 per credit hour. *Financial support:* Federal Work-Study, institutionally sponsored loans, scholarships/grants, and tuition waivers (full and partial) available. Support available to part-time students. Financial award applicants required to submit FAFSA. *Unit head:* Tommy Sanders, Director, 214-333-6851, Fax: 214-333-6955, E-mail: graduate@dbu.edu. *Application contact:* Kit P. Montgomery, Director of Graduate Programs, 214-333-5242, Fax: 214-333-5579, E-mail: graduate@dbu.edu.

Dallas Baptist University, Gary Cook School of Leadership and Christian Education, Program in Christian Education: Student Ministry, Dallas, TX 75211-9299. Offers MA. Part-time and evening/weekend programs available. *Faculty:* 55 full-time (22 women), 114 part-time/adjunct (44 women). *Students:* 1 full-time, 9 part-time. 3 applicants, 100% accepted, 3 enrolled. *Entrance requirements:* For master's, minimum GPA of 3.0. Additional exam requirements/recommendations for international students: Required—TOEFL, IELTS. Application fee: $25. *Expenses:* Tuition: Full-time $9,144; part-time $508 per credit hour. *Financial support:* Federal Work-Study, institutionally sponsored loans, scholarships/grants, and tuition waivers (full and partial) available. Support available to part-time students. Financial award applicants required to submit FAFSA. *Unit head:* Dr. Dwayne Ulmer, Director, 214-333-6851, Fax: 214-333-6955, E-mail: graduate@dbu.edu. *Application contact:* Kit P. Montgomery, Director of Graduate Programs, 214-333-5242, Fax: 214-333-5579, E-mail: graduate@dbu.edu.

Dallas Baptist University, Gary Cook School of Leadership and Christian Education, Program in Global Leadership, Dallas, TX 75211-9299. Offers business communication (MA); Christian education/missions (MA); ESL (MA); general studies (MA); global studies (MA); international business (MA); missions (MA); worship/missions (MA). Part-time and evening/weekend programs available. *Faculty:* 55 full-time (22 women), 114 part-time/adjunct (44 women). *Students:* 2 full-time, 21 part-time. 20 applicants, 65% accepted, 13 enrolled. *Entrance requirements:* For master's, minimum GPA 3.0. Additional exam requirements/recommendations for international students: Required—TOEFL, IELTS. Application fee: $25. *Expenses:* Tuition: Full-time $9,144; part-time $508 per credit hour. *Financial support:* Federal Work-Study, institutionally sponsored loans, scholarships/grants, and tuition waivers (full and partial) available. Support available to part-time students. Financial award applicants required to submit FAFSA. *Unit head:* Dr. Jim Lemons, Director, 214-333-5506, Fax: 214-333-6955, E-mail: graduate@dbu.edu. *Application contact:* Kit P. Montgomery, Director of Graduate Programs, 214-333-5242, Fax: 214-333-5579, E-mail: graduate@dbu.edu.

Dallas Baptist University, Gary Cook School of Leadership and Christian Education, Program in Worship Leadership, Dallas, TX 75211-9299. Offers MA. Part-time and evening/weekend programs available. *Faculty:* 55 full-time (22 women), 114 part-time/adjunct (44 women). *Students:* 17 full-time, 25 part-time. 13 applicants, 62% accepted, 8 enrolled. In 2007, 9 degrees awarded. *Entrance requirements:* For master's, minimum GPA of 3.0. Additional exam requirements/recommendations for international students: Required—TOEFL, IELTS. Application fee: $25. *Expenses:* Tuition: Full-time $9,144; part-time $508 per credit hour. *Financial support:* Federal Work-Study, institutionally sponsored loans, scholarships/grants, and tuition waivers (full and partial) available. Support available to part-time students. Financial award applicants required to submit FAFSA. *Unit head:* Dr. Jim Lemons, Director, 214-333-5454, Fax: 214-333-6955, E-mail: graduate@dbu.edu. *Application contact:* Kit P. Montgomery, Director of Graduate Programs, 214-333-5242, Fax: 214-333-5579, E-mail: graduate@dbu.edu.

Dallas Theological Seminary, Graduate Programs, Dallas, TX 75204-6499. Offers academic ministries (Th M); Bible translation (Th M); biblical and theological studies (CGS); biblical counseling (MA, Th M); biblical exegesis and linguistics (MA); biblical exposition (PhD); biblical studies (MA); Christian education (MA, D Min); cross-cultural ministries (MA, Th M); educational leadership (Th M); evangelism and discipleship (Th M); interdisciplinary studies (Th M); media and communication (MA); media arts in ministry (Th M); ministry (D Min); New Testament studies (Th M, PhD); Old Testament studies (PhD); parachurch ministries (Th M); pastoral ministries (Th M); sacred theology (STM); theological studies (PhD); women's ministry (Th M). *Accreditation:* ATS (one or more programs are accredited). Part-time and evening/weekend programs available. *Degree requirements:* For master's, variable foreign language requirement, thesis (for some programs); for doctorate, 2 foreign languages, thesis/dissertation. *Entrance requirements:* Additional exam requirements/recommendations for international students: Required—TOEFL, TWE. *Application deadline:* For fall admission, 7/1 priority date for domestic students; for winter admission, 11/1 priority date for domestic students; for spring admission, 11/15 priority date for domestic students. Applications are processed on a rolling basis. Application fee: $30. Electronic applications accepted. *Financial support:* Career-related internships or fieldwork, institutionally sponsored loans, scholarships/grants, and tuition waivers (full and partial) available. Financial award application deadline: 2/28. *Unit head:* Dr. Mark L. Bailey, President, 214-841-3676, Fax: 214-841-3565. *Application contact:* Josh Bleeker, Director of Admissions, 214-841-3661, Fax: 214-841-3664, E-mail: admissions@dts.edu.

Denver Seminary, Graduate and Professional Programs, Littleton, CO 80120. Offers apologetics (Certificate); biblical studies (MA); Christian formation and soul care (MA, Certificate); Christian studies (MA, Certificate); church and parachurch leadership (D Min); counseling licensure (MA); counseling ministry (MA); intercultural ministry (Certificate); leadership (MA, Certificate); marriage and family counseling (D Min); pastoral ministry (D Min); philosophy of religion (MA); spiritual guidance (Certificate); theology (M Div, Certificate); worship (Certificate); youth and family ministry (MA). *Accreditation:* ACA; ACIPE; ATS (one or more programs are accredited). Part-time and evening/weekend programs available. Postbaccalaureate distance learning degree programs offered. *Faculty:* 23 full-time (4 women), 94 part-time/adjunct (39 women). *Students:* 517 full-time (154 women), 283 part-time (130 women); includes 47 minority (15 African Americans, 1 American Indian/Alaska Native, 22 Asian Americans or Pacific Islanders, 9 Hispanic Americans), 43 international. Average age 34. 333 applicants, 76% accepted, 166 enrolled. In 2007, 41 first professional degrees, 77 master's, 8 doctorates, 9 other advanced degrees awarded. *Degree requirements:* For master's, 2 foreign languages, thesis (for some programs); for doctorate, 2 foreign languages, thesis/dissertation; for M Div, 2 foreign languages. *Entrance requirements:* For M Div, minimum undergraduate GPA of 2.5; for master's, minimum undergraduate GPA of 3.0; for doctorate, M Div, 3 years of ministry experience. Additional exam requirements/recommendations for international students: Required—TOEFL (minimum score 575 paper-based; 233 computer-based; 90 iBT). *Application deadline:* For fall admission, 7/15 priority date for domestic students; for spring admission, 12/15 priority date for domestic students. Applications are processed on a rolling basis. Application fee: $35. Electronic applications accepted. *Expenses:* Tuition: Part-time $495 per semester hour. One-time fee: $150 part-time. Part-time tuition and fees vary according to course load. *Financial support:* In 2007–08, 220 students received support. Career-related internships or fieldwork, Federal Work-Study, scholarships/grants, and unspecified assistantships available. Support available to part-time students. Financial award application deadline: 4/1; financial award applicants required to submit FAFSA. *Unit head:* Dr. Randy MacFarland, Vice President and Dean, 303-762-6980, Fax: 303-761-8020, E-mail: randy.macfarland@denverseminary.edu. *Application contact:* Nathan Lamb, Director of Admissions, 303-357-5801, Fax: 303-783-3122, E-mail: info@denverseminary.edu.

Eastern Mennonite University, Eastern Mennonite Seminary, Harrisonburg, VA 22802-2462. Offers church leadership (MA); divinity (M Div); ministry studies (Certificate); online theological studies (Certificate); religion (MA); theological studies (Certificate). *Accreditation:* ATS. Part-time programs available. *Faculty:* 9 full-time (2 women), 16 part-time/adjunct (5 women). *Students:* 42 full-time (15 women), 29 part-time (13 women); includes 2 minority (both African Americans), 6 international. Average age 40. 43 applicants, 100% accepted. In 2007, 19 first professional degrees, 4 master's awarded. *Degree requirements:* For master's, thesis (for some programs); for M Div, thesis/dissertation (for some programs), supervised field education. *Entrance requirements:* For M Div and master's, minimum GPA of 2.5. Additional exam requirements/recommendations for international students: Required—TOEFL (minimum score 550 paper-based; 213 computer-based). *Application deadline:* For fall admission, 6/15 priority date for domestic and international students; for winter admission, 11/15 priority date for domestic and international students; for spring admission, 3/15 priority date for domestic and international students. Applications are processed on a rolling basis. Application fee: $25. *Expenses: Contact institution.* Tuition and fees vary according to program. *Financial support:* In 2007–08, 43 students received support. Application deadline: 6/30; *Faculty research:* Spiritual direction and 'culture of call"; leadership coaching: an approach to leadership in a culture of call; clarity of call in the probationary process for United Methodist clergy in Virginia; EMS women's experiences of culture of call efforts; practices of excellent and fruitful Mennonite pastoral ministry. Total annual research expenditures: $45,000. *Unit head:* Dr. Ervin R. Stutzman, Seminary Dean, 540-432-4261, Fax: 540-432-4444, E-mail: stutzerv@emu.edu. *Application contact:* Don A. Yoder, Director of Seminary and Graduate Admissions, 540-432-4257, Fax: 540-432-4598, E-mail: yoderda@emu.edu.

Eastern Mennonite University, Program in Counseling, Harrisonburg, VA 22802-2462. Offers MA, M Div/MA. *Accreditation:* ACA (one or more programs are accredited); ACIPE. Part-time programs available. *Faculty:* 1 full-time (0 women), 5 part-time/adjunct (3 women). *Students:* 32 full-time (26 women), 6 part-time (all women); includes 3 minority (2 African Americans, 1 Asian American or Pacific Islander). Average age 33. 45 applicants, 64% accepted, 21

Pastoral Ministry and Counseling

Eastern Mennonite University (continued)

enrolled. In 2007, 15 degrees awarded. *Degree requirements:* For master's, practicum, internship. *Entrance requirements:* For master's, minimum GPA of 3.0. Additional exam requirements/recommendations for international students: Required—TOEFL (minimum score 550 paper-based). *Application deadline:* For fall admission, 3/1 for domestic students. Application fee: $25. *Expenses: Contact institution.* Tuition and fees vary according to program. *Financial support:* In 2007–08, 7 students received support. Scholarships/grants available. Financial award application deadline: 6/30; financial award applicants required to submit FAFSA. *Faculty research:* Career and gender, empathy and consciousness, pastoral counseling, education models. *Unit head:* Dr. P. David Glanzer, Professor of Counselor Education, 540-432-4244, Fax: 540-432-4444, E-mail: glanzerd@emu.edu. *Application contact:* Brenda C. Fairweather, Administrative Assistant for Masters in Counseling Program, 540-432-4243, Fax: 540-432-4444, E-mail: fairweat@emu.edu.

Eastern University, Palmer Theological Seminary, Program in Ministry, St. Davids, PA 19087-3696. Offers marriage and family (D Min). *Accreditation:* ACIPE. Part-time programs available. *Degree requirements:* For doctorate, thesis/dissertation. *Entrance requirements:* For doctorate, 3 years of experience, involvement in ministry, church endorsement. Expenses: Contact institution.

Ecumenical Theological Seminary, Program in Ministry, Detroit, MI 48201. Offers D Min. *Accreditation:* ACIPE.

Episcopal Theological Seminary of the Southwest, Graduate and Professional Programs, Austin, TX 78768-2247. Offers Anglican studies (Advanced Diploma); chaplaincy (MAPM); counseling (MAC); discipleship (MAPM); divinity (M Div); religion (MAR); spiritual formation (MAPM); theological studies (Advanced Diploma). *Accreditation:* ACIPE; ATS (one or more programs are accredited). Part-time and evening/weekend programs available. *Faculty:* 9 full-time (2 women), 20 part-time/adjunct (6 women). *Students:* 60 full-time (39 women), 37 part-time (27 women); includes 7 minority (4 African Americans, 1 Asian American or Pacific Islander, 2 Hispanic Americans), 1 international. Average age 46. 41 applicants, 98% accepted, 35 enrolled. In 2007, 24 first professional degrees, 9 master's, 2 other advanced degrees awarded. *Degree requirements:* For master's, thesis (for some programs). *Entrance requirements:* For M Div and master's, GRE, MAT, interview; for Advanced Diploma, interview. *Application deadline:* For fall admission, 7/1 for domestic students; for spring admission, 11/1 for domestic students. Applications are processed on a rolling basis. Application fee: $50. *Expenses:* Tuition: Full-time $13,150; part-time $390 per hour. Required fees: $75. One-time fee: $20 part-time. *Financial support:* Career-related internships or fieldwork and scholarships/grants available. Support available to part-time students. Financial award application deadline: 6/17. *Unit head:* Very Rev. Douglas Travis, Dean and President, 512-472-4133 Ext. 307, Fax: 512-472-3098, E-mail: dtravis@etss.edu. *Application contact:* Rev. Ken Malcolm, Director of Admissions, 512-472-4133 Ext. 375, Fax: 512-472-3098, E-mail: kmalcolm@etss.edu.

Evangelical Theological Seminary, Graduate and Professional Programs, Myerstown, PA 17067-1212. Offers divinity (M Div); marriage and family therapy (MA); ministry (Certificate); religion (MA). *Accreditation:* ATS (one or more programs are accredited). Part-time programs available. Postbaccalaureate distance learning degree programs offered (minimal on-campus study). *Faculty:* 7 full-time (2 women), 21 part-time/adjunct (3 women). *Students:* 22 full-time (0 women), 152 part-time (66 women). Average age 33. 60 applicants, 77% accepted, 46 enrolled. In 2007, 11 first professional degrees, 22 master's awarded. *Degree requirements:* For master's, 2 foreign languages; for M Div, 2 foreign languages, ministry internship. *Entrance requirements:* For M Div and master's, minimum GPA of 2.5. Additional exam requirements/recommendations for international students: Required—TOEFL (minimum score 550 paper-based; 213 computer-based). *Application deadline:* For fall admission, 6/1 priority date for domestic students, 4/1 priority date for international students; for spring admission, 11/1 priority date for domestic students, 9/1 priority date for international students. Applications are processed on a rolling basis. Application fee: $35. *Expenses:* Tuition: Full-time $10,440; part-time $435 per credit. Required fees: $25 per semester. One-time fee: $125. *Financial support:* Career-related internships or fieldwork, scholarships/grants, and tuition waivers (full) available. Support available to part-time students. Financial award application deadline: 6/1; financial award applicants required to submit FAFSA. *Faculty research:* Literary form and structure within the Hebrew and Greek scriptures, Wesley studies, esoteric biblical languages, the Mosaic law and the Christian, ethics. *Unit head:* Rev. Dr. John V. Tornfelt, Vice President, Academic Affairs, 717-866-5775 Ext. 140, Fax: 717-866-4667, E-mail: jtornfelt@evangelical.edu. *Application contact:* Tom M. Maiello, Dean of Admissions, 800-532-5775 Ext. 109, Fax: 717-866-4667, E-mail: admissions@evangelical.edu.

Faith Baptist Bible College and Theological Seminary, Graduate Program, Ankeny, IA 50021. Offers biblical studies (MA); pastoral studies (M Div); pastoral training (MA); religion (MA); theological studies (MA). Part-time programs available. *Faculty:* 4 full-time (0 women), 7 part-time/adjunct (0 women). *Students:* 28 full-time (3 women), 28 part-time (2 women); includes 1 minority (Hispanic American), 1 international. Average age 29. In 2007, 9 first professional degrees, 12 master's awarded. *Degree requirements:* For master's, thesis or alternative; for M Div, 2 foreign languages. *Entrance requirements:* Additional exam requirements/recommendations for international students: Required—TOEFL (minimum score 550 paper-based; 197 computer-based). *Application deadline:* For fall admission, 8/1 priority date for domestic students, 8/1 for international students; for spring admission, 12/15 for domestic and international students. Applications are processed on a rolling basis. Application fee: $25. *Expenses:* Tuition: Full-time $10,228; part-time $392 per credit hour. Required fees: $95 per semester. One-time fee: $50. Tuition and fees vary according to class time and course load. *Financial support:* In 2007–08, 70 students received support. Career-related internships or fieldwork and scholarships/grants available. Support available to part-time students. Financial award application deadline: 3/1; financial award applicants required to submit FAFSA. *Faculty research:* Baptist theology, American church history. *Unit head:* Dr. Ernest Schmidt, Dean of Seminary, 515-964-0601, Fax: 514-964-1638, E-mail: schmidte@faith.edu. *Application contact:* Pat Odle, Vice President of Enrollment, 888-FAITH4U, Fax: 515-964-1638, E-mail: odlep@faith.edu.

Fordham University, Graduate School of Religion and Religious Education, New York, NY 10458. Offers pastoral counseling and spiritual care (MA); pastoral ministry/spirituality/pastoral counseling (D Min); religion and religious education (MA); religious education (MS, PhD, PD); spiritual direction (Certificate). Part-time programs available. Terminal master's awarded for partial completion of doctoral program. *Degree requirements:* For master's, research paper; for doctorate, comprehensive exam, thesis/dissertation. *Entrance requirements:* For doctorate, MAT. Electronic applications accepted. Expenses: Contact institution. *Faculty research:* Spirituality and spiritual direction, pastoral care and counseling, adult family and community, growth and young adult.

Freed-Hardeman University, School of Biblical Studies, Program in Ministry, Henderson, TN 38340-2399. Offers M Min. Part-time programs available. *Faculty:* 5 full-time (0 women), 1 part-time/adjunct (0 women). *Students:* 30. Average age 29. In 2007, 12 degrees awarded. *Degree requirements:* For master's, comprehensive exam, internship. *Entrance requirements:* For master's, GRE General Test or MAT. Additional exam requirements/recommendations for international students: Required—TOEFL (minimum score 500 paper-based; 173 computer-based). *Application deadline:* For fall admission, 8/1 priority date for domestic students; for spring admission, 12/1 for domestic students. Applications are processed on a rolling basis. Application fee: $32. *Expenses:* Tuition: Full-time $6,012; part-time $334 per credit hour. Required fees: $10 per hour. *Financial support:* Career-related internships or fieldwork, Federal Work-Study, tuition waivers (partial), and unspecified assistantships available. Support available to part-time students. Financial award application deadline: 8/1; financial award applicants required to submit FAFSA. *Unit head:* Dr. Earl Edwards, Director of Graduate Studies, School of Biblical Studies, 731-989-6626, Fax: 731-989-6059, E-mail: eedwards@fhu.edu.

Gannon University, School of Graduate Studies, College of Humanities, Business, and Education, School of Humanities, Program in Pastoral Studies, Erie, PA 16541-0001. Offers MA, Certificate. Part-time and evening/weekend programs available. *Students:* 5 full-time (3 women), 6 part-time (5 women); includes 2 minority (1 African American, 1 Hispanic American). Average age 31. 8 applicants, 75% accepted, 4 enrolled. In 2007, 5 degrees awarded. *Degree requirements:* For master's, comprehensive exam, thesis. *Entrance requirements:* For master's, GRE General Test, interview; minimum 10 credits of course work in philosophy, religious studies, or theology. Additional exam requirements/recommendations for international students: Required—TOEFL (minimum score 500 paper-based; 173 computer-based). *Application deadline:* Applications are processed on a rolling basis. Application fee: $25. *Expenses:* Tuition: Full-time $13,050; part-time $725 per credit. Required fees: $502; $16 per credit. Tuition and fees vary according to course load, degree level, campus/location and program. *Financial support:* Career-related internships or fieldwork and unspecified assistantships available. Financial award application deadline: 7/1; financial award applicants required to submit FAFSA. *Unit head:* Dr. Mary Anne Rivera, Director, 814-871-5646, E-mail: rivera006@gannon.edu. *Application contact:* Debra Meszaros, Director of Graduate Recruitment, 814-871-5819, Fax: 814-871-5827, E-mail: cfal@gannon.edu.

Gardner-Webb University, M. Christopher White School of Divinity, Boiling Springs, NC 28017. Offers Christian education (M Div); ministry (D Min); missiology (M Div); pastoral care and counseling (M Div); pastoral ministry (M Div); M Div/MA. *Accreditation:* ACIPE; ATS. Part-time programs available. *Degree requirements:* For M Div, 2 foreign languages. *Entrance requirements:* For M Div, minimum GPA of 2.0; for doctorate, minimum GPA of 2.75. Expenses: Contact institution. *Faculty research:* Jewish Christian dialogue, Islam.

Garrett-Evangelical Theological Seminary, Graduate and Professional Programs, Evanston, IL 60201-3298. Offers Bible and culture (PhD); Christian education (MA); Christian education and congregational studies (PhD); contemporary theology and culture (PhD); divinity (M Div); ethics, church, and society (MA); liturgical studies (PhD); ministry (D Min); music ministry (MA); pastoral care and counseling (MA); pastoral theology, personality, and culture (PhD); spiritual formation and evangelism (MA); theological studies (MTS); M Div/MSW. *Accreditation:* ACIPE; ATS (one or more programs are accredited). Part-time programs available. *Degree requirements:* For master's, thesis (for some programs); for doctorate, thesis/dissertation. *Entrance requirements:* For doctorate, GRE (PhD). Additional exam requirements/recommendations for international students: Required—TOEFL (minimum score 560 paper-based; 230 computer-based). Electronic applications accepted.

George Fox University, George Fox Evangelical Seminary, Newberg, OR 97132-2697. Offers divinity (M Div); ministry (D Min), including leadership and spiritual formation, leadership in the emerging culture; ministry leadership (MA); spiritual formation (MA); spiritual formation and discipleship (Certificate); theological studies (MA). *Accreditation:* ACIPE; ATS. Part-time programs available. Postbaccalaureate distance learning degree programs offered (minimal on-campus study). *Faculty:* 7 full-time (2 women), 13 part-time/adjunct (4 women). *Students:* 105 full-time (27 women), 215 part-time (76 women); includes 27 minority (5 African Americans, 2 American Indian/Alaska Native, 12 Asian Americans or Pacific Islanders, 8 Hispanic Americans), 5 international. Average age 42. 135 applicants, 85% accepted, 109 enrolled. In 2007, 11 first professional degrees, 18 master's, 20 doctorates, 1 other advanced degree awarded. *Degree requirements:* For master's, variable foreign language requirement, thesis optional, internship. *Entrance requirements:* Additional exam requirements/recommendations for international students: Required—TOEFL (minimum score 550 paper-based; 213 computer-based). *Application deadline:* For fall admission, 7/1 for domestic and international students; for spring admission, 11/1 for domestic and international students. Applications are processed on a rolling basis. Application fee: $40. Electronic applications accepted. *Expenses: Contact institution.* *Financial support:* In 2007–08, 33 students received support. Career-related internships or fieldwork and scholarships/grants available. Financial award application deadline: 5/1; financial award applicants required to submit FAFSA. *Unit head:* Dr. Chuck Conniry, Vice President and Dean, 503-554-6163, E-mail: cconniry@georgefox.edu. *Application contact:* Sheila Bartlett, Admissions Counselor, 800-631-0921, Fax: 503-554-6111, E-mail: sbartlett@georgefox.edu.

Georgian Court University, School of Arts and Humanities, Lakewood, NJ 08701-2697. Offers Catholic school leadership (Certificate); parish business management (Certificate); pastoral administration (Certificate); pastoral ministry (Certificate); religious education (Certificate); theology (MA, Certificate). Part-time and evening/weekend programs available. *Faculty:* 3 full-time (2 women). *Students:* Average age 51. 10 applicants, 60% accepted, 2 enrolled. In 2007, 9 master's, 1 other advanced degree awarded. *Degree requirements:* For master's, thesis (for some programs). *Entrance requirements:* For master's, 3 letters of recommendation. Additional exam requirements/recommendations for international students: Required—TOEFL (minimum score 550 paper-based; 213 computer-based). *Application deadline:* For fall admission, 8/1 priority date for domestic students, 4/1 for international students; for spring admission, 1/1 priority date for domestic students, 7/1 for international students. Applications are processed on a rolling basis. Application fee: $40. Electronic applications accepted. *Expenses:* Tuition: Full-time $15,456; part-time $644 per credit. Required fees: $760; $200 per term. Tuition and fees vary according to campus/location. *Financial support:* Scholarships/grants, health care benefits, and unspecified assistantships available. Financial award application deadline: 4/15; financial award applicants required to submit FAFSA. *Unit head:* Dr. Linda James, Dean, 732-987-2617, Fax: 732-987-2007. *Application contact:* Eugene Soltys, Director of Graduate Admissions, 732-987-2770, Fax: 732-987-2084, E-mail: graduateadmissions@georgian.edu.

Golden Gate Baptist Theological Seminary, Graduate and Professional Programs, Mill Valley, CA 94941-3197. Offers divinity (M Div); early childhood education (Certificate); education leadership (MAEL, Diploma); ministry (D Min); theological studies (MTS); theology (Th M); youth ministry (Certificate). *Accreditation:* ACIPE; ATS (one or more programs are accredited). Part-time and evening/weekend programs available. *Degree requirements:* For master's, thesis (for some programs); for doctorate, 2 foreign languages, thesis/dissertation; for M Div, 2 foreign languages. *Entrance requirements:* For doctorate, MAT. Additional exam requirements/recommendations for international students: Required—TOEFL (minimum score 550 paper-based; 213 computer-based). Electronic applications accepted.

Gonzaga University, College of Arts and Sciences, Department of Religious Studies, Spokane, WA 99258. Offers pastoral ministry (MA); religious studies (MA); spirituality (MA). *Faculty:* 9 full-time (6 women). *Students:* 4 full-time (3 women), 25 part-time (12 women); includes 3 minority (1 American Indian/Alaska Native, 2 Hispanic Americans). Average age 44. 15 applicants, 87% accepted, 13 enrolled. In 2007, 8 degrees awarded. *Degree requirements:* For master's, comprehensive exam. *Entrance requirements:* For master's, GRE General Test or MAT, minimum GPA of 3.0. Additional exam requirements/recommendations for international students: Required—TOEFL. *Application deadline:* For fall admission, 7/20 priority date for domestic students; for spring admission, 11/1 for domestic students. Applications are processed on a rolling basis. Application fee: $40. *Financial support:* Application deadline: 3/1. *Unit head:* Dr. Ron Large, Chairperson, 509-328-4220 Ext. 6782, E-mail: jennings@gonzaga.edu.

Gordon-Conwell Theological Seminary, Graduate and Professional Programs, South Hamilton, MA 01982. Offers Christian education (MACE); church history (MACH); counseling (MACO); ministry (D Min); missions/evangelism (MAME); New Testament (MANT); Old Testament (MAOT); religion (MAR); theology (M Div, MATH, Th M). *Accreditation:* ACIPE; ATS (one or more programs are accredited). Part-time and evening/weekend programs available. *Degree requirements:* For master's, one foreign language, thesis optional; for doctorate, 2 foreign languages, thesis/dissertation; for M Div, 2 foreign languages. *Entrance requirements:* For M Div and master's, minimum GPA of 2.5; for doctorate, minimum GPA of 3.0.

Graceland University, Community of Christ Seminary, Lamoni, IA 50140. Offers Christian ministry (MACM); religion (MAR). Part-time programs available. Postbaccalaureate distance learning degree programs offered (minimal on-campus study). *Faculty:* 4 full-time (1 woman), 13 part-time/adjunct (5 women). *Students:* 9 full-time (2 women), 21 part-time (8 women);

includes 1 minority (American Indian/Alaska Native), 3 international. Average age 43. 21 applicants, 76% accepted, 15 enrolled. In 2007, 10 degrees awarded. *Degree requirements:* For master's, thesis optional, integrated project. *Entrance requirements:* For master's, minimum cumulative GPA of 3.0. *Application deadline:* For fall admission, 8/15 priority date for domestic students; for winter admission, 10/15 priority date for domestic students; for spring admission, 4/15 priority date for domestic students. Applications are processed on a rolling basis. Application fee: $50. *Expenses: Contact institution.* Part-time tuition and fees vary according to program. *Financial support:* Scholarships/grants available. Financial award application deadline: 12/15; financial award applicants required to submit FAFSA. *Faculty research:* Theology. *Unit head:* Dr. Don H. Compier, Dean, 800-833-0524 Ext. 4900, Fax: 816-833-2990, E-mail: dcompier@graceland.edu. *Application contact:* Tere E. Naylor, Executive Assistant, 816-833-0524 Ext. 4903, Fax: 816-833-2990, E-mail: tnaylor@graceland.edu.

Grace Theological Seminary, Graduate and Professional Programs, Winona Lake, IN 46590-9907. Offers biblical studies (Certificate, Diploma); counseling (M Div); ministry (MA); missions (M Div, MA); theology (M Div, MA, D Min). *Accreditation:* ATS. Part-time programs available. Postbaccalaureate distance learning degree programs offered (no on-campus study). *Degree requirements:* For master's, thesis optional; for doctorate, 2 foreign languages, thesis/dissertation; for M Div, 2 foreign languages, thesis/dissertation optional. *Entrance requirements:* For M Div and master's, MAT, minimum GPA of 2.5. Electronic applications accepted. *Faculty research:* Biblical theology, language, and church ministries.

Grace University, College of Graduate Studies, Counseling Program, Omaha, NE 68108. Offers MA. *Entrance requirements:* For master's, minimum undergraduate GPA of 3.0.

Grand Rapids Theological Seminary of Cornerstone University, Graduate Programs, Grand Rapids, MI 49525-5897. Offers biblical counseling (MA); Biblical counseling (M Div); chaplaincy (M Div); Christian education (M Div, MA); intercultural studies (M Div, MA); New Testament (MA, Th M); Old Testament (MA, Th M); pastoral studies (M Div); systematic theology (MA); theology (Th M). *Accreditation:* ATS. Part-time programs available. Postbaccalaureate distance learning degree programs offered (minimal on-campus study). *Faculty:* 9 full-time (1 woman), 10 part-time/adjunct (1 woman). *Students:* 102 full-time (35 women), 126 part-time (42 women); includes 36 minority (28 African Americans, 2 American Indian/Alaska Native, 3 Asian Americans or Pacific Islanders, 3 Hispanic Americans), 7 international. Average age 35. 160 applicants, 91% accepted, 107 enrolled. *Entrance requirements:* Additional exam requirements/recommendations for international students: Required—TOEFL (minimum score 577 paper-based; 233 computer-based; 90 iBT). *Application deadline:* For fall admission, 8/15 for domestic students; for spring admission, 1/10 for domestic students. Applications are processed on a rolling basis. Electronic applications accepted. *Expenses:* Tuition: Full-time $6,930; part-time $385 per credit hour. Required fees: $520; $10 per credit hour. $170 per semester. Tuition and fees vary according to course load and degree level. *Financial support:* Career-related internships or fieldwork, scholarships/grants, and health care benefits available. Support available to part-time students. Financial award application deadline: 8/15; financial award applicants required to submit FAFSA. *Unit head:* Dr. Douglas L. Fagerstrom, President, 616-222-1422, Fax: 616-222-1502, E-mail: douglas_fagerstrom@cornerstone.edu. *Application contact:* Tara Danielle Kram, 800-697-1133, Fax: 616-254-1623, E-mail: tara_kram@cornerstone.edu.

Greenville College, Program in Leadership and Ministry, Greenville, IL 62246-0159. Offers MA. Part-time programs available. *Degree requirements:* For master's, 6 hours of research/practicum in applied ministry, minimum GPA of 3.0. *Entrance requirements:* For master's, 1 year of work experience in Christian ministry, interview. Additional exam requirements/recommendations for international students: Required—TOEFL (minimum score 525 paper-based; 197 computer-based). Electronic applications accepted.

Harding University, College of Bible and Religion, Program in Ministry, Searcy, AR 72149-0001. Offers M Min. Part-time and evening/weekend programs available. Postbaccalaureate distance learning degree programs offered. *Faculty:* 6 part-time/adjunct (0 women). *Students:* 2 full-time (0 women), 24 part-time (2 women); includes 4 minority (2 African Americans, 1 American Indian/Alaska Native, 1 Hispanic American), 1 international. Average age 37. 3 applicants, 100% accepted, 3 enrolled. In 2007, 4 degrees awarded. *Degree requirements:* For master's, 3 practica (1 hour each), portfolio, capstone project. *Entrance requirements:* For master's, 16 hours course work in Bible, minimum GPA of 2.75. *Application deadline:* For fall admission, 8/1 priority date for domestic and international students; for spring admission, 12/15 priority date for domestic and international students. Applications are processed on a rolling basis. Application fee: $25. Electronic applications accepted. *Expenses:* Tuition: Part-time $485 per credit hour. Required fees: $21 per credit hour. *Financial support:* Career-related internships or fieldwork, institutionally sponsored loans, scholarships/grants, and unspecified assistantships available. *Unit head:* Dr. Bill Richardson, Director/Associate Professor, 501-279-4250, Fax: 501-279-4042, E-mail: mmin@harding.edu. *Application contact:* Debbie Stewart, Information Contact, 501-279-4252, E-mail: dstewart@harding.edu.

Harding University Graduate School of Religion, Graduate Programs, Memphis, TN 38117-5499. Offers Christian ministry (MA); counseling (MA); ministry (M Div, D Min); religion (MA). *Accreditation:* ATS. Part-time programs available. Postbaccalaureate distance learning degree programs offered (minimal on-campus study). *Degree requirements:* For master's, variable foreign language requirement, thesis (for some programs); for doctorate, one foreign language, thesis/dissertation; for M Div, 2 foreign languages, thesis/dissertation optional. *Entrance requirements:* For M Div, GRE General Test (for graduates of non-accredited schools), minimum GPA of 2.5; for master's, minimum GPA of 2.7; for doctorate, minimum GPA of 3.0. Additional exam requirements/recommendations for international students: Required—TOEFL (minimum score 550 paper-based; 213 computer-based; 79 iBT). Electronic applications accepted.

Hardin-Simmons University, Graduate School, Logsdon School of Theology, Logsdon Seminary, Program in Family Ministry, Abilene, TX 79698-0001. Offers MA. Part-time programs available. *Faculty:* 3 full-time (1 woman). *Students:* 15 full-time (7 women), 4 part-time (1 woman); includes 1 minority (Hispanic American) Average age 26. 10 applicants, 80% accepted, 7 enrolled. In 2007, 1 degree awarded. *Degree requirements:* For master's, comprehensive exam, clinical experience, project. *Entrance requirements:* For master's, minimum undergraduate GPA of 3.0 in major, 2.7 overall; 6 hours of course work in psychology; interview; writing sample; 6 hours of course work in Old and New Testament; references. Additional exam requirements/recommendations for international students: Required—TOEFL (minimum score 555 paper-based; 213 computer-based). *Application deadline:* For fall admission, 8/15 priority date for domestic students; for spring admission, 1/5 priority date for domestic students. Applications are processed on a rolling basis. Application fee: $50 ($100 for international students). *Expenses:* Tuition: Full-time $9,810; part-time $545 per hour. Required fees: $590; $75 per semester. One-time fee: $50 part-time. *Financial support:* In 2007–08, 21 students received support, including 2 fellowships (averaging $1,200 per year); career-related internships or fieldwork and scholarships/grants also available. Support available to part-time students. Financial award application deadline: 6/30; financial award applicants required to submit FAFSA. *Unit head:* Dr. Randall Maurer, Director, 325-670-1599, Fax: 325-670-1406, E-mail: rmaurer@hsutx.edu. *Application contact:* Dr. Gary Stanlake, Dean of Graduate Studies, 325-670-1298, Fax: 325-670-1564, E-mail: gradoff@hsutx.edu.

Hartford Seminary, Graduate Programs, Hartford, CT 06105-2279. Offers black ministry (Certificate); Islamic studies (MA); ministerios Hispanos (Certificate); ministry (D Min); religious studies (MA); women's leadership institute (Certificate). *Accreditation:* ATS (one or more programs are accredited). Part-time and evening/weekend programs available. Postbaccalaureate distance learning degree programs offered (no on-campus study). *Faculty:* 12 full-time (5 women), 19 part-time/adjunct (7 women). *Students:* 39 full-time (23 women), 120 part-time (72 women); includes 35 minority (27 African Americans, 5 Asian Americans or Pacific Islanders, 3 Hispanic Americans), 25 international. *Degree requirements:* For master's, thesis optional, oral exam; for doctorate, thesis/dissertation, oral exam. *Entrance requirements:* For doctorate, experience in ministry, M Div. Additional exam requirements/recommendations for international students: Required—TOEFL (minimum score 550 paper-based; 213 computer-based; 80 iBT). *Application deadline:* For fall admission, 7/15 priority date for domestic students, 5/1 priority date for international students; for winter admission, 12/1 priority date for domestic students, 4/1 priority date for international students; for spring admission, 4/5 priority date for domestic students, 3/1 priority date for international students. Applications are processed on a rolling basis. Application fee: $50. *Expenses:* Tuition: Full-time $12,400; part-time $1,550 per unit. *Financial support:* In 2007–08, 74 students received support. Scholarships/grants and tuition waivers (partial) available. Support available to part-time students. Financial award application deadline: 6/1. *Faculty research:* Liturgy and social justice, professional leadership in ministry, congregational studies, Christian-Muslim relations, American religion. *Unit head:* Dr. Efrain Agosto, Academic Dean, 860-509-9554, E-mail: eagosto@hartsem.edu. *Application contact:* Dr. Vanessa Avery-Wall, Admissions Manager, 860-509-9552, Fax: 860-509-9509, E-mail: vaw@hartsem.edu.

Heritage Christian University, Graduate Programs, Florence, AL 35630. Offers counseling (MM); Greek (MA); ministry (MM); New Testament (MA). *Degree requirements:* For master's, practicum (MM), major research paper (MA). *Entrance requirements:* For master's, MAT or GRE, bachelor's degree in Bible from an accredited college or university, minimum GPA of 2.75, 3 letters of recommendation.

Hillsdale Free Will Baptist College, Department of Bible Studies, Moore, OK 73160-1208. Offers ministry (MA). Part-time and evening/weekend programs available. *Degree requirements:* For master's, thesis optional. *Entrance requirements:* Additional exam requirements/recommendations for international students: Recommended—TOEFL (minimum score 500 paper-based).

Holmes Institute, Graduate Program, Burbank, CA 91505. Offers consciousness studies (MS). *Degree requirements:* For master's, comprehensive exam, 1 colloquium, 2 spiritual retreats per year, internship, 2 spiritual conferences. *Entrance requirements:* For master's, 3 letters of recommendation, interview.

Holy Names University, Graduate Division, Department of Counseling Psychology, Oakland, CA 94619-1699. Offers counseling psychology (MA); forensic psychology (MA, Certificate); pastoral counseling (MA, Certificate). Part-time and evening/weekend programs available. *Faculty:* 3 full-time (1 woman), 11 part-time/adjunct (6 women). *Students:* 36 full-time (33 women), 16 part-time (15 women); includes 32 minority (23 African Americans, 3 Asian Americans or Pacific Islanders, 6 Hispanic Americans), 2 international. Average age 35. 21 applicants, 81% accepted, 16 enrolled. In 2007, 13 master's awarded. *Degree requirements:* For master's, comprehensive paper, seminars. *Entrance requirements:* For master's, minimum undergraduate GPA of 2.6 overall, 3.0 in major. Additional exam requirements/recommendations for international students: Required—TOEFL. *Application deadline:* For fall admission, 8/1 priority date for domestic students; for spring admission, 12/1 priority date for domestic students. Applications are processed on a rolling basis. Application fee: $65. *Expenses:* Tuition: Part-time $635 per unit. One-time fee: $340 part-time. Tuition and fees vary according to program. *Financial support:* In 2007–08, 34 students received support. Available to part-time students. Application deadline: 3/2; *Faculty research:* Cognitive psychology, anger management, grief and grief counseling, post-modernism and psychotherapy, spirituality and psychology. *Unit head:* Helen Shoemaker, Program Director, 510-436-1543, E-mail: shoemaker@hnu.edu. *Application contact:* 800-430-1351, Fax: 510-436-1325, E-mail: admissions@hnu.edu.

Holy Names University, Graduate Division, Program in Pastoral Ministries, Oakland, CA 94619-1699. Offers MA, Certificate. *Faculty:* 1 full-time (0 women), 2 part-time/adjunct (both women). *Students:* Average age 45. 19 applicants, 89% accepted, 12 enrolled. In 2007, 1 master's, 8 other advanced degrees awarded. *Degree requirements:* For master's, ministry project. Application fee: $65. *Expenses:* Tuition: Part-time $635 per unit. One-time fee: $340 part-time. Tuition and fees vary according to program. *Financial support:* In 2007–08, 6 students received support. Applicants required to submit FAFSA. *Faculty research:* Ethics, cross-cultural management, faith development through liturgy, multi-cultural community building. *Unit head:* Dr. Robert Lassalle-Klein, Director, 510-436-1074. *Application contact:* Graduate Admissions Office, 800-430-1321, Fax: 510-436-1325, E-mail: hall@hnu.edu.

Houston Baptist University, College of Education and Behavioral Sciences, Program in Christian Counseling, Houston, TX 77074-3298. Offers MACC. *Faculty:* 3 full-time (2 women), 1 (woman) part-time/adjunct. *Students:* 5 full-time (4 women), 7 part-time (all women); includes 4 minority (all African Americans) Average age 36. 16 applicants, 50% accepted, 1 enrolled. In 2007, 6 degrees awarded. *Degree requirements:* For master's, comprehensive exam. *Entrance requirements:* For master's, GRE General Test, minimum GPA of 3.0. Additional exam requirements/recommendations for international students: Required—TOEFL (minimum score 550 paper-based; 213 computer-based). *Application deadline:* For fall admission, 7/1 priority date for domestic and international students; for winter admission, 10/1 priority date for domestic and international students; for spring admission, 1/1 priority date for domestic and international students. Applications are processed on a rolling basis. Application fee: $25 ($100 for international students). *Expenses:* Tuition: Part-time $1,416 per course. Required fees: $190 per quarter. *Financial support:* Federal Work-Study available. Support available to part-time students. Financial award application deadline: 3/1; financial award applicants required to submit FAFSA. *Unit head:* Dr. Renata Nero, Director, 281-649-3000 Ext. 2436, Fax: 281-649-3361, E-mail: rnero@hbu.edu. *Application contact:* Becky Greer, Secretary, 281-649-3000 Ext. 3095, Fax: 281-649-3361, E-mail: bgreer@hbu.edu.

Houston Graduate School of Theology, Graduate School, Houston, TX 77092. Offers counseling (MA); pastoral ministry (M Div, D Min); theology (MA). *Accreditation:* ATS (one or more programs are accredited). Part-time and evening/weekend programs available. *Degree requirements:* For master's, thesis (for some programs); for doctorate, thesis/dissertation; for M Div, thesis/dissertation optional. *Entrance requirements:* For doctorate, GRE General Test or MAT, M Div or equivalent. Additional exam requirements/recommendations for international students: Required—TOEFL (minimum score 550 paper-based; 213 computer-based). *Faculty research:* Hermeneutics, spirituality, religion of Eastern Europe.

Huntington University, Graduate School of Christian Ministries, Huntington, IN 46750-1299. Offers counseling ministries (MA); discipling ministries (MA); pastoral ministries (MA); youth ministry leadership (MA). Part-time programs available. Postbaccalaureate distance learning degree programs offered (minimal on-campus study). *Degree requirements:* For master's, thesis. *Entrance requirements:* Additional exam requirements/recommendations for international students: Required—TOEFL. Electronic applications accepted. *Faculty research:* Outreach, family ministry outreach, leadership, evangelism, youth ministry.

Iliff School of Theology, Graduate and Professional Programs, Denver, CO 80210-4798. Offers biblical studies (MA); church history (MA); religion (MA); religion and social change (MA); specialized ministry (MASM), including justice and peace, pastoral theology and care, religious leadership; theology (M Div, MTS, D Min, PhD), including Biblical studies (PhD), religion and psychological studies (PhD), religion and social change (PhD), theology, philosophy and culture (PhD); theology/ethics (MA). *Accreditation:* ACIPE; ATS. Part-time and evening/weekend programs available. *Degree requirements:* For master's, one foreign language, thesis (for some programs); for doctorate, 2 foreign languages, comprehensive exam, thesis/dissertation; for M Div, thesis/dissertation optional. *Entrance requirements:* For M Div, minimum GPA of 2.75, references; for master's, minimum GPA of 3.0, writing sample, references; for doctorate, GRE General Test, minimum GPA of 3.0, writing sample, letters of recommendation. Additional exam requirements/recommendations for international students: Required—TOEFL (minimum score 550 paper-based). Electronic applications accepted. *Faculty research:* Pastoral care, history, church music, contemporary church, biblical studies.

International Baptist College, Program in Ministry, Tempe, AZ 85282. Offers M Min, D Min.

Iona College, School of Arts and Science, Department of Family and Pastoral Counseling, New Rochelle, NY 10801-1890. Offers family counseling (MS, Certificate); pastoral counseling (MS).

Pastoral Ministry and Counseling

Iona College (continued)

Part-time and evening/weekend programs available. *Faculty:* 7 full-time (2 women), 1 (woman) part-time/adjunct. *Students:* 30 full-time (23 women), 21 part-time (16 women); includes 13 minority (8 African Americans, 5 Hispanic Americans), 1 international. Average age 33. 27 applicants, 74% accepted, 13 enrolled. In 2007, 5 degrees awarded. *Degree requirements:* For master's, thesis, project. *Entrance requirements:* For master's, draw-a-person test, sentence completion test, interview, minimum GPA of 3.0. *Application deadline:* Applications are processed on a rolling basis. Application fee: $50. Electronic applications accepted. *Expenses:* Contact institution. *Financial support:* Career-related internships or fieldwork, tuition waivers (partial), and unspecified assistantships available. Support available to part-time students. *Faculty research:* Marriage counseling. *Unit head:* Dr. Robert Burns, Chair, 914-633-2418, E-mail: rburns@iona.edu. *Application contact:* Veronica Jarek-Prinz, Director of Graduate Admissions, 914-633-2420, Fax: 914-633-2277, E-mail: vjarekprinz@iona.edu.

Jewish University of America, Graduate School, Abrams Institute of Pastoral Counseling, Skokie, IL 60077-3248. Offers counseling (MA); pastoral counseling (MPC, DPC). *Degree requirements:* For master's, thesis optional; for doctorate, one foreign language, thesis/dissertation. *Entrance requirements:* For master's and doctorate, interview.

John Brown University, Graduate Studies Division of Christian Ministry, Siloam Springs, AR 72761-2121. Offers MA. Part-time and evening/weekend programs available. *Faculty:* 4 full-time (0 women), 9 part-time/adjunct (3 women). *Students:* 27 full-time (19 women), 26 part-time (12 women); includes 10 minority (9 African Americans, 1 Hispanic American). Average age 37. 8 applicants, 88% accepted, 7 enrolled. In 2007, 2 degrees awarded. *Entrance requirements:* For master's, GRE General Test, MAT, minimum GPA of 3.0. Additional exam requirements/recommendations for international students: Required—TOEFL (minimum score 550 paper-based; 173 computer-based). *Application deadline:* For fall admission, 8/11 priority date for domestic students; for spring admission, 1/12 priority date for domestic students. Applications are processed on a rolling basis. Application fee: $35 ($100 for international students). Electronic applications accepted. *Financial support:* Application deadline: 3/1. *Unit head:* Dr. Cary Balzer, Director, 479-524-7242, Fax: 479-238-8574, E-mail: cbalzer@jbu.edu. *Application contact:* Chris Ray, Associate Director of Graduate Recruitment, 479-631-4665, E-mail: cray@jbu.edu.

The Johns Hopkins University, School of Education, Department of Counseling and Human Services, Baltimore, MD 21218-2699. Offers addictions counseling (Certificate); clinical community counseling (Certificate); clinical supervision (Certificate); contemporary trauma (Certificate); counseling (MS, CAGS); counseling at-risk youth (Certificate); organizational counseling (Certificate); play therapy (Certificate); spiritual and existential counseling and therapy (Certificate). Part-time and evening/weekend programs available. *Students:* 51 full-time (45 women), 389 part-time (330 women); includes 103 minority (77 African Americans, 2 American Indian/Alaska Native, 13 Asian Americans or Pacific Islanders, 11 Hispanic Americans), 10 international. Average age 33. 142 applicants, 80% accepted, 77 enrolled. In 2007, 110 master's, 31 other advanced degrees awarded. *Entrance requirements:* For master's, minimum GPA of 3.0, interview, resumé, letters of recommendation; for other advanced degree, master's or doctoral degree, interview, resumé, minimum GPA of 3.0, letters of recommendation. Additional exam requirements/recommendations for international students: Required—TOEFL (minimum score 600 paper-based; 250 computer-based; 100 iBT). *Application deadline:* For fall admission, 5/1 for international students; for spring admission, 10/15 for international students. Applications are processed on a rolling basis. Application fee: $60. *Financial support:* Scholarships/grants available. Support available to part-time students. Financial award application deadline: 6/1; financial award applicants required to submit FAFSA. *Unit head:* Dr. Mary Guindon, Chair, 301-294-7040. *Application contact:* Carol Herrman, Admissions Coordinator, 410-872-1234, Fax: 410-872-1251, E-mail: onestop.admissions@jhu.edu.

Knox Theological Seminary, Graduate Programs, Program in Ministry, Fort Lauderdale, FL 33308. Offers D Min. Part-time programs available. *Faculty:* 2 part-time/adjunct (0 women). *Students:* 11 full-time (0 women), 4 part-time; includes 1 African American. Average age 48. 2 applicants, 100% accepted, 2 enrolled. In 2007, 10 degrees awarded. *Median time to degree:* Of those who began their doctoral program in fall 1999, 100% received their degree in 8 years or less. *Degree requirements:* For doctorate, thesis/dissertation. *Entrance requirements:* For doctorate, M Div or equivalent. Additional exam requirements/recommendations for international students: Required—TOEFL, TWE (minimum score 5). *Application deadline:* For fall admission, 6/1 priority date for domestic and international students; for winter admission, 12/1 priority date for domestic and international students; for spring admission, 1/1 priority date for domestic and international students. Applications are processed on a rolling basis. Application fee: $50. *Application contact:* Jim Dietz, Director of Student Services, 800-344-5669, Fax: 954-351-3343, E-mail: jdietz@knoxseminary.edu.

Lancaster Bible College, Graduate School, Lancaster, PA 17608-3403. Offers Bible (MA); consulting resource teacher (M Ed); counseling (MA); ministry (MA); school counseling (M Ed). Part-time and evening/weekend programs available. *Degree requirements:* For master's, comprehensive exam (for some programs), thesis (for some programs). *Entrance requirements:* For master's, bachelor's degree with a minimum of 30 credits of course work in Bible, minimum undergraduate GPA of 3.0, interview. Additional exam requirements/recommendations for international students: Required—TOEFL.

La Salle University, School of Arts and Sciences, Program in Theological, Pastoral and Liturgical Studies, Philadelphia, PA 19141-1199. Offers pastoral studies (MA); religion (MA); theological studies (MA). Part-time and evening/weekend programs available. *Faculty:* 5 full-time (1 woman), 6 part-time/adjunct (3 women). *Students:* 3 full-time (2 women), 47 part-time (24 women); includes 9 minority (4 African Americans, 2 Asian Americans or Pacific Islanders, 3 Hispanic Americans). Average age 47. 9 applicants, 89% accepted, 5 enrolled. In 2007, 20 degrees awarded. *Entrance requirements:* For master's, 26 credits in humanistic subjects, religion, theology, or ministry-related work. *Application deadline:* Applications are processed on a rolling basis. Application fee: $35. *Expenses:* Tuition: Full-time $16,300; part-time $550 per credit. Required fees: $85 per term. Tuition and fees vary according to program. *Financial support:* In 2007–08, 12 students received support. Scholarships/grants available. Financial award applicants required to submit FAFSA. *Unit head:* Rev. Francis Berna, OFM, Director, 215-951-1335, Fax: 215-951-1665, E-mail: berna@lasalle.edu.

Liberty University, College of Arts and Sciences, Lynchburg, VA 24502. Offers counseling (MA); nursing (MSN); pastoral care and counseling (PhD); professional counseling (PhD). *Accreditation:* AACN. Part-time programs available. Postbaccalaureate distance learning degree programs offered (minimal on-campus study). *Faculty:* 15 full-time (5 women), 74 part-time/adjunct (31 women). *Students:* 783 full-time (575 women), 2,031 part-time (1,505 women); includes 721 minority (610 African Americans, 12 American Indian/Alaska Native, 26 Asian Americans or Pacific Islanders, 73 Hispanic Americans), 69 international. Average age 36. In 2007, 164 master's, 2 doctorates awarded. *Degree requirements:* For master's, comprehensive exam (for some programs); for doctorate, comprehensive exam, thesis/dissertation. *Entrance requirements:* For master's, GRE General Test (MSN), minimum undergraduate GPA of 3.0; for doctorate, GRE General Test, minimum master's GPA of 3.25. Additional exam requirements/recommendations for international students: Required—TOEFL (minimum score 600 paper-based; 250 computer-based). *Application deadline:* For fall admission, 6/1 priority date for domestic students; for spring admission, 11/1 priority date for domestic students. Applications are processed on a rolling basis. Application fee: $50. Electronic applications accepted. *Expenses:* Tuition: Full-time $7,110; part-time $395 per credit. Required fees: $950. Tuition and fees vary according to program. *Financial support:* In 2007–08, 817 students received support, including 9 teaching assistantships with tuition reimbursements available; Federal Work-Study also available. *Faculty research:* God concept and adult attachment, building marital strength, image of God and gender, breastfeeding behavior among adolescent mothers, osteoporosis. *Unit head:* Dr. Ronald E. Hawkins, Dean, 434-592-4030, Fax: 434-522-0416, E-mail: rehawkin@liberty.edu. *Application contact:* Kyle A Falce, Director of Graduate Admissions, 800-424-9596, Fax: 800-628-7977, E-mail: gradadmissions@liberty.edu.

Lincoln Christian Seminary, Graduate and Professional Programs, Lincoln, IL 62656-2167. Offers Bible and theology (MA); Bible translation (MA); counseling ministry (MA); divinity (M Div); leadership ministry (MA, D Min). MA in Bible translation offered jointly with Pioneer Bible Translators (Dallas, TX). *Accreditation:* ACIPE; ATS. Part-time programs available. *Faculty:* 12 full-time (2 women), 13 part-time/adjunct (3 women). *Students:* 117 full-time (38 women), 233 part-time (67 women); includes 12 minority (8 African Americans, 2 American Indian/Alaska Native, 2 Hispanic Americans), 14 international. Average age 26. 125 applicants, 92% accepted, 88 enrolled. In 2007, 15 first professional degrees, 37 master's awarded. *Degree requirements:* For master's, 2 foreign languages, thesis; for doctorate, thesis/dissertation; for M Div, 2 foreign languages. *Entrance requirements:* For M Div and master's, minimum GPA of 2.5; for doctorate, MDiv or equivalent. Additional exam requirements/recommendations for international students: Required—TOEFL (minimum score 550 paper-based; 213 computer-based). *Application deadline:* Applications are processed on a rolling basis. Application fee: $20. Electronic applications accepted. *Expenses:* Tuition: Full-time $7,182; part-time $399 per hour. *Financial support:* In 2007–08, 150 students received support, including 5 teaching assistantships (averaging $2,000 per year); career-related internships or fieldwork, Federal Work-Study, and scholarships/grants also available. Support available to part-time students. Financial award application deadline: 3/1; financial award applicants required to submit FAFSA. *Unit head:* Dr. Thomas Tanner, Vice President of Academics, 217-732-3168 Ext. 2240, Fax: 217-732-5718, E-mail: ttanner@lccs.edu. *Application contact:* David Harmon, Director of Admissions, 217-732-3168 Ext. 2275, Fax: 217-732-5914, E-mail: semadmis@lccs.edu.

Loma Linda University, Faculty of Religion, Program in Clinical Ministry, Loma Linda, CA 92350. Offers MA, Certificate. *Faculty:* 19 full-time (2 women), 16 part-time/adjunct (15 women). *Degree requirements:* For master's, comprehensive exam, thesis optional. *Entrance requirements:* For master's, baccalaureate degree, minimum 3.0 GPA. Additional exam requirements/recommendations for international students: Required—TOEFL. *Application deadline:* For fall admission, 8/1 for domestic and international students; for winter admission, 11/1 for domestic and international students; for spring admission, 2/1 for domestic and international students. Application fee: $60. Electronic applications accepted. *Unit head:* Dr. Gerald Winslow, Dean, 909-824-4536.

Loras College, Graduate Division, Program in Theology and Ministry, Dubuque, IA 52004-0178. Offers ministry (MA); theology (MA). Part-time and evening/weekend programs available. *Faculty:* 2 full-time (0 women). *Students:* 2 full-time (1 woman), 23 part-time (20 women), 1 international. Average age 45. 8 applicants, 88% accepted, 7 enrolled. In 2007, 10 degrees awarded. *Degree requirements:* For master's, comprehensive exam (for some programs), thesis (for some programs). *Entrance requirements:* For master's, bachelor's degree or undergraduate minor in religious studies or equivalent, minimum undergraduate GPA of 2.75. *Application deadline:* Applications are processed on a rolling basis. Application fee: $25. *Expenses:* Tuition: Full-time $7,920; part-time $440 per credit. *Financial support:* Applicants required to submit FAFSA. *Unit head:* Dr. Douglas Wathier, Graduate Coordinator, 563-588-7013, E-mail: douglas.wathier@loras.edu. *Application contact:* Graduate Admissions Coordinator, 563-588-7139, Fax: 563-588-4962.

Loyola College in Maryland, Graduate Programs, College of Arts and Sciences, Department of Pastoral Counseling, Program in Pastoral Counseling, Baltimore, MD 21210-2699. Offers MS, PhD, CAS. Part-time and evening/weekend programs available. *Entrance requirements:* For master's, doctorate, and CAS, GRE General Test, GRE Subject Test (recommended). Additional exam requirements/recommendations for international students: Required—TOEFL (minimum score 550 paper-based; 213 computer-based).

Loyola College in Maryland, Graduate Programs, College of Arts and Sciences, Department of Pastoral Counseling, Program in Spiritual and Pastoral Care, Baltimore, MD 21210-2699. Offers MA. Part-time and evening/weekend programs available. *Entrance requirements:* For master's, GRE General Test, GRE Subject Test (recommended). Additional exam requirements/recommendations for international students: Required—TOEFL (minimum score 550 paper-based; 213 computer-based).

See Close-Up on page 697.

Loyola Marymount University, Graduate Division, College of Liberal Arts, Department of Theological Studies, Program in Pastoral Theology, Los Angeles, CA 90045-2659. Offers MA. Part-time and evening/weekend programs available. *Faculty:* 22 full-time (6 women), 8 part-time/adjunct (1 woman). *Students:* 15 full-time (10 women), 40 part-time (28 women); includes 14 minority (4 Asian Americans or Pacific Islanders, 10 Hispanic Americans), 3 international. Average age 45. 43 applicants, 67% accepted, 28 enrolled. In 2007, 4 degrees awarded. *Degree requirements:* For master's, one foreign language, comprehensive exam, thesis or alternative. *Entrance requirements:* For master's, GRE General Test. Additional exam requirements/recommendations for international students: Required—TOEFL. *Application deadline:* For fall admission, 5/1 priority date for domestic students; for spring admission, 11/15 priority date for domestic students. Application fee: $50. Electronic applications accepted. *Financial support:* In 2007–08, research assistantships (averaging $12,370 per year); scholarships/grants and unspecified assistantships also available. Support available to part-time students. Financial award application deadline: 6/1; financial award applicants required to submit FAFSA. *Unit head:* Dr. Douglas S. Burton-Christie, Director, Department of Theological Studies, 310-338-1921, Fax: 310-338-1948, E-mail: dburton@lmu.edu.

Loyola University Chicago, Institute of Pastoral Studies, Program in Pastoral Counseling, Chicago, IL 60611-2196. Offers pastoral counseling (MA); pastoral studies (MA); spiritual development (Certificate); M Div/MA. *Accreditation:* ACIPE. Part-time programs available. *Faculty:* 6 full-time (2 women), 12 part-time/adjunct (7 women). *Students:* 47 full-time (31 women), 20 part-time (14 women); includes 9 minority (5 African Americans, 1 Asian American or Pacific Islander, 3 Hispanic Americans), 5 international. Average age 43. 31 applicants, 77% accepted, 17 enrolled. In 2007, 13 degrees awarded. *Degree requirements:* For master's, thesis or alternative, integration project. *Application deadline:* For fall admission, 2/15 priority date for domestic students. Applications are processed on a rolling basis. Application fee: $50. Electronic applications accepted. *Expenses:* Tuition: Full-time $12,780; part-time $710 per credit hour. Required fees: $55 per semester. Full-time tuition and fees vary according to program. *Financial support:* In 2007–08, 7 students received support. Career-related internships or fieldwork, Federal Work-Study, and institutionally sponsored loans available. Support available to part-time students. Financial award application deadline: 3/1; financial award applicants required to submit FAFSA. *Faculty research:* Pastoral psychotherapy, enrichment outcome, marriage and family therapy, marriage and family spirituality, gender and ethnicity issues, theological anthropology. *Unit head:* Dr. Paul R. Giblin, Associate Professor, 312-915-7483, Fax: 312-915-7410, E-mail: pgibli@luc.edu.

Loyola University Chicago, Institute of Pastoral Studies, Program in Pastoral Studies, Chicago, IL 60611-2196. Offers MA. *Accreditation:* ACIPE. *Faculty:* 6 full-time (2 women). *Students:* 84 full-time (48 women), 71 part-time (50 women); includes 8 minority (5 African Americans, 1 Asian American or Pacific Islander, 2 Hispanic Americans), 8 international. Average age 44. 35 applicants, 86% accepted, 24 enrolled. In 2007, 30 degrees awarded. *Application deadline:* For fall admission, 8/1 priority date for domestic students; for spring admission, 12/1 for domestic students. Applications are processed on a rolling basis. Application fee: $50. *Expenses:* Tuition: Full-time $12,780; part-time $710 per credit hour. Required fees: $55 per semester. Full-time tuition and fees vary according to program. *Financial support:* Career-related internships or fieldwork, Federal Work-Study, institutionally sponsored loans, and scholarships/grants available. Support available to part-time students. Financial award application deadline: 3/1. *Unit head:* Dr. Peter Gilmour, Director, 312-915-7400, Fax: 312-915-7410, E-mail: pgilmou@luc.edu.

Lutheran School of Theology at Chicago, Graduate and Professional Programs, Chicago, IL 60615-5199. Offers ministry (D Min); ministry, pastoral care, and counseling (D Min PCC); theological studies (MA, PhD); theology (M Div, Th M). *Accreditation:* ACIPE; ATS (one or more programs are accredited). Part-time programs available. *Faculty:* 22 full-time, 15 part-time/adjunct. *Students:* 177 full-time, 188 part-time. Terminal master's awarded for partial completion of doctoral program. *Degree requirements:* For master's, variable foreign language requirement; for doctorate, variable foreign language requirement, thesis/dissertation. *Entrance requirements:* For master's, GRE (Th M), M Div or equivalent (Th M); for doctorate, GRE, M Div or equivalent, 3 years of professional experience (D Min, D Min PCC). Additional exam requirements/recommendations for international students: Required—TOEFL, TOEFL (Th M). *Application deadline:* Applications are processed on a rolling basis. Application fee: $50. *Expenses:* Tuition: Full-time $10,890. Part-time tuition and fees vary according to degree level. *Financial support:* Career-related internships or fieldwork and scholarships/grants available. Support available to part-time students. *Unit head:* Dr. Kathleen Billman, Dean, 773-256-0721, Fax: 773-256-0782, E-mail: kbillman@lstc.edu. *Application contact:* Dorothy C. Dominiak, Assistant Director of Admissions and Financial Aid, 773-256-0726, Fax: 773-256-0782, E-mail: ddominia@lstc.edu.

Lutheran Theological Seminary, Graduate and Professional Programs, Saskatoon, SK S7N 0X3, Canada. Offers history (MTS, STM); New Testament (MTS, STM); Old Testament (MTS, STM); pastoral counseling (MTS, STM); systematics (MTS, STM). *Accreditation:* ATS.Part-time programs available. *Degree requirements:* For master's, thesis; for M Div, Greek, Hebrew.

Lutheran Theological Seminary at Gettysburg, Graduate and Professional Programs, Gettysburg, PA 17325-1795. Offers divinity (M Div); ministerial studies (MAMS); outdoor ministry (MAR); parish ministry (D Min); theology (STM). *Accreditation:* ACIPE; ATS (one or more programs are accredited). Part-time programs available. Postbaccalaureate distance learning degree programs offered (no on-campus study). *Degree requirements:* For master's, thesis (for some programs); for M Div, one foreign language. Electronic applications accepted.

The Lutheran Theological Seminary at Philadelphia, Graduate School, Philadelphia, PA 19119-1794. Offers divinity (M Div); ministry (D Min); religion (MAR); social ministry (Certificate); theology (STM). *Accreditation:* ACIPE; ATS. Part-time and evening/weekend programs available. *Faculty:* 22 full-time (6 women), 26 part-time/adjunct (11 women). *Students:* 144 full-time (74 women), 263 part-time (127 women); includes 92 minority (80 African Americans, 2 Asian Americans or Pacific Islanders, 10 Hispanic Americans), 14 international. Average age 43. 123 applicants, 86% accepted, 84 enrolled. In 2007, 44 first professional degrees, 10 master's, 15 doctorates awarded. *Median time to degree:* Of those who began their doctoral program in fall 1999, 70% received their degree in 8 years or less. *Degree requirements:* For master's, one foreign language, comprehensive exam (for some programs), thesis (for some programs); for doctorate, thesis/dissertation; for M Div, 2 foreign languages. *Entrance requirements:* For M Div and master's, minimum undergraduate GPA of 2.8; for doctorate, minimum first professional GPA of 3.0. Additional exam requirements/recommendations for international students: Required—TOEFL (minimum score 550 paper-based; 213 computer-based), TWE. *Application deadline:* For fall admission, 6/1 priority date for domestic students. Applications are processed on a rolling basis. Application fee: $35. Electronic applications accepted. *Expenses:* Tuition: Part-time $1,260 per unit. Part-time tuition and fees vary according to program. *Financial support:* In 2007–08, 102 students received support, including 1 research assistantship with tuition reimbursement available (averaging $2,250 per year), 3 teaching assistantships with tuition reimbursements available (averaging $1,200 per year); career-related internships or fieldwork and Federal Work-Study also available. Financial award application deadline: 7/1; financial award applicants required to submit FAFSA. *Unit head:* Dr. J. Paul Rajashekar, Dean, 215-248-6379, Fax: 215-248-4577, E-mail: rajashekar@ltsp.edu. *Application contact:* Rev. Louise Johnson, Director of Admissions, 800-286-4616 Ext. 6321, Fax: 215-248-7315, E-mail: admissions@ltsp.edu.

Luther Rice University, Graduate Programs, Lithonia, GA 30038-2454. Offers Bible/theology (M Div); Christian education (M Div); Christian studies (MA); church ministry (D Min); counseling (M Div); discipleship counseling (MA); ministry (M Div, MA); missions/evangelism (M Div). Part-time programs available. Postbaccalaureate distance learning degree programs offered (no on-campus study). *Degree requirements:* For doctorate, thesis/dissertation. *Entrance requirements:* Additional exam requirements/recommendations for international students: Required—TOEFL (minimum score 500 paper-based; 173 computer-based).

Madonna University, Program in Religious Studies, Livonia, MI 48150-1173. Offers pastoral ministry (MA).

Malone College, School of Theology, Graduate Program in Christian Ministries, Canton, OH 44709-3897. Offers Christian leadership in sports ministry (MA); Christian ministries (MA); leadership in the Christian church (MA). Part-time and evening/weekend programs available. *Faculty:* 5 full-time (1 woman), 6 part-time/adjunct (1 woman). *Students:* 7 full-time (3 women), 30 part-time (9 women); includes 7 minority (4 African Americans, 1 American Indian/Alaska Native, 1 Asian American or Pacific Islander, 1 Hispanic American). Average age 41. In 2007, 14 degrees awarded. *Entrance requirements:* For master's, minimum GPA of 3.0. *Application deadline:* Applications are processed on a rolling basis. Application fee: $25. *Expenses: Contact institution.* Part-time tuition and fees vary according to program. *Financial support:* Tuition waivers (partial) and unspecified assistantships available. Support available to part-time students. Financial award application deadline: 6/30. *Faculty research:* The Book of Ezekiel, Jeremiah and Lamentations, socio-rhetorical criticism, Pauline Theology, Theological Hermeneutics. *Unit head:* Dr. Joel R. Soza, Director, 330-471-8217, Fax: 330-471-8478, E-mail: jsoza@malone.edu. *Application contact:* Dr. David L. Kleffman, Assistant Director of Graduate Admissions, 330-471-8447, Fax: 330-471-8343, E-mail: dkleffman@malone.edu.

Maple Springs Baptist Bible College and Seminary, Graduate and Professional Programs, Capitol Heights, MD 20743. Offers biblical studies (MA, Certificate); Christian counseling (MA); church administration (MA); divinity (M Div); ministry (D Min); religious education (MA).

Maranatha Baptist Bible College, Program in Biblical Counseling, Watertown, WI 53094. Offers MA. Part-time programs available. Postbaccalaureate distance learning degree programs offered. *Faculty:* 5 full-time (0 women), 2 part-time/adjunct (0 women). *Students:* 5 full-time (3 women), 3 part-time (1 woman); includes 1 minority (Asian American or Pacific Islander) Average age 26. 4 applicants, 100% accepted, 4 enrolled. In 2007, 4 degrees awarded. *Application deadline:* Applications are processed on a rolling basis. Application fee: $50. *Expenses:* Tuition: Full-time $3,360; part-time $210 per credit. Required fees: $300; $19 per credit. *Financial support:* In 2007–08, 2 students received support. Scholarships/grants and tuition waivers (full and partial) available. Support available to part-time students. *Unit head:* Dr. Larry Oats, Chair of Graduate School of Theology, 920-206-2324, Fax: 920-261-9109, E-mail: loats@mbbc.edu. *Application contact:* Dr. Jim Harrison, Director of Admissions, 920-206-2327, Fax: 920-261-9109, E-mail: admissions@mbbc.edu.

Martin University, Graduate School of Urban Ministry, Indianapolis, IN 46218-3867. Offers urban ministry studies (MA). Part-time and evening/weekend programs available. *Degree requirements:* For master's, Greek, oral and written comprehensive exam or thesis. *Faculty research:* How to bridge the gap between black theology and the black church.

Marygrove College, Graduate Division, Department of Pastoral Ministry, Detroit, MI 48221-2599. Offers MA. Part-time and evening/weekend programs available. *Degree requirements:* For master's, internship. *Entrance requirements:* For master's, interview, minimum undergraduate GPA of 3.0, work experience in field.

Marymount University, School of Education and Human Services, Program in Pastoral Counseling, Arlington, VA 22207-4299. Offers pastoral and spiritual care (MA); pastoral counseling (MA, Certificate). Part-time and evening/weekend programs available. *Students:* 1 (woman) full-time, 14 part-time (12 women); includes 3 minority (2 African Americans, 1 Hispanic American). Average age 46. 5 applicants, 100% accepted, 2 enrolled. In 2007, 2 degrees awarded. *Degree requirements:* For master's, thesis or alternative. *Entrance requirements:* For master's, GRE, interview, 2 letters of recommendation, resumé. Additional exam requirements/recommendations for international students: Required—TOEFL (minimum score 600 paper-based; 250 computer-based; 100 iBT). *Application deadline:* For fall admission, 2/15 for domestic students; for spring admission, 9/21 for domestic students. Application fee: $40. *Expenses:* Tuition: Full-time $11,790; part-time $655 per credit. Required fees: $121; $6.7 per credit. *Financial support:* Research assistantships with full tuition reimbursements, career-related internships or fieldwork, scholarships/grants, and unspecified assistantships available. Support available to part-time students. Financial award applicants required to submit FAFSA. *Unit head:* Dr. Lisa Jackson-Cherry, Chair, 703-284-1633, Fax: 703-284-5708, E-mail: lisa.jackson-cherry@marymount.edu.

The Master's College and Seminary, The Master's Seminary, Santa Clarita, CA 91321-1200. Offers biblical counseling (MABC); New Testament (Th D); Old Testament (Th D); preaching (D Min); theology (M Div, M Th, Th D). Part-time programs available. *Faculty:* 18 full-time (0 women), 11 part-time/adjunct (0 women). *Students:* 200 full-time (0 women), 168 part-time; includes 58 minority (9 African Americans, 35 Asian Americans or Pacific Islanders, 14 Hispanic Americans), 30 international. Average age 28. 136 applicants, 82% accepted, 80 enrolled. In 2007, 60 first professional degrees, 9 master's, 11 doctorates awarded. *Degree requirements:* For master's, 2 foreign languages, thesis; for doctorate, 4 foreign languages, thesis/dissertation; for M Div, 2 foreign languages, thesis/dissertation. *Entrance requirements:* For M Div, minimum 2 years of college; for master's, minimum GPA of 2.75; for doctorate, Th M, minimum GPA of 3.5. Additional exam requirements/recommendations for international students: Required—TOEFL (minimum score 550 paper-based). *Application deadline:* For fall admission, 6/1 priority date for domestic and international students; for winter admission, 10/1 priority date for domestic and international students; for spring admission, 1/1 for domestic and international students. Applications are processed on a rolling basis. Application fee: $30. *Expenses:* Tuition: Full-time $8,000; part-time $300 per unit. Required fees: $370. One-time fee: $100 full-time. Tuition and fees vary according to program. *Financial support:* In 2007–08, 121 students received support, including 10 teaching assistantships (averaging $4,000 per year); career-related internships or fieldwork, scholarships/grants, and tuition waivers (partial) also available. Support available to part-time students. Financial award application deadline: 6/1; financial award applicants required to submit FAFSA. *Unit head:* Dr. Richard L. Mayhue, Senior Vice President and Dean, 818-782-6488 Ext. 5632, E-mail: mayhue@tms.edu. *Application contact:* Ray Mehringer, Director of Admissions and Placement, 818-792-6488, Fax: 818-909-5725, E-mail: rmehringer@tms.edu.

McCormick Theological Seminary, Graduate and Professional Programs, Chicago, IL 60615. Offers ministry (D Min); theological studies (MATS, Certificate); theology (M Div); M Div/MSW. *Accreditation:* ACIPE; ATS (one or more programs are accredited). Part-time and evening/weekend programs available. *Degree requirements:* For master's, thesis (for some programs); for doctorate, thesis/dissertation. *Entrance requirements:* For M Div and master's, minimum GPA of 3.0; for doctorate, M Div, minimum 3 years in pastorate. *Faculty research:* Faith formation, families, biblical literature, Dead Sea scrolls, women in antiquity.

McMaster University, McMaster Divinity College, Hamilton, ON L8S 4M2, Canada. Offers biblical studies (M Div); Biblical studies (MA, MTS, Diploma); Christian interpretation/history (M Div, MA, MTS, Diploma); Christian ministry (M Div, MA, MTS, Diploma); Christian Studies (Certificate); Christian theology (PhD). Affiliated with the Toronto School of Theology. *Accreditation:* ATS. Part-time programs available. *Degree requirements:* For master's, one foreign language, thesis optional; for doctorate, 3 foreign languages, comprehensive exam, thesis/dissertation; for other advanced degree, 2 foreign languages, thesis. *Entrance requirements:* For master's, minimum B average in undergraduate course work, 3 letters of reference; for doctorate, minimum B+ average in bachelor's and master's, appropriate modern/ancient language, interview; for other advanced degree, 6 units of related Biblical language, minimum B+ average in undergraduate course work, minimum 15 units of course work in related area of study, 3 letters of recommendation. Additional exam requirements/recommendations for international students: Required—TOEFL (minimum score 550 paper-based; 237 computer-based). *Faculty research:* Ethics, Biblical studies, language studies, church history, Christian ministry.

Meadville Lombard Theological School, Graduate and Professional Programs, Chicago, IL 60637-1602. Offers divinity (M Div); ministry (D Min); religion (MA); M Div/MSW. *Accreditation:* ACIPE; ATS. Part-time programs available. Postbaccalaureate distance learning degree programs offered (minimal on-campus study). *Faculty:* 3 full-time (2 women), 15 part-time/adjunct (6 women). *Students:* 37 full-time (21 women), 31 part-time (19 women); includes 7 minority (2 African Americans, 1 American Indian/Alaska Native, 4 Hispanic Americans), 3 international. Average age 45. 41 applicants, 68% accepted, 17 enrolled. In 2007, 22 first professional degrees, 2 master's, 2 doctorates awarded. *Median time to degree:* Of those who began their doctoral program in fall 1999, 100% received their degree in 8 years or less. *Entrance requirements:* For M Div and master's, bachelor's degree; for doctorate, bachelor's and masters degrees, 3 years of ministry. *Application deadline:* For fall admission, 3/1 priority date for domestic students. Applications are processed on a rolling basis. Application fee: $45. *Financial support:* Career-related internships or fieldwork, Federal Work-Study, institutionally sponsored loans, scholarships/grants, health care benefits, and tuition waivers (full and partial) available. Support available to part-time students. Financial award application deadline: 3/15; financial award applicants required to submit FAFSA. *Unit head:* Rev. Lee C. Barker, President, 773-256-3000, Fax: 773-753-1323. *Application contact:* E. Chavez, Director of Admissions, 773-256-3000 Ext. 0250, Fax: 773-753-1323, E-mail: echavez@meadville.edu.

Mennonite Brethren Biblical Seminary, School of Theology, Program in Christian Ministry, Fresno, CA 93727-5097. Offers MA. Part-time programs available. Postbaccalaureate distance learning degree programs offered (minimal on-campus study). *Students:* Average age 30. 15 applicants, 93% accepted, 12 enrolled. In 2007, 10 degrees awarded. *Entrance requirements:* Additional exam requirements/recommendations for international students: Required—TOEFL (minimum score 550 paper-based; 213 computer-based). *Application deadline:* For fall admission, 8/1 for domestic students; for spring admission, 12/1 for domestic students. Application fee: $35. *Financial support:* Institutionally sponsored loans and scholarships/grants available. Support available to part-time students. Financial award application deadline: 5/1. *Application contact:* Andy Johnson, Director of Recruitment, 559-452-1714, Fax: 559-251-7212, E-mail: ajohnson@mbseminary.edu.

Midwestern Baptist Theological Seminary, Graduate and Professional Programs, Kansas City, MO 64118-4697. Offers Biblical studies (MA); Christian education (MACE); divinity/ministry (M Div); ministry (D Min); sacred music (MCM). *Accreditation:* ATS. Part-time programs available. Postbaccalaureate distance learning degree programs offered (minimal on-campus study). *Degree requirements:* For doctorate, thesis/dissertation; for M Div, 2 foreign languages. *Entrance requirements:* For doctorate, MAT. Electronic applications accepted. *Faculty research:* Ministerial studies, Biblical and theological studies, missions, counseling.

Missouri Baptist University, Graduate Programs, St. Louis, MO 63141-8660. Offers business administration (MBA); Christian ministries (MACM); counseling (MAC); education (MSE); education administration (MEA); educational leadership (MSE, Ed S); teaching (MAT).

Mount Marty College, Graduate Studies Division, Yankton, SD 57078-3724. Offers business administration (MBA); nurse anesthesia (MS); pastoral ministries (MPM). *Accreditation:* AANA/CANAEP (one or more programs are accredited). *Degree requirements:* For master's, thesis or alternative. *Entrance requirements:* For master's, GRE General Test, minimum GPA of 3.0. Electronic applications accepted. *Faculty research:* Clinical anesthesia, professional characteristics, motivations of applicants.

Multnomah Bible College and Biblical Seminary, Multnomah Biblical Seminary, Program in Pastoral Studies, Portland, OR 97220-5898. Offers MA. Part-time programs available. *Faculty:* 8 full-time (0 women), 15 part-time/adjunct (4 women). *Students:* 38 full-time (20 women), 26

Pastoral Ministry and Counseling

Multnomah Bible College and Biblical Seminary (continued)
part-time (12 women); includes 12 minority (4 African Americans, 3 Asian Americans or Pacific Islanders, 5 Hispanic Americans), 5 international. Average age 35. 27 applicants, 63% accepted, 14 enrolled. In 2007, 19 degrees awarded. *Entrance requirements:* For master's, interview. Additional exam requirements/recommendations for international students: Required—TOEFL (minimum score 550 paper-based; 213 computer-based). *Application deadline:* For fall admission, 7/15 priority date for domestic and international students; for spring admission, 11/15 priority date for domestic and international students. Applications are processed on a rolling basis. Application fee: $40. *Financial support:* Career-related internships or fieldwork and scholarships/grants available. Support available to part-time students. Financial award application deadline: 7/15; financial award applicants required to submit FAFSA. *Faculty research:* Counseling as a teaching discipline, New Testament principles for church growth. *Application contact:* Penny Rader, Seminary Admissions Counselor, 503-251-6485, Fax: 503-254-1268, E-mail: admiss@multnomah.edu.

Neumann College, Program in Pastoral Counseling, Aston, PA 19014-1298. Offers pastoral counseling (MS, CAS); spiritual direction (CSD). Part-time and evening/weekend programs available. *Faculty:* 3 full-time (2 women), 7 part-time/adjunct (5 women). *Students:* 5 full-time (all women), 92 part-time (68 women); includes 15 minority (12 African Americans, 2 Asian Americans or Pacific Islanders, 1 Hispanic American). Average age 47. 50 applicants, 100% accepted, 45 enrolled. In 2007, 23 degrees awarded. *Degree requirements:* For master's, clinical case study. *Entrance requirements:* Additional exam requirements/recommendations for international students: Required—TOEFL. *Application deadline:* Applications are processed on a rolling basis. Application fee: $50. *Financial support:* In 2007–08, 8 students received support. Available to part-time students. Application deadline: 3/15; *Faculty research:* Development of an integrated model of religion/psychology for remediation and prevention of emotional disturbance. *Unit head:* Dr. Leonard DiPaul, Executive Director, 610-558-5220, Fax: 610-459-1370, E-mail: dipall@neumann.edu. *Application contact:* Kittie D. Pain, Associate Director of Admissions, Graduate and Adult Programs, 610-558-5613, Fax: 610-558-5652, E-mail: paink@neumann.edu.

New Brunswick Theological Seminary, Graduate and Professional Programs, Program in Metro-Urban Ministry, New Brunswick, NJ 08901-1196. Offers theological studies (D Min). Part-time programs available. *Degree requirements:* For doctorate, thesis/dissertation. *Entrance requirements:* For doctorate, M Div. *Faculty research:* Urban-land use planning, theology of the city.

New Orleans Baptist Theological Seminary, Graduate and Professional Programs, Division of Pastoral Ministries, New Orleans, LA 70126-4858. Offers M Div, MAMFC, D Min, PhD. *Accreditation:* ACIPE. *Degree requirements:* For doctorate, thesis/dissertation; for M Div, project report. *Entrance requirements:* For master's and doctorate, GRE General Test.

Northern Baptist Theological Seminary, Graduate and Professional Programs, Lombard, IL 60148-5698. Offers Bible (MA); Christian ministries (MACM); divinity (M Div); ethics (MA); history (MA); ministry (D Min); theology (MA); worship/spirituality (MAWS); youth ministry (MAYM). *Accreditation:* ATS. Part-time programs available. *Faculty:* 6 full-time (1 woman), 29 part-time/adjunct (6 women). *Students:* 98 full-time (22 women), 91 part-time (32 women); includes 67 minority (51 African Americans, 12 Asian Americans or Pacific Islanders, 4 Hispanic Americans), 3 international. Average age 40. 71 applicants, 90% accepted. In 2007, 21 first professional degrees, 10 master's, 13 doctorates awarded. *Degree requirements:* For doctorate, thesis/dissertation; for M Div, field experience. *Entrance requirements:* For doctorate, 3 years in the ministry post-M Div. Additional exam requirements/recommendations for international students: Required—TOEFL. *Application deadline:* For fall admission, 9/1 priority date for domestic students, 2/1 priority date for international students; for winter admission, 12/1 priority date for domestic students; for spring admission, 3/1 priority date for domestic students. Applications are processed on a rolling basis. Application fee: $35. Electronic applications accepted. *Expenses:* Tuition: Full-time $11,340; part-time $420 per hour. Required fees: $300. Tuition and fees vary according to degree level. *Financial support:* In 2007–08, 68 students received support. Career-related internships or fieldwork and scholarships/grants available. Support available to part-time students. Financial award application deadline: 9/1. *Faculty research:* Theology, worship studies, church history, evangelism, Bible. *Unit head:* Dr. Charles Hambrick-Stowe, Dean, 630-620-2103, Fax: 630-620-2190. *Application contact:* Greg Henson, Director of Enrollment Management, 630-620-2191, Fax: 630-620-2190, E-mail: admissions@seminary.edu.

North Greenville University, T. Walter Brashier Graduate School, Tigerville, SC 29688-1892. Offers business administration (MBA); Christian ministry (MCM). Part-time and evening/weekend programs available. *Faculty:* 3 full-time (1 woman), 8 part-time/adjunct (0 women). *Students:* 44 full-time (19 women), 59 part-time (16 women); includes 17 minority (14 African Americans, 3 Hispanic Americans), 4 international. Average age 32. 128 applicants, 88% accepted, 103 enrolled. In 2007, 36 degrees awarded. *Degree requirements:* For master's, comprehensive exam (for some programs), thesis or alternative, capstone course. *Entrance requirements:* For master's, GMAT, GRE, minimum GPA of 2.25 overall, 2.5 in major. Additional exam requirements/recommendations for international students: Required—TOEFL (minimum score 550 paper-based; 213 computer-based). *Application deadline:* Applications are processed on a rolling basis. Application fee: $30. Electronic applications accepted. *Expenses:* Tuition: Full-time $4,500; part-time $250 per hour. *Financial support:* In 2007–08, 35 students received support. Federal Work-Study, institutionally sponsored loans, scholarships/grants, and tuition waivers (partial) available. Support available to part-time students. Financial award applicants required to submit FAFSA. *Faculty research:* Organizational behavior, church growth, homiletics. *Unit head:* Dr. J. Samuel Isgett, Vice President and Dean for Graduate Studies, 864-877-3052, Fax: 864-877-1653, E-mail: sisgett@ngu.edu. *Application contact:* Tawana P. Scott, Director of Graduate Enrollment, 864-877-1598, Fax: 864-877-1653, E-mail: tscott@ngu.edu.

Northwest Nazarene University, Graduate Studies, Program in Religion, Nampa, ID 83686-5897. Offers Christian education (MA); missional leadership (MA); pastoral ministry (MA); religion (M Div); spiritual formation (MA). Part-time and evening/weekend programs available. Postbaccalaureate distance learning degree programs offered (no on-campus study). *Faculty:* 9 full-time (3 women), 15 part-time/adjunct (3 women). *Students:* 131 full-time (35 women), 12 part-time (5 women); includes 9 minority (1 African American, 1 American Indian/Alaska Native, 5 Asian Americans or Pacific Islanders, 2 Hispanic Americans), 3 international. In 2007, 29 degrees awarded. *Application deadline:* Applications are processed on a rolling basis. Application fee: $50. Electronic applications accepted. *Unit head:* Dr. Jay Akkerman, Director, Graduate Studies, 208-467-8437, Fax: 208-467-8252.

Notre Dame College, Graduate Studies, South Euclid, OH 44121-4293. Offers accounting (Certificate); creative critical thinking (M Ed); financial services management (Certificate); information systems (Certificate); learning disabilities (M Ed); management (Certificate); paralegal (Certificate); pastoral ministry (Certificate); reading (M Ed); teacher education (Certificate). Part-time and evening/weekend programs available. *Degree requirements:* For master's, thesis. *Entrance requirements:* For master's, GRE General Test, MAT, minimum GPA of 2.75, valid teaching certificate. *Faculty research:* Cognitive psychology, teaching critical thinking in the classroom.

Oblate School of Theology, Graduate and Professional Programs, San Antonio, TX 78216-6693. Offers divinity (M Div); Hispanic ministry (D Min); pastoral ministry (MAP Min); pastoral studies (Certificate); spirituality (MA Sp); supervision (D Min), including clinical pastoral education, general supervision; theology (MA Th); M Div/MA Th. *Accreditation:* ACIPE; ATS (one or more programs are accredited). Part-time programs available. *Faculty:* 19 full-time (4 women), 3 part-time/adjunct (0 women). *Students:* 91 full-time (9 women), 70 part-time (29 women); includes 67 minority (9 African Americans, 1 American Indian/Alaska Native, 11 Asian Americans or Pacific Islanders, 46 Hispanic Americans), 33 international. Average age 39. 58 applicants, 100% accepted, 55 enrolled. In 2007, 15 first professional degrees, 8 master's, 9 Certificates awarded. *Degree requirements:* For master's, thesis (for some programs), practicum; for doctorate, paper, practicum; for M Div, one foreign language, seminar. *Entrance requirements:* For M Div, MAT, interview, course work in philosophy and theology; for master's, MAT, interview, course work in theology or religious studies, minimum GPA of 2.5; for doctorate, M Div. Additional exam requirements/recommendations for international students: Required—TOEFL (minimum score 197 computer-based; 71 iBT). *Application deadline:* For fall admission, 6/15 priority date for domestic and international students; for spring admission, 12/30 for domestic and international students. Applications are processed on a rolling basis. Application fee: $45. *Expenses:* Tuition: Full-time $11,232; part-time $432 per credit. Required fees: $160 per semester. One-time fee: $85 full-time. Tuition and fees vary according to course load and degree level. *Financial support:* Scholarships/grants available. Support available to part-time students. Financial award application deadline: 8/1; financial award applicants required to submit FAFSA. *Unit head:* Sr. Elaine Brothers, Academic Dean, 210-341-1366, Fax: 214-341-4519, E-mail: ebrothers@ost.edu. *Application contact:* James Oberhausen, Director of Admission/Registrar, 210-341-1366 Ext. 212, Fax: 210-341-4519, E-mail: registrar@ost.edu.

Oklahoma Christian University, Graduate School of Bible, Oklahoma City, OK 73136-1100. Offers family life ministry (MA); ministry (M Div, MA); youth ministry (MA). Part-time programs available. Postbaccalaureate distance learning degree programs offered (minimal on-campus study). *Faculty:* 12 full-time (0 women). *Students:* 11 full-time (3 women), 44 part-time (4 women); includes 3 minority (2 African Americans, 1 American Indian/Alaska Native), 3 international. Average age 30. 23 applicants, 100% accepted, 16 enrolled. In 2007, 8 degrees awarded. *Degree requirements:* For master's, one foreign language, comprehensive exam, field experience; for M Div, 2 foreign languages, comprehensive exam, field experience. *Entrance requirements:* For M Div and master's, minimum undergraduate GPA of 3.0. Additional exam requirements/recommendations for international students: Required—TOEFL (minimum score 550 paper-based; 213 computer-based). *Application deadline:* For fall admission, 8/15 priority date for domestic and international students; for spring admission, 1/3 priority date for domestic and international students. Applications are processed on a rolling basis. Application fee: $25. Electronic applications accepted. *Expenses:* Tuition: Full-time $6,300; part-time $350 per hour. One-time fee: $25. *Financial support:* In 2007–08, 49 students received support. Career-related internships or fieldwork, Federal Work-Study, scholarships/grants, and tuition waivers (partial) available. Support available to part-time students. Financial award application deadline: 3/1. *Faculty research:* Early marriage adjustment, new religions, Ethiopic language, church health, Hebrew rhetoric. *Unit head:* Dr. John Harrison, Chair, 405-425-5377, Fax: 405-425-5076, E-mail: john.harrison@oc.edu. *Application contact:* Dustin Crawford, Graduate Bible Recruiter, 405-425-5485, Fax: 405-425-5076, E-mail: dustin.crawford@oc.edu.

Olivet Nazarene University, Graduate School, Institute for Church Management, Bourbonnais, IL 60914-2271. Offers church management (MCM); pastoral counseling (MPC). Part-time programs available. *Degree requirements:* For master's, thesis or alternative. Expenses: Contact institution.

Oral Roberts University, School of Theology and Missions, Tulsa, OK 74171-0001. Offers biblical literature (MA), including advanced languages, Judaic-Christian studies; Christian counseling (MA), including marriage and family therapy; Christian education (MA); divinity (M Div); missions (MA); practical theology (MA); theological/historical studies (MA); theology (D Min). *Accreditation:* ATS; NASM. Part-time programs available. Postbaccalaureate distance learning degree programs offered (minimal on-campus study). *Faculty:* 17 full-time (2 women). *Students:* 371 full-time (156 women), 110 part-time (65 women); includes 177 minority (127 African Americans, 5 American Indian/Alaska Native, 20 Asian Americans or Pacific Islanders, 25 Hispanic Americans), 82 international. Average age 36. 159 applicants, 95% accepted, 124 enrolled. In 2007, 38 first professional degrees, 52 master's, 10 doctorates awarded. *Degree requirements:* For master's, thesis (for some programs), practicum/internship; for doctorate, thesis/dissertation, applied research project; for M Div, one foreign language, field experience. *Entrance requirements:* For M Div and master's, GRE General Test or MAT, minimum GPA of 2.5; for doctorate, M Div, minimum GPA of 3.0, 3 years of full-time ministry experience. Additional exam requirements/recommendations for international students: Required—TOEFL (minimum score 500 paper-based; 213 computer-based; 79 iBT). *Application deadline:* For fall admission, 7/1 priority date for domestic and international students; for spring admission, 12/1 priority date for domestic students, 10/1 priority date for international students. Applications are processed on a rolling basis. Application fee: $35. Electronic applications accepted. *Expenses:* Tuition: Part-time $450 per hour. Required fees: $125 per semester. Tuition and fees vary according to class time, degree level and program. *Financial support:* In 2007–08, teaching assistantships (averaging $3,600 per year); scholarships/grants and employment assistantships also available. Financial award application deadline: 6/1; financial award applicants required to submit FAFSA. *Unit head:* Dr. Thomson K. Mathew, Dean, 918-495-7016, Fax: 918-495-6259, E-mail: tmathew@oru.edu. *Application contact:* Debra E. Watkins, Graduate Theology Representative, 918-495-6618, Fax: 918-495-7965, E-mail: owatkins@oru.edu.

Ottawa University, Graduate Studies-Arizona, Program in Professional Counseling, Ottawa, KS 66067-3399. Offers Christian counseling (MA); expressive arts therapy (MA); marriage and family therapy (MA); treatment of trauma, abuse and deprivation (MA). Programs offered in Mesa, Phoenix, Tempe and West Valley, AZ. Part-time and evening/weekend programs available. Postbaccalaureate distance learning degree programs offered. *Degree requirements:* For master's, comprehensive exam, thesis or alternative, field experience, practicum. *Entrance requirements:* For master's, minimum undergraduate GPA of 3.0; course work in theories of personality, abnormal psychology, and human growth and development. Additional exam requirements/recommendations for international students: Required—TOEFL (minimum score 550 paper-based; 213 computer-based).

Philadelphia Biblical University, School of Church and Community Ministries, Langhorne, PA 19047-2990. Offers Christian counseling (MSCC). Part-time and evening/weekend programs available. *Faculty:* 4 full-time (1 woman), 9 part-time/adjunct (6 women). *Students:* 5 full-time (all women), 124 part-time (90 women); includes 38 minority (31 African Americans, 6 Asian Americans or Pacific Islanders, 1 Hispanic American). Average age 37. 77 applicants, 61% accepted, 38 enrolled. In 2007, 39 degrees awarded. *Entrance requirements:* Additional exam requirements/recommendations for international students: Required—TOEFL (minimum score 550 paper-based; 213 computer-based). *Application deadline:* Applications are processed on a rolling basis. Application fee: $25. Electronic applications accepted. *Expenses:* Tuition: Full-time $8,924; part-time $525 per credit. Tuition and fees vary according to program. *Financial support:* In 2007–08, 63 students received support. Scholarships/grants available. Support available to part-time students. Financial award applicants required to submit FAFSA. *Unit head:* Donald Cheyney, Dean, 215-702-4546, E-mail: dcheyney@pbu.edu. *Application contact:* Gwen Dorsey, Enrollment Counselor, Graduate Counseling, 800-572-2472, Fax: 215-702-4248, E-mail: gdorsey@pbu.edu.

Phillips Theological Seminary, Programs in Theology, Doctor of Ministry Program, Tulsa, OK 74116. Offers parish ministry (D Min); pastoral counseling (D Min); practices of ministry (D Min). *Accreditation:* ATS. Part-time programs available. *Degree requirements:* For doctorate, thesis/dissertation. *Entrance requirements:* For doctorate, M Div, minimum GPA of 3.0, 3 years of post-M Div pastoral experience. Expenses: Contact institution. *Faculty research:* Politics and theology, media and theology, ecology and theology.

Providence College, Graduate Studies, Department of Religious Studies, Providence, RI 02918. Offers biblical studies (MA); pastoral ministry (MA); religious education (MA); religious studies (MA). Part-time and evening/weekend programs available. *Faculty:* 7 full-time (0 women). *Students:* 6 full-time (0 women), 21 part-time (6 women). Average age 40. 8 applicants, 75% accepted. In 2007, 9 degrees awarded. *Degree requirements:* For master's, comprehensive exam, Greek and Hebrew (biblical studies). *Entrance requirements:* Additional exam requirements/recommendations for international students: Required—TOEFL (minimum score 550 paper-based; 213 computer-based; 79 iBT). *Application deadline:* For fall admission, 8/1 for domestic students; for spring admission, 12/1 for domestic students. Applications are processed on a rolling basis. Application fee: $55. *Expenses:* Tuition: Full-time $6,783; part-time $969 per course. *Financial support:* In 2007–08, 5 research assistantships with full tuition reimbursements (averaging $8,400 per year) were awarded; career-related internships or fieldwork and unspecified assistantships also available. Support available to part-time students. Financial award application deadline: 8/1; financial award applicants required to submit FAFSA. *Unit head:* Dr. Gary M. Culpepper, Director, 401-865-2863, Fax: 401-865-1449, E-mail: garyculp@providence.edu.

Providence College and Theological Seminary, Theological Seminary, Otterburne, MB R0A 1G0, Canada. Offers children's ministry (Certificate); Christian studies (MA, Certificate); counseling (MA); cross-cultural discipleship (Certificate); divinity (M Div); educational studies (MA), including counseling psychology, educational ministries, student development, teaching English to speakers of other languages, training teachers of English to speakers of other languages; global studies (MA); lay counseling (Diploma); ministry (D Min); teaching English to speakers of other languages (Certificate); theological studies (MA); training teacher of English to speakers of other languages (Certificate); youth ministry (Certificate). *Accreditation:* ATS. Part-time programs available. *Degree requirements:* For master's, variable foreign language requirement, thesis (for some programs); for doctorate, thesis/dissertation; for M Div, 2 foreign languages, comprehensive exam, thesis/dissertation (for some programs). *Entrance requirements:* Additional exam requirements/recommendations for international students: Recommended—TOEFL (minimum score 550 paper-based; 213 computer-based). *Faculty research:* Studies in Isaiah, theology of sin.

Reformed Theological Seminary–Charlotte Campus, Graduate and Professional Programs, Charlotte, NC 28226-6318. Offers biblical studies (MA); ministry (M Div, D Min); theological studies (MA). Part-time programs available. *Faculty:* 10 full-time, 4 part-time/adjunct. *Students:* 109. 53 applicants, 98% accepted, 40 enrolled. In 2007, 20 first professional degrees, 4 master's, 2 doctorates awarded. *Degree requirements:* For master's, comprehensive exam; for doctorate, thesis/dissertation; for M Div, 2 foreign languages, comprehensive exam. *Entrance requirements:* For master's, minimum GPA of 2.6; for doctorate, minimum GPA of 3.0. Additional exam requirements/recommendations for international students: Required—TOEFL (minimum score 550 paper-based; 213 computer-based). *Application deadline:* For fall admission, 7/15 priority date for domestic students; for winter admission, 11/15 priority date for domestic students; for spring admission, 12/15 priority date for domestic students. Applications are processed on a rolling basis. Application fee: $55. Electronic applications accepted. *Expenses:* Tuition: Full-time $12,025; part-time $325 per semester hour. Required fees: $65 per semester. *Financial support:* In 2007–08, teaching assistantships (averaging $1,600 per year); career-related internships or fieldwork and scholarships/grants also available. Financial award application deadline: 5/1. *Application contact:* Stephane Jeanrenaud, Director of Admissions, 800-755-2429, E-mail: admissions.charlotte@rts.edu.

Reformed Theological Seminary–Jackson Campus, Graduate and Professional Programs, Jackson, MS 39209-3099. Offers Bible, theology, and missions (Certificate); biblical studies (MA); Christian education (M Div, MA); counseling (M Div); divinity (M Div, Diploma); marriage and family therapy (MA); ministry (D Min); missions (M Div, MA, D Min); New Testament (Th M); Old Testament (Th M); theological studies (MA); theology (Th M); M Div/MA. *Accreditation:* AAMFT/COAMFTE (one or more programs are accredited); ATS (one or more programs are accredited). *Degree requirements:* For master's, thesis (for some programs), fieldwork; for doctorate, 2 foreign languages, thesis/dissertation; for M Div, 2 foreign languages, thesis/dissertation (for some programs). *Entrance requirements:* For M Div and master's, minimum GPA of 2.6; for doctorate, minimum GPA of 3.0. Additional exam requirements/recommendations for international students: Required—TOEFL.

Reformed Theological Seminary–Orlando Campus, Graduate Program, Oviedo, FL 32765-7197. Offers biblical studies (MA); Christian thought (MA); counseling (MA); ministry (D Min); reformation studies (Th M); theological studies (MA); theology (M Div); MA/Certificate. Part-time programs available. Postbaccalaureate distance learning degree programs offered (minimal on-campus study). *Faculty:* 15 full-time (0 women), 5 part-time/adjunct (0 women). *Students:* 428; includes 45 minority (15 African Americans, 19 Asian Americans or Pacific Islanders, 11 Hispanic Americans), 30 international. 203 applicants, 75% accepted, 107 enrolled. In 2007, 40 first professional degrees, 45 master's, 2 doctorates awarded. *Entrance requirements:* For M Div and master's, minimum GPA of 2.6. *Application deadline:* For fall admission, 5/21 priority date for domestic students; for winter admission, 10/3 priority date for domestic students; for spring admission, 11/5 priority date for domestic students. Applications are processed on a rolling basis. Application fee: $60. Electronic applications accepted. *Unit head:* Dr. Frank A. James, President, 407-366-9493, Fax: 407-366-9425, E-mail: fjames@rts.edu. *Application contact:* Thomas G. Nelson, Director of Admissions, 800-752-4382, Fax: 407-366-9425, E-mail: tnelson@rts.edu.

Regent University, Graduate School, School of Divinity, Virginia Beach, VA 23464-9800. Offers biblical studies (MA); leadership and renewal (D Min); missiology (M Div, MA); practical theology (M Div, MA); renewal studies (PhD); M Div/M Ed; M Div/MA; M Div/MBA; M Ed/MA; MBA/MA. *Accreditation:* ACIPE; ATS. Part-time programs available. Postbaccalaureate distance learning degree programs offered (minimal on-campus study). *Faculty:* 18 full-time (4 women), 22 part-time/adjunct (7 women). *Students:* 186 full-time (76 women), 437 part-time (163 women); includes 249 minority (212 African Americans, 2 American Indian/Alaska Native, 13 Asian Americans or Pacific Islanders, 22 Hispanic Americans), 61 international. Average age 38. 302 applicants, 70% accepted, 114 enrolled. In 2007, 56 first professional degrees, 16 master's, 62 doctorates awarded. *Degree requirements:* For master's, comprehensive exam, thesis or alternative, internship; for doctorate, thesis/dissertation or alternative; for M Div, internship. *Entrance requirements:* For M Div, GRE General Test or MAT, minimum undergraduate GPA of 3.0, minimum 3 years of ministry experience, transcripts, recommendations; for master's, GRE General Test or MAT, minimum undergraduate GPA of 2.75, writing sample, clergy recommendation, transcripts ; for doctorate, M Div or theological master's degree, minimum graduate GPA of 3.5 (PhD), 3.0 (D Min), recommendations, writing sample, transcripts . Additional exam requirements/recommendations for international students: Required—TOEFL (minimum score 577 paper-based; 233 computer-based). *Application deadline:* For fall admission, 5/1 priority date for domestic students. Applications are processed on a rolling basis. Application fee: $50. Electronic applications accepted. *Expenses: Contact institution. Financial support:* In 2007–08, 500 students received support; fellowships with full and partial tuition reimbursements available, career-related internships or fieldwork, scholarships/grants, tuition waivers (full and partial), and unspecified assistantships available. Support available to part-time students. Financial award application deadline: 9/1; financial award applicants required to submit FAFSA. *Faculty research:* Greek and Hebrew etymology. *Unit head:* Dr. Michael Palmer, Dean, 757-226-4406, Fax: 757-226-4597, E-mail: mpalmer@regent.edu. *Application contact:* Althea Bishard, Registrar and Executive Director of Enrollment and Academic Services, 800-373-5504, Fax: 757-226-4381, E-mail: admissions@regent.edu.

Regis College, Graduate and Professional Programs, Toronto, ON M4Y 2R5, Canada. Offers ministry (D Min); ministry and spirituality (MAMS); sacred theology (STB, STM, STD, STL); theological study (MTS); theology (M Div, MA, Th M, PhD, Th D); M Div/MA. *Accreditation:* ATS (one or more programs are accredited). *Faculty:* 15 full-time (4 women), 12 part-time/adjunct (2 women). *Students:* 88 full-time (30 women), 131 part-time (78 women); includes 74 minority (16 African Americans, 1 American Indian/Alaska Native, 48 Asian Americans or Pacific Islanders, 9 Hispanic Americans). Average age 45. 73 applicants, 88% accepted, 52 enrolled. In 2007, 10 first professional degrees, 13 master's, 5 other advanced degrees awarded. Terminal master's awarded for partial completion of doctoral program. *Degree requirements:* For master's, 2 foreign languages, thesis; for doctorate, 3 foreign languages, comprehensive exam, thesis/dissertation; for first professional degree, comprehensive exam. *Entrance requirements:* For first professional degree, minimum GPA of 3.0; for master's, minimum GPA of 3.3; for doctorate, minimum GPA of 3.7. Additional exam requirements/recommendations for international students: Required—TOEFL (minimum score 580 paper-based; 237 computer-based; 93 iBT), TWE (minimum score 5). *Application deadline:* For fall admission, 3/15 priority date for domestic and international students; for winter admission, 12/1 for domestic and international students; for spring admission, 3/15 for domestic and international students. Applications are processed on a rolling basis. Application fee: $25. Tuition charges are reported in Canadian dollars. *Expenses:* Tuition: Part-time $455 Canadian dollars per credit. Tuition and fees vary according to program and student level. *Financial support:* In 2007–08, 58 students received support. Career-related internships or fieldwork and scholarships/grants available. Support available to part-time students. Financial award application deadline: 3/15. *Unit head:* Dr. Gordon Rixon, Dean, 416-922-5474 Ext. 225, Fax: 416-922-2898, E-mail: gordon.rixon@utoronto.ca. *Application contact:* Elaine Chu, Registrar, 416-922-5474 Ext. 226, Fax: 416-922-2898, E-mail: regis.registrar@utoronto.ca.

Roberts Wesleyan College, Division of Social Sciences, Rochester, NY 14624-1997. Offers counseling in ministry (MA); school counseling (MS); school psychology (MS).

Sacred Heart Major Seminary, School of Theology, Detroit, MI 48206-1799. Offers pastoral studies (MAPS); theology (M Div, MA). *Accreditation:* ACIPE; ATS. Part-time and evening/weekend programs available. *Faculty:* 21 full-time (4 women), 10 part-time/adjunct (0 women). *Students:* 75 full-time (3 women), 129 part-time (48 women); includes 39 minority (15 African Americans, 1 American Indian/Alaska Native, 13 Asian Americans or Pacific Islanders, 10 Hispanic Americans), 4 international. Average age 50. In 2007, 4 first professional degrees, 11 master's awarded. *Degree requirements:* For master's, one foreign language, thesis optional, integrating project; for M Div, integrating seminar. *Entrance requirements:* For M Div and master's, GRE, previous course work in philosophy and theology. *Application deadline:* For fall admission, 9/5 for domestic students; for winter admission, 12/20 priority date for domestic students. Application fee: $30. *Expenses:* Tuition: Full-time $17,695; part-time $430 per hour. Required fees: $80; $40 per term. Full-time tuition and fees vary according to program. *Financial support:* Institutionally sponsored loans and scholarships/grants available. Financial award application deadline: 9/1; financial award applicants required to submit FAFSA. *Faculty research:* Local church history, patristics, spirituality, religious education. *Unit head:* Rev. Todd J. Lajiness, Dean of Studies, 313-883-8500, Fax: 313-868-6440, E-mail: lajiness.todd@shms.edu. *Application contact:* John Lajiness, Director of Admissions and Enrollment Management, 313-883-8500, Fax: 313-868-6440, E-mail: lajiness.john@shms.edu.

St. Ambrose University, College of Arts and Sciences, Program in Pastoral Studies, Davenport, IA 52803-2898. Offers MPS. Part-time programs available. *Faculty:* 2 full-time (1 woman), 1 part-time/adjunct (0 women). *Students:* Average age 50. 2 applicants, 100% accepted, 0 enrolled. *Degree requirements:* For master's, integration project. *Entrance requirements:* For master's, minimum GPA of 2.6, prior pastoral experience, 9 credits of course work in theology. Additional exam requirements/recommendations for international students: Required—TOEFL. *Application deadline:* For fall admission, 8/15 priority date for domestic students; for winter admission, 12/15 priority date for domestic students; for spring admission, 1/1 priority date for domestic students. Applications are processed on a rolling basis. Application fee: $25. Electronic applications accepted. *Expenses: Contact institution.* Tuition and fees vary according to course load, degree level, campus/location, program and reciprocity agreements. *Financial support:* In 2007–08, 2 students received support. Career-related internships or fieldwork, scholarships/grants, and tuition waivers (partial) available. Support available to part-time students. Financial award application deadline: 8/15; financial award applicants required to submit FAFSA. *Faculty research:* Theological education, ecclesiology, spirituality and liturgy, medical ethics. *Unit head:* Fr. Bud Grant, Director, 563-333-6419, Fax: 563-333-6243, E-mail: grantrobert@sau.edu. *Application contact:* Elizabeth Berridge, Director of Graduate Student Recruitment, 563-333-6271, Fax: 563-333-6268, E-mail: berridgeelizabethb@sau.edu.

St. Augustine's Seminary of Toronto, Graduate and Professional Programs, Scarborough, ON M1M 1M3, Canada. Offers divinity (M Div); lay ministry (Diploma); religious education (MRE); theological studies (MTS, Diploma). *Accreditation:* ATS. Part-time and evening/weekend programs available. *Faculty:* 11 full-time (4 women), 20 part-time/adjunct (4 women). *Students:* 57 full-time (2 women), 120 part-time (49 women), 14 international. Average age 41. 25 applicants, 96% accepted, 23 enrolled. In 2007, 10 first professional degrees, 6 master's awarded. *Degree requirements:* For M Div, comprehensive exam (for some programs), thesis/dissertation optional, field education. *Entrance requirements:* Course work in philosophy. Additional exam requirements/recommendations for international students: Required—TOEFL (minimum score 580 paper-based; 237 computer-based), TWE (minimum score 5). *Application deadline:* For fall admission, 7/15 priority date for domestic and international students; for winter admission, 11/15 priority date for domestic and international students; for spring admission, 4/15 priority date for domestic and international students. Application fee: $25 Canadian dollars. *Expenses:* Tuition: Part-time $572 per course. Required fees: $57 per term. Tuition and fees vary according to course load. *Unit head:* Rev. Tadeusz J. Nowak, Acting Dean of Studies, 416-261-7207, Fax: 416-261-2529. *Application contact:* Theresa Mary Vicioso, Registrar/Administrative Assistant to the Dean of Studies, 416-261-7207 Ext. 230, Fax: 416-261-2529, E-mail: t.vicioso@utoronto.ca.

Saint Bernard's School of Theology and Ministry, Graduate and Professional Programs, Rochester, NY 14618. Offers pastoral studies (MA, Certificate); theological studies (MA); theology (M Div). *Accreditation:* ATS (one or more programs are accredited). Part-time and evening/weekend programs available. *Faculty:* 7 full-time (3 women), 4 part-time/adjunct (1 woman). *Students:* 3 full-time (2 women), 126 part-time (55 women); includes 13 minority (7 African Americans, 1 American Indian/Alaska Native, 2 Asian Americans or Pacific Islanders, 3 Hispanic Americans). Average age 50. 40 applicants, 50% accepted, 20 enrolled. In 2007, 4 first professional degrees, 37 master's awarded. *Degree requirements:* For master's, variable foreign language requirement, thesis (for some programs). *Entrance requirements:* For M Div, minimum GPA of 2.0; for master's, minimum GPA of 2.5. *Application deadline:* Applications are processed on a rolling basis. Application fee: $75. *Expenses:* Tuition: Full-time $8,220; part-time $1,370 per course. Required fees: $30 per semester. *Financial support:* In 2007–08, 33 students received support; fellowships, research assistantships, teaching assistantships, career-related internships or fieldwork, scholarships/grants, and tuition waivers (partial) available. Support available to part-time students. Financial award application deadline: 4/15; financial award applicants required to submit FAFSA. *Unit head:* Dr. Patricia Schoelles, President, 585-271-3657 Ext. 276, Fax: 585-271-2045, E-mail: pschoelles@stbernards.edu. *Application contact:* Charmel Trinidad, Director of Admissions and Financial Aid, 585-271-3657 Ext. 289, Fax: 585-271-2045, E-mail: strinidad@stbernards.edu.

Saint Francis Seminary, Graduate and Professional Programs, St. Francis, WI 53235-3795. Offers M Div, MAPS. *Accreditation:* ACIPE; ATS. Part-time programs available. *Degree requirements:* For master's, comprehensive exam; for M Div, thesis/dissertation. *Entrance requirements:* For M Div and master's, Otis IQ Test, Terman Concept Mastery Test, interview. Additional exam requirements/recommendations for international students: Required—TOEFL (minimum score 550 paper-based).

St. John's Seminary, Graduate and Professional Programs, Camarillo, CA 93012-2598. Offers divinity (M Div); pastoral ministry (MAPM); theology (MA). *Accreditation:* ATS. Part-time programs available. *Faculty:* 23 full-time (4 women), 8 part-time/adjunct (1 woman). *Students:* 84 full-time (1 woman), 11 part-time (5 women); includes 49 minority (28 Asian Americans or Pacific Islanders, 21 Hispanic Americans), 15 international. Average age 34. 24 applicants, 100% accepted, 21 enrolled. In 2007, 11 first professional degrees, 6 master's awarded. *Degree requirements:* For master's, comprehensive exam (for some programs), thesis optional; for M Div, parish internship. *Entrance requirements:* For M Div, GRE General Test, bishop's approbation; for master's, GRE General Test, minimum GPA of 3.5. Additional exam requirements/recommendations for international students: Required—TOEFL (minimum score 550 paper-based). *Application deadline:* For fall admission, 7/15 priority date for domestic students. Applications are processed on a rolling basis. Application fee: $0. *Expenses:* Tuition: Full-time $12,250; part-time $408 per unit. *Faculty research:* Biblical studies, moral theology, historical studies, systematic theology, spiritual theology. *Unit head:* Rev. Richard Benson, CM, Academic Dean, 805-482-2755, Fax: 805-482-3470, E-mail: rbensoncm@stjohnsem.edu.

Pastoral Ministry and Counseling

St. John's Seminary (continued)

Application contact: Esmé M. Takahashi, Registrar, 805-482-2755 Ext. 1014, Fax: 805-482-3470, E-mail: registrar-sjs@stjohnsem.edu.

St. John's University, St. John's College of Liberal Arts and Sciences, Department of Theology and Religious Studies, Queens, NY 11439. Offers pastoral ministry (Certificate); priestly studies (M Div); theology (MA, Certificate). *Accreditation:* ACIPE. Part-time and evening/weekend programs available. *Faculty:* 20 full-time (6 women), 43 part-time/adjunct (18 women). *Students:* 3 full-time (1 woman), 52 part-time (31 women); includes 10 minority (6 African Americans, 1 Asian American or Pacific Islander, 3 Hispanic Americans), 10 international. Average age 44. 35 applicants, 51% accepted, 7 enrolled. In 2007, 10 degrees awarded. *Degree requirements:* For master's, thesis optional; for M Div, thesis/dissertation optional. *Entrance requirements:* For master's, minimum GPA of 3.0. Additional exam requirements/recommendations for international students: Required—TOEFL (minimum score 500 paper-based; 173 computer-based; 61 iBT), IELTS (minimum score 6). *Application deadline:* For fall admission, 5/1 priority date for domestic and international students; for spring admission, 11/1 priority date for domestic and international students. Applications are processed on a rolling basis. Application fee: $40. Electronic applications accepted. *Financial support:* Research assistantships, scholarships/grants available. Support available to part-time students. Financial award application deadline: 3/1; financial award applicants required to submit FAFSA. *Faculty research:* Systematic theology, moral theory, biblical studies, pastoral theology, church history. *Unit head:* Fr. Michael Whalen, Chair, 718-990-5431, E-mail: whalenm@stjohns.edu. *Application contact:* Beth Evans, Associate Vice President and Executive Director, Enrollment Management, 718-990-6999, Fax: 718-990-5686, E-mail: gradhelp@stjohns.edu.

Saint John's University, Saint John's School of Theology and Seminary, Collegeville, MN 56321. Offers divinity (M Div); liturgical music (MA); liturgical studies (MA); pastoral ministry (MA); theology (MA), including church history, liturgy, monastic studies, scripture, spirituality, systematics; M Div/MA. *Accreditation:* ATS. Part-time programs available. Postbaccalaureate distance learning degree programs offered (no on-campus study). *Degree requirements:* For master's, one foreign language, comprehensive exam (for some programs), thesis (for some programs). *Entrance requirements:* For master's, GRE General Test or MAT. Electronic applications accepted. *Faculty research:* Religious education, biblical literature.

Saint Joseph College, Graduate Division, Department of Counselor Education, West Hartford, CT 06117-2700. Offers community counseling (MA), including child welfare, pastoral counseling, school counseling; spirituality (Certificate). Part-time and evening/weekend programs available. *Degree requirements:* For master's, comprehensive exam, thesis optional, Capstone project. *Entrance requirements:* For master's, PRAXIS I (school counseling), 2 letters of recommendation. Electronic applications accepted.

Saint Leo University, Graduate Pastoral Studies, Saint Leo, FL 33574-6665. Offers MA. Part-time and evening/weekend programs available. *Faculty:* 8 full-time (0 women), 1 (woman) part-time/adjunct. *Students:* 15 full-time (6 women), 65 part-time (11 women); includes 8 minority (6 African Americans, 1 Asian American or Pacific Islander, 1 Hispanic American), 1 international. Average age 53. In 2007, 9 degrees awarded. *Entrance requirements:* For master's, minimum GPA of 3.0, letter of recommendation. Additional exam requirements/recommendations for international students: Required—TOEFL (minimum score 550 paper-based; 213 computer-based). *Application deadline:* For fall admission, 7/1 priority date for domestic and international students; for spring admission, 11/1 priority date for domestic and international students. Applications are processed on a rolling basis. Application fee: $45. Electronic applications accepted. *Expenses:* Tuition: Full-time $9,900; part-time $550 per semester hour. Required fees: $660; $110 per course. Tuition and fees vary according to campus/location and program. *Financial support:* In 2007–08, 66 students received support. Federal Work-Study and scholarships/grants available. Support available to part-time students. *Faculty research:* Ecclesiology and the Second Vatican Council, sacramental theology and the liturgical movement, Christian and Eastern religious traditions, Ecumenism, ministry and technology. *Unit head:* Dr. William Ditewig, Director, 352-588-7389, Fax: 352-588-8300, E-mail: william.ditewig@saintleo.edu. *Application contact:* Jared Welling, Director, Graduate/Weekend and Evening Admission, 800-707-8846, Fax: 352-588-7873, E-mail: grad.admissions@saintleo.edu.

Saint Mary-of-the-Woods College, Program in Pastoral Theology, Saint Mary-of-the-Woods, IN 47876. Offers pastoral theology (MA); youth ministry (Graduate Certificate). Part-time and evening/weekend programs available. Postbaccalaureate distance learning degree programs offered (minimal on-campus study). *Degree requirements:* For master's, thesis, qualifying exam.

St. Mary's University, Graduate School, Department of Theology, San Antonio, TX 78228-8507. Offers pastoral ministry (MA); theology (MA); JD/MA. Part-time and evening/weekend programs available. Postbaccalaureate distance learning degree programs offered (no on-campus study). *Students:* 4 full-time (1 woman), 32 part-time (16 women); includes 7 minority (all Hispanic Americans), 1 international. Average age 41. In 2007, 14 degrees awarded. *Degree requirements:* For master's, thesis optional, practicum (pastoral administration). *Entrance requirements:* For master's, GRE General Test, MAT, 12 credit hours in theology/philosophy. Additional exam requirements/recommendations for international students: Required—TOEFL (minimum score 550 paper-based; 213 computer-based). *Application deadline:* For fall admission, 8/1 for domestic students. Application fee: $0. *Financial support:* Research assistantships, career-related internships or fieldwork, Federal Work-Study, institutionally sponsored loans, scholarships/grants, health care benefits, and unspecified assistantships available. Financial award application deadline: 3/31; financial award applicants required to submit FAFSA. *Faculty research:* Bioethics; perceptions of ministry; Marian doctrines and the contemporary church; Jaspers, peace, and justice. *Unit head:* Rev. Daniel Thompson, Director, 210-436-3310, E-mail: dthompson@stmarytx.edu.

Saint Mary's University of Minnesota, Schools of Graduate and Professional Programs, Graduate School of Health and Human Services, Institute in Pastoral Ministries, Winona, MN 55987-1399. Offers Canon law (Certificate); pastoral administration (MA); pastoral ministries (MA). *Unit head:* Dr. Gregory Sobolewski, Director, 507-457-1767, Fax: 507-457-1752, E-mail: gsobolew@smumn.edu. *Application contact:* Jami Spitzer, Information Contact, 507-457-7500, E-mail: jspitzer@smumn.edu.

Saint Paul University, Faculty of Canon Law, Ottawa, ON K1S 1C4, Canada. Offers canon law (MCL, JCD, PhD, Graduate Certificate, JCL); canonical practice (Graduate Certificate); ecclesiastical administration (Graduate Certificate). Part-time programs available. *Faculty:* 10 full-time (1 woman), 4 part-time/adjunct (3 women). *Students:* 56 full-time (6 women), 1 (woman) part-time; includes 30 minority (14 African Americans, 15 Asian Americans or Pacific Islanders, 1 Hispanic American). Average age 40. 43 applicants, 86% accepted, 32 enrolled. In 2007, 17 master's, 3 doctorates, 16 other advanced degrees awarded. *Degree requirements:* For master's, one foreign language; for doctorate, one foreign language, comprehensive exam, thesis/dissertation; for other advanced degree, one foreign language, comprehensive exam (for some programs), comprehensive exam and seminar paper (JCL). *Entrance requirements:* For master's, appropriate bachelor's degree, 18 credits in theology; for doctorate, JCL or MCL; for other advanced degree, B Th or equivalent (JCL), appropriate bachelor's degree, 18 credits in theology. *Application deadline:* For fall admission, 8/15 priority date for domestic students, 5/15 priority date for international students. Applications are processed on a rolling basis. Application fee: $60 Canadian dollars. *Financial support:* In 2007–08, 3 students received support. Scholarships/grants and bursaries available. *Faculty research:* All questions related to Church law. *Unit head:* Dr. Roland Jacques, Dean, 613-751-4035, Fax: 613-751-4036, E-mail: rjacques@ustpaul.ca. *Application contact:* Beverly Ruth Kavanaugh, Administrative Assistant, 613-751-4018, Fax: 613-751-4036, E-mail: bkavanaugh@ustpaul.ca.

Saint Paul University, Faculty of Human Sciences, Program in Counseling and Spirituality, Ottawa, ON K1S 1C4, Canada. Offers individual or marital/couple counseling (MA); spiritual care (MA). Part-time programs available. *Students:* 57 applicants, 72% accepted, 32 enrolled. In 2007, 18 degrees awarded. *Degree requirements:* For master's, research project or thesis. *Entrance requirements:* For master's, honors BA in human sciences, minimum B average, 12 theology credits. *Application deadline:* For fall admission, 3/31 priority date for domestic and international students; for spring admission, 5/1 priority date for domestic students. Application fee: $60. *Unit head:* Manal Guirguis-Younger, Head, 613-236-1393 Ext. 2390, E-mail: jlowe@ustpaul.ca. *Application contact:* Diane Boudroault, Head, 613-236-1393 Ext. 2292, E-mail: dboudreault@ustpaul.ca.

St. Petersburg Theological Seminary, Graduate Programs, St. Petersburg, FL 33708. Offers Biblical studies (MA); counseling (MA); divinity (M Div); education (MA); Judaic studies (MA); ministry (MA, D Min); religious teacher (MA). Part-time and evening/weekend programs available. Postbaccalaureate distance learning degree programs offered (minimal on-campus study). *Faculty:* 8 full-time (4 women), 15 part-time/adjunct (6 women). *Students:* 32 full-time (16 women), 33 part-time (15 women). In 2007, 1 first professional degree, 5 master's, 1 doctorate awarded. *Degree requirements:* For master's, thesis; for doctorate, thesis/dissertation. *Entrance requirements:* For M Div and master's, Bachelor degree; for doctorate, Master degree. *Application deadline:* For fall admission, 8/15 priority date for domestic students; for winter admission, 12/31 priority date for domestic students. Application fee: $50. Electronic applications accepted. *Expenses:* Tuition: Part-time $140 per credit. Required fees: $15 per semester. Part-time tuition and fees vary according to program. *Financial support:* In 2007–08, 3 students received support. *Unit head:* Dr. George Pierce, Head of the Graduate Program, E-mail: gpierce3@tampabay.rr.com. *Application contact:* Dr. Amy Mormino, Registrar, 727-399-0276, Fax: 727-399-1324, E-mail: registrar@sptseminary.edu.

Saints Cyril and Methodius Seminary, Graduate and Professional Programs, Orchard Lake, MI 48324. Offers pastoral ministry (MAPM); religious education (MARE); theology (M Div, MA). *Accreditation:* ATS. Part-time programs available.

St. Stephen's College, Programs in Theology, Edmonton, AB T6G 2J6, Canada. Offers ministry (D Min); pastoral counseling (MA); social transformation ministry (MA); spirituality and liturgy (MA); theological studies (MTS); theology (M Th). Part-time and evening/weekend programs available. Postbaccalaureate distance learning degree programs offered (minimal on-campus study). Terminal master's awarded for partial completion of doctoral program. *Degree requirements:* For master's, thesis; for doctorate, thesis/dissertation. *Entrance requirements:* Additional exam requirements/recommendations for international students: Required—TOEFL. Electronic applications accepted. *Faculty research:* Methodology for theological education, practice and supervision for ministry.

St. Thomas University, School of Theology and Ministry, Institute for Pastoral Ministries, Miami Gardens, FL 33054-6459. Offers pastoral ministries (MA, Certificate); practical theology (PhD). Part-time and evening/weekend programs available. *Students:* 3 full-time (2 women), 17 part-time (12 women); includes 11 minority (1 African American, 10 Hispanic Americans), 1 international. Average age 41. In 2007, 8 degrees awarded. *Degree requirements:* For master's, comprehensive exam; for doctorate, comprehensive exam, thesis/dissertation. *Entrance requirements:* For master's, interview, minimum GPA of 3.0 or GRE; for doctorate, GRE, MA in theology. Additional exam requirements/recommendations for international students: Required—TOEFL (minimum score 550 paper-based; 213 computer-based; 79 iBT). *Application deadline:* For fall admission, 6/15 priority date for domestic students; for spring admission, 11/15 for domestic students. Applications are processed on a rolling basis. Application fee: $40. Electronic applications accepted. *Financial support:* Career-related internships or fieldwork and unspecified assistantships available. Support available to part-time students. Financial award application deadline: 4/15; financial award applicants required to submit FAFSA. *Unit head:* Dr. Joseph A. Iannone, Dean, 305-474-6973. *Application contact:* Marilyn Carballosa, Assistant Director of Admissions, 305-628-6546, Fax: 305-628-6591, E-mail: graduate@stu.edu.

Santa Clara University, School of Education, Counseling Psychology, and Pastoral Ministries, Program in Pastoral Ministries, Program in Pastoral Liturgy, Santa Clara, CA 95053. Offers MA. Part-time and evening/weekend programs available. *Students:* Average age 48. In 2007, 3 degrees awarded. *Degree requirements:* For master's, comprehensive exam, thesis. *Entrance requirements:* Additional exam requirements/recommendations for international students: Required—TOEFL. *Application deadline:* Applications are processed on a rolling basis. *Financial support:* Application deadline: 3/1; *Unit head:* Fr. Tom Powers, S.J., Director, Program in Pastoral Ministries, 408-554-4322.

Seattle University, School of Theology and Ministry, Program in Pastoral Counseling, Seattle, WA 98122-1090. Offers MA.

Seattle University, School of Theology and Ministry, Program in Pastoral Studies, Seattle, WA 98122-1090. Offers MAPS. Part-time and evening/weekend programs available. *Degree requirements:* For master's, project. *Entrance requirements:* For master's, interview, minimum GPA of 2.75, 2 years of experience in field.

Seminary of the Immaculate Conception, School of Theology, Huntington, NY 11743-1696. Offers pastoral studies (MA); theology (M Div, MA, D Min, Certificate). *Accreditation:* ATS (one or more programs are accredited). Part-time and evening/weekend programs available. *Faculty:* 8 full-time (2 women), 11 part-time/adjunct (4 women). *Students:* 37 full-time (0 women), 128 part-time (54 women); includes 19 minority (9 African Americans, 1 Asian American or Pacific Islander, 9 Hispanic Americans), 6 international. Average age 49. 21 applicants, 100% accepted, 19 enrolled. In 2007, 12 first professional degrees, 37 master's, 6 doctorates awarded. *Degree requirements:* For master's, comprehensive exam; for doctorate, thesis/dissertation; for M Div, one foreign language, thesis/dissertation. *Entrance requirements:* For M Div, college degree in philosophy-theology; for master's, undergraduate degree; for doctorate, MA plus 30 credits or M Div; for Certificate, MA in theology. *Application deadline:* For fall admission, 8/30 priority date for domestic students; for spring admission, 1/20 priority date for domestic students. Applications are processed on a rolling basis. Application fee: $75. *Expenses:* Tuition: Full-time $12,000; part-time $450 per credit. Required fees: $1,000; $50 per semester. One-time fee: $200 part-time. *Financial support:* Scholarships/grants available. Financial award applicants required to submit FAFSA. *Unit head:* Sr. Mary Louise Brink, SC, Associate Dean/Director of Graduate Studies, 631-423-0483 Ext. 130, Fax: 631-432-2346, E-mail: mlbrink@icseminary.edu. *Application contact:* Kathryn L. Zahner, Registrar, 631-423-0483 Ext. 147, Fax: 631-423-2346, E-mail: kzahner@icseminary.edu.

Seton Hall University, Immaculate Conception Seminary School of Theology, South Orange, NJ 07079-2697. Offers pastoral ministry (M Div, MA); theology (MA, Certificate). *Accreditation:* ACIPE; ATS (one or more programs are accredited). Part-time and evening/weekend programs available. *Degree requirements:* For master's, one foreign language, comprehensive exam, thesis, final project; for M Div, final project and seminar, field education, spiritual formation. *Entrance requirements:* For M Div, GRE, MAT; for master's, GRE General Test or MAT. Electronic applications accepted. Expenses: Contact institution.

Shasta Bible College, Program in Biblical Counseling, Redding, CA 96002. Offers biblical counseling and Christian family life education (MA). Part-time programs available. *Faculty:* 1 full-time (0 women), 3 part-time/adjunct (1 woman). *Students:* 4 full-time (2 women), 11 part-time (5 women); includes 2 minority (1 African American, 1 Hispanic American), 2 international. 3 applicants, 100% accepted, 3 enrolled. In 2007, 2 degrees awarded. *Degree requirements:* For master's, comprehensive exam (for some programs), thesis or alternative. *Entrance requirements:* For master's, minimum GPA of 2.5. Additional exam requirements/recommendations for international students: Required—TOEFL (minimum score 550 paper-based; 213 computer-based). *Application deadline:* For fall admission, 8/22 priority date for domestic and international students; for spring admission, 12/19 priority date for domestic and international students. Applications are processed on a rolling basis. Application fee: $35. *Expenses:* Tuition: Full-time $4,050; part-time $225 per unit. Required fees: $480. *Unit head:* Dr. Harlon Confer, Professor of Christian Education and Counseling, 530-529-3550, Fax:

530-221-6929, E-mail: hrlncnfr@yahoo.com. *Application contact:* Mark A. Mueller, Registrar, 530-221-4275 Ext. 206, Fax: 530-221-6929, E-mail: registrar@shasta.edu.

Shasta Bible College, Program in Christian Ministry, Redding, CA 96002. Offers MA. Part-time programs available. Postbaccalaureate distance learning degree programs offered (minimal on-campus study). *Faculty:* 1 full-time (0 women), 2 part-time/adjunct (1 woman). *Students:* 1 (woman) full-time. Average age 52. 1 applicant, 100% accepted, 1 enrolled. *Entrance requirements:* Additional exam requirements/recommendations for international students: Required—TOEFL (minimum score 550 paper-based; 213 computer-based). *Application deadline:* For fall admission, 8/22 priority date for domestic and international students; for spring admission, 12/19 priority date for domestic and international students. Applications are processed on a rolling basis. Application fee: $35. *Expenses:* Tuition: Full-time $4,050; part-time $225 per unit. Required fees: $480.

Simpson University, A.W. Tozer Theological Seminary, Redding, CA 96003-8606. Offers Christian leadership (MA); Christian studies (MA); intercultural studies (MA); ministry (M Div). Part-time and evening/weekend programs available. Postbaccalaureate distance learning degree programs offered (minimal on-campus study). *Faculty:* 6 part-time/adjunct (0 women). *Students:* 6 full-time (0 women), 49 part-time (13 women); includes 7 minority (3 African Americans, 2 Asian Americans or Pacific Islanders, 2 Hispanic Americans), 1 international. Average age 38. 22 applicants, 73% accepted, 16 enrolled. In 2007, 5 degrees awarded. *Degree requirements:* For master's, student portfolio. *Entrance requirements:* For master's, GRE General Test (if undergraduate GPA is below 2.5), 2 letters of reference, Christian Experience statement. Additional exam requirements/recommendations for international students: Required—TOEFL. *Application deadline:* For fall admission, 9/4 priority date for domestic students, 9/4 for international students; for spring admission, 1/8 priority date for domestic students, 1/8 for international students. Applications are processed on a rolling basis. Application fee: $20. Electronic applications accepted. *Expenses: Contact institution. Financial support:* Scholarships/grants available. Support available to part-time students. Financial award application deadline: 3/20; financial award applicants required to submit FAFSA. *Unit head:* Dr. Robert Redman, Dean, 530-226-4144, Fax: 530-326-4871, E-mail: rredman@simpsonuniversity.edu. *Application contact:* Jeff Williams, Director of Enrollment Development, 530-226-4611, Fax: 530-226-4861, E-mail: jwilliams@simpsonuniversity.edu.

Sioux Falls Seminary, Graduate and Professional Programs, Professional Program in Pastoral Ministry, Sioux Falls, SD 57105-1599. Offers M Div. *Accreditation:* ACIPE. Part-time programs available. *Students:* 50 full-time (7 women), 16 part-time (4 women). *Entrance requirements:* Minimum GPA of 2.5. *Application deadline:* For fall admission, 8/1 priority date for domestic students; for spring admission, 1/1 priority date for domestic students. Applications are processed on a rolling basis. Application fee: $35. *Financial support:* Career-related internships or fieldwork and scholarships/grants available. Support available to part-time students. *Application contact:* Bryce H. Eben, Director of Enrollment Development, 605-336-6588, Fax: 605-335-9090, E-mail: beben@sfseminary.edu.

Sioux Falls Seminary, Graduate and Professional Programs, Program in Counseling, Sioux Falls, SD 57105-1599. Offers MA. Part-time programs available. *Students:* 4 full-time (1 woman), 1 part-time. *Entrance requirements:* For master's, minimum GPA of 2.5. *Application deadline:* For fall admission, 8/1 priority date for domestic students; for spring admission, 1/1 priority date for domestic students. Applications are processed on a rolling basis. Application fee: $35. *Unit head:* Dr. Del Donaldson, Professor of Marriage and Family Therapy, 605-336-6588, Fax: 605-335-9090. *Application contact:* Bryce H. Eben, Director of Enrollment Development, 605-336-6588, Fax: 605-335-9090, E-mail: beben@sfseminary.edu.

Southern Baptist Theological Seminary, Billy Graham School of Missions, Evangelism, and Church Growth, Louisville, KY 40280-0004. Offers Christian mission/world religion (PhD); evangelism/church growth (PhD); ministry (D Min); missiology (MA, D Miss); missions, evangelism, and church growth (M Div); theology (Th M). *Accreditation:* ATS. Part-time and evening/weekend programs available. Postbaccalaureate distance learning degree programs offered (minimal on-campus study). *Degree requirements:* For master's and M Div, 2 foreign languages; for doctorate, 4 foreign languages, thesis/dissertation. *Entrance requirements:* For doctorate, GRE General Test, MAT, field essay, M Div. Additional exam requirements/recommendations for international students: Required—TOEFL, TWE. *Faculty research:* Assimilation of church congregants, effective methodologies of evangelism, expectations of church members, spiritual warfare literature, formative church discipline.

Southern Evangelical Seminary, Graduate School of Ministry and Missions, Matthews, NC 28105. Offers apologetics (Certificate); Christian education (MA); church ministry (MA, Certificate); divinity (Certificate), including apologetics (M Div, Certificate); Islamic studies (Certificate); theology (M Div), including apologetics (M Div, Certificate), Biblical studies; youth ministry (MA). Part-time and evening/weekend programs available. Postbaccalaureate distance learning degree programs offered. In 2007, 3 degrees awarded. *Degree requirements:* For master's, thesis (for some programs); for M Div, one foreign language. *Entrance requirements:* Additional exam requirements/recommendations for international students: Required—TOEFL (minimum score 600 paper-based; 250 computer-based). *Application deadline:* For fall admission, 8/15 priority date for domestic students, 8/5 priority date for international students; for winter admission, 12/15 priority date for domestic and international students; for spring admission, 1/15 priority date for domestic and international students. Applications are processed on a rolling basis. Application fee: $25. *Financial support:* Scholarships/grants available. *Unit head:* Dr. Barry R. Leventhal, Dean, 704-847-5600 Ext. 204, Fax: 704-845-1747, E-mail: dean@ses.edu.

Southern Wesleyan University, Program in Christian Ministries, Central, SC 29630-1020. Offers M Min. Evening/weekend programs available. *Faculty:* 6 full-time (1 woman), 4 part-time/adjunct (1 woman). *Students:* 12 full-time (6 women); includes 6 minority (all African Americans) Average age 33. In 2007, 4 degrees awarded. *Degree requirements:* For master's, paper. *Entrance requirements:* For master's, GRE General Test or MAT. *Application deadline:* Applications are processed on a rolling basis. Application fee: $25. *Expenses:* Tuition: Full-time $8,295. Required fees: $1,470. *Financial support:* Tuition waivers (full) available. *Unit head:* Amanda Young, Assistant Director of Admissions, 864-644-5562, Fax: 864-644-5972, E-mail: ayoung@swu.edu.

Southwestern Christian University, Program in Ministry, Bethany, OK 73008-0340. Offers M Min. Part-time programs available. *Degree requirements:* For master's, thesis. *Entrance requirements:* For master's, minimum GPA of 2.5. Additional exam requirements/recommendations for international students: Required—TOEFL (minimum score 500 paper-based). Electronic applications accepted.

Southwestern College, Fifth-Year Graduate Programs, Winfield, KS 67156-2499. Offers leadership (MS); management (MBA); specialized ministries (MA). Part-time programs available. *Faculty:* 12 part-time/adjunct (4 women). *Students:* 19 full-time (5 women), 6 part-time (3 women); includes 4 minority (2 African Americans, 2 Hispanic Americans). Average age 24. 28 applicants, 96% accepted, 25 enrolled. In 2007, 11 degrees awarded. *Degree requirements:* For master's, practicum (MS). *Entrance requirements:* For master's, baccalaureate degree, minimum GPA of 3.0. Additional exam requirements/recommendations for international students: Required—TOEFL (minimum score 550 paper-based). *Application deadline:* For fall admission, 8/24 priority date for domestic students; for spring admission, 12/1 priority date for domestic students. Applications are processed on a rolling basis. Application fee: $25. Electronic applications accepted. *Expenses:* Tuition: Part-time $435 per credit hour. *Financial support:* In 2007–08, 22 students received support. Federal Work-Study, tuition waivers (partial), and unspecified assistantships available. Financial award application deadline: 4/1. *Unit head:* Dr. James Sheppard, Vice President for Academic Affairs, 620-229-6227, Fax: 620-229-6224, E-mail: james.sheppard@sckans.edu. *Application contact:* Stephanie Humphries, Admission Counselor, 800-846-1543 Ext. 6230, Fax: 620-229-6344, E-mail: stephanie.humphries@sckans.edu.

Spring Arbor University, School of Arts and Sciences, Spring Arbor, MI 49283-9799. Offers communication (MA); spiritual formation and leadership (MA). Part-time programs available. Postbaccalaureate distance learning degree programs offered (no on-campus study). *Faculty:* 6 full-time (1 woman), 8 part-time/adjunct (3 women). *Students:* 69 full-time (46 women), 57 part-time (36 women); includes 10 minority (all African Americans), 1 international. In 2007, 3 degrees awarded. *Degree requirements:* For master's, thesis (for some programs). *Entrance requirements:* For master's, GRE (taken within the last 5 years), writing sample, 3 recommendations, personal goals statement. Additional exam requirements/recommendations for international students: Required—TOEFL (minimum score 550 paper-based; 220 computer-based). Application fee: $40. *Expenses: Contact institution.* One-time fee: $40 part-time. Tuition and fees vary according to course load and program. *Financial support:* Applicants required to submit FAFSA. *Unit head:* Dr. Wally Metts, Chair of the Department of Communication, 517-750-1200 Ext. 1491, E-mail: wmetts@arbor.edu. *Application contact:* Carol Bunnell, Secretary, Department of Communication, 517-750-6483, E-mail: cbunnell@arbor.edu.

Trinity Baptist College, Graduate Programs, Jacksonville, FL 32221. Offers Bible (M Ed); Christian school administration (M Ed); classroom practices (M Ed); ministry (M Min); special education (M Ed). Postbaccalaureate distance learning degree programs offered. *Entrance requirements:* For master's, GRE (M Ed), 2 letters of recommendation; minimum GPA of 2.5 (M Min) or 3.0 (M Ed); computer proficiency.

Trinity Episcopal School for Ministry, Graduate Programs, Ambridge, PA 15003-2397. Offers Anglican studies (Diploma); basic Christian studies (Diploma); divinity (M Div); ministry (D Min); mission and evangelism (MAME, Diploma); religion (MAR); youth ministry (Diploma). *Accreditation:* ATS (one or more programs are accredited). Part-time programs available. *Degree requirements:* For master's, thesis optional; for doctorate, thesis/dissertation; for M Div, thesis/dissertation optional, Greek and Hebrew. *Entrance requirements:* Additional exam requirements/recommendations for international students: Required—TOEFL. *Faculty research:* Pauline Epistles, contemporary theology, history of Anglican liturgy, book of Ruth, biblical theology.

Trinity International University, Trinity Evangelical Divinity School, Deerfield, IL 60015-1284. Offers Biblical and Near Eastern archaeology and languages (MA); Christian studies (MA, Certificate); Christian thought (MA); church history (MA, Th M); congregational ministry: pastor-teacher (M Div); congregational ministry: team ministry (M Div); counseling ministries (MA); counseling psychology (MA); cross-cultural ministry (M Div); educational studies (PhD); evangelism (MA); history of Christianity in America (MA); intercultural studies (MA, PhD); leadership and ministry management (D Min); military chaplaincy (D Min); ministry (MA); mission and evangelism (Th M); missions and evangelism (D Min); New Testament (MA, Th M); Old Testament (Th M); Old Testament and Semitic languages (MA); pastoral care (M Div); pastoral care and counseling (D Min); pastoral counseling and psychology (Th M); pastoral theology (Th M); philosophy of religion (MA); preaching (D Min); religion (MA); research ministry (M Div); systematic theology (Th M); theological studies (PhD); urban ministry (MA). *Accreditation:* ATS (one or more programs are accredited). Part-time programs available. Postbaccalaureate distance learning degree programs offered (minimal on-campus study). *Faculty:* 41 full-time (4 women), 77 part-time/adjunct (17 women). *Students:* 578 full-time (141 women), 711 part-time (202 women). In 2007, 92 first professional degrees, 78 master's, 47 doctorates, 23 other advanced degrees awarded. *Degree requirements:* For master's, comprehensive exam, thesis, fieldwork; for doctorate, comprehensive exam (for some programs), thesis/dissertation; for M Div, 2 foreign languages, fieldwork; for Certificate, comprehensive exam, integrative papers. *Entrance requirements:* For M Div, GRE, MAT; for master's, GRE, MAT, minimum cumulative undergraduate GPA of 3.0; for doctorate, GRE, minimum cumulative graduate GPA of 3.2; for Certificate, GRE, MAT, minimum undergraduate GPA of 2.5. Additional exam requirements/recommendations for international students: Required—TOEFL (minimum score 580 paper-based; 237 computer-based), TWE (minimum score 4). *Application deadline:* For fall admission, 7/15 priority date for domestic and international students. Applications are processed on a rolling basis. Application fee: $25. Electronic applications accepted. *Expenses:* Tuition: Full-time $13,200; part-time $630 per credit. Required fees: $170. *Financial support:* In 2007–08, 770 students received support, including 10 fellowships with partial tuition reimbursements available (averaging $6,920 per year); teaching assistantships with partial tuition reimbursements available, career-related internships or fieldwork, Federal Work-Study, scholarships/grants, and tuition waivers (partial) also available. Financial award application deadline: 4/1; financial award applicants required to submit FAFSA. *Unit head:* Dr. Tite Tiénou, Academic Dean, 847-317-8086, Fax: 847-317-8014, E-mail: ttienou@teds.edu. *Application contact:* Ron Campbell, Director of Admissions, 800-345-8337, Fax: 847-317-8097, E-mail: rcampbel@tiu.edu.

Trinity Western University, ACTS Seminaries, Langley, BC V2Y 1Y1, Canada. Offers Christian studies (MA); church ministries (MA); cross cultural ministries (MA); theology (M Div, M Th, MAMFT, MLE, MTS, D Min). *Accreditation:* ATS. Part-time programs available. *Faculty:* 13 full-time (0 women), 20 part-time/adjunct (3 women). *Students:* 129 full-time (58 women), 190 part-time (68 women). Average age 35. In 2007, 81 degrees awarded. *Degree requirements:* For master's, thesis (for some programs), internship. *Entrance requirements:* For master's, BA or equivalent; for doctorate, MDiv or equivalent. Additional exam requirements/recommendations for international students: Required—TOEFL. *Application deadline:* Applications are processed on a rolling basis. Application fee: $75. *Expenses: Contact institution. Financial support:* Research assistantships, career-related internships or fieldwork, Federal Work-Study, and institutionally sponsored loans available. Financial award application deadline: 3/1; financial award applicants required to submit FAFSA. *Faculty research:* Theology of leadership. *Unit head:* Dr. Ron Toews, Principal, 604-588-7531, Fax: 604-513-2045. *Application contact:* Liisa Polkki, Director of Admissions, 604-513-2019, Fax: 604-513-2045, E-mail: acts@twu.ca.

Tyndale University College & Seminary, Graduate Programs, Toronto, ON M2M 4B3, Canada. Offers Biblical studies (M Div); Christian foundations (MTS); Christian studies (Diploma); counseling (M Div); educational ministry (M Div); missions (M Div, Diploma); pastoral and Chinese ministry (M Div); pastoral ministry (M Div); Pentecostal studies (MTS); spiritual formation (M Div, Diploma); theological studies (M Div); theology (Th M); worship and liturgy (M Div, MTS); youth and family ministry (M Div). *Accreditation:* ATS. Part-time programs available. Postbaccalaureate distance learning degree programs offered (no on-campus study). *Degree requirements:* For M Div, one foreign language, thesis/dissertation optional. *Entrance requirements:* For M Div, master's, and Diploma, minimum C+ average in undergraduate course work. Additional exam requirements/recommendations for international students: Required—TOEFL (minimum score 570 paper-based; 230 computer-based), TWE (minimum score 5). Electronic applications accepted. *Faculty research:* Canadian church history, Chinese church history, Old Testament, counseling ministries (narrative therapy), world religions.

United Theological Seminary of the Twin Cities, Graduate and Professional Programs, Program in Ministry, New Brighton, MN 55112-2598. Offers D Min. *Accreditation:* ACIPE; ATS. Part-time programs available. *Faculty:* 12 full-time (7 women), 22 part-time/adjunct (10 women). *Students:* 10 applicants, 100% accepted, 8 enrolled. In 2007, 4 degrees awarded. *Degree requirements:* For doctorate, comprehensive exam, thesis/dissertation. *Entrance requirements:* For doctorate, M Div or equivalent, minimum GPA of 3.0, 3 years experience in professional ministry. Additional exam requirements/recommendations for international students: Required—TOEFL. *Application deadline:* For fall admission, 8/1 priority date for domestic students; for winter admission, 12/1 priority date for domestic students; for spring admission, 1/1 priority date for domestic students. Applications are processed on a rolling basis. Application fee: $50. *Expenses: Contact institution. Financial support:* Application deadline: 5/1; *Unit head:* Dr. Jean Morris Trumbauer, Director, 651-255-6127, Fax: 651-633-4315, E-mail: jtrumbauer@unitedseminary.edu. *Application contact:* Rev. Glen Herrington-Hall, Director of Admissions, 651-255-6107, Fax: 651-633-4315, E-mail: gherrington-hall@unitedseminary.edu.

United Theological Seminary of the Twin Cities, Graduate and Professional Programs, Program in Religious Leadership, New Brighton, MN 55112-2598. Offers MARL. *Accreditation:* ACIPE; ATS. Part-time programs available. *Faculty:* 12 full-time (7 women), 22 part-time/

Pastoral Ministry and Counseling

United Theological Seminary of the Twin Cities (continued)
adjunct (10 women). *Students:* 1 (woman) full-time, 5 part-time (2 women). Average age 43. 3 applicants, 100% accepted, 3 enrolled. *Degree requirements:* For master's, integrative notebook, spiritual chronicle. *Entrance requirements:* For master's, minimum GPA of 2.75. *Application deadline:* For fall admission, 8/1 priority date for domestic students; for winter admission, 12/1 priority date for domestic students; for spring admission, 1/1 priority date for domestic students. Applications are processed on a rolling basis. Application fee: $40. *Expenses:* Tuition: Part-time $373 per credit hour. *Financial support:* Career-related internships or fieldwork, institutionally sponsored loans, and scholarships/grants available. Support available to part-time students. Financial award application deadline: 5/1; financial award applicants required to submit FAFSA. *Application contact:* Rev. Glen Herrington-Hall, Director of Admissions, 651-255-6107, Fax: 651-633-4315, E-mail: gherrington-hall@unitedseminary.edu.

University of Dallas, Braniff Graduate School of Liberal Arts, Institute for Religious and Pastoral Studies, Irving, TX 75062-4736. Offers MCSL, MPM, MRE, MTS. *Accreditation:* ACIPE. Part-time and evening/weekend programs available. Postbaccalaureate distance learning degree programs offered (no on-campus study). *Faculty:* 7 full-time (0 women), 12 part-time/adjunct (2 women). *Students:* 10 full-time (6 women), 83 part-time (49 women); includes 20 minority (1 African American, 7 Asian Americans or Pacific Islanders, 12 Hispanic Americans). Average age 45. 27 applicants, 100% accepted, 20 enrolled. In 2007, 12 degrees awarded. *Application deadline:* For fall admission, 7/15 for domestic students; for spring admission, 11/15 for domestic students. Application fee: $50. *Expenses:* Tuition: Part-time $600 per credit. Required fees: $15 per credit. *Financial support:* In 2007–08, 81 students received support. Scholarships/grants available. Financial award application deadline: 2/15. *Faculty research:* Scripture, pastoral theology, ecclesiology, systematic theology, theological anthropology. *Unit head:* Dr. Brian Schmisek, Director, 972-721-4068, Fax: 972-721-4076, E-mail: schmisek@acad.udallas.edu. *Application contact:* Program Coordinator, 972-721-5105, Fax: 972-721-4076, E-mail: irps@acad.udallas.edu.

University of Dayton, Graduate School, College of Arts and Sciences, Department of Religious Studies, Dayton, OH 45469-1300. Offers pastoral ministry (MA); theological studies (MA); theology (PhD). Part-time and evening/weekend programs available. *Faculty:* 15 full-time (5 women), 11 part-time/adjunct (4 women). *Students:* 43 full-time (19 women), 20 part-time (14 women); includes 4 minority (2 African Americans, 1 Asian American or Pacific Islander, 1 Hispanic American), 2 international. Average age 39. 83 applicants, 64% accepted, 12 enrolled. In 2007, 17 master's, 1 doctorate awarded. Terminal master's awarded for partial completion of doctoral program. *Degree requirements:* For master's, thesis or alternative; for doctorate, 2 foreign languages, comprehensive exam, thesis/dissertation. *Entrance requirements:* For master's, minimum undergraduate GPA of 3.0, 24 semester credits of course work in philosophy/theology/religion; for doctorate, GRE General Test, minimum GPA of 3.5, academic writing sample. Additional exam requirements/recommendations for international students: Required—TOEFL (minimum score 550 paper-based; 213 computer-based; 80 iBT). *Application deadline:* For fall admission, 3/1 priority date for domestic and international students; for winter admission, 7/1 priority date for international students; for spring admission, 1/1 priority date for international students. Applications are processed on a rolling basis. Application fee: $0 ($50 for international students). Electronic applications accepted. *Expenses:* Contact institution. *Financial support:* In 2007–08, 17 fellowships with full tuition reimbursements (averaging $13,711 per year), 8 research assistantships with full tuition reimbursements (averaging $9,382 per year), 1 teaching assistantship with full tuition reimbursement were awarded; career-related internships or fieldwork, institutionally sponsored loans, scholarships/grants, health care benefits, tuition waivers (full), and unspecified assistantships also available. Support available to part-time students. Financial award application deadline: 3/1; financial award applicants required to submit FAFSA. *Faculty research:* Religion and science; U.S. Catholicism/Christianity; theological ethics; methodologies in biblical studies; practical/constructive theology. *Unit head:* Dr. Sandra Yocum-Mize, Chair, 937-229-4321, Fax: 937-229-4330, E-mail: mizes@notes.udayton.edu. *Application contact:* Angela Jones-Glukhov, Associate Director of Graduate Admissions, 937-229-4305, Fax: 937-229-4729.

University of Portland, Graduate School, College of Arts and Sciences, Department of Theology, Portland, OR 97203-5798. Offers pastoral ministry (MA). *Students:* 10 applicants, 60% accepted, 5 enrolled. In 2007, 6 degrees awarded. *Entrance requirements:* For master's, GRE or MAT, 3 letters of recommendation, minimum GPA of 3.0, statement of goals, official transcripts. Additional exam requirements/recommendations for international students: Required—TOEFL (minimum score 550 paper-based; 80 iBT), IELTS (minimum score 7). *Application deadline:* For fall admission, 7/15 priority date for domestic and international students. Application fee: $45. *Expenses:* Tuition: Part-time $775 per semester hour. *Financial support:* Federal Work-Study and scholarships/grants available. Financial award application deadline: 3/1; financial award applicants required to submit FAFSA. *Unit head:* Dr. Matt Baasten, Head, 503-943-7160. *Application contact:* Dr. Mary Labarre, Director, 503-943-7365, E-mail: labarre@up.edu.

University of Puget Sound, Graduate Studies, School of Education, Program in Counseling, Tacoma, WA 98416. Offers agency counseling (M Ed); pastoral counseling (M Ed); school counseling (M Ed). *Accreditation:* NCATE. Part-time programs available. *Faculty:* 2 full-time (both women), 1 (woman) part-time/adjunct. *Students:* 2 full-time (both women), 19 part-time (13 women); includes 4 minority (3 African Americans, 1 American Indian/Alaska Native), 1 international. Average age 32. 27 applicants, 59% accepted, 7 enrolled. In 2007, 19 degrees awarded. *Entrance requirements:* For master's, GRE General Test, minimum GPA of 3.0. Additional exam requirements/recommendations for international students: Required—TOEFL (minimum score 550 paper-based; 213 computer-based; 80 iBT). *Application deadline:* For fall admission, 3/1 priority date for domestic and international students. Applications are processed on a rolling basis. Application fee: $65. Electronic applications accepted. *Expenses:* Contact institution. Tuition and fees vary according to course load. *Financial support:* In 2007–08, 1 teaching assistantship with tuition reimbursement (averaging $14,204 per year) was awarded; career-related internships or fieldwork and tuition waivers (full) also available. Financial award application deadline: 3/31; financial award applicants required to submit FAFSA. *Faculty research:* Cross-role professional preparation, suicide prevention. *Application contact:* Dr. George H. Mills, Vice President for Enrollment, 253-879-3211, Fax: 253-879-3993, E-mail: admission@ups.edu.

University of Saint Francis, Graduate School, Department of Psychology and Counseling, Fort Wayne, IN 46808-3994. Offers general psychology (MS); mental health counseling (MS); pastoral counseling (MS); school counseling (MS Ed). Part-time and evening/weekend programs available. *Faculty:* 4 full-time (1 woman), 3 part-time/adjunct (0 women). *Students:* 28 full-time (24 women), 41 part-time (35 woman); includes 7 minority (3 African Americans, 4 Hispanic Americans). Average age 35. 16 applicants, 88% accepted. In 2007, 8 degrees awarded. *Entrance requirements:* For master's, interview, minimum undergraduate GPA of 3.0. *Application deadline:* For fall admission, 7/1 for domestic students; for spring admission, 11/1 for domestic students. Applications are processed on a rolling basis. Application fee: $20. *Financial support:* In 2007–08, 4 students received support. Federal Work-Study, scholarships/grants, and unspecified assistantships available. *Unit head:* Dr. Rolf Daniel, Dean, 260-399-7700 Ext. 8403, Fax: 260-399-8170, E-mail: rdaniel@sf.edu. *Application contact:* Michelle Kuhlhorst, Admissions Counselor, 260-434-7748, Fax: 260-434-7590, E-mail: mkuhlhorst@st.edu.

University of St. Michael's College, Faculty of Theology, Toronto, ON M5S 1J4, Canada. Offers Catholic leadership (MA); eastern Christian studies (Certificate, Diploma); religious education (Diploma); theological studies (Diploma); theology (M Div, MA, MRE, MTS, D Min, PhD, Th D); theology and ecology (Certificate); theology and Jewish studies (MA). *Accreditation:* ATS (one or more programs are accredited). Part-time programs available. *Faculty:* 10 full-time (3 women), 13 part-time/adjunct (5 women). *Students:* 111 full-time (35 women), 101 part-time (64 women); includes 7 African Americans, 19 Asian Americans or Pacific Islanders, 21 international. Average age 40. 90 applicants, 79% accepted, 51 enrolled. In 2007, 11 first professional degrees, 6 master's, 6 doctorates, 14 other advanced degrees awarded. *Degree requirements:* For master's, thesis (for some programs), 1 foreign language (MA), 2 foreign languages (Th M); for doctorate, 3 foreign languages, comprehensive exam, thesis/dissertation; for M Div, thesis/dissertation optional; for other advanced degree, thesis optional. *Entrance requirements:* For M Div and other advanced degree, minimum GPA of 2.7; for master's, M Div or BA, course work in an ancient or modern language, minimum GPA of 3.3; for doctorate, MA in theology, Th M, or M Div with thesis, minimum GPA of 3.7. Additional exam requirements/recommendations for international students: Required—TOEFL (minimum score 600 paper-based; 250 computer-based). *Application deadline:* For fall admission, 1/15 for domestic and international students. Applications are processed on a rolling basis. Application fee: $25 Canadian dollars. Electronic applications accepted. *Financial support:* In 2007–08, 58 students received support, including fellowships with partial tuition reimbursements available (averaging $2,500 per year), research assistantships with partial tuition reimbursements available (averaging $2,500 per year), 9 teaching assistantships with partial tuition reimbursements available (averaging $2,400 per year); scholarships/grants, tuition waivers (partial), and bursaries also available. Financial award application deadline: 2/1. *Faculty research:* Patristics, eastern Christianity, ecology and theology, ecumenism, Jewish Christian studies. *Unit head:* Dr. Anne Anderson, CSJ, Dean, 416-926-7265, Fax: 416-926-7294, E-mail: anne.anderson@utoronto.ca. *Application contact:* Mehra Taylor.

University of St. Thomas, Graduate Studies, Saint Paul Seminary School of Divinity, Program in Theology/Pastoral Studies, St. Paul, MN 55105-1096. Offers religious education (MARE); theology (MA). *Accreditation:* ACIPE; ATS. Part-time and evening/weekend programs available. *Degree requirements:* For master's, one foreign language, comprehensive exam, thesis or alternative. *Entrance requirements:* For master's, GRE, interview, 3 letters of recommendation. Additional exam requirements/recommendations for international students: Required—TOEFL (minimum score 550 paper-based; 213 computer-based). Electronic applications accepted. Expenses: Contact institution. *Faculty research:* Theological education.

University of San Diego, College of Arts and Sciences, Program in Pastoral Care and Counseling, San Diego, CA 92110-2492. Offers MA, CAS. Part-time and evening/weekend programs available. *Faculty:* 1 (woman) full-time, 1 (woman) part-time/adjunct. *Students:* 4 full-time (3 women), 8 part-time (6 women); includes 4 minority (1 African American, 3 Hispanic Americans). Average age 39. 6 applicants, 33% accepted, 2 enrolled. In 2007, 3 degrees awarded. *Degree requirements:* For master's, final paper. *Entrance requirements:* For master's, GRE General Test, writing assessment, minimum GPA of 3.0, 12 units of course work in religious studies, interview, affiliation with institutionally-endorsed ministry. Additional exam requirements/recommendations for international students: Required—TOEFL (minimum score 580 paper-based; 237 computer-based), TWE. *Application deadline:* For fall admission, 5/1 priority date for domestic students; for spring admission, 11/15 priority date for domestic students. Applications are processed on a rolling basis. Application fee: $45. Electronic applications accepted. *Expenses:* Tuition: Part-time $1,095 per unit. Tuition and fees vary according to degree level and program. *Financial support:* Federal Work-Study, scholarships/grants, tuition waivers (partial), and unspecified assistantships available. Support available to part-time students. Financial award application deadline: 5/1; financial award applicants required to submit FAFSA. *Faculty research:* Social ethics, popular religions, women in scripture, church history, spirituality. *Unit head:* Dr. Ellen Colangelo, Director, 619-260-4784, Fax: 619-260-2260, E-mail: colangelo@sandiego.edu. *Application contact:* Stephen Pultz, Director of Admissions, 619-260-4524, Fax: 619-260-4158, E-mail: grads@sandiego.edu.

University of South Africa, College of Human Sciences, Pretoria, South Africa. Offers adult education (M Ed); African languages (MA, PhD); African politics (MA, PhD); Afrikaans (MA, PhD); ancient history (MA, PhD); ancient Near Eastern studies (MA, PhD); anthropology (MA, PhD); applied linguistics (MA); Arabic (MA, PhD); archaeology (MA); art history (MA); Biblical archaeology (MA); Biblical studies (M Th, D Th, PhD); Christian spirituality (M Th, D Th); church history (M Th, D Th); classical studies (MA, PhD); clinical psychology (MA); communication (MA, PhD); comparative education (M Ed, Ed D); consulting psychology (D Admin, D Com, PhD); curriculum studies (M Ed, Ed D); development studies (M Admin, MA, D Admin, PhD); didactics (M Ed, Ed D); education (M Tech); education management (M Ed, Ed D); educational psychology (M Ed); English (MA); environmental education (M Ed); French (MA, PhD); German (MA, PhD); Greek (MA); guidance and counseling (M Ed); health studies (MA, PhD), including health sciences education (MA), health services management (MA), medical and surgical nursing science (critical care general) (MA), midwifery and neonatal nursing science (MA), trauma and emergency care (MA); history (MA, PhD); history of education (Ed D); inclusive education (M Ed, Ed D); information and communications technology policy and regulation (MA); information science (MA, MIS, PhD); international politics (MA, PhD); Islamic studies (MA, PhD); Italian (MA, PhD); Judaica (MA, PhD); linguistics (MA, PhD); mathematical education (M Ed); mathematics education (MA); missiology (M Th, D Th); modern Hebrew (MA, PhD); musicology (MA, MMus, D Mus, PhD); natural science education (M Ed); New Testament (M Th, D Th); Old Testament (D Th); pastoral therapy (M Th, D Th); philosophy (MA); philosophy of education (M Ed, Ed D); politics (MA, PhD); Portuguese (MA, PhD); practical theology (M Th, D Th); psychology (MA, MS, PhD); psychology of education (M Ed, Ed D); public health (MA); religious studies (MA, D Th, PhD); Romance languages (MA); Russian (MA, PhD); Semitic languages (MA, PhD); social behavior studies in HIV/AIDS (MA); social science (mental health) (MA); social science in development studies (MA); social science in psychology (MA); social science in social work (MA); social science in sociology (MA); social work (MSW, DSW, PhD); socio-education (M Ed, Ed D); sociolinguistics (MA); sociology (MA, PhD); Spanish (MA, PhD); systematic theology (M Th, D Th); TESOL (teaching English to speakers of other languages) (MA); theological ethics (M Th, D Th); theory of literature (MA, PhD); urban ministries (D Th); urban ministry (M Th).

University of Trinity College, Faculty of Divinity, Toronto, ON M5S 1H8, Canada. Offers ministry (Diploma); ministry for church musicians (Diploma); theology (M Div, MTS, Th M, D Min, PhD, Th D, Diploma, L Th); M Div/MA. *Accreditation:* ATS. Part-time programs available. *Degree requirements:* For master's, 2 foreign languages, thesis (for some programs); for doctorate, 3 foreign languages, comprehensive exam, thesis/dissertation; for M Div, thesis/dissertation optional; for other advanced degree, thesis (for some programs). *Entrance requirements:* For M Div, interview; for master's, 1 language (modern or ancient), interview; for doctorate, 2 languages (modern and ancient). Additional exam requirements/recommendations for international students: Required—TOEFL, TWE. *Faculty research:* Interreligious dialogue, feminist theology, systematic theology, philosophy of religion, pastoral theology.

Warner Pacific College, Graduate Programs, Portland, OR 97215-4099. Offers biblical and theological studies (MA); biblical studies (M Rel); education (M Ed); management/organizational leadership (MS); pastoral ministries (M Rel); religion and ethics (M Rel); teaching (MA); theology (M Rel). Part-time programs available. *Faculty:* 20 part-time/adjunct (6 women). *Students:* 57 full-time (26 women), 4 part-time (2 women); includes 5 minority (4 African Americans, 1 Asian American or Pacific Islander). *Degree requirements:* For master's, thesis or alternative, Presentation of Defense. *Entrance requirements:* For master's, interview, minimum GPA of 2.5, letters of recommendations. *Application deadline:* Applications are processed on a rolling basis. *Expenses:* Tuition: Full-time $15,642. Required fees: $150. *Financial support:* Career-related internships or fieldwork and Federal Work-Study available. Financial award application deadline: 7/1; financial award applicants required to submit FAFSA. *Faculty research:* New Testament studies, nineteenth-century Wesleyan theology, preaching and church growth, Christian ethics. *Unit head:* Director, 503-517-1045, Fax: 503-517-1350, E-mail: kazio@warnerpacific.edu.

Wayland Baptist University, Graduate Programs, Programs in Religion, Plainview, TX 79072-6998. Offers Christian ministry (MCM); religion (MA). Part-time and evening/weekend programs available. Postbaccalaureate distance learning degree programs offered (no on-campus study). *Faculty:* 5 full-time (1 woman), 1 part-time/adjunct (0 women). *Students:* 1 full-time (0 women), 12 part-time (4 women); includes 2 minority (both Hispanic Americans) Average age 32. 1 applicant, 100% accepted, 1 enrolled. In 2007, 1 degree awarded. *Degree* *requirements:* For master's, comprehensive exam. *Entrance requirements:* For master's, GRE or MAT. Additional exam requirements/recommendations for international students: Required—TOEFL (minimum score 500 paper-based; 173 computer-based). *Application deadline:* Applications are processed on a rolling basis. Application fee: $35. *Expenses:* Tuition: Full-time $6,390; part-time $355 per credit hour. Required fees: $600; $50 per term. Full-time tuition and fees vary according to course load. *Financial support:* Federal Work-Study, institutionally sponsored loans, and scholarships/grants available. Support available to part-time students. Financial award application deadline: 5/1; financial award applicants required to submit FAFSA. *Unit head:* Dr. Paul Sadler, Chairman, 806-291-1160, Fax: 806-291-1969, E-mail: sadlerp@wbu.edu.

Wesley Biblical Seminary, Graduate Programs, Jackson, MS 39206. Offers Biblical literature (MA); Christian studies (MA); evangelism (M Div); family life ministry (M Div); honors research (M Div); missions (M Div); pastoral ministry (M Div); teaching (M Div); theology (MA). *Accreditation:* ATS. Part-time programs available. *Degree requirements:* For master's, thesis. *Entrance requirements:* Additional exam requirements/recommendations for international students: Required—TOEFL. *Application deadline:* For fall admission, 7/1 priority date for domestic students; for spring admission, 12/1 priority date for domestic students. Applications are processed on a rolling basis. Application fee: $25. Electronic applications accepted. *Financial support:* Scholarships/grants available. Support available to part-time students. *Faculty research:* Patristics, missiology, culture, hermeneutics. *Unit head:* Dr. Ray R. Easley, Vice President for Academic Affairs, 601-366-8880 Ext. 112, Fax: 601-366-8832. *Application contact:* Megan Tirrill, Assistant to the Vice President for Student Development, 800-366-8880 Ext. 110, Fax: 601-366-8832, E-mail: mtirrill@wbs.edu.

Western Seminary, Graduate Programs, Program in Counseling Ministry, Portland, OR 97215-3367. Offers counseling (MA); hospital chaplaincy (Certificate); pastoral counseling (M Div); M Div/MA. Part-time programs available. *Degree requirements:* For master's, practicum; for M Div, 2 foreign languages, practicum. Expenses: Contact institution.

Western Seminary, Graduate Programs, Program in Intercultural Ministry, Portland, OR 97215-3367. Offers M Div, MA, D Miss, Certificate. Part-time programs available. *Degree requirements:* For master's, practicum; for doctorate, 2 foreign languages, thesis/dissertation; for M Div, 2 foreign languages, practicum.

Western Seminary, Graduate Programs, Program in Women's Ministries, Portland, OR 97215-3367. Offers MA, Certificate. *Degree requirements:* For master's, practicum.

Western Seminary–Sacramento Campus, Graduate Programs, Sacramento, CA 95821. Offers exegetical theology (MA); marital and family therapy (MA); ministry (M Div); specialized ministry (MA). Postbaccalaureate distance learning degree programs offered. *Entrance requirements:* For M Div, minimum GPA of 2.5; for master's, minimum GPA of 3.0.

Western Seminary–San Jose Campus, Graduate Programs, Los Gatos, CA 95032-4520. Offers exegetical theology (MA); expositional ministry (M Div); marital and family therapy (MA); ministry (M Div); pastoral ministry (M Div); specialized ministry (MA). Postbaccalaureate distance learning degree programs offered. *Degree requirements:* For master's, 2 foreign languages; for M Div, 3 foreign languages. *Entrance requirements:* For M Div, minimum GPA of 2.5; for master's, minimum GPA of 3.0.

Westminster Theological Seminary, Graduate and Professional Programs, Philadelphia, PA 19118. Offers apologetics (Th M); Biblical and urban studies (Certificate); Biblical counseling (MA); biblical studies (MAR); Christian studies (Certificate); church history (Th M); counseling (M Div); general studies (M Div, MAR); hermeneutics and Bible interpretations (PhD); historical and theological studies (PhD); historical theology (Th M); New Testament (Th M); Old Testament (Th M); pastoral counseling (D Min); pastoral ministry (M Div, D Min); systematic theology (Th M); theological studies (MAR); urban missions (M Div, MA, MAR, D Min). *Accreditation:* ATS. Part-time programs available. Terminal master's awarded for partial completion of doctoral program. *Degree requirements:* For master's, thesis (for some programs); for doctorate, 4 foreign languages, comprehensive exam (for some programs), thesis/dissertation; for M Div, 2 foreign languages. *Entrance requirements:* For doctorate, GRE General Test. Additional exam requirements/recommendations for international students: Required—TOEFL, TWE.

Wheaton College, Graduate School, Department of Psychology, Wheaton, IL 60187-5593. Offers clinical psychology (MA, Psy D); counseling ministries (MA). *Accreditation:* APA (one or more programs are accredited). *Faculty:* 18 full-time (9 women), 10 part-time/adjunct (3 women). *Students:* 141. 159 applicants, 52% accepted, 54 enrolled. In 2007, 44 master's, 13 doctorates awarded. Terminal master's awarded for partial completion of doctoral program. *Degree requirements:* For master's, thesis or alternative; for doctorate, thesis/dissertation, internship. *Entrance requirements:* For master's, GRE General Test, 18 hours of course work in psychology; for doctorate, GRE General Test. *Financial support:* In 2007–08, 3 research assistantships (averaging $4,800 per year) were awarded; career-related internships or fieldwork, Federal Work-Study, scholarships/grants, and unspecified assistantships also available. Financial award application deadline: 6/1; financial award applicants required to submit FAFSA. *Unit head:* Dr. Robert Gregory, Chair, 630-752-7053. *Application contact:* Julie A. Huebner, Director of Graduate Admissions, 630-752-5195, Fax: 630-752-5935, E-mail: gradadm@wheaton.edu.

Wilfrid Laurier University, Waterloo Lutheran Seminary, Waterloo, ON N2L 3C5, Canada. Offers Christian ethics (M Th); divinity (M Div); homiletics (M Th); ministry (D Min); pastoral counseling (M Th); spirituality in a health care setting (Diploma); theological studies (MTS); theology (Diploma); M Div/MTS/MSW. *Accreditation:* ATS. Part-time programs available. *Faculty:* 8 full-time (2 women), 6 part-time/adjunct (2 women). *Students:* 51 full-time (33 women), 57 part-time (33 women); includes 10 minority (3 African Americans, 1 American Indian/Alaska Native, 6 Asian Americans or Pacific Islanders). Average age 42. 23 applicants, 100% accepted, 20 enrolled. In 2007, 1 first professional degree, 8 master's awarded. *Degree requirements:* For master's, one foreign language, thesis (for some programs); for doctorate, thesis/dissertation; for M Div, one foreign language, thesis/dissertation. *Entrance requirements:* For M Div, denominational endorsement; for master's, M Div, 2 units of clinical pastoral education (M Th); for doctorate, M Div, 3 years of ministry experience, proficiency in a foreign language, basic training in clinical pastoral education. Additional exam requirements/recommendations for international students: Required—TOEFL (minimum score 573 paper-based; 230 computer-based; 89 iBT), IELTS (minimum score 7). *Application deadline:* For fall admission, 7/1 priority date for domestic students, 3/1 priority date for international students; for winter admission, 11/1 priority date for domestic students, 6/1 priority date for international students; for spring admission, 3/1 priority date for domestic students, 11/1 priority date for international students. Applications are processed on a rolling basis. Application fee: $50. Electronic applications accepted. *Expenses: Contact institution. Financial support:* In 2007–08, 51 students received support. Career-related internships or fieldwork, institutionally sponsored loans, and scholarships/grants available. Financial award application deadline: 10/1. *Faculty research:* Biblical study, church history, systematic theology. *Unit head:* Dr. David Pfrimmer, Principal/Dean, 519-884-0710, E-mail: dpfrimme@wlu.ca. *Application contact:* Sarina Wheeler, Student Advisor and Admissions Coordinator, 519-884-0710 Ext. 3498, Fax: 519-725-2434, E-mail: swheeler@wlu.ca.

Xavier University of Louisiana, Graduate School, Institute for Black Catholic Studies, New Orleans, LA 70125-1098. Offers pastoral theology (Th M). Part-time programs available. *Degree requirements:* For master's, comprehensive exam, practicum. *Entrance requirements:* For master's, GRE General Test, MAT, minimum GPA of 2.5. Additional exam requirements/recommendations for international students: Required—TOEFL.

Religion

Amridge University, Graduate and Professional Programs, Montgomery, AL 36117. Offers behavioral leadership and management (MA); biblical studies (MA, D Min, PhD); Christian ministry (M Div); family therapy (D Min, PhD), including marriage and family therapy (PhD), professional counseling (PhD); leadership and management (MS); marriage and family therapy (M Div, MA); ministerial leadership (M Div, MS); pastoral counseling (M Div, MS); practical theology (MA); professional counseling (M Div, MA). *Accreditation:* ATS. Part-time and evening/weekend programs available. Postbaccalaureate distance learning degree programs offered (no on-campus study). *Faculty:* 50 full-time (12 women), 36 part-time/adjunct (10 women). *Students:* 165 full-time (85 women), 212 part-time (111 women); includes 174 minority (164 African Americans, 1 American Indian/Alaska Native, 1 Asian American or Pacific Islander, 8 Hispanic Americans). Average age 35. In 2007, 8 first professional degrees, 35 master's, 5 doctorates awarded. *Degree requirements:* For master's, one foreign language, comprehensive exam (for some programs), thesis (for some programs); for doctorate, comprehensive exam (for some programs), thesis/dissertation; for M Div, comprehensive exam (for some programs). *Entrance requirements:* For M Div, master's, and doctorate, GRE General Test or MAT. Additional exam requirements/recommendations for international students: Required—TOEFL. *Application deadline:* For fall admission, 9/1 priority date for domestic students; for spring admission, 1/1 priority date for domestic students. Applications are processed on a rolling basis. Application fee: $50. Electronic applications accepted. *Expenses:* Tuition: Full-time $9,180; part-time $510 per semester hour. Required fees: $400 per term. Tuition and fees vary according to course load and degree level. *Financial support:* Federal Work-Study and scholarships/grants available. Support available to part-time students. Financial award applicants required to submit FAFSA. *Faculty research:* Homiletics, hermeneutics, ancient Near Eastern history. *Unit head:* Rick Johnson, Director of Enrollment Management, 800-351-4040 Ext. 7513, Fax: 334-387-3878, E-mail: rickjohnson@amridgeuniversity.edu. *Application contact:* Ora Davis, Admissions Officer, 334-387-3877 Ext. 7524, Fax: 334-387-3878, E-mail: oradavis@amridgeuniversity.edu.

Arizona State University, Graduate College, College of Liberal Arts and Sciences, Division of Humanities, Department of Religious Studies, Tempe, AZ 85287. Offers MA, PhD. *Degree requirements:* For master's, thesis or alternative. *Entrance requirements:* For master's, GRE.

Azusa Pacific University, Haggard School of Theology, Program in Christian Education, Azusa, CA 91702-7000. Offers MAR.

Baptist Bible College of Pennsylvania, Baptist Bible Seminary, Clarks Summit, PA 18411-1297. Offers biblical studies (PhD); church planting (M Div); global missions (M Div); military chaplaincy (M Div); ministry (M Min, D Min); pastor of church education (M Div); pastor of outreach (M Div); pastoral counseling (M Div); pastoral leadership (M Div); theology (M Div, Th M); youth pastor (M Div). Part-time and evening/weekend programs available. Postbaccalaureate distance learning degree programs offered (minimal on-campus study). *Faculty:* 10 full-time (0 women). *Students:* 102 full-time (0 women), 104 part-time; includes 14 minority (6 African Americans, 4 Asian Americans or Pacific Islanders, 4 Hispanic Americans), 2 international. Average age 38. Terminal master's awarded for partial completion of doctoral program. *Degree requirements:* For master's, 2 foreign languages, thesis; for doctorate, 2 foreign languages, comprehensive exam (for some programs), thesis/dissertation, oral exam; for M Div, 2 foreign languages, thesis/dissertation, oral exam. *Entrance requirements:* For doctorate, Greek and Hebrew entrance exams (PhD). *Application deadline:* Applications are processed on a rolling basis. Application fee: $30. Electronic applications accepted. *Expenses:* Tuition: Full-time $6,516; part-time $362 per credit. Required fees: $468; $232 per semester. *Financial support:* Career-related internships or fieldwork and scholarships/grants available. Support available to part-time students. *Unit head:* Dr. Michael Stallard, Seminary Academic Dean, 570-585-9348, Fax: 570-585-4057, E-mail: mstallard@bbc.edu. *Application contact:* Paul Golden, Director of Seminary Admissions, 570-586-9396, E-mail: pgolden@bbc.edu.

Baylor University, Graduate School, College of Arts and Sciences, Department of Religion, Waco, TX 76798. Offers MA, PhD. *Students:* 67 full-time (11 women), 4 part-time; includes 7 minority (1 African American, 1 American Indian/Alaska Native, 2 Asian Americans or Pacific Islanders, 3 Hispanic Americans), 7 international. In 2007, 1 master's, 7 doctorates awarded. Terminal master's awarded for partial completion of doctoral program. *Degree requirements:* For master's, one foreign language, thesis; for doctorate, 2 foreign languages, thesis/dissertation. *Entrance requirements:* For master's and doctorate, GRE General Test. *Application deadline:* Applications are processed on a rolling basis. Application fee: $25. *Financial support:* Fellowships, research assistantships, teaching assistantships, Federal Work-Study, institutionally sponsored loans, and scholarships/grants available. *Unit head:* Dr. Bill Bellinger, Graduate Program Director, 254-710-3742, Fax: 254-710-3740, E-mail: bill_bellinger@baylor.edu. *Application contact:* Suzanne Keener, Administrative Assistant, 254-710-3588, Fax: 254-710-3870.

Baylor University, Graduate School, College of Arts and Sciences, J. M. Dawson Institute of Church-State Studies, Waco, TX 76798. Offers MA, PhD. *Students:* 36 full-time (10 women), 1 (woman) part-time; includes 4 minority (2 Asian Americans or Pacific Islanders, 2 Hispanic Americans), 5 international. In 2007, 3 master's, 2 doctorates awarded. *Degree requirements:* For master's, thesis, oral exam; for doctorate, one foreign language, thesis/dissertation, preliminary exams. *Entrance requirements:* For master's, GRE General Test; for doctorate, GRE General Test, MA or equivalent. *Application deadline:* For fall admission, 3/1 for domestic students. Applications are processed on a rolling basis. Application fee: $25. *Financial support:* Fellowships, research assistantships, teaching assistantships, Federal Work-Study and institutionally sponsored loans available. Financial award application deadline: 3/1. *Faculty research:* Religion and politics, religion and public education, religious freedom and international politics, First Amendment jurisprudence. *Unit head:* Dr. Derek H. Davis, Director, 254-710-1510, Fax: 254-710-1571, E-mail: derek_davis@baylor.edu. *Application contact:* Suzanne Keener, Administrative Assistant, 254-710-3588, Fax: 254-710-3870.

Bellarmine University, Bellarmine College of Arts and Sciences, Louisville, KY 40205-0671. Offers spirituality (MA). *Faculty:* 2 full-time (1 woman), 2 part-time/adjunct (1 woman). *Students:* Average age 50. In 2007, 9 degrees awarded. *Entrance requirements:* For master's, minimum GPA of 2.8, letter of recommendation, spirituality autobiography. Additional exam requirements/recommendations for international students: Required—TOEFL (minimum score 550 paper-based; 213 computer-based; 80 iBT). Application fee: $25. *Expenses: Contact institution. Unit head:* Dr. Robert Kingsolver, Dean, 502-452-8359, E-mail: kingsolver@bellarmine.edu. *Application contact:* Pat Allen, Office Receptionist, 502-452-8188, E-mail: pallen@bellarmine.edu.

Bethany Theological Seminary, Graduate and Professional Programs, Richmond, IN 47374-4019. Offers biblical studies (MA Th); ministry studies (M Div); peace studies (M Div, MA Th); theological studies (MA Th, CATS); youth ministry (M Div). *Accreditation:* ACIPE; ATS. Part-time

Religion

Bethany Theological Seminary (continued)
programs available. Postbaccalaureate distance learning degree programs offered (minimal on-campus study). *Degree requirements:* For master's, thesis. *Entrance requirements:* For M Div, letters of reference, minimum GPA of 2.75; for master's, letters of reference, minimum GPA of 3.0. Additional exam requirements/recommendations for international students: Required—TOEFL (minimum score 550 paper-based; 218 computer-based).

Bethesda Christian University, Graduate and Professional Programs, Anaheim, CA 92801. Offers biblical studies (MA); theology (M Div). *Entrance requirements:* For M Div and master's, interview.

Beulah Heights University, Graduate School, Atlanta, GA 30316. Offers biblical studies (MA); leadership studies (MA). *Entrance requirements:* Additional exam requirements/recommendations for international students: Required—TOEFL (minimum score 500 paper-based). Electronic applications accepted.

Biola University, Talbot School of Theology, La Mirada, CA 90639-0001. Offers Bible exposition (MA); biblical and theological studies (MA); Christian education (MACE); Christian ministry and leadership (MA); divinity (M Div); education (PhD); ministry (MA Min); New Testament (MA); Old Testament (MA); philosophy of religion and ethics (MA); spiritual formation (MA); spiritual formation and soul care (MA); theology (MA, Th M, D Min). *Accreditation:* ATS. Part-time and evening/weekend programs available. *Degree requirements:* For master's, variable foreign language requirement, thesis or alternative; for doctorate, variable foreign language requirement, thesis/dissertation; for M Div, thesis/dissertation or alternative. *Entrance requirements:* For M Div, minimum GPA of 2.6; for master's, minimum undergraduate GPA of 3.0; for doctorate, minimum GPA of 3.25. Additional exam requirements/recommendations for international students: Required—TOEFL (minimum score 550 paper-based; 213 computer-based). *Faculty research:* Moral development; biological, medical, and social ethics; ancient Near Eastern historical philosophy.

Bob Jones University, Graduate Programs, Greenville, SC 29614. Offers accountancy (MS); Bible (MA); Bible translation (MA); Biblical studies (Certificate); broadcast management (MS); business administration (MBA); church history (MA, PhD); church ministries (MA); church music (MM); cinema and video production (MA); counseling (MS); curriculum and instruction (Ed D); divinity (M Div); dramatic production (MA); educational leadership (MS, Ed D, Ed S); elementary education (M Ed, MAT); English (M Ed, MA, MAT); fine arts (MA); graphic design (MA); history (M Ed, MA); illustration (MA); interpretative speech (MA); mathematics (M Ed, MAT); medical missions (Certificate); ministry (MM, D Min); multi-categorical special education (M Ed, MAT); music (M Ed); New Testament interpretation (PhD); Old Testament interpretation (PhD); orchestral instrument performance (MM); organ performance (MM); pastoral studies (MA); personnel services (MS, Ed S); piano pedagogy (MM); piano performance (MM); platform arts (MA); radio and television broadcasting (MS); rhetoric and public address (MA); secondary education (M Ed); studio art (MA); teaching Bible (MA); theology (MA, PhD); voice performance (MM); youth ministries (MA); M Div/MM.

Boston University, Graduate School of Arts and Sciences, Division of Religious and Theological Studies, Boston, MA 02215. Offers MA, PhD. *Students:* 80 full-time (29 women), 10 part-time (4 women); includes 9 minority (2 African Americans, 6 Asian Americans or Pacific Islanders, 1 Hispanic American), 8 international. Average age 35. 148 applicants, 26% accepted, 14 enrolled. In 2007, 16 master's, 13 doctorates awarded. Terminal master's awarded for partial completion of doctoral program. *Degree requirements:* For master's, one foreign language, comprehensive exam, thesis; for doctorate, 2 foreign languages, comprehensive exam, thesis/dissertation. *Entrance requirements:* For master's and doctorate, GRE General Test, 3 letters of recommendation, academic writing sample. Additional exam requirements/recommendations for international students: Required—TOEFL (minimum score 550 paper-based; 213 computer-based). *Application deadline:* For fall admission, 1/15 for domestic and international students. Application fee: $70. *Expenses:* Tuition: Full-time $34,930; part-time $1,092 per credit. Tuition and fees vary according to class time, course level and program. *Financial support:* In 2007–08, 46 students received support, including 2 fellowships with full tuition reimbursements available (averaging $18,000 per year), 1 research assistantship with full tuition reimbursement available (averaging $16,500 per year), 5 teaching assistantships with full tuition reimbursements available (averaging $16,500 per year); career-related internships or fieldwork, Federal Work-Study, tuition waivers (partial), and unspecified assistantships also available. Support available to part-time students. Financial award application deadline: 1/15; financial award applicants required to submit FAFSA. *Unit head:* Stephen Prothero, Chairman, 617-353-4426, Fax: 617-353-5441, E-mail: prothero@bu.edu. *Application contact:* Karen Nardella, Department Administrator, 617-353-2636, Fax: 617-353-5441, E-mail: kcn@bu.edu.

Briercrest Seminary, Graduate Programs, Program in Christian Ministries, Caronport, SK S0H 0S0, Canada. Offers leadership (MA); marriage and family counseling (MA); missions (MA); pastoral counseling (MA); worship (MA); youth and family ministry (MA). Part-time programs available. *Degree requirements:* For master's, comprehensive exam, thesis optional. *Entrance requirements:* Additional exam requirements/recommendations for international students: Required—TOEFL (minimum score 550 paper-based; 213 computer-based).

Briercrest Seminary, Graduate Programs, Program in Theology, Caronport, SK S0H 0S0, Canada. Offers Biblical studies (M Div); leadership and management (M Div); New Testament (MATS); Old Testament (MATS); pastoral counseling (M Div); pastoral ministry (M Div); theological studies (M Div); theology (MATS); worship (M Div); youth and family ministry (M Div). *Accreditation:* ATS. Part-time programs available. *Degree requirements:* For master's, comprehensive exam, thesis optional. *Entrance requirements:* Additional exam requirements/recommendations for international students: Required—TOEFL (minimum score 550 paper-based; 213 computer-based).

Brown University, Graduate School, Department of Religious Studies, Program in Religious Studies, Providence, RI 02912. Offers AM, PhD. *Degree requirements:* For master's, one foreign language, thesis; for doctorate, 2 foreign languages, thesis/dissertation. *Entrance requirements:* For master's and doctorate, GRE General Test.

Bryn Athyn College of the New Church, Academy of the New Church Theological School, Bryn Athyn, PA 19009-0717. Offers divinity (M Div); religious studies (MA). Part-time programs available. Postbaccalaureate distance learning degree programs offered (minimal on-campus study). *Faculty:* 12. *Students:* 7 full-time (0 women), 19 part-time (13 women), 10 international. Average age 37. 26 applicants, 100% accepted. In 2007, 4 first professional degrees, 2 master's awarded. *Degree requirements:* For master's, thesis; for M Div, 3 foreign languages, thesis/dissertation. *Entrance requirements:* Additional exam requirements/recommendations for international students: Required—TOEFL. *Application deadline:* For fall admission, 1/31 for domestic students. Applications are processed on a rolling basis. *Financial support:* In 2007–08, 7 students received support. Career-related internships or fieldwork, Federal Work-Study, and institutionally sponsored loans available. Financial award application deadline: 1/31. *Unit head:* Andrew Dibb, Dean, 267-502-2640, E-mail: andrew.dibb@ancts.org.

California Institute of Integral Studies, Graduate Programs, School of Consciousness and Transformation, San Francisco, CA 94103. Offers cultural anthropology and social transformation (MA); East-West psychology (MA, PhD); integrative health studies (MA); philosophy and religion (MA, PhD), including Asian and comparative studies, philosophy, cosmology, and consciousness, social and cultural anthropology (PhD), transformative leadership (MA), transformative studies (PhD), women's spirituality, women's spirituality flex format; social and cultural anthropology (PhD); transformative leadership (MA); transformative studies (PhD). Part-time and evening/weekend programs available. Postbaccalaureate distance learning degree programs offered (minimal on-campus study). *Faculty:* 30 full-time, 28 part-time/adjunct. *Students:* 456; includes 92 minority (32 African Americans, 3 American Indian/Alaska Native, 40 Asian Americans or Pacific Islanders, 17 Hispanic Americans), 1 international. Average age 37. 206 applicants, 93% accepted, 114 enrolled. In 2007, 26 degrees awarded. Terminal master's awarded for partial completion of doctoral program. *Degree requirements:* For master's, comprehensive exam (for some programs), thesis optional; for doctorate, comprehensive exam, thesis/dissertation. *Entrance requirements:* For master's, minimum GPA of 3.0, letters of recommendation, writing sample; for doctorate, master's degree, minimum GPA of 3.0, letters of recommendation, writing sample. Additional exam requirements/recommendations for international students: Required—TOEFL. *Application deadline:* For fall admission, 2/15 priority date for domestic and international students; for spring admission, 10/15 priority date for domestic and international students. Applications are processed on a rolling basis. Application fee: $65. Electronic applications accepted. *Expenses:* Tuition: Full-time $16,930; part-time $780 per unit. Tuition and fees vary according to course load and program. *Financial support:* In 2007–08, 292 students received support; research assistantships, teaching assistantships, career-related internships or fieldwork, Federal Work-Study, institutionally sponsored loans, scholarships/grants, and tuition waivers (partial) available. Support available to part-time students. Financial award application deadline: 3/15; financial award applicants required to submit FAFSA. *Faculty research:* Altered states of consciousness, dreams, cosmology, postcolonial studies, integrative health studies. *Application contact:* Allyson Werner, Senior Admissions Counselor, 415-575-6155, Fax: 415-575-1268.

See Close-Up on page 445.

California State University, Long Beach, Graduate Studies, College of Liberal Arts, Department of Religious Studies, Long Beach, CA 90840. Offers MA. Part-time and evening/weekend programs available. *Faculty:* 10 full-time (2 women), 8 part-time/adjunct (0 women). *Students:* 15 full-time (7 women), 16 part-time (4 women); includes 15 minority (2 African Americans, 5 Asian Americans or Pacific Islanders, 8 Hispanic Americans). *Entrance requirements:* Additional exam requirements/recommendations for international students: Required—TOEFL. *Application deadline:* For fall admission, 7/1 for domestic and international students; for spring admission, 12/1 for domestic and international students. Applications are processed on a rolling basis. Application fee: $55. Electronic applications accepted. *Financial support:* Application deadline: 3/2; *Unit head:* Dr. Carlos Piar, Chair, 562-985-5341, Fax: 562-985-5540, E-mail: crpiar@csulb.edu. *Application contact:* Dr. Tony Battaglia, Graduate Advisor, 562-985-7982, Fax: 562-985-5540, E-mail: battagli@csulb.edu.

Cardinal Stritch University, College of Arts and Sciences, Department of Religious Studies, Milwaukee, WI 53217-3985. Offers lay ministries (MA); ministry (MA); religious studies (MA). Part-time and evening/weekend programs available. *Degree requirements:* For master's, comprehensive exam, thesis, faculty recommendation, research project. *Entrance requirements:* For master's, interview, minimum GPA of 2.75.

The Catholic University of America, School of Arts and Sciences, Program in Early Christian Studies, Washington, DC 20064. Offers MA, PhD, Certificate. Part-time programs available. *Faculty:* 1 full-time (0 women). *Students:* 1 full-time (0 women), 8 part-time (2 women), 1 international. Average age 39. Terminal master's awarded for partial completion of doctoral program. *Degree requirements:* For master's, 2 foreign languages, comprehensive exam, thesis optional; for doctorate, 3 foreign languages, comprehensive exam, thesis/dissertation. *Entrance requirements:* For master's and doctorate, GRE General Test, 3 letters of recommendation. Additional exam requirements/recommendations for international students: Required—TOEFL (minimum score 580 paper-based; 237 computer-based). *Application deadline:* For fall admission, 2/1 priority date for domestic students; for spring admission, 11/15 priority date for domestic students. Applications are processed on a rolling basis. Application fee: $55. Electronic applications accepted. *Financial support:* Fellowships, career-related internships or fieldwork, Federal Work-Study, scholarships/grants, tuition waivers (full and partial), and unspecified assistantships available. Support available to part-time students. Financial award application deadline: 2/1; financial award applicants required to submit FAFSA. *Faculty research:* Greek, Latin, Semitic languages and civilization in late antiquity and early Middle Ages. *Unit head:* Dr. Philip Rousseau, Director, 202-319-5795, E-mail: rousseau@cua.edu.

The Catholic University of America, School of Theology and Religious Studies, Washington, DC 20064. Offers M Div, STB, MA, MRE, D Min, PhD, STD, STL, MSLS/MA. *Accreditation:* ATS (one or more programs are accredited). Part-time programs available. *Faculty:* 38 full-time (4 women), 8 part-time/adjunct (2 women). *Students:* 170 full-time (29 women), 197 part-time (57 women); includes 33 minority (9 African Americans, 1 American Indian/Alaska Native, 13 Asian Americans or Pacific Islanders, 10 Hispanic Americans), 64 international. Average age 36. 262 applicants, 77% accepted, 102 enrolled. In 2007, 19 first professional degrees, 16 master's, 16 doctorates awarded. Terminal master's awarded for partial completion of doctoral program. *Degree requirements:* For master's, comprehensive exam; for doctorate, comprehensive exam, thesis/dissertation; for first professional degree, one foreign language; for STL, one foreign language, comprehensive exam, thesis. *Entrance requirements:* For first professional degree and master's, GRE General Test, 3 letters of recommendation; for doctorate and STL, GRE, 3 letters of recommendation. Additional exam requirements/recommendations for international students: Required—TOEFL (minimum score 580 paper-based; 237 computer-based). *Application deadline:* For fall admission, 2/1 priority date for domestic students; for spring admission, 11/15 priority date for domestic students. Applications are processed on a rolling basis. Application fee: $55. Electronic applications accepted. *Financial support:* Fellowships, research assistantships, teaching assistantships, career-related internships or fieldwork, Federal Work-Study, scholarships/grants, tuition waivers (full and partial), and unspecified assistantships available. Support available to part-time students. Financial award application deadline: 2/1; financial award applicants required to submit FAFSA. *Faculty research:* Biblical studies, canon law, church history, liturgical studies, religion and religious education. *Unit head:* Msgr. Kevin W. Irwin, Dean, 202-319-5683, Fax: 202-319-4967, E-mail: irwin@cua.edu.

Chestnut Hill College, School of Graduate Studies, Department of Religious Studies and Philosophy, Philadelphia, PA 19118-2693. Offers holistic spirituality (MA); holistic spirituality and healthcare (MA); holistic spirituality and spiritual direction (MA); holistic spirituality/health care (CAS); spiritual direction (CAS); spirituality (CAS); supervision of spiritual directors (CAS). Part-time and evening/weekend programs available. *Faculty:* 4 full-time (all women), 1 (woman) part-time/adjunct. *Students:* Average age 51. 2 applicants, 100% accepted. In 2007, 13 degrees awarded. *Degree requirements:* For master's, thesis optional, practicum for spiritual direction and healthcare tracks. *Entrance requirements:* For master's, MAT or GRE, transcripts, letters of recommendation, statement of professional goals writing sample. Additional exam requirements/recommendations for international students: Required—TOEFL (minimum score 500 paper-based; 213 computer-based). *Application deadline:* For fall admission, 7/17 priority date for domestic and international students; for spring admission, 12/15 priority date for domestic and international students. Applications are processed on a rolling basis. Application fee: $50. *Faculty research:* Spirituality and health care, spirituality and theology, contemplation and spiritual direction, feminism and ecological spirituality, mysticism and social transformation. *Unit head:* Dr. Marie Conn, Department Chair, 215-248-7044, Fax: 215-248-7155, E-mail: mconn@chc.edu. *Application contact:* Amy Boorse, Administrative Assistant, School of Graduate Studies Office, 215-248-7170, Fax: 215-248-7161, E-mail: gradadmissions@chc.edu.

Chicago Theological Seminary, Graduate and Professional Programs, Chicago, IL 60637-1507. Offers clinical pastoral education (D Min); Jewish-Christian studies (PhD); pastoral counseling (D Min); preaching (D Min); religious studies (MA); spiritual leadership (D Min); theology (M Div); theology and the human sciences (PhD), including theology and society, theology and the personality sciences; M Div/MSW. *Accreditation:* ACIPE; ATS. Part-time programs available. *Faculty:* 13 full-time (5 women). *Students:* 83 full-time (40 women), 135 part-time (66 women); includes 54 minority (45 African Americans, 6 Asian Americans or Pacific Islanders, 3 Hispanic Americans), 33 international. 78 applicants, 94% accepted, 50 enrolled. In 2007, 15 first professional degrees, 8 master's, 22 doctorates awarded. *Degree requirements:* For master's, thesis; for doctorate, 2 foreign languages, comprehensive exam, thesis/dissertation; for M Div, thesis/dissertation. *Entrance requirements:* For doctorate, GRE General Test. Additional exam requirements/recommendations for international students: Required—TOEFL (minimum score 217 computer-based). *Application deadline:* For fall admission, 2/15 priority date for domestic and international students; for spring admission,

11/1 for domestic and international students. Application fee: $50. *Financial support:* In 2007–08, 103 students received support, including 12 fellowships (averaging $10,000 per year); institutionally sponsored loans, scholarships/grants, and tuition waivers (partial) also available. Support available to part-time students. Financial award application deadline: 3/1; financial award applicants required to submit FAFSA. *Faculty research:* Bible, culture and hermeneutics/theology, gender & sexuality/black faith and life/spirituality and psychology/practical theology. Total annual research expenditures: $150,000. *Unit head:* Dr. Theodore W. Jennings, Acting Dean, 773-752-5757, Fax: 773-752-1903, E-mail: tjennings@ctschicago.edu. *Application contact:* Rev. Lin Sanford Keppert, Director of Admissions, Recruitment and Financial Aid, E-mail: lkeppert@ctschicago.edu.

Christian Brothers University, Graduate Programs, School of Arts, Memphis, TN 38104-5581. Offers Catholic studies (MACS); curriculum and instruction (M Ed); educational leadership (MSEL); teacher-leadership (M Ed); teaching (MAT). Part-time and evening/weekend programs available. *Faculty:* 7 full-time (5 women), 14 part-time/adjunct (6 women). *Students:* 73 full-time (48 women), 144 part-time (107 women); includes 86 minority (81 African Americans, 5 Hispanic Americans), 2 international. Average age 33. In 2007, 68 degrees awarded. *Entrance requirements:* For master's, GRE, MAT. *Application deadline:* Applications are processed on a rolling basis. Application fee: $25. *Expenses:* Contact institution. *Financial support:* Institutionally sponsored loans available. Support available to part-time students. *Unit head:* Dr. Marius Carriere, Dean, 901-321-3366, Fax: 901-321-4340, E-mail: mcarrier@cbu.edu. *Application contact:* Dr. Talana L. Vogel, Director, 901-321-4101, Fax: 901-321-3408, E-mail: tvogel@cbu.edu.

Christian Theological Seminary, Graduate and Professional Programs, Indianapolis, IN 46208-3301. Offers marriage and family (MA); pastoral care and counseling (D Min); practical theology (D Min); psychotherapy and faith (MA); sacred theology (STM); specialized ministries (MA); theological studies (MTS); theology (M Div). *Accreditation:* AAMFT/COAMFTE (one or more programs are accredited); ACIPE; ATS. Part-time programs available. Terminal master's awarded for partial completion of doctoral program. *Degree requirements:* For master's, comprehensive exam (for some programs), thesis (for some programs); for doctorate, comprehensive exam, thesis/dissertation; for M Div, comprehensive exam, thesis/dissertation (for some programs), missionary and cross-cultural experience. *Entrance requirements:* For master's, GRE General Test, MAT; for doctorate, M Div or BD. Electronic applications accepted. *Faculty research:* Faith formation, peer learning post graduation.

Cincinnati Christian University, Graduate School, Cincinnati, OH 45204-3200. Offers biblical studies (MA); church history (MA); counseling (MAC); divinity (M Div); ministry (M Min); practical ministries (MA); theological studies (MA). *Accreditation:* ATS. Part-time programs available. *Degree requirements:* For master's, thesis (for some programs); for M Div, 2 foreign languages, oral exam. *Entrance requirements:* For master's, GRE General Test. Additional exam requirements/recommendations for international students: Required—TOEFL. Electronic applications accepted.

Claremont Graduate University, Graduate Programs, School of Religion, Claremont, CA 91711-6160. Offers Hebrew Bible (MA, PhD); history of Christianity and religions of North America (MA, PhD); New Testament (MA, PhD); philosophy of religion and theology (MA, PhD); theology, ethics and culture (MA, PhD); women's studies in religion (MA, PhD); MA/PhD; MBA/PhD. Part-time programs available. *Faculty:* 6 full-time (2 women), 9 part-time/adjunct (5 women). *Students:* 221 full-time (89 women), 7 part-time (2 women); includes 36 minority (15 African Americans, 12 Asian Americans or Pacific Islanders, 9 Hispanic Americans), 33 international. Average age 37. In 2007, 13 master's, 18 doctorates awarded. Terminal master's awarded for partial completion of doctoral program. *Degree requirements:* For master's, one foreign language, comprehensive exam (for some programs), thesis; for doctorate, 2 foreign languages, comprehensive exam, thesis/dissertation. *Entrance requirements:* For master's and doctorate, GRE General Test. *Application deadline:* For fall admission, 2/15 priority date for domestic students. Applications are processed on a rolling basis. Electronic applications accepted. *Expenses:* Tuition: Full-time $31,640; part-time $1,376 per unit. Required fees: $145 per semester. Tuition and fees vary according to course load, degree level and program. *Financial support:* Fellowships, research assistantships, teaching assistantships, Federal Work-Study and institutionally sponsored loans available. Support available to part-time students. Financial award application deadline: 2/15; financial award applicants required to submit FAFSA. *Unit head:* Karen Torjesen, Dean, 909-607-3214, Fax: 909-621-9587, E-mail: karen.torjesen@cgu.edu. *Application contact:* Patrick Horn, Associate Dean, 909-607-8411, Fax: 909-607-9587, E-mail: patrick.horn@cgu.edu.

Claremont School of Theology, Graduate and Professional Programs, Program in Religion, Claremont, CA 91711-3199. Offers practical theology (PhD); religion and theology (MA); religious education (MARE). *Accreditation:* ACIPE; ATS. Terminal master's awarded for partial completion of doctoral program. *Degree requirements:* For master's, thesis; for doctorate, 2 foreign languages, thesis/dissertation. *Entrance requirements:* For doctorate, GRE General Test. Additional exam requirements/recommendations for international students: Required—TOEFL (minimum score 250 computer-based). Electronic applications accepted.

College of the Humanities and Sciences, Harrison Middleton University, Graduate Program, Tempe, AZ 85282. Offers education (MA, Ed D); humanities (MA); imaginative literature (MA); jurisprudence (MA); natural science (MA); philosophy and religion (MA); social science (MA). Part-time and evening/weekend programs available. Postbaccalaureate distance learning degree programs offered (no on-campus study).

Columbia University, Graduate School of Arts and Sciences, Division of Humanities, Department of Religion, New York, NY 10027. Offers M Phil, MA, PhD. *Faculty:* 25 full-time, 5 part-time/adjunct. *Students:* 52 full-time (29 women), 9 part-time (2 women). Average age 33. 112 applicants, 41% accepted. In 2007, 3 master's, 8 doctorates awarded. *Degree requirements:* For master's, 2 foreign languages, thesis, oral and written exams; for doctorate, variable foreign language requirement, thesis/dissertation. *Entrance requirements:* For master's and doctorate, GRE General Test. Additional exam requirements/recommendations for international students: Required—TOEFL. Application fee: $90. *Expenses:* Tuition: Part-time $1,452 per credit. Required fees: $152 per term. One-time fee: $75 part-time. Full-time tuition and fees vary according to course level, course load, degree level and program. *Financial support:* Fellowships, teaching assistantships, Federal Work-Study and institutionally sponsored loans available. Support available to part-time students. Financial award application deadline: 1/5; financial award applicants required to submit FAFSA. *Unit head:* Mark Taylor, Chair, 212-851-4131, Fax: 212-851-4126, E-mail: mct2z@columbia.edu.

Concordia University, School of Graduate Studies, Faculty of Arts and Science, Department of Religion, Program in History and Philosophy of Religion, Montréal, QC H3G 1M8, Canada. Offers MA. *Degree requirements:* For master's, comprehensive exam, thesis optional. *Entrance requirements:* For master's, honors degree in religion or equivalent. *Faculty research:* Comparative ethics, social theory and political society, Judaic studies.

Concordia University, School of Graduate Studies, Faculty of Arts and Science, Department of Religion, Program in Religion, Montréal, QC H3G 1M8, Canada. Offers PhD. *Degree requirements:* For doctorate, one foreign language, comprehensive exam, thesis/dissertation.

Concordia University Chicago, College of Arts and Sciences, Program in Religion, River Forest, IL 60305-1499. Offers MA. Part-time and evening/weekend programs available. *Degree requirements:* For master's, comprehensive exam, thesis. *Entrance requirements:* For master's, minimum GPA of 2.9. Additional exam requirements/recommendations for international students: Required—TOEFL (minimum score 550 paper-based; 195 computer-based). Electronic applications accepted. *Faculty research:* Dead Sea Scrolls, cultural construction of gender in early modern Europe, Luther, Luther's theology of the cross, gospels of Mark and John.

Cornell University, Graduate School, Graduate Fields of Arts and Sciences, Field of Asian Religions, Ithaca, NY 14853-0001. Offers PhD. *Faculty:* 9 full-time (3 women). *Students:* 6 full-time (1 woman), 1 international. Average age 32. 11 applicants, 9% accepted, 1 enrolled. *Degree requirements:* For doctorate, comprehensive exam, thesis/dissertation. *Entrance requirements:* For doctorate, GRE General Test, academic writing sample, 3 letters of recommendation. Additional exam requirements/recommendations for international students: Required—TOEFL (minimum score 600 paper-based; 250 computer-based; 77 iBT). *Application deadline:* For fall admission, 1/15 for domestic students. Application fee: $70. Electronic applications accepted. *Financial support:* In 2007–08, 5 students received support, including 4 fellowships with full tuition reimbursements available, 1 teaching assistantship with full tuition reimbursement available; research assistantships with full tuition reimbursements available, institutionally sponsored loans, scholarships/grants, health care benefits, and unspecified assistantships also available. *Unit head:* Director of Graduate Studies, 607-255-9099, Fax: 607-255-1345. *Application contact:* Graduate Field Assistant, 607-255-9099, Fax: 607-255-1345, E-mail: asian-religions@cornell.edu.

Denver Seminary, Graduate and Professional Programs, Littleton, CO 80120. Offers apologetics (Certificate); biblical studies (MA); Christian formation and soul care (MA, Certificate); Christian studies (MA, Certificate); church and parachurch leadership (D Min); counseling licensure (MA); counseling ministry (MA); intercultural ministry (Certificate); leadership (MA, Certificate); marriage and family counseling (D Min); pastoral ministry (D Min); philosophy of religion (MA); spiritual guidance (Certificate); theology (M Div, Certificate); worship (Certificate); youth and family ministry (MA). *Accreditation:* ACA; ACIPE; ATS (one or more programs are accredited). Part-time and evening/weekend programs available. Postbaccalaureate distance learning degree programs offered. *Faculty:* 23 full-time (4 women), 94 part-time/adjunct (39 women). *Students:* 517 full-time (154 women), 283 part-time (130 women); includes 47 minority (15 African Americans, 1 American Indian/Alaska Native, 22 Asian Americans or Pacific Islanders, 9 Hispanic Americans), 43 international. Average age 34. 333 applicants, 76% accepted, 166 enrolled. In 2007, 41 first professional degrees, 77 master's, 8 doctorates, 9 other advanced degrees awarded. *Degree requirements:* For master's, 2 foreign languages, thesis (for some programs); for doctorate, 2 foreign languages, thesis/dissertation; for M Div, 2 foreign languages. *Entrance requirements:* For M Div, minimum undergraduate GPA of 2.5; for master's, minimum undergraduate GPA of 3.0; for doctorate, M Div, 3 years of ministry experience. Additional exam requirements/recommendations for international students: Required—TOEFL (minimum score 575 paper-based; 233 computer-based; 90 iBT). *Application deadline:* For fall admission, 7/15 priority date for domestic students; for spring admission, 12/15 priority date for domestic students. Applications are processed on a rolling basis. Application fee: $35. Electronic applications accepted. *Expenses:* Tuition: Part-time $495 per semester hour. One-time fee: $150 part-time. Part-time tuition and fees vary according to course load. *Financial support:* In 2007–08, 220 students received support. Career-related internships or fieldwork, Federal Work-Study, scholarships/grants, and unspecified assistantships available. Support available to part-time students. Financial award application deadline: 4/1; financial award applicants required to submit FAFSA. *Unit head:* Dr. Randy MacFarland, Vice President and Dean, 303-762-6980, Fax: 303-761-8020, E-mail: randy.macfarland@denverseminary.edu. *Application contact:* Nathan Lamb, Director of Admissions, 303-357-5801, Fax: 303-783-3122, E-mail: info@denverseminary.edu.

Drew University, Caspersen School of Graduate Studies, Program in Biblical Studies and Early Christianity, Madison, NJ 07940-1493. Offers religion in ancient Israel (MA, PhD); the New Testament and early Christianity (MA, PhD). Part-time programs available. Terminal master's awarded for partial completion of doctoral program. *Degree requirements:* For master's, one foreign language, thesis; for doctorate, 2 foreign languages, comprehensive exam, thesis/dissertation. *Entrance requirements:* For master's and doctorate, GRE General Test. *Faculty research:* Folk religions of ancient Israel, New Testament exegesis and apocrypha, Near East archaeology, Hebrew Bible.

Drew University, Caspersen School of Graduate Studies, Program in Liturgical Studies, Madison, NJ 07940-1493. Offers MA, PhD. Part-time programs available. Terminal master's awarded for partial completion of doctoral program. *Degree requirements:* For master's, one foreign language, thesis; for doctorate, 2 foreign languages, comprehensive exam, thesis/dissertation. *Entrance requirements:* For master's and doctorate, GRE General Test. *Faculty research:* Historical liturgical development, especially early Christian and Reformation; contemporary liturgical practice; homiletics.

Drew University, Caspersen School of Graduate Studies, Program in Religion and Society, Madison, NJ 07940-1493. Offers anthropology of religion (MA, PhD); Christian social ethics (MA, PhD); psychology and religion (MA, PhD); sociology of religion (MA, PhD). Part-time programs available. Terminal master's awarded for partial completion of doctoral program. *Degree requirements:* For master's, one foreign language, thesis; for doctorate, 2 foreign languages, comprehensive exam, thesis/dissertation. *Entrance requirements:* For master's and doctorate, GRE General Test. *Faculty research:* Liberation theory, feminist critique, social science critique of religion.

Drew University, Caspersen School of Graduate Studies, Program in Theological and Religious Studies, Madison, NJ 07940-1493. Offers historical studies (MA, PhD); Methodist studies (PhD); philosophy of religion (MA, PhD); systematic theology (MA, PhD); theological ethics (MA, PhD). *Accreditation:* ATS. Part-time programs available. Terminal master's awarded for partial completion of doctoral program. *Degree requirements:* For master's, one foreign language, thesis; for doctorate, 2 foreign languages, comprehensive exam, thesis/dissertation. *Entrance requirements:* For master's and doctorate, GRE General Test. *Faculty research:* History and theology of religion, postmodern theologies, patristics.

Drew University, Caspersen School of Graduate Studies, Program in Wesleyan and Methodist Studies, Madison, NJ 07940-1493. Offers MA, PhD. *Entrance requirements:* For master's and doctorate, GRE General Test. Additional exam requirements/recommendations for international students: Required—TOEFL, TWE.

Duke University, Graduate School, Department of Religion, Durham, NC 27708. Offers MA, PhD. Part-time programs available. *Faculty:* 38 full-time. *Students:* 79 full-time (30 women); includes 10 minority (4 African Americans, 4 Asian Americans or Pacific Islanders, 2 Hispanic Americans), 12 international. Average age 31. 275 applicants, 11% accepted, 14 enrolled. In 2007, 11 master's, 14 doctorates awarded. Terminal master's awarded for partial completion of doctoral program. *Degree requirements:* For master's, one foreign language, thesis or alternative; for doctorate, 2 foreign languages, thesis/dissertation. *Entrance requirements:* For master's and doctorate, GRE General Test. Additional exam requirements/recommendations for international students: Required—TOEFL (minimum score 550 paper-based; 213 computer-based; 83 iBT), IELTS (minimum score 7). *Application deadline:* For fall admission, 12/15 priority date for domestic and international students. Application fee: $75. Electronic applications accepted. *Financial support:* In 2007–08, 32 fellowships (averaging $8,000 per year), 12 research assistantships (averaging $2,000 per year), 60 teaching assistantships (averaging $2,000 per year) were awarded; Federal Work-Study also available. Financial award application deadline: 12/31; financial award applicants required to submit FAFSA. *Unit head:* Grant Wacker, Director of Graduate Studies, 919-660-3512, Fax: 919-660-3530. *Application contact:* Gay C. Trotter, Staff Assistant, 919-660-3512, Fax: 919-660-3530, E-mail: gtrotter@duke.edu.

Earlham School of Religion, Graduate Programs, Richmond, IN 47374-5360. Offers religion (MA); theology (M Div, M Min). *Accreditation:* ACIPE; ATS. Part-time programs available. Postbaccalaureate distance learning degree programs offered (minimal on-campus study). *Faculty:* 8 full-time (3 women), 6 part-time/adjunct (4 women). *Students:* 108 full-time (63 women); includes 6 minority (3 African Americans, 1 American Indian/Alaska Native, 1 Asian American or Pacific Islander, 1 Hispanic American), 6 international. Average age 43. 37 applicants, 97% accepted, 34 enrolled. In 2007, 10 first professional degrees, 1 master's awarded. *Degree requirements:* For master's, one foreign language, comprehensive exam, thesis; for M Div, project. *Entrance requirements:* For M Div and master's, 3 references. Additional exam requirements/recommendations for international students: Required—TOEFL (minimum score 550 paper-based; 218 computer-based; 82 iBT). *Application deadline:* For fall admission, 7/31

Religion

Earlham School of Religion (continued)
priority date for domestic students; for winter admission, 12/12 priority date for domestic students. Applications are processed on a rolling basis. Application fee: $35. Electronic applications accepted. *Expenses:* Tuition: Full-time $8,802; part-time $326 per credit. Required fees: $466; $150 per term. *Financial support:* Scholarships/grants and tuition waivers (full and partial) available. Financial award application deadline: 4/15; financial award applicants required to submit FAFSA. *Faculty research:* Digitizing Quaker texts, vital Quaker ministry. *Unit head:* Jay W. Marshall, Dean, 800-432-1377, Fax: 765-983-1688, E-mail: marshja@earlham.edu. *Application contact:* Susan G. Axtell, Director of Admissions, 800-432-1377, Fax: 765-983-1688, E-mail: axtelsu@earlham.edu.

Eastern Mennonite University, Eastern Mennonite Seminary, Harrisonburg, VA 22802-2462. Offers church leadership (MA); divinity (M Div); ministry studies (Certificate); online theological studies (Certificate); religion (MA); theological studies (Certificate). *Accreditation:* ATS.Part-time programs available. *Faculty:* 9 full-time (2 women), 16 part-time/adjunct (5 women). *Students:* 42 full-time (15 women), 29 part-time (13 women); includes 2 minority (both African Americans), 6 international. Average age 40. 43 applicants, 100% accepted. In 2007, 19 first professional degrees, 4 master's awarded. *Degree requirements:* For master's, thesis (for some programs); for M Div, thesis/dissertation (for some programs), supervised field education. *Entrance requirements:* For M Div and master's, minimum GPA of 2.5. Additional exam requirements/recommendations for international students: Required—TOEFL (minimum score 550 paper-based; 213 computer-based). *Application deadline:* For fall admission, 6/15 priority date for domestic and international students; for winter admission, 11/15 priority date for domestic and international students; for spring admission, 3/15 priority date for domestic and international students. Applications are processed on a rolling basis. Application fee: $25. *Expenses:* Contact institution. Tuition and fees vary according to program. *Financial support:* In 2007–08, 43 students received support. Application deadline: 6/30; *Faculty research:* Spiritual direction and 'culture of call"; leadership coaching: an approach to leadership in a culture of call; clarity of call in the probationary process for United Methodist clergy in Virginia; EMS women's experiences of culture of call efforts; practices of excellent and fruitful Mennonite pastoral ministry. Total annual research expenditures: $45,000. *Unit head:* Dr. Ervin R. Stutzman, Seminary Dean, 540-432-4261, Fax: 540-432-4444, E-mail: stutzerv@emu.edu. *Application contact:* Don A. Yoder, Director of Seminary and Graduate Admissions, 540-432-4257, Fax: 540-432-4598, E-mail: yoderda@emu.edu.

Edgewood College, Program in Religious Studies, Madison, WI 53711-1997. Offers MA. Part-time and evening/weekend programs available. *Students:* Average age 48. In 2007, 2 degrees awarded. *Entrance requirements:* For master's, minimum GPA of 2.75, 2 letters of reference, personal statement. Additional exam requirements/recommendations for international students: Required—TOEFL (minimum score 213 computer-based). *Application deadline:* For fall admission, 8/24 for domestic students, 8/1 for international students; for spring admission, 1/10 for domestic students, 10/1 for international students. Applications are processed on a rolling basis. Application fee: $25. Electronic applications accepted. *Expenses:* Tuition: Part-time $655 per credit. *Financial support:* Career-related internships or fieldwork, institutionally sponsored loans, scholarships/grants, and tuition waivers (partial) available. *Faculty research:* Interpretation theory and New Testament, women and religion, theology and literature, Hebrew poetry. *Unit head:* Dr. John Leonard, Chairperson, 608-663-2823, Fax: 608-663-3291, E-mail: jleonard@edgewood.edu. *Application contact:* Paula O'Malley, Director of Graduate and Professional Studies, 608-663-2217, Fax: 608-663-3496, E-mail: gps@edgewood.edu.

Elms College, Religious Studies Department, Chicopee, MA 01013-2839. Offers MAAT. Part-time and evening/weekend programs available. *Faculty:* 2 full-time (1 woman), 2 part-time/adjunct (0 women). *Students:* Average age 35. 1 applicant, 100% accepted, 1 enrolled. In 2007, 7 degrees awarded. *Degree requirements:* For master's, thesis. *Entrance requirements:* For master's, minimum GPA of 3.0. Additional exam requirements/recommendations for international students: Required—TOEFL. *Application deadline:* For fall admission, 7/1 priority date for domestic students; for spring admission, 11/1 priority date for domestic students. Applications are processed on a rolling basis. Application fee: $30. *Expenses:* Tuition: Full-time $9,630; part-time $535 per credit. Required fees: $40; $20 per term. *Financial support:* Tuition waivers (partial) available. Financial award application deadline: 4/15; financial award applicants required to submit FAFSA. *Unit head:* Dr. Martin Pion, Director of MALA/MAAT Programs, 413-265-3581, Fax: 413-594-3951, E-mail: pionm@elms.edu.

Emmanuel School of Religion, Graduate and Professional Programs, Johnson City, TN 37601-9438. Offers M Div, MAR, D Min. *Accreditation:* ACIPE; ATS. Part-time programs available. *Faculty:* 12 full-time (1 woman), 3 part-time/adjunct (0 women). *Students:* 99 full-time (33 women), 20 part-time (5 women); includes 3 minority (all African Americans), 11 international. Average age 32. 50 applicants, 94% accepted. In 2007, 18 first professional degrees, 7 master's, 2 doctorates awarded. *Degree requirements:* For master's, 2 foreign languages, thesis; for M Div, 2 foreign languages, thesis/dissertation or alternative. *Entrance requirements:* For doctorate, GRE General Test, Minnesota Multiphasic Personality Inventory. *Application deadline:* For fall admission, 8/1 priority date for domestic students. Applications are processed on a rolling basis. Application fee: $25. *Expenses:* Tuition: Full-time $7,800; part-time $325 per hour. Required fees: $400; $75 per term. *Financial support:* In 2007–08, 100 students received support, including teaching assistantships (averaging $3,600 per year); career-related internships or fieldwork, Federal Work-Study, institutionally sponsored loans, scholarships/grants, and tuition waivers (partial) also available. Support available to part-time students. Financial award application deadline: 4/1. *Unit head:* Dr. Robert F. Hull, Dean and Professor of New Testament, 423-461-1524, Fax: 423-926-6198, E-mail: hullr@esr.edu. *Application contact:* David Fulks, Director of Admissions, 423-461-1536, Fax: 423-926-6198, E-mail: fulksd@esr.edu.

Emory University, Graduate School of Arts and Sciences, Department of Comparative Literature, Atlanta, GA 30322-1100. Offers comparative literature (PhD); English (Certificate); French (Certificate); Middle Eastern studies (PhD); philosophy (Certificate); psychoanalytic studies (PhD); religion (PhD); Spanish (Certificate); women studies (Certificate). *Degree requirements:* For doctorate, 2 foreign languages, comprehensive exam, thesis/dissertation. *Entrance requirements:* For doctorate, GRE General Test, minimum GPA of 3.0. Additional exam requirements/recommendations for international students: Required—TOEFL. Electronic applications accepted. *Faculty research:* Literary theory, psychoanalysis trauma and testimony, literature and religion, literature and technology, literature and philosophy, politics and global culture, literature and aesthetics.

Emory University, Graduate School of Arts and Sciences, Division of Religion, Atlanta, GA 30322-1100. Offers PhD. *Degree requirements:* For doctorate, 2 foreign languages, comprehensive exam, thesis/dissertation. *Entrance requirements:* For doctorate, GRE General Test, minimum GPA of 3.0. Additional exam requirements/recommendations for international students: Required—TOEFL. Electronic applications accepted. *Faculty research:* Systematic and historical theology, biblical studies.

Episcopal Theological Seminary of the Southwest, Graduate and Professional Programs, Austin, TX 78768-2247. Offers Anglican studies (Advanced Diploma); chaplaincy (MAPM); counseling (MAC); discipleship (MAPM); divinity (M Div); religion (MAR); spiritual formation (MAPM); theological studies (Advanced Diploma). *Accreditation:* ACIPE; ATS (one or more programs are accredited). Part-time and evening/weekend programs available. *Faculty:* 9 full-time (2 women), 20 part-time/adjunct (6 women). *Students:* 60 full-time (39 women), 37 part-time (27 women); includes 7 minority (4 African Americans, 1 Asian American or Pacific Islander, 2 Hispanic Americans), 1 international. Average age 46. 41 applicants, 98% accepted, 35 enrolled. In 2007, 24 first professional degrees, 9 master's, 2 other advanced degrees awarded. *Degree requirements:* For master's, thesis (for some programs). *Entrance requirements:* For M Div and master's, GRE, MAT, interview; for Advanced Diploma, interview. *Application deadline:* For fall admission, 7/1 for domestic students; for spring admission, 11/1 for domestic students. Applications are processed on a rolling basis. Application fee: $50. *Expenses:* Tuition: Full-time $13,150; part-time $390 per hour. Required fees: $75. One-time fee: $20 part-time. *Financial support:* Career-related internships or fieldwork and scholarships/grants available. Support available to part-time students. Financial award application deadline: 6/17. *Unit head:* Very Rev. Douglas Travis, Dean and President, 512-472-4133 Ext. 307, Fax: 512-472-3098, E-mail: dtravis@etss.edu. *Application contact:* Rev. Ken Malcolm, Director of Admissions, 512-472-4133 Ext. 375, Fax: 512-472-3098, E-mail: kmalcolm@etss.edu.

Evangelical Theological Seminary, Graduate and Professional Programs, Myerstown, PA 17067-1212. Offers divinity (M Div); marriage and family therapy (MA); ministry (Certificate); religion (MA). *Accreditation:* ATS (one or more programs are accredited). Part-time programs available. Postbaccalaureate distance learning degree programs offered (minimal on-campus study). *Faculty:* 7 full-time (2 women), 21 part-time/adjunct (3 women). *Students:* 22 full-time (0 women), 152 part-time (66 women). Average age 33. 60 applicants, 77% accepted, 46 enrolled. In 2007, 11 first professional degrees, 22 master's awarded. *Degree requirements:* For master's, 2 foreign languages; for M Div, 2 foreign languages, ministry internship. *Entrance requirements:* For M Div and master's, minimum GPA of 2.5. Additional exam requirements/recommendations for international students: Required—TOEFL (minimum score 550 paper-based; 213 computer-based). *Application deadline:* For fall admission, 6/1 priority date for domestic students, 4/1 priority date for international students; for spring admission, 11/1 priority date for domestic students, 9/1 priority date for international students. Applications are processed on a rolling basis. Application fee: $35. *Expenses:* Tuition: Full-time $10,440; part-time $435 per credit. Required fees: $25 per semester. One-time fee: $125. *Financial support:* Career-related internships or fieldwork, scholarships/grants, and tuition waivers (full) available. Support available to part-time students. Financial award application deadline: 6/1; financial award applicants required to submit FAFSA. *Faculty research:* Literary form and structure within the Hebrew and Greek scriptures, Wesley studies, esoteric biblical languages, the Mosaic law and the Christian, ethics. *Unit head:* Rev. Dr. John V. Tornfelt, Vice President, Academic Affairs, 717-866-5775 Ext. 140, Fax: 717-866-4667, E-mail: jtornfelt@evangelical.edu. *Application contact:* Tom M. Maiello, Dean of Admissions, 800-532-5775 Ext. 109, Fax: 717-866-4667, E-mail: admissions@evangelical.edu.

Faith Baptist Bible College and Theological Seminary, Graduate Program, Ankeny, IA 50021. Offers biblical studies (MA); pastoral studies (M Div); pastoral training (MA); religion (MA); theological studies (MA). Part-time programs available. *Faculty:* 4 full-time (0 women), 7 part-time/adjunct (0 women). *Students:* 28 full-time (3 women), 28 part-time (2 women); includes 1 minority (Hispanic American), 1 international. Average age 29. In 2007, 9 first professional degrees, 12 master's awarded. *Degree requirements:* For master's, thesis or alternative; for M Div, 2 foreign languages. *Entrance requirements:* Additional exam requirements/recommendations for international students: Required—TOEFL (minimum score 550 paper-based; 197 computer-based). *Application deadline:* For fall admission, 8/1 priority date for domestic students, 8/1 for international students; for spring admission, 12/15 for domestic and international students. Applications are processed on a rolling basis. Application fee: $25. *Expenses:* Tuition: Full-time $10,228; part-time $392 per credit hour. Required fees: $95 per semester. One-time fee: $50. Tuition and fees vary according to class time and course load. *Financial support:* In 2007–08, 70 students received support. Career-related internships or fieldwork and scholarships/grants available. Support available to part-time students. Financial award application deadline: 3/1; financial award applicants required to submit FAFSA. *Faculty research:* Baptist theology, American church history. *Unit head:* Dr. Ernest Schmidt, Dean of Seminary, 515-964-0601, Fax: 514-964-1638, E-mail: schmidte@faith.edu. *Application contact:* Pat Odle, Vice President of Enrollment, 888-FAITH4U, Fax: 515-964-1638, E-mail: odlep@faith.edu.

Florida International University, College of Arts and Sciences, Department of Religious Studies, Miami, FL 33199. Offers MA. Part-time and evening/weekend programs available. *Faculty:* 10 full-time (2 women). *Students:* 16 full-time (10 women), 9 part-time (5 women); includes 15 minority (3 African Americans, 1 Asian American or Pacific Islander, 11 Hispanic Americans), 6 international. Average age 36. 18 applicants, 94% accepted, 12 enrolled. In 2007, 7 degrees awarded. *Degree requirements:* For master's, thesis. *Entrance requirements:* For master's, GRE General Test, minimum GPA of 3.0, 2 letters of recommendation. Additional exam requirements/recommendations for international students: Required—TOEFL (minimum score 550 paper-based; 213 computer-based). *Application deadline:* For fall admission, 2/15 for domestic and international students; for spring admission, 10/1 for domestic students, 9/1 for international students. Applications are processed on a rolling basis. Application fee: $30. Electronic applications accepted. *Expenses:* Tuition, state resident: full-time $6,106. Tuition, nonresident: full-time $15,528. Required fees: $284. *Financial support:* Teaching assistantships, scholarships/grants available. *Unit head:* Dr. Christine Gudorf, Chairperson, 305-348-2729, Fax: 305-348-1879, E-mail: christine.gudorf@fiu.edu.

Florida State University, Graduate Studies, College of Arts and Sciences, Department of Religion, Tallahassee, FL 32306. Offers humanities (PhD), including religion; religion (MA, PhD). Part-time programs available. *Faculty:* 18 full-time (5 women), 3 part-time/adjunct (2 women). *Students:* 49 full-time (19 women), 5 part-time (3 women); includes 6 minority (1 African American, 1 American Indian/Alaska Native, 1 Asian American or Pacific Islander, 3 Hispanic Americans). Average age 25. 72 applicants, 32% accepted, 15 enrolled. In 2007, 11 master's, 5 doctorates awarded. Terminal master's awarded for partial completion of doctoral program. *Degree requirements:* For master's, one foreign language, thesis (for some programs); for doctorate, 3 foreign languages, thesis/dissertation. *Entrance requirements:* For master's, GRE General Test, minimum GPA of 3.0; for doctorate, GRE General Test, MA in religion. Additional exam requirements/recommendations for international students: Required—TOEFL. *Application deadline:* For fall admission, 1/15 for domestic students. Applications are processed on a rolling basis. Application fee: $30. Electronic applications accepted. *Expenses:* Tuition, state resident: part-time $248 per credit hour. Tuition, nonresident: part-time $880 per credit hour. Tuition and fees vary according to program. *Financial support:* In 2007–08, 49 students received support, including 2 fellowships with partial tuition reimbursements available (averaging $6,300 per year), 1 research assistantship with partial tuition reimbursement available (averaging $6,935 per year), 31 teaching assistantships with partial tuition reimbursements available (averaging $9,074 per year); Federal Work-Study, institutionally sponsored loans, and unspecified assistantships also available. Financial award application deadline: 3/15; financial award applicants required to submit FAFSA. *Faculty research:* Wisdom literature, Hindu goddesses, feminist theology and medical ethics, Tibetan Buddhism, religion and emotion. *Unit head:* Dr. John Corrigan, Chair, 850-644-1020, Fax: 850-644-7225, E-mail: john.corrigan@fsu.edu. *Application contact:* Dr. Amanda Porterfield, Director of Graduate Studies, 850-644-5433, Fax: 850-644-7225, E-mail: aporterf@mailer.fsu.edu.

Fordham University, Graduate School of Religion and Religious Education, New York, NY 10458. Offers pastoral counseling and spiritual care (MA); pastoral ministry/spirituality/pastoral counseling (D Min); religion and religious education (MA); religious education (MS, PhD, PD); spiritual direction (Certificate). Part-time programs available. Terminal master's awarded for partial completion of doctoral program. *Degree requirements:* For master's, research paper; for doctorate, comprehensive exam, thesis/dissertation. *Entrance requirements:* For doctorate, MAT. Electronic applications accepted. Expenses: Contact institution. *Faculty research:* Spirituality and spiritual direction, pastoral care and counseling, adult family and community, growth and young adult.

George Fox University, George Fox Evangelical Seminary, Newberg, OR 97132-2697. Offers divinity (M Div); ministry (D Min), including leadership and spiritual formation, leadership in the emerging culture; ministry leadership (MA); spiritual formation (MA); spiritual formation and discipleship (Certificate); theological studies (MA). *Accreditation:* ACIPE; ATS. Part-time programs available. Postbaccalaureate distance learning degree programs offered (minimal on-campus study). *Faculty:* 7 full-time (2 women), 13 part-time/adjunct (4 women). *Students:* 105 full-time (27 women), 215 part-time (76 women); includes 27 minority (5 African Americans, 2 American Indian/Alaska Native, 12 Asian Americans or Pacific Islanders, 8 Hispanic Americans),

5 international. Average age 42. 135 applicants, 85% accepted, 109 enrolled. In 2007, 11 first professional degrees, 18 master's, 20 doctorates, 1 other advanced degree awarded. *Degree requirements:* For master's, variable foreign language requirement, thesis optional, internship. *Entrance requirements:* Additional exam requirements/recommendations for international students: Required—TOEFL (minimum score 550 paper-based; 213 computer-based). *Application deadline:* For fall admission, 7/1 for domestic and international students; for spring admission, 11/1 for domestic and international students. Applications are processed on a rolling basis. Application fee: $40. Electronic applications accepted. *Expenses: Contact institution. Financial support:* In 2007–08, 33 students received support. Career-related internships or fieldwork and scholarships/grants available. Financial award application deadline: 5/1; financial award applicants required to submit FAFSA. *Unit head:* Dr. Chuck Conniry, Vice President and Dean, 503-554-6163, E-mail: cconniry@georgefox.edu. *Application contact:* Sheila Bartlett, Admissions Counselor, 800-631-0921, Fax: 503-554-6111, E-mail: sbartlett@georgefox.edu.

George Mason University, College of Humanities and Social Sciences, Interdisciplinary Studies Program, Fairfax, VA 22030. Offers anthropology (MAIS); community college teaching (MAIS); folklore (MAIS); higher education (MAIS); individualized studies (MAIS); religion, cultures, and values (MAIS); video-based production (MAIS); women's studies (MAIS); zoo and aquarium leadership (MAIS). Part-time and evening/weekend programs available. *Faculty:* 6 full-time (4 women), 6 part-time/adjunct (5 women). *Students:* 25 full-time (17 women), 90 part-time (76 women); includes 24 minority (5 African Americans, 1 American Indian/Alaska Native, 7 Asian Americans or Pacific Islanders, 11 Hispanic Americans), 3 international. Average age 33. 68 applicants, 72% accepted, 35 enrolled. In 2007, 19 degrees awarded. *Degree requirements:* For master's, thesis optional. *Entrance requirements:* For master's, GRE, GMAT, or MAT, interview, minimum GPA of 3.0 in last 60 hours of course work. *Application deadline:* For fall admission, 5/1 priority date for domestic students; for spring admission, 11/1 for domestic students. Applications are processed on a rolling basis. Application fee: $60 ($75 for international students). Electronic applications accepted. *Financial support:* Fellowships, teaching assistantships, career-related internships or fieldwork, Federal Work-Study, and institutionally sponsored loans available. Support available to part-time students. Financial award application deadline: 3/1; financial award applicants required to submit FAFSA. *Unit head:* John Burns, Chair, 703-993-1291, Fax: 703-993-1297, E-mail: mais@gmu.edu. *Application contact:* Dr. Johannes D. Bergmann, Information Contact, 703-993-8762, E-mail: mais@gmu.edu.

The George Washington University, Columbian College of Arts and Sciences, Department of Religion, Washington, DC 20052. Offers Hinduism and Islam (MA). Part-time and evening/weekend programs available. *Degree requirements:* For master's, one foreign language, comprehensive exam, thesis. *Entrance requirements:* For master's, GRE General Test, interview, minimum GPA of 3.0. Additional exam requirements/recommendations for international students: Required—TOEFL (minimum score 550 paper-based; 213 computer-based). Electronic applications accepted.

Georgia State University, College of Arts and Sciences, Department of Religious Studies, Atlanta, GA 30303-3083. Offers MA. Part-time programs available. *Faculty:* 5 full-time (1 woman). *Students:* 11 full-time (7 women), 5 part-time (1 woman); includes 1 minority (African American) 13 applicants, 54% accepted, 6 enrolled. In 2007, 10 degrees awarded. *Degree requirements:* For master's, thesis. *Entrance requirements:* For master's, GRE, 3 letters of recommendation, writing sample. *Application deadline:* For fall admission, 4/15 for domestic and international students. Application fee: $50. Electronic applications accepted. *Expenses:* Tuition, state resident: part-time $221 per credit hour. *Financial support:* In 2007–08, 22 students received support, including 8 research assistantships with tuition reimbursements available (averaging $4,000 per year), 9 teaching assistantships with tuition reimbursements available (averaging $6,000 per year); unspecified assistantships also available. Financial award application deadline: 4/15. *Faculty research:* Comparative religions; history of religions; religious ethics; comparative religious ritual; Islam, Judaism, and the Middle East. Total annual research expenditures: $80,000. *Unit head:* Dr. Timothy M. Renick, Chair, 404-413-5573, E-mail: trenick@gsu.edu. *Application contact:* Dr. Kathryn Mc Clymond, Director of Graduate Studies, 404-413-6119, E-mail: kmcclymond@gsu.edu.

Gonzaga University, College of Arts and Sciences, Department of Religious Studies, Spokane, WA 99258. Offers pastoral ministry (MA); religious studies (MA); spirituality (MA). *Faculty:* 9 full-time (6 women). *Students:* 4 full-time (3 women), 25 part-time (12 women); includes 3 minority (1 American Indian/Alaska Native, 2 Hispanic Americans). Average age 44. 15 applicants, 87% accepted, 13 enrolled. In 2007, 8 degrees awarded. *Degree requirements:* For master's, comprehensive exam. *Entrance requirements:* For master's, GRE General Test or MAT, minimum GPA of 3.0. Additional exam requirements/recommendations for international students: Required—TOEFL. *Application deadline:* For fall admission, 7/20 priority date for domestic students; for spring admission, 11/1 for domestic students. Applications are processed on a rolling basis. Application fee: $40. *Financial support:* Application deadline: 3/1. *Unit head:* Dr. Ron Large, Chairperson, 509-328-4220 Ext. 6782, E-mail: jennings@gonzaga.edu.

Gordon-Conwell Theological Seminary, Graduate and Professional Programs, South Hamilton, MA 01982. Offers Christian education (MACE); church history (MACH); counseling (MACO); ministry (D Min); missions/evangelism (MAME); New Testament (MANT); Old Testament (MAOT); religion (MAR); theology (M Div, MATH, Th M). *Accreditation:* ACIPE; ATS (one or more programs are accredited). Part-time and evening/weekend programs available. *Degree requirements:* For master's, one foreign language, thesis optional; for doctorate, 2 foreign languages, thesis/dissertation; for M Div, 2 foreign languages. *Entrance requirements:* For M Div and master's, minimum GPA of 2.5; for doctorate, minimum GPA of 3.0.

Graceland University, Community of Christ Seminary, Lamoni, IA 50140. Offers Christian ministry (MACM); religion (MAR). Part-time programs available. Postbaccalaureate distance learning degree programs offered (minimal on-campus study). *Faculty:* 4 full-time (1 woman), 13 part-time/adjunct (5 women). *Students:* 9 full-time (2 women), 21 part-time (8 women); includes 1 minority (American Indian/Alaska Native), 3 international. Average age 43. 21 applicants, 76% accepted, 15 enrolled. In 2007, 10 degrees awarded. *Degree requirements:* For master's, thesis optional, integrated project. *Entrance requirements:* For master's, minimum cumulative GPA of 3.0. *Application deadline:* For fall admission, 8/15 priority date for domestic students; for winter admission, 10/15 priority date for domestic students; for spring admission, 4/15 priority date for domestic students. Applications are processed on a rolling basis. Application fee: $50. *Expenses: Contact institution.* Part-time tuition and fees vary according to program. *Financial support:* Scholarships/grants available. Financial award application deadline: 12/15; financial award applicants required to submit FAFSA. *Faculty research:* Theology. *Unit head:* Dr. Don H. Compier, Dean, 800-833-0524 Ext. 4900, Fax: 816-833-2990, E-mail: dcompier@graceland.edu. *Application contact:* Tere E. Naylor, Executive Assistant, 816-833-0524 Ext. 4903, Fax: 816-833-2990, E-mail: tnaylor@graceland.edu.

Graduate Theological Union, Graduate Programs, Berkeley, CA 94709-1212. Offers art and religion (MA, PhD); biblical languages (MA); biblical studies (Old and New Testament) (MA, PhD, Th D); Buddhist studies (MA); Christian spirituality (MA, PhD); cultural and historical studies of religions (MA, PhD); ethics and social theory (PhD); history (MA, PhD, Th D); homiletics (MA, PhD, Th D); interdisciplinary studies (PhD, Th D); Jewish studies (MA, PhD, Certificate); liturgical studies (MA, PhD, Th D); Near Eastern religions (PhD); Orthodox Christian studies (MA); Orthodox studies (Certificate); religion and psychology (MA, PhD); religion and society/ethics and social theory (MA); systematic and philosophical theology (MA, PhD, Th D); women's studies in religion (Certificate); MA/M Div. *Accreditation:* ATS. *Faculty:* 119 full-time (44 women), 34 part-time/adjunct (9 women). *Students:* 317 full-time (152 women), 35 part-time (19 women); includes 49 minority (15 African Americans, 2 American Indian/Alaska Native, 21 Asian Americans or Pacific Islanders, 11 Hispanic Americans), 74 international. Average age 38. 257 applicants, 59% accepted, 79 enrolled. In 2007, 45 master's, 22 doctorates awarded. Terminal master's awarded for partial completion of doctoral program. *Median time to degree:* Of those who began their doctoral program in fall 1999, 52% received their degree in 8 years or less. *Degree requirements:* For master's, one foreign language, thesis; for doctorate, one foreign language, comprehensive exam, thesis/dissertation. *Entrance requirements:* For master's, GRE General Test; for doctorate, GRE General Test, MA or M Div. Additional exam requirements/recommendations for international students: Required—TOEFL. *Application deadline:* For fall admission, 12/15 for domestic and international students; for winter admission, 2/15 for domestic and international students; for spring admission, 9/30 for domestic and international students. Application fee: $40. Electronic applications accepted. *Expenses:* Tuition: Full-time $13,310. Tuition and fees vary according to degree level and program. *Financial support:* In 2007–08, 122 students received support, including 109 fellowships (averaging $11,581 per year), 1 research assistantship (averaging $3,000 per year), 22 teaching assistantships (averaging $3,500 per year); Federal Work-Study, scholarships/grants, and tuition waivers (partial) also available. Support available to part-time students. Financial award application deadline: 2/1; financial award applicants required to submit FAFSA. *Unit head:* Dr. Arthur G. Holder, Dean, 510-649-2440, Fax: 510-649-1417, E-mail: aholder@gtu.edu. *Application contact:* Dr. Kathleen Kook, Assistant Dean for Admissions, 800-826-4488, Fax: 510-649-1730, E-mail: gtuadm@gtu.edu.

Grand Rapids Theological Seminary of Cornerstone University, Graduate Programs, Grand Rapids, MI 49525-5897. Offers biblical counseling (MA); Biblical counseling (M Div); chaplaincy (M Div); Christian education (M Div, MA); intercultural studies (M Div, MA); New Testament (MA, Th M); Old Testament (MA, Th M); pastoral studies (M Div); systematic theology (MA); theology (Th M). *Accreditation:* ATS. Part-time programs available. Postbaccalaureate distance learning degree programs offered (minimal on-campus study). *Faculty:* 9 full-time (1 woman), 10 part-time/adjunct (1 woman). *Students:* 102 full-time (35 women), 126 part-time (42 women); includes 36 minority (28 African Americans, 2 American Indian/Alaska Native, 3 Asian Americans or Pacific Islanders, 3 Hispanic Americans), 7 international. Average age 35. 160 applicants, 91% accepted, 107 enrolled. *Entrance requirements:* Additional exam requirements/recommendations for international students: Required—TOEFL (minimum score 577 paper-based; 233 computer-based; 90 iBT). *Application deadline:* For fall admission, 8/15 for domestic students; for spring admission, 1/10 for domestic students. Applications are processed on a rolling basis. Electronic applications accepted. *Expenses:* Tuition: Full-time $6,930; part-time $385 per credit hour. Required fees: $520; $10 per credit hour. $170 per semester. Tuition and fees vary according to course load and degree level. *Financial support:* Career-related internships or fieldwork, scholarships/grants, and health care benefits available. Support available to part-time students. Financial award application deadline: 8/15; financial award applicants required to submit FAFSA. *Unit head:* Dr. Douglas L. Fagerstrom, President, 616-222-1422, Fax: 616-222-1502, E-mail: douglas_fagerstrom@cornerstone.edu. *Application contact:* Tara Danielle Kram, 800-697-1133, Fax: 616-254-1623, E-mail: tara_kram@cornerstone.edu.

Harding University Graduate School of Religion, Graduate Programs, Memphis, TN 38117-5499. Offers Christian ministry (MA); counseling (MA); ministry (M Div, D Min); religion (MA). *Accreditation:* ATS. Part-time programs available. Postbaccalaureate distance learning degree programs offered (minimal on-campus study). *Degree requirements:* For master's, variable foreign language requirement, thesis (for some programs); for doctorate, one foreign language, thesis/dissertation; for M Div, 2 foreign languages, thesis/dissertation optional. *Entrance requirements:* For M Div, GRE General Test (for graduates of non-accredited schools), minimum GPA of 2.5; for master's, minimum GPA of 2.7; for doctorate, minimum GPA of 3.0. Additional exam requirements/recommendations for international students: Required—TOEFL (minimum score 550 paper-based; 213 computer-based; 79 iBT). Electronic applications accepted.

Hardin-Simmons University, Graduate School, Logsdon School of Theology, Program in Religion, Abilene, TX 79698-0001. Offers MA. Part-time programs available. *Faculty:* 12 full-time (1 woman), 13 part-time/adjunct (2 women). *Students:* 5 full-time (1 woman), 3 part-time. Average age 30. 3 applicants, 100% accepted, 2 enrolled. In 2007, 4 degrees awarded. *Degree requirements:* For master's, one foreign language, comprehensive exam, thesis or alternative. *Entrance requirements:* For master's, minimum undergraduate GPA of 3.0 in major, 2.7 overall, 18 hours of course work in religious studies, interview. Additional exam requirements/recommendations for international students: Required—TOEFL (minimum score 550 paper-based; 213 computer-based). *Application deadline:* For fall admission, 8/15 priority date for domestic students; for spring admission, 1/5 priority date for domestic students. Applications are processed on a rolling basis. Application fee: $50 ($100 for international students). *Expenses:* Tuition: Full-time $9,810; part-time $545 per hour. Required fees: $590; $75 per semester. One-time fee: $50 part-time. *Financial support:* In 2007–08, 7 students received support; fellowships, scholarships/grants available. Support available to part-time students. Financial award application deadline: 6/30; financial award applicants required to submit FAFSA. *Faculty research:* Archaeology research in Christian origins, Hebrew grammar, history of Christian education, training of ministers into the twenty-first century, role of women in the Old Testament, contemporary ethical issues. *Unit head:* Dr. Travis Frampton, Director, 325-670-1270, Fax: 325-670-1406, E-mail: frampton@hsutx.edu. *Application contact:* Dr. Gary Stanlake, Dean of Graduate Studies, 325-670-1298, Fax: 325-670-1564, E-mail: gradoff@hsutx.edu.

Hartford Seminary, Graduate Programs, Hartford, CT 06105-2279. Offers black ministry (Certificate); Islamic studies (MA); ministerios Hispanos (Certificate); ministry (D Min); religious studies (MA); women's leadership institute (Certificate). *Accreditation:* ATS (one or more programs are accredited). Part-time and evening/weekend programs available. Postbaccalaureate distance learning degree programs offered (no on-campus study). *Faculty:* 12 full-time (5 women), 19 part-time/adjunct (7 women). *Students:* 39 full-time (23 women), 120 part-time (72 women); includes 35 minority (27 African Americans, 5 Asian Americans or Pacific Islanders, 3 Hispanic Americans), 25 international. *Degree requirements:* For master's, thesis optional, oral exam; for doctorate, thesis/dissertation, oral exam. *Entrance requirements:* For doctorate, experience in ministry, M Div. Additional exam requirements/recommendations for international students: Required—TOEFL (minimum score 550 paper-based; 213 computer-based; 80 iBT). *Application deadline:* For fall admission, 7/15 priority date for domestic students, 5/1 priority date for international students; for winter admission, 12/1 priority date for domestic students, 4/1 priority date for international students; for spring admission, 4/5 priority date for domestic students, 3/1 priority date for international students. Applications are processed on a rolling basis. Application fee: $50. *Expenses:* Tuition: Full-time $12,400; part-time $1,550 per unit. *Financial support:* In 2007–08, 74 students received support. Scholarships/grants and tuition waivers (partial) available. Support available to part-time students. Financial award application deadline: 6/1. *Faculty research:* Liturgy and social justice, professional leadership in ministry, congregational studies, Christian-Muslim relations, American religion. *Unit head:* Dr. Efrain Agosto, Academic Dean, 860-509-9554, E-mail: eagosto@hartsem.edu. *Application contact:* Dr. Vanessa Avery-Wall, Admissions Manager, 860-509-9552, Fax: 860-509-9509, E-mail: vaw@hartsem.edu.

Harvard University, Graduate School of Arts and Sciences, Committee on the Study of Religion, Cambridge, MA 02138. Offers PhD. *Degree requirements:* For doctorate, 2 foreign languages, thesis/dissertation. *Entrance requirements:* For doctorate, GRE General Test. Additional exam requirements/recommendations for international students: Required—TOEFL. *Expenses:* Tuition: Full-time $31,456. Full-time tuition and fees vary according to program and student level.

Hebrew Union College–Jewish Institute of Religion, School of Graduate Studies, Cincinnati, OH 45220-2488. Offers Bible and the ancient Near East (M Phil, MA, PhD); Hebrew letters (DHL); history of biblical interpretation (M Phil, MA, PhD); Jewish and Christian studies in the Greco-Roman period (M Phil, PhD); Jewish and cognate studies (M Phil); Judaic and cognate studies (MA, PhD); modern Jewish history (M Phil, MA, PhD); philosophy and Jewish religious thought (M Phil, MA, PhD); rabbinics (M Phil, MA, PhD). Part-time programs available. Terminal master's awarded for partial completion of doctoral program. *Degree requirements:* For master's, one foreign language, thesis optional; for doctorate, 3 foreign languages, comprehensive exam, thesis/dissertation. *Entrance requirements:* For master's and doctorate, GRE General

Religion

Hebrew Union College–Jewish Institute of Religion (continued)
Test, knowledge of Hebrew. Additional exam requirements/recommendations for international students: Required—TOEFL. *Faculty research:* Aramaic lexicon translations, German-Jewish history, neo-Babylonian texts.

Heritage Christian University, Graduate Programs, Florence, AL 35630. Offers counseling (MM); Greek (MA); ministry (MM); New Testament (MA). *Degree requirements:* For master's, practicum (MM), major research paper (MA). *Entrance requirements:* For master's, MAT or GRE, bachelor's degree in Bible from an accredited college or university, minimum GPA of 2.75, 3 letters of recommendation.

Holy Names University, Graduate Division, Sophia Center in Culture and Spirituality, Oakland, CA 94619-1699. Offers MA, Certificate. *Faculty:* 1 full-time (0 women), 13 part-time/adjunct (7 women). *Students:* 11 full-time (8 women), 32 part-time (27 women); includes 5 minority (1 African American, 1 Asian American or Pacific Islander, 3 Hispanic Americans), 10 international. Average age 54. 21 applicants, 95% accepted, 16 enrolled. In 2007, 19 master's, 4 other advanced degrees awarded. *Degree requirements:* For master's, thesis or alternative. *Entrance requirements:* For master's, minimum undergraduate GPA of 2.6 overall, 3.0 in major. Additional exam requirements/recommendations for international students: Required—TOEFL. *Application deadline:* For fall admission, 8/1 priority date for domestic students; for spring admission, 12/1 priority date for domestic students. Applications are processed on a rolling basis. Application fee: $65. *Expenses:* Tuition: Part-time $635 per unit. One-time fee: $340 part-time. Tuition and fees vary according to program. *Financial support:* In 2007–08, 6 students received support. Available to part-time students. Application deadline: 3/2; *Faculty research:* Medieval mystics, environmental justice, work and spirituality. *Unit head:* Dr. James Conlon, Program Director, 510-436-1046. *Application contact:* 800-430-1351, Fax: 510-436-1325, E-mail: admissions@hnu.edu.

Hope International University, School of Graduate Studies, Programs in Ministry, Fullerton, CA 92831-3138. Offers Christian leadership (MCM); church music (MA); church music (Korean track) (MCM); church planting (MCM); intercultural studies (MCM); worship (MCM). Part-time and evening/weekend programs available. Postbaccalaureate distance learning degree programs offered (minimal on-campus study). *Faculty:* 25. *Students:* 12 full-time (2 women), 42 part-time (15 women); includes 11 minority (2 African Americans, 7 Asian Americans or Pacific Islanders, 2 Hispanic Americans), 9 international. Average age 38. 16 applicants, 94% accepted, 14 enrolled. In 2007, 28 degrees awarded. *Degree requirements:* For master's, thesis (for some programs), project. *Entrance requirements:* For master's, minimum GPA of 3.0, MCM program requires an undergraduate degree in music, application, official transcripts, 2 references, statement of purpose. Additional exam requirements/recommendations for international students: Required—TOEFL (minimum score 550 paper-based; 213 computer-based; 86 iBT); Recommended—IELTS (minimum score 7). *Application deadline:* For fall admission, 8/3 priority date for domestic and international students; for winter admission, 12/14 priority date for domestic and international students; for spring admission, 1/4 priority date for domestic and international students. Applications are processed on a rolling basis. Application fee: $75. Electronic applications accepted. *Expenses: Contact institution. Financial support:* Scholarships/grants, health care benefits, and tuition waivers (partial) available. Support available to part-time students. Financial award applicants required to submit FAFSA. *Faculty research:* Church dynamics, growth methodologies. *Unit head:* Dr. David Timms, Chair, 714-879-3401 Ext. 2720, Fax: 714-681-7450, E-mail: djtimms@hiu.edu. *Application contact:* Ed Bort, Assistant Director of Admissions, 800-762-1294 Ext. 2322, Fax: 714-681-7450, E-mail: ebort@hiu.edu.

Iliff School of Theology, Graduate and Professional Programs, Denver, CO 80210-4798. Offers biblical studies (MA); church history (MA); religion (MA); religion and social change (MA); specialized ministry (MASM), including justice and peace, pastoral theology and care, religions leadership; theology (M Div, MTS, D Min, PhD), including Biblical studies (PhD), religion and psychological studies (PhD), religion and social change (PhD), theology, philosophy and culture (PhD); theology/ethics (MA). *Accreditation:* ACIPE; ATS. Part-time and evening/weekend programs available. *Degree requirements:* For master's, one foreign language, thesis (for some programs); for doctorate, 2 foreign languages, comprehensive exam, thesis/dissertation; for M Div, thesis/dissertation optional. *Entrance requirements:* For M Div, minimum GPA of 2.75, references; for master's, minimum GPA of 3.0, writing sample, references; for doctorate, GRE General Test, minimum GPA of 3.0, writing sample, letters of recommendation. Additional exam requirements/recommendations for international students: Required—TOEFL (minimum score 550 paper-based). Electronic applications accepted. *Faculty research:* Pastoral care, history, church music, contemporary church, biblical studies.

Indiana University Bloomington, University Graduate School, College of Arts and Sciences, Department of Religious Studies, Bloomington, IN 47405-7000. Offers MA, PhD. Part-time programs available. *Faculty:* 7 full-time (2 women). *Students:* 21 full-time (11 women), 6 part-time (3 women); includes 4 minority (3 Asian Americans or Pacific Islanders, 1 Hispanic American), 4 international. Average age 31. 91 applicants, 12% accepted, 7 enrolled. In 2007, 3 master's, 3 doctorates awarded. Terminal master's awarded for partial completion of doctoral program. *Degree requirements:* For master's, variable foreign language requirement, thesis or alternative; for doctorate, 2 foreign languages, thesis/dissertation. *Entrance requirements:* For master's, GRE General Test; for doctorate, GRE, MA, writing sample. Additional exam requirements/recommendations for international students: Required—TOEFL. *Application deadline:* For fall admission, 1/15 priority date for domestic students, 12/15 for international students; for spring admission, 9/1 for domestic and international students. Application fee: $50 ($60 for international students). *Financial support:* Fellowships, research assistantships, teaching assistantships, Federal Work-Study and institutionally sponsored loans available. Financial award application deadline: 2/1. *Unit head:* David Brakke, Chair, 812-855-3531. *Application contact:* Debra Melsheimer, Graduate Secretary, 812-855-3531, E-mail: dmelshei@indiana.edu.

The Jewish Theological Seminary, The Graduate School, New York, NY 10027-4649. Offers ancient Judaism (MA, DHL, PhD); Bible (MA, DHL, PhD); Jewish education (PhD); Jewish history (MA, DHL, PhD); Jewish literature (MA, DHL, PhD); Jewish philosophy (MA, DHL, PhD); liturgy (MA, DHL, PhD); medieval Jewish studies (MA, DHL, PhD); Midrash (MA, DHL, PhD); modern Jewish studies (MA, DHL, PhD); Talmud and rabbinics (MA, DHL, PhD); MA/MSW. *Accreditation:* ACIPE. Part-time programs available. *Faculty:* 62 full-time (21 women), 69 part-time/adjunct (33 women). *Students:* 100 full-time (54 women), 26 part-time (12 women); includes 1 minority (Asian American or Pacific Islander), 1 international. Average age 38. 79 applicants, 78% accepted, 28 enrolled. In 2007, 40 master's, 3 doctorates awarded. Terminal master's awarded for partial completion of doctoral program. *Degree requirements:* For master's, one foreign language, comprehensive exam (for some programs), thesis (for some programs); for doctorate, 3 foreign languages, comprehensive exam (for some programs), thesis/dissertation. *Entrance requirements:* For master's, GRE or MAT, 3 letters of recommendation, writing sample; for doctorate, GRE or MAT, 3 letters of recommendation, writing research sample. Additional exam requirements/recommendations for international students: Required—TOEFL (minimum score 100 computer-based). *Application deadline:* For fall admission, 1/15 priority date for domestic students. Applications are processed on a rolling basis. Application fee: $50. *Expenses:* Tuition: Full-time $20,340; part-time $950 per credit. Required fees: $380 per semester. Full-time tuition and fees vary according to degree level, program and student level. *Financial support:* In 2007–08, 49 fellowships (averaging $13,681 per year) were awarded; career-related internships or fieldwork and tuition waivers (full and partial) also available. Support available to part-time students. Financial award application deadline: 3/1; financial award applicants required to submit FAFSA. *Unit head:* Dr. Stephen Garfinkel, Dean, 212-678-8024, Fax: 212-678-8947, E-mail: gradschool@jtsa.edu. *Application contact:* Alayne Birnhak, Director, Graduate School of Admissions, 212-678-8032, Fax: 212-280-6022, E-mail: albirnhak@jtsa.edu.

See Close-Up on page 693.

John Carroll University, Graduate School, Department of Religious Studies, University Heights, OH 44118-4581. Offers MA. Part-time and evening/weekend programs available. *Faculty:* 11 full-time (2 women). *Students:* 6 full-time (3 women), 13 part-time (7 women); includes 1 minority (African American) Average age 38. 17 applicants, 71% accepted, 8 enrolled. In 2007, 7 degrees awarded. *Degree requirements:* For master's, comprehensive exam, thesis (for some programs), research essay or thesis, foreign language proficiency. *Entrance requirements:* For master's, GRE General Test or MAT, minimum 2.5 GPA. Additional exam requirements/recommendations for international students: Required—TOEFL. *Application deadline:* For fall admission, 8/30 priority date for domestic students; for spring admission, 1/11 priority date for domestic students. Applications are processed on a rolling basis. Application fee: $25 ($35 for international students). Electronic applications accepted. *Financial support:* In 2007–08, 8 students received support, including 4 teaching assistantships with full tuition reimbursements available (averaging $8,400 per year); scholarships/grants, tuition waivers (partial), and unspecified assistantships also available. Support available to part-time students. Financial award application deadline: 3/1; financial award applicants required to submit FAFSA. *Faculty research:* Ethics, women's studies, contemporary theology, Bible studies, Latin American theology. *Unit head:* Dr. John R. Spencer, Chairperson, 216-397-4705, Fax: 216-397-4518, E-mail: spencer@jcu.edu.

Kentucky Christian University, Graduate School, Grayson, KY 41143-2205. Offers Christian leadership (MA); New Testament (MA). Part-time programs available. *Faculty:* 6 part-time/adjunct (0 women). *Students:* 2 full-time (0 women), 17 part-time (3 women), 3 international. Average age 33. 14 applicants, 86% accepted, 11 enrolled. In 2007, 6 degrees awarded. *Degree requirements:* For master's, comprehensive exam (for some programs), thesis optional. *Entrance requirements:* For master's, minimum cumulative GPA of 2.75 in major or 2.5 overall; 6 additional hours in Bible (for non-Biblical undergraduate majors). Additional exam requirements/recommendations for international students: Required—TOEFL (minimum score 550 paper-based; 213 computer-based). *Application deadline:* Applications are processed on a rolling basis. Application fee: $35. Electronic applications accepted. *Expenses:* Tuition: Full-time $4,050; part-time $225 per credit hour. *Financial support:* Teaching assistantships with full tuition reimbursements, scholarships/grants and unspecified assistantships available. Support available to part-time students. *Unit head:* Dr. David Fiensy, Graduate Dean, 606-474-3263, Fax: 606-474-3189, E-mail: dfiensy@kcu.edu. *Application contact:* Jane Shick, Academic Office Manager, 877-811-6391, Fax: 606-474-3189, E-mail: gradstudies@kcu.edu.

Knox Theological Seminary, Graduate Programs, Program in Christianity and Culture, Fort Lauderdale, FL 33308. Offers MA. Part-time and evening/weekend programs available. *Faculty:* 3 full-time (0 women). *Students:* 1 (woman) full-time, 33 part-time (16 women); includes 2 African Americans, 1 Asian American or Pacific Islander, 3 Hispanic Americans. Average age 40. 5 applicants, 100% accepted, 5 enrolled. In 2007, 13 degrees awarded. *Entrance requirements:* Additional exam requirements/recommendations for international students: Required—TOEFL, TWE. *Application deadline:* For fall admission, 6/1 priority date for domestic and international students; for winter admission, 12/1 priority date for domestic and international students; for spring admission, 1/1 priority date for domestic and international students. Applications are processed on a rolling basis. Application fee: $50. *Financial support:* In 2007–08, 19 students received support. Scholarships/grants available. Support available to part-time students. Financial award application deadline: 6/1. *Application contact:* Jim Dietz, Director of Student Services, 800-344-5669, Fax: 954-351-3343, E-mail: jdietz@knoxseminary.edu.

La Salle University, School of Arts and Sciences, Program in Theological, Pastoral and Liturgical Studies, Philadelphia, PA 19141-1199. Offers pastoral studies (MA); religion (MA); theological studies (MA). Part-time and evening/weekend programs available. *Faculty:* 5 full-time (1 woman), 6 part-time/adjunct (3 women). *Students:* 3 full-time (2 women), 47 part-time (24 women); includes 9 minority (4 African Americans, 2 Asian Americans or Pacific Islanders, 3 Hispanic Americans). Average age 47. 9 applicants, 89% accepted, 5 enrolled. In 2007, 20 degrees awarded. *Entrance requirements:* For master's, 26 credits in humanistic subjects, religion, theology, or ministry-related work. *Application deadline:* Applications are processed on a rolling basis. Application fee: $35. *Expenses:* Tuition: Full-time $16,300; part-time $550 per credit. Required fees: $85 per term. Tuition and fees vary according to program. *Financial support:* In 2007–08, 12 students received support. Scholarships/grants available. Financial award applicants required to submit FAFSA. *Unit head:* Rev. Francis Berna, OFM, Director, 215-951-1335, Fax: 215-951-1665, E-mail: berna@lasalle.edu.

La Sierra University, School of Religion, Riverside, CA 92515. Offers religion (MA); religious education (MA); religious studies (MA). *Accreditation:* ATS. Part-time programs available. *Degree requirements:* For master's, one foreign language, thesis or alternative. *Entrance requirements:* For master's, GRE General Test, minimum GPA of 3.0.

Lee University, Program in Religion, Cleveland, TN 37320-3450. Offers biblical studies (MA); theological studies (MA); youth and family ministry (MA). *Faculty:* 19 full-time (4 women), 1 (woman) part-time/adjunct. *Students:* 21 full-time (11 women), 23 part-time (8 women); includes 3 minority (1 African American, 1 American Indian/Alaska Native, 1 Hispanic American). Average age 26. 21 applicants, 81% accepted, 13 enrolled. In 2007, 14 degrees awarded. *Degree requirements:* For master's, comprehensive exam, thesis. *Entrance requirements:* For master's, GRE or MAT, minimum GPA of 3.0, 2 letters of recommendation, interview. Additional exam requirements/recommendations for international students: Required—TOEFL. *Application deadline:* For fall admission, 4/1 for domestic students; for spring admission, 10/1 for domestic students. Application fee: $25. *Expenses:* Tuition: Full-time $10,392; part-time $433 per credit. Required fees: $65 per term. Tuition and fees vary according to course load. *Financial support:* Career-related internships or fieldwork, Federal Work-Study, institutionally sponsored loans, scholarships/grants, and unspecified assistantships available. Financial award application deadline: 3/1; financial award applicants required to submit FAFSA. *Faculty research:* Book of Isaiah, Gospel of Mark, school of St. Victor of 12th century, spirit Christology, people groups of New Testament and Greek. Total annual research expenditures: $3,000. *Unit head:* Dr. Michael Fuller, Director, 423-614-8338, E-mail: mfuller@leeuniversity.edu. *Application contact:* Vicki Glasscock, Graduate Admissions Director, 423-614-8059, E-mail: vglasscock@leeuniversity.edu.

Liberty University, Liberty Theological Seminary and Graduate School, Lynchburg, VA 24502. Offers religious studies (M Div, MA, MAR, MRE, D Min); theology (Th M). Part-time programs available. Postbaccalaureate distance learning degree programs offered (minimal on-campus study). *Faculty:* 15 full-time (0 women), 48 part-time/adjunct (0 women). *Students:* 1,060 full-time (209 women), 1,933 part-time (331 women); includes 523 minority (356 African Americans, 19 American Indian/Alaska Native, 51 Asian Americans or Pacific Islanders, 97 Hispanic Americans), 173 international. Average age 38. In 2007, 25 first professional degrees, 210 master's, 8 doctorates awarded. *Degree requirements:* For master's, 2 foreign languages, thesis (for some programs); for doctorate, 2 foreign languages, thesis/dissertation. *Entrance requirements:* For M Div, minimum undergraduate GPA of 2.0; for master's, minimum undergraduate GPA of 2.0, 9 credit hours of course work in Greek, 9 credit hours of course work in Hebrew (Th M); for doctorate, GRE General Test or MAT. Additional exam requirements/recommendations for international students: Required—TOEFL (minimum score 550 paper-based; 213 computer-based). *Application deadline:* For fall admission, 6/1 priority date for domestic students; for spring admission, 11/1 for domestic students. Applications are processed on a rolling basis. Application fee: $50. Electronic applications accepted. *Expenses: Contact institution.* Tuition and fees vary according to program. *Financial support:* In 2007–08, 844 students received support, including 5 teaching assistantships with tuition reimbursements available; career-related internships or fieldwork and Federal Work-Study also available. *Unit head:* Dr. Ergun Caner, Dean, 434-582-2099, Fax: 434-522-0415, E-mail: ecaner@liberty.edu. *Application contact:* Kyle A Falce, Director of Graduate Admissions, 800-424-9596, Fax: 800-628-7977, E-mail: gradadmissions@liberty.edu.

Lipscomb University, Hazelip School of Theology, Nashville, TN 37204-3951. Offers biblical studies (MA); Christian studies (MA); divinity (M Div); ministry (MA); New Testament (MA); Old

Testament (MA); theological studies (MTS); theology (MA). *Accreditation:* ATS. Part-time and evening/weekend programs available. *Faculty:* 7 full-time (0 women), 3 part-time/adjunct (0 women). *Students:* 19 full-time (1 woman), 66 part-time (9 women); includes 5 minority (all African Americans), 2 international. Average age 34. 30 applicants, 80% accepted, 21 enrolled. In 2007, 4 first professional degrees, 12 master's awarded. *Degree requirements:* For master's, 2 foreign languages, comprehensive exam (for some programs); for M Div, 2 foreign languages. *Entrance requirements:* For M Div and master's, 2 references. Additional exam requirements/recommendations for international students: Required—TOEFL (minimum score 570 paper-based; 230 computer-based). *Application deadline:* For fall admission, 8/14 priority date for domestic students; for spring admission, 12/31 for domestic students. Applications are processed on a rolling basis. Application fee: $0 ($75 for international students). Electronic applications accepted. *Expenses:* Tuition: Part-time $599 per semester hour. *Financial support:* Scholarships/grants available. Support available to part-time students. Financial award application deadline: 3/1; financial award applicants required to submit FAFSA. *Faculty research:* Status of Churches of Christ in foreign nations, Hebrew grammar, marriage and family. *Unit head:* Dr. Mark Black, Director, 615-966-1000 Ext. 5799, Fax: 615-966-1808, E-mail: mark.black@lipscomb.edu. *Application contact:* Audrey Everson, Information Contact, 615-966-6051, Fax: 615-966-6052, E-mail: audrey.everson@lipscomb.edu.

Loma Linda University, Faculty of Religion, Program in Religion and Science, Loma Linda, CA 92350. Offers MA. *Degree requirements:* For master's, comprehensive exam, thesis optional. *Entrance requirements:* Additional exam requirements/recommendations for international students: Required—TOEFL. *Application deadline:* For fall admission, 8/1 for domestic and international students; for winter admission, 11/1 for domestic and international students; for spring admission, 2/1 for domestic and international students. Electronic applications accepted. *Unit head:* Dr. Gerald Winslow, Dean, 909-824-4536.

Louisville Presbyterian Theological Seminary, Graduate and Professional Programs, Louisville, KY 40205-1798. Offers Bible (MAR); divinity (M Div); ministry (D Min); religious thought (MAR); theology (Th M); JD/M Div; M Div/MBA; M Div/MS; M Div/MSW. *Accreditation:* AAMFT/COAMFTE (one or more programs are accredited); ACIPE; ATS (one or more programs are accredited). Part-time programs available. *Faculty:* 21 full-time (10 women), 30 part-time/adjunct (11 women). *Students:* 148 full-time (81 women), 62 part-time (34 women); includes 37 minority (30 African Americans, 1 American Indian/Alaska Native, 2 Asian Americans or Pacific Islanders, 4 Hispanic Americans), 7 international. Average age 37. 121 applicants, 78% accepted, 62 enrolled. In 2007, 22 first professional degrees, 10 master's, 6 doctorates awarded. *Degree requirements:* For master's, one foreign language; for doctorate, thesis/dissertation; for M Div, 2 foreign languages. *Entrance requirements:* For master's, interview; for doctorate, M Div. Additional exam requirements/recommendations for international students: Required—TOEFL (minimum score 550 paper-based; 213 computer-based). *Application deadline:* For fall admission, 6/15 priority date for domestic students, 6/1 priority date for international students; for spring admission, 11/15 priority date for domestic and international students. Applications are processed on a rolling basis. Application fee: $60. Electronic applications accepted. *Expenses:* Tuition: Full-time $9,300; part-time $310 per credit. Required fees: $227. *Financial support:* Career-related internships or fieldwork, Federal Work-Study, institutionally sponsored loans, and scholarships/grants available. Financial award application deadline: 4/15; financial award applicants required to submit CSS PROFILE or FAFSA. *Unit head:* Dr. David Hester, Dean, 502-895-3411 Ext. 294, Fax: 502-895-1096, E-mail: dhester@lpts.edu. *Application contact:* Cheri Harper, Director of Admissions, 502-895-3411 Ext. 371, Fax: 502-895-1096, E-mail: charper@lpts.edu.

Loyola University Chicago, Institute of Pastoral Studies, Chicago, IL 60611-2196. Offers divinity (M Div); pastoral counseling (MA, Certificate), including pastoral counseling (MA), pastoral studies (MA), spiritual development (Certificate); pastoral studies (MA); religious education (Certificate); social justice (MA); spiritual direction (Certificate); spirituality (MA); M Div/MA; M Div/MSN; M Div/MSW. *Accreditation:* ACIPE. Part-time and evening/weekend programs available. *Faculty:* 6 full-time (1 woman), 33 part-time/adjunct (16 women). *Students:* 154 full-time (91 women), 103 part-time (74 women); includes 19 minority (11 African Americans, 2 Asian Americans or Pacific Islanders, 6 Hispanic Americans), 13 international. Average age 42. 136 applicants, 83% accepted, 86 enrolled. In 2007, 3 first professional degrees, 54 master's awarded. *Degree requirements:* For master's, thesis optional, project; for M Div, project. *Entrance requirements:* For master's, interview. Additional exam requirements/recommendations for international students: Required—TOEFL. *Application deadline:* Applications are processed on a rolling basis. Application fee: $50. Electronic applications accepted. *Expenses: Contact institution.* Full-time tuition and fees vary according to program. *Financial support:* In 2007–08, 84 students received support. Career-related internships or fieldwork, Federal Work-Study, institutionally sponsored loans, scholarships/grants, and tuition waivers (partial) available. Support available to part-time students. Financial award application deadline: 3/1; financial award applicants required to submit FAFSA. *Faculty research:* Catholic theology, skills of religious ministry, family ministries, spirituality and divorced men. *Unit head:* Dr. Robert A. Ludwig, Director, 312-915-7467, Fax: 312-915-7410, E-mail: rludwig@luc.edu. *Application contact:* Randy Gibbons, Administrative Assistant, 312-915-7450, Fax: 312-915-7410, E-mail: rgibbon@luc.edu.

Lutheran Theological Seminary at Gettysburg, Graduate and Professional Programs, Gettysburg, PA 17325-1795. Offers divinity (M Div); ministerial studies (MAMS); outdoor ministry (MAR); parish ministry (D Min); theology (STM). *Accreditation:* ACIPE; ATS (one or more programs are accredited). Part-time programs available. Postbaccalaureate distance learning degree programs offered (no on-campus study). *Degree requirements:* For master's, thesis (for some programs); for M Div, one foreign language. Electronic applications accepted.

The Lutheran Theological Seminary at Philadelphia, Graduate School, Philadelphia, PA 19119-1794. Offers divinity (M Div); ministry (D Min); religion (MAR); social ministry (Certificate); theology (STM). *Accreditation:* ACIPE; ATS. Part-time and evening/weekend programs available. *Faculty:* 22 full-time (6 women), 26 part-time/adjunct (11 women). *Students:* 144 full-time (74 women), 263 part-time (127 women); includes 92 minority (80 African Americans, 2 Asian Americans or Pacific Islanders, 10 Hispanic Americans), 14 international. Average age 43. 123 applicants, 86% accepted, 84 enrolled. In 2007, 44 first professional degrees, 10 master's, 15 doctorates awarded. *Median time to degree:* Of those who began their doctoral program in fall 1999, 70% received their degree in 8 years or less. *Degree requirements:* For master's, one foreign language, comprehensive exam (for some programs), thesis (for some programs); for doctorate, thesis/dissertation; for M Div, 2 foreign languages. *Entrance requirements:* For M Div and master's, minimum undergraduate GPA of 2.8; for doctorate, minimum first professional GPA of 3.0. Additional exam requirements/recommendations for international students: Required—TOEFL (minimum score 550 paper-based; 213 computer-based), TWE. *Application deadline:* For fall admission, 6/1 priority date for domestic students. Applications are processed on a rolling basis. Application fee: $35. Electronic applications accepted. *Expenses:* Tuition: Part-time $1,260 per unit. Part-time tuition and fees vary according to program. *Financial support:* In 2007–08, 102 students received support, including 1 research assistantship with tuition reimbursement available (averaging $2,250 per year), 3 teaching assistantships with tuition reimbursements available (averaging $1,200 per year); career-related internships or fieldwork and Federal Work-Study also available. Financial award application deadline: 7/1; financial award applicants required to submit FAFSA. *Unit head:* Dr. J. Paul Rajashekar, Dean, 215-248-6379, Fax: 215-248-4577, E-mail: rajashekar@ltsp.edu. *Application contact:* Rev. Louise Johnson, Director of Admissions, 800-286-4616 Ext. 6321, Fax: 215-248-7315, E-mail: admissions@ltsp.edu.

McGill University, Faculty of Graduate and Postdoctoral Studies, Faculty of Religious Studies, Montréal, QC H3A 2T5, Canada. Offers MA, STM, PhD. *Accreditation:* ATS. *Faculty:* 15 full-time (4 women), 26 part-time/adjunct (9 women). *Students:* 59 full-time (21 women), 9 part-time. 63 applicants, 52% accepted, 11 enrolled. In 2007, 8 master's, 5 doctorates awarded.

McMaster University, School of Graduate Studies, Faculty of Social Sciences, Department of Religious Studies, Hamilton, ON L8S 4M2, Canada. Offers MA, PhD. Part-time programs available. *Faculty:* 13 full-time, 4 part-time/adjunct. *Students:* 59 full-time, 6 part-time. 52 applicants, 25% accepted. *Degree requirements:* For master's, one foreign language, thesis; for doctorate, 2 foreign languages, comprehensive exam, thesis/dissertation. *Entrance requirements:* For master's, minimum B+ average. Additional exam requirements/recommendations for international students: Required—TOEFL (minimum score 580 paper-based; 237 computer-based). *Application deadline:* For fall admission, 1/31 priority date for domestic students. Applications are processed on a rolling basis. Application fee: $90. *Financial support:* In 2007–08, 31 fellowships, teaching assistantships (averaging $8,440 per year) were awarded; scholarships/grants also available. *Faculty research:* Hellenistic Judaism, religious biographies in Asia, medieval India, synoptic gospels, ritual and belief systems. *Unit head:* Dr. Eileen Schuller, Chair, 905-525-9140, Fax: 905-525-8161. *Application contact:* Doreen Drew, Graduate Secretary, 905-525-9140 Ext. 23399, Fax: 905-525-8161, E-mail: relstud@mcmaster.ca.

Memorial University of Newfoundland, School of Graduate Studies, Department of Religious Studies, St. John's, NL A1C 5S7, Canada. Offers MA. Part-time programs available. *Degree requirements:* For master's, one foreign language, thesis. *Entrance requirements:* For master's, honors degree in religious studies or equivalent. Electronic applications accepted. *Faculty research:* Biblical studies, Christian thought and history, world religions, ethics, contemporary spirituality.

Miami University, Graduate School, College of Arts and Sciences, Department of Comparative Religion, Oxford, OH 45056. Offers MA. Part-time programs available. *Degree requirements:* For master's, one foreign language, thesis, final exam. *Entrance requirements:* For master's, minimum undergraduate GPA of 3.0 during previous 2 years or 2.75 overall. Additional exam requirements/recommendations for international students: Required—TOEFL (minimum score 550 paper-based; 213 computer-based), TWE (minimum score 4). Electronic applications accepted.

Missouri State University, Graduate College, College of Humanities and Public Affairs, Department of Religious Studies, Springfield, MO 65804-0094. Offers MA. Part-time and evening/weekend programs available. *Faculty:* 11 full-time (4 women). *Students:* 13 full-time (5 women), 15 part-time (6 women); includes 2 minority (1 American Indian/Alaska Native, 1 Asian American or Pacific Islander). Average age 35. 12 applicants, 100% accepted, 5 enrolled. In 2007, 5 degrees awarded. *Degree requirements:* For master's, one foreign language, comprehensive exam, thesis or alternative. *Entrance requirements:* For master's, GRE, minimum GPA of 3.2. Additional exam requirements/recommendations for international students: Required—TOEFL (minimum score 550 paper-based; 213 computer-based; 79 iBT). *Application deadline:* For fall admission, 7/20 priority date for domestic students; for spring admission, 12/20 priority date for domestic students. Applications are processed on a rolling basis. Application fee: $35. Electronic applications accepted. *Expenses:* Tuition, state resident: full-time $3,708; part-time $206 per credit hour. Tuition, nonresident: full-time $7,236; part-time $206 per credit hour. Required fees: $622. Full-time tuition and fees vary according to course level, course load, program and reciprocity agreements. *Financial support:* Research assistantships with full tuition reimbursements, teaching assistantships with full tuition reimbursements, Federal Work-Study, scholarships/grants, and unspecified assistantships available. Financial award application deadline: 3/31; financial award applicants required to submit FAFSA. *Unit head:* Dr. J. E. Llewellyn, Head, 417-836-5514, Fax: 417-836-4757.

Mount St. Mary's College, Graduate Division, Program in Religious Studies, Los Angeles, CA 90049-1599. Offers MA. Part-time and evening/weekend programs available. *Faculty:* 3 part-time/adjunct (2 women). *Students:* 4 full-time (3 women), 19 part-time (15 women); includes 9 minority (1 African American, 2 Asian Americans or Pacific Islanders, 6 Hispanic Americans). Average age 43. In 2007, 6 degrees awarded. *Degree requirements:* For master's, thesis. *Entrance requirements:* For master's, MAT, minimum GPA of 3.0. *Application deadline:* For fall admission, 7/15 priority date for international students; for spring admission, 11/15 priority date for international students. Application fee: $50 ($75 for international students). *Expenses:* Tuition: Part-time $662 per unit. *Financial support:* Institutionally sponsored loans and tuition waivers (partial) available. Support available to part-time students. Financial award application deadline: 3/15. *Faculty research:* Scripture, systematics, ethics, religious education for Mexican-Americans. *Unit head:* Fr. Guillermo Garcia, Director, Graduate Religious Studies, 213-477-2641, E-mail: ggarcia@msmc.la.edu. *Application contact:* Jessica M. Bibeau, Director of Graduate Admission, 213-477-2800 Ext. 2798, Fax: 213-477-2797, E-mail: jbibeau@msmc.la.edu.

Naropa University, Graduate Programs, Program in Indo-Tibetan Buddhism, Boulder, CO 80302-6697. Offers MA. *Faculty:* 6 full-time (2 women), 19 part-time/adjunct (8 women). *Students:* 7 full-time (5 women), 3 part-time (1 woman); includes 2 minority (both Asian Americans or Pacific Islanders), 2 international. Average age 37. 6 applicants, 83% accepted, 4 enrolled. In 2007, 5 degrees awarded. *Degree requirements:* For master's, comprehensive exam, thesis. *Entrance requirements:* For master's, writing sample, interview (by phone or in-person). Additional exam requirements/recommendations for international students: Required—TOEFL (minimum score 600 paper-based; 250 computer-based). *Application deadline:* For fall admission, 1/15 priority date for domestic and international students; for spring admission, 10/15 priority date for domestic students. Applications are processed on a rolling basis. Application fee: $60. Electronic applications accepted. *Expenses:* Tuition: Full-time $15,070; part-time $685 per credit. Required fees: $250 per semester. Tuition and fees vary according to course load. *Financial support:* In 2007–08, 5 students received support, including 1 research assistantship with partial tuition reimbursement available (averaging $3,000 per year), teaching assistantships with partial tuition reimbursements available (averaging $3,000 per year); career-related internships or fieldwork, Federal Work-Study, scholarships/grants, health care benefits, tuition waivers (partial), and unspecified assistantships also available. Support available to part-time students. Financial award application deadline: 3/1; financial award applicants required to submit FAFSA. *Unit head:* Phillip Stanley, Co-Chair, 303-245-4728. *Application contact:* Donna McIntyre, Admissions Counselor, 303-546-3555, Fax: 303-546-3583, E-mail: donna@naropa.edu.

See Close-Up on page 1449.

Naropa University, Graduate Programs, Program in Indo-Tibetan Buddhism with Language, Boulder, CO 80302-6697. Offers MA. *Faculty:* 6 full-time (2 women), 19 part-time/adjunct (8 women). *Students:* 12 full-time (3 women), 3 part-time (2 women); includes 1 minority (Hispanic American), 1 international. Average age 32. 20 applicants, 70% accepted, 7 enrolled. In 2007, 5 degrees awarded. *Degree requirements:* For master's, comprehensive exam, thesis. *Entrance requirements:* For master's, writing sample, interview (by phone or in-person). Additional exam requirements/recommendations for international students: Required—TOEFL (minimum score 600 paper-based; 250 computer-based). *Application deadline:* For fall admission, 1/15 priority date for domestic and international students; for spring admission, 10/15 priority date for domestic students. Applications are processed on a rolling basis. Application fee: $60. Electronic applications accepted. *Expenses:* Tuition: Full-time $15,070; part-time $685 per credit. Required fees: $250 per semester. Tuition and fees vary according to course load. *Financial support:* In 2007–08, 11 students received support, including 1 research assistantship with partial tuition reimbursement available (averaging $3,000 per year), 5 teaching assistantships with partial tuition reimbursements available (averaging $3,000 per year); career-related internships or fieldwork, Federal Work-Study, scholarships/grants, tuition waivers (partial), and unspecified assistantships also available. Support available to part-time students. Financial award application deadline: 3/1; financial award applicants required to submit FAFSA. *Unit head:* Roger Dorris, Co-Chair, 303-546-0937. *Application contact:* Donna McIntyre, Admissions Counselor, 303-546-3555, Fax: 303-546-3583, E-mail: donna@naropa.edu.

See Close-Up on page 1449.

Naropa University, Graduate Programs, Program in Religious Studies, Boulder, CO 80302-6697. Offers MA. *Faculty:* 6 full-time (2 women), 19 part-time/adjunct (8 women). *Students:* 9 full-time (3 women), 7 part-time (4 women); includes 1 minority (Asian American or Pacific

Religion

Naropa University (continued)

Islander) Average age 33. 12 applicants, 75% accepted, 3 enrolled. In 2007, 6 degrees awarded. *Degree requirements:* For master's, thesis. *Entrance requirements:* For master's, interview (by phone or in-person), writing sample. Additional exam requirements/recommendations for international students: Required—TOEFL (minimum score 600 paper-based; 250 computer-based). *Application deadline:* For fall admission, 1/15 priority date for domestic and international students; for spring admission, 10/15 priority date for domestic students. Applications are processed on a rolling basis. Application fee: $60. Electronic applications accepted. *Expenses:* Tuition: Full-time $15,070; part-time $685 per credit. Required fees: $250 per semester. Tuition and fees vary according to course load. *Financial support:* In 2007–08, 12 students received support, including 1 research assistantship with partial tuition reimbursement available (averaging $3,000 per year), 1 teaching assistantship with partial tuition reimbursement available (averaging $3,000 per year); career-related internships or fieldwork, Federal Work-Study, scholarships/grants, tuition waivers (partial), and unspecified assistantships also available. Support available to part-time students. Financial award application deadline: 3/1; financial award applicants required to submit FAFSA. *Unit head:* Phillip Stanley, Co-Chair, 303-245-4728. *Application contact:* Donna McIntyre, Admissions Counselor, 303-546-3555, Fax: 303-546-3583, E-mail: donna@naropa.edu.

See Close-Up on page 1449.

Naropa University, Graduate Programs, Program in Religious Studies with Language, Boulder, CO 80302-6697. Offers MA. *Faculty:* 6 full-time (2 women), 19 part-time/adjunct (8 women). *Students:* 6 full-time (2 women), 2 part-time; includes 1 minority (Asian American or Pacific Islander), 1 international. Average age 27. 11 applicants, 82% accepted, 4 enrolled. In 2007, 1 degree awarded. *Degree requirements:* For master's, thesis, off campus language intensive. *Entrance requirements:* For master's, interview, writing sample. *Expenses:* Tuition: Full-time $15,070; part-time $685 per credit. Required fees: $250 per semester. Tuition and fees vary according to course load. *Financial support:* In 2007–08, 4 students received support, including research assistantships with partial tuition reimbursements available (averaging $3,000 per year), teaching assistantships with partial tuition reimbursements available (averaging $3,000 per year); Federal Work-Study, scholarships/grants, health care benefits, tuition waivers (partial), and unspecified assistantships also available. Support available to part-time students. Financial award applicants required to submit FAFSA. *Unit head:* Dr. Roger Dorris, Co-Chair, 303-245-4730. *Application contact:* Donna McIntyre, Admissions Counselor, 303-546-3555, Fax: 303-546-3583, E-mail: donna@naropa.edu.

See Close-Up on page 1449.

New Life Theological Seminary, Graduate Program, Charlotte, NC 28206-7901. Offers urban Christian ministry (MA), including Biblical studies, church planting, divinity, youth/music. Part-time and evening/weekend programs available. *Faculty:* 4 full-time (0 women), 4 part-time/adjunct (1 woman). *Students:* 10 full-time (2 women), 5 part-time (2 women); includes 6 minority (all African Americans), 5 international. Average age 40. 6 applicants, 100% accepted, 6 enrolled. In 2007, 3 degrees awarded. *Degree requirements:* For master's, thesis. *Application deadline:* For fall admission, 8/22 for domestic and international students; for spring admission, 1/22 for domestic and international students. Application fee: $40 ($140 for international students). Electronic applications accepted. *Expenses:* Tuition: Part-time $770 per course. Required fees: $110 per semester. Tuition and fees vary according to course load. *Financial support:* Federal Work-Study and scholarships/grants available. Financial award application deadline: 4/1; financial award applicants required to submit FAFSA.

New York University, Graduate School of Arts and Science, Draper Interdisciplinary Program in Humanities and Social Thought, New York, NY 10012-1019. Offers humanities and social thought (MA); religion (Advanced Certificate); social theory (Advanced Certificate). Part-time programs available. *Faculty:* 6 full-time (3 women). *Students:* 87 full-time (58 women), 130 part-time (85 women); includes 32 minority (7 African Americans, 13 Asian Americans or Pacific Islanders, 12 Hispanic Americans), 12 international. Average age 28. 259 applicants, 56% accepted, 88 enrolled. In 2007, 64 degrees awarded. *Degree requirements:* For master's, thesis, comprehensive exam or essay. *Entrance requirements:* For degree, master's degree. Additional exam requirements/recommendations for international students: Required—TOEFL. *Application deadline:* For fall admission, 7/1 for domestic students; for spring admission, 12/1 for domestic students. Applications are processed on a rolling basis. Application fee: $85. *Financial support:* Teaching assistantships with tuition reimbursements, Federal Work-Study, institutionally sponsored loans, and tuition waivers (partial) available. Financial award application deadline: 7/1; financial award applicants required to submit FAFSA. *Faculty research:* Art world, gender politics, global histories, literary cultures, the city. *Unit head:* Robin Nagle, Director, 212-998-8070, Fax: 212-995-4691, E-mail: draper.program@nyu.edu. *Application contact:* Robert Dimit, Associate Director, 212-998-8070, Fax: 212-995-4691, E-mail: draper.program@nyu.edu.

New York University, Graduate School of Arts and Science, Program in Religious Studies, New York, NY 10012-1019. Offers MA. Part-time programs available. *Faculty:* 3 full-time (0 women), 5 part-time/adjunct. *Students:* 4 full-time (2 women), 5 part-time (all women), 1 international. Average age 27. 25 applicants, 52% accepted, 7 enrolled. In 2007, 1 degree awarded. *Degree requirements:* For master's, one foreign language, thesis. *Entrance requirements:* For master's, GRE General Test. Additional exam requirements/recommendations for international students: Required—TOEFL. *Application deadline:* For fall admission, 1/4 priority date for domestic students. Application fee: $55. *Financial support:* Teaching assistantships with tuition reimbursements, Federal Work-Study and institutionally sponsored loans available. Financial award application deadline: 4/15; financial award applicants required to submit FAFSA. *Faculty research:* Biblical and rabbinic Judaism, New Testament and early Christianity, comparative mysticism, gender and embodiment, East Asian religions. *Unit head:* Angela Zito, Director, 212-998-3756, Fax: 212-995-4827, E-mail: religious.studies@nyu.edu. *Application contact:* Michael West, Information Contact, 212-998-3756, Fax: 212-995-4827, E-mail: religious.studies@nyu.edu.

Northern Baptist Theological Seminary, Graduate and Professional Programs, Lombard, IL 60148-5698. Offers Bible (MA); Christian ministries (MACM); divinity (M Div); ethics (MA); history (MA); ministry (D Min); theology (MA); worship/spirituality (MAWS); youth ministry (MAYM). *Accreditation:* ATS. Part-time programs available. *Faculty:* 6 full-time (1 woman), 29 part-time/adjunct (6 women). *Students:* 98 full-time (22 women), 91 part-time (32 women); includes 67 minority (51 African Americans, 12 Asian Americans or Pacific Islanders, 4 Hispanic Americans), 3 international. Average age 40. 71 applicants, 90% accepted. In 2007, 21 first professional degrees, 10 master's, 13 doctorates awarded. *Degree requirements:* For doctorate, thesis/dissertation; for M Div, field experience. *Entrance requirements:* For doctorate, 3 years in the ministry post-M Div. Additional exam requirements/recommendations for international students: Required—TOEFL. *Application deadline:* For fall admission, 9/1 priority date for domestic students, 2/1 priority date for international students; for winter admission, 12/1 priority date for domestic students; for spring admission, 3/1 priority date for domestic students. Applications are processed on a rolling basis. Application fee: $35. Electronic applications accepted. *Expenses:* Tuition: Full-time $11,340; part-time $420 per hour. Required fees: $300. Tuition and fees vary according to degree level. *Financial support:* In 2007–08, 68 students received support. Career-related internships or fieldwork and scholarships/grants available. Support available to part-time students. Financial award application deadline: 9/1. *Faculty research:* Theology, worship studies, church history, evangelism, Bible. *Unit head:* Dr. Charles Hambrick-Stowe, Dean, 630-620-2103, Fax: 630-620-2190. *Application contact:* Greg Henson, Director of Enrollment Management, 630-620-2191, Fax: 630-620-2190, E-mail: admissions@seminary.edu.

Northwest Nazarene University, Graduate Studies, Program in Religion, Nampa, ID 83686-5897. Offers Christian education (MA); missional leadership (MA); pastoral ministry (MA); religion (M Div); spiritual formation (MA). Part-time and evening/weekend programs available. Postbaccalaureate distance learning degree programs offered (no on-campus study). *Faculty:* 9 full-time (3 women), 15 part-time/adjunct (3 women). *Students:* 131 full-time (35 women), 12 part-time (5 women); includes 9 minority (1 African American, 1 American Indian/Alaska Native, 5 Asian Americans or Pacific Islanders, 2 Hispanic Americans), 3 international. In 2007, 29 degrees awarded. *Application deadline:* Applications are processed on a rolling basis. Application fee: $50. Electronic applications accepted. *Unit head:* Dr. Jay Akkerman, Director, Graduate Studies, 208-467-8437, Fax: 208-467-8252.

Oblate School of Theology, Graduate and Professional Programs, San Antonio, TX 78216-6693. Offers divinity (M Div); Hispanic ministry (D Min); pastoral ministry (MAP Min); pastoral studies (Certificate); spirituality (MA Sp); supervision (D Min), including clinical pastoral education, general supervision; theology (MA Th); M Div/MA Th. *Accreditation:* ACIPE; ATS (one or more programs are accredited). Part-time programs available. *Faculty:* 19 full-time (4 women), 3 part-time/adjunct (0 women). *Students:* 91 full-time (9 women), 70 part-time (29 women); includes 67 minority (9 African Americans, 1 American Indian/Alaska Native, 11 Asian Americans or Pacific Islanders, 46 Hispanic Americans), 33 international. Average age 39. 58 applicants, 100% accepted, 55 enrolled. In 2007, 15 first professional degrees, 8 master's, 9 Certificates awarded. *Degree requirements:* For master's, thesis (for some programs), practicum; for doctorate, paper, practicum; for M Div, one foreign language, seminar. *Entrance requirements:* For M Div, MAT, interview, course work in philosophy and theology; for master's, MAT, interview, course work in theology or religious studies, minimum GPA of 2.5; for doctorate, M Div. Additional exam requirements/recommendations for international students: Required—TOEFL (minimum score 197 computer-based; 71 iBT). *Application deadline:* For fall admission, 6/15 priority date for domestic and international students; for spring admission, 12/30 for domestic and international students. Applications are processed on a rolling basis. Application fee: $45. *Expenses:* Tuition: Full-time $11,232; part-time $432 per credit. Required fees: $160 per semester. One-time fee: $85 full-time. Tuition and fees vary according to course load and degree level. *Financial support:* Scholarships/grants available. Support available to part-time students. Financial award application deadline: 8/1; financial award applicants required to submit FAFSA. *Unit head:* Sr. Elaine Brothers, Academic Dean, 210-341-1366, Fax: 214-341-4519, E-mail: ebrothers@ost.edu. *Application contact:* James Oberhausen, Director of Admission/Registrar, 210-341-1366 Ext. 212, Fax: 210-341-4519, E-mail: registrar@ost.edu.

Oklahoma City University, Wimberly School of Religion and Graduate Theological Center, Oklahoma City, OK 73106-1402. Offers M Rel, MAR. Part-time and evening/weekend programs available. *Faculty:* 4 full-time (2 women), 5 part-time/adjunct (2 women). *Students:* 5 full-time (4 women), 1 (woman) part-time; includes 2 minority (both African Americans), 1 international. Average age 32. 3 applicants, 67% accepted. *Degree requirements:* For master's, thesis. *Entrance requirements:* For master's, minimum GPA of 2.7. Additional exam requirements/recommendations for international students: Required—TOEFL. *Application deadline:* For fall admission, 8/22 for domestic students; for spring admission, 1/9 for domestic students. Applications are processed on a rolling basis. Application fee: $30 ($70 for international students). *Expenses:* Tuition: Full-time $14,040; part-time $780 per hour. Required fees: $881; $32 per hour. *Financial support:* Fellowships with partial tuition reimbursements, career-related internships or fieldwork, Federal Work-Study, institutionally sponsored loans, and tuition waivers (partial) available. Support available to part-time students. Financial award applicants required to submit FAFSA. *Faculty research:* Biblical studies, church history, social ethics, world religions. *Unit head:* Dr. Mark Davies, Dean, 405-208-5284, Fax: 405-208-6046, E-mail: mdavies@okcu.edu. *Application contact:* Leslie Mckenzie, Director, Graduate Admissions, 800-633-7242, Fax: 405-208-5356, E-mail: gadmissions@okcu.edu.

Olivet Nazarene University, Graduate School, Division of Religion and Philosophy, Bourbonnais, IL 60914-2271. Offers biblical literature (MA); religion (MA); theology (MA). Part-time programs available. *Degree requirements:* For master's, thesis or alternative.

Oxford Graduate School, Graduate Programs, Dayton, TN 37321-6736. Offers family life education (M Litt); organizational leadership in nonprofits (M Litt); religion and society (D Phil).

Pacific School of Religion, Graduate and Professional Programs, Berkeley, CA 94709-1323. Offers M Div, MA, MTS, D Min, PhD, Th D, CAPS, CMS, CSS, CTS. *Accreditation:* ACIPE; ATS (one or more programs are accredited). Part-time programs available. *Degree requirements:* For master's, one foreign language, thesis (for some programs); for doctorate, thesis/dissertation. *Entrance requirements:* For M Div and master's, minimum GPA of 3.0; for doctorate, M Div, minimum GPA of 3.0 (D Min); for other advanced degree, M Div, minimum GPA of 3.0 (CAPS). Additional exam requirements/recommendations for international students: Required—TOEFL (minimum score 550 paper-based; 213 computer-based). Electronic applications accepted. *Faculty research:* Medical ethics, gay/lesbian studies in religion, Asian-American religion, race, culture and theology, theology in context.

Pepperdine University, Seaver College, Division of Religion, Malibu, CA 90263. Offers ministry (MS); religion (M Div, MA). Part-time and evening/weekend programs available. *Degree requirements:* For master's, 2 foreign languages, thesis (for some programs). *Entrance requirements:* For master's, GRE General Test. Additional exam requirements/recommendations for international students: Required—TOEFL.

Point Loma Nazarene University, Graduate Studies, Program in Religion, San Diego, CA 92106-2899. Offers M Min, MA. Part-time programs available. Postbaccalaureate distance learning degree programs offered (minimal on-campus study). *Students:* 10 full-time (3 women), 16 part-time (5 women); includes 9 minority (1 African American, 1 American Indian/Alaska Native, 1 Asian American or Pacific Islander, 6 Hispanic Americans). Average age 38. In 2007, 8 degrees awarded. *Degree requirements:* For master's, thesis optional. *Entrance requirements:* For master's, GRE General Test, letters of recommendation, writing sample. *Application deadline:* For fall admission, 5/15 priority date for domestic students; for spring admission, 11/1 for domestic students. Applications are processed on a rolling basis. Application fee: $35. *Expenses:* Tuition: Full-time $2,790. Tuition and fees vary according to campus/location and program. *Financial support:* Available to part-time students. Application deadline: 4/10. *Faculty research:* Theology, Christian education, church administration. *Unit head:* Dr. Sam Powell, Dean, 619-849-2334, Fax: 619-849-7008.

Princeton Theological Seminary, Graduate and Professional Programs, Princeton, NJ 08542-0803. Offers M Div, MA, Th M, D Min, PhD. *Accreditation:* ACIPE; ATS. Part-time programs available. Terminal master's awarded for partial completion of doctoral program. *Degree requirements:* For doctorate, 2 foreign languages, thesis/dissertation, comprehensive exam (PhD), French and German. *Entrance requirements:* For doctorate, GRE General Test. Additional exam requirements/recommendations for international students: Required—TOEFL. Electronic applications accepted.

Princeton University, Graduate School, Department of Religion, Princeton, NJ 08544-1019. Offers PhD. *Degree requirements:* For doctorate, variable foreign language requirement, comprehensive exam, thesis/dissertation. *Entrance requirements:* For doctorate, GRE General Test. Additional exam requirements/recommendations for international students: Required—TOEFL (minimum score 600 paper-based; 250 computer-based). Electronic applications accepted.

Providence College, Graduate Studies, Department of Religious Studies, Providence, RI 02918. Offers biblical studies (MA); pastoral ministry (MA); religious education (MA); religious studies (MA). Part-time and evening/weekend programs available. *Faculty:* 7 full-time (0 women). *Students:* 6 full-time (0 women), 21 part-time (6 women). Average age 40. 8 applicants, 75% accepted. In 2007, 9 degrees awarded. *Degree requirements:* For master's, comprehensive exam, Greek and Hebrew (biblical studies). *Entrance requirements:* Additional exam requirements/recommendations for international students: Required—TOEFL (minimum score 550 paper-based; 213 computer-based; 79 iBT). *Application deadline:* For fall admission, 8/1 for domestic students; for spring admission, 12/1 for domestic students. Applications are processed on a rolling basis. Application fee: $55. *Expenses:* Tuition: Full-time $6,783; part-time

$969 per course. *Financial support:* In 2007–08, 5 research assistantships with full tuition reimbursements (averaging $8,400 per year) were awarded; career-related internships or fieldwork and unspecified assistantships also available. Support available to part-time students. Financial award application deadline: 8/1; financial award applicants required to submit FAFSA. *Unit head:* Dr. Gary M. Culpepper, Director, 401-865-2863, Fax: 401-865-1449, E-mail: garyculp@providence.edu.

Queen's University at Kingston, School of Graduate Studies and Research, Faculty of Arts and Sciences, Department of Religious Studies, Kingston, ON K7L 3N6, Canada. Offers MA. *Degree requirements:* For master's, one foreign language, essay. *Entrance requirements:* For master's, honors BA in religious studies or equivalent. Additional exam requirements/recommendations for international students: Required—TOEFL (minimum score 600 paper-based; 250 computer-based). *Faculty research:* Modernity, culture, feminism, world religions, traditions.

Reformed Theological Seminary–Charlotte Campus, Graduate and Professional Programs, Charlotte, NC 28226-6318. Offers biblical studies (MA); ministry (M Div, D Min); theological studies (MA). Part-time programs available. *Faculty:* 10 full-time, 4 part-time/adjunct. *Students:* 109. 53 applicants, 98% accepted, 40 enrolled. In 2007, 20 first professional degrees, 4 master's, 2 doctorates awarded. *Degree requirements:* For master's, comprehensive exam; for doctorate, thesis/dissertation; for M Div, 2 foreign languages, comprehensive exam. *Entrance requirements:* For master's, minimum GPA of 2.6; for doctorate, minimum GPA of 3.0. Additional exam requirements/recommendations for international students: Required—TOEFL (minimum score 550 paper-based; 213 computer-based). *Application deadline:* For fall admission, 7/15 priority date for domestic students; for winter admission, 11/15 priority date for domestic students; for spring admission, 12/15 priority date for domestic students. Applications are processed on a rolling basis. Application fee: $55. Electronic applications accepted. *Expenses:* Tuition: Full-time $12,025; part-time $325 per semester hour. Required fees: $65 per semester. *Financial support:* In 2007–08, teaching assistantships (averaging $1,600 per year); career-related internships or fieldwork and scholarships/grants also available. Financial award application deadline: 5/1. *Application contact:* Stephane Jeanrenaud, Director of Admissions, 800-755-2429, E-mail: admissions.charlotte@rts.edu.

Reformed Theological Seminary–Washington D.C., Graduate and Professional Programs, McLean, VA 22101. Offers bible (M Div); practical theology (M Div); religion (MA); theology (M Div). Part-time and evening/weekend programs available. *Faculty:* 23 part-time/adjunct (0 women). *Students:* 7 full-time (0 women), 94 part-time (18 women); includes 1 African American, 17 Asian Americans or Pacific Islanders. Average age 35. 41 applicants, 129% accepted. *Degree requirements:* For master's, integrative paper. *Entrance requirements:* For master's, minimum undergraduate GPA of 2.6. *Application deadline:* Applications are processed on a rolling basis. Application fee: $50. Electronic applications accepted. *Expenses:* Tuition: Part-time $345 per semester hour. Required fees: $50 per semester. One-time fee: $100 part-time. *Financial support:* In 2007–08, 55 students received support, including 7 fellowships (averaging $1,000 per year); institutionally sponsored loans, scholarships/grants, tuition waivers (partial), and unspecified assistantships also available. Support available to part-time students. Financial award application deadline: 6/15. *Faculty research:* Theology, biblical studies, cultural studies. *Unit head:* Hugh C. Whelchel, Executive Director, 703-448-3393, E-mail: hwhelchel@rts.edu. *Application contact:* Geoff M. Sackett, Director of Admissions, 800-639-0226, E-mail: gsackett@rts.edu.

Rice University, Graduate Programs, School of Humanities, Department of Religious Studies, Houston, TX 77251-1892. Offers PhD. *Degree requirements:* For doctorate, 2 foreign languages, comprehensive exam, thesis/dissertation. *Entrance requirements:* For doctorate, GRE General Test, minimum GPA of 3.0, writing sample. Additional exam requirements/recommendations for international students: Required—TOEFL. Electronic applications accepted. *Faculty research:* Religion and contemporary cultures; scriptural interpretation; ethics and philosophy of religion; mysticism; psychology and religious practices.

Sacred Heart University, Graduate Programs, College of Arts and Sciences, Department of Philosophy and Religious Studies, Fairfield, CT 06825-1000. Offers religious studies (MA). Part-time programs available. *Faculty:* 6 full-time (2 women). *Students:* 3 full-time (all women), 24 part-time (16 women); includes 3 minority (2 African Americans, 1 Asian American or Pacific Islander). Average age 37. 7 applicants, 100% accepted, 7 enrolled. In 2007, 3 degrees awarded. *Degree requirements:* For master's, comprehensive exam. *Entrance requirements:* Additional exam requirements/recommendations for international students: Required—TOEFL (minimum score 550 paper-based; 213 computer-based). *Application deadline:* Applications are processed on a rolling basis. Application fee: $50 ($100 for international students). Electronic applications accepted. *Expenses: Contact institution.* Tuition and fees vary according to program. *Financial support:* Career-related internships or fieldwork, institutionally sponsored loans, and unspecified assistantships available. Support available to part-time students. Financial award applicants required to submit FAFSA. *Unit head:* Dr. Christel Manning, Graduate Program Director, 203-371-7733. *Application contact:* Alexis Haakonsen, Dean of Graduate Admissions, 203-365-7619, Fax: 203-365-4732, E-mail: haakonsena@sacredheart.edu.

St. Charles Borromeo Seminary, Overbrook, Graduate and Professional Programs, Division of Religious Studies, Wynnewood, PA 19096. Offers MA. Part-time programs available. *Faculty:* 4 full-time (1 woman), 2 part-time/adjunct (0 women). *Students:* Average age 44. 5 applicants, 100% accepted, 5 enrolled. In 2007, 20 degrees awarded. *Degree requirements:* For master's, comprehensive exam. *Entrance requirements:* For master's, 18 undergraduate credits in theology and/or philosophy or the equivalent. *Application deadline:* For fall admission, 7/15 for domestic students; for spring admission, 11/15 for domestic students. Applications are processed on a rolling basis. Application fee: $0. *Expenses:* Tuition: Full-time $13,616; part-time $1,228 per credit. *Unit head:* Dr. Carmina Magnuson Chapp, Academic Dean, 610-785-6287, Fax: 610-667-4122, E-mail: academicdtdscs@adphila.org.

Saint John's Seminary, Graduate Programs, Brighton, MA 02135. Offers M Div, MA Th, MAM. *Accreditation:* ATS. *Faculty:* 11 full-time (1 woman), 16 part-time/adjunct (8 women). *Students:* 100 full-time (16 women), 59 part-time (37 women). *Application deadline:* Applications are processed on a rolling basis. Application fee: $0. *Expenses:* Tuition: Full-time $11,250; part-time $1,500 per course. One-time fee: $325 part-time. *Unit head:* Fr. Arthur L. Kennedy, Rector, 617-254-2610, Fax: 617-787-2336. *Application contact:* Sr. M. Pierre Jean Wilson, RSM, Dean of Admissions and Records, 617-779-4369, Fax: 617-787-2336, E-mail: admissionsandrecords@sjs.edu.

Santa Clara University, School of Education, Counseling Psychology, and Pastoral Ministries, Program in Pastoral Ministries, Program in Catechetics, Santa Clara, CA 95053. Offers MA. Part-time and evening/weekend programs available. *Students:* Average age 44. 3 applicants, 67% accepted, 2 enrolled. In 2007, 7 degrees awarded. *Degree requirements:* For master's, comprehensive exam, thesis. *Entrance requirements:* Additional exam requirements/recommendations for international students: Required—TOEFL. *Application deadline:* Applications are processed on a rolling basis. *Financial support:* Application deadline: 3/1; *Unit head:* Fr. Tom Powers, S.J., Director, Program in Pastoral Ministries, 408-554-4322.

Santa Clara University, School of Education, Counseling Psychology, and Pastoral Ministries, Program in Pastoral Ministries, Program in Spirituality, Santa Clara, CA 95053. Offers MA. Part-time and evening/weekend programs available. *Students:* 3 full-time (all women), 12 part-time (8 women); includes 4 minority (2 Asian Americans or Pacific Islanders, 2 Hispanic Americans), 1 international. Average age 43. 4 applicants, 100% accepted, 4 enrolled. In 2007, 5 degrees awarded. *Degree requirements:* For master's, comprehensive exam, thesis. *Entrance requirements:* Additional exam requirements/recommendations for international students: Required—TOEFL. *Application deadline:* Applications are processed on a rolling basis. *Financial support:* Application deadline: 3/1; *Unit head:* Fr. Tom Powers, S.J., Director, Program in Pastoral Ministries, 408-554-4322.

Seton Hall University, College of Arts and Sciences, Department of Jewish-Christian Studies, South Orange, NJ 07079-2697. Offers MA. Part-time and evening/weekend programs available. *Degree requirements:* For master's, one foreign language, thesis or alternative. Electronic applications accepted. *Faculty research:* Jewish-Christian issues, biblical studies.

See Close-Up on page 699.

Simpson University, A.W. Tozer Theological Seminary, Redding, CA 96003-8606. Offers Christian leadership (MA); Christian studies (MA); intercultural studies (MA); ministry (M Div). Part-time and evening/weekend programs available. Postbaccalaureate distance learning degree programs offered (minimal on-campus study). *Faculty:* 6 part-time/adjunct (0 women). *Students:* 6 full-time (0 women), 49 part-time (13 women); includes 7 minority (3 African Americans, 2 Asian Americans or Pacific Islanders, 2 Hispanic Americans), 1 international. Average age 38. 22 applicants, 73% accepted, 16 enrolled. In 2007, 5 degrees awarded. *Degree requirements:* For master's, student portfolio. *Entrance requirements:* For master's, GRE General Test (if undergraduate GPA is below 2.5), 2 letters of reference, Christian Experience statement. Additional exam requirements/recommendations for international students: Required—TOEFL. *Application deadline:* For fall admission, 9/4 priority date for domestic students, 9/4 for international students; for spring admission, 1/8 priority date for domestic students, 1/8 for international students. Applications are processed on a rolling basis. Application fee: $20. Electronic applications accepted. *Expenses: Contact institution. Financial support:* Scholarships/grants available. Support available to part-time students. Financial award application deadline: 3/20; financial award applicants required to submit FAFSA. *Unit head:* Dr. Robert Redman, Dean, 530-226-4144, Fax: 530-326-4871, E-mail: rredman@simpsonuniversity.edu. *Application contact:* Jeff Williams, Director of Enrollment Development, 530-226-4611, Fax: 530-226-4861, E-mail: jwilliams@simpsonuniversity.edu.

Sioux Falls Seminary, Graduate and Professional Programs, Program in Christian Leadership, Sioux Falls, SD 57105-1599. Offers MA. *Students:* 5 full-time (2 women), 7 part-time (5 women). *Application contact:* Bryce H. Eben, Director of Enrollment Development, 605-336-6188, Fax: 605-335-9090.

Sioux Falls Seminary, Graduate and Professional Programs, Program in Religious Studies, Sioux Falls, SD 57105-1599. Offers MA. Part-time programs available. *Entrance requirements:* For master's, minimum GPA of 2.5. *Application deadline:* For fall admission, 8/1 priority date for domestic students; for spring admission, 1/1 priority date for domestic students. Applications are processed on a rolling basis. Application fee: $35. *Financial support:* Scholarships/grants available. *Application contact:* Bryce H. Eben, Director of Enrollment Development, 605-336-6588, Fax: 605-335-9090, E-mail: beben@sfseminary.edu.

Southern Adventist University, School of Religion, Collegedale, TN 37315-0370. Offers Biblical and theological studies (MA); church leadership and management (MA); church ministry and homiletics (MA); evangelism and world mission (MA); religious studies (MA). Summer program only. Part-time programs available. *Faculty:* 5 full-time (0 women). *Students:* 2 full-time (0 women), 1 part-time; includes 1 minority (Asian American or Pacific Islander) Average age 36. 9 applicants, 100% accepted. In 2007, 6 degrees awarded. *Degree requirements:* For master's, comprehensive exam, thesis (for some programs). *Entrance requirements:* For master's, GRE. Additional exam requirements/recommendations for international students: Required—TOEFL (minimum score 550 paper-based). *Application deadline:* For spring admission, 4/30 priority date for domestic students, 12/30 for international students. Applications are processed on a rolling basis. Application fee: $25. *Financial support:* In 2007–08, 4 students received support. Tuition waivers (full) available. Support available to part-time students. Financial award application deadline: 4/1; financial award applicants required to submit FAFSA. *Faculty research:* Biblical archaeology. *Unit head:* Dr. Greg A. King, Dean, 423-236-2975, Fax: 423-236-1976, E-mail: gking@southern.edu. *Application contact:* Susan L. Brown, Administrative Assistant, 423-236-2977, Fax: 423-236-1977, E-mail: sbrown@southern.edu.

Southern California Seminary, Graduate and Professional Programs, El Cajon, CA 92019. Offers biblical studies (MA); counseling psychology (MACP); psychology (Psy D); religious studies (MRS); theology (M Div). Part-time and evening/weekend programs available. Postbaccalaureate distance learning degree programs offered (minimal on-campus study). *Faculty:* 7 full-time (0 women), 17 part-time/adjunct (2 women). *Students:* 56 full-time (21 women), 68 part-time (30 women); includes 44 minority (24 African Americans, 2 Asian Americans or Pacific Islanders, 18 Hispanic Americans), 4 international. Average age 38. In 2007, 42 degrees awarded. *Degree requirements:* For master's, thesis (for some programs); for doctorate, thesis/dissertation; for M Div, 2 foreign languages. *Entrance requirements:* For doctorate, master's degree in psychology. Additional exam requirements/recommendations for international students: Required—TOEFL (minimum score 550 paper-based). *Application deadline:* For fall admission, 8/13 for domestic and international students; for spring admission, 12/11 for domestic students, 12/15 for international students. Applications are processed on a rolling basis. Application fee: $27 ($109 for international students). Electronic applications accepted. *Expenses:* Tuition: Part-time $290 per unit. Tuition and fees vary according to campus/location and program. *Financial support:* In 2007–08, 14 students received support. Federal Work-Study, scholarships/grants, and tuition waivers (partial) available. Financial award application deadline: 3/1; financial award applicants required to submit FAFSA. *Unit head:* Dr. Al Letting, Vice-President of Academics, 619-590-2131, E-mail: aletting@socalsem.edu. *Application contact:* Steve Perdue, Director of Admissions, 888-389-7244, E-mail: sperdue@socalsem.edu.

Southern Evangelical Seminary, Graduate School of Ministry and Missions, Matthews, NC 28105. Offers apologetics (Certificate); Christian education (MA); church ministry (MA, Certificate); divinity (Certificate), including apologetics (M Div, Certificate); Islamic studies (Certificate); theology (M Div), including apologetics (M Div, Certificate), Biblical studies; youth ministry (MA). Part-time and evening/weekend programs available. Postbaccalaureate distance learning degree programs offered. In 2007, 3 degrees awarded. *Degree requirements:* For master's, thesis (for some programs); for M Div, one foreign language. *Entrance requirements:* Additional exam requirements/recommendations for international students: Required—TOEFL (minimum score 600 paper-based; 250 computer-based). *Application deadline:* For fall admission, 8/15 priority date for domestic students, 8/5 priority date for international students; for winter admission, 12/15 priority date for domestic and international students; for spring admission, 1/15 priority date for domestic and international students. Applications are processed on a rolling basis. Application fee: $25. *Financial support:* Scholarships/grants available. *Unit head:* Dr. Barry R. Leventhal, Dean, 704-847-5600 Ext. 204, Fax: 704-845-1747, E-mail: dean@ses.edu.

Southern Evangelical Seminary, Veritas Graduate School of Apologetics and Counter-Cult Ministry, Matthews, NC 28105. Offers apologetics (MA, D Min, PhD, Certificate); Islamic studies (MA); Jewish studies (MA); philosophy (MA); religion (MA). *Accreditation:* ATS.Part-time and evening/weekend programs available. Postbaccalaureate distance learning degree programs offered (minimal on-campus study). In 2007, 18 master's, 2 doctorates awarded. *Degree requirements:* For master's, thesis optional; for doctorate, comprehensive exam (for some programs), thesis/dissertation. *Entrance requirements:* Additional exam requirements/recommendations for international students: Required—TOEFL (minimum score 600 paper-based; 250 computer-based). *Application deadline:* For fall admission, 8/5 priority date for domestic and international students; for winter admission, 12/15 priority date for domestic and international students; for spring admission, 1/15 priority date for domestic and international students. Applications are processed on a rolling basis. Application fee: $25. *Financial support:* Scholarships/grants available. *Unit head:* Dr. Thomas A. Howe, Director, Apologetics Program, 704-847-5600 Ext. 209, Fax: 704-845-1747, E-mail: thowe@ses.edu.

Southern Methodist University, Dedman College, Program in Religious Studies, Dallas, TX 75275. Offers MA, PhD. *Faculty:* 38 full-time (11 women). *Students:* 30 full-time (11 women); includes 1 minority (African American), 3 international. Average age 34. 70 applicants, 16% accepted, 6 enrolled. In 2007, 4 degrees awarded. *Median time to degree:* Of those who

Religion

Southern Methodist University (continued)

began their doctoral program in fall 1999, 60% received their degree in 8 years or less. *Degree requirements:* For master's, one foreign language, thesis, oral exam, written exams; for doctorate, 2 foreign languages, thesis/dissertation, oral and written exams. *Entrance requirements:* For master's and doctorate, GRE General Test, minimum GPA of 3.0, course work in religion. Additional exam requirements/recommendations for international students: Required—TOEFL (minimum score 550 paper-based; 210 computer-based; 79 iBT). *Application deadline:* For fall admission, 2/1 for domestic and international students. Application fee: $75. Electronic applications accepted. *Financial support:* In 2007–08, 23 fellowships with full and partial tuition reimbursements (averaging $8,177 per year), 5 research assistantships with full and partial tuition reimbursements (averaging $2,500 per year), 6 teaching assistantships with full and partial tuition reimbursements (averaging $2,000 per year) were awarded; institutionally sponsored loans, scholarships/grants, and tuition waivers (full and partial) also available. Financial award application deadline: 2/1; financial award applicants required to submit FAFSA. *Faculty research:* Theology and ethics, biblical studies, history of Christian doctrine, philosophy of religion. *Unit head:* Prof. Charles M. Wood, Director, 214-768-2432, Fax: 214-768-2117. *Application contact:* Lucy Cobbe, Assistant to Director of Graduate Program, 214-768-2432, Fax: 214-768-2117, E-mail: gradreli@mail.smu.edu.

Southern Nazarene University, Graduate College, Department of Philosophy and Religion, Bethany, OK 73008. Offers theology (MA). Part-time programs available. *Degree requirements:* For master's, one foreign language, thesis optional. *Entrance requirements:* For master's, GMAT, English proficiency exam, minimum GPA of 3.0 in last 60 hours/major, 2.7 overall.

Stanford University, School of Humanities and Sciences, Department of Religious Studies, Stanford, CA 94305-9991. Offers MA, PhD. Terminal master's awarded for partial completion of doctoral program. *Degree requirements:* For master's, one foreign language, thesis optional; for doctorate, 2 foreign languages, thesis/dissertation, qualifying exam. *Entrance requirements:* For master's and doctorate, GRE General Test. Additional exam requirements/recommendations for international students: Required—TOEFL. Electronic applications accepted.

Syracuse University, Graduate School, College of Arts and Sciences, Department of Religion, Syracuse, NY 13244. Offers MA, PhD. Part-time programs available. *Students:* 40 full-time (21 women), 6 part-time (1 woman); includes 2 minority (both Hispanic Americans), 7 international. 87 applicants, 20% accepted, 10 enrolled. In 2007, 3 master's, 3 doctorates awarded. Terminal master's awarded for partial completion of doctoral program. *Degree requirements:* For master's, one foreign language, comprehensive exam, thesis optional; for doctorate, 2 foreign languages, comprehensive exam, thesis/dissertation. *Entrance requirements:* For master's and doctorate, GRE General Test. Additional exam requirements/recommendations for international students: Required—TOEFL. *Application deadline:* For fall admission, 1/10 priority date for domestic students. Applications are processed on a rolling basis. Application fee: $75. Electronic applications accepted. *Expenses:* Tuition: Full-time $18,216; part-time $1,012 per credit. Required fees: $980. Tuition and fees vary according to program. *Financial support:* Fellowships with full tuition reimbursements, teaching assistantships with full tuition reimbursements, tuition waivers (partial) available. Financial award applicants required to submit FAFSA. *Unit head:* Dr. Tazim Kassam, Chair, 315-443-3863, Fax: 315-443-3958, E-mail: tkassam@syr.edu. *Application contact:* Jackie Borowre, Recruiting Contact, 315-443-3861, E-mail: jborowre@syr.edu.

Temple University, Graduate School, College of Liberal Arts, Department of Religion, Philadelphia, PA 19122-6096. Offers MA, PhD. Part-time programs available. *Degree requirements:* For doctorate, variable foreign language requirement, thesis/dissertation. *Entrance requirements:* For doctorate, GRE General Test, minimum GPA of 3.0. Additional exam requirements/recommendations for international students: Required—TOEFL (minimum score 550 paper-based; 213 computer-based; 79 iBT). Electronic applications accepted. *Faculty research:* Textural and historical origins; philosophy of religion and religious thought; religion, culture, and society.

Trevecca Nazarene University, Graduate Division, Graduate Religion Programs, Nashville, TN 37210-2877. Offers biblical studies (MA); preaching and practical theology (MA); systematic theology/historical theology (MA). Part-time programs available. *Faculty:* 3 full-time (0 women), 4 part-time/adjunct (0 women). *Students:* 23 full-time (4 women), 29 part-time (7 women); includes 8 minority (all African Americans), 1 international. Average age 37. In 2007, 9 degrees awarded. *Degree requirements:* For master's, comprehensive exam, thesis optional. *Entrance requirements:* For master's, GRE General Test or MAT, minimum GPA of 2.7, 2 letters of recommendation, philosophy of ministry statement. Additional exam requirements/recommendations for international students: Required—TOEFL (minimum score 550 paper-based; 213 computer-based). *Application deadline:* Applications are processed on a rolling basis. Application fee: $25. Electronic applications accepted. *Expenses:* Contact institution. Tuition and fees vary according to degree level and program. *Financial support:* Applicants required to submit FAFSA. *Unit head:* Dr. Tim Green, Dean/Director, 615-248-1378, Fax: 615-248-7417, E-mail: tgreen@trevecca.edu. *Application contact:* Sherry Crutchfield, Secretary, 615-248-1378, Fax: 615-248-7417, E-mail: admissions_rel@trevecca.edu.

Trinity Episcopal School for Ministry, Graduate Programs, Ambridge, PA 15003-2397. Offers Anglican studies (Diploma); basic Christian studies (Diploma); divinity (M Div); ministry (D Min); mission and evangelism (MAME, Diploma); religion (MAR); youth ministry (Diploma). *Accreditation:* ATS (one or more programs are accredited). Part-time programs available. *Degree requirements:* For master's, thesis optional; for doctorate, thesis/dissertation; for M Div, thesis/dissertation optional, Greek and Hebrew. *Entrance requirements:* Additional exam requirements/recommendations for international students: Required—TOEFL. *Faculty research:* Pauline Epistles, contemporary theology, history of Anglican liturgy, book of Ruth, biblical theology.

Trinity International University, South Florida Campus, Program in Religion, Miami, FL 33132-1996. Offers MA.

Union University, School of Christian Studies, Jackson, TN 38305-3697. Offers MCS. *Unit head:* Dr. Gregory Thornburg, Dean, 731-661-5082, E-mail: gthornbu@uu.edu.

United Theological Seminary of the Twin Cities, Graduate and Professional Programs, Program in Theological and Religious Studies, New Brighton, MN 55112-2598. Offers Certificate. Part-time programs available. *Faculty:* 12 full-time (7 women), 22 part-time/adjunct (10 women). In 2007, 4 degrees awarded. *Application deadline:* For fall admission, 8/1 priority date for domestic students; for winter admission, 12/1 priority date for domestic students; for spring admission, 1/1 priority date for domestic students. Applications are processed on a rolling basis. Application fee: $40. *Expenses:* Tuition: Part-time $373 per credit hour. *Application contact:* Rev. Glen Herrington-Hall, Director of Admissions, 651-255-6107, Fax: 651-633-4315, E-mail: gherrington-hall@unitedseminary.edu.

United Theological Seminary of the Twin Cities, Graduate and Professional Programs, Program in Theology, New Brighton, MN 55112-2598. Offers religion and theology (MA); theology and the arts (MA); women's studies (MA). Part-time programs available. *Faculty:* 12 full-time (7 women), 22 part-time/adjunct (10 women). *Students:* 9 full-time (4 women), 16 part-time (12 women). Average age 43. 13 applicants, 100% accepted, 12 enrolled. In 2007, 1 degree awarded. *Degree requirements:* For master's, thesis. *Entrance requirements:* For master's, minimum GPA of 2.75. *Application deadline:* For fall admission, 8/1 priority date for domestic students; for winter admission, 12/1 priority date for domestic students; for spring admission, 1/1 priority date for domestic students. Application fee: $40. *Expenses:* Tuition: Part-time $373 per credit hour. *Financial support:* Career-related internships or fieldwork, institutionally sponsored loans, and scholarships/grants available. Support available to part-time students. *Application contact:* Rev. Glen Herrington-Hall, Director of Admissions, 651-255-6107, Fax: 651-633-4315, E-mail: gherrington-hall@unitedseminary.edu.

Université de Sherbrooke, Faculty of Theology, Ethics and Philosophy, Sherbrooke, QC J1K 2R1, Canada. Offers applied ethics (Diploma); human science of religions (MA); intercultural training (Diploma); philosophy (MA, PhD); spiritual anthropology (Diploma); theology (MA, PhD, Diploma). Part-time and evening/weekend programs available. Postbaccalaureate distance learning degree programs offered. Terminal master's awarded for partial completion of doctoral program. *Entrance requirements:* For master's, bachelor's degree in related discipline; for doctorate, master's degree in related discipline. *Faculty research:* Faith and culture interrelation.

Université du Québec à Montréal, Graduate Programs, Program in Religious Sciences, Montréal, QC H3C 3P8, Canada. Offers MA, PhD. Part-time programs available. *Degree requirements:* For master's, thesis; for doctorate, thesis/dissertation. *Entrance requirements:* For master's, appropriate bachelor's degree or equivalent, proficiency in French; for doctorate, appropriate master's degree or equivalent, proficiency in French.

Université Laval, Faculty of Theology and Religious Sciences, Programs in Human Sciences of Religion, Québec, QC G1K 7P4, Canada. Offers MA, PhD. Terminal master's awarded for partial completion of doctoral program. *Degree requirements:* For master's, thesis (for some programs); for doctorate, comprehensive exam, thesis/dissertation. *Entrance requirements:* For master's, knowledge of French, comprehension of a second language; for doctorate, knowledge of French and English. Electronic applications accepted.

The University of British Columbia, Faculty of Arts and Faculty of Graduate Studies, Department of Classical, Near Eastern and Religious Studies, Program in Religious Studies, Vancouver, BC V6T 1Z1, Canada. Offers MA, PhD. Part-time programs available. *Faculty:* 7 full-time (2 women). *Students:* 10 full-time (7 women); includes 2 minority (both Asian Americans or Pacific Islanders) 8 applicants, 88% accepted, 3 enrolled. In 2007, 1 degree awarded. *Degree requirements:* For master's, 2 foreign languages, comprehensive exam, thesis optional; for doctorate, 2 foreign languages, comprehensive exam, thesis/dissertation. *Entrance requirements:* For master's, upper second class standing; for doctorate, MA degree. Additional exam requirements/recommendations for international students: Required—TOEFL (minimum score 600 paper-based; 250 computer-based), IELTS. *Application deadline:* For fall admission, 1/31 for domestic and international students. Applications are processed on a rolling basis. Application fee: $90 Canadian dollars ($150 Canadian dollars for international students). Electronic applications accepted. *Financial support:* In 2007–08, 6 students received support, including 2 fellowships with tuition reimbursements available, 5 teaching assistantships with partial tuition reimbursements available (averaging $10,500 per year); scholarships/grants and health care benefits also available. Financial award application deadline: 1/1. *Faculty research:* Hebrew Bible in ancient Near Eastern context, Christian scriptures in Greco-Roman context, mystical aspects of religion, the feminine in western traditions, modern Jewish experience. *Application contact:* Christine R. Dawson, Information Contact, 604-822-2515, Fax: 604-822-9431, E-mail: crdawson@interchange.ubc.ca.

The University of British Columbia, Faculty of Arts and Faculty of Graduate Studies, Department of Classical, Near Eastern and Religious Studies, Programmes in Classics, Vancouver, BC V6T 1Z1, Canada. Offers ancient culture, religion, and ethnicity (MA); classical and near eastern archaeology (MA); classics (MA, PhD). Part-time programs available. *Faculty:* 7 full-time (4 women). *Students:* 16 full-time (7 women); includes 1 minority (Asian American or Pacific Islander) 19 applicants, 95% accepted, 7 enrolled. In 2007, 2 master's awarded. *Median time to degree:* Of those who began their doctoral program in fall 1999, 100% received their degree in 8 years or less. *Degree requirements:* For master's, 2 foreign languages, comprehensive exam, thesis, thesis or comprehensive exam; for doctorate, 2 foreign languages, comprehensive exam, thesis/dissertation. *Entrance requirements:* For master's, upper second class standing; for doctorate, MA degree. Additional exam requirements/recommendations for international students: Required—TOEFL (minimum score 600 paper-based; 250 computer-based), IELTS (minimum score 8). *Application deadline:* For fall admission, 1/31 for domestic and international students. Applications are processed on a rolling basis. Application fee: $90 Canadian dollars ($150 Canadian dollars for international students). Electronic applications accepted. *Financial support:* In 2007–08, 12 students received support, including 5 fellowships with tuition reimbursements available, 12 teaching assistantships with partial tuition reimbursements available (averaging $10,500 per year); scholarships/grants and health care benefits also available. Financial award application deadline: 1/1. *Faculty research:* Classical archaeology, ancient historians, late antiquity, ancient prose fiction, epigraphy. *Application contact:* Christine R. Dawson, Information Contact, 604-822-2515, Fax: 604-822-9431, E-mail: crdawson@interchange.ubc.ca.

University of Calgary, Faculty of Graduate Studies, Faculty of Humanities, Department of Religious Studies, Calgary, AB T2N 1N4, Canada. Offers MA, PhD. Part-time programs available. *Faculty:* 16 full-time (5 women). *Students:* 31 (16 women); includes 6 minority (all Asian Americans or Pacific Islanders) Average age 34. 18 applicants, 56% accepted, 6 enrolled. In 2007, 5 master's awarded. *Median time to degree:* Of those who began their doctoral program in fall 1999, 100% received their degree in 8 years or less. *Degree requirements:* For master's, one foreign language, thesis; for doctorate, 2 foreign languages, thesis/dissertation, candidacy exam. *Entrance requirements:* For master's, minimum GPA of 3.3; for doctorate, minimum GPA of 3.5. Additional exam requirements/recommendations for international students: Required—TOEFL (minimum score 550 paper-based; 213 computer-based). *Application deadline:* For fall admission, 1/7 priority date for domestic and international students. Applications are processed on a rolling basis. Application fee: $100 ($130 for international students). *Financial support:* In 2007–08, 24 students received support, including research assistantships (averaging $4,100 per year), teaching assistantships (averaging $3,510 per year); fellowships also available. Financial award application deadline: 2/1. *Faculty research:* Eastern religions, Western religions, nature of religion. *Unit head:* Dr. Virginia Tumasz, Head, 403-220-5886, Fax: 403-210-0801, E-mail: rels@ucalgary.ca.

University of California, Berkeley, Graduate Division, College of Letters and Science, Department of Near Eastern Studies, Program in Near Eastern Religions, Berkeley, CA 94720-1500. Offers PhD. *Degree requirements:* For doctorate, 2 foreign languages, thesis/dissertation, qualifying exam. *Entrance requirements:* For doctorate, GRE General Test, MA or equivalent in Near Eastern studies or related field; minimum GPA of 3.0, 3 letters of recommendation. *Application deadline:* For fall admission, 12/15 for domestic students. Application fee: $70 ($90 for international students). *Financial support:* Fellowships, research assistantships, teaching assistantships, unspecified assistantships available. *Application contact:* Judy Shattuck, Graduate Assistant, 510-642-6162, Fax: 510-643-8430, E-mail: nes@berkeley.edu.

University of California, Berkeley, Graduate Division, Group in Buddhist Studies, Berkeley, CA 94720-1500. Offers PhD. *Faculty:* 9 full-time. *Degree requirements:* For doctorate, 4 foreign languages, thesis/dissertation, dissertation defense, qualifying exam. *Entrance requirements:* For doctorate, GRE General Test, MA in Japanese, Chinese, or Sanskrit; minimum GPA of 3.0, 3 letters of recommendation. *Application deadline:* For fall admission, 12/8 for domestic students. Application fee: $70 ($90 for international students). Electronic applications accepted. *Financial support:* Unspecified assistantships available. *Unit head:* Robert Sharf, Chair, 510-642-6369, E-mail: rsharf@berkeley.edu. *Application contact:* Information Contact, 510-642-3480, E-mail: gbs@berkeley.edu.

University of California, Santa Barbara, Graduate Division, College of Letters and Sciences, Division of Humanities and Fine Arts, Department of Religious Studies, Santa Barbara, CA 93106. Offers MA, PhD, MA/PhD. *Faculty:* 18 full-time (8 women), 11 part-time/adjunct (5 women). *Students:* 80 full-time (35 women); includes 13 minority (1 African American, 2 American Indian/Alaska Native, 8 Asian Americans or Pacific Islanders, 2 Hispanic Americans), 1 international. Average age 31. 175 applicants, 31% accepted, 15 enrolled. In 2007, 7 master's, 13 doctorates awarded. Terminal master's awarded for partial completion of doctoral program. *Median time to degree:* Of those who began their doctoral program in fall 1999, 53% received their degree in 8 years or less. *Degree requirements:* For master's, one foreign language, comprehensive exam (for some programs), thesis (for some programs), 3 seminars with 3 different faculty, 3 colloquium units ; for doctorate, one foreign language, thesis/dissertation, methodology course, 3 colloquium units. *Entrance requirements:* For master's,

GRE General Test; for doctorate, GRE General Test, MA in related field. Additional exam requirements/recommendations for international students: Required—TOEFL (minimum score 550 paper-based; 213 computer-based; 80 iBT). *Application deadline:* For fall admission, 12/1 for domestic and international students. Application fee: $60. Electronic applications accepted. *Expenses:* Tuition, nonresident: full-time $14,888. Required fees: $10,108. *Financial support:* In 2007–08, 76 students received support, including 23 fellowships with full and partial tuition reimbursements available (averaging $10,900 per year), 43 teaching assistantships with partial tuition reimbursements available (averaging $8,000 per year); career-related internships or fieldwork, Federal Work-Study, institutionally sponsored loans, scholarships/grants, health care benefits, and teaching associate also available. Financial award application deadline: 12/1; financial award applicants required to submit FAFSA. *Faculty research:* Religion and politics, religion and violence, contemporary spirituality, religious traditions, theoretical approaches to the study of religion, area studies. *Unit head:* Prof. Catherine L. Albanese, Chair, 805-893-3564, Fax: 805-893-2059, E-mail: albanese@religion.ucsb.edu. *Application contact:* Sally Lombrozo, Graduate Program Assistant, 805-893-2744, Fax: 805-893-2059, E-mail: lombrozo@religion.ucsb.edu.

University of Chicago, Divinity School, Chicago, IL 60637-1513. Offers M Div, AM, AMRS, PhD, JD/M Div, JD/MA, JD/PhD, MPP/M Div, MSW/M Div. *Accreditation:* ATS (one or more programs are accredited). Part-time programs available. *Degree requirements:* For master's and M Div, one foreign language; for doctorate, 2 foreign languages, comprehensive exam, thesis/dissertation. *Entrance requirements:* For M Div, master's, and doctorate, GRE General Test. Additional exam requirements/recommendations for international students: Required—TOEFL (minimum score 600 paper-based; 250 computer-based). Electronic applications accepted. Expenses: Contact institution. *Faculty research:* Theology, history of religion, ethics, biblical studies, philosophy of religion.

University of Colorado at Boulder, Graduate School, College of Arts and Sciences, Department of Religious Studies, Boulder, CO 80309. Offers MA. *Faculty:* 9. *Students:* 27 full-time (13 women), 11 part-time (5 women); includes 1 minority (American Indian/Alaska Native), 2 international. Average age 29. 13 applicants, 92% accepted. In 2007, 4 degrees awarded. *Degree requirements:* For master's, one foreign language, comprehensive exam, thesis. *Entrance requirements:* For master's, minimum undergraduate GPA of 2.75. *Application deadline:* For fall admission, 1/15 priority date for domestic students, 1/31 for international students; for spring admission, 10/15 for domestic students, 9/15 for international students. Applications are processed on a rolling basis. Application fee: $50 ($60 for international students). *Financial support:* In 2007–08, 13 fellowships (averaging $6,250 per year) were awarded; tuition waivers (full) also available. Financial award application deadline: 1/15. *Faculty research:* Comparative studies in religion, methodologies in the study of religion, religion and dance, history of religions (including Hinduism, Buddhism and religions of China and Japan), Islam, Christianity. *Unit head:* Rodney Taylor, Chair, 303-735-4768, Fax: 303-735-2080, E-mail: rodney.taylor@colorado.edu. *Application contact:* Irene Hesse, Graduate Program Assistant, 303-492-8041, Fax: 303-735-2080, E-mail: rlst@colorado.edu.

University of Denver, Faculty of Arts and Humanities/Social Sciences, Department of Religious Studies, Denver, CO 80208. Offers MA. *Faculty:* 6 full-time (2 women). *Students:* 4 full-time (3 women), 9 part-time (6 women). Average age 25. In 2007, 3 degrees awarded. *Entrance requirements:* For master's, GRE. *Application deadline:* Applications are processed on a rolling basis. Application fee: $50. Electronic applications accepted. *Application contact:* Information Contact, 303-371-2249, E-mail: rlgs01@du.edu.

University of Denver, Graduate Studies, Joint Program in Religious and Theological Studies, Denver, CO 80208. Offers PhD. *Students:* 50 full-time (18 women), 24 part-time (8 women); includes 9 minority (4 African Americans, 1 American Indian/Alaska Native, 2 Asian Americans or Pacific Islanders, 2 Hispanic Americans), 10 international. Average age 40. *Entrance requirements:* For doctorate, GRE. *Application deadline:* For fall admission, 1/15 for domestic students. Application fee: $50. *Unit head:* Dr. Frank Seeburger, Head, 303-871-2766.

University of Detroit Mercy, College of Liberal Arts and Education, Department of Religious Studies, Detroit, MI 48221. Offers MA. *Degree requirements:* For master's, thesis or alternative. *Entrance requirements:* For master's, minimum GPA of 3.0. *Faculty research:* History of religions, textual studies (Old and New Testaments), ethical and cultural studies.

University of Florida, Graduate School, College of Liberal Arts and Sciences, Department of Religion, Gainesville, FL 32611. Offers religion (MA, PhD), including religion and nature (PhD), religion in the Americas (PhD), religions of Asia (PhD). Part-time programs available. *Faculty:* 17 full-time (6 women). *Students:* 31 (17 women); includes 3 minority (1 Asian American or Pacific Islander, 2 Hispanic Americans) 2 international. *Degree requirements:* For master's, one foreign language, thesis. *Entrance requirements:* For master's, GRE General Test, minimum GPA of 3.0. Additional exam requirements/recommendations for international students: Required—TOEFL (minimum score 550 paper-based; 213 computer-based). *Application deadline:* For fall admission, 6/1 priority date for domestic students. Applications are processed on a rolling basis. Application fee: $30. Electronic applications accepted. *Expenses:* Tuition, state resident: full-time $7,478. Tuition, nonresident: full-time $22,603. *Financial support:* In 2007–08, 2 research assistantships (averaging $18,549 per year), 17 teaching assistantships (averaging $16,174 per year) were awarded; fellowships, Federal Work-Study and unspecified assistantships also available. *Faculty research:* Religion in America, Christian thought, Islam, religions of India, comparative religion. *Unit head:* David Hackett, Chair, 352-392-1625 Ext. 232. *Application contact:* Dr. Bron Taylor, Coordinator, 352-392-1625, Fax: 352-392-7395, E-mail: bron@religion.ufl.edu.

University of Georgia, Graduate School, College of Arts and Sciences, Department of Religion, Athens, GA 30602. Offers MA. *Faculty:* 9 full-time (1 woman). *Students:* 22 full-time (13 women), 6 part-time (3 women); includes 2 minority (both Hispanic Americans), 1 international. 43 applicants, 51% accepted, 10 enrolled. In 2007, 10 degrees awarded. *Degree requirements:* For master's, one foreign language, thesis. *Entrance requirements:* For master's, GRE General Test. *Application deadline:* For fall admission, 7/1 priority date for domestic students; for spring admission, 11/15 for domestic students. Application fee: $50. Electronic applications accepted. *Financial support:* Fellowships, research assistantships, teaching assistantships, unspecified assistantships available. *Unit head:* Dr. Sandy D. Martin, Head, 706-542-1485, E-mail: martin@uga.edu. *Application contact:* Dr. Carolyn Medine, Graduate Coordinator, 706-543-0308, Fax: 706-542-6724, E-mail: medine@uga.edu.

University of Hawaii at Manoa, Graduate Division, Colleges of Arts and Sciences, College of Arts and Humanities, Department of Religion, Honolulu, HI 96822. Offers MA. Part-time programs available. *Faculty:* 7 full-time (1 woman). *Students:* 19 full-time (4 women), 1 part-time; includes 4 minority (all Asian Americans or Pacific Islanders) Average age 31. 18 applicants, 44% accepted, 4 enrolled. *Degree requirements:* For master's, one foreign language, thesis optional. *Entrance requirements:* For master's, GRE General Test. Additional exam requirements/recommendations for international students: Required—TOEFL (minimum score 600 paper-based; 250 computer-based; 100 iBT), IELTS (minimum score 7). *Application deadline:* For fall admission, 3/1 for domestic students, 1/15 for international students; for spring admission, 10/1 for domestic students, 9/1 for international students. Applications are processed on a rolling basis. Application fee: $50. *Financial support:* In 2007–08, 1 research assistantship (averaging $16,176 per year), 8 teaching assistantships (averaging $13,430 per year) were awarded; fellowships, career-related internships or fieldwork, scholarships/grants, and tuition waivers (full and partial) also available. Financial award application deadline: 3/1. *Faculty research:* Buddhism, East Asian religion, South Asian religion, Polynesian religion, Western religions. *Application contact:* Poul Andersen, Graduate Field Chairperson, 808-956-8299, Fax: 808-956-9894, E-mail: poul@hawaii.edu.

The University of Iowa, Graduate College, College of Liberal Arts and Sciences, Department of Religious Studies, Iowa City, IA 52242-1316. Offers MA, PhD, JD/MA. *Faculty:* 12 full-time, 7 part-time/adjunct. *Students:* 22 full-time (11 women), 24 part-time (7 women); includes 2 minority (1 Asian American or Pacific Islander, 1 Hispanic American), 2 international. 55 applicants, 29% accepted, 3 enrolled. In 2007, 4 master's, 7 doctorates awarded. Terminal master's awarded for partial completion of doctoral program. *Degree requirements:* For master's, thesis optional, exam; for doctorate, comprehensive exam, thesis/dissertation. *Entrance requirements:* For master's and doctorate, GRE General Test, minimum GPA of 3.0. Additional exam requirements/recommendations for international students: Required—TOEFL (minimum score 550 paper-based; 213 computer-based; 81 iBT). *Application deadline:* For fall admission, 5/1 priority date for domestic students; for spring admission, 11/1 priority date for domestic students. Applications are processed on a rolling basis. Application fee: $60 ($85 for international students). Electronic applications accepted. *Expenses:* Tuition, state resident: part-time $349 per hour. Tuition, nonresident: part-time $349 per hour. Tuition and fees vary according to course load and program. *Financial support:* In 2007–08, 4 fellowships, 25 teaching assistantships with partial tuition reimbursements were awarded; research assistantships with partial tuition reimbursements, tuition waivers (partial) also available. Financial award applicants required to submit FAFSA. *Faculty research:* Eastern and Western religion. *Unit head:* Raymond Mentzer, Chair, 319-335-2164, Fax: 319-335-3716.

University of Kansas, Research and Graduate Studies, College of Liberal Arts and Sciences, Department of Religious Studies, Lawrence, KS 66045. Offers MA. Part-time programs available. *Faculty:* 9. *Students:* 14 full-time (7 women), 8 part-time (6 women); includes 2 minority (both African Americans) Average age 30. 11 applicants, 91% accepted, 9 enrolled. In 2007, 3 degrees awarded. *Degree requirements:* For master's, comprehensive exam, thesis optional. *Entrance requirements:* For master's, GRE (preferred), minimum GPA of 3.0. Additional exam requirements/recommendations for international students: Required—TOEFL. *Application deadline:* For fall admission, 1/10 priority date for domestic and international students; for spring admission, 12/1 priority date for domestic and international students. Applications are processed on a rolling basis. Application fee: $55 ($60 for international students). Electronic applications accepted. *Expenses:* Tuition, state resident: full-time $5,838. Tuition, nonresident: full-time $13,409. Tuition and fees vary according to program. *Financial support:* Fellowships, teaching assistantships with full and partial tuition reimbursements, unspecified assistantships available. Financial award application deadline: 1/1. *Faculty research:* Judaism and Christianity, Islam, religions in Asia, methods and theories, American and Native American religion. *Unit head:* Daniel B. Stevenson, Chair, 785-864-7258, Fax: 785-864-5205, E-mail: rstudies@ku.edu. *Application contact:* Paul Mirecki, Graduate Director, 785-864-7258, Fax: 785-864-5205, E-mail: pmirecki@ku.edu.

University of Lethbridge, School of Graduate Studies, Lethbridge, AB T1K 3M4, Canada. Offers accounting (MScM); addictions counseling (M Sc); agricultural biotechnology (M Sc); agricultural studies (M Sc, MA); anthropology (MA); archaeology (MA); art (MA); biochemistry (M Sc); biological sciences (M Sc); biomolecular science (PhD); biosystems and biodiversity (PhD); Canadian studies (MA); chemistry (M Sc); computer science (M Sc); computer science and geographical information science (M Sc); counseling psychology (M Ed); dramatic arts (MA); earth, space, and physical science (PhD); economics (MA); educational leadership (M Ed); English (MA); environmental science (M Sc); evolution and behavior (PhD); exercise science (M Sc); finance (MScM); French (MA); French/German (MA); French/Spanish (MA); general education (M Ed); general management (MScM); geography (M Sc, MA); German (MA); health sciences (M Sc, MA); history (MA); human resource management and labour relations (MScM); individualized multidisciplinary (M Sc, MA); information systems (MScM); international management (MScM); kinesiology (M Sc, MA); management (M Sc, MA); marketing (MScM); mathematics (M Sc); music (MA); Native American studies (MA); neuroscience (M Sc, PhD); new media (MA); nursing (M Sc); philosophy (MA); physics (M Sc); policy and strategy (MScM); political science (MA); psychology (M Sc, MA); religious studies (MA); sociology (MA); theoretical and computational science (PhD); urban and regional studies (MA). Part-time and evening/weekend programs available. *Students:* 215 full-time, 98 part-time. In 2007, 87 master's, 1 doctorate awarded. *Degree requirements:* For doctorate, comprehensive exam, thesis/dissertation. *Entrance requirements:* For master's, GMAT (M Sc in management), bachelor's degree in related field, minimum GPA of 3.0 during previous 20 graded semester courses, 2 years teaching or related experience (M Ed); for doctorate, master's degree, minimum graduate GPA of 3.5. Additional exam requirements/recommendations for international students: Required—TOEFL. Application fee: $60 Canadian dollars. *Financial support:* Fellowships, research assistantships, teaching assistantships, scholarships/grants, health care benefits, and unspecified assistantships available. *Faculty research:* Movement and brain plasticity, gibberellin physiology, photosynthesis, carbon cycling, molecular properties of main-group ring components. *Unit head:* Dr. Jo-Anne Fiske, Interim Dean, 403-329-2121, Fax: 403-329-2097. *Application contact:* Jennifer Geddes, Graduate Liaison Officer, 403-329-2762, Fax: 403-329-5159, E-mail: jennifer.geddes@uleth.ca.

University of Manitoba, Faculty of Graduate Studies, Faculty of Arts, Department of Religion, Winnipeg, MB R3T 2N2, Canada. Offers MA, PhD. *Degree requirements:* For master's, one foreign language, thesis or alternative.

University of Minnesota, Twin Cities Campus, Graduate School, College of Liberal Arts, Department of Classical and Near Eastern Studies, Minneapolis, MN 55455-0213. Offers ancient and medieval art and archaeology (MA, PhD); classics (MA, PhD); Greek (MA, PhD); Latin (MA, PhD); religions in antiquity (MA). Part-time programs available. *Faculty:* 12 full-time (2 women), 3 part-time/adjunct (2 women). *Students:* 24 full-time (10 women), 8 part-time (2 women); includes 1 minority (African American), 1 international. Average age 29. 37 applicants, 32% accepted, 9 enrolled. In 2007, 4 master's, 1 doctorate awarded. Terminal master's awarded for partial completion of doctoral program. *Degree requirements:* For master's, 2 foreign languages, comprehensive exam, thesis or alternative; for doctorate, variable foreign language requirement, comprehensive exam, thesis/dissertation. *Entrance requirements:* For master's and doctorate, GRE, 3 letters of recommendation, department application, writing sample, copies of transcripts, personal statement. Additional exam requirements/recommendations for international students: Required—TOEFL. *Application deadline:* For fall admission, 1/4 for domestic students. Application fee: $55 ($75 for international students). Electronic applications accepted. *Financial support:* In 2007–08, 10 fellowships with full and partial tuition reimbursements (averaging $11,165 per year), 4 research assistantships (averaging $23,166 per year), 20 teaching assistantships (averaging $23,357 per year) were awarded; career-related internships or fieldwork, Federal Work-Study, institutionally sponsored loans, and tuition waivers (full and partial) also available. Support available to part-time students. Financial award application deadline: 1/4. *Faculty research:* Greek and Latin literature, archaeology, religions in antiquity, ancient Near East. Total annual research expenditures: $14,849. *Unit head:* George A. Sheets, Chair, 612-625-3326, Fax: 612-624-4894, E-mail: gasheets@umn.edu. *Application contact:* Victoria Keller, Administrative Assistant, Fax: 612-624-4894, E-mail: kell0801@umn.edu.

University of Missouri–Columbia, Graduate School, College of Arts and Sciences, Department of Religious Studies, Columbia, MO 65211. Offers MA. *Entrance requirements:* For master's, GRE General Test, minimum GPA of 3.0.

University of Mobile, Graduate Programs, Program in Religious Studies, Mobile, AL 36613. Offers biblical/theological studies (MA); marriage and family counseling (MA). Part-time and evening/weekend programs available. *Faculty:* 6 full-time (0 women), 2 part-time/adjunct (0 women). *Students:* 18 full-time (16 women), 35 part-time (18 women); includes 15 minority (13 African Americans, 2 American Indian/Alaska Native). Average age 27. In 2007, 15 degrees awarded. *Degree requirements:* For master's, one foreign language, comprehensive exam, thesis optional. *Entrance requirements:* For master's, GRE General Test. Additional exam requirements/recommendations for international students: Required—TOEFL. *Application deadline:* For fall admission, 8/3 priority date for domestic students; for spring admission, 12/23 for domestic students. Applications are processed on a rolling basis. Application fee: $40 ($50 for international students). *Financial support:* Federal Work-Study available. Support available to part-time students. Financial award application deadline: 8/1. *Unit head:* Dr. Cecil Taylor, Dean, School of Christian Studies, 251-442-2255, Fax: 251-442-2523, E-mail: ctaylor@

Religion

University of Mobile (continued)
mail.umobile.edu. *Application contact:* Tammy C. Eubanks, Administrative Assistant to Dean of Graduate Programs, 251-442-2270, Fax: 251-442-2523, E-mail: teubanks@umobile.edu.

The University of North Carolina at Chapel Hill, Graduate School, College of Arts and Sciences, Department of Religious Studies, Chapel Hill, NC 27599. Offers MA, PhD. *Degree requirements:* For master's, one foreign language, comprehensive exam, thesis; for doctorate, 2 foreign languages, comprehensive exam, thesis/dissertation. *Entrance requirements:* For master's and doctorate, GRE General Test, minimum GPA of 3.0. Additional exam requirements/recommendations for international students: Required—TOEFL. *Faculty research:* Religion.

The University of North Carolina at Charlotte, Graduate School, College of Arts and Sciences, Department of Religious Studies, Charlotte, NC 28223-0001. Offers MA. *Faculty:* 8 full-time (3 women). *Students:* 1 full-time (0 women), 16 part-time (7 women); includes 1 minority (African American) Average age 33. 6 applicants, 100% accepted, 2 enrolled. In 2007, 1 degree awarded. *Entrance requirements:* For master's, GRE or MAT, 3 letters of reference. Additional exam requirements/recommendations for international students: Required—TOEFL (minimum score 557 paper-based; 220 computer-based). *Application deadline:* For fall admission, 7/15 for domestic students, 5/1 for international students; for spring admission, 11/15 for domestic students, 10/1 for international students. Applications are processed on a rolling basis. Application fee: $55. Electronic applications accepted. *Expenses:* Tuition, state resident: full-time $2,855. Tuition, nonresident: full-time $13,062. Required fees: $1,692. *Financial support:* In 2007–08, 4 teaching assistantships (averaging $9,000 per year) were awarded; fellowships, research assistantships, career-related internships or fieldwork, Federal Work-Study, institutionally sponsored loans, scholarships/grants, and unspecified assistantships also available. Support available to part-time students. Financial award application deadline: 4/1; financial award applicants required to submit FAFSA. *Unit head:* Dr. James D. Tabor, Chair, 704-687-4598, Fax: 704-687-3002, E-mail: jdtabor@email.uncc.edu. *Application contact:* Kathy B. Giddings, Director of Graduate Admissions, 704-687-3366, Fax: 704-687-3279, E-mail: agidding@uncc.edu.

University of North Texas, Robert B. Toulouse School of Graduate Studies, College of Arts and Sciences, Department of Philosophy and Religion Studies, Denton, TX 76203. Offers philosophy (MA, PhD). *Faculty:* 11 full-time (1 woman). *Students:* 15 full-time (8 women), 18 part-time (6 women); includes 4 minority (1 African American, 2 Asian Americans or Pacific Islanders, 1 Hispanic American), 3 international. Average age 31. 27 applicants, 37% accepted, 8 enrolled. In 2007, 5 degrees awarded. *Degree requirements:* For master's, one foreign language, thesis or alternative. *Entrance requirements:* For master's, GRE General Test. Additional exam requirements/recommendations for international students: Required—proof of English language proficiency required for non-native English speakers; Recommended—TOEFL (minimum score 550 paper-based; 213 computer-based). *Application deadline:* For fall admission, 7/15 for domestic students; for spring admission, 11/15 for domestic students. Application fee: $50 ($75 for international students). *Unit head:* Dr. Robert Frodeman, Chair, 940-565-2266, Fax: 940-565-4448, E-mail: frodeman@unt.edu.

University of Notre Dame, Graduate School, College of Arts and Letters, Division of Humanities, Program in Early Christian Studies, Notre Dame, IN 46556. Offers MA. *Faculty:* 26 full-time (6 women). *Students:* 6 full-time (2 women), 1 international. 36 applicants, 14% accepted, 5 enrolled. In 2007, 3 degrees awarded. *Degree requirements:* For master's, 3 foreign languages, comprehensive exam. *Entrance requirements:* For master's, GRE General Test. Additional exam requirements/recommendations for international students: Required—TOEFL (minimum score 600 paper-based; 250 computer-based; 80 iBT). *Application deadline:* For fall admission, 2/1 priority date for domestic students, 2/1 for international students. Application fee: $50. Electronic applications accepted. *Financial support:* In 2007–08, 2 teaching assistantships (averaging $12,000 per year) were awarded; fellowships, research assistantships with full tuition reimbursements, tuition waivers (full) also available. Financial award application deadline: 2/1. *Faculty research:* Early Christian theology, worship and scriptural interpretation; late antique and Byzantine history; art and culture; Greek and Latin literature. *Unit head:* Dr. Blake Leyerle, SJ, Director of Graduate Studies, 574-631-7195, Fax: 574-631-4183. *Application contact:* Dr. Jarren Gonzales, Director of Graduate Admissions, 574-631-7706, Fax: 574-631-4183.

University of Ottawa, Faculty of Graduate and Postdoctoral Studies, Faculty of Arts, Department of Classics and Religious Studies, Ottawa, ON K1N 6N5, Canada. Offers classical studies (MA); religious studies (PhD). *Degree requirements:* For master's, comprehensive exam, thesis or alternative; for doctorate, comprehensive exam, thesis/dissertation. *Entrance requirements:* For master's, honors degree or equivalent, minimum B average; for doctorate, master's degree, minimum B+ average. Electronic applications accepted. *Faculty research:* Religions in Canada, including Amerindian and Inuit religions; religion and culture; late antiquity.

University of Pennsylvania, School of Arts and Sciences, Graduate Group in Religious Studies, Philadelphia, PA 19104. Offers PhD. *Degree requirements:* For doctorate, thesis/dissertation, approved specialty languages, preliminary and final exams. *Entrance requirements:* For doctorate, GRE. Additional exam requirements/recommendations for international students: Required—TOEFL. Electronic applications accepted. *Faculty research:* Judaism and Christianity (ancient, medieval, modern), Islam, Hinduism, Buddhism, modern religious thought.

University of Pittsburgh, School of Arts and Sciences, Cooperative Doctoral Program in Religion, Pittsburgh, PA 15260. Offers PhD. *Faculty:* 11 full-time (3 women), 1 (woman) part-time/adjunct. *Students:* 11 full-time (5 women); includes 1 minority (Asian American or Pacific Islander) Average age 39. 16 applicants, 25% accepted, 3 enrolled. *Degree requirements:* For doctorate, 2 foreign languages, comprehensive exam, thesis/dissertation, preliminary exam. *Entrance requirements:* For doctorate, GRE General Test, sample of research or written work, 3 letters of recommendation, transcripts. Additional exam requirements/recommendations for international students: Required—TOEFL (minimum score 600 paper-based; 250 computer-based; 100 iBT). *Application deadline:* For fall admission, 1/15 for domestic and international students. Application fee: $50. Electronic applications accepted. *Financial support:* In 2007–08, 7 students received support, including 3 fellowships with full tuition reimbursements available (averaging $15,070 per year), 3 teaching assistantships with full tuition reimbursements available (averaging $14,485 per year); research assistantships, tuition waivers (partial) and unspecified assistantships also available. Financial award application deadline: 1/15. *Faculty research:* Contemporary Catholicism and religion in America, Buddhism and East Asian religions, philosophy and religion and religious thought and language, medieval to modern Jewish history, theories and methods in the study of religion. *Unit head:* Dr. Linda Penkower, Chair, 412-624-2277, Fax: 412-624-5994, E-mail: penkower@pitt.edu. *Application contact:* Judy Macey, Administrator III, 412-624-5990, Fax: 412-624-5994, E-mail: relgst@pitt.edu.

University of Pittsburgh, School of Arts and Sciences, Department of Religious Studies, Pittsburgh, PA 15260. Offers MA. *Faculty:* 9 full-time (3 women), 1 (woman) part-time/adjunct. *Students:* 5 full-time (all women). Average age 27. 10 applicants, 40% accepted, 4 enrolled. In 2007, 1 degree awarded. *Degree requirements:* For master's, comprehensive exam, thesis. *Entrance requirements:* For master's, GRE General Test, sample of written work, 3 letters of recommendation, transcripts. Additional exam requirements/recommendations for international students: Required—TOEFL (minimum score 600 paper-based; 250 computer-based; 100 iBT). *Application deadline:* For fall admission, 1/15 for domestic and international students. Application fee: $50. Electronic applications accepted. *Financial support:* In 2007–08, 3 students received support, including fellowships (averaging $15,070 per year), 3 teaching assistantships with full tuition reimbursements available (averaging $14,485 per year); research assistantships with full tuition reimbursements available, tuition waivers (partial) also available. Financial award application deadline: 1/15. *Faculty research:* Contemporary Catholicism and religion in America, Buddhism and East Asian religions, philosophy and religion and religious thought and language, Medieval to modern Jewish history, theories and methods in the study of religion. *Unit head:* Dr. Linda Penkower, Chair, 412-624-2277, Fax: 412-624-5994, E-mail: penkower@pitt.edu. *Application contact:* Judy Macey, Administrator III, 412-624-5990, Fax: 412-624-5994, E-mail: relgst@pitt.edu.

University of Regina, Faculty of Graduate Studies and Research, Faculty of Arts, Department of Religious Studies, Regina, SK S4S 0A2, Canada. Offers MA, PhD. Part-time programs available. *Faculty:* 10 full-time (3 women), 2 part-time/adjunct (0 women). *Students:* 8 full-time (6 women), 4 part-time (3 women). 4 applicants, 100% accepted, 3 enrolled. In 2007, 2 degrees awarded. *Degree requirements:* For master's, thesis. *Entrance requirements:* Additional exam requirements/recommendations for international students: Required—TOEFL (minimum score 580 paper-based; 237 computer-based; 88 iBT). *Application deadline:* Applications are processed on a rolling basis. Application fee: $85 ($100 for international students). Electronic applications accepted. *Financial support:* In 2007–08, 4 students received support, including 4 fellowships (averaging $15,750 per year), research assistantships (averaging $13,875 per year), 1 teaching assistantship (averaging $13,060 per year); scholarships/grants also available. Financial award application deadline: 6/15. *Faculty research:* Christianity, Hinduism, Buddhism, Islam, Judaism. *Unit head:* Dr. Leona Anderson, Head, 306-585-4580, Fax: 306-585-4815, E-mail: leona.anderson@uregina.ca.

University of St. Thomas, Graduate Studies, College of Arts and Sciences, Program in Catholic Studies, St. Paul, MN 55105-1096. Offers MA. Part-time and evening/weekend programs available. *Degree requirements:* For master's, thesis. *Entrance requirements:* For master's, bachelor's degree with minimum GPA of 3.0, writing sample, 3 letters of recommendation. Additional exam requirements/recommendations for international students: Required—TOEFL (minimum score 550 paper-based).

University of Saskatchewan, College of Graduate Studies and Research, College of Arts and Sciences, Department of Religious Studies and Anthropology, Saskatoon, SK S7N 5A2, Canada. Offers MA. *Degree requirements:* For master's, thesis. *Entrance requirements:* Additional exam requirements/recommendations for international students: Required—TOEFL.

University of South Africa, College of Human Sciences, Pretoria, South Africa. Offers adult education (M Ed); African languages (MA, PhD); African politics (MA, PhD); Afrikaans (MA, PhD); ancient history (MA, PhD); ancient Near Eastern studies (MA, PhD); anthropology (MA, PhD); applied linguistics (MA); Arabic (MA, PhD); archaeology (MA); art history (MA); Biblical archaeology (MA); Biblical studies (M Th, D Th, PhD); Christian spirituality (M Th, D Th); church history (M Th, D Th); classical studies (MA, PhD); clinical psychology (MA); communication (MA, PhD); comparative education (M Ed, Ed D); consulting psychology (D Admin, D Com, PhD); curriculum studies (M Ed, Ed D); development studies (M Admin, MA, D Admin, PhD); didactics (M Ed, Ed D); education (M Tech); education management (M Ed, Ed D); educational psychology (M Ed); English (MA); environmental education (M Ed); French (MA, PhD); German (MA, PhD); Greek (MA); guidance and counseling (M Ed); health studies (MA, PhD), including health sciences education (MA), health services management (MA), medical and surgical nursing science (critical care general) (MA), midwifery and neonatal nursing science (MA), trauma and emergency care (MA); history (MA, PhD); history of education (Ed D); inclusive education (M Ed, Ed D); information and communications technology policy and regulation (MA); information science (MA, MIS, PhD); international politics (MA, PhD); Islamic studies (MA, PhD); Italian (MA, PhD); Judaica (MA, PhD); linguistics (MA, PhD); mathematical education (M Ed); mathematics education (MA); missiology (M Th, D Th); modern Hebrew (MA, PhD); musicology (MA, MMus, D Mus, PhD); natural science education (M Ed); New Testament (M Th, D Th); Old Testament (D Th); pastoral therapy (M Th, D Th); philosophy (MA); philosophy of education (M Ed, Ed D); politics (MA, PhD); Portuguese (MA, PhD); practical theology (M Th, D Th); psychology (MA, MS, PhD); psychology of education (M Ed, Ed D); public health (MA); religious studies (MA, D Th, PhD); Romance languages (MA); Russian (MA, PhD); Semitic languages (MA, PhD); social behavior studies in HIV/AIDS (MA); social science (mental health) (MA); social science in development studies (MA); social science in psychology (MA); social science in social work (MA); social science in sociology (MA); social work (MSW, DSW, PhD); socio-education (M Ed, Ed D); sociolinguistics (MA); sociology (MA, PhD); Spanish (MA, PhD); systematic theology (M Th, D Th); TESOL (teaching English to speakers of other languages) (MA); theological ethics (M Th, D Th); theory of literature (MA, PhD); urban ministries (D Th); urban ministry (M Th).

University of South Carolina, The Graduate School, College of Arts and Sciences, Department of Religious Studies, Columbia, SC 29208. Offers MA. Part-time programs available. *Faculty:* 6 full-time (1 woman), 2 part-time/adjunct (0 women). *Students:* 10 full-time (5 women), 1 part-time. Average age 35. 11 applicants, 55% accepted, 4 enrolled. In 2007, 2 degrees awarded. *Degree requirements:* For master's, one foreign language, comprehensive exam, thesis. *Entrance requirements:* For master's, GRE General Test or MAT. Additional exam requirements/recommendations for international students: Required—TOEFL. *Application deadline:* For winter admission, 3/1 for domestic students; for spring admission, 5/1 for domestic students. Application fee: $40. Electronic applications accepted. *Expenses:* Tuition, state resident: part-time $440 per hour. Tuition, nonresident: part-time $936 per hour. Required fees: $17 per hour. Tuition and fees vary according to program. *Financial support:* In 2007–08, 4 students received support, including 2 research assistantships with partial tuition reimbursements available (averaging $8,085 per year); Federal Work-Study, institutionally sponsored loans, scholarships/grants, and unspecified assistantships also available. Financial award application deadline: 3/1. *Faculty research:* Biblical and Near Eastern studies, theology and religious thought, religion and culture, South Asian religions, Islamic studies. Total annual research expenditures: $1,000. *Unit head:* Dr. Steve Lynn, Chair, 803-777-4997, Fax: 803-777-0213, E-mail: lynns@gwm.sc.edu. *Application contact:* Dr. Kevin Lewis, Director of Graduate Studies, 803-777-2561, Fax: 803-777-0213, E-mail: kevin@sc.edu.

University of Southern California, Graduate School, College of Letters, Arts and Sciences, School of Religion, Los Angeles, CA 90089. Offers social ethics (MA, PhD); JD/MA. *Students:* 5 full-time (2 women); includes 2 minority (1 African American, 1 Asian American or Pacific Islander). In 2007, 3 degrees awarded. Terminal master's awarded for partial completion of doctoral program. *Degree requirements:* For master's, thesis optional; for doctorate, one foreign language, thesis/dissertation. *Entrance requirements:* For master's and doctorate, GRE General Test. *Application deadline:* For fall admission, 12/1 priority date for domestic students. Applications are processed on a rolling basis. Application fee: $85. *Financial support:* In 2007–08, research assistantships (averaging $18,500 per year), teaching assistantships with full tuition reimbursements (averaging $18,500 per year) were awarded; Federal Work-Study, institutionally sponsored loans, and scholarships/grants also available. Financial award application deadline: 2/15; financial award applicants required to submit FAFSA. *Faculty research:* Religion in America, religions of immigrants, ancient Near Eastern archaeology and religion, religious pluralism, religion and popular culture, and religion and science. *Unit head:* Dr. Donald Miller, Chair, 213-740-0270. *Application contact:* William May, Information Contact, 213-740-0276, E-mail: wmay@usc.edu.

University of South Florida, Graduate School, College of Arts and Sciences, Department of Religious Studies, Tampa, FL 33620-9951. Offers MA. Part-time and evening/weekend programs available. *Faculty:* 10 full-time (2 women). *Students:* 19 full-time (10 women), 14 part-time (8 women); includes 5 minority (1 African American, 4 Hispanic Americans). 13 applicants, 85% accepted, 6 enrolled. In 2007, 5 degrees awarded. *Degree requirements:* For master's, comprehensive exam, thesis. *Entrance requirements:* For master's, GRE General Test, minimum GPA of 3.0 in last 60 hours. *Application deadline:* For fall admission, 3/15 priority date for domestic and international students; for spring admission, 10/15 priority date for domestic and international students. Applications are processed on a rolling basis. Application fee: $30. Electronic applications accepted. *Financial support:* In 2007–08, 9 teaching assistantships with full tuition reimbursements (averaging $8,000 per year) were awarded; unspecified assistantships also available. Financial award applicants required to submit FAFSA. *Faculty research:* Scripture and history of Judaism, Christianity, and Islam; religion and society; new religions; comparative religious ethics; narrative and religion. *Unit head:* Mozella Mitchell,

Chairperson, 813-974-1852, Fax: 813-974-1853, E-mail: mmitchel@cas.usf.edu. *Application contact:* Wei Zhang, Associate Professor, 813-974-1882, Fax: 813-974-1853, E-mail: wzhang5@cas.usf.edu.

The University of Tennessee, Graduate School, College of Arts and Sciences, Department of Philosophy, Knoxville, TN 37996. Offers medical ethics (MA, PhD); philosophy (MA, PhD); religious studies (MA). Part-time programs available. *Degree requirements:* For master's, thesis or alternative; for doctorate, one foreign language, thesis/dissertation. *Entrance requirements:* For master's and doctorate, GRE General Test, minimum GPA of 2.7. Additional exam requirements/recommendations for international students: Required—TOEFL. Electronic applications accepted.

University of the Incarnate Word, School of Graduate Studies and Research, College of Humanities, Arts, and Social Sciences, Program in Religious Studies, San Antonio, TX 78209-6397. Offers MA. Part-time programs available. *Students:* Average age 43. In 2007, 5 degrees awarded. *Degree requirements:* For master's, practicum. *Entrance requirements:* For master's, GRE General Test or MAT. Additional exam requirements/recommendations for international students: Required—TOEFL. *Application deadline:* Applications are processed on a rolling basis. Application fee: $20. Electronic applications accepted. *Expenses:* Tuition: Part-time $605 per credit hour. Required fees: $58 per credit hour. Tuition and fees vary according to degree level. *Financial support:* Federal Work-Study, scholarships/grants, and tuition waivers (partial) available. Financial award applicants required to submit FAFSA. *Faculty research:* Ministry with Hispanics, spirituality, religious education, pastoral ministry. *Unit head:* Sr. Eilish Ryan, Chair, 210-829-3871, Fax: 210-829-3880, E-mail: eryan@uiwtx.edu. *Application contact:* Andrea Cyterski-Acosta, Dean of Enrollment, 210-829-6005, Fax: 210-829-3921, E-mail: admis@uiwtx.edu.

University of the West, Department of Religious Studies, Rosemead, CA 91770. Offers Buddhist studies (MA, DBS); comparative religions (MA); religious studies (PhD). Part-time and evening/weekend programs available. *Degree requirements:* For master's, thesis or comprehensive exam, competency in language associated with Buddhist Canon literature; for doctorate, one foreign language, comprehensive exam, thesis/dissertation.

University of Toronto, School of Graduate Studies, Humanities Division, Centre for the Study of Religion, Toronto, ON M5S 1A1, Canada. Offers MA, PhD. Part-time programs available. *Faculty:* 50 full-time, 12 part-time/adjunct. *Students:* 67 full-time (32 women), 4 part-time, 14 international. 93 applicants, 44% accepted. In 2007, 2 master's, 3 doctorates awarded. *Degree requirements:* For master's, one foreign language, research paper, language requirement examination; for doctorate, 2 foreign languages, thesis/dissertation, language examinations, general examinations, oral examination. *Entrance requirements:* For master's, BA in religion or a related field; minimum A- average in final year, 3 letters of recommendation, resumé; for doctorate, MA in religion, minimum average of A- in MA courses with no individual grade below a B, 3 letters of recommendation, resumé, brief writing sample. Additional exam requirements/recommendations for international students: Required—TOEFL (minimum score 600 paper-based; 250 computer-based), TWE (minimum score 5). Application fee: $100 Canadian dollars. *Financial support:* Fellowships with full tuition reimbursements, teaching assistantships with full tuition reimbursements available. *Unit head:* Prof. John Kloppenborg, Chair and Graduate Chair, 416-978-3173, Fax: 416-978-3963, E-mail: chair.religion@utoronto.ca. *Application contact:* Secretary, 416-978-3057, Fax: 416-978-1610, E-mail: religion.grad@utoronto.ca.

University of Virginia, College and Graduate School of Arts and Sciences, Department of Religious Studies, Charlottesville, VA 22903. Offers MA, PhD. *Faculty:* 30 full-time (11 women), 1 part-time/adjunct (0 women). *Students:* 83 full-time (30 women), 4 part-time (2 women); includes 4 minority (3 African Americans, 1 Asian American or Pacific Islander), 9 international. Average age 32. 206 applicants, 40% accepted, 22 enrolled. In 2007, 10 master's, 12 doctorates awarded. *Degree requirements:* For master's, one foreign language, thesis optional; for doctorate, 2 foreign languages, comprehensive exam, thesis/dissertation. *Entrance requirements:* For master's and doctorate, GRE General Test. *Application deadline:* Applications are processed on a rolling basis. Application fee: $60. Electronic applications accepted. *Financial support:* Applicants required to submit FAFSA. *Unit head:* Paul Groner, Chair, 434-924-3741, Fax: 434-924-1467, E-mail: groner@virginia.edu.

University of Washington, Graduate School, College of Arts and Sciences, Henry M. Jackson School of International Studies, Comparative Religion Program, Seattle, WA 98195. Offers MAIS. *Faculty:* 21 full-time (9 women). *Students:* 23 full-time (11 women); includes 2 minority (1 Asian American or Pacific Islander, 1 Hispanic American). 39 applicants, 59% accepted, 9 enrolled. In 2007, 3 degrees awarded. *Degree requirements:* For master's, 2 foreign languages. *Entrance requirements:* For master's, GRE General Test, minimum GPA of 3.0. Additional exam requirements/recommendations for international students: Required—TOEFL (minimum score 500 paper-based; 213 computer-based). *Application deadline:* For fall admission, 1/3 for domestic students. Application fee: $50. Electronic applications accepted. *Financial support:* In 2007–08, 1 fellowship with full tuition reimbursement, 2 teaching assistantships with full tuition reimbursements were awarded; research assistantships, career-related internships or fieldwork, Federal Work-Study, and institutionally sponsored loans also available. Financial award application deadline: 1/15; financial award applicants required to submit FAFSA. *Unit head:* Prof. James K. Wellman, Chair, 206-543-0339, E-mail: jwellman@u.washington.edu. *Application contact:* 206-543-6001, Fax: 206-616-3170, E-mail: jsisinfo@u.washington.edu.

University of Waterloo, Graduate Studies, Faculty of Arts, Department of Religious Studies, Waterloo, ON N2L 3G1, Canada. Offers religious diversity in North America (PhD). *Faculty:* 27. *Students:* 10. *Degree requirements:* For doctorate, thesis/dissertation. *Entrance requirements:* Additional exam requirements/recommendations for international students: Required—TOEFL. Application fee: $75. Electronic applications accepted. *Financial support:* Fellowships, research assistantships, teaching assistantships available. *Faculty research:* Religious diversity in North America. *Application contact:* Dr. Doug Cowan, Graduate Officer, E-mail: decowan@uwaterloo.ca.

The University of Winnipeg, Graduate Studies, Department of Religious Studies, Winnipeg, MB R3B 2E9, Canada. Offers MA. Part-time programs available. *Faculty research:* Religion and culture, social ethics, religious liberalism, history of Canaanite and Israelite religion, literary criticism of the Hebrew Bible.

Vanderbilt University, Graduate School, Department of Religion, Nashville, TN 37240-1001. Offers MA, PhD. *Faculty:* 23 full-time (6 women). *Students:* 127 full-time (63 women); includes 24 minority (18 African Americans, 1 American Indian/Alaska Native, 3 Asian Americans or Pacific Islanders, 2 Hispanic Americans), 11 international. Average age 35. 258 applicants, 14% accepted, 17 enrolled. In 2007, 13 master's, 9 doctorates awarded. *Degree requirements:* For master's, one foreign language, thesis; for doctorate, 2 foreign languages, thesis/dissertation, final and qualifying exams. *Entrance requirements:* For master's and doctorate, GRE General Test. *Application deadline:* For fall admission, 1/15 for domestic and international students. Application fee: $0. Electronic applications accepted. *Financial support:* Fellowships with full and partial tuition reimbursements, teaching assistantships with full and partial tuition reimbursements, Federal Work-Study, institutionally sponsored loans, health care benefits, and tuition waivers (full and partial) available. Support available to part-time students. Financial award application deadline: 1/15; financial award applicants required to submit CSS PROFILE or FAFSA. *Faculty research:* Hebrew Bible, New Testament, church history, theology, ethics. *Unit head:* John S. McClure, Chair, 615-343-3977, Fax: 615-343-5449, E-mail: john.s.mcclure@vanderbilt.edu. *Application contact:* James P. Byrd, Director of Graduate Studies, 615-343-3977, Fax: 615-343-5449, E-mail: james.p.byrd@vanderbilt.edu.

Vanguard University of Southern California, School of Religion, Costa Mesa, CA 92626-9601. Offers leadership studies (MA); religion (MA), including biblical studies; theological studies (MTS). Part-time and evening/weekend programs available. *Faculty:* 7 full-time (1 woman), 4 part-time/adjunct (0 women). *Students:* 16 full-time (5 women), 72 part-time (20 women); includes 24 minority (3 African Americans, 1 American Indian/Alaska Native, 5 Asian Americans or Pacific Islanders, 15 Hispanic Americans), 3 international. Average age 38. 39 applicants, 79% accepted, 26 enrolled. In 2007, 25 degrees awarded. *Degree requirements:* For master's, one foreign language, comprehensive exam, thesis (for some programs). *Entrance requirements:* For master's, minimum GPA of 3.0; course work in humanities, religion, and social sciences (MA); minimum GPA of 2.5 (MTS). Additional exam requirements/recommendations for international students: Required—TOEFL (minimum score 550 paper-based; 213 computer-based). *Application deadline:* For fall admission, 4/1 priority date for domestic and international students; for spring admission, 10/1 priority date for domestic and international students. Applications are processed on a rolling basis. Application fee: $45. Electronic applications accepted. *Expenses: Contact institution.* Full-time tuition and fees vary according to course load and program. *Financial support:* In 2007–08, 28 students received support, including 6 teaching assistantships (averaging $1,800 per year); scholarships/grants, tuition waivers (partial), and unspecified assistantships also available. Financial award application deadline: 3/2. *Faculty research:* Apocalyptic literature, narrative theology, ecumenism and Pentecost. *Unit head:* Dr. Andrew Stenhouse, Associate Dean, 714-556-3610 Ext. 3223, Fax: 714-957-9317. *Application contact:* John Sim, Graduate Religion Coordinator, 714-556-3610 Ext. 3285, Fax: 714-957-9317, E-mail: jsim@vanguard.edu.

Virginia University of Lynchburg, Graduate Programs, Lynchburg, VA 24501-6417. Offers M Div.

Wake Forest University, Graduate School of Arts and Sciences, Department of Religion, Winston-Salem, NC 27109. Offers MA. *Accreditation:* ACIPE. Part-time programs available. *Faculty:* 9 full-time (2 women), 2 part-time/adjunct (0 women). *Students:* 13 full-time (7 women), 1 international. Average age 28. 20 applicants, 55% accepted, 8 enrolled. In 2007, 5 master's awarded. *Degree requirements:* For master's, one foreign language, thesis. *Entrance requirements:* For master's, GRE General Test. Additional exam requirements/recommendations for international students: Required—TOEFL (minimum score 213 computer-based; 79 iBT). *Application deadline:* For fall admission, 1/15 for domestic and international students. Application fee: $45 ($55 for international students). Electronic applications accepted. *Financial support:* In 2007–08, 10 students received support, including 1 fellowship with full tuition reimbursement available (averaging $4,000 per year), 1 teaching assistantship with full tuition reimbursement available (averaging $8,000 per year); scholarships/grants, tuition waivers (full and partial), and unspecified assistantships also available. Support available to part-time students. Financial award application deadline: 1/15; financial award applicants required to submit FAFSA. *Faculty research:* Christian origins, biblical archaeology, psychology and religion, religion and literature. *Unit head:* Dr. Simeon Ilesanmi, Director, 336-758-5459, Fax: 336-758-4462, E-mail: ilesanmi@wfu.edu.

Warner Pacific College, Graduate Programs, Portland, OR 97215-4099. Offers biblical and theological studies (MA); biblical studies (M Rel); education (M Ed); management/organizational leadership (MS); pastoral ministries (M Rel); religion and ethics (M Rel); teaching (MA); theology (M Rel). Part-time programs available. *Faculty:* 20 part-time/adjunct (6 women). *Students:* 57 full-time (26 women), 4 part-time (2 women); includes 5 minority (4 African Americans, 1 Asian American or Pacific Islander). *Degree requirements:* For master's, thesis or alternative, Presentation of Defense. *Entrance requirements:* For master's, interview, minimum GPA of 2.5, letters of recommendations. *Application deadline:* Applications are processed on a rolling basis. *Expenses:* Tuition: Full-time $15,642. Required fees: $150. *Financial support:* Career-related internships or fieldwork and Federal Work-Study available. Financial award application deadline: 7/1; financial award applicants required to submit FAFSA. *Faculty research:* New Testament studies, nineteenth-century Wesleyan theology, preaching and church growth, Christian ethics. *Unit head:* Director, 503-517-1045, Fax: 503-517-1350, E-mail: kazio@warnerpacific.edu.

Washington University in St. Louis, Graduate School of Arts and Sciences, Department of History, Program in Jewish, Islamic, and Near Eastern Studies, St. Louis, MO 63130-4899. Offers Islamic and Near Eastern studies (MA); Jewish studies (MA). *Degree requirements:* For master's, one foreign language, thesis (for some programs). *Entrance requirements:* For master's, GRE General Test. Electronic applications accepted.

Wayland Baptist University, Graduate Programs, Programs in Religion, Plainview, TX 79072-6998. Offers Christian ministry (MCM); religion (MA). Part-time and evening/weekend programs available. Postbaccalaureate distance learning degree programs offered (no on-campus study). *Faculty:* 5 full-time (1 woman), 1 part-time/adjunct (0 women). *Students:* 1 full-time (0 women), 12 part-time (4 women); includes 2 minority (both Hispanic Americans) Average age 32. 1 applicant, 100% accepted, 1 enrolled. In 2007, 1 degree awarded. *Degree requirements:* For master's, comprehensive exam. *Entrance requirements:* For master's, GRE or MAT. Additional exam requirements/recommendations for international students: Required—TOEFL (minimum score 500 paper-based; 173 computer-based). *Application deadline:* Applications are processed on a rolling basis. Application fee: $35. *Expenses:* Tuition: Full-time $6,390; part-time $355 per credit hour. Required fees: $600; $50 per term. Full-time tuition and fees vary according to course load. *Financial support:* Federal Work-Study, institutionally sponsored loans, and scholarships/grants available. Support available to part-time students. Financial award application deadline: 5/1; financial award applicants required to submit FAFSA. *Unit head:* Dr. Paul Sadler, Chairman, 806-291-1160, Fax: 806-291-1969, E-mail: sadlerp@wbu.edu.

Western Michigan University, Graduate College, College of Arts and Sciences, Department of Comparative Religion, Kalamazoo, MI 49008-5202. Offers MA, PhD. *Degree requirements:* For master's, one foreign language, thesis optional, oral exam; for doctorate, 2 foreign languages, thesis/dissertation. *Entrance requirements:* For doctorate, GRE General Test.

Western Seminary, Graduate Programs, Programs in Theology, Portland, OR 97215-3367. Offers biblical studies (Certificate); theology (MA, Th M). *Accreditation:* ATS. Part-time programs available. *Degree requirements:* For master's, thesis or alternative, practicum.

Westminster Seminary California, Programs in Theology, Escondido, CA 92027-4128. Offers Biblical studies (MA); historical theology (MA); theological studies (M Div, MA). *Accreditation:* ATS. Part-time and evening/weekend programs available. *Faculty:* 11 full-time (0 women), 10 part-time/adjunct (1 woman). *Students:* 88 full-time (9 women), 45 part-time (6 women); includes 45 minority (2 African Americans, 34 Asian Americans or Pacific Islanders, 9 Hispanic Americans), 9 international. Average age 30. 104 applicants, 64% accepted, 49 enrolled. In 2007, 22 first professional degrees, 11 master's awarded. *Degree requirements:* For master's, 2 foreign languages, thesis (for some programs); for M Div, 2 foreign languages, internship. *Entrance requirements:* For M Div and master's, 2 letters of reference. Additional exam requirements/recommendations for international students: Required—TOEFL (minimum score 570 paper-based; 230 computer-based; 89 iBT), TWE (minimum score 4.5). *Application deadline:* For fall admission, 6/30 priority date for domestic students, 3/15 priority date for international students; for spring admission, 11/30 priority date for domestic students. Applications are processed on a rolling basis. Application fee: $30. *Expenses:* Tuition: Full-time $11,500; part-time $30 per credit. Required fees: $25 per semester. One-time fee: $100 full-time. *Financial support:* In 2007–08, 68 students received support. Career-related internships or fieldwork, institutionally sponsored loans, and scholarships/grants available. Financial award application deadline: 6/30; financial award applicants required to submit FAFSA. *Faculty research:* Neo-paganism, New Testament background, eschatology, Protestant scholasticism, Ezekiel. *Unit head:* Dr. Dennis E. Johnson, Academic Dean, 760-480-8474, Fax: 760-480-0252. *Application contact:* Mark MacVey, Director of Recruiting, 760-480-8474, Fax: 760-480-0252, E-mail: mmacvey@wscal.edu.

Westminster Theological Seminary, Graduate and Professional Programs, Philadelphia, PA 19118. Offers apologetics (Th M); Biblical and urban studies (Certificate); Biblical counseling (MA); biblical studies (MAR); Christian studies (Certificate); church history (Th M); counseling (M Div); general studies (M Div, MAR); hermeneutics and Bible interpretations (PhD); historical

Religion

Westminster Theological Seminary (continued)
and theological studies (PhD); historical theology (Th M); New Testament (Th M); Old Testament (Th M); pastoral counseling (D Min); pastoral ministry (M Div, D Min); systematic theology (Th M); theological studies (MAR); urban missions (M Div, MA, MAR, D Min). *Accreditation:* ATS. Part-time programs available. Terminal master's awarded for partial completion of doctoral program. *Degree requirements:* For master's, thesis (for some programs); for doctorate, 4 foreign languages, comprehensive exam (for some programs), thesis/dissertation; for M Div, 2 foreign languages. *Entrance requirements:* For doctorate, GRE General Test. Additional exam requirements/recommendations for international students: Required—TOEFL, TWE.

Wheaton College, Graduate School, Department of Biblical and Theological Studies, Program in Religion in American Life, Wheaton, IL 60187-5593. Offers MA. Part-time programs available. *Students:* 6 applicants, 83% accepted, 4 enrolled. *Degree requirements:* For master's, thesis optional. *Entrance requirements:* For master's, GRE General Test, MAT. *Application deadline:* For fall admission, 3/1 priority date for domestic students; for spring admission, 11/1 for domestic students. Applications are processed on a rolling basis. Application fee: $30. Electronic applications accepted. *Financial support:* Scholarships/grants and unspecified assistantships available. Financial award application deadline: 3/1; financial award applicants required to submit FAFSA. *Unit head:* Dr. Timothy Larsen, Head, 630-752-5177. *Application contact:* Julie A. Huebner, Director of Graduate Admissions, 630-752-5195, Fax: 630-752-5935, E-mail: gradadm@wheaton.edu.

Wilfrid Laurier University, Faculty of Graduate Studies, Faculty of Arts, Department of Religion and Culture, Waterloo, ON N2L 3C5, Canada. Offers MA, PhD. *Faculty:* 9 full-time, 11 part-time/adjunct. *Students:* 20 full-time, 1 part-time. 43 applicants, 49% accepted, 13 enrolled. In 2007, 9 degrees awarded. *Degree requirements:* For master's, thesis optional; for doctorate, thesis/dissertation. *Entrance requirements:* For master's, honors BA or the equivalent in religious studies or other interdisciplinary social science or humanities program, minimum B average in overall undergraduate course work, B+ average in the undergraduate major; for doctorate, MA in religious studies, minimum A- average. Additional exam requirements/recommendations for international students: Required—TOEFL (minimum score 230 computer-based; 89 iBT). *Application deadline:* For fall admission, 2/1 priority date for domestic students. Application fee: $75. Electronic applications accepted. *Financial support:* Fellowships, research assistantships, teaching assistantships available. *Faculty research:* Religious diversity in North America. *Unit head:* Dr. Carol Duncan, Chairperson, 519-884-0710 Ext. 3692. *Application contact:* Jennifer Poppe, Student Contact, 519-884-0710 Ext. 3536, Fax: 519-884-1020, E-mail: gradstudies@wlu.ca.

Wycliffe College, Division of Advanced Degree Studies, Toronto, ON M5S 1H7, Canada. Offers MA, Th M, D Min, PhD, Th D. *Accreditation:* ATS (one or more programs are accredited). Part-time programs available. Terminal master's awarded for partial completion of doctoral program. *Degree requirements:* For master's, 2 foreign languages, thesis (for some programs); for doctorate, 3 foreign languages, thesis/dissertation. *Entrance requirements:* Additional exam requirements/recommendations for international students: Required—TOEFL (minimum score 600 paper-based; 250 computer-based). Expenses: Contact institution. *Faculty research:* Old and New Testament, doctrine, ethics, philosophy, history.

Wycliffe College, Division of Basic Degree Studies, Toronto, ON M5S 1H7, Canada. Offers Christian Studies (Diploma); theology (M Div, M Rel, MTS). *Accreditation:* ATS. Part-time programs available. *Degree requirements:* For master's, one foreign language, thesis; for M Div, thesis/dissertation optional. *Entrance requirements:* Additional exam requirements/recommendations for international students: Required—TOEFL (minimum score 580 paper-based).

Yale University, Graduate School of Arts and Sciences, Department of Religious Studies, New Haven, CT 06520. Offers PhD. *Degree requirements:* For doctorate, 2 foreign languages, thesis/dissertation. *Entrance requirements:* For doctorate, GRE General Test.

Theology

Abilene Christian University, Graduate School, College of Biblical Studies, Graduate School of Theology, Program in Divinity, Abilene, TX 79699-9100. Offers M Div. *Accreditation:* ATS. *Students:* 54 full-time (8 women), 17 part-time (3 women); includes 7 minority (3 African Americans, 2 Asian Americans or Pacific Islanders, 2 Hispanic Americans), 2 international. 19 applicants, 68% accepted, 11 enrolled. In 2007, 14 degrees awarded. *Degree requirements:* For M Div, one foreign language, comprehensive exam. *Entrance requirements:* GMAT, GRE, or MAT. *Application deadline:* For fall admission, 4/1 priority date for domestic students; for spring admission, 11/1 for domestic students. Applications are processed on a rolling basis. Application fee: $40 ($45 for international students). Electronic applications accepted. *Expenses:* Tuition: Full-time $13,368; part-time $557 per hour. Required fees: $700; $34 per hour. $10 per semester. Tuition and fees vary according to degree level and campus/location. *Unit head:* Dr. Tim Sensing, Graduate Advisor, 325-674-3792, Fax: 325-674-6717, E-mail: sensingt@acu.edu. *Application contact:* William Horn, Graduate Admissions Counselor, 325-674-2656, Fax: 325-674-6717, E-mail: gradinfo@acu.edu.

Abilene Christian University, Graduate School, College of Biblical Studies, Graduate School of Theology, Program in History and Theology, Abilene, TX 79699-9100. Offers MA. *Students:* 6 full-time (0 women), 2 part-time; includes 1 minority (Hispanic American) 4 applicants, 50% accepted, 1 enrolled. In 2007, 1 degree awarded. *Degree requirements:* For master's, comprehensive exam, thesis. *Application deadline:* For fall admission, 4/1 priority date for domestic students; for spring admission, 11/1 for domestic students. Applications are processed on a rolling basis. Application fee: $40 ($45 for international students). Electronic applications accepted. *Expenses:* Tuition: Full-time $13,368; part-time $557 per hour. Required fees: $700; $34 per hour. $10 per semester. Tuition and fees vary according to degree level and campus/location. *Financial support:* Application deadline: 4/1. *Application contact:* William Horn, Graduate Admissions Counselor, 325-674-2656, Fax: 325-674-6717, E-mail: gradinfo@acu.edu.

Abilene Christian University, Graduate School, College of Biblical Studies, Graduate School of Theology, Program in New Testament, Abilene, TX 79699-9100. Offers MA. *Accreditation:* ATS. *Students:* 2 full-time (1 woman), 2 part-time. 5 applicants, 60% accepted, 2 enrolled. In 2007, 1 degree awarded. *Degree requirements:* For master's, comprehensive exam, thesis. *Entrance requirements:* For master's, GRE General Test or MAT. *Application deadline:* For fall admission, 4/1 priority date for domestic students; for spring admission, 11/1 for domestic students. Applications are processed on a rolling basis. Application fee: $40 ($45 for international students). Electronic applications accepted. *Expenses:* Tuition: Full-time $13,368; part-time $557 per hour. Required fees: $700; $34 per hour. $10 per semester. Tuition and fees vary according to degree level and campus/location. *Unit head:* Dr. James Thompson, Graduate Advisor, 325-674-3781, Fax: 325-674-2417, E-mail: thompsonja@acu.edu. *Application contact:* William Horn, Graduate Admissions Counselor, 325-674-2656, Fax: 325-674-6717, E-mail: gradinfo@acu.edu.

Abilene Christian University, Graduate School, College of Biblical Studies, Graduate School of Theology, Program in Old Testament, Abilene, TX 79699-9100. Offers MA. *Students:* 2 full-time (0 women), 2 part-time (1 woman). In 2007, 1 degree awarded. *Degree requirements:* For master's, comprehensive exam, thesis. *Application deadline:* For fall admission, 4/1 priority date for domestic students; for spring admission, 11/1 for domestic students. Applications are processed on a rolling basis. Application fee: $40 ($45 for international students). Electronic applications accepted. *Expenses:* Tuition: Full-time $13,368; part-time $557 per hour. Required fees: $700; $34 per hour. $10 per semester. Tuition and fees vary according to degree level and campus/location. *Unit head:* Dr. Mark Hamilton, Graduate Advisor, 325-674-3765, Fax: 325-674-6108, E-mail: wmh00c@acu.edu. *Application contact:* William Horn, Graduate Admissions Counselor, 325-674-2656, Fax: 325-674-6717, E-mail: gradinfo@acu.edu.

Acadia University, Divinity College, Wolfville, NS B4P 2R6, Canada. Offers divinity (M Div); theology (MA, D Min), including biblical studies (MA), church history (MA), theology (MA). *Accreditation:* ATS. Part-time programs available. *Faculty:* 12 full-time (2 women), 12 part-time/adjunct (1 woman). *Students:* 42 full-time (11 women), 92 part-time (24 women); includes 15 minority (8 African Americans, 1 American Indian/Alaska Native, 6 Asian Americans or Pacific Islanders), 1 international. Average age 43. 20 applicants, 95% accepted, 15 enrolled. In 2007, 15 master's, 2 doctorates awarded. *Degree requirements:* For master's, one foreign language, thesis (for some programs); for doctorate, one foreign language, comprehensive exam, thesis/dissertation. *Entrance requirements:* For M Div, minimum GPA of 2.0; for master's, minimum GPA of 3.0 (MA theology), minimum GPA of 2.0 (M Div); for doctorate, minimum GPA of 3.0, 3 years ministry experience. Additional exam requirements/recommendations for international students: Required—TOEFL. *Application deadline:* For fall admission, 6/30 priority date for domestic students, 4/1 priority date for international students; for spring admission, 4/30 priority date for domestic students. Applications are processed on a rolling basis. Application fee: $25. *Expenses: Contact institution. Financial support:* In 2007–08, 8 teaching assistantships (averaging $1,000 per year) were awarded; career-related internships or fieldwork, institutionally sponsored loans, and scholarships/grants also available. Support available to part-time students. Financial award application deadline: 8/12. *Faculty research:* Biblical canon, Jesus, Dead Sea Scroll, Baptist studies, old testament-Septuagint. *Unit head:* Dr. Harry M. Gardner, President, 902-585-2212, Fax: 902-585-2233, E-mail: harry.gardner@acadiau.ca. *Application contact:* Shawna Peverill, Manager of Student Services, 902-585-2215, Fax: 902-585-2233, E-mail: shawna.peverill@acadiau.ca.

Alliance Theological Seminary, Graduate and Professional Programs, Nyack, NY 10960. Offers Christian ministry (MPS); counseling (MA); intercultural studies (MA); missions (MPS); New Testament (MA); Old Testament (MA); theology (M Div); urban ministry (MPS). *Accreditation:* ATS. Part-time programs available. *Faculty:* 19 full-time (3 women), 9 part-time/adjunct (1 woman). *Students:* 195 full-time (66 women), 452 part-time (207 women); includes 505 minority (239 African Americans, 1 American Indian/Alaska Native, 113 Asian Americans or Pacific Islanders, 152 Hispanic Americans), 35 international. Average age 39. 224 applicants, 98% accepted, 200 enrolled. In 2007, 63 first professional degrees, 46 master's awarded. *Degree requirements:* For master's, comprehensive exam (for some programs), thesis optional, internships; for M Div, 2 foreign languages, internship. *Entrance requirements:* Proficiency in New Testament Greek, minimum GPA of 2.5 (undergraduate). Additional exam requirements/recommendations for international students: Required—TOEFL (minimum score 550 paper-based; 213 computer-based). *Application deadline:* For fall admission, 6/1 priority date for international students; for spring admission, 11/1 priority date for international students. Applications are processed on a rolling basis. *Expenses:* Tuition: Part-time $450 per credit. Required fees: $20 per term. Tuition and fees vary according to course load. *Financial support:* Research assistantships, career-related internships or fieldwork, Federal Work-Study, and scholarships/grants available. Financial award applicants required to submit FAFSA. *Unit head:* Bennett Schepens, Assistant Vice President and Academic Dean, 845-353-2020, Fax: 845-358-2651. *Application contact:* Karen Shaffstall, Director of Admissions, 845-353-2020, Fax: 845-348-3912, E-mail: admissions.ats@nyack.edu.

Ambrose University College, Ambrose Seminary, Calgary, AB T2P 3T5, Canada. Offers biblical/theological studies (MA); Chinese ministries (Certificate); Christian studies (Diploma); church education (M Div); intercultural ministries (M Div, MA, Certificate, Diploma); leadership and ministry (MA, Certificate, Diploma); pastoral ministries (M Div). *Accreditation:* ATS (one or more programs are accredited). Part-time programs available. *Faculty:* 6 full-time (0 women), 28 part-time/adjunct (4 women). *Students:* 44 full-time (13 women), 118 part-time (45 women); includes 59 minority (2 African Americans, 2 American Indian/Alaska Native, 54 Asian Americans or Pacific Islanders, 1 Hispanic American). Average age 41. 45 applicants, 82% accepted, 37 enrolled. In 2007, 7 first professional degrees, 17 master's, 2 other advanced degrees awarded. *Degree requirements:* For master's, 2 foreign languages, internship; for M Div, one foreign language, internship. *Entrance requirements:* For master's, bachelor degree. Additional exam requirements/recommendations for international students: Required—TOEFL or IELTS. *Application deadline:* For fall admission, 7/31 priority date for domestic students, 3/1 priority date for international students; for winter admission, 11/30 priority date for domestic students, 6/1 priority date for international students. Applications are processed on a rolling basis. Application fee: $50. Electronic applications accepted. Tuition and fees charges are reported in Canadian dollars. *Expenses:* Tuition: Part-time $281 Canadian dollars per credit hour. Required fees: $16 Canadian dollars per credit hour. *Financial support:* In 2007–08, 40 students received support. Career-related internships or fieldwork and scholarships/grants available. Support available to part-time students. Financial award application deadline: 3/30. *Faculty research:* Evangelicalism and sociology, missiological trends, chaplaincy, intertestamental studies, postmodernism. *Unit head:* Dr. Paul Spilsbury, Academic Dean, 403-410-2000 Ext. 6905, Fax: 403-571-2556, E-mail: pspilsbu@ambrose.edu.

American Baptist Seminary of the West, Graduate and Professional Programs, Berkeley, CA 94704-3029. Offers community leadership (MA); theology (M Div, MA). *Accreditation:* ACIPE; ATS (one or more programs are accredited). Part-time and evening/weekend programs available. *Faculty:* 4 full-time (all women), 8 part-time/adjunct (2 women). *Students:* 58 (32 women); includes 50 minority (44 African Americans, 6 Asian Americans or Pacific Islanders). In 2007, 15 degrees awarded. *Entrance requirements:* For M Div, minimum GPA of 2.5; for master's, minimum GPA of 3.0. Additional exam requirements/recommendations for international students: Required—TOEFL (minimum score 550 paper-based; 250 computer-based). *Application deadline:* For fall admission, 4/15 priority date for domestic students, 4/15 for international students; for spring admission, 11/1 for international students. Applications are processed on a rolling basis. Application fee: $25. Electronic applications accepted. *Expenses:* Tuition: Full-time $13,000; part-time $500 per unit. Required fees: $240 per semester. One-time fee: $250. *Financial support:* In 2007–08, 38 students received support. Career-related internships or fieldwork, institutionally sponsored loans, scholarships/grants, tuition waivers (partial), and tuition discount available. Support available to part-time students. Financial award application deadline: 4/15; financial award applicants required to submit FAFSA. *Unit head:* Dr. Paul M. Martin, President for the Interim, 510-841-1905 Ext. 224, Fax: 510-841-2446, E-mail: pmartin@absw.edu. *Application contact:* Rev. Michelle M. Holmes, Vice President, 510-841-1905 Ext. 225, Fax: 510-841-2446, E-mail: mmholmes@absw.edu.

American Jewish University, Graduate School, Ziegler School of Rabbinic Studies, Bel Air, CA 90077-1599. Offers MARS. *Degree requirements:* For master's, one foreign language. *Entrance requirements:* For master's, GRE General Test, interview. Additional exam requirements/recommendations for international students: Required—TOEFL.

Amridge University, Graduate and Professional Programs, Montgomery, AL 36117. Offers behavioral leadership and management (MA); biblical studies (MA, D Min, PhD); Christian ministry (M Div); family therapy (D Min, PhD), including marriage and family therapy (PhD), professional counseling (PhD); leadership and management (MS); marriage and family therapy (M Div, MA); ministerial leadership (M Div, MS); pastoral counseling (M Div, MS); practical theology (MA); professional counseling (M Div, MA). *Accreditation:* ATS. Part-time and evening/weekend programs available. Postbaccalaureate distance learning degree programs offered (no on-campus study). *Faculty:* 50 full-time (12 women), 36 part-time/adjunct (10 women). *Students:* 165 full-time (85 women), 212 part-time (111 women); includes 174 minority (164 African Americans, 1 American Indian/Alaska Native, 1 Asian American or Pacific Islander, 8 Hispanic Americans). Average age 35. In 2007, 8 first professional degrees, 35 master's, 5 doctorates awarded. *Degree requirements:* For master's, one foreign language, comprehensive exam (for some programs), thesis (for some programs); for doctorate, comprehensive exam (for some programs), thesis/dissertation; for M Div, comprehensive exam (for some programs). *Entrance requirements:* For M Div, master's, and doctorate, GRE General Test or MAT. Additional exam requirements/recommendations for international students: Required—TOEFL. *Application deadline:* For fall admission, 9/1 priority date for domestic students; for spring admission, 1/1 priority date for domestic students. Applications are processed on a rolling basis. Application fee: $50. Electronic applications accepted. *Expenses:* Tuition: Full-time $9,180; part-time $510 per semester hour. Required fees: $400 per term. Tuition and fees vary according to course load and degree level. *Financial support:* Federal Work-Study and scholarships/grants available. Support available to part-time students. Financial award applicants required to submit FAFSA. *Faculty research:* Homiletics, hermeneutics, ancient Near Eastern history. *Unit head:* Rick Johnson, Director of Enrollment Management, 800-351-4040 Ext. 7513, Fax: 334-387-3878, E-mail: rickjohnson@amridgeuniversity.edu. *Application contact:* Ora Davis, Admissions Officer, 334-387-3877 Ext. 7524, Fax: 334-387-3878, E-mail: oradavis@amridgeuniversity.edu.

Anderson University, School of Theology, Anderson, IN 46012-3495. Offers missions (MA); theology (M Div, MTS, D Min). *Accreditation:* ACIPE; ATS. Part-time programs available. *Degree requirements:* For master's, one foreign language, thesis, integrative senior seminar; for doctorate, thesis/dissertation; for M Div, thesis/dissertation (for some programs). *Faculty research:* Small-church/bivocational ministry, women in ministry.

Andover Newton Theological School, Graduate and Professional Programs, Newton Centre, MA 02459-2243. Offers divinity (M Div); general (MA); psychology and religion (MA); religious education (MA); research (MA); sacred theology (STM); theology (D Min); theology and the arts (MA). *Accreditation:* ACIPE; ATS. Part-time programs available. *Degree requirements:* For master's, comprehensive exam (for some programs), thesis (for some programs); for doctorate, comprehensive exam, thesis/dissertation. *Entrance requirements:* For doctorate, M Div or equivalent. Additional exam requirements/recommendations for international students: Required—TOEFL (minimum score 550 paper-based; 213 computer-based). Electronic applications accepted.

Andrews University, School of Graduate Studies, Seventh-day Adventist Theological Seminary, Berrien Springs, MI 49104. Offers ministry (M Div, D Min); pastoral ministry (MA); religious education (MA, Ed D, PhD, Ed S); theology (M Th, Th D). *Accreditation:* ATS. *Degree requirements:* For master's, thesis optional; for doctorate, variable foreign language requirement, thesis/dissertation; for M Div, one foreign language, thesis/dissertation optional. *Entrance requirements:* For master's, GRE Subject Test, minimum GPA of 2.0.

Apex School of Theology, Graduate Programs, Durham, NC 27713. Offers M Div, MCE. *Faculty research:* Sociology, educational sciences, economics.

Aquinas Institute of Theology, Graduate and Professional Programs, St. Louis, MO 63108. Offers biblical studies (Certificate); health care mission (MAHCM); ministry (M Div); pastoral care (Certificate); pastoral ministry (MAPM); pastoral studies (MAPS); preaching (D Min); spiritual direction (Certificate); theology (M Div, MA); Thomistic studies (Certificate); M Div/MA; MAPS/MSW. *Accreditation:* ATS (one or more programs are accredited). Part-time and evening/weekend programs available. Postbaccalaureate distance learning degree programs offered (minimal on-campus study). *Faculty:* 15 full-time (8 women), 4 part-time/adjunct (2 women). *Students:* 55 full-time (22 women), 190 part-time (117 women); includes 31 minority (14 African Americans, 1 American Indian/Alaska Native, 5 Asian Americans or Pacific Islanders, 11 Hispanic Americans), 10 international. Average age 41. 39 applicants, 92% accepted, 32 enrolled. In 2007, 18 first professional degrees, 14 master's, 4 doctorates, 7 other advanced degrees awarded. *Degree requirements:* For master's, one foreign language, comprehensive exam, thesis or major paper; for doctorate, thesis/dissertation. *Entrance requirements:* For M Div and master's, MAT; for doctorate, 3 years of ministerial experience, 6 hours of graduate course work in homiletics, M Div or the equivalent, minimum GPA of 3.0. Additional exam requirements/recommendations for international students: Required—TOEFL. *Application deadline:* For fall admission, 3/15 priority date for domestic and international students; for spring admission, 11/15 priority date for domestic and international students. Applications are processed on a rolling basis. Application fee: $50. *Expenses:* Tuition: Full-time $14,208; part-time $3,552 per term. Required fees: $195 per term. Tuition and fees vary according to course load. *Financial support:* In 2007–08, 4 research assistantships with full tuition reimbursements (averaging $3,000 per year) were awarded; career-related internships or fieldwork, scholarships/grants, health care benefits, and tuition waivers (partial) also available. Support available to part-time students. Financial award application deadline: 3/15; financial award applicants required to submit CSS PROFILE or FAFSA. *Faculty research:* Theology of preaching, hermeneutics, lay ecclesiastical ministry, pastoral and practical theology. *Unit head:* Fr. Gregory Heille, Academic Dean, 314-256-8800, Fax: 314-256-8888, E-mail: heille@ai.edu. *Application contact:* David Werthmann, Director of Admissions, 314-256-8806, Fax: 314-256-8888, E-mail: admissions@ai.edu.

Asbury Theological Seminary, Graduate and Professional Programs, School of Practical Theology, Wilmore, KY 40390-1199. Offers Christian education (MACE); Christian leadership (MACL); Christian ministries (MAXM); Christian studies (Certificate); counseling (MAC); pastoral counseling (MAPC); youth ministry (MAYM). *Accreditation:* ACIPE; ATS. *Entrance requirements:* Additional exam requirements/recommendations for international students: Required—TOEFL (minimum score 550 paper-based; 79 iBT), IELTS (minimum score 7). *Application deadline:* For fall admission, 1/31 priority date for international students; for spring admission, 3/31 priority date for international students. Applications are processed on a rolling basis. Application fee: $50. Electronic applications accepted. *Expenses:* Tuition: Part-time $444 per hour. One-time fee: $100 part-time. *Unit head:* Dr. Catherine Stonehouse, Dean, 859-858-3581. *Application contact:* Janelle Vernon, Admissions Director, 859-858-2211, Fax: 859-858-2287, E-mail: admissions_office@asburyseminary.edu.

Asbury Theological Seminary, Program in Ministry, Wilmore, KY 40390-1199. Offers D Min. Part-time programs available. *Entrance requirements:* For doctorate, MAT. *Expenses:* Tuition: Part-time $444 per hour. One-time fee: $100 part-time. *Unit head:* Dr. Leslie A. Andrews, Provost, 859-858-2206, Fax: 859-858-2025, E-mail: leslie_andrews@asburyseminary.edu. *Application contact:* Janelle Vernon, Admissions Director, 859-858-2211, Fax: 859-858-2287, E-mail: admissions_office@asburyseminary.edu.

Asbury Theological Seminary, School of Biblical Interpretation and Proclamation, Wilmore, KY 40390-1199. Offers MABS. *Expenses:* Tuition: Part-time $444 per hour. One-time fee: $100 part-time. *Unit head:* Dr. David R. Bauer, Dean, 859-858-3581. *Application contact:* Janelle Vernon, Admissions Director, 859-858-2211, Fax: 859-858-2287, E-mail: admissions_office@asburyseminary.edu.

Asbury Theological Seminary, School of Theology and Formation, Wilmore, KY 40390-1199. Offers MATS. *Students:* 735 applicants, 63% accepted, 306 enrolled. In 2007, 132 master's awarded. *Entrance requirements:* For master's, minimum GPA of 2.75. Additional exam requirements/recommendations for international students: Required—IELTS. *Application deadline:* For fall admission, 7/1 priority date for domestic students, 1/31 priority date for international students; for spring admission, 12/1 priority date for domestic students, 3/31 priority date for international students. Application fee: $50. *Expenses:* Tuition: Part-time $444 per hour. One-time fee: $100 part-time. *Financial support:* Application deadline: 3/1. *Faculty research:* Church history, theology, philosophy, ethics, doctrine. *Unit head:* Dr. C. Reginald Johnson, Dean, 859-858-3581. *Application contact:* Janelle Vernon, Admissions Director, 859-858-2211, Fax: 859-858-2287, E-mail: admissions_office@asburyseminary.edu.

Ashland Theological Seminary, Graduate Programs, Ashland, OH 44805. Offers biblical and theological studies (MA, MAR), including New Testament (MA), Old Testament (MA); Christian ministry (MAPT); Christian studies (Diploma); clinical pastoral counseling (MACPC); historical studies (MA); ministry (D Min); pastoral counseling (MAPC); pastoral ministry (M Div); theological studies (MA). *Accreditation:* ATS. Part-time programs available. *Degree requirements:* For master's, comprehensive exam (for some programs), thesis (for some programs); for doctorate, thesis/dissertation; for M Div, 2 foreign languages. *Entrance requirements:* For M Div, minimum GPA of 2.75; for master's, minimum undergraduate GPA of 2.75; for doctorate, M Div, minimum undergraduate GPA of 3.0. Additional exam requirements/recommendations for international students: Required—TOEFL (minimum score 550 paper-based). Electronic applications accepted. *Faculty research:* Semitic languages and linguistics, rhetorical and social-scientific criticism, Anabaptist studies, inner spiritual healing, African-American clergy in film and literature.

Assemblies of God Theological Seminary, Graduate and Professional Programs, Springfield, MO 65802. Offers Christian ministries (MA); counseling (MA); divinity (M Div); intercultural ministries (MA); intercultural studies (D Miss); relief and development (D Miss); theological studies (MA); vocational ministry (D Min). *Accreditation:* ATS. Part-time and evening/weekend programs available. Postbaccalaureate distance learning degree programs offered (minimal on-campus study). *Faculty:* 16 full-time (3 women), 21 part-time/adjunct (4 women). *Students:* 212 full-time (59 women), 236 part-time (51 women); includes 49 minority (11 African Americans, 5 American Indian/Alaska Native, 11 Asian Americans or Pacific Islanders, 22 Hispanic Americans), 7 international. Average age 36. 181 applicants, 72% accepted, 91 enrolled. In 2007, 28 first professional degrees, 66 master's, 13 doctorates awarded. *Degree requirements:* For master's, analytical reflection paper or comprehensive exam; for doctorate, thesis/dissertation; for M Div, one foreign language, analytical reflection paper. *Entrance requirements:* For M Div, minimum GPA of 2.0; for master's, minimum GPA of 2.5; for doctorate, minimum GPA of 3.0. Additional exam requirements/recommendations for international students: Required—TOEFL (minimum score 550 paper-based; 213 computer-based; 80 iBT). *Application deadline:* For fall admission, 7/1 priority date for domestic students, 6/1 priority date for international students; for spring admission, 12/1 priority date for domestic students, 11/1 priority date for international students. Applications are processed on a rolling basis. Application fee: $35. Electronic applications accepted. *Expenses:* Tuition: Part-time $465 per credit hour. *Financial support:* Career-related internships or fieldwork, Federal Work-Study, and scholarships/grants available. Support available to part-time students. Financial award application deadline: 7/15; financial award applicants required to submit FAFSA. *Unit head:* Stephen Lim, Academic Dean, 417-268-1000, Fax: 417-268-1001, E-mail: slim@agts.edu.

Associated Mennonite Biblical Seminary, Graduate and Professional Programs, Elkhart, IN 46517-1999. Offers Christian formation (MA); divinity (M Div); mission and evangelism (MA); peace studies (MA); theological studies (MA, Certificate). *Accreditation:* ACIPE; ATS. Part-time programs available. *Degree requirements:* For master's, comprehensive exam, thesis optional; for M Div, integration paper. *Entrance requirements:* For M Div, master's, and Certificate, 3 letters of reference. Additional exam requirements/recommendations for international students: Required—TOEFL (minimum score 550 paper-based; 213 computer-based). Electronic applications accepted. *Faculty research:* Biblical studies, theology, church history, church leadership.

The Athenaeum of Ohio, Graduate Programs, Cincinnati, OH 45230-5900. Offers biblical studies (MABS); divinity (M Div); pastoral counseling (MAPC); religion (MAR); theology (MA Th); M Div/MA Th; M Div/MABS; M Div/MAPC. *Accreditation:* ATS (one or more programs are accredited). Part-time and evening/weekend programs available. *Degree requirements:* For master's, one foreign language, comprehensive exam (for some programs), thesis optional; for M Div, comprehensive exam.

Atlantic School of Theology, Graduate and Professional Programs, Halifax, NS B3H 3B5, Canada. Offers M Div, MTS, Graduate Certificate. *Accreditation:* ATS. Part-time programs available. Postbaccalaureate distance learning degree programs offered (minimal on-campus study). *Degree requirements:* For master's, thesis. *Entrance requirements:* For M Div, master's, and Graduate Certificate, minimum B average in undergraduate course work. *Faculty research:* Ethics and biology; death, dying and pastoral care; theology and the economy; adult education; John and anti-Judaism.

Austin Graduate School of Theology, Program in Theological Studies, Austin, TX 78705-5610. Offers MATS. Part-time programs available. *Degree requirements:* For master's, 2 foreign languages, comprehensive exam, faculty forums. *Entrance requirements:* For master's, 3 letters of reference. Additional exam requirements/recommendations for international students: Required—TOEFL (minimum score 550 paper-based). *Faculty research:* Revelation, synoptic problem, acadian, biblical archaeology, worship.

Austin Presbyterian Theological Seminary, Graduate and Professional Programs, Austin, TX 78705-5797. Offers divinity (M Div); ministry (D Min); theological studies (MA); M Div/MATS; M Div/MSSW. *Accreditation:* ACIPE; ATS. Part-time programs available. *Faculty:* 20 full-time (6 women), 3 part-time/adjunct (0 women). *Students:* 123 full-time (60 women), 97 part-time (36 women); includes 27 minority (15 African Americans, 1 American Indian/Alaska Native, 5 Asian Americans or Pacific Islanders, 6 Hispanic Americans), 6 international. Average age 41. 89 applicants, 61% accepted, 41 enrolled. In 2007, 52 first professional degrees, 10 master's, 5 doctorates awarded. *Degree requirements:* For doctorate, thesis/dissertation; for M Div, Greek, Hebrew. *Entrance requirements:* References. Additional exam requirements/recommendations for international students: Required—TOEFL (minimum score 550 paper-based; 213 computer-based; 79 iBT). *Application deadline:* For fall admission, 5/15 priority date for domestic students; for spring admission, 11/15 for domestic students. Applications are processed on a rolling basis. Application fee: $65. *Financial support:* In 2007–08, 130 students received support, including 6 research assistantships (averaging $1,040 per year), 6 teaching assistantships (averaging $1,040 per year); career-related internships or fieldwork, institutionally sponsored loans, scholarships/grants, and tutorships also available. Support available to part-time students. Financial award application deadline: 6/1; financial award applicants required to submit FAFSA. *Faculty research:* Mystical theology, religious pluralism, narrative preaching, social ethics, pastoral care and healing. *Unit head:* Rev. Dr. Michael Jinkins, Academic Dean, 512-404-4821, Fax: 512-479-0738, E-mail: mjinkins@austinseminary.edu. *Application contact:* Jack Barden, Director of Admissions, 512-404-4827, Fax: 512-479-0738, E-mail: jbarden@austinseminary.edu.

Ave Maria University, Graduate Programs, Ave Maria, FL 34142. Offers pastoral theology (MTS); theology (MA, PhD). Terminal master's awarded for partial completion of doctoral program. *Degree requirements:* For master's, one foreign language, thesis; for doctorate, 3 foreign languages, comprehensive exam, thesis/dissertation. *Entrance requirements:* For master's, GRE; for doctorate, GRE, M Div or equivalent; MA or MTS in religion, theology, or philosophy; bachelor's degree with strong background in religion, theology, and/or philosophy.

Ave Maria University, Institute for Pastoral Theology, Ave Maria, FL 34142. Offers MTS. Part-time and evening/weekend programs available.

Azusa Pacific University, Haggard School of Theology, Program in Ministry, Azusa, CA 91702-7000. Offers D Min.

Azusa Pacific University, Haggard School of Theology, Program in Non-Profit Leadership and Theology, Azusa, CA 91702-7000. Offers Christian non-profit leadership (MA).

Theology

Azusa Pacific University, Haggard School of Theology, Program in Religion: Biblical Studies, Azusa, CA 91702-7000. Offers MAR.

Azusa Pacific University, Haggard School of Theology, Program in Religion: Theology and Ethics, Azusa, CA 91702-7000. Offers MAR.

Bangor Theological Seminary, Professional Program, Bangor, ME 04401-4699. Offers M Div, MA, MTS, D Min. M Div not offered at Portland, ME campus. *Accreditation:* ACIPE; ATS. Part-time programs available. *Faculty:* 8 full-time (2 women), 15 part-time/adjunct (5 women). *Students:* 32 full-time (24 women), 97 part-time (73 women); includes 2 minority (1 African American, 1 Asian American or Pacific Islander), 2 international. Average age 47. 52 applicants, 63% accepted, 33 enrolled. In 2007, 17 first professional degrees, 5 master's, 1 doctorate awarded. *Degree requirements:* For master's, thesis optional; for doctorate, project, report; for M Div, thesis/dissertation optional. *Entrance requirements:* For M Div and master's, Bachelor degree; for doctorate, M Div, 3 years in ministry. Additional exam requirements/recommendations for international students: Required—TOEFL (minimum score 550 paper-based; 213 computer-based; 80 iBT). *Application deadline:* For fall admission, 7/15 priority date for domestic students, 4/1 priority date for international students; for spring admission, 12/15 for domestic students. Applications are processed on a rolling basis. Application fee: $40. *Expenses:* Tuition: Part-time $390 per credit. Required fees: $25 per semester. *Financial support:* In 2007–08, 71 students received support, including 2 research assistantships (averaging $2,500 per year); career-related internships or fieldwork, Federal Work-Study, institutionally sponsored loans, and scholarships/grants also available. Support available to part-time students. Financial award application deadline: 5/1; financial award applicants required to submit FAFSA. *Faculty research:* Formation of the New Testament canon, critical pedagogy, history of theological education, human sexuality, the Isaiah Scroll. *Unit head:* Dr. Glenn T. Miller, Academic Dean, 207-942-6781 Ext. 125, Fax: 207-990-1267, E-mail: gmiller@bts.edu. *Application contact:* Michael K. Huddy, Director of Admissions, 207-942-6781 Ext. 126, Fax: 207-990-1267, E-mail: enrollment@bts.edu.

Baptist Bible College, Graduate School of Theology, Springfield, MO 65803-3498. Offers biblical counseling (MA); biblical studies (MA); church ministries (MA); intercultural studies (MA); theology (M Div). Part-time programs available. *Degree requirements:* For master's, 2 foreign languages, thesis (for some programs); for M Div, 2 foreign languages, thesis/dissertation (for some programs). *Entrance requirements:* For master's, outcomes test. Electronic applications accepted.

Baptist Bible College of Pennsylvania, Baptist Bible Seminary, Clarks Summit, PA 18411-1297. Offers biblical studies (PhD); church planting (M Div); global missions (M Div); military chaplaincy (M Div); ministry (M Min, D Min); pastor of church education (M Div); pastor of outreach (M Div); pastoral counseling (M Div); pastoral leadership (M Div); theology (M Div, Th M); youth pastor (M Div). Part-time and evening/weekend programs available. Postbaccalaureate distance learning degree programs offered (minimal on-campus study). *Faculty:* 10 full-time (0 women). *Students:* 102 full-time (0 women), 104 part-time; includes 14 minority (6 African Americans, 4 Asian Americans or Pacific Islanders, 4 Hispanic Americans), 2 international. Average age 38. Terminal master's awarded for partial completion of doctoral program. *Degree requirements:* For master's, 2 foreign languages, thesis; for doctorate, 2 foreign languages, comprehensive exam (for some programs), thesis/dissertation, oral exam; for M Div, 2 foreign languages, thesis/dissertation, oral exam. *Entrance requirements:* For doctorate, Greek and Hebrew entrance exams (PhD). *Application deadline:* Applications are processed on a rolling basis. Application fee: $30. Electronic applications accepted. *Expenses:* Tuition: Full-time $6,516; part-time $362 per credit. Required fees: $468; $232 per semester. *Financial support:* Career-related internships or fieldwork and scholarships/grants available. Support available to part-time students. *Unit head:* Dr. Michael Stallard, Seminary Academic Dean, 570-585-9348, Fax: 570-585-4057, E-mail: mstallard@bbc.edu. *Application contact:* Paul Golden, Director of Seminary Admissions, 570-586-9396, E-mail: pgolden@bbc.edu.

Baptist Missionary Association Theological Seminary, Graduate and Professional Programs, Jacksonville, TX 75766-5407. Offers M Div, MAR. *Accreditation:* ATS. Part-time programs available. *Degree requirements:* For master's, thesis optional; for M Div, 2 foreign languages, thesis/dissertation optional. *Entrance requirements:* Additional exam requirements/recommendations for international students: Required—TOEFL (minimum score 550 paper-based; 213 computer-based). Electronic applications accepted. *Faculty research:* Education, Biblical studies.

Baptist Theological Seminary at Richmond, Graduate and Professional Program, Richmond, VA 23227. Offers children and family ministry (M Div); Christian education (M Div); church music (M Div); theology (D Min); youth and student ministry (M Div); M Div/MS; M Div/MSW. *Accreditation:* ATS. Part-time programs available. Postbaccalaureate distance learning degree programs offered (minimal on-campus study). *Faculty:* 14 full-time (6 women), 8 part-time/adjunct (1 woman). *Students:* 117 full-time (64 women), 17 part-time (7 women); includes 10 minority (6 African Americans, 1 Asian American or Pacific Islander, 3 Hispanic Americans), 1 international. Average age 46. In 2007, 37 first professional degrees, 6 doctorates awarded. *Median time to degree:* Of those who began their doctoral program in fall 1999, 92% received their degree in 8 years or less. *Degree requirements:* For doctorate, one foreign language, comprehensive exam, thesis/dissertation, field study, independent study; for M Div, one foreign language, comprehensive exam (for some programs), thesis/dissertation optional, mission immersion experience, internship. *Entrance requirements:* For doctorate, MAT, M Div, 3 years of full-time ministry experience. Additional exam requirements/recommendations for international students: Required—TOEFL (minimum score 481 paper-based; 213 computer-based). *Application deadline:* For fall admission, 8/1 priority date for domestic students, 5/1 priority date for international students; for winter admission, 12/1 priority date for domestic students, 9/1 priority date for international students; for spring admission, 1/1 priority date for domestic students, 10/1 priority date for international students. Applications are processed on a rolling basis. Application fee: $35. *Expenses:* Tuition: Full-time $7,500; part-time $750 per credit. Required fees: $45 per term. Full-time tuition and fees vary according to degree level. *Financial support:* In 2007–08, 98 students received support, including 16 teaching assistantships (averaging $1,300 per year); scholarships/grants and tuition waivers (partial) also available. Financial award application deadline: 2/1. *Faculty research:* New Testament studies, Old Testament studies, pastoral care, church history, theology. *Unit head:* Dr. Ronald W. Crawford, President, 804-355-8135, Fax: 804-355-8182. *Application contact:* Director of Admissions, 804-355-8135, Fax: 804-355-8182.

Barry University, School of Arts and Sciences, Department of Theology and Philosophy, Miami Shores, FL 33161-6695. Offers ministry (D Min); pastoral ministry for Hispanics (MA); pastoral theology (MA); practical theology (MA). *Accreditation:* ATS. Part-time and evening/weekend programs available. *Degree requirements:* For master's, comprehensive exam, thesis optional; for doctorate, thesis/dissertation. *Entrance requirements:* For master's, GRE General Test or MAT, minimum GPA of 3.0. *Application deadline:* Applications are processed on a rolling basis. Application fee: $30. Electronic applications accepted. *Financial support:* Research assistantships, career-related internships or fieldwork, institutionally sponsored loans, and tuition waivers (partial) available. Support available to part-time students. Financial award application deadline: 5/1; financial award applicants required to submit FAFSA. *Faculty research:* Fundamental morals, bioethics, social ethics, liturgical and sacramental theology, biblical studies. *Unit head:* Fr. Mark Wedig, Chair, 305-899-3378, Fax: 305-899-3385, E-mail: mwedig@mail.barry.edu. *Application contact:* Dave Fletcher, Director of Graduate Admissions, 305-899-3113, Fax: 305-899-2971, E-mail: dfletcher@mail.barry.edu.

Bayamón Central University, Graduate Programs, Program in Theology, Bayamón, PR 00960-1725. Offers biblical studies (MA); divinity (M Div); pastoral theology (MA); theological studies (MA); theology (MA). Part-time and evening/weekend programs available. *Entrance requirements:* For master's, EXADEP, bachelor's degree in theology or related field.

Baylor University, George W. Truett Seminary, Waco, TX 76798. Offers M Div, MTS, D Min, M Div/MM, M Div/MS Ed, M Div/MSW, MTS/MSW. *Accreditation:* ATS. *Faculty:* 17 full-time (3 women), 7 part-time/adjunct (1 woman). *Students:* 323 full-time (97 women), 78 part-time (21 women); includes 64 minority (36 African Americans, 2 American Indian/Alaska Native, 4 Asian Americans or Pacific Islanders, 22 Hispanic Americans), 25 international. Average age 29. 144 applicants, 94% accepted, 102 enrolled. In 2007, 73 first professional degrees, 4 master's, 9 doctorates awarded. *Degree requirements:* For M Div, Greek and Hebrew. *Entrance requirements:* For M Div, minimum GPA of 2.75; for doctorate, minimum M Div GPA of 3.0. Additional exam requirements/recommendations for international students: Required—TOEFL. *Application deadline:* For fall admission, 5/1 priority date for domestic students, 5/1 for international students; for spring admission, 11/1 priority date for domestic students, 11/1 for international students. Applications are processed on a rolling basis. Application fee: $25. *Expenses:* Contact institution. *Financial support:* In 2007–08, 207 students received support, including 1 research assistantship, 12 teaching assistantships; career-related internships or fieldwork, institutionally sponsored loans, scholarships/grants, tuition waivers (partial), and unspecified assistantships also available. Support available to part-time students. Financial award application deadline: 8/1; financial award applicants required to submit FAFSA. Total annual research expenditures: $10,000. *Unit head:* Dr. David E. Garland, Dean, 254-710-3755, Fax: 254-710-3753. *Application contact:* Dr. Grear Howard, Director of Student Services, 254-710-3755, Fax: 254-710-7233, E-mail: grear_howard@baylor.edu.

Beacon University, Graduate Programs, Columbus, GA 31909. Offers cell church development (MAPM); counseling ministry (MAPM); military chaplaincy (MAPM); organizational leadership (MAPM); pastoral ministry (MAPM); theology (M Div, MABS). Part-time and evening/weekend programs available. Postbaccalaureate distance learning degree programs offered (minimal on-campus study). *Faculty:* 35 part-time/adjunct (5 women). *Students:* 57 full-time (34 women), 37 part-time (21 women); includes 56 minority (47 African Americans, 1 Asian American or Pacific Islander, 8 Hispanic Americans), 4 international. 30 applicants, 90% accepted, 19 enrolled. In 2007, 3 first professional degrees, 28 master's awarded. *Degree requirements:* For master's and M Div, comprehensive exam. *Entrance requirements:* For M Div, MAT or GRE or GMAT or MTE, official undergrad and/or transf.; for master's, MAT or GRE or NTE or GMAT, official undergrad and/or trsfr. Additional exam requirements/recommendations for international students: Required—TOEFL (minimum score 500 paper-based; 173 computer-based; 61 iBT); Recommended—IELTS (minimum score 6). Application fee: $90. *Expenses:* Tuition: Full-time $4,608; part-time $256 per credit hour. Required fees: $105 per term. *Financial support:* In 2007–08, 69 students received support. Scholarships/grants available. Financial award application deadline: 7/1. *Unit head:* Dr. Ian A.H. Bond, President, 706-323-5364, E-mail: ian.bond@beacon.edu. *Application contact:* Cindy G. Winkles, Admissions Officer, 706-323-5364 Ext. 258, Fax: 706-323-5891, E-mail: cindy.winkles@beacon.edu.

Bethany Theological Seminary, Graduate and Professional Programs, Richmond, IN 47374-4019. Offers biblical studies (MA Th); ministry studies (M Div); peace studies (M Div, MA Th); theological studies (MA Th, CATS); youth ministry (M Div). *Accreditation:* ACIPE; ATS. Part-time programs available. Postbaccalaureate distance learning degree programs offered (minimal on-campus study). *Degree requirements:* For master's, thesis. *Entrance requirements:* For M Div, letters of reference, minimum GPA of 2.75; for master's, letters of reference, minimum GPA of 3.0. Additional exam requirements/recommendations for international students: Required—TOEFL (minimum score 550 paper-based; 218 computer-based).

Beth Benjamin Academy of Connecticut, Graduate and Professional Programs, Stamford, CT 06901-1202.

Bethel College, Division of Graduate Studies, Program in Theological Studies, Mishawaka, IN 46545-5591. Offers MATS. *Faculty:* 5 part-time/adjunct (0 women). *Students:* 4 full-time (1 woman), 8 part-time (3 women); includes 1 minority (African American) 11 applicants, 100% accepted, 11 enrolled. In 2007, 2 degrees awarded. *Entrance requirements:* Additional exam requirements/recommendations for international students: Required—TOEFL (minimum score 540 paper-based; 207 computer-based). *Application deadline:* For fall admission, 5/1 for international students; for spring admission, 10/1 for international students. Applications are processed on a rolling basis. Application fee: $25. Electronic applications accepted. *Expenses:* Tuition: Full-time $5,940; part-time $330 per credit. Tuition and fees vary according to program. *Financial support:* Career-related internships or fieldwork available. Financial award applicants required to submit FAFSA. *Unit head:* Dr. Gene Carpenter, Director, 574-257-3332, E-mail: carpeng@bethelcollege.edu. *Application contact:* Dr. Robert Morris, Advisor, 574-257-2667.

Bethel Seminary, Graduate and Professional Programs, St. Paul, MN 55112-6998. Offers adult developments and generativity (Certificate); biblical studies (MATS, Certificate); children's and family ministry (MACFM); Christian education (MACE); Christian thought (M Div, MACT); church leadership (D Min); congregation and family care (D Min); global and contextual studies (MA); global missions (Certificate); lay ministry (Certificate); marriage and family studies (M Div); marriage and family therapy (MAMFT); missions (MATS); pastoral counseling (Certificate); pastoral ministries (M Div); spiritual formation (Certificate); theological studies (MATS, Certificate); transformational leadership (MATL); youth ministries (MACE). *Accreditation:* ACIPE; ATS (one or more programs are accredited). Part-time and evening/weekend programs available. Postbaccalaureate distance learning degree programs offered (minimal on-campus study). *Faculty:* 26 full-time (3 women), 73 part-time/adjunct (21 women). *Students:* 374 full-time (115 women), 669 part-time (268 women); includes 183 minority (90 African Americans, 2 American Indian/Alaska Native, 65 Asian Americans or Pacific Islanders, 26 Hispanic Americans). Average age 36. 417 applicants, 86% accepted, 223 enrolled. In 2007, 62 first professional degrees, 102 master's, 14 doctorates awarded. *Degree requirements:* For master's, variable foreign language requirement, thesis (for some programs); for doctorate, thesis/dissertation; for M Div, one foreign language. *Entrance requirements:* For M Div, letters of reference; for master's, letters of reference, transcripts, personal statement; for doctorate, M Div, letters of reference, essays, organizational support. Additional exam requirements/recommendations for international students: Required—TOEFL (minimum score 550 paper-based; 213 computer-based). *Application deadline:* For fall admission, 8/1 priority date for domestic students, 3/1 for international students; for winter admission, 12/1 priority date for domestic students; for spring admission, 3/1 priority date for domestic students. Applications are processed on a rolling basis. Application fee: $20. Electronic applications accepted. *Expenses:* Tuition: Part-time $325 per credit. Required fees: $10 per quarter. *Financial support:* In 2007–08, 661 students received support, including 20 teaching assistantships; career-related internships or fieldwork, Federal Work-Study, scholarships/grants, and tuition waivers (full) also available. Financial award application deadline: 7/15; financial award applicants required to submit FAFSA. *Faculty research:* Nature of theology, ethics, biblical commentaries, nature of God, science and theology. *Unit head:* Dr. Leland Eliason, Executive Vice President and Provost, 651-638-6182. *Application contact:* Joseph V. Dworak, Director of Admissions, 651-638-6288, Fax: 651-638-6002, E-mail: j-dworak@bethel.edu.

Bethesda Christian University, Graduate and Professional Programs, Anaheim, CA 92801. Offers biblical studies (MA); theology (M Div). *Entrance requirements:* For M Div and master's, interview.

Beth HaMedrash Shaarei Yosher Institute, Graduate Programs, Brooklyn, NY 11204. *Accreditation:* AARTS.

Beth Hatalmud Rabbinical College, Graduate Programs, Brooklyn, NY 11214. *Accreditation:* AARTS.

Beth Medrash Govoha, Graduate Programs, Lakewood, NJ 08701-2797. *Accreditation:* AARTS.

Bethune-Cookman University, School of Graduate and Professional Studies, Daytona Beach, FL 32114-3099. Offers transformative leadership (MS). Postbaccalaureate distance learning degree programs offered (minimal on-campus study). *Faculty:* 6 full-time (5 women). *Students:* 11 full-time (8 women); includes 19 African Americans, 1 international. Average age 35. 36 applicants, 69% accepted, 24 enrolled. *Degree requirements:* For master's, thesis. *Entrance* *requirements:* For master's, GRE or MAT, minimum GPA of 2.75 in the last 60 semester hours; 3 letters of recommendation. Additional exam requirements/recommendations for international students: Required—TOEFL (minimum score 550 paper-based; 213 computer-based). *Application deadline:* For fall admission, 7/15 priority date for domestic and international students; for spring admission, 11/15 priority date for domestic and international students. Applications are processed on a rolling basis. Application fee: $50. Electronic applications accepted. *Expenses:* Tuition: Full-time $4,500. *Financial support:* In 2007–08, 156 students received support. Scholarships/grants available. Financial award application deadline: 7/15. *Faculty research:* Civic engagement, communication ethics, service learning in higher education women in leadership. *Unit head:* Dr. Anne M. McCulloch, Dean, School of Graduate and Professional Studies, 386-481-2073, Fax: 386-481-2380, E-mail: mcculloa@cookman.edu. *Application contact:* Sonja Lewis Lucas, Director of Marketing and Public Relations, 386-481-2344, Fax: 386-481-2380, E-mail: lewiss@cookman.edu.

Bexley Hall Episcopal Seminary, Graduate Programs, Columbus, OH 43209-2325. Offers M Div, MA. *Accreditation:* ATS.

Biblical Theological Seminary, Graduate and Professional Programs, Hatfield, PA 19440-2499. Offers counseling (MA); ministry (MA); theology (M Div, D Min). *Accreditation:* ATS.Part-time programs available. *Degree requirements:* For M Div, thesis/dissertation. *Entrance requirements:* Additional exam requirements/recommendations for international students: Required—TOEFL (minimum score 550 paper-based; 213 computer-based). *Faculty research:* Old Testament narrative, Old Testament historiography, Hebrew syntax, parables, addictions.

Biola University, School of Professional Studies, La Mirada, CA 90639-0001. Offers Christian apologetics (MA); organizational leadership (MA). Part-time and evening/weekend programs available. *Entrance requirements:* For master's, minimum undergraduate GPA of 3.0. Additional exam requirements/recommendations for international students: Required—TOEFL (minimum score 550 paper-based; 213 computer-based).

Biola University, Talbot School of Theology, La Mirada, CA 90639-0001. Offers Bible exposition (MA); biblical and theological studies (MA); Christian education (MACE); Christian ministry and leadership (MA); divinity (M Div); education (PhD); ministry (MA Min); New Testament (MA); Old Testament (MA); philosophy of religion and ethics (MA); spiritual formation (MA); spiritual formation and soul care (MA); theology (MA, Th M, D Min). *Accreditation:* ATS. Part-time and evening/weekend programs available. *Degree requirements:* For master's, variable foreign language requirement, thesis or alternative; for doctorate, variable foreign language requirement, thesis/dissertation; for M Div, thesis/dissertation or alternative. *Entrance requirements:* For M Div, minimum GPA of 2.6; for master's, minimum undergraduate GPA of 3.0; for doctorate, minimum GPA of 3.25. Additional exam requirements/recommendations for international students: Required—TOEFL (minimum score 550 paper-based; 213 computer-based). *Faculty research:* Moral development; biological, medical, and social ethics; ancient Near Eastern historical philosophy.

Blessed John XXIII National Seminary, School of Theology, Weston, MA 02493-2618. Offers M Div. *Accreditation:* ATS. *Faculty:* 9 full-time (0 women), 19 part-time/adjunct (3 women). *Students:* 60 full-time (0 women); includes 12 minority (3 African Americans, 1 American Indian/Alaska Native, 4 Asian Americans or Pacific Islanders, 4 Hispanic Americans). Average age 45. In 2007, 15 degrees awarded. *Entrance requirements:* Bachelor's degree or equivalent in life experience. *Application deadline:* For fall admission, 7/15 priority date for domestic students. Applications are processed on a rolling basis. Application fee: $0. *Financial support:* Career-related internships or fieldwork available. *Unit head:* Rev. Peter J. Uglietto, President and Rector, 781-899-5500, Fax: 781-891-9057, E-mail: rev.uglietto@blessedjohnxxiii.edu.

Bob Jones University, Graduate Programs, Greenville, SC 29614. Offers accountancy (MS); Bible (MA); Bible translation (MA); Biblical studies (Certificate); broadcast management (MS); business administration (MBA); church history (MA, PhD); church ministries (MA); church music (MM); cinema and video production (MA); counseling (MS); curriculum and instruction (Ed D); divinity (M Div); dramatic production (MA); educational leadership (MS, Ed D, Ed S); elementary education (M Ed, MAT); English (M Ed, MA, MAT); fine arts (MA); graphic design (MA); history (M Ed, MA); illustration (MA); interpretative speech (MA); mathematics (M Ed, MAT); medical missions (Certificate); ministry (MM, D Min); multi-categorical special education (M Ed, MAT); music (M Ed); New Testament interpretation (PhD); Old Testament interpretation (PhD); orchestral instrument performance (MM); organ performance (MM); pastoral studies (MA); personnel services (MS, Ed S); piano pedagogy (MM); piano performance (MM); platform arts (MA); radio and television broadcasting (MS); rhetoric and public address (MA); secondary education (M Ed); studio art (MA); teaching Bible (MA); theology (MA, PhD); voice performance (MM); youth ministries (MA); M Div/MM.

Boston College, Graduate School of Arts and Sciences, Department of Theology, Chestnut Hill, MA 02467-3800. Offers PhD. *Accreditation:* ATS. Part-time programs available. *Students:* 138 full-time (60 women), 92 part-time (65 women); includes 22 minority (4 African Americans, 2 American Indian/Alaska Native, 4 Asian Americans or Pacific Islanders, 12 Hispanic Americans), 38 international. 223 applicants, 9% accepted, 14 enrolled. In 2007, 17 doctorates awarded. Terminal master's awarded for partial completion of doctoral program. *Degree requirements:* For doctorate, thesis/dissertation. *Entrance requirements:* For doctorate, GRE General Test. Additional exam requirements/recommendations for international students: Required—TOEFL (minimum score 590 paper-based; 250 computer-based; 91 iBT). *Application deadline:* For fall admission, 1/2 for domestic students. Application fee: $70. Electronic applications accepted. *Financial support:* Fellowships with full tuition reimbursements, research assistantships with full tuition reimbursements, teaching assistantships with full tuition reimbursements, Federal Work-Study and scholarships/grants available. Support available to part-time students. Financial award application deadline: 3/1; financial award applicants required to submit FAFSA. *Faculty research:* Roman Catholic theology, Christian social ethics, Bible, history of Christian life and thought. *Unit head:* Dr. Kenneth Himes, Chairperson, 617-552-8440, E-mail: kenneth.himes@bc.edu. *Application contact:* Dr. John Darr, Graduate Program Director, 617-552-4602, E-mail: john.darr@bc.edu.

See Close-Up on page 691.

Boston College, Graduate School of Arts and Sciences, School of Theology and Ministry, Chestnut Hill, MA 02467-3800. Offers church leadership (MA); divinity (M Div); pastoral ministry (MA), including Hispanic ministry, liturgy and worship, pastoral care and counseling, spirituality; religious education (MA, PhD); sacred theology (STD, STL); social justice/social ministry (MA); spiritual direction (MA); theological studies (MTS); theology (Th M, PhD); youth ministry (MA); MA/MA; MS/MA; MSW/MA. Part-time programs available. *Students:* 103 applicants, 54% accepted, 46 enrolled. In 2007, 37 master's, 4 doctorates awarded. *Degree requirements:* For doctorate, one foreign language, thesis/dissertation. *Entrance requirements:* For doctorate, GRE. Additional exam requirements/recommendations for international students: Required—TOEFL (minimum score 550 paper-based; 213 computer-based). *Application deadline:* For fall admission, 3/1 priority date for domestic students. Application fee: $70. Electronic applications accepted. *Financial support:* Fellowships with tuition reimbursements, career-related internships or fieldwork, Federal Work-Study, and tuition waivers (full and partial) available. Support available to part-time students. Financial award application deadline: 3/1; financial award applicants required to submit FAFSA. *Faculty research:* Philosophy and practice of religious education, pastoral psychology, liturgical and spiritual theology, spiritual formation for the practice of ministry. *Unit head:* Dr. Thomas Groome, Chairperson, 617-552-8449, Fax: 617-552-0811. *Application contact:* Dr. Jennifer Bader, Assistant Director, Academic Affairs, 617-552-4478, Fax: 617-552-0811, E-mail: jennifer.bader@bc.edu.

Boston University, School of Theology, Boston, MA 02215. Offers M Div, MSM, MTS, STM, D Min, Th D, D Min/MSW, M Div/MSM, M Div/MSW, MTS/MSW. *Accreditation:* ACIPE; ATS. Part-time programs available. *Faculty:* 24 full-time (10 women), 18 part-time/adjunct (5 women). *Students:* 266 full-time (129 women), 36 part-time (17 women); includes 41 minority (20 African Americans, 11 Asian Americans or Pacific Islanders, 10 Hispanic Americans), 75 international. Average age 35. 229 applicants, 70% accepted. In 2007, 24 first professional degrees, 44 master's, 8 doctorates awarded. *Degree requirements:* For master's, comprehensive exam; for doctorate, 2 foreign languages, comprehensive exam, thesis/dissertation. *Entrance requirements:* For M Div and master's, GRE General Test or MAT, minimum GPA of 3.0; for doctorate, GRE General Test or MAT, minimum GPA of 3.3. *Application deadline:* For fall admission, 1/15 priority date for domestic students; for spring admission, 10/1 priority date for domestic students. Applications are processed on a rolling basis. Application fee: $70. Electronic applications accepted. *Expenses:* Contact institution. Tuition and fees vary according to class time, course level and program. *Financial support:* Fellowships, research assistantships, teaching assistantships, Federal Work-Study, institutionally sponsored loans, and scholarships/grants available. Support available to part-time students. Financial award application deadline: 7/15; financial award applicants required to submit FAFSA. *Faculty research:* Israelite literature in its social and cultural context, New Testament literature in its social and cultural context, Reformation history, women in the church, social ethics. *Unit head:* Dr. Ray Hart, Interim Dean, 617-353-3050, Fax: 617-353-3061. *Application contact:* Rev. Earl R. Beane, Director of Admissions, 617-353-3036, Fax: 617-358-0140, E-mail: sthadmis@bu.edu.

Briercrest Seminary, Graduate Programs, Program in Theology, Caronport, SK S0H 0S0, Canada. Offers Biblical studies (M Div); leadership and management (M Div); New Testament (MATS); Old Testament (MATS); pastoral counseling (M Div); pastoral ministry (M Div); theological studies (M Div); theology (MATS); worship (M Div); youth and family ministry (M Div). *Accreditation:* ATS. Part-time programs available. *Degree requirements:* For master's, comprehensive exam, thesis optional. *Entrance requirements:* Additional exam requirements/recommendations for international students: Required—TOEFL (minimum score 550 paper-based; 213 computer-based).

Bryn Athyn College of the New Church, Academy of the New Church Theological School, Bryn Athyn, PA 19009-0717. Offers divinity (M Div); religious studies (MA). Part-time programs available. Postbaccalaureate distance learning degree programs offered (minimal on-campus study). *Faculty:* 12. *Students:* 7 full-time (0 women), 19 part-time (13 women), 10 international. Average age 37. 26 applicants, 100% accepted. In 2007, 4 first professional degrees, 2 master's awarded. *Degree requirements:* For master's, thesis; for M Div, 3 foreign languages, thesis/dissertation. *Entrance requirements:* Additional exam requirements/recommendations for international students: Required—TOEFL. *Application deadline:* For fall admission, 1/31 for domestic students. Applications are processed on a rolling basis. *Financial support:* In 2007–08, 7 students received support. Career-related internships or fieldwork, Federal Work-Study, and institutionally sponsored loans available. Financial award application deadline: 1/31. *Unit head:* Andrew Dibb, Dean, 267-502-2640, E-mail: andrew.dibb@ancts.org.

California Institute of Integral Studies, Graduate Programs, School of Consciousness and Transformation, San Francisco, CA 94103. Offers cultural anthropology and social transformation (MA); East-West psychology (MA, PhD); integrative health studies (MA); philosophy and religion (MA, PhD), including Asian and comparative studies, philosophy, cosmology, and consciousness, social and cultural anthropology (PhD), transformative leadership (MA), transformative studies (PhD), women's spirituality, women's spirituality flex format; social and cultural anthropology (PhD); transformative leadership (MA); transformative studies (PhD). Part-time and evening/weekend programs available. Postbaccalaureate distance learning degree programs offered (minimal on-campus study). *Faculty:* 30 full-time, 28 part-time/adjunct. *Students:* 456; includes 92 minority (32 African Americans, 3 American Indian/Alaska Native, 40 Asian Americans or Pacific Islanders, 17 Hispanic Americans), 1 international. Average age 37. 206 applicants, 93% accepted, 114 enrolled. In 2007, 26 degrees awarded. Terminal master's awarded for partial completion of doctoral program. *Degree requirements:* For master's, comprehensive exam (for some programs), thesis optional; for doctorate, comprehensive exam, thesis/dissertation. *Entrance requirements:* For master's, minimum GPA of 3.0, letters of recommendation, writing sample; for doctorate, master's degree, minimum GPA of 3.0, letters of recommendation, writing sample. Additional exam requirements/recommendations for international students: Required—TOEFL. *Application deadline:* For fall admission, 2/15 priority date for domestic and international students; for spring admission, 10/15 priority date for domestic and international students. Applications are processed on a rolling basis. Application fee: $65. Electronic applications accepted. *Expenses:* Tuition: Full-time $16,930; part-time $780 per unit. Tuition and fees vary according to course load and program. *Financial support:* In 2007–08, 292 students received support; research assistantships, teaching assistantships, career-related internships or fieldwork, Federal Work-Study, institutionally sponsored loans, scholarships/grants, and tuition waivers (partial) available. Support available to part-time students. Financial award application deadline: 3/15; financial award applicants required to submit FAFSA. *Faculty research:* Altered states of consciousness, dreams, cosmology, postcolonial studies, integrative health studies. *Application contact:* Allyson Werner, Senior Admissions Counselor, 415-575-6155, Fax: 415-575-1268.

See Close-Up on page 445.

Calvary Bible College and Theological Seminary, Calvary Theological Seminary, Kansas City, MO 64147-1341. Offers Bible and theology (MS); biblical counseling (MA); biblical studies (MA); Christian ministry (MA); Christian studies (MS); Christian theology (MA); New Testament (MA); Old Testament (MA); pastoral studies (M Div). Part-time and evening/weekend programs available. *Faculty:* 3 full-time (0 women), 2 part-time/adjunct (0 women). *Students:* 19 full-time (7 women), 36 part-time (11 women); includes 12 minority (9 African Americans, 1 Asian American or Pacific Islander, 2 Hispanic Americans), 2 international. Average age 37. In 2007, 3 first professional degrees, 15 master's awarded. *Degree requirements:* For master's, one foreign language, comprehensive exam, thesis; for M Div, 2 foreign languages, comprehensive exam, thesis/dissertation. *Entrance requirements:* For M Div and master's, GRE, minimum GPA of 2.5, 50 semester hours of course work in liberal arts, BA or BS degree, doctrine agreement. Additional exam requirements/recommendations for international students: Required—TOEFL (minimum score 550 paper-based; 213 computer-based). *Application deadline:* For fall admission, 7/15 priority date for domestic and international students; for spring admission, 12/1 priority date for domestic and international students. Application fee: $25. *Financial support:* In 2007–08, 13 students received support. Scholarships/grants available. Financial award application deadline: 11/5. *Unit head:* Dr. Thomas Baurain, Academic Dean, 816-322-0110 Ext. 1504, Fax: 816-331-4474. *Application contact:* Damon Horton, Director of Admissions, 800-326-3960 Ext. 1320, Fax: 816-331-4474.

Calvin Theological Seminary, Graduate and Professional Programs, Grand Rapids, MI 49546-4387. Offers divinity (M Div); educational ministry (MA); historical theology (PhD); missions: church growth (MA); philosophical and moral theology (PhD); systematic theology (PhD); theological studies (MTS); theology (Th M). *Accreditation:* ACIPE; ATS. Part-time programs available. *Students:* 235 full-time (35 women), 70 part-time (14 women); includes 39 minority (11 African Americans, 1 American Indian/Alaska Native, 19 Asian Americans or Pacific Islanders, 8 Hispanic Americans), 93 international. Average age 31. 159 applicants, 77% accepted, 96 enrolled. In 2007, 21 first professional degrees, 43 master's, 1 doctorate awarded. *Median time to degree:* Of those who began their doctoral program in fall 1999, 80% received their degree in 8 years or less. *Degree requirements:* For master's, thesis (for some programs); for doctorate, 4 foreign languages, comprehensive exam, thesis/dissertation; for M Div, 2 foreign languages. *Entrance requirements:* For doctorate, GRE General Test, Hebrew, Greek, and a modern foreign language. Additional exam requirements/recommendations for international students: Required—TOEFL (minimum score 550 paper-based; 213 computer-based), TWE (minimum score 4). *Application deadline:* For fall admission, 3/1 priority date for domestic and international students. Applications are processed on a rolling basis. Application fee: $25. Electronic applications accepted. *Expenses:* Tuition: Full-time $9,875; part-time $250 per credit hour. *Financial support:* In 2007–08, 187 students received support, including 4 fellowships with full tuition reimbursements available (averaging $8,405 per year), 4 teaching assistantships with full tuition reimbursements available (averaging $5,760 per year); career-related internships or fieldwork, institutionally sponsored loans, scholarships/grants, and tuition

Theology

Calvin Theological Seminary (continued)
waivers (full) also available. Support available to part-time students. Financial award application deadline: 3/1; financial award applicants required to submit FAFSA. *Faculty research:* Recent Trinity theory, Christian anthropology, Proverbs, reformed confessions, Paul's view of law. *Unit head:* Dr. Cornelius Plantinga, Head, 616-957-6024, Fax: 616-957-6536, E-mail: sempres@calvinseminary.edu. *Application contact:* Rev. Gregory Janke, Director of Admissions, 616-957-7035, Fax: 616-957-8621, E-mail: gjanke@calvinseminary.edu.

Campbellsville University, School of Theology, Campbellsville, KY 42718-2799. Offers theology (M Th). Part-time programs available. *Degree requirements:* For master's, comprehensive exam, thesis optional. *Entrance requirements:* For master's, GRE General Test, minimum GPA of 3.0 in major, minimum GPA of 2.75 overall, 18 hours of undergraduate coursework in Christian studies. Electronic applications accepted. *Faculty research:* Clergy needing graduate theology education, trinity and Christian faith, Old Testament David narratives, leadership Principles on Christian University integration of Christian principles in counseling process.

Campbell University, Graduate and Professional Programs, Divinity School, Buies Creek, NC 27506. Offers Christian education (MA); divinity (M Div); ministry (D Min); M Div/MA; M Div/MBA. *Accreditation:* ATS. *Degree requirements:* For doctorate, final project. *Entrance requirements:* For master's, minimum GPA of 2.5; for doctorate, MAT, M Div, minimum graduate GPA of 3.0. Additional exam requirements/recommendations for international students: Required—TOEFL (minimum score 580 paper-based; 237 computer-based). Expenses: Contact institution. *Faculty research:* New Testament, theology, spiritual formation, Old Testament, Christian leadership.

Canadian Southern Baptist Seminary, Graduate Programs, Cochrane, AB T4C 2G1, Canada. Offers ministry (M Div); religious education (MRE). *Accreditation:* ATS. Part-time programs available. *Faculty:* 8 full-time (0 women), 3 part-time/adjunct (1 woman). *Students:* 23 full-time (4 women), 20 part-time (6 women); includes 9 minority (1 African American, 5 Asian Americans or Pacific Islanders, 3 Hispanic Americans), 12 international. Average age 30. 14 applicants, 100% accepted, 14 enrolled. In 2007, 14 degrees awarded. *Entrance requirements:* Additional exam requirements/recommendations for international students: Required—TOEFL (minimum score 560 paper-based; 220 computer-based), IELTS (minimum score 7). *Application deadline:* For fall admission, 7/1 priority date for domestic and international students; for winter admission, 11/15 priority date for domestic and international students. Applications are processed on a rolling basis. Application fee: $50. Tuition and fees charges are reported in Canadian dollars. *Expenses:* Tuition: Full-time $4,440 Canadian dollars; part-time $185 Canadian dollars per credit. Required fees: $530 Canadian dollars; $20 Canadian dollars per credit. Tuition and fees vary according to course load and program. *Application contact:* Kathleen McNaughton, Registrar, E-mail: registrar@csbs.ca.

Capital Bible Seminary, Graduate and Professional Programs, Lanham, MD 20706-3599. Offers biblical studies (MA, Certificate); Christian counseling (MA); Christian counseling and discipleship (Certificate); ministry leadership (MA); theology (M Div, Th M). *Accreditation:* ATS (one or more programs are accredited). Part-time and evening/weekend programs available. *Degree requirements:* For master's, 2 foreign languages, comprehensive exam, thesis (for some programs); for M Div, 2 foreign languages, comprehensive exam. *Entrance requirements:* For M Div and master's, GRE General Test, Greek exam for those with 2 years of Greek, proficiency exam in theology, previous course work in Biblical studies. Additional exam requirements/recommendations for international students: Required—TOEFL (minimum score 550 paper-based; 213 computer-based). *Faculty research:* Dead Sea Scrolls, spiritual gifts, hermeneutics.

Carey Theological College, Graduate Programs, Vancouver, BC V6T 1J6, Canada. Offers MPM, D Min. *Accreditation:* ATS. Part-time programs available. *Faculty:* 7 full-time (2 women), 2 part-time/adjunct (0 women). *Students:* 1 full-time (0 women), 103 part-time (23 women); includes 38 minority (1 African American, 31 Asian Americans or Pacific Islanders, 6 Hispanic Americans). Average age 45. 26 applicants, 77% accepted, 20 enrolled. In 2007, 10 master's, 4 doctorates awarded. *Median time to degree:* Of those who began their doctoral program in fall 1999, 100% received their degree in 8 years or less. *Degree requirements:* For doctorate, thesis/dissertation. *Entrance requirements:* For master's, undergraduate degree with minimum GPA of 2.7; for doctorate, M Div degree with minimum GPA of 3.5. Additional exam requirements/recommendations for international students: Required—TOEFL (minimum score 577 paper-based; 233 computer-based; 90 iBT). *Application deadline:* Applications are processed on a rolling basis. Application fee: $60. Tuition charges are reported in Canadian dollars. *Expenses:* Tuition: Part-time $240 Canadian dollars per credit. *Faculty research:* Missional church, new monasticism, women in leadership, spiritual formation, preaching. *Unit head:* Dr. Barbara Mutch, Academic Vice President, 604-224-4308, Fax: 604-224-5014, E-mail: barmutch@careytheologicalcollege.ca. *Application contact:* Myrna Sears, Registrar, 604-224-4308, Fax: 604-224-5014, E-mail: msears@careytheologicalcollege.ca.

The Catholic Distance University, Graduate Programs, Hamilton, VA 20158. Offers religious studies (MRS); theology (MA). Part-time and evening/weekend programs available. Postbaccalaureate distance learning degree programs offered (no on-campus study). *Degree requirements:* For master's, comprehensive exam, capstone paper or project.

Catholic Theological Union at Chicago, Graduate and Professional Programs, Chicago, IL 60615-5698. Offers biblical spirituality (Certificate); cross-cultural ministries (D Min); cross-cultural missions (Certificate); divinity (M Div); liturgical studies (Certificate); liturgy (D Min); pastoral studies (MAPS, Certificate); spiritual formation (Certificate); spirituality (D Min); theology (MA); M Div/MA; M Div/MSW; M Div/PhD. *Accreditation:* ACIPE; ATS (one or more programs are accredited). Part-time and evening/weekend programs available. *Degree requirements:* For master's, one foreign language, comprehensive exam (for some programs), thesis (for some programs); for doctorate, thesis/dissertation. *Entrance requirements:* For doctorate, master's degree, 5 years of active ministry. *Faculty research:* Doctrine, sacraments, ethics, Bible.

The Catholic University of America, School of Canon Law, Washington, DC 20064. Offers JCD, JCL, JD/JCL. *Faculty:* 6 full-time (1 woman). *Students:* 36 full-time (6 women), 41 part-time (10 women); includes 9 minority (3 African Americans, 3 Asian Americans or Pacific Islanders, 3 Hispanic Americans), 16 international. Average age 44. 49 applicants, 84% accepted, 35 enrolled. In 2007, 3 doctorates awarded. *Degree requirements:* For doctorate, 2 foreign languages, thesis/dissertation. *Entrance requirements:* For doctorate, GRE General Test, 2 letters of recommendation. Additional exam requirements/recommendations for international students: Required—TOEFL (minimum score 580 paper-based; 237 computer-based). *Application deadline:* For fall admission, 2/1 priority date for domestic students; for spring admission, 11/15 priority date for domestic students. Applications are processed on a rolling basis. Application fee: $55. Electronic applications accepted. *Financial support:* Fellowships, research assistantships, teaching assistantships, career-related internships or fieldwork, Federal Work-Study, scholarships/grants, tuition waivers (full and partial), and unspecified assistantships available. Support available to part-time students. Financial award application deadline: 2/1; financial award applicants required to submit FAFSA. *Unit head:* Rev. Msgr. Brian Ferme, Dean, 202-319-5492, Fax: 202-319-4187, E-mail: ferme@cua.edu.

The Catholic University of America, School of Theology and Religious Studies, Washington, DC 20064. Offers M Div, STB, MA, MRE, D Min, PhD, STD, STL, MSLS/MA. *Accreditation:* ATS (one or more programs are accredited). Part-time programs available. *Faculty:* 38 full-time (4 women), 8 part-time/adjunct (2 women). *Students:* 170 full-time (29 women), 197 part-time (57 women); includes 33 minority (9 African Americans, 1 American Indian/Alaska Native, 13 Asian Americans or Pacific Islanders, 10 Hispanic Americans), 64 international. Average age 36. 262 applicants, 77% accepted, 102 enrolled. In 2007, 19 first professional degrees, 16 master's, 16 doctorates awarded. Terminal master's awarded for partial completion of doctoral program. *Degree requirements:* For master's, comprehensive exam; for doctorate, comprehensive exam, thesis/dissertation; for first professional degree, one foreign language; for STL, one foreign language, comprehensive exam, thesis. *Entrance requirements:* For first professional degree and master's, GRE General Test, 3 letters of recommendation; for doctorate and STL, GRE, 3 letters of recommendation. Additional exam requirements/recommendations for international students: Required—TOEFL (minimum score 580 paper-based; 237 computer-based). *Application deadline:* For fall admission, 2/1 priority date for domestic students; for spring admission, 11/15 priority date for domestic students. Applications are processed on a rolling basis. Application fee: $55. Electronic applications accepted. *Financial support:* Fellowships, research assistantships, teaching assistantships, career-related internships or fieldwork, Federal Work-Study, scholarships/grants, tuition waivers (full and partial), and unspecified assistantships available. Support available to part-time students. Financial award application deadline: 2/1; financial award applicants required to submit FAFSA. *Faculty research:* Biblical studies, canon law, church history, liturgical studies, religion and religious education. *Unit head:* Msgr. Kevin W. Irwin, Dean, 202-319-5683, Fax: 202-319-4967, E-mail: irwin@cua.edu.

Central Baptist Theological Seminary, Graduate and Professional Programs, Shawnee, KS 66226. Offers missional church studies (MA); theological studies (MA); theology (M Div, Diploma). *Accreditation:* ACIPE; ATS (one or more programs are accredited). Part-time programs available. *Faculty:* 3 full-time (0 women), 13 part-time/adjunct (5 women). *Students:* 33 full-time (13 women), 69 part-time (34 women); includes 28 minority (25 African Americans, 2 American Indian/Alaska Native, 1 Hispanic American), 2 international. Average age 44. 46 applicants, 48% accepted, 21 enrolled. In 2007, 11 first professional degrees, 2 master's awarded. *Degree requirements:* For master's, thesis optional, MMPI, Myers-Briggs, Enneagram; for M Div, thesis/dissertation optional. *Entrance requirements:* For master's, accredited bachelor's degree with minimum GPA of 2.3. Additional exam requirements/recommendations for international students: Required—TOEFL (minimum score 547 paper-based; 210 computer-based; 77 iBT). *Application deadline:* For fall admission, 8/1 priority date for domestic students; for winter admission, 12/5 priority date for domestic students; for spring admission, 1/2 priority date for domestic students. Applications are processed on a rolling basis. Application fee: $0. Electronic applications accepted. *Expenses:* Tuition: Part-time $330 per credit hour. *Financial support:* In 2007–08, 42 students received support. Career-related internships or fieldwork, scholarships/grants, and tuition waivers (full and partial) available. Support available to part-time students. Financial award application deadline: 6/21; financial award applicants required to submit FAFSA. *Unit head:* Dr. Paul W. Stevens, Interim Academic Dean, 913-667-5704, Fax: 913-371-8110, E-mail: pwstevens@cbts.edu. *Application contact:* Steve Guinn, Director of Enrollment Services, 913-667-5707, Fax: 913-371-8110, E-mail: sguinn@cbts.edu.

Central Baptist Theological Seminary of Virginia Beach, Graduate Programs, Virginia Beach, VA 23464. Offers M Div, MBS, Th M. *Entrance requirements:* For M Div, GRE, interview, M Div or equivalent from an accredited seminary, minimum cumulative GPA of 2.7, church endorsement, 4 recommendations; for master's, GRE, interview, minimum cumulative GPA of 2.4, church endorsement, 4 recommendations. Electronic applications accepted.

Central Yeshiva Tomchei Tmimim-Lubavitch, Graduate Programs, Brooklyn, NY 11230. *Accreditation:* AARTS.

Chaminade University of Honolulu, Graduate Services, Program in Pastoral Theology, Honolulu, HI 96816-1578. Offers MPT. Part-time and evening/weekend programs available. Postbaccalaureate distance learning degree programs offered. *Faculty:* 3 full-time (1 woman), 2 part-time/adjunct (1 woman). *Students:* 2 full-time (0 women), 13 part-time (7 women); includes 9 minority (8 Asian Americans or Pacific Islanders, 1 Hispanic American), 1 international. 7 applicants, 71% accepted, 4 enrolled. In 2007, 5 degrees awarded. *Degree requirements:* For master's, capstone course. *Entrance requirements:* For master's, 2 letters of recommendation. Additional exam requirements/recommendations for international students: Required—TOEFL (minimum score 550 paper-based). *Application deadline:* For fall admission, 9/15 for domestic students; for winter admission, 12/15 for domestic students; for spring admission, 3/15 for domestic students. Applications are processed on a rolling basis. Application fee: $50. Electronic applications accepted. *Expenses:* Tuition: Part-time $490 per credit hour. *Unit head:* Regina Pfeiffer, Assistant Director, 808-735-4700, E-mail: rpfeiffe@chaminade.edu. *Application contact:* Regina Pfeiffer, Director, 808-735-4700, Fax: 808-739-8328, E-mail: mpt@chaminade.edu.

Chicago Theological Seminary, Graduate and Professional Programs, Chicago, IL 60637-1507. Offers clinical pastoral education (D Min); Jewish-Christian studies (PhD); pastoral counseling (D Min); preaching (D Min); religious studies (MA); spiritual leadership (D Min); theology (M Div); theology and the human sciences (PhD), including theology and society, theology and the personality sciences; M Div/MSW. *Accreditation:* ACIPE; ATS. Part-time programs available. *Faculty:* 13 full-time (5 women). *Students:* 83 full-time (40 women), 135 part-time (66 women); includes 54 minority (45 African Americans, 6 Asian Americans or Pacific Islanders, 3 Hispanic Americans), 33 international. 78 applicants, 94% accepted, 50 enrolled. In 2007, 15 first professional degrees, 8 master's, 22 doctorates awarded. *Degree requirements:* For master's, thesis; for doctorate, 2 foreign languages, comprehensive exam, thesis/dissertation; for M Div, thesis/dissertation. *Entrance requirements:* For doctorate, GRE General Test. Additional exam requirements/recommendations for international students: Required—TOEFL (minimum score 217 computer-based). *Application deadline:* For fall admission, 2/15 priority date for domestic and international students; for spring admission, 11/1 for domestic and international students. Application fee: $50. *Financial support:* In 2007–08, 103 students received support, including 12 fellowships (averaging $10,000 per year); institutionally sponsored loans, scholarships/grants, and tuition waivers (partial) also available. Support available to part-time students. Financial award application deadline: 3/1; financial award applicants required to submit FAFSA. *Faculty research:* Bible, culture and hermeneutics/theology, gender & sexuality/black faith and life/spirituality and psychology/practical theology. Total annual research expenditures: $150,000. *Unit head:* Dr. Theodore W. Jennings, Acting Dean, 773-752-5757, Fax: 773-752-1903, E-mail: tjennings@ctschicago.edu. *Application contact:* Rev. Lin Sanford Keppert, Director of Admissions, Recruitment and Financial Aid, E-mail: lkeppert@ctschicago.edu.

Christendom College, Notre Dame Graduate School, Front Royal, VA 22630-5103. Offers theological studies (MA). Part-time and evening/weekend programs available. *Degree requirements:* For master's, one foreign language, thesis or alternative. Electronic applications accepted.

Christian Theological Seminary, Graduate and Professional Programs, Indianapolis, IN 46208-3301. Offers marriage and family (MA); pastoral care and counseling (D Min); practical theology (D Min); psychotherapy and faith (MA); sacred theology (STM); specialized ministries (MA); theological studies (MTS); theology (M Div). *Accreditation:* AAMFT/COAMFTE (one or more programs are accredited); ACIPE; ATS. Part-time programs available. Terminal master's awarded for partial completion of doctoral program. *Degree requirements:* For master's, comprehensive exam (for some programs); thesis (for some programs); for doctorate, comprehensive exam, thesis/dissertation; for M Div, comprehensive exam, thesis/dissertation (for some programs), missionary and cross-cultural experience. *Entrance requirements:* For master's, GRE General Test, MAT; for doctorate, M Div or BD. Electronic applications accepted. *Faculty research:* Faith formation, peer learning post graduation.

Christ the King Seminary, Graduate and Professional Programs, East Aurora, NY 14052. Offers divinity (M Div); pastoral ministry (MA); pastoral studies (Certificate); theology (MA). *Accreditation:* ATS. Part-time and evening/weekend programs available. *Degree requirements:* For master's, comprehensive exam, thesis; for M Div, comprehensive exam. *Entrance requirements:* For M Div and master's, previous course work in philosophy and religious studies.

Church Divinity School of the Pacific, Graduate and Professional Programs, Berkeley, CA 94709-1217. Offers M Div, MA, MTS, D Min, Certificate. *Accreditation:* ACIPE; ATS (one or more programs are accredited). Part-time programs available. *Faculty:* 9 full-time (5 women), 13 part-time/adjunct (2 women). *Students:* 68 full-time (42 women), 48 part-time (27 women); includes 12 minority (3 African Americans, 2 American Indian/Alaska Native, 3 Asian Americans or Pacific Islanders, 4 Hispanic Americans), 5 international. Average age 44. 60 applicants, 92% accepted, 49 enrolled. In 2007, 18 first professional degrees, 2 master's, 1 doctorate awarded.

Degree requirements: For master's, one foreign language, thesis; for doctorate, thesis/dissertation; for M Div, one foreign language. *Entrance requirements:* For M Div, master's, and Certificate, GRE General Test, letters of reference; for doctorate, letters of reference. Additional exam requirements/recommendations for international students: Required—TOEFL. *Application deadline:* For fall admission, 5/1 for domestic students. Applications are processed on a rolling basis. Application fee: $30. Electronic applications accepted. *Expenses:* Tuition: Full-time $14,000; part-time $250 per unit. Required fees: $25 per semester. *Financial support:* Career-related internships or fieldwork, Federal Work-Study, and scholarships/grants available. Support available to part-time students. Financial award application deadline: 3/1; financial award applicants required to submit FAFSA. *Unit head:* Dr. Donn F. Morgan, President and Dean, 510-204-0733. *Application contact:* Kathleen Crisp, Director of Admissions and Recruitment, 510-204-0715, Fax: 510-644-0712, E-mail: admissions@cdsp.edu.

Church of God Theological Seminary, Graduate and Professional Programs, Cleveland, TN 37320-3330. Offers church ministries (MA), including counseling, discipleship and Christian formations, missions, pastoral ministry; discipleship and Christian formations (MA); theology (M Div). *Accreditation:* ACIPE; ATS. Part-time programs available. *Degree requirements:* For M Div, 2 foreign languages, thesis/dissertation, internship. *Faculty research:* Biblical exegesis.

Cincinnati Christian University, Graduate School, Cincinnati, OH 45204-3200. Offers biblical studies (MA); church history (MA); counseling (MAC); divinity (M Div); ministry (M Min); practical ministries (MA); theological studies (MA). *Accreditation:* ATS. Part-time programs available. *Degree requirements:* For master's, thesis (for some programs); for M Div, 2 foreign languages, oral exam. *Entrance requirements:* For master's, GRE General Test. Additional exam requirements/recommendations for international students: Required—TOEFL. Electronic applications accepted.

Claremont Graduate University, Graduate Programs, School of Religion, Claremont, CA 91711-6160. Offers Hebrew Bible (MA, PhD); history of Christianity and religions of North America (MA, PhD); New Testament (MA, PhD); philosophy of religion and theology (MA, PhD); theology, ethics and culture (MA, PhD); women's studies in religion (MA, PhD); MA/PhD; MBA/PhD. Part-time programs available. *Faculty:* 6 full-time (2 women), 9 part-time/adjunct (5 women). *Students:* 221 full-time (89 women), 7 part-time (2 women); includes 36 minority (15 African Americans, 12 Asian Americans or Pacific Islanders, 9 Hispanic Americans), 33 international. Average age 37. In 2007, 13 master's, 18 doctorates awarded. Terminal master's awarded for partial completion of doctoral program. *Degree requirements:* For master's, one foreign language, comprehensive exam (for some programs), thesis; for doctorate, 2 foreign languages, comprehensive exam, thesis/dissertation. *Entrance requirements:* For master's and doctorate, GRE General Test. *Application deadline:* For fall admission, 2/15 priority date for domestic students. Applications are processed on a rolling basis. Electronic applications accepted. *Expenses:* Tuition: Full-time $31,640; part-time $1,376 per unit. Required fees: $145 per semester. Tuition and fees vary according to course load, degree level and program. *Financial support:* Fellowships, research assistantships, teaching assistantships, Federal Work-Study and institutionally sponsored loans available. Support available to part-time students. Financial award application deadline: 2/15; financial award applicants required to submit FAFSA. *Unit head:* Karen Torjesen, Dean, 909-607-3214, Fax: 909-621-9587, E-mail: karen.torjesen@cgu.edu. *Application contact:* Patrick Horn, Associate Dean, 909-607-8411, Fax: 909-607-9587, E-mail: patrick.horn@cgu.edu.

Claremont School of Theology, Graduate and Professional Programs, Master of Divinity Program, Claremont, CA 91711-3199. Offers M Div. *Accreditation:* ACIPE; ATS. Part-time programs available. *Entrance requirements:* Additional exam requirements/recommendations for international students: Required—TOEFL (minimum score 230 computer-based). Electronic applications accepted.

Claremont School of Theology, Graduate and Professional Programs, Program in Religion, Claremont, CA 91711-3199. Offers practical theology (PhD); religion and theology (MA); religious education (MARE). *Accreditation:* ACIPE; ATS. Terminal master's awarded for partial completion of doctoral program. *Degree requirements:* For master's, thesis; for doctorate, 2 foreign languages, thesis/dissertation. *Entrance requirements:* For doctorate, GRE General Test. Additional exam requirements/recommendations for international students: Required—TOEFL (minimum score 250 computer-based). Electronic applications accepted.

Colgate Rochester Crozer Divinity School, Graduate and Professional Programs, Rochester, NY 14620-2530. Offers M Div, MA, D Min, Certificate. *Accreditation:* ACIPE; ATS (one or more programs are accredited). Part-time programs available. *Faculty:* 8 full-time (5 women), 15 part-time/adjunct (7 women). *Students:* 91 full-time, 28 part-time; includes 33 minority (28 African Americans, 1 Asian American or Pacific Islander, 4 Hispanic Americans), 6 international. Average age 43. 51 applicants, 92% accepted, 38 enrolled. In 2007, 19 first professional degrees, 1 master's, 4 doctorates awarded. *Degree requirements:* For master's, thesis; for doctorate, thesis/dissertation. *Entrance requirements:* For M Div and master's, BA/BS, personal statement; for doctorate, M Div, 3 years professional experience. Additional exam requirements/recommendations for international students: Required—TOEFL (minimum score 600 paper-based). *Application deadline:* For fall admission, 7/1 priority date for domestic students, 3/1 for international students; for spring admission, 12/1 priority date for domestic students. Applications are processed on a rolling basis. Application fee: $35. *Expenses:* Tuition: Full-time $8,250; part-time $458 per credit hour. Required fees: $125; $17 per course. *Financial support:* In 2007–08, 60 students received support. Career-related internships or fieldwork and scholarships/grants available. Financial award application deadline: 9/1; financial award applicants required to submit FAFSA. *Faculty research:* Old Testament, New Testament, Christian ethics, Black Church studies, woman and gender studies. *Unit head:* Dr. Eugene C. Bay, President, 585-271-1320 Ext. 680, Fax: 585-271-8013, E-mail: gbay@crcds.edu. *Application contact:* Rev. Melissa M. Morral, Vice President for Enrollment Services, 585-340-9500, Fax: 585-340-9644, E-mail: mmorral@crcds.edu.

Collège Dominicain de Philosophie et de Théologie, Graduate Programs, Programs in Theology, Ottawa, ON K1R 7G3, Canada. Offers M Th, MA Th, PhD, Th D, L Th. Part-time and evening/weekend programs available. *Faculty:* 7 full-time (2 women), 12 part-time/adjunct (2 women). *Students:* 21 full-time (5 women), 4 part-time (1 woman); includes 12 minority (6 African Americans, 1 Asian American or Pacific Islander, 5 Hispanic Americans). Average age 48. 4 applicants, 100% accepted, 4 enrolled. In 2007, 2 master's, 1 doctorate awarded. *Degree requirements:* For master's, 3 foreign languages, research paper; for doctorate, 3 foreign languages, thesis/dissertation, candidacy exam. *Entrance requirements:* For master's, B Th or the equivalent, minimum A- average in undergraduate course work; for doctorate, MA Th or equivalent, minimum A- average in graduate course work. *Application deadline:* For fall admission, 6/1 priority date for domestic students, 3/1 priority date for international students; for winter admission, 11/18 priority date for domestic and international students. Applications are processed on a rolling basis. Application fee: $40. *Expenses:* Tuition: Full-time $3,300; part-time $130 per credit. Required fees: $125. One-time fee: $105 part-time. Tuition and fees vary according to reciprocity agreements. *Financial support:* In 2007–08, 7 fellowships (averaging $1,250 per year) were awarded. *Unit head:* Marie-Therese Nadeau, Dean of the Faculty, 613-233-5696. *Application contact:* Fr. Herve Tremblay, Registrar, 613-233-5696, Fax: 613-233-6064, E-mail: registrar@collegedominicain.ca.

College of Emmanuel and St. Chad, Bachelor of Theology Program, Saskatoon, SK S7N 0W6, Canada. Offers B Th. Part-time programs available. Postbaccalaureate distance learning degree programs offered (minimal on-campus study). *Degree requirements:* For B Th, internship. *Entrance requirements:* 1 year of university level work or equivalent. Additional exam requirements/recommendations for international students: Required—TOEFL. *Faculty research:* Pauline studies, New Testament, ethics, congregational development, trauma and spirituality.

College of Emmanuel and St. Chad, Graduate Programs, Saskatoon, SK S7N 0W6, Canada. Offers M Div, MTS, STM. Part-time programs available. *Degree requirements:* For master's, thesis optional. *Entrance requirements:* For master's, M Div or MTS (STM). Additional exam requirements/recommendations for international students: Required—TOEFL. *Faculty research:* New Testament, systematics, Christian education, theology, ethics.

College of Mount St. Joseph, Graduate Program in Religious Studies, Cincinnati, OH 45233-1670. Offers spiritual and pastoral care (MA). Part-time and evening/weekend programs available. *Faculty:* 3 full-time (1 woman), 3 part-time/adjunct (2 women). *Students:* 1 (woman) full-time, 27 part-time (25 women); includes 1 minority (African American) Average age 47. 18 applicants, 100% accepted, 11 enrolled. In 2007, 13 degrees awarded. *Degree requirements:* For master's, comprehensive exam, integrating project. *Entrance requirements:* For master's, 3 letters of recommendation, interview, essay, minimum GPA of 2.7. Additional exam requirements/recommendations for international students: Required—TOEFL (minimum score 560 paper-based; 220 computer-based). *Application deadline:* Applications are processed on a rolling basis. Application fee: $50. Electronic applications accepted. *Expenses: Contact institution. Financial support:* In 2007–08, 21 students received support. Career-related internships or fieldwork and scholarships/grants available. Support available to part-time students. Financial award application deadline: 6/1; financial award applicants required to submit FAFSA. *Faculty research:* Contextual/cultural/systematic theology, historical/spiritual theology, business/economics ethics, social justice, Biblical/cultural/pastoral theology. *Unit head:* Dr. John Trokan, Chair, 513-244-4272, Fax: 513-244-4222, E-mail: john_trokan@mail.msj.edu. *Application contact:* Marilyn Hoskins, Assistant Director of Admissions for Graduate Recruitment, 513-244-4723, Fax: 513-244-4629, E-mail: marilyn_hoskins@mail.msj.edu.

College of St. Catherine, Graduate Programs, Program in Theology, St. Paul, MN 55105-1789. Offers MA. Part-time and evening/weekend programs available. *Faculty:* 7 full-time (2 women). *Students:* 10 full-time (9 women), 31 part-time (26 women); includes 2 minority (both African Americans) Average age 46. 11 applicants, 82% accepted, 9 enrolled. In 2007, 13 degrees awarded. *Degree requirements:* For master's, comprehensive exam, thesis (for some programs). *Entrance requirements:* For master's, MAT, minimum GPA of 3.0. Additional exam requirements/recommendations for international students: Required—Michigan English Language Assessment Battery or TOEFL (minimum paper-based score 600; computer 250; iBT 100). *Application deadline:* For fall admission, 8/1 priority date for domestic students. Applications are processed on a rolling basis. Application fee: $35. *Expenses: Contact institution. Financial support:* In 2007–08, 9 students received support; research assistantships, career-related internships or fieldwork and institutionally sponsored loans available. Support available to part-time students. Financial award application deadline: 4/1. *Faculty research:* Feminist scholarship, historical theology, symbols, rites of purification, spirituality. *Unit head:* Dr. Chatherine Michaud, CSJ, Director, 651-690-6017, Fax: 651-690-6024. *Application contact:* 651-690-6933, Fax: 651-690-6064.

College of Saint Elizabeth, Department of Theology, Morristown, NJ 07960-6989. Offers MA. Part-time and evening/weekend programs available. *Faculty:* 2 full-time (both women), 1 part-time/adjunct (0 women). *Students:* Average age 58. In 2007, 8 degrees awarded. *Degree requirements:* For master's, thesis or alternative, 3 essays, oral exam. *Entrance requirements:* For master's, interview, minimum GPA of 3.0. *Application deadline:* For fall admission, 3/1 priority date for domestic students; for spring admission, 9/1 for domestic students. Applications are processed on a rolling basis. Application fee: $35. Electronic applications accepted. *Expenses:* Tuition: Full-time $17,016; part-time $709 per credit. Required fees: $1,300; $370 per term. Full-time tuition and fees vary according to program and student's religious affiliation. Part-time tuition and fees vary according to campus/location and student's religious affiliation. *Financial support:* Tuition waivers (partial) and unspecified assistantships available. Support available to part-time students. Financial award applicants required to submit FAFSA. *Unit head:* Sr. Kathleen Flanagan, Director of the Graduate Program in Theology, 973-290-4336, Fax: 973-290-4312, E-mail: kflanagan@cse.edu. *Application contact:* Michael Szarek, Director of Enrollment Management, 973-290-4112, Fax: 973-290-4167, E-mail: mszarek@cse.edu.

Columbia International University, Columbia Biblical Seminary and School of Missions, Columbia, SC 29230-3122. Offers academic ministries (M Div); bible exposition (M Div, MABE); biblical studies (Certificate); counseling ministries (Certificate); divinity (M Div); educational ministries (M Div, MAEM, Certificate); intercultural studies (M Div, MAIS, Certificate); leadership (D Min); leadership for evangelism/mobilization (MALM); member care (D Min); ministry (Certificate); missions (D Min); pastoral counseling and spiritual formation (M Div, MAPS); preaching (D Min); theology (MA). *Accreditation:* ATS (one or more programs are accredited). Part-time and evening/weekend programs available. *Degree requirements:* For master's, integrative seminar; for doctorate, comprehensive exam, thesis/dissertation; for M Div, internship. *Entrance requirements:* For master's, minimum GPA of 2.7; for doctorate, 3 years of ministerial experience, M Div. Additional exam requirements/recommendations for international students: Required—TOEFL. Electronic applications accepted.

Columbia Theological Seminary, Graduate and Professional Programs, Decatur, GA 30031-0520. Offers M Div, MATS, Th M, D Min, Th D. *Accreditation:* ACIPE; ATS (one or more programs are accredited). Terminal master's awarded for partial completion of doctoral program. *Degree requirements:* For master's, thesis (for some programs); for doctorate, one foreign language, thesis/dissertation; for M Div, 2 foreign languages. *Entrance requirements:* For doctorate, M Div or equivalent, 3 years practice of ministry. Additional exam requirements/recommendations for international students: Required—TOEFL.

Concordia Lutheran Seminary, Graduate and Professional Programs, Edmonton, AB T5B 4E3, Canada. Offers M Div, MTS. *Accreditation:* ATS (one or more programs are accredited). Part-time programs available. *Degree requirements:* For master's, thesis or alternative; for M Div, 2 foreign languages, thesis/dissertation. *Entrance requirements:* For M Div, GRE General Test, 1 year of Greek, 1 year of Hebrew, minimum GPA of 2.0; for master's, GRE General Test. Additional exam requirements/recommendations for international students: Required—TOEFL. *Faculty research:* Lutheran Pietism, Christianity and culture, missiology, Christian worship, homiletics.

Concordia Seminary, Graduate Programs, St. Louis, MO 63105-3199. Offers M Div, MA, STM, D Min, PhD, Certificate. *Accreditation:* ACIPE; ATS (one or more programs are accredited). Terminal master's awarded for partial completion of doctoral program. *Degree requirements:* For master's, 3 foreign languages, thesis optional; for doctorate, 4 foreign languages, thesis/dissertation; for M Div, 2 foreign languages, comprehensive exam (for some programs), thesis/dissertation (for some programs). *Entrance requirements:* For M Div, GRE General Test, previous course work in public speaking, Greek, Hebrew, Old Testament, New Testament, and Christian Doctrine; for master's and doctorate, GRE General Test, theological essay in English (foreign students only). Additional exam requirements/recommendations for international students: Required—TOEFL. *Faculty research:* Family counseling, educational administration, contemporary theology, pastoral office, humanism and education.

Concordia Theological Seminary, Graduate and Professional Programs, Fort Wayne, IN 46825-4996. Offers M Div, MA, STM, D Min, D Miss. *Accreditation:* ATS. Part-time programs available. *Degree requirements:* For master's, 2 foreign languages, thesis, oral exam, language exam, comprehensive exam (STM); for doctorate, comprehensive exam, thesis/dissertation, oral exam; for M Div, one foreign language, 1 year of vicarage. *Entrance requirements:* GRE General Test, minimum GPA of 2.25.

Concordia University, School of Graduate Studies, Faculty of Arts and Science, Department of Theological Studies, Montréal, QC H3G 1M8, Canada. Offers MA. *Degree requirements:* For master's, one foreign language, research papers or thesis. *Entrance requirements:* For master's, minimum B average in theology. *Faculty research:* Interpretation theory, theological methodology.

Concordia University, School of Theology, Irvine, CA 92612-3299. Offers MA. Part-time programs available. *Faculty:* 11 full-time, 5 part-time/adjunct. *Students:* 25 full-time (1 woman), 4 part-time (2 women); includes 2 minority (1 Asian American or Pacific Islander, 1 Hispanic American), 6 international. Average age 32. In 2007, 5 degrees awarded. *Degree requirements:* For master's, one foreign language, thesis. *Entrance requirements:* For master's, GRE, MAT.

Theology

Concordia University (continued)

Additional exam requirements/recommendations for international students: Required—TOEFL (minimum score 550 paper-based; 213 computer-based). *Application deadline:* For fall admission, 7/1 priority date for domestic students; for spring admission, 11/30 priority date for domestic students. Application fee: $100 ($300 for international students). *Financial support:* In 2007–08, 1 research assistantship with full tuition reimbursement was awarded; tuition waivers (partial) also available. *Unit head:* Rev. Dr. James V. Bachman, Dean, 949-854-8002 Ext. 1751, Fax: 949-854-6854, E-mail: james.bachman@cui.edu.

Concordia University, St. Paul, College of Vocation and Ministry, St. Paul, MN 55104-5494. Offers Christian education (Certificate); Christian outreach (MA). Part-time and evening/weekend programs available. Postbaccalaureate distance learning degree programs offered (minimal on-campus study). *Faculty:* 3 full-time (0 women), 5 part-time/adjunct (3 women). *Students:* 6 full-time (5 women), 13 part-time (9 women), 1 international. Average age 35. In 2007, 7 other advanced degrees awarded. *Entrance requirements:* Additional exam requirements/recommendations for international students: Required—TOEFL. *Application deadline:* Applications are processed on a rolling basis. Application fee: $50. Electronic applications accepted. *Financial support:* Federal Work-Study and scholarships/grants available. Financial award applicants required to submit FAFSA. *Application contact:* Kimberly Craig, Director of Graduate and Cohort Admission, 651-603-6223, Fax: 651-603-6320, E-mail: craig@csp.edu.

Covenant Theological Seminary, Graduate and Professional Programs, St. Louis, MO 63141-8697. Offers M Div, MA, MAC, MAEM, Th M, D Min, Certificate. *Accreditation:* ATS (one or more programs are accredited). Part-time and evening/weekend programs available. Postbaccalaureate distance learning degree programs offered (minimal on-campus study). *Faculty:* 23 full-time (0 women), 23 part-time/adjunct (8 women). *Students:* 361 full-time (74 women), 431 part-time (142 women); includes 99 minority (41 African Americans, 2 American Indian/Alaska Native, 50 Asian Americans or Pacific Islanders, 6 Hispanic Americans), 17 international. Average age 34. 230 applicants, 99% accepted, 189 enrolled. In 2007, 80 first professional degrees, 68 master's, 6 doctorates awarded. *Degree requirements:* For master's, 2 foreign languages, thesis (for some programs); for doctorate, 2 foreign languages, thesis/dissertation; for M Div and Certificate, 2 foreign languages. *Entrance requirements:* For doctorate and Certificate, M Div. Additional exam requirements/recommendations for international students: Required—TOEFL (minimum score 550 paper-based; 213 computer-based). *Application deadline:* Applications are processed on a rolling basis. Application fee: $50. Electronic applications accepted. *Expenses:* Tuition: Part-time $380 per credit hour. *Financial support:* In 2007–08, 588 students received support. Career-related internships or fieldwork, institutionally sponsored loans, scholarships/grants, and tuition waivers (full and partial) available. Support available to part-time students. Financial award application deadline: 4/15; financial award applicants required to submit FAFSA. *Unit head:* Dr. Sean Lucas, Chief Academic Officer, 314-434-4044. *Application contact:* Jeremy Kicklighter, Director of Admissions, 314-434-4044, Fax: 314-434-4819, E-mail: admissions@covenantseminary.edu.

Creighton University, Graduate School, College of Arts and Sciences, Department of Theology, Omaha, NE 68178-0001. Offers Christian spirituality (MA); ministry (MA); theology (MA). Part-time and evening/weekend programs available. *Faculty:* 13 full-time. *Students:* 1 full-time (0 women), 8 part-time (5 women), 1 international. 3 applicants, 67% accepted, 2 enrolled. In 2007, 45 degrees awarded. *Entrance requirements:* For master's, GRE General Test, 9 hours of theology coursework, 3 letters of recommendation. Additional exam requirements/recommendations for international students: Required—TOEFL (minimum score 550 paper-based; 213 computer-based; 80 iBT). *Application deadline:* For fall admission, 3/1 for domestic and international students. Applications are processed on a rolling basis. Application fee: $50. *Financial support:* Scholarships/grants and tuition waivers (partial) available. Support available to part-time students. Financial award applicants required to submit FAFSA. *Unit head:* Dr. Susan Calef, Director, 402-280-5807, E-mail: scalef@creighton.edu. *Application contact:* LuAnn M. Schwery, Assistant Dean, 402-280-2870, Fax: 402-280-5762, E-mail: schwery@creighton.edu.

The Criswell College, Graduate School of the Bible, Dallas, TX 75246-1537. Offers biblical studies (M Div, MA); Christian leadership (MA); ministry (MA); New Testament (MA); Old Testament (MA); theological studies (MA); theology (MA). Part-time programs available. *Degree requirements:* For master's, 2 foreign languages, thesis optional; for M Div, 2 foreign languages, thesis/dissertation optional. *Entrance requirements:* For M Div and master's, GRE General Test, minimum GPA of 2.5. Electronic applications accepted. *Faculty research:* Emphasis on biblical languages (Hebrew and Greek), expository preaching and evangelism in the local church.

Crown College, Graduate Studies, St. Bonifacius, MN 55375-9001. Offers Christian studies (MA); educational leadership (MA); intercultural leadership (MA); ministry leadership (MA); organizational leadership (MA). Part-time and evening/weekend programs available. *Faculty:* 7 full-time (1 woman), 17 part-time/adjunct (3 women). *Students:* 87 full-time (39 women), 36 part-time (16 women); includes 14 minority (9 African Americans, 3 Asian Americans or Pacific Islanders, 2 Hispanic Americans). Average age 38. 75 applicants, 77% accepted, 43 enrolled. In 2007, 13 degrees awarded. *Degree requirements:* For master's, thesis optional. *Entrance requirements:* For master's, 12 credits in foundational studies, minimum GPA of 2.5. Additional exam requirements/recommendations for international students: Required—TOEFL (minimum score 500 paper-based). *Application deadline:* For fall admission, 8/1 priority date for domestic students; for winter admission, 1/1 priority date for domestic students; for spring admission, 6/1 priority date for domestic students. Applications are processed on a rolling basis. Application fee: $20. *Financial support:* Scholarships/grants available. *Faculty research:* Religious functionalism, Latin American social criticism, Indonesian ethnomusicology, church growth strategies. *Unit head:* Don Bouchard, Director of Adult and Graduate Studies, 952-446-4224, Fax: 952-416-4349, E-mail: grad@crown.edu. *Application contact:* Nate Erickson, Enrollment Coordinator, 952-446-4370, Fax: 952-446-4349, E-mail: grad@crown.edu.

Dallas Theological Seminary, Graduate Programs, Dallas, TX 75204-6499. Offers academic ministries (Th M); Bible translation (Th M); biblical and theological studies (CGS); biblical counseling (MA, Th M); biblical exegesis and linguistics (MA); biblical exposition (PhD); biblical studies (MA); Christian education (MA, D Min); cross-cultural ministries (MA, Th M); educational leadership (Th M); evangelism and discipleship (Th M); interdisciplinary studies (Th M); media and communication (MA); media arts in ministry (Th M); ministry (D Min); New Testament studies (Th M, PhD); Old Testament studies (PhD); parachurch ministries (Th M); pastoral ministries (Th M); sacred theology (STM); theological studies (PhD); women's ministry (Th M). *Accreditation:* ATS (one or more programs are accredited). Part-time and evening/weekend programs available. *Degree requirements:* For master's, variable foreign language requirement, thesis (for some programs); for doctorate, 2 foreign languages, thesis/dissertation. *Entrance requirements:* Additional exam requirements/recommendations for international students: Required—TOEFL, TWE. *Application deadline:* For fall admission, 7/1 priority date for domestic students; for winter admission, 11/1 priority date for domestic students; for spring admission, 11/15 priority date for domestic students. Applications are processed on a rolling basis. Application fee: $30. Electronic applications accepted. *Financial support:* Career-related internships or fieldwork, institutionally sponsored loans, scholarships/grants, and tuition waivers (full and partial) available. Financial award application deadline: 2/28. *Unit head:* Dr. Mark L. Bailey, President, 214-841-3676, Fax: 214-841-3565. *Application contact:* Josh Bleeker, Director of Admissions, 214-841-3661, Fax: 214-841-3664, E-mail: admissions@dts.edu.

Darkei Noam Rabbinical College, Graduate Programs, Brooklyn, NY 11210.

Denver Seminary, Graduate and Professional Programs, Littleton, CO 80120. Offers apologetics (Certificate); biblical studies (MA); Christian formation and soul care (MA, Certificate); Christian studies (MA, Certificate); church and parachurch leadership (D Min); counseling licensure (MA); counseling ministry (MA); intercultural ministry (Certificate); leadership (MA, Certificate); marriage and family counseling (D Min); pastoral ministry (D Min); philosophy of religion (MA); spiritual guidance (Certificate); theology (M Div, Certificate); worship (Certificate); youth and family ministry (MA). *Accreditation:* ACA; ACIPE; ATS (one or more programs are accredited). Part-time and evening/weekend programs available. Postbaccalaureate distance learning degree programs offered. *Faculty:* 23 full-time (4 women), 94 part-time/adjunct (39 women). *Students:* 517 full-time (154 women), 283 part-time (130 women); includes 47 minority (15 African Americans, 1 American Indian/Alaska Native, 22 Asian Americans or Pacific Islanders, 9 Hispanic Americans), 43 international. Average age 34. 333 applicants, 76% accepted, 166 enrolled. In 2007, 41 first professional degrees, 77 master's, 8 doctorates, 9 other advanced degrees awarded. *Degree requirements:* For master's, 2 foreign languages, thesis (for some programs); for doctorate, 2 foreign languages, thesis/dissertation; for M Div, 2 foreign languages. *Entrance requirements:* For M Div, minimum undergraduate GPA of 2.5; for master's, minimum undergraduate GPA of 3.0; for doctorate, M Div, 3 years of ministry experience. Additional exam requirements/recommendations for international students: Required—TOEFL (minimum score 575 paper-based; 233 computer-based; 90 iBT). *Application deadline:* For fall admission, 7/15 priority date for domestic students; for spring admission, 12/15 priority date for domestic students. Applications are processed on a rolling basis. Application fee: $35. Electronic applications accepted. *Expenses:* Tuition: Part-time $495 per semester hour. One-time fee: $150 part-time. Part-time tuition and fees vary according to course load. *Financial support:* In 2007–08, 220 students received support. Career-related internships or fieldwork, Federal Work-Study, scholarships/grants, and unspecified assistantships available. Support available to part-time students. Financial award application deadline: 4/1; financial award applicants required to submit FAFSA. *Unit head:* Dr. Randy MacFarland, Vice President and Dean, 303-762-6980, Fax: 303-761-8020, E-mail: randy.macfarland@denverseminary.edu. *Application contact:* Nathan Lamb, Director of Admissions, 303-357-5801, Fax: 303-783-3122, E-mail: info@denverseminary.edu.

Dominican House of Studies, Pontifical Faculty of the Immaculate Conception, Graduate and Professional Programs in Theology, Washington, DC 20017-1585. Offers M Div, STB, MA, STL. *Accreditation:* ATS (one or more programs are accredited). Part-time programs available. *Faculty:* 10 full-time (1 woman), 9 part-time/adjunct (2 women). *Students:* 63 full-time (2 women), 22 part-time (7 women); includes 5 minority (2 Asian Americans or Pacific Islanders, 3 Hispanic Americans), 21 international. Average age 36. 25 applicants, 80% accepted, 11 enrolled. In 2007, 3 first professional degrees, 1 master's, 1 other advanced degree awarded. *Degree requirements:* For master's, one foreign language, thesis, thesis defense; for first professional degree, 2 foreign languages, comprehensive exam; for STL, 3 foreign languages, thesis, lecture. *Entrance requirements:* For first professional degree, 18 credits of philosophy (36 for STB); reading knowledge of Latin; BA with minimum GPA of 3.0 (3.25 for STB); for master's, 18 credits of philosophy; reading knowledge of Latin; BA with minimum GPA of 3.0. Additional exam requirements/recommendations for international students: Required—TOEFL (minimum score 550 paper-based; 215 computer-based; 79 iBT). *Application deadline:* For fall admission, 7/1 priority date for domestic and international students; for spring admission, 12/1 priority date for domestic and international students. Applications are processed on a rolling basis. Application fee: $50. *Expenses:* Tuition: Full-time $12,240; part-time $510 per credit hour. *Financial support:* In 2007–08, 1 student received support. Career-related internships or fieldwork and scholarships/grants available. Financial award application deadline: 4/1. *Faculty research:* Sacred scripture, moral theology, systematic theology. Total annual research expenditures: $21,550. *Unit head:* Fr. Gabriel O'Donnell, OP, Academic Dean, 202-529-5300, Fax: 202-636-1700, E-mail: dean@dhs.edu. *Application contact:* Tobias John Nathe, Registrar, 202-529-5300 Ext. 122, Fax: 202-636-1700, E-mail: registrar@dhs.edu.

Dominican School of Philosophy and Theology, Graduate Programs, Department of Theology, Berkeley, CA 94708. Offers M Div, Certificate, M Div/MA, MA/MA. *Accreditation:* ATS (one or more programs are accredited). Part-time programs available. *Students:* 49 full-time (9 women), 25 part-time (11 women); includes 39 minority (1 African American, 1 American Indian/Alaska Native, 26 Asian Americans or Pacific Islanders, 11 Hispanic Americans). Average age 35. 33 applicants, 91% accepted, 23 enrolled. In 2007, 1 first professional degree awarded. *Entrance requirements:* Minimum GPA of 2.5. Additional exam requirements/recommendations for international students: Required—TOEFL (minimum score 550 paper-based; 68 computer-based). *Application deadline:* For fall admission, 3/15 priority date for domestic and international students; for spring admission, 10/15 priority date for domestic and international students. Applications are processed on a rolling basis. Application fee: $40. *Expenses:* Tuition: Full-time $11,880; part-time $495 per unit. Required fees: $100. *Financial support:* In 2007–08, 15 students received support. Institutionally sponsored loans, scholarships/grants, health care benefits, and tuition waivers (partial) available. Financial award application deadline: 4/1; financial award applicants required to submit FAFSA. *Faculty research:* Literary and historical study of scripture, Christianity in late antiquity, homiletic theory, religion and art, Christology. *Unit head:* Dr. Edward Krasevac, Chair, 510-883-2082, Fax: 510-849-1372, E-mail: ekrasevac@dspt.edu. *Application contact:* John D. Knutsen, Director of Admissions, 510-883-2073, Fax: 510-849-1372, E-mail: admissions@dspt.edu.

Drew University, Caspersen School of Graduate Studies, Program in Theological and Religious Studies, Madison, NJ 07940-1493. Offers historical studies (MA, PhD); Methodist studies (PhD); philosophy of religion (MA, PhD); systematic theology (MA, PhD); theological ethics (MA, PhD). *Accreditation:* ATS. Part-time programs available. Terminal master's awarded for partial completion of doctoral program. *Degree requirements:* For master's, one foreign language, thesis; for doctorate, 2 foreign languages, comprehensive exam, thesis/dissertation. *Entrance requirements:* For master's and doctorate, GRE General Test. *Faculty research:* History and theology of religion, postmodern theologies, patristics.

Drew University, Caspersen School of Graduate Studies, Program in Wesleyan and Methodist Studies, Madison, NJ 07940-1493. Offers MA, PhD. *Entrance requirements:* For master's and doctorate, GRE General Test. Additional exam requirements/recommendations for international students: Required—TOEFL, TWE.

Drew University, The Theological School, Madison, NJ 07940-1493. Offers M Div, MTS, STM, D Min, Certificate. *Accreditation:* ACIPE; ATS. Part-time programs available. Postbaccalaureate distance learning degree programs offered (minimal on-campus study). *Faculty:* 25 full-time (11 women), 24 part-time/adjunct (12 women). *Students:* 200 full-time (114 women), 165 part-time (81 women); includes 111 minority (85 African Americans, 1 American Indian/Alaska Native, 15 Asian Americans or Pacific Islanders, 10 Hispanic Americans), 73 international. Average age 35. 242 applicants, 40% accepted, 70 enrolled. In 2007, 68 master's, 22 doctorates awarded. *Degree requirements:* For doctorate, thesis/dissertation. *Entrance requirements:* For M Div, 3 years professional ministry experience; for master's, minimum GPA of 3.0. Additional exam requirements/recommendations for international students: Required—TOEFL (minimum score 516 paper-based; 230 computer-based; 88 iBT), TWE. *Application deadline:* For fall admission, 3/1 priority date for domestic and international students; for spring admission, 12/1 priority date for domestic students, 10/1 priority date for international students. Applications are processed on a rolling basis. Application fee: $35. Electronic applications accepted. *Expenses:* Contact institution. *Financial support:* Fellowships, career-related internships or fieldwork, Federal Work-Study, institutionally sponsored loans, and scholarships/grants available. Support available to part-time students. Financial award application deadline: 4/15. *Faculty research:* Biblical studies, constructive theology, ecology and religion, gender and religion, race/ethnicity and religion. *Unit head:* Dr. Maxine Beach, Dean, 973-408-3258, Fax: 973-408-3534, E-mail: mbeach@drew.edu. *Application contact:* Rev. Kevin D. Miller, Director of Admissions, 973-408-3111, Fax: 973-408-3242, E-mail: kmiller@drew.edu.

Duke University, Divinity School, Durham, NC 27708-0586. Offers M Div, MTS, Th M, Th D, JD/MTS, M Div/MSW. *Accreditation:* ACIPE; ATS. Part-time programs available. *Faculty:* 40 full-time (11 women), 19 part-time/adjunct (6 women). *Students:* 491 full-time (223 women), 36 part-time (20 women); includes 115 minority (78 African Americans, 4 American Indian/Alaska Native, 24 Asian Americans or Pacific Islanders, 9 Hispanic Americans). Average age 30. 619 applicants, 50% accepted, 197 enrolled. In 2007, 124 first professional degrees, 37 master's awarded. *Degree requirements:* For master's, thesis optional; for doctorate, 2 foreign languages, thesis/dissertation; for M Div, field experience, spiritual formation, faculty evaluation. *Entrance requirements:* For M Div and master's, 5 letters of reference, 2 essays; for doctorate, GRE, 4 letters of reference, 2-page statement of purpose, one sample of academic writing. Additional exam requirements/recommendations for international students: Required—TOEFL (minimum score 580 paper-based; 237 computer-based; 93 iBT). *Application deadline:* For fall admission, 4/1 for domestic students, 3/1 for international students. Application fee: $50. Electronic applications accepted. *Expenses: Contact institution. Financial support:* In 2007–08, 472 students received support. Career-related internships or fieldwork, Federal Work-Study, institutionally sponsored loans, scholarships/grants, and field education stipends available. Financial award application deadline: 5/2; financial award applicants required to submit FAFSA. *Faculty research:* Biblical studies, historical church studies, theological studies, church ministry studies. Total annual research expenditures: $3.4 million. *Unit head:* Dr. L. Gregory Jones, Dean, 919-660-3434, Fax: 919-660-3474, E-mail: gjones@div.duke.edu. *Application contact:* Rev. Cheryl Brown, Director of Admissions, 919-660-3436, Fax: 919-660-3535, E-mail: admissions@div.duke.edu.

Duquesne University, Graduate School of Liberal Arts, Department of Theology, Pittsburgh, PA 15282-0001. Offers pastoral ministry (MA); religious education (MA); systematic theology (PhD); theology (MA). Part-time and evening/weekend programs available. *Faculty:* 13 full-time (4 women). *Students:* 56 full-time (34 women), 76 part-time (54 women). Average age 35. In 2007, 22 master's, 9 doctorates awarded. *Degree requirements:* For master's, comprehensive exam; for doctorate, 2 foreign languages, comprehensive exam, thesis/dissertation. *Entrance requirements:* For master's and doctorate, GRE General Test. Additional exam requirements/recommendations for international students: Required—TOEFL. *Application deadline:* For fall admission, 2/1 for domestic and international students. Application fee: $50. *Expenses:* Tuition: Part-time $774 per credit. Required fees: $74 per credit. Tuition and fees vary according to program. *Financial support:* In 2007–08, 8 teaching assistantships with full tuition reimbursements (averaging $9,900 per year) were awarded; career-related internships or fieldwork, scholarships/grants, tuition waivers (partial), and unspecified assistantships also available. Support available to part-time students. Financial award application deadline: 5/1. *Unit head:* Dr. George Worgul, Chair, 412-396-6530. *Application contact:* Dr. Marie Baird, Director, 412-396-6000.

Earlham School of Religion, Graduate Programs, Richmond, IN 47374-5360. Offers religion (MA); theology (M Div, M Min). *Accreditation:* ACIPE; ATS. Part-time programs available. Postbaccalaureate distance learning degree programs offered (minimal on-campus study). *Faculty:* 8 full-time (3 women), 6 part-time/adjunct (4 women). *Students:* 108 full-time (63 women); includes 6 minority (3 African Americans, 1 American Indian/Alaska Native, 1 Asian American or Pacific Islander, 1 Hispanic American), 6 international. Average age 43. 37 applicants, 97% accepted, 34 enrolled. In 2007, 10 first professional degrees, 1 master's awarded. *Degree requirements:* For master's, one foreign language, comprehensive exam, thesis; for M Div, project. *Entrance requirements:* For M Div and master's, 3 references. Additional exam requirements/recommendations for international students: Required—TOEFL (minimum score 550 paper-based; 218 computer-based; 82 iBT). *Application deadline:* For fall admission, 7/31 priority date for domestic students; for winter admission, 12/12 priority date for domestic students. Applications are processed on a rolling basis. Application fee: $35. Electronic applications accepted. *Expenses:* Tuition: Full-time $8,802; part-time $326 per credit. Required fees: $466; $150 per term. *Financial support:* Scholarships/grants and tuition waivers (full and partial) available. Financial award application deadline: 4/15; financial award applicants required to submit FAFSA. *Faculty research:* Digitizing Quaker texts, vital Quaker ministry. *Unit head:* Jay W. Marshall, Dean, 800-432-1377, Fax: 765-983-1688, E-mail: marshja@earlham.edu. *Application contact:* Susan G. Axtell, Director of Admissions, 800-432-1377, Fax: 765-983-1688, E-mail: axtelsu@earlham.edu.

Eastern Mennonite University, Eastern Mennonite Seminary, Harrisonburg, VA 22802-2462. Offers church leadership (MA); divinity (M Div); ministry studies (Certificate); online theological studies (Certificate); religion (MA); theological studies (Certificate). *Accreditation:* ATS.Part-time programs available. *Faculty:* 9 full-time (2 women), 16 part-time/adjunct (5 women). *Students:* 42 full-time (15 women), 29 part-time (13 women); includes 2 minority (both African Americans), 6 international. Average age 40. 43 applicants, 100% accepted. In 2007, 19 first professional degrees, 4 master's awarded. *Degree requirements:* For master's, thesis (for some programs); for M Div, thesis/dissertation (for some programs), supervised field education. *Entrance requirements:* For M Div and master's, minimum GPA of 2.5. Additional exam requirements/recommendations for international students: Required—TOEFL (minimum score 550 paper-based; 213 computer-based). *Application deadline:* For fall admission, 6/15 priority date for domestic and international students; for winter admission, 11/15 priority date for domestic and international students; for spring admission, 3/15 priority date for domestic and international students. Applications are processed on a rolling basis. Application fee: $25. *Expenses: Contact institution.* Tuition and fees vary according to program. *Financial support:* In 2007–08, 43 students received support. Application deadline: 6/30; *Faculty research:* Spiritual direction and "culture of call"; leadership coaching: an approach to leadership in a culture of call; clarity of call in the probationary process for United Methodist clergy in Virginia; EMS women's experiences of culture of call efforts; practices of excellent and fruitful Mennonite pastoral ministry. Total annual research expenditures: $45,000. *Unit head:* Dr. Ervin R. Stutzman, Seminary Dean, 540-432-4261, Fax: 540-432-4444, E-mail: stutzerv@emu.edu. *Application contact:* Don A. Yoder, Director of Seminary and Graduate Admissions, 540-432-4257, Fax: 540-432-4598, E-mail: yoderda@emu.edu.

Eastern University, Palmer Theological Seminary, Wynnewood, PA 19096-3430. Offers M Div, MTS, D Min, M Div/MBA, M Div/MS. *Accreditation:* ACIPE; ATS; MSA/CIHE. Part-time and evening/weekend programs available. *Entrance requirements:* Additional exam requirements/recommendations for international students: Required—TOEFL.

Ecumenical Theological Seminary, Professional Program, Detroit, MI 48201. Offers M Div. *Accreditation:* ACIPE; ATS.

Eden Theological Seminary, Graduate and Professional Programs, St. Louis, MO 63119-3192. Offers M Div, MAPS, MTS, D Min. *Accreditation:* ACIPE; ATS. *Degree requirements:* For master's, comprehensive exam (for some programs), thesis (for some programs), 2 oral exams; for doctorate, professional essay, supervised in-service projects; for M Div, thesis/dissertation optional, 2 oral exams. *Entrance requirements:* For M Div and master's, interview, minimum GPA of 2.7; for doctorate, interview, minimum GPA of 3.0. Additional exam requirements/recommendations for international students: Required—TOEFL (minimum score 550 paper-based). Electronic applications accepted. *Faculty research:* Psalms, pastoral ethics, historical Jesus, leadership roles, congregational life.

Emmanuel School of Religion, Graduate and Professional Programs, Johnson City, TN 37601-9438. Offers M Div, MAR, D Min. *Accreditation:* ACIPE; ATS. Part-time programs available. *Faculty:* 12 full-time (1 woman), 3 part-time/adjunct (0 women). *Students:* 99 full-time (33 women), 20 part-time (5 women); includes 3 minority (all African Americans), 11 international. Average age 32. 50 applicants, 94% accepted. In 2007, 18 first professional degrees, 7 master's, 2 doctorates awarded. *Degree requirements:* For master's, 2 foreign languages, thesis; for M Div, 2 foreign languages, thesis/dissertation or alternative. *Entrance requirements:* For doctorate, GRE General Test, Minnesota Multiphasic Personality Inventory. *Application deadline:* For fall admission, 8/1 priority date for domestic students. Applications are processed on a rolling basis. Application fee: $25. *Expenses:* Tuition: Full-time $7,800; part-time $325 per hour. Required fees: $400; $75 per term. *Financial support:* In 2007–08, 100 students received support, including teaching assistantships (averaging $3,600 per year); career-related internships or fieldwork, Federal Work-Study, institutionally sponsored loans, scholarships/grants, and tuition waivers (partial) also available. Support available to part-time students. Financial award application deadline: 4/1. *Unit head:* Dr. Robert F. Hull, Dean and Professor of New Testament, 423-461-1524, Fax: 423-926-6198, E-mail: hullr@esr.edu. *Application contact:* David Fulks, Director of Admissions, 423-461-1536, Fax: 423-926-6198, E-mail: fulksd@esr.edu.

Emory University, Candler School of Theology, Atlanta, GA 30322-1100. Offers M Div, MTS, Th M, Th D, JD/M Div, JD/MTS, M Div/MBA. *Accreditation:* ACIPE; ATS. Part-time programs available. *Degree requirements:* For master's, thesis optional; for doctorate, thesis/dissertation; for M Div, thesis/dissertation optional. *Entrance requirements:* For M Div, minimum undergraduate GPA of 2.75; for master's, minimum undergraduate GPA of 3.0; for doctorate, M Div and 8 units of course work in clinical pastoral education. Additional exam requirements/recommendations for international students: Required—TOEFL (minimum score 213 computer-based). Expenses: Contact institution. *Faculty research:* Biblical studies, church history, ministry practice, pastoral care and ethics.

Episcopal Divinity School, Graduate and Professional Programs, Cambridge, MA 02138-3494. Offers M Div, MATS, D Min, CTS. *Accreditation:* ACIPE; ATS (one or more programs are accredited). Part-time programs available. *Degree requirements:* For master's, thesis optional; for doctorate, thesis/dissertation, project; for M Div, thesis/dissertation optional, fieldwork. *Entrance requirements:* For M Div and master's, GRE General Test or MAT, 2 interviews; for doctorate, 2 interviews, M Div or equivalent; for CTS, GRE General Test, MAT, or advanced degree; 2 interviews. Additional exam requirements/recommendations for international students: Required—TOEFL. *Faculty research:* Anglican, global, and ecumenical studies; congregational studies; feminist liberation theologies.

Episcopal Theological Seminary of the Southwest, Graduate and Professional Programs, Austin, TX 78768-2247. Offers Anglican studies (Advanced Diploma); chaplaincy (MAPM); counseling (MAC); discipleship (MAPM); divinity (M Div); religion (MAR); spiritual formation (MAPM); theological studies (Advanced Diploma). *Accreditation:* ACIPE; ATS (one or more programs are accredited). Part-time and evening/weekend programs available. *Faculty:* 9 full-time (2 women), 20 part-time/adjunct (6 women). *Students:* 60 full-time (39 women), 37 part-time (27 women); includes 7 minority (4 African Americans, 1 Asian American or Pacific Islander, 2 Hispanic Americans), 1 international. Average age 46. 41 applicants, 98% accepted, 35 enrolled. In 2007, 24 first professional degrees, 9 master's, 2 other advanced degrees awarded. *Degree requirements:* For master's, thesis (for some programs). *Entrance requirements:* For M Div and master's, GRE, MAT, interview; for Advanced Diploma, interview. *Application deadline:* For fall admission, 7/1 for domestic students; for spring admission, 11/1 for domestic students. Applications are processed on a rolling basis. Application fee: $50. *Expenses:* Tuition: Full-time $13,150; part-time $390 per hour. Required fees: $75. One-time fee: $20 part-time. *Financial support:* Career-related internships or fieldwork and scholarships/grants available. Support available to part-time students. Financial award application deadline: 6/17. *Unit head:* Very Rev. Douglas Travis, Dean and President, 512-472-4133 Ext. 307, Fax: 512-472-3098, E-mail: dtravis@etss.edu. *Application contact:* Rev. Ken Malcolm, Director of Admissions, 512-472-4133 Ext. 375, Fax: 512-472-3098, E-mail: kmalcolm@etss.edu.

Erskine Theological Seminary, Graduate and Professional Programs, Due West, SC 29639-0668. Offers M Div, MACE, MACM, MAPM, MATS, MCM, D Min. *Accreditation:* ATS. Part-time and evening/weekend programs available. *Degree requirements:* For doctorate, thesis/dissertation; for M Div, 2 foreign languages. *Entrance requirements:* For master's, Myers Briggs Type Indicator, Taylor Johnson Temperament Analysis, Ministry Specialties Test (MACM), minimum GPA of 3.0, interview with committee (MACM); for doctorate, minimum GPA of 3.0 during M Div. Additional exam requirements/recommendations for international students: Required—TOEFL (minimum score 550 paper-based). Electronic applications accepted. *Faculty research:* Church administration, biblical studies.

Evangelical Seminary of Puerto Rico, Graduate and Professional Programs, San Juan, PR 00925-2207. Offers M Div, MAR, D Min. *Accreditation:* ATS. Part-time programs available. *Degree requirements:* For master's, comprehensive exam; for M Div, integration essay. *Entrance requirements:* For M Div, Admission Test for Graduate Studies, denominational endorsement; for master's, Admission Test for Graduate Studies; for doctorate, 3 years experience in ministry service. Additional exam requirements/recommendations for international students: Required—TOEFL, EXADEP. *Faculty research:* Protestantism in Puerto Rico.

Evangelical Theological Seminary, Graduate and Professional Programs, Myerstown, PA 17067-1212. Offers divinity (M Div); marriage and family therapy (MA); ministry (Certificate); religion (MA). *Accreditation:* ATS (one or more programs are accredited). Part-time programs available. Postbaccalaureate distance learning degree programs offered (minimal on-campus study). *Faculty:* 7 full-time (2 women), 21 part-time/adjunct (3 women). *Students:* 22 full-time (0 women), 152 part-time (66 women). Average age 33. 60 applicants, 77% accepted, 46 enrolled. In 2007, 11 first professional degrees, 22 master's awarded. *Degree requirements:* For master's, 2 foreign languages; for M Div, 2 foreign languages, ministry internship. *Entrance requirements:* For M Div and master's, minimum GPA of 2.5. Additional exam requirements/recommendations for international students: Required—TOEFL (minimum score 550 paper-based; 213 computer-based). *Application deadline:* For fall admission, 6/1 priority date for domestic students, 4/1 priority date for international students; for spring admission, 11/1 priority date for domestic students, 9/1 priority date for international students. Applications are processed on a rolling basis. Application fee: $35. *Expenses:* Tuition: Full-time $10,440; part-time $435 per credit. Required fees: $25 per semester. One-time fee: $125. *Financial support:* Career-related internships or fieldwork, scholarships/grants, and tuition waivers (full) available. Support available to part-time students. Financial award application deadline: 6/1; financial award applicants required to submit FAFSA. *Faculty research:* Literary form and structure within the Hebrew and Greek scriptures, Wesley studies, esoteric biblical languages, the Mosaic law and the Christian, ethics. *Unit head:* Rev. Dr. John V. Tornfelt, Vice President, Academic Affairs, 717-866-5775 Ext. 140, Fax: 717-866-4667, E-mail: jtornfelt@evangelical.edu. *Application contact:* Tom M. Maiello, Dean of Admissions, 800-532-5775 Ext. 109, Fax: 717-866-4667, E-mail: admissions@evangelical.edu.

Faith Baptist Bible College and Theological Seminary, Graduate Program, Ankeny, IA 50021. Offers biblical studies (MA); pastoral studies (M Div); pastoral training (MA); religion (MA); theological studies (MA). Part-time programs available. *Faculty:* 4 full-time (0 women), 7 part-time/adjunct (0 women). *Students:* 28 full-time (3 women), 28 part-time (2 women); includes 1 minority (Hispanic American), 1 international. Average age 29. In 2007, 9 first professional degrees, 12 master's awarded. *Degree requirements:* For master's, thesis or alternative; for M Div, 2 foreign languages. *Entrance requirements:* Additional exam requirements/recommendations for international students: Required—TOEFL (minimum score 550 paper-based; 197 computer-based). *Application deadline:* For fall admission, 8/1 priority date for domestic students, 8/1 for international students; for spring admission, 12/15 for domestic and international students. Applications are processed on a rolling basis. Application fee: $25. *Expenses:* Tuition: Full-time $10,228; part-time $392 per credit hour. Required fees: $95 per semester. One-time fee: $50. Tuition and fees vary according to class time and course load. *Financial support:* In 2007–08, 70 students received support. Career-related internships or fieldwork and scholarships/grants available. Support available to part-time students. Financial award application deadline: 3/1; financial award applicants required to submit FAFSA. *Faculty research:* Baptist theology, American church history. *Unit head:* Dr. Ernest Schmidt, Dean of Seminary, 515-964-0601, Fax: 514-964-1638, E-mail: schmidte@faith.edu. *Application contact:* Pat Odle, Vice President of Enrollment, 888-FAITH4U, Fax: 515-964-1638, E-mail: odlep@faith.edu.

Faith Evangelical Lutheran Seminary, Graduate and Professional Programs, Tacoma, WA 98407. Offers B Th, M Div, MCM, MTS, D Min. Part-time and evening/weekend programs available. Postbaccalaureate distance learning degree programs offered (minimal on-campus study). *Degree requirements:* For master's, thesis optional; for doctorate, thesis/dissertation; for first professional degree, thesis/dissertation (for some programs). *Entrance requirements:* For first professional degree and master's, minimum undergraduate GPA of 2.7; for doctorate, minimum graduate GPA of 3.0. Additional exam requirements/recommendations for international students: Required—TOEFL (minimum score 550 paper-based; 213 computer-based).

Fordham University, Graduate School of Arts and Sciences, Department of Theology, New York, NY 10458. Offers MA, PhD. Part-time and evening/weekend programs available. *Faculty:*

Theology

Fordham University (continued)
22 full-time (7 women). *Students:* 17 full-time (8 women), 44 part-time (17 women); includes 3 minority (2 African Americans, 1 Asian American or Pacific Islander), 3 international. Average age 36. 66 applicants, 41% accepted, 7 enrolled. In 2007, 9 master's, 4 doctorates awarded. Terminal master's awarded for partial completion of doctoral program. *Median time to degree:* Of those who began their doctoral program in fall 1999, 30% received their degree in 8 years or less. *Degree requirements:* For master's, one foreign language, comprehensive exam; for doctorate, 2 foreign languages, comprehensive exam, thesis/dissertation. *Entrance requirements:* For master's and doctorate, GRE General Test. Additional exam requirements/recommendations for international students: Required—TOEFL (minimum score 650 paper-based; 280 computer-based). *Application deadline:* For fall admission, 1/4 priority date for domestic students; for spring admission, 11/1 for domestic students. Application fee: $70. Electronic applications accepted. *Expenses:* Tuition: Full-time $23,880; part-time $995 per credit. *Financial support:* In 2007–08, 29 students received support, including 5 fellowships with tuition reimbursements available (averaging $16,310 per year), 15 research assistantships with tuition reimbursements available (averaging $17,145 per year), 9 teaching assistantships with tuition reimbursements available (averaging $13,111 per year); institutionally sponsored loans, tuition waivers (full and partial), and unspecified assistantships also available. Support available to part-time students. Financial award application deadline: 1/4. *Faculty research:* History of Christian tradition, contemporary systematic theology, theological/feminist ethics, American Catholicism, biblical exegesis and theology. Total annual research expenditures: $10,000. *Unit head:* Dr. Terrence Tilley, Chair, 718-817-3245, E-mail: ttilley@fordham.edu. *Application contact:* Charlene Dundie, Director of Graduate Admissions, 718-817-4420, Fax: 718-817-3566, E-mail: dundie@fordham.edu.

Franciscan School of Theology, Graduate and Professional Programs, Berkeley, CA 94709-1294. Offers M Div, MA, MAMC, MTS. *Accreditation:* ATS (one or more programs are accredited). Part-time programs available. *Faculty:* 8 full-time (4 women), 8 part-time/adjunct (0 women). *Students:* 50 full-time (22 women), 30 part-time (16 women); includes 16 minority (8 Asian Americans or Pacific Islanders, 8 Hispanic Americans), 19 international. Average age 43. In 2007, 3 first professional degrees, 14 master's awarded. *Degree requirements:* For master's, one foreign language, thesis. *Entrance requirements:* For master's, GRE General Test (MA). Additional exam requirements/recommendations for international students: Required—TOEFL (minimum score 550 paper-based; 213 computer-based). *Application deadline:* For fall admission, 4/1 priority date for domestic and international students; for spring admission, 10/1 priority date for domestic and international students. Applications are processed on a rolling basis. Application fee: $40. *Expenses:* Tuition: Part-time $625 per unit. Required fees: $60 per semester. *Financial support:* In 2007–08, 40 students received support. Career-related internships or fieldwork, scholarships/grants, and tuition waivers (full and partial) available. Financial award application deadline: 5/1; financial award applicants required to submit FAFSA. *Faculty research:* Church history, multicultural ministries, ethics and morality, catechesis, biblical studies. *Unit head:* Dr. Mario DiCicco, President, 510-848-5232, Fax: 510-549-9466, E-mail: mdicicco@fst.edu. *Application contact:* Pat Morgan, Admissions Coordinator, 510-848-5232 Ext. 15, Fax: 510-549-9466, E-mail: pmorgan@fst.edu.

Franciscan University of Steubenville, Graduate Programs, Department of Theology, Steubenville, OH 43952-1763. Offers theology and Christian ministry (MA). Part-time programs available. Postbaccalaureate distance learning degree programs offered (minimal on-campus study). *Degree requirements:* For master's, comprehensive exam. *Entrance requirements:* For master's, minimum undergraduate GPA of 3.0.

Freed-Hardeman University, School of Biblical Studies, Program in Divinity, Henderson, TN 38340-2399. Offers M Div. *Students:* 18; includes 1 African American. Application fee: $32. *Expenses:* Tuition: Full-time $6,012; part-time $334 per credit hour. Required fees: $10 per hour. *Unit head:* Dr. Earl Edwards, Director of Graduate Studies, School of Biblical Studies, 731-989-6626, E-mail: eedwards@fhu.edu.

Freed-Hardeman University, School of Biblical Studies, Program in New Testament, Henderson, TN 38340-2399. Offers MA. Part-time programs available. *Faculty:* 5 full-time (0 women), 1 part-time/adjunct (0 women). *Students:* 31. Average age 29. In 2007, 8 degrees awarded. *Degree requirements:* For master's, one foreign language, comprehensive exam, thesis. *Entrance requirements:* For master's, GRE General Test or MAT. Additional exam requirements/recommendations for international students: Required—TOEFL (minimum score 500 paper-based; 173 computer-based). *Application deadline:* For fall admission, 8/1 priority date for domestic students; for spring admission, 12/1 for domestic students. Applications are processed on a rolling basis. Application fee: $32. *Expenses:* Tuition: Full-time $6,012; part-time $334 per credit hour. Required fees: $10 per hour. *Financial support:* Career-related internships or fieldwork, Federal Work-Study, tuition waivers (partial), and unspecified assistantships available. Support available to part-time students. Financial award application deadline: 8/1; financial award applicants required to submit FAFSA. *Unit head:* Dr. Earl Edwards, Director of Graduate Studies, School of Biblical Studies, 731-989-6626, Fax: 731-989-6059, E-mail: eedwards@fhu.edu.

Friends University, Graduate School, Division of Science, Arts, and Education, Program in Christian Ministry, Wichita, KS 67213. Offers MACM. Evening/weekend programs available. *Faculty:* 1 full-time (0 women), 4 part-time/adjunct (1 woman). *Students:* 28 full-time. In 2007, 13 degrees awarded. *Entrance requirements:* Additional exam requirements/recommendations for international students: Required—TOEFL (minimum score 560 paper-based; 220 computer-based). *Application deadline:* For fall admission, 8/15 priority date for domestic students, 7/15 priority date for international students; for spring admission, 12/15 priority date for domestic students, 11/15 priority date for international students. Applications are processed on a rolling basis. Application fee: $45 ($65 for international students). Electronic applications accepted. *Unit head:* Dr. Christian Kettler, Director, 800-794-6945 Ext. 5876, E-mail: kettler@friends.edu. *Application contact:* Craig Davis, Director of Graduate Admissions, 800-794-6945 Ext. 5573, Fax: 316-295-5050, E-mail: cdavis@friends.edu.

Fuller Theological Seminary, Graduate School of Theology, Pasadena, CA 91182. Offers M Div, MACL, MAT, Th M, D Min, PhD, MACL/PhD, MACL/Psy D. M Div offered jointly with Denver Conservative Baptist Seminary. *Accreditation:* ACIPE; ATS (one or more programs are accredited). Part-time and evening/weekend programs available. *Degree requirements:* For doctorate, variable foreign language requirement, thesis/dissertation; for M Div, 2 foreign languages. *Entrance requirements:* For doctorate, GRE General Test. *Faculty research:* New Testament, Old Testament, systematic theology, history, practical theology.

Gardner-Webb University, M. Christopher White School of Divinity, Boiling Springs, NC 28017. Offers Christian education (M Div); ministry (D Min); missiology (M Div); pastoral care and counseling (M Div); pastoral ministry (M Div); M Div/MA. *Accreditation:* ACIPE; ATS. Part-time programs available. *Degree requirements:* For M Div, 2 foreign languages. *Entrance requirements:* For M Div, minimum GPA of 2.0; for doctorate, minimum GPA of 2.75. Expenses: Contact institution. *Faculty research:* Jewish Christian dialogue, Islam.

Garrett-Evangelical Theological Seminary, Graduate and Professional Programs, Evanston, IL 60201-3298. Offers Bible and culture (PhD); Christian education (MA); Christian education and congregational studies (PhD); contemporary theology and culture (PhD); divinity (M Div); ethics, church, and society (MA); liturgical studies (PhD); ministry (D Min); music ministry (MA); pastoral care and counseling (MA); pastoral theology, personality, and culture (PhD); spiritual formation and evangelism (MA); theological studies (MTS); M Div/MSW. *Accreditation:* ACIPE; ATS (one or more programs are accredited). Part-time programs available. *Degree requirements:* For master's, thesis (for some programs); for doctorate, thesis/dissertation. *Entrance requirements:* For doctorate, GRE (PhD). Additional exam requirements/recommendations for international students: Required—TOEFL (minimum score 560 paper-based; 230 computer-based). Electronic applications accepted.

General Theological Seminary, Graduate and Professional Programs, New York, NY 10011-4977. Offers Anglican studies (STM, Th D); divinity (M Div); spiritual direction (MASD, STM); theology (MA); STM/Th D. *Accreditation:* ACIPE; ATS. Part-time and evening/weekend programs available. Terminal master's awarded for partial completion of doctoral program. *Degree requirements:* For master's, thesis; for doctorate, 2 foreign languages, thesis/dissertation. *Entrance requirements:* For M Div, GRE General Test, bishop's endorsement; for master's, GRE General Test; for doctorate, GRE, M Div or MA. Additional exam requirements/recommendations for international students: Required—TOEFL. *Faculty research:* Liturgy, New Testament, ethics, history, ecumenical relations.

George Fox University, George Fox Evangelical Seminary, Newberg, OR 97132-2697. Offers divinity (M Div); ministry (D Min), including leadership and spiritual formation, leadership in the emerging culture; ministry leadership (MA); spiritual formation (MA); spiritual formation and discipleship (Certificate); theological studies (MA). *Accreditation:* ACIPE; ATS. Part-time programs available. Postbaccalaureate distance learning degree programs offered (minimal on-campus study). *Faculty:* 7 full-time (2 women), 13 part-time/adjunct (4 women). *Students:* 105 full-time (27 women), 215 part-time (76 women); includes 27 minority (5 African Americans, 2 American Indian/Alaska Native, 12 Asian Americans or Pacific Islanders, 8 Hispanic Americans), 5 international. Average age 42. 135 applicants, 85% accepted, 109 enrolled. In 2007, 11 first professional degrees, 18 master's, 20 doctorates, 1 other advanced degree awarded. *Degree requirements:* For master's, variable foreign language requirement, thesis optional, internship. *Entrance requirements:* Additional exam requirements/recommendations for international students: Required—TOEFL (minimum score 550 paper-based; 213 computer-based). *Application deadline:* For fall admission, 7/1 for domestic and international students; for spring admission, 11/1 for domestic and international students. Applications are processed on a rolling basis. Application fee: $40. Electronic applications accepted. *Expenses:* Contact institution. *Financial support:* In 2007–08, 33 students received support. Career-related internships or fieldwork and scholarships/grants available. Financial award application deadline: 5/1; financial award applicants required to submit FAFSA. *Unit head:* Dr. Chuck Conniry, Vice President and Dean, 503-554-6163, E-mail: cconniry@georgefox.edu. *Application contact:* Sheila Bartlett, Admissions Counselor, 800-631-0921, Fax: 503-554-6111, E-mail: sbartlett@georgefox.edu.

Georgian Court University, School of Arts and Humanities, Lakewood, NJ 08701-2697. Offers Catholic school leadership (Certificate); parish business management (Certificate); pastoral administration (Certificate); pastoral ministry (Certificate); religious education (Certificate); theology (MA, Certificate). Part-time and evening/weekend programs available. *Faculty:* 3 full-time (2 women). *Students:* Average age 51. 10 applicants, 60% accepted, 2 enrolled. In 2007, 9 master's, 1 other advanced degree awarded. *Degree requirements:* For master's, thesis (for some programs). *Entrance requirements:* For master's, 3 letters of recommendation. Additional exam requirements/recommendations for international students: Required—TOEFL (minimum score 550 paper-based; 213 computer-based). *Application deadline:* For fall admission, 8/1 priority date for domestic students, 4/1 for international students; for spring admission, 1/1 priority date for domestic students, 7/1 for international students. Applications are processed on a rolling basis. Application fee: $40. Electronic applications accepted. *Expenses:* Tuition: Full-time $15,456; part-time $644 per credit. Required fees: $760; $200 per term. Tuition and fees vary according to campus/location. *Financial support:* Scholarships/grants, health care benefits, and unspecified assistantships available. Financial award application deadline: 4/15; financial award applicants required to submit FAFSA. *Unit head:* Dr. Linda James, Dean, 732-987-2617, Fax: 732-987-2007. *Application contact:* Eugene Soltys, Director of Graduate Admissions, 732-987-2770, Fax: 732-987-2084, E-mail: graduateadmissions@georgian.edu.

Global University, Graduate School of Theology, Springfield, MO 65804. Offers biblical studies (MA); divinity (M Div); ministerial studies (MA), including education, leadership, missions, New Testament, Old Testament. Part-time and evening/weekend programs available. Postbaccalaureate distance learning degree programs offered (no on-campus study). *Faculty:* 10 full-time (1 woman), 83 part-time/adjunct (10 women). *Students:* 255 full-time (42 women), 297 part-time (55 women). Average age 41. 148 applicants, 94% accepted, 139 enrolled. In 2007, 28 degrees awarded. *Degree requirements:* For master's, thesis (for some programs). *Entrance requirements:* For M Div, minimum undergraduate GPA of 3.0; for master's, minimum undergraduate GPA of 3.0, 15 undergraduate credit hours of course work in Bible or theology. *Application deadline:* Applications are processed on a rolling basis. Application fee: $50. Electronic applications accepted. *Faculty research:* Higher education, cross-cultural missions. *Unit head:* Dr. Carl Chrisner, Dean, 417-862-9533 Ext. 2237, Fax: 417-869-5623, E-mail: cchrisner@globaluniversity.edu. *Application contact:* Jody Patterson, Graduate Student Enrollment Representative, 417-862-9533 Ext. 2347, Fax: 417-862-0863, E-mail: gradenroll@globaluniversity.edu.

Golden Gate Baptist Theological Seminary, Graduate and Professional Programs, Mill Valley, CA 94941-3197. Offers divinity (M Div); early childhood education (Certificate); education leadership (MAEL, Diploma); ministry (D Min); theological studies (MTS); theology (Th M); youth ministry (Certificate). *Accreditation:* ACIPE; ATS (one or more programs are accredited). Part-time and evening/weekend programs available. *Degree requirements:* For master's, thesis (for some programs); for doctorate, 2 foreign languages, thesis/dissertation; for M Div, 2 foreign languages. *Entrance requirements:* For doctorate, MAT. Additional exam requirements/recommendations for international students: Required—TOEFL (minimum score 550 paper-based; 213 computer-based). Electronic applications accepted.

Gordon-Conwell Theological Seminary, Graduate and Professional Programs, South Hamilton, MA 01982. Offers Christian education (MACE); church history (MACH); counseling (MACO); ministry (D Min); missions/evangelism (MAME); New Testament (MANT); Old Testament (MAOT); religion (MAR); theology (M Div, MATH, Th M). *Accreditation:* ACIPE; ATS (one or more programs are accredited). Part-time and evening/weekend programs available. *Degree requirements:* For master's, one foreign language, thesis optional; for doctorate, 2 foreign languages, thesis/dissertation; for M Div, 2 foreign languages. *Entrance requirements:* For M Div and master's, minimum GPA of 2.5; for doctorate, minimum GPA of 3.0.

Grace Theological Seminary, Graduate and Professional Programs, Winona Lake, IN 46590-9907. Offers biblical studies (Certificate, Diploma); counseling (M Div); ministry (MA); missions (M Div, MA); theology (M Div, MA, D Min). *Accreditation:* ATS. Part-time programs available. Postbaccalaureate distance learning degree programs offered (no on-campus study). *Degree requirements:* For master's, thesis optional; for doctorate, 2 foreign languages, thesis/dissertation; for M Div, 2 foreign languages, thesis/dissertation optional. *Entrance requirements:* For M Div and master's, MAT, minimum GPA of 2.5. Electronic applications accepted. *Faculty research:* Biblical theology, language, and church ministries.

Grace University, College of Graduate Studies, Bible Department, Omaha, NE 68108. Offers MA. *Degree requirements:* For master's, thesis optional. *Entrance requirements:* For master's, minimum undergraduate GPA of 3.0. Electronic applications accepted.

Graduate Theological Union, Graduate Programs, Berkeley, CA 94709-1212. Offers art and religion (MA, PhD); biblical languages (MA); biblical studies (Old and New Testament) (MA, PhD, Th D); Buddhist studies (MA); Christian spirituality (MA, PhD); cultural and historical studies of religions (MA, PhD); ethics and social theory (PhD); history (MA, PhD, Th D); homiletics (MA, PhD, Th D); interdisciplinary studies (PhD, Th D); Jewish studies (MA, PhD, Certificate); liturgical studies (MA, PhD, Th D); Near Eastern religions (PhD); Orthodox Christian studies (MA); Orthodox studies (Certificate); religion and psychology (MA, PhD); religion and society/ethics and social theory (MA); systematic and philosophical theology (MA, PhD, Th D); women's studies in religion (Certificate); MA/M Div. *Accreditation:* ATS. *Faculty:* 119 full-time (44 women), 34 part-time/adjunct (9 women). *Students:* 317 full-time (152 women), 35 part-time (19 women); includes 49 minority (15 African Americans, 2 American Indian/Alaska Native, 21 Asian Americans or Pacific Islanders, 11 Hispanic Americans), 74 international. Average age 38. 257 applicants, 59% accepted, 79 enrolled. In 2007, 45 master's, 22 doctorates awarded. Terminal master's awarded for partial completion of doctoral program. *Median time to degree:*

Of those who began their doctoral program in fall 1999, 52% received their degree in 8 years or less. *Degree requirements:* For master's, one foreign language, thesis; for doctorate, one foreign language, comprehensive exam, thesis/dissertation. *Entrance requirements:* For master's, GRE General Test; for doctorate, GRE General Test, MA or M Div. Additional exam requirements/recommendations for international students: Required—TOEFL. *Application deadline:* For fall admission, 12/15 for domestic and international students; for winter admission, 2/15 for domestic and international students; for spring admission, 9/30 for domestic and international students. Application fee: $40. Electronic applications accepted. *Expenses:* Tuition: Full-time $13,310. Tuition and fees vary according to degree level and program. *Financial support:* In 2007–08, 122 students received support, including 109 fellowships (averaging $11,581 per year), 1 research assistantship (averaging $3,000 per year), 22 teaching assistantships (averaging $3,500 per year); Federal Work-Study, scholarships/grants, and tuition waivers (partial) also available. Support available to part-time students. Financial award application deadline: 2/1; financial award applicants required to submit FAFSA. *Unit head:* Dr. Arthur G. Holder, Dean, 510-649-2440, Fax: 510-649-1417, E-mail: aholder@gtu.edu. *Application contact:* Dr. Kathleen Kook, Assistant Dean for Admissions, 800-826-4488, Fax: 510-649-1730, E-mail: gtuadm@gtu.edu.

Grand Rapids Theological Seminary of Cornerstone University, Graduate Programs, Grand Rapids, MI 49525-5897. Offers biblical counseling (MA); Biblical counseling (M Div); chaplaincy (M Div, MA); Christian education (M Div, MA); intercultural studies (M Div, MA); New Testament (MA, Th M); Old Testament (MA, Th M); pastoral studies (M Div); systematic theology (MA); theology (Th M). *Accreditation:* ATS. Part-time programs available. Postbaccalaureate distance learning degree programs offered (minimal on-campus study). *Faculty:* 9 full-time (1 woman), 10 part-time/adjunct (1 woman). *Students:* 102 full-time (35 women), 126 part-time (42 women); includes 36 minority (28 African Americans, 2 American Indian/Alaska Native, 3 Asian Americans or Pacific Islanders, 3 Hispanic Americans), 7 international. Average age 35. 160 applicants, 91% accepted, 107 enrolled. *Entrance requirements:* Additional exam requirements/recommendations for international students: Required—TOEFL (minimum score 577 paper-based; 233 computer-based; 90 iBT). *Application deadline:* For fall admission, 8/15 for domestic students; for spring admission, 1/10 for domestic students. Applications are processed on a rolling basis. Electronic applications accepted. *Expenses:* Tuition: Full-time $6,930; part-time $385 per credit hour. Required fees: $520; $10 per credit hour. $170 per semester. Tuition and fees vary according to course load and degree level. *Financial support:* Career-related internships or fieldwork, scholarships/grants, and health care benefits available. Support available to part-time students. Financial award application deadline: 8/15; financial award applicants required to submit FAFSA. *Unit head:* Dr. Douglas L. Fagerstrom, President, 616-222-1422, Fax: 616-222-1502, E-mail: douglas_fagerstrom@cornerstone.edu. *Application contact:* Tara Danielle Kram, 800-697-1133, Fax: 616-254-1623, E-mail: tara_kram@cornerstone.edu.

Harding University Graduate School of Religion, Graduate Programs, Memphis, TN 38117-5499. Offers Christian ministry (MA); counseling (MA); ministry (M Div, D Min); religion (MA). *Accreditation:* ATS. Part-time programs available. Postbaccalaureate distance learning degree programs offered (minimal on-campus study). *Degree requirements:* For master's, variable foreign language requirement, thesis (for some programs); for doctorate, one foreign language, thesis/dissertation; for M Div, 2 foreign languages, thesis/dissertation optional. *Entrance requirements:* For M Div, GRE General Test (for graduates of non-accredited schools), minimum GPA of 2.5; for master's, minimum GPA of 2.7; for doctorate, minimum GPA of 3.0. Additional exam requirements/recommendations for international students: Required—TOEFL (minimum score 550 paper-based; 213 computer-based; 79 iBT). Electronic applications accepted.

Hardin-Simmons University, Graduate School, Logsdon School of Theology, Abilene, TX 79698-0001. Offers M Div, MA. Part-time and evening/weekend programs available. *Faculty:* 15 full-time (2 women), 13 part-time/adjunct (2 women). *Students:* 72 full-time (19 women), 46 part-time (8 women); includes 14 minority (4 African Americans, 1 American Indian/Alaska Native, 9 Hispanic Americans), 2 international. Average age 30. 44 applicants, 91% accepted, 33 enrolled. In 2007, 15 first professional degrees, 5 master's awarded. *Entrance requirements:* Additional exam requirements/recommendations for international students: Required—TOEFL (minimum score 550 paper-based; 213 computer-based). *Application deadline:* For fall admission, 8/15 priority date for domestic students; for spring admission, 1/5 priority date for domestic students. Applications are processed on a rolling basis. Application fee: $50 ($100 for international students). *Expenses:* Tuition: Full-time $9,810; part-time $545 per hour. Required fees: $590; $75 per semester. One-time fee: $50 part-time. *Financial support:* In 2007–08, 105 students received support, including 12 fellowships (averaging $1,200 per year); scholarships/grants also available. Support available to part-time students. Financial award application deadline: 6/30; financial award applicants required to submit FAFSA. *Unit head:* Dr. Thomas V. Brisco, Dean, 325-670-1266, Fax: 325-670-1406, E-mail: tbrisco@hsutx.edu.

Hardin-Simmons University, Graduate School, Logsdon School of Theology, Logsdon Seminary, Program in Theology, Abilene, TX 79698-0001. Offers M Div. *Accreditation:* ATS. Part-time programs available. *Faculty:* 12 full-time (1 woman), 13 part-time/adjunct (2 women). *Students:* 52 full-time (11 women), 39 part-time (7 women); includes 13 minority (4 African Americans, 1 American Indian/Alaska Native, 8 Hispanic Americans), 2 international. Average age 33. 31 applicants, 94% accepted, 24 enrolled. In 2007, 15 degrees awarded. *Degree requirements:* For M Div, 2 foreign languages, chapel/spiritual formations, colloquium, ministry retreat and formation conferences. *Entrance requirements:* Minimum GPA of 2.0, interview, 3 letters of recommendation. Additional exam requirements/recommendations for international students: Required—TOEFL (minimum score 550 paper-based; 213 computer-based). *Application deadline:* For fall admission, 8/15 priority date for domestic students; for spring admission, 1/5 priority date for domestic students. Applications are processed on a rolling basis. Application fee: $50 ($100 for international students). *Expenses:* Tuition: Full-time $9,810; part-time $545 per hour. Required fees: $590; $75 per semester. One-time fee: $50 part-time. *Financial support:* In 2007–08, 77 students received support, including 10 fellowships (averaging $1,200 per year); career-related internships or fieldwork and scholarships/grants also available. Support available to part-time students. Financial award application deadline: 6/30; financial award applicants required to submit FAFSA. *Faculty research:* Hebrew grammar, history of Christian education, training of ministers into the twenty-first century, role of women in Old Testament, contemporary ethical issues, Ricouer in contemporary theology. *Unit head:* Dr. Robert Ellis, Director, 325-670-5841, E-mail: rellis@hsutx.edu. *Application contact:* Dr. Gary Stanlake, Dean of Graduate Studies, 325-670-1298, Fax: 325-670-1564, E-mail: gradoff@hsutx.edu.

Hartford Seminary, Graduate Programs, Hartford, CT 06105-2279. Offers black ministry (Certificate); Islamic studies (MA); ministerios Hispanos (Certificate); ministry (D Min); religious studies (MA); women's leadership institute (Certificate). *Accreditation:* ATS (one or more programs are accredited). Part-time and evening/weekend programs available. Postbaccalaureate distance learning degree programs offered (no on-campus study). *Faculty:* 12 full-time (5 women), 19 part-time/adjunct (7 women). *Students:* 39 full-time (23 women), 120 part-time (72 women); includes 35 minority (27 African Americans, 5 Asian Americans or Pacific Islanders, 3 Hispanic Americans), 25 international. *Degree requirements:* For master's, thesis optional, oral exam; for doctorate, thesis/dissertation, oral exam. *Entrance requirements:* For doctorate, experience in ministry, M Div. Additional exam requirements/recommendations for international students: Required—TOEFL (minimum score 550 paper-based; 213 computer-based; 80 iBT). *Application deadline:* For fall admission, 7/15 priority date for domestic students, 5/1 priority date for international students; for winter admission, 12/1 priority date for domestic students, 4/1 priority date for international students; for spring admission, 4/5 priority date for domestic students, 3/1 priority date for international students. Applications are processed on a rolling basis. Application fee: $50. *Expenses:* Tuition: Full-time $12,400; part-time $1,550 per unit. *Financial support:* In 2007–08, 74 students received support. Scholarships/grants and tuition waivers (partial) available. Support available to part-time students. Financial award application deadline: 6/1. *Faculty research:* Liturgy and social justice, professional leadership in ministry, congregational studies, Christian-Muslim relations, American religion. *Unit head:* Dr. Efrain Agosto, Academic Dean, 860-509-9554, E-mail: eagosto@hartsem.edu. *Application contact:* Dr. Vanessa Avery-Wall, Admissions Manager, 860-509-9552, Fax: 860-509-9509, E-mail: vaw@hartsem.edu.

Harvard University, Divinity School, Cambridge, MA 02138. Offers M Div, MTS, Th M, PhD, Th D. *Accreditation:* ACIPE; ATS. *Faculty:* 36 full-time (15 women), 81 part-time/adjunct (35 women). *Students:* 453 full-time (235 women); includes 68 minority (22 African Americans, 4 American Indian/Alaska Native, 26 Asian Americans or Pacific Islanders, 16 Hispanic Americans), 45 international. Average age 26. 606 applicants, 43% accepted, 171 enrolled. In 2007, 47 first professional degrees, 100 master's, 1 doctorate awarded. *Median time to degree:* Of those who began their doctoral program in fall 1999, 40% received their degree in 8 years or less. *Degree requirements:* For master's, one foreign language, thesis (for some programs); for doctorate, 3 foreign languages, comprehensive exam, thesis/dissertation; for M Div, one foreign language, thesis/dissertation, field education. *Entrance requirements:* For doctorate, GRE General Test. Additional exam requirements/recommendations for international students: Required—TOEFL (minimum score 600 paper-based; 250 computer-based). *Application deadline:* For fall admission, 1/11 priority date for domestic and international students. Application fee: $75. Electronic applications accepted. *Expenses: Contact institution.* Full-time tuition and fees vary according to program and student level. *Financial support:* In 2007–08, 418 students received support, including 398 fellowships with tuition reimbursements available (averaging $21,469 per year); teaching assistantships, career-related internships or fieldwork, Federal Work-Study, and scholarships/grants also available. Support available to part-time students. Financial award application deadline: 2/1; financial award applicants required to submit FAFSA. *Faculty research:* Theology, Women's Studies, history, comparative religion. *Unit head:* William A. Graham, Dean, 917-495-4513, Fax: 617-496-8026. *Application contact:* Maritza Hernandez, Director of Admissions and Financial Aid, 617-495-5796, Fax: 617-495-0345, E-mail: mhernandez@hds.harvard.edu.

Hebrew College, Rabbinical School, Newton Centre, MA 02459. Offers MA. *Entrance requirements:* For master's, interview. Additional exam requirements/recommendations for international students: Required—TOEFL.

Hebrew Theological College, Department of Talmud and Rabbinics, Skokie, IL 60077-3263. Offers Rabbi.

Hebrew Union College–Jewish Institute of Religion, Rabbinical School, New York, NY 10012-1186. Offers MAHL. *Degree requirements:* For MAHL, one foreign language, thesis/dissertation, fieldwork, sermons. *Entrance requirements:* GRE, language exam, minimum GPA of 3.0, minimum 2 years of college-level Hebrew. Additional exam requirements/recommendations for international students: Required—TOEFL. *Faculty research:* Philosophy and theology, Bible, Hebrew, pastoral care, history and Rabbinics.

Hebrew Union College–Jewish Institute of Religion, Rabbinic School, Cincinnati, OH 45220-2488. Offers MAHL. *Accreditation:* ACIPE. *Degree requirements:* For MAHL, one foreign language, thesis/dissertation. *Entrance requirements:* GRE General Test, Hebrew competency exam, interview, psychological test. *Faculty research:* Comprehensive Aramaic lexicon, four-volume history (German Jews and modern times).

Hebrew Union College–Jewish Institute of Religion, School of Graduate Studies, Program in Pastoral Counseling, New York, NY 10012-1186. Offers D Min. *Accreditation:* ACIPE. *Degree requirements:* For doctorate, thesis/dissertation. *Entrance requirements:* For doctorate, M Div (or higher), ordination/certification for ministry. Additional exam requirements/recommendations for international students: Required—TOEFL. Expenses: Contact institution. *Faculty research:* Philosophy and theology, Bible, Hebrew, pastoral care, history and Rabbinics.

Hebrew Union College–Jewish Institute of Religion, School of Rabbinical Studies, Los Angeles, CA 90007-3796. Offers MAHL. *Accreditation:* ACIPE. *Faculty:* 11 full-time (5 women), 12 part-time/adjunct (4 women). *Students:* 57 full-time (41 women), 2 part-time (both women), 2 international. Average age 32. 55 applicants, 73% accepted, 38 enrolled. In 2007, 14 MAHLs awarded. *Degree requirements:* For MAHL, one foreign language, thesis/dissertation, Hebrew. *Entrance requirements:* GRE General Test, interview, minimum undergraduate GPA of 3.0, 2 years of college-level Hebrew. Additional exam requirements/recommendations for international students: Required—TOEFL (minimum score 550 paper-based). *Application deadline:* For fall admission, 11/1 for domestic and international students; for winter admission, 1/2 for domestic and international students. Application fee: $75. Electronic applications accepted. *Financial support:* Career-related internships or fieldwork and scholarships/grants available. Financial award application deadline: 3/15; financial award applicants required to submit FAFSA. *Unit head:* Rabbi Richard Levy, Director, 213-749-3424 Ext. 4203, Fax: 213-747-6128, E-mail: rlevy@huc.edu. *Application contact:* Deborah Shapiro Abelson, Director of Admissions and Recruitment, 213-749-3424, Fax: 213-747-6128, E-mail: admissions@huc.edu.

Heritage Baptist College and Heritage Theological Seminary, Program in Theological Studies, Cambridge, ON N3C 3T2, Canada. Offers divinity (MA); theological studies (MA, Certificate). *Accreditation:* ATS.

Holy Apostles College and Seminary, Department of Theology, Cromwell, CT 06416-2005. Offers bioethics (MA, Certificate, Post Master's Certificate); church history (MA, Certificate, Post Master's Certificate); dogmatic theology (MA, Certificate, Post Master's Certificate); liturgical music (MA, Certificate, Post Master's Certificate); liturgy (MA, Certificate, Post Master's Certificate); moral theology (MA, Certificate, Post Master's Certificate); philosophical theology (MA, Certificate, Post Master's Certificate); religious education (MA, Certificate, Post Master's Certificate); sacred scripture (MA, Post Master's Certificate); sacred scriptures (Certificate); theology (M Div). Part-time and evening/weekend programs available. Postbaccalaureate distance learning degree programs offered (no on-campus study). *Faculty:* 10 full-time (3 women), 16 part-time/adjunct (5 women). *Students:* 79 full-time (1 woman), 147 part-time (55 women); includes 27 minority (3 African Americans, 9 Asian Americans or Pacific Islanders, 15 Hispanic Americans), 17 international. Average age 43. In 2007, 7 first professional degrees, 32 master's awarded. *Degree requirements:* For master's, one foreign language, comprehensive exam, thesis optional; for other advanced degree, culminating paper. *Entrance requirements:* For M Div, interview; for master's, minimum undergraduate GPA of 3.0; for other advanced degree, minimum graduate GPA of 3.0. *Application deadline:* For fall admission, 8/15 priority date for domestic and international students; for spring admission, 1/15 priority date for domestic and international students. Applications are processed on a rolling basis. Application fee: $50. Electronic applications accepted. *Expenses:* Tuition: Full-time $4,770; part-time $265 per credit. One-time fee: $125 full-time. *Financial support:* In 2007–08, 25 students received support. Career-related internships or fieldwork and scholarships/grants available. Support available to part-time students. Financial award applicants required to submit FAFSA. *Faculty research:* Roman Catholic theology, philosophy. *Unit head:* Rev. Maurice Sheehan, OFM, Academic Dean, 860-632-3001, Fax: 860-632-3030. *Application contact:* Very Rev. Douglas L. Mosey, President and Rector, 860-632-3012, Fax: 860-632-3030, E-mail: rector@holyapostles.edu.

Holy Cross Greek Orthodox School of Theology, Theological Programs, Brookline, MA 02445-7496. Offers M Div, MTS, Th M. *Accreditation:* ATS. Part-time programs available. *Degree requirements:* For master's, 2 foreign languages, thesis (for some programs); for M Div, 2 foreign languages, thesis/dissertation (for some programs). *Entrance requirements:* For M Div and master's, GRE General Test, interview, written submission. Additional exam requirements/recommendations for international students: Required—TOEFL (minimum score 550 paper-based; 213 computer-based). *Faculty research:* Spirituality, liturgies, ecumenism, church history.

Hood Theological Seminary, Graduate and Professional Programs, Salisbury, NC 28144. Offers M Div, MTS, D Min. *Accreditation:* ATS. Evening/weekend programs available. *Degree requirements:* For master's, thesis optional; for doctorate, thesis/dissertation; for M Div, thesis/

Theology

Hood Theological Seminary (continued)
dissertation optional. *Faculty research:* Old Testament human sexuality, preaching and the vulnerable, socio-historical issues, Pauline studies, multiculturalism/African-American studies.

Houston Baptist University, College of Arts and Humanities, Program in Theological Studies, Houston, TX 77074-3298. Offers MATS. Part-time and evening/weekend programs available. *Faculty:* 6 full-time (0 women), 2 part-time/adjunct (0 women). *Students:* 11 full-time (3 women), 8 part-time (2 women); includes 6 minority (all African Americans), 1 international. Average age 36. 17 applicants, 88% accepted, 12 enrolled. In 2007, 11 degrees awarded. *Degree requirements:* For master's, comprehensive exam. *Entrance requirements:* For master's, GRE General Test, 6 hours of course work in Greek or Hebrew (optional), interview, minimum GPA of 2.5. Additional exam requirements/recommendations for international students: Required—TOEFL (minimum score 550 paper-based; 213 computer-based). *Application deadline:* For fall admission, 7/1 priority date for domestic and international students; for winter admission, 10/1 priority date for domestic and international students; for spring admission, 1/1 priority date for domestic and international students. Applications are processed on a rolling basis. Application fee: $25 ($100 for international students). *Expenses:* Contact institution. *Financial support:* Federal Work-Study available. Support available to part-time students. Financial award application deadline: 3/1; financial award applicants required to submit FAFSA. *Unit head:* Dr. Joe Blair, Director, 281-649-3288, Fax: 281-649-3012, E-mail: jblair@hbu.edu. *Application contact:* Sharon Wiser, Secretary, 281-649-3000 Ext. 2212, E-mail: swiser@hbu.edu.

Houston Graduate School of Theology, Graduate School, Houston, TX 77092. Offers counseling (MA); pastoral ministry (M Div, D Min); theology (MA). *Accreditation:* ATS (one or more programs are accredited). Part-time and evening/weekend programs available. *Degree requirements:* For master's, thesis (for some programs); for doctorate, thesis/dissertation; for M Div, thesis/dissertation optional. *Entrance requirements:* For doctorate, GRE General Test or MAT, M Div or equivalent. Additional exam requirements/recommendations for international students: Required—TOEFL (minimum score 550 paper-based; 213 computer-based). *Faculty research:* Hermeneutics, spirituality, religion of Eastern Europe.

Howard University, School of Divinity, Washington, DC 20017. Offers M Div, MARS, D Min. *Accreditation:* ACIPE; ATS. Part-time and evening/weekend programs available. *Degree requirements:* For master's, thesis; for doctorate, thesis/dissertation; for M Div, thesis/dissertation optional. *Entrance requirements:* For M Div, minimum GPA of 2.0; for master's and doctorate, minimum GPA of 3.0. Electronic applications accepted. *Expenses:* Tuition: Full-time $16,175; part-time $899 per credit hour. Required fees: $805. *Faculty research:* African-American religious experience, women in ministry, ecumenics, biblical studies.

Iliff School of Theology, Graduate and Professional Programs, Denver, CO 80210-4798. Offers biblical studies (MA); church history (MA); religion (MA); religion and social change (MA); specialized ministry (MASM), including justice and peace, pastoral theology and care, religious leadership; theology (M Div, MTS, D Min, PhD), including Biblical studies (PhD), religion and psychological studies (PhD), religion and social change (PhD), theology, philosophy and culture (PhD); theology/ethics (MA). *Accreditation:* ACIPE; ATS. Part-time and evening/weekend programs available. *Degree requirements:* For master's, one foreign language, thesis (for some programs); for doctorate, 2 foreign languages, comprehensive exam, thesis/dissertation; for M Div, thesis/dissertation optional. *Entrance requirements:* For M Div, minimum GPA of 2.75, references; for master's, minimum GPA of 3.0, writing sample, references; for doctorate, GRE General Test, minimum GPA of 3.0, writing sample, letters of recommendation. Additional exam requirements/recommendations for international students: Required—TOEFL (minimum score 550 paper-based). Electronic applications accepted. *Faculty research:* Pastoral care, history, church music, contemporary church, biblical studies.

Indiana Wesleyan University, College of Graduate Studies, Program in Ministry, Marion, IN 46953-4974. Offers ministerial education (MA); ministry (MA). Part-time programs available. Postbaccalaureate distance learning degree programs offered. *Faculty:* 5 part-time/adjunct (0 women). *Students:* 124 full-time (21 women), 6 part-time (3 women); includes 21 minority (20 African Americans, 1 Hispanic American). Average age 36. In 2007, 53 degrees awarded. *Degree requirements:* For master's, practicum or project. *Application deadline:* Applications are processed on a rolling basis. Application fee: $0. Electronic applications accepted. *Expenses:* Contact institution. *Financial support:* Career-related internships or fieldwork available. *Faculty research:* History of worship innovation, history of New Testament afterlife traditions, second century Mantanism, cross-cultural ministry. *Unit head:* Dr. Russ Gunsalus, Chair, 765-677 Ext. 2259, E-mail: russ.gunsalus@indwes.edu. *Application contact:* David McMillan, Assistant Director of Enrollment Management, 765-677-2688, E-mail: david.mcmillan@indwes.edu.

Institute for Christian Studies, Graduate Programs, Toronto, ON M5T 1R4, Canada. Offers education (M Phil F, PhD); history of philosophy (M Phil F, PhD); philosophical aesthetics (M Phil F, PhD); philosophy of religion (M Phil F, PhD); political theory (M Phil F, PhD); systematic philosophy (M Phil F, PhD); theology (M Phil F, PhD); worldview studies (MWS). Part-time programs available. Postbaccalaureate distance learning degree programs offered (minimal on-campus study). *Degree requirements:* For master's, one foreign language, thesis; for doctorate, 2 foreign languages, thesis/dissertation. *Entrance requirements:* For master's and doctorate, philosophy background. Additional exam requirements/recommendations for international students: Required—TOEFL (minimum score 600 paper-based; 250 computer-based). *Faculty research:* Human rights, anthropology of self, medieval discourse, gender and body, post-modern thought; biblical hermeneutics, creational aesthetics, ecumenism, epistemology, political theory and public policy, relational psychotherapy.

Inter American University of Puerto Rico, Metropolitan Campus, Faculty of Liberal Arts, Program in Theological Studies, San Juan, PR 00919-1293. Offers PhD.

Interdenominational Theological Center, Graduate and Professional Programs, Atlanta, GA 30314-4112. Offers M Div, MACE, MACM, D Min, Th D, M Div/MACE, M Div/MACM, MACM/MACE. *Accreditation:* ACIPE; ATS (one or more programs are accredited). Part-time and evening/weekend programs available. Postbaccalaureate distance learning degree programs offered (minimal on-campus study). *Faculty:* 21 full-time (6 women), 23 part-time/adjunct (11 women). *Students:* 259 full-time (111 women), 183 part-time (76 women); includes 411 minority (409 African Americans, 2 Hispanic Americans), 18 international. Average age 40. 178 applicants, 77% accepted, 105 enrolled. In 2007, 77 first professional degrees, 10 master's, 7 doctorates awarded. *Degree requirements:* For doctorate, thesis/dissertation. *Entrance requirements:* For M Div, bachelor's degree; for doctorate, master's degree. *Application deadline:* For fall admission, 7/1 for domestic students; for spring admission, 11/15 for domestic and international students. Applications are processed on a rolling basis. Application fee: $50. *Expenses:* Tuition: Full-time $10,365; part-time $608 per credit. *Financial support:* In 2007–08, 375 students received support, including 4 research assistantships; career-related internships or fieldwork and Federal Work-Study also available. Support available to part-time students. Financial award application deadline: 6/15; financial award applicants required to submit FAFSA. *Unit head:* Dr. Michael A. Battle, President, 404-527-7702, Fax: 404-527-7770, E-mail: mbattle@itc.edu. *Application contact:* Walter Cabassa, Office of Admission and Recruitment, 404-527-7792, E-mail: wcabassa@itc.edu.

International Baptist College, Program in Biblical Studies, Tempe, AZ 85282. Offers MA.

Jesuit School of Theology at Berkeley, Programs in Theology, Berkeley, CA 94709-1193. Offers M Div, MA, MABL, MTS, Th M, STD, STL, MA/M Div. *Accreditation:* ATS (one or more programs are accredited). Part-time programs available. *Degree requirements:* For master's, one foreign language, thesis; for doctorate, 2 foreign languages, comprehensive exam, thesis/dissertation; for M Div, comprehensive exam. *Entrance requirements:* For M Div, GRE, undergraduate course work in philosophy; for master's, GRE. Additional exam requirements/recommendations for international students: Required—TOEFL, TWE.

The Jewish Theological Seminary, The Graduate School, New York, NY 10027-4649. Offers ancient Judaism (MA, DHL, PhD); Bible (MA, DHL, PhD); Jewish education (PhD); Jewish history (MA, DHL, PhD); Jewish literature (MA, DHL, PhD); Jewish philosophy (MA, DHL, PhD); liturgy (MA, DHL, PhD); medieval Jewish studies (MA, DHL, PhD); Midrash (MA, DHL, PhD); modern Jewish studies (MA, DHL, PhD); Talmud and rabbinics (MA, DHL, PhD); MA/MSW. *Accreditation:* ACIPE. Part-time programs available. *Faculty:* 62 full-time (21 women), 69 part-time/adjunct (33 women). *Students:* 100 full-time (54 women), 26 part-time (12 women); includes 1 minority (Asian American or Pacific Islander), 1 international. Average age 38. 79 applicants, 78% accepted, 28 enrolled. In 2007, 40 master's, 3 doctorates awarded. Terminal master's awarded for partial completion of doctoral program. *Degree requirements:* For master's, one foreign language, comprehensive exam (for some programs), thesis (for some programs); for doctorate, 3 foreign languages, comprehensive exam (for some programs), thesis/dissertation. *Entrance requirements:* For master's, GRE or MAT, 3 letters of recommendation, writing sample; for doctorate, GRE or MAT, 3 letters of recommendation, writing research sample. Additional exam requirements/recommendations for international students: Required—TOEFL (minimum score 100 computer-based). *Application deadline:* For fall admission, 1/15 priority date for domestic students. Applications are processed on a rolling basis. Application fee: $50. *Expenses:* Tuition: Full-time $20,340; part-time $950 per credit. Required fees: $380 per semester. Full-time tuition and fees vary according to degree level, program and student level. *Financial support:* In 2007–08, 49 fellowships (averaging $13,681 per year) were awarded; career-related internships or fieldwork and tuition waivers (full and partial) also available. Support available to part-time students. Financial award application deadline: 3/1; financial award applicants required to submit FAFSA. *Unit head:* Dr. Stephen Garfinkel, Dean, 212-678-8024, Fax: 212-678-8947, E-mail: gradschool@jtsa.edu. *Application contact:* Alayne Birnhak, Director, Graduate School of Admissions, 212-678-8032, Fax: 212-280-6022, E-mail: albirnhak@jtsa.edu.

See Close-Up on page 693.

The Jewish Theological Seminary, The Rabbinical School, New York, NY 10027-4649. Offers MA, Rabbi. *Accreditation:* ACIPE. *Faculty:* 62 full-time (21 women), 69 part-time/adjunct (33 women). *Students:* 123 full-time (47 women), 15 part-time (5 women); includes 1 minority (Hispanic American) Average age 29. 64 applicants, 56% accepted, 26 enrolled. In 2007, 10 master's, 18 other advanced degrees awarded. *Degree requirements:* For master's and Rabbi, one foreign language, competency exams. *Entrance requirements:* For master's and Rabbi, GRE, interview, writing sample. Additional exam requirements/recommendations for international students: Required—TOEFL. *Application deadline:* For fall admission, 12/31 for domestic students. Applications are processed on a rolling basis. Application fee: $65. *Expenses:* Contact institution. Full-time tuition and fees vary according to degree level, program and student level. *Financial support:* In 2007–08, 68 fellowships (averaging $9,931 per year) were awarded; career-related internships or fieldwork also available. Support available to part-time students. Financial award application deadline: 3/1; financial award applicants required to submit FAFSA. *Unit head:* Rabbi William Lebeau, Dean, 212-678-8067, Fax: 212-678-8947, E-mail: wilebeau@jtsa.edu. *Application contact:* Rabbi Charles Savenor, Associate Dean of the Rabbinical School/Admissions Director, 212-678-8807, Fax: 212-678-8947, E-mail: chsavenor@jtsa.edu.

See Close-Up on page 695.

Johnson Bible College, Program in New Testament, Knoxville, TN 37998-1001. Offers preaching (MA); research (MA). Part-time and evening/weekend programs available. Postbaccalaureate distance learning degree programs offered (no on-campus study). *Faculty:* 1 full-time (0 women), 5 part-time/adjunct (0 women). *Students:* 73 (4 women). Average age 38. In 2007, 8 degrees awarded. *Degree requirements:* For master's, one foreign language, comprehensive exam, thesis (for some programs). *Entrance requirements:* For master's, minimum GPA of 2.5. Additional exam requirements/recommendations for international students: Required—TOEFL. *Application deadline:* For fall admission, 6/1 priority date for domestic students; for spring admission, 11/15 for domestic students. Applications are processed on a rolling basis. Application fee: $50. *Financial support:* Career-related internships or fieldwork and institutionally sponsored loans available. Financial award application deadline: 8/1. *Application contact:* Marsha Ketchen, Application Contact, 800-669-7884, Fax: 865-251-2285, E-mail: mketchen@jbc.edu.

Kehilath Yakov Rabbinical Seminary, Graduate Programs, Brooklyn, NY 11211-7207. *Accreditation:* AARTS.

Kenrick-Glennon Seminary, Graduate and Professional Programs, St. Louis, MO 63119-4330. Offers M Div, MA, Certificate. *Accreditation:* ATS. *Degree requirements:* For master's, thesis optional. *Entrance requirements:* MAT.

Kentucky Christian University, Graduate School, Grayson, KY 41143-2205. Offers Christian leadership (MA); New Testament (MA). Part-time programs available. *Faculty:* 6 part-time/adjunct (0 women). *Students:* 2 full-time (0 women), 17 part-time (3 women), 3 international. Average age 33. 14 applicants, 86% accepted, 11 enrolled. In 2007, 6 degrees awarded. *Degree requirements:* For master's, comprehensive exam (for some programs), thesis optional. *Entrance requirements:* For master's, minimum cumulative GPA of 2.75 in major or 2.5 overall; 6 additional hours in Bible (for non-Biblical undergraduate majors). Additional exam requirements/recommendations for international students: Required—TOEFL (minimum score 550 paper-based; 213 computer-based). *Application deadline:* Applications are processed on a rolling basis. Application fee: $35. Electronic applications accepted. *Expenses:* Tuition: Full-time $4,050; part-time $225 per credit hour. *Financial support:* Teaching assistantships with full tuition reimbursements, scholarships/grants and unspecified assistantships available. Support available to part-time students. *Unit head:* Dr. David Fiensy, Graduate Dean, 606-474-3263, Fax: 606-474-3189, E-mail: dfiensy@kcu.edu. *Application contact:* Jane Shick, Academic Office Manager, 877-811-6391, Fax: 606-474-3189, E-mail: gradstudies@kcu.edu.

Knox College, College of Theology, Toronto, ON M5S 2E6, Canada. Offers M Div, MRE, MTS, Th M, D Min, Th D. Applicants for D Min, Th M, and Th D must apply to Toronto School of Theology. *Accreditation:* ATS. Part-time programs available. *Degree requirements:* For master's, one foreign language, thesis (for some programs); for doctorate, 2 foreign languages, thesis/dissertation. *Entrance requirements:* For doctorate, M Div. Additional exam requirements/recommendations for international students: Required—TOEFL (minimum score 580 paper-based; 237 computer-based), TWE (minimum score 5). *Faculty research:* Nineteenth century theologians.

Knox Theological Seminary, Graduate Programs, Program in Biblical Studies, Fort Lauderdale, FL 33308. Offers CBS. *Accreditation:* ATS. Part-time and evening/weekend programs available. *Faculty:* 5 full-time (0 women), 2 part-time/adjunct (0 women). *Students:* Average age 37. 1 applicant, 100% accepted, 1 enrolled. *Entrance requirements:* Additional exam requirements/recommendations for international students: Required—TOEFL, TWE (minimum score 5). *Application deadline:* For fall admission, 6/1 priority date for domestic and international students; for winter admission, 12/1 priority date for domestic and international students; for spring admission, 1/1 priority date for domestic and international students. Applications are processed on a rolling basis. Application fee: $50. *Financial support:* In 2007–08, 2 students received support. Scholarships/grants available. Support available to part-time students. Financial award application deadline: 6/1. *Application contact:* Jim Dietz, Director of Student Services, 800-344-5669, Fax: 954-351-3343, E-mail: jdietz@knoxseminary.edu.

Knox Theological Seminary, Graduate Programs, Program in Divinity, Fort Lauderdale, FL 33308. Offers M Div. *Accreditation:* ATS. Part-time and evening/weekend programs available. *Faculty:* 5 full-time (0 women), 2 part-time/adjunct (0 women). *Students:* 10 full-time (0 women), 35 part-time; includes 9 African Americans, 5 Hispanic Americans. Average age 36. 8 applicants, 88% accepted, 7 enrolled. In 2007, 5 degrees awarded. *Entrance requirements:* Additional exam requirements/recommendations for international students: Required—TOEFL,

TWE (minimum score 5). *Application deadline:* For fall admission, 6/1 priority date for domestic and international students; for winter admission, 12/1 priority date for domestic and international students; for spring admission, 1/1 priority date for domestic and international students. Applications are processed on a rolling basis. Application fee: $50. *Financial support:* In 2007–08, 28 students received support. Scholarships/grants available. Support available to part-time students. Financial award application deadline: 6/1. *Application contact:* Jim Dietz, Director of Student Services, 800-344-5669, Fax: 954-351-3343, E-mail: jdietz@knoxseminary.edu.

Knox Theological Seminary, Graduate Programs, Program in New and Old Testament, Fort Lauderdale, FL 33308. Offers MBT. *Accreditation:* ATS. Part-time and evening/weekend programs available. *Faculty:* 5 full-time (0 women), 2 part-time/adjunct (0 women). *Students:* 3 full-time (2 women), 10 part-time (3 women); includes 2 African Americans, 1 Hispanic American. Average age 34. 5 applicants, 100% accepted, 5 enrolled. *Degree requirements:* For master's, one foreign language, thesis. *Entrance requirements:* Additional exam requirements/recommendations for international students: Required—TOEFL, TWE (minimum score 5). *Application deadline:* For fall admission, 6/1 priority date for domestic and international students; for winter admission, 12/1 priority date for domestic and international students; for spring admission, 1/1 priority date for domestic and international students. Applications are processed on a rolling basis. Application fee: $50. *Financial support:* In 2007–08, 8 students received support. Scholarships/grants available. Support available to part-time students. Financial award application deadline: 6/1. *Application contact:* Jim Dietz, Director of Student Services, 800-344-5669, Fax: 954-351-3343, E-mail: jdietz@knoxseminary.edu.

Kol Yaakov Torah Center, Graduate Program, Monsey, NY 10952-2954. Offers Advanced Rabbinic Degree. *Accreditation:* AARTS. Part-time and evening/weekend programs available. *Faculty research:* Talmud, Jewish law.

Lakeland College, Graduate Studies Division, Program in Theology, Sheboygan, WI 53082-0359. Offers MAT.

Lancaster Bible College, Graduate School, Lancaster, PA 17608-3403. Offers Bible (MA); consulting resource teacher (M Ed); counseling (MA); ministry (MA); school counseling (M Ed). Part-time and evening/weekend programs available. *Degree requirements:* For master's, comprehensive exam (for some programs), thesis (for some programs). *Entrance requirements:* For master's, bachelor's degree with a minimum of 30 credits of course work in Bible, minimum undergraduate GPA of 3.0, interview. Additional exam requirements/recommendations for international students: Required—TOEFL.

Lancaster Theological Seminary, Graduate and Professional Programs, Lancaster, PA 17603-2812. Offers biblical studies (M Div, MAR); church life and work (M Div, MAR); historical studies (M Div, MAR); integrated ministry studies (M Div, MAR); lay leadership (Certificate); theological studies (M Div, MAR); theology (D Min). *Accreditation:* ACIPE; ATS. *Degree requirements:* For doctorate, thesis/dissertation; for M Div, one foreign language.

La Salle University, School of Arts and Sciences, Program in Theological, Pastoral and Liturgical Studies, Philadelphia, PA 19141-1199. Offers pastoral studies (MA); religion (MA); theological studies (MA). Part-time and evening/weekend programs available. *Faculty:* 5 full-time (1 woman), 6 part-time/adjunct (3 women). *Students:* 3 full-time (2 women), 47 part-time (24 women); includes 9 minority (4 African Americans, 2 Asian Americans or Pacific Islanders, 3 Hispanic Americans). Average age 47. 9 applicants, 89% accepted, 5 enrolled. In 2007, 20 degrees awarded. *Entrance requirements:* For master's, 26 credits in humanistic subjects, religion, theology, or ministry-related work. *Application deadline:* Applications are processed on a rolling basis. Application fee: $35. *Expenses:* Tuition: Full-time $16,300; part-time $550 per credit. Required fees: $85 per term. Tuition and fees vary according to program. *Financial support:* In 2007–08, 12 students received support. Scholarships/grants available. Financial award applicants required to submit FAFSA. *Unit head:* Rev. Francis Berna, OFM, Director, 215-951-1335, Fax: 215-951-1665, E-mail: berna@lasalle.edu.

Lee University, Program in Religion, Cleveland, TN 37320-3450. Offers biblical studies (MA); theological studies (MA); youth and family ministry (MA). *Faculty:* 19 full-time (4 women), 1 (woman) part-time/adjunct. *Students:* 21 full-time (11 women), 23 part-time (8 women); includes 3 minority (1 African American, 1 American Indian/Alaska Native, 1 Hispanic American). Average age 26. 21 applicants, 81% accepted, 13 enrolled. In 2007, 14 degrees awarded. *Degree requirements:* For master's, comprehensive exam, thesis. *Entrance requirements:* For master's, GRE or MAT, minimum GPA of 3.0, 2 letters of recommendation, interview. Additional exam requirements/recommendations for international students: Required—TOEFL. *Application deadline:* For fall admission, 4/1 for domestic students; for spring admission, 10/1 for domestic students. Application fee: $25. *Expenses:* Tuition: Full-time $10,392; part-time $433 per credit. Required fees: $65 per term. Tuition and fees vary according to course load. *Financial support:* Career-related internships or fieldwork, Federal Work-Study, institutionally sponsored loans, scholarships/grants, and unspecified assistantships available. Financial award application deadline: 3/1; financial award applicants required to submit FAFSA. *Faculty research:* Book of Isaiah, Gospel of Mark, school of St. Victor of 12th century, spirit Christology, people groups of New Testament and work. Total annual research expenditures: $3,000. *Unit head:* Dr. Michael Fuller, Director, 423-614-8338, E-mail: mfuller@leeuniversity.edu. *Application contact:* Vicki Glasscock, Graduate Admissions Director, 423-614-8059, E-mail: vglasscock@leeuniversity.edu.

Lexington Theological Seminary, Graduate and Professional Programs, Lexington, KY 40508-3218. Offers M Div, MA, MAPS, D Min, M Div/MSW. *Accreditation:* ACIPE; ATS. Part-time and evening/weekend programs available. *Degree requirements:* For master's, thesis; for doctorate, thesis/dissertation. *Entrance requirements:* Additional exam requirements/recommendations for international students: Required—TOEFL (minimum score 600 paper-based; 250 computer-based). *Faculty research:* History of biblical interpretation, biblical apocalyptic, psalms, history of Stone-Campbell traditions.

Liberty University, Liberty Theological Seminary and Graduate School, Lynchburg, VA 24502. Offers religious studies (M Div, MA, MAR, MRE, D Min); theology (Th M). Part-time programs available. Postbaccalaureate distance learning degree programs offered (minimal on-campus study). *Faculty:* 15 full-time (0 women), 48 part-time/adjunct (0 women). *Students:* 1,060 full-time (209 women), 1,933 part-time (331 women); includes 523 minority (356 African Americans, 19 American Indian/Alaska Native, 51 Asian Americans or Pacific Islanders, 97 Hispanic Americans), 173 international. Average age 38. In 2007, 25 first professional degrees, 210 master's, 8 doctorates awarded. *Degree requirements:* For master's, 2 foreign languages, thesis (for some programs); for doctorate, 2 foreign languages, thesis/dissertation. *Entrance requirements:* For M Div, minimum undergraduate GPA of 2.0; for master's, minimum undergraduate GPA of 2.0, 9 credit hours of course work in Greek, 9 credit hours of course work in Hebrew (Th M); for doctorate, GRE General Test or MAT. Additional exam requirements/recommendations for international students: Required—TOEFL (minimum score 550 paper-based; 213 computer-based). *Application deadline:* For fall admission, 6/1 priority date for domestic students; for spring admission, 11/1 for domestic students. Applications are processed on a rolling basis. Application fee: $50. Electronic applications accepted. *Expenses: Contact institution.* Tuition and fees vary according to program. *Financial support:* In 2007–08, 844 students received support, including 5 teaching assistantships with tuition reimbursements available; career-related internships or fieldwork and Federal Work-Study also available. *Unit head:* Dr. Ergun Caner, Dean, 434-582-2099, Fax: 434-522-0415, E-mail: ecaner@liberty.edu. *Application contact:* Kyle A Falce, Director of Graduate Admissions, 800-424-9596, Fax: 800-628-7977, E-mail: gradadmissions@liberty.edu.

Lincoln Christian Seminary, Graduate and Professional Programs, Lincoln, IL 62656-2167. Offers Bible and theology (MA); Bible translation (MA); counseling ministry (MA); divinity (M Div); leadership ministry (MA, D Min). MA in Bible translation offered jointly with Pioneer Bible Translators (Dallas, TX). *Accreditation:* ACIPE; ATS. Part-time programs available. *Faculty:* 12 full-time (2 women), 13 part-time/adjunct (3 women). *Students:* 117 full-time (38 women), 233 part-time (67 women); includes 12 minority (8 African Americans, 2 American Indian/Alaska Native, 2 Hispanic Americans), 14 international. Average age 26. 125 applicants, 92% accepted, 88 enrolled. In 2007, 15 first professional degrees, 37 master's awarded. *Degree requirements:* For master's, 2 foreign languages, thesis; for doctorate, thesis/dissertation; for M Div, 2 foreign languages. *Entrance requirements:* For M Div and master's, minimum GPA of 2.5; for doctorate, MDiv or equivalent. Additional exam requirements/recommendations for international students: Required—TOEFL (minimum score 550 paper-based; 213 computer-based). *Application deadline:* Applications are processed on a rolling basis. Application fee: $20. Electronic applications accepted. *Expenses:* Tuition: Full-time $7,182; part-time $399 per hour. *Financial support:* In 2007–08, 150 students received support, including 5 teaching assistantships (averaging $2,000 per year); career-related internships or fieldwork, Federal Work-Study, and scholarships/grants also available. Support available to part-time students. Financial award application deadline: 3/1; financial award applicants required to submit FAFSA. *Unit head:* Dr. Thomas Tanner, Vice President of Academics, 217-732-3168 Ext. 2240, Fax: 217-732-5718, E-mail: ttanner@lccs.edu. *Application contact:* David Harmon, Director of Admissions, 217-732-3168 Ext. 2275, Fax: 217-732-5914, E-mail: semadmis@lccs.edu.

Lipscomb University, Hazelip School of Theology, Nashville, TN 37204-3951. Offers biblical studies (MA); Christian studies (MA); divinity (M Div); ministry (MA); New Testament (MA); Old Testament (MA); theological studies (MTS); theology (MA). *Accreditation:* ATS. Part-time and evening/weekend programs available. *Faculty:* 7 full-time (0 women), 3 part-time/adjunct (0 women). *Students:* 19 full-time (1 woman), 66 part-time (9 women); includes 5 minority (all African Americans), 2 international. Average age 34. 30 applicants, 80% accepted, 21 enrolled. In 2007, 4 first professional degrees, 12 master's awarded. *Degree requirements:* For master's, 2 foreign languages, comprehensive exam (for some programs); for M Div, 2 foreign languages. *Entrance requirements:* For M Div and master's, 2 references. Additional exam requirements/recommendations for international students: Required—TOEFL (minimum score 570 paper-based; 230 computer-based). *Application deadline:* For fall admission, 8/14 priority date for domestic students; for spring admission, 12/31 for domestic students. Applications are processed on a rolling basis. Application fee: $0 ($75 for international students). Electronic applications accepted. *Expenses:* Tuition: Part-time $599 per semester hour. *Financial support:* Scholarships/grants available. Support available to part-time students. Financial award application deadline: 3/1; financial award applicants required to submit FAFSA. *Faculty research:* Status of Churches of Christ in foreign nations, Hebrew grammar, marriage and family. *Unit head:* Dr. Mark Black, Director, 615-966-1000 Ext. 5799, Fax: 615-966-1808, E-mail: mark.black@lipscomb.edu. *Application contact:* Audrey Everson, Information Contact, 615-966-6051, Fax: 615-966-6052, E-mail: audrey.everson@lipscomb.edu.

Logos Evangelical Seminary, Graduate Programs, El Monte, CA 91731. Offers M Div, MA, Th M, D Min. *Accreditation:* ATS (one or more programs are accredited). Part-time programs available. *Faculty:* 11 full-time (2 women), 9 part-time/adjunct (1 woman). *Students:* 69 full-time (33 women), 59 part-time (25 women); includes 127 minority (all Asian Americans or Pacific Islanders) In 2007, 15 first professional degrees, 7 master's, 4 doctorates awarded. *Median time to degree:* Of those who began their doctoral program in fall 1999, 60% received their degree in 8 years or less. *Degree requirements:* For master's, comprehensive exam, thesis; for doctorate, thesis/dissertation. *Entrance requirements:* For M Div, BA with a minimum GPA of 2.66, 2 recommendations, 3 years post-baptism; for master's, MA in biblical studies with a minimum GPA of 3.33, 1.5 year of a biblical language, 2 recommendations, 1 research paper; for doctorate, M Div with a minimum GPA of 3.0, 3 years ministry experience, 2 recommendations. Additional exam requirements/recommendations for international students: Required—TOEFL (minimum score 450 paper-based; 133 computer-based; 45 iBT). *Application deadline:* For fall admission, 7/15 for domestic students, 5/15 for international students; for spring admission, 12/15 for domestic students, 10/15 for international students. Applications are processed on a rolling basis. Application fee: $25 ($50 for international students). Electronic applications accepted. *Expenses:* Tuition: Full-time $8,000; part-time $250 per unit. Tuition and fees vary according to degree level. *Financial support:* Application deadline: 3/1. *Faculty research:* Asian-American hermaneutics, narrative theology, Biblical application on Song of Songs. *Unit head:* Dr. Jeffrey Lu, Academic Dean, 626-571-5110 Ext. 26, Fax: 626-571-5119, E-mail: jefl@les.edu. *Application contact:* Becky Perng, Admission Officer, 626-571-5110 Ext. 12, Fax: 626-571-5119, E-mail: admission@les.edu.

Loras College, Graduate Division, Program in Theology and Ministry, Dubuque, IA 52004-0178. Offers ministry (MA); theology (MA). Part-time and evening/weekend programs available. *Faculty:* 2 full-time (0 women). *Students:* 2 full-time (1 woman), 23 part-time (20 women), 1 international. Average age 45. 8 applicants, 88% accepted, 7 enrolled. In 2007, 10 degrees awarded. *Degree requirements:* For master's, comprehensive exam (for some programs), thesis (for some programs). *Entrance requirements:* For master's, bachelor's degree or undergraduate minor in religious studies or equivalent, minimum undergraduate GPA of 2.75. *Application deadline:* Applications are processed on a rolling basis. Application fee: $25. *Expenses:* Tuition: Full-time $7,920; part-time $440 per credit. *Financial support:* Applicants required to submit FAFSA. *Unit head:* Dr. Douglas Wathier, Graduate Coordinator, 563-588-7013, E-mail: douglas.wathier@loras.edu. *Application contact:* Graduate Admissions Coordinator, 563-588-7139, Fax: 563-588-4962.

Louisville Presbyterian Theological Seminary, Graduate and Professional Programs, Louisville, KY 40205-1798. Offers Bible (MAR); divinity (M Div); ministry (D Min); religious thought (MAR); theology (Th M); JD/M Div; M Div/MBA; M Div/MS; M Div/MSW. *Accreditation:* AAMFT/COAMFTE (one or more programs are accredited); ACIPE; ATS (one or more programs are accredited). Part-time programs available. *Faculty:* 21 full-time (10 women), 30 part-time/adjunct (11 women). *Students:* 148 full-time (81 women), 62 part-time (34 women); includes 37 minority (30 African Americans, 1 American Indian/Alaska Native, 2 Asian Americans or Pacific Islanders, 4 Hispanic Americans), 7 international. Average age 37. 121 applicants, 78% accepted, 62 enrolled. In 2007, 22 first professional degrees, 10 master's, 6 doctorates awarded. *Degree requirements:* For master's, one foreign language; for doctorate, thesis/dissertation; for M Div, 2 foreign languages. *Entrance requirements:* For master's, interview; for doctorate, M Div. Additional exam requirements/recommendations for international students: Required—TOEFL (minimum score 550 paper-based; 213 computer-based). *Application deadline:* For fall admission, 6/15 priority date for domestic students, 6/1 priority date for international students; for spring admission, 11/15 priority date for domestic and international students. Applications are processed on a rolling basis. Application fee: $60. Electronic applications accepted. *Expenses:* Tuition: Full-time $9,300; part-time $310 per credit. Required fees: $227. *Financial support:* Career-related internships or fieldwork, Federal Work-Study, institutionally sponsored loans, and scholarships/grants available. Financial award application deadline: 4/15; financial award applicants required to submit CSS PROFILE or FAFSA. *Unit head:* Dr. David Hester, Dean, 502-895-3411 Ext. 294, Fax: 502-895-1096, E-mail: dhester@lpts.edu. *Application contact:* Cheri Harper, Director of Admissions, 502-895-3411 Ext. 371, Fax: 502-895-1096, E-mail: charper@lpts.edu.

Loyola Marymount University, Graduate Division, College of Liberal Arts, Department of Theological Studies, Program in Theology, Los Angeles, CA 90045-2659. Offers MA. *Accreditation:* ATS. *Faculty:* 22 full-time (6 women), 8 part-time/adjunct (1 woman). *Students:* 22 full-time (13 women), 19 part-time (6 women); includes 13 minority (2 African Americans, 4 Asian Americans or Pacific Islanders, 7 Hispanic Americans), 2 international. Average age 37. 13 applicants, 54% accepted, 7 enrolled. In 2007, 9 degrees awarded. *Degree requirements:* For master's, one foreign language, comprehensive exam, thesis or alternative. *Entrance requirements:* For master's, GRE General Test. Additional exam requirements/recommendations for international students: Required—TOEFL (minimum score 600 paper-based; 250 computer-based). *Application deadline:* For fall admission, 5/1 priority date for domestic students; for spring admission, 11/15 priority date for domestic students. Application fee: $50. Electronic applications accepted. *Financial support:* In 2007–08, 32 students received support, including 4 research assistantships (averaging $12,370 per year); Federal Work-Study, scholarships/grants, and unspecified assistantships also available. Support available to part-time students. Financial award application deadline: 6/1; financial award applicants required to submit FAFSA.

Theology

Loyola Marymount University (continued)

Unit head: Dr. Douglas S. Burton-Christie, Director, Department of Theological Studies, 310-338-1921, Fax: 310-338-1948, E-mail: dburton@lmu.edu.

Loyola University Chicago, Graduate School, Department of Theology, Chicago, IL 60611-2196. Offers MA, PhD. Part-time and evening/weekend programs available. *Faculty:* 23 full-time (9 women). *Students:* 74 full-time (23 women), 13 part-time (4 women); includes 5 minority (2 African Americans, 3 Hispanic Americans), 10 international. Average age 36. 84 applicants, 55% accepted, 14 enrolled. In 2007, 12 master's, 3 doctorates awarded. Terminal master's awarded for partial completion of doctoral program. *Degree requirements:* For master's, comprehensive exam; for doctorate, 2 foreign languages, comprehensive exam, thesis/dissertation. *Entrance requirements:* For master's, GRE General Test, minimum GPA of 3.0, 9 hours of course work in theology; for doctorate, GRE General Test, minimum GPA of 3.0, master's degree or equivalent. Additional exam requirements/recommendations for international students: Required—TOEFL. *Application deadline:* For fall admission, 1/15 for domestic students; for spring admission, 12/1 for domestic students. Application fee: $50. Electronic applications accepted. *Expenses:* Tuition: Full-time $12,780; part-time $710 per credit hour. Required fees: $55 per semester. Full-time tuition and fees vary according to program. *Financial support:* In 2007–08, 12 research assistantships (averaging $14,000 per year) were awarded; fellowships, teaching assistantships, institutionally sponsored loans also available. Financial award application deadline: 1/15; financial award applicants required to submit FAFSA. *Faculty research:* Systematics, historical theology, constructive theology, scripture, theological ethics. *Unit head:* Dr. Susan Ross, Department Chair, 773-508-2364, Fax: 773-508-2386, E-mail: sross@luc.edu. *Application contact:* Dr. Robert A. Divito, Graduate Program Director, 773-508-8453, Fax: 773-508-2386, E-mail: rdivito@luc.edu.

Loyola University Chicago, Institute of Pastoral Studies, Professional Program in Divinity, Chicago, IL 60611-2196. Offers M Div, M Div/MA, M Div/MSN, M Div/MSW. *Accreditation:* ACIPE. *Faculty:* 8 full-time (2 women), 26 part-time/adjunct (12 women). *Students:* 16 full-time (8 women), 6 part-time (5 women); includes 2 minority (1 African American, 1 Hispanic American). Average age 30. 13 applicants, 85% accepted, 6 enrolled. In 2007, 3 degrees awarded. *Degree requirements:* For M Div, project, CPE. *Entrance requirements:* Minimum GPA of 3.0, 1 year of ministry experience. Additional exam requirements/recommendations for international students: Required—TOEFL. *Application deadline:* For fall admission, 8/1 priority date for domestic students; for spring admission, 12/1 priority date for domestic students. Applications are processed on a rolling basis. Application fee: $50. Electronic applications accepted. *Expenses: Contact institution.* Full-time tuition and fees vary according to program. *Financial support:* In 2007–08, 9 students received support. Career-related internships or fieldwork, Federal Work-Study, institutionally sponsored loans, and scholarships/grants available. Support available to part-time students. Financial award application deadline: 2/1; financial award applicants required to submit FAFSA. *Faculty research:* Women leadership development for professionals in ministry, religious memoirs, passing on the values of Jesus, justice. *Unit head:* Dr. Robert T. O'Gorman, Professor, 312-915-7485, Fax: 312-915-7410, E-mail: rogorma@luc.edu.

Loyola University Chicago, Institute of Pastoral Studies, Program in Pastoral Counseling, Chicago, IL 60611-2196. Offers pastoral counseling (MA); pastoral studies (MA); spiritual development (Certificate); M Div/MA. *Accreditation:* ACIPE. Part-time programs available. *Faculty:* 6 full-time (2 women), 12 part-time/adjunct (7 women). *Students:* 47 full-time (31 women), 20 part-time (14 women); includes 9 minority (5 African Americans, 1 Asian American or Pacific Islander, 3 Hispanic Americans), 5 international. Average age 43. 31 applicants, 77% accepted, 17 enrolled. In 2007, 13 degrees awarded. *Degree requirements:* For master's, thesis or alternative, integration project. *Application deadline:* For fall admission, 2/15 priority date for domestic students. Applications are processed on a rolling basis. Application fee: $50. Electronic applications accepted. *Expenses:* Tuition: Full-time $12,780; part-time $710 per credit hour. Required fees: $55 per semester. Full-time tuition and fees vary according to program. *Financial support:* In 2007–08, 7 students received support. Career-related internships or fieldwork, Federal Work-Study, and institutionally sponsored loans available. Support available to part-time students. Financial award application deadline: 3/1; financial award applicants required to submit FAFSA. *Faculty research:* Pastoral psychotherapy, enrichment outcome, marriage and family therapy, marriage and family spirituality, gender and ethnicity issues, theological anthropology. *Unit head:* Dr. Paul R. Giblin, Associate Professor, 312-915-7483, Fax: 312-915-7410, E-mail: pgibli@luc.edu.

Loyola University New Orleans, College of Social Sciences, Loyola Institute for Ministry, New Orleans, LA 70118-6195. Offers pastoral studies (MPS); religious education (MRE); theology and ministry (Certificate). Part-time and evening/weekend programs available. Postbaccalaureate distance learning degree programs offered (no on-campus study). *Students:* 13 full-time (1 woman), 329 part-time (238 women); includes 49 minority (17 African Americans, 1 American Indian/Alaska Native, 2 Asian Americans or Pacific Islanders, 29 Hispanic Americans), 1 international. Average age 48. 82 applicants, 100% accepted. In 2007, 114 degrees awarded. *Entrance requirements:* For master's, minimum GPA of 2.5, resumé, 2 letters of recommendation, transcript, essay, work experience. Additional exam requirements/recommendations for international students: Required—TOEFL (minimum score 550 paper-based; 213 computer-based). *Application deadline:* Applications are processed on a rolling basis. Application fee: $20. Electronic applications accepted. *Financial support:* Career-related internships or fieldwork, scholarships/grants, health care benefits, tuition waivers (partial), and room and board assistance available. Support available to part-time students. Financial award application deadline: 5/1; financial award applicants required to submit FAFSA. *Faculty research:* Practical theology, ministry education, small Christian communities, religion and ecology, Christian spirituality. *Unit head:* Dr. Tom Ryan, Director, 504-865-2069, Fax: 504-865-2066, E-mail: tfryan@loyno.edu. *Application contact:* Dr. Cecelia M. Bennett, Associate Director, 504-865-3728, Fax: 504-865-2066, E-mail: abennett@loyno.edu.

Lubbock Christian University, Graduate Biblical Studies, Lubbock, TX 79407-2099. Offers Bible and ministry (MS); biblical interpretation (MA). Part-time programs available. *Degree requirements:* For master's, one foreign language, thesis (for some programs). *Entrance requirements:* For master's, GRE General Test or MAT. *Faculty research:* Commentary on John, commentary on First and Second Thessalonians, mission teams, church leadership, family systems.

Lutheran School of Theology at Chicago, Graduate and Professional Programs, Chicago, IL 60615-5199. Offers ministry (D Min); ministry, pastoral care, and counseling (D Min PCC); theological studies (MA, PhD); theology (M Div, Th M). *Accreditation:* ACIPE; ATS (one or more programs are accredited). Part-time programs available. *Faculty:* 22 full-time, 15 part-time/adjunct. *Students:* 177 full-time, 188 part-time. Terminal master's awarded for partial completion of doctoral program. *Degree requirements:* For master's, variable foreign language requirement; for doctorate, variable foreign language requirement, thesis/dissertation. *Entrance requirements:* For master's, GRE (Th M), M Div or equivalent (Th M); for doctorate, GRE, M Div or equivalent, 3 years of professional experience (D Min, D Min PCC). Additional exam requirements/recommendations for international students: Required—TOEFL, TOEFL (Th M). *Application deadline:* Applications are processed on a rolling basis. Application fee: $50. *Expenses:* Tuition: Full-time $10,890. Part-time tuition and fees vary according to degree level. *Financial support:* Career-related internships or fieldwork and scholarships/grants available. Support available to part-time students. *Unit head:* Dr. Kathleen Billman, Dean, 773-256-0721, Fax: 773-256-0782, E-mail: kbillman@lstc.edu. *Application contact:* Dorothy C. Dominiak, Assistant Director of Admissions and Financial Aid, 773-256-0726, Fax: 773-256-0782, E-mail: ddominia@lstc.edu.

Lutheran Theological Seminary, Graduate and Professional Programs, Saskatoon, SK S7N 0X3, Canada. Offers history (MTS, STM); New Testament (MTS, STM); Old Testament (MTS, STM); pastoral counseling (MTS, STM); systematics (MTS, STM). *Accreditation:* ATS. Part-time programs available. *Degree requirements:* For master's, thesis; for M Div, Greek, Hebrew.

Lutheran Theological Seminary at Gettysburg, Graduate and Professional Programs, Gettysburg, PA 17325-1795. Offers divinity (M Div); ministerial studies (MAMS); outdoor ministry (MAR); parish ministry (D Min); theology (STM). *Accreditation:* ACIPE; ATS (one or more programs are accredited). Part-time programs available. Postbaccalaureate distance learning degree programs offered (no on-campus study). *Degree requirements:* For master's, thesis (for some programs); for M Div, one foreign language. Electronic applications accepted.

The Lutheran Theological Seminary at Philadelphia, Graduate School, Philadelphia, PA 19119-1794. Offers divinity (M Div); ministry (D Min); religion (MAR); social ministry (Certificate); theology (STM). *Accreditation:* ACIPE; ATS. Part-time and evening/weekend programs available. *Faculty:* 22 full-time (6 women), 26 part-time/adjunct (11 women). *Students:* 144 full-time (74 women), 263 part-time (127 women); includes 92 minority (80 African Americans, 2 Asian Americans or Pacific Islanders, 10 Hispanic Americans), 14 international. Average age 43. 123 applicants, 86% accepted, 84 enrolled. In 2007, 44 first professional degrees, 10 master's, 15 doctorates awarded. *Median time to degree:* Of those who began their doctoral program in fall 1999, 70% received their degree in 8 years or less. *Degree requirements:* For master's, one foreign language, comprehensive exam (for some programs), thesis (for some programs); for doctorate, thesis/dissertation; for M Div, 2 foreign languages. *Entrance requirements:* For M Div and master's, minimum undergraduate GPA of 2.8; for doctorate, minimum first professional GPA of 3.0. Additional exam requirements/recommendations for international students: Required—TOEFL (minimum score 550 paper-based; 213 computer-based), TWE. *Application deadline:* For fall admission, 6/1 priority date for domestic students. Applications are processed on a rolling basis. Application fee: $35. Electronic applications accepted. *Expenses:* Tuition: Part-time $1,260 per unit. Part-time tuition and fees vary according to program. *Financial support:* In 2007–08, 102 students received support, including 1 research assistantship with tuition reimbursement available (averaging $2,250 per year), 3 teaching assistantships with tuition reimbursements available (averaging $1,200 per year); career-related internships or fieldwork and Federal Work-Study also available. Financial award application deadline: 7/1; financial award applicants required to submit FAFSA. *Unit head:* Dr. J. Paul Rajashekar, Dean, 215-248-6379, Fax: 215-248-4577, E-mail: rajashekar@ltsp.edu. *Application contact:* Rev. Louise Johnson, Director of Admissions, 800-286-4616 Ext. 6321, Fax: 215-248-7315, E-mail: admissions@ltsp.edu.

Lutheran Theological Southern Seminary, Graduate and Professional Programs, Columbia, SC 29203. Offers M Div, MAR, STM, D Min. *Accreditation:* ACIPE; ATS. Part-time programs available. *Degree requirements:* For master's, comprehensive exam (for some programs), thesis (for some programs); for M Div, 2 foreign languages. *Faculty research:* Theology in 21st century, Biblical interpretation.

Luther Rice University, Graduate Programs, Lithonia, GA 30038-2454. Offers Bible/theology (M Div); Christian education (M Div); Christian studies (MA); church ministry (D Min); counseling (M Div); discipleship counseling (MA); ministry (M Div, MA); missions/evangelism (M Div). Part-time programs available. Postbaccalaureate distance learning degree programs offered (no on-campus study). *Degree requirements:* For doctorate, thesis/dissertation. *Entrance requirements:* Additional exam requirements/recommendations for international students: Required—TOEFL (minimum score 500 paper-based; 173 computer-based).

Luther Seminary, Graduate and Professional Programs, St. Paul, MN 55108-1445. Offers M Div, M Th, MA, MSM, D Min, PhD. *Accreditation:* ACIPE; ATS. *Faculty:* 46. *Students:* 830, 48 international. Average age 30. *Degree requirements:* For master's, thesis or alternative; for doctorate, 2 foreign languages, thesis/dissertation; for M Div, 2 foreign languages, 1 year internship. *Entrance requirements:* For M Div, minimum GPA of 3.0; for master's, minimum GPA of 2.8; for doctorate, GRE General Test. *Application deadline:* For fall admission, 7/1 priority date for domestic students. Applications are processed on a rolling basis. Application fee: $50. Electronic applications accepted. *Expenses:* Tuition: Part-time $1,020 per course. Tuition and fees vary according to degree level and program. *Financial support:* Career-related internships or fieldwork, Federal Work-Study, institutionally sponsored loans, and scholarships/grants available. Support available to part-time students. Financial award application deadline: 6/1; financial award applicants required to submit FAFSA. *Faculty research:* Theology, psychology (pastoral care), church history, Bible, Islamic studies. *Unit head:* Dr. David Lose, Dean of Academic Affairs, 651-641-3471, Fax: 651-641-1609, E-mail: dlose@luthersem.edu. *Application contact:* Ron Olson, Director of Admissions, 612-641-3521, Fax: 612-641-3497, E-mail: rdolson@luthersem.edu.

Machzikei Hadath Rabbinical College, Graduate Programs, Brooklyn, NY 11204-1805. Offers First Talmudic Degree. *Accreditation:* AARTS.

Madonna University, Program in Religious Studies, Livonia, MI 48150-1173. Offers pastoral ministry (MA).

Malone College, School of Theology, Graduate Program in Christian Ministries, Canton, OH 44709-3897. Offers Christian leadership in sports ministry (MA); Christian ministries (MA); leadership in the Christian church (MA). Part-time and evening/weekend programs available. *Faculty:* 5 full-time (1 woman), 6 part-time/adjunct (1 woman). *Students:* 7 full-time (3 women), 30 part-time (9 women); includes 7 minority (4 African Americans, 1 American Indian/Alaska Native, 1 Asian American or Pacific Islander, 1 Hispanic American). Average age 41. In 2007, 14 degrees awarded. *Entrance requirements:* For master's, minimum GPA of 3.0. *Application deadline:* Applications are processed on a rolling basis. Application fee: $25. *Expenses: Contact institution.* Part-time tuition and fees vary according to program. *Financial support:* Tuition waivers (partial) and unspecified assistantships available. Support available to part-time students. Financial award application deadline: 6/30. *Faculty research:* The Book of Ezekiel, Jeremiah and Lamentations, socio-rhetorical criticism, Pauline Theology, Theological Hermeneutics. *Unit head:* Dr. Joel R. Soza, Director, 330-471-8217, Fax: 330-471-8478, E-mail: jsoza@malone.edu. *Application contact:* Dr. David L. Kleffman, Assistant Director of Graduate Admissions, 330-471-8447, Fax: 330-471-8343, E-mail: dkleffman@malone.edu.

Maple Springs Baptist Bible College and Seminary, Graduate and Professional Programs, Capitol Heights, MD 20743. Offers biblical studies (MA, Certificate); Christian counseling (MA); church administration (MA); divinity (M Div); ministry (D Min); religious education (MA).

Maranatha Baptist Bible College, Program in Biblical Studies, Watertown, WI 53094. Offers MA. Part-time programs available. Postbaccalaureate distance learning degree programs offered (minimal on-campus study). *Faculty:* 5 full-time (0 women), 2 part-time/adjunct (0 women). *Students:* 14 full-time (0 women), 10 part-time. Average age 27. 11 applicants, 82% accepted, 9 enrolled. In 2007, 6 degrees awarded. *Degree requirements:* For master's, one foreign language, fieldwork. *Application deadline:* Applications are processed on a rolling basis. Application fee: $40. *Expenses:* Tuition: Full-time $3,360; part-time $210 per credit. Required fees: $300; $19 per credit. *Financial support:* In 2007–08, 8 students received support. Scholarships/grants and tuition waivers (full and partial) available. Support available to part-time students. *Faculty research:* Bible structure, counseling techniques, church history. *Unit head:* Dr. Larry Oats, Chair of Graduate School of Theology, 920-206-2324, Fax: 920-261-9109, E-mail: loats@mbbc.edu. *Application contact:* Dr. Jim Harrison, Director of Admissions, 920-206-2327, Fax: 920-261-9109, E-mail: admissions@mbbc.edu.

Maranatha Baptist Bible College, Program in Theology, Watertown, WI 53094. Offers MA. *Faculty:* 5 full-time (0 women), 2 part-time/adjunct (0 women). *Students:* 2 full-time (0 women), 1 part-time. Average age 27. 1 applicant, 100% accepted, 1 enrolled. *Expenses:* Tuition: Full-time $3,360; part-time $210 per credit. Required fees: $300; $19 per credit. *Unit head:* Dr. Larry Oats, Chair of Graduate School of Theology, 920-206-2324, Fax: 920-261-9109, E-mail: loats@mbbc.edu. *Application contact:* Dr. Jim Harrison, Director of Admissions, 920-206-2327, Fax: 920-261-9109, E-mail: admissions@mbbc.edu.

Marquette University, Graduate School, College of Arts and Sciences, Department of Theology, Milwaukee, WI 53201-1881. Offers ethics (PhD); historical theology (MA, PhD); religious studies (PhD), including scriptural theology (MA, PhD); systematic theology (MA, PhD); theology

(MA), including scriptural theology (MA, PhD); theology and society (PhD). Part-time programs available. *Faculty:* 32 full-time (7 women), 18 part-time/adjunct (2 women). *Students:* 83 full-time (21 women), 52 part-time (17 women); includes 7 minority (3 African Americans, 2 Asian Americans or Pacific Islanders, 2 Hispanic Americans), 11 international. Average age 36. 156 applicants, 38% accepted, 21 enrolled. In 2007, 3 master's, 7 doctorates awarded. Terminal master's awarded for partial completion of doctoral program. *Degree requirements:* For master's, one foreign language, comprehensive exam, thesis or alternative; for doctorate, 2 foreign languages, thesis/dissertation, qualifying exam. *Entrance requirements:* For master's and doctorate, GRE General Test. Additional exam requirements/recommendations for international students: Required—TOEFL. Application fee: $40. *Financial support:* In 2007–08, 5 fellowships, 5 research assistantships, 14 teaching assistantships were awarded; Federal Work-Study, institutionally sponsored loans, scholarships/grants, and tuition waivers (full and partial) also available. Support available to part-time students. Financial award application deadline: 2/15. *Faculty research:* Old Testament theology, New Testament theology, church history, Christian ethics. Total annual research expenditures: $81,775. *Unit head:* Rev. John Laurance, Acting Chair, 414-288-7170, Fax: 414-288-5548. *Application contact:* Dr. Christine Hinze, Director of Graduate Studies, 414-288-6802.

Marylhurst University, Department of Religious StudiesûApplied Theology Program, Marylhurst, OR 97036-0261. Offers applied theology (MA). Part-time and evening/weekend programs available. *Faculty:* 1 full-time (0 women), 12 part-time/adjunct (6 women). *Students:* 2 full-time (1 woman), 32 part-time (25 women). Average age 45. In 2007, 5 degrees awarded. *Degree requirements:* For master's, thesis. *Entrance requirements:* For master's, MAT, resumé, 3 letters of recommendation, interview, autobiography, personal statement. Additional exam requirements/recommendations for international students: Recommended—TOEFL (minimum score 530 paper-based). *Application deadline:* For fall admission, 6/30 priority date for domestic students; for winter admission, 11/30 priority date for domestic students; for spring admission, 3/30 priority date for domestic students. Applications are processed on a rolling basis. Application fee: $40 ($50 for international students). Electronic applications accepted. *Expenses:* Tuition: Part-time $419 per credit. One-time fee: $85 part-time. Tuition and fees vary according to course load and program. *Financial support:* Fellowships, research assistantships, teaching assistantships, Federal Work-Study and scholarships/grants available. Support available to part-time students. Financial award applicants required to submit FAFSA. *Faculty research:* Pastoral care, scripture, world religions. *Unit head:* Dr. Jerry Roussell, Chair, 503-636-8141, Fax: 503-697-5597, E-mail: jroussell@marylhurst.edu. *Application contact:* Kathleen Schneff, Admissions Specialist, 800-634-9982 Ext. 3322, Fax: 503-635-6585, E-mail: admissions@marylhurst.edu.

Marylhurst University, Department of Religious StudiesûDivinity Program, Marylhurst, OR 97036-0261. Offers M Div. Part-time and evening/weekend programs available. *Faculty:* 1 full-time (0 women), 12 part-time/adjunct (6 women). *Students:* 9 full-time (8 women), 23 part-time (20 women). Average age 47. In 2007, 3 degrees awarded. *Degree requirements:* For M Div, thesis/dissertation. *Entrance requirements:* MAT, resumé, 3 letters of recommendation, interview. *Application deadline:* For fall admission, 6/30 for domestic students; for winter admission, 11/30 for domestic students; for spring admission, 3/30 for domestic students. Applications are processed on a rolling basis. Application fee: $40 ($50 for international students). Electronic applications accepted. *Expenses:* Tuition: Part-time $419 per credit. One-time fee: $85 part-time. Tuition and fees vary according to course load and program. *Financial support:* Fellowships, research assistantships, teaching assistantships, Federal Work-Study and scholarships/grants available. Support available to part-time students. *Faculty research:* Scripture-biblical studies, theology, history, ministry, spirituality. *Unit head:* Dr. Jerry Roussell, Chair, 503-636-8141, Fax: 503-697-5597, E-mail: jroussell@marylhurst.edu. *Application contact:* Kathleen Schneff, Admissions Specialist, 800-634-9982 Ext. 3322, Fax: 503-635-6585, E-mail: admissions@marylhurst.edu.

The Master's College and Seminary, The Master's Seminary, Santa Clarita, CA 91321-1200. Offers biblical counseling (MABC); New Testament (Th D); Old Testament (Th D); preaching (D Min); theology (M Div, M Th, Th D). Part-time programs available. *Faculty:* 18 full-time (0 women), 11 part-time/adjunct (0 women). *Students:* 200 full-time (0 women), 168 part-time; includes 58 minority (9 African Americans, 35 Asian Americans or Pacific Islanders, 14 Hispanic Americans), 30 international. Average age 28. 136 applicants, 82% accepted, 80 enrolled. In 2007, 60 first professional degrees, 9 master's, 11 doctorates awarded. *Degree requirements:* For master's, 2 foreign languages, thesis; for doctorate, 4 foreign languages, thesis/dissertation; for M Div, 2 foreign languages, thesis/dissertation. *Entrance requirements:* For M Div, minimum 2 years of college; for master's, minimum GPA of 2.75; for doctorate, Th M, minimum GPA of 3.5. Additional exam requirements/recommendations for international students: Required—TOEFL (minimum score 550 paper-based). *Application deadline:* For fall admission, 6/1 priority date for domestic and international students; for winter admission, 10/1 priority date for domestic and international students; for spring admission, 1/1 for domestic and international students. Applications are processed on a rolling basis. Application fee: $30. *Expenses:* Tuition: Full-time $8,000; part-time $300 per unit. Required fees: $370. One-time fee: $100 full-time. Tuition and fees vary according to program. *Financial support:* In 2007–08, 121 students received support, including 10 teaching assistantships (averaging $4,000 per year); career-related internships or fieldwork, scholarships/grants, and tuition waivers (partial) also available. Support available to part-time students. Financial award application deadline: 6/1; financial award applicants required to submit FAFSA. *Unit head:* Dr. Richard L. Mayhue, Senior Vice President and Dean, 818-782-6488 Ext. 5632, E-mail: mayhue@tms.edu. *Application contact:* Ray Mehringer, Director of Admissions and Placement, 818-792-6488, Fax: 818-909-5725, E-mail: rmehringer@tms.edu.

McCormick Theological Seminary, Graduate and Professional Programs, Chicago, IL 60615. Offers ministry (D Min); theological studies (MATS, Certificate); theology (M Div); M Div/MSW. *Accreditation:* ACIPE; ATS (one or more programs are accredited). Part-time and evening/weekend programs available. *Degree requirements:* For master's, thesis (for some programs); for doctorate, thesis/dissertation. *Entrance requirements:* For M Div and master's, minimum GPA of 3.0; for doctorate, M Div, minimum 3 years in pastorate. *Faculty research:* Faith formation, families, biblical literature, Dead Sea scrolls, women in antiquity.

McGill University, Faculty of Graduate and Postdoctoral Studies, Faculty of Religious Studies, Montréal, QC H3A 2T5, Canada. Offers MA, STM, PhD. *Accreditation:* ATS. *Faculty:* 15 full-time (4 women), 26 part-time/adjunct (9 women). *Students:* 59 full-time (21 women), 9 part-time. 63 applicants, 52% accepted, 11 enrolled. In 2007, 8 master's, 5 doctorates awarded.

McMaster University, McMaster Divinity College, Hamilton, ON L8S 4M2, Canada. Offers biblical studies (M Div); Biblical studies (MA, MTS, Diploma); Christian interpretation/history (M Div, MA, MTS, Diploma); Christian ministry (M Div, MA, MTS, Diploma); Christian Studies (Certificate); Christian theology (PhD). Affiliated with the Toronto School of Theology. *Accreditation:* ATS. Part-time programs available. *Degree requirements:* For master's, one foreign language, thesis optional; for doctorate, 3 foreign languages, comprehensive exam, thesis/dissertation; for other advanced degree, 2 foreign languages, thesis. *Entrance requirements:* For master's, minimum B average in undergraduate course work, 3 letters of reference; for doctorate, minimum B+ average in bachelor's and master's, appropriate modern/ancient language, interview; for other advanced degree, 6 units of related Biblical language, minimum B+ average in undergraduate course work, minimum 15 units of course work in related area of study, 3 letters of recommendation. Additional exam requirements/recommendations for international students: Required—TOEFL (minimum score 550 paper-based; 237 computer-based). *Faculty research:* Ethics, Biblical studies, language studies, church history, Christian ministry.

Meadville Lombard Theological School, Graduate and Professional Programs, Chicago, IL 60637-1602. Offers divinity (M Div); ministry (D Min); religion (MA); M Div/MSW. *Accreditation:* ACIPE; ATS. Part-time programs available. Postbaccalaureate distance learning degree programs offered (minimal on-campus study). *Faculty:* 3 full-time (2 women), 15 part-time/adjunct (6 women). *Students:* 37 full-time (21 women), 31 part-time (19 women); includes 7 minority (2 African Americans, 1 American Indian/Alaska Native, 4 Hispanic Americans), 3 international. Average age 45. 41 applicants, 68% accepted, 17 enrolled. In 2007, 22 first professional degrees, 2 master's, 2 doctorates awarded. *Median time to degree:* Of those who began their doctoral program in fall 1999, 100% received their degree in 8 years or less. *Entrance requirements:* For M Div and master's, bachelor's degree; for doctorate, bachelor's and masters degrees, 3 years of ministry. *Application deadline:* For fall admission, 3/1 priority date for domestic students. Applications are processed on a rolling basis. Application fee: $45. *Financial support:* Career-related internships or fieldwork, Federal Work-Study, institutionally sponsored loans, scholarships/grants, health care benefits, and tuition waivers (full and partial) available. Support available to part-time students. Financial award application deadline: 3/15; financial award applicants required to submit FAFSA. *Unit head:* Rev. Lee C. Barker, President, 773-256-3000, Fax: 773-753-1323. *Application contact:* E. Chavez, Director of Admissions, 773-256-3000 Ext. 0250, Fax: 773-753-1323, E-mail: echavez@meadville.edu.

Memphis Theological Seminary, Graduate and Professional Programs, Memphis, TN 38104-4395. Offers M Div, MAR, D Min. *Accreditation:* ATS. Part-time programs available. *Degree requirements:* For doctorate, thesis/dissertation. *Entrance requirements:* For doctorate, M Div, 3 years in ministry.

Mennonite Brethren Biblical Seminary, School of Theology, Program in Divinity, Fresno, CA 93727-5097. Offers M Div. *Accreditation:* ATS. *Students:* Average age 30. 37 applicants, 97% accepted, 23 enrolled. In 2007, 3 degrees awarded. *Degree requirements:* For M Div, one foreign language. *Application deadline:* For fall admission, 8/1 for domestic students; for spring admission, 12/1 for domestic students. Application fee: $35. *Financial support:* Application deadline: 5/1. *Application contact:* Andy Johnson, Director of Recruitment, 559-452-1714, Fax: 559-251-7212, E-mail: ajohnson@mbseminary.edu.

Mennonite Brethren Biblical Seminary, School of Theology, Programs in New Testament, Old Testament, and Theology, Fresno, CA 93727-5097. Offers New Testament (MA); Old Testament (MA); theology (MA). Part-time programs available. *Students:* Average age 36. 15 applicants, 93% accepted, 12 enrolled. In 2007, 2 degrees awarded. *Entrance requirements:* Additional exam requirements/recommendations for international students: Required—TOEFL (minimum score 550 paper-based; 213 computer-based). *Application deadline:* For fall admission, 8/1 for domestic students; for spring admission, 12/1 for domestic students. Application fee: $35. *Financial support:* Application deadline: 5/1. *Unit head:* Tim Geddert, Head, 559-452-1716. *Application contact:* Andy Johnson, Director of Recruitment, 559-452-1714, Fax: 559-251-7212, E-mail: ajohnson@mbseminary.edu.

Mercer University, Graduate Studies, Cecil B. Day Campus, James and Carolyn McAfee School of Theology, Macon, GA 31207-0003. Offers M Div, D Min. *Accreditation:* ATS.Part-time programs available. *Faculty:* 12 full-time (3 women), 7 part-time/adjunct (4 women). *Students:* 151 full-time (83 women), 84 part-time (40 women); includes 77 minority (74 African Americans, 3 Hispanic Americans), 4 international. Average age 35. 114 applicants, 78% accepted, 48 enrolled. In 2007, 42 degrees awarded. *Degree requirements:* For doctorate, thesis/dissertation, fieldwork, seminars; for M Div, 2 foreign languages. *Entrance requirements:* For M Div, letters of recommendation, minimum B+ average in undergraduate course work; for doctorate, MAT, minimum B+ average in undergraduate course work, letters of recommendation. *Application deadline:* Applications are processed on a rolling basis. Application fee: $35. *Expenses:* Contact institution. *Financial support:* In 2007–08, 30 students received support. Career-related internships or fieldwork, Federal Work-Study, institutionally sponsored loans, and scholarships/grants available. Support available to part-time students. Financial award applicants required to submit FAFSA. *Faculty research:* Biblical studies, Baptist heritage, Christian heritage, theology, pastoral care. *Unit head:* Dr. R. Alan Culpepper, Dean, 678-547-6470, Fax: 678-547-6478, E-mail: culpepper_ra@mercer.edu. *Application contact:* Ryan A. Clark, Director of Admissions, 678-547-6451, Fax: 678-547-6478, E-mail: clark_ra@mercer.edu.

Mesivta of Eastern Parkway Rabbinical Seminary, Graduate Programs, Brooklyn, NY 11218-5559. *Accreditation:* AARTS.

Mesivta Tifereth Jerusalem of America, Graduate Programs, New York, NY 10002-6301. *Accreditation:* AARTS.

Mesivta Torah Vodaath Rabbinical Seminary, Graduate Programs, Brooklyn, NY 11218-5299. *Accreditation:* AARTS.

Methodist Theological School in Ohio, Graduate and Professional Programs, Delaware, OH 43015-8004. Offers M Div, MACE, MACM, MTS, D Min, M Div/MACE, M Div/MACM, M Div/MTS. *Accreditation:* ACIPE; ATS. Part-time programs available. *Faculty:* 17 full-time (6 women), 19 part-time/adjunct (5 women). *Students:* 233 (127 women); includes 43 minority (33 African Americans, 1 American Indian/Alaska Native, 6 Asian Americans or Pacific Islanders, 3 Hispanic Americans) 5 international. 120 applicants, 77% accepted, 70 enrolled. In 2007, 38 first professional degrees, 20 master's awarded. *Entrance requirements:* For master's, official transcripts, 3 letters of recommendation. Additional exam requirements/recommendations for international students: Required—TOEFL (minimum score 577 paper-based; 233 computer-based; 90 iBT). *Application deadline:* For fall admission, 8/15 priority date for domestic students, 1/1 for international students; for spring admission, 7/1 for international students. Applications are processed on a rolling basis. Application fee: $35. *Expenses:* Tuition: Full-time $13,176; part-time $488 per credit hour. One-time fee: $135 full-time. Full-time tuition and fees vary according to course load. *Financial support:* Career-related internships or fieldwork, Federal Work-Study, institutionally sponsored loans, and scholarships/grants available. Support available to part-time students. Financial award application deadline: 4/1; financial award applicants required to submit FAFSA. *Unit head:* Rev. Jay A. Rundell, President, 740-362-3122, Fax: 740-362-3175, E-mail: jrundell@mtso.edu. *Application contact:* Molly Hoffman, Assistant Director of Admissions, 740-362-3373, Fax: 740-362-3135, E-mail: mhoffman@mtso.edu.

Michigan Theological Seminary, Graduate Programs, Plymouth, MI 48170. Offers Christian education (MA); counseling psychology (MA); divinity (M Div); expository communication (D Min); theological studies (MA). *Accreditation:* ATS. Part-time and evening/weekend programs available. *Degree requirements:* For master's, one foreign language, thesis; for doctorate, 2 foreign languages, thesis/dissertation; for M Div, 2 foreign languages. *Faculty research:* Judaism, cults, world religions.

Mid-America Baptist Theological Seminary, Graduate and Professional Programs, Cordova, TN 38016. Offers M Div, MACE, MCE, MM, D Min, PhD. *Degree requirements:* For doctorate, 4 foreign languages, thesis/dissertation; for M Div, 2 foreign languages. *Entrance requirements:* For doctorate, MAT. Additional exam requirements/recommendations for international students: Required—TOEFL (minimum score 600 paper-based; 250 computer-based). Electronic applications accepted.

Mid-America Baptist Theological Seminary Northeast Branch, Program in Theology, Schenectady, NY 12303-3463. Offers M Div. Part-time and evening/weekend programs available. *Faculty:* 5 full-time (0 women), 6 part-time/adjunct (1 woman). *Students:* 20 full-time (0 women), 23 part-time (1 woman); includes 3 minority (1 African American, 2 Asian Americans or Pacific Islanders), 1 international. In 2007, 2 degrees awarded. *Degree requirements:* For M Div, 2 foreign languages. *Entrance requirements:* Additional exam requirements/recommendations for international students: Required—TOEFL. *Application deadline:* For fall admission, 7/28 priority date for domestic students; for winter admission, 12/11 priority date for domestic students. Applications are processed on a rolling basis. Application fee: $25. Electronic applications accepted. *Expenses:* Tuition: Full-time $3,600; part-time $330 per course. *Unit head:* Dr. Timothy K. Christian, Interim Director, 518-355-9000 Ext. 21, Fax: 518-355-8298, E-mail: mjohn@mabtsne.edu. *Application contact:* Molly J. St. John, Administrative Assistant, 518-355-4000 Ext. 11, Fax: 518-355-8298, E-mail: mjohn@mabtsne.edu.

Theology

Mid-America Reformed Seminary, Graduate Programs, Dyer, IN 46311. Offers M Div, MTS. *Accreditation:* ATS. *Degree requirements:* For M Div, comprehensive exam. *Entrance requirements:* Additional exam requirements/recommendations for international students: Required—TOEFL (minimum score 550 paper-based). *Application deadline:* For fall admission, 5/1 for domestic students. Application fee: $15. *Expenses:* Tuition: Full-time $4,500; part-time $200 per hour. *Financial support:* Scholarships/grants available.

Midwestern Baptist Theological Seminary, Graduate and Professional Programs, Kansas City, MO 64118-4697. Offers Biblical studies (MA); Christian education (MACE); divinity/ministry (M Div); ministry (D Min); sacred music (MCM). *Accreditation:* ATS. Part-time programs available. Postbaccalaureate distance learning degree programs offered (minimal on-campus study). *Degree requirements:* For doctorate, thesis/dissertation; for M Div, 2 foreign languages. *Entrance requirements:* For doctorate, MAT. Electronic applications accepted. *Faculty research:* Ministerial studies, Biblical and theological studies, missions, counseling.

Midwest University, Graduate Programs, Wentzville, MO 63385. Offers social work (DSW); teaching English to speakers of other languages (MA); theology (M Div, MA, D Min). Part-time programs available. Postbaccalaureate distance learning degree programs offered (minimal on-campus study). *Faculty:* 16 full-time (2 women), 47 part-time/adjunct (10 women). *Students:* 210 full-time (61 women), 118 part-time (42 women); includes 2 African Americans, 23 Asian Americans or Pacific Islanders, 96 international. Average age 40. 40 applicants. In 2007, 17 first professional degrees, 11 master's, 14 doctorates awarded. *Degree requirements:* For master's, thesis (for some programs); for doctorate, thesis/dissertation; for M Div, thesis/dissertation (for some programs). *Entrance requirements:* Additional exam requirements/recommendations for international students: Recommended—TOEFL (minimum score 550 paper-based). Application fee: $100. *Financial support:* Federal Work-Study and scholarships/grants available. Financial award application deadline: 6/25; financial award applicants required to submit FAFSA. *Unit head:* Dr. Myeong Hwan Oh, Dean of Academic Affairs, 636-327-4645, Fax: 636-327-4715, E-mail: sta@midwest.edu. *Application contact:* Jeoung H. Ham, Director of Admissions, 636-327-4645, Fax: 636-327-4715, E-mail: reg@midwest.edu.

Mirrer Yeshiva, Graduate Programs, Brooklyn, NY 11223-2010. *Accreditation:* AARTS.

Moody Bible Institute, Graduate School, Chicago, IL 60610-3284. Offers biblical studies (MABS, Certificate); intercultural studies (MAIS); ministry (M Div, MA Min, MAUM); spiritual formation (MASF); teaching English to speakers of other languages (Certificate); urban ministry (MAUM). Part-time programs available. *Degree requirements:* For master's, 2 foreign languages, fieldwork (MABS); colloquium, field research project (MA Min). *Entrance requirements:* For master's, 30 hours in Bible/theology, 2 years of ministry experience (MA Min).

Moravian Theological Seminary, Graduate and Professional Programs, Bethlehem, PA 18018-6614. Offers M Div, MAPC, MATS. *Accreditation:* ACIPE; ATS (one or more programs are accredited). Part-time programs available. *Faculty:* 7 full-time (3 women), 11 part-time/adjunct (5 women). *Students:* 35 full-time (20 women), 53 part-time (40 women); includes 3 minority (all African Americans), 8 international. Average age 42. 28 applicants, 82% accepted, 20 enrolled. In 2007, 5 M Divs, 10 master's awarded. *Degree requirements:* For master's, thesis. *Entrance requirements:* Additional exam requirements/recommendations for international students: Required—TOEFL. *Application deadline:* For fall admission, 4/1 priority date for international students; for spring admission, 9/1 priority date for international students. Applications are processed on a rolling basis. Application fee: $25. *Expenses:* Tuition: Full-time $11,178; part-time $460 per credit. Required fees: $60; $30 per term. *Financial support:* In 2007–08, 68 students received support. Career-related internships or fieldwork, Federal Work-Study, and scholarships/grants available. Support available to part-time students. Financial award application deadline: 5/1; financial award applicants required to submit FAFSA. *Unit head:* Rev. Dr. Frank L. Crouch, Dean and Vice President, 610-861-1516. *Application contact:* Rev. Melissa L. Johnson, Director of Admissions and Student Life, 610-861-1525, Fax: 610-861-1569, E-mail: melissajohnson@moravian.edu.

Mount Angel Seminary, Program in Theology, Saint Benedict, OR 97373. Offers M Div, MA. *Accreditation:* ACIPE; ATS. Part-time programs available. *Degree requirements:* For master's, thesis optional.

Mount St. Mary's University, Graduate Seminary, Emmitsburg, MD 21727-7799. Offers M Div, MA. *Accreditation:* ATS. *Faculty:* 9 full-time (1 woman), 10 part-time/adjunct (2 women). *Students:* 149 full-time (0 women), 3 part-time; includes 13 minority (2 African Americans, 5 Asian Americans or Pacific Islanders, 6 Hispanic Americans), 18 international. Average age 30. 64 applicants, 92% accepted, 59 enrolled. In 2007, 21 first professional degrees, 9 master's awarded. *Degree requirements:* For master's, one foreign language, comprehensive exam, thesis, language proficiency exams. *Entrance requirements:* For M Div, 24 credits in philosophy; for master's, 18 credits of course work in philosophy. Additional exam requirements/recommendations for international students: Required—TOEFL (minimum score 550 paper-based; 213 computer-based). *Application deadline:* Applications are processed on a rolling basis. Application fee: $25. *Expenses: Contact institution.* Tuition and fees vary according to program. *Financial support:* In 2007–08, 58 students received support. Career-related internships or fieldwork and scholarships/grants available. Financial award applicants required to submit FAFSA. *Faculty research:* Mariology, biomedical ethics, Old Testament translations, Carolingian Church History, Patristic Theology. *Unit head:* Rev. Steven P. Rohlfs, Vice President/Rector, 301-447-5295, Fax: 301-447-5636, E-mail: rohlfs@msmary.edu. *Application contact:* Paula Smaldone, Seminary Admissions, 301-447-5295, Fax: 301-447-5636, E-mail: psmaldone@msmary.edu.

Mount Vernon Nazarene University, Program in Ministry, Mount Vernon, OH 43050-9500. Offers M Min. Part-time and evening/weekend programs available. *Degree requirements:* For master's, project. *Faculty research:* Pastoral effectiveness and professional development.

Multnomah Bible College and Biblical Seminary, Multnomah Biblical Seminary, Master of Divinity Program, Portland, OR 97220-5898. Offers M Div. *Accreditation:* ATS. Part-time programs available. *Faculty:* 8 full-time (0 women), 15 part-time/adjunct (4 women). *Students:* 101 full-time (9 women), 27 part-time (6 women); includes 14 minority (3 African Americans, 9 Asian Americans or Pacific Islanders, 2 Hispanic Americans), 9 international. Average age 32. 79 applicants, 78% accepted, 46 enrolled. In 2007, 25 degrees awarded. *Degree requirements:* For M Div, 2 foreign languages, thesis/dissertation (for some programs). *Entrance requirements:* Interview. Additional exam requirements/recommendations for international students: Required—TOEFL (minimum score 550 paper-based; 213 computer-based). *Application deadline:* For fall admission, 7/15 priority date for domestic and international students; for spring admission, 11/15 priority date for domestic and international students. Applications are processed on a rolling basis. Application fee: $40. *Financial support:* Career-related internships or fieldwork and scholarships/grants available. Support available to part-time students. Financial award application deadline: 7/15; financial award applicants required to submit FAFSA. *Application contact:* Penny Rader, Seminary Admissions Counselor, 503-251-6485, Fax: 503-254-1268, E-mail: admiss@multnomah.edu.

Multnomah Bible College and Biblical Seminary, Multnomah Biblical Seminary, Programs in Biblical Studies, Portland, OR 97220-5898. Offers MA, Certificate. *Accreditation:* ATS.Part-time programs available. *Faculty:* 8 full-time (0 women), 15 part-time/adjunct (4 women). *Students:* 10 full-time (2 women), 7 part-time (all women); includes 1 Hispanic American. Average age 33. 57 applicants, 95% accepted. In 2007, 5 master's, 33 other advanced degrees awarded. *Degree requirements:* For master's, thesis (for some programs). *Entrance requirements:* For master's, interview. Additional exam requirements/recommendations for international students: Required—TOEFL (minimum score 550 paper-based; 213 computer-based). *Application deadline:* For fall admission, 7/15 priority date for domestic and international students; for spring admission, 11/15 priority date for domestic and international students. Applications are processed on a rolling basis. Application fee: $40. *Financial support:* Career-related internships or fieldwork and scholarships/grants available. Support available to part-time students. Financial award application deadline: 7/15; financial award applicants required to submit FAFSA. *Faculty research:* Old Testament biblical theology, dispensational theology. *Application contact:* Penny Rader, Seminary Admissions Counselor, 503-251-6485, Fax: 503-254-1268, E-mail: admiss@multnomah.edu.

Naropa University, Graduate Programs, Program in Divinity, Boulder, CO 80302-6697. Offers M Div. *Faculty:* 6 full-time (2 women), 19 part-time/adjunct (8 women). *Students:* 19 full-time (12 women), 6 part-time (1 woman); includes 1 minority (Asian American or Pacific Islander) Average age 37. 22 applicants, 59% accepted, 8 enrolled. In 2007, 3 degrees awarded. *Degree requirements:* For M Div, thesis/dissertation, internship. *Entrance requirements:* In-person interview, writing sample. Additional exam requirements/recommendations for international students: Required—TOEFL (minimum score 600 paper-based; 250 computer-based). *Application deadline:* For fall admission, 1/15 priority date for domestic and international students; for spring admission, 10/15 priority date for domestic students. Applications are processed on a rolling basis. Application fee: $60. Electronic applications accepted. *Expenses:* Tuition: Full-time $15,070; part-time $685 per credit. Required fees: $250 per semester. Tuition and fees vary according to course load. *Financial support:* In 2007–08, 16 students received support, including 1 research assistantship with partial tuition reimbursement available (averaging $3,000 per year), 5 teaching assistantships with partial tuition reimbursements available (averaging $3,000 per year); career-related internships or fieldwork, Federal Work-Study, scholarships/grants, tuition waivers (partial), and unspecified assistantships also available. Support available to part-time students. Financial award application deadline: 3/1; financial award applicants required to submit FAFSA. *Unit head:* Phillip Stanley, Co-Chair, 303-245-4728. *Application contact:* Donna McIntyre, Admissions Counselor, 303-546-3555, Fax: 303-546-3583, E-mail: donna@naropa.edu.

See Close-Up on page 1449.

Nashotah House, School of Theology, Nashotah, WI 53058-9793. Offers M Div, MTS, STM, Certificate. *Accreditation:* ACIPE; ATS (one or more programs are accredited). Part-time programs available. *Degree requirements:* For master's, thesis optional; for M Div, 2 foreign languages, thesis/dissertation optional, clinical experience. *Entrance requirements:* For M Div, master's, and Certificate, GRE General Test or MAT, interview. Additional exam requirements/recommendations for international students: Required—TOEFL. *Faculty research:* Formation for parochial ministry, ancient Semitic epigraphy.

Nazarene Theological Seminary, Graduate and Professional Programs, Kansas City, MO 64131-1263. Offers Christian education (MA); intercultural studies (MA); theological studies (MA); theology (M Div, D Min). *Accreditation:* ACIPE; ATS. Part-time programs available. *Faculty:* 19 full-time (3 women), 12 part-time/adjunct (2 women). *Students:* 154 full-time (43 women), 156 part-time (38 women); includes 21 minority (5 African Americans, 3 American Indian/Alaska Native, 5 Asian Americans or Pacific Islanders, 8 Hispanic Americans), 16 international. Average age 31. 129 applicants, 77% accepted, 71 enrolled. In 2007, 40 first professional degrees, 22 master's, 2 doctorates awarded. *Degree requirements:* For master's, comprehensive exam (for some programs), thesis (for some programs); for doctorate, thesis/dissertation. *Entrance requirements:* Additional exam requirements/recommendations for international students: Required—TOEFL. *Application deadline:* For fall admission, 8/1 priority date for domestic students; for spring admission, 12/1 for domestic students. Applications are processed on a rolling basis. Application fee: $25 ($200 for international students). Electronic applications accepted. *Expenses:* Tuition: Full-time $8,544; part-time $356 per credit. Required fees: $75 per semester. *Financial support:* In 2007–08, 235 students received support, including 15 teaching assistantships (averaging $1,400 per year); institutionally sponsored loans and scholarships/grants also available. Support available to part-time students. Financial award application deadline: 3/1; financial award applicants required to submit FAFSA. *Unit head:* Dr. Roger L. Hahn, Dean of the Faculty, 816-268-5412, Fax: 816-268-5500, E-mail: rlhahn@nts.edu. *Application contact:* Jay A. Sandbloom, Director of Admissions, 816-268-5451, Fax: 816-268-5500, E-mail: jasandbloom@nts.edu.

Ner Israel Rabbinical College, Graduate Programs, Baltimore, MD 21208. Offers MTL, DTL, Professional Certificate. *Accreditation:* AARTS. *Faculty:* 10 full-time (0 women), 8 part-time/adjunct (0 women). *Students:* 173 full-time (0 women), 20 part-time. In 2007, 31 master's, 5 doctorates, 22 Professional Certificates awarded. *Application deadline:* Applications are processed on a rolling basis. Application fee: $50. *Expenses:* Tuition: Full-time $8,500. *Application contact:* Rabbi Ezra Neuberger, Information Contact, 410-484-7200, Fax: 410-484-3060.

Ner Israel Yeshiva College of Toronto, Graduate Programs, Thornhill, ON L4J 8A7, Canada. *Accreditation:* AARTS.

New Brunswick Theological Seminary, Graduate and Professional Programs, New Brunswick, NJ 08901-1196. Offers metro-urban ministry (D Min), including theological studies; theological studies (M Div, MA); M Div/MA. *Accreditation:* ACIPE; ATS. Part-time and evening/weekend programs available. *Degree requirements:* For master's, thesis optional. *Entrance requirements:* For M Div, minimum GPA of 2.0; for master's, minimum GPA of 3.0; for doctorate, M Div. Additional exam requirements/recommendations for international students: Required—TOEFL. Electronic applications accepted.

Newman Theological College, Theology Program, Edmonton, AB T6V 1H3, Canada. Offers M Div, M Th, MTS. *Accreditation:* ATS. Part-time programs available. *Degree requirements:* For master's, comprehensive exam, thesis; for M Div, comprehensive exam, thesis/dissertation. *Entrance requirements:* For M Div, bachelor's degree including 12 credits in philosophy; for master's, M Div. Additional exam requirements/recommendations for international students: Required—TOEFL (minimum score 560 paper-based; 220 computer-based).

New Orleans Baptist Theological Seminary, Graduate and Professional Programs, Division of Biblical Studies, New Orleans, LA 70126-4858. Offers M Div, D Min, PhD. *Accreditation:* ACIPE; ATS (one or more programs are accredited). *Degree requirements:* For doctorate, thesis/dissertation. *Entrance requirements:* For doctorate, GRE General Test.

New Orleans Baptist Theological Seminary, Graduate and Professional Programs, Division of Theological and Historical Studies, New Orleans, LA 70126-4858. Offers M Div, D Min, PhD. *Accreditation:* ACIPE; ATS (one or more programs are accredited). *Degree requirements:* For doctorate, thesis/dissertation. *Entrance requirements:* For doctorate, GRE General Test.

New York Theological Seminary, Graduate and Professional Programs, New York, NY 10115. Offers M Div, MPS, MSW, D Min. *Accreditation:* ACIPE; ATS (one or more programs are accredited). Part-time programs available. *Degree requirements:* For doctorate, thesis/dissertation; for M Div, thesis/dissertation, supervised ministry. *Entrance requirements:* For M Div, interview; for doctorate, M Div, 3 years of ministry experience, interview. Additional exam requirements/recommendations for international students: Required—TOEFL. *Faculty research:* Women in leadership; crime and punishment; church history; culture, politics and theology.

The Nigerian Baptist Theological Seminary, Graduate Studies, Ogbomoso, Nigeria. Offers church music (Diploma); divinity (M Div); theological studies (MATS); theology (M Th). Part-time programs available. *Degree requirements:* For master's, thesis, 2 Nigerian languages; for M Div, thesis/dissertation (for some programs), 2 biblical languages; for Diploma, thesis or alternative.

Northeastern Seminary at Roberts Wesleyan College, Graduate and Professional Programs, Rochester, NY 14624. Offers ministry (D Min); theological studies (MA); theology (M Div); M Div/MSW. *Accreditation:* ATS. Evening/weekend programs available. *Faculty:* 7 full-time (1 woman), 27 part-time/adjunct (9 women). *Students:* 92 full-time (38 women), 33 part-time (10 women); includes 34 minority (28 African Americans, 1 American Indian/Alaska Native, 2 Asian Americans or Pacific Islanders, 3 Hispanic Americans). Average age 43. 37

applicants, 73% accepted, 24 enrolled. In 2007, 9 first professional degrees, 11 master's, 4 doctorates awarded. *Degree requirements:* For master's, thesis (for some programs); for doctorate, one foreign language, thesis/dissertation. *Entrance requirements:* For doctorate, M Div, 3 years of full-time ministry experience. Additional exam requirements/recommendations for international students: Required—TOEFL (minimum score 550 paper-based). *Application deadline:* For fall admission, 8/1 priority date for domestic and international students; for spring admission, 12/15 priority date for domestic and international students. Applications are processed on a rolling basis. Application fee: $35. Electronic applications accepted. *Expenses:* Tuition: Full-time $8,280. One-time fee: $450 full-time. *Financial support:* In 2007–08, 125 students received support, including teaching assistantships with partial tuition reimbursements available (averaging $1,700 per year); career-related internships or fieldwork, institutionally sponsored loans, scholarships/grants, and tuition waivers (partial) also available. Financial award applicants required to submit FAFSA. *Faculty research:* Historical theology, spiritual formation, biblical theology, counseling education. *Unit head:* Dr. Wayne G. McCown, Dean, 585-594-6800, Fax: 585-594-6801. *Application contact:* Louis Colon, Director of Admissions, 585-594-6804, Fax: 585-594-6801, E-mail: colon_louis@nes.edu.

Northern Baptist Theological Seminary, Graduate and Professional Programs, Lombard, IL 60148-5698. Offers Bible (MA); Christian ministries (MACM); divinity (M Div); ethics (MA); history (MA); ministry (D Min); theology (MA); worship/spirituality (MAWS); youth ministry (MAYM). *Accreditation:* ATS. Part-time programs available. *Faculty:* 6 full-time (1 woman), 29 part-time/adjunct (6 women). *Students:* 98 full-time (22 women), 91 part-time (32 women); includes 67 minority (51 African Americans, 12 Asian Americans or Pacific Islanders, 4 Hispanic Americans), 3 international. Average age 40. 71 applicants, 90% accepted. In 2007, 21 first professional degrees, 10 master's, 13 doctorates awarded. *Degree requirements:* For doctorate, thesis/dissertation; for M Div, field experience. *Entrance requirements:* For doctorate, 3 years in the ministry post-M Div. Additional exam requirements/recommendations for international students: Required—TOEFL. *Application deadline:* For fall admission, 9/1 priority date for domestic students, 2/1 priority date for international students; for winter admission, 12/1 priority date for domestic students; for spring admission, 3/1 priority date for domestic students. Applications are processed on a rolling basis. Application fee: $35. Electronic applications accepted. *Expenses:* Tuition: Full-time $11,340; part-time $420 per hour. Required fees: $300. Tuition and fees vary according to degree level. *Financial support:* In 2007–08, 68 students received support. Career-related internships or fieldwork and scholarships/grants available. Support available to part-time students. Financial award application deadline: 9/1. *Faculty research:* Theology, worship studies, church history, evangelism, Bible. *Unit head:* Dr. Charles Hambrick-Stowe, Dean, 630-620-2103, Fax: 630-620-2190. *Application contact:* Greg Henson, Director of Enrollment Management, 630-620-2191, Fax: 630-620-2190, E-mail: admissions@seminary.edu.

North Park Theological Seminary, Graduate and Professional Programs, Professional Program, Chicago, IL 60625-4895. Offers M Div, M Div/MBA, M Div/MM. *Accreditation:* ACIPE; ATS. Part-time programs available. *Degree requirements:* For M Div, 2 foreign languages. *Entrance requirements:* Minimum GPA of 2.5. Additional exam requirements/recommendations for international students: Required—TOEFL.

North Park Theological Seminary, Graduate and Professional Programs, Program in Christian Studies, Chicago, IL 60625-4895. Offers Certificate. *Accreditation:* ACIPE. Part-time programs available. *Entrance requirements:* For degree, minimum GPA of 2.5. Additional exam requirements/recommendations for international students: Required—TOEFL.

North Park Theological Seminary, Graduate and Professional Programs, Program in Preaching, Chicago, IL 60625-4895. Offers D Min. *Accreditation:* ACIPE; ATS. *Degree requirements:* For doctorate, thesis/dissertation. *Entrance requirements:* For doctorate, 3 years of preaching experience.

North Park Theological Seminary, Graduate and Professional Programs, Program in Theological Studies, Chicago, IL 60625-4895. Offers MATS, MATS/MBA, MATS/MM, MATS/MSN. *Accreditation:* ACIPE; ATS. Part-time programs available. *Degree requirements:* For master's, comprehensive exam or thesis. *Entrance requirements:* For master's, minimum GPA of 2.5. Additional exam requirements/recommendations for international students: Required—TOEFL.

Northwest Baptist Seminary, Programs in Theology, Tacoma, WA 98407. Offers M Div, M Min, MTS, STM, Th M, D Min, Certificate. Part-time and evening/weekend programs available. *Degree requirements:* For master's, thesis; for M Div, thesis/dissertation (for some programs). *Entrance requirements:* Greek placement exam. Additional exam requirements/recommendations for international students: Required—TOEFL (minimum score 550 paper-based; 213 computer-based), IELTS (minimum score 6).

Notre Dame Seminary, Graduate School of Theology, New Orleans, LA 70118-4391. Offers M Div, MA. *Accreditation:* ACIPE; ATS. Part-time programs available. *Degree requirements:* For master's, one foreign language, comprehensive exam, thesis. *Entrance requirements:* For M Div, GRE, previous course work in philosophy; for master's, GRE. Additional exam requirements/recommendations for international students: Required—TOEFL.

Oakland City University, Chapman Seminary, Oakland City, IN 47660-1099. Offers M Div, D Min. *Accreditation:* ATS. Part-time programs available. *Faculty:* 4 full-time (0 women), 4 part-time/adjunct (1 woman). *Students:* 7 full-time (0 women), 7 part-time (2 women); includes 1 minority (African American) Average age 33. 11 applicants, 100% accepted, 8 enrolled. In 2007, 2 degrees awarded. *Degree requirements:* For doctorate, thesis/dissertation. *Entrance requirements:* For M Div, GRE General Test, minimum GPA of 2.75 in undergraduate major or 2.5 overall; for doctorate, GRE, MAT, letters of recommendation. Additional exam requirements/recommendations for international students: Required—TOEFL. *Application deadline:* Applications are processed on a rolling basis. Application fee: $35. *Expenses:* Contact institution. One-time fee: $35 full-time. *Financial support:* In 2007–08, 10 students received support. Career-related internships or fieldwork and Federal Work-Study available. Support available to part-time students. Financial award applicants required to submit FAFSA. *Faculty research:* Pastoral ministry, Christian education, missions. *Unit head:* Dr. Ray Barber, Dean, 812-749-1298, Fax: 812-749-1446, E-mail: rbarber@oak.edu. *Application contact:* Counselor for Graduate Admissions, 812-749-1241, Fax: 812-749-1233.

Oblate School of Theology, Graduate and Professional Programs, San Antonio, TX 78216-6693. Offers divinity (M Div); Hispanic ministry (D Min); pastoral ministry (MAP Min); pastoral studies (Certificate); spirituality (MA Sp); supervision (D Min), including clinical pastoral education, general supervision; theology (MA Th); M Div/MA Th. *Accreditation:* ACIPE; ATS (one or more programs are accredited). Part-time programs available. *Faculty:* 19 full-time (4 women), 3 part-time/adjunct (0 women). *Students:* 91 full-time (9 women), 70 part-time (29 women); includes 67 minority (9 African Americans, 1 American Indian/Alaska Native, 11 Asian Americans or Pacific Islanders, 46 Hispanic Americans), 33 international. Average age 39. 58 applicants, 100% accepted, 55 enrolled. In 2007, 15 first professional degrees, 8 master's, 9 Certificates awarded. *Degree requirements:* For master's, thesis (for some programs), practicum; for doctorate, paper, practicum; for M Div, one foreign language, seminar. *Entrance requirements:* For M Div, MAT, interview, course work in philosophy and theology; for master's, MAT, interview, course work in theology or religious studies, minimum GPA of 2.5; for doctorate, M Div. Additional exam requirements/recommendations for international students: Required—TOEFL (minimum score 197 computer-based; 71 iBT). *Application deadline:* For fall admission, 6/15 priority date for domestic and international students; for spring admission, 12/30 for domestic and international students. Applications are processed on a rolling basis. Application fee: $45. *Expenses:* Tuition: Full-time $11,232; part-time $432 per credit. Required fees: $160 per semester. One-time fee: $85 full-time. Tuition and fees vary according to course load and degree level. *Financial support:* Scholarships/grants available. Support available to part-time students. Financial award application deadline: 8/1; financial award applicants required to submit FAFSA. *Unit head:* Sr. Elaine Brothers, Academic Dean, 210-341-1366, Fax: 214-341-4519, E-mail: ebrothers@ost.edu. *Application contact:* James Oberhausen, Director of Admission/Registrar, 210-341-1366 Ext. 212, Fax: 210-341-4519, E-mail: registrar@ost.edu.

Ohio Dominican University, Graduate Programs, Division of Theology, Arts and Ideas, Columbus, OH 43219-2099. Offers theology (MA). Part-time and evening/weekend programs available. *Students:* 8 full-time (6 women), 29 part-time (18 women); includes 5 minority (4 African Americans, 1 Hispanic American). Average age 40. In 2007, 9 degrees awarded. *Degree requirements:* For master's, thesis or alternative. *Entrance requirements:* For master's, 20 undergraduate semester hours of theology or the equivalent, 3 letters of recommendation, interview. Additional exam requirements/recommendations for international students: Required—TOEFL (minimum score 550 paper-based; 213 computer-based). *Application deadline:* For fall admission, 7/15 priority date for domestic and international students; for spring admission, 12/15 priority date for domestic and international students. Applications are processed on a rolling basis. Application fee: $25. *Expenses:* Tuition: Part-time $450 per credit hour. Required fees: $10 per semester. *Financial support:* Applicants required to submit FAFSA. *Unit head:* Dr. Barbara Finan, Director, MA in Theology, 614-251-4721, E-mail: finanb@ohiodominican.edu. *Application contact:* Jill M. Westerfeld, Graduate Admissions Recruiter, 614-251-4725, Fax: 614-251-4634, E-mail: westerfj@ohiodominican.edu.

Ohr Hameir Theological Seminary, Graduate Programs, Peekskill, NY 10566. *Accreditation:* AARTS.

Oklahoma Christian University, Graduate School of Bible, Oklahoma City, OK 73136-1100. Offers family life ministry (MA); ministry (M Div, MA); youth ministry (MA). Part-time programs available. Postbaccalaureate distance learning degree programs offered (minimal on-campus study). *Faculty:* 12 full-time (0 women). *Students:* 11 full-time (3 women), 44 part-time (4 women); includes 3 minority (2 African Americans, 1 American Indian/Alaska Native), 3 international. Average age 30. 23 applicants, 100% accepted, 16 enrolled. In 2007, 8 degrees awarded. *Degree requirements:* For master's, one foreign language, comprehensive exam, field experience; for M Div, 2 foreign languages, comprehensive exam, field experience. *Entrance requirements:* For M Div and master's, minimum undergraduate GPA of 3.0. Additional exam requirements/recommendations for international students: Required—TOEFL (minimum score 550 paper-based; 213 computer-based). *Application deadline:* For fall admission, 8/15 priority date for domestic and international students; for spring admission, 1/3 priority date for domestic and international students. Applications are processed on a rolling basis. Application fee: $25. Electronic applications accepted. *Expenses:* Tuition: Full-time $6,300; part-time $350 per hour. One-time fee: $25. *Financial support:* In 2007–08, 49 students received support. Career-related internships or fieldwork, Federal Work-Study, scholarships/grants, and tuition waivers (partial) available. Support available to part-time students. Financial award application deadline: 3/1. *Faculty research:* Early marriage adjustment, new religions, Ethiopic language, church health, Hebrew rhetoric. *Unit head:* Dr. John Harrison, Chair, 405-425-5377, Fax: 405-425-5076, E-mail: john.harrison@oc.edu. *Application contact:* Dustin Crawford, Graduate Bible Recruiter, 405-425-5485, Fax: 405-425-5076, E-mail: dustin.crawford@oc.edu.

Olivet Nazarene University, Graduate School, Department of Practical Ministries, Bourbonnais, IL 60914-2271. Offers MPM. Part-time programs available. *Degree requirements:* For master's, thesis or alternative.

Olivet Nazarene University, Graduate School, Division of Religion and Philosophy, Bourbonnais, IL 60914-2271. Offers biblical literature (MA); religion (MA); theology (MA). Part-time programs available. *Degree requirements:* For master's, thesis or alternative.

Oral Roberts University, School of Theology and Missions, Tulsa, OK 74171-0001. Offers biblical literature (MA), including advanced languages, Judaic-Christian studies; Christian counseling (MA), including marriage and family therapy; Christian education (MA); divinity (M Div); missions (MA); practical theology (MA); theological/historical studies (MA); theology (D Min). *Accreditation:* ATS; NASM. Part-time programs available. Postbaccalaureate distance learning degree programs offered (minimal on-campus study). *Faculty:* 17 full-time (2 women). *Students:* 371 full-time (156 women), 110 part-time (65 women); includes 177 minority (127 African Americans, 5 American Indian/Alaska Native, 20 Asian Americans or Pacific Islanders, 25 Hispanic Americans), 82 international. Average age 36. 159 applicants, 95% accepted, 124 enrolled. In 2007, 38 first professional degrees, 52 master's, 10 doctorates awarded. *Degree requirements:* For master's, thesis (for some programs), practicum/internship; for doctorate, thesis/dissertation, applied research project; for M Div, one foreign language, field experience. *Entrance requirements:* For M Div and master's, GRE General Test or MAT, minimum GPA of 2.5; for doctorate, M Div, minimum GPA of 3.0, 3 years of full-time ministry experience. Additional exam requirements/recommendations for international students: Required—TOEFL (minimum score 500 paper-based; 213 computer-based; 79 iBT). *Application deadline:* For fall admission, 7/1 priority date for domestic and international students; for spring admission, 12/1 priority date for domestic students, 10/1 priority date for international students. Applications are processed on a rolling basis. Application fee: $35. Electronic applications accepted. *Expenses:* Tuition: Part-time $450 per hour. Required fees: $125 per semester. Tuition and fees vary according to class time, degree level and program. *Financial support:* In 2007–08, teaching assistantships (averaging $3,600 per year); scholarships/grants and employment assistantships also available. Financial award application deadline: 6/1; financial award applicants required to submit FAFSA. *Unit head:* Dr. Thomson K. Mathew, Dean, 918-495-7016, Fax: 918-495-6259, E-mail: tmathew@oru.edu. *Application contact:* Debra E. Watkins, Graduate Theology Representative, 918-495-6618, Fax: 918-495-7965, E-mail: owatkins@oru.edu.

Pacific Lutheran Theological Seminary, Graduate and Professional Programs, Berkeley, CA 94708-1597. Offers M Div, MA, MCM, MTS, PhD, Th D, Certificate, M Div/MA. *Accreditation:* ACIPE; ATS (one or more programs are accredited). Part-time programs available. *Degree requirements:* For master's, variable foreign language requirement, thesis or alternative; for M Div, one foreign language. *Entrance requirements:* Minimum cumulative GPA of 2.5, two semesters of Greek. *Faculty research:* Theology and genetics, power and prayer, liturgy and ethics, Christianity and Confucianism, religion and abuse.

Pacific School of Religion, Graduate and Professional Programs, Berkeley, CA 94709-1323. Offers M Div, MA, MTS, D Min, PhD, Th D, CAPS, CMS, CSS, CTS. *Accreditation:* ACIPE; ATS (one or more programs are accredited). Part-time programs available. *Degree requirements:* For master's, one foreign language, thesis (for some programs); for doctorate, thesis/dissertation. *Entrance requirements:* For M Div and master's, minimum GPA of 3.0; for doctorate, M Div, minimum GPA of 3.0 (D Min); for other advanced degree, M Div, minimum GPA of 3.0 (CAPS). Additional exam requirements/recommendations for international students: Required—TOEFL (minimum score 550 paper-based; 213 computer-based). Electronic applications accepted. *Faculty research:* Medical ethics, gay/lesbian studies in religion, Asian-American religion, race, culture and theology, theology in context.

Payne Theological Seminary, Program in Theology, Wilberforce, OH 45384-3474. Offers M Div. *Accreditation:* ACIPE; ATS. Part-time and evening/weekend programs available. Postbaccalaureate distance learning degree programs offered (minimal on-campus study). *Faculty:* 3 full-time (0 women), 14 part-time/adjunct (4 women). *Students:* 87 full-time (41 women), 40 part-time (23 women); includes 125 African Americans, 1 Hispanic American. Average age 40. 26 applicants, 88% accepted, 20 enrolled. In 2007, 8 degrees awarded. *Degree requirements:* For M Div, 2 foreign languages, thesis/dissertation. *Application deadline:* For fall admission, 6/15 priority date for domestic and international students; for spring admission, 12/31 for domestic and international students. Applications are processed on a rolling basis. Application fee: $50. *Expenses:* Tuition: Full-time $6,960; part-time $240 per credit hour. Tuition and fees vary according to campus/location and program. *Financial support:* In 2007–08, 90 students received support. Career-related internships or fieldwork and scholarships/grants available. Support available to part-time students. Financial award application deadline: 5/30; financial award applicants required to submit FAFSA. *Unit head:* Dr. Jerrie McGill, Interim Academic Dean,

Theology

Payne Theological Seminary (continued)
937-376-2946 Ext. 211, Fax: 937-376-2888. *Application contact:* Scott Carpenter, Registrar/ Enrollment Manager, 937-376-2946 Ext. 200, Fax: 937-376-2888, E-mail: scarpenter@ payne.edu.

Philadelphia Biblical University, School of Biblical Studies, Langhorne, PA 19047-2990. Offers M Div, MSB. Part-time and evening/weekend programs available. *Faculty:* 5 full-time (0 women), 6 part-time/adjunct (0 women). *Students:* 18 full-time (2 women), 76 part-time (18 women); includes 33 minority (26 African Americans, 6 Asian Americans or Pacific Islanders, 1 Hispanic American), 3 international. Average age 39. 59 applicants, 47% accepted, 28 enrolled. In 2007, 1 M Div, 9 master's awarded. *Entrance requirements:* Additional exam requirements/ recommendations for international students: Required—TOEFL (minimum score 550 paper-based; 213 computer-based). *Application deadline:* Applications are processed on a rolling basis. Application fee: $25. Electronic applications accepted. *Expenses:* Tuition: Full-time $8,924; part-time $525 per credit. Tuition and fees vary according to program. *Financial support:* In 2007–08, 50 students received support. Scholarships/grants available. Support available to part-time students. Financial award applicants required to submit FAFSA. *Unit head:* Dr. O. Herbert Hirt, Dean, 215-702-4354, Fax: 215-702-4359, E-mail: bible@pbu.edu. *Application contact:* Binu Abraham, Assistant Director, Graduate Admissions, 800-572-2472, Fax: 215-702-4248, E-mail: babraham@pbu.edu.

Phillips Theological Seminary, Programs in Theology, Tulsa, OK 74116. Offers administration of church agencies (M Div); campus ministry (M Div); church-related social work (M Div); college and seminary teaching (M Div); global mission work (M Div); institutional chaplaincy (M Div); ministerial vocations in Christian education (M Div); ministry (D Min), including parish ministry, pastoral counseling, practices of ministry; ministry and culture (MAMC), including Christian education, congregational leadership, history and practice of Christian spirituality, theology, ethics, and culture; ministry of music (M Div); pastoral care and counseling (M Div); pastoral ministry (M Div); theological studies (MTS). *Accreditation:* ATS. Part-time programs available. Postbaccalaureate distance learning degree programs offered (minimal on-campus study). *Degree requirements:* For master's, thesis (for some programs); for doctorate, thesis/dissertation. *Entrance requirements:* For master's, minimum GPA of 2.5; for doctorate, M Div, minimum GPA of 3.0. *Faculty research:* Biblical studies, historical studies, theology and culture, practical theology, theology and film.

Piedmont Baptist College and Graduate School, Piedmont Baptist Graduate School, Winston-Salem, NC 27101-5197. Offers chaplaincy track (MABS); non-language track (MABS); PhD preparation track (MABS); theology (M Min, PhD). Part-time programs available. Postbaccalaureate distance learning degree programs offered (no on-campus study). *Faculty:* 5 full-time (0 women), 8 part-time/adjunct (1 woman). *Students:* 84; includes 3 minority (2 African Americans, 1 Asian American or Pacific Islander). Average age 35. 12 applicants, 100% accepted. In 2007, 18 degrees awarded. *Degree requirements:* For master's, 2 foreign languages, comprehensive exam, thesis or alternative; for doctorate, 2 foreign languages, comprehensive exam. *Entrance requirements:* For master's, GRE General Test, BA/BS; for doctorate, Hebrew and Greek proficiency, MA. *Application deadline:* For fall admission, 8/15 priority date for domestic students; for spring admission, 1/1 for domestic students. Applications are processed on a rolling basis. Application fee: $30. Electronic applications accepted. *Expenses:* Tuition: Part-time $325 per credit hour. *Financial support:* Career-related internships or fieldwork available. Support available to part-time students. Financial award applicants required to submit CSS PROFILE. *Faculty research:* Theological and biblical studies. *Unit head:* Dr. Barkev Trachian, School Director, 336-714-7910, Fax: 336-714-2715, E-mail: trachianb@pbc.edu. *Application contact:* Kathy Holritz, Director of Graduate Admissions, 336-714-7927, Fax: 336-725-5522, E-mail: holritzk@pbc.edu.

Pittsburgh Theological Seminary, Graduate and Professional Programs, Pittsburgh, PA 15206-2596. Offers divinity (M Div); ministry (D Min); theology (MA, STM); JD/M Div; M Div/ MS; M Div/MSW. *Accreditation:* ATS (one or more programs are accredited). Part-time and evening/weekend programs available. *Faculty:* 19 full-time (5 women), 7 part-time/adjunct (2 women). *Students:* 282 full-time (93 women), 70 part-time (36 women); includes 58 minority (52 African Americans, 1 American Indian/Alaska Native, 4 Asian Americans or Pacific Islanders, 1 Hispanic American), 9 international. Average age 36. 149 applicants, 70% accepted, 90 enrolled. In 2007, 51 first professional degrees, 6 master's, 29 doctorates awarded. *Degree requirements:* For master's, comprehensive exam (for some programs), thesis (for some programs); for doctorate, thesis/dissertation; for M Div, one foreign language. *Entrance requirements:* For M Div, master's, and doctorate, interview, references. Additional exam requirements/recommendations for international students: Required—TOEFL (minimum score 570 paper-based). *Application deadline:* For fall admission, 6/15 priority date for domestic students, 12/1 for international students; for winter admission, 10/15 priority date for domestic students; for spring admission, 1/15 priority date for domestic students. Applications are processed on a rolling basis. Application fee: $40. *Expenses:* Tuition: Part-time $295 per credit. Required fees: $46 per term. Tuition and fees vary according to course load. *Financial support:* Career-related internships or fieldwork and scholarships/grants available. Financial award application deadline: 4/15; financial award applicants required to submit FAFSA. *Unit head:* Dr. Byron H. Jackson, Dean of Faculty and Vice President for Academic Affairs, 412-362-5610 Ext. 2118, Fax: 412-363-3260, E-mail: bjackson@pts.edu. *Application contact:* Sherry Sparks, Director of Admissions, 412-362-5610 Ext. 2115, Fax: 412-363-3260, E-mail: ssparks@ pts.edu.

Pontifical Catholic University of Puerto Rico, College of Arts and Humanities, Department of Theology and Philosophy, Ponce, PR 00717-0777. Offers M Div.

Pontifical College Josephinum, School of Theology, Columbus, OH 43235-1498. Offers M Div, MA. *Accreditation:* ATS. Part-time programs available. *Faculty:* 17 full-time (1 woman), 5 part-time/adjunct (2 women). *Students:* 49 full-time (0 women), 2 part-time; includes 5 minority (2 Asian Americans or Pacific Islanders, 3 Hispanic Americans), 10 international. Average age 28. 16 applicants, 88% accepted, 14 enrolled. In 2007, 15 first professional degrees, 5 master's awarded. *Degree requirements:* For master's, 3 foreign languages, comprehensive exam, thesis; for M Div, 2 foreign languages, thesis/dissertation. *Entrance requirements:* For M Div, GRE General Test, 24 credit hours of course work in philosophy, 12 credit hours of course work in theology; for master's, GRE General Test, 15 credit hours of course work in philosophy, 6 credit hours of course work in scripture. Additional exam requirements/ recommendations for international students: Required—TOEFL (minimum score 600 paper-based; 250 computer-based). *Application deadline:* For fall admission, 8/15 for domestic students. Applications are processed on a rolling basis. Application fee: $35. *Expenses:* Tuition: Full-time $19,282; part-time $606 per credit hour. Required fees: $680; $268 per semester. *Financial support:* Career-related internships or fieldwork and Federal Work-Study available. Financial award application deadline: 8/15; financial award applicants required to submit FAFSA. *Unit head:* Rev. Msgr. Nevin Klinger, Vice Rector, 614-885-5585, Fax: 614-885-2307. *Application contact:* Dr. Perry Cahall, Director of Admissions, 614-885-5585, Fax: 614-885-2307, E-mail: pcahall@pcj.edu.

Princeton Theological Seminary, Graduate and Professional Programs, Princeton, NJ 08542-0803. Offers M Div, MA, Th M, D Min, PhD. *Accreditation:* ACIPE; ATS. Part-time programs available. Terminal master's awarded for partial completion of doctoral program. *Degree requirements:* For doctorate, 2 foreign languages, thesis/dissertation, comprehensive exam (PhD), French and German. *Entrance requirements:* For doctorate, GRE General Test. Additional exam requirements/recommendations for international students: Required—TOEFL. Electronic applications accepted.

The Protestant Episcopal Theological Seminary in Virginia, Graduate and Professional Programs, Alexandria, VA 22304. Offers M Div, MACE, MTS, D Min. *Accreditation:* ACIPE; ATS. Part-time programs available. *Faculty:* 26 full-time (11 women), 29 part-time/adjunct (11 women). *Students:* 220. *Degree requirements:* For master's, 2 foreign languages, thesis; for doctorate, thesis/dissertation. *Entrance requirements:* For M Div, master's, and doctorate, GRE General Test. *Application deadline:* For fall admission, 5/1 for domestic students. Application fee: $0. *Financial support:* Career-related internships or fieldwork, Federal Work-Study, and institutionally sponsored loans available. *Application contact:* Jan Sienkiewicz, Coordinator for Admissions and Community Life, 703-370-6600.

Providence College, Graduate Studies, Department of Religious Studies, Providence, RI 02918. Offers biblical studies (MA); pastoral ministry (MA); religious education (MA); religious studies (MA). Part-time and evening/weekend programs available. *Faculty:* 7 full-time (0 women). *Students:* 6 full-time (0 women), 21 part-time (6 women). Average age 40. 8 applicants, 75% accepted. In 2007, 9 degrees awarded. *Degree requirements:* For master's, comprehensive exam, Greek and Hebrew (biblical studies). *Entrance requirements:* Additional exam requirements/recommendations for international students: Required—TOEFL (minimum score 550 paper-based; 213 computer-based; 79 iBT). *Application deadline:* For fall admission, 8/1 for domestic students; for spring admission, 12/1 for domestic students. Applications are processed on a rolling basis. Application fee: $55. *Expenses:* Tuition: Full-time $6,783; part-time $969 per course. *Financial support:* In 2007–08, 5 research assistantships with full tuition reimbursements (averaging $8,400 per year) were awarded; career-related internships or fieldwork and unspecified assistantships also available. Support available to part-time students. Financial award application deadline: 8/1; financial award applicants required to submit FAFSA. *Unit head:* Dr. Gary M. Culpepper, Director, 401-865-2863, Fax: 401-865-1449, E-mail: garyculp@providence.edu.

Providence College and Theological Seminary, Theological Seminary, Otterburne, MB R0A 1G0, Canada. Offers children's ministry (Certificate); Christian studies (MA, Certificate); counseling (MA); cross-cultural discipleship (Certificate); divinity (M Div); educational studies (MA), including counseling psychology, educational ministries, student development, teaching English to speakers of other languages, training teachers of English to speakers of other languages; global studies (MA); lay counseling (Diploma); ministry (D Min); teaching English to speakers of other languages (Certificate); theological studies (MA); training teacher of English to speakers of other languages (Certificate); youth ministry (Certificate). *Accreditation:* ATS. Part-time programs available. *Degree requirements:* For master's, variable foreign language requirement, thesis (for some programs); for doctorate, thesis/dissertation; for M Div, 2 foreign languages, comprehensive exam, thesis/dissertation (for some programs). *Entrance requirements:* Additional exam requirements/recommendations for international students: Recommended—TOEFL (minimum score 550 paper-based; 213 computer-based). *Faculty research:* Studies in Isaiah, theology of sin.

Queen's University at Kingston, Queen's Theological College, Kingston, ON K7L 3N6, Canada. Offers M Div, MTS. *Accreditation:* ATS. Part-time programs available. *Degree requirements:* For master's, thesis (for some programs); for M Div, 2 foreign languages. *Entrance requirements:* For master's, minimum undergraduate B average. Additional exam requirements/ recommendations for international students: Required—TOEFL (minimum score 580 paper-based). *Faculty research:* Early Christian group formations, pastoral care and spiritual direction, feminist theology, public religion, interpretation of Biblical texts using psychologies of shame and trauma.

Quincy University, Program in Theological Studies, Quincy, IL 62301-2699. Offers MTS. Part-time and evening/weekend programs available. Postbaccalaureate distance learning degree programs offered. *Faculty:* 3 full-time (1 woman). *Students:* Average age 49. In 2007, 13 degrees awarded. *Degree requirements:* For master's, comprehensive exam. *Entrance requirements:* For master's, MAT. *Application deadline:* Applications are processed on a rolling basis. Application fee: $25. *Financial support:* In 2007–08, 1 student received support. Applicants required to submit FAFSA. *Unit head:* Dr. Ed Maniscalco, Director, 217-228-5432 Ext. 2201, E-mail: manised@quincy.edu. *Application contact:* Syndi Peck, Director of Admissions, 217-228-5211, Fax: 217-228-5479, E-mail: admissions@quincy.edu.

Rabbi Isaac Elchanan Theological Seminary, Graduate Program, New York, NY 10033-1807. Offers Certificate of Advanced Ordination, Certificate of Ordination. *Degree requirements:* For other advanced degree, one foreign language, comprehensive exam. *Entrance requirements:* For degree, oral exam, 2 interview, undergraduate major in Jewish studies or equivalent. *Faculty research:* Talmud, rabbinics.

Rabbinical Academy Mesivta Rabbi Chaim Berlin, Graduate Program, Brooklyn, NY 11230-4715. Offers Advanced Talmudic Degree, Second Talmudic Degree. *Accreditation:* AARTS. *Faculty:* 10 full-time (0 women). *Students:* 40 full-time (0 women), 3 international. Average age 25. 25 applicants, 80% accepted. In 2007, 30 degrees awarded. *Degree requirements:* For other advanced degree, 2 foreign languages. *Entrance requirements:* For degree, must be a graduate of a rabbinical school. *Financial support:* In 2007–08, 20 research assistantships, 10 teaching assistantships were awarded; fellowships, career-related internships or fieldwork also available. Financial award application deadline: 9/30. *Unit head:* Rabbi Aaron Schechter, Dean, 718-377-0777, Fax: 718-338-5578. *Application contact:* Rabbi Eli Rabinowitz, Registrar, 718-377-0777, Fax: 718-338-5578, E-mail: eli.rabinowitz@myrcb.org.

Rabbinical College Beth Shraga, Graduate Programs, Monsey, NY 10952-3035. *Accreditation:* AARTS.

Rabbinical College Bobover Yeshiva B'nei Zion, Graduate Programs, Brooklyn, NY 11219. *Accreditation:* AARTS.

Rabbinical College Ch'san Sofer, Graduate Programs, Brooklyn, NY 11204. *Accreditation:* AARTS.

Rabbinical College of Long Island, Graduate Programs, Long Beach, NY 11561-3305. *Accreditation:* AARTS.

Rabbinical Seminary M'kor Chaim, Graduate Programs, Brooklyn, NY 11219. *Accreditation:* AARTS.

Rabbinical Seminary of America, Graduate Programs, Flushing, NY 11367. School offers a master's and first professional degree. *Accreditation:* AARTS. *Faculty:* 7 full-time, 4 part-time/ adjunct. *Students:* 223 full-time (0 women). *Application contact:* Abraham Semnel, Registrar, 718-268-4700 Ext. 122.

Reconstructionist Rabbinical College, Graduate Program, Wyncote, PA 19095-1898. Offers MAHL, MAJS, DHL, Certificate. Part-time programs available. *Faculty:* 8 full-time (4 women), 25 part-time/adjunct (14 women). *Students:* 65 full-time (45 women), 1 (woman) part-time. Average age 32. 25 applicants, 52% accepted, 11 enrolled. In 2007, 14 degrees awarded. *Degree requirements:* For master's, one foreign language, thesis (MAJS), completion of rabbinical program (MAHL); for doctorate and MAHL, one foreign language. *Entrance requirements:* For MAHL and doctorate, GRE General Test, placement examinations in Hebrew and Judaism; for master's, GRE General Test. *Application deadline:* For spring admission, 4/30 priority date for domestic and international students. Applications are processed on a rolling basis. Application fee: $50. *Expenses:* Tuition: Full-time $15,000. Required fees: $36. *Financial support:* In 2007–08, 46 students received support, including 4 fellowships with full tuition reimbursements available (averaging $11,000 per year), 1 research assistantship with partial tuition reimbursement available (averaging $5,500 per year), 5 teaching assistantships (averaging $5,500 per year); career-related internships or fieldwork, institutionally sponsored loans, and scholarships/grants also available. Financial award application deadline: 4/15. *Faculty research:* Bible, Hebrew Semitic texts, contemporary Judaism. *Unit head:* Rabbi Dan Ehrenkrantz, President, 215-576-0800 Ext. 129, Fax: 215-576-6143, E-mail: dehrenkrantz@ rrc.edu. *Application contact:* Rabbi Amber Powers, Dean of Recruitment and Admissions, 215-576-0800 Ext. 145, Fax: 215-576-6143, E-mail: apowers@rrc.edu.

Reformed Presbyterian Theological Seminary, Graduate and Professional Programs, Pittsburgh, PA 15208-2594. Offers M Div, MTS, D Min. *Accreditation:* ATS. Part-time and evening/weekend programs available. Electronic applications accepted. *Faculty research:* Prayer.

Reformed Theological Seminary–Charlotte Campus, Graduate and Professional Programs, Charlotte, NC 28226-6318. Offers biblical studies (MA); ministry (M Div, D Min); theological studies (MA). Part-time programs available. *Faculty:* 10 full-time, 4 part-time/adjunct. *Students:* 109. 53 applicants, 98% accepted, 40 enrolled. In 2007, 20 first professional degrees, 4 master's, 2 doctorates awarded. *Degree requirements:* For master's, comprehensive exam; for doctorate, thesis/dissertation; for M Div, 2 foreign languages, comprehensive exam. *Entrance requirements:* For master's, minimum GPA of 2.6; for doctorate, minimum GPA of 3.0. Additional exam requirements/recommendations for international students: Required—TOEFL (minimum score 550 paper-based; 213 computer-based). *Application deadline:* For fall admission, 7/15 priority date for domestic students; for winter admission, 11/15 priority date for domestic students; for spring admission, 12/15 priority date for domestic students. Applications are processed on a rolling basis. Application fee: $55. Electronic applications accepted. *Expenses:* Tuition: Full-time $12,025; part-time $325 per semester hour. Required fees: $65 per semester. *Financial support:* In 2007–08, teaching assistantships (averaging $1,600 per year); career-related internships or fieldwork and scholarships/grants also available. Financial award application deadline: 5/1. *Application contact:* Stephane Jeanrenaud, Director of Admissions, 800-755-2429, E-mail: admissions.charlotte@rts.edu.

Reformed Theological Seminary–Jackson Campus, Graduate and Professional Programs, Jackson, MS 39209-3099. Offers Bible, theology, and missions (Certificate); biblical studies (MA); Christian education (M Div, MA); counseling (M Div); divinity (M Div, Diploma); marriage and family therapy (MA); ministry (D Min); missions (M Div, MA, D Min); New Testament (Th M); Old Testament (Th M); theological studies (MA); theology (Th M); M Div/MA. *Accreditation:* AAMFT/COAMFTE (one or more programs are accredited); ATS (one or more programs are accredited). *Degree requirements:* For master's, thesis (for some programs), fieldwork; for doctorate, 2 foreign languages, thesis/dissertation; for M Div, 2 foreign languages, thesis/dissertation (for some programs). *Entrance requirements:* For M Div and master's, minimum GPA of 2.6; for doctorate, minimum GPA of 3.0. Additional exam requirements/recommendations for international students: Required—TOEFL.

Reformed Theological Seminary–Orlando Campus, Graduate Program, Oviedo, FL 32765-7197. Offers biblical studies (MA); Christian thought (MA); counseling (MA); ministry (D Min); reformation studies (Th M); theological studies (MA); theology (M Div); MA/Certificate. Part-time programs available. Postbaccalaureate distance learning degree programs offered (minimal on-campus study). *Faculty:* 15 full-time (0 women), 5 part-time/adjunct (0 women). *Students:* 428; includes 45 minority (15 African Americans, 19 Asian Americans or Pacific Islanders, 11 Hispanic Americans), 30 international. 203 applicants, 75% accepted, 107 enrolled. In 2007, 40 first professional degrees, 45 master's, 2 doctorates awarded. *Entrance requirements:* For M Div and master's, minimum GPA of 2.6. *Application deadline:* For fall admission, 5/21 priority date for domestic students; for winter admission, 10/3 priority date for domestic students; for spring admission, 11/5 priority date for domestic students. Applications are processed on a rolling basis. Application fee: $60. Electronic applications accepted. *Unit head:* Dr. Frank A. James, President, 407-366-9493, Fax: 407-366-9425, E-mail: fjames@rts.edu. *Application contact:* Thomas G. Nelson, Director of Admissions, 800-752-4382, Fax: 407-366-9425, E-mail: tnelson@rts.edu.

Reformed Theological Seminary–Washington D.C., Graduate and Professional Programs, McLean, VA 22101. Offers bible (M Div); practical theology (M Div); religion (MA); theology (M Div). Part-time and evening/weekend programs available. *Faculty:* 23 part-time/adjunct (0 women). *Students:* 7 full-time (0 women), 94 part-time (18 women); includes 1 African American, 17 Asian Americans or Pacific Islanders. Average age 35. 41 applicants, 129% accepted. *Degree requirements:* For master's, integrative paper. *Entrance requirements:* For master's, minimum undergraduate GPA of 2.6. *Application deadline:* Applications are processed on a rolling basis. Application fee: $50. Electronic applications accepted. *Expenses:* Tuition: Part-time $345 per semester hour. Required fees: $50 per semester. One-time fee: $100 part-time. *Financial support:* In 2007–08, 55 students received support, including 7 fellowships (averaging $1,000 per year); institutionally sponsored loans, scholarships/grants, tuition waivers (partial), and unspecified assistantships also available. Support available to part-time students. Financial award application deadline: 6/15. *Faculty research:* Theology, biblical studies, cultural studies. *Unit head:* Hugh C. Whelchel, Executive Director, 703-448-3393, E-mail: hwhelchel@rts.edu. *Application contact:* Geoff M. Sackett, Director of Admissions, 800-639-0226, E-mail: gsackett@rts.edu.

Regent College, Program in Theology, Vancouver, BC V6T 2E4, Canada. Offers M Div, MCS, Th M, Dip CS. *Accreditation:* ATS (one or more programs are accredited). Part-time and evening/weekend programs available. *Faculty:* 21 full-time (4 women), 17 part-time/adjunct (6 women). *Students:* 267 full-time (89 women), 298 part-time (112 women); includes 156 minority (4 African Americans, 1 American Indian/Alaska Native, 151 Asian Americans or Pacific Islanders). Average age 33. 231 applicants, 94% accepted, 148 enrolled. In 2007, 46 first professional degrees, 87 master's, 21 Dip CSs awarded. *Degree requirements:* For master's, thesis (for some programs). *Entrance requirements:* For M Div and Dip CS, minimum GPA of 2.8; for master's, minimum GPA of 2.8 (MCS), 3.5 (Th M). Additional exam requirements/recommendations for international students: Required—TOEFL (minimum score 575 paper-based; 230 computer-based; 90 iBT), TWE (minimum score 5). *Application deadline:* For fall admission, 2/1 priority date for domestic students, 1/1 priority date for international students; for winter admission, 7/1 priority date for domestic and international students; for spring admission, 2/1 priority date for domestic students, 1/1 priority date for international students. Application fee: $60 Canadian dollars. Tuition and fees charges are reported in Canadian dollars. *Expenses:* Tuition: Full-time $16,056 Canadian dollars; part-time $446 Canadian dollars per credit. Required fees: $135 Canadian dollars per term. One-time fee: $207 Canadian dollars full-time. *Financial support:* In 2007–08, 90 students received support, including 150 teaching assistantships (averaging $2,500 Canadian dollars per year); career-related internships or fieldwork, scholarships/grants, and health care benefits also available. Financial award application deadline: 3/1. *Faculty research:* Integration of theology with secular life, biblical studies. *Unit head:* Dr. Rod Wilson, President, 604-221-3318, Fax: 604-224-3097, E-mail: presidentsoffice@regent-college.edu. *Application contact:* Cindy Y. Aalders, Assistant Registrar, 604-224-3245 Ext. 335, Fax: 604-224-3097, E-mail: admissions@regent-college.edu.

Regent University, Graduate School, School of Divinity, Virginia Beach, VA 23464-9800. Offers biblical studies (MA); leadership and renewal (D Min); missiology (M Div, MA); practical theology (M Div, MA); renewal studies (PhD); M Div/M Ed; M Div/MA; M Div/MBA; M Ed/MA; MBA/MA. *Accreditation:* ACIPE; ATS. Part-time programs available. Postbaccalaureate distance learning degree programs offered (minimal on-campus study). *Faculty:* 18 full-time (4 women), 22 part-time/adjunct (7 women). *Students:* 186 full-time (76 women), 437 part-time (163 women); includes 249 minority (212 African Americans, 2 American Indian/Alaska Native, 13 Asian Americans or Pacific Islanders, 22 Hispanic Americans), 61 international. Average age 38. 302 applicants, 70% accepted, 114 enrolled. In 2007, 56 first professional degrees, 16 master's, 62 doctorates awarded. *Degree requirements:* For master's, comprehensive exam, thesis or alternative, internship; for doctorate, thesis/dissertation or alternative; for M Div, internship. *Entrance requirements:* For M Div, GRE General Test or MAT, minimum undergraduate GPA of 3.0, minimum 3 years of ministry experience, transcripts, recommendations; for master's, GRE General Test or MAT, minimum undergraduate GPA of 2.75, writing sample, clergy recommendation, transcripts ; for doctorate, M Div or theological master's degree, minimum graduate GPA of 3.5 (PhD), 3.0 (D Min), recommendations, writing sample, transcripts . Additional exam requirements/recommendations for international students: Required—TOEFL (minimum score 577 paper-based; 233 computer-based). *Application deadline:* For fall admission, 5/1 priority date for domestic students. Applications are processed on a rolling basis. Application fee: $50. Electronic applications accepted. *Expenses:* Contact institution. *Financial support:* In 2007–08, 500 students received support; fellowships with full and partial tuition reimbursements available, career-related internships or fieldwork, scholarships/grants, tuition waivers (full and partial), and unspecified assistantships available. Support available to part-time students. Financial award application deadline: 9/1; financial award applicants required to submit FAFSA. *Faculty research:* Greek and Hebrew etymology. *Unit head:* Dr. Michael Palmer, Dean, 757-226-4406, Fax: 757-226-4597, E-mail: mpalmer@regent.edu. *Application contact:* Althea Bishard, Registrar and Executive Director of Enrollment and Academic Services, 800-373-5504, Fax: 757-226-4381, E-mail: admissions@regent.edu.

Regis College, Graduate and Professional Programs, Toronto, ON M4Y 2R5, Canada. Offers ministry (D Min); ministry and spirituality (MAMS); sacred theology (STB, STM, STD, STL); theological study (MTS); theology (M Div, MA, Th M, PhD, Th D); M Div/MA. *Accreditation:* ATS (one or more programs are accredited). *Faculty:* 15 full-time (4 women), 12 part-time/adjunct (2 women). *Students:* 88 full-time (30 women), 131 part-time (78 women); includes 74 minority (16 African Americans, 1 American Indian/Alaska Native, 48 Asian Americans or Pacific Islanders, 9 Hispanic Americans). Average age 45. 73 applicants, 88% accepted, 52 enrolled. In 2007, 10 first professional degrees, 13 master's, 5 other advanced degrees awarded. Terminal master's awarded for partial completion of doctoral program. *Degree requirements:* For master's, 2 foreign languages, thesis; for doctorate, 3 foreign languages, comprehensive exam, thesis/dissertation; for first professional degree, comprehensive exam. *Entrance requirements:* For first professional degree, minimum GPA of 3.0; for master's, minimum GPA of 3.3; for doctorate, minimum GPA of 3.7. Additional exam requirements/recommendations for international students: Required—TOEFL (minimum score 580 paper-based; 237 computer-based; 93 iBT), TWE (minimum score 5). *Application deadline:* For fall admission, 3/15 priority date for domestic and international students; for winter admission, 12/1 for domestic and international students; for spring admission, 3/15 for domestic and international students. Applications are processed on a rolling basis. Application fee: $25. Tuition charges are reported in Canadian dollars. *Expenses:* Tuition: Part-time $455 Canadian dollars per credit. Tuition and fees vary according to program and student level. *Financial support:* In 2007–08, 58 students received support. Career-related internships or fieldwork and scholarships/grants available. Support available to part-time students. Financial award application deadline: 3/15. *Unit head:* Dr. Gordon Rixon, Dean, 416-922-5474 Ext. 225, Fax: 416-922-2898, E-mail: gordon.rixon@utoronto.ca. *Application contact:* Elaine Chu, Registrar, 416-922-5474 Ext. 226, Fax: 416-922-2898, E-mail: regis.registrar@utoronto.ca.

Sacred Heart Major Seminary, School of Theology, Detroit, MI 48206-1799. Offers pastoral studies (MAPS); theology (M Div, MA). *Accreditation:* ACIPE; ATS. Part-time and evening/weekend programs available. *Faculty:* 21 full-time (4 women), 10 part-time/adjunct (0 women). *Students:* 75 full-time (3 women), 129 part-time (48 women); includes 39 minority (15 African Americans, 1 American Indian/Alaska Native, 13 Asian Americans or Pacific Islanders, 10 Hispanic Americans), 4 international. Average age 50. In 2007, 4 first professional degrees, 11 master's awarded. *Degree requirements:* For master's, one foreign language, thesis optional, integrating project; for M Div, integrating seminar. *Entrance requirements:* For M Div and master's, GRE, previous course work in philosophy and theology. *Application deadline:* For fall admission, 9/5 for domestic students; for winter admission, 12/20 priority date for domestic students. Application fee: $30. *Expenses:* Tuition: Full-time $17,695; part-time $430 per hour. Required fees: $80; $40 per term. Full-time tuition and fees vary according to program. *Financial support:* Institutionally sponsored loans and scholarships/grants available. Financial award application deadline: 9/1; financial award applicants required to submit FAFSA. *Faculty research:* Local church history, patristics, spirituality, religious education. *Unit head:* Rev. Todd J. Lajiness, Dean of Studies, 313-883-8500, Fax: 313-868-6440, E-mail: lajiness.todd@shms.edu. *Application contact:* John Lajiness, Director of Admissions and Enrollment Management, 313-883-8500, Fax: 313-868-6440, E-mail: lajiness.john@shms.edu.

Sacred Heart School of Theology, Graduate and Professional Programs, Hales Corners, WI 53130-0429. Offers theology (M Div, MA). *Accreditation:* ACIPE; ATS. Part-time programs available. *Faculty:* 29 full-time (6 women), 14 part-time/adjunct (6 women). *Students:* 79 full-time (0 women), 24 part-time (13 women); includes 4 minority (1 African American, 1 Asian American or Pacific Islander, 2 Hispanic Americans), 20 international. Average age 47. 20 applicants, 100% accepted, 20 enrolled. In 2007, 11 first professional degrees, 3 master's awarded. *Degree requirements:* For master's, essay or comprehensive exam; for M Div, integrating seminar. *Entrance requirements:* For master's, MAT, 6 hours of course work each in philosophy and theology, letter of recommendation. *Application deadline:* For fall admission, 8/1 for domestic students; for spring admission, 12/1 for domestic students. Application fee: $50. *Expenses:* Tuition: Part-time $420 per credit. One-time fee: $50 part-time. Tuition and fees vary according to program and student level. *Financial support:* In 2007–08, 10 students received support. Career-related internships or fieldwork and scholarships/grants available. Financial award application deadline: 9/30; financial award applicants required to submit FAFSA. *Unit head:* Very Rev. Jan de Jong, President-Rector, 414-425-8300, Fax: 414-529-6999, E-mail: jdejong@shst.edu. *Application contact:* Rev. Thomas L. Knoebel, Director of Admissions, 414-425-8300 Ext. 6984, Fax: 414-529-6999, E-mail: tknoebel@shst.edu.

St. Andrew's College in Winnipeg, Graduate Programs, Winnipeg, MB R3T 2M7, Canada. Offers M Div. *Degree requirements:* For M Div, one foreign language, thesis/dissertation. *Faculty research:* Church history, doctrine, liturgical theology.

St. Augustine's Seminary of Toronto, Graduate and Professional Programs, Scarborough, ON M1M 1M3, Canada. Offers divinity (M Div); lay ministry (Diploma); religious education (MRE); theological studies (MTS, Diploma). *Accreditation:* ATS. Part-time and evening/weekend programs available. *Faculty:* 11 full-time (4 women), 20 part-time/adjunct (4 women). *Students:* 57 full-time (2 women), 120 part-time (49 women), 14 international. Average age 41. 25 applicants, 96% accepted, 23 enrolled. In 2007, 10 first professional degrees, 6 master's awarded. *Degree requirements:* For M Div, comprehensive exam (for some programs), thesis/dissertation optional, field education. *Entrance requirements:* Course work in philosophy. Additional exam requirements/recommendations for international students: Required—TOEFL (minimum score 580 paper-based; 237 computer-based), TWE (minimum score 5). *Application deadline:* For fall admission, 7/15 priority date for domestic and international students; for winter admission, 11/15 priority date for domestic and international students; for spring admission, 4/15 priority date for domestic and international students. Application fee: $25 Canadian dollars. *Expenses:* Tuition: Part-time $572 per course. Required fees: $57 per term. Tuition and fees vary according to course load. *Unit head:* Rev. Tadeusz J. Nowak, Acting Dean of Studies, 416-261-7207, Fax: 416-261-2529. *Application contact:* Theresa Mary Vicioso, Registrar/Administrative Assistant to the Dean of Studies, 416-261-7207 Ext. 230, Fax: 416-261-2529, E-mail: t.vicioso@utoronto.ca.

Saint Bernard's School of Theology and Ministry, Graduate and Professional Programs, Rochester, NY 14618. Offers pastoral studies (MA, Certificate); theological studies (MA); theology (M Div). *Accreditation:* ATS (one or more programs are accredited). Part-time and evening/weekend programs available. *Faculty:* 7 full-time (3 women), 4 part-time/adjunct (1 woman). *Students:* 3 full-time (2 women), 126 part-time (55 women); includes 13 minority (7 African Americans, 1 American Indian/Alaska Native, 2 Asian Americans or Pacific Islanders, 3 Hispanic Americans). Average age 50. 40 applicants, 50% accepted, 20 enrolled. In 2007, 4 first professional degrees, 37 master's awarded. *Degree requirements:* For master's, variable foreign language requirement, thesis (for some programs). *Entrance requirements:* For M Div, minimum GPA of 2.0; for master's, minimum GPA of 2.5. *Application deadline:* Applications are processed on a rolling basis. Application fee: $75. *Expenses:* Tuition: Full-time $8,220; part-time $1,370 per course. Required fees: $30 per semester. *Financial support:* In 2007–08, 33 students received support; fellowships, research assistantships, teaching assistantships, career-related internships or fieldwork, scholarships/grants, and tuition waivers (partial) available. Support available to part-time students. Financial award application deadline: 4/15; financial award applicants required to submit FAFSA. *Unit head:* Dr. Patricia Schoelles, President, 585-271-3657 Ext. 276, Fax: 585-271-2045, E-mail: pschoelles@stbernards.edu. *Application*

Theology

Saint Bernard's School of Theology and Ministry (continued)
contact: Charmel Trinidad, Director of Admissions and Financial Aid, 585-271-3657 Ext. 289, Fax: 585-271-2045, E-mail: strinidad@stbernards.edu.

St. Bonaventure University, School of Graduate Studies, School of Franciscan Studies, St. Bonaventure, NY 14778-2284. Offers MA, Adv C. Part-time programs available. *Degree requirements:* For master's, thesis optional, integration seminar and paper.

St. Charles Borromeo Seminary, Overbrook, Graduate and Professional Programs, Division of Theology, Wynnewood, PA 19096. Offers M Div, MA. *Accreditation:* ATS. Part-time programs available. *Faculty:* 15 full-time (7 women), 7 part-time/adjunct (4 women). *Students:* 71 full-time (0 women); includes 4 minority (1 African American, 1 American Indian/Alaska Native, 1 Asian American or Pacific Islander, 1 Hispanic American), 4 international. Average age 29. 29 applicants, 100% accepted, 29 enrolled. In 2007, 13 first professional degrees, 13 master's awarded. *Degree requirements:* For master's, comprehensive exam, research papers; for M Div, comprehensive exam. *Entrance requirements:* For M Div, previous course work in philosophy and theology; for master's, M Div. *Application deadline:* For fall admission, 7/15 for domestic students. Applications are processed on a rolling basis. Application fee: $0. *Expenses:* Tuition: Full-time $13,616; part-time $1,228 per credit. *Financial support:* Federal Work-Study and scholarships/grants available. *Unit head:* Rev. Robert A. Pesarchick, Academic Dean, 610-785-6204, Fax: 610-667-1422, E-mail: academicdcdscs@adphila.org. *Application contact:* Rev. David E. Diamond, Vice Rector, 610-785-6271, Fax: 610-617-9267, E-mail: frdd@adphila.org.

Saint Francis Seminary, Graduate and Professional Programs, St. Francis, WI 53235-3795. Offers M Div, MAPS. *Accreditation:* ACIPE; ATS. Part-time programs available. *Degree requirements:* For master's, comprehensive exam; for M Div, thesis/dissertation. *Entrance requirements:* For M Div and master's, Otis IQ Test, Terman Concept Mastery Test, interview. Additional exam requirements/recommendations for international students: Required—TOEFL (minimum score 550 paper-based).

St. John's Seminary, Graduate and Professional Programs, Camarillo, CA 93012-2598. Offers divinity (M Div); pastoral ministry (MAPM); theology (MA). *Accreditation:* ATS. Part-time programs available. *Faculty:* 23 full-time (4 women), 8 part-time/adjunct (1 woman). *Students:* 84 full-time (1 woman), 11 part-time (5 women); includes 49 minority (28 Asian Americans or Pacific Islanders, 21 Hispanic Americans), 15 international. Average age 34. 24 applicants, 100% accepted, 21 enrolled. In 2007, 11 first professional degrees, 6 master's awarded. *Degree requirements:* For master's, comprehensive exam (for some programs), thesis optional; for M Div, parish internship. *Entrance requirements:* For M Div, GRE General Test, bishop's approbation; for master's, GRE General Test, minimum GPA of 3.5. Additional exam requirements/recommendations for international students: Required—TOEFL (minimum score 550 paper-based). *Application deadline:* For fall admission, 7/15 priority date for domestic students. Applications are processed on a rolling basis. Application fee: $0. *Expenses:* Tuition: Full-time $12,250; part-time $408 per unit. *Faculty research:* Biblical studies, moral theology, historical studies, systematic theology, spiritual theology. *Unit head:* Rev. Richard Benson, CM, Academic Dean, 805-482-2755, Fax: 805-482-3470, E-mail: rbensoncm@stjohnsem.edu. *Application contact:* Esmé M. Takahashi, Registrar, 805-482-2755 Ext. 1014, Fax: 805-482-3470, E-mail: registrar-sjs@stjohnsem.edu.

Saint John's Seminary, Graduate Programs, Brighton, MA 02135. Offers M Div, MA Th, MAM. *Accreditation:* ATS. *Faculty:* 11 full-time (1 woman), 16 part-time/adjunct (8 women). *Students:* 100 full-time (16 women), 59 part-time (37 women). *Application deadline:* Applications are processed on a rolling basis. Application fee: $0. *Expenses:* Tuition: Full-time $11,250; part-time $1,500 per course. One-time fee: $325 part-time. *Unit head:* Fr. Arthur L. Kennedy, Rector, 617-254-2610, Fax: 617-787-2336. *Application contact:* Sr. M. Pierre Jean Wilson, RSM, Dean of Admissions and Records, 617-779-4369, Fax: 617-787-2336, E-mail: admissionsandrecords@sjs.edu.

St. John's University, St. John's College of Liberal Arts and Sciences, Department of Theology and Religious Studies, Queens, NY 11439. Offers pastoral ministry (Certificate); priestly studies (M Div); theology (MA, Certificate). *Accreditation:* ACIPE. Part-time and evening/weekend programs available. *Faculty:* 20 full-time (6 women), 43 part-time/adjunct (18 women). *Students:* 3 full-time (1 woman), 52 part-time (31 women); includes 10 minority (6 African Americans, 1 Asian American or Pacific Islander, 3 Hispanic Americans), 10 international. Average age 44. 35 applicants, 51% accepted, 7 enrolled. In 2007, 10 degrees awarded. *Degree requirements:* For master's, thesis optional; for M Div, thesis/dissertation optional. *Entrance requirements:* For master's, minimum GPA of 3.0. Additional exam requirements/recommendations for international students: Required—TOEFL (minimum score 500 paper-based; 173 computer-based; 61 iBT), IELTS (minimum score 6). *Application deadline:* For fall admission, 5/1 priority date for domestic and international students; for spring admission, 11/1 priority date for domestic and international students. Applications are processed on a rolling basis. Application fee: $40. Electronic applications accepted. *Financial support:* Research assistantships, scholarships/grants available. Support available to part-time students. Financial award application deadline: 3/1; financial award applicants required to submit FAFSA. *Faculty research:* Systematic theology, moral theory, biblical studies, pastoral theology, church history. *Unit head:* Fr. Michael Whalen, Chair, 718-990-5431, E-mail: whalenm@stjohns.edu. *Application contact:* Beth Evans, Associate Vice President and Executive Director, Enrollment Management, 718-990-6999, Fax: 718-990-5686, E-mail: gradhelp@stjohns.edu.

Saint John's University, Saint John's School of Theology and Seminary, Collegeville, MN 56321. Offers divinity (M Div); liturgical music (MA); liturgical studies (MA); pastoral ministry (MA); theology (MA), including church history, liturgy, monastic studies, scripture, spirituality, systematics; M Div/MA. *Accreditation:* ATS. Part-time programs available. Postbaccalaureate distance learning degree programs offered (no on-campus study). *Degree requirements:* For master's, one foreign language, comprehensive exam (for some programs), thesis (for some programs). *Entrance requirements:* For master's, GRE General Test or MAT. Electronic applications accepted. *Faculty research:* Religious education, biblical literature.

St. Joseph's Seminary, Institute of Religious Studies, Yonkers, NY 10704. Offers MA. *Accreditation:* ATS. Part-time and evening/weekend programs available. *Degree requirements:* For master's, comprehensive exam. *Entrance requirements:* For master's, 18 hours in theology and/or philosophy. Electronic applications accepted. Expenses: Contact institution. *Faculty research:* Medical ethics, mystical theology of Karl Rahner, medieval church history.

St. Joseph's Seminary, Professional Program, Yonkers, NY 10704. Offers divinity (M Div); theology (MA). *Accreditation:* ATS. *Degree requirements:* For master's, one foreign language, thesis; for M Div, comprehensive exam. *Entrance requirements:* For M Div and master's, 27 credits in philosophy and 9 in theology.

Saint Louis University, Graduate School, College of Arts and Sciences and Graduate School, Department of Theological Studies, St. Louis, MO 63103-2097. Offers historical theology (MA, PhD); theology (MA). Part-time programs available. *Faculty:* 19 full-time (2 women), 2 part-time/adjunct (0 women). *Students:* 29 full-time (9 women), 23 part-time (7 women); includes 4 minority (1 African American, 1 Asian American or Pacific Islander, 2 Hispanic Americans), 3 international. Average age 34. 55 applicants, 58% accepted, 10 enrolled. In 2007, 6 master's, 3 doctorates awarded. *Degree requirements:* For master's, comprehensive exam; for doctorate, 4 foreign languages, comprehensive exam, thesis/dissertation, preliminary exams. *Entrance requirements:* For master's and doctorate, GRE General Test, letters of recommendation, resumé, interview, transcripts, goal statement . Additional exam requirements/recommendations for international students: Required—TOEFL (minimum score 550 paper-based; 213 computer-based). *Application deadline:* For fall admission, 2/1 for domestic and international students; for spring admission, 11/1 for domestic and international students. Applications are processed on a rolling basis. Application fee: $40. Electronic applications accepted. *Expenses:* Tuition: Part-time $845 per credit hour. Required fees: $105 per semester. *Financial support:* In 2007–08, 46 students received support, including 5 research assistantships with full tuition reimbursements available (averaging $12,800 per year), 11 teaching assistantships with full tuition reimbursements available (averaging $12,000 per year); Federal Work-Study, scholarships/grants, traineeships, health care benefits, tuition waivers, and unspecified assistantships also available. Support available to part-time students. Financial award application deadline: 2/1; financial award applicants required to submit FAFSA. *Faculty research:* Biblical and early church studies, medieval and renaissance studies, modern and American Christianity, comparative and interreligious studies, moral and ethical theology. *Unit head:* Fr. J.A. Wayne Hellmann, Chairperson, 314-977-2885, Fax: 314-977-2947, E-mail: hellmann@slu.edu. *Application contact:* Gary U. Behrman, Associate Dean of Graduate School Admissions, 314-977-3827, Fax: 314-977-3943, E-mail: behrmang@slu.edu.

Saint Mary-of-the-Woods College, Program in Pastoral Theology, Saint Mary-of-the-Woods, IN 47876. Offers pastoral theology (MA); youth ministry (Graduate Certificate). Part-time and evening/weekend programs available. Postbaccalaureate distance learning degree programs offered (minimal on-campus study). *Degree requirements:* For master's, thesis, qualifying exam.

Saint Mary Seminary and Graduate School of Theology, School of Theology, Wickliffe, OH 44092-2527. Offers M Div, MA, D Min. *Accreditation:* ATS. Part-time programs available. *Degree requirements:* For master's, comprehensive exam, symposium; for doctorate, thesis/dissertation, final project, symposium; for M Div, one foreign language, evaluation by faculty for ordination. *Entrance requirements:* For M Div, GRE General Test, previous course work in religion and philosophy; for master's, GRE General Test, previous course work in religion; for doctorate, M Div or equivalent, 3 years in full-time ministry, interviews, ministry profile report. *Faculty research:* Pastoral ministry, theology of ministry, ecclesiology, American Catholics.

St. Mary's Seminary and University, Ecumenical Institute of Theology, Baltimore, MD 21210-1994. Offers church ministries (MA); theology (MA Th, Certificate). *Accreditation:* ACIPE; ATS. Part-time and evening/weekend programs available. *Degree requirements:* For master's, thesis or alternative, comprehensive exam or colloquium. Expenses: Contact institution. *Faculty research:* Scripture and ethics, theology and literature, early Christianity and Judaism, medical and social ethics.

Announcement: St. Mary's Ecumenical Institute of Theology offers part-time, accredited theological education for laypeople and clergy from all faith traditions. Students may pursue the MA in theology or the MA in church ministries (with 7 different tracks), certificates in 6 areas, or the post-master's Certificate of Advanced Studies.

St. Mary's Seminary and University, School of Theology, Baltimore, MD 21210-1994. Offers M Div, STB, MA Th, STD, STL. *Accreditation:* ACIPE; ATS (one or more programs are accredited). Part-time programs available. Terminal master's awarded for partial completion of doctoral program. *Degree requirements:* For master's and first professional degree, comprehensive exam. *Entrance requirements:* For master's, Computerized Adaptive Placement Assessment and Support System.

St. Mary's University, Graduate School, Department of Theology, San Antonio, TX 78228-8507. Offers pastoral ministry (MA); theology (MA); JD/MA. Part-time and evening/weekend programs available. Postbaccalaureate distance learning degree programs offered (no on-campus study). *Students:* 4 full-time (1 woman), 32 part-time (16 women); includes 7 minority (all Hispanic Americans), 1 international. Average age 41. In 2007, 14 degrees awarded. *Degree requirements:* For master's, thesis optional, practicum (pastoral administration). *Entrance requirements:* For master's, GRE General Test, MAT, 12 credit hours in theology/philosophy. Additional exam requirements/recommendations for international students: Required—TOEFL (minimum score 550 paper-based; 213 computer-based). *Application deadline:* For fall admission, 8/1 for domestic students. Application fee: $0. *Financial support:* Research assistantships, career-related internships or fieldwork, Federal Work-Study, institutionally sponsored loans, scholarships/grants, health care benefits, and unspecified assistantships available. Financial award application deadline: 3/31; financial award applicants required to submit FAFSA. *Faculty research:* Bioethics; perceptions of ministry; Marian doctrines and the contemporary church; Jaspers, peace, and justice. *Unit head:* Rev. Daniel Thompson, Director, 210-436-3310, E-mail: dthompson@stmarytx.edu.

Saint Meinrad School of Theology, Professional Program, Saint Meinrad, IN 47577. Offers M Div. *Accreditation:* ACIPE; ATS. *Faculty:* 21 full-time (2 women), 7 part-time/adjunct (1 woman). *Students:* 69 full-time (0 women); includes 22 minority (10 African Americans, 4 Asian Americans or Pacific Islanders, 8 Hispanic Americans), 2 international. Average age 32. In 2007, 20 degrees awarded. *Entrance requirements:* 30 credits in philosophy, 12 credits in theology. Additional exam requirements/recommendations for international students: Required—TOEFL (minimum score 550 paper-based). *Application deadline:* For fall admission, 7/31 for domestic and international students; for winter admission, 11/15 for domestic and international students. Applications are processed on a rolling basis. Application fee: $0. *Financial support:* In 2007–08, 64 students received support. Career-related internships or fieldwork, Federal Work-Study, institutionally sponsored loans, and scholarships/grants available. Support available to part-time students. Financial award application deadline: 7/31; financial award applicants required to submit FAFSA. *Unit head:* Dr. Thomas P. Walters, Academic Dean, 812-357-6543, Fax: 812-357-6792, E-mail: twalters@saintmeinrad.edu. *Application contact:* Rev. Jonathan Fassero, OSB, Director of Enrollment, 812-357-6762, Fax: 812-357-6462, E-mail: jfassero@saintmeinrad.edu.

Saint Meinrad School of Theology, Program in Catholic Philosophical Studies, Saint Meinrad, IN 47577. Offers MA. *Faculty:* 21 full-time (2 women), 7 part-time/adjunct (1 woman). *Students:* 15 full-time (0 women); includes 4 minority (1 African American, 1 Asian American or Pacific Islander, 2 Hispanic Americans). *Entrance requirements:* Additional exam requirements/recommendations for international students: Required—TOEFL (minimum score 550 paper-based). *Application deadline:* For fall admission, 7/31 for domestic and international students; for winter admission, 11/15 for domestic and international students. Applications are processed on a rolling basis. *Unit head:* Dr. Thomas P. Walters, Academic Dean, 812-357-6543, Fax: 812-357-6792, E-mail: twalters@saintmeinrad.edu. *Application contact:* Rev. Jonathan Fassero, OSB, Director of Enrollment, 812-357-6762, Fax: 812-357-6462, E-mail: jfassero@saintmeinrad.edu.

Saint Meinrad School of Theology, Program in Catholic Thought and Life, Saint Meinrad, IN 47577. Offers MA. *Accreditation:* ACIPE; ATS. Part-time and evening/weekend programs available. *Faculty:* 21 full-time (2 women), 7 part-time/adjunct (1 woman). *Students:* 5 full-time (1 woman), 19 part-time (7 women). In 2007, 9 degrees awarded. *Degree requirements:* For master's, comprehensive exam. *Application deadline:* For fall admission, 7/31 for domestic and international students; for winter admission, 11/15 for domestic and international students. Applications are processed on a rolling basis. *Financial support:* In 2007–08, 8 students received support. Federal Work-Study, institutionally sponsored loans, and scholarships/grants available. Support available to part-time students. Financial award application deadline: 7/31; financial award applicants required to submit FAFSA. *Unit head:* Kyle Kramer, Director of Lay Degree Programs, 812-357-6678, Fax: 812-357-6792, E-mail: kkramer@saintmeinrad.edu.

Saint Meinrad School of Theology, Program in Theological Studies, Saint Meinrad, IN 47577. Offers MTS. *Accreditation:* ACIPE; ATS. Part-time and evening/weekend programs available. *Faculty:* 21 full-time (2 women), 7 part-time/adjunct (1 woman). *Students:* 3 full-time (2 women), 38 part-time (17 women). In 2007, 18 degrees awarded. *Degree requirements:* For master's, thesis. *Application deadline:* For fall admission, 7/31 for domestic and international students; for winter admission, 11/15 for domestic and international students. Applications are processed on a rolling basis. *Financial support:* In 2007–08, 26 students received support. Federal Work-Study, institutionally sponsored loans, and scholarships/grants available. Support available to part-time students. Financial award application deadline: 7/31; financial award applicants required to submit FAFSA. *Unit head:* Kyle Kramer, Director of Lay Degree Programs, 812-357-6678, Fax: 812-357-6792, E-mail: kkramer@saintmeinrad.edu.

Saint Michael's College, Graduate Programs, Program in Theology and Pastoral Ministry, Colchester, VT 05439. Offers theology (MA, CAS, Certificate). Part-time and evening/weekend programs available. *Faculty:* 16 part-time/adjunct (6 women). *Students:* Average age 48. 4 applicants, 100% accepted, 3 enrolled. In 2007, 7 degrees awarded. *Degree requirements:* For master's, thesis optional, 1 foreign language if thesis option selected. *Entrance requirements:* For master's, bachelor's degree in arts, science, philosophy, theology, or education; minimum GPA of 3.0; 24 hours of course work in theology and other humanistic disciplines. Additional exam requirements/recommendations for international students: Required—TOEFL (minimum score 550 paper-based; 213 computer-based; 80 iBT), IELTS (minimum score 6). *Application deadline:* Applications are processed on a rolling basis. Application fee: $35. Electronic applications accepted. *Expenses: Contact institution. Financial support:* Federal Work-Study available. Support available to part-time students. Financial award applicants required to submit FAFSA. *Unit head:* Dr. Edward J. Mahoney, Director, 802-654-2579, Fax: 802-654-2664, E-mail: emahoney@smcvt.edu.

St. Norbert College, Program in Theological Studies, De Pere, WI 54115-2099. Offers MTS. Part-time programs available. *Faculty:* 5 full-time (1 woman), 2 part-time/adjunct (0 women). *Students:* 8 applicants, 88% accepted, 7 enrolled. In 2007, 11 degrees awarded. *Degree requirements:* For master's, comprehensive exam, thesis. *Entrance requirements:* For master's, minimum of 8 credits of course work in theology/religious studies, BA degree from an accredited institution. *Application deadline:* Applications are processed on a rolling basis. Application fee: $50. Electronic applications accepted. *Expenses:* Tuition: Part-time $335 per credit hour. Required fees: $19 per course. One-time fee: $100 part-time. *Financial support:* In 2007–08, 8 students received support. Scholarships/grants available. Support available to part-time students. *Faculty research:* Practical theology, Holocaust, Rahner, women in the Bible and Christian ethics. *Unit head:* Dr. Howard Ebert, Director, 920-403-3956, Fax: 920-403-4086, E-mail: howard.ebert@snc.edu. *Application contact:* DeEtte L. Radant, Program Coordinator, 920-403-3957, Fax: 920-403-4086, E-mail: deette.radant@snc.edu.

St. Patrick's Seminary & University, School of Theology, Menlo Park, CA 94025-3596. Offers M Div, STB, MA. *Accreditation:* ATS (one or more programs are accredited). Part-time programs available. *Degree requirements:* For master's, comprehensive exam, thesis or alternative. *Entrance requirements:* For first professional degree, GRE General Test or MAT, minimum GPA of 2.0, interview; for master's, GRE General Test, minimum GPA of 3.0, interview. Additional exam requirements/recommendations for international students: Required—TOEFL (minimum score 550 paper-based; 215 computer-based; 80 iBT), TWE. *Faculty research:* Systematic theology, sacred scripture, moral theology, liturgy.

Saint Paul School of Theology, Graduate and Professional Programs, Kansas City, MO 64127-2440. Offers M Div, MTS, D Min. *Accreditation:* ACIPE; ATS. Part-time programs available. *Degree requirements:* For doctorate, thesis/dissertation. *Entrance requirements:* For M Div and master's, minimum GPA of 2.75; for doctorate, minimum GPA of 3.0. Additional exam requirements/recommendations for international students: Required—TOEFL. *Faculty research:* Religion and aging; leadership development; feminist, African-American, and liberation theology; rural ministry; worship and the arts.

Saint Paul University, Faculty of Canon Law, Ottawa, ON K1S 1C4, Canada. Offers canon law (MCL, JCD, PhD, Graduate Certificate, JCL); canonical practice (Graduate Certificate); ecclesiastical administration (Graduate Certificate). Part-time programs available. *Faculty:* 10 full-time (1 woman), 4 part-time/adjunct (3 women). *Students:* 56 full-time (6 women), 1 (woman) part-time; includes 30 minority (14 African Americans, 15 Asian Americans or Pacific Islanders, 1 Hispanic American). Average age 40. 43 applicants, 86% accepted, 32 enrolled. In 2007, 17 master's, 3 doctorates, 16 other advanced degrees awarded. *Degree requirements:* For master's, one foreign language; for doctorate, one foreign language, comprehensive exam, thesis/dissertation; for other advanced degree, one foreign language, comprehensive exam (for some programs), comprehensive exam and seminar paper (JCL). *Entrance requirements:* For master's, appropriate bachelor's degree, 18 credits in theology; for doctorate, JCL or MCL; for other advanced degree, B Th or equivalent (JCL), appropriate bachelor's degree, 18 credits in theology. *Application deadline:* For fall admission, 8/15 priority date for domestic students, 5/15 priority date for international students. Applications are processed on a rolling basis. Application fee: $60 Canadian dollars. *Financial support:* In 2007–08, 3 students received support. Scholarships/grants and bursaries available. *Faculty research:* All questions related to Church law. *Unit head:* Dr. Roland Jacques, Dean, 613-751-4035, Fax: 613-751-4036, E-mail: rjacques@ustpaul.ca. *Application contact:* Beverly Ruth Kavanaugh, Administrative Assistant, 613-751-4018, Fax: 613-751-4036, E-mail: bkavanaugh@ustpaul.ca.

Saint Paul University, Faculty of Human Sciences, Program in Counseling and Spirituality, Ottawa, ON K1S 1C4, Canada. Offers individual or marital/couple counseling (MA); spiritual care (MA). Part-time programs available. *Students:* 57 applicants, 72% accepted, 32 enrolled. In 2007, 18 degrees awarded. *Degree requirements:* For master's, research project or thesis. *Entrance requirements:* For master's, honors BA in human sciences, minimum B average, 12 theology credits. *Application deadline:* For fall admission, 3/31 priority date for domestic and international students; for spring admission, 5/1 priority date for domestic students. Application fee: $60. *Unit head:* Manal Guirguis-Younger, Head, 613-236-1393 Ext. 2390, E-mail: jlowe@ustpaul.ca. *Application contact:* Diane Boudreault, Head, 613-236-1393 Ext. 2292, E-mail: dboudreault@ustpaul.ca.

Saint Paul University, Faculty of Theology, Ottawa, ON K1S 1C4, Canada. Offers MA Th, MP Th, MRE, D Min, D Th, PhD, L Th. *Faculty:* 25 full-time (7 women), 7 part-time/adjunct (0 women). *Students:* 71 full-time (23 women), 16 part-time (9 women), 20 international. In 2007, 7 master's, 2 doctorates, 2 other advanced degrees awarded. *Degree requirements:* For master's and L Th, one foreign language; for doctorate, one foreign language, comprehensive exam, thesis/dissertation. *Entrance requirements:* For master's, B Th; for doctorate, MA Th, L Th, MP TH, M Div. *Application deadline:* For fall admission, 6/15 priority date for domestic students; for winter admission, 10/15 for domestic students. Applications are processed on a rolling basis. Application fee: $60. *Faculty research:* Biblical studies, systematic and historical theology, ethics, spirituality, Eastern Christian studies, applied theology. *Unit head:* Dr. Andrea Spatáfora, Dean, 613-236-1393 Ext. 2277, Fax: 613-751-4016, E-mail: doyenFTdean@ustapaul.ca. *Application contact:* Francine Forgues, Associate Registrar, 613-236-1393 Ext. 2237, Fax: 613-782-3014, E-mail: fforgues@ustpaul.ca.

St. Petersburg Theological Seminary, Graduate Programs, St. Petersburg, FL 33708. Offers Biblical studies (MA); counseling (MA); divinity (M Div); education (MA); Judaic studies (MA); ministry (MA, D Min); religious teacher (MA). Part-time and evening/weekend programs available. Postbaccalaureate distance learning degree programs offered (minimal on-campus study). *Faculty:* 8 full-time (4 women), 15 part-time/adjunct (6 women). *Students:* 32 full-time (16 women), 33 part-time (15 women). In 2007, 1 first professional degree, 5 master's, 1 doctorate awarded. *Degree requirements:* For master's, thesis; for doctorate, thesis/dissertation. *Entrance requirements:* For M Div and master's, Bachelor degree; for doctorate, Master degree. *Application deadline:* For fall admission, 8/15 priority date for domestic students; for winter admission, 12/31 priority date for domestic students. Application fee: $50. Electronic applications accepted. *Expenses:* Tuition: Part-time $140 per credit. Required fees: $15 per semester. Part-time tuition and fees vary according to program. *Financial support:* In 2007–08, 3 students received support. *Unit head:* Dr. George Pierce, Head of the Graduate Program, E-mail: gpierce3@tampabay.rr.com. *Application contact:* Dr. Amy Mormino, Registrar, 727-399-0276, Fax: 727-399-1324, E-mail: registrar@sptseminary.edu.

St. Peter's Seminary, Department of Theology, London, ON N6A 3Y1, Canada. Offers M Div, MTS. *Accreditation:* ATS.

Saints Cyril and Methodius Seminary, Graduate and Professional Programs, Orchard Lake, MI 48324. Offers pastoral ministry (MAPM); religious education (MARE); theology (M Div, MA). *Accreditation:* ATS. Part-time programs available.

St. Stephen's College, Programs in Theology, Edmonton, AB T6G 2J6, Canada. Offers ministry (D Min); pastoral counseling (MA); social transformation ministry (MA); spirituality and liturgy (MA); theological studies (MTS); theology (M Th). Part-time and evening/weekend programs available. Postbaccalaureate distance learning degree programs offered (minimal on-campus study). Terminal master's awarded for partial completion of doctoral program. *Degree requirements:* For master's, thesis; for doctorate, thesis/dissertation. *Entrance requirements:* Additional exam requirements/recommendations for international students: Required—TOEFL. Electronic applications accepted. *Faculty research:* Methodology for theological education, practice and supervision for ministry.

St. Thomas University, School of Theology and Ministry, Institute for Pastoral Ministries, Miami Gardens, FL 33054-6459. Offers pastoral ministries (MA, Certificate); practical theology (PhD). Part-time and evening/weekend programs available. *Students:* 3 full-time (2 women), 17 part-time (12 women); includes 11 minority (1 African American, 10 Hispanic Americans), 1 international. Average age 41. In 2007, 8 degrees awarded. *Degree requirements:* For master's, comprehensive exam; for doctorate, comprehensive exam, thesis/dissertation. *Entrance requirements:* For master's, interview, minimum GPA of 3.0 or GRE; for doctorate, GRE, MA in theology. Additional exam requirements/recommendations for international students: Required—TOEFL (minimum score 550 paper-based; 213 computer-based; 79 iBT). *Application deadline:* For fall admission, 6/15 priority date for domestic students; for spring admission, 11/15 for domestic students. Applications are processed on a rolling basis. Application fee: $40. Electronic applications accepted. *Financial support:* Career-related internships or fieldwork and unspecified assistantships available. Support available to part-time students. Financial award application deadline: 4/15; financial award applicants required to submit FAFSA. *Unit head:* Dr. Joseph A. Iannone, Dean, 305-474-6973. *Application contact:* Marilyn Carballosa, Assistant Director of Admissions, 305-628-6546, Fax: 305-628-6591, E-mail: graduate@stu.edu.

St. Tikhon's Orthodox Theological Seminary, Divinity Program, South Canaan, PA 18459. Offers M Div. *Accreditation:* ATS. *Faculty:* 8 full-time (1 woman), 6 part-time/adjunct (0 women). *Students:* 51 full-time (0 women), 6 part-time; includes 3 minority (1 African American, 2 Hispanic Americans), 4 international. 35 applicants, 80% accepted, 28 enrolled. In 2007, 11 degrees awarded. *Degree requirements:* For M Div, one foreign language, thesis/dissertation optional. *Entrance requirements:* Letters of recommendation. *Application deadline:* For fall admission, 7/30 for domestic students, 6/30 for international students. Applications are processed on a rolling basis. Application fee: $15. *Expenses:* Tuition: Part-time $85 per credit. *Financial support:* Fellowships with partial tuition reimbursements, career-related internships or fieldwork, institutionally sponsored loans, scholarships/grants, and tuition waivers (partial) available. *Faculty research:* Church history, patristics, scripture, spirituality. *Unit head:* Bp. Tikhon Mollard, Rector, 570-937-4411, Fax: 570-937-4139, E-mail: bp.tikhon@stots.edu. *Application contact:* Fr. Michael Dahulich, Dean, Director of Admissions, 570-937-4411, Fax: 570-937-3100, E-mail: fr.michael@stots.edu.

Saint Vincent de Paul Regional Seminary, Graduate and Professional Programs, Boynton Beach, FL 33436-4899. Offers theology (M Div, MA Th). *Accreditation:* ATS. Part-time programs available. *Faculty:* 17 full-time (5 women), 9 part-time/adjunct (1 woman). *Students:* 60 full-time (0 women), 13 part-time (4 women); includes 26 minority (7 African Americans, 2 Asian Americans or Pacific Islanders, 17 Hispanic Americans). Average age 36. 21 applicants, 86% accepted, 18 enrolled. In 2007, 11 M Divs, 1 master's awarded. *Degree requirements:* For master's, comprehensive exam (for some programs), thesis optional; for M Div, one foreign language. *Entrance requirements:* For M Div and master's, GRE General Test, MAT. Additional exam requirements/recommendations for international students: Required—TOEFL. *Application deadline:* For fall admission, 7/1 priority date for domestic students. Applications are processed on a rolling basis. Application fee: $0. *Financial support:* Applicants required to submit FAFSA. *Unit head:* Rev. Steven O'Hala, Academic Dean, 561-732-4424 Ext. 161, Fax: 561-732-8808, E-mail: sohala@svdp.edu. *Application contact:* Rev. Keith Brennan, Rector/President, 561-732-4424, Fax: 561-737-2205.

Saint Vincent Seminary, School of Theology, Latrobe, PA 15650-2690. Offers M Div, MA. *Accreditation:* ATS. Part-time programs available. *Faculty:* 7 full-time (0 women), 17 part-time/adjunct (2 women). *Students:* 65 full-time (1 woman), 9 part-time (3 women); includes 7 minority (1 African American, 3 Asian Americans or Pacific Islanders, 3 Hispanic Americans), 13 international. Average age 39. 26 applicants, 92% accepted, 22 enrolled. In 2007, 13 first professional degrees, 9 master's awarded. *Degree requirements:* For master's, one foreign language, comprehensive exam; for M Div, one foreign language. *Entrance requirements:* For M Div, minimum GPA of 2.5; for master's, minimum GPA of 3.0. Additional exam requirements/recommendations for international students: Required—TOEFL (minimum score 550 paper-based; 220 computer-based). *Application deadline:* For fall admission, 8/1 priority date for domestic students, 8/1 for international students. Applications are processed on a rolling basis. Application fee: $39. Electronic applications accepted. *Expenses:* Tuition: Part-time $588 per credit. Required fees: $164 per semester. One-time fee: $33 part-time. *Financial support:* In 2007–08, 68 students received support. Scholarships/grants available. Support available to part-time students. Financial award application deadline: 8/1; financial award applicants required to submit FAFSA. *Faculty research:* Church history, preaching, psychology of religion, Biblical studies, moral theology. *Unit head:* Very Rev. Justin Matro, President/Rector, 724-537-4592, Fax: 724-532-5052, E-mail: justin.matro@email.stvincent.edu. *Application contact:* Dr. Kathleen Borres, Academic Dean, 724-805-2324, Fax: 724-805-2880, E-mail: kathleen.borres@email.stvincent.edu.

St. Vladimir's Orthodox Theological Seminary, Graduate School of Theology, Crestwood, NY 10707-1699. Offers general theological studies (MA); liturgical music (MA); religious education (MA); theology (M Div, M Th, D Min); M Div/MA. MA in general theological studies, M Div offered jointly with St. Nersess Seminary. *Accreditation:* ATS. Part-time programs available. *Degree requirements:* For master's, one foreign language, thesis, fieldwork; for doctorate, thesis/dissertation, fieldwork; for M Div, one foreign language, thesis/dissertation, fieldwork. *Entrance requirements:* For doctorate, M Div, minimum GPA of 3.0. Additional exam requirements/recommendations for international students: Required—TOEFL (minimum score 250 computer-based).

Samford University, Beeson School of Divinity, Birmingham, AL 35229. Offers M Div, MTS, D Min, JD/M Div, JD/MTS, M Div/MBA, M Div/MM, M Div/MSE. *Accreditation:* ATS. *Faculty:* 15 full-time (3 women), 2 part-time/adjunct (0 women). *Students:* 172 full-time (34 women), 22 part-time (7 women); includes 26 minority (23 African Americans, 1 Asian American or Pacific Islander, 2 Hispanic Americans), 2 international. Average age 31. 85 applicants, 69% accepted, 31 enrolled. In 2007, 46 first professional degrees, 13 master's, 8 doctorates awarded. *Median time to degree:* Of those who began their doctoral program in fall 1999, 75% received their degree in 8 years or less. *Degree requirements:* For master's, one foreign language; for doctorate, thesis/dissertation; for M Div, 2 foreign languages. *Entrance requirements:* For M Div and master's, minimum GPA of 2.0; for doctorate, minimum GPA of 3.0. Additional exam requirements/recommendations for international students: Required—TOEFL (minimum score 550 paper-based; 213 computer-based). *Application deadline:* For fall admission, 3/1 for domestic and international students; for spring admission, 10/1 for domestic and international students. Application fee: $25. *Expenses: Contact institution. Financial support:* In 2007–08, 140 students received support. Scholarships/grants and tuition waivers (full and partial) available. Financial award applicants required to submit FAFSA. *Faculty research:* New Testament theology, exegesis of Psalms, doctrinal preaching, history of Anglicanism, racial reconciliation. *Unit head:* Dr. Timothy George, Dean, 205-726-2632, E-mail: tfgeorge@samford.edu.

San Francisco Theological Seminary, Graduate and Professional Programs, San Anselmo, CA 94960-2997. Offers M Div, MA, MATS, D Min, PhD, Th D, M Div/MA. *Accreditation:* ACIPE; ATS (one or more programs are accredited). Part-time programs available. *Degree requirements:* For master's, one foreign language, thesis (for some programs); for doctorate, thesis/dissertation; for M Div, one foreign language, internship. *Entrance requirements:* For master's,

Theology

San Francisco Theological Seminary (continued)
minimum GPA of 3.0; for doctorate, M Div. Additional exam requirements/recommendations for international students: Required—TOEFL.

Seabury-Western Theological Seminary, School of Theology, Evanston, IL 60201-2976. Offers Anglican ministries (D Min); congregational development (MTS, D Min); preaching (D Min); theological studies (MTS); theology (M Div, L Th). MTS and D Min (congregational development) offered in summer only. *Accreditation:* ACIPE; ATS (one or more programs are accredited). Part-time programs available. *Degree requirements:* For master's, thesis; for doctorate, thesis/dissertation; for L Th, thesis (for some programs). *Entrance requirements:* For M Div and master's, interview, sample of written work. *Faculty research:* Liturgical interpretations of baptism, trinitarian theology, congregational development, post modern biblical criticism-Matthew.

Seattle University, School of Theology and Ministry, Program in Divinity, Seattle, WA 98122-1090. Offers M Div. *Accreditation:* ATS. Part-time and evening/weekend programs available. *Degree requirements:* For M Div, project. *Entrance requirements:* Interview, minimum GPA of 2.75.

Seattle University, School of Theology and Ministry, Program in Transforming Spirituality, Seattle, WA 98122-1090. Offers MATS, Certificate. *Accreditation:* ATS. Part-time and evening/weekend programs available. *Degree requirements:* For master's, project. *Entrance requirements:* For master's, interview, minimum GPA of 2.75.

Seminary of the Immaculate Conception, School of Theology, Huntington, NY 11743-1696. Offers pastoral studies (MA); theology (M Div, MA, D Min, Certificate). *Accreditation:* ATS (one or more programs are accredited). Part-time and evening/weekend programs available. *Faculty:* 8 full-time (2 women), 11 part-time/adjunct (4 women). *Students:* 37 full-time (0 women), 128 part-time (54 women); includes 19 minority (9 African Americans, 1 Asian American or Pacific Islander, 9 Hispanic Americans), 6 international. Average age 49. 21 applicants, 100% accepted, 19 enrolled. In 2007, 12 first professional degrees, 37 master's, 6 doctorates awarded. *Degree requirements:* For master's, comprehensive exam; for doctorate, thesis/dissertation; for M Div, one foreign language, thesis/dissertation. *Entrance requirements:* For M Div, college degree in philosophy-theology; for master's, undergraduate degree; for doctorate, MA plus 30 credits or M Div; for Certificate, MA in theology. *Application deadline:* For fall admission, 8/30 priority date for domestic students; for spring admission, 1/20 priority date for domestic students. Applications are processed on a rolling basis. Application fee: $75. *Expenses:* Tuition: Full-time $12,000; part-time $450 per credit. Required fees: $1,000; $50 per semester. One-time fee: $200 part-time. *Financial support:* Scholarships/grants available. Financial award applicants required to submit FAFSA. *Unit head:* Sr. Mary Louise Brink, SC, Associate Dean/Director of Graduate Studies, 631-423-0483 Ext. 130, Fax: 631-432-2346, E-mail: mlbrink@icseminary.edu. *Application contact:* Kathryn L. Zahner, Registrar, 631-423-0483 Ext. 147, Fax: 631-423-2346, E-mail: kzahner@icseminary.edu.

Seton Hall University, Immaculate Conception Seminary School of Theology, South Orange, NJ 07079-2697. Offers pastoral ministry (M Div, MA); theology (MA, Certificate). *Accreditation:* ACIPE; ATS (one or more programs are accredited). Part-time and evening/weekend programs available. *Degree requirements:* For master's, one foreign language, comprehensive exam, thesis, final project; for M Div, final project and seminar, field education, spiritual formation. *Entrance requirements:* For M Div, GRE, MAT; for master's, GRE General Test or MAT. Electronic applications accepted. Expenses: Contact institution.

Sewanee: The University of the South, School of Theology, Sewanee, TN 37383-1000. Offers M Div, MA, STM, D Min. MA open to foreign students. *Accreditation:* ACIPE; ATS. Part-time programs available. *Faculty:* 12 full-time (4 women), 8 part-time/adjunct (3 women). *Students:* 75 full-time (34 women), 11 part-time (8 women); includes 5 minority (3 African Americans, 1 American Indian/Alaska Native, 1 Hispanic American). Average age 43. 44 applicants, 82% accepted, 31 enrolled. In 2007, 29 first professional degrees, 3 master's, 7 doctorates awarded. *Median time to degree:* Of those who began their doctoral program in fall 1999, 50% received their degree in 8 years or less. *Degree requirements:* For master's, thesis; for doctorate, thesis/dissertation. *Entrance requirements:* For M Div, GRE General Test, interview; for master's, GRE General Test, M Div (STM); for doctorate, M Div. Additional exam requirements/recommendations for international students: Required—TOEFL (minimum score 550 paper-based). *Application deadline:* For fall admission, 4/1 priority date for domestic students, 4/1 for international students. Applications are processed on a rolling basis. Application fee: $25. *Expenses:* Tuition: Full-time $15,804; part-time $660 per credit hour. Required fees: $576. *Financial support:* Institutionally sponsored loans and scholarships/grants available. Support available to part-time students. Financial award application deadline: 5/1; financial award applicants required to submit FAFSA. *Unit head:* Very Rev. William S. Stafford, Dean, 931-598-1288, Fax: 931-598-1412, E-mail: wstafford@sewanee.edu. *Application contact:* Roslyn Dianne Weaver, Director of Admissions/Registrar, 931-598-1283, Fax: 931-598-1852, E-mail: rweaver@sewanee.edu.

Shaw University, Divinity School, Raleigh, NC 27601-2399. Offers M Div, MRE. *Accreditation:* ATS. Part-time and evening/weekend programs available. *Faculty:* 13 full-time (3 women), 10 part-time/adjunct (3 women). *Students:* 150 full-time (71 women), 55 part-time (25 women); includes 189 minority (188 African Americans, 1 American Indian/Alaska Native). Average age 46. 66 applicants, 89% accepted, 43 enrolled. In 2007, 25 first professional degrees, 8 master's awarded. *Degree requirements:* For master's, thesis; for M Div, thesis/dissertation. *Entrance requirements:* For M Div and master's, letters of reference. *Application deadline:* For fall admission, 7/30 priority date for domestic students, 1/30 priority date for international students; for spring admission, 11/30 priority date for domestic students, 8/30 priority date for international students. Applications are processed on a rolling basis. Application fee: $50. Electronic applications accepted. *Expenses:* Tuition: Full-time $7,920; part-time $440 per credit hour. Required fees: $1,640. *Financial support:* In 2007–08, 111 students received support. Federal Work-Study, scholarships/grants, and tuition waivers (full) available. Support available to part-time students. Financial award applicants required to submit FAFSA. *Faculty research:* HIV/AIDS awareness through faith-based curriculum, domestic abuse and violence prevention, pedagogy for non-traditional theology education, health disparities in the African-American community, technology and theological education. *Unit head:* Dr. James T. Robeson, Dean, 919-546-8570, Fax: 919-546-8271, E-mail: jtrob@shawu.edu. *Application contact:* Stella Goldston, Secretary, 919-546-3570, Fax: 919-546-8271, E-mail: sgoldston@shawu.edu.

Sh'or Yoshuv Rabbinical College, Graduate Programs, Far Rockaway, NY 11691-4002. *Accreditation:* AARTS.

Sioux Falls Seminary, Graduate and Professional Programs, Professional Program in Ministry, Sioux Falls, SD 57105-1599. Offers D Min. *Accreditation:* ACIPE. Part-time programs available. *Degree requirements:* For doctorate, thesis/dissertation. *Entrance requirements:* For doctorate, M Div, 3 years of ministry. *Application deadline:* Applications are processed on a rolling basis. Application fee: $35. *Financial support:* Career-related internships or fieldwork and scholarships/grants available. Support available to part-time students. *Unit head:* Dr. Gary Strickland, Interim Director of Doctoral Studies, 605-336-6588, Fax: 605-335-9090, E-mail: gstrickland@sfseminary.edu. *Application contact:* Bryce H. Eben, Director of Enrollment Development, 605-336-6588, Fax: 605-335-9090, E-mail: beben@sfseminary.edu.

Sioux Falls Seminary, Graduate and Professional Programs, Program in Bible and Theology, Sioux Falls, SD 57105-1599. Offers MA. *Accreditation:* ACIPE; ATS. Part-time programs available. *Students:* 1 (woman) full-time, 5 part-time (2 women). *Degree requirements:* For master's, 2 foreign languages, thesis or alternative. *Entrance requirements:* For master's, minimum GPA of 2.5. *Application deadline:* For fall admission, 8/1 priority date for domestic students; for spring admission, 1/1 priority date for domestic students. Applications are processed on a rolling basis. Application fee: $35. *Financial support:* Scholarships/grants available. *Application contact:* Bryce H. Eben, Director of Enrollment Development, 605-336-6588, Fax: 605-335-9090, E-mail: beben@sfseminary.edu.

Sioux Falls Seminary, Graduate and Professional Programs, Program in Theological Studies, Sioux Falls, SD 57105-1599. Offers Certificate. *Application deadline:* For fall admission, 8/1 priority date for domestic students; for spring admission, 1/1 priority date for domestic students. Applications are processed on a rolling basis. Application fee: $35. *Application contact:* Bryce H. Eben, Director of Enrollment Development, 605-336-6588, Fax: 605-335-9090, E-mail: beben@sfseminary.edu.

Southeastern Baptist Theological Seminary, Graduate and Professional Programs, Wake Forest, NC 27588-1889. Offers advanced biblical studies (M Div); Christian education (M Div, MACE); Christian ethics (PhD); Christian ministry (M Div); Christian planting (M Div); church music (MACM); counseling (MACO); evangelism (PhD); language (M Div); ministry (D Min); New Testament (PhD); Old Testament (PhD); philosophy (PhD); theology (Th M, PhD); women's studies (M Div). *Accreditation:* ACIPE; ATS (one or more programs are accredited). *Degree requirements:* For master's, thesis (for some programs), oral exam; for doctorate, thesis/dissertation, fieldwork; for M Div, supervised ministry. *Entrance requirements:* For master's, Cooperative English Test, minimum GPA of 2.0, M Div or equivalent (Th M); for doctorate, GRE General Test or MAT, Cooperative English Test, M Div or equivalent, 3 years of professional experience.

Southern Adventist University, School of Religion, Collegedale, TN 37315-0370. Offers Biblical and theological studies (MA); church leadership and management (MA); church ministry and homiletics (MA); evangelism and world mission (MA); religious studies (MA). Summer program only. Part-time programs available. *Faculty:* 5 full-time (0 women). *Students:* 2 full-time (0 women), 1 part-time; includes 1 minority (Asian American or Pacific Islander) Average age 36. 9 applicants, 100% accepted. In 2007, 6 degrees awarded. *Degree requirements:* For master's, comprehensive exam, thesis (for some programs). *Entrance requirements:* For master's, GRE. Additional exam requirements/recommendations for international students: Required—TOEFL (minimum score 550 paper-based). *Application deadline:* For spring admission, 4/30 priority date for domestic students, 12/30 for international students. Applications are processed on a rolling basis. Application fee: $25. *Financial support:* In 2007–08, 4 students received support. Tuition waivers (full) available. Support available to part-time students. Financial award application deadline: 4/1; financial award applicants required to submit FAFSA. *Faculty research:* Biblical archaeology. *Unit head:* Dr. Greg A. King, Dean, 423-236-2975, Fax: 423-236-1976, E-mail: gking@southern.edu. *Application contact:* Susan L. Brown, Administrative Assistant, 423-236-2977, Fax: 423-236-1977, E-mail: sbrown@southern.edu.

Southern Baptist Theological Seminary, Billy Graham School of Missions, Evangelism, and Church Growth, Louisville, KY 40280-0004. Offers Christian mission/world religion (PhD); evangelism/church growth (PhD); ministry (D Min); missiology (MA, D Miss); missions, evangelism, and church growth (M Div); theology (Th M). *Accreditation:* ATS. Part-time and evening/weekend programs available. Postbaccalaureate distance learning degree programs offered (minimal on-campus study). *Degree requirements:* For master's and M Div, 2 foreign languages; for doctorate, 4 foreign languages, thesis/dissertation. *Entrance requirements:* For doctorate, GRE General Test, MAT, field essay, M Div. Additional exam requirements/recommendations for international students: Required—TOEFL, TWE. *Faculty research:* Assimilation of church congregants, effective methodologies of evangelism, expectations of church members, spiritual warfare literature, formative church discipline.

Southern Baptist Theological Seminary, School of Theology, Louisville, KY 40280-0004. Offers M Div, Th M, D Min, PhD. *Accreditation:* ATS. Part-time and evening/weekend programs available. Postbaccalaureate distance learning degree programs offered (minimal on-campus study). *Degree requirements:* For master's, 2 foreign languages, thesis; for doctorate, 4 foreign languages, thesis/dissertation; for M Div, 2 foreign languages. *Entrance requirements:* For master's, GRE General Test, MAT, M Div; for doctorate, GRE General Test, MAT, interview, M Div, field essay. Additional exam requirements/recommendations for international students: Required—TOEFL, TWE. *Faculty research:* Biblical studies, contemporary theology, church history, pastoral care, ministry/missions studies.

Southern California Seminary, Graduate and Professional Programs, El Cajon, CA 92019. Offers biblical studies (MA); counseling psychology (MACP); psychology (Psy D); religious studies (MRS); theology (M Div). Part-time and evening/weekend programs available. Postbaccalaureate distance learning degree programs offered (minimal on-campus study). *Faculty:* 7 full-time (0 women), 17 part-time/adjunct (2 women). *Students:* 56 full-time (21 women), 68 part-time (30 women); includes 44 minority (24 African Americans, 2 Asian Americans or Pacific Islanders, 18 Hispanic Americans), 4 international. Average age 38. In 2007, 42 degrees awarded. *Degree requirements:* For master's, thesis (for some programs); for doctorate, thesis/dissertation; for M Div, 2 foreign languages. *Entrance requirements:* For doctorate, master's degree in psychology. Additional exam requirements/recommendations for international students: Required—TOEFL (minimum score 550 paper-based). *Application deadline:* For fall admission, 8/13 for domestic and international students; for spring admission, 12/11 for domestic students, 12/15 for international students. Applications are processed on a rolling basis. Application fee: $27 ($109 for international students). Electronic applications accepted. *Expenses:* Tuition: Part-time $290 per unit. Tuition and fees vary according to campus/location and program. *Financial support:* In 2007–08, 14 students received support. Federal Work-Study, scholarships/grants, and tuition waivers (partial) available. Financial award application deadline: 3/1; financial award applicants required to submit FAFSA. *Unit head:* Dr. Al Letting, Vice-President of Academics, 619-590-2131, E-mail: aletting@socalsem.edu. *Application contact:* Steve Perdue, Director of Admissions, 888-389-7244, E-mail: sperdue@socalsem.edu.

Southern Evangelical Seminary, Graduate School of Ministry and Missions, Matthews, NC 28105. Offers apologetics (Certificate); Christian education (MA); church ministry (MA, Certificate); divinity (Certificate), including apologetics (M Div, Certificate); Islamic studies (Certificate); theology (M Div), including apologetics (M Div, Certificate), Biblical studies; youth ministry (MA). Part-time and evening/weekend programs available. Postbaccalaureate distance learning degree programs offered. In 2007, 3 degrees awarded. *Degree requirements:* For master's, thesis (for some programs); for M Div, one foreign language. *Entrance requirements:* Additional exam requirements/recommendations for international students: Required—TOEFL (minimum score 600 paper-based; 250 computer-based). *Application deadline:* For fall admission, 8/15 priority date for domestic students, 8/5 priority date for international students; for winter admission, 12/15 priority date for domestic and international students; for spring admission, 1/15 priority date for domestic and international students. Applications are processed on a rolling basis. Application fee: $25. *Financial support:* Scholarships/grants available. *Unit head:* Dr. Barry R. Leventhal, Dean, 704-847-5600 Ext. 204, Fax: 704-845-1747, E-mail: dean@ses.edu.

Southern Evangelical Seminary, Veritas Graduate School of Apologetics and Counter-Cult Ministry, Matthews, NC 28105. Offers apologetics (MA, D Min, PhD, Certificate); Islamic studies (MA); Jewish studies (MA); philosophy (MA); religion (MA). *Accreditation:* ATS.Part-time and evening/weekend programs available. Postbaccalaureate distance learning degree programs offered (minimal on-campus study). In 2007, 18 master's, 2 doctorates awarded. *Degree requirements:* For master's, thesis optional; for doctorate, comprehensive exam (for some programs), thesis/dissertation. *Entrance requirements:* Additional exam requirements/recommendations for international students: Required—TOEFL (minimum score 600 paper-based; 250 computer-based). *Application deadline:* For fall admission, 8/15 priority date for domestic and international students; for winter admission, 12/15 priority date for domestic and international students; for spring admission, 1/15 priority date for domestic and international students. Applications are processed on a rolling basis. Application fee: $25. *Financial support:* Scholarships/grants available. *Unit head:* Dr. Thomas A. Howe, Director, Apologetics Program, 704-847-5600 Ext. 209, Fax: 704-845-1747, E-mail: thowe@ses.edu.

Southern Methodist University, Perkins School of Theology, Dallas, TX 75275. Offers M Div, CMM, MSM, MTS, D Min. *Accreditation:* ACIPE; ATS. Part-time programs available. *Faculty:* 27 full-time (10 women), 11 part-time/adjunct (1 woman). *Students:* 274 full-time (132 women), 150 part-time (94 women); includes 106 minority (76 African Americans, 2 American Indian/Alaska Native, 8 Asian Americans or Pacific Islanders, 20 Hispanic Americans), 8 international. Average age 39. 192 applicants, 68% accepted, 81 enrolled. In 2007, 60 first professional degrees, 15 master's, 11 doctorates awarded. *Degree requirements:* For master's and M Div, internship; for doctorate, internship, oral exam, professional project. *Entrance requirements:* For M Div and master's, minimum GPA of 2.75, course work in theology or liberal arts (recommended); for doctorate, minimum graduate GPA of 3.0, M Div or equivalent, 3 years of ministry experience. Additional exam requirements/recommendations for international students: Required—TOEFL (minimum score 600 paper-based; 250 computer-based), TWE. *Application deadline:* For fall admission, 5/1 for domestic students, 12/15 for international students; for spring admission, 11/1 for domestic students. Applications are processed on a rolling basis. Application fee: $50. *Expenses: Contact institution. Financial support:* In 2007–08, 204 students received support, including 1 fellowship with full tuition reimbursement available (averaging $10,000 per year); career-related internships or fieldwork, Federal Work-Study, scholarships/grants, and minister's family tuition awards also available. Support available to part-time students. Financial award application deadline: 3/1; financial award applicants required to submit FAFSA. Total annual research expenditures: $271,008. *Unit head:* Dr. William B. Lawrence, Dean, 214-768-2534, Fax: 214-768-2966. *Application contact:* Rev. Herbert S. Coleman, Director, Recruitment and Admissions, 214-768-2139, Fax: 214-768-4245, E-mail: theology@smu.edu.

Southern Nazarene University, Graduate College, Department of Philosophy and Religion, Bethany, OK 73008. Offers theology (MA). Part-time programs available. *Degree requirements:* For master's, one foreign language, thesis optional. *Entrance requirements:* For master's, GMAT, English proficiency exam, minimum GPA of 3.0 in last 60 hours/major, 2.7 overall.

Southwestern Assemblies of God University, Thomas F. Harrison School of Graduate Studies, Program in Theological Studies, Waxahachie, TX 75165-5735. Offers Bible and theology (MS); MS/MA. Postbaccalaureate distance learning degree programs offered. *Degree requirements:* For master's, comprehensive written and oral exams. *Entrance requirements:* For master's, GRE General Test, minimum GPA of 2.5. Electronic applications accepted.

Southwestern Baptist Theological Seminary, School of Theology, Fort Worth, TX 76122-0000. Offers M Div, MA Islamic, MA Miss, MA Th, Th M, D Min, PhD, SPTH. *Accreditation:* ACIPE; ATS (one or more programs are accredited). Part-time and evening/weekend programs available. Terminal master's awarded for partial completion of doctoral program. *Degree requirements:* For master's, 2 foreign languages, thesis (for some programs); for doctorate, 2 foreign languages, comprehensive exam, thesis/dissertation, oral exams; for M Div, 2 foreign languages, thesis/dissertation (for some programs). *Entrance requirements:* For doctorate, GRE, M Div or equivalent. Additional exam requirements/recommendations for international students: Required—TOEFL (minimum score 550 paper-based; 213 computer-based). Electronic applications accepted. *Faculty research:* Backgrounds to the New Testament, methods of teaching ancient Biblical languages, geography of the New Testament world, Baptist history.

Spring Arbor University, School of Arts and Sciences, Spring Arbor, MI 49283-9799. Offers communication (MA); spiritual formation and leadership (MA). Part-time programs available. Postbaccalaureate distance learning degree programs offered (no on-campus study). *Faculty:* 6 full-time (1 woman), 8 part-time/adjunct (3 women). *Students:* 69 full-time (46 women), 57 part-time (36 women); includes 10 minority (all African Americans), 1 international. In 2007, 3 degrees awarded. *Degree requirements:* For master's, thesis (for some programs). *Entrance requirements:* For master's, GRE (taken within the last 5 years), writing sample, 3 recommendations, personal goals statement. Additional exam requirements/recommendations for international students: Required—TOEFL (minimum score 550 paper-based; 220 computer-based). Application fee: $40. *Expenses: Contact institution.* One-time fee: $40 part-time. Tuition and fees vary according to course load and program. *Financial support:* Applicants required to submit FAFSA. *Unit head:* Dr. Wally Metts, Chair of the Department of Communication, 517-750-1200 Ext. 1491, E-mail: wmetts@arbor.edu. *Application contact:* Carol Bunnell, Secretary, Department of Communication, 517-750-6483, E-mail: cbunnell@arbor.edu.

Spring Hill College, Graduate Programs, Program in Theology, Mobile, AL 36608-1791. Offers MA, MPS, MTS. Part-time and evening/weekend programs available. Postbaccalaureate distance learning degree programs offered (no on-campus study). *Faculty:* 5 full-time (0 women), 5 part-time/adjunct (2 women). *Students:* 1 full-time (0 women), 60 part-time (30 women); includes 7 minority (2 African Americans, 1 Asian American or Pacific Islander, 4 Hispanic Americans). Average age 47. In 2007, 13 degrees awarded. *Degree requirements:* For master's, variable foreign language requirement, comprehensive exam, thesis (for some programs). *Entrance requirements:* For master's, minimum undergraduate GPA of 3.0; 6 hours of undergraduate course work in theology (religious studies). Additional exam requirements/recommendations for international students: Required—TOEFL (minimum score 550 paper-based; 213 computer-based). *Application deadline:* For fall admission, 8/1 priority date for domestic students, 6/1 priority date for international students; for spring admission, 12/1 priority date for domestic students, 11/1 priority date for international students. Applications are processed on a rolling basis. Application fee: $25 ($35 for international students). Electronic applications accepted. *Expenses: Contact institution. Financial support:* In 2007–08, 14 students received support. Career-related internships or fieldwork and scholarships/grants available. Support available to part-time students. Financial award applicants required to submit FAFSA. *Unit head:* Dr. Timothy R. Carmody, Director of Graduate Theology Programs, 251-380-4665, Fax: 251-460-2194, E-mail: carmody@shc.edu. *Application contact:* Joyce Genz, Dean of Continuing Studies and Director of Graduate Programs, 251-380-3094, Fax: 251-460-2190, E-mail: grad@shc.edu.

Starr King School for the Ministry, Professional Program, Berkeley, CA 94709-1209. Offers M Div. *Accreditation:* ACIPE; ATS.

Talmudic College of Florida, Program in Talmudic Law, Miami Beach, FL 33139. Offers MRE, Master of Talmudic Law, Doctor of Talmudic Law. *Accreditation:* AARTS. Terminal master's awarded for partial completion of doctoral program. *Degree requirements:* For master's, 2 foreign languages; for doctorate, 2 foreign languages, thesis/dissertation. *Entrance requirements:* For master's, oral exam, undergraduate Judaic studies degree; for doctorate, oral exam, Judaic studies degree.

Taylor University College and Seminary, Graduate and Professional Programs, Edmonton, AB T6J 4T3, Canada. Offers Christian studies (Diploma); intercultural studies (MA, Diploma); theology (M Div, MTS). *Accreditation:* ATS. Part-time programs available. *Degree requirements:* For master's, comprehensive exam, thesis optional. *Entrance requirements:* Additional exam requirements/recommendations for international students: Required—TOEFL (minimum score 550 paper-based; 213 computer-based), IELTS (minimum score 7). *Faculty research:* Biblical studies, administration and organization, world religions.

Temple Baptist Seminary, Program in Theology, Chattanooga, TN 37404-3530. Offers M Div, MABS, MM, MRE, D Min. Part-time and evening/weekend programs available. Postbaccalaureate distance learning degree programs offered (minimal on-campus study). *Degree requirements:* For doctorate, thesis/dissertation; for M Div, proficiency in Greek and Hebrew. *Entrance requirements:* For doctorate, minimum GPA of 3.0, M Div.

Toronto School of Theology, Graduate Programs, Toronto, ON M5S 2C3, Canada. Offers M Div, M Rel, MA, MAMS, MPS, MRE, MTS, Th M, D Min, PhD, Th D. Federation of seven Toronto-area theological colleges; basic degrees offered through the member colleges co-jointly with the University of Toronto. *Accreditation:* ATS. Postbaccalaureate distance learning degree programs offered (minimal on-campus study). *Faculty:* 92 full-time (20 women), 153 part-time/adjunct (47 women). *Students:* 603 full-time (218 women), 628 part-time (333 women). Average age 43. In 2007, 168 first professional degrees, 16 master's, 17 doctorates awarded. Terminal master's awarded for partial completion of doctoral program. *Degree requirements:* For master's, 2 foreign languages, thesis; for doctorate, 3 foreign languages, comprehensive exam, thesis/dissertation. *Entrance requirements:* For master's, language exams, minimum B+ average in undergraduate course work; for doctorate, language exams, first-class standing in master's program. Additional exam requirements/recommendations for international students: Required—TOEFL. *Application deadline:* For fall admission, 1/15 priority date for domestic and international students. Applications are processed on a rolling basis. Application fee: $100 Canadian dollars. Electronic applications accepted. Tuition and fees charges are reported in Canadian dollars. *Expenses:* Tuition: Full-time $4,526 Canadian dollars; part-time $452 Canadian dollars per course. Required fees: $126 Canadian dollars per term. One-time fee: $35 Canadian dollars. Tuition and fees vary according to course level, course load, degree level, program and student level. *Financial support:* Career-related internships or fieldwork available. *Unit head:* Dr. Alan L. Hayes, Director, 416-978-7822, Fax: 416-978-7821, E-mail: alan.hayes@utoronto.ca. *Application contact:* Jonathan Weverink, Advanced Degree Administrator, 416-978-4050, Fax: 416-978-7821, E-mail: inquiries@tst.edu.

Trevecca Nazarene University, Graduate Division, Graduate Religion Programs, Nashville, TN 37210-2877. Offers biblical studies (MA); preaching and practical theology (MA); systematic theology/historical theology (MA). Part-time programs available. *Faculty:* 3 full-time (0 women), 4 part-time/adjunct (0 women). *Students:* 23 full-time (4 women), 29 part-time (7 women); includes 8 minority (all African Americans), 1 international. Average age 37. In 2007, 9 degrees awarded. *Degree requirements:* For master's, comprehensive exam, thesis optional. *Entrance requirements:* For master's, GRE General Test or MAT, minimum GPA of 2.7, 2 letters of recommendation, philosophy of ministry statement. Additional exam requirements/recommendations for international students: Required—TOEFL (minimum score 550 paper-based; 213 computer-based). *Application deadline:* Applications are processed on a rolling basis. Application fee: $25. Electronic applications accepted. *Expenses: Contact institution.* Tuition and fees vary according to degree level and program. *Financial support:* Applicants required to submit FAFSA. *Unit head:* Dr. Tim Green, Dean/Director, 615-248-1378, Fax: 615-248-7417, E-mail: tgreen@trevecca.edu. *Application contact:* Sherry Crutchfield, Secretary, 615-248-1378, Fax: 615-248-7417, E-mail: admissions_rel@trevecca.edu.

Trinity Episcopal School for Ministry, Graduate Programs, Ambridge, PA 15003-2397. Offers Anglican studies (Diploma); basic Christian studies (Diploma); divinity (M Div); ministry (D Min); mission and evangelism (MAME, Diploma); religion (MAR); youth ministry (Diploma). *Accreditation:* ATS (one or more programs are accredited). Part-time programs available. *Degree requirements:* For master's, thesis optional; for doctorate, thesis/dissertation; for M Div, thesis/dissertation optional, Greek and Hebrew. *Entrance requirements:* Additional exam requirements/recommendations for international students: Required—TOEFL. *Faculty research:* Pauline Epistles, contemporary theology, history of Anglican liturgy, book of Ruth, biblical theology.

Trinity International University, Trinity Evangelical Divinity School, Deerfield, IL 60015-1284. Offers Biblical and Near Eastern archaeology and languages (MA); Christian studies (MA, Certificate); Christian thought (MA); church history (MA, Th M); congregational ministry: pastor-teacher (M Div); congregational ministry: team ministry (M Div); counseling ministries (MA); counseling psychology (MA); cross-cultural ministry (M Div); educational studies (PhD); evangelism (MA); history of Christianity in America (MA); intercultural studies (MA, PhD); leadership and ministry management (D Min); military chaplaincy (D Min); ministry (MA); mission and evangelism (Th M); missions and evangelism (D Min); New Testament (MA, Th M); Old Testament (Th M); Old Testament and Semitic languages (MA); pastoral care (M Div); pastoral care and counseling (D Min); pastoral counseling and psychology (Th M); pastoral theology (Th M); philosophy of religion (MA); preaching (D Min); religion (MA); research ministry (M Div); systematic theology (Th M); theological studies (PhD); urban ministry (MA). *Accreditation:* ATS (one or more programs are accredited). Part-time programs available. Postbaccalaureate distance learning degree programs offered (minimal on-campus study). *Faculty:* 41 full-time (4 women), 77 part-time/adjunct (17 women). *Students:* 578 full-time (141 women), 711 part-time (202 women). In 2007, 92 first professional degrees, 78 master's, 47 doctorates, 23 other advanced degrees awarded. *Degree requirements:* For master's, comprehensive exam, thesis, fieldwork; for doctorate, comprehensive exam (for some programs), thesis/dissertation; for M Div, 2 foreign languages, fieldwork; for Certificate, comprehensive exam, integrative papers. *Entrance requirements:* For M Div, GRE, MAT; for master's, GRE, MAT, minimum cumulative undergraduate GPA of 3.0; for doctorate, GRE, minimum cumulative graduate GPA of 3.2; for Certificate, GRE, MAT, minimum undergraduate GPA of 2.5. Additional exam requirements/recommendations for international students: Required—TOEFL (minimum score 580 paper-based; 237 computer-based), TWE (minimum score 4). *Application deadline:* For fall admission, 7/15 priority date for domestic and international students. Applications are processed on a rolling basis. Application fee: $25. Electronic applications accepted. *Expenses:* Tuition: Full-time $13,200; part-time $630 per credit. Required fees: $170. *Financial support:* In 2007–08, 770 students received support, including 10 fellowships with partial tuition reimbursements available (averaging $6,920 per year); teaching assistantships with partial tuition reimbursements available, career-related internships or fieldwork, Federal Work-Study, scholarships/grants, and tuition waivers (partial) also available. Financial award application deadline: 4/1; financial award applicants required to submit FAFSA. *Unit head:* Dr. Tite Tiénou, Academic Dean, 847-317-8086, Fax: 847-317-8014, E-mail: ttienou@teds.edu. *Application contact:* Ron Campbell, Director of Admissions, 800-345-8337, Fax: 847-317-8097, E-mail: rcampbel@tiu.edu.

Trinity Lutheran Seminary, Graduate and Professional Programs, Columbus, OH 43209-2334. Offers church music (MA); divinity (M Div); lay ministry (MA); sacred theology (STM); theological studies (MTS); MSN/MTS; MTS/JD. *Accreditation:* ACIPE; ATS. Part-time programs available. *Faculty:* 20 full-time (9 women), 15 part-time/adjunct (5 women). *Students:* 114 full-time (51 women), 46 part-time (18 women); includes 13 minority (9 African Americans, 3 Asian Americans or Pacific Islanders, 1 Hispanic American), 3 international. Average age 36. 95 applicants, 64% accepted, 53 enrolled. In 2007, 28 first professional degrees, 13 master's awarded. *Degree requirements:* For master's, thesis (for some programs); for M Div, 2 foreign languages, internship. *Entrance requirements:* For master's, M Div or equivalent (STM). Additional exam requirements/recommendations for international students: Required—TOEFL (minimum score 500 paper-based). *Application deadline:* For fall admission, 7/15 priority date for domestic students. Applications are processed on a rolling basis. Application fee: $25. *Expenses:* Tuition: Full-time $10,560. One-time fee: $100 full-time. Tuition and fees vary according to course load. *Financial support:* In 2007–08, 115 students received support. Career-related internships or fieldwork, Federal Work-Study, institutionally sponsored loans, and scholarships/grants available. Support available to part-time students. Financial award application deadline: 5/1; financial award applicants required to submit FAFSA. *Unit head:* Dr. Donald L. Huber, Dean, 614-235-4136, Fax: 614-236-3129, E-mail: dhuber@trinitylutheranseminary.edu. *Application contact:* Rev. Sheri L. Ayers, Director of Admissions, 614-235-4136 Ext. 4614, Fax: 866-610-8572, E-mail: sayers@trinitylutheranseminary.edu.

Trinity Western University, ACTS Seminaries, Langley, BC V2Y 1Y1, Canada. Offers Christian studies (MA); church ministries (MA); cross cultural ministries (MA); theology (M Div, M Th, MAMFT, MLE, MTS, D Min). *Accreditation:* ATS. Part-time programs available. *Faculty:* 13 full-time (0 women), 20 part-time/adjunct (3 women). *Students:* 129 full-time (58 women), 190 part-time (68 women). Average age 35. In 2007, 81 degrees awarded. *Degree requirements:* For master's, thesis (for some programs), internship. *Entrance requirements:* For master's, BA or equivalent; for doctorate, MDiv or equivalent. Additional exam requirements/recommendations for international students: Required—TOEFL. *Application deadline:* Applications are processed on a rolling basis. Application fee: $75. *Expenses: Contact institution. Financial support:* Research assistantships, career-related internships or fieldwork, Federal Work-Study, and institutionally sponsored loans available. Financial award application deadline: 3/1; financial award applicants required to submit FAFSA. *Faculty research:* Theology of leadership. *Unit*

Theology

Trinity Western University (continued)

head: Dr. Ron Toews, Principal, 604-588-7531, Fax: 604-513-2045. *Application contact:* Liisa Polkki, Director of Admissions, 604-513-2019, Fax: 604-513-2045, E-mail: acts@twu.ca.

Trinity Western University, Faculty of Graduate Studies, Program in Biblical Studies, Langley, BC V2Y 1Y1, Canada. Offers MA. *Accreditation:* ATS. Part-time programs available. *Faculty:* 9 part-time/adjunct (0 women). *Students:* 27 full-time (4 women), 8 part-time (1 woman); includes 10 Asian Americans or Pacific Islanders, 3 international. Average age 28. 18 applicants, 56% accepted. In 2007, 2 degrees awarded. *Degree requirements:* For master's, 2 foreign languages, thesis, 2 years Greek; 2 years Hebrew. *Entrance requirements:* For master's, minimum GPA of 3.0, degree in biblical studies, master of divinity or 42 hours Biblical Study credit. Additional exam requirements/recommendations for international students: Required—TOEFL (minimum score 600 paper-based; 250 computer-based). *Application deadline:* For fall admission, 5/1 priority date for domestic and international students; for spring admission, 11/1 priority date for domestic and international students. Applications are processed on a rolling basis. Application fee: $0 Canadian dollars. Electronic applications accepted. *Financial support:* In 2007–08, 15 students received support, including 5 research assistantships with full and partial tuition reimbursements available (averaging $1,500 per year), 7 teaching assistantships (averaging $1,500 per year); institutionally sponsored loans, scholarships/grants, and unspecified assistantships also available. Financial award application deadline: 5/1; financial award applicants required to submit FAFSA. *Faculty research:* Intertestamental literature, Dead Sea Scrolls, Biblical literature, history of Jesus, ancient languages. *Unit head:* Dr. Tony Cummins, Director, 604-888-7511 Ext. 3102, Fax: 604-513-2094, E-mail: tony.cummins@twu.ca. *Application contact:* Vic Cornish, Director, Graduate Admissions, 604-888-7511 Ext. 3130, Fax: 604-513-2064, E-mail: vic.cornish@twu.edu.

Tyndale University College & Seminary, Graduate Programs, Toronto, ON M2M 4B3, Canada. Offers Biblical studies (M Div); Christian foundations (MTS); Christian studies (Diploma); counseling (M Div); educational ministry (M Div); missions (M Div, Diploma); pastoral and Chinese ministry (M Div); pastoral ministry (M Div); Pentecostal studies (MTS); spiritual formation (M Div, Diploma); theological studies (M Div); theology (Th M); worship and liturgy (M Div, MTS); youth and family ministry (M Div). *Accreditation:* ATS. Part-time programs available. Postbaccalaureate distance learning degree programs offered (no on-campus study). *Degree requirements:* For M Div, one foreign language, thesis/dissertation optional. *Entrance requirements:* For M Div, master's, and Diploma, minimum C+ average in undergraduate course work. Additional exam requirements/recommendations for international students: Required—TOEFL (minimum score 570 paper-based; 230 computer-based), TWE (minimum score 5). Electronic applications accepted. *Faculty research:* Canadian church history, Chinese church history, Old Testament, counseling ministries (narrative therapy), world religions.

Unification Theological Seminary, Graduate Program, Main Campus, Barrytown, NY 12507. Offers M Div, MRE, D Min. Part-time programs available. *Faculty:* 8 full-time (2 women), 5 part-time/adjunct (0 women). *Students:* 83 full-time (16 women), 12 part-time (6 women). Average age 37. In 2007, 13 first professional degrees, 22 master's awarded. *Degree requirements:* For master's, one foreign language, project; for doctorate, thesis/dissertation; for M Div, one foreign language, thesis/dissertation. *Entrance requirements:* Additional exam requirements/recommendations for international students: Required—TOEFL (minimum score 450 paper-based; 133 computer-based). *Application deadline:* For fall admission, 8/15 priority date for domestic students; for spring admission, 1/15 priority date for domestic students. Applications are processed on a rolling basis. Application fee: $30. *Expenses:* Tuition: Part-time $410 per credit. Required fees: $127 per term. *Financial support:* Teaching assistantships, career-related internships or fieldwork, institutionally sponsored loans, scholarships/grants, and tuition waivers (partial) available. Financial award applicants required to submit FAFSA. *Faculty research:* Church leadership, church history, world religions, ecumenism, interfaith peacebuilding. *Unit head:* Dr. Andrew Wilson, Academic Dean, 845-752-3000 Ext. 228, Fax: 845-752-3014, E-mail: wilson@uts.edu. *Application contact:* Henry Christopher, Director of Admissions, 845-752-3000 Ext. 200, Fax: 845-752-3016, E-mail: admissions@uts.edu.

Unification Theological Seminary, Graduate Program, New York Extension, New York, NY 10036. Offers M Div, MRE. Part-time and evening/weekend programs available. *Faculty:* 2 full-time (0 women), 8 part-time/adjunct (2 women). *Students:* 24 full-time (9 women), 45 part-time (20 women). Average age 41. In 2007, 4 first professional degrees, 5 master's awarded. *Degree requirements:* For master's, project; for M Div, thesis/dissertation. *Entrance requirements:* Additional exam requirements/recommendations for international students: Required—TOEFL (minimum score 450 paper-based; 133 computer-based). *Application deadline:* For fall admission, 8/15 priority date for domestic students; for spring admission, 1/15 priority date for domestic students. Applications are processed on a rolling basis. Application fee: $30. *Expenses:* Tuition: Part-time $410 per credit. Required fees: $127 per term. *Financial support:* Career-related internships or fieldwork, institutionally sponsored loans, scholarships/grants, and tuition waivers (partial) available. Financial award applicants required to submit FAFSA. *Faculty research:* Service learning. *Unit head:* Dr. Kathy Winings, Dean of the Extension Center, 212-563-6647 Ext. 104, Fax: 212-563-6649, E-mail: irffint@aol.com. *Application contact:* Rev. Leander Hardaway, Admissions Officer, 212-563-6647 Ext. 15, Fax: 212-563-6649, E-mail: lwhardaway@aol.com.

Union Theological Seminary and Presbyterian School of Christian Education, School of Theological Studies, Richmond, VA 23227-4597. Offers M Div, Th M, D Min, PhD, M Div/MA. *Accreditation:* ACIPE; ATS. Terminal master's awarded for partial completion of doctoral program. *Degree requirements:* For master's, oral and written exams; for doctorate, 2 foreign languages, comprehensive exam, thesis/dissertation; for M Div, 2 foreign languages. *Entrance requirements:* For doctorate, GRE General Test. Additional exam requirements/recommendations for international students: Required—TOEFL, TWE.

Union Theological Seminary in the City of New York, Graduate and Professional Programs, New York, NY 10027-5710. Offers M Div, MA, STM, Ed D, PhD, M Div/MSSW. *Accreditation:* ACIPE; ATS (one or more programs are accredited). Part-time programs available. *Degree requirements:* For master's, one foreign language, thesis; for doctorate, 2 foreign languages, thesis/dissertation; for M Div, one foreign language, thesis/dissertation. *Entrance requirements:* For doctorate, GRE General Test, sample of written work. *Faculty research:* American religious history, psychiatry and religion, Christian ethics, New Testament.

United Talmudical Seminary, Graduate Programs, Brooklyn, NY 11211-7900. *Accreditation:* AARTS.

United Theological Seminary, Graduate and Professional Programs, Trotwood, OH 45426. Offers M Div, MA, MATS, D Min, M Div/MA. *Accreditation:* ATS. Part-time and evening/weekend programs available. *Faculty:* 13 full-time (5 women), 35 part-time/adjunct (8 women). *Students:* 220 full-time (101 women), 28 part-time (15 women); includes 116 minority (111 African Americans, 4 Asian Americans or Pacific Islanders, 1 Hispanic American), 5 international. Average age 46. 63 applicants, 90% accepted, 54 enrolled. In 2007, 18 first professional degrees, 6 master's, 54 doctorates awarded. *Degree requirements:* For master's, thesis (for some programs), comprehensive evaluation; for doctorate, thesis/dissertation, final exam; for M Div, comprehensive evaluation. *Entrance requirements:* For M Div, minimum GPA of 2.5, 5 letters of recommendation, interview; for master's, minimum GPA of 2.5, interview, 5 letters of recommendation; for doctorate, minimum GPA of 3.0, 2 letters of recommendation, interview. Additional exam requirements/recommendations for international students: Required—TOEFL (minimum score 550 paper-based; 213 computer-based). *Application deadline:* For fall admission, 8/1 for domestic students, 1/15 for international students; for spring admission, 1/1 for domestic students. Applications are processed on a rolling basis. Application fee: $40. Electronic applications accepted. *Expenses:* Tuition: Full-time $9,064; part-time $412 per credit. Required fees: $866; $80 per semester. *Financial support:* In 2007–08, 87 students received support. Career-related internships or fieldwork, Federal Work-Study, and scholarships/grants available. Financial award application deadline: 4/1; financial award applicants required to submit CSS PROFILE or FAFSA. *Unit head:* Rev. Julie M. Hostetter, Director of Academic and Student Services, 937-529-2201 Ext. 330, Fax: 937-529-2292, E-mail: jhostetter@united.edu. *Application contact:* Linda Rice, Admissions Officer, 937-529-2201 Ext. 3307, Fax: 937-529-2292, E-mail: utsadmis@united.edu.

United Theological Seminary of the Twin Cities, Graduate and Professional Programs, Professional Program, New Brighton, MN 55112-2598. Offers M Div. *Accreditation:* ACIPE; ATS. Part-time programs available. *Faculty:* 9 full-time (6 women), 21 part-time/adjunct (10 women). *Students:* 56 full-time (36 women), 48 part-time (30 women). Average age 45. 21 applicants, 95% accepted, 19 enrolled. In 2007, 17 degrees awarded. *Degree requirements:* For M Div, integrative notebook, spiritual chronicle. *Entrance requirements:* Minimum GPA of 2.75. *Application deadline:* For fall admission, 8/1 priority date for domestic students; for winter admission, 12/1 priority date for domestic students; for spring admission, 1/1 priority date for domestic students. Applications are processed on a rolling basis. Application fee: $40. *Expenses:* Tuition: Part-time $373 per credit hour. *Financial support:* Career-related internships or fieldwork, institutionally sponsored loans, and scholarships/grants available. Support available to part-time students. Financial award application deadline: 5/1; financial award applicants required to submit FAFSA. *Application contact:* Rev. Glen Herrington-Hall, Director of Admissions, 651-255-6107, Fax: 651-633-4315, E-mail: gherrington-hall@unitedseminary.edu.

United Theological Seminary of the Twin Cities, Graduate and Professional Programs, Program in Advanced Theological Studies, New Brighton, MN 55112-2598. Offers Diploma. *Faculty:* 12 full-time (7 women), 22 part-time/adjunct (10 women). In 2007, 1 degree awarded. *Entrance requirements:* Additional exam requirements/recommendations for international students: Required—TOEFL (minimum score 550 paper-based). *Application deadline:* For fall admission, 8/1 priority date for domestic students, 12/1 priority date for international students; for winter admission, 12/1 priority date for domestic students; for spring admission, 1/1 priority date for domestic students. Applications are processed on a rolling basis. Application fee: $40. *Expenses:* Tuition: Part-time $373 per credit hour. *Financial support:* Career-related internships or fieldwork, scholarships/grants, health care benefits, and housing and stipend available. Financial award application deadline: 5/1. *Application contact:* Rev. Glen Herrington-Hall, Director of Admissions, 651-255-6107, Fax: 651-633-4315, E-mail: gherrington-hall@unitedseminary.edu.

United Theological Seminary of the Twin Cities, Graduate and Professional Programs, Program in Ministry Renewal and Professional Development, New Brighton, MN 55112-2598. Offers Certificate. Part-time programs available. *Faculty:* 12 full-time (7 women), 22 part-time/adjunct (10 women). *Entrance requirements:* For degree, M Div or equivalent. Additional exam requirements/recommendations for international students: Required—TOEFL. *Application deadline:* For fall admission, 8/1 priority date for domestic students; for winter admission, 12/1 priority date for domestic students; for spring admission, 1/1 priority date for domestic students. Applications are processed on a rolling basis. Application fee: $50. *Expenses:* Tuition: Part-time $373 per credit hour. *Financial support:* Application deadline: 5/1; *Unit head:* Dr. Jean Morris Trumbauer, Director, 651-255-6127, Fax: 651-633-4315, E-mail: jtrumbauer@unitedseminary.edu. *Application contact:* Rev. Glen Herrington-Hall, Director of Admissions, 651-255-6107, Fax: 651-633-4315, E-mail: gherrington-hall@unitedseminary.edu.

United Theological Seminary of the Twin Cities, Graduate and Professional Programs, Program in Theological and Religious Studies, New Brighton, MN 55112-2598. Offers Certificate. Part-time programs available. *Faculty:* 12 full-time (7 women), 22 part-time/adjunct (10 women). In 2007, 4 degrees awarded. *Application deadline:* For fall admission, 8/1 priority date for domestic students; for winter admission, 12/1 priority date for domestic students; for spring admission, 1/1 priority date for domestic students. Applications are processed on a rolling basis. Application fee: $40. *Expenses:* Tuition: Part-time $373 per credit hour. *Application contact:* Rev. Glen Herrington-Hall, Director of Admissions, 651-255-6107, Fax: 651-633-4315, E-mail: gherrington-hall@unitedseminary.edu.

United Theological Seminary of the Twin Cities, Graduate and Professional Programs, Program in Theology, New Brighton, MN 55112-2598. Offers religion and theology (MA); theology and the arts (MA); women's studies (MA). Part-time programs available. *Faculty:* 12 full-time (7 women), 22 part-time/adjunct (10 women). *Students:* 9 full-time (4 women), 16 part-time (12 women). Average age 43. 13 applicants, 100% accepted, 12 enrolled. In 2007, 1 degree awarded. *Degree requirements:* For master's, thesis. *Entrance requirements:* For master's, minimum GPA of 2.75. *Application deadline:* For fall admission, 8/1 priority date for domestic students; for winter admission, 12/1 priority date for domestic students; for spring admission, 1/1 priority date for domestic students. Application fee: $40. *Expenses:* Tuition: Part-time $373 per credit hour. *Financial support:* Career-related internships or fieldwork, institutionally sponsored loans, and scholarships/grants available. Support available to part-time students. *Application contact:* Rev. Glen Herrington-Hall, Director of Admissions, 651-255-6107, Fax: 651-633-4315, E-mail: gherrington-hall@unitedseminary.edu.

Université de Montréal, Faculty of Theology and Sciences of Religions, Montréal, QC H3C 3J7, Canada. Offers MA, D Th, PhD, Certificate, DESS, L Th. *Faculty:* 23 full-time (7 women), 4 part-time/adjunct (1 woman). *Students:* 80 full-time (24 women), 25 part-time (12 women). 50 applicants, 44% accepted, 19 enrolled. In 2007, 11 master's, 4 doctorates, 1 other advanced degree awarded. *Degree requirements:* For master's, one foreign language; for doctorate, 2 foreign languages, thesis/dissertation, general exam. *Application deadline:* For fall admission, 2/1 priority date for domestic students; for winter admission, 11/1 priority date for domestic students; for spring admission, 2/1 priority date for domestic students. Application fee: $100. Electronic applications accepted. *Financial support:* Research assistantships, teaching assistantships, institutionally sponsored loans and tuition waivers (partial) available. *Unit head:* Jean Duhaime, Dean, 514-343-7160, Fax: 514-343-5738, E-mail: jean.duhaime@umontreal.ca. *Application contact:* Alain Gignac, Vice Dean of Graduate Studies, 514-343-6840, Fax: 514-343-5738, E-mail: alain.gignac@umontreal.ca.

Université de Sherbrooke, Faculty of Theology, Ethics and Philosophy, Sherbrooke, QC J1K 2R1, Canada. Offers applied ethics (Diploma); human science of religions (MA); intercultural training (Diploma); philosophy (MA, PhD); spiritual anthropology (Diploma); theology (MA, PhD, Diploma). Part-time and evening/weekend programs available. Postbaccalaureate distance learning degree programs offered. Terminal master's awarded for partial completion of doctoral program. *Entrance requirements:* For master's, bachelor's degree in related discipline; for doctorate, master's degree in related discipline. *Faculty research:* Faith and culture interrelation.

Université du Québec à Chicoutimi, Graduate Programs, Program in Theology (Pastoral Studies), Chicoutimi, QC G7H 2B1, Canada. Offers MA, PhD. Part-time programs available. *Degree requirements:* For doctorate, thesis/dissertation. *Entrance requirements:* For master's, appropriate bachelor's degree, proficiency in French; for doctorate, appropriate master's degree, proficiency in French.

Université Laval, Faculty of Theology and Religious Sciences, Program in Practical Theology, Québec, QC G1K 7P4, Canada. Offers D Th P. Part-time programs available. *Degree requirements:* For doctorate, comprehensive exam, thesis/dissertation. *Entrance requirements:* For doctorate, knowledge of French and English. Electronic applications accepted.

Université Laval, Faculty of Theology and Religious Sciences, Programs in Theology, Québec, QC G1K 7P4, Canada. Offers MA, PhD. Terminal master's awarded for partial completion of doctoral program. *Degree requirements:* For master's, thesis (for some programs); for doctorate, comprehensive exam, thesis/dissertation. *Entrance requirements:* For master's and doctorate, knowledge of French and English. Electronic applications accepted.

University of Chicago, Divinity School, Chicago, IL 60637-1513. Offers M Div, AM, AMRS, PhD, JD/M Div, JD/MA, JD/PhD, MPP/M Div, MSW/M Div. *Accreditation:* ATS (one or more programs are accredited). Part-time programs available. *Degree requirements:* For master's and M Div, one foreign language; for doctorate, 2 foreign languages, comprehensive exam, thesis/dissertation. *Entrance requirements:* For M Div, master's, and doctorate, GRE General Test. Additional exam requirements/recommendations for international students: Required—TOEFL (minimum score 600 paper-based; 250 computer-based). Electronic applications accepted. Expenses: Contact institution. *Faculty research:* Theology, history of religion, ethics, biblical studies, philosophy of religion.

University of Dallas, Braniff Graduate School of Liberal Arts, Department of Theology, Irving, TX 75062-4736. Offers M Th, MA. Part-time programs available. *Faculty:* 1 full-time (0 women), 1 part-time/adjunct (0 women). *Students:* 17 full-time (3 women), 9 part-time (1 woman); includes 1 minority (Asian American or Pacific Islander), 1 international. Average age 28. 10 applicants, 100% accepted, 7 enrolled. In 2007, 7 degrees awarded. *Degree requirements:* For master's, one foreign language, comprehensive exam, thesis (for some programs). *Entrance requirements:* For master's, GRE General Test. *Application deadline:* For fall admission, 2/15 priority date for domestic students; for spring admission, 11/15 for domestic students. Applications are processed on a rolling basis. Application fee: $50. *Expenses:* Tuition: Part-time $600 per credit. Required fees: $15 per credit. *Financial support:* In 2007–08, 25 students received support. Scholarships/grants available. Financial award application deadline: 2/15. *Faculty research:* Patristics, justice in the Old and New Testament, Pauline literature, Christology, theology of the Trinity. *Unit head:* Dr. Mark D. Lowery, Chair, Chair, 972-721-5357, Fax: 972-721-4007. *Application contact:* Graduate Coordinator, 972-721-5106, Fax: 972-721-5280, E-mail: graduate@acad.udallas.edu.

University of Dayton, Graduate School, College of Arts and Sciences, Department of Religious Studies, Dayton, OH 45469-1300. Offers pastoral ministry (MA); theological studies (MA); theology (PhD). Part-time and evening/weekend programs available. *Faculty:* 15 full-time (5 women), 11 part-time/adjunct (4 women). *Students:* 43 full-time (19 women), 20 part-time (14 women); includes 4 minority (2 African Americans, 1 Asian American or Pacific Islander, 1 Hispanic American), 2 international. Average age 39. 83 applicants, 64% accepted, 12 enrolled. In 2007, 17 master's, 1 doctorate awarded. Terminal master's awarded for partial completion of doctoral program. *Degree requirements:* For master's, thesis or alternative; for doctorate, 2 foreign languages, comprehensive exam, thesis/dissertation. *Entrance requirements:* For master's, minimum undergraduate GPA of 3.0, 24 semester credits of course work in philosophy/theology/religion; for doctorate, GRE General Test, minimum GPA of 3.5, academic writing sample. Additional exam requirements/recommendations for international students: Required—TOEFL (minimum score 550 paper-based; 213 computer-based; 80 iBT). *Application deadline:* For fall admission, 3/1 priority date for domestic and international students; for winter admission, 7/1 priority date for international students; for spring admission, 1/1 priority date for international students. Applications are processed on a rolling basis. Application fee: $0 ($50 for international students). Electronic applications accepted. *Expenses: Contact institution. Financial support:* In 2007–08, 17 fellowships with full tuition reimbursements (averaging $13,711 per year), 8 research assistantships with full tuition reimbursements (averaging $9,382 per year), 1 teaching assistantship with full tuition reimbursement were awarded; career-related internships or fieldwork, institutionally sponsored loans, scholarships/grants, health care benefits, tuition waivers (full), and unspecified assistantships also available. Support available to part-time students. Financial award application deadline: 3/1; financial award applicants required to submit FAFSA. *Faculty research:* Religion and science; U.S. Catholicism/Christianity; theological ethics; methodologies in biblical studies; practical/constructive theology. *Unit head:* Dr. Sandra Yocum-Mize, Chair, 937-229-4321, Fax: 937-229-4330, E-mail: mizes@notes.udayton.edu. *Application contact:* Angela Jones-Glukhov, Associate Director of Graduate Admissions, 937-229-4305, Fax: 937-229-4729.

University of Denver, Graduate Studies, Joint Program in Religious and Theological Studies, Denver, CO 80208. Offers PhD. *Students:* 50 full-time (18 women), 24 part-time (8 women); includes 9 minority (4 African Americans, 1 American Indian/Alaska Native, 2 Asian Americans or Pacific Islanders, 2 Hispanic Americans), 10 international. Average age 40. *Entrance requirements:* For doctorate, GRE. *Application deadline:* For fall admission, 1/15 for domestic students. Application fee: $50. *Unit head:* Dr. Frank Seeburger, Head, 303-871-2766.

University of Dubuque, Theological Seminary, Dubuque, IA 52001-5099. Offers M Div, MAR, D Min. *Accreditation:* ACIPE; ATS. Postbaccalaureate distance learning degree programs offered (minimal on-campus study). *Faculty:* 9 full-time (1 woman), 16 part-time/adjunct (8 women). *Students:* 111 full-time (53 women), 63 part-time (26 women); includes 7 minority (2 African Americans, 1 American Indian/Alaska Native, 2 Asian Americans or Pacific Islanders, 2 Hispanic Americans), 6 international. Average age 48. 75 applicants, 93% accepted, 54 enrolled. In 2007, 33 master's, 11 doctorates awarded. *Degree requirements:* For doctorate, thesis/dissertation. *Entrance requirements:* Additional exam requirements/recommendations for international students: Recommended—TOEFL (minimum score 550 paper-based; 220 computer-based; 80 iBT). *Application deadline:* For fall admission, 4/15 priority date for domestic students, 12/1 priority date for international students; for spring admission, 11/1 priority date for domestic students. Applications are processed on a rolling basis. Application fee: $30. *Financial support:* In 2007–08, 100 fellowships (averaging $8,551 per year) were awarded; career-related internships or fieldwork, Federal Work-Study, institutionally sponsored loans, scholarships/grants, and tuition waivers (full and partial) also available. Support available to part-time students. Financial award application deadline: 6/1; financial award applicants required to submit FAFSA. *Faculty research:* Biblical archaeology, biblical theology, reformed history and theology, pastoral theology, homiletics. Total annual research expenditures: $7,987. *Unit head:* Dr. Bradley Longfield, Dean, 319-589-3122, Fax: 319-589-3110, E-mail: blongfie@dbq.edu. *Application contact:* Peggy Sell, Director, Seminary Admissions, E-mail: psell@dbq.edu.

University of Mobile, Graduate Programs, Program in Religious Studies, Mobile, AL 36613. Offers biblical/theological studies (MA); marriage and family counseling (MA). Part-time and evening/weekend programs available. *Faculty:* 6 full-time (0 women), 2 part-time/adjunct (0 women). *Students:* 18 full-time (16 women), 35 part-time (18 women); includes 15 minority (13 African Americans, 2 American Indian/Alaska Native). Average age 27. In 2007, 15 degrees awarded. *Degree requirements:* For master's, one foreign language, comprehensive exam, thesis optional. *Entrance requirements:* For master's, GRE General Test. Additional exam requirements/recommendations for international students: Required—TOEFL. *Application deadline:* For fall admission, 8/3 priority date for domestic students; for spring admission, 12/23 for domestic students. Applications are processed on a rolling basis. Application fee: $40 ($50 for international students). *Financial support:* Federal Work-Study available. Support available to part-time students. Financial award application deadline: 8/1. *Unit head:* Dr. Cecil Taylor, Dean, School of Christian Studies, 251-442-2255, Fax: 251-442-2523, E-mail: ctaylor@mail.umobile.edu. *Application contact:* Tammy C. Eubanks, Administrative Assistant to Dean of Graduate Programs, 251-442-2270, Fax: 251-442-2523, E-mail: teubanks@umobile.edu.

University of Notre Dame, Graduate School, College of Arts and Letters, Division of Humanities, Department of Theology, Notre Dame, IN 46556. Offers M Div, MA, MSM, MTS, PhD. *Accreditation:* ACIPE; ATS. *Faculty:* 54 full-time (14 women), 3 part-time/adjunct (0 women). *Students:* 226 full-time (94 women), 14 part-time (5 women); includes 797 minority (4 African Americans, 1 American Indian/Alaska Native, 720 Asian Americans or Pacific Islanders, 72 Hispanic Americans), 13 international. 431 applicants, 18% accepted, 59 enrolled. In 2007, 9 first professional degrees, 59 master's, 12 doctorates awarded. Terminal master's awarded for partial completion of doctoral program. *Median time to degree:* Of those who began their doctoral program in fall 1999, 86% received their degree in 8 years or less. *Degree requirements:* For master's, one foreign language, comprehensive exam, thesis or alternative; for doctorate, 3 foreign languages, comprehensive exam, thesis/dissertation, candidacy exam. *Entrance requirements:* For M Div, master's, and doctorate, GRE General Test. Additional exam requirements/recommendations for international students: Required—TOEFL (minimum score 600 paper-based; 250 computer-based; 80 iBT). *Application deadline:* For fall admission, 1/2 for domestic and international students. Application fee: $50. Electronic applications accepted. *Financial support:* In 2007–08, 13 fellowships with full tuition reimbursements (averaging $22,000 per year), 1 research assistantship with full tuition reimbursement (averaging $16,000 per year), 44 teaching assistantships with full tuition reimbursements (averaging $16,000 per year) were awarded; tuition waivers (full) also available. Financial award application deadline: 2/1. *Faculty research:* Liturgy, ethics, historical studies, biblical studies, systematic theology. *Unit head:* Dr. John Cavadini, Chair of Theology Department, 574-631-5732, E-mail: theodgs@nd.edu. *Application contact:* Dr. Jarren Gonzales, Director of Graduate Admissions, 574-631-7706, Fax: 574-631-4183.

University of Saint Mary of the Lake–Mundelein Seminary, School of Theology, Mundelein, IL 60060. Offers M Div, STB, MA, D Min, Certificate, STL. *Accreditation:* ATS (one or more programs are accredited). *Faculty:* 45 full-time (5 women), 11 part-time/adjunct (1 woman). *Students:* 236 full-time (4 women); includes 7 minority (1 African American, 2 Asian Americans or Pacific Islanders, 4 Hispanic Americans), 102 international. Average age 30. 95 applicants, 75% accepted, 71 enrolled. In 2007, 49 first professional degrees, 4 master's, 3 doctorates, 10 other advanced degrees awarded. *Degree requirements:* For doctorate, thesis/dissertation; for first professional degree, thesis/dissertation (for some programs). *Entrance requirements:* For first professional degree, master's, doctorate, and other advanced degree, bachelor's degree. Additional exam requirements/recommendations for international students: Required—TOEFL. *Application deadline:* Applications are processed on a rolling basis. Application fee: $0. Electronic applications accepted. *Financial support:* Career-related internships or fieldwork available. *Unit head:* Rev. Raymond J. Webb, Academic Dean, 847-566-6401.

University of St. Michael's College, Faculty of Theology, Toronto, ON M5S 1J4, Canada. Offers Catholic leadership (MA); eastern Christian studies (Certificate, Diploma); religious education (Diploma); theological studies (Diploma); theology (M Div, MA, MRE, MTS, D Min, PhD, Th D); theology and ecology (Certificate); theology and Jewish studies (MA). *Accreditation:* ATS (one or more programs are accredited). Part-time programs available. *Faculty:* 10 full-time (3 women), 13 part-time/adjunct (5 women). *Students:* 111 full-time (35 women), 101 part-time (64 women); includes 7 African Americans, 19 Asian Americans or Pacific Islanders, 21 international. Average age 40. 90 applicants, 79% accepted, 51 enrolled. In 2007, 11 first professional degrees, 6 master's, 6 doctorates, 14 other advanced degrees awarded. *Degree requirements:* For master's, thesis (for some programs), 1 foreign language (MA), 2 foreign languages (Th M); for doctorate, 3 foreign languages, comprehensive exam, thesis/dissertation; for M Div, thesis/dissertation optional; for other advanced degree, thesis optional. *Entrance requirements:* For M Div and other advanced degree, minimum GPA of 2.7; for master's, M Div or BA, course work in an ancient or modern language, minimum GPA of 3.3; for doctorate, MA in theology, Th M, or M Div with thesis, minimum GPA of 3.7. Additional exam requirements/recommendations for international students: Required—TOEFL (minimum score 600 paper-based; 250 computer-based). *Application deadline:* For fall admission, 1/15 for domestic and international students. Applications are processed on a rolling basis. Application fee: $25 Canadian dollars. Electronic applications accepted. *Financial support:* In 2007–08, 58 students received support, including fellowships with partial tuition reimbursements available (averaging $2,500 per year), research assistantships with partial tuition reimbursements available (averaging $2,500 per year), 9 teaching assistantships with partial tuition reimbursements available (averaging $2,400 per year); scholarships/grants, tuition waivers (partial), and bursaries also available. Financial award application deadline: 2/1. *Faculty research:* Patristics, eastern Christianity, ecology and theology, ecumenism, Jewish Christian studies. *Unit head:* Dr. Anne Anderson, CSJ, Dean, 416-926-7265, Fax: 416-926-7294, E-mail: anne.anderson@utoronto.ca. *Application contact:* Mehra Taylor.

University of St. Thomas, Graduate Studies, Saint Paul Seminary School of Divinity, Program in Divinity, St. Paul, MN 55105-1096. Offers M Div. *Accreditation:* ACIPE; ATS. Part-time programs available. *Entrance requirements:* MAT, interview, 3 letters of recommendation. Additional exam requirements/recommendations for international students: Required—TOEFL (minimum score 550 paper-based; 213 computer-based). *Faculty research:* Theological education.

University of St. Thomas, Graduate Studies, Saint Paul Seminary School of Divinity, Program in Theology/Pastoral Studies, St. Paul, MN 55105-1096. Offers religious education (MARE); theology (MA). *Accreditation:* ACIPE; ATS. Part-time and evening/weekend programs available. *Degree requirements:* For master's, one foreign language, comprehensive exam, thesis or alternative. *Entrance requirements:* For master's, GRE, interview, 3 letters of recommendation. Additional exam requirements/recommendations for international students: Required—TOEFL (minimum score 550 paper-based; 213 computer-based). Electronic applications accepted. Expenses: Contact institution. *Faculty research:* Theological education.

University of St. Thomas, School of Theology, Houston, TX 77006-4696. Offers M Div, MAPS, MAT. *Accreditation:* ACIPE; ATS. Part-time programs available. *Faculty:* 11 full-time (3 women), 5 part-time/adjunct (1 woman). *Students:* 76 full-time (4 women), 116 part-time (45 women); includes 41 minority (7 African Americans, 12 Asian Americans or Pacific Islanders, 22 Hispanic Americans), 20 international. Average age 41. 49 applicants, 100% accepted, 44 enrolled. In 2007, 13 M Divs, 24 master's awarded. *Degree requirements:* For master's, comprehensive exam (MAT). *Entrance requirements:* For M Div, minimum GPA of 2.0; for master's, minimum GPA of 2.3 (MAPS); minimum GPA of 3.0, 18 hours in theology, philosophy, or religious studies (MAT). Additional exam requirements/recommendations for international students: Required—TOEFL (minimum score 550 paper-based). *Application deadline:* Applications are processed on a rolling basis. Application fee: $35. *Expenses: Contact institution. Financial support:* In 2007–08, 16 students received support. Federal Work-Study and scholarships/grants available. Support available to part-time students. Financial award application deadline: 3/1; financial award applicants required to submit FAFSA. *Unit head:* Dr. Sandra C. Magie, Dean, 713-686-4345 Ext. 242, Fax: 713-683-8673, E-mail: smagie@stthom.edu.

University of San Francisco, College of Arts and Sciences, Department of Theology and Religious Studies, San Francisco, CA 94117-1080. Offers theology (MA). Part-time and evening/weekend programs available. *Faculty:* 3 full-time (2 women), 3 part-time/adjunct (0 women). *Students:* 26 full-time (13 women), 1 part-time; includes 8 minority (1 African American, 4 Asian Americans or Pacific Islanders, 3 Hispanic Americans). Average age 37. 35 applicants, 69% accepted, 13 enrolled. In 2007, 4 degrees awarded. *Degree requirements:* For master's, thesis or alternative. *Entrance requirements:* For master's, minimum GPA of 2.7. *Application deadline:* For fall admission, 5/15 priority date for domestic students. Applications are processed on a rolling basis. Application fee: $55 ($65 for international students). *Expenses:* Tuition: Part-time $1,005 per unit. Tuition and fees vary according to degree level, campus/location and program. *Financial support:* In 2007–08, 26 students received support. Federal Work-Study, institutionally sponsored loans, scholarships/grants, and tuition waivers (partial) available. Support available to part-time students. Financial award application deadline: 3/2; financial award applicants required to submit FAFSA. *Faculty research:* World religions, sacraments, psychology and religion, Bible, liberation theology, moral theology. *Unit head:* Dr. James Bretzke, S.J., Chair, 415-422-6601.

The University of Scranton, Graduate School, Program in Theology, Scranton, PA 18510. Offers MA. Part-time and evening/weekend programs available. *Degree requirements:* For master's, thesis (for some programs), capstone experience. *Entrance requirements:* For master's, minimum GPA of 2.75. Additional exam requirements/recommendations for international students: Required—TOEFL (minimum score 500 paper-based; 173 computer-based), IELTS (minimum score 6). Expenses: Contact institution.

University of South Africa, College of Human Sciences, Pretoria, South Africa. Offers adult education (M Ed); African languages (MA, PhD); African politics (MA, PhD); Afrikaans (MA, PhD); ancient history (MA, PhD); ancient Near Eastern studies (MA, PhD); anthropology (MA, PhD); applied linguistics (MA); Arabic (MA, PhD); archaeology (MA); art history (MA); Biblical archaeology (MA); Biblical studies (M Th, D Th, PhD); Christian spirituality (M Th, D Th); church history (M Th, D Th); classical studies (MA, PhD); clinical psychology (MA); communication (MA, PhD); comparative education (M Ed, Ed D); consulting psychology (D Admin, D Com, PhD); curriculum studies (M Ed, Ed D); development studies (M Admin, MA, D Admin, PhD); didactics (M Ed, Ed D); education (M Tech); education management (M Ed, Ed D);

Theology

University of South Africa (continued)
educational psychology (M Ed); English (MA); environmental education (M Ed); French (MA, PhD); German (MA, PhD); Greek (MA); guidance and counseling (M Ed); health studies (MA, PhD), including health sciences education (MA), health services management (MA), medical and surgical nursing science (critical care general) (MA), midwifery and neonatal nursing science (MA), trauma and emergency care (MA); history (MA, PhD); history of education (Ed D); inclusive education (M Ed, Ed D); information and communications technology policy and regulation (MA); information science (MA, MIS, PhD); international politics (MA, PhD); Islamic studies (MA, PhD); Italian (MA, PhD); Judaica (MA, PhD); linguistics (MA, PhD); mathematical education (M Ed); mathematics education (MA); missiology (M Th, D Th); modern Hebrew (MA, PhD); musicology (MA, MMus, D Mus, PhD); natural science education (M Ed); New Testament (M Th, D Th); Old Testament (D Th); pastoral therapy (M Th, D Th); philosophy (MA); philosophy of education (M Ed, Ed D); politics (MA, PhD); Portuguese (MA, PhD); practical theology (M Th, D Th); psychology (MA, MS, PhD); psychology of education (M Ed, Ed D); public health (MA); religious studies (MA, D Th, PhD); Romance languages (MA); Russian (MA, PhD); Semitic languages (MA, PhD); social behavior studies in HIV/AIDS (MA); social science (mental health) (MA); social science in development studies (MA); social science in psychology (MA); social science in social work (MA); social science in sociology (MA); social work (MSW, DSW, PhD); socio-education (M Ed, Ed D); sociolinguistics (MA); sociology (MA, PhD); Spanish (MA, PhD); systematic theology (M Th, D Th); TESOL (teaching English to speakers of other languages) (MA); theological ethics (M Th, D Th); theory of literature (MA, PhD); urban ministries (D Th); urban ministry (M Th).

University of Trinity College, Faculty of Divinity, Toronto, ON M5S 1H8, Canada. Offers ministry (Diploma); ministry for church musicians (Diploma); theology (M Div, MTS, Th M, D Min, PhD, Th D, Diploma, L Th); M Div/MA. *Accreditation:* ATS. Part-time programs available. *Degree requirements:* For master's, 2 foreign languages, thesis (for some programs); for doctorate, 3 foreign languages, comprehensive exam, thesis/dissertation; for M Div, thesis/dissertation optional; for other advanced degree, thesis (for some programs). *Entrance requirements:* For M Div, interview; for master's, 1 language (modern or ancient), interview; for doctorate, 2 languages (modern and ancient). Additional exam requirements/recommendations for international students: Required—TOEFL, TWE. *Faculty research:* Interreligious dialogue, feminist theology, systematic theology, philosophy of religion, pastoral theology.

The University of Winnipeg, Faculty of Theology, Winnipeg, MB R3B 2E9, Canada. Offers marriage and family therapy (MMFT, Certificate); sacred theology (STM); theology (M Div). *Accreditation:* AAMFT/COAMFTE; ATS. Part-time programs available. *Degree requirements:* For M Div, thesis/dissertation optional.

Ursuline College, School of Graduate Studies, Graduate Program in Ministry, Pepper Pike, OH 44124-4398. Offers MA. Part-time programs available. *Faculty:* 1 (woman) full-time, 1 (woman) part-time/adjunct. *Students:* Average age 47. 3 applicants, 100% accepted, 3 enrolled. In 2007, 2 degrees awarded. *Degree requirements:* For master's, thesis. *Entrance requirements:* For master's, minimum undergraduate GPA of 3.0, interview. Additional exam requirements/recommendations for international students: Required—TOEFL (minimum score 500 paper-based; 173 computer-based). *Application deadline:* For fall admission, 8/1 priority date for domestic students. Applications are processed on a rolling basis. Application fee: $25. *Expenses: Contact institution.* Tuition and fees vary according to program. *Financial support:* In 2007–08, 15 students received support. Federal Work-Study available. Financial award application deadline: 3/1; financial award applicants required to submit FAFSA. *Unit head:* Dr. Linda Martin, Co-Director, 440-646-8191, Fax: 440-684-6088, E-mail: lmartin@ursuline.edu. *Application contact:* Jo Mann, Secretary, 440-646-8119, Fax: 440-684-6088, E-mail: gradsch@ursuline.edu.

Valparaiso University, Graduate Division, Program in Liberal Studies, Concentration in Theology, Valparaiso, IN 46383. Offers MALS, Post-Master's Certificate, JD/MALS. Part-time and evening/weekend programs available. *Students:* 1 (woman) full-time, 1 (woman) part-time; includes 1 minority (African American) Average age 35. In 2007, 3 degrees awarded. *Entrance requirements:* For master's, minimum GPA of 3.0. Additional exam requirements/recommendations for international students: Required—TOEFL (minimum score 550 paper-based; 213 computer-based). *Application deadline:* Applications are processed on a rolling basis. Application fee: $30 ($50 for international students). Electronic applications accepted. *Financial support:* Available to part-time students. Applicants required to submit FAFSA. *Application contact:* Jamie Haney, Coordinator of Recruitment Activities, 219-464-5313, Fax: 219-464-5381, E-mail: jamie.haney@valpo.edu.

Valparaiso University, Graduate Division, Program in Liberal Studies, Concentration in Theology and Ministry, Valparaiso, IN 46383. Offers MALS, Post-Master's Certificate. Part-time and evening/weekend programs available. *Entrance requirements:* For master's, minimum GPA of 3.0. Additional exam requirements/recommendations for international students: Required—TOEFL (minimum score 550 paper-based; 213 computer-based). *Application deadline:* Applications are processed on a rolling basis. Application fee: $30 ($50 for international students). Electronic applications accepted. *Financial support:* Available to part-time students. Applicants required to submit FAFSA. *Application contact:* Jamie Haney, Coordinator of Recruitment Activities, 219-464-5313, Fax: 219-464-5381, E-mail: jamie.haney@valpo.edu.

Vancouver School of Theology, Graduate and Professional Programs, Vancouver, BC V6T 1L4, Canada. Offers spiritual direction (Graduate Diploma); theological studies (MATS); theology (M Div, Th M, D Min, Dip CS). *Accreditation:* ATS. Part-time programs available. *Faculty:* 9 full-time (5 women), 8 part-time/adjunct (5 women). *Students:* 137 (86 women); includes 46 minority (22 American Indian/Alaska Native, 24 Asian Americans or Pacific Islanders) 9 international. Average age 46. 33 applicants, 79% accepted, 23 enrolled. In 2007, 18 first professional degrees, 8 master's awarded. *Degree requirements:* For master's, comprehensive exam (for some programs), thesis (for some programs); for M Div, thesis/dissertation (for some programs); for other advanced degree, one foreign language, thesis. *Entrance requirements:* Additional exam requirements/recommendations for international students: Required—TOEFL. *Application deadline:* Applications are processed on a rolling basis. Application fee: $75 Canadian dollars. Electronic applications accepted. *Financial support:* In 2007–08, 60 students received support, including 5 fellowships (averaging $8,000 per year), 3 research assistantships with partial tuition reimbursements available (averaging $1,200 per year), 11 teaching assistantships with partial tuition reimbursements available (averaging $1,200 per year); career-related internships or fieldwork, scholarships/grants, and tuition waivers (partial) also available. Support available to part-time students. Financial award application deadline: 3/30. *Faculty research:* Old Testament studies, pastoral theology, New Testament studies, field education, church history, systematic theology, spirituality. *Unit head:* Dr. Wendy Fletcher, Principal and Dean, 604-822-9808, Fax: 604-822-9212, E-mail: wfletcher@vst.edu. *Application contact:* Anita Fast, Registrar, 604-822-9563, Fax: 604-822-9212, E-mail: afast@vst.edu.

Vanderbilt University, Divinity School, Nashville, TN 37240-1001. Offers M Div, MTS, JD/M Div, JD/MTS, MBA/M Div, MBA/MTS, MD/M Div, MD/MTS, MSN/M Div, MSN/MTS. *Accreditation:* ACIPE; ATS. Part-time programs available. *Faculty:* 30 full-time (11 women), 9 part-time/adjunct (3 women). *Students:* 222 full-time (104 women); includes 45 minority (38 African Americans, 1 American Indian/Alaska Native, 3 Asian Americans or Pacific Islanders, 3 Hispanic Americans). Average age 26. 177 applicants, 77% accepted, 72 enrolled. In 2007, 41 first professional degrees, 25 master's awarded. *Entrance requirements:* Additional exam requirements/recommendations for international students: Required—TOEFL (minimum score 630 paper-based; 250 computer-based; 100 iBT). *Application deadline:* For fall admission, 5/1 for domestic students, 4/1 for international students. Applications are processed on a rolling basis. Application fee: $50. Electronic applications accepted. *Expenses: Contact institution.* *Financial support:* In 2007–08, 200 students received support. Career-related internships or fieldwork, Federal Work-Study, institutionally sponsored loans, scholarships/grants, and tuition waivers (full and partial) available. Financial award application deadline: 5/1; financial award applicants required to submit CSS PROFILE or FAFSA. *Unit head:* Dr. James Hudnut-Beumler, Dean, 615-322-2776, Fax: 615-343-9957, E-mail: james.hudnut-beumler@vanderbilt.edu. *Application contact:* Becky Eberhart.

Vanguard University of Southern California, School of Religion, Costa Mesa, CA 92626-9601. Offers leadership studies (MA); religion (MA), including biblical studies; theological studies (MTS). Part-time and evening/weekend programs available. *Faculty:* 7 full-time (1 woman), 4 part-time/adjunct (0 women). *Students:* 16 full-time (5 women), 72 part-time (20 women); includes 24 minority (3 African Americans, 1 American Indian/Alaska Native, 5 Asian Americans or Pacific Islanders, 15 Hispanic Americans), 3 international. Average age 38. 39 applicants, 79% accepted, 26 enrolled. In 2007, 25 degrees awarded. *Degree requirements:* For master's, one foreign language, comprehensive exam, thesis (for some programs). *Entrance requirements:* For master's, minimum GPA of 3.0; course work in humanities, religion, and social sciences (MA); minimum GPA of 2.5 (MTS). Additional exam requirements/recommendations for international students: Required—TOEFL (minimum score 550 paper-based; 213 computer-based). *Application deadline:* For fall admission, 4/1 priority date for domestic and international students; for spring admission, 10/1 priority date for domestic and international students. Applications are processed on a rolling basis. Application fee: $45. Electronic applications accepted. *Expenses: Contact institution.* Full-time tuition and fees vary according to course load and program. *Financial support:* In 2007–08, 28 students received support, including 6 teaching assistantships (averaging $1,800 per year); scholarships/grants, tuition waivers (partial), and unspecified assistantships also available. Financial award application deadline: 3/2. *Faculty research:* Apocalyptic literature, narrative theology, ecumenism and Pentecost. *Unit head:* Dr. Andrew Stenhouse, Associate Dean, 714-556-3610 Ext. 3223, Fax: 714-957-9317. *Application contact:* John Sim, Graduate Religion Coordinator, 714-556-3610 Ext. 3285, Fax: 714-957-9317, E-mail: jsim@vanguard.edu.

Victoria University, Emmanuel College, Toronto, ON M5S 1K7, Canada. Offers M Div, MA, MPS, MRE, MTS, Th M, D Min, PhD, Th D, Certificate, Diploma, L Th, M Div/MA, M Div/MPS, M Div/MRE. *Accreditation:* ATS. Part-time programs available. Terminal master's awarded for partial completion of doctoral program. *Degree requirements:* For master's, 2 foreign languages, thesis (for some programs); for doctorate, 2 foreign languages, thesis/dissertation; for M Div, thesis/dissertation optional. *Entrance requirements:* For M Div and other advanced degree, BA, B Sc; for doctorate, M Div, MAOP, MTS. Additional exam requirements/recommendations for international students: Required—TOEFL, TWE. *Faculty research:* New Testament and Old Testament hermeneutics, religious symbolism, Reformation, liberation theology, Canadian church history.

Villanova University, Graduate School of Liberal Arts and Sciences, Department of Theology, Villanova, PA 19085-1699. Offers MA. Part-time and evening/weekend programs available. *Faculty:* 5 full-time (0 women), 1 (woman) part-time/adjunct. *Students:* 12 full-time (3 women), 15 part-time (8 women); includes 3 minority (2 Asian Americans or Pacific Islanders, 1 Hispanic American), 1 international. Average age 33. 19 applicants, 100% accepted. In 2007, 9 degrees awarded. *Degree requirements:* For master's, one foreign language, comprehensive exam, thesis optional. *Entrance requirements:* For master's, GRE, minimum GPA of 3.0. *Application deadline:* For fall admission, 8/1 for domestic and international students; for spring admission, 12/1 for domestic and international students. Applications are processed on a rolling basis. Application fee: $50. Electronic applications accepted. *Financial support:* Research assistantships, Federal Work-Study and scholarships/grants available. Financial award applicants required to submit FAFSA. *Unit head:* Dr. Bernard Prusak, Chair, 610-519-7423.

Virginia Union University, School of Theology, Richmond, VA 23220-1170. Offers M Div, D Min. *Accreditation:* ACIPE; ATS. Part-time and evening/weekend programs available. *Entrance requirements:* Additional exam requirements/recommendations for international students: Required—TOEFL.

Walsh University, Graduate Programs, Program in Theology, North Canton, OH 44720-3396. Offers MA. *Faculty:* 3 full-time (1 woman), 2 part-time/adjunct (both women). *Students:* 3 full-time (1 woman), 15 part-time (8 women). Average age 43. 5 applicants, 100% accepted, 5 enrolled. In 2007, 6 degrees awarded. *Degree requirements:* For master's, thesis (for some programs). *Entrance requirements:* For master's, MAT, minimum GPA of 3.0. *Application deadline:* For fall admission, 7/15 priority date for domestic students. Applications are processed on a rolling basis. Application fee: $25. Electronic applications accepted. *Expenses:* Tuition: Full-time $9,270; part-time $575 per credit. *Financial support:* In 2007–08, 15 students received support, including 2 research assistantships with tuition reimbursements available (averaging $4,380 per year). Financial award application deadline: 12/31. *Faculty research:* Hispanic immigration; Hispanic acculturation; cultural pluralism; service learning; agents of change. *Unit head:* Msgr. Lew Gaetano, Coordinator, 330-490-7277, E-mail: lgaetano@walsh.edu. *Application contact:* Linda Suffron, Graduate Admissions, 830-490-7174, E-mail: lsuffron@walsh.edu.

Warner Pacific College, Graduate Programs, Portland, OR 97215-4099. Offers biblical and theological studies (MA); biblical studies (M Rel); education (M Ed); management/organizational leadership (MS); pastoral ministries (M Rel); religion and ethics (M Rel); teaching (MA); theology (M Rel). Part-time programs available. *Faculty:* 20 part-time/adjunct (6 women). *Students:* 57 full-time (26 women), 4 part-time (2 women); includes 5 minority (4 African Americans, 1 Asian American or Pacific Islander). *Degree requirements:* For master's, thesis or alternative, Presentation of Defense. *Entrance requirements:* For master's, interview, minimum GPA of 2.5, letters of recommendations. *Application deadline:* Applications are processed on a rolling basis. *Expenses:* Tuition: Full-time $15,642. Required fees: $150. *Financial support:* Career-related internships or fieldwork and Federal Work-Study available. Financial award application deadline: 7/1; financial award applicants required to submit FAFSA. *Faculty research:* New Testament studies, nineteenth-century Wesleyan theology, preaching and church growth, Christian ethics. *Unit head:* Director, 503-517-1045, Fax: 503-517-1350, E-mail: kazio@warnerpacific.edu.

Wartburg Theological Seminary, Graduate and Professional Programs, Dubuque, IA 52004-5004. Offers diaconal ministry (MA); theology (M Div, MA, MATDE, STM). *Accreditation:* ACIPE; ATS. *Faculty:* 19 full-time (6 women), 9 part-time/adjunct (3 women). *Students:* 154 full-time (73 women), 30 part-time (16 women); includes 6 minority (1 American Indian/Alaska Native, 1 Asian American or Pacific Islander, 4 Hispanic Americans), 9 international. Average age 34. 93 applicants, 75% accepted, 48 enrolled. In 2007, 39 first professional degrees, 14 master's awarded. *Degree requirements:* For master's, thesis (for some programs); for M Div, thesis/dissertation optional. *Entrance requirements:* For M Div, minimum GPA of 2.5; for master's, minimum GPA of 3.0 (STM). Additional exam requirements/recommendations for international students: Required—TOEFL (minimum score 500 paper-based; 173 computer-based; 80 iBT). *Application deadline:* For fall admission, 5/15 priority date for domestic students, 10/1 priority date for international students; for winter admission, 10/1 for international students; for spring admission, 12/15 priority date for domestic students, 10/1 for international students. Applications are processed on a rolling basis. Application fee: $0. Electronic applications accepted. *Expenses:* Tuition: Full-time $10,400; part-time $505 per credit. Required fees: $437; $50 per semester. *Financial support:* In 2007–08, 90 students received support, including 17 research assistantships with partial tuition reimbursements available (averaging $1,088 per year); career-related internships or fieldwork, Federal Work-Study, institutionally sponsored loans, and scholarships/grants also available. Support available to part-time students. Financial award application deadline: 6/15; financial award applicants required to submit FAFSA. *Unit head:* Dr. Craig L. Nessan, Academic Dean, 563-589-0207, Fax: 563-589-0333. *Application contact:* Heather McClintock, Director of Admissions, 563-589-0298, Fax: 563-589-0333, E-mail: admissions@wartburgseminary.edu.

Washington Theological Union, Graduate and Professional Programs, Washington, DC 20012. Offers M Div, MA, MAPS, MTS, D Min, M Div/MA. *Accreditation:* ACIPE; ATS. Part-time programs available. Postbaccalaureate distance learning degree programs offered. *Faculty:* 14 full-time (3 women), 15 part-time/adjunct (5 women). *Students:* 59 full-time (11 women), 182 part-time (87 women). Average age 32. 149 applicants, 95% accepted. In 2007, 19 first professional degrees, 22 master's awarded. *Degree requirements:* For master's, one foreign language, comprehensive exam, thesis. *Entrance requirements:* For M Div, 18 hours of course work in philosophy; for master's, 18 hours of course work in philosophy and religious studies. *Application deadline:* For fall admission, 4/1 priority date for domestic students; for spring admission, 11/15 priority date for domestic students. Applications are processed on a rolling basis. Application fee: $50. *Expenses:* Tuition: Full-time $12,500; part-time $625 per credit. Required fees: $400; $225 per semester. *Financial support:* In 2007–08, 40 students received support. Career-related internships or fieldwork and scholarships/grants available. Support available to part-time students. Financial award application deadline: 3/15; financial award applicants required to submit FAFSA. *Unit head:* Rev. John Burkhard, President/Academic Dean, 202-541-5228, Fax: 202-726-1716. *Application contact:* Christine Palmer, Admissions Assistant, 202-541-5210, Fax: 202-726-1716, E-mail: admissions@wtu.edu.

Wesley Biblical Seminary, Graduate Programs, Jackson, MS 39206. Offers Biblical literature (MA); Christian studies (MA); evangelism (M Div); family life ministry (M Div); honors research (M Div); missions (M Div); pastoral ministry (M Div); teaching (M Div); theology (MA). *Accreditation:* ATS. Part-time programs available. *Degree requirements:* For master's, thesis. *Entrance requirements:* Additional exam requirements/recommendations for international students: Required—TOEFL. *Application deadline:* For fall admission, 7/1 priority date for domestic students; for spring admission, 12/1 priority date for domestic students. Applications are processed on a rolling basis. Application fee: $25. Electronic applications accepted. *Financial support:* Scholarships/grants available. Support available to part-time students. *Faculty research:* Patristics, missiology, culture, hermeneutics. *Unit head:* Dr. Ray R. Easley, Vice President for Academic Affairs, 601-366-8880 Ext. 112, Fax: 601-366-8832. *Application contact:* Megan Tirrill, Assistant to the Vice President for Student Development, 800-366-8880 Ext. 110, Fax: 601-366-8832, E-mail: mtirrill@wbs.edu.

Wesley Theological Seminary, Graduate and Professional Programs, Washington, DC 20016-5690. Offers M Div, MA, MRE, MTS, D Min, M Div/MRE, M Div/MTS. *Accreditation:* ACIPE; ATS. Part-time programs available. *Degree requirements:* For master's, thesis; for doctorate, thesis/dissertation; for M Div, thesis/dissertation or alternative. *Entrance requirements:* For M Div and master's, minimum GPA of 2.7; for doctorate, minimum GPA of 3.0.

Western Seminary, Graduate Programs, Programs in Theology, Portland, OR 97215-3367. Offers biblical studies (Certificate); theology (MA, Th M). *Accreditation:* ATS. Part-time programs available. *Degree requirements:* For master's, thesis or alternative, practicum.

Western Seminary–Sacramento Campus, Graduate Programs, Sacramento, CA 95821. Offers exegetical theology (MA); marital and family therapy (MA); ministry (M Div); specialized ministry (MA). Postbaccalaureate distance learning degree programs offered. *Entrance requirements:* For M Div, minimum GPA of 2.5; for master's, minimum GPA of 3.0.

Western Seminary–San Jose Campus, Graduate Programs, Los Gatos, CA 95032-4520. Offers exegetical theology (MA); expositional ministry (M Div); marital and family therapy (MA); ministry (M Div); pastoral ministry (M Div); specialized ministry (MA). Postbaccalaureate distance learning degree programs offered. *Degree requirements:* For master's, 2 foreign languages; for M Div, 3 foreign languages. *Entrance requirements:* For M Div, minimum GPA of 2.5; for master's, minimum GPA of 3.0.

Western Theological Seminary, Graduate and Professional Programs, Holland, MI 49423-3622. Offers M Div, M Th, D Min. *Accreditation:* ACIPE; ATS. Part-time programs available. Postbaccalaureate distance learning degree programs offered (minimal on-campus study). *Degree requirements:* For doctorate, 2 foreign languages, thesis/dissertation; for M Div, 2 foreign languages. *Entrance requirements:* For doctorate, 5 years of experience in the ministry (must be ordained). Additional exam requirements/recommendations for international students: Required—TOEFL.

Westminster Seminary California, Programs in Theology, Escondido, CA 92027-4128. Offers Biblical studies (MA); historical theology (MA); theological studies (M Div, MA). *Accreditation:* ATS. Part-time and evening/weekend programs available. *Faculty:* 11 full-time (0 women), 10 part-time/adjunct (1 woman). *Students:* 88 full-time (9 women), 45 part-time (6 women); includes 45 minority (2 African Americans, 34 Asian Americans or Pacific Islanders, 9 Hispanic Americans), 9 international. Average age 30. 104 applicants, 64% accepted, 49 enrolled. In 2007, 22 first professional degrees, 11 master's awarded. *Degree requirements:* For master's, 2 foreign languages, thesis (for some programs); for M Div, 2 foreign languages, internship. *Entrance requirements:* For M Div and master's, 2 letters of reference. Additional exam requirements/recommendations for international students: Required—TOEFL (minimum score 570 paper-based; 230 computer-based; 89 iBT), TWE (minimum score 4.5). *Application deadline:* For fall admission, 6/30 priority date for domestic students, 3/15 priority date for international students; for spring admission, 11/30 priority date for domestic students. Applications are processed on a rolling basis. Application fee: $30. *Expenses:* Tuition: Full-time $11,500; part-time $30 per credit. Required fees: $25 per semester. One-time fee: $100 full-time. *Financial support:* In 2007–08, 68 students received support. Career-related internships or fieldwork, institutionally sponsored loans, and scholarships/grants available. Financial award application deadline: 6/30; financial award applicants required to submit FAFSA. *Faculty research:* Neo-paganism, New Testament background, eschatology, Protestant scholasticism, Ezekiel. *Unit head:* Dr. Dennis E. Johnson, Academic Dean, 760-480-8474, Fax: 760-480-0252. *Application contact:* Mark MacVey, Director of Recruiting, 760-480-8474, Fax: 760-480-0252, E-mail: mmacvey@wscal.edu.

Westminster Theological Seminary, Graduate and Professional Programs, Philadelphia, PA 19118. Offers apologetics (Th M); Biblical and urban studies (Certificate); Biblical counseling (MA); biblical studies (MAR); Christian studies (Certificate); church history (Th M); counseling (M Div); general studies (M Div, MAR); hermeneutics and Bible interpretations (PhD); historical and theological studies (PhD); historical theology (Th M); New Testament (Th M); Old Testament (Th M); pastoral counseling (D Min); pastoral ministry (M Div, D Min); systematic theology (Th M); theological studies (MAR); urban missions (M Div, MA, MAR, D Min). *Accreditation:* ATS. Part-time programs available. Terminal master's awarded for partial completion of doctoral program. *Degree requirements:* For master's, thesis (for some programs); for doctorate, 4 foreign languages, comprehensive exam (for some programs), thesis/dissertation; for M Div, 2 foreign languages. *Entrance requirements:* For doctorate, GRE General Test. Additional exam requirements/recommendations for international students: Required—TOEFL, TWE.

Wheaton College, Graduate School, Department of Biblical and Theological Studies, Program in Biblical and Theological Studies, Wheaton, IL 60187-5593. Offers PhD. *Students:* 18. 57 applicants, 19% accepted, 7 enrolled. *Degree requirements:* For doctorate, thesis/dissertation. *Entrance requirements:* For doctorate, GRE. *Application deadline:* For fall admission, 1/1 for domestic and international students. Application fee: $50. Electronic applications accepted. *Unit head:* Dr. Daniel Block, Head, 650-752-5272. *Application contact:* Julie A. Huebner, Director of Graduate Admissions, 630-752-5195, Fax: 630-752-5935, E-mail: gradadm@wheaton.edu.

Wheaton College, Graduate School, Department of Biblical and Theological Studies, Program in Biblical Archaeology, Wheaton, IL 60187-5593. Offers MA. *Faculty:* 2 full-time (0 women). *Students:* 3. 4 applicants, 50% accepted, 2 enrolled. *Degree requirements:* For master's, thesis or alternative, semester of study in Israel. *Entrance requirements:* For master's, GRE General Test or MAT. *Application deadline:* For fall admission, 3/1 priority date for domestic students, 1/1 for international students. Applications are processed on a rolling basis. Application fee: $30. Electronic applications accepted. *Financial support:* Scholarships/grants available. Financial award application deadline: 3/1; financial award applicants required to submit FAFSA. *Unit head:* John Monson, Coordinator, 630-752-5706. *Application contact:* Julie A. Huebner, Director of Graduate Admissions, 630-752-5195, Fax: 630-752-5935, E-mail: gradadm@wheaton.edu.

Wheaton College, Graduate School, Department of Biblical and Theological Studies, Program in Biblical Exegesis, Wheaton, IL 60187-5593. Offers MA. *Students:* 55 applicants, 89% accepted, 31 enrolled. *Degree requirements:* For master's, 2 foreign languages, thesis or alternative. *Entrance requirements:* For master's, GRE General Test or MAT. *Application deadline:* For fall admission, 1/1 for domestic students. Application fee: $30. Electronic applications accepted. *Financial support:* Application deadline: 3/1. *Unit head:* Dr. Gregory Beale, Coordinator, 630-752-5280. *Application contact:* Julie A. Huebner, Director of Graduate Admissions, 630-752-5195, Fax: 630-752-5935, E-mail: gradadm@wheaton.edu.

Wheaton College, Graduate School, Department of Biblical and Theological Studies, Program in Biblical Studies, Wheaton, IL 60187-5593. Offers MA. Part-time programs available. *Students:* 19 applicants, 68% accepted, 4 enrolled. *Degree requirements:* For master's, one foreign language, thesis optional. *Entrance requirements:* For master's, GRE General Test, MAT. *Application deadline:* For fall admission, 3/1 priority date for domestic students; for spring admission, 11/1 for domestic students. Applications are processed on a rolling basis. Application fee: $30. Electronic applications accepted. *Financial support:* Scholarships/grants and unspecified assistantships available. Financial award application deadline: 3/1; financial award applicants required to submit FAFSA. *Unit head:* Dr. Nicholas Perrin, Coordinator, 630-752-5933. *Application contact:* Julie A. Huebner, Director of Graduate Admissions, 630-752-5195, Fax: 630-752-5935, E-mail: gradadm@wheaton.edu.

Wheaton College, Graduate School, Department of Biblical and Theological Studies, Program in General History of Christianity, Wheaton, IL 60187-5593. Offers biblical and theological studies (MA). Part-time and evening/weekend programs available. *Students:* 8 applicants, 75% accepted, 2 enrolled. *Degree requirements:* For master's, thesis optional. *Entrance requirements:* For master's, GRE General Test, MAT. *Application deadline:* For fall admission, 3/1 priority date for domestic students; for spring admission, 11/1 for domestic students. Applications are processed on a rolling basis. Application fee: $30. *Financial support:* Scholarships/grants and unspecified assistantships available. Financial award application deadline: 3/1; financial award applicants required to submit FAFSA. *Unit head:* Dr. Timothy Larsen, Head, 630-752-5177. *Application contact:* Julie A. Huebner, Director of Graduate Admissions, 630-752-5195, Fax: 630-752-5935, E-mail: gradadm@wheaton.edu.

Wheaton College, Graduate School, Department of Biblical and Theological Studies, Program in Historical and Systematic Theology, Wheaton, IL 60187-5593. Offers biblical and theological studies (MA). *Students:* 16 applicants, 75% accepted, 9 enrolled. *Application deadline:* For fall admission, 3/1 priority date for domestic students, 1/1 for international students. Applications are processed on a rolling basis. Application fee: $30. Electronic applications accepted. *Financial support:* Application deadline: 3/1. *Unit head:* Dr. Stephen Spencer, Head, 630-752-5931. *Application contact:* Julie A. Huebner, Director of Graduate Admissions, 630-752-3195, Fax: 630-752-5935, E-mail: gradadm@wheaton.edu.

Wilfrid Laurier University, Waterloo Lutheran Seminary, Waterloo, ON N2L 3C5, Canada. Offers Christian ethics (M Th); divinity (M Div); homiletics (M Th); ministry (D Min); pastoral counseling (M Th); spirituality in a health care setting (Diploma); theological studies (MTS); theology (Diploma); M Div/MTS/MSW. *Accreditation:* ATS. Part-time programs available. *Faculty:* 8 full-time (2 women), 6 part-time/adjunct (2 women). *Students:* 51 full-time (33 women), 57 part-time (33 women); includes 10 minority (3 African Americans, 1 American Indian/Alaska Native, 6 Asian Americans or Pacific Islanders). Average age 42. 23 applicants, 100% accepted, 20 enrolled. In 2007, 1 first professional degree, 8 master's awarded. *Degree requirements:* For master's, one foreign language, thesis (for some programs); for doctorate, thesis/dissertation; for M Div, one foreign language, thesis/dissertation. *Entrance requirements:* For M Div, denominational endorsement; for master's, M Div, 2 units of clinical pastoral education (M Th); for doctorate, M Div, 3 years of ministry experience, proficiency in a foreign language, basic training in clinical pastoral education. Additional exam requirements/recommendations for international students: Required—TOEFL (minimum score 573 paper-based; 230 computer-based; 89 iBT), IELTS (minimum score 7). *Application deadline:* For fall admission, 7/1 priority date for domestic students, 3/1 priority date for international students; for winter admission, 11/1 priority date for domestic students, 6/1 priority date for international students; for spring admission, 3/1 priority date for domestic students, 11/1 priority date for international students. Applications are processed on a rolling basis. Application fee: $50. Electronic applications accepted. *Expenses: Contact institution. Financial support:* In 2007–08, 51 students received support. Career-related internships or fieldwork, institutionally sponsored loans, and scholarships/grants available. Financial award application deadline: 10/1. *Faculty research:* Biblical study, church history, systematic theology. *Unit head:* Dr. David Pfrimmer, Principal/Dean, 519-884-0710, E-mail: dpfrimme@wlu.ca. *Application contact:* Sarina Wheeler, Student Advisor and Admissions Coordinator, 519-884-0710 Ext. 3498, Fax: 519-725-2434, E-mail: swheeler@wlu.ca.

Winebrenner Theological Seminary, Graduate Programs, Findlay, OH 45840. Offers church development (MA); family ministry (MA); theological study (MA); theological/ministerial studies (D Min); theology/ministerial studies (M Div). *Accreditation:* ATS (one or more programs are accredited). Part-time and evening/weekend programs available. *Faculty:* 7 full-time (1 woman), 5 part-time/adjunct (3 women). *Students:* 63 full-time (22 women), 49 part-time (18 women); includes 15 minority (11 African Americans, 3 Asian Americans or Pacific Islanders, 1 Hispanic American), 1 international. Average age 38. 28 applicants, 100% accepted, 26 enrolled. In 2007, 14 first professional degrees, 11 master's, 3 doctorates awarded. *Degree requirements:* For master's, supervised ministry, theological summit; for doctorate, thesis/dissertation, research project; for M Div, 2 foreign languages, supervised ministry, theological summit. *Entrance requirements:* For doctorate, 3 years of post-M Div full-time ministry. Additional exam requirements/recommendations for international students: Required—TOEFL (minimum score 550 paper-based; 213 computer-based). *Application deadline:* For fall admission, 8/15 priority date for domestic students; for winter admission, 12/15 priority date for domestic students; for spring admission, 4/15 priority date for domestic students. Applications are processed on a rolling basis. Application fee: $25. Electronic applications accepted. *Expenses:* Tuition: Full-time $10,050; part-time $395 per credit hour. Required fees: $110 per trimester. *Financial support:* In 2007–08, 62 students received support. Institutionally sponsored loans, scholarships/grants, and tuition waivers (partial) available. Support available to part-time students. Financial award application deadline: 7/1; financial award applicants required to submit FAFSA. *Faculty research:* Evangelical postconservative theological epistemology, coaching, creation theology, Colossians, shared governance. *Unit head:* Dr. M. John Nissley, Vice President for Academic Advancement, 419-434-4247, Fax: 419-434-4267, E-mail: jnissley@winebrenner.edu. *Application contact:* Jim Wilder, Regional Coordinator, 419-434-4220, Fax: 419-434-4267, E-mail: admissions@winebrenner.edu.

Wycliffe College, Division of Advanced Degree Studies, Toronto, ON M5S 1H7, Canada. Offers MA, Th M, D Min, PhD, Th D. *Accreditation:* ATS (one or more programs are accredited). Part-time programs available. Terminal master's awarded for partial completion of doctoral program. *Degree requirements:* For master's, 2 foreign languages, thesis (for some programs); for doctorate, 3 foreign languages, thesis/dissertation. *Entrance requirements:* Additional exam requirements/recommendations for international students: Required—TOEFL (minimum score 600 paper-based; 250 computer-based). Expenses: Contact institution. *Faculty research:* Old and New Testament, doctrine, ethics, philosophy, history.

Wycliffe College, Division of Basic Degree Studies, Toronto, ON M5S 1H7, Canada. Offers Christian Studies (Diploma); theology (M Div, M Rel, MTS). *Accreditation:* ATS. Part-time programs available. *Degree requirements:* For master's, one foreign language, thesis; for M Div, thesis/dissertation optional. *Entrance requirements:* Additional exam requirements/recommendations for international students: Required—TOEFL (minimum score 580 paper-based).

Xavier University, College of Arts and Sciences, Department of Theology, Cincinnati, OH 45207. Offers MA. Part-time and evening/weekend programs available. *Faculty:* 14 full-time (6 women). *Students:* 1 full-time (0 women), 33 part-time (16 women); includes 2 minority (both African Americans) Average age 37. 9 applicants, 100% accepted, 9 enrolled. In 2007, 7 degrees awarded. *Degree requirements:* For master's, thesis optional, research paper. *Entrance*

Theology

Xavier University (continued)
requirements: For master's, MAT or GRE, minimum GPA of 2.7. Additional exam requirements/recommendations for international students: Required—TOEFL (minimum score 550 paper-based; 213 computer-based). *Application deadline:* For fall admission, 8/15 priority date for domestic students. Applications are processed on a rolling basis. Application fee: $35. *Financial support:* Scholarships/grants and unspecified assistantships available. Support available to part-time students. Financial award applicants required to submit FAFSA. *Faculty research:* Anti-Jewish elements in scripture; Christian ethics; war, peace, and world religions; process theology, issues in theology. *Unit head:* Dr. Marie Giblin, Chair, 513-745-2021, Fax: 513-745-3215, E-mail: giblin@xavier.edu. *Application contact:* Roger Bosse, Interim Director of Graduate Studies, 513-745-3357, Fax: 513-745-1048, E-mail: bosse@xavier.edu.

Xavier University of Louisiana, Graduate School, Institute for Black Catholic Studies, New Orleans, LA 70125-1098. Offers pastoral theology (Th M). Part-time programs available. *Degree requirements:* For master's, comprehensive exam, practicum. *Entrance requirements:* For master's, GRE General Test, MAT, minimum GPA of 2.5. Additional exam requirements/recommendations for international students: Required—TOEFL.

Yale University, Divinity School, New Haven, CT 06511. Offers M Div, MAR, STM, JD/M Div, JD/MAR, M Div/MBA, M Div/MF, M Div/MSN, M Div/MSW, MAR/MF, MAR/MSN, MAR/MSW, MD/M Div, MD/MAR. *Accreditation:* ACIPE; ATS. Part-time programs available. *Faculty:* 35 full-time, 15 part-time/adjunct. *Students:* 342 full-time (165 women), 45 part-time (30 women); includes 57 minority (36 African Americans, 15 Asian Americans or Pacific Islanders, 6 Hispanic Americans), 40 international. Average age 26. 486 applicants, 59% accepted, 136 enrolled. In 2007, 71 first professional degrees, 53 master's awarded. *Entrance requirements:* Additional exam requirements/recommendations for international students: Required—IELTS (minimum score 7). *Application deadline:* For fall admission, 2/6 for domestic students. Application fee: $75. Electronic applications accepted. *Expenses:* Contact institution. *Financial support:* In 2007–08, 301 fellowships (averaging $12,679 per year) were awarded; career-related internships or fieldwork, Federal Work-Study, and scholarships/grants also available. Support available to part-time students. Financial award application deadline: 3/1; financial award applicants required to submit FAFSA. *Unit head:* Dr. Harold W. Attridge, Dean, 203-432-5306, Fax: 203-432-9712, E-mail: harold.attridge@yale.edu. *Application contact:* Anna T. Ramirez, Associate Dean of Admissions and Financial Aid, 203-432-9802, Fax: 203-432-7475, E-mail: anna.ramirez@yale.edu.

Yeshiva Beth Moshe, Graduate Programs, Scranton, PA 18505-2124. Offers Second Talmudical Degree, Talmudic Fellow Degree. *Accreditation:* AARTS.

Yeshiva Karlin Stolin Rabbinical Institute, Graduate Programs, Brooklyn, NY 11204. Offers Advanced Rabbinical Degree. *Accreditation:* AARTS.

Yeshiva of Nitra Rabbinical College, Graduate Programs, Mount Kisco, NY 10549. *Accreditation:* AARTS.

Yeshiva Shaar Hatorah Talmudic Research Institute, Graduate Programs, Kew Gardens, NY 11418-1469. *Accreditation:* AARTS.

Yeshivath Zichron Moshe, Graduate Programs, South Fallsburg, NY 12779. Offers Advanced Talmudic Degree, Talmudic Scholar Degree. *Accreditation:* AARTS. Part-time programs available.

Yeshiva Toras Chaim Talmudical Seminary, Graduate Programs, Denver, CO 80204-1415.

BOSTON COLLEGE

Department of Theology

Programs of Study

The doctoral program in theology has as its goal the formation of theologians who intellectually excel in the church, the academy, and society. It is confessional in nature and envisions theology as "faith seeking understanding." Accordingly, the program aims at nourishing a community of faith, scholarly conversation, and research and teaching centered in the study of Christian life and thought, past and present, in ways that contribute to this goal. It recognizes that creative theological discussion and specialized research today require serious and in-depth appropriation of the great philosophical and theological traditions of the past, as well as ecumenical, interdisciplinary, interreligious, and cross-cultural cooperation.

The program is designed and taught by an ecumenical joint faculty drawn from the Department, Andover Newton Theological School, and Weston Jesuit School of Theology, each of which is rooted in and committed to a theological tradition—the Reformed tradition at Andover Newton Theological School and the Roman Catholic tradition at Boston College and Weston Jesuit School of Theology. The creation of this faculty represents a unique degree of Catholic and ecumenical cooperation at the doctoral level, bringing together teachers and students from diversified cultural and religious backgrounds. Indeed, one of the intrinsic components of the program is a call for a wise appropriation of Catholic and/or Protestant theological and doctrinal traditions, as well as critical and constructive dialogue with other major religions, with other Christian theological positions, and with contemporary cultures.

The program is rigorous in its expectation that students master Catholic and/or Protestant theological traditions and critically probe the foundations of various theological positions. Students are expected to master the tools and techniques of research and to organize and integrate their knowledge so as to make an original contribution to theological discussion.

Because the program includes faculty members who are expert in the Hindu, Buddhist, Muslim, and Jewish traditions, it also offers a context in which the issues raised by religious pluralism can be explored, responsibly and in detail, and in which a Christian comparative theology can be pursued seriously.

Students focus their studies in one of five major areas: the history of Christian life and thought, systematic theology, Biblical studies, theological ethics, or comparative theology. A student may also minor in any one of these areas or in pastoral theology. The faculty in each major area determines requirements regarding course distribution, language requirements, comprehensive examinations, and minors. A minimum of two years of full-time course work is required of all. Each doctoral student must pass examinations in at least two languages. Upon completion of course work, doctoral students typically serve as teaching assistants for two years and as teaching fellows for one year.

The Department cooperates with Boston College's Institute for Religious Education and Pastoral Ministry and the graduate schools of education and social work in offering the M.Ed. in religious education, the Certificate of Advanced Educational Specialization in Religious Education, the M.A. in pastoral ministry, the joint Master of Arts in pastoral ministry/Master of Social Work, and the Ph.D. in religion and education. In conjunction with the Ph.D. program in theology, the Department of Theology is also linked to Boston College's Institute of Medieval Philosophy and Theology.

The Boston College Department of Theology is a member of the Boston Theological Institute, a consortium of theology faculties primarily in the Boston-Newton-Cambridge area. Constituent members include Andover Newton Theological School, Boston University School of Theology, Episcopal Divinity School, Gordon-Conwell Theological Seminary, Harvard Divinity School, Holy Cross Greek Orthodox Seminary, St. John's Seminary, and the Weston Jesuit School of Theology. This consortium offers complete cross-registration in several hundred courses, the use of library facilities, and joint seminars and programs.

Research Facilities

Boston College provides its students with state-of-the-art facilities for learning, including a full range of computer services, online access to databases, and a library system with more than 1.9 million books, periodicals, and government documents and 3.4 million microform units. The library's membership in the Boston Library Consortium provides access to ten major research libraries in the Boston area, and an interlibrary loan system provides further resources.

Financial Aid

Academic awards are available through the Graduate School to ensure that outstanding, academically qualified students have financial support while they work toward their degrees. Stipends and scholarships are offered in the form of graduate assistantships, research assistantships, teaching assistantships, teaching fellowships, university fellowships, and tuition scholarships. The amounts of the awards and the number of years for which they are renewable may vary by department. A list of funding sources for students studying theology at the graduate level is available at http://www.bc.edu/schools/cas/theology/gradpage/grants.html.

Cost of Study

For the 2008–09 academic year, tuition and fees for a full-time student are $1148 per credit.

Living and Housing Costs

The Housing Office provides an extensive list of off-campus housing options. Most graduate students rent rooms or apartments near Chestnut Hill. Average monthly expenses, including rent, food, and utilities, are $800 for students.

Student Group

The enrollment at Boston College is 14,500, including 4,200 students enrolled in the various graduate schools. The Department of Theology has 133 full-time and 102 part-time graduate students, 138 of whom are women. This includes 10 students who are members of minority groups and 24 international students.

Location

Boston College is located in the Chestnut Hill section of Newton, an attractive residential area about 6 miles from the heart of Boston with easy access to the city by public transportation. The Boston area, with its numerous educational and biomedical research institutions, offers countless outstanding seminars, lectures, colloquiums, and concerts throughout the year. A wide variety of cultural and recreational opportunities can be found close to the campus.

The College

Founded in Massachusetts in 1863, Boston College currently includes the Graduate School of Arts and Sciences and graduate schools of law, social work, management, nursing, and education. Its expanding campus is graced with many attractive Gothic buildings. Boston College has a strong tradition of academic excellence and service to the community.

Applying

Students should have completed the M.Div. or equivalent degree; a master's degree in religion, theology, or philosophy; or a bachelor's program with a strong background in religion, theology, and/or philosophy. Applicants must submit the completed application, the $70 application fee, an abstract of courses, official transcripts, three letters of recommendation, a statement of purpose (about three pages on the student's interest in the program and academic goals), a writing sample (no more than 25 pages), a resume or curriculum vitae, and GRE scores. International students must also send in official TOEFL scores. All application materials must be submitted directly to the Graduate School of Arts and Sciences by January 1.

Correspondence and Information

Claudette Picklesimer, Graduate Programs Assistant
Department of Theology
Boston College
140 Commonwealth Avenue
Chestnut Hill, Massachusetts 02467

Phone: 617-552-3880
Fax: 617-552-0794
E-mail: claudette.picklesimer.1@bc.edu
Web site: http://www.bc.edu/schools/cas/theology

Boston College

THE FACULTY AND THEIR RESEARCH

Stephen F. Brown, Professor; Ph.D., Louvain (Belgium). Medieval philosophy and theology, especially thirteenth and fourteenth centuries.
Lisa Sowle Cahill, J. Donald Monan Professor; Ph.D., Chicago. History of Christian ethics, New Testament and ethics, Catholic social ethics, feminist theology and sex and gender ethics, bioethics, ethics of war and peace.
Boyd Taylor Coolman, Assistant Professor; Ph.D., Notre Dame. History of Christian theology, particularly in the medieval period; life and thought of the Victorines in the first half of the twelfth century; developments in early thirteenth-century scholastic theology at the Universities of Paris and Oxford.
M. Shawn Copeland, Associate Professor; Ph.D., Boston College. Theological and philosophical anthropology and political theology, African and African-derived religious and cultural experience, African American intellectual history.
Catherine Cornille, Associate Professor; Ph.D., Leuven (Belgium). Theology of religions, the theory of interreligious dialogue, concrete questions in the Hindu-Christian and Buddhist-Christian dialogues, and the phenomenon of enculturation and intercultural theology; theories and methods in the comparative study of religions, women in world religions, and Asian new religious movements.
Robert Daly, S.J., Professor Emeritus; Dr.Theol., Catholic University. Christian sacrifice.
John A. Darr, Associate Professor; Ph.D., Vanderbilt. The Gospel of Luke and Acts of the Apostles, literary criticism and theory, Biblical characters and characterization, Synoptic relations.
Donald J. Dietrich, Professor; Ph.D., Minnesota. Theological aspects relevant to Holocaust studies and the Catholic human rights conversation.
Harvey Egan, S.J., Professor; Dr.Theol., Münster (Germany). Karl Rahner as mystical theologian, Christian mystics.
Jeffrey Geoghegan, Associate Professor; Ph.D., California, San Diego. History and religion of ancient Israel, cultural influences on the development of early Israelite religious expression and belief.
Yonder Gillihan, Assistant Professor; Ph.D., Chicago. Dead Sea Scrolls, Matthew and Paul, apocalypticism, Christian origins within the context of Jewish sectarianism in the late Second Temple period.
Roberto Goizueta, Professor; Ph.D., Marquette. U.S. Latino/a theologies, theology and culture, theological aesthetics, Christology.
Thomas H. Groome, Professor; Ed.D., Columbia. History, theory, and practice of religious education.
Charles C. Hefling, Associate Professor; Ph.D., Boston College. Christology, incarnation, and atonement; theological methodology; Bernard Lonergan and J. H. Newman; Anglican theology, Austin Farrer, and Charles Williams.
Kenneth Himes, O.F.M., Chairperson; Ph.D., Duke. History of Catholic social teaching, role of the U.S. Catholic community in American social reform, ethics of warfare, relationship of religion and politics in the nation's public life.
Michael J. Himes, Professor; Ph.D., Chicago.
Mary Ann Hinsdale, I.H.M., Associate Professor; Ph.D., St. Michael's (Toronto). Ecclesiology, Christology, theological anthropology, feminist theologies.
David Hollenbach, S.J., University Chair in Human Rights and International Justice and Director, Center for Human Rights and International Justice; Ph.D., Yale. Foundation of Christian social ethics, particularly in the areas of human rights, theory of justice, the common good, and the role of religion in social and political life.
Robert P. Imbelli, Associate Professor; Ph.D., Yale. Christology, Trinitarian theology, spirituality.
James Keenan, S.J., Professor; S.T.L., S.T.D., Gregorian. Fundamental moral theology, history of theological ethics, Thomas Aquinas, virtue ethics, HIV/AIDS, genetics, church leadership ethics.
Paul R. Kolbet, Assistant Professor; Ph.D., Notre Dame. Early Christian homilies, exegesis, doctrine, ministry, and spirituality; use of Hellenistic philosophy by early Christians as well as their relationship with Jews; use of early Christian sources in contemporary systematic theology.
Ruth Langer, Associate Professor; Ph.D., Hebrew Union. Jewish liturgy, Christian-Jewish relations.
Frederick Lawrence, Professor; D.Th., Ph.D., Basel (Switzerland).
John Makransky, Associate Professor; Ph.D., Wisconsin–Madison. How doctrines of enlightenment (buddhahood) have developed in connection with diverse forms of Buddhist meditation, philosophical analysis, and ritual practice; theoretical and practical connections between transcendental insight, compassion, and devotion in Tibetan and Indian Buddhist traditions; Buddhist and Christian anthropology and soteriology.
H. John McDargh, Associate Professor; Ph.D., Harvard. Psychological study of religious development, integration of spirituality and psychotherapy, contemporary psychoanalytic theory and theological anthropology.
Bruce T. Morrill, S.J., Associate Professor; Ph.D., Emory. Systematic theology, liturgical theology, political theology, pneumatology, ritual studies.
James W. Morris, Professor; Ph.D., Harvard.
John Paris, S.J., Walsh Professor of Bioethics; Ph.D., USC. Legal and medical ethics.
Pheme Perkins, Professor; Ph.D., Harvard. Greco-Roman cultural setting of early Christianity, Hellenistic philosophy, Pauline epistles, Johannine writings, resurrection and early Christian eschatology, Nag Hammadi corpus, Gnosticism, Irenaeus.
Nancy Pineda-Madrid, Ph.D., Graduate Theological Union. Systematic theology, method in practical/pastoral theologies, U.S. Latino/Latina theologies, feminist reconstructions of redemption/salvation, U.S. and North American pragmatism and religious thought.
Stephen J. Pope, Professor; Ph.D., Chicago. Christian ethics and evolutionary theory, love and justice in contemporary Christian ethics, charity and natural law in Aquinas, Roman Catholic social teachings.
Jane Regan, Associate Professor; Ph.D., Catholic University. Adult faith formation at the parish level.
Louis Roy, O.P., Associate Professor; Ph.D., Cambridge. Thomas Aquinas and Lonergan; mystical and intellectual approaches to God, religious experience and revelation, theology of religions.
Margaret Amy Schatkin, Associate Professor; Ph.D., Fordham; Th.D., Princeton. Critical edition of works of Chrysostom, patristic bibliography, patristic theology.
Francis A. Sullivan, S.J., Adjunct Professor; S.T.D., Gregorian. Ecclesiology, ecumenism, church history.
David Vanderhooft, Associate Professor; Ph.D., Harvard. Hebrew Scriptures, especially the former and latter prophets; historical, cultural, theological, and comparative analyses of ancient Israel's literature; relationship between Israel and the ancient empires of Assyria and Babylonia.
Thomas E. Wangler, Associate Professor; Ph.D., Marquette. Religious history of American Catholicism, specifically, how Catholics believed and lived the Catholic faith, e.g., catechisms, hymnals, devotional books and practices, and faith assertions relative to the American nation.
James M. Weiss, Associate Professor; Ph.D., Chicago. Contemporary spirituality since 1900, Renaissance and Reformation Church history, biography as a literary form, spirituality of work and vocation.

THE JEWISH THEOLOGICAL SEMINARY

The Graduate School

Programs of Study The Graduate School offers the most comprehensive program of advanced Jewish studies available in North America. Through specialized courses of study, students prepare to pursue careers in academia, Jewish art, or communal leadership. Programs of study leading to the M.A. and doctoral (D.H.L. and Ph.D.) degrees are offered in the following fields except as noted: ancient Judaism, Bible and ancient Semitic languages, interdepartmental studies (M.A. only), Jewish art and visual culture (M.A. only), Jewish history, Jewish literature, Jewish thought, Jewish women's studies (M.A. only), liturgy, medieval Jewish studies, midrash and scriptural interpretation, modern Jewish studies, and Talmud and Rabbinics. In addition, The Graduate School offers dual-degree programs with the Columbia University School of Social Work leading to the M.A./M.S.S.W. degrees and with Columbia University's School of International and Public Affairs leading to the M.A./M.P.A. degrees to prepare students to enter the field of communal service.

Research Facilities The Library of The Jewish Theological Seminary houses the most complete collection of Judaica in the Western Hemisphere. With more than 380,000 volumes on open shelves, it is ideally suited for the research needs of graduate students. The Library's special collection, with more than 30,000 items, affords ample opportunities for original scholarship. Students also benefit from the library resources of neighboring Columbia University and Union Theological Seminary. M.A. and Ph.D. students also have access to the courses and facilities of several universities through a special consortial agreement.

Financial Aid Financial aid based on need is available to U.S. and Canadian matriculated M.A. students in the form of scholarships, grants, and loans. There are also competitive merit awards available for outstanding M.A. candidates who apply by March 1. Moreover, some M.A. programs offer their own designated merit fellowships. Prospective Ph.D. students who complete their applications by January 2 are automatically considered for merit-based, five-year fellowships consisting of tuition, an annual stipend, pedagogic training, health insurance, and other benefits. Advanced doctoral students may be awarded teaching assistantships. Students may obtain information and applications for need-based aid from the Office of Financial Aid, 100 Schiff Building (212-678-8007; financialaid@jtsa.edu).

Cost of Study For the 2008–09 academic year, tuition is $26,600 for full-time Ph.D. study and $21,200 for full-time M.A. study. Part-time students are charged $1000 per credit. In addition to tuition, a fee of $400 is charged per semester.

Living and Housing Costs Residence hall rooms are available to single students at a cost of approximately $8800 to $9800 per academic year. Apartments of various sizes and costs are also available to married students. The housing application deadline for all new students entering the following fall semester is May 15. For more information, prospective students should contact the Office of Residence Life (212-678-8035; reslife@jtsa.edu).

Student Group The Graduate School enrolled 175 students in fall 2008. Fifty-five percent of the students are women, and approximately 65 percent of all students receive financial aid.

Location JTS is located on the vibrant Upper West Side of New York City. Its proximity to Columbia University, Teachers College, Union Theological Seminary, and the Manhattan School of Music puts The Graduate School in the heart of a dynamic academic community. Students are encouraged to explore the wealth of cultural activities New York City offers—from music and dance at Lincoln Center to theater on and off Broadway, from art at the Metropolitan and Whitney museums to the galleries in Chelsea and Williamsburg.

The Seminary The Jewish Theological Seminary is a premier academic center consisting of five schools and a world-renowned library. Students flourish in an intellectual environment of warmth and creativity located in the heart of New York City's vibrant Jewish community. Academic departments of unparalleled range and depth offer a rich selection of courses in nearly every field of Judaic studies. Founded in 1886, its original mission was to preserve the knowledge and practice of Conservative Judaism. That mission has blossomed and expanded, and today JTS is a prestigious hub of Jewish learning. JTS grants undergraduate, graduate, and professional degrees through its schools; offers enriching programs for the Jewish community in the United States, Israel, and around the world; and enriches Jewish academic scholarship with its Hebraic and Judaic collection housed in The Library, the Western Hemisphere's most significant and outstanding repository of texts from the tenth century to the present.

Applying Application for admission to degree programs should be made as early as possible. Although applications are accepted and reviewed all year, The Graduate School sets deadlines for those who wish to receive fellowship consideration (January 2 for Ph.D. applicants and March 1 for M.A. applicants). Ph.D. applicants must submit a $50 application fee; official college transcripts; three letters of academic reference; GRE or MAT scores; and a sample of academic research in the field of study, written in English. M.A. applicants must submit a $50 application fee; official college transcripts; three letters of reference, at least two of which must be academic; GRE or MAT scores; and a sample of written English. Applicants whose native language is other than English and who have not been educated at a college where English is the language of instruction should submit official scores of the Test of English as a Foreign Language (TOEFL) in lieu of the GRE or MAT. A minimum TOEFL score of 100 (Internet-based) is required. The Graduate School may also require nonnative English speakers to demonstrate oral/aural English proficiency; for details, students should contact the Admissions Office. For M.A. and doctoral programs, an interview with a members of the admissions committee and/or the department chair is recommended and may be required. Ph.D. candidates may begin their studies in the fall only, whereas M.A. candidates enter The Graduate School in either the fall or the spring. Students who wish to attend The Graduate School on a nonmatriculated basis may do so by submitting a nonmatriculated status application form, accompanied by a $35 application fee and an official college transcript indicating receipt of a B.A. degree. The Graduate School accepts nonmatriculated applications until one month prior to either the fall or spring semester. Two summer sessions are also available. The Graduate School is open to all men and women without regard to age, race, religion, sexual orientation, or national origin.

Correspondence and Information
The Graduate School
The Jewish Theological Seminary
3080 Broadway
Box 74
New York, New York 10027-4649
Phone: 212-678-8022
Fax: 212-280-6022
E-mail: gradschool@jtsa.edu
Web site: http://www.jtsa.edu/graduate

The Jewish Theological Seminary

THE FACULTY

Arnold Eisen, Chancellor.
Michael B. Greenbaum, Vice Chancellor.
Alan M. Cooper, Provost.
Stephen Garfinkel, Dean of The Graduate School and Dean of Academic Affairs.

Ancient Judaism Program
Stephen A. Geller, Professor.
Richard Kalmin, Professor and Program Adviser (fall 2008).
Seth Schwartz, Professor and Program Adviser (spring 2009).

Department of Bible and Ancient Semitic Languages
Alan M. Cooper, Professor.
Stephen A. Geller, Professor.
David Marcus, Professor.
Benjamin Sommer, Professor.
Robert Alan Harris, Associate Professor and Chair.
Stephen Garfinkel, Assistant Professor.
Walter Herzberg, Assistant Professor.
Amy Kalmanofsky, Assistant Professor.
Sharon Keller, Assistant Professor.
David Sperling, Adjunct Professor.
Elizabeth Bloch-Smith, Adjunct Associate Professor.
Miles Cohen, Adjunct Lecturer.

Department of Hebrew Language
Joel Roth, Chair.
Edna Nahshon, Associate Professor.
Nitza Krohn, Senior Lecturer.
Sarah Pelee, Lecturer.
Allon Pratt, Lecturer.
Shlomit Shraybom-Shivtiel, Adjunct Assistant Professor.

Interdepartmental Studies Program
Neil Danzig, Professor.
Edna Nahshon, Associate Professor.
Eitan Fishbane, Assistant Professor.
Maud Kozodoy, Assistant Professor and Program Adviser.

Jewish Art and Visual Culture Program
Vivian B. Mann, Adjunct Professor and Program Adviser.
Susan Chevlowe, Adjunct Assistant Professor.

Department of Jewish History
Daphna Canetti-Nisim, Schusterman Professor of Israel Studies.
David Fishman, Professor.
Ismar Schorsch, Professor.
Seth Schwartz, Professor.
Jack Wertheimer, Professor.
Benjamin R. Gampel, Associate Professor and Chair.
Shuly Rubin Schwartz, Associate Professor.
Stefanie Siegmund, Associate Professor.
Michael Stanislawski, Adjunct Professor.

Department of Jewish Literature
Alan Mintz, Professor and Chair (fall 2008).
David G. Roskies, Professor.
Raymond P. Scheindlin, Professor.
Barbara Mann, Associate Professor and Chair (spring 2009).
Debra Reed Blank, Assistant Professor.
Jeffrey Hoffman, Assistant Professor.
Maud Kozodoy, Assistant Professor.
Anne Lapidus Lerner, Assistant Professor.
Kenneth Berger, Adjunct Assistant Professor.

Department of Jewish Thought
Arnold Eisen, Professor.
Neil Gillman, Professor.
Alan Mittleman, Professor and Chair.
Eitan Fishbane, Assistant Professor.
Leonard Levin, Assistant Professor.
Richard Cohen, Adjunct Professor.
Alfredo Borodowski, Adjunct Assistant Professor.
Gordon Tucker, Adjunct Assistant Professor.

Jewish Professional Leadership: Jewish Studies and Social Work; Jewish Studies and Public Administration
Mayer Rabinowitz, Professor.
Aryeh Davidson, Assistant Professor.
Anne Lapidus Lerner, Assistant Professor.
Ilene Scholnick, Program Adviser.

Jewish Women's Studies Program
David C. Kraemer, Professor.
Stefanie Siegmund, Associate Professor and Program Adviser.
Barbara Mann, Associate Professor.
Anne Lapidus Lerner, Assistant Professor and Program Adviser.

Liturgy Program
Alan Mintz, Professor.
Raymond P. Scheindlin, Professor.
Eliezer Diamond, Associate Professor.
Boaz Tarsi, Associate Professor and Program Adviser.
Jeffrey Hoffman, Assistant Professor.

Medieval Jewish Studies Program
Raymond P. Scheindlin, Professor and Program Adviser (spring 2009).
Benjamin R. Gampel, Associate Professor and Program Adviser (fall 2008).
Robert Harris, Associate Professor.
Eitan Fishbane, Assistant Professor.
Evyatar Marienberg, Assistant Professor.

Midrash and Scriptural Interpretation Program
Alan M. Cooper, Professor.
Judith Hauptman, Professor.
David C. Kraemer, Professor.
Burton L. Visotzky, Professor and Program Adviser.
Robert Harris, Associate Professor.
Rachel Mikva, Assistant Professor.

Modern Jewish Studies Program
David Fishman, Professor and Program Adviser.
Alan Mintz, Professor.
David G. Roskies, Professor and Program Adviser.
Barbara Mann, Associate Professor.

Department of Talmud and Rabbinics
Neil Danzig, Professor.
Israel Francus, Professor.
Shamma Friedman, Professor.
Judith Hauptman, Professor and Chair.
Richard Kalmin, Professor.
David C. Kraemer, Professor.
Joel Roth, Professor.
Burton L. Visotzky, Professor.
Eliezer Diamond, Associate Professor.
Mayer E. Rabinowitz, Associate Professor.
Beth Berkowitz, Assistant Professor.
Marjorie Lehman, Assistant Professor.
Evyatar Marienberg, Assistant Professor.
Jonathan Milgram, Assistant Professor.
Jay Rovner, Adjunct Assistant Professor.

Students in the courtyard at The Jewish Theological Seminary.

The Library of The Jewish Theological Seminary.

THE JEWISH THEOLOGICAL SEMINARY

The Rabbinical School

Program of Study

The Rabbinical School of The Jewish Theological Seminary (JTS) offers a five-year program of study and field experience that leads to rabbinical ordination under the auspices of the Conservative Movement. The third year is spent in Jerusalem at the Schechter Institute of Jewish Studies, JTS's Israeli affiliate. Through a consortium academia agreement, rabbinical students can enroll in courses at Union Theological Seminary and Hebrew Union College. A Master of Arts (M.A.) is earned during the program in a variety of concentrations that students choose from. Concentrations include Bible, rabbinics, Jewish history, Jewish women's studies, Jewish literature, liturgy, Midrash, Jewish education, and pastoral care.

Studying at JTS affords rabbinical students the opportunity to earn another graduate degree through the Graduate School or William Davidson Graduate School of Jewish Education. Students need to be accepted to these programs, and there is a dual-enrollment charge.

The Mekhinah (preparatory) year program is for accepted candidates who need to acquire textual skills in the areas of Bible and Talmud. The Rabbinical School also offers Tokhnit Yesod, the Pre-Rabbinical Program, enabling students to take classes in The Rabbinical School for credit before applying for full admission.

Research Facilities

Rabbinical students regularly study in havruta (in pairs) in the Eisenfeld/Duker Beit Midrash. In addition, the library of The Jewish Theological Seminary houses the most complete collection of Judaica in the Western Hemisphere. With more than 340,000 volumes on open shelves, it is ideally suited for the research needs of graduate students. The library's special collection, with more than 30,000 items, affords ample opportunity for original scholarship. All students also benefit from the resources of neighboring Columbia University and Union Theological Seminary.

Financial Aid

The program at The Rabbinical School offers a significant number of merit-based fellowships. Applicants may obtain applications for merit-based fellowships directly from The Rabbinical School office. Candidates are encouraged to apply for the Wexner Graduate Fellowship from the Wexner Foundation.

Cost of Study

For the 2007–08 academic year, tuition was $20,340 for full-time study. Part-time students were charged $950 per credit.

Living and Housing Costs

Rooms and apartments (150 units) are available to single students at a cost of approximately $8000 per academic year. Apartments of various costs are available to married students. The housing application deadline for incoming students is May 12. For more information, students should contact the Office of Residence Life by calling 212-678-8035 or by sending an e-mail to reslife@jtsa.edu.

Student Group

In fall 2007, 140 students were enrolled in The Rabbinical School. Approximately 40 percent are women. A majority of students receive generous merit-based fellowships.

Location

JTS is located on the vibrant Upper West Side of New York City. Its proximity to Columbia University, Teachers College, Union Theological Seminary, and the Manhattan School of Music puts The Rabbinical School in the heart of a dynamic academic community. Students are encouraged to explore the wealth of cultural activities New York City offers—from music and dance at Lincoln Center to theater on and off Broadway, from art at the Metropolitan and Whitney museums to the galleries in SoHo and Greenwich Village.

The Seminary and The School

Founded in 1886, The Jewish Theological Seminary is the academic and spiritual center of Conservative Judaism worldwide. In1904, it established The Jewish Museum. The New York campus includes five separate yet integrated schools: Albert A. List College of Jewish Studies, The Graduate School (the largest division), H. L. Miller Cantorial School and College of Jewish Music, The Rabbinical School, and William Davidson Graduate School of Jewish Education.

Applying

Applications for regular admission should be submitted by December 31 for the following fall. JTS accepts late applications on case-by-case basis. A $65 application fee, application, essays, official college transcripts, three letters of recommendation, and GRE or LSAT scores are required. All candidates are considered for merit-based fellowships. The deadline for the Tokhnit Yesod program is May 31.

Correspondence and Information

Charles Savenor, Director of Admissions
The Rabbinical School
The Jewish Theological Seminary
3080 Broadway
New York, New York 10027-4649

Phone: 212-678-8807
E-mail: rabschool@jtsa.edu
Web site: http://www.jtsa.edu

The Jewish Theological Seminary

THE FACULTY AND THEIR RESEARCH

The Rabbinical School Administration
Daniel Nevins, Pearl Resnick Dean.
Lisa Gelber, Associate Dean and Rabbi of the Women's League Seminary Synagogue.
Charles Savenor, Associate Dean and Director of Admissions.
Mychal Springer, Associate Dean and Director of Field Education.
Ed Feld, Rabbi in Residence.

The Rabbinical School Faculty
Beth Berkowitz, Ph.D. (religious studies), Columbia. Rabbinic literature, Judaism and Christianity in late antiquity, ritual studies, theories and methods in the study of religion, cultural criticism.
Debra Reed Blank, Ph.D. (liturgy and rabbinics), Jewish Theological Seminary. Liturgy.
Joseph Brodie, Ph.D. (hon.), Jewish Theological Seminary.
Steve Brown, Ed.D. (curriculum development and teaching), Columbia Teachers College. Curriculum development and instruction.
Burton Cohen, Ph.D. (education), Chicago. Informal settings for Jewish education, preparation of teachers and principals for Jewish schools, teaching rabbinic literature to adults, use of computers in Jewish learning and educational research.
Miles B. Cohen, Ph.D. (hon.), Jewish Theological Seminary. Synagogue skills, such as chanting the Torah, Megillot, and prayers of the weekday, Shabbat, holiday services, and special life-cycle occasions; Hebrew grammar.
Alan Cooper, Ph.D. (religious studies), Yale. Linguistic structure of biblical poetry, the Bible.
Aryeh Davidson, Ph.D. (special education and developmental psychology), Columbia. Teacher preparation, leadership development, program evaluation, identity development of Jewish professionals.
Eliezer Diamond, Ph.D. (Talmud), Jewish Theological Seminary. Rabbinic literature; introductory, intermediate, and advanced Talmud study.
Arnold Eisen, Ph.D. (history of Jewish thought), Hebrew University. Jewish identity, revitalization of Jewish tradition, redefinition of the American Jewish community.
Shira Epstein, Ph.D. (curriculum and teaching), Columbia Teachers College. Gender and Jewish education, drama as pedagogy.
Eitan Fishbane, Ph.D., Brandeis. Near Eastern and Judaic studies, history and literature of Jewish mysticism.
David Fishman, Ph.D., Harvard. Modern Jewish history.
Israel Francus, Ph.D., Hebrew University. Talmud and rabbinics.
Shamma Friedman, Ph.D., Jewish Theological Seminary. Talmudic studies, including literary and conceptual development, stratification of the Talmudic sugya, linguistic studies in Hebrew and Aramaic, and the nature of variant readings of the Talmudic texts.
Benjamin Gampel, Ph.D. Columbia. Medieval and early modern Jewish history.
Stephen Garfinkel, Ph.D. (Middle East languages and cultures), Columbia. Early popular perceptions of Moses as a divine figure.
Stephen A. Geller, Ph.D., Harvard. Biblical literature, with special emphasis on the Book of Psalms, biblical poetry, and the prophets.
Neil Gillman, Ph.D., Columbia. Jewish philosophy.
Michael Greenbaum, Ph.D. (higher education administration), Columbia. Nonprofit management, leadership theory and practice, history of the Conservative Movement.
Robert Harris, Ph.D., Jewish Theological Seminary. Literature and commentary, particularly medieval Jewish biblical exegesis.
Judith Hauptman, Ph.D., Jewish Theological Seminary. Talmud, Talmudic research.
Barry Holtz, Ph.D., Brandeis. Classical texts, professional development for teachers, philosophy of Jewish education, current issues confronting Jewish education.
Carol Ingall, Ed.D., Boston University. Curriculum and instruction.
Richard Kalmin, Ph.D. Interpretation of rabbinic stories, ancient Jewish history, and the development of rabbinic literature.
Sharon Keller, Ph.D. (Hebrew and Judaic studies), NYU. Biblical literature, ancient Egyptian art, the Exodus, the afterlife, women's studies.
David Kraemer, Ph.D., Jewish Theological Seminary. Talmud and rabbinics.
Jeffrey Kress, Ph.D., Rutgers. Building Jewish values and identity by using principles of social and emotional learning to augment Jewish education.
Nitza Krohn. Hebrew language.
Marjorie Lehman, Ph.D., Columbia. Religion, Talmud and rabbinics.
Anne Lapidus Lerner, Ph.D., Harvard. Hebrew and American Jewish poetry, modern Jewish literature, portrayal of women in Jewish literature.
Michelle Lynn-Sachs, Ph.D., NYU. Educational leadership, congregational studies, sociology of education, sociology of religion.
Barbara Mann, Ph.D. (comparative literature), Berkeley. Israeli and Jewish literature, cultural studies, modern poetry, urban studies, literary modernism, fine arts.
Vivian Mann, Ph.D. Art history.
David Marcus, Ph.D., Columbia. Middle East languages and cultures; Bible and ancient languages, including Babylonian Aramaic and biblical Hebrew.
Evyatar Marienberg, Ph.D., École des Hautes Études en Sciences Sociale. Talmud, study of beliefs and practices of lay Jews and Christians from various periods.
Jonathan Milgram, Ph.D. (Talmud), Bar Ilan (Israel). Talmud criticism and medieval Jewish law.
Alan Mintz, Ph.D., Columbia. Hebrew literature and language.
Alan Mittleman, Ph.D., Temple. Jewish philosophy.
Edna Nahshon, Ph.D. (performance studies), NYU. Hebrew language.
Daniel Nevins, M.A., Jewish Theological Seminary. Homiletics.
Adina Ofek, Ph.D., Jewish Theological Seminary. Jewish education, Hebrew language.
Sarah Pelee, M.A. (educational counseling), Northwestern. Hebrew language.
Mayer Rabinowitz, Ph.D., Jewish Theological Seminary. Talmud and rabbinics.
Henry Rosenblum. Jewish music, hazzanut.
David Roskies, Ph.D. Brandeis. Jewish literature.
Joel Roth, Ph.D. (Talmud), Jewish Theological Seminary. Talmud and rabbinics.
Raymond Scheindlin, Ph.D., Columbia. Encounter of Hebrew and Arabic cultures in Spain, especially as embodied in the poetry of the two traditions.
Menahem Schmelzer, Ph.D. (Hebrew letters), Jewish Theological Seminary. Medieval Jewish literature.
Ismar Schorsch, Ph.D. (Jewish history), Columbia. Jewish history.
Seth Schwartz, Ph.D., (ancient history), Columbia. Jewish history.
Shuly Rubin Schwartz, Ph.D., Jewish Theological Seminary. American Jewish life, the Jewish family, Jewish women's studies.
Boaz Tarsi, Ph.D., Cornell. Theory of Ashkenazi liturgical music and the music theory of Western common-practice.
Burton Visotzky, Ph.D., Jewish Theological Seminary. Talmud and rabbinics.
Jack Wertheimer, Ph.D. Modern Jewish history, with a particular focus on the religious, communal, and organizational experiences of American Jews since World War II.

LOYOLA COLLEGE IN MARYLAND

Programs in Pastoral Counseling and Spiritual Care

Programs of Study

The pastoral counseling and spiritual care programs at Loyola College are the only advanced degree programs in the United States that integrate religious philosophy with practical behavioral science. The programs prepare students to utilize person-centered, cognitive-behavioral, psychodynamic, and family systems approaches that integrate the psychological, intellectual, emotional, social, and spiritual realms.

The Certificate of Advanced Study (CAS) is designed for those who already have a master's degree in counseling or psychology and are seeking additional course work for professional and/or licensure reasons. The program requires completion of 30 credits and provides an opportunity to become a member of the American Association of Pastoral Counselors.

The goal of the Master of Science (M.S.) in pastoral counseling program is to develop counselors who are able to employ counseling practices with a spiritual dimension. The degree requires 42 credits, including four courses in clinical case supervision.

The Master of Arts in spiritual care prepares qualified persons for ministry using the skills of empathetic listening and responding, crisis intervention strategies, and other tools. The degree requires 39 credits, including courses in crisis intervention, loss and bereavement, and spiritual guidance.

The Ph.D. program is designed for those who wish to further their training as clinicians, supervisors, educators, and researchers. The curriculum consists of 45 credits, including 12 credits in core courses, 12 credits in research courses, 6 credits in clinical courses, and 9 credits in integration courses. Students may elect to complete an academic, clinical, education, or supervision concentration; each concentration requires 12 credits.

A combined M.S./Ph.D. accelerated program awards a master's degree and a Ph.D. in 5 to 6 years of full-time, year-round study.

Research Facilities

The Center for the Study of Spirituality, Trauma, Loss, and Violence offers a holistic approach to healing in an effort to determine how religion and spirituality facilitate healing from trauma, loss, and violence. The center integrates spiritual and religious interventions with evidence-based psychological and social treatments, creating a community of scholars, clinicians, researchers, and students who possess expertise in this niche area.

The Loyola Notre Dame Library contains approximately 463,000 books and bound periodical volumes; over 11,000 videos, DVDs, and CDs; and 989 print periodical subscriptions. The library's Web site serves as a gateway to a variety of Internet resources, including numerous databases such as ERIC, Lexis-Nexis Academic Universe, Maryland Digital Library, Cambridge Scientific, and Business Source Premier, as well as full-text articles from over 23,000 periodicals.

Financial Aid

A variety of financial assistance is available to graduate students. Graduate assistants work 10–20 hours per week in faculty and administrative departments in exchange for a stipend and tuition remission. A number of scholarships are available from the College; award amounts, entry requirements, and eligibility criteria vary. Federal Stafford Loans provide up to $8500 per year in subsidized loans or $20,500 in unsubsidized loans. The Federal Graduate PLUS Loan Program allows students to borrow up to the full cost of attendance, less other aid received. Other loans may be available from alternative sources. Some students may be eligible for federal work-study.

Cost of Study

In 2007–08, master's students spend $440 per credit hour, plus clinical fees of $1128 per course. Ph.D. students spend $550 per credit for 900-level courses, as well as a doctoral dissertations fee of $1400 per semester. All students also pay an Advanced Individual Supervisory Fee of $250 per semester.

Living and Housing Costs

The College does not offer on-campus housing for graduate students, except those who work as resident assistants as part of their financial aid package. However, off-campus housing is available. Students can expect to spend $400–$1000 per month for a 1-bedroom apartment and $850–$1300 for a 2-bedroom apartment, depending on size and location.

Student Group

Approximately 350 students are enrolled in the master's programs each year, 225 in pastoral counseling and 55–60 in spiritual and pastoral care. Another 30 are enrolled in the doctoral program, and 20–30 are enrolled in the remaining programs. Some students are in the ministry or lay ministry. Most doctoral candidates hold master's degrees from a CACREP-approved counseling program and have had prior clinical experience.

Student Outcomes

Graduates of the program are prepared to make contributions to empirical research on the integration of spirituality and faith and the theory and techniques of psychology and counseling. Many alumni are working as licensed counselors at nonprofit organizations, social justice agencies, and faith and poverty-focused organizations or as educators and researchers.

Location

Baltimore is one of the most visited cities in the nation, with 12 million visitors each year. The city has a variety of museums, art galleries, theaters, and music venues, as well as festivals like the annual Showcase of Nations Ethnic Festivals. The Inner Harbor, a popular waterfront attraction, is surrounded by historic neighborhoods with unique shops and restaurants for every style and taste.

The University

Founded by Jesuits in 1852, Loyola College remains committed to the ideals embodied by the priests and brothers of the Society of Jesus, which include an emphasis on academic excellence, the importance of the liberal arts, and the education of the whole person. The College enrolls approximately 6,100 students in a broad spectrum of programs that are practitioner-oriented and designed for professionals seeking a greater level of expertise and satisfaction in their careers.

Applying

To be considered for admission, prospective students must submit a completed application form; official transcripts from each college attended; a current resume; three letters of recommendation from faith community leaders, teachers, or supervisors familiar with the applicant's background; a 3–4 page essay describing personal strengths, faith identity, and career goals; and a $50 nonrefundable application fee. Some programs require submission of official GRE scores; ideally, verbal and quantitative scores should each fall between 500 and 800.

Correspondence and Information

Office of Graduate Admission
Loyola College in Maryland
4501 North Charles Street
Baltimore, Maryland 21210
Phone: 410-617-2587
800-221-9107 Ext. 5020 (toll-free)
Fax: 410-617-2002
E-mail: graduate@loyola.edu
Web site: http://graduate.loyola.edu/pcgrad/info

Loyola College in Maryland

THE FACULTY AND THEIR RESEARCH

Sharon E. Cheston, Professor and Director of Ph.D. Admissions; Ed.D., Northern Illinois. Childhood abuse, spirituality, working with adults who were abused as children.

Joseph Ciarrocchi, Professor; Ph.D., Catholic University. Compulsive behaviors, anxiety disorders, integration of psychology and spirituality.

Geraldine Fialkowski, Assistant Professor and Director of M.S. Admissions; Ph.D., Loyola (Baltimore). Women's issues, loss and bereavement, couples counseling, working with adult survivors of trauma.

C. Kevin Gillespie, Assistant Professor and Director of M.A. Admissions; Ph.D., Boston University. Integration of psychology and spirituality, issues of sexual abuse and trauma.

Joanne Greer, Professor Emerita; Ph.D., Maryland. Psychoanalytic theory, mental health, public health.

Danielle Lasure-Bryant, Adjunct Faculty and Director of M.S./CAS Clinical Education; Ed.D., Cincinnati. Counseling older adults, community mental health counseling, counselor supervision.

Kelly Murray, Assistant Professor and Director of Ph.D. Clinical Education; Ph.D., California School of Professional Psychology. Women's health, post-traumatic stress disorder.

K. Elizabeth Oakes, Assistant Professor; Ph.D., Loyola (Baltimore). Treatment of substance and behavioral addictions.

Ralph L. Piedmont, Professor; Ph.D., Boston University. Taxonomic models of personality and their relevance for understanding mental and physical health outcomes, measurement of spiritual transcendence.

Thomas E. Rodgerson, Affiliate Faculty; Ph.D., Loyola (Baltimore). Clergy and clergy burnout, sexual compulsivity, multifaith counseling, conflict mediation in religious organizations, supervision.

Joseph Stewart-Sicking, Assistant Professor; Ed.D., Cincinnati. Spiritual practices and personal transformation, research methods in the social sciences, faith community's role in the prevention and treatment of mental illness.

Robert Wicks, Professor; Psy.D., MCP Hahnemann. Prevention of secondary stress, the integration of psychology and spirituality from a world religion perspective.

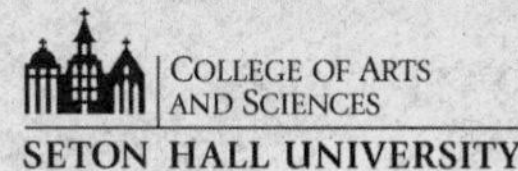

SETON HALL UNIVERSITY

Department of Jewish-Christian Studies

Programs of Study

Seton Hall University's Graduate Department of Jewish-Christian Studies offers a Master of Arts (M.A.) degree and a certificate in Jewish-Christian studies, which cover all aspects of the historical relationships between Jews and Christians—their respective values and traditions. The programs serve as a model for eliminating prejudice through mutual understanding.

Students working toward a degree normally gain an elementary knowledge of Hebrew early in the program, allowing them to enter the Hebrew mind-set of the writers. Courses provide critical study of foundational sources in their social world contexts, tracing how these traditions developed within diverse local settings. Students examine the religious, ethical, and social issues central for understanding Christians and Jews today against the background of anti-Semitism and the Holocaust.

The Department requires that M.A. students choose from either of two programs of study—the thesis or the nonthesis option—in consultation with an adviser. Students in the thesis program complete 27 credits offered by the Department and 6 credits in the reading of Hebrew texts. An adviser's approval must be obtained for all courses chosen. Three credits must be completed in JCST 9001 Thesis (with the topic approved by the Thesis Committee). The thesis must make a contribution to continuing research in some aspect of Jewish-Christian studies. After consultation with the faculty members, students with a strong background in research may choose to do a more extensive investigation of an approved topic and produce a thesis for 6 credits (JCST 9002). Students in the nonthesis program complete 36 credits in Jewish-Christian studies, selecting courses with the approval of the Departmental adviser. Students must demonstrate a basic knowledge of biblical Hebrew.

In the 12-credit Certificate in Jewish-Christian Studies program, students take a required class, Christian Jewish Encounter, and then select three other courses in consultation with the chair of the Department.

For further details, students should see the Department's Web site at: http://www.shu.edu/academics/artsci/ma-jewish-christian-studies/index.cfm.

Research Facilities

The Institute of Judaeo-Christian Studies, founded in 1953, is primarily a center for research and publication. Its area of study is the Church's rootedness in Judaism and the relationship between the Church and the Jewish people through the ages. Its work includes an annual series of lectures, study days, and conferences. These are intended to inform the general public about various facets of Christian-Jewish relations.

The Walsh Library, a state-of-the-art 155,000-square-foot building, houses 500,000 titles, 1,875 current periodicals, and an extensive collection of microform and other nonprint items that include videotapes, CD-ROM music, and other electronic media. Fahy Hall has twenty-eight classrooms, two TV studios, a Macintosh and IBM graphics lab, two classroom amphitheaters, and language and statistics labs. McNulty Hall has well-equipped science labs. The College of Nursing Building contains a multipurpose practice-demonstration room, with twelve hospital beds, an amphitheater, an independent study area, and a computer laboratory. Completed in 1997, Jubilee Hall, a six-story facility with 126,000 square feet of academic space, features high-tech classrooms with computer and multimedia capabilities.

Financial Aid

The H. Suzanne Jobert Scholarship Fund assists students pursuing the M.A. in Jewish-Christian Studies. Inquiries about this tuition scholarship may be made through the Department chair. The Sister Rose Thering Endowment, established in 1993 in honor of Sister Rose's work as an educator and advocate for improving relations between Christians and Jews, provides scholarships for teachers who want to learn more about promoting interreligious understanding and cooperation through education. Scholarships are available to teachers who wish to enroll as nonmatriculated students and take up to 12 credits to receive a certificate of completion.

Cost of Study

In 2008–09, tuition is $875 per credit. Full-time students pay $305 per semester in University and technology fees; part-time students pay $185.

Living and Housing Costs

Housing and living costs in South Orange and surrounding towns are comparable to most suburban cities, with studio and one-bedroom apartments renting for $750 to $1000 per month.

Student Group

Most students in the Jewish-Christian Studies degree and certificate programs are teachers in public, private, or parochial schools; education and ecumenical administrators; or clergy and seminarians. However, the programs also attract educational generalists who seek the means to explore Jewish and Christian studies for personal or career enrichment.

Location

Seton Hall is located on 58 acres in the village of South Orange, New Jersey, a suburban residential area 14 miles southwest of New York City. The town center is a 10-minute walk from the campus and features bookstores, coffee shops, and restaurants. The heart of midtown Manhattan is about 30 minutes away by train; students can take advantage of everything this exciting city has to offer while still living in a suburban area.

The University

Founded in 1856, Seton Hall is a private coeducational Catholic institution—the nation's oldest diocesan institution of higher education in the United States. With a total enrollment of about 10,000, including approximately 4,500 graduate students, the University comprises nine colleges and schools. Seton Hall is accredited by the Middle States Association of Colleges and Schools. Through the incorporation of technology into the curriculum, the College of Arts and Sciences seeks to enhance and enliven the learning environment. Rooted in tradition, yet looking to the future, the College offers a rich set of opportunities for intellectual discovery. Graduate students are guided by scholars and specialists toward the mastery of academic and professional areas.

Applying

In addition to the general University requirements for admission, the Department of Jewish-Christian Studies strongly recommends an interview or suitable correspondence with the Department chair to determine the objectives of the student in relation to the resources of the Department. Students must submit the completed application (available online at http://www.shu.edu/academics/artsci/apply-graduate.cfm), the $50 application fee, and transcripts from all previously attended universities and colleges. The deadlines for fall and spring admission are July 1 and November 1, respectively. Applications are processed on a rolling basis.

Correspondence and Information

The Rev. Lawrence Frizzell, Department Chair
Department of Jewish-Christian Studies
240 Fahy Hall
Seton Hall University
400 South Orange Avenue
South Orange, New Jersey 07079
Phone: 973-761-9751
E-mail: jcst@shu.edu
Web site: http://www.shu.edu/academics/artsci/ma-jewish-christian-studies/index.cfm

Seton Hall University

THE FACULTY AND THEIR RESEARCH

David M. Bossman, Director of the Sister Rose Thering Endowment and Professor; Ph.D., Saint Louis. Editor of the *Biblical Theology Bulletin* since 1981, Dr. Bossman applies cross-cultural analysis to the study of Christian and Jewish sources, contemporizing Jewish and Christian values and fostering cooperative partnerships. He is the founding director of the Sister Rose Thering Endowment for Jewish-Christian Studies.

Alan Brill; Ph.D., Fordham. Teaches modern Jewish studies and is engaged in interfaith dialogue. Rabbi Brill holds a rabbinical degree from Yeshiva.

Asher Finkel, Professor; Ph.D., Tübingen (Germany). Postbiblical Judaism, Jewish thinkers, early Christianity. Rabbi Finkel holds a rabbinical degree from Yeshiva.

Lawrence Frizzell, Associate Professor and Director of the Institute of Judaeo-Christian Studies; S.T.L., S.S.L., D.Phil., Oxford. Jewish literature of the Second Temple Period, Paul and John, Bible and liturgy.

John Morley, Associate Professor and Department Adjunct; Ph.D., NYU. The Holocaust: history and interpretation.

Section 13
Writing

This section contains a directory of institutions offering graduate work in writing, followed by in-depth entries submitted by institutions that chose to prepare detailed program descriptions. Additional information about programs listed in the directory but not augmented by an in-depth entry may be obtained by writing directly to the dean of a graduate school or chair of a department at the address given in the directory.

For programs offering related work, see also in this book *Communication and Media* and *Language and Literature*.

CONTENTS

Program Directories

Announcement

Close-Ups

See also:

Technical Writing

Carnegie Mellon University, College of Humanities and Social Sciences, Department of English, Program in Professional Writing, Pittsburgh, PA 15213-3891. Offers design (MAPW); professional writing (MAPW); research (MAPW); rhetorical theory (MAPW); science writing (MAPW); technical (MAPW). Part-time programs available. *Entrance requirements:* For master's, GRE General Test. Additional exam requirements/recommendations for international students: Required—TOEFL, TWE.

See Close-Up on page 723.

Colorado State University, Graduate School, College of Liberal Arts, Department of Journalism and Technical Communication, Fort Collins, CO 80523-0015. Offers technical communication (MS). Part-time programs available. *Faculty:* 17 full-time (6 women). *Students:* 17 full-time (12 women), 26 part-time (19 women); includes 8 minority (2 American Indian/Alaska Native, 1 Asian American or Pacific Islander, 5 Hispanic Americans), 2 international. Average age 34. 24 applicants, 67% accepted, 7 enrolled. In 2007, 9 master's awarded. *Degree requirements:* For master's, thesis (for some programs). *Entrance requirements:* For master's, GRE General Test, samples of written work, letters of recommendation, resumé or curriculum vita, 3 writing/communication projects. Additional exam requirements/recommendations for international students: Required—TOEFL (minimum score 600 paper-based; 250 computer-based). *Application deadline:* For fall admission, 4/1 priority date for domestic students, 4/1 for international students. Applications are processed on a rolling basis. Application fee: $50. Electronic applications accepted. *Expenses:* Tuition, state resident: full-time $4,887; part-time $272 per credit. Tuition, nonresident: full-time $16,425; part-time $913 per credit. Required fees: $1,379; $75 per credit. *Financial support:* In 2007–08, 18 students received support, including 3 research assistantships with full and partial tuition reimbursements available (averaging $7,694 per year), 11 teaching assistantships with partial tuition reimbursements available (averaging $7,474 per year); fellowships with partial tuition reimbursements available, career-related internships or fieldwork, Federal Work-Study, institutionally sponsored loans, scholarships/grants, traineeships, and unspecified assistantships also available. Support available to part-time students. Financial award application deadline: 3/1; financial award applicants required to submit FAFSA. *Faculty research:* Technical/science communication, public relations, health/risk communication, web/new media technologies, environmental communication. Total annual research expenditures: $332,610. *Unit head:* Greg Luft, Chair, 970-491-6310, Fax: 970-491-2908. *Application contact:* Cindy Christen, Associate Professor and Graduate Program Coordinator, 970-491-6319, Fax: 970-491-2908, E-mail: cindy.christen@colostate.edu.

Drexel University, College of Arts and Sciences, Department of Culture and Communication, Philadelphia, PA 19104-2875. Offers communication (MS); publication management (MS). Part-time and evening/weekend programs available. *Degree requirements:* For master's, internship, professional portfolio. *Entrance requirements:* Additional exam requirements/recommendations for international students: Required—TOEFL. Electronic applications accepted. *Faculty research:* Science information and attitudes, science influence on literature, process of technical writing, document design, software documentation.

Fitchburg State College, Division of Graduate and Continuing Education, Program in Applied Communications, Fitchburg, MA 01420-2697. Offers applied communications (MS, Certificate); library media (MS); technical and professional writing (MS). Part-time and evening/weekend programs available. *Students:* 3 full-time (2 women), 13 part-time (11 women); includes 1 minority (African American), 1 international. Average age 32. 6 applicants, 100% accepted, 4 enrolled. In 2007, 13 degrees awarded. *Entrance requirements:* For master's, GRE General Test or MAT, minimum 2 years of related experience, letters of recommendation, resumé. Additional exam requirements/recommendations for international students: Required—TOEFL (minimum score 550 paper-based; 213 computer-based; 79 iBT). *Application deadline:* Applications are processed on a rolling basis. Application fee: $25 ($50 for international students). *Expenses:* Tuition, nonresident: part-time $150 per credit. Required fees: $109 per credit. *Financial support:* In 2007–08, research assistantships with partial tuition reimbursements (averaging $5,500 per year); Federal Work-Study, scholarships/grants, and unspecified assistantships also available. Support available to part-time students. Financial award application deadline: 3/1; financial award applicants required to submit FAFSA. *Unit head:* Dr. John Chetro-Szivos, Chair, 978-665-3261, Fax: 978-665-3658, E-mail: gce@fsc.edu. *Application contact:* Director of Admissions, 978-665-3144, Fax: 978-665-4540, E-mail: admissions@fsc.edu.

Illinois Institute of Technology, Graduate College, College of Science and Letters, Lewis Department of Humanities, Chicago, IL 60616-3793. Offers information architecture (MS); technical communication (PhD); technical communication and information design (MS). Part-time and evening/weekend programs available. *Faculty:* 18 full-time (7 women), 13 part-time/adjunct (7 women). *Students:* 23 full-time (14 women), 36 part-time (26 women); includes 22 minority (16 African Americans, 3 Asian Americans or Pacific Islanders, 3 Hispanic Americans), 8 international. Average age 34. 71 applicants, 68% accepted, 27 enrolled. In 2007, 12 master's awarded. *Degree requirements:* For master's, comprehensive exam, thesis or alternative, project; for doctorate, comprehensive exam, thesis/dissertation, qualifying exam. *Entrance requirements:* For master's, GRE General Test; for doctorate, GRE General Test, bachelor's degree in technical communication or other relevant field. Additional exam requirements/recommendations for international students: Required—TOEFL (minimum score 550 paper-based; 213 computer-based; 80 iBT). *Application deadline:* For fall admission, 5/1 for domestic and international students; for spring admission, 1/5 for domestic and international students. Applications are processed on a rolling basis. Application fee: $40. Electronic applications accepted. *Expenses:* Tuition: Full-time $14,004; part-time $778 per credit. Required fees: $7 per credit. $235 per term. Tuition and fees vary according to class time, course level, course load, program and student level. *Financial support:* In 2007–08, 15 teaching assistantships with partial tuition reimbursements (averaging $9,000 per year) were awarded; career-related internships or fieldwork, Federal Work-Study, institutionally sponsored loans, scholarships/grants, health care benefits, tuition waivers (partial), and unspecified assistantships also available. Support available to part-time students. Financial award applicants required to submit FAFSA. *Faculty research:* Discourse analysis, linguistics, readability, ethics in professions, instructional and document design, knowledge management, usability testing and evaluation, history and philosophy of science. Total annual research expenditures: $1,343. *Unit head:* Kathryn Riley, Professor and Chair, 312-567-3566, Fax: 312-567-5187, E-mail: riley@iit.edu. *Application contact:* Morgan Frederick, Assistant Director of Graduate Communications, 866-472-3448, Fax: 312-567-3138, E-mail: inquiry.grad@iit.edu.

James Madison University, The Graduate School, College of Arts and Letters, Institute of Technical and Scientific Communication, Harrisonburg, VA 22807. Offers MA, MS. Part-time programs available. *Faculty:* 3 full-time (2 women), 1 (woman) part-time/adjunct. *Students:* 12 full-time (9 women), 7 part-time (5 women); includes 2 minority (1 African American, 1 Hispanic American). Average age 27. In 2007, 7 degrees awarded. *Degree requirements:* For master's, one foreign language, thesis, internship, practicum. *Entrance requirements:* For master's, GRE General Test, GRE Subject Test, TSC application dossier, 3 letters of recommendation, 20-30 page writing samples. Additional exam requirements/recommendations for international students: Required—TOEFL (minimum score 550 paper-based). *Application deadline:* For fall admission, 5/31 priority date for domestic students; for spring admission, 8/31 priority date for domestic students. Applications are processed on a rolling basis. Application fee: $55. Electronic applications accepted. *Expenses:* Tuition, state resident: full-time $6,720; part-time $280 per credit hour. Tuition, nonresident: full-time $19,104; part-time $796 per credit hour. *Financial support:* In 2007–08, 9 students received support, including 1 teaching assistantship with full tuition reimbursement available (averaging $8,494 per year); Federal Work-Study, unspecified assistantships, and 8 assistantships ($7,237) also available. Financial award application deadline: 3/1; financial award applicants required to submit FAFSA. *Unit head:* Dr. Alice I. Philbin, Director and Coordinator, 540-568-8018.

The Johns Hopkins University, Zanvyl Krieger School of Arts and Sciences, The Writing Seminars, Baltimore, MD 21218-2699. Offers fiction writing (MFA); poetry (MFA); science writing (MA). *Faculty:* 6 full-time (3 women). *Students:* 26 full-time (13 women); includes 2 minority (1 Asian American or Pacific Islander, 1 Hispanic American), 1 international. Average age 27. 292 applicants, 6% accepted, 12 enrolled. In 2007, 12 degrees awarded. *Degree requirements:* For master's, one foreign language, thesis, foreign language exam (for MFA). *Entrance requirements:* For master's, GRE General Test, GRE Subject Test (recommended), foreign language exam, sample of written work, 3 letters of recommendation, official college transcripts, GRE scores, and goal statement. Additional exam requirements/recommendations for international students: Required—TOEFL (minimum score 600 paper-based; 250 computer-based). *Application deadline:* For fall admission, 1/15 for domestic and international students. Application fee: $75. Electronic applications accepted. *Financial support:* In 2007–08, 25 students received support, including 1 fellowship (averaging $5,000 per year), 1 research assistantship with full tuition reimbursement available (averaging $17,000 per year), 20 teaching assistantships with full tuition reimbursements available (averaging $17,000 per year); Federal Work-Study, institutionally sponsored loans, scholarships/grants, health care benefits, and tuition waivers (partial) also available. Financial award application deadline: 4/15; financial award applicants required to submit FAFSA. *Faculty research:* Film theory, literary criticism, contemporary fiction. *Unit head:* Prof. Dave Smith, Chair, 410-516-3409, Fax: 410-516-6828, E-mail: davesmith@jhu.edu. *Application contact:* Gina Woloszyn, Contact, 410-516-6286, Fax: 410-516-6828, E-mail: regina@jhu.edu.

See Close-Up on page 727.

Massachusetts Institute of Technology, School of Humanities, Arts, and Social Sciences, Program in Writing and Humanistic Studies, Graduate Program in Science Writing, Cambridge, MA 02139-4307. Offers SM. *Faculty:* 7 full-time (2 women), 1 part-time/adjunct (0 women). *Students:* 7 full-time (6 women), 1 international. Average age 24. 37 applicants, 30% accepted, 7 enrolled. In 2007, 6 degrees awarded. *Degree requirements:* For master's, thesis, internship. *Entrance requirements:* For master's, GRE General Test. Additional exam requirements/recommendations for international students: Required—TOEFL (minimum score 600 paper-based; 250 computer-based). *Application deadline:* For fall admission, 1/15 for domestic and international students. Application fee: $70. Electronic applications accepted. *Expenses:* Tuition: Full-time $34,760; part-time $545 per unit. Required fees: $236. *Financial support:* In 2007–08, 7 students received support, including 7 fellowships with tuition reimbursements available (averaging $28,560 per year); career-related internships or fieldwork, Federal Work-Study, institutionally sponsored loans, scholarships/grants, health care benefits, and unspecified assistantships also available. *Unit head:* Prof. Robert Kanigel, Director, 617-253-6668, Fax: 617-452-5100, E-mail: sciwrite-www@mit.edu. *Application contact:* Graduate Admissions, 617-253-6668, Fax: 617-452-5100, E-mail: sciwrite-www@mit.edu.

Metropolitan State University, College of Arts and Sciences, St. Paul, MN 55106-5000. Offers computer science (MS); liberal studies (MA); technical communication (MS). Part-time and evening/weekend programs available. *Faculty:* 12 full-time (7 women), 4 part-time/adjunct (3 women). *Students:* 17 full-time (13 women), 51 part-time (31 women); includes 8 minority (2 African Americans, 2 American Indian/Alaska Native, 2 Asian Americans or Pacific Islanders, 2 Hispanic Americans), 6 international. Average age 39. In 2007, 21 degrees awarded. *Entrance requirements:* For master's, BA/BS; 2.75 GPA; resum&e. Additional exam requirements/recommendations for international students: Required—TOEFL (minimum score 550 paper-based; 213 computer-based). *Application deadline:* For fall admission, 8/1 priority date for domestic students, 3/15 for international students; for winter admission, 10/15 for international students; for spring admission, 12/1 priority date for domestic students, 3/15 for international students. Application fee: $20. *Expenses:* Tuition, state resident: full-time $5,080; part-time $254 per credit. Tuition, nonresident: full-time $10,160; part-time $508 per credit. Required fees: $189; $34 per credit. *Financial support:* Applicants required to submit FAFSA. *Faculty research:* Computer security, software engineering, distributed systems, document design, diffusing of innovations, social issues and communication technology. *Unit head:* Dr. Ed Malecki, Dean, 651-793-1443, Fax: 651-793-1446, E-mail: ed.malecki@metrostate.edu.

Miami University, Graduate School, College of Arts and Sciences, Department of English, Program in Technical and Scientific Communication, Oxford, OH 45056. Offers MTSC. Part-time programs available. *Degree requirements:* For master's, thesis, final exam. *Entrance requirements:* For master's, minimum undergraduate GPA of 3.0 during previous 2 years or 2.75 overall. Additional exam requirements/recommendations for international students: Required—TOEFL (minimum score 550 paper-based; 213 computer-based), TWE (minimum score 4). Electronic applications accepted.

Oklahoma State University, College of Arts and Sciences, Department of English, Stillwater, OK 74078. Offers creative writing (MA, PhD); literature (MA, PhD); technical writing (MA, PhD). *Faculty:* 51 full-time (29 women), 8 part-time/adjunct (3 women). *Students:* 15 full-time (8 women), 115 part-time (75 women); includes 11 minority (3 African Americans, 6 American Indian/Alaska Native, 2 Hispanic Americans), 20 international. Average age 32. 123 applicants, 45% accepted, 36 enrolled. In 2007, 4 master's, 6 doctorates awarded. *Degree requirements:* For master's, one foreign language, thesis; for doctorate, thesis/dissertation. *Entrance requirements:* For master's, GRE General Test or GMAT, GRE Subject Test, minimum GPA of 3.0; for doctorate, GRE General Test or GMAT, GRE Subject Test, minimum GPA of 3.5, writing sample. Additional exam requirements/recommendations for international students: Required—TOEFL. *Application deadline:* For fall admission, 3/1 priority date for international students; for spring admission, 8/1 priority date for international students. Applications are processed on a rolling basis. Application fee: $40 ($75 for international students). Electronic applications accepted. *Expenses:* Tuition, state resident: full-time $4,993; part-time $148 per credit hour. Tuition, nonresident: full-time $14,755; part-time $555 per credit hour. Tuition and fees vary according to program. *Financial support:* In 2007–08, 8 research assistantships (averaging $4,613 per year), 75 teaching assistantships (averaging $14,116 per year) were awarded; career-related internships or fieldwork, Federal Work-Study, scholarships/grants, health care benefits, tuition waivers (partial), and unspecified assistantships also available. Support available to part-time students. Financial award application deadline: 3/1. *Faculty research:* American and British novel, poetry, and autobiography; Native American languages and literature; institutional history of American film, history, and adaptations; rhetoric and theories of human communication; learning strategies of second language learners. *Unit head:* Dr. Carol Moder, Head, 405-744-9474, Fax: 405-744-6326, E-mail: epu@okstate.edu.

Polytechnic Institute of NYU, Department of Humanities and Social Sciences, Major in Technical Writing and Specialized Journalism, Brooklyn, NY 11201-2990. Offers MS. *Students:* 1 full-time (0 women), 5 part-time (1 woman); includes 2 minority (1 African American, 1 Asian American or Pacific Islander). 6 applicants, 67% accepted, 3 enrolled. *Degree requirements:* For master's, comprehensive exam (for some programs), thesis (for some programs). *Entrance requirements:* Additional exam requirements/recommendations for international students: Required—TOEFL (minimum score 550 paper-based; 213 computer-based); Recommended—IELTS (minimum score 7). *Application deadline:* For fall admission, 7/15 priority date for domestic students, 4/1 priority date for international students; for spring admission, 12/15 priority date for domestic students, 10/1 priority date for international students. Applications are processed on a rolling basis. Application fee: $55. Electronic applications accepted. *Expenses:* Tuition: Full-time $18,486; part-time $1,027 per credit. Required fees: $352 per semester. *Application contact:* Anthea Jeffrey, Graduate Admissions, 718-260-3200, Fax: 718-260-3624, E-mail: gradinfo@poly.edu.

See Close-Up on page 921.

Technical Writing

Regis University, College for Professional Studies, MA Program, Denver, CO 80221-1099. Offers criminology (MA); fine arts administration (Certificate); language and communication (MA); mediation (Certificate); psychology (MA); self-designed major (MA); social justice, peace, and reconciliation (Certificate); social science (MA); technical communication (Certificate). Program also offered in Henderson and Las Vegas (Summerlin), NV. Part-time and evening/weekend programs available. Postbaccalaureate distance learning degree programs offered (minimal on-campus study). *Faculty:* 84. *Students:* 218 (167 women). Average age 41. In 2007, 52 degrees awarded. *Degree requirements:* For master's, thesis, research project. *Entrance requirements:* For master's, resumé, recommendations, essays. Additional exam requirements/recommendations for international students: Required—TOEFL (minimum score 213 computer-based), TWE (minimum score 5). *Application deadline:* For fall admission, 8/13 priority date for domestic students, 7/13 priority date for international students; for winter admission, 10/8 priority date for domestic students, 9/8 priority date for international students; for spring admission, 12/17 priority date for domestic students, 11/17 for international students. Applications are processed on a rolling basis. Application fee: $75. Electronic applications accepted. *Expenses: Contact institution. Financial support:* Federal Work-Study available. Support available to part-time students. Financial award application deadline: 3/15; financial award applicants required to submit FAFSA. *Faculty research:* Independent/nonresidential graduate study: new methods and models, adult learning and the capstone experience, Goal Setting, behavior of Adult students, Innovative Studies for Community Colleges. *Unit head:* Dr. Robert Collins, Chair, 303-458-4302, Fax: 303-964-5538. *Application contact:* Graduate Admissions, 800-677-9270 Ext. 4080, Fax: 303-964-5538, E-mail: masters@regis.edu.

Texas Tech University, Graduate School, College of Arts and Sciences, Department of English, Lubbock, TX 79409. Offers English (MA, PhD); technical communication (MA); technical communication and rhetoric (PhD). Part-time programs available. *Faculty:* 38 full-time (13 women), 2 part-time/adjunct (both women). *Students:* 114 full-time (64 women), 84 part-time (56 women); includes 21 minority (4 African Americans, 3 American Indian/Alaska Native, 3 Asian Americans or Pacific Islanders, 11 Hispanic Americans), 13 international. Average age 34. 155 applicants, 49% accepted, 47 enrolled. In 2007, 18 master's, 11 doctorates awarded. *Degree requirements:* For master's, one foreign language, thesis (for some programs); for doctorate, thesis/dissertation. *Entrance requirements:* For master's and doctorate, GRE General Test. Additional exam requirements/recommendations for international students: Required—TOEFL (minimum score 550 paper-based; 213 computer-based). *Application deadline:* For fall admission, 3/1 priority date for international students; for spring admission, 11/1 priority date for international students. Applications are processed on a rolling basis. Application fee: $50 ($60 for international students). Electronic applications accepted. *Expenses:* Tuition, state resident: part-time $373 per credit hour. Tuition, nonresident: part-time $651 per credit hour. Tuition and fees vary according to program. *Financial support:* In 2007–08, 101 students received support, including 98 teaching assistantships with partial tuition reimbursements available (averaging $14,187 per year); research assistantships with partial tuition reimbursements available, Federal Work-Study and institutionally sponsored loans also available. Support available to part-time students. Financial award application deadline: 4/15; financial award applicants required to submit FAFSA. *Faculty research:* Southwestern literature and language; computers and writing; technical communication and rhetoric; creative writing; nineteenth century studies. Total annual research expenditures: $18,946. *Unit head:* Dr. Sam Dragga, Chair, 806-742-2501, Fax: 806-742-0989, E-mail: sam.dragga@ttu.edu. *Application contact:* Dr. Sean Grass, Director of Graduate Studies, 806-742-2501, Fax: 806-742-0989, E-mail: english.gradadvisor@ttu.edu.

The University of Alabama in Huntsville, School of Graduate Studies, College of Liberal Arts, Department of English, Huntsville, AL 35899. Offers English (MA); teaching of English to speakers of other languages (Certificate); technical communications (Certificate). Part-time and evening/weekend programs available. *Faculty:* 17 full-time (9 women). *Students:* 25 full-time (20 women), 50 part-time (34 women); includes 12 minority (9 African Americans, 1 American Indian/Alaska Native, 2 Hispanic Americans), 1 international. Average age 33. 49 applicants, 80% accepted, 32 enrolled. In 2007, 11 master's, 9 other advanced degrees awarded. *Degree requirements:* For master's, one foreign language, comprehensive exam, thesis or alternative, oral and written exams. *Entrance requirements:* For master's, GRE General Test, minimum GPA of 3.0. Additional exam requirements/recommendations for international students: Required—TOEFL (minimum score 500 paper-based; 173 computer-based; 62 iBT). *Application deadline:* For fall admission, 7/18 for domestic students, 4/1 for international students; for spring admission, 11/30 for domestic students, 9/1 for international students. Applications are processed on a rolling basis. Application fee: $40 ($50 for international students). Electronic applications accepted. *Expenses:* Tuition, state resident: full-time $6,548; part-time $276 per credit hour. Tuition, nonresident: full-time $13,466; part-time $565 per credit hour. *Financial support:* In 2007–08, 10 students received support, including 7 teaching assistantships with full and partial tuition reimbursements available (averaging $8,357 per year); fellowships with full and partial tuition reimbursements available, research assistantships with full and partial tuition reimbursements available, career-related internships or fieldwork, Federal Work-Study, institutionally sponsored loans, scholarships/grants, health care benefits, and unspecified assistantships also available. Support available to part-time students. Financial award application deadline: 4/1; financial award applicants required to submit FAFSA. *Faculty research:* American and British literature, linguistics, technical writing, women's studies, rhetoric. *Unit head:* Dr. Rose Norman, Chair, 256-824-6320, Fax: 256-824-6949, E-mail: normanr@uah.edu.

University of Arkansas at Little Rock, Graduate School, College of Arts, Humanities, and Social Science, Department of Rhetoric and Writing, Little Rock, AR 72204-1099. Offers professional and technical writing (MA). Part-time and evening/weekend programs available. *Students:* Average age 34. *Degree requirements:* For master's, thesis or alternative, oral defense of final project. *Entrance requirements:* For master's, GRE, minimum GPA of 3.0, writing portfolio. *Application deadline:* Applications are processed on a rolling basis. *Financial support:* Research assistantships with tuition reimbursements, teaching assistantships with tuition reimbursements, career-related internships or fieldwork, Federal Work-Study, institutionally sponsored loans, and unspecified assistantships available. Support available to part-time students. *Faculty research:* Writing for industry, science, business, and government; composition and rhetorical theory; writing nonfiction; teaching of writing. *Unit head:* Dr. George H. Jensen, Chairperson, 501-569-3160, E-mail: ghjensen@ualr.edu. *Application contact:* Dr. Cynthia A. Nahrwold, Coordinator, 501-569-3316, Fax: 501-569-8279, E-mail: canahrwold@ualr.edu.

University of California, Santa Cruz, Division of Graduate Studies, Division of Physical and Biological Sciences, Program in Science Communication, Santa Cruz, CA 95064. Offers science illustration (Certificate); science writing (Certificate). *Faculty:* 8 full-time (4 women). *Students:* 11 full-time (9 women); includes 3 minority (all Asian Americans or Pacific Islanders), 2 international. In 2007, 19 degrees awarded. *Entrance requirements:* For degree, GRE General Test, GRE Subject Test, bachelor's degree in science. Application fee: $60. Electronic applications accepted. *Expenses:* Tuition, nonresident: full-time $14,694. Required fees: $11,360. *Financial support:* Fellowships, research assistantships, teaching assistantships, career-related internships or fieldwork, Federal Work-Study, institutionally sponsored loans, and scholarships/grants available. Financial award application deadline: 2/1. *Unit head:* Robert Irion, Director, 831-459-4475. *Application contact:* Andrea Michels, Department Assistant, 831-459-4475, E-mail: scicom@ucsc.edu.

University of Central Florida, College of Arts and Humanities, Department of English, Orlando, FL 32816. Offers English (MA, MFA), including creative writing (MFA), English (MA); literature (MA); professional writing (Certificate); rhetoric and composition (MA); technical communication (MA); texts and technology (PhD). Part-time and evening/weekend programs available. *Faculty:* 73 full-time (41 women), 31 part-time/adjunct (21 women). *Students:* Average age 33. *Degree requirements:* For master's, one foreign language, thesis or alternative. *Entrance requirements:* For master's, GRE General Test, minimum GPA of 3.0 in last 60 hours of course work. Additional exam requirements/recommendations for international students: Required—TOEFL. *Application deadline:* For fall admission, 6/15 for domestic students; for spring admission, 12/1 for domestic students. Application fee: $30. Electronic applications accepted. *Expenses:* Tuition, state resident: full-time $6,484. Tuition, nonresident: full-time $23,938. Tuition and fees vary according to program. *Financial support:* Fellowships with partial tuition reimbursements, research assistantships with partial tuition reimbursements, teaching assistantships with partial tuition reimbursements, career-related internships or fieldwork, Federal Work-Study, institutionally sponsored loans, tuition waivers (partial), and unspecified assistantships available. Financial award application deadline: 3/1; financial award applicants required to submit FAFSA. *Unit head:* Dr. Dawn Trouard, Interim Chair, 407-823-1159, E-mail: dtrouard@mail.ucf.edu.

The University of North Carolina at Greensboro, Graduate School, College of Arts and Sciences, Department of English, Greensboro, NC 27412-5001. Offers creative writing (MFA); English (M Ed, MA, PhD, Certificate), including American literature (PhD), English (M Ed, MA), English literature (PhD), rhetoric and composition (PhD), technical writing (Certificate), women's studies (Certificate). *Faculty:* 29 full-time (16 women), 6 part-time/adjunct (2 women). *Students:* 108 full-time (71 women), 35 part-time (24 women); includes 16 minority (14 African Americans, 1 American Indian/Alaska Native, 1 Asian American or Pacific Islander). 277 applicants, 22% accepted. *Degree requirements:* For master's, comprehensive exam; for doctorate, variable foreign language requirement, thesis/dissertation, preliminary exam. *Entrance requirements:* For master's, GRE General Test, minimum GPA of 3.0; for doctorate, GRE General Test, GRE Subject Test, critical writing sample, minimum GPA of 3.0. Additional exam requirements/recommendations for international students: Required—TOEFL. *Application deadline:* For fall admission, 1/20 priority date for domestic students; for spring admission, 11/1 for domestic students. Applications are processed on a rolling basis. Electronic applications accepted. *Financial support:* Fellowships, research assistantships, teaching assistantships, career-related internships or fieldwork, Federal Work-Study, scholarships/grants, traineeships, and unspecified assistantships available. Support available to part-time students. *Unit head:* Dr. Anne Wallace, Head, 336-334-5311, Fax: 336-334-3281, E-mail: adwallace@uncg.edu. *Application contact:* Michelle Harkleroad, Director of Graduate Admissions, 336-334-4884, Fax: 336-334-4424, E-mail: mbharkle@uncg.edu.

University of North Texas, Robert B. Toulouse School of Graduate Studies, College of Arts and Sciences, Department of English, Denton, TX 76203. Offers creative writing (MA); English (MA, PhD); English as a second language (MA); linguistics (MA); Technical writing (MA). *Faculty:* 60 full-time (36 women). *Students:* 82 full-time (46 women), 91 part-time (65 women); includes 19 minority (4 African Americans, 1 American Indian/Alaska Native, 6 Asian Americans or Pacific Islanders, 8 Hispanic Americans), 13 international. Average age 30. 91 applicants, 47% accepted, 21 enrolled. In 2007, 38 master's, 5 doctorates awarded. Terminal master's awarded for partial completion of doctoral program. *Degree requirements:* For master's, one foreign language, comprehensive exam, thesis optional; for doctorate, one foreign language, comprehensive exam, thesis/dissertation. *Entrance requirements:* For master's, GRE General Test, 3.0 GPA, personal statement, current vita/resumé, writing sample for creative writing program; for doctorate, GRE General Test, 3.5 GPA, 3 letters of recommendation, personal statement, writing sample. Additional exam requirements/recommendations for international students: Required—proof of English language proficiency required for non-native English speakers; Recommended—TOEFL (minimum score 550 paper-based; 213 computer-based). *Application deadline:* For fall admission, 7/15 priority date for domestic students; for spring admission, 11/15 for domestic students. Application fee: $50 ($75 for international students). *Financial support:* In 2007–08, 8 students received support, including 2 fellowships with full tuition reimbursements available (averaging $20,000 per year), 42 teaching assistantships (averaging $11,000 per year); career-related internships or fieldwork, Federal Work-Study, institutionally sponsored loans, scholarships/grants, health care benefits, and unspecified assistantships also available. Financial award application deadline: 4/1. *Faculty research:* Creative writing, British and American literature, composition and rhetoric. Total annual research expenditures: $25,000. *Unit head:* Dr. David Holdeman, Chair, 940-565-2050, Fax: 940-565-4355, E-mail: holdeman@cas1.unt.edu. *Application contact:* Dr. Robert K. Upchuerch, Chair of Graduate Studies, 940-565-2114, Fax: 940-565-4355, E-mail: robertu@unt.edu.

University of the Sciences in Philadelphia, College of Graduate Studies, Program in Biomedical Writing, Philadelphia, PA 19104-4495. Offers biomedical writing (MS); medical marketing writing (Certificate); regulatory affairs writing (Certificate). Part-time and evening/weekend programs available. Postbaccalaureate distance learning degree programs offered (minimal on-campus study). *Faculty:* 2 full-time (1 woman), 14 part-time/adjunct (5 women). *Students:* 2 full-time (1 woman), 39 part-time (29 women), 1 international. Average age 37. In 2007, 8 master's, 3 other advanced degrees awarded. *Entrance requirements:* For master's, GRE General Test. Additional exam requirements/recommendations for international students: Required—TOEFL, TWE. *Application deadline:* For fall admission, 5/1 for international students; for winter admission, 10/1 for international students; for spring admission, 3/1 for international students. Applications are processed on a rolling basis. Application fee: $50. *Expenses: Contact institution. Financial support:* In 2007–08, 7 students received support; teaching assistantships with full tuition reimbursements available, tuition waivers (partial) available. Support available to part-time students. Financial award application deadline: 5/1. *Faculty research:* History of medical writing and publishing, compliance, regulatory. *Unit head:* Dr. Susanna Dodgson, Director, 215-596-8512, E-mail: s.dodgso@usp.edu. *Application contact:* Joyce D'Angelo, Administrative Assistant, 215-596-8937, E-mail: j.dangel@usp.edu.

University of Waterloo, Graduate Studies, Faculty of Arts, Department of English, Language and Literature, Waterloo, ON N2L 3G1, Canada. Offers English language and literature (PhD); literary studies (MA); rhetoric and communication design (MA). Part-time programs available. *Faculty:* 20 full-time (8 women), 19 part-time/adjunct (9 women). *Students:* 105. 106 applicants, 25% accepted, 26 enrolled. In 2007, 12 master's, 4 doctorates awarded. *Degree requirements:* For master's, one foreign language, thesis optional; for doctorate, 2 foreign languages, thesis/dissertation. *Entrance requirements:* For master's, honors degree, minimum B+ average; for doctorate, master's degree, minimum A- average. Additional exam requirements/recommendations for international students: Required—TOEFL, TWE. *Application deadline:* For fall admission, 2/1 for domestic students. Application fee: $75 Canadian dollars. Electronic applications accepted. *Financial support:* Teaching assistantships, career-related internships or fieldwork and scholarships/grants available. Financial award application deadline: 2/1. *Faculty research:* Shakespeare, American literature, rhetoric, Romantics, moderns. *Unit head:* Dr. M. McArthur, Chair, 519-888-4567 Ext. 33359, Fax: 519-746-5788, E-mail: mmcarthu@watarts.uwaterloo.ca. *Application contact:* Dr. V. Lamont, Graduate Officer, 519-888-4567 Ext. 33318, Fax: 519-746-5788, E-mail: vlamont@uwaterloo.ca.

Writing

Abilene Christian University, Graduate School, College of Arts and Sciences, Department of English, Abilene, TX 79699-9100. Offers composition/rhetoric (MA); literature (MA); writing (MA). Part-time programs available. *Faculty:* 15 part-time/adjunct (5 women). *Students:* 12 full-time (7 women), 3 part-time (all women); includes 1 minority (Hispanic American), 1 international. 4 applicants, 225% accepted, 8 enrolled. In 2007, 5 degrees awarded. *Degree requirements:* For master's, one foreign language, comprehensive exam, thesis optional. *Entrance requirements:* For master's, GRE General Test. *Application deadline:* For fall admission, 4/1 priority date for domestic students; for spring admission, 11/1 for domestic students. Applications are processed on a rolling basis. Application fee: $40 ($45 for international students). Electronic applications accepted. *Expenses:* Tuition: Full-time $13,368; part-time $557 per hour. Required fees: $700; $34 per hour. $10 per semester. Tuition and fees vary according to degree level and campus/location. *Financial support:* Teaching assistantships, Federal Work-Study available. Support available to part-time students. Financial award application deadline: 4/1. *Faculty research:* Feminism, Shakespearean dimensions of new literature, poetic consciousness, deconstruction myths. *Unit head:* Dr. Bill Rankin, Graduate Adviser, 325-674-2253, Fax: 325-674-2408, E-mail: rankinw@acu.edu. *Application contact:* William Horn, Graduate Admissions Counselor, 325-674-2656, Fax: 325-674-6717, E-mail: gradinfo@acu.edu.

Adelphi University, Graduate School of Arts and Sciences, Program in Creative Writing, Garden City, NY 11530-0701. Offers MFA. Part-time and evening/weekend programs available. *Students:* 1 (woman) full-time, 12 part-time (8 women); includes 2 minority (both African Americans) Average age 41. *Degree requirements:* For master's, thesis. *Entrance requirements:* For master's, 3 letters of reference, manuscript in chosen genre (poetry, fiction, playwriting). Additional exam requirements/recommendations for international students: Required—TOEFL (minimum score 550 paper-based; 213 computer-based). *Application deadline:* For fall admission, 1/15 for domestic students; for spring admission, 9/15 for domestic students. Applications are processed on a rolling basis. Application fee: $50. Electronic applications accepted. *Financial support:* Fellowships, Federal Work-Study available. *Unit head:* Judith Baumel, Director, 516-877-4031, E-mail: baumel@adelphi.edu. *Application contact:* Christine Murphy, Director of Admissions, 516-877-3050, Fax: 516-877-3039, E-mail: graduateadmissions@adelphi.edu.

See Close-Up on page 721.

American University, College of Arts and Sciences, Department of Literature, Program in Creative Writing, Washington, DC 20016-8001. Offers MFA. Part-time and evening/weekend programs available. *Students:* 38 full-time (28 women), 23 part-time (11 women); includes 8 minority (4 African Americans, 1 Asian American or Pacific Islander, 3 Hispanic Americans), 1 international. Average age 29. In 2007, 15 degrees awarded. *Degree requirements:* For master's, comprehensive exam, thesis. *Entrance requirements:* For master's, GRE, sample of written work. *Application deadline:* For fall admission, 2/1 priority date for domestic students. Application fee: $50. *Expenses:* Tuition: Full-time $19,998; part-time $1,111 per credit hour. Required fees: $380. Tuition and fees vary according to program. *Financial support:* Fellowships, research assistantships, teaching assistantships, career-related internships or fieldwork, institutionally sponsored loans, and tuition waivers (full and partial) available. Support available to part-time students. Financial award application deadline: 2/1. *Unit head:* Richard McCann, Co-Director, 202-885-2978, Fax: 202-885-2938. *Application contact:* Nicki Miller, Graduate Program Assistant, 202-885-2973.

Antioch University Los Angeles, Graduate Programs, Program in Creative Writing, Culver City, CA 90230. Offers creative writing (MFA); pedagogy of creative writing (Certificate). Postbaccalaureate distance learning degree programs offered (minimal on-campus study). *Degree requirements:* For master's, thesis. *Entrance requirements:* For master's, sample of written work. Additional exam requirements/recommendations for international students: Required—TOEFL. *Faculty research:* Creative nonfiction, fiction, poetry.

Antioch University McGregor, Graduate Programs, Individualized Liberal and Professional Studies Program, Yellow Springs, OH 45387-1609. Offers liberal and professional studies (MA), including counseling, creative writing, education, film studies, liberal studies, management, modern literature, psychology, theatre, visual arts. Part-time and evening/weekend programs available. Postbaccalaureate distance learning degree programs offered (minimal on-campus study). *Faculty:* 2 full-time (1 woman), 3 part-time/adjunct (2 women). *Students:* Average age 40. 35 applicants, 63% accepted, 17 enrolled. In 2007, 31 degrees awarded. *Degree requirements:* For master's, thesis or alternative. *Entrance requirements:* For master's, resumé, 2 letters of reference. *Application deadline:* For fall admission, 8/25 for domestic students; for winter admission, 12/5 for domestic students; for spring admission, 3/8 for domestic students. Applications are processed on a rolling basis. Application fee: $50. Electronic applications accepted. *Expenses:* Contact institution. *Financial support:* Federal Work-Study available. Financial award applicants required to submit FAFSA. *Unit head:* Suzanne Fest, Chair, 937-769-1876, Fax: 937-769-1807, E-mail: sfest@mcgregor.edu. *Application contact:* Seth Gordon, Assistant Director of Admissions, 937-769-1800 Ext. 1825, Fax: 937-769-1804, E-mail: sgordon@mcgregor.edu.

See Close-Up on page 443.

Arizona State University, Graduate College, College of Liberal Arts and Sciences, Division of Humanities, Interdisciplinary Program in Creative Writing, Tempe, AZ 85287. Offers MFA. *Entrance requirements:* For master's, GRE.

Asbury College, Graduate Programs, Wilmore, KY 40390-1198. Offers biology: alternative certificate (MA Ed); chemistry: alternative certificate (MA Ed); English (Certificate); English as a second language (MA Ed); ESL (Certificate); French (Certificate); mathematics: alternative certificate (MA Ed); reading / writing (MA Ed); social studies (Certificate); Spanish (Certificate); special education (MA Ed); special education: alternative certificate (MA Ed). *Accreditation:* NCATE. Part-time programs available. *Faculty:* 8 full-time (7 women), 9 part-time/adjunct (4 women). *Students:* Average age 36. 14 applicants, 100% accepted, 14 enrolled. In 2007, 10 degrees awarded. *Degree requirements:* For master's, action research project, portfolio. *Entrance requirements:* For master's, PRAXIS/NTE, minimum GPA of 2.75, letters of recommendation. Additional exam requirements/recommendations for international students: Required—TOEFL (minimum score 550 paper-based). *Application deadline:* Applications are processed on a rolling basis. Application fee: $25. *Expenses:* Tuition: Part-time $353 per credit hour. *Financial support:* Scholarships/grants and traineeships available. Financial award applicants required to submit FAFSA. *Unit head:* Dr. Bonnie J. Banker, Director, 859-858-3511 Ext. 2221, Fax: 859-858-3921, E-mail: bonnie.banker@asbury.edu. *Application contact:* Melanie S. Kinnell, Graduate Program Assistant and Certification Specialist, 859-858-3511 Ext. 2304, Fax: 859-858-3921, E-mail: graded@asbury.edu.

Ashland University, College of Arts and Sciences, Program in Creative Writing, Ashland, OH 44805-3702. Offers MFA. Postbaccalaureate distance learning degree programs offered (minimal on-campus study). *Faculty:* 1 full-time (0 women), 3 part-time/adjunct (2 women). *Students:* 16 full-time (12 women). Average age 37. *Degree requirements:* For master's, thesis. *Entrance requirements:* For master's, writing sample, minimum GPA of 2.75. *Application deadline:* For fall admission, 3/1 priority date for domestic students; for winter admission, 12/1 priority date for domestic students. *Expenses:* Tuition: Part-time $419 per credit. Tuition and fees vary according to degree level and program. *Financial support:* In 2007–08, 12 students received support. Career-related internships or fieldwork, Federal Work-Study, and institutionally sponsored loans available. *Unit head:* Dr. Stephen Haven, Director, MFA Program, 419-289-5979, E-mail: shaven@ashland.edu. *Application contact:* Sarah Marie Wells, Administrative Director, MFA Program, 419-289-5957, E-mail: swells@ashland.edu.

Ball State University, Graduate School, College of Sciences and Humanities, Department of English, Muncie, IN 47306-1099. Offers English (MA, PhD), including composition, creative writing (MA), general (MA), literature; linguistics (MA, PhD), including applied linguistics (PhD); linguistics and teaching English to speakers of other languages (MA); teaching English to speakers of other languages (MA). *Faculty:* 38. *Students:* 42 full-time (27 women), 31 part-time (18 women), 20 international. Average age 27. 99 applicants, 52% accepted, 26 enrolled. In 2007, 22 master's, 6 doctorates awarded. *Degree requirements:* For doctorate, variable foreign language requirement, thesis/dissertation. *Entrance requirements:* For master's, GRE General Test, writing sample; for doctorate, GRE General Test, GRE Subject Test, minimum graduate GPA of 3.2, writing sample. Application fee: $25 ($35 for international students). *Expenses:* Tuition, state resident: full-time $6,864. Tuition, nonresident: full-time $17,932. Required fees: $1,866. *Financial support:* In 2007–08, 2 fellowships with full tuition reimbursements (averaging $15,500 per year), 48 teaching assistantships with full tuition reimbursements (averaging $15,314 per year) were awarded; research assistantships with full tuition reimbursements, career-related internships or fieldwork and unspecified assistantships also available. Financial award application deadline: 3/1. *Faculty research:* American literature; literary editing; Medieval, Renaissance, and eighteenth century British literature; rhetoric. *Unit head:* Dr. Kecia McBride, Chairperson, 765-285-8535, Fax: 765-285-3765.

Belmont University, College of Arts and Sciences, Department of English, Nashville, TN 37212-3757. Offers literature (MA); writing (MA). Part-time and evening/weekend programs available. *Faculty:* 17 full-time (13 women). *Students:* 1 (woman) full-time, 37 part-time (30 women); includes 5 minority (4 African Americans, 1 Hispanic American). Average age 31. 15 applicants, 73% accepted, 10 enrolled. In 2007, 10 degrees awarded. *Degree requirements:* For master's, one foreign language, comprehensive exam (for some programs), thesis optional. *Entrance requirements:* For master's, GRE, letters of recommendation, writing sample. Additional exam requirements/recommendations for international students: Required—TOEFL. *Application deadline:* For fall admission, 8/1 for domestic students; for spring admission, 12/1 for domestic students. Applications are processed on a rolling basis. Application fee: $50. Electronic applications accepted. *Expenses:* Contact institution. *Financial support:* In 2007–08, 20 students received support. Federal Work-Study and scholarships/grants available. Financial award applicants required to submit FAFSA. *Faculty research:* Gender, autobiography, folklore. *Unit head:* Dr. James Wells, Director, 615-460-6239, Fax: 615-460-5720, E-mail: wellsj@mail.belmont.edu.

Bennington College, Graduate Programs, Program in Writing and Literature, Bennington, VT 05201. Offers creative writing (MFA). Postbaccalaureate distance learning degree programs offered (minimal on-campus study). *Faculty:* 14 full-time (8 women), 9 part-time/adjunct (4 women). *Students:* 104 full-time (75 women); includes 6 minority (1 African American, 5 Asian Americans or Pacific Islanders), 3 international. Average age 40. 157 applicants, 27% accepted, 28 enrolled. In 2007, 43 degrees awarded. *Degree requirements:* For master's, thesis, collection of essays or poems, or collection of short stories and/or a novel. *Entrance requirements:* For master's, manuscript. *Application deadline:* For fall admission, 3/1 for domestic students; for spring admission, 9/1 for domestic students. Application fee: $60. *Expenses:* Contact institution. One-time fee: $75 full-time. Tuition and fees vary according to program. *Financial support:* In 2007–08, 6 students received support. Scholarships/grants available. Financial award application deadline: 4/1; financial award applicants required to submit FAFSA. *Unit head:* Sven Birkerts, Director, Writing Seminars, 802-440-4452, Fax: 802-440-4453, E-mail: writing@bennington.edu. *Application contact:* Victoria Clausi, Associate Director of Writing Seminars, 802-440-4454, Fax: 802-440-4453, E-mail: writing@bennington.edu.

Boise State University, Graduate College, College of Arts and Sciences, Department of English, Program in Creative Writing, Boise, ID 83725-0399. Offers MFA. *Degree requirements:* For master's, thesis. *Entrance requirements:* For master's, GRE General Test, minimum GPA of 3.0.

Boston University, Graduate School of Arts and Sciences, Creative Writing Program, Boston, MA 02215. Offers MFA. *Students:* 21 full-time (12 women), 4 part-time (3 women); includes 2 minority (both Hispanic Americans), 1 international. Average age 31. In 2007, 17 degrees awarded. *Expenses:* Tuition: Full-time $34,930; part-time $1,092 per credit. Tuition and fees vary according to class time, course level and program. *Financial support:* In 2007–08, 22 students received support, including teaching assistantships with partial tuition reimbursements available (averaging $16,500 per year); Federal Work-Study and unspecified assistantships also available. Support available to part-time students. Financial award applicants required to submit FAFSA. *Unit head:* Leslie Epstein, Director, 617-353-2510, Fax: 617-353-3653, E-mail: leslieep@bu.edu. *Application contact:* Matthew Yost, Administrative Coordinator, 617-353-2510, Fax: 617-353-3653, E-mail: crwr@bu.edu.

Boston University, Graduate School of Arts and Sciences, Department of English, Boston, MA 02215. Offers creative writing (MA); English (MA, PhD). *Students:* 51 full-time (33 women), 11 part-time (6 women), 1 international. Average age 30. 665 applicants, 14% accepted, 40 enrolled. In 2007, 16 master's, 7 doctorates awarded. Terminal master's awarded for partial completion of doctoral program. *Degree requirements:* For master's, one foreign language, thesis; for doctorate, 2 foreign languages, comprehensive exam, thesis/dissertation, qualifying/oral exam. *Entrance requirements:* For master's and doctorate, GRE General Test, GRE Subject Test, sample of written work, 2 letters of recommendation. Additional exam requirements/recommendations for international students: Required—TOEFL (minimum score 550 paper-based; 213 computer-based). *Application deadline:* For fall admission, 1/15 for domestic students, 2/15 for international students. Application fee: $70. *Expenses:* Tuition: Full-time $34,930; part-time $1,092 per credit. Tuition and fees vary according to class time, course level and program. *Financial support:* In 2007–08, 39 students received support, including 2 fellowships with full tuition reimbursements available (averaging $18,000 per year), 25 teaching assistantships with partial tuition reimbursements available (averaging $16,500 per year); Federal Work-Study, scholarships/grants, and unspecified assistantships also available. Financial award application deadline: 1/15; financial award applicants required to submit FAFSA. *Unit head:* Laurence Breiner, Interim Chairman, 617-353-2509, Fax: 617-353-3653, E-mail: lbrei@bu.edu. *Application contact:* Harriet T. Lane, Administrative Assistant, 617-353-2509, Fax: 617-353-3653, E-mail: hlane@bu.edu.

Boston University, Graduate School of Arts and Sciences, Editorial Institute, Boston, MA 02215. Offers MA, PhD. *Students:* 13 full-time (8 women), 2 part-time; includes 1 minority (Hispanic American) Average age 34. 11 applicants, 64% accepted, 7 enrolled. *Degree requirements:* For master's, one foreign language, thesis; for doctorate, one foreign language, comprehensive exam, thesis/dissertation. *Entrance requirements:* For master's and doctorate, GRE General Test, thesis proposal, 3 letters of recommendation. Additional exam requirements/recommendations for international students: Required—TOEFL (minimum score 550 paper-based; 213 computer-based). *Application deadline:* For fall admission, 3/30 for domestic and international students. Application fee: $70. *Expenses:* Tuition: Full-time $34,930; part-time $1,092 per credit. Tuition and fees vary according to class time, course level and program. *Financial support:* In 2007–08, 12 students received support, including 3 teaching assistantships with full tuition reimbursements available (averaging $16,500 per year); Federal Work-Study, scholarships/grants, and unspecified assistantships also available. Support available to part-time students. Financial award application deadline: 1/15; financial award applicants required to submit FAFSA. *Unit head:* Archie Burnett, Co-Director, 617-353-6631, E-mail: burnetta@bu.edu. *Application contact:* Alex Effgen, Administrative Assistant, 617-353-6631, Fax: 617-353-6917, E-mail: editinst@bu.edu.

Bowling Green State University, Graduate College, College of Arts and Sciences, Department of English, Program in Creative Writing, Bowling Green, OH 43403. Offers fiction (MFA); poetry (MFA). Part-time programs available. *Students:* 19 full-time (11 women), 1 part-time; includes 2 African Americans. Average age 27. 108 applicants, 10% accepted, 9 enrolled. In 2007, 11 degrees awarded. *Degree requirements:* For master's, thesis or alternative. *Entrance requirements:* For master's, GRE General Test. Additional exam requirements/recommendations for international students: Required—TOEFL. *Application deadline:* For fall admission, 2/15 priority date for domestic students. Applications are processed on a rolling basis. Application fee: $30. Electronic applications accepted. *Financial support:* In 2007–08, 2 research assistantships with full tuition reimbursements (averaging $8,404 per year), 18 teaching assistantships with full tuition reimbursements (averaging $8,404 per year) were awarded; Federal Work-Study and unspecified assistantships also available. Financial award applicants required to submit FAFSA. *Faculty research:* Poetry, criticism, novels, translation, travel writing. *Unit head:* Larissa Szporluk, Director, 419-372-8370.

Bowling Green State University, Graduate College, College of Arts and Sciences, Department of English, Program in English, Bowling Green, OH 43403. Offers English (MA, PhD); literature (MA); rhetoric and writing (PhD); scientific and technical communication (MA). Part-time programs available. *Students:* 49 full-time (36 women), 12 part-time (9 women); includes 1 African American, 3 Asian Americans or Pacific Islanders, 1 Hispanic American, 9 international. Average age 31. 64 applicants, 67% accepted, 21 enrolled. In 2007, 14 master's, 6 doctorates awarded. *Degree requirements:* For master's, thesis or alternative; for doctorate, comprehensive exam, thesis/dissertation, foreign language or proficiency in Old English. *Entrance requirements:* For master's and doctorate, GRE General Test. Additional exam requirements/recommendations for international students: Required—TOEFL. *Application deadline:* For fall admission, 2/15 priority date for domestic students. Applications are processed on a rolling basis. Application fee: $30. Electronic applications accepted. *Financial support:* In 2007–08, 3 fellowships with full tuition reimbursements (averaging $14,707 per year), 8 research assistantships with full tuition reimbursements (averaging $9,664 per year), 34 teaching assistantships with full tuition reimbursements (averaging $10,480 per year) were awarded; Federal Work-Study and unspecified assistantships also available. Financial award applicants required to submit FAFSA. *Faculty research:* Postmodern literary theory, rhetorical theory, ethnic American literature, literature and culture, composition pedagogy.

Brooklyn College of the City University of New York, Division of Graduate Studies, Department of English, Program in Creative Writing, Brooklyn, NY 11210-2889. Offers fiction (MFA); playwriting (MFA); poetry (MFA). Part-time and evening/weekend programs available. *Students:* 12 full-time (5 women), 57 part-time (37 women); includes 12 minority (5 African Americans, 4 Asian Americans or Pacific Islanders, 3 Hispanic Americans). 305 applicants, 15% accepted, 31 enrolled. In 2007, 21 degrees awarded. *Degree requirements:* For master's, comprehensive exam, thesis or alternative, 36 credits. *Entrance requirements:* For master's, 12 undergraduate advanced credits in English, writing sample, 2 letters of recommendation, manuscript. Additional exam requirements/recommendations for international students: Required—TOEFL. *Application deadline:* For fall admission, 2/1 for domestic and international students. Applications are processed on a rolling basis. Application fee: $125. Electronic applications accepted. *Financial support:* Federal Work-Study, institutionally sponsored loans, and scholarships/grants available. Support available to part-time students. Financial award application deadline: 5/1; financial award applicants required to submit FAFSA. *Faculty research:* Postmodern fiction. *Unit head:* Dr. Mark Patkowski, Graduate Deputy Chairperson, 718-951-5195, E-mail: mpatkowski@brooklyn.cuny.edu. *Application contact:* Hernan Sierra, Graduate Admissions Coordinator, 718-951-4536, Fax: 718-951-4506, E-mail: grads@brooklyn.cuny.edu.

Brown University, Graduate School, Department of English, Program in Creative Writing, Providence, RI 02912. Offers MFA. *Degree requirements:* For master's, thesis. *Entrance requirements:* For master's, GRE General Test, GRE Subject Test.

California College of the Arts, Graduate Programs, Program in Writing, San Francisco, CA 94107. Offers MFA. *Faculty:* 3 full-time (1 woman), 29 part-time/adjunct (17 women). *Students:* 62 full-time (37 women), 3 part-time (2 women). 102 applicants, 87% accepted, 33 enrolled. In 2007, 31 degrees awarded. *Degree requirements:* For master's, thesis, exhibit. *Entrance requirements:* For master's, appropriate bachelor's degree, portfolio. Additional exam requirements/recommendations for international students: Required—TOEFL (minimum score 600 paper-based; 250 computer-based). *Application deadline:* For fall admission, 1/15 for domestic and international students. Application fee: $50. Electronic applications accepted. *Expenses:* Tuition: Part-time $1,017 per unit. *Financial support:* In 2007–08, 3 fellowships (averaging $10,000 per year), 10 teaching assistantships (averaging $2,000 per year) were awarded; career-related internships or fieldwork, Federal Work-Study, scholarships/grants, and health care benefits also available. Financial award application deadline: 3/2; financial award applicants required to submit FAFSA. *Unit head:* Joseph Lease, Chair, 415-551-9285, E-mail: jlease@cca.edu. *Application contact:* Kathryn Ward, Assistant Director of Graduate Admissions, 415-703-9523 Ext. 9593, Fax: 415-703-9539, E-mail: graduateprograms@cca.edu.

See Close-Up on page 233.

California Institute of the Arts, School of Critical Studies, Valencia, CA 91355-2340. Offers writing (MFA, Adv C). *Entrance requirements:* For master's, portfolio. Additional exam requirements/recommendations for international students: Required—TOEFL.

California Institute of the Arts, School of Theatre, Valencia, CA 91355-2340. Offers acting (MFA, Adv C); design and technology (Adv C); directing (MFA); performing arts design and technology (MFA); theater management (Adv C); theatre management (MFA); writing for performance (MFA). *Accreditation:* NAST. *Degree requirements:* For master's, thesis (for some programs), faculty review, performance or portfolio. *Entrance requirements:* For master's, audition or portfolio, interview. Additional exam requirements/recommendations for international students: Required—TOEFL. Electronic applications accepted.

California State University, Fresno, Division of Graduate Studies, College of Arts and Humanities, Department of English, Fresno, CA 93740-8027. Offers composition theory (MA); creative writing (MFA); literature (MA). Part-time and evening/weekend programs available. *Faculty:* 27 full-time (13 women). *Students:* 102; includes 30 minority (1 African American, 1 American Indian/Alaska Native, 4 Asian Americans or Pacific Islanders, 24 Hispanic Americans), 1 international. Average age 28. 22 applicants. In 2007, 18 degrees awarded. *Degree requirements:* For master's, one foreign language, thesis. *Entrance requirements:* For master's, GRE General Test, minimum GPA of 3.0, writing sample. Additional exam requirements/recommendations for international students: Required—TOEFL. *Application deadline:* For fall admission, 5/1 for domestic and international students; for spring admission, 10/1 for domestic and international students. Applications are processed on a rolling basis. Application fee: $55. Electronic applications accepted. *Financial support:* In 2007–08, 32 teaching assistantships were awarded; career-related internships or fieldwork, Federal Work-Study, and scholarships/grants also available. Support available to part-time students. Financial award application deadline: 3/1; financial award applicants required to submit FAFSA. *Faculty research:* American literature, Renaissance literature, foreign literature. *Unit head:* Dr. James Walton, Chair, 559-278-2553, Fax: 559-278-7143, E-mail: james_walton@csufresno.edu. *Application contact:* Dr. James Lyn Johnson, Graduate Program Coordinator, 559-278-2553, Fax: 559-278-7143, E-mail: james_johnson@csufresno.edu.

California State University, Long Beach, Graduate Studies, College of Liberal Arts, Department of English, Long Beach, CA 90840. Offers creative writing (MFA); English (MA). Part-time programs available. *Faculty:* 50 full-time (24 women), 78 part-time/adjunct (45 women). *Students:* 60 full-time (42 women), 114 part-time (78 women); includes 43 minority (5 African Americans, 1 American Indian/Alaska Native, 17 Asian Americans or Pacific Islanders, 20 Hispanic Americans). Average age 34. *Degree requirements:* For master's, one foreign language, comprehensive exam or thesis. *Entrance requirements:* For master's, GRE Subject Test, minimum GPA of 3.0 in English. *Application deadline:* For fall admission, 7/1 for domestic students; for spring admission, 12/1 for domestic students. Applications are processed on a rolling basis. Application fee: $55. Electronic applications accepted. *Financial support:* Federal Work-Study, institutionally sponsored loans, and scholarships/grants available. Financial award application deadline: 3/2. *Faculty research:* English and American literature, literary theory, linguistics, rhetoric and composition. *Unit head:* Dr. Eileen S. Klink, Chair, 562-985-4223, Fax: 562-985-2369, E-mail: eklink@csulb.edu. *Application contact:* Dr. George Hart, Graduate Adviser, 562-985-4235, Fax: 562-985-2369, E-mail: ghart@csulb.edu.

California State University, Northridge, Graduate Studies, College of Humanities, Department of English, Northridge, CA 91330. Offers creative writing (MA); literature (MA); rhetoric and composition theory (MA). Part-time and evening/weekend programs available. *Faculty:* 37 full-time (19 women), 85 part-time/adjunct (69 women). *Students:* 40 full-time (29 women), 125 part-time (92 women); includes 38 minority (3 African Americans, 1 American Indian/Alaska Native, 13 Asian Americans or Pacific Islanders, 21 Hispanic Americans). Average age 34. 99 applicants, 75% accepted, 40 enrolled. In 2007, 38 degrees awarded. *Degree requirements:* For master's, thesis or alternative. *Entrance requirements:* For master's, writing proficiency test, GRE General Test or minimum GPA of 3.0. Additional exam requirements/recommendations for international students: Required—TOEFL. *Application deadline:* For fall admission, 11/30 for domestic students. Application fee: $55. *Financial support:* Teaching assistantships available. Financial award application deadline: 3/1. *Faculty research:* Reading improvement, professional writing, Dickens, Shaw, English as a second language. *Unit head:* Dr. George Uba, Chair, 818-677-3434, E-mail: george.uba@csun.edu. *Application contact:* Dr. Marjie Seagoe, Graduate Studies Secretary, 818-677-3433.

California State University, Sacramento, Graduate Studies, College of Arts and Letters, Department of English, Sacramento, CA 95819-6048. Offers creative writing (MA); teaching English to speakers of other languages (MA). Part-time programs available. *Students:* 66 full-time (47 women), 89 part-time (57 women); includes 21 minority (3 African Americans, 2 American Indian/Alaska Native, 3 Asian Americans or Pacific Islanders, 13 Hispanic Americans), 3 international. Average age 32. 96 applicants, 74% accepted, 49 enrolled. *Degree requirements:* For master's, thesis, project, or comprehensive exam; writing proficiency exam. *Entrance requirements:* For master's, portfolio (creative writing); minimum GPA of 3.0 in English, 2.75 overall during previous 2 years. Additional exam requirements/recommendations for international students: Required—TOEFL. *Application deadline:* Applications are processed on a rolling basis. Application fee: $55. Electronic applications accepted. *Expenses:* Tuition, state resident: full-time $3,414. Tuition, nonresident: full-time $13,584; part-time $339 per unit. Required fees: $786; $393 per semester. *Financial support:* Research assistantships, teaching assistantships, career-related internships or fieldwork and Federal Work-Study available. Support available to part-time students. Financial award application deadline: 3/1. *Faculty research:* Teaching composition, remedial writing. *Unit head:* Dr. Sheree Meyer, Chairman, 916-278-6586, Fax: 916-278-4588.

California State University, San Marcos, College of Arts and Sciences, Program in Literature and Writing Studies, San Marcos, CA 92096-0001. Offers MA. Part-time and evening/weekend programs available. *Faculty:* 11 full-time (6 women), 13 part-time/adjunct (8 women). *Students:* 21 full-time (15 women), 18 part-time (13 women); includes 8 minority (1 African American, 2 Asian Americans or Pacific Islanders, 5 Hispanic Americans), 2 international. Average age 36. In 2007, 2 degrees awarded. *Degree requirements:* For master's, one foreign language, thesis. *Entrance requirements:* For master's, GRE General Test, minimum GPA of 3.0, writing sample. *Application deadline:* For fall admission, 3/15 priority date for domestic students; for spring admission, 11/15 priority date for domestic students. Applications are processed on a rolling basis. Application fee: $55. *Financial support:* Teaching assistantships with partial tuition reimbursements available. *Faculty research:* Postcolonialism, feminism rhetoric, cultural studies, creative writing, critical theory. *Unit head:* Dr. Dawn Fomo, Department Chair, 760-750-4199, Fax: 760-750-4082, E-mail: scassel@csusm.edu. *Application contact:* Anita Nix, Administrative Coordinator, 760-750-4147, E-mail: anix@csusm.edu.

California State University, Stanislaus, College of Humanities and Social Sciences, Department of English, Turlock, CA 95382. Offers English (MA); literature (MA); rhetoric and teaching of writing (MA); TESOL (MA, Certificate). Part-time programs available. *Faculty:* 21. *Students:* 11 full-time (8 women), 42 part-time (27 women); includes 11 minority (1 Asian American or Pacific Islander, 10 Hispanic Americans). Average age 32. 28 applicants, 100% accepted, 16 enrolled. In 2007, 12 degrees awarded. *Degree requirements:* For master's, one foreign language, comprehensive exam, thesis. *Entrance requirements:* For master's, GRE General Test, minimum GPA of 3.0, 2 letters of reference, personal statement; for Certificate, minimum GPA of 3.0, 2 letters of reference. Additional exam requirements/recommendations for international students: Required—TOEFL (minimum score 550 paper-based; 213 computer-based), TWE (minimum score 4). *Application deadline:* For fall admission, 7/1 for domestic and international students; for winter admission, 10/1 for domestic and international students; for spring admission, 11/1 for domestic and international students. Application fee: $55. Electronic applications accepted. *Expenses:* Tuition, nonresident: full-time $10,170; part-time $339 per unit. Required fees: $3,972; $2,538 per term. $1,165 per semester. *Financial support:* Fellowships, research assistantships, teaching assistantships, career-related internships or fieldwork and Federal Work-Study available. Financial award application deadline: 3/2; financial award applicants required to submit FAFSA. *Faculty research:* Transnational literacies, Renaissance and Medieval literature, abolition writings and slave narratives, qualitative writing. *Application contact:* Dr. Mark Thompson, Chair, 209-667-3361, Fax: 209-667-3720.

Carlow University, Humanities Division, Pittsburgh, PA 15213-3165. Offers creative writing (MFA), including fiction, nonfiction, poetry. Part-time and evening/weekend programs available. *Degree requirements:* For master's, thesis or alternative. *Entrance requirements:* For master's, minimum GPA of 3.0, resumé. Additional exam requirements/recommendations for international students: Required—TOEFL (minimum score 550 paper-based; 213 computer-based).

Carnegie Mellon University, College of Humanities and Social Sciences, Department of English, Program in Professional Writing, Pittsburgh, PA 15213-3891. Offers design (MAPW); professional writing (MAPW); research (MAPW); rhetorical theory (MAPW); science writing (MAPW); technical (MAPW). Part-time programs available. *Entrance requirements:* For master's, GRE General Test. Additional exam requirements/recommendations for international students: Required—TOEFL, TWE.

See Close-Up on page 723.

Central Michigan University, College of Graduate Studies, College of Humanities and Social and Behavioral Sciences, Department of English Language and Literature, Mount Pleasant, MI 48859. Offers composition and communication (MA); creative writing (MA); English language and literature (MA); teaching English to speakers of other languages (MA). *Degree requirements:* For master's, thesis or alternative. *Entrance requirements:* For master's, minimum GPA of 2.7, portfolio. Additional exam requirements/recommendations for international students: Required—TOEFL, Michigan English Language Assessment Battery. *Faculty research:* Composition theory, science fiction history and bibliography, medieval studies, nineteenth century American literature, applied linguistics.

See Close-Up on page 565.

Chapman University, Graduate Studies, Wilkinson College of Social Sciences and Humanities, Program in Creative Writing, Orange, CA 92866. Offers MFA. Part-time and evening/weekend programs available. *Faculty:* 19 full-time (8 women), 19 part-time/adjunct (11 women). *Students:* 33 full-time (21 women), 25 part-time (13 women); includes 7 minority (1 African American, 2 Asian Americans or Pacific Islanders, 4 Hispanic Americans). Average age 29. 40 applicants, 80% accepted, 22 enrolled. In 2007, 19 degrees awarded. *Degree requirements:* For master's, thesis, project. *Entrance requirements:* For master's, GRE General Test or MAT, minimum undergraduate GPA of 3.0, sample of creative writing. Additional exam requirements/recommendations for international students: Required—TOEFL (minimum score 550 paper-based). *Application deadline:* Applications are processed on a rolling basis. Application fee: $55. Electronic applications accepted. *Expenses:* Contact institution. *Financial support:* Fellowships, Federal Work-Study and scholarships/grants available. Financial award application deadline: 6/30; financial award applicants required to submit FAFSA. *Unit head:* Dr. Richard

Writing

Chapman University (continued)

Ruppel, Chair, 714-997-6754, E-mail: ruppel@chapman.edu. *Application contact:* Jim Blaylock, Coordinator, 714-997-6750, E-mail: blaylock@chapman.edu.

Chatham University, Program in Writing, Pittsburgh, PA 15232-2826. Offers creative writing (MFA); fiction (MFA); non-fiction (MFA); poetry (MFA); professional writing (MAPW). Part-time and evening/weekend programs available. Postbaccalaureate distance learning degree programs offered. *Students:* 48 full-time (38 women), 26 part-time (23 women). Average age 31. 38 applicants, 87% accepted, 21 enrolled. In 2007, 43 degrees awarded. *Degree requirements:* For master's, thesis. *Entrance requirements:* For master's, minimum GPA of 3.0, writing sample, recommendation letters. Additional exam requirements/recommendations for international students: Recommended—TOEFL (minimum score 600 paper-based; 250 computer-based; 100 iBT), IELTS (minimum score 7). *Application deadline:* For fall admission, 5/1 priority date for domestic and international students; for winter admission, 10/1 priority date for domestic and international students. Applications are processed on a rolling basis. Application fee: $45. Electronic applications accepted. *Financial support:* Career-related internships or fieldwork available. Financial award applicants required to submit FAFSA. *Faculty research:* Ecopoetics; environment and culture; wilderness and literature; literature of exploration, exile, and home. *Unit head:* Dr. Sheryl St. Germain, Director, 412-365-1190, Fax: 412-365-1505, E-mail: sstgermain@chatham.edu. *Application contact:* 412-365-1825, Fax: 412-365-1609, E-mail: admissions@chatham.edu.

Chicago State University, School of Graduate and Professional Studies, College of Arts and Sciences, Department of English, Chicago, IL 60628. Offers creative writing (MFA); English (MA). *Degree requirements:* For master's, comprehensive exam. *Entrance requirements:* For master's, minimum GPA of 2.75.

City College of the City University of New York, Graduate School, College of Liberal Arts and Science, Division of the Humanities and Arts, Department of English, Program in Creative Writing, New York, NY 10031-9198. Offers MA, MFA. *Students:* 117. 56 applicants, 73% accepted, 28 enrolled. In 2007, 23 degrees awarded. *Degree requirements:* For master's, one foreign language, comprehensive exam, thesis. *Entrance requirements:* For master's, GRE, minimum GPA of 3.0, 10-15 poems or 30-50 pages of fiction (short stories or novel excerpt). Additional exam requirements/recommendations for international students: Required—TOEFL (minimum score 600 paper-based; 250 computer-based). *Application deadline:* For fall admission, 5/1 for domestic students; for spring admission, 11/1 for domestic students. Application fee: $125. *Unit head:* Lindsay Abrams, Head, 212-650-6694, Fax: 212-650-5410, E-mail: gradenglish@ccny.cuny.edu.

Claremont Graduate University, Graduate Programs, School of Arts and Humanities, Department of English, Claremont, CA 91711-6160. Offers American studies (MA, PhD); critical theory (MA, PhD); early modern studies (MA, PhD); English (M Phil, MA, PhD); literary theory (PhD); literature (MA, PhD); literature and creative writing (MA); literature and film (MA); MBA/MA; MBA/PhD. Part-time programs available. *Faculty:* 2 full-time (1 woman), 2 part-time/adjunct (0 women). *Students:* 81 full-time (49 women), 14 part-time (10 women); includes 18 minority (3 American Indian/Alaska Native, 10 Asian Americans or Pacific Islanders, 5 Hispanic Americans), 3 international. Average age 35. In 2007, 14 master's, 5 doctorates awarded. *Degree requirements:* For master's, one foreign language, comprehensive exam; for doctorate, 2 foreign languages, comprehensive exam, thesis/dissertation. *Entrance requirements:* For master's, GRE General Test; for doctorate, GRE General Test, MA in literature. *Application deadline:* For fall admission, 2/15 priority date for domestic students; for spring admission, 11/15 for domestic students. Applications are processed on a rolling basis. Electronic applications accepted. *Expenses:* Tuition: Full-time $31,640; part-time $1,376 per unit. Required fees: $145 per semester. Tuition and fees vary according to course load, degree level and program. *Financial support:* Fellowships, Federal Work-Study and institutionally sponsored loans available. Support available to part-time students. Financial award application deadline: 2/15; financial award applicants required to submit FAFSA. *Faculty research:* American, comparative, and English Renaissance literature; modernism; feminist literature and theory. *Unit head:* Wendy Martin, Chair, 909-621-8612, Fax: 909-607-1221, E-mail: wendy.martin@cgu.edu.

Clemson University, Graduate School, College of Architecture, Arts, and Humanities, Department of English, Program in Professional Communication, Clemson, SC 29634. Offers MA. Part-time programs available. *Students:* 33 full-time (22 women), 9 part-time (8 women); includes 6 minority (3 African Americans, 1 Asian American or Pacific Islander, 2 Hispanic Americans), 1 international. Average age 26. 31 applicants, 65% accepted, 14 enrolled. In 2007, 18 degrees awarded. *Degree requirements:* For master's, one foreign language, thesis optional, oral exam. *Entrance requirements:* For master's, GRE General Test, minimum GPA of 3.0. Additional exam requirements/recommendations for international students: Required—TOEFL, IELTS. *Application deadline:* For fall admission, 6/1 priority date for domestic students, 4/15 for international students; for spring admission, 12/1 for domestic students, 9/15 for international students. Applications are processed on a rolling basis. Application fee: $55. *Financial support:* In 2007–08, 14 research assistantships were awarded; teaching assistantships. Financial award application deadline: 4/1; financial award applicants required to submit FAFSA. *Faculty research:* Usability testing, rhetoric, communication across the curriculum, intercultural communication. Total annual research expenditures: $120,000. *Unit head:* Dr. Summer Taylor, Coordinator, 864-656-6689, Fax: 864-656-1345, E-mail: slsmith@clemson.edu.

Cleveland State University, College of Graduate Studies, College of Liberal Arts and Social Sciences, Department of English, Cleveland, OH 44115. Offers creative writing (MFA); English (MA). Part-time and evening/weekend programs available. *Faculty:* 17 full-time (6 women), 2 part-time/adjunct (1 woman). *Students:* 21 full-time (11 women), 63 part-time (46 women); includes 4 minority (all African Americans), 1 international. Average age 35. 56 applicants, 50% accepted, 15 enrolled. In 2007, 18 degrees awarded. *Degree requirements:* For master's, comprehensive exam, thesis. *Entrance requirements:* For master's, minimum GPA of 2.75, undergraduate concentration in English, writing sample, portfolio. Additional exam requirements/recommendations for international students: Required—TOEFL (525 paper-based; 197 computer-based) or IELTS (6 paper-based). *Application deadline:* For fall admission, 7/18 priority date for domestic students, 5/15 for international students; for spring admission, 12/15 for domestic students, 11/1 for international students. Applications are processed on a rolling basis. Application fee: $30. Electronic applications accepted. *Financial support:* In 2007–08, 20 students received support, including 1 fellowship (averaging $1,000 per year), 5 research assistantships with full and partial tuition reimbursements available (averaging $3,480 per year), 7 teaching assistantships with full and partial tuition reimbursements available (averaging $3,480 per year); Federal Work-Study, institutionally sponsored loans, tuition waivers (full and partial), and unspecified assistantships also available. Support available to part-time students. Financial award application deadline: 2/15. *Faculty research:* Literary history and criticism, linguistics, literature. Total annual research expenditures: $5,000. *Unit head:* Dr. David M. Larson, Chairperson, 216-687-3951, Fax: 216-687-6943, E-mail: d.larson@csuohio.edu. *Application contact:* Dr. Jennifer M. Jeffers, Graduate Director, 216-687-3975, Fax: 216-687-6943, E-mail: j.m.jeffers53@csuohio.edu.

Colorado State University, Graduate School, College of Liberal Arts, Department of English, Fort Collins, CO 80523-0015. Offers creative writing (MFA); English (MA). Part-time programs available. *Faculty:* 31 full-time (20 women), 1 part-time/adjunct (0 women). *Students:* 96 full-time (68 women), 51 part-time (35 women); includes 15 minority (1 African American, 3 American Indian/Alaska Native, 2 Asian Americans or Pacific Islanders, 9 Hispanic Americans), 17 international. Average age 31. 270 applicants, 42% accepted, 52 enrolled. In 2007, 36 degrees awarded. *Degree requirements:* For master's, comprehensive exam (for some programs), thesis (for some programs), exams. *Entrance requirements:* For master's, writing sample, BA/BS with minimum GPA of 3.0. Additional exam requirements/recommendations for international students: Required—TOEFL (minimum score 550 paper-based), TOEFL paper-based score of 575 required for creative writing. *Application deadline:* For fall admission, 1/15 for domestic students; for spring admission, 10/15 priority date for domestic students. Applications are processed on a rolling basis. Application fee: $50. Electronic applications accepted. *Expenses:* Tuition, state resident: full-time $4,887; part-time $272 per credit. Tuition, nonresident: full-time $16,425; part-time $913 per credit. Required fees: $1,379; $75 per credit. *Financial support:* In 2007–08, 38 teaching assistantships with full tuition reimbursements (averaging $11,806 per year) were awarded; fellowships, research assistantships, career-related internships or fieldwork, Federal Work-Study, institutionally sponsored loans, scholarships/grants, traineeships, and unspecified assistantships also available. Support available to part-time students. Financial award application deadline: 5/1; financial award applicants required to submit FAFSA. *Faculty research:* Computers and writing, environmental writing, cultural studies, new historicism, performance and identity. Total annual research expenditures: $47,578. *Unit head:* Dr. Bruce Ronda, Chair, 970-491-6428, Fax: 970-491-5601, E-mail: bruce.ronda@colostate.edu. *Application contact:* Marnie Leonard, Administrative Assistant, 970-491-2403, Fax: 970-491-7541, E-mail: marnie.leonard@colostate.edu.

Columbia College Chicago, Graduate School, Department of Fiction Writing, Chicago, IL 60605-1996. Offers creative writing (MFA); teaching of writing (MA); MFA/MA. Part-time programs available. *Students:* 1 (woman) full-time, 88 part-time (47 women); includes 26 minority (16 African Americans, 1 American Indian/Alaska Native, 2 Asian Americans or Pacific Islanders, 7 Hispanic Americans), 1 international. Average age 34. In 2007, 7 degrees awarded. *Degree requirements:* For master's, thesis, novel-length manuscript. *Entrance requirements:* For master's, minimum GPA of 3.0, portfolio of writing. Additional exam requirements/recommendations for international students: Required—TOEFL (minimum score 550 paper-based; 213 computer-based). *Application deadline:* For fall admission, 2/1 for domestic and international students; for spring admission, 10/3 for domestic students. Application fee: $50. Electronic applications accepted. *Financial support:* Fellowships, career-related internships or fieldwork, Federal Work-Study, and scholarships/grants available. Support available to part-time students. Financial award application deadline: 8/13; financial award applicants required to submit FAFSA. *Unit head:* Randall Albers, Chairperson, 312-344-6710 Ext. 5260, Fax: 312-344-8043, E-mail: ralbers@colum.edu. *Application contact:* Keith Cleveland, Acting Dean of the Graduate School, 312-344-7261, Fax: 312-344-8047, E-mail: kcleveland@colum.edu.

Columbia College Chicago, Graduate School, Program in Poetry, Chicago, IL 60605-1996. Offers MFA. Part-time programs available. *Students:* 9 full-time (6 women), 15 part-time (8 women); includes 6 minority (all African Americans) Average age 28. In 2007, 10 degrees awarded. *Degree requirements:* For master's, thesis. *Entrance requirements:* For master's, interview, writing sample, minimum GPA of 3.0. Additional exam requirements/recommendations for international students: Required—TOEFL (minimum score 550 paper-based; 213 computer-based). *Application deadline:* For fall admission, 2/3 for domestic and international students. Application fee: $50. Electronic applications accepted. *Financial support:* Fellowships, Federal Work-Study and scholarships/grants available. Support available to part-time students. Financial award application deadline: 8/13; financial award applicants required to submit FAFSA. *Unit head:* David Trinidad, Graduate Coordinator, 312-344-8139, Fax: 312-344-8001, E-mail: dtrinidad@colum.edu. *Application contact:* Keith Cleveland, Acting Dean of the Graduate School, 312-344-7261, Fax: 312-344-8047, E-mail: kcleveland@colum.edu.

Columbia University, School of the Arts, Writing Division, New York, NY 10027. Offers fiction (MFA); nonfiction (MFA); poetry (MFA). *Faculty:* 12 full-time (3 women), 24 part-time/adjunct (12 women). *Students:* 382 full-time (253 women); includes 57 minority (11 African Americans, 26 Asian Americans or Pacific Islanders, 20 Hispanic Americans). Average age 29. 643 applicants, 19% accepted, 88 enrolled. In 2007, 54 degrees awarded. *Degree requirements:* For master's, thesis. *Entrance requirements:* For master's, 3 letters of recommendation, writing sample. Additional exam requirements/recommendations for international students: Required—TOEFL (minimum score 600 paper-based; 250 computer-based). *Application deadline:* For fall admission, 1/2 for domestic and international students. Application fee: $120. Electronic applications accepted. *Expenses:* Tuition: Part-time $1,452 per credit. Required fees: $152 per term. One-time fee: $75 part-time. Full-time tuition and fees vary according to course level, course load, degree level and program. *Financial support:* In 2007–08, 135 fellowships (averaging $5,544 per year), 8 research assistantships (averaging $11,236 per year) were awarded; career-related internships or fieldwork, Federal Work-Study, institutionally sponsored loans, and scholarships/grants also available. Financial award applicants required to submit FAFSA. *Unit head:* Ben Marcus, Chair, 212-854-4391, E-mail: writing@columbia.edu. *Application contact:* Director of Admissions, 212-854-2134, E-mail: admissions-arts@columbia.edu.

See Close-Up on page 347.

Concordia University, School of Graduate Studies, Faculty of Arts and Science, Department of English, Program in Creative Writing, Montréal, QC H3G 1M8, Canada. Offers MA. *Degree requirements:* For master's, one foreign language, thesis. *Entrance requirements:* For master's, honors degree in English, minimum GPA of 3.3 in English literature, portfolio. *Faculty research:* Fiction, poetry, prose, drama.

Cornell University, Graduate School, Graduate Fields of Arts and Sciences, Field of English Language and Literature, Ithaca, NY 14853-0001. Offers African-American literature (PhD); American literature after 1865 (PhD); American literature to 1865 (PhD); American studies (PhD); colonial and postcolonial literature (PhD); creative writing (MFA); cultural studies (PhD); dramatic literature (PhD); English poetry (PhD); English Renaissance to 1660 (PhD); lesbian, bisexual, and gay literature studies (PhD); literary criticism and theory (PhD); nineteenth century (PhD); Old and Middle English (PhD); prose fiction (PhD); Restoration and eighteenth century (PhD); twentieth century (PhD); women's literature (PhD); MFA/PhD. *Faculty:* 59 full-time (28 women). *Students:* 97 full-time (53 women); includes 20 minority (7 African Americans, 3 American Indian/Alaska Native, 5 Asian Americans or Pacific Islanders, 5 Hispanic Americans), 13 international. Average age 28. 759 applicants, 7% accepted, 21 enrolled. In 2007, 29 master's, 8 doctorates awarded. Terminal master's awarded for partial completion of doctoral program. *Degree requirements:* For master's, one foreign language, thesis; for doctorate, one foreign language, comprehensive exam, thesis/dissertation, teaching experience. *Entrance requirements:* For master's, GRE General Test, 3 letters of recommendation, creative writing sample; for doctorate, GRE General Test, GRE Subject Test (English), 3 letters of recommendation, writing sample. Additional exam requirements/recommendations for international students: Required—TOEFL (minimum score 600 paper-based; 250 computer-based; 77 iBT). *Application deadline:* For fall admission, 1/10 for domestic students. Application fee: $70. Electronic applications accepted. *Financial support:* In 2007–08, 92 students received support, including 32 fellowships with full tuition reimbursements available, 60 teaching assistantships with full tuition reimbursements available; research assistantships with full tuition reimbursements available, institutionally sponsored loans, scholarships/grants, health care benefits, tuition waivers (full and partial), and unspecified assistantships also available. Financial award applicants required to submit FAFSA. *Faculty research:* English and American literature, women's writing, ethnic and post-colonial literature, critical theory, medievalism. *Unit head:* Director of Graduate Studies, 607-255-7989, Fax: 607-255-6661. *Application contact:* Graduate Field Assistant, 607-255-7989, Fax: 607-255-6661, E-mail: english_grad@cornell.edu.

DePaul University, College of Liberal Arts and Sciences, Department of English, Chicago, IL 60604-2287. Offers English (MA); writing (MA). Part-time and evening/weekend programs available. *Faculty:* 29 full-time (12 women). *Students:* 129 full-time (96 women), 81 part-time (62 women); includes 28 minority (11 African Americans, 4 Asian Americans or Pacific Islanders, 13 Hispanic Americans). Average age 27. 95 applicants, 56% accepted. In 2007, 100 degrees awarded. *Degree requirements:* For master's, written exam. *Entrance requirements:* Additional exam requirements/recommendations for international students: Required—TOEFL. *Application deadline:* For fall admission, 7/1 priority date for domestic students; for winter admission, 10/1 priority date for domestic students; for spring admission, 2/1 priority date for domestic students. Applications are processed on a rolling basis. Application fee: $40. Electronic applications accepted. *Financial support:* In 2007–08, 2 research assistantships with full tuition reimbursements, 7 teaching assistantships with full tuition reimbursements (averaging $7,500 per year) were awarded; fellowships with partial tuition reimbursements, career-related internships or fieldwork, institutionally sponsored loans, scholarships/grants, tuition waivers (partial), and unspecified assistantships also available. Support available to part-time students. Financial award application deadline: 4/1. *Faculty research:* Rhetoric and composition, technical writing, creative writing, linguistics, literacy theory. *Unit head:* Dr. William Fahrenbach, Chairperson, 773-325-1776, E-mail: bfahrenb@depaul.edu. *Application contact:* Dr. Lesley Kordecki, Director, 773-325-1786, Fax: 773-325-8607, E-mail: lkordeck@depaul.edu.

Eastern Kentucky University, The Graduate School, College of Arts and Sciences, Department of English and Theatre, Richmond, KY 40475-3102. Offers creative writing (MFA); English (MA). Part-time and evening/weekend programs available. *Faculty:* 13 full-time (11 women), 1 (woman) part-time/adjunct. *Students:* 19 full-time (11 women), 18 part-time (12 women). Average age 28. 45 applicants, 33% accepted, 8 enrolled. In 2007, 24 degrees awarded. *Degree requirements:* For master's, thesis optional. *Entrance requirements:* For master's, GRE General Test, minimum GPA of 2.5, minor in English with 3.0 GPA. Application fee: $35. *Financial support:* In 2007–08, 21 students received support, including 5 teaching assistantships (averaging $7,500 per year); career-related internships or fieldwork, Federal Work-Study, institutionally sponsored loans, and proctorships, writing laboratory tutorships, computer laboratory tutorships also available. Support available to part-time students. *Faculty research:* Old English, Victorian studies, women's studies, rhetoric, popular culture, novel studies. Total annual research expenditures: $35,000. *Unit head:* Dr. Jim Keller, Interim Chair, 859-622-5861, Fax: 859-622-3156, E-mail: james.keller@eku.edu. *Application contact:* Dr. Susan Krucg, MD Program Coordinator, 859-622-2282, Fax: 859-622-3156, E-mail: susan.krucg@eku.edu.

Eastern Michigan University, Graduate School, College of Arts and Sciences, Department of English Language and Literature, Program in Creative Writing, Ypsilanti, MI 48197. Offers MA. Part-time and evening/weekend programs available. Postbaccalaureate distance learning degree programs offered (minimal on-campus study). *Students:* 6 full-time (3 women), 13 part-time (8 women); includes 4 minority (2 African Americans, 1 American Indian/Alaska Native, 1 Hispanic American). Average age 28. In 2007, 5 degrees awarded. *Entrance requirements:* Additional exam requirements/recommendations for international students: Required—TOEFL. *Application deadline:* Applications are processed on a rolling basis. Application fee: $35. *Expenses:* Tuition, state resident: full-time $8,952; part-time $373 per credit hour. Tuition, nonresident: full-time $17,634; part-time $735 per credit hour. Required fees: $896; $34 per credit hour. Tuition and fees vary according to course level, degree level and program. *Financial support:* Fellowships, research assistantships with full tuition reimbursements, teaching assistantships with full tuition reimbursements, career-related internships or fieldwork, Federal Work-Study, institutionally sponsored loans, scholarships/grants, tuition waivers (partial), and unspecified assistantships available. Support available to part-time students. Financial award applicants required to submit FAFSA. *Application contact:* Dr. Janet Kauffman, Program Advisor, 734-487-1310, Fax: 734-483-9744, E-mail: jkauffman@emich.edu.

Eastern Michigan University, Graduate School, College of Arts and Sciences, Department of English Language and Literature, Program in Teaching of Writing, Ypsilanti, MI 48197. Offers MA, Graduate Certificate. Application fee: $35. *Expenses:* Tuition, state resident: full-time $8,952; part-time $373 per credit hour. Tuition, nonresident: full-time $17,634; part-time $735 per credit hour. Required fees: $896; $34 per credit hour. Tuition and fees vary according to course level, degree level and program. *Application contact:* Steve Krause, Program Advisor.

Eastern Michigan University, Graduate School, College of Arts and Sciences, Department of English Language and Literature, Program in Written and Technical Communications, Ypsilanti, MI 48197. Offers technical communications (MA, Graduate Certificate); written communications (MA). Part-time and evening/weekend programs available. Postbaccalaureate distance learning degree programs offered (minimal on-campus study). *Students:* 8 full-time (3 women), 39 part-time (29 women); includes 6 minority (4 African Americans, 2 Asian Americans or Pacific Islanders). Average age 33. In 2007, 19 degrees awarded. *Entrance requirements:* Additional exam requirements/recommendations for international students: Required—TOEFL. *Application deadline:* Applications are processed on a rolling basis. Application fee: $35. *Expenses:* Tuition, state resident: full-time $8,952; part-time $373 per credit hour. Tuition, nonresident: full-time $17,634; part-time $735 per credit hour. Required fees: $896; $34 per credit hour. Tuition and fees vary according to course level, degree level and program. *Financial support:* Fellowships, research assistantships with full tuition reimbursements, teaching assistantships with full tuition reimbursements, career-related internships or fieldwork, Federal Work-Study, institutionally sponsored loans, scholarships/grants, tuition waivers (partial), and unspecified assistantships available. Support available to part-time students. Financial award applicants required to submit FAFSA. *Application contact:* Prof. Steven Krause, Program Advisor, 734-487-1363, Fax: 734-483-9744, E-mail: skrause@emich.edu.

Eastern Washington University, Graduate Studies, College of Arts and Letters, Department of Creative Writing, Cheney, WA 99004-2431. Offers MFA. *Degree requirements:* For master's, comprehensive exam, thesis. *Entrance requirements:* For master's, GRE General Test, minimum GPA of 3.0, sample of written work.

Emerson College, Graduate Studies, School of the Arts, Department of Writing, Literature and Publishing, Program in Creative Writing, Boston, MA 02116-4624. Offers MFA. Part-time programs available. *Students:* 116 full-time (64 women), 24 part-time (12 women); includes 14 minority (2 African Americans, 1 American Indian/Alaska Native, 8 Asian Americans or Pacific Islanders, 3 Hispanic Americans). Average age 27. 291 applicants, 40% accepted, 47 enrolled. In 2007, 46 degrees awarded. *Degree requirements:* For master's, thesis. *Entrance requirements:* For master's, GRE General Test, 15 page writing sample. Additional exam requirements/recommendations for international students: Required—TOEFL (minimum score 550 paper-based; 213 computer-based; 80 iBT), IELTS (minimum score 7). *Application deadline:* For fall admission, 1/5 for domestic students. Application fee: $60 ($75 for international students). Electronic applications accepted. *Expenses:* Tuition: Full-time $16,800; part-time $840 per credit. Required fees: $60 per semester. One-time fee: $160. *Financial support:* In 2007–08, 4 fellowships with partial tuition reimbursements (averaging $16,000 per year), 19 research assistantships with partial tuition reimbursements (averaging $10,000 per year) were awarded; career-related internships or fieldwork, Federal Work-Study, institutionally sponsored loans, scholarships/grants, and unspecified assistantships also available. Support available to part-time students. Financial award application deadline: 2/1; financial award applicants required to submit FAFSA. *Unit head:* Prof. Douglas Whynott, Director, 617-824-8750. *Application contact:* 617-824-8610, Fax: 617-824-8614, E-mail: gradapp@emerson.edu.

See Close-Up on page 725.

Emerson College, Graduate Studies, School of the Arts, Department of Writing, Literature and Publishing, Program in Publishing and Writing, Boston, MA 02116-4624. Offers MA. Part-time programs available. *Students:* 95 full-time (79 women), 19 part-time (17 women); includes 15 minority (1 African American, 1 American Indian/Alaska Native, 7 Asian Americans or Pacific Islanders, 6 Hispanic Americans), 3 international. Average age 27. 204 applicants, 38% accepted, 48 enrolled. In 2007, 31 degrees awarded. *Degree requirements:* For master's, thesis or alternative. *Entrance requirements:* For master's, GRE General Test, 15 page writing sample. Additional exam requirements/recommendations for international students: Required—TOEFL (minimum score 550 paper-based; 213 computer-based; 80 iBT), IELTS (minimum score 7). *Application deadline:* For fall admission, 1/5 for domestic students. Applications are processed on a rolling basis. Application fee: $60 ($75 for international students). *Expenses:* Tuition: Full-time $16,800; part-time $840 per credit. Required fees: $60 per semester. One-time fee: $160. *Financial support:* In 2007–08, 2 fellowships with partial tuition reimbursements (averaging $14,000 per year), 24 research assistantships with partial tuition reimbursements (averaging $10,000 per year) were awarded; career-related internships or fieldwork, Federal Work-Study, institutionally sponsored loans, scholarships/grants, and unspecified assistantships also available. Support available to part-time students. Financial award application deadline: 2/1; financial award applicants required to submit FAFSA. *Faculty research:* Publishing. *Unit head:* Prof. Lisa Diercks, Director, 617-824-8750. *Application contact:* 617-824-8610, Fax: 617-824-8614, E-mail: gradapp@emerson.edu.

See Close-Up on page 897.

Fairfield University, College of Arts and Sciences, Fairfield, CT 06824-5195. Offers American studies (MA); communications (MA); creative writing (MFA); mathematics (MS). Part-time and evening/weekend programs available. *Faculty:* 40 full-time (15 women), 2 part-time/adjunct (0 women). *Students:* 7 full-time (3 women), 73 part-time (42 women); includes 5 minority (2 African Americans, 1 American Indian/Alaska Native, 1 Asian American or Pacific Islander, 1 Hispanic American), 1 international. 18 applicants, 61% accepted, 7 enrolled. In 2007, 21 degrees awarded. *Degree requirements:* For master's, capstone research course. *Entrance requirements:* For master's, minimum GPA of 3.0, 2 letters of recommendation, resumé, essay. Additional exam requirements/recommendations for international students: Required—TOEFL (minimum score 550 paper-based; 213 computer-based). *Application deadline:* For fall admission, 7/1 for domestic students, 6/15 priority date for international students; for spring admission, 12/1 for domestic students, 10/15 priority date for international students. Applications are processed on a rolling basis. Application fee: $60. *Financial support:* Tuition waivers (partial) and unspecified assistantships available. Financial award applicants required to submit FAFSA. *Unit head:* Dr. Robbin Crabtree, Dean, 203-254-4000 Ext. 3263, Fax: 203-254-4119, E-mail: rcrabtree@mail.fairfield.edu. *Application contact:* Marianne Gumpper, Director of Graduate and Continuing Studies Admissions, 203-254-4184, Fax: 203-254-4073, E-mail: gradadmis@mail.fairfield.edu.

Fairleigh Dickinson University, College at Florham, Maxwell Becton College of Arts and Sciences, Department of English, Communication and Philosophy, Program in Creative Writing, Madison, NJ 07940-1099. Offers MFA. *Students:* 37 full-time (10 women), 5 part-time (2 women), 3 international. Average age 38. 41 applicants, 41% accepted, 14 enrolled. In 2007, 6 degrees awarded. *Application deadline:* Applications are processed on a rolling basis. Application fee: $40. *Expenses:* Tuition: Part-time $869 per credit. *Unit head:* Dr. Martin Green, Chairperson, Department of English, Communication and Philosophy, 973-443-8712.

Florida Atlantic University, Dorothy F. Schmidt College of Arts and Letters, Department of English, Boca Raton, FL 33431-0991. Offers American literature (MA); creative writing (MFA); English literature (MA); fantasy and science fiction (MA); multicultural literature (MA). Part-time programs available. *Degree requirements:* For master's, one foreign language, thesis. *Entrance requirements:* For master's, GRE General Test, minimum GPA of 3.0, writing samples, 2 letters of recommendation. Electronic applications accepted. *Faculty research:* African-American writers, critical theory, British American, Asian American.

Florida International University, College of Arts and Sciences, Department of English, Program in Creative Writing, Miami, FL 33199. Offers MFA. Part-time and evening/weekend programs available. *Students:* 18 full-time (11 women), 23 part-time (14 women); includes 11 minority (3 African Americans, 8 Hispanic Americans), 1 international. Average age 38. 40 applicants, 30% accepted, 9 enrolled. In 2007, 10 degrees awarded. *Degree requirements:* For master's, thesis. *Entrance requirements:* For master's, GRE General Test, minimum GPA of 3.0 writing sample. Additional exam requirements/recommendations for international students: Required—TOEFL (minimum score 550 paper-based; 213 computer-based). *Application deadline:* For fall admission, 1/5 for domestic students, 1/15 for international students. Application fee: $30. Electronic applications accepted. *Expenses:* Tuition, state resident: full-time $6,106. Tuition, nonresident: full-time $15,528. Required fees: $284. *Financial support:* Teaching assistantships available. *Unit head:* Dr. Carmela Pinto McIntire, Chairperson, Department of English, 305-348-2048, Fax: 305-348-3766, E-mail: carmela.pinto_mcintire@fiu.edu.

Florida State University, Graduate Studies, College of Arts and Sciences, Department of English, Tallahassee, FL 32306. Offers creative writing (MFA, PhD); literature (MA, PhD); rhetoric and composition (MA, PhD). Part-time programs available. *Faculty:* 57 full-time (25 women), 14 part-time/adjunct (9 women). *Students:* 148 full-time (105 women), 20 part-time (10 women); includes 30 minority (13 African Americans, 1 American Indian/Alaska Native, 8 Asian Americans or Pacific Islanders, 8 Hispanic Americans). Average age 30. 427 applicants, 17% accepted, 57 enrolled. In 2007, 25 master's, 18 doctorates awarded. *Median time to degree:* Of those who began their doctoral program in fall 1999, 80% received their degree in 8 years or less. *Degree requirements:* For master's, one foreign language, thesis or alternative; for doctorate, 2 foreign languages, thesis/dissertation. *Entrance requirements:* For master's, GRE General Test, GRE Subject Test (literature), sample of written work, 3 letters of recommendation; for doctorate, GRE General Test, sample of written work, 3 letters of recommendation. *Application deadline:* For fall admission, 2/1 priority date for domestic students. Application fee: $30. Electronic applications accepted. *Expenses:* Tuition, state resident: part-time $248 per credit hour. Tuition, nonresident: part-time $880 per credit hour. Tuition and fees vary according to program. *Financial support:* In 2007–08, 155 students received support, including 5 fellowships, 150 teaching assistantships (averaging $11,375 per year); career-related internships or fieldwork, Federal Work-Study, and institutionally sponsored loans also available. Financial award application deadline: 2/1; financial award applicants required to submit FAFSA. *Faculty research:* British literature, American literature, creative writing, rhetoric, multiethnic literature. *Unit head:* Dr. Ralph Berry, Chairman, 850-644-5158, Fax: 850-644-0811, E-mail: rberry@fsu.edu. *Application contact:* Dr. Stan Gontarski, Director, 850-644-6038, Fax: 850-644-0811, E-mail: sgontarski@fsu.edu.

George Mason University, College of Humanities and Social Sciences, Department of English, Program in Creative Writing, Fairfax, VA 22030. Offers MFA. *Faculty:* 73 full-time (39 women), 52 part-time/adjunct (35 women). *Students:* 30 full-time (25 women), 70 part-time (44 women); includes 10 minority (4 African Americans, 1 American Indian/Alaska Native, 4 Asian Americans or Pacific Islanders, 1 Hispanic American), 1 international. Average age 29. 183 applicants, 43% accepted, 38 enrolled. In 2007, 31 degrees awarded. *Degree requirements:* For master's, one foreign language, thesis, exam or project. *Entrance requirements:* For master's, minimum GPA of 3.0 in last 60 hours, portfolio. *Application deadline:* For fall admission, 5/1 for domestic students; for spring admission, 11/1 for domestic students. Application fee: $60 ($75 for international students). Electronic applications accepted. *Financial support:* Fellowships available. Support available to part-time students. Financial award application deadline: 3/1; financial award applicants required to submit FAFSA. *Unit head:* William B. Miller, Director, 703-993-2763, Fax: 703-993-1161, E-mail: writing@gmu.edu.

Georgia College & State University, Graduate School, School of Liberal Arts and Sciences, Department of English, Speech, and Journalism, Program in Creative Writing, Milledgeville, GA 31061. Offers MFA. *Students:* 12 full-time (5 women), 10 part-time (4 women); includes 1 minority (African American) Average age 29. 42 applicants, 33% accepted, 10 enrolled. In 2007, 9 degrees awarded. *Degree requirements:* For master's, thesis. *Entrance requirements:* For master's, GRE or MAT, writing portfolio, letters of recommendation, official transcripts and statement of purpose. Additional exam requirements/recommendations for international students: Required—TOEFL. *Expenses:* Tuition, state resident: full-time $3,726. Tuition, nonresident: full-time $14,868. Required fees: $858. Tuition and fees vary according to campus/location. *Financial support:* In 2007–08, 18 research assistantships were awarded. *Unit head:* Dr. Martin Lammon, Head, 478-445-3508, E-mail: mga@gcsu.edu.

Georgia State University, College of Arts and Sciences, Department of English, Program in Creative Writing, Atlanta, GA 30303-3083. Offers MA, MFA, PhD. *Students:* 10 full-time (5 women), 6 part-time (3 women); includes 1 minority (Asian American or Pacific Islander) In 2007, 2 degrees awarded. *Degree requirements:* For master's, variable foreign language requirement, comprehensive exam, thesis; for doctorate, 2 foreign languages, comprehensive exam, thesis/dissertation. *Entrance requirements:* For master's and doctorate, GRE General Test, portfolio. Additional exam requirements/recommendations for international students: Required—TOEFL. *Application deadline:* For fall admission, 2/15 for domestic students. Applications are processed on a rolling basis. Application fee: $50. Electronic applications accepted.

Writing

Georgia State University (continued)

Expenses: Tuition, state resident: part-time $221 per credit hour. *Financial support:* Teaching assistantships with full tuition reimbursements available. *Application contact:* Dr. Thomas McHaney, Director of Graduate Studies, E-mail: tmchaney@gsu.edu.

Goddard College, Graduate Program, Program in Writing, Plainfield, VT 05667-9432. Offers MFA. Program residency available in Plainfield, VT or Port Townsend, WA. Postbaccalaureate distance learning degree programs offered (minimal on-campus study). *Faculty:* 20 part-time/adjunct (17 women). *Students:* 160 full-time. Average age 39. 96 applicants, 71% accepted, 60 enrolled. *Degree requirements:* For master's, thesis, publishable paper. *Entrance requirements:* For master's, 3 letters of recommendation, preliminary bibliography and study plan. *Application deadline:* Applications are processed on a rolling basis. Application fee: $40. Electronic applications accepted. *Expenses: Contact institution. Financial support:* In 2007–08, 150 students received support. . Applicants required to submit FAFSA. *Unit head:* Paul Selig, Director, 802-454-8311, Fax: 802-454-8017, E-mail: paul.selig@goddard.edu. *Application contact:* David DeLucca, Admissions Counselor, 800-906-8312 Ext. 248, Fax: 802-454-1029, E-mail: david.delucca@goddard.edu.

Goucher College, Program in Creative Nonfiction, Baltimore, MD 21204-2794. Offers MFA. Part-time and evening/weekend programs available. Postbaccalaureate distance learning degree programs offered (minimal on-campus study). *Students:* 43 full-time (35 women). Average age 40. In 2007, 14 degrees awarded. *Degree requirements:* For master's, manuscript, portfolio. *Entrance requirements:* For master's, writing sample. *Application deadline:* For fall admission, 3/5 for domestic students. Application fee: $50. *Expenses: Contact institution. Financial support:* Career-related internships or fieldwork and institutionally sponsored loans available. Financial award application deadline: 2/15; financial award applicants required to submit FAFSA. *Unit head:* Patsy Sims, Director, 410-337-6200, Fax: 410-337-6085, E-mail: psims@goucher.edu.

Hofstra University, College of Liberal Arts and Sciences, Department of English, Hempstead, NY 11549. Offers English and creative writing (MA); English literature (MA). Part-time programs available. *Faculty:* 9 full-time (5 women), 2 part-time/adjunct (both women). *Students:* 17 full-time (11 women), 19 part-time (13 women); includes 4 minority (2 African Americans, 1 Asian American or Pacific Islander, 1 Hispanic American). Average age 28. 39 applicants, 67% accepted, 13 enrolled. In 2007, 7 degrees awarded. *Degree requirements:* For master's, thesis optional. *Entrance requirements:* For master's, writing sample, essay, minimum GPA of 3.0 in Literature courses. Additional exam requirements/recommendations for international students: Required—TOEFL (minimum score 550 paper-based; 213 computer-based). *Application deadline:* Applications are processed on a rolling basis. Application fee: $60. Electronic applications accepted. *Expenses:* Tuition: Full-time $14,220; part-time $820 per credit. Required fees: $970; $165 per term. Tuition and fees vary according to program. *Financial support:* In 2007–08, 18 students received support, including 1 fellowship with tuition reimbursement available (averaging $3,000 per year), 3 research assistantships with full and partial tuition reimbursements available (averaging $8,880 per year); Federal Work-Study, institutionally sponsored loans, scholarships/grants, and tuition waivers (full and partial) also available. Support available to part-time students. Financial award applicants required to submit FAFSA. *Faculty research:* Herman Melville, disability studies, Early American Literature; Queer Theory; Twentieth-Century Popular culture. *Unit head:* Dr. Joseph A. Fichtelberg, Chairperson, 516-463-6279, Fax: 516-463-6395, E-mail: engjaf@hofstra.edu. *Application contact:* Carol Drummer, Dean of Graduate Admissions, 516-463-4876, Fax: 516-463-4664, E-mail: gradstudent@hofstra.edu.

Hollins University, Graduate Programs, Program in Creative Writing, Roanoke, VA 24020-1603. Offers MFA. *Faculty:* 7 full-time (2 women), 3 part-time/adjunct (2 women). *Students:* 24 full-time (14 women); includes 5 minority (3 African Americans, 2 Asian Americans or Pacific Islanders). Average age 26. 191 applicants, 12% accepted, 13 enrolled. In 2007, 12 degrees awarded. *Degree requirements:* For master's, comprehensive exam, thesis. *Entrance requirements:* For master's, manuscripts, 3 letters of recommendation. Additional exam requirements/recommendations for international students: Required—TOEFL (minimum score 550 paper-based; 213 computer-based). *Application deadline:* For fall admission, 1/6 for domestic and international students. Application fee: $40. Electronic applications accepted. *Expenses: Contact institution.* Tuition and fees vary according to course load and program. *Financial support:* In 2007–08, 32 students received support, including 24 fellowships with full and partial tuition reimbursements available (averaging $15,244 per year), 8 teaching assistantships (averaging $6,000 per year); scholarships/grants and unspecified assistantships also available. Support available to part-time students. Financial award application deadline: 2/2; financial award applicants required to submit FAFSA. *Faculty research:* Poetry, fiction, creative nonfiction, literary criticism, literary theory. *Unit head:* Cathryn Hankla, Director, 540-362-6317, Fax: 540-362-6097, E-mail: creative.writing@hollins.edu. *Application contact:* Cathy S. Koon, Manager of Graduate Services, 540-362-6326, Fax: 540-362-6288, E-mail: ckoon@hollins.edu.

Hunter College of the City University of New York, Graduate School, School of Arts and Sciences, Department of English, Program in Creative Writing, New York, NY 10021-5085. Offers creative writing (MFA); fiction (MFA); nonfiction (MFA); poetry (MFA). Part-time and evening/weekend programs available. *Faculty:* 10 full-time (6 women). *Students:* 36; includes 1 minority (African American) Average age 32. 285 applicants, 6% accepted, 17 enrolled. In 2007, 16 degrees awarded. *Degree requirements:* For master's, thesis. *Entrance requirements:* For master's, creative writing manuscript (up to 10 pages of poetry or 25-30 pages of fiction or nonfiction); 500-word personal statement; nonfiction proposal (for nonfiction applicants only). *Application deadline:* For fall admission, 2/1 for domestic and international students. Application fee: $125. *Expenses:* Tuition, state resident: full-time $6,400; part-time $270 per credit. Tuition, nonresident: part-time $500 per credit. One-time fee: $125 full-time. Tuition and fees vary according to program. *Financial support:* In 2007–08, 18 students received support, including 12 fellowships (averaging $5,000 per year); Federal Work-Study and tuition waivers (partial) also available. Support available to part-time students. Financial award application deadline: 4/15. *Unit head:* Sue Nacey, Coordinator, 212-772-5164, Fax: 212-772-5076, E-mail: mfa@hunter.cuny.edu. *Application contact:* Elena Georgiou, Coordinator, 212-772-5164, Fax: 212-772-5076, E-mail: egeorgio@hunter.cuny.edu.

Illinois State University, Graduate School, College of Arts and Sciences, Department of English, Program in Writing, Normal, IL 61790-2200. Offers MA, MS. *Students:* 5 full-time (3 women), 6 part-time (4 women); includes 1 minority (American Indian/Alaska Native). 5 applicants, 40% accepted. *Degree requirements:* For master's, comprehensive exam, internship or practicum. *Entrance requirements:* For master's, GRE General Test, minimum GPA of 3.0 in last 60 hours. *Application deadline:* Applications are processed on a rolling basis. Application fee: $40. *Expenses:* Tuition, state resident: full-time $3,492; part-time $194 per credit hour. Tuition, nonresident: full-time $7,272; part-time $404 per credit hour. Required fees: $1,024; $57 per credit hour. *Financial support:* Tuition waivers (full) available. Financial award application deadline: 4/1. *Unit head:* Dr. Timothy Hunt, Chairperson, Department of English, 309-438-3667.

Indiana State University, School of Graduate Studies, College of Arts and Sciences, Department of English, Terre Haute, IN 47809-1401. Offers English teaching (MA); history (MA); literature (MA). Part-time and evening/weekend programs available. *Faculty:* 16 full-time (4 women), 7 part-time/adjunct (2 women). *Students:* 12 full-time (10 women), 16 part-time (11 women); includes 1 minority (African American) Average age 32. 11 applicants, 100% accepted, 6 enrolled. In 2007, 14 degrees awarded. *Degree requirements:* For master's, one foreign language, thesis optional. *Entrance requirements:* For master's, minimum GPA of 2.75 in all English courses above freshman level. Additional exam requirements/recommendations for international students: Required—TOEFL (minimum score 550 paper-based). *Application deadline:* For fall admission, 7/1 priority date for domestic students; for spring admission, 11/1 priority date for domestic students. Applications are processed on a rolling basis. Application fee: $35. Electronic applications accepted. *Expenses:* Tuition, state resident: full-time $7,056; part-time $294 per semester hour. Tuition, nonresident: full-time $14,016; part-time $584 per semester hour. Required fees: $175 per semester. *Financial support:* In 2007–08, 11 teaching assistantships with partial tuition reimbursements (averaging $3,000 per year) were awarded; career-related internships or fieldwork, Federal Work-Study, and tuition waivers (partial) also available. Support available to part-time students. Financial award application deadline: 3/1; financial award applicants required to submit FAFSA. *Unit head:* Dr. Robert Perrin, Interim Chairperson, 812-237-3160.

Indiana University Bloomington, University Graduate School, College of Arts and Sciences, Department of English, Bloomington, IN 47405-7000. Offers composition, literacy, and culture (PhD); creative writing (MA, MFA), including fiction, poetry; language (MA); literature (MA, PhD); writing (MA). Part-time programs available. *Faculty:* 51 full-time (23 women). *Students:* 148 full-time (89 women), 52 part-time (34 women); includes 20 minority (8 African Americans, 7 Asian Americans or Pacific Islanders, 5 Hispanic Americans), 9 international. Average age 29. 560 applicants, 6% accepted, 32 enrolled. In 2007, 34 master's, 12 doctorates awarded. Terminal master's awarded for partial completion of doctoral program. *Median time to degree:* Of those who began their doctoral program in fall 1999, 30% received their degree in 8 years or less. *Degree requirements:* For master's, one foreign language, thesis (for some programs); for doctorate, 2 foreign languages, thesis/dissertation. *Entrance requirements:* For master's, GRE General Test, minimum GPA of 3.5; for doctorate, GRE General Test, minimum GPA of 3.7. Additional exam requirements/recommendations for international students: Required—TOEFL. *Application deadline:* For fall admission, 1/15 priority date for domestic students, 12/15 for international students; for spring admission, 9/1 for domestic and international students. Application fee: $50 ($60 for international students). *Financial support:* Fellowships, research assistantships, teaching assistantships, career-related internships or fieldwork available. Financial award application deadline: 2/1. *Unit head:* George Hutchinson, Chair, 812-855-8225, E-mail: gbhutchi@indiana.edu. *Application contact:* Patricia Ingham, Director of Admissions, 812-855-0521, Fax: 812-855-9535, E-mail: pingham@indiana.edu.

Indiana University of Pennsylvania, School of Graduate Studies and Research, College of Humanities and Social Sciences, Department of English, Program in Composition and Teaching English to Speakers of Other Languages, Indiana, PA 15705-1087. Offers composition and teaching English to speakers of other languages (PhD); teaching English (MAT); teaching English to speakers of other languages (MA). *Faculty:* 32 full-time (16 women). *Students:* 49 full-time (29 women), 125 part-time (75 women); includes 9 minority (3 African Americans, 1 American Indian/Alaska Native, 2 Asian Americans or Pacific Islanders, 3 Hispanic Americans), 64 international. Average age 38. 213 applicants, 42% accepted, 38 enrolled. In 2007, 17 master's, 10 doctorates awarded. *Degree requirements:* For master's, thesis optional; for doctorate, one foreign language, comprehensive exam, thesis/dissertation. *Entrance requirements:* For master's and doctorate, 2 letters of recommendation. Additional exam requirements/recommendations for international students: Required—TOEFL. *Application deadline:* For fall admission, 7/1 priority date for domestic students; for spring admission, 11/1 for domestic students. Applications are processed on a rolling basis. Application fee: $30. *Expenses:* Tuition, state resident: full-time $6,214; part-time $345 per credit. Tuition, nonresident: full-time $9,944; part-time $552 per credit. Required fees: $43 per credit. One-time fee: $140 part-time. Tuition and fees vary according to course load. *Financial support:* In 2007–08, 5 fellowships (averaging $5,000 per year), 18 research assistantships with full and partial tuition reimbursements (averaging $6,170 per year), 10 teaching assistantships with partial tuition reimbursements (averaging $17,001 per year) were awarded. Financial award application deadline: 3/15; financial award applicants required to submit FAFSA. *Unit head:* Dr. Ben Rafoth, Graduate Coordinator, 724-357-2272.

The Johns Hopkins University, Zanvyl Krieger School of Arts and Sciences, Advanced Academic Programs, Program in Writing, Washington, DC 20036. Offers MA. Part-time and evening/weekend programs available. *Faculty:* 8 full-time, 15 part-time/adjunct. *Students:* 73 applicants, 62% accepted, 41 enrolled. *Degree requirements:* For master's, thesis. *Entrance requirements:* For master's, writing samples. Additional exam requirements/recommendations for international students: Required—TOEFL (minimum score 600 paper-based; 250 computer-based; 100 iBT). *Application deadline:* For fall admission, 5/31 priority date for domestic students, 4/30 for international students; for spring admission, 10/31 priority date for domestic students, 10/31 for international students. Application fee: $70. *Financial support:* Applicants required to submit FAFSA. *Unit head:* Prof. David Everett, Associate Program Chair, 202-452-0758, Fax: 202-452-8713, E-mail: deverett@jhu.edu. *Application contact:* Rachel C. Jenkins, Admissions Manager, 202-452-1941, Fax: 202-452-1970, E-mail: aapadmissions@jhu.edu.

See Close-Up on page 727.

The Johns Hopkins University, Zanvyl Krieger School of Arts and Sciences, The Writing Seminars, Baltimore, MD 21218-2699. Offers fiction writing (MFA); poetry (MFA); science writing (MA). *Faculty:* 6 full-time (3 women). *Students:* 26 full-time (13 women); includes 2 minority (1 Asian American or Pacific Islander, 1 Hispanic American), 1 international. Average age 27. 292 applicants, 6% accepted, 12 enrolled. In 2007, 12 degrees awarded. *Degree requirements:* For master's, one foreign language, thesis, foreign language exam (for MFA). *Entrance requirements:* For master's, GRE General Test, GRE Subject Test (recommended), foreign language exam, sample of written work, 3 letters of recommendation, official college transcripts, GRE scores, and goal statement. Additional exam requirements/recommendations for international students: Required—TOEFL (minimum score 600 paper-based; 250 computer-based). *Application deadline:* For fall admission, 1/15 for domestic and international students. Application fee: $75. Electronic applications accepted. *Financial support:* In 2007–08, 25 students received support, including 1 fellowship (averaging $5,000 per year), 1 research assistantship with full tuition reimbursement available (averaging $17,000 per year), 20 teaching assistantships with full tuition reimbursements available (averaging $17,000 per year); Federal Work-Study, institutionally sponsored loans, scholarships/grants, health care benefits, and tuition waivers (partial) also available. Financial award application deadline: 4/15; financial award applicants required to submit FAFSA. *Faculty research:* Film theory, literary criticism, contemporary fiction. *Unit head:* Prof. Dave Smith, Chair, 410-516-3409, Fax: 410-516-6828, E-mail: davesmith@jhu.edu. *Application contact:* Gina Woloszyn, Contact, 410-516-6286, Fax: 410-516-6828, E-mail: regina@jhu.edu.

See Close-Up on page 727.

Kennesaw State University, College of Humanities and Social Sciences, Program in Professional Writing, Kennesaw, GA 30144-5591. Offers MAPW. Part-time and evening/weekend programs available. *Faculty:* 18 full-time (9 women), 2 part-time/adjunct (1 woman). *Students:* 26 full-time (20 women), 69 part-time (55 women); includes 9 minority (all African Americans), 1 international. Average age 33. 38 applicants, 71% accepted, 14 enrolled. In 2007, 28 degrees awarded. *Entrance requirements:* For master's, GRE General Test, minimum GPA of 2.5, writing sample. Additional exam requirements/recommendations for international students: Required—TOEFL (minimum score 550 paper-based; 213 computer-based; 80 iBT), IELTS (minimum score 6). *Application deadline:* For fall admission, 3/1 for domestic and international students. Application fee: $50. Electronic applications accepted. *Financial support:* In 2007–08, 2 research assistantships with full tuition reimbursements (averaging $15,000 per year) were awarded; Federal Work-Study also available. Support available to part-time students. Financial award application deadline: 6/15; financial award applicants required to submit FAFSA. *Unit head:* Dr. Jim Elledge, Director, 678-797-2039, E-mail: jellege1@kennesaw.edu. *Application contact:* Vilma Marquez, Admissions Counselor, 770-420-4377, Fax: 770-423-6885, E-mail: ksugrad@kennesaw.edu.

Kent State University, College of Arts and Sciences, Department of English, Kent, OH 44242-0001. Offers comparative literature (MA); creative writing (MFA); English (PhD); English for teachers (MA); literature and writing (MA); rhetoric and composition (PhD); teaching English as a second language (MA). Part-time programs available. *Faculty:* 46 full-time (23 women). *Students:* 107 full-time (59 women), 15 part-time (8 women); includes 19 minority (1 African American, 17 Asian Americans or Pacific Islanders, 1 Hispanic American). Average age 33. 105 applicants, 80% accepted, 35 enrolled. In 2007, 34 master's, 1 doctorate awarded.

Terminal master's awarded for partial completion of doctoral program. *Median time to degree:* Of those who began their doctoral program in fall 1999, 50% received their degree in 8 years or less. *Degree requirements:* For master's, one foreign language, thesis optional; for doctorate, one foreign language, thesis/dissertation, qualifying exams. *Entrance requirements:* For master's and doctorate, GRE General Test, writing sample, letters of recommendation. Additional exam requirements/recommendations for international students: Required—TOEFL (minimum score 600 paper-based). *Application deadline:* For fall admission, 2/1 priority date for domestic and international students. Applications are processed on a rolling basis. Application fee: $30. Electronic applications accepted. *Financial support:* In 2007–08, 2 fellowships with full tuition reimbursements (averaging $12,000 per year), 55 teaching assistantships with full tuition reimbursements (averaging $11,020 per year) were awarded; research assistantships with full tuition reimbursements, Federal Work-Study, institutionally sponsored loans, scholarships/grants, traineeships, health care benefits, and unspecified assistantships also available. Financial award application deadline: 2/1. *Faculty research:* British and American literature, textual editing, rhetoric and composition, cultural studies, linguistic and critical theories. *Unit head:* Ronald Corthell, Chair, 330-672-3211, Fax: 330-672-3152, E-mail: rcorthel@kent.edu. *Application contact:* Ray Craig, Information Contact, 330-672-1755, E-mail: rcraig2@kent.edu.

See Close-Up on page 567.

Lesley University, Graduate School of Arts and Social Sciences, Program in Creative Writing, Cambridge, MA 02138-2790. Offers MFA. Part-time programs available. Postbaccalaureate distance learning degree programs offered (minimal on-campus study). *Faculty:* 1 full-time (0 women). *Students:* 81 full-time (63 women), 26 part-time (19 women); includes 10 minority (6 African Americans, 2 Asian Americans or Pacific Islanders, 2 Hispanic Americans), 4 international. Average age 37. 95 applicants, 61% accepted, 30 enrolled. In 2007, 33 degrees awarded. *Degree requirements:* For master's, intensive residency. *Entrance requirements:* For master's, writing sample. Additional exam requirements/recommendations for international students: Required—TOEFL (minimum score 550 paper-based; 213 computer-based; 80 iBT). *Application deadline:* Applications are processed on a rolling basis. Application fee: $50. *Expenses: Contact institution. Financial support:* In 2007–08, 3 students received support, including research assistantships (averaging $3,400 per year), teaching assistantships (averaging $3,400 per year); Federal Work-Study, scholarships/grants, and unspecified assistantships also available. Support available to part-time students. Financial award application deadline: 4/15; financial award applicants required to submit FAFSA. *Unit head:* Steven Cramer, Program Coordinator, 617-349-8357, E-mail: scramer@lesley.edu. *Application contact:* Jana Vanderveer, Assistant Director, Advising and Student Services, 617-349-8369, E-mail: jvanderv@lesley.edu.

See Close-Up on page 729.

Lindenwood University, Graduate Programs, Programs in Individualized Education, St. Charles, MO 63301-1695. Offers administration (MSA); business administration (MBA); communication (MS); communications (MA); criminal justice and administration (MS); gerontology (MA); health management (MS); human resource management (MS); information technology (MBA, Certificate); management (MSA); managing information technology (MS); marketing (MSA); writing (MFA). Part-time and evening/weekend programs available. *Faculty:* 13 full-time (7 women), 54 part-time/adjunct (32 women). *Students:* 774 full-time (495 women), 55 part-time (32 women); includes 226 minority (213 African Americans, 9 Asian Americans or Pacific Islanders, 4 Hispanic Americans), 17 international. Average age 35. In 2007, 299 degrees awarded. *Degree requirements:* For master's, thesis (for some programs), minimum GPA of 3.0, 1 colloquium per term. *Entrance requirements:* For master's, interview, minimum GPA of 3.0. Additional exam requirements/recommendations for international students: Required—TOEFL (minimum score 550 paper-based; 213 computer-based; 80 iBT). *Application deadline:* For fall admission, 9/30 priority date for domestic and international students; for winter admission, 12/30 priority date for domestic and international students; for spring admission, 3/30 priority date for domestic and international students. Applications are processed on a rolling basis. Application fee: $30 ($100 for international students). *Expenses:* Tuition: Full-time $12,400; part-time $350 per hour. Full-time tuition and fees vary according to degree level and program. *Financial support:* Career-related internships or fieldwork, institutionally sponsored loans, tuition waivers (partial), and unspecified assistantships available. Financial award application deadline: 6/30; financial award applicants required to submit FAFSA. *Unit head:* Dan Kemper, Dean of Lindenwood College for Individual Education, 636-949-4501, Fax: 636-949-4505, E-mail: dkemper@lindenwood.edu. *Application contact:* Brett Barger, Dean of Evening Admissions and Extension Campuses, 636-949-4934, Fax: 636-949-4109, E-mail: adultadmissions@lindenwood.edu.

Long Island University, Brooklyn Campus, Richard L. Conolly College of Liberal Arts and Sciences, Department of English, Brooklyn, NY 11201-8423. Offers English literature (MA); professional and creative writing (MA); teaching of writing (MA). Part-time and evening/weekend programs available. *Degree requirements:* For master's, thesis or alternative. *Entrance requirements:* For master's, 2 letters of recommendation. Additional exam requirements/recommendations for international students: Required—TOEFL (minimum score 550 paper-based; 173 computer-based). Electronic applications accepted.

See Close-Up on page 569.

Longwood University, Office of Graduate Studies, Department of English and Modern Languages, Farmville, VA 23909. Offers 6-12 initial teaching/licensure (MA); creative writing (MA); English education and writing (MA); literature (MA). Part-time programs available. *Degree requirements:* For master's, comprehensive exam (for some programs), thesis (for some programs). *Entrance requirements:* For master's, minimum GPA of 2.75. Additional exam requirements/recommendations for international students: Required—TOEFL (minimum score 550 paper-based; 213 computer-based).

Louisiana State University and Agricultural and Mechanical College, Graduate School, College of Arts and Sciences, Department of English, Baton Rouge, LA 70803. Offers creative writing (MFA); English (MA, PhD). Part-time programs available. *Faculty:* 53 full-time (22 women). *Students:* 76 full-time (41 women), 6 part-time (3 women); includes 6 minority (2 African Americans, 1 American Indian/Alaska Native, 1 Asian American or Pacific Islander, 2 Hispanic Americans), 8 international. Average age 30. 138 applicants, 14% accepted, 18 enrolled. In 2007, 10 master's, 7 doctorates awarded. Terminal master's awarded for partial completion of doctoral program. *Degree requirements:* For master's, comprehensive exam; for doctorate, one foreign language, comprehensive exam, thesis/dissertation. *Entrance requirements:* For master's, GRE General Test, minimum GPA of 3.0; for doctorate, GRE General Test, GRE Subject Test, minimum GPA of 3.0. Additional exam requirements/recommendations for international students: Required—TOEFL (minimum score 550 paper-based; 213 computer-based; 79 iBT). *Application deadline:* For fall admission, 5/15 priority date for domestic students, 5/15 for international students; for spring admission, 10/15 priority date for domestic students, 10/15 for international students. Applications are processed on a rolling basis. Application fee: $25. Electronic applications accepted. *Financial support:* In 2007–08, 75 students received support, including 1 fellowship with full tuition reimbursement available (averaging $17,429 per year), 2 research assistantships with partial tuition reimbursements available (averaging $13,500 per year), 71 teaching assistantships with partial tuition reimbursements available (averaging $16,510 per year); career-related internships or fieldwork, Federal Work-Study, traineeships, and health care benefits also available. Financial award application deadline: 2/1; financial award applicants required to submit FAFSA. *Faculty research:* American literature, British literature, cultural studies, rhetoric and composition, folklore. Total annual research expenditures: $206,310. *Unit head:* Dr. Anna Nardo, Chair, 225-578-0812, Fax: 225-578-2214, E-mail: english@lsu.edu. *Application contact:* Dr. Carl Freedman, Director of Graduate Studies, 225-578-7803, Fax: 225-578-4129, E-mail: egs@lsu.edu.

Loyola Marymount University, Graduate Division, School of Film and Television, Program in Screen Writing, Los Angeles, CA 90045-2659. Offers MFA. *Faculty:* 5 full-time (2 women). *Students:* 23 full-time (8 women), 2 part-time (1 woman); includes 6 minority (1 African American, 2 Asian Americans or Pacific Islanders, 3 Hispanic Americans), 3 international. Average age 28. 41 applicants, 24% accepted, 5 enrolled. In 2007, 15 degrees awarded. *Degree requirements:* For master's, thesis, project or script. *Entrance requirements:* For master's, GRE General Test, writing sample. *Application deadline:* For fall admission, 3/15 for domestic students. Application fee: $50. Electronic applications accepted. *Financial support:* In 2007–08, 26 students received support, including 3 research assistantships (averaging $12,370 per year); career-related internships or fieldwork and scholarships/grants also available. Support available to part-time students. Financial award application deadline: 6/1; financial award applicants required to submit FAFSA. *Application contact:* Dr. Eric Xavier, Graduate Director, 310-338-2779, Fax: 310-338-3030, E-mail: exavier@lmu.edu.

Manhattanville College, Graduate Programs, Humanities and Social Sciences Programs, Program in Writing, Purchase, NY 10577-2132. Offers MA. Part-time and evening/weekend programs available. *Degree requirements:* For master's, thesis. *Entrance requirements:* For master's, interview, 2 letters of recommendation. *Faculty research:* Published writers: fiction, poetry, essay.

Massachusetts Institute of Technology, School of Humanities, Arts, and Social Sciences, Program in Writing and Humanistic Studies, Graduate Program in Science Writing, Cambridge, MA 02139-4307. Offers SM. *Faculty:* 7 full-time (2 women), 1 part-time/adjunct (0 women). *Students:* 7 full-time (6 women), 1 international. Average age 24. 37 applicants, 30% accepted, 7 enrolled. In 2007, 6 degrees awarded. *Degree requirements:* For master's, thesis, internship. *Entrance requirements:* For master's, GRE General Test. Additional exam requirements/recommendations for international students: Required—TOEFL (minimum score 600 paper-based; 250 computer-based). *Application deadline:* For fall admission, 1/15 for domestic and international students. Application fee: $70. Electronic applications accepted. *Expenses:* Tuition: Full-time $34,760; part-time $545 per unit. Required fees: $236. *Financial support:* In 2007–08, 7 students received support, including 7 fellowships with tuition reimbursements available (averaging $28,560 per year); career-related internships or fieldwork, Federal Work-Study, institutionally sponsored loans, scholarships/grants, health care benefits, and unspecified assistantships also available. *Unit head:* Prof. Robert Kanigel, Director, 617-253-6668, Fax: 617-452-5100, E-mail: sciwrite-www@mit.edu. *Application contact:* Graduate Admissions, 617-253-6668, Fax: 617-452-5100, E-mail: sciwrite-www@mit.edu.

McNeese State University, Graduate School, College of Liberal Arts, Department of English and Foreign Languages, Program in Creative Writing, Lake Charles, LA 70609. Offers MFA. Evening/weekend programs available. *Faculty:* 14 full-time (7 women). *Students:* 17 full-time (9 women), 1 (woman) part-time; includes 1 minority (African American) In 2007, 4 degrees awarded. *Degree requirements:* For master's, thesis, public reading. *Entrance requirements:* For master's, GRE, writing sample. *Application deadline:* For fall admission, 5/15 priority date for domestic students. Applications are processed on a rolling basis. Application fee: $20 ($30 for international students). *Expenses:* Tuition, state resident: full-time $2,226; part-time $193 per hour. Required fees: $935; $110 per hour. Tuition and fees vary according to course load. *Financial support:* Teaching assistantships available. Financial award application deadline: 5/1.

Miami University, Graduate School, College of Arts and Sciences, Department of English, Oxford, OH 45056. Offers composition and rhetoric (MA, PhD); creative writing (MA); criticism (PhD); English and American literature and language (PhD); English education (MAT); library theory (PhD); literature (MA, MAT, PhD); technical and scientific communication (MTSC). Part-time programs available. *Degree requirements:* For master's, final exam; for doctorate, 2 foreign languages, comprehensive exam, thesis/dissertation, final exams. *Entrance requirements:* For master's, minimum undergraduate GPA of 3.0 during previous 2 years or 2.75 overall; for doctorate, GRE General Test, GRE Subject Test, minimum GPA of 2.75 (undergraduate), 3.0 (graduate). Additional exam requirements/recommendations for international students: Required—TOEFL (minimum score 550 paper-based; 213 computer-based), TWE (minimum score 4). Electronic applications accepted.

Michigan State University, The Graduate School, College of Arts and Letters, Program in Rhetoric and Writing, East Lansing, MI 48824. Offers critical studies in literacy and pedagogy (MA); digital rhetoric and professional writing (MA); rhetoric and writing (PhD). *Entrance requirements:* Additional exam requirements/recommendations for international students: Required—TOEFL. Electronic applications accepted. *Expenses:* Tuition, state resident: part-time $379 per credit hour. Tuition, nonresident: part-time $800 per credit hour. Tuition and fees vary according to program. *Faculty research:* Rhetoric, writing and communication studies; media studies; technical communication, writing for digital environments.

Mills College, Graduate Studies, Department of English, Oakland, CA 94613-1000. Offers creative writing (MFA); English (MFA); English and American literature (MA). Part-time programs available. *Faculty:* 9 full-time (7 women), 20 part-time/adjunct (17 women). *Students:* 82 full-time (68 women), 6 part-time (all women); includes 28 minority (12 African Americans, 10 Asian Americans or Pacific Islanders, 6 Hispanic Americans). Average age 32. 137 applicants, 83% accepted, 46 enrolled. In 2007, 49 degrees awarded. *Degree requirements:* For master's, comprehensive exam, thesis. *Entrance requirements:* For master's, manuscript, writing sample. Additional exam requirements/recommendations for international students: Required—TOEFL. *Application deadline:* For fall admission, 2/1 priority date for domestic students; for spring admission, 11/1 for domestic students. Applications are processed on a rolling basis. Application fee: $50. Electronic applications accepted. *Expenses:* Tuition: Full-time $22,792; part-time $5,702 per credit. Required fees: $828. Part-time tuition and fees vary according to course load and program. *Financial support:* In 2007–08, 72 fellowships (averaging $7,517 per year), 22 teaching assistantships with partial tuition reimbursements (averaging $2,655 per year) were awarded; career-related internships or fieldwork, institutionally sponsored loans, scholarships/grants, tuition waivers (partial), and residence awards also available. Support available to part-time students. Financial award application deadline: 2/1; financial award applicants required to submit CSS PROFILE or FAFSA. *Faculty research:* Creative writing, African-American literature, Victorian women writers, theories of sexuality, Shakespeare. *Unit head:* Cynthia Scheinberg, Chair, 510-430-2213, E-mail: cyns@mills.edu. *Application contact:* Linda Guzman, Graduate Admission Specialist, 510-430-3309, Fax: 510-430-2159, E-mail: grad-studies@mills.edu.

Minnesota State University Mankato, College of Graduate Studies, College of Arts and Humanities, Department of English, Mankato, MN 56001. Offers creative writing (MFA); English (MA, MS); English literature (MA); teaching English (MS, MT); teaching English as a second language (MA); technical communication (Certificate). Part-time programs available. *Students:* 51 full-time (35 women), 78 part-time (54 women). Average age 32. In 2007, 29 degrees awarded. *Degree requirements:* For master's, one foreign language, comprehensive exam, thesis or alternative. *Entrance requirements:* For master's, minimum GPA of 3.0 during previous 2 years, writing sample (MFA). *Application deadline:* Applications are processed on a rolling basis. Application fee: $40. Electronic applications accepted. *Financial support:* Research assistantships with full tuition reimbursements, teaching assistantships with full tuition reimbursements, career-related internships or fieldwork, Federal Work-Study, and unspecified assistantships available. Financial award application deadline: 3/15; financial award applicants required to submit FAFSA. *Faculty research:* Keats and Christianity. *Unit head:* Dr. John Banschbach, Chairperson, 507-389-2117. *Application contact:* 507-389-2321, E-mail: grad@mnsu.edu.

Minnesota State University Moorhead, Graduate Studies, College of Arts and Humanities, Program in Creative Writing, Moorhead, MN 56563-0002. Offers MFA. Part-time programs available. *Degree requirements:* For master's, thesis, final manuscript, final oral exam. *Entrance requirements:* For master's, manuscript, minimum GPA of 2.75, 3 letters of recommendation. Additional exam requirements/recommendations for international students: Required—TOEFL (minimum score 550 paper-based; 213 computer-based). Electronic applications accepted.

Writing

Murray State University, College of Humanities and Fine Arts, Department of English and Philosophy, Program in Creative Writing, Murray, KY 42071. Offers MFA.

Naropa University, Graduate Programs, Program in Creative Writing, Boulder, CO 80302-6697. Offers MFA. Program is offered online only. Part-time programs available. Postbaccalaureate distance learning degree programs offered (minimal on-campus study). *Faculty:* 4 part-time/adjunct (3 women). *Students:* 1 (woman) full-time, 42 part-time (30 women); includes 7 minority (3 African Americans, 3 Asian Americans or Pacific Islanders, 1 Hispanic American). Average age 33. 40 applicants, 70% accepted, 19 enrolled. In 2007, 14 degrees awarded. *Degree requirements:* For master's, manuscript. *Entrance requirements:* For master's, manuscript/writing sample; supplemental application. *Application deadline:* For fall admission, 1/15 for domestic students; for spring admission, 10/15 for domestic students. Application fee: $60. *Expenses:* Tuition: Full-time $15,070; part-time $685 per credit. Required fees: $250 per semester. Tuition and fees vary according to course load. *Financial support:* In 2007–08, 3 students received support. Scholarships/grants and health care benefits available. Support available to part-time students. Financial award applicants required to submit FAFSA. *Unit head:* Junior Burke, Chair, 303-245-4820.

See Close-Up on page 1449.

Naropa University, Graduate Programs, Program in Writing and Poetics, Boulder, CO 80302-6697. Offers MFA. *Faculty:* 8 full-time (3 women), 15 part-time/adjunct (11 women). *Students:* 50 full-time (32 women), 8 part-time (6 women); includes 2 minority (both Hispanic Americans), 1 international. Average age 28. 80 applicants, 73% accepted, 25 enrolled. In 2007, 18 degrees awarded. *Degree requirements:* For master's, thesis. *Entrance requirements:* For master's, manuscript; supplemental application. Additional exam requirements/recommendations for international students: Required—TOEFL (minimum score 600 paper-based; 250 computer-based). *Application deadline:* For fall admission, 1/15 priority date for domestic and international students; for spring admission, 10/15 priority date for domestic and international students. Applications are processed on a rolling basis. Application fee: $60. Electronic applications accepted. *Expenses:* Tuition: Full-time $15,070; part-time $685 per credit. Required fees: $250 per semester. Tuition and fees vary according to course load. *Financial support:* In 2007–08, 47 students received support, including 3 research assistantships with partial tuition reimbursements available (averaging $2,500 per year), 7 teaching assistantships with partial tuition reimbursements available (averaging $2,500 per year); career-related internships or fieldwork, Federal Work-Study, scholarships/grants, health care benefits, tuition waivers (partial), and unspecified assistantships also available. Support available to part-time students. Financial award application deadline: 3/1; financial award applicants required to submit FAFSA. *Unit head:* Junior Burke, Chair, 303-245-4820. *Application contact:* Kate Levene, Assistant Director of Admissions, 303-245-4657, Fax: 303-546-3583, E-mail: klevene@naropa.edu.

See Close-Up on page 1449.

National-Louis University, College of Arts and Sciences, Program in Written Communication, Chicago, IL 60603. Offers MS. Part-time programs available. *Students:* Average age 42. In 2007, 9 degrees awarded. *Degree requirements:* For master's, thesis. *Entrance requirements:* For master's, GRE, MAT, or Watson-Glaser Critical Thinking Appraisal, interview, minimum GPA of 3.0. *Application deadline:* Applications are processed on a rolling basis. *Expenses:* Tuition: Full-time $18,900; part-time $630 per credit hour. Required fees: $20 per term. One-time fee: $40 part-time. Tuition and fees vary according to course load, campus/location and program. *Financial support:* Federal Work-Study, institutionally sponsored loans, scholarships/grants, and tuition waivers available. Support available to part-time students. Financial award applicants required to submit FAFSA. *Unit head:* Steven Masello, Professor, 224-233-2247, Fax: 224-233-2247, E-mail: smasello@nl.edu. *Application contact:* Dr. Larry Poselli, Vice President of Enrollment and Student Services, 800-443-5522 Ext. 5718, Fax: 312-261-.3550, E-mail: larry.polselli@nl.edu.

National University, Academic Affairs, College of Letters and Sciences, Department of Art and Humanities, La Jolla, CA 92037-1011. Offers creative writing (MFA); English (MA). Part-time and evening/weekend programs available. Postbaccalaureate distance learning degree programs offered (no on-campus study). *Faculty:* 18 full-time (6 women), 219 part-time/adjunct (120 women). *Students:* 139 full-time (101 women), 353 part-time (250 women); includes 91 minority (41 African Americans, 4 American Indian/Alaska Native, 15 Asian Americans or Pacific Islanders, 31 Hispanic Americans). Average age 37. 371 applicants, 330 enrolled. In 2007, 100 degrees awarded. *Degree requirements:* For master's, thesis (for some programs). *Entrance requirements:* For master's, interview, minimum GPA of 2.5. Additional exam requirements/recommendations for international students: Required—TOEFL (minimum score 550 paper-based; 213 computer-based; 80 iBT), IELTS (minimum score 6). *Application deadline:* Applications are processed on a rolling basis. Application fee: $60 ($65 for international students). Electronic applications accepted. *Expenses:* Tuition: Full-time $8,262; part-time $306 per unit. One-time fee: $60. *Financial support:* Career-related internships or fieldwork, institutionally sponsored loans, scholarships/grants, and tuition waivers (partial) available. Support available to part-time students. Financial award application deadline: 6/30; financial award applicants required to submit FAFSA. *Unit head:* Dr. Janet Baker, Chair, 858-642-8472, Fax: 858-642-8715, E-mail: jbaker@nu.edu. *Application contact:* Dominick Giovanniello, Associate Regional Dean—San Diego, 800-NAT-UNIV, Fax: 858-642-8709, E-mail: dgiovann@nu.edu.

New England College, Program in Creative Writing, Henniker, NH 03242-3293. Offers poetry (MFA). Part-time and evening/weekend programs available. Electronic applications accepted. *Faculty research:* Poetry collections.

New Mexico Highlands University, Graduate Studies, College of Arts and Sciences, Department of Humanities, Las Vegas, NM 87701. Offers English (MA), including creative writing, language, rhetoric and composition, literature. *Faculty:* 6 full-time (3 women). *Students:* 11 full-time (5 women), 7 part-time (5 women); includes 5 minority (all Hispanic Americans) Average age 32. 17 applicants, 82% accepted, 7 enrolled. In 2007, 3 degrees awarded. *Degree requirements:* For master's, comprehensive exam, thesis. *Entrance requirements:* For master's, minimum undergraduate GPA of 3.0. Additional exam requirements/recommendations for international students: Required—TOEFL (minimum score 540 paper-based; 190 computer-based). *Application deadline:* For fall admission, 8/1 priority date for domestic students. Applications are processed on a rolling basis. Application fee: $15. *Expenses:* Tuition, state resident: full-time $2,642; part-time $110 per credit hour. Tuition, nonresident: full-time $3,964; part-time $165 per credit hour. International tuition: $5,285 full-time. One-time fee: $20 full-time. *Financial support:* In 2007–08, 8 students received support, including teaching assistantships with full and partial tuition reimbursements available (averaging $6,500 per year); career-related internships or fieldwork, Federal Work-Study, institutionally sponsored loans, scholarships/grants, tuition waivers (full and partial), and unspecified assistantships also available. Support available to part-time students. Financial award application deadline: 3/1; financial award applicants required to submit FAFSA. *Faculty research:* Motivation, self-actualization, humanistic psychology, stand up comedy, language and cognition. *Unit head:* Dr. Barbara Risch, Chair, 505-454-3451, Fax: 505-454-3389, E-mail: brisch55@yahoo.com. *Application contact:* Diane Trujillo, Administrative Assistant Graduate Studies, 505-454-3266, Fax: 505-454-3558, E-mail: dtrujillo@nmhu.edu.

New Mexico State University, Graduate School, College of Arts and Sciences, Department of English, Las Cruces, NM 88003-8001. Offers creative writing (MFA); English (MA); rhetoric and professional communication (PhD). Part-time programs available. *Faculty:* 17 full-time (9 women), 1 part-time/adjunct (0 women). *Students:* 70 full-time (37 women), 23 part-time (12 women); includes 12 minority (1 African American, 1 American Indian/Alaska Native, 10 Hispanic Americans), 6 international. Average age 33. 55 applicants, 45% accepted, 19 enrolled. In 2007, 25 master's, 5 doctorates awarded. *Median time to degree:* Of those who began their doctoral program in fall 1999, 80% received their degree in 8 years or less. *Degree requirements:* For master's, one foreign language, comprehensive exam (for some programs), thesis (for some programs); for doctorate, comprehensive exam, thesis/dissertation, internship. *Entrance requirements:* For master's and doctorate, sample of written work. *Application deadline:* For fall admission, 2/1 for domestic and international students. Application fee: $30 ($50 for international students). Electronic applications accepted. *Expenses:* Tuition, state resident: full-time $3,602; part-time $199 per credit. Tuition, nonresident: full-time $13,380; part-time $607 per credit. Required fees: $1,178. *Financial support:* In 2007–08, 3 fellowships, 3 research assistantships, 50 teaching assistantships were awarded; career-related internships or fieldwork, Federal Work-Study, institutionally sponsored loans, scholarships/grants, health care benefits, and unspecified assistantships also available. Financial award application deadline: 2/1; financial award applicants required to submit FAFSA. *Faculty research:* Composition research, history and theory of rhetoric, technical/professional communication, creative writing, English and American literature. *Unit head:* Dr. Harriet Kramer Linkin, Head, 575-646-3931, Fax: 575-646-7725. *Application contact:* Dr. Monica Torres, Director of Graduate Studies, 575-646-3931, E-mail: mftorres@nmsu.edu.

The New School: A University, The New School for General Studies, Program in Creative Writing, New York, NY 10011. Offers MFA. Evening/weekend programs available. *Faculty:* 2 full-time (1 woman), 27 part-time/adjunct (15 women). *Students:* 202 full-time (121 women), 3 part-time (2 women); includes 19 minority (8 African Americans, 5 Asian Americans or Pacific Islanders, 6 Hispanic Americans), 14 international. Average age 29. In 2007, 104 degrees awarded. *Degree requirements:* For master's, thesis. *Entrance requirements:* For master's, portfolio. Additional exam requirements/recommendations for international students: Required—TOEFL (minimum score 600 paper-based; 250 computer-based; 100 iBT). *Application deadline:* For fall admission, 1/15 for domestic students. Applications are processed on a rolling basis. Application fee: $50. *Expenses:* Contact institution. *Financial support:* Research assistantships, teaching assistantships with partial tuition reimbursements, Federal Work-Study, scholarships/grants, and tuition waivers (partial) available. Financial award application deadline: 3/1; financial award applicants required to submit FAFSA. *Unit head:* Dr. Robert Polito, Director, 212-229-5611, Fax: 212-645-0661. *Application contact:* David Norris, Director of Admissions, 212-229-5630, Fax: 212-989-3887, E-mail: nsadmissions@newschool.edu.

See Close-Up on page 731.

New York University, Graduate School of Arts and Science, Department of English, Program in Creative Writing, New York, NY 10012-1019. Offers MA, MFA. Part-time and evening/weekend programs available. *Faculty:* 4 full-time (2 women), 12 part-time/adjunct. *Students:* 72 full-time (39 women), 24 part-time (14 women); includes 13 minority (4 African Americans, 1 American Indian/Alaska Native, 6 Asian Americans or Pacific Islanders, 2 Hispanic Americans), 10 international. Average age 30. 637 applicants, 10% accepted, 45 enrolled. In 2007, 41 degrees awarded. *Degree requirements:* For master's, one foreign language, thesis or alternative. *Entrance requirements:* For master's, GRE General Test, sample of written work. Additional exam requirements/recommendations for international students: Required—TOEFL. *Application deadline:* For fall admission, 12/18 for domestic students. Application fee: $85. *Financial support:* Fellowships with tuition reimbursements, teaching assistantships with tuition reimbursements, Federal Work-Study, institutionally sponsored loans, scholarships/grants, health care benefits, tuition waivers (full and partial), and unspecified assistantships available. Financial award application deadline: 12/18; financial award applicants required to submit FAFSA. *Faculty research:* Fiction, poetry. *Unit head:* Deborah Landau, Director, 212-998-9916, Fax: 212-995-4864, E-mail: creative.writing@nyu.edu. *Application contact:* Russell Carmony, Information Contact, 212-998-8816, Fax: 212-995-4864, E-mail: creative.writing@nyu.edu.

New York University, Tisch School of the Arts Asia, Singapore, NY 248923, Singapore. Offers animation and digital arts (MFA); dramatic writing (MFA); film production (MFA). *Faculty:* 6 full-time (3 women). *Students:* 33 full-time (16 women); includes 6 minority (1 African American, 5 Asian Americans or Pacific Islanders), 13 international. 55 applicants, 22% accepted. *Entrance requirements:* Additional exam requirements/recommendations for international students: Required—TOEFL (minimum score 610 paper-based; 250 computer-based; 105 iBT). *Application deadline:* For fall admission, 2/1 priority date for domestic and international students. Application fee: $60. Electronic applications accepted. *Financial support:* Fellowships with full and partial tuition reimbursements, research assistantships, teaching assistantships, Federal Work-Study, institutionally sponsored loans, and unspecified assistantships available. Financial award application deadline: 2/15; financial award applicants required to submit FAFSA.

See Close-Up on page 291.

New York University, Tisch School of the Arts, Rita and Burton Goldberg Department of Dramatic Writing, New York, NY 10012-1019. Offers MFA. *Faculty:* 15 full-time, 16 part-time/adjunct. *Students:* 42 full-time (17 women); includes 13 minority (3 African Americans, 1 American Indian/Alaska Native, 3 Asian Americans or Pacific Islanders, 6 Hispanic Americans), 3 international. Average age 30. 233 applicants, 13% accepted, 20 enrolled. In 2007, 20 degrees awarded. *Degree requirements:* For master's, thesis, play or screenplay, internship. *Entrance requirements:* For master's, writing sample. Additional exam requirements/recommendations for international students: Required—TOEFL or IELTS. *Application deadline:* For fall admission, 1/8 for domestic and international students. Application fee: $60. Electronic applications accepted. *Financial support:* In 2007–08, 19 students received support, including 5 fellowships with full and partial tuition reimbursements available; career-related internships or fieldwork, Federal Work-Study, institutionally sponsored loans, and scholarships/grants also available. Financial award application deadline: 2/15; financial award applicants required to submit FAFSA. *Faculty research:* Craft of screenwriting film story analysis, production elements in film and theatre. *Unit head:* Richard Wesley, Chair, 212-998-1940, Fax: 212-995-4069. *Application contact:* Dan Sandford, Director of Graduate Admissions, 212-998-1918, Fax: 212-995-4060, E-mail: tisch.gradadmissions@nyu.edu.

North Carolina State University, Graduate School, College of Humanities and Social Sciences, Department of English, Program in Creative Writing, Raleigh, NC 27695. Offers MFA. *Degree requirements:* For master's, thesis optional. *Entrance requirements:* For master's, GRE. Electronic applications accepted. *Faculty research:* Science fiction, Asian poetry, translation, Southern writers, satiric fiction.

Northeastern Illinois University, Graduate College, College of Arts and Sciences, Department of English, Programs in English, Chicago, IL 60625-4699. Offers composition/writing (MA); literature (MA). Part-time and evening/weekend programs available. *Faculty:* 14 full-time (4 women). *Students:* 7 full-time (6 women), 44 part-time (28 women); includes 4 minority (2 African Americans, 2 Hispanic Americans), 2 international. Average age 40. 25 applicants, 52% accepted. In 2007, 7 degrees awarded. *Degree requirements:* For master's, comprehensive exam, thesis optional, minimum GPA of 3.0. *Entrance requirements:* For master's, 30 hours of undergraduate course work in literature and composition (literature), BA in English or approval (composition/writing), minimum GPA of 2.75. Additional exam requirements/recommendations for international students: Required—TOEFL (minimum score 550 paper-based; 213 computer-based; 80 iBT). *Application deadline:* Applications are processed on a rolling basis. Application fee: $25. Electronic applications accepted. *Expenses:* Tuition, state resident: part-time $243 per credit hour. Tuition, nonresident: part-time $443 per credit hour. *Financial support:* In 2007–08, 13 students received support, including 4 research assistantships with full tuition reimbursements available (averaging $6,600 per year); career-related internships or fieldwork, Federal Work-Study, institutionally sponsored loans, scholarships/grants, tuition waivers (full and partial), and unspecified assistantships also available. Support available to part-time students. Financial award applicants required to submit FAFSA. *Faculty research:* Arthurian literature, Southern American literature, rhetoric and theories of authorship. *Unit head:* Dr. Timothy Libretti, Graduate Adviser, 773-442-5820, Fax: 773-442-5490, E-mail: t-libretti@neiu.edu. *Application contact:* Dr. Mohan K. Sood, Dean of the Graduate College, 773-442-6010, Fax: 773-442-6020, E-mail: m-sood@neiu.edu.

Northern Arizona University, Graduate College, College of Arts and Letters, Department of English, Program in English, Flagstaff, AZ 86011. Offers creative writing (MA); English education

(MA); general English (MA); literature (MA); rhetoric (MA). *Degree requirements:* For master's, departmental qualifying exam. *Entrance requirements:* For master's, GRE General Test, GRE Subject Test.

Northern Michigan University, College of Graduate Studies, College of Arts and Sciences, Department of English, Marquette, MI 49855-5301. Offers creative writing (MFA); literature (MA); pedagogy (MA); writing (MA). Part-time programs available. *Degree requirements:* For master's, thesis or alternative. *Entrance requirements:* For master's, minimum GPA of 2.75.

Northwestern University, Medill School of Journalism, Evanston, IL 60208. Offers broadcast journalism (MSJ); integrated marketing communications (MSIMC), including advertising/sales promotion, direct database and e-commerce marketing, general studies, public relations; magazine publishing (MSJ); new media (MSJ); reporting and writing (MSJ). *Accreditation:* ACEJMC (one or more programs are accredited). *Entrance requirements:* For master's, GRE General Test, GMAT or LSAT (MSJ). Additional exam requirements/recommendations for international students: Required—TOEFL. Electronic applications accepted. Expenses: Contact institution. *Faculty research:* Web business journalism, cultural stereotypes, voter apathy, digital television.

Oklahoma City University, Petree College of Arts and Sciences, Program in Liberal Arts, Oklahoma City, OK 73106-1402. Offers art (MLA); general studies (MLA); leadership/management (MLA); literature (MLA); mass communications (MLA); philosophy (MLA); writing (MLA). Part-time and evening/weekend programs available. *Faculty:* 18 full-time (7 women), 14 part-time/adjunct (4 women). *Students:* 24 full-time (18 women), 23 part-time (17 women); includes 6 minority (3 African Americans, 1 American Indian/Alaska Native, 1 Asian American or Pacific Islander, 1 Hispanic American), 14 international. Average age 31. 20 applicants, 95% accepted. In 2007, 13 degrees awarded. *Degree requirements:* For master's, comprehensive exam, thesis optional. *Entrance requirements:* Additional exam requirements/recommendations for international students: Required—TOEFL. *Application deadline:* For fall admission, 8/22 for domestic students; for spring admission, 1/15 for domestic students. Applications are processed on a rolling basis. Application fee: $30 ($70 for international students). *Expenses:* Tuition: Full-time $14,040; part-time $780 per hour. Required fees: $881; $32 per hour. *Financial support:* Fellowships with partial tuition reimbursements, career-related internships or fieldwork, Federal Work-Study, institutionally sponsored loans, and tuition waivers (partial) available. Support available to part-time students. Financial award application deadline: 8/1; financial award applicants required to submit FAFSA. *Unit head:* Dr. Regina Benuett, Director, 405-208-5178, Fax: 405-208-5451, E-mail: rebeunett@okcu.edu. *Application contact:* Leslie McKenzie, Director, Graduate Admissions, 800-633-7242, Fax: 405-208-5356, E-mail: gadmissions@okcu.edu.

Oklahoma State University, College of Arts and Sciences, Department of English, Stillwater, OK 74078. Offers creative writing (MA, PhD); literature (MA, PhD); technical writing (MA, PhD). *Faculty:* 51 full-time (29 women), 8 part-time/adjunct (3 women). *Students:* 15 full-time (8 women), 115 part-time (75 women); includes 11 minority (3 African Americans, 6 American Indian/Alaska Native, 2 Hispanic Americans), 20 international. Average age 32. 123 applicants, 45% accepted, 36 enrolled. In 2007, 4 master's, 6 doctorates awarded. *Degree requirements:* For master's, one foreign language, thesis; for doctorate, thesis/dissertation. *Entrance requirements:* For master's, GRE General Test or GMAT, GRE Subject Test, minimum GPA of 3.0; for doctorate, GRE General Test or GMAT, GRE Subject Test, minimum GPA of 3.5, writing sample. Additional exam requirements/recommendations for international students: Required—TOEFL. *Application deadline:* For fall admission, 3/1 priority date for international students; for spring admission, 8/1 priority date for international students. Applications are processed on a rolling basis. Application fee: $40 ($75 for international students). Electronic applications accepted. *Expenses:* Tuition, state resident: full-time $4,993; part-time $148 per credit hour. Tuition, nonresident: full-time $14,755; part-time $555 per credit hour. Tuition and fees vary according to program. *Financial support:* In 2007–08, 8 research assistantships (averaging $4,613 per year), 75 teaching assistantships (averaging $14,116 per year) were awarded; career-related internships or fieldwork, Federal Work-Study, scholarships/grants, health care benefits, tuition waivers (partial), and unspecified assistantships also available. Support available to part-time students. Financial award application deadline: 3/1. *Faculty research:* American and British novel, poetry, and autobiography; Native American languages and literature; institutional history of American film, history, and adaptations; rhetoric and theories of human communication; learning strategies of second language learners. *Unit head:* Dr. Carol Moder, Head, 405-744-9474, Fax: 405-744-6326, E-mail: epu@okstate.edu.

Old Dominion University, College of Arts and Letters, Program in Creative Writing, Norfolk, VA 23529. Offers MFA. Part-time programs available. *Faculty:* 6 full-time (3 women). *Students:* 16 full-time (12 women), 10 part-time (7 women); includes 2 minority (both African Americans), 1 international. Average age 33. 39 applicants, 41% accepted, 9 enrolled. In 2007, 6 degrees awarded. *Entrance requirements:* For master's, GRE General Test, 24 hours previous course work in English, minimum B average, sample of written work. Additional exam requirements/recommendations for international students: Required—TOEFL. *Application deadline:* For fall admission, 2/15 for domestic students. Applications are processed on a rolling basis. Application fee: $40. Electronic applications accepted. *Expenses:* Tuition, state resident: part-time $304 per credit hour. Tuition, nonresident: part-time $761 per credit hour. *Financial support:* In 2007–08, 13 students received support, including 1 fellowship with tuition reimbursement available (averaging $13,000 per year), 3 research assistantships with tuition reimbursements available (averaging $10,000 per year), 8 teaching assistantships with tuition reimbursements available (averaging $10,000 per year); career-related internships or fieldwork and scholarships/grants also available. Support available to part-time students. Financial award application deadline: 2/15. *Faculty research:* Literary fiction, nonfiction, poetry. Total annual research expenditures: $35,000. *Unit head:* Sheri Reynolds, Graduate Program Director, 757-683-4770, Fax: 757-683-3241, E-mail: cwgpd@odu.edu.

Otis College of Art and Design, Program in Writing, Los Angeles, CA 90045-9785. Offers MFA. *Faculty:* 1 full-time (0 women), 5 part-time/adjunct (1 woman). *Students:* 14 full-time (11 women), 13 part-time (7 women); includes 13 minority (6 African Americans, 4 Asian Americans or Pacific Islanders, 3 Hispanic Americans). Average age 34. 35 applicants, 57% accepted, 8 enrolled. In 2007, 4 degrees awarded. *Degree requirements:* For master's, thesis. *Entrance requirements:* For master's, writing sample. *Application deadline:* For fall admission, 2/15 for domestic and international students. Application fee: $50. Electronic applications accepted. *Expenses:* Tuition: Full-time $30,764; part-time $1,026 per unit. Required fees: $700. *Financial support:* Federal Work-Study, scholarships/grants, and tuition waivers (partial) available. Financial award applicants required to submit FAFSA. *Unit head:* Paul Vangelisti, Chair, 310-665-6891, Fax: 310-665-6890, E-mail: pvangel@otis.edu. *Application contact:* Information Contact, 310-665-6820, Fax: 310-665-6821, E-mail: admissions@otis.edu.

Pacific Lutheran University, Division of Graduate Studies, Division of Humanities, Tacoma, WA 98447. Offers creative writing (MFA). Offered during summer only. Part-time programs available. *Faculty:* 1 full-time (0 women). *Students:* Average age 45. 39 applicants, 72% accepted, 19 enrolled. In 2007, 20 degrees awarded. *Degree requirements:* For master's, thesis, final residency including teaching class. *Entrance requirements:* For master's, portfolio, book review. Additional exam requirements/recommendations for international students: Required—TOEFL. *Application deadline:* For winter admission, 2/15 for domestic and international students. Application fee: $40. Electronic applications accepted. *Expenses: Contact institution.* Tuition and fees vary according to course load and program. *Financial support:* In 2007–08, 23 students received support, including 1 fellowship (averaging $2,000 per year); unspecified assistantships also available. Financial award application deadline: 3/1; financial award applicants required to submit FAFSA. *Unit head:* Dr. Douglas E. Oakman, Dean, 253-535-7317, Fax: 253-536-7132, E-mail: oakmande@plu.edu. *Application contact:* Stan Sanvel Rubin, Director of MFA in Creative Writing Program, 253-535-7221, E-mail: mfa@plu.edu.

Penn State University Park, Graduate School, College of the Liberal Arts, Department of English, State College, University Park, PA 16802-1503. Offers MA, MFA, PhD. *Expenses:* Tuition, state resident: full-time $14,738; part-time $614 per credit. Tuition, nonresident: full-time $26,050; part-time $1,085 per credit. Tuition and fees vary according to course load, program and student level. *Unit head:* Dr. Robin G. Schulze, Director of Graduate Studies, 814-863-2626, Fax: 814-863-7285. *Application contact:* Information Contact, 814-863-3069, E-mail: englgradoffice@psu.edu.

Purdue University, Graduate School, College of Liberal Arts, Department of English, West Lafayette, IN 47907. Offers creative writing (MFA); literature (MA, PhD), including linguistics, literature and philosophy (PhD), rhetoric and composition, theory and cultural studies (PhD). Part-time programs available. *Degree requirements:* For master's, one foreign language; for doctorate, one foreign language, thesis/dissertation. *Entrance requirements:* For master's and doctorate, GRE General Test, sample of written work. Additional exam requirements/recommendations for international students: Required—TOEFL. Electronic applications accepted. *Faculty research:* Cultural studies, postmodern narrative, contemporary women writers, composition theory, slave narratives.

Queens College of the City University of New York, Division of Graduate Studies, Arts and Humanities Division, Department of English, Flushing, NY 11367-1597. Offers creative writing (MA); English language and literature (MA). Part-time and evening/weekend programs available. *Faculty:* 53 full-time (25 women). *Students:* 3 full-time (1 woman), 114 part-time (80 women). 111 applicants, 81% accepted, 67 enrolled. In 2007, 43 degrees awarded. *Degree requirements:* For master's, one foreign language, thesis (for some programs), oral exam (English language and literature). *Entrance requirements:* For master's, manuscript (creative writing), minimum GPA of 3.0. Additional exam requirements/recommendations for international students: Required—TOEFL. *Application deadline:* For fall admission, 4/1 for domestic students; for spring admission, 11/1 for domestic students. Applications are processed on a rolling basis. Application fee: $125. *Financial support:* Career-related internships or fieldwork, Federal Work-Study, institutionally sponsored loans, tuition waivers (partial), and adjunct lectureships available. Support available to part-time students. Financial award application deadline: 4/1; financial award applicants required to submit FAFSA. *Unit head:* Dr. Nancy Comley, Chairperson, 718-997-4600, E-mail: nancy_comley@qc.edu. *Application contact:* Dr. Talia Schaffer, Graduate Adviser, 718-997-4600, E-mail: talia_schaffer@qc.edu.

Queens University of Charlotte, College of Arts and Sciences, Charlotte, NC 28274-0002. Offers creative writing (MFA). Part-time programs available. Postbaccalaureate distance learning degree programs offered (minimal on-campus study). Electronic applications accepted.

Rhode Island College, School of Graduate Studies, Faculty of Arts and Sciences, Department of English, Providence, RI 02908-1991. Offers creative writing (MA); English (MA). Part-time and evening/weekend programs available. *Faculty:* 15 full-time (8 women). *Students:* 5 full-time (4 women), 16 part-time (11 women). Average age 36. In 2007, 4 degrees awarded. *Degree requirements:* For master's, thesis (for some programs). *Entrance requirements:* For master's, GRE General Test, 3 letters of recommendation, interview. *Application deadline:* For fall admission, 4/1 for domestic students; for spring admission, 11/1 for domestic students. Applications are processed on a rolling basis. Application fee: $50. *Expenses:* Tuition, state resident: full-time $6,240; part-time $260 per credit hour. Tuition, nonresident: full-time $13,104; part-time $546 per credit hour. Required fees: $332; $14 per credit hour. One-time fee: $66 part-time. *Financial support:* In 2007–08, 1 teaching assistantship with full tuition reimbursement (averaging $4,000 per year) was awarded; career-related internships or fieldwork, Federal Work-Study, scholarships/grants, health care benefits, and unspecified assistantships also available. Support available to part-time students. Financial award application deadline: 5/15; financial award applicants required to submit FAFSA. *Unit head:* Dr. Maureen Reddy, Chair, 401-456-8028, E-mail: mreddy@ric.edu.

Rivier College, School of Graduate Studies, Department of English, Nashua, NH 03060. Offers English (MA, MAT); writing and literature (MA); MA/MAT. Part-time and evening/weekend programs available. *Degree requirements:* For master's, comprehensive exam (for some programs). *Entrance requirements:* For master's, GRE Subject Test.

Roosevelt University, Graduate Division, College of Arts and Sciences, Department of Literature and Languages, Program in Creative Writing, Chicago, IL 60605-1394. Offers MFA. Part-time and evening/weekend programs available. *Students:* 12 full-time (8 women), 14 part-time (6 women); includes 3 minority (2 African Americans, 1 Hispanic American). Average age 31. 52 applicants, 21% accepted, 7 enrolled. In 2007, 6 degrees awarded. *Application deadline:* For fall admission, 6/1 priority date for domestic students. Applications are processed on a rolling basis. Application fee: $25 ($35 for international students). *Financial support:* Application deadline: 2/15. *Faculty research:* Poetry, fiction, nonfiction, script writing. *Unit head:* Janet Wondra, Head, 312-341-3670. *Application contact:* Joanne Canyon-Heller, Coordinator of Graduate Admission, 877-APPLY RU, Fax: 312-281-3356, E-mail: applyru@roosevelt.edu.

Rosemont College, Graduate School, Program in Creative Writing, Rosemont, PA 19010-1699. Offers MFA. *Expenses:* Tuition: Part-time $525 per credit. Tuition and fees vary according to program. *Unit head:* Elizabeth Corcoran, Director, 610-527-0200, Fax: 610-526-2964.

Rowan University, Graduate School, College of Communication, Program in Writing, Glassboro, NJ 08028-1701. Offers MA. Part-time and evening/weekend programs available. *Faculty:* 7 full-time (3 women). *Students:* 7 full-time (3 women), 19 part-time (13 women); includes 3 minority (1 African American, 1 Asian American or Pacific Islander, 1 Hispanic American). Average age 34. 8 applicants, 88% accepted, 6 enrolled. In 2007, 22 degrees awarded. *Degree requirements:* For master's, comprehensive exam, thesis. *Entrance requirements:* Additional exam requirements/recommendations for international students: Required—TOEFL. *Application deadline:* Applications are processed on a rolling basis. Application fee: $50. Electronic applications accepted. *Expenses:* Tuition, nonresident: full-time $9,882; part-time $549 per credit. Required fees: $104,385 per credit. *Financial support:* Career-related internships or fieldwork and unspecified assistantships available. Support available to part-time students. *Unit head:* Dr. Diane Penrod, Adviser, 856-256-4330. *Application contact:* Chair, 856-256-4096.

Rutgers, The State University of New Jersey, New Brunswick, Mason Gross School of the Arts, Department of Theater Arts, New Brunswick, NJ 08901-1281. Offers acting (MFA); design (MFA); directing (MFA); playwriting (MFA); stage management (MFA). *Degree requirements:* For master's, thesis (for some programs), performance project. *Entrance requirements:* For master's, audition, interview, portfolio. Electronic applications accepted. *Faculty research:* Faculty of working professional.

Saint Joseph's University, College of Arts and Sciences, Program in Writing Studies, Philadelphia, PA 19131-1395. Offers MA. *Students:* 1 full-time (0 women), 40 part-time (26 women); includes 6 minority (all African Americans), 1 international. Average age 30. In 2007, 22 degrees awarded. *Entrance requirements:* For master's, 2 letters of recommendation, resumé, 2 writing samples, application, official transcripts, personal statement. Additional exam requirements/recommendations for international students: Required—TOEFL (minimum score 550 paper-based; 213 computer-based; 79 iBT). *Application deadline:* For fall admission, 7/15 priority date for domestic students, 4/15 priority date for international students; for winter admission, 1/15 priority date for international students; for spring admission, 11/15 priority date for domestic students, 10/15 priority date for international students. Applications are processed on a rolling basis. Application fee: $35. Electronic applications accepted. *Expenses:* Tuition: Part-time $738 per credit. Tuition and fees vary according to degree level and program. *Financial support:* Unspecified assistantships available. *Unit head:* Dr. Owen Gilman, Director, 610-660-1891.

Saint Mary's College of California, School of Liberal Arts, Program in Creative Writing, Moraga, CA 94575. Offers MFA. *Faculty:* 6 full-time (3 women), 4 part-time/adjunct (3 women). *Students:* 44 full-time (27 women); includes 7 minority (1 African American, 3 Asian Americans or Pacific Islanders, 3 Hispanic Americans). Average age 28. 160 applicants, 28% accepted,

Writing

Saint Mary's College of California (continued)
21 enrolled. In 2007, 21 degrees awarded. *Degree requirements:* For master's, thesis. *Entrance requirements:* For master's, sample of written work. *Application deadline:* For fall admission, 2/15 for domestic and international students. Application fee: $45. *Financial support:* In 2007–08, 3 fellowships (averaging $6,000 per year), 20 teaching assistantships (averaging $2,000 per year) were awarded; career-related internships or fieldwork and Federal Work-Study also available. Support available to part-time students. Financial award applicants required to submit FAFSA. *Faculty research:* Poetry, fiction, nonfiction. *Unit head:* Dr. Graham W. Foust, Director, 925-631-4457, Fax: 925-631-4471, E-mail: gwf1@stmarys-ca.edu. *Application contact:* Thomas Cooney, MFA Program Coordinator, 925-631-4762, Fax: 925-631-4471, E-mail: writers@stmarys-ca.edu.

Saint Xavier University, Graduate Studies, School of Arts and Sciences, Department of English, Chicago, IL 60655-3105. Offers English (CAS); literary studies (MA); teaching of writing (MA); writing pedagogy (CAS). Part-time and evening/weekend programs available. In 2007, 14 degrees awarded. *Entrance requirements:* For master's, MAT or GRE, minimum GPA of 3.0. *Application deadline:* For fall admission, 8/15 priority date for domestic students. Applications are processed on a rolling basis. Application fee: $35. *Financial support:* Applicants required to submit FAFSA. *Unit head:* Dr. Nelson Hathcock, Director, 773-298-3235, Fax: 773-779-9061, E-mail: hathcock@sxu.edu. *Application contact:* Beth Gierach, Managing Director of Admission, 773-298-3053, Fax: 773-298-3076, E-mail: gierach@sxu.edu.

Salisbury University, Graduate Division, Program in English, Salisbury, MD 21801-6837. Offers composition, language and rhetoric (MA); literature (MA); teaching English to speakers of other languages (MA). Part-time programs available. *Faculty:* 10 full-time (5 women), 1 part-time/adjunct (0 women). *Students:* 7 full-time (5 women), 26 part-time (18 women); includes 4 minority (2 African Americans, 2 Hispanic Americans). Average age 29. 25 applicants, 72% accepted, 13 enrolled. In 2007, 22 degrees awarded. *Degree requirements:* For master's, thesis optional. *Entrance requirements:* For master's, GRE General Test, MAT or PRAXIS, minimum GPA of 3.0, 2 letters of recommendation. Additional exam requirements/recommendations for international students: Required—TOEFL (minimum score 550 paper-based; 213 computer-based). *Application deadline:* For fall admission, 8/1 for domestic students; for spring admission, 1/1 for domestic students. Applications are processed on a rolling basis. Application fee: $45. Electronic applications accepted. *Expenses:* Tuition, state resident: part-time $260 per credit hour. Tuition, nonresident: part-time $556 per credit hour. *Financial support:* Teaching assistantships with full tuition reimbursements, career-related internships or fieldwork and scholarships/grants available. Support available to part-time students. Financial award applicants required to submit FAFSA. *Faculty research:* Shakespeare, Keats, J. D. Salinger, feminist theory, film, folklore. *Unit head:* Dr. Elizabeth H. Curtin, Director, 410-548-5594, Fax: 410-548-2142, E-mail: ehcurtin@salisbury.edu.

San Diego State University, Graduate and Research Affairs, College of Arts and Letters, Department of English and Comparative Literature, San Diego, CA 92182. Offers creative writing (MFA); English (MA). *Students:* 86 full-time (54 women), 59 part-time (36 women); includes 35 minority (6 African Americans, 8 Asian Americans or Pacific Islanders, 21 Hispanic Americans), 2 international. 154 applicants, 62% accepted, 40 enrolled. In 2007, 38 degrees awarded. *Degree requirements:* For master's, one foreign language, comprehensive exam (for some programs), thesis (for some programs). *Entrance requirements:* For master's, GRE General Test, minimum GPA of 2.85, writing sample, 3 letters of recommendation. Additional exam requirements/recommendations for international students: Required—TOEFL. *Application deadline:* For fall admission, 4/1 for domestic and international students; for spring admission, 10/1 for domestic and international students. Applications are processed on a rolling basis. Application fee: $55. Electronic applications accepted. *Financial support:* In 2007–08, 22 teaching assistantships were awarded; fellowships, research assistantships, career-related internships or fieldwork also available. Financial award applicants required to submit FAFSA. Total annual research expenditures: $105,868. *Unit head:* Sherry Little, Chair, 619-594-5237, Fax: 619-594-4998, E-mail: slittle@mail.sdsu.edu. *Application contact:* Dr. Claire E. Colquitt, Graduate Adviser, 619-594-6219, Fax: 619-594-4998, E-mail: colquitt@mail.sdsu.edu.

San Diego State University, Graduate and Research Affairs, College of Arts and Letters, Department of Rhetoric and Writing, San Diego, CA 92182. Offers MA. Part-time programs available. *Students:* 17 full-time (14 women), 15 part-time (10 women); includes 8 minority (2 African Americans, 1 American Indian/Alaska Native, 2 Asian Americans or Pacific Islanders, 3 Hispanic Americans). 21 applicants, 90% accepted, 15 enrolled. In 2007, 11 degrees awarded. *Degree requirements:* For master's, thesis. *Entrance requirements:* For master's, GRE General Test, writing sample, 3 letters of reference. Additional exam requirements/recommendations for international students: Required—TOEFL. *Application deadline:* For fall admission, 4/1 for domestic and international students; for spring admission, 10/1 for domestic and international students. Application fee: $55. Electronic applications accepted. *Financial support:* Teaching assistantships available. Financial award applicants required to submit FAFSA. *Unit head:* Dr. Glenn McClish, Chair, 619-594-6515, Fax: 619-594-6530, E-mail: gmcclish@mail.sdsu.edu. *Application contact:* Jane Robinett, Graduate Advisor, 619-594-0966, Fax: 619-594-6530, E-mail: jrobinett@mail.sdsu.edu.

San Francisco State University, Division of Graduate Studies, College of Humanities, Department of Creative Writing, San Francisco, CA 94132-1722. Offers MA, MFA. Part-time programs available. *Degree requirements:* For master's, thesis. *Financial support:* Career-related internships or fieldwork and Federal Work-Study available. *Unit head:* Maxine Chernoff, Chair, 415-338-1891, Fax: 415-405-2142, E-mail: cwriting@sfsu.edu. *Application contact:* Barbara Eaton, Academic Office Coordinator, 415-338-1891, E-mail: cwriting@sfsu.edu.

San Jose State University, Graduate Studies and Research, College of Humanities and the Arts, Department of English and Comparative Literature, San Jose, CA 95192-0001. Offers creative writing (MFA); literature (MA); secondary English education (Certificate). *Students:* 37 full-time (23 women), 57 part-time (37 women); includes 22 minority (5 African Americans, 1 American Indian/Alaska Native, 11 Asian Americans or Pacific Islanders, 5 Hispanic Americans), 2 international. Average age 33. 95 applicants, 68% accepted, 42 enrolled. In 2007, 18 degrees awarded. *Degree requirements:* For master's, one foreign language, thesis or alternative. *Entrance requirements:* For master's, GRE. Additional exam requirements/recommendations for international students: Required—TOEFL. *Application deadline:* For fall admission, 6/29 for domestic students; for spring admission, 11/30 for domestic students. Applications are processed on a rolling basis. Application fee: $59. Electronic applications accepted. *Financial support:* Applicants required to submit FAFSA. *Unit head:* John Engell, Chair, 408-924-4499, Fax: 408-924-4580, E-mail: john.engell@email.sjsu.edu. *Application contact:* Dr. Noelle Brada-Williams, Graduate Coordinator, 408-924-4439.

Sarah Lawrence College, Graduate Studies, Program in Writing, Bronxville, NY 10708-5999. Offers creative non-fiction (MFA); fiction (MFA); poetry (MFA). Part-time programs available. *Faculty:* 43 part-time/adjunct (25 women). *Students:* 115 full-time (93 women), 36 part-time (31 women); includes 21 minority (8 African Americans, 1 American Indian/Alaska Native, 6 Asian Americans or Pacific Islanders, 6 Hispanic Americans), 1 international. Average age 31. 364 applicants, 43% accepted, 69 enrolled. In 2007, 62 degrees awarded. *Degree requirements:* For master's, thesis. *Entrance requirements:* For master's, sample of creative writing, minimum B average in undergraduate course work. Additional exam requirements/recommendations for international students: Required—TOEFL (minimum score 600 paper-based). *Application deadline:* For fall admission, 1/15 for domestic students. Application fee: $60. *Expenses:* Tuition: Part-time $1,034 per credit. Required fees: $430 per year. Tuition and fees vary according to program. *Financial support:* In 2007–08, 78 fellowships (averaging $3,791 per year) were awarded; scholarships/grants and unspecified assistantships also available. Support available to part-time students. Financial award application deadline: 3/1. *Unit head:* Kate Johnson, Co-Director, 914-395-2373. *Application contact:* Susan Guma, Dean of Graduate Studies, 914-395-2373, E-mail: sguma@mail.slc.edu.

See Close-Up on page 355.

Savannah College of Art and Design, Graduate School, Program in Professional Writing, Savannah, GA 31402-3146. Offers MFA. Part-time programs available. *Faculty:* 1 (woman) full-time. *Students:* 4 full-time (2 women), 1 (woman) part-time. 22 applicants, 55% accepted, 5 enrolled. *Degree requirements:* For master's, thesis. *Entrance requirements:* Additional exam requirements/recommendations for international students: Required—TOEFL (minimum score 450 paper-based; 133 computer-based). *Application deadline:* For fall admission, 4/1 priority date for domestic and international students. Applications are processed on a rolling basis. Electronic applications accepted. *Expenses:* Tuition: Full-time $24,840; part-time $552 per credit. One-time fee: $500 full-time. *Financial support:* Fellowships, career-related internships or fieldwork, Federal Work-Study, and scholarships/grants available. Financial award application deadline: 4/1; financial award applicants required to submit FAFSA. *Unit head:* Dr. Desirè Houngues, Acting Chair, 912-525-5816, Fax: 912-525-5886, E-mail: dhoungue@scad.edu. *Application contact:* Darrell Tutchton, Director of Graduate and International Enrollment, 912-525-5961, Fax: 912-525-5985, E-mail: admission@scad.edu.

School of the Art Institute of Chicago, Graduate Division, Program in Writing, Chicago, IL 60603-3103. Offers MFA. *Entrance requirements:* Additional exam requirements/recommendations for international students: Required—TOEFL.

See Close-Up on page 259.

Seattle Pacific University, Graduate School, College of Arts and Sciences, Program in Creative Writing, Seattle, WA 98119-1997. Offers MFA. Part-time programs available. *Students:* Average age 37. 65 applicants, 11% accepted, 7 enrolled. In 2007, 5 degrees awarded. *Entrance requirements:* For master's, GRE. Application fee: $50. *Expenses:* Tuition: Part-time $522 per credit hour. Tuition and fees vary according to program. *Financial support:* Applicants required to submit FAFSA. *Unit head:* Dr. Gregory Wolfe, Director, 206-281-2109, E-mail: gwolfe@spu.edu. *Application contact:* Beth Bevis, Coordinator, 206-281-2727.

Seton Hill University, Program in Writing Popular Fiction, Greensburg, PA 15601. Offers MA. Part-time programs available. Postbaccalaureate distance learning degree programs offered (minimal on-campus study). *Faculty:* 3 full-time (1 woman), 16 part-time/adjunct (8 women). *Students:* 1 (woman) full-time, 68 part-time (52 women); includes 5 minority (2 African Americans, 1 Asian American or Pacific Islander, 2 Hispanic Americans), 1 international. Average age 36. 28 applicants, 75% accepted, 18 enrolled. In 2007, 19 degrees awarded. *Degree requirements:* For master's, thesis or alternative. *Entrance requirements:* For master's, writing sample. Additional exam requirements/recommendations for international students: Required—TOEFL (minimum score 600 paper-based; 250 computer-based). *Application deadline:* For fall admission, 6/1 for domestic students; for spring admission, 12/15 for domestic students. Applications are processed on a rolling basis. Application fee: $35. Electronic applications accepted. *Expenses:* Tuition: Full-time $17,955; part-time $665 per credit. Tuition and fees vary according to program. *Financial support:* In 2007–08, 59 students received support. Scholarships/grants, tuition waivers (partial), and unspecified assistantships available. Support available to part-time students. Financial award application deadline: 8/15; financial award applicants required to submit FAFSA. *Faculty research:* Romance novels, science fiction novels, children's fiction, mystery, horror. *Unit head:* Dr. Lee McClain, Director, 724-830-1040, Fax: 724-830-1294, E-mail: mcclain@setonhill.edu. *Application contact:* Dane Zimmer, Advisor, 724-838-4209, Fax: 724-830-1891, E-mail: zimmer@setonhill.edu.

Sewanee: The University of the South, Sewanee School of Letters, Sewanee, TN 37383-1000. Offers American literature and English literature (MA); creative writing (MFA). Programs offered only during the summer. Part-time programs available. *Faculty:* 7 full-time (3 women). *Students:* 41 full-time (20 women); includes 1 minority (African American) Average age 31. 43 applicants, 100% accepted, 41 enrolled. *Degree requirements:* For master's, thesis (for some programs). *Entrance requirements:* For master's, writing sample, 2 letters of recommendation. *Application deadline:* For spring admission, 2/1 priority date for domestic and international students. Applications are processed on a rolling basis. Application fee: $40. Electronic applications accepted. *Expenses:* Contact institution. *Financial support:* Application deadline: 4/1; *Unit head:* Dr. John M Grammer, Director, 931-598-1483, Fax: 931-598-3303, E-mail: jgrammer@sewanee.edu. *Application contact:* Margaret D Binnicker, Coordinator, 931-598-1636, Fax: 931-598-3303, E-mail: mbinnick@sewanee.edu.

See Close-Up on page 579.

Sonoma State University, School of Arts and Humanities, Department of English, Rohnert Park, CA 94928-3609. Offers American literature (MA); creative writing (MA); English literature (MA); world literature (MA). Part-time and evening/weekend programs available. *Students:* 19 full-time (15 women), 6 part-time (5 women); includes 2 minority (1 Asian American or Pacific Islander, 1 Hispanic American). Average age 35. 14 applicants, 93% accepted, 6 enrolled. In 2007, 14 degrees awarded. *Degree requirements:* For master's, one foreign language, thesis or alternative. *Entrance requirements:* For master's, minimum GPA of 2.5. *Application deadline:* For fall admission, 11/30 priority date for domestic students. Application fee: $55. *Financial support:* In 2007–08, 9 teaching assistantships with partial tuition reimbursements were awarded; career-related internships or fieldwork and Federal Work-Study also available. Financial award application deadline: 3/2. *Faculty research:* Women writers, international literature in English, literature of fantasy. *Unit head:* Dr. Greta Vollmer, Chair, 707-661-2140, E-mail: vollmer@sonoma.edu.

Southern Illinois University Carbondale, Graduate School, College of Liberal Arts, Department of English, Program in Creative Writing, Carbondale, IL 62901-4701. Offers MFA. *Faculty:* 5 full-time (3 women). *Students:* 6 full-time (4 women), 25 part-time (8 women); includes 4 minority (1 African American, 1 Asian American or Pacific Islander, 2 Hispanic Americans), 1 international. 67 applicants, 27% accepted, 9 enrolled. In 2007, 15 degrees awarded. *Degree requirements:* For master's, one foreign language, thesis. *Entrance requirements:* For master's, GRE General Test, GRE Subject Test, minimum GPA of 2.7. Additional exam requirements/recommendations for international students: Required—TOEFL. *Application deadline:* For fall admission, 2/15 for domestic students; for spring admission, 11/15 for domestic students. Applications are processed on a rolling basis. Application fee: $20. *Financial support:* In 2007–08, 28 students received support, including 1 fellowship with full tuition reimbursement available, 1 research assistantship with full tuition reimbursement available, 24 teaching assistantships with full tuition reimbursements available; career-related internships or fieldwork, Federal Work-Study, institutionally sponsored loans, and tuition waivers (full) also available. Support available to part-time students. *Application contact:* Donna Schumaier, Administrative Clerk, 618-453-6894, Fax: 618-453-3253, E-mail: gradengl@siu.edu.

Announcement: The MFA in Creative Writing is a three-year studio/academic program. The student-teacher ratio is 5:1, so workshops are small and faculty members provide an unusual degree of both formal and informal mentoring. Most students receive assistantships and teach composition, literature, and/or creative writing, and many intern with the *Crab Orchard Review.*

See Close-Up on page 733.

Southern Illinois University Edwardsville, Graduate Studies and Research, College of Arts and Sciences, Department of English Language and Literature, Program in Creative Writing, Edwardsville, IL 62026-0001. Offers MA. *Students:* 3 full-time (2 women), 16 part-time (10 women); includes 1 minority (American Indian/Alaska Native). In 2007, 1 degree awarded. *Degree requirements:* For master's, one foreign language, thesis. *Entrance requirements:* Additional exam requirements/recommendations for international students: Required—TOEFL. *Application deadline:* For fall admission, 7/20 for domestic students, 6/1 for international students; for spring admission, 12/14 for domestic students, 10/1 for international students. Application fee: $30. Electronic applications accepted. *Financial support:* Fellowships with full tuition reimbursements, research assistantships with full tuition reimbursements, teaching assistantships with full tuition reimbursements available. *Unit head:* Dr. Eileen Joy, Director, 618-650-3971, E-mail: ejoy@siue.edu.

Southern New Hampshire University, School of Liberal Arts, Manchester, NH 03106-1045. Offers clinical services for adults psychiatric disabilities (Certificate); clinical services for children and adolescents with psychiatric disabilities (Certificate); clinical services for persons with co-occurring substance abuse and psychiatric disabilities (Certificate); community mental health (MS); fiction writing (MFA); non-fiction writing (MFA); teaching English as a foreign language (MS). Part-time and evening/weekend programs available. *Faculty:* 18 full-time. *Students:* 187 full-time, 12 part-time. Average age 35. In 2007, 35 degrees awarded. *Degree requirements:* For master's, one foreign language, thesis. *Entrance requirements:* For master's, minimum GPA of 2.75: MS-TEFL, 3.0: MFA. Additional exam requirements/recommendations for international students: Required—TOEFL (minimum score 550 paper-based; 213 computer-based; 79 iBT), IELTS (minimum score 7), TWE (minimum score 5). *Application deadline:* For fall admission, 7/1 priority date for domestic students; for winter admission, 11/1 priority date for domestic students; for spring admission, 6/1 priority date for domestic students. Applications are processed on a rolling basis. Application fee: $40. Electronic applications accepted. *Expenses:* Contact institution. *Financial support:* In 2007–08, 4 research assistantships were awarded; career-related internships or fieldwork and scholarships/grants also available. Financial award applicants required to submit FAFSA. *Faculty research:* Action research, state of the art practice in behavioral health services, wraparound approaches to working with youth, learning styles. *Unit head:* Dr. Karen Erickson, Dean, 603-668-2211, E-mail: k.erickson@snhu.edu. *Application contact:* Scott Durand, Director of Graduate Enrollment Services, 603-644-3102 Ext. 3338, Fax: 603-644-3144, E-mail: s.durand@snhu.edu.

Spalding University, Graduate Studies, College of Social Sciences and Humanities, Program in Writing, Louisville, KY 40203-2188. Offers MFA. Postbaccalaureate distance learning degree programs offered (minimal on-campus study). *Degree requirements:* For master's, thesis. *Entrance requirements:* For master's, writing sample, letters of recommendation. Additional exam requirements/recommendations for international students: Required—TOEFL. Electronic applications accepted. *Faculty research:* Fiction, creative nonfiction, poetry, writing for children, playwriting/screenwriting.

Stony Brook University, State University of New York, Stony Brook Southampton, Program in Writing and Literature, Stony Brook, NY 11794. Offers fiction (MFA); poetry (MFA); scientific writing (MFA), including environmental, medical, technological; scriptwriting (MFA). *Application contact:* Joyce Tuttle, Director of Graduate Admissions and Program Administration, 631-287-8010, Fax: 631-287-8253, E-mail: joyce.tuttle@liu.edu.

See Close-Up on page 735.

Syracuse University, Graduate School, College of Arts and Sciences, Department of English, Program in Creative Writing, Syracuse, NY 13244. Offers MFA. *Students:* 35 full-time (20 women); includes 9 minority (1 African American, 1 American Indian/Alaska Native, 5 Asian Americans or Pacific Islanders, 2 Hispanic Americans), 1 international. 367 applicants, 6% accepted, 12 enrolled. In 2007, 10 degrees awarded. *Degree requirements:* For master's, thesis. *Entrance requirements:* For master's, GRE General Test, sample of written work. Additional exam requirements/recommendations for international students: Required—TOEFL. *Application deadline:* For fall admission, 1/10 priority date for domestic students. Application fee: $75. *Expenses:* Tuition: Full-time $18,216; part-time $1,012 per credit. Required fees: $980. Tuition and fees vary according to program. *Financial support:* Fellowships with full tuition reimbursements, teaching assistantships with full tuition reimbursements, tuition waivers (partial) available. *Unit head:* Christopher Kennedy, Director, 315-443-3755, Fax: 315-443-3660, E-mail: ckennedy@syr.edu. *Application contact:* Terri Zollo, Information Contact, 315-443-2174.

Syracuse University, Graduate School, College of Arts and Sciences, The Writing Program, Program in Composition and Cultural Rhetoric, Syracuse, NY 13244. Offers PhD. *Students:* 24 full-time (20 women), 8 part-time (2 women); includes 3 African Americans, 1 international. 19 applicants, 47% accepted, 4 enrolled. *Entrance requirements:* For doctorate, GRE. *Application deadline:* For fall admission, 2/1 priority date for domestic students. Application fee: $75. Electronic applications accepted. *Expenses:* Tuition: Full-time $18,216; part-time $1,012 per credit. Required fees: $980. Tuition and fees vary according to program. *Financial support:* Fellowships with full tuition reimbursements, teaching assistantships with full tuition reimbursements available. *Unit head:* Collin Brooke, Graduate Director, 315-443-1067.

Temple University, Graduate School, College of Liberal Arts, Department of English, Program in Creative Writing, Philadelphia, PA 19122-6096. Offers MA. Part-time programs available. *Degree requirements:* For master's, comprehensive exam, manuscript. *Entrance requirements:* For master's, GRE General Test, minimum GPA of 3.0. Additional exam requirements/recommendations for international students: Required—TOEFL (minimum score 550 paper-based; 213 computer-based; 79 iBT). Electronic applications accepted. *Faculty research:* Poetry, fiction, cultural studies.

Texas State University–San Marcos, Graduate School, College of Liberal Arts, Department of English, Program in Creative Writing, San Marcos, TX 78666. Offers MFA. Part-time and evening/weekend programs available. *Faculty:* 6 full-time (2 women), 1 part-time/adjunct (0 women). *Students:* 48 full-time (24 women), 15 part-time (7 women); includes 11 minority (1 Asian American or Pacific Islander, 10 Hispanic Americans), 1 international. Average age 30. 106 applicants, 37% accepted, 19 enrolled. In 2007, 14 degrees awarded. *Degree requirements:* For master's, comprehensive exam, thesis. *Entrance requirements:* For master's, 24 hours of undergraduate course work in English (12 advanced) with minimum GPA of 3.25, 6 hours of course work in foreign language, minimum GPA of 2.75 in last 60 hours, writing portfolios. Additional exam requirements/recommendations for international students: Required—TOEFL (minimum score 550 paper-based; 213 computer-based). *Application deadline:* For fall admission, 1/15 priority date for domestic students, 1/15 for international students; for spring admission, 11/1 priority date for domestic students, 10/1 for international students. Applications are processed on a rolling basis. Application fee: $40 ($90 for international students). Electronic applications accepted. *Expenses:* Tuition, state resident: full-time $3,780; part-time $210 per credit hour. Tuition, nonresident: full-time $8,784; part-time $488 per credit hour. Required fees: $493 per semester. Full-time tuition and fees vary according to course load. *Financial support:* In 2007–08, 53 students received support, including 38 teaching assistantships (averaging $5,556 per year); research assistantships, Federal Work-Study and institutionally sponsored loans also available. Support available to part-time students. Financial award application deadline: 4/1; financial award applicants required to submit FAFSA. *Unit head:* Tom Grimes, Graduate Adviser, 512-245-2163, Fax: 512-245-8546, E-mail: tg02@txstate.edu.

Towson University, College of Graduate Studies and Research, Program in Professional Writing, Towson, MD 21252-0001. Offers MS. Part-time and evening/weekend programs available. *Faculty:* 14 full-time (6 women), 1 (woman) part-time/adjunct. *Students:* 16 full-time (11 women), 54 part-time (39 women); includes 15 minority (all African Americans), 1 international. Average age 32. 31 applicants, 97% accepted, 20 enrolled. In 2007, 22 degrees awarded. *Degree requirements:* For master's, thesis optional, exam. *Entrance requirements:* For master's, sample of written work (obtain instructions from English dept), minimum GPA of 3.0, (2) letters of recommendation, official transcripts. *Application deadline:* For fall admission, 3/1 for domestic students; for spring admission, 10/1 for domestic students. Application fee: $50. Electronic applications accepted. *Expenses:* Tuition, state resident: part-time $286 per credit. Tuition, nonresident: part-time $600 per credit. Required fees: $75 per credit. *Financial support:* Federal Work-Study and unspecified assistantships available. Financial award application deadline: 4/1; financial award applicants required to submit FAFSA. *Faculty research:* Creative writing, essay writing, sociopsychological linguistics, interdisciplinary rhetoric, global communication. *Unit head:* Prof. Geoffrey Becker, Graduate Program Director, 410-704-5196, Fax: 410-704-3434, E-mail: prwr@towson.edu. *Application contact:* 410-704-2501, Fax: 410-704-4675, E-mail: grads@towson.edu.

Union Institute & University, Online MA Programs, Cincinnati, OH 45206-1925. Offers health and wellness (MA); history and culture (MA); leadership (MA); literature and writing (MA); psychology (MA). Part-time programs available. Postbaccalaureate distance learning degree programs offered (no on-campus study). *Faculty:* 3 full-time (1 woman), 15 part-time/adjunct (11 women). *Students:* 204 full-time (143 women); includes 19 minority (14 African Americans, 2 American Indian/Alaska Native, 3 Hispanic Americans). Average age 39. In 2007, 46 degrees awarded. *Degree requirements:* For master's, thesis. *Application deadline:* Applications are processed on a rolling basis. Application fee: $50. *Expenses:* Contact institution. *Financial support:* Career-related internships or fieldwork and tuition waivers available. Financial award applicants required to submit FAFSA. *Unit head:* Dr. Brian Webb, Assistant Vice President, Academic Affairs, 802-828-8777, E-mail: brian.webb@tui.edu.

The University of Akron, Graduate School, Buchtel College of Arts and Sciences, Department of English, Akron, OH 44325. Offers composition (MA); creative writing (MFA); literature (MA). Part-time programs available. *Faculty:* 19 full-time (8 women), 1 part-time/adjunct (0 women). *Students:* 39 full-time (22 women), 32 part-time (20 women); includes 4 minority (3 African Americans, 1 Hispanic American), 1 international. Average age 35. 44 applicants, 89% accepted, 26 enrolled. In 2007, 14 master's awarded. *Degree requirements:* For master's, thesis optional. *Entrance requirements:* For master's, BA in English, minimum GPA of 2.75, writing portfolio, letters of recommendation. Additional exam requirements/recommendations for international students: Required—TOEFL (minimum score 580 paper-based; 237 computer-based; 92 iBT). *Application deadline:* For fall admission, 2/15 priority date for domestic students; for spring admission, 10/15 priority date for domestic students. Applications are processed on a rolling basis. Application fee: $30 ($40 for international students). Electronic applications accepted. *Expenses:* Tuition, state resident: full-time $6,164; part-time $342 per credit. Tuition, nonresident: full-time $10,575; part-time $588 per credit. Required fees: $806; $43 per credit. $12 per term. Tuition and fees vary according to course load, degree level and program. *Financial support:* In 2007–08, 6 research assistantships with full tuition reimbursements, 17 teaching assistantships with full tuition reimbursements were awarded; scholarships/grants and unspecified assistantships also available. *Faculty research:* British and American literary studies, literary theory, creative writing, applied linguistics. Total annual research expenditures: $29,305. *Unit head:* Dr. Diana Reep, Chair, 330-972-6873, E-mail: dreep@uakron.edu. *Application contact:* Dr. Hillary Nunn, Director of Graduate Studies, 330-972-7601, E-mail: nunn@uakron.edu.

The University of Alabama, Graduate School, College of Arts and Sciences, Department of English, Tuscaloosa, AL 35487. Offers composition and rhetoric (PhD); creative writing (MFA), including fiction, poetry; literature (MA, PhD); rhetoric and composition (MA); teaching English as a second language (MATESOL). *Faculty:* 30 full-time (12 women). *Students:* 119 full-time (66 women), 16 part-time (12 women); includes 18 minority (11 African Americans, 2 American Indian/Alaska Native, 3 Asian Americans or Pacific Islanders, 2 Hispanic Americans), 7 international. Average age 28. 252 applicants, 20% accepted, 31 enrolled. In 2007, 28 master's, 7 doctorates awarded. *Median time to degree:* Of those who began their doctoral program in fall 1999, 100% received their degree in 8 years or less. *Degree requirements:* For master's, one foreign language, comprehensive exam, thesis (for some programs); for doctorate, 2 foreign languages, comprehensive exam, thesis/dissertation. *Entrance requirements:* For master's and doctorate, GRE, minimum GPA of 3.0, critical writing sample. Additional exam requirements/recommendations for international students: Required—TOEFL. *Application deadline:* For fall admission, 1/15 priority date for domestic students, 1/15 for international students. Application fee: $30. Electronic applications accepted. *Expenses:* Tuition, state resident: full-time $5,700. Tuition, nonresident: full-time $16,518. *Financial support:* In 2007–08, 7 fellowships with full tuition reimbursements (averaging $15,000 per year), 1 research assistantship (averaging $11,708 per year), 106 teaching assistantships with full tuition reimbursements (averaging $11,708 per year) were awarded; career-related internships or fieldwork, scholarships/grants, health care benefits, and unspecified assistantships also available. Financial award application deadline: 1/15. *Faculty research:* Critical theory; modern, Renaissance, and African-American literature. *Unit head:* Dr. Catherine E. Davies, Director of Graduate Studies, 205-348-8499, E-mail: cdavies@bama.ua.edu. *Application contact:* Vernita W. James, Office Assistant II, 205-348-0766, Fax: 205-348-1388, E-mail: vwjames@bama.ua.edu.

University of Alaska Anchorage, College of Arts and Sciences, Program in Creative Writing and Literary Arts, Anchorage, AK 99508-8060. Offers MFA. Part-time programs available. *Degree requirements:* For master's, comprehensive exam, thesis or alternative. *Entrance requirements:* For master's, portfolio, minimum GPA of 3.0. Additional exam requirements/recommendations for international students: Required—TOEFL (minimum score 550 paper-based; 213 computer-based). *Faculty research:* Alaska Quarterly Review publications, feminist studies, ecocriticism and native writing, poetry.

University of Alaska Fairbanks, College of Liberal Arts, Department of English, Fairbanks, AK 99775-7520. Offers creative writing (MFA); English (MA). Part-time programs available. *Degree requirements:* For master's, comprehensive exam, thesis or alternative, oral exams. *Entrance requirements:* For master's, GRE General Test. Additional exam requirements/recommendations for international students: Required—TOEFL (minimum score 550 paper-based; 213 computer-based). Electronic applications accepted. *Faculty research:* Traditional Alaskan native literature, British literature, pedagogy, American literature, rhetoric/composition history.

The University of Arizona, Graduate College, College of Humanities, Department of English, Program in Creative Writing, Tucson, AZ 85721. Offers MFA. *Students:* 278 applicants, 23% accepted. In 2007, 22 degrees awarded. *Entrance requirements:* For master's, minimum GPA of 3.0. Additional exam requirements/recommendations for international students: Required—TOEFL. *Application deadline:* For fall admission, 1/1 for domestic students, 12/1 for international students. Applications are processed on a rolling basis. Application fee: $50. Electronic applications accepted. *Financial support:* In 2007–08, fellowships with tuition reimbursements (averaging $3,000 per year), 35 teaching assistantships with partial tuition reimbursements (averaging $12,000 per year) were awarded; career-related internships or fieldwork, institutionally sponsored loans, health care benefits, tuition waivers (partial), and unspecified assistantships also available. *Unit head:* Aurelie Sheehan, Director, 520-621-3880, E-mail: sheehan@email.arizona.edu. *Application contact:* Marlene Cooksey, Graduate Secretary, 520-621-3880, Fax: 520-621-7397, E-mail: mcooksey@email.arizona.edu.

University of Arkansas, Graduate School, J. William Fulbright College of Arts and Sciences, Department of English, Program in Creative Writing, Fayetteville, AR 72701-1201. Offers MFA. *Students:* 14 full-time (4 women), 19 part-time (12 women); includes 3 minority (1 Asian American or Pacific Islander, 2 Hispanic Americans), 1 international. In 2007, 9 degrees awarded. *Degree requirements:* For master's, thesis. Application fee: $40 ($50 for international students). *Financial support:* In 2007–08, 23 fellowships with tuition reimbursements, 28 teaching assistantships were awarded; research assistantships, career-related internships or fieldwork and Federal Work-Study also available. Support available to part-time students. Financial award application deadline: 4/1; financial award applicants required to submit FAFSA. *Unit head:* Dr. Davis McCombs, Director, 479-575-4301, Fax: 479-575-5919, E-mail: dmccomb@uark.edu.

University of Arkansas at Little Rock, Graduate School, College of Arts, Humanities, and Social Science, Department of Rhetoric and Writing, Little Rock, AR 72204-1099. Offers professional and technical writing (MA). Part-time and evening/weekend programs available. *Students:* Average age 34. *Degree requirements:* For master's, thesis or alternative, oral defense of final project. *Entrance requirements:* For master's, GRE, minimum GPA of 3.0, writing portfolio. *Application deadline:* Applications are processed on a rolling basis. *Financial support:* Research assistantships with tuition reimbursements, teaching assistantships with tuition reimbursements, career-related internships or fieldwork, Federal Work-Study, institutionally sponsored loans, and unspecified assistantships available. Support available to part-time students. *Faculty research:* Writing for industry, science, business, and government; composition and rhetorical theory; writing nonfiction; teaching of writing. *Unit head:* Dr. George

Writing

University of Arkansas at Little Rock (continued)
H. Jensen, Chairperson, 501-569-3160, E-mail: ghjensen@ualr.edu. *Application contact:* Dr. Cynthia A. Nahrwold, Coordinator, 501-569-3316, Fax: 501-569-8279, E-mail: canahrwold@ualr.edu.

University of Baltimore, Graduate School, The Yale Gordon College of Liberal Arts, School of Communications Design, Program in Creative Writing and Publishing Arts, Baltimore, MD 21201-5779. Offers MFA. *Students:* 16 full-time (12 women), 24 part-time (15 women); includes 11 minority (5 African Americans, 1 American Indian/Alaska Native, 3 Asian Americans or Pacific Islanders, 2 Hispanic Americans). Average age 29. *Entrance requirements:* Additional exam requirements/recommendations for international students: Required—TOEFL. *Application deadline:* For fall admission, 3/31 for domestic and international students. Application fee: $45. *Expenses:* Tuition, state resident: part-time $518 per credit. Tuition, nonresident: part-time $751 per credit. Tuition and fees vary according to program. *Unit head:* Kendra Kopelke, Director, MFA in Creative Writing and Publishing Arts, 410-837-6026, E-mail: kkopelke@ubalt.edu. *Application contact:* Wendy Bolyard.

University of Baltimore, Graduate School, The Yale Gordon College of Liberal Arts, School of Communications Design, Program in Publications Design, Baltimore, MD 21201-5779. Offers MA. Part-time and evening/weekend programs available. *Faculty:* 6 full-time (3 women), 10 part-time/adjunct (6 women). *Students:* 42 full-time (35 women), 138 part-time (108 women); includes 41 minority (28 African Americans, 1 American Indian/Alaska Native, 5 Asian Americans or Pacific Islanders, 7 Hispanic Americans), 4 international. Average age 30. 102 applicants, 83% accepted, 78 enrolled. In 2007, 42 degrees awarded. *Degree requirements:* For master's, seminar project. *Entrance requirements:* For master's, minimum GPA of 3.0, portfolio, interview. Additional exam requirements/recommendations for international students: Required—TOEFL (minimum score 550 paper-based; 213 computer-based). *Application deadline:* For fall admission, 8/1 priority date for domestic students, 6/1 for international students; for spring admission, 12/15 for domestic students, 11/1 for international students. Applications are processed on a rolling basis. Application fee: $45. Electronic applications accepted. *Expenses:* Tuition, state resident: part-time $518 per credit. Tuition, nonresident: part-time $751 per credit. Tuition and fees vary according to program. *Financial support:* In 2007–08, 9 research assistantships were awarded; fellowships, career-related internships or fieldwork and Federal Work-Study also available. Support available to part-time students. Financial award application deadline: 4/1; financial award applicants required to submit FAFSA. *Faculty research:* Communication theory, graphic design, media technology. *Unit head:* Dr. Stephanie Gibson, Director, Main Publications Design, 410-837-6050, E-mail: sgibson@ubalt.edu. *Application contact:* Wendy Bolyard.

The University of British Columbia, Faculty of Arts, Creative Writing Program, Vancouver, BC V6T 1Z1, Canada. Offers creative writing (MFA); creative writing and film (MFA); creative writing and theatre (MFA). Part-time programs available. Postbaccalaureate distance learning degree programs offered (minimal on-campus study). *Faculty:* 7 full-time (4 women), 14 part-time/adjunct (7 women). *Students:* 57 full-time (41 women), 90 part-time (67 women). 308 applicants, 22% accepted, 62 enrolled. In 2007, 24 degrees awarded. *Degree requirements:* For master's, thesis. *Entrance requirements:* For master's, sample of written work. Additional exam requirements/recommendations for international students: Required—TOEFL (minimum score 550 paper-based; 213 computer-based). *Application deadline:* For fall admission, 11/7 for domestic and international students; for winter admission, 9/12 for domestic and international students. Application fee: $90 Canadian dollars ($150 Canadian dollars for international students). Electronic applications accepted. *Expenses:* Contact institution. *Financial support:* In 2007–08, 13 students received support, including 5 fellowships (averaging $16,000 per year), research assistantships (averaging $1,500 per year), 2 teaching assistantships (averaging $3,000 per year); Federal Work-Study, institutionally sponsored loans, and unspecified assistantships also available. *Faculty research:* Writing of fiction; poetry, creative nonfiction, plays for stage, screen, television, radio, writing for children and translation, song lyrics and libretto. *Unit head:* Keith Maillard, Chair, 604-822-3058, Fax: 604-822-3616. *Application contact:* Bryan Wade, Residential Graduate Adviser, 604-822-3023, Fax: 604-822-3616, E-mail: bwade@interchange.ubc.ca.

The University of British Columbia, Faculty of Arts and Faculty of Graduate Studies, Department of Theatre and Film, Film Program, Vancouver, BC V6T 1Z1, Canada. Offers creative writing and film production (MFA); film production (MFA, Diploma); film studies (MA). *Faculty:* 5 full-time (2 women). *Students:* 12 full-time (8 women). Average age 25. 22 applicants, 14% accepted, 2 enrolled. In 2007, 4 degrees awarded. *Degree requirements:* For master's, thesis (MA), thesis or project (MFA). *Entrance requirements:* For master's, bachelor's degree in film production or equivalent, BA in film studies. Additional exam requirements/recommendations for international students: Required—TOEFL (minimum score 600 paper-based). *Application deadline:* For fall admission, 2/1 for domestic and international students. Application fee: $90 Canadian dollars ($150 Canadian dollars for international students). Electronic applications accepted. *Financial support:* In 2007–08, 4 fellowships (averaging $18,000 per year), 2 research assistantships (averaging $4,000 per year), 9 teaching assistantships (averaging $9,933 per year) were awarded. Financial award application deadline: 1/1. *Faculty research:* Film history, theory, criticism; producing; experimental film. *Unit head:* Prof. Sharon McGowan, Chair, 604-822-9201, Fax: 604-822-0508, E-mail: sharonmcgowan@ubc.ca. *Application contact:* Zanna Downes, Secretary, 604-822-6037, Fax: 604-822-0508, E-mail: film@interchange.ubc.ca.

University of California, Davis, Graduate Studies, Program in English, Davis, CA 95616. Offers creative writing (MA); English (MA, PhD). Terminal master's awarded for partial completion of doctoral program. *Degree requirements:* For master's, one foreign language, thesis optional; for doctorate, 2 foreign languages, thesis/dissertation. *Entrance requirements:* For master's and doctorate, GRE General Test, GRE Subject Test, minimum GPA of 3.0, writing sample. Additional exam requirements/recommendations for international students: Required—TOEFL (minimum score 550 paper-based; 213 computer-based). Electronic applications accepted. *Faculty research:* Feminist theory, ethnic literature, literary theory, history of literature, literature of nature.

University of California, Irvine, Office of Graduate Studies, School of Humanities, Department of English and Comparative Literature, Program in Writing, Irvine, CA 92697. Offers creative writing (MFA), including fiction, poetry. *Faculty:* 4 full-time (1 woman), 2 part-time/adjunct (1 woman). *Students:* 30 full-time (16 women); includes 2 minority (1 Asian American or Pacific Islander, 1 Hispanic American). Average age 31. 319 applicants, 5% accepted, 10 enrolled. In 2007, 8 degrees awarded. *Degree requirements:* For master's, thesis. *Entrance requirements:* For master's, minimum GPA of 3.0, sample of written work. *Application deadline:* For fall admission, 1/15 for domestic students. Application fee: $60. Electronic applications accepted. *Financial support:* In 2007–08, research assistantships (averaging $15,000 per year), teaching assistantships with partial tuition reimbursements (averaging $14,145 per year) were awarded; fellowships with full and partial tuition reimbursements, institutionally sponsored loans and tuition waivers (full and partial) also available. Financial award application deadline: 3/2; financial award applicants required to submit FAFSA. *Unit head:* Director, 949-824-6718, Fax: 949-824-2916. *Application contact:* Arielle Read, Graduate Administrator, 949-824-6718, Fax: 949-824-2916, E-mail: eclgradapp@uci.edu.

University of California, Riverside, Graduate Division, Department of Creative Writing, Riverside, CA 92521-0102. Offers creative writing and writing for the performing arts (MFA). *Faculty:* 13 full-time (3 women). *Students:* 36 full-time (22 women); includes 10 minority (1 African American, 1 American Indian/Alaska Native, 4 Asian Americans or Pacific Islanders, 4 Hispanic Americans). Average age 34. In 2007, 13 degrees awarded. *Degree requirements:* For master's, thesis, final project. *Entrance requirements:* For master's, GRE General Test, writing sample. Additional exam requirements/recommendations for international students: Required—TOEFL (minimum score 550 paper-based; 213 computer-based; 80 iBT). *Application deadline:* For fall admission, 2/1 for domestic and international students; for winter admission, 9/1 for domestic students, 7/1 for international students; for spring admission, 12/1 for domestic students, 10/1 for international students. Applications are processed on a rolling basis. Application fee: $60 ($75 for international students). Electronic applications accepted. *Financial support:* In 2007–08, 1 fellowship with partial tuition reimbursement (averaging $12,000 per year) was awarded; research assistantships, teaching assistantships with partial tuition reimbursements. *Faculty research:* Non-fiction, playwriting, screenwriting. *Unit head:* Andrew Winer, Graduate Adviser, 951-827-3343, Fax: 951-827-4651, E-mail: andrew.winer@ucr.edu. *Application contact:* Cassee Cortez, Graduate Program Assistant, 951-827-3343, E-mail: performingarts@ucr.edu.

University of California, Santa Cruz, Division of Graduate Studies, Division of Social Sciences, Program in Social Documentation, Santa Cruz, CA 95064. Offers MA. *Students:* 7 full-time (3 women); includes 1 minority (Hispanic American), 2 international. *Entrance requirements:* For master's, writing sample, resumè or curriculum vitae, sample of documentary production work. *Application deadline:* For fall admission, 1/15 for domestic students. Electronic applications accepted. *Expenses:* Tuition, nonresident: full-time $14,694. Required fees:$11,360. *Unit head:* B. Ruby Rich, Director, 831-459-2428, Fax: 831-459-4979, E-mail: brrich@ucsc.edu. *Application contact:* Jessica Hayden, Graduate Program Coordinator, 831-459-4706, E-mail: jhayden@ucsc.edu.

University of Central Florida, College of Arts and Humanities, Department of English, Program in English, Orlando, FL 32816. Offers creative writing (MFA); English (MA). *Expenses:* Tuition, state resident: full-time $6,484. Tuition, nonresident: full-time $23,938. Tuition and fees vary according to program. *Financial support:* Fellowships, research assistantships, teaching assistantships available.

University of Central Oklahoma, College of Graduate Studies and Research, College of Liberal Arts, Department of English, Edmond, OK 73034-5209. Offers composition skills (MA); contemporary literature (MA); creative writing (MA); teaching English as a second language (MA); traditional studies (MA). Part-time programs available. *Faculty:* 18 full-time (9 women), 5 part-time/adjunct (2 women). *Students:* 31 full-time (16 women), 57 part-time (42 women); includes 11 minority (6 African Americans, 2 Asian Americans or Pacific Islanders, 3 Hispanic Americans), 3 international. Average age 33. 25 applicants, 100% accepted. In 2007, 17 degrees awarded. *Degree requirements:* For master's, one foreign language. *Entrance requirements:* For master's, 24 hours of course work in English language and literature. Additional exam requirements/recommendations for international students: Required—TOEFL (minimum score 550 paper-based; 213 computer-based). *Application deadline:* For fall admission, 7/1 for international students; for spring admission, 11/1 for international students. Applications are processed on a rolling basis. Application fee: $25. Electronic applications accepted. *Expenses:* Tuition, state resident: full-time $3,516; part-time $147 per hour. Tuition, nonresident: full-time $9,054; part-time $377 per hour. Required fees: $433; $18 per hour. *Financial support:* In 2007–08, 6 teaching assistantships with partial tuition reimbursements were awarded; career-related internships or fieldwork, Federal Work-Study, and unspecified assistantships also available. Financial award application deadline: 3/31; financial award applicants required to submit FAFSA. *Faculty research:* John Milton, Harriet Beecher Stowe. *Unit head:* Dr. David Macey, Chairman, 405-974-5894, Fax: 405-974-3823. *Application contact:* Dr. Kurt Hochènauer, Director, 405-974-5607 Ext. 5607, Fax: 405-974-3823.

University of Colorado at Boulder, Graduate School, College of Arts and Sciences, Department of English, Boulder, CO 80309. Offers literature (MA, PhD), including creative writing (MA). Part-time programs available. *Faculty:* 41. *Students:* 101 full-time (62 women), 23 part-time (15 women); includes 18 minority (2 African Americans, 5 Asian Americans or Pacific Islanders, 11 Hispanic Americans), 4 international. Average age 30. 43 applicants, 81% accepted. In 2007, 20 master's, 4 doctorates awarded. *Degree requirements:* For master's, one foreign language, comprehensive exam, thesis or alternative; for doctorate, 2 foreign languages, comprehensive exam, thesis/dissertation. *Entrance requirements:* For master's, GRE General Test, GRE Subject Test, minimum undergraduate GPA of 3.0; for doctorate, GRE General Test, GRE Subject Test. *Application deadline:* For fall admission, 1/1 for domestic students, 12/1 for international students. Application fee: $50 ($60 for international students). *Financial support:* In 2007–08, 24 fellowships (averaging $5,514 per year) were awarded; Federal Work-Study and tuition waivers (full) also available. Financial award application deadline: 1/1; financial award applicants required to submit FAFSA. *Faculty research:* Creative writing (MA), language, critical theory, literature. *Unit head:* Katherine Eggert, Chair, 303-492-7382, Fax: 303-492-8904, E-mail: katherine.eggert@colorado.edu. *Application contact:* Graduate Programs Assistant, 303-492-6434, Fax: 303-492-8904, E-mail: ssengl@colorado.edu.

University of Florida, Graduate School, College of Liberal Arts and Sciences, Department of English, Gainesville, FL 32611. Offers creative writing (MFA); English (MA, PhD). *Faculty:* 54 full-time (18 women), 1 (woman) part-time/adjunct. *Students:* 173 (99 women); includes 21 minority (9 African Americans, 6 Asian Americans or Pacific Islanders, 6 Hispanic Americans) 11 international. In 2007, 31 master's, 21 doctorates awarded. *Degree requirements:* For master's, variable foreign language requirement, thesis or alternative; for doctorate, thesis/dissertation. *Entrance requirements:* For master's and doctorate, GRE General Test, minimum GPA of 3.0. Additional exam requirements/recommendations for international students: Required—TOEFL (minimum score 550 paper-based; 213 computer-based). *Application deadline:* For fall admission, 1/15 for domestic students. Application fee: $30. Electronic applications accepted. *Expenses:* Tuition, state resident: full-time $7,478. Tuition, nonresident: full-time $22,603. *Financial support:* In 2007–08, 4 research assistantships with tuition reimbursements (averaging $14,050 per year), 61 teaching assistantships with tuition reimbursements (averaging $13,833 per year) were awarded; fellowships with tuition reimbursements, unspecified assistantships also available. Financial award application deadline: 1/15. *Unit head:* John Leavey, Chair, 352-392-6650 Ext. 230, Fax: 352-392-0860, E-mail: jpl@english.ufl.edu. *Application contact:* Dr. Pamela Gilbert, Coordinator, 352-392-6650 Ext. 231, Fax: 352-392-0860, E-mail: pgilbert@english.ufl.edu.

University of Georgia, Graduate School, College of Arts and Sciences, Department of English, Athens, GA 30602. Offers creative writing (MFA, PhD); English (MA, MAT, PhD). *Faculty:* 37 full-time (16 women). *Students:* 107 full-time (64 women), 18 part-time (12 women); includes 5 minority (all African Americans) 241 applicants, 33% accepted, 23 enrolled. In 2007, 25 master's, 4 doctorates awarded. *Degree requirements:* For master's, one foreign language, thesis (MA); for doctorate, 2 foreign languages, thesis/dissertation. *Entrance requirements:* For master's and doctorate, GRE General Test. Additional exam requirements/recommendations for international students: Required—TWE. *Application deadline:* For fall admission, 7/1 priority date for domestic students; for spring admission, 11/15 for domestic students. Application fee: $50. Electronic applications accepted. *Financial support:* Fellowships, research assistantships, teaching assistantships, unspecified assistantships available. *Unit head:* Dr. Valerie Babb, Head, 706-543-0378, Fax: 706-542-2181, E-mail: vbabb@uga.edu. *Application contact:* Dr. Kris Boudreau, Graduate Coordinator, 706-542-3110, E-mail: boudreau@uga.edu.

University of Houston, College of Liberal Arts and Social Sciences, Department of English, Houston, TX 77204. Offers applied English linguistics (MA); English and American literature (MA, PhD); literature and creative writing (MA, MFA, PhD). Postbaccalaureate distance learning degree programs offered. *Faculty:* 26 full-time (9 women), 6 part-time/adjunct (3 women). *Students:* 85 full-time (39 women), 65 part-time (51 women); includes 17 minority (3 African Americans, 6 Asian Americans or Pacific Islanders, 8 Hispanic Americans), 6 international. Average age 32. 63 applicants, 73% accepted, 29 enrolled. In 2007, 19 master's, 14 doctorates awarded. *Degree requirements:* For master's, one foreign language, thesis (for some programs); for doctorate, 2 foreign languages, comprehensive exam, thesis/dissertation. *Entrance requirements:* For master's, GRE General Test, GRE Subject Test, minimum GPA of 3.0 in last 60 hours of course work; for doctorate, GRE General Test, GRE Subject Test, writing sample. Additional exam requirements/recommendations for international students: Required—TOEFL. *Application deadline:* For fall admission, 1/1 priority date for domestic students. Applications are processed on a rolling basis. Application fee: $50. *Expenses:* Tuition, state resident: full-time $6,297; part-time $262 per credit. Tuition, nonresident: full-time $12,969; part-time $540 per credit. Required fees: $2,696. *Financial support:* In 2007–08, 2 fellowships with full tuition reimbursements (averaging $1,700 per year), 72 teaching assistantships with full tuition reimbursements (averaging $1,200 per year) were awarded; research assistantships with full tuition reimbursements, career-related internships or fieldwork, Federal Work-Study, institutionally sponsored loans, scholarships/grants, health care benefits, and unspecified assistantships also available. Support available to part-time students. Financial award application deadline: 2/1. *Unit head:* Wyman Henderson, Chairperson, 713-743-3004, Fax: 713-743-3215, E-mail: whh@uh.edu. *Application contact:* Ruby Jones, Advising Assistant, 713-743-2941, Fax: 713-743-3215, E-mail: rjones@uh.edu.

University of Houston–Downtown, Graduate Programs, College of Humanities and Social Sciences, Department of English, Houston, TX 77002-1001. Offers professional writing and technical communication (MS). Part-time and evening/weekend programs available. *Faculty:* 5 full-time (4 women). *Students:* 4 full-time (3 women), 23 part-time (19 women); includes 14 minority (9 African Americans, 3 Asian Americans or Pacific Islanders, 2 Hispanic Americans). Average age 40. In 2007, 4 degrees awarded. *Degree requirements:* For master's, thesis (for some programs). *Entrance requirements:* For master's, GRE, resumé, personal statement, writing sample, 3 letters of recommendation. Additional exam requirements/recommendations for international students: Required—TOEFL (minimum score 600 paper-based; 250 computer-based; 86 iBT). *Application deadline:* For fall admission, 3/31 for domestic and international students; for spring admission, 11/30 for domestic and international students. Applications are processed on a rolling basis. Application fee: $35 ($60 for international students). Electronic applications accepted. *Expenses:* Tuition, state resident: full-time $3,060; part-time $170 per credit. Tuition, nonresident: full-time $7,434; part-time $413 per credit. Required fees: $704. *Financial support:* Application deadline: 4/1; *Unit head:* Dr. William Gilbert, Chair, 713-221-8013, Fax: 713-226-5205, E-mail: gilbertw@uhd.edu. *Application contact:* Traneshia Parker, Assistant Director of Admissions, Graduate and International Admissions, 713-221-8910, Fax: 713-223-7984, E-mail: parkert@uhd.edu.

University of Idaho, College of Graduate Studies, College of Letters, Arts and Social Sciences, Department of English, Program in Creative Writing, Moscow, ID 83844-2282. Offers MFA. *Students:* 36 (20 women). Average age 32. In 2007, 11 degrees awarded. *Entrance requirements:* For master's, minimum GPA of 2.8. *Application deadline:* For fall admission, 8/1 for domestic students; for spring admission, 12/15 for domestic students. Application fee: $55 ($60 for international students). *Financial support:* Application deadline: 2/15. *Unit head:* Dr. Kurt Olsson, Chair, Department of English, 208-883-6156.

University of Illinois at Chicago, Graduate College, College of Liberal Arts and Sciences, Department of English, Chicago, IL 60607-7128. Offers English (MA, PhD), including creative writing, language, literacy and rhetoric (PhD), literature, teaching of English (MA); language, literacy, and rhetoric (PhD); linguistics (MA), including applied linguistics (teaching English as a second language). Part-time and evening/weekend programs available. *Degree requirements:* For doctorate, variable foreign language requirement, thesis/dissertation, written and oral exams. *Entrance requirements:* For master's, GRE General Test, GRE Subject Test; for doctorate, GRE General Test, GRE Subject Test, minimum GPA of 2.0. Additional exam requirements/recommendations for international students: Required—TOEFL. Electronic applications accepted. *Faculty research:* Literary history and theory.

University of Illinois at Urbana–Champaign, Graduate College, College of Liberal Arts and Sciences, Department of English, Champaign, IL 61820. Offers creative writing (MFA); English (MA, PhD). *Faculty:* 60 full-time (25 women), 1 (woman) part-time/adjunct. *Students:* 84 full-time (54 women), 69 part-time (42 women); includes 14 minority (6 African Americans, 1 American Indian/Alaska Native, 5 Asian Americans or Pacific Islanders, 2 Hispanic Americans), 15 international. 323 applicants, 8% accepted, 24 enrolled. In 2007, 19 master's, 8 doctorates awarded. *Degree requirements:* For master's, one foreign language, area exams; for doctorate, one foreign language, thesis/dissertation, special field exam. *Entrance requirements:* For master's and doctorate, GRE General Test, GRE Subject Test, minimum GPA of 3.0. *Application deadline:* For fall admission, 1/5 for domestic students; for spring admission, 1/5 for domestic students. Applications are processed on a rolling basis. Application fee: $60 ($75 for international students). Electronic applications accepted. *Financial support:* In 2007–08, 65 fellowships, 9 research assistantships, 124 teaching assistantships were awarded. Financial award application deadline: 2/15. *Faculty research:* English and American literature, cultural studies and critical theory. *Unit head:* Martin Camargo, Head, 217-333-2390, Fax: 217-333-4321, E-mail: mcamargo@uiuc.edu. *Application contact:* Stephanie Shockey, Secretary, 217-244-3646, Fax: 217-333-4321, E-mail: shockey@uiuc.edu.

The University of Iowa, Graduate College, College of Liberal Arts and Sciences, Department of English, Iowa City, IA 52242-1316. Offers English (PhD); literary criticism (PhD); literary history (PhD); literary studies (MA); nonfiction writing (MFA); rhetorical theory and stylistics (PhD); writer's workshop (MFA); JD/PhD. *Faculty:* 54 full-time, 41 part-time/adjunct. *Students:* 158 full-time (90 women), 89 part-time (53 women); includes 40 minority (16 African Americans, 3 American Indian/Alaska Native, 13 Asian Americans or Pacific Islanders, 8 Hispanic Americans), 11 international. 1,337 applicants, 9% accepted, 72 enrolled. In 2007, 72 master's, 12 doctorates awarded. *Degree requirements:* For master's, thesis (for some programs), exam; for doctorate, comprehensive exam, thesis/dissertation. *Entrance requirements:* For master's and doctorate, GRE General Test, minimum GPA of 3.0. Additional exam requirements/recommendations for international students: Required—TOEFL (minimum score 640 paper-based; 273 computer-based; 112 iBT). Application fee: $60 ($85 for international students). Electronic applications accepted. *Expenses:* Tuition, state resident: part-time $349 per hour. Tuition, nonresident: part-time $349 per hour. Tuition and fees vary according to course load and program. *Financial support:* In 2007–08, 31 fellowships, 21 research assistantships with partial tuition reimbursements, 160 teaching assistantships with partial tuition reimbursements were awarded. Financial award applicants required to submit FAFSA. *Unit head:* Jonathan Wilcox, Chair, 319-335-0454, Fax: 319-335-2535.

University of Kansas, Research and Graduate Studies, College of Liberal Arts and Sciences, Department of English, Lawrence, KS 66045. Offers creative writing (MFA); English (MA, PhD). Part-time programs available. *Faculty:* 39. *Students:* 80 full-time (55 women), 31 part-time (21 women); includes 8 minority (4 African Americans, 4 Hispanic Americans), 6 international. Average age 33. 148 applicants, 31% accepted, 27 enrolled. In 2007, 19 master's, 4 doctorates awarded. *Degree requirements:* For master's, one foreign language, comprehensive exam (for some programs), thesis or alternative; for doctorate, 2 foreign languages, comprehensive exam, thesis/dissertation. *Entrance requirements:* For master's and doctorate, GRE General Test, minimum GPA of 3.3. Additional exam requirements/recommendations for international students: Required—TOEFL. *Application deadline:* For fall admission, 1/1 priority date for domestic and international students. Applications are processed on a rolling basis. Application fee: $55 ($60 for international students). Electronic applications accepted. *Expenses:* Tuition, state resident: full-time $5,838. Tuition, nonresident: full-time $13,409. Tuition and fees vary according to program. *Financial support:* Fellowships, research assistantships, teaching assistantships with full and partial tuition reimbursements, unspecified assistantships available. Financial award application deadline: 1/1. *Faculty research:* African-American literature, 20th century American literature, renaissance literature, creative writing. *Unit head:* Dorice Elliott, Chair, 785-864-4520, E-mail: delliott@ku.edu. *Application contact:* Byron Caminero-Santangelo, Director of Graduate Studies, 785-864-2522, E-mail: bsantang@ku.edu.

University of Louisiana at Lafayette, Graduate School, College of Liberal Arts, Department of English, Lafayette, LA 70504. Offers British and American literature (MA), including creative writing, folklore, rhetoric; creative writing (PhD); literature (PhD); rhetoric (PhD). Part-time programs available. Terminal master's awarded for partial completion of doctoral program. *Degree requirements:* For master's, one foreign language, thesis or alternative; for doctorate, 2 foreign languages, comprehensive exam, thesis/dissertation. *Entrance requirements:* For master's, GRE General Test, minimum GPA of 2.75; for doctorate, GRE General Test, minimum GPA of 3.0. Additional exam requirements/recommendations for international students: Required—TOEFL (minimum score 550 paper-based; 213 computer-based). Electronic applications accepted. *Faculty research:* Composition theory, Southern literature, medieval literature.

University of Maryland, College Park, Graduate Studies, College of Arts and Humanities, Department of English, Creative Writing Program, College Park, MD 20742. Offers MA, MFA, PhD. *Students:* 30 full-time (19 women), 13 part-time (6 women); includes 7 minority (3 African Americans, 3 Asian Americans or Pacific Islanders, 1 Hispanic American), 1 international. 141 applicants, 28% accepted, 14 enrolled. In 2007, 16 degrees awarded. *Degree requirements:* For master's, thesis optional, written exam; for doctorate, one foreign language, oral and written exams. *Entrance requirements:* For master's, GRE General Test, minimum GPA of 3.5, writing sample, 3 letters of recommendation. Additional exam requirements/recommendations for international students: Required—TOEFL. *Application deadline:* For fall admission, 1/15 for domestic students, 2/1 for international students. Applications are processed on a rolling basis. Application fee: $60. Electronic applications accepted. *Financial support:* In 2007–08, 2 fellowships (averaging $14,000 per year), 17 teaching assistantships (averaging $15,326 per year) were awarded; research assistantships. Financial award applicants required to submit FAFSA. *Faculty research:* Early British literature, American literature. *Application contact:* Dean of Graduate School, 301-405-4190, Fax: 301-314-9305.

University of Massachusetts Amherst, Graduate School, College of Humanities and Fine Arts, Department of English, Amherst, MA 01003. Offers creative writing (MFA); English and American literature (MA, PhD). Part-time programs available. *Faculty:* 42 full-time (20 women). *Students:* 97 full-time (50 women), 94 part-time (55 women); includes 27 minority (11 African Americans, 1 American Indian/Alaska Native, 7 Asian Americans or Pacific Islanders, 8 Hispanic Americans), 8 international. Average age 30. 878 applicants, 16% accepted, 52 enrolled. In 2007, 32 master's, 12 doctorates awarded. Terminal master's awarded for partial completion of doctoral program. *Degree requirements:* For master's, one foreign language, thesis optional; for doctorate, one foreign language, thesis/dissertation. *Entrance requirements:* For master's, GRE General Test, GRE Subject Test (MA), writing sample (MFA); for doctorate, GRE General Test, GRE Subject Test. Additional exam requirements/recommendations for international students: Required—TOEFL (minimum score 530 paper-based; 197 computer-based). *Application deadline:* For fall admission, 1/15 priority date for domestic and international students. Applications are processed on a rolling basis. Application fee: $50 ($65 for international students). Electronic applications accepted. *Expenses:* Tuition, state resident: full-time $2,640; part-time $110 per credit. Tuition, nonresident: full-time $9,936; part-time $414 per credit. Required fees: $7,455. One-time fee: $332. Tuition and fees vary according to course load, campus/location, program and reciprocity agreements. *Financial support:* In 2007–08, 4 fellowships with full tuition reimbursements (averaging $5,766 per year), 7 research assistantships with full tuition reimbursements (averaging $7,803 per year), 41 teaching assistantships with full tuition reimbursements (averaging $8,477 per year) were awarded; career-related internships or fieldwork, Federal Work-Study, scholarships/grants, traineeships, and unspecified assistantships also available. Support available to part-time students. Financial award application deadline: 1/15. *Unit head:* Dr. Joseph Bartolomeo, Head, 413-545-2575, Fax: 413-545-3880. *Application contact:* 413-545-0643.

University of Massachusetts Dartmouth, Graduate School, College of Arts and Sciences, Program in Professional Writing, North Dartmouth, MA 02747-2300. Offers MA, Post-baccalaureate Certificate. Part-time programs available. *Faculty:* 24 full-time (9 women), 37 part-time/adjunct (26 women). *Students:* 10 full-time (4 women), 17 part-time (16 women); includes 1 minority (African American), 2 international. Average age 34. 20 applicants, 75% accepted, 5 enrolled. In 2007, 8 degrees awarded. *Degree requirements:* For master's, thesis. *Entrance requirements:* For master's, MAT or GRE, portfolio or writing sample (10-30 pages), 3 letters of recommendation. Additional exam requirements/recommendations for international students: Required—TOEFL (minimum score 500 paper-based). *Application deadline:* For fall admission, 4/1 for domestic students, 2/1 for international students; for spring admission, 11/1 for domestic students, 9/1 for international students. Application fee: $40 ($60 for international students). Electronic applications accepted. *Expenses:* Tuition, state resident: full-time $2,071; part-time $86 per credit. Tuition, nonresident: full-time $8,099; part-time $337 per credit. Part-time tuition and fees vary according to course load and program. *Financial support:* In 2007–08, 1 research assistantship (averaging $9,800 per year), 12 teaching assistantships with full tuition reimbursements (averaging $10,450 per year) were awarded; career-related internships or fieldwork, Federal Work-Study, and unspecified assistantships also available. Support available to part-time students. Financial award application deadline: 3/1; financial award applicants required to submit FAFSA. *Unit head:* Dr. Jerry Blitefield, Director, 508-910-6601, Fax: 508-999-9325, E-mail: jblitefield@umassd.edu. *Application contact:* Carol Novo, Graduate Admissions Officer, 508-999-8604, Fax: 508-999-8183, E-mail: graduate@umassd.edu.

University of Memphis, Graduate School, College of Arts and Sciences, Department of English, Memphis, TN 38152. Offers creative writing (MFA); English (MA); writing and language studies (PhD). Part-time programs available. *Faculty:* 33 full-time (17 women), 1 (woman) part-time/adjunct. *Students:* 46 full-time (32 women), 65 part-time (50 women); includes 24 minority (18 African Americans, 5 Asian Americans or Pacific Islanders, 1 Hispanic American), 4 international. Average age 34. 117 applicants, 74% accepted, 28 enrolled. In 2007, 28 master's, 3 doctorates awarded. Terminal master's awarded for partial completion of doctoral program. *Degree requirements:* For master's, one foreign language, comprehensive exam, thesis or alternative; for doctorate, 2 foreign languages, comprehensive exam, thesis/dissertation. *Entrance requirements:* For master's, GRE General Test or MAT, minimum GPA of 2.5; for doctorate, GRE General Test, minimum GPA of 3.0. *Application deadline:* For fall admission, 8/1 for domestic students; for spring admission, 12/1 for domestic students. Applications are processed on a rolling basis. Application fee: $35 ($60 for international students). *Expenses:* Tuition, state resident: full-time $6,990; part-time $377 per hour. Tuition, nonresident: full-time $17,818; part-time $830 per hour. Tuition and fees vary according to course load and program. *Financial support:* In 2007–08, 9 research assistantships with full tuition reimbursements (averaging $3,450 per year), 42 teaching assistantships with full tuition reimbursements (averaging $3,650 per year) were awarded. *Faculty research:* American literature, cultural studies, ESL/linguistics, composition studies/professional writing. *Unit head:* Dr. Steve E. Tabachnick, Chair, 901-678-2651, Fax: 901-678-2226, E-mail: stbchnck@memphis.edu. *Application contact:* Dr. Verner D. Mitchell, Director, Graduate Studies, 901-678-3099, Fax: 901-678-2226, E-mail: vdmtchll@memphis.edu.

University of Miami, Graduate School, College of Arts and Sciences, Department of English, Coral Gables, FL 33124. Offers creative writing (MFA); English (MA, PhD). Part-time programs available. *Faculty:* 30 full-time (14 women), 1 (woman) part-time/adjunct. *Students:* 56 full-time (38 women), 2 part-time (both women); includes 16 minority (5 African Americans, 1 Asian American or Pacific Islander, 10 Hispanic Americans), 7 international. Average age 30. 109 applicants, 26% accepted, 18 enrolled. In 2007, 17 master's, 6 doctorates awarded. Terminal master's awarded for partial completion of doctoral program. *Median time to degree:* Of those who began their doctoral program in fall 1999, 63% received their degree in 8 years or less. *Degree requirements:* For master's, one foreign language, thesis optional; for doctorate, one foreign language, thesis/dissertation. *Entrance requirements:* For master's and doctorate, GRE General Test. *Application deadline:* For fall admission, 2/1 priority date for domestic students. Applications are processed on a rolling basis. Application fee: $50. Electronic applications accepted. *Financial support:* In 2007–08, 47 students received support, including 6 fellowships with full tuition reimbursements available (averaging $20,000 per year), 41 teaching assistantships with full tuition reimbursements available (averaging $16,000 per year); institutionally sponsored loans and unspecified assistantships also available. Financial award application deadline: 2/1; financial award applicants required to submit FAFSA. *Faculty research:* Anglo-Irish literature, feminist criticism and theory, Caribbean literature, early modern literature and culture, postcolonial and ethnic studies. *Unit head:* Prof. Patrick A. McCarthy, Department Chair, 305-284-3840. *Application contact:* Prof. Mihoko Suzuki, Director of Graduate Studies, 305-284-3840, E-mail: englishgrad@miami.edu.

University of Michigan, Horace H. Rackham School of Graduate Studies, College of Literature, Science, and the Arts, Department of English Language and Literature, Creative Writing

Writing

University of Michigan (continued)
Program, Ann Arbor, MI 48109. Offers MFA. *Faculty:* 8 full-time (5 women). *Students:* 47 full-time (36 women); includes 7 minority (all Asian Americans or Pacific Islanders), 3 international. 349 applicants, 7% accepted, 24 enrolled. In 2007, 24 degrees awarded. *Degree requirements:* For master's, comprehensive exam, thesis. *Entrance requirements:* For master's, writing sample. Additional exam requirements/recommendations for international students: Required—TOEFL (minimum score 620 paper-based; 260 computer-based; 106 iBT). *Application deadline:* For fall admission, 1/1 for domestic and international students. Application fee: $60 ($75 for international students). Electronic applications accepted. *Financial support:* Fellowships with tuition reimbursements, teaching assistantships with tuition reimbursements, health care benefits available. *Faculty research:* Prose, poetry. *Unit head:* Eileen Pollack, Director, 734-764-1817. *Application contact:* Graduate Admissions Office, 734-936-2274, Fax: 734-763-3128, E-mail: grad.eng.admis@um.cc.umich.edu.

University of Missouri–St. Louis, College of Arts and Sciences, Department of English, St. Louis, MO 63121. Offers American literature (MA); creative writing (MFA); English (MA); English literature (MA); linguistics (MA); teaching of writing (Graduate Certificate). *Faculty:* 19 full-time (12 women), 1 part-time/adjunct (0 women). *Students:* 16 full-time (12 women), 90 part-time (68 women); includes 9 minority (5 African Americans, 3 Asian Americans or Pacific Islanders, 1 Hispanic American). Average age 32. In 2007, 30 degrees awarded. *Degree requirements:* For master's, thesis optional. *Entrance requirements:* For master's, GRE General Test, writing sample. Additional exam requirements/recommendations for international students: Required—TOEFL (minimum score 550 paper-based; 213 computer-based). *Application deadline:* For fall admission, 7/15 priority date for domestic students; for spring admission, 12/15 priority date for domestic students. Applications are processed on a rolling basis. Application fee: $35 ($40 for international students). Electronic applications accepted. *Financial support:* In 2007–08, 1 research assistantship (averaging $9,000 per year), 6 teaching assistantships with full and partial tuition reimbursements (averaging $9,000 per year) were awarded. *Faculty research:* Victorian literature, Shakespeare and Renaissance literature, eighteenth century literature, composition theory. *Unit head:* Dr. Richard Cook, Director of Graduate Studies, 314-516-5516, Fax: 314-516-5415, E-mail: rcook@umsl.edu. *Application contact:* 314-516-5458, Fax: 314-516-5310, E-mail: gradadm@umsl.edu.

The University of Montana, Graduate School, College of Arts and Sciences, Department of English, Program in Creative Writing, Missoula, MT 59812-0002. Offers fiction (MFA); nonfiction (MFA); poetry (MFA). *Degree requirements:* For master's, final creative paper. *Entrance requirements:* For master's, GRE General Test, sample of written work. Additional exam requirements/recommendations for international students: Required—TOEFL. *Faculty research:* Fiction, poetry, nonfiction.

University of Nebraska at Kearney, College of Graduate Study, College of Fine Arts and Humanities, Department of English, Kearney, NE 68849-0001. Offers creative writing (MA); literature (MA). Part-time and evening/weekend programs available. *Degree requirements:* For master's, thesis optional. *Entrance requirements:* For master's, GRE General Test, writing samples. Additional exam requirements/recommendations for international students: Required—TOEFL (minimum score 550 paper-based; 213 computer-based). Electronic applications accepted. *Faculty research:* Narrative theory, popular culture, western and plains literature, women's studies, media studies.

University of Nebraska at Omaha, Graduate Studies and Research, College of Arts and Sciences, Department of English, Omaha, NE 68182. Offers advanced writing (Certificate); English (MA); teaching English to speakers of other languages (Certificate); technical communication (Certificate). Part-time and evening/weekend programs available. *Faculty:* 17 full-time (9 women). *Students:* 11 full-time (8 women), 49 part-time (33 women); includes 3 minority (1 African American, 1 Asian American or Pacific Islander, 1 Hispanic American), 2 international. Average age 34. 39 applicants, 72% accepted, 20 enrolled. In 2007, 13 master's, 9 other advanced degrees awarded. *Degree requirements:* For master's, comprehensive exam, thesis (for some programs). *Entrance requirements:* For master's, minimum GPA of 3.0, statement of purpose, 3 letters of recommendation, writing sample. Additional exam requirements/recommendations for international students: Required—TOEFL (minimum score 600 paper-based; 250 computer-based; 100 iBT). *Application deadline:* For fall admission, 8/1 priority date for domestic students; for spring admission, 12/1 priority date for domestic students. Applications are processed on a rolling basis. Application fee: $45. Electronic applications accepted. *Financial support:* In 2007–08, 30 students received support; fellowships, teaching assistantships with tuition reimbursements available, Federal Work-Study, institutionally sponsored loans, scholarships/grants, tuition waivers (partial), and unspecified assistantships available. Support available to part-time students. Financial award application deadline: 3/1; financial award applicants required to submit FAFSA. *Unit head:* Dr. Susan Maher, Chairperson, 402-554-3636. *Application contact:* Dr. Joan Latchaw, Student Contact, 402-554-3636.

University of Nebraska at Omaha, Graduate Studies and Research, Program in Writing, Omaha, NE 68182. Offers MFA. Postbaccalaureate distance learning degree programs offered (no on-campus study). *Students:* 35 full-time (22 women); includes 1 minority (Asian American or Pacific Islander) Average age 36. 26 applicants, 73% accepted, 9 enrolled. In 2007, 18 degrees awarded. *Degree requirements:* For master's, comprehensive exam. *Entrance requirements:* For master's, portfolio, letters of recommendation. Additional exam requirements/recommendations for international students: Required—TOEFL (minimum score 550 paper-based; 213 computer-based; 80 iBT). *Application deadline:* For fall admission, 2/15 priority date for domestic students; for spring admission, 7/15 priority date for domestic students. Applications are processed on a rolling basis. Application fee: $45. Electronic applications accepted. *Financial support:* In 2007–08, 27 students received support. Scholarships/grants and tuition waivers (partial) available. Financial award application deadline: 3/1; financial award applicants required to submit FAFSA. *Unit head:* Dr. Richard Duggin, Director, 402-554-4801.

University of Nevada, Las Vegas, Graduate College, College of Liberal Arts, Department of English, Las Vegas, NV 89154-9900. Offers creative writing (MFA); English (PhD); language/composition theory study (MA); literature study (MA). Part-time programs available. *Faculty:* 37 full-time (12 women), 1 part-time/adjunct (0 women). *Students:* 63 full-time (29 women), 27 part-time (15 women); includes 6 minority (3 Asian Americans or Pacific Islanders, 3 Hispanic Americans), 4 international. 118 applicants, 22% accepted, 18 enrolled. In 2007, 16 master's, 5 doctorates awarded. *Degree requirements:* For master's, one foreign language, comprehensive exam, thesis (for some programs); for doctorate, 2 foreign languages, comprehensive exam, thesis/dissertation. *Entrance requirements:* For master's, GRE General Test, GRE Subject Test, minimum GPA of 3.0 during previous 2 years, 2.75 overall; for doctorate, GRE General Test, GRE Subject Test, MA in English, minimum GPA of 3.5. Additional exam requirements/recommendations for international students: Required—TOEFL (minimum score 550 paper-based; 213 computer-based; 80 iBT). *Application deadline:* For fall admission, 2/15 for domestic and international students. Application fee: $60 ($75 for international students). Electronic applications accepted. *Expenses:* Tuition, state resident: part-time $198 per credit. Tuition, nonresident: part-time $416 per credit. Required fees: $256 per semester. Tuition and fees vary according to course load and reciprocity agreements. *Financial support:* In 2007–08, 2 research assistantships with partial tuition reimbursements (averaging $10,000 per year), 52 teaching assistantships with partial tuition reimbursements (averaging $11,000 per year) were awarded; career-related internships or fieldwork, Federal Work-Study, institutionally sponsored loans, scholarships/grants, health care benefits, and unspecified assistantships also available. Support available to part-time students. Financial award application deadline: 3/1. *Unit head:* Dr. Chris Hudgins, Chair, 702-895-3533. *Application contact:* Graduate College Admissions Evaluator, 702-895-3320, Fax: 702-895-4180, E-mail: gradcollege@unlv.edu.

University of New Hampshire, Graduate School, College of Liberal Arts, Department of English, Durham, NH 03824. Offers English (MFA, PhD); English education (MST); language and linguistics (MA); literature (MA); writing (MA). Part-time programs available. *Faculty:* 44 full-time. *Students:* 38 full-time (21 women), 64 part-time (43 women); includes 6 minority (1 American Indian/Alaska Native, 3 Asian Americans or Pacific Islanders, 2 Hispanic Americans), 3 international. Average age 34. 251 applicants, 45% accepted, 31 enrolled. In 2007, 25 master's, 6 doctorates awarded. *Degree requirements:* For master's, one foreign language; for doctorate, 2 foreign languages, thesis/dissertation. *Entrance requirements:* For master's, GRE General Test, sample of written work; for doctorate, GRE General Test, GRE Subject Test, sample of written work. Additional exam requirements/recommendations for international students: Required—TOEFL (minimum score 550 paper-based; 213 computer-based; 80 iBT). *Application deadline:* For fall admission, 2/15 priority date for domestic students, 2/15 for international students. Applications are processed on a rolling basis. Application fee: $60. Electronic applications accepted. *Financial support:* In 2007–08, 1 fellowship, 1 research assistantship, 43 teaching assistantships were awarded; career-related internships or fieldwork, Federal Work-Study, scholarships/grants, and tuition waivers (full and partial) also available. Support available to part-time students. Financial award application deadline: 2/15. *Unit head:* Dr. Andrew Merton, Chairperson, 603-862-3977. *Application contact:* Sue Smith, Administrative Assistant, 603-862-3963, E-mail: engl.grad@unh.edu.

University of New Mexico, Graduate School, College of Arts and Sciences, Department of English, Albuquerque, NM 87131-2039. Offers creative writing (MFA); English (MA, PhD). Part-time programs available. *Faculty:* 46 full-time (24 women), 37 part-time/adjunct (28 women). *Students:* 81 full-time (62 women), 28 part-time (19 women); includes 26 minority (2 African Americans, 3 American Indian/Alaska Native, 4 Asian Americans or Pacific Islanders, 17 Hispanic Americans), 3 international. Average age 36. 191 applicants, 27% accepted, 28 enrolled. In 2007, 14 master's, 15 doctorates awarded. *Degree requirements:* For master's, one foreign language, comprehensive exam (for some programs), thesis (for some programs), portfolio; for doctorate, 2 foreign languages, comprehensive exam, thesis/dissertation. *Entrance requirements:* For master's, GRE General Test, GRE Subject Test (literature MA), writing sample; for doctorate, GRE General Test, GRE Subject Test, writing sample. *Application deadline:* For fall admission, 1/15 for domestic students; for spring admission, 11/1 for domestic students. Application fee: $50. Electronic applications accepted. *Financial support:* In 2007–08, 3 fellowships (averaging $11,283 per year), 75 teaching assistantships with full tuition reimbursements (averaging $13,184 per year) were awarded; career-related internships or fieldwork, scholarships/grants, health care benefits, and unspecified assistantships also available. Financial award application deadline: 2/1; financial award applicants required to submit FAFSA. *Faculty research:* American literature, Native American literature, Chicana/o literature, British and Irish literature, creative writing, rhetoric and writing. Total annual research expenditures: $3,000. *Unit head:* Dr. David Richard Jones, Chair, 505-277-6347, Fax: 505-277-0021, E-mail: djones@unm.edu. *Application contact:* N. Ezra Meier, Graduate Advisor, 505-277-4437, Fax: 505-277-0021, E-mail: english@unm.edu.

University of New Mexico, Graduate School, College of Arts and Sciences, Program in Creative Writing, Albuquerque, NM 87131-2039. Offers MFA. *Students:* 28 full-time (19 women), 9 part-time (7 women); includes 12 minority (1 African American, 1 American Indian/Alaska Native, 2 Asian Americans or Pacific Islanders, 8 Hispanic Americans). Average age 34. 109 applicants, 17% accepted, 11 enrolled. *Degree requirements:* For master's, comprehensive exam, thesis. *Entrance requirements:* For master's, writing sample. *Application deadline:* For fall admission, 1/15 for domestic students. Application fee: $50. *Financial support:* In 2007–08, 75 teaching assistantships with full tuition reimbursements were awarded. Financial award application deadline: 1/15. *Faculty research:* Creative writing, fiction, creative non-fiction, poetry. *Application contact:* Vicki Hall, Academic Administrator III, 505-277-6131, Fax: 505-277-0351, E-mail: vhall@unm.edu.

University of New Mexico, Graduate School, College of Fine Arts, Department of Theatre and Dance, Albuquerque, NM 87131-2039. Offers dramatic writing (MFA); theater and dance (MA). *Accreditation:* NASD; NAST. *Faculty:* 12 full-time (7 women), 28 part-time/adjunct (18 women). *Students:* 16 full-time (11 women), 5 part-time (3 women); includes 7 minority (2 American Indian/Alaska Native, 1 Asian American or Pacific Islander, 4 Hispanic Americans), 1 international. Average age 35. 22 applicants, 200% accepted, 6 enrolled. In 2007, 1 master's awarded. *Degree requirements:* For master's, comprehensive exam (for some programs), thesis (for some programs). *Entrance requirements:* For master's, minimum GPA of 3.0, undergraduate major in theatre, dance or closely related field, 3 letters of recommendation, letter of intent. *Application deadline:* For fall admission, 4/15 for domestic students; for spring admission, 11/10 for domestic students. Application fee: $50. Electronic applications accepted. *Financial support:* In 2007–08, 14 students received support, including 5 research assistantships with partial tuition reimbursements available (averaging $8,000 per year), 6 teaching assistantships with partial tuition reimbursements available (averaging $8,000 per year); Federal Work-Study, health care benefits, tuition waivers (partial), and unspecified assistantships also available. Financial award application deadline: 3/1; financial award applicants required to submit FAFSA. *Faculty research:* Theater education and outreach, choreography, dramatic writing, dance history/criticism. *Unit head:* Susan Pearson, Chair, 505-277-4332, Fax: 505-277-8921, E-mail: speardav@unm.edu. *Application contact:* Christina Squire, Graduate Coordinator, 505-277-7362, Fax: 505-277-8921, E-mail: csquire@unm.edu.

The University of North Carolina at Greensboro, Graduate School, College of Arts and Sciences, Department of English, Program in Creative Writing, Greensboro, NC 27412-5001. Offers MFA. *Students:* 26 full-time (15 women); includes 1 minority (African American) *Degree requirements:* For master's, comprehensive exam, thesis. *Entrance requirements:* For master's, GRE General Test, minimum GPA of 3.0, writing sample. Additional exam requirements/recommendations for international students: Required—TOEFL. *Application deadline:* For fall admission, 3/15 for domestic students. Application fee: $45. Electronic applications accepted. *Financial support:* Fellowships with full tuition reimbursements, research assistantships with full tuition reimbursements, teaching assistantships with full tuition reimbursements, career-related internships or fieldwork, Federal Work-Study, institutionally sponsored loans, scholarships/grants, and traineeships available. Support available to part-time students. *Faculty research:* Fiction, poetry, science fiction, film studies. *Unit head:* Jim Clark, Director, 336-334-5459, E-mail: jlclark@uncg.edu. *Application contact:* Michelle Harkleroad, Director of Graduate Admissions, 336-334-4884, Fax: 336-334-4424, E-mail: mbharkle@uncg.edu.

The University of North Carolina Wilmington, College of Arts and Sciences, Department of Creative Writing, Wilmington, NC 28403-3297. Offers MFA. *Students:* 43 full-time (22 women), 18 part-time (15 women); includes 5 minority (2 African Americans, 2 Asian Americans or Pacific Islanders, 1 Hispanic American), 2 international. Average age 29. 257 applicants, 27% accepted, 23 enrolled. In 2007, 18 degrees awarded. *Degree requirements:* For master's, comprehensive exam, thesis. *Entrance requirements:* For master's, GRE General Test. *Application deadline:* For fall admission, 3/1 for domestic students. Application fee: $45. *Expenses:* Tuition, state resident: full-time $2,714. Tuition, nonresident: full-time $12,579. Required fees: $1,985. *Financial support:* In 2007–08, 16 teaching assistantships were awarded; career-related internships or fieldwork and Federal Work-Study also available. Support available to part-time students. Financial award application deadline: 3/15. *Unit head:* Dr. Philip Gerard, Chair, 910-962-3329, Fax: 910-962-7461, E-mail: gerardp@uncw.edu. *Application contact:* Dr. Robert D. Roer, Dean, Graduate School, 910-962-4117, Fax: 910-962-3787, E-mail: roer@uncw.edu.

See Close-Up on page 737.

University of North Florida, College of Arts and Sciences, Department of English, Jacksonville, FL 32224-2645. Offers MA. Part-time and evening/weekend programs available. *Faculty:* 11 full-time (2 women). *Students:* 19 full-time (16 women), 48 part-time (37 women); includes 8 minority (5 African Americans, 3 Hispanic Americans). Average age 31. 32 applicants, 75% accepted, 19 enrolled. In 2007, 27 degrees awarded. *Degree requirements:* For master's, comprehensive exam, thesis optional. *Entrance requirements:* For master's, GRE General Test, minimum GPA of 3.0 in last 60 hours, writing sample. Additional exam requirements/recommendations for international students: Required—TOEFL (minimum score 500 paper-based; 173 computer-based). *Application deadline:* For fall admission, 7/6 priority date for domestic students, 5/1 for international students; for spring admission, 11/1 priority date for domestic students, 10/1 for international students. Applications are processed on a rolling basis. Application fee: $30. Electronic applications accepted. *Expenses:* Tuition, state resident: part-time $266 per credit hour. Tuition, nonresident: part-time $858 per credit hour. One-time fee: $35 part-time. Tuition and fees vary according to program. *Financial support:* In 2007–08, 43 students received support; research assistantships, Federal Work-Study and tuition waivers (partial) available. Support available to part-time students. Financial award application deadline: 4/1; financial award applicants required to submit FAFSA. *Faculty research:* Genre, period, and individual author studies in British, American, and world literature; literary criticism and theory—psychological, new historical and cultural, deconstructive, feminist, narrative, mythic; film and popular culture; online poetry publishing. *Unit head:* Dr. Samuel A. Kimball, Chair, 904-620-2273, Fax: 904-620-3949, E-mail: skimball@unf.edu. *Application contact:* Dr. Christopher Gababard, Graduate Coordinator, 904-620-1254, Fax: 904-620-3940, E-mail: cgabbard@unf.edu.

University of North Texas, Robert B. Toulouse School of Graduate Studies, College of Arts and Sciences, Department of English, Denton, TX 76203. Offers creative writing (MA); English (MA, PhD); English as a second language (MA); linguistics (MA); Technical writing (MA). *Faculty:* 60 full-time (36 women). *Students:* 82 full-time (46 women), 91 part-time (65 women); includes 19 minority (4 African Americans, 1 American Indian/Alaska Native, 6 Asian Americans or Pacific Islanders, 8 Hispanic Americans), 13 international. Average age 30. 91 applicants, 47% accepted, 21 enrolled. In 2007, 38 master's, 5 doctorates awarded. Terminal master's awarded for partial completion of doctoral program. *Degree requirements:* For master's, one foreign language, comprehensive exam, thesis optional; for doctorate, one foreign language, comprehensive exam, thesis/dissertation. *Entrance requirements:* For master's, GRE General Test, 3.0 GPA, personal statement, current vita/resumè, writing sample for creative writing program; for doctorate, GRE General Test, 3.5 GPA, 3 letters of recommendation, personal statement, writing sample. Additional exam requirements/recommendations for international students: Required—proof of English language proficiency required for non-native English speakers; Recommended—TOEFL (minimum score 550 paper-based; 213 computer-based). *Application deadline:* For fall admission, 7/15 priority date for domestic students; for spring admission, 11/15 for domestic students. Application fee: $50 ($75 for international students). *Financial support:* In 2007–08, 8 students received support, including 2 fellowships with full tuition reimbursements available (averaging $20,000 per year), 42 teaching assistantships (averaging $11,000 per year); career-related internships or fieldwork, Federal Work-Study, institutionally sponsored loans, scholarships/grants, health care benefits, and unspecified assistantships also available. Financial award application deadline: 4/1. *Faculty research:* Creative writing, British and American literature, composition and rhetoric. Total annual research expenditures: $25,000. *Unit head:* Dr. David Holdeman, Chair, 940-565-2050, Fax: 940-565-4355, E-mail: holdeman@cas1.unt.edu. *Application contact:* Dr. Robert K. Upchuerch, Chair of Graduate Studies, 940-565-2114, Fax: 940-565-4355, E-mail: robertu@unt.edu.

University of Notre Dame, Graduate School, College of Arts and Letters, Division of Humanities, Department of English, Creative Writing Program, Notre Dame, IN 46556. Offers MFA. *Faculty:* 7 full-time (2 women), 2 part-time/adjunct (1 woman). *Students:* 22 full-time (10 women); includes 5 minority (1 American Indian/Alaska Native, 1 Asian American or Pacific Islander, 3 Hispanic Americans), 3 international. 221 applicants, 11% accepted, 11 enrolled. In 2007, 11 degrees awarded. *Degree requirements:* For master's, thesis. *Entrance requirements:* For master's, GRE General Test, minimum GPA of 3.0. Additional exam requirements/recommendations for international students: Required—TOEFL (minimum score 600 paper-based; 250 computer-based; 80 iBT). *Application deadline:* For fall admission, 1/2 for domestic and international students. Application fee: $50. Electronic applications accepted. *Financial support:* In 2007–08, 2 fellowships with full tuition reimbursements (averaging $12,000 per year), 7 teaching assistantships with full tuition reimbursements (averaging $12,000 per year) were awarded; research assistantships, tuition waivers (full) also available. Financial award application deadline: 2/1. *Faculty research:* Novels, stories, poetry. *Unit head:* Prof. Cornelius Eady, Director, 574-631-6618, Fax: 574-631-4795, E-mail: creativewriting@nd.edu. *Application contact:* Dr. Jarren Gonzales, Director of Graduate Admissions, 574-631-7706, Fax: 574-631-4183.

University of Oklahoma, Graduate College, Gaylord College of Journalism and Mass Communication, Program in Journalism and Mass Communication, Norman, OK 73019-0390. Offers advertising and public relations (MA); information gathering and distribution (MA); mass communication management and policy (MA); professional writing (MA); telecommunication and new technology (MA). Part-time programs available. *Students:* 33 full-time (22 women), 41 part-time (27 women); includes 15 minority (5 African Americans, 5 American Indian/Alaska Native, 1 Asian American or Pacific Islander, 4 Hispanic Americans), 12 international. 29 applicants, 90% accepted, 15 enrolled. In 2007, 12 degrees awarded. *Degree requirements:* For master's, thesis optional. *Entrance requirements:* For master's, GRE General Test, minimum GPA of 3.2, 9 hours of course work in journalism, course work in statistics. Additional exam requirements/recommendations for international students: Required—TOEFL (minimum score 600 paper-based; 250 computer-based), TWE (minimum score 5). *Application deadline:* For fall admission, 2/1 for domestic students, 4/1 for international students; for spring admission, 11/1 for domestic students, 9/1 for international students. Application fee: $40 ($90 for international students). Electronic applications accepted. *Expenses:* Tuition, state resident: full-time $3,451; part-time $144 per credit hour. Tuition, nonresident: full-time $12,432; part-time $518 per credit hour. Required fees: $1,925; $70 per credit hour. $122 per semester. *Financial support:* In 2007–08, 26 students received support. Career-related internships or fieldwork, scholarships/grants, health care benefits, and unspecified assistantships available. *Faculty research:* Organizational management; rhetorical analysis; international public relations; digital production; normative theory. *Application contact:* Kelly Storm, Graduate Advisor, 405-325-2722, Fax: 405-325-7565, E-mail: kstorm@ou.edu.

University of Oklahoma, Graduate College, Gaylord College of Journalism and Mass Communication, Program in Professional Writing, Norman, OK 73019-0390. Offers MPW. Part-time programs available. *Students:* 14 full-time (10 women), 7 part-time (2 women), 1 international. 3 applicants, 100% accepted, 2 enrolled. In 2007, 8 degrees awarded. *Degree requirements:* For master's, project. *Entrance requirements:* For master's, GRE General Test, 2 letters of recommendation, resumé, writing sample. Additional exam requirements/recommendations for international students: Required—TOEFL (minimum score 600 paper-based; 250 computer-based), TWE (minimum score 5). *Application deadline:* For fall admission, 7/1 for domestic students, 4/1 for international students; for spring admission, 11/1 for domestic students, 9/1 for international students. Application fee: $40 ($90 for international students). Electronic applications accepted. *Expenses:* Tuition, state resident: full-time $3,451; part-time $144 per credit hour. Tuition, nonresident: full-time $12,432; part-time $518 per credit hour. Required fees: $1,925; $70 per credit hour. $122 per semester. *Financial support:* In 2007–08, 6 students received support. Career-related internships or fieldwork, scholarships/grants, health care benefits, and unspecified assistantships available. Financial award applicants required to submit FAFSA. *Faculty research:* Creative writing; script writing; nonfiction. *Application contact:* Kelly Storm, Graduate Advisor, 405-325-2722, Fax: 405-325-7565, E-mail: kstorm@ou.edu.

University of Oregon, Graduate School, College of Arts and Sciences, Department of Creative Writing, Eugene, OR 97403. Offers MFA. *Faculty:* 4 full-time (2 women), 1 part-time/adjunct (0 women). *Students:* 23 full-time (13 women); includes 4 minority (1 African American, 3 Hispanic Americans), 1 international. 12 applicants, 100% accepted. In 2007, 9 degrees awarded. *Degree requirements:* For master's, thesis, exam. *Entrance requirements:* For master's, minimum GPA of 3.0. Additional exam requirements/recommendations for international students: Required—TOEFL. *Application deadline:* For fall admission, 2/1 for domestic students. Application fee: $50. *Financial support:* In 2007–08, 21 teaching assistantships were awarded; fellowships, Federal Work-Study and institutionally sponsored loans also available. Financial award application deadline: 2/1. *Faculty research:* Poetry, fiction, literary nonfiction. *Unit head:* Karen Ford, Acting Director, 541-346-0552. *Application contact:* Julia Schewanick, Admissions Contact, 541-346-0549, Fax: 541-346-0537, E-mail: jas@uoregon.edu.

University of Pennsylvania, Graduate School of Education, Division of Language in Education, Program in Reading, Writing, and Literacy, Philadelphia, PA 19104. Offers MS Ed, Ed D, PhD. Part-time programs available. *Degree requirements:* For master's, comprehensive exam; for doctorate, one foreign language, thesis/dissertation, preliminary exam. *Entrance requirements:* For master's and doctorate, GRE General Test or MAT. Additional exam requirements/recommendations for international students: Required—TOEFL. Electronic applications accepted. Expenses: Contact institution. *Faculty research:* Reading and writing relationships, classroom teachers as researchers, comprehension processes.

University of Pittsburgh, School of Arts and Sciences, Department of English, Pittsburgh, PA 15260. Offers cultural and critical studies (PhD); English (MA); writing (MFA). Part-time programs available. *Faculty:* 55 full-time (23 women). *Students:* 197 full-time (119 women), 37 part-time (34 women); includes 33 minority (11 African Americans, 6 Asian Americans or Pacific Islanders, 16 Hispanic Americans), 4 international. 363 applicants, 29% accepted, 35 enrolled. In 2007, 31 master's, 13 doctorates awarded. *Degree requirements:* For master's, one foreign language; for doctorate, 2 foreign languages, comprehensive exam, thesis/dissertation. *Entrance requirements:* For master's and doctorate, GRE General Test, writing sample. Additional exam requirements/recommendations for international students: Required—TOEFL. *Application deadline:* For fall admission, 12/12 for domestic and international students. Application fee: $50. *Financial support:* In 2007–08, 100 students received support, including 24 fellowships with full tuition reimbursements available (averaging $17,162 per year), 6 research assistantships with full and partial tuition reimbursements available (averaging $11,830 per year), 68 teaching assistantships with full tuition reimbursements available (averaging $14,485 per year); Federal Work-Study, tuition waivers (full and partial), and unspecified assistantships also available. Financial award application deadline: 12/12. *Faculty research:* Cultural studies, literary history and theory, film, composition. *Unit head:* Dr. David Bartholomae, Chairman, 412-624-6509, Fax: 412-624-6639, E-mail: barth@pitt.edu. *Application contact:* Connie Arelt, Graduate Administrator, 412-624-6549, Fax: 412-624-6639, E-mail: car100@pitt.edu.

University of San Francisco, College of Arts and Sciences, Program in Writing, San Francisco, CA 94117-1080. Offers MA, MFA. Part-time and evening/weekend programs available. *Faculty:* 2 full-time (1 woman), 12 part-time/adjunct (6 women). *Students:* 68 full-time (44 women), 5 part-time (2 women); includes 10 minority (3 African Americans, 6 Asian Americans or Pacific Islanders, 1 Hispanic American), 1 international. Average age 35. 233 applicants, 36% accepted, 34 enrolled. In 2007, 13 degrees awarded. *Degree requirements:* For master's, thesis. *Entrance requirements:* For master's, minimum GPA of 3.0, writing sample. *Application deadline:* For fall admission, 2/2 priority date for domestic students. Applications are processed on a rolling basis. Application fee: $55 ($65 for international students). *Expenses:* Tuition: Part-time $1,005 per unit. Tuition and fees vary according to degree level, campus/location and program. *Financial support:* In 2007–08, 51 students received support; fellowships, institutionally sponsored loans available. Support available to part-time students. Financial award application deadline: 3/2; financial award applicants required to submit FAFSA. *Faculty research:* Techniques of teaching the novel to writers, oral history. *Unit head:* Dr. Deborah Lichtman, Director, 415-422-6066, Fax: 415-422-6996, E-mail: mfaw@usfca.edu.

University of South Carolina, The Graduate School, College of Arts and Sciences, Department of English Language and Literature, Columbia, SC 29208. Offers creative writing (MFA); English (MA, PhD); English education (MAT); MLIS/MA. MAT offered in cooperation with the College of Education. Part-time programs available. *Faculty:* 53 full-time (23 women). *Students:* 147 full-time (86 women); includes 18 minority (10 African Americans, 2 American Indian/Alaska Native, 5 Asian Americans or Pacific Islanders, 1 Hispanic American), 1 international. Average age 32. 179 applicants, 21% accepted. In 2007, 8 master's, 14 doctorates awarded. *Degree requirements:* For master's, one foreign language, comprehensive exam, thesis; for doctorate, 2 foreign languages, comprehensive exam, thesis/dissertation. *Entrance requirements:* For master's, GRE General Test (MFA), GRE Subject Test (MA, MAT), sample of written work; for doctorate, GRE General Test, GRE Subject Test, sample of written work. Additional exam requirements/recommendations for international students: Required—TOEFL. *Application deadline:* For fall admission, 1/30 priority date for domestic and international students. Applications are processed on a rolling basis. Application fee: $40. Electronic applications accepted. *Expenses:* Tuition, state resident: part-time $440 per hour. Tuition, nonresident: part-time $936 per hour. Required fees: $17 per hour. Tuition and fees vary according to program. *Financial support:* In 2007–08, 123 students received support, including 17 fellowships with full tuition reimbursements available (averaging $3,000 per year), 10 research assistantships with full tuition reimbursements available (averaging $3,000 per year), 80 teaching assistantships with full tuition reimbursements available (averaging $12,000 per year); institutionally sponsored loans, scholarships/grants, health care benefits, unspecified assistantships, and graders, tutors also available. Financial award application deadline: 1/31. *Faculty research:* American literature, British literature, composition and rhetoric, linguistics, speech communication. Total annual research expenditures: $230,000. *Unit head:* Dr. William Rivers, Interim Chair, 803-777-7120, Fax: 803-777-9064, E-mail: riversw@gwm.sc.edu. *Application contact:* Dr. Lawrence Rhu, Director of Graduate Studies, 803-777-5063, Fax: 803-777-9064, E-mail: rhul@gwm.sc.edu.

University of Southern California, Graduate School, College of Letters, Arts and Sciences, Department of English, Los Angeles, CA 90089. Offers English and American literature (MA, PhD); English literature and creative writing (PhD). *Faculty:* 34 full-time (17 women). *Students:* 110 full-time (72 women), 2 part-time (both women); includes 25 minority (3 African Americans, 2 American Indian/Alaska Native, 9 Asian Americans or Pacific Islanders, 11 Hispanic Americans), 9 international. 236 applicants, 10% accepted. In 2007, 4 master's, 9 doctorates awarded. Terminal master's awarded for partial completion of doctoral program. *Degree requirements:* For doctorate, one foreign language, thesis/dissertation. *Entrance requirements:* For doctorate, GRE General Test, GRE Subject Test. *Application deadline:* For fall admission, 12/1 priority date for domestic students. Application fee: $85. *Financial support:* In 2007–08, 89 students received support, including fellowships with full tuition reimbursements available (averaging $19,000 per year), teaching assistantships with full tuition reimbursements available (averaging $19,532 per year); scholarships/grants also available. Support available to part-time students. Financial award application deadline: 2/15; financial award applicants required to submit FAFSA. *Faculty research:* Creative writing and literature, early modern studies, gender and sexuality, narrative studies, poetry and poetics, media, film and popular culture. *Unit head:* Dr. Bruce Smith, Chair, 213-740-2808. *Application contact:* William Handley, Information Contact, 213-740-2311.

University of Southern California, Graduate School, College of Letters, Arts and Sciences, Program in Professional Writing, Los Angeles, CA 90089. Offers MPW. Part-time and evening/weekend programs available. *Students:* 81 full-time (49 women), 80 part-time (43 women); includes 35 minority (10 African Americans, 1 American Indian/Alaska Native, 14 Asian Americans or Pacific Islanders, 10 Hispanic Americans), 4 international. 78 applicants, 72% accepted. In 2007, 61 degrees awarded. *Degree requirements:* For master's, thesis. *Entrance requirements:* For master's, GRE General Test. *Application deadline:* For fall admission, 12/1 priority date for domestic students. Applications are processed on a rolling basis. Application fee: $85. *Financial support:* In 2007–08, 35 students received support, including research assistantships (averaging $18,500 per year), teaching assistantships with full tuition reimbursements available (averaging $18,500 per year); fellowships with partial tuition reimbursements available, career-related internships or fieldwork, Federal Work-Study, institutionally sponsored loans, scholarships/grants, and unspecified assistantships also available. Support available to part-time students. Financial award application deadline: 2/15; financial award applicants required to submit FAFSA. *Faculty research:* Screenplays, teleplays, fiction, non-fiction, plays, poetry, journalism and publishing, magazine and book publishing. *Unit head:* Dr. John Holland, Chair, E-mail: cwphd@usc.edu.

Writing

University of Southern Maine, College of Arts and Sciences, Program in Creative Writing, Portland, ME 04104. Offers MFA. *Faculty:* 20 full-time (2 women). *Students:* 90 full-time (75 women). Application fee: $50. *Unit head:* Annie Finch, Director, 207-780-5973, Fax: 207-780-5795, E-mail: afinch@usm.maine.edu. *Application contact:* Robin Talbot, Associate Director, 207-780-5262, E-mail: stonecoastmfa@usm.maine.edu.

The University of Texas at Austin, Graduate School, Program in Writing, Austin, TX 78712-1111. Offers MFA. Electronic applications accepted.

The University of Texas at El Paso, Graduate School, College of Liberal Arts, Department of English, El Paso, TX 79968-0001. Offers English and American literature (MA); professional writing and rhetoric (MA); teaching English (MAT). Part-time and evening/weekend programs available. *Degree requirements:* For master's, thesis optional. *Entrance requirements:* For master's, GRE General Test, minimum GPA of 3.0. Additional exam requirements/recommendations for international students: Required—TOEFL. Electronic applications accepted. *Faculty research:* Literature, creative writing, literary theory.

The University of Texas at El Paso, Graduate School, College of Liberal Arts, Interdisciplinary Program in Creative Writing, El Paso, TX 79968-0001. Offers creative writing in English (MFA); creative writing in Spanish (MFA). Part-time and evening/weekend programs available. *Degree requirements:* For master's, thesis. *Entrance requirements:* For master's, departmental exam (creative writing in Spanish), minimum GPA of 3.0. Additional exam requirements/recommendations for international students: Required—TOEFL. Electronic applications accepted.

University of the Sacred Heart, Graduate Programs, Department of Communication, San Juan, PR 00914-0383. Offers advertising (MA); contemporary culture and means (MA); journalism and mass communication (MA); literary creation (MA); public relations (MA). Part-time and evening/weekend programs available. *Degree requirements:* For master's, thesis.

University of the Sacred Heart, Graduate Programs, Program in Creative Writing, San Juan, PR 00914-0383. Offers MA.

The University of Toledo, College of Graduate Studies, College of Arts and Sciences, Department of English Language and Literature, Toledo, OH 43606-3390. Offers English as a second language (MA); literature (MA); teaching of writing (Certificate). Part-time programs available. *Faculty:* 21. *Students:* 36 full-time (27 women), 12 part-time (7 women); includes 4 minority (3 African Americans, 1 Hispanic American), 5 international. Average age 31. 34 applicants, 76% accepted, 19 enrolled. In 2007, 13 degrees awarded. *Degree requirements:* For master's, one foreign language. *Entrance requirements:* For master's, minimum GPA of 2.7. *Application deadline:* For fall admission, 1/15 priority date for domestic students. Applications are processed on a rolling basis. Application fee: $45. Electronic applications accepted. *Financial support:* In 2007–08, 36 teaching assistantships with full tuition reimbursements (averaging $8,200 per year) were awarded; research assistantships, Federal Work-Study, institutionally sponsored loans, scholarships/grants, tuition waivers (full), and unspecified assistantships also available. Support available to part-time students. Financial award application deadline: 4/1; financial award applicants required to submit FAFSA. *Faculty research:* Literary criticism, linguistics, creative writing, folklore and cultural studies. *Unit head:* Dr. Sara Lundquist, Interim Chair, 419-530-2506, Fax: 419-530-2590, E-mail: sara.lundquist@utoledo.edu.

University of Utah, The Graduate School, College of Humanities, Department of English, Program in Creative Writing, Salt Lake City, UT 84112-1107. Offers MFA. *Students:* 8 full-time (5 women), 7 part-time (4 women); includes 3 minority (1 African American, 1 American Indian/Alaska Native, 1 Asian American or Pacific Islander). In 2007, 6 degrees awarded. *Unit head:* Dr. Katharine Coles, Head, 801-581-7200.

University of Victoria, Faculty of Graduate Studies, Faculty of Fine Arts, Department of Writing, Victoria, BC V8W 2Y2, Canada. Offers MFA. *Entrance requirements:* For master's, portfolio, 400-word statement of purpose, 2 letters of reference. *Expenses:* Tuition, state resident: full-time $3,110. International tuition: $3,700 full-time. Tuition and fees vary according to program. *Unit head:* Lorna Crozier, Chair, 250-721-7306, E-mail: lcrozier@finearts.uvic.ca. *Application contact:* Dr. Lynne Van Luven, Graduate Advisor, 250-721-7307, E-mail: lvluven@finearts.uvic.ca.

University of Virginia, College and Graduate School of Arts and Sciences, Department of English Language and Literature, Program in Creative Writing, Charlottesville, VA 22903. Offers MFA. *Faculty:* 7 full-time (5 women). *Students:* 26 full-time (14 women). Average age 25. 551 applicants, 2% accepted, 10 enrolled. In 2007, 11 degrees awarded. *Degree requirements:* For master's, comprehensive exam, thesis. *Entrance requirements:* For master's, GRE General Test, GRE Subject Test. *Application deadline:* Applications are processed on a rolling basis. Application fee: $60. Electronic applications accepted. *Financial support:* Applicants required to submit FAFSA. *Unit head:* Sydney Blair, Director, 434-924-6675, Fax: 434-924-1478, E-mail: shb7f@virginia.edu.

University of West Florida, College of Arts and Sciences: Arts, Department of English and Foreign Languages, Pensacola, FL 32514-5750. Offers creative writing (MA); literature (MA). Part-time and evening/weekend programs available. *Faculty:* 6 full-time (3 women), 1 (woman) part-time/adjunct. *Students:* 2 full-time (1 woman), 23 part-time (17 women); includes 4 minority (1 African American, 1 American Indian/Alaska Native, 2 Asian Americans or Pacific Islanders). Average age 29. 14 applicants, 64% accepted, 8 enrolled. In 2007, 1 degree awarded. *Degree requirements:* For master's, thesis. *Entrance requirements:* For master's, GRE General Test, minimum GPA of 3.0. Additional exam requirements/recommendations for international students: Required—TOEFL (minimum score 550 paper-based; 213 computer-based). *Application deadline:* For fall admission, 6/1 for domestic students, 5/15 for international students; for spring admission, 11/1 for domestic students, 10/1 for international students. Applications are processed on a rolling basis. Application fee: $30. *Expenses:* Tuition, state resident: full-time $6,054; part-time $252 per credit. Tuition, nonresident: full-time $21,886; part-time $912 per credit. *Financial support:* In 2007–08, 8 research assistantships with partial tuition reimbursements (averaging $1,570 per year), 1 teaching assistantship with partial tuition reimbursement (averaging $2,826 per year) were awarded; fellowships, scholarships/grants, tuition waivers (partial), and unspecified assistantships also available. Support available to part-time students. Financial award application deadline: 4/15; financial award applicants required to submit FAFSA. *Faculty research:* Faulkner, Shakespeare, American humor, women's studies, poetry. *Unit head:* Dr. Bob Yeager, Chairperson, 850-474-2923.

University of Windsor, Faculty of Graduate Studies, Faculty of Arts and Social Sciences, Department of English Language, Literature and Creative Writing, Windsor, ON N9B 3P4, Canada. Offers English: creative writing and language and literature (MA); English: language and literature (MA). Part-time programs available. *Faculty:* 14 full-time (7 women). *Students:* 29 full-time (17 women), 2 part-time (1 woman). 50 applicants, 58% accepted. In 2007, 6 degrees awarded. *Degree requirements:* For master's, thesis. *Entrance requirements:* For master's, minimum B average, portfolio. Additional exam requirements/recommendations for international students: Required—TOEFL (minimum score 600 paper-based; 250 computer-based). *Application deadline:* For fall admission, 7/1 priority date for domestic students; for winter admission, 11/1 for domestic students; for spring admission, 3/1 for domestic students. Applications are processed on a rolling basis. Application fee: $55. Electronic applications accepted. *Financial support:* In 2007–08, 19 teaching assistantships (averaging $8,901 per year) were awarded; Federal Work-Study, scholarships/grants, tuition waivers (full and partial), unspecified assistantships, and bursaries also available. Financial award application deadline: 2/15. *Faculty research:* Use of gender-related terms in popular culture; international and Aboriginal literatures: expression of cultural identity; critical analysis of authors: Pope, Munroe, Lady Morgan, Orwell, Thomas; the 'feminine" voice in literature and contemporary culture. *Unit head:* Dr. Karl Jirgens, Head, 519-253-3000 Ext. 2289, Fax: 519-971-3676, E-mail: jirgens@uwindsor.ca. *Application contact:* Applicant Services, 519-253-3000 Ext. 6459, Fax: 519-971-3653, E-mail: gradadmit@uwindsor.ca.

University of Wyoming, Graduate School, College of Arts and Sciences, Department of English, Laramie, WY 82070. Offers creative writing (MFA); English (MA). Part-time programs available. *Faculty:* 25 full-time (11 women). *Students:* 35 full-time (19 women), 10 part-time (8 women); includes 4 minority (1 African American, 3 Hispanic Americans), 1 international. Average age 32. 58 applicants, 34% accepted. In 2007, 15 degrees awarded. *Degree requirements:* For master's, one foreign language, thesis or alternative. *Entrance requirements:* For master's, GRE General Test, minimum GPA of 3.0. *Application deadline:* For fall admission, 3/1 priority date for domestic students; for spring admission, 12/1 for domestic students. Applications are processed on a rolling basis. Application fee: $50. Electronic applications accepted. *Financial support:* In 2007–08, 14 teaching assistantships were awarded; institutionally sponsored loans also available. Financial award application deadline: 3/1. *Faculty research:* Literature and theory, creative writing, English as a second language, ethnic and women's studies, composition. *Unit head:* Janice Harris, Chair, 307-766-6453, Fax: 307-766-3189, E-mail: jharris@uwyo.edu.

Utah State University, School of Graduate Studies, College of Humanities, Arts and Social Sciences, Department of English, Logan, UT 84322. Offers American studies (MA, MS), including folklore, western American literature and culture; English (MA, MS), including literature and writing, technical writing. Part-time and evening/weekend programs available. *Degree requirements:* For master's, thesis or alternative. *Entrance requirements:* For master's, GRE General Test or MAT, minimum GPA of 3.0, recommendation letters, writing samples. Additional exam requirements/recommendations for international students: Required—TOEFL. *Faculty research:* Scottish enlightenment, material culture, composition theory, creative nonfiction, literary criticism.

Vanderbilt University, Graduate School, Program in Creative Writing, Nashville, TN 37240-1001. Offers MFA. *Faculty:* 7 full-time (3 women). *Students:* 10 full-time (6 women). Average age 27. 95 applicants, 11% accepted, 5 enrolled. *Entrance requirements:* For master's, GRE General Test, sample of written work. *Application deadline:* For fall admission, 1/15 for domestic and international students. Application fee: $0. Electronic applications accepted. *Financial support:* Fellowships with full and partial tuition reimbursements, teaching assistantships with full and partial tuition reimbursements, Federal Work-Study, institutionally sponsored loans, and health care benefits available. Financial award application deadline: 1/15; financial award applicants required to submit CSS PROFILE or FAFSA. *Unit head:* Mark Jarman, Director, 615-322-2618, E-mail: mark.jarman@vanderbilt.edu.

Virginia Commonwealth University, Graduate School, College of Humanities and Sciences, Department of English, Program in Creative Writing, Richmond, VA 23284-9005. Offers fiction (MFA); fictional poetry (MFA); poetry (MFA). *Entrance requirements:* For master's, portfolio. *Application deadline:* For fall admission, 2/1 for domestic students; for spring admission, 11/15 for domestic students. Applications are processed on a rolling basis. Application fee: $50. *Expenses:* Tuition, state resident: full-time $7,224; part-time $401 per credit. Tuition, nonresident: full-time $16,072; part-time $891 per credit. Required fees: $1,679; $63 per credit. Tuition and fees vary according to campus/location. *Unit head:* David Wojahn, Program Director, 804-828-1329.

See Close-Up on page 457.

Virginia Commonwealth University, Graduate School, College of Humanities and Sciences, Department of English, Program in English, Richmond, VA 23284-9005. Offers literature (MA); writing and rhetoric (MA). *Application deadline:* For fall admission, 2/1 for domestic students; for spring admission, 11/15 for domestic students. Applications are processed on a rolling basis. Application fee: $50. *Expenses:* Tuition, state resident: full-time $7,224; part-time $401 per credit. Tuition, nonresident: full-time $16,072; part-time $891 per credit. Required fees: $1,679; $63 per credit. Tuition and fees vary according to campus/location. *Unit head:* Katherine Bassard, Program Director, E-mail: kcbassar@vcu.edu.

See Close-Up on page 457.

Warren Wilson College, MFA Program for Writers, Swannanoa, Asheville, NC 28815-9000. Offers MFA. Postbaccalaureate distance learning degree programs offered (minimal on-campus study). *Faculty:* 24 full-time (11 women). *Students:* 77 full-time (58 women); includes 9 minority (3 African Americans, 2 Asian Americans or Pacific Islanders, 4 Hispanic Americans), 1 international. Average age 37. 162 applicants, 11% accepted, 18 enrolled. In 2007, 23 degrees awarded. *Degree requirements:* For master's, thesis, public reading, teaching experience. *Entrance requirements:* For master's, manuscript of creative work. *Application deadline:* For fall admission, 9/1 for domestic and international students; for spring admission, 3/1 for domestic and international students. Application fee: $70. *Expenses:* Tuition: Full-time $12,600. *Financial support:* In 2007–08, 32 students received support. Scholarships/grants available. Financial award application deadline: 3/1; financial award applicants required to submit FAFSA. *Faculty research:* Analytic writing, creative and analytic study of literature. *Unit head:* Peter Turchi, Director, 828-771-3715, Fax: 828-771-7005. *Application contact:* Amy Grimm, Assistant to the Director, 828-771-3715, Fax: 828-771-7005, E-mail: agrimm@warren-wilson.edu.

Washington University in St. Louis, Graduate School of Arts and Sciences, Department of English and American Literature, Writing Program, St. Louis, MO 63130-4899. Offers MFAW. *Degree requirements:* For master's, thesis or written exam. *Entrance requirements:* For master's, GRE General Test, sample of written work. Electronic applications accepted.

Wayne State University, College of Liberal Arts and Sciences, Department of English, Detroit, MI 48202. Offers comparative literature (MA); English (MA, PhD). *Students:* 84 full-time (55 women), 37 part-time (24 women); includes 11 minority (9 African Americans, 1 Asian American or Pacific Islander, 1 Hispanic American), 10 international. Average age 34. 73 applicants, 48% accepted, 12 enrolled. In 2007, 10 master's, 3 doctorates awarded. *Degree requirements:* For master's, one foreign language, essay or thesis; for doctorate, one foreign language, thesis/dissertation. *Entrance requirements:* For master's, GRE General Test, minimum GPA of 3.25 in English, 3.0 overall, statement of purpose; references; sample essay; for doctorate, GRE General Test, GRE Subject Test, statement of purpose, references, sample essay. Additional exam requirements/recommendations for international students: Required—TOEFL (minimum score 550 paper-based; 213 computer-based); Recommended—TWE (minimum score 6). *Application deadline:* For fall admission, 6/1 for international students; for winter admission, 10/1 for international students; for spring admission, 2/1 for international students. Applications are processed on a rolling basis. Application fee: $30 ($50 for international students). Electronic applications accepted. *Expenses:* Tuition, state resident: part-time $403 per credit hour. Tuition, nonresident: part-time $890 per credit hour. *Financial support:* In 2007–08, 40 students received support, including 2 fellowships (averaging $13,001 per year), 32 teaching assistantships (averaging $12,922 per year); research assistantships, career-related internships or fieldwork, institutionally sponsored loans, and tuition waivers (full and partial) also available. Support available to part-time students. Financial award application deadline: 3/1. *Faculty research:* English and American literature, cultural studies, composition, linguistics, film. *Unit head:* Dr. Richard Grusin, Chair, 313-577-7692, Fax: 313-577-8618, E-mail: aj4671@wayne.edu. *Application contact:* Ross Pudaloff, Graduate Director, 313-577-7699, E-mail: r.pudaloff@wayne.edu.

Western Connecticut State University, Division of Graduate Studies, School of Arts and Sciences, Department of English, Danbury, CT 06810-6885. Offers English (MA); literature option (MA); TESOL option (MA); writing option (MA). Part-time and evening/weekend programs available. *Faculty:* 10 full-time (4 women). *Students:* 3 full-time (1 woman), 30 part-time (22 women); includes 2 minority (1 African American, 1 Asian American or Pacific Islander), 1 international. Average age 41. 18 applicants, 83% accepted, 11 enrolled. In 2007, 12 degrees awarded. *Degree requirements:* For master's, thesis or comprehensive exam. *Entrance requirements:* For master's, minimum GPA of 2.5, writing sample. *Application deadline:* For fall admission, 8/5 priority date for domestic students; for spring admission, 1/5 priority date for domestic students. Applications are processed on a rolling basis. Application fee: $50.

Expenses: Tuition, state resident: full-time $4,169. Tuition, nonresident: full-time $11,614. Required fees: $3,278. *Financial support:* Teaching assistantships, career-related internships or fieldwork available. Support available to part-time students. Financial award application deadline: 5/1; financial award applicants required to submit FAFSA. *Unit head:* Dr. Oscar De Los Santos, Associate Professor, 203-837-9044. *Application contact:* Chris Shankle, Associate Director of Graduate Admissions, 203-837-8244, Fax: 203-837-8338, E-mail: shanklec@wcsu.edu.

Western Connecticut State University, Division of Graduate Studies, School of Arts and Sciences, Department of Writing, Linguistics, and Creative Process, Danbury, CT 06810-6885. Offers professional writing (MFA). *Students:* 23 full-time (14 women), 13 part-time (8 women); includes 3 minority (all African Americans) Average age 38. 29 applicants, 45% accepted, 10 enrolled. In 2007, 6 degrees awarded. *Entrance requirements:* For master's, 2 writing samples; a 20-50 page portfolio of previous writing; brief essay. *Application deadline:* For fall admission, 8/5 priority date for domestic students; for spring admission, 1/5 priority date for domestic students. Application fee: $50. *Expenses:* Tuition, state resident: full-time $4,169. Tuition, nonresident: full-time $11,614. Required fees: $3,278. *Unit head:* Dr. Brian Clements, Associate Professor/MFA Coordinator, 203-837-8876. *Application contact:* Chris Shankle, Associate Director of Graduate Admissions, 203-837-8244, Fax: 203-837-8338, E-mail: shanklec@wcsu.edu.

Western Illinois University, School of Graduate Studies, College of Arts and Sciences, Department of English and Journalism, Macomb, IL 61455-1390. Offers literature and language (MA); writing (MA). Part-time programs available. *Students:* 14 full-time (10 women), 31 part-time (21 women); includes 2 minority (1 Asian American or Pacific Islander, 1 Hispanic American), 4 international. Average age 31. 21 applicants, 90% accepted. In 2007, 13 degrees awarded. *Degree requirements:* For master's, thesis or alternative. *Entrance requirements:* For master's, minimum GPA of 2.75. Additional exam requirements/recommendations for international students: Required—TOEFL (minimum score 550 paper-based; 213 computer-based; 80 iBT). *Application deadline:* Applications are processed on a rolling basis. Application fee: $30. Electronic applications accepted. *Expenses:* Tuition, state resident: part-time $217 per credit hour. Tuition, nonresident: part-time $433 per credit hour. Required fees: $54 per credit hour. *Financial support:* In 2007–08, 14 students received support, including 7 research assistantships with full tuition reimbursements available (averaging $6,800 per year), 7 teaching assistantships with full tuition reimbursements available (averaging $7,840 per year). Financial award applicants required to submit FAFSA. *Unit head:* Dr. David Boocker, Chairperson, 309-298-1103. *Application contact:* Dr. Barbara Baily, Director of Graduate Studies/Associate Provost, 309-298-1806, Fax: 309-298-2345, E-mail: grad-office@wiu.edu.

Western Kentucky University, Graduate Studies, Potter College of Arts and Letters, Department of English, Bowling Green, KY 42101. Offers education (MA); English (MA Ed); literature (MA), including American literature, British literature, literary theory, women writers, world literature; teaching English as a second language (MA); writing (MA). Part-time and evening/weekend programs available. *Degree requirements:* For master's, comprehensive exam, thesis optional, final exam. *Entrance requirements:* For master's, GRE General Test, minimum GPA of 2.75. Additional exam requirements/recommendations for international students: Required—TOEFL (minimum score 555 paper-based; 213 computer-based; 79 iBT). *Faculty research:* Improving writing, linking teacher knowledge and performance, Victorian women writers, Kentucky women writers, Kentucky poets.

Western Michigan University, Graduate College, College of Arts and Sciences, Department of English, Kalamazoo, MI 49008-5202. Offers creative writing (MFA); English (MA, PhD); English education (MA, PhD); professional writing (MA). *Degree requirements:* For master's, oral exams; for doctorate, one foreign language, thesis/dissertation, oral exam, written exams. *Entrance requirements:* For master's and doctorate, GRE General Test, GRE Subject Test.

Westminster College, Program in Professional Communication, Salt Lake City, UT 84105-3697. Offers MPC. Part-time and evening/weekend programs available. *Faculty:* 6 full-time (4 women), 2 part-time/adjunct (0 women). *Students:* 10 full-time (2 women), 59 part-time (42 women); includes 2 minority (1 American Indian/Alaska Native, 1 Asian American or Pacific Islander). Average age 34. 47 applicants, 72% accepted, 23 enrolled. In 2007, 16 degrees awarded. *Degree requirements:* For master's, field project. *Entrance requirements:* For master's, personal resumé, sample of professional writing. Additional exam requirements/recommendations for international students: Required—TOEFL (minimum score 600 paper-based; 213 computer-based). *Application deadline:* For fall admission, 8/1 priority date for domestic students. Applications are processed on a rolling basis. Application fee: $40. Electronic applications accepted. *Expenses:* Tuition: Part-time $1,003 per credit hour. Tuition and fees vary according to program and student level. *Financial support:* In 2007–08, 29 students received support. Career-related internships or fieldwork and tuition remissions available. Support available to part-time students. Financial award applicants required to submit FAFSA. *Unit head:* Dr. Helen Hodgson, Director, 801-832-2821, Fax: 801-832-3102, E-mail: hhodgson@westminstercollege.edu. *Application contact:* Joel Bauman, Vice President of Enrollment Services, 801-832-2200, Fax: 801-832-3101, E-mail: admission@westminstercollege.edu.

West Virginia University, Eberly College of Arts and Sciences, Department of English, Program in Creative Writing, Morgantown, WV 26506. Offers MFA. Part-time and evening/weekend programs available. *Students:* 23 full-time (15 women), 4 part-time (3 women), 1 international. Average age 29. 56 applicants, 27% accepted, 8 enrolled. In 2007, 10 degrees awarded. *Application deadline:* For fall admission, 2/1 for domestic students. Application fee: $50. *Expenses:* Tuition, state resident: full-time $5,196; part-time $292 per credit hour. Tuition, nonresident: full-time $15,064; part-time $840 per credit hour. Tuition and fees vary according to program. *Financial support:* In 2007–08, 25 students received support, including 10 teaching assistantships with full tuition reimbursements available (averaging $12,000 per year); research assistantships. *Unit head:* Dr. Mark Brazaitis, Coordinator, 304-293-9707, Fax: 304-293-5380, E-mail: mark.brazaitis@mail.wvu.edu. *Application contact:* Amanda Riley, Graduate Secretary, 304-293-2947, Fax: 304-293-5380, E-mail: amanda.riley@mail.wvu.edu.

Wichita State University, Graduate School, Fairmount College of Liberal Arts and Sciences, Department of English, Wichita, KS 67260. Offers creative writing (MA, MFA); English (MA, MFA). Part-time and evening/weekend programs available. *Degree requirements:* For master's, comprehensive exam. *Entrance requirements:* For master's, GRE, writing sample (MFA). Additional exam requirements/recommendations for international students: Required—TOEFL. Electronic applications accepted.

Wilkes University, Graduate Studies and Continued Learning, College of Arts, Humanities and Social Sciences, Program in Creative Writing, Wilkes-Barre, PA 18766-0002. Offers MA, MFA. *Students:* 73 full-time (37 women), 19 part-time (11 women); includes 2 minority (both American Indian/Alaska Native). Average age 37. In 2007, 31 degrees awarded. *Entrance requirements:* Additional exam requirements/recommendations for international students: Required—TOEFL (minimum score 500 paper-based; 173 computer-based; 79 iBT). Application fee: $45. *Expenses:* Contact institution. *Financial support:* Application deadline: 3/1. *Unit head:* Dr. Bonnie Culver, Director, 570-408-4527, E-mail: bonnie.culver@wilkes.edu. *Application contact:* Kathleen Houlihan, Director of Graduate Studies, 570-408-3235, Fax: 570-408-7846, E-mail: kathleen.houlihan@wilkes.edu.

Wright State University, School of Graduate Studies, College of Liberal Arts, Department of English Language and Literatures, Dayton, OH 45435. Offers composition and rhetoric (MA); English (MA); literature (MA); teaching English to speakers of other languages (MA). *Degree requirements:* For master's, thesis optional, portfolio. *Entrance requirements:* For master's, 20 hours in upper-level English. Additional exam requirements/recommendations for international students: Required—TOEFL. *Faculty research:* American literature, world literature in English, applied linguistics, writing theory and pedagogy.

ADELPHI UNIVERSITY

College of the Arts and Sciences
Program in Creative Writing

Program of Study

The Master of Fine Arts (M.F.A.) in creative writing offers students the opportunity to specialize in three major genres—fiction, poetry, and playwriting. This cross-genre program is distinctive from the traditional two-genre M.F.A. programs in which students study either fiction or poetry. Its unique Professional Development Practicum introduces students to the professional and practical life of writers across many disciplines.

Taught by distinguished faculty members who have published extensively, the program prepares students for careers in writing, teaching, and/or more advanced graduate studies through training in creative writing, language and literary studies, research, and teaching. Most classes are seminars that are held in the evenings once a week, either from 4 to 6:30 p.m. or from 7 to 9:30 p.m. Students must complete 37 credits in a plan of study that includes writing workshops (16 credits) and literature classes (12 credits). Students must also complete an 8-credit thesis colloquium. The 1-credit Professional Development Practicum meets once a week in the spring semester of the first year. Through meetings with writers and agents, students learn firsthand about the professional life of a writer. They also learn the practical procedures of submitting a manuscript or applying for a grant. Students and their advisers determine the appropriate plan of study. A student thesis is required in all programs.

Research Facilities

The University's primary research holdings are at Swirbul Library and include 667,383 volumes (including bound periodicals and government publications), 805,179 items in microformats, 23,230 audiovisual items, 1,635 periodical subscriptions, and access to over 27,000 electronic journal titles. Online access is provided to 233 research databases.

Financial Aid

All applicants are eligible for financial aid and are automatically considered for one of six partial (one-half) tuition remissions. Second-year students and students entering with a previous M.A. degree are eligible for graduate teaching fellowships in the Department of English. There are also opportunities for work-study positions, for community service teaching grants, or for positions at the Writing Center and the Learning Center.

Cost of Study

For the 2007–08 academic year, the tuition rate was $755 per credit. University fees ranged from $300 to $500 per semester.

Living and Housing Costs

The University assists single and married students in finding suitable accommodations whenever possible. The cost of living is dependent upon location and the number of rooms rented.

Location

Located in historic Garden City, New York, 45 minutes from Manhattan and 20 minutes from Queens, Adelphi's 75-acre suburban campus is known for the beauty of its landscape and architecture. The campus is a short walk from the Long Island Rail Road and is convenient to New York's major airports and several major highways. Off-campus centers are located in Manhattan, Hauppauge, and Poughkeepsie.

The University and The College

Founded in 1896, Adelphi is a fully accredited, private university with more than 8,300 undergraduate, graduate, and returning-adult students in the arts and sciences, business, clinical psychology, education, nursing, and social work. Students come from thirty-seven states and from forty-five countries. *The Princeton Review* named Adelphi University a Best College in the Northeastern Region, and *Fiske Guide to Colleges* recognized Adelphi as a "Best Buy" in higher education for two years in a row. The University is the only private institution on Long Island and one of only twenty-six in the nation to earn this recognition.

Mindful of the cultural inheritance of the past, the College of Arts and Sciences encompasses those realms of inquiry that have characterized the modern pursuit of knowledge. The faculty members of the College place a high priority on their students' intellectual development in and out of the classroom and structure programs and opportunities to foster that growth. Students analyze original research or other creative work, develop firsthand facility with creative or research methodologies, undertake collaborative work with peers and mentors, engage in serious internships, and hone communicative skills.

Applying

A baccalaureate degree is required for admission (the degree does not have to be in English or literature). A student must submit the completed application form, the $50 application fee, official college transcripts, two letters of reference from people familiar with the student's writing, a personal statement (of no more than 1,000 words and about the student's writing life and goals), and a manuscript in one genre only (poetry, fiction, or playwriting). The application deadlines are January 15 for fall enrollment and September 15 for spring enrollment. After those dates, rolling admissions are made on a space-available basis.

Correspondence and Information

Judith Baumel, Director of the M.F.A. Program
Harvey Hall, Room 212
College of Arts and Sciences
Adelphi University
Garden City, New York 11530-0701

Phone: 516-877-4031
Fax: 516-877-3039
E-mail: baumel@adelphi.edu
Web site: http://academics.adelphi.edu/artsci/creativewriting/

Adelphi University

THE FACULTY AND THEIR RESEARCH

CREATIVE WRITING

Calvin Baker, Visiting Assistant Professor; B.A., Amherst, 1994.

Judith Baumel, Associate Professor; M.A., Johns Hopkins, 1978. Contemporary poetry.

Martha Cooley, Assistant Professor; B.A., Trinity, 1977. Creative writing, modern and contemporary American literature, world literatures in translation (particularly Italian).

Anton Dudley, Assistant Professor; M.F.A., NYU, 2001. Dramatic writing.

Kermit Frazier, Associate Professor; M.F.A., NYU, 1977; M.A., Syracuse, 1970. Playwriting, television writing, contemporary drama, African American drama, the literature of AIDS.

Jacqueline Jones LaMon, Assistant Professor; J.D., UCLA, 1987; M.F.A., Indiana, 2006.

Igor Webb, Professor; Ph.D., Stanford, 1971. The nineteenth-century novel. *The Short Prose Reader: Annotated Instructor's Edition*, 9th ed. (Boston: McGraw-Hill, 2000).

LITERATURE

Jennifer Fleischner, Professor; Ph.D., Columbia, 1988. Twentieth-century American literature. *Mrs. Lincoln and Mrs. Keckly: The Remarkable Story of the Friendship Between a First Lady and a Former Slave* (New York: Broadway Books, 2003).

Michael Matto, Assistant Professor; Ph.D., NYU, 1998. History of the English language, history of rhetoric, Old English literature and culture, theories of metaphor, history of subjectivity.

Christopher Mayo, Assistant Professor; Ph.D., Brandeis, 2004. Restoration and eighteenth-century British literature and culture. "'A Lord Among Wits': Lord Chesterfield and his Reception of Johnson's Letter." In *Johnsonian News Letter* 56(2):38–42, September 2005.

Adam McKeown, Assistant Professor; Ph.D., NYU, 2000. Shakespeare, early modern visual culture. "Looking at Britomart Looking at Pictures." In *Studies in English Literature* 45:43–64 (2005).

Lahney Preston-Matto, Assistant Professor; Ph.D., NYU, 2000. Twentieth-century medievalism, translation theory, gender, twentieth-century Irish poetry, cultural studies. "Staking in Tongues: Speech-Act as Weapon in *Buffy the Vampire Slayer*." In *Fighting the Forces: What's at Stake in Buffy the Vampire Slayer*, eds. R. V. Wilcox and D. Lavery (Lanham, MD: Rowman and Littlefield, 2002).

Susan Weisser, Professor; Ph.D., Columbia, 1987. The nineteenth-century novel, autobiography, romantic love and gender. Introduction and notes to Jane Austen's *Persuasion* (New York: Barnes & Noble Classics, 2003).

Peter West, Assistant Professor.

Carnegie Mellon

CARNEGIE MELLON UNIVERSITY

Department of English
Graduate Programs in Professional Writing and Communication Design

Programs of Study

The Department of English at Carnegie Mellon offers two graduate degree programs in professional communication: the Master of Arts in Professional Writing (MAPW) and, in conjunction with Carnegie Mellon's School of Design, the joint Master of Design in Communication Planning and Information Design (CPID). Both programs prepare students to directly enter the world of professional communication in print and electronic media and provide the balanced integration of theory, practice, and production needed in these fields The programs vary in the degree to which they emphasize the visual and verbal aspects of communication. The MAPW program foregrounds writing as its foundational skill while offering significant instruction in the complementary skill of visual design for print and electronic texts. The CPID program consistently foregrounds the creative potential of the interplay between words and images in traditional and interactive media and is unique in cross-training writers and designers in the same cohort. Students interested in the CPID program should contact the School of Design directly for detailed information on the program (phone: 412-268-2828).

The MAPW is a flexible and customizable program that prepares students for careers as technical and professional writers, communications specialists, and information designers and managers in a range of traditional and emerging fields. MAPW students study the basics of print and electronic communication in six foundations courses and then specialize through student-selected concentrations. The core curriculum includes professional and technical writing, grammar, style, rhetoric, graphic and document design, and organizational management. Electives and concentrations include technical writing (particularly for the software industry), communication design (including online and multimedia), corporate and business communications, journalism, editing, and science and health-care communications. Beginning in fall 2008, a concentration in investigative journalism is offered through study abroad at Strathclyde University in Scotland during the third semester. A second study-abroad option in technical communication and usability studies via a third semester at the University of Twente in the Netherlands (all classes taught in English) should be available in fall 2009.

Students gain extensive experience in planning, creating, testing, and revising professional documents. Students develop important project management and interpersonal skills through work with clients and team-based projects. In addition, they are prepared to research and understand the communication needs and practices of organizations, to use the latest research in writing and document design, and to develop facility in mastering emerging technologies.

The MAPW program requires three semesters, or 40 credit hours, of course work plus a three- to six-month professional internship generally completed between the second and third semesters. The CPID program requires two years of course work and a master's thesis and project, completed during the second year.

Research Facilities

More than 400 UNIX, Macintosh, and Windows computers are available in public clusters on the Carnegie Mellon campus. In addition, the Department of English maintains a cluster reserved for MAPW and CPID students, with dedicated computers and desktop publishing equipment. This cluster is equipped with current software for word processing, page layout, drawing, imaging, and Web authoring. Cluster hardware features high-end Macintosh machines and a few Windows machines. Additional equipment includes laser printers and scanners. The English department's usability testing lab allows students to conduct user tests of software and print documents, capturing user performance with digital video for subsequent analysis and editing. Students also have access to Carnegie Mellon's on-site print shop, which provides a full range of printing services.

Financial Aid

All students accepted full-time into the MAPW program receive a scholarship that directly reduces tuition by a significant amount. Qualified MAPW applicants who apply by February 15 of each year may also be eligible for additional merit-based scholarship funds. Graduate student loans are available through Carnegie Mellon's Office of Financial Aid, and MAPW students may apply for research assistantships within the Department. Students applying to the CPID program should contact the School of Design (phone: 412-268-2828) for financial aid information.

Cost of Study

Fees and expenses for full-time graduate students in 2008–09 are tuition, $33,810; activity fees, $400; and books and supplies, about $500. Part-time students are charged tuition at a unit rate.

Living and Housing Costs

There is a wide range of affordable housing options close to the Carnegie Mellon campus. Housing costs in Pittsburgh are typically lower than those in other urban settings. Room and board for a single graduate student average around $7000 for a full year. Carnegie Mellon does not provide housing for graduate students.

Student Group

Carnegie Mellon is a national research university of about 10,000 students and 4,000 faculty, research, and administrative staff members. Students come from all fifty states and forty-eight other countries. Nine percent are members of ethnic minority groups; about 20 percent are international students. Of the 95 graduate students enrolled in the Department of English, about 35 are in the literary and cultural studies program, 29 in rhetoric, 32 in the MAPW program, and 15 in the Master of Design program. The ratio of men to women is approximately even.

Student Outcomes

The programs produce graduates who are resourceful, multidimensional professionals with strong career potential. Graduates typically seek communications-based careers in government, business, nonprofits, and industry. Recent graduates have moved directly into positions in organizations such as IBM, NIH, Apple, Ketchum, Bank of New York Mellon, Catapult, Google, Compunetix, Fitch Richardson-Smith, Alcoa, MediaSite, and SiegelGale.

Location

Pittsburgh, Pennsylvania, was rated the number one "Most Livable City" by *Places Rated Almanac* in 2007. The city offers good public transportation, a lively arts and theater scene, diverse outdoor recreation, and an appealing geographical setting. The University is in the Oakland section near Schenley Park, the Carnegie Museums, and the University of Pittsburgh and its medical center. Adjacent neighborhoods offer housing, local shopping, and interesting restaurants and coffee shops. New York City, Philadelphia, Toronto, and Washington, D.C., are all within driving distance.

The University and The Department

Carnegie Mellon comprises a diverse blend of academic disciplines, including nationally recognized programs in cognitive psychology, computer science, design, human-computer interaction, management and public policy, robotics, writing and rhetoric, and applied history. The English department offers undergraduate majors in English, creative writing, professional writing, and technical writing. Carnegie Mellon is recognized as one of the most-wired of U.S. campuses and a pioneer in the use of computing in education.

Applying

MAPW applicants should submit transcripts, three letters of recommendation, a statement of intent, writing samples, a resume, GRE scores, and a nonrefundable fee of $50. Applicants not educated in the United States, Canada, Great Britain, Australia, or New Zealand must also submit TOEFL scores. Interviews, either face-to-face or by telephone, may be required. Applications for the MAPW program are accepted on a rolling basis, with admission closing when enrollment goals are met. MAPW applicants should submit their materials as early as possible and no later than February 15 to be considered for financial aid beyond the usual tuition remission scholarship. Applicants for the CPID program should contact the School of Design (phone: 412-268-2828) for specific application instructions.

Correspondence and Information

MAPW
Director of Graduate Studies
Department of English
Carnegie Mellon University
Pittsburgh, Pennsylvania 15213
Phone: 412-268-2850
Fax: 412-268-7989
E-mail: info@english.hss.cmu.edu
Web site: http://english.cmu.edu

Anita Kulina Smith
CPID Graduate Program Coordinator
Phone: 412-268-6843
E-mail: grad-info@design.cmu.edu
Web site: http://www.design.cmu.edu/ (follow the program link)

Carnegie Mellon University

THE FACULTY AND THEIR RESEARCH

Marian Aguiar, Assistant Professor of English and Literary and Cultural Studies; Ph.D., Massachusetts. Postcolonial and modernism.
Jane Bernstein, Professor of English and Creative Writing; M.F.A., Columbia. Fiction, nonfiction, screenwriting.
Claudia Carlos, Assistant Professor of Rhetoric; Ph.D., Illinois at Urbana-Champaign. Style, argument theory and practice, history of rhetoric, rhetoric of indirection.
Gerald P. Costanzo, Professor of English and Creative Writing; M.A., M.A.T., Johns Hopkins. Poetry, literature.
James Daniels, Thomas S. Baker Professor of English and Creative Writing; M.F.A., Bowling Green State. Poetry, fiction.
Sharon Dilworth, Associate Professor of English and Creative Writing; M.F.A., Michigan. Fiction, screenwriting.
Linda Flower, Professor of English and Rhetoric; Ph.D., Rutgers. Environmental rhetoric, cognitive rhetoric, community literacy.
Terrance Hayes, Professor of Creative Writing; M.F.A., Pittsburgh. Poetry, contemporary literature.
Paul Hopper, Paul Mellon Distinguished Professor of the Humanities and Professor of Rhetoric and Linguistics; Ph.D., Texas. Grammar, discourse studies, linguistics.
Suguru Ishizaki, Associate Professor of Rhetoric and Visual Design; Ph.D., MIT. Visual and document design, writing and design for new media.
Barbara Johnstone, Professor of English and Rhetoric; Ph.D., Michigan. Discourse studies, sociolinguistics.
David S. Kaufer, Professor of English and Rhetoric and Head; Ph.D., Wisconsin. Argument theory, technology and writing, professional communication.
Alan Kennedy, Professor of English; Ph.D., Edinburgh. Modern and Victorian fiction, theories of fiction, poststructural and cultural theory.
Jon P. Klancher, Associate Professor of English; Ph.D., UCLA. Sociology of culture, history of critical theory, Victorian studies, history of the book.
Peggy Knapp, Professor of English; Ph.D., Pittsburgh. Medieval, Renaissance, early modern English studies.
Hilary Masters, Professor of English and Creative Writing; A.B., Brown. Fiction, essays.
Jane McCafferty, Associate Professor of Creative Writing; M.F.A., Pittsburgh. Fiction, magazine writing, literary nonfiction.
Christine Neuwirth, Professor of English and Human-Computer Interaction; Ph.D., Carnegie Mellon. Computer tools for reading and writing, policy arguments, collaborative writing, technical and professional communication, Web and multimedia design.
Kathleen Newman, Associate Professor of English; Ph.D., Yale. American studies, media studies.
Richard Purcell, Assistant Professor of English; Ph.D., Pittsburgh. African American literature, history of Western humanism.
Andreea Deciu Ritivoi, Associate Professor of Rhetoric; Ph.D., Minnesota. Intercultural communication, rhetoric of public policy, professional and technical communication.
Karen Rossi Schnakenberg, Teaching Professor of Rhetoric and Professional Writing; Ph.D., Carnegie Mellon. Technical and professional communication, pedagogy of writing, instructional design, history of writing instruction.
David R. Shumway, Professor of English and Literary and Cultural Studies; Ph.D., Indiana. Organization of power, history of the discipline of English, film and media studies.
Kristina Straub, Professor of English and Associate Head; Ph.D., Emory. Feminist theory, cultural studies, lesbian and gay history and theory, eighteenth-century studies.
Danielle Wetzel, Assistant Professor of Rhetoric and Writing; Ph.D., Carnegie Mellon. Discourse analysis, composition pedagogies and second-language writing.
Jeffrey Williams, Professor of English; Ph.D., SUNY at Stony Brook. History of English departments, critical history and theory, nineteenth-century literature.
James Wynn, Assistant Professor of English; Ph.D., Maryland. Rhetoric of science, professional communication, science writing.

EMERSON COLLEGE

School of the Arts
Master of Fine Arts Program in Creative Writing

Program of Study Ranked by *U.S. News & World Report* among the top programs of its kind, the Emerson College M.F.A. in creative writing program, one of the nation's largest, gives students the breadth and depth of experience and instruction that smaller programs cannot. As part of a distinguished community of students and faculty members, M.F.A. candidates grow in sophistication as writers.

Students concentrate in one literary genre (fiction, nonfiction, or poetry), but may elect to take workshops in topics such as playwriting, screenwriting, memoir, and novel writing. With workshops capped at a dozen participants, students receive personal attention from the College's accomplished faculty members. A graduate's goal is to publish, and Emerson strives to expose students to writing as both an art form and professional pursuit.

For more information about Emerson's M.F.A. in creative writing, interested students should visit http://admission.emerson.edu/admission/graduate/academics/cw.cfm.

Research Facilities The Emerson College library has more than 200,000 volumes, 20,000 journals (paper and electronic), 8,000 e-books, 10,000 nonprint materials, and 10,000 microforms in its collection that focus on the communication studies and performing arts. Through membership in the Fenway Consortium, graduate students have access to more than 2 million volumes. Computer-assisted reference services provide bibliographic databases through Dialog, BRS, and other online services. The Online Computer Library Center is used for student research support.

M.F.A. candidates gain valuable hands-on experience in the Media Services Center, which provides students with access to approximately 2,400 films, videos, laser discs, and DVDs. The center is the home of audio, video, and multimedia production facilities; a video studio; and several nonlinear editing suites comparable to those of any television studio in a major U.S. city.

Financial Aid Emerson College offers several financial assistance programs that make graduate education possible: merit-based awards (domestic and international applicants), low-interest federal loans (domestic applicants only), federal work-study (domestic applicants only), private loans (domestic and international applicants), student employment (domestic and international applicants), and alternative payment plans (domestic and international applicants). For detailed information, students should visit the Office of Student Financial Services Web site at http://www.emerson.edu/financial_services.

Cost of Study Tuition for the 2008–09 academic year is $886 per credit hour. Other fees vary and may apply.

Living and Housing Costs Though on-campus housing is not available for its graduate students, the Emerson College Office of Off-Campus Student Services offers assistance in finding housing, including: local apartment listings, realtor lists, temporary accommodations, search tips, pertinent neighborhood information, a roommate networking service, and more. Costs for housing are comparable to those of rental properties available in larger East Coast cities.

Student Group More than 950 graduate students representing forty-five states and sixty countries are enrolled in Emerson programs.

Student Outcomes Emerson's creative writing graduates are award-winning writers who have published stories, plays, critical essays, and novels. Many teach in colleges and universities across the country and have had their work featured in literary and popular magazines. Recent employers of Emerson students include *The Atlantic Monthly*, Beacon Press, *Boston Book Review*, David R. Godine Publisher, Houghton Mifflin, Pearson Education, *Ploughshares*, *Walking Magazine*, and Yankee Publishing.

Location Situated in the heart of downtown Boston, Emerson offers access to the vast resources of a city that is the home of the nation's finest educational institutions and an international hub of culture, media production, writing, publishing, communication, commerce, and medical innovation. Boston is a career launching pad for Emerson's students, many of whom intern or work at world-renowned organizations throughout the city. Emerson students from around the country and world absorb the city's unique blend of local and global culture, and many find that Boston is an education in itself.

The College Emerson College, founded in 1880 by Charles Wesley Emerson, has expanded upon its original mission of promoting the study of oratory and the performing arts by offering some of the nation's most distinctive graduate programs in communication.

Applying Emerson's graduate programs welcome applicants from across the United States and around the world. Admission is competitive and selective. Emerson is looking for students whose academic and professional backgrounds, communication skills, and passion for the field meet the demands of their chosen program and promise a successful career.

The application deadline is January 5 for domestic and international applicants. Applications that are not complete by the final deadline are not reviewed by the admission committee. Applicants are responsible for ensuring the completion of their application. Application fees are nonrefundable; application forms and supporting materials become the property of the Office of Graduate Admission once they are sent to the office, and they will not be returned.

All application materials, with the exception of GRE test scores, must be submitted together in one package to ensure timely review. A complete application includes the application, either online or printed (PDF download); the application fee ($60 for domestic applicants, $75 for international applicants); official transcripts from all colleges/universities previously attended; three letters of recommendation (by persons best able to assess academic and professional qualifications, including motivation and goals); the essay; official GRE scores; a 15-page writing sample; and a professional resume.

Applicants whose native language is not English must provide evidence of English proficiency by submitting official TOEFL or IELTS test results. (Applicants from India and the Philippines are considered nonnative English speakers and are required to take the TOEFL.) Emerson College's school code for the TOEFL is 3367; no department code is needed. For more information about these tests, prospective student can visit http://www.toefl.org or http://www.ielts.org. Minimum TOEFL scores are 550 paper-based, 213 computer-based, and 80 Internet-based. The minimum IELTS score is 6.5. Applicants who do not meet this requirement are not reviewed for admission.

Decisions are made on complete applications within six to eight weeks.

Deadlines for merit-based and federal aid applications for fall are January 5 and April 1, respectively. Students seeking additional information about financing their graduate education should visit http://www.emerson.edu/financial_services/info-grad.cfm/.

Correspondence and Information

Office of Graduate Admission
Emerson College
120 Boylston Street
Boston, Massachusetts 02116-4624

Phone: 617-824-8610
Fax: 617-824-8614
E-mail: gradapp@emerson.edu
Web site: http://admission.emerson.edu/admission/graduate

Emerson College

THE FACULTY

Daniel Tobin, Professor and Chair; M.T.S., Harvard; M.F.A., Warren Wilson; Ph.D., Virginia. Dr. Tobin is the author of many volumes of poetry. He has received The Discovery/The Nation Award, the Robert Penn Warren Award, the Robert Frost Fellowship, the Katherine Bakeless Nason Prize, and a fellowship from the National Endowment for the Arts, among other prizes for his poetry.

Lisa Diercks, Assistant Professor and Graduate Program Director, M.A. Program; M.S., Boston University. Ms. Diercks is a publishing industry veteran, working primarily in book design. She began her career at Houghton Mifflin/Trade and later established her own design studio. Her publishing clients have included *The Atlantic Monthly;* Beacon Press; Boston Common Press; Candlewick Press; HarperCollins; Little, Brown; and the Museum of Fine Arts. She began teaching as an adjunct in 1996, joining the full-time faculty in 2001. Both she and her students have received multiple awards for design work.

Douglas Whynott, Associate Professor and Graduate Program Director, M.F.A. Program; M.F.A., Massachusetts Amherst. Mr. Whynott is the author of *A Country Practice–Scenes from the Veterinary Life, Following the Bloom–Across America with the Migratory Beekeepers, Giant Bluefin,* and *A Unit of Water, A Unit of Time–Joel White's Last Boat.* He has written extensively for many magazines and journals.

Jonathan Aaron, Associate Professor; Ph.D., Yale. Dr. Aaron is the author of 3 books of poems: *Second Sight, Corridor,* and *Journey to the Lost City.* He has received grants from the National Endowment for the Arts and the Massachusetts Artists Foundation. Aaron has published poetry and criticism in *Paris Review, Partisan Review,* the *London Review of Books,* and others.

Bill Beuttler, Instructor; M.S., Columbia. Mr. Beuttler is a *Boston Globe* correspondent whose writing has appeared recently in *The Atlantic Online, Best Life, Boston* magazine, and *Chicago* magazine, among others. He has worked as an editor for *The Discovery Channel, Men's Journal, Boston, Down Beat,* and *American Way* magazines.

Ben Brooks, Writer-in-Residence; M.F.A., Iowa. Ben Brooks is the author of the novel, *The Icebox* and over seventy-five published short stories. His stories have won an O. Henry Prize and a Nelson Algren Award and have been published in many journals and magazines. In addition, he is the author of numerous published essays on art, history, building design, and travel. He has received awards and fellowships for his fiction from the Fine Arts Work Center in Provincetown, the Massachusetts Artists Foundation, the Arizona Commission on the Arts, the Ingram Merrill Foundation, and elsewhere.

Christine Casson, Scholar/Writer-in-Residence; M.F.A., Warren Wilson. Ms. Casson's scholarly interests include environmental literature, Native American literature, and modern and contemporary poetry in English. She has published recent essays on the work of Linda Hogan and Leslie Marmon Silko. Her poetry has appeared many journals and anthologies.

Yu-Jin Chang, Assistant Professor; Ph.D., Yale. Yu-Jin Chang is a specialist in European comparative literature and philosophy and has recently completed a study of Walter Benjamin and Maurice Blanchot titled *Disaster and Hope.* This study examines the closely related aesthetic conceptions of time and history by these two writers, arguably the two most influential literary theorists of the last century, down to their philosophical origins in, respectively, Leibniz's monadology and Nietzsche's doctrine of eternal return. A former professor of French and German, Dr. Chang has also studied Korean and classical Chinese.

William Donoghue, Associate Professor; Ph.D., Stanford. Dr. Donoghue is a specialist in the novel and the author of *Enlightenment Fiction in England, France and America.* He has published articles and book reviews on British and French eighteenth-century fiction, written and directed a short film with the National Film Board of Canada, translated a volume of French poetry entitled *Lead Blues,* and published his own short fiction in *TriQuarterly, Grain,* and elsewhere. His interests are in philosophy and literature and the theory of the novel.

David Emblidge, Associate Professor; Ph.D., Minnesota. Dr. Emblidge has nearly two decades of experience as a book editor, publisher, and author. His articles and essays have appeared in many journals, magazines, newspapers, and other periodicals. He won a Fulbright Teaching Fellowship, a National Endowment for the Humanities fellowship, and a grant from the Massachusetts Foundation for the Humanities and Public Policy.

Robin Riley Fast, Associate Professor; Ph.D., Minnesota. Dr. Fast's interests include nineteenth-century American literature, American poetry, women writers, and Native American literature. She has published a book titled *The Heart as a Drum: Continuance and Resistance in American Indian Poetry* and articles on poetry and coedited *Approaches to Teaching Dickinson's Poetry.*

Maria Flook, Writer-in-Residence; M.F.A., Iowa. Ms. Flook is the author of nonfiction books, fiction, (which received a PEN American/Ernest Hemingway Foundation Special Citation), and a collection of stories. She has also published two collections of poetry, (winner of the Houghton Mifflin New Poetry Series and the G.L.C.A. New Writers Award). Her work has appeared in many periodicals.

Flora M. González, Professor; Ph.D., Yale. Dr. Gonzalez received her Ph.D. in Hispanic literature and has taught at Dartmouth, Middlebury, and the University of Chicago. Her teaching interests include Latin American fiction and nonfiction, the literatures of the Caribbean, and feminist writing. She has published widely on the topic of the Latin American novel since the 1960s and coedited and translated selected poetry of Excilia Saldana. She has published nonfiction in several journals and reviews. In 1997 and 1998, she was a Fellow at the W. E. B. DuBois Institute at Harvard University and is presently an affiliate of the David Rockefeller Center of Latin American Studies at Harvard.

Lise Haines, Writer-in-Residence; M.F.A., Bennington. Lise Haines is the author of the novels *In My Sister's Country* and *Small Acts of Sex and Electricity.* Her work has appeared in journals, including *Ploughshares, Agni, Crosscurrents, Third Rail,* and *Post Road.* She was a finalist for the 2003 Peterson Fiction Prize and the PEN Nelson Algren Fiction Award. Her teaching credits include UCLA, UCSB, and Stonecoast. The *Boston Globe* called *In My Sister's Country* "an authoritative fictional debut."

DeWitt Henry, Professor; Ph.D., Harvard. Dr. Henry is cofounder and executive director of *Ploughshares,* for which he received a 1993 Commonwealth Award. He has edited four anthologies (one a winner of the Editors' Book Award) and recently published a novel titled *The Marriage of Anna Maye Potts.* He has won the Peter Taylor Prize, a National Endowment for the Arts Fellowship, the Boulevard Fiction Award, and a St. Botolph Foundation Award.

Richard Hoffman, Writer-in-Residence; M.F.A., Goddard. Mr. Hoffman is the author of *Half the House: a Memoir* and a collection of poems, *Without Paradise.* His work has been published in magazines such as *Agni, Ascent,* the *Boston Globe, Harvard Review, Hudson Review, The Literary Review, Poetry, Shenandoah, The Marlboro Review, Witness,* and others, as well as in several anthologies.

Roy Kamada, Assistant Professor; M.F.A., Virginia; Ph.D., California, Davis. Dr. Kamada's work has appeared in several journals. Dr. Kamada is a specialist in British and multiethnic American literatures whose interests include poetry, contemporary poetics, and postcolonial and diasporic studies. He has received grants from the James Irvine Foundation, Poets and Writers, the Vermont Studio Center, and Bread Loaf. He has received the Celeste Turner Wright award from the Academy of American Poets and has been the recipient of the David Noel Miller Fellowship at the University of California, Davis, and a Henry Hoyns Fellowship at the University of Virginia

Bill Knott, Associate Professor; M.F.A., Norwich. Mr. Knott is the author of numerous books of poetry and has been featured in most major journals and poetry magazines. His book, *Selected and Collected Poems,* was the 1979 winner of the Elliston Prize. His publications include *Poems 1963–1988, Outremer, The Quicken Tree, Laugh at the End of the World: Collected Comic Poems 1969–1999,* and, most recently, *The Unsubscriber.*

Maria Koundoura, Associate Professor; Ph.D., Stanford. Dr. Koundoura is a specialist in contemporary literary theory, in particular, postcolonial and transnational culture studies. Among her recent publications are articles on nationalism, multiculturalism, and globality. She is one of the founding editors of the *Stanford Humanities Review.* Currently she is at work on a book on global cities.

Margot Livesey, Writer-in-Residence; B.A., York (UK). Ms. Livesey is the author of *Banishing Verona, Eva Moves the Furniture, The Missing World, Criminals, Homework, Writing About Literature,* and *Learning By Heart.* She has written extensively for journals, magazines, and newspapers.

Gian Lombardo, Publisher-in-Residence and Coordinator, Certificate in Publishing program; M.A., Boston University. Mr. Lombardo has had more than twenty-five years of experience in a wide range of publishing environments—trade, association, and literary and consumer magazines as well as professional, literary, and textbook publishing. He is also the author of *Between Islands,* a collection of poems and verse translations and three collections of prose poetry: *Standing Room, Sky Open Again,* and *Of All the Corners to Forget.* He also directs Quale Press.

Megan Marshall, Assistant Professor; A.B., Harvard. Marshall is the author of *The Peabody Sisters,* a landmark biography of three women who made American intellectual history. *The Peabody Sisters* was a finalist for the Pulitzer Prize for Biography, the recipient of the Francis Parkman Prize from the Society of American Historians, and the Mark Lynton History Prize. She has written for *The New Yorker,* the *Atlantic, Slate,* and the *New York Times Book Review.*

Gail Mazur, Writer-in-Residence; M.A., Lesley. Ms. Mazur is the author of five books of poetry: *Nightfire, The Pose of Happiness, The Common, They Can't Take That Away from Me* (a finalist for the National Book Award in 2001), and *Zeppo's First Wife: New & Selected Poems* (finalist for the Los Angeles Times Book Prize). She has published reviews and essays in the *Chicago Tribune,* the *Boston Globe, Salmagundi,* the *Mississippi Review, Field,* the *Atlantic,* and other publications.

Kim McLarin, Writer-In-Residence; B.A., Duke. Ms. McLarin is the author of the novels *Jump At the Sun, Meeting of the Waters,* and *Taming It Down* and coauthor of the memoir *Growing Up X,* with Ilyasah Shabazz. She is a former staff writer for several newspapers, publications, and the Associated Press.

Pamela Painter, Professor; M.A., Illinois at Chicago. Professor Painter is the author of two collections of short fiction, *Getting to Know the Weather* and *The Long and Short of It.* She is the coauthor, with Anne Bernays, of *WHAT IF? Fiction Exercises for Fiction Writers.* Her work has appeared in numerous literary journals and magazines. She is a founding editor of *StoryQuarterly* and has received grants from the Massachusetts' Artists Foundation and the National Endowment for the Arts.

Frederick Reiken, Associate Professor; M.F.A., California, Irvine. Mr. Reiken is the author of two novels. *The Odd Sea* is a winner of the Hackney Literary Award for a first novel and is listed as one of the "20 best first novels of 1998" by *Booklist.* His second book, *The Lost Legends of New Jersey,* was published in 2000.

Murray Schwartz, Professor; Ph.D., Berkeley. Dr. Schwartz is a specialist in Shakespeare. His interests include literary theory, psychoanalysis, and Holocaust studies as editor, coeditor, and author, as well as many essays on Shakespeare, theoretical and applied psychoanalysis, and poets such as Sylvia Plath. "Morning and Its Vicissitudes: The Shakespearean Community and Shakespearean Romance," appeared in *Psyart,* an online journal. He is currently at work on a psychoanalytic study of the Holocaust and an essay on theories of trauma.

Jeffrey Seglin, Associate Professor; M.T.S., Harvard. Mr. Seglin has extensive experience in magazine and book publishing. He is the author of *The Right Thing: Conscience, Profit and Personal Responsibility in Today's Business; The Good, The Bad, And Your Business: Choosing Right When Ethical Dilemmas Pull You Apart;* and other books. He has written extensively for magazines, newspapers, and other publications.

John Skoyles, Professor; M.F.A., Iowa. Professor Skoyles is the author of three books of poems: *A Little Faith, Permanent Change,* and *Definition of the Soul.* He has also published a book of nonfiction, *Generous Strangers;* a memoir, *Secret Frequencies: A New York Education;* and reviews of books for the Associated Press. He has been awarded two individual fellowships from the National Endowment for the Arts, as well as grants from the New York State and North Carolina Arts Councils.

Tracy L. Strauss, Lecturer of Expository Writing; M.F.A., Boston University. Ms. Strauss was the 2005 recipient of the Somerville Arts Council Literary Fellowship Award for poetry and the 2003 recipient of the International Radio and Television Society (IRTS) Foundation Faculty Award. Her short fiction has been published in *Solas Literary Journal,* and she has written obituaries and on-air promotions for American Movie Classics. Her writing appears in many publications.

Jessica Treadway, Associate Professor; M.A., Boston University. Ms. Treadway is the author of the novel *And Give You Peace.* Her collection *Absent Without Leave and Other Stories* won the John C. Zacharis First Book Award in 1993. A former fellow at Radcliffe's Bunting Institute and recipient of a grant from the National Endowment for the Arts, she also reviews fiction for the *Boston Globe* and the *Chicago Tribune.*

John Trimbur, Professor; Ph.D., Buffalo, SUNY. Dr. Trimbur is a specialist in rhetoric and writing studies, with interests in cultural studies of literacy and the politics of language in the United States and South Africa. He received the Richard Braddock Award for Outstanding Article (2003) for *English Only and U.S. College Composition,* the James L. Kinneavy Award (2001) for *Agency and the Death of the Author: A Partial Defense of Modernism,* and the College Composition and Communication Outstanding Book Award (1993) for *The Politics of Writing Instruction: Postsecondary.* He has also published three textbooks.

Wendy Walters, Associate Professor; Ph.D., California, San Diego. Dr. Walters teaches courses in literatures of the African diaspora, as well as multicultural American literatures. In 2001–02 she was a nonresident fellow at the W. E. B. Du Bois Institute for Afro-American Research at Harvard University, where she finished her manuscript on black international writing. She has published articles in the journals *African American Review, Novel, Critical Arts,* and *MELUS* (Multi-Ethnic Literature of the U.S.), and she has published a chapter in the book *Borders, Exiles, Diasporas.* Her contributor credits include several publications. She is the author of *At Home in Diaspora: Black International Writing.*

Daniel Weaver, Editor-in-Residence; B.A., Earlham. Most recently he was editor in chief and director of Faber & Faber, Inc. and editor in chief of Nation Books, affiliated with *The Nation* magazine. He has been a senior editor at McGraw-Hill and Viking Penguin in New York City. He has edited and published works by Vincent Bugliosi, Gore Vidal, Ved Mehta, Phyllis Chesler, John Sayles, Garry Marshall, Julian Barnes, Alan Lelchuk, Norman Lewis, and Carolyn See, among others.

Mako Yoshkawa, Assistant Professor; M.A., Oxford. Ms. Yoshikawa is the author of two novels: *One Hundred and One Ways,* a national bestseller published in 1999 and translated into six languages, and *Once Removed.* Among her awards for writing are fellowships from the Bunting Institute at Harvard University and from the Massachusetts Cultural Council. She holds a master's in Shakespeare and renaissance drama from Lincoln College, Oxford, and is currently finishing a Ph.D. in incest and miscegenation in twentieth-century American literature at the University of Michigan. Her publications also include scholarly articles on incest and race in American literature.

THE JOHNS HOPKINS UNIVERSITY

Zanvyl Krieger School of Arts and Sciences
Advanced Academic Programs
Master of Arts in Writing

Program of Study

Through intensive writing, thoughtful revision, and careful reading, students in Johns Hopkins University's Master of Arts in Writing Program develop as writers while maintaining jobs or fulfilling other obligations. Experienced faculty members, all of whom are practicing writers or editors, provide expert guidance in four concentrations: fiction, nonfiction, poetry, and science–medical writing. Regardless of the concentration, students receive practical direction and constructive criticism to help them write successful short stories, articles, essays, poems, or books.

The M.A. in Writing Program is the University's part-time alternative to its famous Writing Seminars, the full-time M.F.A program in creative writing. The M.A. program is available in Washington and Baltimore; the Writing Seminars courses are available only in Baltimore.

Students in the Writing Program learn primarily through the practice of writing; literature is studied to clarify approaches to the craft. Classes are kept small, especially in the writing workshops required of all participants. Within the realm of literary writing, students have the flexibility to develop individual styles and pursue specialized subjects. The program's goal is to create a nurturing yet demanding environment where creative writers of diverse promise and purpose are challenged to work toward publication at the highest levels possible.

Nine courses, including a final thesis course, are required for a degree. Courses are offered on weekday evenings or Saturdays to accommodate working adults. Students complete the program at their own pace—usually in two to five years—and nearly all attend on a part-time basis. The full degree program is available at Johns Hopkins University's center at Dupont Circle in Washington, D.C., and at the main Homewood campus in Baltimore. Students may take courses at either or both campuses. The full curriculum and course descriptions, plus biographies of instructors, are available online at http://writing.jhu.edu.

Writing Program students can earn full graduate credit at the annual Hopkins Conference on Craft, which features an enriching, intense summer workshop experience at an exotic location. The 2006 and 2007 conferences were in Florence, Italy, featuring nationally prominent writers such as novelist Alice McDermott, winner of the National Book Award; poets Mary Jo Salter, Dave Smith, and John Irwin; fiction writer Jean McGarry; biographer and editor Robert Wilson; and Pulitzer Prize–winning journalist Wayne Biddle. Program alumni and select outside participants also attend the conference. For more information, students should visit http://advanced.jhu.edu/academic/writing/craftconference/2009/.

The Writing Program often allows working professionals and others who may not be interested in a graduate degree to take a course or two of personal or professional interest. For instance, accomplished fiction writers have taken courses in screenwriting or playwriting to learn those crafts. Likewise, many working editors or writers sample a course or two in the program to read and learn from classics in their field. The program offers a streamlined admissions process to these special attendees; students should contact the program for details.

Research Facilities

Part-time students in Baltimore have full access to the 2.6-million-volume Eisenhower Library and the many other libraries and research resources at Hopkins, one of the world's best-known research institutions. Students in Washington are welcome at the Library Resource Center at 1717 Massachusetts Avenue, NW. The center's staff facilitates interlibrary loans, reserve services, and a collection of program-specific reference materials, books, and videos. The Library Resource Center has eleven workstations in the electronic research room that connect to the Eisenhower Library's online catalog search tool and a vast array of electronic databases, journals, and periodicals. Writing Program students, regardless of campus, can access many of the Hopkins Library System resources online from their homes. This access includes use of thousands of online databases, journals, and listings.

Financial Aid

The Writing Program offers limited, annual scholarships to current students who have taken at least one course. The scholarships, which pay for all or part of one course, are awarded competitively on the basis of merit and need. Federal financial aid in the form of student loans is available on a limited basis to degree candidates who are enrolled in two or more courses per semester or term. More information is available from the Office of Student Financial Services. Certain private alternative loans are available to students who take only one course per term.

Cost of Study

The 2008–09 tuition is $2080 per course. Nine courses are required to complete the degree.

Living and Housing Costs

Most Writing Program students are working adults with their own housing.

Student Group

The Writing Program includes students of all ages and from all walks of life. A typical class includes students in their twenties and their fifties, with others in between or older. Some students cultivate skills to prepare for a career; others are seasoned writers who want to change focus; still others favor artistic exploration over professional ambition. The program has more than 200 students at the two campuses.

Student Outcomes

Writing Program students and alumni have been published in or edit magazines, Web sites, newspapers, newsletters, literary journals, trade publications, and many other venues. Since 1994, their success includes hundreds of articles, short stories, poems, essays, and other work online or in print, plus sixty books and counting—novels, essay/short story/poetry collections, history, travel, memoir, science, narrative journalism, consumer, nature, creative nonfiction, medicine, and architecture. Student or graduate work has appeared in *National Geographic*, the *Washington Post*, *Smithsonian*, *GQ*, the *New York Times*, Salon.com, *Esquire*, *USA Today*, National Public Radio, *Preservation* magazine, *Moment* magazine, ABC News/*Nightline*, WebMD, the *Los Angeles Times*, *USA Weekend*, and *Washingtonian*, as well as literary journals such as the *Florida Review*, *Green Mountains Review*, *Story Quarterly*, the *Haight Ashbury Literary Journal*, *Gargoyle*, *North American Poetry Review*, *Potomac Review*, *Antioch Review*, *Baltimore Review*, *Barrelhouse*, the *Sun*, *Mississippi Review*, *Phoebe*, the *Connecticut Review*, *Exquisite Corpse*, and dozens of others. Program graduates regularly earn adjunct teaching jobs in composition, writing, and journalism at a range of universities, including Maryland, Florida State, American, Ohio, George Washington, Towson, Georgetown, and many others. Select graduates move on to M.F.A. or Ph.D. programs and have earned full-time teaching jobs, including tenure-track jobs at community colleges, four-year colleges, and universities. Students and graduates also have landed writing or editing jobs at the *Washington Post*, *National Geographic*, *Smithsonian*, NPR, and *USA Today*, as well as AARP, the Bureau of National Affairs, National Institutes of Health, Brookings Institution, American Red Cross, National Education Association, American Association for the Advancement of Science, Johns Hopkins University, and many other private companies and nonprofit organizations—plus Congress, federal departments, and government agencies.

Location

The program's headquarters is at the Hopkins Washington Center at Dupont Circle in Washington, D.C., near the Dupont Circle Metro (subway) station, with an auxiliary office at the Homewood campus in Baltimore. The full degree program is offered at both campuses, and students can complete their degrees without commuting to the other campus.

The University and The School

Privately endowed, the Johns Hopkins University was founded in 1876 as the first true American university based on the European model—a graduate institution with an associated preparatory college, a place where knowledge would be created and assembled as well as taught. The Zanvyl Krieger School of Arts and Sciences is at the heart of a small but unusually diverse coeducational university. The core institution of the Johns Hopkins complex of schools, centers, and institutes, the School recognizes the intellectual strength and education requirements of working adults. Through the Advanced Academic Programs (AAP), the School offers a Hopkins education to those wishing to attend graduate school. Most of the AAP programs are designed for part-time study by working adults.

Applying

Admission is based on a competitive evaluation of writing samples and other materials. Students must submit a completed application, the application fee, official transcripts of all college work, a statement of purpose explaining the applicant's aspirations as a writer and describing the applicant's recent reading, and recent writing samples in the chosen concentration, demonstrating the applicant's promise as a writer. The writing samples should be 20 to 40 typed pages or their published equivalent and may include multiple samples; the sample does not have to be a single piece of writing. Applicants also may submit up to three recommendation letters directly relating to their experience or promise as a writer. The letters and resume are optional.

Applications to the M.A. in Writing Program are allowed year-round; accepted students may begin study in the fall, spring, or summer terms. Applications should be submitted two to four months before the beginning of the desired term. For more information, students should visit http://advanced.jhu.edu/admissions.

Correspondence and Information

Master of Arts in Writing Program
Zanvyl Krieger School of Arts and Sciences
The Johns Hopkins University
1717 Massachusetts Avenue, NW, Suite 101
Washington, D.C. 20036-1717

Phone: 800-847-3330 (toll-free)
E-mail: advanced@jhu.edu
Web site: http://writing.jhu.edu

The Johns Hopkins University

THE FACULTY

Primary Instructors

Cathy Alter is a successful freelance writer and author whose feature articles, essays, and reviews have appeared in local and national newspapers and magazines, including the *Washington Post, Washingtonian, Self, Prevention, Fitness, McSweeney's, Spin, Preservation,* and *Might.* Alter also has been a Washington correspondent for *People* magazine. Her book, *Virgin Territory: Stories from the Road to Womanhood* (Three Rivers Press), was released in 2004, and her memoir, *Up for Renewal: What Magazines Taught Me About Love, Sex, and Starting Over* (Atria), was released in July 2008. She has been a frequent lecturer in the nonfiction program at Johns Hopkins and has lectured for Washington Independent Writers, the Junior League of Washington, the Bethesda Literary Festival, and Georgetown University's Bunn Student Journalism Awards. Cathy received an M.A. from Johns Hopkins University.

David Everett (Academic Director) spent twenty-two years as a news journalist and editor, reporting from twenty-six states and eleven other countries. He worked for the *Detroit Free Press* and Knight-Ridder Newspapers, including the Washington, D.C., bureau. His reporting, writing, and essays have won national, state, and local awards, including national honors from the Society of Professional Journalists, National Press Club, Overseas Press Club, and University of Missouri. A contributing author to three nonfiction books, Everett's humor, essays, and reporting appear online and in print in the United States and internationally, and he has published fiction in several literary journals and anthologies. He has lectured at many venues nationwide. He also directs the annual Hopkins Conference on Craft. He has an M.A. in writing (fiction) from Johns Hopkins.

Karen Houppert, an author and freelance writer covering social and political issues, became a Writing Program instructor in late 2007. A staff writer for the *Village Voice* for nearly ten years, she has won several awards for her coverage of gender politics, including a National Women's Political Caucus Award, a Casey Journalism Fellowship, and a 2003 Newswomen's Club of New York Front Page Award. Houppert contributes to a wide variety of publications, from *Glamour, Redbook,* and *Self* to *Mother Jones,* the *Nation,* and *Newsday.* Her work also has appeared in five anthologies, the *New York Times,* and, soon, the *Washington Post Magazine.* She is the author of *The Curse: Confronting the Last Unmentionable Taboo, Menstruation* (Farrar, Straus, and Giroux, 2000); *Home Fires Burning: Married to the Military—For Better or Worse* (Ballantine, 2005); and the Obie Award–winning play *Boys in the Basement,* based on her trial coverage of a real-life rape in Glen Ridge, New Jersey, as well as several other plays. She previously taught graduate writing at New York University and drama at Towson University.

Mary Knudson is a medical writer and editor who is cowriting a book on heart failure that will be published in 2009. She was a medical and science writer for the *Baltimore Sun* for seventeen years. She won one of the top two national awards for science writing, a Science-in-Society Award from the National Association of Science Writers (NASW). Awarded the Harvard Journalism Fellowship for Advanced Studies in Public Health, Knudson coedited both editions of *A Field Guide for Science Writers.* Other work includes a series of children's books on female scientists and various freelance articles. Knudson served on the board of NASW for ten years and helped create the NASW's annual professional workshops. She is a former president of the D.C. Science Writers Association (DCSWA), was Freedom Forum Medical Journalist-in-Residence at Ithaca College in New York, and sits on the Managing Committee for the American Association for the Advancement of Science (AAAS) Science Journalism Awards.

William Loizeaux is the program's Writer in Residence. His latest project is his second novel for young people, *Clarence Cochran, A Human Boy,* which will be published soon by Farrar, Straus, and Giroux. His last young person's book, *Wings* (Farrar, Straus, and Giroux, 2006), won national awards and was named to four national "best of" lists. Previously, Loizeaux published two widely reviewed works of nonfiction. *Anna: A Daughter's Life* was named a 1993 *New York Times* Notable Book of the Year, and *The Shooting of Rabbit Wells* (1998) was optioned for a film by Perimeter Pictures. His essays have appeared in the *American Scholar* and *Christian Science Monitor* and have been cited in *Best American Essays.* His short fiction has appeared in *Triquarterly, Massachusetts Review, Witness,* and elsewhere, plus several anthologies. He recently completed a novella and short-story collection. His degree is from the University of Michigan (M.A.).

Paul Maliszewski is an experienced writing teacher with extensive publications in fiction and nonfiction. He has recently published articles in *Harper's, Smithsonian, Granta, Oxford American, BookForum, McSweeney's,* and *Wilson Quarterly,* among many other magazines. His short stories have been published in the *Paris Review, Gettysburg Review, Boulevard, Mississippi Review, Story Quarterly, Chicago Review, Mid-American Review, McSweeney's,* and the *Antioch Review,* among others. His stories have been reprinted in *Harper's* and have been awarded two Pushcart Prizes. He has edited four collections of writing, including *Paper Placemats,* an anthology of writing and artwork about the significance of place; an issue of *McSweeney's;* and two recent issues of *Denver Quarterly.* He received an M.F.A. in creative writing from Syracuse University.

Susan Muaddi-Darraj is Senior Editor of the *Baltimore Review,* a national journal of fiction, poetry, and creative nonfiction. She earned her M.A. in English literature from Rutgers University, where she also taught classes in fiction. Her collection of short stories, *The Inheritance of Exile,* was named a finalist in the 2003 AWP Book Awards Series, judged by Joan Silber, and published in 2007 by University of Notre Dame Press. She previously edited *Scheherazade's Legacy: Arab and Arab American Women on Writing* for Greenwood/Praeger Press (2004). Susan's fiction has appeared or is forthcoming in *New York Stories,* the *Orchid Literary Review, Mizna,* and elsewhere. Her articles, essays, and reviews have appeared in *City Paper, Full Circle,* the *Philadelphia Inquirer, Pages Magazine, Sojourner, Calyx,* the *Christian Science Monitor, Jouvert,* and many other publications. She has contributed book chapters to several anthologies and collections. She has spoken about fiction writing and publishing at the Rutgers Summer and Spring Writer's Conferences, the Baltimore Writer's Conference, the Saint Joseph's University Reading Series, and other forums. She is co-organizer (along with the editors of the *Potomac Review* and *Barrelhouse*) of Conversations & Connections, an annual conference aimed at helping writers improve their craft.

Madeleine Mysko, a poet and novelist, has previously taught literature and writing at Towson University, the Baltimore Actors' Theater Conservatory, and Johns Hopkins University. She has been the recipient of two individual artist grants from the state of Maryland (poetry and fiction), as well as scholarships from Sewanee Writers' Conference (both poetry and fiction) and Wesleyan Writers' Conference (poetry). Among her honors are an Artscape Prize in Fiction from the city of Baltimore and the Howard Nemerov Award for her sonnet "Incipient Fireworks," chosen by Donald Justice. For years, her poems and short stories have been published in literary journals, including the *Hudson Review, Shenandoah, River Styx,* the *Formalist,* the *Christian Century,* and *Bellevue Literary Review,* among others. Her poetry collection, *Crucial Blue,* is due for release by Rager Media in 2008, and her first novel, *Bringing Vincent Home,* was released in September 2007 by Plain View Press. Recently, the *Baltimore Sun* has been running her short "real-life" reflections on people and places. Mysko is a graduate of George Washington University (M.A., English literature) and Johns Hopkins University (M.A., the Writing Seminars).

Richard Peabody, a prolific poet, fiction writer, and editor, is an experienced teacher and important activist in the Washington, D.C., community of letters. He is the founder and coeditor of *Gargoyle* magazine and editor (or coeditor) of ten anthologies, including *Mondo Barbie, Conversations with Gore Vidal, A Different Beat: Writings by Women of the Beat Generation, Alice Redux,* and *Grace and Gravity: Fiction by Washington Area Women.* He is the author of the novella *Sugar Mountain* (Argonne Hotel Press), two short-story collections, and six poetry collections, including *Last of the Red Hot Magnetos* and *I'm in Love with the Morton Salt Girl* (Paycock Press). Peabody holds an M.A. in literature from American University. He has taught at the University of Virginia, Georgetown University, the Writer's Center, and Johns Hopkins University, where he has been presented the Faculty Award for Distinguished Professional Achievement.

Leslie Pietrzyk is the author of *Year and a Day* (William Morrow, 2004), which was selected for the Borders Bookstores' "Original Voices" series and the Book of the Month Club, and *Pears on a Willow Tree* (Avon Books, 1998). Her short fiction has appeared in many literary journals, including *Iowa Review, Gettysburg Review,* and *New England Review.* Her work has been nominated for the Pushcart Prize, and she has won a number of writing awards, including Shenandoah's Jean Charpiot Goodheart Prize for Fiction. She has received fellowships from Bread Loaf Writers' Conference, Sewanee Writers' Conference, Virginia Center for the Creative Arts, and KHN Center for the Arts. She has an M.F.A. in creative writing from American University.

Nancy Shute is an award-winning journalist who has written news, feature articles, essays, and op-eds for a wide variety of national publications, from *Outside* and *Smithsonian* magazines to the *New York Times, New Republic,* and *National Journal.* She is currently a senior writer at *U.S. News & World Report,* where she covers science and medicine. Shute previously was assistant managing editor at *U.S. News & World Report,* in charge of science and technology coverage. She frequently writes for the Web and appears on radio and television in major markets, including NPR, CNN, CBS, and NBC. She is on the executive board of the National Association of Science Writers and has lectured on journalism and science writing at Columbia University; Johns Hopkins University; University of Maryland; University of California, Santa Cruz; and University of Wisconsin. She authored a chapter in *A Field Guide for Science Writers* (Oxford, 2005). While serving as a Fulbright Scholar in Kamchatka, Russia, she founded the region's first independent bilingual newspaper. Shute holds a master's degree in law from Yale University.

Joanne Cavanaugh Simpson, a writer, a lecturer, and the faculty adviser for Homewood/Baltimore students in the Writing Program, is a freelance writer and former staff writer for the *Miami Herald* and *Johns Hopkins Magazine.* Her literary essays have appeared in the journal *Creative Nonfiction* and the essay collection *Letters to J.D. Salinger.* Her writing textbook, *Literature on Deadline,* was published in 2006. Her M.A. in nonfiction was earned at the Writing Seminars at Johns Hopkins University.

Tim Wendel is an award-winning novelist and journalist. His books include the novel *Castro's Curveball* (Ballantine) and *The New Face of Baseball* (Rayo/HarperCollins), which was named Top History Book for 2004 in the Latino Literary Awards. His articles have appeared in the *New York Times, Washington Post, Esquire, Washingtonian,* and *GQ,* and his columns appear on the *USA Today* op-ed page, where he is on the Board of Contributors. Wendel also cowrote one of the 2005 finalists for the *Good Morning America* national memoir contest. One of the founders of *USA Today Baseball Weekly,* where he was an editor and writer, Wendel has earned two Virginia Literary nominations, a *USA Today* Luminary Award and a Knight-Wallace Fellowship. He has been a Tennessee Williams Scholar to the Sewanee Writing Conference and Pen/Faulkner visiting writer to the Washington, D.C., Public Schools. His latest novel, *Red Rain,* will be published in late 2008. He has a graduate degree in fiction from Johns Hopkins University.

Program Faculty

William Black, M.F.A., Writer, Arts Activist, Lecturer.
Glenn Blake, M.A., Instructor, the Writing Seminars; Managing Editor, the *Johns Hopkins Review;* Lecturer.
Ann Marie Blum, M.A., Poet; Lecturer, Bureau of Human Resources, U.S. State Department.
Rick E. Borchelt, Lecturer; Executive Director of Communications, Johns Hopkins Genetics and Public Policy Center.
Elizabeth J. Cooper, Ph.D., Associate Professor of English (ret.), Virginia Commonwealth University; Lecturer.
Tristan Davies, M.A., Senior Lecturer, the Writing Seminars, Johns Hopkins University.
Ellen M. Dudley, M.A., Author, Editor, Essayist, Lecturer.
David Everett, M.A., Senior Associate Program Chair, Master of Arts in Writing; Essayist; Journalist; Fiction Writer.
Mark Farrington, M.F.A., Faculty Advisor in Fiction, Master of Arts in Writing; Fiction Writer.
Suzanne Fierston, M.A., Writer and Painter, Suzanne Fierston Studios.
Margaret Guroff, M.A., Features Editor, *AARP, The Magazine.*
Ruth Levy Guyer, Ph.D., Author; Bioethicist; Visiting Professor, Haverford College.
Melissa Hendricks, M.A., Freelance Writer, Lecturer.
Arthur Hirsch, M.S., Feature Writer, the *Baltimore Sun.*
Karen Houppert, Author; Special Correspondent, *Washington Post Magazine.*
John Irwin, Ph.D., Decker Professor in the Humanities and the Writing Seminars and Program Chair, Master of Arts in Writing, Johns Hopkins University.
Dale Keiger, Associate Editor, Johns Hopkins Publishing Group; Associate Editor, *Johns Hopkins Magazine.*
Mary Knudson, Faculty Advisor in Science–Medical Writing, Master of Arts in Writing; Freelance Writer; Author; Editor.
Marc Lapadula, M.A., M.F.A., Visiting Associate Professor, the Writing Seminars, Johns Hopkins University.
Paul Maliszewski, M.F.A., Freelance Writer, Author, Fiction Writer, Lecturer.
Margaret Meyers, M.F.A., Fiction Writer, Essayist, Lecturer.
Susan Muaddi-Darraj, M.A., Fiction Writer; Author; Senior Editor, the *Baltimore Review;* Lecturer.
Madeleine Mysko, M.A., Poet, Novelist, Lecturer.
Richard Peabody, M.A., Editor, *Gargoyle* magazine; Poet; Fiction Writer; Lecturer.
W. Edward Perlman, M.A., Faculty Advisor in Poetry, Master of Arts in Writing; Poet; Founder, Entasis Press.
Leslie Pietrzyk, M.F.A., Novelist, Lecturer.
Nancy Shute, M.A., Senior Writer, *U.S. News & World Report;* Lecturer.
Joanne Cavanaugh Simpson, M.A., Instructor, the Writing Seminars, and Faculty Advisor, Master of Arts in Writing, Johns Hopkins University.
Nolan J. Walters, M.A., Writer, Journalist, Lecturer.
Tim Wendel, M.A., Author, Novelist, Sportswriter, Op-Ed Columnist, Lecturer.
Laura Wexler, M.A., Writer, Editor, Lecturer.
Greg Williamson, M.A., Senior Lecturer, the Writing Seminars, Johns Hopkins University.
Robert Wilson, Editor, the *American Scholar;* Author; Lecturer.

LESLEY UNIVERSITY Let's wake up the world.℠

LESLEY UNIVERSITY

Master of Fine Arts in Creative Writing

Program of Study

The Master of Fine Arts (M.F.A.) in creative writing at Lesley University is a two-year, low-residency program in which students, under the guidance of a faculty mentor, design their own concentrations in fiction, nonfiction, poetry, writing for stage and screen, or writing for young people. A nine-day residency begins each semester with an invigorating program of seminars, workshops, readings, and individual conferences to develop the semester's program of study. Students then work independently during the semester under the direction of their faculty mentors—the program's flexibility allowing all participants to work from wherever they live.

Over a four-semester period, students attend four full residencies and take 12 credits per semester, as outlined in each semester's study-plan contract. Following the fourth semester—focused primarily on the creative thesis—graduating students spend a portion of a fifth residency to present a craft seminar, the final requirement for graduation. They may also give a reading from their creative thesis. Grades for each semester are pass-fail, accompanied by narrative evaluations by faculty mentors.

Lesley's M.F.A. in creative writing differs from other low-residency programs in a number of ways. The interdisciplinary component encourages students to expand their abilities as writers by widening their aesthetic experience and deepening their creative thinking. While the multigenre expertise of the M.F.A. faculty is the student's key resource, those with an interest in the visual arts have the opportunity to work with faculty members from the Art Institute of Boston at Lesley (AIB), and those seeking to integrate their writing with such disciplines as art therapy, psychology, and education have the resources of Lesley's Graduate School of Art and Social Sciences and the Lesley Seminars. The interdisciplinary component also offers opportunities for real-world literary experience, including paid and unpaid internships or assistantships in editing, publishing, and teaching at such organizations as Beacon Press; the Concord Poetry Center; David R. Godine, Publisher; Harvard Extension School; *Harvard Review;* the Horn Book; and Lesley University's Humanities Division and Academic Resource Center. Students also have the opportunity to participate in independent studies in an Art of the Author Interview project, book reviewing, magazine writing, photography, and writing the 10-minute play. Some students' interdisciplinary projects have led to full-time publishing jobs, paid teaching assistantships, professional Web sites, book publication, and publications in such journals as the *AWP Writer's Chronicle, Gettysburg Review, Harvard Review,* and *Massachusetts Review.*

Moreover, with its residencies taking place in Cambridge, Massachusetts, Lesley's program draws energy from one of the literary and historic capitals of the United States. Many of the core and visiting faculty members have thrived for years in this epicenter of writing and publishing. Their experiences make them uniquely astute advisers for student writers who need to understand the complexities and opportunities of contemporary literary culture.

Given these advantages, graduates of Lesley's M.F.A. Program in Creative Writing are equipped for new challenges as they continue to write, explore new genres and art forms, and participate in a serious community of writers and artists.

Research Facilities

Lesley University's Ludcke Library holds a working collection of books, periodicals, microfilm, microfiche, nonprint materials, and software resources that are readily available to students. The library provides Internet resources and database access to general and subject-specific resources that are appropriate to the subject focuses of the University. Through the Fenway Consortium, students can access thirteen other institutional libraries in the Boston-Cambridge area.

Financial Aid

A limited number of scholarships are available for students in the M.F.A. in creative writing program; however, the Financial Aid Office assists students as needed in obtaining various types of educational assistance, including Federal Pell Grants, Federal Stafford Student Loans, and Federal Perkins Loans. Some teaching assistantships are also available on a limited basis to M.F.A. candidates with other advanced degrees. In addition, funds from Lesley's Graduate Assistantship Program are available to M.F.A. students. Moreover, a senior teaching fellowship in the undergraduate Humanities Division is available every two years to a qualified Lesley M.F.A. alumnus or alumna.

Cost of Study

The flat tuition for the 2008–09 year is $7140 per semester for the program, plus a residency fee of $350 per residency session. A student requiring accommodations for the residency should plan on an additional cost of approximately $500 to $700 for each nine-day residency, plus the cost of travel to and from Boston.

Living and Housing Costs

For the summer residency, on-campus housing is available to nonlocal students in the M.F.A. in creative writing program. For the winter residency, the program's staff members help nonlocal students arrange housing at off-season rates. Information on local housing and assistance in obtaining housing are available upon request from the M.F.A. program's Assistant Director.

Student Group

The graduate on-campus and off-campus enrollment at Lesley University consists of more than 5,000 students who range in age from their mid-20s to their early 70s—in all stages of professional development. Students come from fifty states and thirty-two countries. Most are currently employed or have worked in the professional field of their choice and have returned to graduate school to enhance their training, learn new skills, or change careers.

Location

Lesley University is located in the historic city of Cambridge, Massachusetts, between Harvard University and Porter Squares in Cambridge, in the greater Boston metropolitan area. The Art Institute of Boston at Lesley University occupies a campus in Kenmore Square in Boston. The University is conveniently connected to downtown Boston by public transportation. Numerous historical sites and cultural attractions are easily accessed by train or bus or on foot, including theaters, museums, concerts, and professional sports events.

The University

Lesley University, founded in 1909 as a women's teaching college, continues its commitment to educating undergraduates while also offering graduate and Ph.D. programs in the fields of education, environmental studies, human services, counseling and psychology, and the arts. With today's student in mind, Lesley University has successfully pioneered a wide variety of flexible programs for adult learners that share a commitment to quality, innovation, and the integration of theory with practice.

Lesley offers degree programs for learners at all levels. The University also supports several centers and hosts a variety of academic and professional conferences and institutes. Lesley programs operate throughout Massachusetts and in twenty-three other states as well as at an affiliated site in Israel.

Applying

The deadline for applying for fall semester (residency in June/July) is March 1. The deadline for applying for spring semester (residency in January) is September 1. Applications are reviewed after these dates on a space-available basis.

A writing sample is a required part of the application. Applicants in fiction or creative nonfiction should submit approximately 20 double-spaced pages of prose. Applicants in poetry should submit up to 10 single-spaced pages of poetry. Applicants for writing for stage and screen should submit 15–20 double-spaced pages of script. Applicants in writing for young people should submit 15 double-spaced pages of Young Adult or Middle-Grade prose or two to three picture-book stories. Applicants must submit three copies of their writing sample with their application. If applying in more than one genre, applicants should submit three copies of the writing sample for each genre. Applicants should clearly indicate, on the title page of their writing samples, the genre to which they are applying.

Correspondence and Information

Office of Graduate and Adult Bachelor's Admissions
Lesley University
29 Everett Street
Cambridge, Massachusetts 02138-2790
Phone: 617-349-8300
888.LESLEY.U (toll-free)
E-mail: info@lesley.edu
Web site: http://www.lesley.edu/oncampus

Lesley University

THE FACULTY AND THEIR RESEARCH

At the heart of the Lesley M.F.A. in creative writing program are its faculty mentors and visiting writers. Included among them are 2 former U.S. Poet Laureates; former fellows from the Mary Ingraham Bunting Institute of Radcliffe College; a recipient of the Commonwealth Prize for Poetry and Canada's Governor General's Award for Literature; winners of the Flannery O'Connor Award, Guggenheim fellowships, the Koret Foundation Book Prize, NEA fellowships, the Norma Farber First Book Award, the Parents' Choice Award, the Parenting's Reading Magic Award, Pushcart Prizes, Whiting awards, numerous state arts council awards, Ingram Merrill Foundation grants, and the PEN Discovery Award; and winners of, or nominees for, the National Book Award and the Pulitzer Prize. In addition, several books by the faculty mentors have been named "notable books" by the *Los Angeles Times,* the *New York Times,* and the *Washington Post.* Many faculty members have published their work in the *New York Times Magazine, The Atlantic Monthly, The New Yorker, The American Poetry Review, Antaeus, Paris Review, Smithsonian, Poetry, The Nation, Grand Street, Kenyon Review, Best American Poetry, The Best American Essays, Triquarterly,* and hundreds of other important journals and anthologies.

Faculty Mentors

Steven Cramer, Program Director. Poetry. Author of *Goodbye to the Orchard, Dialogue for the Left and Right Hand, The World Book,* and *The Eye That Desires to Look Upward.*

Anne Bernays. Fiction and Nonfiction. Author of nine novels, including *Growing Up Rich, Professor Romeo,* and *Trophy House.*

Brian Bouldrey. Fiction. Author of *Honorable Bandit: A Walk Across Corsica; Monster: Adventures in American Machismo; The Genius of Desire; Love, the Magician;* and *The Boom Economy.*

Jami Brandli, Writing for Stage and Screen. Author of published and produced plays *Normal, Moon Man, Flooding,* and *Looking for Bruce.*

Barry Brodsky, Writing for Stage and Screen. Author of published and produced plays and screenplays, including *All Other Nights, The Twelve-forty, The Surrender,* and *The Boys of Winter.*

Wayne Brown. Fiction, Nonfiction, and Poetry. Author of *Landscape with Heron: Stories and Remembrances, The Child of the Sea: Stories and Remembrances, Voyages* (poems), *Edna Manley: The Private Years,* and *On The Coast* (poems).

Jane Brox. Nonfiction. Author of *Clearing Land: Legacies of the American Farm, Five Thousand Days Like This One,* and *Here and Nowhere Else.*

Teresa Cader. Poetry. Author of *Guests* and *The Paper Wasp.*

Rafael Campo. Poetry. Author of *The Enemy; Landscape with Human Figure; The Other Man Was Me; What the Body Told; Diva; The Desire to Heal: A Doctor's Education in Empathy, Identity, and Poetry;* and *The Healing Art: A Doctor's Black Bag of Poetry.*

Leah Hager Cohen, Nonfiction and Poetry. Author of *Train Go Sorry: Inside a Deaf World; Glass, Paper , Beans: Revelations on the Nature and Value of Ordinary Things; Heat Lightening;* and *Heart, You Bully, You Punk.*

Pat Lowery Collins. Writing for Young People. Author of numerous works for children, including *The Fattening Hut, Schooner, Just Imagine, Signs and Wonders,* and *Come Out Come Out.* (http://www.patlowerycollins.com)

David Elliott. Writing for Young People. Author of *Evangeline Mudd and the Great Mink Escapade, Hazel Nutt, Mad Scientist, And Here's to You!, Evangeline Mudd and the Golden-haired Apes of the Ikkinasti Jungle, The Transmogrification of Roscoe Wizzle, Cool Crazy Crickets,* and *Cool Crazy Crickets to the Rescue.*

Thomas Sayers Ellis. Poetry. Author of *The Maverick Room, The Genuine Negro Hero,* and *Good Junk* and coeditor of *On the Verge: Emerging Poets and Artists.*

Tony Eprile. Fiction. Author of the novel *The Persistence of Memory* and *Temporary Sojourner and Other South African Stories.*

Laurie Foos. Fiction. Author of the novels *Ex Utero, Portrait of the Walrus by a Young Artist, Twinship, Bingo Under the Crucifix,* and *Before Elvis There Was Nothing.*

Susan Goodman. Writing for Young People. Author of *The Ultimate Field Trip* series and the *Brave Kids* series as well as *On This Spot: An Expedition Back Through Time; Choppers; The Truth About Poop; Skyscraper; All in Just One Cookie; Gee, Whiz! It's All About Pee;* and other books.

Marcie Hershman, Fiction and Nonfiction. Author of the novels *Tales of the Master Race* and *Safe in America* and the memoir *Speak to Me: Grief, Love and What Endures.*

Alexandra Johnson. Nonfiction. Author of *Leaving a Trace: On Keeping a Journal* and *The Hidden Writer: Diaries and the Creative Life.*

Rachel Kadish. Fiction and Nonfiction. Author of the novels *Tolstoy Lied: A Love Story* and *From a Sealed Room.*

Hester Kaplan. Fiction. Author of *The Edge of Marriage,* a short story collection and *Kinship Theory,* a novel.

Michael Lowenthal. Fiction. Author of the novels *Charity Girl, Avoidance,* and *The Same Embrace.*

William Lychack. Fiction. Author of the novel *The Wasp Eater* and *The Architect of Flowers,* a collection of stories.

Chris Lynch. Writing for Young People. Author of *Inexcusable; Free Will; Me, Dead Dad & Alcatraz; Shadow Boxer;* and *Slot Machine.*

Rachel Manley. Nonfiction. Author of *Slipstream: A Daughter Remembers* and *Drumblair: Memories of a Jamaican Childhood.*

Cate Marvin. Poetry. Author of *Fragment of the Head of a Queen* and *World's Tallest Disaster* and coeditor of *Legitimate Dangers: American Poets of the New Century.*

Kyoko Mori. Fiction and Nonfiction. Author of *Stone Field, True Arrow; Polite Lies: On Being a Woman Caught Between Cultures; The Dream of Water: A Memoir; One Bird; Fallout* (poems); and *Shizuko's Daughter.*

Spencer Reece, Poetry. Author of *The Clerk's Tale* and *Remembering James Merrill.*

Katherine Russell Rich, Nonfiction. Author of *The Red Devil* and *Unspeakable: Life in Another Language.*

Anita Riggio. Writing for Young People. Author and illustrator of *Smack Dab in the Middle, Beware the Brindlebeast, Secret Signs, A Moon in My Teacup,* and *Jitterbug,* a novel for middle-grade readers, as well as illustrator of *The Whispering Cloth* and other picture books.

Christina Shea. Fiction. Author of the novel *Moira's Crossing.*

Kate Snodgrass, Writing for Stage and Screen. Author of published and produced plays *Haiku; Que Sera, Sera;* and *Critics Circle* and produced plays *Observatory, The Glider,* and *How I Saw the Light.*

Janet Sylvester. Poetry. Author of *That Mulberry Wine, A Visitor at the Gate,* and *The Mark of Flesh.*

A. J. Verdelle. Fiction. Author of the novel *The Good Negress.*

Visiting Writers and Artists: A Selection

Ellen Driscoll, sculptor and installation artist, with numerous solo exhibitions, including New York City's Whitney Museum of American Art and the Contemporary Arts Center, Cincinnati. In 2001, she completed a major public commission, "As Above, So Below," for Grand Central Station.

Andre Dubus III, author of *House of Sand and Fog; Bluesman, The Cage Keeper and Other Stories;* and *We Don't Live Here Anymore.*

David Ferry, author of *No Country I Know: New and Selected Poems and Translation* and translator of *The Epistles of Horace, The Georgics of Virgil, Gilgamesh,* and *The Odes of Horace.*

Louise Glück, former Poet Laureate of the United States; winner of the Bollingen Prize, the Pulitzer Prize, and the National Book Critics Circle Award; and author of eleven collections—including *Averno, The Seven Ages, Vita Nova, Meadowlands, The Wild Iris, Ararat, The Triumph of Achilles, Descending Figure, and The House on Marshland*—as well as *Proofs and Theories: Essays on Poetry.*

Robie H. Harris, author of numerous books for young people, including *It's So Amazing! A Book About Eggs, Sperm, Birth, Babies, and Families; Happy Birth Day!; Don't Forget to Come Back; Goodbye, Mousie;* and *It's Perfectly Normal: Changing Bodies, Growing Up, Sex, and Sexual Health.*

Emily Hiestand, author of *Angela the Upside-Down Girl: and Other Domestic Travels* and *The Very Rich Hours: Travels in Orkney, Belize, the Everglades, and Greece;* also a highly regarded poet and photographer. (http://www.elementsboston.net/about/emily.htm)

Richard Hoffman, author of *Half the House: A Memoir* and *Without Paradise* (poems).

Marie Howe, author of *The Good Thief* (National Poetry Series winner, 1988) and *What the Living Do.*

Major Jackson, author of *Hoops* and *Leaving Saturn.*

Lois Lowry, award-winning author of numerous books for young readers, including *Messenger, The Silent Boy, Gathering Blue, The Giver, Looking Back: A Book of Memories,* and the *Anastasia Krupkik* series.

Gail Mazur, author of five poetry collections including *Nightfire, The Pose of Happiness, The Common, They Can't Take that Away from Me* (National Book Award finalist), and *Zeppo's First Wife: New and Selected Poems.*

Roland Merullo, author of the novels *Leaving Losapas; A Russian Requiem; Revere Beach Boulevard;* and *In Revere, in Those Days* as well as *Revere Beach Elegy: A Memoir of Home and Beyond* and *A Passion for Golf: In Pursuit of the Innermost Game.*

Sue Miller, author of six novels: *The Good Mother, Family Pictures, For Love, The Distinguished Guest, While I Was Gone,* and *The World Below* and the story collection, *Inventing the Abbotts.*

Leslea Newman, author of numerous books for children and adults, including *Hachiko Waits, Heather Has Two Mommies, A Letter to Harvey Milk,* and *Write from the Heart.*

Deborah Noyes, author of *When the Wolf Girls Came, Prudence and Moxie,* and *Red Butterfly* and editor of and contributor to the young adult fiction anthology, *Gothic! Ten Original Dark Tales.*

Tom Perrotta, author of the novels *Little Children, Joe College,* and *Election.*

Robert Pinsky, former Poet Laureate of the United States and author of twelve books of poetry, translation, and criticism, most recently *The Figured Wheel: New and Collected Poems, 1966–1996* and *Jersey Rain.*

David Rivard, author of the poetry collections *Torque, Wise Poison, Bewitched Playground,* and *Sugar Town.*

Lloyd Schwartz, Pulitzer Prize winner for music criticism; author of three books of poetry, *These People; Goodnight, Gracie;* and *Cairo Traffic;* and editor of *Elizabeth Bishop and Her Art.*

Maurice Sendak, renowned author and illustrator and winner of countless honors for his achievements, including the Hans Christian Andersen International Medal for his body of illustration work, the Laura Ingalls Wilder Award for his "substantial and lasting contribution to children's literature," and the National Medal of Arts, awarded by President Clinton.

Tom Sleigh, author of five books of poetry, *After One, Waking, The Chain, The Dreamhouse,* and *Far Side of the Earth*—a translation of Euripides' *Herakles,* and a play, *Rubber.*

THE NEW SCHOOL: A UNIVERSITY

Graduate Writing Program

Program of Study

The New School has been a vital center for writing and writing instruction since 1931, when Gorham Munson, a Manhattan editor and influential member of Alfred Stieglitz's circle, introduced his workshop in creative writing. Since 1996, The New School has offered a Master of Fine Arts (M.F.A.) in creative writing, with concentrations in fiction, nonfiction, poetry, and writing for children. Founded by poet and biographer Robert Polito, the M.F.A. program marks the latest transformation in the University's commitment to creative writing. Both in the classroom and through the participation of distinguished visitors, the Graduate Writing Program aims to help students fully engage with the vibrant, diverse world of writing in New York City and beyond.

The M.F.A. program is a full-time course of study balancing writing workshops with seminars in the reading of literature. The program is designed to be completed in four semesters. During each of their first three terms, students enroll in one writing workshop (4 credits) in their area of concentration and one literature seminar (4 credits) and must participate in the Writer's Life Colloquium (1 credit). During their final term of residence, students continue to participate in the Writer's Life Colloquium but no longer enroll in writing workshops or literature seminars. Instead, they work closely with one or more New School writer-teacher advisers in independent study leading to the creation of a writing thesis (4 credits) and a literature project (4 credits), both within their area of concentration. Because of the intensive nature of the Graduate Writing Program, transfer credits are not accepted.

Research Facilities

The Raymond Fogelman Library contains books, standard references, pamphlets, and periodicals used by graduate students in all programs. Graduate students also have access to facilities of the Research Library Association of South Manhattan, which includes Cooper Union and New York University. It is one of the largest interuniversity library consortia in the country. Beyond the consortium are the rich resources of New York City, including 250 METRO member libraries and the public library system of the five boroughs. The University Computing Center is also available to students for their research and writing.

Financial Aid

M.F.A. students are eligible for state and federal grants and loans, and departmental scholarships are awarded to new and continuing students. The committee considers both merit and need in granting available funds. A University scholars' fund also allocates grants to incoming students from underrepresented groups. The University offers an extended payment plan that involves monthly billing throughout the year.

Cost of Study

Tuition for the 2008–09 academic year is $1220 per credit. A University services fee of $100 and a $15 student activities fee are charged each term. For more information, students should visit http://www.newschool.edu/tuition.

Living and Housing Costs

The University Housing Office maintains a comprehensive resource center with apartment listings. University-run apartments and residence halls are also available. The cost of housing, food, transportation, books, and living expenses averages $17,000 annually. For more information, students can visit http://www.newschool.edu/studentservices.

Student Group

M.F.A. students bring to the program a variety of academic backgrounds and types of professional experience. Many continue to work while attending the program. Sixty percent of the students are women; 23 percent are from underrepresented groups. The average age is 26 years. The program currently enrolls approximately 200 students.

Location

The New School writing program reflects the diversity and breadth of the writer's life in New York City. All writing workshops and literature seminar instructors are themselves published writers and experienced teachers, and guests from the city's vast publishing industry—including magazine and book editors, publishers, literary agents, and prominent teachers of writing—are invited to speak at dozens of events organized each semester.

The University

The New School is a leading university in New York City, offering distinguished programs in design, liberal arts, the performing arts, and social and political science, leading to 70 graduate and undergraduate degrees. To learn more, students should visit http://www.newschool.edu/degreeprograms. A privately supported institution, The New School is accredited by the Commission on Higher Education of the Middle States Association of Colleges and Schools and chartered as a university by the Regents of the State of New York.

The eight schools that make up The New School are The New School for General Studies, The New School for Social Research, Milano The New School for Management and Urban Policy, Parsons The New School for Design, Eugene Lang College The New School for Liberal Arts, Mannes College The New School for Music, The New School for Drama, and The New School for Jazz and Contemporary Music.

Applying

The Graduate Writing Program welcomes applications from aspiring writers of diverse academic backgrounds and life experiences. They must hold a bachelor's degree from an accredited college or university. Applications are reviewed by an admissions committee consisting of the director of the writing program and members of the faculty. The writing sample is the most important factor in this review, but letters of recommendation, academic transcripts, and the student's statement of purpose are all carefully evaluated. The deadline for fall admission is January 15. For more information and an application, students can visit http://www.writing.newschool.edu, attend an information session at The New School, or contact the Office of Admissions and Student Services.

Correspondence and Information

Graduate Writing Program
Office of Admissions and Student Services
The New School
66 West 12th Street, Room 401
New York, New York 10011

Phone: 212-229-5630
E-mail: nsadmissions@newschool.edu
Web site: http://www.newschool.edu/writing

The New School: A University

THE FACULTY

Many of America's most important poets, novelists, literary critics, and editors have been part of The New School's writing faculty, including Robert Frost, W. H. Auden, Robert Lowell, LeRoi Jones (Amiri Baraka), Frank O'Hara, Kenneth Koch, Kay Boyle, Marguerite Young, and Alfred Kazin.

Along with Robert Polito, director, and David Lehman, the current M.F.A. faculty includes Jeffery Renard Allen, Jonathan Ames, Susan Bell, Mark Bibbins, Susan Cheever, Jonathan Dee, Elaine Equi, David Gates, Vivian Gornick, Shelley Jackson, Zia Jaffrey, Joyce Johnson, Hettie Jones, James Lasdun, David Lehman, Suzannah Lessard, Philip Lopate, Honor Moore, Maggie Nelson, Sigrid Nunez, Dale Peck, Francine Prose, Liam Rector, Helen Schulman, Tor Seidler, Dani Shapiro, Prageeta Sharma, Laurie Sheck, Darcey Steinke, Benjamin Taylor, Abigail Thomas, Paul Violi, Sarah Weeks, Susan Wheeler, and Stephen Wright.

For a complete list of faculty members and courses, students should visit http://www.writing.newschool.edu.

SOUTHERN ILLINOIS UNIVERSITY CARBONDALE

Department of English
M.F.A. in Creative Writing

Programs of Study

The Master of Fine Arts (M.F.A.) in creative writing at Southern Illinois University Carbondale (SIUC) is a studio-academic program designed to assist talented students in developing their skills as poets or fiction writers. While the M.F.A. is the accepted credential for teachers of creative writing, the program gives primary emphasis to the development of students as writers. The fundamental elements of the program are writing workshops, in which students read and critique the writing of their peers under the guidance of a faculty writer, intensive tutorial work with the thesis director on the student's writing, and the study of the traditions, forms, and theories of literature from a writer's stance. The faculty members (3 poets and 3 fiction writers) work closely with the students and ensure that each student has exposure to a variety of styles and personalities from traditional to experimental. The small program size provides an excellent student-teacher ratio and encourages both formal and informal apprenticeship and tutorial relationships. While no academic program can promise to create writers, the M.F.A. program strives to provide committed, talented writers the guidance, instruction, support, and community that help them produce their best work. The M.F.A. in creative writing program requires satisfactory completion of 48 semester hours. M.F.A. students may elect to focus their studies in fiction or poetry or in a combination of the two genres.

Research Facilities

SIUC's Morris Library contains more than 2.5 million volumes, 3 million microfilms, and more than 12,000 current serial subscriptions. Library users have electronic access to a statewide automated catalog system and nearly 600 electronic data files and CD-ROM products via workstations located throughout the building. The library's special collections are extensive in areas pertinent to graduate students and research and include papers, manuscripts, letters, and research materials in American and British expatriate literature; twentieth-century philosophy, especially John Dewey and the Open Court press; the Irish literary renaissance; literary modernism, with an especially strong collection of James Joyce materials; and proletariat theater. The Humanities Library is particularly rich in both traditional and contemporary monographs and periodicals.

Financial Aid

SIUC offers a number of competitive fellowships to full-time graduate students. Awards are made by the Graduate School on the recommendation of the Graduate Studies Committee. For further information, students should contact the Graduate School. The deadline for applicants for fellowships is usually one month earlier than the deadline for graduate assistantships. Almost all M.F.A. students hold graduate assistantships that provide stipends for the academic year and full remission of tuition. The application deadline for admission with assistantship support is early February, with student notification before April 1.

Cost of Study

In-state graduate tuition is $313.90 per credit hour in 2008–09. Out-of-state tuition is 2.5 times the in-state tuition rate ($784.75 per credit hour). Graduate students with at least a 25 percent appointment as a graduate assistant receive a tuition scholarship. Fees vary from $511.26 (1 credit hour) to $1416.05 (12 credit hours). Students with a graduate assistantship receive a 25 percent reduction in the Primary Care Medical Fee.

Living and Housing Costs

For married couples, students with families, and single graduate students, the University has 690 efficiency and one-, two-, three-, and four-bedroom apartments that rent for $484 to $686 per month in 2008–09. Residence halls for single graduate students are also available, as are accessible residence hall rooms and apartments for students with disabilities.

Student Group

University enrollment exceeds 21,000, including more than 4,000 graduate students. Men and women come from all fifty states and more than 100 other countries. About 53 percent of the graduate students are women, 23 percent are international, and 13 percent are members of American minority groups.

Location

SIUC is 350 miles south of Chicago and 100 miles southeast of St. Louis. Nestled in rolling hills bordered by the Ohio and Mississippi Rivers and enhanced by a mild climate, the area has state parks, national forests and wildlife refuges, and large lakes for outdoor recreation. Cultural offerings include theater, opera, concerts, art exhibits, and cinema. Educational facilities for the families of students are excellent.

The University

Southern Illinois University Carbondale is a comprehensive public university with a variety of general and professional education programs. The University offers bachelor's, associate, master's, and doctoral degrees; the J.D. degree; and the M.D. degree. The University is fully accredited by the North Central Association of Colleges and Schools. The Graduate School has an essential role in the development and coordination of graduate instruction and research programs. The Graduate Council has academic responsibility for determining graduate standards, recommending new graduate programs and research centers, and establishing policies to facilitate the research effort. Southern Illinois University Carbondale is a state-funded university founded in 1869.

Applying

Applicants to the M.F.A. program must complete all forms in the application package, including a separate application for admission to the Graduate School, a nonrefundable processing fee of $40, three letters of recommendation, a statement of purpose, and a writing sample. International students must submit TOEFL scores and a statement showing sufficient financial support at the time of application. The minimum GPA for admission to SIUC's Graduate School is 2.7 (out of 4.0). Application materials for admission, including graduate assistantship support, are available from the Department of English. Application material is also available online at the Departmental Web site. Separate application forms for fellowships are available from the Graduate School.

Correspondence and Information

M.F.A. in Creative Writing Program
Department of English
Southern Illinois University Carbondale
Carbondale, Illinois 62901-4503

Phone: 618-453-6894
E-mail: gradengl@siu.edu
Web site: http://www.siu.edu/departments/English

Southern Illinois University Carbondale

THE FACULTY AND THEIR RESEARCH

Kent Haruf, Professor Emeritus; M.F.A., Iowa, 1973. Fiction writing.
Rodney Jones, Professor; M.F.A., North Carolina at Greensboro, 1973. Poetry writing.
Judy Jordan, Assistant Professor; M.F.A., Utah, 2000. Creative writing, poetry.
Allison E. Joseph, Associate Professor; M.F.A., Indiana, 1992. Poetry writing.
E. Beth Lordan, Professor and Assistant to the Chair; M.F.A., Cornell, 1987. Fiction writing.
Michael Magnuson, Associate Professor and Director of Creative Writing; M.F.A., Florida, 1997. Fiction writing.

STONY BROOK UNIVERSITY, STATE UNIVERSITY OF NEW YORK

M.F.A. Program in Writing and Literature

Program of Study

The Master of Fine Arts (M.F.A.) Program in Writing and Literature at Stony Brook Southampton emphasizes creative work in fiction, poetry, and scriptwriting, but it also extends its emphasis beyond the familiar categories of creative expression to treat all forms of writing as equally relevant to understanding and mastering a world constructed out of words. Students work and publish in many genres, but they are also encouraged to write outside their genres, in the belief that this practice informs their primary area of interest.

Courses are taught by a full-time core faculty and a body of part-time faculty members comprising distinguished visiting writers who provide creative breadth to the program and offer coverage in areas of writing that are essential in contemporary society, in particular fiction, nonfiction, scriptwriting, scientific writing, and writing for the media. These teachers provide instruction and guidance that is friendly, rigorous, professionally useful, and intellectually challenging.

The M.F.A. degree requires 33 credits of course work and a 9-credit thesis for a total of 42 credits. All students take the 3-credit Introduction to Graduate Writing course. This is followed by six writing workshops representing a range of disciplines, including creative nonfiction, scriptwriting, and professional and scientific writing; three special-topic writing and literature seminars; and a 3-credit practicum in arts administration, teaching writing, or publishing and editing. Students also write an M.F.A. thesis, which is intended to be a publishable, book-length work.

The program comprises two academic semesters, two six-week summer sessions, and a credit-bearing writers conference.

Research Facilities

The East and West Campus University libraries contain nearly 2.1 million bound volumes, 130,000 maps and atlases, and 5,800 videos. With nearly 4 million publications in microformat, they have one of the country's largest microfilm collections. The collections represent at least twenty-five languages, and the libraries' Special Collections Department contains 16,000 rare books and 150 collections, including the William Butler Yeats Microfilmed Manuscripts Collection. The University's electronic resources, which are available to students on all campuses, include more than 30,000 Web-accessible journals, hundreds of databases, and several collections of online books, including reference material.

Financial Aid

Qualified graduate students in their second year are eligible to apply for teaching assistantships in writing that include a tuition waiver and stipend. The Stony Brook Southampton Writers Conference Scholarship offers a partial award to matriculated M.F.A. students attending the conference. Full-time M.F.A. students who submit an original work of fiction may apply for the Deborah Hecht Memorial Prize in Fiction. Applicants are also encouraged to explore opportunities for external funding independent of departmental and University resources. Federal loans or loans from private lenders may be available to students in financial need, and some students may find part-time employment.

Cost of Study

In 2008–09, full-time tuition (12 credits) is $3450 for residents and $5460 for nonresidents. Part-time tuition is $288 and $455, respectively. Other costs include a student activity fee of $22, a college fee of $12.50, an infirmary fee of $115.50, a technology fee of $173.50, and a transportation fee of $105. Fees for part-time students vary according to the number of credits a student takes.

Living and Housing Costs

Campus housing is not available for graduate students. However, apartments and houses are available within walking or biking distance of campus. Apartment rentals range from $525 to $800 per month for one bedroom and $1000 to $1500 for two bedrooms.

Student Group

Students in the program display a range of interests and experiences. The student body includes recent college graduates, postcareer professionals, working journalists, secondary school teachers, editors, and professors. Their writing portfolios, whether published or unpublished, encompass a wide range of styles, genres, and subject matter.

Student Outcomes

Graduates of the program continue to work and publish in many genres, including short and long fiction, poetry, creative nonfiction, essay, playwriting, screenwriting, and memoir.

Location

The town of Southampton is located approximately 80 miles from New York City on the South Fork of Long Island. Though home to nearly 55,000 people year-round, the summer population can swell to twice that number, thanks to a multitude of summer activities. The Atlantic Ocean offers surfing, swimming, and fishing, while nearby bays, islands, and inlets are perfect for boating, windsurfing, and waterskiing.

The University

Stony Brook was founded in 1957 as part of the State University of New York system. The Southampton campus, the newest extension of the school, has a curriculum organized around an interdisciplinary core that allows students to explore how political, economic, and social issues relate to the environment. Stony Brook has been ranked by *U.S. News & World Report* and the London *Times* as one of the top universities in the nation and has been named one of the best values by *Kiplinger's* personal finance magazine.

Applying

Applicants must submit a completed application for admission, official transcripts from all colleges previously attended, three letters of recommendation from writing instructors or professionals familiar with the applicant's work, official GRE scores, a one- to two-page statement discussing the reasons for attending the program, a writing sample of ten to thirty pages in any genre, a current resume, and a nonrefundable $60 application fee. The deadline to apply is January 15 for fall admission or October 1 for spring admission.

Correspondence and Information

M.F.A. Program in Writing and Literature
Chancellors Hall, Room 238
Stony Brook University, State University of New York
239 Montauk Highway
Southampton, New York 11968

Phone: 631-632-5030
Fax: 631-632-2576
E-mail: southamptonwriters@notes.cc.sunysb.edu
Web site: http://www.stonybrook.edu/sb/southampton/mfa/index.shtml

Stony Brook University, State University of New York

THE FACULTY AND THEIR RESEARCH

Core Faculty

Carla Caglioti, Associate Director, M.F.A. in Writing and Literature, and Assistant Dean. Caglioti is the founding Associate Director of the Stony Brook Southampton M.F.A. Program in Writing and Literature as well as a longtime associate of the Southampton Writers Conference. Caglioti has a B.A. in English literature and writing and an M.S. in English education; she is a doctoral candidate in English literature. Her dissertation focuses on the rise of the field of creative writing in higher education. Her interests in writing and literature range from Old English riddles to the influence of technology on the writing process (from the quill to the computer).

Robert Reeves, Professor and Director, M.F.A. in Writing and Literature. Reeves is the author of two critically acclaimed novels, both published by Crown, as well as short fiction, essays, and literary criticism. *Kirkus Review* hailed *Doubting Thomas* as "a zesty, classy original," and Patricia Holt of the *San Francisco Chronicle* called *Peeping Thomas* "funny, disturbing, and brilliant." Reeves, director of the Southampton Writers Conference, has also taught writing at Harvard and Princeton.

Roger Rosenblatt, Professor, essayist, and novelist. Rosenblatt's essays for *Time* magazine and PBS's *NewsHour* have won two George Polk Awards, a Peabody, and an Emmy. He is the author of five off-Broadway plays and eleven books, including *Children of War*, which won the Robert F. Kennedy Book Prize and was a finalist for the National Book Critics Circle Award; the national bestseller *Rules for Aging*; and the novel *Lapham Rising*, also a national bestseller. His second novel, *Beet*, was published in early 2008.

Julie Sheehan, Assistant Professor and Curator, "Writers Speak" Lecture Series. Sheehan won the Barnard Women Poets Prize for her second book, *Orient Point*. Other honors include Poets Out Loud prizes for her first book, *Thaw*; the Poetry Society of American's Robert H. Winner Prize; and *The Paris Review*'s Bernard F. Connors Prize. Sheehan's poems have appeared in *Parnassus, Ploughshares, Prairie Schooner, Kenyon Review,* and *Yale Review*, among many others. Her work has been anthologized, most recently in *The Best American Poetry 2005* and *180 More: Extraordinary Poems for Every Day*. She holds a B.A. from Yale and an M.F.A. from Columbia.

Adrienne C. Unger, Administrative Coordinator, M.F.A. in Writing and Literature. Unger received her B.A. in English/creative writing and literature from Long Island University, Southampton, and her M.F.A. in creative writing from George Mason University. Her work for arts and publishing organizations includes stints at the Associated Writing Programs, the Alvin Ailey Dance Theatre Foundation, and Crain Communications Inc. Formerly a freelance writer for various trade and specialty magazines, Unger was also an administrator for the Johns Hopkins Children's Center and the Stony Brook University Humanities Institute.

Lou Ann Walker, Professor and Editor-in-Chief, *The Southampton Review*. Walker's book *A Loss for Words*, a memoir, won a Christopher Award. Her other books include *Hand, Heart & Mind*. Her fiction and nonfiction works have appeared in many publications, including the *New York Times Magazine; Esquire; Life; Allure; Parade*; the *Chicago Sun-Times;* the *New York Times Book Review; O, The Oprah Magazine; The Writer;* and *Hopewell Review*. Formerly an editor at *Esquire* and *New York Magazine*, Walker has lectured on writing at Smith College and Yale University and taught at Marymount Manhattan College, Southampton College, and Columbia University. The author of several screenplays, she is a member of the Writers Guild of America.

Adjunct Faculty

Alan Alda. Screenwriter and memoirist.
Melissa Bank. Novelist and short story writer.
Billy Collins. Poet.
Christopher Durang. Playwright.
Jules Feiffer. Cartoonist, playwright, and screenwriter.
Ursula Hegi. Novelist.
Kaylie Jones. Novelist.
Matthew Klam. Fiction writer and journalist.
Frank McCourt. Memoirist.
Marsha Norman. Playwright.
David Rakoff. Essayist and humorist.
Meg Wolitzer. Novelist and short story writer.

UNIVERSITY OF NORTH CAROLINA WILMINGTON

Master of Fine Arts in Creative Writing Program

Programs of Study

The Department of Creative Writing at the University of North Carolina Wilmington (UNCW) offers a 48-hour (three-year), intensive studio-academic apprenticeship in the writing of fiction, poetry, and creative nonfiction, leading to the Master of Fine Arts (M.F.A.) degree in creative writing. Courses include workshops in the three genres, special topics and forms courses, and a range of courses in literature. While students are expected to demonstrate mastery of one genre, cross-genre study is encouraged. Students, in consultation with their advisers, tailor schedules to their interests, selecting from workshop, literature, criticism, and applicable cultural studies courses. Requirements include 21 hours in writing and 21 hours in literature or forms, with an option of substituting up to 6 of those hours of study in a related discipline. Six thesis hours lead to completion of a substantial book-length manuscript of literary merit and publishable quality. Course work in publishing and editing is also offered in the Publishing Laboratory, along with a fully functioning micropress that issues original works over its own imprint and supports University projects such as perfect-bound course packets, books, and anthologies. Course work in magazine production is also offered in conjunction with publication of *Ecotone,* the department's national literary magazine.

The community spirit begins with a belief in the individual's commitment to other individuals—the desire to help others fulfill their aspirations even while pursuing one's own. Dedicated educators strongly believe in the value of art to the individual life and the collective culture. Though the M.F.A. is a terminal degree designed for writers wishing to pursue various career paths in teaching, writing, publishing, and community arts organization, students are urged to pursue the degree primarily as a way of mastering their art by rigorous study and practice among a community of other dedicated writers.

Research Facilities

UNCW's Randall Library is a 132,823-square-foot facility holding 872,986 bound volumes and more than 1 million items on microfiche/microfilm. The library subscribes to 4,280 journals and numerous online databases and houses a separate computer laboratory that is available only to graduate students. The department sponsors the Center for Visiting Writers at Wrightsville Beach, a residence for visiting authors and a site for curricular activities, in particular an annual Writers' Week Symposium, featuring a week of panels, workshops, lectures, manuscript conferences, and readings by visiting writers, literary agents, and editors. In the Publishing Laboratory, M.F.A. students select and oversee publishing projects through the editing, design, production, and marketing processes. The Publishing Laboratory offers Mac computers equipped with Quark and other editing and publishing programs, as well as binding machinery. Other opportunities for graduate creative activity and experience include community service programs such as Writers in Action—volunteer teachers in local schools—and an annual summer Young Writers' Workshop for regional high school students.

Financial Aid

Beyond federal aid and loan programs, limited scholarship and fellowship funds are available from both the Graduate School and the department. All interested applicants are considered for assistantships, fellowships, and scholarships, which are awarded on a competitive basis. Applicants seeking assistantships are urged to complete their applications well before the deadline. The program has twenty-six teaching assistant positions, all of which include stipends and most of which include tuition remission during the first year for out-of-state students. Though approximately 40 percent of current students receive some level of direct assistance, this number is expected to increase dramatically.

Cost of Study

In-state tuition and fees for 2008–09 are $2419 per semester ($4838 per year for 9 or more credit hours). Out-of-state tuition and fees are $7449 per semester ($14,898 per year for 9 or more credit hours). Because the curriculum includes 1-credit and 2-credit courses, full-time enrollment is not always necessary for program completion.

Living and Housing Costs

Local one-bedroom apartments average $500 per month; two-bedroom apartments average $750 per month. Many students choose to share apartments or houses, particularly in the historic downtown and beach areas, making for a strong sense of off-campus community. For more information, students should visit the program's Web site.

Student Group

The program receives 250–300 applications per year. Yearly enrollment ranges from 20 to 25 students, keeping the program at a total of 60 to 70 students. Most students are enrolled full-time. Approximately 50 percent to 60 percent of students enroll from out of state, including international students from Croatia, Cyprus, Nepal, and England. Student ages currently range from 22 to 67 years of age, many students having returned to school after other jobs and experiences.

Student Outcomes

Since 1999, M.F.A. students and alumni have published numerous books with major commercial and university presses (Crown, Random House, Algonquin, St. Martin's, University of Nebraska Press) and dozens of poems, stories, articles, essays, and reviews in many of the nation's finest periodicals, including *Boulevard, Oxford American, Virginia Quarterly Review, Ms., GQ, Minnesota Review, Ontario Review, The Journal, Cimarron Review, Mississippi Review, Puerto del Sol, The Vermont Literary Review, Princeton Arts Review,* and *North Carolina Literary Review.*

Location

A well-known resort and vacation destination, Wilmington is located on the beautiful and temperate North Carolina coast, with gorgeous beaches and a striking blend of pine and palmetto trees. The area has begun to blossom as a haven for writers, and local theatrical and film projects, including Screen Gems Studio, the largest film studio east of Hollywood, have added to its ambiance.

The University and The Department

One of the few independent creative writing departments in the nation, the department enjoys high-priority status within the University. It is a rigorous and innovative but nurturing community that believes that the ultimate measure of worth is not a faculty's published work but the artistic, personal, and academic evolution of each of the students in its charge. Devoted to the pursuit of excellence through the study and application of craft, faculty members and students value the cross-fertilization of aesthetics and methods across genre lines.

Applying

Applicants submit the following five items to the Graduate School: a typed manuscript in the applicant's primary genre (15 pages of poetry, or 30 pages of fiction or 30 pages of creative nonfiction), an online application for graduate admission, official college transcripts, three recommendations, and an essay on the applicant's goals. No GRE is required. The deadline for receiving applications is February 1. Applications are submitted directly to the Graduate School and forwarded to the M.F.A. program when complete.

Correspondence and Information

M.F.A. Coordinator
Department of Creative Writing
University of North Carolina Wilmington
601 South College Road
Wilmington, North Carolina 28403-5938
Phone: 910-962-7063
Fax: 910-962-7461
E-mail: mfa@uncw.edu
Web site: http://www.uncw.edu/writers

University of North Carolina Wilmington

THE FACULTY AND THEIR RESEARCH

Lavonne Adams, Poetry. Eighth Persephone Book Publication Award for *Everyday Still Life;* Randall Jarrell/Harperprints Poetry Chapbook Prize for *In the Shadow of the Mountain.*

Wendy Brenner, Fiction and Creative Nonfiction. *Large Animals in Everyday Life,* Norton; *Phone Calls from the Dead,* Algonquin. Flannery O'Connor Award, NEA Fellowship, Henfield Award.

Mark Cox, Poetry. *Smoulder,* Godine; *Thirty-Seven Years from the Stone;* and *Natural Causes,* Pitt Poetry Series. Whiting Writers' Award, Oklahoma Book Award, Pulitzer Prize nominee.

Clyde Edgerton, Fiction. Seven novels, most recently, *Lunch at the Piccadilly,* and a memoir, *Solo: My Adventures in the Air,* Algonquin. Guggenheim Fellowship, Walter Raleigh Award.

Phil Furia, Creative Nonfiction. Five books, including *Irving Berlin: A Life in Song,* Schirmer Books; *Ira Gershwin: The Art of the Lyricist,* Oxford; *Skylark: The Life and Times of Johnny Mercer,* St. Martin's.

Philip Gerard, Fiction and Creative Nonfiction. Three novels, including *Desert Kill,* Morrow, and four nonfiction books, including *Secret Soldiers,* Dutton, and *Creative Nonfiction: Researching and Crafting Stories of Real Life,* Story Press.

David Gessner, Creative Nonfiction. Six books, including *Soaring With Fidel,* Beacon; *Return of the Osprey,* Ballantine; and *Sick of Nature,* Dartmouth College Press. Pushcart Prize.

Rebecca Lee, Fiction and Creative Nonfiction. *The City is a Rising Tide,* Simon & Schuster. Short fiction and essays in *Atlantic Monthly, Zoetrope: All Story,* and on National Public Radio's "Selected Shorts." National Magazine Award, Rona Jaffe Award, Bunting Fellow.

Sarah Messer, Creative Nonfiction and Poetry. *Bandit Letters,* New Issues Press; *Red House,* Viking. Fellowships from Provincetown Fine Arts Work Center, the Wisconsin Center for Creative Writers, and the NEA.

Malena Mörling, Poetry. *Ocean Avenue,* New Issues Press Poetry Prize; *Astoria,* University of Pittsburgh Press; poems in *The New York Times, The New Republic, Ploughshares.* Guggenheim Fellowship, Rona Jaffe Award, Academy of American Poets Prize.

Robert Siegel, Fiction, editing, and publishing. *All the Money in the World,* Random House; *All Will Be Revealed,* MacAdam Cage. Michener-Engle Fellowship, Provincetown Fine Arts Work Center Fellowship.

Michael White, Poetry. *The Island,* Copper Canyon; *Palma Cathedral,* University Press of Colorado; *Re-Entry,* University of North Texas. NEA Fellowship, Colorado Poetry Prize, Vassar Miller Prize.

The department hosts an average of 12 visiting writers per year, many of whom teach for one-week, one-month, or one-semester periods. Recent visiting faculty members include Rick Bass, Richard Bausch, Karen Bender, Sharon Bryan, Robert Creeley, Mark Doty, Carolyn Forché, Denise Gess, Albert Goldbarth, Allan Gurganus, Brenda Hillman, Virginia Holman, Philip Levine, Timothy Liu, Alison Lurie, Jill McCorkle, Heather McHugh, Z. Z. Packer, Charles Siebert, Gerald Stern, John Jeremiah Sullivan, Donna Tartt, Terry Tempest-Williams, Daniel Wallace, Joy Williams, and David Wright.

The department also offers an annual 1-credit course, the Writers' Week Symposium, a week of panels, workshops, lectures, manuscript conferences, and readings by visiting writers, literary agents, and editors. Designed to serve both students and the larger Wilmington community, recent Writers' Week Symposia have featured Ben Anastas, Andrea Barrett, Adrienne Brodeur, Jan Deblieu, Kathy Fagan, Nick Flynn, Jonathan Franzen, Robin Hemley, Mary Hood, John Holman, Richard Jackson, Tracy Kidder, Haven Kimmel, Galway Kinnell, Sydney Lea, William Least Heat-Moon, Jane Mead, Jack Myers, Thisbe Nissen, Susan Orlean, Lia Purpura, and Bill Roorbach. Other recent visiting authors include Ken Burns, Fred Chappell, Michael Chitwood, Ted Conover, Stuart Dischell, Tony Hoagland, Tony Hillerman, Bret Lott, Michael McFee, Bob Reiss, Jacob Slichter, and Mark Strand.

ACADEMIC AND PROFESSIONAL PROGRAMS IN INTERDISCIPLINARY STUDIES

Section 14
Interdisciplinary Studies

This section contains a directory of institutions offering graduate work in interdisciplinary studies, followed by in-depth entries submitted by institutions that chose to prepare detailed program descriptions. Additional information about programs listed in the directory but not augmented by an in-depth entry may be obtained by writing directly to the dean of a graduate school or chair of a department at the address given in the directory.

For programs offering related work, see also in this book *Comparative and Interdisciplinary Arts, Humanities,* and *Social Sciences.*

CONTENTS

Program Directory

Close-Ups

See also:

Interdisciplinary Studies

Alaska Pacific University, Graduate Programs, Liberal Studies Department, Self-Designed Programs, Anchorage, AK 99508-4672. Offers MA. Part-time and evening/weekend programs available. *Faculty:* 4 full-time (3 women), 1 (woman) part-time/adjunct. *Students:* 6 full-time (all women), 13 part-time (11 women); includes 1 minority (American Indian/Alaska Native), 1 international. Average age 43. In 2007, 7 degrees awarded. *Degree requirements:* For master's, thesis or project. *Entrance requirements:* For master's, MAT (preferred), GRE General Test or GMAT. *Application deadline:* For fall admission, 4/1 priority date for domestic students. Applications are processed on a rolling basis. Application fee: $25. *Expenses:* Contact institution. One-time fee: $110 full-time. *Financial support:* Research assistantships, teaching assistantships, career-related internships or fieldwork, Federal Work-Study, and unspecified assistantships available. Support available to part-time students. Financial award application deadline: 4/15; financial award applicants required to submit FAFSA. *Unit head:* Dr. Karen McCain, Director, 907-564-8243, E-mail: mccain@alaskapacific.edu. *Application contact:* Michael Warner, Director of Admissions, 907-564-8248, Fax: 907-564-8317, E-mail: mikew@alaskapacific.edu.

Amberton University, Graduate School, Program in Professional Development, Garland, TX 75041-5595. Offers MA. *Faculty:* 11 full-time (6 women), 30 part-time/adjunct (15 women). *Students:* 49 full-time (24 women), 100 part-time (50 women); includes 29 minority (20 African Americans, 2 American Indian/Alaska Native, 2 Asian Americans or Pacific Islanders, 5 Hispanic Americans). Average age 35. *Entrance requirements:* For master's, minimum GPA of 3.0. *Application deadline:* Applications are processed on a rolling basis. *Expenses:* Tuition: Full-time $5,400; part-time $225 per hour. *Application contact:* Adviser, 972-279-6511 Ext. 180, Fax: 972-279-9773, E-mail: advisor@amberton.edu.

American University, College of Arts and Sciences, Interdisciplinary Programs, Washington, DC 20016-8001. Offers applied science: biotechnology (MA); environmental policy (MA); multi-disciplinary (MA). *Students:* 1 (woman) full-time. 1 applicant, 0% accepted. In 2007, 1 degree awarded. *Expenses:* Tuition: Full-time $19,998; part-time $1,111 per credit hour. Required fees: $380. Tuition and fees vary according to program.

Angelo State University, College of Graduate Studies, Program in Interdisciplinary Studies, San Angelo, TX 76909. Offers MA, MS. Part-time and evening/weekend programs available. *Students:* 1 full-time (0 women), 1 (woman) part-time. Average age 48. 2 applicants, 100% accepted, 1 enrolled. In 2007, 2 degrees awarded. *Degree requirements:* For master's, comprehensive exam. *Entrance requirements:* For master's, GRE General Test. Additional exam requirements/recommendations for international students: Required—TOEFL or IELTS. *Application deadline:* For fall admission, 7/15 priority date for domestic students, 6/10 for international students; for spring admission, 12/8 for domestic students, 11/1 for international students. Applications are processed on a rolling basis. Application fee: $25 ($50 for international students). Electronic applications accepted. *Financial support:* Federal Work-Study and scholarships/grants available. Support available to part-time students. Financial award application deadline: 3/1; financial award applicants required to submit FAFSA. *Application contact:* Brenda Stewart, Assistant to the Dean, College of Graduate Studies, 325-942-2169, Fax: 325-942-2194, E-mail: brenda.stewart@angelo.edu.

Antioch University New England, Graduate School, Department of Environmental Studies, Individualized Program, Keene, NH 03431-3552. Offers MS. *Students:* 13 (9 women). *Degree requirements:* For master's, practicum, seminar, thesis or project. *Entrance requirements:* For master's, detailed proposal. *Expenses:* Tuition: Full-time $20,000; part-time $600 per credit. Required fees: $1,050; $300 per semester. Tuition and fees vary according to degree level, program and student level. *Unit head:* Dr. Rachel Thiet, Director, 603-283-2337, E-mail: rachel_thiet@antiochne.edu.

Arizona State University at the West campus, New College of Interdisciplinary Arts and Sciences, Phoenix, AZ 85069-7100. Offers interdisciplinary studies (MA); social justice and human rights (MA). Part-time and evening/weekend programs available. *Faculty:* 15 full-time (7 women), 4 part-time/adjunct (2 women). *Students:* 7 full-time (5 women), 19 part-time (13 women); includes 8 minority (3 African Americans, 2 American Indian/Alaska Native, 2 Asian Americans or Pacific Islanders, 1 Hispanic American), 2 international. Average age 37. In 2007, 4 degrees awarded. *Degree requirements:* For master's, applied project. *Entrance requirements:* For master's, GRE, letter of recommendation, writing sample, personal statement. Additional exam requirements/recommendations for international students: Required—TOEFL (minimum score 550 paper-based; 213 computer-based; 83 iBT), IELTS (minimum score 7). *Application deadline:* For fall admission, 6/1 for domestic and international students; for spring admission, 11/1 for domestic and international students. Applications are processed on a rolling basis. Application fee: $65 ($80 for international students). Electronic applications accepted. *Expenses:* Tuition, state resident: full-time $6,227. Tuition, nonresident: full-time $17,920. Required fees: $146. *Financial support:* Federal Work-Study, scholarships/grants, and tuition waivers (full and partial) available. Support available to part-time students. Financial award applicants required to submit FAFSA. *Unit head:* Dr. Elizabeth Langland, Vice President and Dean, 602-543-6033, Fax: 602-543-6032, E-mail: elizabeth.langland@asu.edu. *Application contact:* Sheryl Gordon, Coordinator, Student Support Services, 602-543-6241, Fax: 602-543-6032, E-mail: sheryl.gordon@asu.edu.

Athabasca University, Centre for Integrated Studies, Athabasca, AB T9S 3A3, Canada. Offers adult education (MA); community studies (MA); cultural studies (MA); educational studies (MA); global change (MA); work, organization, and leadership (MA). Part-time and evening/weekend programs available. Postbaccalaureate distance learning degree programs offered (no on-campus study). *Faculty:* 8 full-time (3 women), 16 part-time/adjunct (13 women). *Students:* Average age 36. 150 applicants, 87% accepted, 112 enrolled. In 2007, 39 degrees awarded. *Degree requirements:* For master's, project. *Entrance requirements:* For master's, 3- or 4-year BA. Additional exam requirements/recommendations for international students: Required—TOEFL (minimum score 560 paper-based; 220 computer-based). *Application deadline:* For fall admission, 3/1 for domestic and international students; for winter admission, 10/1 for domestic and international students. Application fee: $65. Electronic applications accepted. Tuition and fee charges are reported in Canadian dollars. *Expenses:* Tuition, state resident: part-time $1,795 Canadian dollars per credit. Required fees: $70 Canadian dollars per year. One-time fee: $360 Canadian dollars part-time. Part-time tuition and fees vary according to program. *Faculty research:* Women's history, literature and culture studies, sustainable development, labor and education. *Unit head:* Dr. Michael Gismondi, Program Director, 780-675-6218, Fax: 780-675-6921, E-mail: mikeg@athabascau.ca. *Application contact:* Derek Stovin, Program Administrator, 780-675-6236, Fax: 780-675-6921, E-mail: dereks@athabascau.ca.

Baylor University, Graduate School, College of Arts and Sciences, J. M. Dawson Institute of Church-State Studies, Waco, TX 76798. Offers MA, PhD. *Students:* 36 full-time (10 women), 1 (woman) part-time; includes 4 minority (2 Asian Americans or Pacific Islanders, 2 Hispanic Americans), 5 international. In 2007, 3 master's, 2 doctorates awarded. *Degree requirements:* For master's, thesis, oral exam; for doctorate, one foreign language, thesis/dissertation, preliminary exams. *Entrance requirements:* For master's, GRE General Test; for doctorate, GRE General Test, MA or equivalent. *Application deadline:* For fall admission, 3/1 for domestic students. Applications are processed on a rolling basis. Application fee: $25. *Financial support:* Fellowships, research assistantships, teaching assistantships, Federal Work-Study and institutionally sponsored loans available. Financial award application deadline: 3/1. *Faculty research:* Religion and politics, religion and public education, religious freedom and international politics, First Amendment jurisprudence. *Unit head:* Dr. Derek H. Davis, Director, 254-710-1510, Fax: 254-710-1571, E-mail: derek_davis@baylor.edu. *Application contact:* Suzanne Keener, Administrative Assistant, 254-710-3588, Fax: 254-710-3870.

Boise State University, Graduate College, College of Arts and Sciences, Program in Interdisciplinary Studies, Boise, ID 83725-0399. Offers MA, MS. Part-time programs available. *Degree requirements:* For master's, thesis. *Entrance requirements:* For master's, minimum GPA of 3.0. Electronic applications accepted.

Boston University, Metropolitan College (Continuing Education), Department of Liberal Studies, Boston, MA 02215. Offers interdisciplinary studies (MLA). Part-time and evening/weekend programs available. *Students:* Average age 29. 4 applicants, 100% accepted, 4 enrolled. *Degree requirements:* For master's, thesis. *Entrance requirements:* For master's, interview. Additional exam requirements/recommendations for international students: Required—TOEFL (minimum score 560 paper-based). *Application deadline:* Applications are processed on a rolling basis. Application fee: $70. Electronic applications accepted. *Expenses:* Tuition: Full-time $34,930; part-time $1,092 per credit. Tuition and fees vary according to class time, course level and program. *Financial support:* Research assistantships with partial tuition reimbursements, scholarships/grants available. Support available to part-time students. *Faculty research:* Arts and gastronomy. *Unit head:* Daniel Ranall, Interim Chair, 617-358-0005, Fax: 617-358-1230, E-mail: dranalli@bu.edu.

Bowling Green State University, Graduate College, Interdisciplinary Studies, Bowling Green, OH 43403. Offers M Ed, MA, MS, PhD. Part-time programs available. *Degree requirements:* For master's, thesis or alternative; for doctorate, comprehensive exam, thesis/dissertation. *Entrance requirements:* For master's and doctorate, GRE General Test. Additional exam requirements/recommendations for international students: Required—TOEFL. Application fee: $30. Electronic applications accepted. *Financial support:* Fellowships with full tuition reimbursements, research assistantships with full tuition reimbursements, teaching assistantships with full tuition reimbursements, Federal Work-Study and unspecified assistantships available. Financial award applicants required to submit FAFSA. *Application contact:* Dr. Terry L. Lawrence, Assistant Dean for Graduate Admissions and Studies, 419-372-7713, Fax: 419-372-8569, E-mail: tlawren@bgnet.bgsu.edu.

Buffalo State College, State University of New York, Graduate Studies and Research, Program in Multidisciplinary Studies, Buffalo, NY 14222-1095. Offers MA, MS. Part-time and evening/weekend programs available. *Degree requirements:* For master's, thesis or project. *Entrance requirements:* For master's, minimum GPA of 2.5. Additional exam requirements/recommendations for international students: Required—TOEFL (minimum score 550 paper-based; 213 computer-based).

California State University, Bakersfield, Division of Graduate Studies, Program in Interdisciplinary Studies, Bakersfield, CA 93311-1022. Offers MA. *Degree requirements:* For master's, thesis or project. *Entrance requirements:* For master's, minimum GPA of 3.0 in last 90 quarter units. Additional exam requirements/recommendations for international students: Required—TOEFL (minimum score 550 paper-based; 213 computer-based). *Faculty research:* Ethics, physical education and health.

California State University, Chico, Graduate School, Interdisciplinary Programs, Chico, CA 95929-0234. Offers interdisciplinary studies (MA, MS); science teaching (MS); simulation science (MS). Part-time programs available. *Students:* 13 full-time (7 women), 13 part-time (6 women); includes 6 minority (2 American Indian/Alaska Native, 2 Asian Americans or Pacific Islanders, 2 Hispanic Americans), 3 international. Average age 35. 10 applicants, 40% accepted, 4 enrolled. In 2007, 7 degrees awarded. *Degree requirements:* For master's, thesis or alternative, oral exam. *Entrance requirements:* For master's, GRE General Test or MAT, 3 letters of recommendation, purposed program plan, statement of purpose. Additional exam requirements/recommendations for international students: Required—TOEFL (minimum score 550 paper-based; 213 computer-based; 80 iBT), IELTS (minimum score 7). *Application deadline:* For fall admission, 3/1 priority date for domestic students, 3/1 for international students; for spring admission, 9/15 priority date for domestic students, 9/15 for international students. Applications are processed on a rolling basis. Application fee: $55. *Financial support:* Fellowships, Federal Work-Study available. Support available to part-time students. *Unit head:* Dr. Sara Trechter, Graduate Coordinator, 530-898-5447.

California State University, East Bay, Academic Programs and Graduate Studies, Interdisciplinary Programs, Hayward, CA 94542-3000. Offers MA, MS, Certificate. Part-time programs available. *Students:* 1 full-time (0 women), 6 part-time (3 women); includes 3 minority (1 African American, 1 Asian American or Pacific Islander, 1 Hispanic American). Average age 40. 1 applicant, 100% accepted, 0 enrolled. In 2007, 8 degrees awarded. *Degree requirements:* For master's, comprehensive exam, project or thesis. *Entrance requirements:* Additional exam requirements/recommendations for international students: Required—TOEFL (minimum score 550 paper-based; 213 computer-based). *Application deadline:* For fall admission, 5/13 for domestic students, 4/30 for international students; for winter admission, 9/30 for domestic and international students; for spring admission, 12/31 for domestic students, 11/30 for international students. Applications are processed on a rolling basis. Application fee: $55. Electronic applications accepted. *Expenses:* Required fees: $3,987; $851 per quarter. *Financial support:* Fellowships, teaching assistantships, Federal Work-Study, institutionally sponsored loans, and scholarships/grants available. Support available to part-time students. Financial award application deadline: 3/2. *Unit head:* Dr. Carl Bellone, Associate Vice President, 510-885-3716, Fax: 510-885-4777, E-mail: carl.bellone@csueastbay.edu. *Application contact:* My Huynh, Graduate Prospect Specialist, 510-885-2989, Fax: 510-885-4059, E-mail: my.huynh@csueastbay.edu.

California State University, Long Beach, Graduate Studies, Interdisciplinary Studies Program, Long Beach, CA 90840. Offers MA, MS. Part-time programs available. *Students:* 4 full-time (2 women), 4 part-time (3 women); includes 2 Hispanic Americans. Average age 39. *Degree requirements:* For master's, thesis. *Entrance requirements:* For master's, minimum undergraduate GPA of 3.0. *Application deadline:* For fall admission, 7/1 for domestic students; for spring admission, 12/1 for domestic students. Applications are processed on a rolling basis. Application fee: $55. Electronic applications accepted. *Financial support:* Federal Work-Study, institutionally sponsored loans, and scholarships/grants available. Financial award application deadline: 3/2. *Unit head:* Dr. Cecile Lindsay, Director, 562-985-8225, Fax: 562-985-1680, E-mail: clindsay@csulb.edu.

California State University, Northridge, Graduate Studies, Interdisciplinary Studies, Northridge, CA 91330. Offers MA, MS. *Students:* 5 full-time (4 women), 25 part-time (13 women); includes 13 minority (10 African Americans, 1 American Indian/Alaska Native, 2 Hispanic Americans). Average age 43. In 2007, 9 degrees awarded. *Entrance requirements:* For master's, GRE if cumulative undergraduate GPA below 3.0. Additional exam requirements/recommendations for international students: Required—TOEFL. *Application deadline:* For fall admission, 11/30 for domestic students. Application fee: $55. *Financial support:* Federal Work-Study available. Financial award application deadline: 3/1. *Unit head:* Hedy Carpenter, Associate Director of Graduate Programs, 818-677-2138.

California State University, San Bernardino, Graduate Studies, Interdisciplinary Programs, San Bernardino, CA 92407-2397. Offers MA. Part-time and evening/weekend programs available. *Faculty:* 59 full-time (21 women), 25 part-time/adjunct (7 women). *Students:* 1 (woman) full-time, 5 part-time (3 women); includes 1 African American. Average age 43. 2 applicants, 0% accepted. In 2007, 6 degrees awarded. *Degree requirements:* For master's, thesis or alternative. *Application deadline:* For fall admission, 8/31 priority date for domestic students. Application fee: $55. *Financial support:* Career-related internships or fieldwork, Federal Work-Study, and institutionally sponsored loans available. Support available to part-time students. Financial award application deadline: 3/1. *Unit head:* Dr. Sandra Kamusikiri, Dean of Graduate Studies, 909-537-5188, Fax: 909-537-7034, E-mail: skamusik@csusb.edu.

Interdisciplinary Studies

California State University, Stanislaus, Programs in Interdisciplinary Studies, Turlock, CA 95382. Offers MA, MS. Part-time and evening/weekend programs available. *Students:* 1 (woman) full-time, 14 part-time (10 women); includes 2 minority (1 Asian American or Pacific Islander, 1 Hispanic American). Average age 43. 6 applicants, 83% accepted, 0 enrolled. In 2007, 5 degrees awarded. *Degree requirements:* For master's, thesis. *Entrance requirements:* For master's, GRE, minimum GPA of 3.0, personal statement. *Application deadline:* Applications are processed on a rolling basis. Application fee: $55. Electronic applications accepted. *Expenses:* Tuition, nonresident: full-time $10,170; part-time $339 per unit. Required fees: $3,972; $2,538 per term. $1,165 per semester. *Financial support:* Research assistantships, teaching assistantships, Federal Work-Study available. Financial award application deadline: 3/2; financial award applicants required to submit FAFSA. *Unit head:* Dr. Dennis Sayer, Program Director, 209-667-3129, E-mail: dsayers@csustan.edu.

Campbell University, Graduate and Professional Programs, School of Education, Buies Creek, NC 27506. Offers administration (MSA); community counseling (MA); elementary education (M Ed); English education (M Ed); interdisciplinary studies (M Ed); mathematics education (M Ed); middle grades education (M Ed); physical education (M Ed); school counseling (M Ed); secondary education (M Ed); social science education (M Ed). *Accreditation:* NCATE. Part-time and evening/weekend programs available. *Degree requirements:* For master's, comprehensive exam. *Entrance requirements:* For master's, GRE General Test, minimum GPA of 2.7. *Faculty research:* Spiritual values and wellness issues in counseling, stress and professional burnout among counselors, thinking strategies, leadership, adaptive technology.

Central Washington University, Graduate Studies, Research and Continuing Education, Individual Studies Program, Ellensburg, WA 98926. Offers M Ed, MA, MS. Part-time programs available. *Faculty:* 318 full-time (114 women). *Students:* 2 applicants, 50% accepted, 0 enrolled. In 2007, 2 degrees awarded. *Degree requirements:* For master's, thesis. *Entrance requirements:* For master's, GRE General Test, minimum GPA of 3.0. Additional exam requirements/recommendations for international students: Required—TOEFL (minimum score 550 paper-based; 213 computer-based; 79 iBT). *Application deadline:* For fall admission, 4/1 priority date for domestic students; for winter admission, 10/1 for domestic students; for spring admission, 1/1 for domestic students. Applications are processed on a rolling basis. Application fee: $50. *Expenses:* Tuition, state resident: full-time $2,209; part-time $221 per credit. Tuition, nonresident: full-time $4,939; part-time $442 per credit. Required fees: $207 per quarter. Tuition and fees vary according to degree level. *Financial support:* Research assistantships with partial tuition reimbursements available. Financial award application deadline: 3/1; financial award applicants required to submit FAFSA. *Unit head:* Dr. Wayne S. Quirk, Associate Vice President for Graduate Studies, Research and Continuing Education, 509-963-3101, Fax: 509-963-1799, E-mail: masters@cwu.edu. *Application contact:* Justine Eason, Admissions Program Coordinator, 509-963-3103, Fax: 509-963-1799, E-mail: masters@cwu.edu.

Clemson University, Graduate School, Interdisciplinary Studies, Clemson, SC 29634. Offers PhD, Certificate. *Application contact:* Dr. Tristam Aldridge, Interim Associate Dean, 864-656-2561, Fax: 864-656-5344, E-mail: saldrid@clemson.edu.

Columbia University, Graduate School of Arts and Sciences, Program in Liberal Studies, New York, NY 10027. Offers American studies (MA); East Asian studies (MA); human rights studies (MA); Islamic culture studies (MA); Jewish studies (MA); medieval studies (MA); modern European studies (MA); South Asian studies (MA). Part-time and evening/weekend programs available. *Faculty:* 5 part-time/adjunct (2 women). *Students:* 7 full-time (2 women), 75 part-time (51 women); includes 5 minority (1 African American, 3 Asian Americans or Pacific Islanders, 1 Hispanic American), 8 international. Average age 41. 39 applicants, 77% accepted. In 2007, 20 degrees awarded. *Degree requirements:* For master's, thesis. Application fee: $90. *Expenses:* Tuition: Part-time $1,452 per credit. Required fees: $152 per term. One-time fee: $75 part-time. Full-time tuition and fees vary according to course level, course load, degree level and program. *Unit head:* Kristin Balicki, Program Coordinator, 212-854-4932, Fax: 212-854-4912, E-mail: knb2110@columbia.edu.

Dalhousie University, Faculty of Graduate Studies, Program in Interdisciplinary Studies, Halifax, NS B3H 4R2, Canada. Offers PhD. *Students:* 11 full-time (7 women). In 2007, 1 degree awarded. *Degree requirements:* For doctorate, thesis/dissertation. *Entrance requirements:* Additional exam requirements/recommendations for international students: Required—TOEFL. *Application deadline:* For fall admission, 1/31 for domestic students. Applications are processed on a rolling basis. Application fee: $60. *Expenses: Contact institution. Financial support:* Fellowships available. *Unit head:* Dr. Sunny Marche, Associate Dean, 902-494-8078, Fax: 902-494-8797, E-mail: idph@dal.ca. *Application contact:* Dr. Jack Duffy, Graduate Coordinator, 902-494-1838, Fax: 902-494-8797, E-mail: jack.duffy@dal.ca.

Dallas Baptist University, College of Adult Education, Professional Development Program, Dallas, TX 75211-9299. Offers accounting (MA); business (MA); church leadership (MA); corporate management (MA); counseling (MA); criminal justice (MA); English as a second language (MA); finance (MA); higher education (MA); leadership studies (MA); management (MA); management information systems (MA); marketing (MA); missions (MA). Part-time and evening/weekend programs available. *Faculty:* 55 full-time (22 women), 114 part-time/adjunct (44 women). *Students:* 19 full-time, 72 part-time. 35 applicants, 46% accepted, 12 enrolled. In 2007, 37 degrees awarded. *Entrance requirements:* For master's, minimum GPA of 3.0. Additional exam requirements/recommendations for international students: Required—TOEFL, IELTS. Application fee: $25. *Expenses:* Tuition: Full-time $9,144; part-time $508 per credit hour. *Financial support:* Federal Work-Study, institutionally sponsored loans, scholarships/grants, and tuition waivers (full and partial) available. Support available to part-time students. Financial award applicants required to submit FAFSA. *Unit head:* Dr. David Stricklin, Acting Director, 214-333-5496, Fax: 214-333-5558, E-mail: graduate@dbu.edu. *Application contact:* Kit P. Montgomery, Director of Graduate Programs, 214-333-5242, Fax: 214-333-5579, E-mail: graduate@dbu.edu.

DePaul University, College of Liberal Arts and Sciences, Department of Interdisciplinary Studies, Chicago, IL 60604-2287. Offers MA, MS. Part-time and evening/weekend programs available. *Students:* 31 full-time (17 women), 32 part-time (21 women); includes 13 minority (6 African Americans, 2 Asian Americans or Pacific Islanders, 5 Hispanic Americans), 4 international. Average age 31. 10 applicants, 90% accepted. In 2007, 10 master's awarded. *Degree requirements:* For master's, thesis optional. *Application deadline:* Applications are processed on a rolling basis. Application fee: $25. *Unit head:* Dr. Fassil Demissie, Director, 773-325-7356, E-mail: fdemissie@depaul.edu.

Drew University, Caspersen School of Graduate Studies, Program in Arts and Letters, Madison, NJ 07940-1493. Offers holocaust and genocide studies (Certificate); interdisciplinary studies (M Litt, D Litt). Part-time and evening/weekend programs available. Terminal master's awarded for partial completion of doctoral program. *Degree requirements:* For master's, thesis optional; for doctorate, thesis/dissertation. Expenses: Contact institution. *Faculty research:* Interdisciplinary studies across art, literature, music, philosophy, religion, and history.

Eastern Washington University, Graduate Studies, Interdisciplinary Studies, Cheney, WA 99004-2431. Offers MA, MS. *Degree requirements:* For master's, comprehensive exam, thesis or alternative. *Entrance requirements:* For master's, minimum GPA of 3.0.

Emory University, Graduate School of Arts and Sciences, Graduate Institute of Liberal Arts, Atlanta, GA 30322-1100. Offers PhD. *Degree requirements:* For doctorate, one foreign language, comprehensive exam, thesis/dissertation. *Entrance requirements:* For doctorate, GRE General Test. Electronic applications accepted. *Faculty research:* American cultural criticism, intellectual history, psychoanalysis, history of science, popular culture.

Fitchburg State College, Division of Graduate and Continuing Education, Program in Interdisciplinary Studies, Fitchburg, MA 01420-2697. Offers CAGS. Part-time and evening/weekend programs available. *Students:* 6 full-time (5 women), 41 part-time (33 women), 1 international. Average age 40. 23 applicants, 100% accepted, 11 enrolled. In 2007, 19 degrees awarded. *Entrance requirements:* For degree, master's degree, letters of recommendation, resumé. Additional exam requirements/recommendations for international students: Required—TOEFL (minimum score 550 paper-based; 213 computer-based; 79 iBT). *Application deadline:* Applications are processed on a rolling basis. Application fee: $25 ($50 for international students). *Expenses:* Tuition, nonresident: part-time $150 per credit. Required fees: $109 per credit. *Financial support:* In 2007–08, research assistantships with partial tuition reimbursements (averaging $5,500 per year); Federal Work-Study, scholarships/grants, and unspecified assistantships also available. Support available to part-time students. Financial award application deadline: 3/1; financial award applicants required to submit FAFSA. *Unit head:* Dr. Harry Semerjian, Chair, 978-665-3279, Fax: 978-665-3658, E-mail: gce@fsc.edu. *Application contact:* Director of Admissions, 978-665-3144, Fax: 978-665-4540, E-mail: admissions@fsc.edu.

Fresno Pacific University, Graduate Programs, Individualized Study Program, Fresno, CA 93702-4709. Offers MA. Part-time and evening/weekend programs available. *Faculty:* 3 full-time (1 woman), 3 part-time/adjunct (1 woman). *Students:* Average age 37. 5 applicants, 60% accepted, 0 enrolled. In 2007, 4 degrees awarded. *Degree requirements:* For master's, thesis. *Entrance requirements:* For master's, GMAT, GRE General Test, or MAT, 2 writing samples, interview. Additional exam requirements/recommendations for international students: Required—TOEFL (minimum score 550 paper-based; 213 computer-based). *Application deadline:* For fall admission, 7/15 for domestic and international students; for spring admission, 11/15 for domestic and international students. Applications are processed on a rolling basis. Application fee: $90. Electronic applications accepted. *Expenses:* Tuition: Full-time $7,470; part-time $415 per unit. *Financial support:* In 2007–08, 10 students received support. Scholarships/grants and tuition waivers (full and partial) available. Support available to part-time students. Financial award applicants required to submit FAFSA. *Unit head:* Dr. Jeanne Janzen, Director, 559-453-5550, Fax: 559-453-2001, E-mail: jjanzen@fresno.edu.

Frostburg State University, Graduate School, College of Education, Department of Educational Professions, Program in Interdisciplinary Education, Frostburg, MD 21532-1099. Offers M Ed. Part-time and evening/weekend programs available. *Students:* 16 full-time (7 women), 24 part-time (18 women); includes 3 minority (2 African Americans, 1 Hispanic American). Average age 32. 21 applicants, 76% accepted, 14 enrolled. In 2007, 24 degrees awarded. *Degree requirements:* For master's, thesis or alternative. *Application deadline:* For fall admission, 7/15 priority date for domestic students. Applications are processed on a rolling basis. Application fee: $30. Electronic applications accepted. *Expenses:* Tuition, state resident: full-time $5,706; part-time $317 per credit hour. Tuition, nonresident: full-time $6,552; part-time $364 per credit hour. Required fees: $77 per credit hour. $11 per term. *Financial support:* In 2007–08, 1 research assistantship with full tuition reimbursement (averaging $5,000 per year) was awarded; career-related internships or fieldwork also available. Financial award application deadline: 4/1; financial award applicants required to submit FAFSA. *Unit head:* Dr. Thomas Palardy, Coordinator, 301-687-4294. *Application contact:* Vickie Mazer, Director, Graduate Services, 301-687-7053, Fax: 301-687-4597, E-mail: vmmazer@frostburg.edu.

George Mason University, College of Humanities and Social Sciences, Interdisciplinary Studies Program, Fairfax, VA 22030. Offers anthropology (MAIS); community college teaching (MAIS); folklore (MAIS); higher education (MAIS); individualized studies (MAIS); religion, cultures, and values (MAIS); video-based production (MAIS); women's studies (MAIS); zoo and aquarium leadership (MAIS). Part-time and evening/weekend programs available. *Faculty:* 6 full-time (4 women), 6 part-time/adjunct (5 women). *Students:* 25 full-time (17 women), 90 part-time (76 women); includes 24 minority (5 African Americans, 1 American Indian/Alaska Native, 7 Asian Americans or Pacific Islanders, 11 Hispanic Americans), 3 international. Average age 33. 68 applicants, 72% accepted, 35 enrolled. In 2007, 19 degrees awarded. *Degree requirements:* For master's, thesis optional. *Entrance requirements:* For master's, GRE, GMAT, or MAT, interview, minimum GPA of 3.0 in last 60 hours of course work. *Application deadline:* For fall admission, 5/1 priority date for domestic students; for spring admission, 11/1 for domestic students. Applications are processed on a rolling basis. Application fee: $60 ($75 for international students). Electronic applications accepted. *Financial support:* Fellowships, teaching assistantships, career-related internships or fieldwork, Federal Work-Study, and institutionally sponsored loans available. Support available to part-time students. Financial award application deadline: 3/1; financial award applicants required to submit FAFSA. *Unit head:* John Burns, Chair, 703-993-1291, Fax: 703-993-1297, E-mail: mais@gmu.edu. *Application contact:* Dr. Johannes D. Bergmann, Information Contact, 703-993-8762, E-mail: mais@gmu.edu.

Goddard College, Graduate Program, Individually Designed Liberal Arts Program, Plainfield, VT 05667-9432. Offers consciousness studies (MA); environmental studies (MA); transformative language arts (MA). Postbaccalaureate distance learning degree programs offered (minimal on-campus study). *Faculty:* 10 part-time/adjunct (6 women). *Students:* 42. Average age 39. 30 applicants, 83% accepted, 18 enrolled. *Degree requirements:* For master's, thesis. *Entrance requirements:* For master's, 3 letters of recommendation, study plan, bibliography. *Application deadline:* Applications are processed on a rolling basis. Application fee: $40. Electronic applications accepted. *Expenses: Contact institution. Financial support:* In 2007–08, 38 students received support. Applicants required to submit FAFSA. *Unit head:* Margo MacLeod, Director, 802-454-8311, Fax: 802-454-8017, E-mail: macleodm@goddard.edu. *Application contact:* Brenda J. Hawkins, Director of Admissions, 800-906-8311 Ext. 240, Fax: 802-454-1029, E-mail: brenda.hawkins@goddard.edu.

Graduate School and University Center of the City University of New York, Graduate Studies, Interdisciplinary Studies, New York, NY 10016-4039. Offers language in social context (PhD); medieval studies (PhD); public policy (MA, PhD); urban studies (MA, PhD); women's studies (MA, PhD). Terminal master's awarded for partial completion of doctoral program. *Degree requirements:* For master's, thesis; for doctorate, comprehensive exam, thesis/dissertation. *Entrance requirements:* For master's and doctorate, GRE General Test. *Application deadline:* For fall admission, 2/1 for domestic students. Application fee: $40. *Financial support:* Application deadline: 2/1. *Unit head:* Chairman, 212-642-2430.

Hodges University, Graduate Programs, Naples, FL 34119. Offers business administration (MBA); computer information technology (MS); criminal justice (MCJ); education (MPS); information systems management (MIS); interdisciplinary (MPS); law (MPS); management (MSM); professional studies (MPS); psychology (MPS); public administration (MPA). Part-time and evening/weekend programs available. Postbaccalaureate distance learning degree programs offered (no on-campus study). *Faculty:* 16 full-time (4 women), 2 part-time/adjunct (1 woman). *Students:* 37 full-time (25 women), 175 part-time (104 women); includes 64 minority (29 African Americans, 2 Asian Americans or Pacific Islanders, 33 Hispanic Americans). Average age 36. In 2007, 75 degrees awarded. *Degree requirements:* For master's, comprehensive exam (for some programs). *Entrance requirements:* For master's, in-house entrance exam. *Application deadline:* Applications are processed on a rolling basis. Application fee: $50. Electronic applications accepted. *Expenses:* Tuition: Full-time $10,260; part-time $570 per credit hour. Required fees: $190 per trimester. *Financial support:* In 2007–08, 181 students received support. Federal Work-Study and scholarships/grants available. Financial award application deadline: 7/8; financial award applicants required to submit FAFSA. *Unit head:* Terry McMahan, President, 239-513-1122, Fax: 239-598-6253, E-mail: tmcmahan@hodges.edu. *Application contact:* Rita Lampus, Vice President of Student Enrollment Management, 239-513-1122, Fax: 239-598-6253, E-mail: rlampus@internationalcollege.edu.

Hofstra University, New College, Hempstead, NY 11549. Offers interdisciplinary studies (MA). Part-time and evening/weekend programs available. *Students:* 1 applicant, 0% accepted. In 2007, 1 degree awarded. *Degree requirements:* For master's, thesis. *Entrance requirements:* For master's, minimum undergraduate GPA of 3.0, bachelor's degree. Additional exam requirements/recommendations for international students: Required—TOEFL (minimum score 550 paper-based; 213 computer-based). *Application deadline:* Applications are processed on

Interdisciplinary Studies

Hofstra University (continued)
a rolling basis. Application fee: $60. Electronic applications accepted. *Expenses:* *Contact institution.* Tuition and fees vary according to program. *Financial support:* Fellowships with tuition reimbursements, research assistantships with full and partial tuition reimbursements, Federal Work-Study, institutionally sponsored loans, scholarships/grants, tuition waivers (full and partial), and unspecified assistantships available. Support available to part-time students. Financial award applicants required to submit FAFSA. *Faculty research:* Anthropology, religion, ethics, human rights, literature, history. *Unit head:* Dr. Barry Nass, Vice Dean, 516-463-5820, Fax: 516-463-4832, E-mail: barry.n.nass@hofstra.edu. *Application contact:* Carol Drummer, Dean of Graduate Admissions, 516-463-4876, Fax: 516-463-4664, E-mail: gradstudent@hofstra.edu.

Hollins University, Graduate Programs, Program in Liberal Studies, Roanoke, VA 24020-1603. Offers humanities (MALS); interdisciplinary studies (MALS); justice and legal studies (MALS); liberal studies (CAS); social science (MALS); visual and performing arts (MALS). Part-time and evening/weekend programs available. *Faculty:* 9 full-time (2 women), 12 part-time/adjunct (5 women). *Students:* 20 full-time (17 women), 89 part-time (74 women); includes 15 minority (11 African Americans, 1 American Indian/Alaska Native, 2 Asian Americans or Pacific Islanders, 1 Hispanic American). Average age 39. 30 applicants, 93% accepted, 20 enrolled. In 2007, 48 degrees awarded. *Degree requirements:* For master's, thesis. *Entrance requirements:* For master's, letters of recommendation, interview. Additional exam requirements/recommendations for international students: Required—TOEFL (minimum score 550 paper-based; 213 computer-based). *Application deadline:* For fall admission, 7/1 priority date for domestic and international students; for spring admission, 12/10 priority date for domestic and international students. Applications are processed on a rolling basis. Application fee: $40. Electronic applications accepted. *Expenses:* Tuition: Part-time $265 per credit hour. Tuition and fees vary according to course load and program. *Financial support:* In 2007–08, 53 students received support, including 4 fellowships (averaging $1,060 per year); Federal Work-Study and scholarships/grants also available. Support available to part-time students. Financial award application deadline: 7/15; financial award applicants required to submit FAFSA. *Faculty research:* Elderly blacks, film, feminist economics, U.S. voting patterns, Wagner, diversity. *Unit head:* Dr. Edward A. Lynch, Director, 540-362-6475, Fax: 540-362-6288, E-mail: elynch@hollins.edu. *Application contact:* Cathy S. Koon, Manager of Graduate Services, 540-362-6326, Fax: 540-362-6288, E-mail: ckoon@hollins.edu.

Idaho State University, Office of Graduate Studies, Department of Interdisciplinary Studies, Pocatello, ID 83209. Offers general interdisciplinary (M Ed, MA, MNS); waste management and environmental science (MS). Part-time programs available. *Faculty:* 2 full-time (1 woman). In 2007, 2 degrees awarded. *Degree requirements:* For master's, comprehensive exam, thesis optional. *Entrance requirements:* For master's, GRE General Test or MAT, minimum GPA of 3.0. Additional exam requirements/recommendations for international students: Required—TOEFL (minimum score 550 paper-based; 213 computer-based; 80 iBT). *Application deadline:* For fall admission, 7/1 for domestic students, 6/1 for international students; for spring admission, 12/1 for domestic students, 11/1 for international students. Applications are processed on a rolling basis. Application fee: $55. *Expenses:* Tuition, state resident: full-time $2,882; part-time $259 per credit hour. Tuition, nonresident: full-time $11,566; part-time $379 per credit hour. Required fees: $2,278. Full-time tuition and fees vary according to program. Part-time tuition and fees vary according to course load. *Financial support:* Career-related internships or fieldwork, Federal Work-Study, scholarships/grants, and unspecified assistantships available. Support available to part-time students. Financial award application deadline: 1/1; financial award applicants required to submit FAFSA. *Unit head:* Dr. Pamela Crowell, Vice President for Research, 208-282-2714, Fax: 208-282-4529.

Iowa State University of Science and Technology, Graduate College, Interdisciplinary Programs, Program in Interdisciplinary Graduate Studies, Ames, IA 50011. Offers MA, MS. *Students:* 37 full-time (18 women), 37 part-time (26 women); includes 18 minority (12 African Americans, 1 American Indian/Alaska Native, 1 Asian American or Pacific Islander, 4 Hispanic Americans), 19 international. 42 applicants, 69% accepted, 22 enrolled. In 2007, 16 degrees awarded. *Degree requirements:* For master's, thesis or alternative. *Entrance requirements:* Additional exam requirements/recommendations for international students: Required—TOEFL (paper-based 550; computer-based 213; iBT 79) or IELTS (6.5). *Application deadline:* For fall admission, 5/1 priority date for domestic and international students; for spring admission, 10/1 for domestic and international students. Application fee: $30 ($70 for international students). Electronic applications accepted. *Financial support:* In 2007–08, 17 research assistantships with full and partial tuition reimbursements (averaging $16,089 per year), 7 teaching assistantships with full and partial tuition reimbursements (averaging $18,832 per year) were awarded; fellowships, scholarships/grants, health care benefits, and unspecified assistantships also available. *Unit head:* Dr. George A. Jackson, Assistant Dean, 515-294-1170.

John F. Kennedy University, Graduate School of Holistic Studies, Department of Integral Studies, Program in Consciousness Studies, Pleasant Hill, CA 94523-4817. Offers MA. Part-time and evening/weekend programs available. *Degree requirements:* For master's, thesis or alternative. *Entrance requirements:* For master's, interview. Additional exam requirements/recommendations for international students: Required—TOEFL.

Lesley University, Graduate School of Arts and Social Sciences, Self-Designed Master's Program in Interdisciplinary Studies, Cambridge, MA 02138-2790. Offers individualized studies (MA); integrative holistic health (MA); women's studies (MA). Part-time and evening/weekend programs available. Postbaccalaureate distance learning degree programs offered (no on-campus study). *Faculty:* 3 full-time (all women), 5 part-time/adjunct (3 women). *Students:* 12 full-time (11 women), 14 part-time (12 women); includes 3 minority (2 African Americans, 1 Hispanic American), 1 international. Average age 35. 10 applicants, 100% accepted, 9 enrolled. In 2007, 20 degrees awarded. *Entrance requirements:* For master's, 3 letters of recommendation. Additional exam requirements/recommendations for international students: Required—TOEFL (minimum score 550 paper-based; 213 computer-based; 80 iBT). Application fee: $50. *Financial support:* In 2007–08, 1 student received support, including research assistantships (averaging $3,400 per year), teaching assistantships (averaging $3,400 per year); Federal Work-Study, scholarships/grants, and unspecified assistantships also available. Support available to part-time students. Financial award application deadline: 4/15; financial award applicants required to submit FAFSA. *Unit head:* Sharlene Cochrane, Director, 617-349-8477, E-mail: cochrane@lesley.edu. *Application contact:* Lisa Lombardi, Assistant Director, Advising and Student Services, 617-349-8454, E-mail: lombardi@lesley.edu.

Long Island University, C.W. Post Campus, College of Liberal Arts and Sciences, Program in Interdisciplinary Studies, Brookville, NY 11548-1300. Offers MA, MS. Part-time and evening/weekend programs available. *Students:* 5 full-time (2 women), 19 part-time (14 women), 2 international. Average age 33. 19 applicants, 74% accepted, 4 enrolled. In 2007, 6 degrees awarded. *Degree requirements:* For master's, thesis. *Entrance requirements:* For master's, minimum GPA of 3.0. *Application deadline:* Applications are processed on a rolling basis. Application fee: $30. Electronic applications accepted. *Expenses:* Tuition: Part-time $825 per credit. Tuition and fees vary according to course load. *Financial support:* In 2007–08, 3 students received support. Federal Work-Study available. Support available to part-time students. Financial award application deadline: 5/15; financial award applicants required to submit CSS PROFILE or FAFSA. *Unit head:* Dr. Katherine Hill-Miller, Dean, 516-299-2710, Fax: 516-299-4140.

Marquette University, Graduate School, Interdisciplinary PhD Program, Milwaukee, WI 53201-1881. Offers PhD. *Students:* 2 full-time (0 women), 7 part-time (all women); includes 1 minority (African American), 2 international. Average age 40. 1 applicant, 100% accepted, 1 enrolled. In 2007, 3 degrees awarded. *Degree requirements:* For doctorate, thesis/dissertation. *Entrance requirements:* For doctorate, GRE General Test. Additional exam requirements/recommendations for international students: Required—TOEFL. Application fee: $40. *Financial support:* Fellowships, research assistantships, teaching assistantships, career-related internships or fieldwork, Federal Work-Study, institutionally sponsored loans, scholarships/grants, and tuition waivers (full and partial) available. Support available to part-time students. Financial award application deadline: 2/15. *Application contact:* Craig Pierce, Director of Admissions, Graduate School, 414-288-7137, Fax: 414-288-1902, E-mail: craig.pierce@marquette.edu.

Marylhurst University, Department of Interdisciplinary Studies, Marylhurst, OR 97036-0261. Offers MA. Part-time and evening/weekend programs available. *Faculty:* 1 (woman) full-time, 4 part-time/adjunct (1 woman). *Students:* 3 full-time (2 women), 36 part-time (27 women); includes 2 minority (1 Asian American or Pacific Islander, 1 Hispanic American), 1 international. Average age 46. In 2007, 12 degrees awarded. *Degree requirements:* For master's, thesis. *Entrance requirements:* For master's, 2 letters of recommendation, writing sample, personal statement, interview. Additional exam requirements/recommendations for international students: Recommended—TOEFL (minimum score 550 paper-based). *Application deadline:* Applications are processed on a rolling basis. Application fee: $40 ($50 for international students). Electronic applications accepted. *Expenses:* Tuition: Part-time $419 per credit. One-time fee: $85 part-time. Tuition and fees vary according to course load and program. *Financial support:* Federal Work-Study and scholarships/grants available. Support available to part-time students. Financial award applicants required to submit FAFSA. *Faculty research:* World religions, spirituality and literature, philosophy, humanities. *Unit head:* Dr. Debrah B. Bokowski, Chair, 503-636-8141, Fax: 503-697-5597, E-mail: dbokowski@marylhurst.edu. *Application contact:* Kathleen Schneff, Admissions Specialist, 800-634-9982 Ext. 3322, Fax: 503-635-6585, E-mail: admissions@marylhurst.edu.

Marywood University, Academic Affairs, Insalaco College of Creative Arts and Management, Department of Communication Arts, Program in Communication Arts, Scranton, PA 18509-1598. Offers corporate communication (Certificate); e-business (Certificate); health communication (Certificate); instructional technology (Certificate); interdisciplinary (MA); library science/information specialist (Certificate); media management (MA); production (MA). *Students:* 10 full-time (6 women), 22 part-time (15 women); includes 4 minority (1 African American, 3 Hispanic Americans). Average age 28. In 2007, 8 degrees awarded. Application fee: $30. *Expenses:* Tuition: Full-time $15,290; part-time $695 per credit. Required fees: $990; $370 per term. Tuition and fees vary according to degree level.

Minnesota State University Mankato, College of Graduate Studies, Program in Cross-disciplinary Studies, Mankato, MN 56001. Offers MS. Part-time and evening/weekend programs available. *Students:* 1 full-time (0 women), 7 part-time (3 women). Average age 32. In 2007, 11 degrees awarded. *Degree requirements:* For master's, comprehensive exam, thesis or alternative. *Entrance requirements:* For master's, GRE General Test, minimum GPA of 3.0 during previous 2 years. Additional exam requirements/recommendations for international students: Required—TOEFL. *Application deadline:* For fall admission, 7/1 priority date for domestic students; for spring admission, 11/1 for domestic students. Applications are processed on a rolling basis. Application fee: $40. Electronic applications accepted. *Financial support:* Research assistantships with full tuition reimbursements, teaching assistantships with full tuition reimbursements, career-related internships or fieldwork, Federal Work-Study, and unspecified assistantships available. Support available to part-time students. Financial award application deadline: 3/15; financial award applicants required to submit FAFSA. *Unit head:* Chris Mickle, Graduate Coordinator, 507-389-2321. *Application contact:* 507-389-2321, E-mail: grad@mnsu.edu.

Montana State University–Billings, College of Education, Department of Educational Theory and Practice, Option in Interdisciplinary Studies, Billings, MT 59101-0298. Offers M Ed. *Students:* 59. 24 applicants, 100% accepted, 24 enrolled. In 2007, 13 degrees awarded. *Degree requirements:* For master's, thesis or alternative. *Entrance requirements:* For master's, GRE General Test or MAT, minimum GPA of 3.0 (undergraduate), 3.25 (graduate). *Application deadline:* For fall admission, 7/15 for domestic students; for spring admission, 12/1 for domestic students. Applications are processed on a rolling basis. Application fee: $40. *Expenses:* Tuition, state resident: full-time $4,665. Tuition, nonresident: full-time $11,096. *Financial support:* Teaching assistantships, career-related internships or fieldwork, Federal Work-Study, institutionally sponsored loans, scholarships/grants, tuition waivers (partial), and unspecified assistantships available. Support available to part-time students. Financial award application deadline: 5/1; financial award applicants required to submit FAFSA. *Application contact:* David M. Sullivan, Graduate Studies Counselor, 406-657-2053, Fax: 406-657-2299, E-mail: dsullivan@msubillings.edu.

Mountain State University, Graduate Studies, Program in Interdisciplinary Studies, Beckley, WV 25802-9003. Offers MA, MS. Part-time and evening/weekend programs available. Postbaccalaureate distance learning degree programs offered (no on-campus study). *Faculty:* 10 full-time (4 women), 8 part-time/adjunct (4 women). *Students:* 30 full-time (23 women), 14 part-time (8 women); includes 10 minority (7 African Americans, 1 American Indian/Alaska Native, 1 Asian American or Pacific Islander, 1 Hispanic American), 1 international. Average age 37. 80 applicants, 71% accepted. In 2007, 6 degrees awarded. *Degree requirements:* For master's, thesis or alternative. *Entrance requirements:* Additional exam requirements/recommendations for international students: Required—TOEFL (minimum score 550 paper-based; 213 computer-based); Recommended—IELTS (minimum score 7). *Application deadline:* For fall admission, 5/31 priority date for domestic and international students. Applications are processed on a rolling basis. Application fee: $25 ($50 for international students). Electronic applications accepted. *Financial support:* Federal Work-Study, scholarships/grants, and unspecified assistantships available. Support available to part-time students. Financial award applicants required to submit FAFSA. *Unit head:* Dr. Brian Holloway, Dean of Graduate Studies, 304-929-1438, Fax: 304-929-1637, E-mail: holloway@mountainstate.edu. *Application contact:* Dinah Rock, Coordinator of Graduate Academic Services, 304-929-1588, Fax: 304-929-1637, E-mail: drock@mountainstate.edu.

See Close-Up on page 751.

New Mexico State University, Graduate School, Interdisciplinary Program, Las Cruces, NM 88003-8001. Offers MA, MS, PhD. Part-time programs available. Postbaccalaureate distance learning degree programs offered (minimal on-campus study). *Students:* 37 full-time (19 women), 146 part-time (105 women); includes 89 minority (9 African Americans, 2 American Indian/Alaska Native, 2 Asian Americans or Pacific Islanders, 76 Hispanic Americans), 10 international. Average age 37. 104 applicants, 97% accepted, 76 enrolled. *Degree requirements:* For master's, comprehensive exam, thesis; for doctorate, comprehensive exam, thesis/dissertation. *Entrance requirements:* For master's, GRE General Test, minimum GPA of 2.5; for doctorate, GRE General Test, minimum GPA of 3.0. Additional exam requirements/recommendations for international students: Required—TOEFL (minimum score 550 paper-based; 213 computer-based; 79 iBT), IELTS. *Application deadline:* Applications are processed on a rolling basis. Application fee: $30 ($50 for international students). *Expenses:* Tuition, state resident: full-time $3,602; part-time $199 per credit. Tuition, nonresident: full-time $13,380; part-time $607 per credit. Required fees: $1,178. *Financial support:* In 2007–08, 2 research assistantships with full tuition reimbursements, 2 teaching assistantships with full tuition reimbursements were awarded; fellowships, career-related internships or fieldwork, Federal Work-Study, and health care benefits also available. Financial award application deadline: 3/1. *Faculty research:* Bioinformatics, molecular genetics, plant pathology. *Unit head:* Dr. Linda Lacey, Dean, 575-646-5746, Fax: 575-646-7721, E-mail: lacey@nmsu.edu. *Application contact:* Elena Luna, Coordinator, 575-646-3498, Fax: 575-646-7721, E-mail: rosluna@nmsu.edu.

New York University, Gallatin School of Individualized Study, New York, NY 10012-1019. Offers MA. Part-time programs available. *Faculty:* 27 full-time (14 women), 15 part-time/adjunct (3 women). *Students:* 46 full-time (36 women), 144 part-time (120 women); includes 43 minority (20 African Americans, 2 American Indian/Alaska Native, 9 Asian Americans or Pacific Islanders, 12 Hispanic Americans), 5 international. 239 applicants, 51% accepted, 56 enrolled. In 2007, 46 degrees awarded. *Degree requirements:* For master's, thesis. *Entrance requirements:* Additional exam requirements/recommendations for international students:

Required—TOEFL. *Application deadline:* For fall admission, 2/1 for domestic and international students; for spring admission, 11/1 for domestic and international students. Application fee: $50. *Expenses:* *Contact institution.* *Financial support:* In 2007–08, 71 students received support, including 3 fellowships (averaging $15,000 per year), 3 research assistantships with full tuition reimbursements available (averaging $16,000 per year); career-related internships or fieldwork, Federal Work-Study, institutionally sponsored loans, and scholarships/grants also available. Financial award application deadline: 2/1; financial award applicants required to submit FAFSA. *Faculty research:* Arts and culture, gender studies, political and social thought, literature, classical studies. *Unit head:* Dr. Ali Mirsepassi, Interim Dean, 212-998-7370. *Application contact:* Frances R. Levin, Director of Graduate Admissions, 212-998-7370, Fax: 212-995-4150, E-mail: gallatin.gradadmissions@nyu.edu.

See Close-Up on page 753.

Niagara University, Graduate Division of Arts and Sciences, Program in Interdisciplinary Studies, Niagara Falls, Niagara University, NY 14109. Offers MA. *Faculty:* 1 full-time (0 women). *Students:* 3 full-time (all women), 12 part-time (8 women); includes 2 minority (1 African American, 1 Hispanic American). *Expenses:* Tuition: Full-time $11,790; part-time $655 per credit. Required fees: $50; $25 per term. *Unit head:* Dr. Thomas A. Chambers, Director, Interdisciplinary Studies, 716-286-8091, E-mail: chambers@niagara.edu.

Nova Southeastern University, Graduate School of Humanities and Social Sciences, Department of Multi-Disciplinary Studies, Fort Lauderdale, FL 33314-7796. Offers college student affairs (MS); college student personnel administration (Certificate); cross-disciplinary studies (MA). Part-time programs available. Postbaccalaureate distance learning degree programs offered (no on-campus study). *Faculty:* 4 part-time/adjunct (2 women). *Students:* 24 full-time (15 women), 35 part-time (29 women); includes 24 minority (20 African Americans, 4 Hispanic Americans), 2 international. 45 applicants, 67% accepted, 30 enrolled. In 2007, 7 master's awarded. *Degree requirements:* For master's, comprehensive exam, thesis optional, portfolio. *Entrance requirements:* For master's, interview, minimum GPA of 3.0. Additional exam requirements/recommendations for international students: Required—TOEFL. *Application deadline:* For fall admission, 7/1 priority date for domestic and international students; for winter admission, 11/1 priority date for domestic and international students; for spring admission, 3/1 priority date for domestic and international students. Applications are processed on a rolling basis. Electronic applications accepted. *Financial support:* In 2007–08, 20 research assistantships with tuition reimbursements (averaging $13,000 per year) were awarded; career-related internships or fieldwork, Federal Work-Study, institutionally sponsored loans, and scholarships/grants also available. Financial award applicants required to submit CSS PROFILE. *Unit head:* Dr. Judith McKay, Senior Associate Dean, 954-262-3060, Fax: 954-262-3893, E-mail: mckayj@nsu.nova.edu. *Application contact:* Marcia Arango, Student Recruitment Coordinator, 954-262-3006, Fax: 954-262-3968, E-mail: marango@nsu.nova.edu.

See Close-Up on page 953.

The Ohio State University, Graduate School, College of Humanities, Department of Comparative Studies, Columbus, OH 43210. Offers MA, PhD. *Faculty:* 71. *Students:* 18 full-time (14 women), 6 part-time (5 women); includes 2 minority (both African Americans), 5 international. Average age 35. In 2007, 11 degrees awarded. *Entrance requirements:* For master's and doctorate, GRE General Test. Additional exam requirements/recommendations for international students: Required—TOEFL (minimum score 600 paper-based; 250 computer-based). *Application deadline:* For fall admission, 8/15 priority date for domestic students, 7/1 priority date for international students; for winter admission, 12/1 priority date for domestic students, 11/1 priority date for international students; for spring admission, 3/1 priority date for domestic students, 2/1 priority date for international students. Applications are processed on a rolling basis. Application fee: $40 ($50 for international students). Electronic applications accepted. *Financial support:* Fellowships, research assistantships, teaching assistantships, Federal Work-Study, institutionally sponsored loans, and unspecified assistantships available. Support available to part-time students. *Unit head:* Maurice E. Stevens, Graduate Studies Committee Chair, 614-292-2559, Fax: 614-292-6707, E-mail: stevens.368@osu.edu. *Application contact:* 614-292-9444, Fax: 614-292-3895, E-mail: domestic.grad@osu.edu.

Oregon State University, Graduate School, Program in Interdisciplinary Studies, Corvallis, OR 97331. Offers MAIS. Program focuses on three areas of study and must include at least one area of study in liberal arts. Part-time programs available. *Students:* 43 full-time (27 women), 16 part-time (11 women); includes 11 minority (1 African American, 1 American Indian/Alaska Native, 2 Asian Americans or Pacific Islanders, 7 Hispanic Americans), 2 international. Average age 31. In 2007, 22 degrees awarded. *Degree requirements:* For master's, thesis optional. *Entrance requirements:* For master's, minimum GPA of 3.0 in last 90 hours of course work. Additional exam requirements/recommendations for international students: Required—TOEFL. *Application deadline:* For fall admission, 3/1 for domestic students. Applications are processed on a rolling basis. Application fee: $50. *Expenses:* Tuition, state resident: full-time $9,126; part-time $338 per credit. Tuition, nonresident: full-time $14,796; part-time $548 per credit. Required fees: $1,447. *Financial support:* Fellowships, research assistantships, teaching assistantships, career-related internships or fieldwork, Federal Work-Study, and institutionally sponsored loans available. Support available to part-time students. Financial award application deadline: 2/1. *Unit head:* Dr. Mary Ann Matzke, Head Advisor, 541-737-3880, Fax: 541-737-1009, E-mail: maryann.matzke@oregonstate.edu.

Regis University, College for Professional Studies, MA Program, Denver, CO 80221-1099. Offers criminology (MA); fine arts administration (Certificate); language and communication (MA); mediation (Certificate); psychology (MA); self-designed major (MA); social justice, peace, and reconciliation (Certificate); social science (MA); technical communication (Certificate). Program also offered in Henderson and Las Vegas (Summerlin), NV. Part-time and evening/weekend programs available. Postbaccalaureate distance learning degree programs offered (minimal on-campus study). *Faculty:* 84. *Students:* 218 (167 women). Average age 41. In 2007, 52 degrees awarded. *Degree requirements:* For master's, thesis, research project. *Entrance requirements:* For master's, resumé, recommendations, essays. Additional exam requirements/recommendations for international students: Required—TOEFL (minimum score 213 computer-based), TWE (minimum score 5). *Application deadline:* For fall admission, 8/13 priority date for domestic students, 7/13 priority date for international students; for winter admission, 10/8 priority date for domestic students, 9/8 priority date for international students; for spring admission, 12/17 priority date for domestic students, 11/17 for international students. Applications are processed on a rolling basis. Application fee: $75. Electronic applications accepted. *Expenses:* *Contact institution.* *Financial support:* Federal Work-Study available. Support available to part-time students. Financial award application deadline: 3/15; financial award applicants required to submit FAFSA. *Faculty research:* Independent/nonresidential graduate study: new methods and models, adult learning and the capstone experience, Goal Setting, behavior of Adult students, Innovative Studies for Community Colleges. *Unit head:* Dr. Robert Collins, Chair, 303-458-4302, Fax: 303-964-5538. *Application contact:* Graduate Admissions, 800-677-9270 Ext. 4080, Fax: 303-964-5538, E-mail: masters@regis.edu.

Rensselaer Polytechnic Institute, Graduate School, School of Science, Program in Multidisciplinary Science, Troy, NY 12180-3590. Offers MS, PhD. Part-time programs available. *Students:* 6 applicants, 33% accepted, 1 enrolled.Terminal master's awarded for partial completion of doctoral program. *Degree requirements:* For master's, comprehensive exam (for some programs), thesis optional; for doctorate, comprehensive exam, thesis/dissertation. *Entrance requirements:* For master's and doctorate, GRE General Test. Additional exam requirements/recommendations for international students: Required—TOEFL. *Application deadline:* For fall admission, 1/15 priority date for domestic and international students. Applications are processed on a rolling basis. Application fee: $75. Electronic applications accepted. *Expenses:* Tuition: Full-time $34,900; part-time $1,454 per credit. Required fees: $1,802. *Financial support:* In 2007–08, 1 research assistantship with tuition reimbursement (averaging $14,500 per year) was awarded; career-related internships or fieldwork and institutionally sponsored loans also available. Financial award application deadline: 2/1. *Faculty research:* Bioinformatics, polymer science, biocomputation. *Unit head:* Dr. Samuel C. Wait, Associate Dean, 518-276-6305, Fax: 518-276-2825, E-mail: waitc@rpi.edu.

Rochester Institute of Technology, Graduate Enrollment Services, College of Applied Science and Technology, Center for Multidisciplinary Studies, Program in Professional Studies, Rochester, NY 14623-5603. Offers MS. *Students:* 32 full-time (13 women), 71 part-time (40 women); includes 16 minority (10 African Americans, 2 Asian Americans or Pacific Islanders, 4 Hispanic Americans), 19 international. 42 applicants, 74% accepted, 24 enrolled. In 2007, 31 degrees awarded. *Entrance requirements:* For master's, minimum GPA of 3.0. Additional exam requirements/recommendations for international students: Required—TOEFL (minimum score 550 paper-based; 213 computer-based; 79 iBT). *Application deadline:* For fall admission, 3/1 priority date for domestic students. Applications are processed on a rolling basis. Application fee: $50. *Expenses:* Tuition: Full-time $28,491; part-time $800 per credit hour. Required fees: $201; $67 per term. *Financial support:* Career-related internships or fieldwork and institutionally sponsored loans available. Support available to part-time students. Financial award applicants required to submit FAFSA. *Unit head:* Dr. Samuel McQuade, Head, 585-475-5230, E-mail: scmcms@rit.edu.

Rosalind Franklin University of Medicine and Science, College of Health Professions, Department of Interprofessional Healthcare Studies, Interprofessional Healthcare Studies Program, North Chicago, IL 60064-3095. Offers D Sc, PhD. *Faculty:* 1 (woman) full-time, 6 part-time/adjunct (4 women). *Unit head:* Dr. Judith Stoecker, Vice Dean and Program Director, 847-578-8694, Fax: 847-578-8623, E-mail: judith.stoecker@rosalindfranklin.edu. *Application contact:* Laura Nelson, Administrative Assistant, 847-578-3310, Fax: 847-578-8623, E-mail: laura.nelson@rosalindfranklin.edu.

Rutgers, The State University of New Jersey, New Brunswick, Graduate School, BioMaPS Institute for Quantitative Biology, New Brunswick, NJ 08901-1281. Offers computational biology and molecular biophysics (PhD). *Degree requirements:* For doctorate, comprehensive exam, thesis/dissertation. *Entrance requirements:* For doctorate, GRE. Additional exam requirements/recommendations for international students: Required—TOEFL. Electronic applications accepted. *Faculty research:* Protein folding; nucleic acid structure; systems biology; transcriptional regulation; signal transduction.

San Diego State University, Graduate and Research Affairs, Interdisciplinary Studies, San Diego, CA 92182. Offers MA, MS. Part-time programs available. *Students:* 11 full-time (5 women), 19 part-time (11 women); includes 5 minority (1 American Indian/Alaska Native, 2 Asian Americans or Pacific Islanders, 2 Hispanic Americans). 14 applicants, 64% accepted, 8 enrolled. In 2007, 21 degrees awarded. *Degree requirements:* For master's, thesis. *Entrance requirements:* For master's, GRE General Test. Additional exam requirements/recommendations for international students: Required—TOEFL. *Application deadline:* For fall admission, 5/1 for domestic and international students; for spring admission, 11/1 for domestic students, 10/1 for international students. Applications are processed on a rolling basis. Application fee: $55. Electronic applications accepted. *Financial support:* Applicants required to submit FAFSA. *Application contact:* Graduate Admissions, 619-594-0884, E-mail: gra@mail.sdsu.edu.

San Jose State University, Graduate Studies and Research, Graduate Studies Program, Program in Interdisciplinary Studies, San Jose, CA 95192-0001. Offers MA, MS. *Application deadline:* For fall admission, 6/29 for domestic students; for spring admission, 11/30 for domestic students. Applications are processed on a rolling basis. Electronic applications accepted. *Financial support:* Applicants required to submit FAFSA. *Unit head:* Dr. Rhea Williamson, Associate Dean, 408-924-2481, Fax: 408-924-2477.

Sarah Lawrence College, Graduate Studies, Individualized Study Program, Bronxville, NY 10708-5999. Offers MA. Part-time programs available. *Degree requirements:* For master's, thesis. Application fee: $60. *Expenses:* Tuition: Part-time $1,034 per credit. Required fees: $430 per year. Tuition and fees vary according to program. *Financial support:* Career-related internships or fieldwork, scholarships/grants, and unspecified assistantships available. Support available to part-time students. Financial award application deadline: 3/1; financial award applicants required to submit FAFSA. *Unit head:* Susan Guma, Dean of Graduate Studies, 914-395-2373, E-mail: sguma@mail.slc.edu.

Sonoma State University, Institute of Interdisciplinary Studies/Special Major, Rohnert Park, CA 94928-3609. Offers special major (MA, MS). Part-time programs available. *Faculty:* 7 full-time (all women), 1 (woman) part-time/adjunct. *Students:* 15 full-time (12 women), 12 part-time (8 women); includes 2 minority (1 American Indian/Alaska Native, 1 Hispanic American), 1 international. Average age 37. 8 applicants, 63% accepted, 4 enrolled. In 2007, 9 degrees awarded. *Degree requirements:* For master's, thesis or alternative. *Entrance requirements:* For master's, written English proficiency test, minimum GPA of 3.0 in last 60 hours. *Application deadline:* For fall admission, 1/31 for domestic students; for spring admission, 10/31 for domestic students. Application fee: $55. *Financial support:* Career-related internships or fieldwork, Federal Work-Study, and institutionally sponsored loans available. Support available to part-time students. *Unit head:* Dr. Ellen Carlton, Coordinator, 707-664-3918, E-mail: ellen.carlton@sonoma.edu.

Southern Methodist University, School of Education and Human Development, Program in Liberal Studies, Dallas, TX 75275. Offers MLS. Part-time and evening/weekend programs available. *Faculty:* 47 part-time/adjunct (16 women). *Students:* 10 full-time (9 women), 158 part-time (109 women); includes 49 minority (23 African Americans, 2 American Indian/Alaska Native, 6 Asian Americans or Pacific Islanders, 18 Hispanic Americans), 3 international. Average age 40. 57 applicants, 100% accepted. In 2007, 63 master's awarded. *Degree requirements:* For master's, thesis optional. *Application deadline:* For fall admission, 8/15 priority date for domestic students; for spring admission, 1/1 priority date for domestic students. Applications are processed on a rolling basis. Application fee: $50. *Expenses:* *Contact institution.* *Financial support:* In 2007–08, 96 students received support. Available to part-time students. *Unit head:* Dr. David J. Chard, Dean, 214-768-5465, Fax: 214-768-1797. *Application contact:* Michelle Mrak, Director of Graduate Liberal Studies, 214-768-1012, Fax: 214-768-2104, E-mail: mmrak@smu.edu.

Stanford University, School of Education, Program in Social Sciences, Policy, and Educational Practice, Stanford, CA 94305-9991. Offers administration and policy analysis (Ed D, PhD); anthropology of education (PhD); economics of education (PhD); educational linguistics (PhD); evaluation (MA), including interdisciplinary studies; higher education (PhD); history of education (PhD); interdisciplinary studies (PhD); international comparative education (MA, PhD); international education administration and policy analysis (MA); philosophy of education (PhD); policy analysis (MA); prospective principal's program (MA); sociology of education (PhD). *Degree requirements:* For master's, thesis (for some programs); for doctorate, thesis/dissertation. *Entrance requirements:* For master's and doctorate, GRE General Test. Electronic applications accepted.

State University of New York at Fredonia, Graduate Studies, Graduate Programs in Interdisciplinary Studies, Fredonia, NY 14063-1136. Offers MA, MS. Part-time and evening/weekend programs available. *Degree requirements:* For master's, thesis optional.

State University of New York at New Paltz, Graduate School, Faculty of Fine and Performing Arts, Department of Fine Arts, New Paltz, NY 12561. Offers ceramics (MA, MFA); interdisciplinary (MA); metal (MA, MFA); painting (MA, MFA); printmaking (MA, MFA); sculpture (MA, MFA). *Accreditation:* NASAD (one or more programs are accredited). Part-time and evening/weekend programs available. *Faculty:* 29 full-time (20 women), 37 part-time/adjunct (18 women). *Students:* 61 full-time (44 women), 23 part-time (11 women); includes 6 minority (2 Asian Americans or Pacific Islanders, 4 Hispanic Americans), 10 international. Average age 29. 107 applicants. In 2007, 27 degrees awarded. *Degree requirements:* For master's, thesis, portfolio. *Entrance requirements:* For master's, minimum GPA of 3.0, portfolio. Additional exam requirements/recommendations for international students: Required—TOEFL (minimum score 550 paper-based; 213 computer-based; 80 iBT). *Application deadline:* For fall admission, 2/15 for domestic and international students. Application fee: $50. Electronic applications accepted.

Interdisciplinary Studies

State University of New York at New Paltz (continued)

Expenses: Tuition, state resident: full-time $6,900; part-time $288 per credit hour. Tuition, nonresident: full-time $10,920; part-time $455 per credit hour. Required fees: $1,040; $30 per credit hour. $153 per credit hour. Tuition and fees vary according to program. *Financial support:* In 2007–08, 13 students received support, including 2 research assistantships with partial tuition reimbursements available (averaging $5,000 per year), 8 teaching assistantships with partial tuition reimbursements available (averaging $5,000 per year); Federal Work-Study and institutionally sponsored loans also available. *Unit head:* Prof. Francois Deschamps, Chair, 845-257-2787, E-mail: deschamf@newpaltz.edu. *Application contact:* Dr. Anat Shiftan, Coordinator, 845-257-3834, E-mail: shiftana@newpaltz.edu.

Stephen F. Austin State University, Graduate School, College of Applied Arts and Science, Program in Interdisciplinary Studies, Nacogdoches, TX 75962. Offers MIS. Part-time programs available. *Degree requirements:* For master's, comprehensive exam, thesis optional. *Entrance requirements:* For master's, GRE General Test. Additional exam requirements/recommendations for international students: Required—TOEFL (minimum score 550 paper-based; 213 computer-based).

Teachers College, Columbia University, Graduate Faculty of Education, Interdisciplinary Programs, New York, NY 10027-6696. Offers Ed M, MA, Ed D. Part-time programs available. *Students:* 6 full-time (5 women), 16 part-time (6 women); includes 5 minority (3 African Americans, 1 Asian American or Pacific Islander, 1 Hispanic American), 2 international. Average age 39. 3 applicants, 33% accepted, 0 enrolled. In 2007, 3 master's, 3 doctorates awarded. Terminal master's awarded for partial completion of doctoral program. *Degree requirements:* For doctorate, thesis/dissertation. *Application deadline:* For fall admission, 5/15 for domestic students. Application fee: $70. *Financial support:* Fellowships, career-related internships or fieldwork, Federal Work-Study, institutionally sponsored loans, and tuition waivers (full and partial) available. Support available to part-time students. Financial award application deadline: 2/1. *Application contact:* Director of Admissions, 212-678-3083, Fax: 212-678-4171.

Texas A&M University, Interdisciplinary Programs, College Station, TX 77843. Offers MAB, MBIOT, ME, MS, PhD. *Students:* 277 full-time (152 women), 51 part-time (21 women); includes 27 minority (7 African Americans, 9 Asian Americans or Pacific Islanders, 11 Hispanic Americans), 160 international. 191 applicants, 47% accepted, 64 enrolled. In 2007, 221 master's, 58 doctorates awarded. *Expenses:* Tuition, state resident: full-time $6,129. Tuition, nonresident: full-time $11,689. Tuition and fees vary according to course load.

Texas A&M University–Texarkana, Graduate Studies and Research, College of Arts and Sciences and Education, Texarkana, TX 75505-5518. Offers adult education (MS); curriculum and instruction (MS); education (MS); educational administration (M Ed); English (MA); history (MS); instructional technology (MS); interdisciplinary studies (MS); special education (M Ed, MS). Part-time and evening/weekend programs available. *Students:* 273. Average age 32. In 2007, 86 degrees awarded. *Degree requirements:* For master's, comprehensive exam (for some programs), thesis optional. *Entrance requirements:* For master's, minimum GPA of 2.5 on last 60 hours of bachelor's degree. Additional exam requirements/recommendations for international students: Required—TOEFL. *Application deadline:* For fall admission, 7/15 priority date for domestic students; for spring admission, 12/1 priority date for domestic students. Applications are processed on a rolling basis. Application fee: $0 ($25 for international students). Electronic applications accepted. *Financial support:* Career-related internships or fieldwork and scholarships/grants available. Financial award applicants required to submit FAFSA. *Application contact:* Patricia E. Black, Director of Admissions and Registrar, 903-223-3068, Fax: 903-223-3140, E-mail: pat.black@tamut.edu.

Texas State University–San Marcos, Graduate School, Interdisciplinary Studies in Political Science, San Marcos, TX 78666. Offers MAIS. *Degree requirements:* For master's, comprehensive exam. *Application deadline:* For fall admission, 6/15 priority date for domestic students; for spring admission, 10/15 priority date for domestic students. Applications are processed on a rolling basis. Application fee: $40 ($90 for international students). *Expenses:* Tuition, state resident: full-time $3,780; part-time $210 per credit hour. Tuition, nonresident: full-time $8,784; part-time $488 per credit hour. Required fees: $493 per semester. Full-time tuition and fees vary according to course load. *Financial support:* Application deadline: 4/1; *Unit head:* Dr. Cecilia Castillio, Graduate Advisor, 512-245-3255, Fax: 512-345-7815, E-mail: cr09@txstate.edu.

Texas State University–San Marcos, Graduate School, Interdisciplinary Studies Program in Applied Sociology, San Marcos, TX 78666. Offers MAIS. Part-time and evening/weekend programs available. *Students:* 1 full-time (0 women); minority (Hispanic American) Average age 28. 5 applicants, 100% accepted. In 2007, 3 degrees awarded. *Degree requirements:* For master's, comprehensive exam. *Entrance requirements:* For master's, 3.0 GPA on last 60 hrs. of undergraduate, 3 letters of reference, letter of intent. Additional exam requirements/recommendations for international students: Required—TOEFL (minimum score 550 paper-based; 213 computer-based). *Application deadline:* For fall admission, 6/15 priority date for domestic students; for spring admission, 10/15 priority date for domestic students. Applications are processed on a rolling basis. Application fee: $40 ($90 for international students). Electronic applications accepted. *Expenses:* Tuition, state resident: full-time $3,780; part-time $210 per credit hour. Tuition, nonresident: full-time $8,784; part-time $488 per credit hour. Required fees: $493 per semester. Full-time tuition and fees vary according to course load. *Financial support:* In 2007–08, 1 student received support, including 1 teaching assistantship (averaging $5,076 per year). Financial award application deadline: 4/1; financial award applicants required to submit FAFSA. *Unit head:* Dr. Audwin Anderson, Head, 512-245-2113, E-mail: aa04@txstate.edu.

Texas State University–San Marcos, Graduate School, Interdisciplinary Studies Program in Biology, San Marcos, TX 78666. Offers MSIS. *Students:* 4 applicants, 25% accepted. *Degree requirements:* For master's, comprehensive exam. *Application deadline:* For fall admission, 6/15 priority date for domestic students; for spring admission, 10/15 priority date for domestic students. Applications are processed on a rolling basis. Application fee: $40 ($90 for international students). *Expenses:* Tuition, state resident: full-time $3,780; part-time $210 per credit hour. Tuition, nonresident: full-time $8,784; part-time $488 per credit hour. Required fees: $493 per semester. Full-time tuition and fees vary according to course load. *Financial support:* Application deadline: 4/1; *Unit head:* Dr. David Lemker, Graduate Advisor, 512-245-2178, E-mail: dl10@txstate.edu.

Texas State University–San Marcos, Graduate School, Interdisciplinary Studies Program in Criminal Justice, San Marcos, TX 78666. Offers MSIS. Part-time and evening/weekend programs available. *Degree requirements:* For master's, comprehensive exam. *Application deadline:* For fall admission, 6/15 priority date for domestic students; for spring admission, 10/15 priority date for domestic students. Applications are processed on a rolling basis. Application fee: $40 ($90 for international students). *Expenses:* Tuition, state resident: full-time $3,780; part-time $210 per credit hour. Tuition, nonresident: full-time $8,784; part-time $488 per credit hour. Required fees: $493 per semester. Full-time tuition and fees vary according to course load. *Financial support:* Application deadline: 4/1; *Unit head:* Dr. Gini Deibert, Advisor, 512-245-2174, Fax: 512-245-8063, E-mail: gd11@txstate.edu.

Texas State University–San Marcos, Graduate School, Interdisciplinary Studies Program in Educational Administration and Psychological Services, San Marcos, TX 78666. Offers MAIS. *Students:* 1 full-time (0 women), 1 (woman) part-time. Average age 27. *Degree requirements:* For master's, comprehensive exam. *Application deadline:* For fall admission, 6/15 priority date for domestic students; for spring admission, 10/15 priority date for domestic students. Applications are processed on a rolling basis. Application fee: $40 ($90 for international students). *Expenses:* Tuition, state resident: full-time $3,780; part-time $210 per credit hour. Tuition, nonresident: full-time $8,784; part-time $488 per credit hour. Required fees: $493 per semester. Full-time tuition and fees vary according to course load. *Financial support:* Application deadline: 4/1; *Unit head:* Dr. Stan Carpenter, Dean, 512-245-2575, Fax: 512-245-8345, E-mail: sc33@txstate.edu.

Texas State University–San Marcos, Graduate School, Interdisciplinary Studies Program in Elementary Mathematics, Science, and Technology, San Marcos, TX 78666. Offers MSIS. *Students:* 1 (woman) full-time, 1 (woman) part-time. Average age 34. 1 applicant, 100% accepted, 0 enrolled. In 2007, 2 degrees awarded. *Degree requirements:* For master's, comprehensive exam. *Entrance requirements:* Additional exam requirements/recommendations for international students: Required—TOEFL (minimum score 550 paper-based; 213 computer-based). *Application deadline:* For fall admission, 6/15 priority date for domestic students, 6/1 priority date for international students; for spring admission, 10/15 priority date for domestic students, 10/1 priority date for international students. Applications are processed on a rolling basis. Application fee: $40 ($90 for international students). Electronic applications accepted. *Expenses:* Tuition, state resident: full-time $3,780; part-time $210 per credit hour. Tuition, nonresident: full-time $8,784; part-time $488 per credit hour. Required fees: $493 per semester. Full-time tuition and fees vary according to course load. *Financial support:* In 2007–08, 2 students received support, including 1 research assistantship (averaging $5,058 per year). Financial award application deadline: 4/1; financial award applicants required to submit FAFSA. *Unit head:* Dr. Sandra Mody, Acting Dean, 512-245-3360, Fax: 512-245-8095, E-mail: sw04@txstate.edu.

Texas State University–San Marcos, Graduate School, Interdisciplinary Studies Program in Health, Physical Education, and Recreation, San Marcos, TX 78666. Offers MAIS. Part-time and evening/weekend programs available. In 2007, 1 degree awarded. *Degree requirements:* For master's, comprehensive exam, thesis or alternative. *Entrance requirements:* For master's, GRE General Test, minimum GPA of 2.75 in last 60 hours of course work. Additional exam requirements/recommendations for international students: Required—TOEFL. *Application deadline:* For fall admission, 6/15 priority date for domestic students; for spring admission, 10/15 priority date for domestic students. Applications are processed on a rolling basis. Application fee: $40 ($90 for international students). *Expenses:* Tuition, state resident: full-time $3,780; part-time $210 per credit hour. Tuition, nonresident: full-time $8,784; part-time $488 per credit hour. Required fees: $493 per semester. Full-time tuition and fees vary according to course load. *Financial support:* Career-related internships or fieldwork, Federal Work-Study, and institutionally sponsored loans available. Support available to part-time students. Financial award application deadline: 4/1; financial award applicants required to submit FAFSA. *Unit head:* Dr. John Walker, Head, 512-245-2561, Fax: 512-245-8678, E-mail: jw18@txstate.edu. *Application contact:* Dr. J. Michael Willoughby, Dean of Graduate School, 512-245-2581, Fax: 512-245-8365, E-mail: gradcollege@txstate.edu.

Texas State University–San Marcos, Graduate School, Interdisciplinary Studies Program in Modern Languages, San Marcos, TX 78666. Offers MAIS. *Students:* 1 applicant, 100% accepted. *Degree requirements:* For master's, comprehensive exam. *Application deadline:* For fall admission, 6/15 priority date for domestic students; for spring admission, 10/15 priority date for domestic students. Applications are processed on a rolling basis. Application fee: $40 ($90 for international students). *Expenses:* Tuition, state resident: full-time $3,780; part-time $210 per credit hour. Tuition, nonresident: full-time $8,784; part-time $488 per credit hour. Required fees: $493 per semester. Full-time tuition and fees vary according to course load. *Financial support:* Application deadline: 4/1; *Unit head:* Dr. Catherine Jaffe, Advisor, 512-245-2360, Fax: 512-245-8298, E-mail: cj10@txstate.edu.

Texas State University–San Marcos, Graduate School, Interdisciplinary Studies Program in Occupational Education, San Marcos, TX 78666. Offers MAIS, MSIS. *Faculty:* 1 full-time (0 women), 1 part-time/adjunct (0 women). *Students:* 2 full-time (1 woman), 42 part-time (23 women); includes 3 African Americans, 1 Asian American or Pacific Islander, 17 Hispanic Americans, 2 international. Average age 40. 19 applicants, 100% accepted, 12 enrolled. In 2007, 1 degree awarded. *Degree requirements:* For master's, comprehensive exam. *Entrance requirements:* For master's, GPA 2.75 for undergraduate work, statement of personal goals. Additional exam requirements/recommendations for international students: Required—TOEFL (minimum score 550 paper-based; 213 computer-based). *Application deadline:* For fall admission, 6/15 priority date for domestic students, 6/1 priority date for international students; for spring admission, 10/15 priority date for domestic students, 10/1 priority date for international students. Applications are processed on a rolling basis. Application fee: $40 ($90 for international students). *Expenses:* Tuition, state resident: full-time $3,780; part-time $210 per credit hour. Tuition, nonresident: full-time $8,784; part-time $488 per credit hour. Required fees: $493 per semester. Full-time tuition and fees vary according to course load. *Financial support:* In 2007–08, 35 students received support. Application deadline: 4/1; *Unit head:* Dr. Stephen Springer, Director, 512-245-2115, E-mail: ss01@txstate.edu.

Texas State University–San Marcos, Graduate School, Interdisciplinary Studies Program in Psychology, San Marcos, TX 78666. Offers MAIS. *Students:* Average age 49. *Degree requirements:* For master's, comprehensive exam. *Application deadline:* For fall admission, 6/15 priority date for domestic students; for spring admission, 10/15 priority date for domestic students. Applications are processed on a rolling basis. Application fee: $40 ($90 for international students). *Expenses:* Tuition, state resident: full-time $3,780; part-time $210 per credit hour. Tuition, nonresident: full-time $8,784; part-time $488 per credit hour. Required fees: $493 per semester. Full-time tuition and fees vary according to course load. *Financial support:* In 2007–08, 1 student received support. Application deadline: 4/1; *Unit head:* Dr. Francisco Barrios, Advisor, 512-245-3159, Fax: 512-245-3153, E-mail: fb12@txstate.edu.

Texas Tech University, Graduate School, Program in Interdisciplinary Studies, Lubbock, TX 79409. Offers MA, MS. Part-time and evening/weekend programs available. *Students:* 41 full-time (18 women), 47 part-time (30 women); includes 24 minority (5 African Americans, 2 American Indian/Alaska Native, 2 Asian Americans or Pacific Islanders, 15 Hispanic Americans), 10 international. Average age 33. 83 applicants, 94% accepted, 29 enrolled. In 2007, 25 degrees awarded. *Degree requirements:* For master's, comprehensive exam, thesis or alternative. *Entrance requirements:* For master's, GRE General Test. Additional exam requirements/recommendations for international students: Required—TOEFL (minimum score 550 paper-based; 213 computer-based). *Application deadline:* For fall admission, 3/1 priority date for international students; for spring admission, 11/1 priority date for international students. Applications are processed on a rolling basis. Application fee: $50 ($60 for international students). Electronic applications accepted. *Expenses:* Tuition, state resident: part-time $373 per credit hour. Tuition, nonresident: part-time $651 per credit hour. Tuition and fees vary according to program. *Financial support:* In 2007–08, 75 students received support; teaching assistantships with partial tuition reimbursements available, career-related internships or fieldwork, Federal Work-Study, and institutionally sponsored loans available. Support available to part-time students. Financial award application deadline: 4/15; financial award applicants required to submit FAFSA. *Faculty research:* Literature-short story; comparative literature. *Unit head:* Dr. Wendell Aycock, Associate Dean, 806-742-2781 Ext. 228, E-mail: wendell.aycock@ttu.edu. *Application contact:* Graduate Adviser, 806-742-2781 Ext. 228.

Trinity Western University, Faculty of Graduate Studies, Program in Interdisciplinary Humanities, Langley, BC V2Y 1Y1, Canada. Offers general humanities (MAIH); specialized (MAIH), including English, history, philosophy. Part-time and evening/weekend programs available. Postbaccalaureate distance learning degree programs offered (minimal on-campus study). *Faculty:* 19 full-time (6 women), 3 part-time/adjunct (0 women). *Students:* 9 full-time (4 women), 24 part-time (13 women). Average age 30. 16 applicants, 75% accepted, 9 enrolled. In 2007, 2 degrees awarded. *Degree requirements:* For master's, 36 semester hours. *Entrance requirements:* For master's, strong undergraduate degree in Humanities or English, History or Philosophy. *Application deadline:* For fall admission, 5/15 priority date for domestic students; for winter admission, 11/1 priority date for domestic students. Application fee: $40. *Financial support:* In 2007–08, 12 students received support, including 3 fellowships (averaging $17,500 per year), 1 research assistantship (averaging $12,000 per year); career-related internships or fieldwork, scholarships/grants, and traineeships also available. Financial award application deadline: 4/1. *Faculty research:* Literary theory, gender, medieval and early modern literature, philosophy of religion, Thomas Merton's poetics. Total annual research expenditures: $145,000 Canadian dollars. *Unit head:* Dr. Bob Burkinshaw, Director, 604-888-7511 Ext. 3111, Fax: 604-513-2143, E-mail: burkinsh@twu.ca. *Application contact:* Vic Cornish, Director, Graduate Admissions, 604-888-7511 Ext. 3130, Fax: 604-513-2064, E-mail: vic.cornish@twu.edu.

Union Institute & University, Online MA Programs, Cincinnati, OH 45206-1925. Offers health and wellness (MA); history and culture (MA); leadership (MA); literature and writing (MA); psychology (MA). Part-time programs available. Postbaccalaureate distance learning degree programs offered (no on-campus study). *Faculty:* 3 full-time (1 woman), 15 part-time/adjunct (11 women). *Students:* 204 full-time (143 women); includes 19 minority (14 African Americans, 2 American Indian/Alaska Native, 3 Hispanic Americans). Average age 39. In 2007, 46 degrees awarded. *Degree requirements:* For master's, thesis. *Application deadline:* Applications are processed on a rolling basis. Application fee: $50. *Expenses: Contact institution. Financial support:* Career-related internships or fieldwork and tuition waivers available. Financial award applicants required to submit FAFSA. *Unit head:* Dr. Brian Webb, Assistant Vice President, Academic Affairs, 802-828-8777, E-mail: brian.webb@tui.edu.

Union Institute & University, PhD Program in Interdisciplinary Studies, Cincinnati, OH 45206-1925. Offers interdisciplinary studies (PhD), including ethical and creative leadership, humanities and society, public policy and social issues;). Individually-designed interdisciplinary programs. Postbaccalaureate distance learning degree programs offered (minimal on-campus study). *Faculty:* 16 full-time (6 women), 9 part-time/adjunct (7 women). *Students:* 207 full-time (138 women), 60 part-time (37 women); includes 87 minority (71 African Americans, 1 American Indian/Alaska Native, 3 Asian Americans or Pacific Islanders, 12 Hispanic Americans). Average age 46. In 2007, 111 degrees awarded. *Degree requirements:* For doctorate, thesis/dissertation, internship, residency. *Entrance requirements:* For doctorate, master's degree, letters of recommendation, interview. *Application deadline:* Applications are processed on a rolling basis. Application fee: $50. *Expenses:* Tuition: Full-time $20,176; part-time $760 per credit hour. Tuition and fees vary according to course load, degree level and program. *Financial support:* Federal Work-Study, scholarships/grants, and tuition waivers (partial) available. Financial award application deadline: 5/1; financial award applicants required to submit FAFSA. *Faculty research:* Women's studies, adult education, spirituality. *Unit head:* Dr. Larry Preston, Dean, 513-861-6400 Ext. 1151, E-mail: larry.preston@tui.edu.

University of Alaska Anchorage, College of Arts and Sciences, Program in Interdisciplinary Studies, Anchorage, AK 99508-8060. Offers MA, MS. Part-time programs available. *Entrance requirements:* For master's, GRE General Test, GRE Subject Test, minimum GPA of 3.0. Additional exam requirements/recommendations for international students: Required—TOEFL (minimum score 550 paper-based; 213 computer-based).

University of Alaska Fairbanks, Graduate School for Interdisciplinary Studies, Fairbanks, AK 99775-7520. Offers MA, MS, PhD. Part-time programs available. Terminal master's awarded for partial completion of doctoral program. *Degree requirements:* For master's, comprehensive exam (for some programs), thesis (for some programs); for doctorate, one foreign language, comprehensive exam, thesis/dissertation. *Entrance requirements:* For master's and doctorate, GRE General Test. Additional exam requirements/recommendations for international students: Required—TOEFL (minimum score 550 paper-based; 213 computer-based). Electronic applications accepted.

The University of Arizona, Graduate College, Graduate Interdisciplinary Programs, Tucson, AZ 85721. Offers American Indian studies (MA, PhD); applied mathematics (MS, PMS, PhD), including applied mathematics (MS, PhD), mathematical sciences (PMS); biomedical engineering (MS, PhD); cancer biology (PhD); genetics (MS, PhD); insect science (PhD); neuroscience (PhD); physiological sciences (PhD); second language acquisition and teaching (PhD); statistics (MS, PhD); JD/MA. Part-time programs available. *Faculty:* 573. *Students:* 269 full-time (158 women), 57 part-time (27 women); includes 73 minority (5 African Americans, 27 American Indian/Alaska Native, 11 Asian Americans or Pacific Islanders, 30 Hispanic Americans), 71 international. Average age 32. 393 applicants, 17% accepted, 54 enrolled. In 2007, 27 master's, 36 doctorates awarded. *Entrance requirements:* Additional exam requirements/recommendations for international students: Required—TOEFL. Application fee: $50. *Financial support:* Fellowships, research assistantships, teaching assistantships, career-related internships or fieldwork, Federal Work-Study, institutionally sponsored loans, scholarships/grants, and tuition waivers (full and partial) available. Support available to part-time students. Total annual research expenditures: $540,000. *Application contact:* Jolene M. Gruener, Associate Director, 520-621-8368, E-mail: gidp@email.arizona.edu.

University of Arkansas, Graduate School, Interdisciplinary Program in Comparative Literature and Cultural Studies, Fayetteville, AR 72701-1201. Offers classical studies (MA); comparative literature (PhD). *Students:* 7 full-time (6 women), 19 part-time (13 women); includes 4 minority (1 American Indian/Alaska Native, 3 Hispanic Americans), 12 international. In 2007, 2 master's, 1 doctorate awarded. *Degree requirements:* For master's, one foreign language, comprehensive exam, thesis optional; for doctorate, 2 foreign languages, comprehensive exam, thesis/dissertation. *Entrance requirements:* For master's and doctorate, GRE General Test. Application fee: $40 ($50 for international students). *Financial support:* In 2007–08, 1 fellowship, 5 research assistantships, 9 teaching assistantships were awarded; Federal Work-Study and institutionally sponsored loans also available. *Faculty research:* Literary and cultural theory, cultural studies, postcolonial theory, gender studies, world literature. *Unit head:* Luis Fernando Restrepo, Director, 479-575-2951, Fax: 479-575-6795, E-mail: lrestr@uark.edu.

University of Arkansas, Graduate School, Interdisciplinary Program in Environmental Dynamics, Fayetteville, AR 72701-1201. Offers PhD. *Students:* 2 full-time (both women), 33 part-time (11 women); includes 2 minority (1 African American, 1 Hispanic American), 11 international. In 2007, 4 degrees awarded. *Degree requirements:* For doctorate, thesis/dissertation. Application fee: $40 ($50 for international students). *Financial support:* In 2007–08, 11 fellowships with tuition reimbursements, 7 research assistantships, 10 teaching assistantships were awarded. Financial award application deadline: 4/1. *Unit head:* Dr. Stephen Boss, Head, 479-575-6603, Fax: 479-575-3469, E-mail: sboss@uark.edu.

University of Central Florida, Division of Graduate Studies, Program in Interdisciplinary Studies, Orlando, FL 32816. Offers MA, MS. *Degree requirements:* For master's, thesis or alternative. *Entrance requirements:* For master's, GRE General Test, minimum GPA of 3.0 in last 60 hours. Additional exam requirements/recommendations for international students: Required—TOEFL. Application fee: $30. Electronic applications accepted. *Expenses:* Tuition, state resident: full-time $6,484. Tuition, nonresident: full-time $23,938. Tuition and fees vary according to program. *Financial support:* Fellowships, research assistantships, teaching assistantships available.

University of Chicago, Division of the Biological Sciences, The Interdisciplinary Scientist Training Program, Chicago, IL 60637-1513. Offers PhD. *Students:* 1 full-time (0 women). Average age 25. 5 applicants, 40% accepted, 1 enrolled. *Financial support:* In 2007–08, 1 student received support, including fellowships (averaging $27,942 per year), research assistantships (averaging $27,942 per year). *Unit head:* Dr. Harinder Singh, Head; E-mail: hsingh@uchicago.edu. *Application contact:* Michele Seidl, Student Contact, E-mail: mseidl@bsd.uchicago.edu.

University of Cincinnati, Graduate School, McMicken College of Arts and Sciences, Interdisciplinary Studies Program, Cincinnati, OH 45221. Offers PhD. In 2007, 1 degree awarded. *Entrance requirements:* For doctorate, GRE General Test. *Application deadline:* For fall admission, 2/15 priority date for domestic students. Application fee: $30. Electronic applications accepted. *Financial support:* Application deadline: 2/1. *Unit head:* Dr. Robert A. Frank, Head, 513-556-4343, Fax: 513-556-0128, E-mail: judith.trent@uc.edu.

University of Houston–Victoria, School of Arts and Sciences, Program in Interdisciplinary Studies, Victoria, TX 77901-4450. Offers MAIS. Part-time and evening/weekend programs available. Postbaccalaureate distance learning degree programs offered (no on-campus study). *Faculty:* 22 full-time (3 women). *Students:* 13 full-time (8 women), 52 part-time (35 women); includes 26 minority (8 African Americans, 1 American Indian/Alaska Native, 1 Asian American or Pacific Islander, 16 Hispanic Americans), 3 international. In 2007, 28 degrees awarded. *Degree requirements:* For master's, comprehensive exam or thesis. *Entrance requirements:* For master's, GRE General Test. Additional exam requirements/recommendations for international students: Required—TOEFL (minimum score 550 paper-based; 213 computer-based). *Application deadline:* Applications are processed on a rolling basis. Application fee: $0. *Expenses:* Tuition, state resident: full-time $3,492; part-time $194 per semester hour. Tuition, nonresident: full-time $7,596; part-time $422 per semester hour. Required fees: $774; $43 per semester hour. Tuition and fees vary according to course load. *Financial support:* In 2007–08, research assistantships with partial tuition reimbursements (averaging $2,000 per year), teaching assistantships with partial tuition reimbursements (averaging $2,000 per year) were awarded; career-related internships or fieldwork, Federal Work-Study, scholarships/grants, and unspecified assistantships also available. Support available to part-time students. Financial award application deadline: 4/15. *Unit head:* Dr. Horace Fairlamb, Head, 361-570-4204, Fax: 361-570-4229, E-mail: fairlambh@uhv.edu. *Application contact:* Admissions and Records, E-mail: admissions@uhv.edu.

University of Idaho, College of Graduate Studies, Program in Interdisciplinary Studies, Moscow, ID 83844-2282. Offers MA, MS. *Students:* 2. In 2007, 1 degree awarded. *Entrance requirements:* For master's, minimum GPA of 2.8. *Application deadline:* For fall admission, 8/1 for domestic students; for spring admission, 12/15 for domestic students. Application fee: $55 ($60 for international students). *Financial support:* Application deadline: 2/15.

University of Illinois at Springfield, Graduate Programs, College of Liberal Arts and Sciences, Individual Option Program, Springfield, IL 62703-5407. Offers MA. Part-time and evening/weekend programs available. *Faculty:* 4 full-time (3 women). *Students:* 8 full-time (5 women), 26 part-time (19 women); includes 2 minority (1 American Indian/Alaska Native, 1 Asian American or Pacific Islander). Average age 39. 26 applicants, 46% accepted, 9 enrolled. In 2007, 10 degrees awarded. *Degree requirements:* For master's, project or thesis. *Entrance requirements:* For master's, interview, 2 letters of reference, minimum undergraduate GPA of 2.5, academic and vocational goals statement. Additional exam requirements/recommendations for international students: Required—TOEFL (minimum score 550 paper-based; 213 computer-based). *Application deadline:* For fall admission, 4/15 for domestic and international students; for spring admission, 10/15 for domestic and international students. Applications are processed on a rolling basis. Application fee: $50 ($60 for international students). *Expenses:* Tuition, state resident: full-time $5,424; part-time $226 per credit hour. Tuition, nonresident: part-time $553 per credit hour. Required fees: $618 per term. *Financial support:* In 2007–08, research assistantships with full tuition reimbursements (averaging $7,988 per year), teaching assistantships with full tuition reimbursements (averaging $7,988 per year) were awarded; career-related internships or fieldwork, Federal Work-Study, scholarships/grants, health care benefits, and unspecified assistantships also available. Support available to part-time students. Financial award application deadline: 11/15; financial award applicants required to submit FAFSA. *Unit head:* Dr. Annette Van Dyke, Program Administrator, 217-206-7420, Fax: 217-206-6217.

University of Kansas, Graduate Studies Medical Center, Interdisciplinary Graduate Program in Biomedical Sciences, Kansas City, KS 66160-7836. Offers MA, MPH, MS, PhD, MD/MPH, MD/MS, MD/PhD. Part-time and evening/weekend programs available. *Students:* 20 full-time (7 women), 4 part-time (2 women); includes 1 minority (Hispanic American), 15 international. Average age 25. 216 applicants, 19% accepted, 21 enrolled.Terminal master's awarded for partial completion of doctoral program. *Median time to degree:* Of those who began their doctoral program in fall 1999, 62% received their degree in 8 years or less. *Degree requirements:* For master's, thesis; for doctorate, comprehensive exam, thesis/dissertation. *Entrance requirements:* For master's and doctorate, GRE. Additional exam requirements/recommendations for international students: Required—TOEFL. *Application deadline:* For fall admission, 1/15 priority date for domestic and international students. Applications are processed on a rolling basis. Application fee: $0. Electronic applications accepted. *Expenses:* Tuition, state resident: full-time $5,838. Tuition, nonresident: full-time $13,409. Tuition and fees vary according to program. *Financial support:* In 2007–08, 21 students received support; fellowships with full tuition reimbursements available, research assistantships with full tuition reimbursements available, teaching assistantships with full tuition reimbursements available, Federal Work-Study available. Support available to part-time students. Financial award application deadline: 3/30; financial award applicants required to submit FAFSA. *Faculty research:* Cardiovascular biology, neurosciences, signal transduction and cancer biology, molecular biology and genetics, and developmental biology. *Unit head:* Dr. Michael J. Werle, Graduate Adviser, 913-588-7491, Fax: 913-588-2710, E-mail: mwerle@kumc.edu. *Application contact:* Miranda Rudloff, Coordinator, 913-588-2719, Fax: 913-588-5242, E-mail: mrudloff@kumc.edu.

University of Louisville, Graduate School, Interdisciplinary Studies, Louisville, KY 40292-0001. Offers MA, MS. *Students:* 3 full-time (1 woman), 5 part-time (1 woman); includes 2 minority (both African Americans) Average age 38. *Degree requirements:* For master's, thesis. *Entrance requirements:* For master's, GRE General Test. *Application deadline:* Applications are processed on a rolling basis. Application fee: $50.

University of Maine, Graduate School, Interdisciplinary Doctoral Program, Orono, ME 04469. Offers PhD. Part-time and evening/weekend programs available. *Students:* 28 full-time (16 women), 14 part-time (8 women); includes 3 minority (all Asian Americans or Pacific Islanders), 4 international. Average age 37. 10 applicants, 30% accepted, 2 enrolled. *Degree requirements:* For doctorate, comprehensive exam, thesis/dissertation. *Entrance requirements:* For doctorate, GRE General Test. Additional exam requirements/recommendations for international students: Required—TOEFL. *Application deadline:* For fall admission, 4/1 for domestic students; for spring admission, 11/1 for domestic students. Applications are processed on a rolling basis. Application fee: $60. Electronic applications accepted.

University of Manitoba, Faculty of Graduate Studies, Interdisciplinary Programs, Individual Interdisciplinary Programs, Winnipeg, MB R3T 2N2, Canada. Offers M Sc, MA, PhD.

University of Maryland, College Park, Graduate Studies, Interdepartmental Programs, College Park, MD 20742. Offers PhD, MA/MLS, MBA/MPM. *Students:* 66 full-time (43 women), 4 part-time (3 women); includes 12 minority (6 African Americans, 1 American Indian/Alaska Native, 4 Asian Americans or Pacific Islanders, 1 Hispanic American), 21 international. 116 applicants, 30% accepted, 21 enrolled. In 2007, 4 degrees awarded. *Entrance requirements:* For doctorate, GRE General Test. Additional exam requirements/recommendations for international students: Required—TOEFL. *Application deadline:* For fall admission, 5/1 for domestic students, 2/1 for international students; for spring admission, 10/1 for domestic students, 6/1 for international students. Applications are processed on a rolling basis. Application fee: $60. Electronic applications accepted. *Financial support:* In 2007–08, 9 fellowships (averaging $14,553 per year), 1 research assistantship (averaging $15,542 per year), 7 teaching assistantships (averaging $14,569 per year) were awarded; Federal Work-Study and scholarships/grants also available. Support available to part-time students. *Application contact:* Dean of Graduate School, 301-405-0358, Fax: 301-314-9305.

University of Medicine and Dentistry of New Jersey, School of Health Related Professions, Department of Interdisciplinary Studies, Program in Health Sciences, Newark, NJ 07107-1709. Offers cardiopulmonary sciences (PhD); clinical laboratory sciences (PhD); health sciences (MS); interdisciplinary studies (PhD); nutrition (PhD); physical therapy/movement science (PhD). *Degree requirements:* For doctorate, thesis/dissertation. *Entrance requirements:* For doctorate, interview, writing sample. Additional exam requirements/recommendations for international students: Required—TOEFL. *Application deadline:* For fall admission, 3/1 for domestic students. Applications are processed on a rolling basis. Application fee: $50. Electronic applica-

Interdisciplinary Studies

University of Medicine and Dentistry of New Jersey (continued)
tions accepted. *Unit head:* Dr. Margaret Kildoff, Director, 973-972-4989, Fax: 973-972-7854, E-mail: ms-phd-hs@umdnj.edu.

University of Minnesota, Twin Cities Campus, Graduate School, College of Liberal Arts, Department of Cultural Studies and Comparative Literature, Program in Comparative Studies in Discourse and Society, Minneapolis, MN 55455-0213. Offers PhD. *Faculty:* 14 full-time (2 women), 9 part-time/adjunct (7 women). *Students:* 25 full-time (15 women); includes 1 Asian American or Pacific Islander, 1 Hispanic American, 1 international. Average age 26. 67 applicants, 10% accepted, 3 enrolled. In 2007, 1 doctorate awarded. *Degree requirements:* For doctorate, 2 foreign languages, thesis/dissertation. *Entrance requirements:* For doctorate, GRE General Test, sample of written work. Additional exam requirements/recommendations for international students: Required—TOEFL. *Application deadline:* For fall admission, 12/10 for domestic students. Application fee: $55 ($75 for international students). *Financial support:* In 2007–08, 30 students received support, including 1 fellowship with full tuition reimbursement available (averaging $16,000 per year), 1 research assistantship with full tuition reimbursement available (averaging $6,232 per year), 25 teaching assistantships with full tuition reimbursements available (averaging $12,465 per year); Federal Work-Study, institutionally sponsored loans, and tuition waivers (full and partial) also available. Financial award application deadline: 12/10. *Faculty research:* Cultural theory; music; architecture, space, and urbanism; body and gender; film and popular culture. *Unit head:* Liz Kotz, Director, 612-625-4571, Fax: 612-626-0228, E-mail: complit@tc.umn.edu. *Application contact:* Elizabeth Wilson, Executive Secretary, 612-624-7896, Fax: 312-626-0228, E-mail: ejwilson@umn.edu.

University of Missouri–Kansas City, School of Graduate Studies, Kansas City, MO 64110-2499. Offers interdisciplinary studies (PhD), including art history, cell biology and biophysics, chemistry, computer and electrical engineering, computer science and informatics, economics, education, engineering, English, geosciences, health psychology, history, mathematics and statistics, molecular biology and biochemistry, music education, oral biology, pharmaceutical sciences, pharmacology, physics, political science, psychology, public affairs and administration, religious studies, sociology, telecommunications and computer networking, urban leadership and policy studies in education. Students select two or more subjects. *Students:* 66 full-time (29 women), 257 part-time (102 women); includes 27 minority (11 African Americans, 10 Asian Americans or Pacific Islanders, 6 Hispanic Americans), 124 international. Average age 35. 280 applicants, 31% accepted, 8 enrolled. In 2007, 43 degrees awarded. *Median time to degree:* Of those who began their doctoral program in fall 1999, 61.2% received their degree in 8 years or less. *Degree requirements:* For doctorate, comprehensive exam, thesis/dissertation, residency. *Entrance requirements:* For doctorate, GRE General Test, minimum GPA of 2.75 (undergraduate), 3.0 (graduate). Additional exam requirements/recommendations for international students: Required—TOEFL (minimum score 550 paper-based; 213 computer-based), TWE (minimum score 4). *Application deadline:* For fall admission, 1/15 priority date for domestic and international students. Applications are processed on a rolling basis. Application fee: $35 ($50 for international students). Electronic applications accepted. *Expenses:* Tuition, state resident: part-time $287 per hour. Tuition, nonresident: part-time $741 per hour. Required fees: $31 per hour. Tuition and fees vary according to program. *Financial support:* In 2007–08, 1 research assistantship with partial tuition reimbursement (averaging $12,000 per year) was awarded; fellowships with partial tuition reimbursements, teaching assistantships with partial tuition reimbursements, career-related internships or fieldwork, Federal Work-Study, tuition waivers (partial), and unspecified assistantships also available. Support available to part-time students. Financial award application deadline: 3/1; financial award applicants required to submit FAFSA. *Unit head:* Dr. Ronald MacQuarrie, Dean, 816-235-1301, Fax: 816-235-1310, E-mail: macquarrier@umkc.edu. *Application contact:* Qunicy Bennett, Administrative Assistant, 816-235-1559, Fax: 816-235-1310, E-mail: bennettq@umkc.edu.

The University of Montana, Graduate School, Program in Interdisciplinary Studies, Missoula, MT 59812-0002. Offers individual interdisciplinary programs (IIP) (PhD); interdisciplinary studies (MIS). *Degree requirements:* For doctorate, thesis/dissertation. *Entrance requirements:* For master's, GRE General Test. Additional exam requirements/recommendations for international students: Required—TOEFL.

University of New Brunswick Fredericton, School of Graduate Studies, Interdisciplinary Studies Program, Fredericton, NB E3B 5A3, Canada. Offers MA, PhD. *Faculty:* 27 full-time (17 women), 5 part-time/adjunct (2 women). *Students:* 24 full-time (17 women), 5 part-time (2 women). *Degree requirements:* For master's, thesis; for doctorate, comprehensive exam, thesis/dissertation. *Entrance requirements:* For master's, honors degree with A- average, minimum GPA of 3.5; for doctorate, master's degree with A- average, minimum GPA of 3.5. Application fee: $50 Canadian dollars. *Financial support:* In 2007–08, 21 research assistantships, 1 teaching assistantship (averaging $4,400 per year) were awarded; fellowships also available. *Faculty research:* Support needs of young adults with cancer; risk analysis, cervical cancer; treatment of persons with disabilities; tourism strategy; farm-related injuries. *Unit head:* Dr. Gwen Davies, Dean of Graduate Studies, 506-458-7150, Fax: 506-453-4817, E-mail: daviesg@unb.ca. *Application contact:* Janet Amurault, Graduate Secretary, 506-458-7558, Fax: 506-453-4817, E-mail: jamiraul@unb.ca.

University of Northern British Columbia, Office of Graduate Studies, Prince George, BC V2N 4Z9, Canada. Offers business administration (Diploma); community health science (M Sc); disability management (MA); education (M Ed); first nations studies (MA); gender studies (MA); history (MA); interdisciplinary studies (MA); international studies (MA); mathematical, computer and physical sciences (M Sc); natural resources and environmental studies (M Sc, MA, MNRES, PhD); political science (MA); psychology (M Sc, PhD); social work (MSW). Part-time and evening/weekend programs available. Postbaccalaureate distance learning degree programs offered (no on-campus study). *Degree requirements:* For master's, thesis; for doctorate, thesis/dissertation. *Entrance requirements:* For master's, GRE, minimum B average in undergraduate course work; for doctorate, candidacy exam, minimum A average in graduate course work.

University of Northern Colorado, Graduate School, Graduate Interdisciplinary Degree Program, Greeley, CO 80639. Offers MA. Part-time programs available. *Degree requirements:* For master's, comprehensive exam, thesis or alternative. Electronic applications accepted. *Expenses:* Tuition, state resident: part-time $222 per credit. Tuition, nonresident: part-time $627 per credit. Required fees: $36 per credit.

University of North Texas, Robert B. Toulouse School of Graduate Studies, Interdisciplinary Studies, Denton, TX 76203. Offers MA, MS. Part-time programs available. *Students:* 5 full-time (all women), 8 part-time (4 women); includes 6 minority (4 African Americans, 1 Asian American or Pacific Islander, 1 Hispanic American). Average age 35. 10 applicants, 40% accepted, 4 enrolled. In 2007, 4 degrees awarded. *Degree requirements:* For master's, comprehensive exam, thesis optional. *Entrance requirements:* For master's, GRE General Test, minimum GPA of 2.8, 3 letters of reference, personal statement, degree plan. Additional exam requirements/recommendations for international students: Required—proof of English language proficiency required for non-native English speakers; Recommended—TOEFL (minimum score 550 paper-based; 213 computer-based; 80 iBT). *Application deadline:* For fall admission, 7/15 for domestic students; for winter admission, 11/15 for domestic students. Application fee: $50 ($75 for international students). *Financial support:* In 2007–08, 1 student received support, including 1 fellowship (averaging $2,000 per year); career-related internships or fieldwork, Federal Work-Study, and institutionally sponsored loans also available. Financial award application deadline: 4/1. *Unit head:* Donna Hughes, Head, 940-565-2383, Fax: 940-565-2141, E-mail: hughesd@unt.edu.

University of Oklahoma, Graduate College, Program in Interdisciplinary Studies, Norman, OK 73019-0390. Offers MA, MS, PhD. Part-time and evening/weekend programs available. *Students:* 114 full-time (54 women), 386 part-time (159 women); includes 131 minority (70 African Americans, 13 American Indian/Alaska Native, 18 Asian Americans or Pacific Islanders, 30 Hispanic Americans), 15 international. 115 applicants, 96% accepted, 71 enrolled. In 2007, 66 master's, 8 doctorates awarded. *Entrance requirements:* Additional exam requirements/recommendations for international students: Recommended—TOEFL (minimum score 550 paper-based; 213 computer-based). *Application deadline:* For fall admission, 6/1 for domestic students, 4/1 for international students; for spring admission, 11/1 for domestic students, 9/1 for international students. Applications are processed on a rolling basis. Application fee: $40 ($90 for international students). Electronic applications accepted. *Expenses:* Tuition, state resident: full-time $3,451; part-time $144 per credit hour. Tuition, nonresident: full-time $12,432; part-time $518 per credit hour. Required fees: $1,925; $70 per credit hour. $122 per semester. *Financial support:* In 2007–08, 6 research assistantships with partial tuition reimbursements (averaging $11,163 per year) were awarded; tuition waivers (full and partial) and unspecified assistantships also available. Financial award applicants required to submit FAFSA. Total annual research expenditures: $56,240. *Unit head:* Lee Williams, Dean/Vice President of Research, 405-325-3811, Fax: 405-325-5346, E-mail: lwilliams@ou.edu. *Application contact:* Angela Castillo, Academic Counselor II, 405-325-3841, Fax: 405-325-5346, E-mail: acastillo@ou.edu.

University of Oregon, Graduate School, Interdisciplinary Program in Applied Information Management, Eugene, OR 97403. Offers MS. Part-time and evening/weekend programs available. *Students:* 2 applicants, 100% accepted. In 2007, 20 degrees awarded. *Degree requirements:* For master's, project. *Entrance requirements:* For master's, GMAT, GRE, or MAT. Additional exam requirements/recommendations for international students: Required—TOEFL. *Application deadline:* For winter admission, 10/1 for domestic students. Application fee: $50. Electronic applications accepted. *Expenses:* Contact institution. *Financial support:* Institutionally sponsored loans available. Support available to part-time students. Financial award application deadline: 2/1. *Faculty research:* Business management, information design. *Unit head:* Linda F. Ettinger, Director, 800-824-2714, E-mail: aim@continue.uoregon.edu. *Application contact:* Janet Cormack, Coordinator, 800-824-2714, Fax: 503-725-2289, E-mail: aim@continue.uoregon.edu.

University of Ottawa, Faculty of Graduate and Postdoctoral Studies, Interdisciplinary Programs, Ottawa, ON K1N 6N5, Canada. Offers e-business (Certificate); e-commerce (Certificate); finance (Certificate); health services and policies research (Diploma); population health (PhD); population health risk assessment and management (Certificate); public management and governance (Certificate); systems science (Certificate).

University of Pittsburgh, School of Medicine, Graduate Programs in Medicine, Interdisciplinary Biomedical Sciences Program, Pittsburgh, PA 15260. Offers PhD. *Faculty:* 286 full-time (67 women). *Students:* 25 full-time (18 women); includes 2 African Americans, 2 Asian Americans or Pacific Islanders, 9 international. Average age 27. 550 applicants, 16% accepted, 34 enrolled. *Degree requirements:* For doctorate, comprehensive exam, thesis/dissertation. *Entrance requirements:* For doctorate, GRE General Test, GRE Subject Test, minimum QPA of 3.0. Additional exam requirements/recommendations for international students: Required—TOEFL (minimum score 600 paper-based; 250 computer-based; 100 iBT), IELTS (minimum score 7). *Application deadline:* For fall admission, 12/15 priority date for domestic and international students. Application fee: $40. Electronic applications accepted. *Financial support:* In 2007–08, 25 research assistantships with full tuition reimbursements (averaging $24,000 per year) were awarded; teaching assistantships, institutionally sponsored loans, scholarships/grants, traineeships, and unspecified assistantships also available. *Faculty research:* Biochemistry and molecular genetics, cell biology and molecular physiology, cellular and molecular pathology, immunology, molecular pharmacology. *Application contact:* Graduate Studies Administrator, 412-648-8957, Fax: 412-648-1077, E-mail: gradstudies@medschool.pitt.edu.

The University of South Dakota, Graduate School, Interdisciplinary Studies Program, Vermillion, SD 57069-2390. Offers interdisciplinary studies (MA). Part-time programs available. Postbaccalaureate distance learning degree programs offered. *Students:* 30 (15 women). In 2007, 10 degrees awarded. *Degree requirements:* For master's, thesis or alternative. *Entrance requirements:* For master's, minimum GPA of 2.7; supplemental packet. Additional exam requirements/recommendations for international students: Required—TOEFL (minimum score 550 paper-based; 213 computer-based; 79 iBT). *Application deadline:* Applications are processed on a rolling basis. Application fee: $35. Electronic applications accepted. *Financial support:* In 2007–08, research assistantships with partial tuition reimbursements (averaging $4,626 per year); Federal Work-Study and unspecified assistantships also available. Financial award applicants required to submit FAFSA.

The University of Texas at Arlington, Graduate School, College of Science, Department of Interdisciplinary Science, Arlington, TX 76019. Offers MA. Part-time and evening/weekend programs available. *Students:* 1 full-time (0 women), 20 part-time (13 women); includes 7 minority (3 African Americans, 1 American Indian/Alaska Native, 3 Hispanic Americans). In 2007, 1 degree awarded. *Entrance requirements:* For master's, GRE. Additional exam requirements/recommendations for international students: Required—TOEFL (minimum score 550 paper-based; 213 computer-based). *Application deadline:* For fall admission, 6/15 for domestic students. Application fee: $35 ($50 for international students). *Expenses:* Tuition, state resident: full-time $5,934. Tuition, nonresident: full-time $10,938. *Application contact:* Edward T. Morton, Graduate Adviser, 817-272-2309, Fax: 817-272-3511, E-mail: morton@uta.edu.

The University of Texas at Arlington, Graduate School, Interdisciplinary Studies, Arlington, TX 76019. Offers MA, MS. Part-time programs available. In 2007, 1 degree awarded. *Degree requirements:* For master's, comprehensive exam, thesis optional. *Entrance requirements:* For master's, GRE General Test, 3 letters of recommendation, minimum GPA of 3.0 in last 60 hours of undergraduate course work. Additional exam requirements/recommendations for international students: Required—TOEFL (minimum score 550 paper-based; 213 computer-based). *Application deadline:* For fall admission, 6/16 for domestic students. Applications are processed on a rolling basis. Application fee: $35 ($50 for international students). *Expenses:* Tuition, state resident: full-time $5,934. Tuition, nonresident: full-time $10,938. *Financial support:* Application deadline: 6/1; *Unit head:* Dr. Allen F. Repko, Graduate Program Adviser and Coordinator, 817-272-2338, Fax: 817-272-3156, E-mail: repko@uta.edu.

The University of Texas at Brownsville, Graduate Studies, College of Liberal Arts, Department of English, Brownsville, TX 78520-4991. Offers English (MA); interdisciplinary studies (MAIS). Part-time and evening/weekend programs available. *Degree requirements:* For master's, comprehensive exam or thesis. *Entrance requirements:* For master's, GRE General Test. Additional exam requirements/recommendations for international students: Required—TOEFL. *Faculty research:* Sandra Cisneros, Nathaniel Hawthorne, Rodolfo Araya, Isabel Allende, linguistics.

The University of Texas at Brownsville, Graduate Studies, College of Liberal Arts, Department of Modern Languages, Brownsville, TX 78520-4991. Offers interdisciplinary studies (MAIS); Spanish (MA). Part-time and evening/weekend programs available. *Degree requirements:* For master's, comprehensive exam, thesis optional. *Entrance requirements:* For master's, GRE General Test, letters of recommendation, interview. Additional exam requirements/recommendations for international students: Required—TOEFL. *Faculty research:* Children's literature, Hispanic folklore, translation.

The University of Texas at Dallas, School of General Studies, Richardson, TX 75083-0688. Offers interdisciplinary studies (MA). Part-time and evening/weekend programs available. *Faculty:* 3 full-time (2 women). *Students:* 9 full-time (8 women), 30 part-time (22 women); includes 17 minority (11 African Americans, 1 American Indian/Alaska Native, 2 Asian Americans or Pacific Islanders, 3 Hispanic Americans), 2 international. Average age 40. 16 applicants, 94% accepted, 10 enrolled. In 2007, 19 degrees awarded. *Degree requirements:* For master's, research project, seminar. *Entrance requirements:* For master's, GRE General Test, minimum GPA of 3.0. Additional exam requirements/recommendations for international students: Required—TOEFL (minimum score 550 paper-based; 213 computer-based). *Application deadline:* For fall admission, 7/15 for domestic students; for spring admission, 11/15 for domestic students. Applications are processed on a rolling basis. Application fee: $50 ($100 for international students). Electronic applications accepted. *Expenses:* Tuition, state resident: full-time $7,052. Tuition, nonresident: full-time $12,632. Tuition and fees vary according to course load. *Financial support:* Fellowships, research assistantships, teaching assistantships with tuition reimbursements, career-related internships or fieldwork, Federal Work-Study, institutionally sponsored loans, and scholarships/grants available. Support available to part-time students. Financial award application deadline: 4/30; financial award applicants required to submit FAFSA. *Faculty research:* Biomedical ethics, history and philosophy of science, social control and regulation, national security, education policy. *Unit head:* Dr. George Fair, Dean, 972-883-2350, Fax: 972-883-2440, E-mail: gwfair@utdallas.edu. *Application contact:* Janet Carden, Administrative Assistant, 972-883-2350, Fax: 972-883-2440, E-mail: gs-grad-info@utdallas.edu.

The University of Texas at El Paso, Graduate School, College of Liberal Arts, Interdisciplinary Program in Liberal Arts, El Paso, TX 79968-0001. Offers MAIS. Part-time and evening/weekend programs available. *Degree requirements:* For master's, thesis or alternative. *Entrance requirements:* For master's, GRE General Test, minimum GPA of 3.0 in major. Additional exam requirements/recommendations for international students: Required—TOEFL. Electronic applications accepted.

The University of Texas at El Paso, Graduate School, College of Science, Interdisciplinary Studies Program, El Paso, TX 79968-0001. Offers MSIS. Part-time and evening/weekend programs available. *Degree requirements:* For master's, thesis optional. *Entrance requirements:* For master's, GRE General Test. Additional exam requirements/recommendations for international students: Required—TOEFL. Electronic applications accepted.

The University of Texas at San Antonio, College of Education and Human Development, Department of Interdisciplinary Learning and Teaching, San Antonio, TX 78249-0617. Offers curriculum and instruction (MA); early childhood and elementary education (MA); educational psychology/special education (MA); instructional technology (MA); reading and literacy (MA). Part-time and evening/weekend programs available. *Faculty:* 23 full-time (22 women), 3 part-time/adjunct (1 woman). *Students:* 34 full-time (29 women), 227 part-time (195 women); includes 142 minority (26 African Americans, 1 American Indian/Alaska Native, 6 Asian Americans or Pacific Islanders, 109 Hispanic Americans), 3 international. Average age 34. 94 applicants, 100% accepted, 94 enrolled. In 2007, 147 degrees awarded. *Degree requirements:* For master's, comprehensive exam, thesis optional. *Entrance requirements:* For master's, GRE General Test. Additional exam requirements/recommendations for international students: Required—TOEFL (minimum score 500 paper-based; 173 computer-based). *Application deadline:* For fall admission, 7/1 for domestic students, 4/1 for international students; for spring admission, 11/1 for domestic students, 9/1 for international students. Applications are processed on a rolling basis. Application fee: $45 ($80 for international students). Electronic applications accepted. *Financial support:* Research assistantships, career-related internships or fieldwork, Federal Work-Study, scholarships/grants, and unspecified assistantships available. *Faculty research:* Early childhood, reading, special education, foundations, curriculum and instruction. Total annual research expenditures: $1.9 million. *Unit head:* Dr. Belinda B. Flores, Chair, 210-458-5969, Fax: 210-458-7281, E-mail: belinda.flores@utsa.edu.

The University of Texas at Tyler, College of Arts and Sciences, Department of Biology, Tyler, TX 75799-0001. Offers biology (MS); interdisciplinary studies (MSIS). *Faculty:* 11 full-time (4 women), 4 part-time/adjunct (2 women). *Students:* 10 full-time (2 women), 9 part-time (4 women); includes 7 minority (1 African American, 5 Asian Americans or Pacific Islanders, 1 Hispanic American). Average age 27. 8 applicants, 88% accepted, 7 enrolled. In 2007, 6 degrees awarded. *Degree requirements:* For master's, comprehensive exam, thesis, oral qualifying exam, thesis defense. *Entrance requirements:* For master's, GRE General Test, GRE Subject Test, bachelor's degree in biology or equivalent. *Application deadline:* Applications are processed on a rolling basis. Application fee: $25 ($50 for international students). Electronic applications accepted. *Expenses:* Tuition, state resident: part-time $627 per semester hour. Tuition, nonresident: part-time $908 per semester hour. Required fees: $107 per semester hour. Tuition and fees vary according to course load. *Financial support:* In 2007–08, 2 research assistantships (averaging $10,000 per year), 10 teaching assistantships (averaging $10,000 per year) were awarded; scholarships/grants also available. Financial award application deadline: 7/1; financial award applicants required to submit FAFSA. *Faculty research:* Phenotypic plasticity and heritability of life history traits, invertebrate ecology and genetics, systematics and phylogenetics of reptiles, hibernation physiology in turtles, landscape ecology, host-microbe interaction; outer membrane proteins in bacteria. Total annual research expenditures: $200,000. *Unit head:* Dr. Neil Ford, Department Graduate Coordinator, 903-566-7249, E-mail: nford@uttyler.edu. *Application contact:* Pam Morrow, Assistant to Dean for Enrollment Management, 903-566-7205, Fax: 903-566-7068, E-mail: pmorrow@uttyler.edu.

The University of Texas at Tyler, College of Arts and Sciences, Department of Literature and Languages, Tyler, TX 75799-0001. Offers English (MA); interdisciplinary studies (MAIS). Part-time and evening/weekend programs available. *Faculty:* 8 full-time (5 women). *Students:* 7 full-time (2 women), 14 part-time (11 women); includes 5 minority (2 African Americans, 1 Asian American or Pacific Islander, 2 Hispanic Americans). Average age 37. 10 applicants, 100% accepted, 7 enrolled. In 2007, 2 degrees awarded. *Degree requirements:* For master's, one foreign language, comprehensive exam, thesis optional. *Entrance requirements:* For master's, GRE General Test, minimum GPA of 3.0, four semesters—or the equivalent—of one foreign language. *Application deadline:* For fall admission, 8/21 for domestic students; for spring admission, 1/13 for domestic students. Applications are processed on a rolling basis. Application fee: $0. Electronic applications accepted. *Expenses:* Tuition, state resident: part-time $627 per semester hour. Tuition, nonresident: part-time $908 per semester hour. Required fees: $107 per semester hour. Tuition and fees vary according to course load. *Financial support:* In 2007–08, fellowships with full and partial tuition reimbursements (averaging $1,000 per year), 1 research assistantship with full and partial tuition reimbursement (averaging $6,000 per year) were awarded; teaching assistantships with full and partial tuition reimbursements, Federal Work-Study, institutionally sponsored loans, scholarships/grants, tuition waivers, unspecified assistantships, and writing center teaching staff also available. Financial award application deadline: 7/1; financial award applicants required to submit FAFSA. *Faculty research:* Medieval and Tudor drama, Shakespeare, British Romanticism, British and Irish modernism, American Realism, Greek drama, Nineteenth Century American Lit. *Unit head:* Dr. Victor I. Scherb, Chair, 903-566-7374, Fax: 903-565-5700, E-mail: vscherb@mail.uttyl.edu. *Application contact:* Pam Morrow, Assistant to Dean for Enrollment Management, 903-566-7205, Fax: 903-566-7068, E-mail: pmorrow@uttyler.edu.

The University of Texas at Tyler, College of Education and Psychology, Department of Psychology, Tyler, TX 75799-0001. Offers clinical psychology (MS), including neuropsychology, school psychology; counseling psychology (MA), including general, marriage and family; interdisciplinary studies (MSIS); school counseling (MA). Part-time and evening/weekend programs available. *Faculty:* 10 full-time (2 women), 8 part-time/adjunct (5 women). *Students:* 67 full-time (50 women), 60 part-time (50 women); includes 12 minority (4 African Americans, 1 American Indian/Alaska Native, 2 Asian Americans or Pacific Islanders, 5 Hispanic Americans). 37 applicants, 97% accepted, 32 enrolled. In 2007, 16 degrees awarded. *Degree requirements:* For master's, comprehensive exam, thesis optional. *Entrance requirements:* For master's, GRE General Test, minimum GPA of 3.0. *Application deadline:* For fall admission, 2/1 for domestic students; for spring admission, 10/1 for domestic students. Application fee: $0 ($50 for international students). Electronic applications accepted. *Expenses:* Tuition, state resident: part-time $627 per semester hour. Tuition, nonresident: part-time $908 per semester hour. Required fees: $107 per semester hour. Tuition and fees vary according to course load. *Financial support:* In 2007–08, fellowships with partial tuition reimbursements (averaging $3,000 per year), research assistantships (averaging $5,000 per year), teaching assistantships (averaging $1,500 per year) were awarded; career-related internships or fieldwork, Federal Work-Study, and institutionally sponsored loans also available. Support available to part-time students. Financial award application deadline: 7/1. *Faculty research:* Neuropsychology, child abuse, psychometric properties of psychological instruments, maternal behavior, clinical practice issues, victimization of women, post-traumatic stress disorder. *Unit head:* Dr. Charles B. Barke, Interim Chair, 903-565-5875, Fax: 903-565-5560, E-mail: cbarke@uttyler.edu. *Application contact:* Pam Morrow, Assistant to Dean for Enrollment Management, 903-566-7205, Fax: 903-566-7068, E-mail: pmorrow@uttyler.edu.

The University of Texas at Tyler, College of Engineering and Computer Science, Department of Computer Science, Tyler, TX 75799-0001. Offers computer science (MS); interdisciplinary studies (MSIS). *Faculty:* 6 full-time (0 women). *Students:* 19 full-time (5 women), 7 part-time; includes 1 Asian American or Pacific Islander, 14 international. Average age 24. 24 applicants, 100% accepted, 7 enrolled. In 2007, 8 degrees awarded. *Degree requirements:* For master's, comprehensive exam, thesis optional. *Entrance requirements:* For master's, GRE General Test, previous course work in data structures and computer organization, 6 hours of course work in calculus and statistics. *Application deadline:* For fall admission, 6/15 priority date for domestic students; for spring admission, 10/15 priority date for domestic students. Applications are processed on a rolling basis. Application fee: $0. Electronic applications accepted. *Expenses:* Tuition, state resident: part-time $627 per semester hour. Tuition, nonresident: part-time $908 per semester hour. Required fees: $107 per semester hour. Tuition and fees vary according to course load. *Financial support:* In 2007–08, 5 research assistantships (averaging $2,590 per year), 5 teaching assistantships (averaging $3,090 per year) were awarded; scholarships/grants also available. Financial award application deadline: 7/1; financial award applicants required to submit FAFSA. *Faculty research:* Database design, software engineering, client-server architecture, visual programming, data mining, computer security, digital image processing, simulation and modeling, comp science education. Total annual research expenditures:$20,000. *Unit head:* Dr. Stephen Rainwater, Interim Chair, 903-566-7235, Fax: 903-565-5607, E-mail: srainwater@uttyler.edu. *Application contact:* Pam Morrow, Assistant to Dean for Enrollment Management, 903-566-7205, Fax: 903-566-7068, E-mail: pmorrow@uttyler.edu.

The University of Texas–Pan American, College of Arts and Humanities, Program in Interdisciplinary Studies, Edinburg, TX 78541-2999. Offers MAIS, MSIS. Part-time and evening/weekend programs available. *Degree requirements:* For master's, comprehensive exam, thesis or alternative. *Entrance requirements:* For master's, GRE General Test, minimum GPA of 3.0.

University of the Incarnate Word, School of Graduate Studies and Research, College of Humanities, Arts, and Social Sciences, Program in Multidisciplinary Studies, San Antonio, TX 78209-6397. Offers MA. Part-time and evening/weekend programs available. *Students:* 1 (woman) full-time, 1 (woman) part-time; both minorities (both African Americans) Average age 43. *Degree requirements:* For master's, thesis or alternative. *Entrance requirements:* For master's, GRE General Test or MAT, GMAT. *Application deadline:* Applications are processed on a rolling basis. Application fee: $20. Electronic applications accepted. *Expenses:* Tuition: Part-time $605 per credit hour. Required fees: $58 per credit hour. Tuition and fees vary according to degree level. *Financial support:* Federal Work-Study and scholarships/grants available. Financial award applicants required to submit FAFSA. *Application contact:* Andrea Cyterski-Acosta, Dean of Enrollment, 210-829-6005, Fax: 210-829-3921, E-mail: admis@uiwtx.edu.

University of the Incarnate Word, School of Graduate Studies and Research, School of Mathematics, Science, and Engineering, Program in Multidisciplinary Sciences, San Antonio, TX 78209-6397. Offers MA. Part-time and evening/weekend programs available. *Students:* Average age 37. In 2007, 6 degrees awarded. *Degree requirements:* For master's, capstone. *Entrance requirements:* For master's, GRE, BA or BS Education with Teaching Certification and teaching experience. Additional exam requirements/recommendations for international students: Required—TOEFL. *Application deadline:* Applications are processed on a rolling basis. Application fee: $20. Electronic applications accepted. *Expenses:* Tuition: Part-time $605 per credit hour. Required fees: $58 per credit hour. Tuition and fees vary according to degree level. *Financial support:* Federal Work-Study, scholarships/grants, and tuition waivers (partial) available. Financial award applicants required to submit FAFSA. *Unit head:* Dr. Alakananda Chaudhuri, 210-829-3145, Fax: 210-829-3153, E-mail: alakanan@uiwtx.edu. *Application contact:* Andrea Cyterski-Acosta, Dean of Enrollment, 210-829-6005, Fax: 210-829-3921, E-mail: admis@uiwtx.edu.

University of Virginia, College and Graduate School of Arts and Sciences, Program in Art and Architectural History, Charlottesville, VA 22903. Offers MA, PhD. *Students:* 50 full-time (35 women), 3 international. Average age 33. 83 applicants, 31% accepted, 13 enrolled. In 2007, 11 degrees awarded. *Degree requirements:* For master's, 2 foreign languages, comprehensive exam, thesis; for doctorate, 2 foreign languages, thesis/dissertation, oral exam. *Unit head:* Lawrence O. Goedde, Chair, 434-924-6123, Fax: 434-924-3647, E-mail: artdept@virginia.edu.

University of Washington, Tacoma, Graduate Programs, Tacoma, WA 98402-3100. Offers accounting (MBA); certified financial analyst (MBA); computing and software systems (MS); educational administrator (M Ed); interdisciplinary studies (MA); K-8 teacher education (M Ed); nursing (MN); professional certification (M Ed); secondary science education (M Ed); social work (MSW); special education (M Ed). Part-time programs available. *Students:* 160 full-time (107 women), 312 part-time (233 women); includes 90 minority (19 African Americans, 8 American Indian/Alaska Native, 35 Asian Americans or Pacific Islanders, 28 Hispanic Americans). Average age 35. 308 applicants, 61% accepted, 149 enrolled. In 2007, 156 degrees awarded. *Degree requirements:* For master's, comprehensive exam (for some programs), thesis (for some programs), minimum GPA of 2.7 in all courses. *Entrance requirements:* For master's, GRE, GMAT, minimum GPA of 3.0 in last 90 graded credits. Additional exam requirements/recommendations for international students: Required—TOEFL (minimum score 550 paper-based; 237 computer-based; 70 iBT), MLT. *Application deadline:* For fall admission, 5/15 priority date for domestic students, 5/15 for international students; for winter admission, 1/12 priority date for domestic students; for spring admission, 2/25 priority date for domestic students. Applications are processed on a rolling basis. Application fee: $50. Electronic applications accepted. *Expenses:* Tuition, area resident: Part-time $890 per unit. Tuition, nonresident: part-time $2,087 per unit. Tuition and fees vary according to degree level and program. *Financial support:* Federal Work-Study, institutionally sponsored loans, and scholarships/grants available. Support available to part-time students. *Faculty research:* Aids Patient Care (social work), impact of globalization on international urban areas (urban studies), water quality (environmental science), community based healthcare (rural). Total annual research expenditures: $550,000.

The University of Western Ontario, Faculty of Graduate Studies, Center for the Study of Theory and Criticism, London, ON N6A 5B8, Canada. Offers MA, PhD. *Faculty:* 21. *Students:* 25 full-time (13 women). 37 applicants, 41% accepted. In 2007, 8 degrees awarded. *Degree requirements:* For master's, one foreign language, thesis; for doctorate, one foreign language, comprehensive exam, thesis/dissertation. *Entrance requirements:* For master's, honors degree or equivalent, minimum B+ average, 2 samples of written work; for doctorate, MA in humanitites or social sciences. *Application deadline:* For fall admission, 1/15 for domestic and international students. Application fee: $30 Canadian dollars. *Financial support:* In 2007–08, 18 teaching assistantships with full tuition reimbursements (averaging $8,264 Canadian dollars per year) were awarded; research assistantships with tuition reimbursements, scholarships/grants also available. Financial award application deadline: 4/1. *Unit head:* Prof. Clive Thomson, Acting Dean, 519-661-2111 Ext. 85169, E-mail: theory@uwo.ca. *Application contact:* Melanie Caldwell, Information Contact, 519-661-2111 Ext. 83442, E-mail: theory@uwo.ca.

University of Wisconsin–Milwaukee, Graduate School, Program in Multidisciplinary Studies, Milwaukee, WI 53201-0413. Offers PhD. *Students:* 3 full-time (2 women). *Degree requirements:* For doctorate, thesis/dissertation. *Application deadline:* For fall admission, 1/1 priority date for domestic students; for spring admission, 9/1 for domestic students. Applications are processed on a rolling basis. Application fee: $45 ($75 for international students). *Expenses:* Tuition, state resident: part-time $530 per credit. Tuition, nonresident: part-time $1,428 per credit. Required fees: $19 per credit. $229 per term. Tuition and fees vary according to course load and program. *Financial support:* Fellowships, research assistantships, teaching assistantships, career-

Interdisciplinary Studies

University of Wisconsin–Milwaukee (continued)

related internships or fieldwork and unspecified assistantships available. Support available to part-time students. Financial award application deadline: 4/15. *Unit head:* Gwat-Yong Lie, Associate Professor, 414-229-4100, E-mail: gwatlie@uwm.edu. *Application contact:* Wendy Fall, Director of Student Services, 414-229-6569, Fax: 414-229-6967, E-mail: wendyf@uwm.edu.

Virginia Commonwealth University, Graduate School, Program in Interdisciplinary Studies, Richmond, VA 23284-9005. Offers MIS. Part-time programs available. *Students:* 5 applicants, 80% accepted, 3 enrolled. In 2007, 13 degrees awarded. *Degree requirements:* For master's, thesis optional. *Entrance requirements:* For master's, GRE General Test, minimum GPA of 2.8. *Application deadline:* For fall admission, 7/1 for domestic students; for spring admission, 12/1 for domestic students. Applications are processed on a rolling basis. Application fee: $50. *Expenses:* Tuition, state resident: full-time $7,224; part-time $401 per credit. Tuition, nonresident: full-time $16,072; part-time $891 per credit. Required fees: $1,679; $63 per credit. Tuition and fees vary according to campus/location. *Financial support:* Federal Work-Study and institutionally sponsored loans available. Support available to part-time students. *Unit head:* Associate Dean, 804-827-4546, Fax: 804-828-6949, E-mail: ssandham@vcu.edu. *Application contact:* Carole Harwell, Administrative Assistant, 804-827-4546, Fax: 804-827-6949, E-mail: charwell@vcu.edu.

See Close-Up on page 755.

Virginia Polytechnic Institute and State University, Graduate School, Intercollege, Blacksburg, VA 24061. Offers MIT, MS, PhD. *Entrance requirements:* Additional exam requirements/recommendations for international students: Required—TOEFL.

Virginia State University, School of Graduate Studies, Research, and Outreach, Program in Interdisciplinary Studies, Petersburg, VA 23806-0001. Offers MIS. *Degree requirements:* For master's, thesis optional.

Washington State University, Graduate School, Individual Interdisciplinary Doctoral Program, Pullman, WA 99164. Offers PhD. *Students:* 4 full-time (1 woman), 5 part-time (2 women); includes 2 minority (both African Americans), 2 international. 9 applicants, 44% accepted, 4 enrolled. In 2007, 8 degrees awarded. *Degree requirements:* For doctorate, comprehensive exam, thesis/dissertation. *Entrance requirements:* For doctorate, minimum GPA of 3.5, master's degree from an accredited institution. Additional exam requirements/recommendations for international students: Required—TOEFL. *Application deadline:* For fall admission, 2/15 for domestic students, 3/1 for international students; for spring admission, 9/15 for domestic students, 7/1 for international students. Application fee: $50. *Financial support:* In 2007–08, 8 students received support, including 1 fellowship (averaging $4,000 per year), 2 research assistantships with tuition reimbursements available (averaging $13,917 per year), 2 teaching assistantships with tuition reimbursements available (averaging $13,056 per year). *Unit head:* Dr. Lori Wiest, Coordinator, 509-335-1337, Fax: 509-335-1949, E-mail: lwiest@wsu.edu. *Application contact:* Graduate School Admissions, 800-GRADWSU, Fax: 509-335-1949, E-mail: gradsch@wsu.edu.

Wayland Baptist University, Graduate Programs, Program in Multidisciplinary Science, Plainview, TX 79072-6998. Offers MS. Part-time and evening/weekend programs available. *Faculty:* 1 full-time (0 women). *Students:* Average age 37. 2 applicants, 100% accepted, 2 enrolled. In 2007, 1 degree awarded. *Degree requirements:* For master's, comprehensive exam. *Entrance requirements:* For master's, GRE or MAT. Additional exam requirements/recommendations for international students: Required—TOEFL (minimum score 500 paper-based; 173 computer-based). *Application deadline:* Applications are processed on a rolling basis. Application fee: $35. *Expenses:* Tuition: Full-time $6,390; part-time $355 per credit hour. Required fees: $600; $50 per term. Full-time tuition and fees vary according to course load. *Financial support:* Federal Work-Study, institutionally sponsored loans, and scholarships/grants available. Support available to part-time students. Financial award application deadline: 5/1; financial award applicants required to submit FAFSA. *Unit head:* Dr. Vaughn Ross, Chairman, Division of Mathematics and Science, 806-291-1115, Fax: 806-291-1968, E-mail: vross@wpu.edu.

Western Kentucky University, Graduate Studies, College of Education and Behavioral Sciences, Department of Special Instructional Programs, Bowling Green, KY 42101. Offers exceptional child education (MAE); interdisciplinary early child education (MAE); library media education (MS); literacy (MAE). Part-time and evening/weekend programs available. Postbaccalaureate distance learning degree programs offered (minimal on-campus study). *Degree requirements:* For master's, comprehensive exam. *Entrance requirements:* For master's, GRE General Test. Additional exam requirements/recommendations for international students: Required—TOEFL (minimum score 555 paper-based; 213 computer-based; 79 iBT). *Faculty research:* Teacher preparation in moderate/severe disabilities.

Western New Mexico University, Graduate Division, Interdisciplinary Studies, Silver City, NM 88062-0680. Offers MA. Part-time programs available. *Degree requirements:* For master's, comprehensive exam (for some programs), thesis optional. *Entrance requirements:* For master's, GRE General Test, GRE Subject Test, minimum GPA of 3.2 in last 64 hours of undergraduate study. Additional exam requirements/recommendations for international students: Required—TOEFL (minimum score 550 paper-based; 213 computer-based). *Application deadline:* For fall admission, 6/1 priority date for domestic and international students; for spring admission, 10/1 priority date for domestic and international students. Application fee: $0. *Application contact:* Dan Tressler, Director of Admissions, 505-538-6106, Fax: 505-538-6127, E-mail: tresslerd@wnmu.edu.

West Texas A&M University, Program in Interdisciplinary Studies, Canyon, TX 79016-0001. Offers MA, MS. Part-time and evening/weekend programs available. Postbaccalaureate distance learning degree programs offered (minimal on-campus study). *Degree requirements:* For master's, comprehensive exam, thesis or alternative. *Entrance requirements:* For master's, GRE General Test, interview with graduate Dean. Additional exam requirements/recommendations for international students: Required—TOEFL (minimum score 550 paper-based). Electronic applications accepted.

Worcester Polytechnic Institute, Graduate Studies and Research, Programs in Interdisciplinary Studies, Worcester, MA 01609-2280. Offers bioscience administration (MS); impact engineering (MS); manufacturing engineering management (MS); power systems management (MS); social science (PhD); systems engineering (MS); systems modeling (MS). Part-time and evening/weekend programs available. *Faculty:* 1 part-time/adjunct (0 women). *Students:* 2 full-time (1 woman), 75 part-time (19 women); includes 10 minority (4 African Americans, 6 Asian Americans or Pacific Islanders), 3 international. 115 applicants, 57% accepted, 44 enrolled. In 2007, 19 master's, 1 doctorate awarded. *Degree requirements:* For master's, thesis; for doctorate, comprehensive exam, thesis/dissertation. *Entrance requirements:* For master's and doctorate, 3 letters of recommendation. Additional exam requirements/recommendations for international students: Required—TOEFL (minimum score 550 paper-based; 213 computer-based; 79 iBT), IELTS (minimum score 7). *Application deadline:* For fall admission, 1/15 priority date for domestic students; for spring admission, 10/15 priority date for domestic students. Application fee: $70. *Expenses:* Tuition: Part-time $1,089 per credit hour. *Financial support:* In 2007–08, 1 student received support, including 1 research assistantship with full tuition reimbursement available; unspecified assistantships also available. Financial award application deadline:1/15. Total annual research expenditures: $108,817. *Unit head:* Dr. Fred J. Looft, Head, 508-831-5231, Fax: 508-831-5491, E-mail: fjlooft@wpi.edu. *Application contact:* Lynne Dougherty, Administrative Assistant, 508-831-5301, Fax: 508-831-5717, E-mail: grad@wpi.edu.

Wright State University, School of Graduate Studies, Interdisciplinary Programs, Program in Interdisciplinary Studies, Dayton, OH 45435. Offers MA, MS. *Degree requirements:* For master's, thesis optional. *Entrance requirements:* Additional exam requirements/recommendations for international students: Required—TOEFL.

York University, Faculty of Graduate Studies, Program in Interdisciplinary Studies, Toronto, ON M3J 1P3, Canada. Offers MA. Part-time programs available. *Degree requirements:* For master's, thesis or alternative. Electronic applications accepted.

Mountain State University™

MOUNTAIN STATE UNIVERSITY

Graduate Program in Interdisciplinary Studies

Programs of Study

The Graduate Program in Interdisciplinary Studies at Mountain State University (MSU) is offered through individualized study by the School of Graduate Studies. A graduate degree in interdisciplinary studies allows students to create programs of study incorporating the work of different domains of knowledge. It provides a useful approach for those whose interests fall between traditional areas. Students can integrate a variety of disciplines and incorporate fieldwork, directed research, mentored learning, and other forms of study.

The 36-semester-hour degree program is divided into three phases: methodology, content, and perspective.

In the methodology phase (3 hours), the student develops a detailed degree plan for proposal to the program. This proposal, based on the student's research, tells what he or she plans to learn in the content phase and details a plan to demonstrate that learning in the perspective phase.

Once the program has approved the degree plan, the student begins the content phase (25 hours). The content phase typically includes graduate-level courses, directed study, field experience and research, and a major project.

The culminating element in the degree program is the perspective project (8 hours) in which the student demonstrates mastery of the program content in a work featuring analysis, synthesis, and evaluation. The perspective project may be a traditional thesis; however, it may instead take the form of an extended written document or project.

Although students may structure their studies around different areas of specific interest, standardized curricula are provided for those who wish to pursue graduate study in selected fields: disability studies (M.S.), liberal studies (M.A.), psychology studies (M.A.), and social and behavioral studies (M.S.). These programs incorporate the University course work to fulfill the content phase of the program.

In addition to master's degree options, the Graduate Program in Interdisciplinary Studies offers two 15-credit-hour certificates. Certificate programs are designed for those who wish to strengthen their workplace credentials or to pursue knowledge outside the structure of a degree program. The certificate programs offered are Professional Communication, which is a blend of written and Web presentation, grant writing, teaching, and training, all underpinned by a study of great presenters; and Cultures and Social Concepts, in which the student pursues interdisciplinary understanding of the relationship between cultural concepts and social movements. The Graduate Program in Interdisciplinary Studies also offers an 18-credit-hour certificate in Psychology Studies.

Research Facilities

Learning resources include multimedia classrooms, computer laboratories, computer-assisted instruction, nursing and health assessment labs, and laboratories for the basic sciences. The Robert C. Byrd Learning Resource Center includes a student-centered library and media center. The collection comprises more than 95,000 titles, supplemented both by interlibrary loan and by extensive electronic resources, including ProQuest, CINAHL (Cumulative Index to Nursing and Allied Health Literature), Social Issues Resources Series (SIRS), EBSCOhost, Westlaw, Wilson Web, Newsbank, and Medline. Technology resources include state-of-the-art telecommunication links, technology equipment, high-speed access and software, and a 3-D immersion module.

Financial Aid

Eligible graduate students may qualify for Federal Stafford Student Loans. Prospective students must submit the Free Application for Federal Student Aid (FAFSA) for determination of eligibility. Most graduate students receive some sort of financial assistance.

Cost of Study

Tuition for 2008–09 is $325 per credit hour. Payment plans are available.

Living and Housing Costs

Many affordable housing opportunities are available in the neighborhoods surrounding the campus and in other nearby areas, which range from suburban to rural. Graduate students may also live in the residence hall on campus. Residence hall fees for 2008–09 are $1500 per semester for double occupancy and $2150 per semester for a private room. Students living on campus are required to purchase one of the University's meal plans.

Student Group

Mountain State University serves more than 8,000 students a year. Graduate enrollment and programming have grown steadily since the University's first graduate program was launched in 1998.

Location

Mountain State University's main campus is located near downtown Beckley, West Virginia, a small city that serves as a regional center for business, health care, education, and tourism in the heart of the southern West Virginia mountains. The Beckley area offers the quiet of a small town with a wealth of recreational and cultural opportunities. Nearby recreational opportunities include white-water rafting on the famed New and Gauley Rivers, skiing, hiking, biking, climbing and rappelling, and other outdoor pursuits. Beckley is an hour's drive from the state capital of Charleston and just a few hours from Pittsburgh, Pennsylvania; Washington, D.C.; and other eastern metropolitan areas.

The University

For seventy-five years, Mountain State University has been a leader in overcoming barriers to higher education and in offering academic programs that combine a liberal arts foundation with career-oriented studies. The University features innovative programming, flexible learning arrangements, well-qualified and deeply committed faculty members, and outstanding student services, all in a relaxed atmosphere.

Applying

Admission to the Graduate Program in Interdisciplinary Studies is open to students with a bachelor's degree from a regionally accredited college or university. There are no standardized test requirements, although on admission, a writing sample may be required for advising and assessment purposes. Students intending a psychology studies emphasis should refer to the online graduate catalog for additional admission requirements.

Applicants should submit a graduate application and arrange for official transcripts of all undergraduate studies and any graduate work to be sent directly to the School of Graduate Studies. Students can apply, enroll, and begin their studies at any time during the academic year.

Because of the individualized nature of the program, it is recommended that applicants discuss their educational goals with a program representative either before they apply or as soon as possible after acceptance.

Correspondence and Information

Mountain State University
Box 9003
Beckley, West Virginia 25802-9003
Phone: 304-929-INFO (4636)
866-FOR-MSU1 (866-367-6781) (toll-free)
E-mail: gomsu@mountainstate.edu
Web site: http://www.mountainstate.edu

Mountain State University

THE GRADUATE FACULTY

Jeffrey Atwood, Associate Professor and Lead Leadership Faculty Member, MSU Orlando; Ed.D., Central Florida.
Jonnathan Bailey, Instructor of Nurse Anesthesia; M.S., Mountain State; CRNA.
Vincent Beach, Professor and Dean, School of Arts and Sciences; Ph.D., CUNY Graduate Center.
M. Susan Bonifer, Professor of English and Communication; Ph.D., Indiana of Pennsylvania.
Loretta Ann Bostic, Instructor and Assistant Director, Nurse Anesthesia; M.S., Marshall, CRNA.
Debra Campbell, Instructor and Director, Physician Assistant Program; M.H.S., Mountain State; PA-C.
Wayne Ellis, Professor and Director, Nurse Anesthesia; Ph.D., Texas A&M; RN, CRNA, ARNP.
Diana Foley, Associate Professor and Director, Nursing, MSU Martinsburg; Ed.D., Wilmington (Delaware); RN.
Robert Hayes, Assistant Professor and Lead Graduate Faculty Member, Psychology; Ph.D., Capella.
Frank Hitt, Associate Professor of Leadership and Director, Leadership Programs; Ed.D., Sarasota.
James E. Hodge, Professor of Mathematics; Ed.D., West Virginia.
Brian Holloway, Professor of English and Dean, School of Graduate Studies; Ph.D., Illinois.
Michael Kane, Assistant Professor and Director, Justice Studies; Ph.D., Union (Ohio).
Melissa Lilly, Instructor and Clinical Coordinator, Physician Assistant Program; M.S.P.A., Alderson-Broaddus; PA-C.
Matthew Lonam, Assistant Professor of Leadership; Ph.D., Missouri.
William Martin, Jr., Assistant Professor (part-time) of Physician Assistant Program; Ph.D., Minnesota.
James McCoy, Assistant Professor of English; Ph.D., Florida State.
Michael McMillion, Instructor of Physician Assistant Program; M.S.P.A., Mountain State; PA-C.
Mark Miller, Professor and Senior Academic Officer, Experiential Learning; Ph.D., Virginia Tech.
Nada Najjar, Assistant Professor of English; Ph.D., Toledo.
Jennifer Pack, Instructor of Physician Assistant Program; M.M.S., Alderson-Broaddus; PA-C.
Gary Poling, Assistant Professor and Medical Director, Physician Assistant Program; D.O., West Virginia School of Osteopathic Medicine.
Gail Zell Serdoz, Associate Professor of Nursing; M.S.N., West Virginia; RN.
Jessica Sharp, Professor of Nursing and Senior Academic Officer, Graduate Nursing; Ph.D., George Mason; RN, FNP-C, BC-APN.
John Sidor, Associate Professor of Leadership and Lead Leadership Faculty Member, MSU Martinsburg; Ph.D., Pittsburgh.
Arnold Simonse, Professor of Social Work; D.S.W., Catholic University.
Richard Weil, Assistant Professor of Leadership and Lead Leadership Faculty Member, MSU Center Township; D.B.A., Argosy.
William M. White, Dean, School of Leadership and Professional Development; Ed.D., Fielding Institute.
Shewana Workman, Instructor of Nurse Anesthesia; M.S., Bellarmine; CRNA.
Ruth G. Wylie, Associate Dean, School of Leadership and Professional Development; Ph.D., West Virginia.

NEW YORK UNIVERSITY

Gallatin School of Individualized Study

Program of Study

The Gallatin School offers an M.A. degree in individualized study. Working closely with a faculty adviser, self-motivated students have the opportunity to develop an individually tailored, interdisciplinary educational program. Students master an area of concentration that integrates study in several disciplines. For example, a student who is interested in the arts and community could combine courses in educational theater, arts administration, and sociology; a student with an interest in the cultural history of the United States might combine English with history and museum studies; a student with an interest in communications might develop a program to include course work in cinema studies, gender studies, and media ecology; and a student wishing to study the European Union might combine course work in politics, history, and social policy. A student's course of study is not limited to these examples. Students are encouraged to design a program according to their individual needs and interests. With the adviser, the student designs a 40-credit M.A. program consisting of course work and other options that may include independent study, tutorials, internships, and private lessons in the arts.

The course work is taken in the various graduate schools of NYU, such as the Graduate School of Arts and Science; the Stern School of Business; the Wagner Graduate School of Public Service; the Steinhardt School of Culture, Education, and Human Development; the Silver School of Social Work; and the Tisch School of the Arts (selected courses). In addition to course work, independent study and tutorials allow students to pursue in-depth research, while internships and private lessons enable students to take advantage of the resources of New York City. The program requires 40 credits; students may apply for a maximum of 12 transfer credits and/or course-equivalency credits, which are based on previous work experience or training. A thesis is required and can be a traditional research paper, an applied project, or an artistic endeavor, such as a performance, a novel, or a work of visual art.

During the first year and a half, the curriculum for full-time students consists primarily of course work along with independent study, tutorials, and internships (if desired). Students may combine courses from the various schools of NYU in preparation for the thesis. Students may attend on a full-time or part-time basis. Full-time students usually complete the program in 2½ years; part-time students generally complete the program in three to four years but are given up to six years.

Research Facilities

NYU's Bobst Library, one of the largest open-stack research libraries in the nation, houses nearly 3.9 million volumes. Bobst is one of nine NYU libraries. Casa Italiana Zerilli-Marimò, Glucksman Ireland House, Bronfman Center for Jewish Student Life, King Juan Carlos I of Spain Center, La Maison Française, Deutsches Haus, and Hagop Kevorkian Center are available for student use. The Grey Art Gallery, the University's fine arts museum, presents innovative exhibitions each year that encompass all aspects of the visual arts.

Financial Aid

Scholarships, work-study opportunities, loans, and a deferred-payment plan are available. Financial aid is awarded on the basis of merit and demonstrated financial need to both full-time and part-time students. Resident assistantships and student employment are also available.

In 2007–08, 61 percent of graduate students received some form of aid; of those receiving aid, 67 percent received scholarships/grants, 77 percent received loans, and 7 percent received work-study. The range of scholarship/grant packages was $275–$35,500. The range of loan packages was $4000–$52,454.

Sources of financial support include the NYU Reynolds Program in Social Entrepreneurship. This program is a comprehensive initiative designed to equip the next generation of social entrepreneurial leaders and infrastructure developers and managers with the skills, resources, and networking opportunities needed to help solve society's most intractable problems in sustainable and scalable ways. The program offers twenty graduate fellowships each year to students across the University. The graduate fellowship provides up to $50,000 over two years and dedicated curricular and cocurricular activities. For more information, students should visit http://www.nyu.edu/reynolds.

Other financial includes Foreign Language and Area Studies (FLAS) Fellowships (http://www.nyu.edu/gsas/dept/europe, http://www.nyu.edu/gsas/dept/latin, or http://www.nyu.edu/gsas/program/neareas); Residential Education Assistantship Opportunities (http://www.nyu.edu/residential.education/staff/studentselection/index.html); NYU America Reads/America Counts (http://www.steinhardt.nyu.edu/americareads); and New York State Tuition Assistance Program (http://www.nyu.edu/financial.aid/tap.html).

Part-time and international students should visit http://www.nyu.edu/financial.aid for more information about financial aid.

Cost of Study

Tuition for the 2007–08 academic year at Gallatin was $1107 per credit per term, plus additional nonrefundable registration and services fees. Tuition is paid per credit, per term. The University offers a comprehensive health insurance benefit plan at $2228 per year. Full-time and international students are automatically enrolled in this plan unless they already have comparable coverage.

Living and Housing Costs

Graduate student housing at NYU provides the advantages of apartment-style living with the convenience, security, activities, and supportive environment of residence hall life. Several types of accommodations are offered to suit different preferences and budgets, including shared studios, double rooms in one- and two-bedroom apartments, and a limited number of private rooms in two- and three-person suites. Off-campus housing is also available at market rates. Meal plans are available but not required. For further information, students may visit http://www.nyu.edu/housing.

Student Group

There are approximately 200 graduate students in the Gallatin School. Half of the students are from the New York metropolitan area, whereas the other half come from across the country as well as from international locations. Because of the diversity offered in the Gallatin School, students come from a wide range of undergraduate disciplines.

Student Outcomes

Because of the individualized nature of Gallatin, graduates embark on a wide variety of professions. In the arts, graduates include choreographers, artistic directors of dance and theater companies, performers, writers, arts administrators, curators, and museum directors. Graduates in the arts often remain in academia, teaching the arts at all levels, from elementary to university. In the field of finance, Gallatin graduates hold positions in such firms as Oppenheimer & Company, the Bank of America, and Citigroup. Others enter the fields of nutrition, psychotherapy, journalism, education, and communications, while many have obtained positions in government, social, and environmental agencies. Graduates have also entered Ph.D. programs in such areas as literature, sociology, cinema, performance studies, cultural studies, educational theater, history, music composition, and political science.

Location

NYU's Gallatin School is located in historic Greenwich Village, which is known for its small-scale, European style of living. NYU's campus is within minutes of Broadway and off-Broadway drama and dance, art galleries, coffeehouses, restaurants, clubs, bookstores, and world-renowned museums and libraries. The Jerome S. Coles Sports and Recreation Center and the Palladium Athletic Facility serve the recreational needs of all students.

The University

NYU is a private university, comprising fourteen schools and colleges. The University was founded in 1831 by Albert Gallatin, Treasury Secretary under Thomas Jefferson, and other prominent New Yorkers, who believed that the place for a university was not in "the seclusion of cloistered halls but in the throbbing heart of a great city." In this spirit, the Gallatin School was founded in 1972.

Applying

Students may be admitted for the fall, spring, or summer terms. In addition to official transcripts, two letters of recommendation and a statement of purpose are required.

Correspondence and Information

Director of Graduate Admissions
Gallatin School of Individualized Study
New York University
715 Broadway, 6th Floor
New York, New York 10003-6806
Phone: 212-998-7370
Web site: http://www.nyu.edu/gallatin/gallatin08

New York University

THE FACULTY AND THEIR RESEARCH

Students in the Gallatin School take courses in the various graduate schools of New York University. Essentially, the entire graduate faculty of the University instructs Gallatin students. The following is a list of Gallatin faculty members.

Susanne Wofford, Dean, Gallatin School of Individualized Study; Ph.D., Yale. Shakespeare, Spenser, Renaissance and classical epic, comparative European drama, narrative and literary theory.

Sinan Antoon, Ph.D., Harvard. Premodern Arabo-Islamic culture, contemporary Arab culture and politics.
Nina Cornyetz, Ph.D., Columbia. Critical, literary, and film theory; intellectual history; gender and sexuality; cultural studies; psychoanalytic and materialist-feminist methodologies; area specialization in Japan.
Michael D. Dinwiddie, M.F.A., NYU. African American culture and politics, theater history and criticism, dramatic writing, filmmaking and cinema studies, nineteenth- and twentieth-century music.
Stephen Duncombe, Ph.D., CUNY Graduate Center. Media and cultural studies; history of the mass media, advertising, and consumer society; theory and politics of alternative culture; media activism and cultural resistance.
Sharon Friedman, Ph.D., NYU. Modern drama, literary interpretation, women and literature, critical writing.
Lisa Goldfarb, Ph.D., CUNY Graduate Center. Nineteenth- and twentieth-century European and American poetry and fiction, music and literature, questions of belief in literature.
Jean Graybeal, Ph.D., Syracuse. Philosophy and psychology of religion, religion and culture, women and religion, philosophies of the body, feminist spirituality.
Karen Hornick, Ph.D., Columbia. Literature, cultural history, feminism and gender studies, popular culture.
Kristin Horton, M.F.A., Iowa. Directing, Shakespeare, new play development, theater and cross-cultural dialogue, ritual studies, puppetry.
Steven Hutkins, Ph.D., NYU. Renaissance literature, spirituality, technology of writing, documentary and independent feature films, classic texts, phenomenology of place, intellectual autobiography.
Bradley Lewis, Ph.D., George Washington; M.D., Tennessee. Science studies, cultural studies of science, disability studies, medical humanities, psychology.
Julie Malnig, Ph.D., NYU. Popular theater and drama, theater history and criticism, history of American and British social dance, early twentieth-century American culture and the arts, feminist and cultural studies, contemporary playwriting.
Eve Meltzer, Ph.D., Berkeley. Contemporary art, theory, and criticism; psychoanalytic, structuralist, and poststructuralist thought; photography; discourses on materiality and material culture; theories of information; rhetorics of digitality; phenomenology.
M. Bella Mirabella, Ph.D., Rutgers. Classic texts; Shakespeare and Renaissance literature; role of dance in English drama; history of the Italian Renaissance; the origins of Christianity; Dante, Boccaccio, and the Italian Renaissance.
Ali Mirsepassi, Ph.D., American. Middle Eastern studies, social theory, sociology of religion, Islam and modernity, intellectual history, Iranian studies.
David Thornton Moore, Ed.D., Harvard. History of social thought and contemporary social issues, work reform and experiential education, innovations in higher education.
Kimberly Phillips-Fein, Ph.D., Columbia. American political, business, and labor history; history of economic thought; the role of business in the development of the modern conservative movement in the second half of the twentieth century; the centrality of economic ideas in the rise of the right.
Stacy Pies, Ph.D., CUNY Graduate Center. Comparative literature and critical theory, poetry (post-1600s), relationship of visual arts and literature, narrative and psychoanalysis.
René Francisco Poitevin, Ph.D., California, Davis. Urban theory, geographic information systems, social movements, race and ethnic relations in the United States.
Millery Polyné, Ph.D., Michigan–Ann Arbor. History of African American and African Caribbean/African Latino cultural, political, and economic initiatives in the nineteenth and twentieth centuries; U.S. empire building in the Americas; cultural studies; dance; jazz.
Laurin Raiken, M.A., Adelphi. Sociology of the arts and culture; analysis of American social, political, and economic institutions; arts management and cultural policy; arts professions; Native American culture.
George Shulman, Ph.D., Berkeley. History of European and American social thought, including relevant literary works; American political culture; urban politics and culture in Paris (1750–1900) and New York (1900–present); the Bible in Western politics and thought.
Laura M. Slatkin, Ph.D., Harvard. Classical philology, Homeric studies, women and gender in antiquity, metaphor and social order.
Alycia Smith-Howard, Ph.D., Shakespeare Institute, Birmingham (England). Shakespeare, feminist theory in performance, modern American drama and nineteenth-century studies (drama, literature, and cultural studies).
Clyde R. Taylor, Ph.D., Wayne State. Politics of representation, vernacular modernisms, cinema and society, African American and African literature, cultural symbolism.
John Kuo Wei Tchen, Ph.D., NYU. Cross-cultural studies, history and public policy of New York City, mapping identities and imagining communities, practices and theories of educational and cultural institutions, radical pedagogy, Asian/Pacific American studies.
Alejandro Velasco, Ph.D., Duke. History of modern Latin America, social movements, urban culture, democratization.
E. Frances White, Ph.D., Boston University. African and African American history, study of gender and sexuality.

A Gallatin professor talks with students.

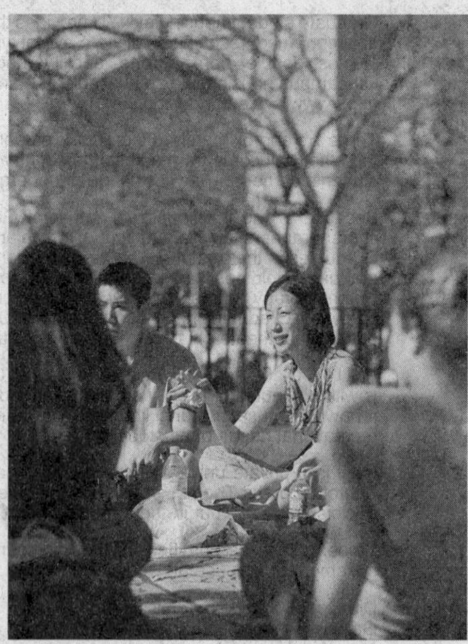

Gallatin students use Washington Square Park as an outdoor classroom.

VIRGINIA COMMONWEALTH UNIVERSITY

Master of Interdisciplinary Studies

Programs of Study

Virginia Commonwealth University (VCU) offers the Master of Interdisciplinary Studies (M.I.S.). This degree program provides an opportunity for the highly motivated student to pursue a unique course of study that combines graduate course work with a learner-centered approach. The student is an active participant in proposing a curriculum that supports an individualized and scholastically rigorous academic goal in a clearly defined, multidisciplinary program. To expand the program's range of options and interdisciplinary perspectives, the program allows for cooperative ventures with other approved colleges and universities.

In addition to an individualized program of study, two other options for the M.I.S. are available—an interdisciplinary arts/off-campus program with a focus in studio art and a mathematics and science leadership/K–8 mathematics specialist program. The School of the Arts and the Office of Community Programs jointly administer the M.I.S. interdisciplinary arts program, providing an opportunity for the off-campus student to earn a graduate degree by combining art courses, both studio and academic, within established guidelines. The program is not the equivalent of a Master of Fine Arts degree; it does, however, provide an additional option for qualified persons, especially art teachers, who are interested in studio art classes. Focus areas include crafts, computers and the arts, painting, photography, printmaking, drawing, and sculpture, among others. The mathematics and science leadership/K–8 mathematics specialist program is designed for in-service teachers of mathematics for kindergarten through eighth grades. Students select courses offered by VCU's mathematics, science, and education departments and courses offered by other collaborating Virginia colleges and universities.

Students enrolled in M.I.S. programs of study must complete a minimum of 39 graduate semester credits. These include at least 9, and not more than 15, graduate semester credits in each of at least two focus areas. No more than 15 credits in any one focus area (exclusive of directed research, independent study, special project, or thesis requirements) may be applied toward the degree. Students must complete a minimum of 3 credits in a research methods course relevant to the final research project as well as 3–6 credits of approved directed research, independent study, special project, or thesis work.

Research Facilities

VCU libraries provide a combined capacity of more than 1.7 million volumes, 10,200 periodical titles, and an online bibliographic search service accessing hundreds of databases. In addition, the Virginia state and Richmond public libraries are within walking distance of both VCU campuses. Academic Computing provides a variety of microcomputer, minicomputer, and mainframe computing services to support the research and instructional endeavors of its faculty and students, including consultation, instruction, and computer acquisition.

Financial Aid

In addition to need-based financial aid awarded through the Office of Financial Aid, graduate students at VCU are eligible for a number of University-sponsored financing options, including scholarships, employment opportunities, and fellowships and teaching assistantships. All forms of graduate student support are reported to the Office of Financial Aid and are considered when determining need-based support.

A number of assistantships, fellowships, and scholarships are awarded each year to new and continuing graduate students on the basis of a variety of criteria. Awards vary by program, and selection is made at the department level; therefore, inquiry about such awards should be made directly to the director of the program.

Students may contact the Office of Financial Aid at 804-828-6669 (Monroe Park Campus) or 804-828-2702 (MCV Campus) or visit http://www.vcu.edu/enroll/finaid/ for current information on financial aid programs, policies, and procedures.

Cost of Study

For full-time graduate study (9–15 credits) in 2008–09, Virginia residents pay tuition and fees of $4739 per semester; nonresidents, $9106 per semester. For part-time graduate study, Virginia residents pay tuition and fees of $495 per hour; nonresidents, $978 per hour.

For full-time doctoral study (9–15 credits) in 2008–09, Virginia residents pay tuition and fees of $4523 per semester; nonresidents, $8947 per semester. For part-time graduate study, Virginia residents pay tuition and fees of $471 per hour; nonresidents, $960 per hour.

Some programs require additional fees. On the Medical College of Virginia (MCV) campus, tuition, fees, and other expenses vary in the Medicine, Pharmacy, Nurse Anesthesia, Dentistry, and School of Allied Health programs.

Living and Housing Costs

Graduate student housing is available on both the MCV campus and the academic campus of Virginia Commonwealth University. Many graduate students live in off-campus housing, which is reasonably priced and readily available in a variety of styles and settings in nearby residential areas or within easy commuting distance. On-campus housing information is available on the Web at http://www.housing.vcu.edu/. Off-campus housing information is available at http://www.usca.vcu.edu/offcampus/.

Student Group

VCU enrolls nearly 32,000 students, 8,149 of whom are graduate students. More than 200 clubs and organizations reflect the diverse social, recreational, educational, political, and religious interests of the student body.

Location

Richmond is Virginia's capital and a major East Coast financial and manufacturing center that offers students a wide range of cultural, educational, and recreational activities. Richmond is located in central Virginia at the intersection of Interstates 95 and 64, 2 hours south of Washington, D.C., and nestled between the Blue Ridge Mountains and the Atlantic coast. The Richmond region is easily accessible by plane, car, and train. With nearly 1 million residents, the historic city of Richmond combines big-city offerings with small-town hospitality. Applicants are encouraged to explore http://www.visit.richmond.com/ for more information on the city.

The University

Virginia Commonwealth University is a state-supported coeducational university with a graduate school, a major teaching hospital, and twelve academic and professional units that offer sixty-two undergraduate, sixty-nine master's, forty postbaccalaureate and post-master's certificate programs, and thirty-one Ph.D. programs. VCU also offers M.D., D.D.S., D.P.T., and Pharm.D. programs as well as cooperative degree programs with other major Virginia colleges and universities. The academic campus is located in Richmond's historic Fan District. The health sciences campus and hospital are located 2 miles east in the downtown business district. A University bus service provides free intercampus transportation for faculty members and students.

With more than $211 million in annual research funding, VCU is classified as one of the nation's top research universities by the Carnegie Foundation for the Advancement of Teaching. More than 32,000 undergraduate, certificate, graduate, post-master's, professional, and doctoral students are enrolled in 205 academic programs, sixty-five of which are unique in the commonwealth of Virginia. The faculty members represent the finest American and international graduate institutions and enhance the University's position among the important institutions of higher learning in the United States and the world via their work in the classroom, laboratory, studio, and clinic and in their scholarly publications.

Applying

Admission procedures and program requirements are detailed in the *Graduate Bulletin*. Application deadlines and materials, including the application and the *Graduate Bulletin*, are available online at the Graduate School Web site at http://www.graduate.vcu.edu. Virginia Commonwealth University is an equal opportunity/affirmative action institution providing access to education and employment without regard to age, race, color, national origin, gender, religion, sexual orientation, veteran's status, political affiliation, or disability.

Correspondence and Information

Sherry T. Sandkam, Director
Master of Interdisciplinary Studies
Graduate School
1001 Grove Avenue
Virginia Commonwealth University
P.O. Box 843051
Richmond, Virginia 23284-3051

Phone: 804-828-6916
Fax: 804-828-6949
E-mail: ssandkam@vcu.edu
Web site: http://www.vcu.edu/graduate/ps/master_inter.html

Virginia Commonwealth University

THE FACULTY

Dr. Sherry T. Sandkam, Assistant Professor, Department of Educational Leadership, School of Education; Associate Dean, Graduate School; and Director, Master of Interdisciplinary Studies Program. ssandkam@vcu.edu

Carole E. Harwell, Enrollment Services Coordinator, Graduate School, Master of Interdisciplinary Studies–Individual Programs of Study. charwell@vcu.edu

Sue F. Munro, Program Director, Master of Interdisciplinary Studies Program–Interdisciplinary Arts. sfmunro@vcu.edu

Reuben W. Farley, Professor, Department of Mathematics and Applied Mathematics, College of Humanities and Sciences and Director, Interdisciplinary Track in Mathematics and Science Leadership. rwfarley@vcu.edu

ACADEMIC AND PROFESSIONAL PROGRAMS IN THE SOCIAL SCIENCES

Section 15
Area and Cultural Studies

This section contains a directory of institutions offering graduate work in area and cultural studies, followed by in-depth entries submitted by institutions that chose to prepare detailed program descriptions. Additional information about programs listed in the directory but not augmented by an in-depth entry may be obtained by writing directly to the dean of a graduate school or chair of a department at the address given in the directory.

For programs offering related work, see also in this book *Geography, History, Language and Literature, Political Science and International Affairs,* and *Sociology, Anthropology, and Archaeology.*

CONTENTS

Program Directories

Close-Ups

See also:

African-American Studies

Boston University, Graduate School of Arts and Sciences, Program in African American Studies, Boston, MA 02215. Offers MA. *Students:* 2 full-time (both women), 1 international. Average age 26. 10 applicants, 50% accepted. In 2007, 1 degree awarded. *Degree requirements:* For master's, one foreign language, comprehensive exam. *Entrance requirements:* For master's, GRE General Test, 2 letters of recommendation. Additional exam requirements/recommendations for international students: Required—TOEFL (minimum score 550 paper-based; 213 computer-based). *Application deadline:* For fall admission, 7/1 for domestic and international students. Application fee: $70. *Expenses:* Tuition: Full-time $34,930; part-time $1,092 per credit. Tuition and fees vary according to class time, course level and program. *Financial support:* In 2007–08, 1 student received support. Career-related internships or fieldwork, Federal Work-Study, scholarships/grants, and unspecified assistantships available. Support available to part-time students. Financial award application deadline: 1/15; financial award applicants required to submit FAFSA. *Unit head:* Ronald K. Richardson, Director, 617-353-2796, Fax: 617-353-4975, E-mail: rrichard@bu.edu. *Application contact:* Christine J. Loken-Kim, Program Administrator, 617-358-1421, Fax: 617-353-0455, E-mail: lokenkim@bu.edu.

Clark Atlanta University, School of Arts and Sciences, Department of African-American Studies, Atlanta, GA 30314. Offers MA, DAH. Part-time programs available. *Faculty:* 1 full-time (0 women), 1 (woman) part-time/adjunct. *Students:* 11 full-time (7 women), 26 part-time (11 women); includes 33 minority (all African Americans), 2 international. Average age 37. 11 applicants, 82% accepted, 1 enrolled. In 2007, 6 master's, 1 doctorate awarded. *Degree requirements:* For master's, one foreign language, thesis. *Entrance requirements:* For master's, GRE General Test, minimum GPA of 2.5. Additional exam requirements/recommendations for international students: Required—TOEFL (minimum score 500 paper-based; 173 computer-based). *Application deadline:* For fall admission, 4/1 for domestic and international students; for spring admission, 11/1 for domestic and international students. Applications are processed on a rolling basis. Application fee: $40 ($55 for international students). Electronic applications accepted. *Expenses:* Tuition: Full-time $11,664; part-time $648 per credit hour. Required fees: $550; $275 per semester. *Financial support:* Scholarships/grants available. Financial award application deadline: 4/30; financial award applicants required to submit FAFSA. *Unit head:* Dr. Josephine Bradley, Chairperson, 404-880-6810, E-mail: jbradley@cau.edu. *Application contact:* Michelle Clark-Davis, Graduate Program Admissions, 404-880-8709, E-mail: mdowis@cau.edu.

Clark Atlanta University, School of Arts and Sciences, Department of Africana Women's Studies, Atlanta, GA 30314. Offers MA, DAH. Part-time programs available. *Faculty:* 1 (woman) full-time. *Students:* 7 full-time (6 women), 6 part-time (5 women); includes 11 minority (all African Americans), 1 international. 5 applicants, 100% accepted, 0 enrolled. In 2007, 2 master's, 5 doctorates awarded. *Degree requirements:* For master's, one foreign language, thesis; for doctorate, 2 foreign languages, thesis/dissertation. *Entrance requirements:* For master's, GRE General Test, minimum GPA of 2.5; for doctorate, GRE General Test, minimum graduate GPA of 3.0. Additional exam requirements/recommendations for international students: Required—TOEFL (minimum score 500 paper-based; 173 computer-based). *Application deadline:* For fall admission, 4/1 for domestic and international students; for spring admission, 11/1 for domestic and international students. Applications are processed on a rolling basis. Application fee: $40 ($55 for international students). Electronic applications accepted. *Expenses:* Tuition: Full-time $11,664; part-time $648 per credit hour. Required fees: $550; $275 per semester. *Financial support:* Scholarships/grants available. Financial award application deadline: 4/30; financial award applicants required to submit FAFSA. *Faculty research:* Concerns of women of African descent globally. *Unit head:* Dr. Josephine Bradley, Chairperson, 404-880-6810, E-mail: jbradley@cau.edu. *Application contact:* Michelle Clark-Davis, Graduate Program Admissions, 404-880-8709, E-mail: mdowis@cau.edu.

Columbia University, Graduate School of Arts and Sciences, Program in African-American Studies, New York, NY 10027. Offers MA. Part-time programs available. Application fee: $90. *Expenses:* Tuition: Part-time $1,452 per credit. Required fees: $152 per term. One-time fee: $75 part-time. Full-time tuition and fees vary according to course level, course load, degree level and program. *Unit head:* Steven Gregory, Program Director, 212-854-4552, Fax: 212-854-7060, E-mail: sg820@columbia.edu.

Cornell University, Graduate School, Graduate Fields of Arts and Sciences, Field of African and African-American Studies, Ithaca, NY 14853-0001. Offers African studies (MPS); African-American studies (MPS). *Faculty:* 13 full-time (5 women). *Students:* 14 full-time (7 women); includes 11 minority (all African Americans) Average age 26. 39 applicants, 23% accepted, 7 enrolled. In 2007, 6 degrees awarded. *Degree requirements:* For master's, thesis. *Entrance requirements:* For master's, GRE General Test (recommended), 3 letters of recommendation. Additional exam requirements/recommendations for international students: Required—TOEFL (minimum score 550 paper-based; 213 computer-based; 77 iBT). *Application deadline:* For fall admission, 1/30 for domestic students. Application fee: $70. Electronic applications accepted. *Financial support:* In 2007–08, 14 students received support, including 7 fellowships with full tuition reimbursements available, 7 research assistantships; teaching assistantships with full tuition reimbursements available, institutionally sponsored loans, scholarships/grants, health care benefits, tuition waivers (full and partial), and unspecified assistantships also available. Financial award applicants required to submit FAFSA. *Faculty research:* African-American literature, art, cinema and theater; African-American politics and public policy; African history, politics and art; Caribbean politics and Africana Diaspora. *Unit head:* Director of Graduate Studies, 607-255-4625, Fax: 607-255-0784. *Application contact:* Graduate Field Assistant, 607-255-4625, Fax: 607-255-0784, E-mail: spt1@cornell.edu.

Cornell University, Graduate School, Graduate Fields of Arts and Sciences, Field of English Language and Literature, Ithaca, NY 14853-0001. Offers African-American literature (PhD); American literature after 1865 (PhD); American literature to 1865 (PhD); American studies (PhD); colonial and postcolonial literature (PhD); creative writing (MFA); cultural studies (PhD); dramatic literature (PhD); English poetry (PhD); English Renaissance to 1660 (PhD); lesbian, bisexual, and gay literature studies (PhD); literary criticism and theory (PhD); nineteenth century (PhD); Old and Middle English (PhD); prose fiction (PhD); Restoration and eighteenth century (PhD); twentieth century (PhD); women's literature (PhD); MFA/PhD. *Faculty:* 59 full-time (28 women). *Students:* 97 full-time (53 women); includes 20 minority (7 African Americans, 3 American Indian/Alaska Native, 5 Asian Americans or Pacific Islanders, 5 Hispanic Americans), 13 international. Average age 28. 759 applicants, 7% accepted, 21 enrolled. In 2007, 29 master's, 8 doctorates awarded. Terminal master's awarded for partial completion of doctoral program. *Degree requirements:* For master's, one foreign language, thesis; for doctorate, one foreign language, comprehensive exam, thesis/dissertation, teaching experience. *Entrance requirements:* For master's, GRE General Test, 3 letters of recommendation, creative writing sample; for doctorate, GRE General Test, GRE Subject Test (English), 3 letters of recommendation, writing sample. Additional exam requirements/recommendations for international students: Required—TOEFL (minimum score 600 paper-based; 250 computer-based; 77 iBT). *Application deadline:* For fall admission, 1/10 for domestic students. Application fee: $70. Electronic applications accepted. *Financial support:* In 2007–08, 92 students received support, including 32 fellowships with full tuition reimbursements available, 60 teaching assistantships with full tuition reimbursements available; research assistantships with full tuition reimbursements available, institutionally sponsored loans, scholarships/grants, health care benefits, tuition waivers (full and partial), and unspecified assistantships also available. Financial award applicants required to submit FAFSA. *Faculty research:* English and American literature, women's writing, ethnic and post-colonial literature, critical theory, medievalism. *Unit head:* Director of Graduate Studies, 607-255-7989, Fax: 607-255-6661. *Application contact:* Graduate Field Assistant, 607-255-7989, Fax: 607-255-6661, E-mail: english_grad@cornell.edu.

Eastern Michigan University, Graduate School, College of Arts and Sciences, Department of African-American Studies, Ypsilanti, MI 48197. Offers Graduate Certificate. *Faculty:* 4 full-time (0 women). *Students:* Average age 35. In 2007, 2 degrees awarded. Application fee: $35. *Expenses:* Tuition, state resident: full-time $8,952; part-time $373 per credit hour. Tuition, nonresident: full-time $17,634; part-time $735 per credit hour. Required fees: $896; $34 per credit hour. Tuition and fees vary according to course level, degree level and program. *Unit head:* Dr. Victor Okafor, Interim Department Head, 734-487-3460, Fax: 734-487-6891, E-mail: victor.okafor@emich.edu. *Application contact:* Dr. Robert Perry, Graduate Advisor, 734-487-3460, Fax: 734-487-6891, E-mail: robert.perry@emich.edu.

Florida Agricultural and Mechanical University, Division of Graduate Studies, Research, and Continuing Education, College of Arts and Sciences, Division of History and Political Sciences, Program in Applied Social Science, Tallahassee, FL 32307-3200. Offers African American history (MASS); criminal justice (MASS); economics (MASS); history (MASS); political science (MASS); public administration (MASS); public management (MASS); social work (MASS); sociology (MASS). Part-time programs available. *Degree requirements:* For master's, thesis optional. *Entrance requirements:* For master's, GRE General Test, minimum GPA of 3.0. *Faculty research:* Southern history, black history, election trends, presidential history.

Harvard University, Graduate School of Arts and Sciences, Department of African and African American Studies, Cambridge, MA 02138. Offers PhD. *Expenses:* Tuition: Full-time $31,456. Full-time tuition and fees vary according to program and student level.

Indiana University Bloomington, University Graduate School, College of Arts and Sciences, Department of African American and African Diaspora Studies, Bloomington, IN 47405-7000. Offers MA. Part-time programs available. *Faculty:* 3 full-time (1 woman). *Students:* 15 full-time (9 women), 5 part-time; includes 13 minority (all African Americans), 4 international. Average age 30. 16 applicants, 69% accepted, 6 enrolled. In 2007, 3 degrees awarded. *Entrance requirements:* For master's, GRE, minimum GPA of 3.0. Additional exam requirements/recommendations for international students: Required—TOEFL. *Application deadline:* For fall admission, 1/15 priority date for domestic students, 12/15 for international students; for spring admission, 9/1 for domestic and international students. Applications are processed on a rolling basis. Application fee: $50 ($60 for international students). Electronic applications accepted. *Financial support:* Fellowships with tuition reimbursements, research assistantships with tuition reimbursements, teaching assistantships with tuition reimbursements available. *Unit head:* Dr. Valerie Grim, Chair, 812-855-3875. *Application contact:* Yunika Jackson, Department Secretary, 812-855-3875, E-mail: ytjackso@indiana.edu.

Michigan State University, The Graduate School, College of Arts and Letters, Program in African-American and African Studies, East Lansing, MI 48824. Offers MA, PhD. *Entrance requirements:* Additional exam requirements/recommendations for international students: Required—TOEFL. Electronic applications accepted. *Expenses:* Tuition, state resident: part-time $379 per credit hour. Tuition, nonresident: part-time $800 per credit hour. Tuition and fees vary according to program. *Faculty research:* Black American and diasporic studies, comparative communities of color.

Morgan State University, School of Graduate Studies, College of Liberal Arts, Department of History and Geography, Baltimore, MD 21251. Offers African-American studies (MA); history (MA, PhD). Part-time and evening/weekend programs available. *Faculty:* 8 full-time. *Students:* 34 (16 women); includes 30 minority (all African Americans) 20 applicants, 75% accepted. *Degree requirements:* For master's, comprehensive exam, thesis; for doctorate, comprehensive exam, thesis/dissertation. *Entrance requirements:* For master's, minimum GPA of 2.5; for doctorate, GRE or MAT. Additional exam requirements/recommendations for international students: Required—TOEFL (minimum score 550 paper-based; 213 computer-based). *Application deadline:* For fall admission, 2/1 priority date for domestic students; for spring admission, 10/1 priority date for domestic students. Applications are processed on a rolling basis. Application fee: $0. *Financial support:* In 2007–08, 2 fellowships were awarded; research assistantships. Financial award application deadline: 2/1. *Faculty research:* Women's history, African diaspora history, urban history. *Unit head:* Dr. Annette Palmer, Chair, 443-885-3190, E-mail: annette.palmer@morgan.edu. *Application contact:* Dr. Mark Garrison, Associate Dean, 443-885-3185, Fax: 443-885-8226, E-mail: mark.garrison@morgan.edu.

North Carolina Agricultural and Technical State University, Graduate School, College of Arts and Sciences, Department of English, Program in English and Afro-American Literature, Greensboro, NC 27411. Offers MA. Part-time and evening/weekend programs available. *Degree requirements:* For master's, comprehensive exam, qualifying exam. *Entrance requirements:* For master's, GRE General Test, minimum GPA of 3.0.

The Ohio State University, Graduate School, College of Humanities, Department of African-American and African Studies, Columbus, OH 43210. Offers MA. *Faculty:* 18. *Students:* 15 full-time (13 women), 4 part-time (3 women); includes 15 minority (all African Americans), 1 international. Average age 26. In 2007, 6 degrees awarded. *Degree requirements:* For master's, comprehensive exam, internship or thesis. *Entrance requirements:* For master's, GRE General Test. Additional exam requirements/recommendations for international students: Required—TOEFL (minimum score 600 paper-based; 250 computer-based). *Application deadline:* For fall admission, 8/15 priority date for domestic students, 7/1 priority date for international students; for winter admission, 12/1 priority date for domestic students, 11/1 priority date for international students; for spring admission, 3/1 priority date for domestic students, 2/1 priority date for international students. Applications are processed on a rolling basis. Application fee: $40 ($50 for international students). Electronic applications accepted. *Financial support:* In 2007–08, 9 teaching assistantships were awarded; fellowships, research assistantships, Federal Work-Study, institutionally sponsored loans, and unspecified assistantships also available. Support available to part-time students. *Unit head:* Isaac J. Mowoe, Graduate Studies Committee Chair, 614-292-3700, Fax: 614-292-2293, E-mail: mowoe.2@osu.edu. *Application contact:* 614-292-9444, Fax: 614-292-3895, E-mail: domestic.grad@osu.edu.

Rutgers, The State University of New Jersey, New Brunswick, Graduate School, Program in History, New Brunswick, NJ 08901-1281. Offers African-American history (PhD); early American history (PhD); early modern European history (PhD); east Asian history (PhD); global and comparative history (PhD); history (PhD); history of diplomacy and foreign relations (PhD); history of technology, environment and health (PhD); history of the Atlantic cultures and African diaspora (PhD); Latin American history (PhD); medieval history (PhD); modern European history (PhD); nineteenth and twentieth century American history (PhD); women's and gender history (PhD). *Degree requirements:* For doctorate, thesis/dissertation. *Entrance requirements:* For doctorate, GRE General Test, sample of written work. Electronic applications accepted. *Faculty research:* American history, European history, Afro-American history, women's history, Latin American history.

Syracuse University, Graduate School, College of Arts and Sciences, Department of African-American Studies, Program in Pan-African Studies, Syracuse, NY 13244. Offers MA. *Students:* 14 full-time (8 women); includes 9 minority (all African Americans), 5 international. 13 applicants, 69% accepted, 8 enrolled. In 2007, 1 degree awarded. *Entrance requirements:* For master's, GRE General Test. Additional exam requirements/recommendations for international students: Required—TOEFL. *Application deadline:* For fall admission, 1/10 priority date for domestic students. Application fee: $75. Electronic applications accepted. *Expenses:* Tuition: Full-time $18,216; part-time $1,012 per credit. Required fees: $980. Tuition and fees vary according to program. *Financial support:* Fellowships with tuition reimbursements available. *Unit head:* Dr. Winston Grady Willis, Director, 315-443-3005. *Application contact:* Aja Brown, Information Contact, 315-443-3097, E-mail: aabrow02@syr.edu.

Temple University, Graduate School, College of Liberal Arts, Department of African American Studies, Philadelphia, PA 19122-6096. Offers MA, PhD. Terminal master's awarded for partial completion of doctoral program. *Degree requirements:* For master's, comprehensive exam; for doctorate, one foreign language, thesis/dissertation, oral and written qualifying exams. *Entrance requirements:* For doctorate, MA in African American studies. Additional exam requirements/recommendations for international students: Required—TOEFL (minimum score 550 paper-based; 213 computer-based; 79 iBT). Electronic applications accepted. *Faculty research:* Afrocentric theory; African-American youth; centered drama, literature, and history; comparative analysis; South and West Africa; Nile Valley.

University at Albany, State University of New York, College of Arts and Sciences, Department of Africana Studies, Albany, NY 12222-0001. Offers African studies (MA); Afro-American studies (MA). Part-time and evening/weekend programs available. *Students:* 24 full-time (16 women), 6 part-time (4 women). Average age 27. In 2007, 10 degrees awarded. *Entrance requirements:* Additional exam requirements/recommendations for international students: Required—TOEFL (minimum score 550 paper-based; 213 computer-based). *Application deadline:* For fall admission, 5/15 for international students; for spring admission, 11/1 for international students. Applications are processed on a rolling basis. Application fee: $75. Electronic applications accepted. *Expenses:* Tuition, state resident: part-time $576 per credit. Tuition, nonresident: part-time $910 per credit. Tuition and fees vary according to program. *Financial support:* Fellowships, teaching assistantships, Federal Work-Study available. Financial award application deadline: 5/1. *Faculty research:* The black family, Afro-centricity in poetry, black women in U.S. literature, African economic development, African American history. *Unit head:* Dr. Marcia Sutherland, Director, 518-442-4730.

University of California, Berkeley, Graduate Division, College of Letters and Science, Department of African American Studies, Berkeley, CA 94720-1500. Offers PhD. *Faculty:* 4 full-time. *Degree requirements:* For doctorate, one foreign language, thesis/dissertation. *Entrance requirements:* For doctorate, minimum GPA of 3.0, 3 letters of recommendation. Additional exam requirements/recommendations for international students: Required—TOEFL (paper-based 570; computer-based 230) or IELTS (paper-based 7). *Application deadline:* For fall admission, 12/15 for domestic students. Application fee: $70 ($90 for international students). *Financial support:* Fellowships with full tuition reimbursements, research assistantships with partial tuition reimbursements, teaching assistantships with partial tuition reimbursements, unspecified assistantships available. Financial award applicants required to submit FAFSA. *Faculty research:* Black influence on U.S. foreign policy, black intellectuals, ethnic space in urban society, representation in museums of African-Americans and British Americans during slavery. *Unit head:* Prof. Stephen Small, Chair, 510-643-7972, Fax: 510-642-7089, E-mail: small@berkeley.edu. *Application contact:* Margaret B. Wilkerson, Professor, 510-642-7084, E-mail: africam@berkeley.edu.

University of California, Los Angeles, Graduate Division, College of Letters and Science, Program in Afro-American Studies, Los Angeles, CA 90095. Offers MA, MA/JD. *Students:* 25 full-time (14 women); includes 23 minority (all African Americans) Average age 28. 35 applicants, 57% accepted, 12 enrolled. In 2007, 6 degrees awarded. *Degree requirements:* For master's, one foreign language, comprehensive exam or thesis. *Entrance requirements:* For master's, GRE General Test, minimum GPA of 3.0, sample of written work. *Application deadline:* For fall admission, 12/15 for domestic students. Application fee: $60. Electronic applications accepted. *Expenses:* Tuition, nonresident: full-time $5,728. Required fees: $8,966. Full-time tuition and fees vary according to program and student level. *Financial support:* In 2007–08, 13 fellowships with full and partial tuition reimbursements, 2 teaching assistantships with full and partial tuition reimbursements were awarded; research assistantships with full and partial tuition reimbursements, Federal Work-Study, institutionally sponsored loans, and tuition waivers (full and partial) also available. Financial award application deadline: 3/1; financial award applicants required to submit FAFSA. *Unit head:* Brenda Stevenson, Chair, 310-825-7403. *Application contact:* Departmental Office, 310-825-9821, E-mail: idpstaff@bunche.ucla.edu.

The University of Iowa, Graduate College, College of Liberal Arts and Sciences, Program in African American World Studies, Iowa City, IA 52242-1316. Offers MA. In 2007, 1 degree awarded. *Degree requirements:* For master's, thesis optional, exam. *Entrance requirements:* For master's, GRE General Test, minimum GPA of 3.0. Additional exam requirements/recommendations for international students: Required—TOEFL (minimum score 550 paper-based; 213 computer-based; 81 iBT). Application fee: $60 ($85 for international students). Electronic applications accepted. *Expenses:* Tuition, state resident: part-time $349 per hour. Tuition, nonresident: part-time $349 per hour. Tuition and fees vary according to course load and program. *Financial support:* Fellowships, research assistantships with partial tuition reimbursements, teaching assistantships with partial tuition reimbursements available. Financial award applicants required to submit FAFSA. *Unit head:* Richard Turner, Coordinator, 319-335-0285, Fax: 319-384-3293.

University of Massachusetts Amherst, Graduate School, College of Humanities and Fine Arts, Department of Afro-American Studies, Amherst, MA 01003. Offers MA, PhD. *Faculty:* 11 full-time (3 women). *Students:* 25 full-time (10 women), 2 part-time (both women); includes 20 minority (18 African Americans, 1 Asian American or Pacific Islander, 1 Hispanic American), 1 international. Average age 32. 49 applicants, 16% accepted, 3 enrolled. In 2007, 8 master's, 8 doctorates awarded. *Degree requirements:* For master's, thesis or alternative; for doctorate, thesis/dissertation. *Entrance requirements:* For doctorate, writing sample. Additional exam requirements/recommendations for international students: Required—TOEFL (minimum score 530 paper-based; 197 computer-based). *Application deadline:* For fall admission, 1/15 for domestic and international students. Applications are processed on a rolling basis. Application fee: $50 ($65 for international students). Electronic applications accepted. *Expenses:* Tuition, state resident: full-time $2,640; part-time $110 per credit. Tuition, nonresident: full-time $9,936; part-time $414 per credit. Required fees: $7,455. One-time fee: $332. Tuition and fees vary according to course load, campus/location, program and reciprocity agreements. *Financial support:* In 2007–08, 12 research assistantships with full tuition reimbursements (averaging $10,002 per year), 1 teaching assistantship with full tuition reimbursement (averaging $11,510 per year) were awarded; fellowships with full tuition reimbursements, career-related internships or fieldwork, Federal Work-Study, scholarships/grants, traineeships, and unspecified assistantships also available. Support available to part-time students. Financial award application deadline: 2/1. *Unit head:* Dr. Amilcar Shabazz, Chair, 413-545-2751, Fax: 413-545-0628.

University of Wisconsin–Madison, Graduate School, College of Letters and Science, Department of Afro-American Studies, Madison, WI 53706-1380. Offers MA. *Degree requirements:* For master's, thesis or alternative. *Entrance requirements:* For master's, bachelor's degree in related field, minimum GPA of 3.0. Additional exam requirements/recommendations for international students: Required—TOEFL. Electronic applications accepted. *Faculty research:* Afro American art, history, music, literature, and culture.

West Virginia University, Eberly College of Arts and Sciences, Department of History, Morgantown, WV 26506. Offers African history (MA, PhD); African-American history (MA, PhD); American history (MA, PhD); Appalachian/regional history (MA, PhD); East Asian history (MA, PhD); European history (MA, PhD); history of science and technology (MA, PhD); Latin American history (MA). Part-time programs available. *Faculty:* 19 full-time (5 women), 12 part-time/adjunct (4 women). *Students:* 43 full-time (17 women), 30 part-time (11 women); includes 5 minority (1 African American, 1 American Indian/Alaska Native, 2 Asian Americans or Pacific Islanders, 1 Hispanic American), 7 international. Average age 33. 70 applicants, 59% accepted, 17 enrolled. In 2007, 8 master's, 3 doctorates awarded. *Median time to degree:* Of those who began their doctoral program in fall 1999, 75% received their degree in 8 years or less. *Degree requirements:* For master's, one foreign language, thesis (for some programs), oral exam, thesis defense; for doctorate, one foreign language, comprehensive exam, thesis/dissertation, dissertation defense. *Entrance requirements:* For master's, GRE General Test, minimum GPA of 3.0; for doctorate, GRE General Test. Additional exam requirements/recommendations for international students: Required—TOEFL (minimum score 550 paper-based), IELTS (minimum score 7). *Application deadline:* For fall admission, 12/31 for domestic students; for spring admission, 10/1 for domestic students. Applications are processed on a rolling basis. Application fee: $45. Electronic applications accepted. *Expenses:* Tuition, state resident: full-time $5,196; part-time $292 per credit hour. Tuition, nonresident: full-time $15,064; part-time $840 per credit hour. Tuition and fees vary according to program. *Financial support:* In 2007–08, 60 students received support, including 5 fellowships with full tuition reimbursements available (averaging $3,000 per year), 1 research assistantship with full tuition reimbursement available (averaging $7,200 per year), 8 teaching assistantships with full tuition reimbursements available (averaging $12,000 per year); career-related internships or fieldwork, Federal Work-Study, institutionally sponsored loans, health care benefits, tuition waivers (full and partial), and graduate administrative assistantships also available. Financial award application deadline: 12/31; financial award applicants required to submit FAFSA. *Faculty research:* U.S., Appalachia, modern Europe, Africa, colonial and post-colonial societies. Total annual research expenditures: $93,327. *Unit head:* Dr. Steven M. Zdatny, Chair, 304-293-2421 Ext. 5241, Fax: 304-293-3616, E-mail: steve.zdatny@mail.wvu.edu. *Application contact:* Dr. Greg A. Good, Director of Graduate Studies, 304-293-2421 Ext. 5247, Fax: 304-293-3616, E-mail: greg.good@mail.wvu.edu.

Yale University, Graduate School of Arts and Sciences, Interdisciplinary Program in African-American Studies, New Haven, CT 06520. Offers MA, PhD. *Degree requirements:* For master's, one foreign language, thesis. *Entrance requirements:* For master's and doctorate, GRE General Test.

African Studies

Boston University, Graduate School of Arts and Sciences, Department of International Relations, Boston, MA 02215. Offers African studies (Certificate); international relations (MA); international relations and environmental policy management (MA); international relations and international communication (MA); JD/MA; MBA/MA. *Students:* 60 full-time (33 women), 28 part-time (19 women); includes 12 minority (4 African Americans, 6 Asian Americans or Pacific Islanders, 2 Hispanic Americans), 13 international. Average age 29. 337 applicants, 64% accepted, 48 enrolled. In 2007, 36 degrees awarded. *Degree requirements:* For master's, one foreign language, comprehensive exam, thesis. *Entrance requirements:* For master's, GRE General Test, 3 letters of recommendation; for Certificate, GRE General Test. Additional exam requirements/recommendations for international students: Required—TOEFL (minimum score 600 paper-based; 250 computer-based). *Application deadline:* For fall admission, 4/15 for domestic and international students; for spring admission, 10/15 for domestic and international students. Application fee: $70. *Expenses:* Tuition: Full-time $34,930; part-time $1,092 per credit. Tuition and fees vary according to class time, course level and program. *Financial support:* In 2007–08, 17 students received support. Federal Work-Study, scholarships/grants, and unspecified assistantships available. Support available to part-time students. Financial award application deadline: 1/15; financial award applicants required to submit FAFSA. *Unit head:* Dr. Erik Goldstein, Chairman, 617-353-9280, Fax: 617-353-9290, E-mail: goldstee@bu.edu. *Application contact:* Michael Williams, Graduate Program Administrator, 617-353-9349, Fax: 617-353-9290, E-mail: mawillia@bu.edu.

Claremont Graduate University, Graduate Programs, School of Arts and Humanities, Department of History, Claremont, CA 91711-6160. Offers Africana history (Certificate); American studies and U.S. history (MA, PhD); archival studies (MA, PhD); early modern studies (MA, PhD); European studies (MA, PhD); oral history (MA, PhD); MBA/MA; MBA/PhD. *Faculty:* 3 full-time (2 women), 1 part-time/adjunct (0 women). *Students:* 74 full-time (40 women), 8 part-time (3 women); includes 15 minority (1 African American, 2 Asian Americans or Pacific Islanders, 12 Hispanic Americans), 2 international. Average age 37. In 2007, 8 master's, 8 doctorates awarded. *Degree requirements:* For master's, 2 foreign languages, thesis; for doctorate, 2 foreign languages, comprehensive exam, thesis/dissertation. *Entrance requirements:* For master's and doctorate, GRE General Test. *Application deadline:* For fall admission, 2/15 priority date for domestic students. Applications are processed on a rolling basis. Electronic applications accepted. *Expenses:* Tuition: Full-time $31,640; part-time $1,376 per unit. Required fees: $145 per semester. Tuition and fees vary according to course load, degree level and program. *Financial support:* Fellowships, research assistantships, Federal Work-Study and institutionally sponsored loans available. Support available to part-time students. Financial award application deadline: 2/15; financial award applicants required to submit FAFSA. *Faculty research:* Intellectual and social history, cultural studies, gender studies, Western history, Chicano history. *Unit head:* Janet Farrell Brodie, Chair, 909-621-8880, Fax: 909-621-8609, E-mail: janet.brodie@cgu.edu.

Claremont Graduate University, Graduate Programs, School of Educational Studies, Claremont, CA 91711-6160. Offers Africana education (Certificate); education and policy (MA, PhD); higher education/student affairs (MA, PhD); human development (MA, PhD); public school administration (MA, PhD); quantitative evaluation (MA, PhD); special education (MA, PhD); teacher education (MA); teaching and learning (MA, PhD); urban leadership (PhD); MBA/PhD. Part-time programs available. *Faculty:* 17 full-time (11 women), 22 part-time/adjunct (14 women). *Students:* 272 full-time (182 women), 172 part-time (115 women); includes 171 minority (39 African Americans, 1 American Indian/Alaska Native, 38 Asian Americans or Pacific Islanders, 93 Hispanic Americans), 8 international. Average age 37. In 2007, 79 master's, 28 doctorates awarded. Terminal master's awarded for partial completion of doctoral program. *Degree requirements:* For master's, comprehensive exam (for some programs), thesis or alternative; for doctorate, comprehensive exam, thesis/dissertation. *Entrance requirements:* For master's and doctorate, GRE General Test. *Application deadline:* For fall admission, 2/15 priority date for domestic students. Applications are processed on a rolling basis. Electronic applications accepted. *Expenses:* Tuition: Full-time $31,640; part-time $1,376 per unit. Required fees: $145 per semester. Tuition and fees vary according to course load, degree level and program. *Financial support:* Fellowships, research assistantships, Federal Work-Study and institutionally sponsored loans available. Support available to part-time students. Financial award application deadline: 2/15; financial award applicants required to submit FAFSA. *Faculty research:* Education administration, K–12 and higher education, multicultural education, education policy, diversity in higher education, faculty issues. *Unit head:* Barbara Hart, Interim Dean, 909-621-8317, Fax: 909-621-8734, E-mail: barbara.hart@cgu.edu. *Application contact:* Cece Gaddy, Administrative Director, 909-621-8317, Fax: 909-621-8734, E-mail: cece.gaddy@cgu.edu.

Columbia University, School of International and Public Affairs, Institute of African Studies, New York, NY 10027. Offers Certificate. Students must be enrolled in a separate graduate degree program at Columbia University. *Application deadline:* For fall admission, 1/4 priority date for domestic students; for spring admission, 10/1 priority date for domestic students. Application fee: $85. Electronic applications accepted. *Expenses:* Tuition: Part-time $1,452 per credit. Required fees: $152 per term. One-time fee: $75 part-time. Full-time tuition and fees

African Studies

Columbia University (continued)

vary according to course level, course load, degree level and program. *Financial support:* Application deadline: 1/15. *Unit head:* Mamadou Diouf, Director, 212-854-4633, Fax: 212-854-4639. *Application contact:* Matt Clemons, Director of Admissions and Financial Aid, 212-854-6216, Fax: 212-854-3010, E-mail: mc2793@columbia.edu.

Cornell University, Graduate School, Graduate Fields of Arts and Sciences, Field of African and African-American Studies, Ithaca, NY 14853-0001. Offers African studies (MPS); African-American studies (MPS). *Faculty:* 13 full-time (5 women). *Students:* 14 full-time (7 women); includes 11 minority (all African Americans) Average age 26. 39 applicants, 23% accepted, 7 enrolled. In 2007, 6 degrees awarded. *Degree requirements:* For master's, thesis. *Entrance requirements:* For master's, GRE General Test (recommended), 3 letters of recommendation. Additional exam requirements/recommendations for international students: Required—TOEFL (minimum score 550 paper-based; 213 computer-based; 77 iBT). *Application deadline:* For fall admission, 1/30 for domestic students. Application fee: $70. Electronic applications accepted. *Financial support:* In 2007–08, 14 students received support, including 7 fellowships with full tuition reimbursements available, 7 research assistantships; teaching assistantships with full tuition reimbursements available, institutionally sponsored loans, scholarships/grants, health care benefits, tuition waivers (full and partial), and unspecified assistantships also available. Financial award applicants required to submit FAFSA. *Faculty research:* African-American literature, art, cinema and theater; African-American politics and public policy; African history, politics and art; Caribbean politics and Africana Diaspora. *Unit head:* Director of Graduate Studies, 607-255-4625, Fax: 607-255-0784. *Application contact:* Graduate Field Assistant, 607-255-4625, Fax: 607-255-0784, E-mail: spt1@cornell.edu.

Cornell University, Graduate School, Graduate Fields of Arts and Sciences, Field of History, Ithaca, NY 14853-0001. Offers African history (MA, PhD); American history (MA, PhD); ancient history (MA, PhD); early modern European history (MA, PhD); English history (MA, PhD); French history (MA, PhD); German history (MA, PhD); history of science (MA, PhD); Latin American history (MA, PhD); medieval Chinese history (MA, PhD); medieval history (MA, PhD); modern Chinese history (MA, PhD); modern European history (MA, PhD); modern Japanese history (MA, PhD); premodern Islamic history (MA, PhD); premodern Japanese history (MA, PhD); Renaissance history (MA, PhD); Russian history (MA, PhD); Southeast Asian history (MA, PhD). *Faculty:* 56 full-time (14 women). *Students:* 63 full-time (29 women); includes 11 minority (6 African Americans, 2 Asian Americans or Pacific Islanders, 3 Hispanic Americans), 20 international. Average age 31. 201 applicants, 6% accepted, 10 enrolled. In 2007, 11 master's, 11 doctorates awarded. Terminal master's awarded for partial completion of doctoral program. *Degree requirements:* For master's, thesis; for doctorate, 2 foreign languages, comprehensive exam, thesis/dissertation, 1 year of teaching experience. *Entrance requirements:* For master's and doctorate, GRE General Test, writing sample, 3 letters of recommendation. Additional exam requirements/recommendations for international students: Required—TOEFL (minimum score 550 paper-based; 213 computer-based; 77 iBT). *Application deadline:* For fall admission, 1/15 for domestic students. Application fee: $70. Electronic applications accepted. *Financial support:* In 2007–08, 54 students received support, including 26 fellowships with full tuition reimbursements available, 28 teaching assistantships with full tuition reimbursements available; research assistantships with full tuition reimbursements available, institutionally sponsored loans, scholarships/grants, health care benefits, tuition waivers (full and partial), and unspecified assistantships also available. Financial award applicants required to submit FAFSA. *Unit head:* Director of Graduate Studies, 607-255-6738, Fax: 607-255-0469. *Application contact:* Graduate Field Assistant, 607-255-6738, Fax: 607-255-0469, E-mail: history_grad_info@cornell.edu.

Florida International University, College of Arts and Sciences, Program in African-New World Studies, Miami, FL 33199. Offers MA. Part-time and evening/weekend programs available. *Faculty:* 3 full-time (1 woman). *Students:* 8 full-time (5 women), 6 part-time (5 women); includes 13 minority (10 African Americans, 1 Asian American or Pacific Islander, 2 Hispanic Americans). Average age 28. 6 applicants, 100% accepted, 4 enrolled. In 2007, 1 degree awarded. *Degree requirements:* For master's, one foreign language, thesis optional. *Entrance requirements:* For master's, GRE General Test, minimum GPA of 3.0, letters of recommendation. Additional exam requirements/recommendations for international students: Required—TOEFL. *Application deadline:* For fall admission, 6/1 for domestic students, 4/1 for international students; for spring admission, 10/1 for domestic students, 9/1 for international students. Application fee: $30. *Expenses:* Tuition, state resident: full-time $6,106. Tuition, nonresident: full-time $15,528. Required fees: $284. *Financial support:* Teaching assistantships available. *Unit head:* Dr. Akin Ogundiran, Director, 305-919-5529, Fax: 305-919-5267, E-mail: akin.ogundiran@fiu.edu.

Harvard University, Graduate School of Arts and Sciences, Department of African and African American Studies, Cambridge, MA 02138. Offers PhD. *Expenses:* Tuition: Full-time $31,456. Full-time tuition and fees vary according to program and student level.

Howard University, Graduate School, Department of African Studies, Washington, DC 20059-0002. Offers MA, PhD. Part-time programs available. *Faculty:* 9 full-time (2 women), 1 part-time/adjunct (0 women). *Students:* 48 full-time (29 women), 2 part-time (both women); includes 47 minority (all African Americans) Average age 26. In 2007, 5 master's, 2 doctorates awarded. *Median time to degree:* Of those who began their doctoral program in fall 1999, 70% received their degree in 8 years or less. *Degree requirements:* For master's, one foreign language, comprehensive exam, thesis, internship; for doctorate, 2 foreign languages, comprehensive exam, thesis/dissertation, field research for some. *Entrance requirements:* For master's, GRE General Test, minimum GPA of 3.0; for doctorate, GRE General Test, minimum GPA of 3.5. *Application deadline:* For fall admission, 4/1 for domestic and international students; for spring admission, 11/1 for domestic and international students. Applications are processed on a rolling basis. Application fee: $45. Electronic applications accepted. *Expenses:* Tuition: Full-time $16,175; part-time $899 per credit hour. Required fees: $805. *Financial support:* In 2007–08, 2 students received support, including 6 fellowships with full and partial tuition reimbursements available (averaging $16,000 per year), 17 research assistantships with full and partial tuition reimbursements available (averaging $16,000 per year); teaching assistantships with full and partial tuition reimbursements available, career-related internships or fieldwork, Federal Work-Study, institutionally sponsored loans, scholarships/grants, tuition waivers (full and partial), and unspecified assistantships also available. Support available to part-time students. Financial award application deadline: 4/1. *Faculty research:* African literature and film, economics of Africa, international relations, public policy analysis, gender. *Unit head:* Dr. Mbye Cham, Chair, 202-238-2328, Fax: 202-238-2326, E-mail: mcham@howard.edu.

Indiana University Bloomington, University Graduate School, College of Arts and Sciences, African Studies Program, Bloomington, IN 47405-7000. Offers MA. *Students:* 1 (woman) full-time, 1 part-time; includes 1 minority (African American) Average age 43. 8 applicants, 38% accepted, 1 enrolled.Application fee: $50 ($60 for international students). *Unit head:* Dr. Samuel Obeng, Director, 812-855-8284, E-mail: sobeng@indiana.edu. *Application contact:* Sue Hanson, Graduate Secretary, 812-855-8284, E-mail: shanson@indiana.edu.

The Johns Hopkins University, Paul H. Nitze School of Advanced International Studies, Washington, DC 20036. Offers international development (Certificate); international public policy (MIPP); international relations (MA, PhD), including African studies (MA), American foreign policy (MA), Asian studies (MA), Canadian studies (MA), conflict management (MA), European studies (MA), global theory and history (MA), international development (MA), international law, and organizations (MA), international policy (MA), international relations (general) (MA), Latin American studies (MA), Middle East studies (MA), Russian and Eurasian studies (MA), strategic studies (MA); international studies (Certificate); JD/MA; MBA/MA; MHS/MA. *Faculty:* 66 full-time (22 women), 158 part-time/adjunct (54 women). *Students:* 578 full-time (256 women), 46 part-time (16 women); includes 85 minority (18 African Americans, 1 American Indian/Alaska Native, 51 Asian Americans or Pacific Islanders, 15 Hispanic Americans), 193 international. Average age 27. In 2007, 359 master's, 13 doctorates awarded. Terminal master's awarded for partial completion of doctoral program. *Degree requirements:* For master's, one foreign language, 16 non-language courses (8 for MIPP), 2 core examinations, comprehensive oral exam, paper (for some programs); for doctorate, 2 foreign languages, thesis/dissertation, 3 comprehensive exams, defense. *Entrance requirements:* For master's, GMAT or GRE General Test, previous course work in economics, foreign language, undergraduate degree; for doctorate, GRE General Test, master's degree. Additional exam requirements/recommendations for international students: Required—TOEFL (minimum paper-based score of 600, computer-based 250, iBT 100) or IELTS (minimum 7.0). *Application deadline:* For fall admission, 1/7 for domestic students. Application fee: $80. Electronic applications accepted. *Expenses: Contact institution. Financial support:* In 2007–08, 350 students received support, including fellowships (averaging $7,500 per year); career-related internships or fieldwork, Federal Work-Study, and scholarships/grants also available. Financial award application deadline: 2/15; financial award applicants required to submit FAFSA. *Faculty research:* Regional studies and functional fields of international relations, international economics, conflict management, global theory and history, international law and organizations, international policy, strategic studies. *Unit head:* Tara Campbell, Associate Director of Admissions, 202-663-5700, Fax: 202-663-7788. *Application contact:* Dr. Belinda A. Yeomans, Director of Admissions, 202-663-5700, Fax: 202-663-7788, E-mail: admissions.sais@jhu.edu.

Michigan State University, The Graduate School, College of Arts and Letters, Program in African-American and African Studies, East Lansing, MI 48824. Offers MA, PhD. *Entrance requirements:* Additional exam requirements/recommendations for international students: Required—TOEFL. Electronic applications accepted. *Expenses:* Tuition, state resident: part-time $379 per credit hour. Tuition, nonresident: part-time $800 per credit hour. Tuition and fees vary according to program. *Faculty research:* Black American and diasporic studies, comparative communities of color.

New York University, Graduate School of Arts and Science, Department of History, New York, NY 10012-1019. Offers African diaspora (PhD); African history (PhD); archival management and historical editing (Advanced Certificate); Atlantic history (PhD); French studies/history (PhD); Hebrew and Judaic studies/history (PhD); history (MA, PhD), including Europe (PhD), Latin American and the Caribbean (PhD), United States (PhD), women's history (MA); Middle Eastern history (MA); Middle Eastern studies/history (PhD); public history (Advanced Certificate); world history (MA); JD/MA; MA/Advanced Certificate. Part-time programs available. *Faculty:* 43 full-time (19 women), 18 part-time/adjunct. *Students:* 106 full-time (68 women), 48 part-time (34 women); includes 29 minority (18 African Americans, 4 Asian Americans or Pacific Islanders, 7 Hispanic Americans), 26 international. Average age 31. 413 applicants, 19% accepted, 40 enrolled. In 2007, 17 master's, 7 doctorates awarded. Terminal master's awarded for partial completion of doctoral program. *Degree requirements:* For master's, seminar paper; for doctorate, one foreign language, thesis/dissertation, oral and written exams; for Advanced Certificate, internship. *Entrance requirements:* For master's, GRE General Test, minimum GPA of 3.0, writing sample; for doctorate, GRE. Additional exam requirements/recommendations for international students: Required—TOEFL. *Application deadline:* For fall admission, 12/12 for domestic students. Application fee: $85. *Financial support:* Fellowships with tuition reimbursements, research assistantships, teaching assistantships with tuition reimbursements, career-related internships or fieldwork, Federal Work-Study, institutionally sponsored loans, scholarships/grants, health care benefits, and unspecified assistantships available. Financial award application deadline: 12/12; financial award applicants required to submit FAFSA. *Faculty research:* African, East Asian, Medieval, early modern, and modern European history; U.S. history; African and African diaspora; Latin American history; Atlantic World. *Unit head:* Michael Gomez, Chair, 212-998-8600, Fax: 212-995-4017, E-mail: history.dept@nyu.edu. *Application contact:* Gregory Grandin, Director of Graduate Studies, 212-998-8600, Fax: 212-995-4017, E-mail: history.dept@nyu.edu.

New York University, Graduate School of Arts and Science, Program in Africana Studies, New York, NY 10012-1019. Offers MA. *Faculty:* 3 full-time (1 woman), 3 part-time/adjunct. *Students:* 9 full-time (7 women), 2 part-time (both women); includes 6 minority (all African Americans), 2 international. Average age 29. 21 applicants, 71% accepted, 6 enrolled. In 2007, 12 degrees awarded. *Degree requirements:* For master's, thesis or alternative. *Entrance requirements:* For master's, GRE, sample of written work. Additional exam requirements/recommendations for international students: Required—TOEFL. *Application deadline:* For fall admission, 1/4 priority date for domestic students. Application fee: $85. *Financial support:* Fellowships with tuition reimbursements, Federal Work-Study and institutionally sponsored loans available. Financial award application deadline: 1/4; financial award applicants required to submit FAFSA. *Faculty research:* Pan-Africanism, black urban studies, film and literature of black diaspora, cultural politics and theory, politics of identity. *Unit head:* Swam Amkpa, Director, 212-998-2130, Fax: 212-995-4109, E-mail: africana@nyu.edu. *Application contact:* Adam Green, Director of Graduate Studies, 212-998-2130, Fax: 212-995-4109, E-mail: africana@nyu.edu.

New York University, Graduate School of Arts and Science, Program in Museum Studies, New York, NY 10012-1019. Offers museum studies (MA, Advanced Certificate), including Africana studies (MA), Hebrew and Judaic studies (MA), Latin American and Caribbean studies (MA), Near Eastern studies (MA). Part-time and evening/weekend programs available. *Faculty:* 4 full-time (1 woman), 6 part-time/adjunct. *Students:* 55 full-time (46 women), 26 part-time (23 women); includes 11 minority (1 American Indian/Alaska Native, 5 Asian Americans or Pacific Islanders, 5 Hispanic Americans), 19 international. Average age 28. 141 applicants, 66% accepted, 35 enrolled. In 2007, 25 master's awarded. *Entrance requirements:* For degree, master's or PhD. *Application deadline:* For fall admission, 2/1 for domestic students; for spring admission, 11/1 for domestic students. Application fee: $85. *Financial support:* Application deadline: 2/1. *Faculty research:* Modern and contemporary art, history of museums and exhibitions, conservation of cultural materials, museum anthropology, ethnography. *Unit head:* Bruce Altshuler, Director, 212-998-8080, Fax: 212-995-4185, E-mail: museum.studies@nyu.edu. *Application contact:* Tatiana Kamorina, Information Contact, 212-998-8080, Fax: 212-995-4185, E-mail: museum.studies@nyu.edu.

Northwestern University, The Graduate School, Program of African Studies, Evanston, IL 60208. Offers Certificate. *Degree requirements:* For Certificate, one foreign language. *Faculty research:* Collapsing states in Africa, HIV/AIDS in Africa, Islam in Africa, African philosophy.

The Ohio State University, Graduate School, College of Humanities, Department of African-American and African Studies, Columbus, OH 43210. Offers MA. *Faculty:* 18. *Students:* 15 full-time (13 women), 4 part-time (3 women); includes 15 minority (all African Americans), 1 international. Average age 26. In 2007, 6 degrees awarded. *Degree requirements:* For master's, comprehensive exam, internship or thesis. *Entrance requirements:* For master's, GRE General Test. Additional exam requirements/recommendations for international students: Required—TOEFL (minimum score 600 paper-based; 250 computer-based). *Application deadline:* For fall admission, 8/15 priority date for domestic students, 7/1 priority date for international students; for winter admission, 12/1 priority date for domestic students, 11/1 priority date for international students; for spring admission, 3/1 priority date for domestic students, 2/1 priority date for international students. Applications are processed on a rolling basis. Application fee: $40 ($50 for international students). Electronic applications accepted. *Financial support:* In 2007–08, 9 teaching assistantships were awarded; fellowships, research assistantships, Federal Work-Study, institutionally sponsored loans, and unspecified assistantships also available. Support available to part-time students. *Unit head:* Isaac J. Mowoe, Graduate Studies Committee Chair, 614-292-3700, Fax: 614-292-2293, E-mail: mowoe.2@osu.edu. *Application contact:* 614-292-9444, Fax: 614-292-3895, E-mail: domestic.grad@osu.edu.

Ohio University, Graduate College, Center for International Studies, Program in African Studies, Athens, OH 45701-2979. Offers MA. Part-time programs available. *Faculty:* 21 full-time (7 women). *Students:* 24 full-time (13 women); includes 3 minority (all African Americans), 18 international. 88 applicants, 58% accepted, 19 enrolled. In 2007, 23 degrees awarded. *Degree requirements:* For master's, one foreign language, thesis optional. *Entrance* *requirements:* For master's, GRE, minimum GPA of 3.0. Additional exam requirements/recommendations for international students: Required—TOEFL (minimum score 550 paper-based; 213 computer-based). *Application deadline:* For fall admission, 1/1 for domestic and international students. Application fee: $50 ($55 for international students). *Financial support:* In 2007–08, 5 fellowships with tuition reimbursements (averaging $11,000 per year), 12 research assistantships with tuition reimbursements (averaging $10,000 per year), 1 teaching assistantship with tuition reimbursement (averaging $10,000 per year) were awarded; Federal Work-Study, institutionally sponsored loans, scholarships/grants, and tuition waivers (full) also available. Financial award application deadline: 1/1. *Faculty research:* African social sciences and the humanities. Total annual research expenditures: $110,000. *Unit head:* Dr. William Stephen Howard, Director, 740-593-1834, Fax: 740-593-1837, E-mail: showard1@ohio.edu. *Application contact:* Joan Kraynanski, Administrative Assistant, 740-593-1840, Fax: 740-593-1837, E-mail: kraynans@ohio.edu.

Rutgers, The State University of New Jersey, New Brunswick, Graduate School, Program in History, New Brunswick, NJ 08901-1281. Offers African-American history (PhD); early American history (PhD); early modern European history (PhD); east Asian history (PhD); global and comparative history (PhD); history (PhD); history of diplomacy and foreign relations (PhD); history of technology, environment and health (PhD); history of the Atlantic cultures and African diaspora (PhD); Latin American history (PhD); medieval history (PhD); modern European history (PhD); nineteenth and twentieth century American history (PhD); women's and gender history (PhD). *Degree requirements:* For doctorate, thesis/dissertation. *Entrance requirements:* For doctorate, GRE General Test, sample of written work. Electronic applications accepted. *Faculty research:* American history, European history, Afro-American history, women's history, Latin American history.

St. John's University, St. John's College of Liberal Arts and Sciences, Institute of Asian Studies, Queens, NY 11439. Offers Asian and African cultural studies (Adv C); Asian studies (Adv C); Chinese studies (MA, Adv C); East Asian culture studies (Adv C); East Asian studies (MA). Part-time and evening/weekend programs available. *Faculty:* 2 full-time (1 woman), 11 part-time/adjunct (9 women). *Students:* 6 full-time (2 women), 5 part-time (all women); includes 3 minority (all Asian Americans or Pacific Islanders), 6 international. Average age 30. 19 applicants, 84% accepted, 4 enrolled. In 2007, 14 degrees awarded. *Degree requirements:* For master's, one foreign language, comprehensive exam, thesis optional. *Entrance requirements:* For master's, 18 hours of course work in the field, minimum GPA of 3.0. Additional exam requirements/recommendations for international students: Required—TOEFL (minimum score 500 paper-based; 173 computer-based; 61 iBT), IELTS (minimum score 6). *Application deadline:* For fall admission, 5/1 priority date for domestic and international students; for spring admission, 11/1 priority date for domestic and international students. Applications are processed on a rolling basis. Application fee: $40. Electronic applications accepted. *Financial support:* Research assistantships, scholarships/grants available. Support available to part-time students. Financial award application deadline: 3/1; financial award applicants required to submit FAFSA. *Faculty research:* East Asian philosophy and religion, Chinese language and literature, Japanese language, modern Japan, Chinese art and history. *Unit head:* Dr. Bernadette Li, Chair, 718-990-1657, E-mail: lib@stjohns.edu. *Application contact:* Beth Evans, Associate Vice President and Executive Director, Enrollment Management, 718-990-6999, Fax: 718-990-5686, E-mail: gradhelp@stjohns.edu.

Stony Brook University, State University of New York, Graduate School, College of Arts and Sciences, Department of Africana Studies, Stony Brook, NY 11794. Offers MA. *Faculty:* 10 full-time, 21 part-time/adjunct. *Degree requirements:* For master's, research thesis project, research seminar. *Entrance requirements:* For master's, GRE General Test, minimum GPA of 3.0, 3 letters of recommendation. *Unit head:* Floris Cash, Chairperson, 631-632-7472. *Application contact:* Anthony Hurley, Graduate Program Director, 631-632-1366.

See Close-Up on page 811.

Syracuse University, Graduate School, College of Arts and Sciences, Department of African-American Studies, Program in Pan-African Studies, Syracuse, NY 13244. Offers MA. *Students:* 14 full-time (8 women); includes 9 minority (all African Americans), 5 international. 13 applicants, 69% accepted, 8 enrolled. In 2007, 1 degree awarded. *Entrance requirements:* For master's, GRE General Test. Additional exam requirements/recommendations for international students: Required—TOEFL. *Application deadline:* For fall admission, 1/10 priority date for domestic students. Application fee: $75. Electronic applications accepted. *Expenses:* Tuition: Full-time $18,216; part-time $1,012 per credit. Required fees: $980. Tuition and fees vary according to program. *Financial support:* Fellowships with tuition reimbursements available. *Unit head:* Dr. Winston Grady Willis, Director, 315-443-3005. *Application contact:* Aja Brown, Information Contact, 315-443-3097, E-mail: aabrow02@syr.edu.

University at Albany, State University of New York, College of Arts and Sciences, Department of Africana Studies, Albany, NY 12222-0001. Offers African studies (MA); Afro-American studies (MA). Part-time and evening/weekend programs available. *Students:* 24 full-time (16 women), 6 part-time (4 women). Average age 27. In 2007, 10 degrees awarded. *Entrance requirements:* Additional exam requirements/recommendations for international students: Required—TOEFL (minimum score 550 paper-based; 213 computer-based). *Application deadline:* For fall admission, 5/15 for international students; for spring admission, 11/1 for international students. Applications are processed on a rolling basis. Application fee: $75. Electronic applications accepted. *Expenses:* Tuition, state resident: part-time $576 per credit. Tuition, nonresident: part-time $910 per credit. Tuition and fees vary according to program. *Financial support:* Fellowships, teaching assistantships, Federal Work-Study available. Financial award application deadline: 5/1. *Faculty research:* The black family, Afro-centricity in poetry, black women in U.S. literature, African economic development, African American history. *Unit head:* Dr. Marcia Sutherland, Director, 518-442-4730.

University of California, Los Angeles, Graduate Division, College of Letters and Science, Program in African Studies, Los Angeles, CA 90095. Offers MA, MPH/MA. *Students:* 18 full-time (14 women); includes 7 minority (6 African Americans, 1 Asian American or Pacific Islander), 2 international. Average age 27. 17 applicants, 82% accepted, 9 enrolled. In 2007, 3 degrees awarded. *Degree requirements:* For master's, one foreign language, comprehensive exam or thesis. *Entrance requirements:* For master's, GRE General Test, minimum GPA of 3.0, sample of research writing. *Application deadline:* For fall admission, 12/15 for domestic students. Application fee: $60. Electronic applications accepted. *Expenses:* Tuition, nonresident: full-time $5,728. Required fees: $8,966. Full-time tuition and fees vary according to program and student level. *Financial support:* In 2007–08, 6 fellowships with full and partial tuition reimbursements, 3 research assistantships with full and partial tuition reimbursements, 1 teaching assistantship with full and partial tuition reimbursement were awarded; Federal Work-Study, institutionally sponsored loans, scholarships/grants, and tuition waivers (full and partial) also available. Financial award application deadline: 3/1; financial award applicants required to submit FAFSA. *Unit head:* Katrina Thompson, Chair, 310-206-6571. *Application contact:* Departmental Office, 310-206-6571, E-mail: idpgrads@international.ucla.edu.

University of Connecticut, Graduate School, College of Liberal Arts and Sciences, Field of International Studies, Program in African Studies, Storrs, CT 06269. Offers MA. *Faculty:* 40 full-time (22 women). *Students:* 2 full-time (both women), (both international). Average age 41. 1 applicant, 0% accepted. In 2007, 2 degrees awarded. *Degree requirements:* For master's, comprehensive exam. *Entrance requirements:* For master's, GRE General Test. Additional exam requirements/recommendations for international students: Required—TOEFL (minimum score 550 paper-based; 213 computer-based). *Application deadline:* For fall admission, 2/1 priority date for domestic and international students; for spring admission, 11/1 for domestic students, 10/1 for international students. Applications are processed on a rolling basis. Application fee: $55. Electronic applications accepted. *Expenses:* Tuition, state resident: part-time $469 per credit hour. Tuition, nonresident: part-time $1,218 per credit hour. *Financial support:* In 2007–08, 2 research assistantships with full tuition reimbursements were awarded; teaching assistantships with full tuition reimbursements, Federal Work-Study, scholarships/grants, health care benefits, and unspecified assistantships also available. Financial award application deadline: 2/1; financial award applicants required to submit FAFSA.

University of Florida, Graduate School, College of Liberal Arts and Sciences, Center for African Studies, Gainesville, FL 32611. Offers Certificate. Part-time programs available. *Faculty:* 4 full-time (2 women). *Application deadline:* For fall admission, 6/1 priority date for domestic students; for spring admission, 11/1 for domestic students. *Expenses:* Tuition, state resident: full-time $7,478. Tuition, nonresident: full-time $22,603. *Financial support:* In 2007–08, 4 research assistantships (averaging $17,864 per year) were awarded; fellowships, teaching assistantships, Federal Work-Study and institutionally sponsored loans also available. Financial award application deadline: 2/15. *Faculty research:* Governance, human rights, African archaeology, southern African history, wildlife conservation and natural resources. *Unit head:* Dr. Leonardo Villalon, Director, 352-392-2183, Fax: 352-392-2435, E-mail: villalon@africa.ufl.edu. *Application contact:* Corinna Greene, Office Manager, 352-392-2183, Fax: 352-392-2435, E-mail: cgreene@africa.ufl.edu.

University of Illinois at Urbana–Champaign, Graduate College, College of Liberal Arts and Sciences, Center for African Studies, Champaign, IL 61820. Offers MA. *Students:* 10 full-time (6 women), 1 (woman) part-time; includes 4 minority (all African Americans), 2 international. 16 applicants, 44% accepted, 5 enrolled. In 2007, 3 degrees awarded. *Degree requirements:* For master's, one foreign language, thesis optional. *Entrance requirements:* For master's, minimum GPA of 3.0. *Application deadline:* Applications are processed on a rolling basis. Application fee: $60 ($75 for international students). Electronic applications accepted. *Financial support:* In 2007–08, 9 fellowships, 2 teaching assistantships were awarded; research assistantships, career-related internships or fieldwork, Federal Work-Study, institutionally sponsored loans, and tuition waivers (partial) also available. Financial award application deadline: 2/15. *Unit head:* Merle Bowen, Director, 217-333-6335, Fax: 217-244-2429, E-mail: bowen@uiuc.edu. *Application contact:* Sue Swisher, Administrative Aide, 217-244-4713, Fax: 217-244-2429, E-mail: swisher@uiuc.edu.

University of Louisville, Graduate School, College of Arts and Sciences, Department of Pan-African Studies, Louisville, KY 40292-0001. Offers MA. *Students:* 11 full-time (8 women), 4 part-time (3 women); includes 13 minority (all African Americans) Average age 28. In 2007, 6 degrees awarded. *Degree requirements:* For master's, thesis (for some programs). *Entrance requirements:* For master's, GRE General Test. Application fee: $50. *Financial support:* In 2007–08, 8 teaching assistantships with tuition reimbursements (averaging $12,000 per year) were awarded. *Unit head:* Dr. Ricky L. Jones, Chair, 502-852-0027, Fax: 502-852-5954, E-mail: rljones01@louisville.edu. *Application contact:* Dr. Theresa Rajack-Talley, Graduate Studies Director, 502-852-4192, Fax: 502-852-5954, E-mail: tatall01@louisville.edu.

University of Pittsburgh, University Center for International Studies, Pittsburgh, PA 15260. Offers African studies (Certificate); Asian studies (Certificate); European Union studies (Certificate); global studies (Certificate); Latin American studies (Certificate); Russian and East European studies (Certificate); West European studies (Certificate). *Unit head:* Lawrence F. Feick, Director, University Center for International Studies, 412-648-7374, Fax: 412-624-4672, E-mail: feick@pitt.edu.

University of South Florida, Graduate School, College of Arts and Sciences, Department of Africana Studies, Tampa, FL 33620-9951. Offers MLA. *Faculty:* 3 full-time (1 woman), 3 part-time/adjunct (2 women). *Students:* 6 applicants, 83% accepted, 5 enrolled. *Entrance requirements:* For master's, GRE, 3 letters of recommendation. *Application deadline:* For fall admission, 6/1 for domestic students; for spring admission, 10/15 for domestic students. Application fee: $30. *Financial support:* Tuition waivers (full) available. Financial award applicants required to submit FAFSA. *Unit head:* Trevor Purcell, Faculty Member, 813-974-4441, Fax: 813-974-2668, E-mail: purcell@chumai.crs.usf.edu.

University of Wisconsin–Madison, Graduate School, College of Letters and Science, Department of African Languages and Literature, Madison, WI 53706-1380. Offers MA, PhD. Part-time programs available. *Degree requirements:* For master's, one foreign language, thesis; for doctorate, 2 foreign languages, comprehensive exam, thesis/dissertation. *Entrance requirements:* For master's, BA in African language and literature; for doctorate, MA in African language and literature. Electronic applications accepted. *Faculty research:* Oral traditions, language pedagogy, stylistics, sociolinguistics, literary criticism.

West Virginia University, Eberly College of Arts and Sciences, Department of History, Morgantown, WV 26506. Offers African history (MA, PhD); African-American history (MA, PhD); American history (MA, PhD); Appalachian/regional history (MA, PhD); East Asian history (MA, PhD); European history (MA, PhD); history of science and technology (MA, PhD); Latin American history (MA). Part-time programs available. *Faculty:* 19 full-time (5 women), 12 part-time/adjunct (4 women). *Students:* 43 full-time (17 women), 30 part-time (11 women); includes 5 minority (1 African American, 1 American Indian/Alaska Native, 2 Asian Americans or Pacific Islanders, 1 Hispanic American), 7 international. Average age 33. 70 applicants, 59% accepted, 17 enrolled. In 2007, 8 master's, 3 doctorates awarded. *Median time to degree:* Of those who began their doctoral program in fall 1999, 75% received their degree in 8 years or less. *Degree requirements:* For master's, one foreign language, thesis (for some programs), oral exam, thesis defense; for doctorate, one foreign language, comprehensive exam, thesis/dissertation, dissertation defense. *Entrance requirements:* For master's, GRE General Test, minimum GPA of 3.0; for doctorate, GRE General Test. Additional exam requirements/recommendations for international students: Required—TOEFL (minimum score 550 paper-based), IELTS (minimum score 7). *Application deadline:* For fall admission, 12/31 for domestic students; for spring admission, 10/1 for domestic students. Applications are processed on a rolling basis. Application fee: $45. Electronic applications accepted. *Expenses:* Tuition, state resident: full-time $5,196; part-time $292 per credit hour. Tuition, nonresident: full-time $15,064; part-time $840 per credit hour. Tuition and fees vary according to program. *Financial support:* In 2007–08, 60 students received support, including 5 fellowships with full tuition reimbursements available (averaging $3,000 per year), 1 research assistantship with full tuition reimbursement available (averaging $7,200 per year), 8 teaching assistantships with full tuition reimbursements available (averaging $12,000 per year); career-related internships or fieldwork, Federal Work-Study, institutionally sponsored loans, health care benefits, tuition waivers (full and partial), and graduate administrative assistantships also available. Financial award application deadline: 12/31; financial award applicants required to submit FAFSA. *Faculty research:* U.S., Appalachia, modern Europe, Africa, colonial and post-colonial societies. Total annual research expenditures: $93,327. *Unit head:* Dr. Steven M. Zdatny, Chair, 304-293-2421 Ext. 5241, Fax: 304-293-3616, E-mail: steve.zdatny@mail.wvu.edu. *Application contact:* Dr. Greg A. Good, Director of Graduate Studies, 304-293-2421 Ext. 5247, Fax: 304-293-3616, E-mail: greg.good@mail.wvu.edu.

Yale University, Graduate School of Arts and Sciences, Interdisciplinary Program in African Studies, New Haven, CT 06520. Offers MA. *Degree requirements:* For master's, one foreign language, thesis. *Entrance requirements:* For master's, GRE General Test.

American Indian/Native American Studies

Montana State University, College of Graduate Studies, College of Letters and Science, Department of Native American Studies, Bozeman, MT 59717. Offers MA. Part-time programs available. *Faculty:* 6 full-time (1 woman), 1 part-time/adjunct (0 women). *Students:* 3 full-time (all women), 2 part-time; includes 1 minority (American Indian/Alaska Native), 1 international. Average age 40. 6 applicants, 67% accepted, 4 enrolled. In 2007, 2 degrees awarded. *Degree requirements:* For master's, comprehensive exam. *Entrance requirements:* For master's, GRE General Test. Additional exam requirements/recommendations for international students: Required—TOEFL (minimum score 550 paper-based; 213 computer-based). *Application deadline:* For fall admission, 7/15 priority date for domestic students, 5/15 priority date for international students; for spring admission, 12/1 priority date for domestic students, 10/1 priority date for international students. Applications are processed on a rolling basis. Application fee: $30. Electronic applications accepted. *Expenses:* Tuition, state resident: full-time $5,176. Tuition, nonresident: full-time $13,070. *Financial support:* In 2007–08, 4 students received support, including 10,010 teaching assistantships with full tuition reimbursements available. Financial award application deadline: 3/1; financial award applicants required to submit FAFSA. *Faculty research:* Ethnoecology, American Indian cultural studies, Federal Indian law and policy, indigenous political theory, American Indian literature. *Unit head:* Dr. Walter Fleming, Head, 406-994-3881, Fax: 406-994-6879, E-mail: wfleming@montana.edu.

Trent University, Graduate Studies, Program in Canadian Studies and Native Studies, Peterborough, ON K9J 7B8, Canada. Offers MA. Part-time programs available. *Degree requirements:* For master's, thesis. *Entrance requirements:* For master's, honors degree. *Faculty research:* Native community-based socioeconomic development, environmental and social impact inventory, regional studies.

Trent University, Graduate Studies, Program in Native Studies, Peterborough, ON K9J 7B8, Canada. Offers PhD. Part-time programs available. *Degree requirements:* For doctorate, thesis/dissertation. *Entrance requirements:* For doctorate, master's degree.

The University of Arizona, Graduate College, Graduate Interdisciplinary Programs, Graduate Interdisciplinary Program in American Indian Studies, Tucson, AZ 85721. Offers MA, PhD, JD/MA. Part-time programs available. *Faculty:* 28. *Students:* 30 full-time (20 women), 9 part-time (7 women); includes 24 minority (23 American Indian/Alaska Native, 1 Hispanic American), 4 international. Average age 37. 31 applicants, 61% accepted, 12 enrolled. In 2007, 6 master's, 4 doctorates awarded. *Degree requirements:* For master's, thesis; for doctorate, one foreign language, comprehensive exam, thesis/dissertation. *Entrance requirements:* For master's and doctorate, minimum GPA of 3.0. Additional exam requirements/recommendations for international students: Required—TOEFL. *Application deadline:* For fall admission, 1/15 for domestic and international students. Application fee: $50. *Financial support:* In 2007–08, fellowships with partial tuition reimbursements (averaging $2,000 per year), teaching assistantships with partial tuition reimbursements (averaging $6,000 per year) were awarded; research assistantships with partial tuition reimbursements, institutionally sponsored loans, scholarships/grants, health care benefits, tuition waivers (partial), and unspecified assistantships also available. Support available to part-time students. Financial award application deadline: 1/15. *Faculty research:* Indian law and policy, Indian societies, Indian language and literature, Indian education. Total annual research expenditures: $155,000. *Unit head:* Dr. K. Tsianina Lomawaima, Head, 520-621-7108, Fax: 520-621-7952, E-mail: lomawaim@email.arizona.edu. *Application contact:* Graduate Education Program Facilitator, 520-621-7108, Fax: 520-621-7952, E-mail: aisp@email.arizona.edu.

University of California, Davis, Graduate Studies, Program in Native American Studies, Davis, CA 95616. Offers MA, PhD. Terminal master's awarded for partial completion of doctoral program. *Degree requirements:* For master's, comprehensive exam (for some programs), thesis (for some programs); for doctorate, thesis/dissertation. *Entrance requirements:* For doctorate, GRE. Additional exam requirements/recommendations for international students: Required—TOEFL (minimum score 550 paper-based; 213 computer-based).

University of California, Los Angeles, Graduate Division, College of Letters and Science, Program in American Indian Studies, Los Angeles, CA 90095. Offers MA, JD/MA. *Students:* 23 full-time (12 women); includes 16 minority (15 American Indian/Alaska Native, 1 Hispanic American). Average age 29. 35 applicants, 57% accepted, 9 enrolled. In 2007, 2 degrees awarded. *Degree requirements:* For master's, comprehensive exam or thesis. *Entrance requirements:* For master's, GRE General Test (recommended), minimum GPA of 3.0, sample of written work. *Application deadline:* For fall admission, 12/15 for domestic students. Application fee: $60. Electronic applications accepted. *Expenses:* Tuition, nonresident: full-time $5,728. Required fees: $8,966. Full-time tuition and fees vary according to program and student level. *Financial support:* In 2007–08, 10 fellowships with full and partial tuition reimbursements, 3 teaching assistantships with full and partial tuition reimbursements were awarded; research assistantships with full and partial tuition reimbursements, Federal Work-Study, institutionally sponsored loans, and tuition waivers (full and partial) also available. Financial award application deadline: 3/1; financial award applicants required to submit FAFSA. *Unit head:* Dr. Felicia Hodge, Chair, 310-825-7315. *Application contact:* Departmental Office, 310-825-7315, E-mail: aisc@ucla.edu.

University of Kansas, Research and Graduate Studies, College of Liberal Arts and Sciences, Center for Indigenous Nations Studies, Lawrence, KS 66045. Offers MA. Part-time programs available. *Students:* 21 full-time (16 women), 17 part-time (10 women); includes 26 minority (all American Indian/Alaska Native). Average age 34. 15 applicants, 67% accepted, 5 enrolled. In 2007, 4 degrees awarded. *Degree requirements:* For master's, thesis or alternative. *Entrance requirements:* For master's, GRE, resumé, writing sample, minimum GPA of 3.0, preferred, three recommendations, personal statement, application fee. Additional exam requirements/recommendations for international students: Required—TOEFL. *Application deadline:* For fall admission, 1/15 priority date for domestic students; for winter admission, 1/15 priority date for domestic students; for spring admission, 5/15 for domestic students. Application fee: $55 ($60 for international students). Electronic applications accepted. *Expenses:* Tuition, state resident: full-time $5,838. Tuition, nonresident: full-time $13,409. Tuition and fees vary according to program. *Financial support:* Fellowships, teaching assistantships, Federal Work-Study, institutionally sponsored loans, and scholarships/grants available. Support available to part-time students. Financial award application deadline: 3/15; financial award applicants required to submit FAFSA. *Faculty research:* American Indian history, religion, literature, law, languages, decolonization, sovereignty, and pre-Columbian cultures of Latin America. *Unit head:* Dr. John Hoopes, Director, 785-864-2660, Fax: 785-864-0370, E-mail: insp@ku.edu. *Application contact:* Prof. Sharon O'Brien, Graduate Advisor, 785-864-9057, Fax: 785-864-0370, E-mail: insp@ku.edu.

University of Lethbridge, School of Graduate Studies, Lethbridge, AB T1K 3M4, Canada. Offers accounting (MScM); addictions counseling (M Sc); agricultural biotechnology (M Sc); agricultural studies (M Sc, MA); anthropology (MA); archaeology (MA); art (MA); biochemistry (M Sc); biological sciences (M Sc); biomolecular science (PhD); biosystems and biodiversity (PhD); Canadian studies (MA); chemistry (M Sc); computer science (M Sc); computer science and geographical information science (M Sc); counseling psychology (M Ed); dramatic arts (MA); earth, space, and physical science (PhD); economics (MA); educational leadership (M Ed); English (MA); environmental science (M Sc); evolution and behavior (PhD); exercise science (M Sc); finance (MScM); French (MA); French/German (MA); French/Spanish (MA); general education (M Ed); general management (MScM); geography (M Sc, MA); German (MA); health sciences (M Sc, MA); history (MA); human resource management and labour relations (MScM); individualized multidisciplinary (M Sc, MA); information systems (MScM); international management (MScM); kinesiology (M Sc, MA); management (M Sc, MA); marketing (MScM); mathematics (M Sc); music (MA); Native American studies (MA); neuroscience (M Sc, PhD); new media (MA); nursing (M Sc); philosophy (MA); physics (M Sc); policy and strategy (MScM); political science (MA); psychology (M Sc, MA); religious studies (MA); sociology (MA); theoretical and computational science (PhD); urban and regional studies (MA). Part-time and evening/weekend programs available. *Students:* 215 full-time, 98 part-time. In 2007, 87 master's, 1 doctorate awarded. *Degree requirements:* For doctorate, comprehensive exam, thesis/dissertation. *Entrance requirements:* For master's, GMAT (M Sc in management), bachelor's degree in related field, minimum GPA of 3.0 during previous 20 graded semester courses, 2 years teaching or related experience (M Ed); for doctorate, master's degree, minimum graduate GPA of 3.5. Additional exam requirements/recommendations for international students: Required—TOEFL. Application fee: $60 Canadian dollars. *Financial support:* Fellowships, research assistantships, teaching assistantships, scholarships/grants, health care benefits, and unspecified assistantships available. *Faculty research:* Movement and brain plasticity, gibberellin physiology, photosynthesis, carbon cycling, molecular properties of main-group ring components. *Unit head:* Dr. Jo-Anne Fiske, Interim Dean, 403-329-2121, Fax: 403-329-2097. *Application contact:* Jennifer Geddes, Graduate Liaison Officer, 403-329-2762, Fax: 403-329-5159, E-mail: jennifer.geddes@uleth.ca.

University of Manitoba, Faculty of Graduate Studies, Interdisciplinary Programs, Department of Native Studies, Winnipeg, MB R3T 2N2, Canada. Offers M Sc, MA.

University of Oklahoma, Graduate College, College of Arts and Sciences, Department of Native American Studies, Norman, OK 73019-0390. Offers MA. Part-time programs available. *Faculty:* 3 full-time (1 woman). *Students:* 7 full-time (5 women), 4 part-time (1 woman); includes 7 minority (all American Indian/Alaska Native), 1 international. 7 applicants, 71% accepted, 3 enrolled. In 2007, 1 degree awarded. *Degree requirements:* For master's, thesis. *Entrance requirements:* For master's, minimum undergraduate GPA of 3.0, 3 letters of recommendation. *Application deadline:* For fall admission, 2/1 for domestic students, 4/1 for international students; for spring admission, 11/1 for domestic students, 9/1 for international students. Applications are processed on a rolling basis. Application fee: $40 ($90 for international students). Electronic applications accepted. *Expenses:* Tuition, state resident: full-time $3,451; part-time $144 per credit hour. Tuition, nonresident: full-time $12,432; part-time $518 per credit hour. Required fees: $1,925; $70 per credit hour. $122 per semester. *Financial support:* In 2007–08, 13 students received support, including 6 teaching assistantships with partial tuition reimbursements available (averaging $12,235 per year); fellowships, research assistantships with partial tuition reimbursements available, tuition waivers (partial) and unspecified assistantships also available. Financial award application deadline: 2/1; financial award applicants required to submit FAFSA. *Faculty research:* Indians; race and identity politics among Cherokees, American Indian contemporary literature, Seminoles, Native American women, American Indian history, ethics and value conflicts in archaeology, native American literature, aesthetic understanding of native American art. Total annual research expenditures: $8,083. *Unit head:* Joe Watkins, Director, 405-325-2312, Fax: 405-325-0842, E-mail: jwatkins@ou.edu. *Application contact:* Barbara Hobson, Assistant Director, 405-325-2324, Fax: 405-325-0842, E-mail: bhobson@ou.edu.

University of Regina, Faculty of Graduate Studies and Research, Faculty of Arts, Program in Indigenous Studies, Regina, SK S4S 0A2, Canada. Offers MA. Offered as special case program. Part-time programs available. *Faculty:* 10 full-time (3 women). *Degree requirements:* For master's, thesis. *Entrance requirements:* For master's, honors degree in Indian studies or related field. Additional exam requirements/recommendations for international students: Required—TOEFL (minimum score 580 paper-based; 237 computer-based; 88 iBT). *Application deadline:* For fall admission, 3/15 for domestic students. Application fee: $85 ($100 for international students). Electronic applications accepted. *Financial support:* In 2007–08, fellowships (averaging $15,750 per year), research assistantships (averaging $13,875 per year), teaching assistantships (averaging $13,060 per year) were awarded; scholarships/grants also available. Financial award application deadline: 6/15.

American Studies

American University, School of International Service, Washington, DC 20016-8001. Offers comparative and regional studies (MA); cross-cultural communication (Certificate); development management (MS); environmental policy (MA); ethics, peace, and global affairs (MA); global environmental policy (MA); international communication (MA); international development (MA); international development management (Certificate); international economic policy (MA); international economic relations (Certificate); international peace and conflict resolution (MA); international politics (MA); international relations (PhD); international service (MIS); the Americas (Certificate); U.S. foreign policy (MA); JD/MA; MBA/MA. Part-time and evening/weekend programs available. *Faculty:* 73 full-time (27 women), 34 part-time/adjunct (15 women). *Students:* 528 full-time (339 women), 355 part-time (218 women); includes 137 minority (39 African Americans, 2 American Indian/Alaska Native, 45 Asian Americans or Pacific Islanders, 51 Hispanic Americans), 119 international. Average age 27. 1,840 applicants, 66% accepted, 321 enrolled. In 2007, 347 master's, 5 doctorates, 12 other advanced degrees awarded. Terminal master's awarded for partial completion of doctoral program. *Degree requirements:* For master's, one foreign language, comprehensive exam, thesis or alternative; for doctorate, one foreign language, comprehensive exam, thesis/dissertation, research practicum; for Certificate, minimum 15 credit hours related course work. *Entrance requirements:* For master's, GRE General Test, 24 credits of course work in related social sciences, minimum GPA of 3.5, 2 letters of recommendation, bachelor's Degree, resumé, statement of purpose; for doctorate, GRE General Test, 2 letters of recommendation, 24 credits in related social sciences. Additional exam requirements/recommendations for international students: Required—TOEFL (minimum score 550 paper-based; 213 computer-based). *Application deadline:* For fall admission, 1/15 priority date for domestic students; for spring admission, 10/1 priority date for domestic students. Applications are processed on a rolling basis. Application fee: $50. *Expenses:* Tuition: Full-time $19,998; part-time $1,111 per credit hour. Required fees: $380. Tuition and fees vary according to program. *Financial support:* Career-related internships or fieldwork, Federal Work-Study, and institutionally sponsored loans available. Financial award application deadline: 1/15. *Faculty research:* International intellectual property, international environmental issues, international law and legal order, international telecommunications/technology, international sustainable development. *Unit head:* Dr. Louis W. Goodman, Dean, 202-885-1600, Fax: 202-885-2494. *Application contact:* Amanda Taylor, Director of Graduate Admissions and Financial Aid, 202-885-1599, Fax: 202-885-2494.

See Close-Up on page 1139.

American Studies

Appalachian State University, Cratis D. Williams Graduate School, Center for Appalachian Studies, Boone, NC 28608. Offers MA. Part-time programs available. *Faculty:* 7 full-time (4 women). *Students:* 15 full-time (11 women), 6 part-time (4 women). Average age 27. 14 applicants, 86% accepted, 10 enrolled. In 2007, 6 degrees awarded. *Degree requirements:* For master's, one foreign language, comprehensive exam, thesis optional. *Entrance requirements:* For master's, GRE General Test, 3 letters of recommendation. Additional exam requirements/recommendations for international students: Required—TOEFL (minimum score 570 paper-based; 230 computer-based; 79 iBT), IELTS (minimum score 7), TOEFL or IELTS. *Application deadline:* For fall admission, 7/1 for domestic students, 1/1 for international students; for spring admission, 11/1 for domestic students, 6/1 for international students. Applications are processed on a rolling basis. Application fee: $50. Electronic applications accepted. *Expenses:* Tuition, state resident: part-time $127 per semester hour. Tuition, nonresident: part-time $597 per semester hour. Required fees: $18 per semester. *Financial support:* In 2007–08, 8 research assistantships (averaging $7,000 per year) were awarded; fellowships, teaching assistantships, career-related internships or fieldwork, Federal Work-Study, scholarships/grants, and unspecified assistantships also available. Financial award application deadline: 4/1. *Faculty research:* Appalachian culture, sustainable development. Total annual research expenditures: $17,000. *Unit head:* Dr. Pat Beaver, Director, 828-262-2550, E-mail: beaverpd@appstate.edu. *Application contact:* Dr. Edwin Arnold, Program Coordinator, 828-262-4089, E-mail: arnoldet@appstate.edu.

Baylor University, Graduate School, College of Arts and Sciences, Program in American Studies, Waco, TX 76798. Offers MA. *Students:* 4 full-time (3 women), 1 (woman) part-time; includes 1 minority (African American) In 2007, 2 degrees awarded. *Degree requirements:* For master's, thesis, final oral exam. *Entrance requirements:* For master's, GRE General Test, 24 semester hours of course work in subjects with American content. *Application deadline:* For fall admission, 8/1 for domestic students. Applications are processed on a rolling basis. Application fee: $25. *Financial support:* Fellowships, Federal Work-Study and institutionally sponsored loans available. Financial award application deadline: 4/15. *Unit head:* Dr. Donald Greco, Graduate Program Director, 254-710-6043, Fax: 254-710-3600, E-mail: donald_greco@baylor.edu. *Application contact:* Suzanne Keener, Administrative Assistant, 254-710-3588, Fax: 254-710-3870.

Boston University, Graduate School of Arts and Sciences, Program in American and New England Studies, Boston, MA 02215. Offers PhD. *Students:* 36 full-time (26 women), 10 part-time (5 women); includes 4 minority (all African Americans), 1 international. Average age 35. 73 applicants, 18% accepted, 6 enrolled. In 2007, 6 doctorates awarded. *Degree requirements:* For doctorate, one foreign language, comprehensive exam, thesis/dissertation. *Entrance requirements:* For doctorate, GRE General Test, scholarly writing sample, 3 letters of recommendation. Additional exam requirements/recommendations for international students: Required—TOEFL (minimum score 550 paper-based; 213 computer-based). *Application deadline:* For fall admission, 1/15 for domestic and international students. Application fee: $70. *Expenses:* Tuition: Full-time $34,930; part-time $1,092 per credit. Tuition and fees vary according to class time, course level and program. *Financial support:* In 2007–08, 15 students received support, including 1 fellowship with full tuition reimbursement available (averaging $18,000 per year), 1 research assistantship with full tuition reimbursement available (averaging $16,500 per year), 4 teaching assistantships with full tuition reimbursements available (averaging $16,500 per year); career-related internships or fieldwork, Federal Work-Study, scholarships/grants, and unspecified assistantships also available. Support available to part-time students. Financial award application deadline: 1/15; financial award applicants required to submit FAFSA. *Unit head:* Marilyn Halter, Director, 617-353-9912, Fax: 617-353-2556, E-mail: mhalter@bu.edu. *Application contact:* Jordan Hertzberg, Senior Program Coordinator, 617-353-2948, Fax: 617-353-2556, E-mail: jhertz@bu.edu.

Bowling Green State University, Graduate College, College of Arts and Sciences, American Culture Studies Program, Bowling Green, OH 43403. Offers MA, PhD. Part-time programs available. *Faculty:* 15 part-time/adjunct (7 women). *Students:* 50 full-time (31 women), 21 part-time (11 women); includes 15 minority (10 African Americans, 5 Hispanic Americans), 7 international. Average age 33. 76 applicants, 36% accepted, 14 enrolled. In 2007, 10 master's, 12 doctorates awarded. *Degree requirements:* For master's, thesis or alternative; for doctorate, comprehensive exam, thesis/dissertation. *Entrance requirements:* For master's and doctorate, GRE General Test. Additional exam requirements/recommendations for international students: Required—TOEFL. *Application deadline:* For fall admission, 2/1 for domestic students. Application fee: $30. Electronic applications accepted. *Financial support:* In 2007–08, 2 fellowships with full tuition reimbursements (averaging $14,707 per year), 10 research assistantships with full tuition reimbursements (averaging $8,908 per year), 34 teaching assistantships with full tuition reimbursements (averaging $10,702 per year) were awarded; Federal Work-Study and unspecified assistantships also available. Financial award applicants required to submit FAFSA. *Faculty research:* Race and ethnicity, gender, popular culture. *Unit head:* Dr. Don McQuarie, Chair, 419-372-0586.

Bowling Green State University, Graduate College, College of Arts and Sciences, Department of Popular Culture, Bowling Green, OH 43403. Offers MA. Part-time programs available. *Faculty:* 7 full-time (5 women), 2 part-time/adjunct (1 woman). *Students:* 16 full-time (7 women), 2 part-time (both women). Average age 27. 27 applicants, 48% accepted, 9 enrolled. In 2007, 10 degrees awarded. *Degree requirements:* For master's, thesis or alternative. *Entrance requirements:* For master's, GRE General Test. Additional exam requirements/recommendations for international students: Required—TOEFL. *Application deadline:* For fall admission, 2/15 priority date for domestic students. Application fee: $30. Electronic applications accepted. *Financial support:* In 2007–08, 1 research assistantship with full tuition reimbursement (averaging $8,404 per year), 15 teaching assistantships with full tuition reimbursements (averaging $8,404 per year) were awarded; career-related internships or fieldwork, Federal Work-Study, institutionally sponsored loans, and unspecified assistantships also available. Financial award applicants required to submit FAFSA. *Faculty research:* Mass media (popular film, TV, and music); folklore/folklife; ritual, festival, celebration, and holidays; global, international, and popular culture; nineteenth century everyday life. *Unit head:* Dr. Angela Nelson, Chair, 419-372-0284. *Application contact:* Dr. Jeffrey Brown, Graduate Coordinator, 419-372-2982.

Brandeis University, Graduate School of Arts and Sciences, Department of History, Program in American History, Waltham, MA 02454-9110. Offers MA, PhD. Part-time programs available. *Faculty:* 15 full-time (4 women), 1 part-time/adjunct (0 women). *Students:* 33 full-time (15 women), 3 international. Average age 30. 58 applicants, 29% accepted, 7 enrolled. In 2007, 6 master's, 3 doctorates awarded. Terminal master's awarded for partial completion of doctoral program. *Degree requirements:* For master's, one foreign language, thesis, colloquia, directed research, seminars; for doctorate, one foreign language, comprehensive exam, thesis/dissertation, colloquia, directed research, seminars. *Entrance requirements:* For master's and doctorate, GRE General Test, resumé, writing sample, letters of recommendation, statement of purpose. Additional exam requirements/recommendations for international students: Required—TOEFL (minimum score 600 paper-based; 250 computer-based; 100 iBT), IELTS (minimum score 7). *Application deadline:* For fall admission, 1/15 for domestic students. Application fee: $55. Electronic applications accepted. *Financial support:* In 2007–08, 19 students received support, including 14 fellowships with full tuition reimbursements available (averaging $18,500 per year), 5 teaching assistantships (averaging $3,000 per year); research assistantships, scholarships/grants, health care benefits, and tuition waivers (full and partial) also available. Support available to part-time students. Financial award application deadline: 4/15; financial award applicants required to submit CSS PROFILE or FAFSA. *Faculty research:* American polity, social history, cultural, legal, colonial. *Unit head:* Dr. Michael Willrich, Program Chair, 781-736-2292, Fax: 781-736-2273, E-mail: willrich@brandeis.edu.

Brown University, Graduate School, Department of American Civilization, Providence, RI 02912. Offers AM, PhD. *Degree requirements:* For doctorate, thesis/dissertation, preliminary exam.

California State University, Fullerton, Graduate Studies, College of Humanities and Social Sciences, Department of American Studies, Fullerton, CA 92834-9480. Offers MA. Part-time programs available. *Students:* 14 full-time (8 women), 29 part-time (18 women); includes 13 minority (4 Asian Americans or Pacific Islanders, 9 Hispanic Americans). Average age 26. 29 applicants, 72% accepted, 18 enrolled. In 2007, 14 degrees awarded. *Degree requirements:* For master's, comprehensive exam or thesis. *Entrance requirements:* For master's, minimum GPA of 3.0 in major, 2.5 in last 60 hours. Application fee: $55. *Financial support:* Teaching assistantships, Federal Work-Study, institutionally sponsored loans, and scholarships/grants available. Support available to part-time students. Financial award application deadline: 3/1. *Unit head:* Dr. Jesse Battan, Chair, 714-278-2441. *Application contact:* Dr. John Ibson, Adviser, 714-278-3625.

Claremont Graduate University, Graduate Programs, School of Arts and Humanities, Department of English, Claremont, CA 91711-6160. Offers American studies (MA, PhD); critical theory (MA, PhD); early modern studies (MA, PhD); English (M Phil, MA, PhD); literary theory (PhD); literature (MA, PhD); literature and creative writing (MA); literature and film (MA); MBA/MA; MBA/PhD. Part-time programs available. *Faculty:* 2 full-time (1 woman), 2 part-time/adjunct (0 women). *Students:* 81 full-time (49 women), 14 part-time (10 women); includes 18 minority (3 American Indian/Alaska Native, 10 Asian Americans or Pacific Islanders, 5 Hispanic Americans), 3 international. Average age 35. In 2007, 14 master's, 5 doctorates awarded. *Degree requirements:* For master's, one foreign language, comprehensive exam; for doctorate, 2 foreign languages, comprehensive exam, thesis/dissertation. *Entrance requirements:* For master's, GRE General Test; for doctorate, GRE General Test, MA in literature. *Application deadline:* For fall admission, 2/15 priority date for domestic students; for spring admission, 11/15 for domestic students. Applications are processed on a rolling basis. Electronic applications accepted. *Expenses:* Tuition: Full-time $31,640; part-time $1,376 per unit. Required fees: $145 per semester. Tuition and fees vary according to course load, degree level and program. *Financial support:* Fellowships, Federal Work-Study and institutionally sponsored loans available. Support available to part-time students. Financial award application deadline: 2/15; financial award applicants required to submit FAFSA. *Faculty research:* American, comparative, and English Renaissance literature; modernism; feminist literature and theory. *Unit head:* Wendy Martin, Chair, 909-621-8612, Fax: 909-607-1221, E-mail: wendy.martin@cgu.edu.

Claremont Graduate University, Graduate Programs, School of Arts and Humanities, Department of History, Claremont, CA 91711-6160. Offers Africana history (Certificate); American studies and U.S. history (MA, PhD); archival studies (MA); early modern studies (MA, PhD); European studies (MA, PhD); oral history (MA, PhD); MBA/MA; MBA/PhD. *Faculty:* 3 full-time (2 women), 1 part-time/adjunct (0 women). *Students:* 74 full-time (40 women), 8 part-time (3 women); includes 15 minority (1 African American, 2 Asian Americans or Pacific Islanders, 12 Hispanic Americans), 2 international. Average age 37. In 2007, 8 master's, 8 doctorates awarded. *Degree requirements:* For master's, 2 foreign languages, thesis; for doctorate, 2 foreign languages, comprehensive exam, thesis/dissertation. *Entrance requirements:* For master's and doctorate, GRE General Test. *Application deadline:* For fall admission, 2/15 priority date for domestic students. Applications are processed on a rolling basis. Electronic applications accepted. *Expenses:* Tuition: Full-time $31,640; part-time $1,376 per unit. Required fees: $145 per semester. Tuition and fees vary according to course load, degree level and program. *Financial support:* Fellowships, research assistantships, Federal Work-Study and institutionally sponsored loans available. Support available to part-time students. Financial award application deadline: 2/15; financial award applicants required to submit FAFSA. *Faculty research:* Intellectual and social history, cultural studies, gender studies, Western history, Chicano history. *Unit head:* Janet Farrell Brodie, Chair, 909-621-8880, Fax: 909-621-8609, E-mail: janet.brodie@cgu.edu.

The College of William and Mary, Faculty of Arts and Sciences, Program in American Studies, Williamsburg, VA 23187-8795. Offers MA, PhD, JD/MA. Part-time programs available. *Faculty:* 5 full-time (2 women). *Students:* 44 full-time (27 women), 7 part-time (5 women); includes 10 minority (9 African Americans, 1 Asian American or Pacific Islander), 3 international. Average age 32. 8,327 applicants, 0% accepted, 45 enrolled. In 2007, 4 master's, 5 doctorates awarded. Terminal master's awarded for partial completion of doctoral program. *Median time to degree:* Of those who began their doctoral program in fall 1999, 28% received their degree in 8 years or less. *Degree requirements:* For master's, thesis; for doctorate, one foreign language, comprehensive exam, thesis/dissertation. *Entrance requirements:* For master's, BA Degree; for doctorate, MA Degree. Additional exam requirements/recommendations for international students: Required—TOEFL. *Application deadline:* For fall admission, 1/15 for domestic and international students. Application fee: $30. Electronic applications accepted. *Expenses:* Tuition, state resident: full-time $6,250; part-time $275 per credit hour. Tuition, nonresident: part-time $760 per credit hour. Required fees: $3,550. Tuition and fees vary according to program. *Financial support:* In 2007–08, 23 fellowships with full tuition reimbursements (averaging $10,849 per year) were awarded; career-related internships or fieldwork, tuition waivers (full and partial), and unspecified assistantships also available. Financial award application deadline: 3/15; financial award applicants required to submit FAFSA. *Faculty research:* Native American literature and environment, Guada canal and memory, 20th century African-American celebrity, African-American's relation to war, American religious nationalism. Total annual research expenditures: $48,384. *Unit head:* Dr. Maureen F. Fitzgerald, Director/Dean, 757-221-1281, Fax: 757-221-1287, E-mail: mafitz@wm.edu. *Application contact:* Jean Brown, Program Administrator, 757-221-1275, Fax: 757-221-1287, E-mail: jxbrow@wm.edu.

Columbia University, Graduate School of Arts and Sciences, Program in Liberal Studies, New York, NY 10027. Offers American studies (MA); East Asian studies (MA); human rights studies (MA); Islamic culture studies (MA); Jewish studies (MA); medieval studies (MA); modern European studies (MA); South Asian studies (MA). Part-time and evening/weekend programs available. *Faculty:* 5 part-time/adjunct (2 women). *Students:* 7 full-time (2 women), 75 part-time (51 women); includes 5 minority (1 African American, 3 Asian Americans or Pacific Islanders, 1 Hispanic American), 8 international. Average age 41. 39 applicants, 77% accepted. In 2007, 20 degrees awarded. *Degree requirements:* For master's, thesis. Application fee: $90. *Expenses:* Tuition: Part-time $1,452 per credit. Required fees: $152 per term. One-time fee: $75 part-time. Full-time tuition and fees vary according to course level, course load, degree level and program. *Unit head:* Kristin Balicki, Program Coordinator, 212-854-4932, Fax: 212-854-4912, E-mail: knb2110@columbia.edu.

Cornell University, Graduate School, Graduate Fields of Arts and Sciences, Field of English Language and Literature, Ithaca, NY 14853-0001. Offers African-American literature (PhD); American literature after 1865 (PhD); American literature to 1865 (PhD); American studies (PhD); colonial and postcolonial literature (PhD); creative writing (MFA); cultural studies (PhD); dramatic literature (PhD); English poetry (PhD); English Renaissance to 1660 (PhD); lesbian, bisexual, and gay literature studies (PhD); literary criticism and theory (PhD); nineteenth century (PhD); Old and Middle English (PhD); prose fiction (PhD); Restoration and eighteenth century (PhD); twentieth century (PhD); women's literature (PhD); MFA/PhD. *Faculty:* 59 full-time (28 women). *Students:* 97 full-time (53 women); includes 20 minority (7 African Americans, 3 American Indian/Alaska Native, 5 Asian Americans or Pacific Islanders, 5 Hispanic Americans), 13 international. Average age 28. 759 applicants, 7% accepted, 21 enrolled. In 2007, 29 master's, 8 doctorates awarded. Terminal master's awarded for partial completion of doctoral program. *Degree requirements:* For master's, one foreign language, thesis; for doctorate, one foreign language, comprehensive exam, thesis/dissertation, teaching experience. *Entrance requirements:* For master's, GRE General Test, 3 letters of recommendation, creative writing sample; for doctorate, GRE General Test, GRE Subject Test (English), 3 letters of recommendation, writing sample. Additional exam requirements/recommendations for international students: Required—TOEFL (minimum score 600 paper-based; 250 computer-based; 77 iBT). *Application deadline:* For fall admission, 1/10 for domestic students. Application fee: $70. Electronic applications accepted. *Financial support:* In 2007–08, 92 students received support, including 32 fellowships with full tuition reimbursements available, 60 teaching assistantships with full tuition reimbursements available; research assistantships with full tuition reimbursements available, institutionally sponsored loans, scholarships/grants, health care benefits,

American Studies

Cornell University (continued)

tuition waivers (full and partial), and unspecified assistantships also available. Financial award applicants required to submit FAFSA. *Faculty research:* English and American literature, women's writing, ethnic and post-colonial literature, critical theory, medievalism. *Unit head:* Director of Graduate Studies, 607-255-7989, Fax: 607-255-6661. *Application contact:* Graduate Field Assistant, 607-255-7989, Fax: 607-255-6661, E-mail: english_grad@cornell.edu.

Cornell University, Graduate School, Graduate Fields of Arts and Sciences, Field of History, Ithaca, NY 14853-0001. Offers African history (MA, PhD); American history (MA, PhD); ancient history (MA, PhD); early modern European history (MA, PhD); English history (MA, PhD); French history (MA, PhD); German history (MA, PhD); history of science (MA, PhD); Latin American history (MA, PhD); medieval Chinese history (MA, PhD); medieval history (MA, PhD); modern Chinese history (MA, PhD); modern European history (MA, PhD); modern Japanese history (MA, PhD); premodern Islamic history (MA, PhD); premodern Japanese history (MA, PhD); Renaissance history (MA, PhD); Russian history (MA, PhD); Southeast Asian history (MA, PhD). *Faculty:* 56 full-time (14 women). *Students:* 63 full-time (29 women); includes 11 minority (6 African Americans, 2 Asian Americans or Pacific Islanders, 3 Hispanic Americans), 20 international. Average age 31. 201 applicants, 6% accepted, 10 enrolled. In 2007, 11 master's, 11 doctorates awarded. Terminal master's awarded for partial completion of doctoral program. *Degree requirements:* For master's, thesis; for doctorate, 2 foreign languages, comprehensive exam, thesis/dissertation, 1 year of teaching experience. *Entrance requirements:* For master's and doctorate, GRE General Test, writing sample, 3 letters of recommendation. Additional exam requirements/recommendations for international students: Required—TOEFL (minimum score 550 paper-based; 213 computer-based; 77 iBT). *Application deadline:* For fall admission, 1/15 for domestic students. Application fee: $70. Electronic applications accepted. *Financial support:* In 2007–08, 54 students received support, including 26 fellowships with full tuition reimbursements available, 28 teaching assistantships with full tuition reimbursements available; research assistantships with full tuition reimbursements available, institutionally sponsored loans, scholarships/grants, health care benefits, tuition waivers (full and partial), and unspecified assistantships also available. Financial award applicants required to submit FAFSA. *Unit head:* Director of Graduate Studies, 607-255-6738, Fax: 607-255-0469. *Application contact:* Graduate Field Assistant, 607-255-6738, Fax: 607-255-0469, E-mail: history_grad_info@cornell.edu.

Cornell University, Graduate School, Graduate Fields of Arts and Sciences, Field of History of Art and Archaeology, Ithaca, NY 14853. Offers American art (PhD); ancient art and archaeology (PhD); Asian art (PhD); baroque art (PhD); medieval art (PhD); modern art (PhD); Renaissance art (PhD); Southeast Asian art (PhD); theory and criticism (PhD). *Faculty:* 21 full-time (14 women). *Students:* 22 full-time (17 women); includes 6 minority (2 African Americans, 2 Asian Americans or Pacific Islanders, 2 Hispanic Americans), 6 international. Average age 32. 61 applicants, 15% accepted, 4 enrolled. In 2007, 2 doctorates awarded. *Degree requirements:* For doctorate, one foreign language, comprehensive exam, thesis/dissertation, general exams in 3 areas. *Entrance requirements:* For doctorate, GRE General Test, sample of written work, 3 letters of recommendation. Additional exam requirements/recommendations for international students: Required—TOEFL (minimum score 550 paper-based; 213 computer-based; 77 iBT). *Application deadline:* For fall admission, 1/15 for domestic students. Application fee: $70. Electronic applications accepted. *Financial support:* In 2007–08, 17 students received support, including 10 fellowships with full tuition reimbursements available, 7 teaching assistantships with full tuition reimbursements available; research assistantships with full tuition reimbursements available, institutionally sponsored loans, scholarships/grants, health care benefits, tuition waivers (full and partial), and unspecified assistantships also available. Financial award applicants required to submit FAFSA. *Unit head:* Director of Graduate Studies, 607-255-4905, Fax: 607-255-0566, E-mail: art_history@cornell.edu. *Application contact:* Director of Graduate Studies, 607-255-4905, Fax: 607-255-0566, E-mail: art_history@cornell.edu.

Drake University, School of Education, Department of Teaching and Learning, Program in Secondary Education, Des Moines, IA 50311-4516. Offers art (MAT); biology (MAT); business (MAT); chemistry (MAT); English (MAT); general science (MAT); history-American (MAT); history-world (MAT); journalism (MAT); mathematics (MAT); physical science (MAT); physics (MAT); sociology (MAT); speech (MAT); speech communication (MAT); theatre (MAT). Part-time programs available. *Faculty:* 10 full-time (3 women), 28 part-time/adjunct (16 women). *Students:* 13 full-time (7 women), 33 part-time (20 women). 41 applicants, 56% accepted. In 2007, 12 degrees awarded. *Degree requirements:* For master's, comprehensive exam, thesis (for some programs), internships (for some programs). *Entrance requirements:* For master's, GRE General Test, MAT, or Drake Writing Assessment, resumé, 2 letters of recommendation. Additional exam requirements/recommendations for international students: Required—TOEFL (minimum score 550 paper-based; 213 computer-based). *Application deadline:* For fall admission, 7/1 priority date for domestic students, 6/1 priority date for international students; for spring admission, 11/1 priority date for domestic students, 10/1 priority date for international students. Applications are processed on a rolling basis. Application fee: $25. Electronic applications accepted. *Expenses:* Tuition: Full-time $26,030; part-time $370 per credit hour. Required fees: $406; $40 per semester. Tuition and fees vary according to program. *Financial support:* Career-related internships or fieldwork and unspecified assistantships available. Support available to part-time students. *Faculty research:* Counseling and rehabilitation, behavioral supports, inquiry-based science methods, teacher quality enhancement. Total annual research expenditures: $1.5 million. *Application contact:* Ann J. Martin, Graduate Coordinator, 515-271-2034, Fax: 515-271-2831, E-mail: ann.martin@drake.edu.

East Carolina University, Graduate School, Thomas Harriot College of Arts and Sciences, Department of History, Greenville, NC 27858-4353. Offers American history (MA); European history (MA); maritime history (MA). Part-time and evening/weekend programs available. *Faculty:* 27 full-time (4 women). *Students:* 30 full-time (14 women), 26 part-time (14 women); includes 4 minority (2 African Americans, 2 Hispanic Americans), 3 international. Average age 31. 14 applicants, 50% accepted, 3 enrolled. In 2007, 13 degrees awarded. *Degree requirements:* For master's, one foreign language, comprehensive exam, thesis. *Entrance requirements:* For master's, GRE General Test, GRE Subject Test. Additional exam requirements/recommendations for international students: Required—TOEFL. *Application deadline:* For fall admission, 6/1 priority date for domestic students; for spring admission, 10/15 for domestic students. Applications are processed on a rolling basis. Application fee: $50. *Financial support:* Fellowships, research assistantships with partial tuition reimbursements, teaching assistantships with partial tuition reimbursements, Federal Work-Study available. Support available to part-time students. Financial award application deadline: 6/1. *Unit head:* Dr. Michael Palmer, Chair, 252-328-1046, E-mail: palmerm@ecu.edu. *Application contact:* Dr. Carl Swanson, Director of Graduate Studies, 252-328-6485, E-mail: swansonc@ecu.edu.

Eastern Michigan University, Graduate School, College of Arts and Sciences, Department of History and Philosophy, Program in Social Science, Ypsilanti, MI 48197. Offers social science (MA, Graduate Certificate); social science and American culture (MLS). Part-time and evening/weekend programs available. Postbaccalaureate distance learning degree programs offered (minimal on-campus study). *Students:* 3 full-time (2 women), 19 part-time (12 women); includes 3 minority (all African Americans) Average age 36. In 2007, 13 degrees awarded. *Degree requirements:* For master's, thesis optional. *Entrance requirements:* Additional exam requirements/recommendations for international students: Required—TOEFL. *Application deadline:* Applications are processed on a rolling basis. Application fee: $35. *Expenses:* Tuition, state resident: full-time $8,952; part-time $373 per credit hour. Tuition, nonresident: full-time $17,634; part-time $735 per credit hour. Required fees: $896; $34 per credit hour. Tuition and fees vary according to course level, degree level and program. *Financial support:* Fellowships, research assistantships with full tuition reimbursements, teaching assistantships with full tuition reimbursements, career-related internships or fieldwork, Federal Work-Study, institutionally sponsored loans, scholarships/grants, tuition waivers (partial), and unspecified assistantships available. Support available to part-time students. Financial award applicants required to submit FAFSA. *Application contact:* Dr. Jill Dieterle, Advisor, 734-487-0053, Fax: 734-487-6835, E-mail: jdieterle@emich.edu.

Emory & Henry College, Graduate Programs, Emory, VA 24327-0947. Offers American history (MA Ed); professional studies (M Ed); reading specialist (MA Ed). Part-time and evening/weekend programs available. *Faculty:* 3 full-time (1 woman). *Students:* Average age 37. 15 applicants, 100% accepted, 15 enrolled. In 2007, 68 degrees awarded. *Entrance requirements:* For master's, GRE or PRAXIS I, recommendations, writing sample, official transcripts. *Application deadline:* Applications are processed on a rolling basis. Application fee: $30. *Expenses:* Tuition: Part-time $285 per semester hour. *Financial support:* Applicants required to submit FAFSA. *Unit head:* Dr. Jack Roper, Director of Graduate Studies, 276-944-6188, Fax: 276-944-5223, E-mail: jroper@ehc.edu.

Fairfield University, College of Arts and Sciences, Fairfield, CT 06824-5195. Offers American studies (MA); communications (MA); creative writing (MFA); mathematics (MS). Part-time and evening/weekend programs available. *Faculty:* 40 full-time (15 women), 2 part-time/adjunct (0 women). *Students:* 7 full-time (3 women), 73 part-time (42 women); includes 5 minority (2 African Americans, 1 American Indian/Alaska Native, 1 Asian American or Pacific Islander, 1 Hispanic American), 1 international. 18 applicants, 61% accepted, 7 enrolled. In 2007, 21 degrees awarded. *Degree requirements:* For master's, capstone research course. *Entrance requirements:* For master's, minimum GPA of 3.0, 2 letters of recommendation, resumé, essay. Additional exam requirements/recommendations for international students: Required—TOEFL (minimum score 550 paper-based; 213 computer-based). *Application deadline:* For fall admission, 7/1 for domestic students, 6/15 priority date for international students; for spring admission, 12/1 for domestic students, 10/15 priority date for international students. Applications are processed on a rolling basis. Application fee: $60. *Financial support:* Tuition waivers (partial) and unspecified assistantships available. Financial award applicants required to submit FAFSA. *Unit head:* Dr. Robbin Crabtree, Dean, 203-254-4000 Ext. 3263, Fax: 203-254-4119, E-mail: rcrabtree@mail.fairfield.edu. *Application contact:* Marianne Gumpper, Director of Graduate and Continuing Studies Admissions, 203-254-4184, Fax: 203-254-4073, E-mail: gradadmis@mail.fairfield.edu.

Florida State University, Graduate Studies, College of Arts and Sciences, Department of Interdisciplinary Humanities, Program in American and Florida Studies, Tallahassee, FL 32306. Offers MA, Certificate. Part-time programs available. *Faculty:* 7 full-time (3 women). *Students:* 13 full-time (8 women); includes 1 minority (Hispanic American) Average age 25. 3 applicants, 100% accepted, 3 enrolled. In 2007, 1 master's, 1 other advanced degree awarded. *Degree requirements:* For master's, one foreign language, thesis or alternative. *Entrance requirements:* For master's, GRE General Test, minimum GPA of 3.0. *Application deadline:* For fall admission, 7/1 priority date for domestic students; for spring admission, 11/1 priority date for domestic students. Applications are processed on a rolling basis. Application fee: $30. Electronic applications accepted. *Expenses:* Tuition, state resident: part-time $248 per credit hour. Tuition, nonresident: part-time $880 per credit hour. Tuition and fees vary according to program. *Financial support:* In 2007–08, 4 students received support, including fellowships with tuition reimbursements available (averaging $20,000 per year), 1 research assistantship with tuition reimbursement available (averaging $7,500 per year), 3 teaching assistantships with tuition reimbursements available (averaging $7,500 per year); career-related internships or fieldwork, Federal Work-Study, and unspecified assistantships also available. Support available to part-time students. Financial award applicants required to submit FAFSA. *Faculty research:* American intellectual history, religion in America, Hemingway, consumer culture, Florida history, Florida culture, development of communities.

The George Washington University, Columbian College of Arts and Sciences, Department of American Studies, Washington, DC 20052. Offers American studies (MA, PhD); historic preservation (MA); material culture (MA). Part-time and evening/weekend programs available. Terminal master's awarded for partial completion of doctoral program. *Degree requirements:* For master's, comprehensive exam; for doctorate, one foreign language, thesis/dissertation, general exam. *Entrance requirements:* For master's and doctorate, GRE General Test, minimum GPA of 3.0. Additional exam requirements/recommendations for international students: Required—TOEFL (minimum score 550 paper-based; 213 computer-based).

Harvard University, Graduate School of Arts and Sciences, Committee on History of American Civilization, Cambridge, MA 02138. Offers PhD. *Degree requirements:* For doctorate, 2 foreign languages, thesis/dissertation. *Entrance requirements:* For doctorate, GRE General Test, GRE Subject Test (recommended). Additional exam requirements/recommendations for international students: Required—TOEFL. *Expenses:* Tuition: Full-time $31,456. Full-time tuition and fees vary according to program and student level. *Faculty research:* American history, literature, and religion in the Colonial era; twentieth century American history, literature, and law; Southern literature, history, and sociology.

Lehigh University, College of Arts and Sciences, Program in American Studies, Bethlehem, PA 18015-3094. Offers MA. Part-time programs available. *Students:* 11 full-time (9 women), 5 part-time (2 women), 3 international. Average age 30. 16 applicants, 81% accepted, 10 enrolled. In 2007, 3 degrees awarded. *Degree requirements:* For master's, thesis. *Entrance requirements:* For master's, GRE. Additional exam requirements/recommendations for international students: Required—TOEFL. *Application deadline:* For spring admission, 12/1 for domestic students. Application fee: $65. Electronic applications accepted. *Financial support:* In 2007–08, 1 fellowship with full tuition reimbursement was awarded; tuition waivers (full) and unspecified assistantships also available. *Unit head:* Prof. John Pettegrew, Director, 610-758-3355, Fax: 610-758-6554, E-mail: jcp5@lehigh.edu. *Application contact:* Prof. John Pettegrew, Director, 610-758-3355, Fax: 610-758-6554, E-mail: jcp5@lehigh.edu.

Lindenwood University, Graduate Programs, Division of Humanities, St. Charles, MO 63301-1695. Offers American studies (MA). Part-time programs available. *Faculty:* 2 full-time (both women). *Students:* 1 (woman) full-time, 1 (woman) part-time. Average age 41. *Degree requirements:* For master's, minimum GPA of 3.0. *Entrance requirements:* For master's, minimum GPA of 2.5, essay. Additional exam requirements/recommendations for international students: Required—TOEFL (minimum score 550 paper-based; 213 computer-based; 80 iBT). *Application deadline:* For fall admission, 8/30 priority date for domestic and international students; for spring admission, 12/30 for domestic students, 12/30 priority date for international students. Applications are processed on a rolling basis. Application fee: $30 ($100 for international students). Electronic applications accepted. *Expenses:* Tuition: Full-time $12,400; part-time $350 per hour. Full-time tuition and fees vary according to degree level and program. *Financial support:* Career-related internships or fieldwork, institutionally sponsored loans, tuition waivers (partial), and unspecified assistantships available. Financial award application deadline: 6/30; financial award applicants required to submit FAFSA. *Unit head:* Dr. Don Heidenreich, Dean of Humanities, 636-949-4414, E-mail: dheidenreich@lindenwood.edu. *Application contact:* Brett Barger, Dean of Evening Admissions and Extension Campuses, 636-949-4934, Fax: 636-949-4109, E-mail: adultadmissions@lindenwood.edu.

Michigan State University, The Graduate School, College of Arts and Letters, Program in American Studies, East Lansing, MI 48824. Offers MA, PhD. *Entrance requirements:* Additional exam requirements/recommendations for international students: Required—TOEFL. Electronic applications accepted. *Expenses:* Tuition, state resident: part-time $379 per credit hour. Tuition, nonresident: part-time $800 per credit hour. Tuition and fees vary according to program.

New Mexico Highlands University, Graduate Studies, College of Arts and Sciences, Program in Southwest Studies, Las Vegas, NM 87701. Offers anthropology (MA). Program is interdisciplinary. Part-time programs available. *Faculty:* 14 full-time (7 women), 1 (woman) part-time/adjunct. *Students:* 4 full-time (3 women), 13 part-time (9 women); includes 5 minority (1 American Indian/Alaska Native, 4 Hispanic Americans). Average age 35. 13 applicants, 77% accepted, 3 enrolled. In 2007, 2 degrees awarded. *Degree requirements:* For master's, comprehensive exam, thesis or alternative. *Entrance requirements:* For master's, minimum undergraduate GPA of 3.0. Additional exam requirements/recommendations for international students: Required—TOEFL (minimum score 540 paper-based; 190 computer-based). *Application deadline:* For fall admission, 8/1 priority date for domestic students. Applications are processed on a rolling basis. Application fee: $15. *Expenses:* Tuition, state resident: full-time $2,642; part-time $110 per credit hour. Tuition, nonresident: full-time $3,964; part-time $165 per credit hour. International tuition: $5,285 full-time. One-time fee: $20 full-time. *Financial support:* In 2007–08, 4 students received support, including teaching assistantships (averaging $6,500 per year); career-related internships or fieldwork, Federal Work-Study, institutionally sponsored loans, scholarships/grants, tuition waivers (full and partial), and unspecified assistantships also available. Support available to part-time students. Financial award application deadline: 3/1; financial award applicants required to submit FAFSA. *Faculty research:* Southwest Indians, applied anthropology, Hispanic Southwest, archaeology, physical anthropology. *Application contact:* Diane Trujillo, Administrative Assistant Graduate Studies, 505-454-3266, Fax: 505-454-3558, E-mail: dtrujillo@nmhu.edu.

New York University, Graduate School of Arts and Science, Program in American Studies, New York, NY 10012-1019. Offers MA, PhD. Part-time programs available. *Faculty:* 4 full-time (1 woman), 2 part-time/adjunct. *Students:* 52 full-time (32 women), 2 part-time (both women); includes 22 minority (12 African Americans, 7 Asian Americans or Pacific Islanders, 3 Hispanic Americans), 2 international. Average age 33. 175 applicants, 6% accepted, 7 enrolled. In 2007, 3 master's, 6 doctorates awarded. *Degree requirements:* For master's, one foreign language, thesis; for doctorate, 2 foreign languages, thesis/dissertation. *Entrance requirements:* For master's and doctorate, GRE General Test, writing sample. Additional exam requirements/recommendations for international students: Required—TOEFL. *Application deadline:* For fall admission, 12/18 for domestic students. Application fee: $85. *Financial support:* Fellowships with tuition reimbursements, teaching assistantships with tuition reimbursements, Federal Work-Study, institutionally sponsored loans, and unspecified assistantships available. Financial award application deadline: 12/18; financial award applicants required to submit FAFSA. *Faculty research:* Cultural politics; race, gender, and sexuality studies; nationalism and transnationalism; science and technology; urban and suburban studies. *Unit head:* Carolyn Dinshaw, Chair, 212-998-8538, Fax: 212-995-4371, E-mail: amstudies@nyu.edu. *Application contact:* Adam Green, Director of Graduate Studies, 212-998-8538, Fax: 212-995-4371, E-mail: amstudies@nyu.edu.

New York University, Graduate School of Arts and Science, Program in Irish and Irish American Studies, New York, NY 10012-1019. Offers MA. Part-time programs available. *Students:* 4 full-time (2 women), 4 part-time (2 women), 1 international. Average age 35. 9 applicants, 100% accepted, 7 enrolled. *Degree requirements:* For master's, one foreign language. *Entrance requirements:* For master's, GRE General Test. Additional exam requirements/recommendations for international students: Required—TOEFL. *Application deadline:* For fall admission, 4/15 priority date for domestic students. Application fee: $85. *Financial support:* Federal Work-Study, scholarships/grants, health care benefits, and unspecified assistantships available. Financial award application deadline: 4/15.

Northeastern State University, Graduate College, College of Liberal Arts, Program in American Studies, Tahlequah, OK 74464-2399. Offers MA. Part-time and evening/weekend programs available. *Students:* 4 full-time (1 woman), 8 part-time (4 women); includes 4 minority (1 African American, 3 American Indian/Alaska Native). In 2007, 7 degrees awarded. *Degree requirements:* For master's, thesis, written and oral examinations. *Entrance requirements:* For master's, GRE, minimum GPA of 2.5. Additional exam requirements/recommendations for international students: Required—TOEFL (minimum score 213 computer-based). *Application deadline:* For fall admission, 6/1 priority date for domestic students. Applications are processed on a rolling basis. Application fee: $0 ($25 for international students). Electronic applications accepted. *Financial support:* Teaching assistantships, Federal Work-Study available. Financial award application deadline: 3/1. *Unit head:* Dr. Chris Owen, Coordinator, 918-456-5511, Fax: 918-458-2390, E-mail: owen@nsuok.edu.

Penn State Harrisburg, Graduate School, School of Humanities, Middletown, PA 17057-4898. Offers American studies (MA); humanities (MA). Evening/weekend programs available. *Unit head:* Kathryn Robinson, Director, 717-948-6189, E-mail: kdr12@psu.edu.

Pepperdine University, Seaver College, Humanities Division, Malibu, CA 90263. Offers American studies (MA); history (MA). *Degree requirements:* For master's, oral and written exams. *Entrance requirements:* For master's, GRE General Test, undergraduate major or 15 upper-division units in history. Additional exam requirements/recommendations for international students: Required—TOEFL.

Purdue University, Graduate School, College of Liberal Arts, Program in American Studies, West Lafayette, IN 47907. Offers MA, PhD. *Degree requirements:* For master's, essay; for doctorate, one foreign language, thesis/dissertation. *Entrance requirements:* For master's and doctorate, GRE General Test, sample of written work. Additional exam requirements/recommendations for international students: Required—TOEFL, TWE. Electronic applications accepted. *Faculty research:* American history, literature, politics, sociology, women's studies, African-American studies, mass culture.

Saint Louis University, Graduate School, College of Arts and Sciences and Graduate School, Department of American Studies, St. Louis, MO 63103-2097. Offers MA, MA-R, PhD. Part-time programs available. *Faculty:* 4 full-time (1 woman). *Students:* 26 full-time (16 women), 18 part-time (5 women); includes 6 minority (3 African Americans, 1 Asian American or Pacific Islander, 2 Hispanic Americans), 3 international. Average age 36. 24 applicants, 75% accepted, 8 enrolled. In 2007, 2 master's, 2 doctorates awarded. *Degree requirements:* For master's, thesis optional, comprehensive written and oral exams; for doctorate, one foreign language, comprehensive exam, thesis/dissertation, preliminary exams. *Entrance requirements:* For master's and doctorate, GRE General Test, letters of recommendation, resumé, goal statement, transcripts. Additional exam requirements/recommendations for international students: Required—TOEFL (minimum score 525 paper-based; 194 computer-based). *Application deadline:* For fall admission, 2/15 priority date for domestic and international students; for spring admission, 11/1 for domestic and international students. Applications are processed on a rolling basis. Application fee: $40. Electronic applications accepted. *Expenses:* Tuition: Part-time $845 per credit hour. Required fees: $105 per semester. *Financial support:* In 2007–08, 24 students received support, including 2 research assistantships with full tuition reimbursements available (averaging $12,000 per year), 11 teaching assistantships with full tuition reimbursements available (averaging $12,000 per year); Federal Work-Study, scholarships/grants, traineeships, health care benefits, tuition waivers (partial), and unspecified assistantships also available. Support available to part-time students. Financial award application deadline: 2/1; financial award applicants required to submit FAFSA. *Faculty research:* Urban studies, American religion, intellectual history, southern culture, African-American literature. *Unit head:* Dr. Matthew J. Mancini, Chairperson, 314-977-2990, Fax: 314-977-1806, E-mail: mancini@slu.edu. *Application contact:* Gary U. Behrman, Associate Dean of Graduate School Admissions, 314-977-3827, Fax: 314-977-3943, E-mail: behrmang@slu.edu.

State University of New York College at Cortland, Graduate Studies, School of Arts and Sciences, Program in American Civilization and Culture, Cortland, NY 13045. Offers CAS. Part-time and evening/weekend programs available. *Entrance requirements:* Additional exam requirements/recommendations for international students: Required—TOEFL.

Trinity College, Graduate Programs, Program in American Studies, Hartford, CT 06106-3100. Offers MA. Part-time and evening/weekend programs available. *Degree requirements:* For master's, thesis or alternative. *Entrance requirements:* For master's, minimum GPA of 3.0.

Universidad de las Américas–Puebla, Division of Graduate Studies, School of Social Sciences, Program in American Studies, Puebla, Mexico. Offers MA. Part-time and evening/weekend programs available. *Degree requirements:* For master's, one foreign language, thesis. *Faculty research:* NAFTA, technology, culture, politics and economics in NAFTA region.

University at Buffalo, the State University of New York, Graduate School, College of Arts and Sciences, Department of American Studies, Buffalo, NY 14260. Offers MA, PhD. Post-baccalaureate distance learning degree programs offered (minimal on-campus study). Terminal master's awarded for partial completion of doctoral program. *Degree requirements:* For master's, comprehensive exam, thesis (for some programs); for doctorate, comprehensive exam, thesis/dissertation. *Entrance requirements:* For master's, minimum GPA of 3.0; for doctorate, GRE, minimum GPA of 3.0. Additional exam requirements/recommendations for international students: Required—TOEFL (minimum score 550 paper-based; 213 computer-based). Electronic applications accepted. *Faculty research:* Native American studies, intercultural studies, indigenous people's studies, multiculturalism, border theory, cultural studies, American popular culture.

The University of Alabama, Graduate School, College of Arts and Sciences, Department of American Studies, Tuscaloosa, AL 35487. Offers MA. Part-time programs available. *Faculty:* 6 full-time (2 women). *Students:* 12 full-time (9 women), 3 part-time (2 women); includes 2 minority (both African Americans), 1 international. Average age 25. 13 applicants, 85% accepted, 6 enrolled. In 2007, 6 degrees awarded. *Degree requirements:* For master's, comprehensive exam, thesis optional. *Entrance requirements:* For master's, GRE or MAT. Additional exam requirements/recommendations for international students: Required—TOEFL. *Application deadline:* For fall admission, 1/15 priority date for domestic and international students; for spring admission, 11/30 priority date for domestic and international students. Applications are processed on a rolling basis. Application fee: $30. Electronic applications accepted. *Expenses:* Tuition, state resident: full-time $5,700. Tuition, nonresident: full-time $16,518. *Financial support:* In 2007–08, 12 students received support, including 5 teaching assistantships with full tuition reimbursements available (averaging $10,291 per year); Federal Work-Study, tuition waivers (full), and unspecified assistantships also available. *Faculty research:* Social and cultural history, popular music, African-American arts, the south, women's history, Asian-American studies, sports, Latino Studies. *Unit head:* Dr. Lynne M. Adrian, Associate Professor, 205-348-5940, Fax: 205-348-9766, E-mail: ladrian@tenhoor.as.ua.edu.

University of Central Oklahoma, College of Graduate Studies and Research, College of Liberal Arts, Department of History, Edmond, OK 73034-5209. Offers history (MA); museum studies (MA); social studies teaching (MA); Southwestern studies (MA). Part-time programs available. *Faculty:* 12 full-time (3 women). *Students:* 12 full-time (6 women), 15 part-time (9 women); includes 1 minority (Hispanic American) Average age 32. 10 applicants, 100% accepted. In 2007, 8 degrees awarded. *Degree requirements:* For master's, thesis optional. *Entrance requirements:* Additional exam requirements/recommendations for international students: Required—TOEFL (minimum score 550 paper-based; 213 computer-based). *Application deadline:* For fall admission, 7/1 for international students; for spring admission, 11/1 for international students. Applications are processed on a rolling basis. Application fee: $25. Electronic applications accepted. *Expenses:* Tuition, state resident: full-time $3,516; part-time $147 per hour. Tuition, nonresident: full-time $9,054; part-time $377 per hour. Required fees: $433; $18 per hour. *Financial support:* Career-related internships or fieldwork, Federal Work-Study, and unspecified assistantships available. Financial award application deadline: 3/31; financial award applicants required to submit FAFSA. *Faculty research:* China, Russia, civil war, American naval logistics. *Unit head:* Dr. Stanley Adamial, Chairman, 405-974-5451, Fax: 405-974-3823. *Application contact:* Dr. Carolyn Pool, Director, 405-974-5671, Fax: 405-974-3823, E-mail: cpool@ucok.edu.

University of Dallas, Braniff Graduate School of Liberal Arts, Program in American Studies, Irving, TX 75062-4736. Offers MAS. Part-time programs available. *Faculty:* 1 full-time (0 women), 2 part-time/adjunct (0 women). *Students:* 4 full-time (all women), 4 part-time (2 women). Average age 35. 2 applicants, 100% accepted, 1 enrolled. In 2007, 2 degrees awarded. *Degree requirements:* For master's, comprehensive exam. *Entrance requirements:* For master's, GRE General Test. *Application deadline:* For fall admission, 2/15 priority date for domestic students; for spring admission, 11/15 for domestic students. Applications are processed on a rolling basis. Application fee: $50. *Expenses:* Tuition: Part-time $600 per credit. Required fees: $15 per credit. *Financial support:* In 2007–08, 8 students received support. Scholarships/grants available. Financial award application deadline: 2/15. *Faculty research:* Shakespeare, Milton, Melville, Hawthorne, liberty and American literature. *Unit head:* Dr. John Alvis, Director, 972-721-5365, Fax: 972-721-4007, E-mail: alvis@udallas.edu. *Application contact:* Graduate Coordinator, 972-721-5106, Fax: 972-721-5280, E-mail: graduate@acad.udallas.edu.

University of Delaware, College of Arts and Sciences, Winterthur Program in Early American Culture, Newark, DE 19716. Offers MA. *Faculty:* 18 full-time (12 women), 13 part-time/adjunct (9 women). *Students:* 18 full-time (15 women). Average age 26. 39 applicants, 23% accepted, 8 enrolled. In 2007, 10 degrees awarded. *Degree requirements:* For master's, thesis. *Entrance requirements:* For master's, GRE General Test, minimum GPA of 3.0. *Application deadline:* For fall admission, 1/15 for domestic students. Application fee: $60. Electronic applications accepted. *Financial support:* In 2007–08, 18 students received support, including 16 fellowships with full tuition reimbursements available (averaging $17,250 per year); career-related internships or fieldwork also available. Financial award application deadline: 1/15. *Faculty research:* American material culture, American studies, decorative arts. *Unit head:* Dr. J. Ritchie Garrison, Director, 302-831-2678, Fax: 302-831-8057, E-mail: jrg@udel.edu.

University of Hawaii at Manoa, Graduate Division, Colleges of Arts and Sciences, College of Arts and Humanities, Department of American Studies, Honolulu, HI 96822. Offers American studies (MA, PhD); historic preservation (Graduate Certificate); museum studies (Graduate Certificate). Part-time programs available. *Faculty:* 11 full-time (3 women), 3 part-time/adjunct (1 woman). *Students:* 28 full-time (18 women), 22 part-time (13 women); includes 15 minority (1 American Indian/Alaska Native, 12 Asian Americans or Pacific Islanders, 2 Hispanic Americans), 8 international. Average age 38. 41 applicants, 66% accepted, 15 enrolled. *Median time to degree:* Of those who began their doctoral program in fall 1999, 33% received their degree in 8 years or less. *Degree requirements:* For master's, comprehensive exam (for some programs), thesis (for some programs); for doctorate, comprehensive exam, thesis/dissertation. *Entrance requirements:* For master's and doctorate, GRE General Test. Additional exam requirements/recommendations for international students: Required—TOEFL (minimum score 600 paper-based; 250 computer-based; 100 iBT), IELTS (minimum score 7). *Application deadline:* For fall admission, 2/1 for domestic students, 1/15 for international students; for spring admission, 9/1 for domestic and international students. Application fee: $50. *Financial support:* In 2007–08, 7 teaching assistantships (averaging $14,154 per year) were awarded; institutionally sponsored loans and tuition waivers (full and partial) also available. Support available to part-time students. Financial award application deadline: 3/31. *Faculty research:* Ethnicity and race, popular culture, historic preservation, arts and culture, international relations. Total annual research expenditures: $6,584. *Application contact:* Robert Perkinson, Graduate Chairperson, 808-956-8570, Fax: 808-956-4733, E-mail: perk@hawaii.edu.

The University of Iowa, Graduate College, College of Liberal Arts and Sciences, Department of American Studies, Iowa City, IA 52242-1316. Offers MA, PhD. *Faculty:* 3 full-time, 3 part-time/adjunct. *Students:* 5 full-time (2 women), 32 part-time (15 women); includes 4 minority (2 African Americans, 1 American Indian/Alaska Native, 1 Asian American or Pacific Islander), 5 international. 50 applicants, 26% accepted, 6 enrolled. In 2007, 9 master's, 1 doctorate awarded. *Degree requirements:* For master's, thesis optional, exam; for doctorate, comprehensive exam, thesis/dissertation. *Entrance requirements:* For master's and doctorate, GRE General Test, minimum GPA of 3.0. Additional exam requirements/recommendations for international students: Required—TOEFL (minimum score 550 paper-based; 213 computer-based; 81 iBT). *Application deadline:* For fall admission, 1/10 for domestic and international students. Application fee: $60 ($85 for international students). Electronic applications accepted. *Expenses:* Tuition, state resident: part-time $349 per hour. Tuition, nonresident: part-time $349 per hour. Tuition and fees vary according to course load and program. *Financial support:* In 2007–08, 4 fellowships, 5 research assistantships with partial tuition reimbursements, 21 teaching assistantships with partial tuition reimbursements were awarded. Financial award applicants required to submit FAFSA. *Unit head:* Dr. Lauren Rabinovitz, Chair, 319-335-0320, Fax: 319-335-0314.

American Studies

University of Kansas, Research and Graduate Studies, College of Liberal Arts and Sciences, Program in American Studies, Lawrence, KS 66045. Offers MA, PhD, MUP/MA. Part-time programs available. *Faculty:* 13. *Students:* 35 full-time (23 women), 18 part-time (11 women); includes 7 minority (4 African Americans, 1 American Indian/Alaska Native, 2 Hispanic Americans), 14 international. Average age 33. 31 applicants, 55% accepted, 6 enrolled. In 2007, 7 master's, 4 doctorates awarded. Terminal master's awarded for partial completion of doctoral program. *Degree requirements:* For master's, thesis or alternative; for doctorate, 2 foreign languages, comprehensive exam, thesis/dissertation. *Entrance requirements:* For master's and doctorate, GRE General Test. Additional exam requirements/recommendations for international students: Required—TOEFL. *Application deadline:* For fall admission, 5/1 for domestic students. Applications are processed on a rolling basis. Application fee: $55 ($60 for international students). Electronic applications accepted. *Expenses:* Tuition, state resident: full-time $5,838. Tuition, nonresident: full-time $13,409. Tuition and fees vary according to program. *Financial support:* Fellowships with full tuition reimbursements, research assistantships with partial tuition reimbursements, teaching assistantships with full and partial tuition reimbursements, Federal Work-Study and unspecified assistantships available. Financial award application deadline: 12/21. *Faculty research:* Race and ethnicity, popular culture, contemporary America, gender, social and cultural theory. *Unit head:* Cheryl Lester, Director, 785-864-2309, Fax: 785-864-5772, E-mail: chlester@ku.edu. *Application contact:* Kay Isbell, Information Contact, 785-864-2306, Fax: 785-864-5772, E-mail: amerst@ku.edu.

University of Louisiana at Lafayette, Graduate School, College of Liberal Arts, Department of Modern Languages, Program in Francophone Studies, Lafayette, LA 70504. Offers PhD. *Degree requirements:* For doctorate, 2 foreign languages, comprehensive exam, thesis/dissertation. *Entrance requirements:* For doctorate, GRE General Test, minimum GPA of 2.75. Additional exam requirements/recommendations for international students: Required—TOEFL (minimum score 550 paper-based; 213 computer-based). Electronic applications accepted. *Faculty research:* Louisiana folklore, eighteenth century French literature, contemporary criticism.

University of Maryland, College Park, Graduate Studies, College of Arts and Humanities, Department of American Studies, College Park, MD 20742. Offers MA, PhD. *Faculty:* 49 full-time (23 women), 4 part-time/adjunct (1 woman). *Students:* 55 full-time (39 women), 12 part-time (8 women); includes 26 minority (18 African Americans, 3 Asian Americans or Pacific Islanders, 5 Hispanic Americans), 5 international. 95 applicants, 25% accepted, 9 enrolled. In 2007, 6 master's, 5 doctorates awarded. *Median time to degree:* Of those who began their doctoral program in fall 1999, 11% received their degree in 8 years or less. *Degree requirements:* For master's, thesis optional, thesis or scholarly paper and exam; for doctorate, thesis/dissertation, 3 comprehensive exams. *Entrance requirements:* For master's, GRE General Test, minimum GPA of 3.0, writing sample, 3 letters of recommendation; for doctorate, GRE General Test. Additional exam requirements/recommendations for international students: Required—TOEFL. *Application deadline:* For fall admission, 12/15 for domestic students, 2/1 for international students. Applications are processed on a rolling basis. Application fee: $60. Electronic applications accepted. *Financial support:* In 2007–08, 4 fellowships with full tuition reimbursements (averaging $10,919 per year), 32 teaching assistantships with tuition reimbursements (averaging $16,144 per year) were awarded; research assistantships, career-related internships or fieldwork, Federal Work-Study, and scholarships/grants also available. Support available to part-time students. Financial award applicants required to submit FAFSA. *Faculty research:* Material culture, modes of culture, cultural movements, popular culture, ethnography. Total annual research expenditures: $1,500. *Unit head:* Nancy L. Struna, Chairperson, 301-405-7183, Fax: 301-314-9453, E-mail: nlstruna@umd.edu. *Application contact:* Dean of Graduate School, 301-405-4190, Fax: 301-314-9305.

University of Massachusetts Boston, Office of Graduate Studies, College of Liberal Arts, Program in American Studies, Boston, MA 02125-3393. Offers MA. Part-time and evening/weekend programs available. *Degree requirements:* For master's, thesis or capstone project. *Entrance requirements:* For master's, minimum GPA of 2.75. *Faculty research:* War in American culture, immigration history, Latin Americans, history of race and popular music, education and Asian Americans.

University of Michigan, Horace H. Rackham School of Graduate Studies, College of Literature, Science, and the Arts, Interdepartmental Program in American Culture, Ann Arbor, MI 48109. Offers AM, PhD. *Faculty:* 37 full-time (19 women). *Students:* 59 full-time (34 women); includes 33 minority (9 African Americans, 2 American Indian/Alaska Native, 12 Asian Americans or Pacific Islanders, 10 Hispanic Americans), 2 international. 90 applicants, 10% accepted, 7 enrolled. In 2007, 3 master's, 6 doctorates awarded. Terminal master's awarded for partial completion of doctoral program. *Degree requirements:* For doctorate, field and preliminary exams, oral defense of dissertation. *Entrance requirements:* For master's, GRE General Test; for doctorate, GRE General Test, sample of written work. Additional exam requirements/recommendations for international students: Required—TOEFL. *Application deadline:* For fall admission, 12/1 for domestic and international students. Application fee: $60 ($75 for international students). Electronic applications accepted. *Financial support:* In 2007–08, 7 fellowships with tuition reimbursements (averaging $18,000 per year), 15 teaching assistantships with tuition reimbursements (averaging $18,000 per year) were awarded; research assistantships, Federal Work-Study and tuition waivers also available. *Faculty research:* Cultural studies; ethnic studies, American culture methodology, literature, history. *Unit head:* Gregory Dowd, Director, 734-763-1460, Fax: 734-936-1967, E-mail: ac.inq@umich.edu. *Application contact:* Marlene Moore, Graduate Student Coordinator, 734-647-9533, Fax: 734-936-1967, E-mail: ac.inq@umich.edu.

University of Michigan–Flint, Graduate Programs, Program in American Culture, Flint, MI 48502-1950. Offers MLS. Part-time programs available. *Faculty:* 2 full-time (0 women). *Students:* 6 full-time (3 women), 30 part-time (17 women); includes 7 minority (4 African Americans, 2 Asian Americans or Pacific Islanders, 1 Hispanic American). Average age 43. 6 applicants, 100% accepted, 4 enrolled. In 2007, 14 degrees awarded. *Degree requirements:* For master's, thesis. *Entrance requirements:* For master's, minimum GPA of 3.0, 24 undergraduate credits in humanities and social sciences. Additional exam requirements/recommendations for international students: Required—TOEFL (minimum score 560 paper-based; 220 computer-based; 84 iBT), IELTS (minimum score 7). *Application deadline:* For fall admission, 8/1 for domestic students, 3/1 for international students; for winter admission, 11/15 for domestic students, 7/1 for international students; for spring admission, 3/15 for domestic students, 11/1 for international students. Application fee: $55. Electronic applications accepted. *Financial support:* In 2007–08, 3 fellowships (averaging $1,000 per year), 1 research assistantship (averaging $3,850 per year) were awarded; Federal Work-Study, scholarships/grants, and unspecified assistantships also available. Support available to part-time students. Financial award application deadline: 6/1; financial award applicants required to submit FAFSA. *Unit head:* Dr. Robert L. Houbeck, Director, 810-762-3018, E-mail: rhoubeck@umflint.edu. *Application contact:* Bradley T. Maki, Director of Graduate Admissions, 810-762-3171, Fax: 810-766-6789, E-mail: bmaki@umflint.edu.

University of Minnesota, Twin Cities Campus, Graduate School, College of Liberal Arts, Department of American Studies, Minneapolis, MN 55455-0213. Offers PhD. *Degree requirements:* For doctorate, one foreign language, comprehensive exam, thesis/dissertation. *Entrance requirements:* For doctorate, GRE General Test, sample of written work, 3 letters of recommendation. Additional exam requirements/recommendations for international students: Required—TOEFL (minimum score 550 paper-based; 213 computer-based). *Faculty research:* American Indian history, nationalism/transnationalism, gender and sexuality, race and ethnicity.

University of Mississippi, Graduate School, College of Liberal Arts, Interdisciplinary Program in Southern Studies, Oxford, University, MS 38677. Offers MA. *Faculty:* 1 full-time (0 women). *Students:* 17 full-time (9 women), 7 part-time (4 women); includes 3 minority (2 African Americans, 1 American Indian/Alaska Native), 1 international. In 2007, 5 degrees awarded. *Entrance requirements:* For master's, GRE General Test, minimum GPA of 3.0. Additional exam requirements/recommendations for international students: Required—TOEFL. *Application deadline:* For fall admission, 2/1 for domestic students; for spring admission, 10/1 for domestic students. Applications are processed on a rolling basis. Application fee: $25. Electronic applications accepted. *Expenses:* Tuition, state resident: full-time $4,932. Tuition, nonresident: full-time $11,436. *Financial support:* Scholarships/grants available. Financial award application deadline: 3/1; financial award applicants required to submit FAFSA. *Unit head:* Dr. Ted Ownby, Interim Director, 662-915-5993, Fax: 662-915-5814, E-mail: cssc@olemiss.edu.

University of New Mexico, Graduate School, College of Arts and Sciences, Department of American Studies, Albuquerque, NM 87131-2039. Offers MA, PhD. Part-time programs available. *Faculty:* 5 full-time (2 women), 3 part-time/adjunct (2 women). *Students:* 38 full-time (30 women), 15 part-time (11 women); includes 20 minority (3 African Americans, 4 American Indian/Alaska Native, 13 Hispanic Americans), 1 international. Average age 37. 49 applicants, 35% accepted, 8 enrolled. In 2007, 3 master's, 6 doctorates awarded. Terminal master's awarded for partial completion of doctoral program. *Degree requirements:* For master's, comprehensive exam (for some programs), thesis (for some programs); for doctorate, one foreign language, comprehensive exam, thesis/dissertation. *Entrance requirements:* For master's, BA in related field; for doctorate, MA in related field, complete dossier. Additional exam requirements/recommendations for international students: Required—TOEFL. *Application deadline:* For fall admission, 2/1 for domestic students. Application fee: $50. Electronic applications accepted. *Financial support:* In 2007–08, 29 students received support, including 24 teaching assistantships with tuition reimbursements available (averaging $6,024 per year); research assistantships, career-related internships or fieldwork, health care benefits, tuition waivers (full), and unspecified assistantships also available. Support available to part-time students. Financial award application deadline: 3/1; financial award applicants required to submit FAFSA. *Faculty research:* Culture studies environment/science/technology, gender, race/class/ethnicity, popular culture, Southwest studies. Total annual research expenditures: $13,755. *Unit head:* Dr. Alex Lubin, Chair, 505-277-3929, Fax: 505-277-1208, E-mail: alubin@unm.edu. *Application contact:* Dr. Sandy Rodrigue, Department Administrator, 505-277-3929, Fax: 505-277-1208, E-mail: amstudy@unm.edu.

University of Pennsylvania, School of Arts and Sciences, Graduate Group in American Civilization, Philadelphia, PA 19104. Offers AM, PhD, JD/AM, JD/PhD. Electronic applications accepted. *Faculty research:* Cultural history, historic ethnography, material culture studies.

University of Southern California, Graduate School, College of Letters, Arts and Sciences, Department of American Studies and Ethnicity, Los Angeles, CA 90089. Offers PhD. *Faculty:* 38 full-time (21 women). *Students:* 48 full-time (31 women); includes 38 minority (12 African Americans, 1 American Indian/Alaska Native, 13 Asian Americans or Pacific Islanders, 12 Hispanic Americans), 2 international. 77 applicants, 13% accepted. In 2007, 2 doctorates awarded. Terminal master's awarded for partial completion of doctoral program. *Degree requirements:* For doctorate, one foreign language, thesis/dissertation. *Entrance requirements:* For doctorate, GRE. *Application deadline:* For fall admission, 12/1 priority date for domestic students. Application fee: $85. *Financial support:* In 2007–08, 40 students received support, including fellowships with full tuition reimbursements available (averaging $17,270 per year), research assistantships with full tuition reimbursements available (averaging $18,570 per year), teaching assistantships with full tuition reimbursements available (averaging $18,570 per year); tuition waivers (full) also available. *Faculty research:* Race, ethnicity, culture, gender, sexuality. *Unit head:* Dr. Ruth Gilmore, Chair, 213-740-2426, E-mail: aseinfo@usc.edu.

University of Southern Maine, College of Arts and Sciences, Program in American and New England Studies, Portland, ME 04104-9300. Offers MA. Part-time and evening/weekend programs available. *Degree requirements:* For master's, thesis optional. *Entrance requirements:* For master's, GRE General Test or MAT. Additional exam requirements/recommendations for international students: Required—TOEFL. *Faculty research:* Social history, regional culture, landscape of literature, material culture, art and architecture.

University of South Florida, Graduate School, College of Arts and Sciences, Department of Humanities and American Studies, Tampa, FL 33620-9951. Offers American studies (MA); liberal arts (MLA). Part-time and evening/weekend programs available. *Faculty:* 8 full-time (4 women). *Students:* 17 full-time (11 women), 23 part-time (10 women); includes 9 minority (7 African Americans, 2 Hispanic Americans). 20 applicants, 75% accepted, 12 enrolled. In 2007, 6 degrees awarded. *Degree requirements:* For master's, thesis. *Entrance requirements:* For master's, GRE General Test, minimum GPA of 3.0 in last 60 hours, academic writing sample. *Application deadline:* For fall admission, 6/1 priority date for domestic students, 3/1 for international students; for spring admission, 10/15 priority date for domestic students, 8/1 for international students. Application fee: $30. *Financial support:* In 2007–08, 4 teaching assistantships with tuition reimbursements were awarded; scholarships/grants also available. Financial award application deadline: 4/4. *Faculty research:* American South, American autobiography, material culture, critical theory, cultural studies. *Unit head:* Daniel Belgrad, Program Director, 813-974-9388, Fax: 813-974-9409, E-mail: ams@cas.usf.edu. *Application contact:* Sarah Challis, Information Contact, 813-974-9388, Fax: 813-974-9409, E-mail: ams@cas.usf.edu.

The University of Texas at Austin, Graduate School, College of Liberal Arts, Department of American Studies, Austin, TX 78712-1111. Offers MA, PhD. Part-time programs available. *Degree requirements:* For master's, thesis; for doctorate, one foreign language, thesis/dissertation, qualifying oral exam. *Entrance requirements:* For master's and doctorate, GRE General Test, minimum GPA of 3.5. Electronic applications accepted. *Faculty research:* Race, gender, and ethnicity; history of the American West; American design and archaeology; literary cultural history; religion and psychology in American culture.

University of Utah, The Graduate School, College of Humanities, Department of English, Salt Lake City, UT 84112-1107. Offers American studies (MA, PhD); British American literature (MA, PhD); creative writing (MFA, PhD); literature (PhD); rhetoric and composition (PhD). *Faculty:* 39 full-time (16 women). *Students:* 59 full-time (39 women), 23 part-time (14 women); includes 5 minority (2 African Americans, 1 American Indian/Alaska Native, 2 Asian Americans or Pacific Islanders), 1 international. Average age 33. 177 applicants, 23% accepted, 22 enrolled. In 2007, 14 master's, 7 doctorates awarded. *Median time to degree:* Of those who began their doctoral program in fall 1999, 83% received their degree in 8 years or less. *Degree requirements:* For master's, one foreign language, thesis (for some programs), written exam; for doctorate, 2 foreign languages, comprehensive exam, thesis/dissertation. *Entrance requirements:* For master's and doctorate, GRE General Test, minimum GPA of 3.2. Additional exam requirements/recommendations for international students: Required—TOEFL (minimum score 500 paper-based; 173 computer-based; 120 iBT). *Application deadline:* For fall admission, 12/15 for domestic and international students. Applications are processed on a rolling basis. Application fee: $45 ($65 for international students). Electronic applications accepted. *Financial support:* In 2007–08, 49 students received support, including 8 fellowships with full tuition reimbursements available (averaging $12,000 per year), 41 teaching assistantships with full tuition reimbursements available (averaging $12,000 per year); research assistantships, health care benefits also available. Financial award application deadline: 12/15; financial award applicants required to submit FAFSA. *Faculty research:* Poetics and modern poetry, 19th and 20th century British and American literature, the American west, environmental studies, critical theory and race and gender studies. Total annual research expenditures: $36,210. *Unit head:* Prof. Vincent P. Pecora, Chair, 801-581-6168, E-mail: v.pecora@utah.edu. *Application contact:* Prof. Matthew Potolsky, Director of Graduate Studies, 801-581-5245, E-mail: m.potolsky@utah.edu.

University of Wyoming, Graduate School, College of Arts and Sciences, American Studies Program, Laramie, WY 82070. Offers MA. Part-time programs available. *Faculty:* 3 full-time (1 woman). *Students:* 10 full-time (4 women), 9 part-time (5 women), 5 international. Average age 29. 14 applicants, 57% accepted. In 2007, 10 degrees awarded. *Degree requirements:* For master's, thesis optional. *Entrance requirements:* For master's, GRE General Test, minimum GPA of 3.0. *Application deadline:* For fall admission, 4/1 priority date for domestic students. Applications are processed on a rolling basis. Application fee: $50. *Financial support:* In

2007–08, 10 research assistantships with tuition reimbursements, 7 teaching assistantships with tuition reimbursements were awarded; career-related internships or fieldwork, Federal Work-Study, and tuition waivers (partial) also available. Financial award application deadline: 3/1. *Faculty research:* Material culture, American culture, ethnicity, cultural environments, public culture. Total annual research expenditures: $25,000. *Unit head:* Dr. Eric Sandeen, Director, 307-766-3898.

Utah State University, School of Graduate Studies, College of Humanities, Arts and Social Sciences, Department of English and Department of History, Program in American Studies, Logan, UT 84322. Offers folklore (MA, MS); western American literature and culture (MA, MS). Part-time and evening/weekend programs available. *Degree requirements:* For master's, thesis or alternative. *Entrance requirements:* For master's, GRE General Test or MAT, minimum GPA of 3.0, 3 letters of recommendation, writing sample. Additional exam requirements/recommendations for international students: Required—TOEFL. *Faculty research:* Folklore and folklife, American culture, regional studies, material culture, Jewish folklore, Native American folklore.

Washington State University, Graduate School, College of Liberal Arts, Department of History, Pullman, WA 99164. Offers early and modern European history (MA, PhD); environmental history (MA, PhD); Latin American history (MA, PhD); modern East Asia history (MA, PhD); public history (MA, PhD); US history (MA, PhD); women's history (MA, PhD); world history (MA, PhD). Part-time programs available. *Faculty:* 24. *Students:* 45 full-time (28 women), 8 part-time (4 women); includes 2 minority (both Hispanic Americans), 2 international. Average age 33. 64 applicants, 41% accepted, 15 enrolled. In 2007, 8 master's, 2 doctorates awarded. *Degree requirements:* For master's, comprehensive exam (for some programs), thesis, oral exam; for doctorate, one foreign language, comprehensive exam, thesis/dissertation, oral and written exam. *Entrance requirements:* For master's, GRE General Test, minimum GPA of 3.3, language background form, writing sample; for doctorate, GRE General Test, minimum GPA of 3.5, language background form, writing sample. Additional exam requirements/recommendations for international students: Required—TOEFL (minimum score 550 paper-based). *Application deadline:* For fall admission, 2/1 for domestic and international students; for spring admission, 11/1 for domestic and international students. Applications are processed on a rolling basis. Application fee: $50. Electronic applications accepted. *Financial support:* In 2007–08, 30 students received support, including 1 fellowship with partial tuition reimbursement available (averaging $3,000 per year), research assistantships with full and partial tuition reimbursements available (averaging $13,917 per year), 28 teaching assistantships with full and partial tuition reimbursements available (averaging $13,056 per year); career-related internships or fieldwork, Federal Work-Study, institutionally sponsored loans, scholarships/grants, and health care benefits also available. Financial award application deadline: 4/1; financial award applicants required to submit FAFSA. *Faculty research:* Public, world, environmental, women and U.S. history. Total annual research expenditures: $44,501. *Unit head:* Dr. John Kicza, Co-Chair, 509-335-5002, Fax: 509-335-4171, E-mail: jekicza@wsu.edu. *Application contact:* Graduate Studies Director, 509-335-4030, Fax: 509-335-4171, E-mail: kale@wsu.edu.

Washington State University, Graduate School, College of Liberal Arts, Program in American Studies, Pullman, WA 99164. Offers ethnic studies (MA, PhD); feminist studies (MA, PhD); history (MA, PhD); literature (MA, PhD). *Faculty:* 39. *Students:* 27 full-time (19 women), 4 part-time (2 women); includes 17 minority (6 African Americans, 4 American Indian/Alaska Native, 2 Asian Americans or Pacific Islanders, 5 Hispanic Americans), 3 international. Average age 35. 78 applicants, 15% accepted, 12 enrolled. In 2007, 5 master's, 1 doctorate awarded. *Degree requirements:* For master's, one foreign language, comprehensive exam (for some programs), thesis optional, oral exam; for doctorate, one foreign language, comprehensive exam (for some programs), thesis/dissertation, oral exam. *Entrance requirements:* For master's and doctorate, GRE General Test, minimum GPA of 3.0, writing sample, 3 letters of recommendation. Additional exam requirements/recommendations for international students: Required—TOEFL. *Application deadline:* For fall admission, 2/1 priority date for domestic students, 3/1 for international students; for spring admission, 7/1 for international students. Applications are processed on a rolling basis. Application fee: $50. *Financial support:* In 2007–08, 24 students received support, including 1 fellowship (averaging $6,950 per year), 3 research assistantships with full and partial tuition reimbursements available (averaging $13,917 per year), 17 teaching assistantships with full and partial tuition reimbursements available (averaging $13,056 per year); career-related internships or fieldwork, Federal Work-Study, institutionally sponsored loans, tuition waivers (partial), and teaching associateships also available. Financial award application deadline: 3/1; financial award applicants required to submit FAFSA. *Faculty research:* The American West in multicultural perspective; nineteenth century historical, literary, and cultural studies; comparative American ethnic literatures and cultures; American cultures and the environment; American rhetoric. *Unit head:* Dr. Noel Sturgeon, Director, 509-335-1560, E-mail: reedtv@wsu.edu. *Application contact:* Graduate School Admissions, 800-GRADWSU, Fax: 509-335-1949, E-mail: gradsch@wsu.edu.

West Virginia University, Eberly College of Arts and Sciences, Department of History, Morgantown, WV 26506. Offers African history (MA, PhD); African-American history (MA, PhD); American history (MA, PhD); Appalachian/regional history (MA, PhD); East Asian history (MA, PhD); European history (MA, PhD); history of science and technology (MA, PhD); Latin American history (MA). Part-time programs available. *Faculty:* 19 full-time (5 women), 12 part-time/adjunct (4 women). *Students:* 43 full-time (17 women), 30 part-time (11 women); includes 5 minority (1 African American, 1 American Indian/Alaska Native, 2 Asian Americans or Pacific Islanders, 1 Hispanic American), 7 international. Average age 33. 70 applicants, 59% accepted, 17 enrolled. In 2007, 8 master's, 3 doctorates awarded. *Median time to degree:* Of those who began their doctoral program in fall 1999, 75% received their degree in 8 years or less. *Degree requirements:* For master's, one foreign language, thesis (for some programs), oral exam, thesis defense; for doctorate, one foreign language, comprehensive exam, thesis/dissertation, dissertation defense. *Entrance requirements:* For master's, GRE General Test, minimum GPA of 3.0; for doctorate, GRE General Test. Additional exam requirements/recommendations for international students: Required—TOEFL (minimum score 550 paper-based), IELTS (minimum score 7). *Application deadline:* For fall admission, 12/31 for domestic students; for spring admission, 10/1 for domestic students. Applications are processed on a rolling basis. Application fee: $45. Electronic applications accepted. *Expenses:* Tuition, state resident: full-time $5,196; part-time $292 per credit hour. Tuition, nonresident: full-time $15,064; part-time $840 per credit hour. Tuition and fees vary according to program. *Financial support:* In 2007–08, 60 students received support, including 5 fellowships with full tuition reimbursements available (averaging $3,000 per year), 1 research assistantship with full tuition reimbursement available (averaging $7,200 per year), 8 teaching assistantships with full tuition reimbursements available (averaging $12,000 per year); career-related internships or fieldwork, Federal Work-Study, institutionally sponsored loans, health care benefits, tuition waivers (full and partial), and graduate administrative assistantships also available. Financial award application deadline: 12/31; financial award applicants required to submit FAFSA. *Faculty research:* U.S., Appalachia, modern Europe, Africa, colonial and post-colonial societies. Total annual research expenditures: $93,327. *Unit head:* Dr. Steven M. Zdatny, Chair, 304-293-2421 Ext. 5241, Fax: 304-293-3616, E-mail: steve.zdatny@mail.wvu.edu. *Application contact:* Dr. Greg A. Good, Director of Graduate Studies, 304-293-2421 Ext. 5247, Fax: 304-293-3616, E-mail: greg.good@mail.wvu.edu.

Wheaton College, Graduate School, Department of Biblical and Theological Studies, Program in Religion in American Life, Wheaton, IL 60187-5593. Offers MA. Part-time programs available. *Students:* 6 applicants, 83% accepted, 4 enrolled. *Degree requirements:* For master's, thesis optional. *Entrance requirements:* For master's, GRE General Test, MAT. *Application deadline:* For fall admission, 3/1 priority date for domestic students; for spring admission, 11/1 for domestic students. Applications are processed on a rolling basis. Application fee: $30. Electronic applications accepted. *Financial support:* Scholarships/grants and unspecified assistantships available. Financial award application deadline: 3/1; financial award applicants required to submit FAFSA. *Unit head:* Dr. Timothy Larsen, Head, 630-752-5177. *Application contact:* Julie A. Huebner, Director of Graduate Admissions, 630-752-5195, Fax: 630-752-5935, E-mail: gradadm@wheaton.edu.

Yale University, Graduate School of Arts and Sciences, Interdisciplinary Program in American Studies, New Haven, CT 06520. Offers MA, PhD. *Degree requirements:* For doctorate, one foreign language, thesis/dissertation. *Entrance requirements:* For doctorate, GRE General Test.

Asian-American Studies

California State University, Long Beach, Graduate Studies, College of Liberal Arts, Department of Asian and Asian American Studies, Long Beach, CA 90840. Offers Asian American studies (Certificate); Asian studies (MA). Part-time programs available. *Faculty:* 11 full-time (7 women), 12 part-time/adjunct (7 women). *Students:* 10 full-time (6 women), 13 part-time (9 women); includes 19 Asian Americans or Pacific Islanders. Average age 41. *Degree requirements:* For master's, one foreign language, comprehensive exam or thesis. *Application deadline:* For fall admission, 7/1 for domestic students; for spring admission, 12/1 for domestic students. Applications are processed on a rolling basis. Application fee: $55. Electronic applications accepted. *Financial support:* Federal Work-Study, institutionally sponsored loans, and scholarships/grants available. Financial award application deadline: 3/2. *Faculty research:* South Asia, China, Japan, Southeast Asia, Asian-American in the U.S. *Unit head:* Dr. John N Tsuchida, Chair, 562-985-7530, Fax: 562-985-1535, E-mail: jtsuchid@csulb.edu. *Application contact:* Dr. Hsin-Sheng Cassandra Kao, Graduate Advisor, 562-985-7530, Fax: 562-985-1535, E-mail: ckao@csulb.edu.

San Francisco State University, Division of Graduate Studies, College of Ethnic Studies, Program in Asian American Studies, San Francisco, CA 94132-1722. Offers MA. *Unit head:* Dr. Morlon Hom, Unit Head, 415-338-2968. *Application contact:* Ben Kobashigawa, Coordinator, 415-338-2698, E-mail: aas@sfsu.edu.

University of California, Los Angeles, Graduate Division, College of Letters and Science, Program in Asian-American Studies, Los Angeles, CA 90095. Offers MA, MA/MPH, MA/MSW. *Students:* 14 full-time (9 women); includes 9 minority (8 Asian Americans or Pacific Islanders, 1 Hispanic American). Average age 26. 22 applicants, 41% accepted, 7 enrolled. In 2007, 15 degrees awarded. *Degree requirements:* For master's, one foreign language, comprehensive exam or thesis, research tool. *Entrance requirements:* For master's, minimum GPA of 3.0, sample of written work. *Application deadline:* For fall admission, 12/15 for domestic students. Application fee: $60. Electronic applications accepted. *Expenses:* Tuition, nonresident: full-time $5,728. Required fees: $8,966. Full-time tuition and fees vary according to program and student level. *Financial support:* In 2007–08, 16 fellowships with full and partial tuition reimbursements, 4 research assistantships with full and partial tuition reimbursements, 12 teaching assistantships with full and partial tuition reimbursements were awarded; tuition waivers (full and partial) also available. Financial award application deadline: 3/1; financial award applicants required to submit FAFSA. *Unit head:* Dr. Lane Hirabayashi, Chair, 310-267-5592. *Application contact:* Departmental Office, 310-267-5592, E-mail: maprogram@asianam.ucla.edu.

Asian Studies

California Institute of Integral Studies, Graduate Programs, School of Consciousness and Transformation, San Francisco, CA 94103. Offers cultural anthropology and social transformation (MA); East-West psychology (MA, PhD); integrative health studies (MA); philosophy and religion (MA, PhD), including Asian and comparative studies, philosophy, cosmology, and consciousness, social and cultural anthropology (PhD), transformative leadership (MA), transformative studies (PhD), women's spirituality, women's spirituality flex format; social and cultural anthropology (PhD); transformative leadership (MA); transformative studies (PhD). Part-time and evening/weekend programs available. Postbaccalaureate distance learning degree programs offered (minimal on-campus study). *Faculty:* 30 full-time, 28 part-time/adjunct. *Students:* 456; includes 92 minority (32 African Americans, 3 American Indian/Alaska Native, 40 Asian Americans or Pacific Islanders, 17 Hispanic Americans), 1 international. Average age 37. 206 applicants, 93% accepted, 114 enrolled. In 2007, 26 degrees awarded. Terminal master's awarded for partial completion of doctoral program. *Degree requirements:* For master's, comprehensive exam (for some programs), thesis optional; for doctorate, comprehensive exam, thesis/dissertation. *Entrance requirements:* For master's, minimum GPA of 3.0, letters of recommendation, writing sample; for doctorate, master's degree, minimum GPA of 3.0, letters of recommendation, writing sample. Additional exam requirements/recommendations for international students: Required—TOEFL. *Application deadline:* For fall admission, 2/15 priority date for domestic and international students; for spring admission, 10/15 priority date for domestic and international students. Applications are processed on a rolling basis. Application fee: $65. Electronic applications accepted. *Expenses:* Tuition: Full-time $16,930; part-time $780 per unit. Tuition and fees vary according to course load and program. *Financial support:* In 2007–08, 292 students received support; research assistantships, teaching assistantships, career-related internships or fieldwork, Federal Work-Study, institutionally sponsored loans, scholarships/grants, and tuition waivers (partial) available. Support available to part-time students. Financial award application deadline: 3/15; financial award applicants required to

Asian Studies

California Institute of Integral Studies (continued)
submit FAFSA. *Faculty research:* Altered states of consciousness, dreams, cosmology, postcolonial studies, integrative health studies. *Application contact:* Allyson Werner, Senior Admissions Counselor, 415-575-6155, Fax: 415-575-1268.

See Close-Up on page 445.

California State University, Long Beach, Graduate Studies, College of Liberal Arts, Department of Asian and Asian American Studies, Long Beach, CA 90840. Offers Asian American studies (Certificate); Asian studies (MA). Part-time programs available. *Faculty:* 11 full-time (7 women), 12 part-time/adjunct (7 women). *Students:* 10 full-time (6 women), 13 part-time (9 women); includes 19 Asian Americans or Pacific Islanders. Average age 41. *Degree requirements:* For master's, one foreign language, comprehensive exam or thesis. *Application deadline:* For fall admission, 7/1 for domestic students; for spring admission, 12/1 for domestic students. Applications are processed on a rolling basis. Application fee: $55. Electronic applications accepted. *Financial support:* Federal Work-Study, institutionally sponsored loans, and scholarships/grants available. Financial award application deadline: 3/2. *Faculty research:* South Asia, China, Japan, Southeast Asia, Asian-American in the U.S. *Unit head:* Dr. John N Tsuchida, Chair, 562-985-7530, Fax: 562-985-1535, E-mail: jtsuchid@csulb.edu. *Application contact:* Dr. Hsin-Sheng Cassandra Kao, Graduate Advisor, 562-985-7530, Fax: 562-985-1535, E-mail: ckao@csulb.edu.

Columbia University, Graduate School of Arts and Sciences, Division of Humanities, Department of East Asian Languages and Cultures, New York, NY 10027. Offers East Asian languages and cultures (M Phil, MA, PhD); Oriental studies (M Phil, MA, PhD). *Faculty:* 17 full-time, 17 part-time/adjunct. *Students:* 68 full-time (39 women), 5 part-time (3 women); includes 9 minority (all Asian Americans or Pacific Islanders), 15 international. Average age 32. 162 applicants, 31% accepted. In 2007, 11 master's, 7 doctorates awarded. *Degree requirements:* For master's, one foreign language, comprehensive exam, thesis; for doctorate, 2 foreign languages, thesis/dissertation. *Entrance requirements:* For master's and doctorate, GRE General Test. Additional exam requirements/recommendations for international students: Required—TOEFL. Application fee: $90. *Expenses:* Tuition: Part-time $1,452 per credit. Required fees: $152 per term. One-time fee: $75 part-time. Full-time tuition and fees vary according to course level, course load, degree level and program. *Financial support:* Fellowships, teaching assistantships, institutionally sponsored loans available. Support available to part-time students. Financial award application deadline: 1/5; financial award applicants required to submit FAFSA. *Unit head:* Robert Hymes, Chair, 212-854-2574, Fax: 212-678-8629, E-mail: hymes@columbia.edu.

Columbia University, Graduate School of Arts and Sciences, Division of Humanities, Department of Middle East Languages and Cultures, New York, NY 10027. Offers Hebrew language and literature (M Phil, MA, PhD); Middle Eastern languages and cultures (M Phil, MA, PhD); South Asian languages and cultures (M Phil, MA, PhD). Part-time programs available. *Faculty:* 22 full-time, 11 part-time/adjunct. *Students:* 52 full-time (25 women), 4 part-time (3 women); includes 4 minority (3 Asian Americans or Pacific Islanders, 1 Hispanic American), 12 international. Average age 35. 42 applicants, 48% accepted. In 2007, 2 master's, 5 doctorates awarded. *Degree requirements:* For master's, thesis, oral and written exams; for doctorate, 3 foreign languages, thesis/dissertation. *Entrance requirements:* For master's and doctorate, GRE General Test. Additional exam requirements/recommendations for international students: Required—TOEFL. Application fee: $90. *Expenses:* Tuition: Part-time $1,452 per credit. Required fees: $152 per term. One-time fee: $75 part-time. Full-time tuition and fees vary according to course level, course load, degree level and program. *Financial support:* Fellowships, teaching assistantships, Federal Work-Study and institutionally sponsored loans available. Support available to part-time students. Financial award application deadline: 1/5; financial award applicants required to submit FAFSA. *Faculty research:* Indo-Iranian, Turkish, central Asian, and Armenian studies; Arabic and ancient Semitics. *Unit head:* Sheldon Pollock, Chair, 212-854-6781, Fax: 212-854-5517, E-mail: sp2356@columbia.edu.

Columbia University, Graduate School of Arts and Sciences, Program in East Asian Regional Studies, New York, NY 10027. Offers MA. *Degree requirements:* For master's, 2 foreign languages. *Entrance requirements:* For master's, GRE General Test. Application fee: $90. *Expenses:* Tuition: Part-time $1,452 per credit. Required fees: $152 per term. One-time fee: $75 part-time. Full-time tuition and fees vary according to course level, course load, degree level and program. *Unit head:* Myron Cohen, Chair, 212-854-1739, E-mail: mlc5@columbia.edu.

Columbia University, Graduate School of Arts and Sciences, Program in Liberal Studies, New York, NY 10027. Offers American studies (MA); East Asian studies (MA); human rights studies (MA); Islamic culture studies (MA); Jewish studies (MA); medieval studies (MA); modern European studies (MA); South Asian studies (MA). Part-time and evening/weekend programs available. *Faculty:* 5 part-time/adjunct (2 women). *Students:* 7 full-time (2 women), 75 part-time (51 women); includes 5 minority (1 African American, 3 Asian Americans or Pacific Islanders, 1 Hispanic American), 8 international. Average age 41. 39 applicants, 77% accepted. In 2007, 20 degrees awarded. *Degree requirements:* For master's, thesis. Application fee: $90. *Expenses:* Tuition: Part-time $1,452 per credit. Required fees: $152 per term. One-time fee: $75 part-time. Full-time tuition and fees vary according to course level, course load, degree level and program. *Unit head:* Kristin Balicki, Program Coordinator, 212-854-4932, Fax: 212-854-4912, E-mail: knb2110@columbia.edu.

Columbia University, School of International and Public Affairs, Southern Asian Institute, New York, NY 10027. Offers Certificate. Students must be enrolled in a separate graduate degree program at Columbia University. *Application deadline:* For fall admission, 1/4 for domestic students; for spring admission, 10/1 for domestic students. Application fee: $85. Electronic applications accepted. *Expenses:* Tuition: Part-time $1,452 per credit. Required fees: $152 per term. One-time fee: $75 part-time. Full-time tuition and fees vary according to course level, course load, degree level and program. *Financial support:* Application deadline: 1/15. *Unit head:* Dr. Vidya Dehejia, Director, 212-854-3616, Fax: 212-854-6987, E-mail: sipa_admission@columbia.edu. *Application contact:* Matt Clemons, Director of Admissions and Financial Aid, 212-854-6216, Fax: 212-854-3010, E-mail: mc2793@columbia.edu.

Columbia University, School of International and Public Affairs, Weatherhead East Asian Institute, New York, NY 10027. Offers Asian studies (Certificate). Students must be enrolled in a separate graduate degree program at Columbia University. *Entrance requirements:* For degree, proficiency in East Asian language. *Application deadline:* For fall admission, 1/4 for domestic students; for spring admission, 10/1 for domestic students. Application fee: $85. Electronic applications accepted. *Expenses:* Tuition: Part-time $1,452 per credit. Required fees: $152 per term. One-time fee: $75 part-time. Full-time tuition and fees vary according to course level, course load, degree level and program. *Financial support:* Application deadline: 1/15. *Unit head:* Myron Cohen, Director, 212-854-7912, E-mail: sipa_admission@columbia.edu. *Application contact:* Matt Clemons, Director of Admissions and Financial Aid, 212-854-6216, Fax: 212-854-3010, E-mail: mc2793@columbia.edu.

Cornell University, Graduate School, Graduate Fields of Arts and Sciences, Field of Asian Religions, Ithaca, NY 14853-0001. Offers PhD. *Faculty:* 9 full-time (3 women). *Students:* 6 full-time (1 woman), 1 international. Average age 32. 11 applicants, 9% accepted, 1 enrolled. *Degree requirements:* For doctorate, comprehensive exam, thesis/dissertation. *Entrance requirements:* For doctorate, GRE General Test, academic writing sample, 3 letters of recommendation. Additional exam requirements/recommendations for international students: Required—TOEFL (minimum score 600 paper-based; 250 computer-based; 77 iBT). *Application deadline:* For fall admission, 1/15 for domestic students. Application fee: $70. Electronic applications accepted. *Financial support:* In 2007–08, 5 students received support, including 4 fellowships with full tuition reimbursements available, 1 teaching assistantship with full tuition reimbursement available; research assistantships with full tuition reimbursements available, institutionally sponsored loans, scholarships/grants, health care benefits, and unspecified assistantships also available. *Unit head:* Director of Graduate Studies, 607-255-9099, Fax: 607-255-1345. *Application contact:* Graduate Field Assistant, 607-255-9099, Fax: 607-255-1345, E-mail: asian-religions@cornell.edu.

Cornell University, Graduate School, Graduate Fields of Arts and Sciences, Field of Asian Studies, Ithaca, NY 14853-0001. Offers East Asian linguistics (MA); East Asian studies (MA); South Asian linguistics (MA); South Asian studies (MA); Southeast Asian linguistics (MA); Southeast Asian studies (MA). *Faculty:* 52 full-time (17 women). *Students:* 18 full-time (0 women); includes 5 minority (3 African Americans, 1 Asian American or Pacific Islander, 1 Hispanic American), 2 international. Average age 26. 64 applicants, 61% accepted, 13 enrolled. In 2007, 10 degrees awarded. *Degree requirements:* For master's, one foreign language, thesis. *Entrance requirements:* For master's, GRE General Test, 3 letters of recommendation. Additional exam requirements/recommendations for international students: Required—TOEFL (minimum score 550 paper-based; 213 computer-based; 77 iBT). *Application deadline:* Applications are processed on a rolling basis. Application fee: $70. Electronic applications accepted. *Financial support:* In 2007–08, 4 students received support, including 4 fellowships with full tuition reimbursements available; research assistantships with full tuition reimbursements available, teaching assistantships with full tuition reimbursements available, institutionally sponsored loans, scholarships/grants, health care benefits, tuition waivers (full and partial), and unspecified assistantships also available. Financial award applicants required to submit FAFSA. *Faculty research:* East Asian studies, South Asian studies, Southeast Asian studies. *Unit head:* Director of Graduate Studies, 607-255-9099, Fax: 607-255-1345. *Application contact:* Graduate Field Assistant, 607-255-9099, Fax: 607-255-1345, E-mail: asian@cornell.edu.

Cornell University, Graduate School, Graduate Fields of Arts and Sciences, Field of East Asian Literature, Ithaca, NY 14853-0001. Offers Asian religions (MA, PhD); Chinese linguistics (MA, PhD); Chinese philology (MA, PhD); classical Chinese literature (MA, PhD); classical Japanese literature (MA, PhD); Japanese linguistics (MA, PhD); Korean literature (MA, PhD); modern Chinese literature (MA, PhD); modern Japanese literature (MA, PhD). *Faculty:* 12 full-time (4 women). *Students:* 20 full-time (10 women); includes 4 minority (all Asian Americans or Pacific Islanders), 11 international. Average age 32. 41 applicants, 15% accepted, 3 enrolled. In 2007, 1 master's, 4 doctorates awarded. *Degree requirements:* For master's, 2 foreign languages, thesis, teaching experience; for doctorate, 2 foreign languages, comprehensive exam, thesis/dissertation, teaching experience. *Entrance requirements:* For master's and doctorate, GRE General Test, 3 years of study in Chinese, Japanese, Korean, or Vietnamese, 3 letters of recommendation, academic writing sample. Additional exam requirements/recommendations for international students: Required—TOEFL (minimum score 600 paper-based; 250 computer-based; 77 iBT). *Application deadline:* For fall admission, 1/10 priority date for domestic students. Application fee: $70. Electronic applications accepted. *Financial support:* In 2007–08, 19 students received support, including 15 fellowships with full tuition reimbursements available, 4 teaching assistantships with full tuition reimbursements available; research assistantships with full tuition reimbursements available, institutionally sponsored loans, scholarships/grants, health care benefits, tuition waivers (full and partial), and unspecified assistantships also available. Financial award applicants required to submit FAFSA. *Faculty research:* Vietnamese literature; Chinese literature, drama, and film; Japanese theater and literature; popular culture in East Asia; Korean literature; Asian linguistics. *Unit head:* Director of Graduate Studies, 607-255-9099. *Application contact:* Graduate Field Assistant, 607-255-9099, E-mail: east_asian_lit@cornell.edu.

Cornell University, Graduate School, Graduate Fields of Arts and Sciences, Field of History, Ithaca, NY 14853-0001. Offers African history (MA, PhD); American history (MA, PhD); ancient history (MA, PhD); early modern European history (MA, PhD); English history (MA, PhD); French history (MA, PhD); German history (MA, PhD); history of science (MA, PhD); Latin American history (MA, PhD); medieval Chinese history (MA, PhD); medieval history (MA, PhD); modern Chinese history (MA, PhD); modern European history (MA, PhD); modern Japanese history (MA, PhD); premodern Islamic history (MA, PhD); premodern Japanese history (MA, PhD); Renaissance history (MA, PhD); Russian history (MA, PhD); Southeast Asian history (MA, PhD). *Faculty:* 56 full-time (14 women). *Students:* 63 full-time (29 women); includes 11 minority (6 African Americans, 2 Asian Americans or Pacific Islanders, 3 Hispanic Americans), 20 international. Average age 31. 201 applicants, 6% accepted, 10 enrolled. In 2007, 11 master's, 11 doctorates awarded. Terminal master's awarded for partial completion of doctoral program. *Degree requirements:* For master's, thesis; for doctorate, 2 foreign languages, comprehensive exam, thesis/dissertation, 1 year of teaching experience. *Entrance requirements:* For master's and doctorate, GRE General Test, writing sample, 3 letters of recommendation. Additional exam requirements/recommendations for international students: Required—TOEFL (minimum score 550 paper-based; 213 computer-based; 77 iBT). *Application deadline:* For fall admission, 1/15 for domestic students. Application fee: $70. Electronic applications accepted. *Financial support:* In 2007–08, 54 students received support, including 26 fellowships with full tuition reimbursements available, 28 teaching assistantships with full tuition reimbursements available; research assistantships with full tuition reimbursements available, institutionally sponsored loans, scholarships/grants, health care benefits, tuition waivers (full and partial), and unspecified assistantships also available. Financial award applicants required to submit FAFSA. *Unit head:* Director of Graduate Studies, 607-255-6738, Fax: 607-255-0469. *Application contact:* Graduate Field Assistant, 607-255-6738, Fax: 607-255-0469, E-mail: history_grad_info@cornell.edu.

Cornell University, Graduate School, Graduate Fields of Arts and Sciences, Field of History of Art and Archaeology, Ithaca, NY 14853. Offers American art (PhD); ancient art and archaeology (PhD); Asian art (PhD); baroque art (PhD); medieval art (PhD); modern art (PhD); Renaissance art (PhD); Southeast Asian art (PhD); theory and criticism (PhD). *Faculty:* 21 full-time (14 women). *Students:* 22 full-time (17 women); includes 6 minority (2 African Americans, 2 Asian Americans or Pacific Islanders, 2 Hispanic Americans), 6 international. Average age 32. 61 applicants, 15% accepted, 4 enrolled. In 2007, 2 doctorates awarded. *Degree requirements:* For doctorate, one foreign language, comprehensive exam, thesis/dissertation, general exams in 3 areas. *Entrance requirements:* For doctorate, GRE General Test, sample of written work, 3 letters of recommendation. Additional exam requirements/recommendations for international students: Required—TOEFL (minimum score 550 paper-based; 213 computer-based; 77 iBT). *Application deadline:* For fall admission, 1/15 for domestic students. Application fee: $70. Electronic applications accepted. *Financial support:* In 2007–08, 17 students received support, including 10 fellowships with full tuition reimbursements available, 7 teaching assistantships with full tuition reimbursements available; research assistantships with full tuition reimbursements available, institutionally sponsored loans, scholarships/grants, health care benefits, tuition waivers (full and partial), and unspecified assistantships also available. Financial award applicants required to submit FAFSA. *Unit head:* Director of Graduate Studies, 607-255-4905, Fax: 607-255-0566, E-mail: art_history@cornell.edu. *Application contact:* Director of Graduate Studies, 607-255-4905, Fax: 607-255-0566, E-mail: art_history@cornell.edu.

Cornell University, Graduate School, Graduate Fields of Arts and Sciences, Field of Linguistics, Ithaca, NY 14853-0001. Offers applied linguistics (MA, PhD); East Asian linguistics (MA, PhD); English linguistics (MA, PhD); general linguistics (MA, PhD); Germanic linguistics (MA, PhD); Indo-European linguistics (MA, PhD); phonetics (MA, PhD); phonological theory (MA, PhD); Romance linguistics (MA, PhD); second language acquisition (MA, PhD); semantics (MA, PhD); Slavic linguistics (MA, PhD); sociolinguistics (MA, PhD); South Asian linguistics (MA, PhD); Southeast Asian linguistics (MA, PhD); syntactic theory (MA, PhD). *Faculty:* 19 full-time. *Students:* 31 full-time (16 women); includes 1 minority (Hispanic American), 19 international. Average age 28. 89 applicants, 17% accepted, 8 enrolled. In 2007, 2 master's, 1 doctorate awarded. Terminal master's awarded for partial completion of doctoral program. *Degree requirements:* For master's, one foreign language, thesis; for doctorate, one foreign language, comprehensive exam, thesis/dissertation. *Entrance requirements:* For master's and doctorate, GRE General Test, 2 letters of recommendation. Additional exam requirements/recommendations for international students: Required—TOEFL (minimum score 600 paper-based; 250 computer-based; 77 iBT). *Application deadline:* For fall admission, 1/15 for domestic students. Application fee: $70. Electronic applications accepted. *Financial support:* In 2007–08,

30 students received support, including 14 fellowships with full tuition reimbursements available, 2 research assistantships with full tuition reimbursements available, 14 teaching assistantships with full tuition reimbursements available; institutionally sponsored loans, scholarships/grants, health care benefits, tuition waivers (full and partial), and unspecified assistantships also available. Financial award applicants required to submit FAFSA. *Faculty research:* Phonology and phonetics; syntax and semantics; historical linguistics; philosophy of language; language acquisition. *Unit head:* Director of Graduate Studies, 607-255-1105. *Application contact:* Graduate Field Assistant, 607-255-1105, E-mail: lingfield@cornell.edu.

Duke University, Graduate School, Department of East Asian Studies, Durham, NC 27708. Offers AM, Certificate. Part-time programs available. *Faculty:* 33 full-time. *Students:* 13 full-time (8 women); includes 2 minority (1 Asian American or Pacific Islander, 1 Hispanic American), 2 international. 30 applicants, 67% accepted, 7 enrolled. In 2007, 8 degrees awarded. *Entrance requirements:* For master's, GRE General Test. Additional exam requirements/recommendations for international students: Required—TOEFL (minimum score 550 paper-based; 213 computer-based; 83 iBT), IELTS (minimum score 7). *Application deadline:* For fall admission, 12/15 priority date for domestic and international students; for spring admission, 11/1 for domestic students. Application fee: $75. Electronic applications accepted. *Financial support:* Application deadline: 12/31. *Unit head:* Nan Lin, Director, 919-684-2604, Fax: 919-681-6247, E-mail: sjholsey@duke.edu.

Florida International University, College of Arts and Sciences, Program in Asian Studies, Miami, FL 33199. Offers MA. Part-time and evening/weekend programs available. *Students:* 8 full-time (5 women), 5 part-time (2 women); includes 8 minority (3 Asian Americans or Pacific Islanders, 5 Hispanic Americans), 1 international. Average age 30. 8 applicants, 75% accepted, 6 enrolled. In 2007, 4 degrees awarded. *Degree requirements:* For master's, thesis. *Entrance requirements:* For master's, minimum GPA of 3.0, letters of recommendation. Additional exam requirements/recommendations for international students: Required—TOEFL (minimum score 550 paper-based; 213 computer-based). *Application deadline:* For fall admission, 6/1 for domestic students, 4/1 for international students; for spring admission, 10/1 for domestic students, 9/1 for international students. Applications are processed on a rolling basis. Application fee: $30. Electronic applications accepted. *Expenses:* Tuition, state resident: full-time $6,106. Tuition, nonresident: full-time $15,528. Required fees: $284. *Financial support:* Teaching assistantships, scholarships/grants available. *Unit head:* Dr. Steven Heine, 305-348-1914, Fax: 305-348-6586, E-mail: asian@fiu.edu.

Florida State University, Graduate Studies, College of Social Sciences, Program in Asian Studies, Tallahassee, FL 32306. Offers MA. Part-time programs available. *Students:* 1 (woman) full-time, 9 part-time (4 women); includes 2 minority (1 African American, 1 Asian American or Pacific Islander), 3 international. Average age 26. 16 applicants, 100% accepted, 7 enrolled. In 2007, 1 degree awarded. *Degree requirements:* For master's, one foreign language, comprehensive exam, thesis optional. *Entrance requirements:* For master's, GRE General Test, minimum GPA of 3.0. Additional exam requirements/recommendations for international students: Required—TOEFL (minimum score 550 paper-based; 213 computer-based; 80 iBT). *Application deadline:* For fall admission, 7/1 for domestic and international students; for spring admission, 11/1 for domestic and international students. Applications are processed on a rolling basis. Application fee: $30. Electronic applications accepted. *Expenses:* Tuition, state resident: part-time $248 per credit hour. Tuition, nonresident: part-time $880 per credit hour. Tuition and fees vary according to program. *Financial support:* In 2007–08, research assistantships with full tuition reimbursements (averaging $5,000 per year); fellowships with full tuition reimbursements, Federal Work-Study and institutionally sponsored loans also available. Financial award application deadline: 2/15; financial award applicants required to submit FAFSA. *Faculty research:* Art history of the Orient, Asian history and politics. *Unit head:* Dr. Lee K. Metcalf, Director, 850-644-7327, Fax: 850-645-4981, E-mail: lmetcalf@fsu.edu. *Application contact:* Patty Lollis, Program Assistant, 850-644-4418, Fax: 850-645-4981, E-mail: plollis@mailer.fsu.edu.

The George Washington University, Elliott School of International Affairs, Program in Asian Studies, Washington, DC 20052. Offers MA, JD/MA, MBA/MA, MPH/MA. Part-time and evening/weekend programs available. *Degree requirements:* For master's, one foreign language, capstone project. *Entrance requirements:* For master's, GRE General Test, 2 years (or the equivalent) of an approved Asian language. Additional exam requirements/recommendations for international students: Required—TOEFL. Electronic applications accepted. *Faculty research:* Sino-Soviet studies, Japanese-U.S. relations, Chinese foreign policy, economic development in China.

Harvard University, Graduate School of Arts and Sciences, Committee on Inner Asian and Altaic Studies, Cambridge, MA 02138. Offers PhD. *Degree requirements:* For doctorate, 2 foreign languages, thesis/dissertation, oral general exam. *Entrance requirements:* For doctorate, GRE General Test, proficiency in a related foreign language. Additional exam requirements/recommendations for international students: Required—TOEFL. *Expenses:* Tuition: Full-time $31,456. Full-time tuition and fees vary according to program and student level.

Harvard University, Graduate School of Arts and Sciences, Committee on Regional Studies–East Asia, Cambridge, MA 02138. Offers Chinese studies (AM); Japanese studies (AM); Korean studies (AM); Mongolian studies (AM); Vietnamese studies (AM). *Degree requirements:* For master's, one foreign language, seminar paper. *Entrance requirements:* For master's, GRE General Test. Additional exam requirements/recommendations for international students: Required—TOEFL. *Expenses:* Tuition: Full-time $31,456. Full-time tuition and fees vary according to program and student level.

Harvard University, Graduate School of Arts and Sciences, Department of Sanskrit and Indian Studies, Cambridge, MA 02138. Offers Indian philosophy (AM, PhD); Pali (AM, PhD); Sanskrit (AM, PhD); Tibetan (AM, PhD); Urdu (AM, PhD). Terminal master's awarded for partial completion of doctoral program. *Degree requirements:* For master's, 3 foreign languages; for doctorate, 3 foreign languages, thesis/dissertation. *Entrance requirements:* For master's, GRE General Test; for doctorate, GRE General Test, proficiency in French and German. Additional exam requirements/recommendations for international students: Required—TOEFL. *Expenses:* Tuition: Full-time $31,456. Full-time tuition and fees vary according to program and student level.

Indiana University Bloomington, University Graduate School, College of Arts and Sciences, Department of Central Eurasian Studies, Bloomington, IN 47405-7000. Offers MA, PhD. *Faculty:* 11 full-time (0 women). *Students:* 39 full-time (12 women), 13 part-time (6 women); includes 3 minority (1 American Indian/Alaska Native, 2 Asian Americans or Pacific Islanders), 12 international. Average age 32. 38 applicants, 71% accepted, 8 enrolled. In 2007, 8 master's, 4 doctorates awarded. Terminal master's awarded for partial completion of doctoral program. *Median time to degree:* Of those who began their doctoral program in fall 1999, 50% received their degree in 8 years or less. *Degree requirements:* For master's, one foreign language, thesis; for doctorate, 2 foreign languages, thesis/dissertation, qualifying exams. *Entrance requirements:* For master's, minimum GPA of 3.0, 2 years of a foreign language; for doctorate, minimum GPA of 3.5, 1 research language. Additional exam requirements/recommendations for international students: Required—TOEFL. *Application deadline:* For fall admission, 1/15 priority date for domestic students, 12/15 for international students; for spring admission, 9/1 priority date for domestic students, 9/1 for international students. Applications are processed on a rolling basis. Application fee: $50 ($60 for international students). Electronic applications accepted. *Financial support:* Fellowships with full tuition reimbursements, research assistantships with full tuition reimbursements, teaching assistantships with full tuition reimbursements, Federal Work-Study available. Financial award application deadline: 2/16. *Faculty research:* Central Asia, Hungarian civilization, Tibetan civilization, Turkish studies, Mongolian philology. *Unit head:* Christopher Atwood, Chair, 812-855-2233, E-mail: catwood@indiana.edu. *Application contact:* April Younger, Graduate Secretary, 812-855-2233, E-mail: ayounger@indiana.edu.

Indiana University Bloomington, University Graduate School, College of Arts and Sciences, Department of East Asian Languages and Cultures, Bloomington, IN 47405-7000. Offers Chinese (MA, PhD); East Asian languages and cultures (PhD); East Asian studies (MA); Japanese (MA, PhD); language pedagogy (MA). Part-time programs available. *Faculty:* 7 full-time (2 women). *Students:* 19 full-time (12 women), 6 part-time (3 women); includes 3 minority (1 African American, 1 Asian American or Pacific Islander, 1 Hispanic American), 6 international. Average age 32. 77 applicants, 25% accepted, 10 enrolled. In 2007, 7 master's, 1 doctorate awarded. *Degree requirements:* For master's, 2 foreign languages, thesis; for doctorate, 2 foreign languages, thesis/dissertation. *Entrance requirements:* Additional exam requirements/recommendations for international students: Required—TOEFL. *Application deadline:* For fall admission, 1/15 for domestic students, 12/15 for international students; for spring admission, 9/1 for domestic and international students. Applications are processed on a rolling basis. Application fee: $50 ($60 for international students). Electronic applications accepted. *Financial support:* Fellowships, teaching assistantships, Federal Work-Study and tuition waivers (full) available. Financial award application deadline: 3/1. *Faculty research:* Postwar/postmodern Japanese fiction, modern Chinese film and literature, classical Chinese literature and philosophy, Chinese and Japanese linguistics and pedagogy, East Asian politics. *Unit head:* Robert Eno, Chair, 812-855-0856, E-mail: eno@indiana.edu. *Application contact:* Edith Sarra, Director of Graduate Studies, 812-855-4031, Fax: 812-855-6402, E-mail: eserra@indiana.edu.

The Johns Hopkins University, Paul H. Nitze School of Advanced International Studies, Washington, DC 20036. Offers international development (Certificate); international public policy (MIPP); international relations (MA, PhD), including African studies (MA), American foreign policy (MA), Asian studies (MA), Canadian studies (MA), conflict management (MA), European studies (MA), global theory and history (MA), international development (MA), international law, and organizations (MA), international policy (MA), international relations (general) (MA), Latin American studies (MA), Middle East studies (MA), Russian and Eurasian studies (MA), strategic studies (MA); international studies (Certificate); JD/MA; MBA/MA; MHS/MA. *Faculty:* 66 full-time (22 women), 158 part-time/adjunct (54 women). *Students:* 578 full-time (256 women), 46 part-time (16 women); includes 85 minority (18 African Americans, 1 American Indian/Alaska Native, 51 Asian Americans or Pacific Islanders, 15 Hispanic Americans), 193 international. Average age 27. In 2007, 359 master's, 13 doctorates awarded. Terminal master's awarded for partial completion of doctoral program. *Degree requirements:* For master's, one foreign language, 16 non-language courses (8 for MIPP), 2 core examinations, comprehensive oral exam, paper (for some programs); for doctorate, 2 foreign languages, thesis/dissertation, 3 comprehensive exams, defense. *Entrance requirements:* For master's, GMAT or GRE General Test, previous course work in economics, foreign language, undergraduate degree; for doctorate, GRE General Test, master's degree. Additional exam requirements/recommendations for international students: Required—TOEFL (minimum paper-based score of 600, computer-based 250, iBT 100) or IELTS (minimum 7.0). *Application deadline:* For fall admission, 1/7 for domestic students. Application fee: $80. Electronic applications accepted. *Expenses:* Contact institution. *Financial support:* In 2007–08, 350 students received support, including fellowships (averaging $7,500 per year); career-related internships or fieldwork, Federal Work-Study, and scholarships/grants also available. Financial award application deadline: 2/15; financial award applicants required to submit FAFSA. *Faculty research:* Regional studies and functional fields of international relations, international economics, conflict management, global theory and history, international law and organizations, international policy, strategic studies. *Unit head:* Tara Campbell, Associate Director of Admissions, 202-663-5700, Fax: 202-663-7788. *Application contact:* Dr. Belinda A. Yeomans, Director of Admissions, 202-663-5700, Fax: 202-663-7788, E-mail: admissions.sais@jhu.edu.

Maharishi University of Management, Graduate Studies, Program in Maharishi Vedic Science, Fairfield, IA 52557. Offers MA, PhD. Evening/weekend programs available. *Faculty:* 7 full-time (1 woman), 2 part-time/adjunct (1 woman). *Students:* 51 full-time (29 women), 2 part-time (both women); includes 1 minority (Asian American or Pacific Islander), 24 international. Average age 48. In 2007, 5 master's, 4 doctorates awarded. *Degree requirements:* For master's, thesis; for doctorate, thesis/dissertation. *Entrance requirements:* For master's, minimum GPA of 3.0; for doctorate, GRE, minimum GPA of 3.0. Additional exam requirements/recommendations for international students: Required—TOEFL. *Application deadline:* For fall admission, 4/15 priority date for domestic students. Applications are processed on a rolling basis. *Expenses:* Tuition: Full-time $24,000; part-time $350 per unit. Required fees: $430; $350 per unit. Tuition and fees vary according to class time, course load, degree level and program. *Financial support:* Career-related internships or fieldwork, Federal Work-Study, and tuition waivers (full) available. Support available to part-time students. *Faculty research:* Modern science and Vedic science, unification of knowledge, philosophy of science, Sanskrit. *Unit head:* Dr. Frederick Travis, Chair, 515-472-7000 Ext. 3309, E-mail: ftravis@mum.edu.

McGill University, Faculty of Graduate and Postdoctoral Studies, Faculty of Arts, Department of East Asian Studies, Montréal, QC H3A 2T5, Canada. Offers MA, PhD. *Faculty:* 11 full-time (5 women), 5 part-time/adjunct (1 woman). *Students:* 15 full-time (9 women). 35 applicants, 29% accepted, 5 enrolled. In 2007, 2 master's, 2 doctorates awarded. *Application contact:* Suan Ong, Administrative Assistant, 514-398-6742, Fax: 514-398-1882, E-mail: suan.ong@mcgill.ca.

New York University, Graduate School of Arts and Science, Department of East Asian Studies, New York, NY 10012-1019. Offers MA, PhD. Part-time programs available. *Students:* 7 full-time (5 women), 4 part-time (2 women); includes 1 Asian American or Pacific Islander, 6 international. Average age 31. 74 applicants, 5% accepted, 1 enrolled. In 2007, 3 degrees awarded. *Degree requirements:* For master's and doctorate, one foreign language. *Entrance requirements:* For master's and doctorate, GRE General Test. Additional exam requirements/recommendations for international students: Required—TOEFL. Application fee: $85. Electronic applications accepted. *Financial support:* Fellowships with tuition reimbursements, teaching assistantships with tuition reimbursements, Federal Work-Study, institutionally sponsored loans, scholarships/grants, health care benefits, and unspecified assistantships available. Financial award application deadline: 1/4. *Application contact:* Roberta Popik, Associate Dean of Enrollment, 212-998-8050, Fax: 212-995-4557, E-mail: gsas.admissions@nyu.edu.

Ohio University, Graduate College, Center for International Studies, Program in Southeast Asian Studies, Athens, OH 45701-2979. Offers MA. *Faculty:* 37 full-time (10 women), 9 part-time/adjunct (4 women). *Students:* 21 full-time (11 women), 2 part-time (both women), 18 international. Average age 26. 22 applicants, 77% accepted, 10 enrolled. In 2007, 14 degrees awarded. *Degree requirements:* For master's, one foreign language, thesis optional. *Entrance requirements:* For master's, minimum GPA of 3.0. Additional exam requirements/recommendations for international students: Required—TOEFL (minimum score 550 paper-based; 213 computer-based). *Application deadline:* For fall admission, 1/1 for domestic and international students. Application fee: $50 ($55 for international students). *Financial support:* In 2007–08, 9 fellowships with full tuition reimbursements (averaging $11,000 per year), 12 research assistantships with full tuition reimbursements (averaging $10,000 per year), 2 teaching assistantships with full tuition reimbursements (averaging $10,000 per year) were awarded; career-related internships or fieldwork, Federal Work-Study, institutionally sponsored loans, scholarships/grants, tuition waivers (full), and unspecified assistantships also available. Financial award application deadline: 1/1. *Faculty research:* Indonesian and Malaysian: political, history, literature, media, Islam, and environmental problems. Total annual research expenditures: $36,000. *Application contact:* Joan Kraynanski, Administrative Assistant, 740-593-1840, Fax: 740-593-1837, E-mail: kraynans@ohio.edu.

Princeton University, Graduate School, Department of East Asian Studies, Princeton, NJ 08544-1019. Offers Chinese and Japanese art and archaeology (PhD); East Asian civilizations (PhD); East Asian studies (PhD). *Degree requirements:* For doctorate, 2 foreign languages, thesis/dissertation. *Entrance requirements:* For doctorate, GRE General Test, fluency in Japanese and/or Chinese. Additional exam requirements/recommendations for international students: Required—TOEFL (minimum score 600 paper-based; 250 computer-based). Electronic

Asian Studies

Princeton University (continued)
applications accepted. *Faculty research:* Modern and classical Japanese literature, premodern Chinese and Japanese history, Chinese narrative and poetry.

Rutgers, The State University of New Jersey, New Brunswick, Graduate School, Program in History, New Brunswick, NJ 08901-1281. Offers African-American history (PhD); early American history (PhD); early modern European history (PhD); east Asian history (PhD); global and comparative history (PhD); history (PhD); history of diplomacy and foreign relations (PhD); history of technology, environment and health (PhD); history of the Atlantic cultures and African diaspora (PhD); Latin American history (PhD); medieval history (PhD); modern European history (PhD); nineteenth and twentieth century American history (PhD); women's and gender history (PhD). *Degree requirements:* For doctorate, thesis/dissertation. *Entrance requirements:* For doctorate, GRE General Test, sample of written work. Electronic applications accepted. *Faculty research:* American history, European history, Afro-American history, women's history, Latin American history.

St. John's College, Graduate Institute in Liberal Education, Program in Eastern Classics, Santa Fe, NM 87505-4599. Offers MA. Part-time and evening/weekend programs available. *Entrance requirements:* For master's, 2 letters of recommendation. Additional exam requirements/recommendations for international students: Required—TOEFL, TWE. Expenses: Contact institution.

St. John's University, St. John's College of Liberal Arts and Sciences, Institute of Asian Studies, Queens, NY 11439. Offers Asian and African cultural studies (Adv C); Asian studies (Adv C); Chinese studies (MA, Adv C); East Asian culture studies (Adv C); East Asian studies (MA). Part-time and evening/weekend programs available. *Faculty:* 2 full-time (1 woman), 11 part-time/adjunct (9 women). *Students:* 6 full-time (2 women), 5 part-time (all women); includes 3 minority (all Asian Americans or Pacific Islanders), 6 international. Average age 30. 19 applicants, 84% accepted, 4 enrolled. In 2007, 14 degrees awarded. *Degree requirements:* For master's, one foreign language, comprehensive exam, thesis optional. *Entrance requirements:* For master's, 18 hours of course work in the field, minimum GPA of 3.0. Additional exam requirements/recommendations for international students: Required—TOEFL (minimum score 500 paper-based; 173 computer-based; 61 iBT), IELTS (minimum score 6). *Application deadline:* For fall admission, 5/1 priority date for domestic and international students; for spring admission, 11/1 priority date for domestic and international students. Applications are processed on a rolling basis. Application fee: $40. Electronic applications accepted. *Financial support:* Research assistantships, scholarships/grants available. Support available to part-time students. Financial award application deadline: 3/1; financial award applicants required to submit FAFSA. *Faculty research:* East Asian philosophy and religion, Chinese language and literature, Japanese language, modern Japan, Chinese art and history. *Unit head:* Dr. Bernadette Li, Chair, 718-990-1657, E-mail: lib@stjohns.edu. *Application contact:* Beth Evans, Associate Vice President and Executive Director, Enrollment Management, 718-990-6999, Fax: 718-990-5686, E-mail: gradhelp@stjohns.edu.

San Diego State University, Graduate and Research Affairs, College of Arts and Letters, Center for Asian Studies, San Diego, CA 92182. Offers MA. *Students:* 2 full-time (1 woman), 2 part-time; includes 1 minority (Asian American or Pacific Islander) In 2007, 2 degrees awarded. *Degree requirements:* For master's, one foreign language, thesis. *Entrance requirements:* For master's, GRE General Test, 3 letters of reference, writing sample. Additional exam requirements/recommendations for international students: Required—TOEFL. *Application deadline:* For fall admission, 5/1 for domestic and international students; for spring admission, 11/1 for domestic students, 10/1 for international students. Applications are processed on a rolling basis. Application fee: $55. Electronic applications accepted. *Financial support:* Career-related internships or fieldwork available. Financial award applicants required to submit FAFSA. *Faculty research:* Language acquisition process, social organization of Asia, economic development. *Unit head:* Dr. Linda Holler, Interim Chair, 619-594-5164, Fax: 619-594-0257, E-mail: lholler@mail.sdsu.edu.

Seton Hall University, College of Arts and Sciences, Department of Asian Studies, South Orange, NJ 07079-2697. Offers MA. Part-time and evening/weekend programs available. *Degree requirements:* For master's, thesis optional. Electronic applications accepted. *Faculty research:* Modern Chinese history, contemporary Chinese politics, ancient Chinese history, Hinduism, Asian business.

See Close-Up on page 807.

Stanford University, School of Humanities and Sciences, Center for East Asian Studies, Stanford, CA 94305-9991. Offers MA. *Degree requirements:* For master's, one foreign language, thesis. *Entrance requirements:* For master's, GRE General Test. Additional exam requirements/recommendations for international students: Required—TOEFL. Electronic applications accepted.

University of Alberta, Faculty of Graduate Studies and Research, Department of East Asian Studies, Edmonton, AB T6G 2E1, Canada. Offers Chinese literature (MA); East Asian interdisciplinary studies (MA); Japanese literature (MA). Part-time programs available. *Degree requirements:* For master's, one foreign language, thesis. *Entrance requirements:* Additional exam requirements/recommendations for international students: Required—TOEFL. Electronic applications accepted. *Faculty research:* Classical Chinese poetry and poetics, Chinese philosophy, modern/contemporary Chinese literature, modern Japanese literature and culture, Japanese women's writing.

The University of Arizona, Graduate College, College of Humanities, Department of East Asian Studies, Tucson, AZ 85721. Offers MA, PhD. Part-time programs available. *Faculty:* 14. *Students:* 17 full-time (12 women), 16 part-time (11 women); includes 5 minority (1 African American, 1 American Indian/Alaska Native, 2 Asian Americans or Pacific Islanders, 1 Hispanic American), 19 international. Average age 32. 42 applicants, 19% accepted, 8 enrolled. In 2007, 3 master's, 4 doctorates awarded. Terminal master's awarded for partial completion of doctoral program. *Degree requirements:* For master's, one foreign language; for doctorate, 2 foreign languages. *Entrance requirements:* For master's, GRE General Test, 2 letters of recommendation, minimum GPA of 3.0, statement of purpose; for doctorate, GRE General Test, 2 letters of recommendation, minimum GPA of 3.0, statement of purpose, writing sample. Additional exam requirements/recommendations for international students: Required—TOEFL (minimum score 550 paper-based). *Application deadline:* For fall admission, 2/1 for domestic students, 12/1 for international students. Applications are processed on a rolling basis. Application fee: $50. Electronic applications accepted. *Financial support:* In 2007–08, 2 fellowships with partial tuition reimbursements (averaging $5,000 per year), 1 research assistantship (averaging $7,622 per year), 28 teaching assistantships with full tuition reimbursements (averaging $10,061 per year) were awarded; tuition waivers (partial) also available. Financial award application deadline: 2/1. *Faculty research:* Chinese history, Chinese/Japanese linguistics, Chinese/Japanese literature, Chinese/Japanese religion. *Unit head:* Dr. J. Philip Gabriel, Head, 520-621-7505, Fax: 520-621-1149, E-mail: jgabriel@u.arizona.edu. *Application contact:* Janet Kania, Administrative Associate, 520-621-5452, Fax: 520-621-1149, E-mail: kaniaj@u.arizona.edu.

The University of British Columbia, Faculty of Arts, Department of Asian Studies, Vancouver, BC V6T 1Z1, Canada. Offers MA, PhD. *Faculty:* 22 full-time (9 women). *Students:* 57 full-time (28 women). 48 applicants, 40% accepted, 12 enrolled. In 2007, 3 master's, 3 doctorates awarded. *Degree requirements:* For master's, one foreign language, thesis; for doctorate, 2 foreign languages, thesis/dissertation. *Entrance requirements:* For master's, BA degree; for doctorate, master's degree in Asian studies or equivalent. Additional exam requirements/recommendations for international students: Required—TOEFL (minimum score 570 paper-based; 230 computer-based; 85 iBT). *Application deadline:* For fall admission, 12/6 for domestic and international students. Applications are processed on a rolling basis. Application fee: $90 Canadian dollars ($150 Canadian dollars for international students). Electronic applications accepted. *Financial support:* In 2007–08, 3 fellowships with full tuition reimbursements (averaging $7,500 Canadian dollars per year), 5 research assistantships with full and partial tuition reimbursements (averaging $3,000 Canadian dollars per year), 28 teaching assistantships with full and partial tuition reimbursements (averaging $10,000 Canadian dollars per year) were awarded. *Faculty research:* Language; linguistics; literature; religion and philosophy; premodern history of China, Japan, Korea, South and South East Asia. *Unit head:* Dr. Ross King, Head, 604-822-9240, Fax: 604-822-8937, E-mail: asiahead@interchange.ubc.ca. *Application contact:* Jasmina Miodragovic, Graduate Secretary, 604-822-5728, Fax: 604-822-8937, E-mail: asiagrad@interchange.ubc.ca.

The University of British Columbia, Faculty of Graduate Studies, Institute of Asian Research, Vancouver, BC V6T 1Z1, Canada. Offers MAPPS. Part-time programs available. *Faculty:* 9 full-time (1 woman), 2 part-time/adjunct (0 women). *Students:* 28 full-time (16 women). Average age 30. 60 applicants, 42% accepted, 14 enrolled. In 2007, 15 degrees awarded. *Degree requirements:* For master's, thesis optional. *Entrance requirements:* Additional exam requirements/recommendations for international students: Required—TOEFL (minimum score 600 paper-based; 250 computer-based; 100 iBT), GRE (recommended). *Application deadline:* For fall admission, 3/30 for domestic students, 3/1 for international students. Application fee: $90 ($150 for international students). Electronic applications accepted. *Financial support:* In 2007–08, 7 fellowships with tuition reimbursements (averaging $70,000 Canadian dollars per year), 16 research assistantships (averaging $3,500 Canadian dollars per year) were awarded; career-related internships or fieldwork, institutionally sponsored loans, scholarships/grants, and tuition waivers (partial) also available. *Faculty research:* Social cohesion, globalization, social safety nets, research and development alliances, knowledge-based workshops. *Unit head:* Pitman B. Potter, Director and Professor of Law, 604-822-4686, Fax: 604-822-5207, E-mail: potter@interchg.ubc.ca. *Application contact:* Marietta T. Lao, Administrator, 604-822-2746, Fax: 604-822-5207, E-mail: mlao@interchg.ubc.ca.

University of California, Berkeley, Graduate Division, College of Letters and Science, Department of South and Southeast Asian Studies, Berkeley, CA 94720-1500. Offers Hindi (MA, PhD); Indonesian (MA, PhD); Sanskrit (MA, PhD); Tamil (MA, PhD). *Faculty:* 6 full-time, 14 part-time/adjunct. Terminal master's awarded for partial completion of doctoral program. *Degree requirements:* For master's, 2 foreign languages, thesis; for doctorate, 2 foreign languages, thesis/dissertation, oral qualifying exam. *Entrance requirements:* For master's and doctorate, GRE General Test, minimum GPA of 3.0, 3 letters of recommendation. *Application deadline:* For fall admission, 12/3 for domestic students. Application fee: $70 ($90 for international students). Electronic applications accepted. *Financial support:* Fellowships, research assistantships, teaching assistantships, unspecified assistantships available. *Unit head:* George Hart, Chair, 510-642-8169, E-mail: ghart@socrates.berkeley.edu. *Application contact:* Lee Amazonas, Student Affairs Officer, 510-642-4219, E-mail: casmauga@berkeley.edu.

University of California, Berkeley, Graduate Division, Group in Asian Studies, Berkeley, CA 94720-1500. Offers Asian studies (PhD); East Asian studies (MA); Northeast Asian studies (MA); South Asian studies (MA); Southeast Asian studies (MA); JD/MA; MBA/MA; MJ/MA. *Degree requirements:* For master's, one foreign language, comprehensive exam or thesis; for doctorate, 2 foreign languages, thesis/dissertation, qualifying exam. *Entrance requirements:* For master's and doctorate, GRE General Test, minimum GPA of 3.0, 3 letters of recommendation. *Application deadline:* For fall admission, 12/1 for domestic students. Application fee: $70 ($90 for international students). *Financial support:* Fellowships, research assistantships, teaching assistantships, Federal Work-Study and unspecified assistantships available. Financial award applicants required to submit FAFSA. *Unit head:* Bonnie Wade, Chair, 510-642-0333, E-mail: bcwade@berkeley.edu. *Application contact:* Hilary Vanessa Finchum-Sung, Student Affairs Officer, 510-642-0333, Fax: 510-643-7062, E-mail: hfinchum_sung@berkeley.edu.

University of California, Berkeley, Graduate Division, Group in Buddhist Studies, Berkeley, CA 94720-1500. Offers PhD. *Faculty:* 9 full-time. *Degree requirements:* For doctorate, 4 foreign languages, thesis/dissertation, dissertation defense, qualifying exam. *Entrance requirements:* For doctorate, GRE General Test, MA in Japanese, Chinese, or Sanskrit; minimum GPA of 3.0, 3 letters of recommendation. *Application deadline:* For fall admission, 12/8 for domestic students. Application fee: $70 ($90 for international students). Electronic applications accepted. *Financial support:* Unspecified assistantships available. *Unit head:* Robert Sharf, Chair, 510-642-6369, E-mail: rsharf@berkeley.edu. *Application contact:* Information Contact, 510-642-3480, E-mail: gbs@berkeley.edu.

University of California, Los Angeles, Graduate Division, College of Letters and Science, Department of Asian Languages and Cultures, Los Angeles, CA 90095. Offers MA, PhD. *Faculty:* 15. *Students:* 34 full-time (20 women); includes 20 minority (all Asian Americans or Pacific Islanders), 19 international. Average age 26. 70 applicants, 21% accepted, 8 enrolled. In 2007, 1 master's, 7 doctorates awarded. Terminal master's awarded for partial completion of doctoral program. *Degree requirements:* For master's, one foreign language, comprehensive exam, comprehensive exam or thesis; for doctorate, 2 foreign languages, thesis/dissertation, oral and written qualifying exams. *Entrance requirements:* For master's, GRE General Test, minimum GPA of 3.0, sample of written work; for doctorate, GRE General Test, minimum undergraduate GPA of 3.0, sample of research writing or thesis in English. Additional exam requirements/recommendations for international students: Required—TOEFL. *Application deadline:* For fall admission, 12/15 for domestic students. Application fee: $60. Electronic applications accepted. *Expenses:* Tuition, nonresident: full-time $5,728. Required fees:$8,966. Full-time tuition and fees vary according to program and student level. *Financial support:* In 2007–08, 6 fellowships with full and partial tuition reimbursements, 20 research assistantships with full and partial tuition reimbursements, 27 teaching assistantships with full and partial tuition reimbursements were awarded; Federal Work-Study, institutionally sponsored loans, and tuition waivers (full and partial) also available. Financial award application deadline: 3/1; financial award applicants required to submit FAFSA. *Unit head:* Dr. John Duncan, Chair, 310-206-8235. *Application contact:* Departmental Office, 310-206-8235, E-mail: alcgen@humnet.ucla.edu.

University of California, Los Angeles, Graduate Division, College of Letters and Science, Interdepartmental Program in East Asian Studies, Los Angeles, CA 90095. Offers MA. *Students:* 8 full-time (6 women); includes 5 minority (all Asian Americans or Pacific Islanders), 2 international. Average age 27. 45 applicants, 60% accepted, 6 enrolled. In 2007, 4 degrees awarded. *Degree requirements:* For master's, one foreign language, comprehensive exam. *Entrance requirements:* For master's, GRE General Test, minimum undergraduate GPA of 3.0. *Application deadline:* For fall admission, 12/15 for domestic students. Application fee: $60. *Expenses:* Tuition, nonresident: full-time $5,728. Required fees: $8,966. Full-time tuition and fees vary according to program and student level. *Financial support:* In 2007–08, 2 fellowships with full and partial tuition reimbursements, 3 teaching assistantships with full and partial tuition reimbursements were awarded; research assistantships with full and partial tuition reimbursements, tuition waivers (full and partial) also available. Financial award application deadline: 3/1; financial award applicants required to submit FAFSA. *Unit head:* David Schaberg, Director, 310-206-6571. *Application contact:* Program Office, 310-206-6571, E-mail: idgrads@international.ucla.edu.

University of California, Riverside, Graduate Division, Program in Southeast Asian Studies, Riverside, CA 92521-0102. Offers MA. *Faculty:* 11 full-time (6 women). *Students:* 1 full-time (0 women); minority (Asian American or Pacific Islander) *Degree requirements:* For master's, one foreign language, thesis. *Application deadline:* For fall admission, 5/1 for domestic students, 2/1 for international students; for winter admission, 9/1 for domestic students, 7/1 for international students; for spring admission, 12/1 for domestic students, 10/1 for international students. Application fee: $60 ($75 for international students). *Financial support:* In 2007–08, teaching assistantships with tuition reimbursements (averaging $16,500 per year). *Faculty research:* Southeast Asian texts, rituals and performance, music and technoculture, dance ethnography, ethnomusicology. *Unit head:* Dr. Hendrick Maier, Director, 951-827-7057, Fax: 951-827-2160, E-mail: hendrick.maier@ucr.edu.

University of California, Santa Barbara, Graduate Division, College of Letters and Sciences, Division of Humanities and Fine Arts, Department of East Asian Languages and Cultural Studies, Santa Barbara, CA 93106. Offers Asian studies (MA), including East Asian languages and cultural studies; East Asian languages and cultural studies (PhD). *Faculty:* 10 full-time (5 women), 6 part-time/adjunct (2 women). *Students:* 12 full-time (8 women); includes 2 minority (both Asian Americans or Pacific Islanders), 5 international. Average age 28. 73 applicants, 30% accepted, 5 enrolled. In 2007, 7 degrees awarded. *Degree requirements:* For master's, one foreign language, thesis or alternative. *Entrance requirements:* For master's and doctorate, GRE. Additional exam requirements/recommendations for international students: Required—TOEFL (minimum score 550 paper-based; 213 computer-based; 80 iBT). *Application deadline:* For fall admission, 4/1 for domestic and international students. Application fee: $60. Electronic applications accepted. *Expenses:* Tuition, nonresident: full-time $14,888. Required fees: $10,108. *Financial support:* In 2007–08, 11 students received support, including 5 fellowships with full and partial tuition reimbursements available (averaging $15,300 per year), 6 teaching assistantships with partial tuition reimbursements available; research assistantships, Federal Work-Study, institutionally sponsored loans, scholarships/grants, health care benefits, and unspecified assistantships also available. Financial award application deadline: 12/15; financial award applicants required to submit FAFSA. *Faculty research:* Chinese literature, Chinese film, Japanese society, Japanese literature, East Asian cultural studies. *Unit head:* Dr. William Powell, Chair, 805-893-4455, Fax: 805-893-3011, E-mail: bpowell@religion.ucsb.edu. *Application contact:* Dr. Ronald Egan, Faculty Graduate Advisor, 805-893-3770, Fax: 805-893-3011, E-mail: ronegan@eastasian.ucsb.edu.

University of Chicago, Division of the Humanities, Department of East Asian Languages and Civilizations, Chicago, IL 60637-1513. Offers AM, PhD. *Students:* 48. 65 applicants, 14% accepted, 4 enrolled.Terminal master's awarded for partial completion of doctoral program. *Degree requirements:* For master's, one foreign language, thesis; for doctorate, 2 foreign languages, thesis/dissertation. *Entrance requirements:* For master's and doctorate, GRE General Test. Additional exam requirements/recommendations for international students: Required—TOEFL. *Application deadline:* For fall admission, 12/15 for domestic students. Application fee: $55. *Financial support:* Fellowships, Federal Work-Study available. Financial award application deadline: 12/15; financial award applicants required to submit FAFSA. *Unit head:* Dr. Edward Shaughnessy, Chair, 773-702-1255.

University of Chicago, Division of the Humanities, Department of South Asian Languages and Civilizations, Chicago, IL 60637-1513. Offers South Asian languages and civilizations (AM, PhD), including Bengali (PhD), Hindi (PhD), Sanskrit (PhD), Tamil (PhD), Urdu (PhD). *Students:* 27. 27 applicants, 33% accepted, 5 enrolled.Terminal master's awarded for partial completion of doctoral program. *Degree requirements:* For master's, one foreign language, thesis; for doctorate, 2 foreign languages, thesis/dissertation. *Entrance requirements:* For master's and doctorate, GRE General Test. Additional exam requirements/recommendations for international students: Required—TOEFL. *Application deadline:* For fall admission, 12/15 for domestic students. Application fee: $55. *Financial support:* Fellowships, Federal Work-Study available. Financial award application deadline: 12/15; financial award applicants required to submit FAFSA. *Unit head:* Dr. Steven Collins, Chair, 773-702-8373.

University of Colorado at Boulder, Graduate School, College of Arts and Sciences, Department of East Asian Languages and Civilizations, Boulder, CO 80309. Offers Chinese (MA, PhD); Japanese (MA, PhD). Part-time programs available. *Faculty:* 9. *Students:* 29 full-time (15 women), 6 part-time (4 women); includes 5 minority (all Asian Americans or Pacific Islanders), 12 international. Average age 29. 25 applicants, 64% accepted. In 2007, 6 degrees awarded. *Degree requirements:* For master's, comprehensive exam. *Entrance requirements:* For master's, BA in Chinese or Japanese, minimum undergraduate GPA of 3.0. Additional exam requirements/recommendations for international students: Required—TOEFL. *Application deadline:* For fall admission, 1/1 priority date for domestic students, 12/1 for international students; for spring admission, 10/1 for domestic students, 9/1 for international students. Applications are processed on a rolling basis. Application fee: $50 ($60 for international students). *Financial support:* In 2007–08, 12 fellowships (averaging $3,372 per year), 2 research assistantships (averaging $10,564 per year) were awarded; career-related internships or fieldwork and Federal Work-Study also available. Financial award application deadline: 2/1. *Faculty research:* Chinese and Japanese modern and classical literature, religions, linguistics, language pedagogy, pre-modern and contemporary fiction, sociolinguistics. Total annual research expenditures: $1.1 million. *Unit head:* Michael Breed, Chair, 303-492-7241, Fax: 303-492-7272, E-mail: michael.breed@colorado.edu. *Application contact:* Graduate Secretary, 303-492-6639, Fax: 303-492-7272, E-mail: ealc@colorado.edu.

University of Hawaii at Manoa, Graduate Division, School of Pacific and Asian Studies, Program in Asian Studies, Concentration in Korean Studies, Honolulu, HI 96822. Offers Graduate Certificate. Part-time programs available. *Students:* 2 full-time (1 woman), 1 part-time; includes 1 minority (Asian American or Pacific Islander), 1 international. *Degree requirements:* For Graduate Certificate, one foreign language. *Entrance requirements:* For degree, GRE. Additional exam requirements/recommendations for international students: Required—TOEFL (minimum score 560 paper-based; 220 computer-based; 83 iBT), IELTS (minimum score 5). *Application contact:* Ho-Min Sohn, Director, 808-956-7041, Fax: 808-956-2213, E-mail: homin@hawaii.edu.

University of Hawaii at Manoa, Graduate Division, School of Pacific and Asian Studies, Program in Asian Studies, Concentration in Southeast Asian Studies, Honolulu, HI 96822. Offers Graduate Certificate. Part-time programs available. *Degree requirements:* For Graduate Certificate, one foreign language. *Entrance requirements:* For degree, GRE. Additional exam requirements/recommendations for international students: Required—TOEFL (minimum score 560 paper-based; 220 computer-based; 83 iBT), IELTS (minimum score 5). *Application contact:* Barbara Andaya, Director, 808-956-2688, Fax: 808-956-6345, E-mail: dirseas@hawaii.edu.

University of Illinois at Urbana–Champaign, Graduate College, College of Liberal Arts and Sciences, School of Literatures, Cultures and Linguistics, Department of East Asian Languages and Cultures, Champaign, IL 61820. Offers Asian studies (MA); East Asian languages and cultures (PhD). *Faculty:* 15 full-time (5 women), 1 (woman) part-time/adjunct. *Students:* 28 full-time (23 women), 11 part-time (8 women); includes 5 minority (1 American Indian/Alaska Native, 4 Asian Americans or Pacific Islanders), 25 international. 59 applicants, 19% accepted, 8 enrolled. In 2007, 4 master's awarded. *Degree requirements:* For master's, one foreign language; for doctorate, thesis/dissertation. *Entrance requirements:* For master's, GRE General Test, minimum GPA of 3.0. Additional exam requirements/recommendations for international students: Required—TOEFL. *Application deadline:* For fall admission, 1/16 for domestic students; for spring admission, 1/16 for domestic students. Application fee: $60 ($75 for international students). Electronic applications accepted. *Financial support:* In 2007–08, 8 fellowships, 3 research assistantships, 27 teaching assistantships were awarded; tuition waivers (full and partial) also available. Financial award application deadline: 2/15. *Unit head:* Karen Kelsky, Head, 217-244-9077, Fax: 217-244-2223, E-mail: kelsky@uiuc.edu. *Application contact:* Brian Ruppert, Director of Graduate Studies, 217-244-4012, Fax: 217-244-2223, E-mail: ruppert@uiuc.edu.

The University of Iowa, Graduate College, College of Liberal Arts and Sciences, Program in Asian Languages and Literature, Iowa City, IA 52242-1316. Offers MA. *Faculty:* 11 full-time, 10 part-time/adjunct. *Students:* 14 full-time (12 women), 1 (woman) part-time, 13 international. 10 applicants, 60% accepted, 5 enrolled. In 2007, 4 degrees awarded. *Degree requirements:* For master's, thesis optional, exam. *Entrance requirements:* For master's, GRE General Test, minimum GPA of 3.0. Additional exam requirements/recommendations for international students: Required—TOEFL (minimum score 590 paper-based; 243 computer-based; 96 iBT). *Application deadline:* For fall admission, 4/15 for domestic students; for spring admission, 10/1 for domestic students. Application fee: $60 ($85 for international students). Electronic applications accepted. *Expenses:* Tuition, state resident: part-time $349 per hour. Tuition, nonresident: part-time $349 per hour. Tuition and fees vary according to course load and program. *Financial support:* In 2007–08, 1 research assistantship with partial tuition reimbursement, 7 teaching assistantships with partial tuition reimbursements were awarded; fellowships also available. Financial award applicants required to submit FAFSA. *Unit head:* Margaret Mills, Chair, 219-335-2151, Fax: 319-353-2207.

University of Kansas, Research and Graduate Studies, College of Liberal Arts and Sciences, Department of East Asian Languages and Cultures, Lawrence, KS 66045. Offers MA. Part-time programs available. *Faculty:* 8. *Students:* 8 full-time (2 women), 3 part-time (all women); includes 1 minority (Asian American or Pacific Islander), 2 international. Average age 30. 15 applicants, 53% accepted, 4 enrolled. In 2007, 2 degrees awarded. *Degree requirements:* For master's, one foreign language, thesis. *Entrance requirements:* For master's, GRE. Additional exam requirements/recommendations for international students: Required—TOEFL. *Application deadline:* For fall admission, 5/1 priority date for domestic students; for spring admission, 11/30 priority date for domestic students. Applications are processed on a rolling basis. Application fee: $55 ($60 for international students). Electronic applications accepted. *Expenses:* Tuition, state resident: full-time $5,838. Tuition, nonresident: full-time $13,409. Tuition and fees vary according to program. *Financial support:* Fellowships, teaching assistantships with full and partial tuition reimbursements, unspecified assistantships available. Financial award application deadline: 2/1. *Faculty research:* Gender relations in literature, ancient Chinese law, visual culture of modern Japan, Japanese language pedagogy, Chinese paleography, Korean shananism, folklore, traditional Chinese and Japenese literature, Chinese linguistics and language pedagogy. *Unit head:* Keith McMahon, Chair and Graduate Director, 785-864-3100, E-mail: kmcmahon@ku.edu. *Application contact:* Georgia Damis, Graduate Secretary, 785-864-3100, Fax: 785-864-4298, E-mail: ealc@ku.edu.

University of Michigan, Horace H. Rackham School of Graduate Studies, College of Literature, Science, and the Arts, Center for Chinese Studies, Ann Arbor, MI 48109. Offers Asian studies: China (AM, Graduate Certificate); JD/AM; MBA/AM; MPP/AM. Part-time programs available. *Faculty:* 30 full-time. *Students:* 12 full-time. In 2007, 5 degrees awarded. *Degree requirements:* For master's, one foreign language, thesis. *Entrance requirements:* For master's, GRE General Test. Additional exam requirements/recommendations for international students: Required—TOEFL. *Application deadline:* For winter admission, 1/15 for domestic and international students. Application fee: $60 ($75 for international students). Electronic applications accepted. *Financial support:* Fellowships, Federal Work-Study available. *Faculty research:* Economic reform in China, Chinese religion, history of late Imperial China, Chinese foreign policy, Chinese music and music history. *Unit head:* Mary Gallagher, Director, 734-764-6308, Fax: 734-764-5540. *Application contact:* Maryellen Bartolome, Student Services Coordinator, 734-936-1603, Fax: 734-764-5540, E-mail: mbartolo@umich.edu.

University of Michigan, Horace H. Rackham School of Graduate Studies, College of Literature, Science, and the Arts, Center for Japanese Studies, Ann Arbor, MI 48109. Offers AM, JD/AM, MBA/AM. Part-time programs available. *Faculty:* 41 full-time (22 women), 9 part-time/adjunct (1 woman). *Students:* 15 full-time (9 women), 3 part-time (all women); includes 7 minority (2 African Americans, 1 American Indian/Alaska Native, 4 Asian Americans or Pacific Islanders), 1 international. Average age 27. 30 applicants, 73% accepted, 12 enrolled. In 2007, 2 degrees awarded. *Degree requirements:* For master's, one foreign language, thesis or alternative. *Entrance requirements:* For master's, GRE General Test. Additional exam requirements/recommendations for international students: Required—TOEFL (minimum score 560 paper-based; 220 computer-based; 84 iBT). *Application deadline:* For fall admission, 1/15 for domestic and international students. Application fee: $60 ($75 for international students). Electronic applications accepted. *Financial support:* In 2007–08, 14 students received support, including 2 fellowships with full tuition reimbursements available (averaging $12,500 per year); career-related internships or fieldwork, Federal Work-Study, scholarships/grants, health care benefits, and tuition waivers (full and partial) also available. Support available to part-time students. Financial award application deadline: 2/1; financial award applicants required to submit FAFSA. *Faculty research:* Japanese literature; Japanese history; Japanese linguistics and language pedagogy; gender and sexuality in Japan. *Unit head:* Mark D. West, Director, 734-764-6307, Fax: 734-936-2948, E-mail: umcjs@umich.edu. *Application contact:* Azumi Ann Takata, PhD, Student Services Coordinator, 734-647-3766, Fax: 734-936-2948, E-mail: cjsadmissions@umich.edu.

University of Michigan, Horace H. Rackham School of Graduate Studies, College of Literature, Science, and the Arts, Center for South Asian Studies, Ann Arbor, MI 48109. Offers MA, Certificate, MBA/MA. Part-time programs available. *Faculty:* 38 full-time (13 women), 1 (woman) part-time/adjunct. *Students:* 10 full-time (6 women); includes 6 minority (all Asian Americans or Pacific Islanders) Average age 31. 12 applicants, 83% accepted, 1 enrolled. In 2007, 4 master's, 2 other advanced degrees awarded. *Degree requirements:* For master's, one foreign language, thesis, 24 credits area studies; for Certificate, one foreign language, 15 credits area studies. *Entrance requirements:* For master's, GRE General Test, GMAT (MA/MBA), LSAT (law), 3 transcripts; for Certificate, GRE General Test, GMAT (MA/MBA), LSAT (law), 2 transcripts. Additional exam requirements/recommendations for international students: Required—TOEFL (minimum score 560 paper-based; 220 computer-based; 84 iBT). *Application deadline:* For fall admission, 1/15 for domestic and international students; for winter admission, 1/15 priority date for domestic and international students. Application fee: $60 ($75 for international students). Electronic applications accepted. *Financial support:* In 2007–08, 1 fellowship with full tuition reimbursement (averaging $15,000 per year) was awarded; career-related internships or fieldwork, Federal Work-Study, institutionally sponsored loans, scholarships/grants, and health care benefits also available. Financial award application deadline: 2/1; financial award applicants required to submit FAFSA. *Faculty research:* History of Islam and South Asia; ethnicity and nationalism; global and transnational feminism; South Asian architecture and urbanism; mysticism and politics in Indian religions. *Unit head:* Dr. William J. Glover, Director, 734-764-0352, Fax: 734-936-0996, E-mail: wglover@umich.edu. *Application contact:* Nancy A. Becker, Center for South Asian Studies Student Services Assistant, 734-764-0448, Fax: 734-936-0996, E-mail: nbecker@umich.edu.

University of Michigan, Horace H. Rackham School of Graduate Studies, College of Literature, Science, and the Arts, Center for Southeast Asian Studies, Ann Arbor, MI 48109. Offers MA, Graduate Certificate, MBA/MA, MPP/MA. Part-time programs available. *Faculty:* 26 full-time (12 women), 4 part-time/adjunct (0 women). *Students:* 7 full-time (2 women); includes 3 minority (all Asian Americans or Pacific Islanders) Average age 30. 11 applicants, 45% accepted, 2 enrolled. In 2007, 5 degrees awarded. *Degree requirements:* For master's, one foreign language, thesis, 24 credits area studies; for Graduate Certificate, one foreign language, 15 credits area studies. *Entrance requirements:* For master's, GRE General Test, GMAT (MA/MBA), LSAT (dual degree law), 3 recommendations; transcripts; statement of purpose; for Graduate Certificate, GRE General Test, GMAT (MA/MBA), LSAT (dual degree law), 2 recommendations; transcripts; statement of purpose. Additional exam requirements/recommendations for international students: Required—TOEFL (minimum score 560 paper-based; 220 computer-based; 84 iBT). *Application deadline:* For fall admission, 1/15 for domestic and international students; for winter admission, 1/15 priority date for domestic and international students. Application fee: $60 ($75 for international students). Electronic applications accepted. *Financial support:* In 2007–08, 3 fellowships with full tuition reimbursements (averaging $15,000 per year) were awarded; career-related internships or fieldwork, Federal Work-Study, institutionally sponsored loans, scholarships/grants, and health care benefits also available. Financial award application deadline: 2/1; financial award applicants required to submit FAFSA. *Faculty research:* Modern Southeast Asia political economy and policy-making; media, ritual, and religion; technology and colonialism in Southeast Asia; urbanization in developing countries; modernity and mase culture in Southeast Asia. *Unit head:* Dr. Allen Hicken, Director, 734-764-0352, Fax: 734-936-0996, E-mail: ahicken@umich.edu. *Application contact:* Gigi Bosch Gates, Student Services Coordinator, 734-764-0352, Fax: 734-936-0996, E-mail: gigib@umich.edu.

University of Michigan, Horace H. Rackham School of Graduate Studies, College of Literature, Science, and the Arts, Department of Asian Languages and Cultures, Ann Arbor, MI 48109. Offers MA, PhD. Terminal master's awarded for partial completion of doctoral program. *Degree*

Asian Studies

University of Michigan (continued)
requirements: For master's, variable foreign language requirement, thesis; for doctorate, 2 foreign languages, thesis/dissertation, oral defense of dissertation, preliminary exam. *Entrance requirements:* For master's and doctorate, GRE General Test. Additional exam requirements/ recommendations for international students: Required—TOEFL (minimum score 600 paper-based; 250 computer-based). Electronic applications accepted. *Faculty research:* Literature, linguistics, religion, philosophy, music, cinema.

University of Minnesota, Twin Cities Campus, Graduate School, College of Liberal Arts, Department of Asian Languages and Literatures, Minneapolis, MN 55455-0213. Offers Asian literatures, cultures, and media (PhD). *Faculty:* 9 full-time (4 women), 5 part-time/adjunct (all women). *Students:* 10 full-time (3 women); includes 2 minority (1 African American, 1 Hispanic American), 8 international. Average age 23. 40 applicants, 23% accepted, 5 enrolled. *Degree requirements:* For doctorate, comprehensive exam, thesis/dissertation. *Entrance requirements:* For doctorate, GRE, 3 letters of recommendation. Additional exam requirements/ recommendations for international students: Required—TOEFL (minimum score 550 paper-based; 213 computer-based), IELTS (minimum score 7). *Application deadline:* For fall admission, 1/2 for domestic and international students. Application fee: $55 ($75 for international students). Electronic applications accepted. *Financial support:* In 2007–08, 2 students received support, including 2 fellowships with full tuition reimbursements available (averaging $16,000 per year). Financial award application deadline: 1/5. *Faculty research:* Gender studies, post-colonial theory, poetics and poetic theory, film studies, post modernist thought. Total annual research expenditures: $2,500. *Unit head:* Ray Wakefield, Interim Chair, 612-625-0122, E-mail: allchair@umn.edu. *Application contact:* Prof. Paul Rouzer, Director of Graduate Studies, 612-625-2564, Fax: 612-624-5513, E-mail: prouzer@umn.edu.

University of Oregon, Graduate School, College of Arts and Sciences, Program in Asian Studies, Eugene, OR 97403. Offers MA. Part-time programs available. *Students:* 5 full-time (2 women), 2 international. 12 applicants, 42% accepted. In 2007, 7 degrees awarded. *Degree requirements:* For master's, one foreign language, thesis or alternative. *Entrance requirements:* For master's, GRE General Test. Additional exam requirements/recommendations for international students: Required—TOEFL. *Application deadline:* For fall admission, 2/15 for domestic students; for winter admission, 9/15 for domestic students. Application fee: $50. *Financial support:* In 2007–08, 10 teaching assistantships were awarded; fellowships, Federal Work-Study also available. Financial award application deadline: 2/15. *Faculty research:* East and Southeast Asia, Pacific Islands. *Unit head:* Ina Asim, Head, 541-346-4867. *Application contact:* Daniel Gorman, Coordinator, 541-346-2850, Fax: 541-346-0802, E-mail: dqgorman@uoregon.edu.

University of Pennsylvania, School of Arts and Sciences, Graduate Group in East Asian Languages and Civilization, Philadelphia, PA 19104. Offers AM, PhD.

University of Pennsylvania, School of Arts and Sciences, Graduate Group in South Asian Regional Studies, Philadelphia, PA 19104. Offers AM, PhD. Terminal master's awarded for partial completion of doctoral program. *Degree requirements:* For master's, one foreign language, thesis, written exam; for doctorate, 3 foreign languages, thesis/dissertation, written exam. *Entrance requirements:* For master's, GRE General Test. Additional exam requirements/ recommendations for international students: Required—TOEFL. Electronic applications accepted. *Faculty research:* South Asian linguistics, literature, and history; economic history.

University of Pittsburgh, School of Arts and Sciences, Department of East Asian Languages and Literatures, Pittsburgh, PA 15260. Offers East Asian studies (MA). Part-time programs available. *Faculty:* 7 full-time (3 women), 6 part-time/adjunct (4 women). *Students:* 8 full-time (4 women), 1 part-time, 4 international. Average age 28. 18 applicants, 44% accepted, 2 enrolled. In 2007, 2 degrees awarded. *Degree requirements:* For master's, one foreign language, thesis, oral comprehensive exam. *Entrance requirements:* For master's, GRE General Test, 2 years of Chinese or Japanese, minimum QPA of 3.0. Additional exam requirements/recommendations for international students: Required—TOEFL (minimum score 600 paper-based). *Application deadline:* For fall admission, 1/15 for domestic and international students. Application fee: $50. Electronic applications accepted. *Financial support:* In 2007–08, 6 students received support, including 3 fellowships with full and partial tuition reimbursements available (averaging $15,070 per year), teaching assistantships with full and partial tuition reimbursements available (averaging $4,000 per year); Federal Work-Study, scholarships/grants, health care benefits, tuition waivers (full and partial), and unspecified assistantships also available. Financial award application deadline: 1/30. *Faculty research:* Chinese literature, film, and poetry; Japanese literature, film, and theater; Chinese society and culture; East Asian foreign policy, security studies, and economic history; Japanese performing arts and fine arts. *Unit head:* Dr. Hiroshi Nara, Chairman, 412-624-5568, Fax: 412-624-3458, E-mail: hnara@pitt.edu. *Application contact:* Paula Locante, Administrator, 412-624-5568, Fax: 412-624-3458, E-mail: plocante@pitt.edu.

University of Pittsburgh, University Center for International Studies, Pittsburgh, PA 15260. Offers African studies (Certificate); Asian studies (Certificate); European Union studies (Certificate); global studies (Certificate); Latin American studies (Certificate); Russian and East European studies (Certificate); West European studies (Certificate). *Unit head:* Lawrence F. Feick, Director, University Center for International Studies, 412-648-7374, Fax: 412-624-4672, E-mail: feick@pitt.edu.

University of San Francisco, College of Arts and Sciences, Program in Asia Pacific Studies, San Francisco, CA 94117-1080. Offers MA. Part-time and evening/weekend programs available. *Faculty:* 1 full-time (0 women), 6 part-time/adjunct (3 women). *Students:* 42 full-time (27 women); includes 11 minority (1 African American, 8 Asian Americans or Pacific Islanders, 2 Hispanic Americans), 12 international. Average age 27. 42 applicants, 100% accepted, 22 enrolled. In 2007, 20 degrees awarded. *Degree requirements:* For master's, one foreign language, thesis. *Entrance requirements:* For master's, minimum GPA of 3.0. *Application deadline:* Applications are processed on a rolling basis. Application fee: $55 ($65 for international students). *Expenses:* Tuition: Part-time $1,005 per unit. Tuition and fees vary according to degree level, campus/location and program. *Financial support:* In 2007–08, 27 students received support. Career-related internships or fieldwork, Federal Work-Study, and institutionally sponsored loans available. Financial award application deadline: 3/2; financial award applicants required to submit FAFSA. *Faculty research:* History of Christianity in China, U.S.-China policy, East Asian economies and political systems, sociolinguistic aspects of Japanese. *Unit head:* Dr. John Nelson, Director, 415-422-2226, Fax: 415-422-5933.

University of Southern California, Graduate School, College of Letters, Arts and Sciences, Department of East Asian Languages and Cultures, Los Angeles, CA 90089. Offers MA, PhD. *Faculty:* 13 full-time (5 women). *Students:* 20 full-time (14 women); includes 5 minority (1 African American, 4 Asian Americans or Pacific Islanders), 11 international. 45 applicants, 24% accepted. In 2007, 3 master's, 1 doctorate awarded. *Degree requirements:* For master's, one foreign language, thesis; for doctorate, 2 foreign languages, thesis/dissertation. *Entrance requirements:* For master's and doctorate, GRE General Test. *Application deadline:* For fall admission, 12/20 for domestic students. Application fee: $85. *Financial support:* In 2007–08, 18 students received support, including fellowships with tuition reimbursements available (averaging $19,000 per year), teaching assistantships with tuition reimbursements available (averaging $18,570 per year); scholarships/grants also available. Financial award application deadline: 2/15; financial award applicants required to submit FAFSA. *Faculty research:* Premodern Chinese history, modern and classical Chinese literature, Japanese, Korea. *Unit head:* Dr. Xiabing Tang, Chair, 213-740-3707, Fax: 213-740-9295, E-mail: ealc@usc.edu. *Application contact:* Josephine Le, Information Contact, 213-740-2311.

University of Southern California, Graduate School, College of Letters, Arts and Sciences, Department of East Asian Studies, Los Angeles, CA 90089. Offers MA, MBA/MA. Part-time programs available. *Faculty:* 3 full-time (1 woman). *Students:* 10 full-time (6 women); includes 4 minority (all Asian Americans or Pacific Islanders), 3 international. 38 applicants, 37% accepted. In 2007, 3 degrees awarded. *Degree requirements:* For master's, thesis. *Entrance requirements:* For master's, GRE General Test. *Application deadline:* For fall admission, 1/7 for domestic students. Application fee: $85. *Financial support:* In 2007–08, 6 students received support, including teaching assistantships with full tuition reimbursements available (averaging $18,570 per year). Financial award application deadline: 2/15; financial award applicants required to submit FAFSA. *Faculty research:* China, Japan, Korea, film/cinema in East Asia, geography. *Unit head:* Dr. Stanley Rosen, Chair, 213-740-2991, E-mail: easc@usc.edu.

The University of Texas at Austin, Graduate School, College of Liberal Arts, Center for Asian Studies, Austin, TX 78712-1111. Offers MA, MBA/MA, MP Aff/MA. Part-time programs available. *Degree requirements:* For master's, one foreign language, thesis. *Entrance requirements:* For master's, GRE General Test. Electronic applications accepted.

The University of Texas at Austin, Graduate School, College of Liberal Arts, Department of Asian Studies, Austin, TX 78712-1111. Offers Asian cultures and languages (MA, PhD). Part-time programs available. *Degree requirements:* For master's, thesis; for doctorate, 3 foreign languages, thesis/dissertation. *Entrance requirements:* For master's and doctorate, GRE General Test. Electronic applications accepted. *Faculty research:* Modern Taiwanese fiction, modern Japanese literature, religious studies in South Asia during classical period.

University of Toronto, School of Graduate Studies, Humanities Division, Centre for South Asian Studies, Toronto, ON M5S 1A1, Canada. Offers MA, PhD. Students who wish to be admitted into the Collaborative Program in South Asian Studies must apply to one of the following units: anthropology, English, history, geography, political science (PhD only), religious studies, social work. Part-time programs available. *Students:* 1 applicant, 100% accepted. *Degree requirements:* For master's, thesis optional; for doctorate, one foreign language, thesis/dissertation. Application fee: $100 Canadian dollars. *Unit head:* Prof. C. Kanaganayakam, Interim Director, 416-978-4294, Fax: 416-978-8744. *Application contact:* Secretary, 416-978-4294, Fax: 416-978-8744, E-mail: south.asian@utoronto.ca.

University of Toronto, School of Graduate Studies, Humanities Division, Department of East Asian Studies, Toronto, ON M5S 1A1, Canada. Offers MA, PhD. Part-time programs available. *Faculty:* 16 full-time, 4 part-time/adjunct. *Students:* 32 full-time (19 women), 9 international. 61 applicants, 36% accepted. In 2007, 10 master's, 1 doctorate awarded. *Degree requirements:* For master's, thesis optional; for doctorate, 2 foreign languages, comprehensive exam, thesis/ dissertation. *Entrance requirements:* For master's, writing sample, 2 letters of recommendation, BA in a specialist or East Asian studies program, minimum B+ average in final year; for doctorate, writing sample, 3 letters of recommendation, MA in East Asian studies. Additional exam requirements/recommendations for international students: Required—TOEFL (minimum score 600 paper-based), TWE (minimum score 5). *Application deadline:* For fall admission, 1/31 for domestic students. Application fee: $100 Canadian dollars. Electronic applications accepted. *Unit head:* Prof. Vincent Shen, Chair and Graduate Chair, 416-978-0685, E-mail: vincent.shen@utoronto.ca. *Application contact:* Norma Escobar, Secretary, 416-946-3625, Fax: 416-978-5711, E-mail: easgen.escobar@utoronto.ca.

University of Victoria, Faculty of Graduate Studies, Faculty of Humanities, Department of Pacific and Asian Studies, Victoria, BC V8W 2Y2, Canada. Offers MA. *Faculty:* 9 full-time (3 women). *Students:* 9 full-time (all women), 1 international. Average age 25. 9 applicants, 33% accepted, 2 enrolled. *Degree requirements:* For master's, thesis. *Entrance requirements:* For master's, minimum B+ average, writing sample. Additional exam requirements/recommendations for international students: Required—TOEFL (minimum score 575 paper-based; 233 computer-based), IELTS (minimum score 7). *Application deadline:* For fall admission, 1/15 for domestic students, 12/15 for international students. Application fee: $75 Canadian dollars ($125 Canadian dollars for international students). Electronic applications accepted. *Expenses:* Tuition, state resident: full-time $3,110. International tuition: $3,700 full-time. Tuition and fees vary according to program. *Financial support:* In 2007–08, 2 fellowships (averaging $2,500 Canadian dollars per year), 2 teaching assistantships (averaging $3,000 Canadian dollars per year) were awarded; scholarships/grants and health care benefits also available. Financial award application deadline: 2/15. *Faculty research:* Culture, ethnicity and identity; economy and society; gender studies; languages and linguistics; literature. *Unit head:* Dr. M. Cody Poulton, Chair, 250-721-8707, Fax: 250-721-7219, E-mail: cpoulton@uvic.ca. *Application contact:* Dr. Leslie Butt, Graduate Advisor, 250-721-6647, Fax: 250-721-7219, E-mail: lbutt@uvic.ca.

University of Virginia, College and Graduate School of Arts and Sciences, Department of East Asian Languages, Literatures, and Cultures, Charlottesville, VA 22903. Offers East Asian studies (MA); MBA/MA. *Faculty:* 12 full-time (10 women), 2 part-time/adjunct (both women). *Students:* 3 full-time (1 woman); includes 1 minority (American Indian/Alaska Native). Average age 24. 20 applicants, 30% accepted, 2 enrolled. In 2007, 2 degrees awarded. *Degree requirements:* For master's, one foreign language, comprehensive exam, thesis. *Entrance requirements:* For master's, GRE General Test. *Application deadline:* Applications are processed on a rolling basis. Application fee: $60. Electronic applications accepted. *Financial support:* Applicants required to submit FAFSA. *Unit head:* Daniel Lefkowitz, Chair, 434-924-3452, Fax: 434-924-6977, E-mail: dl2h@virginia.edu.

University of Washington, Graduate School, College of Arts and Sciences, Henry M. Jackson School of International Studies, China Studies Program, Seattle, WA 98195. Offers MAIS. *Faculty:* 32. *Students:* 16 full-time (7 women); includes 3 minority (1 African American, 2 Asian Americans or Pacific Islanders). Average age 25. 43 applicants, 49% accepted, 5 enrolled. In 2007, 10 degrees awarded. *Degree requirements:* For master's, one foreign language, thesis optional. *Entrance requirements:* For master's, GRE General Test, minimum GPA of 3.0. Additional exam requirements/recommendations for international students: Required—TOEFL (minimum score 500 paper-based; 213 computer-based). Application fee: $50. Electronic applications accepted. *Financial support:* In 2007–08, 4 fellowships with full tuition reimbursements were awarded; research assistantships, teaching assistantships, career-related internships or fieldwork, Federal Work-Study, and institutionally sponsored loans also available. Financial award application deadline: 1/15; financial award applicants required to submit FAFSA. *Unit head:* Prof. Yue Dong, Chair, 206-543-4999. *Application contact:* 206-543-6001, Fax: 206-616-3170, E-mail: jsisinfo@u.washington.edu.

University of Washington, Graduate School, College of Arts and Sciences, Henry M. Jackson School of International Studies, Japan Studies Program, Seattle, WA 98195. Offers MAIS. *Faculty:* 19 full-time (9 women). *Students:* 14 full-time (8 women); includes 1 minority (Asian American or Pacific Islander), 2 international. 25 applicants, 60% accepted, 7 enrolled. In 2007, 7 degrees awarded. *Degree requirements:* For master's, one foreign language. *Entrance requirements:* For master's, GRE General Test, minimum GPA of 3.0. Additional exam requirements/recommendations for international students: Required—TOEFL (minimum score 500 paper-based; 213 computer-based). Application fee: $45. Electronic applications accepted. *Financial support:* In 2007–08, 1 fellowship with full tuition reimbursement, 2 research assistantships with full tuition reimbursements, 1 teaching assistantship were awarded; career-related internships or fieldwork, Federal Work-Study, and institutionally sponsored loans also available. Financial award application deadline: 1/15; financial award applicants required to submit FAFSA. *Unit head:* Prof. Robert Pekkanen, Chair, 206-685-1527. *Application contact:* 206-543-6001, Fax: 206-616-3170, E-mail: jsisinfo@u.washington.edu.

University of Washington, Graduate School, College of Arts and Sciences, Henry M. Jackson School of International Studies, Korea Studies Program, Seattle, WA 98195. Offers MAIS. *Faculty:* 7 full-time (4 women). *Students:* 13 full-time (7 women); includes 2 minority (both Asian Americans or Pacific Islanders), 4 international. 14 applicants, 93% accepted, 10 enrolled. In 2007, 5 degrees awarded. *Degree requirements:* For master's, one foreign language. *Entrance requirements:* For master's, GRE General Test, minimum GPA of 3.0. Additional exam requirements/recommendations for international students: Required—TOEFL (minimum score 500 paper-based; 213 computer-based). Application fee: $50. Electronic applications accepted. *Financial support:* In 2007–08, 1 fellowship with full tuition reimbursement was awarded; research assistantships, career-related internships or fieldwork, Federal Work-

Study, institutionally sponsored loans, and summer language study awards also available. Financial award application deadline: 1/15; financial award applicants required to submit FAFSA. *Unit head:* Prof. Clark W. Sorensen, Chair, 206-543-1696, E-mail: sangok@u.washington.edu. *Application contact:* 206-543-6001, Fax: 206-616-3170, E-mail: jsisinfo@u.washington.edu.

University of Washington, Graduate School, College of Arts and Sciences, Henry M. Jackson School of International Studies, Russian, East European and Central Asian Studies Program, Seattle, WA 98195. Offers Central Asian studies (MAIS); East European studies (MAIS); Russian studies (MAIS). *Faculty:* 56 full-time (25 women). *Students:* 23 full-time (13 women); includes 3 minority (1 Asian American or Pacific Islander, 2 Hispanic Americans), 3 international. 29 applicants, 66% accepted, 9 enrolled. In 2007, 13 degrees awarded. *Degree requirements:* For master's, one foreign language, thesis. *Entrance requirements:* For master's, GRE General Test, 2 years of relevant language, minimum GPA of 3.0. Additional exam requirements/recommendations for international students: Required—TOEFL (minimum score 500 paper-based; 213 computer-based). Application fee: $50. Electronic applications accepted. *Financial support:* In 2007–08, 5 fellowships with full tuition reimbursements were awarded; research assistantships, teaching assistantships, career-related internships or fieldwork, Federal Work-Study, institutionally sponsored loans, and summer language study awards also available. Financial award application deadline: 1/15. *Unit head:* Prof. Stephen E. Hanson, Chair, 206-543-9460, Fax: 206-685-0668, E-mail: shanson@u.washington.edu. *Application contact:* 206-543-6001, Fax: 206-616-3170, E-mail: jsisinfo@u.washington.edu.

University of Washington, Graduate School, College of Arts and Sciences, Henry M. Jackson School of International Studies, South Asian Studies Program, Seattle, WA 98195. Offers MAIS. *Faculty:* 22 full-time (10 women). *Students:* 6 full-time (3 women); includes 3 minority (all Asian Americans or Pacific Islanders) 12 applicants, 100% accepted, 3 enrolled. In 2007, 4 degrees awarded. *Degree requirements:* For master's, one foreign language, thesis optional. *Entrance requirements:* For master's, GRE General Test, minimum GPA of 3.0. Additional exam requirements/recommendations for international students: Required—TOEFL (minimum score 500 paper-based; 213 computer-based). Application fee: $50. Electronic applications accepted. *Financial support:* In 2007–08, 3 fellowships with full tuition reimbursements were awarded; research assistantships, career-related internships or fieldwork, Federal Work-Study, institutionally sponsored loans, and summer language study awards also available. Financial award application deadline: 1/15; financial award applicants required to submit FAFSA. *Unit head:* Prof. Priti Ramamurthy, Chair, 206-543-6984, E-mail: priti@u.washington.edu. *Application contact:* 206-543-6001, Fax: 206-616-3170, E-mail: jsisinfo@u.washington.edu.

University of Wisconsin–Madison, Graduate School, College of Letters and Science, Center for Southeast Asian Studies, Madison, WI 53706. Offers MA. Part-time programs available. *Degree requirements:* For master's, one foreign language, oral defense of seminar paper. Electronic applications accepted. *Faculty research:* Economic development, censorship, political change, pedagogical developments in Indonesia, Philippine historical demography, environment photography.

University of Wisconsin–Madison, Graduate School, College of Letters and Science, Department of Languages and Cultures of Asia, Madison, WI 53706-1380. Offers MA, PhD. Part-time programs available. Terminal master's awarded for partial completion of doctoral program. *Degree requirements:* For master's, one foreign language, thesis or alternative; for doctorate, 2 foreign languages, thesis/dissertation. *Entrance requirements:* For master's, minimum GPA of 3.0; for doctorate, minimum GPA of 3.25, master's degree. Electronic applications accepted. *Faculty research:* Literature, folklore, religion.

Valparaiso University, Graduate Division, Program in Chinese Studies, Valparaiso, IN 46383. Offers MA, JD/MA. Part-time and evening/weekend programs available. *Students:* 2 full-time (0 women), 1 part-time; includes 1 minority (Hispanic American) Average age 26. In 2007, 5 degrees awarded. *Entrance requirements:* For master's, minimum GPA of 3.0, Chinese language proficiency. Additional exam requirements/recommendations for international students: Required—TOEFL (minimum score 550 paper-based; 213 computer-based). *Application deadline:* Applications are processed on a rolling basis. Application fee: $30 ($50 for international students). Electronic applications accepted. *Financial support:* Scholarships/grants and unspecified assistantships available. Support available to part-time students. Financial award applicants required to submit FAFSA. *Application contact:* Jamie Haney, Coordinator of Recruitment Activities, 219-464-5313, Fax: 219-464-5381, E-mail: jamie.haney@valpo.edu.

Washington State University, Graduate School, College of Liberal Arts, Department of History, Pullman, WA 99164. Offers early and modern European history (MA, PhD); environmental history (MA, PhD); Latin American history (MA, PhD); modern East Asia history (MA, PhD); public history (MA, PhD); US history (MA, PhD); women's history (MA, PhD); world history (MA, PhD). Part-time programs available. *Faculty:* 24. *Students:* 45 full-time (28 women), 8 part-time (4 women); includes 2 minority (both Hispanic Americans), 2 international. Average age 33. 64 applicants, 41% accepted, 15 enrolled. In 2007, 8 master's, 2 doctorates awarded. *Degree requirements:* For master's, comprehensive exam (for some programs), thesis, oral exam; for doctorate, one foreign language, comprehensive exam, thesis/dissertation, oral and written exam. *Entrance requirements:* For master's, GRE General Test, minimum GPA of 3.3, language background form, writing sample; for doctorate, GRE General Test, minimum GPA of 3.5, language background form, writing sample. Additional exam requirements/recommendations for international students: Required—TOEFL (minimum score 550 paper-based). *Application deadline:* For fall admission, 2/1 for domestic and international students; for spring admission, 11/1 for domestic and international students. Applications are processed on a rolling basis. Application fee: $50. Electronic applications accepted. *Financial support:* In 2007–08, 30 students received support, including 1 fellowship with partial tuition reimbursement available (averaging $3,000 per year), research assistantships with full and partial tuition reimbursements available (averaging $13,917 per year), 28 teaching assistantships with full and partial tuition reimbursements available (averaging $13,056 per year); career-related internships or fieldwork, Federal Work-Study, institutionally sponsored loans, scholarships/grants, and health care benefits also available. Financial award application deadline: 4/1; financial award applicants required to submit FAFSA. *Faculty research:* Public, world, environmental, women and U.S. history. Total annual research expenditures: $44,501. *Unit head:* Dr. John Kicza, Co-Chair, 509-335-5002, Fax: 509-335-4171, E-mail: jekicza@wsu.edu. *Application contact:* Graduate Studies Director, 509-335-4030, Fax: 509-335-4171, E-mail: kale@wsu.edu.

Washington University in St. Louis, Graduate School of Arts and Sciences, Department of Asian and Near Eastern Languages and Literatures, St. Louis, MO 63130-4899. Offers Asian language (MA); Asian studies (MA); Chinese (PhD); comparative literature (MA, PhD); Japanese (PhD). Terminal master's awarded for partial completion of doctoral program. *Degree requirements:* For master's, thesis optional; for doctorate, thesis/dissertation. *Entrance requirements:* For master's and doctorate, GRE General Test. Electronic applications accepted.

Washington University in St. Louis, Graduate School of Arts and Sciences, Program in East Asian Studies, St. Louis, MO 63130-4899. Offers art history (PhD); Chinese (MA); Chinese and comparative literature (PhD); East Asian studies (MA); history (PhD); Japanese (MA); Japanese and comparative literature (PhD); JD/MA; MBA/MA. PhD offered through specific departments. *Entrance requirements:* For master's and doctorate, GRE General Test. Electronic applications accepted.

See Close-Up on page 815.

West Virginia University, Eberly College of Arts and Sciences, Department of History, Morgantown, WV 26506. Offers African history (MA, PhD); African-American history (MA, PhD); American history (MA, PhD); Appalachian/regional history (MA, PhD); East Asian history (MA, PhD); European history (MA, PhD); history of science and technology (MA, PhD); Latin American history (MA). Part-time programs available. *Faculty:* 19 full-time (5 women), 12 part-time/adjunct (4 women). *Students:* 43 full-time (17 women), 30 part-time (11 women); includes 5 minority (1 African American, 1 American Indian/Alaska Native, 2 Asian Americans or Pacific Islanders, 1 Hispanic American), 7 international. Average age 33. 70 applicants, 59% accepted, 17 enrolled. In 2007, 8 master's, 3 doctorates awarded. *Median time to degree:* Of those who began their doctoral program in fall 1999, 75% received their degree in 8 years or less. *Degree requirements:* For master's, one foreign language, thesis (for some programs), oral exam, thesis defense; for doctorate, one foreign language, comprehensive exam, thesis/dissertation, dissertation defense. *Entrance requirements:* For master's, GRE General Test, minimum GPA of 3.0; for doctorate, GRE General Test. Additional exam requirements/recommendations for international students: Required—TOEFL (minimum score 550 paper-based), IELTS (minimum score 7). *Application deadline:* For fall admission, 12/31 for domestic students; for spring admission, 10/1 for domestic students. Applications are processed on a rolling basis. Application fee: $45. Electronic applications accepted. *Expenses:* Tuition, state resident: full-time $5,196; part-time $292 per credit hour. Tuition, nonresident: full-time $15,064; part-time $840 per credit hour. Tuition and fees vary according to program. *Financial support:* In 2007–08, 60 students received support, including 5 fellowships with full tuition reimbursements available (averaging $3,000 per year), 1 research assistantship with full tuition reimbursement available (averaging $7,200 per year), 8 teaching assistantships with full tuition reimbursements available (averaging $12,000 per year); career-related internships or fieldwork, Federal Work-Study, institutionally sponsored loans, health care benefits, tuition waivers (full and partial), and graduate administrative assistantships also available. Financial award application deadline: 12/31; financial award applicants required to submit FAFSA. *Faculty research:* U.S., Appalachia, modern Europe, Africa, colonial and post-colonial societies. Total annual research expenditures: $93,327. *Unit head:* Dr. Steven M. Zdatny, Chair, 304-293-2421 Ext. 5241, Fax: 304-293-3616, E-mail: steve.zdatny@mail.wvu.edu. *Application contact:* Dr. Greg A. Good, Director of Graduate Studies, 304-293-2421 Ext. 5247, Fax: 304-293-3616, E-mail: greg.good@mail.wvu.edu.

Yale University, Graduate School of Arts and Sciences, Program in East Asian Studies, New Haven, CT 06520. Offers MA. *Degree requirements:* For master's, one foreign language. *Entrance requirements:* For master's, GRE General Test.

Canadian Studies

Carleton University, Faculty of Graduate Studies, Faculty of Arts and Social Sciences, School of Canadian Studies, Ottawa, ON K1S 5B6, Canada. Offers MA, PhD. *Degree requirements:* For master's, one foreign language, thesis optional; for doctorate, one foreign language, thesis/dissertation. *Entrance requirements:* For master's, honors degree. Additional exam requirements/recommendations for international students: Required—TOEFL. *Application deadline:* Applications are processed on a rolling basis. Application fee: $77. Electronic applications accepted. *Financial support:* Fellowships, research assistantships, teaching assistantships, career-related internships or fieldwork, institutionally sponsored loans, scholarships/grants, and unspecified assistantships available. *Faculty research:* Modern Canada, cultural studies, women's studies, aboriginal studies and the north, heritage conservation. *Unit head:* André Loiselle, Director, 613-520-2600 Ext. 2366, Fax: 613-520-3903, E-mail: director_canadian_studies@carleton.ca. *Application contact:* Mary Casaubon, Graduate Supervisor, 613-520-2600 Ext. 4034, Fax: 613-520-3903, E-mail: canadian_studies@carleton.ca.

Collège universitaire de Saint-Boniface, Program in Canadian Studies, Saint-Boniface, MB R2H 0H7, Canada. Offers MA.

The Johns Hopkins University, Paul H. Nitze School of Advanced International Studies, Washington, DC 20036. Offers international development (Certificate); international public policy (MIPP); international relations (MA, PhD), including African studies (MA), American foreign policy (MA), Asian studies (MA), Canadian studies (MA), conflict management (MA), European studies (MA), global theory and history (MA), international development (MA), international law, and organizations (MA), international policy (MA), international relations (general) (MA), Latin American studies (MA), Middle East studies (MA), Russian and Eurasian studies (MA), strategic studies (MA); international studies (Certificate); JD/MA; MBA/MA; MHS/MA. *Faculty:* 66 full-time (22 women), 158 part-time/adjunct (54 women). *Students:* 578 full-time (256 women), 46 part-time (16 women); includes 85 minority (18 African Americans, 1 American Indian/Alaska Native, 51 Asian Americans or Pacific Islanders, 15 Hispanic Americans), 193 international. Average age 27. In 2007, 359 master's, 13 doctorates awarded. Terminal master's awarded for partial completion of doctoral program. *Degree requirements:* For master's, one foreign language, 16 non-language courses (8 for MIPP), 2 core examinations, comprehensive oral exam, paper (for some programs); for doctorate, 2 foreign languages, thesis/dissertation, 3 comprehensive exams, defense. *Entrance requirements:* For master's, GMAT or GRE General Test, previous course work in economics, foreign language, undergraduate degree; for doctorate, GRE General Test, master's degree. Additional exam requirements/recommendations for international students: Required—TOEFL (minimum paper-based score of 600, computer-based 250, iBT 100) or IELTS (minimum 7.0). *Application deadline:* For fall admission, 1/7 for domestic students. Application fee: $80. Electronic applications accepted. *Expenses:* Contact institution. *Financial support:* In 2007–08, 350 students received support, including fellowships (averaging $7,500 per year); career-related internships or fieldwork, Federal Work-Study, and scholarships/grants also available. Financial award application deadline: 2/15; financial award applicants required to submit FAFSA. *Faculty research:* Regional studies and functional fields of international relations, international economics, conflict management, global theory and history, international law and organizations, international policy, strategic studies. *Unit head:* Tara Campbell, Associate Director of Admissions, 202-663-5700, Fax: 202-663-7788. *Application contact:* Dr. Belinda A. Yeomans, Director of Admissions, 202-663-5700, Fax: 202-663-7788, E-mail: admissions.sais@jhu.edu.

Saint Mary's University, Faculty of Arts, Program in Atlantic Canada Studies, Halifax, NS B3H 3C3, Canada. Offers MA. Part-time and evening/weekend programs available. *Degree requirements:* For master's, thesis. *Entrance requirements:* For master's, honors degree. Expenses: Contact institution.

Trent University, Graduate Studies, Program in Canadian Studies and Native Studies, Peterborough, ON K9J 7B8, Canada. Offers MA. Part-time programs available. *Degree requirements:* For master's, thesis. *Entrance requirements:* For master's, honors degree. *Faculty research:* Native community-based socioeconomic development, environmental and social impact inventory, regional studies.

Université de Sherbrooke, Faculty of Letters and Human Sciences, Department of Letters and Communications, Sherbrooke, QC J1K 2R1, Canada. Offers comparative Canadian literature (MA, PhD); French literature (MA, PhD); linguistics (MA); lit&erature de crèation (MA, PhD);

Canadian Studies

Université de Sherbrooke (continued)

theatre (MA). *Degree requirements:* For master's, thesis or alternative; for doctorate, thesis/dissertation. *Entrance requirements:* For master's, minimum GPA of 2.8; for doctorate, minimum GPA of 3.0.

Université du Québec à Chicoutimi, Graduate Programs, Program in Regional Studies, Chicoutimi, QC G7H 2B1, Canada. Offers MA. Part-time programs available. *Degree requirements:* For master's, thesis. *Entrance requirements:* For master's, appropriate bachelor's degree, proficiency in French.

Université du Québec à Trois-Rivières, Graduate Programs, Program in Quebec Studies, Trois-Rivières, QC G9A 5H7, Canada. Offers MA, PhD. Part-time programs available. *Degree requirements:* For master's, thesis optional; for doctorate, thesis/dissertation. *Entrance requirements:* For master's, appropriate bachelor's degree, proficiency in French; for doctorate, appropriate master's degree, proficiency in French.

University of Lethbridge, School of Graduate Studies, Lethbridge, AB T1K 3M4, Canada. Offers accounting (MScM); addictions counseling (M Sc); agricultural biotechnology (M Sc); agricultural studies (M Sc, MA); anthropology (MA); archaeology (MA); art (MA); biochemistry (M Sc); biological sciences (M Sc); biomolecular science (PhD); biosystems and biodiversity (PhD); Canadian studies (MA); chemistry (M Sc); computer science (M Sc); computer science and geographical information science (M Sc); counseling psychology (M Ed); dramatic arts (MA); earth, space, and physical science (PhD); economics (MA); educational leadership (M Ed); English (MA); environmental science (M Sc); evolution and behavior (PhD); exercise science (M Sc); finance (MScM); French (MA); French/German (MA); French/Spanish (MA); general education (M Ed); general management (MScM); geography (M Sc, MA); German (MA); health sciences (M Sc, MA); history (MA); human resource management and labour relations (MScM); individualized multidisciplinary (M Sc, MA); information systems (MScM); international management (MScM); kinesiology (M Sc, MA); management (M Sc, MA); marketing (MScM); mathematics (M Sc); music (MA); Native American studies (MA); neuroscience (M Sc, PhD); new media (MA); nursing (M Sc); philosophy (MA); physics (M Sc); policy and strategy (MScM); political science (MA); psychology (M Sc, MA); religious studies (MA); sociology (MA); theoretical and computational science (PhD); urban and regional studies (MA). Part-time and evening/weekend programs available. *Students:* 215 full-time, 98 part-time. In 2007, 87 master's, 1 doctorate awarded. *Degree requirements:* For doctorate, comprehensive exam, thesis/dissertation. *Entrance requirements:* For master's, GMAT (M Sc in management), bachelor's degree in related field, minimum GPA of 3.0 during previous 20 graded semester courses, 2 years teaching or related experience (M Ed); for doctorate, master's degree, minimum graduate GPA of 3.5. Additional exam requirements/recommendations for international students: Required—TOEFL. Application fee: $60 Canadian dollars. *Financial support:* Fellowships, research assistantships, teaching assistantships, scholarships/grants, health care benefits, and unspecified assistantships available. *Faculty research:* Movement and brain plasticity, gibberellin physiology, photosynthesis, carbon cycling, molecular properties of main-group ring components. *Unit head:* Dr. Jo-Anne Fiske, Interim Dean, 403-329-2121, Fax: 403-329-2097. *Application contact:* Jennifer Geddes, Graduate Liaison Officer, 403-329-2762, Fax: 403-329-5159, E-mail: jennifer.geddes@uleth.ca.

University of Manitoba, Faculty of Graduate Studies, College Universitaire de Saint Boniface, Program in Canadian Studies, Winnipeg, MB R3T 2N2, Canada. Offers MA.

University of Ottawa, Faculty of Graduate and Postdoctoral Studies, Faculty of Arts, Institute of Canadian Studies, Ottawa, ON K1N 6N5, Canada. Offers economics (PhD); English (PhD); geography (PhD); history (PhD); lettres Françaises (PhD); linguistics (PhD); philosophy (PhD); political science (PhD); psychology (PhD); religious studies (PhD); translation studies (PhD). *Degree requirements:* For doctorate, comprehensive exam, thesis/dissertation.

University of Regina, Faculty of Graduate Studies and Research, Faculty of Arts, Canadian Plains Studies Program, Regina, SK S4S 0A2, Canada. Offers MA, PhD. Offered as special case program. Part-time programs available. *Faculty:* 1 full-time (0 women). *Students:* 3 full-time (2 women), 2 part-time (both women). 1 applicant, 100% accepted, 1 enrolled. In 2007, 1 degree awarded. *Degree requirements:* For master's, thesis; for doctorate, thesis/dissertation. *Entrance requirements:* Additional exam requirements/recommendations for international students: Required—TOEFL (minimum score 580 paper-based; 237 computer-based; 88 iBT). *Application deadline:* Applications are processed on a rolling basis. Application fee: $85 ($100 for international students). Electronic applications accepted. *Financial support:* In 2007–08, 1 fellowship (averaging $15,750 per year), 1 research assistantship (averaging $13,875 per year), 1 teaching assistantship (averaging $13,060 per year) were awarded; scholarships/grants also available. Financial award application deadline: 6/15. *Faculty research:* Prairie region. *Unit head:* Dr. Harry Diaz, Graduate Program Coordinator, 306-585-4758, Fax: 306-585-4699, E-mail: canadian.plains@uregina.ca.

University of Saskatchewan, College of Graduate Studies and Research, College of Arts and Sciences, Department of Native Studies, Saskatoon, SK S7N 5A2, Canada. Offers MA, PhD. *Degree requirements:* For master's, thesis; for doctorate, thesis/dissertation. *Entrance requirements:* Additional exam requirements/recommendations for international students: Required—TOEFL.

Cultural Studies

Ambrose University College, Ambrose Seminary, Calgary, AB T2P 3T5, Canada. Offers biblical/theological studies (MA); Chinese ministries (Certificate); Christian studies (Diploma); church education (M Div); intercultural ministries (M Div, MA, Certificate, Diploma); leadership and ministry (MA, Certificate, Diploma); pastoral ministries (M Div). *Accreditation:* ATS (one or more programs are accredited). Part-time programs available. *Faculty:* 6 full-time (0 women), 28 part-time/adjunct (4 women). *Students:* 44 full-time (13 women), 118 part-time (45 women); includes 59 minority (2 African Americans, 2 American Indian/Alaska Native, 54 Asian Americans or Pacific Islanders, 1 Hispanic American). Average age 41. 45 applicants, 82% accepted, 37 enrolled. In 2007, 7 first professional degrees, 17 master's, 2 other advanced degrees awarded. *Degree requirements:* For master's, 2 foreign languages, internship; for M Div, one foreign language, internship. *Entrance requirements:* For master's, bachelor degree. Additional exam requirements/recommendations for international students: Required—TOEFL or IELTS. *Application deadline:* For fall admission, 7/31 priority date for domestic students, 3/1 priority date for international students; for winter admission, 11/30 priority date for domestic students, 6/1 priority date for international students. Applications are processed on a rolling basis. Application fee: $50. Electronic applications accepted. Tuition and fees charges are reported in Canadian dollars. *Expenses:* Tuition: Part-time $281 Canadian dollars per credit hour. Required fees: $16 Canadian dollars per credit hour. *Financial support:* In 2007–08, 40 students received support. Career-related internships or fieldwork and scholarships/grants available. Support available to part-time students. Financial award application deadline: 3/30. *Faculty research:* Evangelicalism and sociology, missiological trends, chaplaincy, intertestamental studies, postmodernism. *Unit head:* Dr. Paul Spilsbury, Academic Dean, 403-410-2000 Ext. 6905, Fax: 403-571-2556, E-mail: pspilsbu@ambrose.edu.

Asbury Theological Seminary, Graduate and Professional Programs, E. Stanley Jones School of World Mission and Evangelism, Wilmore, KY 40390-1199. Offers intercultural studies (MA); world mission and evangelism (MA). *Accreditation:* ATS. *Faculty:* 9 full-time (1 woman), 8 part-time/adjunct (1 woman). *Entrance requirements:* Additional exam requirements/recommendations for international students: Required—TOEFL (minimum score 550 paper-based; 79 iBT), IELTS (minimum score 7). *Application deadline:* For fall admission, 7/1 priority date for domestic students, 1/31 priority date for international students; for spring admission, 12/1 priority date for domestic students, 3/31 priority date for international students. Applications are processed on a rolling basis. Application fee: $50. Electronic applications accepted. *Expenses: Contact institution.* One-time fee: $100 part-time. *Faculty research:* Missiology, anthropology, evangelization, contextual theology, religious studies. *Unit head:* Dr. Ronald K. Crandall, Dean, 859-858-2252, Fax: 859-858-2375, E-mail: ron_crandall@asburyseminary.edu. *Application contact:* Janelle Vernon, Admissions Director, 859-858-2211, Fax: 859-858-2287, E-mail: admissions_office@asburyseminary.edu.

Athabasca University, Centre for Integrated Studies, Athabasca, AB T9S 3A3, Canada. Offers adult education (MA); community studies (MA); cultural studies (MA); educational studies (MA); global change (MA); work, organization, and leadership (MA). Part-time and evening/weekend programs available. Postbaccalaureate distance learning degree programs offered (no on-campus study). *Faculty:* 8 full-time (3 women), 16 part-time/adjunct (13 women). *Students:* Average age 36. 150 applicants, 87% accepted, 112 enrolled. In 2007, 39 degrees awarded. *Degree requirements:* For master's, project. *Entrance requirements:* For master's, 3- or 4-year BA. Additional exam requirements/recommendations for international students: Required—TOEFL (minimum score 560 paper-based; 220 computer-based). *Application deadline:* For fall admission, 3/1 for domestic and international students; for winter admission, 10/1 for domestic and international students. Application fee: $65. Electronic applications accepted. Tuition and fees charges are reported in Canadian dollars. *Expenses:* Tuition, state resident: part-time $1,795 Canadian dollars per credit. Required fees: $70 Canadian dollars per year. One-time fee: $360 Canadian dollars part-time. Part-time tuition and fees vary according to program. *Faculty research:* Women's history, literature and culture studies, sustainable development, labor and education. *Unit head:* Dr. Michael Gismondi, Program Director, 780-675-6218, Fax: 780-675-6921, E-mail: mikeg@athabascau.ca. *Application contact:* Derek Stovin, Program Administrator, 780-675-6236, Fax: 780-675-6921, E-mail: dereks@athabascau.ca.

Baptist Bible College, Graduate School of Theology, Springfield, MO 65803-3498. Offers biblical counseling (MA); biblical studies (MA); church ministries (MA); intercultural studies (MA); theology (M Div). Part-time programs available. *Degree requirements:* For master's, 2 foreign languages, thesis (for some programs); for M Div, 2 foreign languages, thesis/dissertation (for some programs). *Entrance requirements:* For master's, outcomes test. Electronic applications accepted.

Biola University, School of Intercultural Studies, La Mirada, CA 90639-0001. Offers applied linguistics (MA); intercultural education (PhD); intercultural studies (MAICS); missiology (D Miss); missions (MA); teaching English to speakers of other languages (MA, Certificate). Part-time and evening/weekend programs available. Terminal master's awarded for partial completion of doctoral program. *Degree requirements:* For master's, one foreign language, comprehensive exam; for doctorate, one foreign language, comprehensive exam, thesis/dissertation. *Entrance requirements:* For master's, minimum undergraduate GPA of 3.0; for doctorate, MA, 3 years of ministry experience, minimum graduate GPA of 3.3. Additional exam requirements/recommendations for international students: Required—TOEFL (minimum score 550 paper-based; 213 computer-based). Electronic applications accepted.

Brandeis University, Graduate School of Arts and Sciences, Program in Cultural Production, Waltham, MA 02454-9110. Offers MA. Part-time programs available. *Faculty:* 6 full-time (2 women), 2 part-time/adjunct (both women). *Students:* 15 full-time (14 women), 3 part-time (2 women); includes 3 minority (1 African American, 1 Asian American or Pacific Islander, 1 Hispanic American), 4 international. 27 applicants, 81% accepted, 9 enrolled. *Entrance requirements:* For master's, GRE (recommended), statement of purpose, 2 letters of recommendation, official transcripts, resumé, portfolio/writing sample. Additional exam requirements/recommendations for international students: Required—TOEFL (minimum score 650 paper-based; 250 computer-based; 100 iBT), IELTS (minimum score 7). *Application deadline:* For fall admission, 1/15 priority date for domestic students. Applications are processed on a rolling basis. Application fee: $55. Electronic applications accepted. *Financial support:* Scholarships/grants and tuition waivers (partial) available. Support available to part-time students. Financial award application deadline: 4/15; financial award applicants required to submit CSS PROFILE. *Unit head:* Dr. Mark Auslander, Program Chair, 781-736-2214, E-mail: mausland@brandeis.edu.

Brock University, Faculty of Graduate Studies, Faculty of Social Sciences, Program in Popular Culture, St. Catharines, ON L2S 3A1, Canada. Offers MA. Part-time programs available. *Degree requirements:* For master's, thesis optional. *Entrance requirements:* For master's, honors BA. Additional exam requirements/recommendations for international students: Required—TOEFL (minimum score 550 paper-based; 213 computer-based; 80 iBT), IELTS (minimum score 7), TWE (minimum score 4). Electronic applications accepted. *Faculty research:* Film and television studies, popular music, historical aspects of popular culture, popular literature.

Chapman University, Graduate Studies, School of Education, Program in Education: Cultural and Curricular Studies, Orange, CA 92866. Offers PhD. *Faculty:* 19 full-time (13 women), 20 part-time/adjunct (12 women). *Students:* 8 full-time (6 women), 1 part-time; includes 5 minority (2 African Americans, 3 Hispanic Americans). Average age 34. 21 applicants, 43% accepted, 9 enrolled. *Degree requirements:* For doctorate, thesis/dissertation. *Financial support:* Federal Work-Study and scholarships/grants available. *Unit head:* Dr. Joel Colbert, Director, 714-744-7076.

Claremont Graduate University, Graduate Programs, School of Arts and Humanities, Department of Cultural Studies, Claremont, CA 91711-6160. Offers Africana studies (Certificate); cultural studies (MA, PhD); media studies (MA, PhD); museum studies (MA). Part-time programs available. *Faculty:* 2 full-time (1 woman), 2 part-time/adjunct (0 women). *Students:* 48 full-time (33 women), 10 part-time (4 women); includes 19 minority (10 African Americans, 5 Asian Americans or Pacific Islanders, 4 Hispanic Americans), 5 international. Average age 35. In 2007, 7 master's, 4 doctorates awarded. *Degree requirements:* For master's, one foreign language, thesis; for doctorate, 2 foreign languages, comprehensive exam, thesis/dissertation. *Entrance requirements:* For master's and doctorate, GRE General Test. *Application deadline:* For fall admission, 2/15 priority date for domestic students. Applications are processed on a rolling basis. Electronic applications accepted. *Expenses:* Tuition: Full-time $31,640; part-time $1,376 per unit. Required fees: $145 per semester. Tuition and fees vary according to course load, degree level and program. *Financial support:* Fellowships, research assistantships, career-related internships or fieldwork, Federal Work-Study, and institutionally sponsored loans available. Support available to part-time students. Financial award application deadline: 2/15; financial award applicants required to submit FAFSA. *Unit head:* Henry Krips, Chair, 909-607-7803, Fax: 909-621-8609, E-mail: henry.krips@cgu.edu.

Columbia International University, Columbia Biblical Seminary and School of Missions, Columbia, SC 29230-3122. Offers academic ministries (M Div); bible exposition (M Div, MABE);

biblical studies (Certificate); counseling ministries (Certificate); divinity (M Div); educational ministries (M Div, MAEM, Certificate); intercultural studies (M Div, MAIS, Certificate); leadership (D Min); leadership for evangelism/mobilization (MALM); member care (D Min); ministry (Certificate); missions (D Min); pastoral counseling and spiritual formation (M Div, MAPS); preaching (D Min); theology (MA). *Accreditation:* ATS (one or more programs are accredited). Part-time and evening/weekend programs available. *Degree requirements:* For master's, integrative seminar; for doctorate, comprehensive exam, thesis/dissertation; for M Div, internship. *Entrance requirements:* For master's, minimum GPA of 2.7; for doctorate, 3 years of ministerial experience, M Div. Additional exam requirements/recommendations for international students: Required—TOEFL. Electronic applications accepted.

Cornell University, Graduate School, Graduate Fields of Arts and Sciences, Field of English Language and Literature, Ithaca, NY 14853-0001. Offers African-American literature (PhD); American literature after 1865 (PhD); American literature to 1865 (PhD); American studies (PhD); colonial and postcolonial literature (PhD); creative writing (MFA); cultural studies (PhD); dramatic literature (PhD); English poetry (PhD); English Renaissance to 1660 (PhD); lesbian, bisexual, and gay literature studies (PhD); literary criticism and theory (PhD); nineteenth century (PhD); Old and Middle English (PhD); prose fiction (PhD); Restoration and eighteenth century (PhD); twentieth century (PhD); women's literature (PhD); MFA/PhD. *Faculty:* 59 full-time (28 women). *Students:* 97 full-time (53 women); includes 20 minority (7 African Americans, 3 American Indian/Alaska Native, 5 Asian Americans or Pacific Islanders, 5 Hispanic Americans), 13 international. Average age 28. 759 applicants, 7% accepted, 21 enrolled. In 2007, 29 master's, 8 doctorates awarded. Terminal master's awarded for partial completion of doctoral program. *Degree requirements:* For master's, one foreign language, thesis; for doctorate, one foreign language, comprehensive exam, thesis/dissertation, teaching experience. *Entrance requirements:* For master's, GRE General Test, 3 letters of recommendation, creative writing sample; for doctorate, GRE General Test, GRE Subject Test (English), 3 letters of recommendation, writing sample. Additional exam requirements/recommendations for international students: Required—TOEFL (minimum score 600 paper-based; 250 computer-based; 77 iBT). *Application deadline:* For fall admission, 1/10 for domestic students. Application fee: $70. Electronic applications accepted. *Financial support:* In 2007–08, 92 students received support, including 32 fellowships with full tuition reimbursements available, 60 teaching assistantships with full tuition reimbursements available; research assistantships with full tuition reimbursements available, institutionally sponsored loans, scholarships/grants, health care benefits, tuition waivers (full and partial), and unspecified assistantships also available. Financial award applicants required to submit FAFSA. *Faculty research:* English and American literature, women's writing, ethnic and post-colonial literature, critical theory, medievalism. *Unit head:* Director of Graduate Studies, 607-255-7989, Fax: 607-255-6661. *Application contact:* Graduate Field Assistant, 607-255-7989, Fax: 607-255-6661, E-mail: english_grad@cornell.edu.

George Mason University, College of Humanities and Social Sciences, Program in Cultural Studies, Fairfax, VA 22030. Offers PhD. Part-time and evening/weekend programs available. *Faculty:* 24 full-time (13 women). *Students:* 5 full-time (2 women), 57 part-time (33 women); includes 3 minority (2 African Americans, 1 Asian American or Pacific Islander), 15 international. Average age 35. 63 applicants, 46% accepted, 15 enrolled. In 2007, 4 degrees awarded. *Degree requirements:* For doctorate, one foreign language, comprehensive exam, thesis/dissertation, foreign language exams. *Entrance requirements:* For doctorate, GRE General Test, sample of written work, MA or simultaneous application to related MA program at George Mason University. Additional exam requirements/recommendations for international students: Required—TOEFL. *Application deadline:* For fall admission, 1/15 for domestic students. Application fee: $60 ($75 for international students). Electronic applications accepted. *Financial support:* In 2007–08, 14 students received support, including 2 fellowships (averaging $10,000 per year), 1 research assistantship with tuition reimbursement available (averaging $18,000 per year), 4 teaching assistantships with tuition reimbursements available (averaging $11,000 per year); unspecified assistantships and tuition remissions also available. Support available to part-time students. Financial award application deadline: 1/15; financial award applicants required to submit FAFSA. *Unit head:* Roger N. Lancaster, Director, 703-993-2851, Fax: 703-993-2852, E-mail: cultural@gmu.edu.

See Close-Up on page 803.

Graduate Theological Union, Graduate Programs, Berkeley, CA 94709-1212. Offers art and religion (MA, PhD); biblical languages (MA); biblical studies (Old and New Testament) (MA, PhD, Th D); Buddhist studies (MA); Christian spirituality (MA, PhD); cultural and historical studies of religions (MA, PhD); ethics and social theory (PhD); history (MA, PhD, Th D); homiletics (MA, PhD, Th D); interdisciplinary studies (PhD, Th D); Jewish studies (MA, PhD, Certificate); liturgical studies (MA, PhD, Th D); Near Eastern religions (PhD); Orthodox Christian studies (MA); Orthodox studies (Certificate); religion and psychology (MA, PhD); religion and society/ethics and social theory (MA); systematic and philosophical theology (MA, PhD, Th D); women's studies in religion (Certificate); MA/M Div. *Accreditation:* ATS. *Faculty:* 119 full-time (44 women), 34 part-time/adjunct (9 women). *Students:* 317 full-time (152 women), 35 part-time (19 women); includes 49 minority (15 African Americans, 2 American Indian/Alaska Native, 21 Asian Americans or Pacific Islanders, 11 Hispanic Americans), 74 international. Average age 38. 257 applicants, 59% accepted, 79 enrolled. In 2007, 45 master's, 22 doctorates awarded. Terminal master's awarded for partial completion of doctoral program. *Median time to degree:* Of those who began their doctoral program in fall 1999, 52% received their degree in 8 years or less. *Degree requirements:* For master's, one foreign language, thesis; for doctorate, one foreign language, comprehensive exam, thesis/dissertation. *Entrance requirements:* For master's, GRE General Test; for doctorate, GRE General Test, MA or M Div. Additional exam requirements/recommendations for international students: Required—TOEFL. *Application deadline:* For fall admission, 12/15 for domestic and international students; for winter admission, 2/15 for domestic and international students; for spring admission, 9/30 for domestic and international students. Application fee: $40. Electronic applications accepted. *Expenses:* Tuition: Full-time $13,310. Tuition and fees vary according to degree level and program. *Financial support:* In 2007–08, 122 students received support, including 109 fellowships (averaging $11,581 per year), 1 research assistantship (averaging $3,000 per year), 22 teaching assistantships (averaging $3,500 per year); Federal Work-Study, scholarships/grants, and tuition waivers (partial) also available. Support available to part-time students. Financial award application deadline: 2/1; financial award applicants required to submit FAFSA. *Unit head:* Dr. Arthur G. Holder, Dean, 510-649-2440, Fax: 510-649-1417, E-mail: aholder@gtu.edu. *Application contact:* Dr. Kathleen Kook, Assistant Dean for Admissions, 800-826-4488, Fax: 510-649-1730, E-mail: gtuadm@gtu.edu.

Lewis & Clark College, Graduate School of Education and Counseling, Department of Counseling Psychology, Portland, OR 97219-7899. Offers addictions treatment (MA); counseling psychology (MA, MS); marriage, couple and family therapy (MA); psychological and cultural studies (MA); school psychology (MS, Ed S). Part-time and evening/weekend programs available. *Faculty:* 6 full-time (2 women), 26 part-time/adjunct (15 women). *Students:* 98 full-time (80 women), 127 part-time (102 women); includes 19 minority (4 African Americans, 5 Asian Americans or Pacific Islanders, 10 Hispanic Americans). Average age 31. 162 applicants, 81% accepted, 70 enrolled. In 2007, 57 master's, 14 other advanced degrees awarded. *Degree requirements:* For master's, thesis proposal (MS). *Entrance requirements:* For master's, GRE General Test, minimum undergraduate GPA of 2.75. Additional exam requirements/recommendations for international students: Required—TOEFL (minimum score 575 paper-based; 233 computer-based). *Application deadline:* For fall admission, 2/1 priority date for domestic and international students; for spring admission, 10/1 priority date for domestic and international students. Application fee: $50. Electronic applications accepted. *Expenses:* Tuition: Part-time $645 per credit. Tuition and fees vary according to campus/location. *Financial support:* In 2007–08, 183 students received support, including fellowships (averaging $22,000 per year); career-related internships or fieldwork, Federal Work-Study, institutionally sponsored loans, scholarships/grants, health care benefits, and tuition waivers (partial) also available. Support available to part-time students. Financial award applicants required to submit FAFSA. *Faculty research:* Treatment of depression, substance abuse, child-family problems, health psychology, marital relations. *Unit head:* Dr. Tod Sloan, Chair, 503-768-6060, Fax: 503-768-6065, E-mail: cpsy@lclark.edu. *Application contact:* Becky Haas, Director of Admissions, 503-768-6200, Fax: 503-768-6205, E-mail: gseadmit@lclark.edu.

Maranatha Baptist Bible College, Program in Cross-Cultural Studies, Watertown, WI 53094. Offers MA. Part-time programs available. Postbaccalaureate distance learning degree programs offered. *Faculty:* 5 full-time (0 women), 2 part-time/adjunct (0 women). *Students:* 2 full-time (0 women). Average age 25. 1 applicant, 100% accepted, 1 enrolled. *Application deadline:* Applications are processed on a rolling basis. Application fee: $50. *Expenses:* Tuition: Full-time $3,360; part-time $210 per credit. Required fees: $300; $19 per credit. *Financial support:* Scholarships/grants and tuition waivers (full and partial) available. Support available to part-time students. *Unit head:* Dr. Larry Oats, Chair of Graduate School of Theology, 920-206-2324, Fax: 920-261-9109, E-mail: loats@mbbc.edu. *Application contact:* Dr. Jim Harrison, Director of Admissions, 920-206-2327, Fax: 920-261-9109, E-mail: admissions@mbbc.edu.

McMaster University, School of Graduate Studies, Faculty of Humanities, Department of English and Cultural Studies, Hamilton, ON L8S 4M2, Canada. Offers cultural studies and critical theory (MA); English (MA, PhD). Part-time programs available. *Faculty:* 25 full-time. *Students:* 97 full-time. 116 applicants, 20% accepted. *Degree requirements:* For master's, one foreign language, thesis; for doctorate, one foreign language, comprehensive exam, thesis/dissertation. *Entrance requirements:* For master's, honors degree, minimum B+ average in at least 6 full courses of English beyond year 1; for doctorate, MA; minimum A- average in two of three courses. Additional exam requirements/recommendations for international students: Required—TOEFL (minimum score 580 paper-based; 237 computer-based). *Application deadline:* For fall admission, 2/15 for domestic students. Applications are processed on a rolling basis. Application fee: $90. *Financial support:* In 2007–08, fellowships (averaging $7,500 per year), teaching assistantships (averaging $8,440 per year) were awarded; research assistantships, scholarships/grants also available. *Faculty research:* Literary theory, feminist theory, literature of migration, Bakhting globalization. *Unit head:* Dr. Mary O'Connor, Chair, 905-525-9140 Ext. 23731, Fax: 905-777-8316, E-mail: moconnor@mcmaster.ca. *Application contact:* Dr. Grace Kehler, Chair, Graduate Studies, 905-525-9140 Ext. 23723, Fax: 905-777-8316, E-mail: kehlerg@mcmaster.ca.

New York University, Steinhardt School of Culture, Education and Human Development, New York, NY 10012-1019. Offers MA, MFA, MM, MPH, MS, DA, DPS, DPT, Ed D, PhD, Advanced Certificate. *Accreditation:* Teacher Education Accreditation Council. Part-time and evening/weekend programs available. *Faculty:* 261 full-time (156 women), 687 part-time/adjunct (369 women). *Students:* 2,076 full-time (1,665 women), 1,446 part-time (1,131 women); includes 740 minority (242 African Americans, 5 American Indian/Alaska Native, 280 Asian Americans or Pacific Islanders, 213 Hispanic Americans), 559 international. Average age 32. 5,422 applicants, 52% accepted, 1251 enrolled. In 2007, 1,330 master's, 93 doctorates, 22 other advanced degrees awarded. *Degree requirements:* For doctorate, comprehensive exam (for some programs), thesis/dissertation. *Entrance requirements:* For doctorate, GRE General Test, interview. Additional exam requirements/recommendations for international students: Required—TOEFL. *Application deadline:* For fall admission, 2/1 priority date for domestic students, 2/1 for international students; for spring admission, 12/1 for domestic and international students. Applications are processed on a rolling basis. Application fee: $50. *Expenses: Contact institution. Financial support:* In 2007–08, fellowships with full and partial tuition reimbursements (averaging $15,000 per year); research assistantships with full and partial tuition reimbursements, teaching assistantships with full and partial tuition reimbursements, career-related internships or fieldwork, Federal Work-Study, institutionally sponsored loans, scholarships/grants, traineeships, tuition waivers (partial), and unspecified assistantships also available. Support available to part-time students. Financial award application deadline: 2/1; financial award applicants required to submit FAFSA. *Faculty research:* Equity, urban adolescents, arts in education, globalization, community and public health. Total annual research expenditures: $21.3 million. *Unit head:* Dr. Mary Brabeck, Dean, 212-998-5000. *Application contact:* 212-998-5030, Fax: 212-995-4328, E-mail: steinhardt.gradadmissions@nyu.edu.

St. Francis Xavier University, Graduate Studies, Department of Celtic Studies, Antigonish, NS B2G 2W5, Canada. Offers MA. *Faculty:* 3 full-time (2 women). *Degree requirements:* For master's, thesis. *Entrance requirements:* Additional exam requirements/recommendations for international students: Required—TOEFL (minimum score 580 paper-based; 236 computer-based). Application fee: $40. *Faculty research:* Scottish Gaelic in Nova Scotia. *Unit head:* Dr. Kenneth E. Nilsen, Chair, 902-867-2116, Fax: 902-867-5395, E-mail: knilsen@stfx.ca.

San Francisco State University, Division of Graduate Studies, College of Behavioral and Social Sciences, Human Sexuality Studies Program, San Francisco, CA 94132-1722. Offers MA. *Unit head:* Dr. Gilbert Herdt, Chair, 415-405-3570, E-mail: hmsxdept@sfsu.edu. *Application contact:* Prof. Rita Melendez, Graduate Coordinator, 415-405-3571, E-mail: rmelende@sfsu.edu.

Simmons College, College of Arts and Sciences Graduate Studies, Program in Gender/Cultural Studies, Boston, MA 02115. Offers MA, MA/MAT, MA/MS. Part-time programs available. *Faculty:* 19 full-time (17 women), 1 part-time/adjunct (0 women). *Students:* 2 full-time (both women), 31 part-time (28 women); includes 3 minority (all African Americans) Average age 26. 41 applicants, 63% accepted, 14 enrolled. In 2007, 12 degrees awarded. *Degree requirements:* For master's, project, thesis, internship, or fieldwork (one is required). *Entrance requirements:* For master's, academic writing sample. Additional exam requirements/recommendations for international students: Required—TOEFL (minimum score 600 paper-based; 250 computer-based; 100 iBT). *Application deadline:* For fall admission, 8/1 priority date for domestic and international students; for spring admission, 12/15 priority date for domestic and international students. Applications are processed on a rolling basis. Application fee: $35. Electronic applications accepted. *Expenses:* Tuition: Full-time $8,500. Tuition and fees vary according to degree level and program. *Financial support:* In 2007–08, 6 students received support. Scholarships/grants available. Financial award application deadline: 3/1; financial award applicants required to submit FAFSA. *Faculty research:* Obscenity, gender and film, media studies, gender and sexuality, race, postcolonialism. *Unit head:* Jyoti Puri, Director, 617-521-2593, E-mail: jyoti.puri@simmons.edu. *Application contact:* Kristen Haack, Director, Graduate Studies Admission, 617-521-2917, Fax: 617-521-3058, E-mail: gsa@simmons.edu.

Simpson University, A.W. Tozer Theological Seminary, Redding, CA 96003-8606. Offers Christian leadership (MA); Christian studies (MA); intercultural studies (MA); ministry (M Div). Part-time and evening/weekend programs available. Postbaccalaureate distance learning degree programs offered (minimal on-campus study). *Faculty:* 6 part-time/adjunct (0 women). *Students:* 6 full-time (0 women), 49 part-time (13 women); includes 7 minority (3 African Americans, 2 Asian Americans or Pacific Islanders, 2 Hispanic Americans), 1 international. Average age 38. 22 applicants, 73% accepted, 16 enrolled. In 2007, 5 degrees awarded. *Degree requirements:* For master's, student portfolio. *Entrance requirements:* For master's, GRE General Test (if undergraduate GPA is below 2.5), 2 letters of reference, Christian Experience statement. Additional exam requirements/recommendations for international students: Required—TOEFL. *Application deadline:* For fall admission, 9/4 priority date for domestic students, 9/4 for international students; for spring admission, 1/8 priority date for domestic students, 1/8 for international students. Applications are processed on a rolling basis. Application fee: $20. Electronic applications accepted. *Expenses: Contact institution. Financial support:* Scholarships/grants available. Support available to part-time students. Financial award application deadline: 3/20; financial award applicants required to submit FAFSA. *Unit head:* Dr. Robert Redman, Dean, 530-226-4144, Fax: 530-326-4871, E-mail: rredman@simpsonuniversity.edu. *Application contact:* Jeff Williams, Director of Enrollment Development, 530-226-4611, Fax: 530-226-4861, E-mail: jwilliams@simpsonuniversity.edu.

Southern Illinois University Carbondale, Graduate School, College of Liberal Arts, Department of Foreign Languages and Literatures, Carbondale, IL 62901-4701. Offers MA. Part-time programs available. *Faculty:* 18 full-time (5 women), 1 (woman) part-time/adjunct. *Students:* 5

Cultural Studies

Southern Illinois University Carbondale (continued)
full-time (4 women), 13 part-time (10 women); includes 5 minority (1 American Indian/Alaska Native, 4 Hispanic Americans), 5 international. Average age 24. 7 applicants, 71% accepted, 2 enrolled. *Degree requirements:* For master's, one foreign language, thesis. *Entrance requirements:* For master's, minimum GPA of 2.7. Additional exam requirements/recommendations for international students: Required—TOEFL. *Application deadline:* Applications are processed on a rolling basis. Application fee: $0. *Financial support:* In 2007–08, 9 students received support; fellowships with full tuition reimbursements available, research assistantships with full tuition reimbursements available, teaching assistantships with full tuition reimbursements available, career-related internships or fieldwork, Federal Work-Study, institutionally sponsored loans, scholarships/grants, and tuition waivers (full) available. Support available to part-time students. Financial award application deadline: 5/15. *Faculty research:* Bibliography, historical linguistics, language pedagogy, philology, commercial facets. *Unit head:* Dr. Anne Winston-Allen, Chairperson, 618-453-5435, E-mail: winston@siu.edu. *Application contact:* Kitty Mabus, Administrative Clerk, 618-453-5430, E-mail: mabus@siu.edu.

State University of New York at Binghamton, Graduate School, School of Arts and Sciences, Philosophy, Interpretation and Culture Program, Binghamton, NY 13902-6000. Offers MA, PhD. *Students:* 22 full-time (13 women), 30 part-time (10 women); includes 12 minority (6 African Americans, 3 Asian Americans or Pacific Islanders, 3 Hispanic Americans), 21 international. Average age 35. 32 applicants, 34% accepted, 4 enrolled. In 2007, 5 master's, 11 doctorates awarded. *Unit head:* Dr. William Haver, Director, 607-777-3827.

Stony Brook University, State University of New York, Graduate School, College of Arts and Sciences, Department of Comparative Literary and Cultural Studies, Stony Brook, NY 11794. Offers comparative literature (MA, PhD); cultural studies (PhD). Evening/weekend programs available. *Faculty:* 7 full-time (2 women). *Students:* 28 full-time (21 women), 9 part-time (8 women); includes 6 minority (1 African American, 5 Asian Americans or Pacific Islanders), 15 international. Average age 30. 58 applicants, 17% accepted. In 2007, 3 master's, 2 doctorates awarded. Terminal master's awarded for partial completion of doctoral program. *Degree requirements:* For master's, 2 foreign languages, exam; for doctorate, 3 foreign languages, comprehensive exam, thesis/dissertation. *Entrance requirements:* For master's and doctorate, GRE General Test, minimum GPA of 3.5 in major, 3.0 overall. Additional exam requirements/recommendations for international students: Required—TOEFL. *Application deadline:* For fall admission, 1/15 for domestic students. Application fee: $60. *Financial support:* In 2007–08, 17 teaching assistantships were awarded; fellowships, research assistantships also available. *Faculty research:* Literary theory, interdisciplinary studies, literary history. *Unit head:* Dr. Robert Harvey, Chairman, 631-632-7456.

See Close-Up on page 583.

Taylor University College and Seminary, Graduate and Professional Programs, Edmonton, AB T6J 4T3, Canada. Offers Christian studies (Diploma); intercultural studies (MA, Diploma); theology (M Div, MTS). *Accreditation:* ATS. Part-time programs available. *Degree requirements:* For master's, comprehensive exam, thesis optional. *Entrance requirements:* Additional exam requirements/recommendations for international students: Required—TOEFL (minimum score 550 paper-based; 213 computer-based), IELTS (minimum score 7). *Faculty research:* Biblical studies, administration and organization, world religions.

Union Institute & University, Online MA Programs, Cincinnati, OH 45206-1925. Offers health and wellness (MA); history and culture (MA); leadership (MA); literature and writing (MA); psychology (MA). Part-time programs available. Postbaccalaureate distance learning degree programs offered (no on-campus study). *Faculty:* 3 full-time (1 woman), 15 part-time/adjunct (11 women). *Students:* 204 full-time (143 women); includes 19 minority (14 African Americans, 2 American Indian/Alaska Native, 3 Hispanic Americans). Average age 39. In 2007, 46 degrees awarded. *Degree requirements:* For master's, thesis. *Application deadline:* Applications are processed on a rolling basis. Application fee: $50. *Expenses:* Contact institution. *Financial support:* Career-related internships or fieldwork and tuition waivers available. Financial award applicants required to submit FAFSA. *Unit head:* Dr. Brian Webb, Assistant Vice President, Academic Affairs, 802-828-8777, E-mail: brian.webb@tui.edu.

Union University, Institute for International and Intercultural Studies, Jackson, TN 38305-3697. Offers MAIS. Part-time and evening/weekend programs available. *Faculty:* 5 full-time (2 women), 2 part-time/adjunct (both women). *Students:* 33 full-time (23 women); includes 2 minority (1 African American, 1 Asian American or Pacific Islander), 3 international. 30 applicants, 70% accepted, 21 enrolled. In 2007, 9 master's awarded. *Degree requirements:* For master's, capstone course. *Entrance requirements:* For master's, GRE, minimum undergraduate GPA of 3.0, 3 letters of reference. Additional exam requirements/recommendations for international students: Required—TOEFL (minimum score 560 paper-based; 220 computer-based). *Application deadline:* For fall admission, 8/15 priority date for domestic and international students. Applications are processed on a rolling basis. Application fee: $25 ($50 for international students). Electronic applications accepted. *Faculty research:* International education, ethnographic field research, intercultural training for professionals and students, language and culture. *Unit head:* Dr. Cynthia Powell Jayne, Director, 731-661-5358, Fax: 731-661-5175, E-mail: cjayne@uu.edu. *Application contact:* Carol Johnson, MAIS Program Coordinator, 731-661-5057, Fax: 731-661-5175, E-mail: cljohnso@uu.edu.

University of Alaska Fairbanks, College of Liberal Arts, Department of Alaska Native Studies, Fairbanks, AK 99775-7520. Offers cross cultural studies (MA). *Degree requirements:* For master's, comprehensive exam, thesis or alternative. *Entrance requirements:* For master's, GRE General Test. Additional exam requirements/recommendations for international students: Required—TOEFL (minimum score 550 paper-based; 213 computer-based). *Faculty research:* Alaska native literature, oral traditions, history, law and policy; Alaska native cultures, art, native American religion and philosophy.

University of California, Davis, Graduate Studies, Graduate Group in Cultural Studies, Davis, CA 95616. Offers MA, PhD. *Degree requirements:* For master's, thesis; for doctorate, thesis/dissertation. *Entrance requirements:* For doctorate, GRE. Additional exam requirements/recommendations for international students: Required—TOEFL (minimum score 550 paper-based; 213 computer-based). Electronic applications accepted.

University of Hawaii at Manoa, Graduate Division, East-West Center, Honolulu, HI 96822. Offers international cultural studies (Graduate Certificate). Part-time programs available. *Students:* 22 full-time (14 women), 5 part-time (4 women); includes 7 minority (6 Asian Americans or Pacific Islanders, 1 Hispanic American), 11 international. 8 applicants, 13% accepted, 1 enrolled. *Entrance requirements:* For degree, GRE General Test. Additional exam requirements/recommendations for international students: Required—TOEFL (minimum score 540 paper-based; 207 computer-based; 76 iBT), IELTS (minimum score 5). *Application deadline:* For fall admission, 3/1 for domestic and international students; for spring admission, 9/1 for domestic and international students. Application fee: $50. *Financial support:* In 2007–08, 2 research assistantships (averaging $17,847 per year), 6 teaching assistantships (averaging $14,574 per year) were awarded. *Application contact:* Mari Yoshihara, Graduate Chairperson, 808-956-8542, Fax: 808-956-4733, E-mail: myoshiha@hawaii.edu.

University of Houston–Clear Lake, School of Human Sciences and Humanities, Programs in Human Sciences, Houston, TX 77058-1098. Offers behavioral sciences (MA), including behavioral sciences-general, behavioral sciences-psychology, behavioral sciences-sociology; clinical psychology (MA); criminology (MA); cross-cultural studies (MA); family therapy (MA); fitness and human performance (MA); school psychology (MA). *Accreditation:* AAMFT/COAMFTE. Part-time and evening/weekend programs available. Postbaccalaureate distance learning degree programs offered (minimal on-campus study). *Degree requirements:* For master's, thesis or alternative. *Entrance requirements:* For master's, GRE General Test. Additional exam requirements/recommendations for international students: Required—TOEFL (minimum score 550 paper-based; 213 computer-based). Electronic applications accepted. *Faculty research:* Smoking cessation, adolescent sexuality, white collar crime, serial murder, human factors/human computer interaction.

University of Minnesota, Twin Cities Campus, Graduate School, College of Liberal Arts, Department of Cultural Studies and Comparative Literature, Program in Comparative Studies in Discourse and Society, Minneapolis, MN 55455-0213. Offers PhD. *Faculty:* 14 full-time (2 women), 9 part-time/adjunct (7 women). *Students:* 25 full-time (15 women); includes 1 Asian American or Pacific Islander, 1 Hispanic American, 1 international. Average age 26. 67 applicants, 10% accepted, 3 enrolled. In 2007, 1 doctorate awarded. *Degree requirements:* For doctorate, 2 foreign languages, thesis/dissertation. *Entrance requirements:* For doctorate, GRE General Test, sample of written work. Additional exam requirements/recommendations for international students: Required—TOEFL. *Application deadline:* For fall admission, 12/10 for domestic students. Application fee: $55 ($75 for international students). *Financial support:* In 2007–08, 30 students received support, including 1 fellowship with full tuition reimbursement available (averaging $16,000 per year), 1 research assistantship with full tuition reimbursement available (averaging $6,232 per year), 25 teaching assistantships with full tuition reimbursements available (averaging $12,465 per year); Federal Work-Study, institutionally sponsored loans, and tuition waivers (full and partial) also available. Financial award application deadline: 12/10. *Faculty research:* Cultural theory; music; architecture, space, and urbanism; body and gender; film and popular culture. *Unit head:* Liz Kotz, Director, 612-625-4571, Fax: 612-626-0228, E-mail: complit@tc.umn.edu. *Application contact:* Elizabeth Wilson, Executive Secretary, 612-624-7896, Fax: 312-626-0228, E-mail: ejwilson@umn.edu.

University of Pittsburgh, School of Arts and Sciences, Department of English, Pittsburgh, PA 15260. Offers cultural and critical studies (PhD); English (MA); writing (MFA). Part-time programs available. *Faculty:* 55 full-time (23 women). *Students:* 197 full-time (119 women), 37 part-time (34 women); includes 33 minority (11 African Americans, 6 Asian Americans or Pacific Islanders, 16 Hispanic Americans), 4 international. 363 applicants, 29% accepted, 35 enrolled. In 2007, 31 master's, 13 doctorates awarded. *Degree requirements:* For master's, one foreign language; for doctorate, 2 foreign languages, comprehensive exam, thesis/dissertation. *Entrance requirements:* For master's and doctorate, GRE General Test, writing sample. Additional exam requirements/recommendations for international students: Required—TOEFL. *Application deadline:* For fall admission, 12/12 for domestic and international students. Application fee: $50. *Financial support:* In 2007–08, 100 students received support, including 24 fellowships with full tuition reimbursements available (averaging $17,162 per year), 6 research assistantships with full and partial tuition reimbursements available (averaging $11,830 per year), 68 teaching assistantships with full tuition reimbursements available (averaging $14,485 per year); Federal Work-Study, tuition waivers (full and partial), and unspecified assistantships also available. Financial award application deadline: 12/12. *Faculty research:* Cultural studies, literary history and theory, film, composition. *Unit head:* Dr. David Bartholomae, Chairman, 412-624-6509, Fax: 412-624-6639, E-mail: barth@pitt.edu. *Application contact:* Connie Arelt, Graduate Administrator, 412-624-6549, Fax: 412-624-6639, E-mail: car100@pitt.edu.

The University of Texas at San Antonio, College of Education and Human Development, Division of Bicultural-Bilingual Studies, San Antonio, TX 78249-0617. Offers bicultural studies (MA); bicultural-bilingual studies (MA); culture, literacy, and language (PhD); teaching English as a second language (MA). Part-time and evening/weekend programs available. *Faculty:* 13 full-time (8 women), 1 part-time/adjunct (0 women). *Students:* 42 full-time (39 women), 105 part-time (85 women); includes 100 minority (2 African Americans, 3 Asian Americans or Pacific Islanders, 95 Hispanic Americans), 12 international. Average age 33. 63 applicants, 75% accepted, 44 enrolled. In 2007, 36 master's, 4 doctorates awarded. *Degree requirements:* For master's, one foreign language, comprehensive exam, thesis optional; for doctorate, one foreign language, comprehensive exam, thesis/dissertation. *Entrance requirements:* For master's and doctorate, GRE General Test. Additional exam requirements/recommendations for international students: Required—TOEFL (minimum score 500 paper-based; 173 computer-based). *Application deadline:* For fall admission, 7/1 for domestic students, 4/1 for international students; for spring admission, 11/1 for domestic students, 9/1 for international students. Applications are processed on a rolling basis. Application fee: $45 ($80 for international students). Electronic applications accepted. *Financial support:* In 2007–08, 1 fellowship (averaging $45,000 per year), 5 research assistantships (averaging $4,735 per year), 13 teaching assistantships (averaging $9,108 per year) were awarded; career-related internships or fieldwork and Federal Work-Study also available. Support available to part-time students. *Faculty research:* Spanish-English bilingualism, cultural transmission in bilingual communities, literacy in bilingual settings, content-based ESL, second language acquisition in classroom contexts. Total annual research expenditures: $566,708. *Unit head:* Dr. Robert D. Milk, Director, 210-458-4426, Fax: 210-458-5962, E-mail: rmilk@utsa.edu.

University of the Sacred Heart, Graduate Programs, Department of Communication, Program in Contemporary Culture and Means, San Juan, PR 00914-0383. Offers MA. *Degree requirements:* For master's, thesis.

Washington State University, Graduate School, College of Liberal Arts, Edward R. Murrow College of Communication, Pullman, WA 99164. Offers health communications (MA, PhD); intercultural and international communications (MA, PhD); media and society (MA, PhD); media process and effects (MA, PhD); organizational communications (MA, PhD). *Faculty:* 30. *Students:* 43 full-time (26 women), 6 part-time (4 women); includes 2 minority (1 Asian American or Pacific Islander, 1 Hispanic American), 19 international. Average age 30. 120 applicants, 22% accepted, 19 enrolled. In 2007, 22 master's, 1 doctorate awarded. *Degree requirements:* For master's, comprehensive exam (for some programs), thesis optional, oral exam; for doctorate, comprehensive exam, thesis/dissertation. *Entrance requirements:* For master's, GRE General Test, minimum GPA of 3.25, 3 letters of recommendation; for doctorate, GRE General Test, minimum undergraduate GPA of 3.25, graduate 3.5; MA in communication; 3 letters of recommendation. Additional exam requirements/recommendations for international students: Required—TOEFL (minimum score 580 paper-based; 237 computer-based). *Application deadline:* For fall admission, 1/15 priority date for domestic students, 3/1 for international students. Applications are processed on a rolling basis. Application fee: $50. Electronic applications accepted. *Financial support:* In 2007–08, 46 students received support, including 2 fellowships (averaging $4,477 per year), 7 research assistantships with full and partial tuition reimbursements available (averaging $13,917 per year), 34 teaching assistantships with full and partial tuition reimbursements available (averaging $13,056 per year); career-related internships or fieldwork, Federal Work-Study, institutionally sponsored loans, tuition waivers (partial), and teaching associateships also available. Financial award application deadline: 4/1; financial award applicants required to submit FAFSA. *Faculty research:* Advocacy communication, mediated communication in decision making, communication technology policy and effects, multicultural and international psychology and physiology of communication. Total annual research expenditures: $550,455. *Unit head:* Dr. Erica Austin, Interim Director, 509-335-1556, E-mail: eaustin@wsu.edu. *Application contact:* Graduate School Admissions, 800-GRADWSU, Fax: 509-335-1949, E-mail: gradsch@wsu.edu.

Wheaton College, Graduate School, Department of Intercultural Studies, Wheaton, IL 60187-5593. Offers evangelism (MA); intercultural studies (MA); intercultural studies/teaching English as a second language (MA); missions (MA); teaching English as a second language (Certificate). Part-time programs available. *Faculty:* 5 full-time (2 women), 4 part-time/adjunct (2 women). *Students:* 76. 69 applicants, 75% accepted, 33 enrolled. In 2007, 29 degrees awarded. *Degree requirements:* For master's, thesis or alternative. *Entrance requirements:* For master's, GRE General Test, MAT. *Application deadline:* For fall admission, 3/1 priority date for domestic students; for spring admission, 11/1 for domestic students. Applications are processed on a rolling basis. Application fee: $30. Electronic applications accepted. *Financial support:* Career-related internships or fieldwork, scholarships/grants, and unspecified assistantships available. Financial award application deadline: 3/1; financial award applicants required to submit FAFSA. *Unit head:* Dr. Evvy Campbell, Chair, 630-752-5258. *Application contact:* Julie A. Huebner,

Director of Graduate Admissions, 630-752-5195, Fax: 630-752-5935, E-mail: gradadm@wheaton.edu.

Wilfrid Laurier University, Faculty of Graduate Studies, Faculty of Arts, Cultural Analysis and Social Theory Program, Waterloo, ON N2L 3C5, Canada. Offers MA. *Faculty:* 13 full-time. *Students:* 8 full-time. 31 applicants, 42% accepted, 8 enrolled. *Entrance requirements:* For master's, honours BA in humanities, social science or interdisciplinary program with social theory, minimum B+ in final year of full-time study. Additional exam requirements/recommendations for international students: Required—TOEFL (minimum score 230 computer-based; 89 iBT). *Application deadline:* For fall admission, 2/1 priority date for domestic students. Application fee: $75. Electronic applications accepted. *Financial support:* Fellowships, research assistantships, teaching assistantships available. *Faculty research:* Globalization, identify and social movements, body politics: gender, sexuality and embodiment, cultural representation and social theory. *Unit head:* Dr. Herbert Pimlott, Head, 519-884-1970 Ext. 2522. *Application contact:* Jennifer Poppe, Student Contact, 519-884-0710 Ext. 3536, Fax: 519-884-1020, E-mail: gradstudies@wlu.ca.

East European and Russian Studies

Boston College, Graduate School of Arts and Sciences, Department of Slavic and Eastern Languages, Program in Slavic Studies, Chestnut Hill, MA 02467-3800. Offers MA, MA/JD, MBA/MA. Part-time programs available. *Degree requirements:* For master's, 3 foreign languages, comprehensive exam, thesis or alternative. *Entrance requirements:* Additional exam requirements/recommendations for international students: Required—TOEFL (minimum score 550 paper-based; 213 computer-based). *Application deadline:* For fall admission, 1/15 for domestic students. Application fee: $70. Electronic applications accepted. *Financial support:* Application deadline: 3/1.

Carleton University, Faculty of Graduate Studies, Faculty of Public Affairs and Management, Institute of European and Russian Studies, Ottawa, ON K1S 5B6, Canada. Offers European and European Union studies (MA); European integration studies (Diploma); Russian, Eurasian and transition studies (MA). *Degree requirements:* For master's, one foreign language, thesis optional. *Entrance requirements:* For master's, honors degree or equivalent; 2 years of Russian, German or other central east European language. Additional exam requirements/recommendations for international students: Required—TOEFL. *Application deadline:* Applications are processed on a rolling basis. Application fee: $77 Canadian dollars. *Financial support:* Fellowships, teaching assistantships, institutionally sponsored loans, scholarships/grants, and unspecified assistantships available. *Faculty research:* East-West relations, minority rights in Russia and Eastern Europe. *Unit head:* Andrea Chandler, Director, 613-520-2600 Ext. 2888, Fax: 613-520-2889, E-mail: eurus@carleton.ca. *Application contact:* Ginette Lafleur, Graduate Secretary, 613-520-2600 Ext. 2888, Fax: 613-520-2889, E-mail: eurus@carleton.ca.

Columbia University, Graduate School of Arts and Sciences, Program in Russian, Eurasian and East European Regional Studies, New York, NY 10027. Offers MA. Part-time programs available. Application fee: $90. *Expenses:* Tuition: Part-time $1,452 per credit. Required fees: $152 per term. One-time fee: $75 part-time. Full-time tuition and fees vary according to course level, course load, degree level and program. *Unit head:* Dr. Catherine Theimer Nepomnyashchy, Advisor, 212-854-6213, Fax: 212-666-3481, E-mail: cn29@columbia.edu.

Columbia University, School of International and Public Affairs, The East Central Europe Center, New York, NY 10027. Offers Certificate. Students must be enrolled in a separate graduate degree program at Columbia University. *Application deadline:* For fall admission, 1/4 for domestic students; for spring admission, 10/1 for domestic students. Application fee: $85. Electronic applications accepted. *Expenses:* Tuition: Part-time $1,452 per credit. Required fees: $152 per term. One-time fee: $75 part-time. Full-time tuition and fees vary according to course level, course load, degree level and program. *Financial support:* In 2007–08, 1 research assistantship was awarded; fellowships, career-related internships or fieldwork and Federal Work-Study also available. Financial award application deadline: 1/15. *Faculty research:* Ethnic politics, modern East Central European history, post-Communist economic and political transitions, East Central European language and literature. *Unit head:* Dr. John Micgiel, Director, 212-854-4008, Fax: 212-854-8577, E-mail: jsm6@columbia.edu. *Application contact:* Matt Clemons, Director of Admissions and Financial Aid, 212-854-6216, Fax: 212-854-3010, E-mail: mc2793@columbia.edu.

Columbia University, School of International and Public Affairs, The Harriman Institute, New York, NY 10027. Offers Certificate. Students must be enrolled in a separate graduate degree program at Columbia University. Part-time programs available. *Degree requirements:* For Certificate, one foreign language, thesis. *Entrance requirements:* For degree, minimum 2 years of Russian. *Application deadline:* For fall admission, 1/4 for domestic students; for spring admission, 10/1 for domestic students. Application fee: $85. Electronic applications accepted. *Expenses:* Tuition: Part-time $1,452 per credit. Required fees: $152 per term. One-time fee: $75 part-time. Full-time tuition and fees vary according to course level, course load, degree level and program. *Financial support:* Fellowships, career-related internships or fieldwork and Federal Work-Study available. Financial award application deadline: 1/15. *Unit head:* Dr. Catherine Theimer Nepomnyashchy, Director, 212-854-6213, Fax: 212-666-3481, E-mail: cn29@columbia.edu. *Application contact:* Matt Clemons, Director of Admissions and Financial Aid, 212-854-6216, Fax: 212-854-3010, E-mail: mc2793@columbia.edu.

Cornell University, Graduate School, Graduate Fields of Arts and Sciences, Field of History, Ithaca, NY 14853-0001. Offers African history (MA, PhD); American history (MA, PhD); ancient history (MA, PhD); early modern European history (MA, PhD); English history (MA, PhD); French history (MA, PhD); German history (MA, PhD); history of science (MA, PhD); Latin American history (MA, PhD); medieval Chinese history (MA, PhD); medieval history (MA, PhD); modern Chinese history (MA, PhD); modern European history (MA, PhD); modern Japanese history (MA, PhD); premodern Islamic history (MA, PhD); premodern Japanese history (MA, PhD); Renaissance history (MA, PhD); Russian history (MA, PhD); Southeast Asian history (MA, PhD). *Faculty:* 56 full-time (14 women). *Students:* 63 full-time (29 women); includes 11 minority (6 African Americans, 2 Asian Americans or Pacific Islanders, 3 Hispanic Americans), 20 international. Average age 31. 201 applicants, 6% accepted, 10 enrolled. In 2007, 11 master's, 11 doctorates awarded. Terminal master's awarded for partial completion of doctoral program. *Degree requirements:* For master's, thesis; for doctorate, 2 foreign languages, comprehensive exam, thesis/dissertation, 1 year of teaching experience. *Entrance requirements:* For master's and doctorate, GRE General Test, writing sample, 3 letters of recommendation. Additional exam requirements/recommendations for international students: Required—TOEFL (minimum score 550 paper-based; 213 computer-based; 77 iBT). *Application deadline:* For fall admission, 1/15 for domestic students. Application fee: $70. Electronic applications accepted. *Financial support:* In 2007–08, 54 students received support, including 26 fellowships with full tuition reimbursements available, 28 teaching assistantships with full tuition reimbursements available; research assistantships with full tuition reimbursements available, institutionally sponsored loans, scholarships/grants, health care benefits, tuition waivers (full and partial), and unspecified assistantships also available. Financial award applicants required to submit FAFSA. *Unit head:* Director of Graduate Studies, 607-255-6738, Fax: 607-255-0469. *Application contact:* Graduate Field Assistant, 607-255-6738, Fax: 607-255-0469, E-mail: history_grad_info@cornell.edu.

Florida State University, Graduate Studies, College of Social Sciences, Program in Russian and East European Studies, Tallahassee, FL 32306. Offers MA. Part-time programs available. *Students:* 2 full-time (both women), 2 part-time. Average age 28. 5 applicants, 100% accepted, 2 enrolled. In 2007, 1 degree awarded. *Degree requirements:* For master's, one foreign language, comprehensive exam, thesis optional. *Entrance requirements:* For master's, GRE General Test, minimum GPA of 3.0. Additional exam requirements/recommendations for international students: Required—TOEFL (minimum score 550 paper-based; 213 computer-based; 80 iBT). *Application deadline:* For fall admission, 7/1 for domestic and international students; for spring admission, 11/1 for domestic and international students. Applications are processed on a rolling basis. Application fee: $30. Electronic applications accepted. *Expenses:* Tuition, state resident: part-time $248 per credit hour. Tuition, nonresident: part-time $880 per credit hour. Tuition and fees vary according to program. *Financial support:* In 2007–08, research assistantships with full tuition reimbursements (averaging $5,000 per year); fellowships, career-related internships or fieldwork, Federal Work-Study, and institutionally sponsored loans also available. Financial award application deadline: 2/15; financial award applicants required to submit FAFSA. *Unit head:* Dr. Lee K. Metcalf, Director, 850-644-7327, Fax: 850-645-4981, E-mail: lmetcalf@fsu.edu. *Application contact:* Patty Lollis, Program Assistant, 850-644-4418, Fax: 850-645-4981, E-mail: plollis@mailer.fsu.edu.

Georgetown University, Graduate School of Arts and Sciences, Program in Russian and East European Studies, Washington, DC 20057. Offers MA, MA/PhD. *Degree requirements:* For master's, one foreign language, comprehensive exam, thesis optional. *Entrance requirements:* For master's, GRE General Test. Additional exam requirements/recommendations for international students: Required—TOEFL. *Faculty research:* East-West trade.

The George Washington University, Elliott School of International Affairs, Program in European and Eurasian Studies, Washington, DC 20052. Offers MA, JD/MA, MBA/MA. Part-time and evening/weekend programs available. *Degree requirements:* For master's, one foreign language, capstone project. *Entrance requirements:* For master's, GRE General Test, 2 years (or the equivalent) of a modern European language (or Russian), 2 semesters of introductory economics (macro or micro economics). Additional exam requirements/recommendations for international students: Required—TOEFL. Electronic applications accepted. *Faculty research:* NATO, European economics, European history, European Union.

Harvard University, Graduate School of Arts and Sciences, Committee on Regional Studies-Russia, Eastern Europe, and Central Asia, Cambridge, MA 02138. Offers AM. *Degree requirements:* For master's, one foreign language. *Entrance requirements:* For master's, GRE General Test. Additional exam requirements/recommendations for international students: Required—TOEFL. *Expenses:* Tuition: Full-time $31,456. Full-time tuition and fees vary according to program and student level. *Faculty research:* Strategic policy, ethnography and demography of U.S.S.R., non-Russian nationality language training.

Indiana University Bloomington, University Graduate School, College of Arts and Sciences, Russian and East European Institute, Bloomington, IN 47405-7000. Offers MA, Certificate, MBA/MA, MIS/MA, MLS/MA, MPA/MA. Part-time programs available. *Students:* 28 full-time (13 women), 3 part-time; includes 4 minority (1 Asian American or Pacific Islander, 3 Hispanic Americans). Average age 27. 30 applicants, 80% accepted, 10 enrolled. In 2007, 7 degrees awarded. *Degree requirements:* For master's, one foreign language, essay, proficiency and written exams; for Certificate, one foreign language, oral and proficiency exams. *Entrance requirements:* For master's, GRE General Test, minimum 2 years of college Russian (Russian area studies); for Certificate, GRE General Test. Additional exam requirements/recommendations for international students: Required—TOEFL. *Application deadline:* For fall admission, 1/15 priority date for domestic students, 12/15 for international students; for spring admission, 9/1 priority date for domestic students, 9/1 for international students. Applications are processed on a rolling basis. Application fee: $50 ($60 for international students). *Financial support:* Fellowships, research assistantships with full tuition reimbursements, teaching assistantships, career-related internships or fieldwork, Federal Work-Study, and institutionally sponsored loans available. Financial award application deadline: 2/15; financial award applicants required to submit FAFSA. *Faculty research:* Political and economic transition of former Soviet Union and Eastern Europe, Russian and Soviet history, Slavic literature and linguistics, education and mass media of former Soviet Union and Eastern Europe. *Unit head:* David Ransel, Director, 812-855-7309, Fax: 812-855-6411, E-mail: ransel@indiana.edu. *Application contact:* Marianne Davis, Administrative Secretary, 812-855-3869, Fax: 812-855-6411, E-mail: marwdavi@indiana.edu.

The Johns Hopkins University, Paul H. Nitze School of Advanced International Studies, Washington, DC 20036. Offers international development (Certificate); international public policy (MIPP); international relations (MA, PhD), including African studies (MA), American foreign policy (MA), Asian studies (MA), Canadian studies (MA), conflict management (MA), European studies (MA), global theory and history (MA), international development (MA), international law, and organizations (MA), international policy (MA), international relations (general) (MA), Latin American studies (MA), Middle East studies (MA), Russian and Eurasian studies (MA), strategic studies (MA); international studies (Certificate); JD/MA; MBA/MA; MHS/MA. *Faculty:* 66 full-time (22 women), 158 part-time/adjunct (54 women). *Students:* 578 full-time (256 women), 46 part-time (16 women); includes 85 minority (18 African Americans, 1 American Indian/Alaska Native, 51 Asian Americans or Pacific Islanders, 15 Hispanic Americans), 193 international. Average age 27. In 2007, 359 master's, 13 doctorates awarded. Terminal master's awarded for partial completion of doctoral program. *Degree requirements:* For master's, one foreign language, 16 non-language courses (8 for MIPP), 2 core examinations, comprehensive oral exam, paper (for some programs); for doctorate, 2 foreign languages, thesis/dissertation, 3 comprehensive exams, defense. *Entrance requirements:* For master's, GMAT or GRE General Test, previous course work in economics, foreign language, undergraduate degree; for doctorate, GRE General Test, master's degree. Additional exam requirements/recommendations for international students: Required—TOEFL (minimum paper-based score of 600, computer-based 250, iBT 100) or IELTS (minimum 7.0). *Application deadline:* For fall admission, 1/7 for domestic students. Application fee: $80. Electronic applications accepted. *Expenses: Contact institution. Financial support:* In 2007–08, 350 students received support, including fellowships (averaging $7,500 per year); career-related internships or fieldwork, Federal Work-Study, and scholarships/grants also available. Financial award application deadline: 2/15; financial award applicants required to submit FAFSA. *Faculty research:* Regional studies and functional fields of international relations, international economics, conflict management, global theory and history, international law and organizations, international policy, strategic studies. *Unit head:* Tara Campbell, Associate Director of Admissions, 202-663-5700, Fax: 202-663-7788. *Application contact:* Dr. Belinda A. Yeomans, Director of Admissions, 202-663-5700, Fax: 202-663-7788, E-mail: admissions.sais@jhu.edu.

La Salle University, School of Arts and Sciences, Central and Eastern European Studies Program, Philadelphia, PA 19141-1199. Offers MA. Part-time and evening/weekend programs available. *Faculty:* 5 part-time/adjunct (1 woman). *Students:* 11 full-time (6 women), 29 part-time (17 women); includes 5 minority (3 African Americans, 1 American Indian/Alaska Native, 1 Asian American or Pacific Islander), 9 international. Average age 31. 15 applicants,

East European and Russian Studies

La Salle University (continued)
93% accepted, 9 enrolled. In 2007, 6 degrees awarded. *Degree requirements:* For master's, one foreign language, thesis or alternative. *Entrance requirements:* For master's, MAT. Additional exam requirements/recommendations for international students: Required—TOEFL. *Application deadline:* Applications are processed on a rolling basis. Application fee: $35. *Expenses: Contact institution.* Tuition and fees vary according to program. *Financial support:* In 2007–08, 19 students received support. Career-related internships or fieldwork, Federal Work-Study, and scholarships/grants available. Financial award applicants required to submit FAFSA. *Faculty research:* Ukrainian culture, Russian studies, business in Central and Eastern European countries. *Unit head:* Dr. Berhhardt G. Blumenthal, Director, 215-951-7201, E-mail: blumenth@lasalle.edu.

The Ohio State University, Graduate School, College of Humanities, Department of Slavic and East European Languages and Literatures, Program in Slavic and East European Studies, Columbus, OH 43210. Offers MA. *Faculty:* 39. *Students:* 13 full-time (4 women), 2 part-time (both women); includes 1 minority (Asian American or Pacific Islander) Average age 25. In 2007, 9 degrees awarded. *Degree requirements:* For master's, thesis optional. *Entrance requirements:* For master's, GRE General Test. Additional exam requirements/recommendations for international students: Required—TOEFL (paper-based 550; computer-based 213) or IELTS (7) or Michigan English Language Assessment Battery (82). *Application deadline:* For fall admission, 8/15 priority date for domestic students, 7/1 priority date for international students; for winter admission, 12/1 priority date for domestic students, 11/1 priority date for international students; for spring admission, 3/1 priority date for domestic students, 2/1 priority date for international students. Applications are processed on a rolling basis. Application fee: $40 ($50 for international students). Electronic applications accepted. *Financial support:* Fellowships, Federal Work-Study and institutionally sponsored loans available. Support available to part-time students. *Unit head:* Halina Stephan, Graduate Studies Committee Chair, 614-292-8770, Fax: 614-292-4273, E-mail: stephan.31@osu.edu. *Application contact:* 614-292-9444, Fax: 614-292-3895, E-mail: domestic.grad@osu.edu.

Stanford University, School of Humanities and Sciences, Center for Russian and East European Studies, Stanford, CA 94305-9991. Offers MA. *Degree requirements:* For master's, one foreign language. *Entrance requirements:* For master's, GRE General Test. Additional exam requirements/recommendations for international students: Required—TOEFL. Electronic applications accepted.

University of Alberta, Faculty of Graduate Studies and Research, Department of Modern Languages and Cultural Studies, Edmonton, AB T6G 2E1, Canada. Offers applied linguistics (Germanic, Romance, Slavic) (MA); French language, literatures and linguistics (PhD); French language, literatures, and linguistics (MA); Germanic languages, literatures and linguistics (PhD); Germanic languages, literatures, and linguistics (MA); Italian studies (MA); Slavic languages and literatures (Russian, Ukrainian) (MA, PhD); Slavic linguistics (Russian, Ukrainian) (MA, PhD); Spanish and Latin American studies (MA, PhD); Ukrainian folklore (MA, PhD). Part-time programs available. *Degree requirements:* For master's, one foreign language, thesis; for doctorate, 2 foreign languages, comprehensive exam, thesis/dissertation. *Entrance requirements:* For master's and doctorate, 1 language other than English. Additional exam requirements/recommendations for international students: Required—Michigan English Language Assessment Battery or TOEFL (paper score 550; computer score 213). Electronic applications accepted. *Faculty research:* Russian/Ukrainian studies; German studies; contemporary Latin American, French and Francophone studies; Italian studies.

The University of British Columbia, Faculty of Arts and Faculty of Graduate Studies, Department of Central, Eastern and Northern European Studies, Vancouver, BC V6T 1Z1, Canada. Offers Germanic studies (MA, PhD). Part-time programs available. *Faculty:* 8 full-time (2 women). *Students:* 15 full-time (10 women). 6 applicants, 50% accepted. In 2007, 2 master's, 2 doctorates awarded. *Median time to degree:* Of those who began their doctoral program in fall 1999, 100% received their degree in 8 years or less. *Degree requirements:* For master's, one foreign language, thesis optional, exam; for doctorate, comprehensive exam, thesis/dissertation. *Entrance requirements:* For master's, BA in German; for doctorate, MA in German. Additional exam requirements/recommendations for international students: Required—TOEFL (minimum score 550 paper-based; 213 computer-based). *Application deadline:* For fall admission, 1/15 for domestic students, 2/15 for international students. Applications are processed on a rolling basis. Application fee: $90 Canadian dollars ($150 Canadian dollars for international students). Electronic applications accepted. *Financial support:* In 2007–08, 10 students received support, including 5 fellowships with partial tuition reimbursements available (averaging $3,300 per year), 4 research assistantships with partial tuition reimbursements available (averaging $5,000 per year), 10 teaching assistantships with full tuition reimbursements available (averaging $10,000 per year); career-related internships or fieldwork, Federal Work-Study, scholarships/grants, and tuition waivers (full and partial) also available. Support available to part-time students. Financial award application deadline: 1/15. *Faculty research:* Second language acquisition, media theory, performance theory, gender studies, cultural studies. *Unit head:* Dr. Thomas Salumets, Head, 604-822-6403, Fax: 604-822-9344, E-mail: german@interchange.ubc.ca. *Application contact:* Dr. Gaby Pailer, Graduate Admissions, 604-822-4042, Fax: 604-822-9344, E-mail: german@interchange.ubc.ca.

University of Illinois at Chicago, Graduate College, College of Liberal Arts and Sciences, Department of Slavic and Baltic Languages and Literatures, Chicago, IL 60607-7128. Offers Slavic languages and literatures (PhD); Slavic studies (MA). Evening/weekend programs available. Terminal master's awarded for partial completion of doctoral program. *Degree requirements:* For doctorate, one foreign language, thesis/dissertation. *Entrance requirements:* For master's and doctorate, GRE General Test, minimum GPA of 3.0. Additional exam requirements/recommendations for international students: Required—TOEFL. Electronic applications accepted.

University of Illinois at Urbana–Champaign, Graduate College, College of Liberal Arts and Sciences, Russian, East European and Eurasian Center, Champaign, IL 61820. Offers MA. *Students:* 8 full-time (1 woman); includes 1 minority (African American) 16 applicants, 44% accepted, 5 enrolled. In 2007, 6 degrees awarded. *Application deadline:* Applications are processed on a rolling basis. Application fee: $60 ($75 for international students). Electronic applications accepted. *Financial support:* In 2007–08, 8 fellowships were awarded; research assistantships, teaching assistantships. Financial award application deadline: 2/15. *Unit head:* Richard Tempest, Head, 217-344-3066, Fax: 217-333-7310, E-mail: rtempest@uiuc.edu. *Application contact:* Merrily Shaw, Assistant to the Director, 217-244-4721, Fax: 217-333-1582, E-mail: mshaw2@uiuc.edu.

University of Kansas, Research and Graduate Studies, College of Liberal Arts and Sciences, Center for Russian, East European and Eurasian Studies, Lawrence, KS 66045. Offers MA. Part-time programs available. *Faculty:* 45 full-time (11 women). *Students:* 10 full-time (2 women), 1 part-time. Average age 28. 13 applicants, 100% accepted, 3 enrolled. In 2007, 8 master's awarded. *Degree requirements:* For master's, one foreign language, comprehensive exam, interdisciplinary capstone seminar. *Entrance requirements:* For master's, GRE General Test, 3 letters of recommendation. Additional exam requirements/recommendations for international students: Required—TOEFL. *Application deadline:* For fall admission, 5/1 priority date for domestic students, 2/14 priority date for international students; for spring admission, 10/1 priority date for domestic students, 9/1 priority date for international students. Applications are processed on a rolling basis. Application fee: $55 ($60 for international students). Electronic applications accepted. *Expenses:* Tuition, state resident: full-time $5,838. Tuition, nonresident: full-time $13,409. Tuition and fees vary according to program. *Financial support:* In 2007–08, 8 fellowships with full tuition reimbursements, 2 research assistantships with full and partial tuition reimbursements were awarded; scholarships/grants and tuition waivers (partial) also available. Financial award application deadline: 1/31; financial award applicants required to submit FAFSA. *Faculty research:* Transition studies, Russian history and philosophy, Ukrainian and Russian domestic and foreign policies, Slavic languages and literatures, security policies in Central Asia and the Caucasus. *Unit head:* Dr. William Comer, Director, 785-864-4236, Fax: 785-864-3800, E-mail: crees@ku.edu. *Application contact:* Ray C. Finch, Graduate Advisor, Assistant Director, 785-864-4248, Fax: 785-864-3800, E-mail: rayfin3@ku.edu.

University of Michigan, Horace H. Rackham School of Graduate Studies, College of Literature, Science, and the Arts, Interdepartmental Program in Russian and East European Studies, Ann Arbor, MI 48109. Offers AM, Certificate, JD/AM, MBA/AM, MPP/AM. Part-time programs available. *Faculty:* 76. *Students:* 18 full-time (13 women), 1 part-time. Average age 26. 38 applicants, 66% accepted, 7 enrolled. In 2007, 4 degrees awarded. *Degree requirements:* For master's, one foreign language, thesis. *Entrance requirements:* For master's, GRE General Test. Additional exam requirements/recommendations for international students: Required—TOEFL. *Application deadline:* For fall admission, 2/1 for domestic and international students. Application fee: $60 ($75 for international students). Electronic applications accepted. *Financial support:* In 2007–08, 11 students received support, including 8 fellowships with tuition reimbursements available (averaging $15,000 per year), 3 teaching assistantships with tuition reimbursements available (averaging $8,000 per year); career-related internships or fieldwork, Federal Work-Study, scholarships/grants, health care benefits, and unspecified assistantships also available. Financial award application deadline: 2/1. *Unit head:* Dr. Michael D Kennedy, Director, 734-764-0351, Fax: 734-763-4765, E-mail: crees@umich.edu. *Application contact:* Rachel Facey, Student Services Associate, 734-764-0351, Fax: 734-763-4765, E-mail: crees.admissions@umich.edu.

The University of North Carolina at Chapel Hill, Graduate School, Curriculum in Russian and East European Studies, Chapel Hill, NC 27599. Offers MA. Part-time programs available. *Degree requirements:* For master's, one foreign language, thesis. *Entrance requirements:* For master's, GRE General Test. Additional exam requirements/recommendations for international students: Required—TOEFL. Electronic applications accepted. *Faculty research:* Language, area studies, social sciences, sciences, professional schools.

University of Pittsburgh, University Center for International Studies, Pittsburgh, PA 15260. Offers African studies (Certificate); Asian studies (Certificate); European Union studies (Certificate); global studies (Certificate); Latin American studies (Certificate); Russian and East European studies (Certificate); West European studies (Certificate). *Unit head:* Lawrence F. Feick, Director, University Center for International Studies, 412-648-7374, Fax: 412-624-4672, E-mail: feick@pitt.edu.

University of Saskatchewan, College of Graduate Studies and Research, College of Arts and Sciences, Department of Languages and Linguistics, Saskatoon, SK S7N 5A2, Canada. Offers MA. *Degree requirements:* For master's, 2 foreign languages, thesis. *Entrance requirements:* Additional exam requirements/recommendations for international students: Required—TOEFL.

The University of Texas at Austin, Graduate School, Program in Russian, East European and Eurasian Studies, Austin, TX 78712-1111. Offers MA, JD/MA, MBA/MA, MP Aff/MA. Part-time programs available. *Degree requirements:* For master's, one foreign language, report or thesis. *Entrance requirements:* For master's, GRE General Test, 3 years of formal language training or equivalent, minimum GPA of 3.0. Electronic applications accepted. *Faculty research:* East European gypsies, elite transformation and democracy in Eastern Europe, elite partisanship as an intervening variable in Russian politics, post-Soviet youth in Russia.

University of Toronto, School of Graduate Studies, Social Sciences Division, Centre for European, Russian and Eurasian Studies, Toronto, ON M5S 1A1, Canada. Offers MA. *Faculty:* 35 full-time, 13 part-time/adjunct. *Students:* 29 full-time (22 women), 9 international. 41 applicants, 73% accepted. *Degree requirements:* For master's, one foreign language, language proficiency test. *Entrance requirements:* For master's, minimum B+ average in final year, coursework in Russian/East European subjects, 2 years of study in a relevant language. *Application deadline:* For fall admission, 2/1 priority date for domestic students. Application fee: $100 Canadian dollars. *Financial support:* Fellowships available. *Unit head:* Prof. Peter Solomon, Director, 416-946-8938, Fax: 416-978-8939, E-mail: peter.solomon@utoronto.ca. *Application contact:* Jana Oldfield, Business Officer, 416-946-8938, Fax: 416-978-8939, E-mail: jana.oldfield@utoronto.ca.

University of Washington, Graduate School, College of Arts and Sciences, Henry M. Jackson School of International Studies, Russian, East European and Central Asian Studies Program, Seattle, WA 98195. Offers Central Asian studies (MAIS); East European studies (MAIS); Russian studies (MAIS). *Faculty:* 56 full-time (25 women). *Students:* 23 full-time (13 women); includes 3 minority (1 Asian American or Pacific Islander, 2 Hispanic Americans), 3 international. 29 applicants, 66% accepted, 9 enrolled. In 2007, 13 degrees awarded. *Degree requirements:* For master's, one foreign language, thesis. *Entrance requirements:* For master's, GRE General Test, 2 years of relevant language, minimum GPA of 3.0. Additional exam requirements/recommendations for international students: Required—TOEFL (minimum score 500 paper-based; 213 computer-based). Application fee: $50. Electronic applications accepted. *Financial support:* In 2007–08, 5 fellowships with full tuition reimbursements were awarded; research assistantships, teaching assistantships, career-related internships or fieldwork, Federal Work-Study, institutionally sponsored loans, and summer language study awards also available. Financial award application deadline: 1/15. *Unit head:* Prof. Stephen E. Hanson, Chair, 206-543-9460, Fax: 206-685-0668, E-mail: shanson@u.washington.edu. *Application contact:* 206-543-6001, Fax: 206-616-3170, E-mail: jsisinfo@u.washington.edu.

Yale University, Graduate School of Arts and Sciences, Program in Russian and East European Studies, New Haven, CT 06520. Offers MA. *Degree requirements:* For master's, 2 foreign languages. *Entrance requirements:* For master's, GRE General Test.

Ethnic Studies

Cornell University, Graduate School, Graduate Fields of Arts and Sciences, Field of Sociology, Ithaca, NY 14853-0001. Offers economy and society (MA, PhD); gender and life course (MA, PhD); methodology (MA, PhD); organizations (MA, PhD); policy analysis (MA, PhD); political sociology/social movements (MA, PhD); racial and ethnic relations (MA, PhD); social networks (MA, PhD); social psychology (MA, PhD); social stratification (MA, PhD). *Faculty:* 37 full-time (12 women). *Students:* 46 full-time (20 women); includes 10 minority (2 African Americans, 6 Asian Americans or Pacific Islanders, 2 Hispanic Americans), 10 international. Average age 30. 149 applicants, 7% accepted, 5 enrolled. In 2007, 4 master's, 6 doctorates awarded. Terminal master's awarded for partial completion of doctoral program. *Degree requirements:* For master's, thesis; for doctorate, thesis/dissertation, 1 year of teaching experience. *Entrance requirements:* For master's and doctorate, GRE General Test, 2 letters of recommendation, writing sample. Additional exam requirements/recommendations for international students: Required—TOEFL (minimum score 550 paper-based; 213 computer-based; 77 iBT). *Application deadline:* For fall admission, 1/15 for domestic students. Application fee: $70. Electronic applications accepted. *Financial support:* In 2007–08, 40 students received support, including 16 fellowships with full tuition reimbursements available, 8 research assistantships with full tuition reimbursements available, 16 teaching assistantships with full tuition reimbursements available; institutionally sponsored loans, scholarships/grants, health care benefits, tuition waivers (full and partial), and unspecified assistantships also available. Financial award applicants required to submit FAFSA. *Faculty research:* Comparative societal analysis, work and family, simulations, social class and mobility, racial segregation and inequality. *Unit head:* Director of Graduate Studies, 607-255-4266. *Application contact:* Graduate Field Assistant, 607-255-4266, E-mail: sociology@cornell.edu.

Minnesota State University Mankato, College of Graduate Studies, College of Social and Behavioral Sciences, Department of Ethnic Studies, Mankato, MN 56001. Offers MS. *Students:* 10 full-time (7 women), 11 part-time (4 women). *Unit head:* Dr. Maricela DeMirjyn, Graduate Coordinator, 507-389-2798.

San Francisco State University, Division of Graduate Studies, College of Ethnic Studies, Program in Ethnic Studies, San Francisco, CA 94132-1722. Offers MA. *Unit head:* Dr. Laureen Chew, Associate Dean, 415-338-1693, E-mail: ethnicst@sfsu.edu. *Application contact:* Dr. Nancy Mirabel, Graduate Coordinator, 415-338-1693, E-mail: ethnicst@sfsu.edu.

Université Laval, Faculty of Letters, Department of History, Programs in Ethnology of French-Speaking People in North America, Québec, QC G1K 7P4, Canada. Offers MA, PhD. Terminal master's awarded for partial completion of doctoral program. *Degree requirements:* For master's, thesis; for doctorate, comprehensive exam, thesis/dissertation. *Entrance requirements:* For master's and doctorate, English exam (comprehension of written English), knowledge of French. Electronic applications accepted.

University of California, Berkeley, Graduate Division, Group in Ethnic Studies, Berkeley, CA 94720-1500. Offers PhD. *Faculty:* 17 full-time. *Degree requirements:* For doctorate, one foreign language, thesis/dissertation, qualifying exam. *Entrance requirements:* For doctorate, minimum GPA of 3.0, 3 letters of recommendation. *Application deadline:* For fall admission, 12/15 for domestic students. Application fee: $70 ($90 for international students). *Financial support:* Fellowships with full tuition reimbursements, research assistantships with partial tuition reimbursements, teaching assistantships with partial tuition reimbursements, unspecified assistantships available. *Faculty research:* Gender and race, Asian American visual art, racial theory and politics, Chicana/o literature and visual arts, history of Native North Americans. *Unit head:* Beatriz Manz, Chair, 510-642-2088, E-mail: bmanz@berkeley.edu. *Application contact:* Information Contact, 510-642-6643, Fax: 510-642-6456, E-mail: ethnicst@berkeley.edu.

University of California, Riverside, Graduate Division, Department of Ethnic Studies, Riverside, CA 92521-0102. Offers PhD. *Faculty:* 11 full-time (4 women). *Degree requirements:* For doctorate, comprehensive exam, thesis/dissertation. *Entrance requirements:* Additional exam requirements/recommendations for international students: Required—TOEFL (minimum score 550 paper-based; 213 computer-based; 80 iBT). *Application deadline:* For fall admission, 5/1 for domestic students, 2/1 for international students; for winter admission, 9/1 for domestic students, 7/1 for international students; for spring admission, 12/1 for domestic students, 10/1 for international students. Application fee: $60 ($75 for international students). *Faculty research:* The political economy of race, class, gender, sexuality, cultural production, the state, law, criminal justice and grass roots responses. *Unit head:* Dr. Alfredo Mirande, Chair, 951-827-1012. *Application contact:* Dr. Edward Chang, Information Contact, 951-827-1825, E-mail: edward.chang@ucr.edu.

University of California, San Diego, Office of Graduate Studies, Department of Ethnic Studies, La Jolla, CA 92093. Offers MA, PhD. Electronic applications accepted.

Washington State University, Graduate School, College of Liberal Arts, Program in American Studies, Pullman, WA 99164. Offers ethnic studies (MA, PhD); feminist studies (MA, PhD); history (MA, PhD); literature (MA, PhD). *Faculty:* 39. *Students:* 27 full-time (19 women), 4 part-time (2 women); includes 17 minority (6 African Americans, 4 American Indian/Alaska Native, 2 Asian Americans or Pacific Islanders, 5 Hispanic Americans), 3 international. Average age 35. 78 applicants, 15% accepted, 12 enrolled. In 2007, 5 master's, 1 doctorate awarded. *Degree requirements:* For master's, one foreign language, comprehensive exam (for some programs), thesis optional, oral exam; for doctorate, one foreign language, comprehensive exam (for some programs), thesis/dissertation, oral exam. *Entrance requirements:* For master's and doctorate, GRE General Test, minimum GPA of 3.0, writing sample, 3 letters of recommendation. Additional exam requirements/recommendations for international students: Required—TOEFL. *Application deadline:* For fall admission, 2/1 priority date for domestic students, 3/1 for international students; for spring admission, 7/1 for international students. Applications are processed on a rolling basis. Application fee: $50. *Financial support:* In 2007–08, 24 students received support, including 1 fellowship (averaging $6,950 per year), 3 research assistantships with full and partial tuition reimbursements available (averaging $13,917 per year), 17 teaching assistantships with full and partial tuition reimbursements available (averaging $13,056 per year); career-related internships or fieldwork, Federal Work-Study, institutionally sponsored loans, tuition waivers (partial), and teaching associateships also available. Financial award application deadline: 3/1; financial award applicants required to submit FAFSA. *Faculty research:* The American West in multicultural perspective; nineteenth century historical, literary, and cultural studies; comparative American ethnic literatures and cultures; American cultures and the environment; American rhetoric. *Unit head:* Dr. Noel Sturgeon, Director, 509-335-1560, E-mail: reedtv@wsu.edu. *Application contact:* Graduate School Admissions, 800-GRADWSU, Fax: 509-335-1949, E-mail: gradsch@wsu.edu.

Folklore

George Mason University, College of Humanities and Social Sciences, Interdisciplinary Studies Program, Fairfax, VA 22030. Offers anthropology (MAIS); community college teaching (MAIS); folklore (MAIS); higher education (MAIS); individualized studies (MAIS); religion, cultures, and values (MAIS); video-based production (MAIS); women's studies (MAIS); zoo and aquarium leadership (MAIS). Part-time and evening/weekend programs available. *Faculty:* 6 full-time (4 women), 6 part-time/adjunct (5 women). *Students:* 25 full-time (17 women), 90 part-time (76 women); includes 24 minority (5 African Americans, 1 American Indian/Alaska Native, 7 Asian Americans or Pacific Islanders, 11 Hispanic Americans), 3 international. Average age 33. 68 applicants, 72% accepted, 35 enrolled. In 2007, 19 degrees awarded. *Degree requirements:* For master's, thesis optional. *Entrance requirements:* For master's, GRE, GMAT, or MAT, interview, minimum GPA of 3.0 in last 60 hours of course work. *Application deadline:* For fall admission, 5/1 priority date for domestic students; for spring admission, 11/1 for domestic students. Applications are processed on a rolling basis. Application fee: $60 ($75 for international students). Electronic applications accepted. *Financial support:* Fellowships, teaching assistantships, career-related internships or fieldwork, Federal Work-Study, and institutionally sponsored loans available. Support available to part-time students. Financial award application deadline: 3/1; financial award applicants required to submit FAFSA. *Unit head:* John Burns, Chair, 703-993-1291, Fax: 703-993-1297, E-mail: mais@gmu.edu. *Application contact:* Dr. Johannes D. Bergmann, Information Contact, 703-993-8762, E-mail: mais@gmu.edu.

The George Washington University, Columbian College of Arts and Sciences, Department of Anthropology, Concentration in Folklife, Washington, DC 20052. Offers MA. *Degree requirements:* For master's, comprehensive exam, thesis or alternative. *Entrance requirements:* For master's, GRE General Test, minimum GPA of 3.0.

Indiana University Bloomington, University Graduate School, College of Arts and Sciences, Department of Folklore and Ethnomusicology, Bloomington, IN 47408-3890. Offers folklore (MA, PhD), including ethnomusicology. Part-time programs available. *Faculty:* 12 full-time (5 women), 11 part-time/adjunct (6 women). *Students:* 97 full-time (67 women), 21 part-time (12 women); includes 25 minority (11 African Americans, 1 American Indian/Alaska Native, 6 Asian Americans or Pacific Islanders, 7 Hispanic Americans), 23 international. Average age 34. 81 applicants, 53% accepted, 18 enrolled. In 2007, 11 master's, 7 doctorates awarded. *Median time to degree:* Of those who began their doctoral program in fall 1999, 33% received their degree in 8 years or less. *Degree requirements:* For master's, one foreign language, comprehensive exam, thesis or alternative, project or thesis; for doctorate, 2 foreign languages, comprehensive exam, thesis/dissertation, registration is required for candidacy. *Entrance requirements:* For master's and doctorate, GRE General Test, minimum GPA of 3.0. Additional exam requirements/recommendations for international students: Required—TOEFL (minimum score 550 paper-based; 213 computer-based; 79 iBT). *Application deadline:* For fall admission, 1/15 for domestic students, 12/1 for international students. Application fee: $50 ($60 for international students). Electronic applications accepted. *Financial support:* In 2007–08, 27 students received support; fellowships with full tuition reimbursements available, research assistantships with full tuition reimbursements available, teaching assistantships with full tuition reimbursements available, Federal Work-Study and unspecified assistantships available. Financial award application deadline: 3/1; financial award applicants required to submit FAFSA. *Faculty research:* Narrative, performance studies, material culture, popular culture, music. *Unit head:* Dr. Portia Maultsby, Chair, 812-855-0395, Fax: 812-855-4008, E-mail: maultsby@indiana.edu. *Application contact:* Christopher Roush, Graduate Secretary, 812-855-0389, Fax: 812-855-4008, E-mail: croush@indiana.edu.

Memorial University of Newfoundland, School of Graduate Studies, Department of Folklore, St. John's, NL A1C 5S7, Canada. Offers MA, PhD. Part-time programs available. *Degree requirements:* For master's, thesis optional; for doctorate, one foreign language, comprehensive exam, thesis/dissertation, oral thesis defense. *Entrance requirements:* For master's, 36 credit hours of course work in folklore, humanities, or social studies; honors degree; for doctorate, MA in folklore or related field. Electronic applications accepted. *Faculty research:* Narrative, folklife, belief theory, methodology, popular culture.

University of Alberta, Faculty of Graduate Studies and Research, Department of Modern Languages and Cultural Studies, Edmonton, AB T6G 2E1, Canada. Offers applied linguistics (Germanic, Romance, Slavic) (MA); French language, literatures and linguistics (PhD); French language, literatures, and linguistics (MA); Germanic languages, literatures and linguistics (PhD); Germanic languages, literatures, and linguistics (MA); Italian studies (MA); Slavic languages and literatures (Russian, Ukrainian) (MA, PhD); Slavic linguistics (Russian, Ukrainian) (MA, PhD); Spanish and Latin American studies (MA, PhD); Ukrainian folklore (MA, PhD). Part-time programs available. *Degree requirements:* For master's, one foreign language, thesis; for doctorate, 2 foreign languages, comprehensive exam, thesis/dissertation. *Entrance requirements:* For master's and doctorate, 1 language other than English. Additional exam requirements/recommendations for international students: Required—Michigan English Language Assessment Battery or TOEFL (paper score 550; computer score 213). Electronic applications accepted. *Faculty research:* Russian/Ukrainian studies; German studies; contemporary Latin American, French and Francophone studies; Italian studies.

University of California, Berkeley, Graduate Division, Group in Folklore, Berkeley, CA 94720-1500. Offers MA. *Entrance requirements:* For master's, GRE General Test, minimum GPA of 3.0, 3 letters of recommendation. *Application deadline:* For fall admission, 12/15 for domestic students. Application fee: $70 ($90 for international students). *Unit head:* Charles Briggs, Chair, E-mail: clbriggs@berkeley.edu. *Application contact:* Information Contact, 510-643-7934, E-mail: folklore@socrates.berkeley.edu.

University of Louisiana at Lafayette, Graduate School, College of Liberal Arts, Department of English, Lafayette, LA 70504. Offers British and American literature (MA), including creative writing, folklore, rhetoric; creative writing (PhD); literature (PhD); rhetoric (PhD). Part-time programs available. Terminal master's awarded for partial completion of doctoral program. *Degree requirements:* For master's, one foreign language, thesis or alternative; for doctorate, 2 foreign languages, comprehensive exam, thesis/dissertation. *Entrance requirements:* For master's, GRE General Test, minimum GPA of 2.75; for doctorate, GRE General Test, minimum GPA of 3.0. Additional exam requirements/recommendations for international students: Required—TOEFL (minimum score 550 paper-based; 213 computer-based). Electronic applications accepted. *Faculty research:* Composition theory, Southern literature, medieval literature.

The University of North Carolina at Chapel Hill, Graduate School, College of Arts and Sciences, Curriculum in Folklore, Chapel Hill, NC 27599. Offers MA. *Degree requirements:* For master's, one foreign language, comprehensive exam, thesis. *Entrance requirements:* For master's, GRE General Test, minimum GPA of 3.0, writing sample. Electronic applications accepted. *Faculty research:* Public folklore, politics of culture, folklore and feminist theory, belief and health systems, Southern culture.

University of Oregon, Graduate School, College of Arts and Sciences, Folklore Program, Eugene, OR 97403. Offers independent study: folklore (MA, MS). Part-time programs available. *Students:* 21 full-time (14 women), 3 part-time (1 woman); includes 1 American Indian/Alaska Native, 1 international. 17 applicants, 71% accepted. In 2007, 5 degrees awarded. *Degree requirements:* For master's, one foreign language, project or thesis. *Entrance requirements:* For master's, GRE General Test, minimum GPA of 3.0. Additional exam requirements/recommendations for international students: Required—TOEFL. *Application deadline:* For fall

Folklore

University of Oregon (continued)
admission, 2/15 for domestic students. Application fee: $50. *Financial support:* In 2007–08, 6 teaching assistantships were awarded; career-related internships or fieldwork and Federal Work-Study also available. *Faculty research:* American folklore, East European folklore, film and folklore, folk religion and belief, ballad. *Unit head:* Dan Wojcik, Director, 541-346-3946, Fax: 541-346-5026. *Application contact:* Cathy O'Grady, Admissions Contact, 541-346-1505, E-mail: ogrady@uoregon.edu.

University of Pennsylvania, School of Arts and Sciences, Graduate Group in Folklore and Folklife, Philadelphia, PA 19104. Offers AM, PhD. Part-time programs available. Terminal master's awarded for partial completion of doctoral program. *Degree requirements:* For master's, one foreign language, thesis or alternative; for doctorate, 2 foreign languages, thesis/dissertation. *Entrance requirements:* For master's and doctorate, GRE General Test. Electronic applications accepted. *Faculty research:* Material culture, narrative and poetics of language, alternative health systems, public display of events.

The University of Texas at Austin, Graduate School, College of Liberal Arts, Department of Anthropology, Program in Folklore and Public Culture, Austin, TX 78712-1111. Offers MA, PhD. Part-time programs available. Terminal master's awarded for partial completion of doctoral program. *Degree requirements:* For master's, one foreign language, thesis, report; for doctorate, one foreign language, thesis/dissertation. *Entrance requirements:* For master's and doctorate, GRE General Test. Electronic applications accepted. *Faculty research:* Expressive culture, gender, genre, folklore and culture of British Isles, ethnography of speaking.

Utah State University, School of Graduate Studies, College of Humanities, Arts and Social Sciences, Department of English and Department of History, Program in American Studies, Logan, UT 84322. Offers folklore (MA, MS); western American literature and culture (MA, MS). Part-time and evening/weekend programs available. *Degree requirements:* For master's, thesis or alternative. *Entrance requirements:* For master's, GRE General Test or MAT, minimum GPA of 3.0, 3 letters of recommendation, writing sample. Additional exam requirements/recommendations for international students: Required—TOEFL. *Faculty research:* Folklore and folklife, American culture, regional studies, material culture, Jewish folklore, Native American folklore.

Gender Studies

Central European University, Graduate Studies, School of Social Sciences and Humanities, Budapest, Hungary. Offers economics (MA, PhD); gender studies (MA, PhD); international relations and European studies (MA, PhD); mathematics and its applications (MS, PhD); medieval studies (MA, PhD); nationalism studies (MA, PhD); philosophy (MA, PhD); political science (MA, PhD); public policy (MA, PhD); sociology and social anthropology (MA, PhD). *Faculty:* 75 full-time (25 women), 46 part-time/adjunct (10 women). *Students:* 625 full-time (355 women). Average age 26. 2,500 applicants, 31% accepted, 540 enrolled. In 2007, 325 master's, 20 doctorates awarded. Terminal master's awarded for partial completion of doctoral program. *Degree requirements:* For master's, one foreign language, thesis; for doctorate, one foreign language, comprehensive exam, thesis/dissertation. *Entrance requirements:* For master's, CEU subject tests, interview; for doctorate, GRE, CEU subject test, interview. Additional exam requirements/recommendations for international students: Required—TOEFL (minimum score 570 paper-based; 230 computer-based). *Application deadline:* For fall admission, 1/15 priority date for domestic and international students. Application fee: $0. Electronic applications accepted. Tuition charges are reported in euros. *Expenses:* Tuition: Full-time 10,000 euros; part-time 315 euros per credit. *Financial support:* In 2007–08, 402 students received support, including 350 fellowships with full and partial tuition reimbursements available (averaging $5,000 per year); career-related internships or fieldwork, institutionally sponsored loans, and scholarships/grants also available. Financial award application deadline: 1/5. *Faculty research:* Civil society, fiscal decentralization, party politics, political philosophy (especially Liberalism, theory of Democracy). Total annual research expenditures: $35,000. *Unit head:* Dr. Howard Michael Robinson, Provost, 361-327-3003, Fax: 361-327-3211, E-mail: robinson@ceu.hu. *Application contact:* Zsuzsanna Jaszberenyi, Admissions Officer, 361-327-3009, Fax: 361-327-3211, E-mail: admissions@ceu.hu.

See Close-Up on page 447.

Cornell University, Graduate School, Graduate Fields of Arts and Sciences, Field of Sociology, Ithaca, NY 14853-0001. Offers economy and society (MA, PhD); gender and life course (MA, PhD); methodology (MA, PhD); organizations (MA, PhD); policy analysis (MA, PhD); political sociology/social movements (MA, PhD); racial and ethnic relations (MA, PhD); social networks (MA, PhD); social psychology (MA, PhD); social stratification (MA, PhD). *Faculty:* 37 full-time (12 women). *Students:* 46 full-time (20 women); includes 10 minority (2 African Americans, 6 Asian Americans or Pacific Islanders, 2 Hispanic Americans), 10 international. Average age 30. 149 applicants, 7% accepted, 5 enrolled. In 2007, 4 master's, 6 doctorates awarded. Terminal master's awarded for partial completion of doctoral program. *Degree requirements:* For master's, thesis; for doctorate, thesis/dissertation, 1 year of teaching experience. *Entrance requirements:* For master's and doctorate, GRE General Test, 2 letters of recommendation, writing sample. Additional exam requirements/recommendations for international students: Required—TOEFL (minimum score 550 paper-based; 213 computer-based; 77 iBT). *Application deadline:* For fall admission, 1/15 for domestic students. Application fee: $70. Electronic applications accepted. *Financial support:* In 2007–08, 40 students received support, including 16 fellowships with full tuition reimbursements available, 8 research assistantships with full tuition reimbursements available, 16 teaching assistantships with full tuition reimbursements available; institutionally sponsored loans, scholarships/grants, health care benefits, tuition waivers (full and partial), and unspecified assistantships also available. Financial award applicants required to submit FAFSA. *Faculty research:* Comparative societal analysis, work and family, simulations, social class and mobility, racial segregation and inequality. *Unit head:* Director of Graduate Studies, 607-255-4266. *Application contact:* Graduate Field Assistant, 607-255-4266, E-mail: sociology@cornell.edu.

Eastern Michigan University, Graduate School, College of Arts and Sciences, Department of Women's and Gender Studies, Ypsilanti, MI 48197. Offers MLS. Part-time and evening/weekend programs available. Postbaccalaureate distance learning degree programs offered (minimal on-campus study). *Students:* 4 full-time (3 women), 9 part-time (all women); includes 3 minority (all African Americans) Average age 30. In 2007, 8 degrees awarded. *Degree requirements:* For master's, thesis optional. *Entrance requirements:* Additional exam requirements/recommendations for international students: Required—TOEFL. *Application deadline:* Applications are processed on a rolling basis. Application fee: $35. *Expenses:* Tuition, state resident: full-time $8,952; part-time $373 per credit hour. Tuition, nonresident: full-time $17,634; part-time $735 per credit hour. Required fees: $896; $34 per credit hour. Tuition and fees vary according to course level, degree level and program. *Financial support:* Fellowships, research assistantships with full tuition reimbursements, teaching assistantships with full tuition reimbursements, career-related internships or fieldwork, Federal Work-Study, institutionally sponsored loans, scholarships/grants, tuition waivers (partial), and unspecified assistantships available. Support available to part-time students. Financial award applicants required to submit FAFSA. *Unit head:* Dr. Linda Schott, Director, 734-487-1177, Fax: 734-487-5029, E-mail: lschott@emich.edu. *Application contact:* Dr. Kate Mehuron, Program Advisor, 734-487-1177, Fax: 734-487-5029, E-mail: kmehuron@emich.edu.

Indiana University Bloomington, University Graduate School, College of Arts and Sciences, Gender Studies Program, Bloomington, IN 47405-7000. Offers PhD. *Faculty:* 4 full-time (all women). *Students:* 14 full-time (11 women); includes 2 minority (1 American Indian/Alaska Native, 1 Hispanic American), 2 international. Average age 27. 60 applicants, 8% accepted, 5 enrolled. *Application deadline:* For fall admission, 1/12 priority date for domestic students, 12/1 priority date for international students. Application fee: $50 ($60 for international students). *Financial support:* Fellowships with tuition reimbursements, research assistantships with tuition reimbursements, teaching assistantships with tuition reimbursements available. *Unit head:* Helen Gremillion, Director of Graduate Studies, 812-855-0101, E-mail: hgremill@indiana.edu. *Application contact:* Nina Taylor, Graduate Secretary, 812-855-4848, E-mail: nitaylor@indiana.edu.

Indiana University–Purdue University Indianapolis, School of Liberal Arts, Department of Sociology, Indianapolis, IN 46202-2896. Offers family/gender studies (MA); medical sociology (MA); work/occupations (MA). *Faculty:* 17 full-time (8 women). *Students:* 13 full-time (11 women), 7 part-time (4 women); includes 3 minority (all African Americans), 1 international. Average age 27. In 2007, 5 degrees awarded. Application fee: $50 ($60 for international students). *Expenses:* Tuition, state resident: full-time $5,818; part-time $242 per credit hour. Tuition, nonresident: full-time $17,106; part-time $713 per credit hour. Required fees: $629. Tuition and fees vary according to course load, campus/location and program. *Financial support:* In 2007–08, 2 fellowships (averaging $9,500 per year), 2 teaching assistantships (averaging $6,309 per year) were awarded. *Unit head:* Carrie Foote, Director of Graduate Studies, 317-274-8981, E-mail: sociology@iupui.edu.

Memorial University of Newfoundland, School of Graduate Studies, Department of Sociology, St. John's, NL A1C 5S7, Canada. Offers gender (PhD); maritime sociology (PhD); sociology (M Phil, MA); work and development (PhD). Part-time programs available. *Degree requirements:* For master's, comprehensive exam, thesis optional, program journal (M Phil); for doctorate, one foreign language, comprehensive exam, thesis/dissertation, oral defense of thesis. *Entrance requirements:* For master's, 2nd class degree from university of recognized standing in area of study; for doctorate, MA, M Phil, or equivalent. Electronic applications accepted. *Faculty research:* Work and development, gender, maritime sociology.

Northwestern University, The Graduate School, Program in Gender Studies, Evanston, IL 60208. Offers PhD/Certificate. *Faculty research:* Anthropology, gender in Victorian period, autobiography, performance ethnographies, Slavic literature, women in the law.

Roosevelt University, Graduate Division, College of Arts and Sciences, Department of Literature and Languages, Program in Women's and Gender Studies, Chicago, IL 60605-1394. Offers MA, Certificate. Part-time and evening/weekend programs available. *Students:* 8 full-time (all women), 7 part-time (all women); includes 2 minority (both African Americans) Average age 32. 29 applicants, 28% accepted, 8 enrolled. In 2007, 6 degrees awarded. *Degree requirements:* For master's, thesis. *Entrance requirements:* For master's, minimum GPA of 2.7. *Application deadline:* For fall admission, 6/1 priority date for domestic students. Applications are processed on a rolling basis. Application fee: $25 ($35 for international students). *Financial support:* Application deadline: 2/15. *Faculty research:* Feminist economics; philosophy of feminism; race, class, and gender; women and art; women's history. *Unit head:* Ann Brigham, Head, 312-341-3725, Fax: 312-341-3680, E-mail: abrigham@roosevelt.edu. *Application contact:* Joanne Canyon-Heller, Coordinator of Graduate Admission, 877-APPLY RU, Fax: 312-281-3356, E-mail: applyru@roosevelt.edu.

Rutgers, The State University of New Jersey, New Brunswick, Graduate School, Program in Women's and Gender Studies, New Brunswick, NJ 08901-1281. Offers MA, PhD. Part-time programs available. *Degree requirements:* For master's, thesis or alternative; for doctorate, comprehensive exam, thesis/dissertation. *Entrance requirements:* For master's and doctorate, GRE General Test, writing sample, 3 letters of recommendation. Additional exam requirements/recommendations for international students: Required—TOEFL. *Faculty research:* Feminist theory, gender and sexuality, global and cultural studies, women in history, literature, and politics, feminist politics.

Simmons College, College of Arts and Sciences Graduate Studies, Program in Gender/Cultural Studies, Boston, MA 02115. Offers MA, MA/MAT, MA/MS. Part-time programs available. *Faculty:* 19 full-time (17 women), 1 part-time/adjunct (0 women). *Students:* 2 full-time (both women), 31 part-time (28 women); includes 3 minority (all African Americans) Average age 26. 41 applicants, 63% accepted, 14 enrolled. In 2007, 12 degrees awarded. *Degree requirements:* For master's, project, thesis, internship, or fieldwork (one is required). *Entrance requirements:* For master's, academic writing sample. Additional exam requirements/recommendations for international students: Required—TOEFL (minimum score 600 paper-based; 250 computer-based; 100 iBT). *Application deadline:* For fall admission, 8/1 priority date for domestic and international students; for spring admission, 12/15 priority date for domestic and international students. Applications are processed on a rolling basis. Application fee: $35. Electronic applications accepted. *Expenses:* Tuition: Full-time $8,500. Tuition and fees vary according to degree level and program. *Financial support:* In 2007–08, 6 students received support. Scholarships/grants available. Financial award application deadline: 3/1; financial award applicants required to submit FAFSA. *Faculty research:* Obscenity, gender and film, media studies, gender and sexuality, race, postcolonialism. *Unit head:* Jyoti Puri, Director, 617-521-2593, E-mail: jyoti.puri@simmons.edu. *Application contact:* Kristen Haack, Director, Graduate Studies Admission, 617-521-2917, Fax: 617-521-3058, E-mail: gsa@simmons.edu.

University of Florida, Graduate School, College of Liberal Arts and Sciences, Center for Women's Studies and Gender Research, Gainesville, FL 32611. Offers gender and development (Graduate Certificate); women's studies (MA, MWS, Graduate Certificate); MA/JD; MA/MA. *Faculty:* 2 full-time (both women). *Students:* 10 (9 women); includes 3 minority (1 African American, 2 Hispanic Americans) 1 international. In 2007, 2 master's awarded. *Expenses:* Tuition, state resident: full-time $7,478. Tuition, nonresident: full-time $22,603. *Financial support:* In 2007–08, 5 teaching assistantships (averaging $9,439 per year) were awarded; research assistantships. *Unit head:* Milagros Pefiilde;a, Director, 352-392-3365 Ext. 273, Fax: 352-392-6568, E-mail: mpena@soc.ufl.edu. *Application contact:* Kendal L. Broad, Graduate Coordinator, 352-392-0251 Ext. 257, Fax: 352-392-6568, E-mail: kendal@soc.ufl.edu.

University of Memphis, Graduate School, College of Arts and Sciences, Women's and Gender Studies Program, Memphis, TN 38152. Offers MA. *Students:* 7 full-time (all women), 3 part-time (all women); includes 5 African Americans. Average age 32. 12 applicants, 58% accepted, 4 enrolled. In 2007, 3 degrees awarded. *Degree requirements:* For master's, comprehensive exam, thesis or alternative. *Entrance requirements:* For master's, Letters of Reference. Application fee: $35 ($60 for international students). *Expenses:* Tuition, state resident: full-time $6,990; part-time $377 per hour. Tuition, nonresident: full-time $17,818; part-time $830 per hour. Tuition and fees vary according to course load and program. *Financial support:* In 2007–08, 3 research assistantships with full tuition reimbursements (averaging $6,667 per year), 1 teaching assistantship (averaging $4,000 per year) were awarded. Financial award application deadline: 2/15. *Unit head:* Dr. Wanda Rushing, Program Director, 901-678-3550, Fax: 901-678-4206, E-mail: wrushing@memphis.edu.

The University of North Carolina at Greensboro, Graduate School, College of Arts and Sciences, Program in Women's and Gender Studies, Greensboro, NC 27412-5001. Offers MA, Certificate. *Students:* 10 full-time (9 women), 3 part-time (all women); includes 6 minority (5 African Americans, 1 Asian American or Pacific Islander). 14 applicants, 71% accepted. Application fee: $45. Electronic applications accepted. *Unit head:* Katherine Jamieson, Director, 336-334-5273, E-mail: rmjamies@uncg.edu. *Application contact:* Michelle Harkleroad, Director of Graduate Admissions, 336-334-4884, Fax: 336-334-4424, E-mail: mbharkle@uncg.edu.

University of Northern British Columbia, Office of Graduate Studies, Prince George, BC V2N 4Z9, Canada. Offers business administration (Diploma); community health science (M Sc); disability management (MA); education (M Ed); first nations studies (MA); gender studies (MA); history (MA); interdisciplinary studies (MA); international studies (MA); mathematical, computer and physical sciences (M Sc); natural resources and environmental studies (M Sc, MA, MNRES, PhD); political science (MA); psychology (M Sc, PhD); social work (MSW). Part-time and evening/weekend programs available. Postbaccalaureate distance learning degree programs offered (no on-campus study). *Degree requirements:* For master's, thesis; for doctorate, thesis/dissertation. *Entrance requirements:* For master's, GRE, minimum B average in undergraduate course work; for doctorate, candidacy exam, minimum A average in graduate course work.

University of Northern Iowa, Graduate College, Program in Women's and Gender Studies, Cedar Falls, IA 50614. Offers MA. *Students:* 9 full-time (all women), 3 part-time (all women); includes 1 minority (African American), 2 international. 19 applicants, 84% accepted, 5 enrolled. In 2007, 5 degrees awarded. *Degree requirements:* For master's, comprehensive exam (for some programs), thesis or alternative. *Entrance requirements:* For master's, minimum GPA of 3.0. Additional exam requirements/recommendations for international students: Required—TOEFL (minimum score 500 paper-based; 180 computer-based; 61 iBT). *Application deadline:* Applications are processed on a rolling basis. Application fee: $30 ($50 for international students). Electronic applications accepted. *Expenses:* Tuition, state resident: full-time $6,246; part-time $694 per credit hour. Tuition, nonresident: full-time $14,554; part-time $694 per credit hour. Required fees: $838; $119 per semester. *Financial support:* Application deadline: 2/1. *Unit head:* Dr. Phyllis Baker, Head/Graduate Coordinator, 319-273-2109, Fax: 319-273-3053, E-mail: phyllis.baker@uni.edu.

University of Saskatchewan, College of Graduate Studies and Research, College of Arts and Sciences, Department of Women's and Gender Studies, Saskatoon, SK S7N 5A2, Canada. Offers MA, PhD. *Degree requirements:* For master's, thesis; for doctorate, thesis/dissertation. *Entrance requirements:* Additional exam requirements/recommendations for international students: Required—TOEFL.

Virginia Commonwealth University, Graduate School, College of Humanities and Sciences, Wilder School of Government and Public Affairs, Department of Sociology, Program in Gender Violence Intervention, Richmond, VA 23284-9005. Offers Certificate, MSW/Certificate. *Application deadline:* For fall admission, 7/1 for domestic students; for spring admission, 11/15 for domestic students. Application fee: $50. *Expenses:* Tuition, state resident: full-time $7,224; part-time $401 per credit. Tuition, nonresident: full-time $16,072; part-time $891 per credit. Required fees: $1,679; $63 per credit. Tuition and fees vary according to campus/location. *Application contact:* Dr. Sarah Jane Brubaker, Director, Graduate Programs in Sociology, 804-827-2400, Fax: 804-828-1027, E-mail: sbrubaker@vcu.edu.

See Close-Up on page 457.

Hispanic Studies

Brown University, Graduate School, Department of Hispanic Studies, Providence, RI 02912. Offers AM, PhD. *Degree requirements:* For master's, one foreign language, thesis; for doctorate, 2 foreign languages, thesis/dissertation, preliminary exam.

California State University, Los Angeles, Graduate Studies, College of Natural and Social Sciences, Department of Chicano Studies, Los Angeles, CA 90032-8530. Offers Mexican-American studies (MA). Part-time and evening/weekend programs available. *Faculty:* 2 full-time (1 woman). *Students:* 6 full-time (3 women), 16 part-time (11 women); includes 20 minority (2 African Americans, 18 Hispanic Americans). Average age 34. In 2007, 7 degrees awarded. *Degree requirements:* For master's, one foreign language, comprehensive exam or thesis. *Entrance requirements:* For master's, undergraduate major in Mexican-American studies or related area, 12 units in Chicano studies. Additional exam requirements/recommendations for international students: Required—TOEFL. *Application deadline:* For fall admission, 6/30 for domestic students; for spring admission, 2/1 for domestic students. Applications are processed on a rolling basis. Application fee: $55. *Financial support:* Career-related internships or fieldwork and Federal Work-Study available. Support available to part-time students. Financial award application deadline: 3/1. *Faculty research:* U.S.-Mexican relations, Chicano literature, community organization among Chicanos and Hispanics, Spanish language in the American Southwest. *Unit head:* Dr. Michael Soldatenko, Chair, 323-343-2400, Fax: 323-343-5609, E-mail: msoldat@calstatela.edu.

California State University, Northridge, Graduate Studies, College of Humanities, Department of Chicana and Chicano Studies, Northridge, CA 91330. Offers MA. *Faculty:* 22 full-time (13 women), 45 part-time/adjunct (18 women). *Students:* 15 full-time (8 women), 24 part-time (12 women); includes 37 minority (all Hispanic Americans), 1 international. Average age 28. 17 applicants, 82% accepted, 9 enrolled. In 2007, 3 degrees awarded. *Degree requirements:* For master's, thesis, project. *Entrance requirements:* Additional exam requirements/recommendations for international students: Required—TOEFL. *Application deadline:* For fall admission, 11/30 for domestic students. Application fee: $55. *Financial support:* Application deadline: 3/1. *Unit head:* Dr. David Rodriguez, Chair, 818-677-2734.

Eastern Michigan University, Graduate School, College of Arts and Sciences, Department of Foreign Languages and Bilingual Studies, Program in Foreign Languages, Ypsilanti, MI 48197. Offers French (MA); German (MA); German for business (Graduate Certificate); Hispanic language and cultures (Graduate Certificate); Japanese business practices (Graduate Certificate); Spanish (MA). Part-time and evening/weekend programs available. Postbaccalaureate distance learning degree programs offered (minimal on-campus study). *Students:* 1 (woman) full-time, 18 part-time (17 women); includes 2 minority (1 Asian American or Pacific Islander, 1 Hispanic American). Average age 35. In 2007, 8 master's, 2 other advanced degrees awarded. *Degree requirements:* For master's, one foreign language, thesis optional. *Entrance requirements:* Additional exam requirements/recommendations for international students: Required—TOEFL. *Application deadline:* Applications are processed on a rolling basis. Application fee: $35. *Expenses:* Tuition, state resident: full-time $8,952; part-time $373 per credit hour. Tuition, nonresident: full-time $17,634; part-time $735 per credit hour. Required fees: $896; $34 per credit hour. Tuition and fees vary according to course level, degree level and program. *Financial support:* Fellowships, research assistantships with full tuition reimbursements, teaching assistantships with full tuition reimbursements, career-related internships or fieldwork, Federal Work-Study, institutionally sponsored loans, scholarships/grants, tuition waivers (partial), and unspecified assistantships available. Support available to part-time students. Financial award applicants required to submit FAFSA. *Application contact:* Dr. Genevieve Peden, Program Advisor, 734-487-2283, Fax: 734-487-3411, E-mail: gpeden@emich.edu.

La Salle University, School of Arts and Sciences, Program in Bilingual/Bicultural Studies (Spanish), Philadelphia, PA 19141-1199. Offers MA. Part-time and evening/weekend programs available. *Faculty:* 1 full-time (0 women), 4 part-time/adjunct (0 women). *Students:* 3 full-time (all women), 62 part-time (49 women); includes 28 minority (13 African Americans, 2 Asian Americans or Pacific Islanders, 13 Hispanic Americans). Average age 36. 16 applicants, 81% accepted, 12 enrolled. In 2007, 9 degrees awarded. *Degree requirements:* For master's, one foreign language, thesis or alternative, project. *Entrance requirements:* For master's, GRE or MAT. *Application deadline:* Applications are processed on a rolling basis. Application fee: $35. *Expenses:* Contact institution. Tuition and fees vary according to program. *Financial support:* In 2007–08, 37 students received support. Scholarships/grants and tuition waivers (partial) available. Support available to part-time students. Financial award application deadline: 5/16; financial award applicants required to submit FAFSA. *Faculty research:* Puerto Rican literature, cross-cultural communication, English as a second language methodology, Spanish language. *Unit head:* Dr. Luis Gomez, Director, 215-951-1209.

Louisiana State University and Agricultural and Mechanical College, Graduate School, College of Arts and Sciences, Department of Foreign Languages and Literatures, Baton Rouge, LA 70803. Offers Hispanic studies (MA). Part-time programs available. *Faculty:* 20 full-time (9 women). *Students:* 9 full-time (6 women), 2 part-time (1 woman); includes 2 Hispanic Americans, 2 international. Average age 30. 3 applicants, 100% accepted, 3 enrolled. In 2007, 10 degrees awarded. *Degree requirements:* For master's, 2 foreign languages, thesis optional. *Entrance requirements:* For master's, GRE General Test, minimum GPA of 3.0. Additional exam requirements/recommendations for international students: Required—TOEFL (minimum score 550 paper-based; 213 computer-based; 79 iBT). *Application deadline:* For fall admission, 1/25 priority date for domestic students, 5/15 for international students; for spring admission, 10/15 for international students. Applications are processed on a rolling basis. Application fee: $25. Electronic applications accepted. *Financial support:* In 2007–08, 8 students received support, including 8 teaching assistantships with partial tuition reimbursements available (averaging $10,500 per year); fellowships with full tuition reimbursements available, research assistantships with partial tuition reimbursements available, Federal Work-Study, scholarships/grants, health care benefits, and tuition waivers (full and partial) also available. Financial award application deadline: 4/1; financial award applicants required to submit FAFSA. *Faculty research:* Hispanic cultural studies, linguistics, literary and cultural theory, peninsular and Latin American literature. *Unit head:* Dr. Emily E. Batinski, Chair, 225-578-6616, Fax: 225-578-5074, E-mail: slbati@lsu.edu. *Application contact:* Dr. Alejandro Cortazar, Graduate Adviser, 225-578-5169, Fax: 225-578-5074, E-mail: acorta1@lsu.edu.

McGill University, Faculty of Graduate and Postdoctoral Studies, Faculty of Arts, Department of Hispanic Studies, Montréal, QC H3A 2T5, Canada. Offers MA, PhD. *Faculty:* 6 full-time (3 women), 15 part-time/adjunct (12 women). *Students:* 11 full-time (9 women), 4 part-time (all women). 14 applicants, 71% accepted, 3 enrolled. In 2007, 3 master's awarded.

Michigan State University, The Graduate School, College of Arts and Letters, Department of Spanish and Portuguese, East Lansing, MI 48824. Offers applied Spanish linguistics (MA); Hispanic cultural studies (PhD); Hispanic literatures (MA). *Entrance requirements:* Additional exam requirements/recommendations for international students: Required—TOEFL. Electronic applications accepted. *Expenses:* Tuition, state resident: part-time $379 per credit hour. Tuition, nonresident: part-time $800 per credit hour. Tuition and fees vary according to program.

Pontifical Catholic University of Puerto Rico, College of Arts and Humanities, Department of Hispanic Studies, Ponce, PR 00717-0777. Offers grammar and writing (Professional Certificate); Hispanic studies (MA). Part-time and evening/weekend programs available. *Degree requirements:* For master's, variable foreign language requirement, comprehensive exam, thesis or alternative. *Entrance requirements:* For master's, GRE General Test, 2 letters of recommendation, interview, minimum GPA of 2.75. Electronic applications accepted.

St. Thomas University, School of Leadership Studies, Program in Hispanic Media, Miami Gardens, FL 33054-6459. Offers MA, Certificate. Part-time and evening/weekend programs available. *Students:* 3 full-time (all women), 13 part-time (11 women); includes 14 minority (1 African American, 13 Hispanic Americans), 2 international. Average age 29. 7 applicants, 57% accepted. *Degree requirements:* For master's, comprehensive exam. *Entrance requirements:* Additional exam requirements/recommendations for international students: Required—TOEFL (minimum score 550 paper-based; 213 computer-based; 79 iBT). *Application deadline:* Applications are processed on a rolling basis. Application fee: $40. Electronic applications accepted. *Financial support:* Unspecified assistantships available. Financial award applicants required to submit FAFSA. *Unit head:* Dr. Andrea Campbell, Coordinator, 305-628-6508, Fax: 305-628-6757. *Application contact:* Marilyn Carballosa, Assistant Director of Admissions, 305-628-6546, Fax: 305-628-6591, E-mail: graduate@stu.edu.

San Jose State University, Graduate Studies and Research, College of Social Sciences, Department of Mexican-American Studies, San Jose, CA 95192-0001. Offers MA. *Students:* 10 full-time (7 women), 13 part-time (6 women); includes 21 minority (all Hispanic Americans) Average age 27. 14 applicants, 79% accepted, 9 enrolled. In 2007, 5 degrees awarded. *Application deadline:* For fall admission, 6/29 for domestic students; for spring admission, 11/30 for domestic students. Applications are processed on a rolling basis. Application fee: $59. Electronic applications accepted. *Financial support:* Application deadline: 5/31; *Unit head:* Dr. Lou Holscher, Chair, 408-924-5837, Fax: 408-924-5700, E-mail: holscher@sjsu.edu. *Application contact:* Dr. Marcos Pizarro, Graduate Coordinator, 408-924-5584.

Stony Brook University, State University of New York, Graduate School, College of Arts and Sciences, Department of Hispanic Languages and Literature, Stony Brook, NY 11794. Offers MA, PhD. Evening/weekend programs available. *Faculty:* 10 full-time (4 women), 1 part-time/adjunct (0 women). *Students:* 39 full-time (25 women), 10 part-time (7 women); includes 17 minority (1 African American, 16 Hispanic Americans), 20 international. Average age 33. 26 applicants, 85% accepted. In 2007, 2 master's, 2 doctorates awarded. *Degree requirements:* For master's, one foreign language, thesis or alternative; for doctorate, 2 foreign languages, thesis/dissertation. *Entrance requirements:* For master's, GRE General Test, BA in Spanish; for doctorate, GRE General Test, MA in Spanish. Additional exam requirements/recommendations for international students: Required—TOEFL. *Application deadline:* For fall admission, 1/15 for domestic students. Application fee: $60. *Expenses:* Contact institution. *Financial support:* In 2007–08, 21 teaching assistantships were awarded; fellowships, research assistantships, tuition waivers and unspecified assistantships also available. *Faculty research:* Spanish language and literature. *Unit head:* Dr. Victoriano Roncero-Lopez, Chair, 631-632-6959. *Application contact:* Dr. Lou Charnon-Deutsch, Director of Graduate Studies, 631-632-6935, Fax: 631-632-9724, E-mail: ldeutsch@notes.cc.sunysb.edu.

See Close-Up on page 809.

Hispanic Studies

Texas A&M International University, Office of Graduate Studies and Research, College of Arts and Sciences, Department of Language and Literature, Laredo, TX 78041-1900. Offers English (MA); Hispanic studies (PhD); Spanish (MA). *Faculty:* 5 full-time (1 woman). *Students:* 2 full-time (1 woman), 19 part-time (13 women); includes 19 minority (all Hispanic Americans) Average age 29. 17 applicants, 76% accepted, 7 enrolled. In 2007, 1 degree awarded. *Entrance requirements:* For master's, GRE General Test. Additional exam requirements/recommendations for international students: Required—TOEFL (minimum score 550 paper-based; 213 computer-based). *Application deadline:* For fall admission, 7/15 priority date for domestic students; for spring admission, 11/12 for domestic students. Applications are processed on a rolling basis. Application fee: $25. *Financial support:* In 2007–08, 5 students received support. Application deadline: 11/1. *Unit head:* Dr. Sean Chadwell, Chair, 956-326-2471, E-mail: schadwell@tamiu.edu. *Application contact:* Rosie Espinoza-Dickinson, Director of Admissions, 956-326-2200, Fax: 956-326-2199, E-mail: enroll@tamiu.edu.

Université de Montréal, Faculty of Arts and Sciences, Department of Literatures and Modern Languages, Montréal, QC H3C 3J7, Canada. Offers German literature (PhD); German studies (MA); Hispanic literature (PhD); Hispanic studies (MA); literature and cinema (PhD). *Faculty:* 13 full-time (5 women), 1 (woman) part-time/adjunct. *Students:* 44 full-time (30 women), 5 part-time (4 women). 28 applicants, 79% accepted, 19 enrolled. In 2007, 7 degrees awarded. Terminal master's awarded for partial completion of doctoral program. *Degree requirements:* For master's, 2 foreign languages, thesis; for doctorate, 2 foreign languages, thesis/dissertation, general exam. *Application deadline:* For fall admission, 2/1 priority date for domestic students; for winter admission, 11/1 priority date for domestic students; for spring admission, 2/1 priority date for domestic students. Application fee: $100. Electronic applications accepted. *Financial support:* Teaching assistantships available. *Unit head:* Monique Moser, Director, 514-343-7050, Fax: 514-343-2255, E-mail: monique.moser@umontreal.ca. *Application contact:* Nikola von Merveldt, Responsible for German Studies Program, 514-343-5905, Fax: 514-343-2255, E-mail: n.von.merveldt@umontreal.ca.

University of Alberta, Faculty of Graduate Studies and Research, Department of Modern Languages and Cultural Studies, Edmonton, AB T6G 2E1, Canada. Offers applied linguistics (Germanic, Romance, Slavic) (MA); French language, literatures and linguistics (PhD); French language, literatures, and linguistics (MA); Germanic languages, literatures and linguistics (PhD); Germanic languages, literatures, and linguistics (MA); Italian studies (MA); Slavic languages and literatures (Russian, Ukrainian) (MA, PhD); Slavic linguistics (Russian, Ukrainian) (MA, PhD); Spanish and Latin American studies (MA, PhD); Ukrainian folklore (MA, PhD). Part-time programs available. *Degree requirements:* For master's, one foreign language, thesis; for doctorate, 2 foreign languages, comprehensive exam, thesis/dissertation. *Entrance requirements:* For master's and doctorate, 1 language other than English. Additional exam requirements/recommendations for international students: Required—Michigan English Language Assessment Battery or TOEFL (paper score 550; computer score 213). Electronic applications accepted. *Faculty research:* Russian/Ukrainian studies; German studies; contemporary Latin American, French and Francophone studies; Italian studies.

The University of British Columbia, Faculty of Arts and Faculty of Graduate Studies, Department of French, Hispanic and Italian Studies, Vancouver, BC V6T 1Z1, Canada. Offers French (MA, PhD); Hispanic studies (MA, PhD). Part-time programs available. *Faculty:* 20 full-time (9 women). *Students:* 45 full-time (29 women), 1 (woman) part-time. 35 applicants, 77% accepted, 18 enrolled. In 2007, 5 master's, 1 doctorate awarded. *Degree requirements:* For master's, thesis optional; for doctorate, 2 foreign languages, comprehensive exam, thesis/dissertation. *Entrance requirements:* For master's, BA degree; for doctorate, MA degree. Additional exam requirements/recommendations for international students: Required—TOEFL (minimum score 550 paper-based; 213 computer-based; 80 iBT). *Application deadline:* For fall admission, 4/1 priority date for domestic students, 3/1 priority date for international students; for winter admission, 9/1 priority date for domestic students, 8/1 priority date for international students. Applications are processed on a rolling basis. Application fee: $90 Canadian dollars ($150 Canadian dollars for international students). Electronic applications accepted. *Financial support:* In 2007–08, 5 fellowships with partial tuition reimbursements (averaging $16,000 per year), 6 research assistantships (averaging $1,328 per year), 28 teaching assistantships (averaging $10,700 per year) were awarded; Federal Work-Study and tuition waivers (partial) also available. Financial award application deadline: 2/15. *Faculty research:* Medieval and Renaissance literature, modern literature, romance philology and linguistics, cultural studies, women's literature. *Unit head:* Dr. André C. Lamontagne, Head, 604-822-5746, Fax: 604-822-6675, E-mail: andrelam@interchange.ubc.ca. *Application contact:* Dr. Christine Rouget, Graduate Advisor, 604-822-4035, Fax: 604-822-6675, E-mail: roug@interchange.ubc.ca.

University of California, Berkeley, Graduate Division, College of Letters and Science, Department of Hispanic Languages and Literature, Berkeley, CA 94720-1500. Offers PhD. *Faculty:* 16 full-time (6 women). *Degree requirements:* For doctorate, thesis/dissertation, qualifying exam. *Entrance requirements:* For doctorate, GRE General Test, minimum GPA of 3.0, 3 letters of recommendation. Additional exam requirements/recommendations for international students: Required—TOEFL (minimum score 570 paper-based; 230 computer-based). *Application deadline:* For fall admission, 12/15 for domestic students. Application fee: $70 ($90 for international students). *Financial support:* Fellowships with full tuition reimbursements, research assistantships, teaching assistantships with partial tuition reimbursements, unspecified assistantships available. Financial award applicants required to submit FAFSA. *Unit head:* Jose Rabasa, Chair, 510-642—2105, E-mail: jrabasa@berkeley.edu. *Application contact:* Veronica Lopez, Student Affairs Officer, 510-642-8037, Fax: 510-8037, E-mail: spanga@berkeley.edu.

University of California, Los Angeles, Graduate Division, College of Letters and Science, Department of Spanish and Portuguese, Program in Hispanic Languages and Literature, Los Angeles, CA 90095. Offers PhD. *Students:* 49 full-time (38 women); includes 24 minority (1 African American, 3 Asian Americans or Pacific Islanders, 20 Hispanic Americans), 5 international. Average age 33. 27 applicants, 41% accepted, 8 enrolled. In 2007, 4 degrees awarded. *Median time to degree:* Of those who began their doctoral program in fall 1999, 39% received their degree in 8 years or less. *Degree requirements:* For doctorate, 2 foreign languages, thesis/dissertation, oral and written exams. *Entrance requirements:* For doctorate, GRE General Test, minimum undergraduate GPA of 3.0, sample of written work (recommended), Master's degree. *Application deadline:* For fall admission, 12/31 for domestic students. Application fee: $60. Electronic applications accepted. *Expenses:* Tuition, nonresident: full-time $5,728. Required fees: $8,966. Full-time tuition and fees vary according to program and student level. *Financial support:* In 2007–08, 48 fellowships with full and partial tuition reimbursements, 6 research assistantships with full and partial tuition reimbursements, 30 teaching assistantships with full and partial tuition reimbursements were awarded; tuition waivers (full and partial) also available. Financial award applicants required to submit FAFSA. *Application contact:* Departmental Office, 310-825-1036, E-mail: peinado@humnet.ucla.edu.

University of California, Riverside, Graduate Division, Department of Hispanic Studies, Riverside, CA 92521-0102. Offers Spanish (MA, PhD). *Faculty:* 8 full-time (3 women). *Students:* 22 full-time (14 women), 1 part-time; includes 16 minority (all Hispanic Americans), 2 international. Average age 34. 14 applicants, 21% accepted, 3 enrolled. In 2007, 6 master's, 1 doctorate awarded. Terminal master's awarded for partial completion of doctoral program. *Degree requirements:* For master's, one foreign language, comprehensive exam; for doctorate, one foreign language, thesis/dissertation, qualifying exams, 1 quarter of teaching experience. *Entrance requirements:* For master's and doctorate, GRE General Test, minimum GPA of 3.2. Additional exam requirements/recommendations for international students: Required—TOEFL (minimum score 550 paper-based; 213 computer-based; 80 iBT). *Application deadline:* For fall admission, 1/5 for domestic students, 2/1 for international students; for winter admission, 9/1 for domestic students, 7/1 for international students; for spring admission, 12/1 for domestic students, 10/1 for international students. Applications are processed on a rolling basis. Application fee: $60 ($75 for international students). Electronic applications accepted. *Financial support:* In 2007–08, fellowships with tuition reimbursements (averaging $12,000 per year), teaching assistantships with tuition reimbursements (averaging $16,500 per year) were awarded; career-related internships or fieldwork, Federal Work-Study, institutionally sponsored loans, scholarships/grants, health care benefits, and tuition waivers (full and partial) also available. Financial award application deadline: 1/5; financial award applicants required to submit FAFSA. *Faculty research:* Spanish literature of sixteenth, seventeenth and twentieth century; pre-Columbian and colonial Latin American literature; nineteenth and twentieth century Latin American literature. *Unit head:* Dr. David E. Hevzberger, Chair, 951-827-5007 Ext. 11462, Fax: 951-827-2160, E-mail: david.herzberger@ucr.edu. *Application contact:* Dr. Susan Antebi, Graduate Advisor, 951-827-1969, Fax: 951-827-2294, E-mail: clhsgrad@ucr.edu.

University of California, Santa Barbara, Graduate Division, College of Letters and Sciences, Division of Humanities and Fine Arts, Department of Spanish and Portuguese, Santa Barbara, CA 93106. Offers Hispanic languages and literature (PhD); Portuguese (MA); Spanish (MA). Spanish Language Institute available during summer sessions. *Faculty:* 16 full-time (6 women). *Students:* 27 full-time (12 women); includes 6 minority (all Hispanic Americans), 8 international. Average age 31. 34 applicants, 62% accepted, 9 enrolled. In 2007, 3 master's, 4 doctorates awarded. *Median time to degree:* Of those who began their doctoral program in fall 1999, 60% received their degree in 8 years or less. *Degree requirements:* For master's, 2 foreign languages, thesis optional; for doctorate, 2 foreign languages, comprehensive exam, thesis/dissertation. *Entrance requirements:* For master's, GRE, 2 writing samples, undergraduate major in Spanish or equivalent; for doctorate, GRE, 2 writing samples, Master's degree. Additional exam requirements/recommendations for international students: Required—TOEFL (minimum score 550 paper-based; 213 computer-based; 80 iBT). *Application deadline:* For fall admission, 3/1 for domestic and international students; for winter admission, 11/1 for domestic and international students; for spring admission, 2/1 for domestic and international students. Applications are processed on a rolling basis. Application fee: $60. Electronic applications accepted. *Expenses:* Tuition, nonresident: full-time $14,888. Required fees: $10,108. *Financial support:* In 2007–08, 27 students received support, including 6 fellowships with full tuition reimbursements available (averaging $15,500 per year), 4 research assistantships, 26 teaching assistantships with full and partial tuition reimbursements available (averaging $16,390 per year); career-related internships or fieldwork, Federal Work-Study, scholarships/grants, health care benefits, tuition waivers (full and partial), and unspecified assistantships also available. Financial award application deadline: 1/7; financial award applicants required to submit FAFSA. *Faculty research:* 19th century Spanish and Portuguese literature, Spanish and Spanish American literature, 19th and 20th century Portuguese and Brazilian literatures, Mexican literature, Catalan language and culture. *Unit head:* Prof. Francisco P. Lomeli, Chair, 805-893-2798, E-mail: rap@spanport.ucsb.edu. *Application contact:* Carol Conley, Graduate Program Assistant, 805-893-3162, Fax: 805-893-8341, E-mail: cconley@spanport.ucsb.edu.

University of California, Santa Barbara, Graduate Division, College of Letters and Sciences, Division of Social Sciences, Department of Chicana and Chicano Studies, Santa Barbara, CA 93106. Offers PhD, MA/PhD. *Faculty:* 8 full-time (4 women), 4 part-time/adjunct (2 women). *Students:* 18 full-time (9 women); includes 17 minority (1 American Indian/Alaska Native, 16 Hispanic Americans). Average age 29. 30 applicants, 30% accepted, 4 enrolled. *Degree requirements:* For doctorate, one foreign language, comprehensive exam, thesis/dissertation. *Entrance requirements:* For doctorate, GRE, writing sample. Additional exam requirements/recommendations for international students: Required—TOEFL (minimum score 550 paper-based; 213 computer-based; 80 iBT). *Application deadline:* For fall admission, 1/1 for domestic and international students. Application fee: $60. Electronic applications accepted. *Expenses:* Tuition, nonresident: full-time $14,888. Required fees: $10,108. *Financial support:* In 2007–08, 17 students received support, including 15 fellowships with full and partial tuition reimbursements available (averaging $5,613 per year), 4 research assistantships with full and partial tuition reimbursements available (averaging $1,500 per year), 7 teaching assistantships with partial tuition reimbursements available (averaging $15,000 per year); career-related internships or fieldwork, Federal Work-Study, institutionally sponsored loans, scholarships/grants, health care benefits, tuition waivers (full and partial), and unspecified assistantships also available. Financial award application deadline: 12/15. *Faculty research:* Global, postcolonial and border studies; literature, culture and representation; political history and community; critical and cultural theory; gender and sexuality studies. *Unit head:* Dr. Juan Vincente Palerm, Chair, 805-893-3601, E-mail: palerm@anth.ucsb.edu. *Application contact:* Katherine G. Morales, Graduate Academic Assistant, 805-893-5269, Fax: 805-893-4076, E-mail: kmoreales@chicst.ucsb.edu.

University of Illinois at Chicago, Graduate College, College of Liberal Arts and Sciences, Department of Spanish and French, Program in Hispanic Studies, Chicago, IL 60607-7128. Offers MA, PhD. Part-time programs available. Terminal master's awarded for partial completion of doctoral program. *Degree requirements:* For master's, one foreign language, departmental qualifying exam. *Entrance requirements:* For master's, GRE General Test, minimum GPA of 2.75, undergraduate major in Spanish. Additional exam requirements/recommendations for international students: Required—TOEFL. Electronic applications accepted.

University of Kentucky, Graduate School, College of Arts and Sciences, Program in Hispanic Studies, Lexington, KY 40506-0032. Offers MA, PhD. *Faculty:* 9 full-time (6 women). *Students:* 46 full-time (32 women), 5 part-time (4 women); includes 8 minority (1 African American, 7 Hispanic Americans), 11 international. Average age 31. 38 applicants, 63% accepted, 12 enrolled. In 2007, 3 master's, 5 doctorates awarded. *Median time to degree:* Of those who began their doctoral program in fall 1999, 0% received their degree in 8 years or less. *Degree requirements:* For master's, one foreign language, comprehensive exam, thesis optional; for doctorate, 2 foreign languages, comprehensive exam, thesis/dissertation. *Entrance requirements:* For master's, GRE General Test, minimum undergraduate GPA of 2.75; for doctorate, GRE General Test, minimum graduate GPA of 3.0. Additional exam requirements/recommendations for international students: Required—TOEFL (minimum score 550 paper-based; 213 computer-based). *Application deadline:* For fall admission, 7/17 priority date for domestic students, 2/1 priority date for international students; for spring admission, 12/13 priority date for domestic students, 6/15 priority date for international students. Application fee: $50 ($65 for international students). Electronic applications accepted. *Expenses:* Tuition, state resident: part-time $437 per credit hour. Tuition, nonresident: part-time $931 per credit hour. *Financial support:* In 2007–08, 37 students received support, including 7 fellowships with full tuition reimbursements available (averaging $3,000 per year), 36 teaching assistantships with full tuition reimbursements available (averaging $12,000 per year); research assistantships, Federal Work-Study, institutionally sponsored loans, scholarships/grants, traineeships, health care benefits, tuition waivers (partial), and unspecified assistantships also available. Support available to part-time students. Financial award application deadline: 3/15. *Faculty research:* Hispanic linguistics, medieval Spanish literature and civilization, Renaissance and Golden Age literature and civilization, Spanish American literature and civilization. *Unit head:* Dr. Susan Carvalho, Director of Graduate Studies, 859-257-1565, Fax: 859-323-9077. *Application contact:* Dr. Brian Jackson, Senior Associate Dean, 859-257-4667, Fax: 859-257-4676, E-mail: brian.jackson@uky.edu.

The University of North Carolina at Greensboro, Graduate School, College of Arts and Sciences, Department of Romance Languages, Program in Spanish, Greensboro, NC 27412-5001. Offers advanced Spanish language and Hispanic cultural studies (Certificate); Spanish (MA). *Faculty:* 10 full-time (7 women), 1 part-time/adjunct (0 women). *Students:* 2 full-time (1 woman), 3 part-time (all women). *Degree requirements:* For master's, one foreign language, comprehensive exam, thesis or alternative. *Entrance requirements:* For master's, GRE General Test, 3-5 minute tape demonstrating foreign language proficiency, composition in Spanish, sample paper in English. Additional exam requirements/recommendations for international students: Required—TOEFL. *Application deadline:* For spring admission, 11/1 for domestic students. Applications are processed on a rolling basis. Application fee: $45. Electronic applications accepted. *Financial support:* Research assistantships, teaching assistantships, unspecified assistantships available. *Application contact:* Michelle Harkleroad, Director of Graduate Admissions, 336-334-4884, Fax: 336-334-4424, E-mail: mbharkle@uncg.edu.

The University of North Carolina Wilmington, College of Arts and Sciences, Department of Foreign Languages and Literature, Wilmington, NC 28403-3297. Offers Hispanic studies

(Graduate Certificate). *Students:* Average age 41. 2 applicants, 100% accepted, 1 enrolled. Application fee: $45. *Expenses:* Tuition, state resident: full-time $2,714. Tuition, nonresident: full-time $12,579. Required fees: $1,985. *Financial support:* In 2007–08, 4 teaching assistantships were awarded. *Unit head:* Dr. Raymond Burt, Chair, 910-962-4095, E-mail: burtr@uncw.edu. *Application contact:* Dr. Robert D. Roer, Dean, Graduate School, 910-962-4117, Fax: 910-962-3787, E-mail: roer@uncw.edu.

University of Pittsburgh, School of Arts and Sciences, Department of Hispanic Languages and Literatures, Pittsburgh, PA 15260. Offers MA, PhD. Part-time programs available. *Faculty:* 9 full-time (2 women). *Students:* 44 full-time (29 women); includes 13 minority (2 African Americans, 2 Asian Americans or Pacific Islanders, 9 Hispanic Americans), 27 international. Average age 30. 41 applicants, 54% accepted, 11 enrolled. In 2007, 8 master's, 5 doctorates awarded. Terminal master's awarded for partial completion of doctoral program. *Median time to degree:* Of those who began their doctoral program in fall 1999, 57% received their degree in 8 years or less. *Degree requirements:* For master's, one foreign language, comprehensive exam (for some programs), thesis or alternative, research paper; for doctorate, 2 foreign languages, comprehensive exam, thesis/dissertation. *Entrance requirements:* Additional exam requirements/recommendations for international students: Required—TOEFL (minimum score 550 paper-based; 213 computer-based; 80 iBT). *Application deadline:* For fall admission, 1/15 priority date for domestic and international students. Application fee: $50. Electronic applications accepted. *Financial support:* In 2007–08, 32 students received support, including 7 fellowships with full tuition reimbursements available (averaging $15,500 per year), 24 teaching assistantships with full tuition reimbursements available (averaging $14,500 per year); scholarships/grants, health care benefits, and tuition waivers (partial) also available. Financial award application deadline: 1/15. *Faculty research:* Latin American, Luso-Brazilian, and peninsular literature; cultural theory; cultural studies; race, ethnicity, and post-colonial studies. *Unit head:* Dr. Elizabeth Monasterios, Chair, 412-624-5226, Fax: 412-624-8505, E-mail: elm15@pitt.edu. *Application contact:* Dr. Juan Duchesne-Winter, Director of Graduate Studies, 412-624-0141, Fax: 412-624-8505, E-mail: duchesne@pitt.edu.

University of Puerto Rico, Mayagüez Campus, Graduate Studies, College of Arts and Sciences, Department of Hispanic Studies, Mayagüez, PR 00681-9000. Offers MA. Part-time programs available. *Faculty:* 22 full-time (15 women). *Students:* 9 full-time (8 women), 14 part-time (13 women); includes 22 minority (all Hispanic Americans), 1 international. 11 applicants, 82% accepted, 7 enrolled. In 2007, 2 degrees awarded. *Degree requirements:* For master's, comprehensive exam, thesis. *Entrance requirements:* For master's, minimum GPA of 2.75, BA degree in Hispanic studies or its equivalent. *Application deadline:* For fall admission, 2/15 for domestic and international students; for spring admission, 9/15 for domestic and international students. Applications are processed on a rolling basis. Application fee: $25. *Financial support:* In 2007–08, 4 students received support, including fellowships (averaging $12,000 per year), research assistantships (averaging $15,000 per year), 4 teaching assistantships (averaging $8,500 per year); Federal Work-Study and institutionally sponsored loans also available. *Faculty research:* Spanish literature, Hispanic-American literature, Puerto Rican literature, stylistics, linguistics. *Unit head:* Dr. Jaime Martell, Director, 787-265-3843, Fax: 787-265-3843, E-mail: jmartell@uprm.edu. *Application contact:* Dr. Maribel Acosta, Graduate Program Coordinator, 787-832-4040 Ext. 3334, Fax: 787-265-3843, E-mail: macostalugo@gmail.com.

University of Puerto Rico, Río Piedras, College of Humanities, Department of Hispanic Studies, San Juan, PR 00931-3300. Offers MA, PhD. Part-time programs available. *Students:* 65 full-time (54 women), 78 part-time (57 women). Average age 36. In 2007, 5 master's, 7 doctorates awarded. *Degree requirements:* For master's, one foreign language, comprehensive exam, thesis; for doctorate, one foreign language, comprehensive exam, thesis/dissertation. *Entrance requirements:* For master's, PAEG or GRE, interview, minimum GPA of 3.0, letter of recommendation (2); for doctorate, PAEG or GRE, interview, master's degree, minimum GPA of 3.0, letter of recommendation (2). *Application deadline:* For fall admission, 2/1 for domestic and international students. Application fee: $17. *Expenses:* Tuition, state resident: full-time $1,808; part-time $113 per credit. Tuition, nonresident: full-time $5,248; part-time $328 per credit. Required fees: $72 per term. *Financial support:* Fellowships, research assistantships, teaching assistantships, Federal Work-Study, institutionally sponsored loans, and tuition waivers (partial) available. Financial award application deadline: 5/31. *Faculty research:* Poetry of Luis Palés Matos, short stories in Puerto Rico, language in the social process, 'Decima Popular", Anglicism. *Unit head:* Dr. Matilda Albert, Director, 787-764-0000 Ext. 2486, Fax: 787-763-5899.

The University of Texas at San Antonio, College of Liberal and Fine Arts, Department of Modern Languages and Literatures, San Antonio, TX 78249-0617. Offers Hispanic culture (MA); Spanish (MA). Part-time and evening/weekend programs available. *Faculty:* 5 full-time (3 women), 1 (woman) part-time/adjunct. *Students:* 5 full-time (4 women), 26 part-time (20 women); includes 28 minority (1 Asian American or Pacific Islander, 27 Hispanic Americans), 1 international. Average age 38. 17 applicants, 88% accepted, 14 enrolled. In 2007, 10 degrees awarded. *Degree requirements:* For master's, one foreign language, comprehensive exam, thesis optional. *Entrance requirements:* For master's, GRE, minimum GPA of 3.0, sample of written and spoken work. Additional exam requirements/recommendations for international students: Required—TOEFL (minimum score 500 paper-based; 173 computer-based). *Application deadline:* For fall admission, 7/1 for domestic students, 4/1 for international students; for spring admission, 11/1 for domestic students, 9/1 for international students. Applications are processed on a rolling basis. Application fee: $45 ($80 for international students). Electronic applications accepted. *Financial support:* In 2007–08, 1 teaching assistantship (averaging $7,676 per year) was awarded; career-related internships or fieldwork, Federal Work-Study, and institutionally sponsored loans also available. Support available to part-time students. Total annual research expenditures: $18,771. *Unit head:* Dr. Ritva M. Nummikoski, Chair, 210-458-4373, Fax: 210-458-5672, E-mail: mnummikoski@utsa.edu. *Application contact:* Dr. Jack Himelblau, Graduate Advisor, 210-458-5218, E-mail: jhimelblau@utsa.edu.

University of Victoria, Faculty of Graduate Studies, Faculty of Humanities, Department of Hispanic and Italian Studies, Victoria, BC V8W 2Y2, Canada. Offers Hispanic and Italian studies (MA); Hispanic studies (MA). *Faculty:* 4 full-time (1 woman). *Students:* 6 full-time, 1 international. Average age 25. 6 applicants, 33% accepted, 2 enrolled. *Degree requirements:* For master's, one foreign language, comprehensive exam, thesis (for some programs). *Entrance requirements:* For master's, undergraduate major in Hispanic studies, minimum B+ average. Additional exam requirements/recommendations for international students: Required—TOEFL (minimum score 575 paper-based; 233 computer-based), IELTS (minimum score 7). *Application deadline:* For fall admission, 4/1 priority date for domestic students, 12/15 priority date for international students. Applications are processed on a rolling basis. Application fee: $75 ($125 for international students). Electronic applications accepted. *Expenses:* Tuition, state resident: full-time $3,110. International tuition: $3,700 full-time. Tuition and fees vary according to program. *Financial support:* In 2007–08, 3 students received support, including teaching assistantships (averaging $5,000 per year); fellowships, scholarships/grants also available. Financial award application deadline: 2/15. *Faculty research:* Medieval/Renaissance Spanish and Italian literature, Golden Age literature, Latin American literature. Total annual research expenditures: $1,000. *Unit head:* Dr. Pablo Restrepo-Gautier, Chair, 250-721-7413, Fax: 250-721-6608, E-mail: spanit@uvic.ca. *Application contact:* Donna Fleming, Graduate Secretary, 250-721-7413, Fax: 250-721-6608, E-mail: spanit@uvic.ca.

University of Washington, Graduate School, College of Arts and Sciences, Department of Romance Languages and Literature, Division of Spanish and Portuguese Studies, Seattle, WA 98195. Offers Hispanic literary and cultural studies (MA). *Faculty:* 6 full-time (3 women), 2 part-time/adjunct (1 woman). *Students:* 16 full-time (10 women); includes 3 minority (all Hispanic Americans), 6 international. 25 applicants, 52% accepted, 9 enrolled. In 2007, 4 degrees awarded. *Degree requirements:* For master's, 2 foreign languages, thesis optional, exam. *Entrance requirements:* For master's, GRE General Test, minimum GPA of 3.0. Additional exam requirements/recommendations for international students: Required—TOEFL. *Application deadline:* For fall admission, 1/15 priority date for domestic students, 11/1 priority date for international students. Application fee: $50. Electronic applications accepted. *Financial support:* In 2007–08, 1 fellowship with full tuition reimbursement (averaging $4,677 per year), 16 teaching assistantships with full tuition reimbursements (averaging $13,059 per year) were awarded; Federal Work-Study, institutionally sponsored loans, scholarships/grants, health care benefits, and unspecified assistantships also available. Financial award application deadline: 1/15; financial award applicants required to submit FAFSA. *Faculty research:* Medieval through modern Spanish literature and film, Latin American literature, poetry and essay, pan-Hispanic ballad, Hispanic cultural studies, second language acquisition and applied linguistics. *Unit head:* Prof. Anthony Geist, Chair, 206-543-2020, Fax: 206-685-7054, E-mail: tgeist@u.washington.edu. *Application contact:* Suzanna Martinez, Academic Counselor, 206-543-2075, Fax: 206-685-7054, E-mail: spsadv@u.washington.edu.

Villanova University, Graduate School of Liberal Arts and Sciences, Department of Classical and Modern Languages and Literature, Villanova, PA 19085-1699. Offers classics (MA); Hispanic studies (MA). Part-time and evening/weekend programs available. *Faculty:* 4 full-time (3 women), 1 part-time/adjunct (0 women). *Students:* 15 full-time (9 women), 12 part-time (11 women); includes 12 minority (1 Asian American or Pacific Islander, 11 Hispanic Americans), 7 international. Average age 33. 16 applicants, 94% accepted. In 2007, 7 degrees awarded. *Degree requirements:* For master's, one foreign language, comprehensive exam, thesis optional. *Entrance requirements:* For master's, minimum GPA of 3.0. Additional exam requirements/recommendations for international students: Required—TOEFL. *Application deadline:* For fall admission, 8/1 for domestic and international students; for spring admission, 12/1 for domestic and international students. Applications are processed on a rolling basis. Application fee: $50. Electronic applications accepted. *Financial support:* Teaching assistantships with tuition reimbursements, Federal Work-Study and scholarships/grants available. Financial award applicants required to submit FAFSA. *Unit head:* Silvia Nagy-Zekmi, Chair, 610-519-7478.

Holocaust Studies

Clark University, Graduate School, Department of History, Program in Holocaust History, Worcester, MA 01610-1477. Offers PhD. *Students:* 29 applicants, 17% accepted, 5 enrolled. *Degree requirements:* For doctorate, thesis/dissertation. *Entrance requirements:* Additional exam requirements/recommendations for international students: Required—TOEFL. Application fee: $55. *Expenses:* Tuition: Full-time $32,600; part-time $1,019 per credit. Required fees: $30. Tuition and fees vary according to program. *Financial support:* In 2007–08, fellowships with full and partial tuition reimbursements (averaging $11,850 per year), research assistantships with full and partial tuition reimbursements (averaging $11,850 per year), teaching assistantships with full and partial tuition reimbursements (averaging $11,850 per year) were awarded; tuition waivers (partial) also available. *Faculty research:* Jewish persecution, children and survivors, Germany's role in the holocaust. *Unit head:* Deborah Dwork, Professor, 508-421-3745. *Application contact:* Tatyana Macaulay, Program Officer, 508-793-7764, Fax: 508-793-8827, E-mail: chgs@clarku.edu.

Drew University, Caspersen School of Graduate Studies, Program in Arts and Letters, Madison, NJ 07940-1493. Offers holocaust and genocide studies (Certificate); interdisciplinary studies (M Litt, D Litt). Part-time and evening/weekend programs available. Terminal master's awarded for partial completion of doctoral program. *Degree requirements:* For master's, thesis optional; for doctorate, thesis/dissertation. Expenses: Contact institution. *Faculty research:* Interdisciplinary studies across art, literature, music, philosophy, religion, and history.

Kean University, Nathan Weiss Graduate College, Program in Holocaust and Genocide Studies, Union, NJ 07083. Offers MA. Part-time and evening/weekend programs available. *Students:* 2 full-time (1 woman), 12 part-time (9 women); includes 1 minority (Hispanic American) Average age 34. 9 applicants, 100% accepted, 9 enrolled. *Degree requirements:* For master's, comprehensive exam, thesis. *Entrance requirements:* For master's, GRE General Test or MAT, minimum GPA of 3.0 or equivalent experience, 3 letters of recommendation, interview. *Application deadline:* For fall admission, 5/1 for domestic students; for spring admission, 11/1 for domestic students. Application fee: $60 ($150 for international students). Electronic applications accepted. *Expenses:* Tuition, state resident: full-time $9,384; part-time $391 per credit. Tuition, nonresident: full-time $12,720; part-time $530 per credit. Required fees: $2,382; $99 per credit. Part-time tuition and fees vary according to course load. *Financial support:* In 2007–08, 1 research assistantship with full tuition reimbursement (averaging $3,217 per year) was awarded; unspecified assistantships also available. *Unit head:* Dr. Bernard Weinstein, Program Coordinator, 908-737-0399, E-mail: bweinste@kean.edu. *Application contact:* Joanne Morris, Director of Graduate Admissions, 908-737-3355, Fax: 908-737-3354, E-mail: grad-adm@kean.edu.

Laura and Alvin Siegal College of Judaic Studies, Graduate Programs, Beachwood, OH 44122-7116. Offers humanities (MA), including Holocaust studies; religious education (MAJS), including Jewish education, Judaic studies. Part-time and evening/weekend programs available. Postbaccalaureate distance learning degree programs offered (no on-campus study). *Degree requirements:* For master's, one foreign language, thesis. *Entrance requirements:* For master's, interview.

The Richard Stockton College of New Jersey, School of Graduate and Continuing Education, Program in Holocaust and Genocide Studies, Pomona, NJ 08240-0195. Offers MA. Part-time programs available. *Faculty:* 2 full-time (1 woman), 4 part-time/adjunct (2 women). *Students:* 6 full-time (all women), 13 part-time (8 women); includes 4 minority (3 African Americans, 1 Asian American or Pacific Islander). Average age 32. 19 applicants, 411% accepted, 7 enrolled. In 2007, 9 degrees awarded. *Entrance requirements:* Additional exam requirements/recommendations for international students: Required—TOEFL. *Application deadline:* For fall admission, 8/15 for domestic and international students; for spring admission, 1/5 for domestic and international students. Applications are processed on a rolling basis. Application fee: $50. *Expenses:* Tuition, state resident: part-time $439 per credit. Required fees: $105 per credit. Tuition and fees vary according to course load and degree level. *Financial support:* Career-related internships or fieldwork and unspecified assistantships available. Financial award application deadline: 3/1; financial award applicants required to submit FAFSA. *Faculty research:* Women and the Holocaust, survivor perspectives, liberty and persecution. *Unit head:* Dr. Carol Rittner, Interim Director, 609-652-4553, Fax: 609-748-5541, E-mail: mahg@stockton.edu. *Application contact:* Alison Henry, Associate Director of Admissions, 609-652-4261, Fax: 609-626-5541, E-mail: admissions@stockton.edu.

Seton Hill University, Program in Genocide and Holocaust Studies, Greensburg, PA 15601. Offers Certificate. *Expenses:* Tuition: Full-time $17,955; part-time $665 per credit. Tuition and

Holocaust Studies

Seton Hill University (continued)

fees vary according to program. *Unit head:* Dr. Terrance DePasquale, Dean of Graduate and International Programs, 724-838-4256, E-mail: depasquale@setonhill.edu. *Application contact:* Christine Schaeffer, Director of Graduate and Adult Studies, 724-838-4283, Fax: 724-830-1891, E-mail: schaeffer@setonhill.edu.

West Chester University of Pennsylvania, Office of Graduate Studies and Extended Education, College of Arts and Sciences, Department of History, West Chester, PA 19383. Offers history (M Ed, MA); holocaust and genocide studies (MA, Certificate). Part-time and evening/weekend programs available. *Students:* 13 full-time (6 women), 27 part-time (12 women); includes 3 minority (1 African American, 2 Hispanic Americans). Average age 31. 35 applicants, 100% accepted, 14 enrolled. In 2007, 17 degrees awarded. *Degree requirements:* For master's, comprehensive exam, thesis optional. *Entrance requirements:* Additional exam requirements/recommendations for international students: Required—TOEFL (minimum score 550 paper-based; 213 computer-based; 80 iBT). *Application deadline:* For fall admission, 4/15 priority date for domestic students; for spring admission, 10/15 for domestic students. Applications are processed on a rolling basis. Application fee: $35. *Expenses:* Tuition, state resident: part-time $345 per credit. Tuition, nonresident: part-time $552 per credit. Tuition and fees vary according to course load. *Financial support:* In 2007–08, 4 research assistantships with full and partial tuition reimbursements (averaging $5,000 per year) were awarded; unspecified assistantships also available. Support available to part-time students. Financial award application deadline: 2/15. *Faculty research:* Oral histories, siege of Leningrad. *Unit head:* Dr. Thomas Legg, Chair, 610-436-2201, E-mail: tlegg@wcupa.edu. *Application contact:* Dr. Maria Boes, Graduate Coordinator, 610-436-2201, E-mail: mboes@wcupa.edu.

Jewish Studies

American Jewish University, Graduate School, Bel Air, CA 90077-1599. Offers MA Ed, MAJCS, MARS, MBA. Part-time and evening/weekend programs available. *Entrance requirements:* For master's, interview, minimum undergraduate GPA of 3.0. Additional exam requirements/recommendations for international students: Required—TOEFL.

American Jewish University, Graduate School, David Lieber School of Graduate Studies, Program in Jewish Communal Studies, Bel Air, CA 90077-1599. Offers MAJCS. *Degree requirements:* For master's, thesis. *Entrance requirements:* For master's, GMAT or GRE General Test, interview.

Baltimore Hebrew University, Peggy Meyerhoff Pearlstone School of Graduate Studies, Program in Jewish Communal Service, Baltimore, MD 21215-3996. Offers MAJCS. Part-time programs available. *Degree requirements:* For master's, one foreign language, thesis or alternative. *Entrance requirements:* Additional exam requirements/recommendations for international students: Required—TOEFL (minimum score 213 computer-based).

Baltimore Hebrew University, Peggy Meyerhoff Pearlstone School of Graduate Studies, Program in Jewish Education, Baltimore, MD 21215-3996. Offers MAJE. Part-time programs available. *Degree requirements:* For master's, one foreign language, thesis or alternative. *Entrance requirements:* For master's, minimum GPA of 3.0. Additional exam requirements/recommendations for international students: Required—TOEFL (minimum score 213 computer-based).

Baltimore Hebrew University, Peggy Meyerhoff Pearlstone School of Graduate Studies, Program in Jewish Studies, Baltimore, MD 21215-3996. Offers MAJS, PhD. Part-time programs available. Terminal master's awarded for partial completion of doctoral program. *Degree requirements:* For master's, one foreign language, comprehensive exam (for some programs), thesis or alternative; for doctorate, 3 foreign languages, comprehensive exam, thesis/dissertation. *Entrance requirements:* For master's, minimum GPA of 3.0; for doctorate, GRE General Test, minimum GPA of 3.5, master's thesis or equivalent. Additional exam requirements/recommendations for international students: Required—TOEFL.

Brandeis University, Graduate School of Arts and Sciences, Department of Near Eastern and Judaic Studies, Waltham, MA 02454-9110. Offers Near Eastern and Judaic studies (MA, PhD); Near Eastern and Judaic studies and sociology (PhD); Near Eastern and Judaic studies and women's studies (MA); teaching of Hebrew (MAT). Part-time programs available. *Faculty:* 25 full-time (11 women), 5 part-time/adjunct (3 women). *Students:* 44 full-time (21 women), 4 part-time; includes 1 minority (African American), 10 international. Average age 33. 62 applicants, 53% accepted, 15 enrolled. In 2007, 7 master's, 4 doctorates awarded. Terminal master's awarded for partial completion of doctoral program. *Degree requirements:* For master's, one foreign language, comprehensive exam, thesis or alternative; for doctorate, 3 foreign languages, comprehensive exam, thesis/dissertation. *Entrance requirements:* For master's and doctorate, GRE General Test (recommended), letters of recommendation, transcripts, statement of purpose. Additional exam requirements/recommendations for international students: Required—TOEFL (minimum score 600 paper-based; 250 computer-based; 100 iBT), IELTS (minimum score 7). *Application deadline:* For fall admission, 1/15 priority date for domestic and international students. Applications are processed on a rolling basis. Application fee: $55. Electronic applications accepted. *Financial support:* In 2007–08, 15 students received support, including 14 fellowships with full and partial tuition reimbursements available (averaging $17,000 per year), 1 teaching assistantship with partial tuition reimbursement available (averaging $3,000 per year); research assistantships with full and partial tuition reimbursements available, scholarships/grants, health care benefits, and tuition waivers (full and partial) also available. Support available to part-time students. Financial award application deadline: 4/15; financial award applicants required to submit CSS PROFILE or FAFSA. *Faculty research:* Ancient Near East and Bible, philosophy, history, modern Middle East, Islamic studies. *Unit head:* Dr. David Wright, Chair, 781-736-2954, Fax: 781-736-2070, E-mail: wright@brandeis.edu. *Application contact:* Dr. Eugene Sheppard, Graduate Advisor, 781-736-2965, Fax: 781-736-2070, E-mail: sheppard@brandeis.edu.

Brandeis University, Graduate School of Arts and Sciences, Hornstein: The Jewish Professional Leadership Program, Waltham, MA 02454-9110. Offers MA/MA, MBA/MA, MPP/MA. Part-time programs available. *Faculty:* 3 full-time (0 women), 5 part-time/adjunct (3 women). *Students:* 19 full-time (9 women), 1 (woman) part-time, 3 international. Average age 25. 17 applicants, 88% accepted, 10 enrolled. *Entrance requirements:* Additional exam requirements/recommendations for international students: Required—TOEFL (minimum score 600 paper-based; 250 computer-based; 100 iBT), IELTS (minimum score 7). *Application deadline:* For fall admission, 2/15 priority date for domestic and international students. Applications are processed on a rolling basis. Application fee: $55. Electronic applications accepted. *Financial support:* In 2007–08, 20 students received support, including 10 fellowships; research assistantships, career-related internships or fieldwork, institutionally sponsored loans, scholarships/grants, tuition waivers (full), and living expense stipends also available. Support available to part-time students. Financial award application deadline: 3/30; financial award applicants required to submit CSS PROFILE. *Faculty research:* Leadership, informal education, demography, Jewish identity, Israel-Diaspora relations. *Unit head:* Dr. Jonathan D. Sarna, Director, 781-736-2990, Fax: 781-736-2070, E-mail: hornstein@brandeis.edu. *Application contact:* Carol Hengerle, Program Administrator, 781-736-2990, Fax: 781-736-2070, E-mail: hornstein@brandeis.edu.

Brooklyn College of the City University of New York, Division of Graduate Studies, Department of Judaic Studies, Brooklyn, NY 11210-2889. Offers MA. Part-time and evening/weekend programs available. *Degree requirements:* For master's, 2 foreign languages, comprehensive exam, thesis or alternative, comprehensive exam or thesis. *Entrance requirements:* For master's, 18 upper-level credits in Judaic studies, interview, 2 letters of recommendation, interview. Additional exam requirements/recommendations for international students: Required—TOEFL. *Application deadline:* For fall admission, 3/1 priority date for domestic students, 2/1 priority date for international students; for spring admission, 11/1 priority date for domestic students, 10/1 priority date for international students. Applications are processed on a rolling basis. Application fee: $125. Electronic applications accepted. *Financial support:* Federal Work-Study, institutionally sponsored loans, and scholarships/grants available. Support available to part-time students. Financial award application deadline: 5/1; financial award applicants required to submit FAFSA. *Faculty research:* Biblical studies, Talmud and Midrash, modern Jewish history and thought. *Unit head:* Dr. Sara Reguer, Chairperson, 718-951-5229, Fax: 718-951-4703, E-mail: sreguer@brooklyn.cuny.edu. *Application contact:* Hernan Sierra, Graduate Admissions Coordinator, 718-951-4536, Fax: 718-951-4506, E-mail: grads@brooklyn.cuny.edu.

Brown University, Graduate School, Department of Religious Studies, Program in Judaic Studies, Providence, RI 02912. Offers AM, PhD. *Degree requirements:* For master's, one foreign language, thesis; for doctorate, 2 foreign languages, thesis/dissertation. *Entrance requirements:* For master's, GRE General Test, proficiency in Hebrew; for doctorate, GRE General Test, proficiency in Hebrew and Aramaic.

Chicago Theological Seminary, Graduate and Professional Programs, Chicago, IL 60637-1507. Offers clinical pastoral education (D Min); Jewish-Christian studies (PhD); pastoral counseling (D Min); preaching (D Min); religious studies (MA); spiritual leadership (D Min); theology (M Div); theology and the human sciences (PhD), including theology and society, theology and the personality sciences; M Div/MSW. *Accreditation:* ACIPE; ATS. Part-time programs available. *Faculty:* 13 full-time (5 women). *Students:* 83 full-time (40 women), 135 part-time (66 women); includes 54 minority (45 African Americans, 6 Asian Americans or Pacific Islanders, 3 Hispanic Americans), 33 international. 78 applicants, 94% accepted, 50 enrolled. In 2007, 15 first professional degrees, 8 master's, 22 doctorates awarded. *Degree requirements:* For master's, thesis; for doctorate, 2 foreign languages, comprehensive exam, thesis/dissertation; for M Div, thesis/dissertation. *Entrance requirements:* For doctorate, GRE General Test. Additional exam requirements/recommendations for international students: Required—TOEFL (minimum score 217 computer-based). *Application deadline:* For fall admission, 2/15 priority date for domestic and international students; for spring admission, 11/1 for domestic and international students. Application fee: $50. *Financial support:* In 2007–08, 103 students received support, including 12 fellowships (averaging $10,000 per year); institutionally sponsored loans, scholarships/grants, and tuition waivers (partial) also available. Support available to part-time students. Financial award application deadline: 3/1; financial award applicants required to submit FAFSA. *Faculty research:* Bible, culture and hermeneutics/theology, gender & sexuality/black faith and life/spirituality and psychology/practical theology. Total annual research expenditures: $150,000. *Unit head:* Dr. Theodore W. Jennings, Acting Dean, 773-752-5757, Fax: 773-752-1903, E-mail: tjennings@ctschicago.edu. *Application contact:* Rev. Lin Sanford Keppert, Director of Admissions, Recruitment and Financial Aid, E-mail: lkeppert@ctschicago.edu.

Columbia University, Graduate School of Arts and Sciences, Division of Humanities, Program in Jewish Studies, New York, NY 10027. Offers M Phil, MA, PhD. *Students:* 1 applicant, 0% accepted. *Degree requirements:* For master's, variable foreign language requirement; for doctorate, variable foreign language requirement, thesis/dissertation. *Entrance requirements:* For master's and doctorate, GRE General Test. Additional exam requirements/recommendations for international students: Required—TOEFL. Application fee: $90. *Expenses:* Tuition: Part-time $1,452 per credit. Required fees: $152 per term. One-time fee: $75 part-time. Full-time tuition and fees vary according to course level, course load, degree level and program. *Financial support:* Available to part-time students. Application deadline: 1/5; *Faculty research:* Jewish history, culture, and institutions; Hebrew, Yiddish, and Jewish languages and literatures; history of Jewish philosophy and religion. *Unit head:* Yosef Yerushalmi, Chair, 212-854-2581, Fax: 212-854-2590, E-mail: yhy1@columbia.edu.

Columbia University, Graduate School of Arts and Sciences, Interdepartmental Committee on Yiddish Studies, New York, NY 10027. Offers MA. Applicants must apply for admission to one of the participating departments: Germanic Languages, History, Middle East Languages and Cultures, Religion. *Entrance requirements:* For master's, high degree of proficiency in Yiddish. Application fee: $90. *Expenses:* Tuition: Part-time $1,452 per credit. Required fees: $152 per term. One-time fee: $75 part-time. Full-time tuition and fees vary according to course level, course load, degree level and program. *Unit head:* Michael F. Stanislawski, Chair, 212-854-2482, E-mail: mfs3@columbia.edu.

Columbia University, Graduate School of Arts and Sciences, Program in Liberal Studies, New York, NY 10027. Offers American studies (MA); East Asian studies (MA); human rights studies (MA); Islamic culture studies (MA); Jewish studies (MA); medieval studies (MA); modern European studies (MA); South Asian studies (MA). Part-time and evening/weekend programs available. *Faculty:* 5 part-time/adjunct (2 women). *Students:* 7 full-time (2 women), 75 part-time (51 women); includes 5 minority (1 African American, 3 Asian Americans or Pacific Islanders, 1 Hispanic American), 8 international. Average age 41. 39 applicants, 77% accepted. In 2007, 20 degrees awarded. *Degree requirements:* For master's, thesis. Application fee: $90. *Expenses:* Tuition: Part-time $1,452 per credit. Required fees: $152 per term. One-time fee: $75 part-time. Full-time tuition and fees vary according to course level, course load, degree level and program. *Unit head:* Kristin Balicki, Program Coordinator, 212-854-4932, Fax: 212-854-4912, E-mail: knb2110@columbia.edu.

Concordia University, School of Graduate Studies, Faculty of Arts and Science, Department of Religion, Program in Judaic Studies, Montréal, QC H3G 1M8, Canada. Offers MA. *Degree requirements:* For master's, one foreign language, comprehensive exam, thesis optional. *Entrance requirements:* For master's, Hebrew exam, honors degree in Judaic studies or equivalent. Additional exam requirements/recommendations for international students: Required—TOEFL. *Faculty research:* Jewish religious reflections and modern philosophy of religion, Judaism and modernity, Judaism in late antiquity.

Cornell University, Graduate School, Graduate Fields of Arts and Sciences, Field of Near Eastern Studies, Ithaca, NY 14853-0001. Offers ancient Near Eastern studies (MA, PhD); Arabic and Islamic studies (MA, PhD); biblical studies (MA, PhD); Hebrew and Judaic studies (MA, PhD). *Faculty:* 13 full-time. *Students:* 4 full-time (3 women), 2 international. Average age 26. 14 applicants, 14% accepted, 1 enrolled.Terminal master's awarded for partial completion of doctoral program. *Degree requirements:* For master's, one foreign language, thesis; for doctorate, 2 foreign languages, comprehensive exam, thesis/dissertation. *Entrance requirements:* For master's and doctorate, GRE General Test, 2 years of 1 Near Eastern language, 3 letters of recommendation, writing sample. Additional exam requirements/recommendations for international students: Required—TOEFL (minimum score 550 paper-based; 213 computer-based; 77 iBT). *Application deadline:* For fall admission, 2/1 for domestic students. Application fee: $70. Electronic applications accepted. *Financial support:* In 2007–08, 4 students received support, including 3 fellowships with full tuition reimbursements available, 1 teaching assistantship with full tuition reimbursement available; research assistantships with full tuition reimbursements available, institutionally sponsored loans, scholarships/grants, health care benefits, tuition waivers (full and partial), and unspecified assistantships also available. Financial award applicants required to submit FAFSA. *Faculty research:* Ancient Near East (including archeology), Hebrew and Judaic studies (including bible), early Christianity, Arabic and Islamic studies, modern Middle East. *Unit head:* Director of Graduate Studies, 607-255-1329, Fax: 607-255-6450. *Application contact:* Graduate Field Assistant, 607-255-1329, Fax: 607-255-6450, E-mail: neareastern@cornell.edu.

Emory University, Graduate School of Arts and Sciences, Program in Jewish Studies, Atlanta, GA 30322-1100. Offers MA. *Degree requirements:* For master's, one foreign language, thesis optional. *Entrance requirements:* For master's, GRE General Test, 2 years of course work in Hebrew or equivalent, writing sample. Additional exam requirements/recommendations for international students: Required—TOEFL. Electronic applications accepted. *Faculty research:* Medieval Jewish history and culture, Hebrew language and linguistics, Jewish law, Jewish ethics, Holocaust studies.

Graduate Theological Union, Graduate Programs, Berkeley, CA 94709-1212. Offers art and religion (MA, PhD); biblical languages (MA); biblical studies (Old and New Testament) (MA, PhD, Th D); Buddhist studies (MA); Christian spirituality (MA, PhD); cultural and historical studies of religions (MA, PhD); ethics and social theory (PhD); history (MA, PhD, Th D); homiletics (MA, PhD, Th D); interdisciplinary studies (PhD, Th D); Jewish studies (MA, PhD, Certificate); liturgical studies (MA, PhD, Th D); Near Eastern religions (PhD); Orthodox Christian studies (MA); Orthodox studies (Certificate); religion and psychology (MA, PhD); religion and society/ethics and social theory (MA); systematic and philosophical theology (MA, PhD, Th D); women's studies in religion (Certificate); MA/M Div. *Accreditation:* ATS. *Faculty:* 119 full-time (44 women), 34 part-time/adjunct (9 women). *Students:* 317 full-time (152 women), 35 part-time (19 women); includes 49 minority (15 African Americans, 2 American Indian/Alaska Native, 21 Asian Americans or Pacific Islanders, 11 Hispanic Americans), 74 international. Average age 38. 257 applicants, 59% accepted, 79 enrolled. In 2007, 45 master's, 22 doctorates awarded. Terminal master's awarded for partial completion of doctoral program. *Median time to degree:* Of those who began their doctoral program in fall 1999, 52% received their degree in 8 years or less. *Degree requirements:* For master's, one foreign language, thesis; for doctorate, one foreign language, comprehensive exam, thesis/dissertation. *Entrance requirements:* For master's, GRE General Test; for doctorate, GRE General Test, MA or M Div. Additional exam requirements/recommendations for international students: Required—TOEFL. *Application deadline:* For fall admission, 12/15 for domestic and international students; for winter admission, 2/15 for domestic and international students; for spring admission, 9/30 for domestic and international students. Application fee: $40. Electronic applications accepted. *Expenses:* Tuition: Full-time $13,310. Tuition and fees vary according to degree level and program. *Financial support:* In 2007–08, 122 students received support, including 109 fellowships (averaging $11,581 per year), 1 research assistantship (averaging $3,000 per year), 22 teaching assistantships (averaging $3,500 per year); Federal Work-Study, scholarships/grants, and tuition waivers (partial) also available. Support available to part-time students. Financial award application deadline: 2/1; financial award applicants required to submit FAFSA. *Unit head:* Dr. Arthur G. Holder, Dean, 510-649-2440, Fax: 510-649-1417, E-mail: aholder@gtu.edu. *Application contact:* Dr. Kathleen Kook, Assistant Dean for Admissions, 800-826-4488, Fax: 510-649-1730, E-mail: gtuadm@gtu.edu.

Gratz College, Graduate Programs, Program in Jewish Studies, Melrose Park, PA 19027. Offers classical studies (MA); Jewish studies (MA); modern studies (MA). Part-time programs available. *Degree requirements:* For master's, one foreign language, comprehensive exam, thesis optional.

Harvard University, Graduate School of Arts and Sciences, Department of Near Eastern Languages and Civilizations, Cambridge, MA 02138. Offers Akkadian and Sumerian (AM, PhD); Arabic (AM, PhD); Armenian (AM, PhD); biblical history (AM, PhD); Hebrew (AM, PhD); Indo-Muslim culture (AM, PhD); Iranian (AM, PhD); Jewish history and literature (AM, PhD); Persian (AM, PhD); Semitic philology (AM, PhD); Syro-Palestinian archaeology (AM, PhD); Turkish (AM, PhD). *Degree requirements:* For doctorate, variable foreign language requirement, thesis/dissertation, general exams. *Entrance requirements:* For master's, GRE General Test; for doctorate, GRE General Test, proficiency in a Near Eastern language. Additional exam requirements/recommendations for international students: Required—TOEFL. *Expenses:* Tuition: Full-time $31,456. Full-time tuition and fees vary according to program and student level.

Hebrew College, Cantor Educator Program, Newton Centre, MA 02459. Offers MJ Ed. *Entrance requirements:* For master's, GRE, interview. Additional exam requirements/recommendations for international students: Required—TOEFL.

Hebrew College, Program in Jewish Studies, Newton Centre, MA 02459. Offers Jewish liturgical music (Certificate); Jewish music education (Certificate); Jewish studies (MA). Part-time and evening/weekend programs available. Postbaccalaureate distance learning degree programs offered (minimal on-campus study). *Degree requirements:* For master's, one foreign language. *Entrance requirements:* For master's, GRE, interview. Additional exam requirements/recommendations for international students: Required—TOEFL.

Hebrew Union College–Jewish Institute of Religion, Edgar F. Magnin School of Graduate Studies, Los Angeles, CA 90007-3796. Offers MAJS, DHL, DHS. Part-time programs available. *Students:* 2 full-time (1 woman), 2 part-time, 1 international. Average age 39. In 2007, 3 degrees awarded. Terminal master's awarded for partial completion of doctoral program. *Degree requirements:* For master's, one foreign language, thesis, Hebrew; for doctorate, one foreign language, thesis/dissertation, Hebrew. *Entrance requirements:* For master's, GRE General Test, Hebrew Language Test, interview, minimum undergraduate GPA of 3.0; for doctorate, GRE General Test, Hebrew Language Test, interview, minimum graduate GPA of 3.0. Additional exam requirements/recommendations for international students: Required—TOEFL (minimum score 550 paper-based). *Application deadline:* For fall admission, 4/1 for domestic and international students. Applications are processed on a rolling basis. Application fee: $75. Electronic applications accepted. *Financial support:* In 2007–08, 2 students received support, including teaching assistantships (averaging $12,000 per year); fellowships, career-related internships or fieldwork, scholarships/grants, and unspecified assistantships also available. Financial award application deadline: 3/2; financial award applicants required to submit FAFSA. *Unit head:* Dr. Sharon Gillerman, Director, 213-749-3424 Ext. 4241, Fax: 213-747-6128, E-mail: sgillerman@huc.edu. *Application contact:* Deborah Shapiro Abelson, Director of Admissions and Recruitment, 213-749-3424, Fax: 213-747-6128, E-mail: admissions@huc.edu.

Hebrew Union College–Jewish Institute of Religion, Rabbinic School, Cincinnati, OH 45220-2488. Offers MAHL. *Accreditation:* ACIPE. *Degree requirements:* For MAHL, one foreign language, thesis/dissertation. *Entrance requirements:* GRE General Test, Hebrew competency exam, interview, psychological test. *Faculty research:* Comprehensive Aramaic lexicon, four-volume history (German Jews and modern times).

Hebrew Union College–Jewish Institute of Religion, School of Graduate Studies, Cincinnati, OH 45220-2488. Offers Bible and the ancient Near East (M Phil, MA, PhD); Hebrew letters (DHL); history of biblical interpretation (M Phil, MA, PhD); Jewish and Christian studies in the Greco-Roman period (M Phil, PhD); Jewish and cognate studies (M Phil); Judaic and cognate studies (MA, PhD); modern Jewish history (M Phil, MA, PhD); philosophy and Jewish religious thought (M Phil, MA, PhD); rabbinics (M Phil, MA, PhD). Part-time programs available. Terminal master's awarded for partial completion of doctoral program. *Degree requirements:* For master's, one foreign language, thesis optional; for doctorate, 3 foreign languages, comprehensive exam, thesis/dissertation. *Entrance requirements:* For master's and doctorate, GRE General Test, knowledge of Hebrew. Additional exam requirements/recommendations for international students: Required—TOEFL. *Faculty research:* Aramaic lexicon translations, German-Jewish history, neo-Babylonian texts.

Hebrew Union College–Jewish Institute of Religion, School of Graduate Studies, Program in Judaic Studies, New York, NY 10012-1186. Offers MAJS. Part-time programs available. *Degree requirements:* For master's, one foreign language, thesis. *Entrance requirements:* For master's, GRE, minimum 2 years of college-level Hebrew. *Faculty research:* Philosophy and theology, Bible, Hebrew, history and Rabbinics.

The Jewish Theological Seminary, The Graduate School, New York, NY 10027-4649. Offers ancient Judaism (MA, DHL, PhD); Bible (MA, DHL, PhD); Jewish education (PhD); Jewish history (MA, DHL, PhD); Jewish literature (MA, DHL, PhD); Jewish philosophy (MA, DHL, PhD); liturgy (MA, DHL, PhD); medieval Jewish studies (MA, DHL, PhD); Midrash (MA, DHL, PhD); modern Jewish studies (MA, DHL, PhD); Talmud and rabbinics (MA, DHL, PhD); MA/MSW. *Accreditation:* ACIPE. Part-time programs available. *Faculty:* 62 full-time (21 women), 69 part-time/adjunct (33 women). *Students:* 100 full-time (54 women), 26 part-time (12 women); includes 1 minority (Asian American or Pacific Islander), 1 international. Average age 38. 79 applicants, 78% accepted, 28 enrolled. In 2007, 40 master's, 3 doctorates awarded. Terminal master's awarded for partial completion of doctoral program. *Degree requirements:* For master's, one foreign language, comprehensive exam (for some programs), thesis (for some programs); for doctorate, 3 foreign languages, comprehensive exam (for some programs), thesis/dissertation. *Entrance requirements:* For master's, GRE or MAT, 3 letters of recommendation, writing sample; for doctorate, GRE or MAT, 3 letters of recommendation, writing research sample. Additional exam requirements/recommendations for international students: Required—TOEFL (minimum score 100 computer-based). *Application deadline:* For fall admission, 1/15 priority date for domestic students. Applications are processed on a rolling basis. Application fee: $50. *Expenses:* Tuition: Full-time $20,340; part-time $950 per credit. Required fees: $380 per semester. Full-time tuition and fees vary according to degree level, program and student level. *Financial support:* In 2007–08, 49 fellowships (averaging $13,681 per year) were awarded; career-related internships or fieldwork and tuition waivers (full and partial) also available. Support available to part-time students. Financial award application deadline: 3/1; financial award applicants required to submit FAFSA. *Unit head:* Dr. Stephen Garfinkel, Dean, 212-678-8024, Fax: 212-678-8947, E-mail: gradschool@jtsa.edu. *Application contact:* Alayne Birnhak, Director, Graduate School of Admissions, 212-678-8032, Fax: 212-280-6022, E-mail: albimhak@jtsa.edu.

See Close-Up on page 693.

The Jewish Theological Seminary, William Davidson Graduate School of Jewish Education, New York, NY 10027-4649. Offers MA, Ed D. Offered in conjunction with Rabbinical School; H. L. Miller Cantorial School and College of Jewish Music; Teacher's College, Columbia University; and Union Theological Seminary. Part-time programs available. Postbaccalaureate distance learning degree programs offered (minimal on-campus study). *Faculty:* 62 full-time (21 women), 69 part-time/adjunct (33 women). *Students:* 78 full-time (52 women), 28 part-time (13 women); includes 2 minority (both Hispanic Americans) Average age 29. 35 applicants, 80% accepted, 27 enrolled. In 2007, 43 master's awarded. *Degree requirements:* For master's, one foreign language, thesis optional; for doctorate, one foreign language, comprehensive exam, thesis/dissertation. *Entrance requirements:* For master's, GRE or MAT, 3 letters of recommendation; for doctorate, GRE or MAT, writing sample, 3 letters of recommendation. *Application deadline:* For fall admission, 7/15 priority date for domestic students. Applications are processed on a rolling basis. Application fee: $50. *Expenses:* Tuition: Full-time $20,340; part-time $950 per credit. Required fees: $380 per semester. Full-time tuition and fees vary according to degree level, program and student level. *Financial support:* In 2007–08, 88 fellowships (averaging $12,341 per year) were awarded; career-related internships or fieldwork also available. Financial award application deadline: 3/1. *Unit head:* Dr. Steven Brown, Dean, 212-678-8030, Fax: 212-749-9085, E-mail: stbrown@jtsa.edu. *Application contact:* Leora Skolnik, Admissions Coordinator, 212-678-8866, Fax: 212-749-9085, E-mail: leskolnik@jtsa.edu.

Jewish University of America, Graduate School, Graduate Research Division, Skokie, IL 60077-3248. Offers Bible (MHL, DHL); Hebrew (MHL, DHL); history (MHL, DHL); Jewish studies (MHL, DHL); philosophy (MHL, DHL); rabbinics (MHL, DHL). Part-time programs available. *Degree requirements:* For doctorate, one foreign language, thesis/dissertation; for MHL, thesis/dissertation optional. *Entrance requirements:* For MHL and doctorate, interview.

Laura and Alvin Siegal College of Judaic Studies, Graduate Programs, Program in Religious Education, Beachwood, OH 44122-7116. Offers Jewish education (MAJS); Judaic studies (MAJS). Part-time and evening/weekend programs available. Postbaccalaureate distance learning degree programs offered (minimal on-campus study). *Degree requirements:* For master's, one foreign language, thesis. *Entrance requirements:* For master's, interview.

McGill University, Faculty of Graduate and Postdoctoral Studies, Faculty of Arts, Department of Jewish Studies, Montréal, QC H3A 2T5, Canada. Offers MA. *Faculty:* 10 full-time (3 women), 3 part-time/adjunct (2 women). *Students:* 2 full-time (1 woman). 10 applicants, 20% accepted, 1 enrolled. In 2007, 2 degrees awarded.

New York University, Graduate School of Arts and Science, Program in Museum Studies, New York, NY 10012-1019. Offers museum studies (MA, Advanced Certificate), including Africana studies (MA), Hebrew and Judaic studies (MA), Latin American and Caribbean studies (MA), Near Eastern studies (MA). Part-time and evening/weekend programs available. *Faculty:* 4 full-time (1 woman), 6 part-time/adjunct. *Students:* 55 full-time (46 women), 26 part-time (23 women); includes 11 minority (1 American Indian/Alaska Native, 5 Asian Americans or Pacific Islanders, 5 Hispanic Americans), 19 international. Average age 28. 141 applicants, 66% accepted, 35 enrolled. In 2007, 25 master's awarded. *Entrance requirements:* For degree, master's or PhD. *Application deadline:* For fall admission, 2/1 for domestic students; for spring admission, 11/1 for domestic students. Application fee: $85. *Financial support:* Application deadline: 2/1. *Faculty research:* Modern and contemporary art, history of museums and exhibitions, conservation of cultural materials, museum anthropology, ethnography. *Unit head:* Bruce Altshuler, Director, 212-998-8080, Fax: 212-995-4185, E-mail: museum.studies@nyu.edu. *Application contact:* Tatiana Kamorina, Information Contact, 212-998-8080, Fax: 212-995-4185, E-mail: museum.studies@nyu.edu.

New York University, Graduate School of Arts and Science, Skirball Department of Hebrew and Judaic Studies, New York, NY 10012-1019. Offers Hebrew and Judaic studies (MA, PhD); Hebrew and Judaic studies/museum studies (MA). Part-time programs available. *Faculty:* 12 full-time (4 women), 11 part-time/adjunct. *Students:* 45 full-time (24 women), 38 part-time (25 women); includes 2 minority (1 Asian American or Pacific Islander, 1 Hispanic American), 23 international. Average age 31. 92 applicants, 34% accepted, 13 enrolled. In 2007, 10 master's, 4 doctorates awarded. Terminal master's awarded for partial completion of doctoral program. *Degree requirements:* For master's, 2 foreign languages, comprehensive exam, thesis optional; for doctorate, 4 foreign languages, comprehensive exam, thesis/dissertation. *Entrance requirements:* For master's, GRE General Test, minimum 2 years of undergraduate course work in Hebrew; for doctorate, GRE General Test. Additional exam requirements/recommendations for international students: Required—TOEFL. *Application deadline:* For fall admission, 12/18 priority date for domestic students. Application fee: $85. *Financial support:* Fellowships with tuition reimbursements, teaching assistantships with tuition reimbursements, Federal Work-Study and institutionally sponsored loans available. Financial award application deadline: 1/4; financial award applicants required to submit FAFSA. *Faculty research:* Post-biblical and Talmudic literature and history, mysticism, Bible and ancient Near East, medieval and modern Jewish history, medieval and modern Jewish philosophy. *Unit head:* Lawrence Schiffman, Chair, 212-98-8980, E-mail: gsas.hebrewjudaic@nyu.edu. *Application contact:* Shayne Figueroa, Graduate Secretary, 212-998-8980, Fax: 212-995-4178, E-mail: gsas.hebrewjudaic@nyu.edu.

Jewish Studies

New York University, Steinhardt School of Culture, Education and Human Development, Department of Humanities and Social Sciences in the Professions, Program in Education and Jewish Studies, New York, NY 10012-1019. Offers PhD. Part-time and evening/weekend programs available. *Faculty:* 1 full-time (0 women). *Students:* 8 full-time (6 women), 7 part-time (3 women); includes 1 minority (Hispanic American), 2 international. 9 applicants, 89% accepted, 4 enrolled. In 2007, 1 degree awarded. *Degree requirements:* For doctorate, thesis/dissertation. *Entrance requirements:* For doctorate, GRE General Test, interview. Additional exam requirements/recommendations for international students: Required—TOEFL. *Application deadline:* For fall admission, 12/15 priority date for domestic and international students; for spring admission, 11/1 for domestic and international students. Applications are processed on a rolling basis. Application fee: $50. *Financial support:* Fellowships with full and partial tuition reimbursements, teaching assistantships with partial tuition reimbursements, career-related internships or fieldwork, Federal Work-Study, institutionally sponsored loans, scholarships/grants, tuition waivers (partial), and unspecified assistantships available. Support available to part-time students. Financial award application deadline: 2/1; financial award applicants required to submit FAFSA. *Faculty research:* Jewish education, educational history, Judaic studies. *Unit head:* Dr. Harold Wechsler, Director, 212-992-9475, Fax: 212-995-4178. *Application contact:* 212-998-5023, Fax: 212-995-4328, E-mail: steinhardt.gradadmissions@nyu.edu.

St. Petersburg Theological Seminary, Graduate Programs, St. Petersburg, FL 33708. Offers Biblical studies (MA); counseling (MA); divinity (M Div); education (MA); Judaic studies (MA); ministry (MA, D Min); religious teacher (MA). Part-time and evening/weekend programs available. Postbaccalaureate distance learning degree programs offered (minimal on-campus study). *Faculty:* 8 full-time (4 women), 15 part-time/adjunct (6 women). *Students:* 32 full-time (16 women), 33 part-time (15 women). In 2007, 1 first professional degree, 5 master's, 1 doctorate awarded. *Degree requirements:* For master's, thesis; for doctorate, thesis/dissertation. *Entrance requirements:* For M Div and master's, Bachelor degree; for doctorate, Master degree. *Application deadline:* For fall admission, 8/15 priority date for domestic students; for winter admission, 12/31 priority date for domestic students. Application fee: $50. Electronic applications accepted. *Expenses:* Tuition: Part-time $140 per credit. Required fees: $15 per semester. Part-time tuition and fees vary according to program. *Financial support:* In 2007–08, 3 students received support. *Unit head:* Dr. George Pierce, Head of the Graduate Program, E-mail: gpierce3@tampabay.rr.com. *Application contact:* Dr. Amy Mormino, Registrar, 727-399-0276, Fax: 727-399-1324, E-mail: registrar@sptseminary.edu.

Seton Hall University, College of Arts and Sciences, Department of Jewish-Christian Studies, South Orange, NJ 07079-2697. Offers MA. Part-time and evening/weekend programs available. *Degree requirements:* For master's, one foreign language, thesis or alternative. Electronic applications accepted. *Faculty research:* Jewish-Christian issues, biblical studies.

See Close-Up on page 699.

Southern Evangelical Seminary, Veritas Graduate School of Apologetics and Counter-Cult Ministry, Matthews, NC 28105. Offers apologetics (MA, D Min, PhD, Certificate); Islamic studies (MA); Jewish studies (MA); philosophy (MA); religion (MA). *Accreditation:* ATS.Part-time and evening/weekend programs available. Postbaccalaureate distance learning degree programs offered (minimal on-campus study). In 2007, 18 master's, 2 doctorates awarded. *Degree requirements:* For master's, thesis optional; for doctorate, comprehensive exam (for some programs), thesis/dissertation. *Entrance requirements:* Additional exam requirements/recommendations for international students: Required—TOEFL (minimum score 600 paper-based; 250 computer-based). *Application deadline:* For fall admission, 8/5 priority date for domestic and international students; for winter admission, 12/15 priority date for domestic and international students; for spring admission, 1/15 priority date for domestic and international students. Applications are processed on a rolling basis. Application fee: $25. *Financial support:* Scholarships/grants available. *Unit head:* Dr. Thomas A. Howe, Director, Apologetics Program, 704-847-5600 Ext. 209, Fax: 704-845-1747, E-mail: thowe@ses.edu.

Spertus Institute of Jewish Studies, Graduate Programs, Program in Jewish Studies, Chicago, IL 60605-1901. Offers MAJS, MSJE, MSJS, DJS, DSJS. Part-time and evening/weekend programs available. Postbaccalaureate distance learning degree programs offered (minimal on-campus study). *Degree requirements:* For master's, one foreign language, thesis (for some programs); for doctorate, one foreign language, thesis/dissertation. *Entrance requirements:* For master's, interview, BAJS (MAJS); for doctorate, MAJS.

Telshe Yeshiva–Chicago, Graduate Program, Chicago, IL 60625-5598. Offers Second Talmudic Degree. *Accreditation:* AARTS.

Touro College, School of Jewish Studies, New York, NY 10010. Offers MA. Part-time programs available. *Degree requirements:* For master's, one foreign language, thesis. *Entrance requirements:* For master's, previous course work in Jewish studies, proficiency in Hebrew. *Faculty research:* Medieval and modern Jewish history, Jewish philosophy, holocaust studies, Jewish education.

University of California, Berkeley, Graduate Division, Program in Jewish Studies, Berkeley, CA 94720-1500. Offers PhD. *Entrance requirements:* For doctorate, GRE General Test, 3 letters of recommendation. *Application deadline:* For fall admission, 12/15 for domestic students. Application fee: $70 ($90 for international students). *Unit head:* Robert Alter, Chair, 510-643-2995, E-mail: altcos@berkeley.edu. *Application contact:* Sandra J. B. Richmond, Program Analyst, 510-643-2995, Fax: 510-643-3927, E-mail: info@jewishstudies.berkeley.edu.

University of California, San Diego, Office of Graduate Studies, Department of History, La Jolla, CA 92093. Offers history (MA, PhD); Judaic studies (MA); science studies (PhD). *Degree requirements:* For doctorate, thesis/dissertation. *Entrance requirements:* For master's and doctorate, GRE General Test. Electronic applications accepted.

University of Connecticut, Graduate School, College of Liberal Arts and Sciences, Field of International Studies, Program in Judaic Studies, Storrs, CT 06269. Offers MA. *Faculty:* 38 full-time (21 women). *Students:* 2 full-time (1 woman), 3 part-time (all women). Average age 33. 6 applicants, 50% accepted, 3 enrolled. In 2007, 3 degrees awarded. *Entrance requirements:* Additional exam requirements/recommendations for international students: Required—TOEFL (minimum score 550 paper-based; 213 computer-based). *Application deadline:* For fall admission, 2/1 priority date for domestic and international students; for spring admission, 11/1 for domestic students, 10/1 for international students. Applications are processed on a rolling basis. Electronic applications accepted. *Expenses:* Tuition, state resident: part-time $469 per credit hour. Tuition, nonresident: part-time $1,218 per credit hour. *Financial support:* In 2007–08, 2 research assistantships were awarded; teaching assistantships, Federal Work-Study, scholarships/grants, health care benefits, and unspecified assistantships also available. Financial award application deadline: 2/1. *Unit head:* Arnold Dashefsky, Director, 860-486-4289, Fax: 860-486-6332, E-mail: arnold.dashefsky@uconn.edu.

University of Maryland, College Park, Graduate Studies, College of Arts and Humanities, Program in Jewish Studies, College Park, MD 20742. Offers MA. *Faculty:* 3 full-time (all women), 3 part-time/adjunct (1 woman). *Students:* 5 applicants, 40% accepted, 2 enrolled. *Degree requirements:* For master's, thesis or 2 major research papers. *Entrance requirements:* For master's, GRE General Test, 3 letters of recommendation, writing sample. Additional exam requirements/recommendations for international students: Required—TOEFL. *Application deadline:* For fall admission, 12/15 for domestic students, 2/1 for international students. Application fee: $60. *Financial support:* In 2007–08, 2 teaching assistantships (averaging $16,025 per year) were awarded; fellowships also available. *Application contact:* Dean of Graduate Studies, 301-405-0358, Fax: 301-314-9305.

University of Michigan, Jean and Samuel Frankel Center for Judaic Studies, Ann Arbor, MI 48109. Offers MA, Graduate Certificate. Part-time programs available. *Faculty:* 25 full-time (10 women). *Students:* 8 full-time (7 women), 1 (woman) part-time, 1 international. Average age 30. 8 applicants, 75% accepted, 2 enrolled. *Degree requirements:* For master's, one foreign language, thesis, foreign language must be either Hebrew or Yiddish. *Entrance requirements:* For master's, GRE General Test; for Graduate Certificate, Admission to a U-M doctoral program. Additional exam requirements/recommendations for international students: Required—TOEFL (minimum score 540 paper-based; 220 computer-based). *Application deadline:* For fall admission, 1/10 for domestic and international students; for winter admission, 9/1 for domestic and international students. Application fee: $60 ($75 for international students). Electronic applications accepted. *Financial support:* In 2007–08, 14 fellowships were awarded. *Faculty research:* Jewish history (antique to modern); Jewish literature; Yiddish language and literature; Jewish cultural studies; Jewish political and social studies. *Unit head:* Prof. Deborah Dash Moore, Director, 734-763-9047, Fax: 734-936-2186, E-mail: ddmoore@umich.edu. *Application contact:* Tracy Ann Darnell, Student/Fellow Coordinator, 734-615-6097, Fax: 734-936-2186, E-mail: tdarnell@umich.edu.

The University of Montana, Graduate School, School of Fine Arts, Department of Art, Missoula, MT 59812-0002. Offers fine arts (MA, MFA), including art (MA), art history (MA), ceramics (MFA), integrated arts and education (MA), media arts (MFA), painting and drawing (MFA), photography (MFA), printmaking (MFA), sculpture (MFA). *Accreditation:* NASAD (one or more programs are accredited). *Degree requirements:* For master's, thesis exhibit. *Entrance requirements:* For master's, GRE General Test, portfolio.

University of St. Michael's College, Faculty of Theology, Toronto, ON M5S 1J4, Canada. Offers Catholic leadership (MA); eastern Christian studies (Certificate, Diploma); religious education (Diploma); theological studies (Diploma); theology (M Div, MA, MRE, MTS, D Min, PhD, Th D); theology and ecology (Certificate); theology and Jewish studies (MA). *Accreditation:* ATS (one or more programs are accredited). Part-time programs available. *Faculty:* 10 full-time (3 women), 13 part-time/adjunct (5 women). *Students:* 111 full-time (35 women), 101 part-time (64 women); includes 7 African Americans, 19 Asian Americans or Pacific Islanders, 21 international. Average age 40. 90 applicants, 79% accepted, 51 enrolled. In 2007, 11 first professional degrees, 6 master's, 6 doctorates, 14 other advanced degrees awarded. *Degree requirements:* For master's, thesis (for some programs), 1 foreign language (MA), 2 foreign languages (Th M); for doctorate, 3 foreign languages, comprehensive exam, thesis/dissertation; for M Div, thesis/dissertation optional; for other advanced degree, thesis optional. *Entrance requirements:* For M Div and other advanced degree, minimum GPA of 2.7; for master's, M Div or BA, course work in an ancient or modern language, minimum GPA of 3.3; for doctorate, MA in theology, Th M, or M Div with thesis, minimum GPA of 3.7. Additional exam requirements/recommendations for international students: Required—TOEFL (minimum score 600 paper-based; 250 computer-based). *Application deadline:* For fall admission, 1/15 for domestic and international students. Applications are processed on a rolling basis. Application fee: $25 Canadian dollars. Electronic applications accepted. *Financial support:* In 2007–08, 58 students received support, including fellowships with partial tuition reimbursements available (averaging $2,500 per year), research assistantships with partial tuition reimbursements available (averaging $2,500 per year), 9 teaching assistantships with partial tuition reimbursements available (averaging $2,400 per year); scholarships/grants, tuition waivers (partial), and bursaries also available. Financial award application deadline: 2/1. *Faculty research:* Patristics, eastern Christianity, ecology and theology, ecumenism, Jewish Christian studies. *Unit head:* Dr. Anne Anderson, CSJ, Dean, 416-926-7265, Fax: 416-926-7294, E-mail: anne.anderson@utoronto.ca. *Application contact:* Mehra Taylor.

University of Wisconsin–Madison, Graduate School, College of Letters and Science, Department of Hebrew and Semitic Studies, Madison, WI 53706-1380. Offers MA, PhD. Terminal master's awarded for partial completion of doctoral program. *Degree requirements:* For master's, 2 foreign languages; for doctorate, thesis/dissertation. *Entrance requirements:* For master's and doctorate, GRE. Electronic applications accepted. *Faculty research:* Biblical language and literature, Northwest Semitic languages.

University of Wisconsin–Milwaukee, Graduate School, College of Letters and Sciences, Interdepartmental Program in Foreign Language and Literature, Milwaukee, WI 53201-0413. Offers classics and Hebrew studies (MAFLL); comparative literature (MAFLL); French and Italian (MAFLL); German (MAFLL); Slavic studies (MAFLL); Spanish (MAFLL). Part-time programs available. *Faculty:* 39 full-time (17 women). *Students:* 29 full-time (21 women), 31 part-time (23 women); includes 8 minority (1 Asian American or Pacific Islander, 7 Hispanic Americans), 22 international. 54 applicants, 67% accepted, 26 enrolled. In 2007, 34 degrees awarded. *Degree requirements:* For master's, 2 foreign languages, thesis or alternative. *Application deadline:* For fall admission, 1/1 priority date for domestic students; for spring admission, 9/1 for domestic students. Applications are processed on a rolling basis. Application fee: $45 ($75 for international students). *Expenses:* Tuition, state resident: part-time $530 per credit. Tuition, nonresident: part-time $1,428 per credit. Required fees: $19 per credit. $229 per term. Tuition and fees vary according to course load and program. *Financial support:* In 2007–08, 44 teaching assistantships were awarded; fellowships, research assistantships, career-related internships or fieldwork and unspecified assistantships also available. Support available to part-time students. Financial award application deadline: 4/15. *Unit head:* Gabrielle Verdier, Representative, 414-229-3346, Fax: 414-229-2741, E-mail: verdier@uwm.edu.

Washington University in St. Louis, Graduate School of Arts and Sciences, Department of History, Program in Jewish, Islamic, and Near Eastern Studies, St. Louis, MO 63130-4899. Offers Islamic and Near Eastern studies (MA); Jewish studies (MA). *Degree requirements:* For master's, one foreign language, thesis (for some programs). *Entrance requirements:* For master's, GRE General Test. Electronic applications accepted.

Yeshiva University, Bernard Revel Graduate School of Jewish Studies, New York, NY 10033-3201. Offers MA, PhD. Part-time programs available. Terminal master's awarded for partial completion of doctoral program. *Degree requirements:* For master's, comprehensive exam; for doctorate, 2 foreign languages, comprehensive exam, thesis/dissertation. *Entrance requirements:* For master's and doctorate, GRE General Test (recommended), reading knowledge of Hebrew, minimum GPA of 3.0. *Faculty research:* Bible, Jewish history, Jewish philosophy and mysticism, Talmud, Semitic languages.

Latin American Studies

American University, College of Arts and Sciences, Department of Language and Foreign Studies, Program in Spanish: Latin American Studies, Washington, DC 20016-8001. Offers Spanish: Latin American studies (MA); translation (Certificate). Part-time and evening/weekend programs available. *Students:* 17 full-time (14 women), 13 part-time (9 women); includes 8 minority (3 African Americans, 1 Asian American or Pacific Islander, 4 Hispanic Americans), 1 international. Average age 28. In 2007, 8 master's, 14 other advanced degrees awarded. *Degree requirements:* For master's, one foreign language, comprehensive exam, thesis or alternative, research requirement. *Entrance requirements:* For master's, GRE, bachelor's degree in language or equivalent, essay in Spanish; 3.2 GPA; statement of purpose; for Certificate, Bachelor's degree in Spanish or BA any field and Spanish proficiency. *Application deadline:* For fall admission, 2/1 for domestic students; for spring admission, 10/1 for domestic students. Application fee: $50. *Expenses:* Tuition: Full-time $19,998; part-time $1,111 per credit hour. Required fees: $380. Tuition and fees vary according to program. *Financial support:* Fellowships with full and partial tuition reimbursements, career-related internships or fieldwork, Federal Work-Study, and institutionally sponsored loans available. Financial award application deadline: 2/1. *Faculty research:* Latin American culture; literature, and history; computer-aided instruction.

Arizona State University, Graduate College, College of Liberal Arts and Sciences, Division of Humanities, Department of History, Tempe, AZ 85287. Offers Asian history (MA, PhD); British history (MA, PhD); European history (MA, PhD); Latin American studies (MA, PhD); public history (MA); U.S. history (PhD); U.S. western history (MA). *Degree requirements:* For master's, thesis or alternative; for doctorate, 2 foreign languages, thesis/dissertation. *Entrance requirements:* For master's and doctorate, GRE.

Boricua College, Program in Latin American and Caribbean Studies (Brooklyn Campus), New York, NY 10032-1560. Offers MA. Evening/weekend programs available. *Degree requirements:* For master's, thesis, 40 credits. *Entrance requirements:* For master's, interview by the faculty, essay. Additional exam requirements/recommendations for international students: Required—Boricua College's exam. *Application deadline:* Applications are processed on a rolling basis. Application fee: $100. *Financial support:* Career-related internships or fieldwork and Federal Work-Study available. Financial award applicants required to submit FAFSA. *Unit head:* Dr. Maria Montes, Chair, 718-782-2200 Ext. 222.

Boricua College, Program in Latin American and Caribbean Studies (Manhattan Campus), New York, NY 10032-1560. Offers MA. Evening/weekend programs available. *Degree requirements:* For master's, thesis, 40 credits. *Entrance requirements:* For master's, interview by the faculty, essay. Additional exam requirements/recommendations for international students: Required—Boricua College's exam. *Application deadline:* Applications are processed on a rolling basis. Application fee: $100. *Financial support:* Career-related internships or fieldwork and Federal Work-Study available. Financial award applicants required to submit FAFSA. *Unit head:* Dr. Shivaji Sengupta, Head, 212-694-1000 Ext. 617, E-mail: ssengupta@boricuacollege.edu. *Application contact:* Abraham Cruz, Director of Student Services (Manhattan), 212-694-1000 Ext. 650, Fax: 212-694-1015, E-mail: acruz@boricuacollege.edu.

Brown University, Graduate School, Center for Portuguese and Brazilian Studies, Providence, RI 02912. Offers Brazilian studies (AM); Luso-Brazilian studies (PhD); Portuguese studies and bilingual education (AM). *Degree requirements:* For doctorate, thesis/dissertation.

California State University, Los Angeles, Graduate Studies, College of Natural and Social Sciences, Program in Latin American Studies, Los Angeles, CA 90032-8530. Offers MA. Part-time and evening/weekend programs available. *Faculty:* 1 (woman) full-time. *Students:* 13 full-time (9 women), 19 part-time (10 women); includes 19 minority (all Hispanic Americans), 4 international. Average age 31. In 2007, 6 degrees awarded. *Degree requirements:* For master's, one foreign language, comprehensive exam, thesis. *Entrance requirements:* For master's, minimum GPA of 2.5. Additional exam requirements/recommendations for international students: Required—TOEFL. *Application deadline:* For fall admission, 6/30 for domestic students; for spring admission, 2/1 for domestic students. Applications are processed on a rolling basis. Application fee: $55. *Financial support:* Federal Work-Study available. Support available to part-time students. Financial award application deadline: 3/1. *Faculty research:* Central America, Cuba, Third World development, labor history, redemocratization. *Unit head:* Dr. Marjorie W. Bray, Coordinator, 323-343-2180, Fax: 323-343-5485, E-mail: mbray@calstatela.edu.

Centro de Estudios Avanzados de Puerto Rico y el Caribe, Graduate Program in Puerto Rican and Caribbean Studies, Old San Juan, PR 00902-3970. Offers Puerto Rican and Caribbean history (MA, PhD); Puerto Rican and Caribbean literature (MA, PhD); Puerto Rican studies (MA). Part-time and evening/weekend programs available. *Degree requirements:* For master's, comprehensive exam, thesis; for doctorate, 2 foreign languages, comprehensive exam, thesis/dissertation. *Entrance requirements:* For master's and doctorate, interview. *Faculty research:* Literature, history, art, folklore, and culture of Puerto Rico and Caribbean countries.

Columbia University, School of International and Public Affairs, Institute of Latin American Studies, New York, NY 10027. Offers Certificate. Students must also be enrolled in a separate graduate degree program at Columbia University. *Application deadline:* For fall admission, 1/4 priority date for domestic students; for spring admission, 10/1 priority date for domestic students. Application fee: $85. Electronic applications accepted. *Expenses:* Tuition: Part-time $1,452 per credit. Required fees: $152 per term. One-time fee: $75 part-time. Full-time tuition and fees vary according to course level, course load, degree level and program. *Financial support:* Application deadline: 1/15. *Faculty research:* Rights vs. efficiency in a globalized era, citizenship and governance in Latin America and Western Europe. *Application contact:* Matt Clemons, Director of Admissions and Financial Aid, 212-854-6216, Fax: 212-854-3010, E-mail: mc2793@columbia.edu.

Cornell University, Graduate School, Graduate Fields of Arts and Sciences, Field of Archaeology, Ithaca, NY 14853-0001. Offers environmental archaeology (MA); historical archaeology (MA); Latin American archaeology (MA); medieval archaeology (MA); Mediterranean and Near Eastern archaeology (MA); Stone Age archaeology (MA). *Faculty:* 14 full-time (3 women). *Students:* 2 full-time (both women). Average age 26. 19 applicants, 5% accepted, 1 enrolled. In 2007, 2 degrees awarded. *Degree requirements:* For master's, one foreign language, thesis. *Entrance requirements:* For master's, GRE General Test, 3 letters of recommendation, sample of written work. Additional exam requirements/recommendations for international students: Required—TOEFL (minimum score 550 paper-based; 213 computer-based; 77 iBT). *Application deadline:* For fall admission, 1/15 for domestic students. Application fee: $70. Electronic applications accepted. *Financial support:* In 2007–08, 2 students received support, including 2 teaching assistantships with full tuition reimbursements available; fellowships with full tuition reimbursements available, research assistantships with full tuition reimbursements available, institutionally sponsored loans, scholarships/grants, health care benefits, tuition waivers (full and partial), and unspecified assistantships also available. Financial award applicants required to submit FAFSA. *Faculty research:* Anatolia, Lydia, Sardis, classical and Hellenistic Greece; science in archaeology; North American Indians; Stone Age Africa; Maya trade. *Unit head:* Director of Graduate Studies, 607-255-6768, E-mail: blj7@cornell.edu. *Application contact:* Graduate Field Assistant, 607-255-6768, E-mail: dsd6@cornell.edu.

Cornell University, Graduate School, Graduate Fields of Arts and Sciences, Field of History, Ithaca, NY 14853-0001. Offers African history (MA, PhD); American history (MA, PhD); ancient history (MA, PhD); early modern European history (MA, PhD); English history (MA, PhD); French history (MA, PhD); German history (MA, PhD); history of science (MA, PhD); Latin American history (MA, PhD); medieval Chinese history (MA, PhD); medieval history (MA, PhD); modern Chinese history (MA, PhD); modern European history (MA, PhD); modern Japanese history (MA, PhD); premodern Islamic history (MA, PhD); premodern Japanese history (MA, PhD); Renaissance history (MA, PhD); Russian history (MA, PhD); Southeast Asian history (MA, PhD). *Faculty:* 56 full-time (14 women). *Students:* 63 full-time (29 women); includes 11 minority (6 African Americans, 2 Asian Americans or Pacific Islanders, 3 Hispanic Americans), 20 international. Average age 31. 201 applicants, 6% accepted, 10 enrolled. In 2007, 11 master's, 11 doctorates awarded. Terminal master's awarded for partial completion of doctoral program. *Degree requirements:* For master's, thesis; for doctorate, 2 foreign languages, comprehensive exam, thesis/dissertation, 1 year of teaching experience. *Entrance requirements:* For master's and doctorate, GRE General Test, writing sample, 3 letters of recommendation. Additional exam requirements/recommendations for international students: Required—TOEFL (minimum score 550 paper-based; 213 computer-based; 77 iBT). *Application deadline:* For fall admission, 1/15 for domestic students. Application fee: $70. Electronic applications accepted. *Financial support:* In 2007–08, 54 students received support, including 26 fellowships with full tuition reimbursements available, 28 teaching assistantships with full tuition reimbursements available; research assistantships with full tuition reimbursements available, institutionally sponsored loans, scholarships/grants, health care benefits, tuition waivers (full and partial), and unspecified assistantships also available. Financial award applicants required to submit FAFSA. *Unit head:* Director of Graduate Studies, 607-255-6738, Fax: 607-255-0469. *Application contact:* Graduate Field Assistant, 607-255-6738, Fax: 607-255-0469, E-mail: history_grad_info@cornell.edu.

Duke University, Graduate School, Center for Latin American and Caribbean Studies, Durham, NC 27708-0586. Offers Certificate. *Faculty:* 30 full-time, 15 part-time/adjunct. *Application deadline:* For fall admission, 12/31 for domestic students. Application fee: $75. *Financial support:* Fellowships, scholarships/grants available. Financial award application deadline: 12/31. *Faculty research:* Political economy of development, social transformations in Central America, Colonial literature, history and fiscal policies, comparative Spanish-American literature and poetry. *Unit head:* Diane Nelson, Director, 919-684-2069, Fax: 919-681-8483, E-mail: dmnelson@duke.edu.

Duke University, Graduate School, Department of History, Durham, NC 27708. Offers history (AM, PhD); Latin American studies (PhD); JD/AM; MD/PhD. *Faculty:* 37 full-time. *Students:* 63 full-time (34 women); includes 10 minority (8 African Americans, 1 American Indian/Alaska Native, 1 Asian American or Pacific Islander), 15 international. 204 applicants, 11% accepted, 10 enrolled. In 2007, 10 master's, 10 doctorates awarded. *Degree requirements:* For doctorate, 2 foreign languages, thesis/dissertation. *Entrance requirements:* For doctorate, GRE General Test. Additional exam requirements/recommendations for international students: Required—TOEFL (minimum score 550 paper-based; 213 computer-based; 83 iBT), IELTS (minimum score 7). *Application deadline:* For fall admission, 12/15 priority date for domestic and international students. Application fee: $75. Electronic applications accepted. *Financial support:* Fellowships, research assistantships, teaching assistantships, Federal Work-Study available. Financial award application deadline: 12/31. *Unit head:* John Thompson, Director of Graduate Studies, 919-681-5746, Fax: 919-681-7670, E-mail: rmennis@duke.edu.

Florida International University, College of Arts and Sciences, Latin American and Caribbean Studies Center, Miami, FL 33199. Offers MA. *Faculty:* 1 full-time (0 women). *Students:* 20 full-time (12 women), 13 part-time (6 women); includes 15 minority (1 African American, 1 Asian American or Pacific Islander, 13 Hispanic Americans), 3 international. Average age 30. 31 applicants, 68% accepted, 10 enrolled. In 2007, 22 degrees awarded. *Degree requirements:* For master's, one foreign language, thesis or alternative. *Entrance requirements:* For master's, GRE General Test, minimum GPA of 3.0, 3 letters of recommendation. Additional exam requirements/recommendations for international students: Required—TOEFL (minimum score 550 paper-based; 213 computer-based). *Application deadline:* For fall admission, 2/1 for domestic and international students; for spring admission, 10/1 for domestic students, 9/1 for international students. Applications are processed on a rolling basis. Application fee: $30. Electronic applications accepted. *Expenses:* Tuition, state resident: full-time $6,106. Tuition, nonresident: full-time $15,528. Required fees: $284. *Financial support:* Teaching assistantships available. *Unit head:* Dr. Cristina Eguizabal, Director, 305-348-2894, Fax: 305-348-3593, E-mail: cristina.eguizabal@fiu.edu.

Fordham University, Graduate School of Arts and Sciences, Program in Latin American and Latino Studies, New York, NY 10458. Offers MA, Certificate. *Students:* 11 full-time (all women); all minorities (all Hispanic Americans) 1 applicant, 100% accepted, 1 enrolled. In 2007, 1 degree awarded. *Entrance requirements:* Additional exam requirements/recommendations for international students: Required—TOEFL (minimum score 650 paper-based; 280 computer-based). *Application deadline:* For fall admission, 1/4 priority date for domestic students; for spring admission, 11/1 for domestic students. Application fee: $65. Electronic applications accepted. *Expenses:* Tuition: Full-time $23,880; part-time $995 per credit. *Financial support:* Application deadline: 1/4; *Faculty research:* Latinos and Hollywood, Puerto Rican women and labor history, education and the state in El Salvador, Avant-garde literature in 20th century Latin America. *Unit head:* Dr. Arnaldo Cruz-Malave, Director, 718-817-6571, E-mail: lalsi@fordham.edu. *Application contact:* Charlene Dundie, Director of Graduate Admissions, 718-817-4420, Fax: 718-817-3566, E-mail: dundie@fordham.edu.

Georgetown University, Graduate School of Arts and Sciences, Center for Latin American Studies, Washington, DC 20057-1026. Offers MA, MA/PhD. *Degree requirements:* For master's, one foreign language, comprehensive exam, thesis optional. *Entrance requirements:* For master's, GRE General Test, minimum B average. Additional exam requirements/recommendations for international students: Required—TOEFL.

The George Washington University, Elliott School of International Affairs, Program in Latin American and Hemispheric Studies, Washington, DC 20052. Offers MA, JD/MA, MBA/MA. Part-time and evening/weekend programs available. *Degree requirements:* For master's, one foreign language, capstone project. *Entrance requirements:* For master's, GRE General Test, 2 years (or the equivalent) of Spanish or Portuguese. Additional exam requirements/recommendations for international students: Required—TOEFL. Electronic applications accepted. *Faculty research:* Democracy and change in Andean nations, rural economic development, peasant cooperatives and political change.

Georgia State University, College of Arts and Sciences, Department of History, Atlanta, GA 30303-3083. Offers heritage preservation (MHP, Certificate); history (MA, PhD); Latin American studies (Certificate). Part-time and evening/weekend programs available. *Faculty:* 30 full-time (10 women), 7 part-time/adjunct (2 women). *Students:* 37 full-time (16 women), 86 part-time (33 women); includes 14 minority (12 African Americans, 1 Asian American or Pacific Islander, 1 Hispanic American), 5 international. Average age 37. 59 applicants, 59% accepted, 19 enrolled. In 2007, 7 master's, 7 doctorates awarded. *Median time to degree:* Of those who began their doctoral program in fall 1999, 20% received their degree in 8 years or less. *Degree requirements:* For master's, one foreign language, comprehensive exam, thesis, exam; for doctorate, 2 foreign languages, comprehensive exam, thesis/dissertation, exam. *Entrance requirements:* For master's, GRE General Test; for doctorate, GRE General Test, sample of written work. Additional exam requirements/recommendations for international students: Required—TOEFL. *Application deadline:* For fall admission, 4/15 for domestic students; for spring admission, 11/15 for domestic students. Applications are processed on a rolling basis. Application fee: $50. Electronic applications accepted. *Expenses:* Tuition, state resident: part-time $221 per credit hour. *Financial support:* In 2007–08, 30 students received support, including research assistantships with full tuition reimbursements available (averaging $6,750 per year), 23 teaching assistantships with full tuition reimbursements available (averaging $14,250 per year); fellowships with full tuition reimbursements available, career-related internships or fieldwork, Federal Work-Study, institutionally sponsored loans, health care benefits, and unspecified assistantships also available. Support available to part-time students. Financial award application deadline: 3/1; financial award applicants required to submit FAFSA. *Faculty*

Latin American Studies

Georgia State University (continued)

research: Historic preservation, labor history, twentieth-century U.S. history, American South, world history. Total annual research expenditures: $160,000. *Unit head:* Dr. Hugh Hudson, Chair, 404-413-6380, Fax: 404-413-6384, E-mail: hhudson@gsu.edu. *Application contact:* Dr. David McCreery, Director of Graduate Studies, 404-413-6364, Fax: 404-413-6384, E-mail: dmccreery@gsu.edu.

Indiana University Bloomington, University Graduate School, College of Arts and Sciences, Center for Latin American and Caribbean Studies, Bloomington, IN 47405-7000. Offers MA, MBA/MA, MLS/MA, MPA/MA. Students working on a PhD in other departments may qualify for a PhD certificate or minor in Latin American and Caribbean Studies. Part-time programs available. *Students:* 9 full-time (6 women), 3 part-time (2 women); includes 5 minority (1 American Indian/Alaska Native, 1 Asian American or Pacific Islander, 3 Hispanic Americans), 1 international. Average age 36. 18 applicants, 72% accepted, 7 enrolled. In 2007, 3 degrees awarded. *Degree requirements:* For master's, one foreign language, oral and written exam. *Entrance requirements:* For master's, GRE General Test. Additional exam requirements/recommendations for international students: Required—TOEFL. *Application deadline:* For fall admission, 1/15 priority date for domestic students, 12/15 for international students; for spring admission, 9/1 priority date for domestic students, 9/1 for international students. Applications are processed on a rolling basis. Application fee: $50 ($60 for international students). *Financial support:* Fellowships with tuition reimbursements, research assistantships with tuition reimbursements, teaching assistantships with tuition reimbursements, career-related internships or fieldwork, Federal Work-Study, institutionally sponsored loans, scholarships/grants, and unspecified assistantships available. Financial award application deadline: 7/15; financial award applicants required to submit FAFSA. *Unit head:* Dr. Jeffrey Gould, Director, 812-855-9098, Fax: 812-855-5345, E-mail: gouldj@indiana.edu. *Application contact:* Amy Belcher, Information Contact, 812-855-9097, Fax: 812-855-5345, E-mail: clacs@indiana.edu.

The Johns Hopkins University, Paul H. Nitze School of Advanced International Studies, Washington, DC 20036. Offers international development (Certificate); international public policy (MIPP); international relations (MA, PhD), including African studies (MA), American foreign policy (MA), Asian studies (MA), Canadian studies (MA), conflict management (MA), European studies (MA), global theory and history (MA), international development (MA), international law, and organizations (MA), international policy (MA), international relations (general) (MA), Latin American studies (MA), Middle East studies (MA), Russian and Eurasian studies (MA), strategic studies (MA); international studies (Certificate); JD/MA; MBA/MA; MHS/MA. *Faculty:* 66 full-time (22 women), 158 part-time/adjunct (54 women). *Students:* 578 full-time (256 women), 46 part-time (16 women); includes 85 minority (18 African Americans, 1 American Indian/Alaska Native, 51 Asian Americans or Pacific Islanders, 15 Hispanic Americans), 193 international. Average age 27. In 2007, 359 master's, 13 doctorates awarded. Terminal master's awarded for partial completion of doctoral program. *Degree requirements:* For master's, one foreign language, 16 non-language courses (8 for MIPP), 2 core examinations, comprehensive oral exam, paper (for some programs); for doctorate, 2 foreign languages, thesis/dissertation, 3 comprehensive exams, defense. *Entrance requirements:* For master's, GMAT or GRE General Test, previous course work in economics, foreign language, undergraduate degree; for doctorate, GRE General Test, master's degree. Additional exam requirements/recommendations for international students: Required—TOEFL (minimum paper-based score of 600, computer-based 250, iBT 100) or IELTS (minimum 7.0). *Application deadline:* For fall admission, 1/7 for domestic students. Application fee: $80. Electronic applications accepted. *Expenses: Contact institution. Financial support:* In 2007–08, 350 students received support, including fellowships (averaging $7,500 per year); career-related internships or fieldwork, Federal Work-Study, and scholarships/grants also available. Financial award application deadline: 2/15; financial award applicants required to submit FAFSA. *Faculty research:* Regional studies and functional fields of international relations, international economics, conflict management, global theory and history, international law and organizations, international policy, strategic studies. *Unit head:* Tara Campbell, Associate Director of Admissions, 202-663-5700, Fax: 202-663-7788. *Application contact:* Dr. Belinda A. Yeomans, Director of Admissions, 202-663-5700, Fax: 202-663-7788, E-mail: admissions.sais@jhu.edu.

La Salle University, School of Arts and Sciences, Program in Bilingual/Bicultural Studies (Spanish), Philadelphia, PA 19141-1199. Offers MA. Part-time and evening/weekend programs available. *Faculty:* 1 full-time (0 women), 4 part-time/adjunct (0 women). *Students:* 3 full-time (all women), 62 part-time (49 women); includes 28 minority (13 African Americans, 2 Asian Americans or Pacific Islanders, 13 Hispanic Americans). Average age 36. 16 applicants, 81% accepted, 12 enrolled. In 2007, 9 degrees awarded. *Degree requirements:* For master's, one foreign language, thesis or alternative, project. *Entrance requirements:* For master's, GRE or MAT. *Application deadline:* Applications are processed on a rolling basis. Application fee: $35. *Expenses: Contact institution.* Tuition and fees vary according to program. *Financial support:* In 2007–08, 37 students received support. Scholarships/grants and tuition waivers (partial) available. Support available to part-time students. Financial award application deadline: 5/16; financial award applicants required to submit FAFSA. *Faculty research:* Puerto Rican literature, cross-cultural communication, English as a second language methodology, Spanish language. *Unit head:* Dr. Luis Gomez, Director, 215-951-1209.

Michigan State University, The Graduate School, College of Social Science, Program in Chicano/Latino Studies, East Lansing, MI 48824. Offers PhD. *Entrance requirements:* Additional exam requirements/recommendations for international students: Required—TOEFL. Electronic applications accepted. *Expenses:* Tuition, state resident: part-time $379 per credit hour. Tuition, nonresident: part-time $800 per credit hour. Tuition and fees vary according to program.

New York University, Graduate School of Arts and Science, Center for Latin American and Caribbean Studies, New York, NY 10012-1019. Offers MA, JD/MA. Part-time programs available. *Faculty:* 2 full-time (0 women), 5 part-time/adjunct. *Students:* 21 full-time (14 women), 26 part-time (17 women); includes 18 minority (2 African Americans, 1 American Indian/Alaska Native, 15 Hispanic Americans), 5 international. Average age 28. 67 applicants, 75% accepted, 17 enrolled. In 2007, 20 degrees awarded. *Degree requirements:* For master's, one foreign language, thesis or alternative, major project. *Entrance requirements:* For master's, GRE General Test, knowledge of Portuguese or Spanish. Additional exam requirements/recommendations for international students: Required—TOEFL. *Application deadline:* For fall admission, 1/4 priority date for domestic students. Application fee: $85. *Financial support:* Fellowships with tuition reimbursements, teaching assistantships with tuition reimbursements, Federal Work-Study, institutionally sponsored loans, scholarships/grants, health care benefits, and unspecified assistantships available. Financial award application deadline: 1/4; financial award applicants required to submit FAFSA. *Faculty research:* Latin American politics, Caribbean societies, Andean history, political economy of cultural policies. *Unit head:* Tom Abercrombie, Director, 212-998-8686, Fax: 212-995-4163, E-mail: clacs.info@nyu.edu. *Application contact:* Maritza Colon, Department Administrator, 212-998-8686, Fax: 212-995-4163, E-mail: clacs.info@nyu.edu.

New York University, Graduate School of Arts and Science, Program in Museum Studies, New York, NY 10012-1019. Offers museum studies (MA, Advanced Certificate), including Africana studies (MA), Hebrew and Judaic studies (MA), Latin American and Caribbean studies (MA), Near Eastern studies (MA). Part-time and evening/weekend programs available. *Faculty:* 4 full-time (1 woman), 6 part-time/adjunct. *Students:* 55 full-time (46 women), 26 part-time (23 women); includes 11 minority (1 American Indian/Alaska Native, 5 Asian Americans or Pacific Islanders, 5 Hispanic Americans), 19 international. Average age 28. 141 applicants, 66% accepted, 35 enrolled. In 2007, 25 master's awarded. *Entrance requirements:* For degree, master's or PhD. *Application deadline:* For fall admission, 2/1 for domestic students; for spring admission, 11/1 for domestic students. Application fee: $85. *Financial support:* Application deadline: 2/1. *Faculty research:* Modern and contemporary art, history of museums and exhibitions, conservation of cultural materials, museum anthropology, ethnography. *Unit head:* Bruce Altshuler, Director, 212-998-8080, Fax: 212-995-4185, E-mail: museum.studies@nyu.edu. *Application contact:* Tatiana Kamorina, Information Contact, 212-998-8080, Fax: 212-995-4185, E-mail: museum.studies@nyu.edu.

Ohio University, Graduate College, Center for International Studies, Program in Latin American Studies, Athens, OH 45701-2979. Offers MA. Part-time programs available. *Faculty:* 24 full-time (5 women). *Students:* 21 full-time (11 women), 2 part-time (1 woman); includes 3 minority (all Hispanic Americans), 10 international. 23 applicants, 74% accepted, 12 enrolled. In 2007, 14 degrees awarded. *Degree requirements:* For master's, one foreign language, thesis optional. *Entrance requirements:* For master's, minimum GPA of 3.0. Additional exam requirements/recommendations for international students: Required—TOEFL (minimum score 550 paper-based; 213 computer-based). *Application deadline:* For fall admission, 1/1 for domestic and international students. Applications are processed on a rolling basis. Application fee: $50 ($55 for international students). *Financial support:* In 2007–08, 23 students received support, including 4 research assistantships with full tuition reimbursements available (averaging $10,000 per year); career-related internships or fieldwork, Federal Work-Study, institutionally sponsored loans, scholarships/grants, tuition waivers (full), unspecified assistantships, and stipends also available. Financial award application deadline: 1/1. *Faculty research:* Central America, Ecuador, Brazil, transnational migration, microfinance. *Unit head:* Dr. Brad Jokisch, Director, 740-593-1835, Fax: 740-593-1837, E-mail: jokisch@ohio.edu. *Application contact:* Joan Kraynanski, Administrative Assistant, 740-593-1840, Fax: 740-593-1837, E-mail: kraynans@ohio.edu.

San Diego State University, Graduate and Research Affairs, College of Arts and Letters, Center for Latin American Studies, San Diego, CA 92182. Offers MA, MBA/MA. *Students:* 15 full-time (9 women), 18 part-time (9 women); includes 16 minority (1 Asian American or Pacific Islander, 15 Hispanic Americans), 3 international. Average age 30. 26 applicants, 65% accepted, 11 enrolled. In 2007, 14 degrees awarded. *Degree requirements:* For master's, 2 foreign languages, thesis or alternative. *Entrance requirements:* For master's, GRE General Test, 3 letters of reference. Additional exam requirements/recommendations for international students: Required—TOEFL. *Application deadline:* For fall admission, 5/1 for domestic and international students; for spring admission, 11/1 for domestic students, 10/1 for international students. Applications are processed on a rolling basis. Application fee: $55. Electronic applications accepted. *Financial support:* In 2007–08, 2 research assistantships were awarded; career-related internships or fieldwork, Federal Work-Study, and institutionally sponsored loans also available. Financial award applicants required to submit FAFSA. *Faculty research:* Latin American politics and economics. *Unit head:* Dr. James B. Gerber, Graduate Coordinator, 619-594-5532, Fax: 619-594-6281, E-mail: jgerber@mail.sdsu.edu. *Application contact:* Dr. James B. Gerber, Graduate Coordinator, 619-594-5532, Fax: 619-594-6281, E-mail: jgerber@mail.sdsu.edu.

Simon Fraser University, Graduate Studies, Faculty of Arts and Social Sciences, Latin American Studies Program, Burnaby, BC V5A 1S6, Canada. Offers MA. *Degree requirements:* For master's, thesis. *Entrance requirements:* For master's, minimum GPA of 3.0. Additional exam requirements/recommendations for international students: Required—TOEFL or IELTS. *Faculty research:* Sociology theory, social and cultural anthropology, political sociology, religion and society, Canadian native people.

Tulane University, School of Liberal Arts, Roger Thayer Stone Center for Latin American Studies, New Orleans, LA 70118-5669. Offers MA, PhD, MBA/MA, MCL/MA. Terminal master's awarded for partial completion of doctoral program. *Degree requirements:* For master's, one foreign language, thesis optional; for doctorate, 2 foreign languages, thesis/dissertation. *Entrance requirements:* For master's, GRE General Test, minimum B average in undergraduate course work; for doctorate, GRE General Test. Additional exam requirements/recommendations for international students: Required—TOEFL. Electronic applications accepted.

See Close-Up on page 813.

University at Albany, State University of New York, College of Arts and Sciences, Latin American, Caribbean, and US Latino Studies, Albany, NY 12222-0001. Offers MA, Certificate. Part-time programs available. *Students:* 11 full-time (10 women), 2 part-time (both women). Average age 31. 7 applicants, 86% accepted, 4 enrolled. In 2007, 3 degrees awarded. *Degree requirements:* For master's, thesis. *Entrance requirements:* For master's, ability to read and write Spanish. Additional exam requirements/recommendations for international students: Required—TOEFL (minimum score 550 paper-based; 213 computer-based). *Application deadline:* For fall admission, 3/15 for domestic students, 5/1 for international students; for spring admission, 11/1 for international students. Applications are processed on a rolling basis. Application fee: $75. Electronic applications accepted. *Expenses:* Tuition, state resident: part-time $576 per credit. Tuition, nonresident: part-time $910 per credit. Tuition and fees vary according to program. *Financial support:* Fellowships, research assistantships, teaching assistantships available. Financial award application deadline: 3/15. *Faculty research:* Meso-American anthropology, Latin American women's studies, Latinos in the U.S. *Unit head:* Glyne Griffith, Chair, 518-442-4890.

The University of Arizona, Graduate College, College of Social and Behavioral Sciences, Center for Latin American Studies, Tucson, AZ 85721. Offers MA. Part-time programs available. *Faculty:* 3. *Students:* 31 full-time (22 women), 2 part-time (both women); includes 7 minority (1 African American, 6 Hispanic Americans), 3 international. Average age 30. 46 applicants, 67% accepted, 8 enrolled. In 2007, 9 degrees awarded. *Degree requirements:* For master's, 2 foreign languages, comprehensive exam, thesis optional. *Entrance requirements:* For master's, GRE, minimum GPA of 3.0, resumè or curriculum vitae, 2 letters of recommendation, statement of purpose. Additional exam requirements/recommendations for international students: Required—TOEFL (minimum score 550 paper-based). *Application deadline:* For fall admission, 2/15 for domestic students, 12/1 for international students. Application fee: $50. *Financial support:* In 2007–08, 31 students received support; fellowships with partial tuition reimbursements available, research assistantships with partial tuition reimbursements available, teaching assistantships with partial tuition reimbursements available, career-related internships or fieldwork, Federal Work-Study, institutionally sponsored loans, scholarships/grants, tuition waivers (full and partial), and unspecified assistantships available. *Faculty research:* Comparative analyses of national identities and of democratization across Latin America, environmental problems and management along the U.S.—Mexican border, integration efforts along the Peru/Ecuador border, social justice issues in Guatemala. Total annual research expenditures: $499,606. *Unit head:* Dr. Scott Whiteford, Director, 520-626-7207, Fax: 520-626-7248, E-mail: eljete@email.arizona.edu. *Application contact:* Dr. Marla Schoen, Information Contact, 520-626-3317, Fax: 520-626-7248, E-mail: marlas@email.arizona.edu.

University of California, Berkeley, Graduate Division, Group in Latin American Studies, Berkeley, CA 94720-1500. Offers MA, MJ/MA. *Degree requirements:* For master's, 2 foreign languages. *Entrance requirements:* For master's, GRE General Test, minimum GPA of 3.0, reading knowledge of Spanish or Portuguese, 3 letters of recommendation. Additional exam requirements/recommendations for international students: Required—TOEFL. *Application deadline:* For fall admission, 12/15 for domestic students. Application fee: $70 ($90 for international students). Electronic applications accepted. *Financial support:* Fellowships, teaching assistantships with tuition reimbursements, unspecified assistantships available. *Faculty research:* Rural development, border communities, political economy, geography, history. *Unit head:* John Lie, Chair, 510-642-0656, E-mail: iasone@berkeley.edu. *Application contact:* Information Contact, 510-642-4466, E-mail: lasgrad@berkeley.edu.

University of California, Los Angeles, Graduate Division, College of Letters and Science, Program in Latin American Studies, Los Angeles, CA 90095. Offers MA, M Ed/MA, MA/MA, MBA/MA, MLIS/MA, MPH/MA. *Students:* 21 full-time (15 women); includes 17 minority (2 Asian Americans or Pacific Islanders, 15 Hispanic Americans), 1 international. Average age 30. 46 applicants, 48% accepted, 10 enrolled. In 2007, 12 degrees awarded. *Degree requirements:* For master's, 2 foreign languages, comprehensive exam, comprehensive exam or thesis. *Entrance requirements:* For master's, GRE General Test, minimum GPA of 3.0. *Application deadline:* For fall admission, 12/15 for domestic students. Application fee: $60. Electronic applications accepted. *Expenses:* Tuition, nonresident: full-time $5,728. Required fees:$8,966. Full-time tuition and fees vary according to program and student level. *Financial support:* In 2007–08, 6 fellowships with full and partial tuition reimbursements, 5 research assistantships with full and partial tuition reimbursements, 8 teaching assistantships with full and partial tuition reimbursements were awarded; Federal Work-Study, institutionally sponsored loans, scholarships/grants, and tuition waivers (full and partial) also available. Financial award application deadline: 3/1; financial award applicants required to submit FAFSA. *Unit head:* Dr. Kevin Terraciano, Chair, 310-206-6571. *Application contact:* Departmental Office, 310-206-6571, E-mail: idpgrads@international.ucla.edu.

University of California, San Diego, Office of Graduate Studies, Department of Political Science, Latin American Studies Program, La Jolla, CA 92093. Offers MA. *Entrance requirements:* For master's, GRE General Test, GRE Subject Test. Electronic applications accepted.

University of California, Santa Barbara, Graduate Division, College of Letters and Sciences, Division of Humanities and Fine Arts, Department of Spanish and Portuguese, Santa Barbara, CA 93106. Offers Hispanic languages and literature (PhD); Portuguese (MA); Spanish (MA). Spanish Language Institute available during summer sessions. *Faculty:* 16 full-time (6 women). *Students:* 27 full-time (12 women); includes 6 minority (all Hispanic Americans), 8 international. Average age 31. 34 applicants, 62% accepted, 9 enrolled. In 2007, 3 master's, 4 doctorates awarded. *Median time to degree:* Of those who began their doctoral program in fall 1999, 60% received their degree in 8 years or less. *Degree requirements:* For master's, 2 foreign languages, thesis optional; for doctorate, 2 foreign languages, comprehensive exam, thesis/dissertation. *Entrance requirements:* For master's, GRE, 2 writing samples, undergraduate major in Spanish or equivalent; for doctorate, GRE, 2 writing samples, Master's degree. Additional exam requirements/recommendations for international students: Required—TOEFL (minimum score 550 paper-based; 213 computer-based; 80 iBT). *Application deadline:* For fall admission, 3/1 for domestic and international students; for winter admission, 11/1 for domestic and international students; for spring admission, 2/1 for domestic and international students. Applications are processed on a rolling basis. Application fee: $60. Electronic applications accepted. *Expenses:* Tuition, nonresident: full-time $14,888. Required fees: $10,108. *Financial support:* In 2007–08, 27 students received support, including 6 fellowships with full tuition reimbursements available (averaging $15,500 per year), 4 research assistantships, 26 teaching assistantships with full and partial tuition reimbursements available (averaging $16,390 per year); career-related internships or fieldwork, Federal Work-Study, scholarships/grants, health care benefits, tuition waivers (full and partial), and unspecified assistantships also available. Financial award application deadline: 1/7; financial award applicants required to submit FAFSA. *Faculty research:* 19th century Spanish and Portuguese literature, Spanish and Spanish American literature, 19th and 20th century Portuguese and Brazilian literatures, Mexican literature, Catalan language and culture. *Unit head:* Prof. Francisco P. Lomeli, Chair, 805-893-2798, E-mail: rap@spanport.ucsb.edu. *Application contact:* Carol Conley, Graduate Program Assistant, 805-893-3162, Fax: 805-893-8341, E-mail: cconley@spanport.ucsb.edu.

University of California, Santa Barbara, Graduate Division, College of Letters and Sciences, Division of Humanities and Fine Arts, Program in Latin American and Iberian Studies, Santa Barbara, CA 93106. Offers Latin American studies (MA). *Faculty:* 56 part-time/adjunct (26 women). *Students:* 12 full-time (7 women); includes 4 minority (all Hispanic Americans) Average age 29. 24 applicants, 75% accepted, 4 enrolled. In 2007, 4 degrees awarded. *Degree requirements:* For master's, one foreign language, comprehensive exam (for some programs), thesis. *Entrance requirements:* For master's, GRE, 2 writing samples, BA. Additional exam requirements/recommendations for international students: Required—TOEFL (minimum score 550 paper-based; 213 computer-based; 80 iBT). *Application deadline:* For fall admission, 5/1 for domestic and international students; for winter admission, 11/1 for domestic and international students; for spring admission, 2/1 for domestic and international students. Application fee: $60. *Expenses:* Tuition, nonresident: full-time $14,888. Required fees: $10,108. *Financial support:* In 2007–08, 10 students received support, including 10 fellowships with full and partial tuition reimbursements available (averaging $3,000 per year), 4 teaching assistantships with partial tuition reimbursements available (averaging $25,000 per year); Federal Work-Study, institutionally sponsored loans, scholarships/grants, and health care benefits also available. Financial award application deadline: 1/15; financial award applicants required to submit FAFSA. *Faculty research:* Political science, anthropology, history, sociology, Portuguese. *Unit head:* Dr. Kate Bruhn, Chair, 805-893-2999, E-mail: laisdirector@spanport.ucsb.edu. *Application contact:* Carol Conley, Graduate Program Assistant, 805-893-3162, Fax: 805-893-8341, E-mail: cconley@spanport.ucsb.edu.

University of Central Florida, College of Sciences, Department of Sociology, Orlando, FL 32816. Offers applied sociology (MA); domestic violence (MA, Certificate); Maya studies (Certificate); sociology (PhD). Part-time and evening/weekend programs available. *Faculty:* 21 full-time (12 women), 3 part-time/adjunct (2 women). *Degree requirements:* For master's, comprehensive written exam or thesis. *Entrance requirements:* For master's, GRE General Test, minimum GPA of 3.0 in last 60 hours of course work. Additional exam requirements/recommendations for international students: Required—TOEFL. *Application deadline:* For fall admission, 7/15 for domestic students; for spring admission, 12/1 for domestic students. Application fee: $30. Electronic applications accepted. *Expenses:* Tuition, state resident: full-time $6,484. Tuition, nonresident: full-time $23,938. Tuition and fees vary according to program. *Financial support:* Fellowships with partial tuition reimbursements, research assistantships with partial tuition reimbursements, teaching assistantships with partial tuition reimbursements, career-related internships or fieldwork, Federal Work-Study, institutionally sponsored loans, tuition waivers (partial), and unspecified assistantships available. Financial award application deadline: 3/1; financial award applicants required to submit FAFSA. *Faculty research:* Religious subcultures, attitudes toward abortion, population, sport research, stratification. *Unit head:* Dr. Jay Corzine, Chair, 407-823-2227, Fax: 407-823-5156, E-mail: hcorzine@mail.ucf.edu.

University of Chicago, Division of Social Sciences and Division of the Humanities, Latin American and Caribbean Studies Program, Chicago, IL 60637-1513. Offers AM, MBA/AM. *Students:* 9. In 2007, 2 degrees awarded. *Degree requirements:* For master's, one foreign language, thesis. *Entrance requirements:* For master's, GRE General Test. Additional exam requirements/recommendations for international students: Required—TOEFL. *Application deadline:* For fall admission, 12/28 for domestic students. Application fee: $55. Electronic applications accepted. *Financial support:* Federal Work-Study, institutionally sponsored loans, and scholarships/grants available. Financial award application deadline: 12/28. *Unit head:* Prof. Dain Borges, Director, 773-702-9741. *Application contact:* Office of the Dean of Students, 773-702-8415.

University of Connecticut, Graduate School, College of Liberal Arts and Sciences, Field of International Studies, Program in Latin American Studies, Storrs, CT 06269. Offers MA. *Faculty:* 53 full-time (28 women). *Students:* 9 full-time (5 women), 3 part-time (2 women); includes 6 minority (all Hispanic Americans), 3 international. Average age 29. 11 applicants, 45% accepted, 5 enrolled. In 2007, 4 degrees awarded. *Degree requirements:* For master's, comprehensive exam. *Entrance requirements:* For master's, GRE General Test. Additional exam requirements/recommendations for international students: Required—TOEFL (minimum score 550 paper-based; 213 computer-based). *Application deadline:* For fall admission, 2/1 priority date for domestic students, 2/1 for international students; for spring admission, 11/1 for domestic students, 10/1 for international students. Applications are processed on a rolling basis. Application fee: $55. Electronic applications accepted. *Expenses:* Tuition, state resident: part-time $469 per credit hour. Tuition, nonresident: part-time $1,218 per credit hour. *Financial support:* In 2007–08, 6 research assistantships with full tuition reimbursements were awarded; fellowships, teaching assistantships with full tuition reimbursements, Federal Work-Study, scholarships/grants, health care benefits, and unspecified assistantships also available. Financial award application deadline: 2/1; financial award applicants required to submit FAFSA. *Unit head:* Tricia Gabany-Guerrero, Chairperson, 860-486-2814, Fax: 860-486-2963, E-mail: t.gabany_guerrero@uconn.edu. *Application contact:* Ludmilla Burns, Administrative Assistant, 860-486-5888, Fax: 860-486-0641, E-mail: ludmilla.burns@uconn.edu.

University of Florida, Graduate School, College of Liberal Arts and Sciences, Center for Latin American Studies, Gainesville, FL 32611. Offers MA, Certificate, JD/MA. Part-time programs available. *Faculty:* 6 full-time (4 women). *Students:* 34 (27 women); includes 11 minority (1 African American, 10 Hispanic Americans) 8 international. In 2007, 6 degrees awarded. *Degree requirements:* For master's, thesis. *Entrance requirements:* For master's, GRE General Test, minimum GPA of 3.0. Additional exam requirements/recommendations for international students: Required—TOEFL (minimum score 550 paper-based; 213 computer-based). *Application deadline:* For fall admission, 6/1 priority date for domestic students. Applications are processed on a rolling basis. Application fee: $30. Electronic applications accepted. *Expenses:* Tuition, state resident: full-time $7,478. Tuition, nonresident: full-time $22,603. *Financial support:* In 2007–08, 16 research assistantships (averaging $20,217 per year) were awarded; fellowships, teaching assistantships, career-related internships or fieldwork, Federal Work-Study, institutionally sponsored loans, and unspecified assistantships also available. Financial award application deadline: 3/1. *Faculty research:* Tropical conservation and development; ethnicity in the Americas, Brazil, and Cuba; North American Free Trade Agreement. *Unit head:* Carmen Diana Deere, Director, 352-392-0375, Fax: 352-392-7682, E-mail: deere@latam.ufl.edu. *Application contact:* Dr. M. Cristina Espinosa, Coordinator, 352-392-0375, Fax: 352-392-7682, E-mail: espinosa@latam.ufl.edu.

University of Illinois at Urbana–Champaign, Graduate College, College of Liberal Arts and Sciences, Center for Latin American and Caribbean Studies, Champaign, IL 61820. Offers Latin American studies (MA). *Students:* 5 full-time (4 women), 2 part-time (1 woman); includes 2 minority (1 African American, 1 Hispanic American). 10 applicants, 60% accepted, 3 enrolled. In 2007, 6 degrees awarded. *Entrance requirements:* For master's, GRE, minimum GPA of 3.0. *Application deadline:* For fall admission, 1/15 for domestic students. Applications are processed on a rolling basis. Application fee: $60 ($75 for international students). Electronic applications accepted. *Financial support:* In 2007–08, 4 fellowships were awarded; research assistantships, teaching assistantships. Financial award application deadline: 2/15. *Unit head:* Nils Jacobson, Director, 217-333-3182, Fax: 217-244-7333, E-mail: njacobse@uiuc.edu. *Application contact:* Angelina Cotler, Associate Director, 217-244-2790, Fax: 217-244-7333, E-mail: cotler@uiuc.edu.

University of Kansas, Research and Graduate Studies, College of Liberal Arts and Sciences, Center of Latin American Studies, Lawrence, KS 66045. Offers Brazilian studies (Certificate); Central American and Mexican studies (Certificate); Latin American studies (MA). Part-time programs available. *Faculty:* 31. *Students:* 10 full-time (7 women), 7 part-time (4 women); includes 2 minority (both Hispanic Americans), 1 international. Average age 26. 11 applicants, 73% accepted, 6 enrolled. In 2007, 7 degrees awarded. *Degree requirements:* For master's, 2 foreign languages, comprehensive exam, thesis optional. *Entrance requirements:* For master's, GRE, minimum GPA of 3.0, references, writing sample. Additional exam requirements/recommendations for international students: Required—TOEFL. *Application deadline:* For spring admission, 2/1 priority date for domestic students. Applications are processed on a rolling basis. Application fee: $55 ($60 for international students). Electronic applications accepted. *Expenses:* Tuition, state resident: full-time $5,838. Tuition, nonresident: full-time $13,409. Tuition and fees vary according to program. *Financial support:* Fellowships with full tuition reimbursements, research assistantships with full and partial tuition reimbursements, teaching assistantships with full and partial tuition reimbursements, scholarships/grants and unspecified assistantships available. Financial award application deadline: 2/1. *Faculty research:* Democracy, ethnicity, literature, environment, gender. *Unit head:* Peter Herlihy, Graduate Advisor, 785-864-4213, Fax: 785-864-3800, E-mail: herlihy@ku.edu. *Application contact:* Judy Farmer, Office Manager, 785-864-4213, Fax: 785-864-3800, E-mail: jfarmer@ku.edu.

University of Massachusetts Dartmouth, Graduate School, College of Arts and Sciences, Department of Portuguese, North Dartmouth, MA 02747-2300. Offers Portuguese (MA); WSO-Afro-Brazilian studies (PhD). *Faculty:* 6 full-time (2 women), 1 part-time/adjunct (0 women). *Students:* 8 full-time (6 women), 11 part-time (5 women); includes 6 minority (1 African American, 1 Asian American or Pacific Islander, 4 Hispanic Americans), 3 international. Average age 35. 18 applicants, 89% accepted, 12 enrolled. In 2007, 3 degrees awarded. *Degree requirements:* For master's, comprehensive exam (for some programs). *Entrance requirements:* For master's, GRE (recommended), 10-page writing sample; for doctorate, GRE. Additional exam requirements/recommendations for international students: Required—TOEFL (minimum score 500 paper-based). *Application deadline:* For fall admission, 4/20 priority date for domestic students, 2/20 priority date for international students; for spring admission, 11/15 priority date for domestic students, 9/15 priority date for international students. Applications are processed on a rolling basis. Application fee: $40 ($60 for international students). Electronic applications accepted. *Expenses:* Tuition, state resident: full-time $2,071; part-time $86 per credit. Tuition, nonresident: full-time $8,099; part-time $337 per credit. Part-time tuition and fees vary according to course load and program. *Financial support:* In 2007–08, 2 research assistantships with full tuition reimbursements (averaging $14,875 per year), 8 teaching assistantships with full tuition reimbursements (averaging $15,000 per year) were awarded; unspecified assistantships also available. Financial award application deadline: 3/1; financial award applicants required to submit FAFSA. *Unit head:* Victor J Mendes, Director, Graduate Studies, 508-999-8338, Fax: 508-999-9272, E-mail: vmendes@umassd.edu. *Application contact:* Carol Novo, Graduate Admissions Officer, 508-999-8604, Fax: 508-999-8183, E-mail: graduate@umassd.edu.

University of Miami, Graduate School, College of Arts and Sciences, Department of Latin American and Caribbean Studies, Coral Gables, FL 33124. Offers Latin American studies (MA). Part-time programs available. *Faculty:* 69 full-time (24 women), 4 part-time/adjunct (0 women). *Students:* 10 full-time (all women), 1 (woman) part-time; includes 3 minority (1 African American, 2 Hispanic Americans), 1 international. Average age 26. 24 applicants, 58% accepted, 7 enrolled. In 2007, 1 degree awarded. *Degree requirements:* For master's, comprehensive exam (for some programs), thesis, linguistic competency in Spanish or Portuguese, reading competency in a second Latin American language. *Entrance requirements:* For master's, GRE, 3 letters of recommendation. Additional exam requirements/recommendations for international students: Required—TOEFL. *Application deadline:* For fall admission, 2/1 for domestic and international students. Applications are processed on a rolling basis. Application fee: $50. Electronic applications accepted. *Financial support:* In 2007–08, 11 students received support, including 4 teaching assistantships with full and partial tuition reimbursements available (averaging $12,200 per year); fellowships, research assistantships, career-related internships or fieldwork, institutionally sponsored loans, scholarships/grants, health care benefits, and unspecified assistantships also available. Financial award application deadline: 3/1. *Faculty research:* Literary, media, religious, visual and cultural studies, environment and tourism studies, US-Latin American Relations and drug trafficking, migration, globalization, and social movements, democratization, regime transitions, and citizenship. *Unit head:* Dr. Lillian Manzor, Director, Degree Programs in Latin American Studies, 305-284-2017, Fax: 305-284-2796, E-mail: lmanzor@miami.edu.

University of New Mexico, Graduate School, College of Arts and Sciences, Committee on Latin American Studies, Albuquerque, NM 87131-2039. Offers MA, PhD, JD/MA, MBA/MA, MCRP/MA, MSN/MA. *Students:* 27 full-time (13 women), 5 part-time (2 women); includes 9 minority (1 American Indian/Alaska Native, 8 Hispanic Americans), 3 international. Average age 31. 56 applicants, 61% accepted, 12 enrolled. In 2007, 16 master's, 2 doctorates awarded. *Degree requirements:* For master's, one foreign language, comprehensive exam (for some programs), thesis (for some programs); for doctorate, 2 foreign languages, comprehensive exam, thesis/dissertation. *Entrance requirements:* For master's, GRE General Test, intermediate competence in Spanish, Portuguese or indigenous Latin American Language, background in LAS-related coursework; for doctorate, GRE General Test, master's degree in related field, one Latin American language. Additional exam requirements/recommendations for international students: Required—TOEFL. *Application deadline:* For fall admission, 2/1 priority date

Latin American Studies

University of New Mexico (continued)
for domestic students; for spring admission, 11/1 for domestic students. Application fee: $50. Electronic applications accepted. *Financial support:* In 2007–08, 27 students received support, including 8 research assistantships with full tuition reimbursements available (averaging $12,223 per year), 2 teaching assistantships with full tuition reimbursements available (averaging $12,223 per year); fellowships, Federal Work-Study, scholarships/grants, health care benefits, tuition waivers (full), and unspecified assistantships also available. Financial award application deadline: 2/1; financial award applicants required to submit FAFSA. *Unit head:* Dr. Kimberly Gauderman, Director, 505-277-7042, Fax: 505-277-5989, E-mail: kgaud@unm.edu. *Application contact:* Amanda Kay Wolfe, Academic Project Manager, 505-277-7044, Fax: 505-277-5989, E-mail: akwolfe@unm.edu.

The University of North Carolina at Chapel Hill, Graduate School, College of Arts and Sciences, Department of Political Science, Chapel Hill, NC 27599. Offers Latin American studies (Certificate); political science (MA, PhD); trans-Atlantic studies (MA). *Degree requirements:* For master's, comprehensive exam; for doctorate, one foreign language, comprehensive exam, thesis/dissertation. *Entrance requirements:* For master's and doctorate, GRE General Test, minimum GPA of 3.0 recommended. Electronic applications accepted.

University of Notre Dame, Graduate School, College of Arts and Letters, Division of Humanities, Department of Romance Languages and Literatures, Notre Dame, IN 46556. Offers French and Francophone studies (MA); Iberian and Latin American studies (MA); Italian studies (MA); Romance literatures (MA). Part-time programs available. *Faculty:* 25 full-time (10 women), 4 part-time/adjunct (all women). *Students:* 18 full-time (12 women); includes 4 minority (all Hispanic Americans), 3 international. 28 applicants, 61% accepted, 9 enrolled. In 2007, 12 degrees awarded. *Degree requirements:* For master's, 2 foreign languages, comprehensive exam, thesis optional. *Entrance requirements:* For master's, GRE General Test, BA in target language. Additional exam requirements/recommendations for international students: Required—TOEFL (minimum score 600 paper-based; 250 computer-based; 80 iBT). *Application deadline:* For fall admission, 2/1 priority date for domestic students, 2/1 for international students. Application fee: $50. Electronic applications accepted. *Financial support:* In 2007–08, 1 fellowship (averaging $15,000 per year), 10 teaching assistantships with full tuition reimbursements (averaging $12,000 per year) were awarded; research assistantships, tuition waivers (full) also available. Financial award application deadline: 2/1. *Faculty research:* Literature of discovery and exploration, modern literature, literary criticism, medieval literature, feminist critical theory. *Unit head:* Dr. John Welle, Director of Graduate Studies, 574-631-6887, Fax: 574-631-3493, E-mail: al.romland.1@nd.edu. *Application contact:* Dr. Jarren Gonzales, Director of Graduate Admissions, 574-631-7706, Fax: 574-631-4183.

University of Pittsburgh, University Center for International Studies, Pittsburgh, PA 15260. Offers African studies (Certificate); Asian studies (Certificate); European Union studies (Certificate); global studies (Certificate); Latin American studies (Certificate); Russian and East European studies (Certificate); West European studies (Certificate). *Unit head:* Lawrence F. Feick, Director, University Center for International Studies, 412-648-7374, Fax: 412-624-4672, E-mail: feick@pitt.edu.

University of South Florida, Graduate School, College of Arts and Sciences, Institute for the Study of Latin America and the Caribbean, Tampa, FL 33620-9951. Offers Cuban studies (Graduate Certificate); Latin American and Caribbean studies (Graduate Certificate); Latin American, Caribbean and Latino studies (MA).

The University of Texas at Austin, Graduate School, College of Liberal Arts, Center for Latin American Studies, Austin, TX 78712-1111. Offers MA, PhD, JD/MA, MBA/MA, MP Aff/MA, MSCRP/MA. *Entrance requirements:* For master's and doctorate, GRE General Test.

University of Wisconsin–Madison, Graduate School, College of Letters and Science, Latin American, Caribbean and Iberian Studies Program, Madison, WI 53706-1380. Offers MA. *Degree requirements:* For master's, 2 foreign languages, thesis. *Entrance requirements:* For master's, minimum GPA of 3.0. Electronic applications accepted. *Faculty research:* Development, gender, social movements, cultural studies, history.

Vanderbilt University, Graduate School, Program in Latin American Studies, Nashville, TN 37240-1001. Offers MA, MBA/MA. *Faculty:* 24 full-time (5 women). *Students:* 13 full-time (5 women); includes 4 minority (all Hispanic Americans), 2 international. Average age 26. 26 applicants, 42% accepted, 9 enrolled. In 2007, 4 degrees awarded. *Degree requirements:* For master's, 2 foreign languages, thesis or alternative. *Entrance requirements:* For master's, GRE General Test. *Application deadline:* For fall admission, 1/15 for domestic and international students. Application fee: $0. Electronic applications accepted. *Financial support:* Teaching assistantships with full tuition reimbursements, Federal Work-Study, institutionally sponsored loans, and health care benefits available. Financial award application deadline: 1/15; financial award applicants required to submit CSS PROFILE or FAFSA. *Faculty research:* Latin American and Iberian studies, anthropology, history, Spanish and Portuguese, social and political science. *Unit head:* Edward Fischer, Director, 615-322-2527, Fax: 615-343-0230, E-mail: edward.f.fischer@vanderbilt.edu.

West Virginia University, Eberly College of Arts and Sciences, Department of History, Morgantown, WV 26506. Offers African history (MA, PhD); African-American history (MA, PhD); American history (MA, PhD); Appalachian/regional history (MA, PhD); East Asian history (MA, PhD); European history (MA, PhD); history of science and technology (MA, PhD); Latin American history (MA). Part-time programs available. *Faculty:* 19 full-time (5 women), 12 part-time/adjunct (4 women). *Students:* 43 full-time (17 women), 30 part-time (11 women); includes 5 minority (1 African American, 1 American Indian/Alaska Native, 2 Asian Americans or Pacific Islanders, 1 Hispanic American), 7 international. Average age 33. 70 applicants, 59% accepted, 17 enrolled. In 2007, 8 master's, 3 doctorates awarded. *Median time to degree:* Of those who began their doctoral program in fall 1999, 75% received their degree in 8 years or less. *Degree requirements:* For master's, one foreign language, thesis (for some programs), oral exam, thesis defense; for doctorate, one foreign language, comprehensive exam, thesis/dissertation, dissertation defense. *Entrance requirements:* For master's, GRE General Test, minimum GPA of 3.0; for doctorate, GRE General Test. Additional exam requirements/recommendations for international students: Required—TOEFL (minimum score 550 paper-based), IELTS (minimum score 7). *Application deadline:* For fall admission, 12/31 for domestic students; for spring admission, 10/1 for domestic students. Applications are processed on a rolling basis. Application fee: $45. Electronic applications accepted. *Expenses:* Tuition, state resident: full-time $5,196; part-time $292 per credit hour. Tuition, nonresident: full-time $15,064; part-time $840 per credit hour. Tuition and fees vary according to program. *Financial support:* In 2007–08, 60 students received support, including 5 fellowships with full tuition reimbursements available (averaging $3,000 per year), 1 research assistantship with full tuition reimbursement available (averaging $7,200 per year), 8 teaching assistantships with full tuition reimbursements available (averaging $12,000 per year); career-related internships or fieldwork, Federal Work-Study, institutionally sponsored loans, health care benefits, tuition waivers (full and partial), and graduate administrative assistantships also available. Financial award application deadline: 12/31; financial award applicants required to submit FAFSA. *Faculty research:* U.S., Appalachia, modern Europe, Africa, colonial and post-colonial societies. Total annual research expenditures: $93,327. *Unit head:* Dr. Steven M. Zdatny, Chair, 304-293-2421 Ext. 5241, Fax: 304-293-3616, E-mail: steve.zdatny@mail.wvu.edu. *Application contact:* Dr. Greg A. Good, Director of Graduate Studies, 304-293-2421 Ext. 5247, Fax: 304-293-3616, E-mail: greg.good@mail.wvu.edu.

Near and Middle Eastern Studies

The American University in Cairo, Graduate Studies and Research, School of Humanities and Social Sciences, Department of Arabic Studies, Cairo, Egypt. Offers Arab language and literature (MA); Islamic art and architecture (MA); Islamic studies (Diploma); Middle East studies (MA, Diploma); Middle Eastern history (MA). Part-time programs available. *Degree requirements:* For master's, thesis optional, proficiency in French or German. *Entrance requirements:* Additional exam requirements/recommendations for international students: Required—English entrance exam and/or TOEFL. Electronic applications accepted. *Faculty research:* History of early Islam, Ayubbid, and Mamluk periods; nineteenth- and twentieth-century Middle East Islamic jurisprudence; contemporary Arabic literary criticism.

American University of Beirut, Graduate Programs, Faculty of Arts and Sciences, Beirut, Lebanon. Offers anthropology (MA); Arabic language and literature (MA); archaeology (MA); biology (MS); chemistry (MS); computer science (MS); economics (MA); education (MA); English language (MA); English literature (MA); environmental policy planning (MSES); financial economics (MAFE); geology (MS); history (MA); mathematics (MA, MS); Middle Eastern studies (MA); philosophy (MA); physics (MS); political studies (MA); psychology (MA); public administration (MA); sociology (MA); statistics (MA, MS). Part-time programs available. *Faculty:* 108 full-time (29 women), 5 part-time/adjunct (3 women). *Students:* 134 full-time (92 women), 228 part-time (167 women). Average age 25. 319 applicants, 67% accepted, 91 enrolled. In 2007, 144 degrees awarded. *Degree requirements:* For master's, one foreign language, comprehensive exam, thesis (for some programs). *Entrance requirements:* For master's, GRE, letter of recommendation. Additional exam requirements/recommendations for international students: Required—TOEFL (minimum score 600 paper-based; 250 computer-based; 100 iBT), IELTS (minimum score 8). *Application deadline:* For fall admission, 4/30 for domestic and international students; for spring admission, 11/1 for domestic and international students. Application fee: $50. *Expenses:* Tuition: Full-time $9,954; part-time $553 per credit. Tuition and fees vary according to course load and program. *Financial support:* In 2007–08, 28 students received support. Career-related internships or fieldwork, institutionally sponsored loans, scholarships/grants, health care benefits, and unspecified assistantships available. Financial award application deadline: 2/4; financial award applicants required to submit FAFSA. *Faculty research:* String theory and supergravity; computer graphics; algebra and number theory; popular Arabic literature; marine and freshwater biology; integrating science, math and technology. Total annual research expenditures: $132,270. *Unit head:* Khalil Bitar, Dean, 961-1374374 Ext. 3800, Fax: 961-1744461, E-mail: kmb@aub.edu.lb. *Application contact:* Dr. Salim Kanaan, Director, Admissions Office, 961-1350000 Ext. 2594, Fax: 961-1750775, E-mail: sk00@aub.edu.lb.

The American University of Paris, Graduate Programs, Paris, France. Offers finance (MSF); global communications (MAGC); international affairs, conflict resolution and civil society development (MA); Middle Eastern and Islamic studies (MA); public administration (MPA). *Degree requirements:* For master's, thesis. *Entrance requirements:* For master's, minimum undergraduate GPA of 3.0.

Brandeis University, Graduate School of Arts and Sciences, Department of Near Eastern and Judaic Studies, Waltham, MA 02454-9110. Offers Near Eastern and Judaic studies (MA, PhD); Near Eastern and Judaic studies and sociology (PhD); Near Eastern and Judaic studies and women's studies (MA); teaching of Hebrew (MAT). Part-time programs available. *Faculty:* 25 full-time (11 women), 5 part-time/adjunct (3 women). *Students:* 44 full-time (21 women), 4 part-time; includes 1 minority (African American), 10 international. Average age 33. 62 applicants, 53% accepted, 15 enrolled. In 2007, 7 master's, 4 doctorates awarded. Terminal master's awarded for partial completion of doctoral program. *Degree requirements:* For master's, one foreign language, comprehensive exam, thesis or alternative; for doctorate, 3 foreign languages, comprehensive exam, thesis/dissertation. *Entrance requirements:* For master's and doctorate, GRE General Test (recommended), letters of recommendation, transcripts, statement of purpose. Additional exam requirements/recommendations for international students: Required—TOEFL (minimum score 600 paper-based; 250 computer-based; 100 iBT), IELTS (minimum score 7). *Application deadline:* For fall admission, 1/15 priority date for domestic and international students. Applications are processed on a rolling basis. Application fee: $55. Electronic applications accepted. *Financial support:* In 2007–08, 15 students received support, including 14 fellowships with full and partial tuition reimbursements available (averaging $17,000 per year), 1 teaching assistantship with partial tuition reimbursement available (averaging $3,000 per year); research assistantships with full and partial tuition reimbursements available, scholarships/grants, health care benefits, and tuition waivers (full and partial) also available. Support available to part-time students. Financial award application deadline: 4/15; financial award applicants required to submit CSS PROFILE or FAFSA. *Faculty research:* Ancient Near East and Bible, philosophy, history, modern Middle East, Islamic studies. *Unit head:* Dr. David Wright, Chair, 781-736-2954, Fax: 781-736-2070, E-mail: wright@brandeis.edu. *Application contact:* Dr. Eugene Sheppard, Graduate Advisor, 781-736-2965, Fax: 781-736-2070, E-mail: sheppard@brandeis.edu.

Columbia University, Graduate School of Arts and Sciences, Division of Humanities, Department of Middle East Languages and Cultures, New York, NY 10027. Offers Hebrew language and literature (M Phil, MA, PhD); Middle Eastern languages and cultures (M Phil, MA, PhD); South Asian languages and cultures (M Phil, MA, PhD). Part-time programs available. *Faculty:* 22 full-time, 11 part-time/adjunct. *Students:* 52 full-time (25 women), 4 part-time (3 women); includes 4 minority (3 Asian Americans or Pacific Islanders, 1 Hispanic American), 12 international. Average age 35. 42 applicants, 48% accepted. In 2007, 2 master's, 5 doctorates awarded. *Degree requirements:* For master's, thesis, oral and written exams; for doctorate, 3 foreign languages, thesis/dissertation. *Entrance requirements:* For master's and doctorate, GRE General Test. Additional exam requirements/recommendations for international students: Required—TOEFL. Application fee: $90. *Expenses:* Tuition: Part-time $1,452 per credit. Required fees: $152 per term. One-time fee: $75 part-time. Full-time tuition and fees vary according to course level, course load, degree level and program. *Financial support:* Fellowships, teaching assistantships, Federal Work-Study and institutionally sponsored loans available. Support available to part-time students. Financial award application deadline: 1/5; financial award applicants required to submit FAFSA. *Faculty research:* Indo-Iranian, Turkish, central Asian, and Armenian studies; Arabic and ancient Semitics. *Unit head:* Sheldon Pollock, Chair, 212-854-6781, Fax: 212-854-5517, E-mail: sp2356@columbia.edu.

Columbia University, Graduate School of Arts and Sciences, Program in Liberal Studies, New York, NY 10027. Offers American studies (MA); East Asian studies (MA); human rights studies (MA); Islamic culture studies (MA); Jewish studies (MA); medieval studies (MA); modern European studies (MA); South Asian studies (MA). Part-time and evening/weekend programs available. *Faculty:* 5 part-time/adjunct (2 women). *Students:* 7 full-time (2 women), 75 part-time (51 women); includes 5 minority (1 African American, 3 Asian Americans or Pacific Islanders, 1 Hispanic American), 8 international. Average age 41. 39 applicants, 77% accepted.

In 2007, 20 degrees awarded. *Degree requirements:* For master's, thesis. Application fee: $90. *Expenses:* Tuition: Part-time $1,452 per credit. Required fees: $152 per term. One-time fee: $75 part-time. Full-time tuition and fees vary according to course level, course load, degree level and program. *Unit head:* Kristin Balicki, Program Coordinator, 212-854-4932, Fax: 212-854-4912, E-mail: knb2110@columbia.edu.

Columbia University, School of International and Public Affairs, Middle East Institute, New York, NY 10027. Offers Certificate. Students must also be enrolled in a separate graduate degree program at Columbia University. *Application deadline:* For fall admission, 1/4 priority date for domestic students; for spring admission, 10/1 priority date for domestic students. Application fee: $85. Electronic applications accepted. *Expenses:* Tuition: Part-time $1,452 per credit. Required fees: $152 per term. One-time fee: $75 part-time. Full-time tuition and fees vary according to course level, course load, degree level and program. *Financial support:* Application deadline: 1/5. *Unit head:* Dr. Rashidi Khalidi, Director, 212-854-2584, Fax: 212-854-1413, E-mail: sipa_admission@columbia.edu. *Application contact:* Matt Clemons, Director of Admissions and Financial Aid, 212-854-6216, Fax: 212-854-3010, E-mail: mc2793@columbia.edu.

Cornell University, Graduate School, Graduate Fields of Arts and Sciences, Field of Archaeology, Ithaca, NY 14853-0001. Offers environmental archaeology (MA); historical archaeology (MA); Latin American archaeology (MA); medieval archaeology (MA); Mediterranean and Near Eastern archaeology (MA); Stone Age archaeology (MA). *Faculty:* 14 full-time (3 women). *Students:* 2 full-time (both women). Average age 26. 19 applicants, 5% accepted, 1 enrolled. In 2007, 2 degrees awarded. *Degree requirements:* For master's, one foreign language, thesis. *Entrance requirements:* For master's, GRE General Test, 3 letters of recommendation, sample of written work. Additional exam requirements/recommendations for international students: Required—TOEFL (minimum score 550 paper-based; 213 computer-based; 77 iBT). *Application deadline:* For fall admission, 1/15 for domestic students. Application fee: $70. Electronic applications accepted. *Financial support:* In 2007–08, 2 students received support, including 2 teaching assistantships with full tuition reimbursements available; fellowships with full tuition reimbursements available, research assistantships with full tuition reimbursements available, institutionally sponsored loans, scholarships/grants, health care benefits, tuition waivers (full and partial), and unspecified assistantships also available. Financial award applicants required to submit FAFSA. *Faculty research:* Anatolia, Lydia, Sardis, classical and Hellenistic Greece; science in archaeology; North American Indians; Stone Age Africa; Maya trade. *Unit head:* Director of Graduate Studies, 607-255-6768, E-mail: blj7@cornell.edu. *Application contact:* Graduate Field Assistant, 607-255-6768, E-mail: dsd6@cornell.edu.

Cornell University, Graduate School, Graduate Fields of Arts and Sciences, Field of History, Ithaca, NY 14853-0001. Offers African history (MA, PhD); American history (MA, PhD); ancient history (MA, PhD); early modern European history (MA, PhD); English history (MA, PhD); French history (MA, PhD); German history (MA, PhD); history of science (MA, PhD); Latin American history (MA, PhD); medieval Chinese history (MA, PhD); medieval history (MA, PhD); modern Chinese history (MA, PhD); modern European history (MA, PhD); modern Japanese history (MA, PhD); premodern Islamic history (MA, PhD); premodern Japanese history (MA, PhD); Renaissance history (MA, PhD); Russian history (MA, PhD); Southeast Asian history (MA, PhD). *Faculty:* 56 full-time (14 women). *Students:* 63 full-time (29 women); includes 11 minority (6 African Americans, 2 Asian Americans or Pacific Islanders, 3 Hispanic Americans), 20 international. Average age 31. 201 applicants, 6% accepted, 10 enrolled. In 2007, 11 master's, 11 doctorates awarded. Terminal master's awarded for partial completion of doctoral program. *Degree requirements:* For master's, thesis; for doctorate, 2 foreign languages, comprehensive exam, thesis/dissertation, 1 year of teaching experience. *Entrance requirements:* For master's and doctorate, GRE General Test, writing sample, 3 letters of recommendation. Additional exam requirements/recommendations for international students: Required—TOEFL (minimum score 550 paper-based; 213 computer-based; 77 iBT). *Application deadline:* For fall admission, 1/15 for domestic students. Application fee: $70. Electronic applications accepted. *Financial support:* In 2007–08, 54 students received support, including 26 fellowships with full tuition reimbursements available, 28 teaching assistantships with full tuition reimbursements available; research assistantships with full tuition reimbursements available, institutionally sponsored loans, scholarships/grants, health care benefits, tuition waivers (full and partial), and unspecified assistantships also available. Financial award applicants required to submit FAFSA. *Unit head:* Director of Graduate Studies, 607-255-6738, Fax: 607-255-0469. *Application contact:* Graduate Field Assistant, 607-255-6738, Fax: 607-255-0469, E-mail: history_grad_info@cornell.edu.

Cornell University, Graduate School, Graduate Fields of Arts and Sciences, Field of Near Eastern Studies, Ithaca, NY 14853-0001. Offers ancient Near Eastern studies (MA, PhD); Arabic and Islamic studies (MA, PhD); biblical studies (MA, PhD); Hebrew and Judaic studies (MA, PhD). *Faculty:* 13 full-time. *Students:* 4 full-time (3 women), 2 international. Average age 26. 14 applicants, 14% accepted, 1 enrolled.Terminal master's awarded for partial completion of doctoral program. *Degree requirements:* For master's, one foreign language, thesis; for doctorate, 2 foreign languages, comprehensive exam, thesis/dissertation. *Entrance requirements:* For master's and doctorate, GRE General Test, 2 years of 1 Near Eastern language, 3 letters of recommendation, writing sample. Additional exam requirements/recommendations for international students: Required—TOEFL (minimum score 550 paper-based; 213 computer-based; 77 iBT). *Application deadline:* For fall admission, 2/1 for domestic students. Application fee: $70. Electronic applications accepted. *Financial support:* In 2007–08, 4 students received support, including 3 fellowships with full tuition reimbursements available, 1 teaching assistantship with full tuition reimbursement available; research assistantships with full tuition reimbursements available, institutionally sponsored loans, scholarships/grants, health care benefits, tuition waivers (full and partial), and unspecified assistantships also available. Financial award applicants required to submit FAFSA. *Faculty research:* Ancient Near East (including archeology), Hebrew and Judaic studies (including bible), early Christianity, Arabic and Islamic studies, modern Middle East. *Unit head:* Director of Graduate Studies, 607-255-1329, Fax: 607-255-6450. *Application contact:* Graduate Field Assistant, 607-255-1329, Fax: 607-255-6450, E-mail: neareastern@cornell.edu.

Drew University, Caspersen School of Graduate Studies, Program in Biblical Studies and Early Christianity, Madison, NJ 07940-1493. Offers religion in ancient Israel (MA, PhD); the New Testament and early Christianity (MA, PhD). Part-time programs available. Terminal master's awarded for partial completion of doctoral program. *Degree requirements:* For master's, one foreign language, thesis; for doctorate, 2 foreign languages, comprehensive exam, thesis/dissertation. *Entrance requirements:* For master's and doctorate, GRE General Test. *Faculty research:* Folk religions of ancient Israel, New Testament exegesis and apocrypha, Near East archaeology, Hebrew Bible.

Emory University, Graduate School of Arts and Sciences, Department of Comparative Literature, Atlanta, GA 30322-1100. Offers comparative literature (PhD); English (Certificate); French (Certificate); Middle Eastern studies (PhD); philosophy (Certificate); psychoanalytic studies (PhD); religion (PhD); Spanish (Certificate); women studies (Certificate). *Degree requirements:* For doctorate, 2 foreign languages, comprehensive exam, thesis/dissertation. *Entrance requirements:* For doctorate, GRE General Test, minimum GPA of 3.0. Additional exam requirements/recommendations for international students: Required—TOEFL. Electronic applications accepted. *Faculty research:* Literary theory, psychoanalysis trauma and testimony, literature and religion, literature and technology, literature and philosophy, politics and global culture, literature and aesthetics.

Georgetown University, Graduate School of Arts and Sciences, Arab Studies Program, Washington, DC 20057. Offers MA, Certificate, MA/PhD. *Degree requirements:* For master's, one foreign language, comprehensive exam, proficiency in Arabic. *Entrance requirements:* For master's, GRE, minimum GPA of 3.0. Additional exam requirements/recommendations for international students: Required—TOEFL. *Faculty research:* Contemporary Arab world.

Gratz College, Graduate Programs, Program in Israel Studies, Melrose Park, PA 19027. Offers Certificate. Part-time and evening/weekend programs available. *Degree requirements:* For Certificate, one foreign language.

Harvard University, Graduate School of Arts and Sciences, Committee on Middle Eastern Studies, Cambridge, MA 02138. Offers anthropology and Middle Eastern studies (PhD); economics and Middle Eastern studies (PhD); fine arts and Middle Eastern studies (PhD); history and Middle Eastern studies (PhD); regional studies–Middle East (AM). Terminal master's awarded for partial completion of doctoral program. *Degree requirements:* For master's, one foreign language; for doctorate, 2 foreign languages, thesis/dissertation. *Entrance requirements:* For master's, GRE General Test; for doctorate, GRE General Test, 1 year of course work in Middle Eastern regional studies, proficiency in a related language. Additional exam requirements/recommendations for international students: Required—TOEFL. *Expenses:* Tuition: Full-time $31,456. Full-time tuition and fees vary according to program and student level.

Harvard University, Graduate School of Arts and Sciences, Department of Near Eastern Languages and Civilizations, Cambridge, MA 02138. Offers Akkadian and Sumerian (AM, PhD); Arabic (AM, PhD); Armenian (AM, PhD); biblical history (AM, PhD); Hebrew (AM, PhD); Indo-Muslim culture (AM, PhD); Iranian (AM, PhD); Jewish history and literature (AM, PhD); Persian (AM, PhD); Semitic philology (AM, PhD); Syro-Palestinian archaeology (AM, PhD); Turkish (AM, PhD). *Degree requirements:* For doctorate, variable foreign language requirement, thesis/dissertation, general exams. *Entrance requirements:* For master's, GRE General Test; for doctorate, GRE General Test, proficiency in a Near Eastern language. Additional exam requirements/recommendations for international students: Required—TOEFL. *Expenses:* Tuition: Full-time $31,456. Full-time tuition and fees vary according to program and student level.

Hebrew Union College–Jewish Institute of Religion, School of Graduate Studies, Cincinnati, OH 45220-2488. Offers Bible and the ancient Near East (M Phil, MA, PhD); Hebrew letters (DHL); history of biblical interpretation (M Phil, MA, PhD); Jewish and Christian studies in the Greco-Roman period (M Phil, PhD); Jewish and cognate studies (M Phil); Judaic and cognate studies (MA, PhD); modern Jewish history (M Phil, MA, PhD); philosophy and Jewish religious thought (M Phil, MA, PhD); rabbinics (M Phil, MA, PhD). Part-time programs available. Terminal master's awarded for partial completion of doctoral program. *Degree requirements:* For master's, one foreign language, thesis optional; for doctorate, 3 foreign languages, comprehensive exam, thesis/dissertation. *Entrance requirements:* For master's and doctorate, GRE General Test, knowledge of Hebrew. Additional exam requirements/recommendations for international students:. Required—TOEFL. *Faculty research:* Aramaic lexicon translations, German-Jewish history, neo-Babylonian texts.

The Johns Hopkins University, Paul H. Nitze School of Advanced International Studies, Washington, DC 20036. Offers international development (Certificate); international public policy (MIPP); international relations (MA, PhD), including African studies (MA), American foreign policy (MA), Asian studies (MA), Canadian studies (MA), conflict management (MA), European studies (MA), global theory and history (MA), international development (MA), international law, and organizations (MA), international policy (MA), international relations (general) (MA), Latin American studies (MA), Middle East studies (MA), Russian and Eurasian studies (MA), strategic studies (MA); international studies (Certificate); JD/MA; MBA/MA; MHS/MA. *Faculty:* 66 full-time (22 women), 158 part-time/adjunct (54 women). *Students:* 578 full-time (256 women), 46 part-time (16 women); includes 85 minority (18 African Americans, 1 American Indian/Alaska Native, 51 Asian Americans or Pacific Islanders, 15 Hispanic Americans), 193 international. Average age 27. In 2007, 359 master's, 13 doctorates awarded. Terminal master's awarded for partial completion of doctoral program. *Degree requirements:* For master's, one foreign language, 16 non-language courses (8 for MIPP), 2 core examinations, comprehensive oral exam, paper (for some programs); for doctorate, 2 foreign languages, thesis/dissertation, 3 comprehensive exams, defense. *Entrance requirements:* For master's, GMAT or GRE General Test, previous course work in economics, foreign language, undergraduate degree; for doctorate, GRE General Test, master's degree. Additional exam requirements/recommendations for international students: Required—TOEFL (minimum paper-based score of 600, computer-based 250, iBT 100) or IELTS (minimum 7.0). *Application deadline:* For fall admission, 1/7 for domestic students. Application fee: $80. Electronic applications accepted. *Expenses: Contact institution. Financial support:* In 2007–08, 350 students received support, including fellowships (averaging $7,500 per year); career-related internships or fieldwork, Federal Work-Study, and scholarships/grants also available. Financial award application deadline: 2/15; financial award applicants required to submit FAFSA. *Faculty research:* Regional studies and functional fields of international relations, international economics, conflict management, global theory and history, international law and organizations, international policy, strategic studies. *Unit head:* Tara Campbell, Associate Director of Admissions, 202-663-5700, Fax: 202-663-7788. *Application contact:* Dr. Belinda A. Yeomans, Director of Admissions, 202-663-5700, Fax: 202-663-7788, E-mail: admissions.sais@jhu.edu.

The Johns Hopkins University, Zanvyl Krieger School of Arts and Sciences, Department of Near Eastern Studies, Baltimore, MD 21218-2699. Offers PhD. Part-time programs available. *Faculty:* 7 full-time (1 woman), 7 part-time/adjunct (6 women). *Students:* 22 full-time (11 women), 4 international. Average age 26. 64 applicants, 11% accepted, 6 enrolled. In 2007, 2 doctorates awarded. *Median time to degree:* Of those who began their doctoral program in fall 1999, 70% received their degree in 8 years or less. *Degree requirements:* For doctorate, 2 foreign languages, comprehensive exam, thesis/dissertation. *Entrance requirements:* Additional exam requirements/recommendations for international students: Required—TOEFL (minimum score 600 paper-based; 250 computer-based). *Application deadline:* For fall admission, 1/15 for domestic students. Application fee: $75. Electronic applications accepted. *Financial support:* In 2007–08, 16 students received support, including 14 fellowships with full tuition reimbursements available (averaging $15,100 per year), 2 teaching assistantships with full tuition reimbursements available (averaging $15,100 per year); research assistantships with tuition reimbursements available, career-related internships or fieldwork and Federal Work-Study also available. Financial award application deadline: 4/15; financial award applicants required to submit FAFSA. *Faculty research:* Egyptology, Assyriology, religions of ancient Israel and Syria, ancient and biblical law, demotic Egyptian. *Unit head:* Dr. Theodore Lewis, Chair, 410-516-6791, Fax: 410-516-5218, E-mail: tjl@jhu.edu. *Application contact:* Glenda Hogan, Academic Program Coordinator, 410-516-7394, Fax: 410-516-5218, E-mail: ghogan@jhu.edu.

McGill University, Faculty of Graduate and Postdoctoral Studies, Faculty of Arts, Institute of Islamic Studies, Montréal, QC H3A 2T5, Canada. Offers MA, PhD, Diploma. *Faculty:* 13 full-time (6 women), 13 part-time/adjunct (6 women). *Students:* 53 full-time (22 women), 1 (woman) part-time. 81 applicants, 27% accepted, 10 enrolled. In 2007, 14 master's, 6 doctorates awarded.

New York University, Graduate School of Arts and Science, Hagop Kevorkian Center for Near Eastern Studies, Department of Middle Eastern and Islamic Studies, New York, NY 10012-1019. Offers Middle Eastern and Islamic studies (MA, PhD); Middle Eastern and Islamic studies/history (PhD). Part-time programs available. *Faculty:* 17 full-time (6 women), 3 part-time/adjunct. *Students:* 41 full-time (22 women), 2 part-time (both women); includes 5 minority (4 Asian Americans or Pacific Islanders, 1 Hispanic American), 12 international. Average age 31. 127 applicants, 8% accepted, 6 enrolled. In 2007, 1 master's, 3 doctorates awarded. Terminal master's awarded for partial completion of doctoral program. *Degree requirements:* For master's, 2 foreign languages, thesis; for doctorate, 4 foreign languages, comprehensive exam, thesis/dissertation. *Entrance requirements:* For master's and doctorate, GRE General Test. Additional exam requirements/recommendations for international students: Required—TOEFL. *Application deadline:* For fall admission, 12/18 for domestic students. Application fee: $85. *Financial support:* Fellowships with tuition reimbursements, teaching assistantships with tuition reimbursements, Federal Work-Study and institutionally sponsored loans available. Financial award application deadline: 12/18; financial award applicants required to submit FAFSA. *Faculty research:* Middle Eastern history, Arabic/Persian/Turkish language and literature, cultures and societies of Middle East, Islamic studies. *Unit head:* Zachary Lockman, Chairman, 212-

Near and Middle Eastern Studies

New York University (continued)
998-8880, Fax: 212-995-4689, E-mail: mideast.studies@nyu.edu. *Application contact:* Philip Kennedy, Director of Graduate Studies, 212-998-8880, Fax: 212-995-4689, E-mail: mideast.studies@nyu.edu.

New York University, Graduate School of Arts and Science, Hagop Kevorkian Center for Near Eastern Studies, Program in Near Eastern Studies, New York, NY 10012-1019. Offers Near Eastern studies (MA); Near Eastern studies (museum studies) (MA); Near Eastern studies/journalism (MA). Part-time programs available. *Degree requirements:* For master's, one foreign language, thesis. *Entrance requirements:* For master's, GRE General Test. Additional exam requirements/recommendations for international students: Required—TOEFL. *Faculty research:* Politics, political economy, anthropology, history and culture of the Middle East.

New York University, Graduate School of Arts and Science, Program in Museum Studies, New York, NY 10012-1019. Offers museum studies (MA, Advanced Certificate), including Africana studies (MA), Hebrew and Judaic studies (MA), Latin American and Caribbean studies (MA), Near Eastern studies (MA). Part-time and evening/weekend programs available. *Faculty:* 4 full-time (1 woman), 6 part-time/adjunct. *Students:* 55 full-time (46 women), 26 part-time (23 women); includes 11 minority (1 American Indian/Alaska Native, 5 Asian Americans or Pacific Islanders, 5 Hispanic Americans), 19 international. Average age 28. 141 applicants, 66% accepted, 35 enrolled. In 2007, 25 master's awarded. *Entrance requirements:* For degree, master's or PhD. *Application deadline:* For fall admission, 2/1 for domestic students; for spring admission, 11/1 for domestic students. Application fee: $85. *Financial support:* Application deadline: 2/1. *Faculty research:* Modern and contemporary art, history of museums and exhibitions, conservation of cultural materials, museum anthropology, ethnography. *Unit head:* Bruce Altshuler, Director, 212-998-8080, Fax: 212-995-4185, E-mail: museum.studies@nyu.edu. *Application contact:* Tatiana Kamorina, Information Contact, 212-998-8080, Fax: 212-995-4185, E-mail: museum.studies@nyu.edu.

Princeton University, Graduate School, Department of Near Eastern Studies, Princeton, NJ 08544-1019. Offers ancient Near Eastern studies (PhD); Islamic studies (PhD); Near Eastern studies (MA). *Degree requirements:* For master's, one foreign language, thesis; for doctorate, 2 foreign languages, thesis/dissertation. *Entrance requirements:* For master's and doctorate, GRE General Test. Additional exam requirements/recommendations for international students: Required—TOEFL (minimum score 550 paper-based). Electronic applications accepted.

Southern Evangelical Seminary, Veritas Graduate School of Apologetics and Counter-Cult Ministry, Matthews, NC 28105. Offers apologetics (MA, D Min, PhD, Certificate); Islamic studies (MA); Jewish studies (MA); philosophy (MA); religion (MA). *Accreditation:* ATS.Part-time and evening/weekend programs available. Postbaccalaureate distance learning degree programs offered (minimal on-campus study). In 2007, 18 master's, 2 doctorates awarded. *Degree requirements:* For master's, thesis optional; for doctorate, comprehensive exam (for some programs), thesis/dissertation. *Entrance requirements:* Additional exam requirements/recommendations for international students: Required—TOEFL (minimum score 600 paper-based; 250 computer-based). *Application deadline:* For fall admission, 8/5 priority date for domestic and international students; for winter admission, 12/15 priority date for domestic and international students; for spring admission, 1/15 priority date for domestic and international students. Applications are processed on a rolling basis. Application fee: $25. *Financial support:* Scholarships/grants available. *Unit head:* Dr. Thomas A. Howe, Director, Apologetics Program, 704-847-5600 Ext. 209, Fax: 704-845-1747, E-mail: thowe@ses.edu.

The University of Arizona, Graduate College, College of Social and Behavioral Sciences, Department of Near Eastern Studies, Tucson, AZ 85721. Offers MA, PhD. Part-time and evening/weekend programs available. *Faculty:* 13. *Students:* 34 full-time (21 women), 7 part-time (4 women); includes 4 minority (1 African American, 1 American Indian/Alaska Native, 2 Asian Americans or Pacific Islanders), 5 international. Average age 29. 59 applicants, 53% accepted, 15 enrolled. In 2007, 11 master's, 1 doctorate awarded. Terminal master's awarded for partial completion of doctoral program. *Degree requirements:* For master's, one foreign language; for doctorate, 3 foreign languages, thesis/dissertation. *Entrance requirements:* For master's and doctorate, GRE General Test, minimum GPA of 3.0, statement of purpose, curriculum vitae, writing sample. Additional exam requirements/recommendations for international students: Required—TOEFL (minimum score 550 paper-based; 213 computer-based). *Application deadline:* For fall admission, 1/15 for domestic students, 12/1 for international students; for spring admission, 1/1 for domestic students, 6/1 for international students. Applications are processed on a rolling basis. Application fee: $50. Electronic applications accepted. *Financial support:* Fellowships, research assistantships, teaching assistantships, Federal Work-Study, institutionally sponsored loans, and tuition waivers (full) available. Support available to part-time students. *Unit head:* Dr. Michael E. Bonine, Head, 520-626-9140, Fax: 520-621-2333, E-mail: bonine@u.arizona.edu. *Application contact:* Kathleen A. Landeen, Graduate Coordinator, 520-626-8731, Fax: 520-621-2333, E-mail: klandeen@email.arizona.edu.

University of California, Berkeley, Graduate Division, College of Letters and Science, Department of Near Eastern Studies, Program in Near Eastern Religions, Berkeley, CA 94720-1500. Offers PhD. *Degree requirements:* For doctorate, 2 foreign languages, thesis/dissertation, qualifying exam. *Entrance requirements:* For doctorate, GRE General Test, MA or equivalent in Near Eastern studies or related field; minimum GPA of 3.0, 3 letters of recommendation. *Application deadline:* For fall admission, 12/15 for domestic students. Application fee: $70 ($90 for international students). *Financial support:* Fellowships, research assistantships, teaching assistantships, unspecified assistantships available. *Application contact:* Judy Shattuck, Graduate Assistant, 510-642-6162, Fax: 510-643-8430, E-mail: nes@berkeley.edu.

University of California, Berkeley, Graduate Division, College of Letters and Science, Department of Near Eastern Studies, Program in Near Eastern Studies, Berkeley, CA 94720-1500. Offers MA, PhD. *Degree requirements:* For doctorate, 2 foreign languages, thesis/dissertation, qualifying exam. *Entrance requirements:* For master's and doctorate, GRE General Test, minimum GPA of 3.0, 3 letters of recommendation. *Application deadline:* For fall admission, 12/15 for domestic students. Application fee: $70 ($90 for international students). *Financial support:* Unspecified assistantships available. *Application contact:* Judy Shattuck, Graduate Assistant, 510-642-6162, Fax: 510-643-8430, E-mail: nes@berkeley.edu.

University of California, Los Angeles, Graduate Division, College of Letters and Science, Department of Near Eastern Languages and Cultures, Los Angeles, CA 90095. Offers MA, PhD. *Students:* 40 full-time (19 women); includes 6 minority (3 Asian Americans or Pacific Islanders, 3 Hispanic Americans), 1 international. Average age 28. 55 applicants, 31% accepted, 8 enrolled. In 2007, 2 master's, 5 doctorates awarded. *Median time to degree:* Of those who began their doctoral program in fall 1999, 100% received their degree in 8 years or less. *Degree requirements:* For master's, one foreign language, comprehensive exam; for doctorate, 2 foreign languages, thesis/dissertation, oral and written qualifying exams. *Entrance requirements:* For master's and doctorate, GRE General Test, minimum GPA of 3.25, sample of written work recommended. Additional exam requirements/recommendations for international students: Required—TOEFL. *Application deadline:* For fall admission, 12/30 for domestic students. Application fee: $60. Electronic applications accepted. *Expenses:* Tuition, nonresident: full-time $5,728. Required fees: $8,966. Full-time tuition and fees vary according to program and student level. *Financial support:* In 2007–08, 35 fellowships with full and partial tuition reimbursements, 13 research assistantships with full and partial tuition reimbursements, 17 teaching assistantships with full and partial tuition reimbursements were awarded; Federal Work-Study, institutionally sponsored loans, scholarships/grants, and tuition waivers (full and partial) also available. Financial award application deadline: 3/1; financial award applicants required to submit FAFSA. *Unit head:* Dr. William Schniedewind, Chair, 310-825-4165. *Application contact:* Departmental Office, 310-825-4165, E-mail: nreast@humnet.ucla.edu.

University of California, Los Angeles, Graduate Division, College of Letters and Science, Program in Indo-European Studies, Los Angeles, CA 90095. Offers PhD. *Students:* 10 full-time (3 women), 2 international. Average age 28. 12 applicants, 42% accepted, 3 enrolled. In 2007, 1 degree awarded. *Degree requirements:* For doctorate, 2 foreign languages, thesis/dissertation, oral and written qualifying exams. *Entrance requirements:* For doctorate, minimum undergraduate GPA of 3.0, writing sample, competency in Classical Latin. *Application deadline:* For fall admission, 1/15 for domestic students. Application fee: $60. Electronic applications accepted. *Expenses:* Tuition, nonresident: full-time $5,728. Required fees: $8,966. Full-time tuition and fees vary according to program and student level. *Financial support:* In 2007–08, 6 fellowships with full and partial tuition reimbursements, 6 research assistantships with full and partial tuition reimbursements, 3 teaching assistantships with full and partial tuition reimbursements were awarded; Federal Work-Study, institutionally sponsored loans, and tuition waivers (full and partial) also available. Financial award application deadline: 3/1; financial award applicants required to submit FAFSA. *Unit head:* Dr. Stephanie Jamison, Chair, 310-206-1590. *Application contact:* Departmental Office, 310-206-1590, E-mail: dahugheida@humnet.ucla.edu.

University of California, Los Angeles, Graduate Division, College of Letters and Science, Program in Islamic Studies, Los Angeles, CA 90095. Offers MA, PhD, MPH/MA. *Students:* 19 full-time (5 women); includes 2 minority (1 African American, 1 Hispanic American), 4 international. Average age 35. 27 applicants, 44% accepted, 3 enrolled. In 2007, 2 master's awarded. *Degree requirements:* For master's, one foreign language, comprehensive exam; for doctorate, 2 foreign languages, thesis/dissertation, oral and written qualifying exams. *Entrance requirements:* For master's, GRE General Test, minimum GPA of 3.0; for doctorate, GRE General Test, minimum undergraduate GPA of 3.0, Masters degree, advanced level proficiency in Arabic. *Application deadline:* For fall admission, 12/15 for domestic students. Application fee: $60. Electronic applications accepted. *Expenses:* Tuition, nonresident: full-time $5,728. Required fees: $8,966. Full-time tuition and fees vary according to program and student level. *Financial support:* In 2007–08, 7 fellowships with full and partial tuition reimbursements, 4 research assistantships with full and partial tuition reimbursements, 5 teaching assistantships with full and partial tuition reimbursements were awarded; Federal Work-Study, institutionally sponsored loans, scholarships/grants, and tuition waivers (full and partial) also available. Financial award application deadline: 3/1; financial award applicants required to submit FAFSA. *Unit head:* Dr. Michael Morony, Chair, 310-206-6571. *Application contact:* Departmental Office, 310-206-6571, E-mail: idpgrads@international.ucla.edu.

University of Chicago, Division of Social Sciences and Division of the Humanities, Middle Eastern Studies Program, Chicago, IL 60637-1513. Offers AM, MBA/AM, MPP/AM. *Students:* 30. In 2007, 6 degrees awarded. *Degree requirements:* For master's, one foreign language, thesis. *Entrance requirements:* For master's, GRE General Test. Additional exam requirements/recommendations for international students: Required—TOEFL. *Application deadline:* For fall admission, 12/28 for domestic students. Application fee: $55. Electronic applications accepted. *Financial support:* Federal Work-Study, institutionally sponsored loans, and scholarships/grants available. Financial award application deadline: 12/28. *Unit head:* Prof. Holly Shissler, Director, 773-702-8296. *Application contact:* Office of the Dean of Students, 773-702-8415.

University of Chicago, Division of the Humanities, Department of Near Eastern Languages and Civilizations, Chicago, IL 60637-1513. Offers AM, PhD. *Faculty:* 52. *Students:* 149. 113 applicants, 33% accepted, 17 enrolled.Terminal master's awarded for partial completion of doctoral program. *Degree requirements:* For master's, one foreign language, comprehensive exam, thesis; for doctorate, 2 foreign languages, comprehensive exam, thesis/dissertation. *Entrance requirements:* For master's and doctorate, GRE General Test. Additional exam requirements/recommendations for international students: Required—TOEFL. *Application deadline:* For fall admission, 12/15 for domestic students. Application fee: $55. *Financial support:* Fellowships, Federal Work-Study available. Financial award application deadline: 12/15; financial award applicants required to submit FAFSA. *Unit head:* Dr. Theo van den Hout, Chair, 773-702-9512.

University of Kansas, Research and Graduate Studies, College of Liberal Arts and Sciences, Center for Russian, East European and Eurasian Studies, Lawrence, KS 66045. Offers MA. Part-time programs available. *Faculty:* 45 full-time (11 women). *Students:* 10 full-time (2 women), 1 part-time. Average age 28. 13 applicants, 100% accepted, 3 enrolled. In 2007, 8 master's awarded. *Degree requirements:* For master's, one foreign language, comprehensive exam, interdisciplinary capstone seminar. *Entrance requirements:* For master's, GRE General Test, 3 letters of recommendation. Additional exam requirements/recommendations for international students: Required—TOEFL. *Application deadline:* For fall admission, 5/1 priority date for domestic students, 2/14 priority date for international students; for spring admission, 10/1 priority date for domestic students, 9/1 priority date for international students. Applications are processed on a rolling basis. Application fee: $55 ($60 for international students). Electronic applications accepted. *Expenses:* Tuition, state resident: full-time $5,838. Tuition, nonresident: full-time $13,409. Tuition and fees vary according to program. *Financial support:* In 2007–08, 8 fellowships with full tuition reimbursements, 2 research assistantships with full and partial tuition reimbursements were awarded; scholarships/grants and tuition waivers (partial) also available. Financial award application deadline: 1/31; financial award applicants required to submit FAFSA. *Faculty research:* Transition studies, Russian history and philosophy, Ukrainian and Russian domestic and foreign policies, Slavic languages and literatures, security policies in Central Asia and the Caucasus. *Unit head:* Dr. William Comer, Director, 785-864-4236, Fax: 785-864-3800, E-mail: crees@ku.edu. *Application contact:* Ray C. Finch, Graduate Advisor, Assistant Director, 785-864-4248, Fax: 785-864-3800, E-mail: rayfin3@ku.edu.

University of Michigan, Horace H. Rackham School of Graduate Studies, College of Literature, Science, and the Arts, Department of Near Eastern Studies, Ann Arbor, MI 48109. Offers ancient Israel/Hebrew Bible (AM, PhD); Arabic (AM, PhD); Armenian (AM, PhD); early Christian studies (AM, PhD); Egyptology (AM, PhD); Hebrew (AM, PhD); Islamic studies (AM, PhD); Mesopotamian and ancient Near Eastern studies (AM, PhD); Persian (AM, PhD); teaching of Arabic as a foreign Language (AM); Turkish (AM, PhD). Part-time programs available. *Faculty:* 22 full-time (3 women), 8 part-time/adjunct (3 women). *Students:* 45 full-time (21 women); includes 2 minority (both African Americans), 7 international. Average age 27. 88 applicants, 17% accepted, 5 enrolled. In 2007, 2 master's, 3 doctorates awarded. Terminal master's awarded for partial completion of doctoral program. *Degree requirements:* For master's, 2 foreign languages; for doctorate, 4 foreign languages, oral defense of dissertation, preliminary exam. *Entrance requirements:* For master's, GRE General Test; for doctorate, GRE General Test, master's degree. Additional exam requirements/recommendations for international students: Required—TOEFL (minimum score 560 paper-based; 220 computer-based; 84 iBT). *Application deadline:* For fall admission, 12/15 for domestic and international students. Application fee: $60 ($75 for international students). *Financial support:* In 2007–08, 25 students received support, including 14 fellowships with full tuition reimbursements available (averaging $14,400 per year), research assistantships with tuition reimbursements available (averaging $15,200 per year), 16 teaching assistantships with full tuition reimbursements available (averaging $15,200 per year); scholarships/grants, health care benefits, and unspecified assistantships also available. *Faculty research:* Middle and Near Eastern literatures, languages, cultures from ancient times to the present. *Unit head:* Prof. Gary Beckman, Chair, 734-764-0314, Fax: 734-936-2679, E-mail: sidd@umich.edu. *Application contact:* Angela Beskow, Student Services Assistant, 734-763-4539, Fax: 734-936-2679, E-mail: aradjews@umich.edu.

University of Michigan, Horace H. Rackham School of Graduate Studies, Interdepartmental Program in Modern Middle Eastern and North African Studies, Ann Arbor, MI 48109. Offers AM, JD/AM, MBA/AM, MPH/AM. *Degree requirements:* For master's, one foreign language, thesis or alternative. *Entrance requirements:* For master's, GRE General Test. Additional exam requirements/recommendations for international students: Required—TOEFL. Electronic applications accepted. *Faculty research:* Middle east and north Africa.

University of Pennsylvania, School of Arts and Sciences, Graduate Group in Near Eastern Languages and Civilization, Philadelphia, PA 19104. Offers AM, PhD.

University of South Africa, College of Human Sciences, Pretoria, South Africa. Offers adult education (M Ed); African languages (MA, PhD); African politics (MA, PhD); Afrikaans (MA, PhD); ancient history (MA, PhD); ancient Near Eastern studies (MA, PhD); anthropology (MA, PhD); applied linguistics (MA); Arabic (MA, PhD); archaeology (MA); art history (MA); Biblical archaeology (MA); Biblical studies (M Th, D Th, PhD); Christian spirituality (M Th, D Th); church history (M Th, D Th); classical studies (MA, PhD); clinical psychology (MA); communication (MA, PhD); comparative education (M Ed, Ed D); consulting psychology (D Admin, D Com, PhD); curriculum studies (M Ed, Ed D); development studies (M Admin, MA, D Admin, PhD); didactics (M Ed, Ed D); education (M Tech); education management (M Ed, Ed D); educational psychology (M Ed); English (MA); environmental education (M Ed); French (MA, PhD); German (MA, PhD); Greek (MA); guidance and counseling (M Ed); health studies (MA, PhD), including health sciences education (MA), health services management (MA), medical and surgical nursing science (critical care general) (MA), midwifery and neonatal nursing science (MA), trauma and emergency care (MA); history (MA, PhD); history of education (Ed D); inclusive education (M Ed, Ed D); information and communications technology policy and regulation (MA); information science (MA, MIS, PhD); international politics (MA, PhD); Islamic studies (MA, PhD); Italian (MA, PhD); Judaica (MA, PhD); linguistics (MA, PhD); mathematical education (M Ed); mathematics education (MA); missiology (M Th, D Th); modern Hebrew (MA, PhD); musicology (MA, MMus, D Mus, PhD); natural science education (M Ed); New Testament (M Th, D Th); Old Testament (D Th); pastoral therapy (M Th, D Th); philosophy (MA); philosophy of education (M Ed, Ed D); politics (MA, PhD); Portuguese (MA, PhD); practical theology (M Th, D Th); psychology (MA, MS, PhD); psychology of education (M Ed, Ed D); public health (MA); religious studies (MA, D Th, PhD); Romance languages (MA); Russian (MA, PhD); Semitic languages (MA, PhD); social behavior studies in HIV/AIDS (MA); social science (mental health) (MA); social science in development studies (MA); social science in psychology (MA); social science in social work (MA); social science in sociology (MA); social work (MSW, DSW, PhD); socio-education (M Ed, Ed D); sociolinguistics (MA); sociology (MA, PhD); Spanish (MA, PhD); systematic theology (M Th, D Th); TESOL (teaching English to speakers of other languages) (MA); theological ethics (M Th, D Th); theory of literature (MA, PhD); urban ministries (D Th); urban ministry (M Th).

The University of Texas at Austin, Graduate School, College of Liberal Arts, Center for Middle Eastern Studies, Austin, TX 78712-1111. Offers MA, JD/MA, MBA/MA, MLIS/MA, MP Aff/MA. *Degree requirements:* For master's, one foreign language, thesis optional. *Entrance requirements:* For master's, GRE General Test. Electronic applications accepted.

The University of Texas at Austin, Graduate School, College of Liberal Arts, Department of Middle Eastern Studies, Austin, TX 78712-1111. Offers Arabic studies (MA, PhD); Hebrew studies (MA, PhD); Persian studies (MA, PhD). *Degree requirements:* For master's, one foreign language, comprehensive exam, thesis; for doctorate, 2 foreign languages, comprehensive exam, thesis/dissertation. *Entrance requirements:* For master's and doctorate, GRE General Test. Additional exam requirements/recommendations for international students: Required—TOEFL. Electronic applications accepted. *Faculty research:* Islamic studies, Persian language and literature, Hebrew language, Jewish studies, Arabic literature and language.

University of Toronto, School of Graduate Studies, Humanities Division, Department of Near and Middle Eastern Civilizations, Toronto, ON M5S 1A1, Canada. Offers MA, PhD. Part-time programs available. *Faculty:* 25 full-time, 8 part-time/adjunct. *Students:* 89 full-time (44 women), 4 part-time, 28 international. 134 applicants, 51% accepted. In 2007, 3 master's, 1 doctorate awarded. *Degree requirements:* For master's, thesis optional; for doctorate, 2 foreign languages, thesis/dissertation, language proficiency exams. *Entrance requirements:* For master's, BA in relevant area, minimum B+ average in final year, prior coursework in ancient Near Eastern or Islamic civilizations, 2 letters of reference; for doctorate, MA in relevant area with a minimum A– average, 2 letters of reference. Additional exam requirements/recommendations for international students: Required—TOEFL (minimum score 580 paper-based; 237 computer-based), TWE (minimum score 5). *Application deadline:* For fall admission, 1/15 for domestic students. Application fee: $100 Canadian dollars. *Unit head:* Prof. Linda Northrup, Chair, 416-978-0378, Fax: 416-978-3305. *Application contact:* Anna Sousa, Graduate Administrator, 416-978-3181, Fax: 416-978-3305, E-mail: anna.sousa@utoronto.edu.

University of Utah, The Graduate School, College of Humanities, Program in Middle East Studies, Salt Lake City, UT 84112-1107. Offers anthropology (MA); Arabic (MA, PhD); Arabic and linguistics (MA, PhD); Hebrew (MA); history (MA, PhD); Persian (MA, PhD); political science (MA, PhD); Turkish (MA). *Faculty:* 12 full-time (3 women). *Students:* 26 full-time (12 women), 10 part-time (2 women); includes 1 minority (Asian American or Pacific Islander), 10 international. Average age 36. 36 applicants, 78% accepted, 10 enrolled. In 2007, 6 master's awarded. Terminal master's awarded for partial completion of doctoral program. *Median time to degree:* Of those who began their doctoral program in fall 1999, 100% received their degree in 8 years or less. *Degree requirements:* For master's, 2 foreign languages, comprehensive exam, thesis optional; for doctorate, 3 foreign languages, comprehensive exam, thesis/dissertation. *Entrance requirements:* For master's, GRE General Test, minimum GPA of 3.2; for doctorate, GRE General Test, MA in Middle East studies or equivalent, minimum GPA of 3.2. Additional exam requirements/recommendations for international students: Required—TOEFL (minimum score 580 paper-based; 237 computer-based; 92 iBT). *Application deadline:* For fall admission, 1/15 for domestic and international students; for spring admission, 9/15 for domestic and international students. Application fee: $45 ($65 for international students). *Financial support:* In 2007–08, 17 students received support, including 14 fellowships with full tuition reimbursements available (averaging $14,000 per year), 2 teaching assistantships with full tuition reimbursements available (averaging $12,000 per year); unspecified assistantships also available. Financial award application deadline: 1/15. *Faculty research:* Arabic literature and linguistics, Islamic studies, Middle East history, political science, Judaic studies. *Unit head:* Dr. Ibrahim A. Karawan, Director, 801-581-6181, Fax: 801-581-6183, E-mail: ibrahim.karawan@poli-sci.utah.edu. *Application contact:* Peter von Sivers, Director of Graduate Studies, 801-581-8073, Fax: 801-581-6183, E-mail: peter.vonsivers@utah.edu.

University of Washington, Graduate School, College of Arts and Sciences, Department of Near Eastern Languages and Civilization, Seattle, WA 98195. Offers MA. *Degree requirements:* For master's, 2 foreign languages, exams. *Entrance requirements:* For master's, GRE, minimum GPA of 3.0. Additional exam requirements/recommendations for international students: Required—TOEFL. Electronic applications accepted. *Faculty research:* Arabic, Hebrew, Persian, and Turkish literature; Islamic civilization and religion; Central Asian Turkic language and literature; Hebrew Bible and ancient Near East; ancient Christianity.

University of Washington, Graduate School, College of Arts and Sciences, Henry M. Jackson School of International Studies, Middle Eastern Studies Program, Seattle, WA 98195. Offers MAIS. *Faculty:* 35 full-time (14 women). *Students:* 12 full-time (5 women), 1 international. 42 applicants, 36% accepted, 3 enrolled. In 2007, 7 degrees awarded. *Degree requirements:* For master's, one foreign language, thesis optional. *Entrance requirements:* For master's, GRE General Test, minimum GPA of 3.0. Additional exam requirements/recommendations for international students: Required—TOEFL (minimum score 500 paper-based; 213 computer-based). Application fee: $50. Electronic applications accepted. *Financial support:* In 2007–08, 1 fellowship with full tuition reimbursement was awarded; research assistantships, teaching assistantships, career-related internships or fieldwork, Federal Work-Study, institutionally sponsored loans, and summer language study awards also available. Financial award application deadline: 1/15; financial award applicants required to submit FAFSA. *Unit head:* Prof. Philip D. Schuyler, Chair, 206-543-9878. *Application contact:* 206-543-6001, Fax: 206-616-3170, E-mail: jsisinfo@u.washington.edu.

University of Washington, Graduate School, Interdisciplinary Program in Near and Middle Eastern Studies, Seattle, WA 98195. Offers PhD. *Degree requirements:* For doctorate, 3 foreign languages, thesis/dissertation. *Entrance requirements:* For doctorate, GRE General Test, minimum GPA of 3.0. Additional exam requirements/recommendations for international students: Required—TOEFL. Electronic applications accepted.

University of Waterloo, Graduate Studies, Faculty of Arts, Department of Classical Studies, Waterloo, ON N2L 3G1, Canada. Offers ancient Mediterranean cultures (MA). *Degree requirements:* For master's, one foreign language. *Entrance requirements:* For master's, BA, B+. Application fee: $75. *Financial support:* Fellowships, research assistantships, teaching assistantships available. *Faculty research:* Ancient history, philosophy, anthropology, religion, culture. *Unit head:* Dr. Riemer Faber, Chair, Classical Studies, E-mail: rfarber@uwaterloo.ca. *Application contact:* Dr. David Porreca, Graduate Officer, E-mail: dporreca@uwaterloo.ca.

Washington University in St. Louis, Graduate School of Arts and Sciences, Department of History, Program in Jewish, Islamic, and Near Eastern Studies, St. Louis, MO 63130-4899. Offers Islamic and Near Eastern studies (MA); Jewish studies (MA). *Degree requirements:* For master's, one foreign language, thesis (for some programs). *Entrance requirements:* For master's, GRE General Test. Electronic applications accepted.

Wayne State University, College of Liberal Arts and Sciences, Department of Classical and Modern Languages, Literatures, and Cultures, Program in Near Eastern and Asian Studies, Detroit, MI 48202. Offers language learning (MA); Near Eastern studies (MA). *Faculty:* 1 (woman) full-time. *Students:* 4 full-time (1 woman), 5 part-time (3 women); includes 3 minority (1 African American, 2 Asian Americans or Pacific Islanders), 1 international. Average age 31. 6 applicants, 50% accepted, 2 enrolled. *Degree requirements:* For master's, one foreign language. *Entrance requirements:* For master's, GRE General Test. Additional exam requirements/recommendations for international students: Required—TOEFL (minimum score 550 paper-based; 213 computer-based); Recommended—TWE (minimum score 6). *Application deadline:* For fall admission, 7/1 for domestic students, 6/1 for international students; for winter admission, 10/1 for international students; for spring admission, 2/1 for international students. Applications are processed on a rolling basis. Application fee: $30 ($50 for international students). Electronic applications accepted. *Expenses:* Tuition, state resident: part-time $403 per credit hour. Tuition, nonresident: part-time $890 per credit hour. *Financial support:* In 2007–08, 3 teaching assistantships with tuition reimbursements (averaging $12,447 per year) were awarded. *Faculty research:* Modern Middle East history, Arabic language and culture studies, Chinese linguistics, Islamic studies, Judaic studies. *Unit head:* Dr. May Seikaly, Chair, 313-577-6266, Fax: 313-577-3266, E-mail: ad6006@wayne.edu.

Northern Studies

University of Alaska Fairbanks, College of Liberal Arts, Department of Northern Studies, Fairbanks, AK 99775-7520. Offers MA. Part-time programs available. *Degree requirements:* For master's, comprehensive exam, thesis or alternative. *Entrance requirements:* For master's, GRE General Test. Additional exam requirements/recommendations for international students: Required—TOEFL (minimum score 550 paper-based; 213 computer-based). Electronic applications accepted. *Faculty research:* Canadian history, environmental history, Native Alaskan history and art, fetal alcohol syndrome.

University of Manitoba, Faculty of Graduate Studies, Faculty of Arts, Department of Icelandic Studies, Winnipeg, MB R3T 2N2, Canada. Offers MA.

Western European Studies

Boston College, Graduate School of Arts and Sciences, Department of History, Chestnut Hill, MA 02467-3800. Offers European national studies (MA); history (MA, PhD); medieval studies (MA). *Students:* 70 full-time (35 women), 10 part-time (6 women); includes 8 minority (2 African Americans, 3 Asian Americans or Pacific Islanders, 3 Hispanic Americans), 6 international. 192 applicants, 25% accepted, 25 enrolled. In 2007, 16 master's, 7 doctorates awarded. Terminal master's awarded for partial completion of doctoral program. *Degree requirements:* For master's, one foreign language, comprehensive exam, thesis optional; for doctorate, 2 foreign languages, comprehensive exam, thesis/dissertation. *Entrance requirements:* For master's and doctorate, GRE General Test, writing sample. Additional exam requirements/recommendations for international students: Required—TOEFL (minimum score 590 paper-based; 250 computer-based; 91 iBT). *Application deadline:* For fall admission, 1/15 for domestic students. Application fee: $70. Electronic applications accepted. *Financial support:* Fellowships with full tuition reimbursements, research assistantships with full tuition reimbursements, teaching assistantships with full tuition reimbursements, Federal Work-Study and scholarships/grants available. Support available to part-time students. Financial award application deadline: 3/1; financial award applicants required to submit FAFSA. *Faculty research:* Modern and early modern European, U.S., Russian, and Soviet history; European and U.S. intellectual history. *Unit head:* Dr. Marilynn Johnson, Chairperson, 617-552-3781. *Application contact:* Dr. David Quigley, Director of Graduate Studies, 617-552-2267, E-mail: david.quigley@bc.edu.

Brown University, Graduate School, Center for Portuguese and Brazilian Studies, Providence, RI 02912. Offers Brazilian studies (AM); Luso-Brazilian studies (PhD); Portuguese studies and bilingual education (AM). *Degree requirements:* For doctorate, thesis/dissertation.

Carleton University, Faculty of Graduate Studies, Faculty of Public Affairs and Management, Institute of European and Russian Studies, Ottawa, ON K1S 5B6, Canada. Offers European

Western European Studies

Carleton University (continued)
and European Union studies (MA); European integration studies (Diploma); Russian, Eurasian and transition studies (MA). *Degree requirements:* For master's, one foreign language, thesis optional. *Entrance requirements:* For master's, honors degree or equivalent; 2 years of Russian, German or other central east European language. Additional exam requirements/recommendations for international students: Required—TOEFL. *Application deadline:* Applications are processed on a rolling basis. Application fee: $77 Canadian dollars. *Financial support:* Fellowships, teaching assistantships, institutionally sponsored loans, scholarships/grants, and unspecified assistantships available. *Faculty research:* East-West relations, minority rights in Russia and Eastern Europe. *Unit head:* Andrea Chandler, Director, 613-520-2600 Ext. 2888, Fax: 613-520-2889, E-mail: eurus@carleton.ca. *Application contact:* Ginette Lafleur, Graduate Secretary, 613-520-2600 Ext. 2888, Fax: 613-520-2889, E-mail: eurus@carleton.ca.

The Catholic University of America, School of Arts and Sciences, Program in Irish Studies, Washington, DC 20064. Offers MA. Part-time programs available. *Faculty:* 1 (woman) part-time/adjunct. *Students:* 3 full-time (2 women), 1 (woman) part-time. Average age 29. 5 applicants, 60% accepted, 2 enrolled. In 2007, 2 degrees awarded. *Degree requirements:* For master's, one foreign language, comprehensive exam. *Entrance requirements:* For master's, GRE General Test, 3 letters of recommendation, writing sample. Additional exam requirements/recommendations for international students: Required—TOEFL (minimum score 580 paper-based; 237 computer-based). *Application deadline:* For fall admission, 2/1 priority date for domestic students; for spring admission, 11/15 priority date for domestic students. Applications are processed on a rolling basis. Application fee: $55. Electronic applications accepted. *Financial support:* Career-related internships or fieldwork, Federal Work-Study, scholarships/grants, tuition waivers (partial), and unspecified assistantships available. Support available to part-time students. Financial award application deadline: 2/1; financial award applicants required to submit FAFSA. *Faculty research:* Eighteenth and nineteenth century Irish literature, contemporary Irish literature, Irish language, Irish politics, Irish American history. *Unit head:* Christina H. Mahony, Acting Director, 202-319-5458, Fax: 202-319-6076, E-mail: mahonyc@cua.edu.

Claremont Graduate University, Graduate Programs, School of Arts and Humanities, Department of History, Claremont, CA 91711-6160. Offers Africana history (Certificate); American studies and U.S. history (MA, PhD); archival studies (MA); early modern studies (MA, PhD); European studies (MA, PhD); oral history (MA, PhD); MBA/MA; MBA/PhD. *Faculty:* 3 full-time (2 women), 1 part-time/adjunct (0 women). *Students:* 74 full-time (40 women), 8 part-time (3 women); includes 15 minority (1 African American, 2 Asian Americans or Pacific Islanders, 12 Hispanic Americans), 2 international. Average age 37. In 2007, 8 master's, 8 doctorates awarded. *Degree requirements:* For master's, 2 foreign languages, thesis; for doctorate, 2 foreign languages, comprehensive exam, thesis/dissertation. *Entrance requirements:* For master's and doctorate, GRE General Test. *Application deadline:* For fall admission, 2/15 priority date for domestic students. Applications are processed on a rolling basis. Electronic applications accepted. *Expenses:* Tuition: Full-time $31,640; part-time $1,376 per unit. Required fees: $145 per semester. Tuition and fees vary according to course load, degree level and program. *Financial support:* Fellowships, research assistantships, Federal Work-Study and institutionally sponsored loans available. Support available to part-time students. Financial award application deadline: 2/15; financial award applicants required to submit FAFSA. *Faculty research:* Intellectual and social history, cultural studies, gender studies, Western history, Chicano history. *Unit head:* Janet Farrell Brodie, Chair, 909-621-8880, Fax: 909-621-8609, E-mail: janet.brodie@cgu.edu.

Columbia University, Graduate School of Arts and Sciences, Program in Liberal Studies, New York, NY 10027. Offers American studies (MA); East Asian studies (MA); human rights studies (MA); Islamic culture studies (MA); Jewish studies (MA); medieval studies (MA); modern European studies (MA); South Asian studies (MA). Part-time and evening/weekend programs available. *Faculty:* 5 part-time/adjunct (2 women). *Students:* 7 full-time (2 women), 75 part-time (51 women); includes 5 minority (1 African American, 3 Asian Americans or Pacific Islanders, 1 Hispanic American), 8 international. Average age 41. 39 applicants, 77% accepted. In 2007, 20 degrees awarded. *Degree requirements:* For master's, thesis. Application fee: $90. *Expenses:* Tuition: Part-time $1,452 per credit. Required fees: $152 per term. One-time fee: $75 part-time. Full-time tuition and fees vary according to course level, course load, degree level and program. *Unit head:* Kristin Balicki, Program Coordinator, 212-854-4932, Fax: 212-854-4912, E-mail: knb2110@columbia.edu.

Columbia University, School of International and Public Affairs, Institute for the Study of Europe, New York, NY 10027. Offers Certificate. Students must be enrolled in a separate graduate degree program at Columbia University. *Application deadline:* For fall admission, 1/4 for domestic students; for spring admission, 10/1 for domestic students. Application fee: $85. Electronic applications accepted. *Expenses:* Tuition: Part-time $1,452 per credit. Required fees: $152 per term. One-time fee: $75 part-time. Full-time tuition and fees vary according to course level, course load, degree level and program. *Financial support:* Application deadline: 1/15. *Unit head:* Dr. Volker Berghahn, Director, 212-854-4618, Fax: 212-854-8577. *Application contact:* Matt Clemons, Director of Admissions and Financial Aid, 212-854-6216, Fax: 212-854-3010, E-mail: mc2793@columbia.edu.

Cornell University, Graduate School, Graduate Fields of Arts and Sciences, Field of History, Ithaca, NY 14853-0001. Offers African history (MA, PhD); American history (MA, PhD); ancient history (MA, PhD); early modern European history (MA, PhD); English history (MA, PhD); French history (MA, PhD); German history (MA, PhD); history of science (MA, PhD); Latin American history (MA, PhD); medieval Chinese history (MA, PhD); medieval history (MA, PhD); modern Chinese history (MA, PhD); modern European history (MA, PhD); modern Japanese history (MA, PhD); premodern Islamic history (MA, PhD); premodern Japanese history (MA, PhD); Renaissance history (MA, PhD); Russian history (MA, PhD); Southeast Asian history (MA, PhD). *Faculty:* 56 full-time (14 women). *Students:* 63 full-time (29 women); includes 11 minority (6 African Americans, 2 Asian Americans or Pacific Islanders, 3 Hispanic Americans), 20 international. Average age 31. 201 applicants, 6% accepted, 10 enrolled. In 2007, 11 master's, 11 doctorates awarded. Terminal master's awarded for partial completion of doctoral program. *Degree requirements:* For master's, thesis; for doctorate, 2 foreign languages, comprehensive exam, thesis/dissertation, 1 year of teaching experience. *Entrance requirements:* For master's and doctorate, GRE General Test, writing sample, 3 letters of recommendation. Additional exam requirements/recommendations for international students: Required—TOEFL (minimum score 550 paper-based; 213 computer-based; 77 iBT). *Application deadline:* For fall admission, 1/15 for domestic students. Application fee: $70. Electronic applications accepted. *Financial support:* In 2007–08, 54 students received support, including 26 fellowships with full tuition reimbursements available, 28 teaching assistantships with full tuition reimbursements available; research assistantships with full tuition reimbursements available, institutionally sponsored loans, scholarships/grants, health care benefits, tuition waivers (full and partial), and unspecified assistantships also available. Financial award applicants required to submit FAFSA. *Unit head:* Director of Graduate Studies, 607-255-6738, Fax: 607-255-0469. *Application contact:* Graduate Field Assistant, 607-255-6738, Fax: 607-255-0469, E-mail: history_grad_info@cornell.edu.

East Carolina University, Graduate School, Thomas Harriot College of Arts and Sciences, Department of History, Greenville, NC 27858-4353. Offers American history (MA); European history (MA); maritime history (MA). Part-time and evening/weekend programs available. *Faculty:* 27 full-time (4 women). *Students:* 30 full-time (14 women), 26 part-time (14 women); includes 4 minority (2 African Americans, 2 Hispanic Americans), 3 international. Average age 31. 14 applicants, 50% accepted, 3 enrolled. In 2007, 13 degrees awarded. *Degree requirements:* For master's, one foreign language, comprehensive exam, thesis. *Entrance requirements:* For master's, GRE General Test, GRE Subject Test. Additional exam requirements/recommendations for international students: Required—TOEFL. *Application deadline:* For fall admission, 6/1 priority date for domestic students; for spring admission, 10/15 for domestic students. Applications are processed on a rolling basis. Application fee: $50. *Financial support:* Fellowships, research assistantships with partial tuition reimbursements, teaching assistantships with partial tuition reimbursements, Federal Work-Study available. Support available to part-time students. Financial award application deadline: 6/1. *Unit head:* Dr. Michael Palmer, Chair, 252-328-1046, E-mail: palmerm@ecu.edu. *Application contact:* Dr. Carl Swanson, Director of Graduate Studies, 252-328-6485, E-mail: swansonc@ecu.edu.

Georgetown University, Graduate School of Arts and Sciences, BMW Center for German and European Studies, Washington, DC 20057. Offers MA, MA/JD, MA/PhD. *Degree requirements:* For master's, 2 foreign languages, comprehensive exam. *Entrance requirements:* For master's, GRE General Test. Additional exam requirements/recommendations for international students: Required—TOEFL. *Faculty research:* Trans-Atlantic relations, European Union, German and European Studies.

The George Washington University, Elliott School of International Affairs, Program in European and Eurasian Studies, Washington, DC 20052. Offers MA, JD/MA, MBA/MA. Part-time and evening/weekend programs available. *Degree requirements:* For master's, one foreign language, capstone project. *Entrance requirements:* For master's, GRE General Test, 2 years (or the equivalent) of a modern European language (or Russian), 2 semesters of introductory economics (macro or micro economics). Additional exam requirements/recommendations for international students: Required—TOEFL. Electronic applications accepted. *Faculty research:* NATO, European economics, European history, European Union.

Indiana University Bloomington, University Graduate School, College of Arts and Sciences, Department of West European Studies, Bloomington, IN 47405-7000. Offers MA. *Faculty:* 1 full-time (0 women). *Students:* 6 full-time (4 women), 1 (woman) part-time, 2 international. Average age 26. 5 applicants, 60% accepted, 1 enrolled. In 2007, 1 degree awarded. *Degree requirements:* For master's, 2 foreign languages, thesis. *Entrance requirements:* For master's, GRE General Test. Additional exam requirements/recommendations for international students: Required—TOEFL. *Application deadline:* For fall admission, 1/15 priority date for domestic students, 12/15 for international students; for spring admission, 9/1 priority date for domestic students, 9/1 for international students. Applications are processed on a rolling basis. Application fee: $50 ($60 for international students). *Financial support:* Fellowships with full tuition reimbursements, research assistantships with full tuition reimbursements, teaching assistantships with partial tuition reimbursements available. *Faculty research:* European integration, economics of Europe, European union, European culture and identity, expansion of European union. *Unit head:* Dr. Patricia McManus, Director, 812-855-3280, E-mail: pmcmanus@indiana.edu. *Application contact:* Deborah Piston-Hatlen, Associate Director, 812-855-3280, Fax: 812-855-7695, E-mail: weur@indiana.edu.

The Johns Hopkins University, Paul H. Nitze School of Advanced International Studies, Washington, DC 20036. Offers international development (Certificate); international public policy (MIPP); international relations (MA, PhD), including African studies (MA), American foreign policy (MA), Asian studies (MA), Canadian studies (MA), conflict management (MA), European studies (MA), global theory and history (MA), international development (MA), international law, and organizations (MA), international policy (MA), international relations (general) (MA), Latin American studies (MA), Middle East studies (MA), Russian and Eurasian studies (MA), strategic studies (MA); international studies (Certificate); JD/MA; MBA/MA; MHS/MA. *Faculty:* 66 full-time (22 women), 158 part-time/adjunct (54 women). *Students:* 578 full-time (256 women), 46 part-time (16 women); includes 85 minority (18 African Americans, 1 American Indian/Alaska Native, 51 Asian Americans or Pacific Islanders, 15 Hispanic Americans), 193 international. Average age 27. In 2007, 359 master's, 13 doctorates awarded. Terminal master's awarded for partial completion of doctoral program. *Degree requirements:* For master's, one foreign language, 16 non-language courses (8 for MIPP), 2 core examinations, comprehensive oral exam, paper (for some programs); for doctorate, 2 foreign languages, thesis/dissertation, 3 comprehensive exams, defense. *Entrance requirements:* For master's, GMAT or GRE General Test, previous course work in economics, foreign language, undergraduate degree; for doctorate, GRE General Test, master's degree. Additional exam requirements/recommendations for international students: Required—TOEFL (minimum paper-based score of 600, computer-based 250, iBT 100) or IELTS (minimum 7.0). *Application deadline:* For fall admission, 1/7 for domestic students. Application fee: $80. Electronic applications accepted. *Expenses:* Contact institution. *Financial support:* In 2007–08, 350 students received support, including fellowships (averaging $7,500 per year); career-related internships or fieldwork, Federal Work-Study, and scholarships/grants also available. Financial award application deadline: 2/15; financial award applicants required to submit FAFSA. *Faculty research:* Regional studies and functional fields of international relations, international economics, conflict management, global theory and history, international law and organizations, international policy, strategic studies. *Unit head:* Tara Campbell, Associate Director of Admissions, 202-663-5700, Fax: 202-663-7788. *Application contact:* Dr. Belinda A. Yeomans, Director of Admissions, 202-663-5700, Fax: 202-663-7788, E-mail: admissions.sais@jhu.edu.

New York University, Graduate School of Arts and Science, Center for European Studies, New York, NY 10012-1019. Offers MA. *Faculty:* 4 full-time (0 women). *Students:* 7 full-time (6 women), 2 part-time (1 woman); includes 1 minority (African American), 1 international. Average age 24. 21 applicants, 90% accepted, 6 enrolled. In 2007, 14 degrees awarded. *Entrance requirements:* For master's, GRE General Test. Additional exam requirements/recommendations for international students: Required—TOEFL. *Application deadline:* For fall admission, 1/4 priority date for domestic students. Application fee: $55. Electronic applications accepted. *Financial support:* Fellowships with tuition reimbursements, teaching assistantships with tuition reimbursements, career-related internships or fieldwork, Federal Work-Study, institutionally sponsored loans, and scholarships/grants available. Financial award application deadline: 1/4; financial award applicants required to submit FAFSA. *Faculty research:* Xenophobia, migration, and identity politics in Europe; European Union and political economy; Central Eastern Europe. *Unit head:* Katherine Fleming, Director, 212-998-3838, Fax: 212-995-4188, E-mail: european.studies@nyu.edu. *Application contact:* Jennifer Denbo, Department Graduate Administrator, 212-998-3838, Fax: 212-995-4188.

San Diego State University, Graduate and Research Affairs, College of Arts and Letters, Department of European Studies, San Diego, CA 92182. Offers MA. *Students:* 2 full-time (0 women), 3 part-time (all women); includes 2 minority (1 African American, 1 Hispanic American), 1 international. Average age 29. 4 applicants, 75% accepted, 2 enrolled. In 2007, 1 degree awarded. *Degree requirements:* For master's, one foreign language. *Entrance requirements:* For master's, GRE General Test. Additional exam requirements/recommendations for international students: Required—TOEFL. *Application deadline:* For fall admission, 5/1 for domestic and international students; for spring admission, 11/1 for domestic students, 10/1 for international students. Applications are processed on a rolling basis. Application fee: $55. Electronic applications accepted. *Financial support:* Teaching assistantships, career-related internships or fieldwork available. Financial award applicants required to submit FAFSA. *Unit head:* Dr. Edith Benkov, Chair, 619-594-5111, Fax: 619-594-8006, E-mail: ebenkov@mail.sdsu.edu. *Application contact:* Dr. Anne Donadey, Graduate Adviser, 619-594-0815, Fax: 619-594-8006, E-mail: adonadey@mail.sdsu.edu.

University of Connecticut, Graduate School, College of Liberal Arts and Sciences, Field of International Studies, Program in European Studies, Storrs, CT 06269. Offers MA. *Faculty:* 35 full-time (20 women). *Students:* 4 full-time (3 women). Average age 28. 14 applicants, 43% accepted, 4 enrolled. In 2007, 3 degrees awarded. *Degree requirements:* For master's, comprehensive exam. *Entrance requirements:* For master's, GRE General Test. Additional exam requirements/recommendations for international students: Required—TOEFL (minimum score 550 paper-based; 213 computer-based). *Application deadline:* For fall admission, 2/1 priority date for domestic and international students; for spring admission, 11/1 for domestic students, 10/1 for international students. Applications are processed on a rolling basis. Application fee: $40 ($45 for international students). Electronic applications accepted. *Expenses:* Tuition, state resident: part-time $469 per credit hour. Tuition, nonresident: part-time $1,218 per credit hour. *Financial support:* In 2007–08, 3 research assistantships, 1 teaching assistantship with full tuition reimbursement were awarded; Federal Work-Study, scholarships/grants, health care benefits, and unspecified assistantships also available. Financial award application deadline: 2/1; financial award applicants required to submit FAFSA. *Unit head:* John Davis, Chairperson, 860-486-2752, Fax: 860-486-0641, E-mail: john.davis@uconn.edu. *Application contact:* Ludmilla Burns, Administrative Assistant, 860-486-5888, Fax: 860-486-0641, E-mail: ludmilla.burns@uconn.edu.

University of Connecticut, Graduate School, College of Liberal Arts and Sciences, Field of International Studies, Program in Italian History and Culture, Storrs, CT 06269. Offers MA. *Faculty:* 35 full-time (20 women). *Entrance requirements:* Additional exam requirements/recommendations for international students: Required—TOEFL (minimum score 550 paper-based; 213 computer-based). *Application deadline:* For fall admission, 2/1 priority date for domestic and international students; for spring admission, 11/1 for domestic students, 10/1 for international students. Applications are processed on a rolling basis. Electronic applications accepted. *Expenses:* Tuition, state resident: part-time $469 per credit hour. Tuition, nonresident: part-time $1,218 per credit hour. *Financial support:* Research assistantships, teaching assistantships, Federal Work-Study, scholarships/grants, health care benefits, and unspecified assistantships available. Financial award application deadline: 2/1. *Unit head:* John Davis, Chairperson, 860-486-2752, Fax: 860-486-0641, E-mail: john.davis@uconn.edu.

University of Guelph, Graduate Program Services, College of Arts, School of Languages and Literatures, Program in European Studies, Guelph, ON N1G 2W1, Canada. Offers MA. *Faculty:* 27 full-time (10 women). *Students:* 3 full-time (1 woman). 7 applicants, 57% accepted, 3 enrolled. *Degree requirements:* For master's, six semester courses, research paper. *Entrance requirements:* For master's, curriculum vitae, letter of intent, writing sample, 2 letters of recommendation, transcript. *Application deadline:* Applications are processed on a rolling basis. Application fee: $85. *Financial support:* Teaching assistantships, scholarships/grants available. *Application contact:* Dr. Dorothy Odartey-Wellington, Information Contact, 519-824-4120 Ext. 53179, E-mail: dodartey@uoguelph.ca.

University of Nevada, Reno, Graduate School, Interdisciplinary Program in Basque Studies, Reno, NV 89557. Offers PhD. *Faculty:* 7. *Students:* 1 (woman) full-time, 5 part-time (3 women); includes 1 minority (Hispanic American), 3 international. Average age 39. 4 applicants, 50% accepted, 1 enrolled. In 2007, 1 degree awarded. *Degree requirements:* For doctorate, thesis/dissertation. *Entrance requirements:* For doctorate, GRE General Test, master's degree in related field, minimum GPA of 3.0. Additional exam requirements/recommendations for international students: Required—TOEFL. *Application deadline:* For fall admission, 3/1 priority date for domestic students; for spring admission, 11/1 for domestic students. Applications are processed on a rolling basis. Application fee: $60 ($95 for international students). *Expenses:* Tuition, state resident: full-time $2,774; part-time $154 per credit. Tuition, nonresident: full-time $13,578; part-time $330 per credit. Required fees: $49 per semester. *Financial support:* In 2007–08, 3 research assistantships were awarded; teaching assistantships. Financial award application deadline: 3/1. *Faculty research:* Ethnic groups, Basque society, migration studies, symbolic anthropology, terrorism. *Unit head:* Dr. Sandra Ott, Graduate Programs Director, 775-682-5573.

University of Pittsburgh, University Center for International Studies, Pittsburgh, PA 15260. Offers African studies (Certificate); Asian studies (Certificate); European Union studies (Certificate); global studies (Certificate); Latin American studies (Certificate); Russian and East European studies (Certificate); West European studies (Certificate). *Unit head:* Lawrence F. Feick, Director, University Center for International Studies, 412-648-7374, Fax: 412-624-4672, E-mail: feick@pitt.edu.

Washington State University, Graduate School, College of Liberal Arts, Department of History, Pullman, WA 99164. Offers early and modern European history (MA, PhD); environmental history (MA, PhD); Latin American history (MA, PhD); modern East Asia history (MA, PhD); public history (MA, PhD); US history (MA, PhD); women's history (MA, PhD); world history (MA, PhD). Part-time programs available. *Faculty:* 24. *Students:* 45 full-time (28 women), 8 part-time (4 women); includes 2 minority (both Hispanic Americans), 2 international. Average age 33. 64 applicants, 41% accepted, 15 enrolled. In 2007, 8 master's, 2 doctorates awarded. *Degree requirements:* For master's, comprehensive exam (for some programs), thesis, oral exam; for doctorate, one foreign language, comprehensive exam, thesis/dissertation, oral and written exam. *Entrance requirements:* For master's, GRE General Test, minimum GPA of 3.3, language background form, writing sample; for doctorate, GRE General Test, minimum GPA of 3.5, language background form, writing sample. Additional exam requirements/recommendations for international students: Required—TOEFL (minimum score 550 paper-based). *Application deadline:* For fall admission, 2/1 for domestic and international students; for spring admission, 11/1 for domestic and international students. Applications are processed on a rolling basis. Application fee: $50. Electronic applications accepted. *Financial support:* In 2007–08, 30 students received support, including 1 fellowship with partial tuition reimbursement available (averaging $3,000 per year), research assistantships with full and partial tuition reimbursements available (averaging $13,917 per year), 28 teaching assistantships with full and partial tuition reimbursements available (averaging $13,056 per year); career-related internships or fieldwork, Federal Work-Study, institutionally sponsored loans, scholarships/grants, and health care benefits also available. Financial award application deadline: 4/1; financial award applicants required to submit FAFSA. *Faculty research:* Public, world, environmental, women and U.S. history. Total annual research expenditures: $44,501. *Unit head:* Dr. John Kicza, Co-Chair, 509-335-5002, Fax: 509-335-4171, E-mail: jekicza@wsu.edu. *Application contact:* Graduate Studies Director, 509-335-4030, Fax: 509-335-4171, E-mail: kale@wsu.edu.

Women's Studies

Brandeis University, Graduate School of Arts and Sciences, Joint Degree Programs in Women's and Gender Studies, Waltham, MA 02454-9110. Offers anthropology and women's and gender studies (MA); English and women's and gender studies (MA); music and women's and gender studies (MA); Near Eastern and Judaic studies and women's and gender studies (MA); sociology and women's and gender studies (MA); sustainable international development and women's/gender studies (MA). Part-time programs available. *Faculty:* 17 full-time (16 women), 2 part-time/adjunct (both women). *Students:* 10 full-time (8 women); includes 3 minority (1 African American, 1 Asian American or Pacific Islander, 1 Hispanic American), 2 international. Average age 25. 29 applicants, 38% accepted, 5 enrolled. In 2007, 15 degrees awarded. *Degree requirements:* For master's, thesis. *Entrance requirements:* For master's, GRE, sample of written work, resumé. Additional exam requirements/recommendations for international students: Required—TOEFL (minimum score 600 paper-based; 250 computer-based; 100 iBT), IELTS (minimum score 7). *Application deadline:* For fall admission, 1/15 for domestic students. Application fee: $55. Electronic applications accepted. *Financial support:* In 2007–08, 6 students received support, including 4 fellowships with partial tuition reimbursements available (averaging $4,450 per year), 2 teaching assistantships (averaging $3,000 per year); research assistantships, scholarships/grants and tuition waivers (full and partial) also available. Support available to part-time students. Financial award application deadline: 4/15; financial award applicants required to submit CSS PROFILE or FAFSA. *Unit head:* Prof. James Mandrell, Chair, 781-736-3042, Fax: 781-736-3044, E-mail: mandrell@brandeis.edu. *Application contact:* Kathryn Dalton, Program Administrator, 781-736-3045, Fax: 781-736-3044, E-mail: daltonka@brandeis.edu.

California Institute of Integral Studies, Graduate Programs, School of Consciousness and Transformation, San Francisco, CA 94103. Offers cultural anthropology and social transformation (MA); East-West psychology (MA, PhD); integrative health studies (MA); philosophy and religion (MA, PhD), including Asian and comparative studies, philosophy, cosmology, and consciousness, social and cultural anthropology (PhD), transformative leadership (MA), transformative studies (PhD), women's spirituality, women's spirituality flex format; social and cultural anthropology (PhD); transformative leadership (MA); transformative studies (PhD). Part-time and evening/weekend programs available. Postbaccalaureate distance learning degree programs offered (minimal on-campus study). *Faculty:* 30 full-time, 28 part-time/adjunct. *Students:* 456; includes 92 minority (32 African Americans, 3 American Indian/Alaska Native, 40 Asian Americans or Pacific Islanders, 17 Hispanic Americans), 1 international. Average age 37. 206 applicants, 93% accepted, 114 enrolled. In 2007, 26 degrees awarded. Terminal master's awarded for partial completion of doctoral program. *Degree requirements:* For master's, comprehensive exam (for some programs), thesis optional; for doctorate, comprehensive exam, thesis/dissertation. *Entrance requirements:* For master's, minimum GPA of 3.0; letters of recommendation, writing sample; for doctorate, master's degree, minimum GPA of 3.0, letters of recommendation, writing sample. Additional exam requirements/recommendations for international students: Required—TOEFL. *Application deadline:* For fall admission, 2/15 priority date for domestic and international students; for spring admission, 10/15 priority date for domestic and international students. Applications are processed on a rolling basis. Application fee: $65. Electronic applications accepted. *Expenses:* Tuition: Full-time $16,930; part-time $780 per unit. Tuition and fees vary according to course load and program. *Financial support:* In 2007–08, 292 students received support; research assistantships, teaching assistantships, career-related internships or fieldwork, Federal Work-Study, institutionally sponsored loans, scholarships/grants, and tuition waivers (partial) available. Support available to part-time students. Financial award application deadline: 3/15; financial award applicants required to submit FAFSA. *Faculty research:* Altered states of consciousness, dreams, cosmology, postcolonial studies, integrative health studies. *Application contact:* Allyson Werner, Senior Admissions Counselor, 415-575-6155, Fax: 415-575-1268.

See Close-Up on page 445.

Claremont Graduate University, Graduate Programs, School of Arts and Humanities, Program in Applied Women's Studies, Claremont, CA 91711-6160. Offers MA. *Students:* 12 full-time (all women), 4 part-time (all women); includes 4 minority (2 Asian Americans or Pacific Islanders, 2 Hispanic Americans). Average age 28. In 2007, 5 degrees awarded. *Degree requirements:* For master's, internship. *Entrance requirements:* For master's, GRE General Test. *Application deadline:* For fall admission, 2/15 priority date for domestic students. Applications are processed on a rolling basis. Electronic applications accepted. *Expenses:* Tuition: Full-time $31,640; part-time $1,376 per unit. Required fees: $145 per semester. Tuition and fees vary according to course load, degree level and program. *Financial support:* Fellowships, career-related internships or fieldwork and Federal Work-Study available. Support available to part-time students. Financial award application deadline: 2/15; financial award applicants required to submit FAFSA.

Claremont Graduate University, Graduate Programs, School of Religion, Claremont, CA 91711-6160. Offers Hebrew Bible (MA, PhD); history of Christianity and religions of North America (MA, PhD); New Testament (MA, PhD); philosophy of religion and theology (MA, PhD); theology, ethics and culture (MA, PhD); women's studies in religion (MA, PhD); MA/PhD; MBA/PhD. Part-time programs available. *Faculty:* 6 full-time (2 women), 9 part-time/adjunct (5 women). *Students:* 221 full-time (89 women), 7 part-time (2 women); includes 36 minority (15 African Americans, 12 Asian Americans or Pacific Islanders, 9 Hispanic Americans), 33 international. Average age 37. In 2007, 13 master's, 18 doctorates awarded. Terminal master's awarded for partial completion of doctoral program. *Degree requirements:* For master's, one foreign language, comprehensive exam (for some programs), thesis; for doctorate, 2 foreign languages, comprehensive exam, thesis/dissertation. *Entrance requirements:* For master's and doctorate, GRE General Test. *Application deadline:* For fall admission, 2/15 priority date for domestic students. Applications are processed on a rolling basis. Electronic applications accepted. *Expenses:* Tuition: Full-time $31,640; part-time $1,376 per unit. Required fees: $145 per semester. Tuition and fees vary according to course load, degree level and program. *Financial support:* Fellowships, research assistantships, teaching assistantships, Federal Work-Study and institutionally sponsored loans available. Support available to part-time students. Financial award application deadline: 2/15; financial award applicants required to submit FAFSA. *Unit head:* Karen Torjesen, Dean, 909-607-3214, Fax: 909-621-9587, E-mail: karen.torjesen@cgu.edu. *Application contact:* Patrick Horn, Associate Dean, 909-607-8411, Fax: 909-607-9587, E-mail: patrick.horn@cgu.edu.

Clark Atlanta University, School of Arts and Sciences, Department of Africana Women's Studies, Atlanta, GA 30314. Offers MA, DAH. Part-time programs available. *Faculty:* 1 (woman) full-time. *Students:* 7 full-time (6 women), 6 part-time (5 women); includes 11 minority (all African Americans), 1 international. 5 applicants, 100% accepted, 0 enrolled. In 2007, 2 master's, 5 doctorates awarded. *Degree requirements:* For master's, one foreign language, thesis; for doctorate, 2 foreign languages, thesis/dissertation. *Entrance requirements:* For master's, GRE General Test, minimum GPA of 2.5; for doctorate, GRE General Test, minimum graduate GPA of 3.0. Additional exam requirements/recommendations for international students: Required—TOEFL (minimum score 500 paper-based; 173 computer-based). *Application deadline:* For fall admission, 4/1 for domestic and international students; for spring admission, 11/1 for domestic and international students. Applications are processed on a rolling basis. Application fee: $40 ($55 for international students). Electronic applications accepted. *Expenses:* Tuition: Full-time $11,664; part-time $648 per credit hour. Required fees: $550; $275 per semester. *Financial support:* Scholarships/grants available. Financial award application deadline: 4/30; financial award applicants required to submit FAFSA. *Faculty research:* Concerns of women of African descent globally. *Unit head:* Dr. Josephine Bradley, Chairperson, 404-880-6810, E-mail: jbradley@cau.edu. *Application contact:* Michelle Clark-Davis, Graduate Program Admissions, 404-880-8709, E-mail: mdowis@cau.edu.

Cornell University, Graduate School, Graduate Fields of Arts and Sciences, Field of English Language and Literature, Ithaca, NY 14853-0001. Offers African-American literature (PhD); American literature after 1865 (PhD); American literature to 1865 (PhD); American studies (PhD); colonial and postcolonial literature (PhD); creative writing (MFA); cultural studies (PhD); dramatic literature (PhD); English poetry (PhD); English Renaissance to 1660 (PhD); lesbian, bisexual, and gay literature studies (PhD); literary criticism and theory (PhD); nineteenth century (PhD); Old and Middle English (PhD); prose fiction (PhD); Restoration and eighteenth century (PhD); twentieth century (PhD); women's literature (PhD); MFA/PhD. *Faculty:* 59 full-time (28 women). *Students:* 97 full-time (53 women); includes 20 minority (7 African Americans, 3 American Indian/Alaska Native, 5 Asian Americans or Pacific Islanders, 5 Hispanic Americans), 13 international. Average age 28. 759 applicants, 7% accepted, 21 enrolled. In 2007, 29 master's, 8 doctorates awarded. Terminal master's awarded for partial completion of doctoral program. *Degree requirements:* For master's, one foreign language, thesis; for doctorate,

Women's Studies

Cornell University (continued)

one foreign language, comprehensive exam, thesis/dissertation, teaching experience. *Entrance requirements:* For master's, GRE General Test, 3 letters of recommendation, creative writing sample; for doctorate, GRE General Test, GRE Subject Test (English), 3 letters of recommendation, writing sample. Additional exam requirements/recommendations for international students: Required—TOEFL (minimum score 600 paper-based; 250 computer-based; 77 iBT). *Application deadline:* For fall admission, 1/10 for domestic students. Application fee: $70. Electronic applications accepted. *Financial support:* In 2007–08, 92 students received support, including 32 fellowships with full tuition reimbursements available, 60 teaching assistantships with full tuition reimbursements available; research assistantships with full tuition reimbursements available, institutionally sponsored loans, scholarships/grants, health care benefits, tuition waivers (full and partial), and unspecified assistantships also available. Financial award applicants required to submit FAFSA. *Faculty research:* English and American literature, women's writing, ethnic and post-colonial literature, critical theory, medievalism. *Unit head:* Director of Graduate Studies, 607-255-7989, Fax: 607-255-6661. *Application contact:* Graduate Field Assistant, 607-255-7989, Fax: 607-255-6661, E-mail: english_grad@cornell.edu.

Drew University, Caspersen School of Graduate Studies, Women's Studies Program, Madison, NJ 07940-1493. Offers MA. *Degree requirements:* For master's, one foreign language, thesis. *Entrance requirements:* For master's, GRE General Test. *Faculty research:* Feminist theory, feminist literature, gender analysis, social theory and religion.

Duke University, Graduate School, Women's Studies Program, Durham, NC 27708-0586. Offers Certificate. *Faculty:* 125 full-time. *Application deadline:* For fall admission, 12/31 for domestic students. Application fee: $75. *Financial support:* Application deadline: 12/31. *Faculty research:* History of women's studies, feminist pedagogy, higher education, women's health, race/class/gender and sexual orientation. *Unit head:* Kathi Weeks, Director, 919-684-3655, Fax: 919-684-4652, E-mail: ehathaw@duke.edu.

Eastern Michigan University, Graduate School, College of Arts and Sciences, Department of Women's and Gender Studies, Ypsilanti, MI 48197. Offers MLS. Part-time and evening/weekend programs available. Postbaccalaureate distance learning degree programs offered (minimal on-campus study). *Students:* 4 full-time (3 women), 9 part-time (all women); includes 3 minority (all African Americans) Average age 30. In 2007, 8 degrees awarded. *Degree requirements:* For master's, thesis optional. *Entrance requirements:* Additional exam requirements/recommendations for international students: Required—TOEFL. *Application deadline:* Applications are processed on a rolling basis. Application fee: $35. *Expenses:* Tuition, state resident: full-time $8,952; part-time $373 per credit hour. Tuition, nonresident: full-time $17,634; part-time $735 per credit hour. Required fees: $896; $34 per credit hour. Tuition and fees vary according to course level, degree level and program. *Financial support:* Fellowships, research assistantships with full tuition reimbursements, teaching assistantships with full tuition reimbursements, career-related internships or fieldwork, Federal Work-Study, institutionally sponsored loans, scholarships/grants, tuition waivers (partial), and unspecified assistantships available. Support available to part-time students. Financial award applicants required to submit FAFSA. *Unit head:* Dr. Linda Schott, Director, 734-487-1177, Fax: 734-487-5029, E-mail: lschott@emich.edu. *Application contact:* Dr. Kate Mehuron, Program Advisor, 734-487-1177, Fax: 734-487-5029, E-mail: kmehuron@emich.edu.

Emory University, Graduate School of Arts and Sciences, Department of Comparative Literature, Atlanta, GA 30322-1100. Offers comparative literature (PhD); English (Certificate); French (Certificate); Middle Eastern studies (PhD); philosophy (Certificate); psychoanalytic studies (PhD); religion (PhD); Spanish (Certificate); women studies (Certificate). *Degree requirements:* For doctorate, 2 foreign languages, comprehensive exam, thesis/dissertation. *Entrance requirements:* For doctorate, GRE General Test, minimum GPA of 3.0. Additional exam requirements/recommendations for international students: Required—TOEFL. Electronic applications accepted. *Faculty research:* Literary theory, psychoanalysis trauma and testimony, literature and religion, literature and technology, literature and philosophy, politics and global culture, literature and aesthetics.

Emory University, Graduate School of Arts and Sciences, Department of Spanish and Portuguese, Atlanta, GA 30322-1100. Offers comparative literature (Certificate); film studies (Certificate); Spanish (PhD); women's studies (Certificate). *Degree requirements:* For doctorate, 2 foreign languages, comprehensive exam, thesis/dissertation. *Entrance requirements:* For doctorate, GRE General Test. Additional exam requirements/recommendations for international students: Required—TOEFL. Electronic applications accepted. *Faculty research:* Spanish literature, Spanish-American literature, literary theory, criticism, cultural studies.

Emory University, Graduate School of Arts and Sciences, Department of Women's Studies, Atlanta, GA 30322-1100. Offers PhD. *Degree requirements:* For doctorate, comprehensive exam, thesis/dissertation. *Entrance requirements:* For doctorate, GRE General Test, writing sample. Additional exam requirements/recommendations for international students: Required—TOEFL. Electronic applications accepted. *Faculty research:* Feminist theory, women's literature, African-American literature, gender in cross-cultural perspective, public policy and globalization.

Florida Atlantic University, Dorothy F. Schmidt College of Arts and Letters, Women's Studies Center, Boca Raton, FL 33431-0991. Offers MA, Certificate. *Degree requirements:* For master's, comprehensive exam, thesis or alternative. *Entrance requirements:* For master's, GRE General Test, minimum GPA of 3.0. *Faculty research:* Women and science/technology, feminist theory, violence against women, women and international development, feminist medical anthropology.

George Mason University, College of Humanities and Social Sciences, Interdisciplinary Studies Program, Fairfax, VA 22030. Offers anthropology (MAIS); community college teaching (MAIS); folklore (MAIS); higher education (MAIS); individualized studies (MAIS); religion, cultures, and values (MAIS); video-based production (MAIS); women's studies (MAIS); zoo and aquarium leadership (MAIS). Part-time and evening/weekend programs available. *Faculty:* 6 full-time (4 women), 6 part-time/adjunct (5 women). *Students:* 25 full-time (17 women), 90 part-time (76 women); includes 24 minority (5 African Americans, 1 American Indian/Alaska Native, 7 Asian Americans or Pacific Islanders, 11 Hispanic Americans), 3 international. Average age 33. 68 applicants, 72% accepted, 35 enrolled. In 2007, 19 degrees awarded. *Degree requirements:* For master's, thesis optional. *Entrance requirements:* For master's, GRE, GMAT, or MAT, interview, minimum GPA of 3.0 in last 60 hours of course work. *Application deadline:* For fall admission, 5/1 priority date for domestic students; for spring admission, 11/1 for domestic students. Applications are processed on a rolling basis. Application fee: $60 ($75 for international students). Electronic applications accepted. *Financial support:* Fellowships, teaching assistantships, career-related internships or fieldwork, Federal Work-Study, and institutionally sponsored loans available. Support available to part-time students. Financial award application deadline: 3/1; financial award applicants required to submit FAFSA. *Unit head:* John Burns, Chair, 703-993-1291, Fax: 703-993-1297, E-mail: mais@gmu.edu. *Application contact:* Dr. Johannes D. Bergmann, Information Contact, 703-993-8762, E-mail: mais@gmu.edu.

The George Washington University, Columbian College of Arts and Sciences, Department of Women's Studies, Washington, DC 20052. Offers MA, Certificate. Part-time and evening/weekend programs available. *Degree requirements:* For master's, comprehensive exam, thesis or alternative. *Entrance requirements:* For master's, GRE General Test, minimum GPA of 3.0. Additional exam requirements/recommendations for international students: Required—TOEFL (minimum score 550 paper-based; 213 computer-based). Electronic applications accepted.

The George Washington University, Columbian College of Arts and Sciences, School of Public Policy and Public Administration, Washington, DC 20052. Offers public policy (MA, MPP), including environmental and resource policy (MA), philosophy and social policy (MA), women's studies (MA); public policy and administration (PhD); public policy and public administration (MPA), including budget and public finance, federal policy, politics, and management, international development management, managing public organizations, managing state and local governments and urban policy, nonprofit management, policy analysis and evaluation, public administration; JD/MPP; MPA/JD; PhD/MPP. Part-time and evening/weekend programs available. *Degree requirements:* For doctorate, thesis/dissertation, general exam. *Entrance requirements:* For master's, GRE General Test, minimum GPA of 3.0; for doctorate, GRE General Test, interview, minimum GPA of 3.0. Additional exam requirements/recommendations for international students: Required—TOEFL (minimum score 550 paper-based; 213 computer-based). Electronic applications accepted.

The George Washington University, Columbian College of Arts and Sciences, School of Public Policy and Public Administration, Interdisciplinary Programs in Public Policy, Program in Women's Studies, Washington, DC 20052. Offers MA. Part-time and evening/weekend programs available. *Degree requirements:* For master's, comprehensive exam. *Entrance requirements:* For master's, GRE General Test, minimum GPA of 3.0. Additional exam requirements/recommendations for international students: Required—TOEFL (minimum score 550 paper-based; 213 computer-based). Electronic applications accepted.

Georgia State University, College of Arts and Sciences, Women's Studies Institute, Atlanta, GA 30303-3083. Offers MA. Part-time programs available. *Faculty:* 4 full-time (all women). *Students:* 6 full-time (all women), 9 part-time (8 women); includes 9 minority (all African Americans) 22 applicants, 55% accepted, 5 enrolled. In 2007, 9 master's awarded. *Degree requirements:* For master's, one foreign language, comprehensive exam, thesis, portfolio. *Entrance requirements:* For master's, GRE General Test. Additional exam requirements/recommendations for international students: Required—TOEFL. *Application deadline:* For fall admission, 8/1 for domestic students; for spring admission, 12/1 for domestic students. Applications are processed on a rolling basis. Application fee: $50. Electronic applications accepted. *Expenses:* Tuition, state resident: part-time $221 per credit hour. *Financial support:* In 2007–08, 1 fellowship with tuition reimbursement (averaging $3,500 per year), 1 research assistantship with tuition reimbursement (averaging $6,000 per year), teaching assistantships with tuition reimbursements (averaging $6,000 per year) were awarded; career-related internships or fieldwork, Federal Work-Study, institutionally sponsored loans, health care benefits, tuition waivers (partial), and unspecified assistantships also available. Support available to part-time students. Financial award application deadline: 2/15; financial award applicants required to submit FAFSA. *Faculty research:* Globalization and gender, womanism, culture and gender, black feminist thought, feminist theory. *Unit head:* Dr. Susan Talburt, Director, 404-413-6581, E-mail: stalburt@gsu.edu. *Application contact:* Dr. Layli Phillips, Director of Graduate Studies, 404-413-6586, E-mail: layli@gsu.edu.

Graduate School and University Center of the City University of New York, Graduate Studies, Interdisciplinary Studies, New York, NY 10016-4039. Offers language in social context (PhD); medieval studies (PhD); public policy (MA, PhD); urban studies (MA, PhD); women's studies (MA, PhD). Terminal master's awarded for partial completion of doctoral program. *Degree requirements:* For master's, thesis; for doctorate, comprehensive exam, thesis/dissertation. *Entrance requirements:* For master's and doctorate, GRE General Test. *Application deadline:* For fall admission, 2/1 for domestic students. Application fee: $40. *Financial support:* Application deadline: 2/1. *Unit head:* Chairman, 212-642-2430.

Graduate Theological Union, Graduate Programs, Berkeley, CA 94709-1212. Offers art and religion (MA, PhD); biblical languages (MA); biblical studies (Old and New Testament) (MA, PhD, Th D); Buddhist studies (MA); Christian spirituality (MA, PhD); cultural and historical studies of religions (MA, PhD); ethics and social theory (PhD); history (MA, PhD, Th D); homiletics (MA, PhD, Th D); interdisciplinary studies (PhD, Th D); Jewish studies (MA, PhD, Certificate); liturgical studies (MA, PhD, Th D); Near Eastern religions (PhD); Orthodox Christian studies (MA); Orthodox studies (Certificate); religion and psychology (MA, PhD); religion and society/ethics and social theory (MA); systematic and philosophical theology (MA, PhD, Th D); women's studies in religion (Certificate); MA/M Div. *Accreditation:* ATS. *Faculty:* 119 full-time (44 women), 34 part-time/adjunct (9 women). *Students:* 317 full-time (152 women), 35 part-time (19 women); includes 49 minority (15 African Americans, 2 American Indian/Alaska Native, 21 Asian Americans or Pacific Islanders, 11 Hispanic Americans), 74 international. Average age 38. 257 applicants, 59% accepted, 79 enrolled. In 2007, 45 master's, 22 doctorates awarded. Terminal master's awarded for partial completion of doctoral program. *Median time to degree:* Of those who began their doctoral program in fall 1999, 52% received their degree in 8 years or less. *Degree requirements:* For master's, one foreign language, thesis; for doctorate, one foreign language, comprehensive exam, thesis/dissertation. *Entrance requirements:* For master's, GRE General Test; for doctorate, GRE General Test, MA or M Div. Additional exam requirements/recommendations for international students: Required—TOEFL. *Application deadline:* For fall admission, 12/15 for domestic and international students; for winter admission, 2/15 for domestic and international students; for spring admission, 9/30 for domestic and international students. Application fee: $40. Electronic applications accepted. *Expenses:* Tuition: Full-time $13,310. Tuition and fees vary according to degree level and program. *Financial support:* In 2007–08, 122 students received support, including 109 fellowships (averaging $11,581 per year), 1 research assistantship (averaging $3,000 per year), 22 teaching assistantships (averaging $3,500 per year); Federal Work-Study, scholarships/grants, and tuition waivers (partial) also available. Support available to part-time students. Financial award application deadline: 2/1; financial award applicants required to submit FAFSA. *Unit head:* Dr. Arthur G. Holder, Dean, 510-649-2440, Fax: 510-649-1417, E-mail: aholder@gtu.edu. *Application contact:* Dr. Kathleen Kook, Assistant Dean for Admissions, 800-826-4488, Fax: 510-649-1730, E-mail: gtuadm@gtu.edu.

Institute of Transpersonal Psychology, Residential Programs, Palo Alto, CA 94303. Offers clinical psychology (PhD); counseling psychology (MA); transpersonal psychology (MA, PhD); women's spirituality (PhD). Part-time and evening/weekend programs available. *Faculty:* 17 full-time (9 women), 31 part-time/adjunct (18 women). *Students:* 239 full-time (164 women), 48 part-time (33 women); includes 46 minority (8 African Americans, 4 American Indian/Alaska Native, 18 Asian Americans or Pacific Islanders, 16 Hispanic Americans), 16 international. Average age 38. 132 applicants, 80% accepted, 79 enrolled. In 2007, 47 master's, 16 doctorates awarded. Terminal master's awarded for partial completion of doctoral program. *Degree requirements:* For doctorate, thesis/dissertation. *Entrance requirements:* For master's and doctorate, bachelor's degree. *Application deadline:* For fall admission, 2/15 priority date for domestic students. Applications are processed on a rolling basis. Application fee: $55. *Expenses:* Tuition: Full-time $11,877; part-time $3,959 per quarter. Tuition and fees vary according to degree level and student level. *Financial support:* In 2007–08, 178 students received support; teaching assistantships, career-related internships or fieldwork, Federal Work-Study, and scholarships/grants available. Support available to part-time students. Financial award application deadline: 7/1; financial award applicants required to submit FAFSA. *Unit head:* Dr. Paul Roy, Academic Vice President, 650-493-4430 Ext. 243, Fax: 650-493-6835, E-mail: proy@itp.edu. *Application contact:* 650-493-4430 Ext. 16, Fax: 650-493-6835, E-mail: itpinfo@itp.edu.

See Close-Up on page 1439.

Lakehead University, Graduate Studies, Women's Studies Collaborative Program, Thunder Bay, ON P7B 5E1, Canada. Offers M Ed, MA, MSW. Part-time programs available. *Degree requirements:* For master's, thesis (for some programs). *Entrance requirements:* Additional exam requirements/recommendations for international students: Required—TOEFL. *Faculty research:* Feminist thought, feminist pedagogy, women of literature, Canadian women's history, well-being of women.

Lesley University, Graduate School of Arts and Social Sciences, Self-Designed Master's Program in Interdisciplinary Studies, Cambridge, MA 02138-2790. Offers individualized studies (MA); integrative holistic health (MA); women's studies (MA). Part-time and evening/weekend programs available. Postbaccalaureate distance learning degree programs offered (no on-campus study). *Faculty:* 3 full-time (all women), 5 part-time/adjunct (3 women). *Students:* 12 full-time (11 women), 14 part-time (12 women); includes 3 minority (2 African Americans, 1 Hispanic American), 1 international. Average age 35. 10 applicants, 100% accepted, 9 enrolled.

In 2007, 20 degrees awarded. *Entrance requirements:* For master's, 3 letters of recommendation. Additional exam requirements/recommendations for international students: Required—TOEFL (minimum score 550 paper-based; 213 computer-based; 80 iBT). Application fee: $50. *Financial support:* In 2007–08, 1 student received support, including research assistantships (averaging $3,400 per year), teaching assistantships (averaging $3,400 per year); Federal Work-Study, scholarships/grants, and unspecified assistantships also available. Support available to part-time students. Financial award application deadline: 4/15; financial award applicants required to submit FAFSA. *Unit head:* Sharlene Cochrane, Director, 617-349-8477, E-mail: cochrane@lesley.edu. *Application contact:* Lisa Lombardi, Assistant Director, Advising and Student Services, 617-349-8454, E-mail: lombardi@lesley.edu.

Memorial University of Newfoundland, School of Graduate Studies, Interdisciplinary Program in Women's Studies, St. John's, NL A1C 5S7, Canada. Offers MWS.

Minnesota State University Mankato, College of Graduate Studies, College of Social and Behavioral Sciences, Department of Women's Studies, Mankato, MN 56001. Offers MS, Certificate. Part-time programs available. *Students:* 4 full-time (3 women), 7 part-time (all women). Average age 28. In 2007, 6 degrees awarded. *Degree requirements:* For master's, comprehensive exam, thesis or alternative. *Entrance requirements:* For master's, minimum GPA of 3.0 during previous 2 years of course work. Additional exam requirements/recommendations for international students: Required—TOEFL. *Application deadline:* For fall admission, 7/1 priority date for domestic students; for spring admission, 11/1 for domestic students. Applications are processed on a rolling basis. Application fee: $40. *Financial support:* Research assistantships, teaching assistantships with full tuition reimbursements, career-related internships or fieldwork, Federal Work-Study, institutionally sponsored loans, and unspecified assistantships available. Support available to part-time students. Financial award application deadline: 3/15; financial award applicants required to submit FAFSA. *Unit head:* Dr. Maria Bevacqua, Chairperson, 507-389-2077. *Application contact:* 507-389-2321, E-mail: grad@mnsu.edu.

Mount Saint Vincent University, Graduate Programs, Department of Women's Studies, Halifax, NS B3M 2J6, Canada. Offers MA. Part-time programs available. *Degree requirements:* For master's, thesis. Electronic applications accepted.

The Ohio State University, Graduate School, College of Humanities, Department of Women's Studies, Columbus, OH 43210. Offers MA, PhD. *Faculty:* 63. *Students:* 28 full-time (all women), 3 part-time (all women); includes 8 minority (6 African Americans, 1 Asian American or Pacific Islander, 1 Hispanic American), 1 international. Average age 28. In 2007, 8 degrees awarded. *Degree requirements:* For master's, thesis optional. *Entrance requirements:* Additional exam requirements/recommendations for international students: Required—TOEFL (minimum score 600 paper-based; 250 computer-based). *Application deadline:* For fall admission, 8/15 priority date for domestic students, 7/1 priority date for international students; for winter admission, 12/1 priority date for domestic students, 11/1 priority date for international students; for spring admission, 3/1 priority date for domestic students, 2/1 priority date for international students. Applications are processed on a rolling basis. Application fee: $40 ($50 for international students). Electronic applications accepted. *Financial support:* Fellowships, research assistantships, teaching assistantships, career-related internships or fieldwork, Federal Work-Study, institutionally sponsored loans, and unspecified assistantships available. Support available to part-time students. *Unit head:* Claire Robertson, Graduate Studies Committee Chair, 614-292-1021, Fax: 614-292-0276, E-mail: robertson.8@osu.edu. *Application contact:* 614-292-9444, Fax: 614-292-3895, E-mail: domestic.grad@osu.edu.

Roosevelt University, Graduate Division, College of Arts and Sciences, Department of Literature and Languages, Program in Women's and Gender Studies, Chicago, IL 60605-1394. Offers MA, Certificate. Part-time and evening/weekend programs available. *Students:* 8 full-time (all women), 7 part-time (all women); includes 2 minority (both African Americans) Average age 32. 29 applicants, 28% accepted, 8 enrolled. In 2007, 6 degrees awarded. *Degree requirements:* For master's, thesis. *Entrance requirements:* For master's, minimum GPA of 2.7. *Application deadline:* For fall admission, 6/1 priority date for domestic students. Applications are processed on a rolling basis. Application fee: $25 ($35 for international students). *Financial support:* Application deadline: 2/15. *Faculty research:* Feminist economics; philosophy of feminism; race, class, and gender; women and art; women's history. *Unit head:* Ann Brigham, Head, 312-341-3725, Fax: 312-341-3680, E-mail: abrigham@roosevelt.edu. *Application contact:* Joanne Canyon-Heller, Coordinator of Graduate Admission, 877-APPLY RU, Fax: 312-281-3356, E-mail: applyru@roosevelt.edu.

Rutgers, The State University of New Jersey, New Brunswick, Graduate School, Department of Political Science, New Brunswick, NJ 08901-1281. Offers American politics (PhD); comparative politics (PhD); international relations (PhD); political theory (PhD); public law (PhD); women and politics (PhD). *Degree requirements:* For doctorate, one foreign language, comprehensive exam, thesis/dissertation. *Entrance requirements:* For doctorate, GRE General Test. Additional exam requirements/recommendations for international students: Required—TOEFL.

Rutgers, The State University of New Jersey, New Brunswick, Graduate School, Program in Women's and Gender Studies, New Brunswick, NJ 08901-1281. Offers MA, PhD. Part-time programs available. *Degree requirements:* For master's, thesis or alternative; for doctorate, comprehensive exam, thesis/dissertation. *Entrance requirements:* For master's and doctorate, GRE General Test, writing sample, 3 letters of recommendation. Additional exam requirements/recommendations for international students: Required—TOEFL. *Faculty research:* Feminist theory, gender and sexuality, global and cultural studies, women in history, literature, and politics, feminist politics.

Saint Mary's University, Faculty of Arts, Program in Women's Studies, Halifax, NS B3H 3C3, Canada. Offers MA. Part-time programs available. *Degree requirements:* For master's, thesis. *Entrance requirements:* For master's, honors degree.

San Diego State University, Graduate and Research Affairs, College of Arts and Letters, Department of Women's Studies, San Diego, CA 92182. Offers MA. *Students:* 22 full-time (21 women), 11 part-time (all women); includes 8 minority (4 African Americans, 4 Hispanic Americans), 2 international. 30 applicants, 67% accepted, 12 enrolled. In 2007, 9 degrees awarded. *Entrance requirements:* For master's, GRE General Test, 2 letters of reference. Additional exam requirements/recommendations for international students: Required—TOEFL. *Application deadline:* For fall admission, 2/15 priority date for domestic and international students; for spring admission, 11/1 for domestic students, 10/1 for international students. Applications are processed on a rolling basis. Application fee: $55. Electronic applications accepted. *Financial support:* In 2007–08, 20 teaching assistantships were awarded. Financial award applicants required to submit FAFSA. *Unit head:* Bonnie Kime Scott, Chair, 619-594-6524, Fax: 619-594-5218, E-mail: bkscott@mail.sdsu.edu. *Application contact:* Susan Cayleff, Graduate Advisor, 619-594-6460, Fax: 619-594-5218, E-mail: cayleff@mail.sdsu.edu.

San Francisco State University, Division of Graduate Studies, College of Humanities, Department of Women Studies, San Francisco, CA 94132-1722. Offers MA. Part-time and evening/weekend programs available. *Unit head:* Dr. Nan Alamilla Boyd, Chair, 415-338-3065, Fax: 415-405-2428. *Application contact:* Dr. Jillian Sandell, Graduate Coordinator, 415-338-1388.

Sarah Lawrence College, Graduate Studies, Program in Women's History, Bronxville, NY 10708-5999. Offers MA. Part-time programs available. *Faculty:* 9 part-time/adjunct (8 women). *Students:* 16 full-time (14 women), 6 part-time (all women); includes 5 minority (1 African American, 1 Asian American or Pacific Islander, 3 Hispanic Americans). Average age 27. 35 applicants, 80% accepted, 12 enrolled. In 2007, 14 degrees awarded. *Degree requirements:* For master's, thesis. *Entrance requirements:* For master's, previous course work in history, minimum B average in undergraduate course work. Additional exam requirements/recommendations for international students: Required—TOEFL (minimum score 600 paper-based). *Application deadline:* For fall admission, 2/1 priority date for domestic students. Applications are processed on a rolling basis. Application fee: $60. *Expenses:* Tuition: Part-time $1,034 per credit. Required fees: $430 per year. Tuition and fees vary according to program. *Financial support:* In 2007–08, 15 fellowships (averaging $3,433 per year) were awarded; career-related internships or fieldwork also available. Support available to part-time students. Financial award application deadline: 3/1. *Unit head:* Priscilla Murolo, Director, 914-395-2405. *Application contact:* Susan Guma, Dean of Graduate Studies, 914-395-2373, E-mail: sguma@mail.slc.edu.

See Close-Up on page 805.

Shenandoah University, School of Education and Human Development, Winchester, VA 22601-5195. Offers administrative leadership (D Ed); advanced professional teaching English to speakers of other languages (Certificate); education (MSE); elementary education (Certificate); middle school education (Certificate); professional studies (Certificate); professional teaching English to speakers of other languages (Certificate); public management (Certificate); secondary education (Certificate); women's studies (Certificate). Part-time and evening/weekend programs available. Postbaccalaureate distance learning degree programs offered (minimal on-campus study). *Faculty:* 13 full-time (7 women), 4 part-time/adjunct (2 women). *Students:* 10 full-time (6 women), 280 part-time (192 women); includes 7 minority (5 African Americans, 2 Hispanic Americans), 17 international. Average age 45. 169 applicants, 95% accepted, 125 enrolled. In 2007, 100 master's, 7 doctorates, 13 other advanced degrees awarded. *Degree requirements:* For master's, comprehensive exam (for some programs), thesis (for some programs), internship; for doctorate, comprehensive exam, thesis/dissertation. *Entrance requirements:* For master's, minimum GPA of 3.0 or satisfactory GRE, 3 letters of recommendation, valid teaching license, essay; for doctorate, minimum GPA of 3.5 in master's, 3 years of teaching experience, 3 letters of recommendation, writing samples; for Certificate, minimum undergraduate GPA of 3.0, essay, 3 letters of recommendation. Additional exam requirements/recommendations for international students: Required—TOEFL (minimum score 527 paper-based; 197 computer-based; 71 iBT). *Application deadline:* For fall admission, 7/15 for domestic students; for spring admission, 10/15 for domestic students. Application fee: $30. Electronic applications accepted. *Expenses:* Tuition: Part-time $640 per credit. Part-time tuition and fees vary according to degree level and program. *Financial support:* Career-related internships or fieldwork, institutionally sponsored loans, and unspecified assistantships available. Support available to part-time students. Financial award application deadline: 3/15; financial award applicants required to submit FAFSA. *Faculty research:* Nanotechnology, writing pedagogy and writing centers, violence in schools, Virginia/Shenandoah Valley history and culture, stress in children. *Unit head:* Dr. Calvin Allen, Dean, 540-665-4587, Fax: 540-665-4644, E-mail: callen@su.edu. *Application contact:* David Anthony, Dean of Admissions, 540-665-4581, Fax: 540-665-4627, E-mail: admit@su.edu.

Simon Fraser University, Graduate Studies, Faculty of Arts and Social Sciences, Department of Women's Studies, Burnaby, BC V5A 1S6, Canada. Offers MA, PhD. *Degree requirements:* For master's, thesis or alternative. *Entrance requirements:* For master's, minimum GPA of 3.8. Additional exam requirements/recommendations for international students: Required—TOEFL or IELTS. *Faculty research:* Theory development, disability, economics, globalization.

Southeastern Baptist Theological Seminary, Graduate and Professional Programs, Wake Forest, NC 27588-1889. Offers advanced biblical studies (M Div); Christian education (M Div, MACE); Christian ethics (PhD); Christian ministry (M Div); Christian planting (M Div); church music (MACM); counseling (MACO); evangelism (PhD); language (M Div); ministry (D Min); New Testament (PhD); Old Testament (PhD); philosophy (PhD); theology (Th M, PhD); women's studies (M Div). *Accreditation:* ACIPE; ATS (one or more programs are accredited). *Degree requirements:* For master's, thesis (for some programs), oral exam; for doctorate, thesis/dissertation, fieldwork; for M Div, supervised ministry. *Entrance requirements:* For master's, Cooperative English Test, minimum GPA of 2.0, M Div or equivalent (Th M); for doctorate, GRE General Test or MAT, Cooperative English Test, M Div or equivalent, 3 years of professional experience.

Southern Connecticut State University, School of Graduate Studies, School of Arts and Sciences, Program in Women's Studies, New Haven, CT 06515-1355. Offers MA. Part-time and evening/weekend programs available. *Students:* 6 full-time (all women), 13 part-time (all women); includes 2 minority (both Hispanic Americans) 12 applicants, 67% accepted, 7 enrolled. In 2007, 5 degrees awarded. *Degree requirements:* For master's, thesis or alternative. *Entrance requirements:* For master's, interview. *Application deadline:* Applications are processed on a rolling basis. Application fee: $50. Electronic applications accepted. *Financial support:* Application deadline: 4/15. *Unit head:* Dr. Tricia Lin, Director, 203-392-6832, Fax: 203-392-5670, E-mail: lin84@southernct.edu.

Suffolk University, College of Arts and Sciences, Department of Women's Health, Boston, MA 02108-2770. Offers MA. *Faculty:* 5 full-time (4 women), 7 part-time/adjunct (all women). *Students:* 6 full-time (all women), 2 part-time (both women), 1 international. Average age 26. 20 applicants, 50% accepted, 8 enrolled. *Entrance requirements:* Additional exam requirements/recommendations for international students: Required—TOEFL (minimum score 550 paper-based; 213 computer-based; 80 iBT). *Application deadline:* For fall admission, 6/15 priority date for domestic students, 6/15 for international students; for spring admission, 11/1 priority date for domestic students, 11/1 for international students. Applications are processed on a rolling basis. Application fee: $50. Electronic applications accepted. *Financial support:* In 2007–08, 8 students received support, including 8 fellowships (averaging $8,744 per year). *Unit head:* Dr. Amy Agigian, Director, 617-573-8487, Fax: 617-994-4278, E-mail: aagigian@suffolk.edu. *Application contact:* Judith Reynolds, Director of Graduate Admissions, 617-573-8302, Fax: 617-523-0116, E-mail: grad.admission@suffolk.edu.

Texas Woman's University, Graduate School, College of Arts and Sciences, Program in Women's Studies, Denton, TX 76201. Offers MA. *Students:* 11 full-time (all women), 17 part-time (all women); includes 10 minority (4 African Americans, 1 American Indian/Alaska Native, 5 Hispanic Americans), 1 international. Average age 31. In 2007, 10 degrees awarded. *Degree requirements:* For master's, thesis. *Entrance requirements:* For master's, 2 letters of reference, personal essay. Additional exam requirements/recommendations for international students: Required—TOEFL (minimum score 550 paper-based; 213 computer-based; 79 iBT). *Application deadline:* For fall admission, 4/1 for international students; for spring admission, 8/1 for international students. Applications are processed on a rolling basis. Application fee: $30 ($50 for international students). Electronic applications accepted. *Expenses:* Tuition, state resident: full-time $3,294; part-time $183 per credit. Tuition, nonresident: full-time $8,298; part-time $461 per credit. Required fees: $985; $55 per credit. Tuition and fees vary according to degree level. *Financial support:* In 2007–08, 1 teaching assistantship (averaging $10,440 per year) was awarded; career-related internships or fieldwork, Federal Work-Study, institutionally sponsored loans, scholarships/grants, traineeships, health care benefits, and unspecified assistantships also available. Support available to part-time students. Financial award application deadline: 3/1; financial award applicants required to submit FAFSA. *Faculty research:* Feminism and religion, family violence, feminist theory, women of color, feminist ethics. *Unit head:* Dr. Claire L. Sahlin, Director, 940-898-2119, Fax: 940-898-2101, E-mail: csahlin@twu.edu. *Application contact:* Samuel Wheeler, Assistant Director of Admissions, 940-898-3188, Fax: 940-898-3081, E-mail: wheelersr@twu.edu.

Towson University, College of Graduate Studies and Research, Program in Women's Studies, Towson, MD 21252-0001. Offers MS, Certificate. *Faculty:* 3 full-time (all women), 1 (woman) part-time/adjunct. *Students:* 5 full-time (all women), 4 part-time (all women); includes 3 minority (all African Americans), 1 international. Average age 33. 3 applicants, 100% accepted, 1 enrolled. In 2007, 7 master's, 2 other advanced degrees awarded. *Degree requirements:* For master's, thesis optional. *Entrance requirements:* For master's, minimum GPA of 3.0, 9 credits of course work in women's studies and/or the social sciences. *Application deadline:* Applications are processed on a rolling basis. Application fee: $50. Electronic applications accepted. *Expenses:* Tuition, state resident: part-time $286 per credit. Tuition, nonresident: part-time $600 per credit. Required fees: $75 per credit. *Financial support:* Application deadline: 4/1;

Women's Studies

Towson University (continued)

Faculty research: Gender and international relations, health, economics, violence against women, public policy. *Unit head:* Rita Marinho, Graduate Program Director, 410-704-5250, Fax: 410-704-3469, E-mail: rmarinho@towson.edu. *Application contact:* 410-704-2501, Fax: 410-704-4675, E-mail: grads@towson.edu.

United Theological Seminary of the Twin Cities, Graduate and Professional Programs, Program in Theology, New Brighton, MN 55112-2598. Offers religion and theology (MA); theology and the arts (MA); women's studies (MA). Part-time programs available. *Faculty:* 12 full-time (7 women), 22 part-time/adjunct (10 women). *Students:* 9 full-time (4 women), 16 part-time (12 women). Average age 43. 13 applicants, 100% accepted, 12 enrolled. In 2007, 1 degree awarded. *Degree requirements:* For master's, thesis. *Entrance requirements:* For master's, minimum GPA of 2.75. *Application deadline:* For fall admission, 8/1 priority date for domestic students; for winter admission, 12/1 priority date for domestic students; for spring admission, 1/1 priority date for domestic students. Application fee: $40. *Expenses:* Tuition: Part-time $373 per credit hour. *Financial support:* Career-related internships or fieldwork, institutionally sponsored loans, and scholarships/grants available. Support available to part-time students. *Application contact:* Rev. Glen Herrington-Hall, Director of Admissions, 651-255-6107, Fax: 651-633-4315, E-mail: gherrington-hall@unitedseminary.edu.

Université Laval, Faculty of Social Sciences, Program in Feminist Studies, Québec, QC G1K 7P4, Canada. Offers Diploma. Part-time programs available. *Entrance requirements:* For degree, knowledge of French, comprehension of written English. Electronic applications accepted.

University at Albany, State University of New York, College of Arts and Sciences, Department of Women's Studies, Albany, NY 12222-0001. Offers MA, DA. *Students:* 11 full-time (all women), 2 part-time (both women). Average age 29. In 2007, 11 master's, 1 doctorate awarded. *Entrance requirements:* Additional exam requirements/recommendations for international students: Required—TOEFL (minimum score 550 paper-based; 213 computer-based). *Application deadline:* For fall admission, 8/1 for domestic students, 5/1 for international students. Applications are processed on a rolling basis. Application fee: $75. Electronic applications accepted. *Expenses:* Tuition, state resident: part-time $576 per credit. Tuition, nonresident: part-time $910 per credit. Tuition and fees vary according to program. *Faculty research:* Feminist pedagogy, lesbian and gay studies, women in the African diaspora, women's health policy, literature of feminism. *Unit head:* Gwendolyn Moore, Chair, 518-442-4220, Fax: 518-442-4419.

The University of Alabama, Graduate School, College of Arts and Sciences, Department of Women's Studies, Tuscaloosa, AL 35487. Offers MA. *Faculty:* 3 full-time (all women). *Students:* 8 full-time (all women), 3 part-time (all women); includes 1 minority (African American) Average age 29. 4 applicants, 100% accepted, 4 enrolled. In 2007, 1 degree awarded. *Degree requirements:* For master's, comprehensive exam, thesis. *Entrance requirements:* For master's, MAT or GRE. Additional exam requirements/recommendations for international students: Required—TOEFL. *Application deadline:* For fall admission, 3/7 priority date for domestic students, 3/7 for international students. Application fee: $30. Electronic applications accepted. *Expenses:* Tuition, state resident: full-time $5,700. Tuition, nonresident: full-time $16,518. *Financial support:* In 2007–08, 6 students received support, including 3 research assistantships with tuition reimbursements available (averaging $10,908 per year), 3 teaching assistantships with tuition reimbursements available (averaging $10,908 per year); health care benefits and unspecified assistantships also available. Financial award application deadline: 4/1. *Faculty research:* Feminist theory, domestic violence, women's health, women in baseball, women in films. Total annual research expenditures: $28,164. *Unit head:* Dr. Ida M. Johnson, Chair, 205-348-8462, Fax: 205-348-3584, E-mail: ijohnson@bama.ua.edu. *Application contact:* Dr. Carol Pierman, Director of Graduate Studies, 205-348-9841, Fax: 205-348-3584, E-mail: cpierman@bama.ua.edu.

The University of Arizona, Graduate College, College of Social and Behavioral Sciences, Department of Women's Studies, Tucson, AZ 85721. Offers MA, PhD. Part-time programs available. *Faculty:* 12. *Students:* 12 full-time (all women); includes 5 minority (2 Asian Americans or Pacific Islanders, 3 Hispanic Americans). Average age 27. 21 applicants, 38% accepted, 3 enrolled. In 2007, 4 degrees awarded. *Degree requirements:* For master's, thesis/project. *Entrance requirements:* For master's and doctorate, GRE, minimum GPA of 3.0, 3 letters of recommendation. Additional exam requirements/recommendations for international students: Required—TOEFL (minimum score 600 paper-based; 250 computer-based). *Application deadline:* For fall admission, 12/1 for domestic and international students. Applications are processed on a rolling basis. Application fee: $50. Electronic applications accepted. *Financial support:* In 2007–08, 2 fellowships with full tuition reimbursements (averaging $5,000 per year), 7 research assistantships with full tuition reimbursements (averaging $6,145 per year), 6 teaching assistantships with full tuition reimbursements (averaging $6,145 per year) were awarded; career-related internships or fieldwork, scholarships/grants, health care benefits, tuition waivers (full and partial), and unspecified assistantships also available. Financial award application deadline: 1/15. *Faculty research:* Gender race and border studies, sexuality and the body, gender health and science, cultural representation and theory, public policy and social movements. Total annual research expenditures: $115,299. *Unit head:* Dr. Jennifer Croissant, Interim Head, 520-626-0079, Fax: 520-621-1533, E-mail: ilc@email.arizona.edu. *Application contact:* Susan D. Whitworth, Information Contact, 520-626-5657, Fax: 520-621-1533, E-mail: whitwort@email.arizona.edu.

University of California, Los Angeles, Graduate Division, College of Letters and Science, Program in Women's Studies, Los Angeles, CA 90095. Offers MA, PhD. *Students:* 20 full-time (all women); includes 8 minority (2 African Americans, 1 American Indian/Alaska Native, 2 Asian Americans or Pacific Islanders, 3 Hispanic Americans). Average age 30. 47 applicants, 11% accepted, 1 enrolled. In 2007, 10 degrees awarded. Terminal master's awarded for partial completion of doctoral program. *Degree requirements:* For master's, comprehensive exam or thesis; for doctorate, one foreign language, thesis/dissertation, written and oral exams. *Entrance requirements:* For master's, GRE General Test, Degree objective must be Ph.D; for doctorate, GRE General Test, minimum undergraduate GPA of 3.0. *Application deadline:* For fall admission, 12/15 for domestic students. Application fee: $60. Electronic applications accepted. *Expenses:* Tuition, nonresident: full-time $5,728. Required fees: $8,966. Full-time tuition and fees vary according to program and student level. *Financial support:* In 2007–08, 22 fellowships with full and partial tuition reimbursements, 11 research assistantships with full and partial tuition reimbursements, 11 teaching assistantships with full and partial tuition reimbursements were awarded; tuition waivers (full and partial) also available. Financial award applicants required to submit FAFSA. *Unit head:* Dr. Christine Littleton, Chair, 310-206-8101.

University of California, Santa Barbara, Graduate Division, College of Letters and Sciences, Division of Humanities and Fine Arts, Department of Germanic, Slavic, and Semitic Studies, Santa Barbara, CA 93106. Offers Germanic languages and literature (MA, PhD), including applied linguistics (optional emphasis) (PhD), women's studies (optional emphasis) (PhD); MA/PhD. *Faculty:* 3 full-time (2 women). *Students:* 4 full-time (2 women), 2 international. Average age 31. 5 applicants, 80% accepted, 0 enrolled. In 2007, 1 master's, 2 doctorates awarded. Terminal master's awarded for partial completion of doctoral program. *Median time to degree:* Of those who began their doctoral program in fall 1999, 100% received their degree in 8 years or less. *Degree requirements:* For master's, 2 foreign languages, comprehensive exam, thesis, 36 units graduate level coursework; for doctorate, 3 foreign languages, comprehensive exam, thesis/dissertation. *Entrance requirements:* For master's and doctorate, GRE, sample of written work, tape of spoken German and/or English, proficiency in a foreign language. Additional exam requirements/recommendations for international students: Required—TOEFL (minimum score 550 paper-based; 213 computer-based; 80 iBT). *Application deadline:* For fall admission, 12/31 for domestic students, 5/1 for international students; for winter admission, 11/1 for domestic and international students; for spring admission, 2/1 for domestic and international students. Applications are processed on a rolling basis. Application fee: $60. Electronic applications accepted. *Expenses:* Tuition, nonresident: full-time $14,888. Required fees: $10,108. *Financial support:* In 2007–08, 4 students received support, including fellowships with full and partial tuition reimbursements available (averaging $5,400 per year), teaching assistantships with full and partial tuition reimbursements available (averaging $16,389 per year); Federal Work-Study, institutionally sponsored loans, scholarships/grants, and health care benefits also available. Financial award application deadline: 12/15; financial award applicants required to submit FAFSA. *Faculty research:* Critical theory, media-technology, psychoanalysis, German romanticism, Goethe. *Unit head:* Prof. Elisabeth Weber, Chair, 805-893-2295, E-mail: weber@gss.ucsb.edu. *Application contact:* Sierra Gray, Graduate Program Assistant, 805-893-2131, Fax: 805-893-2374, E-mail: sierra@gss.ucsb.edu.

University of California, Santa Barbara, Graduate Division, College of Letters and Sciences, Division of Humanities and Fine Arts, Department of History, Santa Barbara, CA 93106. Offers history (PhD), including European medieval studies, global studies, public history, technology and society, women's studies; MA/PhD. *Faculty:* 44 full-time (19 women), 7 part-time/adjunct (3 women). *Students:* 122 full-time (66 women); includes 26 minority (3 African Americans, 6 Asian Americans or Pacific Islanders, 17 Hispanic Americans), 8 international. Average age 34. 139 applicants, 38% accepted, 21 enrolled. In 2007, 16 doctorates awarded. Terminal master's awarded for partial completion of doctoral program. *Median time to degree:* Of those who began their doctoral program in fall 1999, 47% received their degree in 8 years or less. *Degree requirements:* For doctorate, one foreign language, comprehensive exam, thesis/dissertation, one or more languages depending on field of study. *Entrance requirements:* For doctorate, GRE. Additional exam requirements/recommendations for international students: Required—TOEFL (minimum score 550 paper-based; 213 computer-based; 80 iBT). *Application deadline:* For fall admission, 12/5 for domestic and international students. Application fee: $60. Electronic applications accepted. *Expenses:* Tuition, nonresident: full-time $14,888. Required fees: $10,108. *Financial support:* In 2007–08, 109 students received support, including 44 fellowships with full and partial tuition reimbursements available (averaging $9,600 per year), 40 teaching assistantships with partial tuition reimbursements available (averaging $16,391 per year); research assistantships, Federal Work-Study, scholarships/grants, traineeships, health care benefits, tuition waivers (full and partial), and unspecified assistantships also available. Financial award application deadline: 12/5. *Faculty research:* Europe, U. S., Latin America, Middle East, East Asia. *Unit head:* Kenneth J. Mouré, Chair, 805-893-8156, Fax: 805-893-8795, E-mail: moure@history.ucrb.edu. *Application contact:* Deborah Johnson, Graduate Program Assistant, 805-893-2224, Fax: 805-893-8795, E-mail: deborahj@history.ucsb.edu.

University of California, Santa Barbara, Graduate Division, College of Letters and Sciences, Division of Humanities and Fine Arts, Program in Comparative Literature, Santa Barbara, CA 93106. Offers comparative literature (PhD); East Asian literatures (PhD); women's studies (PhD); MA/PhD. *Faculty:* 22 full-time (18 women). *Students:* 25 full-time (19 women); includes 4 minority (2 Asian Americans or Pacific Islanders, 2 Hispanic Americans), 4 international. Average age 31. 33 applicants, 39% accepted, 8 enrolled. In 2007, 4 doctorates awarded. Terminal master's awarded for partial completion of doctoral program. *Median time to degree:* Of those who began their doctoral program in fall 1999, 25% received their degree in 8 years or less. *Degree requirements:* For doctorate, 2 foreign languages, comprehensive exam, thesis/dissertation. *Entrance requirements:* For doctorate, GRE, samples of written work, study of literature in at least 2 approved languages, demonstration of foreign language proficiency. Additional exam requirements/recommendations for international students: Required—TOEFL (minimum score 550 paper-based; 213 computer-based; 80 iBT). *Application deadline:* For fall admission, 12/15 for domestic and international students. Application fee: $60. Electronic applications accepted. *Expenses:* Tuition, nonresident: full-time $14,888. Required fees: $10,108. *Financial support:* In 2007–08, 25 students received support, including 11 fellowships with full and partial tuition reimbursements available (averaging $13,200 per year), 7 teaching assistantships with full and partial tuition reimbursements available (averaging $16,389 per year); Federal Work-Study, institutionally sponsored loans, scholarships/grants, and health care benefits also available. Financial award application deadline: 12/15; financial award applicants required to submit FAFSA. *Faculty research:* Interdisciplinary studies, literary theory, cultural studies, early-modern and modern literature, critical theory. *Unit head:* Prof. Elisabeth Weber, Chair, 805-893-2295, E-mail: weber@gss.ucsb.edu. *Application contact:* Sierra Gray, Graduate Program Assistant, 805-893-2131, Fax: 805-893-2374, E-mail: sierra@gss.ucsb.edu.

University of California, Santa Barbara, Graduate Division, College of Letters and Sciences, Division of Social Sciences, Department of Anthropology, Santa Barbara, CA 93106. Offers anthropology (MA, PhD), including global studies (PhD), human development (PhD), quantitative methods in social sciences (PhD), technology and society (PhD), women's studies (PhD); North American archaeology (MA); MA/PhD. *Faculty:* 13 full-time (2 women), 2 part-time/adjunct (both women). *Students:* 55 full-time (29 women); includes 10 minority (3 Asian Americans or Pacific Islanders, 7 Hispanic Americans), 10 international. Average age 32. 73 applicants, 25% accepted, 6 enrolled. In 2007, 9 master's, 8 doctorates awarded. Terminal master's awarded for partial completion of doctoral program. *Median time to degree:* Of those who began their doctoral program in fall 1999, 38% received their degree in 8 years or less. *Degree requirements:* For master's, comprehensive exam, thesis; for doctorate, comprehensive exam, thesis/dissertation. *Entrance requirements:* For master's and doctorate, GRE General Test, sample of written work, statement of purpose with completed coversheets (2 copies), post-secondary institutions attended. Additional exam requirements/recommendations for international students: Required—TOEFL (minimum score 550 paper-based; 213 computer-based; 80 iBT). *Application deadline:* For fall admission, 12/1 for domestic and international students. Application fee: $60. Electronic applications accepted. *Expenses:* Tuition, nonresident: full-time $14,888. Required fees: $10,108. *Financial support:* In 2007–08, 56 students received support, including 14 fellowships with full and partial tuition reimbursements available (averaging $9,623 per year), 13 research assistantships with full and partial tuition reimbursements available (averaging $10,000 per year), 32 teaching assistantships with partial tuition reimbursements available (averaging $19,988 per year); career-related internships or fieldwork, Federal Work-Study, institutionally sponsored loans, scholarships/grants, traineeships, health care benefits, and unspecified assistantships also available. Financial award application deadline: 12/1; financial award applicants required to submit FAFSA. *Faculty research:* Evolutionary psychology, archaeology, sociocultural anthropology, biosocial anthropology, evolutionary ecology, bioarchaeology. *Unit head:* Prof. Barbara Voorhies, Chair, 805-896-2519, Fax: 805-893-8707, E-mail: voorhies@anth.oesb.edu. *Application contact:* Larisa Traga, Graduate Program Assistant, 805-893-2516, Fax: 805-893-8707, E-mail: traga@anth.ucsb.edu.

University of Cincinnati, Graduate School, McMicken College of Arts and Sciences, Department of Women's Studies, Cincinnati, OH 45221. Offers MA, Certificate, MA/JD. Part-time programs available. *Faculty:* 8 full-time (all women). *Students:* 31 full-time (30 women), 4 part-time (all women); includes 8 minority (3 African Americans, 4 Asian Americans or Pacific Islanders, 1 Hispanic American), 4 international. Average age 25. In 2007, 8 degrees awarded. *Degree requirements:* For master's, comprehensive exam, final paper/project. *Entrance requirements:* For master's, GRE General Test, Undergraduate degree transcripts, 3 letters of recommendation, completed application. Additional exam requirements/recommendations for international students: Required—TOEFL (minimum score 600 paper-based), IELTS (minimum score 7). *Application deadline:* For fall admission, 1/15 for domestic and international students. Application fee: $40. Electronic applications accepted. *Financial support:* In 2007–08, 17 students received support, including 1 fellowship with full tuition reimbursement available (averaging $12,000 per year), 10 research assistantships with full tuition reimbursements available (averaging $10,500 per year), 6 teaching assistantships with full tuition reimbursements available (averaging $10,500 per year); career-related internships or fieldwork, Federal Work-Study, institutionally sponsored loans, scholarships/grants, tuition waivers (partial), unspecified assistantships, and partial health premium waiver also available. Financial award application deadline: 1/15; financial award applicants required to submit FAFSA. *Faculty research:* Feminist legal, sexuality, international political economy, Latin American, cultural/

literary and environmental studies. Total annual research expenditures: $80,000. *Unit head:* Dr. Anne Sisson Runyan, Director of Graduate Studies, 513-556-6652, Fax: 513-556-6771, E-mail: anne.runyan@uc.edu.

University of Florida, Graduate School, College of Liberal Arts and Sciences, Center for Women's Studies and Gender Research, Gainesville, FL 32611. Offers gender and development (Graduate Certificate); women's studies (MA, MWS, Graduate Certificate); MA/JD; MA/MA. *Faculty:* 2 full-time (both women). *Students:* 10 (9 women); includes 3 minority (1 African American, 2 Hispanic Americans) 1 international. In 2007, 2 master's awarded. *Expenses:* Tuition, state resident: full-time $7,478. Tuition, nonresident: full-time $22,603. *Financial support:* In 2007–08, 5 teaching assistantships (averaging $9,439 per year) were awarded; research assistantships. *Unit head:* Milagros Petiilde;a, Director, 352-392-3365 Ext. 273, Fax: 352-392-6568, E-mail: mpena@soc.ufl.edu. *Application contact:* Kendal L. Broad, Graduate Coordinator, 352-392-0251 Ext. 257, Fax: 352-392-6568, E-mail: kendal@soc.ufl.edu.

University of Georgia, Graduate School, College of Arts and Sciences, Institute for Women's Studies, Athens, GA 30602. Offers Certificate. *Faculty:* 1 (woman) full-time. *Students:* 1 applicant, 100% accepted, 1 enrolled. *Unit head:* Dr. Chris Cuomo, Director, 706-542-2846, E-mail: cuomo@uga.edu. *Application contact:* Dr. Blaise Parker, Assistant Director, 706-542-2846, Fax: 706-542-0049, E-mail: blaze@uga.edu.

University of Hawaii at Manoa, Graduate Division, Colleges of Arts and Sciences, College of Social Sciences, Advanced Women's Studies Program, Honolulu, HI 96822. Offers Graduate Certificate. Part-time programs available. *Students:* 6 full-time (all women), 2 part-time (both women); includes 1 minority (Asian American or Pacific Islander), 1 international. *Entrance requirements:* Additional exam requirements/recommendations for international students: Required—TOEFL (minimum score 500 paper-based; 173 computer-based; 61 iBT), IELTS (minimum score 5). *Application deadline:* For fall admission, 3/1 for domestic and international students. Application fee: $50. *Financial support:* In 2007–08, 1 research assistantship (averaging $16,176 per year), 4 teaching assistantships (averaging $14,670 per year) were awarded. *Application contact:* Susan Hippensteele, Director, 808-956-6313, Fax: 808-956-9616, E-mail: hippenst@hawaii.edu.

The University of Iowa, Graduate College, College of Liberal Arts and Sciences, Department of Women's Studies, Iowa City, IA 52242-1316. Offers PhD. *Faculty:* 1 full-time, 4 part-time/adjunct. *Students:* 2 full-time (both women), 8 part-time (all women), 2 international. 29 applicants, 17% accepted, 1 enrolled. In 2007, 3 degrees awarded. *Degree requirements:* For doctorate, comprehensive exam, thesis/dissertation. *Entrance requirements:* For doctorate, GRE General Test, minimum GPA of 3.0. Additional exam requirements/recommendations for international students: Required—TOEFL (minimum score 550 paper-based; 213 computer-based; 81 iBT). *Application deadline:* For fall admission, 1/15 for domestic and international students. Application fee: $60 ($85 for international students). Electronic applications accepted. *Expenses:* Tuition, state resident: part-time $349 per hour. Tuition, nonresident: part-time $349 per hour. Tuition and fees vary according to course load and program. *Financial support:* In 2007–08, 5 teaching assistantships with partial tuition reimbursements were awarded; fellowships, research assistantships with partial tuition reimbursements also available. Financial award applicants required to submit FAFSA. *Unit head:* Dr. Lauren Rabinovitz, Interim Chair, 319-335-0322, Fax: 319-335-0314.

University of Louisville, Graduate School, College of Arts and Sciences, Department of Women's and Gender Studies, Louisville, KY 40292-0001. Offers MA, Certificate, MSSW/MA. *Students:* 5 full-time (4 women), 6 part-time (all women); includes 1 minority (African American) Average age 33. *Financial support:* In 2007–08, 1 teaching assistantship (averaging $12,000 per year) was awarded. *Unit head:* Nancy M. Theriot, Chairperson, 502-852-8160, Fax: 502-852-4421, E-mail: nancyt@louisville.edu.

University of Maryland, Baltimore County, Graduate School, College of Arts, Humanities and Social Sciences, Program in Gender and Women's Studies, Baltimore, MD 21250. Offers Postbaccalaureate Certificate. Part-time and evening/weekend programs available. *Students:* Average age 22. 1 applicant, 100% accepted, 0 enrolled. *Entrance requirements:* For degree, BA. *Application deadline:* Applications are processed on a rolling basis. Application fee: $50. Electronic applications accepted. *Faculty research:* Reproductive politics, resilience, sexuality, U.S. women's history. *Unit head:* Dr. Anne Brodsky, Coordinator, 410-455-2416. *Application contact:* Carole McCann, Coordinator, 410-455-2161, E-mail: mccann@umbc.edu.

University of Maryland, College Park, Graduate Studies, College of Arts and Humanities, Department of Women's Studies, College Park, MD 20742. Offers MA, PhD. *Faculty:* 71 full-time (67 women), 2 part-time/adjunct (both women). *Students:* 23 full-time (all women), 3 part-time (all women); includes 11 minority (6 African Americans, 3 Asian Americans or Pacific Islanders, 2 Hispanic Americans), 3 international. 77 applicants, 8% accepted, 3 enrolled. In 2007, 2 master's, 2 doctorates awarded. *Degree requirements:* For master's, thesis or alternative; for doctorate, one foreign language, thesis/dissertation or alternative. *Entrance requirements:* For master's, GRE General Test, writing sample, 3 letters of recommendation. Additional exam requirements/recommendations for international students: Required—TOEFL. *Application deadline:* For fall admission, 1/2 for domestic students, 2/1 for international students. Application fee: $60. *Financial support:* In 2007–08, 6 fellowships (averaging $14,202 per year), 15 teaching assistantships with tuition reimbursements (averaging $15,842 per year) were awarded; research assistantships, career-related internships or fieldwork, Federal Work-Study, and scholarships/grants also available. Support available to part-time students. *Faculty research:* Gender roles, national and global diversity, sexuality. Total annual research expenditures: $66,767. *Unit head:* Dr. Bonnie Dill, Chair, 301-405-6877, Fax: 301-314-9190, E-mail: btdill@umd.edu. *Application contact:* Dean of Graduate School, 301-405-0358, Fax: 301-314-9305.

University of Massachusetts Boston, Office of Graduate Studies, Division of Continuing Education and John W. McCormack Graduate School of Policy Studies, Program in Women in Politics and Government, Boston, MA 02125-3393. Offers Certificate. Part-time and evening/weekend programs available. *Degree requirements:* For Certificate, practicum, final project. *Entrance requirements:* For degree, interview, minimum GPA of 2.75.

University of Massachusetts Boston, Office of Graduate Studies, John W. McCormack Graduate School of Policy Studies, Boston, MA 02125-3393. Offers gerontology (MA, MS, PhD, Certificate), including gerontology (MS, PhD, Certificate), gerontology research (MA), management in aging services (MA); public affairs (MS); public policy (PhD); women in politics and government (Certificate). Certificate program in women in politics and government offered jointly with Division of Continuing Education. Part-time and evening/weekend programs available. *Degree requirements:* For doctorate, thesis/dissertation; for Certificate, practicum, final project. *Entrance requirements:* For doctorate, GRE General Test; for Certificate, interview, minimum GPA of 2.5.

University of Memphis, Graduate School, College of Arts and Sciences, Women's and Gender Studies Program, Memphis, TN 38152. Offers MA. *Students:* 7 full-time (all women), 3 part-time (all women); includes 5 African Americans. Average age 32. 12 applicants, 58% accepted, 4 enrolled. In 2007, 3 degrees awarded. *Degree requirements:* For master's, comprehensive exam, thesis or alternative. *Entrance requirements:* For master's, Letters of Reference. Application fee: $35 ($60 for international students). *Expenses:* Tuition, state resident: full-time $6,990; part-time $377 per hour. Tuition, nonresident: full-time $17,818; part-time $830 per hour. Tuition and fees vary according to course load and program. *Financial support:* In 2007–08, 3 research assistantships with full tuition reimbursements (averaging $6,667 per year), 1 teaching assistantship (averaging $4,000 per year) were awarded. Financial award application deadline: 2/15. *Unit head:* Dr. Wanda Rushing, Program Director, 901-678-3550, Fax: 901-678-4206, E-mail: wrushing@memphis.edu.

University of Michigan, Horace H. Rackham School of Graduate Studies, College of Literature, Science, and the Arts, Department of Women's Studies, Ann Arbor, MI 48109. Offers English and women's studies (PhD); history and women's studies (PhD); lesbian, gay, bisexual, transgender, queer (LGBTQ) studies (Certificate); psychology and women's studies (PhD); sociology and women's studies (PhD); women's studies (Certificate). *Faculty:* 71 full-time (68 women). *Students:* 70 full-time (69 women); includes 12 minority (4 African Americans, 5 Asian Americans or Pacific Islanders, 3 Hispanic Americans), 9 international. Average age 30. 140 applicants, 9% accepted. In 2007, 6 doctorates, 5 other advanced degrees awarded. *Degree requirements:* For doctorate, variable foreign language requirement, thesis/dissertation. *Entrance requirements:* For doctorate, GRE General Test, previous undergraduate course work in women's studies. *Application deadline:* For fall admission, 12/15 for domestic students. Application fee: $60 ($75 for international students). Electronic applications accepted. *Financial support:* In 2007–08, 23 fellowships with full tuition reimbursements (averaging $16,000 per year), 19 teaching assistantships with full and partial tuition reimbursements (averaging $15,199 per year) were awarded; career-related internships or fieldwork, institutionally sponsored loans, scholarships/grants, traineeships, health care benefits, and unspecified assistantships also available. *Faculty research:* Gender issues; LGBTQ studies; sexuality; women and science; global feminism. *Unit head:* Valerie Traub, Chair, 734-763-2047, Fax: 734-647-4943, E-mail: traubv@umich.edu. *Application contact:* Jen Sarafin, Graduate Student Services Coordinator, 734-763-2047, Fax: 734-647-4943, E-mail: jsarafin@umich.edu.

University of Minnesota, Twin Cities Campus, Graduate School, College of Liberal Arts, Department of Gender, Women, and Sexuality Studies, Minneapolis, MN 55455-0213. Offers feminist studies (PhD). *Faculty:* 6 full-time (all women). *Students:* 14 full-time (all women), 4 part-time (all women); includes 8 minority (3 African Americans, 3 Asian Americans or Pacific Islanders, 2 Hispanic Americans), 5 international. Average age 25. 32 applicants, 13% accepted, 3 enrolled. *Degree requirements:* For doctorate, comprehensive exam, thesis/dissertation. *Entrance requirements:* For doctorate, GRE. Additional exam requirements/recommendations for international students: Required—TOEFL (minimum score 550 paper-based). *Application deadline:* For fall admission, 12/1 for domestic and international students. Application fee: $55 ($75 for international students). Electronic applications accepted. *Financial support:* In 2007–08, 5 fellowships with full tuition reimbursements, 2 research assistantships with full tuition reimbursements (averaging $15,000 per year), 6 teaching assistantships with full tuition reimbursements (averaging $15,000 per year) were awarded. *Faculty research:* Transnational feminist theories, critical development theory, feminist postcolonialisms, feminist science studies and studying of health, literature, Asian diasporas, sexuality and queer theory. *Unit head:* Susan Craddock, Interim Chair, 612-624-7319.

University of Nevada, Las Vegas, Graduate College, College of Liberal Arts, Women's Studies Department, Las Vegas, NV 89154-9900. Offers Certificate. *Faculty:* 5 full-time (all women), 1 (woman) part-time/adjunct. *Entrance requirements:* Additional exam requirements/recommendations for international students: Required—TOEFL (minimum score 550 paper-based; 213 computer-based; 80 iBT). *Application deadline:* For fall admission, 6/15 for domestic students, 5/1 for international students; for spring admission, 11/15 for domestic students, 10/1 for international students. Application fee: $60 ($75 for international students). Electronic applications accepted. *Expenses:* Tuition, state resident: part-time $198 per credit. Tuition, nonresident: part-time $416 per credit. Required fees: $256 per semester. Tuition and fees vary according to course load and reciprocity agreements. *Financial support:* In 2007–08, 4 research assistantships with partial tuition reimbursements (averaging $10,000 per year) were awarded. *Unit head:* Dr. Lois Helmbold, Chair, 702-895-0837, Fax: 702-895-5055, E-mail: lois.helmbold@unlv.edu.

University of New Mexico, Graduate School, College of Arts and Sciences, Program in Women Studies, Albuquerque, NM 87131-2039. Offers Graduate Certificate. *Degree requirements:* For Graduate Certificate, thesis. *Entrance requirements:* For degree, must be enrolled in degree-granting program before acceptance for Graduate Certification in Women Studies. *Application deadline:* Applications are processed on a rolling basis. Application fee: $50. *Unit head:* Dr. Janet Cramer, Director, 505-277-3854, Fax: 505-277-0267, E-mail: jcramer@unm.edu.

The University of North Carolina at Greensboro, Graduate School, College of Arts and Sciences, Department of English, Greensboro, NC 27412-5001. Offers creative writing (MFA); English (M Ed, MA, PhD, Certificate), including American literature (PhD), English (M Ed, MA), English literature (PhD), rhetoric and composition (PhD), technical writing (Certificate), women's studies (Certificate). *Faculty:* 29 full-time (16 women), 6 part-time/adjunct (2 women). *Students:* 108 full-time (71 women), 35 part-time (24 women); includes 16 minority (14 African Americans, 1 American Indian/Alaska Native, 1 Asian American or Pacific Islander). 277 applicants, 22% accepted. *Degree requirements:* For master's, comprehensive exam; for doctorate, variable foreign language requirement, thesis/dissertation, preliminary exam. *Entrance requirements:* For master's, GRE General Test, minimum GPA of 3.0; for doctorate, GRE General Test, GRE Subject Test, critical writing sample, minimum GPA of 3.0. Additional exam requirements/recommendations for international students: Required—TOEFL. *Application deadline:* For fall admission, 1/20 priority date for domestic students; for spring admission, 11/1 for domestic students. Applications are processed on a rolling basis. Electronic applications accepted. *Financial support:* Fellowships, research assistantships, teaching assistantships, career-related internships or fieldwork, Federal Work-Study, scholarships/grants, traineeships, and unspecified assistantships available. Support available to part-time students. *Unit head:* Dr. Anne Wallace, Head, 336-334-5311, Fax: 336-334-3281, E-mail: adwallace@uncg.edu. *Application contact:* Michelle Harkleroad, Director of Graduate Admissions, 336-334-4884, Fax: 336-334-4424, E-mail: mbharkle@uncg.edu.

The University of North Carolina at Greensboro, Graduate School, College of Arts and Sciences, Program in Women's and Gender Studies, Greensboro, NC 27412-5001. Offers MA, Certificate. *Students:* 10 full-time (9 women), 3 part-time (all women); includes 6 minority (5 African Americans, 1 Asian American or Pacific Islander). 14 applicants, 71% accepted. Application fee: $45. Electronic applications accepted. *Unit head:* Katherine Jamieson, Director, 336-334-5273, E-mail: rmjamies@uncg.edu. *Application contact:* Michelle Harkleroad, Director of Graduate Admissions, 336-334-4884, Fax: 336-334-4424, E-mail: mbharkle@uncg.edu.

University of Northern Iowa, Graduate College, Program in Women's and Gender Studies, Cedar Falls, IA 50614. Offers MA. *Students:* 9 full-time (all women), 3 part-time (all women); includes 1 minority (African American), 2 international. 19 applicants, 84% accepted, 5 enrolled. In 2007, 5 degrees awarded. *Degree requirements:* For master's, comprehensive exam (for some programs), thesis or alternative. *Entrance requirements:* For master's, minimum GPA of 3.0. Additional exam requirements/recommendations for international students: Required—TOEFL (minimum score 500 paper-based; 180 computer-based; 61 iBT). *Application deadline:* Applications are processed on a rolling basis. Application fee: $30 ($50 for international students). Electronic applications accepted. *Expenses:* Tuition, state resident: full-time $6,246; part-time $694 per credit hour. Tuition, nonresident: full-time $14,554; part-time $694 per credit hour. Required fees: $838; $119 per semester. *Financial support:* Application deadline: 2/1. *Unit head:* Dr. Phyllis Baker, Head/Graduate Coordinator, 319-273-2109, Fax: 319-273-3053, E-mail: phyllis.baker@uni.edu.

University of Ottawa, Faculty of Graduate and Postdoctoral Studies, Faculty of Social Sciences, Institute of Women's Studies, Ottawa, ON K1N 6N5, Canada. Offers criminology (MA, MCA); education (MA); English (MA); history (MA); human kinetics (MA); law (LL M); lettres Françaises (MA); nursing (M Sc); pastoral studies (MA); political science (MA); religious studies (MA); sociology (MA). *Degree requirements:* For master's, thesis or alternative.

University of Pittsburgh, School of Arts and Sciences, Program in Women's Studies, Pittsburgh, PA 15260. Offers Doctoral Certificate, Master's Certificate. Part-time programs available. *Faculty:* 67 full-time (60 women). *Students:* 56 full-time (52 women), 4 part-time (all women); includes 10 minority (5 African Americans, 2 Asian Americans or Pacific Islanders, 3 Hispanic Americans), 2 international. Average age 27. 8 applicants, 100% accepted, 8 enrolled. In 2007, 9 degrees awarded. *Application deadline:* Applications are processed on a rolling basis. Application fee: $50. Electronic applications accepted. *Financial support:* In 2007–08, 2 students

Women's Studies

University of Pittsburgh (continued)
received support, including 2 teaching assistantships with full tuition reimbursements available (averaging $13,290 per year); scholarships/grants also available. *Faculty research:* Global feminisms; gender and interpersonal violence; race and gender studies; representation and gender in media, arts, and literature; concepts of the body. *Unit head:* Jean Ferguson Carr, Director, 412-624-6485, Fax: 412-624-6492, E-mail: wstudies@pitt.edu.

University of Regina, Faculty of Graduate Studies and Research, Faculty of Arts, Department of Women's Studies, Regina, SK S4S 0A2, Canada. Offers MA. Offered as a special case program. Part-time programs available. *Faculty:* 2 full-time (both women). *Degree requirements:* For master's, thesis. *Entrance requirements:* Additional exam requirements/recommendations for international students: Required—TOEFL (minimum score 580 paper-based; 237 computer-based). *Application deadline:* Applications are processed on a rolling basis. Application fee: $85 ($100 for international students). Electronic applications accepted. *Financial support:* In 2007–08, fellowships (averaging $15,750 per year), research assistantships (averaging $13,875 per year), teaching assistantships (averaging $13,060 per year) were awarded; scholarships/grants also available. Financial award application deadline: 6/15. *Unit head:* Dr. Wendee Kubik, Graduate Program Coordinator, 306-585-4668, E-mail: wendee.kubik@uregina.ca.

University of Saskatchewan, College of Graduate Studies and Research, College of Arts and Sciences, Department of Women's and Gender Studies, Saskatoon, SK S7N 5A2, Canada. Offers MA, PhD. *Degree requirements:* For master's, thesis; for doctorate, thesis/dissertation. *Entrance requirements:* Additional exam requirements/recommendations for international students: Required—TOEFL.

University of South Carolina, The Graduate School, College of Arts and Sciences, Program in Women's Studies, Columbia, SC 29208. Offers Certificate. Part-time programs available. *Faculty:* 10 full-time (9 women), 79 part-time/adjunct (69 women). *Students:* 4 full-time (2 women), 21 part-time (all women); includes 12 minority (8 African Americans, 3 Asian Americans or Pacific Islanders, 1 Hispanic American). Average age 30. 8 applicants, 100% accepted, 8 enrolled. In 2007, 9 degrees awarded. *Entrance requirements:* For degree, GRE General Test or MAT. Additional exam requirements/recommendations for international students: Required—TOEFL. *Application deadline:* For fall admission, 8/1 priority date for domestic students; for spring admission, 12/1 priority date for domestic students. Applications are processed on a rolling basis. Application fee: $40. Electronic applications accepted. *Expenses:* Tuition, state resident: part-time $440 per hour. Tuition, nonresident: part-time $936 per hour. Required fees: $17 per hour. Tuition and fees vary according to program. *Financial support:* In 2007–08, 6 students received support, including 6 research assistantships with full tuition reimbursements available (averaging $10,000 per year). Financial award application deadline: 4/1. *Faculty research:* Health; pedagogy; intersection of race, class, gender; public policy; politics of culture and representations, feminist political economics. *Unit head:* Dr. Drualla K. Barker, Director, 803-777-4007, Fax: 803-777-9114, E-mail: barkerdk@sc.edu. *Application contact:* Dr. DeAnne K. Messias, Graduate Director, 803-777-4007, Fax: 803-777-9114, E-mail: deanne.messias@sc.edu.

University of South Florida, Graduate School, College of Arts and Sciences, Department of Women's Studies, Tampa, FL 33620-9951. Offers MA. Part-time programs available. *Faculty:* 4 full-time (all women). *Students:* 10 full-time (all women), 6 part-time (5 women); includes 4 minority (3 African Americans, 1 Hispanic American). 11 applicants, 82% accepted, 7 enrolled. In 2007, 3 degrees awarded. *Degree requirements:* For master's, comprehensive exam, thesis (for some programs), thesis or internship. *Entrance requirements:* For master's, GRE General Test, 3 letters of reference, writing sample, minimum GPA 3.0 in last 60 hours. Additional exam requirements/recommendations for international students: Required—TOEFL (minimum score 550 paper-based; 213 computer-based). *Application deadline:* For fall admission, 3/30 for domestic students, 1/1 for international students; for spring admission, 10/15 for domestic students, 7/1 for international students. Applications are processed on a rolling basis. Application fee: $30. *Financial support:* In 2007–08, 7 students received support, including 1 fellowship with full tuition reimbursement available (averaging $13,000 per year), 8 teaching assistantships with full tuition reimbursements available. Financial award application deadline: 3/1. *Unit head:* Dr. Kim Vaz, Chairperson, 813-974-0985, Fax: 813-974-0336, E-mail: vaz@cas.usf.edu. *Application contact:* Dr. Marilyn Myerson, Graduate Director, 813-974-0978, Fax: 813-974-0336, E-mail: myerson@cas.usf.edu.

University of Washington, Graduate School, College of Arts and Sciences, Department of Women Studies, Seattle, WA 98195. Offers MA, PhD. Terminal master's awarded for partial completion of doctoral program. *Degree requirements:* For master's, thesis; for doctorate, one foreign language, thesis/dissertation, exam. *Entrance requirements:* For master's and doctorate, GRE General Test. Additional exam requirements/recommendations for international students: Required—TOEFL. Electronic applications accepted. *Faculty research:* Women's history in U.S. and China; Native American ethnography and identity; women, science, and technology; political economy of development, feminism and nationalism.

Washington State University, Graduate School, College of Liberal Arts, Program in American Studies, Pullman, WA 99164. Offers ethnic studies (MA, PhD); feminist studies (MA, PhD); history (MA, PhD); literature (MA, PhD). *Faculty:* 39. *Students:* 27 full-time (19 women), 4 part-time (2 women); includes 17 minority (6 African Americans, 4 American Indian/Alaska Native, 2 Asian Americans or Pacific Islanders, 5 Hispanic Americans), 3 international. Average age 35. 78 applicants, 15% accepted, 12 enrolled. In 2007, 5 master's, 1 doctorate awarded. *Degree requirements:* For master's, one foreign language, comprehensive exam (for some programs), thesis optional, oral exam; for doctorate, one foreign language, comprehensive exam (for some programs), thesis/dissertation, oral exam. *Entrance requirements:* For master's and doctorate, GRE General Test, minimum GPA of 3.0, writing sample, 3 letters of recommendation. Additional exam requirements/recommendations for international students: Required—TOEFL. *Application deadline:* For fall admission, 2/1 priority date for domestic students, 3/1 for international students; for spring admission, 7/1 for international students. Applications are processed on a rolling basis. Application fee: $50. *Financial support:* In 2007–08, 24 students received support, including 1 fellowship (averaging $6,950 per year), 3 research assistantships with full and partial tuition reimbursements available (averaging $13,917 per year), 17 teaching assistantships with full and partial tuition reimbursements available (averaging $13,056 per year); career-related internships or fieldwork, Federal Work-Study, institutionally sponsored loans, tuition waivers (partial), and teaching associateships also available. Financial award application deadline: 3/1; financial award applicants required to submit FAFSA. *Faculty research:* The American West in multicultural perspective; nineteenth century historical, literary, and cultural studies; comparative American ethnic literatures and cultures; American cultures and the environment; American rhetoric. *Unit head:* Dr. Noel Sturgeon, Director, 509-335-1560, E-mail: reedtv@wsu.edu. *Application contact:* Graduate School Admissions, 800-GRADWSU, Fax: 509-335-1949, E-mail: gradsch@wsu.edu.

West Chester University of Pennsylvania, Office of Graduate Studies and Extended Education, College of Arts and Sciences, Department of Women's Studies, West Chester, PA 19383. Offers leadership for women (MSA, Certificate). Part-time and evening/weekend programs available. *Students:* 1 (woman) full-time. Average age 35. *Degree requirements:* For master's, comprehensive exam. *Entrance requirements:* For master's, GMAT, GRE General Test, or MAT, interview, minimum GPA of 3.0. Additional exam requirements/recommendations for international students: Required—TOEFL (minimum score 550 paper-based; 213 computer-based; 80 iBT). *Application deadline:* For fall admission, 4/15 priority date for domestic students; for spring admission, 10/15 for domestic students. Applications are processed on a rolling basis. Application fee: $35. *Expenses:* Tuition, state resident: part-time $345 per credit. Tuition, nonresident: part-time $552 per credit. Tuition and fees vary according to course load. *Financial support:* In 2007–08, research assistantships with full and partial tuition reimbursements (averaging $5,000 per year); unspecified assistantships also available. Support available to part-time students. Financial award application deadline: 2/15; financial award applicants required to submit FAFSA. *Unit head:* Dr. Lisa Kirschenbaum, Interim Director, 610-436-2464, E-mail: lkirschenbaum@wcupa.edu. *Application contact:* Dr. Linda Millhous, Concentration Advisor, 610-436-2180, E-mail: lmillhous@wcupa.edu.

York University, Faculty of Graduate Studies, Faculty of Arts, Program in Women's Studies, Toronto, ON M3J 1P3, Canada. Offers MA, PhD. *Degree requirements:* For master's, thesis or alternative; for doctorate, comprehensive exam, thesis/dissertation. Electronic applications accepted.

GEORGE MASON UNIVERSITY

College of Arts and Sciences
Ph.D. Program in Cultural Studies

Program of Study

Cultural studies is a new field of scholarly inquiry, emerging in the second half of the twentieth century. Broadly speaking, cultural studies analyzes the production and circulation of meanings in objects of all kinds, including representations in mass media as well as oppositional subcultures, industrial products as well as practices of performance and display. Although cultural studies draws freely on theory and methods from more traditional disciplines (anthropology, history, literary theory, philosophy, political economy, and sociology), it responds to questions not immediately answerable by conventional means. That is, it seeks to account for everyday cultural objects under conditions constrained by power and defined by contestation, conflict, and change. Unlike traditional disciplines, cultural studies also implies social self-reflection, an awareness that the scholar and his or her scholarship are themselves very much caught up in the political currents and in the global circulation of meanings being studied. Finally, cultural studies both draws on and produces the key strands of contemporary cultural theory: semiotics, deconstruction, dialogics, poststructuralism, and neo-Marxism.

The first of its kind at the doctoral level in the United States, the Program in Cultural Studies at George Mason draws on faculty members from ten different departments, programs, and institutes. As a center for advanced graduate training, it is a research-oriented program. The course of study consists of 48 credit hours beyond the M.A. The core curriculum (18 credits) includes an introduction to cultural studies and a research methods course, as well as courses on political economy, gender/sexuality, critical race studies, science/technology, social institutions, and visual/performance culture. The field specializations (18 credit hours) involve intensive research and work in two areas of cultural studies scholarship. Fields of specialization, chosen by the student and crafted under the guidance of faculty advisers, point logically toward the dissertation (12 credit hours) and other forms of professional development. The Colloquium Series, an intellectual centerpiece of the program, is organized by faculty members and students and forms the basis for one of the required core courses. The Colloquium brings to the campus distinguished outside scholars from diverse backgrounds and perspectives to broaden the discussion of issues and debates relevant to contemporary research in cultural studies.

Research Facilities

The University library, which houses more than 600,000 volumes, is pioneering electronic global access to research materials. Every building on campus is linked by a fiber-optics network, and students also have use of state-of-the-art multimedia computer labs and facilities, including a virtual reality lab. The Washington Regional Library Consortium gives students access to 4 million volumes.

Financial Aid

Fellowship aid, teaching and research assistantships, and tuition remission are available to qualified applicants.

Cost of Study

Tuition is $371 per credit hour for in-state students and $929.50 per credit hour for out-of-state students. The normal full-time load is 9 credit hours per semester. Fees are $60 per year.

Living and Housing Costs

Room and board costs for students living on campus average $4840 per year. Housing for graduate students is extremely limited. Most students live off campus. The cost of living is comparable to that in other large northeastern urban areas.

Student Group

Sixty-three students (many are part-time) come from diverse backgrounds and with diverse career plans. The University's total enrollment is 30,000 and growing each year.

Location

The University's main campus in northern Virginia covers nearly 600 wooded acres. Nearby Washington, D.C., offers students access to some of the world's great cultural institutions. Students are entitled to participate in seminars and internships and to use archives and collections at institutions such as the Folger Shakespeare Library, the Smithsonian, and the Library of Congress.

The University and The Program

A young, dynamic institution, George Mason has become known for the development of innovative interdisciplinary programs. The Program in Cultural Studies fits naturally with the University's strengths in information technology, public policy, history and new media, and the arts.

Applying

Students with M.A. degrees in relevant fields are eligible to apply to the Program in Cultural Studies. Students with only a bachelor's degree must apply to an M.A. program in one of the following departments: English, sociology, history, philosophy, foreign languages and literatures, or economics, all of which have established feeder tracks in cultural studies. Students with only a bachelor's degree may apply simultaneously to the Program in Cultural Studies. All applicants must submit grade transcripts, a statement of interest, a writing sample, scores on the General Test of the Graduate Record Examinations, and three academic letters of reference. The statement of interest should include an account of the applicant's intellectual interests as these have been shaped in general studies. It should also provide a general overview of the course of graduate study and in the doctoral dissertation. Applicants who are not native English speakers should also submit TOEFL scores. Students may apply for either full-time or part-time status. The application deadline is January 15.

Correspondence and Information

Roger N. Lancaster, Director
Program in Cultural Studies
MSN 5E4
George Mason University
Fairfax, Virginia 22030-4444
Phone: 703-993-2851
Fax: 703-993-2852
E-mail: cultural@gmu.edu
Web site: http://culturalstudies.gmu.edu/

Applicants should send materials to:
Graduate Admissions Office
MSN 2D2
George Mason University
4400 University Drive
Fairfax, Virginia 22030

George Mason University

THE FACULTY AND THEIR RESEARCH

Denise Albanese, Ph.D., Stanford. Early modern literature and culture, colonialism, early scientific modernity.
Amal Amireh, Ph.D., Boston University. English.
Debra Bergoffen, Ph.D., Georgetown. Feminist theory, women's studies.
Amy Best, Ph.D., Syracuse. Sociology and anthropology.
Andrew Bickford, Ph.D., Rutgers. Sociology and anthropology.
Johanna Bockman, Ph.D., California, San Diego. Global affairs.
Lorraine Brown, Ph.D., Maryland, College Park. Nineteenth- and twentieth-century contemporary drama, focusing on gender and museum studies; American and European studies.
Zofia Burr, Ph.D., Cornell. Twentieth-century poetry, poetic theory, women's studies.
Jack Censer, Dean, College of Humanities and Social Sciences; Ph.D., Johns Hopkins. French history, press and public opinion, political traditions.
Michael Chang, Ph.D., California, San Diego. History and art history.
Dina Copelman, Ph.D., Princeton. European and women's history.
Rick Davis, College of Visual and Performing Arts; Ph.D., Yale.
Marion Deshmukh, Ph.D., Columbia. German and European cultural, intellectual, and art history.
Sheila ffolliott, Ph.D., Pennsylvania. Art collecting and patronage; gender, with focus on queenship images and museum display.
Joel Foreman, Ph.D., George Washington. Online writing instruction systems.
John Foster, Ph.D., Yale. Postmodernism, modes of narrative, comparative literature.
Wayne Froman, Ph.D., Fordham. Hermeneutics, post-Heideggerian French philosophical thought, phenomenology.
Cynthia Fuchs, Ph.D., Pennsylvania. Gender studies, TV and film, postmodern theory.
Timothy Gibson, Ph.D., Simon Fraser. Communication.
Paula Gilbert, Ph.D., Columbia. Gender and women's studies, comparative literature.
Michele Greet, Ph.D., NYU. History and art history.
Gregory Guagnano, Ph.D., California, Davis. Environmental sociology, evolutionary theory.
Hugh Gusterson, Ph.D., Stanford. Sociology and anthropology.
Nancy Weiss Hanrahan, Ph.D., New School for Social Research. Sociology of music, cultural criticism.
Devon Hodges, Ph.D., SUNY at Buffalo. Feminist theory, early modern culture.
Mack Holt, Ph.D., Emory. Popular political culture, Reformation, European history.
Lois Horton, Ph.D., Brandeis. Social history, urban sociology, social welfare policy.
Mark Jacobs, Ph.D., Chicago. Sociological theory, juvenile justice, sociology of culture.
Rosemary Jann, Ph.D., Northwestern. Literary theory, historiography, British fiction and poetry.
Kristin Johnsen-Neshati, M.F.A., Yale. Russian drama, Shakespeare, women playwrights.
Deborah Kaplan, Ph.D., Brandeis. Women's studies, gender studies, performance theory.
Timothy Kaposy, Ph.D., McMaster. Cultural studies.
Matthew Karush, Ph.D., Chicago. History and art history.
David Kaufmann, Ph.D., Yale. Critical theory, contemporary poetry, eighteenth-century and Romantic literature and intellectual history.
Roger Lancaster, Director, Cultural Studies Program; Ph.D., Berkeley. Marxism and critical theory; gender, sexuality, and lesbigay studies; Latin America.
Alison Landsberg, Ph.D., Chicago. English, history, American literature and culture, immigration and mass culture 1890–1935, commemoration and public history in twentieth-century America, film theory and spectatorship.
Jennifer Leeman, Ph.D., Georgetown. Modern and classical languages.
Cynthia Lont, Ph.D., Iowa. Mass communication theory, women and media, women's music and culture.
Peter Mandaville, Co-Director, Center for Global Studies; Ph.D., Kent (England).
Robert Matz, Ph.D., Johns Hopkins. Early modern culture, history of literature, cultural theory.
Char Miller, Ph.D., Johns Hopkins. Public and international affairs.
John O'Connor, Ph.D., Virginia. Collaborative online writing, fiction and nonfiction hypertext, the effects of multimedia on writing.
Michael O'Malley, Ph.D., Berkeley. Nineteenth-century U.S. social and cultural history.
Ann Palkovich, Ph.D., Northwestern. Complex adaptive systems, construction of meaning in material culture.
Lisa M. Rabin, Ph.D., Yale. Spanish-American literature, with emphasis on poetry and the Colonial period; comparative literature; interdisciplinary studies of literature and art; literary theory; women's studies.
John Radner, Ph.D., Harvard. Eighteenth-century British literature, autobiography, utopian literature and practice.
Janine Ricouart, Ph.D., California, Davis. Gay and lesbian studies, Canadian/Quebec studies, women's studies.
Jeanette Roan, Ph.D., Rochester. English.
Karen Rosenblum, Ph.D., Colorado. Sex and gender studies, deviance, language.
Mark Sample, Ph.D., Pennsylvania. English.
Jessica Scarlata, Ph.D., Rutgers. English.
Linda Seligmann, Ph.D., Illinois at Urbana-Champaign. Political economy, anthropological theory and methods, language and culture, Latin America.
Debra Shutika, Ph.D., Pennsylvania. English.
Paul Smith, Ph.D., Kent (England). Theory and pedagogy of cultural studies, modernist poetry, gender studies.
Suzanne E. Smith, Ph.D., Yale. African-American history, twentieth century versus cultural history, film studies.
Peter Stearns, Provost of George Mason University; Ph.D., Harvard. Social history.
Jeffrey Stewart, Ph.D., Yale. U.S. cultural history, history of the 1920s and 1930s, African-American culture.
Ellen Todd, Ph.D., Stanford. Issues of representation, gender, and spectatorship in American art from the Civil War to the present.
Toni-Michelle Travis, Ph.D., Chicago. Public and international affairs, government, African-American studies.
Steven Vallas, Ph.D., Rutgers. Sociology and anthropology.
Alok Yadov, Ph.D., Cornell. Colonial and post-Colonial studies, nations and nationalism, early modern studies.
Margaret Yocom, Ph.D., Massachusetts. Folklore, construction of race and gender, English drama.
Rosemarie Zagarri, Ph.D., Yale. Colonial and Revolutionary America, political and cultural history.

SARAH LAWRENCE COLLEGE

Women's History

Program of Study

Founded in 1972, the Sarah Lawrence master's program in women's history was the first in the nation to offer graduate study in this field. The intellectually challenging program introduces students to the rapidly expanding historical literature on women, feminist theory in its relation to women's history, and research methods and resources in the field.

The program features small seminars, close collaborative work with faculty members, focused and intense immersion in the literature of the field, and immediate research in primary sources. Courses address the impact of gender, social class, race, ethnicity, and sexual orientation on women's experiences in culture and society. While concentrating their efforts on historical issues, students may also pursue related topics in women's studies that are available across the curriculum.

The major emphasis of the program is United States women's history, but interdisciplinary and cross-cultural work is encouraged.

The program, which leads to the Master of Arts degree in women's history, requires two years of study and completion of 36 course credits (24 credits in the first year, 12 in the second). All students write a thesis during their second year.

A joint-degree program in women's history and law is offered in cooperation with Pace University Law School. Students in this program can pursue study leading to a master's degree in women's history and a J.D. By taking courses that are acceptable for transfer credit in each of the schools involved, and through careful course planning, the joint-degree student can complete both degrees in four years of full-time study. This program can also be completed on a part-time basis.

Research Facilities

The College's facilities include classrooms, laboratories, and a computer center; a modern library with 202,265 books and 880 periodicals, which is linked by computer to more than 6,000 other libraries; the Performing Arts Center; a music building, including a music library; and a state-of-the-art sports complex.

Financial Aid

Graduate students are welcome to apply for financial aid. There are two required forms for U.S. citizens (and other federally eligible students) and one form for international students. U.S. citizens should complete the Free Application for Federal Student Aid (FAFSA) and the Financial Aid PROFILE. International students may use the College's International Application for Financial Aid. There are links to all three forms at http://www.sarahlawrence.edu/finaid. March 1 is the College's preferential filing date. It is important that all applicants for financial aid complete either the PROFILE or the international application for aid at the same time as their application for admission. All financial aid is awarded on the basis of need. Students who complete the appropriate forms in a timely manner are automatically considered for all aid resources administered by Sarah Lawrence College. Grants (gift aid) and student loans comprise the two elements of a Sarah Lawrence financial aid package. Every federally eligible aid recipient is offered a student loan. Students are not required to accept the loan in order to receive Sarah Lawrence College gift aid. International students are advised to investigate financing opportunities offered by their government or private institutions. Detailed descriptions and a thorough explanation of financial aid procedures are available in *Financing Your Graduate Education at Sarah Lawrence College,* published and updated by the Office of Graduate Studies. A copy of the booklet is mailed to all students who apply to a graduate studies program.

Cost of Study

For more information about program costs, prospective students should visit http://www.slc.edu/student-accounts/Graduate_Tuition_and_Costs.php.

Living and Housing Costs

Estimated expenses for off-campus housing and food are $15,390 per year.

Student Group

Sarah Lawrence attracts students who seek a creative education within the rigorous discipline of women's history. Work in history trains students in advanced research, writing, and presentation skills applicable to almost any field. Graduates of the program have pursued more advanced work in history and in other social science fields; museum, library, and archival work; teaching; educational administration; public policy; international affairs; law; and advocacy work.

The student body of the entire Sarah Lawrence graduate studies program is diverse, with about 300 students ranging in age from 22 to 55. Students in the women's history program come from across the country and often have extensive work experience.

Location

The College is situated in the Bronxville/Yonkers suburban community in southern Westchester County, just 15 miles north of midtown Manhattan in New York City. Main roads and a commuter railroad make it possible to reach the city in about 30 minutes, enabling students to take advantage of the social, cultural, and intellectual resources of New York.

The College

Founded in 1926, Sarah Lawrence is a small liberal arts college for men and women. It is a lively community of students, scholars, and artists, offering outstanding programs on the graduate level. The College is nationally renowned for its unique academic structure, which combines small classes with individual student-faculty conferences.

Applying

Applicants for graduate studies must have received a B.A. or an equivalent degree from an accredited college or university. Applicants should write to the College address, giving a brief summary of their educational and professional background, and reason for seeking the master's degree. Applicants are asked to complete an application form and to furnish transcripts of all undergraduate work; two letters of recommendation, preferably from former teachers; and a sample of their best academic writing. GRE scores are not required. Applicants are encouraged to visit the campus and to meet with students, faculty members, and the director of graduate studies. The deadline for first consideration is February 1.

To qualify for the joint program, students must apply separately to each school. Financial aid applications also must be made to each school. (Students may receive financial aid from only one school per semester.)

Correspondence and Information

Susan Guma
Dean of Graduate Studies
Sarah Lawrence College
Bronxville, New York 10709-5999
Phone: 914-395-2371
Fax: 914-395-2664
E-mail: grad@sarahlawrence.edu
Web site: http://www.sarahlawrence.edu

Sarah Lawrence College

THE FACULTY AND THEIR RESEARCH

Priscilla Murolo, Director; Ph.D., Yale. U.S. labor history.
Tara James, Associate Director; M.A., Sarah Lawrence.
Eileen Ka-may Cheng, Ph.D., Yale. Nineteenth-century America, with a focus on intellectual and political history.
Rachel Cohen, A.B., Harvard. Writing/creative nonfiction.
Lyde Cullen Sizer, Ph.D., Brown. Women's literary cultures, American popular culture, the American Civil War.
K. Komozi Woodard, Ph.D., Pennsylvania. African American history and culture, with emphasis on the black freedom movement, American urban history, and ghetto formation.

Affiliate Faculty
Julie Abraham, Lesbian and gay studies.
Bella Brodzki, Literature.
Isabelle de Sena, Spanish/literature.
Mary Dillard, History.
Arnold Krupat, Literature.
Chikwenye Ogunyemi, Literature.
David Peritz, Political science.
Mary Porter, Anthropology.
Marilyn Power, Economics.
Kasturi Ray, Global studies
Sandra Robinson, Asian studies.
Judith Rodenbeck, Art history.
Shahnaz Rouse, Sociology.
Barbara Schecter, Psychology.
Pauline Watts, History.
Matilde Zimmermann, History.

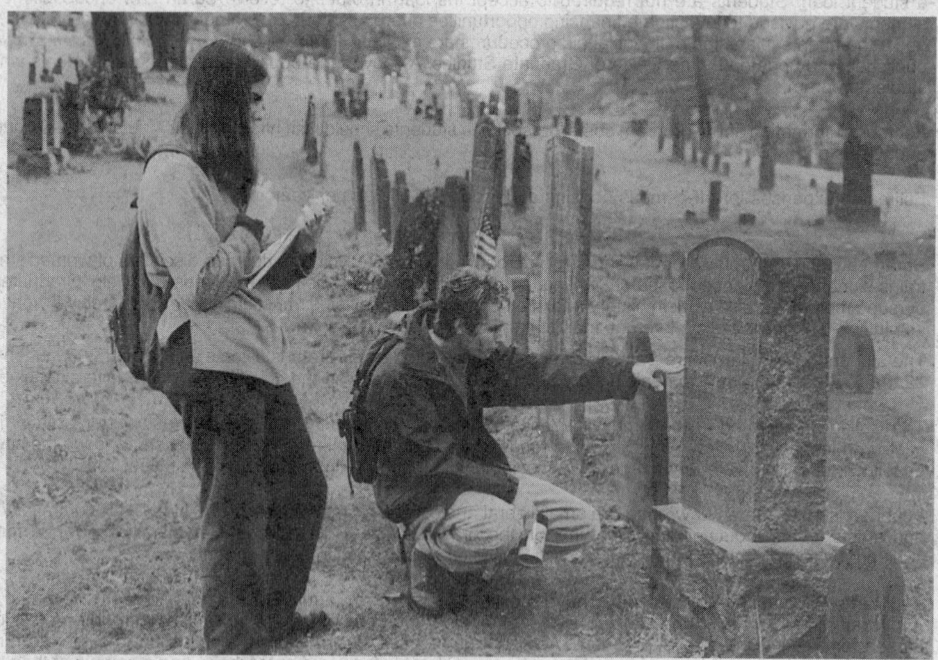

Students visiting a cemetery as part of their course work.

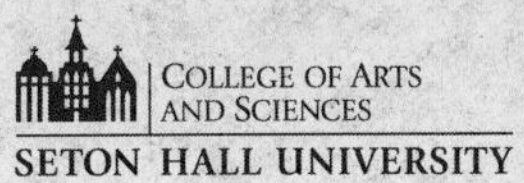

SETON HALL UNIVERSITY

Department of Asian Studies

Programs of Study

The Department of Asian Studies offers graduate courses leading to the Master of Arts (M.A.) degree. The Department also offers a dual master's degree program—the M.A. in Asian Studies/M.A. in Diplomacy and International Relations—with the John C. Whitehead School of Diplomacy and International Relations. The major program provides students with training in the languages and cultures of Asia, leading to careers in government, international services, research, teaching, or business as well as advanced graduate study. Languages offered by the Department are Chinese (Mandarin) and Japanese. Area courses cover the civilizations and affairs of Asia, with emphasis on China, India, and Japan.

M.A. students can complete either 39 credits of course work or 36 credits and a thesis. Core courses total 21 credits; the remaining credits are electives. The 60-credit dual M.A. program requires that students complete 45 credits in core courses (including 18 credits in diplomacy and international relations, 12 credits in traditional East Asia, and 6 credits in modern and contemporary East Asia), 3 credits in free electives, and 9 credits in research and practicum.

The Department of Asian Studies offers a track in Teaching Chinese Language and Culture. The program prepares students to meet the Chinese content area requirement for a New Jersey Certificate of Eligibility (CE). The curriculum includes courses in the Chinese language, literature, theory, civilization, Chinese linguistics, applied linguistics, and teaching methods. Upon successful completion of 39 credits, students receive a Master of Arts in Asian studies and are eligible to enter a New Jersey State Department of Education alternate route program. On completion of the alternate route program, students receive a New Jersey Certificate as teacher of Chinese.

The Department of Asian Studies cooperates with the W. Paul Stillman School of Business in offering a Certificate in International Business and the five-year B.A./M.B.A. program.

For further information about graduate programs in Asian Studies, students should visit the Web site at http://www.shu.edu/academics/artsci/ma-asian-studies/index.cfm.

Research Facilities

In cooperation with the Asia Center, the Department conducts research on Asia, sponsors conferences, conducts summer institutes, and has an impressive program of publication.

The Language Resource Center (LRC) in the College of Arts and Sciences houses the theater-style Screening Room and a state-of-the-art computer workstation area. All computers have keyboards installed in a number of languages, including Arabic, Chinese, and Japanese, and have Internet access, video recording and editing software, and connections to a VCR/DVD combo for viewing. The LRC provides DVDs, videos, and other media in Arabic, Chinese, English, French, German, Italian, Japanese, Spanish, Russian, and other languages and offers self-paced language learning materials for Seton Hall community members who wish to study a language on their own.

The Walsh Library, a state-of-the-art 155,000-square-foot building, houses 500,000 titles, 1,875 current periodicals, and an extensive collection of microform and other nonprint items that include videotapes, CD-ROM music, and other electronic media. Fahy Hall has twenty-eight classrooms, two TV studios, a Macintosh and IBM graphics lab, two classroom amphitheaters, and language and statistics labs. McNulty Hall has well-equipped science labs. The College of Nursing Building contains a multipurpose practice-demonstration room with twelve hospital beds, an amphitheater, an independent study area, and a computer laboratory. Completed in 1997, Jubilee Hall, a six-story facility with 126,000 square feet of academic space, features high-tech classrooms with computer and multimedia capabilities and the Center for Securities Trading and Analysis, commonly referred to as the Trading Room.

Financial Aid

Each year the Department normally awards teaching assistantships to a limited number of qualified graduate students majoring in Asian studies. Full-time teaching assistants receive a monthly stipend for ten months (September–June) in addition to a waiver of the University's tuition (up to 12 credits per semester). Half-time teaching assistants receive half of the stipend and tuition remission for half of their credit hours. During the appointment period, teaching assistants are solely responsible for their travel expenses, room and board, and all other expenses of a personal nature. For general financial aid information, as well as information on graduate assistantships and teaching assistantships and their respective applications, students should visit http://www.shu.edu/applying/graduate/grad-finaid.cfm.

Cost of Study

In 2008–09, tuition is $875 per credit. Full-time students pay $305 per semester in University and technology fees; part-time students pay $185.

Living and Housing Costs

Housing and living costs in South Orange and surrounding towns are comparable to most suburban cities, with studio and one-bedroom apartments renting for $750 to $1000 per month.

Location

Seton Hall is located on 58 acres in the village of South Orange, New Jersey, a suburban residential area 14 miles southwest of New York City. The town center is a 10-minute walk from the campus and features bookstores, coffee shops, and restaurants. The heart of midtown Manhattan is about 30 minutes away by train; students can take advantage of everything this exciting city has to offer while still living in a suburban area.

The University and The Department

Founded in 1856, Seton Hall is a private coeducational Catholic institution—the nation's oldest diocesan institution of higher education in the United States. With a total enrollment of about 10,000, including approximately 4,500 graduate students, the University comprises nine colleges and schools. Seton Hall is accredited by the Middle States Association of Colleges and Schools. Through the incorporation of technology into the curriculum, the College of Arts and Sciences seeks to enhance and enliven the learning environment. Rooted in tradition, yet looking to the future, the College offers a rich set of opportunities for intellectual discovery. Graduate students are guided by scholars and specialists toward the mastery of academic and professional areas.

The Department of Asian Studies at Seton Hall University has long been recognized as a pioneer and leader in the field of Asian studies. Recently, the *Fiske Guide to Colleges,* published by the *New York Times,* cited the Department for excellence in the quality of its faculty and programs. The Department has a more-than-fifty-year tradition in Asian studies. It views itself and its achievements as a clear sign of Seton Hall's dedication to international studies. Purely by chance, when the name Seton Hall University is rendered into Chinese, it translates as "The West-East University." This coincidence proved true when Seton Hall became one of the first American universities to develop exchanges with Asian universities.

Applying

In addition to the general University requirements for admission to graduate studies, candidates should show a strong background in Asian studies or in one of the disciplines in which the Department offers courses. Students must submit the completed application (available online at http://www.shu.edu/academics/artsci/apply-graduate.cfm), the $50 application fee, a resume, a statement of purpose, two letters of recommendation, and transcripts from all previously attended universities or colleges. For the dual master's degree program, students must apply independently to each degree program, preferably indicating at the time of application that they intend to follow the joint Asian studies/diplomacy program when admitted. The deadlines for fall and spring admission are July 1 and November 1, respectively. Applications are processed on a rolling basis.

For the track in Teaching Chinese and Culture, all candidates are required to demonstrate a strong proficiency in both English and Chinese. Nonnative speakers of Chinese are required to take the Hanyu Shuiping Kaoshi (HSK), a national standard Chinese language proficiency test. International students and those who have received their baccalaureate degrees from universities outside the United States are required to submit official TOEFL scores.

Correspondence and Information

Dr. Shigeru Osuka, Director of Graduate Studies
Department of Asian Studies
Fahy Hall 211
Seton Hall University
400 South Orange Avenue
South Orange, New Jersey 07079
Phone: 973-275-2712
Fax: 973-761-9596
E-mail: osukashi@shu.edu
Web site: http://www.shu.edu/academics/artsci/ma-asian-studies/index.cfm

Seton Hall University

THE FACULTY AND THEIR RESEARCH

Full-time Faculty

Deborah Brown, Associate Professor and Undergraduate Adviser; Ph.D., Drew. Asian religions, modern and contemporary Asian history and politics.

Dongdong Chen, Assistant Professor, Chinese Program Director, and Director, Graduate Studies; Ph.D., McGill. Linguistics, language acquisition, Chinese language.

Edwin Pak-wah Leung, Professor and Chair; Ph.D., California, Santa Barbara. Modern Asian, modern Chinese history and politics, international politics and business.

Michael Linderman, Assistant Professor; Ph.D., Pennsylvania.

Shigeru Osuka, Associate Professor and Japanese Program Director; Ed.D., Hawaii. Japanese language, Japanese history, Asian religions, Buddhist studies, Japanese religions.

Adjunct Faculty

Fen-Dow Chu, Ph.D., MIT. Traditional Chinese history.

Claire Diab, M.A., Seton Hall. Asian religions and culture.

Hwa-Soon Meyer, Ed.D., Columbia. Korean history and culture, ethno music and dance, Korean language.

Hiroko Ogino, B.A., Tsuda Women's College. Japanese language and culture.

Mei Zhao, Ph.D., Suzhou. Chinese language and literature.

STONY BROOK UNIVERSITY, STATE UNIVERSITY OF NEW YORK

Department of Hispanic Languages and Literature

Programs of Study

The Department of Hispanic Languages and Literature at Stony Brook awards the Master of Arts in Hispanic languages and literature, the Master of Arts in Romance languages, Master of Arts in teaching, and the Ph.D. in Spanish, Latin American, and U.S. Latino literature. The program focuses on all aspects of Spanish, Latin American, and U.S. Latino literature and culture and their relationship with other cultures. The goals are to offer graduate students the opportunity to conduct theoretically advanced research and develop the necessary analytical and professional skills to pursue a successful career in their specialty. The Department places great emphasis on extensive faculty-student contact outside the classroom. The Department's internationally recognized faculty members work individually with graduate students to provide research materials and professional advice on scholarly publishing, conference papers, job searches, and all other aspects that prepare them for an academic career at the four-year college or research university level, or for other professional careers in humanistic study, research, and writing.

The program offers an integrated curriculum of courses and seminars together with individual reading and research courses. New Ph.D. students take 12 credits the first two semesters, 9 credits in each semester of the second year (or after completing 24 graduate credits), 6 credits in each semester of the third year, while the fourth year normally is dedicated to passing the comprehensive exam and writing a dissertation. At the beginning of the second year, Ph.D. students must pass a qualifying exam, and at the beginning of the spring semester of the third year, they must pass a comprehensive exam. The average duration of the program is four to five years. For M.A. students, three or four semesters of full-time course work is required. For students with an M.A. or its equivalent, a minimum of two consecutive semesters of full-time graduate study in residence is required. The Department believes that learning to teach is an integral part of any graduate program. All graduate students are required to teach 3 to 5 hours a week and are carefully trained and supervised by the Director of Language Instruction and other members of the Department.

Research Facilities

Graduate students have full access to educational facilities designed to encourage and further their research and teaching efforts. The Department is located in the Frank Melville Jr. Memorial Library near the main entrance to the book stacks and adjacent to the offices of faculty members and graduate students. Graduate student offices are equipped with Internet access, and computers are available both in the students' offices and in the graduate student resource room. Also in the library is the Language and Learning Research Center, a state-of-the-art facility devoted to language acquisition in its broadest sense and research in language acquisition. The Center offers graduate-level courses on the intersection between language learning and technology and hosts workshops in language pedagogy. The Spanish language and Spanish and Latin American literatures collection of the library comprises approximately 59,200 volumes. The collection is growing at the rate of nearly 1,400 volumes annually. The Department of Special Collections houses quantities of scarce or unique items of extreme value, including the Amunategui Collection (early nineteenth century), the Columbine (2,000 volumes on Columbus, the discovery of America, and Americus Vespucius), and the Biblioteca Natan from Mexico. Students have round-the-clock access to a state-of-the-art computer facility located adjacent to the Department offices.

Financial Aid

The Department has a yearly allocation of approximately twenty teaching assistantships (TA), which are awarded each year to the most promising applicants or continuing students. The current yearly TA stipend is $12,664, renewable for a maximum of three years for Ph.D. students entering with the M.A. or equivalent, or four years for Ph.D. students entering with a B.A. or equivalent. The teaching stipend is supplemented by a tuition fellowship in the amount of $6900 per year for U.S. residents and $10,500 per year for non-U.S. residents. There is a limited opportunity for summer teaching at an appropriate stipend. Several fellowships are also available, including W. Burghardt Turner Fellowships with a stipend of $10,000, which are awarded every year to promising minority students with American citizenship; the Graduate Council Fellowship; and the Dorothy Pieper Merit Award for Outstanding Entering Doctoral Students.

Cost of Study

In 2008–09, full-time tuition at 12 credits for entering in-state residents is $3450 per semester, while out-of-state residents and international students pay $5460. Additional fees for each semester, including (but not limited to) the infirmary, activity, technology, and transportation fees, total about $875. International students also pay a service fee of approximately $35 per semester and an orientation fee of $50. Fees for the mandatory Student Health Insurance Plan vary depending on citizenship and employment status.

Living and Housing Costs

For 2008–09, Stony Brook calculates the cost of education excluding tuition, fees, and insurance at $14,228 per year. On-campus apartments range in cost from approximately $336 per month to approximately $1456 per month, depending on the size of the unit and the number of students sharing the space. Off-campus housing options include rooms, houses, and apartments that can be rented from approximately $350 to $2500 per month. Costs including books, food, and transportation may vary depending on academic program and/or personal circumstances.

Student Group

Nearly 60 full- and part-time graduate students were enrolled in spring 2005. Of these, 20 were teaching assistants and 3 were W. Burghardt Turner Fellowship recipients. Maintaining an ethnically and regionally diverse student body and faculty is a priority for the Department.

Student Outcomes

The Department is also proud of its postdoctoral placements. Recent graduates have been placed at the University of Connecticut, Marquette University, Illinois Wesleyan University, Brandeis University, Barnard College, University of Texas, Catholic University of Chile, University of São Paulo, and the University of Seville.

Location

Stony Brook University is located on the North Shore of Long Island, about 60 miles east of New York City, and is served by three airports—MacArthur Islip, JFK, and LaGuardia. The Staller Center for the Arts provides Broadway-quality entertainment, and a commuter train runs directly from Manhattan to the campus.

The University and The Department

Although a relatively young university, Stony Brook is quickly becoming a prestigious research institution. The recent invitation to join the Alliance of American Universities shows the recognition of the high quality of the faculty members and students. The Department of Hispanic Languages and Literature has established a climate of cooperation with other departments, maintaining ongoing programmatic links with women's studies, film studies, comparative literature, the Latin American and Caribbean Studies Center, the Humanities Institute, and the American Studies Initiative.

Applying

Besides completing the online application form, students must provide an official transcript of all undergraduate and graduate course work, a minimum TOEFL score of 550 (computer version 213, IBT version 90) for students whose first language is not English, three letters of recommendation, and a nonrefundable $60 fee. The deadline for receipt of all application materials is January 15 for fall admission and October 15 for spring. Scores from the Graduate Record Examinations (GRE), while recommended, are not required for admission.

Correspondence and Information

Department of Hispanic Languages and Literature
Stony Brook University, State University of New York
Stony Brook, New York 11794-3371
Web site: http://www.sunysb.edu/hispanic/

Stony Brook University, State University of New York

THE FACULTY AND THEIR RESEARCH

Lou Charnon-Deutsch, Professor and Director of Graduate Studies; Ph.D., Chicago, 1978. Visual culture in nineteenth-century Spain, applications of feminist theory to women's literature, nineteenth-century realism.
Paul Firbas, Associate Professor; Ph.D., Princeton, 2001. Latin American literature from the sixteenth and seventeenth century.
Daniela Flesler, Assistant Professor; Ph.D., Tulane, 2001. The recent immigration of people from North Africa to modern Spain and the artistic reaction to this social and political phenomenon.
Flora Klein-Andreu, Associate Professor Emeritus; Ph.D., Columbia, 1973. Analysis of meaning in grammar and its many implications.
Francisco Ordóñez, Assistant Professor; Ph.D., CUNY Graduate Center, 1997. Romance syntax and linguistic theory, interface between syntax and morphology, combination of synchronic and diachronic perspectives focusing on clitics.
Adrián Pérez Melgosa, Visiting Assistant Professor; Ph.D., Rochester, 1995. Narrative theory in film and the novel, evolution of intercultural relations in the Americas after WWII and their representation in commercial fictions.
Rachel Price, Visiting Assistant Professor; Ph.D., Duke, 2007. Nineteenth- and twentieth-century Latin American, Caribbean, and comparative literatures; the Atlantic; critical theory, psychoanalysis; poetry.
Malcolm K. Read, Professor; Ph.D., Wales, 1976. The construction of subjectivity in the pre- and early-modern periods and upon the epistemological and ontological dimensions of the human sciences.
Victoriano Roncero-López, Professor; Ph.D., Illinois, 1988. European humanism and its influence in the literature of the sixteenth and seventeenth centuries in Spain.
Lilia Delfina Ruiz-Debbe, Visiting Assistant Professor; Ph.D., Genève, 1996. Interlanguage studies and second language acquisition and its implications for methodology in classroom situations.
José Elías Ulloa, Assistant Professor; Ph.D., Rutgers, 2005. Hispanic linguistics, phonology.
Antonio Vera-León, Associate Professor Emeritus; Ph.D., Princeton, 1987. The formation of a national narrative tradition within a colonial situation, the narrative resources of painting and their connection to literary narrative.
Kathleen Vernon, Associate Professor; Ph.D., Chicago, 1982. Cross-national relations among the cinemas of Spain, Latin America, and the United States during the 1930s and 1940s.

STONY BROOK UNIVERSITY, STATE UNIVERSITY OF NEW YORK

Program in Africana Studies

Program of Study

The Africana Studies Department at Stony Brook University addresses the experiences of persons of African descent throughout the world, exploring African civilizations and their influences on other parts of the "Black Diaspora." The department provides a disciplined intellectual environment to study the histories, literatures, political systems, cultures, arts, and social theories of Africa and the African Diaspora as well as the issues within global black communities from both historical and contemporary perspectives.

The Master of Arts in Africana studies meets the need for academic inquiry into the history, experiences, and perspectives of peoples of African heritage worldwide and enhances professional development in careers in a range of professions where knowledge of the Black experience is increasingly useful, such as law, management, medicine, public health, public service, social welfare, museum curator studies, cinema studies, and education.

The degree requires a total of 30 course credits with an overall minimum GPA of 3.0. Eighteen of these credits come from the graduate core curriculum. A two-semester sequence introduces students to the theoretical and methodological issues of the United States, Africa, and the Caribbean/Latin America, and a required research seminar introduces students to the historiography of the African Diaspora. The remaining 12 credits may be part of an elective mix of graduate courses taken within and outside the department, including a 6-credit research thesis project, tutorials, or a study-abroad program conducted in Africa and/or the Caribbean-Latin America.

Research Facilities

The East and West Campus University libraries contain nearly 2.1 million bound volumes, 130,000 maps and atlases, and 5,800 videos. With nearly 4 million publications in microformat, they have one of the country's largest microfilm collections. The collections represent at least twenty-five languages, and the libraries' Special Collections Department contains 16,000 rare books and 150 collections, including the William Butler Yeats Microfilmed Manuscripts Collection. The University's electronic resources, which are available to students on all campuses, include more than 30,000 Web-accessible journals, hundreds of databases, and several collections of online books, including reference material.

Financial Aid

The W. Burghardt Turner Fellowship is awarded to qualified underrepresented students whose immediate academic plans include obtaining a graduate or professional degree. Graduate Assistance in Areas of National Need fellowships provide stipends covering the student's financial need. Other fellowships may be available from external organizations. Tuition Assistance Program awards of up to $250 are given to New York State residents enrolled full-time and in good academic standing. Students may also borrow up to $10,000 annually under the Federal Stafford Loan Program or up to $6000 under the Federal Perkins Loan Program. Some students work part-time to help cover their educational costs.

Cost of Study

In 2008–09, full-time tuition (12 credits) is $3450 for residents and $5460 for nonresidents. Part-time tuition is $288 and $455, respectively. Other costs include a student activity fee of $22, a college fee of $12.50, an infirmary fee of $115.50, a technology fee of $173.50, and a transportation fee of $105. Fees for part-time students vary according to the number of credits a student takes.

Living and Housing Costs

Campus housing is not available for graduate students. However, apartments and houses are available within walking or biking distance of campus. Apartment rentals range from $525 to $800 per month for one bedroom and $1000 to $1500 for two bedrooms.

Student Group

Students in the program come from a wide range of academic backgrounds. The majority come from Long Island and New York City, but many come from across the country and from other countries.

Student Outcomes

Graduates of the program receive the knowledge and skills necessary to pursue careers in education, law, journalism, international relations, social work, nursing, health care, state and local government, and the nonprofit sector.

Location

The University is located on the North Shore of Long Island, about 60 miles east of New York City. The campus is nestled amid fields and woodlands, with Long Island Sound just minutes to the north and the Atlantic Ocean a 45-minute drive to the south. The Long Island Railroad connects New York City with the Stony Brook campus. Three major highways lead to New York City, and bus service is available on campus and to various points on Long Island.

The University

Stony Brook is a 1,100-acre university where world-renowned faculty members have created a stimulating, highly interactive environment for graduate studies. Campus refurbishment efforts have enhanced the University environment. Bicycle paths, an apple orchard, park benches, a duck pond, and spacious plazas complement the more than 120 modern laboratories and classroom buildings. Diversity is a byword at Stony Brook, where 31 percent of graduate students hail from other countries.

Applying

Applicants must submit a completed online application, official transcripts from all colleges previously attended, three letters of recommendation from instructors or professionals familiar with the applicant's work, official GRE scores, a statement discussing the reasons for attending the program, and a nonrefundable $60 application fee. The deadline to apply is January 15 for fall admission or October 1 for spring admission.

Correspondence and Information

Floris Cash, Department Chair
Department of Africana Studies
Social and Behavioral Sciences Building, Room S-249
Stony Brook University, State University of New York
Stony Brook, New York 11794-4380
Phone: 631-632-7470
Fax: 631-632-5753
E-mail: floris.cash@stonybrook.edu
Web site: http://www.stonybrook.edu/afs/

Stony Brook University, State University of New York

THE FACULTY AND THEIR RESEARCH

Winnifred R. Brown-Glaude, Assistant Professor; Ph.D. (sociology), Temple, 2003. Race and ethnicity in the Caribbean and Latin America, gender and development, intersectionality, women and informal economies, race and race relations in the United States, sociology of the body, black feminism, social research, feminist research methods.

Floris Barnett Cash, Associate Professor and Chair; Ph.D. (African American women's studies), SUNY at Stony Brook, 1986. History, U.S. social and political history, African American history, Latin American history.

David L. Ferguson, Professor; Ph.D. (mathematics and science education), Berkeley, 1968. Quantitative methods; computer applications, especially intelligent tutorial systems and decision support systems; mathematics, science, and engineering education.

Georges Fouron, Professor; Ed.D., Columbia, 1985. Social studies education, bilingual education, identity, Haiti, immigrants' experience in America, transnationalism.

Barbara E. Frank, Associate Professor; Ph.D. (African art history), Indiana, 1988. African art history, especially West Africa; arts of the African Diaspora and ancient Mesoamerica.

E. Anthony Hurley, Associate Professor and Director, Graduate Studies; Ph.D. (French), Rutgers, 1992. Francophone literature of the Caribbean and Africa, Caribbean poetics, AfroCaribbean culture, Caribbean American literature.

Peniel Joseph, Assistant Professor; Ph.D. (American history), Temple, 2000. Civil rights/black power movements, African American history, African American intellectual history, comparative black nationalism, 20th century American social history, black feminism, African Diaspora, pan-Africanism, American popular culture, black urban history.

Leslie H. Owens, Associate Professor; Ph.D., California, Riverside, 1972. African-American social history, black family, civil rights movement, slavery.

Olufemi Vaughan, Professor; D.Phil. (politics), Oxford (England), 1989. Modern African political and social history, international relations, comparative politics, international relations, African Diaspora studies, globalization.

Carlos M. Vidal, Associate Professor; D.S.W., Fordham. Hispanic families, culture, diversity, social movements, social policy.

Tracey Walters, Associate Professor; Ph.D. (English), Howard, 1999. African American literature, Caribbean literature, African literature, pan-African literature, black British literature and culture, 20th century American and British literature, journalism.

TULANE UNIVERSITY

Stone Center for Latin American Studies

Programs of Study

Tulane's Stone Center for Latin American Studies offers one of the world's premier programs for the study of Latin America and the Caribbean. The multidisciplinary M.A. and Ph.D. programs provide basic education and training for both academic and professional careers. In addition, the Center for Latin American Studies offers joint M.A./M.B.A. and M.A./J.D. degrees and joint Ph.D. degree programs with Art History and Political Science. The M.A. degree requires completion of a total of 30 hours of course work distributed over a primary concentration and two supporting concentrations and demonstrated competency in at least one language of the region. Normally, students write an M.A. thesis, although a nonthesis option exists. The M.A. program can be completed in three semesters by students who elect to pursue the nonthesis option, but the Center strongly encourages students to pursue the thesis option and seeks to recruit students who are eager to accept the challenge. These students complete the program in four semesters. Both the M.A./M.B.A and M.A./J.D. joint-degree programs require 24 semester hours of course work in Latin American studies in addition to the requirements of the respective professional school. The Ph.D. requires 54 hours of course work in a primary concentration and two supporting concentrations, demonstrated proficiency in two foreign languages, general preliminary examinations, and a doctoral dissertation. In addition, the joint Ph.D. program requires completion of disciplinary degree requirements.

Research Facilities

The Latin American Library (LAL) at Tulane is one of three free-standing collections of its kind in U.S. universities. It has more than 425,000 volumes, with world-renowned collections of Latin American social sciences and humanities, with particular emphasis on history, anthropology, archaeology, art history, architecture, and cultural studies. It also has a Latin American photographic archive of 35,000 images. Its rare book and manuscript collections are extensive. The LAL is one of the world's leading repositories of colonial and pre-Columbian pictorials (Native American writing). Its collections also include the earliest extant original letter sent by Cortés from Mexico; the Codex Tulane, a large sixteenth-century Mixtec pictorial scroll; and Maya monument rubbings by Merle Greene Robinson. Annually, the Latin American Library hosts the Richard E. Greenleaf fellowship program, which brings scholars from Latin America and the Caribbean to conduct research for up to three months.

Tulane offers foreign study and internship programs in Mexico, Guatemala, Cuba, Brazil, Argentina, and Ecuador. Its Schools of Law and Business offer executive master's and doctoral programs in Mexico, Ecuador, Venezuela, and Chile for residents of those countries. Every summer, an average of 25 to 30 graduate students conduct funded field research in Latin America. The Middle American Research Institute (MARI) is dedicated to research and publication in the social sciences about Mexico and Central America. The School of Public Health and Tropical Medicine operates research and teaching programs on campus and throughout the tropical world, including the Health Office for Latin America in Lima, Peru. The Payson Institute for International Development and Technology Transfer operates a center for disaster mitigation in developing areas and offers an M.S. and a joint J.D./M.S. in international development.

Financial Aid

Superior students received full tuition waivers plus stipends of $16,000 in 2007–08. The Center has a limited number of teaching assistantships reserved for advanced students. There are also several federal FLAS fellowships that require the study of Portuguese or Haitian Creole. The Center funds annual summer research projects in Latin America for a select group of graduate students. There is also funding for a limited number of students to enroll in summer intensive institutes for less commonly taught languages such as Kaqchikel Maya, Portuguese, Haitian Creole, and indigenous Latin American languages.

Cost of Study

In 2008–09, full-time tuition and fees are projected to be $37,100. Students with tuition waivers pay fees of $1624 per year (amount covers academic fee, health services fee, Reilly recreation fee, and a student activities fee). The fee for graduate student health insurance, provided through Tulane University, is $2000.

Living and Housing Costs

There are many apartments close to the main campus. On average, prices range from $500 to $1000 a month. For Tulane-sponsored housing, graduate students have the option of renting at the Papillon Apartments, located uptown, or the Deming Pavilion, located downtown. More information can be found on Tulane's Housing Services Web site at http://housing.tulane.edu.

Student Group

The current interdisciplinary graduate student body numbers 39. In addition, more than 80 graduate students specialize in the study of Latin America while pursuing degrees in such fields as anthropology, history, literature, and public health. Students come from all over the United States, Europe, and Latin America.

Location

Tulane is located in the uptown section of New Orleans, bounded by Audubon Park (which houses the Audubon Zoo), residential areas, and shopping areas where neighborhood restaurants and small shops abound. The French Quarter and Canal Street (downtown) are a short ride away via the St. Charles Avenue streetcar. New Orleans has approximately 400,000 residents; the metropolitan area has more than 1.3 million. Louisiana was a French and Spanish colony and has a legal system and many customs that have a great deal in common with Latin America and the Caribbean. The metropolitan area has a population of more than 50,000 Latin Americans, and the city has many commercial ties with Latin America.

The University and The Program

Tulane University is a private, nonsectarian institution of approximately 12,000 students. From its foundation in 1834, Tulane University has furthered a mission of leading study and research in Latin America. The Middle American Research Institute was founded in 1924 and the Center for Latin American Studies, in 1966. Today, the core faculty of more than 70 Latin Americanists represents the largest contingent of faculty members associated with any department or program at the University. Students and faculty members benefit from the holdings of the Latin American Library and a network of contacts with public officials, nongovernmental organizations, and academic leaders in Latin America.

The program has received numerous accolades. It is currently one of eighteen programs designated on a competitive basis by the U.S. Department of Education as a National Resource Center on Latin America. In addition to the academic program, which includes more than 450 courses plus independent studies, there are frequent lectures, conferences, symposia, and other events of scholarly interest on campus.

Applying

Applicants must provide complete transcripts, three letters of recommendation, and scores from the GRE General Test (taken within the last five years). The complete application packet is due by February 1. Ordinarily, to receive financial aid, students should have at least a 3.5 GPA and a combined verbal/quantitative score of at least 1200 on the GRE. All applicants, including those applying to joint-degree programs, must submit GRE scores. All potential applicants are encouraged to visit the Stone Center Web site (http://stonecenter.tulane.edu/) for more information on applying to the program.

Correspondence and Information

Stone Center for Latin American Studies
Tulane University
100 Jones Hall
New Orleans, Louisiana 70118
Phone: 504-865-5164
Fax: 504-865-6719
E-mail: rtsclas@tulane.edu
Web site: http://stonecenter.tulane.edu/

Tulane University

THE FACULTY AND THEIR RESEARCH

Anthropology: E. Wyllys Andrews V, Director, Middle American Research Institute; Ph.D., Tulane. Central America, archaeology of Central America, eastern Mesoamerica, Yucatan Peninsula, Guatemala, El Salvador, Honduras. William Balée, Ph.D., Columbia. Brazil, ethnoecology, ethnobotany. Dan M. Healan, Ph.D., Missouri. Mexico, archaeological ceramics, household or settlement patterns. Robert Hill, Ph.D., Pennsylvania. Cultural anthropology, ethnohistory, late postclassic and colonial Maya society. Katherine Jack, Ph.D., Alberta. Physical anthropology (primatology), primate behavior in Ecuador and Costa Rica. Judith Maxwell, Ph.D., Chicago. Language and linguistics, Kaqchikel Maya linguistics and culture, bilingual education, discourse analysis. Katherine Nelson, Ph.D., SMU. Archaeology of the American Southwest and Peru. John Verano, Ph.D., UCLA. South American archaeology, forensic anthropology.

Architecture: Eugene Cizek, Ph.D., Tulane, M.C.P., MIT, Dr.Sci., Delft University of Technology. Historic preservation, Guatemala. Robert Gonzalez, Ph.D., Berkeley. Pan-Americanism and its built environment. Carol McMichael Reese, Ph.D., Texas. Argentina, Mexico, urban studies, architecture and urbanism in the Americas, nineteenth and twentieth centuries.

Art History: Florencia Bazzano-Nelson, Ph.D., New Mexico. Modern Latin American art. Elizabeth Boone, Ph.D., Texas. Mexico, pre-Colombian art, colonial art of Mexico, Aztecs. Pamela Franco, Ph.D., Emory. Arts of Africa and the African diaspora. Thomas F. Reese, Director, Center for Latin American Studies; Ph.D., Yale. Argentina, Mexico, art/art history, area studies, Latin American and Iberian art, architecture and urbanism.

Business: John Trapani III, Director, Goldring Institute of International Business; Ph.D., Tulane.

Cell and Molecular Biology: Leonard B. Thien, Ph.D., UCLA. Mexico, pollination biology of ancient plants.

Communication: Ana López, Director, Cuban and Caribbean Studies Institute; Ph.D., Iowa. Mass communication, film, cultural studies, popular culture. Vicki Mayer, Ph.D., California, San Diego. Mexican Americans, mass media, and cultural citizenship. Mauro Pereira Porto, Ph.D., California, San Diego. Brazil, media, and politics.

Earth and Environmental Sciences: Stephen A. Nelson, Ph.D., Berkeley. Volcanology, Mexican volcanoes.

Ecology and Evolutionary Biology: Jeff Chambers, Ph.D., California, Santa Barbara. Terrestrial ecology, physiological ecology, and biogeochemistry. Stephen Darwin, Ph.D., Massachusetts. Mexico, morphology and evolution of vascular plants, vascular flora of the Yucatan Peninsula. Lee Dyer, Ph.D., Colorado. Plant-animal interactions, tropical ecology. Thomas Sherry, Ph.D., UCLA. Neotropical ornithology, population, ecology of migratory birds, site suitability, preemption and the spatial scale of population regulation.

Economics: John Edwards, Ph.D., Maryland. Labor, education. Leandro Magnusson, Ph.D., Brown. Brazil, econometrics.

English: Guarav Desai, Ph.D., Duke. Postcolonial studies; literary, legal, and cultural theory. Supriya M. Nair, Ph.D., Texas at Austin. Cultural studies, feminist theory. Felipe Smith, Ph.D., LSU. Caribbean, African American literature, American literature, diasporan literature.

French: Thomas A. Klingler, Ph.D., Indiana. Caribbean, Haiti, language and linguistics, Creole language and culture. Richard Watts, Ph.D., Yale. French Antilles literature.

History: Rosanne Adderley, Ph.D., Pennsylvania. Caribbean, formation of African diaspora culture, Atlantic slave trade. James Boyden, Ph.D., Texas. Hapsburg Spain, renaissance and reformation, early modern Atlantic world. Colin M. MacLachlan, Ph.D., UCLA. Brazil, Mexico, environment and ecology. Susan Schroeder, Ph.D., UCLA. Mexico, Mesoamerican social history, early Nahuatl philology. Justin Wolfe, Ph.D., UCLA: Central America, race and ethnicity. Gertrude M. Yeager, Ph.D., Texas Christian. South American historiography, Chile, Andes, women, nation-making.

Latin American Studies: James D. Huck, Assistant Director/Graduate Advisor, Stone Center for Latin American Studies; Ph.D., Tulane. Mexican politics. Edith A. G. Wolfe, Assistant Director of Undergraduate Affairs, Stone Center for Latin American Studies; Ph.D., Texas. Modernism, Brazil.

Law: Oliver Houck, J.D., Georgetown. Environmental and natural resources law, Cuba.

Library: Hortensia Calvo, Doris Stone Librarian and Director, Latin American Library; Ph.D., Yale. Spanish and Spanish-American literature. Wilbur E. Meneray, Assistant Dean for Special Collections; Ph.D., North Carolina. Guatemala, Louisiana, colonial Louisiana, history. Lance Query, Dean of Libraries and Academic Information Resources; Ph.D., Indiana. Latin American history.

Payson Center for International Development: William E. Bertrand, Ph.D., Tulane. Public health and medicine, information technology, information and evaluation systems, instructional technology and design, human resource planning. Eamon Kelly, Ph.D., Columbia. Development, planning. S. W. R. deSamarasinghe, Ph.D., Cambridge. Economics, ethnic conflict.

Political Science: Mary Clark, Ph.D., Wisconsin. Costa Rica, comparative politics. Casey Kane-Love, Ph.D., Tulane. Mexico, U.S.-Latin American relations, Mexican politics. Anthony Pereira, Ph.D., Harvard. Southern cone, state reform, civil-military relations, agrarian politics. Aaron Schneider, Ph.D., Berkeley. Brazil, Central America, political economy, public finance. Jeff Stacey, Ph.D., Columbia. Comparative politics, regional integration, international organization. Raymond Taras, Ph.D., Warsaw. Comparative communism, Eastern European relations with Latin America.

Psychology: Enrique Varela, Ph.D., Kansas. Mexico, clinical psychology, posttraumatic stress and anxiety.

Public Health and Tropical Medicine: Pierre Buekens, Ph.D./M.D., Free University of Brussels. Obstetrics and gynecology, epidemiology, general Latin America. Carl Kendall, Ph.D., Rochester. Anthropology, social and cultural factors of community health. Kate Macintyre, Ph.D., North Carolina. Health systems analysis, international health policy analysis. Laura Murphy, Ph.D., North Carolina. Ecuador, planning, development, household livelihoods and well-being, frontier settlement, tropical deforestation. Valerie Paz-Soldán, Ph.D., North Carolina. Public health and tropical medicine, maternal and child health in Peru.

Sociology: Martha Huggins, Ph.D., New Hampshire. Brazil, political policing, torture and violence, urban sociology.

Spanish and Portuguese: Idelber Avelar, Ph.D., Duke. Postdictatorial culture, Southern Cone and Brazilian literature and culture, identity and Latin Americanism. Laura Bass, Ph.D., Princeton. Seventeenth-century Spanish and colonial theater. John Charles, Ph.D., Yale. Colonial Peru, Latin American literature. Christopher Dunn, Ph.D., Brown. Cuba, cultural studies, Brazilian culture, African diaspora studies, popular music. Antonio Gómez, Ph.D., Pittsburgh. Literature of exile, Cuba, Argentina. Amy George Hirons, Ph.D., Tulane. Linguistics, Latin American literature, Mesoamerican art history. Harry Howard, Ph.D., Cornell. Language, neuromimetic modeling of linguistics and allied phenomena. Marilyn Miller, Ph.D., Oregon. Colonial literatures of Latin America, postcolonial theory, Caribbean and trans-American studies. Tatjana Pavlovic, Ph.D., Washington. Film studies, feminism, critical theory. Fernando César Rivera-Díaz, Ph.D., Princeton. Contemporary Latin American narratives. Isabel Sans, Ph.D., Arizona State. Spanish cultural studies, globalization/culture in Latin America. Maureen Shea, Ph.D., Arizona. Literature and culture, Central American and Andean literature, testimonial literature, gender and sexuality. Ari Zighelboim, Ph.D., Tulane. Colonial Latin American literature and culture, Andean studies, Jewish–Latin American cultural expressions.

AFFILIATED RESEARCH FACULTY

Centro de Investigación y Adiestramiento Poli´tico Administrativo (CIAPA), San José, Costa Rica: Rodolfo Cerdas Cruz, Ph.D., Academy of Sciences of the U.S.S.R. Central America, political science and law, human rights, labor organizations, Communist Party. Ludovico Feoli, Chief Executive Director; Ph.D., Tulane. Latin American political economy, state building. Constantino Urcuyo, Doctorat troisieme cycle, Sorbonne. Central America, political science, democratic culture.

Middle American Research Institute: Merle Greene Robertson, Research Associate; M.A., Berkeley. Maya sculpture.

WASHINGTON UNIVERSITY IN ST. LOUIS

Programs in East Asian Studies

Program of Study

Washington University in St. Louis has trained East Asian specialists for careers in scholarship, diplomacy, law, and business for more than forty years. The University has a nationally distinguished faculty and an innovative curriculum in East Asian cultures, business, and law. Because admission to the graduate programs is selective and classes are small, students receive a high degree of individual training. There is considerable latitude in designing programs of study to meet personal and professional objectives.

The Master of Arts (M.A.) degree in East Asian studies offers advanced interdisciplinary training in Chinese or Japanese studies. Major areas of focus include literature, political economy, law, gender, intellectual history, and business organization. The program begins with the core seminar in East Asian Studies, which introduces students to rigorous methodological and analytical tools and approaches, and concludes with a series of exit examinations in the students' chosen fields. Normally requiring three semesters to complete, students may extend their program to allow further language training, overseas study, internships, or thesis writing.

The joint J.D./M.A. program in law and East Asian studies offers an integrated curriculum, combining the School of Law's regular program and strengths in East Asian legal studies with the interdisciplinary East Asian studies program. Coordinated Master of Arts and Master of Business Administration degrees (M.A./M.B.A.) are also available. Students typically complete the J.D./M.A. in seven to eight semesters and the M.A./M.B.A. in six.

Advanced study in East Asia is available through graduate exchange arrangements with major Chinese, Japanese, and Korean institutions and through University language programs in Japan, the People's Republic of China, and Taiwan.

Research Facilities

The East Asian Library contains 145,300 volumes of books and bound periodicals in Chinese, Japanese, and Korean. The Law Library has a major collection on Chinese law, which now includes most Chinese primary legal materials (statutes and cases), supplemented with legal encyclopedias, major law treatises, and monograph series, and it is preparing for a substantial expansion of the Japanese law collection, with a particular emphasis on commercial law. The John M. Olin Library collection includes approximately 21,000 volumes on East Asian subjects in Western languages as well as more than 400 serial holdings on East Asia in Western languages. A member of the OCLC online cataloging system, the Olin Library has access to library holdings in East Asian studies across the country. The East Asian Library terminal has Chinese, Japanese, and Korean capability.

Financial Aid

Most students receive full- or partial-tuition scholarships. Fellowships, Washington University Fellowships, and Spencer T. Olin Fellowships for Women are awarded on a competitive basis. Teaching assistantships are normally reserved for advanced students.

Cost of Study

Graduate tuition for students enrolled in Washington University Graduate School of Arts and Sciences was $34,500 for 18 to 24 units in the academic year 2007–08.

Living and Housing Costs

Living expenses during the 2007–08 academic year were approximately $16,400, including books and medical insurance.

Student Group

In 2007–08, 15 students were pursuing the M.A. in East Asian studies, the joint J.D./M.A., or the joint M.A./M.B.A. The student community also includes East Asian specialists pursuing Ph.D. degrees in such programs as Chinese/Japanese and comparative literature, history, anthropology, and political science.

Student Outcomes

Many M.A. graduates of the programs in East Asian Studies continue for advanced degrees in academe or professional schools. Others report careers in international banking, education, nonprofit organizations, or government service. Graduates of the J.D./M.A. program serve as associates with firms in New York, Chicago, Taipei, Beijing, Tokyo, and Hong Kong; international tax consultants; assistant district attorneys; and as professors with international law schools. M.B.A./M.A. graduates have accepted offers from worldwide electronics companies and other renowned corporations with postings in East Asia.

Location

St. Louis, a metropolitan area of more than 2.5 million, enhances the excellence and innovation of Washington University's international studies. More than 300 firms, including ten Fortune 500 companies, are actively engaged in East Asian business. The city also offers a network of international cultural institutions, including the St. Louis Symphony Orchestra, the Saint Louis Art Museum, the Opera Theatre of St. Louis, the Missouri Botanical Garden (with special Japanese and Chinese gardens), a recently renovated riverfront area, and many fine ethnic restaurants.

The University

Founded in 1853, Washington University is an independent institution dedicated to excellence in graduate and professional education. The East Asian studies programs are located on the 168-acre Danforth Campus, within a few minutes walk of the main library, the East Asian Library, the John M. Olin School of Business, the School of Law, the Center for Political Economy, and other facilities. Graduate students also have access to the East Asian faculty members at the University of Missouri–St. Louis.

Applying

Candidates are required to have their college transcripts and their scores on the Graduate Record Examinations sent to program office. Students whose native language is not English are required to send an official copy of their TOEFL results. Applicants to the joint J.D./M.A. and M.A./M.B.A. programs apply for admission to both East Asian Studies and the relevant professional school.

Correspondence and Information

East Asian Studies
Campus Box 1123
Cupples II, Room 105
Washington University in St. Louis
1 Brookings Drive
St. Louis, Missouri 63130-4899

Phone: 314-935-4448
Fax: 314-935-5485
E-mail: eas@artsci.wustl.edu
Web site: http://artsci.wustl.edu/~eas

Washington University in St. Louis

THE FACULTY AND THEIR RESEARCH

Art History
Gwen Bennett. Chinese Neolithic period archaeology.

History
Steven Miles. Modern Chinese history.
Lori Watt. Modern Japanese history.

Languages and Literatures
Hiroo Aridome. Japanese language.
Letty Lingchei Chen. Modern Chinese literature.
Rebecca Copeland. Modern Japanese literature.
Beata Grant. Chinese literature and religious studies.
Shino Hayashi. Japanese language.
Robert E. Hegel. Chinese vernacular fiction and drama.
M. Mimi Kim. Korean language.
Pauline Chen Lee. Chinese religion and culture.
Xia Liang. Chinese language.
Chun-ying Lin. Chinese language.
Marvin H. Marcus. Modern Japanese literature.
Virginia Marcus. Japanese language.
Robert E. Morrell (Emeritus). Japanese literature and Buddhism.
Judy Zhijun Mu. Chinese language.
Jamie Newhard. Premodern Japanese literature.
Kayo Niimi. Japanese language.
Wei Wang. Chinese language.
Fengtao Wu. Chinese language.

Law
John O. Haley. Comparative law, litigation, Japanese law.
Charles McManis. Intellectual property law in East Asia.
Carl Minzner. Chinese law and politics.

Performing Arts
Mary Jean Cowell. Japanese theater and dance.

Political Science
Andrew Mertha. Chinese politics, international relations, comparative politics.

Section 16
Communication and Media

This section contains a directory of institutions offering graduate work in communication and media, followed by in-depth entries submitted by institutions that chose to prepare detailed program descriptions. Additional information about programs listed in the directory but not augmented by an in-depth entry may be obtained by writing directly to the dean of a graduate school or chair of a department at the address given in the directory.

For programs offering related work, see also in this book *Film, Television, and Video; Language and Literature;* and *Psychology and Counseling.* In the other guides in this series:

Graduate Programs in Engineering & Applied Sciences

See *Computer Science and Information Technology* and *Telecommunications*

Graduate Programs in Business, Education, Health, Information Studies, Law & Social Work

See *Advertising and Public Relations*

CONTENTS

Program Directories

Announcements

Close-Ups

See also:

Communication—General

Abilene Christian University, Graduate School, College of Arts and Sciences, Department of Communication, Abilene, TX 79699-9100. Offers human communication (MA); organizational and human resource development (MS). Part-time programs available. *Faculty:* 7 part-time/adjunct (2 women). *Students:* 37 full-time (24 women), 16 part-time (6 women); includes 10 minority (4 African Americans, 1 Asian American or Pacific Islander, 5 Hispanic Americans), 8 international. 33 applicants, 61% accepted, 13 enrolled. In 2007, 34 degrees awarded. *Degree requirements:* For master's, one foreign language, comprehensive exam, thesis. *Entrance requirements:* For master's, GRE General Test. *Application deadline:* For fall admission, 4/1 priority date for domestic students; for spring admission, 11/1 for domestic students. Applications are processed on a rolling basis. Application fee: $40 ($45 for international students). Electronic applications accepted. *Expenses:* Tuition: Full-time $13,368; part-time $557 per hour. Required fees: $700; $34 per hour. $10 per semester. Tuition and fees vary according to degree level and campus/location. *Financial support:* Teaching assistantships, Federal Work-Study available. Support available to part-time students. Financial award application deadline: 4/1. *Faculty research:* Intercultural communication, family communication, forensics, interpersonal communication. *Unit head:* Dr. Joe Cardot, Chairman, 325-674-2136. *Application contact:* William Horn, Graduate Admissions Counselor, 325-674-2656, Fax: 325-674-6717, E-mail: gradinfo@acu.edu.

American University, School of Communication, Washington, DC 20016-8001. Offers MA, MFA. *Accreditation:* ACEJMC (one or more programs are accredited). Part-time and evening/weekend programs available. *Faculty:* 45 full-time (22 women), 50 part-time/adjunct. *Students:* 132 full-time (92 women), 215 part-time (135 women); includes 74 minority (48 African Americans, 10 Asian Americans or Pacific Islanders, 16 Hispanic Americans), 32 international. Average age 27. 594 applicants, 65% accepted, 177 enrolled. In 2007, 159 degrees awarded. *Degree requirements:* For master's, comprehensive exam, thesis or alternative. *Entrance requirements:* For master's, GRE General Test. Additional exam requirements/recommendations for international students: Required—TOEFL (minimum score: 600 paper-based; 260 computer-based; 100 iBT) or IELTS (7.0). *Application deadline:* For fall admission, 2/1 priority date for domestic students, 4/1 priority date for international students; for spring admission, 11/15 for domestic students. Applications are processed on a rolling basis. Application fee: $50. Electronic applications accepted. *Expenses:* Tuition: Full-time $19,998; part-time $1,111 per credit hour. Required fees: $380. Tuition and fees vary according to program. *Financial support:* In 2007–08, 64 students received support, including 6 fellowships with partial tuition reimbursements available (averaging $23,000 per year), 12 research assistantships with partial tuition reimbursements available (averaging $11,000 per year), 12 teaching assistantships with partial tuition reimbursements available (averaging $11,000 per year); career-related internships or fieldwork, Federal Work-Study, institutionally sponsored loans, scholarships/grants, and tuition waivers (partial) also available. Financial award application deadline: 2/1; financial award applicants required to submit FAFSA. *Faculty research:* New communication technology, documentaries and public broadcasting, litigation and public relations, dissident media, race and gender and the media, international journalism and human rights, social media. *Unit head:* Prof. Larry Kirkman, Dean, 202-885-2058, Fax: 202-885-2099, E-mail: larry@american.edu. *Application contact:* Sharmeen Ahsan-Bracciale, Graduate Admissions Office, 202-885-2040, Fax: 202-885-2019, E-mail: sharmeen@american.edu.

See Close-Up on page 881.

The American University in Cairo, Graduate Studies and Research, School of Business, Economics and Communication, Department of Journalism and Communication, Cairo, Egypt. Offers journalism/mass communication (MA); television journalism (MA, Diploma). Part-time programs available. *Degree requirements:* For master's, thesis (for some programs). *Entrance requirements:* For master's, English entrance exam, GMAT. Electronic applications accepted. *Faculty research:* Mass media and national development/censorship, intercultural photo communication, comparative journalism/television.

The American University of Paris, Graduate Programs, Paris, France. Offers finance (MSF); global communications (MAGC); international affairs, conflict resolution and civil society development (MA); Middle Eastern and Islamic studies (MA); public administration (MPA). *Degree requirements:* For master's, thesis. *Entrance requirements:* For master's, minimum undergraduate GPA of 3.0.

Andrews University, School of Graduate Studies, College of Arts and Sciences, Interdisciplinary Studies in Communication Program, Berrien Springs, MI 49104. Offers MA.

Angelo State University, College of Graduate Studies, College of Liberal and Fine Arts, Department of Communications, Drama, and Journalism, San Angelo, TX 76909. Offers communication systems management (MA). Part-time and evening/weekend programs available. *Faculty:* 2 full-time (0 women). *Students:* Average age 26. 7 applicants, 43% accepted, 3 enrolled. In 2007, 9 degrees awarded. *Degree requirements:* For master's, comprehensive exam, thesis optional. *Entrance requirements:* For master's, GRE General Test. Additional exam requirements/recommendations for international students: Required—TOEFL or IELTS. *Application deadline:* For fall admission, 7/15 priority date for domestic students, 6/10 for international students; for spring admission, 12/8 for domestic students, 11/1 for international students. Applications are processed on a rolling basis. Application fee: $40 ($50 for international students). Electronic applications accepted. *Financial support:* In 2007–08, 5 students received support, including 3 teaching assistantships (averaging $10,251 per year); career-related internships or fieldwork, Federal Work-Study, scholarships/grants, and unspecified assistantships also available. Support available to part-time students. Financial award application deadline: 3/1; financial award applicants required to submit FAFSA. *Unit head:* Dr. June H. Smith, Department Head, 325-942-2031 Ext. 228, E-mail: june.smith@angelo.edu. *Application contact:* Dr. Jeff Boone, Graduate Advisor, 325-942-2343 Ext. 244, E-mail: jeff.boone@angelo.edu.

Arizona State University, Graduate College, College of Liberal Arts and Sciences, Division of Social Sciences, Hugh Downs School of Human Communication, Tempe, AZ 85287. Offers communication (PhD); speech and interpersonal communication (MA). *Degree requirements:* For master's, thesis or alternative; for doctorate, thesis/dissertation.

Arizona State University at the West campus, College of Human Services, Department of Communication Studies, Phoenix, AZ 85069-7100. Offers communication (MA). Part-time and evening/weekend programs available. *Faculty:* 7 full-time (4 women). *Students:* 14 full-time (9 women), 18 part-time (14 women); includes 7 minority (1 African American, 1 American Indian/Alaska Native, 2 Asian Americans or Pacific Islanders, 3 Hispanic Americans), 4 international. Average age 33. In 2007, 5 degrees awarded. *Degree requirements:* For master's, comprehensive exams or thesis. *Entrance requirements:* For master's, GRE if GPA below 3.0 in last 60 hours of undergraduate study, 2 letters of recommendation, minimum GPA of 3.0 in last 2 years of undergraduate study, personal statement, writing sample of scholarly work. Additional exam requirements/recommendations for international students: Required—TOEFL (minimum score 550 paper-based; 213 computer-based; 83 iBT), IELTS (minimum score 7). *Application deadline:* For fall admission, 4/15 for domestic and international students; for spring admission, 10/15 for domestic and international students. Applications are processed on a rolling basis. Application fee: $65 ($80 for international students). Electronic applications accepted. *Expenses:* Tuition, state resident: full-time $6,227. Tuition, nonresident: full-time $17,920. Required fees: $146. *Financial support:* Scholarships/grants and tuition waivers (full) available. Support available to part-time students. Financial award application deadline: 3/15; financial award applicants required to submit FAFSA. *Faculty research:* Research regarding various ways in which communication shapes social contexts, constructs people's realities, and constitutes human relationships. *Unit head:* Dr. Jeffrey Kassing, Chair, 602-543-6631, Fax: 602-543-6612, E-mail: jkassing@asu.edu. *Application contact:* Janis Lacey, Administrative Assistant, 602-543-6631, Fax: 602-543-6612, E-mail: jkassing@asu.edu.

Arkansas State University, Graduate School, College of Communications, Jonesboro, State University, AR 72467. Offers MA, MSMC, SCCT. Part-time programs available. *Faculty:* 13 full-time (5 women), 1 part-time/adjunct (0 women). *Students:* 14 full-time (8 women), 16 part-time (12 women); includes 13 minority (all African Americans), 3 international. Average age 26. 21 applicants, 76% accepted, 16 enrolled. In 2007, 12 degrees awarded. *Degree requirements:* For master's, one foreign language, comprehensive exam, thesis or alternative. *Entrance requirements:* For master's, GRE General Test, appropriate bachelor's degree, letters of reference, official transcript; for SCCT, interview, master's degree, official transcript. Additional exam requirements/recommendations for international students: Required—TOEFL (minimum score 213 computer-based). *Application deadline:* Applications are processed on a rolling basis. Application fee: $30 ($40 for international students). Electronic applications accepted. *Expenses:* Tuition, state resident: full-time $3,528; part-time $196 per hour. Tuition, nonresident: full-time $8,928; part-time $496 per hour. Required fees: $842; $44 per hour. $25 per term. Tuition and fees vary according to course load and program. *Financial support:* Career-related internships or fieldwork, scholarships/grants, and unspecified assistantships available. Financial award application deadline: 7/1; financial award applicants required to submit FAFSA. *Faculty research:* Audience analysis, agenda setting, nonverbal communication, media ethics, political advertising. *Unit head:* Dr. Russell Shain, Dean, 870-972-2468, Fax: 870-972-3856, E-mail: rshain@astate.edu.

Arkansas Tech University, Graduate School, School of Liberal and Fine Arts, Russellville, AR 72801. Offers communication (MLA); English (M Ed, MA); fine arts (MLA); history (MA); multi-media journalism (MA); social science (MLA); social studies (M Ed); Spanish (MA, MLA); teaching English as a second language (MA, MLA). Part-time programs available. *Students:* 54 full-time (43 women), 79 part-time (54 women); includes 11 minority (3 African Americans, 1 American Indian/Alaska Native, 1 Asian American or Pacific Islander, 6 Hispanic Americans), 29 international. Average age 33. In 2007, 71 degrees awarded. *Degree requirements:* For master's, project. *Entrance requirements:* For master's, GRE General Test or MAT. Additional exam requirements/recommendations for international students: Required—TOEFL (minimum score 500 paper-based; 173 computer-based; 61 iBT). *Application deadline:* For fall admission, 3/1 priority date for domestic students, 5/1 priority date for international students; for winter admission, 10/1 priority date for international students; for spring admission, 10/1 priority date for domestic and international students. Applications are processed on a rolling basis. Application fee: $0 ($30 for international students). Electronic applications accepted. *Expenses:* Tuition, state resident: full-time $3,150; part-time $175 per hour. Tuition, nonresident: full-time $6,300; part-time $350 per hour. Required fees: $384; $8 per hour. $120 per term. Tuition and fees vary according to course load. *Financial support:* In 2007–08, teaching assistantships with full tuition reimbursements (averaging $4,000 per year); career-related internships or fieldwork, Federal Work-Study, scholarships/grants, health care benefits, and unspecified assistantships also available. Support available to part-time students. Financial award application deadline: 4/15; financial award applicants required to submit FAFSA. *Unit head:* Dr. Georgena Duncan, Dean, 479-968-0266, Fax: 479-968-0275, E-mail: georgena.duncan@atu.edu. *Application contact:* Dr. Eldon G. Clary, Dean of Graduate School, 479-968-0398, Fax: 479-964-0542, E-mail: graduate.school@atu.edu.

Auburn University, Graduate School, College of Liberal Arts, Department of Communication and Journalism, Auburn University, AL 36849. Offers communication (MA); mass communications (MA). Part-time programs available. *Faculty:* 17 full-time (9 women). *Students:* 15 full-time (10 women), 3 part-time (1 woman), 3 international. Average age 27. 21 applicants, 67% accepted, 10 enrolled. In 2007, 13 degrees awarded. *Degree requirements:* For master's, thesis (for some programs). *Entrance requirements:* For master's, GRE General Test. *Application deadline:* For fall admission, 7/7 for domestic students; for spring admission, 11/24 for domestic students. Applications are processed on a rolling basis. Application fee: $25 ($50 for international students). Electronic applications accepted. *Financial support:* Teaching assistantships, Federal Work-Study available. Support available to part-time students. Financial award application deadline: 3/15. *Unit head:* Dr. Mary Helen Brown, Acting Chair, 334-844-2727. *Application contact:* Dr. Joe Pittman, Interim Dean of the Graduate School, 334-844-4700.

Austin Peay State University, College of Graduate Studies, College of Arts and Letters, Department of Communication and Theatre, Clarksville, TN 37044. Offers communication arts (MA). Part-time and evening/weekend programs available. Postbaccalaureate distance learning degree programs offered (no on-campus study). *Faculty:* 5 full-time (1 woman), 4 part-time/adjunct (2 women). *Students:* 1 full-time (0 women), 73 part-time (54 women); includes 21 minority (17 African Americans, 1 Asian American or Pacific Islander, 3 Hispanic Americans). Average age 32. In 2007, 14 degrees awarded. *Degree requirements:* For master's, comprehensive exam, thesis (for some programs). *Entrance requirements:* For master's, GRE General Test, 3 letters of recommendation. Additional exam requirements/recommendations for international students: Required—TOEFL (minimum score 500 paper-based; 173 computer-based). *Application deadline:* For fall admission, 7/31 priority date for domestic students; for spring admission, 12/17 priority date for domestic students. Applications are processed on a rolling basis. Application fee: $25. Electronic applications accepted. *Expenses:* Tuition, state resident: full-time $5,446; part-time $288 per credit hour. Tuition, nonresident: full-time $15,722; part-time $734 per credit hour. Required fees: $1,180. Part-time tuition and fees vary according to course load. *Financial support:* In 2007–08, research assistantships (averaging $10,368 per year); career-related internships or fieldwork, Federal Work-Study, institutionally sponsored loans, scholarships/grants, and unspecified assistantships also available. Support available to part-time students. Financial award application deadline: 3/1; financial award applicants required to submit FAFSA. *Unit head:* Dr. Mike Gotcher, Chair, 931-221-7378, Fax: 931-221-7265, E-mail: comm@apsu.edu.

Ball State University, Graduate School, College of Communication, Information, and Media, Muncie, IN 47306-1099. Offers MA, MS. *Faculty:* 31. *Students:* 101 full-time (48 women), 72 part-time (47 women); includes 16 minority (8 African Americans, 1 American Indian/Alaska Native, 2 Asian Americans or Pacific Islanders, 5 Hispanic Americans), 39 international. Average age 25. 159 applicants, 75% accepted, 84 enrolled. In 2007, 101 degrees awarded. Application fee: $25 ($35 for international students). *Expenses:* Tuition, state resident: full-time $6,864. Tuition, nonresident: full-time $17,932. Required fees: $1,866. *Financial support:* In 2007–08, 71 teaching assistantships with full tuition reimbursements (averaging $7,728 per year) were awarded; research assistantships with full tuition reimbursements, career-related internships or fieldwork also available. Financial award application deadline: 3/1. *Unit head:* Roger Lavery, Dean, 765-285-6000, Fax: 765-285-6002.

Barry University, School of Arts and Sciences, Department of Communication, Miami Shores, FL 33161-6695. Offers broadcasting (Certificate); communication (MA), including broadcast communication, public relations and corporate communications; organizational communication (MS). Part-time and evening/weekend programs available. *Degree requirements:* For master's, thesis (for some programs). *Entrance requirements:* For master's, GRE General Test, MAT, minimum GPA of 3.0. *Application deadline:* Applications are processed on a rolling basis. Application fee: $30. Electronic applications accepted. *Financial support:* Career-related internships or fieldwork available. Support available to part-time students. Financial award application deadline: 5/1; financial award applicants required to submit FAFSA. *Faculty research:* Organizational communication, broadcast communication, intercultural communication, advertising, leadership. *Unit head:* Dr. Denis Vogel, Chair, 305-899-3468, E-mail: dvogel@mail.barry.edu. *Application contact:* Dave Fletcher, Director of Graduate Admissions, 305-899-3113, Fax: 305-899-2971, E-mail: dfletcher@mail.barry.edu.

Baylor University, Graduate School, College of Arts and Sciences, Department of Communication Studies, Waco, TX 76798. Offers MA. Part-time programs available. *Students:* 19 full-time (10 women), 2 part-time (1 woman); includes 2 minority (1 Asian American or Pacific Islander, 1 Hispanic American), 1 international. Average age 22. In 2007, 16 degrees awarded.

Degree requirements: For master's, thesis or alternative. *Entrance requirements:* For master's, GRE General Test. *Application deadline:* For fall admission, 8/1 for domestic students. Applications are processed on a rolling basis. Application fee: $25. *Financial support:* In 2007–08, 12 teaching assistantships were awarded; career-related internships or fieldwork, Federal Work-Study, institutionally sponsored loans, and scholarships/grants also available. Financial award application deadline: 4/1. *Faculty research:* Rhetoric and debate, organizational communication, media studies, new technology. *Unit head:* Dr. David Schlueter, Graduate Program Director, 254-710-1621, E-mail: david_schlueter@baylor.edu. *Application contact:* Suzanne Keener, Administrative Assistant, 254-710-3588, Fax: 254-710-3870.

Bellevue University, Graduate School, Bellevue, NE 68005-3098. Offers business (MBA); communications studies (MA, MS); computer information systems (MS); health care administration (MS); human services (MS); leadership (MA); management (MA); security management (MS). MA is delivered in an accelerated executive format. Part-time and evening/weekend programs available. Postbaccalaureate distance learning degree programs offered (no on-campus study). *Degree requirements:* For master's, thesis or project. *Entrance requirements:* For master's, minimum GPA of 2.5 in last 60 hours. Additional exam requirements/recommendations for international students: Required—TOEFL (minimum score 538 paper-based; 200 computer-based).

Bethel University, Graduate School, Department of Communication Studies, St. Paul, MN 55112-6999. Offers communication (MA); post-secondary teaching (Certificate). Evening/weekend programs available. *Faculty:* 7 full-time (2 women), 5 part-time/adjunct (2 women). *Students:* 33 full-time (23 women), 3 part-time (2 women). Average age 37. In 2007, 16 master's awarded. *Degree requirements:* For master's, comprehensive exam, thesis. *Entrance requirements:* For master's, MAT, interview, minimum GPA of 3.0, course work in communication and statistics, references. Additional exam requirements/recommendations for international students: Required—TOEFL (minimum score 550 paper-based; 213 computer-based). *Application deadline:* For fall admission, 5/15 priority date for domestic students; for spring admission, 3/15 for domestic students. Applications are processed on a rolling basis. Application fee: $25. Electronic applications accepted. *Expenses:* Tuition: Part-time $415 per credit. Tuition and fees vary according to program. *Financial support:* Institutionally sponsored loans and scholarships/grants available. *Unit head:* Dr. Leta J. Frazier, Director, 651-638-6260, Fax: 651-635-8004, E-mail: leta-frazier@bethel.edu. *Application contact:* Michael Price, Director of Admissions, 651-635-8000 Ext. 8017, Fax: 651-635-8039, E-mail: m-price@bethel.edu.

Boise State University, Graduate College, College of Social Sciences and Public Affairs, Department of Communication, Boise, ID 83725-0399. Offers MA. Part-time programs available. *Degree requirements:* For master's, thesis. *Entrance requirements:* For master's, minimum GPA of 3.0, writing sample. Electronic applications accepted.

Boston University, College of Communication, Boston, MA 02215. Offers MFA, MS, JD/MS, MBA/MS. Part-time programs available. *Faculty:* 57 full-time, 81 part-time/adjunct. *Students:* 336 full-time (238 women), 38 part-time (27 women); includes 41 minority (14 African Americans, 1 American Indian/Alaska Native, 18 Asian Americans or Pacific Islanders, 8 Hispanic Americans), 66 international. Average age 26. 800 applicants, 50% accepted. In 2007, 183 degrees awarded. *Degree requirements:* For master's, thesis. *Entrance requirements:* For master's, GRE General Test. Additional exam requirements/recommendations for international students: Required—TOEFL. *Application deadline:* For fall admission, 2/1 for domestic students. Electronic applications accepted. *Expenses:* Tuition: Full-time $34,930; part-time $1,092 per credit. Tuition and fees vary according to class time, course level and program. *Financial support:* In 2007–08, 290 students received support, including 18 teaching assistantships with partial tuition reimbursements available; career-related internships or fieldwork, Federal Work-Study, institutionally sponsored loans, scholarships/grants, and unspecified assistantships also available. Support available to part-time students. Financial award application deadline: 2/1; financial award applicants required to submit FAFSA. *Unit head:* Dr. Tobe Berkovitz, Dean, 617-353-3450, Fax: 617-358-0399, E-mail: com@bu.edu. *Application contact:* William A. Taylor, Assistant Director, Graduate Services and Financial Aid, 617-353-3481, Fax: 617-358-0399, E-mail: comgrad@bu.edu.

See Close-Up on page 885.

Bowling Green State University, Graduate College, College of Arts and Sciences, School of Communication Studies, Bowling Green, OH 43403. Offers MA, PhD. Part-time programs available. *Faculty:* 24 full-time (12 women), 3 part-time/adjunct (1 woman). *Students:* 46 full-time (26 women), 15 part-time (10 women); includes 8 minority (6 African Americans, 1 Asian American or Pacific Islander, 1 Hispanic American), 16 international. Average age 33. 77 applicants, 36% accepted, 7 enrolled. In 2007, 4 master's, 7 doctorates awarded. Terminal master's awarded for partial completion of doctoral program. *Degree requirements:* For master's, thesis or alternative; for doctorate, comprehensive exam, thesis/dissertation. *Entrance requirements:* For master's and doctorate, GRE General Test. Additional exam requirements/recommendations for international students: Required—TOEFL. *Application deadline:* For fall admission, 1/1 priority date for domestic students. Application fee: $30. Electronic applications accepted. *Financial support:* In 2007–08, 2 fellowships with full tuition reimbursements (averaging $14,707 per year), 8 research assistantships with full tuition reimbursements (averaging $8,788 per year), 34 teaching assistantships with full tuition reimbursements (averaging $11,098 per year) were awarded; career-related internships or fieldwork, Federal Work-Study, and unspecified assistantships also available. Financial award applicants required to submit FAFSA. *Unit head:* Dr. Oliver Boyd-Barrett, Director, 419-372-6018. *Application contact:* Dr. Radhika Gajjala, Assistant Professor, 419-372-0528.

Brandeis University, Rabb School of Continuing Studies, Division of Graduate Professional Studies, Virtual Team Management and Communication Program, Waltham, MA 02454-9110. Offers Graduate Certificate. Part-time and evening/weekend programs available. Postbaccalaureate distance learning degree programs offered (no on-campus study). *Faculty:* 2 full-time (both women), 32 part-time/adjunct (5 women). *Entrance requirements:* For degree, resumé, official transcripts, recommendations. Additional exam requirements/recommendations for international students: Recommended—TOEFL (minimum score 600 paper-based; 250 computer-based; 100 iBT). *Application deadline:* For fall admission, 6/15 priority date for domestic students; for winter admission, 10/15 priority date for domestic students; for spring admission, 2/15 priority date for domestic students. Applications are processed on a rolling basis. Application fee: $50. Electronic applications accepted. *Unit head:* Dr. Aline Yurik, Program Chair, 781-736-8787, Fax: 781-736-3420, E-mail: ayurik@brandeis.edu.

Brigham Young University, Graduate Studies, College of Fine Arts and Communications, Department of Communications, Provo, UT 84602-1001. Offers mass communication (MA). *Faculty:* 15 full-time (2 women). *Students:* 24 full-time (14 women), 18 part-time (7 women); includes 5 minority (1 American Indian/Alaska Native, 4 Hispanic Americans). Average age 30. 33 applicants, 52% accepted, 13 enrolled. In 2007, 5 degrees awarded. *Degree requirements:* For master's, comprehensive exam, thesis. *Entrance requirements:* For master's, GRE, minimum GPA of 3.0 in last 60 hours of course work. Additional exam requirements/recommendations for international students: Required—TOEFL (minimum score 580 paper-based; 237 computer-based). *Application deadline:* For fall admission, 2/28 for domestic and international students. Application fee: $50. Electronic applications accepted. *Financial support:* In 2007–08, 17 students received support, including 23 research assistantships with full and partial tuition reimbursements available (averaging $3,981 per year), 9 teaching assistantships with full tuition reimbursements available (averaging $5,015 per year); career-related internships or fieldwork, institutionally sponsored loans, scholarships/grants, unspecified assistantships, and supplementary awards also available. Financial award application deadline: 5/15; financial award applicants required to submit FAFSA. *Faculty research:* Ethics, international, magazine, newspaper, media effects. *Unit head:* Dr. Edward E. Adams, Chair, 801-422-2997, Fax: 801-422-0160, E-mail: comms.secretary@byu.edu. *Application contact:* Dr. Kevin L. Stoker, Graduate Coordinator, 801-422-1222, Fax: 801-422-0160, E-mail: kevin_stoker@byu.edu.

California State University, Chico, Graduate School, College of Communication and Education, Department of Communication Arts and Sciences, Program in Communication Studies, Chico, CA 95929-0722. Offers MA. *Students:* 9 full-time (7 women), 7 part-time (4 women); includes 3 minority (all Hispanic Americans). Average age 29. 14 applicants, 64% accepted, 9 enrolled. In 2007, 6 degrees awarded. *Degree requirements:* For master's, thesis. *Entrance requirements:* Additional exam requirements/recommendations for international students: Required—TOEFL (minimum score 550 paper-based; 213 computer-based; 80 iBT), IELTS (minimum score 7). *Application deadline:* For fall admission, 3/1 priority date for domestic students, 3/1 for international students; for spring admission, 9/15 priority date for domestic students, 9/15 for international students. Applications are processed on a rolling basis. Application fee: $55. Electronic applications accepted. *Application contact:* Dr. Ruth Guzley, Graduate Coordinator, 530-898-5751.

California State University, East Bay, Academic Programs and Graduate Studies, College of Letters, Arts, and Social Sciences, Department of Communication, Hayward, CA 94542-3000. Offers MA. Part-time programs available. *Faculty:* 10 full-time (3 women). *Students:* 1 (woman) full-time, 12 part-time (8 women); includes 3 minority (2 Asian Americans or Pacific Islanders, 1 Hispanic American). Average age 33. 25 applicants, 52% accepted, 7 enrolled. In 2007, 7 degrees awarded. *Degree requirements:* For master's, comprehensive exam, thesis optional, project or thesis. *Entrance requirements:* For master's, GRE, minimum GPA of 3.0 in field. Additional exam requirements/recommendations for international students: Required—TOEFL (minimum score 550 paper-based; 213 computer-based). *Application deadline:* For fall admission, 5/31 for domestic students, 4/30 for international students; for winter admission, 9/30 for domestic and international students; for spring admission, 12/31 for domestic students, 11/30 for international students. Applications are processed on a rolling basis. Application fee: $55. Electronic applications accepted. *Expenses:* Required fees: $3,987; $851 per quarter. *Financial support:* Fellowships, teaching assistantships, Federal Work-Study, institutionally sponsored loans, and scholarships/grants also available. Support available to part-time students. Financial award application deadline: 3/2. *Unit head:* Dr. Isaac Catt, Chair, 510-885-3292, Fax: 510-885-4099, E-mail: isaac.catt@csueastbay.edu. *Application contact:* My Huynh, Graduate Prospect Specialist, 510-885-2989, Fax: 510-885-4059, E-mail: my.huynh@csueastbay.edu.

California State University, Fresno, Division of Graduate Studies, College of Arts and Humanities, Department of Communication, Fresno, CA 93740-8027. Offers MA. Part-time and evening/weekend programs available. *Faculty:* 9 full-time (4 women). *Students:* 22; includes 5 minority (2 African Americans, 1 American Indian/Alaska Native, 2 Asian Americans or Pacific Islanders). Average age 28. 1 applicant. In 2007, 8 degrees awarded. *Degree requirements:* For master's, thesis or alternative. *Entrance requirements:* For master's, GRE General Test, minimum GPA of 3.1. Additional exam requirements/recommendations for international students: Required—TOEFL. *Application deadline:* For fall admission, 5/1 for domestic and international students; for spring admission, 10/1 for domestic and international students. Applications are processed on a rolling basis. Application fee: $55. Electronic applications accepted. *Financial support:* In 2007–08, 9 teaching assistantships (averaging $5,508 per year) were awarded; career-related internships or fieldwork, Federal Work-Study, and scholarships/grants also available. Support available to part-time students. Financial award application deadline: 3/1; financial award applicants required to submit FAFSA. *Faculty research:* Learning styles, education, critical thinking. *Unit head:* Dr. Katherine Adams, Chair, 559-278-2826, Fax: 559-278-4113, E-mail: kathy_adams@csufresno.edu. *Application contact:* Dr. Kevin J. Ayotte, Graduate Program Coordinator, 559-278-2826, Fax: 559-278-4113, E-mail: kjayotte@csufresno.edu.

California State University, Fullerton, Graduate Studies, College of Communications, Department of Communications, Fullerton, CA 92834-9480. Offers communications—advertising (MA); communications—entertainment and tourism (MA); communications—journalism (MA); communications—public relations (MA). Part-time programs available. *Students:* 25 full-time (22 women), 39 part-time (24 women); includes 19 minority (1 African American, 6 Asian Americans or Pacific Islanders, 12 Hispanic Americans), 11 international. Average age 29. 140 applicants, 41% accepted, 28 enrolled. In 2007, 43 degrees awarded. *Degree requirements:* For master's, project or thesis. *Entrance requirements:* For master's, GRE General Test. Application fee: $55. *Financial support:* Teaching assistantships, career-related internships or fieldwork, Federal Work-Study, institutionally sponsored loans, and scholarships/grants available. Support available to part-time students. Financial award application deadline: 3/1. *Unit head:* Dr. Tony Fellow, Chair, 714-278-3517. *Application contact:* Coordinator, 714-278-3832.

California State University, Long Beach, Graduate Studies, College of Liberal Arts, Department of Communication Studies, Long Beach, CA 90840. Offers MA. Part-time programs available. *Faculty:* 34 full-time (21 women), 48 part-time/adjunct (28 women). *Students:* 12 full-time (6 women), 21 part-time (15 women); includes 8 minority (2 African Americans, 1 American Indian/Alaska Native, 3 Asian Americans or Pacific Islanders, 2 Hispanic Americans). Average age 30. *Degree requirements:* For master's, comprehensive exam or thesis. *Entrance requirements:* For master's, GRE. *Application deadline:* For fall admission, 7/1 for domestic students; for spring admission, 12/1 for domestic students. Applications are processed on a rolling basis. Application fee: $55. Electronic applications accepted. *Financial support:* Federal Work-Study, institutionally sponsored loans, and scholarships/grants available. Financial award application deadline: 3/2. *Faculty research:* Rhetoric, public address, communication theory, interpersonal communication, intercultural communication. *Unit head:* Dr. Sharon Downey, Chair, 562-985-4301, Fax: 562-985-4259, E-mail: sdowney@csulb.edu. *Application contact:* Dr. Amy Bippus, Graduate Adviser, 562-985-7862, Fax: 562-985-4259, E-mail: abippus@csulb.edu.

California State University, Los Angeles, Graduate Studies, College of Arts and Letters, Department of Communication Studies, Los Angeles, CA 90032-8530. Offers speech communication (MA). Part-time and evening/weekend programs available. *Faculty:* 13 full-time (4 women). *Students:* 29 full-time (20 women), 37 part-time (29 women); includes 26 minority (10 African Americans, 7 Asian Americans or Pacific Islanders, 9 Hispanic Americans), 12 international. Average age 31. In 2007, 14 degrees awarded. *Degree requirements:* For master's, comprehensive exam or thesis. *Entrance requirements:* For master's, minimum GPA of 2.75 in last 90 units of course work. Additional exam requirements/recommendations for international students: Required—TOEFL. *Application deadline:* For fall admission, 6/30 for domestic students; for spring admission, 2/1 for domestic students. Applications are processed on a rolling basis. Application fee: $55. *Financial support:* Career-related internships or fieldwork and Federal Work-Study available. Support available to part-time students. Financial award application deadline: 3/1. *Faculty research:* Organizational, interpersonal, intercultural, and instructional communication; rhetorical theories. *Unit head:* Dr. John Ramirez, Chair, 323-343-4200, Fax: 323-343-6467, E-mail: jramire4@calstatela.edu.

California State University, Northridge, Graduate Studies, College of Arts, Media, and Communication, Northridge, CA 91330. Offers MA, MFA, MM. Part-time and evening/weekend programs available. *Faculty:* 85 full-time (36 women), 206 part-time/adjunct (91 women). *Students:* 91 full-time (47 women), 154 part-time (103 women); includes 52 minority (9 African Americans, 3 American Indian/Alaska Native, 16 Asian Americans or Pacific Islanders, 24 Hispanic Americans), 15 international. Average age 34. 297 applicants, 51% accepted, 82 enrolled. In 2007, 71 degrees awarded. *Entrance requirements:* Additional exam requirements/recommendations for international students: Required—TOEFL. *Application deadline:* For fall admission, 11/30 for domestic students. Application fee: $55. *Financial support:* Teaching assistantships, career-related internships or fieldwork, Federal Work-Study, and unspecified assistantships available. Support available to part-time students. Financial award application deadline: 3/1. *Unit head:* Robert Bucker, Dean, 818-677-2246, E-mail: robert.bucker@csun.edu.

California State University, Sacramento, Graduate Studies, College of Arts and Letters, Department of Communication Studies, Sacramento, CA 95819-6048. Offers MA. Part-time programs available. *Students:* 7 full-time (3 women), 43 part-time (32 women); includes 7

Communication—General

California State University, Sacramento (continued)
minority (1 Asian American or Pacific Islander, 6 Hispanic Americans). Average age 29. 43 applicants, 47% accepted, 13 enrolled. *Degree requirements:* For master's, thesis or alternative, writing proficiency exam. *Entrance requirements:* For master's, minimum GPA of 3.25 during previous 2 years. Additional exam requirements/recommendations for international students: Required—TOEFL. *Application deadline:* Applications are processed on a rolling basis. Application fee: $55. Electronic applications accepted. *Expenses:* Tuition, state resident: full-time $3,414. Tuition, nonresident: full-time $13,584; part-time $339 per unit. Required fees: $786; $393 per semester. *Financial support:* Research assistantships, teaching assistantships, career-related internships or fieldwork and Federal Work-Study available. Support available to part-time students. Financial award application deadline: 3/1. *Unit head:* Nick Burnett, Chair, 916-278-6688, Fax: 916-278-4588.

California State University, San Bernardino, Graduate Studies, College of Arts and Letters, Department of Communication Studies, San Bernardino, CA 92407-2397. Offers MA. *Faculty:* 14 full-time, 15 part-time/adjunct. *Students:* 32 full-time (25 women), 19 part-time (14 women); includes 18 minority (8 African Americans, 3 Asian Americans or Pacific Islanders, 7 Hispanic Americans), 9 international. Average age 26. 72 applicants, 40% accepted, 18 enrolled. In 2007, 6 degrees awarded. *Application deadline:* For fall admission, 8/31 priority date for domestic students. Application fee: $55. *Unit head:* Dr. Juan Delgado, Interim Chair, 909-537-5820, Fax: 909-537-7009, E-mail: jdelgado@csusb.edu.

Carleton University, Faculty of Graduate Studies, Faculty of Public Affairs and Management, School of Journalism and Communication, Program in Communication, Ottawa, ON K1S 5B6, Canada. Offers MA, PhD. *Degree requirements:* For master's, thesis optional; for doctorate, comprehensive exam, thesis/dissertation. *Entrance requirements:* For master's, honors degree. Additional exam requirements/recommendations for international students: Required—TOEFL. *Application deadline:* Applications are processed on a rolling basis. Application fee: $77 Canadian dollars. *Financial support:* Fellowships, teaching assistantships, institutionally sponsored loans, scholarships/grants, and unspecified assistantships available. *Faculty research:* History of communication and media systems, communication/information technologies and society, communication and social relations, communication policy and political economy. *Unit head:* Sheryl Hamilton, Graduate Supervisor, 613-520-2600 Ext. 7408. *Application contact:* Carole Crasswell, Graduate Secretary, 613-520-2600 Ext. 7408, Fax: 613-520-6690, E-mail: carole_crasswell@carleton.ca.

Carnegie Mellon University, College of Fine Arts, School of Design, Program in Communication Planning and Information Design, Pittsburgh, PA 15213-3891. Offers M Des. Part-time programs available. *Degree requirements:* For master's, thesis. *Entrance requirements:* For master's, GRE, portfolio of relevant work. Additional exam requirements/recommendations for international students: Required—TOEFL (minimum score 600 paper-based). *Faculty research:* Dynamic information design, communication design, systems design, strategic planning, kinetic typography and emotion.

Carnegie Mellon University, College of Humanities and Social Sciences, Department of English, Pittsburgh, PA 15213-3891. Offers communication planning and design (M Des); English (MA); literary and cultural studies (MA, PhD); professional writing (MAPW), including design, professional writing, research, rhetorical theory, science writing, technical; rhetoric (MA, PhD). Part-time programs available. Terminal master's awarded for partial completion of doctoral program. *Degree requirements:* For doctorate, 2 foreign languages, comprehensive exam, thesis/dissertation. *Entrance requirements:* For master's and doctorate, GRE General Test. Additional exam requirements/recommendations for international students: Required—TOEFL, TWE. *Faculty research:* Cognitive processes in discourse with emphasis on writing, testing, and evaluation.

Central Connecticut State University, School of Graduate Studies, School of Arts and Sciences, Department of Communication, New Britain, CT 06050-4010. Offers organizational communication (MS). Part-time and evening/weekend programs available. *Faculty:* 14 full-time (4 women), 7 part-time/adjunct (2 women). *Students:* 5 full-time (4 women), 25 part-time (15 women); includes 4 minority (3 African Americans, 1 Hispanic American), 2 international. Average age 30. 22 applicants, 50% accepted, 6 enrolled. *Degree requirements:* For master's, comprehensive exam, thesis or alternative. *Entrance requirements:* For master's, minimum GPA of 3.0. Additional exam requirements/recommendations for international students: Required—TOEFL. *Application deadline:* For fall admission, 7/1 for domestic students; for spring admission, 12/1 for domestic students. Applications are processed on a rolling basis. Application fee: $50. Electronic applications accepted. *Expenses:* Tuition, area resident: Full-time $4,169. Tuition, state resident: full-time $6,253. Tuition, nonresident: full-time $11,614; part-time $400 per credit. Required fees: $3,322. One-time fee: $62 part-time. Tuition and fees vary according to degree level and program. *Financial support:* In 2007–08, 2 students received support; research assistantships, career-related internships or fieldwork, Federal Work-Study, scholarships/grants, and unspecified assistantships available. Support available to part-time students. Financial award application deadline: 3/1; financial award applicants required to submit FAFSA. *Faculty research:* Organizational communication, mass communication, intercultural communication, political communication, information management. *Unit head:* Dr. Serafin Mendez-Mendez, Chair, 860-832-2690.

Central Michigan University, College of Graduate Studies, College of Communication and Fine Arts, Department of Speech, Communication and Dramatic Arts, Mount Pleasant, MI 48859. Offers interpersonal and public communication (MA); oral interpretation (MA); theatre (MA). *Degree requirements:* For master's, thesis or alternative. *Entrance requirements:* For master's, minimum GPA of 3.0 in last 15 hours of speech communication and dramatic arts courses, 2.7 in last 60 hours. *Faculty research:* Rhetoric, organizational communication, communication education.

Clarion University of Pennsylvania, Office of Research and Graduate Studies, College of Arts and Sciences, Department of Mass Media Arts, Journalism, and Communication Studies, Clarion, PA 16214. Offers MS. Part-time programs available. *Faculty:* 6 full-time (2 women). *Students:* 9 full-time, 8 part-time. 9 applicants, 44% accepted, 4 enrolled. In 2007, 7 degrees awarded. *Degree requirements:* For master's, comprehensive exam, thesis or alternative. *Entrance requirements:* For master's, minimum QPA of 3.0. Additional exam requirements/recommendations for international students: Required—TOEFL (minimum score 600 paper-based; 250 computer-based; 100 iBT). *Application deadline:* For fall admission, 8/1 priority date for domestic students, 4/15 priority date for international students; for spring admission, 12/1 priority date for domestic students, 9/15 priority date for international students. Applications are processed on a rolling basis. Application fee: $30. Electronic applications accepted. *Financial support:* In 2007–08, 7 research assistantships with full tuition reimbursements (averaging $3,817 per year) were awarded. Support available to part-time students. Financial award application deadline: 3/1. *Unit head:* Dr. Susan Hilton, Graduate Coordinator and Department Chair, 814-393-2245, Fax: 814-393-2186, E-mail: shilton@clarion.edu.

Clark University, Graduate School, College of Professional and Continuing Education, Program in Professional Communication, Worcester, MA 01610-1477. Offers MSPC. *Students:* 33 full-time (22 women), 18 part-time (13 women); includes 2 minority (1 African American, 1 American Indian/Alaska Native), 10 international. Average age 31. 29 applicants, 100% accepted, 29 enrolled. In 2007, 24 degrees awarded. *Degree requirements:* For master's, thesis optional. *Application deadline:* Applications are processed on a rolling basis. Application fee: $40. Electronic applications accepted. *Expenses:* Tuition: Full-time $32,600; part-time $1,019 per credit. Required fees: $30. Tuition and fees vary according to program. *Unit head:* Max E. Hess, Director of Graduate Studies, 508-793-7217, Fax: 508-793-7232. *Application contact:* Julia Parent, Director of Marketing, Communications, and Admissions, 508-793-7217, Fax: 508-793-7232, E-mail: jparent@clarku.edu.

Clemson University, Graduate School, College of Architecture, Arts, and Humanities, Department of English, Program in Professional Communication, Clemson, SC 29634. Offers MA. Part-time programs available. *Students:* 33 full-time (22 women), 9 part-time (8 women); includes 6 minority (3 African Americans, 1 Asian American or Pacific Islander, 2 Hispanic Americans), 1 international. Average age 26. 31 applicants, 65% accepted, 14 enrolled. In 2007, 18 degrees awarded. *Degree requirements:* For master's, one foreign language, thesis optional, oral exam. *Entrance requirements:* For master's, GRE General Test, minimum GPA of 3.0. Additional exam requirements/recommendations for international students: Required—TOEFL, IELTS. *Application deadline:* For fall admission, 6/1 priority date for domestic students, 4/15 for international students; for spring admission, 12/1 for domestic students, 9/15 for international students. Applications are processed on a rolling basis. Application fee: $55. *Financial support:* In 2007–08, 14 research assistantships were awarded; teaching assistantships. Financial award application deadline: 4/1; financial award applicants required to submit FAFSA. *Faculty research:* Usability testing, rhetoric, communication across the curriculum, intercultural communication. Total annual research expenditures: $120,000. *Unit head:* Dr. Summer Taylor, Coordinator, 864-656-6689, Fax: 864-656-1345, E-mail: slsmith@clemson.edu.

Clemson University, Graduate School, College of Architecture, Arts, and Humanities, Department of English, Program in Rhetorics, Communication and Information Design, Clemson, SC 29634. Offers PhD. *Students:* 20 full-time (8 women), 1 part-time; includes 2 minority (1 African American, 1 Asian American or Pacific Islander), 4 international. 21 applicants, 57% accepted, 8 enrolled. *Degree requirements:* For doctorate, thesis/dissertation (for some programs). *Entrance requirements:* For doctorate, GRE, master's degree in English, communications studies, art, professional communication or related field; portfolio; 3 letters of reference; minimum graduate GPA of 3.5. Additional exam requirements/recommendations for international students: Required—TOEFL (minimum score 550 paper-based; 213 computer-based). *Application deadline:* For fall admission, 2/1 priority date for domestic students, 4/15 for international students. Application fee: $55. *Financial support:* Teaching assistantships available. *Unit head:* Dr. Victor Vitanza, Coordinator, 864-656-6411, Fax: 864-656-0599, E-mail: sophist@clemson.edu.

Clemson University, Graduate School, College of Business and Behavioral Science, Department of Graphic Communications, Clemson, SC 29634. Offers MS. *Faculty:* 10 full-time (3 women), 1 part-time/adjunct (0 women). *Students:* 9 full-time (6 women); includes 5 minority (4 African Americans, 1 Asian American or Pacific Islander), 1 international. 5 applicants, 60% accepted, 1 enrolled. In 2007, 4 degrees awarded. *Entrance requirements:* For master's, GRE General Test. Additional exam requirements/recommendations for international students: Required—TOEFL. *Application deadline:* For fall admission, 4/15 for international students; for spring admission, 9/15 for international students. Application fee: $55. *Financial support:* In 2007–08, 1 research assistantship (averaging $10,000 per year), 8 teaching assistantships (averaging $9,000 per year) were awarded. Financial award applicants required to submit FAFSA. *Unit head:* Dr. Samuel T. Ingram, Chair, 864-656-3447.

Cleveland State University, College of Graduate Studies, College of Liberal Arts and Social Sciences, School of Communication, Cleveland, OH 44115. Offers applied communication theory and methodology (MA); culture, communication and health care (Certificate). Part-time and evening/weekend programs available. *Faculty:* 17 full-time (9 women), 1 part-time/adjunct (0 women). *Students:* 14 full-time (13 women), 14 part-time (9 women); includes 3 minority (2 African Americans, 1 Asian American or Pacific Islander), 6 international. Average age 33. 29 applicants, 59% accepted, 10 enrolled. In 2007, 2 degrees awarded. *Degree requirements:* For master's, thesis, project or comprehensive exam. *Entrance requirements:* For master's, GRE or MAT, minimum undergraduate GPA of 2.75, 2 letters of recommendation. Additional exam requirements/recommendations for international students: Required—TOEFL (minimum score 525 paper-based; 197 computer-based). *Application deadline:* For fall admission, 7/15 priority date for domestic and international students; for spring admission, 1/15 priority date for domestic students, 12/15 priority date for international students. Applications are processed on a rolling basis. Application fee: $30. Electronic applications accepted. *Financial support:* In 2007–08, 5 research assistantships with full and partial tuition reimbursements (averaging $3,132 per year), 7 teaching assistantships with full and partial tuition reimbursements (averaging $3,231 per year) were awarded; career-related internships or fieldwork, tuition waivers (full and partial), and unspecified assistantships also available. *Faculty research:* Interpersonal, organizational, and mass communication; health communication. *Unit head:* Dr. Richard M. Perloff, Director, 216-687-4631, Fax: 216-687-5435, E-mail: r.perloff@csuohio.edu.

The College at Brockport, State University of New York, School of Arts and Performance, Department of Communication, Brockport, NY 14420-2997. Offers MA. Part-time and evening/weekend programs available. *Students:* 11 full-time (6 women), 13 part-time (7 women); includes 4 minority (2 African Americans, 1 Asian American or Pacific Islander, 1 Hispanic American), 2 international. 16 applicants, 94% accepted, 8 enrolled. In 2007, 10 degrees awarded. *Degree requirements:* For master's, thesis or alternative, research project. *Entrance requirements:* For master's, minimum GPA of 3.0, letters of recommendation. Additional exam requirements/recommendations for international students: Required—TOEFL (minimum score 550 paper-based; 213 computer-based; 79 iBT). *Application deadline:* For fall admission, 7/15 for domestic and international students; for spring admission, 11/15 for domestic and international students. Application fee: $50. *Expenses:* Tuition, state resident: full-time $6,900; part-time $288 per credit. Tuition, nonresident: full-time $10,920; part-time $455 per credit. Required fees: $738; $31 per credit. *Financial support:* In 2007–08, 3 teaching assistantships with tuition reimbursements (averaging $6,000 per year) were awarded; Federal Work-Study, scholarships/grants, and unspecified assistantships also available. Support available to part-time students. Financial award application deadline: 3/15; financial award applicants required to submit FAFSA. *Faculty research:* Organizational communication, rhetorical theory and criticism, media theory and criticism, interpersonal communication, communication theory. *Unit head:* Dr. Monica Brasted, Chairperson, 585-395-2511, E-mail: mbrasted@brockport.edu. *Application contact:* Dr. Alex Lyon, Graduate Director, 585-395-5772, E-mail: alyon@brockport.edu.

College of Charleston, Graduate School, School of Humanities and Social Sciences, Program in Communication, Charleston, SC 29424-0001. Offers MA. Part-time and evening/weekend programs available. *Faculty:* 19 full-time (11 women). *Degree requirements:* For master's, comprehensive exam or thesis. *Entrance requirements:* For master's, GRE, writing sample; 2 letters of recommendation; minimum GPA of 2.75, 3.0 in major. *Application deadline:* For fall admission, 4/1 for domestic students; for spring admission, 11/1 for domestic students. Applications are processed on a rolling basis. Electronic applications accepted. *Expenses:* Tuition, state resident: full-time $7,778; part-time $324 per hour. Tuition, nonresident: full-time $18,732; part-time $781 per hour. *Unit head:* Dr. Douglas Ferguson, Director, 844-983-7854, E-mail: fergusond@cofc.edu.

The College of New Rochelle, Graduate School, Division of Art and Communication Studies, Program in Communication Studies, New Rochelle, NY 10805-2308. Offers MS, Certificate. Part-time and evening/weekend programs available. *Faculty:* 2 full-time (1 woman), 7 part-time/adjunct (3 women). *Students:* 12 full-time (11 women), 22 part-time (19 women); includes 12 minority (10 African Americans, 2 Hispanic Americans). Average age 35. In 2007, 24 degrees awarded. *Degree requirements:* For master's, thesis or alternative. *Entrance requirements:* For master's, GRE General Test, interview, minimum GPA of 3.0. Additional exam requirements/recommendations for international students: Required—TOEFL. *Application deadline:* For fall admission, 8/1 priority date for domestic students. Applications are processed on a rolling basis. Application fee: $35. *Expenses:* Tuition: Part-time $650 per credit. Required fees: $90 per term. *Financial support:* In 2007–08, 1 research assistantship was awarded; scholarships/grants and tuition waivers (partial) also available. Support available to part-time students. *Unit head:* Head, 914-654-5279.

College of Notre Dame of Maryland, Graduate Studies, Program in Contemporary Communication, Baltimore, MD 21210-2476. Offers MA. Part-time and evening/weekend programs available. *Students:* 4 full-time (all women), 59 part-time (51 women). *Degree* *requirements:* For master's, thesis optional. *Entrance requirements:* For master's, minimum GPA of 3.0. Additional exam requirements/recommendations for international students: Required—TOEFL (minimum score 500 paper-based; 173 computer-based; 61 iBT). *Application deadline:* For fall admission, 7/5 for domestic students; for winter admission, 11/5 for domestic students; for spring admission, 12/5 for domestic students. Applications are processed on a rolling basis. Application fee: $45. Electronic applications accepted. *Financial support:* Application deadline: 6/30; *Unit head:* Barbara Mento, Head, 410-532-5591, Fax: 410-532-5333, E-mail: bmento@ndm.edu. *Application contact:* Erica D. Jones, Graduate Admissions Coordinator, 410-532-5317, Fax: 410-532-5333, E-mail: gradadm@ndm.edu.

Columbia University, Graduate School of Business, Doctoral Program in Business, New York, NY 10027. Offers business (PhD), including accounting, decision, risk, and operations, finance and economics, management, marketing. *Accreditation:* AACSB. *Faculty:* 117 full-time (14 women), 124 part-time/adjunct (18 women). *Students:* 114 full-time (38 women); includes 6 minority (5 Asian Americans or Pacific Islanders, 1 Hispanic American), 87 international. Average age 27. 603 applicants, 6% accepted, 7 enrolled. In 2007, 16 degrees awarded. *Median time to degree:* Of those who began their doctoral program in fall 1999, 76% received their degree in 8 years or less. *Degree requirements:* For doctorate, comprehensive exam, thesis/dissertation, major field exam, research paper, thesis proposal. *Entrance requirements:* For doctorate, GMAT or GRE (finance), 2 letters of reference, resumé. Additional exam requirements/recommendations for international students: Required—TOEFL. *Application deadline:* For fall admission, 1/1 for domestic and international students. Application fee: $75. Electronic applications accepted. *Expenses: Contact institution.* One-time fee: $75 part-time. Full-time tuition and fees vary according to course level, course load, degree level and program. *Financial support:* In 2007–08, 90 students received support, including fellowships with full tuition reimbursements available (averaging $22,000 per year), research assistantships (averaging $4,000 per year); teaching assistantships, career-related internships or fieldwork, institutionally sponsored loans, health care benefits, tuition waivers (full), and unspecified assistantships also available. *Unit head:* Elizabeth Elam Chang, Administrative Director, 212-854-2836, Fax: 212-932-2359, E-mail: phdinfo@gsb.columbia.edu.

Columbia University, Graduate School of Business, MBA Program, New York, NY 10027. Offers accounting (MBA); decision, risk, and operations (MBA); entrepreneurship (MBA); finance and economics (MBA); human resource management (MBA); international business (MBA); management/leadership (MBA); marketing (MBA); media (MBA); real estate (MBA); social enterprise (MBA); DDS/MBA; JD/MBA; MBA/MIA; MBA/MPH; MBA/MS; MD/MBA. *Faculty:* 117 full-time (14 women), 124 part-time/adjunct (18 women). *Students:* 1,226 full-time (420 women); includes 274 minority (75 African Americans, 4 American Indian/Alaska Native, 162 Asian Americans or Pacific Islanders, 33 Hispanic Americans), 409 international. Average age 28. 5,623 applicants, 16% accepted, 711 enrolled. In 2007, 711 degrees awarded. *Entrance requirements:* For master's, GMAT, 2 letters of recommendation, official transcripts, essay, personal statement, completed application. Additional exam requirements/recommendations for international students: Required—TOEFL. *Application deadline:* For fall admission, 4/15 for domestic students, 3/4 for international students; for spring admission, 10/8 for domestic and international students. Applications are processed on a rolling basis. Application fee: $250. Electronic applications accepted. *Expenses:* Tuition: Part-time $1,452 per credit. Required fees: $152 per term. One-time fee: $75 part-time. Full-time tuition and fees vary according to course level, course load, degree level and program. *Financial support:* Fellowships, research assistantships, teaching assistantships, career-related internships or fieldwork, institutionally sponsored loans, scholarships/grants, and unspecified assistantships available. Financial award applicants required to submit FAFSA. *Unit head:* Prof. Amir Ziv, Vice Dean of Students and the MBA Program, 212-854-3485, Fax: 212-932-0545, E-mail: az50@columbia.edu. *Application contact:* Linda B. Meehan, Assistant Dean of Admissions, 212-854-1961, Fax: 212-662-6754, E-mail: apply@gsb.columbia.edu.

Concordia University, School of Graduate Studies, Faculty of Arts and Science, Department of Communication Studies, Montréal, QC H3G 1M8, Canada. Offers communication (PhD); communication studies (Diploma); media studies (MA). *Degree requirements:* For master's, thesis optional; for doctorate, one foreign language, comprehensive exam, thesis/dissertation, research practicum, seminar. *Entrance requirements:* For master's, bachelor's degree in communications, 2 years of media-related experience; for doctorate, MA in communications. *Faculty research:* Communication and development, organizational communication, cultural studies, rhetoric, future studies.

Cornell University, Graduate School, Graduate Fields of Agriculture and Life Sciences, Field of Communication, Ithaca, NY 14853-0001. Offers communication (MPS, MS, PhD); communication research methods (MS, PhD); international communication (MS, PhD); science and environmental communication (MS, PhD); social psychology of communication (MS, PhD); uses and effects of communication (MS, PhD). *Faculty:* 19 full-time (6 women). *Students:* 28 full-time (19 women); includes 6 minority (1 African American, 3 Asian Americans or Pacific Islanders, 2 Hispanic Americans), 11 international. Average age 29. 123 applicants, 12% accepted, 7 enrolled. In 2007, 8 master's, 5 doctorates awarded. *Degree requirements:* For master's, thesis (MS); for doctorate, comprehensive exam, thesis/dissertation. *Entrance requirements:* For master's and doctorate, GRE General Test, 3 letters of recommendation. Additional exam requirements/recommendations for international students: Required—TOEFL (minimum score 600 paper-based; 250 computer-based; 100 iBT). *Application deadline:* For fall admission, 1/15 for domestic students. Application fee: $70. Electronic applications accepted. *Financial support:* In 2007–08, 24 students received support, including 3 fellowships with full tuition reimbursements available, 7 research assistantships with full tuition reimbursements available, 14 teaching assistantships with full tuition reimbursements available; institutionally sponsored loans, scholarships/grants, health care benefits, tuition waivers (full and partial), and unspecified assistantships also available. Financial award applicants required to submit FAFSA. *Faculty research:* Mass communication, communication technologies, science and environmental communication. *Unit head:* Director of Graduate Studies, 607-255-2112. *Application contact:* Graduate Field Assistant, 607-255-2112, E-mail: commgrad@cornell.edu.

DePaul University, College of Communication, Chicago, IL 60604-2287. Offers journalism (MA); media, culture, and society (MA); organizational and multicultural communication (MA); public relations and advertising (MA). Part-time and evening/weekend programs available. *Faculty:* 21 full-time (10 women), 9 part-time/adjunct (4 women). *Students:* 88 full-time (69 women), 43 part-time (38 women); includes 29 minority (16 African Americans, 5 Asian Americans or Pacific Islanders, 8 Hispanic Americans), 2 international. Average age 29. 242 applicants, 47% accepted, 68 enrolled. In 2007, 64 degrees awarded. *Degree requirements:* For master's, final exam or thesis/project. *Entrance requirements:* For master's, GRE General Test (public relations and advertising), minimum GPA of 3.0, writing sample, essay, letters of recommendation, resumé. Additional exam requirements/recommendations for international students: Required—TOEFL (minimum score 590 paper-based; 245 computer-based; 96 iBT). Application fee: $40. Electronic applications accepted. *Financial support:* In 2007–08, 8 students received support, including 2 teaching assistantships with full tuition reimbursements available (averaging $12,000 per year); fellowships with full tuition reimbursements available, research assistantships, career-related internships or fieldwork, scholarships/grants, and tuition waivers (partial) also available. Support available to part-time students. Financial award applicants required to submit FAFSA. *Faculty research:* Intercultural communication, corporate culture, diversity in the working place, organizational socialization, critical cultural studies. *Unit head:* Dr. Jacqueline Taylor, Dean, 773-325-7216, Fax: 773-325-7584, E-mail: jtaylor@depaul.edu. *Application contact:* Ann Spittle, Director of Graduate Admission, 773-325-8369, Fax: 773-325-2395, E-mail: aspittle@depaul.edu.

DeVry University, Keller Graduate School of Management, Oakbrook Terrace, IL 60181. Offers accounting and financial management (MAFM); business administration (MBA); human resources management (MHRM); information systems management (MISM); network and communications management (MNCM); project management (MPM); public administration (MPA). *Faculty:* 22 full-time, 425 part-time/adjunct. *Unit head:* Dr. Sherril Hoel, Academic Dean of Administration and Accreditation, 630-574-1894. *Application contact:* Student Application Contact, 630-571-7700.

Drake University, School of Journalism and Mass Communication, Communication Leadership Program, Des Moines, IA 50311-4516. Offers MCL. *Faculty:* 8 part-time/adjunct (3 women). *Students:* Average age 32. 20 applicants, 55% accepted, 8 enrolled. *Degree requirements:* For master's, comprehensive exam (for some programs), thesis (for some programs), internships (for some programs). Application fee: $25. *Expenses:* Tuition: Full-time $26,030; part-time $370 per credit hour. Required fees: $406; $40 per semester. Tuition and fees vary according to program. *Application contact:* Carla McCrea, Assistant to the Dean, 515-271-2838, E-mail: carla.mccrea@drake.edu.

Drexel University, College of Arts and Sciences, Department of Culture and Communication, Philadelphia, PA 19104-2875. Offers communication (MS); publication management (MS). Part-time and evening/weekend programs available. *Degree requirements:* For master's, internship, professional portfolio. *Entrance requirements:* Additional exam requirements/recommendations for international students: Required—TOEFL. Electronic applications accepted. *Faculty research:* Science information and attitudes, science influence on literature, process of technical writing, document design, software documentation.

Drury University, Program in Communication, Springfield, MO 65802. Offers MA. Part-time and evening/weekend programs available. *Students:* Average age 37. *Entrance requirements:* For master's, GMAT or MAT. Additional exam requirements/recommendations for international students: Required—TOEFL. *Application deadline:* For fall admission, 8/25 priority date for domestic students; for spring admission, 1/15 priority date for domestic students. Applications are processed on a rolling basis. Application fee: $25. Electronic applications accepted. *Expenses: Contact institution. Financial support:* Application deadline: 10/15; *Unit head:* Ron Schie, Director, 417-873-7235, Fax: 417-873-7897, E-mail: rschie@drury.edu. *Application contact:* Kay Lowder, Graduate Programs Office Coordinator, 417-873-6948, Fax: 417-873-6681, E-mail: grad@drury.edu.

Duquesne University, Graduate School of Liberal Arts, Department of Communication and Rhetorical Studies, Pittsburgh, PA 15282-0001. Offers communication (MA); rhetoric (PhD). Part-time and evening/weekend programs available. *Faculty:* 6 full-time (3 women), 5 part-time/adjunct (3 women). *Students:* 72 full-time (39 women), 50 part-time (38 women). Average age 27. In 2007, 19 master's, 6 doctorates awarded. *Degree requirements:* For master's, thesis optional, practicum; for doctorate, 2 foreign languages, comprehensive exam, thesis/dissertation. *Entrance requirements:* For master's, GRE General Test, MAT or GMAT; for doctorate, GRE General Test. Additional exam requirements/recommendations for international students: Required—TOEFL. *Application deadline:* For fall admission, 2/1 priority date for domestic and international students; for spring admission, 11/1 priority date for domestic and international students. Applications are processed on a rolling basis. Application fee: $50. *Expenses:* Tuition: Part-time $774 per credit. Required fees: $74 per credit. Tuition and fees vary according to program. *Financial support:* In 2007–08, 9 research assistantships with full tuition reimbursements (averaging $9,000 per year), 10 teaching assistantships with full tuition reimbursements (averaging $13,000 per year) were awarded; career-related internships or fieldwork, Federal Work-Study, institutionally sponsored loans, scholarships/grants, tuition waivers (full and partial), and unspecified assistantships also available. Financial award application deadline: 5/1. *Unit head:* Dr. Ronald Arnett, Chair, 412-396-5076. *Application contact:* Dr. Janie Fritz, Director, 412-396-6460.

Eastern Michigan University, Graduate School, College of Arts and Sciences, Department of Communication and Theatre Arts, Program in Communication, Ypsilanti, MI 48197. Offers MA. Part-time and evening/weekend programs available. Postbaccalaureate distance learning degree programs offered (minimal on-campus study). *Students:* 8 full-time (7 women), 32 part-time (24 women); includes 12 minority (9 African Americans, 1 American Indian/Alaska Native, 2 Asian Americans or Pacific Islanders), 3 international. Average age 33. In 2007, 35 degrees awarded. *Degree requirements:* For master's, thesis or alternative. *Entrance requirements:* Additional exam requirements/recommendations for international students: Required—TOEFL. *Application deadline:* Applications are processed on a rolling basis. Application fee: $35. *Expenses:* Tuition, state resident: full-time $8,952; part-time $373 per credit hour. Tuition, nonresident: full-time $17,634; part-time $735 per credit hour. Required fees: $896; $34 per credit hour. Tuition and fees vary according to course level, degree level and program. *Financial support:* Fellowships, research assistantships with full tuition reimbursements, teaching assistantships with full tuition reimbursements, career-related internships or fieldwork, Federal Work-Study, institutionally sponsored loans, scholarships/grants, tuition waivers (partial), and unspecified assistantships available. Support available to part-time students. Financial award applicants required to submit FAFSA. *Unit head:* Dr. Dennis Patrick, Coordinator, 734-487-4199, Fax: 734-487-3443, E-mail: dpatrickl@emich.edu. *Application contact:* Dr. Lee Stille, Graduate Coordinator, 734-487-3131, Fax: 734-487-3443, E-mail: lee.stille@emich.edu.

Eastern New Mexico University, Graduate School, College of Liberal Arts and Sciences, Department of Communicative Arts and Sciences, Portales, NM 88130. Offers MA. Part-time programs available. Postbaccalaureate distance learning degree programs offered (minimal on-campus study). *Faculty:* 6 full-time (3 women). *Students:* 3 full-time (2 women), 23 part-time (13 women); includes 5 minority (3 African Americans, 2 Hispanic Americans), 3 international. Average age 30. 14 applicants, 86% accepted. In 2007, 4 degrees awarded. *Degree requirements:* For master's, comprehensive exam, thesis optional. *Entrance requirements:* For master's, minimum GPA of 2.5. *Application deadline:* For fall admission, 8/20 priority date for domestic students. Applications are processed on a rolling basis. Application fee: $0. Electronic applications accepted. *Expenses:* Tuition, state resident: full-time $2,592; part-time $108 per credit hour. Tuition, nonresident: full-time $8,136; part-time $339 per credit hour. Required fees: $3,850 per credit hour. *Financial support:* In 2007–08, research assistantships (averaging $8,200 per year), 13 teaching assistantships (averaging $8,200 per year) were awarded; fellowships, Federal Work-Study also available. Support available to part-time students. Financial award application deadline: 3/1. *Faculty research:* Radio and television production. *Unit head:* Dr. Janet Roehl, Graduate Coordinator, 575-562-2113, E-mail: janet.roehl@enmu.edu.

Eastern Washington University, Graduate Studies, College of Social and Behavioral Sciences, Department of Communication Studies, Cheney, WA 99004-2431. Offers MS. Part-time and evening/weekend programs available. *Degree requirements:* For master's, comprehensive exam, thesis or alternative. *Entrance requirements:* For master's, GRE General Test, minimum GPA of 3.0.

East Tennessee State University, School of Graduate Studies, College of Arts and Sciences, Department of Communication, Johnson City, TN 37614. Offers MA. *Entrance requirements:* For master's, GRE. Additional exam requirements/recommendations for international students: Required—TOEFL (minimum score 550 paper-based; 213 computer-based). *Faculty research:* Political communications, visual communication, depictions of gender and ethnicity in print and online media and online corporate media, presidential rhetoric and newspaper coverage of presidential speeches.

Edinboro University of Pennsylvania, Graduate Studies and Research, School of Liberal Arts, Department of Communications and Media Studies, Edinboro, PA 16444. Offers MA. Part-time and evening/weekend programs available. *Faculty:* 4 full-time (1 woman). *Students:* 23 full-time (17 women), 11 part-time (5 women); includes 4 minority (3 African Americans, 1 Hispanic American), 4 international. Average age 29. In 2007, 26 degrees awarded. *Degree requirements:* For master's, thesis or alternative, competency exam. *Entrance requirements:* For master's, GRE or MAT, minimum QPA of 2.5. *Application deadline:* Applications are processed on a rolling basis. Application fee: $30. Electronic applications accepted. *Expenses:* Tuition, state resident: full-time $6,214; part-time $345 per credit. Tuition, nonresident: full-time $9,944; part-time $552 per credit. Required fees: $46 per credit. *Financial support:* In 2007–08,

Communication—General

Edinboro University of Pennsylvania (continued)
10 research assistantships with full and partial tuition reimbursements (averaging $3,850 per year) were awarded; career-related internships or fieldwork, Federal Work-Study, scholarships/grants, and unspecified assistantships also available. Support available to part-time students. Financial award application deadline: 2/15; financial award applicants required to submit FAFSA. *Unit head:* Dr. Anthony Peyronel, Coordinator, 814-732-2444, E-mail: apeyronel@edinboro.edu. *Application contact:* Dr. R. Scott Baldwin, Dean, 814-732-2752, Fax: 814-732-2268, E-mail: sbaldwin@edinboro.edu.

Emerson College, Graduate Studies, School of Communication, Department of Communication Studies, Boston, MA 02116-4624. Offers communication management (MA). *Entrance requirements:* Additional exam requirements/recommendations for international students: Required—TOEFL. *Application deadline:* Applications are processed on a rolling basis. Electronic applications accepted. *Expenses:* Tuition: Full-time $16,800; part-time $840 per credit. Required fees: $60 per semester. One-time fee: $160.

Fairfield University, College of Arts and Sciences, Fairfield, CT 06824-5195. Offers American studies (MA); communications (MA); creative writing (MFA); mathematics (MS). Part-time and evening/weekend programs available. *Faculty:* 40 full-time (15 women), 2 part-time/adjunct (0 women). *Students:* 7 full-time (3 women), 73 part-time (42 women); includes 5 minority (2 African Americans, 1 American Indian/Alaska Native, 1 Asian American or Pacific Islander, 1 Hispanic American), 1 international. 18 applicants, 61% accepted, 7 enrolled. In 2007, 21 degrees awarded. *Degree requirements:* For master's, capstone research course. *Entrance requirements:* For master's, minimum GPA of 3.0, 2 letters of recommendation, resumé, essay. Additional exam requirements/recommendations for international students: Required—TOEFL (minimum score 550 paper-based; 213 computer-based). *Application deadline:* For fall admission, 7/1 for domestic students, 6/15 priority date for international students; for spring admission, 12/1 for domestic students, 10/15 priority date for international students. Applications are processed on a rolling basis. Application fee: $60. *Financial support:* Tuition waivers (partial) and unspecified assistantships available. Financial award applicants required to submit FAFSA. *Unit head:* Dr. Robbin Crabtree, Dean, 203-254-4000 Ext. 3263, Fax: 203-254-4119, E-mail: rcrabtree@mail.fairfield.edu. *Application contact:* Marianne Gumpper, Director of Graduate and Continuing Studies Admissions, 203-254-4184, Fax: 203-254-4073, E-mail: gradadmis@mail.fairfield.edu.

Fairleigh Dickinson University, Metropolitan Campus, Maxwell Becton College of Arts and Sciences, Department of English, Communication, and Philosophy, Teaneck, NJ 07666-1914. Offers corporate communications (MA). Application fee: $40. *Expenses:* Tuition: Part-time $869 per credit. Tuition and fees vary according to degree level, campus/location and program.

Fairleigh Dickinson University, Metropolitan Campus, University College: Arts, Sciences, and Professional Studies, School of Art and Media Studies, Program in Media and Communications, Teaneck, NJ 07666-1914. Offers MA. *Students:* 8 full-time (3 women), 5 part-time (3 women). Average age 31. 5 applicants, 80% accepted, 1 enrolled. In 2007, 10 degrees awarded. Application fee: $40. *Expenses:* Tuition: Part-time $869 per credit. Tuition and fees vary according to degree level, campus/location and program. *Unit head:* Jason Scorza, Director, School of Art and Media Studies, 201-692-2000.

Fitchburg State College, Division of Graduate and Continuing Education, Program in Applied Communications, Fitchburg, MA 01420-2697. Offers applied communications (MS, Certificate); library media (MS); technical and professional writing (MS). Part-time and evening/weekend programs available. *Students:* 3 full-time (2 women), 13 part-time (11 women); includes 1 minority (African American), 1 international. Average age 32. 6 applicants, 100% accepted, 4 enrolled. In 2007, 13 degrees awarded. *Entrance requirements:* For master's, GRE General Test or MAT, minimum 2 years of related experience, letters of recommendation, resumé. Additional exam requirements/recommendations for international students: Required—TOEFL (minimum score 550 paper-based; 213 computer-based; 79 iBT). *Application deadline:* Applications are processed on a rolling basis. Application fee: $25 ($50 for international students). *Expenses:* Tuition, nonresident: part-time $150 per credit. Required fees: $109 per credit. *Financial support:* In 2007–08, research assistantships with partial tuition reimbursements (averaging $5,500 per year); Federal Work-Study, scholarships/grants, and unspecified assistantships also available. Support available to part-time students. Financial award application deadline: 3/1; financial award applicants required to submit FAFSA. *Unit head:* Dr. John Chetro-Szivos, Chair, 978-665-3261, Fax: 978-665-3658, E-mail: gce@fsc.edu. *Application contact:* Director of Admissions, 978-665-3144, Fax: 978-665-4540, E-mail: admissions@fsc.edu.

Florida Atlantic University, Dorothy F. Schmidt College of Arts and Letters, Department of Communication, Boca Raton, FL 33431-0991. Offers MA. Part-time programs available. *Degree requirements:* For master's, one foreign language, comprehensive exam (for some programs), thesis (for some programs). *Entrance requirements:* For master's, GRE General Test, minimum GPA of 3.0. Electronic applications accepted. *Faculty research:* Cultural studies, gender studies, film, communication theory, journalism, new media.

Florida Institute of Technology, Graduate Programs, College of Psychology and Liberal Arts, Department of Humanities and Communication, Melbourne, FL 32901-6975. Offers communication (MS). Part-time and evening/weekend programs available. *Faculty:* 3 full-time (2 women). *Students:* 5 full-time (4 women), 8 part-time (6 women); includes 3 minority (1 African American, 1 American Indian/Alaska Native, 1 Hispanic American), 1 international. Average age 38. 12 applicants, 100% accepted, 2 enrolled. In 2007, 2 degrees awarded. *Degree requirements:* For master's, comprehensive exam (for some programs), thesis (for some programs). *Entrance requirements:* For master's, GRE General Test, minimum GPA of 3.0, 2 letters of recommendation, writing sample. Additional exam requirements/recommendations for international students: Required—TOEFL (minimum score 550 paper-based; 213 computer-based). *Application deadline:* Applications are processed on a rolling basis. Application fee: $50. Electronic applications accepted. *Expenses:* Tuition: Part-time $945 per credit. *Financial support:* Career-related internships or fieldwork and tuition remissions available. Financial award application deadline: 3/1; financial award applicants required to submit FAFSA. *Faculty research:* Communication of astronomy in the 17th century, persuasion and patronage in 17th century work, technical and cross-cultural communication. Total annual research expenditures: $98,019. *Unit head:* Dr. Robert A. Taylor, Department Head, 321-674-7384, Fax: 321-674-8109, E-mail: rotaylor@fit.edu. *Application contact:* Thomas M. Shea, Director of Graduate Admissions, 321-674-7577, Fax: 321-723-9468, E-mail: tshea@fit.edu.

Florida State University, Graduate Studies, College of Communication, Department of Communication, Tallahassee, FL 32306. Offers corporate and public communication (MA, MS); integrated marketing communication (MA, MS); mass communication (PhD); media and communication studies (MA, MS); speech communication (PhD). Part-time programs available. *Faculty:* 26 full-time (7 women), 2 part-time/adjunct (0 women). *Students:* 96 full-time (66 women), 126 part-time (70 women); includes 92 minority (37 African Americans, 1 American Indian/Alaska Native, 35 Asian Americans or Pacific Islanders, 19 Hispanic Americans), 1 international. Average age 24. 230 applicants, 74% accepted, 80 enrolled. In 2007, 77 master's, 6 doctorates awarded. *Median time to degree:* Of those who began their doctoral program in fall 1999, 67% received their degree in 8 years or less. *Degree requirements:* For master's, thesis (for some programs); for doctorate, comprehensive exam, thesis/dissertation. *Entrance requirements:* For master's, GRE General Test, minimum GPA of 3.0; for doctorate, GRE General Test, minimum GPA of 3.3 in graduate course work. Additional exam requirements/recommendations for international students: Required—TOEFL (minimum score 600 paper-based; 250 computer-based; 100 iBT). *Application deadline:* For fall admission, 7/1 priority date for domestic and international students; for winter admission, 3/1 priority date for domestic and international students; for spring admission, 11/1 priority date for domestic and international students. Applications are processed on a rolling basis. Application fee: $30. *Expenses:* Tuition, state resident: part-time $248 per credit hour. Tuition, nonresident: part-time $880 per credit hour. Tuition and fees vary according to program. *Financial support:* In 2007–08, 49 students received support, including 1 fellowship with full tuition reimbursement available, 8 research assistantships with full tuition reimbursements available (averaging $14,000 per year), 40 teaching assistantships with full tuition reimbursements available (averaging $5,000 per year); career-related internships or fieldwork, Federal Work-Study, institutionally sponsored loans, scholarships/grants, tuition waivers (partial), and unspecified assistantships also available. Support available to part-time students. Financial award application deadline: 2/1; financial award applicants required to submit FAFSA. *Faculty research:* Communication technology and policy, marketing communication, communication content and effect, new communication/information technologies. Total annual research expenditures: $264,208. *Unit head:* Dr. Stephen D. McDowell, Chairperson, 850-644-2276, Fax: 850-644-8642, E-mail: smcdowel@mailer.fsu.edu. *Application contact:* Natashia Hinson-Turner, Graduate Program Assistant, 850-644-8746, Fax: 850-644-8642, E-mail: dc.gradinfo@comm.fsu.edu.

Fordham University, Graduate School of Arts and Sciences, Department of Communication and Media Studies, New York, NY 10458. Offers public communications (MA). Part-time and evening/weekend programs available. *Faculty:* 11 full-time (3 women). *Students:* 23 full-time (10 women), 34 part-time (22 women); includes 11 minority (7 African Americans, 1 Asian American or Pacific Islander, 3 Hispanic Americans), 9 international. Average age 26. 88 applicants, 78% accepted, 22 enrolled. In 2007, 35 degrees awarded. *Degree requirements:* For master's, thesis, internship. *Entrance requirements:* For master's, GRE General Test. Additional exam requirements/recommendations for international students: Required—TOEFL (minimum score 600 paper-based; 250 computer-based). *Application deadline:* For fall admission, 1/4 priority date for domestic students; for spring admission, 11/1 for domestic students. Application fee: $70. Electronic applications accepted. *Expenses:* Tuition: Full-time $23,880; part-time $995 per credit. *Financial support:* In 2007–08, 4 students received support, including 4 research assistantships with tuition reimbursements available (averaging $17,942 per year); fellowships, teaching assistantships with tuition reimbursements available, career-related internships or fieldwork, Federal Work-Study, institutionally sponsored loans, scholarships/grants, tuition waivers (full and partial), and unspecified assistantships also available. Financial award application deadline: 1/4. Total annual research expenditures: $80,000. *Unit head:* Dr. Paul Levinson, Chair, 718-817-4860, Fax: 718-817-4868, E-mail: levinson@fordham.edu. *Application contact:* Charlene Dundie, Director of Graduate Admissions, 718-817-4420, Fax: 718-817-3566, E-mail: dundie@fordham.edu.

Fort Hays State University, Graduate School, College of Arts and Sciences, Department of Communication, Hays, KS 67601-4099. Offers MS. Part-time programs available. *Faculty:* 5 full-time (1 woman). *Students:* 67 full-time (40 women), 17 part-time (15 women); includes 72 minority (71 Asian Americans or Pacific Islanders, 1 Hispanic American). Average age 31. 49 applicants, 84% accepted. In 2007, 9 degrees awarded. *Degree requirements:* For master's, comprehensive exam, thesis optional. *Entrance requirements:* Additional exam requirements/recommendations for international students: Required—TOEFL (minimum score 550 paper-based; 213 computer-based). *Application deadline:* For fall admission, 7/1 priority date for domestic students. Applications are processed on a rolling basis. Application fee: $35. Electronic applications accepted. *Expenses:* Tuition, state resident: part-time $155 per credit hour. Tuition, nonresident: part-time $409 per credit hour. Tuition and fees vary according to class time, course level, course load, degree level, campus/location and program. *Financial support:* Research assistantships, teaching assistantships, institutionally sponsored loans available. Support available to part-time students. *Faculty research:* Listening skills development, oral sensory motor skills, speech, reading, articulation in preschool children. *Unit head:* Dr. Scott Robson, Interim Chair, 785-628-5365, E-mail: sjrobson@fhsu.edu.

George Mason University, College of Humanities and Social Sciences, Program in Communications, Fairfax, VA 22030. Offers MA, PhD. *Faculty:* 33 full-time (15 women), 42 part-time/adjunct (21 women). *Students:* 9 full-time (6 women), 28 part-time (20 women); includes 3 minority (1 African American, 2 Asian Americans or Pacific Islanders), 4 international. Average age 27. 98 applicants, 51% accepted, 33 enrolled. In 2007, 4 degrees awarded. *Entrance requirements:* For master's, GRE or MAT, minimum GPA of 3.0 in last 60 undergraduate hours, 3 letters of recommendation. Application fee: $60 ($75 for international students). *Financial support:* Research assistantships, teaching assistantships available. *Unit head:* Gary Kreps, Chair, 703-993-1094, Fax: 703-993-1096. *Application contact:* Jennifer Furlong, Student Contact, 703-993-1314, E-mail: jfurlong@gmu.edu.

Georgetown University, Graduate School of Arts and Sciences, Program in Communication, Culture, and Technology, Washington, DC 20057. Offers MA. Part-time and evening/weekend programs available. *Degree requirements:* For master's, thesis (for some programs). *Entrance requirements:* For master's, GRE General Test, 3 letters of recommendation, writing sample. Additional exam requirements/recommendations for international students: Required—TOEFL (minimum score 600 paper-based; 250 computer-based). Electronic applications accepted.

See Close-Up on page 899.

Georgia State University, College of Arts and Sciences, Department of Communication, Atlanta, GA 30303-3083. Offers film/video/digital imaging (MA); human communication and social influence (MA); mass communication (MA); moving image studies (PhD); public communication (PhD). Part-time programs available. *Faculty:* 27 full-time (13 women). *Students:* 81 full-time (51 women), 61 part-time (41 women); includes 31 minority (26 African Americans, 2 Asian Americans or Pacific Islanders, 3 Hispanic Americans), 17 international. 179 applicants, 30% accepted, 29 enrolled. In 2007, 23 master's, 10 doctorates awarded. *Degree requirements:* For master's, one foreign language, thesis or alternative; for doctorate, comprehensive exam, thesis/dissertation. *Entrance requirements:* For master's and doctorate, GRE General Test. Additional exam requirements/recommendations for international students: Required—TOEFL (minimum score 80 computer-based). Application fee: $50. Electronic applications accepted. *Expenses:* Tuition, state resident: part-time $221 per credit hour. *Financial support:* In 2007–08, 1 fellowship with tuition reimbursement (averaging $15,000 per year) was awarded; research assistantships, teaching assistantships with tuition reimbursements, career-related internships or fieldwork, Federal Work-Study, institutionally sponsored loans, tuition waivers (partial), and unspecified assistantships also available. Support available to part-time students. Financial award applicants required to submit FAFSA. *Faculty research:* Critical/cultural studies, rhetoric studies, film/media studies, mass communications/journalism, audience studies. *Unit head:* Dr. David Cheshier, Chair, 404-413-5649, E-mail: dcheshier@gsu.edu. *Application contact:* Tawanna Tookes, Administrative Specialist, Managerial, 404-413-5652, E-mail: joutkt@langate.gsu.edu.

Gonzaga University, School of Professional Studies, Program in Communication and Leadership Studies, Spokane, WA 99258. Offers MA. Postbaccalaureate distance learning degree programs offered. *Faculty:* 12 full-time (5 women), 23 part-time/adjunct (7 women). *Students:* 38 full-time (27 women), 172 part-time (132 women); includes 26 minority (9 African Americans, 2 American Indian/Alaska Native, 5 Asian Americans or Pacific Islanders, 10 Hispanic Americans). Average age 34. In 2007, 12 degrees awarded.

Governors State University, College of Arts and Sciences, Program in Communication and Training, University Park, IL 60466-0975. Offers communication studies (MA); instructional and training technology (MA); media communication (MA). Part-time and evening/weekend programs available. *Students:* 30 full-time, 78 part-time. Average age 35. *Degree requirements:* For master's, thesis or alternative. *Application deadline:* For fall admission, 7/15 priority date for domestic students; for spring admission, 11/10 for domestic students. Applications are processed on a rolling basis. Application fee: $25. *Financial support:* Research assistantships, Federal Work-Study, institutionally sponsored loans, and scholarships/grants available. Support available to part-time students. Financial award application deadline: 5/1. *Unit head:* Dr. Eric V. Martin, Dean, College of Arts and Sciences, 708-534-4101.

Grand Valley State University, College of Liberal Arts and Sciences, School of Communications, Allendale, MI 49401-9403. Offers MS. Part-time and evening/weekend programs available. *Faculty:* 5 full-time (0 women), 3 part-time/adjunct (0 women). *Students:* 19 full-time (11 women), 43 part-time (23 women); includes 14 minority (11 African Americans, 3 Hispanic Americans), 3 international. Average age 33. 26 applicants, 100% accepted, 19 enrolled. In 2007, 15 degrees awarded. *Degree requirements:* For master's, thesis or alternative. *Entrance requirements:* For master's, minimum GPA of 3.0 in last 60 hours, 2 letters of recommendation. Additional exam requirements/recommendations for international students: Required—TOEFL (minimum score 550 paper-based; 213 computer-based). *Application deadline:* For fall admission, 8/15 priority date for domestic students; for winter admission, 12/15 priority date for domestic students; for spring admission, 4/15 priority date for domestic students. Applications are processed on a rolling basis. Application fee: $30. Electronic applications accepted. *Financial support:* In 2007–08, 5 research assistantships with tuition reimbursements (averaging $8,000 per year) were awarded; career-related internships or fieldwork, Federal Work-Study, and institutionally sponsored loans also available. Support available to part-time students. Financial award application deadline: 4/15. *Faculty research:* Communication technology, databases, organizational communication, systems theory, public relations and advertising. *Unit head:* Dr. Alex Nesterenko, Director, 616-331-3668, Fax: 616-895-2700, E-mail: nesterea@gvsu.edu. *Application contact:* Dr. William Michael Pritchard, Coordinator, 616-331-3668, Fax: 616-331-2700, E-mail: pritchmi@gvsu.edu.

Harvard University, Extension School, Cambridge, MA 02138-3722. Offers applied sciences (CAS); biotechnology (ALM); educational technologies (ALM); educational technology (CET); English for graduate and professional studies (DGP); environmental management (ALM, CEM); information technology (ALM); journalism (ALM); liberal arts (ALM); management (ALM, CM); mathematics for teaching (ALM); museum studies (ALM); premedical studies (Diploma); publication and communication (CPC). Part-time and evening/weekend programs available. *Faculty:* 242 part-time/adjunct. *Students:* Average age 35. In 2007, 190 master's, 78 other advanced degrees awarded. *Degree requirements:* For master's, thesis. *Entrance requirements:* For master's, 3 completed graduate courses with grade of B or higher. Additional exam requirements/recommendations for international students: Required—TOEFL (minimum score 600 paper-based; 250 computer-based), TWE (minimum score 5). *Application deadline:* Applications are processed on a rolling basis. Application fee: $75. *Expenses:* Contact institution. Full-time tuition and fees vary according to program and student level. *Financial support:* In 2007–08, 198 students received support. Scholarships/grants available. Support available to part-time students. Financial award application deadline: 8/6; financial award applicants required to submit FAFSA. *Unit head:* Michael Shinagel, Dean, 617-495-1000. *Application contact:* Program Director, 617-495-4024, Fax: 617-495-9176.

Hawai'i Pacific University, College of Communication, Honolulu, HI 96813. Offers MA. Part-time and evening/weekend programs available. *Faculty:* 6 full-time (3 women), 6 part-time/adjunct (4 women). *Students:* 101 full-time (74 women), 51 part-time (34 women); includes 40 minority (4 African Americans, 4 American Indian/Alaska Native, 28 Asian Americans or Pacific Islanders, 4 Hispanic Americans), 74 international. Average age 28. 70 applicants, 93% accepted, 43 enrolled. In 2007, 24 degrees awarded. *Degree requirements:* For master's, thesis. *Entrance requirements:* Additional exam requirements/recommendations for international students: Recommended—TOEFL (minimum score 550 paper-based; 213 computer-based; 80 iBT), TWE (minimum score 5). *Application deadline:* For fall admission, 2/15 priority date for domestic students; for spring admission, 10/15 priority date for domestic students. Applications are processed on a rolling basis. Application fee: $50. Electronic applications accepted. *Expenses:* Tuition: Full-time $14,400. Required fees: $1,885. Tuition and fees vary according to course load and program. *Financial support:* In 2007–08, 50 students received support. Career-related internships or fieldwork, Federal Work-Study, scholarships/grants, and unspecified assistantships available. Support available to part-time students. Financial award application deadline: 3/1; financial award applicants required to submit FAFSA. *Unit head:* Dr. Steven Combs, Dean, 808-544-0828, Fax: 808-544-0835, E-mail: scombs@hpu.edu. *Application contact:* Danny Lam, Assistant Director of Graduate Admissions, 808-544-1135, Fax: 808-544-0280, E-mail: graduate@hpu.edu.

See Close-Up on page 901.

Hofstra University, School of Communication, Hempstead, NY 11549. Offers MA, MFA. Part-time and evening/weekend programs available. *Faculty:* 12 full-time (7 women), 2 part-time/adjunct (1 woman). *Students:* 19 full-time (13 women), 27 part-time (17 women); includes 13 minority (7 African Americans, 3 Asian Americans or Pacific Islanders, 3 Hispanic Americans), 3 international. Average age 29. 47 applicants, 89% accepted, 25 enrolled. In 2007, 3 degrees awarded. *Degree requirements:* For master's, comprehensive exam, thesis, Thesis. *Entrance requirements:* For master's, letters of recommendation, interview, minimum GPA. Additional exam requirements/recommendations for international students: Required—TOEFL (minimum score 550 paper-based; 213 computer-based). *Application deadline:* Applications are processed on a rolling basis. Application fee: $60. Electronic applications accepted. *Expenses:* Tuition: Full-time $14,220; part-time $820 per credit. Required fees: $970; $165 per term. Tuition and fees vary according to program. *Financial support:* In 2007–08, 17 students received support, including 2 fellowships with tuition reimbursements available (averaging $2,500 per year), 1 research assistantship with full and partial tuition reimbursement available (averaging $6,660 per year); Federal Work-Study, institutionally sponsored loans, scholarships/grants, tuition waivers (full and partial), and unspecified assistantships also available. Support available to part-time students. Financial award applicants required to submit FAFSA. *Faculty research:* Performance of race and gender, medial literacy and media ecology, cultural issues and social justice, community radio, film theory and aesthetics. Total annual research expenditures: $10,000. *Unit head:* Dr. Sybil A. DelGaudio, Dean, 516-463-5431, Fax: 516-463-4866, E-mail: avfsdg@hofstra.edu. *Application contact:* Carol Drummer, Dean of Graduate Admissions, 516-463-4876, Fax: 516-463-4664, E-mail: gradstudent@hofstra.edu.

Howard University, School of Communications, Washington, DC 20059-0002. Offers MA, MFA, MS, PhD. Part-time and evening/weekend programs available. Terminal master's awarded for partial completion of doctoral program. *Degree requirements:* For master's, comprehensive exam (for some programs), thesis optional; for doctorate, one foreign language, comprehensive exam, thesis/dissertation. *Entrance requirements:* For master's, GRE General Test, minimum GPA of 3.0; for doctorate, GRE General Test, minimum GPA of 3.2. Additional exam requirements/recommendations for international students: Required—TOEFL. Electronic applications accepted. Expenses: Contact institution. *Faculty research:* Communication disorders, intercultural communication, communication skills, race and media.

Illinois Institute of Technology, Graduate College, College of Science and Letters, Lewis Department of Humanities, Chicago, IL 60616-3793. Offers information architecture (MS); technical communication (PhD); technical communication and information design (MS). Part-time and evening/weekend programs available. *Faculty:* 18 full-time (7 women), 13 part-time/adjunct (7 women). *Students:* 23 full-time (14 women), 36 part-time (26 women); includes 22 minority (16 African Americans, 3 Asian Americans or Pacific Islanders, 3 Hispanic Americans), 8 international. Average age 34. 71 applicants, 68% accepted, 27 enrolled. In 2007, 12 master's awarded. *Degree requirements:* For master's, comprehensive exam, thesis or alternative, project; for doctorate, comprehensive exam, thesis/dissertation, qualifying exam. *Entrance requirements:* For master's, GRE General Test; for doctorate, GRE General Test, bachelor's degree in technical communication or other relevant field. Additional exam requirements/recommendations for international students: Required—TOEFL (minimum score 550 paper-based; 213 computer-based; 80 iBT). *Application deadline:* For fall admission, 5/1 for domestic and international students; for spring admission, 1/5 for domestic and international students. Applications are processed on a rolling basis. Application fee: $40. Electronic applications accepted. *Expenses:* Tuition: Full-time $14,004; part-time $778 per credit. Required fees: $7 per credit. $235 per term. Tuition and fees vary according to class time, course level, course load, program and student level. *Financial support:* In 2007–08, 15 teaching assistantships with partial tuition reimbursements (averaging $9,000 per year) were awarded; career-related internships or fieldwork, Federal Work-Study, institutionally sponsored loans, scholarships/grants, health care benefits, tuition waivers (partial), and unspecified assistantships also available. Support available to part-time students. Financial award applicants required to submit FAFSA. *Faculty research:* Discourse analysis, linguistics, readability, ethics in professions, instructional and document design, knowledge management, usability testing and evaluation, history and philosophy of science. Total annual research expenditures: $1,343. *Unit head:* Kathryn Riley, Professor and Chair, 312-567-3566, Fax: 312-567-5187, E-mail: riley@iit.edu. *Application contact:* Morgan Frederick, Assistant Director of Graduate Communications, 866-472-3448, Fax: 312-567-3138, E-mail: inquiry.grad@iit.edu.

Illinois State University, Graduate School, College of Arts and Sciences, School of Communication, Normal, IL 61790-2200. Offers MA, MS. *Faculty:* 21 full-time (4 women), 1 part-time/adjunct (0 women). *Students:* 55 full-time (31 women), 23 part-time (17 women); includes 8 minority (5 African Americans, 3 Hispanic Americans), 6 international. 60 applicants, 68% accepted. In 2007, 23 degrees awarded. *Degree requirements:* For master's, thesis or alternative. *Entrance requirements:* For master's, GRE General Test, minimum GPA of 2.8 in last 60 hours of course work. Additional exam requirements/recommendations for international students: Required—TOEFL. *Application deadline:* Applications are processed on a rolling basis. Application fee: $40. *Expenses:* Tuition, state resident: full-time $3,492; part-time $194 per credit hour. Tuition, nonresident: full-time $7,272; part-time $404 per credit hour. Required fees: $1,024; $57 per credit hour. *Financial support:* In 2007–08, 7 research assistantships (averaging $7,393 per year), 39 teaching assistantships (averaging $7,915 per year) were awarded; tuition waivers (full) and unspecified assistantships also available. Financial award application deadline: 4/1. *Faculty research:* Corporation for public broadcasting, FY2007, community service grant for WGLT-FM, Illinois public broadcasting grant FY2007 for WGLT-FM; WGLT digital conversion fund. Total annual research expenditures: $281,407. *Unit head:* Dr. Larry Long, Chairperson, 309-438-3671.

Indiana State University, School of Graduate Studies, College of Arts and Sciences, Department of Communication, Terre Haute, IN 47809-1401. Offers communication studies (MA, MS); radio, television and film (MA, MS). Part-time programs available. *Faculty:* 11 full-time (4 women), 1 part-time/adjunct (0 women). *Students:* 11 full-time (7 women), 5 part-time (1 woman); includes 2 minority (both African Americans), 5 international. Average age 31. 25 applicants, 84% accepted, 6 enrolled. In 2007, 8 degrees awarded. *Degree requirements:* For master's, thesis (for some programs), oral and written exam. *Entrance requirements:* For master's, GRE General Test. Additional exam requirements/recommendations for international students: Required—TOEFL. *Application deadline:* For fall admission, 3/1 for domestic students; for spring admission, 11/1 priority date for domestic students. Applications are processed on a rolling basis. Application fee: $35. *Expenses:* Tuition, state resident: full-time $7,056; part-time $294 per semester hour. Tuition, nonresident: full-time $14,016; part-time $584 per semester hour. Required fees: $175 per semester. *Financial support:* In 2007–08, 7 teaching assistantships with partial tuition reimbursements (averaging $7,000 per year) were awarded; career-related internships or fieldwork, Federal Work-Study, institutionally sponsored loans, and tuition waivers (partial) also available. Support available to part-time students. Financial award application deadline: 3/1; financial award applicants required to submit FAFSA. *Faculty research:* Women in media, communication apprehension, media history. *Unit head:* Dr. David Worley, Chairperson, 812-237-3245.

Indiana University Bloomington, University Graduate School, College of Arts and Sciences, Department of Telecommunications, Bloomington, IN 47405-7000. Offers mass communications (PhD); telecommunications (MA, MS). *Faculty:* 11 full-time (4 women). *Students:* 61 full-time (26 women), 10 part-time (6 women); includes 6 minority (3 African Americans, 1 Asian American or Pacific Islander, 2 Hispanic Americans), 40 international. Average age 31. 61 applicants, 49% accepted, 23 enrolled. In 2007, 26 master's, 3 doctorates awarded. Terminal master's awarded for partial completion of doctoral program. *Median time to degree:* Of those who began their doctoral program in fall 1999, 33% received their degree in 8 years or less. *Degree requirements:* For master's, thesis (for some programs); for doctorate, thesis/dissertation. *Entrance requirements:* For master's and doctorate, GRE General Test. Additional exam requirements/recommendations for international students: Required—TOEFL. *Application deadline:* For fall admission, 1/15 priority date for domestic students, 12/15 for international students. Applications are processed on a rolling basis. Application fee: $50 ($60 for international students). *Financial support:* Fellowships, research assistantships, teaching assistantships, tuition waivers (full) available. *Faculty research:* Media processes and effects, media law and policy, media management, media design and production. *Unit head:* Tamera Theodore, Graduate Secretary, 812-855-2017, E-mail: ttheodor@indiana.edu.

Announcement: Our goal is to train media experts. The MS degree prepares students for careers in production (games, other interactive media) or management. MA and PhD degrees prepare students for careers in media research as media consultants or academics. The PhD program is ranked among the top 12 in the country. The department offers state-of-the-art teaching, research, and production facilities. Funding is available for all three degrees. Visit www.indiana.edu/~telecom/index.html.

Indiana University–Purdue University Fort Wayne, College of Arts and Sciences, Department of Communication, Fort Wayne, IN 46805-1499. Offers professional communication (MA, MS). Part-time programs available. *Faculty:* 6 full-time (2 women), 2 part-time/adjunct (1 woman). *Students:* 10 full-time (5 women), 20 part-time (12 women); includes 5 minority (2 African Americans, 1 American Indian/Alaska Native, 1 Asian American or Pacific Islander, 1 Hispanic American), 2 international. Average age 32. 9 applicants, 67% accepted, 6 enrolled. In 2007, 8 degrees awarded. *Degree requirements:* For master's, oral exam. *Entrance requirements:* For master's, GRE General Test, minimum GPA of 3.0. Additional exam requirements/recommendations for international students: Required—TOEFL (minimum score 550 paper-based; 213 computer-based; 77 iBT). *Application deadline:* For fall admission, 8/1 for domestic students; for spring admission, 10/1 priority date for domestic students. Applications are processed on a rolling basis. Application fee: $55. Electronic applications accepted. *Expenses:* Tuition, state resident: full-time $4,203; part-time $234 per credit. Tuition, nonresident: full-time $9,761; part-time $542 per credit. Required fees: $466; $26 per credit. Tuition and fees vary according to course load. *Financial support:* In 2007–08, 11 teaching assistantships with partial tuition reimbursements (averaging $11,950 per year) were awarded; scholarships/grants also available. Support available to part-time students. Financial award application deadline: 3/1; financial award applicants required to submit FAFSA. *Faculty research:* Family communication concepts, pedagogical politics, contentious social issues. *Unit head:* Dr. Marcia Dixson, Chair and Associate Professor, 260-481-6558, Fax: 260-481-6183, E-mail: dixson@po.ipfw.edu. *Application contact:* Dr. Steven Carr, Graduate Program Director, 260-481-6825, Fax: 260-481-6183, E-mail: carr@ipfw.edu.

Instituto Tecnológico y de Estudios Superiores de Monterrey, Campus Ciudad Obregón, Programs in Education, Program in Communications, Ciudad Obregón, Mexico. Offers ME.

Instituto Tecnológico y de Estudios Superiores de Monterrey, Campus Monterrey, Graduate and Research Division, Program in Natural and Social Sciences, Monterrey, Mexico. Offers biotechnology (MS); chemistry (MS, PhD); communications (MS); education (MA). Part-time programs available. *Degree requirements:* For master's, one foreign language, thesis; for doctorate, one foreign language, thesis/dissertation. *Entrance requirements:* For master's, EXADEP; for doctorate, EXADEP, master's degree in related field. Additional exam requirements/recommendations for international students: Required—TOEFL. *Faculty research:* Cultural industries, mineral substances, bioremediation, food processing, CQ in industrial chemical processing.

International University in Geneva, Program in Media and Communication, Geneva, Switzerland. Offers MA.

Ithaca College, Graduate Studies, Roy H. Park School of Communications, Program in Communications, Ithaca, NY 14850-7020. Offers MS. Part-time programs available. *Faculty:* 9 full-time (4 women). *Students:* 27 full-time (19 women), 10 part-time (5 women), 10 international. Average age 29. 38 applicants, 71% accepted, 18 enrolled. In 2007, 12 degrees awarded.

Communication—General

Ithaca College (continued)

Degree requirements: For master's, comprehensive exam, thesis optional. *Entrance requirements:* For master's, minimum GPA of 3.0. Additional exam requirements/recommendations for international students: Required—TOEFL (minimum score 550 paper-based; 213 computer-based; 80 iBT). *Application deadline:* For fall admission, 7/1 for domestic students; for spring admission, 12/1 for domestic students. Applications are processed on a rolling basis. Application fee: $40. *Expenses:* Tuition: Full-time $17,310; part-time $577 per credit hour. *Financial support:* In 2007–08, 28 students received support, including 18 teaching assistantships (averaging $9,173 per year); career-related internships or fieldwork, Federal Work-Study, scholarships/grants, and unspecified assistantships also available. Support available to part-time students. Financial award application deadline: 3/1; financial award applicants required to submit FAFSA. *Faculty research:* Interactive multimedia, workforce diversity, instructional design, technology in the workplace, corporate communication systems. *Unit head:* Dr. Howard Kalman, Chairperson, 607-274-3527, Fax: 607-274-1263, E-mail: gps@ithaca.edu.

The Johns Hopkins University, Zanvyl Krieger School of Arts and Sciences, Advanced Academic Programs, Program in Communication in Contemporary Society, Washington, DC 20036. Offers MA, MA/MBA. Part-time and evening/weekend programs available. *Students:* 117 applicants, 65% accepted, 71 enrolled. *Degree requirements:* For master's, thesis. *Entrance requirements:* For master's, minimum GPA of 3.0, strong writing skills. Additional exam requirements/recommendations for international students: Required—TOEFL (minimum score 250 computer-based; 100 iBT). *Application deadline:* For fall admission, 5/31 priority date for domestic students, 4/30 priority date for international students; for spring admission, 10/31 priority date for domestic and international students. Applications are processed on a rolling basis. Application fee: $70. Electronic applications accepted. *Financial support:* Applicants required to submit FAFSA. *Unit head:* Dr. Erika Falk, Associate Program Chair, 202-452-8711, E-mail: erikafalk@jhu.edu. *Application contact:* Rachel C. Jenkins, Admissions Manager, 202-452-1941, Fax: 202-452-1970, E-mail: aapadmissions@jhu.edu.

See Close-Up on page 903.

Kean University, College of Humanities and Social Sciences, Program in Communication Studies, Union, NJ 07083. Offers MA. Part-time and evening/weekend programs available. *Faculty:* 7 full-time (3 women). *Students:* 10 full-time (7 women), 11 part-time (8 women); includes 5 African Americans, 1 Hispanic American, 3 international. Average age 29. 10 applicants, 90% accepted, 7 enrolled. In 2007, 8 degrees awarded. *Degree requirements:* For master's, comprehensive exam, thesis optional. *Entrance requirements:* For master's, GRE General Test, 3 letters of recommendation, interview, personal statement/essay. *Application deadline:* For fall admission, 5/1 for domestic students; for spring admission, 11/1 for domestic students. Applications are processed on a rolling basis. Application fee: $60 ($150 for international students). Electronic applications accepted. *Expenses:* Tuition, state resident: full-time $9,384; part-time $391 per credit. Tuition, nonresident: full-time $12,720; part-time $530 per credit. Required fees: $2,382; $99 per credit. Part-time tuition and fees vary according to course load. *Financial support:* In 2007–08, 5 research assistantships with full tuition reimbursements (averaging $3,217 per year) were awarded; unspecified assistantships also available. *Unit head:* Dr. Jack E. Sargent, Program Coordinator, 408-737-0467, E-mail: jsargent@kean.edu. *Application contact:* Joanne Morris, Director of Graduate Admissions, 908-737-3355, Fax: 908-737-3354, E-mail: grad-adm@kean.edu.

Kent State University, College of Communication and Information, School of Communication Studies, Kent, OH 44242-0001. Offers MA, PhD. *Faculty:* 8 full-time (5 women). *Students:* 28 full-time (23 women), 16 part-time (10 women). Average age 32. 39 applicants, 54% accepted, 7 enrolled. In 2007, 1 degree awarded. *Degree requirements:* For master's, thesis optional; for doctorate, variable foreign language requirement, thesis/dissertation. *Entrance requirements:* For master's and doctorate, GRE General Test, minimum GPA of 3.0. Additional exam requirements/recommendations for international students: Required—TOEFL (minimum score 600 paper-based), TWE (minimum score 5). *Application deadline:* For fall admission, 7/12 for domestic students; for spring admission, 11/29 for domestic students. Applications are processed on a rolling basis. Application fee: $30. Electronic applications accepted. *Financial support:* In 2007–08, 22 students received support, including 1 fellowship with full tuition reimbursement available (averaging $11,500 per year), 2 research assistantships with full tuition reimbursements available (averaging $8,250 per year), 19 teaching assistantships with full tuition reimbursements available; career-related internships or fieldwork, Federal Work-Study, and tuition waivers (full) also available. Financial award application deadline: 2/1. *Faculty research:* Interpersonal communication, organizational communication, mass communication, new technologies and communication. *Unit head:* Stan Wearden, Director, 330-672-2659, E-mail: swearden@kent.edu. *Application contact:* Paul Haridakis, Graduate Coordinator, 330-672-0174, E-mail: pharidak@kent.edu.

Liberty University, School of Communications, Lynchburg, VA 24502. Offers MA. Part-time programs available. *Faculty:* 7 full-time (2 women). *Students:* 22 full-time (13 women), 4 part-time (3 women); includes 1 minority (African American), 7 international. Average age 25. In 2007, 6 degrees awarded. *Degree requirements:* For master's, thesis. *Entrance requirements:* For master's, minimum undergraduate GPA of 3.0, 2 faculty recommendations, 1 pastoral recommendation. Additional exam requirements/recommendations for international students: Required—TOEFL (minimum score 600 paper-based; 250 computer-based). *Application deadline:* For fall admission, 6/1 priority date for domestic students; for spring admission, 11/1 priority date for domestic students. Application fee: $50. Electronic applications accepted. *Expenses:* Tuition: Full-time $7,110; part-time $395 per credit. Required fees: $950. Tuition and fees vary according to program. *Financial support:* In 2007–08, 25 students received support. Federal Work-Study and unspecified assistantships available. *Unit head:* Dr. William G. Gribbin, Dean, 434-582-2466, E-mail: wgribbin@liberty.edu. *Application contact:* Kyle A Falce, Director of Graduate Admissions, 800-424-9596, Fax: 800-628-7977, E-mail: gradadmissions@liberty.edu.

Lindenwood University, Graduate Programs, Programs in Individualized Education, St. Charles, MO 63301-1695. Offers administration (MSA); business administration (MBA); communication (MS); communications (MA); criminal justice and administration (MS); gerontology (MA); health management (MS); human resource management (MS); information technology (MBA, Certificate); management (MSA); managing information technology (MS); marketing (MSA); writing (MFA). Part-time and evening/weekend programs available. *Faculty:* 13 full-time (7 women), 54 part-time/adjunct (32 women). *Students:* 774 full-time (495 women), 55 part-time (32 women); includes 226 minority (213 African Americans, 9 Asian Americans or Pacific Islanders, 4 Hispanic Americans), 17 international. Average age 35. In 2007, 299 degrees awarded. *Degree requirements:* For master's, thesis (for some programs), minimum GPA of 3.0, 1 colloquium per term. *Entrance requirements:* For master's, interview, minimum GPA of 3.0. Additional exam requirements/recommendations for international students: Required—TOEFL (minimum score 550 paper-based; 213 computer-based; 80 iBT). *Application deadline:* For fall admission, 9/30 priority date for domestic and international students; for winter admission, 12/30 priority date for domestic and international students; for spring admission, 3/30 priority date for domestic and international students. Applications are processed on a rolling basis. Application fee: $30 ($100 for international students). *Expenses:* Tuition: Full-time $12,400; part-time $350 per hour. Full-time tuition and fees vary according to degree level and program. *Financial support:* Career-related internships or fieldwork, institutionally sponsored loans, tuition waivers (partial), and unspecified assistantships available. Financial award application deadline: 6/30; financial award applicants required to submit FAFSA. *Unit head:* Dan Kemper, Dean of Lindenwood College for Individual Education, 636-949-4501, Fax: 636-949-4505, E-mail: dkemper@lindenwood.edu. *Application contact:* Brett Barger, Dean of Evening Admissions and Extension Campuses, 636-949-4934, Fax: 636-949-4109, E-mail: adultadmissions@lindenwood.edu.

Louisiana State University and Agricultural and Mechanical College, Graduate School, College of Arts and Sciences, Department of Communication Studies, Baton Rouge, LA 70803. Offers MA, PhD. *Faculty:* 11 full-time (7 women). *Students:* 35 full-time (20 women), 10 part-time (5 women); includes 2 African Americans, 1 Hispanic American, 2 international. Average age 32. 23 applicants, 74% accepted, 11 enrolled. In 2007, 3 master's, 2 doctorates awarded. *Degree requirements:* For master's, thesis; for doctorate, one foreign language, thesis/dissertation. *Entrance requirements:* For master's and doctorate, GRE General Test, minimum GPA of 3.0. Additional exam requirements/recommendations for international students: Required—TOEFL (minimum score 550 paper-based; 213 computer-based; 79 iBT). *Application deadline:* For fall admission, 1/25 priority date for domestic students, 5/15 for international students; for spring admission, 10/15 for international students. Applications are processed on a rolling basis. Application fee: $25. Electronic applications accepted. *Financial support:* In 2007–08, 38 students received support, including 2 fellowships with full and partial tuition reimbursements available (averaging $21,783 per year), 1 research assistantship with full and partial tuition reimbursement available (averaging $25,000 per year), 28 teaching assistantships with full and partial tuition reimbursements available (averaging $11,229 per year); career-related internships or fieldwork, Federal Work-Study, institutionally sponsored loans, scholarships/grants, health care benefits, tuition waivers (full and partial), and unspecified assistantships also available. Support available to part-time students. Financial award applicants required to submit FAFSA. *Faculty research:* Rhetorical theory and criticism, performance studies, interpersonal communication. *Unit head:* Dr. Renee Edwards, Chair, 225-578-4172, Fax: 225-578-4828, E-mail: edwards@lsu.edu. *Application contact:* Dr. Ruth Bowman, Graduate Adviser, 225-578-6812, Fax: 225-578-4828, E-mail: spbowm@lsu.edu.

Marquette University, Graduate School, College of Communication, Milwaukee, WI 53201-1881. Offers advertising and public relations (MA); broadcasting and electronic communications (MA); communications studies (MA); journalism (MA); mass communications (MA); religious communications (MA); science, health and environmental communications (MA). *Accreditation:* ACEJMC. Part-time and evening/weekend programs available. *Faculty:* 31 full-time (17 women), 34 part-time/adjunct (17 women). *Students:* 24 full-time (13 women), 19 part-time (12 women); includes 7 minority (1 African American, 1 American Indian/Alaska Native, 2 Asian Americans or Pacific Islanders, 3 Hispanic Americans), 7 international. Average age 28. 76 applicants, 58% accepted, 15 enrolled. In 2007, 17 degrees awarded. *Degree requirements:* For master's, comprehensive exam. *Entrance requirements:* For master's, GRE. Additional exam requirements/recommendations for international students: Required—TOEFL. Application fee: $40. *Financial support:* In 2007–08, 6 research assistantships, 12 teaching assistantships were awarded; career-related internships or fieldwork, Federal Work-Study, institutionally sponsored loans, scholarships/grants, and tuition waivers (full and partial) also available. Support available to part-time students. Financial award application deadline: 2/15. *Faculty research:* Urban journalism, gender and communication, intercultural communication, religious communication. Total annual research expenditures: $17,806. *Unit head:* Dr. Ana Garner, Dean, 414-288-3588, Fax: 414-288-1578.

Marshall University, Academic Affairs Division, College of Liberal Arts, Department of Communication Studies, Huntington, WV 25755. Offers MA. *Faculty:* 8 full-time (2 women), 19 part-time/adjunct (14 women). *Students:* 17 full-time (10 women), 7 part-time (5 women); includes 2 minority (both African Americans), 4 international. Average age 28. In 2007, 14 degrees awarded. *Degree requirements:* For master's, thesis optional. Application fee: $40. *Financial support:* Fellowships available. *Unit head:* Dr. Robert Bookwalter, Interim Chair, 304-696-2815, E-mail: bookwalt@marshall.edu. *Application contact:* Information Contact, 304-746-1900, Fax: 304-746-1902, E-mail: services@marshall.edu.

Marywood University, Academic Affairs, Insalaco College of Creative Arts and Management, Department of Communication Arts, Program in Communication Arts, Scranton, PA 18509-1598. Offers corporate communication (Certificate); e-business (Certificate); health communication (Certificate); instructional technology (Certificate); interdisciplinary (MA); library science/information specialist (Certificate); media management (MA); production (MA). *Students:* 10 full-time (6 women), 22 part-time (15 women); includes 4 minority (1 African American, 3 Hispanic Americans). Average age 28. In 2007, 8 degrees awarded. Application fee: $30. *Expenses:* Tuition: Full-time $15,290; part-time $695 per credit. Required fees: $990; $370 per term. Tuition and fees vary according to degree level.

McGill University, Faculty of Graduate and Postdoctoral Studies, Faculty of Arts, Department of Art History and Communication Studies, Montréal, QC H3A 2T5, Canada. Offers MA, PhD. *Faculty:* 14 full-time (8 women), 8 part-time/adjunct (4 women). *Students:* 96 full-time (66 women), 10 part-time (7 women). 215 applicants, 18% accepted, 13 enrolled. In 2007, 7 master's, 11 doctorates awarded.

Miami University, Graduate School, College of Arts and Sciences, Department of Communication, Oxford, OH 45056. Offers mass communication (MA); speech communication (MA). Part-time programs available. *Degree requirements:* For master's, final exam. *Entrance requirements:* For master's, minimum undergraduate GPA of 3.0 during previous 2 years or 2.75 overall. Additional exam requirements/recommendations for international students: Required—TOEFL (minimum score 550 paper-based; 213 computer-based), TWE (minimum score 4). Electronic applications accepted.

Michigan State University, The Graduate School, College of Communication Arts and Sciences, Department of Communication, East Lansing, MI 48824. Offers MA, PhD. *Entrance requirements:* Additional exam requirements/recommendations for international students: Required—TOEFL (minimum score 580 paper-based; 237 computer-based). Electronic applications accepted. *Expenses:* Tuition, state resident: part-time $379 per credit hour. Tuition, nonresident: part-time $800 per credit hour. Tuition and fees vary according to program.

Mississippi College, Graduate School, College of Arts and Sciences, School of Christian Studies and the Arts, Department of Communication, Clinton, MS 39058. Offers applied communication (MSC); public relations and corporate communication (MSC). Part-time programs available. *Faculty:* 5 full-time (2 women), 2 part-time/adjunct (0 women). *Students:* 20 full-time (13 women), 11 part-time (10 women); includes 5 minority (all African Americans), 15 international. Average age 27. In 2007, 3 degrees awarded. *Degree requirements:* For master's, comprehensive exam, thesis optional. *Entrance requirements:* For master's, GRE or NTE, minimum GPA of 2.5. Additional exam requirements/recommendations for international students: Recommended—IELTS. *Application deadline:* For fall admission, 4/1 for domestic students. Applications are processed on a rolling basis. Application fee: $25. Electronic applications accepted. *Expenses:* Tuition: Full-time $7,470; part-time $415 per hour. Required fees: $1,160 per term. Part-time tuition and fees vary according to course load and degree level. *Financial support:* Career-related internships or fieldwork, Federal Work-Study, and unspecified assistantships available. Support available to part-time students. Financial award application deadline: 4/1; financial award applicants required to submit FAFSA. *Unit head:* Dr. Cliff Fortenberry, Chair, 601-925-3457, E-mail: fortenbe@mc.edu.

Missouri State University, Graduate College, College of Arts and Letters, Department of Communication and Mass Media, Springfield, MO 65804-0094. Offers MA. Part-time and evening/weekend programs available. *Faculty:* 10 full-time (5 women). *Students:* 16 full-time (10 women), 22 part-time (15 women); includes 2 minority (1 African American, 1 Hispanic American), 1 international. Average age 28. 24 applicants, 96% accepted, 13 enrolled. In 2007, 18 degrees awarded. *Degree requirements:* For master's, comprehensive exam, thesis or alternative. *Entrance requirements:* For master's, GRE General Test, minimum GPA of 3.0. Additional exam requirements/recommendations for international students: Required—TOEFL (minimum score 550 paper-based; 213 computer-based; 79 iBT). *Application deadline:* For fall admission, 7/20 for domestic students; for spring admission, 12/20 for domestic students. Applications are processed on a rolling basis. Application fee: $35. Electronic applications accepted. *Expenses:* Tuition, state resident: full-time $3,708; part-time $206 per credit hour. Tuition, nonresident: full-time $7,236; part-time $206 per credit hour. Required fees: $622. Full-time tuition and fees vary according to course level, course load, program and reciprocity agreements. *Financial support:* In 2007–08, 1 research assistantship with full tuition reimbursement (averaging $7,050 per year), 14 teaching assistantships with full tuition reimbursements (averaging $7,050 per year) were awarded; career-related internships or fieldwork, Federal Work-Study, institutionally sponsored loans, scholarships/grants, tuition waivers (partial), and unspecified assistantships also available. Support available to part-time students. Financial award application deadline: 3/31; financial award applicants required to submit FAFSA. *Unit head:* Dr. Kelly McNeilis, Head, 417-836-4423, Fax: 417-836-4774, E-mail: communication@missouristate.edu.

Missouri State University, Graduate College, Interdisciplinary Program in Administrative Studies, Springfield, MO 65804-0094. Offers applied communication (MSAS); criminal justice (MSAS); environmental management (MSAS); project management (MSAS); sports management (MSAS). Part-time programs available. Postbaccalaureate distance learning degree programs offered (no on-campus study). *Students:* 21 full-time (10 women), 64 part-time (35 women); includes 5 minority (4 African Americans, 1 Hispanic American), 1 international. Average age 35. 17 applicants, 94% accepted, 13 enrolled. In 2007, 21 degrees awarded. *Degree requirements:* For master's, comprehensive exam, thesis or alternative. *Entrance requirements:* For master's, GRE, GMAT, 3 years of work experience. Additional exam requirements/recommendations for international students: Required—TOEFL (minimum score 550 paper-based; 213 computer-based; 79 iBT). *Application deadline:* For fall admission, 7/20 priority date for domestic students; for spring admission, 12/20 priority date for domestic students. Applications are processed on a rolling basis. Application fee: $35. Electronic applications accepted. *Expenses:* Tuition, state resident: full-time $3,708; part-time $206 per credit hour. Tuition, nonresident: full-time $7,236; part-time $206 per credit hour. Required fees: $622. Full-time tuition and fees vary according to course level, course load, program and reciprocity agreements. *Financial support:* In 2007–08, 4 teaching assistantships (averaging $7,050 per year) were awarded; research assistantships, career-related internships or fieldwork, Federal Work-Study, institutionally sponsored loans, scholarships/grants, and unspecified assistantships also available. Support available to part-time students. Financial award application deadline: 3/31; financial award applicants required to submit FAFSA. *Unit head:* John Bourhis, Director, 417-836-6390, E-mail: johnbourhis@missouristate.edu.

Monmouth University, Graduate School, Department of Corporate and Public Communication, West Long Branch, NJ 07764-1898. Offers corporate and public communication (MA); human resources communication (Certificate); media studies (Certificate); public relations (Certificate). *Faculty:* 7 full-time (5 women), 2 part-time/adjunct (1 woman). *Students:* 6 full-time (5 women), 40 part-time (29 women); includes 4 minority (3 African Americans, 1 Hispanic American), 3 international. Average age 30. 22 applicants, 95% accepted, 12 enrolled. In 2007, 18 degrees awarded. *Degree requirements:* For master's, comprehensive exam, project. *Entrance requirements:* For master's, GRE, minimum GPA of 3.0 in major, 2.75 overall. Additional exam requirements/recommendations for international students: Required—TOEFL (minimum score 550 paper-based; 213 computer-based; 79 iBT), IELTS (minimum score 5), MELAB 77, Cambridge A, B, C. *Application deadline:* For fall admission, 7/15 priority date for domestic students, 6/1 for international students; for spring admission, 11/15 priority date for domestic students, 11/1 for international students. Applications are processed on a rolling basis. Application fee: $50. Electronic applications accepted. *Financial support:* In 2007–08, 34 students received support, including 33 fellowships (averaging $1,330 per year), 11 research assistantships (averaging $4,456 per year); scholarships/grants and unspecified assistantships also available. Support available to part-time students. Financial award application deadline: 3/1; financial award applicants required to submit FAFSA. *Faculty research:* Service learning, history of television, feminism and the media, executive communication, public relations pedagogy. *Unit head:* Dr. Eleanor Novek, Program Director, 732-263-5449, Fax: 732-571-3609, E-mail: enovek@monmouth.edu. *Application contact:* Kevin Roane, Director, Office of Graduate Admission, 732-571-3452, Fax: 732-263-5123, E-mail: gradadm@monmouth.edu.

Montana State University–Billings, College of Arts and Sciences, Department of Communication and Theater, Billings, MT 59101-0298. Offers public relations (MS). Part-time programs available. Postbaccalaureate distance learning degree programs offered. *Students:* 36. 12 applicants, 100% accepted, 12 enrolled. In 2007, 11 degrees awarded. *Degree requirements:* For master's, thesis optional. *Entrance requirements:* For master's, GRE General Test, minimum undergraduate GPA of 3.0, 3 letters of recommendation. *Application deadline:* For fall admission, 3/15 for domestic students, 7/15 for international students; for spring admission, 10/15 for domestic students, 12/1 for international students. Applications are processed on a rolling basis. Application fee: $40. *Expenses:* Tuition, state resident: full-time $4,665. Tuition, nonresident: full-time $11,096. *Financial support:* Teaching assistantships, career-related internships or fieldwork, Federal Work-Study, institutionally sponsored loans, and scholarships/grants available. Support available to part-time students. Financial award application deadline: 5/1; financial award applicants required to submit FAFSA. *Unit head:* Dr. David Weiss, Chair, 406-657-2962. *Application contact:* David M. Sullivan, Graduate Studies Counselor, 406-657-2053, Fax: 406-657-2299, E-mail: dsullivan@msubillings.edu.

Montclair State University, The Office of Graduate Admissions and Support Services, School of the Arts, Department of Communication Studies, Montclair, NJ 07043-1624. Offers organizational communication (MA); public relations (MA); speech communication (MA). Part-time and evening/weekend programs available. *Faculty:* 5 full-time (3 women), 39 part-time/adjunct (21 women). *Students:* 8 full-time (6 women), 15 part-time (10 women); includes 3 minority (2 African Americans, 1 Hispanic American), 4 international. 41 applicants, 22% accepted, 6 enrolled. In 2007, 7 degrees awarded. *Degree requirements:* For master's, comprehensive exam. *Entrance requirements:* For master's, GRE General Test, minimum GPA of 3.0; undergraduate degree or work in theatre, oral interpretation, speech communication, media, or broadcasting; 2 letters of recommendation. Additional exam requirements/recommendations for international students: Required—TOEFL (minimum score 83 computer-based). *Application deadline:* For fall admission, 6/1 for international students; for spring admission, 10/1 for international students. Applications are processed on a rolling basis. Application fee: $60. Electronic applications accepted. *Financial support:* In 2007–08, 1 research assistantship with full tuition reimbursement (averaging $7,000 per year) was awarded; Federal Work-Study, scholarships/grants, and unspecified assistantships also available. Support available to part-time students. Financial award application deadline: 3/1; financial award applicants required to submit FAFSA. *Unit head:* Dr. Christine Lemesianou, Chairperson, 973-655-5214. *Application contact:* Dr. Michael Kent, Adviser, 973-655-5130, E-mail: kentm@mail.montclair.edu.

Morehead State University, Graduate Programs, Caudill College of Humanities, Department of Communication and Theatre, Morehead, KY 40351. Offers communication (MA). Part-time and evening/weekend programs available. *Faculty:* 7 full-time (2 women). *Students:* 20 full-time (10 women), 11 part-time (8 women); includes 3 minority (2 African Americans, 1 Hispanic American), 2 international. Average age 28. In 2007, 9 degrees awarded. *Degree requirements:* For master's, comprehensive exam, thesis optional. *Entrance requirements:* For master's, GRE General Test, sample of written work. Additional exam requirements/recommendations for international students: Required—TOEFL (minimum score 500 paper-based; 173 computer-based). *Application deadline:* For fall admission, 8/1 priority date for domestic and international students; for spring admission, 12/1 priority date for domestic and international students. Applications are processed on a rolling basis. Application fee: $0 ($55 for international students). *Financial support:* In 2007–08, 6 teaching assistantships (averaging $6,000 per year) were awarded; career-related internships or fieldwork, Federal Work-Study, and unspecified assistantships also available. Financial award application deadline: 4/1; financial award applicants required to submit FAFSA. *Faculty research:* Mass media effects, organizational communications, advertising/public relations. *Unit head:* Dr. Robert Willenbrink, Chair, 606-783-2134, Fax: 606-783-2457, E-mail: r.willenbrink@moreheadstate.edu. *Application contact:* Michelle Barber, Graduate Admissions Counselor, 606-783-2039, Fax: 606-783-5061, E-mail: m.barber@moreheadstate.edu.

National University, Academic Affairs, School of Media and Communication, La Jolla, CA 92037-1011. Offers MFA, MS. Part-time and evening/weekend programs available. Postbaccalaureate distance learning degree programs offered (no on-campus study). *Faculty:* 11 full-time (5 women), 63 part-time/adjunct (25 women). *Students:* 69 full-time (35 women), 158 part-time (86 women); includes 54 minority (25 African Americans, 2 American Indian/Alaska Native, 7 Asian Americans or Pacific Islanders, 20 Hispanic Americans). Average age 39. 159 applicants, 90% accepted, 167 enrolled. In 2007, 58 degrees awarded. *Degree requirements:* For master's, thesis (for some programs). *Entrance requirements:* For master's, interview, minimum GPA of 2.5. Additional exam requirements/recommendations for international students: Required—TOEFL (minimum score 550 paper-based; 213 computer-based; 80 iBT), IELTS (minimum score 6). *Application deadline:* Applications are processed on a rolling basis. Application fee: $60 ($65 for international students). Electronic applications accepted. *Expenses:* Tuition: Full-time $8,262; part-time $306 per unit. One-time fee: $60. *Financial support:* Career-related internships or fieldwork, institutionally sponsored loans, scholarships/grants, and tuition waivers (partial) available. Support available to part-time students. Financial award application deadline: 6/30; financial award applicants required to submit FAFSA. *Faculty research:* Digital media / film / journalism. *Unit head:* Debra B. Schneiger, Dean, 858-642-8424, Fax: 858-642-8743, E-mail: dschneiger@nu.edu. *Application contact:* Dominick Giovanniello, Associate Regional Dean—San Diego, 800-NAT-UNIV, Fax: 858-642-8709, E-mail: dgiovann@nu.edu.

New Mexico State University, Graduate School, College of Arts and Sciences, Department of Communication Studies, Las Cruces, NM 88003-8001. Offers MA. Part-time programs available. *Faculty:* 5 full-time (3 women), 1 part-time/adjunct (0 women). *Students:* 20 full-time (15 women), 10 part-time (9 women); includes 1 Asian American or Pacific Islander, 7 Hispanic Americans, 6 international. Average age 32. 25 applicants, 68% accepted, 10 enrolled. In 2007, 9 degrees awarded. *Degree requirements:* For master's, comprehensive exam (for some programs), thesis (for some programs). *Entrance requirements:* For master's, minimum GPA of 3.0. *Application deadline:* For fall admission, 7/1 priority date for domestic students; for spring admission, 4/1 priority date for domestic students. Applications are processed on a rolling basis. Application fee: $30 ($50 for international students). Electronic applications accepted. *Expenses:* Tuition, state resident: full-time $3,602; part-time $199 per credit. Tuition, nonresident: full-time $13,380; part-time $607 per credit. Required fees: $1,178. *Financial support:* In 2007–08, 2 fellowships, 1 research assistantship, 14 teaching assistantships with partial tuition reimbursements were awarded; Federal Work-Study and health care benefits also available. Financial award application deadline: 3/1. *Faculty research:* Interpersonal, organizational, intercultural, political, and health communication. *Unit head:* Dr. Anne P. Hubbell, Head, 575-646-2801, Fax: 575-646-1603, E-mail: ahubbell@nmsu.edu.

The New School: A University, The New School for General Studies, Program in Media Studies, New York, NY 10011. Offers communication theory (MA); media studies (MA). Part-time and evening/weekend programs available. *Faculty:* 19 full-time (8 women), 44 part-time/adjunct (16 women). *Students:* 201 full-time (136 women), 230 part-time (138 women); includes 99 minority (42 African Americans, 2 American Indian/Alaska Native, 25 Asian Americans or Pacific Islanders, 30 Hispanic Americans), 76 international. Average age 30. In 2007, 124 degrees awarded. *Degree requirements:* For master's, thesis optional. *Entrance requirements:* For master's, interview. Additional exam requirements/recommendations for international students: Required—TOEFL (minimum score 600 paper-based; 250 computer-based; 100 iBT). *Application deadline:* For fall admission, 4/15 for domestic students; for spring admission, 10/15 for domestic students. Applications are processed on a rolling basis. Application fee: $50. *Financial support:* Fellowships, research assistantships, teaching assistantships, Federal Work-Study, scholarships/grants, and tuition waivers (partial) available. Financial award application deadline: 3/1; financial award applicants required to submit FAFSA. *Faculty research:* Effect of technology on society, effect of U.S. media on international affairs, effect of media on corporate affairs. *Unit head:* Dr. Peter L. Haratonik, Interim Chair, Media Studies and Film, 212-229-8903, Fax: 212-465-0661, E-mail: haraton@newschool.edu. *Application contact:* David Norris, Director of Admissions, 212-229-5630, Fax: 212-989-3887, E-mail: nsadmissions@newschool.edu.

See Close-Up on page 907.

New York Institute of Technology, Graduate Division, School of Arts, Sciences, and Communication, Program in Communication Arts, Old Westbury, NY 11568-8000. Offers MA. Part-time and evening/weekend programs available. *Students:* 75 full-time (52 women), 92 part-time (54 women); includes 29 minority (13 African Americans, 7 Asian Americans or Pacific Islanders, 9 Hispanic Americans), 65 international. Average age 31. 191 applicants, 78% accepted, 100 enrolled. In 2007, 153 degrees awarded. *Degree requirements:* For master's, thesis or alternative. *Entrance requirements:* For master's, minimum QPA of 2.85. Additional exam requirements/recommendations for international students: Required—TOEFL (minimum score 550 paper-based; 213 computer-based). *Application deadline:* For fall admission, 7/1 priority date for domestic students; for spring admission, 12/1 priority date for domestic students. Applications are processed on a rolling basis. Application fee: $50. Electronic applications accepted. *Expenses:* Tuition: Part-time $739 per credit. Required fees: $75 per semester. *Financial support:* Research assistantships with partial tuition reimbursements, career-related internships or fieldwork, Federal Work-Study, institutionally sponsored loans, tuition waivers (partial), and unspecified assistantships available. Support available to part-time students. Financial award applicants required to submit FAFSA. *Faculty research:* Distance learning technology, computer animation, intercultural communication, multimedia technology. *Unit head:* James Fauvell, Director, 516-686-7567, Fax: 516-686-7567. *Application contact:* Jacquelyn Nealon, Dean of Admissions and Financial Aid, 516-686-7925, Fax: 516-686-7613, E-mail: jnealon@nyit.edu.

New York University, Steinhardt School of Culture, Education and Human Development, Department of Media, Culture and Communication, New York, NY 10012-1019. Offers media ecology/culture and communication (PhD); media, culture, and communication (MA). Part-time and evening/weekend programs available. *Faculty:* 24 full-time (11 women), 41 part-time/adjunct (17 women). *Students:* 66 full-time (44 women), 56 part-time (37 women); includes 17 minority (7 African Americans, 8 Asian Americans or Pacific Islanders, 2 Hispanic Americans), 34 international. 321 applicants, 40% accepted, 44 enrolled. In 2007, 78 master's, 3 doctorates awarded. *Entrance requirements:* Additional exam requirements/recommendations for international students: Required—TOEFL. *Application deadline:* For fall admission, 12/15 priority date for domestic and international students; for spring admission, 11/1 for domestic and international students. Applications are processed on a rolling basis. Application fee: $50. *Financial support:* Fellowships with full and partial tuition reimbursements, teaching assistantships with full and partial tuition reimbursements, career-related internships or fieldwork, Federal Work-Study, institutionally sponsored loans, scholarships/grants, tuition waivers (partial), and unspecified assistantships available. Support available to part-time students. Financial award application deadline: 2/1; financial award applicants required to submit FAFSA. *Faculty research:* Digital media, intercultural communication, race and politics, media criticism, media literacy. *Unit head:* Dr. Ted Magder, Chairperson, 212-998-5191, Fax: 212-995-4046, E-mail: ted.magder@nyu.edu. *Application contact:* 212-998-5030, Fax: 212-995-4328, E-mail: steinhardt.gradadmissions@nyu.edu.

Norfolk State University, School of Graduate Studies, School of Liberal Arts, Department of Media and Communication, Norfolk, VA 23504. Offers MA. Part-time programs available. *Degree requirements:* For master's, thesis. *Entrance requirements:* For master's, GRE, minimum GPA of 2.5, letters of recommendation. Additional exam requirements/recommendations for international students: Required—TOEFL.

North Carolina State University, Graduate School, College of Humanities and Social Sciences, Department of Communication, Raleigh, NC 27695. Offers organizational communication (MS). *Degree requirements:* For master's, thesis optional. *Entrance requirements:* For master's, GRE, minimum undergraduate GPA of 3.0 during last 60 hours. Electronic applications accepted. *Faculty research:* Instructional communication, political communication, organizational conflict management, intercultural communication, communication technology.

North Dakota State University, College of Graduate and Interdisciplinary Studies, College of Arts, Humanities and Social Sciences, Department of Communication, Fargo, ND 58105.

Communication—General

North Dakota State University (continued)
Offers communication (PhD); mass communication (MA, MS); speech communication (MA, MS). Part-time programs available. Postbaccalaureate distance learning degree programs offered (no on-campus study). *Faculty:* 11 full-time (5 women), 3 part-time/adjunct (1 woman). *Students:* 42 full-time (24 women), 50 part-time (35 women); includes 2 minority (both Asian Americans or Pacific Islanders), 7 international. Average age 27. 62 applicants, 40% accepted, 19 enrolled. In 2007, 15 master's, 7 doctorates awarded. Terminal master's awarded for partial completion of doctoral program. *Median time to degree:* Of those who began their doctoral program in fall 1999, 25% received their degree in 8 years or less. *Degree requirements:* For master's, thesis (for some programs); for doctorate, comprehensive exam, thesis/dissertation, 2-3 publications referred before comps. *Entrance requirements:* For master's, GRE, minimum undergraduate GPA of 3.25; for doctorate, GRE, minimum undergraduate GPA of 3.5. Additional exam requirements/recommendations for international students: Required—TOEFL (minimum score 600 paper-based; 250 computer-based; 100 iBT), IELTS (minimum score 7). *Application deadline:* For fall admission, 2/15 priority date for domestic students; for winter admission, 10/15 priority date for domestic students. Applications are processed on a rolling basis. Application fee: $45 ($60 for international students). Electronic applications accepted. *Expenses:* Tuition, state resident: full-time $5,376; part-time $224 per credit. Tuition, nonresident: full-time $14,354; part-time $598 per credit. Required fees: $962; $40 per credit. Part-time tuition and fees vary according to course load and reciprocity agreements. *Financial support:* In 2007–08, 38 students received support, including 1 fellowship with full tuition reimbursement available (averaging $16,000 per year), 10 research assistantships with full tuition reimbursements available (averaging $12,000 per year), 10 teaching assistantships with full tuition reimbursements available (averaging $8,100 per year); career-related internships or fieldwork, Federal Work-Study, institutionally sponsored loans, tuition waivers (full), and unspecified assistantships also available. Financial award application deadline: 2/1. *Faculty research:* Communication and rhetorical theory, organizational communication, broadcast and print journalism, international communication, PR and advertising. Total annual research expenditures: $148,496. *Unit head:* Dr. Paul E. Nelson, Chair, 701-231-7705, Fax: 701-231-7784, E-mail: paul.nelson.1@ndsu.edu. *Application contact:* Dr. Judy C. Pearson, Director of Graduate Studies, 701-231-6551, Fax: 701-231-1074, E-mail: judy.pearson@ndsu.edu.

Northeastern State University, Graduate College, College of Liberal Arts, Department of Communication, Tahlequah, OK 74464-2399. Offers MA. Part-time and evening/weekend programs available. *Students:* 5 full-time (all women), 11 part-time (7 women); includes 5 American Indian/Alaska Native. In 2007, 8 degrees awarded. *Degree requirements:* For master's, comprehensive exam. *Entrance requirements:* For master's, GRE, MAT, minimum GPA of 2.5. Additional exam requirements/recommendations for international students: Required—TOEFL (minimum score 213 computer-based). *Application deadline:* For fall admission, 6/1 priority date for domestic students. Applications are processed on a rolling basis. Application fee: $0 ($25 for international students). Electronic applications accepted. *Financial support:* Teaching assistantships, Federal Work-Study available. Financial award application deadline: 3/1. *Unit head:* Dr. Mike Chanselar, Chair, 918-456-5511 Ext. 3600, Fax: 918-458-2348.

Northern Arizona University, Graduate College, College of Social and Behavioral Sciences, School of Communication, Flagstaff, AZ 86011. Offers applied communication (MA).

Northern Illinois University, Graduate School, College of Liberal Arts and Sciences, Department of Communication, De Kalb, IL 60115-2854. Offers communication studies (MA). Part-time programs available. *Faculty:* 24 full-time (11 women), 1 part-time/adjunct (0 women). *Students:* 32 full-time (19 women), 20 part-time (15 women); includes 7 minority (3 African Americans, 2 Asian Americans or Pacific Islanders, 2 Hispanic Americans), 1 international. Average age 29. 42 applicants, 67% accepted, 18 enrolled. In 2007, 29 degrees awarded. *Degree requirements:* For master's, comprehensive exam, thesis optional. *Entrance requirements:* For master's, GRE General Test, minimum GPA of 2.75. Additional exam requirements/recommendations for international students: Required—TOEFL (minimum score 550 paper-based; 213 computer-based). *Application deadline:* For fall admission, 6/1 for domestic students, 5/1 for international students; for spring admission, 11/1 for domestic students, 10/1 for international students. Applications are processed on a rolling basis. Application fee: $30. Electronic applications accepted. *Expenses:* Tuition, area resident: Part-time $226 per credit hour. Tuition, state resident: full-time $5,424; part-time $225 per credit hour. Tuition, nonresident: full-time $10,848. Required fees: $2,416; $64 per credit hour. *Financial support:* In 2007–08, 34 teaching assistantships with full tuition reimbursements were awarded; fellowships with full tuition reimbursements, research assistantships with full tuition reimbursements, career-related internships or fieldwork, Federal Work-Study, scholarships/grants, tuition waivers (full), and unspecified assistantships also available. Support available to part-time students. Financial award applicants required to submit FAFSA. *Faculty research:* Journalism, history film studies, rhetoric or criticism, globalization, mass media law. *Unit head:* Dr. Steven M Ralston, Chair, 815-753-7028, Fax: 815-753-7109, E-mail: sralston@niu.edu. *Application contact:* Dr. Jeffrey Chown, Director, Graduate Studies, 815-753-1711, E-mail: schown@niu.edu.

Northern Kentucky University, Office of Graduate Programs, College of Informatics, Program in Communication, Highland Heights, KY 41099. Offers MA Comm. Part-time and evening/weekend programs available. *Faculty:* 11 full-time (4 women). *Students:* 8 full-time (4 women), 33 part-time (25 women); includes 3 minority (2 African Americans, 1 Asian American or Pacific Islander). Average age 29. 34 applicants, 65% accepted, 14 enrolled. *Degree requirements:* For master's, comprehensive exam (for some programs), thesis (for some programs). *Entrance requirements:* For master's, GRE, minimum GPA of 3.0, 3 letters of recommendation, 500-word statement of interest. Additional exam requirements/recommendations for international students: Required—TOEFL (minimum score 550 paper-based; 213 computer-based; 79 iBT). *Application deadline:* For fall admission, 2/1 priority date for domestic students, 6/1 for international students; for spring admission, 7/1 priority date for domestic students, 10/1 for international students. Applications are processed on a rolling basis. Application fee: $30. Electronic applications accepted. *Financial support:* Unspecified assistantships available. *Faculty research:* Organizational communication, public relations, interpersonal communication, gender communication, communication theory. *Unit head:* Dr. Cady Short-Thompson, Program Director, 859-572-6614, Fax: 859-572-5378, E-mail: shorthomp@nku.edu. *Application contact:* Dr. Peg Griffin, Director of Graduate Programs, 859-572-1555, Fax: 859-572-6670, E-mail: gradprog@nku.edu.

Northwestern University, The Graduate School, School of Communication, Department of Communication Studies, Evanston, IL 60208. Offers communication studies (MA, PhD); communication systems strategy and management (MSC); managerial communication (MSC). MA and PhD admissions and degrees offered through The Graduate School. Terminal master's awarded for partial completion of doctoral program. *Degree requirements:* For doctorate, thesis/dissertation. *Entrance requirements:* For master's and doctorate, GRE General Test. Additional exam requirements/recommendations for international students: Required—TOEFL. Electronic applications accepted.

The Ohio State University, Graduate School, College of Social and Behavioral Sciences, School of Communication, Program in Communication, Columbus, OH 43210. Offers MA, PhD. *Faculty:* 25. *Students:* 40 full-time (25 women), 3 part-time (all women); includes 4 minority (1 African American, 2 Asian Americans or Pacific Islanders, 1 Hispanic American), 14 international. Average age 28. In 2007, 4 degrees awarded. *Degree requirements:* For doctorate, thesis/dissertation. *Entrance requirements:* For master's and doctorate, GRE General Test. Additional exam requirements/recommendations for international students: Required—TOEFL (minimum score 620 paper-based; 250 computer-based). *Application deadline:* For fall admission, 8/15 priority date for domestic students, 7/1 priority date for international students; for winter admission, 12/1 priority date for domestic students, 11/1 priority date for international students; for spring admission, 3/1 priority date for domestic students, 2/1 priority date for international students. Applications are processed on a rolling basis. Application fee: $40 ($50 for international students). Electronic applications accepted. *Financial support:* Fellowships, research assistantships, teaching assistantships, Federal Work-Study and institutionally sponsored loans available. Support available to part-time students. *Unit head:* William P. Eveland, Graduate Studies Committee Chair, 614-292-6004, Fax: 614-292-2055, E-mail: eveland.6@osu.edu. *Application contact:* 614-292-9444, Fax: 614-292-3895, E-mail: domestic.grad@osu.edu.

See Close-Up on page 915.

The Ohio State University, Graduate School, College of Social and Behavioral Sciences, School of Communication, Program in Journalism and Communication, Columbus, OH 43210. Offers MA. *Students:* 2 full-time (both women); both minorities (both African Americans) Average age 22. *Entrance requirements:* For master's, GRE General Test. *Application deadline:* Applications are processed on a rolling basis. Application fee: $40 ($50 for international students). Electronic applications accepted. *Unit head:* William Eveland, Graduate Studies Committee Chair, 614-292-6004, Fax: 614-292-2055, E-mail: eveland.6@osu.edu. *Application contact:* Graduate Admissions, 614-292-9444, Fax: 614-292-2895, E-mail: domestic.grad@osu.edu.

Ohio University, Graduate College, Scripps College of Communication, Athens, OH 45701-2979. Offers MA, MCTP, MS, PhD. Part-time programs available. *Faculty:* 93 full-time (33 women). *Students:* 116 full-time (61 women), 36 part-time (20 women); includes 12 minority (6 African Americans, 3 Asian Americans or Pacific Islanders, 3 Hispanic Americans), 72 international. 316 applicants, 39% accepted, 85 enrolled. In 2007, 39 master's, 13 doctorates awarded. *Degree requirements:* For master's, comprehensive exam (for some programs); for doctorate, comprehensive exam, thesis/dissertation. *Entrance requirements:* For master's and doctorate, GRE General Test. Additional exam requirements/recommendations for international students: Required—TOEFL. *Application deadline:* For fall admission, 2/1 priority date for domestic students, 1/1 priority date for international students. Applications are processed on a rolling basis. Application fee: $50 ($55 for international students). Electronic applications accepted. *Expenses:* Contact institution. *Financial support:* In 2007–08, 64 students received support, including 7 fellowships (averaging $7,000 per year), 22 research assistantships with full and partial tuition reimbursements available (averaging $8,600 per year), 28 teaching assistantships with full tuition reimbursements available (averaging $14,000 per year); career-related internships or fieldwork, Federal Work-Study, institutionally sponsored loans, and tuition waivers (full and partial) also available. Financial award application deadline: 2/1; financial award applicants required to submit FAFSA. *Faculty research:* Health communication, organizational communication, mass communication, media studies, international communication. Total annual research expenditures: $115,000. *Unit head:* Dr. Gregory J. Shepherd, Dean, 740-593-4883, Fax: 740-593-0459, E-mail: shepherg@ohio.edu. *Application contact:* Dr. David H. Mould, Associate Dean, 740-593-4885, Fax: 740-593-0459, E-mail: mould@ohio.edu.

Penn State University Park, Graduate School, College of Communications, State College, University Park, PA 16802-1503. Offers MA, PhD. *Accreditation:* ACEJMC (one or more programs are accredited). *Students:* 63 full-time (35 women), 12 part-time (7 women); includes 11 minority (5 African Americans, 1 American Indian/Alaska Native, 3 Asian Americans or Pacific Islanders, 2 Hispanic Americans), 19 international. Average age 31. 190 applicants, 29% accepted, 22 enrolled. In 2007, 12 master's, 10 doctorates awarded. *Entrance requirements:* For master's and doctorate, GRE General Test. Additional exam requirements/recommendations for international students: Required—TOEFL (minimum score 550 paper-based; 213 computer-based; 80 iBT). *Application deadline:* Applications are processed on a rolling basis. Application fee: $45. Electronic applications accepted. *Expenses:* Tuition, state resident: full-time $14,738; part-time $614 per credit. Tuition, nonresident: full-time $26,050; part-time $1,085 per credit. Tuition and fees vary according to course load, program and student level. *Financial support:* Fellowships, research assistantships, teaching assistantships available. Financial award applicants required to submit FAFSA. *Unit head:* Dr. Douglas A. Anderson, Dean, 814-863-1484, Fax: 814-863-8044, E-mail: doug-anderson@psu.edu. *Application contact:* Cynthia E. Nicosia, Director Graduate Enrollment Services, 814-865-1834, Fax: 814-865-4627, E-mail: cey1@psu.edu.

Penn State University Park, Graduate School, College of the Liberal Arts, Department of Communication Arts and Sciences, State College, University Park, PA 16802-1503. Offers MA, PhD. *Expenses:* Tuition, state resident: full-time $14,738; part-time $614 per credit. Tuition, nonresident: full-time $26,050; part-time $1,085 per credit. Tuition and fees vary according to course load, program and student level. *Unit head:* Dr. James P. Dillard, Head, 814-865-5232, Fax: 814-863-7986, E-mail: jpd16@psu.edu.

Pepperdine University, Seaver College, Division of Communication, Malibu, CA 90263. Offers MA. Part-time programs available. *Degree requirements:* For master's, thesis or alternative. *Entrance requirements:* For master's, GRE General Test, bachelor's degree in communication or related field. Additional exam requirements/recommendations for international students: Required—TOEFL.

Pittsburg State University, Graduate School, College of Arts and Sciences, Department of Communication, Pittsburg, KS 66762. Offers applied communication (MA); communication education (MA); theatre (MA). *Degree requirements:* For master's, thesis or alternative.

Point Park University, School of Arts and Sciences, Department of Journalism and Mass Communication, Pittsburgh, PA 15222-1984. Offers MA. Part-time and evening/weekend programs available. *Faculty:* 9 full-time, 16 part-time/adjunct. *Students:* 26 full-time (18 women), 53 part-time (43 women); includes 18 minority (16 African Americans, 1 Asian American or Pacific Islander, 1 Hispanic American), 2 international. Average age 28. 108 applicants, 57% accepted, 29 enrolled. In 2007, 19 degrees awarded. *Degree requirements:* For master's, thesis or alternative. *Entrance requirements:* For master's, minimum GPA of 2.75, 2 letters of recommendation. Additional exam requirements/recommendations for international students: Required—TOEFL. *Application deadline:* Applications are processed on a rolling basis. Application fee: $30. Electronic applications accepted. *Expenses:* Tuition: Full-time $10,566; part-time $587 per credit. Required fees: $360; $20 per credit. *Financial support:* In 2007–08, 2 students received support, including 2 research assistantships with full tuition reimbursements available (averaging $5,400 per year); career-related internships or fieldwork and scholarships/grants also available. Support available to part-time students. Financial award application deadline: 5/1; financial award applicants required to submit FAFSA. *Unit head:* Helen Fallon, Chair, 412-392-3982, E-mail: hfallon@pointpark.edu. *Application contact:* Marty Paonessa, Associate Director, Graduate and Adult Enrollment, 412-392-3915, Fax: 412-392-6164, E-mail: mpaonessa@pointpark.edu.

See Close-Up on page 919.

Polytechnic Institute of NYU, Department of Electrical and Computer Engineering, Major in Wireless Communications, Brooklyn, NY 11201-2990. Offers Certificate. *Entrance requirements:* Additional exam requirements/recommendations for international students: Required—TOEFL (minimum score 550 paper-based; 213 computer-based); Recommended—IELTS (minimum score 7). *Application deadline:* For fall admission, 7/15 priority date for domestic students, 4/1 priority date for international students; for spring admission, 12/15 priority date for domestic students, 10/1 priority date for international students. Applications are processed on a rolling basis. Application fee: $55. Electronic applications accepted. *Expenses:* Tuition: Full-time $18,486; part-time $1,027 per credit. Required fees: $352 per semester. *Application contact:* Anthea Jeffrey, Graduate Admissions, 718-260-3200, Fax: 718-260-3624, E-mail: gradinfo@poly.edu.

Purdue University, Graduate School, College of Liberal Arts, Department of Communication, West Lafayette, IN 47907. Offers MA, MS, PhD. *Degree requirements:* For master's, comprehensive exams or thesis; for doctorate, thesis/dissertation. *Entrance requirements:* For master's, GRE General Test, writing sample; for doctorate, GRE General Test, master's degree, writing sample. Additional exam requirements/recommendations for international students: Required—TOEFL, TWE. Electronic applications accepted. *Faculty research:* Interpersonal communication, mass communication, organizational communication, public affairs and issue management, rhetorical studies.

Purdue University Calumet, Graduate School, School of Liberal Arts and Sciences, Department of Communication and Creative Arts, Hammond, IN 46323-2094. Offers communication (MA). Part-time and evening/weekend programs available. *Degree requirements:* For master's, comprehensive exam, thesis optional, thesis or extended course work. *Entrance requirements:* For master's, minimum GPA of 3.0. Additional exam requirements/recommendations for international students: Required—TOEFL. Electronic applications accepted. *Faculty research:* International communication, gender studies, political rhetoric, media effects, media accountability.

Quinnipiac University, School of Communications, Hamden, CT 06518-1940. Offers MS. Part-time and evening/weekend programs available. *Faculty:* 10 full-time (3 women), 16 part-time/adjunct (3 women). *Students:* 49 full-time (25 women), 56 part-time (30 women); includes 16 minority (15 African Americans, 1 Hispanic American), 3 international. Average age 29. 79 applicants, 84% accepted, 43 enrolled. In 2007, 32 degrees awarded. *Entrance requirements:* For master's, minimum GPA of 2.8, portfolio or writing sample. Additional exam requirements/recommendations for international students: Required—TOEFL (minimum score 575 paper-based; 233 computer-based; 90 iBT), IELTS (minimum score 7). *Application deadline:* For fall admission, 7/30 priority date for domestic students, 4/30 priority date for international students; for spring admission, 12/15 priority date for domestic students, 9/15 priority date for international students. Applications are processed on a rolling basis. Application fee: $45. Electronic applications accepted. *Expenses:* Tuition: Part-time $675 per credit. Required fees: $30 per credit. Tuition and fees vary according to course load. *Financial support:* In 2007–08, 1 fellowship with full tuition reimbursement was awarded; career-related internships or fieldwork, tuition waivers (partial), and unspecified assistantships also available. Support available to part-time students. Financial award application deadline: 4/15; financial award applicants required to submit FAFSA. *Unit head:* Graduate Admissions Office, 800-462-1944, Fax: 203-582-3443, E-mail: graduate@quinnipiac.edu. *Application contact:* Scott Farber, Information Contact, E-mail: graduate@quinnipiac.edu.

See Close-Up on page 923.

Regent University, Graduate School, School of Communication and the Arts, Virginia Beach, VA 23464-9800. Offers acting and directing (MFA); cinema arts (MA); communication (MA, PhD); fine arts (MFA); journalism (MA); script and screenwriting (MFA); television arts (MA); theatre arts (MA). Part-time programs available. Postbaccalaureate distance learning degree programs offered (minimal on-campus study). *Faculty:* 23 full-time (3 women), 12 part-time/adjunct (3 women). *Students:* 123 full-time (66 women), 145 part-time (83 women); includes 71 minority (54 African Americans, 2 American Indian/Alaska Native, 3 Asian Americans or Pacific Islanders, 12 Hispanic Americans), 14 international. Average age 33. 176 applicants, 66% accepted, 64 enrolled. In 2007, 60 master's, 15 doctorates awarded. *Degree requirements:* For master's, thesis or alternative; for doctorate, thesis/dissertation. *Entrance requirements:* For master's, GRE General Test or MAT, minimum undergraduate GPA of 3.0, writing sample, computer literacy survey, recommendation, resumé, interview, audition (MFA programs); for doctorate, GRE General Test, minimum graduate GPA of 3.0, writing sample, computer literacy survey, recommendation, interview, transcripts. Additional exam requirements/recommendations for international students: Required—TOEFL (minimum score 577 paper-based; 233 computer-based). *Application deadline:* For fall admission, 3/1 priority date for domestic students; for spring admission, 10/1 priority date for domestic students. Applications are processed on a rolling basis. Application fee: $50. Electronic applications accepted. *Expenses: Contact institution. Financial support:* In 2007–08, 247 students received support, including 5 fellowships with full and partial tuition reimbursements available (averaging $7,245 per year); scholarships/grants, tuition waivers (full and partial), and unspecified assistantships also available. Support available to part-time students. Financial award application deadline: 9/1; financial award applicants required to submit FAFSA. *Faculty research:* Southern gospel music, education and entertainment, celebrities and the media, journalism and ethics, C. S. Lewis. *Unit head:* Michael Patrick, Dean, 757-226-4970, Fax: 757-226-4279, E-mail: michpat@regent.edu. *Application contact:* Althea Bishard, Registrar and Executive Director of Enrollment and Academic Services, 800-373-5504, Fax: 757-226-4381, E-mail: admissions@regent.edu.

Regis University, College for Professional Studies, MA Program, Denver, CO 80221-1099. Offers criminology (MA); fine arts administration (Certificate); language and communication (MA); mediation (Certificate); psychology (MA); self-designed major (MA); social justice, peace, and reconciliation (Certificate); social science (MA); technical communication (Certificate). Program also offered in Henderson and Las Vegas (Summerlin), NV. Part-time and evening/weekend programs available. Postbaccalaureate distance learning degree programs offered (minimal on-campus study). *Faculty:* 84. *Students:* 218 (167 women). Average age 41. In 2007, 52 degrees awarded. *Degree requirements:* For master's, thesis, research project. *Entrance requirements:* For master's, resumé, recommendations, essays. Additional exam requirements/recommendations for international students: Required—TOEFL (minimum score 213 computer-based), TWE (minimum score 5). *Application deadline:* For fall admission, 8/13 priority date for domestic students, 7/13 priority date for international students; for winter admission, 10/8 priority date for domestic students, 9/8 priority date for international students; for spring admission, 12/17 priority date for domestic students, 11/17 for international students. Applications are processed on a rolling basis. Application fee: $75. Electronic applications accepted. *Expenses: Contact institution. Financial support:* Federal Work-Study available. Support available to part-time students. Financial award application deadline: 3/15; financial award applicants required to submit FAFSA. *Faculty research:* Independent/nonresidential graduate study; new methods and models, adult learning and the capstone experience, Goal Setting, behavior of Adult students, Innovative Studies for Community Colleges. *Unit head:* Dr. Robert Collins, Chair, 303-458-4302, Fax: 303-964-5538. *Application contact:* Graduate Admissions, 800-677-9270 Ext. 4080, Fax: 303-964-5538, E-mail: masters@regis.edu.

Rensselaer Polytechnic Institute, Graduate School, School of Humanities and Social Sciences, Department of Language, Literature, and Communication, Troy, NY 12180-3590. Offers communication and rhetoric (MS, PhD); human-computer interaction (MS); technical communication (MS). Part-time programs available. Postbaccalaureate distance learning degree programs offered (minimal on-campus study). *Faculty:* 15 full-time (7 women), 1 (woman) part-time/adjunct. *Students:* 53 applicants, 58% accepted, 16 enrolled. In 2007, 14 master's, 3 doctorates awarded. Terminal master's awarded for partial completion of doctoral program. *Median time to degree:* Of those who began their doctoral program in fall 1999, 38% received their degree in 8 years or less. *Degree requirements:* For master's, thesis optional; for doctorate, comprehensive exam, thesis/dissertation. *Entrance requirements:* For master's, GRE General Test, resumé; for doctorate, GRE General Test, writing sample, resumé or curriculum vitae. Additional exam requirements/recommendations for international students: Required—TOEFL (minimum score 570 paper-based; 230 computer-based). *Application deadline:* For fall admission, 1/15 priority date for domestic students; for spring admission, 10/15 priority date for domestic students. Applications are processed on a rolling basis. Application fee: $75. Electronic applications accepted. *Expenses:* Tuition: Full-time $34,900; part-time $1,454 per credit. Required fees: $1,802. *Financial support:* In 2007–08, 18 students received support, including 8 fellowships with full tuition reimbursements available (averaging $14,500 per year), 1 research assistantship with full tuition reimbursement available (averaging $14,500 per year), 9 teaching assistantships with full tuition reimbursements available (averaging $14,500 per year); career-related internships or fieldwork, institutionally sponsored loans, and unspecified assistantships also available. Financial award application deadline: 1/15. *Faculty research:* Human-computer interaction, virtual institutions/communities, media design, theory and culture, usability, digital and visual rhetoric. *Unit head:* Prof. Cheryl Geisler, Head, 518-276-6468, Fax: 518-276-4092, E-mail: geislc@rpi.edu. *Application contact:* Kathy A. Colman, Recruitment Coordinator, 518-276-6469, Fax: 518-276-4092, E-mail: colmak@rpi.edu.

See Close-Up on page 925.

Rochester Institute of Technology, Graduate Enrollment Services, College of Imaging Arts and Sciences, School of Print Media, Rochester, NY 14623-5603. Offers print media (MS). *Students:* 23 full-time (10 women), 22 part-time (11 women); includes 3 minority (1 African American, 1 Asian American or Pacific Islander, 1 Hispanic American), 20 international. 24 applicants, 63% accepted, 14 enrolled. In 2007, 22 degrees awarded. *Entrance requirements:* For master's, minimum GPA of 3.0. Additional exam requirements/recommendations for international students: Required—TOEFL (minimum score 550 paper-based; 213 computer-based; 79 iBT). *Application deadline:* For fall admission, 3/1 priority date for domestic students. Applications are processed on a rolling basis. Application fee: $50. *Expenses:* Tuition: Full-time $28,491; part-time $800 per credit hour. Required fees: $201; $67 per term. *Financial support:* Research assistantships with partial tuition reimbursements, teaching assistantships with partial tuition reimbursements, career-related internships or fieldwork, institutionally sponsored loans, scholarships/grants, and unspecified assistantships available. Support available to part-time students. Financial award applicants required to submit FAFSA. *Unit head:* Dr. Patricia Sorce, Chair, 585-475-2313, E-mail: psorce@mail.rit.edu.

Rochester Institute of Technology, Graduate Enrollment Services, College of Liberal Arts, Department of Communications, Program in Communication and Media Technologies, Rochester, NY 14623-5603. Offers MS. *Students:* 20 full-time (17 women), 15 part-time (11 women); includes 7 minority (6 African Americans, 1 Asian American or Pacific Islander), 4 international. 34 applicants, 71% accepted, 16 enrolled. In 2007, 7 degrees awarded. *Degree requirements:* For master's, thesis. *Entrance requirements:* For master's, minimum GPA of 3.0, writing sample. Additional exam requirements/recommendations for international students: Required—TOEFL (minimum score 600 paper-based; 250 computer-based; 100 iBT). *Application deadline:* For fall admission, 3/1 priority date for domestic students. Applications are processed on a rolling basis. Application fee: $50. Electronic applications accepted. *Expenses:* Tuition: Full-time $28,491; part-time $800 per credit hour. Required fees: $201; $67 per term. *Financial support:* Fellowships with partial tuition reimbursements, research assistantships with partial tuition reimbursements, teaching assistantships with partial tuition reimbursements, career-related internships or fieldwork, institutionally sponsored loans, scholarships/grants, and unspecified assistantships available. Support available to part-time students. Financial award applicants required to submit FAFSA. *Unit head:* Dr. Rudy Pugliese, Head, 585-475-5925, E-mail: rrpgsl@rit.edu.

Roosevelt University, Graduate Division, College of Arts and Sciences, Department of Communication, Chicago, IL 60605-1394. Offers integrated marketing communications (MSIMC); journalism (MSJ). Part-time and evening/weekend programs available. *Students:* 74 full-time (55 women), 143 part-time (117 women); includes 89 minority (69 African Americans, 1 American Indian/Alaska Native, 4 Asian Americans or Pacific Islanders, 15 Hispanic Americans), 26 international. Average age 30. 189 applicants, 59% accepted, 110 enrolled. In 2007, 102 degrees awarded. *Application deadline:* For fall admission, 6/1 priority date for domestic students. Applications are processed on a rolling basis. Application fee: $25 ($35 for international students). *Financial support:* Research assistantships, career-related internships or fieldwork and Federal Work-Study available. Financial award application deadline: 2/15. *Unit head:* Linda Jones, Chair, 312-281-3230. *Application contact:* Joanne Canyon-Heller, Coordinator of Graduate Admission, 877-APPLY RU, Fax: 312-281-3356, E-mail: applyru@roosevelt.edu.

Rutgers, The State University of New Jersey, New Brunswick, School of Communication, Information and Library Studies, Program in Communication, Information and Library Studies, New Brunswick, NJ 08901-1281. Offers PhD. Part-time programs available. *Degree requirements:* For doctorate, comprehensive exam, thesis/dissertation, qualifying exams. *Entrance requirements:* For doctorate, GRE General Test, proficiency in statistics. Additional exam requirements/recommendations for international students: Required—TOEFL (minimum score 600 paper-based; 250 computer-based). Electronic applications accepted. *Faculty research:* Information science, media studies.

Saginaw Valley State University, College of Arts and Behavioral Sciences, Program in Communication and Digital Media Design, University Center, MI 48710. Offers MA. Part-time and evening/weekend programs available. *Students:* 15 full-time (9 women), 27 part-time (10 women); includes 3 minority (1 African American, 1 Asian American or Pacific Islander, 1 Hispanic American), 9 international. Average age 35. 32 applicants, 88% accepted, 19 enrolled. In 2007, 16 degrees awarded. *Degree requirements:* For master's, thesis. *Entrance requirements:* For master's, minimum GPA of 2.75. Additional exam requirements/recommendations for international students: Required—TOEFL. *Application deadline:* Applications are processed on a rolling basis. Application fee: $25. Electronic applications accepted. *Expenses:* Tuition, state resident: full-time $8,264; part-time $344 per credit hour. Tuition, nonresident: full-time $15,853; part-time $661 per credit hour. Required fees: $341; $14 per credit hour. Tuition and fees vary according to course load. *Financial support:* In 2007–08, research assistantships (averaging $5,000 per year); Federal Work-Study also available. Support available to part-time students. Financial award application deadline: 4/1; financial award applicants required to submit FAFSA. *Unit head:* Dr. Steve Erickson, Program Coordinator/Professor of Theatre, 989-964-4147, E-mail: erickson@svsu.edu.

St. John's University, St. John's College of Liberal Arts and Sciences, Department of Speech, Communication Sciences and Theatre, Queens, NY 11439. Offers MA, Au D, Advanced Diploma. *Accreditation:* ASHA. Evening/weekend programs available. *Faculty:* 20 full-time (12 women), 40 part-time/adjunct (25 women). *Students:* 83 full-time (77 women), 75 part-time (71 women); includes 33 minority (15 African Americans, 1 American Indian/Alaska Native, 4 Asian Americans or Pacific Islanders, 13 Hispanic Americans), 2 international. Average age 27. 406 applicants, 26% accepted, 47 enrolled. In 2007, 60 degrees awarded. *Degree requirements:* For master's, comprehensive exam, thesis optional, internship. *Entrance requirements:* For master's, minimum GPA of 3.0. Additional exam requirements/recommendations for international students: Required—TOEFL (minimum score 500 paper-based; 173 computer-based; 61 iBT), IELTS (minimum score 6). *Application deadline:* For fall admission, 2/1 for domestic students, 5/1 priority date for international students; for spring admission, 10/1 for domestic students, 11/1 priority date for international students. Applications are processed on a rolling basis. Application fee: $40. Electronic applications accepted. *Expenses: Contact institution. Financial support:* Research assistantships, career-related internships or fieldwork and scholarships/grants available. Support available to part-time students. Financial award application deadline: 3/1; financial award applicants required to submit FAFSA. *Faculty research:* Bilingualism and adult and child language disorders, dysphagia speech motor control, electrophysiological measurement of hearing, central auditory processing disorders and auditory habilitation and rehabilitation. *Unit head:* Dr. Fredericka Bell-Berti, Chair, 718-990-6450, E-mail: bellf@stjohns.edu. *Application contact:* Beth Evans, Associate Vice President and Executive Director, Enrollment Management, 718-990-6999, Fax: 718-990-5686, E-mail: gradhelp@stjohns.edu.

Saint Louis University, Graduate School, College of Arts and Sciences and Graduate School, Department of Communication, St. Louis, MO 63103-2097. Offers MA, MA-R. Part-time programs available. *Faculty:* 15 full-time (7 women), 1 (woman) part-time/adjunct. *Students:* 16 full-time (13 women), 11 part-time (8 women); includes 1 minority (African American), 1 international. Average age 29. 28 applicants, 68% accepted, 8 enrolled. In 2007, 8 degrees awarded. *Degree requirements:* For master's, thesis (for some programs), comprehensive oral and written exams. *Entrance requirements:* For master's, GRE General Test, letters of recommendation, resumé, interview, transcripts, goal statement. Additional exam requirements/recommendations for international students: Required—TOEFL (minimum score 525 paper-based; 194 computer-based). *Application deadline:* For fall admission, 7/1 for domestic and international students; for spring admission, 11/1 for domestic and international students. Applications are processed on a rolling basis. Application fee: $40. Electronic applications accepted. *Expenses:* Tuition: Part-time $845 per credit hour. Required fees: $105 per semester. *Financial support:* In 2007–08, 18 students received support, including 3 research assistantships with full tuition reimbursements available (averaging $12,000 per year), 7 teaching assistantships with full tuition reimbursements available (averaging $10,000 per year); Federal Work-Study, scholarships/grants, traineeships, health care benefits, and unspecified assistantships also available. Support available to part-time students. Financial award application deadline: 2/1; financial award applicants required to submit FAFSA. *Faculty research:* Media studies, organizational communication, dialogue, intercultural communication,

Communication—General

Saint Louis University (continued)
qualitative research methods. *Unit head:* Dr. Kathleen M. Farrell, Chairperson, 314-977-2065, Fax: 314-977-3195, E-mail: farrellk@slu.edu. *Application contact:* Gary U. Behrman, Associate Dean of Graduate School Admissions, 314-977-3827, Fax: 314-977-3943, E-mail: behrmang@slu.edu.

St. Mary's University, Graduate School, Department of English and Communication Studies, Program in Communication Studies, San Antonio, TX 78228-8507. Offers MA. Part-time programs available. Postbaccalaureate distance learning degree programs offered (minimal on-campus study). *Students:* 6 full-time (5 women), 23 part-time (16 women); includes 16 minority (1 African American, 15 Hispanic Americans), 2 international. Average age 29. In 2007, 9 degrees awarded. *Degree requirements:* For master's, comprehensive exam, thesis. *Entrance requirements:* For master's, GRE General Test, MAT. Additional exam requirements/recommendations for international students: Required—TOEFL (minimum score 550 paper-based; 213 computer-based). *Application deadline:* For fall admission, 8/1 priority date for domestic students. Applications are processed on a rolling basis. Application fee: $0. Electronic applications accepted. *Financial support:* Career-related internships or fieldwork, Federal Work-Study, institutionally sponsored loans, scholarships/grants, and health care benefits available. Financial award application deadline: 3/31; financial award applicants required to submit FAFSA. *Faculty research:* Persuasion and negotiation, group dynamics, language and communication, business communication, organizational communication. *Unit head:* Dr. Elijah Akhahenda, Director, 210-436-3107.

St. Thomas University, School of Leadership Studies, Miami Gardens, FL 33054-6459. Offers MA, MPS, MS, Ed D, Certificate. Part-time and evening/weekend programs available. *Students:* 3 full-time (all women), 13 part-time (11 women); includes 14 minority (1 African American, 13 Hispanic Americans), 2 international. Average age 28. *Entrance requirements:* Additional exam requirements/recommendations for international students: Required—TOEFL (minimum score 550 paper-based; 213 computer-based; 79 iBT). Application fee: $40. *Financial support:* Unspecified assistantships available. Financial award applicants required to submit FAFSA. *Unit head:* Dr. Gloria Ruiz, Interim Dean, 305-628-6508, Fax: 305-628-6757, E-mail: gruiz@stu.edu. *Application contact:* Marilyn Carballosa, Assistant Director of Admissions, 305-628-6546, Fax: 305-628-6591, E-mail: graduate@stu.edu.

San Diego State University, Graduate and Research Affairs, College of Professional Studies and Fine Arts, School of Communication, San Diego, CA 92182. Offers advertising and public relations (MA); critical-cultural studies (MA); interaction studies (MA); intercultural and international studies (MA); new media studies (MA); news and information studies (MA); telecommunications and media management (MA). *Students:* 30 full-time (16 women), 62 part-time (47 women); includes 6 minority (3 African Americans, 2 Asian Americans or Pacific Islanders, 1 Hispanic American), 11 international. 167 applicants, 41% accepted, 45 enrolled. In 2007, 49 degrees awarded. *Degree requirements:* For master's, thesis. *Entrance requirements:* For master's, GRE General Test, 3 letters of recommendation. Additional exam requirements/recommendations for international students: Required—TOEFL. *Application deadline:* For fall admission, 3/1 for domestic and international students; for spring admission, 10/1 for domestic and international students. Applications are processed on a rolling basis. Application fee: $55. Electronic applications accepted. *Financial support:* In 2007–08, 34 teaching assistantships were awarded; career-related internships or fieldwork and unspecified assistantships also available. Financial award applicants required to submit FAFSA. Total annual research expenditures: $153,598. *Unit head:* Diane Borden, Interim Director, 619-594-8098, Fax: 619-594-6246. *Application contact:* Patricia Geist-Martin, Information Contact, 619-594-4182, E-mail: pgeist@mail.sdsu.edu.

San Jose State University, Graduate Studies and Research, College of Social Sciences, Department of Communication Studies, San Jose, CA 95192-0001. Offers MA. *Students:* 13 full-time (11 women), 34 part-time (24 women); includes 9 minority (5 Asian Americans or Pacific Islanders, 4 Hispanic Americans), 6 international. Average age 30. 43 applicants, 51% accepted, 14 enrolled. In 2007, 28 degrees awarded. *Degree requirements:* For master's, comprehensive exam, thesis or alternative, project. *Entrance requirements:* For master's, minimum GPA of 3.0. *Application deadline:* For fall admission, 6/29 for domestic students; for spring admission, 11/30 for domestic students. Applications are processed on a rolling basis. Application fee: $59. Electronic applications accepted. *Financial support:* Applicants required to submit FAFSA. *Unit head:* Dr. Dennis Jaehne, Chair, 408-924-5373, Fax: 408-924-5396, E-mail: djaehne@email.sjsu.edu. *Application contact:* Dr. Deanna L. Fassett, Graduate Coordinator, 408-924-5511, Fax: 408-924-5396, E-mail: deanna.fassett@sjsu.edu.

Seton Hall University, College of Arts and Sciences, Department of Communication, South Orange, NJ 07079-2697. Offers corporate and public communication (MA); strategic communication and leadership (MA). Part-time and evening/weekend programs available. Postbaccalaureate distance learning degree programs offered (minimal on-campus study). *Entrance requirements:* For master's, GRE or GMAT, minimum GPA of 3.0. Electronic applications accepted. *Faculty research:* Managerial communication, communication consulting, communication and development.

See Close-Up on page 927.

Shippensburg University of Pennsylvania, School of Graduate Studies, College of Arts and Sciences, Department of Communication/Journalism, Shippensburg, PA 17257-2299. Offers communication studies (MS). Part-time and evening/weekend programs available. *Faculty:* 7 full-time (2 women), 2 part-time/adjunct (both women). *Students:* 13 full-time (6 women), 23 part-time (17 women); includes 2 minority (1 African American, 1 Asian American or Pacific Islander). Average age 31. 26 applicants, 65% accepted, 10 enrolled. In 2007, 16 degrees awarded. *Degree requirements:* For master's, thesis optional, written comprehensive exam or communications project; candidacy. *Entrance requirements:* For master's, GRE or MAT (if GPA is below 2.75), 2 letters of recommendation, essay or goals statement. Additional exam requirements/recommendations for international students: Required—TOEFL (minimum score 580 paper-based; 237 computer-based). *Application deadline:* For fall admission, 3/1 for international students; for spring admission, 7/1 for international students. Applications are processed on a rolling basis. Application fee: $30. Electronic applications accepted. *Expenses:* Tuition, state resident: part-time $345 per credit. Tuition, nonresident: part-time $552 per credit. Required fees: $28 per credit. Tuition and fees vary according to course load. *Financial support:* In 2007–08, 10 research assistantships with full tuition reimbursements (averaging $3,575 per year) were awarded; career-related internships or fieldwork, scholarships/grants, and unspecified assistantships also available. Support available to part-time students. Financial award application deadline: 3/1; financial award applicants required to submit FAFSA. *Unit head:* Dr. Ted Carlin, Chairperson, 717-477-1521, Fax: 717-477-4013, E-mail: ejcarl@ship.edu. *Application contact:* Renee Payne, Associate Dean of Graduate Admissions, 717-477-1231, Fax: 717-477-4016, E-mail: rmpayn@ship.edu.

Simon Fraser University, Graduate Studies, Faculty of Applied Sciences, School of Communication, Burnaby, BC V5A 1S6, Canada. Offers MA, PhD. *Degree requirements:* For master's, thesis optional; for doctorate, thesis/dissertation. *Entrance requirements:* For master's, minimum GPA of 3.0; for doctorate, minimum GPA of 3.5. Additional exam requirements/recommendations for international students: Required—TOEFL or IELTS. Electronic applications accepted. *Faculty research:* Theory and methodology, policy studies in communication media and telecommunication, international development, journalism studies, telelearning and telework.

South Dakota State University, Graduate School, College of Arts and Science, Department of Journalism and Mass Communication, Brookings, SD 57007. Offers communication studies and journalism (MS). Part-time and evening/weekend programs available. *Degree requirements:* For master's, thesis, oral exam. *Entrance requirements:* Additional exam requirements/recommendations for international students: Required—TOEFL (minimum score 550 paper-based; 213 computer-based; 79 iBT). *Faculty research:* Mass communication applications.

Southeastern Louisiana University, College of Arts, Humanities and Social Sciences, Department of Communication, Hammond, LA 70402. Offers organizational communication (MA). Part-time and evening/weekend programs available. *Faculty:* 2 full-time (1 woman). *Students:* 9 full-time (8 women), 21 part-time (15 women); includes 7 minority (6 African Americans, 1 Hispanic American). Average age 28. 15 applicants, 100% accepted, 10 enrolled. In 2007, 6 degrees awarded. *Degree requirements:* For master's, comprehensive exam. *Entrance requirements:* For master's, GRE General Test, bachelor's degree in communication or related field, minimum GPA of 3.0. Additional exam requirements/recommendations for international students: Required—TOEFL (minimum score 500 paper-based; 173 computer-based). *Application deadline:* For fall admission, 7/15 priority date for domestic students, 6/1 priority date for international students; for spring admission, 12/1 priority date for domestic students, 10/1 priority date for international students. Applications are processed on a rolling basis. Application fee: $20 ($30 for international students). Electronic applications accepted. *Expenses:* Tuition, state resident: full-time $2,216; part-time $123 per credit. Tuition, nonresident: full-time $6,716; part-time $373 per credit. Required fees: $1,105; $61 per credit. *Financial support:* Career-related internships or fieldwork, Federal Work-Study, institutionally sponsored loans, unspecified assistantships, and administrative assistantships available. Support available to part-time students. Financial award application deadline: 5/1; financial award applicants required to submit FAFSA. *Faculty research:* Cross cultural communication in multi-national organizations, health communication among women, leadership communication, new media in organizations, crisis communication in organizations. *Unit head:* Dr. Karen Fontenot, Department Head, 985-549-2105, Fax: 985-549-5014, E-mail: kfontenot@selu.edu. *Application contact:* Sandra Meyers, Graduate Admissions Analyst, 985-549-2066, Fax: 985-549-5632, E-mail: admissions@selu.edu.

Southern Illinois University Carbondale, Graduate School, College of Mass Communication and Media Arts, Carbondale, IL 62901-4701. Offers MA, MFA, PhD, MBA/MA. Part-time programs available. *Faculty:* 35 full-time (9 women), 2 part-time/adjunct (0 women). *Students:* 36 full-time (17 women), 87 part-time (38 women); includes 10 minority (3 African Americans, 2 American Indian/Alaska Native, 1 Asian American or Pacific Islander, 4 Hispanic Americans), 51 international. Average age 28. 118 applicants, 24% accepted, 17 enrolled. In 2007, 17 master's, 4 doctorates awarded. *Degree requirements:* For doctorate, thesis/dissertation. *Entrance requirements:* For doctorate, GRE General Test, minimum GPA of 3.25. Additional exam requirements/recommendations for international students: Required—TOEFL. *Application deadline:* Applications are processed on a rolling basis. Application fee: $20. *Financial support:* In 2007–08, 75 students received support; fellowships, research assistantships, teaching assistantships, career-related internships or fieldwork, Federal Work-Study, institutionally sponsored loans, and tuition waivers (full) available. Support available to part-time students. *Unit head:* Gary Kolb, Interim Dean, 618-453-5794, E-mail: jschool@siu.edu.

Announcement: Students in the MFA program work closely with distinguished faculty members to focus on the creation of high-quality creative works in photography, film, video, sound, new media, and intermedia. Courses in criticism, theory, and history help students to place their work within the context of contemporary arts practice. The College-wide PhD program engages students in the analysis of the fundamentals of media and communication, whether social, economic, political, cultural, historical, legal/regulatory, or international. Its firm grounding in conceptual and methodological debates is designed to educate researchers and instructors who will make significant contributions to the field of media analysis, policies, and practices. The College is home to the Global Media Research Center and Big Muddy Independent Film Festival.

See Close-Ups on pages 929 and 931.

Southern Utah University, College of Humanities and Social Sciences, Program in Communication, Cedar City, UT 84720-2498. Offers MA. *Faculty:* 9 full-time (1 woman). *Students:* 7 full-time (2 women), 26 part-time (13 women); includes 1 American Indian/Alaska Native, 1 Hispanic American. 5 applicants, 100% accepted, 3 enrolled. In 2007, 1 degree awarded. *Application deadline:* Applications are processed on a rolling basis. Application fee: $50 ($65 for international students). Electronic applications accepted. *Financial support:* In 2007–08, 6 research assistantships (averaging $800 per year), 6 teaching assistantships (averaging $4,200 per year) were awarded. *Unit head:* Dr. John Ault, Interim Dean, College of Humanities and Social Sciences, 435-586-7898, Fax: 435-865-8193, E-mail: ault@suu.edu.

Spalding University, Graduate Studies, College of Business and Communication, Louisville, KY 40203-2188. Offers business communication (MS). Part-time and evening/weekend programs available. *Degree requirements:* For master's, project. *Entrance requirements:* For master's, GRE or GMAT, writing sample, interview, letters of recommendation. Additional exam requirements/recommendations for international students: Required—TOEFL (minimum score 535 paper-based). Electronic applications accepted. *Faculty research:* Curriculum development, consumer behavior, interdisciplinary pedagogy.

Spring Arbor University, School of Arts and Sciences, Spring Arbor, MI 49283-9799. Offers communication (MA); spiritual formation and leadership (MA). Part-time programs available. Postbaccalaureate distance learning degree programs offered (no on-campus study). *Faculty:* 6 full-time (1 woman), 8 part-time/adjunct (3 women). *Students:* 69 full-time (46 women), 57 part-time (36 women); includes 10 minority (all African Americans), 1 international. In 2007, 3 degrees awarded. *Degree requirements:* For master's, thesis (for some programs). *Entrance requirements:* For master's, GRE (taken within the last 5 years), writing sample, 3 recommendations, personal goals statement. Additional exam requirements/recommendations for international students: Required—TOEFL (minimum score 550 paper-based; 220 computer-based). Application fee: $40. *Expenses:* *Contact institution.* One-time fee: $40 part-time. Tuition and fees vary according to course load and program. *Financial support:* Applicants required to submit FAFSA. *Unit head:* Dr. Wally Metts, Chair of the Department of Communication, 517-750-1200 Ext. 1491, E-mail: wmetts@arbor.edu. *Application contact:* Carol Bunnell, Secretary, Department of Communication, 517-750-6483, E-mail: cbunnell@arbor.edu.

Stanford University, School of Humanities and Sciences, Department of Communication, Stanford, CA 94305-9991. Offers communication (journalism specialization) (MA); communication theory and research (PhD). *Faculty:* 11 full-time (0 women). *Students:* 55 full-time (31 women). Average age 28. 166 applicants, 20% accepted. In 2007, 17 master's, 4 doctorates awarded. *Degree requirements:* For master's, thesis, project; for doctorate, thesis/dissertation, qualifying examination, area examination, 2 projects. *Entrance requirements:* For master's and doctorate, GRE General Test. Additional exam requirements/recommendations for international students: Required—TOEFL (minimum score 600 paper-based; 250 computer-based). *Application deadline:* For fall admission, 12/2 for domestic and international students. Application fee: $105. Electronic applications accepted. *Financial support:* Research assistantships, teaching assistantships available. *Unit head:* James S. Fishkin, Chair, 650-723-4611. *Application contact:* Student Services Manager, 650-723-2075, Fax: 650-725-2472, E-mail: comm-studentservices@stanford.edu.

State University of New York College at Potsdam, School of Arts and Sciences, Department of English, Potsdam, NY 13676. Offers English and communication (MA). Part-time and evening/weekend programs available. *Faculty:* 4 full-time (3 women), 1 (woman) part-time/adjunct. *Students:* 11 full-time (4 women), 3 part-time (all women). 5 applicants, 80% accepted, 3 enrolled. In 2007, 1 degree awarded. *Degree requirements:* For master's, one foreign language, thesis or alternative. *Entrance requirements:* For master's, minimum GPA of 3.0 in last 60 hours of undergraduate course work. Additional exam requirements/recommendations for international students: Required—TOEFL (minimum score 550 paper-based; 213 computer-based; 80 iBT), IELTS (minimum score 6). *Application deadline:* Applications are processed on a rolling basis. Application fee: $50. *Financial support:* In 2007–08, 1 student received support; teaching assistantships with full tuition reimbursements available, Federal Work-Study and unspecified assistantships available. Support available to part-time students. Financial award application deadline: 3/1; financial award applicants required to submit FAFSA. *Unit head:* Dr. Lisa Wilson, Director of Graduate Studies, English and Communication, 315-267-2004, Fax:

315-267-3256, E-mail: wilsonlm@potsdam.edu. *Application contact:* Peter Cutler, Graduate Admissions Counselor, 315-267-3154, Fax: 315-267-4802, E-mail: cutlerpj@potsdam.edu.

State University of New York College of Environmental Science and Forestry, Faculty of Environmental Studies, Syracuse, NY 13210-2779. Offers environmental and community land planning (MPS, MS, PhD); environmental and natural resources policy (PhD); environmental communication and participatory processes (MPS, MS, PhD); environmental policy and democratic processes (MPS, MS, PhD); environmental systems and risk management (MPS, MS, PhD); water and wetland resource studies (MPS, MS, PhD). Part-time programs available. *Degree requirements:* For master's, thesis (for some programs); for doctorate, comprehensive exam, thesis/dissertation. *Entrance requirements:* For master's and doctorate, GRE General Test, minimum GPA of 3.0. Additional exam requirements/recommendations for international students: Required—TOEFL (minimum score 550 paper-based; 213 computer-based; 80 iBT), IELTS (minimum score 6). *Faculty research:* Environmental education/communications, water resources, land resources, waste management.

Stephen F. Austin State University, Graduate School, College of Applied Arts and Science, Department of Communication, Nacogdoches, TX 75962. Offers communication (MA); mass communication (MA). Part-time programs available. *Degree requirements:* For master's, comprehensive exam, thesis optional. *Entrance requirements:* For master's, GRE General Test. Additional exam requirements/recommendations for international students: Required—TOEFL (minimum score 550 paper-based; 213 computer-based).

Stevens Institute of Technology, Graduate School, Charles V. Schaefer Jr. School of Engineering, Department of Electrical and Computer Engineering, Program in Electrical Engineering, Hoboken, NJ 07030. Offers computer architecture and digital system design (M Eng, PhD, Engr); signal processing for communications (M Eng, PhD, Engr); telecommunications engineering (M Eng, PhD, Engr); telecommunications management (MS, PhD, Certificate). *Degree requirements:* For master's, thesis optional; for doctorate, variable foreign language requirement, thesis/dissertation. *Entrance requirements:* For master's, doctorate, and other advanced degree, GRE. Additional exam requirements/recommendations for international students: Required—TOEFL. Electronic applications accepted.

Suffolk University, College of Arts and Sciences, Department of Communication, Boston, MA 02108-2770. Offers MA. Part-time and evening/weekend programs available. *Faculty:* 16 full-time (8 women). *Students:* 15 full-time (13 women), 25 part-time (16 women), 3 international. Average age 27. 73 applicants, 68% accepted, 15 enrolled. In 2007, 19 degrees awarded. *Entrance requirements:* For master's, GRE General Test, MAT, or GMAT. Additional exam requirements/recommendations for international students: Required—TOEFL (minimum score 550 paper-based; 213 computer-based; 80 iBT). *Application deadline:* For fall admission, 6/15 priority date for domestic students, 6/15 for international students; for spring admission, 11/1 priority date for domestic students, 11/1 for international students. Applications are processed on a rolling basis. Application fee: $50. Electronic applications accepted. *Financial support:* In 2007–08, 28 students received support, including 25 fellowships with partial tuition reimbursements available (averaging $5,458 per year); career-related internships or fieldwork, Federal Work-Study, and institutionally sponsored loans also available. Support available to part-time students. Financial award application deadline: 4/1; financial award applicants required to submit FAFSA. *Faculty research:* New media and new markets for advertising, First Amendment issues with the Internet, gender and intercultural communication, organizational development. *Unit head:* Dr. Robert Rosenthal, Chair, 617-573-8502, E-mail: rrosenth@suffolk.edu. *Application contact:* Judith Reynolds, Director of Graduate Admissions, 617-573-8302, Fax: 617-523-0116, E-mail: grad.admission@suffolk.edu.

Syracuse University, Graduate School, College of Visual and Performing Arts, Department of Communication and Rhetorical Studies, Syracuse, NY 13244. Offers MA, MS. Part-time programs available. *Students:* 10 full-time (4 women), 2 part-time (both women); includes 3 minority (2 African Americans, 1 Asian American or Pacific Islander), 1 international. 15 applicants, 67% accepted, 6 enrolled. In 2007, 11 degrees awarded. *Entrance requirements:* For master's, GRE General Test, writing sample. Additional exam requirements/recommendations for international students: Required—TOEFL. *Application deadline:* For fall admission, 1/1 priority date for domestic students. Applications are processed on a rolling basis. Application fee: $75. Electronic applications accepted. *Expenses:* Tuition: Full-time $18,216; part-time $1,012 per credit. Required fees: $980. Tuition and fees vary according to program. *Financial support:* In 2007–08, 9 students received support; fellowships with tuition reimbursements available, teaching assistantships with full tuition reimbursements available, tuition waivers (partial) available. *Unit head:* Dr. Amos Kiewe, Chair, 315-443-2308, Fax: 315-443-5141, E-mail: akiewe@syr.edu. *Application contact:* Harriett Conti, Associate Director, Graduate Student Services, 315-443-3089, E-mail: hmconti@syr.edu.

Syracuse University, Graduate School, S. I. Newhouse School of Public Communications, Syracuse, NY 13244. Offers MA, MS, PhD, JD/MA, JD/MS, MS/MA. *Accreditation:* ACEJMC (one or more programs are accredited). Postbaccalaureate distance learning degree programs offered (minimal on-campus study). *Faculty:* 51 full-time (17 women), 40 part-time/adjunct (12 women). *Students:* 270 full-time (175 women), 85 part-time (58 women); includes 64 minority (39 African Americans, 12 Asian Americans or Pacific Islanders, 13 Hispanic Americans), 58 international. 837 applicants, 62% accepted, 303 enrolled. In 2007, 211 master's, 6 doctorates awarded. *Degree requirements:* For master's, comprehensive exam (for some programs); for doctorate, thesis/dissertation, qualifying exams. *Entrance requirements:* For master's and doctorate, GRE General Test. Additional exam requirements/recommendations for international students: Required—TOEFL (minimum score 600 paper-based; 250 computer-based; 100 iBT), IELTS (minimum score 7). *Application deadline:* For fall admission, 2/1 for domestic students. Application fee: $75. Electronic applications accepted. *Expenses:* Tuition: Full-time $18,216; part-time $1,012 per credit. Required fees: $980. Tuition and fees vary according to program. *Financial support:* In 2007–08, fellowships with tuition reimbursements (averaging $11,000 per year), teaching assistantships with tuition reimbursements (averaging $7,500 per year) were awarded; research assistantships with tuition reimbursements, career-related internships or fieldwork, Federal Work-Study, scholarships/grants, and tuition waivers (partial) also available. Support available to part-time students. Financial award application deadline: 2/1; financial award applicants required to submit FAFSA. *Faculty research:* Media convergence, political reporting, interactive multimedia, popular television, advertising effectiveness. *Unit head:* David M. Rubin, Dean, 315-443-2302, Fax: 315-443-3946, E-mail: newhouse@syr.edu. *Application contact:* Graduate Records Office, 315-443-4039, Fax: 315-443-1834, E-mail: pcgrad@syr.edu.

Announcement: S.I. Newhouse School of Public Communications is pleased to announce the opening of its new building, Newhouse III. This 74,000-square-foot addition includes a Center for Digital Convergence Suite, a Collaborative Media Room, an expanded Career Development Center, new classrooms, a new auditorium, student meeting rooms, and an expanded café to benefit students, faculty and staff members, and alumni.

See Close-Up on page 935.

Teachers College, Columbia University, Graduate Faculty of Education, Department of Math, Science and Technology, Program in Communications, New York, NY 10027-6696. Offers Ed M, MA, Ed D. Part-time and evening/weekend programs available. *Faculty:* 24 part-time/adjunct. *Students:* 10 full-time (7 women), 29 part-time (19 women); includes 7 minority (3 African Americans, 2 Asian Americans or Pacific Islanders, 2 Hispanic Americans), 7 international. Average age 34. 28 applicants, 75% accepted, 7 enrolled. In 2007, 7 master's, 4 doctorates awarded. Terminal master's awarded for partial completion of doctoral program. *Degree requirements:* For doctorate, thesis/dissertation. *Entrance requirements:* For doctorate, GRE General Test or MAT. *Application deadline:* For fall admission, 5/15 for domestic students; for spring admission, 12/1 for domestic students. Application fee: $70. *Financial support:* Career-related internships or fieldwork, Federal Work-Study, institutionally sponsored loans, and tuition waivers (full and partial) available. Support available to part-time students. Financial award application deadline: 2/1. *Faculty research:* Television and youth, application of digital technology to education reform. *Application contact:* Deanna Ghozati, Assistant Director of Admission, 212-678-4018, Fax: 212-678-4171, E-mail: ghozati@tc.edu.

Temple University, Graduate School, School of Communications and Theater, Philadelphia, PA 19122-6096. Offers MA, MFA, MJ, MS, PhD. Part-time and evening/weekend programs available. *Degree requirements:* For doctorate, one foreign language, thesis/dissertation. *Entrance requirements:* For master's, minimum GPA of 3.0; for doctorate, GRE General Test, minimum GPA of 3.0. Additional exam requirements/recommendations for international students: Required—TOEFL (minimum score 550 paper-based; 213 computer-based; 79 iBT). Electronic applications accepted.

Temple University, Health Sciences Center and Graduate School, College of Health Professions, Department of Communication Sciences, Philadelphia, PA 19122-6096. Offers communication sciences (PhD); linguistics (MA); speech-language-hearing (MA). *Accreditation:* ASHA. Part-time and evening/weekend programs available. *Degree requirements:* For doctorate, thesis/dissertation. *Entrance requirements:* For master's and doctorate, GRE General Test, minimum GPA of 3.0. Additional exam requirements/recommendations for international students: Required—TOEFL (minimum score 550 paper-based; 213 computer-based; 79 iBT). Electronic applications accepted. *Faculty research:* Fluency, infants and families, multilingual/multicultural communication, geriatrics, conflict process, language, health communication.

Texas A&M University, College of Liberal Arts, Department of Communication, College Station, TX 77843. Offers MA, PhD. *Faculty:* 15. *Students:* 49 full-time (34 women), 28 part-time (17 women); includes 9 minority (2 African Americans, 1 Asian American or Pacific Islander, 6 Hispanic Americans), 11 international. Average age 27. 74 applicants, 51% accepted, 23 enrolled. In 2007, 10 master's, 3 doctorates awarded. *Degree requirements:* For master's, thesis or alternative; for doctorate, thesis/dissertation. *Entrance requirements:* For master's, GRE General Test. Additional exam requirements/recommendations for international students: Required—TOEFL. *Application deadline:* For fall admission, 2/15 priority date for domestic students; for spring admission, 10/15 for domestic students. Applications are processed on a rolling basis. Application fee: $50 ($75 for international students). Electronic applications accepted. *Expenses:* Tuition, state resident: full-time $6,129. Tuition, nonresident: full-time $11,689. Tuition and fees vary according to course load. *Financial support:* In 2007–08, fellowships with partial tuition reimbursements (averaging $12,000 per year), research assistantships with partial tuition reimbursements (averaging $11,000 per year), teaching assistantships with partial tuition reimbursements (averaging $11,000 per year) were awarded; institutionally sponsored loans also available. Financial award application deadline: 2/1; financial award applicants required to submit FAFSA. *Faculty research:* Rhetoric and public affairs, communication and health, communication and organizations. *Unit head:* Dr. Richard L. Street, Head, 979-845-5500, Fax: 979-845-6594, E-mail: r-street@tamu.edu. *Application contact:* Barbara F. Sharf, Director of Graduate Studies, 979-845-0625, Fax: 979-845-6594, E-mail: bsharf@tamu.edu.

Texas Southern University, Graduate School, Tavis Smiley School of Communication, Houston, TX 77004-4584. Offers MA. Part-time programs available. *Faculty:* 4 full-time (2 women). *Students:* 16 full-time (14 women), 23 part-time (16 women); includes 34 minority (all African Americans), 5 international. Average age 30. 13 applicants, 92% accepted, 7 enrolled. In 2007, 9 degrees awarded. *Degree requirements:* For master's, comprehensive exam, thesis. *Entrance requirements:* For master's, GRE General Test, minimum GPA of 2.5. Additional exam requirements/recommendations for international students: Required—TOEFL. *Application deadline:* For fall admission, 7/15 priority date for domestic students. Applications are processed on a rolling basis. Application fee: $50 ($75 for international students). *Financial support:* In 2007–08, 4 fellowships were awarded; research assistantships, teaching assistantships, career-related internships or fieldwork, Federal Work-Study, and institutionally sponsored loans also available. Financial award application deadline: 5/1. *Unit head:* Dr. James Ward, Dean, 713-313-7740, E-mail: ward_jw@tsu.edu. *Application contact:* Dr. Louis Browne, Graduate Adviser, 713-313-7024.

Texas State University–San Marcos, Graduate School, College of Fine Arts and Communication, San Marcos, TX 78666. Offers MA, MFA, MM. Part-time and evening/weekend programs available. *Faculty:* 43 full-time (16 women), 6 part-time/adjunct (4 women). *Students:* 116 full-time (75 women), 88 part-time (54 women); includes 40 minority (12 African Americans, 1 American Indian/Alaska Native, 4 Asian Americans or Pacific Islanders, 23 Hispanic Americans), 15 international. Average age 30. 104 applicants, 94% accepted, 73 enrolled. In 2007, 62 degrees awarded. *Degree requirements:* For master's, comprehensive exam. *Entrance requirements:* For master's, GRE General Test (for some programs), minimum GPA of 2.75 in last 60 hours of course work. Additional exam requirements/recommendations for international students: Required—TOEFL (minimum score 550 paper-based; 213 computer-based). *Application deadline:* For fall admission, 6/15 priority date for domestic students; for spring admission, 10/15 priority date for domestic students. Applications are processed on a rolling basis. Application fee: $40 ($90 for international students). Electronic applications accepted. *Expenses:* Tuition, state resident: full-time $3,780; part-time $210 per credit hour. Tuition, nonresident: full-time $8,784; part-time $488 per credit hour. Required fees: $493 per semester. Full-time tuition and fees vary according to course load. *Financial support:* In 2007–08, 162 students received support, including 8 research assistantships (averaging $5,810 per year), 59 teaching assistantships (averaging $4,155 per year); career-related internships or fieldwork, Federal Work-Study, institutionally sponsored loans, scholarships/grants, and unspecified assistantships also available. Support available to part-time students. Financial award application deadline: 4/1; financial award applicants required to submit FAFSA. *Unit head:* Dr. T. Richard Cheatham, Dean, 512-245-2308, Fax: 512-245-8334, E-mail: tc02@txstate.edu. *Application contact:* Dr. J. Michael Willoughby, Dean of Graduate School, 512-245-2581, Fax: 512-245-8365, E-mail: gradcollege@txstate.edu.

Texas State University–San Marcos, Graduate School, College of Fine Arts and Communication, Department of Communication Studies, Program in Communication Studies, San Marcos, TX 78666. Offers MA. Part-time and evening/weekend programs available. *Faculty:* 6 full-time (3 women). *Students:* 35 full-time (26 women), 16 part-time (12 women); includes 14 minority (5 African Americans, 1 American Indian/Alaska Native, 1 Asian American or Pacific Islander, 7 Hispanic Americans), 2 international. Average age 28. 27 applicants, 96% accepted, 22 enrolled. In 2007, 16 degrees awarded. *Degree requirements:* For master's, comprehensive exam. *Entrance requirements:* For master's, minimum GPA of 3.0 in last 60 hours. Additional exam requirements/recommendations for international students: Required—TOEFL (minimum score 550 paper-based; 213 computer-based). *Application deadline:* For fall admission, 6/15 priority date for domestic students; for spring admission, 10/15 priority date for domestic students. Applications are processed on a rolling basis. Application fee: $40 ($90 for international students). Electronic applications accepted. *Expenses:* Tuition, state resident: full-time $3,780; part-time $210 per credit hour. Tuition, nonresident: full-time $8,784; part-time $488 per credit hour. Required fees: $493 per semester. Full-time tuition and fees vary according to course load. *Financial support:* In 2007–08, 48 students received support, including 2 research assistantships (averaging $5,378 per year), 23 teaching assistantships (averaging $5,408 per year); career-related internships or fieldwork, Federal Work-Study, and institutionally sponsored loans also available. Support available to part-time students. Financial award application deadline: 4/1; financial award applicants required to submit FAFSA. *Faculty research:* Speech education, rhetoric and criticism, interpersonal and group communication, communication theory, rhetoric of Sojourner Truth. *Unit head:* Dr. Mary Hoffman, Graduate Adviser, 512-245-2165, Fax: 512-245-3138, E-mail: rm07@txstate.edu.

Texas Tech University, Graduate School, College of Arts and Sciences, Department of Communication Studies, Lubbock, TX 79409. Offers MA. Part-time programs available. *Faculty:* 8 full-time (3 women). *Students:* 22 full-time (13 women), 10 part-time (6 women); includes 4 minority (1 African American, 1 American Indian/Alaska Native, 1 Asian American or Pacific Islander, 1 Hispanic American), 2 international. Average age 26. 14 applicants, 50% accepted,

Communication—General

Texas Tech University (continued)

7 enrolled. In 2007, 8 degrees awarded. *Degree requirements:* For master's, thesis. *Entrance requirements:* For master's, GRE General Test. Additional exam requirements/recommendations for international students: Required—TOEFL (minimum score 550 paper-based; 213 computer-based). *Application deadline:* For fall admission, 3/1 priority date for international students; for spring admission, 11/1 priority date for international students. Applications are processed on a rolling basis. Application fee: $50 ($60 for international students). Electronic applications accepted. *Expenses:* Tuition, state resident: part-time $373 per credit hour. Tuition, nonresident: part-time $651 per credit hour. Tuition and fees vary according to program. *Financial support:* In 2007–08, 22 students received support, including 22 teaching assistantships with partial tuition reimbursements available (averaging $10,231 per year); research assistantships with partial tuition reimbursements available, Federal Work-Study and institutionally sponsored loans also available. Support available to part-time students. Financial award application deadline: 4/15; financial award applicants required to submit FAFSA. *Faculty research:* Computer mediated communication, crisis communication, instructional communication, intercultural communication, health communication. Total annual research expenditures: $14,168. *Unit head:* Dr. Patrick C. Hughes, Chair, 806-742-3911, Fax: 806-742-1025, E-mail: patrick.hughes@ttu.edu. *Application contact:* Dr. Juliann Scholl, Graduate Director, 806-742-1675, Fax: 806-742-1025, E-mail: juliann.scholl@ttu.edu.

Towson University, College of Graduate Studies and Research, Program in Communications Management, Towson, MD 21252-0001. Offers MS. *Students:* 9 full-time (8 women), 24 part-time (19 women); includes 10 minority (9 African Americans, 1 Hispanic American), 1 international. Average age 29. 13 applicants, 100% accepted, 8 enrolled. In 2007, 8 degrees awarded. *Degree requirements:* For master's, thesis. *Entrance requirements:* For master's, 24 credits in mass communications, public relations and/or advertising, writing and statistics; professional experience; minimum GPA of 3.0. *Application deadline:* For fall admission, 1/15 for domestic students. Application fee: $50. Electronic applications accepted. *Expenses:* Tuition, state resident: part-time $286 per credit. Tuition, nonresident: part-time $600 per credit. Required fees: $75 per credit. *Financial support:* Application deadline: 4/1; *Unit head:* Meg Algren, Graduate Program Director, 410-704-5641, E-mail: malgren@towson.edu. *Application contact:* 410-704-2501, Fax: 410-704-4675, E-mail: grads@towson.edu.

Towson University, College of Graduate Studies and Research, Program in Strategic Public Relations and Integrated Communications, Towson, MD 21252-0001. Offers Certificate. Evening/weekend programs available. Postbaccalaureate distance learning degree programs offered (no on-campus study). In 2007, 8 degrees awarded. *Entrance requirements:* For degree, 24 credits in related course work, minimum GPA of 3.0. *Application deadline:* For fall admission, 1/15 for domestic students. Application fee: $50. Electronic applications accepted. *Expenses:* Tuition, state resident: part-time $286 per credit. Tuition, nonresident: part-time $600 per credit. Required fees: $75 per credit. *Financial support:* Fellowships, teaching assistantships, career-related internships or fieldwork, Federal Work-Study, and unspecified assistantships available. Support available to part-time students. Financial award application deadline: 4/1; financial award applicants required to submit FAFSA. *Unit head:* Meg Algren, Graduate Program Director, 410-704-5641, E-mail: malgren@towson.edu. *Application contact:* 410-704-2501, Fax: 410-704-4675, E-mail: grads@towson.edu.

Trinity International University, Trinity Graduate School, Deerfield, IL 60015-1284. Offers bioethics (MA); communication and culture (MA); counseling psychology (MA); instructional leadership (M Ed); teaching (MA). Part-time and evening/weekend programs available. Postbaccalaureate distance learning degree programs offered (minimal on-campus study). *Faculty:* 4 full-time (3 women), 34 part-time/adjunct (12 women). *Students:* 92 full-time (71 women), 91 part-time (52 women). In 2007, 55 degrees awarded. *Degree requirements:* For master's, comprehensive exam. *Entrance requirements:* For master's, GRE General Test or MAT, minimum undergraduate GPA of 3.0. Additional exam requirements/recommendations for international students: Required—TOEFL (minimum score 580 paper-based; 237 computer-based), TWE (minimum score 4). *Application deadline:* For fall admission, 7/15 priority date for domestic and international students. Applications are processed on a rolling basis. Application fee: $25. Electronic applications accepted. *Expenses:* Tuition: Full-time $13,200; part-time $630 per credit. Required fees: $170. *Financial support:* Career-related internships or fieldwork, Federal Work-Study, institutionally sponsored loans, and tuition waivers (partial) available. Support available to part-time students. Financial award application deadline: 4/1; financial award applicants required to submit FAFSA. *Unit head:* Dr. James Stamoolis, Academic Dean, 847-317-7001, Fax: 847-317-4786. *Application contact:* Ken Botton, Director of Enrollment Services for University Records and Graduate Admissions, 800-533-0975, Fax: 847-317-8097, E-mail: kbotton@tiu.edu.

Trinity (Washington) University, School of Professional Studies, Washington, DC 20017-1094. Offers business administration (MBA); communication (MA); information security management (MS); organizational management (MSA), including federal program management, human resource management, nonprofit management, organizational development, public and community health. Part-time and evening/weekend programs available. *Degree requirements:* For master's, thesis (for some programs), capstone project (MSA). *Entrance requirements:* For master's, minimum GPA of 2.5. Additional exam requirements/recommendations for international students: Required—TOEFL (minimum score 550 paper-based; 213 computer-based).

Troy University, Graduate School, College of Communication and Fine Arts, Troy, AL 36082. Offers MS. *Degree requirements:* For master's, comprehensive exam, thesis optional. *Entrance requirements:* For master's, GRE, MAT, or GMAT. Additional exam requirements/recommendations for international students: Required—TOEFL (minimum score 523 paper-based; 200 computer-based). *Application deadline:* For fall admission, 6/1 for international students; for spring admission, 10/15 for international students. Application fee: $50. *Unit head:* Dr. Maryjo Cochran, Dean, 334-670-3869, Fax: 334-670-3547, E-mail: macochran@troy.edu. *Application contact:* Brenda K. Campbell, Director of Graduate Admissions, 334-670-3178, Fax: 334-670-3733, E-mail: bcamp@troy.edu.

Université de Montréal, Faculty of Arts and Sciences, Department of Communication, Montréal, QC H3C 3J7, Canada. Offers communication (PhD); communication in changing organizations (Certificate); communication sciences (M Sc). *Faculty:* 16 full-time (7 women), 4 part-time/adjunct (2 women). *Students:* 113 full-time (64 women), 11 part-time (6 women). 123 applicants, 27% accepted, 31 enrolled. In 2007, 20 master's, 1 doctorate awarded. *Degree requirements:* For master's, thesis; for doctorate, one foreign language, thesis/dissertation, general exam. *Entrance requirements:* For doctorate, proficiency in French. *Application deadline:* For fall admission, 2/1 priority date for domestic students; for winter admission, 11/1 priority date for domestic students; for spring admission, 2/1 priority date for domestic students. Application fee: $100. Electronic applications accepted. *Financial support:* Fellowships, research assistantships, teaching assistantships, career-related internships or fieldwork available. *Faculty research:* Mass media/new communication technologies, organizational communication. *Unit head:* Francois Cooren, Director, 514-343-7819, Fax: 514-343-2298, E-mail: f.cooren@umontreal.ca. *Application contact:* Micheline Frenette, Responsible for the M Sc, 514-343-5799, E-mail: micheline.frenette@umontreal.ca.

Université du Québec à Montréal, Graduate Programs, Program in Communications, Montréal, QC H3C 3P8, Canada. Offers MA, PhD. Part-time programs available. *Degree requirements:* For master's, thesis; for doctorate, thesis/dissertation. *Entrance requirements:* For master's, appropriate bachelor's degree or equivalent, proficiency in French; for doctorate, appropriate master's degree or equivalent, proficiency in French.

University at Albany, State University of New York, College of Arts and Sciences, Department of Communication, Albany, NY 12222-0001. Offers communication (MA); sociology and communication (PhD). Part-time programs available. *Students:* 32 full-time (26 women), 20 part-time (12 women). Average age 31. In 2007, 18 master's, 1 doctorate awarded. *Degree requirements:* For master's, comprehensive exam, thesis or alternative; for doctorate, comprehensive exam, thesis/dissertation. *Entrance requirements:* For master's, minimum GPA of 3.0; for doctorate, GRE, minimum GPA of 3.0. Additional exam requirements/recommendations for international students: Required—TOEFL (minimum score 550 paper-based; 213 computer-based). *Application deadline:* For fall admission, 2/20 priority date for domestic students, 5/1 for international students. Applications are processed on a rolling basis. Application fee: $75. Electronic applications accepted. *Expenses:* Tuition, state resident: part-time $576 per credit. Tuition, nonresident: part-time $910 per credit. Tuition and fees vary according to program. *Financial support:* Fellowships, teaching assistantships, career-related internships or fieldwork and institutionally sponsored loans available. Financial award application deadline: 3/1. *Faculty research:* Language and social interaction, campaign communication, media agenda-setting, high-speed management, organizational boundary-spanning. *Unit head:* Teresa Harrison, Chair, 518-442-4871.

University at Buffalo, the State University of New York, Graduate School, College of Arts and Sciences, Department of Communication, Buffalo, NY 14260. Offers MA, PhD. Part-time programs available. Terminal master's awarded for partial completion of doctoral program. *Degree requirements:* For master's, thesis; for doctorate, comprehensive exam, thesis/dissertation. *Entrance requirements:* For master's and doctorate, GRE General Test, minimum GPA of 3.0. Additional exam requirements/recommendations for international students: Required—TOEFL (minimum score 600 paper-based; 250 computer-based); Recommended—TWE. Electronic applications accepted. *Faculty research:* Technology, health, international, interpersonal.

The University of Akron, Graduate School, College of Fine and Applied Arts, School of Communication, Akron, OH 44325. Offers MA. Part-time and evening/weekend programs available. *Faculty:* 15 full-time (10 women), 1 part-time/adjunct (0 women). *Students:* 26 full-time (19 women), 14 part-time (7 women); includes 5 minority (3 African Americans, 2 Hispanic Americans), 4 international. Average age 32. 18 applicants, 72% accepted, 7 enrolled. In 2007, 8 degrees awarded. *Degree requirements:* For master's, thesis optional, thesis, project or written comprehensive exam. *Entrance requirements:* For master's, undergraduate major in communication or related area, minimum GPA of 2.75. Additional exam requirements/recommendations for international students: Required—TOEFL (minimum score 550 paper-based; 213 computer-based; 79 iBT). *Application deadline:* For fall admission, 5/1 for domestic students. Applications are processed on a rolling basis. Application fee: $30 ($40 for international students). Electronic applications accepted. *Expenses:* Tuition, state resident: full-time $6,164; part-time $342 per credit. Tuition, nonresident: full-time $10,575; part-time $588 per credit. Required fees: $806; $43 per credit. $12 per term. Tuition and fees vary according to course load, degree level and program. *Financial support:* In 2007–08, 2 research assistantships with full tuition reimbursements, 11 teaching assistantships with full tuition reimbursements were awarded; institutionally sponsored loans, tuition waivers (full), and unspecified assistantships also available. *Faculty research:* Communications theory, business and organization communications, criticism of communications, film and video studies, interpersonal and intercultural communications. *Unit head:* Dr. Carolyn Anderson, Director, 330-972-7600, E-mail: canderson@uakron.edu. *Application contact:* Dr. Richard Caplan, Graduate Coordinator, 330-972-5565, E-mail: caplan@uakron.edu.

The University of Alabama, Graduate School, College of Communication and Information Sciences, Tuscaloosa, AL 35487. Offers MA, MFA, MLIS, PhD. *Accreditation:* ACEJMC (one or more programs are accredited at the [master's] level). *Faculty:* 42 full-time (17 women), 2 part-time/adjunct (0 women). *Students:* 194 full-time (144 women), 204 part-time (156 women); includes 36 minority (25 African Americans, 3 American Indian/Alaska Native, 4 Asian Americans or Pacific Islanders, 4 Hispanic Americans), 21 international. Average age 31. 476 applicants, 49% accepted, 92 enrolled. In 2007, 136 master's, 8 doctorates awarded. *Degree requirements:* For master's, comprehensive exam, thesis or alternative; for doctorate, comprehensive exam, thesis/dissertation, must have Masters Degree. *Entrance requirements:* For master's, GRE; for doctorate, GRE, minimum graduate GPA of 3.0. Additional exam requirements/recommendations for international students: Required—TOEFL (minimum score 600 paper-based; 250 computer-based). *Application deadline:* For fall admission, 2/15 priority date for domestic and international students; for winter admission, 11/1 priority date for international students; for spring admission, 11/1 priority date for domestic students. Applications are processed on a rolling basis. Application fee: $30. Electronic applications accepted. *Expenses:* Tuition, state resident: full-time $5,700. Tuition, nonresident: full-time $16,518. *Financial support:* In 2007–08, 78 students received support, including 3 fellowships with tuition reimbursements available (averaging $15,000 per year), 34 research assistantships with tuition reimbursements available (averaging $13,045 per year), 38 teaching assistantships with tuition reimbursements available (averaging $13,045 per year); career-related internships or fieldwork, Federal Work-Study, institutionally sponsored loans, and health care benefits also available. Financial award application deadline: 2/15. *Faculty research:* Media research, broadcast policy and law, political communication, media management, political advertising. Total annual research expenditures: $117,274. *Unit head:* Dr. Jennings Bryant, Associate Dean for Graduate Studies, 205-348-8593, Fax: 205-348-6774. *Application contact:* Diane Shaddix, Information Contact, 205-348-8593, Fax: 205-348-6774, E-mail: dshaddix@bama.ua.edu.

The University of Alabama at Birmingham, School of Arts and Humanities, Department of Communication Studies, Birmingham, AL 35294. Offers communication management (MA). *Students:* 9 full-time (6 women), 20 part-time (16 women); includes 5 minority (all African Americans), 1 international. Average age 29. 16 applicants, 75% accepted. In 2007, 12 degrees awarded. *Unit head:* Dr. Virginia P. Richmond, Chair, 205-996-6522, Fax: 205-934-8916, E-mail: drvprl@uab.edu.

University of Alaska Fairbanks, College of Liberal Arts, Department of Communications, Fairbanks, AK 99775-7520. Offers professional communications (MA). Part-time programs available. *Degree requirements:* For master's, comprehensive exam, thesis or alternative. *Entrance requirements:* For master's, GRE General Test. Additional exam requirements/recommendations for international students: Required—TOEFL (minimum score 550 paper-based; 213 computer-based). Electronic applications accepted. *Faculty research:* Interpersonal communications, health communications, intercultural communications, politeness and face management in conversation, gender communication.

University of Alberta, Faculty of Extension, Edmonton, AB T6G 2E1, Canada. Offers communications and technology (MA).

University of Alberta, Faculty of Graduate Studies and Research, Program in Communications and Technology, Edmonton, AB T6G 2E1, Canada. Offers MACT.

The University of Arizona, Graduate College, College of Social and Behavioral Sciences, Department of Communication, Tucson, AZ 85721. Offers MA, PhD. Part-time programs available. *Faculty:* 10. *Students:* 17 full-time (13 women), 10 part-time (7 women); includes 2 minority (1 Asian American or Pacific Islander, 1 Hispanic American), 5 international. Average age 30. 48 applicants, 21% accepted, 9 enrolled. In 2007, 3 master's, 1 doctorate awarded. Terminal master's awarded for partial completion of doctoral program. *Degree requirements:* For master's, thesis optional; for doctorate, comprehensive exam, thesis/dissertation. *Entrance requirements:* For master's, GRE General Test, minimum GPA of 3.25, writing sample; for doctorate, GRE General Test, minimum GPA of 3.5, writing sample. Additional exam requirements/recommendations for international students: Required—TOEFL (minimum score 550 paper-based; 213 computer-based). *Application deadline:* Applications are processed on a rolling basis. Application fee: $50. Electronic applications accepted. *Financial support:* In 2007–08, 23 students received support; fellowships, research assistantships, teaching assistantships, career-related internships or fieldwork, Federal Work-Study, scholarships/grants, health care benefits, tuition waivers (full), and unspecified assistantships available. *Faculty research:* Health communication, new communication techologies. Total annual research expenditures: $23,565. *Unit head:* Dr. Chris Segrin, Department Head, 520-621-1366, Fax: 520-621-5504,

E-mail: segrin@email.arizona.edu. *Application contact:* Dr. Peggy Flyntz, Graduate Coordinator, 520-307-0695, Fax: 520-621-5504, E-mail: commgrad@email.arizona.edu.

University of Arkansas, Graduate School, J. William Fulbright College of Arts and Sciences, Department of Communication, Fayetteville, AR 72701-1201. Offers MA. Part-time programs available. *Students:* 8 full-time (5 women), 24 part-time (20 women); includes 3 minority (1 African American, 1 American Indian/Alaska Native, 1 Asian American or Pacific Islander), 3 international. In 2007, 15 degrees awarded. *Degree requirements:* For master's, thesis. *Entrance requirements:* For master's, GRE General Test. Application fee: $40 ($50 for international students). *Financial support:* In 2007–08, 20 teaching assistantships were awarded; fellowships, research assistantships, career-related internships or fieldwork and Federal Work-Study also available. Support available to part-time students. Financial award application deadline: 4/1; financial award applicants required to submit FAFSA. *Unit head:* Dr. Robert Brady, Departmental Chairperson, 479-575-3046, Fax: 479-575-6734, E-mail: rbrady@uark.edu. *Application contact:* Dennis Bailey, Graduate Coordinator, 479-575-3046, Fax: 479-575-6734, E-mail: dlb@uark.edu.

University of Baltimore, Graduate School, The Yale Gordon College of Liberal Arts, School of Communications Design, Baltimore, MD 21201-5779. Offers communications design (DCD); creative writing and publishing arts (MFA); integrated design (MFA); publications design (MA). Part-time and evening/weekend programs available. *Faculty:* 6 full-time (3 women), 10 part-time/adjunct (6 women). *Students:* 7 full-time (5 women), 11 part-time (7 women); includes 1 minority (Hispanic American), 4 international. Average age 34. 8 applicants, 38% accepted, 3 enrolled. In 2007, 5 degrees awarded. *Degree requirements:* For doctorate, applied project. *Entrance requirements:* For doctorate, minimum GPA of 3.2, related master's degree, interview. Additional exam requirements/recommendations for international students: Required—TOEFL (minimum score 550 paper-based; 213 computer-based). *Application deadline:* For fall admission, 7/15 for domestic students; for spring admission, 12/15 for domestic students. Applications are processed on a rolling basis. Application fee: $45. Electronic applications accepted. *Expenses: Contact institution.* Tuition and fees vary according to program. *Financial support:* In 2007–08, 2 fellowships with full tuition reimbursements (averaging $15,000 per year) were awarded. Financial award application deadline: 4/1; financial award applicants required to submit FAFSA. *Faculty research:* Information and graphics design, economics, hypermedia communications. *Unit head:* Dr. Edwin Gold, Co-Director, MFA in Integrated Design, 410-837-6022, E-mail: egold@ubalt.edu. *Application contact:* Wendy Bolyard.

See Close-Up on page 937.

University of Calgary, Faculty of Graduate Studies, Faculty of Communication and Culture, Calgary, AB T2N 1N4, Canada. Offers MA, MCS, PhD. Part-time and evening/weekend programs available. *Degree requirements:* For master's, thesis, project (MCS), thesis (MA); for doctorate, thesis/dissertation. *Entrance requirements:* For master's, minimum GPA of 3.0; for doctorate, master's degree, minimum GPA of 3.0, BA degree, min GPA of 3.0. Additional exam requirements/recommendations for international students: Required—TOEFL (minimum score 600 paper-based; 250 computer-based); Recommended—IELTS (minimum score 8). Electronic applications accepted. *Faculty research:* Science communications, structuration theory, organizational communication, communication theory, media law.

University of California, Davis, Graduate Studies, Program in Communication, Davis, CA 95616. Offers MA. *Degree requirements:* For master's, comprehensive exam (for some programs), thesis (for some programs). *Entrance requirements:* For master's, GRE. Additional exam requirements/recommendations for international students: Required—TOEFL (minimum score 550 paper-based; 213 computer-based).

University of California, San Diego, Office of Graduate Studies, Department of Communication, La Jolla, CA 92093. Offers MA, PhD. *Entrance requirements:* For doctorate, GRE General Test. Electronic applications accepted.

University of California, San Diego, Office of Graduate Studies, Interdisciplinary Program in Cognitive Science, La Jolla, CA 92093. Offers cognitive science/anthropology (PhD); cognitive science/communication (PhD); cognitive science/computer science and engineering (PhD); cognitive science/linguistics (PhD); cognitive science/neuroscience (PhD); cognitive science/philosophy (PhD); cognitive science/psychology (PhD); cognitive science/sociology (PhD). Admissions offered through affiliated departments. *Faculty:* 65 full-time (14 women). *Students:* 7 full-time (3 women). Average age 26. 2 applicants, 100% accepted, 2 enrolled. In 2007, 1 degree awarded. *Degree requirements:* For doctorate, thesis/dissertation. *Entrance requirements:* For doctorate, GRE General Test, acceptance into one of the 8 participating departments. *Application deadline:* Applications are processed on a rolling basis. Application fee: $0. *Faculty research:* Language and cognition, philosophy of mind, visual perception, biological anthropology, sociolinguistics. *Unit head:* Gary Cottrell, Director, 858-534-7141, Fax: 858-534-1128, E-mail: gcottrell@ucsd.edu. *Application contact:* Beverley Walton, Coordinator, 858-534-4387, E-mail: bwalton@ucsd.edu.

University of California, Santa Barbara, Graduate Division, College of Letters and Sciences, Division of Social Sciences, Department of Communication, Santa Barbara, CA 93106. Offers PhD, MA/PhD. *Faculty:* 20 full-time (9 women). *Students:* 36 full-time (25 women); includes 10 minority (1 African American, 1 American Indian/Alaska Native, 6 Asian Americans or Pacific Islanders, 2 Hispanic Americans), 3 international. Average age 29. 121 applicants, 15% accepted, 10 enrolled. In 2007, 6 doctorates awarded. *Median time to degree:* Of those who began their doctoral program in fall 1999, 50% received their degree in 8 years or less. *Degree requirements:* For doctorate, comprehensive exam, thesis/dissertation. *Entrance requirements:* For doctorate, GRE General Test. Additional exam requirements/recommendations for international students: Required—TOEFL (minimum score 600 paper-based; 213 computer-based; 80 iBT). *Application deadline:* For fall admission, 1/1 for domestic and international students. Application fee: $60. Electronic applications accepted. *Expenses:* Tuition, nonresident: full-time $14,888. Required fees: $10,108. *Financial support:* In 2007–08, 36 students received support, including 15 fellowships with full tuition reimbursements available (averaging $8,285 per year), 5 research assistantships (averaging $17,000 per year), 31 teaching assistantships with full tuition reimbursements available (averaging $17,000 per year); Federal Work-Study, institutionally sponsored loans, scholarships/grants, health care benefits, tuition waivers (full), and unspecified assistantships also available. Financial award application deadline: 12/15; financial award applicants required to submit FAFSA. *Faculty research:* Interpersonal communication, organizational communication, media/mass communication, intercultural communication, intrapersonal communication. *Unit head:* Michael Stohl, Chair, 805-893-7935, E-mail: mstohl@comm.ucsb.edu. *Application contact:* Nancy Siris-Rawls, Graduate Program Assistant, 805-893-3046, Fax: 805-893-7483, E-mail: nsiris@comm.ucsb.edu.

University of California, Santa Cruz, Division of Graduate Studies, Division of Physical and Biological Sciences, Program in Science Communication, Santa Cruz, CA 95064. Offers science illustration (Certificate); science writing (Certificate). *Faculty:* 8 full-time (4 women). *Students:* 11 full-time (9 women); includes 3 minority (all Asian Americans or Pacific Islanders), 2 international. In 2007, 19 degrees awarded. *Entrance requirements:* For degree, GRE General Test, GRE Subject Test, bachelor's degree in science. Application fee: $60. Electronic applications accepted. *Expenses:* Tuition, nonresident: full-time $14,694. Required fees: $11,360. *Financial support:* Fellowships, research assistantships, teaching assistantships, career-related internships or fieldwork, Federal Work-Study, institutionally sponsored loans, and scholarships/grants available. Financial award application deadline: 2/1. *Unit head:* Robert Irion, Director, 831-459-4475. *Application contact:* Andrea Michels, Department Assistant, 831-459-4475, E-mail: scicom@ucsc.edu.

University of Central Florida, College of Sciences, Nicholson School of Communication, Orlando, FL 32816. Offers MA. Part-time and evening/weekend programs available. *Faculty:* 43 full-time (18 women), 37 part-time/adjunct (18 women). *Degree requirements:* For master's, thesis or comprehensive exam. *Entrance requirements:* For master's, GRE General Test, minimum GPA of 3.0 in last 60 hours of course work. Additional exam requirements/recommendations for international students: Required—TOEFL. *Application deadline:* For fall admission, 7/15 for domestic students; for spring admission, 12/7 for domestic students. Application fee: $30. Electronic applications accepted. *Expenses:* Tuition, state resident: full-time $6,484. Tuition, nonresident: full-time $23,938. Tuition and fees vary according to program. *Financial support:* Fellowships with partial tuition reimbursements, research assistantships with partial tuition reimbursements, teaching assistantships with partial tuition reimbursements, career-related internships or fieldwork, Federal Work-Study, institutionally sponsored loans, tuition waivers (partial), and unspecified assistantships available. Financial award application deadline: 3/1; financial award applicants required to submit FAFSA. *Faculty research:* Persuasion, communication apprehension, nonverbal communication, conflict resolution. *Unit head:* Dr. Mary Alice Shaver, Director, 407-823-2681, Fax: 407-823-5216, E-mail: mshaver@mail.ucf.edu.

University of Central Missouri, The Graduate School, College of Arts, Humanities and Social Sciences, Department of Communication, Warrensburg, MO 64093. Offers communication (MA); speech communication (MA). Part-time programs available. *Faculty:* 15 full-time (7 women). *Students:* 15 full-time (7 women), 39 part-time (26 women); includes 4 minority (2 African Americans, 1 American Indian/Alaska Native, 1 Asian American or Pacific Islander), 11 international. Average age 29. 33 applicants, 55% accepted, 11 enrolled. In 2007, 13 degrees awarded. *Degree requirements:* For master's, comprehensive exam, internship, research papers or thesis. *Entrance requirements:* For master's, minimum GPA of 2.5. Additional exam requirements/recommendations for international students: Required—TOEFL (minimum score 500 paper-based; 173 computer-based). *Application deadline:* For fall admission, 6/1 priority date for domestic students, 5/1 priority date for international students; for spring admission, 10/1 priority date for domestic students, 10/1 for international students. Applications are processed on a rolling basis. Application fee: $30 ($50 for international students). *Expenses:* Tuition, state resident: full-time $6,259; part-time $256 per credit hour. Tuition, nonresident: full-time $11,915; part-time $491 per credit hour. Required fees: $604; $20 per credit hour. *Financial support:* In 2007–08, 14 students received support; teaching assistantships with full tuition reimbursements available, career-related internships or fieldwork, Federal Work-Study, scholarships/grants, unspecified assistantships, and administrative and laboratory assistantships available. Support available to part-time students. Financial award application deadline: 3/1; financial award applicants required to submit FAFSA. *Unit head:* Dr. Terry Cunconan, Chair, 660-543-4890, Fax: 660-543-8006, E-mail: cunconan@ucmo.edu.

University of Cincinnati, Graduate School, McMicken College of Arts and Sciences, Department of Communication, Cincinnati, OH 45221. Offers MA. Part-time programs available. *Faculty:* 9 full-time (5 women). *Students:* 17 full-time (13 women), 2 part-time (1 woman); includes 3 minority (2 African Americans, 1 Asian American or Pacific Islander). Average age 23. 28 applicants, 57% accepted, 16 enrolled. In 2007, 9 degrees awarded. *Degree requirements:* For master's, comprehensive exam, thesis or alternative. *Entrance requirements:* For master's, GRE General Test, undergraduate course work in communication. Additional exam requirements/recommendations for international students: Required—TOEFL. *Application deadline:* For fall admission, 2/1 for domestic students. Application fee: $30. Electronic applications accepted. *Financial support:* In 2007–08, fellowships with full tuition reimbursements (averaging $9,000 per year), research assistantships with full tuition reimbursements (averaging $9,000 per year), teaching assistantships with full tuition reimbursements (averaging $9,000 per year) were awarded; tuition waivers (partial) and unspecified assistantships also available. Financial award application deadline: 5/1. *Faculty research:* Political communication, health communication, organizational communication, interpersonal communication. Total annual research expenditures: $50 million. *Unit head:* Dr. Teresa Sabourin, Head, 513-556-4451, Fax: 513-556-0899. *Application contact:* Dr. Judith S. Trent, Graduate Program Director, 513-556-4460, Fax: 513-556-4493, E-mail: judith.trent@uc.edu.

University of Colorado at Boulder, Graduate School, College of Arts and Sciences, Department of Communication, Boulder, CO 80309. Offers MA, PhD. *Faculty:* 15. *Students:* 44 full-time (31 women), 13 part-time (8 women); includes 7 minority (2 African Americans, 1 Asian American or Pacific Islander, 4 Hispanic Americans), 4 international. Average age 33. 34 applicants, 74% accepted. In 2007, 9 master's, 7 doctorates awarded. *Degree requirements:* For master's, comprehensive exam, thesis optional; for doctorate, comprehensive exam, thesis/dissertation. *Entrance requirements:* For master's and doctorate, GRE General Test, minimum undergraduate GPA of 3.2. *Application deadline:* For fall admission, 12/31 priority date for domestic students, 12/15 for international students; for spring admission, 9/15 for domestic students, 8/15 for international students. Applications are processed on a rolling basis. Application fee: $50 ($60 for international students). *Financial support:* In 2007–08, 18 fellowships (averaging $2,015 per year), 2 research assistantships (averaging $10,835 per year) were awarded; tuition waivers (full) also available. Financial award application deadline: 12/15. *Faculty research:* Organizational communication, computer-mediated communication and new technology, critical cultural studies, rhetoric and civil discourse, interpersonal communication, language and social interaction. Total annual research expenditures: $17,914. *Unit head:* Robert Craig, Chair, 303-492-6498, Fax: 303-492-8411, E-mail: robert.craig@colorado.edu. *Application contact:* Josephine Kapatayes, Administrative Assistant, 303-492-7307, Fax: 303-492-8411, E-mail: commgrad@colorado.edu.

University of Colorado at Boulder, Graduate School, School of Journalism and Mass Communication, Boulder, CO 80309. Offers communication (PhD), including media studies; mass communication research (MA); newsgathering (MA). *Accreditation:* ACEJMC (one or more programs are accredited). Part-time programs available. *Faculty:* 21. *Students:* 83 full-time (56 women), 10 part-time (7 women); includes 9 minority (3 African Americans, 2 Asian Americans or Pacific Islanders, 4 Hispanic Americans), 10 international. Average age 31. 122 applicants, 74% accepted. In 2007, 38 master's, 6 doctorates awarded. *Degree requirements:* For master's, comprehensive exam, thesis or alternative; for doctorate, comprehensive exam, thesis/dissertation. *Entrance requirements:* For master's, GRE General Test, minimum undergraduate GPA of 2.75; for doctorate, GRE General Test, minimum undergraduate GPA of 3.2, 3.5 graduate. *Application deadline:* For fall admission, 2/15 for domestic students, 12/1 for international students. Applications are processed on a rolling basis. Application fee: $50 ($60 for international students). *Financial support:* In 2007–08, 26 fellowships (averaging $2,908 per year), 10 research assistantships with tuition reimbursements (averaging $14,446 per year) were awarded; institutionally sponsored loans and unspecified assistantships also available. Financial award application deadline: 3/1. *Faculty research:* Writing on science and the environment, mass communication and public opinion, minority representation in the media, media and culture. Total annual research expenditures: $326,556. *Unit head:* Paul Voakes, Dean, 303-492-4364, Fax: 303-492-0969, E-mail: paul.voakes@colorado.edu. *Application contact:* Graduate Program Assistant, 303-492-5008, Fax: 303-492-0969, E-mail: sjmcgrad@colorado.edu.

University of Colorado at Colorado Springs, Graduate School, College of Letters, Arts and Sciences, Department of Communications, Colorado Springs, CO 80933-7150. Offers MA. Part-time programs available. *Faculty:* 8 full-time (6 women). *Students:* 40 full-time (30 women), 20 part-time (14 women); includes 12 minority (2 African Americans, 2 Asian Americans or Pacific Islanders, 8 Hispanic Americans). Average age 31. 14 applicants, 93% accepted, 8 enrolled. In 2007, 7 degrees awarded. *Degree requirements:* For master's, thesis optional. *Entrance requirements:* For master's, GRE General Test. *Financial support:* Teaching assistantships, career-related internships or fieldwork, Federal Work-Study, and institutionally sponsored loans available. Support available to part-time students. *Faculty research:* Organizational communication, interpersonal communication, communication education, oral communication, cultural diversity. *Unit head:* Dr. David Nelson, Chair, 719-262-4129, Fax: 719-262-4030, E-mail: drnelson@uccs.edu. *Application contact:* Karen Norris, Program Assistant, 719-262-4114, Fax: 719-262-4030, E-mail: knorris@uccs.edu.

University of Colorado Denver, College of Liberal Arts and Sciences, Department of Communication, Program in Communication, Denver, CO 80217-3364. Offers MA. Part-time and

Communication—General

University of Colorado Denver (continued)

evening/weekend programs available. *Faculty:* 14 full-time (9 women). *Students:* 4 full-time (3 women), 11 part-time (9 women); includes 3 minority (2 African Americans, 1 Hispanic American), 2 international. Average age 28. 21 applicants, 38% accepted, 5 enrolled. In 2007, 2 degrees awarded. *Degree requirements:* For master's, comprehensive exam, thesis or alternative. *Entrance requirements:* For master's, GRE General Test, resumé or curriculum vitae. Additional exam requirements/recommendations for international students: Required—TOEFL (minimum score 525 paper-based; 197 computer-based). *Application deadline:* For fall admission, 6/1 for domestic students. Applications are processed on a rolling basis. Application fee: $50 ($75 for international students). Electronic applications accepted. *Financial support:* Research assistantships, teaching assistantships, Federal Work-Study available. Financial award application deadline: 4/1; financial award applicants required to submit FAFSA. *Application contact:* Sally Thee, Program Assistant, 303-556-2591, Fax: 303-556-6018, E-mail: sally.thee@cudenver.edu.

University of Connecticut, Graduate School, College of Liberal Arts and Sciences, Department of Communication Sciences, Storrs, CT 06269. Offers communication sciences (MA, Au D, PhD), including audiology (Au D, PhD), communication processes (MA), communication processes and marketing communication (PhD), speech-language pathology (MA, PhD); Au D/PhD. *Accreditation:* ASHA (one or more programs are accredited). *Faculty:* 25 full-time (10 women). *Students:* 103 full-time (79 women), 6 part-time (1 woman); includes 2 minority (1 African American, 1 Asian American or Pacific Islander), 11 international. Average age 27. 237 applicants, 18% accepted, 34 enrolled. In 2007, 19 master's, 6 doctorates awarded. Terminal master's awarded for partial completion of doctoral program. *Degree requirements:* For master's, comprehensive exam; for doctorate, thesis/dissertation. *Entrance requirements:* For master's and doctorate, GRE General Test. Additional exam requirements/recommendations for international students: Required—TOEFL (minimum score 550 paper-based; 213 computer-based). *Application deadline:* For fall admission, 2/1 priority date for domestic and international students; for spring admission, 11/1 for domestic students, 10/1 for international students. Applications are processed on a rolling basis. Application fee: $55. Electronic applications accepted. *Expenses:* Tuition, state resident: part-time $469 per credit hour. Tuition, nonresident: part-time $1,218 per credit hour. *Financial support:* In 2007–08, 10 research assistantships with full tuition reimbursements, 42 teaching assistantships with full tuition reimbursements were awarded; fellowships, Federal Work-Study, scholarships/grants, health care benefits, and unspecified assistantships also available. Financial award application deadline: 2/1; financial award applicants required to submit FAFSA. *Unit head:* Carl A. Coelho, Chair, 860-486-2628. *Application contact:* Sue Kiss, Administrative Assistant, 860-486-2628, Fax: 860-486-5422, E-mail: susan.kiss@uconn.edu.

University of Connecticut, Graduate School, College of Liberal Arts and Sciences, Department of Communication Sciences, Field of Communication Sciences, Program in Communication Processes, Storrs, CT 06269. Offers MA. *Faculty:* 13 full-time (7 women). *Students:* 9 full-time (3 women), 1 international. Average age 25. 34 applicants, 6% accepted, 2 enrolled. In 2007, 4 degrees awarded. *Degree requirements:* For master's, comprehensive exam. *Entrance requirements:* For master's, GRE General Test. Additional exam requirements/recommendations for international students: Required—TOEFL (minimum score 550 paper-based; 213 computer-based). *Application deadline:* For fall admission, 2/1 priority date for domestic and international students; for spring admission, 11/1 for domestic students, 10/1 for international students. Applications are processed on a rolling basis. Application fee: $55. Electronic applications accepted. *Expenses:* Tuition, state resident: part-time $469 per credit hour. Tuition, nonresident: part-time $1,218 per credit hour. *Financial support:* In 2007–08, 1 research assistantship with full tuition reimbursement, 8 teaching assistantships with full tuition reimbursements were awarded; Federal Work-Study, scholarships/grants, health care benefits, and unspecified assistantships also available. Financial award application deadline: 2/1; financial award applicants required to submit FAFSA. *Application contact:* Sue Kiss, Administrative Assistant, 860-486-2628, Fax: 860-486-5422, E-mail: susan.kiss@uconn.edu.

University of Dayton, Graduate School, College of Arts and Sciences, Department of Communication, Dayton, OH 45469-1300. Offers MA. Part-time and evening/weekend programs available. *Faculty:* 8 full-time (5 women), 1 part-time/adjunct (0 women). *Students:* 15 full-time (12 women), 1 (woman) part-time; includes 3 minority (1 African American, 2 Asian Americans or Pacific Islanders). Average age 26. 41 applicants, 59% accepted, 3 enrolled. In 2007, 8 degrees awarded. *Degree requirements:* For master's, comprehensive exam, thesis optional. *Entrance requirements:* For master's, GRE General Test, minimum undergraduate GPA of 3.0. Additional exam requirements/recommendations for international students: Required—TOEFL (minimum score 550 paper-based; 213 computer-based; 80 iBT). *Application deadline:* For fall admission, 3/1 priority date for domestic and international students; for winter admission, 7/1 priority date for international students; for spring admission, 1/1 priority date for international students. Applications are processed on a rolling basis. Application fee: $0. Electronic applications accepted. *Financial support:* In 2007–08, 7 teaching assistantships with full tuition reimbursements (averaging $9,000 per year) were awarded; career-related internships or fieldwork, institutionally sponsored loans, health care benefits, and unspecified assistantships also available. Support available to part-time students. Financial award applicants required to submit FAFSA. *Faculty research:* Health communication, organizational communication, mass communication. *Unit head:* Dr. Donald Yoder, Chair, 937-229-2028, E-mail: donald.yoder@notes.udayton.edu. *Application contact:* Angela Jones-Glukhov, Associate Director of Graduate Admissions, 937-229-4305, Fax: 937-229-4729.

University of Delaware, College of Arts and Sciences, Department of Communication, Newark, DE 19716. Offers MA. Part-time and evening/weekend programs available. *Faculty:* 14 full-time (7 women). *Students:* 18 full-time (16 women), 2 part-time (both women); includes 1 minority (African American), 1 international. Average age 26. 22 applicants, 68% accepted, 6 enrolled. In 2007, 4 degrees awarded. *Degree requirements:* For master's, comprehensive exam (for some programs), thesis (for some programs). *Entrance requirements:* For master's, GRE General Test, minimum GPA of 3.0. Additional exam requirements/recommendations for international students: Required—TOEFL (minimum score 600 paper-based; 270 computer-based). *Application deadline:* For fall admission, 3/1 for domestic students. Application fee: $60. Electronic applications accepted. *Financial support:* In 2007–08, 10 students received support, including 10 teaching assistantships with full tuition reimbursements available (averaging $14,600 per year); career-related internships or fieldwork also available. Financial award application deadline: 2/10. *Faculty research:* Politics and the media, online social interaction technologies, mass communication law, media and the perceptions of reality, the role of communication in public opinion processes, small group research, communication during resource dilemmas. *Unit head:* Dr. Elizabeth Perse, Chair, 302-831-8029, Fax: 302-831-1892, E-mail: eperse@udel.edu. *Application contact:* Dr. Nancy Signorielli, Information Contact, 302-831-8041, Fax: 302-831-1892, E-mail: nancys@udel.edu.

University of Denver, Faculty of Arts and Humanities/Social Sciences, School of Communication, Denver, CO 80208. Offers MA, MS, PhD. Part-time programs available. *Faculty:* 20 full-time (12 women). *Students:* 59 full-time (37 women), 48 part-time (35 women); includes 12 minority (6 African Americans, 1 American Indian/Alaska Native, 2 Asian Americans or Pacific Islanders, 3 Hispanic Americans), 10 international. Average age 29. In 2007, 39 master's, 6 doctorates awarded. *Degree requirements:* For doctorate, one foreign language, thesis/dissertation. *Entrance requirements:* For master's, GRE General Test. Additional exam requirements/recommendations for international students: Required—TOEFL, TWE. *Application deadline:* Applications are processed on a rolling basis. Application fee: $50. Electronic applications accepted. *Financial support:* Career-related internships or fieldwork, Federal Work-Study, institutionally sponsored loans, and scholarships/grants available. Support available to part-time students. *Unit head:* Chairperson. *Application contact:* Information Contact, 303-871-2166, E-mail: mcomadm@du.edu.

See Close-Up on page 939.

University of Denver, University College, Denver, CO 80208. Offers applied communication (MAS, MPS, Certificate); computer information systems (MAS, Certificate); environmental policy and management (MAS, Certificate); geographic information systems (MAS, Certificate); human resource administration (MPS, Certificate); knowledge and information technologies (MAS); liberal studies (MLS, Certificate); modern languages (MLS, Certificate); organizational leadership (MPS, Certificate); security management (Certificate); technology management (MAS, Certificate), including 21st century strategic management (MAS), international markets (MAS), project management (MAS), research and development management (MAS); telecommunications (MAS, Certificate), including broadband (MAS), telecommunications management and policy (MAS), telecommunications technology (MAS), wireless networks (MAS). Part-time and evening/weekend programs available. Postbaccalaureate distance learning degree programs offered (no on-campus study). *Students:* 29 full-time (15 women), 524 part-time (304 women); includes 92 minority (37 African Americans, 3 American Indian/Alaska Native, 17 Asian Americans or Pacific Islanders, 35 Hispanic Americans), 53 international. Average age 36. 625 applicants, 97% accepted, 359 enrolled. In 2007, 151 master's, 2 Certificates awarded. *Entrance requirements:* Additional exam requirements/recommendations for international students: Required—TOEFL (minimum score 550 paper-based; 213 computer-based). *Application deadline:* Applications are processed on a rolling basis. Application fee: $75. Electronic applications accepted. *Expenses: Contact institution. Financial support:* Applicants required to submit FAFSA. *Unit head:* Dr. James Davis, Dean, 303-871-2291, Fax: 303-871-4047, E-mail: jdavis@du.edu. *Application contact:* Information Contact, 303-871-3069.

University of Dubuque, Program in Communication, Dubuque, IA 52001-5099. Offers information technologies communication (MAC); leadership and management (MAC); strategic and corporate communication (MAC). Part-time and evening/weekend programs available. *Faculty:* 5 full-time (3 women), 1 part-time/adjunct (0 women). *Students:* 2 full-time (1 woman), 25 part-time (16 women); includes 2 minority (both African Americans) Average age 35. In 2007, 7 degrees awarded. *Degree requirements:* For master's, thesis optional. *Entrance requirements:* For master's, GRE, minimum GPA of 2.5, 3 recommendations. Additional exam requirements/recommendations for international students: Required—TOEFL (minimum score 550 paper-based; 213 computer-based). *Application deadline:* For fall admission, 8/15 priority date for domestic students, 7/15 priority date for international students. Applications are processed on a rolling basis. Application fee: $25. Electronic applications accepted. *Financial support:* Teaching assistantships with full tuition reimbursements, Federal Work-Study available. Support available to part-time students. Financial award application deadline: 4/1. *Faculty research:* Intercultural communication, management communication. *Unit head:* Dr. Robert Reid, Program Director, 563-589-3188, Fax: 563-589-3690, E-mail: rreid@dbq.edu. *Application contact:* Carol A. Knockle, Graduate Program Coordinator, 563-589-3300, Fax: 563-589-3184, E-mail: mac@dbq.edu.

University of Florida, Graduate School, College of Journalism and Communications, Gainesville, FL 32611. Offers advertising (M Adv); journalism (MAMC); mass communication (MAMC, PhD); public relations (MAMC); telecommunication (MAMC); JD/MAMC; JD/PhD. *Accreditation:* ACEJMC (one or more programs are accredited). Part-time programs available. *Faculty:* 48 full-time (26 women). *Students:* 28 (17 women); includes 5 minority (1 African American, 2 Asian Americans or Pacific Islanders, 2 Hispanic Americans) 11 international. In 2007, 14 degrees awarded. Terminal master's awarded for partial completion of doctoral program. *Degree requirements:* For master's, thesis optional; for doctorate, thesis/dissertation. *Entrance requirements:* For master's and doctorate, GRE General Test, minimum GPA of 3.0. Additional exam requirements/recommendations for international students: Required—TOEFL (minimum score 550 paper-based; 213 computer-based). *Application deadline:* For fall admission, 6/1 for domestic students. Applications are processed on a rolling basis. Application fee: $30. Electronic applications accepted. *Expenses:* Tuition, state resident: full-time $7,478. Tuition, nonresident: full-time $22,603. *Financial support:* Fellowships with full and partial tuition reimbursements, research assistantships with full tuition reimbursements, teaching assistantships with full tuition reimbursements, career-related internships or fieldwork, Federal Work-Study, institutionally sponsored loans, and unspecified assistantships available. Support available to part-time students. Financial award application deadline: 4/15. *Faculty research:* Public opinion, law and policy, regulation, environmental communication, international communication. *Unit head:* Dr. John W. Wright, Interim Dean, 352-392-0466. *Application contact:* Dr. Debbie Treise, Associate Dean for Graduate Programs, 352-392-6557, Fax: 352-392-1794, E-mail: dtreise@jou.ufl.edu.

University of Georgia, Graduate School, Grady School of Journalism and Mass Communication, Athens, GA 30602. Offers journalism and mass communication (MA); mass communication (PhD). *Accreditation:* ACEJMC (one or more programs are accredited). *Faculty:* 43 full-time (20 women). *Students:* 80 full-time (49 women), 12 part-time (6 women); includes 8 minority (6 African Americans, 1 Asian American or Pacific Islander, 1 Hispanic American), 23 international. 263 applicants, 34% accepted, 33 enrolled. In 2007, 35 master's, 5 doctorates awarded. *Degree requirements:* For master's, comprehensive exam, thesis (MA); for doctorate, comprehensive exam, thesis/dissertation. *Entrance requirements:* For master's and doctorate, GRE General Test. Additional exam requirements/recommendations for international students: Required—TOEFL, TWE (PhD). *Application deadline:* For spring admission, 2/15 for domestic students. Application fee: $50. Electronic applications accepted. *Financial support:* Research assistantships, teaching assistantships, tuition waivers (full) and unspecified assistantships available. *Unit head:* Dr. E. Culpepper Clark, Dean, 706-542-1704, Fax: 706-542-2183, E-mail: cully@uga.edu. *Application contact:* Dr. Jeffrey K. Springston, Graduate Coordinator, 706-542-5030, E-mail: jspring@uga.edu.

University of Hartford, College of Arts and Sciences, Program in Communication, West Hartford, CT 06117-1599. Offers MA. Part-time and evening/weekend programs available. *Faculty:* 7 full-time (2 women). *Students:* 8 full-time (7 women), 30 part-time (22 women); includes 4 minority (3 African Americans, 1 Hispanic American), 6 international. Average age 29. 28 applicants, 75% accepted, 12 enrolled. In 2007, 20 degrees awarded. *Degree requirements:* For master's, comprehensive exam, thesis optional. *Entrance requirements:* For master's, GRE, 3 letters of recommendation. Additional exam requirements/recommendations for international students: Required—TOEFL (minimum score 550 paper-based; 213 computer-based). *Application deadline:* For fall admission, 4/15 for domestic students; for spring admission, 11/15 for domestic students. Applications are processed on a rolling basis. Application fee: $45. Electronic applications accepted. *Expenses: Contact institution. Financial support:* Teaching assistantships, career-related internships or fieldwork, Federal Work-Study, and unspecified assistantships available. Support available to part-time students. Financial award application deadline: 6/1; financial award applicants required to submit FAFSA. *Faculty research:* Communication reticence, relational communication, media literacy, journalism history, media audience attitude and behavior. *Unit head:* Dr. Sundeep Muppidi, Graduate Director, 860-768-5054, E-mail: muppidi@hartford.edu. *Application contact:* Reneé Murphy, Assistant Director of Graduate Admissions, 860-768-4371, Fax: 860-768-5160, E-mail: rmurphy@hartford.edu.

University of Hawaii at Manoa, Graduate Division, Colleges of Arts and Sciences, College of Social Sciences, School of Communications, Program in Communication, Honolulu, HI 96822. Offers MA. Part-time programs available. *Faculty:* 20 full-time (5 women), 2 part-time/adjunct (0 women). *Students:* 18 full-time (10 women), 14 part-time (11 women); includes 15 minority (1 African American, 13 Asian Americans or Pacific Islanders, 1 Hispanic American), 5 international. 34 applicants, 32% accepted, 9 enrolled. *Degree requirements:* For master's, thesis optional. *Entrance requirements:* Additional exam requirements/recommendations for international students: Required—TOEFL (minimum score 600 paper-based; 250 computer-based; 100 iBT), IELTS (minimum score 7). *Application deadline:* For fall admissión, 2/1 for domestic students, 1/15 for international students. Application fee: $50. *Financial support:* In 2007–08, 2 research assistantships (averaging $16,188 per year), 1 teaching assistantship (averaging $13,296 per year) were awarded. *Application contact:* Dr. Gary Fontaine, Graduate Field Chairperson, 808-956-8715, Fax: 808-956-5396, E-mail: fontaine@hawaii.edu.

University of Houston, College of Liberal Arts and Social Sciences, School of Communication, Houston, TX 77204. Offers mass communication studies (MA); public relations studies (MA); speech communication (MA). Part-time and evening/weekend programs available. *Faculty:* 8 full-time (3 women), 3 part-time/adjunct (2 women). *Students:* 34 full-time (30 women), 53 part-time (40 women); includes 37 minority (24 African Americans, 3 Asian Americans or Pacific Islanders, 10 Hispanic Americans), 11 international. Average age 29. 46 applicants, 80% accepted, 18 enrolled. In 2007, 24 degrees awarded. *Entrance requirements:* For master's, GRE General Test, minimum GPA of 3.0 in last 60 hours of course work. *Application deadline:* For fall admission, 7/3 priority date for domestic students. Applications are processed on a rolling basis. Application fee: $25 ($75 for international students). *Expenses:* Tuition, state resident: full-time $6,297; part-time $262 per credit. Tuition, nonresident: full-time $12,969; part-time $540 per credit. Required fees: $2,696. *Financial support:* In 2007–08, 4 fellowships with full tuition reimbursements (averaging $9,750 per year), 8 teaching assistantships with full tuition reimbursements (averaging $9,750 per year) were awarded; research assistantships with full tuition reimbursements, career-related internships or fieldwork, Federal Work-Study, institutionally sponsored loans, scholarships/grants, health care benefits, and unspecified assistantships also available. Support available to part-time students. Financial award application deadline: 2/1. *Faculty research:* Risk communication, relationship development, critical studies, corporate communication. *Unit head:* Beth Olson, Chairperson, 713-743-2873, Fax: 713-743-2876, E-mail: bolson@uh.edu. *Application contact:* Angela Parrish, Graduate Coordinator, 713-743-2873, Fax: 713-743-2876, E-mail: aparrish@bayou.uh.edu.

University of Illinois at Chicago, Graduate College, College of Liberal Arts and Sciences, Department of Communication, Chicago, IL 60607-7128. Offers communication (MA); mass communication (MA). Evening/weekend programs available. *Degree requirements:* For master's, thesis. *Entrance requirements:* For master's, GRE General Test, minimum GPA of 3.0 in last 90 hours. Additional exam requirements/recommendations for international students: Required—TOEFL. Electronic applications accepted. *Faculty research:* Organizational, political, and interpersonal communication; public relations.

University of Illinois at Springfield, Graduate Programs, College of Liberal Arts and Sciences, Program in Communication, Springfield, IL 62703-5407. Offers MA. Part-time and evening/weekend programs available. *Faculty:* 11 full-time (6 women). *Students:* 14 full-time (13 women), 25 part-time (17 women); includes 4 minority (2 African Americans, 1 Asian American or Pacific Islander, 1 Hispanic American), 1 international. Average age 31. 22 applicants, 59% accepted, 9 enrolled. In 2007, 20 degrees awarded. *Degree requirements:* For master's, comprehensive exam, thesis, or project. *Entrance requirements:* For master's, UIS Graduate Admission Writing Exam, minimum undergraduate GPA of 3.0. Additional exam requirements/recommendations for international students: Required—TOEFL (minimum score 580 paper-based). *Application deadline:* Applications are processed on a rolling basis. Application fee: $50 ($60 for international students). Electronic applications accepted. *Expenses:* Tuition, state resident: full-time $5,424; part-time $226 per credit hour. Tuition, nonresident: part-time $553 per credit hour. Required fees: $618 per term. *Financial support:* In 2007–08, research assistantships with full tuition reimbursements (averaging $7,988 per year), teaching assistantships with full tuition reimbursements (averaging $7,988 per year) were awarded; career-related internships or fieldwork, Federal Work-Study, scholarships/grants, health care benefits, and unspecified assistantships also available. Support available to part-time students. Financial award application deadline: 11/15; financial award applicants required to submit FAFSA. *Unit head:* Dr. Mary Bohlen, Program Administrator, 217-206-7362, Fax: 217-206-6217.

University of Illinois at Urbana–Champaign, Graduate College, College of Communications, Institute of Communications Research, Champaign, IL 61820. Offers communications (PhD). *Faculty:* 7 full-time (2 women). *Students:* 48 full-time (25 women), 11 part-time (9 women); includes 14 minority (6 African Americans, 4 Asian Americans or Pacific Islanders, 4 Hispanic Americans), 17 international. 156 applicants, 6% accepted, 9 enrolled. In 2007, 4 doctorates awarded. *Degree requirements:* For doctorate, thesis/dissertation. *Entrance requirements:* For doctorate, GRE General Test, minimum GPA of 3.0. *Application deadline:* For fall admission, 2/1 for domestic students. Application fee: $60 ($75 for international students). *Financial support:* In 2007–08, 20 fellowships, 15 research assistantships, 38 teaching assistantships were awarded; tuition waivers (full and partial) also available. Financial award application deadline: 2/1. *Faculty research:* Feminist cultural studies, media technology, international communications, Latino studies, economics of media. Total annual research expenditures: $50,000. *Unit head:* Dr. Clifford Christians, Director, 217-333-1549, Fax: 217-244-7695, E-mail: cchrstns@uiuc.edu. *Application contact:* Bonnie Howard, Administrative Secretary, 217-333-7860, Fax: 217-333-7695, E-mail: bbhoward@uiuc.edu.

The University of Iowa, Graduate College, College of Liberal Arts and Sciences, Department of Communication Studies, Iowa City, IA 52242-1316. Offers communication research (MA, PhD); rhetorical studies (MA, PhD). *Faculty:* 11 full-time, 8 part-time/adjunct. *Students:* 27 full-time (18 women), 40 part-time (18 women); includes 8 minority (1 African American, 1 American Indian/Alaska Native, 4 Asian Americans or Pacific Islanders, 2 Hispanic Americans), 18 international. 130 applicants, 18% accepted, 12 enrolled. In 2007, 2 master's, 10 doctorates awarded. *Degree requirements:* For master's, thesis optional, exam; for doctorate, comprehensive exam, thesis/dissertation. *Entrance requirements:* For master's and doctorate, GRE General Test, minimum GPA of 3.0. Additional exam requirements/recommendations for international students: Required—TOEFL (minimum score 550 paper-based; 213 computer-based; 81 iBT). *Application deadline:* For fall admission, 1/1 priority date for domestic and international students. Applications are processed on a rolling basis. Application fee: $60 ($85 for international students). Electronic applications accepted. *Expenses:* Tuition, state resident: part-time $349 per hour. Tuition, nonresident: part-time $349 per hour. Tuition and fees vary according to course load and program. *Financial support:* In 2007–08, 6 fellowships, 3 research assistantships with partial tuition reimbursements, 40 teaching assistantships with partial tuition reimbursements were awarded. Financial award applicants required to submit FAFSA. *Unit head:* Kristine L. Fitch, Chair, 319-353-2264, Fax: 319-335-2930.

University of Kansas, Research and Graduate Studies, College of Liberal Arts and Sciences, Department of Communication Studies, Lawrence, KS 66045. Offers MA, PhD. Evening/weekend programs available. *Faculty:* 18. *Students:* 57 full-time (36 women), 23 part-time (17 women); includes 5 minority (3 African Americans, 1 American Indian/Alaska Native, 1 Asian American or Pacific Islander), 10 international. Average age 33. 96 applicants, 32% accepted, 22 enrolled. In 2007, 11 master's, 11 doctorates awarded. *Degree requirements:* For master's, comprehensive exam (for some programs), thesis or alternative; for doctorate, comprehensive exam, thesis/dissertation. *Entrance requirements:* For master's, GRE General Test, minimum GPA of 3.1; for doctorate, GRE General Test, minimum GPA of 3.2 (undergraduate), 3.6 (graduate). Additional exam requirements/recommendations for international students: Required—TOEFL. *Application deadline:* For fall admission, 1/15 priority date for domestic students, 1/15 for international students; for spring admission, 11/15 for domestic and international students. Applications are processed on a rolling basis. Application fee: $55 ($60 for international students). Electronic applications accepted. *Expenses:* Tuition, state resident: full-time $5,838. Tuition, nonresident: full-time $13,409. Tuition and fees vary according to program. *Financial support:* Fellowships with tuition reimbursements, research assistantships, teaching assistantships with full and partial tuition reimbursements, unspecified assistantships available. Financial award application deadline: 1/15. *Faculty research:* Rhetoric, organizational communication, political communication, interpersonal communication, new technology. *Unit head:* Dr. Robert C. Rowland, Chair, 785-864-9868, Fax: 785-864-5203, E-mail: rrowland@ku.edu. *Application contact:* Dr. Beth Innocenti Manolescu, Graduate Director, 785-864-9018, Fax: 785-864-5203, E-mail: bimanole@ku.edu.

University of Kentucky, Graduate School, College of Communications and Information Studies, Program in Communication, Lexington, KY 40506-0032. Offers MA, PhD. *Faculty:* 29 full-time (7 women), 1 part-time/adjunct (0 women). *Students:* 47 full-time (36 women), 12 part-time (6 women); includes 4 minority (3 African Americans, 1 Hispanic American), 3 international. Average age 34. 84 applicants, 30% accepted, 12 enrolled. In 2007, 8 master's, 5 doctorates awarded. *Median time to degree:* Of those who began their doctoral program in fall 1999, 68% received their degree in 8 years or less. *Degree requirements:* For master's, comprehensive exam, thesis optional; for doctorate, comprehensive exam, thesis/dissertation. *Entrance requirements:* For master's, GRE General Test, minimum undergraduate GPA of 2.75; for doctorate, GRE General Test, minimum graduate GPA of 3.0, minimum undergraduate GPA of 2.75. Additional exam requirements/recommendations for international students: Required—TOEFL (minimum score 550 paper-based; 213 computer-based). *Application deadline:* For fall admission, 7/17 priority date for domestic students, 2/1 priority date for international students; for spring admission, 12/13 priority date for domestic students, 6/15 priority date for international students. Applications are processed on a rolling basis. Application fee: $50 ($65 for international students). Electronic applications accepted. *Expenses:* Tuition, state resident: part-time $437 per credit hour. Tuition, nonresident: part-time $931 per credit hour. *Financial support:* In 2007–08, 36 students received support, including 5 fellowships with full tuition reimbursements available (averaging $3,875 per year), 1 research assistantship with full tuition reimbursement available (averaging $18,500 per year), 34 teaching assistantships with full tuition reimbursements available (averaging $9,500 per year); career-related internships or fieldwork, Federal Work-Study, institutionally sponsored loans, scholarships/grants, traineeships, health care benefits, tuition waivers (partial), and unspecified assistantships also available. Support available to part-time students. Financial award application deadline: 3/15. *Faculty research:* Public service campaigns, health communication, mass media law and public policy, political communication, international and intercultural communication. Total annual research expenditures: $315,000. *Unit head:* Dr. Derek Lane, Director of Graduate Studies, 859-257-7805, Fax: 859-323-9879, E-mail: drlane@uky.edu. *Application contact:* Dr. Brian Jackson, Senior Associate Dean, 859-257-4667, Fax: 859-257-4676, E-mail: brian.jackson@uky.edu.

University of Louisiana at Lafayette, Graduate School, College of Liberal Arts, Department of Communication, Lafayette, LA 70504. Offers mass communications (MS). Part-time programs available. *Degree requirements:* For master's, thesis optional. *Entrance requirements:* For master's, GRE General Test, minimum GPA of 2.75. Additional exam requirements/recommendations for international students: Required—TOEFL (minimum score 550 paper-based; 213 computer-based). Electronic applications accepted. *Faculty research:* Mass media problems, issues and ethics, mass communication, historical studies, conflict of interest and law and ethics in journalism, contemporary issues and trends in publications.

University of Louisiana at Monroe, Graduate Studies and Research, College of Arts and Sciences, Department of Communication, Monroe, LA 71209-0001. Offers MA. *Faculty:* 3 full-time (1 woman). *Students:* 10 full-time (9 women), 9 part-time (6 women); includes 3 African Americans, 1 Asian American or Pacific Islander, 2 Hispanic Americans. Average age 26. In 2007, 2 degrees awarded. *Degree requirements:* For master's, thesis optional. *Entrance requirements:* For master's, GRE (minimum verbal and quantitative score: 900), minimum GPA of 2.5 or GRE General Test. Additional exam requirements/recommendations for international students: Required—TOEFL (minimum score 500 paper-based; 173 computer-based; 61 iBT). *Application deadline:* For fall admission, 8/22 priority date for domestic students, 7/1 for international students; for winter admission, 12/12 priority date for domestic students; for spring admission, 1/17 priority date for domestic students, 11/1 for international students. Applications are processed on a rolling basis. Application fee: $20 ($30 for international students). Electronic applications accepted. *Expenses:* Tuition, state resident: full-time $2,220. Tuition, nonresident: full-time $8,172. *Financial support:* In 2007–08, 2 research assistantships with full tuition reimbursements (averaging $2,500 per year), 2 teaching assistantships with full tuition reimbursements (averaging $2,500 per year) were awarded; career-related internships or fieldwork, Federal Work-Study, and unspecified assistantships also available. Financial award application deadline: 4/1; financial award applicants required to submit FAFSA. *Faculty research:* Interactive media, rhetoric progress, interpersonal, journalism history, gender/multicultural issues, forensics. *Unit head:* Dr. Carl L. Thameling, Interim Head, 318-342-1406, Fax: 318-342-1422, E-mail: thameling@ulm.edu.

University of Maine, Graduate School, College of Liberal Arts and Sciences, Department of Communication and Journalism, Orono, ME 04469. Offers communication (MA). Part-time programs available. *Students:* 22 full-time (16 women), 8 part-time (7 women), 4 international. Average age 28. 22 applicants, 64% accepted, 9 enrolled. In 2007, 9 master's awarded. *Degree requirements:* For master's, thesis or alternative. *Entrance requirements:* For master's, GRE General Test. Additional exam requirements/recommendations for international students: Required—TOEFL. *Application deadline:* For fall admission, 2/1 priority date for domestic students. Applications are processed on a rolling basis. Application fee: $60. Electronic applications accepted. *Financial support:* In 2007–08, 15 teaching assistantships with tuition reimbursements (averaging $9,010 per year) were awarded; career-related internships or fieldwork, Federal Work-Study, institutionally sponsored loans, and tuition waivers (full and partial) also available. Support available to part-time students. Financial award application deadline: 3/1. *Faculty research:* Rhetorical theory, semiotics, discourse analysis, gender and communication, children's talk/communication disorders. *Unit head:* Dr. Nancy Hall, Chair, 207-581-2006, Fax: 207-581-1286. *Application contact:* Scott G. Delcourt, Associate Dean of the Graduate School, 207-581-3219, Fax: 207-581-3232, E-mail: graduate@maine.edu.

University of Maryland, Baltimore County, Graduate School, College of Arts, Humanities and Social Sciences, Department of Modern Languages and Linguistics, Program in Intercultural Communication, Baltimore, MD 21250. Offers MA. Part-time and evening/weekend programs available. *Faculty:* 10 full-time (3 women), 3 part-time/adjunct (2 women). *Students:* 23 full-time (20 women), 14 part-time (10 women); includes 6 minority (1 African American, 2 Asian Americans or Pacific Islanders, 3 Hispanic Americans), 13 international. 29 applicants, 72% accepted, 15 enrolled. In 2007, 17 degrees awarded. *Degree requirements:* For master's, one foreign language, comprehensive exam, thesis. *Entrance requirements:* For master's, GRE General Test, minimum GPA of 3.0, 3 letters of recommendation, self-evaluation and statement of support, resumé. Additional exam requirements/recommendations for international students: Required—TOEFL. *Application deadline:* For fall admission, 1/31 for domestic and international students. Applications are processed on a rolling basis. Application fee: $45. Electronic applications accepted. *Financial support:* In 2007–08, 8 students received support, including 4 teaching assistantships with full tuition reimbursements available (averaging $11,324 per year). Financial award applicants required to submit FAFSA. *Faculty research:* Comparative television research-cross-cultural; cultural studies; social developments in Latin America; intercultural communication; French civilization and cultural studies; language, gender and sexuality; sociolinguistics; African linguistics; immigrants in U. S. and Latin American societies. *Unit head:* Dr. Edward Larkey, Director, 410-455-2104, Fax: 410-455-1025, E-mail: larkey@umbc.edu.

University of Maryland, College Park, Graduate Studies, College of Arts and Humanities, Department of Communication, College Park, MD 20742. Offers MA, PhD. *Faculty:* 28 full-time (17 women), 6 part-time/adjunct (3 women). *Students:* 53 full-time (40 women), 2 part-time (both women); includes 4 minority (2 African Americans, 1 Asian American or Pacific Islander, 1 Hispanic American), 18 international. 203 applicants, 10% accepted, 14 enrolled. In 2007, 10 master's, 7 doctorates awarded. *Degree requirements:* For master's, thesis optional; for doctorate, comprehensive exam, thesis/dissertation. *Entrance requirements:* For master's, GRE General Test, minimum GPA of 3.0, sample of scholarly writing, 3 letters of recommendation; for doctorate, GRE General Test. Additional exam requirements/recommendations for international students: Required—TOEFL. *Application deadline:* For fall admission, 2/1 for domestic and international students. Applications are processed on a rolling basis. Application fee: $60. Electronic applications accepted. *Financial support:* In 2007–08, 3 fellowships with full tuition reimbursements (averaging $7,500 per year), 45 teaching assistantships with tuition reimbursements (averaging $15,163 per year) were awarded; Federal Work-Study, scholarships/grants, and unspecified assistantships also available. Support available to part-time students. Financial award applicants required to submit FAFSA. *Faculty research:* Health communication, interpersonal communication, persuasion, intercultural communication, contemporary rhetoric theory. Total annual research expenditures: $58,984. *Unit head:* Dr. Elizabeth L. Toth, Chair, 301-405-8979, Fax: 301-314-9471, E-mail: eltoth@umd.edu. *Application contact:* Dean of Graduate School, 301-405-4190, Fax: 301-314-9305.

Communication—General

University of Massachusetts Amherst, Graduate School, College of Social and Behavioral Sciences, Department of Communication, Amherst, MA 01003. Offers MA, PhD. Part-time programs available. *Faculty:* 22 full-time (11 women). *Students:* 61 full-time (36 women), 13 part-time (11 women); includes 12 minority (2 African Americans, 4 Asian Americans or Pacific Islanders, 6 Hispanic Americans), 28 international. Average age 35. 179 applicants, 16% accepted, 13 enrolled. In 2007, 3 master's, 5 doctorates awarded. Terminal master's awarded for partial completion of doctoral program. *Degree requirements:* For master's, thesis or alternative; for doctorate, one foreign language, thesis/dissertation. *Entrance requirements:* For master's and doctorate, GRE General Test, 3 letters of recommendation. Additional exam requirements/recommendations for international students: Required—TOEFL (minimum score 530 paper-based; 197 computer-based). *Application deadline:* For fall admission, 1/15 priority date for domestic and international students. Applications are processed on a rolling basis. Application fee: $50 ($65 for international students). Electronic applications accepted. *Expenses:* Tuition, state resident: full-time $2,640; part-time $110 per credit. Tuition, nonresident: full-time $9,936; part-time $414 per credit. Required fees: $7,455. One-time fee: $332. Tuition and fees vary according to course load, campus/location, program and reciprocity agreements. *Financial support:* In 2007–08, 11 research assistantships with full tuition reimbursements (averaging $3,678 per year), 44 teaching assistantships with full tuition reimbursements (averaging $9,438 per year) were awarded; fellowships with full tuition reimbursements, career-related internships or fieldwork, Federal Work-Study, scholarships/grants, traineeships, and unspecified assistantships also available. Support available to part-time students. Financial award application deadline: 12/15. *Unit head:* Dr. Michael Morgan, Head, 413-545-4134, Fax: 413-545-6399.

University of Memphis, Graduate School, College of Communication and Fine Arts, Department of Communication, Memphis, TN 38152. Offers communication (MA); communication arts (PhD); film and video production (MA). Part-time programs available. *Faculty:* 16 full-time (6 women). *Students:* 29 full-time (14 women), 20 part-time (8 women); includes 9 minority (8 African Americans, 1 Asian American or Pacific Islander). Average age 37. 33 applicants, 55% accepted, 9 enrolled. In 2007, 9 master's, 5 doctorates awarded. *Degree requirements:* For master's, comprehensive exam, thesis or alternative; for doctorate, comprehensive exam, thesis/dissertation. *Entrance requirements:* For master's and doctorate, GRE General Test. Additional exam requirements/recommendations for international students: Required—TOEFL (minimum score 550 paper-based; 210 computer-based). *Application deadline:* For fall admission, 8/1 for domestic students. Application fee: $35 ($60 for international students). *Expenses:* Tuition, state resident: full-time $6,990; part-time $377 per hour. Tuition, nonresident: full-time $17,818; part-time $830 per hour. Tuition and fees vary according to course load and program. *Financial support:* In 2007–08, 8 research assistantships with full tuition reimbursements (averaging $5,700 per year), 16 teaching assistantships with full tuition reimbursements (averaging $7,350 per year) were awarded; unspecified assistantships also available. *Faculty research:* Rhetoric, media studies, applied communication (health communication). *Unit head:* Dr. Mike Leff, Chair, 901-678-2565, Fax: 901-678-4331, E-mail: m_leff@bellsouth.net. *Application contact:* Dr. Sandra Sarkela, Coordinator of Graduate Studies, 901-678-3173, Fax: 901-678-4331, E-mail: ssarkela@memphis.edu.

University of Miami, Graduate School, School of Communication, Coral Gables, FL 33124. Offers communication (PhD); communication studies (MA); film studies (MA, PhD); motion pictures (MFA), including production, producing, and screenwriting; print journalism (MA); public relations (MA); Spanish language journalism (MA); television broadcast journalism (MA). *Accreditation:* ACEJMC. Part-time programs available. *Faculty:* 39 full-time (12 women). *Students:* 113 full-time (61 women), 16 part-time (5 women); includes 28 minority (8 African Americans, 1 Asian American or Pacific Islander, 19 Hispanic Americans), 14 international. Average age 27. 374 applicants, 56% accepted, 64 enrolled. In 2007, 48 master's, 2 doctorates awarded. *Degree requirements:* For master's, comprehensive exam (for some programs), thesis (for some programs); for doctorate, comprehensive exam, thesis/dissertation. *Entrance requirements:* For master's, GRE General Test; for doctorate, GRE General Test, master's thesis or scholarly research. Additional exam requirements/recommendations for international students: Required—TOEFL (minimum score 600 paper-based; 250 computer-based; 100 iBT). *Application deadline:* For fall admission, 12/15 priority date for domestic and international students. Applications are processed on a rolling basis. Application fee: $50. Electronic applications accepted. *Financial support:* In 2007–08, 68 students received support, including 10 teaching assistantships with full tuition reimbursements available; fellowships with full tuition reimbursements available, Federal Work-Study, institutionally sponsored loans, scholarships/grants, tuition waivers (partial), and unspecified assistantships also available. Financial award application deadline: 3/1; financial award applicants required to submit FAFSA. *Faculty research:* Communication studies, mass communication, international/interpersonal communication, film studies, journalism. *Unit head:* Dr. Sam L. Grogg, Dean, 305-284-3420, Fax: 305-284-2454, E-mail: sgrogg@miami.edu. *Application contact:* Dr. Leonardo C. Ferreira, Director of Graduate Studies, 305-284-3180, Fax: 305-284-8701, E-mail: lferreira@miami.edu.

See Close-Up on page 943.

University of Michigan, Horace H. Rackham School of Graduate Studies, College of Literature, Science, and the Arts, Department of Communication Studies, Ann Arbor, MI 48104-2523. Offers PhD. *Faculty:* 15 full-time (5 women), 5 part-time/adjunct (1 woman). *Students:* 27 full-time (19 women); includes 4 minority (2 African Americans, 2 Asian Americans or Pacific Islanders), 7 international. Average age 27. 80 applicants, 15% accepted, 6 enrolled. In 2007, 3 degrees awarded. *Degree requirements:* For doctorate, comprehensive exam, thesis/dissertation. *Entrance requirements:* For doctorate, GRE. Additional exam requirements/recommendations for international students: Required—TOEFL (minimum score 560 paper-based; 220 computer-based; 84 iBT). *Application deadline:* For fall admission, 1/15 for domestic and international students. Application fee: $75. Electronic applications accepted. *Financial support:* In 2007–08, 27 students received support, including fellowships with full tuition reimbursements available (averaging $15,600 per year), teaching assistantships with full tuition reimbursements available (averaging $15,199 per year); scholarships/grants, health care benefits, tuition waivers (full and partial), and unspecified assistantships also available. Financial award application deadline: 3/15; financial award applicants required to submit FAFSA. *Faculty research:* Political communication; media, culture and society; media effects; race, gender, and the media; new media, media law and policy. *Unit head:* Prof. Susan J. Douglas, Professor and Chair, 734-764-0420, Fax: 734-764-3288, E-mail: sdoug@umich.edu. *Application contact:* Cornelius Wright, Graduate Program Coordinator, 734-764-0420, Fax: 734-764-3288, E-mail: commphd@umich.edu.

University of Minnesota, Twin Cities Campus, Graduate School, College of Design, Department of Design, Housing, and Apparel, Minneapolis, MN 55455-0213. Offers apparel (MA, MS, PhD); design communication (MA, MS, PhD); housing studies (MA, MS, PhD, Postbaccalaureate Certificate); interactive design (MFA); interior design (MA, MS, PhD). Part-time programs available. *Faculty:* 24 full-time (18 women), 5 part-time/adjunct (4 women). *Students:* 41 full-time (34 women), 28 part-time (21 women); includes 3 minority (1 African American, 1 Asian American or Pacific Islander, 1 Hispanic American), 20 international. 37 applicants, 54% accepted, 15 enrolled. In 2007, 3 master's, 8 doctorates awarded. *Median time to degree:* Of those who began their doctoral program in fall 1999, 100% received their degree in 8 years or less. *Degree requirements:* For master's and Postbaccalaureate Certificate, comprehensive exam, thesis (for some programs); for doctorate, comprehensive exam, thesis/dissertation. *Entrance requirements:* For master's, GRE General Test, minimum GPA of 3.0 (preferred), portfolio, 3 letters of recommendation; for doctorate, GRE General Test, minimum GPA of 3.0 (preferred), portfolio, 3 letters of recommendation, writing sample; for Postbaccalaureate Certificate, GRE General Test, minimum GPA of 3.0 (preferred). Additional exam requirements/recommendations for international students: Required—TOEFL (minimum score 550 paper-based; 213 computer-based; 79 iBT). *Application deadline:* For fall admission, 1/15 for domestic and international students. Application fee: $55 ($75 for international students). Electronic applications accepted. *Financial support:* In 2007–08, 34 students received support, including 13 research assistantships with partial tuition reimbursements available (averaging $12,652 per year), 24 teaching assistantships with partial tuition reimbursements available (averaging $12,652 per year); Federal Work-Study, institutionally sponsored loans, and unspecified assistantships also available. Financial award application deadline: 2/1; financial award applicants required to submit FAFSA. *Faculty research:* Housing policy and community development; consumer behavior; interactive design; design history; social, cultural, and behavioral issues related to designed environments. Total annual research expenditures: $320,058. *Unit head:* Becky Love Yust, Professor and Department Head, 612-624-7461, Fax: 612-624-2750, E-mail: byust@che.umn.edu. *Application contact:* Charleen Klarquist, Student Support Services Assistant, 612-626-1219, Fax: 612-624-2750, E-mail: dhagrad@umn.edu.

University of Minnesota, Twin Cities Campus, Graduate School, College of Liberal Arts, Department of Communication Studies, Minneapolis, MN 55455-0213. Offers MA, PhD. *Faculty:* 12 full-time (6 women), 12 part-time/adjunct (6 women). *Students:* 77 full-time (54 women), 15 part-time (9 women); includes 10 minority (2 African Americans, 6 Asian Americans or Pacific Islanders, 2 Hispanic Americans), 6 international. Average age 26. 112 applicants, 17% accepted, 13 enrolled. In 2007, 8 master's, 3 doctorates awarded. *Median time to degree:* Of those who began their doctoral program in fall 1999, 98% received their degree in 8 years or less. *Degree requirements:* For master's, thesis or alternative; for doctorate, thesis/dissertation. *Entrance requirements:* For master's, GRE General Test, minimum GPA of 3.0; for doctorate, GRE General Test, minimum graduate GPA of 3.5. Additional exam requirements/recommendations for international students: Required—TOEFL. *Application deadline:* For fall admission, 1/15 priority date for domestic and international students. Applications are processed on a rolling basis. Application fee: $55 ($75 for international students). Electronic applications accepted. *Financial support:* In 2007–08, 28 students received support, including 28 teaching assistantships with full tuition reimbursements available (averaging $12,683 per year); fellowships with tuition reimbursements available, research assistantships, Federal Work-Study and institutionally sponsored loans also available. Support available to part-time students. Financial award application deadline: 1/15. *Faculty research:* Rhetorical studies, communication theory, media studies, gender and communication, public address. *Unit head:* Dr. Edward Schiappa, Chair, 612-624-5800, Fax: 612-624-6544, E-mail: schiappa@umn.edu. *Application contact:* Bea Dehler, Graduate Coordinator, 612-624-5800, Fax: 612-624-6544, E-mail: dehle001@tc.umn.edu.

University of Missouri–Columbia, Graduate School, College of Arts and Sciences, Department of Communication, Columbia, MO 65211. Offers MA, PhD. Terminal master's awarded for partial completion of doctoral program. *Degree requirements:* For doctorate, thesis/dissertation. *Entrance requirements:* For master's and doctorate, GRE General Test, minimum GPA of 3.0.

University of Missouri–St. Louis, College of Fine Arts and Communication, Department of Communication, St. Louis, MO 63121. Offers MA. *Faculty:* 7 full-time (5 women). *Students:* 7 full-time (5 women), 20 part-time (16 women); includes 3 minority (2 African Americans, 1 Asian American or Pacific Islander), 3 international. Average age 29. In 2007, 20 degrees awarded. *Entrance requirements:* For master's, 3 letters of recommendation. Additional exam requirements/recommendations for international students: Required—TOEFL (minimum score 550 paper-based; 213 computer-based). *Application deadline:* For fall admission, 7/15 for domestic students; for spring admission, 12/15 for domestic students. Application fee: $35 ($40 for international students). *Financial support:* In 2007–08, 5 teaching assistantships (averaging $12,000 per year) were awarded. *Faculty research:* Theory and methodology: intercultural, interpersonal, and mass organizational. *Unit head:* Dr. Michael Beatty, Director of Graduate Studies, 314-516-5485, Fax: 314-516-5816, E-mail: beatty@umsl.edu. *Application contact:* 314-516-5458, Fax: 314-516-6996, E-mail: gradadm@umsl.edu.

The University of Montana, Graduate School, College of Arts and Sciences, Department of Communication Studies, Missoula, MT 59812-0002. Offers MA. *Degree requirements:* For master's, thesis (for some programs). *Entrance requirements:* For master's, GRE General Test. Additional exam requirements/recommendations for international students: Required—TOEFL (minimum score 525 paper-based; 197 computer-based). *Faculty research:* Conflict management, organizational communication, language, personal relationships, rhetoric.

University of Nebraska at Omaha, Graduate Studies and Research, College of Communication, Fine Arts and Media, School of Communication, Omaha, NE 68182. Offers MA. Part-time and evening/weekend programs available. *Faculty:* 23 full-time (12 women). *Students:* 4 full-time (2 women), 55 part-time (32 women); includes 5 minority (3 African Americans, 2 Asian Americans or Pacific Islanders), 3 international. Average age 30. 45 applicants, 49% accepted, 16 enrolled. In 2007, 14 degrees awarded. *Degree requirements:* For master's, comprehensive exam, thesis (for some programs). *Entrance requirements:* For master's, minimum GPA of 3.25, essay, 15 undergraduate communication courses. Additional exam requirements/recommendations for international students: Required—TOEFL (minimum score 550 paper-based; 213 computer-based; 80 iBT). *Application deadline:* For fall admission, 6/1 priority date for domestic students; for spring admission, 11/1 priority date for domestic students. Applications are processed on a rolling basis. Application fee: $45. Electronic applications accepted. *Financial support:* In 2007–08, 35 students received support; fellowships, research assistantships with tuition reimbursements available, teaching assistantships with tuition reimbursements available, Federal Work-Study, institutionally sponsored loans, scholarships/grants, tuition waivers (partial), and unspecified assistantships available. Support available to part-time students. Financial award application deadline: 3/1; financial award applicants required to submit FAFSA. *Unit head:* Dr. Jeremy Lipschultz, Director, 402-554-2600. *Application contact:* Dr. Barbara Pickering, Student Contact, 402-554-2600.

University of Nebraska–Lincoln, Graduate College, College of Arts and Sciences, Department of Communication Studies, Lincoln, NE 68588. Offers communication studies and theatre arts (PhD); communications studies (MA). *Degree requirements:* For master's, thesis optional; for doctorate, comprehensive exam, thesis/dissertation. *Entrance requirements:* For master's and doctorate, GRE General Test, writing sample. Additional exam requirements/recommendations for international students: Required—TOEFL (minimum score 600 paper-based; 250 computer-based). Electronic applications accepted. *Faculty research:* Message strategies, gender communication, political communication, organizational communication, instructional communication.

University of Nevada, Las Vegas, Graduate College, Greenspun College of Urban Affairs, Department of Communication Studies, Las Vegas, NV 89154-9900. Offers MA. Part-time programs available. *Faculty:* 12 full-time (6 women). *Students:* 14 full-time (9 women), 13 part-time (9 women); includes 5 minority (3 African Americans, 2 Hispanic Americans). 20 applicants, 40% accepted, 6 enrolled. In 2007, 4 degrees awarded. *Degree requirements:* For master's, comprehensive exam (for some programs), thesis (for some programs). *Entrance requirements:* For master's, GRE General Test, minimum GPA of 3.0. Additional exam requirements/recommendations for international students: Required—TOEFL (minimum score 550 paper-based; 213 computer-based; 80 iBT). *Application deadline:* For fall admission, 3/1 for domestic and international students. Application fee: $60 ($75 for international students). Electronic applications accepted. *Expenses:* Tuition, state resident: part-time $198 per credit. Tuition, nonresident: part-time $416 per credit. Required fees: $256 per semester. Tuition and fees vary according to course load and reciprocity agreements. *Financial support:* In 2007–08, 7 research assistantships with partial tuition reimbursements (averaging $10,000 per year), 7 teaching assistantships with partial tuition reimbursements (averaging $10,000 per year) were awarded; career-related internships or fieldwork, Federal Work-Study, institutionally sponsored loans, scholarships/grants, health care benefits, and unspecified assistantships also available. Support available to part-time students. Financial award application deadline: 3/1. *Unit head:* Dr. Tom Burkholder, Chair, 702-895-3325. *Application contact:* Graduate College Admissions Evaluator, 702-895-3320, Fax: 702-895-4180, E-mail: gradcollege@unlv.edu.

University of New Mexico, Graduate School, College of Arts and Sciences, Department of Communication and Journalism, Albuquerque, NM 87131-2039. Offers communication (MA, PhD). Part-time programs available. *Faculty:* 20 full-time (14 women), 16 part-time/adjunct (10 women). *Students:* 48 full-time (36 women), 22 part-time (16 women); includes 17 minority (5 African Americans, 2 American Indian/Alaska Native, 3 Asian Americans or Pacific Islanders, 7 Hispanic Americans), 20 international. Average age 36. 89 applicants, 25% accepted, 15 enrolled. In 2007, 6 master's, 8 doctorates awarded. *Degree requirements:* For master's, comprehensive exam (for some programs), thesis (for some programs), 30 hour class work and 6 hour thesis or project, or 36 hours class work and comprehensive exam; for doctorate, 2 foreign languages, comprehensive exam, thesis/dissertation. *Entrance requirements:* For master's and doctorate, GRE General Test, letters of recommendation, writing sample, letter of intent, vita, transcripts, application fee. Additional exam requirements/recommendations for international students: Required—TOEFL (minimum score 550 paper-based; 213 computer-based). *Application deadline:* For fall admission, 1/15 for domestic students; for spring admission, 10/1 for domestic students. Application fee: $50. Electronic applications accepted. *Financial support:* In 2007–08, 1 fellowship with tuition reimbursement (averaging $12,000 per year), 2 research assistantships (averaging $16,000 per year), 38 teaching assistantships with tuition reimbursements (averaging $13,500 per year) were awarded; career-related internships or fieldwork, scholarships/grants, health care benefits, and unspecified assistantships also available. Financial award application deadline: 3/1; financial award applicants required to submit FAFSA. *Faculty research:* Interpersonal/organizational communication, rhetoric, mass communication, intercultural communication, health communication. Total annual research expenditures: $195. *Unit head:* Dr. John Oetzel, Chair, 505-277-5305, Fax: 505-277-4206, E-mail: joetzel@unm.edu. *Application contact:* Mary Bibeau, Academic Advisor, 505-277-1903, Fax: 505-277-4206, E-mail: cjugrads@unm.edu.

The University of North Carolina at Chapel Hill, Graduate School, College of Arts and Sciences, Department of Communication Studies, Chapel Hill, NC 27599. Offers MA, PhD. *Degree requirements:* For master's, comprehensive exam, thesis; for doctorate, thesis/dissertation. *Entrance requirements:* For master's and doctorate, GRE General Test, minimum GPA of 3.0. Electronic applications accepted.

The University of North Carolina at Charlotte, Graduate School, College of Arts and Sciences, Department of Communication Studies, Charlotte, NC 28223-0001. Offers MA. Part-time and evening/weekend programs available. *Faculty:* 9 full-time (3 women). *Students:* 7 full-time (4 women), 23 part-time (19 women), 5 international. Average age 29. 42 applicants, 45% accepted, 13 enrolled. In 2007, 10 degrees awarded. *Degree requirements:* For master's, thesis or alternative. *Entrance requirements:* For master's, GRE General Test, minimum GPA of 2.75 overall. Additional exam requirements/recommendations for international students: Required—TOEFL (minimum score 557 paper-based; 220 computer-based). *Application deadline:* For fall admission, 3/15 for domestic students, 5/1 for international students; for spring admission, 11/15 for domestic students, 10/1 for international students. Applications are processed on a rolling basis. Application fee: $55. Electronic applications accepted. *Expenses:* Tuition, state resident: full-time $2,855. Tuition, nonresident: full-time $13,062. Required fees: $1,692. *Financial support:* In 2007–08, 5 research assistantships (averaging $5,333 per year), 31 teaching assistantships (averaging $8,000 per year) were awarded; fellowships, career-related internships or fieldwork, Federal Work-Study, institutionally sponsored loans, scholarships/grants, and unspecified assistantships also available. Support available to part-time students. Financial award application deadline: 4/1; financial award applicants required to submit FAFSA. *Faculty research:* Health literacy, systems of care and mental illness, the communication of emotions in gendered workplaces, international constructs of public relations managerial responsibilities, sports culture and the construction of social contracts, African American Oratory. *Unit head:* Dr. Richard W. Leeman, Chair, 704-687-4005, Fax: 704-687-6900, E-mail: rwleeman@email.uncc.edu. *Application contact:* Kathy B. Giddings, Director of Graduate Admissions, 704-687-3366, Fax: 704-687-3279, E-mail: agidding@uncc.edu.

The University of North Carolina at Greensboro, Graduate School, College of Arts and Sciences, Department of Communication, Greensboro, NC 27412-5001. Offers communication studies (MA). Part-time programs available. *Faculty:* 8 full-time (4 women), 2 part-time/adjunct (both women). *Students:* 21 full-time (16 women), 8 part-time (7 women); includes 7 minority (all African Americans) 35 applicants, 46% accepted. *Degree requirements:* For master's, thesis or alternative. *Entrance requirements:* For master's, GRE General Test, MAT, or PRAXIS. Additional exam requirements/recommendations for international students: Required—TOEFL. *Application deadline:* For fall admission, 6/1 priority date for domestic students; for spring admission, 11/1 for domestic students. Applications are processed on a rolling basis. Application fee: $45. Electronic applications accepted. *Financial support:* Fellowships, research assistantships with full tuition reimbursements, teaching assistantships with full tuition reimbursements, career-related internships or fieldwork, scholarships/grants, traineeships, and unspecified assistantships available. *Unit head:* Dr. Pete Kellett, Head, 336-334-5297, E-mail: pmkellet@uncg.edu. *Application contact:* Michelle Harkleroad, Director of Graduate Admissions, 336-334-4884, Fax: 336-334-4424, E-mail: mbharkle@uncg.edu.

University of North Dakota, Graduate School, College of Arts and Sciences, School of Communication, Grand Forks, ND 58202. Offers MA, PhD. Part-time programs available. *Faculty:* 7 full-time (4 women). *Students:* 10 full-time (3 women), 27 part-time (18 women); includes 1 African American, 3 American Indian/Alaska Native, 1 Hispanic American, 7 international. 18 applicants, 33% accepted, 6 enrolled. In 2007, 4 master's, 2 doctorates awarded. *Degree requirements:* For master's, comprehensive exam, thesis or alternative; for doctorate, thesis/dissertation. *Entrance requirements:* For master's and doctorate, GRE General Test, minimum GPA of 3.0. Additional exam requirements/recommendations for international students: Required—TOEFL (minimum score 550 paper-based; 213 computer-based; 79 iBT), IELTS (minimum score 7). *Application deadline:* For fall admission, 2/15 priority date for domestic and international students; for spring admission, 10/15 priority date for domestic and international students. Applications are processed on a rolling basis. Application fee: $35. Electronic applications accepted. *Expenses:* Tuition, state resident: full-time $4,050; part-time $225 per credit. Tuition, nonresident: full-time $10,818; part-time $601 per credit. Required fees: $110 per semester. Tuition and fees vary according to class time, campus/location, program and reciprocity agreements. *Financial support:* In 2007–08, 4 research assistantships with full and partial tuition reimbursements (averaging $6,293 per year), 19 teaching assistantships with full tuition reimbursements (averaging $8,333 per year) were awarded; fellowships with full and partial tuition reimbursements, Federal Work-Study, institutionally sponsored loans, scholarships/grants, health care benefits, tuition waivers (full and partial), and unspecified assistantships also available. Support available to part-time students. Financial award application deadline: 3/15; financial award applicants required to submit FAFSA. *Faculty research:* Communication technologies, mass communication in diverse society, acculturation and socialization functions. *Unit head:* Dr. Mary Lee Horowski, Graduate Director, 701-777-2159, Fax: 701-777-3090, E-mail: maryleehorowski@und.edu. *Application contact:* Staci Wells, Admissions Associate, 701-777-2945, Fax: 701-777-3619, E-mail: gradschool@mail.und.nodak.edu.

University of Northern Colorado, Graduate School, College of Humanities and Social Sciences, School of Communication, Program in Communication Studies, Greeley, CO 80639. Offers MA. Part-time programs available. *Faculty:* 4 full-time (1 woman). *Students:* 15 full-time (9 women), 6 part-time (4 women), 2 international. Average age 30. 8 applicants, 100% accepted, 7 enrolled. In 2007, 7 degrees awarded. *Degree requirements:* For master's, comprehensive exam, thesis or alternative. *Entrance requirements:* For master's, GRE General Test, 3 letters of recommendation. *Application deadline:* Applications are processed on a rolling basis. Application fee: $50 ($60 for international students). Electronic applications accepted. *Expenses:* Tuition, state resident: part-time $222 per credit. Tuition, nonresident: part-time $627 per credit. Required fees: $36 per credit. *Financial support:* In 2007–08, 1 research assistantship (averaging $5,968 per year), 3 teaching assistantships (averaging $4,913 per year) were awarded. Financial award application deadline: 3/1; financial award applicants required to submit FAFSA. *Unit head:* Dr. James Keaton, Program Coordinator, 970-351-2045, Fax: 970-351-2336.

University of Northern Iowa, Graduate College, College of Humanities and Fine Arts, Department of Communication Studies, Cedar Falls, IA 50614. Offers MA. Part-time and evening/weekend programs available. *Students:* 21 full-time (13 women), 19 part-time (15 women); includes 6 minority (5 African Americans, 1 Hispanic American), 6 international. 33 applicants, 55% accepted, 6 enrolled. In 2007, 12 degrees awarded. *Degree requirements:* For master's, comprehensive exam, thesis or alternative. *Entrance requirements:* For master's, minimum GPA of 3.0. Additional exam requirements/recommendations for international students: Required—TOEFL (minimum score 500 paper-based; 180 computer-based; 61 iBT). *Application deadline:* For fall admission, 8/1 priority date for domestic students. Applications are processed on a rolling basis. Application fee: $30 ($50 for international students). Electronic applications accepted. *Expenses:* Tuition, state resident: full-time $6,246; part-time $694 per credit hour. Tuition, nonresident: full-time $14,554; part-time $694 per credit hour. Required fees: $838; $119 per semester. *Financial support:* Career-related internships or fieldwork, Federal Work-Study, scholarships/grants, and tuition waivers (full and partial) available. Support available to part-time students. Financial award application deadline: 2/1. *Unit head:* Dr. John Fritch, Head, 319-273-2217, Fax: 319-273-7356, E-mail: john.fritch@uni.edu.

University of North Texas, Robert B. Toulouse School of Graduate Studies, College of Arts and Sciences, Department of Communication Studies, Denton, TX 76203. Offers MA, MS. Part-time programs available. *Faculty:* 10 full-time (4 women). *Students:* 16 full-time (12 women), 20 part-time (16 women); includes 9 minority (4 African Americans, 2 Asian Americans or Pacific Islanders, 3 Hispanic Americans), 2 international. Average age 27. 34 applicants, 35% accepted, 9 enrolled. In 2007, 8 degrees awarded. *Degree requirements:* For master's, one foreign language, comprehensive exam, thesis optional, internship or problem in lieu of thesis. *Entrance requirements:* For master's, GRE General Test, letter of application, statement of purpose, vital resumè, transcripts. Additional exam requirements/recommendations for international students: Required—proof of English language proficiency required for non-native English speakers; Recommended—TOEFL (minimum score 550 paper-based; 213 computer-based). *Application deadline:* For fall admission, 7/15 for domestic students; for spring admission, 11/15 for domestic students. Application fee: $50 ($75 for international students). *Financial support:* In 2007–08, teaching assistantships (averaging $9,030 per year); career-related internships or fieldwork, Federal Work-Study, and institutionally sponsored loans also available. Financial award application deadline: 4/1. *Faculty research:* Rhetoric, performance studies, interpersonal communication, organizational communication, health communication. Total annual research expenditures: $15,000. *Unit head:* Dr. John M. Allison, Chair and Director of Graduate Studies, 940-565-2588, Fax: 940-565-3630, E-mail: allison@unt.edu.

University of Oklahoma, Graduate College, College of Arts and Sciences, Department of Communication, Norman, OK 73019-0390. Offers MA, PhD. Part-time and evening/weekend programs available. *Faculty:* 15 full-time (7 women), 4 part-time/adjunct (1 woman). *Students:* 47 full-time (27 women), 48 part-time (26 women); includes 14 minority (6 African Americans, 1 American Indian/Alaska Native, 4 Asian Americans or Pacific Islanders, 3 Hispanic Americans), 17 international. 52 applicants, 60% accepted, 18 enrolled. In 2007, 16 master's, 3 doctorates awarded. *Degree requirements:* For master's, comprehensive exam, thesis or alternative; for doctorate, thesis/dissertation, general exam. *Entrance requirements:* For master's, GRE General Test, minimum undergraduate GPA of 3.0; for doctorate, GRE General Test, minimum graduate GPA of 3.5. Additional exam requirements/recommendations for international students: Required—TOEFL (minimum score 550 paper-based; 213 computer-based). *Application deadline:* For fall admission, 4/1 priority date for domestic students, 4/1 for international students; for spring admission, 11/1 for domestic students, 9/1 for international students. Applications are processed on a rolling basis. Application fee: $40 ($90 for international students). Electronic applications accepted. *Expenses:* Tuition, state resident: full-time $3,451; part-time $144 per credit hour. Tuition, nonresident: full-time $12,432; part-time $518 per credit hour. Required fees: $1,925; $70 per credit hour. $122 per semester. *Financial support:* In 2007–08, 36 students received support, including 4 research assistantships with partial tuition reimbursements available (averaging $11,565 per year), 32 teaching assistantships with partial tuition reimbursements available (averaging $11,662 per year); scholarships/grants, health care benefits, unspecified assistantships, and annual graduate student awards also available. Financial award applicants required to submit FAFSA. *Faculty research:* Health communication, language and social interaction, political/mass communication, social influence/interpersonal communication; intercultural/international communication. Total annual research expenditures: $78,388. *Unit head:* Dr. Michael W. Pfau, Chair, 405-325-3111, Fax: 405-325-7625, E-mail: mwpfau@ou.edu. *Application contact:* Brandi Goldman, Academic Advisor, 405-325-7710, Fax: 405-325-7625, E-mail: goldman@ou.edu.

University of Oregon, Graduate School, School of Journalism and Communication, Eugene, OR 97403. Offers MA, MS, PhD. *Accreditation:* ACEJMC (one or more programs are accredited); ASHA. Part-time programs available. *Faculty:* 16 full-time (7 women), 1 (woman) part-time/adjunct. *Students:* 76 full-time (53 women), 16 part-time (7 women); includes 10 minority (1 African American, 1 American Indian/Alaska Native, 3 Asian Americans or Pacific Islanders, 5 Hispanic Americans), 15 international. 66 applicants, 47% accepted. In 2007, 13 master's, 5 doctorates awarded. *Degree requirements:* For master's, thesis or alternative. *Entrance requirements:* For master's, GRE General Test; for doctorate, master's degree. Application fee: $50. *Financial support:* In 2007–08, 37 teaching assistantships were awarded; career-related internships or fieldwork, Federal Work-Study, institutionally sponsored loans, and scholarships/grants also available. Financial award application deadline: 3/31. *Faculty research:* Impact of mass communication, media technology, media accountability, craft attitudes, media economics. *Unit head:* Timothy W. Gleason, Dean, 541-346-3739. *Application contact:* Petra Hagen, Graduate Secretary, 541-346-2136, E-mail: phagen@uoregon.edu.

University of Ottawa, Faculty of Graduate and Postdoctoral Studies, Faculty of Arts, Department of Communication, Ottawa, ON K1N 6N5, Canada. Offers MA. Electronic applications accepted. *Faculty research:* Media studies, organizational communications.

University of Pennsylvania, Annenberg School for Communication, Philadelphia, PA 19104. Offers PhD. *Degree requirements:* For doctorate, thesis/dissertation. *Entrance requirements:* For doctorate, GRE General Test. Electronic applications accepted.

University of Pittsburgh, School of Arts and Sciences, Department of Communication, Pittsburgh, PA 15260. Offers MA, PhD. *Faculty:* 8 full-time (1 woman), 3 part-time/adjunct (2 women). *Students:* 42 full-time (21 women); includes 10 minority (2 African Americans, 3 Asian Americans or Pacific Islanders, 5 Hispanic Americans), 3 international. Average age 31. 81 applicants, 6% accepted. In 2007, 2 master's, 4 doctorates awarded. *Degree requirements:* For master's, comprehensive exam, thesis optional; for doctorate, comprehensive exam, thesis/dissertation. *Entrance requirements:* For master's and doctorate, GRE General Test, sample of written work. Additional exam requirements/recommendations for international students: Required—TOEFL (minimum score 550 paper-based; 213 computer-based; 80 iBT). *Application deadline:* For fall admission, 1/2 priority date for domestic and international students. Application fee: $50. Electronic applications accepted. *Financial support:* In 2007–08, 25 students received support, including 6 fellowships with tuition reimbursements available (averaging $15,070 per year), 16 teaching assistantships with tuition reimbursements available (averaging $14,485 per year); Federal Work-Study, scholarships/grants, health care benefits, tuition waivers (full), and unspecified assistantships also available. Financial award application deadline: 1/2; financial award applicants required to submit FAFSA. *Faculty research:* Media and cultural studies, public argument and discourse, rhetoric of science, history, criticism and theory of rhetoric. *Unit head:* Dr. Barbara Warnick, Department Chair, 412-624-1564, Fax: 412-624-1878, E-mail: bwarnick@pitt.edu. *Application contact:* Dr. Ronald J. Zboray, Director of Graduate Studies, 412-624-6969, Fax: 412-624-1878, E-mail: zboray@pitt.edu.

University of Portland, Graduate School, College of Arts and Sciences, Department of Communication Studies, Portland, OR 97203-5798. Offers communication (MA); management communication (MS). Part-time and evening/weekend programs available. *Faculty:* 7 full-time (2 women), 1 part-time/adjunct (0 women). *Students:* 8 applicants, 63% accepted, 3 enrolled. In 2007, 4 degrees awarded. *Degree requirements:* For master's, thesis optional. *Entrance requirements:* For master's, GRE General Test, minimum GPA of 3.25, 3 letters of recommendation, resumé, statement of goals, official transcripts. Additional exam requirements/recommendations for international students: Required—TOEFL (minimum score 600 paper-

Communication—General

University of Portland (continued)

based; 100 iBT), IELTS (minimum score 8). *Application deadline:* For fall admission, 7/15 priority date for domestic and international students; for spring admission, 12/15 priority date for domestic and international students. Applications are processed on a rolling basis. Application fee: $50. *Expenses:* Tuition: Part-time $775 per semester hour. *Financial support:* Career-related internships or fieldwork, Federal Work-Study, scholarships/grants, and tuition waivers (partial) available. Financial award application deadline: 3/1; financial award applicants required to submit FAFSA. *Unit head:* Dr. Jeffrey Kerssen-Griep, Director, 503-943-7167, E-mail: kerssen@up.edu.

University of Rhode Island, Graduate School, College of Arts and Sciences, Department of Communication Studies, Kingston, RI 02881. Offers MS. *Expenses:* Tuition, state resident: full-time $6,936; part-time $385 per credit. Tuition, nonresident: full-time $19,044; part-time $1,058 per credit. Required fees: $1,508; $48 per credit. $30 per semester. One-time fee: $80 part-time. *Unit head:* Dr. Lynne Derbyshire, Chair, 401-874-2510.

University of South Africa, College of Human Sciences, Pretoria, South Africa. Offers adult education (M Ed); African languages (MA, PhD); African politics (MA, PhD); Afrikaans (MA, PhD); ancient history (MA, PhD); ancient Near Eastern studies (MA, PhD); anthropology (MA, PhD); applied linguistics (MA); Arabic (MA, PhD); archaeology (MA); art history (MA); Biblical archaeology (MA); Biblical studies (M Th, D Th, PhD); Christian spirituality (M Th, D Th); church history (M Th, D Th); classical studies (MA, PhD); clinical psychology (MA); communication (MA, PhD); comparative education (M Ed, Ed D); consulting psychology (D Admin, D Com, PhD); curriculum studies (M Ed, Ed D); development studies (M Admin, MA, D Admin, PhD); didactics (M Ed, Ed D); education (M Tech); education management (M Ed, Ed D); educational psychology (M Ed); English (MA); environmental education (M Ed); French (MA, PhD); German (MA, PhD); Greek (MA); guidance and counseling (M Ed); health studies (MA, PhD), including health sciences education (MA), health services management (MA), medical and surgical nursing science (critical care general) (MA), midwifery and neonatal nursing science (MA), trauma and emergency care (MA); history (MA, PhD); history of education (Ed D); inclusive education (M Ed, Ed D); information and communications technology policy and regulation (MA); information science (MA, MIS, PhD); international politics (MA, PhD); Islamic studies (MA, PhD); Italian (MA, PhD); Judaica (MA, PhD); linguistics (MA, PhD); mathematical education (M Ed); mathematics education (MA); missiology (M Th, D Th); modern Hebrew (MA, PhD); musicology (MA, MMus, D Mus, PhD); natural science education (M Ed); New Testament (M Th, D Th); Old Testament (D Th); pastoral therapy (M Th, D Th); philosophy (MA); philosophy of education (M Ed, Ed D); politics (MA, PhD); Portuguese (MA, PhD); practical theology (M Th, D Th); psychology (MA, MS, PhD); psychology of education (M Ed, Ed D); public health (MA); religious studies (MA, D Th, PhD); Romance languages (MA); Russian (MA, PhD); Semitic languages (MA, PhD); social behavior studies in HIV/AIDS (MA); social science (mental health) (MA); social science in development studies (MA); social science in psychology (MA); social science in social work (MA); social science in sociology (MA); social work (MSW, DSW, PhD); socio-education (M Ed, Ed D); sociolinguistics (MA); sociology (MA, PhD); Spanish (MA, PhD); systematic theology (M Th, D Th); TESOL (teaching English to speakers of other languages) (MA); theological ethics (M Th, D Th); theory of literature (MA, PhD); urban ministries (D Th); urban ministry (M Th).

University of South Alabama, Graduate School, College of Arts and Sciences, Department of Communication, Mobile, AL 36688-0002. Offers MA. *Faculty:* 4 full-time (1 woman), 5 part-time/adjunct (3 women). *Students:* 17 full-time (12 women), 16 part-time (10 women); includes 4 minority (3 African Americans, 1 American Indian/Alaska Native), 3 international. 22 applicants, 86% accepted, 14 enrolled. In 2007, 10 degrees awarded. *Degree requirements:* For master's, comprehensive exam, thesis optional. *Entrance requirements:* For master's, GRE, GMAT, minimum GPA of 3.0, B.A. in communication or 36 semester hours. *Application deadline:* For fall admission, 9/1 priority date for domestic students. Applications are processed on a rolling basis. Application fee: $25. *Expenses:* Tuition, state resident: full-time $4,224; part-time $176 per credit hour. Tuition, nonresident: full-time $8,448; part-time $352 per credit hour. Required fees: $802. Full-time tuition and fees vary according to program and student level. *Financial support:* Research assistantships available. Financial award application deadline: 4/1. *Unit head:* Dr. Gerald Wilson, Chair, 251-380-2800.

The University of South Dakota, Graduate School, College of Arts and Sciences, Department of Communication Studies, Vermillion, SD 57069-2390. Offers MA. Part-time programs available. *Faculty:* 9 full-time (3 women), 1 part-time/adjunct (0 women). *Students:* 15 (9 women). In 2007, 3 degrees awarded. *Degree requirements:* For master's, comprehensive exam (for some programs), thesis (for some programs). *Entrance requirements:* For master's, minimum GPA of 2.7. Additional exam requirements/recommendations for international students: Required—TOEFL (minimum score 575 paper-based; 213 computer-based; 79 iBT). *Application deadline:* Applications are processed on a rolling basis. Application fee: $35. Electronic applications accepted. *Financial support:* In 2007–08, 8 teaching assistantships with partial tuition reimbursements (averaging $8,000 per year) were awarded; career-related internships or fieldwork, Federal Work-Study, and unspecified assistantships also available. Support available to part-time students. Financial award applicants required to submit FAFSA. *Faculty research:* Male/female communication, interpersonal communication, relational communication, rhetoric and public address, organizational communication. *Unit head:* Dr. Terry Robertson, Chair, 605-677-5474, Fax: 605-677-8876, E-mail: troberts@usd.edu. *Application contact:* Dr. Clark Callahan, Graduate Director, 605-677-5474, Fax: 605-677-8876, E-mail: ccallaha@usd.edu.

University of Southern California, Graduate School, Annenberg School for Communication, Los Angeles, CA 90089. Offers MA, MCM, MPD, PhD, JD/MCM, MA/M Sc, MCM/MAJCS. Part-time and evening/weekend programs available. *Faculty:* 74 full-time (24 women), 62 part-time/adjunct (18 women). *Students:* 431 full-time, 85 part-time; includes 134 minority (30 African Americans, 3 American Indian/Alaska Native, 55 Asian Americans or Pacific Islanders, 46 Hispanic Americans), 114 international. Average age 30. 1,020 applicants, 42% accepted, 228 enrolled. In 2007, 239 master's, 16 doctorates awarded. Terminal master's awarded for partial completion of doctoral program. *Degree requirements:* For master's, comprehensive exam; for doctorate, thesis/dissertation. *Entrance requirements:* For master's, GRE General Test or GMAT, resumé, writing samples, letters of recommendation, statement of purpose; for doctorate, GRE General Test, resumé, writing samples, letters of recommendation, statement of purpose, interest survey. Additional exam requirements/recommendations for international students: Required—TOEFL (minimum score 280 computer-based; 114 iBT). *Application deadline:* For fall admission, 12/15 priority date for domestic and international students; for spring admission, 12/1 priority date for domestic students, 12/1 for international students. Applications are processed on a rolling basis. Application fee: $85. Electronic applications accepted. *Financial support:* In 2007–08, 22 fellowships with full tuition reimbursements (averaging $24,845 per year), 33 research assistantships with full tuition reimbursements (averaging $23,939 per year), 41 teaching assistantships with full tuition reimbursements (averaging $21,253 per year) were awarded; career-related internships or fieldwork, Federal Work-Study, institutionally sponsored loans, scholarships/grants, health care benefits, tuition waivers (partial), and unspecified assistantships also available. Support available to part-time students. Financial award application deadline: 1/15; financial award applicants required to submit FAFSA. Total annual research expenditures: $5.6 million. *Unit head:* Ernest Wilson, Dean, 213-740-6180, Fax: 213-740-3772. *Application contact:* Allyson Hill, Director of Admissions, 213-821-0770, E-mail: ascadm@usc.edu.

See Close-Up on page 945.

University of Southern California, Graduate School, Annenberg School for Communication, School of Communication, Program in Communication, Los Angeles, CA 90089. Offers communication (MA, PhD), including interpersonal and social dynamics (PhD), mass communication, technology, and public policy (PhD), organizational communication (PhD), rhetorical and cultural studies (PhD). *Students:* 86 full-time (52 women); includes 16 minority (3 African Americans, 2 American Indian/Alaska Native, 5 Asian Americans or Pacific Islanders, 6 Hispanic Americans), 24 international. Average age 31. 196 applicants, 13% accepted, 19 enrolled. In 2007, 16 degrees awarded. *Median time to degree:* Of those who began their doctoral program in fall 1999, 89% received their degree in 8 years or less. *Degree requirements:* For doctorate, thesis/dissertation. *Entrance requirements:* For master's and doctorate, GRE General Test, resumé, writing samples, 3 letters of recommendation, interest survey questionnaire, statement of purpose. Additional exam requirements/recommendations for international students: Required—TOEFL (minimum score 280 computer-based; 115 iBT); Recommended—TWE. *Application deadline:* For fall admission, 11/30 for domestic and international students. Application fee: $85. Electronic applications accepted. *Financial support:* In 2007–08, 18 students received support, including 18 fellowships with full tuition reimbursements available (averaging $26,500 per year); research assistantships, teaching assistantships, Federal Work-Study, institutionally sponsored loans, scholarships/grants, health care benefits, tuition waivers (partial), and unspecified assistantships also available. Support available to part-time students. Financial award application deadline: 1/1; financial award applicants required to submit FAFSA. *Faculty research:* Computer-mediated communication, public health campaigns, communication democracy and the public sphere, new communication technologies in organizations, communication and community. *Unit head:* Dr. Thomas Goodnight, Director, 213-821-5384. *Application contact:* Allyson Hill, Director of Admissions, 213-821-0770, E-mail: ascadm@usc.edu.

See Close-Up on page 945.

University of Southern California, Graduate School, Annenberg School for Communication, School of Communication, Program in Global Communication, Los Angeles, CA 90089. Offers MA/M Sc. Program offered jointly with London School of Economics. *Students:* 29 full-time (22 women); includes 3 minority (all Asian Americans or Pacific Islanders), 18 international. Average age 24. 179 applicants, 47% accepted, 41 enrolled. *Entrance requirements:* Additional exam requirements/recommendations for international students: Required—TOEFL (minimum score 280 computer-based; 114 iBT). *Application deadline:* For fall admission, 3/1 priority date for domestic and international students. Applications are processed on a rolling basis. Application fee: $85. Electronic applications accepted. *Financial support:* In 2007–08, 16 research assistantships with full and partial tuition reimbursements (averaging $10,000 per year) were awarded; fellowships with full tuition reimbursements, teaching assistantships with full and partial tuition reimbursements, Federal Work-Study, institutionally sponsored loans, scholarships/grants, health care benefits, tuition waivers (partial), and unspecified assistantships also available. Support available to part-time students. Financial award application deadline: 1/15; financial award applicants required to submit FAFSA. *Faculty research:* New technology, audience analysis, globalization, entertainment industry, integrated communication. *Unit head:* Dr. Patricia Riley, Director, 213-740-3949, Fax: 213-740-0013, E-mail: priley@usc.edu. *Application contact:* Allyson Hill, Director of Admissions, 213-821-0770, E-mail: ascadm@usc.edu.

See Close-Up on page 945.

University of South Florida, Graduate School, College of Arts and Sciences, Department of Communication, Tampa, FL 33620-9951. Offers MA, PhD. Part-time and evening/weekend programs available. *Faculty:* 15 full-time (8 women). *Students:* 43 full-time (27 women), 27 part-time (16 women); includes 9 minority (6 African Americans, 1 Asian American or Pacific Islander, 2 Hispanic Americans), 4 international. 96 applicants, 51% accepted, 15 enrolled. In 2007, 5 master's, 4 doctorates awarded. *Degree requirements:* For master's, comprehensive exam, pro-seminar course; for doctorate, comprehensive exam, thesis/dissertation. *Entrance requirements:* For master's, GRE General Test or GMAT, minimum GPA of 3.0. Additional exam requirements/recommendations for international students: Required—TOEFL (minimum score 550 paper-based; 213 computer-based). *Application deadline:* For fall admission, 6/1 priority date for domestic students, 5/1 priority date for international students; for spring admission, 10/15 priority date for domestic students, 8/1 priority date for international students. Applications are processed on a rolling basis. Application fee: $30. Electronic applications accepted. *Financial support:* Career-related internships or fieldwork, Federal Work-Study, and institutionally sponsored loans available. Support available to part-time students. Financial award application deadline: 2/1; financial award applicants required to submit FAFSA. *Faculty research:* Organizational processes, gender relations, media criticism, interpersonal relations, health communication. Total annual research expenditures: $4,778. *Unit head:* Dr. Eric M. Eisenberg, Chairperson, 813-974-6823, Fax: 813-974-6817, E-mail: eisenber@chuma.cas.usf.edu. *Application contact:* Dr. Gil Rodman, Information Contact, 813-974-3025, Fax: 813-974-6817, E-mail: grodman@chuma1.cas.usf.edu.

The University of Tennessee, Graduate School, College of Communication and Information, Knoxville, TN 37996. Offers advertising (MS, PhD); broadcasting (MS, PhD); communications (MS, PhD); information sciences (MS, PhD); journalism (MS, PhD); public relations (MS, PhD); speech communication (MS, PhD). *Accreditation:* ACEJMC (one or more programs are accredited at the [master's] level). Part-time and evening/weekend programs available. Postbaccalaureate distance learning degree programs offered (no on-campus study). *Degree requirements:* For master's, thesis or alternative; for doctorate, thesis/dissertation. *Entrance requirements:* For master's and doctorate, GRE General Test, minimum GPA of 2.7. Additional exam requirements/recommendations for international students: Required—TOEFL. Electronic applications accepted.

The University of Texas at Arlington, Graduate School, College of Liberal Arts, Program in Communication, Arlington, TX 76019. Offers MA. Part-time and evening/weekend programs available. *Students:* 8 full-time (5 women), 28 part-time (22 women); includes 9 minority (8 African Americans, 1 Hispanic American), 5 international. 43 applicants, 28% accepted, 12 enrolled. In 2007, 11 degrees awarded. *Degree requirements:* For master's, comprehensive exam (for some programs), thesis or alternative. *Entrance requirements:* For master's, GRE General Test. Additional exam requirements/recommendations for international students: Required—TOEFL (minimum score 550 paper-based; 213 computer-based). Application fee: $35 ($50 for international students). *Expenses:* Tuition, state resident: full-time $5,934. Tuition, nonresident: full-time $10,938. *Financial support:* In 2007–08, fellowships (averaging $1,000 per year); research assistantships, teaching assistantships. *Unit head:* Dr. Charla Markham-Shaw, Chair, 817-272-2163, E-mail: markham@uta.edu. *Application contact:* Dr. Tom Christie, Graduate Advisor, 817-272-2163, E-mail: christie@uta.edu.

The University of Texas at Austin, Graduate School, College of Communication, Austin, TX 78712-1111. Offers MA, MFA, PhD, MBA/MA, MP Aff/MA. Part-time programs available. *Entrance requirements:* For master's and doctorate, GRE General Test. Electronic applications accepted.

The University of Texas at Dallas, School of Behavioral and Brain Sciences, Program in Communication Sciences, Richardson, TX 75083-0688. Offers PhD. Part-time and evening/weekend programs available. *Faculty:* 18 full-time (10 women), 5 part-time/adjunct (4 women). *Students:* 12 full-time (11 women), 8 part-time (7 women); includes 3 minority (1 African American, 2 Asian Americans or Pacific Islanders), 8 international. Average age 27. 6 applicants, 50% accepted, 1 enrolled. In 2007, 4 doctorates awarded. *Degree requirements:* For doctorate, thesis/dissertation. *Entrance requirements:* For doctorate, GRE General Test, minimum GPA of 3.0 in upper-level course work in field. Additional exam requirements/recommendations for international students: Required—TOEFL (minimum score 550 paper-based; 213 computer-based). *Application deadline:* For fall admission, 7/15 for domestic students; for spring admission, 11/15 for domestic students. Applications are processed on a rolling basis. Application fee: $50 ($100 for international students). Electronic applications accepted. *Expenses:* Tuition, state resident: full-time $7,052. Tuition, nonresident: full-time $12,632. Tuition and fees vary according to course load. *Financial support:* In 2007–08, 3 research assistantships with tuition reimbursements (averaging $15,451 per year), 6 teaching assistantships with tuition reimbursements (averaging $10,395 per year) were awarded; fellowships, Federal Work-Study, institutionally sponsored loans, scholarships/grants, and unspecified assistantships also available. Support available to part-time students. Financial award application deadline: 4/30; financial award applicants required to submit FAFSA. *Faculty research:* Speech perception, auditory processing, language acquisition by young children, language development. *Unit head:* Dr. Robert D. Stillman, Head, 972-883-3106, Fax: 972-883-3022, E-mail: stillman@utdallas.edu.

The University of Texas at El Paso, Graduate School, College of Liberal Arts, Department of Communication, El Paso, TX 79968-0001. Offers communication (MA). Part-time and evening/weekend programs available. *Degree requirements:* For master's, thesis optional. *Entrance requirements:* For master's, GRE General Test, minimum GPA of 3.0. Additional exam requirements/recommendations for international students: Required—TOEFL. Electronic applications accepted. *Faculty research:* Cross-cultural communication, information media, telecommunication technology, trans-border communication, human communication.

The University of Texas at San Antonio, College of Liberal and Fine Arts, Department of Communication, San Antonio, TX 78249-0617. Offers MA. Part-time and evening/weekend programs available. *Faculty:* 8 full-time (3 women). *Students:* 7 full-time (6 women), 24 part-time (18 women); includes 17 minority (3 African Americans, 1 Asian American or Pacific Islander, 13 Hispanic Americans), 2 international. Average age 30. 25 applicants, 60% accepted, 15 enrolled. In 2007, 5 degrees awarded. *Entrance requirements:* Additional exam requirements/recommendations for international students: Required—TOEFL (minimum score 500 paper-based; 173 computer-based). *Application deadline:* For fall admission, 7/1 for domestic students, 4/1 for international students; for spring admission, 11/1 for domestic students, 9/1 for international students. Applications are processed on a rolling basis. Application fee: $45 ($80 for international students). Electronic applications accepted. *Financial support:* In 2007–08, 1 teaching assistantship (averaging $7,980 per year) was awarded; Federal Work-Study, scholarships/grants, and unspecified assistantships also available. *Unit head:* Dr. Steven Levitt, Chair, 210-458-5990, E-mail: steven.levitt@utsa.edu.

The University of Texas at Tyler, College of Arts and Sciences, Department of Communication, Tyler, TX 75799-0001. Offers communication (MA); interdisciplinary studies (MAIS, MSIS). Part-time programs available. *Faculty:* 5 full-time (1 woman). *Students:* Average age 38. 2 applicants, 100% accepted, 2 enrolled. *Degree requirements:* For master's, comprehensive exam. *Entrance requirements:* For master's, GRE General Test, minimum GPA of 2.5. *Application deadline:* Applications are processed on a rolling basis. Application fee: $0. Electronic applications accepted. *Expenses:* Tuition, state resident: part-time $627 per semester hour. Tuition, nonresident: part-time $908 per semester hour. Required fees: $107 per semester hour. Tuition and fees vary according to course load. *Financial support:* Fellowships, research assistantships, teaching assistantships available. Financial award application deadline: 7/1; financial award applicants required to submit FAFSA. *Faculty research:* Organizational communication, feminist criticism, religions communication, mass media. *Unit head:* Dr. Jeffrey Hobbs, Interim Chair, 903-566-5627, Fax: 903-566-7287, E-mail: jhobbs@uttyler.edu. *Application contact:* Pam Morrow, Assistant to Dean for Enrollment Management, 903-566-7205, Fax: 903-566-7068, E-mail: pmorrow@uttyler.edu.

The University of Texas–Pan American, College of Arts and Humanities, Department of Communications, Edinburg, TX 78541-2999. Offers communication (MA); theatre (MA). *Accreditation:* NAST. Part-time and evening/weekend programs available. *Degree requirements:* For master's, comprehensive exam, thesis or alternative. *Entrance requirements:* For master's, minimum GPA of 3.0. Additional exam requirements/recommendations for international students: Required—TOEFL. *Faculty research:* Rhetorical theory, intercultural and mass communication, American theatre, multicultural theatre and drama, television and film.

University of the Incarnate Word, School of Graduate Studies and Research, H-E-B School of Business and Administration, Programs in Administration, San Antonio, TX 78209-6397. Offers adult education (MAA); applied administration (MAA); communication arts (MAA); instructional technology (MAA); international business (Certificate); nutrition (MAA); organizational development (MAA, Certificate); project management (Certificate); sports management (MAA). Part-time and evening/weekend programs available. Postbaccalaureate distance learning degree programs offered (no on-campus study). *Students:* Average age 34. In 2007, 69 degrees awarded. *Degree requirements:* For master's, capstone. *Entrance requirements:* For master's, GMAT. Additional exam requirements/recommendations for international students: Required—TOEFL. *Application deadline:* Applications are processed on a rolling basis. Application fee: $20. Electronic applications accepted. *Expenses:* Tuition: Part-time $605 per credit hour. Required fees: $58 per credit hour. Tuition and fees vary according to degree level. *Financial support:* Federal Work-Study and scholarships/grants available. Financial award applicants required to submit FAFSA. *Unit head:* Dr. Dan Dominguez, MAA Director, 210-829-3180, Fax: 210-805-3564, E-mail: domingue@uiwtx.edu. *Application contact:* Andrea Cyterski-Acosta, Dean of Enrollment, 210-829-6005, Fax: 210-829-3921, E-mail: admis@uiwtx.edu.

University of the Incarnate Word, School of Graduate Studies and Research, School of Interactive Media and Design, Program in Communication Arts, San Antonio, TX 78209-6397. Offers communication arts (MA); instructional technology (MA). Part-time and evening/weekend programs available. *Students:* 4 full-time (3 women), 33 part-time (19 women); includes 25 minority (2 African Americans, 23 Hispanic Americans), 3 international. Average age 31. In 2007, 7 degrees awarded. *Degree requirements:* For master's, thesis or alternative. *Entrance requirements:* For master's, GMAT, GRE General Test. Additional exam requirements/recommendations for international students: Required—TOEFL. *Application deadline:* Applications are processed on a rolling basis. Application fee: $20. Electronic applications accepted. *Expenses:* Tuition: Part-time $605 per credit hour. Required fees: $58 per credit hour. Tuition and fees vary according to degree level. *Financial support:* Federal Work-Study, scholarships/grants, and tuition waivers (partial) available. Financial award applicants required to submit FAFSA. *Unit head:* Dr. Valerie Greenberg, 210-829-3891, Fax: 210-829-3196, E-mail: valprof@aol.com. *Application contact:* Andrea Cyterski-Acosta, Dean of Enrollment, 210-829-6005, Fax: 210-829-3921, E-mail: admis@uiwtx.edu.

University of the Pacific, College of the Pacific, Department of Communication, Stockton, CA 95211-0197. Offers MA. *Faculty:* 9 full-time (2 women), 1 (woman) part-time/adjunct. *Students:* 1 (woman) full-time, 16 part-time (11 women); includes 4 minority (1 African American, 1 Asian American or Pacific Islander, 2 Hispanic Americans), 1 international. Average age 28. 26 applicants, 65% accepted, 11 enrolled. In 2007, 5 degrees awarded. *Degree requirements:* For master's, thesis. *Entrance requirements:* For master's, GRE General Test. Additional exam requirements/recommendations for international students: Required—TOEFL (minimum score 475 paper-based; 150 computer-based). *Application deadline:* For fall admission, 3/1 priority date for domestic students; for spring admission, 10/1 for domestic students. Applications are processed on a rolling basis. Application fee: $75. *Financial support:* In 2007–08, 8 teaching assistantships were awarded. Support available to part-time students. Financial award application deadline: 3/1; financial award applicants required to submit FAFSA. *Unit head:* Dr. Qingwen Dong, Chairman, 209-946-2505, E-mail: qdong@pacific.edu.

University of the Sacred Heart, Graduate Programs, Department of Communication, San Juan, PR 00914-0383. Offers advertising (MA); contemporary culture and means (MA); journalism and mass communication (MA); literary creation (MA); public relations (MA). Part-time and evening/weekend programs available. *Degree requirements:* For master's, thesis.

The University of Toledo, College of Graduate Studies, College of Arts and Sciences, Department of Communications, Toledo, OH 43606-3390. Offers communication studies (Certificate). *Faculty:* 8. *Students:* 2 applicants, 100% accepted, 1 enrolled. In 2007, 1 degree awarded. *Application deadline:* For fall admission, 1/15 priority date for domestic students. Application fee: $45. *Unit head:* Dr. James Benjamin, Chair, 419-530-2051, E-mail: james.benjamin@utoledo.edu.

University of Utah, The Graduate School, College of Humanities, Department of Communication, Salt Lake City, UT 84112-1107. Offers M Phil, MA, MS, PhD. Part-time programs available. *Faculty:* 35 full-time (19 women). *Students:* 47 full-time (23 women), 47 part-time (26 women); includes 8 minority (4 Asian Americans or Pacific Islanders, 4 Hispanic Americans), 4 international. Average age 37. 115 applicants, 33% accepted, 21 enrolled. In 2007, 5 master's, 9 doctorates awarded. *Median time to degree:* Of those who began their doctoral program in fall 1999, 60% received their degree in 8 years or less. *Degree requirements:* For master's, thesis or alternative; for doctorate, comprehensive exam, thesis/dissertation. *Entrance requirements:* For master's and doctorate, GRE General Test, minimum GPA of 3.0. Additional exam requirements/recommendations for international students: Required—TOEFL (minimum score 500 paper-based; 173 computer-based). *Application deadline:* For fall admission, 1/15 for domestic and international students. Application fee: $45 ($65 for international students). Electronic applications accepted. *Financial support:* In 2007–08, 3 fellowships with full tuition reimbursements (averaging $17,500 per year), 14 teaching assistantships with full tuition reimbursements (averaging $12,500 per year) were awarded; career-related internships or fieldwork and health care benefits also available. Financial award application deadline: 1/15; financial award applicants required to submit FAFSA. *Faculty research:* Communication theory and history, rhetoric, mass communications, journalism, public address and forensics. Total annual research expenditures: $168,806. *Unit head:* Dr. Ann L. Darling, Chair, 801-581-3912, Fax: 801-585-6255, E-mail: ann.darling@utah.edu. *Application contact:* Karen L. Ashcraft, Director of Graduate Studies, 801-585-1889, Fax: 801-585-6255, E-mail: k.ashcraft@utah.edu.

University of Vermont, Graduate College, College of Arts and Sciences, Department of Communication Sciences, Burlington, VT 05405. Offers MS. *Accreditation:* ASHA. *Students:* 24 (23 women). 66 applicants, 39% accepted, 7 enrolled. In 2007, 13 degrees awarded. *Entrance requirements:* For master's, GRE General Test. Additional exam requirements/recommendations for international students: Required—TOEFL (minimum score 550 paper-based; 213 computer-based; 80 iBT). *Application deadline:* For fall admission, 2/1 for domestic students. Application fee: $40. Electronic applications accepted. *Financial support:* Fellowships available. Financial award application deadline: 3/1. *Unit head:* Prof. P. Prelock, Chair, 802-656-3861. *Application contact:* Rebecca McCauley, Coordinator, 802-656-3861.

University of Washington, Graduate School, College of Arts and Sciences, Department of Communication, Seattle, WA 98195. Offers MA, MC, PhD. Part-time programs available. Terminal master's awarded for partial completion of doctoral program. *Degree requirements:* For master's, thesis, project (MC); for doctorate, thesis/dissertation. *Entrance requirements:* For master's and doctorate, GRE, minimum GPA of 3.0, writing sample. Additional exam requirements/recommendations for international students: Required—TOEFL. Electronic applications accepted. *Faculty research:* Communication and culture, communication technology and society, international communication, political communication, rhetoric and critical studies.

University of West Florida, College of Arts and Sciences: Arts, Department of Communication Arts, Pensacola, FL 32514-5750. Offers MA. Part-time and evening/weekend programs available. *Faculty:* 2 full-time (both women). *Students:* 6 full-time (4 women), 16 part-time (13 women); includes 3 minority (1 African American, 1 Asian American or Pacific Islander, 1 Hispanic American). Average age 39. 17 applicants, 82% accepted, 12 enrolled. In 2007, 5 degrees awarded. *Degree requirements:* For master's, thesis or alternative. *Entrance requirements:* For master's, GRE General Test, minimum GPA of 3.0. Additional exam requirements/recommendations for international students: Required—TOEFL (minimum score 550 paper-based; 213 computer-based). *Application deadline:* For fall admission, 6/1 for domestic students, 5/15 for international students; for spring admission, 11/1 for domestic students, 10/1 for international students. Applications are processed on a rolling basis. Application fee: $30. *Expenses:* Tuition, state resident: full-time $6,054; part-time $252 per credit. Tuition, nonresident: full-time $21,886; part-time $912 per credit. *Financial support:* In 2007–08, 1 research assistantship with partial tuition reimbursement (averaging $1,880 per year), 4 teaching assistantships with partial tuition reimbursements (averaging $3,760 per year) were awarded; career-related internships or fieldwork, Federal Work-Study, and scholarships/grants also available. Support available to part-time students. Financial award application deadline: 4/15; financial award applicants required to submit FAFSA. *Faculty research:* Equity studies. *Unit head:* Dr. Bruce M. Swain, Chairperson, 850-474-3278.

University of Windsor, Faculty of Graduate Studies, Faculty of Arts and Social Sciences, Department of Communication Studies, Windsor, ON N9B 3P4, Canada. Offers communication and social justice (MA). *Faculty:* 9 full-time (4 women), 1 (woman) part-time/adjunct. *Students:* 25 full-time (13 women). 61 applicants, 33% accepted. In 2007, 2 degrees awarded. *Degree requirements:* For master's, thesis. *Entrance requirements:* For master's, writing sample/media production or multimedia portfolio, minimum B average. Additional exam requirements/recommendations for international students: Required—TOEFL (minimum score 600 paper-based; 250 computer-based). *Application deadline:* For fall admission, 3/15 for domestic students. Applications are processed on a rolling basis. Application fee: $55. Electronic applications accepted. *Financial support:* In 2007–08, 14 teaching assistantships (averaging $8,901 per year) were awarded; Federal Work-Study, scholarships/grants, tuition waivers (full and partial), unspecified assistantships, and bursaries also available. Financial award application deadline: 2/15. *Faculty research:* Sociology of news, media ownership and control, communication networks and social movements, issues of media representation. *Unit head:* Dr. Irvin Goldman, Dean, 519-253-3000 Ext. 2897, Fax: 519-971-3676, E-mail: goldman@uwindsor.ca. *Application contact:* Applicant Services, 519-253-3000 Ext. 6459, Fax: 519-971-3653, E-mail: gradadmit@uwindsor.ca.

University of Wisconsin–Madison, Graduate School, College of Letters and Science, Department of Communication Arts, Madison, WI 53706-1380. Offers MA, PhD. Terminal master's awarded for partial completion of doctoral program. *Degree requirements:* For master's, one foreign language, thesis (for some programs); for doctorate, one foreign language, thesis/dissertation. *Entrance requirements:* For master's and doctorate, GRE General Test, minimum GPA of 3.5. Electronic applications accepted.

University of Wisconsin–Madison, Graduate School, College of Letters and Science, School of Journalism and Mass Communication, Madison, WI 53706-1380. Offers family and consumer journalism (PhD); journalism and mass communication (MA); mass communication (PhD). Part-time programs available. *Degree requirements:* For master's, thesis (for some programs); for doctorate, thesis/dissertation. *Entrance requirements:* For master's, GRE General Test, minimum GPA of 3.0; for doctorate, GRE General Test, minimum GPA of 3.5. Additional exam requirements/recommendations for international students: Required—TOEFL. Electronic applications accepted. *Faculty research:* International/development communication; strategic mass communication; mass communication and the individual; science, technology, and environment communication; mass communication and societal institutions.

University of Wisconsin–Milwaukee, Graduate School, College of Letters and Sciences, Department of Communication, Milwaukee, WI 53201-0413. Offers MA, Certificate. Part-time programs available. *Faculty:* 17 full-time (9 women). *Students:* 9 full-time (7 women), 29 part-time (22 women); includes 4 minority (1 African American, 2 American Indian/Alaska Native, 1 Hispanic American), 6 international. 28 applicants, 71% accepted, 15 enrolled. In 2007, 12 degrees awarded. *Degree requirements:* For master's, thesis or alternative. *Entrance requirements:* For master's, GRE General Test, minimum GPA of 3.0. *Application deadline:* For fall admission, 1/1 priority date for domestic students; for spring admission, 9/1 for domestic students. Applications are processed on a rolling basis. Application fee: $45 ($75 for international students). *Expenses:* Tuition, state resident: part-time $530 per credit. Tuition, nonresident: part-time $1,428 per credit. Required fees: $19 per credit. $229 per term. Tuition and fees vary according to course load and program. *Financial support:* In 2007–08, 24 teaching assistantships were awarded; fellowships, research assistantships, career-related internships or fieldwork and unspecified assistantships also available. Support available to part-time students. Financial award application deadline: 4/15. *Unit head:* Mike Allen, Representative, 414-229-4261, Fax: 414-229-3859.

University of Wisconsin–Stevens Point, College of Fine Arts and Communication, Division of Communication, Stevens Point, WI 54481-3897. Offers interpersonal communication (MA);

Communication—General

University of Wisconsin–Stevens Point (continued)
mass communication (MA); organizational communication (MA); public relations (MA). Part-time programs available. *Degree requirements:* For master's, thesis or alternative. *Entrance requirements:* For master's, GRE. Additional exam requirements/recommendations for international students: Required—TOEFL (minimum score 575 paper-based). *Application deadline:* For fall admission, 3/1 priority date for domestic students. Applications are processed on a rolling basis. Application fee: $45. *Expenses:* Tuition, state resident: full-time $6,161. Tuition, nonresident: full-time $16,771. Required fees: $884. Tuition and fees vary according to course load. *Financial support:* In 2007–08, 9 teaching assistantships were awarded; career-related internships or fieldwork, Federal Work-Study, institutionally sponsored loans, and unspecified assistantships also available. Support available to part-time students. Financial award application deadline: 5/1; financial award applicants required to submit FAFSA. *Faculty research:* Communication theory and research, film history. *Unit head:* Dr. James Haney, Chair, 715-346-3409, E-mail: jhaney@uwsp.edu. *Application contact:* Dr. Chris Sadler, Graduate Coordinator, 715-346-3898, E-mail: csadler@uwsp.edu.

University of Wisconsin–Superior, Graduate Division, Department of Communicating Arts, Superior, WI 54880-4500. Offers mass communication (MA); speech communication (MA); theater (MA). Part-time programs available. *Degree requirements:* For master's, comprehensive exam, thesis or alternative, position paper or project. *Entrance requirements:* For master's, minimum GPA of 2.75. *Faculty research:* Multimedia technology, ethics in journalism, diversity, electronic portfolio assessment.

University of Wisconsin–Whitewater, School of Graduate Studies, College of Arts and Communications, Department of Communication, Whitewater, WI 53190-1790. Offers corporate communication (MS); mass communication (MS). Part-time and evening/weekend programs available. Postbaccalaureate distance learning degree programs offered (no on-campus study). *Faculty:* 35. *Students:* 7 full-time (3 women), 14 part-time (8 women); includes 3 African Americans, 2 Asian Americans or Pacific Islanders, 1 Hispanic American. Average age 31. 13 applicants, 46% accepted, 3 enrolled. In 2007, 8 degrees awarded. *Degree requirements:* For master's, thesis or alternative. *Entrance requirements:* For master's, 2 letters of recommendation. Additional exam requirements/recommendations for international students: Required—TOEFL (minimum score 550 paper-based; 213 computer-based). *Application deadline:* For fall admission, 7/15 priority date for domestic students, 7/15 for international students; for spring admission, 12/1 priority date for domestic students, 12/1 for international students. Applications are processed on a rolling basis. Application fee: $45. Electronic applications accepted. *Expenses:* Tuition, state resident: full-time $3,451; part-time $244 per credit. Tuition, nonresident: full-time $8,756; part-time $560 per credit. *Financial support:* Research assistantships, Federal Work-Study, unspecified assistantships, and out-of-state fee waivers available. Support available to part-time students. Financial award application deadline: 3/15; financial award applicants required to submit FAFSA. *Application contact:* Sally A. Lange, School of Graduate Studies, 262-472-1006, Fax: 262-472-5027, E-mail: gradschl@uww.edu.

University of Wyoming, Graduate School, College of Arts and Sciences, Department of Communication and Journalism, Laramie, WY 82070. Offers communication (MA). Part-time programs available. *Faculty:* 9 full-time (2 women). *Students:* 16 full-time (12 women), 14 part-time (9 women); includes 1 minority (Asian American or Pacific Islander), 4 international. Average age 29. 17 applicants, 59% accepted. In 2007, 5 degrees awarded. *Degree requirements:* For master's, thesis. *Entrance requirements:* For master's, GRE General Test, minimum GPA of 3.0. *Application deadline:* For fall admission, 6/1 priority date for domestic students. Applications are processed on a rolling basis. Application fee: $50. *Financial support:* In 2007–08, 8 teaching assistantships with full tuition reimbursements (averaging $10,062 per year) were awarded; career-related internships or fieldwork, Federal Work-Study, and institutionally sponsored loans also available. Financial award application deadline: 3/1. *Faculty research:* Personal relations, nonverbal behavior, media management, communication technology, conversation analysis. *Unit head:* Dr. Ken L. Smith, Chair, 307-766-6273, Fax: 307-766-3812. *Application contact:* Dr. Michael Brown, Director of Graduate Studies, 307-766-3822, Fax: 307-766-3812, E-mail: mrbrown@uwyo.edu.

Utah State University, School of Graduate Studies, College of Humanities, Arts and Social Sciences, Department of Journalism and Communication, Logan, UT 84322. Offers MA, MS. Part-time programs available. *Degree requirements:* For master's, comprehensive exam, thesis. *Entrance requirements:* For master's, GRE General Test or MAT, minimum GPA of 3.0. Additional exam requirements/recommendations for international students: Required—TOEFL. Electronic applications accepted. *Faculty research:* Race and gender and media, history of censorship, internet design and advertising, technology gap.

Villanova University, Graduate School of Liberal Arts and Sciences, Department of Communication, Villanova, PA 19085-1699. Offers MA. Part-time and evening/weekend programs available. *Faculty:* 6 full-time (3 women). *Students:* 18 full-time (12 women), 30 part-time (22 women); includes 7 minority (3 African Americans, 1 Asian American or Pacific Islander, 3 Hispanic Americans), 2 international. Average age 29. 11 applicants, 27% accepted. In 2007, 12 degrees awarded. *Degree requirements:* For master's, comprehensive exam, thesis optional. *Entrance requirements:* For master's, GRE or GMAT, minimum GPA of 3.0. Additional exam requirements/recommendations for international students: Required—TOEFL. *Application deadline:* For fall admission, 8/1 for domestic and international students; for spring admission, 12/1 for domestic and international students. Applications are processed on a rolling basis. Application fee: $50. Electronic applications accepted. *Financial support:* Research assistantships, Federal Work-Study available. Financial award applicants required to submit FAFSA. *Unit head:* Dr. Emory Woodard, Director of Graduate Studies in Communication, 610-519-4780.

Virginia Commonwealth University, Graduate School, College of Humanities and Sciences, School of Mass Communications, Program in Media, Art, and Text, Richmond, VA 23284-9005. Offers PhD. *Students:* 18 full-time (12 women), 5 part-time (2 women); includes 4 minority (2 African Americans, 2 Hispanic Americans), 1 international. 33 applicants, 52% accepted, 12 enrolled. *Entrance requirements:* For doctorate, GRE, MA, MAE, or MFA in appropriate field of study (English, art history, studio art, poetry, mass communications); 3 letters of recommendation. *Application deadline:* For fall admission, 3/15 for domestic students. *Expenses:* Tuition, state resident: full-time $7,224; part-time $401 per credit. Tuition, nonresident: full-time $16,072; part-time $891 per credit. Required fees: $1,679; $63 per credit. Tuition and fees vary according to campus/location. *Unit head:* Thom Didato, Director, 804-828-1329, E-mail: tndidato@vcu.edu.

See Close-Up on page 457.

Virginia Polytechnic Institute and State University, Graduate School, College of Liberal Arts and Human Sciences, Department of Communication, Blacksburg, VA 24061. Offers MA. *Entrance requirements:* Additional exam requirements/recommendations for international students: Required—TOEFL (minimum score 600 paper-based; 250 computer-based).

Wake Forest University, Graduate School of Arts and Sciences, Department of Communication, Winston-Salem, NC 27109. Offers speech communication (MA). Part-time programs available. *Faculty:* 12 full-time (3 women). *Students:* 16 full-time (10 women), 1 (woman) part-time, 5 international. Average age 23. 28 applicants, 50% accepted, 7 enrolled. In 2007, 7 degrees awarded. *Degree requirements:* For master's, one foreign language, thesis. *Entrance requirements:* For master's, GRE General Test, writing sample. Additional exam requirements/recommendations for international students: Required—TOEFL (minimum score 213 computer-based; 79 iBT). *Application deadline:* For fall admission, 1/15 for domestic and international students. Application fee: $45 ($55 for international students). Electronic applications accepted. *Financial support:* In 2007–08, 17 students received support, including 1 research assistantship with full tuition reimbursement available (averaging $8,000 per year), 15 teaching assistantships with full tuition reimbursements available (averaging $8,000 per year); fellowships with full tuition reimbursements available, scholarships/grants, tuition waivers (full and partial), and unspecified assistantships also available. Support available to part-time students. Financial award application deadline: 1/15; financial award applicants required to submit FAFSA. *Unit head:* Ananda Mitra, Director, 336-758-5134, Fax: 336-758-4691, E-mail: ananda@wfu.edu.

Washington State University, Graduate School, College of Liberal Arts, Edward R. Murrow College of Communication, Pullman, WA 99164. Offers health communications (MA, PhD); intercultural and international communications (MA, PhD); media and society (MA, PhD); media process and effects (MA, PhD); organizational communications (MA, PhD). *Faculty:* 30. *Students:* 43 full-time (26 women), 6 part-time (4 women); includes 2 minority (1 Asian American or Pacific Islander, 1 Hispanic American), 19 international. Average age 30. 120 applicants, 22% accepted, 19 enrolled. In 2007, 22 master's, 1 doctorate awarded. *Degree requirements:* For master's, comprehensive exam (for some programs), thesis optional, oral exam; for doctorate, comprehensive exam, thesis/dissertation. *Entrance requirements:* For master's, GRE General Test, minimum GPA of 3.25, 3 letters of recommendation; for doctorate, GRE General Test, minimum undergraduate GPA of 3.25, graduate 3.5; MA in communication; 3 letters of recommendation. Additional exam requirements/recommendations for international students: Required—TOEFL (minimum score 580 paper-based; 237 computer-based). *Application deadline:* For fall admission, 1/15 priority date for domestic students, 3/1 for international students. Applications are processed on a rolling basis. Application fee: $50. Electronic applications accepted. *Financial support:* In 2007–08, 46 students received support, including 2 fellowships (averaging $4,477 per year), 7 research assistantships with full and partial tuition reimbursements available (averaging $13,917 per year), 34 teaching assistantships with full and partial tuition reimbursements available (averaging $13,056 per year); career-related internships or fieldwork, Federal Work-Study, institutionally sponsored loans, tuition waivers (partial), and teaching associateships also available. Financial award application deadline: 4/1; financial award applicants required to submit FAFSA. *Faculty research:* Advocacy communication, mediated communication in decision making, communication technology policy and effects, multicultural and international psychology and physiology of communication. Total annual research expenditures: $550,455. *Unit head:* Dr. Erica Austin, Interim Director, 509-335-1556, E-mail: eaustin@wsu.edu. *Application contact:* Graduate School Admissions, 800-GRADWSU, Fax: 509-335-1949, E-mail: gradsch@wsu.edu.

Wayne State College, School of Education and Counseling, Department of Educational Foundations and Leadership, Program in Curriculum and Instruction, Wayne, NE 68787. Offers alternative education (MSE); business and information technology education (MSE); communication arts education (MSE); early childhood education (MSE); elementary education (MSE); English as a second language (MSE); English education (MSE); family and consumer sciences education (MSE); industrial technology and vocational education (MSE); learning communities (MSE); mathematics education (MSE); music education (MSE); science education (MSE); social science education (MSE). *Accreditation:* NCATE. Part-time and evening/weekend programs available. *Faculty:* 30 part-time/adjunct (22 women). *Students:* 11 full-time (9 women), 344 part-time (299 women); includes 7 minority (2 African Americans, 1 American Indian/Alaska Native, 1 Asian American or Pacific Islander, 3 Hispanic Americans). Average age 36. In 2007, 130 degrees awarded. *Degree requirements:* For master's, comprehensive exam, thesis optional. *Entrance requirements:* For master's, GRE General Test. Additional exam requirements/recommendations for international students: Required—TOEFL (minimum score 550 paper-based; 213 computer-based). *Application deadline:* Applications are processed on a rolling basis. Application fee: $30. *Expenses:* Tuition, state resident: full-time $3,348; part-time $140 per credit hour. Tuition, nonresident: full-time $6,696; part-time $279 per credit hour. Required fees: $972; $41 per credit hour. Tuition and fees vary according to course load. *Financial support:* Applicants required to submit FAFSA.

Wayne State University, College of Fine, Performing and Communication Arts, Department of Communication, Detroit, MI 48202. Offers communication studies (MA, PhD); public relations and organizational communication (MA); radio-TV-film (MA, PhD); speech communication (MA, PhD). *Students:* 74 full-time (49 women), 128 part-time (94 women); includes 63 minority (51 African Americans, 1 American Indian/Alaska Native, 3 Asian Americans or Pacific Islanders, 8 Hispanic Americans), 14 international. Average age 34. 92 applicants, 62% accepted, 42 enrolled. In 2007, 39 master's, 6 doctorates awarded. *Degree requirements:* For master's, thesis, essay, or comprehensive exam; for doctorate, thesis/dissertation. *Entrance requirements:* For master's, minimum GPA of 3.0, personal statement; sample of academic writing; for doctorate, GRE, minimum GPA of 3.3, MA; letters of recommendation; personal statement; sample of written scholarship. Additional exam requirements/recommendations for international students: Required—TOEFL (minimum score 550 paper-based; 213 computer-based); Recommended—TWE (minimum score 6). *Application deadline:* For fall admission, 4/1 for domestic students, 6/1 for international students; for winter admission, 10/1 for international students; for spring admission, 2/1 for international students. Applications are processed on a rolling basis. Application fee: $30 ($50 for international students). Electronic applications accepted. *Expenses:* Tuition, state resident: part-time $403 per credit hour. Tuition, nonresident: part-time $890 per credit hour. *Financial support:* In 2007–08, 22 students received support, including 2 fellowships with tuition reimbursements available (averaging $14,351 per year), 17 teaching assistantships with tuition reimbursements available (averaging $12,922 per year); research assistantships with tuition reimbursements available, career-related internships or fieldwork also available. Financial award application deadline: 2/1. *Faculty research:* Rhetorical theory and criticism; mass media theory and research; argumentation; organizational communication; risk and crisis communication; interpersonal, family, and health communication. *Unit head:* Dr. Matthew Seeger, Chair, 313-577-2959, Fax: 313-577-6300, E-mail: aa4331@wayne.edu. *Application contact:* Hayg Oshagan, Associate Professor, 313-577-0429, E-mail: ad4570@wayne.edu.

Webster University, School of Communications, St. Louis, MO 63119-3194. Offers MA. Part-time and evening/weekend programs available. Postbaccalaureate distance learning degree programs offered. *Faculty:* 4 full-time (2 women), 19 part-time/adjunct. *Students:* 53 full-time (37 women), 269 part-time (200 women); includes 109 minority (98 African Americans, 3 American Indian/Alaska Native, 3 Asian Americans or Pacific Islanders, 5 Hispanic Americans), 14 international. Average age 31. 58 applicants, 95% accepted, 47 enrolled. In 2007, 68 degrees awarded. *Entrance requirements:* For master's, 36 hours of graduate course work. *Application deadline:* Applications are processed on a rolling basis. Application fee: $35 ($50 for international students). *Expenses:* Tuition: Full-time $9,360; part-time $520 per credit. *Financial support:* Career-related internships or fieldwork and Federal Work-Study available. Support available to part-time students. Financial award application deadline: 4/1; financial award applicants required to submit FAFSA. *Unit head:* Debra Carpenter, Dean, 314-968-7154, Fax: 314-963-6106, E-mail: carpenda@webster.edu. *Application contact:* Director of Graduate and Evening Student Admissions, Fax: 314-968-7116, E-mail: gadmit@webster.edu.

West Chester University of Pennsylvania, Office of Graduate Studies and Extended Education, College of Arts and Sciences, Department of Communication Studies, West Chester, PA 19383. Offers communication studies (MA). Part-time and evening/weekend programs available. *Students:* 9 full-time (7 women), 13 part-time (10 women); includes 4 minority (3 African Americans, 1 Asian American or Pacific Islander). Average age 29. 16 applicants, 94% accepted, 8 enrolled. In 2007, 9 degrees awarded. *Degree requirements:* For master's, comprehensive exam, thesis optional. *Entrance requirements:* For master's, GRE or MAT. Additional exam requirements/recommendations for international students: Required—TOEFL (minimum score 550 paper-based; 213 computer-based; 80 iBT). *Application deadline:* For fall admission, 4/15 priority date for domestic students; for spring admission, 10/15 for domestic students. Applications are processed on a rolling basis. Application fee: $35. *Expenses:* Tuition, state resident: part-time $345 per credit. Tuition, nonresident: part-time $552 per credit. Tuition and fees vary according to course load. *Financial support:* In 2007–08, 5 research assistantships with full and partial tuition reimbursements (averaging $5,000 per year) were awarded; unspecified assistantships also available. Support available to part-time students. Financial award application deadline: 2/15; financial award applicants required to submit FAFSA. *Faculty research:* Documentary of the Dalai Lama. *Unit head:* Dr. Timothy Brown, Chair, 610-436-2500, E-mail: tbrown@wcupa.edu. *Application contact:* Dr. Edward Lordan, Graduate Coordinator, 610-436-2114, E-mail: elordan@wcupa.edu.

Western Illinois University, School of Graduate Studies, College of Fine Arts and Communication, Department of Communication, Macomb, IL 61455-1390. Offers MA. Part-time programs available. *Students:* 13 full-time (6 women), 5 part-time (all women); includes 2 minority (1 African American, 1 Hispanic American), 2 international. Average age 29. 14 applicants, 86% accepted. In 2007, 4 degrees awarded. *Degree requirements:* For master's, comprehensive exam (for some programs), thesis or alternative. *Entrance requirements:* Additional exam requirements/recommendations for international students: Required—TOEFL (minimum score 580 paper-based; 237 computer-based; 92 iBT). *Application deadline:* Applications are processed on a rolling basis. Application fee: $30. Electronic applications accepted. *Expenses:* Tuition, state resident: part-time $217 per credit hour. Tuition, nonresident: part-time $433 per credit hour. Required fees: $54 per credit hour. *Financial support:* In 2007–08, 13 students received support, including 10 research assistantships with full tuition reimbursements available (averaging $6,800 per year), 3 teaching assistantships with full tuition reimbursements available (averaging $7,840 per year). Financial award applicants required to submit FAFSA. *Unit head:* Dr. Roberta Davilla, Chairperson, 309-298-1507. *Application contact:* Dr. Barbara Baily, Director of Graduate Studies/Associate Provost, 309-298-1806, Fax: 309-298-2345, E-mail: grad-office@wiu.edu.

Western Kentucky University, Graduate Studies, Potter College of Arts and Letters, Department of Communication, Bowling Green, KY 42101. Offers communication (MA). Part-time and evening/weekend programs available. *Degree requirements:* For master's, comprehensive exam, thesis optional, final exam. *Entrance requirements:* For master's, GRE General Test, minimum GPA of 2.75. Additional exam requirements/recommendations for international students: Required—TOEFL (minimum score 555 paper-based; 213 computer-based; 79 iBT). *Faculty research:* Public rhetoric and public address organization communication, teamwork in communication, intercultural crisis communication.

Western Michigan University, Graduate College, College of Arts and Sciences, Department of Communication, Kalamazoo, MI 49008-5202. Offers organizational communication (MA).

Westminster College, Program in Professional Communication, Salt Lake City, UT 84105-3697. Offers MPC. Part-time and evening/weekend programs available. *Faculty:* 6 full-time (4 women), 2 part-time/adjunct (0 women). *Students:* 10 full-time (2 women), 59 part-time (42 women); includes 2 minority (1 American Indian/Alaska Native, 1 Asian American or Pacific Islander). Average age 34. 47 applicants, 72% accepted, 23 enrolled. In 2007, 16 degrees awarded. *Degree requirements:* For master's, field project. *Entrance requirements:* For master's, personal resumé, sample of professional writing. Additional exam requirements/recommendations for international students: Required—TOEFL (minimum score 600 paper-based; 213 computer-based). *Application deadline:* For fall admission, 8/1 priority date for domestic students. Applications are processed on a rolling basis. Application fee: $40. Electronic applications accepted. *Expenses:* Tuition: Part-time $1,003 per credit hour. Tuition and fees vary according to program and student level. *Financial support:* In 2007–08, 29 students received support. Career-related internships or fieldwork and tuition remissions available. Support available to part-time students. Financial award applicants required to submit FAFSA. *Unit head:* Dr. Helen Hodgson, Director, 801-832-2821, Fax: 801-832-3102, E-mail: hhodgson@westminstercollege.edu. *Application contact:* Joel Bauman, Vice President of Enrollment Services, 801-832-2200, Fax: 801-832-3101, E-mail: admission@westminstercollege.edu.

West Texas A&M University, College of Fine Arts and Humanities, Department of Art, Communication, and Theater, Program in Communication, Canyon, TX 79016-0001. Offers MA. Part-time programs available. *Degree requirements:* For master's, comprehensive exam, thesis optional. *Entrance requirements:* For master's, GRE General Test, 24 hours of undergraduate communications courses, 1 letter of recommendation, interview with communication advisor. Additional exam requirements/recommendations for international students: Required—TOEFL (minimum score 550 paper-based). Electronic applications accepted. *Faculty research:* Comparison student learning in basic public speaking in traditional versus online format, impact of supervisor immediacy and power on organizational outcomes, storytelling, gender, nonverbal.

West Virginia University, Eberly College of Arts and Sciences, Department of Communication Studies, Morgantown, WV 26506. Offers communication in instruction (MA); communication studies (PhD); communication theory and research (MA); corporate and organizational communication (MA). Part-time programs available. *Faculty:* 13 full-time (5 women), 3 part-time/adjunct (2 women). *Students:* 27 full-time (16 women), 57 part-time (41 women); includes 5 minority (3 African Americans, 1 Asian American or Pacific Islander, 1 Hispanic American), 1 international. Average age 35. 94 applicants, 68% accepted, 44 enrolled. In 2007, 56 master's, 2 doctorates awarded. *Median time to degree:* Of those who began their doctoral program in fall 1999, 100% received their degree in 8 years or less. *Degree requirements:* For master's, comprehensive exam (for some programs), thesis (for some programs); for doctorate, comprehensive exam, thesis/dissertation. *Entrance requirements:* For master's and doctorate, minimum GPA of 3.0. Additional exam requirements/recommendations for international students: Required—TOEFL. *Application deadline:* For fall admission, 2/1 priority date for domestic students. Applications are processed on a rolling basis. Application fee: $50. Electronic applications accepted. *Expenses:* Tuition, state resident: full-time $5,196; part-time $292 per credit hour. Tuition, nonresident: full-time $15,064; part-time $840 per credit hour. Tuition and fees vary according to program. *Financial support:* In 2007–08, 49 students received support, including 20 teaching assistantships with full tuition reimbursements available (averaging $10,000 per year); career-related internships or fieldwork, Federal Work-Study, institutionally sponsored loans, tuition waivers (full and partial), and graduate resident hall assistantships also available. Financial award application deadline: 3/1; financial award applicants required to submit FAFSA. *Faculty research:* Instructional communication, interpersonal communication, health communication, influence, instructional communication, social influence. *Unit head:* Dr. Matthew M. Martin, Chair, 304-293-3905, Fax: 304-293-8667, E-mail: matt.martin@mail.wvu.edu. *Application contact:* Dr. Scott A. Myers, PhD Coordinator, 304-293-3905, E-mail: smyers@mail.wvu.edu.

West Virginia University, Perley Isaac Reed School of Journalism, Program in Integrated Marketing Communications, Morgantown, WV 26506. Offers MS. Part-time programs available. Postbaccalaureate distance learning degree programs offered (no on-campus study). *Students:* 41 full-time (30 women), 146 part-time (95 women); includes 24 minority (12 African Americans, 2 American Indian/Alaska Native, 5 Asian Americans or Pacific Islanders, 5 Hispanic Americans), 2 international. Average age 32. 113 applicants, 84% accepted, 67 enrolled. In 2007, 38 degrees awarded. *Entrance requirements:* For master's, GRE or GMAT. Additional exam requirements/recommendations for international students: Required—TOEFL. *Application deadline:* For fall admission, 6/15 priority date for domestic and international students; for spring admission, 10/15 priority date for domestic and international students. Applications are processed on a rolling basis. Application fee: $50. *Expenses:* Tuition, state resident: full-time $5,196; part-time $292 per credit hour. Tuition, nonresident: full-time $15,064; part-time $840 per credit hour. Tuition and fees vary according to program. *Financial support:* In 2007–08, 90 students received support. *Unit head:* Chad Mezera, Marketing Director, 304-293-3505 Ext. 5415, Fax: 304-293-3072, E-mail: chad.mezera@mail.wvu.edu.

Wichita State University, Graduate School, Fairmount College of Liberal Arts and Sciences, Elliot School of Communication, Wichita, KS 67260. Offers MA. Part-time programs available. *Degree requirements:* For master's, comprehensive exam, research project or thesis. *Entrance requirements:* For master's, GRE. Additional exam requirements/recommendations for international students: Required—TOEFL. Electronic applications accepted. *Faculty research:* Classical roots of rhetoric, gender and communication, communication perspective on suicide, small group communications, theatre studies.

Wilfrid Laurier University, Faculty of Graduate Studies, Faculty of Arts, Department of Communication Studies, Waterloo, ON N2L 3C5, Canada. Offers MA. *Faculty:* 12 full-time. *Students:* 8 full-time. 13 applicants, 62% accepted, 8 enrolled. *Degree requirements:* For master's, thesis optional. *Entrance requirements:* For master's, honours BA in communication studies or a cognate discipline from an approved university with a minimum B+ overall in last two years of study and in undergraduate major. Additional exam requirements/recommendations for international students: Required—TOEFL (minimum score 230 computer-based; 89 iBT). *Application deadline:* For fall admission, 2/1 priority date for domestic students. Application fee: $75. Electronic applications accepted. *Financial support:* Fellowships, research assistantships, teaching assistantships available. *Faculty research:* Visual communication and culture, media, technology and culture. *Unit head:* Dr. Barbara Jenkins, Chairperson, 519-884-0710 Ext. 2997, E-mail: bjenkins@wlu.ca. *Application contact:* Jennifer Poppe, Student Contact, 519-884-0710 Ext. 3536, Fax: 519-884-1020, E-mail: gradstudies@wlu.ca.

William Paterson University of New Jersey, College of the Arts and Communication, Program in Communication and Media Studies, Wayne, NJ 07470-8420. Offers MA. *Students:* 3 full-time (all women), 7 part-time (3 women); includes 2 African Americans, 1 Hispanic American. In 2007, 2 degrees awarded. *Degree requirements:* For master's, comprehensive exam. *Entrance requirements:* For master's, GRE General Test or MAT, minimum GPA of 2.75. *Application deadline:* Applications are processed on a rolling basis. Application fee: $50. Electronic applications accepted. *Financial support:* Research assistantships with full tuition reimbursements, career-related internships or fieldwork, Federal Work-Study, and unspecified assistantships available. Support available to part-time students. Financial award application deadline: 4/1; financial award applicants required to submit FAFSA. *Faculty research:* Cable television, intercultural communication. *Unit head:* Casey Lum, Program Director, 973-720-2342, Fax: 973-720-2483. *Application contact:* Danielle Liautaud, Director, 973-720-3579, Fax: 973-720-2035, E-mail: liautaudd@wpunj.edu.

York University, Faculty of Graduate Studies, Program in Communication and Culture, Toronto, ON M3J 1P3, Canada. Offers MA, PhD. *Degree requirements:* For master's, thesis or alternative; for doctorate, comprehensive exam, thesis/dissertation. Electronic applications accepted.

Arts Journalism

Syracuse University, Graduate School, S. I. Newhouse School of Public Communications, Program in Arts Journalism, Syracuse, NY 13244. Offers MA. *Students:* 18 full-time (13 women), 1 (woman) part-time; includes 1 African American, 1 Hispanic American. 47 applicants, 60% accepted. In 2007, 14 degrees awarded. *Entrance requirements:* For master's, GRE General Test. Additional exam requirements/recommendations for international students: Required—TOEFL (minimum score 600 paper-based; 250 computer-based). *Application deadline:* For fall admission, 2/1 for domestic and international students. Application fee: $75. Electronic applications accepted. *Expenses:* Tuition: Full-time $18,216; part-time $1,012 per credit. Required fees: $980. Tuition and fees vary according to program. *Unit head:* Johanna Keller, Director, 315-443-9251, Fax: 315-443-3946, E-mail: pcgrad@syr.edu. *Application contact:* Graduate Records Office, 315-443-4039, Fax: 315-443-1834, E-mail: pcgrad@syr.edu.

Broadcast Journalism

American University, School of Communication, Program in Journalism and Public Affairs, Washington, DC 20016-8001. Offers broadcast journalism (MA), including economic journalism, international journalism, public policy journalism; print journalism (MA), including economic journalism, international journalism, public policy journalism. *Accreditation:* ACEJMC. Part-time and evening/weekend programs available. *Faculty:* 13 full-time (5 women), 4 part-time/adjunct (all women). *Students:* 36 full-time (31 women); includes 10 minority (7 African Americans, 3 Asian Americans or Pacific Islanders), 10 international. 190 applicants, 63% accepted, 35 enrolled. In 2007, 40 degrees awarded. *Degree requirements:* For master's, comprehensive exam, thesis or alternative. *Entrance requirements:* For master's, GRE General Test. Additional exam requirements/recommendations for international students: Required—TOEFL (minimum score 600 paper-based; 250 computer-based). *Application deadline:* For fall admission, 2/1 priority date for domestic students, 4/1 priority date for international students. Applications are processed on a rolling basis. Application fee: $50. Electronic applications accepted. *Expenses:* Tuition: Full-time $19,998; part-time $1,111 per credit hour. Required fees: $380. Tuition and fees vary according to program. *Financial support:* In 2007–08, 3 fellowships with partial tuition reimbursements (averaging $27,000 per year), 14 research assistantships with tuition reimbursements (averaging $7,000 per year), 3 teaching assistantships with tuition reimbursements (averaging $7,000 per year) were awarded; career-related internships or fieldwork, Federal Work-Study, institutionally sponsored loans, scholarships/grants, tuition waivers (partial), and unspecified assistantships also available. Financial award application deadline: 2/1. *Faculty research:* Government and media effects of journalistic practices and policies, race and gender and the media, investigative reporting, computer assisted reporting. *Unit head:* Wendell

Broadcast Journalism

American University (continued)
Cochran, Division Director, 202-885-2072. *Application contact:* Sharmeen Ahsan-Bracciale, Graduate Admissions Office, 202-885-2040, Fax: 202-885-2019, E-mail: sharmeen@american.edu.

See Close-Up on page 881.

The American University in Cairo, Graduate Studies and Research, School of Business, Economics and Communication, Department of Journalism and Communication, Cairo, Egypt. Offers journalism/mass communication (MA); television journalism (MA, Diploma). Part-time programs available. *Degree requirements:* For master's, thesis (for some programs). *Entrance requirements:* For master's, English entrance exam, GMAT. Electronic applications accepted. *Faculty research:* Mass media and national development/censorship, intercultural photo communication, comparative journalism/television.

Boston University, College of Communication, Department of Journalism, Boston, MA 02215. Offers broadcast journalism (MS); business and economics journalism (MS); photo journalism (MS); print journalism (MS); science journalism (MS). *Faculty:* 23 full-time, 26 part-time/adjunct. *Students:* 122 full-time (90 women), 6 part-time (5 women); includes 18 minority (9 African Americans, 8 Asian Americans or Pacific Islanders, 1 Hispanic American), 23 international. Average age 26. In 2007, 83 degrees awarded. *Degree requirements:* For master's, thesis. *Entrance requirements:* For master's, GRE General Test, sample of written work. Additional exam requirements/recommendations for international students: Required—TOEFL. *Application deadline:* For fall admission, 2/1 for domestic students. Electronic applications accepted. *Expenses:* Tuition: Full-time $34,930; part-time $1,092 per credit. Tuition and fees vary according to class time, course level and program. *Financial support:* Teaching assistantships with partial tuition reimbursements, career-related internships or fieldwork, Federal Work-Study, institutionally sponsored loans, scholarships/grants, and unspecified assistantships available. Support available to part-time students. Financial award application deadline: 2/1; financial award applicants required to submit FAFSA. *Unit head:* Lou Ureneck, Chairman, 617-353-3484, Fax: 617-353-1086, E-mail: lureneck@bu.edu. *Application contact:* William A. Taylor, Assistant Director, Graduate Services and Financial Aid, 617-353-3481, Fax: 617-358-0399, E-mail: comgrad@bu.edu.

See Close-Up on page 885.

Emerson College, Graduate Studies, School of Communication, Department of Journalism, Boston, MA 02116-4624. Offers print/multimedia journalism, broadcast journalism, integrated journalism (MA), including broadcast journalism, integrated journalism, print/multimedia journalism. Part-time programs available. *Faculty:* 13 full-time (6 women). *Students:* 62 full-time (33 women), 3 part-time (2 women); includes 6 Asian Americans or Pacific Islanders, 3 Hispanic Americans, 9 international. Average age 25. 117 applicants, 76% accepted, 33 enrolled. In 2007, 34 degrees awarded. *Entrance requirements:* For master's, GRE General Test. Additional exam requirements/recommendations for international students: Required—TOEFL (minimum score 550 paper-based; 213 computer-based; 80 iBT), IELTS (minimum score 7). *Application deadline:* For fall admission, 3/1 priority date for domestic students, 5/1 for international students; for spring admission, 11/1 priority date for domestic students, 11/1 for international students. Applications are processed on a rolling basis. Application fee: $60 ($75 for international students). Electronic applications accepted. *Expenses:* Tuition: Full-time $16,800; part-time $840 per credit. Required fees: $60 per semester. One-time fee: $160. *Financial support:* In 2007–08, 3 fellowships with partial tuition reimbursements (averaging $14,000 per year), 6 research assistantships with partial tuition reimbursements (averaging $10,000 per year) were awarded; career-related internships or fieldwork, Federal Work-Study, institutionally sponsored loans, scholarships/grants, and unspecified assistantships also available. Support available to part-time students. Financial award application deadline: 3/1; financial award applicants required to submit FAFSA. *Faculty research:* Journalism. *Unit head:* Prof. Janet Kolodzy, Acting Chair, 617-824-8805. *Application contact:* 617-824-8610, Fax: 617-824-8614, E-mail: gradapp@emerson.edu.

See Close-Up on page 893.

Northwestern University, Medill School of Journalism, Evanston, IL 60208. Offers broadcast journalism (MSJ); integrated marketing communications (MSIMC), including advertising/sales promotion, direct database and e-commerce marketing, general studies, public relations; magazine publishing (MSJ); new media (MSJ); reporting and writing (MSJ). *Accreditation:* ACEJMC (one or more programs are accredited). *Entrance requirements:* For master's, GRE General Test, GMAT or LSAT (MSJ). Additional exam requirements/recommendations for international students: Required—TOEFL. Electronic applications accepted. Expenses: Contact institution. *Faculty research:* Web business journalism, cultural stereotypes, voter apathy, digital television.

Syracuse University, Graduate School, S. I. Newhouse School of Public Communications, Department of Broadcast Journalism, Syracuse, NY 13244. Offers MS. *Students:* 35 full-time (18 women), 2 part-time (1 woman); includes 6 African Americans, 3 Asian Americans or Pacific Islanders, 1 Hispanic American, 3 international. 92 applicants, 70% accepted. In 2007, 30 degrees awarded. *Degree requirements:* For master's, capstone course. *Entrance requirements:* For master's, GRE General Test. Additional exam requirements/recommendations for international students: Required—TOEFL. *Application deadline:* For fall admission, 2/1 for domestic and international students. Application fee: $75. *Expenses:* Tuition: Full-time $18,216; part-time $1,012 per credit. Required fees: $980. Tuition and fees vary according to program. *Unit head:* Dona Hayes, Chair, 315-443-1944, Fax: 315-443-3946, E-mail: pcgrad@syr.edu. *Application contact:* Graduate Records Office, 315-443-4039, Fax: 315-443-1834, E-mail: pcgrad@syr.edu.

See Close-Up on page 935.

University of Maryland, College Park, Graduate Studies, Phillip Merrill College of Journalism, College Park, MD 20742. Offers broadcast journalism (MA); journalism (MA); journalism and media studies (PhD); online news (MA); public affairs reporting (MA). *Accreditation:* ACEJMC (one or more programs are accredited). Part-time and evening/weekend programs available. *Faculty:* 28 full-time (13 women), 36 part-time/adjunct (10 women). *Students:* 71 full-time (43 women), 17 part-time (7 women); includes 20 minority (13 African Americans, 1 American Indian/Alaska Native, 4 Asian Americans or Pacific Islanders, 2 Hispanic Americans), 12 international. 243 applicants, 35% accepted, 32 enrolled. In 2007, 23 master's, 2 doctorates awarded. *Degree requirements:* For doctorate, thesis/dissertation, preliminary written and oral comprehensive exams. *Entrance requirements:* For master's and doctorate, GRE General Test, minimum GPA of 3.0, 3 letters of recommendation. Additional exam requirements/recommendations for international students: Required—TOEFL. *Application deadline:* For fall admission, 3/1 for domestic students, 2/1 for international students; for spring admission, 10/1 for domestic students, 6/1 for international students. Applications are processed on a rolling basis. Application fee: $60. Electronic applications accepted. *Financial support:* In 2007–08, 5 fellowships with full tuition reimbursements (averaging $13,925 per year), 2 research assistantships with tuition reimbursements (averaging $16,468 per year), 18 teaching assistantships with tuition reimbursements (averaging $15,744 per year) were awarded; career-related internships or fieldwork, Federal Work-Study, and scholarships/grants also available. Support available to part-time students. Financial award applicants required to submit FAFSA. *Faculty research:* Mass communication theory, specialized journalism, new telecommunication technologies, press integration. Total annual research expenditures: $130,465. *Unit head:* Thomas Kunkel, Dean, 301-405-2383, Fax: 301-314-1978, E-mail: tkunkel@umd.edu. *Application contact:* Dean of Graduate School, 301-405-0358, Fax: 301-314-9305.

See Close-Up on page 941.

University of Miami, Graduate School, School of Communication, Coral Gables, FL 33124. Offers communication (PhD); communication studies (MA); film studies (MA, PhD); motion pictures (MFA), including production, producing, and screenwriting; print journalism (MA); public relations (MA); Spanish language journalism (MA); television broadcast journalism (MA). *Accreditation:* ACEJMC. Part-time programs available. *Faculty:* 39 full-time (12 women). *Students:* 113 full-time (61 women), 16 part-time (5 women); includes 28 minority (8 African Americans, 1 Asian American or Pacific Islander, 19 Hispanic Americans), 14 international. Average age 27. 374 applicants, 56% accepted, 64 enrolled. In 2007, 48 master's, 2 doctorates awarded. *Degree requirements:* For master's, comprehensive exam (for some programs), thesis (for some programs); for doctorate, comprehensive exam, thesis/dissertation. *Entrance requirements:* For master's, GRE General Test; for doctorate, GRE General Test, master's thesis or scholarly research. Additional exam requirements/recommendations for international students: Required—TOEFL (minimum score 600 paper-based; 250 computer-based; 100 iBT). *Application deadline:* For fall admission, 12/15 priority date for domestic and international students. Applications are processed on a rolling basis. Application fee: $50. Electronic applications accepted. *Financial support:* In 2007–08, 68 students received support, including 10 teaching assistantships with full tuition reimbursements available; fellowships with full tuition reimbursements available, Federal Work-Study, institutionally sponsored loans, scholarships/grants, tuition waivers (partial), and unspecified assistantships also available. Financial award application deadline: 3/1; financial award applicants required to submit FAFSA. *Faculty research:* Communication studies, mass communication, international/interpersonal communication, film studies, journalism. *Unit head:* Dr. Sam L. Grogg, Dean, 305-284-3420, Fax: 305-284-2454, E-mail: sgrogg@miami.edu. *Application contact:* Dr. Leonardo C. Ferreira, Director of Graduate Studies, 305-284-3180, Fax: 305-284-8701, E-mail: lferreira@miami.edu.

See Close-Up on page 943.

University of Southern California, Graduate School, Annenberg School for Communication, School of Journalism, Program in Broadcast Journalism, Los Angeles, CA 90089. Offers MA. *Students:* 34 full-time (30 women), 4 part-time (all women); includes 18 minority (3 African Americans, 8 Asian Americans or Pacific Islanders, 7 Hispanic Americans), 2 international. Average age 26. 79 applicants, 48% accepted, 16 enrolled. In 2007, 37 degrees awarded. *Degree requirements:* For master's, comprehensive exam. *Entrance requirements:* For master's, GRE General Test, resumé, writing samples, letters of recommendation, statement of purpose. Additional exam requirements/recommendations for international students: Required—TOEFL (minimum score 280 computer-based; 114 iBT). *Application deadline:* For fall admission, 1/15 for domestic and international students. Application fee: $85. Electronic applications accepted. *Financial support:* Teaching assistantships with full tuition reimbursements, career-related internships or fieldwork, Federal Work-Study, institutionally sponsored loans, scholarships/grants, health care benefits, and unspecified assistantships available. Support available to part-time students. Financial award application deadline: 1/15; financial award applicants required to submit FAFSA. *Application contact:* Allyson Hill, Director of Admissions, 213-821-0770, E-mail: ascadm@usc.edu.

See Close-Up on page 945.

Corporate and Organizational Communication

The American University of Athens, The School of Graduate Studies, Athens, Greece. Offers biomedical sciences (MS); business (MBA); business communication (MA); computer sciences (MS); engineering and applied sciences (MS); politics and policy making (MA); systems engineering (MS); telecommunications (MS). *Faculty:* 15 full-time (2 women), 13 part-time/adjunct (4 women). *Students:* 20 full-time (2 women), 8 part-time, 10 international. *Entrance requirements:* For master's, University Degree/Resum&e, 2 recommendation letters/TOEFL score 550. Additional exam requirements/recommendations for international students: Required—TOEFL (minimum score 550 paper-based; 213 computer-based). Application fee: 100 euros. *Expenses:* Tuition: Part-time $400 per credit. Required fees: $400 per credit. Tuition and fees vary according to program. *Faculty research:* Nanotechnology, environmental sciences, rock mechanics, human skin studies, Monte Carlo algorithms and software. *Unit head:* Dr. Rita Roussos, Director of the School of Graduate Studies, 302-725-9301-3, Fax: 302-10-7259304, E-mail: rroussos@aua.edu.

Antioch University Seattle, Graduate Programs, Center for Creative Change, Seattle, WA 98121-1814. Offers environment and community (MA); management (MS); organizational psychology (MA); strategic communications (MA); whole system design (MA). Evening/weekend programs available. Electronic applications accepted. Expenses: Contact institution.

Barry University, School of Arts and Sciences, Department of Communication, Miami Shores, FL 33161-6695. Offers broadcasting (Certificate); communication (MA), including broadcast communication, public relations and corporate communications; organizational communication (MS). Part-time and evening/weekend programs available. *Degree requirements:* For master's, thesis (for some programs). *Entrance requirements:* For master's, GRE General Test, MAT, minimum GPA of 3.0. *Application deadline:* Applications are processed on a rolling basis. Application fee: $30. Electronic applications accepted. *Financial support:* Career-related internships or fieldwork available. Support available to part-time students. Financial award application deadline: 5/1; financial award applicants required to submit FAFSA. *Faculty research:* Organizational communication, broadcast communication, intercultural communication, advertising, leadership. *Unit head:* Dr. Denis Vogel, Chair, 305-899-3468, E-mail: dvogel@mail.barry.edu. *Application contact:* Dave Fletcher, Director of Graduate Admissions, 305-899-3113, Fax: 305-899-2971, E-mail: dfletcher@mail.barry.edu.

Bernard M. Baruch College of the City University of New York, Weissman School of Arts and Sciences, Program in Corporate Communication, New York, NY 10010-5585. Offers MA.

Bowie State University, Graduate Programs, Program in Organizational Communication, Bowie, MD 20715-9465. Offers MA, Certificate. Part-time and evening/weekend programs available. *Degree requirements:* For master's, comprehensive exam, thesis optional, research paper. *Entrance requirements:* For master's, minimum GPA of 2.5. Electronic applications accepted. *Faculty research:* International telecommunications, developmental communications.

Canisius College, Graduate Division, College of Arts and Sciences, Department of Communication and Leadership, Buffalo, NY 14208-1098. Offers MS. Part-time and evening/weekend programs available. *Faculty:* 10 full-time (4 women). *Students:* 8 full-time (6 women), 32 part-time (26 women); includes 7 minority (3 African Americans, 1 Asian American or Pacific Islander, 3 Hispanic Americans), 3 international. Average age 31. 21 applicants, 62% accepted, 9 enrolled. In 2007, 13 degrees awarded. *Degree requirements:* For master's, thesis. *Entrance requirements:* For master's, GRE General Test or GMAT. *Application deadline:* For fall admission,

7/15 priority date for domestic students; for spring admission, 4/15 priority date for domestic students. Applications are processed on a rolling basis. Application fee: $25. Electronic applications accepted. *Expenses:* Tuition: Full-time $32,574; part-time $651 per credit. Required fees: $222; $19 per credit. Tuition and fees vary according to program. *Financial support:* In 2007–08, 1 research assistantship with tuition reimbursement was awarded. *Faculty research:* Health and communication, conflict and communication. *Unit head:* Dr. Rosanne L. Hartman, Director, 716-888-2589, Fax: 716-888-3118, E-mail: hartmanr@canisius.edu.

Central Connecticut State University, School of Graduate Studies, School of Arts and Sciences, Department of Communication, New Britain, CT 06050-4010. Offers organizational communication (MS). Part-time and evening/weekend programs available. *Faculty:* 14 full-time (4 women), 7 part-time/adjunct (2 women). *Students:* 5 full-time (4 women), 25 part-time (15 women); includes 4 minority (3 African Americans, 1 Hispanic American), 2 international. Average age 30. 22 applicants, 50% accepted, 6 enrolled. *Degree requirements:* For master's, comprehensive exam, thesis or alternative. *Entrance requirements:* For master's, minimum GPA of 3.0. Additional exam requirements/recommendations for international students: Required—TOEFL. *Application deadline:* For fall admission, 7/1 for domestic students; for spring admission, 12/1 for domestic students. Applications are processed on a rolling basis. Application fee: $50. Electronic applications accepted. *Expenses:* Tuition, area resident: Full-time $4,169. Tuition, state resident: full-time $6,253. Tuition, nonresident: full-time $11,614; part-time $400 per credit. Required fees: $3,322. One-time fee: $62 part-time. Tuition and fees vary according to degree level and program. *Financial support:* In 2007–08, 2 students received support; research assistantships, career-related internships or fieldwork, Federal Work-Study, scholarships/grants, and unspecified assistantships available. Support available to part-time students. Financial award application deadline: 3/1; financial award applicants required to submit FAFSA. *Faculty research:* Organizational communication, mass communication, intercultural communication, political communication, information management. *Unit head:* Dr. Serafin Mendez-Mendez, Chair, 860-832-2690.

Central Michigan University, College of Graduate Studies, Program in Administration, Mount Pleasant, MI 48859. Offers acquisitions administration (MSA); general administration (MSA); health services administration (MSA); hospitality and tourism administration (MSA); human resources administration (MSA); information resource management (MSA); international administration (MSA); leadership (MSA); long-term care administration (MSA); organizational communication (MSA); public administration (MSA); recreation and park administration (MSA); sport administration (MSA). *Accreditation:* AACSB. *Degree requirements:* For master's, thesis or alternative. *Entrance requirements:* For master's, minimum undergraduate GPA of 2.5.

College of Charleston, Graduate School, School of Humanities and Social Sciences, Program in Organizational and Corporate Communication, Charleston, SC 29424-0001. Offers Certificate. *Students:* Average age 30. 8 applicants, 75% accepted, 6 enrolled. *Entrance requirements:* For degree, minimum GPA of 2.5. Application fee: $35. Electronic applications accepted. *Expenses:* Tuition, state resident: full-time $7,778; part-time $324 per hour. Tuition, nonresident: full-time $18,732; part-time $781 per hour. *Unit head:* Dr. Douglas Ferguson, Director, 844-983-7854, E-mail: fergusond@cofc.edu. *Application contact:* Susan Hallatt, Assistant Director of Graduate Admissions, 843-953-5614, Fax: 843-953-1434, E-mail: hallatts@cofc.edu.

Columbia University, Graduate School of Business, MBA Program, New York, NY 10027. Offers accounting (MBA); decision, risk, and operations (MBA); entrepreneurship (MBA); finance and economics (MBA); human resource management (MBA); international business (MBA); management/leadership (MBA); marketing (MBA); media (MBA); real estate (MBA); social enterprise (MBA); DDS/MBA; JD/MBA; MBA/MIA; MBA/MPH; MBA/MS; MD/MBA. *Faculty:* 117 full-time (14 women), 124 part-time/adjunct (18 women). *Students:* 1,226 full-time (420 women); includes 274 minority (75 African Americans, 4 American Indian/Alaska Native, 162 Asian Americans or Pacific Islanders, 33 Hispanic Americans), 409 international. Average age 28. 5,623 applicants, 16% accepted, 711 enrolled. In 2007, 711 degrees awarded. *Entrance requirements:* For master's, GMAT, 2 letters of recommendation, official transcripts, essay, personal statement, completed application. Additional exam requirements/recommendations for international students: Required—TOEFL. *Application deadline:* For fall admission, 4/15 for domestic students, 3/4 for international students; for spring admission, 10/8 for domestic and international students. Applications are processed on a rolling basis. Application fee: $250. Electronic applications accepted. *Expenses:* Tuition: Part-time $1,452 per credit. Required fees: $152 per term. One-time fee: $75 part-time. Full-time tuition and fees vary according to course level, course load, degree level and program. *Financial support:* Fellowships, research assistantships, teaching assistantships, career-related internships or fieldwork, institutionally sponsored loans, scholarships/grants, and unspecified assistantships available. Financial award applicants required to submit FAFSA. *Unit head:* Prof. Amir Ziv, Vice Dean of Students and the MBA Program, 212-854-3485, Fax: 212-932-0545, E-mail: az50@columbia.edu. *Application contact:* Linda B. Meehan, Assistant Dean of Admissions, 212-854-1961, Fax: 212-662-6754, E-mail: apply@gsb.columbia.edu.

Columbia University, School of Continuing Education, Program in Strategic Communications, New York, NY 10027. Offers MS. Part-time and evening/weekend programs available. *Faculty:* 3 full-time (2 women), 7 part-time/adjunct (3 women). *Students:* Average age 28. In 2007, 14 degrees awarded. *Degree requirements:* For master's, 36 credits. *Entrance requirements:* For master's, BA/BS 3.0 GPA. Additional exam requirements/recommendations for international students: Required—American Language Program (ALP) placement test. *Application deadline:* For fall admission, 7/11 priority date for domestic students; for spring admission, 11/11 priority date for domestic students. Applications are processed on a rolling basis. Application fee: $50. Electronic applications accepted. *Expenses:* Tuition: Part-time $1,452 per credit. Required fees: $152 per term. One-time fee: $75 part-time. Full-time tuition and fees vary according to course level, course load, degree level and program. *Financial support:* Institutionally sponsored loans available. Financial award applicants required to submit FAFSA. *Faculty research:* Marketing communications, public relations, crisis management. *Unit head:* Trudi Baldwin, Director, 212-854-0541, Fax: 212-854-5861, E-mail: tb293@columbia.edu. *Application contact:* 212-854-9666, E-mail: ce-advis@columbia.edu.

Concordia University Wisconsin, Graduate Programs, School of Business and Legal Studies, MBA Program, Mequon, WI 53097-2402. Offers finance (MBA); health care administration (MBA); human resource management (MBA); international business (MBA); international business-bilingual English/Chinese (MBA); management (MBA); management information systems (MBA); managerial communications (MBA); marketing (MBA); public administration (MBA); risk management (MBA). Postbaccalaureate distance learning degree programs offered (minimal on-campus study). *Degree requirements:* For master's, comprehensive exam, thesis or alternative. *Entrance requirements:* Additional exam requirements/recommendations for international students: Required—TOEFL. Expenses: Contact institution.

Dallas Baptist University, College of Business, Business Administration Program, Dallas, TX 75211-9299. Offers accounting (MBA); business communication (MBA); conflict resolution management (MBA); e-business (MBA); entrepreneurship (MBA); finance (MBA); health care management (MBA); international business (MBA); management (MBA); management information systems (MBA); marketing (MBA); project management (MBA); technology and engineering management (MBA). *Accreditation:* ACBSP. Part-time and evening/weekend programs available. *Faculty:* 55 full-time (22 women), 114 part-time/adjunct (44 women). *Students:* 134 full-time, 335 part-time. 285 applicants, 59% accepted, 115 enrolled. In 2007, 148 degrees awarded. *Entrance requirements:* For master's, GMAT, minimum GPA of 3.0. Additional exam requirements/recommendations for international students: Required—TOEFL, IELTS. *Application deadline:* Applications are processed on a rolling basis. Application fee: $25. Electronic applications accepted. *Expenses:* Tuition: Full-time $9,144; part-time $508 per credit hour. *Financial support:* Federal Work-Study, institutionally sponsored loans, scholarships/grants, and tuition waivers (full and partial) available. Support available to part-time students. Financial award applicants required to submit FAFSA. *Faculty research:* Sports management, services marketing, retailing, strategic management, financial planning/investments. *Unit head:* Dr. Sandra S. Reid, Director, 214-333-5280, Fax: 214-333-5293, E-mail: graduate@dbu.edu. *Application contact:* Kit P. Montgomery, Director of Graduate Programs, 214-333-5242, Fax: 214-333-5579, E-mail: graduate@dbu.edu.

Dallas Baptist University, College of Business, Management Program, Dallas, TX 75211-9299. Offers business communication (MA); conflict resolution management (MA); general management (MA); health care management (MA); human resource management (MA). Part-time and evening/weekend programs available. *Faculty:* 55 full-time (22 women), 114 part-time/adjunct (44 women). *Students:* 20 full-time, 157 part-time. 61 applicants, 62% accepted, 28 enrolled. In 2007, 76 degrees awarded. *Entrance requirements:* For master's, GRE General Test, minimum GPA of 3.0. Additional exam requirements/recommendations for international students: Required—TOEFL, IELTS. *Application deadline:* Applications are processed on a rolling basis. Application fee: $25. Electronic applications accepted. *Expenses:* Tuition: Full-time $9,144; part-time $508 per credit hour. *Financial support:* Federal Work-Study, institutionally sponsored loans, scholarships/grants, and tuition waivers (full and partial) available. Support available to part-time students. Financial award applicants required to submit FAFSA. *Faculty research:* Organizational behavior, conflict personalities. *Unit head:* Candice L Armstrong, Director of Management Program, 214-333-5280, Fax: 214-333-5293, E-mail: graduate@dbu.edu. *Application contact:* Kit P. Montgomery, Director of Graduate Programs, 214-333-5242, Fax: 214-333-5579, E-mail: graduate@dbu.edu.

Dallas Baptist University, Gary Cook School of Leadership and Christian Education, Program in Global Leadership, Dallas, TX 75211-9299. Offers business communication (MA); Christian education/missions (MA); ESL (MA); general studies (MA); global studies (MA); international business (MA); missions (MA); worship/missions (MA). Part-time and evening/weekend programs available. *Faculty:* 55 full-time (22 women), 114 part-time/adjunct (44 women). *Students:* 2 full-time, 21 part-time. 20 applicants, 65% accepted, 13 enrolled. *Entrance requirements:* For master's, minimum GPA 3.0. Additional exam requirements/recommendations for international students: Required—TOEFL, IELTS. Application fee: $25. *Expenses:* Tuition: Full-time $9,144; part-time $508 per credit hour. *Financial support:* Federal Work-Study, institutionally sponsored loans, scholarships/grants, and tuition waivers (full and partial) available. Support available to part-time students. Financial award applicants required to submit FAFSA. *Unit head:* Dr. Jim Lemons, Director, 214-333-5506, Fax: 214-333-6955, E-mail: graduate@dbu.edu. *Application contact:* Kit P. Montgomery, Director of Graduate Programs, 214-333-5242, Fax: 214-333-5579, E-mail: graduate@dbu.edu.

DePaul University, College of Communication, Chicago, IL 60604-2287. Offers journalism (MA); media, culture, and society (MA); organizational and multicultural communication (MA); public relations and advertising (MA). Part-time and evening/weekend programs available. *Faculty:* 21 full-time (10 women), 9 part-time/adjunct (4 women). *Students:* 88 full-time (69 women), 43 part-time (38 women); includes 29 minority (16 African Americans, 5 Asian Americans or Pacific Islanders, 8 Hispanic Americans), 2 international. Average age 29. 242 applicants, 47% accepted, 68 enrolled. In 2007, 64 degrees awarded. *Degree requirements:* For master's, final exam or thesis/project. *Entrance requirements:* For master's, GRE General Test (public relations and advertising), minimum GPA of 3.0, writing sample, essay, letters of recommendation, resumé. Additional exam requirements/recommendations for international students: Required—TOEFL (minimum score 590 paper-based; 245 computer-based; 96 iBT). Application fee: $40. Electronic applications accepted. *Financial support:* In 2007–08, 8 students received support, including 2 teaching assistantships with full tuition reimbursements available (averaging $12,000 per year); fellowships with full tuition reimbursements available, research assistantships, career-related internships or fieldwork, scholarships/grants, and tuition waivers (partial) also available. Support available to part-time students. Financial award applicants required to submit FAFSA. *Faculty research:* Intercultural communication, corporate culture, diversity in the working place, organizational socialization, critical cultural studies. *Unit head:* Dr. Jacqueline Taylor, Dean, 773-325-7216, Fax: 773-325-7584, E-mail: jtaylor@depaul.edu. *Application contact:* Ann Spittle, Director of Graduate Admission, 773-325-8369, Fax: 773-325-2395, E-mail: aspittle@depaul.edu.

Emerson College, Graduate Studies, School of Communication, Department of Communication Studies, Program in Communication Management, Boston, MA 02116-4624. Offers MA. Part-time programs available. *Students:* 44 full-time (37 women), 9 part-time (7 women); includes 1 African American, 1 American Indian/Alaska Native, 2 Asian Americans or Pacific Islanders, 10 international. Average age 26. 38 applicants, 89% accepted, 25 enrolled. In 2007, 22 degrees awarded. *Entrance requirements:* For master's, GMAT or GRE General Test. Additional exam requirements/recommendations for international students: Required—TOEFL (minimum score 550 paper-based; 213 computer-based; 80 iBT), IELTS (minimum score 7). *Application deadline:* For fall admission, 3/1 priority date for domestic students, 5/1 for international students; for spring admission, 11/1 priority date for domestic students. Applications are processed on a rolling basis. Application fee: $60 ($75 for international students). Electronic applications accepted. *Expenses:* Tuition: Full-time $16,800; part-time $840 per credit. Required fees: $60 per semester. One-time fee: $160. *Financial support:* In 2007–08, 2 fellowships with partial tuition reimbursements (averaging $14,000 per year), 5 research assistantships with partial tuition reimbursements (averaging $10,000 per year) were awarded; career-related internships or fieldwork, Federal Work-Study, institutionally sponsored loans, and scholarships/grants also available. Support available to part-time students. Financial award application deadline: 3/1; financial award applicants required to submit FAFSA. *Faculty research:* Organizational management, corporate and organizational communication. *Unit head:* Prof. Linda Gallant, Director, 617-824-8491. *Application contact:* 617-824-8610, Fax: 617-824-8614, E-mail: gradapp@emerson.edu.

See Close-Up on page 891.

Fairleigh Dickinson University, College at Florham, Maxwell Becton College of Arts and Sciences, Department of English, Communication and Philosophy, Program in Corporate and Organizational Communication, Madison, NJ 07940-1099. Offers MA, MA/MBA. *Students:* 18 full-time (17 women), 20 part-time (14 women), 4 international. Average age 31. 19 applicants, 63% accepted, 14 enrolled. In 2007, 12 degrees awarded. *Entrance requirements:* For master's, GRE General Test. *Application deadline:* Applications are processed on a rolling basis. Application fee: $40. *Expenses:* Tuition: Part-time $869 per credit.

Florida State University, Graduate Studies, College of Communication, Department of Communication, Tallahassee, FL 32306. Offers corporate and public communication (MA, MS); integrated marketing communication (MA, MS); mass communication (PhD); media and communication studies (MA, MS); speech communication (PhD). Part-time programs available. *Faculty:* 26 full-time (7 women), 2 part-time/adjunct (0 women). *Students:* 96 full-time (66 women), 126 part-time (70 women); includes 92 minority (37 African Americans, 1 American Indian/Alaska Native, 35 Asian Americans or Pacific Islanders, 19 Hispanic Americans), 1 international. Average age 24. 230 applicants, 74% accepted, 80 enrolled. In 2007, 77 master's, 6 doctorates awarded. *Median time to degree:* Of those who began their doctoral program in fall 1999, 67% received their degree in 8 years or less. *Degree requirements:* For master's, thesis (for some programs); for doctorate, comprehensive exam, thesis/dissertation. *Entrance requirements:* For master's, GRE General Test, minimum GPA of 3.0; for doctorate, GRE General Test, minimum GPA of 3.3 in graduate course work. Additional exam requirements/recommendations for international students: Required—TOEFL (minimum score 600 paper-based; 250 computer-based; 100 iBT). *Application deadline:* For fall admission, 7/1 priority date for domestic and international students; for winter admission, 3/1 priority date for domestic and international students; for spring admission, 11/1 priority date for domestic and international students. Applications are processed on a rolling basis. Application fee: $30. *Expenses:* Tuition, state resident: part-time $248 per credit hour. Tuition, nonresident: part-time $880 per credit hour. Tuition and fees vary according to program. *Financial support:* In 2007–08, 49 students received support, including 1 fellowship with full tuition reimbursement available, 8 research assistantships with full tuition reimbursements available (averaging $14,000 per year), 40 teaching assistantships with full tuition reimbursements available (averaging $5,000

Corporate and Organizational Communication

Florida State University (continued)
per year); career-related internships or fieldwork, Federal Work-Study, institutionally sponsored loans, scholarships/grants, tuition waivers (partial), and unspecified assistantships also available. Support available to part-time students. Financial award application deadline: 2/1; financial award applicants required to submit FAFSA. *Faculty research:* Communication technology and policy, marketing communication, communication content and effect, new communication/information technologies. Total annual research expenditures: $264,208. *Unit head:* Dr. Stephen D. McDowell, Chairperson, 850-644-2276, Fax: 850-644-8642, E-mail: smcdowel@mailer.fsu.edu. *Application contact:* Natashia Hinson-Turner, Graduate Program Assistant, 850-644-8746, Fax: 850-644-8642, E-mail: dc.gradinfo@comm.fsu.edu.

Fordham University, Graduate School of Business Administration, New York, NY 10023. Offers accounting (MBA); communications and media management (MBA); executive business administration (EMBA); finance (MBA, MS); information systems (MBA, MS); management systems (MBA); marketing (MBA); media management (MS); taxation (MS); taxation and accounting (MTA);); JD/MBA; MBA/MIM; MS/MBA. *Accreditation:* AACSB. Part-time and evening/weekend programs available. *Faculty:* 92 full-time (29 women), 95 part-time/adjunct (19 women). *Students:* 365 full-time (143 women), 1,183 part-time (474 women); includes 254 minority (56 African Americans, 2 American Indian/Alaska Native, 137 Asian Americans or Pacific Islanders, 59 Hispanic Americans), 69 international. Average age 28. 1,131 applicants, 64% accepted, 411 enrolled. In 2007, 488 degrees awarded. *Entrance requirements:* For master's, GMAT, official undergraduate transcripts, 2 letters of recommendation, resumé, personal statement. Additional exam requirements/recommendations for international students: Required—TOEFL (minimum score 600 paper-based; 250 computer-based; 100 iBT). *Application deadline:* For fall admission, 6/1 priority date for domestic students, 5/1 priority date for international students; for winter admission, 11/1 priority date for domestic students, 10/1 priority date for international students; for spring admission, 3/1 priority date for domestic students, 2/1 priority date for international students. Applications are processed on a rolling basis. Application fee: $65. Electronic applications accepted. *Expenses: Contact institution. Financial support:* In 2007–08, 37 students received support, including fellowships (averaging $27,000 per year); research assistantships, career-related internships or fieldwork, institutionally sponsored loans, scholarships/grants, and unspecified assistantships also available. Support available to part-time students. Financial award application deadline: 5/1; financial award applicants required to submit FAFSA. *Unit head:* Dr. Howard Tuckman, Dean, 212-636-6165, Fax: 212-307-1779, E-mail: tuckman@fordham.edu. *Application contact:* Cynthia Perez, Director of Admissions and Financial Aid, 212-636-6200, Fax: 212-636-7076, E-mail: admissionsgb@fordham.edu.

Franklin University, Marketing and Communications Program, Columbus, OH 43215-5399. Offers MS. Part-time and evening/weekend programs available. *Faculty:* 1 full-time (0 women), 8 part-time/adjunct (3 women). *Students:* 82 full-time (60 women), 12 part-time (8 women); includes 25 minority (21 African Americans, 3 Asian Americans or Pacific Islanders, 1 Hispanic American), 5 international. Average age 33. In 2007, 55 degrees awarded. *Degree requirements:* For master's, thesis or alternative. *Entrance requirements:* For master's, minimum undergraduate GPA of 2.75, undergraduate course work in marketing and statistics. Additional exam requirements/recommendations for international students: Required—TOEFL (minimum score 600 paper-based; 232 computer-based). *Application deadline:* For fall admission, 8/15 priority date for domestic students; for winter admission, 12/20 priority date for domestic students; for spring admission, 4/4 priority date for domestic students. Applications are processed on a rolling basis. Application fee: $30. Electronic applications accepted. *Expenses:* Tuition: Full-time $4,543; part-time $413 per credit hour. Tuition and fees vary according to campus/location and program. *Financial support:* In 2007–08, 50 students received support. Application deadline: 6/30. *Unit head:* Dr. Doug Ross, Program Chair, 614-947-6149. *Application contact:* Graduate Services Office, 614-797-4700, Fax: 614-224-7723, E-mail: gradschl@franklin.edu.

Hawai'i Pacific University, College of Business Administration, Honolulu, HI 96813. Offers accounting/CPA (MBA); communication (MBA); e-business (MBA); economics (MBA); finance (MBA); human resource management (MBA); information systems (MBA); international business (MBA); management (MBA); marketing (MBA); organizational change (MBA); travel industry management (MBA). Part-time and evening/weekend programs available. *Faculty:* 40 full-time (16 women), 30 part-time/adjunct (10 women). *Students:* 280 full-time (132 women), 193 part-time (91 women); includes 144 minority (11 African Americans, 7 American Indian/Alaska Native, 119 Asian Americans or Pacific Islanders, 7 Hispanic Americans), 219 international. Average age 29. 204 applicants, 95% accepted, 110 enrolled. In 2007, 150 degrees awarded. *Degree requirements:* For master's, thesis. *Entrance requirements:* For master's, GMAT. Additional exam requirements/recommendations for international students: Recommended—TOEFL (minimum score 550 paper-based; 213 computer-based; 80 iBT), TWE (minimum score 5). *Application deadline:* For fall admission, 2/15 priority date for domestic students; for spring admission, 10/15 priority date for domestic students. Applications are processed on a rolling basis. Application fee: $50. Electronic applications accepted. *Expenses:* Tuition: Full-time $14,400. Required fees: $1,885. Tuition and fees vary according to course load and program. *Financial support:* In 2007–08, 107 students received support; research assistantships, career-related internships or fieldwork, Federal Work-Study, scholarships/grants, and unspecified assistantships available. Support available to part-time students. Financial award application deadline: 3/1; financial award applicants required to submit FAFSA. *Faculty research:* Statistical control process as used by management, studies in comparative cross-cultural management styles, not-for-profit management. *Unit head:* Dr. Charles Steilen, Dean, 808-544-9301, Fax: 808-544-0283, E-mail: csteilen@hpu.edu. *Application contact:* Danny Lam, Assistant Director of Graduate Admissions, 808-544-1135, Fax: 808-544-0280, E-mail: graduate@hpu.edu.

HEC Montreal, School of Business Administration, Diploma Programs in Administration, Program in Marketing Communication, Montréal, QC H3T 2A7, Canada. Offers Diploma. All courses are given in French; program offered on part-time basis only. Part-time programs available. *Students:* 105 applicants, 35% accepted, 33 enrolled. In 2007, 19 degrees awarded. *Degree requirements:* For Diploma, one foreign language. *Entrance requirements:* For degree, relevant work experience, letters of recommendation. *Application deadline:* For fall admission, 4/15 for domestic and international students. Application fee: $75 Canadian dollars. Electronic applications accepted. Tuition charges are reported in Canadian dollars. *Expenses:* Tuition, state resident: full-time $5,800 Canadian dollars. Tuition, nonresident: full-time $12,200 Canadian dollars. International tuition: $23,300 Canadian dollars full-time. *Financial support:* Scholarships/grants available. *Application contact:* Francine Blais, Administrative Director, 514-340-6112, Fax: 514-340-6411, E-mail: francine.blais@hec.ca.

Howard University, School of Communications, Department of Communication and Culture, Washington, DC 20059-0002. Offers intercultural communication (MA, PhD); organizational communication (MA, PhD). Offered through the Graduate School of Arts and Sciences. Part-time programs available. Terminal master's awarded for partial completion of doctoral program. *Degree requirements:* For master's, comprehensive exam or thesis; for doctorate, one foreign language, comprehensive exam, thesis/dissertation. *Entrance requirements:* For master's, English proficiency exam, GRE General Test, minimum GPA of 3.0; for doctorate, English proficiency exam, GRE General Test, master's degree in related field, minimum GPA of 3.5. Additional exam requirements/recommendations for international students: Required—TOEFL. *Expenses:* Tuition: Full-time $16,175; part-time $899 per credit hour. Required fees: $805. *Faculty research:* Media effects, black discourse, development communication, African-American organizations.

Illinois Institute of Technology, Stuart School of Business, Program in Marketing Communication, Chicago, IL 60616-3793. Offers MS, JD/MS, MBA/MS. Part-time and evening/weekend programs available. *Faculty:* 1 full-time (0 women), 7 part-time/adjunct (3 women). *Students:* 33 full-time (24 women), 5 part-time (2 women); includes 2 minority (1 African American, 1 Asian American or Pacific Islander), 32 international. Average age 25. 79 applicants, 77% accepted, 19 enrolled. In 2007, 23 degrees awarded. *Entrance requirements:* For master's, GMAT or GRE General Test. Additional exam requirements/recommendations for international students: Required—TOEFL (minimum score 600 paper-based; 250 computer-based; 100 iBT). *Application deadline:* For fall admission, 5/1 for domestic and international students; for spring admission, 1/5 for domestic and international students. Applications are processed on a rolling basis. Application fee: $75. Electronic applications accepted. *Expenses: Contact institution.* Tuition and fees vary according to class time, course level, course load, program and student level. *Financial support:* Career-related internships or fieldwork, Federal Work-Study, institutionally sponsored loans, scholarships/grants, traineeships, health care benefits, and tuition waivers (partial) available. Support available to part-time students. Financial award applicants required to submit FAFSA. *Unit head:* Sanford Bredine, Associate Director and Senior Lecturer, 312-906-6540, Fax: 312-906-6549, E-mail: bredine@stuart.itt.edu. *Application contact:* Brian Jansen, Director of Graduate Admissions, 312-906-6521, Fax: 312-906-6549, E-mail: admission@stuart.iit.edu.

Iowa State University of Science and Technology, Graduate College, College of Liberal Arts and Sciences, Department of English, Ames, IA 50011. Offers English (MA); rhetoric and professional communication (PhD). *Faculty:* 54 full-time (30 women), 4 part-time/adjunct (2 women). *Students:* 96 full-time (57 women), 23 part-time (17 women); includes 4 minority (1 African American, 3 Hispanic Americans), 24 international. 119 applicants, 49% accepted, 37 enrolled. In 2007, 35 master's, 6 doctorates awarded. *Degree requirements:* For master's, thesis or alternative; for doctorate, thesis/dissertation. *Entrance requirements:* For master's, GRE General Test, sample of written work, resumé, portfolio in creative writing; for doctorate, GRE General Test, sample of written work, resumé. Additional exam requirements/recommendations for international students: Required—TOEFL (paper-based 600; computer-based 250; iBT 100) or IELTS (7.0). *Application deadline:* For fall admission, 1/15 priority date for domestic and international students. Application fee: $30 ($70 for international students). Electronic applications accepted. *Financial support:* In 2007–08, 4 research assistantships with partial tuition reimbursements (averaging $18,159 per year), 81 teaching assistantships with partial tuition reimbursements (averaging $18,445 per year) were awarded; fellowships, scholarships/grants, health care benefits, and unspecified assistantships also available. *Faculty research:* Creative writing, literature, rhetoric, composition and professional communication, teaching English as a second language, applied linguistics. *Unit head:* Dr. Charles Kostelnick, Chair, 515-294-2477, Fax: 515-294-2125, E-mail: englgrad@iastate.edu. *Application contact:* Dr. Helen Ewald, Director of Graduate Education, 515-294-2477, E-mail: englgrad@iastate.edu.

John Carroll University, Graduate School, Department of Communications Management, University Heights, OH 44118-4581. Offers MA. Part-time and evening/weekend programs available. *Faculty:* 5 full-time (3 women), 2 part-time/adjunct (0 women). *Students:* 14 full-time (10 women); includes 2 minority (both African Americans) Average age 26. 15 applicants, 33% accepted, 3 enrolled. In 2007, 8 degrees awarded. *Degree requirements:* For master's, comprehensive exam, thesis or project. *Entrance requirements:* For master's, GRE General Test, minimum GPA of 3.0. Additional exam requirements/recommendations for international students: Required—TOEFL. *Application deadline:* For fall admission, 8/15 priority date for domestic students, 8/1 for international students; for spring admission, 1/15 for domestic students, 12/15 for international students. Applications are processed on a rolling basis. Application fee: $25 ($35 for international students). Electronic applications accepted. *Financial support:* In 2007–08, 7 students received support, including 3 teaching assistantships with full tuition reimbursements available (averaging $8,000 per year). Financial award application deadline: 3/1; financial award applicants required to submit FAFSA. *Faculty research:* Communication law, media ethics, international studies, international broadcasting, media history. *Unit head:* Dr. Mary Ann Flannery, Chair, 216-397-4242, Fax: 216-397-1759, E-mail: mflannery@jcu.edu. *Application contact:* Dr. Alan Roger Stephenson, Graduate Director, 216-397-4679, Fax: 216-397-1759, E-mail: astephenson@jcu.edu.

Jones International University, Graduate School of Business Administration, Centennial, CO 80112. Offers accounting (MBA); business communication (MABC); entrepreneurship (MABC, MBA); finance (MBA); global enterprise management (MBA); health care management (MBA); information security management (MBA); information technology management (MBA); leadership and influence (MABC); leading the customer-driven organization (MABC); negotiation and conflict management (MBA); project management (MABC, MBA). Program only offered online. Part-time and evening/weekend programs available. Postbaccalaureate distance learning degree programs offered (no on-campus study). *Degree requirements:* For master's, capstone project. *Entrance requirements:* For master's, minimum cumulative GPA of 2.5. Additional exam requirements/recommendations for international students: Recommended—TOEFL (minimum score 550 paper-based; 213 computer-based). Electronic applications accepted.

La Salle University, School of Arts and Sciences, Program in Professional Communication, Philadelphia, PA 19141-1199. Offers MA. Part-time and evening/weekend programs available. *Faculty:* 7 full-time (4 women), 9 part-time/adjunct (4 women). *Students:* 22 full-time (19 women), 89 part-time (68 women); includes 25 minority (20 African Americans, 1 Asian American or Pacific Islander, 4 Hispanic Americans), 6 international. Average age 31. 40 applicants, 65% accepted, 17 enrolled. In 2007, 46 degrees awarded. *Degree requirements:* For master's, exam or project. *Entrance requirements:* For master's, GRE or MAT. *Application deadline:* Applications are processed on a rolling basis. Application fee: $35. *Expenses: Contact institution.* Tuition and fees vary according to program. *Financial support:* In 2007–08, 52 students received support. Career-related internships or fieldwork, institutionally sponsored loans, and scholarships/grants available. Support available to part-time students. Financial award applicants required to submit FAFSA. *Unit head:* Dr. Michael F. Smith, Director, 215-951-1155, Fax: 215-951-5043.

Loyola University Chicago, Graduate School of Business, Marketing Department, Chicago, IL 60611-2196. Offers integrated marketing communications (MS); marketing (MSIMC). Part-time and evening/weekend programs available. *Faculty:* 8 full-time (4 women), 6 part-time/adjunct (4 women). *Students:* 21 full-time (15 women), 41 part-time (28 women); includes 17 minority (8 African Americans, 6 Asian Americans or Pacific Islanders, 3 Hispanic Americans). In 2007, 15 degrees awarded. *Entrance requirements:* For master's, GMAT, letters of recommendation, personal statement. Additional exam requirements/recommendations for international students: Required—TOEFL (minimum score 550 paper-based; 213 computer-based; 80 iBT). *Application deadline:* For fall admission, 7/15 for domestic and international students; for winter admission, 10/1 for domestic and international students; for spring admission, 1/15 for domestic and international students. Applications are processed on a rolling basis. Application fee: $50. Electronic applications accepted. *Expenses: Contact institution.* Full-time tuition and fees vary according to program. *Financial support:* In 2007–08, 2 students received support, including research assistantships with partial tuition reimbursements available (averaging $5,000 per year); teaching assistantships, career-related internships or fieldwork also available. Support available to part-time students. Financial award application deadline: 3/15; financial award applicants required to submit FAFSA. *Faculty research:* Web performance metrics, new venture marketing strategies over consumption, benefit segmentation strategies. *Unit head:* Dr. Raymond Benton, Chair, E-mail: rbenton@luc.edu. *Application contact:* Olivia Heath, Enrollment Advisor, 312-915-8908, Fax: 312-915-7207, E-mail: oheath@luc.edu.

Manhattanville College, Graduate Programs, Humanities and Social Sciences Programs, Program in Management Communications, Purchase, NY 10577-2132. Offers MS. Part-time programs available. *Entrance requirements:* For master's, 2 letters of recommendation, interview.

Marietta College, Program in Corporate Media, Marietta, OH 45750-4000. Offers MCM. *Faculty:* 5 full-time (4 women), 2 part-time/adjunct (0 women). *Students:* 12 full-time (8 women), 13 part-time (7 women). *Unit head:* Dr. Liane Gray-Starner, Chair, 740-376-4680, E-mail: graystal@marietta.edu. *Application contact:* Cathy J. Brown, Director of Graduate and Continuing Studies, 740-376-4740, Fax: 740-376-4423, E-mail: ce@marietta.edu.

Marist College, Graduate Programs, School of Communication and the Arts, Poughkeepsie, NY 12601-1387. Offers organizational communication and leadership (MA). Part-time programs available. Postbaccalaureate distance learning degree programs offered (no on-campus study). *Faculty:* 2 full-time (both women), 2 part-time/adjunct (1 woman). *Students:* 5 full-time (4 women), 60 part-time (48 women); includes 3 minority (all Hispanic Americans) Average age 35. 88 applicants, 65% accepted, 44 enrolled. In 2007, 25 degrees awarded. *Degree requirements:* For master's, thesis or comprehensive exam. *Entrance requirements:* For master's, GRE, minimum undergraduate GPA of 3.0, resumé, 3 letters of recommendation, transcript, statement of purpose. Additional exam requirements/recommendations for international students: Required—TOEFL (minimum score 550 paper-based; 213 computer-based; 80 iBT); Recommended—IELTS (minimum score 7). *Application deadline:* For fall admission, 8/1 for domestic students, 6/15 for international students; for spring admission, 10/31 for international students. Applications are processed on a rolling basis. Application fee: $50. Electronic applications accepted. *Expenses:* Tuition: Part-time $665 per credit. *Financial support:* In 2007–08, 33 students received support; research assistantships, scholarships/grants available. Support available to part-time students. Financial award application deadline: 8/15; financial award applicants required to submit FAFSA. *Unit head:* Dr. Subir Sengupta, Interim Dean, 845-575-2678, E-mail: subir.sengupta@marist.edu. *Application contact:* Kelly Holmes, Director of Admissions, 845-575-3800, Fax: 845-575-3166, E-mail: graduate@marist.edu.

Marywood University, Academic Affairs, Insalaco College of Creative Arts and Management, Department of Communication Arts, Program in Communication Arts, Scranton, PA 18509-1598. Offers corporate communication (Certificate); e-business (Certificate); health communication (Certificate); instructional technology (Certificate); interdisciplinary (MA); library science/information specialist (Certificate); media management (MA); production (MA). *Students:* 10 full-time (6 women), 22 part-time (15 women); includes 4 minority (1 African American, 3 Hispanic Americans). Average age 28. In 2007, 8 degrees awarded. Application fee: $30. *Expenses:* Tuition: Full-time $15,290; part-time $695 per credit. Required fees: $990; $370 per term. Tuition and fees vary according to degree level.

Marywood University, Academic Affairs, Insalaco College of Creative Arts and Management, Department of Communication Arts, Program in Information Sciences, Scranton, PA 18509-1598. Offers corporate communication (MS); e-business (MS); health communication (MS); instructional technology (MS); library science/information science (MS). *Students:* 2 full-time (both women), 17 part-time (15 women); includes 1 minority (American Indian/Alaska Native). Average age 40.Application fee: $30. *Expenses:* Tuition: Full-time $15,290; part-time $695 per credit. Required fees: $990; $370 per term. Tuition and fees vary according to degree level.

Metropolitan College of New York, Program in Media Management, New York, NY 10013. Offers MBA. Evening/weekend programs available. *Degree requirements:* For master's, thesis, 10 day study abroad. *Entrance requirements:* For master's, GMAT or GRE, appropriate work experience, interview, minimum GPA of 2.7. Additional exam requirements/recommendations for international students: Required—TOEFL (minimum score 600 paper-based; 220 computer-based). Electronic applications accepted. Expenses: Contact institution.

Mississippi College, Graduate School, College of Arts and Sciences, School of Christian Studies and the Arts, Department of Communication, Clinton, MS 39058. Offers applied communication (MSC); public relations and corporate communication (MSC). Part-time programs available. *Faculty:* 5 full-time (2 women), 2 part-time/adjunct (0 women). *Students:* 20 full-time (13 women), 11 part-time (10 women); includes 5 minority (all African Americans), 15 international. Average age 27. In 2007, 3 degrees awarded. *Degree requirements:* For master's, comprehensive exam, thesis optional. *Entrance requirements:* For master's, GRE or NTE, minimum GPA of 2.5. Additional exam requirements/recommendations for international students: Recommended—IELTS. *Application deadline:* For fall admission, 4/1 for domestic students. Applications are processed on a rolling basis. Application fee: $25. Electronic applications accepted. *Expenses:* Tuition: Full-time $7,470; part-time $415 per hour. Required fees: $1,160 per term. Part-time tuition and fees vary according to course load and degree level. *Financial support:* Career-related internships or fieldwork, Federal Work-Study, and unspecified assistantships available. Support available to part-time students. Financial award application deadline: 4/1; financial award applicants required to submit FAFSA. *Unit head:* Dr. Cliff Fortenberry, Chair, 601-925-3457, E-mail: fortenbe@mc.edu.

Monmouth University, Graduate School, Department of Corporate and Public Communication, West Long Branch, NJ 07764-1898. Offers corporate and public communication (MA); human resources communication (Certificate); media studies (Certificate); public relations (Certificate). *Faculty:* 7 full-time (5 women), 2 part-time/adjunct (1 woman). *Students:* 6 full-time (5 women), 40 part-time (29 women); includes 4 minority (3 African Americans, 1 Hispanic American), 3 international. Average age 30. 22 applicants, 95% accepted, 12 enrolled. In 2007, 18 degrees awarded. *Degree requirements:* For master's, comprehensive exam, project. *Entrance requirements:* For master's, GRE, minimum GPA of 3.0 in major, 2.75 overall. Additional exam requirements/recommendations for international students: Required—TOEFL (minimum score 550 paper-based; 213 computer-based; 79 iBT), IELTS (minimum score 5), MELAB 77, Cambridge A, B, C. *Application deadline:* For fall admission, 7/15 priority date for domestic students, 6/1 for international students; for spring admission, 11/15 priority date for domestic students, 11/1 for international students. Applications are processed on a rolling basis. Application fee: $50. Electronic applications accepted. *Financial support:* In 2007–08, 34 students received support, including 33 fellowships (averaging $1,330 per year), 11 research assistantships (averaging $4,456 per year); scholarships/grants and unspecified assistantships also available. Support available to part-time students. Financial award application deadline: 3/1; financial award applicants required to submit FAFSA. *Faculty research:* Service learning, history of television, feminism and the media, executive communication, public relations pedagogy. *Unit head:* Dr. Eleanor Novek, Program Director, 732-263-5449, Fax: 732-571-3609, E-mail: enovek@monmouth.edu. *Application contact:* Kevin Roane, Director, Office of Graduate Admission, 732-571-3452, Fax: 732-263-5123, E-mail: gradadm@monmouth.edu.

Montclair State University, The Office of Graduate Admissions and Support Services, School of the Arts, Department of Communication Studies, Montclair, NJ 07043-1624. Offers organizational communication (MA); public relations (MA); speech communication (MA). Part-time and evening/weekend programs available. *Faculty:* 5 full-time (3 women), 39 part-time/adjunct (21 women). *Students:* 8 full-time (6 women), 15 part-time (10 women); includes 3 minority (2 African Americans, 1 Hispanic American), 4 international. 41 applicants, 22% accepted, 6 enrolled. In 2007, 7 degrees awarded. *Degree requirements:* For master's, comprehensive exam. *Entrance requirements:* For master's, GRE General Test, minimum GPA of 3.0; undergraduate degree or work in theatre, oral interpretation, speech communication, media, or broadcasting; 2 letters of recommendation. Additional exam requirements/recommendations for international students: Required—TOEFL (minimum score 83 computer-based). *Application deadline:* For fall admission, 6/1 for international students; for spring admission, 10/1 for international students. Applications are processed on a rolling basis. Application fee: $60. Electronic applications accepted. *Financial support:* In 2007–08, 1 research assistantship with full tuition reimbursement (averaging $7,000 per year) was awarded; Federal Work-Study, scholarships/grants, and unspecified assistantships also available. Support available to part-time students. Financial award application deadline: 3/1; financial award applicants required to submit FAFSA. *Unit head:* Dr. Christine Lemesianou, Chairperson, 973-655-5214. *Application contact:* Dr. Michael Kent, Adviser, 973-655-5130, E-mail: kentm@mail.montclair.edu.

Murray State University, College of Business and Public Affairs, Program in Organizational Communication, Murray, KY 42071. Offers MA, MS. Part-time programs available. *Degree requirements:* For master's, thesis (for some programs). *Entrance requirements:* For master's, minimum GPA of 2.5 for conditional admittance, 3.0 for unconditional admittance. Additional exam requirements/recommendations for international students: Required—TOEFL (minimum score 550 paper-based; 213 computer-based). *Faculty research:* Organizational learning, organizational culture, leadership, health communication, personality.

New Mexico State University, Graduate School, College of Arts and Sciences, Department of English, Las Cruces, NM 88003-8001. Offers creative writing (MFA); English (MA); rhetoric and professional communication (PhD). Part-time programs available. *Faculty:* 17 full-time (9 women), 1 part-time/adjunct (0 women). *Students:* 70 full-time (37 women), 23 part-time (12 women); includes 12 minority (1 African American, 1 American Indian/Alaska Native, 10 Hispanic Americans), 6 international. Average age 33. 55 applicants, 45% accepted, 19 enrolled. In 2007, 25 master's, 5 doctorates awarded. *Median time to degree:* Of those who began their doctoral program in fall 1999, 80% received their degree in 8 years or less. *Degree requirements:* For master's, one foreign language, comprehensive exam (for some programs), thesis (for some programs); for doctorate, comprehensive exam, thesis/dissertation, internship. *Entrance requirements:* For master's and doctorate, sample of written work. *Application deadline:* For fall admission, 2/1 for domestic and international students. Application fee: $30 ($50 for international students). Electronic applications accepted. *Expenses:* Tuition, state resident: full-time $3,602; part-time $199 per credit. Tuition, nonresident: full-time $13,380; part-time $607 per credit. Required fees: $1,178. *Financial support:* In 2007–08, 3 fellowships, 3 research assistantships, 50 teaching assistantships were awarded; career-related internships or fieldwork, Federal Work-Study, institutionally sponsored loans, scholarships/grants, health care benefits, and unspecified assistantships also available. Financial award application deadline: 2/1; financial award applicants required to submit FAFSA. *Faculty research:* Composition research, history and theory of rhetoric, technical/professional communication, creative writing, English and American literature. *Unit head:* Dr. Harriet Kramer Linkin, Head, 575-646-3931, Fax: 575-646-7725. *Application contact:* Dr. Monica Torres, Director of Graduate Studies, 575-646-3931, E-mail: mftorres@nmsu.edu.

New York University, School of Continuing and Professional Studies, Division of Programs in Business, Program in Public Relations and Corporate Communications, New York, NY 10012-1019. Offers MS. Part-time and evening/weekend programs available. *Faculty:* 1 full-time (0 women), 9 part-time/adjunct (2 women). *Students:* 31 full-time (25 women), 88 part-time (71 women); includes 26 minority (12 African Americans, 4 Asian Americans or Pacific Islanders, 10 Hispanic Americans), 17 international. Average age 27. 119 applicants, 39% accepted, 27 enrolled. In 2007, 4 degrees awarded. *Degree requirements:* For master's, capstone project. *Entrance requirements:* For master's, GRE General Test or GMAT (for recent graduates), related work experience, 2 letters of recommendation, resumé, essay. Additional exam requirements/recommendations for international students: Required—TOEFL (minimum score 600 paper-based; 250 computer-based; 100 iBT), TWE. *Application deadline:* For fall admission, 3/15 priority date for domestic students, 3/15 for international students; for spring admission, 10/15 priority date for domestic students, 8/15 for international students. Applications are processed on a rolling basis. Application fee: $75. Electronic applications accepted. *Financial support:* In 2007–08, 73 students received support, including 73 fellowships (averaging $1,380 per year); institutionally sponsored loans and scholarships/grants also available. Financial award application deadline: 3/1; financial award applicants required to submit FAFSA. *Unit head:* John Doorley, Director, 212-992-3600, Fax: 212-992-3650. *Application contact:* Helen Sapp, Assistant Director, 212-992-3600, Fax: 212-992-3676, E-mail: helen.sapp@nyu.edu.

See Close-Up on page 911.

North Carolina State University, Graduate School, College of Humanities and Social Sciences, Department of Communication, Raleigh, NC 27695. Offers organizational communication (MS). *Degree requirements:* For master's, thesis optional. *Entrance requirements:* For master's, GRE, minimum undergraduate GPA of 3.0 during last 60 hours. Electronic applications accepted. *Faculty research:* Instructional communication, political communication, organizational conflict management, intercultural communication, communication technology.

Northwestern University, The Graduate School, School of Communication, Department of Communication Studies, Managerial Communication Program, Evanston, IL 60208. Offers MSC. *Entrance requirements:* For master's, GRE General Test.

Northwestern University, Medill School of Journalism, Integrated Marketing Communications Program, Evanston, IL 60208. Offers advertising/sales promotion (MSIMC); direct database and e-commerce marketing (MSIMC); general studies (MSIMC); public relations (MSIMC). Part-time programs available. *Entrance requirements:* For master's, GRE General Test or GMAT, full-time work experience (preferred). Additional exam requirements/recommendations for international students: Required—TOEFL. Electronic applications accepted. *Faculty research:* Data mining, business to business marketing, values in advertising, political advertising.

Oklahoma City University, Meinders School of Business, Program in Business Administration, Oklahoma City, OK 73106-1402. Offers finance (MBA); health administration (MBA); information technology (MBA); integrated marketing communications (MBA); international business (MBA); marketing (MBA); JD/MBA. *Accreditation:* ACBSP. Part-time and evening/weekend programs available. *Faculty:* 30 full-time (7 women), 24 part-time/adjunct (5 women). *Students:* 465 full-time (163 women), 194 part-time (70 women); includes 77 minority (42 African Americans, 12 American Indian/Alaska Native, 13 Asian Americans or Pacific Islanders, 10 Hispanic Americans), 376 international. Average age 28. In 2007, 280 degrees awarded. *Degree requirements:* For master's, comprehensive exam. *Entrance requirements:* For master's, minimum GPA of 2.5. Additional exam requirements/recommendations for international students: Required—TOEFL (minimum score 510 paper-based). *Application deadline:* For fall admission, 8/22 for domestic students; for spring admission, 1/15 for domestic students. Applications are processed on a rolling basis. Application fee: $30 ($70 for international students). *Expenses:* Tuition: Full-time $14,040; part-time $780 per hour. Required fees: $881; $32 per hour. *Financial support:* Fellowships with partial tuition reimbursements, career-related internships or fieldwork, Federal Work-Study, institutionally sponsored loans, and tuition waivers (partial) available. Support available to part-time students. Financial award application deadline: 8/1. *Faculty research:* Management information systems, international business strategies. *Unit head:* Dr. Mahmood Shandiz, Senior Associate Dean, 405-208-5130, Fax: 405-208-5098, E-mail: mshandiz@okcu.edu. *Application contact:* Leslie McKenzie, Director, Graduate Admissions, 800-633-7242, Fax: 405-208-5356, E-mail: gadmissions@okcu.edu.

Queens University of Charlotte, Hayworth College, Department of Organizational Communications, Charlotte, NC 28274-0002. Offers MA. Part-time and evening/weekend programs available. *Degree requirements:* For master's, capstone course. *Entrance requirements:* Additional exam requirements/recommendations for international students: Required—TOEFL. Expenses: Contact institution.

Radford University, Graduate College, College of Humanities and Behavioral Sciences, Department of Communication, Radford, VA 24142. Offers corporate and professional communication (MS). Part-time programs available. Postbaccalaureate distance learning degree programs offered. *Faculty:* 7 full-time (4 women). *Students:* Average age 25. 11 applicants, 91% accepted, 5 enrolled. In 2007, 10 degrees awarded. *Degree requirements:* For master's, comprehensive exam, thesis optional. *Entrance requirements:* For master's, GRE. *Application deadline:* For fall admission, 2/1 priority date for domestic students, 12/1 for international students; for spring admission, 9/1 for domestic students, 7/1 for international students. Applications are processed on a rolling basis. Application fee: $40. Electronic applications accepted. *Financial support:* In 2007–08, 11 students received support, including 3 research assistantships with partial tuition reimbursements available (averaging $8,000 per year), 6 teaching assistantships with partial tuition reimbursements available (averaging $8,700 per year); career-related internships or fieldwork, Federal Work-Study, institutionally sponsored loans, and scholarships/grants also available. Financial award application deadline: 3/1; financial award applicants required to submit FAFSA. *Unit head:* Dr. Kristin Froemling, Acting Chair, 540-831-6044, Fax: 540-831-5970, E-mail: kfroemling@radford.edu. *Application contact:* Graduate Admissions Office, 540-831-5431, Fax: 540-831-6061, E-mail: gradcollege@radford.edu.

Regis College, Department of Organizational and Professional Communication, Weston, MA 02493. Offers MS. Part-time and evening/weekend programs available. *Faculty:* 2 full-time (both women), 1 part-time/adjunct (0 women). *Students:* Average age 35. In 2007, 13 degrees awarded. *Degree requirements:* For master's, thesis. *Entrance requirements:* For

Corporate and Organizational Communication

Regis College (continued)

master's, GRE or MAT. *Application deadline:* Applications are processed on a rolling basis. Application fee: $50. *Expenses:* Tuition: Full-time $25,990; part-time $730 per credit hour. *Financial support:* In 2007–08, 9 students received support. Scholarships/grants available. Financial award applicants required to submit FAFSA. *Unit head:* Dr. Joan Murray, Director, 781-768-7416, Fax: 781-768-7159, E-mail: joan.murray@regiscollege.edu.

Roosevelt University, Graduate Division, College of Arts and Sciences, Department of Communication, Program in Integrated Marketing Communications, Chicago, IL 60605-1394. Offers MSIMC. Part-time and evening/weekend programs available. *Students:* 49 full-time (36 women), 119 part-time (98 women); includes 65 minority (52 African Americans, 1 American Indian/Alaska Native, 1 Asian American or Pacific Islander, 11 Hispanic Americans), 24 international. Average age 30. 132 applicants, 58% accepted, 53 enrolled. In 2007, 79 degrees awarded. *Application deadline:* For fall admission, 6/1 priority date for domestic students. Applications are processed on a rolling basis. Application fee: $25 ($35 for international students). *Financial support:* In 2007–08, 2 research assistantships were awarded; career-related internships or fieldwork and Federal Work-Study also available. Financial award application deadline: 2/15. *Faculty research:* Print journalism, urban high school journalism. *Application contact:* Joanne Canyon-Heller, Coordinator of Graduate Admission, 877-APPLY RU, Fax: 312-281-3356, E-mail: applyru@roosevelt.edu.

Royal Roads University, Graduate Studies, Faculty of Management, Victoria, BC V9B 5Y2, Canada. Offers digital technologies management (MBA); executive management (MBA), including global aviation management, knowledge management, leadership; human resources management (MBA); public relations and communications management (MBA). Post-baccalaureate distance learning degree programs offered (minimal on-campus study). *Degree requirements:* For master's, thesis. *Entrance requirements:* For master's, 5-7 years of related work experience. Additional exam requirements/recommendations for international students: Required—TOEFL (paper-based 570; computer-based 233) or IELTS (paper-based 7) (recommended). Electronic applications accepted. Expenses: Contact institution. *Faculty research:* Global venture analysis standards; computer assisted venture opportunity screening; teaching philosophies, instructions and methods.

Schiller International University, Graduate Programs, London, Program in Communications, London, United Kingdom. Offers business communication (MA).

Seton Hall University, College of Arts and Sciences, Department of Communication, South Orange, NJ 07079-2697. Offers corporate and public communication (MA); strategic communication and leadership (MA). Part-time and evening/weekend programs available. Post-baccalaureate distance learning degree programs offered (minimal on-campus study). *Entrance requirements:* For master's, GRE or GMAT, minimum GPA of 3.0. Electronic applications accepted. *Faculty research:* Managerial communication, communication consulting, communication and development.

See Close-Up on page 927.

Simmons College, College of Arts and Sciences Graduate Studies, Program in Communications Management, Boston, MA 02115. Offers MS, MS/MA. Part-time programs available. *Faculty:* 12 part-time/adjunct (6 women). *Students:* Average age 30. 29 applicants, 66% accepted, 14 enrolled. In 2007, 29 degrees awarded. *Degree requirements:* For master's, applied learning project. *Entrance requirements:* For master's, GRE General Test, MAT, or GMAT, 2 years of professional experience. Additional exam requirements/recommendations for international students: Required—TOEFL (minimum score 600 paper-based; 250 computer-based; 100 iBT). *Application deadline:* For fall admission, 8/1 priority date for domestic and international students; for spring admission, 12/15 priority date for domestic and international students. Applications are processed on a rolling basis. Application fee: $35. Electronic applications accepted. *Expenses:* Tuition: Full-time $8,500. Tuition and fees vary according to degree level and program. *Financial support:* In 2007–08, 21 students received support. Scholarships/grants available. Financial award application deadline: 3/1; financial award applicants required to submit FAFSA. *Faculty research:* Diversity in organizations, organizational communications, communications technologies, motivational communication. *Unit head:* Joan C. Abrams, Director, Assistant Professor, 617-521-2845, Fax: 617-521-3149, E-mail: abrams@simmons.edu. *Application contact:* Kristen Haack, Director, Graduate Studies Admission, 617-521-2917, Fax: 617-521-3058, E-mail: gsa@simmons.edu.

Southern Illinois University Edwardsville, Graduate Studies and Research, College of Arts and Sciences, Department of Speech Communication, Program in Corporate and Organizational Communication, Edwardsville, IL 62026-0001. Offers Postbaccalaureate Certificate. Part-time programs available. *Students:* 3 applicants, 33% accepted. *Entrance requirements:* Additional exam requirements/recommendations for international students: Required—TOEFL. *Application deadline:* For fall admission, 7/20 for domestic students, 6/1 for international students; for spring admission, 12/14 for domestic students, 10/1 for international students. Application fee: $30. Electronic applications accepted. *Financial support:* Fellowships with full tuition reimbursements, research assistantships with full tuition reimbursements, teaching assistantships with full tuition reimbursements available. *Unit head:* Dr. Waittsien Cheah, Director, 618-650-5016, E-mail: wcheah@siue.edu.

Southern Polytechnic State University, School of Arts and Sciences, Department of English, Technical Communication, and Media Arts, Marietta, GA 30060-2896. Offers information design and communication (MS); technical and professional communication (Graduate Certificate). Part-time and evening/weekend programs available. Postbaccalaureate distance learning degree programs offered (minimal on-campus study). *Faculty:* 4 full-time (3 women). *Students:* 4 full-time (3 women), 33 part-time (24 women); includes 13 minority (11 African Americans, 2 Hispanic Americans), 2 international. Average age 39. 31 applicants, 58% accepted, 15 enrolled. In 2007, 8 degrees awarded. *Degree requirements:* For master's, thesis optional, students can complete 36-hour requirement through a thesis option (6 hours), an internship option (6 hours) or an advanced coursework option (6 hours); for Graduate Certificate, thesis optional, students can complete 18-hour requirement for advanced certificate through a thesis option (6 hours), an internship option (6 hours) or an advanced coursework option (6 hours). *Entrance requirements:* For master's, GRE, statement of purpose, writing sample, professional recommendations, proctored essay; for Graduate Certificate, statement of purpose, writing sample, professional recommendations, proctored essay. Additional exam requirements/recommendations for international students: Required—TOEFL (minimum score 550 paper-based; 213 computer-based; 79 iBT). *Application deadline:* For fall admission, 5/1 priority date for domestic students, 7/1 priority date for international students; for spring admission, 9/1 priority date for domestic students, 11/1 priority date for international students. Applications are processed on a rolling basis. Application fee: $20. Electronic applications accepted. *Expenses:* Tuition, state resident: full-time $2,544; part-time $159 per credit hour. Tuition, nonresident: full-time $10,176; part-time $636 per credit hour. Required fees: $315 per term. *Financial support:* In 2007–08, 6 students received support, including 2 research assistantships with full tuition reimbursements available (averaging $6,000 per year); career-related internships or fieldwork, Federal Work-Study, scholarships/grants, and unspecified assistantships also available. Support available to part-time students. Financial award application deadline: 5/1; financial award applicants required to submit FAFSA. *Faculty research:* Usability, user-centered design, instructional design, information architecture, information design. *Unit head:* Dr. Mark Nunes, Chair, 678-915-7202, Fax: 678-915-7425, E-mail: mnunes@spsu.edu. *Application contact:* Virginia A. Head, Director of Admissions, 678-915-4188, Fax: 678-915-7292, E-mail: vhead@spsu.edu.

Spalding University, Graduate Studies, College of Business and Communication, Louisville, KY 40203-2188. Offers business communication (MS). Part-time and evening/weekend programs available. *Degree requirements:* For master's, project. *Entrance requirements:* For master's, GRE or GMAT, writing sample, interview, letters of recommendation. Additional exam requirements/recommendations for international students: Required—TOEFL (minimum score 535 paper-based). Electronic applications accepted. *Faculty research:* Curriculum development, consumer behavior, interdisciplinary pedagogy.

Stevens Institute of Technology, Graduate School, Arthur E. Imperatore School of Sciences and Arts, Department of Humanities and Social Sciences, Program in Professional Communications, Hoboken, NJ 07030. Offers Certificate.

Syracuse University, Graduate School, S. I. Newhouse School of Public Communications, Department of Public Relations, Syracuse, NY 13244. Offers communications management (MS); public relations (MS); MS/MA. *Students:* 34 full-time (26 women), 61 part-time (43 women); includes 8 minority (6 African Americans, 1 Asian American or Pacific Islander, 1 Hispanic American), 18 international. 157 applicants, 54% accepted, 52 enrolled. In 2007, 42 degrees awarded. *Degree requirements:* For master's, comprehensive exam, internship. *Entrance requirements:* For master's, GRE General Test. Additional exam requirements/recommendations for international students: Required—TOEFL (minimum score 600 paper-based; 250 computer-based). *Application deadline:* For fall admission, 2/1 for domestic and international students. Application fee: $75. *Expenses:* Tuition: Full-time $18,216; part-time $1,012 per credit. Required fees: $980. Tuition and fees vary according to program. *Unit head:* Maria P. Russell, Chair, 315-443-7401, Fax: 315-443-3946, E-mail: pcgrad@syr.edu. *Application contact:* Graduate Records Office, 315-443-4039, Fax: 315-443-3946, E-mail: pcgrad@syr.edu.

Temple University, Graduate School, School of Communications and Theater, Department of Strategic and Organizational Communication, Philadelphia, PA 19122-6096. Offers communication management (MS); mass media and communication (PhD). *Entrance requirements:* Additional exam requirements/recommendations for international students: Required—TOEFL (minimum score 550 paper-based; 213 computer-based; 79 iBT).

Towson University, College of Graduate Studies and Research, Program in Communications Management, Towson, MD 21252-0001. Offers MS. *Students:* 9 full-time (8 women), 24 part-time (19 women); includes 10 minority (9 African Americans, 1 Hispanic American), 1 international. Average age 29. 13 applicants, 100% accepted, 8 enrolled. In 2007, 8 degrees awarded. *Degree requirements:* For master's, thesis. *Entrance requirements:* For master's, 24 credits in mass communications, public relations and/or advertising, writing and statistics; professional experience; minimum GPA of 3.0. *Application deadline:* For fall admission, 1/15 for domestic students. Application fee: $50. Electronic applications accepted. *Expenses:* Tuition, state resident: part-time $286 per credit. Tuition, nonresident: part-time $600 per credit. Required fees: $75 per credit. *Financial support:* Application deadline: 4/1; *Unit head:* Meg Algren, Graduate Program Director, 410-704-5641, E-mail: malgren@towson.edu. *Application contact:* 410-704-2501, Fax: 410-704-4675, E-mail: grads@towson.edu.

Universidad Autonoma de Guadalajara, Graduate Programs, Guadalajara, Mexico. Offers advertising and corporate communications (MA); architecture (M Arch); business (MBA); computational science (MCC); education (Ed M, Ed D); international business (MIB); international corporate law (LL M); manufacturing systems (MMS); philosophy (MA, PhD); prosecution law (LL M); quality systems (MQS); renewable energy (MS); teaching mathematics (MA).

University of Alaska Fairbanks, College of Liberal Arts, Department of Communications, Fairbanks, AK 99775-7520. Offers professional communications (MA). Part-time programs available. *Degree requirements:* For master's, comprehensive exam, thesis or alternative. *Entrance requirements:* For master's, GRE General Test. Additional exam requirements/recommendations for international students: Required—TOEFL (minimum score 550 paper-based; 213 computer-based). Electronic applications accepted. *Faculty research:* Interpersonal communications, health communications, intercultural communications, politeness and face management in conversation, gender communication.

University of Connecticut, Graduate School, College of Liberal Arts and Sciences, Department of Communication Sciences, Storrs, CT 06269. Offers communication sciences (MA, Au D, PhD), including audiology (Au D, PhD), communication processes (MA), communication processes and marketing communication (PhD), speech-language pathology (MA, PhD); Au D/PhD. *Accreditation:* ASHA (one or more programs are accredited). *Faculty:* 25 full-time (10 women). *Students:* 103 full-time (79 women), 6 part-time (1 woman); includes 2 minority (1 African American, 1 Asian American or Pacific Islander), 11 international. Average age 27. 237 applicants, 18% accepted, 34 enrolled. In 2007, 19 master's, 6 doctorates awarded. Terminal master's awarded for partial completion of doctoral program. *Degree requirements:* For master's, comprehensive exam; for doctorate, thesis/dissertation. *Entrance requirements:* For master's and doctorate, GRE General Test. Additional exam requirements/recommendations for international students: Required—TOEFL (minimum score 550 paper-based; 213 computer-based). *Application deadline:* For fall admission, 2/1 priority date for domestic and international students; for spring admission, 11/1 for domestic students, 10/1 for international students. Applications are processed on a rolling basis. Application fee: $55. Electronic applications accepted. *Expenses:* Tuition, state resident: part-time $469 per credit hour. Tuition, nonresident: part-time $1,218 per credit hour. *Financial support:* In 2007–08, 10 research assistantships with full tuition reimbursements, 42 teaching assistantships with full tuition reimbursements were awarded; fellowships, Federal Work-Study, scholarships/grants, health care benefits, and unspecified assistantships also available. Financial award application deadline: 2/1; financial award applicants required to submit FAFSA. *Unit head:* Carl A. Coelho, Chair, 860-486-2628. *Application contact:* Sue Kiss, Administrative Assistant, 860-486-2628, Fax: 860-486-5422, E-mail: susan.kiss@uconn.edu.

University of Connecticut, Graduate School, College of Liberal Arts and Sciences, Department of Communication Sciences, Field of Communication Sciences, Program in Communication Processes and Marketing Communication, Storrs, CT 06269. Offers PhD. *Faculty:* 16 full-time (6 women). *Students:* 18 full-time (8 women), 6 part-time (1 woman), 5 international. Average age 32. 42 applicants, 2% accepted, 1 enrolled. In 2007, 4 degrees awarded. *Degree requirements:* For doctorate, thesis/dissertation. *Entrance requirements:* For doctorate, GMAT or GRE General Test. Additional exam requirements/recommendations for international students: Required—TOEFL (minimum score 550 paper-based; 213 computer-based). *Application deadline:* For fall admission, 2/1 priority date for domestic and international students; for spring admission, 11/1 for domestic students, 10/1 for international students. Applications are processed on a rolling basis. Application fee: $55. Electronic applications accepted. *Expenses:* Tuition, state resident: part-time $469 per credit hour. Tuition, nonresident: part-time $1,218 per credit hour. *Financial support:* In 2007–08, 4 research assistantships with full tuition reimbursements, 13 teaching assistantships with full tuition reimbursements were awarded; fellowships, Federal Work-Study, scholarships/grants, health care benefits, and unspecified assistantships also available. Financial award application deadline: 2/1; financial award applicants required to submit FAFSA. *Application contact:* Sue Kiss, Administrative Assistant, 860-486-2628, Fax: 860-486-5422, E-mail: susan.kiss@uconn.edu.

University of Portland, Graduate School, College of Arts and Sciences, Department of Communication Studies, Portland, OR 97203-5798. Offers communication (MA); management communication (MS). Part-time and evening/weekend programs available. *Faculty:* 7 full-time (2 women), 1 part-time/adjunct (0 women). *Students:* 8 applicants, 63% accepted, 3 enrolled. In 2007, 4 degrees awarded. *Degree requirements:* For master's, thesis optional. *Entrance requirements:* For master's, GRE General Test, minimum GPA of 3.25, 3 letters of recommendation, resumé, statement of goals, official transcripts. Additional exam requirements/recommendations for international students: Required—TOEFL (minimum score 600 paper-based; 100 iBT), IELTS (minimum score 8). *Application deadline:* For fall admission, 7/15 priority date for domestic and international students; for spring admission, 12/15 priority date for domestic and international students. Applications are processed on a rolling basis. Application fee: $50. *Expenses:* Tuition: Part-time $775 per semester hour. *Financial support:* Career-related internships or fieldwork, Federal Work-Study, scholarships/grants, and tuition waivers (partial) available. Financial award application deadline: 3/1; financial award applicants required to submit FAFSA. *Unit head:* Dr. Jeffrey Kerssen-Griep, Director, 503-943-7167, E-mail: kerssen@up.edu.

University of St. Thomas, Graduate Studies, Opus College of Business, Program in Business Communication, St. Paul, MN 55105-1096. Offers MBC. Part-time and evening/weekend programs available. *Degree requirements:* For master's, thesis, final project. *Entrance requirements:* For master's, GMAT or GRE. Additional exam requirements/recommendations for international students: Required—TOEFL. Electronic applications accepted. Expenses: Contact institution. *Faculty research:* Communication technology.

University of Southern California, Graduate School, Annenberg School for Communication, School of Communication, Program in Communication, Los Angeles, CA 90089. Offers communication (MA, PhD), including interpersonal and social dynamics (PhD), mass communication, technology, and public policy (PhD), organizational communication (PhD), rhetorical and cultural studies (PhD). *Students:* 86 full-time (52 women); includes 16 minority (3 African Americans, 2 American Indian/Alaska Native, 5 Asian Americans or Pacific Islanders, 6 Hispanic Americans), 24 international. Average age 31. 196 applicants, 13% accepted, 19 enrolled. In 2007, 16 degrees awarded. *Median time to degree:* Of those who began their doctoral program in fall 1999, 89% received their degree in 8 years or less. *Degree requirements:* For doctorate, thesis/dissertation. *Entrance requirements:* For master's and doctorate, GRE General Test, resumé, writing samples, 3 letters of recommendation, interest survey questionnaire, statement of purpose. Additional exam requirements/recommendations for international students: Required—TOEFL (minimum score 280 computer-based; 115 iBT); Recommended—TWE. *Application deadline:* For fall admission, 11/30 for domestic and international students. Application fee: $85. Electronic applications accepted. *Financial support:* In 2007–08, 18 students received support, including 18 fellowships with full tuition reimbursements available (averaging $26,500 per year); research assistantships, teaching assistantships, Federal Work-Study, institutionally sponsored loans, scholarships/grants, health care benefits, tuition waivers (partial), and unspecified assistantships also available. Support available to part-time students. Financial award application deadline: 1/1; financial award applicants required to submit FAFSA. *Faculty research:* Computer-mediated communication, public health campaigns, communication democracy and the public sphere, new communication technologies in organizations, communication and community. *Unit head:* Dr. Thomas Goodnight, Director, 213-821-5384. *Application contact:* Allyson Hill, Director of Admissions, 213-821-0770, E-mail: ascadm@usc.edu.

See Close-Up on page 945.

University of Southern California, Graduate School, Annenberg School for Communication, School of Communication, Program in Communication Management, Los Angeles, CA 90089. Offers MCM, JD/MCM, MCM/MAJCS. Part-time and evening/weekend programs available. *Students:* 143 full-time, 73 part-time; includes 59 minority (14 African Americans, 1 American Indian/Alaska Native, 25 Asian Americans or Pacific Islanders, 19 Hispanic Americans), 55 international. Average age 31. 252 applicants, 54% accepted, 78 enrolled. In 2007, 735 degrees awarded. *Degree requirements:* For master's, professional project. *Entrance requirements:* For master's, GRE General Test or GMAT, resumé, writing samples, recommendation letters, statement of purpose. Additional exam requirements/recommendations for international students: Required—TOEFL (minimum score 280 computer-based; 114 iBT). *Application deadline:* For fall admission, 7/1 priority date for domestic students, 3/15 priority date for international students; for spring admission, 11/30 priority date for domestic students, 9/1 priority date for international students. Applications are processed on a rolling basis. Application fee: $85. Electronic applications accepted. *Financial support:* Fellowships, research assistantships, teaching assistantships with full and partial tuition reimbursements, Federal Work-Study, institutionally sponsored loans, scholarships/grants, health care benefits, and tuition waivers (partial) available. Support available to part-time students. Financial award application deadline: 1/15; financial award applicants required to submit FAFSA. *Faculty research:* Global communication, communication law and policy, entertainment management, marketing communication, strategic and corporate communication management. *Unit head:* Dr. Rebecca Weintraub, Director, 213-821-0764, Fax: 213-740-8036, E-mail: weintrau@usc.edu. *Application contact:* Allyson Hill, Director of Admissions, 213-821-0770, E-mail: ascadm@usc.edu.

See Close-Up on page 945.

University of Wisconsin–Stevens Point, College of Fine Arts and Communication, Division of Communication, Stevens Point, WI 54481-3897. Offers interpersonal communication (MA); mass communication (MA); organizational communication (MA); public relations (MA). Part-time programs available. *Degree requirements:* For master's, thesis or alternative. *Entrance requirements:* For master's, GRE. Additional exam requirements/recommendations for international students: Required—TOEFL (minimum score 575 paper-based). *Application deadline:* For fall admission, 3/1 priority date for domestic students. Applications are processed on a rolling basis. Application fee: $45. *Expenses:* Tuition, state resident: full-time $6,161. Tuition, nonresident: full-time $16,771. Required fees: $884. Tuition and fees vary according to course load. *Financial support:* In 2007–08, 9 teaching assistantships were awarded; career-related internships or fieldwork, Federal Work-Study, institutionally sponsored loans, and unspecified assistantships also available. Support available to part-time students. Financial award application deadline: 5/1; financial award applicants required to submit FAFSA. *Faculty research:* Communication theory and research, film history. *Unit head:* Dr. James Haney, Chair, 715-346-3409, E-mail: jhaney@uwsp.edu. *Application contact:* Dr. Chris Sadler, Graduate Coordinator, 715-346-3898, E-mail: csadler@uwsp.edu.

University of Wisconsin–Whitewater, School of Graduate Studies, College of Arts and Communications, Department of Communication, Whitewater, WI 53190-1790. Offers corporate communication (MS); mass communication (MS). Part-time and evening/weekend programs available. Postbaccalaureate distance learning degree programs offered (no on-campus study). *Faculty:* 35. *Students:* 7 full-time (3 women), 14 part-time (8 women); includes 3 African Americans, 2 Asian Americans or Pacific Islanders, 1 Hispanic American. Average age 31. 13 applicants, 46% accepted, 3 enrolled. In 2007, 8 degrees awarded. *Degree requirements:* For master's, thesis or alternative. *Entrance requirements:* For master's, 2 letters of recommendation. Additional exam requirements/recommendations for international students: Required—TOEFL (minimum score 550 paper-based; 213 computer-based). *Application deadline:* For fall admission, 7/15 priority date for domestic students, 7/15 for international students; for spring admission, 12/1 priority date for domestic students, 12/1 for international students. Applications are processed on a rolling basis. Application fee: $45. Electronic applications accepted. *Expenses:* Tuition, state resident: full-time $3,451; part-time $244 per credit. Tuition, nonresident: full-time $8,756; part-time $560 per credit. *Financial support:* Research assistantships, Federal Work-Study, unspecified assistantships, and out-of-state fee waivers available. Support available to part-time students. Financial award application deadline: 3/15; financial award applicants required to submit FAFSA. *Application contact:* Sally A. Lange, School of Graduate Studies, 262-472-1006, Fax: 262-472-5027, E-mail: gradschl@uww.edu.

Washington State University, Graduate School, College of Liberal Arts, Edward R. Murrow College of Communication, Pullman, WA 99164. Offers health communications (MA, PhD); intercultural and international communications (MA, PhD); media and society (MA, PhD); media process and effects (MA, PhD); organizational communications (MA, PhD). *Faculty:* 30. *Students:* 43 full-time (26 women), 6 part-time (4 women); includes 2 minority (1 Asian American or Pacific Islander, 1 Hispanic American), 19 international. Average age 30. 120 applicants, 22% accepted, 19 enrolled. In 2007, 22 master's, 1 doctorate awarded. *Degree requirements:* For master's, comprehensive exam (for some programs), thesis optional, oral exam; for doctorate, comprehensive exam, thesis/dissertation. *Entrance requirements:* For master's, GRE General Test, minimum GPA of 3.25, 3 letters of recommendation; for doctorate, GRE General Test, minimum undergraduate GPA of 3.25, graduate 3.5; MA in communication; 3 letters of recommendation. Additional exam requirements/recommendations for international students: Required—TOEFL (minimum score 580 paper-based; 237 computer-based). *Application deadline:* For fall admission, 1/15 priority date for domestic students, 3/1 for international students. Applications are processed on a rolling basis. Application fee: $50. Electronic applications accepted. *Financial support:* In 2007–08, 46 students received support, including 2 fellowships (averaging $4,477 per year), 7 research assistantships with full and partial tuition reimbursements available (averaging $13,917 per year), 34 teaching assistantships with full and partial tuition reimbursements available (averaging $13,056 per year); career-related internships or fieldwork, Federal Work-Study, institutionally sponsored loans, tuition waivers (partial), and teaching associateships also available. Financial award application deadline: 4/1; financial award applicants required to submit FAFSA. *Faculty research:* Advocacy communication, mediated communication in decision making, communication technology policy and effects, multicultural and international psychology and physiology of communication. Total annual research expenditures: $550,455. *Unit head:* Dr. Erica Austin, Interim Director, 509-335-1556, E-mail: eaustin@wsu.edu. *Application contact:* Graduate School Admissions, 800-GRADWSU, Fax: 509-335-1949, E-mail: gradsch@wsu.edu.

Wayne State University, College of Fine, Performing and Communication Arts, Department of Communication, Detroit, MI 48202. Offers communication studies (MA, PhD); public relations and organizational communication (MA); radio-TV-film (MA, PhD); speech communication (MA, PhD). *Students:* 74 full-time (49 women), 128 part-time (94 women); includes 63 minority (51 African Americans, 1 American Indian/Alaska Native, 3 Asian Americans or Pacific Islanders, 8 Hispanic Americans), 14 international. Average age 34. 92 applicants, 62% accepted, 42 enrolled. In 2007, 39 master's, 6 doctorates awarded. *Degree requirements:* For master's, thesis, essay, or comprehensive exam; for doctorate, thesis/dissertation. *Entrance requirements:* For master's, minimum GPA of 3.0, personal statement; sample of academic writing; for doctorate, GRE, minimum GPA of 3.3, MA; letters of recommendation; personal statement; sample of written scholarship. Additional exam requirements/recommendations for international students: Required—TOEFL (minimum score 550 paper-based; 213 computer-based); Recommended—TWE (minimum score 6). *Application deadline:* For fall admission, 4/1 for domestic students, 6/1 for international students; for winter admission, 10/1 for international students; for spring admission, 2/1 for international students. Applications are processed on a rolling basis. Application fee: $30 ($50 for international students). Electronic applications accepted. *Expenses:* Tuition, state resident: part-time $403 per credit hour. Tuition, nonresident: part-time $890 per credit hour. *Financial support:* In 2007–08, 22 students received support, including 2 fellowships with tuition reimbursements available (averaging $14,351 per year), 17 teaching assistantships with tuition reimbursements available (averaging $12,922 per year); research assistantships with tuition reimbursements available, career-related internships or fieldwork also available. Financial award application deadline: 2/1. *Faculty research:* Rhetorical theory and criticism; mass media theory and research; argumentation; organizational communication; risk and crisis communication; interpersonal, family, and health communication. *Unit head:* Dr. Matthew Seeger, Chair, 313-577-2959, Fax: 313-577-6300, E-mail: aa4331@wayne.edu. *Application contact:* Hayg Oshagan, Associate Professor, 313-577-0429, E-mail: ad4570@wayne.edu.

Webster University, School of Communications, Program in Communications Management, St. Louis, MO 63119-3194. Offers MA. *Expenses:* Tuition: Full-time $9,360; part-time $520 per credit. *Unit head:* Susan Seymour, Director, 314-961-2660 Ext. 7527.

Western Michigan University, Graduate College, College of Arts and Sciences, Department of Communication, Kalamazoo, MI 49008-5202. Offers organizational communication (MA).

West Virginia University, Eberly College of Arts and Sciences, Department of Communication Studies, Morgantown, WV 26506. Offers communication in instruction (MA); communication studies (PhD); communication theory and research (MA); corporate and organizational communication (MA). Part-time programs available. *Faculty:* 13 full-time (5 women), 3 part-time/adjunct (2 women). *Students:* 27 full-time (16 women), 57 part-time (41 women); includes 5 minority (3 African Americans, 1 Asian American or Pacific Islander, 1 Hispanic American), 1 international. Average age 35. 94 applicants, 68% accepted, 44 enrolled. In 2007, 56 master's, 2 doctorates awarded. *Median time to degree:* Of those who began their doctoral program in fall 1999, 100% received their degree in 8 years or less. *Degree requirements:* For master's, comprehensive exam (for some programs), thesis (for some programs); for doctorate, comprehensive exam, thesis/dissertation. *Entrance requirements:* For master's and doctorate, minimum GPA of 3.0. Additional exam requirements/recommendations for international students: Required—TOEFL. *Application deadline:* For fall admission, 2/1 priority date for domestic students. Applications are processed on a rolling basis. Application fee: $50. Electronic applications accepted. *Expenses:* Tuition, state resident: full-time $5,196; part-time $292 per credit hour. Tuition, nonresident: full-time $15,064; part-time $840 per credit hour. Tuition and fees vary according to program. *Financial support:* In 2007–08, 49 students received support, including 20 teaching assistantships with full tuition reimbursements available (averaging $10,000 per year); career-related internships or fieldwork, Federal Work-Study, institutionally sponsored loans, tuition waivers (full and partial), and graduate resident hall assistantships also available. Financial award application deadline: 3/1; financial award applicants required to submit FAFSA. *Faculty research:* Instructional communication, interpersonal communication, health communication, influence, instructional communication, social influence. *Unit head:* Dr. Matthew M. Martin, Chair, 304-293-3905, Fax: 304-293-8667, E-mail: matt.martin@mail.wvu.edu. *Application contact:* Dr. Scott A. Myers, PhD Coordinator, 304-293-3905, E-mail: smyers@mail.wvu.edu.

Health Communication

Cleveland State University, College of Graduate Studies, College of Liberal Arts and Social Sciences, School of Communication, Cleveland, OH 44115. Offers applied communication theory and methodology (MA); culture, communication and health care (Certificate). Part-time and evening/weekend programs available. *Faculty:* 17 full-time (9 women), 1 part-time/adjunct (0 women). *Students:* 14 full-time (13 women), 14 part-time (9 women); includes 3 minority (2 African Americans, 1 Asian American or Pacific Islander), 6 international. Average age 33. 29 applicants, 59% accepted, 10 enrolled. In 2007, 2 degrees awarded. *Degree requirements:* For master's, thesis, project or comprehensive exam. *Entrance requirements:* For master's, GRE or MAT, minimum undergraduate GPA of 2.75, 2 letters of recommendation. Additional exam requirements/recommendations for international students: Required—TOEFL (minimum score 525 paper-based; 197 computer-based). *Application deadline:* For fall admission, 7/15 priority date for domestic and international students; for spring admission, 1/15 priority date for domestic students, 12/15 priority date for international students. Applications are processed on a rolling basis. Application fee: $30. Electronic applications accepted. *Financial*

Health Communication

Cleveland State University (continued)
support: In 2007–08, 5 research assistantships with full and partial tuition reimbursements (averaging $3,132 per year), 7 teaching assistantships with full and partial tuition reimbursements (averaging $3,231 per year) were awarded; career-related internships or fieldwork, tuition waivers (full and partial), and unspecified assistantships also available. *Faculty research:* Interpersonal, organizational, and mass communication; health communication. *Unit head:* Dr. Richard M. Perloff, Director, 216-687-4631, Fax: 216-687-5435, E-mail: r.perloff@csuohio.edu.

East Carolina University, Graduate School, College of Fine Arts and Communication, School of Communication, Greenville, NC 27858-4353. Offers health communication (MA). *Students:* 17 full-time (15 women), 2 part-time (both women); includes 5 minority (3 African Americans, 2 Asian Americans or Pacific Islanders). Average age 24. *Entrance requirements:* For master's, GRE. *Financial support:* Teaching assistantships available. *Unit head:* Dr. Tim Hudson, Head, 252-328-2814, E-mail: hudsont@ecu.edu.

Emerson College, Graduate Studies, School of Communication, Department of Marketing Communication, Program in Health Communication, Boston, MA 02116-4624. Offers MA. Part-time programs available. *Students:* 32 full-time (31 women), 4 part-time (3 women); includes 2 Asian Americans or Pacific Islanders, 2 Hispanic Americans, 1 international. Average age 26. 42 applicants, 83% accepted, 16 enrolled. In 2007, 11 degrees awarded. *Entrance requirements:* For master's, GMAT or GRE General Test. Additional exam requirements/recommendations for international students: Required—TOEFL (minimum score 550 paper-based; 213 computer-based; 80 iBT), IELTS (minimum score 7). *Application deadline:* For fall admission, 3/1 priority date for domestic students, 5/1 for international students; for spring admission, 11/1 priority date for domestic students, 11/1 for international students. Applications are processed on a rolling basis. Application fee: $60 ($75 for international students). Electronic applications accepted. *Expenses:* Tuition: Full-time $16,800; part-time $840 per credit. Required fees: $60 per semester. One-time fee: $160. *Financial support:* In 2007–08, 2 fellowships with partial tuition reimbursements (averaging $14,000 per year), 8 research assistantships with partial tuition reimbursements (averaging $10,000 per year) were awarded; career-related internships or fieldwork, Federal Work-Study, scholarships/grants, and unspecified assistantships also available. Support available to part-time students. Financial award application deadline: 3/1; financial award applicants required to submit FAFSA. *Faculty research:* Health promotion, health communications. *Unit head:* Dr. Timothy Edgar, Director, 617-824-8492. *Application contact:* 617-824-8610, Fax: 617-824-8614, E-mail: gradapp@emerson.edu.

Marquette University, Graduate School, College of Communication, Milwaukee, WI 53201-1881. Offers advertising and public relations (MA); broadcasting and electronic communications (MA); communications studies (MA); journalism (MA); mass communications (MA); religious communications (MA); science, health and environmental communications (MA). *Accreditation:* ACEJMC. Part-time and evening/weekend programs available. *Faculty:* 31 full-time (17 women), 34 part-time/adjunct (17 women). *Students:* 24 full-time (13 women), 19 part-time (12 women); includes 7 minority (1 African American, 1 American Indian/Alaska Native, 2 Asian Americans or Pacific Islanders, 3 Hispanic Americans), 7 international. Average age 28. 76 applicants, 58% accepted, 15 enrolled. In 2007, 17 degrees awarded. *Degree requirements:* For master's, comprehensive exam. *Entrance requirements:* For master's, GRE. Additional exam requirements/recommendations for international students: Required—TOEFL. Application fee: $40. *Financial support:* In 2007–08, 6 research assistantships, 12 teaching assistantships were awarded; career-related internships or fieldwork, Federal Work-Study, institutionally sponsored loans, scholarships/grants, and tuition waivers (full and partial) also available. Support available to part-time students. Financial award application deadline: 2/15. *Faculty research:* Urban journalism, gender and communication, intercultural communication, religious communication. Total annual research expenditures: $17,806. *Unit head:* Dr. Ana Garner, Dean, 414-288-3588, Fax: 414-288-1578.

Marywood University, Academic Affairs, Insalaco College of Creative Arts and Management, Department of Communication Arts, Program in Communication Arts, Scranton, PA 18509-1598. Offers corporate communication (Certificate); e-business (Certificate); health communication (Certificate); instructional technology (Certificate); interdisciplinary (MA); library science/information specialist (Certificate); media management (MA); production (MA). *Students:* 10 full-time (6 women), 22 part-time (15 women); includes 4 minority (1 African American, 3 Hispanic Americans). Average age 28. In 2007, 8 degrees awarded. Application fee: $30. *Expenses:* Tuition: Full-time $15,290; part-time $695 per credit. Required fees: $990; $370 per term. Tuition and fees vary according to degree level.

Marywood University, Academic Affairs, Insalaco College of Creative Arts and Management, Department of Communication Arts, Program in Information Sciences, Scranton, PA 18509-1598. Offers corporate communication (MS); e-business (MS); health communication (MS); instructional technology (MS); library science/information science (MS). *Students:* 2 full-time (both women), 17 part-time (15 women); includes 1 minority (American Indian/Alaska Native). Average age 40.Application fee: $30. *Expenses:* Tuition: Full-time $15,290; part-time $695 per credit. Required fees: $990; $370 per term. Tuition and fees vary according to degree level.

Michigan State University, The Graduate School, College of Communication Arts and Sciences, Program in Health Communication, East Lansing, MI 48824. Offers MA. *Entrance requirements:* Additional exam requirements/recommendations for international students: Required—TOEFL. Electronic applications accepted. *Expenses:* Tuition, state resident: part-time $379 per credit hour. Tuition, nonresident: part-time $800 per credit hour. Tuition and fees vary according to program. *Faculty research:* Mass communication and public health, health communication for diverse populations, descriptive and analytical epidemiology.

Tufts University, School of Medicine, Public Health and Professional Degree Programs, Boston, MA 02111. Offers biomedical sciences (MS); health communication (MS); pain research, education and policy (MS); public health (MPH). *Accreditation:* CEPH (one or more programs are accredited). Part-time and evening/weekend programs available. *Students:* 99 full-time (62 women), 60 part-time (48 women); includes 40 minority (5 African Americans, 1 American Indian/Alaska Native, 30 Asian Americans or Pacific Islanders, 4 Hispanic Americans), 17 international. 512 applicants, 51% accepted, 132 enrolled. In 2007, 47 degrees awarded. *Degree requirements:* For master's, thesis (for some programs). *Entrance requirements:* For master's, GRE General Test. Additional exam requirements/recommendations for international students: Required—TOEFL. *Application deadline:* For fall admission, 4/15 priority date for domestic students, 3/15 for international students; for spring admission, 10/25 priority date for domestic students, 10/25 for international students. Applications are processed on a rolling basis. Application fee: $70. Electronic applications accepted. *Expenses:* Contact institution. *Financial support:* Federal Work-Study and scholarships/grants available. Support available to part-time students. Financial award application deadline: 2/29; financial award applicants required to submit FAFSA. *Faculty research:* Environmental and occupational health, nutrition, epidemiology, health communication, health services management and policy. *Unit head:* Dr. Harris Berman, Dean, Public Health and Professional Degree Programs, 617-636-0935. *Application contact:* Peg Martin, Assistant Director of Admissions and Student Services, 617-636-0935, Fax: 617-636-3949, E-mail: med-phpd@tufts.edu.

Tulane University, School of Public Health and Tropical Medicine, Department of Community Health Sciences, Program in Health Education and Communication, New Orleans, LA 70118-5669. Offers MPH. *Accreditation:* CEPH. *Degree requirements:* For master's, comprehensive exam. *Entrance requirements:* For master's, GRE General Test. Additional exam requirements/recommendations for international students: Required—TOEFL.

University of Florida, Graduate School, College of Health and Human Performance, Department of Health Education and Behavior, Gainesville, FL 32611. Offers health behavior (PhD); health communication (Graduate Certificate); health education and behavior (MS). *Accreditation:* NCATE (one or more programs are accredited). Part-time programs available. *Faculty:* 12 full-time (4 women). Terminal master's awarded for partial completion of doctoral program. *Degree requirements:* For master's, thesis (for some programs); for doctorate, thesis/dissertation. *Entrance requirements:* For master's and doctorate, GRE General Test, minimum GPA of 3.0. Additional exam requirements/recommendations for international students: Required—TOEFL (minimum score 550 paper-based; 213 computer-based). *Application deadline:* For fall admission, 6/1 priority date for domestic students. Applications are processed on a rolling basis. Application fee: $30. Electronic applications accepted. *Expenses:* Tuition, state resident: full-time $7,478. Tuition, nonresident: full-time $22,603. *Financial support:* In 2007–08, 6 research assistantships (averaging $11,364 per year), 10 teaching assistantships (averaging $9,726 per year) were awarded; fellowships, career-related internships or fieldwork and institutionally sponsored loans also available. *Faculty research:* Adolescent health, human sexuality and HIV/AIDS, substance use, nutrition. *Unit head:* Dr. Robert Weiler, Chair, 352-392-0583 Ext. 1282, Fax: 352-392-1909, E-mail: rweiler@hhp.ufl.edu. *Application contact:* Dr. Robert Morgan Pigg, Coordinator, 352-392-0583 Ext. 1281, Fax: 352-392-1909, E-mail: rmpigg@hhp.ufl.edu.

University of Southern California, Keck School of Medicine and Graduate School, Graduate Programs in Medicine, Department of Preventive Medicine, Master of Public Health Program, Los Angeles, CA 90089. Offers biometry/epidemiology (MPH); health communication (MPH); health promotion (MPH); preventive nutrition (MPH). *Accreditation:* CEPH. Part-time programs available. *Faculty:* 22 full-time (12 women), 3 part-time/adjunct (0 women). *Students:* 155 full-time (121 women); includes 83 minority (16 African Americans, 51 Asian Americans or Pacific Islanders, 16 Hispanic Americans), 20 international. Average age 26. 211 applicants, 75% accepted, 68 enrolled. In 2007, 53 degrees awarded. *Degree requirements:* For master's, practicum, final report, oral presentation. *Entrance requirements:* For master's, GRE General Test, MCAT, GMAT, DAT, minimum GPA of 3.0. Additional exam requirements/recommendations for international students: Required—TOEFL (minimum score 600 paper-based; 250 computer-based; 100 iBT). *Application deadline:* For fall admission, 6/1 priority date for domestic and international students; for spring admission, 11/15 priority date for domestic students, 10/1 priority date for international students. Applications are processed on a rolling basis. Application fee: $65 ($75 for international students). Electronic applications accepted. *Financial support:* In 2007–08, 131 students received support, including research assistantships with full tuition reimbursements available (averaging $11,109 per year), teaching assistantships with partial tuition reimbursements available (averaging $11,109 per year); career-related internships or fieldwork, Federal Work-Study, institutionally sponsored loans, scholarships/grants, health care benefits, unspecified assistantships, and staff tuition remission also available. Support available to part-time students. Financial award application deadline: 5/1; financial award applicants required to submit CSS PROFILE or FAFSA. *Faculty research:* Substance abuse prevention, cancer and heart disease prevention, mass media and health communication research, health promotion, treatment compliance. Total annual research expenditures: $93.8 million. *Unit head:* Dr. Thomas W. Valente, Director, 626-457-6678, Fax: 626-457-6699, E-mail: tvalente@usc.edu. *Application contact:* Chrystal Romero, Admissions Counselor, 626-457-6676, Fax: 626-457-4012, E-mail: ccromero@usc.edu.

University of West Florida, College of Arts and Sciences: Sciences, Division of Life and Health Sciences, Pensacola, FL 32514-5750. Offers biology (MS, MST), including biological chemistry (MS), biology (MS), biology education (MST), coastal zone studies (MS), environmental biology (MS); general biology (MS), including biology; health communication (MA), including health care ethics; public health (MPH). Part-time programs available. *Faculty:* 10 full-time (2 women), 3 part-time/adjunct (2 women). *Students:* 16 full-time (11 women), 46 part-time (29 women); includes 12 minority (8 African Americans, 3 Asian Americans or Pacific Islanders, 1 Hispanic American), 6 international. Average age 28. 36 applicants, 58% accepted, 19 enrolled. In 2007, 12 degrees awarded. *Entrance requirements:* For master's, GRE General Test. Additional exam requirements/recommendations for international students: Required—TOEFL (minimum score 550 paper-based; 213 computer-based). *Application deadline:* For fall admission, 6/1 for domestic students, 5/15 for international students; for spring admission, 11/1 for domestic students, 10/1 for international students. Applications are processed on a rolling basis. Application fee: $30. *Expenses:* Tuition, state resident: full-time $6,054; part-time $252 per credit. Tuition, nonresident: full-time $21,886; part-time $912 per credit. *Financial support:* In 2007–08, 6 research assistantships with partial tuition reimbursements (averaging $13,503 per year), 15 teaching assistantships with partial tuition reimbursements (averaging $10,608 per year) were awarded; scholarships/grants and tuition waivers (partial) also available. Financial award application deadline: 4/15; financial award applicants required to submit FAFSA. *Unit head:* Dr. George L. Stewart, Chairperson, 850-474-2748.

Washington State University, Graduate School, College of Liberal Arts, Edward R. Murrow College of Communication, Pullman, WA 99164. Offers health communications (MA, PhD); intercultural and international communications (MA, PhD); media and society (MA, PhD); media process and effects (MA, PhD); organizational communications (MA, PhD). *Faculty:* 30. *Students:* 43 full-time (26 women), 6 part-time (4 women); includes 2 minority (1 Asian American or Pacific Islander, 1 Hispanic American), 19 international. Average age 30. 120 applicants, 22% accepted, 19 enrolled. In 2007, 22 master's, 1 doctorate awarded. *Degree requirements:* For master's, comprehensive exam (for some programs), thesis optional, oral exam; for doctorate, comprehensive exam, thesis/dissertation. *Entrance requirements:* For master's, GRE General Test, minimum GPA of 3.25, 3 letters of recommendation; for doctorate, GRE General Test, minimum undergraduate GPA of 3.25, graduate 3.5; MA in communication; 3 letters of recommendation. Additional exam requirements/recommendations for international students: Required—TOEFL (minimum score 580 paper-based; 237 computer-based). *Application deadline:* For fall admission, 1/15 priority date for domestic students, 3/1 for international students. Applications are processed on a rolling basis. Application fee: $50. Electronic applications accepted. *Financial support:* In 2007–08, 46 students received support, including 2 fellowships (averaging $4,477 per year), 7 research assistantships with full and partial tuition reimbursements available (averaging $13,917 per year), 34 teaching assistantships with full and partial tuition reimbursements available (averaging $13,056 per year); career-related internships or fieldwork, Federal Work-Study, institutionally sponsored loans, tuition waivers (partial), and teaching associateships also available. Financial award application deadline: 4/1; financial award applicants required to submit FAFSA. *Faculty research:* Advocacy communication, mediated communication in decision making, communication technology policy and effects, multicultural and international psychology and physiology of communication. Total annual research expenditures: $550,455. *Unit head:* Dr. Erica Austin, Interim Director, 509-335-1556, E-mail: eaustin@wsu.edu. *Application contact:* Graduate School Admissions, 800-GRADWSU, Fax: 509-335-1949, E-mail: gradsch@wsu.edu.

Internet and Interactive Multimedia

Academy of Art University, Graduate Program, School of Multimedia Communications, San Francisco, CA 94105-3410. Offers MA.

Alfred University, Graduate School, New York State College of Ceramics, School of Art and Design, Alfred, NY 14802-1205. Offers ceramic art (MFA); electronic integrated arts (MFA); glass art (MFA); sculpture (MFA). *Accreditation:* NASAD. *Students:* 34 full-time (19 women). Average age 26. 278 applicants, 6% accepted, 17 enrolled. In 2007, 17 degrees awarded. *Degree requirements:* For master's, exhibit. *Entrance requirements:* For master's, portfolio. Additional exam requirements/recommendations for international students: Required—TOEFL (minimum score 550 paper-based; 213 computer-based; 80 iBT), IELTS (minimum score 6). *Application deadline:* For fall admission, 1/15 for domestic students, 2/1 for international students. Application fee: $50. Electronic applications accepted. *Expenses:* Tuition: Full-time $32,016; part-time $680 per credit hour. Required fees: $850; $140 per year. *Financial support:* In 2007–08, 35 students received support; teaching assistantships with full tuition reimbursements available, tuition waivers (full) available. Financial award applicants required to submit FAFSA. *Faculty research:* Ceramic sculpture, functional ceramics, wood, mixed media, hot and cold glass. *Unit head:* Joseph Lewis, Dean, 607-871-2412, E-mail: lewis@alfred.edu. *Application contact:* Valerie Stephens, Coordinator of Graduate Admissions, 607-871-2141, Fax: 607-871-2198, E-mail: gradinquiry@alfred.edu.

American Academy of Art, Graduate Programs, Program in Digital Media and Design, Chicago, IL 60604-4302. Offers MFA. *Degree requirements:* For master's, thesis, exhibition. *Entrance requirements:* For master's, interview, portfolio, 2 letters of recommendation. Additional exam requirements/recommendations for international students: Required—TOEFL (minimum score 500 paper-based; 173 computer-based). *Faculty research:* Animation, print design, digital film, communication theory.

Brooklyn College of the City University of New York, Division of Graduate Studies, Program in Performance and Interactive Media Arts, Brooklyn, NY 11210-2889. Offers MFA, CAS. *Students:* 9 full-time (6 women), 8 part-time (2 women); includes 7 minority (3 African Americans, 1 Asian American or Pacific Islander, 3 Hispanic Americans). 25 applicants, 76% accepted, 10 enrolled. In 2007, 3 degrees awarded. *Entrance requirements:* For master's, 2 letters of recommendation, resumé, portfolio, interview; for CAS, 2 letters of recommendation. *Application deadline:* For fall admission, 3/1 priority date for domestic students, 2/1 priority date for international students; for spring admission, 11/1 priority date for domestic students, 10/1 priority date for international students. Applications are processed on a rolling basis. Application fee: $125. Electronic applications accepted. *Financial support:* Application deadline: 5/1. *Unit head:* Dr. John Jannone, Director, E-mail: jannone brooklyn.cuny.edu. *Application contact:* Hernan Sierra, Graduate Admissions Coordinator, 718-951-4536, Fax: 718-951-4506, E-mail: grads@brooklyn.cuny.edu.

California State University, East Bay, Academic Programs and Graduate Studies, Multimedia Program, Hayward, CA 94542-3000. Offers MA. *Faculty:* 5 full-time (2 women). *Students:* 18 full-time (10 women), 9 part-time (4 women); includes 10 minority (2 African Americans, 4 Asian Americans or Pacific Islanders, 4 Hispanic Americans), 2 international. Average age 32. 34 applicants, 56% accepted, 14 enrolled. In 2007, 20 degrees awarded. *Entrance requirements:* For master's, minimum GPA of 2.5. Additional exam requirements/recommendations for international students: Required—TOEFL (minimum score 550 paper-based; 213 computer-based). *Application deadline:* For fall admission, 5/31 for domestic students, 4/30 for international students; for winter admission, 9/30 for domestic and international students; for spring admission, 12/31 for domestic students, 11/30 for international students. Application fee: $55. *Expenses:* Required fees: $3,987; $851 per quarter. *Unit head:* Dr. James F. Petrillo, Graduate Coordinator/Program Director, 510-885-3204, Fax: 510-885- Ext. 4301. *Application contact:* My Huynh, Graduate Prospect Specialist, 510-885-2989, Fax: 510-885-4059, E-mail: my.huynh@csueastbay.edu.

Concordia University, School of Graduate Studies, Faculty of Engineering and Computer Science, Concordia Institute for Information Systems Engineering (CIISE), Montréal, QC H3G 1M8, Canada. Offers 3D graphics and game development (Certificate); information systems security (M Eng, MA Sc); quality systems engineering (M Eng, MA Sc); service engineering and network management (Certificate).

Duquesne University, Graduate School of Liberal Arts, Program in Multimedia Technology, Pittsburgh, PA 15282-0001. Offers MS, Certificate. Part-time and evening/weekend programs available. *Faculty:* 10 full-time (1 woman), 3 part-time/adjunct (0 women). *Students:* 21 full-time (15 women), 40 part-time (13 women). Average age 22. In 2007, 20 degrees awarded. *Entrance requirements:* For master's, MAT or GRE General Test, portfolio. Additional exam requirements/recommendations for international students: Required—TOEFL. *Application deadline:* For fall admission, 8/15 for domestic students, 5/1 for international students. Applications are processed on a rolling basis. Application fee: $50. *Expenses:* Tuition: Part-time $774 per credit. Required fees: $74 per credit. Tuition and fees vary according to program. *Financial support:* In 2007–08, 1 research assistantship with full tuition reimbursement (averaging $8,400 per year) was awarded; Federal Work-Study also available. Support available to part-time students. Financial award application deadline: 5/1. *Unit head:* Dr. John Shepherd, Director, 412-396-5772.

Full Sail University, Program in Education Media Design and Technology, Winter Park, FL 32792-7437. Offers MS. Postbaccalaureate distance learning degree programs offered (no on-campus study). *Faculty:* 6 full-time (5 women). *Students:* 17 full-time (12 women). *Entrance requirements:* Additional exam requirements/recommendations for international students: Required—TOEFL (minimum score 550 paper-based; 213 computer-based; 79 iBT). Application fee: $150. *Expenses:* Tuition: Full-time $31,300. *Unit head:* Holly Ludgate, Program Director, 800-226-7625, E-mail: admissions@fullsail.com.

Georgetown University, Graduate School of Arts and Sciences, Program in Communication, Culture, and Technology, Washington, DC 20057. Offers MA. Part-time and evening/weekend programs available. *Degree requirements:* For master's, thesis (for some programs). *Entrance requirements:* For master's, GRE General Test, 3 letters of recommendation, writing sample. Additional exam requirements/recommendations for international students: Required—TOEFL (minimum score 600 paper-based; 250 computer-based). Electronic applications accepted.

See Close-Up on page 899.

Georgia Institute of Technology, Graduate Studies and Research, Ivan Allen College of Policy and International Affairs, Program in Information Design and Technology, Atlanta, GA 30332-0001. Offers human computer interaction (MSHCI); information design and technology (MSIDT). *Degree requirements:* For master's, thesis or alternative. *Entrance requirements:* Additional exam requirements/recommendations for international students: Required—TOEFL. Electronic applications accepted. *Faculty research:* New media studies.

Indiana University–Purdue University Indianapolis, School of Informatics, Indianapolis, IN 46202-2896. Offers informatics (PhD); media arts and science (MS). Part-time and evening/weekend programs available. *Faculty:* 3 full-time (0 women). *Students:* 31 full-time (9 women), 81 part-time (36 women); includes 19 minority (9 African Americans, 9 Asian Americans or Pacific Islanders, 1 Hispanic American), 26 international. Average age 35. In 2007, 39 degrees awarded. *Degree requirements:* For master's, multimedia project. *Entrance requirements:* For master's, minimum undergraduate GPA of 3.0, graduate 3.2; interview; portfolio; BA with demonstrated media arts skills. Additional exam requirements/recommendations for international students: Required—TOEFL. *Application deadline:* For fall admission, 3/15 for domestic students; for spring admission, 11/15 for domestic students. Application fee: $50 ($60 for international students). *Expenses:* Tuition, state resident: full-time $5,818; part-time $242 per credit hour. Tuition, nonresident: full-time $17,106; part-time $713 per credit hour. Required fees: $629. Tuition and fees vary according to course load, campus/location and program. *Financial support:* In 2007–08, 6 fellowships (averaging $17,447 per year), 13 teaching assistantships (averaging $9,392 per year) were awarded; career-related internships or fieldwork, Federal Work-Study, institutionally sponsored loans, and scholarships/grants also available. Support available to part-time students. *Unit head:* Darrell L. Bailey, Executive Associate Dean, 317-278-4636, Fax: 317-278-7769.

Long Island University, C.W. Post Campus, School of Visual and Performing Arts, Department of Theatre, Film, Dance and Arts Management, Brookville, NY 11548-1300. Offers interactive multimedia (MA); theatre (MA). Part-time and evening/weekend programs available. *Faculty:* 2 full-time (both women), 23 part-time/adjunct (13 women). *Students:* 18 full-time (12 women), 18 part-time (9 women); includes 7 minority (1 African American, 5 Asian Americans or Pacific Islanders, 1 Hispanic American), 3 international. Average age 31. 26 applicants, 65% accepted, 11 enrolled. In 2007, 4 degrees awarded. *Degree requirements:* For master's, thesis. *Entrance requirements:* For master's, placement exam. *Application deadline:* Applications are processed on a rolling basis. Application fee: $30. Electronic applications accepted. *Expenses:* Tuition: Part-time $825 per credit. Tuition and fees vary according to course load. *Financial support:* Career-related internships or fieldwork, Federal Work-Study, institutionally sponsored loans, scholarships/grants, and production assistantships available. Support available to part-time students. Financial award application deadline: 5/15; financial award applicants required to submit CSS PROFILE or FAFSA. *Faculty research:* Playwriting, intercultural dance and theatre, translation, Suzuki, set and costume design. *Unit head:* Dr. Cara Gargano, Chair, 516-299-2353, E-mail: cgargano@liu.edu. *Application contact:* Beth Carson, Director of Graduate and International Admissions, 516-299-2900 Ext. 3952, Fax: 516-299-2137, E-mail: enroll@cwpost.liu.edu.

Marlboro College, Graduate Center, Program in Internet Engineering, Brattleboro, VT 05301. Offers MS. Part-time and evening/weekend programs available. Postbaccalaureate distance learning degree programs offered (minimal on-campus study). *Faculty:* 1 full-time (0 women), 4 part-time/adjunct (0 women). *Students:* 2 full-time (0 women), 3 part-time (1 woman). Average age 40. 2 applicants, 50% accepted, 1 enrolled. In 2007, 3 degrees awarded. *Degree requirements:* For master's, capstone project. *Entrance requirements:* For master's, 2 letters of recommendation, transcripts, letter of intent. *Application deadline:* For fall admission, 3/1 priority date for domestic students. Applications are processed on a rolling basis. Application fee: $0. Electronic applications accepted. *Expenses:* Tuition: Full-time $18,900; part-time $630 per credit. Tuition and fees vary according to program. *Financial support:* Applicants required to submit FAFSA. *Unit head:* Mark Francillon, Director, 802-258-9207, Fax: 802-258-9201, E-mail: markf@marlboro.edu. *Application contact:* Joe Heslin, Associate Director of Admissions, 802-258-9209, Fax: 802-258-9201, E-mail: jheslin@gradcenter.marlboro.edu.

Marlboro College, Graduate Center, Program in Teaching with Technology, Brattleboro, VT 05301. Offers MAT. Part-time and evening/weekend programs available. Postbaccalaureate distance learning degree programs offered (minimal on-campus study). *Faculty:* 7 part-time/adjunct (4 women). *Students:* 4 full-time (all women), 1 (woman) part-time. 3 applicants, 67% accepted, 2 enrolled. In 2007, 9 degrees awarded. *Degree requirements:* For master's, capstone project. *Entrance requirements:* For master's, 2 letters of recommendation, transcripts, letter of intent. *Application deadline:* For fall admission, 3/1 priority date for domestic students. Applications are processed on a rolling basis. Application fee: $0. Electronic applications accepted. *Expenses:* Tuition: Full-time $18,900; part-time $630 per credit. Tuition and fees vary according to program. *Financial support:* Applicants required to submit FAFSA. *Unit head:* Kevin Bell, Academic Director, 802-258-9203, Fax: 802-258-9201, E-mail: kbell@gradcenter.marlboro.edu. *Application contact:* Joe Heslin, Associate Director of Admissions, 802-258-9209, Fax: 802-258-9201, E-mail: jheslin@gradcenter.marlboro.edu.

National University, Academic Affairs, School of Media and Communication, Department of Media, La Jolla, CA 92037-1011. Offers digital cinema (MFA); educational and instructional technology (MS); video game production and design (MFA). Part-time and evening/weekend programs available. Postbaccalaureate distance learning degree programs offered (no on-campus study). *Faculty:* 7 full-time (2 women), 55 part-time/adjunct (22 women). *Students:* 69 full-time (35 women), 158 part-time (86 women); includes 54 minority (25 African Americans, 2 American Indian/Alaska Native, 7 Asian Americans or Pacific Islanders, 20 Hispanic Americans). Average age 39. 159 applicants, 143 enrolled. In 2007, 58 degrees awarded. *Degree requirements:* For master's, thesis. *Entrance requirements:* For master's, interview, minimum GPA of 2.5. Additional exam requirements/recommendations for international students: Required—TOEFL (minimum score 550 paper-based; 213 computer-based; 80 iBT), IELTS (minimum score 6). *Application deadline:* Applications are processed on a rolling basis. Application fee: $60 ($65 for international students). Electronic applications accepted. *Expenses:* Tuition: Full-time $8,262; part-time $306 per unit. One-time fee: $60. *Financial support:* Career-related internships or fieldwork, institutionally sponsored loans, scholarships/grants, and tuition waivers (partial) available. Support available to part-time students. Financial award application deadline: 6/30; financial award applicants required to submit FAFSA. *Unit head:* Dr. Timothy Langdell, Department Chair, 858-642-8466, Fax: 858-642-8743, E-mail: tlangdell@nu.edu. *Application contact:* Dominick Giovanniello, Associate Regional Dean—San Diego, 800-NAT-UNIV, Fax: 858-642-8709, E-mail: dgiovann@nu.edu.

New Jersey Institute of Technology, Office of Graduate Studies, Newark College of Engineering, Department of Electrical and Computer Engineering, Program in Internet Engineering, Newark, NJ 07102. Offers MS. Part-time and evening/weekend programs available. *Students:* 6 full-time (3 women), 3 part-time; includes 2 minority (both Hispanic Americans), 6 international. Average age 31. 9 applicants, 22% accepted, 2 enrolled. In 2007, 3 degrees awarded. *Entrance requirements:* For master's, GRE General Test. Additional exam requirements/recommendations for international students: Required—TOEFL (minimum score 550 paper-based; 213 computer-based). *Application deadline:* For fall admission, 6/5 priority date for domestic students; for spring admission, 10/15 for domestic students. Applications are processed on a rolling basis. Application fee: $60. Electronic applications accepted. *Expenses:* Tuition, state resident: full-time $12,730. Tuition, nonresident: full-time $18,090. Tuition and fees vary according to course load and campus/location. *Financial support:* Fellowships with full and partial tuition reimbursements, research assistantships with full and partial tuition reimbursements, teaching assistantships with full and partial tuition reimbursements, career-related internships or fieldwork, Federal Work-Study, institutionally sponsored loans, and unspecified assistantships available. Financial award application deadline: 3/15. *Application contact:* Kathryn Kelly, Director of Admissions, 973-596-3300, Fax: 973-596-3461, E-mail: admissions@njit.edu.

New Mexico Highlands University, Graduate Studies, College of Arts and Sciences, Program in Media Arts and Computer Science, Las Vegas, NM 87701. Offers computer science (MA, MS); media arts (MA). *Faculty:* 5 full-time (1 woman), 1 part-time/adjunct (0 women). *Students:* 21 full-time (7 women), 8 part-time (4 women); includes 9 minority (1 Asian American or Pacific Islander, 8 Hispanic Americans), 12 international. Average age 30. 30 applicants, 70% accepted, 5 enrolled. In 2007, 10 degrees awarded. *Degree requirements:* For master's, comprehensive exam, thesis. *Entrance requirements:* For master's, minimum undergraduate GPA of 3.0. Additional exam requirements/recommendations for international students: Required—TOEFL (minimum score 540 paper-based; 190 computer-based). Application fee: $15. *Expenses:* Tuition, state resident: full-time $2,642; part-time $110 per credit hour. Tuition, nonresident: full-time $3,964; part-time $165 per credit hour. International tuition: $5,285 full-time. One-time fee: $20 full-time. *Financial support:* In 2007–08, 12 students received support, including teaching assistantships (averaging $7,200 per year); career-related internships or fieldwork, Federal Work-Study, institutionally sponsored loans, scholarships/grants, tuition waivers (full and partial), and unspecified assistantships also available. Support available to part-time students. Financial award application deadline: 3/1; financial award applicants required to

Internet and Interactive Multimedia

New Mexico Highlands University (continued)

submit FAFSA. *Application contact:* Diane Trujillo, Administrative Assistant Graduate Studies, 505-454-3266, Fax: 505-454-3558, E-mail: dtrujillo@nmhu.edu.

New York University, Tisch School of the Arts, Interactive Telecommunications Program, New York, NY 10012-1019. Offers MPS. *Faculty:* 9 full-time, 40 part-time/adjunct. *Students:* 214 full-time (91 women), 20 part-time (11 women); includes 33 minority (7 African Americans, 14 Asian Americans or Pacific Islanders, 12 Hispanic Americans), 81 international. Average age 29. 248 applicants, 77% accepted, 121 enrolled. In 2007, 102 degrees awarded. *Degree requirements:* For master's, thesis. *Entrance requirements:* Additional exam requirements/recommendations for international students: Required—TOEFL (minimum score 600 paper-based; 250 computer-based; 100 iBT), IELTS. *Application deadline:* For fall admission, 1/8 priority date for domestic and international students. Application fee: $60. Electronic applications accepted. *Financial support:* In 2007–08, 90 students received support, including 24 fellowships with full and partial tuition reimbursements available; career-related internships or fieldwork, Federal Work-Study, institutionally sponsored loans, scholarships/grants, and tuition waivers (partial) also available. Financial award application deadline: 2/15; financial award applicants required to submit FAFSA. *Faculty research:* Interactive narrative/storytelling, interactive media, web technology, physical computing, ubiquitous computing. *Unit head:* Red Burns, Chair, 212-998-1880, Fax: 212-998-1898, E-mail: itp.inquiries@nyu.edu. *Application contact:* Dan Sandford, Director of Graduate Admissions, 212-998-1918, Fax: 212-995-4060, E-mail: tisch.gradadmissions@nyu.edu.

Polytechnic Institute of NYU, Department of Humanities and Social Sciences, Major in Integrated Digital Media, Brooklyn, NY 11201-2990. Offers MS, Graduate Certificate. *Students:* 18 full-time (5 women), 5 part-time (1 woman); includes 5 minority (2 African Americans, 2 Asian Americans or Pacific Islanders, 1 Hispanic American), 5 international. 28 applicants, 82% accepted, 14 enrolled. In 2007, 11 degrees awarded. *Expenses:* Tuition: Full-time $18,486; part-time $1,027 per credit. Required fees: $352 per semester. *Application contact:* Anthea Jeffrey, Graduate Admissions, 718-260-3200, Fax: 718-260-3624, E-mail: gradinfo@poly.edu.

See Close-Up on page 921.

Pratt Institute, School of Art and Design, Program in Digital Arts, Brooklyn, NY 11205-3899. Offers computer graphics (MFA). *Accreditation:* NASAD. Part-time programs available. *Faculty:* 6 full-time (1 woman), 17 part-time/adjunct (8 women). *Students:* 70 full-time (37 women), 1 part-time; includes 8 minority (3 African Americans, 3 Asian Americans or Pacific Islanders, 2 Hispanic Americans), 34 international. Average age 30. 173 applicants, 22% accepted, 12 enrolled. In 2007, 25 degrees awarded. *Degree requirements:* For master's, thesis, exhibit. *Entrance requirements:* For master's, portfolio or video tape, bachelor's degree, transcripts, letters of recommendation, statement. Additional exam requirements/recommendations for international students: Required—TOEFL (minimum score 550 paper-based; 213 computer-based). *Application deadline:* For fall admission, 2/1 for domestic students; for spring admission, 10/1 for domestic students. Applications are processed on a rolling basis. Application fee: $50 ($90 for international students). Electronic applications accepted. *Expenses:* Tuition: Full-time $25,680. Required fees: $1,106. Tuition and fees vary according to program. *Financial support:* Career-related internships or fieldwork, Federal Work-Study, institutionally sponsored loans, scholarships/grants, health care benefits, and unspecified assistantships available. Support available to part-time students. Financial award application deadline: 2/1; financial award applicants required to submit FAFSA. *Unit head:* Peter Patchen, Chair, 718-636-3693, E-mail: peter.patchen@pratt.edu. *Application contact:* Young Hah, Director of Graduate Admissions, 718-636-3683, Fax: 718-399-4242, E-mail: yhah@pratt.edu.

See Close-Up on page 253.

Quinnipiac University, School of Communications, Program in Interactive Communications, Hamden, CT 06518-1940. Offers MS. Part-time and evening/weekend programs available. *Faculty:* 5 full-time (2 women), 5 part-time/adjunct (0 women). *Students:* 19 full-time (7 women), 35 part-time (18 women); includes 6 minority (all African Americans), 2 international. Average age 30. 29 applicants, 93% accepted, 24 enrolled. In 2007, 13 degrees awarded. *Entrance requirements:* For master's, minimum GPA of 2.8, portfolio or writing sample. Additional exam requirements/recommendations for international students: Required—TOEFL (minimum score 575 paper-based; 233 computer-based; 90 iBT), IELTS (minimum score 7). *Application deadline:* For fall admission, 7/30 priority date for domestic students, 4/30 priority date for international students; for spring admission, 12/15 priority date for domestic students, 9/15 priority date for international students. Applications are processed on a rolling basis. Application fee: $45. Electronic applications accepted. *Expenses:* Tuition: Part-time $675 per credit. Required fees: $30 per credit. Tuition and fees vary according to course load. *Financial support:* Tuition waivers (partial) and unspecified assistantships available. Support available to part-time students. Financial award application deadline: 4/15; financial award applicants required to submit FAFSA. *Faculty research:* Technology and democracy, the role of computing in social change. *Unit head:* Richard Hanley, Director, 203-582-8439, Fax: 203-582-5310, E-mail: rich.hanley@quinnipiac.edu. *Application contact:* 800-462-1944, Fax: 203-582-3443, E-mail: graduate@quinnipiac.edu.

See Close-Up on page 923.

Robert Morris University, Graduate Studies, School of Communications and Information Systems, Moon Township, PA 15108-1189. Offers communication and information systems (MS); competitive intelligence systems (MS); computer information systems (MS); information security and assurance (MS); information systems and communications (D Sc); information technology project management (MS); Internet information systems (MS). Part-time and evening/weekend programs available. *Faculty:* 21 full-time (6 women), 8 part-time/adjunct (2 women). *Students:* Average age 33. 141 applicants, 84% accepted, 78 enrolled. In 2007, 103 master's, 9 doctorates awarded. *Degree requirements:* For doctorate, thesis/dissertation. *Entrance requirements:* For doctorate, employer letter of endorsement, interview. Additional exam requirements/recommendations for international students: Required—TOEFL (minimum score 550 paper-based; 213 computer-based; 79 iBT). *Application deadline:* For fall admission, 7/1 priority date for domestic and international students; for spring admission, 11/1 priority date for domestic and international students. Applications are processed on a rolling basis. Application fee: $35. Electronic applications accepted. *Expenses: Contact institution.* Part-time tuition and fees vary according to course load, degree level and program. *Financial support:* Research assistantships with partial tuition reimbursements, institutionally sponsored loans and unspecified assistantships available. Support available to part-time students. Financial award application deadline: 5/1. *Unit head:* Dr. Barbara J. Levine, Acting Dean, 412-262-8415, Fax: 412-262-8483, E-mail: levine@rmu.edu. *Application contact:* Kellie L. Laurenzi, Dean of Admissions, 412-262-8235, Fax: 412-397-2425, E-mail: laurenzi@rmu.edu.

Rochester Institute of Technology, Graduate Enrollment Services, Golisano College of Computing and Information Sciences, Department of Information Technology, Program in Game Design and Development, Rochester, NY 14623-5603. Offers MS. *Students:* 9 full-time (1 woman), 1 part-time; includes 1 minority (Asian American or Pacific Islander), 1 international. 19 applicants, 47% accepted, 6 enrolled. *Entrance requirements:* Additional exam requirements/recommendations for international students: Required—TOEFL (minimum score 570 paper-based; 230 computer-based; 88 iBT). *Expenses:* Tuition: Full-time $28,491; part-time $800 per credit hour. Required fees: $201; $67 per term. *Financial support:* Research assistantships with partial tuition reimbursements, teaching assistantships with partial tuition reimbursements, career-related internships or fieldwork, institutionally sponsored loans, scholarships/grants, and unspecified assistantships available. Support available to part-time students. Financial award applicants required to submit FAFSA. *Unit head:* Andrew Phelps, Head, 585-475-6758.

Rochester Institute of Technology, Graduate Enrollment Services, Golisano College of Computing and Information Sciences, Department of Information Technology, Program in Interactive Multimedia Development, Rochester, NY 14623-5603. Offers AC. *Students:* 5 applicants, 80% accepted, 4 enrolled. In 2007, 3 degrees awarded. *Entrance requirements:* For degree, GRE, minimum GPA of 3.0. Additional exam requirements/recommendations for international students: Required—TOEFL (minimum score 570 paper-based; 230 computer-based; 88 iBT). *Application deadline:* For fall admission, 3/1 priority date for domestic students. Applications are processed on a rolling basis. Application fee: $50. *Expenses:* Tuition: Full-time $28,491; part-time $800 per credit hour. Required fees: $201; $67 per term. *Financial support:* Research assistantships with partial tuition reimbursements, teaching assistantships with partial tuition reimbursements, career-related internships or fieldwork, institutionally sponsored loans, scholarships/grants, and unspecified assistantships available. Support available to part-time students. Financial award applicants required to submit FAFSA. *Application contact:* Diane Bills, Graduate Coordinator, 585-475-6791, E-mail: dpb@it.rit.edu.

Sacred Heart University, Graduate Programs, College of Arts and Sciences, Department of Computer Science and Information Technology, Fairfield, CT 06825-1000. Offers computer science (MS); database (CPS); information technology (MS, CPS); information technology and network security (CPS); interactive multimedia (CPS); Web development (CPS). Part-time and evening/weekend programs available. *Faculty:* 7 full-time (4 women). *Students:* 7 full-time (1 woman), 61 part-time (27 women); includes 9 minority (2 African Americans, 1 American Indian/Alaska Native, 4 Asian Americans or Pacific Islanders, 2 Hispanic Americans), 14 international. Average age 33. 19 applicants, 95% accepted, 18 enrolled. In 2007, 28 degrees awarded. *Degree requirements:* For master's, thesis optional. *Entrance requirements:* Additional exam requirements/recommendations for international students: Required—TOEFL (minimum score 550 paper-based; 213 computer-based). *Application deadline:* Applications are processed on a rolling basis. Application fee: $50 ($100 for international students). Electronic applications accepted. *Expenses:* Tuition: Part-time $510 per credit. Tuition and fees vary according to program. *Financial support:* Career-related internships or fieldwork, institutionally sponsored loans, and unspecified assistantships available. Support available to part-time students. Financial award applicants required to submit FAFSA. *Faculty research:* Contemporary market software. *Unit head:* Domenick Pinto, Academic Director and Chairperson, 203-371-7789, Fax: 203-371-0506, E-mail: pintod@sacredheart.edu. *Application contact:* Office of Graduate Admissions, 203-365-7619, Fax: 203-365-4732, E-mail: gradstudies@sacredheart.edu.

San Diego State University, Graduate and Research Affairs, College of Professional Studies and Fine Arts, School of Communication, San Diego, CA 92182. Offers advertising and public relations (MA); critical-cultural studies (MA); interaction studies (MA); intercultural and international studies (MA); new media studies (MA); news and information studies (MA); telecommunications and media management (MA). *Students:* 30 full-time (16 women), 62 part-time (47 women); includes 6 minority (3 African Americans, 2 Asian Americans or Pacific Islanders, 1 Hispanic American), 11 international. 167 applicants, 41% accepted, 45 enrolled. In 2007, 49 degrees awarded. *Degree requirements:* For master's, thesis. *Entrance requirements:* For master's, GRE General Test, 3 letters of recommendation. Additional exam requirements/recommendations for international students: Required—TOEFL. *Application deadline:* For fall admission, 3/1 for domestic and international students; for spring admission, 10/1 for domestic and international students. Applications are processed on a rolling basis. Application fee: $55. Electronic applications accepted. *Financial support:* In 2007–08, 34 teaching assistantships were awarded; career-related internships or fieldwork and unspecified assistantships also available. Financial award applicants required to submit FAFSA. Total annual research expenditures: $153,598. *Unit head:* Diane Borden, Interim Director, 619-594-8098, Fax: 619-594-6246. *Application contact:* Patricia Geist-Martin, Information Contact, 619-594-4182, E-mail: pgeist@mail.sdsu.edu.

Savannah College of Art and Design, Graduate School, Program in Interactive Design and Game Development, Savannah, GA 31402-3146. Offers MA, MFA. Part-time programs available. *Faculty:* 8 full-time (1 woman), 1 part-time/adjunct (0 women). *Students:* 43 full-time (16 women), 16 part-time (5 women); includes 6 minority (3 African Americans, 1 Asian American or Pacific Islander, 2 Hispanic Americans), 14 international. Average age 26. 52 applicants, 46% accepted, 11 enrolled. In 2007, 13 degrees awarded. *Degree requirements:* For master's, thesis, internships. *Entrance requirements:* For master's, interview, portfolio. Additional exam requirements/recommendations for international students: Required—TOEFL (minimum score 450 paper-based; 133 computer-based). *Application deadline:* For fall admission, 4/1 priority date for domestic and international students. Applications are processed on a rolling basis. Application fee: $50. Electronic applications accepted. *Expenses:* Tuition: Full-time $24,840; part-time $552 per credit. One-time fee: $500 full-time. *Financial support:* Fellowships, career-related internships or fieldwork, Federal Work-Study, and scholarships/grants available. Financial award application deadline: 4/1; financial award applicants required to submit FAFSA. *Unit head:* Josephine Leong, Chair, 912-525-8523, E-mail: jleong@scad.edu. *Application contact:* Darrell Tutchton, Director of Graduate and International Enrollment, 912-525-5961, Fax: 912-525-5985, E-mail: admission@scad.edu.

School of Visual Arts, Graduate Programs, Program in Photography, Video and Related Media, New York, NY 10010-3994. Offers MFA. *Accreditation:* NASAD. *Faculty:* 1 full-time (0 women), 29 part-time/adjunct (12 women). *Students:* 80 full-time (42 women), 8 part-time (4 women); includes 10 minority (2 African Americans, 1 Asian American or Pacific Islander, 7 Hispanic Americans), 22 international. Average age 29. 246 applicants, 35% accepted, 44 enrolled. In 2007, 28 degrees awarded. *Degree requirements:* For master's, final review, project or thesis. *Entrance requirements:* For master's, portfolio. Additional exam requirements/recommendations for international students: Required—TOEFL (minimum score 550 paper-based; 213 computer-based; 79 iBT). *Application deadline:* For fall admission, 2/1 for domestic students. Application fee: $80. Electronic applications accepted. *Expenses:* Tuition: Full-time $26,120; part-time $870 per credit. Tuition and fees vary according to program. *Financial support:* In 2007–08, 40 students received support. Career-related internships or fieldwork, Federal Work-Study, scholarships/grants, and unspecified assistantships available. Support available to part-time students. Financial award application deadline: 2/1; financial award applicants required to submit FAFSA. *Unit head:* Charles Traub, Chair, 212-592-2360, Fax: 212-592-2366, E-mail: ctraub@sva.edu.

Simon Fraser University, Graduate Studies, Faculty of Applied Sciences, School of Interactive Arts and Technology, Surrey, BC V3T 2W1, Canada. Offers information technology (M Sc, PhD); interactive arts (M Sc, PhD). *Degree requirements:* For master's, thesis; for doctorate, comprehensive exam, thesis/dissertation. *Entrance requirements:* For master's, 2 references, curriculum vitae; for doctorate, 3 references, curriculm vitae, minimum GPA of 3.0. Additional exam requirements/recommendations for international students: Required—TOEFL (minimum score 570 paper-based; 230 computer-based), TWE (minimum score 5). Electronic applications accepted.

Southern Polytechnic State University, School of Arts and Sciences, Department of English, Technical Communication, and Media Arts, Marietta, GA 30060-2896. Offers information design and communication (MS); technical and professional communication (Graduate Certificate). Part-time and evening/weekend programs available. Postbaccalaureate distance learning degree programs offered (minimal on-campus study). *Faculty:* 4 full-time (3 women). *Students:* 4 full-time (3 women), 33 part-time (24 women); includes 13 minority (11 African Americans, 2 Hispanic Americans), 2 international. Average age 39. 31 applicants, 58% accepted, 15 enrolled. In 2007, 8 degrees awarded. *Degree requirements:* For master's, thesis optional, students can complete 36-hour requirement through a thesis option (6 hours), an internship option (6 hours) or an advanced coursework option (6 hours); for Graduate Certificate, thesis optional, students can complete 18-hour requirement for advanced certificate through a thesis option (6 hours), an internship option (6 hours) or an advanced coursework option (6 hours). *Entrance requirements:* For master's, GRE, statement of purpose, writing sample, professional recommendations, proctored essay; for Graduate Certificate, statement of purpose, writing sample, professional recommendations, proctored essay. Additional exam requirements/recommendations for international students: Required—TOEFL (minimum score 550 paper-based; 213 computer-based; 79 iBT). *Application deadline:* For fall admission, 5/1 priority date for domestic students, 7/1 priority date for international students; for spring admission, 9/1 priority date for domestic students, 11/1 priority date for international students. Applications are processed on a rolling basis. Application fee: $20. Electronic applications accepted. *Expenses:* Tuition, state resident: full-time $2,544; part-time $159 per credit hour. Tuition, nonresident: full-time $10,176; part-time $636 per credit hour. Required fees: $315 per term. *Financial support:* In 2007–08, 6 students received support, including 2 research assistantships with full tuition reimbursements available (averaging $6,000 per year); career-related internships or fieldwork, Federal Work-Study, scholarships/grants, and unspecified assistantships also available. Support available to part-time students. Financial award application deadline: 5/1; financial award applicants required to submit FAFSA. *Faculty research:* Usability, user-centered design, instructional design, information architecture, information design. *Unit head:* Dr. Mark Nunes, Chair, 678-915-7202, Fax: 678-915-7425, E-mail: mnunes@spsu.edu. *Application contact:* Virginia A. Head, Director of Admissions, 678-915-4188, Fax: 678-915-7292, E-mail: vhead@spsu.edu.

Stevens Institute of Technology, Graduate School, Charles V. Schaefer Jr. School of Engineering, Department of Computer Science, Hoboken, NJ 07030. Offers computer graphics (Certificate); computer science (MS, PhD); computer systems (Certificate); database management systems (Certificate); distributed systems (Certificate); elements of computer science (Certificate); enterprise computing (Certificate); enterprise security and information assurance (Certificate); health informatics (Certificate); multimedia experience and management (Certificate); networks and systems administration (Certificate); security and privacy (Certificate); service oriented computing (Certificate); software design (Certificate); theoretical computer science (Certificate). Part-time and evening/weekend programs available. Terminal master's awarded for partial completion of doctoral program. *Degree requirements:* For master's, thesis optional; for doctorate, variable foreign language requirement, comprehensive exam, thesis/dissertation. *Entrance requirements:* For master's and doctorate, GRE, minimum GPA of 3.0. Additional exam requirements/recommendations for international students: Required—TOEFL. Electronic applications accepted. *Faculty research:* Semantics, reliability theory, programming language, cyber security.

Syracuse University, Graduate School, S. I. Newhouse School of Public Communications, Department of Visual and Interactive Communications, Program in New Media, Syracuse, NY 13244. Offers MS. *Students:* 14 full-time (10 women), 2 part-time; includes 1 African American, 1 Hispanic American, 4 international. 23 applicants, 83% accepted, 13 enrolled. In 2007, 3 degrees awarded. *Degree requirements:* For master's, capstone course. *Entrance requirements:* For master's, GRE General Test. Additional exam requirements/recommendations for international students: Required—TOEFL (minimum score 600 paper-based; 250 computer-based). *Application deadline:* For fall admission, 2/1 for domestic and international students. Application fee: $75. Electronic applications accepted. *Expenses:* Tuition: Full-time $18,216; part-time $1,012 per credit. Required fees: $980. Tuition and fees vary according to program. *Unit head:* Stephen M. Masiclat, Director, 315-443-2304, Fax: 315-443-3946, E-mail: pcgrad@syr.edu. *Application contact:* Graduate Records Office, 315-443-4039, Fax: 315-443-1834, E-mail: pcgrad@syr.edu.

Towson University, College of Graduate Studies and Research, Program in Applied Information Technology, Towson, MD 21252-0001. Offers applied information technology (D Sc); database management (Certificate); information security and assurance (Certificate); information systems management (Certificate); Internet application development (Certificate); networking technologies (Certificate); software engineering (Certificate). *Students:* 30 full-time (12 women), 184 part-time (69 women); includes 65 minority (49 African Americans, 2 American Indian/Alaska Native, 10 Asian Americans or Pacific Islanders, 4 Hispanic Americans), 27 international. Average age 34. 42 applicants, 98% accepted, 25 enrolled. In 2007, 1 doctorate, 70 other advanced degrees awarded. *Entrance requirements:* For doctorate, minimum GPA 3.0, letter of intent, resumè, 2 letters of recommendation, personal assessment forms, official transcripts. Additional exam requirements/recommendations for international students: Required—TOEFL (minimum score 550 paper-based). *Application deadline:* For fall admission, 4/15 for international students; for spring admission, 10/1 for international students. Applications are processed on a rolling basis. Application fee: $50. Electronic applications accepted. *Expenses:* Tuition, state resident: part-time $286 per credit. Tuition, nonresident: part-time $600 per credit. Required fees: $75 per credit. *Financial support:* Application deadline: 4/1. *Unit head:* Dr. Ramesh Karne, Graduate Program Director, 410-704-3955, Fax: 410-704-3868, E-mail: rkarne@towson.edu. *Application contact:* Lisa Loewe, The Graduate School, 410-704-4309, E-mail: mloewe@towson.edu.

Towson University, College of Graduate Studies and Research, Program in Interactive Media Design, Towson, MD 21252-0001. Offers Certificate. Postbaccalaureate distance learning degree programs offered (no on-campus study). *Faculty:* 1 (woman) full-time. *Students:* Average age 43. 3 applicants, 100% accepted, 3 enrolled. *Entrance requirements:* For degree, minimum GPA of 3.0, resumé, letter of intent, BA in art education or coursework, professional experience in graphic design or art education. Additional exam requirements/recommendations for international students: Required—TOEFL (minimum score 550 paper-based). *Expenses:* Tuition, state resident: part-time $286 per credit. Tuition, nonresident: part-time $600 per credit. Required fees: $75 per credit. *Unit head:* Bridget Z. Sullivan, Director, 410-704-2802, E-mail: bsullivan@towson.edu.

Towson University, College of Graduate Studies and Research, Program in Internet Application Development, Towson, MD 21252-0001. Offers Certificate. Part-time and evening/weekend programs available. *Students:* Average age 30. In 2007, 4 degrees awarded. Application fee: $50. Electronic applications accepted. *Expenses:* Tuition, state resident: part-time $286 per credit. Tuition, nonresident: part-time $600 per credit. Required fees: $75 per credit. *Financial support:* Application deadline: 4/1. *Unit head:* Mike O'Leary, Graduate Program Director, 410-704-4143, E-mail: moleary@towson.edu. *Application contact:* Lisa Loewe, The Graduate School, 410-704-4309, E-mail: mloewe@towson.edu.

University of Central Florida, College of Arts and Humanities, Division of Film and Digital Media, Orlando, FL 32816. Offers entrepreneurial digital cinema (MFA); interactive entertainment (MS); visual language and interactive media (MFA). *Faculty:* 28 full-time (11 women), 8 part-time/adjunct (2 women). *Expenses:* Tuition, state resident: full-time $6,484. Tuition, nonresident: full-time $23,938. Tuition and fees vary according to program. *Financial support:* Fellowships, research assistantships, teaching assistantships available. *Unit head:* Dr. David Vickers, Interim Head, 407-823-1736, E-mail: dvickers@mail.ucf.edu.

University of Florida, Graduate School, College of Fine Arts, School of Art and Art History, Gainesville, FL 32611. Offers art (MFA), including ceramics, creative photography, drawing, electronic intermedia, graphic design, painting, printmaking, sculpture; art education (MA); art history (MA, PhD); digital arts and sciences (MA); museology (museum studies) (MA). *Accreditation:* NASAD. *Faculty:* 29 full-time (14 women), 2 part-time/adjunct (1 woman). *Students:* 82 (48 women); includes 4 minority (2 Asian Americans or Pacific Islanders, 2 Hispanic Americans) 4 international. In 2007, 20 degrees awarded. *Degree requirements:* For master's, variable foreign language requirement, project or thesis (MFA). *Entrance requirements:* For master's, portfolio (MFA), writing sample (MA), GRE General Test or minimum GPA of 3.0. Additional exam requirements/recommendations for international students: Required—TOEFL (minimum score 550 paper-based; 213 computer-based). *Application deadline:* For fall admission, 1/15 priority date for domestic students. Applications are processed on a rolling basis. Application fee: $30. Electronic applications accepted. *Expenses:* Tuition, state resident: full-time $7,478. Tuition, nonresident: full-time $22,603. *Financial support:* In 2007–08, 3 research assistantships with tuition reimbursements (averaging $9,515 per year), 67 teaching assistantships with tuition reimbursements (averaging $9,839 per year) were awarded; fellowships, Federal Work-Study, institutionally sponsored loans, and unspecified assistantships also available. Financial award applicants required to submit FAFSA. *Faculty research:* Studio production, art historical studies of style context. *Unit head:* Glenn Willumson, Program Director, 352-392-0201 Ext. 234. *Application contact:* Prof. Richard Heipp, Coordinator, 352-392-0201 Ext. 239, Fax: 352-392-8453, E-mail: heipp@ufl.edu.

University of Georgia, Graduate School, Terry College of Business, Program in Internet Technology, Athens, GA 30602. Offers MIT. *Students:* 51 applicants, 61% accepted, 23 enrolled. In 2007, 26 degrees awarded. *Application deadline:* For fall admission, 7/1 priority date for domestic students; for spring admission, 11/15 for domestic students. Application fee: $50.

University of Miami, Graduate School, College of Arts and Sciences, Department of Art and Art History, Coral Gables, FL 33124. Offers art history (MA); ceramics/glass (MFA); graphic design/multimedia (MFA); painting (MFA); photography/digital imaging (MFA); printmaking (MFA); sculpture (MFA). Part-time programs available. *Faculty:* 14 full-time (6 women). *Students:* 23 full-time (15 women), 5 part-time (3 women); includes 5 minority (2 African Americans, 3 Hispanic Americans). Average age 29. 55 applicants, 18% accepted, 8 enrolled. In 2007, 8 degrees awarded. *Degree requirements:* For master's, variable foreign language requirement, thesis, exhibit (MFA), comprehensive exam (MA). *Entrance requirements:* For master's, GRE General Test (MA), research paper (MA), slide portfolio (MFA), artist statement (MFA). Additional exam requirements/recommendations for international students: Required—TOEFL. *Application deadline:* For fall admission, 2/15 for domestic students, 1/15 for international students; for winter admission, 9/15 for domestic students. Application fee: $50. Electronic applications accepted. *Financial support:* In 2007–08, 25 students received support, including 17 teaching assistantships with full tuition reimbursements available (averaging $10,000 per year); Federal Work-Study, institutionally sponsored loans, scholarships/grants, and tuition waivers (full) also available. Financial award application deadline: 3/1; financial award applicants required to submit FAFSA. *Faculty research:* Installation art, public art. *Unit head:* Prof. Lise Drost, Chair, 305-284-2542, Fax: 305-284-2115, E-mail: l.drost@miami.edu. *Application contact:* Prof. Brian Curtis, Graduate Secretary, 305-284-2542, Fax: 305-284-2115, E-mail: art-arh@miami.edu.

University of San Francisco, College of Arts and Sciences, Department of Computer Science, Program in Internet Engineering, San Francisco, CA 94117-1080. Offers MS. *Expenses:* Tuition: Part-time $1,005 per unit. Tuition and fees vary according to degree level, campus/location and program. *Unit head:* Terence Parr, Graduate Director, 415-422-6530, Fax: 415-422-5800.

University of Southern California, Graduate School, Annenberg School for Communication, School of Journalism, Program in Online Journalism, Los Angeles, CA 90089. Offers MA. Part-time programs available. *Students:* 8 full-time (5 women); includes 2 minority (1 Asian American or Pacific Islander, 1 Hispanic American). 19 applicants, 68% accepted, 8 enrolled. In 2007, 1 degree awarded. *Degree requirements:* For master's, comprehensive exam, thesis. *Entrance requirements:* For master's, GRE General Test, resumé, writing samples, letters of recommendation, statement of purpose. Additional exam requirements/recommendations for international students: Required—TOEFL (minimum score 280 computer-based; 114 iBT). *Application deadline:* For fall admission, 1/15 for domestic and international students. Application fee: $85. Electronic applications accepted. *Financial support:* Fellowships with full tuition reimbursements available. Financial award applicants required to submit FAFSA. *Application contact:* Allyson Hill, Director of Admissions, 213-821-0770, E-mail: ascadm@usc.edu.

See Close-Up on page 945.

University of Southern California, Graduate School, School of Cinematic Arts, Division of Interactive Media, Los Angeles, CA 90089. Offers interactive media (MFA). *Faculty:* 11 full-time (3 women), 10 part-time/adjunct (1 woman). *Students:* 30 full-time (7 women), 2 part-time (1 woman); includes 10 minority (2 African Americans, 5 Asian Americans or Pacific Islanders, 3 Hispanic Americans), 5 international. 30 applicants, 53% accepted. In 2007, 11 degrees awarded. *Degree requirements:* For master's, thesis. *Entrance requirements:* For master's, GRE. *Application deadline:* For fall admission, 12/1 priority date for domestic students. *Financial support:* In 2007–08, 19 students received support, including fellowships with tuition reimbursements available (averaging $20,000 per year), research assistantships with tuition reimbursements available (averaging $19,000 per year), teaching assistantships with tuition reimbursements available (averaging $19,000 per year); career-related internships or fieldwork, Federal Work-Study, and scholarships/grants also available. *Faculty research:* Mobile media, game design innovation, immersive media. *Unit head:* Dr. Scott Fisher, Head, 213-821-2515, E-mail: uscinteractive@cinema.usc.edu.

University of Southern California, Graduate School, School of Engineering, Department of Computer Science, Los Angeles, CA 90089. Offers computer networks (MS); computer science (MS, PhD); multimedia and creative technologies (MS); robotics and automation (MS); software engineering (MS). Part-time programs available. Postbaccalaureate distance learning degree programs offered. *Students:* 704 full-time (153 women), 335 part-time (61 women); includes 108 minority (6 African Americans, 94 Asian Americans or Pacific Islanders, 8 Hispanic Americans), 780 international. 1,817 applicants, 47% accepted. In 2007, 466 master's, 49 doctorates awarded. Terminal master's awarded for partial completion of doctoral program. *Degree requirements:* For doctorate, thesis/dissertation. *Entrance requirements:* For master's and doctorate, GRE General Test. *Application deadline:* For fall admission, 12/1 priority date for domestic students. Applications are processed on a rolling basis. Application fee: $85. *Financial support:* Application deadline: 2/15; *Faculty research:* Neural computation, molecular composition, multi-media and virtual reality, databases. *Unit head:* Dr. Gerard Medioni, Chair, 213-740-4494, Fax: 213-740-7285, E-mail: csdept@pollux.usc.edu.

University of Southern California, Graduate School, School of Engineering, Department of Electrical Engineering and Department of Computer Science, Program in Multimedia and Creative Technologies, Los Angeles, CA 90089. Offers MS. Part-time programs available. Postbaccalaureate distance learning degree programs offered. *Students:* 8 full-time (1 woman), 12 part-time (1 woman); includes 7 minority (1 African American, 5 Asian Americans or Pacific Islanders, 1 Hispanic American), 11 international. 31 applicants, 84% accepted. In 2007, 7 degrees awarded. Terminal master's awarded for partial completion of doctoral program. *Degree requirements:* For master's, thesis optional. *Entrance requirements:* For master's, GRE General Test. *Application deadline:* For fall admission, 5/1 for domestic students; for spring admission, 10/1 for domestic students. Applications are processed on a rolling basis. Application fee: $85. *Financial support:* Application deadline: 2/15. *Unit head:* Ramesh Govindan, Head, 213-740-2311.

Virginia Commonwealth University, Graduate School, School of the Arts, Department of Graphic Design, Richmond, VA 23284-9005. Offers design/visual communications (MFA); interior environment (MFA); photography and film (MFA). *Accreditation:* NASAD. *Faculty:* 15 full-time (3 women). *Students:* 42 full-time (31 women), 6 part-time (3 women); includes 6 minority (2 African Americans, 1 Asian American or Pacific Islander, 3 Hispanic Americans), 7 international. 80 applicants, 31% accepted, 20 enrolled. In 2007, 17 degrees awarded. *Degree requirements:* For master's, thesis, exhibition. *Entrance requirements:* For master's, portfolio. *Application deadline:* For fall admission, 3/1 for domestic students. Application fee: $50. *Expenses:* Tuition, state resident: full-time $7,224; part-time $401 per credit. Tuition, nonresident: full-time $16,072; part-time $891 per credit. Required fees: $1,679; $63 per credit. Tuition and fees vary according to campus/location. *Financial support:* Fellowships, teaching assistantships, career-related internships or fieldwork, Federal Work-Study, institutionally sponsored loans, and tuition waivers (full and partial) available. Support available to part-time students. Financial award application deadline: 3/15. *Faculty research:* Film, photography, interior environments, visual communication. *Unit head:* John DeMao, Chair, 804-828-7329, E-mail: jdemao@vcu.edu.

See Close-Up on page 275.

Western Illinois University, School of Graduate Studies, College of Education and Human Services, Department of Instructional Design and Technology, Macomb, IL 61455-1390. Offers

Internet and Interactive Multimedia

Western Illinois University (continued)
distance learning (Certificate); graphic applications (Certificate); instructional design and technology (MS); multimedia (Certificate); technology integration in education (Certificate); training development (Certificate). Part-time programs available. Postbaccalaureate distance learning degree programs offered (no on-campus study). *Students:* 19 full-time (5 women), 71 part-time (52 women); includes 8 minority (5 African Americans, 1 Asian American or Pacific Islander, 2 Hispanic Americans), 5 international. Average age 38. 20 applicants, 70% accepted. In 2007, 22 master's, 2 other advanced degrees awarded. *Degree requirements:* For master's, thesis or alternative. *Entrance requirements:* For master's, minimum GPA of 2.75. Additional exam requirements/recommendations for international students: Required—TOEFL (minimum score 550 paper-based; 213 computer-based; 80 iBT). *Application deadline:* Applications are processed on a rolling basis. Application fee: $30. Electronic applications accepted. *Expenses:* Tuition, state resident: part-time $217 per credit hour. Tuition, nonresident: part-time $433 per credit hour. Required fees: $54 per credit hour. *Financial support:* In 2007–08, 9 students received support, including 7 research assistantships with full tuition reimbursements available (averaging $6,800 per year), 2 teaching assistantships with full tuition reimbursements available (averaging $7,840 per year). Financial award applicants required to submit FAFSA. *Unit head:* Dr. Hoyet Hemphill, Chairperson, 309-298-1952. *Application contact:* Dr. Barbara Baily, Director of Graduate Studies/Associate Provost, 309-298-1806, Fax: 309-298-2345, E-mail: grad-office@wiu.edu.

Wilmington University, Division of Information Technology and Advanced Communications, New Castle, DE 19720-6491. Offers corporate training (MS); information assurance (MS); information systems technologies (MS); Internet web design (MS); management information systems (MS). Part-time and evening/weekend programs available. *Faculty:* 1 full-time (0 women). *Students:* 17 full-time (7 women), 55 part-time (19 women); includes 6 minority (2 African Americans, 2 Asian Americans or Pacific Islanders, 2 Hispanic Americans). Average age 36. 37 applicants, 100% accepted, 21 enrolled. In 2007, 35 degrees awarded. *Entrance requirements:* Additional exam requirements/recommendations for international students: Required—TOEFL (minimum score 500 paper-based; 173 computer-based). *Application deadline:* Applications are processed on a rolling basis. Application fee: $25. Electronic applications accepted. *Expenses:* Tuition: Full-time $6,246; part-time $1,041 per course. Tuition and fees vary according to degree level and campus/location. *Unit head:* Dr. Jack Nold, Head, 302-328-9401 Ext. 254.

Journalism

American University, School of Communication, Program in Journalism and Public Affairs, Washington, DC 20016-8001. Offers broadcast journalism (MA), including economic journalism, international journalism, public policy journalism; print journalism (MA), including economic journalism, international journalism, public policy journalism. *Accreditation:* ACEJMC. Part-time and evening/weekend programs available. *Faculty:* 13 full-time (5 women), 4 part-time/adjunct (all women). *Students:* 36 full-time (31 women); includes 10 minority (7 African Americans, 3 Asian Americans or Pacific Islanders), 10 international. 190 applicants, 63% accepted, 35 enrolled. In 2007, 40 degrees awarded. *Degree requirements:* For master's, comprehensive exam, thesis or alternative. *Entrance requirements:* For master's, GRE General Test. Additional exam requirements/recommendations for international students: Required—TOEFL (minimum score 600 paper-based; 250 computer-based). *Application deadline:* For fall admission, 2/1 priority date for domestic students, 4/1 priority date for international students. Applications are processed on a rolling basis. Application fee: $50. Electronic applications accepted. *Expenses:* Tuition: Full-time $19,998; part-time $1,111 per credit hour. Required fees: $380. Tuition and fees vary according to program. *Financial support:* In 2007–08, 3 fellowships with partial tuition reimbursements (averaging $27,000 per year), 14 research assistantships with tuition reimbursements (averaging $7,000 per year), 3 teaching assistantships with tuition reimbursements (averaging $7,000 per year) were awarded; career-related internships or fieldwork, Federal Work-Study, institutionally sponsored loans, scholarships/grants, tuition waivers (partial), and unspecified assistantships also available. Financial award application deadline: 2/1. *Faculty research:* Government and media effects of journalistic practices and policies, race and gender and the media, investigative reporting, computer assisted reporting. *Unit head:* Wendell Cochran, Division Director, 202-885-2072. *Application contact:* Sharmeen Ahsan-Bracciale, Graduate Admissions Office, 202-885-2040, Fax: 202-885-2019, E-mail: sharmeen@american.edu.

See Close-Up on page 881.

American University, School of Communication, Weekend Programs in Communication, Washington, DC 20016-8001. Offers interactive journalism (MA); news media studies (MA); producing for film and video (MA); public communication (MA). *Accreditation:* ACEJMC. Part-time and evening/weekend programs available. *Faculty:* 5 part-time/adjunct (2 women). *Students:* 137 applicants, 61% accepted, 61 enrolled. In 2007, 15 degrees awarded. *Degree requirements:* For master's, comprehensive exam, thesis or alternative. *Entrance requirements:* Additional exam requirements/recommendations for international students: Required—TOEFL (minimum score 600 paper-based; 250 computer-based). *Application deadline:* For fall admission, 8/1 for domestic students. Applications are processed on a rolling basis. Application fee: $50. Electronic applications accepted. *Expenses:* Tuition: Full-time $19,998; part-time $1,111 per credit hour. Required fees: $380. Tuition and fees vary according to program. *Financial support:* In 2007–08, 3 fellowships (averaging $3,500 per year) were awarded; institutionally sponsored loans also available. *Unit head:* Wendell Cochran, Journalism Weekend Program Director, 202-885-2075, E-mail: cochran@american.edu. *Application contact:* Sharmeen Ahsan-Bracciale, Graduate Admissions Office, 202-885-2040, Fax: 202-885-2019, E-mail: sharmeen@american.edu.

See Close-Up on page 881.

The American University in Cairo, Graduate Studies and Research, School of Business, Economics and Communication, Department of Journalism and Communication, Cairo, Egypt. Offers journalism/mass communication (MA); television journalism (MA, Diploma). Part-time programs available. *Degree requirements:* For master's, thesis (for some programs). *Entrance requirements:* For master's, English entrance exam, GMAT. Electronic applications accepted. *Faculty research:* Mass media and national development/censorship, intercultural photo communication, comparative journalism/television.

Angelo State University, College of Graduate Studies, College of Liberal and Fine Arts, Department of Communications, Drama, and Journalism, San Angelo, TX 76909. Offers communication systems management (MA). Part-time and evening/weekend programs available. *Faculty:* 2 full-time (0 women). *Students:* Average age 26. 7 applicants, 43% accepted, 3 enrolled. In 2007, 9 degrees awarded. *Degree requirements:* For master's, comprehensive exam, thesis optional. *Entrance requirements:* For master's, GRE General Test. Additional exam requirements/recommendations for international students: Required—TOEFL or IELTS. *Application deadline:* For fall admission, 7/15 priority date for domestic students, 6/10 for international students; for spring admission, 12/8 for domestic students, 11/1 for international students. Applications are processed on a rolling basis. Application fee: $40 ($50 for international students). Electronic applications accepted. *Financial support:* In 2007–08, 5 students received support, including 3 teaching assistantships (averaging $10,251 per year); career-related internships or fieldwork, Federal Work-Study, scholarships/grants, and unspecified assistantships also available. Support available to part-time students. Financial award application deadline: 3/1; financial award applicants required to submit FAFSA. *Unit head:* Dr. June H. Smith, Department Head, 325-942-2031 Ext. 228, E-mail: june.smith@angelo.edu. *Application contact:* Dr. Jeff Boone, Graduate Advisor, 325-942-2343 Ext. 244, E-mail: jeff.boone@angelo.edu.

Arizona State University, Graduate College, Walter Cronkite School of Journalism and Mass Communication, Tempe, AZ 85287-1305. Offers MMC. *Accreditation:* ACEJMC. *Degree requirements:* For master's, 36 credit hours (includes class work and a professional immersion experience). *Entrance requirements:* For master's, GRE, minimum GPA of 3.0 in the last 60 semester hours or 90 quarter hours of undergraduate coursework; official transcripts; resumé and/or biographical sketch; 350- to 500-word personal statement; 3 letters of recommendation. Additional exam requirements/recommendations for international students: Required—TOEFL. Electronic applications accepted.

See Close-Up on page 883.

Arkansas State University, Graduate School, College of Communications, Department of Journalism, Jonesboro, State University, AR 72467. Offers MSMC. Part-time programs available. *Faculty:* 4 full-time (2 women), 1 part-time/adjunct (0 women). *Students:* 3 full-time (1 woman), 7 part-time (5 women); includes 4 minority (all African Americans), 2 international. Average age 26. 9 applicants, 67% accepted, 6 enrolled. In 2007, 4 degrees awarded. *Degree requirements:* For master's, comprehensive exam, thesis or alternative. *Entrance requirements:* For master's, GRE General Test, appropriate bachelor's degree, letters of reference, recommendations, official transcript. Additional exam requirements/recommendations for international students: Required—TOEFL (minimum score 213 computer-based). *Application deadline:* Applications are processed on a rolling basis. Application fee: $30 ($40 for international students). Electronic applications accepted. *Expenses:* Tuition, state resident: full-time $3,528; part-time $196 per hour. Tuition, nonresident: full-time $8,928; part-time $496 per hour. Required fees: $842; $44 per hour. $25 per term. Tuition and fees vary according to course load and program. *Financial support:* Career-related internships or fieldwork, scholarships/grants, and unspecified assistantships available. Financial award application deadline: 7/1; financial award applicants required to submit FAFSA. *Faculty research:* Campus press issues, communication and culture, digital pre-press workflow, editing specialized publications, media ethics in decision making. *Unit head:* Dr. Osabuohien Amienyi, Chair, 870-972-3070, Fax: 870-972-2997, E-mail: osami@astate.edu.

Arkansas Tech University, Graduate School, School of Liberal and Fine Arts, Russellville, AR 72801. Offers communication (MLA); English (M Ed, MA); fine arts (MLA); history (MA); multi-media journalism (MA); social science (MLA); social studies (M Ed); Spanish (MA, MLA); teaching English as a second language (MA, MLA). Part-time programs available. *Students:* 54 full-time (43 women), 79 part-time (54 women); includes 11 minority (3 African Americans, 1 American Indian/Alaska Native, 1 Asian American or Pacific Islander, 6 Hispanic Americans), 29 international. Average age 33. In 2007, 71 degrees awarded. *Degree requirements:* For master's, project. *Entrance requirements:* For master's, GRE General Test or MAT. Additional exam requirements/recommendations for international students: Required—TOEFL (minimum score 500 paper-based; 173 computer-based; 61 iBT). *Application deadline:* For fall admission, 3/1 priority date for domestic students, 5/1 priority date for international students; for winter admission, 10/1 priority date for international students; for spring admission, 10/1 priority date for domestic and international students. Applications are processed on a rolling basis. Application fee: $0 ($30 for international students). Electronic applications accepted. *Expenses:* Tuition, state resident: full-time $3,150; part-time $175 per hour. Tuition, nonresident: full-time $6,300; part-time $350 per hour. Required fees: $384; $8 per hour. $120 per term. Tuition and fees vary according to course load. *Financial support:* In 2007–08, teaching assistantships with full tuition reimbursements (averaging $4,000 per year); career-related internships or fieldwork, Federal Work-Study, scholarships/grants, health care benefits, and unspecified assistantships also available. Support available to part-time students. Financial award application deadline: 4/15; financial award applicants required to submit FAFSA. *Unit head:* Dr. Georgena Duncan, Dean, 479-968-0266, Fax: 479-968-0275, E-mail: georgena.duncan@atu.edu. *Application contact:* Dr. Eldon G. Clary, Dean of Graduate School, 479-968-0398, Fax: 479-964-0542, E-mail: graduate.school@atu.edu.

Ball State University, Graduate School, College of Communication, Information, and Media, Department of Journalism, Muncie, IN 47306-1099. Offers journalism (MA); public relations (MA). *Faculty:* 14. *Students:* 25 full-time (18 women), 40 part-time (31 women); includes 7 minority (4 African Americans, 1 American Indian/Alaska Native, 1 Asian American or Pacific Islander, 1 Hispanic American), 12 international. Average age 26. 61 applicants, 72% accepted, 28 enrolled. In 2007, 35 degrees awarded. *Entrance requirements:* For master's, resumé. Application fee: $25 ($35 for international students). *Expenses:* Tuition, state resident: full-time $6,864. Tuition, nonresident: full-time $17,932. Required fees: $1,866. *Financial support:* In 2007–08, 16 teaching assistantships with full tuition reimbursements (averaging $7,546 per year) were awarded; research assistantships with full tuition reimbursements, career-related internships or fieldwork also available. Financial award application deadline: 3/1. *Faculty research:* Image studies, readership surveys, audience perception studies. *Unit head:* Marilyn Weaver, Chairperson, 765-285-8200, Fax: 765-285-7997, E-mail: mweaver@bsu.edu. *Application contact:* Dan Waechter, Information Contact, 765-285-8200, Fax: 765-285-7997, E-mail: dwaechter@bsu.edu.

Baylor University, Graduate School, College of Arts and Sciences, Department of Journalism, Waco, TX 76798. Offers international journalism (MIJ); journalism (MA). *Students:* 11 full-time (all women), 10 part-time (8 women); includes 3 minority (2 African Americans, 1 Hispanic American), 2 international. Average age 24. In 2007, 4 degrees awarded. *Degree requirements:* For master's, proficiency in 1 foreign language (MIJ). *Entrance requirements:* For master's, GRE General Test. *Application deadline:* Applications are processed on a rolling basis. Application fee: $25. *Financial support:* Research assistantships, teaching assistantships, career-related internships or fieldwork, Federal Work-Study, and institutionally sponsored loans available. Support available to part-time students. *Faculty research:* International politics, mass media and society, journalism history, editing practices. *Unit head:* Dr. Lianne Fridriksson, Graduate Program Director, 254-710-6346, Fax: 254-710-3363, E-mail: lianne_fridriksson@baylor.edu. *Application contact:* Suzanne Keener, Administrative Assistant, 254-710-3588, Fax: 254-710-3870.

Bob Jones University, Graduate Programs, Greenville, SC 29614. Offers accountancy (MS); Bible (MA); Bible translation (MA); Biblical studies (Certificate); broadcast management (MS); business administration (MBA); church history (MA, PhD); church ministries (MA); church music (MM); cinema and video production (MA); counseling (MS); curriculum and instruction (Ed D); divinity (M Div); dramatic production (MA); educational leadership (MS, Ed D, Ed S); elementary education (M Ed, MAT); English (M Ed, MA, MAT); fine arts (MA); graphic design (MA); history (M Ed, MA); illustration (MA); interpretative speech (MA); mathematics (M Ed, MAT); medical missions (Certificate); ministry (MM, D Min); multi-categorical special education (M Ed, MAT); music (M Ed); New Testament interpretation (PhD); Old Testament interpretation (PhD); orchestral instrument performance (MM); organ performance (MM); pastoral studies (MA); personnel services (MS, Ed S); piano pedagogy (MM); piano performance (MM); platform arts (MA); radio and television broadcasting (MS); rhetoric and public address (MA); secondary education (M Ed); studio art (MA); teaching Bible (MA); theology (MA, PhD); voice performance (MM); youth ministries (MA); M Div/MM.

Boston University, College of Communication, Department of Journalism, Boston, MA 02215. Offers broadcast journalism (MS); business and economics journalism (MS); photo journalism (MS); print journalism (MS); science journalism (MS). *Faculty:* 23 full-time, 26 part-time/adjunct. *Students:* 122 full-time (90 women), 6 part-time (5 women); includes 18 minority (9 African Americans, 8 Asian Americans or Pacific Islanders, 1 Hispanic American), 23 international. Average age 26. In 2007, 83 degrees awarded. *Degree requirements:* For master's, thesis. *Entrance requirements:* For master's, GRE General Test, sample of written work. Additional exam requirements/recommendations for international students: Required—TOEFL. *Application deadline:* For fall admission, 2/1 for domestic students. Electronic applications accepted. *Expenses:* Tuition: Full-time $34,930; part-time $1,092 per credit. Tuition and fees vary according to class time, course level and program. *Financial support:* Teaching assistantships with partial tuition reimbursements, career-related internships or fieldwork, Federal Work-Study, institutionally sponsored loans, scholarships/grants, and unspecified assistantships available. Support available to part-time students. Financial award application deadline: 2/1; financial award applicants required to submit FAFSA. *Unit head:* Lou Ureneck, Chairman, 617-353-3484, Fax: 617-353-1086, E-mail: lureneck@bu.edu. *Application contact:* William A. Taylor, Assistant Director, Graduate Services and Financial Aid, 617-353-3481, Fax: 617-358-0399, E-mail: comgrad@bu.edu.

See Close-Up on page 885.

California State University, Fresno, Division of Graduate Studies, College of Arts and Humanities, Department of Mass Communication and Journalism, Fresno, CA 93740-8027. Offers MA. Part-time and evening/weekend programs available. *Faculty:* 8 full-time (4 women). *Students:* 10; includes 4 minority (2 Asian Americans or Pacific Islanders, 2 Hispanic Americans). Average age 28. 7 applicants. In 2007, 6 degrees awarded. *Degree requirements:* For master's, thesis. *Entrance requirements:* For master's, GRE General Test, minimum GPA of 3.0. Additional exam requirements/recommendations for international students: Required—TOEFL. *Application deadline:* For fall admission, 5/1 for domestic and international students; for spring admission, 10/1 for domestic and international students. Applications are processed on a rolling basis. Application fee: $55. Electronic applications accepted. *Financial support:* In 2007–08, 1 teaching assistantship was awarded; career-related internships or fieldwork, Federal Work-Study, scholarships/grants, and unspecified assistantships also available. Support available to part-time students. Financial award application deadline: 3/1; financial award applicants required to submit FAFSA. *Unit head:* Prof. Donald Priest, Chair, 559-278-2087, Fax: 559-278-4995, E-mail: donald_priest@csufresno.edu. *Application contact:* Dr. Tamyra Pierce, Graduate Program Coordinator, 559-278-2087, Fax: 559-278-4995, E-mail: tpierce@csufresno.edu.

California State University, Fullerton, Graduate Studies, College of Communications, Department of Communications, Fullerton, CA 92834-9480. Offers communications—advertising (MA); communications—entertainment and tourism (MA); communications—journalism (MA); communications—public relations (MA). Part-time programs available. *Students:* 25 full-time (22 women), 39 part-time (24 women); includes 19 minority (1 African American, 6 Asian Americans or Pacific Islanders, 12 Hispanic Americans), 11 international. Average age 29. 140 applicants, 41% accepted, 28 enrolled. In 2007, 43 degrees awarded. *Degree requirements:* For master's, project or thesis. *Entrance requirements:* For master's, GRE General Test. Application fee: $55. *Financial support:* Teaching assistantships, career-related internships or fieldwork, Federal Work-Study, institutionally sponsored loans, and scholarships/grants available. Support available to part-time students. Financial award application deadline: 3/1. *Unit head:* Dr. Tony Fellow, Chair, 714-278-3517. *Application contact:* Coordinator, 714-278-3832.

California State University, Northridge, Graduate Studies, College of Arts, Media, and Communication, Department of Journalism, Northridge, CA 91330. Offers mass communication (MA). Part-time and evening/weekend programs available. *Faculty:* 9 full-time (5 women), 19 part-time/adjunct (6 women). *Students:* 5 full-time (2 women), 29 part-time (23 women); includes 11 minority (3 African Americans, 3 Asian Americans or Pacific Islanders, 5 Hispanic Americans). Average age 32. 46 applicants, 54% accepted, 11 enrolled. In 2007, 13 degrees awarded. *Degree requirements:* For master's, thesis. *Entrance requirements:* For master's, GRE General Test. Additional exam requirements/recommendations for international students: Required—TOEFL. *Application deadline:* For fall admission, 11/30 for domestic students. Application fee: $55. *Financial support:* Career-related internships or fieldwork and Federal Work-Study available. Financial award application deadline: 3/1. *Unit head:* Dr. Kent Kirkton, Chair, 818-677-3135, E-mail: kent.kirkton@csun.edu.

Carleton University, Faculty of Graduate Studies, Faculty of Public Affairs and Management, School of Journalism and Communication, Ottawa, ON K1S 5B6, Canada. Offers communication (MA, PhD); journalism (MJ). *Degree requirements:* For master's, thesis optional; for doctorate, comprehensive exam, thesis/dissertation. *Entrance requirements:* For master's, honors degree. Additional exam requirements/recommendations for international students: Required—TOEFL. *Application deadline:* Applications are processed on a rolling basis. Application fee: $77 Canadian dollars. *Financial support:* Fellowships, teaching assistantships available. *Faculty research:* Specialized print reporting, broadcast journalism, journalism studies. *Unit head:* Karim Karim, Director, 613-520-2600 Ext. 7404, Fax: 613-520-6690, E-mail: journalism@carleton.ca. *Application contact:* Freda Choueiri, Graduate Administrator, 613-520-2600 Ext. 7404, Fax: 613-520-6690, E-mail: freda_choueiri@carleton.ca.

Columbia College Chicago, Graduate School, Department of Journalism, Chicago, IL 60605-1996. Offers public affairs journalism (MA). *Students:* 14 full-time (10 women), 23 part-time (20 women); includes 14 minority (11 African Americans, 3 Hispanic Americans). Average age 27. In 2007, 20 degrees awarded. *Degree requirements:* For master's, thesis. *Entrance requirements:* For master's, interview, minimum GPA of 3.0, writing sample. Additional exam requirements/recommendations for international students: Required—TOEFL (minimum score 550 paper-based; 213 computer-based). *Application deadline:* For fall admission, 4/4 for domestic students, 2/14 for international students. Application fee: $50. *Financial support:* Fellowships, career-related internships or fieldwork, Federal Work-Study, and scholarships/grants available. Support available to part-time students. Financial award application deadline: 8/13; financial award applicants required to submit FAFSA. *Unit head:* Nancy Day, Chairperson, 312-344-7089, Fax: 312-344-8059, E-mail: nday@colum.edu. *Application contact:* Keith Cleveland, Acting Dean of the Graduate School, 312-344-7261, Fax: 312-344-8047, E-mail: kcleveland@colum.edu.

Columbia University, Graduate School of Journalism, New York, NY 10027. Offers MS, PhD, JD/MS, MIA/MS, MS/MBA. *Accreditation:* ACEJMC. Part-time programs available. *Degree requirements:* For master's, thesis; for doctorate, thesis/dissertation. *Entrance requirements:* For master's, writing test, 2-3 samples of journalistic work, minimum typing speed of 50 words per minute; for doctorate, GRE. Additional exam requirements/recommendations for international students: Required—TOEFL. Expenses: Contact institution. One-time fee: $75 part-time. Full-time tuition and fees vary according to course level, course load, degree level and program. *Faculty research:* International communication, communication technologies, ethics in journalism, journalism history.

See Close-Up on page 887.

Concordia University, School of Graduate Studies, Faculty of Arts and Science, Department of Journalism, Montréal, QC H3G 1M8, Canada. Offers Diploma. *Degree requirements:* For Diploma, one foreign language. *Entrance requirements:* Additional exam requirements/recommendations for international students: Required—departmental English test or TOEFL.

CUNY Graduate School of Journalism, Graduate Program, New York, NY 10036. Offers MA. *Degree requirements:* For master's, internship, final or capstone project. *Entrance requirements:* For master's, GRE, 3 letters of recommendation, resumé. Additional exam requirements/recommendations for international students: Required—TOEFL (minimum score 260 computer-based; 105 iBT). Electronic applications accepted.

See Close-Up on page 889.

DePaul University, College of Communication, Chicago, IL 60604-2287. Offers journalism (MA); media, culture, and society (MA); organizational and multicultural communication (MA); public relations and advertising (MA). Part-time and evening/weekend programs available. *Faculty:* 21 full-time (10 women), 9 part-time/adjunct (4 women). *Students:* 88 full-time (69 women), 43 part-time (38 women); includes 29 minority (16 African Americans, 5 Asian Americans or Pacific Islanders, 8 Hispanic Americans), 2 international. Average age 29. 242 applicants, 47% accepted, 68 enrolled. In 2007, 64 degrees awarded. *Degree requirements:* For master's, final exam or thesis/project. *Entrance requirements:* For master's, GRE General Test (public relations and advertising), minimum GPA of 3.0, writing sample, essay, letters of recommendation, resumé. Additional exam requirements/recommendations for international students: Required—TOEFL (minimum score 590 paper-based; 245 computer-based; 96 iBT). Application fee: $40. Electronic applications accepted. *Financial support:* In 2007–08, 8 students received support, including 2 teaching assistantships with full tuition reimbursements available (averaging $12,000 per year); fellowships with full tuition reimbursements available, research assistantships, career-related internships or fieldwork, scholarships/grants, and tuition waivers (partial) also available. Support available to part-time students. Financial award applicants required to submit FAFSA. *Faculty research:* Intercultural communication, corporate culture, diversity in the working place, organizational socialization, critical cultural studies. *Unit head:* Dr. Jacqueline Taylor, Dean, 773-325-7216, Fax: 773-325-7584, E-mail: jtaylor@depaul.edu. *Application contact:* Ann Spittle, Director of Graduate Admission, 773-325-8369, Fax: 773-325-2395, E-mail: aspittle@depaul.edu.

Drake University, School of Education, Department of Teaching and Learning, Program in Secondary Education, Des Moines, IA 50311-4516. Offers art (MAT); biology (MAT); business (MAT); chemistry (MAT); English (MAT); general science (MAT); history-American (MAT); history-world (MAT); journalism (MAT); mathematics (MAT); physical science (MAT); physics (MAT); sociology (MAT); speech (MAT); speech communication (MAT); theatre (MAT). Part-time programs available. *Faculty:* 10 full-time (3 women), 28 part-time/adjunct (16 women). *Students:* 13 full-time (7 women), 33 part-time (20 women). 41 applicants, 56% accepted. In 2007, 12 degrees awarded. *Degree requirements:* For master's, comprehensive exam, thesis (for some programs), internships (for some programs). *Entrance requirements:* For master's, GRE General Test, MAT, or Drake Writing Assessment, resumé, 2 letters of recommendation. Additional exam requirements/recommendations for international students: Required—TOEFL (minimum score 550 paper-based; 213 computer-based). *Application deadline:* For fall admission, 7/1 priority date for domestic students, 6/1 priority date for international students; for spring admission, 11/1 priority date for domestic students, 10/1 priority date for international students. Applications are processed on a rolling basis. Application fee: $25. Electronic applications accepted. *Expenses:* Tuition: Full-time $26,030; part-time $370 per credit hour. Required fees: $406; $40 per semester. Tuition and fees vary according to program. *Financial support:* Career-related internships or fieldwork and unspecified assistantships available. Support available to part-time students. *Faculty research:* Counseling and rehabilitation, behavioral supports, inquiry-based science methods, teacher quality enhancement. Total annual research expenditures: $1.5 million. *Application contact:* Ann J. Martin, Graduate Coordinator, 515-271-2034, Fax: 515-271-2831, E-mail: ann.martin@drake.edu.

Drexel University, School of Journalism, Philadelphia, PA 19104-2875. Offers MA. *Entrance requirements:* Additional exam requirements/recommendations for international students: Required—TOEFL.

Emerson College, Graduate Studies, School of Communication, Department of Journalism, Boston, MA 02116-4624. Offers print/multimedia journalism, broadcast journalism, integrated journalism (MA), including broadcast journalism, integrated journalism, print/multimedia journalism. Part-time programs available. *Faculty:* 13 full-time (6 women). *Students:* 62 full-time (33 women), 3 part-time (2 women); includes 6 Asian Americans or Pacific Islanders, 3 Hispanic Americans, 9 international. Average age 25. 117 applicants, 76% accepted, 33 enrolled. In 2007, 34 degrees awarded. *Entrance requirements:* For master's, GRE General Test. Additional exam requirements/recommendations for international students: Required—TOEFL (minimum score 550 paper-based; 213 computer-based; 80 iBT), IELTS (minimum score 7). *Application deadline:* For fall admission, 3/1 priority date for domestic students, 5/1 for international students; for spring admission, 11/1 priority date for domestic students, 11/1 for international students. Applications are processed on a rolling basis. Application fee: $60 ($75 for international students). Electronic applications accepted. *Expenses:* Tuition: Full-time $16,800; part-time $840 per credit. Required fees: $60 per semester. One-time fee: $160. *Financial support:* In 2007–08, 3 fellowships with partial tuition reimbursements (averaging $14,000 per year), 6 research assistantships with partial tuition reimbursements (averaging $10,000 per year) were awarded; career-related internships or fieldwork, Federal Work-Study, institutionally sponsored loans, scholarships/grants, and unspecified assistantships also available. Support available to part-time students. Financial award application deadline: 3/1; financial award applicants required to submit FAFSA. *Faculty research:* Journalism. *Unit head:* Prof. Janet Kolodzy, Acting Chair, 617-824-8805. *Application contact:* 617-824-8610, Fax: 617-824-8614, E-mail: gradapp@emerson.edu.

See Close-Up on page 893.

Florida Agricultural and Mechanical University, Division of Graduate Studies, Research, and Continuing Education, School of Journalism and Graphic Communication, Tallahassee, FL 32307-3200. Offers journalism (MS). *Degree requirements:* For master's, comprehensive exam, thesis (for some programs). *Entrance requirements:* For master's, GRE General Test, minimum GPA of 3.0. Additional exam requirements/recommendations for international students: Required—TOEFL.

Harvard University, Extension School, Cambridge, MA 02138-3722. Offers applied sciences (CAS); biotechnology (ALM); educational technologies (ALM); educational technology (CET); English for graduate and professional studies (DGP); environmental management (ALM, CEM); information technology (ALM); journalism (ALM); liberal arts (ALM); management (ALM, CM); mathematics for teaching (ALM); museum studies (ALM); premedical studies (Diploma); publication and communication (CPC). Part-time and evening/weekend programs available. *Faculty:* 242 part-time/adjunct. *Students:* Average age 35. In 2007, 190 master's, 78 other advanced degrees awarded. *Degree requirements:* For master's, thesis. *Entrance requirements:* For master's, 3 completed graduate courses with grade of B or higher. Additional exam requirements/recommendations for international students: Required—TOEFL (minimum score 600 paper-based; 250 computer-based), TWE (minimum score 5). *Application deadline:* Applications are processed on a rolling basis. Application fee: $75. *Expenses: Contact institution.* Full-time tuition and fees vary according to program and student level. *Financial support:* In 2007–08, 198 students received support. Scholarships/grants available. Support available to part-time students. Financial award application deadline: 8/6; financial award applicants required to submit FAFSA. *Unit head:* Michael Shinagel, Dean, 617-495-1000. *Application contact:* Program Director, 617-495-4024, Fax: 617-495-9176.

Hofstra University, School of Communication, Department of Journalism, Media Studies, and Public Relations, Hempstead, NY 11549. Offers journalism (MA). Part-time and evening/weekend programs available. *Faculty:* 4 full-time (3 women), 1 part-time/adjunct (0 women). *Students:* 9 full-time (5 women), 12 part-time (7 women); includes 5 minority (2 African Americans, 1 Asian American or Pacific Islander, 2 Hispanic Americans), 1 international. Average age 28. 29 applicants, 83% accepted, 13 enrolled. *Degree requirements:* For master's, thesis. *Entrance requirements:* For master's, minimum GPA of 2.75; bachelor's degree. Additional exam requirements/recommendations for international students: Required—TOEFL (minimum score 550 paper-based; 213 computer-based). *Application deadline:* Applications are processed on a rolling basis. Application fee: $60. Electronic applications accepted.

Journalism

Hofstra University (continued)

Expenses: Tuition: Full-time $14,220; part-time $820 per credit. Required fees: $970; $165 per term. Tuition and fees vary according to program. *Financial support:* In 2007–08, 4 students received support; fellowships with tuition reimbursements available, research assistantships with full and partial tuition reimbursements available, Federal Work-Study, institutionally sponsored loans, scholarships/grants, tuition waivers (full and partial), and unspecified assistantships available. Support available to part-time students. Financial award applicants required to submit FAFSA. *Faculty research:* Media ecology, media literacy, environmental and health journalism, citizen journalism, the future of news; cultural issues and social justice refuting. *Unit head:* Dr. Matthew Sobnosky, Director, 516-463-7141, E-mail: sphmjs@hofstra.edu. *Application contact:* Carol Drummer, Dean of Graduate Admissions, 516-463-4876, Fax: 516-463-4664, E-mail: gradstudent@hofstra.edu.

Indiana University Bloomington, School of Journalism, Bloomington, IN 47405-7000. Offers journalism (MA, MAT); mass communication (PhD); MA/JD; MA/MA. PhD offered through the University Graduate School. *Faculty:* 11 full-time (5 women). *Students:* 39 full-time (22 women), 16 part-time (14 women); includes 8 minority (5 African Americans, 2 Asian Americans or Pacific Islanders, 1 Hispanic American), 8 international. Average age 29. 125 applicants, 62% accepted, 33 enrolled. In 2007, 39 master's awarded. Terminal master's awarded for partial completion of doctoral program. *Median time to degree:* Of those who began their doctoral program in fall 1999, 80% received their degree in 8 years or less. *Degree requirements:* For master's, thesis (for some programs); for doctorate, thesis/dissertation. *Entrance requirements:* For master's and doctorate, GRE General Test. Additional exam requirements/recommendations for international students: Required—TOEFL. *Application deadline:* For fall admission, 1/15 priority date for domestic students; for spring admission, 9/1 priority date for domestic students. Applications are processed on a rolling basis. Application fee: $50 ($60 for international students). *Financial support:* Fellowships, research assistantships with full tuition reimbursements, teaching assistantships with partial tuition reimbursements, career-related internships or fieldwork, Federal Work-Study, institutionally sponsored loans, and tuition waivers (full) available. Financial award application deadline: 1/15. *Faculty research:* Political communication, international communication, communication history, communication law, visual communication. Total annual research expenditures: $165,185. *Unit head:* Bradley Hamm, Dean, 812-855-9247. *Application contact:* Amy Reynolds, Associate Dean of Graduate Studies, 812-855-8111.

Iona College, School of Arts and Science, Department of Mass Communication, New Rochelle, NY 10801-1890. Offers journalism (MS); public relations (MA). *Accreditation:* ACEJMC (one or more programs are accredited). Part-time and evening/weekend programs available. *Faculty:* 8 full-time (0 women), 8 part-time/adjunct (4 women). *Students:* 8 full-time (6 women), 33 part-time (24 women); includes 9 minority (3 African Americans, 1 American Indian/Alaska Native, 1 Asian American or Pacific Islander, 4 Hispanic Americans), 2 international. Average age 28. 31 applicants, 39% accepted, 7 enrolled. In 2007, 16 degrees awarded. *Degree requirements:* For master's, comprehensive exam or thesis. *Entrance requirements:* For master's, GRE General Test, minimum GPA of 3.0. Additional exam requirements/recommendations for international students: Required—TOEFL (minimum score 550 paper-based; 213 computer-based). *Application deadline:* Applications are processed on a rolling basis. Application fee: $50. Electronic applications accepted. *Expenses:* Contact institution. *Financial support:* Career-related internships or fieldwork, tuition waivers (partial), and unspecified assistantships available. Support available to part-time students. *Faculty research:* Media ecology, new media, corporate communication, media images, organizational learning in public relations. *Unit head:* Dr. Orly Shachar, Chair, 914-633-2165, E-mail: oshachar@iona.edu. *Application contact:* Veronica Jarek-Prinz, Director of Graduate Admissions, 914-633-2420, Fax: 914-633-2277, E-mail: vjarekprinz@iona.edu.

Iowa State University of Science and Technology, Graduate College, College of Liberal Arts and Sciences, Greenlee School of Journalism and Mass Communication, Ames, IA 50011. Offers MS. *Faculty:* 17 full-time (5 women), 2 part-time/adjunct (0 women). *Students:* 30 full-time (22 women), 7 part-time (6 women); includes 3 minority (1 African American, 2 Hispanic Americans), 18 international. 51 applicants, 69% accepted, 17 enrolled. In 2007, 15 degrees awarded. *Degree requirements:* For master's, thesis or alternative. *Entrance requirements:* For master's, GRE General Test. Additional exam requirements/recommendations for international students: Required—TOEFL (paper-based 570; computer-based 213; iBT 80) or IELTS (6.5). *Application deadline:* For fall admission, 4/1 priority date for domestic and international students; for spring admission, 11/1 priority date for domestic and international students. Applications are processed on a rolling basis. Application fee: $30 ($70 for international students). Electronic applications accepted. *Financial support:* In 2007–08, 12 research assistantships with full and partial tuition reimbursements (averaging $16,161 per year), 3 teaching assistantships with partial tuition reimbursements (averaging $15,600 per year) were awarded; fellowships, scholarships/grants, health care benefits, and unspecified assistantships also available. *Unit head:* Dr. Michael Bugeja, Chair, 515-294-0481, Fax: 515-294-5108, E-mail: greenlee@iastate.edu. *Application contact:* Dr. Eric Abbott, Director of Graduate Education, 515-294-0492, E-mail: masscomm@iastate.edu.

Kent State University, College of Communication and Information, School of Journalism and Mass Communication, Kent, OH 44242-0001. Offers MA. Part-time programs available. *Faculty:* 19 full-time (6 women), 5 part-time/adjunct (0 women). *Students:* 20 full-time (10 women), 18 part-time (11 women); includes 6 minority (5 African Americans, 1 Asian American or Pacific Islander), 2 international. Average age 35. 34 applicants, 71% accepted, 10 enrolled. In 2007, 10 degrees awarded. *Degree requirements:* For master's, thesis optional. *Entrance requirements:* For master's, GRE General Test, minimum GPA of 3.0. Additional exam requirements/recommendations for international students: Recommended—TOEFL (minimum score 600 paper-based; 250 computer-based). *Application deadline:* For fall admission, 3/1 priority date for domestic and international students; for spring admission, 10/30 priority date for domestic students, 10/30 for international students. Applications are processed on a rolling basis. Application fee: $30. Electronic applications accepted. *Financial support:* In 2007–08, 1 fellowship with full tuition reimbursement (averaging $6,550 per year), 2 research assistantships with full tuition reimbursements (averaging $6,550 per year), 7 teaching assistantships with full tuition reimbursements (averaging $6,550 per year) were awarded; career-related internships or fieldwork, Federal Work-Study, institutionally sponsored loans, scholarships/grants, health care benefits, tuition waivers (full), and unspecified assistantships also available. Financial award application deadline: 2/1; financial award applicants required to submit FAFSA. *Faculty research:* Electronic tablet newspapers, accuracy and ethics in broadcast news, internet credibility, First Amendment, HDTV. Total annual research expenditures: $120,500. *Unit head:* Jeffrey W. Fruit, Director, 330-672-2572, Fax: 330-672-4064, E-mail: jfruit@kent.edu. *Application contact:* Evonne H. Whitmore, Graduate Coordinator, 330-672-8304, E-mail: ewhitmor@kent.edu.

Marquette University, Graduate School, College of Communication, Milwaukee, WI 53201-1881. Offers advertising and public relations (MA); broadcasting and electronic communications (MA); communications studies (MA); journalism (MA); mass communications (MA); religious communications (MA); science, health and environmental communications (MA). *Accreditation:* ACEJMC. Part-time and evening/weekend programs available. *Faculty:* 31 full-time (17 women), 34 part-time/adjunct (17 women). *Students:* 24 full-time (13 women), 19 part-time (12 women); includes 7 minority (1 African American, 1 American Indian/Alaska Native, 2 Asian Americans or Pacific Islanders, 3 Hispanic Americans), 7 international. Average age 28. 76 applicants, 58% accepted, 15 enrolled. In 2007, 17 degrees awarded. *Degree requirements:* For master's, comprehensive exam. *Entrance requirements:* For master's, GRE. Additional exam requirements/recommendations for international students: Required—TOEFL. Application fee: $40. *Financial support:* In 2007–08, 6 research assistantships, 12 teaching assistantships were awarded; career-related internships or fieldwork, Federal Work-Study, institutionally sponsored loans, scholarships/grants, and tuition waivers (full and partial) also available. Support available to part-time students. Financial award application deadline: 2/15. *Faculty research:* Urban journalism, gender and communication, intercultural communication, religious communication. Total annual research expenditures: $17,806. *Unit head:* Dr. Ana Garner, Dean, 414-288-3588, Fax: 414-288-1578.

Marshall University, Academic Affairs Division, School of Journalism and Mass Communications, Huntington, WV 25755. Offers MAJ. *Accreditation:* ACEJMC. *Faculty:* 3 full-time (1 woman), 4 part-time/adjunct (1 woman). *Students:* 23 full-time (16 women), 2 part-time (1 woman); includes 1 minority (American Indian/Alaska Native), 6 international. Average age 27. In 2007, 10 degrees awarded. *Degree requirements:* For master's, thesis optional. *Entrance requirements:* For master's, GRE General Test. Application fee: $40. *Unit head:* Dr. Corley F. Dennison, Dean, 304-696-2809, E-mail: dennisoc@marshall.edu. *Application contact:* Information Contact, 304-746-1900, Fax: 304-746-1902, E-mail: services@marshall.edu.

Michigan State University, The Graduate School, College of Communication Arts and Sciences, School of Journalism, East Lansing, MI 48824. Offers MA. *Entrance requirements:* Additional exam requirements/recommendations for international students: Required—TOEFL. Electronic applications accepted. *Expenses:* Tuition, state resident: part-time $379 per credit hour. Tuition, nonresident: part-time $800 per credit hour. Tuition and fees vary according to program.

New York University, Graduate School of Arts and Science, Department of Biology, New York, NY 10012-1019. Offers biology (PhD); biomedical journalism (MS); cancer and molecular biology (PhD); computational biology (PhD); computers in biological research (MS); developmental genetics (PhD); general biology (MS); immunology and microbiology (PhD); molecular genetics (PhD); neurobiology (PhD); oral biology (MS); plant biology (PhD); recombinant DNA technology (MS); MS/MBA. Part-time programs available. *Faculty:* 24 full-time (5 women), 8 part-time/adjunct. *Students:* 102 full-time (55 women), 43 part-time (24 women); includes 25 minority (2 African Americans, 14 Asian Americans or Pacific Islanders, 9 Hispanic Americans), 68 international. Average age 28. 313 applicants, 53% accepted, 60 enrolled. In 2007, 47 master's, 6 doctorates awarded. Terminal master's awarded for partial completion of doctoral program. *Degree requirements:* For master's, thesis or alternative, qualifying paper; for doctorate, comprehensive exam, thesis/dissertation. *Entrance requirements:* For master's, GRE General Test; for doctorate, GRE General Test, GRE Subject Test. Additional exam requirements/recommendations for international students: Required—TOEFL. *Application deadline:* For fall admission, 12/12 priority date for domestic students. Application fee: $55. *Financial support:* Fellowships with tuition reimbursements, research assistantships with tuition reimbursements, teaching assistantships with tuition reimbursements, career-related internships or fieldwork, Federal Work-Study, institutionally sponsored loans, scholarships/grants, health care benefits, and unspecified assistantships available. Financial award application deadline: 12/12; financial award applicants required to submit FAFSA. *Faculty research:* Genomics, molecular and cell biology, development and molecular genetics, molecular evolution of plants and animals. *Unit head:* Gloria Coruzzi, Chair, 212-998-8200, Fax: 212-995-4015, E-mail: biology@nyu.edu. *Application contact:* Stephen Small, Director of Graduate Studies, 212-998-8200, Fax: 212-995-4015, E-mail: biology@nyu.edu.

New York University, Graduate School of Arts and Science, Department of Journalism, New York, NY 10012-1019. Offers biomedical journalism (MS); cultural reporting and criticism (MA); French studies/journalism (MA); journalism (MA); Latin American and Caribbean studies/journalism (MA); Near Eastern studies/journalism (MA); science and environmental reporting (Advanced Certificate); MA/Advanced Certificate. *Accreditation:* ACEJMC. Part-time programs available. *Faculty:* 18 full-time (6 women), 39 part-time/adjunct. *Students:* 140 full-time (93 women), 61 part-time (41 women); includes 19 minority (6 African Americans, 10 Asian Americans or Pacific Islanders, 3 Hispanic Americans), 41 international. Average age 27. 468 applicants, 46% accepted, 99 enrolled. In 2007, 95 degrees awarded. *Degree requirements:* For master's, written projects. *Entrance requirements:* For master's, GRE General Test, sample of written work. Additional exam requirements/recommendations for international students: Required—TOEFL. *Application deadline:* For fall admission, 1/4 priority date for domestic students. Application fee: $85. *Financial support:* Fellowships with tuition reimbursements, teaching assistantships with tuition reimbursements, Federal Work-Study, institutionally sponsored loans, scholarships/grants, and tuition waivers (partial) available. Financial award application deadline: 1/4; financial award applicants required to submit FAFSA. *Faculty research:* Newspaper, magazine, and broadcast journalism; business and financial reporting; media studies. *Unit head:* Brooke Kraeger, Chair, 212-998-7980, Fax: 212-995-4148, E-mail: graduate.journalism@nyu.edu. *Application contact:* Stephen Solomon, Director of Graduate Studies, 212-998-7980, Fax: 212-995-4148, E-mail: graduate.journalism@nyu.edu.

See Close-Up on page 909.

Northeastern University, College of Arts and Sciences, School of Journalism, Boston, MA 02115-5096. Offers MA. Part-time and evening/weekend programs available. *Faculty:* 13 full-time (5 women). *Students:* 21 full-time (15 women), 7 part-time (5 women). 78 applicants, 60% accepted. In 2007, 7 degrees awarded. *Degree requirements:* For master's, thesis (for some programs). *Entrance requirements:* For master's, GRE General Test, minimum GPA of 3.0. *Application deadline:* For fall admission, 2/1 priority date for domestic students, 5/1 for international students. Applications are processed on a rolling basis. Application fee: $50. Electronic applications accepted. *Financial support:* Career-related internships or fieldwork, Federal Work-Study, institutionally sponsored loans, scholarships/grants, tuition waivers (partial), and unspecified assistantships available. Financial award application deadline: 3/1; financial award applicants required to submit FAFSA. *Faculty research:* Online journalism, broadcast news, foreign reporting, presidential debates, sporting society. *Unit head:* Prof. Belle Adler, Graduate Coordinator, 617-373-3238, Fax: 617-373-8773, E-mail: b.adler@neu.edu. *Application contact:* Carol Medige, Graduate Assistant, 617-373-3236, Fax: 617-373-8773, E-mail: gradjourn@neu.edu.

Northwestern University, Medill School of Journalism, Evanston, IL 60208. Offers broadcast journalism (MSJ); integrated marketing communications (MSIMC), including advertising/sales promotion, direct database and e-commerce marketing, general studies, public relations; magazine publishing (MSJ); new media (MSJ); reporting and writing (MSJ). *Accreditation:* ACEJMC (one or more programs are accredited). *Entrance requirements:* For master's, GRE General Test, GMAT or LSAT (MSJ). Additional exam requirements/recommendations for international students: Required—TOEFL. Electronic applications accepted. Expenses: Contact institution. *Faculty research:* Web business journalism, cultural stereotypes, voter apathy, digital television.

The Ohio State University, Graduate School, College of Social and Behavioral Sciences, School of Communication, Program in Journalism and Communication, Columbus, OH 43210. Offers MA. *Students:* 2 full-time (both women); both minorities (both African Americans) Average age 22. *Entrance requirements:* For master's, GRE General Test. *Application deadline:* Applications are processed on a rolling basis. Application fee: $40 ($50 for international students). Electronic applications accepted. *Unit head:* William Eveland, Graduate Studies Committee Chair, 614-292-6004, Fax: 614-292-2055, E-mail: eveland.6@osu.edu. *Application contact:* Graduate Admissions, 614-292-9444, Fax: 614-292-2895, E-mail: domestic.grad@osu.edu.

Ohio University, Graduate College, Scripps College of Communication, E.W. Scripps School of Journalism, Athens, OH 45701-2979. Offers MS, PhD. *Accreditation:* ACEJMC (one or more programs are accredited). Part-time programs available. *Faculty:* 26 full-time (12 women), 4 part-time/adjunct (1 woman). *Students:* 38 full-time (22 women), 13 part-time (8 women); includes 3 minority (2 African Americans, 1 Hispanic American), 19 international. Average age 26. 137 applicants, 32% accepted, 23 enrolled. In 2007, 16 master's, 4 doctorates awarded. *Degree requirements:* For master's, thesis or alternative; for doctorate, comprehensive exam, thesis/dissertation. *Entrance requirements:* For master's and doctorate, GRE General Test, minimum GPA of 3.0. Additional exam requirements/recommendations for international students: Required—TOEFL (minimum score 600 paper-based; 250 computer-based; 100 iBT). *Application deadline:* For fall admission, 2/1 priority date for domestic students, 2/1 for international students. Applications are processed on a rolling basis. Application fee: $50 ($55 for international students). Electronic applications accepted. *Financial support:* In 2007–08, 30 students received support, including 4 fellowships (averaging $7,000 per year), 8 research assistantships with full tuition reimbursements available (averaging $9,300 per year), 10 teaching assistantships with full tuition reimbursements available (averaging $15,500 per year); career-related internships or fieldwork, Federal Work-Study, institutionally sponsored loans, and tuition waivers (full) also available. Financial award application deadline: 2/1. *Faculty research:* Newspaper, magazine, broadcasting, public relations, advertising. Total annual research expenditures: $120,000. *Unit head:* Thomas Hodson, Director, 740-593-2590, Fax: 740-593-2592, E-mail: hodson@ohio.edu. *Application contact:* Dr. Joseph Bernt, Associate Director, 740-593-2589 Ext. 740, Fax: 740-593-2592, E-mail: berntj@ohio.edu.

Point Park University, School of Arts and Sciences, Department of Journalism and Mass Communication, Pittsburgh, PA 15222-1984. Offers MA. Part-time and evening/weekend programs available. *Faculty:* 9 full-time, 16 part-time/adjunct. *Students:* 26 full-time (18 women), 53 part-time (43 women); includes 18 minority (16 African Americans, 1 Asian American or Pacific Islander, 1 Hispanic American), 2 international. Average age 28. 108 applicants, 57% accepted, 29 enrolled. In 2007, 19 degrees awarded. *Degree requirements:* For master's, thesis or alternative. *Entrance requirements:* For master's, minimum GPA of 2.75, 2 letters of recommendation. Additional exam requirements/recommendations for international students: Required—TOEFL. *Application deadline:* Applications are processed on a rolling basis. Application fee: $30. Electronic applications accepted. *Expenses:* Tuition: Full-time $10,566; part-time $587 per credit. Required fees: $360; $20 per credit. *Financial support:* In 2007–08, 2 students received support, including 2 research assistantships with full tuition reimbursements available (averaging $5,400 per year); career-related internships or fieldwork and scholarships/grants also available. Support available to part-time students. Financial award application deadline: 5/1; financial award applicants required to submit FAFSA. *Unit head:* Helen Fallon, Chair, 412-392-3982, E-mail: hfallon@pointpark.edu. *Application contact:* Marty Paonessa, Associate Director, Graduate and Adult Enrollment, 412-392-3915, Fax: 412-392-6164, E-mail: mpaonessa@pointpark.edu.

See Close-Up on page 919.

Polytechnic Institute of NYU, Department of Humanities and Social Sciences, Major in Technical Writing and Specialized Journalism, Brooklyn, NY 11201-2990. Offers MS. *Students:* 1 full-time (0 women), 5 part-time (1 woman); includes 2 minority (1 African American, 1 Asian American or Pacific Islander). 6 applicants, 67% accepted, 3 enrolled. *Degree requirements:* For master's, comprehensive exam (for some programs), thesis (for some programs). *Entrance requirements:* Additional exam requirements/recommendations for international students: Required—TOEFL (minimum score 550 paper-based; 213 computer-based); Recommended—IELTS (minimum score 7). *Application deadline:* For fall admission, 7/15 priority date for domestic students, 4/1 priority date for international students; for spring admission, 12/15 priority date for domestic students, 10/1 priority date for international students. Applications are processed on a rolling basis. Application fee: $55. Electronic applications accepted. *Expenses:* Tuition: Full-time $18,486; part-time $1,027 per credit. Required fees: $352 per semester. *Application contact:* Anthea Jeffrey, Graduate Admissions, 718-260-3200, Fax: 718-260-3624, E-mail: gradinfo@poly.edu.

See Close-Up on page 921.

Quinnipiac University, School of Communications, Program in Journalism, Hamden, CT 06518-1940. Offers MS. Part-time and evening/weekend programs available. *Faculty:* 5 full-time (1 woman), 11 part-time/adjunct (3 women). *Students:* 30 full-time (18 women), 21 part-time (12 women); includes 10 minority (9 African Americans, 1 Hispanic American), 1 international. Average age 27. 50 applicants, 78% accepted, 19 enrolled. In 2007, 19 degrees awarded. *Degree requirements:* For master's, project. *Entrance requirements:* For master's, minimum GPA of 2.8, portfolio or writing sample. Additional exam requirements/recommendations for international students: Required—TOEFL (minimum score 575 paper-based; 233 computer-based; 90 iBT), IELTS (minimum score 7). *Application deadline:* For fall admission, 7/30 priority date for domestic students, 4/30 priority date for international students; for spring admission, 12/15 priority date for domestic students, 9/15 priority date for international students. Applications are processed on a rolling basis. Application fee: $45. Electronic applications accepted. *Expenses:* Tuition: Part-time $675 per credit. Required fees: $30 per credit. Tuition and fees vary according to course load. *Financial support:* In 2007–08, 1 fellowship with full tuition reimbursement was awarded; career-related internships or fieldwork and unspecified assistantships also available. Support available to part-time students. Financial award application deadline: 4/15; financial award applicants required to submit FAFSA. *Faculty research:* Journalism history, media representation, media and politics, media influence. *Unit head:* Richard Hanley, Director, 203-582-8439, Fax: 203-582-5310, E-mail: rich.hanley@quinnipiac.edu. *Application contact:* 800-462-1944, Fax: 203-582-3443, E-mail: graduate@quinnipiac.edu.

See Close-Up on page 923.

Regent University, Graduate School, School of Communication and the Arts, Virginia Beach, VA 23464-9800. Offers acting and directing (MFA); cinema arts (MA); communication (MA, PhD); fine arts (MFA); journalism (MA); script and screenwriting (MFA); television arts (MA); theatre arts (MA). Part-time programs available. Postbaccalaureate distance learning degree programs offered (minimal on-campus study). *Faculty:* 23 full-time (3 women), 12 part-time/adjunct (3 women). *Students:* 123 full-time (66 women), 145 part-time (83 women); includes 71 minority (54 African Americans, 2 American Indian/Alaska Native, 3 Asian Americans or Pacific Islanders, 12 Hispanic Americans), 14 international. Average age 33. 176 applicants, 66% accepted, 64 enrolled. In 2007, 60 master's, 15 doctorates awarded. *Degree requirements:* For master's, thesis or alternative; for doctorate, thesis/dissertation. *Entrance requirements:* For master's, GRE General Test or MAT, minimum undergraduate GPA of 3.0, writing sample, computer literacy survey, recommendation, resumé, interview, audition (MFA programs); for doctorate, GRE General Test, minimum graduate GPA of 3.0, writing sample, computer literacy survey, recommendation, interview, transcripts. Additional exam requirements/recommendations for international students: Required—TOEFL (minimum score 577 paper-based; 233 computer-based). *Application deadline:* For fall admission, 3/1 priority date for domestic students; for spring admission, 10/1 priority date for domestic students. Applications are processed on a rolling basis. Application fee: $50. Electronic applications accepted. *Expenses: Contact institution. Financial support:* In 2007–08, 247 students received support, including 5 fellowships with full and partial tuition reimbursements available (averaging $7,245 per year); scholarships/grants, tuition waivers (full and partial), and unspecified assistantships also available. Support available to part-time students. Financial award application deadline: 9/1; financial award applicants required to submit FAFSA. *Faculty research:* Southern gospel music, education and entertainment, celebrities and the media, journalism and ethics, C. S. Lewis. *Unit head:* Michael Patrick, Dean, 757-226-4970, Fax: 757-226-4279, E-mail: michpat@regent.edu. *Application contact:* Althea Bishard, Registrar and Executive Director of Enrollment and Academic Services, 800-373-5504, Fax: 757-226-4381, E-mail: admissions@regent.edu.

Roosevelt University, Graduate Division, College of Arts and Sciences, Department of Communication, Program in Journalism, Chicago, IL 60605-1394. Offers MSJ. Part-time and evening/weekend programs available. *Students:* 25 full-time (19 women), 24 part-time (19 women); includes 24 minority (17 African Americans, 3 Asian Americans or Pacific Islanders, 4 Hispanic Americans), 4 international. Average age 30. 57 applicants, 61% accepted, 16 enrolled. In 2007, 23 degrees awarded. *Application deadline:* For fall admission, 6/1 priority date for domestic students. Applications are processed on a rolling basis. Application fee: $25 ($35 for international students). *Financial support:* Application deadline: 2/15. *Application contact:* Joanne Canyon-Heller, Coordinator of Graduate Admission, 877-APPLY RU, Fax: 312-281-3356, E-mail: applyru@roosevelt.edu.

South Dakota State University, Graduate School, College of Arts and Science, Department of Journalism and Mass Communication, Brookings, SD 57007. Offers communication studies and journalism (MS). Part-time and evening/weekend programs available. *Degree requirements:* For master's, thesis, oral exam. *Entrance requirements:* Additional exam requirements/recommendations for international students: Required—TOEFL (minimum score 550 paper-based; 213 computer-based; 79 iBT). *Faculty research:* Mass communication applications.

Southern Illinois University Carbondale, Graduate School, College of Mass Communication and Media Arts, Department of Journalism, Carbondale, IL 62901-4701. Offers PhD. *Unit head:* William Frievogel, Director, 618-453-2121.

Stanford University, School of Humanities and Sciences, Department of Communication, Stanford, CA 94305-9991. Offers communication (journalism specialization) (MA); communication theory and research (PhD). *Faculty:* 11 full-time (0 women). *Students:* 55 full-time (31 women). Average age 28. 166 applicants, 20% accepted. In 2007, 17 master's, 4 doctorates awarded. *Degree requirements:* For master's, thesis, project; for doctorate, thesis/dissertation, qualifying examination, area examination, 2 projects. *Entrance requirements:* For master's and doctorate, GRE General Test. Additional exam requirements/recommendations for international students: Required—TOEFL (minimum score 600 paper-based; 250 computer-based). *Application deadline:* For fall admission, 12/2 for domestic and international students. Application fee: $105. Electronic applications accepted. *Financial support:* Research assistantships, teaching assistantships available. *Unit head:* James S. Fishkin, Chair, 650-723-4611. *Application contact:* Student Services Manager, 650-723-2075, Fax: 650-725-2472, E-mail: comm-studentservices@stanford.edu.

Syracuse University, Graduate School, S. I. Newhouse School of Public Communications, Department of Broadcast Journalism, Syracuse, NY 13244. Offers MS. *Students:* 35 full-time (18 women), 2 part-time (1 woman); includes 6 African Americans, 3 Asian Americans or Pacific Islanders, 1 Hispanic American, 3 international. 92 applicants, 70% accepted. In 2007, 30 degrees awarded. *Degree requirements:* For master's, capstone course. *Entrance requirements:* For master's, GRE General Test. Additional exam requirements/recommendations for international students: Required—TOEFL. *Application deadline:* For fall admission, 2/1 for domestic and international students. Application fee: $75. *Expenses:* Tuition: Full-time $18,216; part-time $1,012 per credit. Required fees: $980. Tuition and fees vary according to program. *Unit head:* Dona Hayes, Chair, 315-443-1944, Fax: 315-443-3946, E-mail: pcgrad@syr.edu. *Application contact:* Graduate Records Office, 315-443-4039, Fax: 315-443-1834, E-mail: pcgrad@syr.edu.

See Close-Up on page 935.

Syracuse University, Graduate School, S. I. Newhouse School of Public Communications, Program in Arts Journalism, Syracuse, NY 13244. Offers MA. *Students:* 18 full-time (13 women), 1 (woman) part-time; includes 1 African American, 1 Hispanic American. 47 applicants, 60% accepted. In 2007, 14 degrees awarded. *Entrance requirements:* For master's, GRE General Test. Additional exam requirements/recommendations for international students: Required—TOEFL (minimum score 600 paper-based; 250 computer-based). *Application deadline:* For fall admission, 2/1 for domestic and international students. Application fee: $75. Electronic applications accepted. *Expenses:* Tuition: Full-time $18,216; part-time $1,012 per credit. Required fees: $980. Tuition and fees vary according to program. *Unit head:* Johanna Keller, Director, 315-443-9251, Fax: 315-443-3946, E-mail: pcgrad@syr.edu. *Application contact:* Graduate Records Office, 315-443-4039, Fax: 315-443-1834, E-mail: pcgrad@syr.edu.

Syracuse University, Graduate School, S. I. Newhouse School of Public Communications, Program in Magazine, Newspaper and Online Journalism, Syracuse, NY 13244. Offers MA. *Students:* 39 full-time (27 women), 3 part-time (all women); includes 18 minority (10 African Americans, 3 Asian Americans or Pacific Islanders, 5 Hispanic Americans), 4 international. 146 applicants, 87% accepted. In 2007, 45 degrees awarded. *Degree requirements:* For master's, capstone course. *Entrance requirements:* For master's, GRE General Test. Additional exam requirements/recommendations for international students: Required—TOEFL (minimum score 600 paper-based; 250 computer-based). *Application deadline:* For fall admission, 2/1 for domestic and international students. Application fee: $75. Electronic applications accepted. *Expenses:* Tuition: Full-time $18,216; part-time $1,012 per credit. Required fees: $980. Tuition and fees vary according to program. *Unit head:* Melissa Chessher, Director, 315-443-4004, Fax: 315-443-3946, E-mail: pcgrad@syr.edu. *Application contact:* Graduate Records Office, 315-443-4039, Fax: 315-443-1834, E-mail: pcgrad@syr.edu.

See Close-Up on page 935.

Temple University, Graduate School, School of Communications and Theater, Department of Journalism, Philadelphia, PA 19122-6096. Offers MJ. Part-time programs available. *Degree requirements:* For master's, written exam. *Entrance requirements:* For master's, GRE General Test, minimum GPA of 3.0. Additional exam requirements/recommendations for international students: Required—TOEFL (minimum score 550 paper-based; 213 computer-based; 79 iBT). Electronic applications accepted. *Faculty research:* Journalism history, advertising research, media law, media institutions.

Texas Christian University, College of Communication, Schieffer School of Journalism, Fort Worth, TX 76129-0002. Offers advertising/public relations (MS); news-editorial (MS). Part-time and evening/weekend programs available. *Degree requirements:* For master's, thesis, written exam. *Entrance requirements:* For master's, GRE General Test. Additional exam requirements/recommendations for international students: Required—TOEFL. *Application deadline:* For fall admission, 3/1 for domestic students; for spring admission, 12/1 for domestic students. Applications are processed on a rolling basis. Application fee: $0. *Expenses:* Tuition: Part-time $865 per credit hour. Required fees: $48 per year. *Financial support:* Application deadline: 3/1. *Unit head:* Dr. Tommy Thomason, Director, 817-257-7425, E-mail: t.thomason@tcu.edu.

Université Laval, Faculty of Letters, Department of Information and Communication, Program in International Journalism, Québec, QC G1K 7P4, Canada. Offers Diploma. Offered jointly with École Supérieure De Journalisme De Lille (France). *Entrance requirements:* For degree, English exam, French exam, test on international current events, interview, knowledge of French, knowledge of English. Electronic applications accepted.

The University of Alabama, Graduate School, College of Communication and Information Sciences, Department of Journalism, Tuscaloosa, AL 35487. Offers MA. *Faculty:* 9 full-time (2 women), 1 part-time/adjunct (0 women). *Students:* 17 full-time (13 women), 4 part-time (3 women); includes 5 minority (3 African Americans, 2 Hispanic Americans). Average age 28. 33 applicants, 70% accepted, 14 enrolled. In 2007, 6 master's awarded. *Degree requirements:* For master's, comprehensive exam, thesis or alternative. *Entrance requirements:* For master's, GRE or MAT, minimum GPA of 3.0. Additional exam requirements/recommendations for international students: Required—TOEFL (minimum score 600 paper-based; 250 computer-based). *Application deadline:* For fall admission, 2/15 priority date for domestic and international students; for winter admission, 11/1 priority date for international students; for spring admission, 11/1 for domestic students. Applications are processed on a rolling basis. Application fee: $30. Electronic applications accepted. *Expenses:* Tuition, state resident: full-time $5,700. Tuition, nonresident: full-time $16,518. *Financial support:* In 2007–08, 7 students received support, including 2 research assistantships with full tuition reimbursements available (averaging $10,908 per year), 2 teaching assistantships with full tuition reimbursements available (averaging $10,908 per year); career-related internships or fieldwork, Federal Work-Study, and institutionally sponsored loans also available. Financial award application deadline: 2/15. *Faculty research:* Law, history, processes and practices, effects and theory. *Unit head:* Dr. Jennifer Greer, Chair, 205-348-6304, Fax: 205-348-2780, E-mail: jdgreer@ua.edu. *Application contact:* Dr. Matthew Bunker, Graduate Coordinator, 205-348-8616, Fax: 205-348-2780, E-mail: bunker@jn.ua.edu.

University of Arkansas, Graduate School, J. William Fulbright College of Arts and Sciences, Department of Journalism, Fayetteville, AR 72701-1201. Offers MA. *Students:* 11 full-time (6 women), 12 part-time (8 women); includes 4 minority (2 African Americans, 2 American Indian/Alaska Native), 3 international. In 2007, 7 degrees awarded. Application fee: $40 ($50

Journalism

University of Arkansas (continued)
for international students). *Financial support:* In 2007–08, 3 teaching assistantships were awarded; fellowships with tuition reimbursements, research assistantships, career-related internships or fieldwork and Federal Work-Study also available. Support available to part-time students. Financial award application deadline: 4/1; financial award applicants required to submit FAFSA. *Unit head:* Patsy Watkins, Departmental Chairperson, 479-575-3601, Fax: 479-575-4314, E-mail: pwatkins@uark.edu. *Application contact:* Jan Wicks, Graduate Coordinator, 479-575-2006, Fax: 479-575-4314, E-mail: jwicks@uark.edu.

University of Arkansas at Little Rock, Graduate School, College of Professional Studies, School of Mass Communication, Little Rock, AR 72204-1099. Offers journalism (MA). Part-time and evening/weekend programs available. *Students:* Average age 30. *Degree requirements:* For master's, comprehensive exam, thesis optional. *Entrance requirements:* For master's, GRE General Test, minimum GPA of 2.7. *Application deadline:* Applications are processed on a rolling basis. *Financial support:* Research assistantships with tuition reimbursements, career-related internships or fieldwork, Federal Work-Study, institutionally sponsored loans, and unspecified assistantships available. Support available to part-time students. *Faculty research:* Theory and practice of mass communication, social role of the mass media. *Unit head:* Dr. Jamie M. Bryne, Chairperson, 501-569-3250, E-mail: jmbryne@ualr.edu. *Application contact:* Dr. Bruce L. Plopper, Coordinator, 501-569-3250, E-mail: blplopper@ualr.edu.

The University of British Columbia, Faculty of Arts and Faculty of Graduate Studies, The School of Journalism, Vancouver, BC V6T 1Z1, Canada. Offers MJ. *Faculty:* 4 full-time (1 woman), 4 part-time/adjunct (1 woman). *Students:* 44 full-time (28 women); includes 13 minority (2 African Americans, 10 Asian Americans or Pacific Islanders, 1 Hispanic American). Average age 24. 118 applicants, 34% accepted, 25 enrolled. In 2007, 24 degrees awarded. *Degree requirements:* For master's, thesis. *Entrance requirements:* For master's, portfolio, resumé with cover letter, letters of reference, transcripts. Additional exam requirements/recommendations for international students: Required—TOEFL (minimum score 615 paper-based; 260 computer-based). *Application deadline:* For fall admission, 1/1 for domestic and international students. Application fee: $90 Canadian dollars ($150 Canadian dollars for international students). Electronic applications accepted. *Expenses: Contact institution. Financial support:* In 2007–08, 21 students received support, including 21 fellowships (averaging $12,200 per year); career-related internships or fieldwork also available. Financial award application deadline: 12/1. *Faculty research:* New media, media coverage, journalistic ethics, audiences, investigative journalism. *Unit head:* Prof. Mary Lynn Young, Director, 604-822-6688, Fax: 604-822-6707. *Application contact:* Barbara R. Wallin, Program Assistant, 604-822-6688, Fax: 604-822-6707, E-mail: journal@interchange.ubc.ca.

University of California, Berkeley, Graduate Division, Graduate School of Journalism, Berkeley, CA 94720-1500. Offers MJ, JD/MJ, MJ/MA. *Accreditation:* ACEJMC. *Faculty:* 12 full-time, 12 part-time/adjunct. *Degree requirements:* For master's, project. *Entrance requirements:* For master's, GRE General Test, 3 work samples, minimum GPA of 3.0, 3 letters of recommendation. Additional exam requirements/recommendations for international students: Required—TOEFL (minimum score 600 paper-based; 250 computer-based). *Application deadline:* For fall admission, 12/1 for domestic students. Application fee: $70 ($90 for international students). *Financial support:* Fellowships, research assistantships, career-related internships or fieldwork, Federal Work-Study, institutionally sponsored loans, scholarships/grants, tuition waivers (full and partial), and unspecified assistantships available. Financial award applicants required to submit FAFSA. *Faculty research:* Documentary, new media, print (newspaper and magazine), broadcast (television and radio), photography. *Application contact:* Information Contact, 510-642-7928, E-mail: applysoj@journalism. berkeley.edu.

University of Colorado at Boulder, Graduate School, School of Journalism and Mass Communication, Boulder, CO 80309. Offers communication (PhD), including media studies; mass communication research (MA); newsgathering (MA). *Accreditation:* ACEJMC (one or more programs are accredited). Part-time programs available. *Faculty:* 21. *Students:* 83 full-time (56 women), 10 part-time (7 women); includes 9 minority (3 African Americans, 2 Asian Americans or Pacific Islanders, 4 Hispanic Americans), 10 international. Average age 31. 122 applicants, 74% accepted. In 2007, 38 master's, 6 doctorates awarded. *Degree requirements:* For master's, comprehensive exam, thesis or alternative; for doctorate, comprehensive exam, thesis/dissertation. *Entrance requirements:* For master's, GRE General Test, minimum undergraduate GPA of 2.75; for doctorate, GRE General Test, minimum undergraduate GPA of 3.2, 3.5 graduate. *Application deadline:* For fall admission, 2/15 for domestic students, 12/1 for international students. Applications are processed on a rolling basis. Application fee: $50 ($60 for international students). *Financial support:* In 2007–08, 26 fellowships (averaging $2,908 per year), 10 research assistantships with tuition reimbursements (averaging $14,446 per year) were awarded; institutionally sponsored loans and unspecified assistantships also available. Financial award application deadline: 3/1. *Faculty research:* Writing on science and the environment, mass communication and public opinion, minority representation in the media, media and culture. Total annual research expenditures: $326,556. *Unit head:* Paul Voakes, Dean, 303-492-4364, Fax: 303-492-0969, E-mail: paul.voakes@colorado.edu. *Application contact:* Graduate Program Assistant, 303-492-5008, Fax: 303-492-0969, E-mail: sjmcgrad@colorado.edu.

University of Florida, Graduate School, College of Journalism and Communications, Department of Journalism, Gainesville, FL 32611. Offers MAMC. *Faculty:* 17 full-time (9 women). *Degree requirements:* For master's, thesis optional. *Entrance requirements:* For master's, GRE General Test, minimum GPA of 3.0. Additional exam requirements/recommendations for international students: Required—TOEFL (minimum score 550 paper-based; 213 computer-based). *Application deadline:* For fall admission, 6/1 for domestic students. Application fee: $30. *Expenses:* Tuition, state resident: full-time $7,478. Tuition, nonresident: full-time $22,603. *Unit head:* Dr. William McKeen, Chair, 352-392-0500, E-mail: wmckeen@jou.ufl.edu. *Application contact:* Dr. Kim Walsh-Childers, Graduate Coordinator, 352-392-3924, E-mail: kwchilders@jou.ufl.edu.

University of Georgia, Graduate School, Grady School of Journalism and Mass Communication, Athens, GA 30602. Offers journalism and mass communication (MA); mass communication (PhD). *Accreditation:* ACEJMC (one or more programs are accredited). *Faculty:* 43 full-time (20 women). *Students:* 80 full-time (49 women), 12 part-time (6 women); includes 8 minority (6 African Americans, 1 Asian American or Pacific Islander, 1 Hispanic American), 23 international. 263 applicants, 34% accepted, 33 enrolled. In 2007, 35 master's, 5 doctorates awarded. *Degree requirements:* For master's, comprehensive exam, thesis (MA); for doctorate, comprehensive exam, thesis/dissertation. *Entrance requirements:* For master's and doctorate, GRE General Test. Additional exam requirements/recommendations for international students: Required—TOEFL, TWE (PhD). *Application deadline:* For spring admission, 2/15 for domestic students. Application fee: $50. Electronic applications accepted. *Financial support:* Research assistantships, teaching assistantships, tuition waivers (full) and unspecified assistantships available. *Unit head:* Dr. E. Culpepper Clark, Dean, 706-542-1704, Fax: 706-542-2183, E-mail: cully@uga.edu. *Application contact:* Dr. Jeffrey K. Springston, Graduate Coordinator, 706-542-5030, E-mail: jspring@uga.edu.

University of Illinois at Springfield, Graduate Programs, College of Public Affairs and Administration, Public Affairs Reporting Program, Springfield, IL 62703-5407. Offers MA. Part-time and evening/weekend programs available. *Faculty:* 1 full-time (0 women). *Students:* 19 full-time (14 women); includes 6 minority (4 African Americans, 1 Asian American or Pacific Islander, 1 Hispanic American). Average age 24. 26 applicants, 81% accepted, 19 enrolled. In 2007, 16 degrees awarded. *Degree requirements:* For master's, internship, professional portfolio. *Entrance requirements:* For master's, interview, writing sample, 3 letters of reference. Additional exam requirements/recommendations for international students: Required—TOEFL (minimum score 550 paper-based; 213 computer-based). *Application deadline:* For fall admission, 4/1 for domestic and international students. Application fee: $50 ($60 for international students). Electronic applications accepted. *Expenses:* Tuition, state resident: full-time $5,424; part-time $226 per credit hour. Tuition, nonresident: part-time $553 per credit hour. Required fees: $618 per term. *Financial support:* Career-related internships or fieldwork, Federal Work-Study, scholarships/grants, and health care benefits available. Support available to part-time students. Financial award application deadline: 11/15; financial award applicants required to submit FAFSA. *Unit head:* Dr. Charles Wheeler, Director, 217-206-6535, Fax: 217-206-7807, E-mail: wheeler.charles@uis.edu.

University of Illinois at Urbana–Champaign, Graduate College, College of Communications, Department of Journalism, Champaign, IL 61820. Offers MS, MS/MBA. *Accreditation:* ACEJMC. *Faculty:* 14 full-time (4 women). *Students:* 18 full-time (8 women), 8 part-time (4 women); includes 2 minority (both Hispanic Americans), 2 international. Average age 23. 81 applicants, 22% accepted, 15 enrolled. In 2007, 20 degrees awarded. *Entrance requirements:* For master's, minimum GPA of 3.0. *Application deadline:* For fall admission, 3/14 for domestic students. Applications are processed on a rolling basis. Application fee: $60 ($75 for international students). *Financial support:* In 2007–08, 1 fellowship, 14 research assistantships, 12 teaching assistantships were awarded; career-related internships or fieldwork, Federal Work-Study, institutionally sponsored loans, and tuition waivers (full and partial) also available. Financial award application deadline: 2/15. *Unit head:* Walter Harrington, Head, 217-333-0709, Fax: 217-333-7931, E-mail: wharring@uiuc.edu. *Application contact:* Diana King-Schwanke, Secretary, 217-333-0709, Fax: 217-333-7931, E-mail: dking6@uiuc.edu.

The University of Iowa, Graduate College, College of Liberal Arts and Sciences, School of Journalism and Mass Communication, Program in Professional Journalism, Iowa City, IA 52242-1316. Offers MA, JD/MA. *Accreditation:* ACEJMC. *Students:* 18 full-time (7 women), 7 part-time (4 women); includes 3 minority (1 African American, 1 American Indian/Alaska Native, 1 Hispanic American), 2 international. 53 applicants, 49% accepted, 12 enrolled. In 2007, 10 master's awarded. *Degree requirements:* For master's, thesis optional, exam. *Entrance requirements:* For master's, GRE General Test, minimum GPA of 3.0. Additional exam requirements/recommendations for international students: Required—TOEFL (minimum score 570 paper-based; 230 computer-based; 89 iBT). *Application deadline:* For fall admission, 1/10 priority date for domestic and international students. Applications are processed on a rolling basis. Application fee: $60 ($85 for international students). Electronic applications accepted. *Expenses:* Tuition, state resident: part-time $349 per hour. Tuition, nonresident: part-time $349 per hour. Tuition and fees vary according to course load and program. *Financial support:* In 2007–08, 6 research assistantships with partial tuition reimbursements, 8 teaching assistantships with partial tuition reimbursements were awarded; fellowships, career-related internships or fieldwork and Federal Work-Study also available. Financial award applicants required to submit FAFSA. *Faculty research:* Verbal and visual aspects of historical, legal, social, and cross-cultural communication. *Unit head:* Marc Armstrong, Interim Director, School of Journalism and Mass Communication, 319-335-3486, Fax: 319-335-3502.

University of Kansas, Research and Graduate Studies, School of Journalism and Mass Communications, Lawrence, KS 66045. Offers journalism (MS). *Accreditation:* ACEJMC.Part-time programs available. *Faculty:* 21. *Students:* 23 full-time (10 women), 54 part-time (44 women); includes 9 minority (3 African Americans, 2 American Indian/Alaska Native, 4 Hispanic Americans), 7 international. Average age 31. 81 applicants, 70% accepted, 27 enrolled. In 2007, 19 degrees awarded. *Degree requirements:* For master's, comprehensive exam, thesis. *Entrance requirements:* For master's, GRE General Test, GMAT (marketing communications), LSAT (MS/JD), minimum GPA of 3.0. Additional exam requirements/recommendations for international students: Required—TOEFL, TOEFL or IELTS. *Application deadline:* For fall admission, 2/1 for domestic and international students; for spring admission, 11/1 for domestic and international students. Application fee: $55 ($60 for international students). Electronic applications accepted. *Expenses:* Tuition, state resident: full-time $5,838. Tuition, nonresident: full-time $13,409. Tuition and fees vary according to program. *Financial support:* Fellowships, research assistantships, teaching assistantships with full and partial tuition reimbursements, career-related internships or fieldwork, scholarships/grants, and unspecified assistantships available. Support available to part-time students. Financial award application deadline: 2/1; financial award applicants required to submit FAFSA. *Faculty research:* Advertising, creativity, media economics, public relations, press law, online journalism, political journalism, marketing communication, new media, visual communication. *Unit head:* Ann Brill, Dean, 785-864-4755, Fax: 785-864-4396, E-mail: abrill@ku.edu. *Application contact:* Cindy Nesvarba, Graduate Records Coordinator, 785-864-7649, Fax: 785-864-5318, E-mail: cnesvarb@ku.edu.

University of Maryland, College Park, Graduate Studies, Phillip Merrill College of Journalism, College Park, MD 20742. Offers broadcast journalism (MA); journalism (MA); journalism and media studies (PhD); online news (MA); public affairs reporting (MA). *Accreditation:* ACEJMC (one or more programs are accredited). Part-time and evening/weekend programs available. *Faculty:* 28 full-time (13 women), 36 part-time/adjunct (10 women). *Students:* 71 full-time (43 women), 17 part-time (7 women); includes 20 minority (13 African Americans, 1 American Indian/Alaska Native, 4 Asian Americans or Pacific Islanders, 2 Hispanic Americans), 12 international. 243 applicants, 35% accepted, 32 enrolled. In 2007, 23 master's, 2 doctorates awarded. *Degree requirements:* For doctorate, thesis/dissertation, preliminary written and oral comprehensive exams. *Entrance requirements:* For master's and doctorate, GRE General Test, minimum GPA of 3.0, 3 letters of recommendation. Additional exam requirements/recommendations for international students: Required—TOEFL. *Application deadline:* For fall admission, 3/1 for domestic students, 2/1 for international students; for spring admission, 10/1 for domestic students, 6/1 for international students. Applications are processed on a rolling basis. Application fee: $60. Electronic applications accepted. *Financial support:* In 2007–08, 5 fellowships with full tuition reimbursements (averaging $13,925 per year), 2 research assistantships with tuition reimbursements (averaging $16,468 per year), 18 teaching assistantships with tuition reimbursements (averaging $15,744 per year) were awarded; career-related internships or fieldwork, Federal Work-Study, and scholarships/grants also available. Support available to part-time students. Financial award applicants required to submit FAFSA. *Faculty research:* Mass communication theory, specialized journalism, new telecommunication technologies, press integration. Total annual research expenditures: $130,465. *Unit head:* Thomas Kunkel, Dean, 301-405-2383, Fax: 301-314-1978, E-mail: tkunkel@umd.edu. *Application contact:* Dean of Graduate School, 301-405-0358, Fax: 301-314-9305.

See Close-Up on page 941.

University of Memphis, Graduate School, College of Communication and Fine Arts, Department of Journalism, Memphis, TN 38152. Offers general journalism (MA); journalism administration (MA). *Accreditation:* ACEJMC. Postbaccalaureate distance learning degree programs offered (no on-campus study). *Faculty:* 8 full-time (3 women), 2 part-time/adjunct (1 woman). *Students:* 16 full-time (15 women), 33 part-time (28 women); includes 11 minority (all African Americans) Average age 30. 28 applicants, 57% accepted, 12 enrolled. In 2007, 10 degrees awarded. *Degree requirements:* For master's, comprehensive exam. *Entrance requirements:* For master's, GRE General Test, MAT. *Application deadline:* For fall admission, 8/1 for domestic students; for spring admission, 12/1 for domestic students. Applications are processed on a rolling basis. Application fee: $35 ($60 for international students). *Expenses:* Tuition, state resident: full-time $6,990; part-time $377 per hour. Tuition, nonresident: full-time $17,818; part-time $830 per hour. Tuition and fees vary according to course load and program. *Financial support:* In 2007–08, 10 research assistantships (averaging $6,100 per year) were awarded; teaching assistantships, scholarships/grants also available. Support available to part-time students. *Faculty research:* Spirit of libel law, statistical software packages, college yearbooks, computer-assisted grammar project, newspaper in education. *Unit head:* Dr. James W. Redmond, Chairman, 901-678-2401, Fax: 901-678-4287, E-mail: jredmond@memphis.edu. *Application contact:* Dr. David Arant, Coordinator of Graduate Studies, 901-678-4596, Fax: 901-678-4913, E-mail: darant@memphis.edu.

University of Miami, Graduate School, School of Communication, Coral Gables, FL 33124. Offers communication (PhD); communication studies (MA); film studies (MA, PhD); motion pictures (MFA), including production, producing, and screenwriting; print journalism (MA);

public relations (MA); Spanish language journalism (MA); television broadcast journalism (MA). *Accreditation:* ACEJMC. Part-time programs available. *Faculty:* 39 full-time (12 women). *Students:* 113 full-time (61 women), 16 part-time (5 women); includes 28 minority (8 African Americans, 1 Asian American or Pacific Islander, 19 Hispanic Americans), 14 international. Average age 27. 374 applicants, 56% accepted, 64 enrolled. In 2007, 48 master's, 2 doctorates awarded. *Degree requirements:* For master's, comprehensive exam (for some programs), thesis (for some programs); for doctorate, comprehensive exam, thesis/dissertation. *Entrance requirements:* For master's, GRE General Test; for doctorate, GRE General Test, master's thesis or scholarly research. Additional exam requirements/recommendations for international students: Required—TOEFL (minimum score 600 paper-based; 250 computer-based; 100 iBT). *Application deadline:* For fall admission, 12/15 priority date for domestic and international students. Applications are processed on a rolling basis. Application fee: $50. Electronic applications accepted. *Financial support:* In 2007–08, 68 students received support, including 10 teaching assistantships with full tuition reimbursements available; fellowships with full tuition reimbursements available, Federal Work-Study, institutionally sponsored loans, scholarships/grants, tuition waivers (partial), and unspecified assistantships also available. Financial award application deadline: 3/1; financial award applicants required to submit FAFSA. *Faculty research:* Communication studies, mass communication, international/interpersonal communication, film studies, journalism. *Unit head:* Dr. Sam L. Grogg, Dean, 305-284-3420, Fax: 305-284-2454, E-mail: sgrogg@miami.edu. *Application contact:* Dr. Leonardo C. Ferreira, Director of Graduate Studies, 305-284-3180, Fax: 305-284-8701, E-mail: lferreira@miami.edu.

See Close-Up on page 943.

University of Mississippi, Graduate School, College of Liberal Arts, Department of Journalism, Oxford, University, MS 38677. Offers MA. *Faculty:* 18 full-time (8 women), 6 part-time/adjunct (1 woman). *Students:* 22 full-time (11 women), 2 part-time (both women); includes 10 minority (all African Americans), 3 international. In 2007, 9 degrees awarded. *Degree requirements:* For master's, thesis. *Entrance requirements:* For master's, GRE General Test, minimum GPA of 3.0. Additional exam requirements/recommendations for international students: Required—TOEFL. *Application deadline:* For fall admission, 8/1 for domestic students. Applications are processed on a rolling basis. Application fee: $25. Electronic applications accepted. *Expenses:* Tuition, state resident: full-time $4,932. Tuition, nonresident: full-time $11,436. *Financial support:* Career-related internships or fieldwork and scholarships/grants available. Financial award application deadline: 3/1; financial award applicants required to submit FAFSA. *Unit head:* Dr. Samir Husni, Chairman, 662-915-7146, Fax: 662-915-7765.

University of Missouri–Columbia, Graduate School, School of Journalism, Columbia, MO 65211. Offers MA, PhD. *Accreditation:* ACEJMC (one or more programs are accredited). Part-time programs available. Terminal master's awarded for partial completion of doctoral program. *Degree requirements:* For master's, thesis (for some programs); for doctorate, 2 foreign languages, thesis/dissertation. *Entrance requirements:* For master's and doctorate, GRE General Test, minimum GPA of 3.0. Additional exam requirements/recommendations for international students: Required—TOEFL (minimum score 600 paper-based; 250 computer-based; 100 iBT).

The University of Montana, Graduate School, School of Journalism, Missoula, MT 59812-0002. Offers MA. *Accreditation:* ACEJMC. *Faculty:* 10 full-time (3 women). *Students:* 20 full-time (16 women), 1 (woman) part-time; includes 1 American Indian/Alaska Native, 1 Asian American or Pacific Islander, 2 international. In 2007, 5 degrees awarded. *Degree requirements:* For master's, thesis or alternative, professional project. *Entrance requirements:* For master's, GRE, statement, essay. Additional exam requirements/recommendations for international students: Required—TOEFL (minimum score 580 paper-based). *Application deadline:* For fall admission, 2/15 priority date for domestic students. Applications are processed on a rolling basis. Application fee: $51. Electronic applications accepted. *Financial support:* In 2007–08, 6 students received support, including 2 teaching assistantships with full tuition reimbursements available (averaging $9,000 per year); career-related internships or fieldwork, Federal Work-Study, and scholarships/grants also available. Financial award application deadline: 2/15; financial award applicants required to submit FAFSA. *Faculty research:* Native American issues, natural resources, public affairs, economy, photojournalism, multimedia, media law. *Unit head:* Peggy Kuhr, Dean, 406-243-4001, Fax: 406-243-5369, E-mail: peggy.kuhr@umontana.edu. *Application contact:* Dennis L. Swibold, Acting Director of Graduate Studies, 406-243-2230, E-mail: dennis.swibold@umontana.edu.

University of Nebraska–Lincoln, Graduate College, College of Journalism and Mass Communications, Lincoln, NE 68588. Offers MA. Postbaccalaureate distance learning degree programs offered (no on-campus study). *Degree requirements:* For master's, thesis. *Entrance requirements:* For master's, samples of work. Additional exam requirements/recommendations for international students: Required—TOEFL (minimum score 600 paper-based; 250 computer-based). Electronic applications accepted. *Faculty research:* Interactive media and the Internet, community newspapers, children's radio, advertising involvement, telecommunications policy.

University of Nevada, Las Vegas, Graduate College, Greenspun College of Urban Affairs, School of Journalism and Media Studies, Las Vegas, NV 89154-9900. Offers MA. *Faculty:* 11 full-time (2 women). *Students:* 11 full-time (7 women), 15 part-time (9 women); includes 4 minority (3 Asian Americans or Pacific Islanders, 1 Hispanic American), 2 international. 19 applicants, 68% accepted, 10 enrolled. In 2007, 2 degrees awarded. *Entrance requirements:* For master's, GRE General Test, minimum 3.0 GPA. Additional exam requirements/recommendations for international students: Required—TOEFL (minimum score 550 paper-based; 213 computer-based; 80 iBT). *Application deadline:* For fall admission, 3/15 for domestic and international students. Application fee: $60 ($75 for international students). Electronic applications accepted. *Expenses:* Tuition, state resident: part-time $198 per credit. Tuition, nonresident: part-time $416 per credit. Required fees: $256 per semester. Tuition and fees vary according to course load and reciprocity agreements. *Financial support:* In 2007–08, 3 research assistantships with partial tuition reimbursements (averaging $10,000 per year), 5 teaching assistantships with partial tuition reimbursements (averaging $9,000 per year) were awarded; career-related internships or fieldwork, Federal Work-Study, institutionally sponsored loans, scholarships/grants, health care benefits, and unspecified assistantships also available. Support available to part-time students. Financial award application deadline: 3/1. *Unit head:* Dr. Ardyth Broadrick Sohn, Director, 702-895-4491. *Application contact:* Graduate College Admissions Evaluator, 702-895-3320, Fax: 702-895-4180, E-mail: gradcollege@unlv.edu.

University of Nevada, Reno, Graduate School, Donald W. Reynolds School of Journalism, Reno, NV 89557. Offers MA. *Accreditation:* ACEJMC. *Faculty:* 11. *Students:* 5 full-time (3 women), 5 part-time (all women); includes 1 minority (American Indian/Alaska Native). Average age 37. 19 applicants, 53% accepted, 2 enrolled. In 2007, 15 degrees awarded. *Degree requirements:* For master's, thesis. *Entrance requirements:* For master's, GRE, minimum GPA of 2.75. Additional exam requirements/recommendations for international students: Required—TOEFL. *Application deadline:* For fall admission, 4/15 priority date for domestic students; for spring admission, 12/1 for domestic students. Applications are processed on a rolling basis. Application fee: $60 ($95 for international students). *Expenses:* Tuition, state resident: full-time $2,774; part-time $154 per credit. Tuition, nonresident: full-time $13,578; part-time $330 per credit. Required fees: $49 per semester. *Financial support:* In 2007–08, 6 research assistantships were awarded; teaching assistantships, Federal Work-Study and institutionally sponsored loans also available. Financial award application deadline: 3/1. *Unit head:* Dr. Donica Mensing, Graduate Program Director, 775-784-4187.

University of North Texas, Robert B. Toulouse School of Graduate Studies, College of Arts and Sciences, Department of Journalism, Denton, TX 76203. Offers MA, MJ. *Accreditation:* ACEJMC (one or more programs are accredited). Part-time programs available. *Faculty:* 17 full-time (6 women). *Students:* 37 full-time (27 women), 24 part-time (18 women); includes 10 minority (5 African Americans, 1 American Indian/Alaska Native, 4 Hispanic Americans), 4 international. Average age 28. 58 applicants, 52% accepted, 23 enrolled. In 2007, 28 degrees awarded. *Degree requirements:* For master's, variable foreign language requirement, comprehensive exam, thesis or alternative. *Entrance requirements:* For master's, GRE General Test, GPC in lieu of verbal GRE, porfolio. Additional exam requirements/recommendations for international students: Recommended—TOEFL (minimum score 550 paper-based; 213 computer-based). *Application deadline:* For fall admission, 7/15 for domestic students; for spring admission, 11/15 for domestic students. Application fee: $50 ($75 for international students). *Financial support:* In 2007–08, 1 research assistantship (averaging $8,640 per year), 5 teaching assistantships (averaging $4,320 per year) were awarded; career-related internships or fieldwork, Federal Work-Study, and institutionally sponsored loans also available. Financial award application deadline: 4/1. *Faculty research:* Mass communication theory, public relations, advertising, mass communication technology, journalism ethics. *Unit head:* Dr. Susan Zavoina, Chair, 940-565-2205, Fax: 940-565-2370, E-mail: zavoina@unt.edu. *Application contact:* Dr. Mitchell Land, Graduate Adviser, 940-565-4564, Fax: 940-369-8959, E-mail: mland@unt.edu.

University of Oklahoma, Graduate College, Gaylord College of Journalism and Mass Communication, Program in Journalism and Mass Communication, Norman, OK 73019-0390. Offers advertising and public relations (MA); information gathering and distribution (MA); mass communication management and policy (MA); professional writing (MA); telecommunication and new technology (MA). Part-time programs available. *Students:* 33 full-time (22 women), 41 part-time (27 women); includes 15 minority (5 African Americans, 5 American Indian/Alaska Native, 1 Asian American or Pacific Islander, 4 Hispanic Americans), 12 international. 29 applicants, 90% accepted, 15 enrolled. In 2007, 12 degrees awarded. *Degree requirements:* For master's, thesis optional. *Entrance requirements:* For master's, GRE General Test, minimum GPA of 3.2, 9 hours of course work in journalism, course work in statistics. Additional exam requirements/recommendations for international students: Required—TOEFL (minimum score 600 paper-based; 250 computer-based), TWE (minimum score 5). *Application deadline:* For fall admission, 2/1 for domestic students, 4/1 for international students; for spring admission, 11/1 for domestic students, 9/1 for international students. Application fee: $40 ($90 for international students). Electronic applications accepted. *Expenses:* Tuition, state resident: full-time $3,451; part-time $144 per credit hour. Tuition, nonresident: full-time $12,432; part-time $518 per credit hour. Required fees: $1,925; $70 per credit hour. $122 per semester. *Financial support:* In 2007–08, 26 students received support. Career-related internships or fieldwork, scholarships/grants, health care benefits, and unspecified assistantships available. *Faculty research:* Organizational management; rhetorical analysis; international public relations; digital production; normative theory. *Application contact:* Kelly Storm, Graduate Advisor, 405-325-2722, Fax: 405-325-7565, E-mail: kstorm@ou.edu.

University of Oregon, Graduate School, School of Journalism and Communication, Eugene, OR 97403. Offers MA, MS, PhD. *Accreditation:* ACEJMC (one or more programs are accredited); ASHA. Part-time programs available. *Faculty:* 16 full-time (7 women), 1 (woman) part-time/adjunct. *Students:* 76 full-time (53 women), 16 part-time (7 women); includes 10 minority (1 African American, 1 American Indian/Alaska Native, 3 Asian Americans or Pacific Islanders, 5 Hispanic Americans), 15 international. 66 applicants, 47% accepted. In 2007, 13 master's, 5 doctorates awarded. *Degree requirements:* For master's, thesis or alternative. *Entrance requirements:* For master's, GRE General Test; for doctorate, master's degree. Application fee: $50. *Financial support:* In 2007–08, 37 teaching assistantships were awarded; career-related internships or fieldwork, Federal Work-Study, institutionally sponsored loans, and scholarships/grants also available. Financial award application deadline: 3/31. *Faculty research:* Impact of mass communication, media technology, media accountability, craft attitudes, media economics. *Unit head:* Timothy W. Gleason, Dean, 541-346-3739. *Application contact:* Petra Hagen, Graduate Secretary, 541-346-2136, E-mail: phagen@uoregon.edu.

University of South Carolina, The Graduate School, College of Mass Communications and Information Studies, School of Journalism and Mass Communications, Columbia, SC 29208. Offers MA, MMC, PhD. *Accreditation:* ACEJMC (one or more programs are accredited). Part-time programs available. *Faculty:* 24 full-time (7 women). *Students:* 39 full-time (28 women), 36 part-time (22 women); includes 7 minority (all African Americans), 12 international. Average age 28. 79 applicants, 56% accepted, 19 enrolled. In 2007, 24 master's, 2 doctorates awarded. *Median time to degree:* Of those who began their doctoral program in fall 1999, 80% received their degree in 8 years or less. *Degree requirements:* For master's, comprehensive exam, thesis (for some programs); for doctorate, one foreign language, comprehensive exam, thesis/dissertation. *Entrance requirements:* For master's and doctorate, GRE General Test, minimum GPA of 3.0. Additional exam requirements/recommendations for international students: Required—TOEFL (minimum score 600 paper-based; 250 computer-based; 75 iBT). *Application deadline:* For fall admission, 7/1 priority date for domestic and international students; for spring admission, 11/15 priority date for domestic and international students. Applications are processed on a rolling basis. Application fee: $40. Electronic applications accepted. *Expenses:* Tuition, state resident: part-time $440 per hour. Tuition, nonresident: part-time $936 per hour. Required fees: $17 per hour. Tuition and fees vary according to program. *Financial support:* In 2007–08, 26 students received support, including 8 research assistantships (averaging $19,000 per year), 1 teaching assistantship (averaging $19,000 per year); fellowships, career-related internships or fieldwork, Federal Work-Study, scholarships/grants, and unspecified assistantships also available. Financial award application deadline: 2/15. *Faculty research:* Ethics, communications law, international communications, science/health/environmental/risk communications, convergent media. Total annual research expenditures: $200,000. *Unit head:* Dr. Erik Collins, Associate Director for Graduate Studies and Research, 803-777-3310, Fax: 803-777-1267, E-mail: erik.collins@sc.edu. *Application contact:* Sandra M. Hughes, Manager, Graduate Student Services, 803-777-5166, Fax: 803-777-1267, E-mail: hughes-sandra@sc.edu.

University of Southern California, Graduate School, Annenberg School for Communication, School of Journalism, Program in Broadcast Journalism, Los Angeles, CA 90089. Offers MA. *Students:* 34 full-time (30 women), 4 part-time (all women); includes 18 minority (3 African Americans, 8 Asian Americans or Pacific Islanders, 7 Hispanic Americans), 2 international. Average age 26. 79 applicants, 48% accepted, 16 enrolled. In 2007, 37 degrees awarded. *Degree requirements:* For master's, comprehensive exam. *Entrance requirements:* For master's, GRE General Test, resumé, writing samples, letters of recommendation, statement of purpose. Additional exam requirements/recommendations for international students: Required—TOEFL (minimum score 280 computer-based; 114 iBT). *Application deadline:* For fall admission, 1/15 for domestic and international students. Application fee: $85. Electronic applications accepted. *Financial support:* Teaching assistantships with full tuition reimbursements, career-related internships or fieldwork, Federal Work-Study, institutionally sponsored loans, scholarships/grants, health care benefits, and unspecified assistantships available. Support available to part-time students. Financial award application deadline: 1/15; financial award applicants required to submit FAFSA. *Application contact:* Allyson Hill, Director of Admissions, 213-821-0770, E-mail: ascadm@usc.edu.

See Close-Up on page 945.

University of Southern California, Graduate School, Annenberg School for Communication, School of Journalism, Program in Print Journalism, Los Angeles, CA 90089. Offers MA. *Students:* 46 full-time, 4 part-time; includes 15 minority (2 African Americans, 6 Asian Americans or Pacific Islanders, 7 Hispanic Americans), 2 international. Average age 26. 124 applicants, 60% accepted, 19 enrolled. In 2007, 21 degrees awarded. *Degree requirements:* For master's, comprehensive exam. *Entrance requirements:* For master's, GRE General Test, resumé, writing samples, letters of recommendation. Additional exam requirements/recommendations for international students: Required—TOEFL (minimum score 280 computer-based; 114 iBT). *Application deadline:* For fall admission, 1/15 for domestic and international students. Application fee: $85. Electronic applications accepted. *Financial support:* Career-related internships or fieldwork, Federal Work-Study, institutionally sponsored loans, scholarships/grants, health care benefits, and unspecified assistantships available. Support available to part-time students. Financial award application deadline: 1/15; financial award applicants required to

Journalism

University of Southern California (continued)
submit FAFSA. *Application contact:* Allyson Hill, Director of Admissions, 213-821-0770, E-mail: ascadm@usc.edu.

See Close-Up on page 945.

University of Southern California, Graduate School, Annenberg School for Communication, School of Journalism, Program in Specialized Journalism, Los Angeles, CA 90089. Offers MA. *Students:* 6 applicants, 0% accepted. *Degree requirements:* For master's, thesis. *Entrance requirements:* For master's, GRE General Test, resumé, professional work samples, letters of recommendation, statement of purpose. Additional exam requirements/recommendations for international students: Required—TOEFL (minimum score 280 computer-based; 114 iBT). *Application deadline:* For fall admission, 6/2 priority date for domestic and international students. Applications are processed on a rolling basis. Application fee: $85. Electronic applications accepted. *Financial support:* In 2007–08, 10 fellowships (averaging $20,000 per year) were awarded; Federal Work-Study also available. Support available to part-time students. Financial award application deadline: 1/15; financial award applicants required to submit FAFSA. *Unit head:* Robert Suro, Director, 213-821-6263, E-mail: suro@usc.edu. *Application contact:* Allyson Hill, Director of Admissions, 213-821-0770, E-mail: ascadm@usc.edu.

See Close-Up on page 945.

The University of Tennessee, Graduate School, College of Communication and Information, Knoxville, TN 37996. Offers advertising (MS, PhD); broadcasting (MS, PhD); communications (MS, PhD); information sciences (MS, PhD); journalism (MS, PhD); public relations (MS, PhD); speech communication (MS, PhD). *Accreditation:* ACEJMC (one or more programs are accredited at the [master's] level). Part-time and evening/weekend programs available. Postbaccalaureate distance learning degree programs offered (no on-campus study). *Degree requirements:* For master's, thesis or alternative; for doctorate, thesis/dissertation. *Entrance requirements:* For master's and doctorate, GRE General Test, minimum GPA of 2.7. Additional exam requirements/recommendations for international students: Required—TOEFL. Electronic applications accepted.

The University of Texas at Austin, Graduate School, College of Communication, School of Journalism, Austin, TX 78712-1111. Offers MA, PhD. Part-time programs available. *Degree requirements:* For master's, thesis; for doctorate, one foreign language, thesis/dissertation. *Entrance requirements:* For master's and doctorate, GRE General Test. Electronic applications accepted. *Faculty research:* Politics of race, gender, and sexuality; visual ethics; media law and ethics; national television violence study; agenda setting and public opinion.

University of the Sacred Heart, Graduate Programs, Department of Communication, Program in Journalism and Mass Communication, San Juan, PR 00914-0383. Offers MA. *Degree requirements:* For master's, thesis.

The University of Western Ontario, Faculty of Graduate Studies, Faculty of Information and Media Studies, Program in Journalism, London, ON N6A 5B8, Canada. Offers MA. *Degree requirements:* For master's, internship. *Entrance requirements:* For master's, honors degree, minimum B average during previous 2 years of course work. Additional exam requirements/recommendations for international students: Required—TOEFL (minimum score 640 paper-based; 273 computer-based), TWE (minimum score 5). Electronic applications accepted.

University of Wisconsin–Madison, Graduate School, College of Agricultural and Life Sciences, Department of Life Sciences Communications, Madison, WI 53706-1380. Offers agricultural journalism (MS); family and consumer journalism (MS); mass communication (PhD). *Degree requirements:* For doctorate, thesis/dissertation.

University of Wisconsin–Madison, Graduate School, College of Letters and Science, School of Journalism and Mass Communication, Program in Journalism and Mass Communication, Madison, WI 53706-1380. Offers MA.

University of Wisconsin–Milwaukee, Graduate School, College of Letters and Sciences, Department of Journalism and Mass Communication, Milwaukee, WI 53201-0413. Offers MA. Part-time programs available. *Faculty:* 12 full-time (3 women). *Students:* 7 full-time (3 women), 25 part-time (20 women), 6 international. 33 applicants, 52% accepted, 10 enrolled. In 2007, 12 degrees awarded. *Degree requirements:* For master's, thesis or alternative. *Entrance requirements:* For master's, GRE General Test, minimum GPA of 3.0. *Application deadline:* For fall admission, 1/1 priority date for domestic students; for spring admission, 9/1 for domestic students. Applications are processed on a rolling basis. Application fee: $45 ($75 for international students). *Expenses:* Tuition, state resident: part-time $530 per credit. Tuition, nonresident: part-time $1,428 per credit. Required fees: $19 per credit. $229 per term. Tuition and fees vary according to course load and program. *Financial support:* In 2007–08, 21 teaching assistantships were awarded; fellowships, research assistantships, career-related internships or fieldwork and unspecified assistantships also available. Support available to part-time students. Financial award application deadline: 4/15. *Unit head:* Paul Brewer, Representative, 414-229-5376, Fax: 414-229-2411, E-mail: prbrewer@uwm.edu.

Virginia Commonwealth University, Graduate School, College of Humanities and Sciences, School of Mass Communications, Program in Mass Communications, Richmond, VA 23284-9005. Offers scholastic journalism (MS); strategic public relations (MS). *Degree requirements:* For master's, comprehensive exam, thesis optional. *Entrance requirements:* For master's, GRE General Test. *Application deadline:* For fall admission, 7/1 for domestic students; for spring admission, 11/15 for domestic students. Applications are processed on a rolling basis. Application fee: $50. *Expenses:* Tuition, state resident: full-time $7,224; part-time $401 per credit. Tuition, nonresident: full-time $16,072; part-time $891 per credit. Required fees: $1,679; $63 per credit. Tuition and fees vary according to campus/location. *Financial support:* Teaching assistantships, career-related internships or fieldwork, Federal Work-Study, institutionally sponsored loans, and tuition waivers (full and partial) available. Support available to part-time students. Financial award applicants required to submit FAFSA.

See Close-Up on page 457.

West Virginia University, Perley Isaac Reed School of Journalism, Morgantown, WV 26506. Offers integrated marketing communications (MS); journalism (MSJ). MS program taught exclusively online. Part-time programs available. Postbaccalaureate distance learning degree programs offered (no on-campus study). *Faculty:* 13 full-time (7 women), 30 part-time/adjunct (15 women). *Students:* 59 full-time (40 women), 163 part-time (107 women); includes 27 minority (14 African Americans, 2 American Indian/Alaska Native, 5 Asian Americans or Pacific Islanders, 6 Hispanic Americans), 3 international. Average age 32. 142 applicants, 75% accepted, 67 enrolled. In 2007, 46 degrees awarded. *Degree requirements:* For master's, thesis or alternative. *Entrance requirements:* For master's, GRE General Test, minimum GPA of 3.0, writing samples. Additional exam requirements/recommendations for international students: Required—TOEFL. *Application deadline:* For fall admission, 3/1 priority date for domestic students, 3/1 for international students. Application fee: $50. Electronic applications accepted. *Expenses:* Tuition, state resident: full-time $5,196; part-time $292 per credit hour. Tuition, nonresident: full-time $15,064; part-time $840 per credit hour. Tuition and fees vary according to program. *Financial support:* In 2007–08, 118 students received support, including 2 research assistantships (averaging $8,500 per year), 5 teaching assistantships with full tuition reimbursements available (averaging $8,500 per year); career-related internships or fieldwork, Federal Work-Study, institutionally sponsored loans, tuition waivers (full and partial), and graduate administrative assistantships also available. Financial award application deadline: 2/1; financial award applicants required to submit FAFSA. *Faculty research:* History, law, and women in media; press management; public opinion; advertising effectiveness; international advertising. Total annual research expenditures: $43,727. *Unit head:* Dr. Maryann Reed, Dean, 304-293-3505 Ext. 5409, Fax: 304-293-3072, E-mail: maryann.reed@mail.wvu.edu. *Application contact:* Dr. Steve Urbanski, Director of Graduate Studies, 304-293-3505 Ext. 5435, Fax: 304-293-3072, E-mail: steve.urbanski@mail.wvu.edu.

Mass Communication

American University, School of Communication, Program in International Media, Washington, DC 20016-8001. Offers MA. *Degree requirements:* For master's, one foreign language, comprehensive exam. *Entrance requirements:* For master's, GRE, bachelor[0092]s degree with minimum cumulative GPA of 3.3, 2 letters of reference. Additional exam requirements/recommendations for international students: Required—TOEFL. *Application deadline:* For fall admission, 6/1 for domestic students. Applications are processed on a rolling basis. *Expenses:* Tuition: Full-time $19,998; part-time $1,111 per credit hour. Required fees: $380. Tuition and fees vary according to program. *Application contact:* Sharmeen Ahsan-Bracciale, Graduate Admissions Office, 202-885-2040, Fax: 202-885-2019, E-mail: sharmeen@american.edu.

American University, School of Communication, Program in Public Communication, Washington, DC 20016-8001. Offers MA. *Accreditation:* ACEJMC. Part-time and evening/weekend programs available. *Faculty:* 11 full-time (6 women), 6 part-time/adjunct (2 women). *Students:* 37 full-time (30 women), 29 part-time (16 women); includes 6 African Americans, 3 Asian Americans or Pacific Islanders, 2 Hispanic Americans, 5 international. 153 applicants, 68% accepted, 43 enrolled. In 2007, 61 degrees awarded. *Degree requirements:* For master's, comprehensive exam, thesis or alternative. *Entrance requirements:* For master's, GRE General Test. Additional exam requirements/recommendations for international students: Required—TOEFL (minimum score 600 paper-based; 250 computer-based). *Application deadline:* For fall admission, 2/1 priority date for domestic students, 4/1 priority date for international students. Applications are processed on a rolling basis. Application fee: $50. Electronic applications accepted. *Expenses:* Tuition: Full-time $19,998; part-time $1,111 per credit hour. Required fees: $380. Tuition and fees vary according to program. *Financial support:* In 2007–08, 10 research assistantships with partial tuition reimbursements (averaging $11,000 per year), 2 teaching assistantships with partial tuition reimbursements (averaging $11,000 per year) were awarded; career-related internships or fieldwork, Federal Work-Study, institutionally sponsored loans, scholarships/grants, and tuition waivers (partial) also available. Financial award application deadline: 2/1. *Faculty research:* Litigation and public relations, cross-cultural and intercultural communication, statistical public relations, African-Americans and women in public communication, international public relations. *Unit head:* Leonard Steinhorn, Director, Public Communication Division, 202-885-2031, E-mail: lsteinh@american.edu. *Application contact:* Sharmeen Ahsan-Bracciale, Graduate Admissions Office, 202-885-2040, Fax: 202-885-2019, E-mail: sharmeen@american.edu.

See Close-Up on page 881.

American University, School of Communication, Weekend Programs in Communication, Washington, DC 20016-8001. Offers interactive journalism (MA); news media studies (MA); producing for film and video (MA); public communication (MA). *Accreditation:* ACEJMC. Part-time and evening/weekend programs available. *Faculty:* 5 part-time/adjunct (2 women). *Students:* 137 applicants, 61% accepted, 61 enrolled. In 2007, 15 degrees awarded. *Degree requirements:* For master's, comprehensive exam, thesis or alternative. *Entrance requirements:* Additional exam requirements/recommendations for international students: Required—TOEFL (minimum score 600 paper-based; 250 computer-based). *Application deadline:* For fall admission, 8/1 for domestic students. Applications are processed on a rolling basis. Application fee: $50. Electronic applications accepted. *Expenses:* Tuition: Full-time $19,998; part-time $1,111 per credit hour. Required fees: $380. Tuition and fees vary according to program. *Financial support:* In 2007–08, 3 fellowships (averaging $3,500 per year) were awarded; institutionally sponsored loans also available. *Unit head:* Wendell Cochran, Journalism Weekend Program Director, 202-885-2075, E-mail: cochran@american.edu. *Application contact:* Sharmeen Ahsan-Bracciale, Graduate Admissions Office, 202-885-2040, Fax: 202-885-2019, E-mail: sharmeen@american.edu.

See Close-Up on page 881.

The American University in Cairo, Graduate Studies and Research, School of Business, Economics and Communication, Department of Journalism and Communication, Cairo, Egypt. Offers journalism/mass communication (MA); television journalism (MA, Diploma). Part-time programs available. *Degree requirements:* For master's, thesis (for some programs). *Entrance requirements:* For master's, English entrance exam, GMAT. Electronic applications accepted. *Faculty research:* Mass media and national development/censorship, intercultural photo communication, comparative journalism/television.

Auburn University, Graduate School, College of Liberal Arts, Department of Communication and Journalism, Auburn University, AL 36849. Offers communication (MA); mass communications (MA). Part-time programs available. *Faculty:* 17 full-time (9 women). *Students:* 15 full-time (10 women), 3 part-time (1 woman), 3 international. Average age 27. 21 applicants, 67% accepted, 10 enrolled. In 2007, 13 degrees awarded. *Degree requirements:* For master's, thesis (for some programs). *Entrance requirements:* For master's, GRE General Test. *Application deadline:* For fall admission, 7/7 for domestic students; for spring admission, 11/24 for domestic students. Applications are processed on a rolling basis. Application fee: $25 ($50 for international students). Electronic applications accepted. *Financial support:* Teaching assistantships, Federal Work-Study available. Support available to part-time students. Financial award application deadline: 3/15. *Unit head:* Dr. Mary Helen Brown, Acting Chair, 334-844-2727. *Application contact:* Dr. Joe Pittman, Interim Dean of the Graduate School, 334-844-4700.

Boston University, College of Communication, Department of Mass Communication, Advertising, and Public Relations, Boston, MA 02215. Offers advertising (MS); communication research (MS); communication studies (MS); public relations (MS); JD/MS. *Faculty:* 21 full-time, 28 part-time/adjunct. *Students:* 99 full-time (85 women), 45 part-time (37 women); includes 15 minority (1 African American, 7 Asian Americans or Pacific Islanders, 7 Hispanic Americans), 29 international. Average age 26. In 2007, 78 degrees awarded. *Degree requirements:* For master's, thesis. *Entrance requirements:* For master's, GRE General Test, samples of written work. Additional exam requirements/recommendations for international students: Required—TOEFL. *Application deadline:* For fall admission, 2/1 for domestic students. Application fee: $60. Electronic applications accepted. *Expenses:* Tuition: Full-time $34,930; part-time $1,092 per credit. Tuition and fees vary according to class time, course level and program. *Financial support:* Research assistantships, teaching assistantships with partial tuition reimbursements, career-related internships or fieldwork, Federal Work-Study, institutionally sponsored loans, scholarships/grants, and unspecified assistantships available. Support available to part-time students. Financial award application deadline: 2/1; financial award applicants required to submit FAFSA. *Unit head:* T. Barton Carter, Chairman, 617-353-3482, E-mail: comlaw@bu.edu. *Application contact:* William A. Taylor, Assistant Director, Graduate Services and Financial Aid, 617-353-3481, Fax: 617-358-0399, E-mail: comgrad@bu.edu.

See Close-Up on page 885.

Brigham Young University, Graduate Studies, College of Fine Arts and Communications, Department of Communications, Provo, UT 84602-1001. Offers mass communication (MA). *Faculty:* 15 full-time (2 women). *Students:* 24 full-time (14 women), 18 part-time (7 women); includes 5 minority (1 American Indian/Alaska Native, 4 Hispanic Americans). Average age 30. 33 applicants, 52% accepted, 13 enrolled. In 2007, 5 degrees awarded. *Degree requirements:* For master's, comprehensive exam, thesis. *Entrance requirements:* For master's, GRE, minimum GPA of 3.0 in last 60 hours of course work. Additional exam requirements/recommendations for international students: Required—TOEFL (minimum score 580 paper-based; 237 computer-based). *Application deadline:* For fall admission, 2/28 for domestic and international students. Application fee: $50. Electronic applications accepted. *Financial support:* In 2007–08, 17 students received support, including 23 research assistantships with full and partial tuition reimbursements available (averaging $3,981 per year), 9 teaching assistantships with full tuition reimbursements available (averaging $5,015 per year); career-related internships or fieldwork, institutionally sponsored loans, scholarships/grants, unspecified assistantships, and supplementary awards also available. Financial award application deadline: 5/15; financial award applicants required to submit FAFSA. *Faculty research:* Ethics, international, magazine, newspaper, media effects. *Unit head:* Dr. Edward E. Adams, Chair, 801-422-2997, Fax: 801-422-0160, E-mail: comms.secretary@byu.edu. *Application contact:* Dr. Kevin L. Stoker, Graduate Coordinator, 801-422-1222, Fax: 801-422-0160, E-mail: kevin_stoker@byu.edu.

California State University, Fresno, Division of Graduate Studies, College of Arts and Humanities, Department of Mass Communication and Journalism, Fresno, CA 93740-8027. Offers MA. Part-time and evening/weekend programs available. *Faculty:* 8 full-time (4 women). *Students:* 10; includes 4 minority (2 Asian Americans or Pacific Islanders, 2 Hispanic Americans). Average age 28. 7 applicants. In 2007, 6 degrees awarded. *Degree requirements:* For master's, thesis. *Entrance requirements:* For master's, GRE General Test, minimum GPA of 3.0. Additional exam requirements/recommendations for international students: Required—TOEFL. *Application deadline:* For fall admission, 5/1 for domestic and international students; for spring admission, 10/1 for domestic and international students. Applications are processed on a rolling basis. Application fee: $55. Electronic applications accepted. *Financial support:* In 2007–08, 1 teaching assistantship was awarded; career-related internships or fieldwork, Federal Work-Study, scholarships/grants, and unspecified assistantships also available. Support available to part-time students. Financial award application deadline: 3/1; financial award applicants required to submit FAFSA. *Unit head:* Prof. Donald Priest, Chair, 559-278-2087, Fax: 559-278-4995, E-mail: donald_priest@csufresno.edu. *Application contact:* Dr. Tamyra Pierce, Graduate Program Coordinator, 559-278-2087, Fax: 559-278-4995, E-mail: tpierce@csufresno.edu.

California State University, Northridge, Graduate Studies, College of Arts, Media, and Communication, Department of Journalism, Northridge, CA 91330. Offers mass communication (MA). Part-time and evening/weekend programs available. *Faculty:* 9 full-time (5 women), 19 part-time/adjunct (6 women). *Students:* 5 full-time (2 women), 29 part-time (23 women); includes 11 minority (3 African Americans, 3 Asian Americans or Pacific Islanders, 5 Hispanic Americans). Average age 32. 46 applicants, 54% accepted, 11 enrolled. In 2007, 13 degrees awarded. *Degree requirements:* For master's, thesis. *Entrance requirements:* For master's, GRE General Test. Additional exam requirements/recommendations for international students: Required—TOEFL. *Application deadline:* For fall admission, 11/30 for domestic students. Application fee: $55. *Financial support:* Career-related internships or fieldwork and Federal Work-Study available. Financial award application deadline: 3/1. *Unit head:* Dr. Kent Kirkton, Chair, 818-677-3135, E-mail: kent.kirkton@csun.edu.

Central Michigan University, College of Graduate Studies, College of Communication and Fine Arts, Department of Speech, Communication and Dramatic Arts, Concentration in Interpersonal and Public Communication, Mount Pleasant, MI 48859. Offers MA. *Degree requirements:* For master's, thesis. *Entrance requirements:* For master's, minimum GPA of 3.0 in last 15 hours of speech communication and dramatic arts courses, 2.7 in last 60 hours. *Faculty research:* Communication in organizations, communication in families, relational communication and conflict, communication education.

The College of Saint Rose, Graduate Studies, School of Arts and Humanities, Department of Public Communications, Albany, NY 12203-1419. Offers MA. Part-time and evening/weekend programs available. *Faculty:* 7 full-time (4 women), 7 part-time/adjunct (2 women). *Students:* 5 full-time (3 women), 20 part-time (18 women); includes 3 minority (2 Asian Americans or Pacific Islanders, 1 Hispanic American). Average age 32. 15 applicants, 87% accepted, 10 enrolled. In 2007, 4 degrees awarded. *Degree requirements:* For master's, final project or thesis. *Entrance requirements:* For master's, minimum undergraduate GPA of 3.0, 2 writing samples. Additional exam requirements/recommendations for international students: Required—TOEFL (minimum score 550 paper-based; 213 computer-based). *Application deadline:* For fall admission, 7/15 priority date for domestic and international students; for spring admission, 11/15 priority date for domestic and international students. Applications are processed on a rolling basis. Application fee: $35. Electronic applications accepted. *Financial support:* Career-related internships or fieldwork, scholarships/grants, tuition waivers (partial), and unspecified assistantships available. Support available to part-time students. Financial award application deadline: 3/1; financial award applicants required to submit FAFSA. *Unit head:* Karen McGrath, Chair, 518-458-2028, Fax: 518-454-2862, E-mail: mcgrathk@strose.edu. *Application contact:* Susan Patterson, Assistant Vice President for Graduate Admission, 518-454-5136, Fax: 518-458-5479, E-mail: ace@strose.edu.

Florida International University, School of Journalism and Mass Communication, Miami, FL 33199. Offers mass communication (MS). *Accreditation:* ACEJMC. Part-time and evening/weekend programs available. *Faculty:* 22 full-time (13 women). *Students:* 66 full-time (47 women), 45 part-time (34 women); includes 75 minority (13 African Americans, 4 Asian Americans or Pacific Islanders, 58 Hispanic Americans), 19 international. Average age 28. 98 applicants, 67% accepted, 39 enrolled. In 2007, 58 degrees awarded. *Degree requirements:* For master's, thesis optional. *Entrance requirements:* For master's, minimum GPA of 3.0, essay, resumé. Additional exam requirements/recommendations for international students: Required—TOEFL. *Application deadline:* For fall admission, 6/1 for domestic students, 4/1 for international students; for spring admission, 10/1 for domestic students, 9/1 for international students. Applications are processed on a rolling basis. Application fee: $30. *Expenses:* Tuition, state resident: full-time $6,106. Tuition, nonresident: full-time $15,528. Required fees: $284. *Financial support:* Scholarships/grants and unspecified assistantships available. *Faculty research:* Post-Hurricane Andrew population studies, Central American journalism, employment discrimination. *Unit head:* Dr. Lillian Kopenhaver, Dean, 305-919-5674, Fax: 305-919-5203, E-mail: kopenha@fiu.edu.

Florida State University, Graduate Studies, College of Communication, Department of Communication, Tallahassee, FL 32306. Offers corporate and public communication (MA, MS); integrated marketing communication (MA, MS); mass communication (PhD); media and communication studies (MA, MS); speech communication (PhD). Part-time programs available. *Faculty:* 26 full-time (7 women), 2 part-time/adjunct (0 women). *Students:* 96 full-time (66 women), 126 part-time (70 women); includes 92 minority (37 African Americans, 1 American Indian/Alaska Native, 35 Asian Americans or Pacific Islanders, 19 Hispanic Americans), 1 international. Average age 24. 230 applicants, 74% accepted, 80 enrolled. In 2007, 77 master's, 6 doctorates awarded. *Median time to degree:* Of those who began their doctoral program in fall 1999, 67% received their degree in 8 years or less. *Degree requirements:* For master's, thesis (for some programs); for doctorate, comprehensive exam, thesis/dissertation. *Entrance requirements:* For master's, GRE General Test, minimum GPA of 3.0; for doctorate, GRE General Test, minimum GPA of 3.3 in graduate course work. Additional exam requirements/recommendations for international students: Required—TOEFL (minimum score 600 paper-based; 250 computer-based; 100 iBT). *Application deadline:* For fall admission, 7/1 priority date for domestic and international students; for winter admission, 3/1 priority date for domestic and international students; for spring admission, 11/1 priority date for domestic and international students. Applications are processed on a rolling basis. Application fee: $30. *Expenses:* Tuition, state resident: part-time $248 per credit hour. Tuition, nonresident: part-time $880 per credit hour. Tuition and fees vary according to program. *Financial support:* In 2007–08, 49 students received support, including 1 fellowship with full tuition reimbursement available, 8 research assistantships with full tuition reimbursements available (averaging $14,000 per year), 40 teaching assistantships with full tuition reimbursements available (averaging $5,000 per year); career-related internships or fieldwork, Federal Work-Study, institutionally sponsored loans, scholarships/grants, tuition waivers (partial), and unspecified assistantships also available. Support available to part-time students. Financial award application deadline: 2/1; financial award applicants required to submit FAFSA. *Faculty research:* Communication technology and policy, marketing communication, communication content and effect, new communication/information technologies. Total annual research expenditures: $264,208. *Unit head:* Dr. Stephen D. McDowell, Chairperson, 850-644-2276, Fax: 850-644-8642, E-mail: smcdowel@mailer.fsu.edu. *Application contact:* Natashia Hinson-Turner, Graduate Program Assistant, 850-644-8746, Fax: 850-644-8642, E-mail: dc.gradinfo@comm.fsu.edu.

Fordham University, Graduate School of Arts and Sciences, Department of Communication and Media Studies, New York, NY 10458. Offers public communications (MA). Part-time and evening/weekend programs available. *Faculty:* 11 full-time (3 women). *Students:* 23 full-time (10 women), 34 part-time (22 women); includes 11 minority (7 African Americans, 1 Asian American or Pacific Islander, 3 Hispanic Americans), 9 international. Average age 26. 88 applicants, 78% accepted, 22 enrolled. In 2007, 35 degrees awarded. *Degree requirements:* For master's, thesis, internship. *Entrance requirements:* For master's, GRE General Test. Additional exam requirements/recommendations for international students: Required—TOEFL (minimum score 600 paper-based; 250 computer-based). *Application deadline:* For fall admission, 1/4 priority date for domestic students; for spring admission, 11/1 for domestic students. Application fee: $70. Electronic applications accepted. *Expenses:* Tuition: Full-time $23,880; part-time $995 per credit. *Financial support:* In 2007–08, 4 students received support, including 4 research assistantships with tuition reimbursements available (averaging $17,942 per year); fellowships, teaching assistantships with tuition reimbursements available, career-related internships or fieldwork, Federal Work-Study, institutionally sponsored loans, scholarships/grants, tuition waivers (full and partial), and unspecified assistantships also available. Financial award application deadline: 1/4. Total annual research expenditures: $80,000. *Unit head:* Dr. Paul Levinson, Chair, 718-817-4860, Fax: 718-817-4868, E-mail: levinson@fordham.edu. *Application contact:* Charlene Dundie, Director of Graduate Admissions, 718-817-4420, Fax: 718-817-3566, E-mail: dundie@fordham.edu.

The George Washington University, Columbian College of Arts and Sciences, School of Media and Public Affairs, Washington, DC 20052. Offers MA. *Degree requirements:* For master's, thesis optional. *Entrance requirements:* For master's, GRE General Test. Additional exam requirements/recommendations for international students: Required—TOEFL (minimum score 550 paper-based; 213 computer-based). Electronic applications accepted.

Georgia State University, College of Arts and Sciences, Department of Communication, Atlanta, GA 30303-3083. Offers film/video/digital imaging (MA); human communication and social influence (MA); mass communication (MA); moving image studies (PhD); public communication (PhD). Part-time programs available. *Faculty:* 27 full-time (13 women). *Students:* 81 full-time (51 women), 61 part-time (41 women); includes 31 minority (26 African Americans, 2 Asian Americans or Pacific Islanders, 3 Hispanic Americans), 17 international. 179 applicants, 30% accepted, 29 enrolled. In 2007, 23 master's, 10 doctorates awarded. *Degree requirements:* For master's, one foreign language, thesis or alternative; for doctorate, comprehensive exam, thesis/dissertation. *Entrance requirements:* For master's and doctorate, GRE General Test. Additional exam requirements/recommendations for international students: Required—TOEFL (minimum score 80 computer-based). Application fee: $50. Electronic applications accepted. *Expenses:* Tuition, state resident: part-time $221 per credit hour. *Financial support:* In 2007–08, 1 fellowship with tuition reimbursement (averaging $15,000 per year) was awarded; research assistantships, teaching assistantships with tuition reimbursements, career-related internships or fieldwork, Federal Work-Study, institutionally sponsored loans, tuition waivers (partial), and unspecified assistantships also available. Support available to part-time students. Financial award applicants required to submit FAFSA. *Faculty research:* Critical/cultural studies, rhetoric studies, film/media studies, mass communications/journalism, audience studies. *Unit head:* Dr. David Cheshier, Chair, 404-413-5649, E-mail: dcheshier@gsu.edu. *Application contact:* Tawanna Tookes, Administrative Specialist, Managerial, 404-413-5652, E-mail: joutkt@langate.gsu.edu.

Grambling State University, School of Graduate Studies and Research, College of Professional Studies, Program in Mass Communication, Grambling, LA 71245. Offers MA. *Accreditation:* ACEJMC. Part-time programs available. *Faculty:* 6 full-time (2 women). *Students:* 12 full-time (8 women), 5 part-time (all women); includes 15 minority (all African Americans), 1 international. Average age 27. In 2007, 8 master's awarded. *Degree requirements:* For master's, comprehensive exam, thesis optional. *Entrance requirements:* For master's, GRE, Minimum of 2.5 on last degree. Additional exam requirements/recommendations for international students: Required—TOEFL. *Application deadline:* For fall admission, 7/1 for domestic students; for spring admission, 12/1 for domestic students. Applications are processed on a rolling basis. Application fee: $20 ($30 for international students). *Expenses:* Tuition, state resident: full-time $1,729. Tuition, nonresident: full-time $3,736. *Financial support:* In 2007–08, 3 research assistantships (averaging $3,083 per year) were awarded; career-related internships or fieldwork, institutionally sponsored loans, and unspecified assistantships also available. Financial award application deadline: 5/31; financial award applicants required to submit FAFSA. *Unit head:* Dr. Anita Flemming-Rife, Director, 318-274-3272, Fax: 318-274-3194, E-mail: rifea@gram.edu. *Application contact:* Dr. Martin Edu, Coordinator, 318-274-3272, Fax: 318-274-3194, E-mail: edum@gram.edu.

Howard University, School of Communications, Division of Mass Communication and Media Studies, Washington, DC 20059-0002. Offers mass communication (MA, PhD); media studies (MA, PhD). Part-time and evening/weekend programs available. *Degree requirements:* For master's, comprehensive exam (for some programs), thesis optional; for doctorate, one foreign language, comprehensive exam, thesis/dissertation. *Entrance requirements:* For master's, GRE, minimum GPA of 3.0; for doctorate, GRE, minimum graduate GPA of 3.5. Additional exam requirements/recommendations for international students: Required—TOEFL. Electronic applications accepted. *Expenses:* Tuition: Full-time $16,175; part-time $899 per credit hour. Required fees: $805. *Faculty research:* Advertising, public relations, journalism new media.

Indiana University Bloomington, School of Journalism, Bloomington, IN 47405-7000. Offers journalism (MA, MAT); mass communication (PhD); MA/JD; MA/MA. PhD offered through the University Graduate School. *Faculty:* 11 full-time (5 women). *Students:* 39 full-time (22 women), 16 part-time (14 women); includes 8 minority (5 African Americans, 2 Asian Americans or Pacific Islanders, 1 Hispanic American), 8 international. Average age 29. 125 applicants, 62% accepted, 33 enrolled. In 2007, 39 master's awarded. Terminal master's awarded for partial completion of doctoral program. *Median time to degree:* Of those who began their doctoral program in fall 1999, 80% received their degree in 8 years or less. *Degree requirements:* For master's, thesis (for some programs); for doctorate, thesis/dissertation. *Entrance requirements:* For master's and doctorate, GRE General Test. Additional exam requirements/recommendations for international students: Required—TOEFL. *Application deadline:* For fall admission, 1/15 priority date for domestic students; for spring admission, 9/1 priority date for domestic students. Applications are processed on a rolling basis. Application fee: $50 ($60 for international students). *Financial support:* Fellowships, research assistantships with full tuition reimbursements, teaching assistantships with partial tuition reimbursements, career-related internships or fieldwork, Federal Work-Study, institutionally sponsored loans, and tuition waivers (full) available. Financial award application deadline: 1/15. *Faculty research:* Political communication, international communication, communication history, communication law, visual communication. Total annual

Mass Communication

Indiana University Bloomington (continued)

research expenditures: $165,185. *Unit head:* Bradley Hamm, Dean, 812-855-9247. *Application contact:* Amy Reynolds, Associate Dean of Graduate Studies, 812-855-8111.

Indiana University Bloomington, University Graduate School, College of Arts and Sciences, Department of Telecommunications, Program in Mass Communications, Bloomington, IN 47405-7000. Offers PhD. In 2007, 3 degrees awarded. *Degree requirements:* For doctorate, comprehensive exam, thesis/dissertation. *Entrance requirements:* For doctorate, GRE General Test, minimum graduate GPA of 3.5, 3 letters of recommendation. Additional exam requirements/recommendations for international students: Required—TOEFL (minimum score 600 paper-based; 250 computer-based). *Application contact:* Mitchell Byler, Assistant Dean, 812-855-4871, E-mail: mbyler@indiana.edu.

Iona College, School of Arts and Science, Department of Mass Communication, New Rochelle, NY 10801-1890. Offers journalism (MS); public relations (MA). *Accreditation:* ACEJMC (one or more programs are accredited). Part-time and evening/weekend programs available. *Faculty:* 8 full-time (0 women), 8 part-time/adjunct (4 women). *Students:* 8 full-time (6 women), 33 part-time (24 women); includes 9 minority (3 African Americans, 1 American Indian/Alaska Native, 1 Asian American or Pacific Islander, 4 Hispanic Americans), 2 international. Average age 28. 31 applicants, 39% accepted, 7 enrolled. In 2007, 16 degrees awarded. *Degree requirements:* For master's, comprehensive exam or thesis. *Entrance requirements:* For master's, GRE General Test, minimum GPA of 3.0. Additional exam requirements/recommendations for international students: Required—TOEFL (minimum score 550 paper-based; 213 computer-based). *Application deadline:* Applications are processed on a rolling basis. Application fee: $50. Electronic applications accepted. *Expenses:* Contact institution. *Financial support:* Career-related internships or fieldwork, tuition waivers (partial), and unspecified assistantships available. Support available to part-time students. *Faculty research:* Media ecology, new media, corporate communication, media images, organizational learning in public relations. *Unit head:* Dr. Orly Shachar, Chair, 914-633-2165, E-mail: oshachar@iona.edu. *Application contact:* Veronica Jarek-Prinz, Director of Graduate Admissions, 914-633-2420, Fax: 914-633-2277, E-mail: vjarekprinz@iona.edu.

Iowa State University of Science and Technology, Graduate College, College of Liberal Arts and Sciences, Greenlee School of Journalism and Mass Communication, Ames, IA 50011. Offers MS. *Faculty:* 17 full-time (5 women), 2 part-time/adjunct (0 women). *Students:* 30 full-time (22 women), 7 part-time (6 women); includes 3 minority (1 African American, 2 Hispanic Americans), 18 international. 51 applicants, 69% accepted, 17 enrolled. In 2007, 15 degrees awarded. *Degree requirements:* For master's, thesis or alternative. *Entrance requirements:* For master's, GRE General Test. Additional exam requirements/recommendations for international students: Required—TOEFL (paper-based 570; computer-based 213; iBT 80) or IELTS (6.5). *Application deadline:* For fall admission, 4/1 priority date for domestic and international students; for spring admission, 11/1 priority date for domestic and international students. Applications are processed on a rolling basis. Application fee: $30 ($70 for international students). Electronic applications accepted. *Financial support:* In 2007–08, 12 research assistantships with full and partial tuition reimbursements (averaging $16,161 per year), 3 teaching assistantships with partial tuition reimbursements (averaging $15,600 per year) were awarded; fellowships, scholarships/grants, health care benefits, and unspecified assistantships also available. *Unit head:* Dr. Michael Bugeja, Chair, 515-294-0481, Fax: 515-294-5108, E-mail: greenlee@iastate.edu. *Application contact:* Dr. Eric Abbott, Director of Graduate Education, 515-294-0492, E-mail: masscomm@iastate.edu.

Jackson State University, Graduate School, School of Liberal Arts, Department of Mass Communications, Jackson, MS 39217. Offers MS. Part-time and evening/weekend programs available. *Degree requirements:* For master's, comprehensive exam, thesis optional. *Entrance requirements:* For master's, GRE General Test. Additional exam requirements/recommendations for international students: Required—TOEFL.

Kansas State University, Graduate School, College of Arts and Sciences, A. Q. Miller School of Journalism and Mass Communications, Manhattan, KS 66506. Offers mass communications (MS). Part-time programs available. *Faculty:* 10 full-time (4 women), 1 part-time/adjunct (0 women). *Students:* 18 full-time (16 women), 7 part-time (6 women); includes 2 minority (both African Americans), 5 international. Average age 27. 23 applicants, 78% accepted, 7 enrolled. In 2007, 17 degrees awarded. *Degree requirements:* For master's, thesis or alternative. *Entrance requirements:* For master's, GRE General Test, minimum GPA of 3.0. Additional exam requirements/recommendations for international students: Required—TOEFL (minimum score 600 paper-based). *Application deadline:* For fall admission, 2/1 priority date for domestic students; for spring admission, 7/1 priority date for domestic students. Applications are processed on a rolling basis. Application fee: $30 ($55 for international students). Electronic applications accepted. *Financial support:* In 2007–08, 7 students received support, including 7 teaching assistantships with full tuition reimbursements available (averaging $8,286 per year); research assistantships, career-related internships or fieldwork, institutionally sponsored loans, and scholarships/grants also available. Support available to part-time students. Financial award application deadline: 3/10; financial award applicants required to submit FAFSA. *Faculty research:* Synergistic effects of integrated marketing communications; risk and hazard communication; leadership in media coverage; political communication; advertising psycholinguistic effects. Total annual research expenditures: $129,735. *Unit head:* Angela Powers, Head, 785-532-3955, Fax: 785-532-5484, E-mail: apowers@ksu.edu. *Application contact:* Bob Meeds, Director, 785-532-3961, Fax: 785-532-5484, E-mail: meeds@ksu.edu.

Kent State University, College of Communication and Information, School of Journalism and Mass Communication, Kent, OH 44242-0001. Offers MA. Part-time programs available. *Faculty:* 19 full-time (6 women), 5 part-time/adjunct (0 women). *Students:* 20 full-time (10 women), 18 part-time (11 women); includes 6 minority (5 African Americans, 1 Asian American or Pacific Islander), 2 international. Average age 35. 34 applicants, 71% accepted, 10 enrolled. In 2007, 10 degrees awarded. *Degree requirements:* For master's, thesis optional. *Entrance requirements:* For master's, GRE General Test, minimum GPA of 3.0. Additional exam requirements/recommendations for international students: Recommended—TOEFL (minimum score 600 paper-based; 250 computer-based). *Application deadline:* For fall admission, 3/1 priority date for domestic and international students; for spring admission, 10/30 priority date for domestic students, 10/30 for international students. Applications are processed on a rolling basis. Application fee: $30. Electronic applications accepted. *Financial support:* In 2007–08, 1 fellowship with full tuition reimbursement (averaging $6,550 per year), 2 research assistantships with full tuition reimbursements (averaging $6,550 per year), 7 teaching assistantships with full tuition reimbursements (averaging $6,550 per year) were awarded; career-related internships or fieldwork, Federal Work-Study, institutionally sponsored loans, scholarships/grants, health care benefits, tuition waivers (full), and unspecified assistantships also available. Financial award application deadline: 2/1; financial award applicants required to submit FAFSA. *Faculty research:* Electronic tablet newspapers, accuracy and ethics in broadcast news, internet credibility, First Amendment, HDTV. Total annual research expenditures: $120,500. *Unit head:* Jeffrey W. Fruit, Director, 330-672-2572, Fax: 330-672-4064, E-mail: jfruit@kent.edu. *Application contact:* Evonne H. Whitmore, Graduate Coordinator, 330-672-8304, E-mail: ewhitmor@kent.edu.

Louisiana State University and Agricultural and Mechanical College, Graduate School, Manship School of Mass Communication, Baton Rouge, LA 70803. Offers MMC, PhD. *Accreditation:* ACEJMC. Part-time programs available. Postbaccalaureate distance learning degree programs offered (minimal on-campus study). *Faculty:* 25 full-time (13 women). *Students:* 39 full-time (24 women), 14 part-time (12 women); includes 6 minority (5 African Americans, 1 Hispanic American), 14 international. Average age 31. 61 applicants, 39% accepted, 17 enrolled. In 2007, 8 master's, 1 doctorate awarded. *Degree requirements:* For master's, thesis. *Entrance requirements:* For master's, GRE General Test, minimum GPA of 3.0. Additional exam requirements/recommendations for international students: Required—TOEFL (minimum score 550 paper-based; 213 computer-based; 79 iBT). *Application deadline:* For fall admission, 1/25 priority date for domestic students, 5/15 for international students; for spring admission, 10/15 for international students. Applications are processed on a rolling basis. Application fee: $25. Electronic applications accepted. *Financial support:* In 2007–08, 44 students received support, including 26 research assistantships with full and partial tuition reimbursements available (averaging $15,415 per year), 4 teaching assistantships with full and partial tuition reimbursements available (averaging $20,250 per year); fellowships, career-related internships or fieldwork, Federal Work-Study, institutionally sponsored loans, scholarships/grants, health care benefits, tuition waivers (full and partial), and unspecified assistantships also available. Support available to part-time students. Financial award application deadline: 3/1; financial award applicants required to submit FAFSA. *Faculty research:* Media effects, political communication, new media technologies, persuasive communication, journalism processes and practice. Total annual research expenditures: $85,046. *Unit head:* Dr. John Maxwell Hamilton, Dean, 225-578-2002, Fax: 225-578-2125, E-mail: jhamilt@lsu.edu. *Application contact:* Dr. Margaret DeFleur, Associate Dean of Graduate Studies and Research, 225-578-9294, Fax: 225-578-2125, E-mail: defleur@lsu.edu.

See Close-Up on page 905.

Lynn University, College of Business and Management, Boca Raton, FL 33431-5598. Offers aviation management (MBA); financial valuation and investment management (MBA); global leadership (PhD); hospitality management (MBA); international business (MBA); marketing (MBA); mass communication and media management (MBA); sports and athletics administration (MBA). Part-time and evening/weekend programs available. Postbaccalaureate distance learning degree programs offered. *Degree requirements:* For master's, project; for doctorate, thesis/dissertation, qualifying paper. *Entrance requirements:* For master's, GMAT or GRE, minimum undergraduate GPA of 3.0, resumé, 2 letters of recommendation; for doctorate, GRE or GMAT, minimum graduate GPA of 3.25, resumé, 2 letters of recommendation. Additional exam requirements/recommendations for international students: Required—TOEFL (minimum score 550 paper-based; 213 computer-based). Electronic applications accepted. *Faculty research:* Labor relations, dynamic balance in leisure-time skills, ethics in athletics, hotel development.

Lynn University, Eugene M. and Christine E. Lynn College of International Communication, Boca Raton, FL 33431-5598. Offers mass communication (MS). Part-time and evening/weekend programs available. *Entrance requirements:* For master's, GRE, resumé, 2 letters of recommendation, minimum GPA of 3.0. Additional exam requirements/recommendations for international students: Required—TOEFL (minimum score 550 paper-based; 213 computer-based).

Marquette University, Graduate School, College of Communication, Milwaukee, WI 53201-1881. Offers advertising and public relations (MA); broadcasting and electronic communications (MA); communications studies (MA); journalism (MA); mass communications (MA); religious communications (MA); science, health and environmental communications (MA). *Accreditation:* ACEJMC. Part-time and evening/weekend programs available. *Faculty:* 31 full-time (17 women), 34 part-time/adjunct (17 women). *Students:* 24 full-time (13 women), 19 part-time (12 women); includes 7 minority (1 African American, 1 American Indian/Alaska Native, 2 Asian Americans or Pacific Islanders, 3 Hispanic Americans), 7 international. Average age 28. 76 applicants, 58% accepted, 15 enrolled. In 2007, 17 degrees awarded. *Degree requirements:* For master's, comprehensive exam. *Entrance requirements:* For master's, GRE. Additional exam requirements/recommendations for international students: Required—TOEFL. Application fee: $40. *Financial support:* In 2007–08, 6 research assistantships, 12 teaching assistantships were awarded; career-related internships or fieldwork, Federal Work-Study, institutionally sponsored loans, scholarships/grants, and tuition waivers (full and partial) also available. Support available to part-time students. Financial award application deadline: 2/15. *Faculty research:* Urban journalism, gender and communication, intercultural communication, religious communication. Total annual research expenditures: $17,806. *Unit head:* Dr. Ana Garner, Dean, 414-288-3588, Fax: 414-288-1578.

Marshall University, Academic Affairs Division, School of Journalism and Mass Communications, Huntington, WV 25755. Offers MAJ. *Accreditation:* ACEJMC. *Faculty:* 3 full-time (1 woman), 4 part-time/adjunct (1 woman). *Students:* 23 full-time (16 women), 2 part-time (1 woman); includes 1 minority (American Indian/Alaska Native), 6 international. Average age 27. In 2007, 10 degrees awarded. *Degree requirements:* For master's, thesis optional. *Entrance requirements:* For master's, GRE General Test. Application fee: $40. *Unit head:* Dr. Corley F. Dennison, Dean, 304-696-2809, E-mail: dennisoc@marshall.edu. *Application contact:* Information Contact, 304-746-1900, Fax: 304-746-1902, E-mail: services@marshall.edu.

Miami University, Graduate School, College of Arts and Sciences, Department of Communication, Program in Mass Communication, Oxford, OH 45056. Offers MA. Part-time programs available. *Degree requirements:* For master's, final exam. *Entrance requirements:* For master's, minimum undergraduate GPA of 3.0 during previous 2 years or 2.75 overall. Additional exam requirements/recommendations for international students: Required—TOEFL (minimum score 550 paper-based; 213 computer-based), TWE (minimum score 4). Electronic applications accepted.

Middle Tennessee State University, College of Graduate Studies, College of Mass Communication, Studies in Mass Communication, Murfreesboro, TN 37132. Offers MS. Part-time and evening/weekend programs available. Postbaccalaureate distance learning degree programs offered. *Faculty:* 17 full-time (2 women). *Students:* 1 (woman) full-time, 53 part-time (41 women); includes 23 minority (17 African Americans, 5 Asian Americans or Pacific Islanders, 1 Hispanic American). Average age 29. 58 applicants, 64% accepted. In 2007, 18 degrees awarded. *Degree requirements:* For master's, comprehensive exam, thesis optional. *Entrance requirements:* For master's, GRE. Additional exam requirements/recommendations for international students: Required—TOEFL (paper-based 525; computer-based 195; IBT 71) or IELTS (6.0). *Financial support:* In 2007–08, 8 students received support. Institutionally sponsored loans available. Support available to part-time students. Financial award application deadline: 5/1. *Faculty research:* Ethics of digital media, communication administration, international media issues. *Unit head:* Dr. Clare Bratten, Director, 615-898-5874.

Murray State University, College of Business and Public Affairs, Program in Mass Communications, Murray, KY 42071. Offers MA, MS. Part-time programs available. *Entrance requirements:* Additional exam requirements/recommendations for international students: Required—TOEFL (minimum score 550 paper-based; 213 computer-based). *Faculty research:* AH media on the Internet, visual communication and learning, persuasion, media framing, history of radio and wireless technology.

The New School: A University, The New School for General Studies, Program in International Affairs, New York, NY 10011. Offers global management, trade, and finance (MA, MS); international development (MA, MS); international media and communication (MA, MS); international politics and diplomacy (MA, MS); service, civic, and non-profit management (MS). Part-time programs available. *Faculty:* 10 full-time (6 women), 26 part-time/adjunct (11 women). *Students:* 192 full-time (129 women), 122 part-time (80 women); includes 67 minority (20 African Americans, 17 Asian Americans or Pacific Islanders, 30 Hispanic Americans), 54 international. Average age 30. In 2007, 78 degrees awarded. *Entrance requirements:* Additional exam requirements/recommendations for international students: Required—TOEFL (minimum score 600 paper-based; 250 computer-based; 100 iBT). *Application deadline:* For fall admission, 4/15 for domestic students; for spring admission, 10/15 for domestic students. Application fee: $50. *Financial support:* Fellowships with partial tuition reimbursements, research assistantships, teaching assistantships with partial tuition reimbursements, career-related internships or fieldwork, Federal Work-Study, scholarships/grants, tuition waivers (partial), and unspecified assistantships available. Support available to part-time students. Financial award application deadline: 3/1; financial award applicants required to submit FAFSA. *Unit head:* Dr. Michael Cohen, Director, 212-206-3524, Fax: 212-645-0661, E-mail: cohenm2@newschool.edu.

Application contact: David Norris, Director of Admissions, 212-229-5630, Fax: 212-989-3887, E-mail: nsadmissions@newschool.edu.

See Close-Up on page 1159.

North Dakota State University, College of Graduate and Interdisciplinary Studies, College of Arts, Humanities and Social Sciences, Department of Communication, Fargo, ND 58105. Offers communication (PhD); mass communication (MA, MS); speech communication (MA, MS). Part-time programs available. Postbaccalaureate distance learning degree programs offered (no on-campus study). *Faculty:* 11 full-time (5 women), 3 part-time/adjunct (1 woman). *Students:* 42 full-time (24 women), 50 part-time (35 women); includes 2 minority (both Asian Americans or Pacific Islanders), 7 international. Average age 27. 62 applicants, 40% accepted, 19 enrolled. In 2007, 15 master's, 7 doctorates awarded. Terminal master's awarded for partial completion of doctoral program. *Median time to degree:* Of those who began their doctoral program in fall 1999, 25% received their degree in 8 years or less. *Degree requirements:* For master's, thesis (for some programs); for doctorate, comprehensive exam, thesis/dissertation, 2-3 publications referred before comps. *Entrance requirements:* For master's, GRE, minimum undergraduate GPA of 3.25; for doctorate, GRE, minimum undergraduate GPA of 3.5. Additional exam requirements/recommendations for international students: Required—TOEFL (minimum score 600 paper-based; 250 computer-based; 100 iBT), IELTS (minimum score 7). *Application deadline:* For fall admission, 2/15 priority date for domestic students; for winter admission, 10/15 priority date for domestic students. Applications are processed on a rolling basis. Application fee: $45 ($60 for international students). Electronic applications accepted. *Expenses:* Tuition, state resident: full-time $5,376; part-time $224 per credit. Tuition, nonresident: full-time $14,354; part-time $598 per credit. Required fees: $962; $40 per credit. Part-time tuition and fees vary according to course load and reciprocity agreements. *Financial support:* In 2007–08, 38 students received support, including 1 fellowship with full tuition reimbursement available (averaging $16,000 per year), 10 research assistantships with full tuition reimbursements available (averaging $12,000 per year), 10 teaching assistantships with full tuition reimbursements available (averaging $8,100 per year); career-related internships or fieldwork, Federal Work-Study, institutionally sponsored loans, tuition waivers (full), and unspecified assistantships also available. Financial award application deadline: 2/1. *Faculty research:* Communication and rhetorical theory, organizational communication, broadcast and print journalism, international communication, PR and advertising. Total annual research expenditures: $148,496. *Unit head:* Dr. Paul E. Nelson, Chair, 701-231-7705, Fax: 701-231-7784, E-mail: paul.nelson.1@ndsu.edu. *Application contact:* Dr. Judy C. Pearson, Director of Graduate Studies, 701-231-6551, Fax: 701-231-1074, E-mail: judy.pearson@ndsu.edu.

Oklahoma City University, Petree College of Arts and Sciences, Program in Liberal Arts, Oklahoma City, OK 73106-1402. Offers art (MLA); general studies (MLA); leadership/management (MLA); literature (MLA); mass communications (MLA); philosophy (MLA); writing (MLA). Part-time and evening/weekend programs available. *Faculty:* 18 full-time (7 women), 14 part-time/adjunct (4 women). *Students:* 24 full-time (18 women), 23 part-time (17 women); includes 6 minority (3 African Americans, 1 American Indian/Alaska Native, 1 Asian American or Pacific Islander, 1 Hispanic American), 14 international. Average age 31. 20 applicants, 95% accepted. In 2007, 13 degrees awarded. *Degree requirements:* For master's, comprehensive exam, thesis optional. *Entrance requirements:* Additional exam requirements/recommendations for international students: Required—TOEFL. *Application deadline:* For fall admission, 8/22 for domestic students; for spring admission, 1/15 for domestic students. Applications are processed on a rolling basis. Application fee: $30 ($70 for international students). *Expenses:* Tuition: Full-time $14,040; part-time $780 per hour. Required fees: $881; $32 per hour. *Financial support:* Fellowships with partial tuition reimbursements, career-related internships or fieldwork, Federal Work-Study, institutionally sponsored loans, and tuition waivers (partial) available. Support available to part-time students. Financial award application deadline: 8/1; financial award applicants required to submit FAFSA. *Unit head:* Dr. Regina Benuett, Director, 405-208-5178, Fax: 405-208-5451, E-mail: rebeunett@okcu.edu. *Application contact:* Leslie McKenzie, Director, Graduate Admissions, 800-633-7242, Fax: 405-208-5356, E-mail: gadmissions@okcu.edu.

Oklahoma State University, College of Arts and Sciences, School of Journalism and Broadcasting, Stillwater, OK 74078. Offers mass communication (MS). *Faculty:* 18 full-time (4 women), 5 part-time/adjunct (0 women). *Students:* 7 full-time (4 women), 14 part-time (6 women). Average age 28. 28 applicants, 36% accepted, 6 enrolled. In 2007, 8 degrees awarded. *Degree requirements:* For master's, thesis, professional project, or professional degree plan. *Entrance requirements:* For master's, GRE or GMAT, minimum GPA of 3.0. Additional exam requirements/recommendations for international students: Required—TOEFL. *Application deadline:* For fall admission, 3/1 priority date for international students; for spring admission, 8/1 priority date for international students. Applications are processed on a rolling basis. Application fee: $40 ($75 for international students). Electronic applications accepted. *Expenses:* Tuition, state resident: full-time $4,993; part-time $148 per credit hour. Tuition, nonresident: full-time $14,755; part-time $555 per credit hour. Tuition and fees vary according to program. *Financial support:* In 2007–08, 1 research assistantship (averaging $7,770 per year), 6 teaching assistantships (averaging $8,325 per year) were awarded; career-related internships or fieldwork, Federal Work-Study, scholarships/grants, health care benefits, tuition waivers (partial), and unspecified assistantships also available. Support available to part-time students. Financial award application deadline: 3/1. *Unit head:* Tom Weir, Director, 405-744-6354.

Penn State University Park, Graduate School, Intercollege Graduate Programs, State College, University Park, PA 16802-1503. Offers acoustics (M Eng, MS, PhD); bioengineering (MS, PhD); ecology (MS, PhD); environmental pollution control (MEPC, MS); genetics (MS, PhD); integrative biosciences (MS, PhD), including integrative biosciences; mass communications (PhD); nutrition (MS, PhD), including nutrition; physiology (MS, PhD); plant physiology (MS, PhD); quality and manufacturing management (MMM). *Entrance requirements:* Additional exam requirements/recommendations for international students: Required—TOEFL (minimum score 550 paper-based; 213 computer-based; 80 iBT). *Application deadline:* Applications are processed on a rolling basis. Application fee: $45. Electronic applications accepted. *Expenses:* Tuition, state resident: full-time $14,738; part-time $614 per credit. Tuition, nonresident: full-time $26,050; part-time $1,085 per credit. Tuition and fees vary according to course load, program and student level. *Financial support:* Fellowships, research assistantships, teaching assistantships available. Financial award applicants required to submit FAFSA. *Unit head:* Dr. Regina Vasilatos-Younken, Senior Associate Dean, 814-865-2516, Fax: 814-863-4627, E-mail: rxv@psu.edu. *Application contact:* Cynthia E. Nicosia, Director, Graduate Enrollment Services, 814-865-1795, Fax: 814-865-4627, E-mail: cey1@psu.edu.

Point Park University, School of Arts and Sciences, Department of Journalism and Mass Communication, Pittsburgh, PA 15222-1984. Offers MA. Part-time and evening/weekend programs available. *Faculty:* 9 full-time, 16 part-time/adjunct. *Students:* 26 full-time (18 women), 53 part-time (43 women); includes 18 minority (16 African Americans, 1 Asian American or Pacific Islander, 1 Hispanic American), 2 international. Average age 28. 108 applicants, 57% accepted, 29 enrolled. In 2007, 19 degrees awarded. *Degree requirements:* For master's, thesis or alternative. *Entrance requirements:* For master's, minimum GPA of 2.75, 2 letters of recommendation. Additional exam requirements/recommendations for international students: Required—TOEFL. *Application deadline:* Applications are processed on a rolling basis. Application fee: $30. Electronic applications accepted. *Expenses:* Tuition: Full-time $10,566; part-time $587 per credit. Required fees: $360; $20 per credit. *Financial support:* In 2007–08, 2 students received support, including 2 research assistantships with full tuition reimbursements available (averaging $5,400 per year); career-related internships or fieldwork and scholarships/grants also available. Support available to part-time students. Financial award application deadline: 5/1; financial award applicants required to submit FAFSA. *Unit head:* Helen Fallon, Chair, 412-392-3982, E-mail: hfallon@pointpark.edu. *Application contact:* Marty Paonessa, Associate Director, Graduate and Adult Enrollment, 412-392-3915, Fax: 412-392-6164, E-mail: mpaonessa@pointpark.edu.

See Close-Up on page 919.

St. Cloud State University, School of Graduate Studies, College of Fine Arts and Humanities, Department of Mass Communication, St. Cloud, MN 56301-4498. Offers MS. *Accreditation:* ACEJMC. *Faculty:* 11 full-time (5 women). *Students:* 19 full-time (9 women), 25 part-time (17 women); includes 4 minority (2 African Americans, 2 Asian Americans or Pacific Islanders), 9 international. 7 applicants, 100% accepted, 2 enrolled. In 2007, 13 degrees awarded. *Degree requirements:* For master's, thesis or alternative. *Entrance requirements:* For master's, GRE General Test, minimum GPA of 2.75. Additional exam requirements/recommendations for international students: Required—MELAB; Recommended—TOEFL (minimum score 550 paper-based; 213 computer-based), IELTS (minimum score 7). *Application deadline:* For fall admission, 6/1 priority date for domestic students, 4/1 for international students; for spring admission, 10/1 priority date for domestic students, 8/1 for international students. Applications are processed on a rolling basis. Application fee: $35. Electronic applications accepted. *Expenses:* Tuition, state resident: part-time $267 per credit. Tuition, nonresident: part-time $418 per credit. Required fees: $28 per credit. *Financial support:* Federal Work-Study, scholarships/grants, and unspecified assistantships available. Financial award application deadline: 3/1. *Unit head:* Dr. Roya Akhavan-Majid, Chairperson, 320-308-3293, E-mail: comm@stcloudstate.edu. *Application contact:* Linda Lou Krueger, School of Graduate Studies, 320-308-2113, Fax: 320-308-5371, E-mail: lekrueger@stcloudstate.edu.

San Jose State University, Graduate Studies and Research, College of Applied Sciences and Arts, School of Journalism and Mass Communications, San Jose, CA 95192-0001. Offers mass communications (MS). *Accreditation:* ACEJMC. Part-time programs available. *Students:* 26 full-time (19 women), 45 part-time (33 women); includes 21 minority (5 African Americans, 1 American Indian/Alaska Native, 6 Asian Americans or Pacific Islanders, 9 Hispanic Americans), 13 international. Average age 30. 59 applicants, 69% accepted, 20 enrolled. In 2007, 22 degrees awarded. *Degree requirements:* For master's, thesis or alternative. *Entrance requirements:* For master's, GRE, minimum GPA of 3.0. *Application deadline:* For fall admission, 6/29 for domestic students; for spring admission, 11/30 for domestic students. Applications are processed on a rolling basis. Application fee: $59. Electronic applications accepted. *Financial support:* Applicants required to submit FAFSA. *Faculty research:* Communications theory, mass media effects, public relations, international communications. *Unit head:* William Briggs, Director, 408-924-3249, Fax: 408-924-3299, E-mail: bbriggs@casa.sjsu.edu.

Seton Hall University, College of Arts and Sciences, Department of Communication, South Orange, NJ 07079-2697. Offers corporate and public communication (MA); strategic communication and leadership (MA). Part-time and evening/weekend programs available. Postbaccalaureate distance learning degree programs offered (minimal on-campus study). *Entrance requirements:* For master's, GRE or GMAT, minimum GPA of 3.0. Electronic applications accepted. *Faculty research:* Managerial communication, communication consulting, communication and development.

See Close-Up on page 927.

Southern Illinois University Carbondale, Graduate School, College of Mass Communication and Media Arts, Department of Mass Communication and Media Arts, Carbondale, IL 62901-4701. Offers MA, MFA. *Students:* 31 full-time (15 women), 62 part-time (26 women); includes 8 minority (2 African Americans, 2 American Indian/Alaska Native, 1 Asian American or Pacific Islander, 3 Hispanic Americans), 39 international. 84 applicants, 14% accepted, 9 enrolled. In 2007, 16 master's awarded. *Unit head:* Prof. Jan Roddy, Director of Graduate Studies, 618-453-5794, E-mail: jroddy@siu.edu.

Southern Illinois University Edwardsville, Graduate Studies and Research, College of Arts and Sciences, Department of Mass Communications, Program in Mass Communications, Edwardsville, IL 62026-0001. Offers MS. *Students:* 7 full-time (5 women), 12 part-time (8 women); includes 3 minority (all African Americans), 1 international. 25 applicants, 52% accepted. In 2007, 7 degrees awarded. *Degree requirements:* For master's, comprehensive exam (for some programs), thesis (for some programs). *Application deadline:* For fall admission, 7/20 for domestic students, 6/1 for international students; for spring admission, 12/14 for domestic students, 10/1 for international students. Application fee: $30. Electronic applications accepted. *Financial support:* In 2007–08, 2 research assistantships with full tuition reimbursements, 3 teaching assistantships with full tuition reimbursements were awarded; fellowships with full tuition reimbursements also available. *Unit head:* Dr. Gary Hicks, Director, 618-650-2242, E-mail: ghicks@siue.edu.

Southern University and Agricultural and Mechanical College, Graduate School, College of Arts and Humanities, Department of Mass Communications, Baton Rouge, LA 70813. Offers MA. *Accreditation:* ACEJMC. *Faculty:* 4 full-time (0 women). *Students:* 20 full-time (16 women), 4 part-time (3 women); all minorities (23 African Americans, 1 Hispanic American). Average age 23. 16 applicants, 75% accepted, 10 enrolled. In 2007, 17 degrees awarded. *Degree requirements:* For master's, comprehensive exam, thesis. *Entrance requirements:* For master's, GRE General Test. Additional exam requirements/recommendations for international students: Required—TOEFL (minimum score 525 paper-based; 193 computer-based). *Application deadline:* For fall admission, 4/15 priority date for domestic and international students; for spring admission, 11/1 priority date for domestic and international students. Applications are processed on a rolling basis. Application fee: $25. *Financial support:* In 2007–08, 5 students received support, including 3 research assistantships (averaging $7,000 per year). Financial award application deadline: 4/15. *Faculty research:* Photojournalism, textbook on broadcast. *Unit head:* Dr. Mahmoud Braima, Chairman, 225-771-5790, Fax: 225-771-4943. *Application contact:* Dr. Joseph Terry Kennedy, Associate Professor, 225-771-5790, E-mail: tken@aol.com.

Stephen F. Austin State University, Graduate School, College of Applied Arts and Science, Department of Communication, Nacogdoches, TX 75962. Offers communication (MA); mass communication (MA). Part-time programs available. *Degree requirements:* For master's, comprehensive exam, thesis optional. *Entrance requirements:* For master's, GRE General Test. Additional exam requirements/recommendations for international students: Required—TOEFL (minimum score 550 paper-based; 213 computer-based).

Syracuse University, Graduate School, S. I. Newhouse School of Public Communications, Department of Public Relations, Program in Communications Management, Syracuse, NY 13244. Offers MS. Postbaccalaureate distance learning degree programs offered. *Students:* 17 applicants, 76% accepted, 12 enrolled. In 2007, 18 degrees awarded. *Degree requirements:* For master's, comprehensive exam, internship. *Entrance requirements:* For master's, GRE General Test. Additional exam requirements/recommendations for international students: Required—TOEFL. *Application deadline:* For fall admission, 5/15 for domestic and international students. Applications are processed on a rolling basis. Application fee: $75. Electronic applications accepted. *Expenses:* Tuition: Full-time $18,216; part-time $1,012 per credit. Required fees: $980. Tuition and fees vary according to program. *Application contact:* Executive Education, 315-443-3368, E-mail: commgt@syr.edu.

See Close-Up on page 935.

Syracuse University, Graduate School, S. I. Newhouse School of Public Communications, Program in Mass Communications, Syracuse, NY 13244. Offers PhD. *Students:* 15 full-time (12 women), 7 part-time (5 women); includes 1 Asian American or Pacific Islander, 9 international. 69 applicants, 10% accepted, 7 enrolled. In 2007, 6 degrees awarded. *Degree requirements:* For doctorate, thesis/dissertation, qualifying exams. *Entrance requirements:* For doctorate, GRE General Test. Additional exam requirements/recommendations for international students: Required—TOEFL. *Application deadline:* For fall admission, 12/10 for domestic and international students. Application fee: $75. Electronic applications accepted. *Expenses:* Tuition: Full-time $18,216; part-time $1,012 per credit. Required fees: $980. Tuition and fees vary according to program. *Financial support:* Fellowships, research assistantships, teaching assistantships, career-related internships or fieldwork and tuition waivers (partial) available.

Mass Communication

Syracuse University (continued)

Unit head: Carol M. Liebler, Director, 315-443-3372, Fax: 315-443-3946, E-mail: masscomm@syr.edu. *Application contact:* Doctoral Office, 315-443-3372, E-mail: masscomm@syr.edu.

See Close-Up on page 935.

Temple University, Graduate School, School of Communications and Theater, Department of Strategic and Organizational Communication, Program in Mass Media and Communication, Philadelphia, PA 19122-6096. Offers PhD. Part-time programs available. *Degree requirements:* For doctorate, one foreign language, thesis/dissertation. *Entrance requirements:* For doctorate, GRE General Test, minimum GPA of 3.0, sample of written work. Additional exam requirements/recommendations for international students: Required—TOEFL (minimum score 550 paper-based; 213 computer-based; 79 iBT). Electronic applications accepted. *Faculty research:* Aesthetics and criticism, media institutions, social theory and processes.

Texas State University–San Marcos, Graduate School, College of Fine Arts and Communication, School of Journalism and Mass Communication, San Marcos, TX 78666. Offers MA. *Faculty:* 8 full-time (5 women), 1 (woman) part-time/adjunct. *Students:* 27 full-time (18 women), 15 part-time (8 women); includes 10 minority (4 African Americans, 1 Asian American or Pacific Islander, 5 Hispanic Americans), 3 international. Average age 28. 17 applicants, 88% accepted, 12 enrolled. In 2007, 15 degrees awarded. *Degree requirements:* For master's, comprehensive exam, thesis or alternative. *Entrance requirements:* For master's, GRE General Test, departmental grammar test, minimum GPA of 3.0 in last 60 hours of course work. Additional exam requirements/recommendations for international students: Required—TOEFL (minimum score 550 paper-based; 213 computer-based). *Application deadline:* For fall admission, 2/1 priority date for domestic students, 2/1 for international students; for spring admission, 10/15 priority date for domestic students, 10/1 for international students. Applications are processed on a rolling basis. Application fee: $40 ($90 for international students). Electronic applications accepted. *Expenses:* Tuition, state resident: full-time $3,780; part-time $210 per credit hour. Tuition, nonresident: full-time $8,784; part-time $488 per credit hour. Required fees: $493 per semester. Full-time tuition and fees vary according to course load. *Financial support:* In 2007–08, 31 students received support, including 5 research assistantships (averaging $6,159 per year), 10 teaching assistantships (averaging $5,089 per year); career-related internships or fieldwork, Federal Work-Study, and institutionally sponsored loans also available. Support available to part-time students. Financial award application deadline: 4/1; financial award applicants required to submit FAFSA. *Unit head:* Dr. Lori Bergen, Director, 512-245-2656, Fax: 512-245-7649, E-mail: lb04@txstate.edu. *Application contact:* Dr. Sandyha Rao, Graduate Adviser, 512-245-3790, Fax: 512-245-7649, E-mail: sr02@txstate.edu.

Texas Tech University, Graduate School, College of Mass Communications, Lubbock, TX 79409. Offers MA, PhD. Part-time programs available. *Faculty:* 14 full-time (2 women). *Students:* 32 full-time (16 women), 13 part-time (8 women); includes 5 minority (1 African American, 1 American Indian/Alaska Native, 3 Hispanic Americans), 7 international. Average age 29. 47 applicants, 64% accepted, 11 enrolled. In 2007, 12 degrees awarded. *Degree requirements:* For master's, thesis or alternative. *Entrance requirements:* For master's, GRE General Test. Additional exam requirements/recommendations for international students: Required—TOEFL (minimum score 550 paper-based; 213 computer-based). *Application deadline:* For fall admission, 3/1 priority date for international students; for spring admission, 11/1 priority date for international students. Applications are processed on a rolling basis. Application fee: $50 ($60 for international students). Electronic applications accepted. *Expenses:* Tuition, state resident: part-time $373 per credit hour. Tuition, nonresident: part-time $651 per credit hour. Tuition and fees vary according to program. *Financial support:* In 2007–08, 31 students received support, including 12 teaching assistantships with partial tuition reimbursements available (averaging $19,725 per year); research assistantships with partial tuition reimbursements available, Federal Work-Study and institutionally sponsored loans also available. Support available to part-time students. Financial award application deadline: 4/15; financial award applicants required to submit FAFSA. *Faculty research:* Contemporary media use and structure; Hispanic media; characteristics of public relations spokesperson credibility; psychological measures of advertising effectiveness; media law. Total annual research expenditures: $33,265. *Unit head:* Dr. Jerry C. Hudson, Dean, 806-742-3385 Ext. 224, Fax: 806-742-1085, E-mail: jerry.hudson@ttu.edu. *Application contact:* Dr. Michael Parkinson, Associate Dean of Graduate Studies, 806-742-3385 Ext. 254, Fax: 806-742-1085, E-mail: michael.parkinson@ttu.edu.

Université Laval, Faculty of Letters, Department of Information and Communication, Program in Public Communication, Québec, QC G1K 7P4, Canada. Offers MA. Part-time programs available. *Degree requirements:* For master's, thesis (for some programs). *Entrance requirements:* For master's, knowledge of French, knowledge of English. Electronic applications accepted.

The University of Alabama, Graduate School, College of Communication and Information Sciences, Program in Mass Communications, Tuscaloosa, AL 35487. Offers PhD. *Students:* 42 full-time (26 women), 11 part-time (8 women); includes 5 minority (4 African Americans, 1 Hispanic American), 15 international. Average age 34. 52 applicants, 40% accepted, 7 enrolled. In 2007, 8 doctorates awarded. Application fee: $30. *Expenses:* Tuition, state resident: full-time $5,700. Tuition, nonresident: full-time $16,518. *Application contact:* Diane Shaddix, Information Contact, 205-348-8593, Fax: 205-348-6774, E-mail: dshaddix@bama.ua.edu.

University of Arkansas at Little Rock, Graduate School, College of Professional Studies, School of Mass Communication, Little Rock, AR 72204-1099. Offers journalism (MA). Part-time and evening/weekend programs available. *Students:* Average age 30. *Degree requirements:* For master's, comprehensive exam, thesis optional. *Entrance requirements:* For master's, GRE General Test, minimum GPA of 2.7. *Application deadline:* Applications are processed on a rolling basis. *Financial support:* Research assistantships with tuition reimbursements, career-related internships or fieldwork, Federal Work-Study, institutionally sponsored loans, and unspecified assistantships available. Support available to part-time students. *Faculty research:* Theory and practice of mass communication, social role of the mass media. *Unit head:* Dr. Jamie M. Bryne, Chairperson, 501-569-3250, E-mail: jmbryne@ualr.edu. *Application contact:* Dr. Bruce L. Plopper, Coordinator, 501-569-3250, E-mail: blplopper@ualr.edu.

University of Central Missouri, The Graduate School, College of Arts, Humanities and Social Sciences, Department of Communication, Warrensburg, MO 64093. Offers communication (MA); speech communication (MA). Part-time programs available. *Faculty:* 15 full-time (7 women). *Students:* 15 full-time (7 women), 39 part-time (26 women); includes 4 minority (2 African Americans, 1 American Indian/Alaska Native, 1 Asian American or Pacific Islander), 11 international. Average age 29. 33 applicants, 55% accepted, 11 enrolled. In 2007, 13 degrees awarded. *Degree requirements:* For master's, comprehensive exam, internship, research papers or thesis. *Entrance requirements:* For master's, minimum GPA of 2.5. Additional exam requirements/recommendations for international students: Required—TOEFL (minimum score 500 paper-based; 173 computer-based). *Application deadline:* For fall admission, 6/1 priority date for domestic students, 5/1 priority date for international students; for spring admission, 10/1 priority date for domestic students, 10/1 for international students. Applications are processed on a rolling basis. Application fee: $30 ($50 for international students). *Expenses:* Tuition, state resident: full-time $6,259; part-time $256 per credit hour. Tuition, nonresident: full-time $11,915; part-time $491 per credit hour. Required fees: $604; $20 per credit hour. *Financial support:* In 2007–08, 14 students received support; teaching assistantships with full tuition reimbursements available, career-related internships or fieldwork, Federal Work-Study, scholarships/grants, unspecified assistantships, and administrative and laboratory assistantships available. Support available to part-time students. Financial award application deadline: 3/1; financial award applicants required to submit FAFSA. *Unit head:* Dr. Terry Cunconan, Chair, 660-543-4890, Fax: 660-543-8006, E-mail: cunconan@ucmo.edu.

University of Colorado at Boulder, Graduate School, School of Journalism and Mass Communication, Boulder, CO 80309. Offers communication (PhD), including media studies; mass communication research (MA); newsgathering (MA). *Accreditation:* ACEJMC (one or more programs are accredited). Part-time programs available. *Faculty:* 21. *Students:* 83 full-time (56 women), 10 part-time (7 women); includes 9 minority (3 African Americans, 2 Asian Americans or Pacific Islanders, 4 Hispanic Americans), 10 international. Average age 31. 122 applicants, 74% accepted. In 2007, 38 master's, 6 doctorates awarded. *Degree requirements:* For master's, comprehensive exam, thesis or alternative; for doctorate, comprehensive exam, thesis/dissertation. *Entrance requirements:* For master's, GRE General Test, minimum undergraduate GPA of 2.75; for doctorate, GRE General Test, minimum undergraduate GPA of 3.2, 3.5 graduate. *Application deadline:* For fall admission, 2/15 for domestic students, 12/1 for international students. Applications are processed on a rolling basis. Application fee: $50 ($60 for international students). *Financial support:* In 2007–08, 26 fellowships (averaging $2,908 per year), 10 research assistantships with tuition reimbursements (averaging $14,446 per year) were awarded; institutionally sponsored loans and unspecified assistantships also available. Financial award application deadline: 3/1. *Faculty research:* Writing on science and the environment, mass communication and public opinion, minority representation in the media, media and culture. Total annual research expenditures: $326,556. *Unit head:* Paul Voakes, Dean, 303-492-4364, Fax: 303-492-0969, E-mail: paul.voakes@colorado.edu. *Application contact:* Graduate Program Assistant, 303-492-5008, Fax: 303-492-0969, E-mail: sjmcgrad@colorado.edu.

University of Denver, Faculty of Arts and Humanities/Social Sciences, School of Communication, Department of Mass Communications, Denver, CO 80208. Offers advertising management (MS); digital media studies (MA); mass communications (MA); public relations (MS); video production (MA). Part-time programs available. *Faculty:* 14 full-time (9 women). *Students:* 7 full-time (5 women), 30 part-time (23 women); includes 5 minority (1 African American, 4 Hispanic Americans), 1 international. Average age 26. In 2007, 19 degrees awarded. *Degree requirements:* For master's, thesis (for some programs). *Entrance requirements:* For master's, GRE General Test. Additional exam requirements/recommendations for international students: Required—TOEFL, TWE. *Application deadline:* Applications are processed on a rolling basis. Application fee: $50. Electronic applications accepted. *Financial support:* In 2007–08, 3 research assistantships with full and partial tuition reimbursements (averaging $8,400 per year), 5 teaching assistantships with full and partial tuition reimbursements (averaging $10,000 per year) were awarded; career-related internships or fieldwork, Federal Work-Study, institutionally sponsored loans, and scholarships/grants also available. Support available to part-time students. Financial award application deadline: 3/1; financial award applicants required to submit FAFSA. *Faculty research:* Youth and civic engagement. Total annual research expenditures: $117,000. *Unit head:* Dr. Diane Waldman, Chair, 303-871-2166. *Application contact:* Information Contact, 303-871-2166, E-mail: mcomadm@du.edu.

See Close-Up on page 939.

University of Florida, Graduate School, College of Journalism and Communications, Gainesville, FL 32611. Offers advertising (M Adv); journalism (MAMC); mass communication (MAMC, PhD); public relations (MAMC); telecommunication (MAMC); JD/MAMC; JD/PhD. *Accreditation:* ACEJMC (one or more programs are accredited). Part-time programs available. *Faculty:* 48 full-time (26 women). *Students:* 28 (17 women); includes 5 minority (1 African American, 2 Asian Americans or Pacific Islanders, 2 Hispanic Americans) 11 international. In 2007, 14 degrees awarded. Terminal master's awarded for partial completion of doctoral program. *Degree requirements:* For master's, thesis optional; for doctorate, thesis/dissertation. *Entrance requirements:* For master's and doctorate, GRE General Test, minimum GPA of 3.0. Additional exam requirements/recommendations for international students: Required—TOEFL (minimum score 550 paper-based; 213 computer-based). *Application deadline:* For fall admission, 6/1 for domestic students. Applications are processed on a rolling basis. Application fee: $30. Electronic applications accepted. *Expenses:* Tuition, state resident: full-time $7,478. Tuition, nonresident: full-time $22,603. *Financial support:* Fellowships with full and partial tuition reimbursements, research assistantships with full tuition reimbursements, teaching assistantships with full tuition reimbursements, career-related internships or fieldwork, Federal Work-Study, institutionally sponsored loans, and unspecified assistantships available. Support available to part-time students. Financial award application deadline: 4/15. *Faculty research:* Public opinion, law and policy, regulation, environmental communication, international communication. *Unit head:* Dr. John W. Wright, Interim Dean, 352-392-0466. *Application contact:* Dr. Debbie Treise, Associate Dean for Graduate Programs, 352-392-6557, Fax: 352-392-1794, E-mail: dtreise@jou.ufl.edu.

University of Georgia, Graduate School, Grady School of Journalism and Mass Communication, Athens, GA 30602. Offers journalism and mass communication (MA); mass communication (PhD). *Accreditation:* ACEJMC (one or more programs are accredited). *Faculty:* 43 full-time (20 women). *Students:* 80 full-time (49 women), 12 part-time (6 women); includes 8 minority (6 African Americans, 1 Asian American or Pacific Islander, 1 Hispanic American), 23 international. 263 applicants, 34% accepted, 33 enrolled. In 2007, 35 master's, 5 doctorates awarded. *Degree requirements:* For master's, comprehensive exam, thesis (MA); for doctorate, comprehensive exam, thesis/dissertation. *Entrance requirements:* For master's and doctorate, GRE General Test. Additional exam requirements/recommendations for international students: Required—TOEFL, TWE (PhD). *Application deadline:* For spring admission, 2/15 for domestic students. Application fee: $50. Electronic applications accepted. *Financial support:* Research assistantships, teaching assistantships, tuition waivers (full) and unspecified assistantships available. *Unit head:* Dr. E. Culpepper Clark, Dean, 706-542-1704, Fax: 706-542-2183, E-mail: cully@uga.edu. *Application contact:* Dr. Jeffrey K. Springston, Graduate Coordinator, 706-542-5030, E-mail: jspring@uga.edu.

University of Houston, College of Liberal Arts and Social Sciences, School of Communication, Houston, TX 77204. Offers mass communication studies (MA); public relations studies (MA); speech communication (MA). Part-time and evening/weekend programs available. *Faculty:* 8 full-time (3 women), 3 part-time/adjunct (2 women). *Students:* 34 full-time (30 women), 53 part-time (40 women); includes 37 minority (24 African Americans, 3 Asian Americans or Pacific Islanders, 10 Hispanic Americans), 11 international. Average age 29. 46 applicants, 80% accepted, 18 enrolled. In 2007, 24 degrees awarded. *Entrance requirements:* For master's, GRE General Test, minimum GPA of 3.0 in last 60 hours of course work. *Application deadline:* For fall admission, 7/3 priority date for domestic students. Applications are processed on a rolling basis. Application fee: $25 ($75 for international students). *Expenses:* Tuition, state resident: full-time $6,297; part-time $262 per credit. Tuition, nonresident: full-time $12,969; part-time $540 per credit. Required fees: $2,696. *Financial support:* In 2007–08, 4 fellowships with full tuition reimbursements (averaging $9,750 per year), 8 teaching assistantships with full tuition reimbursements (averaging $9,750 per year) were awarded; research assistantships with full tuition reimbursements, career-related internships or fieldwork, Federal Work-Study, institutionally sponsored loans, scholarships/grants, health care benefits, and unspecified assistantships also available. Support available to part-time students. Financial award application deadline: 2/1. *Faculty research:* Risk communication, relationship development, critical studies, corporate communication. *Unit head:* Beth Olson, Chairperson, 713-743-2873, Fax: 713-743-2876, E-mail: bolson@uh.edu. *Application contact:* Angela Parrish, Graduate Coordinator, 713-743-2873, Fax: 713-743-2876, E-mail: aparrish@bayou.uh.edu.

University of Illinois at Chicago, Graduate College, College of Liberal Arts and Sciences, Department of Communication, Chicago, IL 60607-7128. Offers communication (MA); mass communication (MA). Evening/weekend programs available. *Degree requirements:* For master's, thesis. *Entrance requirements:* For master's, GRE General Test, minimum GPA of 3.0 in last 90 hours. Additional exam requirements/recommendations for international students: Required—TOEFL. Electronic applications accepted. *Faculty research:* Organizational, political, and interpersonal communication; public relations.

The University of Iowa, Graduate College, College of Liberal Arts and Sciences, School of Journalism and Mass Communication, Iowa City, IA 52242-1316. Offers mass communication (PhD); media communication (MA); professional journalism (MA); JD/MA. *Accreditation:* ACEJMC (one or more programs are accredited). *Faculty:* 15 full-time, 16 part-time/adjunct. *Students:* 23 full-time (10 women), 22 part-time (10 women); includes 7 minority (4 African Americans, 1 American Indian/Alaska Native, 2 Hispanic Americans), 10 international. 78 applicants, 42%

accepted, 14 enrolled. In 2007, 11 master's, 5 doctorates awarded. *Degree requirements:* For master's, thesis optional, exam; for doctorate, comprehensive exam, thesis/dissertation. *Entrance requirements:* For master's and doctorate, GRE General Test, minimum GPA of 3.0. Additional exam requirements/recommendations for international students: Required—TOEFL (minimum score 570 paper-based; 230 computer-based; 89 iBT). *Application deadline:* For fall admission, 1/10 priority date for domestic and international students. Applications are processed on a rolling basis. Application fee: $60 ($85 for international students). Electronic applications accepted. *Expenses:* Tuition, state resident: part-time $349 per hour. Tuition, nonresident: part-time $349 per hour. Tuition and fees vary according to course load and program. *Financial support:* In 2007–08, 3 fellowships, 10 research assistantships with partial tuition reimbursements, 18 teaching assistantships with partial tuition reimbursements were awarded; career-related internships or fieldwork and Federal Work-Study also available. Financial award applicants required to submit FAFSA. *Faculty research:* Verbal and visual aspects of historical, legal, social, and cross-cultural communication. *Unit head:* Marc Armstrong, Interim Director, 319-335-3486, Fax: 319-335-3502.

University of Louisiana at Lafayette, Graduate School, College of Liberal Arts, Department of Communication, Lafayette, LA 70504. Offers mass communications (MS). Part-time programs available. *Degree requirements:* For master's, thesis optional. *Entrance requirements:* For master's, GRE General Test, minimum GPA of 2.75. Additional exam requirements/recommendations for international students: Required—TOEFL (minimum score 550 paper-based; 213 computer-based). Electronic applications accepted. *Faculty research:* Mass media problems, issues and ethics, mass communication, historical studies, conflict of interest and law and ethics in journalism, contemporary issues and trends in publications.

University of Michigan, Horace H. Rackham School of Graduate Studies, College of Literature, Science, and the Arts, Department of Communication Studies, Ann Arbor, MI 48104-2523. Offers PhD. *Faculty:* 15 full-time (5 women), 5 part-time/adjunct (1 woman). *Students:* 27 full-time (19 women); includes 4 minority (2 African Americans, 2 Asian Americans or Pacific Islanders), 7 international. Average age 27. 80 applicants, 15% accepted, 6 enrolled. In 2007, 3 degrees awarded. *Degree requirements:* For doctorate, comprehensive exam, thesis/dissertation. *Entrance requirements:* For doctorate, GRE. Additional exam requirements/recommendations for international students: Required—TOEFL (minimum score 560 paper-based; 220 computer-based; 84 iBT). *Application deadline:* For fall admission, 1/15 for domestic and international students. Application fee: $75. Electronic applications accepted. *Financial support:* In 2007–08, 27 students received support, including fellowships with full tuition reimbursements available (averaging $15,600 per year), teaching assistantships with full tuition reimbursements available (averaging $15,199 per year); scholarships/grants, health care benefits, tuition waivers (full and partial), and unspecified assistantships also available. Financial award application deadline: 3/15; financial award applicants required to submit FAFSA. *Faculty research:* Political communication; media, culture and society; media effects; race, gender, and the media; new media, media law and policy. *Unit head:* Prof. Susan J. Douglas, Professor and Chair, 734-764-0420, Fax: 734-764-3288, E-mail: sdoug@umich.edu. *Application contact:* Cornelius Wright, Graduate Program Coordinator, 734-764-0420, Fax: 734-764-3288, E-mail: commphd@umich.edu.

University of Minnesota, Twin Cities Campus, Graduate School, College of Liberal Arts, School of Journalism and Mass Communication, Minneapolis, MN 55455-0213. Offers health journalism (professional program) (MA); mass communication (MA, PhD); strategic communication (professional program) (MA). *Faculty:* 18 full-time (8 women), 4 part-time/adjunct (1 woman). *Students:* 59 full-time (43 women), 36 part-time (25 women); includes 20 minority (5 African Americans, 14 Asian Americans or Pacific Islanders, 1 Hispanic American), 25 international. Average age 34. 87 applicants, 29% accepted, 16 enrolled. In 2007, 8 master's, 2 doctorates awarded. *Degree requirements:* For master's, thesis; for doctorate, comprehensive exam, thesis/dissertation. *Entrance requirements:* For master's and doctorate, GRE, letters of recommendation, minimum undergraduate GPA of 3.0, writing sample. Additional exam requirements/recommendations for international students: Required—TOEFL. *Application deadline:* For fall admission, 12/31 for domestic and international students. Application fee: $55 ($75 for international students). *Financial support:* In 2007–08, 22 fellowships with full and partial tuition reimbursements (averaging $3,480 per year), 14 research assistantships with full and partial tuition reimbursements (averaging $8,139 per year), 56 teaching assistantships with full and partial tuition reimbursements (averaging $9,891 per year) were awarded; career-related internships or fieldwork, Federal Work-Study, institutionally sponsored loans, and tuition waivers (partial) also available. Support available to part-time students. Financial award application deadline: 12/31; financial award applicants required to submit FAFSA. *Faculty research:* Communication law, regulation, and ethics; history; mass media effects; new media, health communication. Total annual research expenditures: $159,725. *Unit head:* Albert R. Tims, Director, 612-625-1338, Fax: 612-626-8251. *Application contact:* Dr. Ron Faber, Director of Graduate Studies, 612-625-4054, Fax: 612-626-8251, E-mail: sjmcgrad@umn.edu.

University of Nebraska–Lincoln, Graduate College, College of Journalism and Mass Communications, Lincoln, NE 68588. Offers MA. Postbaccalaureate distance learning degree programs offered (no on-campus study). *Degree requirements:* For master's, thesis. *Entrance requirements:* For master's, samples of work. Additional exam requirements/recommendations for international students: Required—TOEFL (minimum score 600 paper-based; 250 computer-based). Electronic applications accepted. *Faculty research:* Interactive media and the Internet, community newspapers, children's radio, advertising involvement, telecommunications policy.

The University of North Carolina at Chapel Hill, Graduate School, School of Journalism and Mass Communication, Chapel Hill, NC 27599. Offers mass communication (MA, PhD). *Accreditation:* ACEJMC (one or more programs are accredited). Part-time programs available. *Faculty:* 46 full-time (18 women). *Students:* 188 applicants, 29% accepted, 32 enrolled. In 2007, 24 master's, 8 doctorates awarded. *Median time to degree:* Of those who began their doctoral program in fall 1999, 90% received their degree in 8 years or less. *Degree requirements:* For master's, comprehensive exam, thesis; for doctorate, comprehensive exam, thesis/dissertation. *Entrance requirements:* For master's and doctorate, GRE General Test, minimum GPA of 3.0. Additional exam requirements/recommendations for international students: Required—TOEFL (minimum score 620 paper-based; 260 computer-based; 105 iBT). *Application deadline:* For fall admission, 1/1 for domestic and international students. Application fee: $73. Electronic applications accepted. *Expenses: Contact institution. Financial support:* In 2007–08, 14 research assistantships with full tuition reimbursements (averaging $14,000 per year), 14 teaching assistantships with full tuition reimbursements (averaging $14,000 per year) were awarded; institutionally sponsored loans and health care benefits also available. Financial award application deadline: 3/1; financial award applicants required to submit FAFSA. *Faculty research:* Media processes and production, legal and regulatory issues, media effects, media history. *Unit head:* Dr. Jean Folkerts, Dean, 919-962-1204, Fax: 919-962-0620. *Application contact:* Dr. Anne Johnston, Associate Dean for Graduate Studies, 919-962-4286, Fax: 919-962-0620, E-mail: jomcgrad@unc.edu.

University of Oklahoma, Graduate College, Gaylord College of Journalism and Mass Communication, Program in Journalism and Mass Communication, Norman, OK 73019-0390. Offers advertising and public relations (MA); information gathering and distribution (MA); mass communication management and policy (MA); professional writing (MA); telecommunication and new technology (MA). Part-time programs available. *Students:* 33 full-time (22 women), 41 part-time (27 women); includes 15 minority (5 African Americans, 5 American Indian/Alaska Native, 1 Asian American or Pacific Islander, 4 Hispanic Americans), 12 international. 29 applicants, 90% accepted, 15 enrolled. In 2007, 12 degrees awarded. *Degree requirements:* For master's, thesis optional. *Entrance requirements:* For master's, GRE General Test, minimum GPA of 3.2, 9 hours of course work in journalism, course work in statistics. Additional exam requirements/recommendations for international students: Required—TOEFL (minimum score 600 paper-based; 250 computer-based), TWE (minimum score 5). *Application deadline:* For fall admission, 2/1 for domestic students, 4/1 for international students; for spring admission, 11/1 for domestic students, 9/1 for international students. Application fee: $40 ($90 for international students). Electronic applications accepted. *Expenses:* Tuition, state resident: full-time $3,451; part-time $144 per credit hour. Tuition, nonresident: full-time $12,432; part-time $518 per credit hour. Required fees: $1,925; $70 per credit hour. $122 per semester. *Financial support:* In 2007–08, 26 students received support. Career-related internships or fieldwork, scholarships/grants, health care benefits, and unspecified assistantships available. *Faculty research:* Organizational management; rhetorical analysis; international public relations; digital production; normative theory. *Application contact:* Kelly Storm, Graduate Advisor, 405-325-2722, Fax: 405-325-7565, E-mail: kstorm@ou.edu.

University of Puerto Rico, Río Piedras, School of Communication, San Juan, PR 00931-3300. Offers MA. Part-time programs available. *Students:* 41 full-time (30 women), 19 part-time (13 women). Average age 29. In 2007, 11 degrees awarded. *Degree requirements:* For master's, comprehensive exam, thesis. *Entrance requirements:* For master's, GRE, PAEG, minimum GPA of 3.0, 2 letters of recommendation, interview. *Application deadline:* For fall admission, 2/1 for domestic students. Application fee: $17. *Expenses:* Tuition, state resident: full-time $1,808; part-time $113 per credit. Tuition, nonresident: full-time $5,248; part-time $328 per credit. Required fees: $72 per term. *Financial support:* Fellowships, research assistantships, teaching assistantships, Federal Work-Study, institutionally sponsored loans, and tuition waivers (partial) available. Financial award application deadline: 5/31. *Unit head:* Dr. Eliseo Colón, Director, 787-764-0000 Ext. 5042, Fax: 787-763-5390. *Application contact:* Information Contact, 787-764-0000 Ext. 5043, Fax: 787-763-5390.

University of Southern California, Graduate School, Annenberg School for Communication, School of Communication, Program in Communication, Los Angeles, CA 90089. Offers communication (MA, PhD), including interpersonal and social dynamics (PhD), mass communication, technology, and public policy (PhD), organizational communication (PhD), rhetorical and cultural studies (PhD). *Students:* 86 full-time (52 women); includes 16 minority (3 African Americans, 2 American Indian/Alaska Native, 5 Asian Americans or Pacific Islanders, 6 Hispanic Americans), 24 international. Average age 31. 196 applicants, 13% accepted, 19 enrolled. In 2007, 16 degrees awarded. *Median time to degree:* Of those who began their doctoral program in fall 1999, 89% received their degree in 8 years or less. *Degree requirements:* For doctorate, thesis/dissertation. *Entrance requirements:* For master's and doctorate, GRE General Test, resumé, writing samples, 3 letters of recommendation, interest survey questionnaire, statement of purpose. Additional exam requirements/recommendations for international students: Required—TOEFL (minimum score 280 computer-based; 115 iBT); Recommended—TWE. *Application deadline:* For fall admission, 11/30 for domestic and international students. Application fee: $85. Electronic applications accepted. *Financial support:* In 2007–08, 18 students received support, including 18 fellowships with full tuition reimbursements available (averaging $26,500 per year); research assistantships, teaching assistantships, Federal Work-Study, institutionally sponsored loans, scholarships/grants, health care benefits, tuition waivers (partial), and unspecified assistantships also available. Support available to part-time students. Financial award application deadline: 1/1; financial award applicants required to submit FAFSA. *Faculty research:* Computer-mediated communication, public health campaigns, communication democracy and the public sphere, new communication technologies in organizations, community and community. *Unit head:* Dr. Thomas Goodnight, Director, 213-821-5384. *Application contact:* Allyson Hill, Director of Admissions, 213-821-0770, E-mail: ascadm@usc.edu.

See Close-Up on page 945.

University of Southern Mississippi, Graduate School, College of Arts and Letters, School of Mass Communication and Journalism, Hattiesburg, MS 39406-0001. Offers mass communication (MA, MS, PhD); public relations (MS). *Faculty:* 14 full-time (4 women), 1 part-time/adjunct (0 women). *Students:* 30 full-time (17 women), 37 part-time (23 women); includes 16 minority (13 African Americans, 3 Asian Americans or Pacific Islanders), 4 international. Average age 33. 54 applicants, 56% accepted, 10 enrolled. In 2007, 14 master's, 5 doctorates awarded. *Degree requirements:* For master's, comprehensive exam, thesis optional; for doctorate, comprehensive exam, thesis/dissertation. *Entrance requirements:* For master's, GRE General Test, minimum GPA of 3.0 in field of study, 2.75 in last 2 years; for doctorate, GRE General Test, minimum GPA of 3.5. Additional exam requirements/recommendations for international students: Required—TOEFL. *Application deadline:* For fall admission, 3/1 priority date for domestic students, 3/1 for international students. Applications are processed on a rolling basis. Application fee: $30. *Financial support:* In 2007–08, 18 students received support, including 12 teaching assistantships with full tuition reimbursements available (averaging $7,483 per year); fellowships with full tuition reimbursements available, research assistantships with full tuition reimbursements available, career-related internships or fieldwork, Federal Work-Study, and unspecified assistantships also available. Financial award application deadline: 3/15. *Unit head:* Dr. Christopher Campbell, Director, 601-266-5650, Fax: 601-266-4263. *Application contact:* Dr. Gene Wiggins, Graduate Coordinator, 601-266-5650, Fax: 601-266-6473.

University of South Florida, Graduate School, College of Arts and Sciences, School of Mass Communications, Tampa, FL 33620-9951. Offers MA. *Accreditation:* ACEJMC. Part-time and evening/weekend programs available. *Faculty:* 8 full-time (3 women). *Students:* 23 full-time (20 women), 29 part-time (25 women); includes 6 minority (3 African Americans, 3 Hispanic Americans), 7 international. 41 applicants, 85% accepted, 18 enrolled. In 2007, 7 degrees awarded. *Degree requirements:* For master's, comprehensive exam, thesis. *Entrance requirements:* For master's, GRE General Test, minimum GPA of 3.0 in last 60 hours of course work. Additional exam requirements/recommendations for international students: Required—TOEFL (minimum score 550 paper-based; 213 computer-based). *Application deadline:* For fall admission, 3/15 for domestic students; for spring admission, 10/15 for domestic students. Application fee: $30. Electronic applications accepted. *Financial support:* Application deadline: 2/28. *Faculty research:* First Amendment analysis, civic journalism, public opinion, media ethics, public relation management. Total annual research expenditures: $121,160. *Unit head:* Dr. Edward Jay Friedlander, Chairperson, 813-974-2591, Fax: 813-974-2592, E-mail: efriedla@luna.cas.usf.edu. *Application contact:* Dr. Ken Killebrew, Application Contact, 813-974-6795, Fax: 813-974-2592, E-mail: kkillebr@luna.cas.usf.edu.

University of the Sacred Heart, Graduate Programs, Department of Communication, Program in Journalism and Mass Communication, San Juan, PR 00914-0383. Offers MA. *Degree requirements:* For master's, thesis.

University of Wisconsin–Madison, Graduate School, College of Letters and Science, School of Journalism and Mass Communication, Program in Journalism and Mass Communication, Madison, WI 53706-1380. Offers MA.

University of Wisconsin–Madison, Graduate School, College of Letters and Science, School of Journalism and Mass Communication, Program in Mass Communication, Madison, WI 53706-1380. Offers PhD. *Degree requirements:* For doctorate, thesis/dissertation.

University of Wisconsin–Milwaukee, Graduate School, College of Letters and Sciences, Department of Journalism and Mass Communication, Milwaukee, WI 53201-0413. Offers MA. Part-time programs available. *Faculty:* 12 full-time (3 women). *Students:* 7 full-time (3 women), 25 part-time (20 women), 6 international. 33 applicants, 52% accepted, 10 enrolled. In 2007, 12 degrees awarded. *Degree requirements:* For master's, thesis or alternative. *Entrance requirements:* For master's, GRE General Test, minimum GPA of 3.0. *Application deadline:* For fall admission, 1/1 priority date for domestic students; for spring admission, 9/1 for domestic students. Applications are processed on a rolling basis. Application fee: $45 ($75 for international students). *Expenses:* Tuition, state resident: part-time $530 per credit. Tuition, nonresident: part-time $1,428 per credit. Required fees: $19 per credit. $229 per term. Tuition and fees vary according to course load and program. *Financial support:* In 2007–08, 21 teaching assistantships were awarded; fellowships, research assistantships, career-related internships or fieldwork and unspecified assistantships also available. Support available to

Mass Communication

University of Wisconsin–Milwaukee (continued)
part-time students. Financial award application deadline: 4/15. *Unit head:* Paul Brewer, Representative, 414-229-5376, Fax: 414-229-2411, E-mail: prbrewer@uwm.edu.

University of Wisconsin–Stevens Point, College of Fine Arts and Communication, Division of Communication, Stevens Point, WI 54481-3897. Offers interpersonal communication (MA); mass communication (MA); organizational communication (MA); public relations (MA). Part-time programs available. *Degree requirements:* For master's, thesis or alternative. *Entrance requirements:* For master's, GRE. Additional exam requirements/recommendations for international students: Required—TOEFL (minimum score 575 paper-based). *Application deadline:* For fall admission, 3/1 priority date for domestic students. Applications are processed on a rolling basis. Application fee: $45. *Expenses:* Tuition, state resident: full-time $6,161. Tuition, nonresident: full-time $16,771. Required fees: $884. Tuition and fees vary according to course load. *Financial support:* In 2007–08, 9 teaching assistantships were awarded; career-related internships or fieldwork, Federal Work-Study, institutionally sponsored loans, and unspecified assistantships also available. Support available to part-time students. Financial award application deadline: 5/1; financial award applicants required to submit FAFSA. *Faculty research:* Communication theory and research, film history. *Unit head:* Dr. James Haney, Chair, 715-346-3409, E-mail: jhaney@uwsp.edu. *Application contact:* Dr. Chris Sadler, Graduate Coordinator, 715-346-3898, E-mail: csadler@uwsp.edu.

University of Wisconsin–Superior, Graduate Division, Department of Communicating Arts, Superior, WI 54880-4500. Offers mass communication (MA); speech communication (MA); theater (MA). Part-time programs available. *Degree requirements:* For master's, comprehensive exam, thesis or alternative, position paper or project. *Entrance requirements:* For master's, minimum GPA of 2.75. *Faculty research:* Multimedia technology, ethics in journalism, diversity, electronic portfolio assessment.

University of Wisconsin–Whitewater, School of Graduate Studies, College of Arts and Communications, Department of Communication, Whitewater, WI 53190-1790. Offers corporate communication (MS); mass communication (MS). Part-time and evening/weekend programs available. Postbaccalaureate distance learning degree programs offered (no on-campus study). *Faculty:* 35. *Students:* 7 full-time (3 women), 14 part-time (8 women); includes 3 African Americans, 2 Asian Americans or Pacific Islanders, 1 Hispanic American. Average age 31. 13 applicants, 46% accepted, 3 enrolled. In 2007, 8 degrees awarded. *Degree requirements:* For master's, thesis or alternative. *Entrance requirements:* For master's, 2 letters of recommendation. Additional exam requirements/recommendations for international students: Required—TOEFL (minimum score 550 paper-based; 213 computer-based). *Application deadline:* For fall admission, 7/15 priority date for domestic students, 7/15 for international students; for spring admission, 12/1 priority date for domestic students, 12/1 for international students. Applications are processed on a rolling basis. Application fee: $45. Electronic applications accepted. *Expenses:* Tuition, state resident: full-time $3,451; part-time $244 per credit. Tuition, nonresident: full-time $8,756; part-time $560 per credit. *Financial support:* Research assistantships, Federal Work-Study, unspecified assistantships, and out-of-state fee waivers available. Support available to part-time students. Financial award application deadline: 3/15; financial award applicants required to submit FAFSA. *Application contact:* Sally A. Lange, School of Graduate Studies, 262-472-1006, Fax: 262-472-5027, E-mail: gradschl@uww.edu.

Virginia Commonwealth University, Graduate School, College of Humanities and Sciences, School of Mass Communications, Program in Mass Communications, Richmond, VA 23284-9005. Offers scholastic journalism (MS); strategic public relations (MS). *Degree requirements:* For master's, comprehensive exam, thesis optional. *Entrance requirements:* For master's, GRE General Test. *Application deadline:* For fall admission, 7/1 for domestic students; for spring admission, 11/15 for domestic students. Applications are processed on a rolling basis. Application fee: $50. *Expenses:* Tuition, state resident: full-time $7,224; part-time $401 per credit. Tuition, nonresident: full-time $16,072; part-time $891 per credit. Required fees: $1,679; $63 per credit. Tuition and fees vary according to campus/location. *Financial support:* Teaching assistantships, career-related internships or fieldwork, Federal Work-Study, institutionally sponsored loans, and tuition waivers (full and partial) available. Support available to part-time students. Financial award applicants required to submit FAFSA.

See Close-Up on page 457.

Media Studies

American University, School of Communication, Film and Electronic Media Program, Washington, DC 20016-8001. Offers MFA. *Faculty:* 14 full-time (6 women). *Students:* 33 full-time (19 women), 42 part-time (22 women). 51 applicants, 73% accepted, 22 enrolled. In 2007, 141 degrees awarded. *Degree requirements:* For master's, comprehensive exam, thesis or alternative. *Entrance requirements:* For master's, GRE General Test. Additional exam requirements/recommendations for international students: Required—TOEFL (minimum score 600 paper-based; 250 computer-based). *Application deadline:* For fall admission, 2/1 priority date for domestic and international students; for spring admission, 11/15 for domestic and international students. Applications are processed on a rolling basis. Application fee: $50. Electronic applications accepted. *Expenses:* Tuition: Full-time $19,998; part-time $1,111 per credit hour. Required fees: $380. Tuition and fees vary according to program. *Financial support:* In 2007–08, 10 students received support, including 2 fellowships with partial tuition reimbursements available (averaging $13,000 per year), 2 research assistantships with partial tuition reimbursements available (averaging $11,000 per year), 4 teaching assistantships with partial tuition reimbursements available (averaging $11,000 per year); career-related internships or fieldwork, Federal Work-Study, institutionally sponsored loans, scholarships/grants, tuition waivers (partial), and unspecified assistantships also available. Financial award application deadline: 2/1. *Faculty research:* Documentary film production, social media, media and public policy, visual literacy, new technology. *Unit head:* Prof. John Douglass, Director, Film and Media Arts Division, 202-885-2045, Fax: 202-885-2019, E-mail: jdougla@american.edu. *Application contact:* Sharmeen Ahsan-Bracciale, Graduate Admissions Office, 202-885-2040, Fax: 202-885-2019, E-mail: sharmeen@american.edu.

Arkansas State University, Graduate School, College of Communications, Department of Radio-Television, Jonesboro, State University, AR 72467. Offers MSMC. Part-time programs available. *Faculty:* 4 full-time (1 woman). *Students:* 5 full-time (2 women), 7 part-time (6 women); includes 7 minority (all African Americans), 1 international. Average age 25. 6 applicants, 83% accepted, 5 enrolled. In 2007, 4 degrees awarded. *Degree requirements:* For master's, one foreign language, comprehensive exam, thesis or alternative. *Entrance requirements:* For master's, GRE General Test, appropriate bachelor's degree, letters of reference, recommendations, official transcript. Additional exam requirements/recommendations for international students: Required—TOEFL (minimum score 213 computer-based). *Application deadline:* Applications are processed on a rolling basis. Application fee: $30 ($40 for international students). Electronic applications accepted. *Expenses:* Tuition, state resident: full-time $3,528; part-time $196 per hour. Tuition, nonresident: full-time $8,928; part-time $496 per hour. Required fees: $842; $44 per hour. $25 per term. Tuition and fees vary according to course load and program. *Financial support:* Career-related internships or fieldwork, scholarships/grants, and unspecified assistantships available. Financial award application deadline: 7/1; financial award applicants required to submit FAFSA. *Faculty research:* Cable and alternative technologies, development communications, Freedom of Information Act, public radio, role of media in national integration. *Unit head:* Dr. Osabuohien Amienyi, Chair, 870-972-3070, Fax: 870-972-2997, E-mail: osami@astate.edu.

Bob Jones University, Graduate Programs, Greenville, SC 29614. Offers accountancy (MS); Bible (MA); Bible translation (MA); Biblical studies (Certificate); broadcast management (MS); business administration (MBA); church history (MA, PhD); church ministries (MA); church music (MM); cinema and video production (MA); counseling (MS); curriculum and instruction (Ed D); divinity (M Div); dramatic production (MA); educational leadership (MS, Ed D, Ed S); elementary education (M Ed, MAT); English (M Ed, MA, MAT); fine arts (MA); graphic design (MA); history (M Ed, MA); illustration (MA); interpretative speech (MA); mathematics (M Ed, MAT); medical missions (Certificate); ministry (MM, D Min); multi-categorical special education (M Ed, MAT); music (M Ed); New Testament interpretation (PhD); Old Testament interpretation (PhD); orchestral instrument performance (MM); organ performance (MM); pastoral studies (MA); personnel services (MS, Ed S); piano pedagogy (MM); piano performance (MM); platform arts (MA); radio and television broadcasting (MS); rhetoric and public address (MA); secondary education (M Ed); studio art (MA); teaching Bible (MA); theology (MA, PhD); voice performance (MM); youth ministries (MA); M Div/MM.

Boston University, College of Communication, Department of Film and Television, Boston, MA 02215. Offers film production (MFA); film studies (MFA); screenwriting (MFA); television (MS); television management (MS); MBA/MS. *Faculty:* 13 full-time, 27 part-time/adjunct. *Students:* 115 full-time (63 women), 17 part-time (12 women); includes 13 minority (4 African Americans, 1 American Indian/Alaska Native, 4 Asian Americans or Pacific Islanders, 4 Hispanic Americans), 14 international. Average age 26. In 2007, 10 degrees awarded. *Degree requirements:* For master's, thesis. *Entrance requirements:* For master's, GMAT (MS in television management), GRE General Test, sample of written or creative work. Additional exam requirements/recommendations for international students: Required—TOEFL. *Application deadline:* For fall admission, 2/1 for domestic students. Electronic applications accepted. *Expenses:* Tuition: Full-time $34,930; part-time $1,092 per credit. Tuition and fees vary according to class time, course level and program. *Financial support:* Teaching assistantships with partial tuition reimbursements, career-related internships or fieldwork, Federal Work-Study, institutionally sponsored loans, scholarships/grants, and unspecified assistantships available. Support available to part-time students. Financial award application deadline: 2/1; financial award applicants required to submit FAFSA. *Unit head:* Charles Merzbacher, Chairman, 617-353-3483, Fax: 617-353-1084, E-mail: ftvchair@bu.edu. *Application contact:* William A. Taylor, Assistant Director, Graduate Services and Financial Aid, 617-353-3481, Fax: 617-358-0399, E-mail: comgrad@bu.edu.

See Close-Up on page 885.

California State University, Fullerton, Graduate Studies, College of Communications, Department of Communications, Fullerton, CA 92834-9480. Offers communications—advertising (MA); communications—entertainment and tourism (MA); communications—journalism (MA); communications—public relations (MA). Part-time programs available. *Students:* 25 full-time (22 women), 39 part-time (24 women); includes 19 minority (1 African American, 6 Asian Americans or Pacific Islanders, 12 Hispanic Americans), 11 international. Average age 29. 140 applicants, 41% accepted, 28 enrolled. In 2007, 43 degrees awarded. *Degree requirements:* For master's, project or thesis. *Entrance requirements:* For master's, GRE General Test. Application fee: $55. *Financial support:* Teaching assistantships, career-related internships or fieldwork, Federal Work-Study, institutionally sponsored loans, and scholarships/grants available. Support available to part-time students. Financial award application deadline: 3/1. *Unit head:* Dr. Tony Fellow, Chair, 714-278-3517. *Application contact:* Coordinator, 714-278-3832.

Carnegie Mellon University, School of Computer Science and College of Fine Arts, Program in Entertainment Technology, Pittsburgh, PA 15213-3891. Offers MET.

Central Michigan University, College of Graduate Studies, College of Communication and Fine Arts, Department of Broadcast and Cinematic Arts, Mount Pleasant, MI 48859. Offers MA. *Degree requirements:* For master's, thesis or alternative. *Entrance requirements:* For master's, GRE, 30 semester hours in broadcasting or related course work, minimum undergraduate GPA of 2.7. *Faculty research:* TV, film history and criticism, writing for the media, international broadcasting and media systems, history of American broadcasting.

City College of the City University of New York, Graduate School, College of Liberal Arts and Science, Division of the Humanities and Arts, Department of Media Arts Production, New York, NY 10031-9198. Offers MFA. *Students:* 41 full-time (15 women); includes 26 minority (7 African Americans, 7 Asian Americans or Pacific Islanders, 12 Hispanic Americans), 9 international. 53 applicants, 38% accepted, 20 enrolled. In 2007, 19 degrees awarded. *Entrance requirements:* For master's, videotape portfolio. Additional exam requirements/recommendations for international students: Required—TOEFL (minimum score 575 paper-based; 233 computer-based). *Application deadline:* For fall admission, 4/1 for domestic students. Application fee: $125. *Unit head:* Andrej Krakowski, Chair, 212-650-5398, Fax: 212-650-7272. *Application contact:* David Davidson, Advisor, 212-650-7235, Fax: 212-650-7272.

Claremont Graduate University, Graduate Programs, School of Arts and Humanities, Department of Cultural Studies, Claremont, CA 91711-6160. Offers Africana studies (Certificate); cultural studies (MA, PhD); media studies (MA, PhD); museum studies (MA). Part-time programs available. *Faculty:* 2 full-time (1 woman), 2 part-time/adjunct (0 women). *Students:* 48 full-time (33 women), 10 part-time (4 women); includes 19 minority (10 African Americans, 5 Asian Americans or Pacific Islanders, 4 Hispanic Americans), 5 international. Average age 35. In 2007, 7 master's, 4 doctorates awarded. *Degree requirements:* For master's, one foreign language, thesis; for doctorate, 2 foreign languages, comprehensive exam, thesis/dissertation. *Entrance requirements:* For master's and doctorate, GRE General Test. *Application deadline:* For fall admission, 2/15 priority date for domestic students. Applications are processed on a rolling basis. Electronic applications accepted. *Expenses:* Tuition: Full-time $31,640; part-time $1,376 per unit. Required fees: $145 per semester. Tuition and fees vary according to course load, degree level and program. *Financial support:* Fellowships, research assistantships, career-related internships or fieldwork, Federal Work-Study, and institutionally sponsored loans available. Support available to part-time students. Financial award application deadline: 2/15; financial award applicants required to submit FAFSA. *Unit head:* Henry Krips, Chair, 909-607-7803, Fax: 909-621-8609, E-mail: henry.krips@cgu.edu.

College of Staten Island of the City University of New York, Graduate Programs, Program in Cinema and Media Studies, Staten Island, NY 10314-6600. Offers MA. Part-time and evening/weekend programs available. *Faculty:* 6 full-time (3 women). *Students:* 1 full-time (0 women), 13 part-time (6 women); includes 1 minority (African American), 4 international. Average age 30. 12 applicants, 83% accepted, 6 enrolled. In 2007, 7 degrees awarded. *Degree requirements:* For master's, comprehensive exam, thesis optional, written thesis, original film or media or production thesis or written examination. *Entrance requirements:* For master's, 10-12 page critical writing sample on film or media topic, minimum GPA of 3.0 in cinema studies or communications, 3 letters of recommendation, personal statement. Additional exam requirements/recommendations for international students: Required—TOEFL (minimum score 550 paper-based; 213 computer-based; 79 iBT). *Application deadline:* For fall admission, 4/15 priority date for domestic and international students. Applications are processed on a rolling basis. Application fee: $125. Electronic applications accepted. *Expenses:* Tuition, state resident: part-time $270 per credit. Tuition, nonresident: part-time $500 per credit. Required fees: $38 per semester. One-time fee: $15 part-time. Tuition and fees vary according to course load. *Financial support:* In 2007–08, 1 student received support, including 7 fellowships (averaging $1,200 per year), 4 teaching assistantships (averaging $1,250 per year). Financial award application deadline: 4/1; financial award applicants required to submit CSS PROFILE or FAFSA. *Faculty research:* The historical, culture, and pedagogical legacy of Dun Mingjins documentary film practice; Australian Chinatowns in comparative perspectives; nickelodeons in Newark, from puppets to pictures; real costs: bringing environmental impact to e-commerce; culture of complaint: media decency book proposal. *Unit head:* Dr. Matthew Solomon, Coordinator, 718-982-2548, E-mail: cinemamasters@mail.csi.cuny.edu. *Application contact:* Sasha Spence, Assistant Director of Graduate Recruitment Admissions, 718-982-2699, Fax: 718-982-2500, E-mail: spence@mail.csi.cuny.edu.

Columbia College Chicago, Graduate School, Department of Arts, Entertainment and Media Management, Chicago, IL 60605-1996. Offers arts, entertainment and media management (MA), including media management, music business, performing arts management, visual arts management. Evening/weekend programs available. *Students:* 117 full-time (84 women), 83 part-time (51 women); includes 50 minority (35 African Americans, 1 American Indian/Alaska Native, 3 Asian Americans or Pacific Islanders, 11 Hispanic Americans), 15 international. Average age 27. In 2007, 50 degrees awarded. *Degree requirements:* For master's, thesis, internship. *Entrance requirements:* For master's, interview, minimum GPA of 3.0. Additional exam requirements/recommendations for international students: Required—TOEFL (minimum score 550 paper-based; 213 computer-based). *Application deadline:* For fall admission, 6/1 for domestic students, 3/1 for international students; for spring admission, 10/3 for domestic students. Applications are processed on a rolling basis. Application fee: $50. Electronic applications accepted. *Financial support:* Fellowships, career-related internships or fieldwork, Federal Work-Study, and scholarships/grants available. Support available to part-time students. Financial award application deadline: 8/13; financial award applicants required to submit FAFSA. *Unit head:* Dr. J. Dennis Rich, Chairperson, 312-344-7659 Ext. 5260, Fax: 312-344-8063, E-mail: drich@colum.edu. *Application contact:* Keith Cleveland, Acting Dean of the Graduate School, 312-344-7261, Fax: 312-344-8047, E-mail: kcleveland@colum.edu.

Concordia University, School of Graduate Studies, Faculty of Arts and Science, Department of Communication Studies, Montréal, QC H3G 1M8, Canada. Offers communication (PhD); communication studies (Diploma); media studies (MA). *Degree requirements:* For master's, thesis optional; for doctorate, one foreign language, comprehensive exam, thesis/dissertation, research practicum, seminar. *Entrance requirements:* For master's, bachelor's degree in communications, 2 years of media-related experience; for doctorate, MA in communications. *Faculty research:* Communication and development, organizational communication, cultural studies, rhetoric, future studies.

Concordia University, School of Graduate Studies, Faculty of Fine Arts, Department of Studio Arts, Montréal, QC H3G 1M8, Canada. Offers studio arts (MFA), including film production, open media, painting, photography, print media, sculpture, ceramics and fibers. *Degree requirements:* For master's, thesis or alternative. *Entrance requirements:* For master's, portfolio.

Dallas Theological Seminary, Graduate Programs, Dallas, TX 75204-6499. Offers academic ministries (Th M); Bible translation (Th M); biblical and theological studies (CGS); biblical counseling (MA, Th M); biblical exegesis and linguistics (MA); biblical exposition (PhD); biblical studies (MA); Christian education (MA, D Min); cross-cultural ministries (MA, Th M); educational leadership (Th M); evangelism and discipleship (Th M); interdisciplinary studies (Th M); media and communication (MA); media arts in ministry (Th M); ministry (D Min); New Testament studies (Th M, PhD); Old Testament studies (PhD); parachurch ministries (Th M); pastoral ministries (Th M); sacred theology (STM); theological studies (PhD); women's ministry (Th M). *Accreditation:* ATS (one or more programs are accredited). Part-time and evening/weekend programs available. *Degree requirements:* For master's, variable foreign language requirement, thesis (for some programs); for doctorate, 2 foreign languages, thesis/dissertation. *Entrance requirements:* Additional exam requirements/recommendations for international students: Required—TOEFL, TWE. *Application deadline:* For fall admission, 7/1 priority date for domestic students; for winter admission, 11/1 priority date for domestic students; for spring admission, 11/15 priority date for domestic students. Applications are processed on a rolling basis. Application fee: $30. Electronic applications accepted. *Financial support:* Career-related internships or fieldwork, institutionally sponsored loans, scholarships/grants, and tuition waivers (full and partial) available. Financial award application deadline: 2/28. *Unit head:* Dr. Mark L. Bailey, President, 214-841-3676, Fax: 214-841-3565. *Application contact:* Josh Bleeker, Director of Admissions, 214-841-3661, Fax: 214-841-3664, E-mail: admissions@dts.edu.

DePaul University, College of Communication, Chicago, IL 60604-2287. Offers journalism (MA); media, culture, and society (MA); organizational and multicultural communication (MA); public relations and advertising (MA). Part-time and evening/weekend programs available. *Faculty:* 21 full-time (10 women), 9 part-time/adjunct (4 women). *Students:* 88 full-time (69 women), 43 part-time (38 women); includes 29 minority (16 African Americans, 5 Asian Americans or Pacific Islanders, 8 Hispanic Americans), 2 international. Average age 29. 242 applicants, 47% accepted, 68 enrolled. In 2007, 64 degrees awarded. *Degree requirements:* For master's, final exam or thesis/project. *Entrance requirements:* For master's, GRE General Test (public relations and advertising), minimum GPA of 3.0, writing sample, essay, letters of recommendation, resumé. Additional exam requirements/recommendations for international students: Required—TOEFL (minimum score 590 paper-based; 245 computer-based; 96 iBT). Application fee: $40. Electronic applications accepted. *Financial support:* In 2007–08, 8 students received support, including 2 teaching assistantships with full tuition reimbursements available (averaging $12,000 per year); fellowships with full tuition reimbursements available, research assistantships, career-related internships or fieldwork, scholarships/grants, and tuition waivers (partial) also available. Support available to part-time students. Financial award applicants required to submit FAFSA. *Faculty research:* Intercultural communication, corporate culture, diversity in the working place, organizational socialization, critical cultural studies. *Unit head:* Dr. Jacqueline Taylor, Dean, 773-325-7216, Fax: 773-325-7584, E-mail: jtaylor@depaul.edu. *Application contact:* Ann Spittle, Director of Graduate Admission, 773-325-8369, Fax: 773-325-2395, E-mail: aspittle@depaul.edu.

Digital Media Arts College, Graduate Programs, Boca Raton, FL 33431. Offers graphic design (MFA); special FX animation (MFA).

Edinboro University of Pennsylvania, Graduate Studies and Research, School of Liberal Arts, Department of Communications and Media Studies, Edinboro, PA 16444. Offers MA. Part-time and evening/weekend programs available. *Faculty:* 4 full-time (1 woman). *Students:* 23 full-time (17 women), 11 part-time (5 women); includes 4 minority (3 African Americans, 1 Hispanic American), 4 international. Average age 29. In 2007, 26 degrees awarded. *Degree requirements:* For master's, thesis or alternative, competency exam. *Entrance requirements:* For master's, GRE or MAT, minimum QPA of 2.5. *Application deadline:* Applications are processed on a rolling basis. Application fee: $30. Electronic applications accepted. *Expenses:* Tuition, state resident: full-time $6,214; part-time $345 per credit. Tuition, nonresident: full-time $9,944; part-time $552 per credit. Required fees: $46 per credit. *Financial support:* In 2007–08, 10 research assistantships with full and partial tuition reimbursements (averaging $3,850 per year) were awarded; career-related internships or fieldwork, Federal Work-Study, scholarships/grants, and unspecified assistantships also available. Support available to part-time students. Financial award application deadline: 2/15; financial award applicants required to submit FAFSA. *Unit head:* Dr. Anthony Peyronel, Coordinator, 814-732-2444, E-mail: apeyronel@edinboro.edu. *Application contact:* Dr. R. Scott Baldwin, Dean, 814-732-2752, Fax: 814-732-2268, E-mail: sbaldwin@edinboro.edu.

Emerson College, Graduate Studies, School of the Arts, Department of Visual and Media Arts, Programs in Audio, Television/Video, and New Media Production, Boston, MA 02116-4624. Offers audio production (MA); new media production (MA); television/video production (MA). Part-time programs available. *Faculty:* 37 full-time (12 women). *Students:* 104 full-time (46 women), 37 part-time (20 women); includes 3 African Americans, 2 Hispanic Americans, 1 international. Average age 25. 148 applicants, 73% accepted, 55 enrolled. In 2007, 41 degrees awarded. *Degree requirements:* For master's, thesis or alternative. *Entrance requirements:* For master's, GRE General Test. Additional exam requirements/recommendations for international students: Required—TOEFL (minimum score 550 paper-based; 213 computer-based; 80 iBT), IELTS (minimum score 7). *Application deadline:* For fall admission, 3/1 priority date for domestic students; for spring admission, 11/1 priority date for domestic students. Applications are processed on a rolling basis. Application fee: $60 ($75 for international students). *Expenses:* Tuition: Full-time $16,800; part-time $840 per credit. Required fees: $60 per semester. One-time fee: $160. *Financial support:* In 2007–08, 1 fellowship with partial tuition reimbursement (averaging $14,000 per year), 14 research assistantships with partial tuition reimbursements (averaging $10,000 per year) were awarded; teaching assistantships with partial tuition reimbursements, career-related internships or fieldwork, scholarships/grants, and unspecified assistantships also available. Support available to part-time students. Financial award application deadline: 3/1; financial award applicants required to submit FAFSA. *Faculty research:* Media studies. *Unit head:* Prof. Jan Roberts Breslin, Director, 617-824-8800. *Application contact:* 617-824-8610, Fax: 617-824-8614, E-mail: gradapp@emerson.edu.

See Close-Up on page 895.

Fairleigh Dickinson University, Metropolitan Campus, University College: Arts, Sciences, and Professional Studies, School of Art and Media Studies, Program in Media and Communications, Teaneck, NJ 07666-1914. Offers MA. *Students:* 8 full-time (3 women), 5 part-time (3 women). Average age 31. 5 applicants, 80% accepted, 1 enrolled. In 2007, 10 degrees awarded. Application fee: $40. *Expenses:* Tuition: Part-time $869 per credit. Tuition and fees vary according to degree level, campus/location and program. *Unit head:* Jason Scorza, Director, School of Art and Media Studies, 201-692-2000.

Florida State University, Graduate Studies, College of Communication, Department of Communication, Tallahassee, FL 32306. Offers corporate and public communication (MA, MS); integrated marketing communication (MA, MS); mass communication (PhD); media and communication studies (MA, MS); speech communication (PhD). Part-time programs available. *Faculty:* 26 full-time (7 women), 2 part-time/adjunct (0 women). *Students:* 96 full-time (66 women), 126 part-time (70 women); includes 92 minority (37 African Americans, 1 American Indian/Alaska Native, 35 Asian Americans or Pacific Islanders, 19 Hispanic Americans), 1 international. Average age 24. 230 applicants, 74% accepted, 80 enrolled. In 2007, 77 master's, 6 doctorates awarded. *Median time to degree:* Of those who began their doctoral program in fall 1999, 67% received their degree in 8 years or less. *Degree requirements:* For master's, thesis (for some programs); for doctorate, comprehensive exam, thesis/dissertation. *Entrance requirements:* For master's, GRE General Test, minimum GPA of 3.0; for doctorate, GRE General Test, minimum GPA of 3.3 in graduate course work. Additional exam requirements/recommendations for international students: Required—TOEFL (minimum score 600 paper-based; 250 computer-based; 100 iBT). *Application deadline:* For fall admission, 7/1 priority date for domestic and international students; for winter admission, 3/1 priority date for domestic and international students; for spring admission, 11/1 priority date for domestic and international students. Applications are processed on a rolling basis. Application fee: $30. *Expenses:* Tuition, state resident: part-time $248 per credit hour. Tuition, nonresident: part-time $880 per credit hour. Tuition and fees vary according to program. *Financial support:* In 2007–08, 49 students received support, including 1 fellowship with full tuition reimbursement available, 8 research assistantships with full tuition reimbursements available (averaging $14,000 per year), 40 teaching assistantships with full tuition reimbursements available (averaging $5,000 per year); career-related internships or fieldwork, Federal Work-Study, institutionally sponsored loans, scholarships/grants, tuition waivers (partial), and unspecified assistantships also available. Support available to part-time students. Financial award application deadline: 2/1; financial award applicants required to submit FAFSA. *Faculty research:* Communication technology and policy, marketing communication, communication content and effect, new communication/information technologies. Total annual research expenditures: $264,208. *Unit head:* Dr. Stephen D. McDowell, Chairperson, 850-644-2276, Fax: 850-644-8642, E-mail: smcdowel@mailer.fsu.edu. *Application contact:* Natashia Hinson-Turner, Graduate Program Assistant, 850-644-8746, Fax: 850-644-8642, E-mail: dc.gradinfo@comm.fsu.edu.

Fordham University, Graduate School of Business Administration, New York, NY 10023. Offers accounting (MBA); communications and media management (MBA); executive business administration (EMBA); finance (MBA, MS); information systems (MBA, MS); management systems (MBA); marketing (MBA); media management (MS); taxation (MS); taxation and accounting (MTA);); JD/MBA; MBA/MIM; MS/MBA. *Accreditation:* AACSB. Part-time and evening/weekend programs available. *Faculty:* 92 full-time (29 women), 95 part-time/adjunct (19 women). *Students:* 365 full-time (143 women), 1,183 part-time (474 women); includes 254 minority (56 African Americans, 2 American Indian/Alaska Native, 137 Asian Americans or Pacific Islanders, 59 Hispanic Americans), 69 international. Average age 28. 1,131 applicants, 64% accepted, 411 enrolled. In 2007, 488 degrees awarded. *Entrance requirements:* For master's, GMAT, official undergraduate transcripts, 2 letters of recommendation, resumé, personal statement. Additional exam requirements/recommendations for international students: Required—TOEFL (minimum score 600 paper-based; 250 computer-based; 100 iBT). *Application deadline:* For fall admission, 6/1 priority date for domestic students, 5/1 priority date for international students; for winter admission, 11/1 priority date for domestic students, 10/1 priority date for international students; for spring admission, 3/1 priority date for domestic students, 2/1 priority date for international students. Applications are processed on a rolling basis. Application fee: $65. Electronic applications accepted. *Expenses:* Contact institution. *Financial support:* In 2007–08, 37 students received support, including fellowships (averaging $27,000 per year); research assistantships, career-related internships or fieldwork, institutionally sponsored loans, scholarships/grants, and unspecified assistantships also available. Support available to part-time students. Financial award application deadline: 5/1; financial award applicants required to submit FAFSA. *Unit head:* Dr. Howard Tuckman, Dean, 212-636-6165, Fax: 212-307-1779, E-mail: tuckman@fordham.edu. *Application contact:* Cynthia Perez, Director of Admissions and Financial Aid, 212-636-6200, Fax: 212-636-7076, E-mail: admissionsgb@fordham.edu.

Governors State University, College of Arts and Sciences, Program in Communication and Training, University Park, IL 60466-0975. Offers communication studies (MA); instructional and training technology (MA); media communication (MA). Part-time and evening/weekend programs available. *Students:* 30 full-time, 78 part-time. Average age 35. *Degree requirements:* For master's, thesis or alternative. *Application deadline:* For fall admission, 7/15 priority date for domestic students; for spring admission, 11/10 for domestic students. Applications are processed on a rolling basis. Application fee: $25. *Financial support:* Research assistantships, Federal Work-Study, institutionally sponsored loans, and scholarships/grants available. Support available to part-time students. Financial award application deadline: 5/1. *Unit head:* Dr. Eric V. Martin, Dean, College of Arts and Sciences, 708-534-4101.

Howard University, School of Communications, Division of Mass Communication and Media Studies, Washington, DC 20059-0002. Offers mass communication (MA, PhD); media studies (MA, PhD). Part-time and evening/weekend programs available. *Degree requirements:* For master's, comprehensive exam (for some programs), thesis optional; for doctorate, one foreign language, comprehensive exam, thesis/dissertation. *Entrance requirements:* For master's, GRE, minimum GPA of 3.0; for doctorate, GRE, minimum graduate GPA of 3.5. Additional exam requirements/recommendations for international students: Required—TOEFL. Electronic applications accepted. *Expenses:* Tuition: Full-time $16,175; part-time $899 per credit hour. Required fees: $805. *Faculty research:* Advertising, public relations, journalism new media.

Media Studies

Hunter College of the City University of New York, Graduate School, School of Arts and Sciences, Department of Film and Media Studies, Program in Integrated Media Arts, New York, NY 10021-5085. Offers MA, MFA. Part-time and evening/weekend programs available. *Faculty:* 10 full-time (4 women), 2 part-time/adjunct (1 woman). *Students:* 7 full-time (4 women), 63 part-time (38 women); includes 9 minority (1 African American, 1 Asian American or Pacific Islander, 7 Hispanic Americans). Average age 35. 70 applicants, 46% accepted, 11 enrolled. In 2007, 6 degrees awarded. *Entrance requirements:* For master's, GRE General Test, 3 letters of recommendation, portfolio of media works, minimum GPA of 3.0. Additional exam requirements/recommendations for international students: Required—TOEFL, TWE. *Application deadline:* For fall admission, 2/1 for domestic students. Application fee: $125. *Expenses:* Tuition, state resident: full-time $6,400; part-time $270 per credit. Tuition, nonresident: part-time $500 per credit. One-time fee: $125 full-time. Tuition and fees vary according to program. *Financial support:* Federal Work-Study and tuition waivers (partial) available. Support available to part-time students. *Faculty research:* Nonfiction production, Internet as medium, public interest journalism, social and historical roots of media arts. *Unit head:* Kelly Anderson, Deputy Chair, 212-772-6008. *Application contact:* Mary Flanagan, New Media Advisor, 212-650-3219, E-mail: maryflanagan@hunter.cuny.edu.

Indiana State University, School of Graduate Studies, College of Arts and Sciences, Department of Communication, Terre Haute, IN 47809-1401. Offers communication studies (MA, MS); radio, television and film (MA, MS). Part-time programs available. *Faculty:* 11 full-time (4 women), 1 part-time/adjunct (0 women). *Students:* 11 full-time (7 women), 5 part-time (1 woman); includes 2 minority (both African Americans), 5 international. Average age 31. 25 applicants, 84% accepted, 6 enrolled. In 2007, 8 degrees awarded. *Degree requirements:* For master's, thesis (for some programs), oral and written exam. *Entrance requirements:* For master's, GRE General Test. Additional exam requirements/recommendations for international students: Required—TOEFL. *Application deadline:* For fall admission, 3/1 for domestic students; for spring admission, 11/1 priority date for domestic students. Applications are processed on a rolling basis. Application fee: $35. *Expenses:* Tuition, state resident: full-time $7,056; part-time $294 per semester hour. Tuition, nonresident: full-time $14,016; part-time $584 per semester hour. Required fees: $175 per semester. *Financial support:* In 2007–08, 7 teaching assistantships with partial tuition reimbursements (averaging $7,000 per year) were awarded; career-related internships or fieldwork, Federal Work-Study, institutionally sponsored loans, and tuition waivers (partial) also available. Support available to part-time students. Financial award application deadline: 3/1; financial award applicants required to submit FAFSA. *Faculty research:* Women in media, communication apprehension, media history. *Unit head:* Dr. David Worley, Chairperson, 812-237-3245.

International University in Geneva, Program in Media and Communication, Geneva, Switzerland. Offers MA.

Kutztown University of Pennsylvania, College of Graduate Studies and Extended Learning, College of Liberal Arts and Sciences, Program in Electronic Media, Kutztown, PA 19530-0730. Offers MS. Part-time and evening/weekend programs available. *Faculty:* 3 full-time (0 women). *Students:* 4 full-time (2 women), 10 part-time (1 woman); includes 1 minority (American Indian/Alaska Native), 3 international. Average age 31. 12 applicants, 67% accepted, 8 enrolled. In 2007, 7 degrees awarded. *Degree requirements:* For master's, thesis. *Entrance requirements:* For master's, GRE General Test. Additional exam requirements/recommendations for international students: Required—TOEFL. *Application deadline:* Applications are processed on a rolling basis. Application fee: $35. Electronic applications accepted. *Expenses:* Tuition, state resident: full-time $6,214; part-time $345 per credit. Tuition, nonresident: full-time $9,944; part-time $552 per credit. Required fees: $1,536; $78 per credit. $65 per semester. *Financial support:* Career-related internships or fieldwork, Federal Work-Study, scholarships/grants, and unspecified assistantships available. Financial award application deadline: 3/15; financial award applicants required to submit FAFSA. *Unit head:* Dr. Joseph Chuk, Chairperson, 610-683-4492, Fax: 610-683-4659, E-mail: chuk@kutztown.edu.

Louisiana State University and Agricultural and Mechanical College, Graduate School, Manship School of Mass Communication, Baton Rouge, LA 70803. Offers MMC, PhD. *Accreditation:* ACEJMC. Part-time programs available. Postbaccalaureate distance learning degree programs offered (minimal on-campus study). *Faculty:* 25 full-time (13 women). *Students:* 39 full-time (24 women), 14 part-time (12 women); includes 6 minority (5 African Americans, 1 Hispanic American), 14 international. Average age 31. 61 applicants, 39% accepted, 17 enrolled. In 2007, 8 master's, 1 doctorate awarded. *Degree requirements:* For master's, thesis. *Entrance requirements:* For master's, GRE General Test, minimum GPA of 3.0. Additional exam requirements/recommendations for international students: Required—TOEFL (minimum score 550 paper-based; 213 computer-based; 79 iBT). *Application deadline:* For fall admission, 1/25 priority date for domestic students, 5/15 for international students; for spring admission, 10/15 for international students. Applications are processed on a rolling basis. Application fee: $25. Electronic applications accepted. *Financial support:* In 2007–08, 44 students received support, including 26 research assistantships with full and partial tuition reimbursements available (averaging $15,415 per year), 4 teaching assistantships with full and partial tuition reimbursements available (averaging $20,250 per year); fellowships, career-related internships or fieldwork, Federal Work-Study, institutionally sponsored loans, scholarships/grants, health care benefits, tuition waivers (full and partial), and unspecified assistantships also available. Support available to part-time students. Financial award application deadline: 3/1; financial award applicants required to submit FAFSA. *Faculty research:* Media effects, political communication, new media technologies, persuasive communication, journalism processes and practice. Total annual research expenditures: $85,046. *Unit head:* Dr. John Maxwell Hamilton, Dean, 225-578-2002, Fax: 225-578-2125, E-mail: jhamilt@lsu.edu. *Application contact:* Dr. Margaret DeFleur, Associate Dean of Graduate Studies and Research, 225-578-9294, Fax: 225-578-2125, E-mail: defleur@lsu.edu.

See Close-Up on page 905.

Lynn University, College of Business and Management, Boca Raton, FL 33431-5598. Offers aviation management (MBA); financial valuation and investment management (MBA); global leadership (PhD); hospitality management (MBA); international business (MBA); marketing (MBA); mass communication and media management (MBA); sports and athletics administration (MBA). Part-time and evening/weekend programs available. Postbaccalaureate distance learning degree programs offered. *Degree requirements:* For master's, project; for doctorate, thesis/dissertation, qualifying paper. *Entrance requirements:* For master's, GMAT or GRE, minimum undergraduate GPA of 3.0, resumé, 2 letters of recommendation; for doctorate, GRE or GMAT, minimum graduate GPA of 3.25, resumé, 2 letters of recommendation. Additional exam requirements/recommendations for international students: Required—TOEFL (minimum score 550 paper-based; 213 computer-based). Electronic applications accepted. *Faculty research:* Labor relations, dynamic balance in leisure-time skills, ethics in athletics, hotel development.

Marquette University, Graduate School, College of Communication, Milwaukee, WI 53201-1881. Offers advertising and public relations (MA); broadcasting and electronic communications (MA); communications studies (MA); journalism (MA); mass communications (MA); religious communications (MA); science, health and environmental communications (MA). *Accreditation:* ACEJMC. Part-time and evening/weekend programs available. *Faculty:* 31 full-time (17 women), 34 part-time/adjunct (17 women). *Students:* 24 full-time (13 women), 19 part-time (12 women); includes 7 minority (1 African American, 1 American Indian/Alaska Native, 2 Asian Americans or Pacific Islanders, 3 Hispanic Americans), 7 international. Average age 28. 76 applicants, 58% accepted, 15 enrolled. In 2007, 17 degrees awarded. *Degree requirements:* For master's, comprehensive exam. *Entrance requirements:* For master's, GRE. Additional exam requirements/recommendations for international students: Required—TOEFL. Application fee: $40. *Financial support:* In 2007–08, 6 research assistantships, 12 teaching assistantships were awarded; career-related internships or fieldwork, Federal Work-Study, institutionally sponsored loans, scholarships/grants, and tuition waivers (full and partial) also available. Support available to part-time students. Financial award application deadline: 2/15. *Faculty research:* Urban journalism, gender and communication, intercultural communication, religious communication. Total annual research expenditures: $17,806. *Unit head:* Dr. Ana Garner, Dean, 414-288-3588, Fax: 414-288-1578.

Marywood University, Academic Affairs, Insalaco College of Creative Arts and Management, Department of Communication Arts, Program in Communication Arts, Scranton, PA 18509-1598. Offers corporate communication (Certificate); e-business (Certificate); health communication (Certificate); instructional technology (Certificate); interdisciplinary (MA); library science/information specialist (Certificate); media management (MA); production (MA). *Students:* 10 full-time (6 women), 22 part-time (15 women); includes 4 minority (1 African American, 3 Hispanic Americans). Average age 28. In 2007, 8 degrees awarded. Application fee: $30. *Expenses:* Tuition: Full-time $15,290; part-time $695 per credit. Required fees: $990; $370 per term. Tuition and fees vary according to degree level.

Massachusetts Institute of Technology, School of Architecture and Planning, Program in Media Arts and Sciences, Cambridge, MA 02139-4307. Offers media arts and sciences (SM, PhD); media technology (SM). *Faculty:* 21 full-time (4 women). *Students:* 116 full-time (23 women); includes 12 minority (3 African Americans, 8 Asian Americans or Pacific Islanders, 1 Hispanic American), 48 international. Average age 28. 367 applicants, 12% accepted, 40 enrolled. In 2007, 34 master's, 11 doctorates awarded. Terminal master's awarded for partial completion of doctoral program. *Degree requirements:* For master's, thesis; for doctorate, comprehensive exam, thesis/dissertation. *Entrance requirements:* Additional exam requirements/recommendations for international students: Required—TOEFL (minimum score 600 paper-based; 250 computer-based). *Application deadline:* For fall admission, 12/15 for domestic and international students. Application fee: $70. Electronic applications accepted. *Expenses:* Tuition: Full-time $34,760; part-time $545 per unit. Required fees: $236. *Financial support:* In 2007–08, 108 students received support, including 2 fellowships with tuition reimbursements available (averaging $10,667 per year), 112 research assistantships with tuition reimbursements available (averaging $25,909 per year); Federal Work-Study, institutionally sponsored loans, scholarships/grants, health care benefits, and unspecified assistantships also available. *Faculty research:* Human machine interaction; communications technologies; new media technologies; physical computing; learning and creativity. Total annual research expenditures: $10.8 million. *Unit head:* Prof. Mitchel J. Resnick, Head, 617-253-5114, Fax: 617-253-8542. *Application contact:* Graduate Admissions, 617-253-5114, Fax: 617-253-8542, E-mail: mas@media.mit.edu.

See Close-Up on page 161.

Massachusetts Institute of Technology, School of Humanities, Arts, and Social Sciences, Program in Comparative Media Studies, Cambridge, MA 02139-4307. Offers SM. *Students:* 21 full-time (13 women); includes 3 minority (all Asian Americans or Pacific Islanders), 6 international. Average age 28. 83 applicants, 18% accepted, 12 enrolled. In 2007, 17 degrees awarded. *Degree requirements:* For master's, thesis. *Entrance requirements:* For master's, GRE General Test. Additional exam requirements/recommendations for international students: Required—TOEFL (minimum score 577 paper-based; 233 computer-based). *Application deadline:* For fall admission, 1/15 for domestic and international students. Application fee: $70. Electronic applications accepted. *Expenses:* Tuition: Full-time $34,760; part-time $545 per unit. Required fees: $236. *Financial support:* In 2007–08, 19 students received support, including 2 fellowships with tuition reimbursements available, 18 research assistantships with tuition reimbursements available (averaging $22,028 per year); Federal Work-Study, institutionally sponsored loans, scholarships/grants, health care benefits, and unspecified assistantships also available. *Faculty research:* Convergence Culture; New Media Literacies; Games and Education; Civic Media; Media History. Total annual research expenditures: $1.4 million. *Unit head:* Prof. Henry Jenkins, Co-Director, 617-253-3599, Fax: 617-258-5133, E-mail: cms@mit.edu. *Application contact:* Graduate Admissions, 617-253-3599, Fax: 617-258-5133, E-mail: cms-admissions@mit.edu.

Metropolitan College of New York, Program in Media Management, New York, NY 10013. Offers MBA. Evening/weekend programs available. *Degree requirements:* For master's, thesis, 10 day study abroad. *Entrance requirements:* For master's, GMAT or GRE, appropriate work experience, interview, minimum GPA of 2.7. Additional exam requirements/recommendations for international students: Required—TOEFL (minimum score 600 paper-based; 220 computer-based). Electronic applications accepted. Expenses: Contact institution.

Michigan State University, The Graduate School, College of Communication Arts and Sciences, Department of Telecommunication, Information Studies, and Media, East Lansing, MI 48824. Offers MA. *Entrance requirements:* Additional exam requirements/recommendations for international students: Required—TOEFL. Electronic applications accepted.

Michigan State University, The Graduate School, College of Communication Arts and Sciences, Program in Media and Information Studies, East Lansing, MI 48824. Offers PhD. *Entrance requirements:* Additional exam requirements/recommendations for international students: Required—TOEFL. Electronic applications accepted. *Expenses:* Tuition, state resident: part-time $379 per credit hour. Tuition, nonresident: part-time $800 per credit hour. Tuition and fees vary according to program. *Faculty research:* Mass media, comparative media.

Monmouth University, Graduate School, Department of Corporate and Public Communication, West Long Branch, NJ 07764-1898. Offers corporate and public communication (MA); human resources communication (Certificate); media studies (Certificate); public relations (Certificate). *Faculty:* 7 full-time (5 women), 2 part-time/adjunct (1 woman). *Students:* 6 full-time (5 women), 40 part-time (29 women); includes 4 minority (3 African Americans, 1 Hispanic American), 3 international. Average age 30. 22 applicants, 95% accepted, 12 enrolled. In 2007, 18 degrees awarded. *Degree requirements:* For master's, comprehensive exam, project. *Entrance requirements:* For master's, GRE, minimum GPA of 3.0 in major, 2.75 overall. Additional exam requirements/recommendations for international students: Required—TOEFL (minimum score 550 paper-based; 213 computer-based; 79 iBT), IELTS (minimum score 5), MELAB 77, Cambridge A, B, C. *Application deadline:* For fall admission, 7/15 priority date for domestic students, 6/1 for international students; for spring admission, 11/15 priority date for domestic students, 11/1 for international students. Applications are processed on a rolling basis. Application fee: $50. Electronic applications accepted. *Financial support:* In 2007–08, 34 students received support, including 33 fellowships (averaging $1,330 per year), 11 research assistantships (averaging $4,456 per year); scholarships/grants and unspecified assistantships also available. Support available to part-time students. Financial award application deadline: 3/1; financial award applicants required to submit FAFSA. *Faculty research:* Service learning, history of television, feminism and the media, executive communication, public relations pedagogy. *Unit head:* Dr. Eleanor Novek, Program Director, 732-263-5449, Fax: 732-571-3609, E-mail: enovek@monmouth.edu. *Application contact:* Kevin Roane, Director, Office of Graduate Admission, 732-571-3452, Fax: 732-263-5123, E-mail: gradadm@monmouth.edu.

National University, Academic Affairs, School of Media and Communication, Department of Media, La Jolla, CA 92037-1011. Offers digital cinema (MFA); educational and instructional technology (MS); video game production and design (MFA). Part-time and evening/weekend programs available. Postbaccalaureate distance learning degree programs offered (no on-campus study). *Faculty:* 7 full-time (2 women), 55 part-time/adjunct (22 women). *Students:* 69 full-time (35 women), 158 part-time (86 women); includes 54 minority (25 African Americans, 2 American Indian/Alaska Native, 7 Asian Americans or Pacific Islanders, 20 Hispanic Americans). Average age 39. 159 applicants, 143 enrolled. In 2007, 58 degrees awarded. *Degree requirements:* For master's, thesis. *Entrance requirements:* For master's, interview, minimum GPA of 2.5. Additional exam requirements/recommendations for international students: Required—TOEFL (minimum score 550 paper-based; 213 computer-based; 80 iBT), IELTS (minimum score 6). *Application deadline:* Applications are processed on a rolling basis. Application fee: $60 ($65 for international students). Electronic applications accepted. *Expenses:* Tuition: Full-time $8,262; part-time $306 per unit. One-time fee: $60. *Financial support:* Career-related internships or fieldwork, institutionally sponsored loans, scholarships/grants, and tuition waivers (partial) available. Support available to part-time students. Financial award application deadline: 6/30; financial award applicants required to submit FAFSA. *Unit head:* Dr. Timothy Langdell, Department Chair, 858-642-8466, Fax: 858-642-8743, E-mail: tlangdell@nu.edu. *Application contact:* Dominick Giovanniello, Associate Regional Dean—San Diego, 800-NAT-UNIV, Fax: 858-642-8709, E-mail: dgiovann@nu.edu.

New Mexico Highlands University, Graduate Studies, College of Arts and Sciences, Program in Media Arts and Computer Science, Las Vegas, NM 87701. Offers computer science (MA, MS); media arts (MA). *Faculty:* 5 full-time (1 woman), 1 part-time/adjunct (0 women). *Students:* 21 full-time (7 women), 8 part-time (4 women); includes 9 minority (1 Asian American or Pacific Islander, 8 Hispanic Americans), 12 international. Average age 30. 30 applicants, 70% accepted, 5 enrolled. In 2007, 10 degrees awarded. *Degree requirements:* For master's, comprehensive exam, thesis. *Entrance requirements:* For master's, minimum undergraduate GPA of 3.0. Additional exam requirements/recommendations for international students: Required—TOEFL (minimum score 540 paper-based; 190 computer-based). Application fee: $15. *Expenses:* Tuition, state resident: full-time $2,642; part-time $110 per credit hour. Tuition, nonresident: full-time $3,964; part-time $165 per credit hour. International tuition: $5,285 full-time. One-time fee: $20 full-time. *Financial support:* In 2007–08, 12 students received support, including teaching assistantships (averaging $7,200 per year); career-related internships or fieldwork, Federal Work-Study, institutionally sponsored loans, scholarships/grants, tuition waivers (full and partial), and unspecified assistantships also available. Support available to part-time students. Financial award application deadline: 3/1; financial award applicants required to submit FAFSA. *Application contact:* Diane Trujillo, Administrative Assistant Graduate Studies, 505-454-3266, Fax: 505-454-3558, E-mail: dtrujillo@nmhu.edu.

The New School: A University, The New School for General Studies, Program in Media Studies, New York, NY 10011. Offers communication theory (MA); media studies (MA). Part-time and evening/weekend programs available. *Faculty:* 19 full-time (8 women), 44 part-time/adjunct (16 women). *Students:* 201 full-time (136 women), 230 part-time (138 women); includes 99 minority (42 African Americans, 2 American Indian/Alaska Native, 25 Asian Americans or Pacific Islanders, 30 Hispanic Americans), 76 international. Average age 30. In 2007, 124 degrees awarded. *Degree requirements:* For master's, thesis optional. *Entrance requirements:* For master's, interview. Additional exam requirements/recommendations for international students: Required—TOEFL (minimum score 600 paper-based; 250 computer-based; 100 iBT). *Application deadline:* For fall admission, 4/15 for domestic students; for spring admission, 10/15 for domestic students. Applications are processed on a rolling basis. Application fee: $50. *Financial support:* Fellowships, research assistantships, teaching assistantships, Federal Work-Study, scholarships/grants, and tuition waivers (partial) available. Financial award application deadline: 3/1; financial award applicants required to submit FAFSA. *Faculty research:* Effect of technology on society, effect of U.S. media on international affairs, effect of media on corporate affairs. *Unit head:* Dr. Peter L. Haratonik, Interim Chair, Media Studies and Film, 212-229-8903, Fax: 212-465-0661, E-mail: haraton@newschool.edu. *Application contact:* David Norris, Director of Admissions, 212-229-5630, Fax: 212-989-3887, E-mail: nsadmissions@newschool.edu.

See Close-Up on page 907.

New York University, Graduate School of Arts and Science, Department of Anthropology, Program in Culture and Media, New York, NY 10012-1019. Offers MA/Advanced Certificate, PhD/Advanced Certificate. Awarded with MA or PhD in anthropology. *Faculty:* 1 (woman) full-time. *Students:* 6 full-time (5 women), 3 part-time (2 women); includes 1 minority (Hispanic American), 1 international. Average age 30. 40 applicants, 3% accepted, 0 enrolled. *Entrance requirements:* Additional exam requirements/recommendations for international students: Required—TOEFL. *Application deadline:* For fall admission, 1/4 priority date for domestic students. Application fee: $55. *Financial support:* Fellowships, research assistantships, teaching assistantships, career-related internships or fieldwork, institutionally sponsored loans, scholarships/grants, health care benefits, and unspecified assistantships available. Financial award application deadline: 1/4. *Faculty research:* Critical history of ethnographic film, ethnography of media, indigenous media, politics of reproduction and disability, social movements. *Unit head:* Faye Ginsburg, Director, 212-998-8558, Fax: 212-995-4014, E-mail: anthropology@nyu.edu.

New York University, Steinhardt School of Culture, Education and Human Development, Department of Media, Culture and Communication, New York, NY 10012-1019. Offers media ecology/culture and communication (PhD); media, culture, and communication (MA). Part-time and evening/weekend programs available. *Faculty:* 24 full-time (11 women), 41 part-time/adjunct (17 women). *Students:* 66 full-time (44 women), 56 part-time (37 women); includes 17 minority (7 African Americans, 8 Asian Americans or Pacific Islanders, 2 Hispanic Americans), 34 international. 321 applicants, 40% accepted, 44 enrolled. In 2007, 78 master's, 3 doctorates awarded. *Entrance requirements:* Additional exam requirements/recommendations for international students: Required—TOEFL. *Application deadline:* For fall admission, 12/15 priority date for domestic and international students; for spring admission, 11/1 for domestic and international students. Applications are processed on a rolling basis. Application fee: $50. *Financial support:* Fellowships with full and partial tuition reimbursements, teaching assistantships with full and partial tuition reimbursements, career-related internships or fieldwork, Federal Work-Study, institutionally sponsored loans, scholarships/grants, tuition waivers (partial), and unspecified assistantships available. Support available to part-time students. Financial award application deadline: 2/1; financial award applicants required to submit FAFSA. *Faculty research:* Digital media, intercultural communication, race and politics, media criticism, media literacy. *Unit head:* Dr. Ted Magder, Chairperson, 212-998-5191, Fax: 212-995-4046, E-mail: ted.magder@nyu.edu. *Application contact:* 212-998-5030, Fax: 212-995-4328, E-mail: steinhardt.gradadmissions@nyu.edu.

Norfolk State University, School of Graduate Studies, School of Liberal Arts, Department of Media and Communication, Norfolk, VA 23504. Offers MA. Part-time programs available. *Degree requirements:* For master's, thesis. *Entrance requirements:* For master's, GRE, minimum GPA of 2.5, letters of recommendation. Additional exam requirements/recommendations for international students: Required—TOEFL.

Northwestern University, The Graduate School, School of Communication, Department of Radio/Television/Film, Evanston, IL 60208. Offers MA, MFA, PhD. Admissions and degrees offered through The Graduate School. Part-time programs available. Terminal master's awarded for partial completion of doctoral program. *Degree requirements:* For master's, comprehensive exam or thesis; for doctorate, thesis/dissertation, qualifying exam. *Entrance requirements:* For master's and doctorate, GRE General Test. Additional exam requirements/recommendations for international students: Required—TOEFL. Electronic applications accepted. *Faculty research:* Art and new media, media theory and criticism, gender, media history, documentary.

Northwestern University, Medill School of Journalism, Evanston, IL 60208. Offers broadcast journalism (MSJ); integrated marketing communications (MSIMC), including advertising/sales promotion, direct database and e-commerce marketing, general studies, public relations; magazine publishing (MSJ); new media (MSJ); reporting and writing (MSJ). *Accreditation:* ACEJMC (one or more programs are accredited). *Entrance requirements:* For master's, GRE General Test, GMAT or LSAT (MSJ). Additional exam requirements/recommendations for international students: Required—TOEFL. Electronic applications accepted. Expenses: Contact institution. *Faculty research:* Web business journalism, cultural stereotypes, voter apathy, digital television.

Ohio University, Graduate College, Scripps College of Communication, School of Media Arts and Studies, Athens, OH 45701-2979. Offers mass communication (PhD); media arts and studies (MA). *Faculty:* 17 full-time (5 women), 2 part-time/adjunct (1 woman). *Students:* 42 full-time (20 women), 9 part-time (4 women); includes 3 minority (2 African Americans, 1 Asian American or Pacific Islander), 34 international. Average age 29. 87 applicants, 39% accepted, 27 enrolled. In 2007, 16 master's, 9 doctorates awarded. *Degree requirements:* For master's, comprehensive exam, thesis or alternative; for doctorate, comprehensive exam, thesis/dissertation. *Entrance requirements:* For master's, GRE General Test or MAT, minimum GPA of 3.0; for doctorate, GRE General Test or MAT. Additional exam requirements/recommendations for international students: Required—TOEFL (minimum score 600 paper-based; 250 computer-based). *Application deadline:* For fall admission, 1/31 for domestic students, 12/31 priority date for international students. Application fee: $50 ($55 for international students). *Financial support:* In 2007–08, 8 research assistantships with full tuition reimbursements, 16 teaching assistantships with full tuition reimbursements were awarded; career-related internships or fieldwork, Federal Work-Study, and institutionally sponsored loans also available. Financial award application deadline: 1/31. *Faculty research:* Children's media, international media, policy and regulation, new technologies, cultural studies. *Unit head:* Dr. Roger Cooper, Director, Fax: 740-593-9184, E-mail: cooperr@ohio.edu. *Application contact:* Dr. Mia L. Consalvo, Director of Graduate Studies, 740-597-1521, Fax: 740-593-9184, E-mail: consaluo@ohio.edu.

Ohio University, Graduate College, Scripps College of Communication, School of Visual Communication, Athens, OH 45701-2979. Offers MA. *Accreditation:* NASAD. *Faculty:* 11 full-time (2 women). *Students:* 26 full-time (15 women), 13 part-time (8 women); includes 5 minority (2 African Americans, 1 Asian American or Pacific Islander, 2 Hispanic Americans), 15 international. In 2007, 7 degrees awarded. *Entrance requirements:* For master's, minimum GPA of 2.5, portfolio. Additional exam requirements/recommendations for international students: Required—TOEFL (minimum score 600 paper-based; 250 computer-based). *Application deadline:* For fall admission, 2/1 for domestic students, 12/15 for international students. Application fee: $50 ($55 for international students). Electronic applications accepted. *Financial support:* In 2007–08, 30 students received support, including 1 fellowship, 2 research assistantships, 4 teaching assistantships with tuition reimbursements available; Federal Work-Study, institutionally sponsored loans, and tuition waivers (partial) also available. Financial award applicants required to submit FAFSA. *Faculty research:* Photographic communication (photojournalism, multimedia, and documentary), photographic illustration (product, editorial, architectural), multimedia (planning and design), media management. *Unit head:* Terry Eiler, Director, 740-595-4895, E-mail: eiler@ohio.edu. *Application contact:* Mike Williams, Associate Director, 740-597-1778, Fax: 740-593-0190, E-mail: william5@ohio.edu.

Rochester Institute of Technology, Graduate Enrollment Services, College of Liberal Arts, Department of Communications, Program in Communication and Media Technologies, Rochester, NY 14623-5603. Offers MS. *Students:* 20 full-time (17 women), 15 part-time (11 women); includes 7 minority (6 African Americans, 1 Asian American or Pacific Islander), 4 international. 34 applicants, 71% accepted, 15 enrolled. In 2007, 7 degrees awarded. *Degree requirements:* For master's, thesis. *Entrance requirements:* For master's, minimum GPA of 3.0, writing sample. Additional exam requirements/recommendations for international students: Required—TOEFL (minimum score 600 paper-based; 250 computer-based; 100 iBT). *Application deadline:* For fall admission, 3/1 priority date for domestic students. Applications are processed on a rolling basis. Application fee: $50. Electronic applications accepted. *Expenses:* Tuition: Full-time $28,491; part-time $800 per credit hour. Required fees: $201; $67 per term. *Financial support:* Fellowships with partial tuition reimbursements, research assistantships with partial tuition reimbursements, teaching assistantships with partial tuition reimbursements, career-related internships or fieldwork, institutionally sponsored loans, scholarships/grants, and unspecified assistantships available. Support available to part-time students. Financial award applicants required to submit FAFSA. *Unit head:* Dr. Rudy Pugliese, Head, 585-475-5925, E-mail: rrpgsl@rit.edu.

Saginaw Valley State University, College of Arts and Behavioral Sciences, Program in Communication and Digital Media Design, University Center, MI 48710. Offers MA. Part-time and evening/weekend programs available. *Students:* 15 full-time (9 women), 27 part-time (10 women); includes 3 minority (1 African American, 1 Asian American or Pacific Islander, 1 Hispanic American), 9 international. Average age 35. 32 applicants, 88% accepted, 19 enrolled. In 2007, 16 degrees awarded. *Degree requirements:* For master's, thesis. *Entrance requirements:* For master's, minimum GPA of 2.75. Additional exam requirements/recommendations for international students: Required—TOEFL. *Application deadline:* Applications are processed on a rolling basis. Application fee: $25. Electronic applications accepted. *Expenses:* Tuition, state resident: full-time $8,264; part-time $344 per credit hour. Tuition, nonresident: full-time $15,853; part-time $661 per credit hour. Required fees: $341; $14 per credit hour. Tuition and fees vary according to course load. *Financial support:* In 2007–08, research assistantships (averaging $5,000 per year); Federal Work-Study also available. Support available to part-time students. Financial award application deadline: 4/1; financial award applicants required to submit FAFSA. *Unit head:* Dr. Steve Erickson, Program Coordinator/Professor of Theatre, 989-964-4147, E-mail: erickson@svsu.edu.

San Diego State University, Graduate and Research Affairs, College of Professional Studies and Fine Arts, School of Communication, San Diego, CA 92182. Offers advertising and public relations (MA); critical-cultural studies (MA); interaction studies (MA); intercultural and international studies (MA); new media studies (MA); news and information studies (MA); telecommunications and media management (MA). *Students:* 30 full-time (16 women), 62 part-time (47 women); includes 6 minority (3 African Americans, 2 Asian Americans or Pacific Islanders, 1 Hispanic American), 11 international. 167 applicants, 41% accepted, 45 enrolled. In 2007, 49 degrees awarded. *Degree requirements:* For master's, thesis. *Entrance requirements:* For master's, GRE General Test, 3 letters of recommendation. Additional exam requirements/recommendations for international students: Required—TOEFL. *Application deadline:* For fall admission, 3/1 for domestic and international students; for spring admission, 10/1 for domestic and international students. Applications are processed on a rolling basis. Application fee: $55. Electronic applications accepted. *Financial support:* In 2007–08, 34 teaching assistantships were awarded; career-related internships or fieldwork and unspecified assistantships also available. Financial award applicants required to submit FAFSA. Total annual research expenditures: $153,598. *Unit head:* Diane Borden, Interim Director, 619-594-8098, Fax: 619-594-6246. *Application contact:* Patricia Geist-Martin, Information Contact, 619-594-4182, E-mail: pgeist@mail.sdsu.edu.

San Diego State University, Graduate and Research Affairs, College of Professional Studies and Fine Arts, School of Theater, Television and Film, Program in Television, Film, and New Media Production, San Diego, CA 92182. Offers MA. *Students:* 9 full-time (3 women), 19 part-time (10 women); includes 4 minority (1 African American, 1 Asian American or Pacific Islander, 2 Hispanic Americans), 6 international. 26 applicants, 42% accepted, 8 enrolled. In 2007, 12 degrees awarded. *Entrance requirements:* For master's, GRE General Test, 3 letters of recommendation, resumé, sample reel, influential book list, influential films list, hobby list. Additional exam requirements/recommendations for international students: Required—TOEFL. *Application deadline:* For fall admission, 3/1 for domestic students, 3/1 priority date for international students; for spring admission, 10/1 for domestic students, 10/1 priority date for international students. Applications are processed on a rolling basis. Application fee: $55. Electronic applications accepted. *Financial support:* Career-related internships or fieldwork available. Financial award applicants required to submit FAFSA. *Faculty research:* Experimental film and television programs, documentary film, television research and production. Total annual research expenditures: $25,000. *Unit head:* Greg Durbin, Graduate Advisor, 619-594-6856, E-mail: gdurbin@sciences.sdsu.edu. *Application contact:* Greg Durbin, Graduate Advisor, 619-594-6856, E-mail: gdurbin@sciences.sdsu.edu.

San Francisco State University, Division of Graduate Studies, College of Creative Arts, Department of Broadcast and Electronic Communication Arts, San Francisco, CA 94132-1722. Offers radio and television (MA). *Unit head:* Dr. Scott Patterson, Chair, 415-338-1788, Fax: 415-338-1688. *Application contact:* Dr. Nancy Reist, Graduate Coordinator, 415-338-1788, E-mail: becagrad@sfsu.edu.

Savannah College of Art and Design, Graduate School, Program in Broadcast Design, Savannah, GA 31402-3146. Offers MA, MFA. Part-time programs available. *Faculty:* 3 full-time

Media Studies

Savannah College of Art and Design (continued)
(0 women), 1 part-time/adjunct (0 women). *Students:* 40 full-time (15 women), 16 part-time (4 women); includes 8 minority (6 African Americans, 1 Asian American or Pacific Islander, 1 Hispanic American), 21 international. 65 applicants, 51% accepted, 17 enrolled. In 2007, 16 degrees awarded. *Degree requirements:* For master's, thesis, internships. *Entrance requirements:* For master's, interview, portfolio. Additional exam requirements/recommendations for international students: Required—TOEFL (minimum score 450 paper-based; 133 computer-based). *Application deadline:* For fall admission, 4/1 priority date for domestic and international students. Applications are processed on a rolling basis. Application fee: $50. Electronic applications accepted. *Expenses:* Tuition: Full-time $24,840; part-time $552 per credit. One-time fee: $500 full-time. *Financial support:* Research assistantships, career-related internships or fieldwork, Federal Work-Study, and scholarships/grants available. Financial award application deadline: 4/1; financial award applicants required to submit FAFSA. *Unit head:* Jill Taffet, Chair, 912-525-8551, E-mail: jtaffet@scad.edu. *Application contact:* Darrell Tutchton, Director of Graduate and International Enrollment, 912-525-5961, Fax: 912-525-5985, E-mail: admission@scad.edu.

Savannah College of Art and Design, Graduate School, Program in Performing Arts, Savannah, GA 31402-3146. Offers MA, MFA. *Faculty:* 8 full-time (3 women), 1 part-time/adjunct (0 women). *Students:* 22 full-time (15 women), 1 (woman) part-time; includes 4 minority (3 African Americans, 1 Asian American or Pacific Islander), 2 international. 28 applicants, 50% accepted, 12 enrolled. In 2007, 3 degrees awarded. *Degree requirements:* For master's, thesis, internship. *Entrance requirements:* For master's, audition, interview. Additional exam requirements/recommendations for international students: Required—TOEFL (minimum score 450 paper-based; 133 computer-based). *Application deadline:* For fall admission, 4/1 priority date for domestic and international students. Applications are processed on a rolling basis. Application fee: $50. Electronic applications accepted. *Expenses:* Tuition: Full-time $24,840; part-time $552 per credit. One-time fee: $500 full-time. *Financial support:* In 2007–08, 3 fellowships were awarded; career-related internships or fieldwork, Federal Work-Study, and scholarships/grants also available. Financial award application deadline: 4/1; financial award applicants required to submit FAFSA. *Unit head:* Dr. Joseph Kline, Chair, 912-525-6648, Fax: 912-525-6935, E-mail: jkline@scad.edu. *Application contact:* Darrell Tutchton, Director of Graduate and International Enrollment, 912-525-5961, Fax: 912-525-5985, E-mail: admission@scad.edu.

See Close-Up on page 257.

Southern Illinois University Carbondale, Graduate School, College of Mass Communication and Media Arts, Department of Mass Communication and Media Arts, Carbondale, IL 62901-4701. Offers MA, MFA. *Students:* 31 full-time (15 women), 62 part-time (26 women); includes 8 minority (2 African Americans, 2 American Indian/Alaska Native, 1 Asian American or Pacific Islander, 3 Hispanic Americans), 39 international. 84 applicants, 14% accepted, 9 enrolled. In 2007, 16 master's awarded. *Unit head:* Prof. Jan Roddy, Director of Graduate Studies, 618-453-5794, E-mail: jroddy@siu.edu.

Southern Illinois University Carbondale, Graduate School, College of Mass Communication and Media Arts, Department of Professional Media and Media Management Studies, Carbondale, IL 62901-4701. Offers MA. *Students:* 5 full-time (2 women), 19 part-time (10 women); includes 2 minority (1 African American, 1 Hispanic American), 9 international. 19 applicants, 68% accepted, 5 enrolled. In 2007, 1 degree awarded. *Unit head:* Prof. Jan Roddy, Director, 618-453-5794.

Southern Illinois University Carbondale, Graduate School, College of Mass Communication and Media Arts, Program in Media Theory and Research, Carbondale, IL 62901-4701. Offers MA. *Students:* 15 applicants, 20% accepted, 3 enrolled. *Unit head:* Prof. Jan Roddy, Director of Graduate Studies, 618-453-5794, E-mail: jroddy@siu.edu.

Southern Illinois University Edwardsville, Graduate Studies and Research, College of Arts and Sciences, Department of Mass Communications, Program in Media Literacy, Edwardsville, IL 62026-0001. Offers Postbaccalaureate Certificate. Part-time programs available. *Students:* 2 applicants, 0% accepted. *Entrance requirements:* Additional exam requirements/recommendations for international students: Required—TOEFL. *Application deadline:* For fall admission, 7/20 for domestic students, 6/1 for international students; for spring admission, 12/14 for domestic students, 10/1 for international students. Application fee: $30. Electronic applications accepted. *Financial support:* Fellowships with full tuition reimbursements, research assistantships with full tuition reimbursements, teaching assistantships with full tuition reimbursements available. Financial award application deadline: 3/1. *Unit head:* Dr. Gary Hicks, Director, 618-650-2242, E-mail: ghicks@siue.edu.

Syracuse University, Graduate School, S. I. Newhouse School of Public Communications, Department of Television, Radio, and Film, Syracuse, NY 13244. Offers documentary film and history (MA). *Students:* 46 full-time (25 women), 2 part-time; includes 9 minority (all African Americans), 3 international. 119 applicants, 68% accepted. In 2007, 44 degrees awarded. *Degree requirements:* For master's, comprehensive exam. *Entrance requirements:* For master's, GRE General Test. Additional exam requirements/recommendations for international students: Required—TOEFL (minimum score 600 paper-based; 250 computer-based). *Application deadline:* For fall admission, 2/1 for domestic and international students. Application fee: $75. Electronic applications accepted. *Expenses:* Tuition: Full-time $18,216; part-time $1,012 per credit. Required fees: $980. Tuition and fees vary according to program. *Unit head:* Michael Schoonmaker, Chair, 315-443-4004, Fax: 315-443-3946, E-mail: pcgrad@syr.edu. *Application contact:* Graduate Records Office, 315-443-4039, Fax: 315-443-1834, E-mail: pcgrad@syr.edu.

See Close-Up on page 935.

Syracuse University, Graduate School, S. I. Newhouse School of Public Communications, Program in Media Management, Syracuse, NY 13244. Offers MS. *Students:* 17 full-time (11 women); includes 3 African Americans, 2 Asian Americans or Pacific Islanders, 1 Hispanic American, 7 international. 43 applicants, 60% accepted. In 2007, 7 degrees awarded. *Degree requirements:* For master's, thesis optional, capstone course. *Entrance requirements:* For master's, GRE General Test or GMAT. Additional exam requirements/recommendations for international students: Required—TOEFL (minimum score 600 paper-based; 250 computer-based). *Application deadline:* For fall admission, 2/1 for domestic and international students. Application fee: $75. Electronic applications accepted. *Expenses:* Tuition: Full-time $18,216; part-time $1,012 per credit. Required fees: $980. Tuition and fees vary according to program. *Unit head:* Robert E. Lloyd, Director, 315-443-2417, Fax: 315-443-3946, E-mail: pcgrad@syr.edu. *Application contact:* Graduate Records Office, 315-443-4039, Fax: 315-334-1834, E-mail: pcgrad@syr.edu.

See Close-Up on page 935.

Syracuse University, Graduate School, S. I. Newhouse School of Public Communications, Program in Media Studies, Syracuse, NY 13244. Offers MA. *Students:* 22 full-time (14 women), 3 part-time (2 women); includes 2 Asian Americans or Pacific Islanders, 1 Hispanic American, 6 international. 45 applicants, 58% accepted, 17 enrolled. In 2007, 8 degrees awarded. *Degree requirements:* For master's, thesis. *Entrance requirements:* For master's, GRE General Test. Additional exam requirements/recommendations for international students: Required—TOEFL (minimum score 600 paper-based; 250 computer-based). *Application deadline:* For fall admission, 2/1 for domestic and international students. Application fee: $75. Electronic applications accepted. *Expenses:* Tuition: Full-time $18,216; part-time $1,012 per credit. Required fees: $980. Tuition and fees vary according to program. *Unit head:* Carol M. Liebler, Director, 315-443-3372, Fax: 315-443-3946, E-mail: masscomm@syr.edu. *Application contact:* Doctoral Office, 315-443-3372, E-mail: masscomm@syr.edu.

Temple University, Graduate School, School of Communications and Theater, Department of Broadcasting, Telecommunications and Mass Media, Philadelphia, PA 19122-6096. Offers MA. Part-time programs available. *Degree requirements:* For master's, thesis optional, written exam. *Entrance requirements:* For master's, GRE General Test, minimum GPA of 3.0. Additional exam requirements/recommendations for international students: Required—TOEFL (minimum score 550 paper-based; 213 computer-based; 79 iBT). Electronic applications accepted. *Faculty research:* Media institutions, international communications, communication policy, media theory.

Temple University, Graduate School, School of Communications and Theater, Department of Strategic and Organizational Communication, Program in Mass Media and Communication, Philadelphia, PA 19122-6096. Offers PhD. Part-time programs available. *Degree requirements:* For doctorate, one foreign language, thesis/dissertation. *Entrance requirements:* For doctorate, GRE General Test, minimum GPA of 3.0, sample of written work. Additional exam requirements/recommendations for international students: Required—TOEFL (minimum score 550 paper-based; 213 computer-based; 79 iBT). Electronic applications accepted. *Faculty research:* Aesthetics and criticism, media institutions, social theory and processes.

University at Buffalo, the State University of New York, Graduate School, College of Arts and Sciences, Department of Media Study, Buffalo, NY 14260. Offers humanities (film studies concentration) (MA); media arts production (MFA); new media design (Certificate); M Arch/MFA. Part-time programs available. *Degree requirements:* For master's, thesis. *Entrance requirements:* For master's, portfolio. Additional exam requirements/recommendations for international students: Required—TOEFL (minimum score 550 paper-based; 213 computer-based), SPEAK (for those awarded assistantships). Electronic applications accepted. *Faculty research:* Digital arts, video, documentary, film, virtual reality, digital poetics, locative media.

The University of Alabama, Graduate School, College of Communication and Information Sciences, Department of Telecommunication and Film, Tuscaloosa, AL 35487. Offers MA. *Faculty:* 7 full-time (2 women). *Students:* 9 full-time (6 women), 1 (woman) part-time; includes 1 minority (Hispanic American), 2 international. Average age 24. 9 applicants, 44% accepted, 4 enrolled. In 2007, 6 degrees awarded. *Degree requirements:* For master's, comprehensive exam, thesis or alternative. *Entrance requirements:* For master's, GRE, minimum GPA of 3.0. Additional exam requirements/recommendations for international students: Required—TOEFL. *Application deadline:* For fall admission, 2/15 priority date for domestic students; for spring admission, 11/1 for domestic students. Applications are processed on a rolling basis. Application fee: $30. Electronic applications accepted. *Expenses:* Tuition, state resident: full-time $5,700. Tuition, nonresident: full-time $16,518. *Financial support:* In 2007–08, 2 research assistantships with tuition reimbursements (averaging $9,825 per year), 2 teaching assistantships with tuition reimbursements (averaging $9,825 per year) were awarded; institutionally sponsored loans also available. Financial award application deadline: 2/15. *Faculty research:* Entertainment theory, news and public affairs, effects of telecommunications, management. Total annual research expenditures: $18,719. *Unit head:* Dr. Loy A. Singleton, Chair, 205-348-6350, Fax: 205-348-5162, E-mail: loy.singleton@ua.edu. *Application contact:* Dr. Gary Copeland, Graduate Coordinator, 205-348-6350, Fax: 205-348-5162, E-mail: copeland@ua.edu.

The University of Arizona, Graduate College, College of Fine Arts, School of Media Arts, Tucson, AZ 85721. Offers MA. Part-time programs available. *Faculty:* 10 full-time (6 women). *Students:* 12 full-time (9 women); includes 1 minority (Hispanic American), 2 international. Average age 24. 22 applicants, 50% accepted, 7 enrolled. *Degree requirements:* For master's, comprehensive exam. *Entrance requirements:* For master's, GRE, minimum GPA of 3.0. Additional exam requirements/recommendations for international students: Required—TOEFL (minimum score 550 paper-based). *Application deadline:* For fall admission, 2/15 for domestic and international students. Applications are processed on a rolling basis. Application fee: $50. Electronic applications accepted. *Financial support:* In 2007–08, 2 fellowships with tuition reimbursements (averaging $4,000 per year) were awarded; teaching assistantships with tuition reimbursements, career-related internships or fieldwork, scholarships/grants, health care benefits, tuition waivers (full and partial), and unspecified assistantships also available. Financial award applicants required to submit FAFSA. Total annual research expenditures: $3,643. *Unit head:* Albert Tucci, Head, 520-621-7007, E-mail: tucci@email.arizona.edu. *Application contact:* Sylvia Jo Miles, Administrative Secretary, 520-626-2847, Fax: 520-621-9662, E-mail: sjmiles@u.arizona.edu.

University of California, Santa Barbara, Graduate Division, College of Letters and Sciences, Division of Humanities and Fine Arts, Department of Media Arts and Technology, Santa Barbara, CA 93106. Offers electronic music and sound design (MA, PhD); multimedia engineering (MS, PhD); visual and spatial arts (MA, PhD). *Faculty:* 1 full-time (0 women), 12 part-time/adjunct (3 women). *Students:* 32 full-time (4 women); includes 3 minority (all Hispanic Americans), 9 international. Average age 30. 66 applicants, 36% accepted, 10 enrolled. In 2007, 11 master's, 1 doctorate awarded. Terminal master's awarded for partial completion of doctoral program. *Degree requirements:* For master's, thesis, 1 project; for doctorate, comprehensive exam, thesis/dissertation. *Entrance requirements:* For master's and doctorate, GRE, portfolios, programming language, calculus-based math, expertise in 1 discipline and experience in another. Additional exam requirements/recommendations for international students: Required—TOEFL (minimum score 550 paper-based; 213 computer-based; 80 iBT). *Application deadline:* For fall admission, 1/15 for domestic students, 3/1 for international students. Application fee: $60. Electronic applications accepted. *Expenses:* Tuition, nonresident: full-time $14,888. Required fees: $10,108. *Financial support:* In 2007–08, 28 students received support, including 11 fellowships with full and partial tuition reimbursements available (averaging $17,400 per year), 16 teaching assistantships; career-related internships or fieldwork, Federal Work-Study, scholarships/grants, health care benefits, and unspecified assistantships also available. Financial award application deadline: 12/15; financial award applicants required to submit FAFSA. *Faculty research:* Networking requirements for multimedia-capable systems, ceration of development of multimedia theatre, graphical user interfaces, distributed programming, speech image and video compression, audio signal processing, wireless communications. *Unit head:* Prof. Matthew Turk, Chair, 805-893-4236, E-mail: mturk@cs.ucsb.edu. *Application contact:* Diane Harden, Graduate Program Assistant, 805-893-2887, Fax: 805-893-2930, E-mail: harden@mat.ucsb.edu.

University of Chicago, Division of the Humanities, Committee on Cinema and Media Studies, Chicago, IL 60637-1513. Offers AM, PhD. *Students:* 39. 136 applicants, 4% accepted, 3 enrolled. *Degree requirements:* For master's, one foreign language, thesis; for doctorate, 2 foreign languages, thesis/dissertation. *Application deadline:* For fall admission, 12/15 for domestic students. *Financial support:* Fellowships available. Financial award application deadline: 12/15; financial award applicants required to submit FAFSA. *Unit head:* Dr. Thomas Gunning, Chair, 773-702-0264.

University of Colorado at Boulder, Alliance for Technology, Learning, and Society, Boulder, CO 80309. Offers technology, media, and society (PhD). *Students:* 2 full-time (both women), 1 part-time. Average age 33. 3 applicants, 100% accepted. *Application deadline:* For fall admission, 1/28 for domestic students, 12/1 for international students. *Financial support:* In 2007–08, 2 fellowships (averaging $9,233 per year), 1 research assistantship (averaging $15,966 per year) were awarded. Financial award application deadline: 1/15. *Faculty research:* Evaluation of the Dissector Tool based on the visible Human Data Project, assessing student outcomes for SENCER (an NSF-sponsored program using civic engagement to increase the interest and learning in undergraduate science at over 300 U.S. universities). *Application contact:* E-mail: cuatlas@colorado.edu.

University of Colorado at Boulder, Graduate School, School of Journalism and Mass Communication, Program in Communication, Boulder, CO 80309. Offers media studies (PhD). *Students:* 18 full-time (10 women), 5 part-time (4 women); includes 5 minority (3 African Americans, 2 Hispanic Americans), 3 international. Average age 35. 21 applicants, 24% accepted. In 2007, 6 degrees awarded. *Entrance requirements:* For doctorate, GRE General Test, minimum undergraduate GPA of 3.25. Additional exam requirements/recommendations for international students: Required—TOEFL. *Application deadline:* For fall admission, 2/15 for domestic and international students. Application fee: $50 ($60 for international students).

Financial support: In 2007–08, 14 fellowships (averaging $3,857 per year), 9 research assistantships (averaging $14,446 per year) were awarded; unspecified assistantships also available. Financial award application deadline: 3/1. *Unit head:* Janice Peck, Director, 303-492-2047, Fax: 303-492-0969, E-mail: janice.peck@colorado.edu. *Application contact:* Graduate Program Assistant, 303-492-5008, Fax: 303-492-0969, E-mail: sjmcgrad@colorado.edu.

University of Denver, Faculty of Arts and Humanities/Social Sciences, School of Communication, Department of Mass Communications, Denver, CO 80208. Offers advertising management (MS); digital media studies (MA); mass communications (MA); public relations (MS); video production (MA). Part-time programs available. *Faculty:* 14 full-time (9 women). *Students:* 7 full-time (5 women), 30 part-time (23 women); includes 5 minority (1 African American, 4 Hispanic Americans), 1 international. Average age 26. In 2007, 19 degrees awarded. *Degree requirements:* For master's, thesis (for some programs). *Entrance requirements:* For master's, GRE General Test. Additional exam requirements/recommendations for international students: Required—TOEFL, TWE. *Application deadline:* Applications are processed on a rolling basis. Application fee: $50. Electronic applications accepted. *Financial support:* In 2007–08, 3 research assistantships with full and partial tuition reimbursements (averaging $8,400 per year), 5 teaching assistantships with full and partial tuition reimbursements (averaging $10,000 per year) were awarded; career-related internships or fieldwork, Federal Work-Study, institutionally sponsored loans, and scholarships/grants also available. Support available to part-time students. Financial award application deadline: 3/1; financial award applicants required to submit FAFSA. *Faculty research:* Youth and civic engagement. Total annual research expenditures: $117,000. *Unit head:* Dr. Diane Waldman, Chair, 303-871-2166. *Application contact:* Information Contact, 303-871-2166, E-mail: mcomadm@du.edu.

See Close-Up on page 939.

University of Florida, Graduate School, College of Journalism and Communications, Department of Telecommunication, Gainesville, FL 32611. Offers MAMC. *Faculty:* 11 full-time (6 women). *Degree requirements:* For master's, thesis optional. *Entrance requirements:* For master's, GRE General Test, minimum GPA of 3.0. *Application deadline:* For fall admission, 6/1 priority date for domestic students. Applications are processed on a rolling basis. Application fee: $20. *Expenses:* Tuition, state resident: full-time $7,478. Tuition, nonresident: full-time $22,603. *Unit head:* Dr. David H. Ostroff, Chair, 352-392-0463, Fax: 352-392-3919, E-mail: dostroff@jou.ufl.edu. *Application contact:* Dr. Sylvia Chan-Olmsted, Coordinator, 352-392-0954, Fax: 352-392-3919, E-mail: chanolmsted@jou.ufl.edu.

The University of Iowa, Graduate College, College of Liberal Arts and Sciences, School of Journalism and Mass Communication, Iowa City, IA 52242-1316. Offers mass communication (PhD); media communication (MA); professional journalism (MA); JD/MA. *Accreditation:* ACEJMC (one or more programs are accredited). *Faculty:* 15 full-time, 16 part-time/adjunct. *Students:* 23 full-time (10 women), 22 part-time (10 women); includes 7 minority (4 African Americans, 1 American Indian/Alaska Native, 2 Hispanic Americans), 10 international. 78 applicants, 42% accepted, 14 enrolled. In 2007, 11 master's, 5 doctorates awarded. *Degree requirements:* For master's, thesis optional, exam; for doctorate, comprehensive exam, thesis/dissertation. *Entrance requirements:* For master's and doctorate, GRE General Test, minimum GPA of 3.0. Additional exam requirements/recommendations for international students: Required—TOEFL (minimum score 570 paper-based; 230 computer-based; 89 iBT). *Application deadline:* For fall admission, 1/10 priority date for domestic and international students. Applications are processed on a rolling basis. Application fee: $60 ($85 for international students). Electronic applications accepted. *Expenses:* Tuition, state resident: part-time $349 per hour. Tuition, nonresident: part-time $349 per hour. Tuition and fees vary according to course load and program. *Financial support:* In 2007–08, 3 fellowships, 10 research assistantships with partial tuition reimbursements, 18 teaching assistantships with partial tuition reimbursements were awarded; career-related internships or fieldwork and Federal Work-Study also available. Financial award applicants required to submit FAFSA. *Faculty research:* Verbal and visual aspects of historical, legal, social, and cross-cultural communication. *Unit head:* Marc Armstrong, Interim Director, 319-335-3486, Fax: 319-335-3502.

University of Lethbridge, School of Graduate Studies, Lethbridge, AB T1K 3M4, Canada. Offers accounting (MScM); addictions counseling (M Sc); agricultural biotechnology (M Sc); agricultural studies (M Sc, MA); anthropology (MA); archaeology (MA); art (MA); biochemistry (M Sc); biological sciences (M Sc); biomolecular science (PhD); biosystems and biodiversity (PhD); Canadian studies (MA); chemistry (M Sc); computer science (M Sc); computer science and geographical information science (M Sc); counseling psychology (M Ed); dramatic arts (MA); earth, space, and physical science (PhD); economics (MA); educational leadership (M Ed); English (MA); environmental science (M Sc); evolution and behavior (PhD); exercise science (M Sc); finance (MScM); French (MA); French/German (MA); French/Spanish (MA); general education (M Ed); general management (MScM); geography (M Sc, MA); German (MA); health sciences (M Sc, MA); history (MA); human resource management and labour relations (MScM); individualized multidisciplinary (M Sc, MA); information systems (MScM); international management (MScM); kinesiology (M Sc, MA); management (M Sc, MA); marketing (MScM); mathematics (M Sc); music (MA); Native American studies (MA); neuroscience (M Sc, PhD); new media (MA); nursing (M Sc); philosophy (MA); physics (M Sc); policy and strategy (MScM); political science (MA); psychology (M Sc, MA); religious studies (MA); sociology (MA); theoretical and computational science (PhD); urban and regional studies (MA). Part-time and evening/weekend programs available. *Students:* 215 full-time, 98 part-time. In 2007, 87 master's, 1 doctorate awarded. *Degree requirements:* For doctorate, comprehensive exam, thesis/dissertation. *Entrance requirements:* For master's, GMAT (M Sc in management), bachelor's degree in related field, minimum GPA of 3.0 during previous 20 graded semester courses, 2 years teaching or related experience (M Ed); for doctorate, master's degree, minimum graduate GPA of 3.5. Additional exam requirements/recommendations for international students: Required—TOEFL. Application fee: $60 Canadian dollars. *Financial support:* Fellowships, research assistantships, teaching assistantships, scholarships/grants, health care benefits, and unspecified assistantships available. *Faculty research:* Movement and brain plasticity, gibberellin physiology, photosynthesis, carbon cycling, molecular properties of main-group ring components. *Unit head:* Dr. Jo-Anne Fiske, Interim Dean, 403-329-2121, Fax: 403-329-2097. *Application contact:* Jennifer Geddes, Graduate Liaison Officer, 403-329-2762, Fax: 403-329-5159, E-mail: jennifer.geddes@uleth.ca.

University of Maryland, College Park, Graduate Studies, Phillip Merrill College of Journalism, College Park, MD 20742. Offers broadcast journalism (MA); journalism (MA); journalism and media studies (PhD); online news (MA); public affairs reporting (MA). *Accreditation:* ACEJMC (one or more programs are accredited). Part-time and evening/weekend programs available. *Faculty:* 28 full-time (13 women), 36 part-time/adjunct (10 women). *Students:* 71 full-time (43 women), 17 part-time (7 women); includes 20 minority (13 African Americans, 1 American Indian/Alaska Native, 4 Asian Americans or Pacific Islanders, 2 Hispanic Americans), 12 international. 243 applicants, 35% accepted, 32 enrolled. In 2007, 23 master's, 2 doctorates awarded. *Degree requirements:* For doctorate, thesis/dissertation, preliminary written and oral comprehensive exams. *Entrance requirements:* For master's and doctorate, GRE General Test, minimum GPA of 3.0, 3 letters of recommendation. Additional exam requirements/recommendations for international students: Required—TOEFL. *Application deadline:* For fall admission, 3/1 for domestic students, 2/1 for international students; for spring admission, 10/1 for domestic students, 6/1 for international students. Applications are processed on a rolling basis. Application fee: $60. Electronic applications accepted. *Financial support:* In 2007–08, 5 fellowships with full tuition reimbursements (averaging $13,925 per year), 2 research assistantships with tuition reimbursements (averaging $16,468 per year), 18 teaching assistantships with tuition reimbursements (averaging $15,744 per year) were awarded; career-related internships or fieldwork, Federal Work-Study, and scholarships/grants also available. Support available to part-time students. Financial award applicants required to submit FAFSA. *Faculty research:* Mass communication theory, specialized journalism, new telecommunication technologies, press integration. Total annual research expenditures: $130,465. *Unit head:* Thomas Kunkel, Dean, 301-405-2383, Fax: 301-314-1978, E-mail: tkunkel@umd.edu. *Application contact:* Dean of Graduate School, 301-405-0358, Fax: 301-314-9305.

See Close-Up on page 941.

University of Michigan, Horace H. Rackham School of Graduate Studies, The School of Music, Theatre, and Dance, Program in Media Arts, Ann Arbor, MI 48109. Offers MA. *Entrance requirements:* For master's, GRE, portfolio. Additional exam requirements/recommendations for international students: Required—TOEFL (minimum score 600 paper-based; 250 computer-based).

University of Nevada, Las Vegas, Graduate College, Greenspun College of Urban Affairs, School of Journalism and Media Studies, Las Vegas, NV 89154-9900. Offers MA. *Faculty:* 11 full-time (2 women). *Students:* 11 full-time (7 women), 15 part-time (9 women); includes 4 minority (3 Asian Americans or Pacific Islanders, 1 Hispanic American), 2 international. 19 applicants, 68% accepted, 10 enrolled. In 2007, 2 degrees awarded. *Entrance requirements:* For master's, GRE General Test, minimum 3.0 GPA. Additional exam requirements/recommendations for international students: Required—TOEFL (minimum score 550 paper-based; 213 computer-based; 80 iBT). *Application deadline:* For fall admission, 3/15 for domestic and international students. Application fee: $60 ($75 for international students). Electronic applications accepted. *Expenses:* Tuition, state resident: part-time $198 per credit. Tuition, nonresident: part-time $416 per credit. Required fees: $256 per semester. Tuition and fees vary according to course load and reciprocity agreements. *Financial support:* In 2007–08, 3 research assistantships with partial tuition reimbursements (averaging $10,000 per year), 5 teaching assistantships with partial tuition reimbursements (averaging $9,000 per year) were awarded; career-related internships or fieldwork, Federal Work-Study, institutionally sponsored loans, scholarships/grants, health care benefits, and unspecified assistantships also available. Support available to part-time students. Financial award application deadline: 3/1. *Unit head:* Dr. Ardyth Broadrick Sohn, Director, 702-895-4491. *Application contact:* Graduate College Admissions Evaluator, 702-895-3320, Fax: 702-895-4180, E-mail: gradcollege@unlv.edu.

The University of North Carolina at Greensboro, Graduate School, College of Arts and Sciences, Department of Broadcasting and Cinema, Greensboro, NC 27412-5001. Offers film and video production (MFA). *Application contact:* Michelle Harkleroad, Director of Graduate Admissions, 336-334-4884, Fax: 336-334-4424, E-mail: mbharkle@uncg.edu.

University of South Carolina, The Graduate School, College of Arts and Sciences, Department of Art, Division of Media Arts, Columbia, SC 29208. Offers MMA. *Faculty:* 7 full-time (4 women), 3 part-time/adjunct (0 women). *Students:* 6 full-time (4 women), 4 part-time (1 woman); includes 1 minority (African American) Average age 33. 9 applicants, 78% accepted. In 2007, 3 degrees awarded. *Degree requirements:* For master's, thesis. *Entrance requirements:* For master's, GRE General Test, interview, portfolio. Additional exam requirements/recommendations for international students: Required—TOEFL. *Application deadline:* For fall admission, 6/30 priority date for domestic students; for spring admission, 11/30 for domestic students. Applications are processed on a rolling basis. Application fee: $35. Electronic applications accepted. *Expenses:* Tuition, state resident: part-time $440 per hour. Tuition, nonresident: part-time $936 per hour. Required fees: $17 per hour. Tuition and fees vary according to program. *Financial support:* In 2007–08, 5 research assistantships with partial tuition reimbursements (averaging $2,000 per year) were awarded; teaching assistantships with partial tuition reimbursements, career-related internships or fieldwork and Federal Work-Study also available. *Faculty research:* Three dimensional imaging, script writing. *Unit head:* Dr. Walter V. Hanclosky, Director of Graduate Studies, 803-777-5212, Fax: 803-777-9355, E-mail: whanclosky@sc.edu. *Application contact:* Kim Roberson, Administrative Assistant, 803-777-6812, Fax: 803-777-9355, E-mail: robersek@gwm.sc.edu.

University of Southern California, Graduate School, Annenberg School for Communication, School of Communication, Program in Communication Management, Los Angeles, CA 90089. Offers MCM, JD/MCM, MCM/MAJCS. Part-time and evening/weekend programs available. *Students:* 143 full-time, 73 part-time; includes 59 minority (14 African Americans, 1 American Indian/Alaska Native, 25 Asian Americans or Pacific Islanders, 19 Hispanic Americans), 55 international. Average age 31. 252 applicants, 54% accepted, 78 enrolled. In 2007, 735 degrees awarded. *Degree requirements:* For master's, professional project. *Entrance requirements:* For master's, GRE General Test or GMAT, resumé, writing samples, recommendation letters, statement of purpose. Additional exam requirements/recommendations for international students: Required—TOEFL (minimum score 280 computer-based; 114 iBT). *Application deadline:* For fall admission, 7/1 priority date for domestic students, 3/15 priority date for international students; for spring admission, 11/30 priority date for domestic students, 9/1 priority date for international students. Applications are processed on a rolling basis. Application fee: $85. Electronic applications accepted. *Financial support:* Fellowships, research assistantships, teaching assistantships with full and partial tuition reimbursements, Federal Work-Study, institutionally sponsored loans, scholarships/grants, health care benefits, and tuition waivers (partial) available. Support available to part-time students. Financial award application deadline: 1/15; financial award applicants required to submit FAFSA. *Faculty research:* Global communication, communication law and policy, entertainment management, marketing communication, strategic and corporate communication management. *Unit head:* Dr. Rebecca Weintraub, Director, 213-821-0764, Fax: 213-740-8036, E-mail: weintrau@usc.edu. *Application contact:* Allyson Hill, Director of Admissions, 213-821-0770, E-mail: ascadm@usc.edu.

See Close-Up on page 945.

University of Southern California, Graduate School, Annenberg School for Communication, School of Journalism, Program in Broadcast Journalism, Los Angeles, CA 90089. Offers MA. *Students:* 34 full-time (30 women), 4 part-time (all women); includes 18 minority (3 African Americans, 8 Asian Americans or Pacific Islanders, 7 Hispanic Americans), 2 international. Average age 26. 79 applicants, 48% accepted, 16 enrolled. In 2007, 37 degrees awarded. *Degree requirements:* For master's, comprehensive exam. *Entrance requirements:* For master's, GRE General Test, resumé, writing samples, letters of recommendation, statement of purpose. Additional exam requirements/recommendations for international students: Required—TOEFL (minimum score 280 computer-based; 114 iBT). *Application deadline:* For fall admission, 1/15 for domestic and international students. Application fee: $85. Electronic applications accepted. *Financial support:* Teaching assistantships with full tuition reimbursements, career-related internships or fieldwork, Federal Work-Study, institutionally sponsored loans, scholarships/grants, health care benefits, and unspecified assistantships available. Support available to part-time students. Financial award application deadline: 1/15; financial award applicants required to submit FAFSA. *Application contact:* Allyson Hill, Director of Admissions, 213-821-0770, E-mail: ascadm@usc.edu.

See Close-Up on page 945.

University of Southern California, Graduate School, School of Cinematic Arts, Division of Animation and Digital Arts, Los Angeles, CA 90089. Offers film, video, and computer animation (MFA); media arts and practice (PhD). *Faculty:* 6 full-time (4 women), 17 part-time/adjunct (4 women). *Degree requirements:* For master's, thesis; for doctorate, thesis/dissertation. *Entrance requirements:* For master's and doctorate, GRE. *Application deadline:* For fall admission, 2/15 for domestic students. *Financial support:* Fellowships, career-related internships or fieldwork, scholarships/grants, and tuition waivers (partial) available. *Faculty research:* Science visualization, visual effects, experimental animation, documentary visualization, motion graphics. *Unit head:* Kathy Smith, Head, 213-740-2311.

The University of Tennessee, Graduate School, College of Communication and Information, Knoxville, TN 37996. Offers advertising (MS, PhD); broadcasting (MS, PhD); communications (MS, PhD); information sciences (MS, PhD); journalism (MS, PhD); public relations (MS, PhD); speech communication (MS, PhD). *Accreditation:* ACEJMC (one or more programs are accredited at the [master's] level). Part-time and evening/weekend programs available. Post-

Media Studies

The University of Tennessee (continued)
baccalaureate distance learning degree programs offered (no on-campus study). *Degree requirements:* For master's, thesis or alternative; for doctorate, thesis/dissertation. *Entrance requirements:* For master's and doctorate, GRE General Test, minimum GPA of 2.7. Additional exam requirements/recommendations for international students: Required—TOEFL. Electronic applications accepted.

The University of Texas at Austin, Graduate School, College of Communication, Department of Radio-Television-Film, Austin, TX 78712-1111. Offers film/video production (MFA); radio-television-film (MA, PhD). *Degree requirements:* For master's, thesis (for some programs); for doctorate, thesis/dissertation. *Entrance requirements:* For master's and doctorate, GRE General Test. Electronic applications accepted. *Faculty research:* International communication, film studies, media and culture, telecommunication and new media, gender and sexuality.

The University of Western Ontario, Faculty of Graduate Studies, Faculty of Information and Media Studies, Programs in Media Studies, London, ON N6A 5B8, Canada. Offers MA, PhD. Part-time programs available. *Degree requirements:* For master's, thesis; for doctorate, comprehensive exam, thesis/dissertation. *Entrance requirements:* For master's, 2 letters of reference; for doctorate, MA in media studies, communications or related field. Additional exam requirements/recommendations for international students: Required—TOEFL (minimum score 625 paper-based), TWE (minimum score 5). Electronic applications accepted. *Faculty research:* Media cultures, media industries, media technologies.

Virginia Commonwealth University, Graduate School, College of Humanities and Sciences, School of Mass Communications, Program in Media, Art, and Text, Richmond, VA 23284-9005. Offers PhD. *Students:* 18 full-time (12 women), 5 part-time (2 women); includes 4 minority (2 African Americans, 2 Hispanic Americans), 1 international. 33 applicants, 52% accepted, 12 enrolled. *Entrance requirements:* For doctorate, GRE, MA, MAE, or MFA in appropriate field of study (English, art history, studio art, poetry, mass communications); 3 letters of recommendation. *Application deadline:* For fall admission, 3/15 for domestic students. *Expenses:* Tuition, state resident: full-time $7,224; part-time $401 per credit. Tuition, nonresident: full-time $16,072; part-time $891 per credit. Required fees: $1,679; $63 per credit. Tuition and fees vary according to campus/location. *Unit head:* Thom Didato, Director, 804-828-1329, E-mail: tndidato@vcu.edu.

See Close-Up on page 457.

Washington State University, Graduate School, College of Liberal Arts, Edward R. Murrow College of Communication, Pullman, WA 99164. Offers health communications (MA, PhD); intercultural and international communications (MA, PhD); media and society (MA, PhD); media process and effects (MA, PhD); organizational communications (MA, PhD). *Faculty:* 30. *Students:* 43 full-time (26 women), 6 part-time (4 women); includes 2 minority (1 Asian American or Pacific Islander, 1 Hispanic American), 19 international. Average age 30. 120 applicants, 22% accepted, 19 enrolled. In 2007, 22 master's, 1 doctorate awarded. *Degree requirements:* For master's, comprehensive exam (for some programs), thesis optional, oral exam; for doctorate, comprehensive exam, thesis/dissertation. *Entrance requirements:* For master's, GRE General Test, minimum GPA of 3.25, 3 letters of recommendation; for doctorate, GRE General Test, minimum undergraduate GPA of 3.25, graduate 3.5; MA in communication; 3 letters of recommendation. Additional exam requirements/recommendations for international students: Required—TOEFL (minimum score 580 paper-based; 237 computer-based). *Application deadline:* For fall admission, 1/15 priority date for domestic students, 3/1 for international students. Applications are processed on a rolling basis. Application fee: $50. Electronic applications accepted. *Financial support:* In 2007–08, 46 students received support, including 2 fellowships (averaging $4,477 per year), 7 research assistantships with full and partial tuition reimbursements available (averaging $13,917 per year), 34 teaching assistantships with full and partial tuition reimbursements available (averaging $13,056 per year); career-related internships or fieldwork, Federal Work-Study, institutionally sponsored loans, tuition waivers (partial), and teaching associateships also available. Financial award application deadline: 4/1; financial award applicants required to submit FAFSA. *Faculty research:* Advocacy communication, mediated communication in decision making, communication technology policy and effects, multicultural and international psychology and physiology of communication. Total annual research expenditures: $550,455. *Unit head:* Dr. Erica Austin, Interim Director, 509-335-1556, E-mail: eaustin@wsu.edu. *Application contact:* Graduate School Admissions, 800-GRADWSU, Fax: 509-335-1949, E-mail: gradsch@wsu.edu.

Wayne State University, College of Fine, Performing and Communication Arts, Department of Communication, Detroit, MI 48202. Offers communication studies (MA, PhD); public relations and organizational communication (MA); radio-TV-film (MA, PhD); speech communication (MA, PhD). *Students:* 74 full-time (49 women), 128 part-time (94 women); includes 63 minority (51 African Americans, 1 American Indian/Alaska Native, 3 Asian Americans or Pacific Islanders, 8 Hispanic Americans), 14 international. Average age 34. 92 applicants, 62% accepted, 42 enrolled. In 2007, 39 master's, 6 doctorates awarded. *Degree requirements:* For master's, thesis, essay, or comprehensive exam; for doctorate, thesis/dissertation. *Entrance requirements:* For master's, minimum GPA of 3.0, personal statement; sample of academic writing; for doctorate, GRE, minimum GPA of 3.3, MA; letters of recommendation; personal statement; sample of written scholarship. Additional exam requirements/recommendations for international students: Required—TOEFL (minimum score 550 paper-based; 213 computer-based); Recommended—TWE (minimum score 6). *Application deadline:* For fall admission, 4/1 for domestic students, 6/1 for international students; for winter admission, 10/1 for international students; for spring admission, 2/1 for international students. Applications are processed on a rolling basis. Application fee: $30 ($50 for international students). Electronic applications accepted. *Expenses:* Tuition, state resident: part-time $403 per credit hour. Tuition, nonresident: part-time $890 per credit hour. *Financial support:* In 2007–08, 22 students received support, including 2 fellowships with tuition reimbursements available (averaging $14,351 per year), 17 teaching assistantships with tuition reimbursements available (averaging $12,922 per year); research assistantships with tuition reimbursements available, career-related internships or fieldwork also available. Financial award application deadline: 2/1. *Faculty research:* Rhetorical theory and criticism; mass media theory and research; argumentation; organizational communication; risk and crisis communication; interpersonal, family, and health communication. *Unit head:* Dr. Matthew Seeger, Chair, 313-577-2959, Fax: 313-577-6300, E-mail: aa4331@wayne.edu. *Application contact:* Hayg Oshagan, Associate Professor, 313-577-0429, E-mail: ad4570@wayne.edu.

Webster University, School of Communications, Program in Media Communications, St. Louis, MO 63119-3194. Offers MA. *Expenses:* Tuition: Full-time $9,360; part-time $520 per credit. *Unit head:* Susan Seymour, Director, 314-961-2660 Ext. 7527.

Webster University, School of Communications, Program in Media Literacy, St. Louis, MO 63119-3194. Offers MA. *Expenses:* Tuition: Full-time $9,360; part-time $520 per credit. *Unit head:* Susan Seymour, Director, 314-961-2660 Ext. 7527.

West Virginia State University, Graduate Programs, Program in Media Studies, Institute, WV 25112-1000. Offers MA. *Entrance requirements:* For master's, GRE, minimum GPA of 3.0, letters of recommendation. Additional exam requirements/recommendations for international students: Required—TOEFL (minimum score 550 paper-based). *Expenses:* Tuition, state resident: full-time $7,760; part-time $253 per hour. Required fees: $160 per semester.

William Paterson University of New Jersey, College of the Arts and Communication, Program in Communication and Media Studies, Wayne, NJ 07470-8420. Offers MA. *Students:* 3 full-time (all women), 7 part-time (3 women); includes 2 African Americans, 1 Hispanic American. In 2007, 2 degrees awarded. *Degree requirements:* For master's, comprehensive exam. *Entrance requirements:* For master's, GRE General Test or MAT, minimum GPA of 2.75. *Application deadline:* Applications are processed on a rolling basis. Application fee: $50. Electronic applications accepted. *Financial support:* Research assistantships with tuition reimbursements, career-related internships or fieldwork, Federal Work-Study, and unspecified assistantships available. Support available to part-time students. Financial award application deadline: 4/1; financial award applicants required to submit FAFSA. *Faculty research:* Cable television, intercultural communication. *Unit head:* Casey Lum, Program Director, 973-720-2342, Fax: 973-720-2483. *Application contact:* Danielle Liautaud, Director, 973-720-3579, Fax: 973-720-2035, E-mail: liautaudd@wpunj.edu.

Publishing

Drexel University, College of Arts and Sciences, Department of Culture and Communication, Program in Publication Management, Philadelphia, PA 19104-2875. Offers MS. Part-time and evening/weekend programs available. *Degree requirements:* For master's, research project. *Entrance requirements:* Additional exam requirements/recommendations for international students: Required—TOEFL. Electronic applications accepted.

Drexel University, College of Media Arts and Design, Philadelphia, PA 19104-2875. Offers architecture (M Arch); design (MS), including fashion design, interior design; media arts (MS); performing arts (MS), including arts administration. *Accreditation:* NASAD. Part-time and evening/weekend programs available. *Entrance requirements:* For master's, interview. Additional exam requirements/recommendations for international students: Required—TOEFL. Electronic applications accepted. Expenses: Contact institution.

Emerson College, Graduate Studies, School of the Arts, Department of Writing, Literature and Publishing, Program in Publishing and Writing, Boston, MA 02116-4624. Offers MA. Part-time programs available. *Students:* 95 full-time (79 women), 19 part-time (17 women); includes 15 minority (1 African American, 1 American Indian/Alaska Native, 7 Asian Americans or Pacific Islanders, 6 Hispanic Americans), 3 international. Average age 27. 204 applicants, 38% accepted, 48 enrolled. In 2007, 31 degrees awarded. *Degree requirements:* For master's, thesis or alternative. *Entrance requirements:* For master's, GRE General Test, 15 page writing sample. Additional exam requirements/recommendations for international students: Required—TOEFL (minimum score 550 paper-based; 213 computer-based; 80 iBT), IELTS (minimum score 7). *Application deadline:* For fall admission, 1/5 for domestic students. Applications are processed on a rolling basis. Application fee: $60 ($75 for international students). *Expenses:* Tuition: Full-time $16,800; part-time $840 per credit. Required fees: $60 per semester. One-time fee: $160. *Financial support:* In 2007–08, 2 fellowships with partial tuition reimbursements (averaging $14,000 per year), 24 research assistantships with partial tuition reimbursements (averaging $10,000 per year) were awarded; career-related internships or fieldwork, Federal Work-Study, institutionally sponsored loans, scholarships/grants, and unspecified assistantships also available. Support available to part-time students. Financial award application deadline: 2/1; financial award applicants required to submit FAFSA. *Faculty research:* Publishing. *Unit head:* Prof. Lisa Diercks, Director, 617-824-8750. *Application contact:* 617-824-8610, Fax: 617-824-8614, E-mail: gradapp@emerson.edu.

See Close-Up on page 897.

The George Washington University, College of Professional Studies, Program in Publishing, Washington, DC 20052. Offers MPS. Program offered at Alexandria, VA education center. *Entrance requirements:* For master's, minimum cumulative GPA of 3.0. Electronic applications accepted.

New York University, School of Continuing and Professional Studies, Division for Media Industry Studies and Design, Center for Publishing, New York, NY 10012-1019. Offers MS. Part-time and evening/weekend programs available. *Faculty:* 44 part-time/adjunct (27 women). *Students:* 34 full-time (23 women), 62 part-time (52 women); includes 6 minority (1 African American, 2 Asian Americans or Pacific Islanders, 3 Hispanic Americans), 7 international. Average age 27. 106 applicants, 59% accepted, 35 enrolled. In 2007, 18 degrees awarded. *Degree requirements:* For master's, thesis. *Entrance requirements:* For master's, GMAT or GRE General Test for recent graduates, work experience, 2 letters of recommendation, resumé, essay. Additional exam requirements/recommendations for international students: Required—TOEFL (minimum score 600 paper-based; 250 computer-based; 100 iBT), TWE. *Application deadline:* For fall admission, 3/15 priority date for domestic and international students; for spring admission, 10/15 priority date for domestic students, 8/15 priority date for international students. Applications are processed on a rolling basis. Application fee: $75. Electronic applications accepted. *Financial support:* In 2007–08, 79 students received support, including 79 fellowships (averaging $2,370 per year); career-related internships or fieldwork, Federal Work-Study, institutionally sponsored loans, and scholarships/grants also available. Support available to part-time students. Financial award application deadline: 3/1; financial award applicants required to submit FAFSA. *Faculty research:* Special marketing and distribution channels. *Unit head:* Andrea L. Chambers, Director, 212-992-3235, Fax: 212-790-3233, E-mail: andrea.chambers@nyu.edu. *Application contact:* Alyssa Léal, Associate Director, 212-790-3236, Fax: 212-790-3233, E-mail: alyssa.leal@nyu.edu.

See Close-Up on page 913.

Northwestern University, Medill School of Journalism, Evanston, IL 60208. Offers broadcast journalism (MSJ); integrated marketing communications (MSIMC), including advertising/sales promotion, direct database and e-commerce marketing, general studies, public relations; magazine publishing (MSJ); new media (MSJ); reporting and writing (MSJ). *Accreditation:* ACEJMC (one or more programs are accredited). *Entrance requirements:* For master's, GRE General Test, GMAT or LSAT (MSJ). Additional exam requirements/recommendations for international students: Required—TOEFL. Electronic applications accepted. Expenses: Contact institution. *Faculty research:* Web business journalism, cultural stereotypes, voter apathy, digital television.

Pace University, Dyson College of Arts and Sciences, Program in Publishing, New York, NY 10038. Offers MS. Part-time and evening/weekend programs available. Postbaccalaureate distance learning degree programs offered. *Faculty:* 2 full-time, 10 part-time/adjunct. *Students:* 53 full-time (46 women), 55 part-time (50 women); includes 25 minority (16 African Americans, 2 Asian Americans or Pacific Islanders, 7 Hispanic Americans), 2 international. Average age 27. 88 applicants, 82% accepted, 45 enrolled. In 2007, 39 degrees awarded. *Degree requirements:* For master's, internship or thesis. *Entrance requirements:* For master's, GRE General Test. *Application deadline:* For fall admission, 7/31 priority date for domestic students; for spring admission, 11/30 priority date for domestic students. Applications are processed on a rolling basis. Application fee: $65. Electronic applications accepted. *Expenses:* Tuition: Part-time $856 per credit. Tuition and fees vary according to degree level and program.

Financial support: Research assistantships, career-related internships or fieldwork available. Support available to part-time students. Financial award applicants required to submit FAFSA. *Unit head:* Prof. Sherman Raskin, Chairperson and Director, 212-346-1417. *Application contact:* Joanna Broda, Director of Admissions, 212-346-1652, Fax: 212-346-1585, E-mail: gradnyc@pace.edu.

See Close-Up on page 917.

Rosemont College, Graduate School, Program in English and Publishing and English Literature, Rosemont, PA 19010-1699. Offers English and publishing (MA); English literature (MA). Part-time programs available. *Faculty:* 13 part-time/adjunct (9 women). *Students:* 21 full-time (16 women), 87 part-time (73 women); includes 8 minority (6 African Americans, 2 Hispanic Americans), 1 international. Average age 30. 39 applicants, 79% accepted, 28 enrolled. In 2007, 41 degrees awarded. *Degree requirements:* For master's, comprehensive exam (for some programs), thesis. *Entrance requirements:* For master's, Baccalaureat Degree 3.0 college GPA, statement of purpose, 3 letters of recommendation. Additional exam requirements/recommendations for international students: Required—TOEFL. *Application deadline:* Applications are processed on a rolling basis. Application fee: $50. Electronic applications accepted. *Expenses:* Tuition: Part-time $525 per credit. Tuition and fees vary according to program. *Financial support:* Institutionally sponsored loans and unspecified assistantships available. *Unit head:* Elizabeth Corcoran, Director, 610-527-0200, Fax: 610-526-2964. *Application contact:* Karen Scales, Director, Enrollment and Student Services, 610-527-0200 Ext. 2187, Fax: 610-526-2964, E-mail: gradstudies@rosemont.edu.

Simon Fraser University, Graduate Studies, Faculty of Arts and Social Sciences, Canadian Centre for Studies in Publishing, Burnaby, BC V5A 1S6, Canada. Offers M Pub. *Degree requirements:* For master's, internship, project report. *Entrance requirements:* For master's, minimum GPA of 3.0. Additional exam requirements/recommendations for international students: Required—TWE, TOEFL or IELTS. Expenses: Contact institution. *Faculty research:* History of publishing, electronic publishing, editing, multimedia, publication design.

University of Baltimore, Graduate School, The Yale Gordon College of Liberal Arts, School of Communications Design, Program in Creative Writing and Publishing Arts, Baltimore, MD 21201-5779. Offers MFA. *Students:* 16 full-time (12 women), 24 part-time (15 women); includes 11 minority (5 African Americans, 1 American Indian/Alaska Native, 3 Asian Americans or Pacific Islanders, 2 Hispanic Americans). Average age 29. *Entrance requirements:* Additional exam requirements/recommendations for international students: Required—TOEFL. *Application deadline:* For fall admission, 3/31 for domestic and international students. Application fee: $45. *Expenses:* Tuition, state resident: part-time $518 per credit. Tuition, nonresident: part-time $751 per credit. Tuition and fees vary according to program. *Unit head:* Kendra Kopelke, Director, MFA in Creative Writing and Publishing Arts, 410-837-6026, E-mail: kkopelke@ubalt.edu. *Application contact:* Wendy Bolyard.

University of Baltimore, Graduate School, The Yale Gordon College of Liberal Arts, School of Communications Design, Program in Publications Design, Baltimore, MD 21201-5779. Offers MA. Part-time and evening/weekend programs available. *Faculty:* 6 full-time (3 women), 10 part-time/adjunct (6 women). *Students:* 42 full-time (35 women), 138 part-time (108 women); includes 41 minority (28 African Americans, 1 American Indian/Alaska Native, 5 Asian Americans or Pacific Islanders, 7 Hispanic Americans), 4 international. Average age 30. 102 applicants, 83% accepted, 78 enrolled. In 2007, 42 degrees awarded. *Degree requirements:* For master's, seminar project. *Entrance requirements:* For master's, minimum GPA of 3.0, portfolio, interview. Additional exam requirements/recommendations for international students: Required—TOEFL (minimum score 550 paper-based; 213 computer-based). *Application deadline:* For fall admission, 8/1 priority date for domestic students, 6/1 for international students; for spring admission, 12/15 for domestic students, 11/1 for international students. Applications are processed on a rolling basis. Application fee: $45. Electronic applications accepted. *Expenses:* Tuition, state resident: part-time $518 per credit. Tuition, nonresident: part-time $751 per credit. Tuition and fees vary according to program. *Financial support:* In 2007–08, 9 research assistantships were awarded; fellowships, career-related internships or fieldwork and Federal Work-Study also available. Support available to part-time students. Financial award application deadline: 4/1; financial award applicants required to submit FAFSA. *Faculty research:* Communication theory, graphic design, media technology. *Unit head:* Dr. Stephanie Gibson, Director, Main Publications Design, 410-837-6050, E-mail: sgibson@ubalt.edu. *Application contact:* Wendy Bolyard.

Rhetoric

Abilene Christian University, Graduate School, College of Arts and Sciences, Department of English, Abilene, TX 79699-9100. Offers composition/rhetoric (MA); literature (MA); writing (MA). Part-time programs available. *Faculty:* 15 part-time/adjunct (5 women). *Students:* 12 full-time (7 women), 3 part-time (all women); includes 1 minority (Hispanic American), 1 international. 4 applicants, 225% accepted, 8 enrolled. In 2007, 5 degrees awarded. *Degree requirements:* For master's, one foreign language, comprehensive exam, thesis optional. *Entrance requirements:* For master's, GRE General Test. *Application deadline:* For fall admission, 4/1 priority date for domestic students; for spring admission, 11/1 for domestic students. Applications are processed on a rolling basis. Application fee: $40 ($45 for international students). Electronic applications accepted. *Expenses:* Tuition: Full-time $13,368; part-time $557 per hour. Required fees: $700; $34 per hour. $10 per semester. Tuition and fees vary according to degree level and campus/location. *Financial support:* Teaching assistantships, Federal Work-Study available. Support available to part-time students. Financial award application deadline: 4/1. *Faculty research:* Feminism, Shakespearean dimensions of new literature, poetic consciousness, deconstruction myths. *Unit head:* Dr. Bill Rankin, Graduate Adviser, 325-674-2253, Fax: 325-674-2408, E-mail: rankinw@acu.edu. *Application contact:* William Horn, Graduate Admissions Counselor, 325-674-2656, Fax: 325-674-6717, E-mail: gradinfo@acu.edu.

Ball State University, Graduate School, College of Communication, Information, and Media, Department of Communication Studies, Muncie, IN 47306-1099. Offers speech, public address, forensics, and rhetoric (MA). *Faculty:* 5. *Students:* 19 full-time (9 women), 9 part-time (8 women); includes 5 minority (2 African Americans, 3 Hispanic Americans), 7 international. Average age 23. 31 applicants, 74% accepted, 13 enrolled. In 2007, 16 degrees awarded. *Entrance requirements:* For master's, GRE General Test. Application fee: $25 ($35 for international students). *Expenses:* Tuition, state resident: full-time $6,864. Tuition, nonresident: full-time $17,932. Required fees: $1,866. *Financial support:* In 2007–08, 28 teaching assistantships with full tuition reimbursements (averaging $8,322 per year) were awarded; research assistantships, career-related internships or fieldwork also available. Financial award application deadline: 3/1. *Unit head:* Glen Stamp, Chairperson, 765-285-1882, Fax: 765-285-2736.

Bob Jones University, Graduate Programs, Greenville, SC 29614. Offers accountancy (MS); Bible (MA); Bible translation (MA); Biblical studies (Certificate); broadcast management (MS); business administration (MBA); church history (MA, PhD); church ministries (MA); church music (MM); cinema and video production (MA); counseling (MS); curriculum and instruction (Ed D); divinity (M Div); dramatic production (MA); educational leadership (MS, Ed D, Ed S); elementary education (M Ed, MAT); English (M Ed, MA, MAT); fine arts (MA); graphic design (MA); history (M Ed, MA); illustration (MA); interpretative speech (MA); mathematics (M Ed, MAT); medical missions (Certificate); ministry (MM, D Min); multi-categorical special education (M Ed, MAT); music (M Ed); New Testament interpretation (PhD); Old Testament interpretation (PhD); orchestral instrument performance (MM); organ performance (MM); pastoral studies (MA); personnel services (MS, Ed S); piano pedagogy (MM); piano performance (MM); platform arts (MA); radio and television broadcasting (MS); rhetoric and public address (MA); secondary education (M Ed); studio art (MA); teaching Bible (MA); theology (MA, PhD); voice performance (MM); youth ministries (MA); M Div/MM.

Bowling Green State University, Graduate College, College of Arts and Sciences, Department of English, Program in English, Bowling Green, OH 43403. Offers English (MA, PhD); literature (MA); rhetoric and writing (PhD); scientific and technical communication (MA). Part-time programs available. *Students:* 49 full-time (36 women), 12 part-time (9 women); includes 1 African American, 3 Asian Americans or Pacific Islanders, 1 Hispanic American, 9 international. Average age 31. 64 applicants, 67% accepted, 21 enrolled. In 2007, 14 master's, 6 doctorates awarded. *Degree requirements:* For master's, thesis or alternative; for doctorate, comprehensive exam, thesis/dissertation, foreign language or proficiency in Old English. *Entrance requirements:* For master's and doctorate, GRE General Test. Additional exam requirements/recommendations for international students: Required—TOEFL. *Application deadline:* For fall admission, 2/15 priority date for domestic students. Applications are processed on a rolling basis. Application fee: $30. Electronic applications accepted. *Financial support:* In 2007–08, 3 fellowships with full tuition reimbursements (averaging $14,707 per year), 8 research assistantships with full tuition reimbursements (averaging $9,664 per year), 34 teaching assistantships with full tuition reimbursements (averaging $10,480 per year) were awarded; Federal Work-Study and unspecified assistantships also available. Financial award applicants required to submit FAFSA. *Faculty research:* Postmodern literary theory, rhetorical theory, ethnic American literature, literature and culture, composition pedagogy.

California State University, Dominguez Hills, College of Arts and Humanities, Department of English, Carson, CA 90747-0001. Offers English (MA); rhetoric and composition (Certificate); teaching English as a second language (Certificate). Part-time and evening/weekend programs available. *Faculty:* 15 full-time (6 women). *Students:* 28 full-time (17 women), 41 part-time (28 women); includes 29 minority (12 African Americans, 5 Asian Americans or Pacific Islanders, 12 Hispanic Americans), 5 international. Average age 36. 34 applicants, 88% accepted, 15 enrolled. In 2007, 27 degrees awarded. *Degree requirements:* For master's, comprehensive exam (for some programs), thesis or alternative. *Entrance requirements:* For master's, minimum GPA of 3.0 in last 60 units. Additional exam requirements/recommendations for international students: Required—TOEFL (minimum score 550 paper-based; 213 computer-based). *Application deadline:* Applications are processed on a rolling basis. Application fee: $55. Electronic applications accepted. *Faculty research:* Gender studies, transnationalism, discourse analysis, visual culture, Shakespeare. *Unit head:* Dr. Cyril Zoerner, Chair, 310-243-3322. *Application contact:* 310-243-3600.

California State University, Northridge, Graduate Studies, College of Humanities, Department of English, Northridge, CA 91330. Offers creative writing (MA); literature (MA); rhetoric and composition theory (MA). Part-time and evening/weekend programs available. *Faculty:* 37 full-time (19 women), 85 part-time/adjunct (69 women). *Students:* 40 full-time (29 women), 125 part-time (92 women); includes 38 minority (3 African Americans, 1 American Indian/Alaska Native, 13 Asian Americans or Pacific Islanders, 21 Hispanic Americans). Average age 34. 99 applicants, 75% accepted, 40 enrolled. In 2007, 38 degrees awarded. *Degree requirements:* For master's, thesis or alternative. *Entrance requirements:* For master's, writing proficiency test, GRE General Test or minimum GPA of 3.0. Additional exam requirements/recommendations for international students: Required—TOEFL. *Application deadline:* For fall admission, 11/30 for domestic students. Application fee: $55. *Financial support:* Teaching assistantships available. Financial award application deadline: 3/1. *Faculty research:* Reading improvement, professional writing, Dickens, Shaw, English as a second language. *Unit head:* Dr. George Uba, Chair, 818-677-3434, E-mail: george.uba@csun.edu. *Application contact:* Dr. Marjie Seagoe, Graduate Studies Secretary, 818-677-3433.

California State University, Stanislaus, College of Humanities and Social Sciences, Department of English, Turlock, CA 95382. Offers English (MA); literature (MA); rhetoric and teaching of writing (MA); TESOL (MA, Certificate). Part-time programs available. *Faculty:* 21. *Students:* 11 full-time (8 women), 42 part-time (27 women); includes 11 minority (1 Asian American or Pacific Islander, 10 Hispanic Americans). Average age 32. 28 applicants, 100% accepted, 16 enrolled. In 2007, 12 degrees awarded. *Degree requirements:* For master's, one foreign language, comprehensive exam, thesis. *Entrance requirements:* For master's, GRE General Test, minimum GPA of 3.0, 2 letters of reference, personal statement; for Certificate, minimum GPA of 3.0, 2 letters of reference. Additional exam requirements/recommendations for international students: Required—TOEFL (minimum score 550 paper-based; 213 computer-based), TWE (minimum score 4). *Application deadline:* For fall admission, 7/1 for domestic and international students; for winter admission, 10/1 for domestic and international students; for spring admission, 11/1 for domestic and international students. Application fee: $55. Electronic applications accepted. *Expenses:* Tuition, nonresident: full-time $10,170; part-time $339 per unit. Required fees: $3,972; $2,538 per term. $1,165 per semester. *Financial support:* Fellowships, research assistantships, teaching assistantships, career-related internships or fieldwork and Federal Work-Study available. Financial award application deadline: 3/2; financial award applicants required to submit FAFSA. *Faculty research:* Transnational literacies, Renaissance and Medieval literature, abolition writings and slave narratives, qualitative writing. *Application contact:* Dr. Mark Thompson, Chair, 209-667-3361, Fax: 209-667-3720.

Carnegie Mellon University, College of Humanities and Social Sciences, Department of English, Program in Professional Writing, Pittsburgh, PA 15213-3891. Offers design (MAPW); professional writing (MAPW); research (MAPW); rhetorical theory (MAPW); science writing (MAPW); technical (MAPW). Part-time programs available. *Entrance requirements:* For master's, GRE General Test. Additional exam requirements/recommendations for international students: Required—TOEFL, TWE.

See Close-Up on page 723.

The Catholic University of America, School of Arts and Sciences, Department of English Language and Literature, Washington, DC 20064. Offers English language and literature (MA, PhD); rhetoric (MA, PhD); MSLS/MA. Part-time and evening/weekend programs available. *Faculty:* 11 full-time (3 women), 4 part-time/adjunct (1 woman). *Students:* 22 full-time (11 women), 38 part-time (22 women), 1 international. Average age 29. 72 applicants, 60% accepted, 21 enrolled. In 2007, 13 master's, 1 doctorate awarded. Terminal master's awarded for partial completion of doctoral program. *Degree requirements:* For master's, one foreign language, comprehensive exam, thesis or alternative; for doctorate, 2 foreign languages, comprehensive exam, thesis/dissertation. *Entrance requirements:* For master's and doctorate, GRE General Test, 3 letters of recommendation, writing sample. Additional exam requirements/recommendations for international students: Required—TOEFL (minimum score 580 paper-based; 237 computer-based). *Application deadline:* For fall admission, 2/1 priority date for domestic students; for spring admission, 11/15 priority date for domestic students. Applications are processed on a rolling basis. Application fee: $55. Electronic applications accepted. *Financial support:* Fellowships, teaching assistantships, career-related internships or fieldwork,

Rhetoric

The Catholic University of America (continued)
Federal Work-Study, scholarships/grants, tuition waivers (full and partial), and unspecified assistantships available. Support available to part-time students. Financial award application deadline: 2/1; financial award applicants required to submit FAFSA. *Faculty research:* Medieval literature, theory and history of rhetoric, modern Irish literature, religion and literature, English and American drama. *Unit head:* Dr. Ernest Suarez, Chair, 202-319-5488, Fax: 202-319-4188, E-mail: suarez@cua.edu.

Clemson University, Graduate School, College of Architecture, Arts, and Humanities, Department of English, Program in Rhetorics, Communication and Information Design, Clemson, SC 29634. Offers PhD. *Students:* 20 full-time (8 women), 1 part-time; includes 2 minority (1 African American, 1 Asian American or Pacific Islander), 4 international. 21 applicants, 57% accepted, 8 enrolled. *Degree requirements:* For doctorate, thesis/dissertation (for some programs). *Entrance requirements:* For doctorate, GRE, master's degree in English, communications studies, art, professional communication or related field; portfolio; 3 letters of reference; minimum graduate GPA of 3.5. Additional exam requirements/recommendations for international students: Required—TOEFL (minimum score 550 paper-based; 213 computer-based). *Application deadline:* For fall admission, 2/1 priority date for domestic students, 4/15 for international students. Application fee: $55. *Financial support:* Teaching assistantships available. *Unit head:* Dr. Victor Vitanza, Coordinator, 864-656-6411, Fax: 864-656-0599, E-mail: sophist@clemson.edu.

Duquesne University, Graduate School of Liberal Arts, Department of Communication and Rhetorical Studies, Pittsburgh, PA 15282-0001. Offers communication (MA); rhetoric (PhD). Part-time and evening/weekend programs available. *Faculty:* 6 full-time (3 women), 5 part-time/adjunct (3 women). *Students:* 72 full-time (39 women), 50 part-time (38 women). Average age 27. In 2007, 19 master's, 6 doctorates awarded. *Degree requirements:* For master's, thesis optional, practicum; for doctorate, 2 foreign languages, comprehensive exam, thesis/dissertation. *Entrance requirements:* For master's, GRE General Test, MAT or GMAT; for doctorate, GRE General Test. Additional exam requirements/recommendations for international students: Required—TOEFL. *Application deadline:* For fall admission, 2/1 priority date for domestic and international students; for spring admission, 11/1 priority date for domestic and international students. Applications are processed on a rolling basis. Application fee: $50. *Expenses:* Tuition: Part-time $774 per credit. Required fees: $74 per credit. Tuition and fees vary according to program. *Financial support:* In 2007–08, 9 research assistantships with full tuition reimbursements (averaging $9,000 per year), 10 teaching assistantships with full tuition reimbursements (averaging $13,000 per year) were awarded; career-related internships or fieldwork, Federal Work-Study, institutionally sponsored loans, scholarships/grants, tuition waivers (full and partial), and unspecified assistantships also available. Financial award application deadline: 5/1. *Unit head:* Dr. Ronald Arnett, Chair, 412-396-5076. *Application contact:* Dr. Janie Fritz, Director, 412-396-6460.

Florida State University, Graduate Studies, College of Arts and Sciences, Department of English, Tallahassee, FL 32306. Offers creative writing (MFA, PhD); literature (MA, PhD); rhetoric and composition (MA, PhD). Part-time programs available. *Faculty:* 57 full-time (25 women), 14 part-time/adjunct (9 women). *Students:* 148 full-time (105 women), 20 part-time (10 women); includes 30 minority (13 African Americans, 1 American Indian/Alaska Native, 8 Asian Americans or Pacific Islanders, 8 Hispanic Americans). Average age 30. 427 applicants, 17% accepted, 57 enrolled. In 2007, 25 master's, 18 doctorates awarded. *Median time to degree:* Of those who began their doctoral program in fall 1999, 80% received their degree in 8 years or less. *Degree requirements:* For master's, one foreign language, thesis or alternative; for doctorate, 2 foreign languages, thesis/dissertation. *Entrance requirements:* For master's, GRE General Test, GRE Subject Test (literature), sample of written work, 3 letters of recommendation; for doctorate, GRE General Test, sample of written work, 3 letters of recommendation. *Application deadline:* For fall admission, 2/1 priority date for domestic students. Application fee: $30. Electronic applications accepted. *Expenses:* Tuition, state resident: part-time $248 per credit hour. Tuition, nonresident: part-time $880 per credit hour. Tuition and fees vary according to program. *Financial support:* In 2007–08, 155 students received support, including 5 fellowships, 150 teaching assistantships (averaging $11,375 per year); career-related internships or fieldwork, Federal Work-Study, and institutionally sponsored loans also available. Financial award application deadline: 2/1; financial award applicants required to submit FAFSA. *Faculty research:* British literature, American literature, creative writing, rhetoric, multiethnic literature. *Unit head:* Dr. Ralph Berry, Chairman, 850-644-5158, Fax: 850-644-0811, E-mail: rberry@fsu.edu. *Application contact:* Dr. Stan Gontarski, Director, 850-644-6038, Fax: 850-644-0811, E-mail: sgontarski@fsu.edu.

Georgia State University, College of Arts and Sciences, Department of English, Atlanta, GA 30303-3083. Offers creative writing (MA, MFA, PhD); English (MA, PhD); fiction (MFA); literary studies and composition (MA, PhD); poetry (MFA); rhetoric (MA, PhD). Part-time and evening/weekend programs available. *Faculty:* 43 full-time (21 women). *Students:* 128 full-time (96 women), 103 part-time (58 women); includes 34 minority (23 African Americans, 2 American Indian/Alaska Native, 4 Asian Americans or Pacific Islanders, 5 Hispanic Americans), 11 international. 232 applicants, 44% accepted, 54 enrolled. In 2007, 20 master's, 9 doctorates awarded. *Degree requirements:* For master's, one foreign language, thesis; for doctorate, 2 foreign languages, comprehensive exam, thesis/dissertation, exam. *Entrance requirements:* For master's and doctorate, GRE General Test. Additional exam requirements/recommendations for international students: Required—TOEFL. *Application deadline:* For fall admission, 2/15 for domestic students. Applications are processed on a rolling basis. Application fee: $50. Electronic applications accepted. *Expenses:* Tuition, state resident: part-time $221 per credit hour. *Financial support:* In 2007–08, 5 research assistantships with tuition reimbursements, 11 teaching assistantships with tuition reimbursements were awarded; Federal Work-Study, institutionally sponsored loans, and unspecified assistantships also available. Support available to part-time students. Financial award application deadline: 2/15; financial award applicants required to submit FAFSA. *Faculty research:* Literary biography, folklore, Southern literature, medieval literature. *Unit head:* Dr. Matthew Roudane, Chair, 404-413-5804, E-mail: engmcr@langate.gsu.edu. *Application contact:* Melissa McLeod, Assistant to Director of Graduate Studies, 404-413-5807, Fax: 404-413-5830, E-mail: engmkm@langate.gsu.edu.

Indiana University of Pennsylvania, School of Graduate Studies and Research, College of Humanities and Social Sciences, Department of English, Indiana, PA 15705-1087. Offers composition and teaching English to speakers of other languages (MA, MAT, PhD), including composition and teaching English to speakers of other languages (PhD), teaching English (MAT), teaching English to speakers of other languages (MA); literature and criticism (MA, PhD), including generalist (MA), literature (MA), literature and criticism (PhD); rhetoric and linguistics (PhD). Part-time programs available. *Faculty:* 32 full-time (16 women). *Students:* 122 full-time (62 women), 211 part-time (136 women); includes 20 minority (11 African Americans, 1 American Indian/Alaska Native, 2 Asian Americans or Pacific Islanders, 6 Hispanic Americans), 93 international. Average age 35. 345 applicants, 48% accepted, 73 enrolled. In 2007, 48 master's, 35 doctorates awarded. *Degree requirements:* For master's, thesis optional; for doctorate, one foreign language, comprehensive exam, thesis/dissertation. *Entrance requirements:* For master's and doctorate, 2 letters of recommendation. Additional exam requirements/recommendations for international students: Required—TOEFL. *Application deadline:* For fall admission, 7/1 priority date for domestic students; for spring admission, 11/1 for domestic students. Applications are processed on a rolling basis. Application fee: $30. *Expenses:* Tuition, state resident: full-time $6,214; part-time $345 per credit. Tuition, nonresident: full-time $9,944; part-time $552 per credit. Required fees: $43 per credit. One-time fee: $140 part-time. Tuition and fees vary according to course load. *Financial support:* In 2007–08, 9 fellowships (averaging $1,200 per year), 42 research assistantships with full and partial tuition reimbursements (averaging $6,180 per year), 20 teaching assistantships with partial tuition reimbursements (averaging $17,001 per year) were awarded. Financial award application deadline: 3/15; financial award applicants required to submit FAFSA. *Unit head:* Dr. Gail I. Berlin, Chairperson, 724-357-2261, E-mail: ivy@iup.edu.

Iowa State University of Science and Technology, Graduate College, College of Liberal Arts and Sciences, Department of English, Ames, IA 50011. Offers English (MA); rhetoric and professional communication (PhD). *Faculty:* 54 full-time (30 women), 4 part-time/adjunct (2 women). *Students:* 96 full-time (57 women), 23 part-time (17 women); includes 4 minority (1 African American, 3 Hispanic Americans), 24 international. 119 applicants, 49% accepted, 37 enrolled. In 2007, 35 master's, 6 doctorates awarded. *Degree requirements:* For master's, thesis or alternative; for doctorate, thesis/dissertation. *Entrance requirements:* For master's, GRE General Test, sample of written work, resumé, portfolio in creative writing; for doctorate, GRE General Test, sample of written work, resumé. Additional exam requirements/recommendations for international students: Required—TOEFL (paper-based 600; computer-based 250; iBT 100) or IELTS (7.0). *Application deadline:* For fall admission, 1/15 priority date for domestic and international students. Application fee: $30 ($70 for international students). Electronic applications accepted. *Financial support:* In 2007–08, 4 research assistantships with partial tuition reimbursements (averaging $18,159 per year), 81 teaching assistantships with partial tuition reimbursements (averaging $18,445 per year) were awarded; fellowships, scholarships/grants, health care benefits, and unspecified assistantships also available. *Faculty research:* Creative writing, literature, rhetoric, composition and professional communication, teaching English as a second language, applied linguistics. *Unit head:* Dr. Charles Kostelnick, Chair, 515-294-2477, Fax: 515-294-2125, E-mail: englgrad@iastate.edu. *Application contact:* Dr. Helen Ewald, Director of Graduate Education, 515-294-2477, E-mail: englgrad@iastate.edu.

Kansas State University, Graduate School, College of Arts and Sciences, Department of Speech, Manhattan, KS 66506. Offers rhetoric/communication (MA); theatre (MA). *Faculty:* 14 full-time (8 women). *Students:* 44 full-time (26 women), 3 part-time (all women); includes 2 minority (1 African American, 1 Hispanic American), 2 international. Average age 23. 35 applicants, 86% accepted, 17 enrolled. In 2007, 1 degree awarded. *Degree requirements:* For master's, thesis or alternative. *Entrance requirements:* For master's, GRE General Test (recommended), minimum GPA of 3.0. Additional exam requirements/recommendations for international students: Required—TOEFL. *Application deadline:* For fall admission, 3/1 for domestic students, 2/1 priority date for international students; for spring admission, 10/1 for domestic students, 8/1 priority date for international students. Applications are processed on a rolling basis. Application fee: $30 ($55 for international students). *Financial support:* In 2007–08, 24 teaching assistantships with full tuition reimbursements (averaging $9,417 per year) were awarded; career-related internships or fieldwork, institutionally sponsored loans, and scholarships/grants also available. Support available to part-time students. Financial award application deadline: 3/1; financial award applicants required to submit FAFSA. *Faculty research:* Interpersonal/intercultural communication, political advertising, political rhetoric, deliberative democracy, persuasion, social influence, compliance-gaining. Total annual research expenditures: $2,748. *Unit head:* Charles Griffin, Head, 785-532-6860, Fax: 785-532-3714, E-mail: charlieg@ksu.edu. *Application contact:* William Schenck-Hamlin, Director, 785-532-6861, Fax: 785-532-3714, E-mail: billsh@ksu.edu.

Kent State University, College of Arts and Sciences, Department of English, Kent, OH 44242-0001. Offers comparative literature (MA); creative writing (MFA); English (PhD); English for teachers (MA); literature and writing (MA); rhetoric and composition (PhD); teaching English as a second language (MA). Part-time programs available. *Faculty:* 46 full-time (23 women). *Students:* 107 full-time (59 women), 15 part-time (8 women); includes 19 minority (1 African American, 17 Asian Americans or Pacific Islanders, 1 Hispanic American). Average age 33. 105 applicants, 80% accepted, 35 enrolled. In 2007, 34 master's, 1 doctorate awarded. Terminal master's awarded for partial completion of doctoral program. *Median time to degree:* Of those who began their doctoral program in fall 1999, 50% received their degree in 8 years or less. *Degree requirements:* For master's, one foreign language, thesis optional; for doctorate, one foreign language, thesis/dissertation, qualifying exams. *Entrance requirements:* For master's and doctorate, GRE General Test, writing sample, letters of recommendation. Additional exam requirements/recommendations for international students: Required—TOEFL (minimum score 600 paper-based). *Application deadline:* For fall admission, 2/1 priority date for domestic and international students. Applications are processed on a rolling basis. Application fee: $30. Electronic applications accepted. *Financial support:* In 2007–08, 2 fellowships with full tuition reimbursements (averaging $12,000 per year), 55 teaching assistantships with full tuition reimbursements (averaging $11,020 per year) were awarded; research assistantships with full tuition reimbursements, Federal Work-Study, institutionally sponsored loans, scholarships/grants, traineeships, health care benefits, and unspecified assistantships also available. Financial award application deadline: 2/1. *Faculty research:* British and American literature, textual editing, rhetoric and composition, cultural studies, linguistic and critical theories. *Unit head:* Ronald Corthell, Chair, 330-672-3211, Fax: 330-672-3152, E-mail: rcorthel@kent.edu. *Application contact:* Ray Craig, Information Contact, 330-672-1755, E-mail: rcraig2@kent.edu.

See Close-Up on page 567.

Miami University, Graduate School, College of Arts and Sciences, Department of English, Oxford, OH 45056. Offers composition and rhetoric (MA, PhD); creative writing (MA); criticism (PhD); English and American literature and language (PhD); English education (MAT); library theory (PhD); literature (MA, MAT, PhD); technical and scientific communication (MTSC). Part-time programs available. *Degree requirements:* For master's, final exam; for doctorate, 2 foreign languages, comprehensive exam, thesis/dissertation, final exams. *Entrance requirements:* For master's, minimum undergraduate GPA of 3.0 during previous 2 years or 2.75 overall; for doctorate, GRE General Test, GRE Subject Test, minimum GPA of 2.75 (undergraduate), 3.0 (graduate). Additional exam requirements/recommendations for international students: Required—TOEFL (minimum score 550 paper-based; 213 computer-based), TWE (minimum score 4). Electronic applications accepted.

Michigan State University, The Graduate School, College of Arts and Letters, Program in Rhetoric and Writing, East Lansing, MI 48824. Offers critical studies in literacy and pedagogy (MA); digital rhetoric and professional writing (MA); rhetoric and writing (PhD). *Entrance requirements:* Additional exam requirements/recommendations for international students: Required—TOEFL. Electronic applications accepted. *Expenses:* Tuition, state resident: part-time $379 per credit hour. Tuition, nonresident: part-time $800 per credit hour. Tuition and fees vary according to program. *Faculty research:* Rhetoric, writing and communication studies; media studies; technical communication, writing for digital environments.

Michigan Technological University, Graduate School, College of Sciences and Arts, Department of Humanities, Program in Rhetoric and Technical Communication, Houghton, MI 49931-1295. Offers MS, PhD. Part-time programs available. *Faculty:* 26 full-time (15 women), 1 part-time/adjunct (0 women). *Students:* 29 full-time (19 women), 34 part-time (20 women); includes 8 minority (3 African Americans, 1 American Indian/Alaska Native, 1 Asian American or Pacific Islander, 3 Hispanic Americans), 1 international. Average age 37. 34 applicants, 53% accepted, 15 enrolled. In 2007, 4 master's, 2 doctorates awarded. Terminal master's awarded for partial completion of doctoral program. *Median time to degree:* Of those who began their doctoral program in fall 1999, 56% received their degree in 8 years or less. *Degree requirements:* For master's, comprehensive exam; for doctorate, one foreign language, comprehensive exam, thesis/dissertation. *Entrance requirements:* Additional exam requirements/recommendations for international students: Required—TOEFL (minimum score 600 paper-based; 250 computer-based). *Application deadline:* Applications are processed on a rolling basis. Application fee: $40 ($45 for international students). Electronic applications accepted. *Financial support:* In 2007–08, 35 students received support, including 1 fellowship with full tuition reimbursement available (averaging $9,542 per year), 2 research assistantships with full tuition reimbursements available (averaging $9,542 per year), 28 teaching assistantships with full tuition reimbursements available (averaging $9,542 per year); career-related internships or fieldwork, Federal Work-Study, scholarships/grants, health care benefits, tuition waivers (partial), and unspecified assistantships also available. Financial award applicants required to submit FAFSA. *Unit head:* Elizabeth Flynn, Director, 906-487-3231, E-mail: eflynn@mtu.edu. *Application contact:* Marjorie L. Lindley, Office Assistant 5, 906-487-2381, Fax: 906-487-3559, E-mail: mlindley@mtu.edu.

New Mexico Highlands University, Graduate Studies, College of Arts and Sciences, Department of Humanities, Las Vegas, NM 87701. Offers English (MA), including creative writing, language, rhetoric and composition, literature. *Faculty:* 6 full-time (3 women). *Students:* 11 full-time (5 women), 7 part-time (5 women); includes 5 minority (all Hispanic Americans) Average age 32. 17 applicants, 82% accepted, 7 enrolled. In 2007, 3 degrees awarded. *Degree requirements:* For master's, comprehensive exam, thesis. *Entrance requirements:* For master's, minimum undergraduate GPA of 3.0. Additional exam requirements/recommendations for international students: Required—TOEFL (minimum score 540 paper-based; 190 computer-based). *Application deadline:* For fall admission, 8/1 priority date for domestic students. Applications are processed on a rolling basis. Application fee: $15. *Expenses:* Tuition, state resident: full-time $2,642; part-time $110 per credit hour. Tuition, nonresident: full-time $3,964; part-time $165 per credit hour. International tuition: $5,285 full-time. One-time fee: $20 full-time. *Financial support:* In 2007–08, 8 students received support, including teaching assistantships with full and partial tuition reimbursements available (averaging $6,500 per year); career-related internships or fieldwork, Federal Work-Study, institutionally sponsored loans, scholarships/grants, tuition waivers (full and partial), and unspecified assistantships also available. Support available to part-time students. Financial award application deadline: 3/1; financial award applicants required to submit FAFSA. *Faculty research:* Motivation, self-actualization, humanistic psychology, stand up comedy, language and cognition. *Unit head:* Dr. Barbara Risch, Chair, 505-454-3451, Fax: 505-454-3389, E-mail: brisch55@yahoo.com. *Application contact:* Diane Trujillo, Administrative Assistant Graduate Studies, 505-454-3266, Fax: 505-454-3558, E-mail: dtrujillo@nmhu.edu.

New Mexico State University, Graduate School, College of Arts and Sciences, Department of English, Las Cruces, NM 88003-8001. Offers creative writing (MFA); English (MA); rhetoric and professional communication (PhD). Part-time programs available. *Faculty:* 17 full-time (9 women), 1 part-time/adjunct (0 women). *Students:* 70 full-time (37 women), 23 part-time (12 women); includes 12 minority (1 African American, 1 American Indian/Alaska Native, 10 Hispanic Americans), 6 international. Average age 33. 55 applicants, 45% accepted, 19 enrolled. In 2007, 25 master's, 5 doctorates awarded. *Median time to degree:* Of those who began their doctoral program in fall 1999, 80% received their degree in 8 years or less. *Degree requirements:* For master's, one foreign language, comprehensive exam (for some programs), thesis (for some programs); for doctorate, comprehensive exam, thesis/dissertation, internship. *Entrance requirements:* For master's and doctorate, sample of written work. *Application deadline:* For fall admission, 2/1 for domestic and international students. Application fee: $30 ($50 for international students). Electronic applications accepted. *Expenses:* Tuition, state resident: full-time $3,602; part-time $199 per credit. Tuition, nonresident: full-time $13,380; part-time $607 per credit. Required fees: $1,178. *Financial support:* In 2007–08, 3 fellowships, 3 research assistantships, 50 teaching assistantships were awarded; career-related internships or fieldwork, Federal Work-Study, institutionally sponsored loans, scholarships/grants, health care benefits, and unspecified assistantships also available. Financial award application deadline: 2/1; financial award applicants required to submit FAFSA. *Faculty research:* Composition research, history and theory of rhetoric, technical/professional communication, creative writing, English and American literature. *Unit head:* Dr. Harriet Kramer Linkin, Head, 575-646-3931, Fax: 575-646-7725. *Application contact:* Dr. Monica Torres, Director of Graduate Studies, 575-646-3931, E-mail: mftorres@nmsu.edu.

Northern Arizona University, Graduate College, College of Arts and Letters, Department of English, Program in English, Flagstaff, AZ 86011. Offers creative writing (MA); English education (MA); general English (MA); literature (MA); rhetoric (MA). *Degree requirements:* For master's, departmental qualifying exam. *Entrance requirements:* For master's, GRE General Test, GRE Subject Test.

Rensselaer Polytechnic Institute, Graduate School, School of Humanities and Social Sciences, Department of Language, Literature, and Communication, Programs in Communication and Rhetoric, Troy, NY 12180-3590. Offers MS, PhD. *Faculty:* 15 full-time (7 women), 1 (woman) part-time/adjunct. *Students:* 37 applicants, 43% accepted, 6 enrolled. In 2007, 3 degrees awarded. Terminal master's awarded for partial completion of doctoral program. *Median time to degree:* Of those who began their doctoral program in fall 1999, 38% received their degree in 8 years or less. *Degree requirements:* For master's, thesis optional; for doctorate, comprehensive exam, thesis/dissertation. *Entrance requirements:* For master's, GRE General Test, resumé; for doctorate, GRE General Test, writing sample, resumé or curriculum vitae. Additional exam requirements/recommendations for international students: Required—TOEFL (minimum score 570 paper-based; 230 computer-based). *Application deadline:* For fall admission, 1/15 priority date for domestic students; for spring admission, 10/15 priority date for domestic students. Applications are processed on a rolling basis. Application fee: $45. Electronic applications accepted. *Expenses:* Tuition: Full-time $34,900; part-time $1,454 per credit. Required fees: $1,802. *Financial support:* In 2007–08, 18 students received support, including 8 fellowships with full tuition reimbursements available (averaging $14,500 per year), 1 research assistantship with full tuition reimbursement available (averaging $14,500 per year), 9 teaching assistantships with full tuition reimbursements available (averaging $14,500 per year); career-related internships or fieldwork, institutionally sponsored loans, and unspecified assistantships also available. Financial award application deadline: 1/15. *Faculty research:* Human-computer interaction, media design and theory, rhetoric and culture, virtual institutions/communities, usability. *Application contact:* Kathy A. Colman, Recruitment Coordinator, 518-276-6469, Fax: 518-276-4092, E-mail: colmak@rpi.edu.

See Close-Up on page 925.

San Diego State University, Graduate and Research Affairs, College of Arts and Letters, Department of Rhetoric and Writing, San Diego, CA 92182. Offers MA. Part-time programs available. *Students:* 17 full-time (14 women), 15 part-time (10 women); includes 8 minority (2 African Americans, 1 American Indian/Alaska Native, 2 Asian Americans or Pacific Islanders, 3 Hispanic Americans). 21 applicants, 90% accepted, 15 enrolled. In 2007, 11 degrees awarded. *Degree requirements:* For master's, thesis. *Entrance requirements:* For master's, GRE General Test, writing sample, 3 letters of reference. Additional exam requirements/recommendations for international students: Required—TOEFL. *Application deadline:* For fall admission, 4/1 for domestic and international students; for spring admission, 10/1 for domestic and international students. Application fee: $55. Electronic applications accepted. *Financial support:* Teaching assistantships available. Financial award applicants required to submit FAFSA. *Unit head:* Dr. Glenn McClish, Chair, 619-594-6515, Fax: 619-594-6530, E-mail: gmcclish@mail.sdsu.edu. *Application contact:* Jane Robinett, Graduate Advisor, 619-594-0966, Fax: 619-594-6530, E-mail: jrobinett@mail.sdsu.edu.

Southern Illinois University Carbondale, Graduate School, College of Liberal Arts, Department of English, Carbondale, IL 62901-4701. Offers composition (MA, PhD), including composition, literature, rhetoric; creative writing (MFA). *Faculty:* 33 full-time (14 women), 1 (woman) part-time/adjunct. *Students:* 30 full-time (15 women), 61 part-time (41 women); includes 3 minority (1 African American, 2 Hispanic Americans), 9 international. 59 applicants, 36% accepted, 8 enrolled. In 2007, 10 master's, 4 doctorates awarded. *Degree requirements:* For master's, one foreign language, thesis; for doctorate, 2 foreign languages, thesis/dissertation. *Entrance requirements:* For master's, GRE General Test, GRE Subject Test, minimum GPA of 2.7; for doctorate, GRE General Test, GRE Subject Test, minimum GPA of 3.25. Additional exam requirements/recommendations for international students: Required—TOEFL. *Application deadline:* For fall admission, 2/15 for domestic students; for spring admission, 11/15 for domestic students. Applications are processed on a rolling basis. Application fee: $20. *Financial support:* In 2007–08, 2 fellowships with full tuition reimbursements, 5 research assistantships with full tuition reimbursements, 72 teaching assistantships with full tuition reimbursements were awarded; career-related internships or fieldwork, Federal Work-Study, institutionally sponsored loans, and tuition waivers (full) also available. Support available to part-time students. *Faculty research:* British literature, English literature, modern Continental literature, literary criticism and theory, film studies, Irish studies. *Unit head:* Dr. Michael Humphries, Chair, 618-453-6854, Fax: 618-453-3253, E-mail: mhumphri@siu.edu. *Application contact:* Donna Schumaier, Administrative Clerk, 618-453-6894, Fax: 618-453-3253, E-mail: gradengl@siu.edu.

See Close-Up on page 581.

Syracuse University, Graduate School, College of Arts and Sciences, The Writing Program, Program in Composition and Cultural Rhetoric, Syracuse, NY 13244. Offers PhD. *Students:* 24 full-time (20 women), 8 part-time (2 women); includes 3 African Americans, 1 international. 19 applicants, 47% accepted, 4 enrolled. *Entrance requirements:* For doctorate, GRE. *Application deadline:* For fall admission, 2/1 priority date for domestic students. Application fee: $75. Electronic applications accepted. *Expenses:* Tuition: Full-time $18,216; part-time $1,012 per credit. Required fees: $980. Tuition and fees vary according to program. *Financial support:* Fellowships with full tuition reimbursements, teaching assistantships with full tuition reimbursements available. *Unit head:* Collin Brooke, Graduate Director, 315-443-1067.

Syracuse University, Graduate School, College of Visual and Performing Arts, Department of Communication and Rhetorical Studies, Syracuse, NY 13244. Offers MA, MS. Part-time programs available. *Students:* 10 full-time (4 women), 2 part-time (both women); includes 3 minority (2 African Americans, 1 Asian American or Pacific Islander), 1 international. 15 applicants, 67% accepted, 6 enrolled. In 2007, 11 degrees awarded. *Entrance requirements:* For master's, GRE General Test, writing sample. Additional exam requirements/recommendations for international students: Required—TOEFL. *Application deadline:* For fall admission, 1/1 priority date for domestic students. Applications are processed on a rolling basis. Application fee: $75. Electronic applications accepted. *Expenses:* Tuition: Full-time $18,216; part-time $1,012 per credit. Required fees: $980. Tuition and fees vary according to program. *Financial support:* In 2007–08, 9 students received support; fellowships with tuition reimbursements available, teaching assistantships with full tuition reimbursements available, tuition waivers (partial) available. *Unit head:* Dr. Amos Kiewe, Chair, 315-443-2308, Fax: 315-443-5141, E-mail: akiewe@syr.edu. *Application contact:* Harriett Conti, Associate Director, Graduate Student Services, 315-443-3089, E-mail: hmconti@syr.edu.

Texas State University–San Marcos, Graduate School, College of Liberal Arts, Department of English, Program in Rhetoric and Composition, San Marcos, TX 78666. Offers MA. Part-time programs available. *Faculty:* 4 full-time (2 women). *Students:* 6 full-time (5 women), 3 part-time (2 women); includes 1 Hispanic American. Average age 33. 2 applicants, 100% accepted, 2 enrolled. *Entrance requirements:* For master's, 3.25 in a minimum of 24 hours of undergrad English, 6 hours foreign language. Additional exam requirements/recommendations for international students: Required—TOEFL (minimum score 550 paper-based; 213 computer-based). *Application deadline:* For fall admission, 6/15 for domestic students, 6/1 for international students; for spring admission, 10/15 for domestic students, 10/1 for international students. Applications are processed on a rolling basis. Application fee: $40 ($90 for international students). Electronic applications accepted. *Expenses:* Tuition, state resident: full-time $3,780; part-time $210 per credit hour. Tuition, nonresident: full-time $8,784; part-time $488 per credit hour. Required fees: $493 per semester. Full-time tuition and fees vary according to course load. *Financial support:* In 2007–08, 7 students received support, including 4 teaching assistantships (averaging $5,076 per year); Federal Work-Study and institutionally sponsored loans also available. Support available to part-time students. Financial award application deadline: 4/1; financial award applicants required to submit FAFSA. *Unit head:* Dr. Rebecca Jackson, Graduate Advisor, 512-245-2163, E-mail: rj10@txstate.edu.

Texas Tech University, Graduate School, College of Arts and Sciences, Department of English, Lubbock, TX 79409. Offers English (MA, PhD); technical communication (MA); technical communication and rhetoric (PhD). Part-time programs available. *Faculty:* 38 full-time (13 women), 2 part-time/adjunct (both women). *Students:* 114 full-time (64 women), 84 part-time (56 women); includes 21 minority (4 African Americans, 3 American Indian/Alaska Native, 3 Asian Americans or Pacific Islanders, 11 Hispanic Americans), 13 international. Average age 34. 155 applicants, 49% accepted, 47 enrolled. In 2007, 18 master's, 11 doctorates awarded. *Degree requirements:* For master's, one foreign language, thesis (for some programs); for doctorate, thesis/dissertation. *Entrance requirements:* For master's and doctorate, GRE General Test. Additional exam requirements/recommendations for international students: Required—TOEFL (minimum score 550 paper-based; 213 computer-based). *Application deadline:* For fall admission, 3/1 priority date for international students; for spring admission, 11/1 priority date for international students. Applications are processed on a rolling basis. Application fee: $50 ($60 for international students). Electronic applications accepted. *Expenses:* Tuition, state resident: part-time $373 per credit hour. Tuition, nonresident: part-time $651 per credit hour. Tuition and fees vary according to program. *Financial support:* In 2007–08, 101 students received support, including 98 teaching assistantships with partial tuition reimbursements available (averaging $14,187 per year); research assistantships with partial tuition reimbursements available, Federal Work-Study and institutionally sponsored loans also available. Support available to part-time students. Financial award application deadline: 4/15; financial award applicants required to submit FAFSA. *Faculty research:* Southwestern literature and language; computers and writing; technical communication and rhetoric; creative writing; nineteenth century studies. Total annual research expenditures: $18,946. *Unit head:* Dr. Sam Dragga, Chair, 806-742-2501, Fax: 806-742-0989, E-mail: sam.dragga@ttu.edu. *Application contact:* Dr. Sean Grass, Director of Graduate Studies, 806-742-2501, Fax: 806-742-0989, E-mail: english.gradadvisor@ttu.edu.

Texas Woman's University, Graduate School, College of Arts and Sciences, Department of English, Speech, and Foreign Languages, Denton, TX 76201. Offers English (MA); rhetoric (PhD). Part-time programs available. *Students:* 9 full-time (7 women), 47 part-time (41 women); includes 10 minority (5 African Americans, 1 American Indian/Alaska Native, 1 Asian American or Pacific Islander, 3 Hispanic Americans), 1 international. Average age 38. In 2007, 7 master's, 4 doctorates awarded. *Degree requirements:* For master's, one foreign language, comprehensive exam, thesis; for doctorate, 2 foreign languages, comprehensive exam, thesis/dissertation. *Entrance requirements:* For master's, GRE General Test, writing sample, 3 letters of reference, interview, minimum GPA of 3.0; for doctorate, GRE General Test, writing sample, 3 letters of reference, interview, 3.0 GPA on previous upper division and graduate work. Additional exam requirements/recommendations for international students: Required—TOEFL (minimum score 550 paper-based; 213 computer-based; 79 iBT). *Application deadline:* For fall admission, 4/1 for international students; for spring admission, 8/1 for international students. Applications are processed on a rolling basis. Application fee: $30 ($50 for international students). Electronic applications accepted. *Expenses:* Tuition, state resident: full-time $3,294; part-time $183 per credit. Tuition, nonresident: full-time $8,298; part-time $461 per credit. Required fees: $985; $55 per credit. Tuition and fees vary according to degree level. *Financial support:* In 2007–08, 9 research assistantships (averaging $10,494 per year), 15 teaching assistantships (averaging $10,746 per year) were awarded; career-related internships or fieldwork, Federal Work-Study, institutionally sponsored loans, scholarships/grants, traineeships, health care benefits, and unspecified assistantships also available. Support available to part-time students. Financial award application deadline: 3/1; financial award applicants required to submit FAFSA. *Faculty research:* British and American literature; rhetoric: historical and applied; composition studies and technology; literary theory and criticism; women's literature and feminist rhetoric. *Unit head:* Dr. Bruce Krajewski, Chair, 940-898-2324, Fax: 940-898-2297, E-mail: bkrajewski@twu.edu. *Application contact:* Samuel Wheeler, Assistant Director of Admissions, 940-898-3188, Fax: 940-898-3081, E-mail: wheelersr@twu.edu.

The University of Alabama, Graduate School, College of Arts and Sciences, Department of English, Tuscaloosa, AL 35487. Offers composition and rhetoric (PhD); creative writing (MFA), including fiction, poetry; literature (MA, PhD); rhetoric and composition (MA); teaching English

Rhetoric

The University of Alabama (continued)

as a second language (MATESOL). *Faculty:* 30 full-time (12 women). *Students:* 119 full-time (66 women), 16 part-time (12 women); includes 18 minority (11 African Americans, 2 American Indian/Alaska Native, 3 Asian Americans or Pacific Islanders, 2 Hispanic Americans), 7 international. Average age 28. 252 applicants, 20% accepted, 31 enrolled. In 2007, 28 master's, 7 doctorates awarded. *Median time to degree:* Of those who began their doctoral program in fall 1999, 100% received their degree in 8 years or less. *Degree requirements:* For master's, one foreign language, comprehensive exam, thesis (for some programs); for doctorate, 2 foreign languages, comprehensive exam, thesis/dissertation. *Entrance requirements:* For master's and doctorate, GRE, minimum GPA of 3.0, critical writing sample. Additional exam requirements/recommendations for international students: Required—TOEFL. *Application deadline:* For fall admission, 1/15 priority date for domestic students, 1/15 for international students. Application fee: $30. Electronic applications accepted. *Expenses:* Tuition, state resident: full-time $5,700. Tuition, nonresident: full-time $16,518. *Financial support:* In 2007–08, 7 fellowships with full tuition reimbursements (averaging $15,000 per year), 1 research assistantship (averaging $11,708 per year), 106 teaching assistantships with full tuition reimbursements (averaging $11,708 per year) were awarded; career-related internships or fieldwork, scholarships/grants, health care benefits, and unspecified assistantships also available. Financial award application deadline: 1/15. *Faculty research:* Critical theory; modern, Renaissance, and African-American literature. *Unit head:* Dr. Catherine E. Davies, Director of Graduate Studies, 205-348-8499, E-mail: cdavies@bama.ua.edu. *Application contact:* Vernita W. James, Office Assistant II, 205-348-0766, Fax: 205-348-1388, E-mail: vwjames@bama.ua.edu.

The University of Arizona, Graduate College, College of Humanities, Department of English, Rhetoric, Composition and the Teaching of English Program, Tucson, AZ 85721. Offers MA, PhD. *Students:* 32 applicants, 28% accepted. In 2007, 3 master's, 1 doctorate awarded. *Degree requirements:* For master's, one foreign language, comprehensive exam; for doctorate, one foreign language, comprehensive exam, thesis/dissertation. *Entrance requirements:* For master's, GRE, 3 letters of recommendation, minimum GPA of 3.0, statement of purpose, writing sample. Additional exam requirements/recommendations for international students: Required—TOEFL (minimum score 550 paper-based). *Application deadline:* For fall admission, 1/1 for domestic students, 12/1 for international students. Applications are processed on a rolling basis. Application fee: $50. Electronic applications accepted. *Unit head:* John Warnock, Director, 520-621-3255, Fax: 520-621-7397, E-mail: johnw@u.arizona.edu. *Application contact:* Alison Miller, Program Assistant, 520-621-7213, Fax: 520-621-7397, E-mail: admiller@u.arizona.edu.

University of Arkansas at Little Rock, Graduate School, College of Arts, Humanities, and Social Science, Department of Rhetoric and Writing, Little Rock, AR 72204-1099. Offers professional and technical writing (MA). Part-time and evening/weekend programs available. *Students:* Average age 34. *Degree requirements:* For master's, thesis or alternative, oral defense of final project. *Entrance requirements:* For master's, GRE, minimum GPA of 3.0, writing portfolio. *Application deadline:* Applications are processed on a rolling basis. *Financial support:* Research assistantships with tuition reimbursements, teaching assistantships with tuition reimbursements, career-related internships or fieldwork, Federal Work-Study, institutionally sponsored loans, and unspecified assistantships available. Support available to part-time students. *Faculty research:* Writing for industry, science, business, and government; composition and rhetorical theory; writing nonfiction; teaching of writing. *Unit head:* Dr. George H. Jensen, Chairperson, 501-569-3160, E-mail: ghjensen@ualr.edu. *Application contact:* Dr. Cynthia A. Nahrwold, Coordinator, 501-569-3316, Fax: 501-569-8279, E-mail: canahrwold@ualr.edu.

University of California, Berkeley, Graduate Division, College of Letters and Science, Department of Rhetoric, Berkeley, CA 94720-1500. Offers PhD. *Degree requirements:* For doctorate, 2 foreign languages, thesis/dissertation, qualifying exam. *Entrance requirements:* For doctorate, GRE General Test, minimum GPA of 3.0, 3 letters of recommendation. *Application deadline:* For fall admission, 12/8 for domestic students. Application fee: $70 ($90 for international students). *Financial support:* Fellowships, research assistantships, teaching assistantships, unspecified assistantships available. *Faculty research:* History and theory of rhetoric, public discourse (law, politics, and science), literature and philosophy, film. *Unit head:* Mark Sandberg, Chair, 510-642-0927, E-mail: sandberg@berkeley.edu. *Application contact:* Maxine Fredericksen, Rhetoric Student Assistant, 510-642-3522, E-mail: trout@berkeley.edu.

University of Illinois at Chicago, Graduate College, College of Liberal Arts and Sciences, Department of English, Chicago, IL 60607-7128. Offers English (MA, PhD), including creative writing, language, literacy and rhetoric (PhD), literature, teaching of English (MA); language, literacy, and rhetoric (PhD); linguistics (MA), including applied linguistics (teaching English as a second language). Part-time and evening/weekend programs available. *Degree requirements:* For doctorate, variable foreign language requirement, thesis/dissertation, written and oral exams. *Entrance requirements:* For master's, GRE General Test, GRE Subject Test; for doctorate, GRE General Test, GRE Subject Test, minimum GPA of 2.0. Additional exam requirements/recommendations for international students: Required—TOEFL. Electronic applications accepted. *Faculty research:* Literary history and theory.

The University of Iowa, Graduate College, College of Liberal Arts and Sciences, Department of Communication Studies, Iowa City, IA 52242-1316. Offers communication research (MA, PhD); rhetorical studies (MA, PhD). *Faculty:* 11 full-time, 8 part-time/adjunct. *Students:* 27 full-time (18 women), 40 part-time (18 women); includes 8 minority (1 African American, 1 American Indian/Alaska Native, 4 Asian Americans or Pacific Islanders, 2 Hispanic Americans), 18 international. 130 applicants, 18% accepted, 12 enrolled. In 2007, 2 master's, 10 doctorates awarded. *Degree requirements:* For master's, thesis optional, exam; for doctorate, comprehensive exam, thesis/dissertation. *Entrance requirements:* For master's and doctorate, GRE General Test, minimum GPA of 3.0. Additional exam requirements/recommendations for international students: Required—TOEFL (minimum score 550 paper-based; 213 computer-based; 81 iBT). *Application deadline:* For fall admission, 1/1 priority date for domestic and international students. Applications are processed on a rolling basis. Application fee: $60 ($85 for international students). Electronic applications accepted. *Expenses:* Tuition, state resident: part-time $349 per hour. Tuition, nonresident: part-time $349 per hour. Tuition and fees vary according to course load and program. *Financial support:* In 2007–08, 6 fellowships, 3 research assistantships with partial tuition reimbursements, 40 teaching assistantships with partial tuition reimbursements were awarded. Financial award applicants required to submit FAFSA. *Unit head:* Kristine L. Fitch, Chair, 319-353-2264, Fax: 319-335-2930.

The University of Iowa, Graduate College, College of Liberal Arts and Sciences, Department of English, Iowa City, IA 52242-1316. Offers English (PhD); literary criticism (PhD); literary history (PhD); literary studies (MA); nonfiction writing (MFA); rhetorical theory and stylistics (PhD); writer's workshop (MFA); JD/PhD. *Faculty:* 54 full-time, 41 part-time/adjunct. *Students:* 158 full-time (90 women), 89 part-time (53 women); includes 40 minority (16 African Americans, 3 American Indian/Alaska Native, 13 Asian Americans or Pacific Islanders, 8 Hispanic Americans), 11 international. 1,337 applicants, 9% accepted, 72 enrolled. In 2007, 72 master's, 12 doctorates awarded. *Degree requirements:* For master's, thesis (for some programs), exam; for doctorate, comprehensive exam, thesis/dissertation. *Entrance requirements:* For master's and doctorate, GRE General Test, minimum GPA of 3.0. Additional exam requirements/recommendations for international students: Required—TOEFL (minimum score 640 paper-based; 273 computer-based; 112 iBT). Application fee: $60 ($85 for international students). Electronic applications accepted. *Expenses:* Tuition, state resident: part-time $349 per hour. Tuition, nonresident: part-time $349 per hour. Tuition and fees vary according to course load and program. *Financial support:* In 2007–08, 31 fellowships, 21 research assistantships with partial tuition reimbursements, 160 teaching assistantships with partial tuition reimbursements were awarded. Financial award applicants required to submit FAFSA. *Unit head:* Jonathan Wilcox, Chair, 319-335-0454, Fax: 319-335-2535.

University of Louisiana at Lafayette, Graduate School, College of Liberal Arts, Department of English, Lafayette, LA 70504. Offers British and American literature (MA), including creative writing, folklore, rhetoric; creative writing (PhD); literature (PhD); rhetoric (PhD). Part-time programs available. Terminal master's awarded for partial completion of doctoral program. *Degree requirements:* For master's, one foreign language, thesis or alternative; for doctorate, 2 foreign languages, comprehensive exam, thesis/dissertation. *Entrance requirements:* For master's, GRE General Test, minimum GPA of 2.75; for doctorate, GRE General Test, minimum GPA of 3.0. Additional exam requirements/recommendations for international students: Required—TOEFL (minimum score 550 paper-based; 213 computer-based). Electronic applications accepted. *Faculty research:* Composition theory, Southern literature, medieval literature.

University of Louisville, Graduate School, College of Arts and Sciences, Department of English, Program in English Rhetoric and Composition, Louisville, KY 40292-0001. Offers PhD. *Students:* 40 full-time (26 women), 2 part-time (both women); includes 5 minority (4 African Americans, 1 Hispanic American), 2 international. Average age 34. In 2007, 6 degrees awarded. *Degree requirements:* For doctorate, 2 foreign languages, thesis/dissertation. *Entrance requirements:* For doctorate, GRE General Test, writing sample. *Application deadline:* For fall admission, 3/1 for domestic students. Applications are processed on a rolling basis. Application fee: $50. *Financial support:* Fellowships with full tuition reimbursements, teaching assistantships with full tuition reimbursements available. Financial award application deadline: 3/1. *Unit head:* Dr. Susan Griffin, Chair, Department of English, 502-852-6801, Fax: 502-852-4182, E-mail: smgriff01@louisville.edu.

The University of North Carolina at Greensboro, Graduate School, College of Arts and Sciences, Department of English, Program in English, Greensboro, NC 27412-5001. Offers American literature (PhD); English (M Ed, MA); English literature (PhD); rhetoric and composition (PhD). *Students:* 82 full-time (56 women), 35 part-time (24 women); includes 15 minority (13 African Americans, 1 American Indian/Alaska Native, 1 Asian American or Pacific Islander). *Degree requirements:* For master's, comprehensive exam, thesis or alternative; for doctorate, variable foreign language requirement, thesis/dissertation, preliminary exam. *Entrance requirements:* For master's, GRE General Test, GRE Subject Test, minimum GPA of 3.0; for doctorate, GRE General Test, GRE Subject Test, critical writing sample, minimum GPA of 3.0. Additional exam requirements/recommendations for international students: Required—TOEFL. *Application deadline:* For fall admission, 1/20 priority date for domestic students; for spring admission, 11/1 for domestic students. Application fee: $45. Electronic applications accepted. *Financial support:* Fellowships, research assistantships, teaching assistantships available. *Unit head:* Dr. Christian Moraru, Director of Graduate Studies, 336-334-3564, E-mail: c_moraru@uncg.edu. *Application contact:* Michelle Harkleroad, Director of Graduate Admissions, 336-334-4884, Fax: 336-334-4424, E-mail: mbharkle@uncg.edu.

The University of Texas at Arlington, Graduate School, College of Liberal Arts, Department of English, Arlington, TX 76019. Offers English (MA); literature (PhD); rhetoric (PhD). Part-time and evening/weekend programs available. *Faculty:* 8 full-time (5 women). *Students:* 18 full-time (15 women), 88 part-time (53 women); includes 17 minority (7 African Americans, 3 Asian Americans or Pacific Islanders, 7 Hispanic Americans), 11 international. 33 applicants, 67% accepted, 19 enrolled. In 2007, 10 master's, 3 doctorates awarded. *Degree requirements:* For master's, thesis or comprehensive exam; for doctorate, one foreign language, comprehensive exam, thesis/dissertation. *Entrance requirements:* For master's, GRE General Test, minimum 5-page writing sample, minimum GPA of 3.0, 3 letters of recommendation; for doctorate, GRE General Test, minimum graduate GPA of 3.5, writing sample, 3 letters of recommendation. Additional exam requirements/recommendations for international students: Required—TOEFL (minimum score 550 paper-based; 213 computer-based). *Application deadline:* For fall admission, 6/16 for domestic students. Applications are processed on a rolling basis. Application fee: $35 ($50 for international students). *Expenses:* Tuition, state resident: full-time $5,934. Tuition, nonresident: full-time $10,938. *Financial support:* In 2007–08, 6 fellowships (averaging $1,000 per year), 2 research assistantships, 26 teaching assistantships (averaging $8,500 per year) were awarded; scholarships/grants also available. Financial award application deadline: 5/1. *Faculty research:* Rhetoric composition, American literature, British literature, cultural studies, women's studies. *Unit head:* Dr. Wendy Faris, Chair, 817-272-2692, Fax: 817-272-2718, E-mail: wbfaris@uta.edu. *Application contact:* Dr. Kevin Gustafson, Associate Chair for Graduate Studies, 817-272-2739, E-mail: gustafson@uta.edu.

The University of Texas at El Paso, Graduate School, College of Liberal Arts, Department of English, El Paso, TX 79968-0001. Offers English and American literature (MA); professional writing and rhetoric (MA); teaching English (MAT). Part-time and evening/weekend programs available. *Degree requirements:* For master's, thesis optional. *Entrance requirements:* For master's, GRE General Test, minimum GPA of 3.0. Additional exam requirements/recommendations for international students: Required—TOEFL. Electronic applications accepted. *Faculty research:* Literature, creative writing, literary theory.

University of Utah, The Graduate School, College of Humanities, Department of English, Salt Lake City, UT 84112-1107. Offers American studies (MA, PhD); British American literature (MA, PhD); creative writing (MFA, PhD); literature (PhD); rhetoric and composition (PhD). *Faculty:* 39 full-time (16 women). *Students:* 59 full-time (39 women), 23 part-time (14 women); includes 5 minority (2 African Americans, 1 American Indian/Alaska Native, 2 Asian Americans or Pacific Islanders), 1 international. Average age 33. 177 applicants, 23% accepted, 22 enrolled. In 2007, 14 master's, 7 doctorates awarded. *Median time to degree:* Of those who began their doctoral program in fall 1999, 83% received their degree in 8 years or less. *Degree requirements:* For master's, one foreign language, thesis (for some programs), written exam; for doctorate, 2 foreign languages, comprehensive exam, thesis/dissertation. *Entrance requirements:* For master's and doctorate, GRE General Test, minimum GPA of 3.2. Additional exam requirements/recommendations for international students: Required—TOEFL (minimum score 500 paper-based; 173 computer-based; 120 iBT). *Application deadline:* For fall admission, 12/15 for domestic and international students. Applications are processed on a rolling basis. Application fee: $45 ($65 for international students). Electronic applications accepted. *Financial support:* In 2007–08, 49 students received support, including 8 fellowships with full tuition reimbursements available (averaging $12,000 per year), 41 teaching assistantships with full tuition reimbursements available (averaging $12,000 per year); research assistantships, health care benefits also available. Financial award application deadline: 12/15; financial award applicants required to submit FAFSA. *Faculty research:* Poetics and modern poetry, 19th and 20th century British and American literature, the American west, environmental studies, critical theory and race and gender studies. Total annual research expenditures: $36,210. *Unit head:* Prof. Vincent P. Pecora, Chair, 801-581-6168, E-mail: v.pecora@utah.edu. *Application contact:* Prof. Matthew Potolsky, Director of Graduate Studies, 801-581-5245, E-mail: m.potolsky@utah.edu.

Virginia Commonwealth University, Graduate School, College of Humanities and Sciences, Department of English, Program in English, Richmond, VA 23284-9005. Offers literature (MA); writing and rhetoric (MA). *Application deadline:* For fall admission, 2/1 for domestic students; for spring admission, 11/15 for domestic students. Applications are processed on a rolling basis. Application fee: $50. *Expenses:* Tuition, state resident: full-time $7,224; part-time $401 per credit. Tuition, nonresident: full-time $16,072; part-time $891 per credit. Required fees: $1,679; $63 per credit. Tuition and fees vary according to campus/location. *Unit head:* Katherine Bassard, Program Director, E-mail: kcbassar@vcu.edu.

See Close-Up on page 457.

Wright State University, School of Graduate Studies, College of Liberal Arts, Department of English Language and Literatures, Dayton, OH 45435. Offers composition and rhetoric (MA); English (MA); literature (MA); teaching English to speakers of other languages (MA). *Degree requirements:* For master's, thesis optional, portfolio. *Entrance requirements:* For master's, 20 hours in upper-level English. Additional exam requirements/recommendations for international students: Required—TOEFL. *Faculty research:* American literature, world literature in English, applied linguistics, writing theory and pedagogy.

Speech and Interpersonal Communication

Abilene Christian University, Graduate School, College of Arts and Sciences, Department of Communication, Program in Human Communication, Abilene, TX 79699-9100. Offers MA. Part-time programs available. *Faculty:* 7 part-time/adjunct (2 women). *Students:* 17 full-time (13 women), 4 part-time (1 woman); includes 2 minority (1 Asian American or Pacific Islander, 1 Hispanic American), 4 international. 14 applicants, 79% accepted, 8 enrolled. In 2007, 11 degrees awarded. *Degree requirements:* For master's, one foreign language, comprehensive exam, thesis optional. *Entrance requirements:* For master's, GRE General Test. *Application deadline:* For fall admission, 4/1 priority date for domestic students; for spring admission, 11/1 for domestic students. Applications are processed on a rolling basis. Application fee: $40 ($45 for international students). Electronic applications accepted. *Expenses:* Tuition: Full-time $13,368; part-time $557 per hour. Required fees: $700; $34 per hour. $10 per semester. Tuition and fees vary according to degree level and campus/location. *Financial support:* Teaching assistantships, Federal Work-Study available. Support available to part-time students. Financial award application deadline: 4/1. *Faculty research:* Intercultural communication, family communication, forensics, organizational communication. *Unit head:* Dr. Paul Lakey, Graduate Adviser, 325-674-2292, Fax: 325-674-6966, E-mail: lakeyp@acu.edu. *Application contact:* William Horn, Graduate Admissions Counselor, 325-674-2656, Fax: 325-674-6717, E-mail: gradinfo@acu.edu.

Arizona State University, Graduate College, College of Liberal Arts and Sciences, Division of Social Sciences, Hugh Downs School of Human Communication, Tempe, AZ 85287. Offers communication (PhD); speech and interpersonal communication (MA). *Degree requirements:* For master's, thesis or alternative; for doctorate, thesis/dissertation.

Arkansas State University, Graduate School, College of Communications, Department of Communication Studies, Jonesboro, State University, AR 72467. Offers speech communications and theater (MA, SCCT). Part-time programs available. *Faculty:* 5 full-time (2 women). *Students:* 6 full-time (5 women), 2 part-time (1 woman); includes 2 minority (both African Americans) Average age 26. 6 applicants, 83% accepted, 5 enrolled. In 2007, 4 degrees awarded. *Degree requirements:* For master's, one foreign language, comprehensive exam, thesis or alternative. *Entrance requirements:* For master's, GRE General Test, appropriate bachelor's degree, writing sample, letter of recommendation, official transcript. Additional exam requirements/recommendations for international students: Required—TOEFL (minimum score 213 computer-based). *Application deadline:* Applications are processed on a rolling basis. Application fee: $30 ($40 for international students). Electronic applications accepted. *Expenses:* Tuition, state resident: full-time $3,528; part-time $196 per hour. Tuition, nonresident: full-time $8,928; part-time $496 per hour. Required fees: $842; $44 per hour. $25 per term. Tuition and fees vary according to course load and program. *Financial support:* Teaching assistantships, career-related internships or fieldwork, scholarships/grants, and unspecified assistantships available. Financial award application deadline: 7/1; financial award applicants required to submit FAFSA. *Faculty research:* Business and professional speech development, communication consulting, speech communication, interpersonal communication, organizational training and development. *Unit head:* Dr. Thomas Bagland, Chair, 870-972-3091, Fax: 870-972-3856, E-mail: tbaglan@astate.edu.

Arkansas State University, Graduate School, College of Fine Arts, Department of Theatre, Jonesboro, State University, AR 72467. Offers speech communication and theater (MA, SCCT). Part-time programs available. *Faculty:* 3 full-time (1 woman). *Students:* 1 (woman) full-time, 2 part-time (both women). Average age 29. In 2007, 1 degree awarded. *Degree requirements:* For master's, comprehensive exam, thesis or alternative; for SCCT, comprehensive exam. *Entrance requirements:* For master's, GRE General Test or MAT, appropriate bachelor's degree, official transcript; for SCCT, GRE General Test or MAT, interview, master's degree, official transcript. Additional exam requirements/recommendations for international students: Required—TOEFL (minimum score 213 computer-based). *Application deadline:* Applications are processed on a rolling basis. Application fee: $30 ($40 for international students). Electronic applications accepted. *Expenses:* Tuition, state resident: full-time $3,528; part-time $196 per hour. Tuition, nonresident: full-time $8,928; part-time $496 per hour. Required fees: $842; $44 per hour. $25 per term. Tuition and fees vary according to course load and program. *Financial support:* Teaching assistantships, scholarships/grants and unspecified assistantships available. Financial award application deadline: 7/1; financial award applicants required to submit FAFSA. *Faculty research:* Acting, costume design and technology, directing and stage, makeup design and technology, voice and movement. *Unit head:* Bobby Simpson, Chair, 870-972-2037, Fax: 870-972-2830, E-mail: bsimpson@astate.edu.

Ball State University, Graduate School, College of Communication, Information, and Media, Department of Communication Studies, Muncie, IN 47306-1099. Offers speech, public address, forensics, and rhetoric (MA). *Faculty:* 5. *Students:* 19 full-time (9 women), 9 part-time (8 women); includes 5 minority (2 African Americans, 3 Hispanic Americans), 7 international. Average age 23. 31 applicants, 74% accepted, 13 enrolled. In 2007, 16 degrees awarded. *Entrance requirements:* For master's, GRE General Test. Application fee: $25 ($35 for international students). *Expenses:* Tuition, state resident: full-time $6,864. Tuition, nonresident: full-time $17,932. Required fees: $1,866. *Financial support:* In 2007–08, 28 teaching assistantships with full tuition reimbursements (averaging $8,322 per year) were awarded; research assistantships, career-related internships or fieldwork also available. Financial award application deadline: 3/1. *Unit head:* Glen Stamp, Chairperson, 765-285-1882, Fax: 765-285-2736.

Bob Jones University, Graduate Programs, Greenville, SC 29614. Offers accountancy (MS); Bible (MA); Bible translation (MA); Biblical studies (Certificate); broadcast management (MS); business administration (MBA); church history (MA, PhD); church ministries (MA); church music (MM); cinema and video production (MA); counseling (MS); curriculum and instruction (Ed D); divinity (M Div); dramatic production (MA); educational leadership (MS, Ed D, Ed S); elementary education (M Ed, MAT); English (M Ed, MA, MAT); fine arts (MA); graphic design (MA); history (M Ed, MA); illustration (MA); interpretative speech (MA); mathematics (M Ed, MAT); medical missions (Certificate); ministry (MM, D Min); multi-categorical special education (M Ed, MAT); music (M Ed); New Testament interpretation (PhD); Old Testament interpretation (PhD); orchestral instrument performance (MM); organ performance (MM); pastoral studies (MA); personnel services (MS, Ed S); piano pedagogy (MM); piano performance (MM); platform arts (MA); radio and television broadcasting (MS); rhetoric and public address (MA); secondary education (M Ed); studio art (MA); teaching Bible (MA); theology (MA, PhD); voice performance (MM); youth ministries (MA); M Div/MM.

Bowling Green State University, Graduate College, College of Arts and Sciences, School of Communication Studies, Program of Communication Studies, Bowling Green, OH 43403. Offers MA, PhD. *Students:* 46 full-time (26 women), 15 part-time (10 women); includes 8 minority (6 African Americans, 1 Asian American or Pacific Islander, 1 Hispanic American), 16 international. Average age 33. 77 applicants, 36% accepted, 7 enrolled. In 2007, 4 master's, 7 doctorates awarded. Terminal master's awarded for partial completion of doctoral program. *Degree requirements:* For master's, thesis or alternative; for doctorate, comprehensive exam, thesis/dissertation. *Entrance requirements:* For master's and doctorate, GRE General Test. Additional exam requirements/recommendations for international students: Required—TOEFL. *Application deadline:* For fall admission, 1/1 priority date for domestic students. Application fee: $30. Electronic applications accepted. *Financial support:* In 2007–08, 2 fellowships with full tuition reimbursements (averaging $14,707 per year), 8 research assistantships with full tuition reimbursements (averaging $8,788 per year), 34 teaching assistantships with full tuition reimbursements (averaging $11,098 per year) were awarded; Federal Work-Study and unspecified assistantships also available. Financial award applicants required to submit FAFSA. *Faculty research:* Rhetorical theory and criticism, culture and communication, interpersonal/organizational communication.

Brooklyn College of the City University of New York, Division of Graduate Studies, Department of Speech Communication Arts and Sciences, Brooklyn, NY 11210-2889. Offers audiology (Au D); speech (MA), including audiology, public communication; speech and hearing sciences (PhD); speech pathology (MS). The department offers courses at Brooklyn College that are creditable towards the CUNY doctoral degree (with permission of the executive officer of the doctoral program); MS in speech pathology has fall admissions only. *Accreditation:* ASHA (one or more programs are accredited). Part-time programs available. *Students:* 34 full-time (33 women), 64 part-time (61 women); includes 10 minority (6 African Americans, 4 Hispanic Americans), 7 international. 238 applicants, 39% accepted, 35 enrolled. In 2007, 43 degrees awarded. Terminal master's awarded for partial completion of doctoral program. *Degree requirements:* For master's, comprehensive exam, National Teacher Exam. *Entrance requirements:* For master's, GRE, minimum GPA of 3.0, interview, essay. Additional exam requirements/recommendations for international students: Required—TOEFL. *Application deadline:* For fall admission, 2/1 for domestic and international students. Applications are processed on a rolling basis. Application fee: $125. Electronic applications accepted. *Financial support:* Career-related internships or fieldwork, Federal Work-Study, institutionally sponsored loans, scholarships/grants, and traineeships available. Support available to part-time students. Financial award application deadline: 5/1; financial award applicants required to submit FAFSA. *Faculty research:* Language and learning disorders, aphasia, auditory disorders, public and business communication, voice and fluency disorders. *Unit head:* Dr. Michele Emmer, Chairperson, 718-951-5225, Fax: 718-951-4167, E-mail: memmer@brooklyn.cuny.edu. *Application contact:* Hernan Sierra, Graduate Admissions Coordinator, 718-951-4536, Fax: 718-951-4506, E-mail: grads@brooklyn.cuny.edu.

California State University, Fullerton, Graduate Studies, College of Communications, Department of Human Communications, Fullerton, CA 92834-9480. Offers communicative disorders (MA); speech communication (MA). *Accreditation:* ASHA. Part-time programs available. *Students:* 69 full-time (62 women), 36 part-time (31 women); includes 32 minority (4 African Americans, 7 Asian Americans or Pacific Islanders, 21 Hispanic Americans), 5 international. Average age 30. 198 applicants, 17% accepted, 26 enrolled. In 2007, 41 degrees awarded. *Degree requirements:* For master's, comprehensive exam, thesis or alternative. *Entrance requirements:* For master's, minimum GPA of 3.0 in major. Application fee: $55. *Financial support:* Teaching assistantships, career-related internships or fieldwork, Federal Work-Study, institutionally sponsored loans, and scholarships/grants available. Support available to part-time students. Financial award application deadline: 3/1. *Faculty research:* Speech therapy. *Unit head:* Dr. John Reinard, Chair, 714-278-3617.

California State University, Fullerton, Graduate Studies, College of Humanities and Social Sciences, Program in Linguistics, Fullerton, CA 92834-9480. Offers analysis of specific language structures (MA); anthropological linguistics (MA); applied linguistics (MA); communication and semantics (MA); disorders of communication (MA); experimental phonetics (MA). Part-time programs available. *Students:* 10 full-time (7 women), 12 part-time (9 women); includes 6 minority (2 Asian Americans or Pacific Islanders, 4 Hispanic Americans), 5 international. Average age 33. 21 applicants, 52% accepted, 6 enrolled. In 2007, 8 degrees awarded. *Degree requirements:* For master's, one foreign language, thesis or alternative, project. *Entrance requirements:* For master's, minimum GPA of 3.0, undergraduate major in linguistics or related field. Application fee: $55. *Financial support:* Career-related internships or fieldwork, Federal Work-Study, institutionally sponsored loans, and scholarships/grants available. Support available to part-time students. Financial award application deadline: 3/1. *Unit head:* Dr. Franz Muller-Gotama, Adviser, 714-278-2441.

California State University, Los Angeles, Graduate Studies, College of Arts and Letters, Department of Communication Studies, Los Angeles, CA 90032-8530. Offers speech communication (MA). Part-time and evening/weekend programs available. *Faculty:* 13 full-time (4 women). *Students:* 29 full-time (20 women), 37 part-time (29 women); includes 26 minority (10 African Americans, 7 Asian Americans or Pacific Islanders, 9 Hispanic Americans), 12 international. Average age 31. In 2007, 14 degrees awarded. *Degree requirements:* For master's, comprehensive exam or thesis. *Entrance requirements:* For master's, minimum GPA of 2.75 in last 90 units of course work. Additional exam requirements/recommendations for international students: Required—TOEFL. *Application deadline:* For fall admission, 6/30 for domestic students; for spring admission, 2/1 for domestic students. Applications are processed on a rolling basis. Application fee: $55. *Financial support:* Career-related internships or fieldwork and Federal Work-Study available. Support available to part-time students. Financial award application deadline: 3/1. *Faculty research:* Organizational, interpersonal, intercultural, and instructional communication; rhetorical theories. *Unit head:* Dr. John Ramirez, Chair, 323-343-4200, Fax: 323-343-6467, E-mail: jramire4@calstatela.edu.

California State University, Northridge, Graduate Studies, College of Arts, Media, and Communication, Department of Communication Studies, Northridge, CA 91330. Offers MA. *Faculty:* 7 full-time (4 women), 26 part-time/adjunct (18 women). *Students:* 15 full-time (11 women), 27 part-time (20 women); includes 12 minority (1 African American, 4 Asian Americans or Pacific Islanders, 7 Hispanic Americans), 2 international. Average age 28. 55 applicants, 44% accepted, 16 enrolled. In 2007, 9 degrees awarded. *Entrance requirements:* For master's, GRE General Test. Additional exam requirements/recommendations for international students: Required—TOEFL. *Application deadline:* For fall admission, 11/30 for domestic students. Application fee: $55. *Financial support:* Teaching assistantships available. Financial award application deadline: 3/1. *Unit head:* Dr. Bernardo Attias, Chair, 818-677-2853.

Central Michigan University, College of Graduate Studies, College of Communication and Fine Arts, Department of Speech, Communication and Dramatic Arts, Concentration in Interpersonal and Public Communication, Mount Pleasant, MI 48859. Offers MA. *Degree requirements:* For master's, thesis. *Entrance requirements:* For master's, minimum GPA of 3.0 in last 15 hours of speech communication and dramatic arts courses, 2.7 in last 60 hours. *Faculty research:* Communication in organizations, communication in families, relational communication and conflict, communication education.

Central Michigan University, College of Graduate Studies, College of Communication and Fine Arts, Department of Speech, Communication and Dramatic Arts, Concentration in Oral Interpretation, Mount Pleasant, MI 48859. Offers MA. *Degree requirements:* For master's, thesis or alternative. *Entrance requirements:* For master's, minimum GPA of 3.0 in last 15 hours of speech communication and dramatic arts courses, 2.7 in last 60 hours.

Colorado State University, Graduate School, College of Liberal Arts, Department of Speech Communication, Fort Collins, CO 80523-0015. Offers MA. *Faculty:* 13 full-time (4 women), 1 part-time/adjunct (0 women). *Students:* 23 full-time (16 women), 4 part-time (3 women); includes 2 minority (1 Asian American or Pacific Islander, 1 Hispanic American), 1 international. Average age 25. 21 applicants, 90% accepted, 12 enrolled. In 2007, 8 master's awarded. *Degree requirements:* For master's, thesis. *Entrance requirements:* For master's, GRE General Test, minimum GPA of 3.0; writing sample. Additional exam requirements/recommendations for international students: Required—TOEFL (minimum score 550 paper-based; 230 computer-based). *Application deadline:* For fall admission, 1/31 priority date for domestic and international students. Applications are processed on a rolling basis. Application fee: $50. Electronic applications accepted. *Expenses:* Tuition, state resident: full-time $4,887; part-time $272 per credit. Tuition, nonresident: full-time $16,425; part-time $913 per credit. Required fees: $1,379; $75 per credit. *Financial support:* In 2007–08, 22 teaching assistantships with full and partial tuition reimbursements (averaging $11,799 per year) were awarded; scholarships/grants and unspecified assistantships also available. Financial award application deadline: 3/1; financial award applicants required to submit FAFSA. *Faculty research:* Rhetorical theory and criticism, media and popular culture, intercultural communication, freedom of speech, communication theory. Total annual research expenditures: $14,989. *Unit head:* Dr. David Vest, Head, 970-491-6140, E-mail: david.vest@colostate.edu. *Application contact:* Dr. Greg Dickinson, Director of Graduate Studies, 970-491-6893, E-mail: greg.dickinson@colostate.edu.

Speech and Interpersonal Communication

Drake University, School of Education, Department of Teaching and Learning, Program in Secondary Education, Des Moines, IA 50311-4516. Offers art (MAT); biology (MAT); business (MAT); chemistry (MAT); English (MAT); general science (MAT); history-American (MAT); history-world (MAT); journalism (MAT); mathematics (MAT); physical science (MAT); physics (MAT); sociology (MAT); speech (MAT); speech communication (MAT); theatre (MAT). Part-time programs available. *Faculty:* 10 full-time (3 women), 28 part-time/adjunct (16 women). *Students:* 13 full-time (7 women), 33 part-time (20 women). 41 applicants, 56% accepted. In 2007, 12 degrees awarded. *Degree requirements:* For master's, comprehensive exam, thesis (for some programs), internships (for some programs). *Entrance requirements:* For master's, GRE General Test, MAT, or Drake Writing Assessment, resumé, 2 letters of recommendation. Additional exam requirements/recommendations for international students: Required—TOEFL (minimum score 550 paper-based; 213 computer-based). *Application deadline:* For fall admission, 7/1 priority date for domestic students, 6/1 priority date for international students; for spring admission, 11/1 priority date for domestic students, 10/1 priority date for international students. Applications are processed on a rolling basis. Application fee: $25. Electronic applications accepted. *Expenses:* Tuition: Full-time $26,030; part-time $370 per credit hour. Required fees: $406; $40 per semester. Tuition and fees vary according to program. *Financial support:* Career-related internships or fieldwork and unspecified assistantships available. Support available to part-time students. *Faculty research:* Counseling and rehabilitation, behavioral supports, inquiry-based science methods, teacher quality enhancement. Total annual research expenditures: $1.5 million. *Application contact:* Ann J. Martin, Graduate Coordinator, 515-271-2034, Fax: 515-271-2831, E-mail: ann.martin@drake.edu.

Eastern Illinois University, Graduate School, College of Arts and Humanities, Department of Communication Studies, Charleston, IL 61920-3099. Offers MA. Part-time programs available. *Faculty:* 11 full-time (2 women). In 2007, 21 degrees awarded. *Degree requirements:* For master's, major paper. *Application deadline:* For fall admission, 7/31 priority date for domestic students. Applications are processed on a rolling basis. Application fee: $30. *Expenses:* Tuition, state resident: part-time $218 per hour. Tuition, nonresident: part-time $654 per hour. *Financial support:* In 2007–08, 1 research assistantship with tuition reimbursement (averaging $7,200 per year), 6 teaching assistantships with tuition reimbursements (averaging $7,200 per year) were awarded. *Unit head:* Dr. Mark Borzi, Chairperson, 217-581-2016, E-mail: cfmgb@eiu.edu. *Application contact:* Dr. Melanie Mills, Coordinator, 217-581-6306, E-mail: mbmills@eiu.edu.

Florida State University, Graduate Studies, College of Communication, Department of Communication, Tallahassee, FL 32306. Offers corporate and public communication (MA, MS); integrated marketing communication (MA, MS); mass communication (PhD); media and communication studies (MA, MS); speech communication (PhD). Part-time programs available. *Faculty:* 26 full-time (7 women), 2 part-time/adjunct (0 women). *Students:* 96 full-time (66 women), 126 part-time (70 women); includes 92 minority (37 African Americans, 1 American Indian/Alaska Native, 35 Asian Americans or Pacific Islanders, 19 Hispanic Americans), 1 international. Average age 24. 230 applicants, 74% accepted, 80 enrolled. In 2007, 77 master's, 6 doctorates awarded. *Median time to degree:* Of those who began their doctoral program in fall 1999, 67% received their degree in 8 years or less. *Degree requirements:* For master's, thesis (for some programs); for doctorate, comprehensive exam, thesis/dissertation. *Entrance requirements:* For master's, GRE General Test, minimum GPA of 3.0; for doctorate, GRE General Test, minimum GPA of 3.3 in graduate course work. Additional exam requirements/recommendations for international students: Required—TOEFL (minimum score 600 paper-based; 250 computer-based; 100 iBT). *Application deadline:* For fall admission, 7/1 priority date for domestic and international students; for winter admission, 3/1 priority date for domestic and international students; for spring admission, 11/1 priority date for domestic and international students. Applications are processed on a rolling basis. Application fee: $30. *Expenses:* Tuition, state resident: part-time $248 per credit hour. Tuition, nonresident: part-time $880 per credit hour. Tuition and fees vary according to program. *Financial support:* In 2007–08, 49 students received support, including 1 fellowship with full tuition reimbursement available, 8 research assistantships with full tuition reimbursements available (averaging $14,000 per year), 40 teaching assistantships with full tuition reimbursements available (averaging $5,000 per year); career-related internships or fieldwork, Federal Work-Study, institutionally sponsored loans, scholarships/grants, tuition waivers (partial), and unspecified assistantships also available. Support available to part-time students. Financial award application deadline: 2/1; financial award applicants required to submit FAFSA. *Faculty research:* Communication technology and policy, marketing communication, communication content and effect, new communication/information technologies. Total annual research expenditures: $264,208. *Unit head:* Dr. Stephen D. McDowell, Chairperson, 850-644-2276, Fax: 850-644-8642, E-mail: smcdowel@mailer.fsu.edu. *Application contact:* Natashia Hinson-Turner, Graduate Program Assistant, 850-644-8746, Fax: 850-644-8642, E-mail: dc.gradinfo@comm.fsu.edu.

Georgia State University, College of Arts and Sciences, Department of Communication, Atlanta, GA 30303-3083. Offers film/video/digital imaging (MA); human communication and social influence (MA); mass communication (MA); moving image studies (PhD); public communication (PhD). Part-time programs available. *Faculty:* 27 full-time (13 women). *Students:* 81 full-time (51 women), 61 part-time (41 women); includes 31 minority (26 African Americans, 2 Asian Americans or Pacific Islanders, 3 Hispanic Americans), 17 international. 179 applicants, 30% accepted, 29 enrolled. In 2007, 23 master's, 10 doctorates awarded. *Degree requirements:* For master's, one foreign language, thesis or alternative; for doctorate, comprehensive exam, thesis/dissertation. *Entrance requirements:* For master's and doctorate, GRE General Test. Additional exam requirements/recommendations for international students: Required—TOEFL (minimum score 80 computer-based). Application fee: $50. Electronic applications accepted. *Expenses:* Tuition, state resident: part-time $221 per credit hour. *Financial support:* In 2007–08, 1 fellowship with tuition reimbursement (averaging $15,000 per year) was awarded; research assistantships, teaching assistantships with tuition reimbursements, career-related internships or fieldwork, Federal Work-Study, institutionally sponsored loans, tuition waivers (partial), and unspecified assistantships also available. Support available to part-time students. Financial award applicants required to submit FAFSA. *Faculty research:* Critical/cultural studies, rhetoric studies, film/media studies, mass communications/journalism, audience studies. *Unit head:* Dr. David Cheshier, Chair, 404-413-5649, E-mail: dcheshier@gsu.edu. *Application contact:* Tawanna Tookes, Administrative Specialist, Managerial, 404-413-5652, E-mail: joutkt@langate.gsu.edu.

Hofstra University, School of Communication, Department of Speech Communication, Rhetoric, and Performance Studies, Hempstead, NY 11549. Offers speech communication and rhetorical studies (MA). Part-time and evening/weekend programs available. *Faculty:* 6 full-time (3 women). *Students:* 7 full-time (5 women), 13 part-time (8 women); includes 5 minority (4 African Americans, 1 Asian American or Pacific Islander), 2 international. Average age 28. 11 applicants, 100% accepted, 7 enrolled. In 2007, 3 degrees awarded. *Degree requirements:* For master's, comprehensive exam, thesis. *Entrance requirements:* For master's, 2 letters of recommendation, interview. Additional exam requirements/recommendations for international students: Required—TOEFL (minimum score 550 paper-based; 213 computer-based). *Application deadline:* Applications are processed on a rolling basis. Application fee: $60. Electronic applications accepted. *Expenses:* Tuition: Full-time $14,220; part-time $820 per credit. Required fees: $970; $165 per term. Tuition and fees vary according to program. *Financial support:* In 2007–08, 10 students received support, including 2 fellowships with tuition reimbursements available (averaging $2,500 per year), 1 research assistantship with full and partial tuition reimbursement available (averaging $6,660 per year); Federal Work-Study, institutionally sponsored loans, scholarships/grants, tuition waivers (full and partial), and unspecified assistantships also available. Support available to part-time students. Financial award applicants required to submit FAFSA. *Faculty research:* Performance of race and gender; public deliberation; public memory; rhetoric and labor; civic engagement and political participation. *Unit head:* Dr. Matthew Sobnosky, Director, 516-463-7141, E-mail: sphmjs@hofstra.edu. *Application contact:* Carol Drummer, Dean of Graduate Admissions, 516-463-4876, Fax: 516-463-4664, E-mail: gradstudent@hofstra.edu.

Idaho State University, Office of Graduate Studies, College of Arts and Sciences, Department of Communication and Rhetorical Studies, Pocatello, ID 83209. Offers speech communication (MA). Part-time programs available. *Faculty:* 4 full-time (1 woman). *Students:* 6 full-time (4 women), 4 part-time (1 woman); includes 2 minority (both Hispanic Americans), 1 international. Average age 32. In 2007, 4 degrees awarded. *Degree requirements:* For master's, comprehensive exam, thesis (for some programs). *Entrance requirements:* For master's, GRE General Test, minimum GPA of 3.0 in all upper level courses. Additional exam requirements/recommendations for international students: Required—TOEFL (minimum score 550 paper-based; 213 computer-based; 80 iBT). *Application deadline:* For fall admission, 7/1 for domestic students, 6/1 for international students; for spring admission, 12/1 for domestic students, 11/1 for international students. Applications are processed on a rolling basis. Application fee: $55. Electronic applications accepted. *Expenses:* Tuition, state resident: full-time $2,882; part-time $259 per credit hour. Tuition, nonresident: full-time $11,566; part-time $379 per credit hour. Required fees: $2,278. Full-time tuition and fees vary according to program. Part-time tuition and fees vary according to course load. *Financial support:* In 2007–08, 3 teaching assistantships with full and partial tuition reimbursements (averaging $9,128 per year) were awarded; career-related internships or fieldwork, Federal Work-Study, institutionally sponsored loans, scholarships/grants, health care benefits, and unspecified assistantships also available. Support available to part-time students. Financial award application deadline: 1/1; financial award applicants required to submit FAFSA. *Faculty research:* Rhetorical studies, organizational communication. *Unit head:* Dr. James DiSanza, Chairman, 208-282-3395, Fax: 208-282-4598, E-mail: disajame@isu.edu. *Application contact:* Ellen Combs, Graduate School Technical Records Specialist, 208-282-2150, Fax: 208-282-4847.

Indiana University Bloomington, University Graduate School, College of Arts and Sciences, Department of Communication and Culture, Bloomington, IN 47405-7000. Offers MA, PhD. *Faculty:* 20 full-time (10 women). *Students:* 70 full-time (40 women), 9 part-time (6 women); includes 7 minority (1 African American, 1 Asian American or Pacific Islander, 5 Hispanic Americans), 8 international. Average age 32. 147 applicants, 24% accepted, 16 enrolled. In 2007, 2 master's, 7 doctorates awarded. *Median time to degree:* Of those who began their doctoral program in fall 1999, 73% received their degree in 8 years or less. *Degree requirements:* For master's, comprehensive exam; for doctorate, one foreign language, comprehensive exam, thesis/dissertation, colloquium, teaching. *Entrance requirements:* For master's and doctorate, GRE General Test (recommended), minimum GPA of 3.0, 3 letters of recommendation, writing sample. Additional exam requirements/recommendations for international students: Required—TOEFL (minimum score 550 paper-based; 213 computer-based). *Application deadline:* For winter admission, 1/15 for domestic students, 12/1 for international students. Application fee: $50 ($60 for international students). Electronic applications accepted. *Financial support:* In 2007–08, 60 students received support; fellowships with tuition reimbursements available, teaching assistantships with full tuition reimbursements available available. Financial award application deadline: 4/15. *Faculty research:* Rhetoric and public culture, film and media studies, performance ethnography. *Unit head:* Prof. Gregory A. Waller, Chair, 812-855-2367, Fax: 812-855-6014, E-mail: cmcl@indiana.edu. *Application contact:* Kathy P. Teige, Graduate Secretary, 812-855-6389, Fax: 812-855-6014, E-mail: ktiege@indiana.edu.

Kansas State University, Graduate School, College of Arts and Sciences, Department of Speech, Manhattan, KS 66506. Offers rhetoric/communication (MA); theatre (MA). *Faculty:* 14 full-time (8 women). *Students:* 44 full-time (26 women), 3 part-time (all women); includes 2 minority (1 African American, 1 Hispanic American), 2 international. Average age 23. 35 applicants, 86% accepted, 17 enrolled. In 2007, 1 degree awarded. *Degree requirements:* For master's, thesis or alternative. *Entrance requirements:* For master's, GRE General Test (recommended), minimum GPA of 3.0. Additional exam requirements/recommendations for international students: Required—TOEFL. *Application deadline:* For fall admission, 3/1 for domestic students, 2/1 priority date for international students; for spring admission, 10/1 for domestic students, 8/1 priority date for international students. Applications are processed on a rolling basis. Application fee: $30 ($55 for international students). *Financial support:* In 2007–08, 24 teaching assistantships with full tuition reimbursements (averaging $9,417 per year) were awarded; career-related internships or fieldwork, institutionally sponsored loans, and scholarships/grants also available. Support available to part-time students. Financial award application deadline: 3/1; financial award applicants required to submit FAFSA. *Faculty research:* Interpersonal/intercultural communication, political advertising, political rhetoric, deliberative democracy, persuasion, social influence, compliance-gaining. Total annual research expenditures: $2,748. *Unit head:* Charles Griffin, Head, 785-532-6860, Fax: 785-532-3714, E-mail: charlieg@ksu.edu. *Application contact:* William Schenck-Hamlin, Director, 785-532-6861, Fax: 785-532-3714, E-mail: billsh@ksu.edu.

Louisiana Tech University, Graduate School, College of Liberal Arts, Department of Speech, Ruston, LA 71272. Offers speech (MA); speech pathology and audiology (MA). *Accreditation:* ASHA. *Degree requirements:* For master's, thesis or alternative. *Entrance requirements:* For master's, GRE General Test. *Application deadline:* For fall admission, 7/29 for domestic students; for spring admission, 2/3 for domestic students. Application fee: $20 ($30 for international students). *Financial support:* In 2007–08, 5 students received support; fellowships, career-related internships or fieldwork, Federal Work-Study, institutionally sponsored loans, and unspecified assistantships available. Financial award application deadline: 2/1. *Unit head:* Dr. Sheryl Shoemaker, Head, 318-257-4764, Fax: 318-257-4492. *Application contact:* Dr. Clarice Dans, Head, 318-257-4764, Fax: 318-257-4492, E-mail: cdans@ltparts.latech.edu.

Marquette University, Graduate School, College of Communication, Milwaukee, WI 53201-1881. Offers advertising and public relations (MA); broadcasting and electronic communications (MA); communications studies (MA); journalism (MA); mass communications (MA); religious communications (MA); science, health and environmental communications (MA). *Accreditation:* ACEJMC. Part-time and evening/weekend programs available. *Faculty:* 31 full-time (17 women), 34 part-time/adjunct (17 women). *Students:* 24 full-time (13 women), 19 part-time (12 women); includes 7 minority (1 African American, 1 American Indian/Alaska Native, 2 Asian Americans or Pacific Islanders, 3 Hispanic Americans), 7 international. Average age 28. 76 applicants, 58% accepted, 15 enrolled. In 2007, 17 degrees awarded. *Degree requirements:* For master's, comprehensive exam. *Entrance requirements:* For master's, GRE. Additional exam requirements/recommendations for international students: Required—TOEFL. Application fee: $40. *Financial support:* In 2007–08, 6 research assistantships, 12 teaching assistantships were awarded; career-related internships or fieldwork, Federal Work-Study, institutionally sponsored loans, scholarships/grants, and tuition waivers (full and partial) also available. Support available to part-time students. Financial award application deadline: 2/15. *Faculty research:* Urban journalism, gender and communication, intercultural communication, religious communication. Total annual research expenditures: $17,806. *Unit head:* Dr. Ana Garner, Dean, 414-288-3588, Fax: 414-288-1578.

Miami University, Graduate School, College of Arts and Sciences, Department of Communication, Program in Speech Communication, Oxford, OH 45056. Offers MA. Part-time programs available. *Degree requirements:* For master's, final exam. *Entrance requirements:* For master's, minimum undergraduate GPA of 3.0 during previous 2 years or 2.75 overall. Additional exam requirements/recommendations for international students: Required—TOEFL (minimum score 550 paper-based; 213 computer-based), TWE (minimum score 4). Electronic applications accepted.

Minnesota State University Mankato, College of Graduate Studies, College of Arts and Humanities, Department of Speech Communication, Mankato, MN 56001. Offers forensics (MFA); speech communication (MA, MS, MT). *Students:* 19 full-time (14 women), 14 part-time (11 women). Average age 29. In 2007, 10 degrees awarded. *Degree requirements:* For master's, one foreign language, comprehensive exam, thesis. *Entrance requirements:* For master's, minimum GPA of 3.0 during previous 2 years, writing sample. *Application deadline:* For fall admission, 7/1 priority date for domestic students; for spring admission, 11/1 for domestic students. Applications are processed on a rolling basis. Application fee: $40. Electronic applications accepted. *Financial support:* Research assistantships, teaching assistantships with full tuition reimbursements, career-related internships or fieldwork, Federal Work-Study, and institutionally sponsored loans available. Support available to part-time students. Financial award application deadline: 3/15; financial award applicants required to submit FAFSA. *Unit head:* Dr. Daniel Cronn-Mills, Chairperson, 507-389-2213. *Application contact:* 507-389-2321, E-mail: grad@mnsu.edu.

Montclair State University, The Office of Graduate Admissions and Support Services, School of the Arts, Department of Communication Studies, Montclair, NJ 07043-1624. Offers organizational communication (MA); public relations (MA); speech communication (MA). Part-time and evening/weekend programs available. *Faculty:* 5 full-time (3 women), 39 part-time/adjunct (21 women). *Students:* 8 full-time (6 women), 15 part-time (10 women); includes 3 minority (2 African Americans, 1 Hispanic American), 4 international. 41 applicants, 22% accepted, 6 enrolled. In 2007, 7 degrees awarded. *Degree requirements:* For master's, comprehensive exam. *Entrance requirements:* For master's, GRE General Test, minimum GPA of 3.0; undergraduate degree or work in theatre, oral interpretation, speech communication, media, or broadcasting; 2 letters of recommendation. Additional exam requirements/recommendations for international students: Required—TOEFL (minimum score 83 computer-based). *Application deadline:* For fall admission, 6/1 for international students; for spring admission, 10/1 for international students. Applications are processed on a rolling basis. Application fee: $60. Electronic applications accepted. *Financial support:* In 2007–08, 1 research assistantship with full tuition reimbursement (averaging $7,000 per year) was awarded; Federal Work-Study, scholarships/grants, and unspecified assistantships also available. Support available to part-time students. Financial award application deadline: 3/1; financial award applicants required to submit FAFSA. *Unit head:* Dr. Christine Lemesianou, Chairperson, 973-655-5214. *Application contact:* Dr. Michael Kent, Adviser, 973-655-5130, E-mail: kentm@mail.montclair.edu.

New York University, Steinhardt School of Culture, Education and Human Development, Department of Media, Culture and Communication, New York, NY 10012-1019. Offers media ecology/culture and communication (PhD); media, culture, and communication (MA). Part-time and evening/weekend programs available. *Faculty:* 24 full-time (11 women), 41 part-time/adjunct (17 women). *Students:* 66 full-time (44 women), 56 part-time (37 women); includes 17 minority (7 African Americans, 8 Asian Americans or Pacific Islanders, 2 Hispanic Americans), 34 international. 321 applicants, 40% accepted, 44 enrolled. In 2007, 78 master's, 3 doctorates awarded. *Entrance requirements:* Additional exam requirements/recommendations for international students: Required—TOEFL. *Application deadline:* For fall admission, 12/15 priority date for domestic and international students; for spring admission, 11/1 for domestic and international students. Applications are processed on a rolling basis. Application fee: $50. *Financial support:* Fellowships with full and partial tuition reimbursements, teaching assistantships with full and partial tuition reimbursements, career-related internships or fieldwork, Federal Work-Study, institutionally sponsored loans, scholarships/grants, tuition waivers (partial), and unspecified assistantships available. Support available to part-time students. Financial award application deadline: 2/1; financial award applicants required to submit FAFSA. *Faculty research:* Digital media, intercultural communication, race and politics, media criticism, media literacy. *Unit head:* Dr. Ted Magder, Chairperson, 212-998-5191, Fax: 212-995-4046, E-mail: ted.magder@nyu.edu. *Application contact:* 212-998-5030, Fax: 212-995-4328, E-mail: steinhardt.gradadmissions@nyu.edu.

North Dakota State University, College of Graduate and Interdisciplinary Studies, College of Arts, Humanities and Social Sciences, Department of Communication, Fargo, ND 58105. Offers communication (PhD); mass communication (MA, MS); speech communication (MA, MS). Part-time programs available. Postbaccalaureate distance learning degree programs offered (no on-campus study). *Faculty:* 11 full-time (5 women), 3 part-time/adjunct (1 woman). *Students:* 42 full-time (24 women), 50 part-time (35 women); includes 2 minority (both Asian Americans or Pacific Islanders), 7 international. Average age 27. 62 applicants, 40% accepted, 19 enrolled. In 2007, 15 master's, 7 doctorates awarded. Terminal master's awarded for partial completion of doctoral program. *Median time to degree:* Of those who began their doctoral program in fall 1999, 25% received their degree in 8 years or less. *Degree requirements:* For master's, thesis (for some programs); for doctorate, comprehensive exam, thesis/dissertation, 2-3 publications referred before comps. *Entrance requirements:* For master's, GRE, minimum undergraduate GPA of 3.25; for doctorate, GRE, minimum undergraduate GPA of 3.5. Additional exam requirements/recommendations for international students: Required—TOEFL (minimum score 600 paper-based; 250 computer-based; 100 iBT), IELTS (minimum score 7). *Application deadline:* For fall admission, 2/15 priority date for domestic students; for winter admission, 10/15 priority date for domestic students. Applications are processed on a rolling basis. Application fee: $45 ($60 for international students). Electronic applications accepted. *Expenses:* Tuition, state resident: full-time $5,376; part-time $224 per credit. Tuition, nonresident: full-time $14,354; part-time $598 per credit. Required fees: $962; $40 per credit. Part-time tuition and fees vary according to course load and reciprocity agreements. *Financial support:* In 2007–08, 38 students received support, including 1 fellowship with full tuition reimbursement available (averaging $16,000 per year), 10 research assistantships with full tuition reimbursements available (averaging $12,000 per year), 10 teaching assistantships with full tuition reimbursements available (averaging $8,100 per year); career-related internships or fieldwork, Federal Work-Study, institutionally sponsored loans, tuition waivers (full), and unspecified assistantships also available. Financial award application deadline: 2/1. *Faculty research:* Communication and rhetorical theory, organizational communication, broadcast and print journalism, international communication, PR and advertising. Total annual research expenditures: $148,496. *Unit head:* Dr. Paul E. Nelson, Chair, 701-231-7705, Fax: 701-231-7784, E-mail: paul.nelson.1@ndsu.edu. *Application contact:* Dr. Judy C. Pearson, Director of Graduate Studies, 701-231-6551, Fax: 701-231-1074, E-mail: judy.pearson@ndsu.edu.

Northeastern Illinois University, Graduate College, College of Arts and Sciences, Department of Communication, Media and Theatre, Program in Communication, Media and Theatre, Chicago, IL 60625-4699. Offers MA. Part-time and evening/weekend programs available. *Faculty:* 12 full-time (6 women), 7 part-time/adjunct (2 women). *Students:* 4 full-time (3 women), 25 part-time (18 women); includes 6 minority (5 African Americans, 1 Asian American or Pacific Islander), 2 international. Average age 34. 21 applicants, 76% accepted. In 2007, 9 degrees awarded. *Degree requirements:* For master's, comprehensive exam, oral exams, thesis or 3 term papers; minimum GPA of 3.0. *Entrance requirements:* For master's, 15 undergraduate hours in speech and performing arts, minimum GPA of 2.75. Additional exam requirements/recommendations for international students: Required—TOEFL (minimum score 550 paper-based; 213 computer-based; 80 iBT). *Application deadline:* Applications are processed on a rolling basis. Application fee: $25. Electronic applications accepted. *Expenses:* Tuition, state resident: part-time $243 per credit hour. Tuition, nonresident: part-time $443 per credit hour. *Financial support:* In 2007–08, 10 students received support, including 1 research assistantship with full tuition reimbursement available (averaging $6,600 per year); career-related internships or fieldwork, Federal Work-Study, institutionally sponsored loans, scholarships/grants, tuition waivers (full and partial), and unspecified assistantships also available. Support available to part-time students. Financial award applicants required to submit FAFSA. *Faculty research:* Creative drama, family communication, fine arts and general education, playwriting techniques, interpersonal communications.

Northeastern University, Bouvé College of Health Sciences Graduate School, Department of Speech-Language Pathology and Audiology, Program in Audiology, Boston, MA 02115-5096. Offers Au D. *Faculty:* 10 full-time (8 women), 7 part-time/adjunct. *Students:* 8 full-time (7 women), 1 (woman) part-time. 38 applicants, 58% accepted. *Entrance requirements:* For doctorate, GRE, minimum 3.2 GPA. *Application deadline:* For fall admission, 2/15 for domestic students. *Unit head:* Dr. Sandra Cleveland, Director, 617-373-2496. *Application contact:* Margaret Schnabel, Director of Graduate Admissions, 617-373-2708, E-mail: bouvegrad@neu.edu.

Northwestern University, The Graduate School, School of Communication, Department of Performance Studies, Evanston, IL 60208. Offers MA, PhD. Admissions and degrees offered through The Graduate School. Part-time programs available. Terminal master's awarded for partial completion of doctoral program. *Degree requirements:* For master's, recital; for doctorate, one foreign language, thesis/dissertation, recital. *Entrance requirements:* For master's and doctorate, GRE General Test. Additional exam requirements/recommendations for international students: Required—TOEFL. *Faculty research:* Adaptation/performance of literature, ethnography of performance, critical cultural studies, performance theory, intercultural performance, gender studies.

Ohio University, Graduate College, Scripps College of Communication, School of Communication Studies, Athens, OH 45701-2979. Offers PhD. *Degree requirements:* For doctorate, comprehensive exam, thesis/dissertation. *Entrance requirements:* For doctorate, GRE General Test, minimum GPA of 3.0. Additional exam requirements/recommendations for international students: Required—TOEFL. Electronic applications accepted. *Faculty research:* Rhetoric and public culture, relating and organizing, health communication.

Portland State University, Graduate Studies, College of Liberal Arts and Sciences, Department of Communication, Portland, OR 97207-0751. Offers general speech communication (MA, MS, Certificate). Part-time programs available. *Faculty:* 12 full-time (8 women), 9 part-time/adjunct (8 women). *Students:* 20 full-time (14 women), 7 part-time (5 women); includes 1 minority (Asian American or Pacific Islander), 6 international. Average age 31. 17 applicants, 65% accepted, 9 enrolled. In 2007, 14 degrees awarded. *Degree requirements:* For master's, thesis. *Entrance requirements:* For master's, GRE General Test, minimum GPA of 3.0 in upper-division course work or 2.75 overall, 3 letters of recommendation. Additional exam requirements/recommendations for international students: Required—TOEFL (minimum score 550 paper-based; 213 computer-based). *Application deadline:* For fall admission, 3/1 for domestic and international students. Application fee: $50. *Expenses:* Tuition, state resident: full-time $7,047. Tuition, nonresident: full-time $11,178. *Financial support:* In 2007–08, 9 teaching assistantships with full tuition reimbursements (averaging $5,694 per year) were awarded; research assistantships with full tuition reimbursements, career-related internships or fieldwork, Federal Work-Study, scholarships/grants, and unspecified assistantships also available. Support available to part-time students. Financial award application deadline: 3/1; financial award applicants required to submit FAFSA. Total annual research expenditures: $20,522. *Unit head:* Cynthia Coleman, Chair, 503-725-3544, Fax: 503-725-5385, E-mail: morganbk@pdx.edu. *Application contact:* Kathleen Morgan, Office Coordinator, 503-725-5384, Fax: 503-725-5385, E-mail: morganbk@pdx.edu.

Rensselaer Polytechnic Institute, Graduate School, School of Humanities and Social Sciences, Department of Language, Literature, and Communication, Programs in Communication and Rhetoric, Troy, NY 12180-3590. Offers MS, PhD. *Faculty:* 15 full-time (7 women), 1 (woman) part-time/adjunct. *Students:* 37 applicants, 43% accepted, 6 enrolled. In 2007, 3 degrees awarded. Terminal master's awarded for partial completion of doctoral program. *Median time to degree:* Of those who began their doctoral program in fall 1999, 38% received their degree in 8 years or less. *Degree requirements:* For master's, thesis optional; for doctorate, comprehensive exam, thesis/dissertation. *Entrance requirements:* For master's, GRE General Test, resumé; for doctorate, GRE General Test, writing sample, resumé or curriculum vitae. Additional exam requirements/recommendations for international students: Required—TOEFL (minimum score 570 paper-based; 230 computer-based). *Application deadline:* For fall admission, 1/15 priority date for domestic students; for spring admission, 10/15 priority date for domestic students. Applications are processed on a rolling basis. Application fee: $45. Electronic applications accepted. *Expenses:* Tuition: Full-time $34,900; part-time $1,454 per credit. Required fees: $1,802. *Financial support:* In 2007–08, 18 students received support, including 8 fellowships with full tuition reimbursements available (averaging $14,500 per year), 1 research assistantship with full tuition reimbursement available (averaging $14,500 per year), 9 teaching assistantships with full tuition reimbursements available (averaging $14,500 per year); career-related internships or fieldwork, institutionally sponsored loans, and unspecified assistantships also available. Financial award application deadline: 1/15. *Faculty research:* Human-computer interaction, media design and theory, rhetoric and culture, virtual institutions/communities, usability. *Application contact:* Kathy A. Colman, Recruitment Coordinator, 518-276-6469, Fax: 518-276-4092, E-mail: colmak@rpi.edu.

See Close-Up on page 925.

San Francisco State University, Division of Graduate Studies, College of Humanities, Department of Communication Studies, San Francisco, CA 94132-1722. Offers MA. Part-time programs available. *Application deadline:* Applications are processed on a rolling basis. *Financial support:* Teaching assistantships available. *Unit head:* Dr. Gerianne Merrigan, Chair, 415-338-1597, E-mail: merrigan@sfsu.edu. *Application contact:* Dr. Mercilee Jenkins, Graduate Coordinator, 415-338-1597, E-mail: leej@sfsu.edu.

San Jose State University, Graduate Studies and Research, College of Social Sciences, Department of History, San Jose, CA 95192-0001. Offers history (MA); history education (MA). *Students:* 10 full-time (4 women), 45 part-time (22 women); includes 6 minority (1 African American, 3 Asian Americans or Pacific Islanders, 2 Hispanic Americans), 1 international. Average age 38. 67 applicants, 78% accepted, 24 enrolled. In 2007, 14 degrees awarded. *Degree requirements:* For master's, comprehensive exam, thesis or alternative. *Entrance requirements:* For master's, bachelor's degree or 15 units of course work in history, minimum GPA of 3.0. *Application deadline:* For fall admission, 2/15 for domestic students. Applications are processed on a rolling basis. Application fee: $59. Electronic applications accepted. *Financial support:* Fellowships available. Financial award applicants required to submit FAFSA. *Unit head:* Jonathan P. Roth, Chair, 408-924-5500, Fax: 408-924-5531. *Application contact:* Patricia Evridge Hill, Graduate Adviser, 408-924-5755.

Seton Hall University, School of Graduate Medical Education, Program in Speech-Language Pathology, South Orange, NJ 07079-2697. Offers MS. *Faculty:* 7 full-time (4 women), 5 part-time/adjunct (3 women). *Students:* 49 full-time (all women); includes 4 minority (3 Asian Americans or Pacific Islanders, 1 Hispanic American), 1 international. Average age 25. 140 applicants, 25% accepted, 28 enrolled. In 2007, 21 degrees awarded. *Entrance requirements:* For master's, GRE, bachelor's degree, clinical experience; minimum GPA of 3.0, undergraduate preprofessional coursework in communication sciences and disorders. *Application deadline:* For fall admission, 3/1 priority date for domestic students. Applications are processed on a rolling basis. Application fee: $75. Electronic applications accepted. *Financial support:* In 2007–08, 1 student received support, including 1 research assistantship with partial tuition reimbursement available (averaging $4,000 per year); unspecified assistantships and student technology assistantships also available. *Faculty research:* Child language disorders, motor speech control, voice disorders, dysphagia, early intervention/teaming. *Unit head:* Dr. Robert F. Orlikoff, Chair, 973-275-2825, Fax: 973-275-2370, E-mail: gradmeded@shu.edu. *Application contact:* Deborah Verderosa, Director of Admissions, 973-275-2062, Fax: 973-275-2370, E-mail: gradmeded@shu.edu.

Southern Illinois University Carbondale, Graduate School, College of Liberal Arts, Department of Speech Communication, Carbondale, IL 62901-4701. Offers speech communication (MA, MS, PhD); speech/theater (PhD). *Faculty:* 16 full-time (8 women). *Students:* 39 full-time (20 women), 42 part-time (23 women); includes 13 minority (8 African Americans, 1 American Indian/Alaska Native, 4 Hispanic Americans), 14 international. 81 applicants, 22% accepted, 5 enrolled. In 2007, 6 master's, 7 doctorates awarded. *Degree requirements:* For master's, one foreign language, thesis or alternative; for doctorate, one foreign language, thesis/dissertation. *Entrance requirements:* For master's, GRE General Test or MAT, minimum GPA of 2.7; for doctorate, GRE General Test or MAT, minimum GPA of 3.25. Additional exam requirements/recommendations for international students: Required—TOEFL. *Application deadline:* For fall admission, 2/1 for domestic students. Application fee: $0. *Financial support:* In 2007–08, 61 students received support, including 4 fellowships with full tuition reimbursements available, 4 research assistantships with full tuition reimbursements available, 50 teaching assistantships with full tuition reimbursements available; Federal Work-Study, institutionally sponsored loans, and tuition waivers (full) also available. Support available to part-time students. *Unit head:* Dr. Nathan Stucky, Chair, 618-453-2291, E-mail: nstucky@siu.edu. *Application contact:* Dr. Ronald Pelias, Graduate Director, 618-453-2291, E-mail: rpelias@siu.edu.

Speech and Interpersonal Communication

Southern Illinois University Carbondale (continued)

Announcement: Known as a program that produces high-quality teachers, the Department of Speech Communication has 100% placement for its graduates. The department offers mentoring for graduate teaching assistants by award-winning and dedicated faculty members who believe teaching matters.

See Close-Up on page 933.

Southern Illinois University Edwardsville, Graduate Studies and Research, College of Arts and Sciences, Department of Speech Communication, Program in Speech Communication, Edwardsville, IL 62026-0001. Offers MA. Part-time and evening/weekend programs available. *Students:* 10 full-time (9 women), 7 part-time (all women); includes 4 minority (3 African Americans, 1 Asian American or Pacific Islander). 12 applicants, 75% accepted. In 2007, 11 degrees awarded. *Degree requirements:* For master's, thesis or alternative, final exam. *Entrance requirements:* Additional exam requirements/recommendations for international students: Required—TOEFL. *Application deadline:* For fall admission, 7/20 for domestic students, 6/1 for international students; for spring admission, 12/14 for domestic students, 10/1 for international students. Application fee: $30. Electronic applications accepted. *Financial support:* In 2007–08, 1 fellowship with full tuition reimbursement, 7 teaching assistantships with full tuition reimbursements were awarded; research assistantships with full tuition reimbursements. *Unit head:* Dr. Waittsien Cheah, Director, 618-650-5016, E-mail: wcheah@siue.edu.

Texas A&M University–Commerce, Graduate School, College of Arts and Sciences, Department of Communication and Theatre, Commerce, TX 75429-3011. Offers theatre (MA, MS). Part-time programs available. *Faculty:* 4 full-time (3 women). *Students:* 7 full-time (3 women), 8 part-time (3 women); includes 6 minority (3 African Americans, 2 American Indian/Alaska Native, 1 Hispanic American). Average age 36. In 2007, 1 degree awarded. *Degree requirements:* For master's, comprehensive exam, thesis (for some programs). *Entrance requirements:* For master's, GRE General Test. *Application deadline:* For fall admission, 6/1 priority date for domestic students; for spring admission, 11/1 priority date for domestic students. Applications are processed on a rolling basis. Application fee: $0 ($25 for international students). Electronic applications accepted. *Financial support:* In 2007–08, research assistantships (averaging $7,875 per year), teaching assistantships (averaging $7,875 per year) were awarded; Federal Work-Study, institutionally sponsored loans, and scholarships/grants also available. Financial award application deadline: 5/1; financial award applicants required to submit FAFSA. *Faculty research:* Theater history. Total annual research expenditures: $45,000. *Unit head:* Dr. John Hanners, Head, 903-886-5346, Fax: 903-468-3250, E-mail: john_hanners@tamu-commerce.edu. *Application contact:* Tammi Thompson, Graduate Admissions Adviser, 843-886-5167, Fax: 843-886-5165, E-mail: tammi_thompson@tamu-commerce.edu.

Texas Christian University, College of Communication, Department of Communication Studies, Fort Worth, TX 76129-0002. Offers communication in human relations (MS). Part-time and evening/weekend programs available. *Entrance requirements:* For master's, GRE General Test. Additional exam requirements/recommendations for international students: Required—TOEFL. *Application deadline:* For fall admission, 3/1 for domestic students; for spring admission, 12/1 for domestic students. Applications are processed on a rolling basis. Application fee: $0. *Expenses:* Tuition: Part-time $865 per credit hour. Required fees: $48 per year. *Financial support:* Unspecified assistantships available. Financial award application deadline: 3/1. *Unit head:* Dr. Chris Sawyer, Chairperson, 817-257-7610.

The University of Alabama, Graduate School, College of Communication and Information Sciences, Department of Communication Studies, Tuscaloosa, AL 35487. Offers MA. *Faculty:* 7 full-time (4 women). *Students:* 15 full-time (8 women), 2 part-time (both women); includes 6 minority (5 African Americans, 1 American Indian/Alaska Native), 1 international. Average age 25. 25 applicants, 64% accepted, 8 enrolled. In 2007, 7 degrees awarded. *Degree requirements:* For master's, comprehensive exam (for some programs), thesis optional, research colloquium presentation, final practicum report. *Entrance requirements:* For master's, GRE. Additional exam requirements/recommendations for international students: Required—TOEFL (minimum score 550 paper-based; 213 computer-based). *Application deadline:* For fall admission, 5/1 for domestic and international students; for spring admission, 11/1 for domestic and international students. Applications are processed on a rolling basis. Application fee: $30. Electronic applications accepted. *Expenses:* Tuition, state resident: full-time $5,700. Tuition, nonresident: full-time $16,518. *Financial support:* In 2007–08, 7 students received support, including 1 research assistantship with full tuition reimbursement available (averaging $10,908 per year), 6 teaching assistantships with full tuition reimbursements available (averaging $10,908 per year); career-related internships or fieldwork and health care benefits also available. Financial award application deadline: 5/1. *Faculty research:* Rhetorical theory, organizational communication, communication theory. *Unit head:* Dr. Beth S. Bennett, Chair and Associate Professor, 205-348-5997, Fax: 205-348-8080, E-mail: bbennett@bama.ua.edu. *Application contact:* Dr. Tom Harris, Graduate Coordinator and Professor, 205-348-5997, Fax: 205-348-8080, E-mail: tharris@ua.edu.

University of Arkansas at Little Rock, Graduate School, College of Professional Studies, Department of Speech Communication, Little Rock, AR 72204-1099. Offers applied communication studies (MA). Part-time and evening/weekend programs available. *Students:* Average age 32. *Degree requirements:* For master's, comprehensive exam, internship, paper, or thesis. *Entrance requirements:* For master's, GRE General Test, MAT, minimum GPA of 2.7. *Application deadline:* Applications are processed on a rolling basis. *Financial support:* Research assistantships, career-related internships or fieldwork, Federal Work-Study, institutionally sponsored loans, and unspecified assistantships available. *Faculty research:* Communication theory and applications, managerial communication, human resource training and development, health communication. *Unit head:* Dr. Robert R. Ulmer, Chairperson, 501-569-3158, E-mail: rrulmer@ualr.edu. *Application contact:* Dr. Linda M. Pledger, Coordinator, 501-569-3158, E-mail: lmpledger@ualr.edu.

University of Central Missouri, The Graduate School, College of Arts, Humanities and Social Sciences, Department of Communication, Warrensburg, MO 64093. Offers communication (MA); speech communication (MA). Part-time programs available. *Faculty:* 15 full-time (7 women). *Students:* 15 full-time (7 women), 39 part-time (26 women); includes 4 minority (2 African Americans, 1 American Indian/Alaska Native, 1 Asian American or Pacific Islander), 11 international. Average age 29. 33 applicants, 55% accepted, 11 enrolled. In 2007, 13 degrees awarded. *Degree requirements:* For master's, comprehensive exam, internship, research papers or thesis. *Entrance requirements:* For master's, minimum GPA of 2.5. Additional exam requirements/recommendations for international students: Required—TOEFL (minimum score 500 paper-based; 173 computer-based). *Application deadline:* For fall admission, 6/1 priority date for domestic students, 5/1 priority date for international students; for spring admission, 10/1 priority date for domestic students, 10/1 for international students. Applications are processed on a rolling basis. Application fee: $30 ($50 for international students). *Expenses:* Tuition, state resident: full-time $6,259; part-time $256 per credit hour. Tuition, nonresident: full-time $11,915; part-time $491 per credit hour. Required fees: $604; $20 per credit hour. *Financial support:* In 2007–08, 14 students received support; teaching assistantships with full tuition reimbursements available, career-related internships or fieldwork, Federal Work-Study, scholarships/grants, unspecified assistantships, and administrative and laboratory assistantships available. Support available to part-time students. Financial award application deadline: 3/1; financial award applicants required to submit FAFSA. *Unit head:* Dr. Terry Cunconan, Chair, 660-543-4890, Fax: 660-543-8006, E-mail: cunconan@ucmo.edu.

University of Central Missouri, The Graduate School, College of Health and Human Services, Department of Communication Disorders, Warrensburg, MO 64093. Offers speech pathology and audiology (MS). Part-time programs available. *Faculty:* 8 full-time (4 women). *Students:* 51 full-time (47 women), 11 part-time (all women); includes 3 minority (1 African American, 2 Hispanic Americans), 1 international. Average age 27. 33 applicants, 79% accepted, 10 enrolled. In 2007, 22 degrees awarded. *Degree requirements:* For master's, project, research paper, or thesis; observation (25 hours); clinical practicum (350 hours); National Examination in Speech Pathology and Audiology (NESPA) exam. *Entrance requirements:* For master's, GRE, minimum GPA of 3.0, clinical practicum. Additional exam requirements/recommendations for international students: Required—TOEFL (minimum score 500 paper-based; 173 computer-based). *Application deadline:* For fall admission, 6/1 priority date for domestic students, 5/1 priority date for international students; for spring admission, 10/1 priority date for domestic students, 10/1 for international students. Applications are processed on a rolling basis. Application fee: $30 ($50 for international students). *Expenses:* Tuition, state resident: full-time $6,259; part-time $256 per credit hour. Tuition, nonresident: full-time $11,915; part-time $491 per credit hour. Required fees: $604; $20 per credit hour. *Financial support:* In 2007–08, 14 students received support; teaching assistantships with partial tuition reimbursements available, Federal Work-Study, scholarships/grants, unspecified assistantships, and administrative and laboratory assistantships available. Support available to part-time students. Financial award application deadline: 3/1; financial award applicants required to submit FAFSA. *Faculty research:* Motor Speech disorders, Autism Intervention, Pediatric Swallowing Disorders, Adult Swallowing Disorders, Clinical Supervision. Total annual research expenditures: $286,898. *Unit head:* Dr. Carl Harlan, Chair, 660-543-4918, Fax: 660-543-4918, E-mail: harlan@ucmo.edu.

University of Denver, Faculty of Arts and Humanities/Social Sciences, School of Communication, Department of Human Communication Studies, Denver, CO 80208. Offers MA, PhD. Part-time programs available. *Faculty:* 11 full-time (8 women). *Students:* 32 full-time (20 women), 8 part-time (6 women); includes 8 minority (4 African Americans, 1 American Indian/Alaska Native, 2 Asian Americans or Pacific Islanders, 1 Hispanic American), 2 international. Average age 33. In 2007, 1 master's, 5 doctorates awarded. *Degree requirements:* For master's, comprehensive exam or thesis; for doctorate, one foreign language, thesis/dissertation. *Entrance requirements:* For master's and doctorate, GRE General Test. Additional exam requirements/recommendations for international students: Required—TOEFL, TWE. *Application deadline:* Applications are processed on a rolling basis. Application fee: $50. *Financial support:* In 2007–08, 30 students received support, including 17 teaching assistantships with full and partial tuition reimbursements available (averaging $11,300 per year); career-related internships or fieldwork, Federal Work-Study, institutionally sponsored loans, and scholarships/grants also available. Support available to part-time students. Financial award application deadline: 2/10; financial award applicants required to submit FAFSA. *Faculty research:* Successful community collaborative efforts, long-term marriages, cross-ethnic friendships, public dialogue about environmental risk, women's international cooperation. Total annual research expenditures: $56,000. *Unit head:* Dr. Roy Wood, Chair, 303-871-2385. *Application contact:* Information Contact, 303-871-4313, E-mail: joasmith@du.edu.

See Close-Up on page 939.

University of Georgia, Graduate School, College of Arts and Sciences, Department of Speech Communication, Athens, GA 30602. Offers MA, PhD. *Faculty:* 13 full-time (6 women). *Students:* 32 full-time (22 women), 1 part-time; includes 3 minority (2 African Americans, 1 Hispanic American), 2 international. 66 applicants, 27% accepted, 10 enrolled. In 2007, 5 master's, 4 doctorates awarded. *Degree requirements:* For master's, thesis; for doctorate, one foreign language, thesis/dissertation. *Entrance requirements:* For master's and doctorate, GRE General Test. *Application deadline:* For fall admission, 7/1 priority date for domestic students; for spring admission, 11/15 for domestic students. Application fee: $50. Electronic applications accepted. *Financial support:* Fellowships, research assistantships, teaching assistantships, unspecified assistantships available. *Unit head:* Dr. Jerold L. Hale, Head, 706-542-4893, Fax: 706-542-3245, E-mail: jhale@uga.edu. *Application contact:* Dr. Jennifer A. Samp, Graduate Coordinator, 706-542-3250.

University of Hawaii at Manoa, Graduate Division, Colleges of Arts and Sciences, College of Arts and Humanities, Department of Speech, Honolulu, HI 96822. Offers MA. Part-time programs available. *Faculty:* 13 full-time (5 women). *Students:* 16 full-time (13 women), 3 part-time (2 women); includes 13 minority (1 African American, 12 Asian Americans or Pacific Islanders), 1 international. Average age 28. 15 applicants, 73% accepted, 10 enrolled. *Degree requirements:* For master's, thesis optional. *Entrance requirements:* For master's, GRE General Test. Additional exam requirements/recommendations for international students: Required—TOEFL (minimum score 600 paper-based; 250 computer-based; 100 iBT), IELTS (minimum score 7). *Application deadline:* For fall admission, 3/1 for domestic students, 1/15 for international students; for spring admission, 9/1 for domestic students, 8/1 for international students. Application fee: $50. *Financial support:* In 2007–08, 1 research assistantship (averaging $15,552 per year), 8 teaching assistantships (averaging $13,430 per year) were awarded; tuition waivers (full) also available. *Faculty research:* Social influence, relational management, message processing, intercultural communication. Total annual research expenditures:$9,500. *Application contact:* Min-Sun Kim, Graduate Chairperson, 808-956-3316, Fax: 808-956-3947, E-mail: kmin@hawaii.edu.

University of Houston, College of Liberal Arts and Social Sciences, School of Communication, Houston, TX 77204. Offers mass communication studies (MA); public relations studies (MA); speech communication (MA). Part-time and evening/weekend programs available. *Faculty:* 8 full-time (3 women), 3 part-time/adjunct (2 women). *Students:* 34 full-time (30 women), 53 part-time (40 women); includes 37 minority (24 African Americans, 3 Asian Americans or Pacific Islanders, 10 Hispanic Americans), 11 international. Average age 29. 46 applicants, 80% accepted, 18 enrolled. In 2007, 24 degrees awarded. *Entrance requirements:* For master's, GRE General Test, minimum GPA of 3.0 in last 60 hours of course work. *Application deadline:* For fall admission, 7/3 priority date for domestic students. Applications are processed on a rolling basis. Application fee: $25 ($75 for international students). *Expenses:* Tuition, state resident: full-time $6,297; part-time $262 per credit. Tuition, nonresident: full-time $12,969; part-time $540 per credit. Required fees: $2,696. *Financial support:* In 2007–08, 4 fellowships with full tuition reimbursements (averaging $9,750 per year), 8 teaching assistantships with full tuition reimbursements (averaging $9,750 per year) were awarded; research assistantships with full tuition reimbursements, career-related internships or fieldwork, Federal Work-Study, institutionally sponsored loans, scholarships/grants, health care benefits, and unspecified assistantships also available. Support available to part-time students. Financial award application deadline: 2/1. *Faculty research:* Risk communication, relationship development, critical studies, corporate communication. *Unit head:* Beth Olson, Chairperson, 713-743-2873, Fax: 713-743-2876, E-mail: bolson@uh.edu. *Application contact:* Angela Parrish, Graduate Coordinator, 713-743-2873, Fax: 713-743-2876, E-mail: aparrish@bayou.uh.edu.

University of Illinois at Urbana–Champaign, Graduate College, College of Liberal Arts and Sciences, Department of Speech Communication, Champaign, IL 61820. Offers MA, PhD. *Faculty:* 26 full-time (12 women). *Students:* 39 full-time (27 women), 20 part-time (9 women); includes 8 minority (2 African Americans, 4 Asian Americans or Pacific Islanders, 2 Hispanic Americans), 2 international. 85 applicants, 34% accepted, 15 enrolled. In 2007, 19 master's, 9 doctorates awarded. *Degree requirements:* For master's, thesis optional; for doctorate, thesis/dissertation. *Entrance requirements:* For master's, GRE, minimum GPA of 3.0. *Application deadline:* For fall admission, 2/1 priority date for domestic students. Applications are processed on a rolling basis. Application fee: $60 ($75 for international students). Electronic applications accepted. *Financial support:* In 2007–08, 4 fellowships, 19 research assistantships, 52 teaching assistantships were awarded. Financial award application deadline: 2/15. *Unit head:* Barbara J. Wilson, Head, 217-333-2683, Fax: 217-244-1598, E-mail: bjwilson@uiuc.edu. *Application contact:* Mary Strum, Graduate Program Secretary, 217-333-2683, Fax: 217-244-1598, E-mail: strum@uiuc.edu.

University of Maryland, College Park, Graduate Studies, College of Behavioral and Social Sciences, Department of Hearing and Speech Sciences, College Park, MD 20742. Offers audiology (MA, PhD); hearing and speech sciences (Au D); language pathology (MA, PhD); neuroscience (PhD); speech (MA, PhD). *Accreditation:* ASHA (one or more programs are accredited). *Faculty:* 19 full-time (all women), 12 part-time/adjunct (9 women). *Students:* 68

full-time (66 women), 22 part-time (all women); includes 18 minority (7 African Americans, 6 Asian Americans or Pacific Islanders, 5 Hispanic Americans), 2 international. 257 applicants, 43% accepted, 30 enrolled. In 2007, 24 master's, 1 doctorate awarded. *Degree requirements:* For master's, thesis optional; for doctorate, thesis/dissertation, written and oral exams. *Entrance requirements:* For master's, GRE General Test, minimum GPA of 3.5, 3 letters of recommendation; for doctorate, GRE General Test, minimum GPA of 3.5. Additional exam requirements/recommendations for international students: Required—TOEFL. *Application deadline:* For fall admission, 1/15 for domestic and international students. Applications are processed on a rolling basis. Application fee: $60. Electronic applications accepted. *Financial support:* In 2007–08, 2 fellowships with full tuition reimbursements (averaging $6,963 per year), 2 research assistantships (averaging $14,371 per year), 19 teaching assistantships with tuition reimbursements (averaging $13,951 per year) were awarded; career-related internships or fieldwork, Federal Work-Study, and scholarships/grants also available. Support available to part-time students. Financial award applicants required to submit FAFSA. *Faculty research:* Speech perception, language acquisition, bilingualism, hearing loss. Total annual research expenditures: $512,784. *Unit head:* Dr. Nan B. Ratner, Chair, 301-405-4213, Fax: 301-314-2023, E-mail: nratner@umd.edu. *Application contact:* Dean of Graduate School, 301-405-4190, Fax: 301-314-9305.

University of Nevada, Reno, Graduate School, College of Liberal Arts, Department of Speech Communications, Reno, NV 89557. Offers MA. *Faculty:* 8. *Students:* 2 full-time (both women), 9 part-time (7 women); includes 1 minority (Hispanic American) Average age 30. 11 applicants, 55% accepted, 6 enrolled. In 2007, 5 degrees awarded. *Degree requirements:* For master's, thesis optional. *Entrance requirements:* For master's, GRE General Test, minimum GPA of 3.0. Additional exam requirements/recommendations for international students: Required—TOEFL. *Application deadline:* For fall admission, 3/1 priority date for domestic students; for spring admission, 11/1 for domestic students. Applications are processed on a rolling basis. Application fee: $60 ($95 for international students). *Expenses:* Tuition, state resident: full-time $2,774; part-time $154 per credit. Tuition, nonresident: full-time $13,578; part-time $330 per credit. Required fees: $49 per semester. *Financial support:* In 2007–08, 4 teaching assistantships were awarded; Federal Work-Study and institutionally sponsored loans also available. Financial award application deadline: 3/1. *Faculty research:* Rhetorical theory and criticism; communications/sex roles; judicial, legal, contextual, and behavioral approaches to communication theory. *Unit head:* Dr. Gwen Hullman, Graduate Program Director, 775-784-4854.

University of South Carolina, The Graduate School, College of Education, Department of Instruction and Teacher Education, Program in Secondary Education, Columbia, SC 29208. Offers art education (IMA, MAT); business education (IMA, MAT); English (MAT); foreign language (MAT); health education (MAT); mathematics (MAT); science (IMA, MAT); secondary (Ed D); secondary education (MT, PhD); social studies (MAT); theatre and speech (MAT). IMA and MT offered jointly with the subject areas. *Accreditation:* NCATE. *Faculty:* 6 full-time (5 women), 7 part-time/adjunct (5 women). *Students:* 93 full-time (61 women), 35 part-time (22 women); includes 14 minority (10 African Americans, 1 American Indian/Alaska Native, 1 Asian American or Pacific Islander, 2 Hispanic Americans). 40 applicants, 50% accepted, 16 enrolled. In 2007, 108 master's, 1 doctorate awarded. *Degree requirements:* For master's, comprehensive exam, thesis (for some programs), foreign language (MA); for doctorate, one foreign language, comprehensive exam, thesis/dissertation. *Entrance requirements:* For master's, GRE General Test or MAT, teaching certificate (IMA, M Ed), interview; for doctorate, GRE General Test or MAT, interview. Application fee: $40. *Expenses:* Tuition, state resident: part-time $440 per hour. Tuition, nonresident: part-time $936 per hour. Required fees: $17 per hour. Tuition and fees vary according to program. *Faculty research:* Middle school programs, professional development, school collaboration. *Unit head:* Dr. Ed Dickey, Professor/Coordinator, 803-777-6235, Fax: 803-777-3193, E-mail: edickey@gwm.sc.edu. *Application contact:* 803-777-6732, Fax: 803-777-3068, E-mail: teach@gwm.sc.edu.

University of Southern California, Graduate School, Annenberg School for Communication, School of Communication, Program in Communication, Los Angeles, CA 90089. Offers communication (MA, PhD), including interpersonal and social dynamics (PhD), mass communication, technology, and public policy (PhD), organizational communication (PhD), rhetorical and cultural studies (PhD). *Students:* 86 full-time (52 women); includes 16 minority (3 African Americans, 2 American Indian/Alaska Native, 5 Asian Americans or Pacific Islanders, 6 Hispanic Americans), 24 international. Average age 31. 196 applicants, 13% accepted, 19 enrolled. In 2007, 16 degrees awarded. *Median time to degree:* Of those who began their doctoral program in fall 1999, 89% received their degree in 8 years or less. *Degree requirements:* For doctorate, thesis/dissertation. *Entrance requirements:* For master's and doctorate, GRE General Test, resumé, writing samples, 3 letters of recommendation, interest survey questionnaire, statement of purpose. Additional exam requirements/recommendations for international students: Required—TOEFL (minimum score 280 computer-based; 115 iBT); Recommended—TWE. *Application deadline:* For fall admission, 11/30 for domestic and international students. Application fee: $85. Electronic applications accepted. *Financial support:* In 2007–08, 18 students received support, including 18 fellowships with full tuition reimbursements available (averaging $26,500 per year); research assistantships, teaching assistantships, Federal Work-Study, institutionally sponsored loans, scholarships/grants, health care benefits, tuition waivers (partial), and unspecified assistantships also available. Support available to part-time students. Financial award application deadline: 1/1; financial award applicants required to submit FAFSA. *Faculty research:* Computer-mediated communication, public health campaigns, communication democracy and the public sphere, new communication technologies in organizations, community and community. *Unit head:* Dr. Thomas Goodnight, Director, 213-821-5384. *Application contact:* Allyson Hill, Director of Admissions, 213-821-0770, E-mail: ascadm@usc.edu.

See Close-Up on page 945.

University of Southern Mississippi, Graduate School, College of Arts and Letters, Department of Speech Communication, Hattiesburg, MS 39406-0001. Offers MA, MS, PhD. *Faculty:* 10 full-time (3 women). *Students:* 7 full-time (5 women), 14 part-time (8 women); includes 4 minority (2 African Americans, 1 Asian American or Pacific Islander, 1 Hispanic American). Average age 37. 13 applicants, 46% accepted, 4 enrolled. In 2007, 4 master's, 4 doctorates awarded. *Degree requirements:* For master's, comprehensive exam, thesis optional; for doctorate, comprehensive exam, thesis/dissertation. *Entrance requirements:* For master's, GRE General Test, minimum GPA of 3.0 last 60 hours, 3.0 in major; for doctorate, GRE General Test, minimum GPA of 3.5. Additional exam requirements/recommendations for international students: Required—TOEFL. *Application deadline:* For fall admission, 3/1 priority date for domestic students, 3/1 for international students. Application fee: $30. *Financial support:* In 2007–08, 2 research assistantships with tuition reimbursements (averaging $12,071 per year), 4 teaching assistantships with tuition reimbursements (averaging $12,071 per year) were awarded; Federal Work-Study, scholarships/grants, and unspecified assistantships also available. Financial award application deadline: 3/15. *Faculty research:* Persuasion and social influence, interpersonal communication, organizational communication, political communication, crisis communication. *Unit head:* Dr. Charles Tardy, Chair, 601-266-4271, Fax: 601-266-4275. *Application contact:* Dr. Lawrence Hosman, Graduate Coordinator, 601-266-4271, Fax: 601-266-4275.

The University of Tennessee, Graduate School, College of Communication and Information, Knoxville, TN 37996. Offers advertising (MS, PhD); broadcasting (MS, PhD); communications (MS, PhD); information sciences (MS, PhD); journalism (MS, PhD); public relations (MS, PhD); speech communication (MS, PhD). *Accreditation:* ACEJMC (one or more programs are accredited at the [master's] level). Part-time and evening/weekend programs available. Postbaccalaureate distance learning degree programs offered (no on-campus study). *Degree requirements:* For master's, thesis or alternative; for doctorate, thesis/dissertation. *Entrance requirements:* For master's and doctorate, GRE General Test, minimum GPA of 2.7. Additional exam requirements/recommendations for international students: Required—TOEFL. Electronic applications accepted.

University of Wisconsin–Stevens Point, College of Fine Arts and Communication, Division of Communication, Stevens Point, WI 54481-3897. Offers interpersonal communication (MA); mass communication (MA); organizational communication (MA); public relations (MA). Part-time programs available. *Degree requirements:* For master's, thesis or alternative. *Entrance requirements:* For master's, GRE. Additional exam requirements/recommendations for international students: Required—TOEFL (minimum score 575 paper-based). *Application deadline:* For fall admission, 3/1 priority date for domestic students. Applications are processed on a rolling basis. Application fee: $45. *Expenses:* Tuition, state resident: full-time $6,161. Tuition, nonresident: full-time $16,771. Required fees: $884. Tuition and fees vary according to course load. *Financial support:* In 2007–08, 9 teaching assistantships were awarded; career-related internships or fieldwork, Federal Work-Study, institutionally sponsored loans, and unspecified assistantships also available. Support available to part-time students. Financial award application deadline: 5/1; financial award applicants required to submit FAFSA. *Faculty research:* Communication theory and research, film history. *Unit head:* Dr. James Haney, Chair, 715-346-3409, E-mail: jhaney@uwsp.edu. *Application contact:* Dr. Chris Sadler, Graduate Coordinator, 715-346-3898, E-mail: csadler@uwsp.edu.

University of Wisconsin–Superior, Graduate Division, Department of Communicating Arts, Superior, WI 54880-4500. Offers mass communication (MA); speech communication (MA); theater (MA). Part-time programs available. *Degree requirements:* For master's, comprehensive exam, thesis or alternative, position paper or project. *Entrance requirements:* For master's, minimum GPA of 2.75. *Faculty research:* Multimedia technology, ethics in journalism, diversity, electronic portfolio assessment.

Wake Forest University, Graduate School of Arts and Sciences, Department of Communication, Winston-Salem, NC 27109. Offers speech communication (MA). Part-time programs available. *Faculty:* 12 full-time (3 women). *Students:* 16 full-time (10 women), 1 (woman) part-time, 5 international. Average age 23. 28 applicants, 50% accepted, 7 enrolled. In 2007, 7 degrees awarded. *Degree requirements:* For master's, one foreign language, thesis. *Entrance requirements:* For master's, GRE General Test, writing sample. Additional exam requirements/recommendations for international students: Required—TOEFL (minimum score 213 computer-based; 79 iBT). *Application deadline:* For fall admission, 1/15 for domestic and international students. Application fee: $45 ($55 for international students). Electronic applications accepted. *Financial support:* In 2007–08, 17 students received support, including 1 research assistantship with full tuition reimbursement available (averaging $8,000 per year), 15 teaching assistantships with full tuition reimbursements available (averaging $8,000 per year); fellowships with full tuition reimbursements available, scholarships/grants, tuition waivers (full and partial), and unspecified assistantships also available. Support available to part-time students. Financial award application deadline: 1/15; financial award applicants required to submit FAFSA. *Unit head:* Ananda Mitra, Director, 336-758-5134, Fax: 336-758-4691, E-mail: ananda@wfu.edu.

Washington University in St. Louis, School of Medicine, Program in Audiology and Communication Sciences, St Louis, MO 63110. Offers audiology (Au D); deaf education (MS); speech and hearing sciences (PhD). *Accreditation:* ASHA (one or more programs are accredited). *Faculty:* 22 full-time (12 women), 18 part-time/adjunct (12 women). *Students:* 75 full-time (74 women); includes 4 minority (1 African American, 2 Asian Americans or Pacific Islanders, 1 Hispanic American), 1 international. Average age 24. 116 applicants, 26% accepted, 30 enrolled. In 2007, 11 master's, 13 doctorates awarded. *Median time to degree:* Of those who began their doctoral program in fall 1999, 100% received their degree in 8 years or less. *Degree requirements:* For master's, comprehensive exam, thesis, independent study project, oral exam; for doctorate, comprehensive exam, thesis/dissertation, capstone project, oral exam. *Entrance requirements:* For master's, GRE General Test, minimum B average in undergraduate course work; for doctorate, GRE General Test, minimum B average. Additional exam requirements/recommendations for international students: Required—TOEFL (minimum score 600 paper-based; 250 computer-based; 100 iBT). *Application deadline:* For fall admission, 2/15 for domestic and international students. Application fee: $50 ($75 for international students). Electronic applications accepted. *Expenses:* Contact institution. *Financial support:* In 2007–08, 75 students received support, including 75 fellowships (averaging $13,129 per year); career-related internships or fieldwork, institutionally sponsored loans, scholarships/grants, health care benefits, tuition waivers (partial), and unspecified assistantships also available. Support available to part-time students. Financial award application deadline: 2/15; financial award applicants required to submit FAFSA. *Faculty research:* Sensory aids, noise, speech perception, biological deafness, audiology. *Unit head:* Dr. William W. Clark, Program Director, 314-747-0104, Fax: 314-747-0105, E-mail: clarkw@wustl.edu. *Application contact:* Elizabeth A. Elliott, Graduate Program Coordinator, 314-747-0104, Fax: 314-747-0105, E-mail: elliottb@wustl.edu.

Wayne State University, College of Fine, Performing and Communication Arts, Department of Communication, Detroit, MI 48202. Offers communication studies (MA, PhD); public relations and organizational communication (MA); radio-TV-film (MA, PhD); speech communication (MA, PhD). *Students:* 74 full-time (49 women), 128 part-time (94 women); includes 63 minority (51 African Americans, 1 American Indian/Alaska Native, 3 Asian Americans or Pacific Islanders, 8 Hispanic Americans), 14 international. Average age 34. 92 applicants, 62% accepted, 42 enrolled. In 2007, 39 master's, 6 doctorates awarded. *Degree requirements:* For master's, thesis, essay, or comprehensive exam; for doctorate, thesis/dissertation. *Entrance requirements:* For master's, minimum GPA of 3.0, personal statement; sample of academic writing; for doctorate, GRE, minimum GPA of 3.3, MA; letters of recommendation; personal statement; sample of written scholarship. Additional exam requirements/recommendations for international students: Required—TOEFL (minimum score 550 paper-based; 213 computer-based); Recommended—TWE (minimum score 6). *Application deadline:* For fall admission, 4/1 for domestic students, 6/1 for international students; for winter admission, 10/1 for international students; for spring admission, 2/1 for international students. Applications are processed on a rolling basis. Application fee: $30 ($50 for international students). Electronic applications accepted. *Expenses:* Tuition, state resident: part-time $403 per credit hour. Tuition, nonresident: part-time $890 per credit hour. *Financial support:* In 2007–08, 22 students received support, including 2 fellowships with tuition reimbursements available (averaging $14,351 per year), 17 teaching assistantships with tuition reimbursements available (averaging $12,922 per year); research assistantships with tuition reimbursements available, career-related internships or fieldwork also available. Financial award application deadline: 2/1. *Faculty research:* Rhetorical theory and criticism; mass media theory and research; argumentation; organizational communication; risk and crisis communication; interpersonal, family, and health communication. *Unit head:* Dr. Matthew Seeger, Chair, 313-577-2959, Fax: 313-577-6300, E-mail: aa4331@wayne.edu. *Application contact:* Hayg Oshagan, Associate Professor, 313-577-0429, E-mail: ad4570@wayne.edu.

Technical Communication

Boise State University, Graduate College, College of Arts and Sciences, Department of English, Program in Technical Communication, Boise, ID 83725-0399. Offers MA. Part-time programs available. *Degree requirements:* For master's, thesis. *Entrance requirements:* For master's, minimum GPA of 3.0. Electronic applications accepted.

Bowling Green State University, Graduate College, College of Arts and Sciences, Department of English, Program in English, Bowling Green, OH 43403. Offers English (MA, PhD); literature (MA); rhetoric and writing (PhD); scientific and technical communication (MA). Part-time programs available. *Students:* 49 full-time (36 women), 12 part-time (9 women); includes 1 African American, 3 Asian Americans or Pacific Islanders, 1 Hispanic American, 9 international. Average age 31. 64 applicants, 67% accepted, 21 enrolled. In 2007, 14 master's, 6 doctorates awarded. *Degree requirements:* For master's, thesis or alternative; for doctorate, comprehensive exam, thesis/dissertation, foreign language or proficiency in Old English. *Entrance requirements:* For master's and doctorate, GRE General Test. Additional exam requirements/recommendations for international students: Required—TOEFL. *Application deadline:* For fall admission, 2/15 priority date for domestic students. Applications are processed on a rolling basis. Application fee: $30. Electronic applications accepted. *Financial support:* In 2007–08, 3 fellowships with full tuition reimbursements (averaging $14,707 per year), 8 research assistantships with full tuition reimbursements (averaging $9,664 per year), 34 teaching assistantships with full tuition reimbursements (averaging $10,480 per year) were awarded; Federal Work-Study and unspecified assistantships also available. Financial award applicants required to submit FAFSA. *Faculty research:* Postmodern literary theory, rhetorical theory, ethnic American literature, literature and culture, composition pedagogy.

Colorado State University, Graduate School, College of Liberal Arts, Department of Journalism and Technical Communication, Fort Collins, CO 80523-0015. Offers technical communication (MS). Part-time programs available. *Faculty:* 17 full-time (6 women). *Students:* 17 full-time (12 women), 26 part-time (19 women); includes 8 minority (2 American Indian/Alaska Native, 1 Asian American or Pacific Islander, 5 Hispanic Americans), 2 international. Average age 34. 24 applicants, 67% accepted, 7 enrolled. In 2007, 9 master's awarded. *Degree requirements:* For master's, thesis (for some programs). *Entrance requirements:* For master's, GRE General Test, samples of written work, letters of recommendation, resumé or curriculum vita, 3 writing/communication projects. Additional exam requirements/recommendations for international students: Required—TOEFL (minimum score 600 paper-based; 250 computer-based). *Application deadline:* For fall admission, 4/1 priority date for domestic students, 4/1 for international students. Applications are processed on a rolling basis. Application fee: $50. Electronic applications accepted. *Expenses:* Tuition, state resident: full-time $4,887; part-time $272 per credit. Tuition, nonresident: full-time $16,425; part-time $913 per credit. Required fees: $1,379; $75 per credit. *Financial support:* In 2007–08, 18 students received support, including 3 research assistantships with full and partial tuition reimbursements available (averaging $7,694 per year), 11 teaching assistantships with partial tuition reimbursements available (averaging $7,474 per year); fellowships with partial tuition reimbursements available, career-related internships or fieldwork, Federal Work-Study, institutionally sponsored loans, scholarships/grants, traineeships, and unspecified assistantships also available. Support available to part-time students. Financial award application deadline: 3/1; financial award applicants required to submit FAFSA. *Faculty research:* Technical/science communication, public relations, health/risk communication, web/new media technologies, environmental communication. Total annual research expenditures: $332,610. *Unit head:* Greg Luft, Chair, 970-491-6310, Fax: 970-491-2908. *Application contact:* Cindy Christen, Associate Professor and Graduate Program Coordinator, 970-491-6319, Fax: 970-491-2908, E-mail: cindy.christen@colostate.edu.

Eastern Michigan University, Graduate School, College of Arts and Sciences, Department of English Language and Literature, Program in Written and Technical Communications, Ypsilanti, MI 48197. Offers technical communications (MA, Graduate Certificate); written communications (MA). Part-time and evening/weekend programs available. Postbaccalaureate distance learning degree programs offered (minimal on-campus study). *Students:* 8 full-time (3 women), 39 part-time (29 women); includes 6 minority (4 African Americans, 2 Asian Americans or Pacific Islanders). Average age 33. In 2007, 19 degrees awarded. *Entrance requirements:* Additional exam requirements/recommendations for international students: Required—TOEFL. *Application deadline:* Applications are processed on a rolling basis. Application fee: $35. *Expenses:* Tuition, state resident: full-time $8,952; part-time $373 per credit hour. Tuition, nonresident: full-time $17,634; part-time $735 per credit hour. Required fees: $896; $34 per credit hour. Tuition and fees vary according to course level, degree level and program. *Financial support:* Fellowships, research assistantships with full tuition reimbursements, teaching assistantships with full tuition reimbursements, career-related internships or fieldwork, Federal Work-Study, institutionally sponsored loans, scholarships/grants, tuition waivers (partial), and unspecified assistantships available. Support available to part-time students. Financial award applicants required to submit FAFSA. *Application contact:* Prof. Steven Krause, Program Advisor, 734-487-1363, Fax: 734-483-9744, E-mail: skrause@emich.edu.

Harvard University, Graduate School of Education, Master's Programs in Education, Cambridge, MA 02138. Offers arts in education (Ed M); education policy and management (Ed M); higher education (Ed M); human development and psychology (Ed M); international education policy (Ed M); language and literacy (Ed M); learning and teaching (Ed M); mid-career mathematics and science (teaching certificate) (Ed M); mind brain and education (Ed M); risk and prevention (Ed M); school leadership (Ed M); special studies (Ed M); teaching and curriculum (teaching certificate) (Ed M); technology innovation and education (Ed M). Part-time programs available. *Faculty:* 67 full-time (34 women), 31 part-time/adjunct (15 women). *Students:* 515 full-time (395 women), 71 part-time (55 women); includes 135 minority (46 African Americans, 1 American Indian/Alaska Native, 55 Asian Americans or Pacific Islanders, 33 Hispanic Americans), 72 international. Average age 28. 1,219 applicants, 61% accepted, 537 enrolled. In 2007, 610 degrees awarded. *Entrance requirements:* For master's, GRE General Test, 3 letters of recommendation, official transcripts, statement of purpose. Additional exam requirements/recommendations for international students: Required—TOEFL (minimum score 600 paper-based; 250 computer-based; 100 iBT), TWE (minimum score 5). *Application deadline:* For fall admission, 1/4 for domestic and international students. Application fee: $85. Electronic applications accepted. *Expenses:* Contact institution. *Financial support:* In 2007–08, 375 students received support, including 31 fellowships with full and partial tuition reimbursements available (averaging $17,189 per year); career-related internships or fieldwork, Federal Work-Study, institutionally sponsored loans, scholarships/grants, health care benefits, tuition waivers (full and partial), and unspecified assistantships also available. Support available to part-time students. Financial award application deadline: 2/1; financial award applicants required to submit FAFSA. *Faculty research:* Learning and development; educational leadership and organizations; educational policy analysis. Total annual research expenditures: $16.7 million. *Unit head:* Jennifer L. Petrallia, Assistant Dean for Master's Studies, 617-495-8445. *Application contact:* Information Contact, 617-495-3414, Fax: 617-496-3577, E-mail: gseadmissions@harvard.edu.

Lawrence Technological University, College of Arts and Sciences, Southfield, MI 48075-1058. Offers computer science (MS); educational technology (MET); science education (MSE); technical communication (MS). Part-time and evening/weekend programs available. *Faculty:* 14 full-time (6 women), 14 part-time/adjunct (4 women). *Students:* 6 full-time (2 women), 144 part-time (65 women); includes 6 minority (5 African Americans, 1 Asian American or Pacific Islander), 66 international. Average age 31. 370 applicants, 61% accepted, 47 enrolled. In 2007, 40 degrees awarded. *Degree requirements:* For master's, thesis (for some programs). *Entrance requirements:* For master's, GRE. Additional exam requirements/recommendations for international students: Required—TOEFL (minimum score 550 paper-based; 213 computer-based; 79 iBT). *Application deadline:* For fall admission, 8/1 priority date for domestic students, 6/1 for international students; for winter admission, 12/1 priority date for domestic students, 10/1 for international students; for spring admission, 5/1 priority date for domestic students, 3/1 for international students. Applications are processed on a rolling basis. Application fee: $50. Electronic applications accepted. *Expenses:* Tuition: Part-time $710 per credit hour. Tuition and fees vary according to campus/location and program. *Financial support:* In 2007–08, 31 students received support. Federal Work-Study available. Financial award application deadline: 4/1; financial award applicants required to submit FAFSA. *Unit head:* Dr. Hsiao-Ping Moore, Dean, 248-204-3500, Fax: 248-204-3518, E-mail: scidean@ltu.edu. *Application contact:* Jane Rohrback, Director of Admissions, 248-204-3160, Fax: 248-204-3188, E-mail: admissions@ltu.edu.

Michigan Technological University, Graduate School, College of Sciences and Arts, Department of Humanities, Program in Rhetoric and Technical Communication, Houghton, MI 49931-1295. Offers MS, PhD. Part-time programs available. *Faculty:* 26 full-time (15 women), 1 part-time/adjunct (0 women). *Students:* 29 full-time (19 women), 34 part-time (20 women); includes 8 minority (3 African Americans, 1 American Indian/Alaska Native, 1 Asian American or Pacific Islander, 3 Hispanic Americans), 1 international. Average age 37. 34 applicants, 53% accepted, 15 enrolled. In 2007, 4 master's, 2 doctorates awarded. Terminal master's awarded for partial completion of doctoral program. *Median time to degree:* Of those who began their doctoral program in fall 1999, 56% received their degree in 8 years or less. *Degree requirements:* For master's, comprehensive exam; for doctorate, one foreign language, comprehensive exam, thesis/dissertation. *Entrance requirements:* Additional exam requirements/recommendations for international students: Required—TOEFL (minimum score 600 paper-based; 250 computer-based). *Application deadline:* Applications are processed on a rolling basis. Application fee: $40 ($45 for international students). Electronic applications accepted. *Financial support:* In 2007–08, 35 students received support, including 1 fellowship with full tuition reimbursement available (averaging $9,542 per year), 2 research assistantships with full tuition reimbursements available (averaging $9,542 per year), 28 teaching assistantships with full tuition reimbursements available (averaging $9,542 per year); career-related internships or fieldwork, Federal Work-Study, scholarships/grants, health care benefits, tuition waivers (partial), and unspecified assistantships also available. Financial award applicants required to submit FAFSA. *Unit head:* Elizabeth Flynn, Director, 906-487-3231, E-mail: eflynn@mtu.edu. *Application contact:* Marjorie L. Lindley, Office Assistant 5, 906-487-2381, Fax: 906-487-3559, E-mail: mlindley@mtu.edu.

Minnesota State University Mankato, College of Graduate Studies, College of Arts and Humanities, Department of English, Mankato, MN 56001. Offers creative writing (MFA); English (MA, MS); English literature (MA); teaching English (MS, MT); teaching English as a second language (MA); technical communication (Certificate). Part-time programs available. *Students:* 51 full-time (35 women), 78 part-time (54 women). Average age 32. In 2007, 29 degrees awarded. *Degree requirements:* For master's, one foreign language, comprehensive exam, thesis or alternative. *Entrance requirements:* For master's, minimum GPA of 3.0 during previous 2 years, writing sample (MFA). *Application deadline:* Applications are processed on a rolling basis. Application fee: $40. Electronic applications accepted. *Financial support:* Research assistantships with full tuition reimbursements, teaching assistantships with full tuition reimbursements, career-related internships or fieldwork, Federal Work-Study, and unspecified assistantships available. Financial award application deadline: 3/15; financial award applicants required to submit FAFSA. *Faculty research:* Keats and Christianity. *Unit head:* Dr. John Banschbach, Chairperson, 507-389-2117. *Application contact:* 507-389-2321, E-mail: grad@mnsu.edu.

Montana Tech of The University of Montana, Graduate School, Department of Technical Communication, Butte, MT 59701-8997. Offers MS. Part-time programs available. *Faculty:* 8 full-time (2 women), 4 part-time/adjunct (1 woman). *Students:* 7 full-time (all women), 2 part-time (both women). 6 applicants, 67% accepted, 4 enrolled. In 2007, 1 degree awarded. *Degree requirements:* For master's, project or thesis. *Entrance requirements:* For master's, GRE General Test, minimum GPA of 3.0. Additional exam requirements/recommendations for international students: Required—TOEFL (minimum score 525 paper-based; 195 computer-based; 71 iBT). *Application deadline:* For fall admission, 4/1 priority date for domestic students, 3/1 priority date for international students; for spring admission, 10/1 priority date for domestic students, 7/1 priority date for international students. Applications are processed on a rolling basis. Application fee: $30. Electronic applications accepted. *Expenses:* Tuition, state resident: part-time $305 per credit hour. Tuition, nonresident: part-time $803 per credit hour. Required fees: $100 per semester. Tuition and fees vary according to program. *Financial support:* In 2007–08, 6 students received support, including 4 teaching assistantships with partial tuition reimbursements available (averaging $6,000 per year); research assistantships with partial tuition reimbursements available, career-related internships or fieldwork, tuition waivers (partial), and unspecified assistantships also available. Financial award application deadline: 4/1; financial award applicants required to submit FAFSA. *Faculty research:* Environmental concerns and the Big Hole River, history of Butte mining, African studies, multicultural communication. *Unit head:* Dr. Henrietta Shirk, Head, 406-496-4297, Fax: 406-496-4510, E-mail: hshirk@mtech.edu. *Application contact:* Cindy Dunstan, Administrator, Graduate School, 406-496-4304, Fax: 406-496-4710, E-mail: cdunstan@mtech.edu.

New Jersey Institute of Technology, Office of Graduate Studies, College of Science and Liberal Arts, Department of Humanities and Social Sciences, Program in Professional and Technical Communication, Newark, NJ 07102. Offers MS. Part-time and evening/weekend programs available. *Students:* 6 full-time (4 women), 26 part-time (15 women); includes 14 minority (9 African Americans, 3 Asian Americans or Pacific Islanders, 2 Hispanic Americans), 1 international. Average age 39. 20 applicants, 65% accepted, 9 enrolled. In 2007, 13 master's awarded. Terminal master's awarded for partial completion of doctoral program. *Degree requirements:* For master's, thesis or alternative. *Entrance requirements:* For master's, GRE General Test. Additional exam requirements/recommendations for international students: Required—TOEFL (minimum score 550 paper-based; 213 computer-based). *Application deadline:* For fall admission, 6/5 priority date for domestic students; for spring admission, 10/15 for domestic students. Applications are processed on a rolling basis. Application fee: $60. Electronic applications accepted. *Expenses:* Tuition, state resident: full-time $12,730. Tuition, nonresident: full-time $18,090. Tuition and fees vary according to course load and campus/location. *Financial support:* Fellowships with full and partial tuition reimbursements, research assistantships with full and partial tuition reimbursements, teaching assistantships with full and partial tuition reimbursements, career-related internships or fieldwork, Federal Work-Study, institutionally sponsored loans, and unspecified assistantships available. Financial award application deadline: 3/15. *Faculty research:* Technology transfer, global sustainability, technology policy, professional ethics. *Unit head:* Dr. Burt Kimmelman, Director, 973-596-3376, Fax: 973-642-4689, E-mail: kimmelman@njit.edu. *Application contact:* Kathryn Kelly, Director of Admissions, 973-596-3300, Fax: 973-596-3461, E-mail: admissions@njit.edu.

North Carolina State University, Graduate School, College of Humanities and Social Sciences, Department of English, Program in Technical Communication, Raleigh, NC 27695. Offers MS. *Degree requirements:* For master's, thesis optional. *Entrance requirements:* For master's, GRE General Test. Electronic applications accepted. *Faculty research:* Workplace writing, organizational socialization and power, integrated and multimedia documentation systems, technical communication management, usability testing theories.

Polytechnic Institute of NYU, Department of Humanities and Social Sciences, Major in Technical Communication, Brooklyn, NY 11201-2990. Offers Graduate Certificate. *Students:* 4 full-time (3 women), 4 part-time (1 woman); includes 5 minority (4 African Americans, 1 Asian American or Pacific Islander). 11 applicants, 82% accepted, 3 enrolled. *Entrance requirements:* Additional exam requirements/recommendations for international students: Required—TOEFL (minimum score 550 paper-based; 213 computer-based); Recommended—IELTS (minimum score 7). *Application deadline:* For fall admission, 7/15 priority date for domestic students, 4/1 priority date for international students; for spring admission, 12/15 priority date for domestic students,

10/1 priority date for international students. Applications are processed on a rolling basis. Application fee: $55. Electronic applications accepted. *Expenses:* Tuition: Full-time $18,486; part-time $1,027 per credit. Required fees: $352 per semester. *Application contact:* Anthea Jeffrey, Graduate Admissions, 718-260-3200, Fax: 718-260-3624, E-mail: gradinfo@poly.edu.

Rensselaer Polytechnic Institute, Graduate School, School of Humanities and Social Sciences, Department of Language, Literature, and Communication, Program in Technical Communication, Troy, NY 12180-3590. Offers MS. Part-time programs available. *Faculty:* 15 full-time (7 women), 1 (woman) part-time/adjunct. *Students:* 2 applicants, 100% accepted, 2 enrolled. In 2007, 9 degrees awarded. *Degree requirements:* For master's, thesis optional. *Entrance requirements:* For master's, GRE General Test, resumé. Additional exam requirements/recommendations for international students: Required—TOEFL (minimum score 570 paper-based; 230 computer-based). *Application deadline:* For fall admission, 1/15 priority date for domestic students; for spring admission, 10/15 priority date for domestic students. Applications are processed on a rolling basis. Application fee: $75. Electronic applications accepted. *Expenses:* Tuition: Full-time $34,900; part-time $1,454 per credit. Required fees: $1,802. *Financial support:* In 2007–08, 1 fellowship with tuition reimbursement (averaging $12,000 per year) was awarded; research assistantships, teaching assistantships, career-related internships or fieldwork and institutionally sponsored loans also available. Financial award application deadline: 1/15. *Faculty research:* Human-computer interaction, media design, theory and culture, teaching and learning in the virtual classroom, usability. *Application contact:* Kathy A. Colman, Recruitment Coordinator, 518-276-6469, Fax: 518-276-4092, E-mail: colmak@rpi.edu.

See Close-Up on page 925.

Rochester Institute of Technology, Graduate Enrollment Services, College of Applied Science and Technology, Center for Multidisciplinary Studies, Program in Technical Information Design, Rochester, NY 14623-5603. Offers AC. *Students:* 1 applicant, 100% accepted, 1 enrolled. *Entrance requirements:* Additional exam requirements/recommendations for international students: Required—TOEFL (minimum score 550 paper-based; 213 computer-based; 79 iBT). *Application deadline:* For fall admission, 3/1 priority date for domestic students. Applications are processed on a rolling basis. Application fee: $50. Electronic applications accepted. *Expenses:* Tuition: Full-time $28,491; part-time $800 per credit hour. Required fees: $201; $67 per term. *Financial support:* Institutionally sponsored loans available. Support available to part-time students. Financial award applicants required to submit FAFSA. *Unit head:* Thomas Moran, Chair, 585-475-4936, E-mail: tfmcad@rit.edu.

Southern Polytechnic State University, School of Arts and Sciences, Department of English, Technical Communication, and Media Arts, Marietta, GA 30060-2896. Offers information design and communication (MS); technical and professional communication (Graduate Certificate). Part-time and evening/weekend programs available. Postbaccalaureate distance learning degree programs offered (minimal on-campus study). *Faculty:* 4 full-time (3 women). *Students:* 4 full-time (3 women), 33 part-time (24 women); includes 13 minority (11 African Americans, 2 Hispanic Americans), 2 international. Average age 39. 31 applicants, 58% accepted, 15 enrolled. In 2007, 8 degrees awarded. *Degree requirements:* For master's, thesis optional, students can complete 36-hour requirement through a thesis option (6 hours), an internship option (6 hours) or an advanced coursework option (6 hours); for Graduate Certificate, thesis optional, students can complete 18-hour requirement for advanced certificate through a thesis option (6 hours), an internship option (6 hours) or an advanced coursework option (6 hours). *Entrance requirements:* For master's, GRE, statement of purpose, writing sample, professional recommendations, proctored essay; for Graduate Certificate, statement of purpose, writing sample, professional recommendations, proctored essay. Additional exam requirements/recommendations for international students: Required—TOEFL (minimum score 550 paper-based; 213 computer-based; 79 iBT). *Application deadline:* For fall admission, 5/1 priority date for domestic students, 7/1 priority date for international students; for spring admission, 9/1 priority date for domestic students, 11/1 priority date for international students. Applications are processed on a rolling basis. Application fee: $20. Electronic applications accepted. *Expenses:* Tuition, state resident: full-time $2,544; part-time $159 per credit hour. Tuition, nonresident: full-time $10,176; part-time $636 per credit hour. Required fees: $315 per term. *Financial support:* In 2007–08, 6 students received support, including 2 research assistantships with full tuition reimbursements available (averaging $6,000 per year); career-related internships or fieldwork, Federal Work-Study, scholarships/grants, and unspecified assistantships also available. Support available to part-time students. Financial award application deadline: 5/1; financial award applicants required to submit FAFSA. *Faculty research:* Usability, user-centered design, instructional design, information architecture, information design. *Unit head:* Dr. Mark Nunes, Chair, 678-915-7202, Fax: 678-915-7425, E-mail: mnunes@spsu.edu. *Application contact:* Virginia A. Head, Director of Admissions, 678-915-4188, Fax: 678-915-7292, E-mail: vhead@spsu.edu.

Texas State University–San Marcos, Graduate School, College of Liberal Arts, Department of English, Program in Technical Communication, San Marcos, TX 78666. Offers MA. *Faculty:* 5 full-time (3 women). *Students:* 4 full-time (3 women), 22 part-time (17 women); includes 4 minority (2 African Americans, 2 Hispanic Americans). Average age 33. 7 applicants, 100% accepted, 6 enrolled. In 2007, 7 degrees awarded. *Degree requirements:* For master's, comprehensive exam, thesis or alternative. *Entrance requirements:* For master's, minimum GPA of 2.75 in last 60 hours of course work, portfolio. Additional exam requirements/recommendations for international students: Required—TOEFL (minimum score 550 paper-based; 213 computer-based). *Application deadline:* For fall admission, 6/15 priority date for domestic students, 6/1 for international students; for spring admission, 11/1 priority date for domestic students, 10/1 for international students. Applications are processed on a rolling basis. Application fee: $40 ($90 for international students). Electronic applications accepted. *Expenses:* Tuition, state resident: full-time $3,780; part-time $210 per credit hour. Tuition, nonresident: full-time $8,784; part-time $488 per credit hour. Required fees: $493 per semester. Full-time tuition and fees vary according to course load. *Financial support:* In 2007–08, 15 students received support, including 4 research assistantships (averaging $5,563 per year), 1 teaching assistantship (averaging $5,076 per year); Federal Work-Study and institutionally sponsored loans also available. Support available to part-time students. Financial award application deadline: 4/1. *Unit head:* Dr. Libby Allison, Graduate Advisor, 512-245-2163, Fax: 512-245-8546.

University of Colorado Denver, College of Liberal Arts and Sciences, Department of Communication, Program in Technical Communication, Denver, CO 80217-3364. Offers MS. Part-time and evening/weekend programs available. *Students:* 1 full-time (0 women), 7 part-time (5 women). Average age 33. 2 applicants, 100% accepted, 2 enrolled. In 2007, 6 degrees awarded. *Degree requirements:* For master's, comprehensive exam, thesis or alternative. *Entrance requirements:* For master's, GRE General Test, GRE Subject Test. Additional exam requirements/recommendations for international students: Required—TOEFL (minimum score 525 paper-based; 197 computer-based). *Application deadline:* For fall admission, 6/1 for domestic students; for spring admission, 11/1 for domestic students. Applications are processed on a rolling basis. Application fee: $50 ($75 for international students). Electronic applications accepted. *Financial support:* Fellowships with partial tuition reimbursements, research assistantships with partial tuition reimbursements, teaching assistantships, Federal Work-Study and institutionally sponsored loans available. Financial award application deadline: 4/1; financial award applicants required to submit FAFSA. *Faculty research:* Web design, interface design and XML single sourcing, comprehensive of legal documents. *Application contact:* Sally Thee, Program Assistant, 303-556-2591, Fax: 303-556-6018, E-mail: sally.thee@cudenver.edu.

University of Houston–Downtown, Graduate Programs, College of Humanities and Social Sciences, Department of English, Houston, TX 77002-1001. Offers professional writing and technical communication (MS). Part-time and evening/weekend programs available. *Faculty:* 5 full-time (4 women). *Students:* 4 full-time (3 women), 23 part-time (19 women); includes 14 minority (9 African Americans, 3 Asian Americans or Pacific Islanders, 2 Hispanic Americans). Average age 40. In 2007, 4 degrees awarded. *Degree requirements:* For master's, thesis (for some programs). *Entrance requirements:* For master's, GRE, resumé, personal statement, writing sample, 3 letters of recommendation. Additional exam requirements/recommendations for international students: Required—TOEFL (minimum score 600 paper-based; 250 computer-based; 86 iBT). *Application deadline:* For fall admission, 3/31 for domestic and international students; for spring admission, 11/30 for domestic and international students. Applications are processed on a rolling basis. Application fee: $35 ($60 for international students). Electronic applications accepted. *Expenses:* Tuition, state resident: full-time $3,060; part-time $170 per credit. Tuition, nonresident: full-time $7,434; part-time $413 per credit. Required fees: $704. *Financial support:* Application deadline: 4/1; *Unit head:* Dr. William Gilbert, Chair, 713-221-8013, Fax: 713-226-5205, E-mail: gilbertw@uhd.edu. *Application contact:* Traneshia Parker, Assistant Director of Admissions, Graduate and International Admissions, 713-221-8910, Fax: 713-223-7984, E-mail: parkert@uhd.edu.

University of Nebraska at Omaha, Graduate Studies and Research, College of Arts and Sciences, Department of English, Omaha, NE 68182. Offers advanced writing (Certificate); English (MA); teaching English to speakers of other languages (Certificate); technical communication (Certificate). Part-time and evening/weekend programs available. *Faculty:* 17 full-time (9 women). *Students:* 11 full-time (8 women), 49 part-time (33 women); includes 3 minority (1 African American, 1 Asian American or Pacific Islander, 1 Hispanic American), 2 international. Average age 34. 39 applicants, 72% accepted, 20 enrolled. In 2007, 13 master's, 9 other advanced degrees awarded. *Degree requirements:* For master's, comprehensive exam, thesis (for some programs). *Entrance requirements:* For master's, minimum GPA of 3.0, statement of purpose, 3 letters of recommendation, writing sample. Additional exam requirements/recommendations for international students: Required—TOEFL (minimum score 600 paper-based; 250 computer-based; 100 iBT). *Application deadline:* For fall admission, 8/1 priority date for domestic students; for spring admission, 12/1 priority date for domestic students. Applications are processed on a rolling basis. Application fee: $45. Electronic applications accepted. *Financial support:* In 2007–08, 30 students received support; fellowships, teaching assistantships with tuition reimbursements available, Federal Work-Study, institutionally sponsored loans, scholarships/grants, tuition waivers (partial), and unspecified assistantships available. Support available to part-time students. Financial award application deadline: 3/1; financial award applicants required to submit FAFSA. *Unit head:* Dr. Susan Maher, Chairperson, 402-554-3636. *Application contact:* Dr. Joan Latchaw, Student Contact, 402-554-3636.

University of Washington, Graduate School, College of Engineering, Department of Technical Communication, Seattle, WA 98195. Offers MSTC, PhD. Part-time and evening/weekend programs available. *Faculty:* 13 full-time (6 women), 6 part-time/adjunct (1 woman). *Students:* 53 full-time (34 women), 7 part-time (4 women); includes 8 minority (1 African American, 6 Asian Americans or Pacific Islanders, 1 Hispanic American), 6 international. Average age 33. 57 applicants, 53% accepted, 24 enrolled. In 2007, 29 degrees awarded. *Degree requirements:* For master's, thesis or alternative; for doctorate, comprehensive exam, thesis/dissertation. *Entrance requirements:* For master's, GRE General Test, minimum GPA of 3.0; for doctorate, GRE, minimum GPA of 3.0. Additional exam requirements/recommendations for international students: Required—TOEFL. *Application deadline:* For fall admission, 2/1 for domestic students, 11/15 priority date for international students. Applications are processed on a rolling basis. Application fee: $50. Electronic applications accepted. *Financial support:* In 2007–08, 2 fellowships with full tuition reimbursements, 10 research assistantships with full tuition reimbursements, 15 teaching assistantships with full tuition reimbursements were awarded; career-related internships or fieldwork, institutionally sponsored loans, and tuition waivers (full) also available. Financial award application deadline: 2/28; financial award applicants required to submit FAFSA. *Faculty research:* Communication design, user interface design and usability, new media design, science news writing, comprehension processes. Total annual research expenditures: $725,000. *Unit head:* Dr. Judith A. Ramey, Chair, 206-543-2567, Fax: 206-543-8858, E-mail: jramey@u.washington.edu. *Application contact:* Gian Bruno, Academic Counselor, 206-543-1798, Fax: 206-543-8858, E-mail: tc@u.washington.edu.

AMERICAN UNIVERSITY

School of Communication

Programs of Study

The School of Communication (SOC) offers professional graduate programs that prepare students for careers in traditional and emerging media. Students work closely with faculty members in small, laboratory environments while also pursuing professional opportunities in Washington, D.C.'s, many world-class media organizations, including Discovery Communications, National Geographic, *USA Today*, and *washingtonpost.com*. Most SOC faculty members are themselves working practitioners who have won Oscars, Emmys, and other professional honors. In addition to professional faculty members, a committed group of alumni works with students individually in a unique mentoring program. All graduate programs emphasize writing, hands-on learning, and analysis of the social, legal, and economic challenges shaping today's media.

SOC offers five full-time and four weekend master's degree programs. The full-time programs include the Master of Arts (M.A.) in journalism and public affairs (33 hours), with tracks in broadcast and print journalism and concentrations in economic, international, and public policy journalism; the M.A. in public communication (30 hours), with concentrations in arts, government, political, and public interest communication as well as corporate and international public relations; the M.A. in international media (45 hours), a joint program with the School of International Service, which offers a combination of theory, research, and professional production skills to provide a global media advantage; the M.A. in film and video (36 hours), with concentrations in film and video production, screenwriting, multimedia, and film history, theory, and criticism; and the Master of Fine Arts (M.F.A.) in film and electronic media, a terminal degree that allows students to pursue collegiate-level teaching careers.

The weekend M.A. programs for working professionals include interactive journalism, news media studies, public communication, and producing for film and video. Students move through the programs with a cohort of fellow students who meet every Saturday for twenty months.

Research Facilities

The SOC Friedheim Journalism Center (FJC) features two fully networked computer classrooms, each with twenty PCs configured for computer-assisted research and reporting, multimedia and Web authoring, and page layout and design. The FJC also contains a third, smaller lab with Mac and Windows computers for students' research, writing, and rich-media authoring. The School also has three fully equipped Mac-based computer labs, all featuring state-of-the-art software applications for graphics production, digital imaging and compositing, layout and design, Web authoring, and digital video editing. A 109-seat theater is equipped with multiformat video projection and interactive videoconferencing capabilities. There are also traditional black-and-white photographic darkroom facilities; small-, medium-, and large-format film cameras; high-quality digital scanning equipment; photo-quality color inkjet printing; and a growing collection of professional digital cameras, all dedicated for exclusive SOC-student use. A separate facility, the Media Production Center, houses a 40-foot by 40-foot, three-camera color television studio; the fully networked Ed Bliss Broadcast Newsroom; three digital audio studios; a large multiuse classroom; a field production equipment check-out facility; and ten digital video postproduction suites for Avid and Final Cut Pro editing.

Financial Aid

SOC offers merit-based financial aid awards on a competitive basis in all of its full-time graduate programs. Awards range from a minimum stipend of $1000 to a maximum of 24 hours of tuition remission with a $9000 stipend for the academic year, involving a service commitment of up to 12 hours per week. In 2007–08, 60 graduate students received merit-based financial aid, with a total value (stipend plus tuition remission) of $900,000. American University also offers need-based financial aid to students who qualify by filing the Free Application for Federal Student Aid (FAFSA) form.

Cost of Study

For the 2008–09 academic year, graduate tuition is $1178 per credit hour. Students may anticipate a 4 percent increase in tuition in each academic year. Full-time graduate study is considered to be at least 9 hours each semester; students in the full-time journalism and public affairs and public communication programs usually complete 12 hours per semester. Special fees are charged for thesis processing, activities, and maintaining matriculation (if the student is not registered for courses). Courses requiring the use of production equipment or computer facilities typically incur additional lab fees.

Living and Housing Costs

Although many graduate students live off campus, the University has some graduate dormitory rooms and apartments available. The Off-Campus Housing Office maintains a referral file of rooms and apartments. Housing costs in Washington, D.C., are comparable to those in other major metropolitan areas.

Student Group

The SOC enrolls approximately 350 students in its graduate programs, divided more or less evenly among its full-time and weekend programs in journalism, public communication, and film and media arts. It also has a full-time program in international media, which it offers with the University's School of International Service. Approximately 65 percent of the graduate students are women, 26 percent are members of minority groups, and 11 percent are international. All of the programs emphasize a strong liberal arts education as a requirement for admission, and none requires students to have majored in communication as undergraduates. Consequently, students selected in the competitive admission process come from diverse educational and professional backgrounds. Many students have worked professionally, and all have shown evidence of their professional and academic commitment.

Location

The School of Communication takes full advantage of the rich professional opportunities of Washington, D.C., as the nation's media capital as well as one of its largest production markets. Nationally recognized journalists, filmmakers, and public relations executives regularly serve as guest lecturers and adjunct professors. The city also offers the cultural resources of the Smithsonian Institution, the National Gallery of Art, the Kennedy Center for the Performing Arts, and the Library of Congress, plus a thriving artistic community of galleries and clubs.

The University and The School

Founded in 1893, American University (AU) is located on an 84-acre site in a residential area of northwest Washington that is accessible by Metro, the region's subway system. As a member of the Consortium of Universities of the Washington Metropolitan Area, AU offers its degree candidates the option of taking courses at other consortium universities for residence credit. SOC has educated communication professionals for forty years. Its journalism and public communication programs are accredited by the Accrediting Council for Education in Journalism and Mass Communications (ACEJMC), and its program in film and media arts is one of only twelve U.S. programs accepted for membership in CILECT, the International Association of Film and Television Schools. The School's faculty members and alumni are working professionals who constitute a valuable network for graduating students seeking career advancement.

Applying

Applicants must have a minimum GPA of 3.0 during their last 60 credits (two years) of undergraduate study for application to all graduate programs, except the M.A. in international media, which requires a minimum GPA of 3.3 in the last 60 credits of undergraduate study. In addition, a 1,000-word statement of purpose, two letters of recommendation, a completed SOC application form, and an application fee of $50 are required for consideration. Recommendations should be submitted on professional letterhead with a business card attached. International students who have learned English as a second language are required to score a minimum of 600 on the paper-based version, 250 on the computer-based version, or 100 on the Internet-based version of the TOEFL. SOC also accepts the IELTS exam for English proficiency from students with a minimum score of 7.0. All applicants for the full-time programs are required to take the GRE. The application deadline for fall admission into all full-time programs is June 1 (February 1 for merit award consideration). The film and video program also admits students in the spring semester, with an application deadline of November 15. Weekend programs' priority deadline for applications is June 1; however, applications are accepted on a rolling admissions basis until the start of the fall semester in mid-August. Applications for financial aid should be submitted before February 1.

Correspondence and Information

Office of Graduate Programs
School of Communication
American University
4400 Massachusetts Avenue, NW
Washington, D.C. 20016-8017
Phone: 202-885-2040
E-mail: gradcomm@american.edu
Web site: http://www.soc.american.edu

American University

THE FACULTY

Larry Kirkman, Professor and Dean; M.A.T., Harvard.
Laird B. Anderson, Professor Emeritus; M.A., American. Journalism.
Patricia Aufderheide, Professor; Ph.D., Minnesota. Film and Media Arts.
Randall Blair, Associate Professor and Director, Weekend Producing for Film and Video Program; M.A., American. Film and Media Arts.
W. Joseph Campbell, Associate Professor; Ph.D., North Carolina. Journalism.
Wendell Cochran, Associate Professor and Director, Journalism Division, Weekend Interactive Journalism and News Media Studies Programs; M.A., Missouri. Journalism.
John Doolittle, Associate Professor; Ph.D., Wisconsin–Madison. Journalism.
John Douglass, Associate Professor and Director, Film and Media Arts Division; M.A., American. Film and Media Arts.
Amy Eisman, Director, Writing Programs; M.A., American. Journalism.
Larry Engel, Assistant Professor; M.F.A., Columbia. Film and Media Arts.
Brooke Fisher Liu, Assistant Professor; Ph.D., North Carolina. Public Communication.
William Gentile, Artist-in-Residence; M.A., Ohio State.
Joseph Graf, Assistant Professor; M.A., Ohio State. Public Communication.
Jane Hall, Associate Professor; M.S.J., Columbia. Journalism.
Darrell Hayes, Assistant Professor and Director, Weekend Public Communication Program; M.A., Oklahoma. Public Communication.
Jerry Hendrix, Professor Emeritus; Ph.D., LSU. Public Communication.
Bagus Himawan, Assistant Professor; M.A., American. Film and Media Arts.
Maria Ivancin, Assistant Professor; M.B.A., Illinois. Public Communication.
Leena Jayaswal, Assistant Professor; M.F.A., Maryland Institute, College of Art. Film and Media Arts.
Iris Krasnow, Assistant Professor; M.A., Georgetown. Washington Journalism Semester.
Charles Lewis, Distinguished-Journalist-in-Residence; M.A., Johns Hopkins. Journalism.
Dotty Lynch, Executive-in-Residence; M.A., Fordham. Public Communication.
Brigid Maher, Assistant Professor; M.F.A., Northwestern. Film and Media Arts.
Sarah Menke-Fish, Assistant Professor; M.A., American. Film and Media Arts.
Kathryn Montgomery, Professor; Ph.D., UCLA. Public Communication.
Matthew Nisbet, Assistant Professor; Ph.D., Cornell. Public Communication.
Jill Olmsted, Associate Professor; M.A., American. Journalism.
Chris Palmer, Distinguished-Film-Producer-in-Residence; M.A., Harvard. Film and Media Arts.
Lynne Perri, Journalist-in-Residence; M.S., Northwestern. Journalism.
Gemma Puglisi, Assistant Professor; M.A., Catholic University. Public Communication.
Rose Ann Robertson, Associate Dean for Student and Academic Affairs; M.S., Southern Illinois. Journalism.
Rick Rockwell, Associate Professor; M.A., USC. Journalism.
Danielle Schwartz, Assistant Professor; Ph.D., McGill. Public Communication.
Chris Simpson, Professor; M.A., Maryland. Journalism.
Rick Stack, Associate Professor; J.D., Missouri. Public Communication.
Leonard Steinhorn, Associate Professor and Director, Public Communication Division; M.A., Johns Hopkins. Public Communication.
Margaret Stogner, Assistant Professor; M.A., Stanford. Film and Media Arts.
Rodger Streitmatter, Professor and Senior Associate Dean; Ph.D., American. Journalism.
John Watson, Associate Professor; J.D., Rutgers; Ph.D., North Carolina. Journalism.
Russell Williams, Artist-in-Residence; B.A., American. Film and Media Arts.
Lewis Wolfson, Professor Emeritus; M.S.J., Columbia; M.A., Harvard. Journalism.
Joanne Yamauchi, Professor Emeritus; Ph.D., Northwestern. Public Communication.
Rhonda Zaharna, Associate Professor; Ed.D., Columbia. Public Communication.
Anne Zelle, Professor Emeritus; M.A., Pius XII (Italy). Film and Media Arts.

ARIZONA STATE UNIVERSITY

Walter Cronkite School of Journalism and Mass Communication
Master of Mass Communication Program

Programs of Study

The Walter Cronkite School of Journalism and Mass Communication at Arizona State University (ASU) offers an innovative, full-immersion master's program that builds on the strengths that have made the School one of the best in the nation. The fifteen-month, full-time Master of Mass Communication degree program is unique in scope, focus, and intensity. It begins with immersion in the journalistic skills, values, and principles embodied by Walter Cronkite, the School's guiding light for the past three decades. It is also designed with the future in mind. Students learn how to navigate a dramatically different twenty-first-century media environment through classes and a symposium specifically focused on the future of journalism. They are able to apply that knowledge through an intensive practical experience in one of the School's signature professional programs.

The Mid-Career Master of Mass Communication track is one of the Cronkite School's newest and most distinctive programs. It is designed specifically for journalists and communications professionals with substantial professional experience who are seeking to develop new and useful skills and knowledge to help them accomplish specific career goals. Each student's course of study is highly individualized and interdisciplinary, with course work tailored to the student's goals. For example, a veteran journalist interested in First Amendment applications in the newsroom may undertake a curriculum that combines traditional courses in journalism ethics and law with courses in the law school; a student interested in digital media entrepreneurship may combine new media courses in the Cronkite School with graduate classes in the W. P. Carey School of Business; or a general assignment reporter who wants to specialize in health and science reporting may take journalism reporting and writing courses as well as courses in the natural sciences.

Each student accepted into the Mid-Career Master of Mass Communication program is paired with a member of the Cronkite faculty who helps develop an appropriate program of study and provides one-on-one guidance and mentorship. Students may pursue their studies part-time or full-time. For more information, students should contact Lisbeth Dambrowkski, graduate student support specialist senior, at lisbeth.dambrowski@asu.edu 480.965.1796.

Students at the Cronkite School of Journalism study under a remarkable faculty that comprises national news media leaders, including former CNN anchor Aaron Brown, former *Minneapolis Star Tribune* editor Tim McGuire, former BET Vice President Retha Hill, Pulitzer Prize–winning investigative reporter Steve Doig, and former *Akron Beacon Journal* publisher Jim Crutchfield. Other veterans head up the School's professional immersion programs, which are a cornerstone of the graduate experience. Graduate students interested in broadcasting may spend their final semester in Cronkite NewsWatch, the School's weekly newscast, under the direction of former television reporter and anchor Mark Lodato. Or they may spend it with former television managing editor Sue Green at Cronkite News Service, producing stories for TV stations across the state. Students interested in print and online journalism may choose Cronkite News Service, working under former Associated Press editor Steve Elliott on daily stories about state government for newspapers around the state. Those interested in digital media may elect the New Media Innovation Lab, or they might decide to develop their own new media products at the Knight Center for Digital Media Entrepreneurship. Other professional experiences include the Southwest Borderlands Initiative and the Public Relations Laboratory.

The program is designed so that each class moves through as a cohort, entering in the fall semester and attending full-time for three semesters (excluding the summer, when many students do internships). In August 2008, the Cronkite School is scheduled to move to the center of downtown Phoenix, where students will learn in a new state-of-the-art building that will be one of the most sophisticated journalism education complexes in the nation.

Research Facilities

The New Media Innovation Lab is a research and development facility designed to help media companies create new and exciting multimedia products. Operated by the Cronkite School, the lab brings together students from across the campus—journalism, business, computer engineering, and design. The New Media Innovation Lab is located in Computing Commons on ASU's Tempe campus. In 2008, it is scheduled to move into the Cronkite School's new building in downtown Phoenix.

Collectively, the ASU University libraries are among the premier research libraries in the country. The collections comprise nearly 4 million volumes, more than 34,000 periodical and serial subscriptions, thousands of sound recordings and videos, and hundreds of thousands of government documents and maps.

Financial Aid

A limited number of fellowships and assistantships are offered to top applicants. These highly competitive awards are given for an academic year and may be renewed for an additional semester. The fellowship covers all tuition and fees and includes a $20,000 annual stipend. Students awarded assistantships are charged the in-state rate for tuition and receive a 50 percent remission of that tuition, and they receive an annual stipend of approximately $12,000. The Phoenix Press Box Association Endowment Scholarship is awarded to a graduate student each year, and additional scholarships are open to all Cronkite School students. Information about additional financial aid from the Graduate College can be found at http://www.asu.edu/graduate/financial/.

Cost of Study

In 2007–08, tuition was $326 per academic credit for residents or $747 per credit for out-of-state students, plus $150 in fees. Students can also expect to spend approximately $2180 for books and supplies, $3090 for transportation, and $2950 in miscellaneous personal costs. Health insurance costs an additional $1264 per year.

Living and Housing Costs

Students living on campus pay $5319 for double occupancy and $6033 for single-occupancy rooms. Meal plans range from $1900 to $3500. Other fees include an annual $30 data connectivity fee and an annual $40 Residence Hall Association fee. Students living off campus typically pay between $680 and $900 per month in rent, depending on the size and location of the apartment.

Student Group

Each year, the School draws students from across the country who are inquisitive, passionate, and diverse. Of the 58 students currently enrolled, 36 are women and 2 are international. The average age is 32.

Location

Tempe, the seventh-largest city in Arizona, has been voted one of the top 10 college towns by the *New York Times*. The city is packed with history, culture, shopping, dining, nightlife, and sports, and Tempe Town Lake provides a haven for kayaking, sailing, rowing, jogging, skating, and picnicking. The Tempe campus is just minutes from downtown Phoenix, Scottsdale, and Phoenix Sky Harbor International Airport.

The University and The School

Since its establishment in 1886, Arizona State University has emerged as a leading national and international research and teaching institution. Its mission is to provide outstanding programs in instruction, research, and creative activity; to promote and support economic development; and to provide service that is appropriate for the nation and the region. The University offers undergraduate and graduate programs for more than 58,000 students through five campuses throughout Arizona and other instructional, research, and public service sites throughout Maricopa County.

The Walter Cronkite School of Journalism and Mass Communication is a nationally recognized professional school that consistently ranks in the top 10 in the annual Hearst intercollegiate journalism competition, often called the Pulitzers of college journalism. The faculty consists of award-winning professional journalists and world-class media scholars.

Applying

For the most part, candidates for the Master of Mass Communication program come with limited or no professional experience, but students interested in the Mid-Career Master of Mass Communication track should be able to demonstrate leadership and expertise in their fields and have specific goals in mind for what they want to study. To be considered for admission to ASU and the Cronkite School, students must have at least a 3.0 GPA (on a 4.0 scale) in the last 60 semester hours or 90 quarter hours of undergraduate course work. Students must submit the completed application, the application fee, official transcripts of all college-level work, GRE scores, a resume and/or a biographical sketch, three letters of recommendation, and a 350- to 500-word personal statement that serves as a writing sample. International applicants must also take the Test of English as a Foreign Language (TOEFL). Students are admitted for the fall semester only. The deadline is February 1. The admission process is conducted on a rolling basis between December and March.

Correspondence and Information

Graduate College Admissions
Stauffer Building, Room A231
Walter Cronkite School of Journalism and Mass Communication
Arizona State University
P.O. Box 871305
Tempe, Arizona 85287-1305

Phone: 480-965-1796
Fax: 480-965-7041
E-mail: masscomm@asu.edu
Web site: http://cronkite.asu.edu/grad/index.php

Arizona State University

THE FACULTY AND THEIR RESEARCH

Craig M. Allen, Associate Professor; Ph.D., Ohio. History, political media, presidential communication, international mass media.
Marianne Barrett, Associate Professor, Solheim Professor, and Associate Dean for Academic Affairs; Ph.D., Michigan State. Media management, economics, policy.
Sharon Bramlett-Solomon, Associate Professor; Ph.D., Indiana. Media construction and depiction of race images.
Aaron Brown, Walter Cronkite Professor of Journalism. Broadcast journalism.
Christopher Callahan, Professor and Dean; M.P.A., Harvard. Journalism ethics, news diversity, press-government relations and investigative reporting.
Serena Carpenter, Professor, Ph.D., Michigan State. Online and new media.
Michael Casavantes, Lecturer; M.A., New Mexico State. Twentieth-century American history.
John E. Craft, Professor; Ph.D., Ohio. TV media.
James N. Crutchfield, Director of Student Media and Weil Family Professor of Journalism; B.A., Duquesne.
Steve Doig, Professor and Knight Chair in Journalism; B.A., Dartmouth.
Steve Elliott, Director, Cronkite News Service; M.B.A., Arizona State.
Mary-Lou Galician, Associate Professor; Ed.D., Memphis State. Media literacy.
Kristin Gilger, Assistant Dean; M.S., Nebraska. Newspaper management, newswriting, journalism ethics.
Dan Gillmor, Director, Knight Center for Digital Media Entrepreneurship; B.A., Vermont. New media, citizen-based journalism, digital media.
Donald G. Godfrey, Professor; Ph.D., Washington (Seattle). Electronic media.
Susan Green, Broadcast Director, Cronkite News Service; B.A., Arizona State.
Retha Hill, Director, New Media Innovation Lab. New digital media products.
Aric Johnson, *Arizona Republic* Editor-in-Residence; B.A., USC.
Frederic "Fritz" Leigh, Clinical Professor and Associate Dean for Student Affairs; Ed.D., Arizona State. Broadcasting.
Mark Lodato, Professor of Practice and News Director; B.J., Missouri.
Fran R. Matera, Associate Professor; Ph.D., Miami (Florida). Hispanic audiences.
Tim McGuire, Professor and Frank Russell Chair of Journalism; J.D., William Mitchell Law. Ethics, spirituality, and values in the workplace.
Bruce D. Merrill, Professor; Ph.D., Michigan. Political behavior and political media communications.
Jim Rush, Lecturer and TV Production Manager; B.S., Arizona State.
Dennis E. Russell, Associate Professor; Ph.D., Utah. Mass-mediated popular culture, critical studies, film, literary and music analysis, First Amendment law.
Joseph Russomanno, Associate Professor; Ph.D., Colorado at Boulder. Broadcast journalism, First Amendment law.
Carol Schwalbe, Assistant Professor; M.A., George Washington. Online journalism.
B. William Silcock, Assistant Professor; Ph.D., Missouri. Global television news cultures.
Edward J. Sylvester, Professor; M.A., CUNY, City College. Science writing.
Leslie-Jean Thornton, Assistant Professor; Ph.D., North Carolina at Chapel Hill. Newspapers, design, technology, spread of information.
George L. Watson, Parents Association Professor of Political Science; Ph.D., Duke. Media and politics.
Xu Wu, Assistant Professor; Ph.D., Florida. China's online media, international public relations, crisis management, political communication, mass communication theories.

BOSTON UNIVERSITY

College of Communication

Programs of Study

The College has three graduate departments: Film and Television; Mass Communication, Advertising, and Public Relations; and Journalism. Master of Science degree programs are available in the major fields of advertising, broadcast journalism, business and economics journalism, journalism, mass communication, public relations, science journalism, television, and television management. A Master of Fine Arts is offered in the areas of film production, film studies, and screenwriting. The College also offers the following dual-degree programs: J.D./M.S. in mass communication and M.B.A./M.S. in television management.

The programs usually require three to four semesters of work. In several sequences, a creative project may be elected in place of a thesis. In the Department of Mass Communication, Advertising, and Public Relations, students may take a comprehensive exam in place of a thesis. A number of elective courses make up degree requirements within each program.

Summer internships are encouraged in all programs. Few summer courses are offered. Degree candidates must complete their work in seven years from the date of first course registration, or they may be required to satisfy additional requirements.

Research Facilities

The College provides opportunities for students to participate actively in ongoing research projects through part-time work and assistantships in the Communication Research Center, a research division organized to accept projects that have academic merit, do not compete directly with available commercial research facilities, and are in keeping with the objectives of the College. Physical facilities include a city room with an Associated Press wire service drop and a copy desk; VDTs; photo labs with fully equipped digital darkrooms; radio taping, recording, and broadcast facilities; AVID editing suites; a closed-circuit TV center; complete film facilities; seminar rooms; a century-old newspaper morgue; and a reading room. The College has several computer labs and a state-of-the-art multimedia lab with both PCs and Macs. The University's Mugar Library has a substantial communication collection.

Financial Aid

The University offers various financial aid options to qualified students. These programs include merit scholarships ranging from $1000 to full tuition, the Federal Work-Study Program, and Federal Stafford Loans. Graduate assistantships are available through the individual departments. The stipends for scholarships and assistantships ranged from $1000 to $6000 per semester in 2007–08. Various loan programs and part-time jobs are also available. Students are urged to use their own initiative in finding support, since the resources of the graduate programs are limited; possible sources of aid include state agencies and private organizations. Library references and online searches are helpful information sources.

Cost of Study

Tuition is $36,540 for the 2008–09 academic year.

Living and Housing Costs

Most graduate students are advised to seek off-campus housing. Limited on-campus graduate housing is available. The cost for room and board is estimated to be about $12,000 for the nine-month academic year. The University maintains apartments for married full-time graduate students and their families.

Student Group

Of the 375 full- and part-time graduate students enrolled in fall 2007, 193 were returning to continue their studies, while 182 were beginning programs. There were several international students in the entering group, and many domestic students were from outside New England. Women make up 75 percent of the graduate class. Alumni of the College are found throughout the United States and in thirty-eight other countries, practicing their communication skills in media, government, industry, social institutions, education, and private business.

Location

Boston, the largest city in New England and one of the largest media markets in the U.S., is a seaport whose character results from a rich blend of historical heritage, active cultural life, and contemporary growth in technology, medicine, and business. Greater Boston, with more than fifty colleges and universities, remains an unrivaled center of learning. Within the city's compact center are the Boston Common and the Public Garden, Faneuil Hall Marketplace, art galleries, Chinatown, and the Freedom Trail, along which are some of the most important landmarks in U.S. history. Admission to the Museum of Fine Arts is free for University students. The Boston Symphony Orchestra, the Opera Company of Boston, and many fine chamber and jazz groups offer annual seasons, as do dance and theater companies. Boston is the home of the New England Patriots, the Red Sox, the Celtics, and the Bruins.

The University and The College

Boston University is an independent, coeducational, nonsectarian university with an enrollment of about 29,000 full-time students and a faculty of more than 2,500. Its academic diversity meets the needs of one of the largest bodies of scholars in the world. Incorporated in 1869, the University today provides students with the advantages of a large, contemporary educational complex while maintaining many traditional priorities. Its sixteen schools and colleges respond to students' occupational needs and the increasingly specialized demands they face in the modern world. The main campus, on the south bank of the Charles River, occupies 64 acres just west of downtown Boston. The University's Medical Center is in the city's south end.

The College of Communication was founded in 1947 to provide professional education in public relations, journalism, broadcasting, and film. Graduate programs have been offered since the founding of the College. An integral part of the central campus, the College has its own building, lending a small-college atmosphere to its programs. The University is accredited by the New England Association of Schools and Colleges.

Applying

Applicants must have a bachelor's degree from an accredited college or university. Various majors are acceptable, but a strong background in social science and the humanities is considered desirable. Scores on the GRE General Test must be filed. M.B.A./M.S. television management students must file scores on the GMAT. Students applying to the J.D./M.S. in mass communication program must take the LSAT. International students must file TOEFL scores; there are minimum score requirements, which can be found on the University's Office of Admissions Web site (http://www.bu.edu/admissions/apply/int_language.html). Consideration is given to academic performance, test scores, recommendations, writing samples, and evidence of motivation in respect to the selected major. Applications with credentials must be received at the College of Communication by February 1. Early applications are encouraged. Incomplete applications cannot be reviewed. Online applications are preferred; applications may be submitted online at http://www.bu.edu/com/grad.

Correspondence and Information

Graduate Services
College of Communication
Boston University
640 Commonwealth Avenue
Boston, Massachusetts 02215

Phone: 617-353-3481
800-992-6514 (toll-free)
Fax: 617-358-0399
E-mail: comgrad@bu.edu
Web site: http://www.bu.edu/com/grad

Boston University

THE FACULTY AND AREAS OF CONCENTRATION

The names of the full-time faculty members are listed below in conjunction with the department in which their major responsibilities lie. Many faculty members teach in several programs. The entire faculty teaches in both the undergraduate and graduate curricula of the College. In addition to possessing excellent academic credentials, most faculty members have had extensive experience as practitioners in their areas of specialization. The Dean ad interim of the College is Tobe L. Berkovitz, B.F.A., M.A., Ph.D. (theater arts, speech communication).

DEPARTMENT OF FILM AND TELEVISION. Charles Merzbacher, M.F.A. (film production), Chairman; Robert Arnold, Ph.D. (film studies); John Bernstein, B.A., Ph.D. (film); Raymond Carney, Ph.D. (American studies); Mary Jane Doherty, M.S. (visual studies); Roy Grundmann, Ph.D. (critical studies); Samuel Kauffmann, M.S. (film production); John R. Kelly, Ph.D. (radio, film, and television); Frederick Lewis, M.A. (creative writing); Jeremy Murray-Brown, M.A. (broadcasting); Cathy Perron, M.S. (mass communication); Geoffrey Poister, Ph.D. (social science); Paul Schneider, M.F.A.; Garland Waller, M.S. (broadcast journalism).

Film Production. Mary Jane Doherty, Director. This two-year program provides thorough, hands-on training in all aspects of film production: scriptwriting, directing, cinematography, postproduction, and distribution. The emphasis is on narrative filmmaking. The curriculum includes courses in critical studies of film masterworks.

Screenwriting. John Bernstein, Director. This two-year program emphasizes a non-formulaic approach to screenwriting and requires students to understand and practice the art of screenwriting, to learn the fundamentals of dramatic production, to understand various models of film structure and film history, and to comprehend the role of the storyteller and the place of the screenplay in the dramatic tradition.

Film Studies. Roy Grundmann, Director. This two-year program prepares students to work as critics, historians, scholars, teachers, librarians, archivists, programmers, or exhibitors. Film studies majors, under faculty supervision, may pursue a variety of critical approaches to film.

Television Management. Cathy Perron, Director. This three-semester program is for students who have decided to pursue management careers in various telecommunications industries. There is also a five-semester dual-degree program in conjunction with the Graduate School of Management.

Television Production. Cathy Perron, Director. This three-semester program combines hands-on production experience with courses in the history and social impact of television and in television management to prepare students for careers in production, management, programming, marketing, teaching, and criticism.

DEPARTMENT OF JOURNALISM. Lou Ureneck, B.A. (English), Chair; Fred Bayles, B.S. (journalism); Keith Botsford, A.M.; Chris Daly, M.A. (American history); Anne Donohue, M.S. (broadcast journalism), M.A. (international relations); Jonathan Klarfeld, A.B. (English); H. Joachim Maitre, Ph.D. (literature); Robert Manoff, M.C.P. (urban studies); Elizabeth Mehren, M.J.; Sasha Norkin, M.S.; Safoura Rafeizadeh, M.F.A. (graphic design); Caryl Rivers, M.S. (journalism); Ellen Ruppel Shell, B.A. (biology); Frank H. Shorr, M.S. (broadcasting and film); Peter Smith, B.S.; Peter Southwick, B.A. (government); Douglas Starr, M.S. (science reporting); James Thistle, B.S. (communication); Susan Walker, B.A.; Mitchell Zuckoff, M.A. (journalism).

Journalism. Jonathan Klarfeld, Director. The program in journalism provides qualified students with an in-depth understanding of the press in its various aspects—its editorial and economic functions, its relation to other social institutions, and its limitations and responsibilities. Competence in research in mass communication problems is one area of emphasis. Another is proficiency in reporting, writing and editing, and other professional practices that prepare graduates for employment in the field. Graduate students may elect the traditional research thesis or a reporting project in a specialized area, designed for publication in the form of magazine articles or as an extended newspaper series.

Broadcast Journalism. James Thistle, Director. The program provides a working knowledge of the organization and structure of broadcasting and its relationship to government, mastery of the techniques of television and radio newswriting, and a survey of the varied aspects of television news programming.

Business and Economics Journalism. Lou Ureneck, Director. This program combines journalism training with instruction in business and economics. Core courses include an introduction to business and economics reporting, advanced business writing, international business and economics reporting, and investigative techniques.

Science Journalism. Douglas Starr and Ellen Ruppel Shell, Co-Directors. This program prepares students to work as reporters, writers, and editors for scientific, engineering, or business newspapers and magazines. Students are also exposed to basic courses in audiovisual subjects, broadcast journalism, and publication management and may select advanced courses and directed-study projects in these professional areas. The three-semester, 48-credit program includes internships of the student's choice with various organizations, including a science news service, scientific and engineering newspapers and magazines, and scientific, industrial, and business institutions. In conjunction with their internships or course work, students also usually prepare a major science communication project for professional production or publication.

DEPARTMENT OF MASS COMMUNICATION, ADVERTISING, AND PUBLIC RELATIONS. T. Barton Carter, J.D. (law), Chair; Judith Austin, B.F.A.; Tobe Berkovitz, Ph.D. (theater arts, speech communication); Christopher Cakebread, Ph.D. (mass communication); John Carroll, A.B. (Latin, Greek, and English); Carolyn Clark, M.S. (marketing); Dorothy Clark, M.S. (mass communication); Jo Doherty, M.S. (mass communication); Edward Downes, M.S. (journalism); Michel Elasmar, Ph.D. (mass communication); Thomas Fauls, M.S. (advertising); Hyun-Yeul Lee, Ph.D.; Joyce Macario, M.F.A. (graphic design); Peter Morrissey, B.S. (communication); Patrice Oppliger, Ph.D.; Susan Parenio, M.A. (English literature); John Schulz, D.Phil. (international relations); John Verret, B.A. (economics); Tammy Vigil, Ph.D. (communication studies); H. Denis Wu, Ph.D.

Advertising. The M.S. in advertising at Boston University is designed to prepare students to work in advertising agencies, media companies, and other marketing communications organizations. Some are prepared for doctoral-level studies. All students must take courses that provide a broad understanding of the advertising industry and of the role of communication in contemporary society. In addition, they focus on developing advertising campaigns or research skills. Students may choose one of three tracks: management track, creative track, or thesis track. The management track prepares students for careers in account management, media, account planning, or advertising research. The creative track prepares students for careers in art direction or copywriting. The thesis track prepares students for careers in marketing research or education.

Mass Communication. The mass communication program is designed to cover the broad range of professional communications studies and industries without specializing in any one area and to provide students with a strong understanding of communications theory, processes, and application, along with basic writing and media skills. Through this generalist approach, students are prepared to practice in such professional areas as advertising agencies, newspapers, publishing houses, television and radio stations, and nonprofit and government agencies. The program incorporates policy, planning, and management studies.

Public Relations. The program in public relations is designed to provide professional instruction for qualified students seeking careers in public relations for business, government, and nonprofit organizations. The program has three foundations: the theory and process of communication, the administrative and policy sciences, and research findings in communication and the social sciences. These foundations are interconnected by a body of knowledge drawn from the liberal arts, particularly the social sciences, and applied to the practical decisions and programs of public relations.

The Journalism School
Columbia University

COLUMBIA UNIVERSITY

The Graduate School of Journalism

Programs of Study

The School offers two intensive master's degrees for students who are pursuing a professional career in journalism and a traditional doctoral program in journalism and communication.

The Master of Science (M.S.) program is designed to provide a thorough grounding in the skills and values that a person needs to be a professional journalist, such as a general-assignment reporter at a newspaper or a producer or on-air reporter at a TV news operation. The program blends study of the arts, new media, and principles of journalism with study of such areas of knowledge as education, health, science, environment, urban problems, economics, international affairs, politics, and society. Candidates working toward the M.S. in journalism cover news and developing stories under the guidance of full-time faculty members and part-time adjunct professors who are drawn from New York City's journalistic community. Most instruction and critique of students' work occurs in small seminars and workshops. The School admits approximately 80 students from overseas. A flexible part-time M.S. program, which begins in late May, is available for students who want to work while continuing their education.

The Toni Stabile Center for Investigative Journalism is dedicated to training students interested in pursuing distinguished careers in investigative journalism. Candidates for the Master of Science degree are able to pursue this specialization, which is platform-neutral and is taken in addition to the traditional M.S. concentrations of broadcast, newspaper, magazine, and new media. In order to graduate with a specialization in investigative journalism, students must apply to the center as part of their application for admission to the School and then take all four courses offered by the Stabile Center.

The Master of Arts (M.A.) program focuses on teaching future leaders in journalism about complicated subjects they might encounter in their careers. The journalism school's founder, Joseph Pulitzer, wrote a manifesto for the school in 1904, in which he said, ". . . in general university courses we may find by-products that would meet the needs of the journalist. Why not divert, deflect, extract, and concentrate them for the journalist as specialist?" That is the goal of the M.A. program—to train students as journalists in the substantive understanding of subject matter. It therefore draws deeply on expertise that resides elsewhere in the University and entails a good deal of academic partnership between the journalism school and the rest of the University. Applicants to the M.A. program are assumed to have attained a high degree of professional competency as journalists. This is demonstrated by either a record of substantial professional achievement or a master's degree in journalism from Columbia or a peer institution.

The Ph.D. program is based on the concept that, at the advanced level, the study of journalism consists largely in interrogating and opening a conversation with other disciplines that are capable of illuminating journalism as a social and political practice. The idea is that journalism is, at root, a form of storytelling, with generic connections to such other forms as Homeric poems, Elizabethan drama, nineteenth-century realistic novels, and twentieth-century film. Successful candidates develop an intimate understanding of journalism as a political and social phenomenon. The program is devoted to journalism as an intellectual craft chronicling contemporary life and times.

Dual-degree programs are offered with the School of Law, the School of Business, the School of International and Public Affairs, the Graduate School of Arts and Sciences' program in earth and environmental sciences, the Scripps Howard Program in Religion, and the School of Journalism at Sciences Po in Paris.

Research Facilities

The Roone Arledge Broadcast Lab, a state-of-the-art facility with up-to-date computer labs, is the backbone of the School's physical plant. Students also do their own end-user searching on LexisNexis and Dow Jones News/Retrieval. The School, as part of a university community of 28,000 students and faculty members, has libraries with more than 6 million volumes and a computer center for academic research projects.

Financial Aid

All admissions decisions are need-blind. The Graduate School of Journalism offers approximately $4.4 million annually in fellowships and scholarships to students who demonstrate high academic achievement, financial need, and exceptional promise for leading careers in journalism. In conjunction with its Student Financial Planning Office, Columbia works with each student to ease the cost of attendance through a combination of scholarships and need-based programs, including grants and federal and private loans. Each year, about 95 percent of the graduate students are assisted through educational loans totaling more than $8 million. All applicants requiring financial aid must fill out a Journalism School Financial Aid Form. In addition to that form, all domestic applicants must fill out a FAFSA. Students should visit the Web site for details. Students in the part-time program may apply for student loans, provided they enroll for a minimum of 6 credits.

Cost of Study

In 2008–09, tuition and fees total $44,782 for the M.S. program and $40,342 for the M.A. and Ph.D. programs. Students in the part-time program pay on a per-point basis. The cost of a point in 2008–09 is $1362.

Living and Housing Costs

In 2008–09, rooms in graduate residence halls for single students range from $7500 to $17,500 per academic year, depending on the size of the apartment, the number of students sharing it, and whether it is furnished. Single rooms off campus start at approximately $850 per month; apartments, at $1050. Single-room rates at International House, which accommodates 500 graduate students, range from $7000 to $11,900 per academic year. Apartment rates at International House range from $954 to $1900 per month. With travel and telephone expenses, the yearly cost of living for a single student usually ranges from $20,370 to $24,000.

Student Group

Students at the School represent a diverse range of interests and aspirations. There are currently 385 students enrolled—229 full-time M.S. students, 92 part-time M.S. students, 39 M.A. students, and 25 Ph.D. students.

Location

In gathering, writing, editing, photographing, and presenting the news, the students' laboratory is New York City—one of the world's great news and media centers.

The University and The School

Established as King's College in 1754, Columbia was given a state charter and a new name after the Revolutionary War. The School of Journalism opened in 1912 as an undergraduate institution but since 1935 has operated exclusively at the graduate level. The University awards the Pulitzer Prizes in Journalism and Letters and administers the Columbia University Seminars on Media and Society, while the School administers the Alfred I. duPont–Columbia University Awards in Broadcast Journalism, the Maria Moors Cabot Prizes for Latin American reporting, the National Magazine Awards, the John Chancellor Award, the John B. Oakes Award for Environmental Reporting, and the Lukas Book Project. The School also publishes the *Columbia Journalism Review.* The Saul and Janice Poliak Center for the Study of First Amendment Issues was established and endowed in 1983 and the George T. Delacorte Center for Magazine Journalism in 1985. The School's 9,451 alumni include scores of publishers, top-ranking editors, foreign correspondents, reporters, and broadcasters.

Applying

The School accepts majors in all disciplines. Emphasis is on academic excellence in a substantive course of study, initiative, curiosity, a passion for journalism, and professional promise. All M.S. applicants are required to take a writing test that helps the admission committee assess their breadth of knowledge and use of English. The GRE is required for the Ph.D. application but not for the M.S. or M.A. programs. Applications must be filed with the $95 application fee. Application deadlines can be found at the School's Web site (http://www.journalism.columbia.edu). Decisions are mailed on or before April 1. The School uses an online application only. Students may check the admission Web site for updates and the recruitment schedule.

All dual-degree applicants must submit an application to the appropriate school in addition to the journalism application.

Correspondence and Information

The Graduate School of Journalism
Columbia University
2950 Broadway, Room 203
New York, New York 10027

Phone: 212-854-8608
Fax: 212-854-2352
E-mail: admissions@jrn.columbia.edu
Web site: http://www.journalism.columbia.edu

Columbia University

THE FACULTY

Nicholas Lemann, Henry R. Luce Professor and Dean; B.A., Harvard. Managing editor, the *Washington Monthly;* associate editor, executive editor, *Texas Monthly;* national staff reporter, the *Washington Post;* national correspondent, the *Atlantic Monthly;* staff writer, the *New Yorker;* author of several books, including *The Last Battle of the Civil War* (2006), *The Big Test: The Secret History of the American Meritocracy* (1999), and *The Promised Land: The Great Black Migration and How It Changed America* (1991).

Helen Benedict, Professor of Journalism; M.S., Berkeley. Reporter, *Weekly News* (London); managing editor, *New Wings;* reporter, the *Independent* and the *Gazette* (California); freelance writer; author, *The Lonely Soldier: The Private War of Women Serving in Iraq,* to be published in spring 2009 by Beacon Press. In May 2008, she had an op-ed in the *New York Times* on this subject and in March 2007 published a piece on the sexual assault of women soldiers in *Salon* magazine, which won the James Aronson Award for Social Justice Journalism. Her other nonfiction books include *Virgin or Vamp: How the Press Covers Sex Crimes* (1992), *Portraits in Print* (1991), and *Recovery: How to Survive Sexual Assault* (1985, 1994). Her novels include *The Opposite of Love* (2007), *The Sailor's Wife* (2000), *Bad Angel* (1996, 1997), and *A World Like This* (1990).

Sheila Coronel, Professor of Professional Practice and Director, Stabile Center for Investigative Journalism; M.S., London School of Economics. Executive Director, Philippine Center for Investigative Journalism; reporter, the *New York Times,* the *Guardian* (London), and the *Manila Chronicle;* author of more than a dozen books, including *The Rulemakers: How the Wealthy and Well-Born Dominate Congress* (2004), *The Memory of Dances* (2002), *Edsa 2: A Nation in Revolt* (2001), and *Coups, Cults and Cannibals* (a collection of reportage, 1993).

June Cross, Associate Professor; B.A., Harvard. Fellow at Carnegie Mellon University's School of Urban and Public Affairs and the W.E.B. DuBois Institute for Afro-American Studies at Harvard; producer, *This Far by Faith,* a six-part PBS series on the African-American religious experience; reporter, PBS's *Frontline, CBS News,* and PBS's *MacNeil/Lehrer NewsHour.* Her reporting for the *NewsHour* on the U.S. invasion of Grenada won a 1983 Emmy; *Secret Daughter,* an autobiographical film, won an Emmy in 1997 and a DuPont–Columbia Award for Excellence in Broadcast Journalism. She is the author of a memoir, *Secret Daughter* (2006).

John Dinges, Associate Professor of Journalism; M.A., Stanford. Reporter, copy editor, the *Des Moines Register* and the *Tribune;* special correspondent, assistant editor (foreign desk), the *Washington Post;* editor and writer, World Bank's *Urban Edge;* foreign editor, managing editor for news, editorial director, National Public Radio; winner, Maria Moors Cabot Prize for excellence in Latin American reporting; juror, Alfred I. duPont–Columbia University Awards; author, *The Condor Years: How Pinochet and His Allies Brought Terrorism to Three Continents* (2004); editor and coauthor, *Sound Reporting* (1992); editor, *Independence and Integrity: A Guidebook for Public Radio Journalism* (1995), *Our Man in Panama: The Shrewd Rise and Brutal Fall of Manuel Noriega* (1990), and *Assassination on Embassy Row* (1980).

Thomas Edsall, Joseph Pulitzer II and Edith Pulitzer Moore Professor of Journalism; B.A., Boston University. Reporter, the *Washington Post;* correspondent for the *New Republic* and the *National Journal;* has reported for the *Baltimore Sun* and the *Providence Journal.* Contributor to *American Prospect,* the *Atlantic Monthly, Civilization, Dissent, Harper's,* the *Nation,* the *New Republic,* the *New York Review of Books,* and *Washington Monthly.* TV and radio commentator for CNN, CSPAN, MSNBC, PBS, FOX, and NPR. Author of *Building Red America* (2006); *Chain Reaction: The Impact of Race, Rights, and Taxes on American Politics* (2005); *Power and Money: Writing About Politics* (1988); and *The New Politics of Inequality* (1984).

Samuel G. Freedman, Professor of Journalism; B.A., Wisconsin. Reporter, Bridgewater (New Jersey) *Courier-News;* reporter, *Chicago Tribune's Suburban Trib;* reporter, the *New York Times;* contributor, *Rolling Stone, Salon,* and the *New York Times;* contributing correspondent, *PBS Religion & Ethics NewsWeekly;* member, *USA Today* Board of Contributors; adjunct professor of theater, Columbia University School of the Arts; winner, numerous literary awards; author, *Jew vs. Jew: The Struggle for the Soul of American Jewry* (2000), *The Inheritance: How Three Families and America Moved from Roosevelt to Reagan and Beyond* (1996), *Upon This Rock: The Miracles of a Black Church* (1993), and *Small Victories: The Real World of a Teacher, Her Students and Their High School* (1990).

Todd Gitlin, Professor of Journalism and Sociology; Ph.D., Berkeley. Contributing writer, *Mother Jones;* winner, numerous literary awards; member, editorial board, *Dissent and the American Scholar;* author, *Letters to a Young Activist* (2003); *Media Unlimited: How the Torrent of Images and Sounds Overwhelms Our Lives* (2002); *Sacrifice* (1999); *The Twilight of Common Dreams: Why America Is Wracked by Culture Wars* (1995); *The Murder of Albert Einstein* (1992); *Watching Television* (editor, 1987); *The Sixties: Years of Hope, Days of Rage* (1987); *Inside Prime Time* (1983); *The Whole World Is Watching: Mass Media in the Making and Unmaking of the Left* (1981); *Busy Being Born* (1974); and *Uptown: Poor Whites in Chicago* (1970).

Ari L. Goldman, Professor of Journalism; M.S., Columbia. Reporter and religion correspondent, the *New York Times;* director, Scripps Howard Program in Religion, Journalism and the Spiritual Life; author, *Living a Year of Kaddish* (2003), *Being Jewish* (2000), and *The Search for God at Harvard* (1991).

David Hajdu, Associate Professor of Journalism. Columnist, the *New Republic;* contributor, the *Atlantic Monthly,* the *New Yorker,* the *New York Review of Books,* the *New York Times Magazine,* and *Vanity Fair;* general editor, *Entertainment Weekly;* editor-at-large, New York Times Magazine Group; editor-in-chief, *Video Review.* Author of several books, including *The Ten-Cent Plague: The Great Comic-Book Scare and How It Changed America* (2008); *Positively 4th Street: The Lives and Times of Joan Baez, Bob Dylan, Mimi Baez Farina and Richard Farina* (2001); and *Lush Life: A Biography of Billy Strayhorn* (1996); the last two were finalists for the National Book Critics Circle Award.

LynNell Hancock, Associate Professor of Journalism; M.A., M.S., Columbia. Assistant editor, Pantheon Books; freelance writer; staff writer, the *Village Voice;* education reporter, the *Daily News* (New York); education editor, *Newsweek;* former director, Prudential Fellowship for Children and the News; National Advisory Board member, Journalism Fellowships in Child and Family Policy; steering committee member, Institute for Child and Family Policy, Columbia University; contributor, *The Public Assault on America's Children: Poverty, Violence and Juvenile Injustice;* author, *Prairie Fires* (2007) and *Hands to Work: The Stories of Three Families Racing the Welfare Clock* (2002).

Marguerite Holloway, Assistant Professor and Director, Science and Environmental Journalism; M.S., Columbia. Codirector of the dual-degree earth and environmental sciences journalism program; contributing editor, *Scientific American;* reporter, *Medical Tribune;* freelance writer, the *Village Voice, Mother Jones, Discover,* the *New York Times, Natural History,* and *Wired.*

Stephen D. Isaacs, Professor of Journalism; B.A., Harvard. Reporter and editor, *Louisville Times* (Kentucky); reporter, the *Economist,* the *Guardian,* and other British publications; copy editor, reporter, city editor, metropolitan editor, Sunday magazine editor, New York bureau chief, national correspondent, the *Washington Post;* director, *Los Angeles Times/Washington Post* News Service; editor and senior vice president, the *Minneapolis Star;* producer, CBS News; producer and consultant, David Hartman; chairman, Private Network Productions; author, *Jews and American Politics* (1974).

Michael Janeway, Professor of Journalism and the Arts; B.A., Harvard. Reporter, *Newsday* and *Newsweek;* associate editor, *New Leader Magazine;* assistant editor, associate editor, managing editor, executive editor, the *Atlantic Monthly;* special assistant to Secretary of State Cyrus Vance; assistant managing editor, managing editor, editor in chief, the *Boston Globe;* executive editor, Trade and Reference Division, Houghton Mifflin Co.; author, *Republic of Denial: Press, Politics, and Public Life* (1999); coeditor, contributor, *A Story of Our Time: American Politics and the Press in an Era of Loss* (1999) and *Who We Are: An Atlantic Chronicle of the United States and Vietnam* (1968).

David A. Klatell, Professor of Professional Practice and Chair of International Studies; M.S., Boston University. News writer, producer, executive producer, WCVB-TV (Boston); senior producer, White House television pool; international station development, *New York Times* Television; consultant, international television news network development, Sweden and Portugal; former chair of the jury, Alfred I. duPont–Columbia University Awards in Broadcast Journalism; associate editor, *Encyclopedia of International Media and Communication;* contributor to the *Washington Post Sunday Magazine* and the *New York Times;* coauthor, *Inside Big-Time Sports* (1996) and *Sports for Sale, Television Money and the Fans* (1988).

Dale Maharidge, Associate Professor. 1988 Nieman Fellow, Harvard; reporter, the *Cleveland Plain Dealer* and the *Sacramento Bee;* contributor, *Rolling Stone, George,* the *Nation, Mother Jones,* and the *New York Times.* Most of his books are illustrated with the work of photographer Michael Williamson. The first book, *Journey to Nowhere: The Saga of the New Underclass* (1985), later inspired Bruce Springsteen to write two songs; it was reissued in 1996 with an introduction by Springsteen. His second book, *And Their Children After Them* (1989), won the Pulitzer Prize for nonfiction in 1990. Other books include *Denison, Iowa: Searching for the Soul of America Through the Secrets of a Midwest Town* (2005); *Homeland* (2004); *The Coming White Minority: California, Multiculturalism & the Nation's Future* (1996, 1999); *The Last Great American Hobo* (1993); and *Yosemite: A Landscape of Life* (1990).

Sylvia Nasar, John S. and James L. Knight Professor of Business Journalism; M.A., NYU. Research scientist, the Institute for Economic Analysis (1977–80); economist, Scientists Institute for Public Information and Control Data Corporation (1981–82); writer, *Fortune* magazine (1983–89); columnist, *U.S. News & World Report* (1990); reporter, the *New York Times* (1991–99); judge, National Book Award and Overseas Press Club Journalism Awards; author, *A Beautiful Mind,* winner of the 1998 National Book Critics Circle Award for Biography and finalist, Pulitzer Prize for Biography.

Victor Navasky, Delacorte Professor of Journalism and Director of the George Delacorte Center for Magazine Journalism; LL.B., Yale. Founder, editor, publisher, *Monocle;* editor, the *New York Times Magazine;* columnist, the *New York Times Book Review;* editor, publisher, editorial director, the *Nation;* author, *A Matter of Opinion* (which won the George Polk Book Award in 2005), *Naming Names* (which won a national Book Award in 1982), and *Kennedy Justice* (1971).

Mirta Ojito, Assistant Professor; M.A., Columbia. Reporter, the *Miami Herald, El Nuevo Herald,* and the *New York Times;* shared Pulitzer Prize for national reporting (2001) and received the American Society of Newspaper Editors' writing award for best foreign reporting (1999); author, *Finding Mañana: A Memoir of a Cuban Exodus* (2005).

Addie Rimmer, Associate Professor of Professional Practice; M.S., Columbia. Reporter, National News Council, Commodity News Services; copy editor, the *Miami Herald* and the *Wall Street Journal;* assistant managing editor, deputy features editor, *Press-Telegram* (Long Beach, California); editor and vice president, the *News* (Boca Raton, Florida); executive editor and vice president, *Daily Camera;* deputy managing editor/news, *Detroit Free Press.*

Michael Schudson, Professor of Journalism; Ph.D., Harvard. Author of six books and editor of two others concerning the history and sociology of the American news media, advertising, popular culture, Watergate, and cultural memory. He has been a Guggenheim fellow; a resident fellow at the Center for Advanced Study in the Behavioral Sciences, Palo Alto; and a MacArthur Foundation "genius" fellow. In 2004, he received the Murray Edelman distinguished career award from the political communication section of the American Political Science Association and the International Communication Association. Schudson's articles have appeared in *Columbia Journalism Review, Wilson Quarterly,* and the *American Prospect,* and he has published op-eds in the *New York Times, Washington Post, Los Angeles Times, Newsday,* the *Financial Times,* and the *San Diego Union.*

Michael Shapiro, Assistant Professor of Journalism; M.A., Missouri. Reporter, Bridgewater (New Jersey) *Courier-News* and *Chicago Tribune's Suburban Trib;* associate editor, *Collector-Investor;* contributor to the *New York Times Magazine,* the *New Yorker, Esquire, Sports Illustrated, New York,* and the *Wall Street Journal;* author, *The Last Good Season: Brooklyn, the Dodgers, and Their Final Pennant Race Together* (2003); *Solomon's Sword* (1999); *Who Will Teach for America?* (1993); *The Shadow in the Sun: A Korean Year of Love and Sorrow* (1990); and *Japan: In the Land of the Brokenhearted* (1989).

Alisa Solomon, Associate Professor and Director, Arts & Culture, M.A. Program; Ph.D., Yale. Staff writer at the *Village Voice;* contributor, the *Nation,* the *Forward,* and the *New York Times;* contributor of theater commentaries, WNYC; contributing editor, *Beyond the Pale: Radical Jewish Culture and Politics* (WBAI); author, *Re-dressing the Canon: Essays on Theatre and Gender* (1997); editor of three anthologies: *Wrestling with Zion: Progressive Jewish-American Responses to the Israeli-Palestinian Conflict* (with Tony Kushner), *Theater and Social Change* (Theater, 31:3), and *The Queerest Art: Essays on Lesbian and Gay Theater* (with Framji Minwalla).

Sreenath Sreenivasan, Professor of Professional Practice and Dean of Student Affairs; M.S., Columbia. Directs the new media department at the School; worked as a journalist in India and Fiji; writes for the *New York Times, Popular Science, Time Digital,* and *BusinessWeek;* cofounder, the South Asian Journalists Association; founding administrator, Online Journalism Awards; technology reporter on air, WNBC, New York; formerly on-air technology reporter, WABC, New York.

James B. Stewart, Bloomberg Professor of Business and Economic Journalism; J.D., Harvard. Associate, Cravath, Swaine & Moore; reporter, executive editor, *American Lawyer;* reporter, *Page One;* editor, the *Wall Street Journal;* contributor, the *New Yorker;* editor at large, *Smart Money;* winner, Pulitzer Prize for explanatory journalism (1988); author, *DisneyWar* (2005), *Follow the Story* (1998), *Blood Sport* (1996), *Den of Thieves* (1991), *The Prosecutors* (1987), and *The Partners* (1984).

Alexander Stille, San Paolo Professor of International Journalism; M.S., Columbia. Contributor, the *New York Times, La Republica,* the *New Yorker,* the *New York Review of Books,* the *New York Times Magazine,* the *Atlantic Monthly,* and the *New Republic;* correspondent, *U.S. News & World Report,* the *Boston Globe,* and the *Toronto Globe and Mail;* winner of numerous literary awards; author, *The Sack of Rome: How a Beautiful European Country with a Fabled History and a Storied Culture Was Taken Over by a Man Named Silvio Berlusconi* (2006), *The Future of the Past* (2002), *Excellent Cadavers: The Mafia and the Death of the First Italian Republic* (1995), and *Benevolence and Betrayal: Five Italian Jewish Families Under Fascism* (1991).

Richard Wald, Fred Friendly Professor of Journalism. Former vice president, ABC News; worked for the *Herald Tribune,* the *Washington Post,* NBC News, and the *Times-Mirror* (Los Angeles).

Jonathan Weiner, Professor of Journalism; M.A., Harvard. Writes for the *New Yorker,* the *New York Times Magazine,* and the *New Republic;* author, *His Brother's Keeper: A Story from the Edge of Medicine* (2004), chosen as one of the most notable books of the year by the *New York Times; Time, Love, Memory: A Great Biologist and His Quest for the Origins of Behavior* (1999), winner of the National Book Critics Circle Award; and *The Beak of the Finch* (1994), winner of the Pulitzer Prize for Nonfiction. In 2000 and 2001, he served as Rockefeller University's first Writer in Residence.

Other Faculty Members
Ann Cooper, Josh M. Friedman, Rhoda Lipton, Laura Muha, Robin Reisig, Duy Linh Tu, Andie Tucher.

Professors Emeriti
W. Phillips Davison, Osborn Elliott, John Foster Jr., Kenneth Goldstein, Luther Jackson, Penn T. Kimball, Joan Konner, Melvin Mencher, Donald Shanor, Seymour Topping, Frederick T. C. Yu.

Visiting and Special Faculty Members
Floyd Abrams, Vincent A. Blasi, Evan Cornog, Sig Gissler, Anthony Lewis, Frank Moretti, Arlene Morgan, Terri Thompson, Betsy West.

Members of the Adjunct Faculty
A list of adjunct faculty members can be found at http://www.jrn.columbia.edu/faculty/.

CUNY GRADUATE SCHOOL OF JOURNALISM

Master of Arts in Journalism

Programs of Study

The Master of Arts degree in journalism at CUNY's Graduate School of Journalism is an intensive, full-time, three-semester program designed to prepare students for a career in journalism. Required courses in the first and second semesters provide a solid grounding in reporting and writing skills needed by all journalists. In the second semester, students select a media track—print (newspaper or magazine), broadcast (radio or TV), or interactive—in which they want to hone their skills. However, all students get a broad introduction to all media platforms, so they are prepared to work in the converged newsroom of the future. Students also choose a subject-matter concentration—arts/culture, business/economics, health/medicine, international reporting, or urban affairs—allowing them to practice deeper reporting skills that can be applied to any beat, even as they develop an expertise in one area. Beyond the core reporting and writing instruction, required courses in the 45-credit program include legal and ethical issues, research techniques, and fundamentals of interactive media. Students have some flexibility in tailoring their course of study to their particular interests and goals.

To graduate, each student must complete a capstone project, which may be a significant print piece, broadcast project, or major Web site package. Students also participate in an 8–10 week paid summer internship between their second and third semesters to give them experience in a working newsroom and to strengthen their resume.

Between the first and second semesters, the School offers optional enrichment seminars in its January Academy. Examples include a workshop on freelance writing, an introduction to sports reporting, or workshops in computer-assisted reporting or broadcast editing. The School's Web-based NYCity News Service provides the opportunity for all students to have their work distributed to professional media outlets for usage. Broadcast students also can have their work distributed through CUNY-TV, a 24-hour cable TV station that reaches 2 million viewers.

Classes are small and instruction is personalized. The faculty includes veteran journalists, including 3 Pulitzer prize winners, as well as professionals working in newsrooms across the city who have chosen to share their expertise with the next generation of journalists.

Research Facilities

The CUNY Graduate School of Journalism's new state-of-the-art facility includes an 80-seat wireless newsroom, digital television and radio studios, editing suites equipped with Final Cut Pro editing software, wireless classrooms that can reach out anywhere in the world, a lecture hall, student café, and student lounges. Students learn on the latest technology and are able to borrow a broad array of audio, video, and photography equipment to carry out their assignments.

A library/research center houses a collection of 2,000 volumes, more than 40 periodical titles, sixty electronic journals, and databases focused on journalism. All electronic material can be accessed by students at the School or at home over the Internet. Through CUNY's university-wide library resources, students and faculty members have access to another 4 million items. The Research Center offers students interlibrary loan privileges as well as research instruction.

Financial Aid

More than 80 percent of the students receive a tuition scholarship from the school, ranging from $1000 to $11,320 over three semesters. These need- and merit-based scholarships funded by supporters of the School include the Arthur "Punch" Sulzberger Scholarship, News Corporation Scholarship, Himan Brown Scholarship, Connie Chung and Maury Povich Scholarship, Daniel Schorr Scholarship, Julius Barnathan Scholarship, and the Irving Rosenthal Scholarship. Many of these scholarship funds provide assistance to multiple students in each academic year.

Approximately 75 percent of students have opted to take advantage of federal student loans to cover their living costs while at School. Many students also qualify for federal work-study programs that pay students to work at the School while pursuing their degree. Many students continue to work while in School, but the School cautions against trying to work more than 12 hours per week.

To be considered for a need-based scholarship from the School of Journalism, students must submit the Application for Financial Assistance and the Free Application for Federal Student Aid (FAFSA) by February 1 (can be filed online). To qualify for federal loan funding, students are asked to complete the FAFSA by February 1.

Cost of Study

The tuition for New York State residents is $3200 per semester. Tuition for the entire three-semester program is $9600, plus fees of $1720, bringing the three-semester total for tuition and fees to $11,320.

The tuition for non–New York State residents is $500 per credit. Assuming 15 credits per semester, the tuition is $7500 per semester. Out-of-state residents who are U.S. citizens or permanent residents may qualify for in-state tuition in their third semester, if they become legal residents of New York State. If so, tuition for the entire three-semester program is $18,200 plus fees of $1720, bringing the three-semester total for tuition and fees to $19,920.

For international students, tuition for the entire three-semester program is $22,500, plus fees of $1720, bringing the three-semester total for tuition and fees to $24,220.

Living and Housing Costs

Estimated costs for room and board are about $8000 for an academic year. To minimize housing costs, many students live in the four boroughs outside Manhattan and share an apartment. Virtually all use public transportation. For those wishing to live in Manhattan, a number of rooms are reserved for graduate journalism students at the CUNY City College Towers dormitory. For more information, students should contact Chris Clarke at cclarke@capstonemail.com or by phone at 917-507-0055. That office can also provide information about other housing options and connect students interested in sharing housing.

Student Group

There are currently 49 students enrolled in the program; 42 percent are members of minority groups, and 68 percent are women. The average age is 26. Students come from a variety of backgrounds: from the journalism profession, from other professions, and straight from an undergraduate school. Although some had never written a journalistic article before, all demonstrated an ability to write and think, a deep curiosity about the world, and a strong interest in making journalism their profession.

Location

The CUNY Graduate School of Journalism is housed at 219 West 40th Street, a block from Times Square, in the former home of the legendary *New York Herald Tribune.* Located in the heart of the media capital of the world, the School is within a short walking distance of many of the nation's largest media companies. The new headquarters for *The New York Times* is next door.

The School and The University

The CUNY Graduate School of Journalism opened in August 2006 under the leadership of Stephen Shepard, who served as editor of *BusinessWeek* for more than twenty years. The School's Board of Advisors includes David Westin, president of ABC News; Richard Stengel, managing editor of *Time;* Mortimer Zuckerman, chairman and publisher of the *New York Daily News* and *U.S. News & World Report;* Mark Whitaker, senior vice president, NBC News; Norman Pearlstine, former editor of the *Wall Street Journal;* Rosanna Rosada, publisher of *El Diario/La Prensa;* Merrill Brown, former editor-in-chief of MSNBC.com and a new media consultant; Matthew Winkler, editor-in-chief of *Bloomberg News;* and Michael Oreskes, editor of the *International Herald Tribune.*

The Graduate School of Journalism operates under the aegis of the CUNY Graduate Center and is one of twenty institutions that comprise the City University of New York, the nation's largest urban university. The CUNY Graduate Center administers thirty doctoral and six master's programs as well as twenty-eight research institutes. The University's origins date back to 1847 to the Free Academy, which grew into City College. Throughout its history, the University has maintained a commitment to academic excellence and to providing access and opportunity to students from diverse ethnic and geographic backgrounds.

Applying

Applications are accepted for the fall semester only. A four-year undergraduate degree is required of all applicants, including international students. International applicants are defined as those who hold or intend to apply for a nonimmigrant visa. They must have the equivalent of a U.S. undergraduate degree and a minimum grade-point average of 3.0 (B) to be considered for admission. In addition to the Graduate Record Exam (GRE), all international applicants are required to take the Test of English as a Foreign Language (TOEFL), including its writing component, the TWE. The deadline for all applications is January 2. The School uses an online application that can be accessed on its Web site. Students may mail supporting application materials to Graduate School of Journalism, Office of Admissions, The Graduate Center, 365 Fifth Avenue, New York, New York 10016-4309.

Correspondence and Information

CUNY Graduate School of Journalism
219 West 40th Street
New York, New York 10018

Phone: 646-758-7700
E-mail: admissions@journalism.cuny.edu
Web site: http://www.journalism.cuny.edu

CUNY Graduate School of Journalism

THE FACULTY

Eric Alterman, Professor; Ph.D., Stanford. Senior fellow at the Center for American Progress; an award-winning author, widely published both in print and other media; writer of *The Nation*'s "Liberal Media" column and MSNBC.com's "Altercation" weblog.
Sarah Bartlett, Professor and Director of the Urban and Business Reporting Programs; M. Phil., Sussex (England). Editor-in-Chief of Oxygen Media; Assistant Managing Editor at *BusinessWeek;* former reporter at *Fortune* and *The New York Times;* author of two books; host of U$A Inc., a weekly show on finance on CUNY-TV.
Roslyn Bernstein, Professor; Ph.D., NYU. Founder of the journalism and business journalism programs at Baruch College; founder and publisher of *Dollars and $ense,* the Baruch College business review.
Jere Hester, Associate Professor and Director of NYCity News Service; B.A., NYU. City Editor of the *New York Daily News;* Editor-in-Chief, *Downtown Express.*
Ruth Hochberger, Editor in Residence; J.D., Boston College. Editor-in-Chief of the *New York Law Journal,* member of the New York Bar, criminal defense lawyer for the Legal Aid Society in Manhattan.
Lonnie Isabel, Associate Professor; B.A., Amherst. Deputy Managing Editor of *Newsday* responsible for supervising the national, foreign, state, Washington, health, and science staffs; Assistant Managing Editor and National Editor of *Newsday.*
Jeff Jarvis, Associate Professor and Director of the Interactive Media Program; B.A., Northwestern. Author of the Buzzmachine.com Web log; new-media columnist and consultant for *The Guardian* in London; President of Advance.net, the online arm of Advance Publications; creator and Managing Editor of *Entertainment Weekly;* critic and Development Editor *TV Guide;* Associate Publisher and Sunday Editor, *New York Daily News.*
Sandeep Junnarkar, Associate Professor; M.S., Columbia. Co-producer of Lives in Focus, a multimedia Web site that features stories on under-reported issues; New York Bureau Chief of CNET News.com; Web producer for New York Times on the Web; recognized by the Society of American Business Editors and Writers for online reporting.
Frederick Kaufman, Associate Professor; Ph.D., CUNY Graduate Center. Magazine journalist published in *The New York Times Sunday Magazine, The New York Times Sunday Book Review, New York Magazine, Harper's, The New Yorker, Gentleman's Quarterly, Interview, Spin, Spy, Aperture, Allure, Publisher's Weekly, The Village Voice Literary Supplement,* and other publications.
Glenn Lewis, Associate Professor; M.A., CUNY, City College. Magazine journalist published in *Publishers Weekly, Car & Driver, US, Seventeen, Family Weekly, Library Journal,* and the *Philadelphia Inquirer;* author of children's book series; co-founder of Book Smart, Inc.; expert commentator on media for Channel 5 News.
Trudy Lieberman, Director of Health/Medicine Reporting Program; B.A., Kansas. Director of the Center for Consumer Health Choices at Consumers Union, contributing editor to the *Columbia Journalism Review* and *The Nation,* consumer writer at the *Detroit Free Press,* author of five nonfiction books.
Anthony Mancini, Professor; B.A., Fordham. Widely published writer of fiction and nonfiction; began journalism career at the *New York Post;* contributed articles to numerous newspapers and magazines, including *The New York Times,* the *Washington Post, New York,* and *Travel & Leisure;* author of seven novels.
Heath Meriwether, Distinguished Writing Coach; M.A., Harvard. Publisher and Executive Editor of the *Detroit Free Press;* Executive Editor, Managing Editor, and reporter for the *Miami Herald.*
Margot Mifflin, Assistant Professor and Interim Director of the Arts/Culture Program; M.A., NYU. Contributing editor at *Elle;* freelance writer on art, pop culture, books, and women's issues published in *The New York Times, Salon.com, The Village Voice, The New Yorker,* and several women's magazines; author of two nonfiction books.
Paul Moses, Professor; M.F.A., Massachusetts Amherst. City Editor at *Newsday*'s New York City edition; lead writer on a New York *Newsday* team that won the Pulitzer Prize for Spot News Reporting; winner of the Silurians' award for breaking news coverage in 1992; Brooklyn Editor, City Hall Bureau Chief, and National Religion Writer during seventeen years at *Newsday.*
Linda Prout, Professor and Director of the Broadcast Program; M.S., Columbia. Writer and producer for PBS and the Bravo Network; Station Director for Harlem Community Radio; producer of award-winning series for television and video including *The Kids' Chronicle* and *WomanSource;* reporter for several print publications including *Newsday, Newsweek,* and the *Star-Ledger.*
Geanne Rosenberg, Associate Professor; M.S., J.D., Columbia. Journalist specializing in coverage of legal, regulatory, and business issues; published in *Columbia Journalism Review, The New York Times, The National Law Journal, Editor and Publisher Magazine, Investor's Business Daily,* and many other newspapers and magazines.
Stephen B. Shepard, Professor and Dean of the Graduate School of Journalism; M.S., Columbia. Editor-in-Chief of *Business Week,* the largest business magazine in the world, for twenty years; Senior Editor for National Affairs at *Newsweek* and editor of the *Saturday Review;* co-founder and Director of Columbia University's Knight-Bagehot Fellowship in Economic and Business Journalism.
Bernard Stein, Professor; B.A., Columbia. Editor and co-publisher of the *Riverdale Press,* an award-winning weekly community newspaper in the Bronx that has won more than 300 state and national awards for excellence; winner of the Pulitzer Prize for editorial writing in 1998.
Steven Strasser, Associate Professor; M.A., Columbia. Managing Editor, National Affairs Editor and senior writer for *Newsweek International;* Moscow Correspondent, Hong Kong Bureau Chief, and Asia Editor for *Newsweek;* recipient of three Oversees Press Club awards; editor of three nonfiction books.
Wayne Svoboda, Associate Professor and Director of the Print Program; M.S., Columbia; M.S., London School of Economics. East Coast Correspondent for *Time* magazine; Africa Editor at *The Economist;* freelance reporter for publications including the *Wall Street Journal* and *Institutional Investor;* Fulbright Scholar who has taught in Russia and the Czech Republic.
Judith Watson, Associate Professor and Associate Dean; B.A., Pomona. New York Bureau Chief of United Press International; New York State Editor and Albany Capitol Bureau Chief, UPI; Director, *Hoosier in Washington* news service; reporter for *The Frankfort Times.*
Scotti Williston, Senior Producer in Residence. Reporter for WPIX-TV, NY; TV producer in the U.S., Europe, the Middle East, Africa, Russia, and China; Cairo Bureau Chief and Rome Bureau Chief for CBS News; producer for CBS Sunday Morning; independent producer and consultant for NBC News, National Hellenic Radio (NYC), and WNET/PBS (NYC).

Adjunct Faculty
Rose Marie Arce, senior producer for CNN.
Michael Arena, former investigative reporter for *Newsday* who shared the Pulitzer Prize for Spot News reporting.
Russell Chun, freelance art and multimedia developer.
Greg David, Editor-in-Chief, *Crain's New York Business.*
David Diaz, veteran TV correspondent for WCBS and WNBC TV.
James Estrin, senior staff photographer for *The New York Times.*
Beth Fertig, senior reporter for WNYC radio.
George Freeman, Vice President and Assistant General Counsel for *The New York Times.*
Timothy Harper, freelance writer and editor with extensive reporting experience around the globe.
Jennifer Johnson Hicks, assistant news editor at The Wall Street Journal Online who oversees breaking news and production for the Web site in the evenings.
Mona Houck, staff editor on the national desk for *The New York Times.*
Susan Kuhn, former associate editor at *Forbes.*
Andrew W. Lehren, reporter at *The New York Times* specializing in computer-assisted reporting.
Rebecca Leung, former freelancer at the *Los Angeles Times* and former producer for CBS News, TheStreet.com, ABC News, and CNET.
Robert B. Levine, freelance journalist who covers music and pop culture for *The New York Times, Fortune,* and many other publications.
David Lewis, president of a documentary production company, former associate producer for *60 Minutes.*
Anne Mintz, Director of Knowledge Management at *Forbes.*
Alan Mirabella, senior editor at Bloomberg News in New York.
Barbara Oliver, Director of News Research for *The New York Times.*
Ivan Oransky, Deputy Editor of *The Scientist: Magazine of the Life Sciences.*
Eric Owles, senior online producer for *The New York Times.*
Tina Pamintuan, media producer and freelance writer, former NPR producer.
Garry Pierre-Pierre, editor and publisher of the *Haitian Times.*
Barbara Raab, senior writer and producer for NBC News.
Laura Sanders, reporter and senior editor at *Forbes* for twenty years.
John Schiumo, host of "The Call" for NY1.
Jan Simpson, former assistant managing editor at *Time* magazine in the Society/Life section.
Jack Styczynski, freelance sports feature writer and researcher for NBC News, *The New York Times,* and *People* magazine.
John Smock, photojournalist for SIPA, a photo agency with offices in New York and in Paris, and the Associated Press.
Indrani Sen, freelance magazine writer, former reporter for *Newsday.*
Dody Tsiantar, freelance magazine writer, veteran reporter for *Time.*
Rob Williams, reporter for *The Star-Ledger,* covering seven communities in Morris County and writing about development, the immigration debate, and related topics.

EMERSON COLLEGE

School of Communication
Master of Arts in Communication Management

Program of Study

The Emerson College M.A. in Communication Management (CM) program allows students to develop skills in speaking, writing, listening, and negotiations, as well as the media expertise necessary for success in the rapidly changing technological environment. As professionals who analyze, strategize, initiate, and evaluate effective communication plans, CM graduates find career success as communication officers, organizational or communication strategists, directors of financial communication, and more. They acquire an understanding of an organization's stakeholders necessary for effective ethical communication campaigns and strategies.

Students enrolled in the communication management program have many career options. As a communication management specialist, Emerson graduates' qualifications transfer across business, government, and nonprofit sectors. The CM degree prepares students for leadership positions in communication, including director of corporate communications or public affairs in the business sector, communications director of press secretary in the political and governmental arena, director of public advocacy campaigns for a nonprofit of nongovernmental organization, independent consultant or trainer, or senior executive in business or government. They help organizations to define and communicate their vision, mission, and strategy, making them invaluable members of any executive team.

Research Facilities

The Emerson College library has more than 200,000 volumes, 20,000 journals (paper and electronic), 8,000 e-books, 10,000 nonprint materials, and 10,000 microforms in its collection that focus on the communication studies and performing arts. Through membership in the Fenway Library Consortium, graduate students have access to more than 2 million volumes. Computer-assisted reference services provide bibliographic databases through Dialog, BRS, and other online services. The Online Computer Library Center is used for student research support.

M.A. candidates gain valuable hands-on experience in the Media Services Center, which provides students with access to approximately 2,400 films, videos, laser discs, and DVDs. The center is the home of audio, video, and multimedia production facilities; a video studio; and several nonlinear editing suites comparable to those of any television studio in a major U.S. city. In addition, a marketing suite opened in 2003 that features a focus group room with an observation booth. There are also fully-mediated classrooms.

Financial Aid

Emerson College offers several financial assistance programs that make graduate education possible: merit-based awards (domestic and international applicants), low-interest federal loans (domestic applicants only), federal work-study (domestic applicants only), private loans (domestic and international applicants), student employment (domestic and international applicants), and alternative payment plans (domestic and international applicants). For detailed information, students should visit the Office of Student Financial Services Web site at http://www.emerson.edu/financial_services.

Cost of Study

Tuition for the 2008–09 academic year is $886 per credit hour. Other fees vary and may apply.

Living and Housing Costs

Though on-campus housing is not available for its graduate students, the Emerson College Office of Off-Campus Student Services offers assistance in finding housing, including: local apartment listings, realtor lists, temporary accommodations, search tips, pertinent neighborhood information, a roommate networking service, and more. Costs for housing are comparable to those of rental properties available in larger East Coast cities.

Student Group

More than 950 graduate students representing forty-five states and sixty countries are enrolled in Emerson programs.

Student Outcomes

Located in the heart of Boston, Emerson has access to nationally renowned organizations in one of the nation's largest media and corporate centers. Recent employers have included the AIDS Action Committee, Arnold Worldwide, Blue Cross & Blue Shield, Fidelity Investments, the Massachusetts State House, and the Polaroid Corporation.

Location

Situated in the heart of downtown Boston, Emerson offers access to the vast resources of a city that is the home of the nation's finest educational institutions and an international hub of culture, media production, writing, publishing, communication, commerce, and medical innovation. Boston is a career launching pad for Emerson's students, many of whom intern or work at world-renowned organizations throughout the city. Emerson students from around the country and world absorb the city's unique blend of local and global culture, and many find that Boston is an education in itself.

The College

Emerson College, founded in 1880 by Charles Wesley Emerson, has expanded upon its original mission of promoting the study of oratory and the performing arts by offering some of the nation's most distinctive graduate programs in communication.

Applying

Emerson's graduate programs welcome applicants from across the United States and around the world. Admission is competitive and selective. Emerson is looking for students whose academic and professional backgrounds, communication skills, and passion for the field meet the demands of their chosen program and promise a successful career.

The application deadline for fall enrollment is June 1 for domestic applicants and May 1 for international applicants. For spring enrollment, the deadline is November 1 for international and domestic applicants. Applications that are not complete by the final deadline are not reviewed by the admission committee. Applicants are responsible for ensuring the completion of their application. Application fees are nonrefundable; application forms and supporting materials become the property of the Office of Graduate Admission once they are sent to the office, and they will not be returned.

All application materials, with the exception of GRE/GMAT test scores, must be submitted together in one package to ensure a timely review. A complete application includes the application form (students may apply online or they may download the PDF version), the application fee ($60 for domestic applicants; $75 for international applicants), official transcripts from all colleges/universities previously attended, three sealed letters of recommendation (by persons best able to assess academic and professional qualifications, including motivation, goals, and potential), GRE/GMAT test scores, two essay responses to questions listed in the application, and a professional resume.

Applicants whose native language is not English must provide evidence of English proficiency by submitting official TOEFL or IELTS test results. (Applicants from India and the Philippines are considered nonnative English speakers and are required to take the TOEFL.) Emerson College's school code for the TOEFL is 3367; no department code is needed. For more information about these tests, prospective student can visit http://www.toefl.org or http://www.ielts.org. Minimum TOEFL scores are 550 paper-based, 213 computer-based, and 80 Internet-based. The minimum IELTS score is 6.5. Applicants who do not meet this requirement are not reviewed for admission.

Decisions are made on complete applications within six to eight weeks.

Deadlines for merit-based and federal aid applications for fall are March 1 and April 1, respectively and November 1 for spring. For more information about financing a graduate education, students should visit: http://www.emerson.edu/financial_services/info-grad.cfm/.

Correspondence and Information

Office of Graduate Admission
Emerson College
120 Boylston Street
Boston, Massachusetts 02116-4624

Phone: 617-824-8610
Fax: 617-824-8614
E-mail: gradapp@emerson.edu
Web site: http://admission.emerson.edu/admission/graduate

Emerson College

THE FACULTY AND THEIR RESEARCH

Linda Peek Schacht, Acting Chair and Scholar-in-Residence; B.A., David Lipscomb. Ms. Peek Schacht has had a three-decade career advising leaders in every sector on strategy and communications, including appointments in the White House Press Office and the U.S. Senate Leadership staff. She retired as vice president, director of public affairs and communications strategy at the Coca-Cola Company in 2002, after eleven years as the company's chief communication strategist. From 1983 to 1988, Ms. Peek Schacht was spokesperson for the U.S. Senate Democratic leader and communications director for the Senate Democratic Policy Committee. She was the first public affairs director of *USA Today,* where she focused on the development, testing, and launch of the newspaper. As communications director and press secretary for the Carter-Mondale re-election campaign, she was the first woman to head a presidential campaign press office. She was a special assistant in the Carter White House office of media liaison, responsible for the President's twice monthly meetings with journalists from outside Washington. She is on the board of International Women's Media Foundation and is the president of the Mike Schacht Foundation, which produces sports-oriented art and writing workshops for children. As a senior fellow at the Kennedy School of Government at Harvard from 2002 to 2006, Ms. Peek Schacht offered workshops on leadership and communication.

Linda Gallant, Assistant Professor and Graduate Program Director; Ph.D., Nebraska–Lincoln. Dr. Gallant investigates how Web-based information and communication technologies can best facilitate human communication to advance social computing and media for personal use as well as internal and external corporate communication. She has publications in *Personal and Ubiquitous Computing, e-Service Journal, Qualitative Research Reports in Communication, DOXA Communication, First Monday, Management Communication Quarterly,* and *Academic Exchange Quarterly.*

John D. Anderson, Associate Professor; Ph.D., Texas at Austin. Dr. Anderson, a National Endowment for the Humanities Fellow, focuses his research in the area of narrative theory and performance. In addition to publishing articles in *Text and Performance Quarterly,* he serves as book review co-editor for the journal. He performs nationally in his one-person shows about Charles Dickens, Henry James, and William Faulkner. He has received Chautauqua grants to present humanities programs on the Civil War and on the 1930s. Dr. Anderson is active in the performance studies divisions of both the Speech Communication Association and the Eastern Communication Association.

Philip Glenn, Associate Professor; Ph.D., Texas at Austin. Dr. Glenn teaches courses in interpersonal communication, mediation, negotiation, conflict management, research methods, and language and social interaction. His research primarily concerns characterizing aspects of sequential organization on routine human interaction in casual and institutional settings.

J. E. Hollingworth, Associate Professor; M.A., Emerson. Mr. Hollingworth is a nationally known speaker, lecturer, and consultant in the public and private sectors. He is also on the staff of the Stanford Institute, the Division of Continuing Education at Harvard University, the New England Institute for Law Enforcement Management, and the WACUBO Fourth Year Program at the University of California, Santa Barbara.

J. Gregory Payne, Associate Professor; M.P.A., Harvard (JFK); Ph.D., Illinois. Dr. Payne is an author, speechwriter, and expert on political communication, ethics, and docudrama. His recent research publications include articles on ethics and the mass media, health communication, and political communication. He is the founding Director of the Emerson College Political Media Study Group, and has been the co-director of the Emerson Center on Ethics in Political and Health Communication. He is the author of *Tom Bradley: The Impossible Dream, Mayday: Kent State,* and the play *Kent State: A Requiem.* Dr. Payne is on the editorial boards of the *Quarterly Journal of Speech,* the *Journal of Health Communication,* and the *Southern Speech Journal.* He was the guest editor of the 1989, 1993, and 1997 special editions on political campaigns for the *American Behavioral Scientist.*

Michael Weiler, Associate Professor; Ph.D., Pittsburgh. Dr. Weiler, formerly a member of the faculty at the University of Massachusetts at Amherst, the University of Pittsburgh, and Baylor University, is an expert in argument, rhetoric, and political communication. His research has appeared in the *Journal of the American Forensic Association* and the *Quarterly Journal of Speech,* and he has coauthored a collection of essays on the rhetoric of Ronald Reagan.

EMERSON COLLEGE

School of Communication
Master of Arts in Journalism

Program of Study

As technology transforms journalism, the need for thoughtful, ethical, and informed news professionals is growing. Today's journalists must employ both traditional and new media practices in order to effectively present news. Across a variety of media, Emerson graduates are covering the news—from local and national radio and television, to print and online publications.

Whether students' interests lie in broadcast, print, or multimedia, the Emerson College M.A. in journalism curriculum and state-of-the-art facilities arm them with the needed skills, while allowing them the freedom to explore their professional potential in specializations that include column writing; political, sports, or environmental reporting; and cultural affairs, among others.

For more information about Emerson's M.A. in journalism, prospective students should visit http://admission.emerson.edu/admission/graduate/academics/jrl.cfm.

Research Facilities

The Emerson College library has more than 200,000 volumes, 20,000 journals (paper and electronic), 8,000 e-books, 10,000 non-print materials, and 10,000 microforms in its collection that focus on communication studies and the performing arts. Students also benefit from the Fenway Libraries Online (FLO) program, which features online catalog access to nine other libraries in the greater Boston area.

M.A. candidates gain valuable, hands-on experience in the Media Services Center, which provides students with access to a video studio, several nonlinear editing suites comparable to those of any television studio in a major U.S. city, and approximately 2,400 films, videos, laser disks, and DVDs. The center is the home of audio, video, and multimedia production facilities.

Financial Aid

Emerson College offers several financial assistance programs that make an Emerson education possible: merit-based awards (domestic and international applicants), low-interest federal loans (domestic applicants only), federal work-study (domestic applicants only), private loans (domestic and international applicants), student employment (domestic and international applicants), and alternative payment plans (domestic and international applicants). For detailed information, students should visit the Office of Student Financial Services Web site at http://www.emerson.edu/financial_services.

Cost of Study

Tuition for the 2008–09 academic year is $886 per credit hour. Other fees vary and may apply.

Living and Housing Costs

Though on-campus housing is not available for its graduate students, the Emerson College Office of Off-Campus Student Services offers assistance in finding housing, including: local apartment listings, realtor lists, temporary accommodations, search tips, pertinent neighborhood information, a roommate networking service, and more. Costs for housing are comparable to those of rental properties available in larger East Coast cities.

Student Group

More than 950 graduate students representing forty-five states and sixty countries are enrolled in Emerson programs.

Student Outcomes

Emerson's journalism graduates are found across the nation and throughout the world investigating, reporting, and editing in a range of media. They are reporters, editors, producers, news directors, and anchors with employers such as *Arizona Republic,* Associated Press, *Dateline NBC,* Lycos News, MSNBC, New England Cable News, *Quincy Patriot Ledger,* and Boston's WGBH-TV.

Location

Situated in the heart of downtown Boston, Emerson offers access to the vast resources of a city that is home to the nation's finest educational institutions and an international hub of culture, media production, writing, publishing, communication, commerce, and medical innovation. Boston is a career launching pad for Emerson's students, many of whom intern or work at world-renowned organizations throughout the city. Emerson students from around the country and the world absorb the city's unique blend of local and global culture, and many find that Boston is an education in itself.

The College

Emerson College, founded in 1880 by Charles Wesley Emerson, has expanded upon its original mission of promoting the study of oratory and the performing arts by offering some of the nation's most distinctive graduate programs in communication.

Applying

Emerson's graduate programs welcome applicants from across the United States and around the world. Admission is competitive and selective. Emerson is looking for students whose academic and professional backgrounds, communication skills, and passion for the field meet the demands of their chosen program and promise a successful career.

The application deadline is June 1 for domestic applicants and May 1 for international applicants. Applications that are not complete by the final deadline are not reviewed by the admission committee. Applicants are responsible for ensuring the completion of their application. Application fees are nonrefundable; application forms and supporting materials become the property of the Office of Graduate Admission once they are sent to the office, and they will not be returned.

All application materials, with the exception of GRE test scores, must be submitted together in one package to ensure a timely review. A complete application includes the application form (students may apply online or they may download the PDF version), the application fee ($60 for domestic applicants; $75 for international applicants), official transcripts from all colleges/universities previously attended, three sealed letters of recommendation (by persons best able to assess academic and professional qualifications, including motivation, goals, and potential), GRE test scores, an essay, and a professional resume.

Applicants whose native language is not English must provide evidence of English proficiency by submitting official TOEFL or IELTS test results. (Applicants from India and the Philippines are considered nonnative English speakers and are required to take the TOEFL.) Emerson College's school code for the TOEFL is 3367; no department code is needed. For more information about these tests, prospective student can visit http://www.toefl.org or http://www.ielts.org. Minimum TOEFL scores are 550 paper-based, 213 computer-based, and 80 Internet-based. The minimum IELTS score is 6.5. Applicants who do not meet this requirement are not reviewed for admission.

Decisions are made on complete applications within six to eight weeks.

Deadlines for merit-based and federal aid applications for fall are March 1 and April 1, respectively. For more information about financing a graduate education, students should visit: http://www.emerson.edu/financial_services/info-grad.cfm/

Correspondence and Information

Office of Graduate Admission
Emerson College
120 Boylston Street
Boston, Massachusetts 02116-4624

Phone: 617-824-8610
Fax: 617-824-8614
E-mail: gradapp@emerson.edu
Web site: http://admission.emerson.edu/admission/graduate/

Emerson College

THE FACULTY AND THEIR RESEARCH

Janet Kolodzy, Acting Chair and Associate Professor; M.S.J., Northwestern. Ms. Kolodzy has been a reporter, writer, and producer, including positions as senior writer/editor at CNN International, senior producer at CNN World Report, and assistant state editor at the *Cleveland Plain Dealer.* She was one of twelve journalists to receive a Michigan Journalism Fellowship in 1990–91 to study at the University of Michigan, where she concentrated on Eastern European history, politics, and culture. Ms. Kolodzy spent the summer of 1999 working for CNN Interactive. Her primary areas of interest are international news and the impact of convergence on journalism.

Emmanuel Paraschos, Professor and Graduate Program Director; Ph.D., Missouri–Columbia. Dr. Paraschos was formerly the Dean of the European Institute for International Communication in Maastricht, the Netherlands, and Chairperson of the Journalism Department at the University of Arkansas, Little Rock. He served as a Fulbright Professor in Scandinavia where he taught at the Norwegian Institute of Journalism, and at universities in Sweden, Denmark, and Norway. He has been published in, among others, *Journalism Quarterly, Journal of Communication, College Press Review,* and *Journalism Educator.* His most recent book is *Media Law and Regulation in the European Union* and his most recent book chapter is "Religion and Freedom of Expression Law in the European Union," from *Religion, Law and Freedom: A Global Perspective.* Since 1994, he has served as copublisher of *Media Ethics* magazine. In 1995, he won Emerson's Irma Mann Stearns Distinguished Faculty Award. His primary areas of research and expertise are media law and ethics, global journalism, print and multimedia journalism, propaganda and the press, news media and foreign policy, and the role of the press in a democratic society.

Paula Childs, Journalist-in-Residence and Internship Coordinator; M.A., Harvard. Ms. Childs has spent her entire professional career as a print and broadcast journalist. She cohosted an Emmy Award-winning weekly news magazine show at Channel 7 in Boston and also worked as a reporter at television stations in Denver and Atlanta. She began her broadcast career as a radio reporter and news director and has also worked as an editorial page columnist for *Tab Community Newspapers.* Her areas of interest include media ethics and the changing world of media convergence.

Marsha Della-Giustina, Associate Professor; Ed.D., Boston University. Dr. Della-Giustina has had a long career as a television news producer. Among her honors are a Gracie Award, a National Commendation Award from American Women in Radio and Television, and awards from the National Education Writers Association and the National Association of Government Communicators. She has two Emmys from the National Academy of Television Arts and Sciences, a Society of Professional Journalists National Advisor Award, a Distinguished Broadcast Journalism Education Achievement Award, and a Curriculum Design Award from the Women's Institute for Freedom of the Press. Her primary areas of interest include media management, political journalism, international affairs, and gender issues.

Michelle Johnson, Journalist-in-Residence; M.S., Columbia. Johnson, a former editor for the *Boston Globe,* was part of the team that launched the *Globe's* award-winning regional news Web site, Boston.com. Prior to moving into new media, she was an editor for the *Globe* for 13 years and later a personal technology columnist. She has extensive experience writing for both print and online media. At the *Globe,* Johnson served as assistant political editor and senior assistant business editor before being named editorial manager of Boston.com. Johnson was awarded a Knight Fellowship in 1993. She has also received awards from the National Association of Black Journalists (NABJ) and the National Lesbian and Gay Journalists Association (NLGJA). She has conducted numerous workshops for a variety of professional journalism associations, including the National Association of Hispanic Journalists; NABJ; NLGJA; the American Society of Newspaper Editors; and UNITY, Journalists of Color, Inc.

Jerry Lanson, Associate Professor; M.A., Missouri–Columbia. A columnist and writing coach, Mr. Lanson joined the faculty at Emerson in 1999 after four years on the faculty at Syracuse University. Mr. Lanson is a former deputy city editor and peninsula bureau chief of the *San Jose Mercury News* in San Jose, California. He was part of the city-desk staff awarded a Pulitzer Prize for its coverage of the Loma Prieta earthquake in 1989. He is the coauthor of two textbooks, *Writing and Reporting the News* and *News in a New Century: Reporting in an Age of Converging Media,* and has coached editors and reporters at newspapers ranging from the *Christian Science Monitor* to the *Boston Globe.* Among his honors is a National Teaching Award from the Poynter Institute for Media Studies. His areas of interest include journalism ethics and the impact of new media on reporting and writing.

Mark Leccese, Assistant Professor; M.A., Boston College. Mr. Leccese spent almost 30 years covering politics and government as a wire service reporter; a daily newspaper reporter; the editor-in-chief of *Tab Community Newspapers,* the largest circulation of weekly newspapers in New England; a correspondent for the *Boston Globe;* and the State House bureau chief for a large chain of Massachusetts newspapers. He has also been a magazine writer and editor, a literary critic, and a writer and editor at bizjournals.com. He recently served as the associate editor for the *Boston Business Journal.* His freelance work has appeared in the *Columbia Journalism Review, The Quill, Boston Magazine, America,* the *Boston Phoenix,* zooba.com, beansprout.net, and Boston.com. His primary area of interest is the effect of the Internet on the public discourse about politics and public policy.

Paul Niwa, Scholar-in-Residence; M.S., Columbia. Mr. Niwa has launched and helped launch two international television networks, six newscasts, and a streaming media newscast for NBC, CNBC, and StockHouse Media, Canada's largest Internet company. As Senior Vice President at StockHouse, Mr. Niwa was responsible for content at the company's eight global editorial centers. In 1999, he helped NBC create *Early Today,* and in 1996 he launched the award winning *NBC Asia Evening News* in Hong Kong. He produced CNBC's *Today's Business* and the nationally syndicated newscast *This Morning's Business.* He has won two Golden Mike awards for radio reporting and documentary.

Melinda Robbins, Associate Professor; Ph.D., Georgia. Dr. Robins has extensive international journalism and media experience. She has been a reporter and editor of the *New Haven Register* and the *Journal-Courier* in Connecticut. She has served as a media consultant for the Jamaican government and a Fulbright Scholar teaching journalism in Uganda and has done research on women journalists in Tanzania. She has conducted workshops for journalists in Tanzania, Zimbabwe, Uganda, and Tonga. Her research interests include media in developing countries, issues of representation, and gender.

Carole Simpson, Leader-in-Residence; B.A., Michigan. Veteran journalist and longtime weekend anchor of *ABC World News Tonight,* Ms. Simpson joined the faculty at Emerson in 2007. The three-time Emmy winner brings four decades of print, radio, and television experience to her teaching and mentoring of students. Ms. Simpson began her career in her native Chicago, working in community newspapers, radio, and local television. She joined ABC News in 1982 and has worked as senior correspondent and weekend anchor. Awards for her work include two DuPont-Columbia Awards, a Peabody Award, and the Milestone in Broadcasting Award from the National Commission of Working Women. Ms. Simpson is also a founder and board member of the International Women's Media Foundation. Her areas of interest include social issues, the First Amendment, and women's leadership in media. She is currently writing a book about her experiences as an African American woman in news.

EMERSON COLLEGE

School of the Arts
Master of Fine Arts in Media Art

Program of Study

Media art professionals are at the forefront of modern culture, helping to shape the way we experience the world. They are natural storytellers who are interested in experimenting with the medium through which the story is told.

The M.F.A. in media art empowers its talented students to develop their creative voice, working with image and sound to entertain, inform, persuade, and challenge. The program offers a truly integrated approach in an increasingly convergent media environment, using state-of-the art equipment and facilities. Students graduate with highly developed skills that allow them to work at advanced levels within the media industries or teach at the university level.

For more information about Emerson's M.F.A. in media arts, prospective students should visit http://admission.emerson.edu/admission/graduate/academics/ma.cfm.

Research Facilities

The Emerson College library has more than 200,000 volumes, 20,000 journals (paper and electronic), 8,000 e-books, 10,000 nonprint materials, and 10,000 microforms in its collection that focus on the communication studies and performing arts. Through membership in the Fenway Library Consortium, graduate students have access to more than 2 million volumes. Computer-assisted reference services provide bibliographic databases through Dialog, BRS, and other online services. The Online Computer Library Center is used for student research support.

M.F.A. candidates gain valuable hands-on experience in the Media Services Center, which provides students with access to approximately 2,400 films, videos, laser discs, and DVDs. The center is the home of audio, video, and multimedia production facilities; a video studio; and several nonlinear editing suites comparable to those of any television studio in a major U.S. city. There is a marketing suite that features a focus group room with an observation booth, and there are also fully mediated classrooms.

Emerson's production and postproduction equipment and facilities include nine digital audio editing rooms, two fully equipped professional television studios, three professional digital audio sound production studios (one with Dolby surround sound), twenty-eight Avid editing stations, digital mix-to-picture studios, a DVD authoring studio, multiple digital production labs dedicated to new media technologies, computer animation, Final Cut Pro video editing, and WERS, Emerson's award-winning, student-run FM radio station.

Financial Aid

Emerson College offers several financial assistance programs that make graduate education possible: merit-based awards (domestic and international applicants), low-interest federal loans (domestic applicants only), federal work-study (domestic applicants only), private loans (domestic and international applicants), student employment (domestic and international applicants), and alternative payment plans (domestic and international applicants). For detailed information, students should visit the Office of Student Financial Services Web site at http://www.emerson.edu/financial_services.

Cost of Study

Tuition for the 2008–09 academic year is $886 per credit hour. Other fees vary and may apply.

Living and Housing Costs

Though on-campus housing is not available for its graduate students, the Emerson College Office of Off-Campus Student Services offers assistance in finding housing, including: local apartment listings, realtor lists, temporary accommodations, search tips, pertinent neighborhood information, a roommate networking service, and more. Costs for housing are comparable to those of rental properties available in larger East Coast cities.

Student Group

More than 950 graduate students representing forty-five states and sixty countries are enrolled in Emerson programs.

Student Outcomes

Emerson alumni are talented and successful media artists—conceiving, writing, directing, producing, and editing video documentaries, video narratives, interactive CDs, and Web sites. Among recent employers are America Online, AT&T New Media Services, AVID Technology, Circle Interactive, Fox Broadcasting Corporation, Hearst-Argyle Television Productions, Pinball Productions, September Productions, and WHDH-TV.

Location

Situated in the heart of downtown Boston, Emerson offers access to the vast resources of a city that is the home of the nation's finest educational institutions and an international hub of culture, media production, writing, publishing, communication, commerce, and medical innovation. Boston is a career launching pad for Emerson's students, many of whom intern or work at world-renowned organizations throughout the city. Emerson students from around the country and world absorb the city's unique blend of local and global culture, and many find that Boston is an education in itself.

The College

Emerson College, founded in 1880 by Charles Wesley Emerson, has expanded upon its original mission of promoting the study of oratory and the performing arts by offering some of the nation's most distinctive graduate programs in communication.

Applying

Emerson's graduate programs welcome applicants from across the United States and around the world. Admission is competitive and selective. Emerson is looking for students whose academic and professional backgrounds, communication skills, and passion for the field meet the demands of their chosen program and promise a successful career.

The priority application deadline (to be considered for merit aid) for fall enrollment is January 5. The final deadline for all applicants is March 1. Applications that are not complete by the final deadline are not reviewed by the admission committee. Applicants are responsible for ensuring the completion of their application. Application fees are nonrefundable; application forms and supporting materials become the property of the Office of Graduate Admission once they are sent to the office and are not returned. Deadlines for merit-based and federal aid applications for fall are January 5 and April 1, respectively.

All application materials must be submitted together in one package to ensure a timely review. A complete application includes the application form (students may apply online or they may download the PDF version), the application fee ($60 for domestic applicants; $75 for international applicants), official transcripts from all colleges/universities previously attended, three sealed letters of recommendation (by persons best able to assess academic and professional qualifications, including motivation, goals, and potential), portfolio of media or other creative work, two essays, and a professional resume. GRE scores are optional, because the School is primarily interested in students' creative and academic achievement and aptitude.

Applicants whose native language is not English must provide evidence of English proficiency by submitting official TOEFL or IELTS test results. (Applicants from India and the Philippines are considered nonnative English speakers and are required to take the TOEFL.) Emerson College's school code for the TOEFL is 3367; no department code is needed. For more information about these tests, prospective student can visit http://www.toefl.org or http://www.ielts.org. Minimum TOEFL scores are 550 paper-based, 213 computer-based, and 80 Internet-based. The minimum IELTS score is 6.5. Applicants who do not meet this requirement are not reviewed for admission.

Decisions are made on complete applications within six to eight weeks. For more information about financing a graduate education, students should visit: http://www.emerson.edu/financial_services/info-grad.cfm/.

Correspondence and Information

Office of Graduate Admission
Emerson College
120 Boylston Street
Boston, Massachusetts 02116-4624

Phone: 617-824-8610
Fax: 617-824-8614
E-mail: gradapp@emerson.edu
Web site: http://admission.emerson.edu/admission/graduate

Emerson College

THE FACULTY AND THEIR RESEARCH

Michael Selig, Associate Professor and Chair; Ph.D., Northwestern. Dr. Selig has taught at the University of Vermont, Rosary College, Northwestern University, and the University of Texas. He has published in *Screen, Wide Angle, Jump Cut,* and other publications. He is a former editor of the *Journal of Film and Video.*

Jan Roberts-Breslin, Associate Professor and Graduate Program Director; M.F.A., Temple. Ms. Roberts-Breslin is an independent media artist whose work has been broadcast on PBS and has received national and international festival awards. She served as video director for the United Church of Christ in New York City and has taught at Temple and Seton Hall universities. She is the author of *Making Media: Foundations of Sound and Image Production.*

Claire Andrade-Watkins, Associate Professor; Ph.D., Boston University. Dr. Andrade-Watkins, a historian and filmmaker, has published extensively on French- and Portuguese-speaking African cinema in leading academic journals and film publications including *Framework, Research in African Literatures, International Journal of African History, Journal of Visual Anthropology,* and the *Independent.* She is coeditor of *Blackframes: Critical Perspectives on Black Independent Cinema.* She was a 1995–1996 Fulbright Scholar in Cape Verde, where she conducted research on indigenous cinema in Cape Verde. With a 1997 grant from the American Philosophical Society, she researched colonial cinema in Lisbon. She recently completed an award-winning "documemoire," *Some Kind of Funny Porto Rican,* about the Cape Verdean community in Providence, Rhode Island. Other documentaries she produced include *The Spirit of Cape Verde,* a half-hour documentary celebrating the bonds between New England, Cape Verde, and President Aristides Periera's historical first visit to the United States in 1983. She was an associate producer on *Odyssey,* a national PBS anthropology and archaeology documentary series, and assistant to the producer on *Sankofa,* an internationally acclaimed feature film on slavery by filmmaker Haile Gerima.

Pierre Archambault, Associate Professor; M.F.A., Art Institute of Chicago. Mr. Archambault is a sound designer, sound art and music composer, and a performer of electronic music. Among others, his credits include sound design for the award winning CD-ROM, *Exotic Japan,* the BBC film *Dear Nelson,* and contributing composer for the PBS series *Our Stories* and *Made-in-Maine.* He also composed the music for the global art exhibit, *C.O.D.* He has taught at the School of the Art Institute of Chicago and the Savannah College of Art and Design.

Martie Cook, Assistant Professor; M.F.A., Emerson. Ms. Cook has worked as a writer/producer for all four television networks and PBS. Her writing credits include *Charles In Charge* and *Full House.* Her producing credits include *Entertainment Tonight, America's Most Wanted, NBC Nightly News,* the *Today* show, and the Emmy-nominated children's show *Zoom.* Ms. Cook's screenplay *Zachary's Truth* was optioned by Universal Studios.

Thomas Cooper, Professor; Ph.D., Toronto. Dr. Cooper is the author of six books and more than a hundred articles and is copublisher of *Media Ethics* magazine. He served as assistant speechwriter in the White House and, as the assistant to Marshall McLuhan, produced some of the first audio-spacebridges between the U.S. and Soviet Union. He has received many fellowships, awards, and grants.

Pierre H. Desir, Assistant Professor; M.A., M.F.A., UCLA. Mr. Desir is an independent filmmaker and cinematographer whose work, including *Zona, Compensation, Cycles,* and *The Gods and the Thief,* has appeared at numerous domestic and international film festivals, including Sundance, Toronto, Amiens, London, Chicago, and New York.

L. Marc Fields, Associate Professor; M.F.A., NYU. Mr. Fields previously taught screenwriting and production at NYU's Tisch School of the Arts, the New School, and Concord Academy. A writer/producer/director of arts and cultural documentaries for PBS, his production credits include four years as a series producer for *State of the Arts,* a weekly arts magazine on New Jersey Public Television, and five regional Emmys. He is the coauthor of *From the Bowery to Broadway: Lew Fields and the Roots of American Popular Theater,* and is a frequent consultant for programs about American popular entertainment. For the recent six-part PBS series, *Broadway: The American Musical,* he wrote the scripts for two episodes.

John (Craig) Freeman, Associate Professor; M.F.A., Colorado at Boulder. Mr. Freeman has taught as an Associate Professor at the University of Massachusetts Lowell and as an Assistant Professor at the University of Florida. His work has been exhibited internationally including at the Contemporary Art Center in Atlanta; the Nickle Arts Museum in Calgary, Çanada; the Centro de la Imagen in Mexico City; the Photographers Gallery in London; the Center for Experimental and Perceptual Art (CEPA) in Buffalo; Mobius in Boston; the Ambrosino Gallery in Miami; and the Friends of Photography's Ansel Adams Center in San Francisco. In 1992 he was awarded an Individual Artist Fellowship from the National Endowment for the Arts. His work has been published in *Leonardo,* the *Journal of Visual Culture, Exposure, Artforum, Ten-8, Z Magazine, Afterimage, Photo Metro, New Art Examiner, Time, Harper's,* and *Der Spiegel.*

Donald Fry, Associate Professor; Ph.D., Ohio State. Dr. Fry's expertise is in mass communication theory, research methods, and media management. He served as Television and Film Head of the Department of Speech Communication, Wichita State University, and has taught at West Virginia University, Ohio State University, and Bowling Green State University. Dr. Fry has published in the *Journal of Communication Inquiry, Communication Yearbook, Critical Studies in Mass Communication, Newspaper Research Journal,* and *Mass Communication Yearbook.*

Daniel Gaucher, Assistant Professor; M.F.A.; Massachusetts College of Art. Mr. Gaucher established himself in the production world as one of the original editors for the hit series, *Blind Date.* Since then he's crafted a series of successes including *5th Wheel, Queer Eye for the Straight Guy,* and *Extreme Engineering.* His work has aired worldwide on NBC, MTV, Bravo, A&E, UPN, Spike, VH-1, TLC, Discovery, PBS and the National Geographic Channel.

John Gianvito, Assistant Professor; B.F.A., California Institute of the Arts; M.S., M.I.T. Mr. Gianvito is a filmmaker, curator, and critic, He has directed three feature films, including the award-winning *The Mad Songs of Fernanda Hussein,* and has recently completed editing of the book *Andrei Tarkovsky: Interviews,* forthcoming from the University Press of Mississippi.

Eric Gordon, Assistant Professor; Ph.D., USC. Dr. Gordon works in the fields of critical urbanism and new media. Before coming to Emerson, he was a Postdoctoral Fellow at the Institute for Multimedia Literacy (IML) at USC's Annenberg Center for Communications, where he was codesigner of a software application called MediaBASE that allows users new opportunities for the exploration and manipulation of media projects. His recent publications include *Towards a Networked Urbanism: Hugh Ferriss, Rockefeller Center and the 'Invisible Empire of the Air',* and *The Database City: Narrative, Interactivity and the Renewal of Hollywood Boulevard.*

Robert Hilliard, Professor; Ph.D., Columbia. Former Dean of Graduate Studies and Dean of Continuing Education at Emerson, Dr. Hilliard teaches courses such as Media Programming, The Media and the Holocaust, Hate.com, Communication Law, and Pictures of Protest. He was formerly chief of the public broadcasting branch of the Federal Communications Commission and chair of the Federal Interagency Media Committee for the White House. A frequent lecturer on media and education on all continents, Dr. Hilliard is the author of more than thirty books on communication, including several leading media texts.

Tom Kingdon, Associate Professor; M.A., Birmingham (UK). Mr. Kingdon is a producer and a director. His credits include *Masterpiece Theater* and the BBC TV's *Eastenders,* in addition to several other network drama series, children's programs, and corporate programs. He is the author of *Total Directing,* which discusses directing camera and actors in film and television.

Brooke A. Knight, Assistant Professor; M.F.A., California Institute of the Arts. Mr. Knight, an artist working in new media, has exhibited his work in more than twenty international festivals and exhibitions in the past four years, including Through the Looking Glass, Art Frankfurt, Medi@terra, Variable Media, Art Interactive, and Experimenta. Primarily working with the medium of the Internet, Mr. Knight's main areas of interest are interactivity, language and meaning, and the landscape.

Cher Krause Knight, Assistant Professor; Ph.D., Temple. Dr. Knight is an art historian focused on modern and contemporary art and architecture. She is also a specialist in museum studies, with an emphasis on curatorial theory. She has published her work in a variety of sources, including *Analecta Husserliana: The Yearbook of Phenomenological Research,* the *Journal of American and Comparative Cultures, Visual Resources,* and the anthology, *Reclaiming the Spiritual in Art: Contemporary Cross-Cultural Perspectives.*

Cristina A. Kotz Cornejo, Assistant Professor; M.A., Antioch; M.F.A., NYU. Ms. Kotz Cornejo is an independent filmmaker currently developing a feature-length film titled *Soledad. Soledad* was a semi-finalist for the 2004 Sundance Screenwriter's Lab and was in the script competition at the 2003 International Festival of New Latin American Cinema in Havana, Cuba. Her personal documentary, *My Argentine Family,* premiered at the 2003 Rhode Island International Film Festival and her digital short *Ocean Waves,* which has screened at the New England Film and Video Festival and the Boston Underground Film Festival, among others, received the Award of Merit from the University Film and Video Association. In 2000 Cristina was awarded a grant from the Partnership for a Drug Free America to direct *Ernesto,* which premiered at the Palm Springs International Short Film Festival. Her short film, *The Appointment,* developed under the advisement of Spike Lee and Nancy Savoca while Ms. Cornejo was a student, was awarded a Warner Brothers Pictures Production Award, a Dean's Post Production Award, and three NYU Craft Awards and was picked up for distribution by Urban Entertainment.

Diane Lake, Assistant Professor; M.A., Massachusetts Amherst. Ms. Lake's film credits include writing assignments for Paramount, Disney, Miramax, and NBC/Davis Entertainment. Her film *Frida* opened the Venice Film Festival in 2002, was named to numerous 10-best lists for the year, and was nominated for six Academy Awards. She has also taught at UCLA.

Jim Macak, Assistant Professor; M.F.A., Yale. Mr. Macak worked as an intern for Emmy and Humanitas winner David Milch and went on to write scripts for three of Milch's shows, including *NYPD Blue.* He was also chosen as a Disney Fellow and wrote a produced sitcom pilot for Disney and CBS, as well as several TV movies for CBS, FOX, and Lifetime. He served as a staff writer for other TV dramas and the daytime serial *General Hospital.* In addition to his career as a TV writer, Mr. Macak is also a playwright. His plays have been seen at The Long Wharf Theater in New Haven, The Coast Playhouse in Los Angeles, and the Tennessee Williams Fine Arts Festival in Key West. He previously taught at Chapman University in Southern California.

Maurice Methot, Assistant Professor; M.A., Brown. Mr. Methot teaches courses in audio for new media, studio recording, and media production. He is a composer, performer, and media artist whose work is devoted to the exploration of sound both as a physical phenomenon and as a metaphorical device. He has performed extensively in a variety of venues ranging from the punk mecca C.B.G.B.'s to the Moscow Conservatory of Music. His work in experimental video has been screened at a numerous conferences and digital media festivals. His professional work includes freelance production for MTV. His projects are available on CD, cassette, vinyl, and on the World Wide Web. He has also taught at Brown University, Southern Illinois University, and Albright College in Pennsylvania.

Kathryn Ramey, Assistant Professor; M.A., M.F.A., Ph.D., Temple. Ms. Ramey is an experimental filmmaker and scholar. Her award-winning films have screened at the Toronto International, Ann Arbor, Athens, Boston Independent, and Philadelphia film festivals, among others. In 2004, she was the recipient of a Pennsylvania Council of the Arts Fellowship for her works in film. In 2003, she was a Social Science Research Council Program on the Arts Fellow for her research on experimental filmmakers. Her most recently published works include "Between Art, Industry and Academia: The Fragile Balancing Act of the Film Avant-Garde" in *Visual Anthropology Review.*

Eric P. Schaefer, Associate Professor; Ph.D., Texas at Austin. Dr. Schaefer's primary research interests are film history, exploitation film, and other marginalized cinemas; popular culture; and postwar film and television. He is the author of a number of articles and the award-winning book *Bold! Daring! Shocking! True!: A History of Exploitation Films, 1919-1959.* He is currently working on *Massacre of Pleasure: A History of Sexploitation Films, 1960-1979.* Dr. Schaefer is also active in the area of film preservation and serves on the editorial board of the *Moving Image,* the journal of the Association of Moving Image Archivists.

Jane Shattuc, Associate Professor; Ph.D., Wisconsin–Madison. Dr. Shattuc has taught at the University of Vermont and the University of Wisconsin–Madison, and was a fellow at Bonn Universität, Bonn, Germany. Dr. Shattuc is the author of *Television, Tabloids, Tears: Fassbinder and Popular Culture* and *The Talking Cure: Television Talk Shows and Women,* and is the editor of *Hop on Pop: The Politics and Pleasures of Popular Cultures.*

James Sheldon, Associate Professor; M.S., MIT. Mr. Sheldon worked for many years as a museum curator and artist active in the media of photography, video, and interactive art. Recently he produced a number of interactive exhibition applications for the Museum of Fine Arts, Boston. Currently, he is working on a series of online interactive documentaries about cultural landscapes funded by the Cultural Landscape Foundation and the National Endowment for the Arts.

Stephen Shipps, Associate Professor; Ed.D., Harvard. Dr. Shipps is an arts educator primarily concerned with the nature and history of "art" as a Western cultural institution, and how best to teach this concept. He has written and spoken widely about those concerns in both national and international forums. An award-winning teacher, he has been a Fellow of the National Endowment of the Humanities and of the Getty Center for Education in the Arts, and is currently Chair of the Education Committee of the College Art Association.

Jean Stawarz, Associate Professor; M.F.A., Goddard. Ms. Stawarz has worked as a screenwriter, story editor, and associate producer. Her production credits include the award-winning films *Powwow Highway* and *Henry & Verlin,* and the television dramas *Spirit Rider* and *North of Sixty.* Her work has been screened at many film festivals including Sundance Film Festival, Montreal Film Festival, and the Munich Film Festival, and has aired on PBS, CBC, and the BBC. The Telluride Indie Fest named her original screenplay, *The Sculptors,* one of the "top thirty screenplays in the world." She has also taught at Southern Illinois University, Carbondale.

Jeff Talman, Assistant Professor; M.A., CUNY, New York. Mr.Talman, award-winning sound artist, has created installations for The Kitchen, NYC; the MIT Media Lab, the Basilica of St. Ulrich in Regensburg, Germany; Eyebeam, NYC, and others. His unique achievement in sound art is the reiterative resonance system in which the resonant frequencies of an installation site become the sole sound source for the work. *The New York Times, WIRED* magazine, and other publications have recognized this important process and work. Recent awards include a New York Foundation for the Arts Award in Computer Arts and a Gunk Foundation Grant. Recent artist residencies include Yaddo, the Virginia Center for the Creative Arts, and the Oberpfälzer Künstlerhaus in Schwandorf, Germany. Mr. Talman has directed orchestras and taught at City College, Columbia University, and Massachusetts College of Art. He produced and hosted a weekly show of new music, *Airwaves,* for six years on WKCR-FM, New York, featuring interviews, live performances, and the latest CD releases. He is currently represented by Bitforms Gallery, NYC.

Robert Todd, Assistant Professor; M.F.A., Tufts. An experimental filmmaker and sound artist, Mr. Todd continually produces short works that resist categorization. His work has screened internationally and received various awards.

Shujen Wang, Associate Professor; Ph.D., Maryland. Dr. Wang is a Research Associate in the Fairbank Center for East Asian Research at Harvard University. Dr. Wang's research interests include global film distribution, piracy and copyright governance, and issues surrounding space, technology, the state, and power. The author of *Framing Piracy: Globalization and Film Distribution in Greater China,* she has published in such journals as *Cinema Journal, Film Quarterly, positions, Theory Culture & Society, Public Culture, Asian Cinema, Text, Visual Anthropology, Journal of Communication Inquiry, Gazette, Asian Journal of Communication,* and *Media Asia.*

EMERSON COLLEGE

School of the Arts
Master of Arts in Publishing and Writing

Program of Study

Words may originate in the minds of writers, but publishing professionals are responsible for cultivating, shaping, and delivering the written word to the world. Other programs focus on the business and editing sides of publishing, but do not also encourage the exploration of literature and creative writing the way the Emerson College M.A. in publishing and writing program does.

Students concentrate in book, magazine, or electronic publishing, gaining insight into diverse aspects of the industry, from writing and editing, to design, production, and distribution. Emerson's graduates have gone on to become literary agents and critics, editorial consultants, book and magazine editors and designers, publicists, print production specialists, and more.

For more information about Emerson's M.A. in publishing and writing, interested students should visit http://admission.emerson.edu/admission/graduate/academics/pw.cfm.

Research Facilities

The Emerson College library has more than 200,000 volumes, 20,000 journals (paper and electronic), 8,000 e-books, 10,000 nonprint materials, and 10,000 microforms in its collection that focus on the communication studies and performing arts. Through membership in the Fenway Library Consortium, graduate students have access to more than 2 million volumes. Computer-assisted reference services provide bibliographic databases through Dialog, BRS, and other online services. The Online Computer Library Center is used for student research support.

M.A. candidates gain valuable hands-on experience in the Media Services Center, which provides students with access to approximately 2,400 films, videos, laser discs, and DVDs. The center is the home of audio, video, and multimedia production facilities; a video studio; and several nonlinear editing suites comparable to those of any television studio in a major U.S. city. In addition, a new marketing suite opened in 2003 that features a focus group room with an observation booth. There are also fully-mediated classrooms.

Financial Aid

Emerson College offers several financial assistance programs that make graduate education possible: merit-based awards (domestic and international applicants), low-interest federal loans (domestic applicants only), federal work-study (domestic applicants only), private loans (domestic and international applicants), student employment (domestic and international applicants), and alternative payment plans (domestic and international applicants). For detailed information, students should visit the Office of Student Financial Services Web site at http://www.emerson.edu/financial_services.

Cost of Study

Tuition for the 2008–09 academic year is $886 per credit hour. Other fees vary and may apply.

Living and Housing Costs

Though on-campus housing is not available for its graduate students, the Emerson College Office of Off-Campus Student Services offers assistance in finding housing, including local apartment listings, realtor lists, temporary accommodations, search tips, pertinent neighborhood information, a roommate networking service, and more. Costs for housing are comparable to those of rental properties available in larger East Coast cities.

Student Group

More than 950 graduate students representing forty-five states and sixty countries are enrolled in Emerson programs.

Location

Situated in the heart of downtown Boston, Emerson offers access to the vast resources of a city that is the home of the nation's finest educational institutions and an international hub of culture, media production, writing, publishing, communication, commerce, and medical innovation. Boston is a career launching pad for Emerson's students, many of whom intern or work at world-renowned organizations throughout the city. Emerson students from around the country and world absorb the city's unique blend of local and global culture, and many find that Boston is an education in itself.

The College

Emerson College, founded in 1880 by Charles Wesley Emerson, has expanded upon its original mission of promoting the study of oratory and the performing arts by offering some of the nation's most distinctive graduate programs in communication.

Applying

Emerson's graduate programs welcome applicants from across the United States and around the world. Admission is competitive and selective. Emerson is looking for students whose academic and professional backgrounds, communication skills, and passion for the field meet the demands of their chosen program and promise a successful career.

The application deadline is January 5 for domestic and international applicants. Applications that are not complete by the final deadline are not reviewed by the admission committee. Applicants are responsible for ensuring the completion of their application. Application fees are nonrefundable; application forms and supporting materials become the property of the Office of Graduate Admission once they are sent to the office, and they will not be returned.

All application materials, with the exception of GRE test scores, must be submitted together in one package to ensure a timely review. A complete application includes the application form (students may apply online or may download the PDF version), the application fee ($60 for domestic applicants; $75 for international applicants), official transcripts from all colleges/universities previously attended, three sealed letters of recommendation (by persons best able to assess academic and professional qualifications, including motivation, goals, and potential), GRE test scores, an essay, a 15-page writing sample, and a professional resume.

Applicants whose native language is not English must provide evidence of English proficiency by submitting official TOEFL or IELTS test results. (Applicants from India and the Philippines are considered nonnative English speakers and are required to take the TOEFL.) Emerson College's school code for the TOEFL is 3367; no department code is needed. For more information about these tests, prospective student can visit http://www.toefl.org or http://www.ielts.org. Minimum TOEFL scores are 550 paper-based, 213 computer-based, and 80 Internet-based. The minimum IELTS score is 6.5. Applicants who do not meet this requirement are not reviewed for admission.

Decisions are made on complete applications within six to eight weeks.

Deadlines for merit-based and federal aid applications for fall are January 5 and April 1, respectively. For more information about financing a graduate education, students should visit: http://www.emerson.edu/financial_services/info-grad.cfm/.

Correspondence and Information

Office of Graduate Admission
Emerson College
120 Boylston Street
Boston, Massachusetts 02116-4624

Phone: 617-824-8610
Fax: 617-824-8614
E-mail: gradapp@emerson.edu
Web site: http://admission.emerson.edu/admission/graduate

Emerson College

THE FACULTY

Daniel Tobin, Professor and Chair; M.T.S., Harvard; M.F.A., Warren Wilson; Ph.D., Virginia. Dr. Tobin is the author of *The Narrows* (poetry), *Double Life* (poetry), *Where the World is Made* (poetry), and *Passage to the Center: Imagination and the Sacred in the Poetry of Seamus Heaney* and two edited works, *The Book of Irish American Poetry from the Eighteenth Century to the Present*, and *In a Dynasty of Fire: The Selected Poems of Lola Ridge*. A fourth book of poems, *Second Things*, will appear in 2008. He has received The Discovery/The Nation Award, the Robert Penn Warren Award, the Robert Frost Fellowship, the Katherine Bakeless Nason Prize, and a fellowship from the National Endowment for the Arts, among other prizes for his poetry.

Lisa Diercks, Assistant Professor and Graduate Program Director, M.A. Program; M.S., Boston University. Ms. Diercks is a publishing industry veteran, working primarily in book design. She began her career at Houghton Mifflin/Trade and later established her own design studio. Her publishing clients have included *The Atlantic Monthly;* Beacon Press; Boston Common Press; Candlewick Press; HarperCollins; Little, Brown; and the Museum of Fine Arts. She began teaching as an adjunct in 1996, joining the full-time faculty in 2001. Both she and her students have received multiple awards for design work.

Douglas Whynott, Associate Professor and Director, M.F.A. Program; M.F.A., Massachusetts Amherst. Mr. Whynott is the author of *A Country Practice-Scenes from the Veterinary Life, Following the Bloom-Across America with the Migratory Beekeepers, Giant Bluefin*, and *A Unit of Water, A Unit of Time-Joel White's Last Boat*. He has written for *The New York Times Book Review, Smithsonian, Discover, Islands, Outside, The Boston Globe Magazine, Reader's Digest, New England Monthly, Orion*, and *The Massachusetts Review*.

Jonathan Aaron, Associate Professor; Ph.D., Yale. Dr. Aaron is the author of three books of poems: *Second Sight, Corridor*, and *Journey to the Lost City*. He has received grants from the National Endowment for the Arts and the Massachusetts Artists Foundation. Aaron has published poetry and criticism in *Paris Review, Partisan Review*, the *London Review of Books*, and others.

Bill Beuttler, Publisher-in-Residence; M.S., Columbia. Mr. Beuttler is a *Boston Globe* correspondent whose writing has appeared recently in *The Atlantic Online, Best Life, Boston* magazine, and *Chicago* magazine, among others. He has worked as an editor for *The Discovery Channel, Men's Journal, Boston, Down Beat*, and *American Way* magazines.

Ben Brooks, Writer-in-Residence; M.F.A., Iowa. Ben Brooks is the author of the novel, *The Icebox* and over 75 published short stories. His stories have won an O. Henry Prize and a Nelson Algren Award and have been published in such journals as *Sewanee Review, Chicago Review, Virginia Quarterly Review, Story Quarterly, American Short Fiction, Notre Dame Review, Epoch, Mississippi Review, Confrontation, Denver Quarterly, Writers' Forum, The Long Story*, and elsewhere. Most recently, stories were published in *The Florida Review* and *Other Voices* and a story is forthcoming in *The Long Story*. In addition, he is the author of numerous published essays on art, history, building design, and travel. He has received awards and fellowships for his fiction from the Fine Arts Work Center in Provincetown, the Massachusetts Artists Foundation, the Arizona Commission on the Arts, the Ingram Merrill Foundation, and elsewhere.

Christine Casson, Scholar/Writer-in-Residence; M.F.A., Warren Wilson. Ms. Casson's scholarly interests include environmental literature, Native American literature, and modern and contemporary poetry in English. She has published recent essays on the work of Linda Hogan and Leslie Marmon Silko. Her poetry has appeared in *Natural Bridge, South Dakota Review, Alabama Literary Review, Agenda, Slant, Fashioned Pleasures*, and in the anthology *Never Before*.

Yu-Jin Chang, Assistant Professor; Ph.D., Yale. Yu-Jin Chang is a specialist in European comparative literature and philosophy and has recently completed a study of Walter Benjamin and Maurice Blanchot titled *Disaster and Hope*. This study examines the closely related aesthetic conceptions of time and history by these two writers, arguably the two most influential literary theorists of the last century, down to their philosophical origins in, respectively, Leibniz's monadology and Nietzsche's doctrine of eternal return. A former professor of French and German, Dr. Chang has also studied Korean and classical Chinese.

William Donoghue, Associate Professor; Ph.D., Stanford. Dr. Donoghue is a specialist in the novel and the author of *Enlightenment Fiction in England, France and America*. He has published articles and book reviews on British and French eighteenth-century fiction, written and directed a short film with the National Film Board of Canada, translated a volume of French poetry entitled *Lead Blues*, and published his own short fiction in *TriQuarterly, Grain*, and elsewhere. His interests are in philosophy and literature and the theory of the novel.

David Emblidge, Associate Professor; Ph.D., Minnesota. Dr. Emblidge has nearly two decades of experience as a book editor and publisher. He edited *My Day: The Best of Eleanor Roosevelt's Acclaimed Newspaper Columns, 1936-1962; The Appalachian Trail Reader;* and the forthcoming *Beneath the Metropolis: The Underground of the World's Great Cities.*. He authored *Exploring the Appalachian Trail: Hikes in Southern New England* and edited four other volumes in this series. He coauthored *Writer's Resource: The Watson-Guptill Guide to Workshops, Conferences, Artists' Colonies and Academic Programs*. His articles and essays have appeared in *Southwest Review, The New Republic, Saturday Review*, the *New York Times*, the *Boston Globe*, and other periodicals. He won a Fulbright Teaching Fellowship, a National Endowment for the Humanities fellowship, and a grant from the Massachusetts Foundation for the Humanities and Public Policy.

Robin Riley Fast, Associate Professor; Ph.D., Minnesota. Dr. Fast's interests include nineteenth-century American literature, American poetry, women writers, and Native American literature. She has published a book titled *The Heart as a Drum: Continuance and Resistance in American Indian Poetry*, articles on poetry, and coedited *Approaches to Teaching Dickinson's Poetry*.

Maria Flook, Writer-in-Residence; M.F.A., Iowa. Ms. Flook is the author of the nonfiction books, *My Sister Life: The Story of My Sister's Disappearance*, and *Invisible Eden: A Story of Love and Murder on Cape Cod*. Her fiction includes the novels *Lux, Open Water, Family Night* (which received a PEN American/Ernest Hemingway Foundation Special Citation) and a collection of stories, *You Have the Wrong Man*. She has also published two collections of poetry, *Sea Room* and *Reckless Wedding* (winner of the Houghton Mifflin New Poetry Series and the G.L.C.A. New Writers Award). Her work has appeared in *The New Yorker, TriQuarterly, The New York Times Book Review*, and elsewhere.

Flora M. González, Professor; Ph.D., Yale. Dr. Gonzalez received her Ph.D. in Hispanic literature and has taught at Dartmouth, Middlebury, and the University of Chicago. Her teaching interests include Latin American fiction and nonfiction, the literatures of the Caribbean, and feminist writing. She has published widely on the topic of the Latin American novel since the 1960s, including her book *Jose Donoso's House of Fiction: A Dramatic Construction of Time and Place*. In collaboration with Rosamond Rosenmeier, she edited and translated *In the Vortex of the Cyclone: Selected Poems by Excilia Saldana*. She has published nonfiction in the *Americas Review* and the *Michigan Quarterly Review*, and has been anthologized in *RE-Membering Cuba*. In 1997 and 1998 she was a Fellow at the W.E.B. DuBois Institute at Harvard University and is presently an affiliate of the David Rockefeller Center of Latin American Studies at Harvard. Her ongoing research project is entitled "Braiding the Tresses of Memory: Autobiography and National Identity by Afro-Cuban Women," soon to be completed. Her most recent book is *Guarding Cultural Memory: Afro-Cuban Women in Literature and the Arts*.

Lise Haines, Writer-in-Residence; M.F.A., Bennington. Lise Haines is the author of the novels, *In My Sister's Country* and *Small Acts of Sex and Electricity*. Her short stories and essays have appeared in journals including: *Ploughshares, Agni, Crosscurrents, Third Rail*, and *Post Road*. She was a finalist for the 2003 Paterson Fiction Prize and the PEN Nelson Algren Fiction Award. Her teaching credits include UCLA, UCSB, and Stonecoast. The *Boston Globe* called *In My Sister's Country* "an authoritative fictional debut." Ms. Haines grew up in Chicago, lived in California for many years, and now resides in Massachusetts.

DeWitt Henry, Professor; Ph.D., Harvard. Dr. Henry is cofounder and executive director of *Ploughshares*, for which he received a 1993 Commonwealth Award. He has edited four anthologies, *The Ploughshares Reader: New Fiction for the 80's* (winner of the Editors' Book Award), *Other Sides of Silence: New Fiction from Ploughshares, Fathering Daughters: Reflections by Men, Sorrow's Company: Writers on Loss and Grief*, and recently published a novel titled *The Marriage of Anna Maye Potts*. He has won, among other awards for his fiction, the Peter Taylor Prize, a National Endowment for the Arts Fellowship, the Boulevard Fiction Award, and a St. Botolph Foundation Award.

Richard Hoffman, Writer-in-Residence; M.F.A., Goddard. Mr. Hoffman is the author of *Half the House: a Memoir* and a collection of poems, *Without Paradise*. His work has been published in magazines such as *Agni, Ascent, The Boston Globe, Harvard Review, Hudson Review, The Literary Review, Poetry, Shenandoah, The Marlboro Review, Witness*, and others, as well as in several anthologies.

Roy Kamada, Assistant Professor; M.F.A., Virginia; Ph.D., California, Davis. Dr. Kamada's work has appeared in *The Diasporic Imagination: Identifying Asian-American Representations in America and Ecological Poetry: A Critical Introduction*. He is currently working on a project tentatively titled, *Postcolonial Romanticisms: Landscape and the Possibilities of Inheritance*. Dr. Kamada is a specialist in British and multi-ethnic American literatures whose interests include poetry, contemporary poetics and postcolonial and diasporic studies. He has received grants from the James Irvine Foundation, Poets and Writers, the Vermont Studio Center, and Bread Loaf. He has received the Celeste Turner Wright award from the Academy of American Poets and has been the recipient of the David Noel Miller Fellowship at UC Davis and a Henry Hoyns Fellowship at the University of Virigina.

Bill Knott, Associate Professor; M.F.A., Norwich. Mr. Knott is the author of numerous books of poetry and has been featured in most major journals and poetry magazines. His book, *Selected and Collected Poems*, was the 1979 winner of the Elliston Prize. His publications include *Poems 1963-1988, Outremer, The Quicken Tree, Laugh at the End of the World: Collected Comic Poems 1969-1999*, and most recently *The Unsubscriber*.

Maria Koundoura, Associate Professor; Ph.D., Stanford. Dr. Koundoura is a specialist in contemporary literary theory, in particular, postcolonial and transnational culture studies. Among her recent publications are articles on nationalism, multiculturalism, and globality in *Multicultural States* and in *Hop on Pop: The Pleasures and Politics of Popular Culture*, modernity and postcoloniality in *Culture Agonistes* and in *The Eighteenth Century: Theory and Interpretation*, and on nation and gender politics in *Colby Quarterly*. She is one of the founding editors of the *Stanford Humanities Review*. Currently she is at work on a book on global cities.

Margot Livesey, Writer-in-Residence; B.A., York (UK). Ms. Livesey is the author of *Banishing Verona, Eva Moves the Furniture, The Missing World, Criminals, Homework, Writing About Literature*, and *Learning By Heart*. She has written for *The New York Times Book Review, The Atlantic Monthly, The New Yorker*, the *Boston Globe, Newsday*, and *The Improper Bostonian*.

Gian Lombardo, Publisher-in-Residence and Coordinator, Certificate in Publishing program; M.A., Boston University. Mr. Lombardo has had more than 25 years of experience in a wide range of publishing environments—trade, association, and literary and consumer magazines as well as professional, literary, and textbook publishing. His clients have included *Reed Business Information, Ploughshares, Agni*, Bedford/St. Martin's, Boston Society of Civil Engineers, and *Transitions Abroad*. He is also the author of *Between Islands*, a collection of poems and verse translations and three collections of prose poetry—*Standing Room, Sky Open Again*, and *Of All the Corners to Forget*. He also directs Quale Press, which publishes both literary and technology-oriented works

Megan Marshall, Assistant Professor; A.B., Harvard. Megan Marshall is the author of *The Peabody Sisters*, a landmark biography of three women who made American intellectual history. *The Peabody Sisters* was a finalist for the Pulitzer Prize for Biography, the recipient of the Francis Parkman Prize from the Society of American Historians, and the Mark Lynton History Prize. She has written for *The New Yorker, the Atlantic, Slate*, and *The New York Times Book Review*.

Gail Mazur, Writer-in-Residence; M.A., Lesley. Ms. Mazur is the author of five books of poetry: *Nightfire, The Pose of Happiness, The Common, They Can't Take That Away from Me* (a finalist for the National Book Award in 2001), and *Zeppos First Wife: New & Selected Poems* (finalist for the Los Angeles Times Book Prize). She has published reviews and essays in the *Chicago Tribune*, the *Boston Globe, Salmagundi, The Mississippi Review, Field, The Atlantic*, and other publications.

Kim McLarin, Writer-in-Residence; B.A., Duke. Ms. McLarin is the author of the novels *Jump At the Sun, Meeting of the Waters*, and *Taming It Down*, and coauthor of the memoir *Growing Up X*, with Ilyasah Shabazz. She is a former staff writer for the *New York Times*, the *Philadelphia Inquirer*, the Greensboro *News & Record*, and the Associated Press. She has written for *The New York Times Sunday Magazine, Black Issues Book Review*, and *Architecture Boston*, among other publications.

Pamela Painter, Professor; M.A., Illinois at Chicago. Professor Painter is the author of two collections of short fiction, *Getting to Know the Weather* and *The Long and Short of It*. She is the coauthor, with Anne Bernays, of *WHAT IF? Fiction Exercises for Fiction Writers*. Her work has appeared in numerous literary journals and magazines, including *The Atlantic Monthly, Harper's, Kenyon Review*, and *Story*. She is a founding editor of *StoryQuarterly*, and has received grants from the Massachusetts' Artists Foundation and the National Endowment for the Arts.

Frederick Reiken, Associate Professor; M.F.A., California, Irvine. Mr. Reiken is the author of two novels. *The Odd Sea* is a winner of the Hackney Literary Award for a first novel and is listed as one of the "20 best first novels of 1998" by *Booklist*. His second book, *The Lost Legends of New Jersey*, was published in 2000.

Murray Schwartz, Professor; Ph.D., Berkeley. Dr. Schwartz is a specialist in Shakespeare. His interests include literary theory, psychoanalysis, and Holocaust studies. He coedited *Representing Shakespeare: New Psychoanalytic Essays*. Other major publications include *Memory and Desire: Psychoanalysis, Literature, Aging, A Thematic Introduction to Shakespeare, Erik Erikson*, and *Where is Literature?*, as well as many essays on Shakespeare, theoretical and applied psychoanalysis, and poets such as Sylvia Plath. "Morning and Its Vicissitudes: The Shakespearean Community and Shakespearean Romance," appeared in *Psyart*, an online journal. He is currently at work on a psychoanalytic study of the Holocaust and an essay on theories of trauma.

Jeffrey Seglin, Associate Professor; M.T.S., Harvard. Mr. Seglin has extensive experience in magazine and book publishing. He is the author of *The Right Thing: Conscience, Profit and Personal Responsibility in Today's Business; The Good, The Bad, And Your Business: Choosing Right When Ethical Dilemmas Pull You Apart;* and other books. He has written for *Fortune, salon.com*, and *Inc.* magazine (where he was an executive editor), and many other publications. He wrote a monthly business ethics column for the Sunday *New York Times* from 1998 to 2004, and currently writes a weekly syndicated column on general ethics for the *New York Times Syndicate*.

John Skoyles, Professor; M.F.A., Iowa. Professor Skoyles is the author of three books of poems: *A Little Faith, Permanent Change*, and *Definition of the Soul*. He has also published a book of nonfiction, *Generous Strangers;* a memoir, *Secret Frequencies: A New York Education;* and reviews of books for the Associated Press. He has been awarded two individual fellowships from the National Endowment for the Arts, as well as grants from the New York State and North Carolina Arts Councils.

Tracy L. Strauss, Lecturer of Expository Writing; M.F.A., Boston University. Ms. Strauss was the 2005 Recipient of the Somerville Arts Council Literary Fellowship Award for poetry and the 2003 Recipient of the International Radio and Television Society (IRTS) Foundation Faculty Award. Her short fiction has been published in *Solas Literary Journal*, and she has written obituaries and on-air promotions for American Movie Classics. Her writing has also appeared in the *Hopkins Quarterly*, the *Writing Center Journal, Through Smoked Glass, Equal Opportunity* magazine, and *The Chronicle of Higher Education*.

Jessica Treadway, Associate Professor; M.A., Boston University. Ms. Treadway is the author of the novel *And Give You Peace*. Her collection *Absent Without Leave and Other Stories* won the John C. Zacharis First Book Award in 1993. A former fellow at Radcliffe's Bunting Institute and recipient of a grant from the National Endowment for the Arts, she also reviews fiction for the *Boston Globe* and the *Chicago Tribune*.

Wendy Walters, Associate Professor; Ph.D., California, San Diego. Dr. Walters teaches courses in literatures of the African diaspora, as well as multicultural American literatures. In 2001–02 she was a non-resident fellow at the W. E. B. Du Bois Institute for Afro-American Research at Harvard University, where she finished her manuscript on black international writing. She has published articles in the journals *African American Review, Novel, Critical Arts*, and *MELUS* (Multi-Ethnic Literature of the U.S.), and has published a chapter in the book *Borders, Exiles, Diasporas*. Her contributor credits include *Black Writers* and the *Oxford Companion to African American Literature*. She is the author of *At Home in Diaspora: Black International Writing*.

Mako Yoshikawa, Assistant Professor; M.A., Oxford. Ms. Yoshikawa is the author of two novels: *One Hundred and One Ways*, a national bestseller published in 1999 and translated into six languages, and *Once Removed*. Among her awards for writing are fellowships from the Bunting Institute at Harvard University and from the Massachusetts Cultural Council. She holds a master's in Shakespeare and renaissance drama from Lincoln College, Oxford, and is currently finishing a Ph.D. in incest and miscegenation in twentieth-century American literature at the University of Michigan. Her publications also include scholarly articles on incest and race in American literature.

GEORGETOWN UNIVERSITY

Graduate School of Arts and Sciences
Communication, Culture & Technology Program

Program of Study

The way people communicate is changing dramatically. The Communication, Culture & Technology (CCT) Program explores how individuals use media and technology to communicate from social, economic, political, and cultural perspectives. The program is designed for those who want to combine their academic interests with studies of the history and future of technology. With this knowledge, students advance within their current careers, take their careers in a new direction, or prepare for further study at the Ph.D. level.

The CCT curriculum prepares students to be critical thinkers and first-rate scholars. Students apply their knowledge in meaningful ways to the problems and challenges of a world perpetually changing and responding in the face of the globalizing forces of communication, information technologies, and international media systems. General areas of study include cultural studies; issues in globalization; networking technology and social change; politics and media; technology and information policy; technology, art, and representation; and technology, business, and the economy.

CCT students must successfully complete a core course and one of two degree sequences with a cumulative GPA of no less than 3.0 to be eligible for the Master of Arts degree in communication, culture, and technology. Students may select a degree sequence of 36 credits culminating in a thesis project, or they may select the 39-credit course work option. Full-time enrollment is strongly encouraged; part-time enrollment is permitted by permission only. All students must complete the program requirements within three years. Full-time students typically graduate in two years.

Research Facilities

The dedicated CCT Student Computer Lab gives CCT students use of the Internet, scanning technology, printers, and major software applications. In addition to the dedicated computer lab, CCT students have access to a wide array of resources at Georgetown. Lauinger Library houses more than 2 million resource materials and provides a variety of electronic information resources, including online subscription databases and journals, computer labs, and a multimedia center. Lauinger Library is also a Federal Depository Library and a depository for the World Bank. In addition, CCT maintains a close relationship with Georgetown's Center for New Designs in Learning and Scholarship (CNDLS), an innovative center for studying, developing, and fostering the integration of pedagogy and technology. CNDLS offers a few paid research assistantships to CCT students.

Financial Aid

In addition to federal loan programs, the CCT Program offers a limited number of merit-based scholarships. These scholarships are partial- or full-tuition scholarships only and do not cover living expenses or fees. Matriculated students are eligible to apply for CCT teaching and research assistantships, which are offered on a competitive basis.

Cost of Study

CCT 2007–08 tuition was $25,056. This assumes a full-time course load of 9 credits per semester at $1392 per credit. The CCT Program also charges an annual mandatory $500 lab fee. This fee goes toward maintenance of and upgrades to the CCT student computer lab and subscriptions to online research resources and helps defray the costs of student printing and copying. Students should expect to spend $300 per semester on books.

Living and Housing Costs

Georgetown University does not provide housing for graduate students. There are an abundance of rental properties in the Washington, D.C., area, which is easily navigated by an efficient bus and subway system. Georgetown University also operates a free student bus service to and from selected stops in Washington and Arlington, Virginia. Students should estimate at least $1400 per month for living costs such as room, board, and personal expenses.

Student Group

CCT enrolls approximately 70 students each year. Total enrollment for 2006–07 was 173, of whom 20 percent were international students and 18 percent were members of minority groups. CCT students hail from diverse undergraduate, cultural, and professional backgrounds. This interdisciplinary foundation is embraced by the CCT Program and cultivated in the CCT curriculum. The result is a cooperative environment that promotes a very high level of intellectual and personal exploration.

Student Outcomes

CCT students find employment in a number of areas, including public relations, consulting, government affairs, research and analysis, marketing, Web site production, media, and advocacy. Approximately 10 percent of CCT graduates pursue further studies in Ph.D. programs in communication, cultural studies, media studies, political science, and other disciplines.

Location

Georgetown University is located in the historic Georgetown neighborhood of Washington, D.C. Washington is a vibrant international city at the center of a metropolitan region of more than 5 million people. The area has a lively art, music, and theater scene; ample outdoor recreation; and a full calendar of events and activities, and, of course, the Smithsonian and the National Mall.

The University and The Program

Georgetown University is a major international university that includes four undergraduate schools, respected graduate programs, a law school, and a medical school. Established in 1789 as the nation's first Jesuit university, Georgetown was founded on the principle that serious and sustained discourse among people of diverse backgrounds promotes intellectual understanding and progress. The CCT Program, a master's degree program in the Graduate School of Arts and Sciences, embodies this principle in its collaborative learning environment and innovative approach.

Applying

The application and financial aid deadline for fall is in late January for scholarship consideration, and the application deadline for students not seeking scholarships is in late February (students should consult the Web site for the exact dates). Spring admissions are offered on a case-by-case basis. GRE scores are required of all applicants. TOEFL or IELTS results are required for applicants who attended a university outside of the U.S. in which English was not the primary language of instruction. Additional required documents include sealed and signed official transcripts and official letters of recommendation, a statement of purpose, and an academic writing sample. An interview is not required. Admissions notifications are made by early April. Students can apply online at http://cct.georgetown.edu.

Correspondence and Information

Admissions Officer
Communication, Culture & Technology Program
Georgetown University
3520 Prospect Street, NW, Suite 311
Washington, D.C. 20057
Phone: 202-687-6618
Fax: 202-687-1720
E-mail: cctprogram@georgetown.edu
Web site: http://cct.georgetown.edu

Georgetown University

THE FACULTY AND THEIR RESEARCH

Michael Coventry, Visiting Assistant Professor; Ph.D. (history), Georgetown. Twentieth-century American popular and visual culture; gender; new media pedagogies; history of American nationalism; war, technology, and media.

Mirjana Dedaic, Visiting Assistant Professor; Ph.D. (sociolinguistics), Georgetown. Political linguistics and communication, intercultural communication, linguistic pragmatics, critical discourse analysis.

D. Linda Garcia, Research Professor and Director; Ph.D. (social informatics), Amsterdam. Network economics, networks in international development, organizational field analysis, communications policy.

Martin Irvine, Associate Professor and Founding Director of CCT; Ph.D. (English), Harvard. Contemporary arts, mediology, social contexts of media and communication technologies.

Michael Macovski, Associate Professor; Ph.D. (English), Berkeley. Hypertextual theory and digital culture.

Diana Owen, Associate Professor of Political Science; Ph.D. (political science), Wisconsin–Madison. Political communication, public opinion, political socialization and culture, mass media and elections, statistical methodology.

Jeffrey Peck, Professor; Ph.D. (comparative literature), Berkeley. Interdisciplinary theory, globalization, construction and representation of national and minority identities, cultural studies, German-Jewish studies.

J. P. Singh, Assistant Professor; Ph.D. (political economy and public policy), USC. International governance, political economy, technology and globalization, international development, politics of cultural representation.

Matthew Tinkcom, Associate Professor; Ph.D. (English), Pittsburgh. Critical theory, cultural studies, popular media, film studies, queer and gender studies.

Jeanine Warisse Turner, Associate Professor; Ph.D. (communication), Ohio State. Computer-mediated communication, virtual organizations, virtual communities, multi-communicating.

Eric Zimmer, S.J., Assistant Professor; Ph.D. (communication), Pennsylvania. Digital Divide, technology in the nonprofit sector, social marketing, political communication.

HAWAI'I PACIFIC UNIVERSITY

College of Communication

Program of Study

The Master of Arts in communication program (M.A./COM) provides students with an interdisciplinary approach integrating skills, theory, and knowledge. Students completing this Hawai'i Pacific University (HPU) program are prepared for careers ranging across the spectrum of business, marketing, advertising, mass media, public relations, entertainment, broadcast or print journalism, the Internet, or education. Technology is emphasized in each course so that graduates are prepared for rapid change in communication industries.

The M.A./COM requires a minimum of 39 semester hours of graduate work composed of 18 semester hours of core courses, 15 semester hours of electives, and 6 semester hours of writing a professional paper, project, or thesis. Assignments and internships use a pragmatic approach to develop marketable skills. Students apply what they learn in the classroom to actual problems faced by organizations and businesses.

Research Facilities

To support graduate studies, University libraries, with a collection exceeding 153,000 volumes, add an average of 2,500 volumes annually. Periodical titles number more than 1,700, and 205,000 pieces of microfiche and 5,300 rolls of microfilm are maintained.

Libraries are electronically linked to the catalogs and databases of Hawaii's major publicly supported library systems, other specialized libraries on Oahu, and remote-site libraries. HPU students are provided with e-mail as well as Internet and online access to state-of-the-art research databases. Laboratory facilities provide computers and software for writing and graphic design.

Financial Aid

The University participates in all federal financial aid programs designated for graduate students. These programs provide aid in the form of subsidized (need-based) and unsubsidized (non-need-based) Federal Stafford Student Loans. Through these loans, funds may be available to cover the student's entire cost of education. To apply for aid, students must submit the Free Application for Federal Student Aid (FAFSA) after January 1. Mailing of student award letters usually begins by the end of March. The University also offers several institutional scholarships and assistantships.

Cost of Study

For the 2007–08 academic year, graduate tuition was $560 per credit hour, and books cost approximately $1500 for the entire program.

Living and Housing Costs

The University has both residence halls and an apartment referral service. Including tuition, books, housing, food, health insurance, and miscellaneous expenses, the cost of living for a typical single student for two semesters (nine months) is approximately $26,280.

Student Group

University enrollment currently stands at nearly 9,000, including more than 1,200 graduate students. All fifty states and more than 100 countries are represented.

Location

The University has three campuses linked by shuttle. Hawai'i Pacific combines the excitement of an urban, downtown campus with the serenity of the windward side of the island. The main campus is located in downtown Honolulu, the business and financial center of the Pacific. The Hawai'i Loa campus is 8 miles away, situated in Kaneohe at the base of the Ko'olau Mountains; it is the site of the School of Nursing, the marine science program, and a variety of other course offerings. The third campus, Oceanic Institute, is an applied aquaculture research facility located on a 56-acre site at Makapu'u Point on the windward coast.

The University

Hawai'i Pacific University is the largest private postsecondary institution in the state of Hawaii. The University is coeducational, with a faculty of more than 300 members, a student-faculty ratio of 18:1, and an average class size of 20. A wide range of counseling and student support services are available. There are more than ninety student organizations, including the Graduate Student Organization.

Applying

Hawai'i Pacific University seeks students with academic promise, outstanding career potential and high motivation. Applicants should complete and forward a graduate admissions application form, have official transcripts sent from all colleges or universities, submit two original and current letters of recommendation, and submit two essays. Admissions decisions are made on a rolling basis, and applicants are notified between one and two weeks after all documents have been submitted. Applicants to Hawai'i Pacific University's graduate program are encouraged to submit applications online at http://www.hpu.edu/grad.

Correspondence and Information

Graduate Admissions
Hawai'i Pacific University
1164 Bishop Street, #911
Honolulu, Hawaii 96813

Phone: 808-544-1135
866-GRAD-HPU (toll-free)
Fax: 808-544-0280
E-mail: graduate@hpu.edu
Web site: http://www.hpu.edu/grad

Hawai'i Pacific University

THE FACULTY

John N. Barnum, Ph.D. (public relations), Texas at Austin.
Brian Cannon, Ph.D. (new media, graphic design, desktop publishing), Regent University (Virginia).
Steven Combs, Ph.D. (rhetoric, organizational communication), USC.
Joanne Gula, Ph.D. (advertising, broadcasting), Massachusetts.
John P. Hart, Ph.D. (persuasion, public relations, mass media), Kansas.
Serena Hashimoto, Ph.D. (communication theory, international communication, film studies), European Graduate School (Switzerland).
Hsuan-Yuan (Jade) Huang, Ph.D. (new media and advertising), North Carolina at Chapel Hill.
Lowell Ing, M.F.A. (multimedia), CUNY.
Minjeong Kim, Ph.D. (communication law and research), North Carolina at Chapel Hill.
Laurence LeDoux, D.A. (journalism, professional writing), Oregon.
Vicky Seiler, Ph.D. (advertising, strategic communication), Western Sydney.
Penny Pence Smith, Ph.D. (public relations), North Carolina at Chapel Hill.
James D. Whitfield, Ed.D. (journalism, public relations), Texas Tech.

THE JOHNS HOPKINS UNIVERSITY

Zanvyl Krieger School of Arts and Sciences
Advanced Academic Programs
Communication in Contemporary Society

Program of Study

The information and influence professions are at the heart of today's new economy and society. From political advertising to health promotion to public and media relations, communication plays a central role. Drawing on current practice, theory, and science, classes are designed to give students usable knowledge that will serve them in their profession. Courses are taught by leading industry experts and by Hopkins scholars so that full- and part-time students can have a competitive advantage in the workplace. The faculty includes tenured Hopkins faculty members, leading consultants, public relations executives, social scientists, government officials, and experts in political and health communication.

The Communication in Contemporary Society Program is designed for students who want to be trained or retrained for the communications and information professions in the new media environment. Classes are offered in the evenings, so students do not need to break stride in their professional careers.

All students in the program earn an M.A. in Communication in Contemporary Society. In addition, they may identify a concentration in one or occasionally two areas. Students do not need to identify a concentration and can pursue a broad curriculum that draws from all areas.

The Concentration in Political Communication addresses issues from campaign strategies to running a press office to influencing public policy. Courses include public affairs, campaign communication, crisis and issues communication, and ethnic politics. Communication is at the heart of politics; this concentration explores how, why, and what works.

The Concentration in Public and Media Relations covers everything from advertising to social marketing to budgeting and executing a comprehensive communication campaign. Courses include public relations, media relations, crisis and issue communication, and ethnic marketing.

The Concentration in Health Communication considers what characterizes an effective public information campaign, how to design campaigns about health, what demands are placed on communications specialists during an emergency, and how drug companies promote drugs. Courses include developing health communication campaigns, health psychology and persuasion, crisis and issue communication, and social marketing.

The Concentration in Digital Technologies addresses privacy, ethics, technological advances, globalization, and other topics that have become increasingly important in the changing media environment. Courses include history of communication technology, Internet strategies, digital security, digital content, and digital rights management.

Research Facilities

Students in Washington use the Library Resource Center at 1717 Massachusetts Avenue, NW. The center's staff arranges interlibrary loans and offers reserve services and a collection of program-specific reference materials. The Library Resource Center has eleven workstations in the electronic research room that connect to the Eisenhower Library's Horizon WebPac, the Hopkins online catalog search tool, and a vast array of electronic databases, journals, and periodicals. A twenty-four-station student computer lab is filled with state-of-the-art econometric software.

Financial Aid

Federal financial aid in the form of student loans is available on a limited basis to degree candidates who are enrolled in two or more courses per semester or term. More information is available from the Office of Student Financial Services.

Cost of Study

Tuition is $2560 per course in 2008–09. Ten courses are required to complete the degree.

Living and Housing Costs

Students make their own arrangements for housing.

Student Group

Students pursuing the M.S. in Communication in Contemporary Society come from private companies, nonprofit organizations, educational institutions, and government agencies.

Location

The program is housed at the Johns Hopkins Washington Center at 1717 Massachusetts Avenue, NW, near Dupont Circle in Washington, D.C.

The University and The School

The Johns Hopkins University Washington, D.C., Center is located at 1717 Massachusetts Avenue, NW, close to the Carey Business School and the School of Advanced International Studies, two other Johns Hopkins divisions. The center is located in Washington's vibrant Dupont Circle neighborhood, a block from the Dupont Circle Metro station.

Applying

Students must submit the completed application form, the nonrefundable application fee, official transcripts of all college work, a resume, and a 1,000-word statement of purpose.

Students may apply throughout the year and begin study during any of the three terms. When an application is received, every effort is made to render a decision and notify an applicant in time for the upcoming term. For more information, students should visit http://advanced.jhu.edu/admissions.

Correspondence and Information

Advanced Academic Programs
Zanvyl Krieger School of Arts and Sciences
The Johns Hopkins University
1717 Massachusetts Avenue, NW, Suite 101
Washington, D.C. 20036-1717
Phone: 800-847-3330 (toll-free)
E-mail: aapadmissions@jhu.edu
Web site: http://communication.jhu.edu

The Johns Hopkins University

THE FACULTY

Distinguished Hopkins scholars team up with industry experts to teach students how to apply the science and theories of effective communication to everyday work situations. The program's entire team of nationally recognized faculty and staff members is approachable, and class sizes are small so that students develop personal relationships with faculty members.

LOUISIANA STATE UNIVERSITY

Manship School of Mass Communication

Programs of Study

The information age is changing the way citizens get information and form opinions about issues. New media expands the arenas of communication, debate, and news reporting. Now, more than ever, there is a need for thoughtful, analytical study about how media influence people and impact democracy.

The Manship School of Mass Communication offers the nation's only graduate program focused exclusively on media and public affairs, with a Master of Mass Communication (M.M.C.) and a Ph.D. in mass communication and public affairs. Students gain experience through studying real-world strategic problems. They explore how political communication, journalism, advertising, and public relations shape perceptions and public discourse locally, nationally, and globally. Collaborative programs with other departments, such as political science, provide access to a broad range of related courses. Students can tailor some courses to focus on a particular area of interest.

Highly selective small classes allow students to work closely with senior faculty members from a wide range of disciplines: journalism to advertising, political science to public relations, sociology to history. Students and faculty members collaborate on innovative research projects; graduate students regularly publish in peer-reviewed journals and present at premier conferences.

The Manship School of Mass Communication faculty includes internationally recognized scholars with solid professional experience. The School has been recognized by the leading journalism education organizations and other academic associations. Recent surveys have placed the Manship School among the top 10 most productive departments nationwide in terms of faculty publication in leading journals. Faculty members have leadership roles in journalism, communications, and political science professional and academic organizations, and they serve on the editorial boards of leading scholarly journals.

The Ph.D. program generally takes three to four years to complete and requires 88 credit hours of study, including 18 hours of dissertation work and a 9-hour externship. The master's program requires 34–37 credit hours of study and generally takes about two years to complete. Students choose between a thesis and a professional project as a capstone.

Research Facilities

The School's commitment to the study of media and public affairs extends beyond the classroom, with a network of resources to support faculty and graduate research, including the Manship School Research Facility. Recent renovations to the School have created a world-class environment, with dedicated office space for graduate students, a $1.5 -million broadcast studio, multimedia classrooms, computer labs, and a state-of-the-art forum that provides space for academic, professional, and community events.

The Manship School Research Facility helps faculty members, graduate students, University departments, state organizations, and businesses conduct research studies through its free-standing facilities. The facility includes the Public Policy Research Lab, which provides advanced quantitative and qualitative research. The new Media Effects Lab is a state-of-the-art experimental lab that allows advanced research into the physical and emotional effects of media messages.

The Reilly Center for Media & Public Affairs within the Manship School is dedicated to tackling ideas and issues that explore the role of the media and democracy. The center brings in visiting professionals and scholars, conducts dynamic symposia, and facilitates training and partnerships with professional and academic organizations. The center also funds important research for faculty members and graduate students.

The Forum on Media Diversity provides universities and professional media organizations with access to research on diversity, a database of articles and books, and directories.

The Center for Computational Technology (CCT) investigates how new technologies can be used by researchers in social science and the humanities and provides new tools, platforms, and environments for artistic expression. CCT's Laboratory for Creative Arts and Technology (LCAT) provides dedicated research labs for audio, video, and other technologies.

Students also have access to outstanding library facilities, including Troy H. Middleton Library (the main library), Hill Memorial Library, Cartographic Information Center, the CEBA Reading Room, the Chemistry Library, and the Design Resource Center. Collectively, these library units house approximately 3 million volumes, more than 3 million microforms, and more than 7 million manuscripts. In addition, the LSU libraries provide access to more than 400 electronic indexes and databases and more than 21,990 current serial titles (including 12,000 electronic serials), maintain two electronic classrooms for instruction, house three computer labs with more than 200 computers, and serve as a regional U.S. Government Document Depository and a U.S. Patent and Trademark Depository.

Financial Aid

The Manship School offers one of the most competitive graduate financial packages in the country. Doctoral students are offered at least $24,000 per year in stipends plus tuition waivers and health insurance. Master's students receive stipends of $10,500 for nine months and can apply for a graduate assistantship with tuition waiver. In addition, students have access to more than $1000 in free software. The University also has a variety of federal financial aid options available through its financial aid office, including Federal Stafford Student Loans and Federal Perkins Loans.

Cost of Study

For 9 credit hours, graduate tuition and fees for fall 2007 were $2266 for Louisiana residents and $6416 for nonresidents. The cost of textbooks and course materials varies depending on a student's class schedule.

Living and Housing Costs

LSU has one-, two-, three-, and four-bedroom apartments available for single, upperclass, and full-time graduate students. Rent ranges from $2040 to $3680 per semester. Married-student housing is also available for families. Rents range from $2775 to $3000 per semester. A wide range of off-campus housing is also available around LSU.

Student Group

The master's program at the Manship School typically admits about 20 students per year, and the doctoral program admits 5 to 7 students each year. The graduate class includes students from across the United States and around the world, with diverse backgrounds and outstanding experience, including a CNN reporter, a Pulitzer Prize winner, and a former executive with the EPA. The majority of master's students come to the program within a year or two of completing their bachelor's degrees; the doctoral students typically have extensive professional experience before entering the program.

Student Outcomes

Students gain the skills required to pursue an academic career or advance in journalism, political consulting, advertising, and public relations or government nonprofit, corporate, or media organizations. Manship School graduates move on to impressive jobs at top universities and with private and nonprofit organizations. They pursue academic careers in teaching and research or work in politics, print, and broadcast journalism; advertising; and public relations.

Location

Louisiana State University is located in Baton Rouge, the state's capital. Louisiana has a long history of fascinating politics and a unique Cajun and Creole heritage. Bordered by the Mississippi River, Baton Rouge boasts a thriving arts community, unique cuisine and outstanding restaurants, outdoor activities, and a comfortable lifestyle. The city is about an hour's drive from New Orleans.

The University and The School

Louisiana State University is the state's flagship university. It offers a wide range of programs, extracurricular activities, and resources. Founded in 1860, the University has grown into a community of more than 34,000 faculty and staff members and students from every state and more than 120 countries.

The School is home to approximately 70 graduate students and 1,100 undergraduates. In 1994, the School became an independent unit of the University. The Manship School is one of just eleven LSU priority programs, reflecting its national reputation, outstanding faculty, and unique contribution to the campus.

Applying

Students can get applications and instructions on the Web site or by contacting the School. Each application must include application forms from the Manship School and LSU's Graduate School, transcripts from all colleges and universities attended, three letters of academic recommendation, a resume, and a letter describing the applicant's objectives. Master's applicants must have a bachelor's degree from an accredited institution, a minimum 3.0 undergraduate GPA, and a combined score of at least 1000 on the GRE, with a verbal score of at least 550. Ph.D. applicants must have a master's degree from an accredited institution, a minimum 3.0 undergraduate GPA, a minimum 3.5 graduate GPA, and a composite GRE score of at least 1000, with a verbal score of at least 500. Students must submit applications by January 25 for consideration for doctoral assistantships and for graduate assistantships. Applications submitted after January 25 may be considered for admission on a space-available basis.

Correspondence and Information

Margaret H. DeFleur
Associate Dean for Graduate Studies and Research
Manship School of Mass Communication
Louisiana State University
Baton Rouge, Louisiana 70803

Phone: 225-578-0334
E-mail: defleur@lsu.edu
Web site: http://www.manship.lsu.edu

Louisiana State Unviersity

THE FACULTY AND THEIR RESEARCH

John Maxwell Hamilton, LSU Foundation Hopkins P. Breazeale Professor and Dean; Ph.D. (American civilization), George Washington, 1983. Journalism, radio, public service, foreign affairs, U.S.–Third World relations.
Margaret DeFleur, Associate Dean for Graduate Studies and Research; Ph.D. (mass communication), Syracuse, 1994. Mass communication theory and research, media effects, health communication.
John B. Breaux, Distinguished Professor and Former U.S. Senator; J.D., LSU, 1967. National public policy.
Jinx C. Broussard, Associate Professor; Ph.D., Southern Mississippi, 2001. Public relations.
Yvonne Cappe, Professional in Residence; M.A. (journalism), Ohio State, 1994. Broadcast news.
Nicole Smith Dahmen, Assistant Professor; Ph.D. (journalism), North Carolina at Chapel Hill. Ethics, technology, visual communication.
Louis A. Day, Professor; Ph.D. (mass communication), Ohio, 1973. Media law and ethics.
Melvin DeFleur, Distinguished Professor; Ph.D. (sociology), Washington (Seattle). Mass communication theory.
William Dickinson, Distinguished Professor; B.A. (English), Kansas, 1953. Journalism, editing, writing.
Johanna Dunaway, Assistant Professor, Ph.D. (political science), Rice, 2006. Mass media and politics, public opinion.
Emily Erickson, Assistant Professor; Ph.D. (mass communication), Alabama, 2002. First Amendment theory and jurisprudence, interactions between media and American society, public opinion and politics.
Craig Freeman, Associate Professor; J.D., LSU, 1998. Media law, freedom of expression, media ethics and broadcasting.
Ronald Garay, F. Walker Lockett Professor; Ph.D. (mass communication), Ohio, 1980. Electronic media history and public policy.
Robert Kirby Goidel, Professor and Director of Public Policy Research; Ph.D., Kentucky, 1993. Political participation, elections and campaign finance, public opinion, media and politics.
Ralph Izard, Sig Mickelson/CBS Professor; Ph.D. (communications), Indiana, 1969. First Amendment, ethics.
Yongick Jeong, Assistant Professor; Ph.D. (advertising and media effects), North Carolina at Chapel Hill, 2007. New media, entertainment media, advertising effectiveness.
David Kurpius, Associate Dean for Undergraduate Studies and Administration; Ph.D. (mass communication), Wisconsin, 1997. Civic journalism and local television news.
Regina Lawrence, Reilly Chair in Political Communication; Ph.D. (political science), Washington (Seattle), 1997. Political communication, mass media and politics.
Laura F. Lindsay, Professor; Ph.D. (organizational communication), LSU, 1976. Organizational communication systems, communication planning, crisis communication.
George Lockwood, Distinguished Professor; M.A. (journalism and political science), Minnesota, 1957.
Lisa Lundy, Assistant Professor; Ph.D. (mass communication), Florida, 2004. Agricultural communication, science communication, public relations.
Jennifer Macha, Instructor; M.A. (advertising), Texas at Austin. Advertising, marketing, visual communication.
Robert Mann, Manship Chair and Senior Fellow; M.A., California State. Public policy, political communication, history.
Andrea Miller, Assistant Professor; Ph.D. (journalism), Missouri–Columbia, 2003. Broadcast news, production.
Richard Alan Nelson, Professor; Ph.D. (communication), Florida State, 1980. Advertising issues, issues management, propaganda.
Tad Odell, Instructor; Ph.D. candidate (telecommunications management), Oregon. Broadcast, documentaries, journalism.
Anne Osborne, Associate Dean of Sponsored Research and Programs; Ph.D. (mass communication), Tennessee, 1999.
Jay L. Perkins, Associate Professor; M.A. (history), LSU, 1988. Investigative reporting, computer-assisted reporting, political-consulting techniques.
Richard Popp, Assistant Professor; Ph.D. (mass media and communication), Temple, 2008. Mass media history, media and identity.
Lance Porter, Assistant Professor; Ph.D. (mass communication), Georgia, 2002. New media, public relations.
Monica Postelnicu, Assistant Professor; Ph.D. (mass communication), Florida. New media, technology, public affairs, political communication.
Billy I. Ross, Distinguished Professor; Ph.D. (journalism), Southern Illinois, 1964. Public relations, advertising, administration.
Meghan Sanders, Assistant Professor; Ph.D. (mass communication), Penn State. Public relations, media effects, communication.
Rosanne Scholl, Assistant Professor; Ph.D. (mass communications), Wisconsin–Madison, 2008. Media effects on economic and political attitudes.
Jay Shelledy, Greer Chair of Media Business and Ethics and Director, Student Media; B.A. (journalism), Gonzaga. News, writing.
Danny Shipka, Assistant Professor; Ph.D. (public relations and film), Florida, 2007. Public relations, popular culture, film.
Felicia Wu Song, Assistant Professor, Ph.D. (sociology), Virginia. New media and technology, Internet in society, mass communication theory.
Judith L. Sylvester, Associate Professor; Ph.D. (journalism), Missouri–Columbia, 1994. Research methods, civic journalism, health-care campaigns, social marketing.
Chris Weber, Assistant Professor; Ph.D. (political science), Stony Brook, SUNY, 2008. Mass media and political persuasion.
Micheal Xenos, Assistant Professor and Director, Media Effects Lab; Ph.D. (political science), Washington (Seattle). Political communication, public opinion.
Jay Yu, Assistant Professor; Ph.D. (advertising), Georgia, 2007. New media, advertising, culture.

Affiliate Faculty

Cecil L. Eubanks, Alumni Professor of Political Science; Ph.D., Michigan, 1970. Contemporary political thought, political theology, the American founding period.
James C. Garand, Emogine Pliner Distinguished Professor of Political Science; Ph.D. (political science), Kentucky, 1984. Legislative politics, electoral politics, public policy, bureaucratic politics, the American presidency, domestic political economy.
Robert E. Hogan, Associate Professor of Political Science; Ph.D., Rice, 1998. Campaigns and elections, political parties and interest groups, state politics, legislative politics.
T. Wayne Parent, Russell B. Long Professor of Political Science; Ph.D., Indiana, 1983. Electoral coalitions, black politics, Southern politics.
James Richardson, Director, Public Administration Institute, E. J. Ourso College of Business; Ph.D. (economics), Michigan, 1971. Economic forecasting, state and local taxation issues.
Dek Terrell, Associate Professor, E. J. Ourso College of Business; Ph.D., Duke, 1991. Microeconomics, applications of Bayesian econometrics.

THE NEW SCHOOL: A UNIVERSITY

Department of Media Studies and Film
Master of Arts in Media Studies

Program of Study

The Master of Arts program in the Department of Media Studies and Film at The New School provides a theoretical and practical course of study for both filmmakers and those interested in exploring other types of media.

The program is highly individualized, and the curriculum includes production classes in video, audio, film, and multimedia technologies as well as academic seminars in communications theory. Students also have the option to complete their degree online through classes offered by The New School. Most students attend part-time and complete the degree in approximately three years. The thesis option requires 36 credits, and the nonthesis option requires 39 credits. In addition, the Department offers a 12-credit graduate certificate in media management; recently, it launched a one-year graduate certificate program in documentary media studies—the only one of its kind in New York City.

Media studies graduates use their degrees to enhance their current careers or build new ones in a broad spectrum of fields such as marketing, public relations, and nonprofit management. Many stay in the world of academia, pursuing Ph.D.'s or working as university professors. Still others seek creative outlets as artists, filmmakers, and designers.

Research Facilities

The Raymond Fogelman Library at The New School contains books, standard references, pamphlets, and periodicals essential to the media studies program. Matriculated students may also use the Elmer Holmes Bobst Library at New York University and the Cooper Union Library, which are members, with The New School, of the Research Library Association of South Manhattan.

Students in the media studies program have access to Macintosh and PCs in the University Computing Center. They may also use the Knowledge Union multimedia lab, which offers state-of-the-art capabilities for multimedia production, including multimedia classrooms equipped for computer, video, and sound presentation; video and audio editing stations and suites; a large open lab with PowerMac, Windows, and Silicon Graphics workstations; and an equipment center. In addition, students often work with faculty members on research and production projects at off-campus sites throughout the New York metropolitan area.

Financial Aid

Nearly half of the full-time and part-time students in the media studies program receive financial aid, ranging from small awards to full scholarships. The Awards Committee considers both merit and need in granting available funds. The New School also offers an extended payment plan that involves monthly billing throughout the semester.

Cost of Study

Tuition for the 2008–09 academic year is $1076 per credit. A $100 University services fee and a $15 student services fee are charged each term. For more information, students should visit http://www.newschool.edu/tuition.

Living and Housing Costs

The University Housing Office maintains a comprehensive resource center with apartment listings. University apartments and residence halls are also available. The cost of housing, food, transportation, and living expenses averages $17,000 annually. More information is available online at http://www.newschool.edu/studentservices.

Student Group

Students in the media studies program are a diverse and creative group—a third come from outside the United States, a third are members of underrepresented groups, and more than half are women. Many students are already professionals and work in media-related jobs while attending the program.

Location

New York City is the communications capital of the world, and the media studies program takes full advantage of what the city has to offer. Broadcast television stations, cable operations, corporate communications facilities, and film, video, and audio production companies provide professional internship opportunities in research, and students also attend special events with media professionals each semester. In addition, students are encouraged to explore the numerous communications activities available only in New York City.

The School and The Department

The New School is a leading university in New York City offering distinguished programs in design, liberal arts, the performing arts, and social and political science, leading to seventy graduate and undergraduate degrees. To learn more, students should visit http://www.newschool.edu/degreeprograms. A privately supported institution, The New School is accredited by the Commission on Higher Education of the Middle States Association of Colleges and Schools and chartered as a university by the Regents of the State of New York.

The guiding mission of the Department of Media Studies and Film at The New School is to help students develop a critical understanding of the mediated culture in which we live and master the skills needed to produce media messages in a variety of forms and genres. Since it was established at The New School in 1975, the program has been committed to strengthening the connection between media theory and practice. Today, in a world defined by rapidly changing information and communications technologies, it remains open to innovation and embraces all forms of media. The media studies program aims to prepare students for success in a competitive marketplace while educating them to be humane and thoughtful citizens in an increasingly mediated world. For more information about the program, prospective students should visit http://www.newschool.edu/mediastudies.

Applying

An applicant to the Media Studies program must hold a bachelor's degree from an accredited college or university. Applications from students in all academic disciplines are invited. A completed application, an application fee, a statement of purpose, official transcripts of all undergraduate and graduate studies, and one academic and one professional letter of recommendation should be submitted to the Media Studies Admissions Office by the stated application deadline. A personal interview may be required of all applicants. This interview may be waived or conducted by telephone under special circumstances. It is the responsibility of the applicant to ensure the receipt of admissions materials by the announced deadline. The application deadline for fall admission is March 15; the application deadline for spring admission is October 15.

To request a catalog and/or an application form, students should visit http://www.mediastudies.newschool.edu or contact the Office of Admissions.

Correspondence and Information

Office of Admissions
The New School
66 West 12th Street, Room 401
New York, New York 10011

Phone: 212-229-5630
E-mail: nsadmissions@newschool.edu
Web site: http://www.newschool.edu/mediastudies

The New School: A University

THE FACULTY

Core Faculty

Deirdre Boyle, M.A., Antioch (Ohio). Video historian, media critic, consultant, and programmer; author of *Subject to Change: Guerrilla Television Revisited, Video Preservation,* and *Video Classics.*

Paolo Carpignano, D.Lett., Rome. Author of *Crisis and Workers' Organization* and *The Formation of the Mass Worker in the USA* as well as numerous articles on international communications.

Sumita Chakravarty, Ph.D., Lucknow (India); Ph.D., Illinois at Urbana-Champaign. Author of *National Identity in Indian Popular Cinema;* articles in the *Quarterly Review of Film and Video, Cine-Tracts, South Asia Bulletin,* and *World Film Directors.*

Elizabeth Ellsworth, Ph.D., Wisconsin. Author of *Teaching Positions: Difference, Pedagogy, and the Power of Address;* architecture and media studies to address issues of time, space, and place in mediated learning environments.

Peter L. Haratonik, M.A., NYU. Acting chair, New School Department of Media Studies and Film; former director, Film/Video/Broadcasting, NYU; chair, Communication Arts Department; director, Television Institute, Hofstra University; past president of the Association of Communication Administration; author and consultant.

Jae Ho Kang, Ph.D., Cambridge. Former Alexander von Humboldt Research Fellow, Institute for Social Research at University of Frankfurt (Germany); social theory of media and mass culture, critical theory of art and technology; new media and political communications.

Lawrence (Kit) Laybourne, M.A., UCLA. A founder of the media studies program and head of animation and special projects at Oxygen Media; created the signature course, Foundations of Media Design.

Shannon Mattern, Ph.D., NYU. Author of *Public Places, Info Spaces: Creating the Modern Urban Library;* relationships between media and spatial theory and practice.

Diane Mitchell, M.F.A., Michigan State. Multimedia producer and designer; artist; awards include NEA, NYSCA, and NYCH grants and industry awards in multimedia production for Fortune 500 companies and the United Nations.

Vlad Nikolic, M.A., New School. Award-winning filmmaker and director for film and TV; films include *The End of the Millennium, Cut, Serendipity,* and the feature documentary *The City.*

Raphael Parra, B.A., CUNY, Hunter. Laureate, University of the Andes (Venezuela); professional AVID editor; owner and senior editor at Timeline Film and Video, a postproduction facility.

Paul Ryan, B.A., NYU. Author of articles in *Leonardo, Afterimage, Millennium, Terra Nova,* and *Semiotica,* among others; author of *Cybernetics of the Sacred* and *Video Mind, Earth Mind;* video art shown internationally and at the Museum of Modern Art.

Barry Salmon, M.A., New School. Composer of scores for numerous films as well as music for dance, theater, radio, and video art; performing and recording guitarist and record and CD producer.

Part-Time Faculty

For a current listing of courses and part-time faculty members, students should visit the Department's Web site at http://www.newschool.edu/mediastudies.

NEW YORK UNIVERSITY

School of Continuing and Professional Studies
Master of Science in Public Relations and Corporate Communications

Program of Study

The Master of Science (M.S.) in Public Relations and Corporate Communications program at the School of Continuing and Professional Studies (SCPS) addresses the industry's need for skilled PR professionals. The role of the communications specialist is rapidly expanding in the public relations, corporate communications, and marketing communities, and the function of both public relations (the management of relationships between an organization and its publics) and its subset, corporate communications (the area responsible for centralized communications on behalf of the organization), is increasingly being integrated with other marketing efforts.

This program prepares students to become the next generation of professionals from whom industry leaders choose their spokespeople and strategists. In this degree program, students acquire a blend of practical and theoretical knowledge that is immediately applicable to the work environment, develop the specialized writing skills they need to advance in the public relations industry through in-depth public relations writing seminars, and gain experience working alongside today's top communications professionals through a practicum that significantly adds to their portfolio.

Faculty members are expert practitioners in public relations and corporate communications, including senior executives at preeminent global public relations firms and leading corporations responsible for crisis and issue management, corporate branding, media relations, event promotion, professional development, business-to-business communications, and corporate reputation management.

The 42-credit master's degree program may be completed part-time or full-time. The curriculum consists of required core courses, concentration courses, a practicum, and the final capstone project (thesis). Concentrations are available in public relations management and corporate and organizational communications. The M.S. in Public Relations and Corporate Communications curriculum is continually reevaluated and updated in response to industry needs to provide the most up-to-date and relevant course of study.

Research Facilities

The Elmer Holmes Bobst Library and Study Center, one of the largest open-stack research libraries in the world, houses more than 3 million of NYU's nearly 4.4 million volumes. In addition to books, journals, and other print materials, the library provides access to many nonprint resources. These include microforms, databases, and other electronic resources that students can connect to from their home or residence hall; extensive video and audio collections; and a variety of computer equipment and software programs.

NYU's central source for computing, information, network, and telecommunications services is Information Technology Services (ITS). ITS maintains four large, modern computer labs with high-end Macintosh and Windows computers, laser printers, multimedia equipment, and a wide variety of up-to-date software. The Client Services division of ITS provides comprehensive help with the materials and equipment available to students via telephone and e-mail, online, and in person.

Financial Aid

There are many financial aid options to consider, including fellowships and low-interest educational loans. NYU's centralized Office of Financial Aid assists students with loan packages, scholarships, and the NYU monthly payment plan, which enables students to spread out their tuition payments. For more information, students should visit http://www.nyu.edu/financial.aid.

Cost of Study

Tuition for part-time students for the 2008–09 academic year is $1326 per credit plus fees. For full-time students (10–12 credits per semester), the cost of tuition and related fees is $13,260 per semester. Fees vary somewhat by program. The Board of Trustees of New York University reserves the right to alter these costs without notice.

Living and Housing Costs

Graduate student housing is available on the University campus and is administered through the Office of Housing and Residence Life. However, students may choose to live off campus. NYU's Off-Campus Housing Office (OCHO) offers assistance to members of the NYU community in their search for non-University housing options. OCHO provides, exclusively to NYU students, listings of available locations for rent through private landlords, property managers, brokers, and real estate agents. Updated daily, these listings are accessible through OCHO's computer terminals or online for members of the NYU community.

Student Group

In 2007–08, there were 125 students enrolled in the Master of Science in Public Relations and Corporate Communications program. The median age was 28 and 83 percent of the students were women. Part-time students accounted for 74 percent of those enrolled.

Location

The Graduate Program in Public Relations and Corporate Communications, offered through the Division of Programs in Business at NYU's School of Continuing and Professional Studies, is located in the Midtown Center at 11 West 42nd Street, in the heart of Manhattan. For public relations, no other city comes close to the wide range of dynamic professional opportunities in New York City.

The University, The School, and The Program

NYU is a private university composed of fourteen schools and colleges. The University was founded in 1831 and the School of Continuing and Professional Studies was founded in 1934. The Graduate Program in Public Relations and Corporate Communications was established in 2005. For more than twenty-five years, SCPS has been a leader in offering an ever-expanding array of courses designed to develop professionals in the public relations, corporate communications, and marketing communities.

Applying

Students may apply for fall or spring admission. Factors that are considered in evaluating an applicant include official transcripts of academic achievement in previous undergraduate and graduate course work, scores from the GRE or GMAT, TOEFL scores (for international students), the nature and extent of previous work experience, professional recommendations, and a statement of purpose.

Correspondence and Information

Office of Admissions
Master of Science in Public Relations and Corporate Communications
New York University
145 Fourth Avenue, Room 219
New York, New York 10003
Phone: 212-998-7200 Ext. 776
Fax: 212-995-4674
E-mail: scps.gradadmissions@nyu.edu
Web site: http://www.scps.nyu.edu/776

New York University

THE ADMINISTRATION

Robert S. Lapiner, Ph.D., Dean, School of Continuing and Professional Studies.
Anthony R. Davidson, M.B.A., Ph.D., Divisional Dean and Clinical Professor, Division of Programs in Business.
John Doorley, M.A., Academic Program Director and Clinical Associate Professor, Graduate Program in Public Relations and Corporate Communications, Division of Programs in Business.

NEW YORK UNIVERSITY

School of Continuing and Professional Studies
Master of Science in Publishing

Program of Study

The Master of Science (M.S.) in Publishing program at the School of Continuing and Professional Studies (SCPS) is a unique program that prepares students for management-level positions in a rapidly changing industry. In addition to providing the core fundamentals of book, magazine, and digital publishing, the program trains future leaders to excel in an era of media convergence in which multiple platforms influence business decisions and strategies. Taught by leading publishing professionals, the program integrates rigorous course work with industry case studies, practical workplace assignments, networking opportunities, and an exploration of critical issues and future trends. Founded on New York University's (NYU) distinctive tradition of academic excellence, the program is designed for students committed to a future in both traditional and new digital media.

The program's faculty members are top executives, leaders, and managers of national and multinational publishing companies. These expert instructors and practitioners represent a diverse cross-section in background and scholarship. Professors bring an insider's viewpoint into the classroom and challenge students' critical-thinking and decision-making abilities.

The 42-credit degree program may be completed on a part-time or full-time basis. The curriculum consists of required core courses, media specializations, and the final capstone course (thesis project). Media specializations are offered in media marketing and distribution, media profitability, and media content development. The capstone course gives students the opportunity to pursue a research project centered in the industry, company, or specific area of most value to them. Through full-time study, students can complete the program in two years; part-time study takes three to four years. The M.S. in Publishing curriculum is continually reevaluated and updated in response to industry needs to provide the most up-to-date and relevant course of study.

Research Facilities

The Elmer Holmes Bobst Library and Study Center, one of the largest open-stack research libraries in the world, houses more than 3 million of NYU's nearly 4.4 million volumes. In addition to books, journals, and other print materials, the library provides access to many nonprint resources. These include microforms, databases, and other electronic resources that students can connect to from their home or residence hall; extensive video and audio collections; and a variety of computer equipment and software programs.

NYU's central source for computing, information, network, and telecommunications services is Information Technology Services (ITS). ITS maintains four large, modern computer labs with high-end Macintosh and Windows computers, laser printers, multimedia equipment, and a wide variety of up-to-date software. Using the telephone, e-mail, the Web, and personal interaction, the client services division of ITS provides comprehensive help on the materials and equipment available to students.

Financial Aid

There are many financial aid options to consider, including fellowships and low-interest educational loans. NYU's centralized Office of Financial Aid assists students with loan packages, scholarships, and the NYU monthly payment plan, which enables students to spread out their tuition payments. Department scholarships are also available. To learn more, interested students should visit http://www.nyu.edu/financial.aid.

Cost of Study

Tuition for part-time students for the 2008–09 academic year is $1326 per credit, plus fees. For full-time students (10–12 credits per semester), the cost of tuition and related fees is $13,260 per semester. Fees vary somewhat by program. The Board of Trustees of New York University reserves the right to alter these costs without notice.

Living and Housing Costs

Graduate student housing is available on the University campus and is administered through the Office of Housing and Residence Life. However, students may choose to live off campus. NYU's Off-Campus Housing Office (OCHO) offers assistance to members of the NYU community in their search for non-University housing options. OCHO provides, exclusively to NYU students, listings of available locations for rent through private landlords, property managers, brokers, and real estate agents. Updated daily, these listings are accessible to members of the NYU community through OCHO's computer terminals or online.

Student Group

In 2007–08, there were 87 students enrolled in the Master of Science in Publishing program. The median age was 29, and 80 percent of the students were women. Part-time students accounted for 62 percent of those enrolled. Most of the students currently work in publishing and enter the graduate program with a minimum of two years' experience.

Location

The M.S. in Publishing is housed at NYU's Midtown Center at 11 West 42nd Street. Classes are held at NYU's Washington Square campus and Midtown Center. Study takes place in the world's publishing capital, New York City, which is home to more than 1,000 publishers as well as twenty-five major global conglomerates. In addition, the industry's top advertising agencies, media corporations, and information technology companies are located and based in New York.

The University and The School

NYU is a private university, composed of fourteen schools and colleges. The University was founded in 1831 and the School of Continuing and Professional Studies in 1934. Since 1943, SCPS has offered an array of programs for the publishing industry, including seminars and workshops, a summer publishing institute, continuing education courses, and certificate programs.

Applying

Students may apply for fall or spring admission. Application packages must include official transcripts, results of the GRE or GMAT, TOEFL scores (for students whose native language is not English), resumes or professional summaries, letters of recommendation, and a statement of purpose.

Correspondence and Information

Office of Admissions
Master of Science in Publishing
New York University
145 Fourth Avenue, Room 219
New York, New York 10003

Phone: 212-998-7200 Ext. 413
Fax: 212-995-4674
E-mail: scps.gradadmissions@nyu.edu
Web site: http://www.scps.nyu.edu/413

New York University

THE ADMINISTRATION

Robert S. Lapiner, Ph.D., Dean, School of Continuing and Professional Studies.
Andrea L. Chambers, M.S., Academic Program Director and Clinical Assistant Professor, Center for Publishing.
Alyssa Léal, M.S., Associate Director, Center for Publishing.

THE OHIO STATE UNIVERSITY

College of Social and Behavioral Sciences
School of Communication

Program of Study

The School pursues studies in communication within an empirical social science framework in a number of areas of communication, including public opinion and political communication, health communication, mass communication, interpersonal communication, communication technology and society, and strategic communication. The School offers degrees in communication at the Ph.D. and M.A. levels.

Strongly rooted in the social sciences, the program is appropriately located within the College of Social and Behavioral Sciences. With nationally ranked programs in such areas as psychology, political science, and sociology, the College provides a stimulating intellectual environment for pursuing graduate studies.

An interdisciplinary social science perspective permeates all programs of the School. Prospective students from all academic backgrounds are encouraged to apply, but students with B.A. and M.A. degrees in journalism, mass communication or communication areas, or other empirical social sciences are especially welcome. The faculty's interdisciplinary approach provides students with a broad appreciation of the factors affecting the communication process.

In addition to theoretical research, the program encourages a relationship between theory and application. Applied communication research that can have a positive impact on society is an integral part of the program.

Research Facilities

Students benefit from Ohio State's extensive library system, one of the most advanced in the nation. It contains more than 4.8 million volumes as well as an advanced computer system known as OhioLink. OhioLink allows easy access to materials at the Ohio State University libraries and also to those of many other research libraries in the state and the State Library in Columbus. In addition to easy interlibrary loans, OhioLink provides a wide range of online data, scholarly and public affairs reference services, and online journals. All students receive free computer accounts from University Technology Services upon registration that provide access to the Internet and e-mail.

Major research institutes housed at Ohio State include the Center for Human Resource Research, Center for Cognitive Science, and the John Glenn Institute for Public Service and Public Policy.

The School has labs for conducting communication research using a variety of instruments and procedures, including physiological and psychological data collection. Labs permit gathering of data from individuals or groups, using face-to-face, computers, Internet, or other media. The School provides access to computers using the Statistical Package for the Social Science and other, more specialized statistical analysis software.

Financial Aid

Fellowships and graduate associateships are available based on academic credentials. Fellowships provide a one-year waiver of tuition and fees and a monthly stipend of $1256 for master's students and $1615 for Ph.D students. There is no work commitment associated with fellowships. Students may apply by indicating an interest on the graduate school application. Many M.A. students are supported with fellowships or assistantships. Assistantships provide a waiver of tuition and fees and a monthly stipend of at least $1250 for 20 hours of work a week. Ph.D. students receive a stipend of approximately $1650 per month.

Cost of Study

University tuition and fees for three quarters of study in 2007–08 were $9972 for Ohio residents and $24,126 for nonresidents. Tuition is waived for students awarded graduate assistantship or fellowship appointments.

Living and Housing Costs

Columbus is a moderate cost area, with many diverse housing opportunities both on and off campus.

Student Group

The School enrolls about 20 to 30 Ph.D. students and about 10 to 15 M.A. students per year from universities all over the world. Ph.D. students typically find employment in academic settings upon graduation. Many students in the M.A. program continue in doctoral studies at Ohio State University or elsewhere.

Location

Ohio State University's main campus is located in Columbus, the capital city of Ohio, with a population of approximately 1.6 million people. Columbus is a thriving metropolitan area with a diverse service-based economy. The city offers a low cost of living and a high quality of life with a lively downtown area, theaters, museums, art galleries, ethnic restaurants, and more movie screens per capita than anywhere in the country. Columbus has a world-class zoo and symphony orchestra as well as an excellent metropolitan parks system and scenic sites for boating, fishing, and sailing.

The University

The Ohio State University is a leading comprehensive teaching and research university and one of the largest in the country, with nearly 50,000 students. The University combines a responsibility for the advancement and dissemination of knowledge with a land-grant heritage of public service, offering an extensive range of academic programs in the liberal arts, the sciences, and the professions. Few universities can match Ohio State's breadth of academic offerings and related interdisciplinary opportunities, including 176 undergraduate majors, 220 graduate fields of study, and professional programs.

Applying

The program is designed for graduate students who seek to blend social science perspectives with the study of communication and have academic promise and demonstrated interest in the field. Applicants are required to submit a graduate admission application form, a statement of purpose, at least three letters of recommendation, transcripts of all colleges and universities attended, the results of the Graduate Record Examinations (GRE), and an application fee ($40 for domestic applicants; $50 for international applicants). All international students, even if they have received prior education at a U.S. institution, must submit results of the Test of English as a Foreign Language (TOEFL) that include the spoken English component. The application deadline for full consideration for all forms of financial aid is January 15.

Correspondence and Information

Director of Graduate Studies
School of Communication
The Ohio State University
3016 Derby Hall
154 North Oval Mall
Columbus, Ohio 43210-1339

Phone: 614-292-6503
Fax: 614-292-2055
E-mail: comm@osu.edu
Web site: http://www.comm.ohio-state.edu

The Ohio State University

THE FACULTY AND THEIR RESEARCH

Osei Appiah, Associate Professor; Ph.D., Stanford. Media effects on ethnic minorities.
Lucy Shelton Caswell, Professor and Curator of Cartoon Research Library; A.M.L.S., Michigan. History of political cartoons and comic strips.
Prabu David, Associate Professor; Ph.D., North Carolina. New media technologies and cognitive processing.
Brenda Dervin, Professor; Ph.D., Michigan State. Development and implementation of a communication-based methodology called Sense-Making.
John W. Dimmick, Associate Professor; Ph.D., Michigan. Media users and gratifications, media economics.
William P. Eveland, Professor; Ph.D., Wisconsin. Political communication and new technologies.
R. Kelly Garrett, Assistant Professor; Ph.D., Michigan. New communication technologies and politics.
Carroll Glynn, Professor and Director; Ph.D., Wisconsin. Public opinion and communication.
Andrew Hayes, Associate Professor; Ph.D., Cornell. Research methodology, psychometrics, data analysis, public opinion.
R. Lance Holbert, Associate Professor; Ph.D., Wisconsin. Political communication and public opinion.
Young Mie Kim, Assistant Professor; Ph.D., Illinois. Political communication, new communication technologies, and mass communication.
Susan Kline, Associate Professor; Ph.D., Illinois. Interpersonal communication, social interaction, and relational competencies; argumentation and social influence.
Silvia Knobloch-Westerwick, Associate Professor; Ph.D., Hanover (Germany). Media effects of news, entertainment, and new communication technologies.
Gerald M. Kosicki, Associate Professor; Ph.D., Wisconsin. Public opinion and communication, survey research methods and analysis, political communication.
Chad Mahood, Assistant Professor; Ph.D., California, Santa Barbara. Traditional and new media effects, with special focus on video games.
Michael McClusky, Assistant Professor; Ph.D., Wisconsin. Political communication, journalism, activism, new communication technologies.
Daniel G. McDonald, Professor; Ph.D., Wisconsin. Psychological and social aspects of mass communication, intra-audience effects.
Emily Moyer-Guse, Assistant Professor; Ph.D., California, Santa Barbara. Media and children, strategic communication.
Amy Nathanson, Associate Professor; Ph.D., Wisconsin. Children and the media.
Erik Nisbet, Assistant Professor; Ph.D., Cornell. Comparative political communication, strategic communication, public opinion.
Ray Pingree, Assistant Professor; Ph.D., Wisconsin. Reasoning, large-group deliberation, political communication, organizational communication.
Janice Raup-Krieger, Assistant Professor; Ph.D., Penn State. Health and interpersonal communication.
Kimberly Rios Morrison, Assistant Professor; Ph.D., Stanford. Social influence, public opinion, organizational communication.
Felecia G. Jones Ross, Associate Professor; Ph.D., Georgia. Mass media and traditionally discriminated groups, especially history of the black press.
Thomas A. Schwartz, Associate Professor; Ph.D., Southern Illinois. Communication law and history.
Michael Slater, Professor; Ph.D., Stanford. Health communication, media and message effects, persuasion.
Dongyoung Sohn, Assistant Professor; Ph.D., Texas at Austin. Communication technology, diffusion process, collective behavior, strategic communication.
Zheng "Joyce" Wang, Assistant Professor; Ph.D., Indiana. Emotion and cognition during message processing, psychophysiology and dynamic modeling methods.
Sharon Crook West, Associate Professor; M.A., Ohio State. Role of news media in Ohio politics.
Axel Westerwick, Assistant Professor; Ph.D., RWTH Aachen (Germany). Communication technology, knowledge management, organizational communication, multicultural communication.

PACE UNIVERSITY

Dyson College of Arts and Sciences
Master of Science in Publishing Program

Program of Study

The Master of Science in publishing program provides leading-edge professional study for students who are seeking management careers in the dynamic book and magazine industry. The 36-credit program is distinguished by the strong support of the publishing community. The advisory board includes many active editors, publishers, designers, and executives, who play an active role in overseeing the curriculum and ensuring its relevancy to the industry's current needs and realities. The curriculum provides a comprehensive education in all aspects of the business, including editorial, production, marketing, finance, acquisitions and subsidiary rights, and new technologies. Students select one or more areas of concentration through elective courses. All students participate in internships with area publishers. The program is offered in the classroom and online. For more information, prospective students should call 212-346-1416, send an e-mail to begidi@pace.edu, or go online to http://www.pace.deu/dyson/mspub.

Research Facilities

The Pace University Library is a comprehensive teaching library and student-learning center, a virtual library that combines strong core collections with ubiquitous access to global Internet resources to support broad and diversified curricula. Reciprocal borrowing and access accords, traditional interlibrary loan services, and commercial document-delivery options supplement the aggregate library. Pace offers Instructional Services Librarians, a state-of-the-art electronic classroom, digital reference services, and multimedia applications. Pace's computer resource centers are linked to high-speed data networks and feature sophisticated hardware and software to facilitate active learning. Recognized as one of America's most wired universities, Pace supports high-speed Internet and Internet2 access on every campus. Residence facilities are wired, and most public areas are enabled for wireless connectivity. Full-motion videoconference facilities enable remote delivery of instruction between campus sites for synchronous learning applications. Many courses are Web assisted with state-of-the-art software, and some courses and programs are completely Web based.

Financial Aid

Pace's comprehensive student financial assistance program includes scholarships, graduate assistantships, student loans, and tuition payment plans. Scholarships are awarded to students in recognition of academic achievement and are available for full- and part-time study. Highly qualified students may be eligible for assistantships awarded by departments, which pay stipends of up to $5100 and tuition remission of up to 24 credits during the 2008–09 academic year. Pace participates in all major federal and state financial aid programs, such as Federal Direct Loans, the New York State Tuition Assistance Program (TAP), and Federal Perkins Loans. All students are encouraged to apply for these programs by filing the Free Application for Federal Student Aid (FAFSA).

Cost of Study

Tuition for graduate courses is $890 per credit in 2008–09.

Living and Housing Costs

Residence facilities are available on campus in both New York City and Westchester. Double-occupancy rooms ranged from approximately $8500 to $12,000 for the 2007–08 academic year. University-operated, off-campus housing is available in proximity of the New York City campus.

Student Group

Pace students represent diverse personal, cultural, and educational backgrounds. Many students are employed and pursue graduate study for personal growth and career advancement. Forty-four percent are enrolled part-time in evening classes. Current enrollment in the graduate publishing program is approximately 65 students.

Location

Pace University is a multicampus institution with campuses in both New York City and Westchester County, New York. All locations are within reach of cultural, business, and social resources and opportunities. The downtown Manhattan campus is adjacent to Wall Street and City Hall. Pace's Midtown Center is a short distance from Times Square, theaters, and Grand Central Station. The Pleasantville/Briarcliff campus is located in a suburban setting, surrounded by towns that offer various forms of recreation. The Graduate Center and the School of Law are located in White Plains, New York, among major retail districts and many corporate headquarters. All locations are accessible by public transportation. The graduate publishing program is available at the Midtown Center.

The University

Founded in 1906, Pace University is a private, nonsectarian, coeducational institution. Originally founded as a school of accounting, Pace Institute was designated Pace College in 1973. Through growth and various successes, it was renamed Pace University, as approved by the New York State Board of Regents. Today, Pace offers comprehensive undergraduate, graduate, doctoral, and professional programs at several campus locations through six schools and colleges.

Applying

Admission to Pace University graduate programs requires successful completion of a U.S. baccalaureate degree or its equivalent from an accredited institution. Students must submit a completed application, application fee, official transcripts from all postsecondary institutions attended, a personal statement, a resume, and two letters of recommendation. Students must demonstrate satisfactory performance on the GRE General Test. International students must submit official TOEFL scores and official transcripts in the native language with a professional English translation. Applications should be submitted by August 1 for the fall semester, December 1 for the spring semester, and May 1 for summer sessions. International applications should be submitted one month prior to these dates.

Correspondence and Information

Office of Graduate Admission
Pace University
1 Pace Plaza
New York, New York 10038
Phone: 212-346-1531
Fax: 212-346-1585
E-mail: gradnyc@pace.edu
Web site: http://www.pace.edu

Office of Graduate Admission
Pace University
1 Martine Avenue
White Plains, New York 10606
Phone: 914-422-4283
Fax: 914-422-4287
E-mail: gradwp@pace.edu
Web site: http://www.pace.edu

Pace University

THE FACULTY

Jodylynn Bachiman, Adjunct Lecturer in Publishing; M.S., Pace.
Andrea Baron, Adjunct Lecturer in Publishing; M.S., Pace.
Edward W. Barry, Adjunct Lecturer in Publishing; B.A., Connecticut.
Vaughn P. Benjamin, Adjunct Lecturer in Publishing; M.B.A., Pace.
Denolyn Carroll, Adjunct Lecturer in Publishing; M.S., Pace.
David R. Delano, Adjunct Lecturer in Publishing; B.A., Loyola.
Heidi A. Freund, Adjunct Lecturer in Publishing; B.A., Macalester.
Steven Garrelts, Adjunct Lecturer in Publishing; M.S., Pace.
David M. Hetherington, Adjunct Lecturer in Publishing; M.B.A., Fairleigh Dickinson.
Shay Humphrey, Adjunct Lecturer in Publishing; J.D., Florida.
Chris Kartchner, Adjunct Lecturer in Publishing; M.B.A., Dowling.
Jane Kinney-Denning, Adjunct Lecturer in Publishing and Director of Internships and Corporate Outreach; M.A., Wisconsin.
Drew Limsky, Adjunct Assistant Professor of English; J.D., NYU.
Kristina Pennella, Adjunct Lecturer in Publishing; B.F.A., Pratt.
Allan M. Rabinowitz, Professor of Accounting and Finance and Associate Director, M.S. in Publishing Program; M.B.A., NYU; CPA.
Sherman Raskin, Professor of English and Director of the M.S. in Publishing Program; M.A., Columbia.
Melissa Rosati, Adjunct Lecturer in Publishing; B.A., Akron.
John Selfridge, Adjunct Lecturer in Publishing; J.D., Rutgers.
Joel Stein, Adjunct Lecturer in Publishing; M.F.A., Iowa.
Ivor A. Whitson, Adjunct Lecturer in Publishing; M.B.A., Fordham.
Veronica R. Whitson, Adjunct Lecturer in Publishing.

The Advisory Board

Anne Adamo, Employee Relations, Pearson Education.
Jodylynn Bachiman, Production Coordinator, Corporate Production, Time, Inc.
Deidre Bair, Ph.D., author and scholar.
Andrea Baron, Manufacturing Manager, American Express Publishing.
Stevan Baron, Vice President, Production, *Aperture.*
Edward W. Barry, former President, Oxford University Press.
Janet K. Behning, Production Manager, Princeton Architectural Press.
Vaughn P. Benjamin, Vice President, MCA/Workforce Diversity, Magazine Publishers of America.
Jeff Bens, Director of Writing Programs, Manhattanville College.
Chip Berry, Director of Magazine Sales, NewsStand.com.
Laura Brown, President, Oxford University Press.
Edgar M. Buttenheim, Emeritus; former Executive Vice President, Springhouse Corporation.
Robert Carter, Emeritus; consultant and author.
Fred Ciporen, President, *Publishers Weekly.*
Richard Curtis, President and CEO, E-rights/E-reads, Ltd.
Al Driver, Editor, The *Metropolitan Corporate Counsel.*
Martha Driver, Publisher, The *Metropolitan Corporate Counsel.*
Michelle Dunn, Managing Director, *Aperture West.*
Charles R. Ellis, Emeritus; President and CEO, John Wiley and Sons.
Rochelle W. Evans, former Human Resources Director, *Times Mirror* Magazines and Broadcasting.
Robert E. Evanson, former President, McGraw-Hill Education.
Christine Ford, Managing Editor, *Working Mother Magazine.*
Paula Freedman, Senior Project Manager, Internet Group, Scholastic, Inc.
Frank R. Gatti, Chief Financial Officer, Vice President, and Treasurer, Educational Testing Service.
Elizabeth A. Geiser, Director, The Denver Publishing Institute.
Thomas H. Guinzburg, Emeritus; former CEO, The Viking Press.
J. J. Hanson, former President and Founding Publisher, *Folio* magazine.
Peter P. Hanson, former Publisher, *Money* and *Home Mechanix.*
Bruce Harris, President, Workman Publishing Co.
Jane Isay, Editor-in-Chief, Harcourt, Harcourt Trade Publishers.
Elizabeth Janice, Reporter, Avon Products, Inc.
Chris Kartchner, Vice President, Ness Technologies.
Elizabeth Krajcsik, Consultant, former Vice President, Media Horizons.
Edwin Lewis, former Vice President and Treasurer, Hearst Corporation.
Xiaochuan Lian, Copyrights and Permissions Administrator, Springer-Verlag, New York.
David Linton, Ph.D., Chair, Division of Humanities, and Professor of Communication Arts, Marymount Manhattan College.
Shirley Lord, Vice President of Content, ibeauty.com; Senior Editor, *Vogue* magazine; and novelist.
Donald McAllister Jr., former Chairman, Geyer-McAllister Publications, Inc.
Riley McDonough, Executive Vice President, Sales and Commerce, Spinner.com–Silicon Valley.
Terilyn McGovern-Mazza, Consultant, Corporate Development, Federal Farm Credit Banks Funding Corp.
Eliot Minsker, Emeritus; CEO, Knowledge Industry Publications, Inc.
Kerry Morris, Sales Assistant, Oxford University Press.
Scott S. Parmelee, Publisher, Mariah Media, Inc.
Betty A. Prashker, Editorial Consultant, former Executive Vice President, Editor-in-Chief, Crown Publishers, Inc.
Allan M. Rabinowitz, Associate Director, M.S. in Publishing Program, and former President, The Scribner Book Companies.
Betty Rockmore, President of Advertising, Director of Tabloids, American Media, Inc,
Michael F. Rooney, Vice President and General Manager, ESPN Outdoors.
Edwin Ruzinsky, Deloitte and Touche Consulting Group.
Erin Scanlon, Partner, Deloitte and Touche LLP.
Budd Schulberg, Emeritus; novelist, screenwriter, and dramatist.
Daniel Shea, Assistant Professor of English; Mount St. Mary's College.
Martha Sledge, Ph.D., Assistant Professor of English, Marymount Manhattan College.
Peggy Smyth, Partner, Arthur Andersen.
Robert Stern, former CEO, Message Plus Corporation.
Laurence Usdin, CFO, Bookazine Co., Inc.
Robert Wesner, President and Publisher, Wesden, Inc.
Ivor A. Whitson, President, CenterLink Information Systems.

POINT PARK UNIVERSITY

Master of Arts in Journalism and Mass Communication

Program of Study

The graduate program in journalism and mass communication at Point Park University leads to the Master of Arts (M.A.) degree. The program admits students with a variety of undergraduate and professional backgrounds. The Point Park M.A. program, with opportunities such as working with the Innocence Institute of Western Pennsylvania and a news service tied to the *Pittsburgh Tribune-Review*, is exceptionally well designed for professionals already working, and planning to continue to work, for mass communication employers. Other matriculants plan to move on to doctoral study or enter mass communication professions for the first time.

Full-time students may easily complete the program within two calendar years, and extraordinarily motivated students may complete the program in one calendar year. Courses are offered during three terms—fall, spring, and summer. Part-time students, who traditionally compose the bulk of the graduate student body, may complete the program within three years. Writing a master's thesis is optional but highly recommended for students planning to pursue any doctoral degree.

The 36-credit program includes a core of four courses; up to three may be waived, based on courses in previous undergraduate programs, and replaced with electives. One course taken outside the department in a related area is required. Two courses are for independent student research, including a thesis option. Other course work is composed of electives that provide a significant concentration in print journalism, broadcasting, public relations, advertising, and/or new media. Up to 9 credits (three courses) toward the M.A. may be completed at another institution.

Research Facilities

The University's library is located in the University Center, a gloriously renovated historic building. The combined holdings number about 125,000 monographs, 16,640 periodical subscriptions, 37 online databases, 650 audio and videocassettes, and a total microform count of 20,000 volumes. The online catalog, wireless Internet access, and printers are available throughout the building.

Students are able to borrow material not held within the system and have it delivered to the University Center through the various interlibrary loan programs.

The library's journalism and mass communication collection, which is the most extensive in western Pennsylvania and the second largest in the state, exceeds those of most research universities in Pennsylvania and other states.

Financial Aid

Students may apply for financial aid, which is granted on the basis of need, and for various state and federal loans. International applicants may seek loans and scholarships from a number of home-country and international agencies.

The department offers three graduate assistantships. The assistant must be a full-time student in the program and be able to work in the department a minimum of 20 hours per week during fall and spring semesters.

Cost of Study

Tuition and fees for 2007–08 were $607 per credit. The cost of books and supplies averaged $350 per term.

Living and Housing Costs

Housing is available in the University's residence halls. The cost in 2007–08 was typically $4000 per term. Apartments are available to students within a short travel distance on Pittsburgh's effective mass transit system. A variety of meal plans are available at the campus student cafeteria.

Student Group

Enrollment in the graduate program in fall 2007 was nearly 90. Many were full-time. Most were employed full-time in the communications industry or elsewhere. Generally, a small contingent of international students adds an exciting multicultural flavor to the classes, which seldom exceed 15 students. During 2007–08, the first Fulbright Scholar entered the program.

Location

Pittsburgh is the thirteenth-largest metropolitan area in the United States and ranks high as a center for corporate headquarters. Newspapers, radio and TV stations, and public relations and advertising agencies are within easy walking distance of the campus. The location is excellent for challenging graduate-level internships. Frequent association with professionals in the media and in the classroom often leads to employment immediately after graduation.

The University

Point Park University is located in the Golden Triangle of downtown Pittsburgh. Founded in 1960, it has grown from a small business school to a four-year institution with graduate programs in journalism and mass communication, curriculum and instruction, engineering management, business administration, educational administration, criminal justice administration, and organizational leadership. It is accredited by the Middle States Association of Colleges and Schools and is a member of the Pittsburgh Council on Higher Education.

Applying

Applicants for the M.A. program must take the GRE if their undergraduate GPA falls below 2.75 overall and/or under 3.0 in their undergraduate major. Those whose first language is not English must take the TOEFL and the TWE. Students may be admitted for the fall, spring, or summer term.

Correspondence and Information

Point Park University
201 Wood Street
Pittsburgh, Pennsylvania 15222-1984
Phone: 412-392-3808
800-321-0129 (toll-free)
Fax: 412-392-6164
E-mail: ptenroll@pointpark.edu
Web site: http://www.pointpark.edu

Point Park University

THE FACULTY

In addition to the full-time faculty members listed below, the program utilizes qualified professionals who represent organizations engaged in the mass communications concentrations of the M.A. program.

Dane S. Claussen, Director; Ph.D., Georgia.

Michael J. Burke, M.A., SUNY at Albany; M.A., Point Park.
David J. Fabilli, M.A., Youngstown State.
Helen M. Fallon, M.A., Duquesne.
Heather Starr Fiedler, Ph.D., Nova Southeastern.
Jan Getz, M.A., Miami (Ohio).
Anthony Moretti, Ph.D., Ohio.
William R. "Bill" Moushey Jr., M.S., Point Park.
Robert O'Gara, M.L.S., Duquesne.
Christopher Rolinson, M.A., Point Park.

POLYTECHNIC INSTITUTE OF NYU

Department of Humanities and Social Sciences
Programs in Integrated Digital Media and Technical Writing

Programs of Study The Master of Science program in integrated digital media combines high standards of creative production with excellent scholarship in the historical, legal, cultural, and strategic aspects of digital media communications. The fundamental approach of the program is to provide a rich and balanced mix of technological innovation, creative experiment, and critical thought. With this in mind, Polytechnic Institute of NYU (NYU-Poly) maintains and encourages full use of its partnerships with leading firms and institutions in New York and around the world. New York City provides access to world leaders across a broad spectrum, from contemporary art to international development agencies to global media enterprises. Students must complete 30 credit hours, including 6 credit hours of a major creative/research thesis project.

Students in the graduate certificate program in integrated digital media must take two graduate digital media theory seminars and three graduate digital media studio seminars for a total of 15 credits. The certificate credits may be applied toward a full Master of Science if academic requirements have been met.

The Master of Science program in technical writing and specialized journalism requires students to complete a minimum of 30 credit hours. Students take a series of core courses, including Introduction to Technical and Professional Communication, Style for the Professional Writer, and Copyediting for Technical, Scientific, and Business Publications. At least 12 credit hours should be in courses in the student's chosen specialization. Students may also take a limited number of related courses in other departments.

Students in the graduate certificate program in technical communication program are trained in the fundamentals of technical communication through a combination of core courses and electives. Five courses, or 15 credit hours, are required. It is possible to complete the certificate on online.

Research Facilities The Integrated Digital Media Institute's facilities include a full recording studio with 7.1 production and postproduction capabilities and a general-purpose lab suitable for development and testing of interactive media installations for cultural, scientific, and commercial applications. The Rumpus Lab offers top-of-the-line workstations equipped with graphics, audio, video, and interactive applications as well as the ability to prototype and develop multi-screen installations. Also available are a nine-screen presentation space and a 340-seat auditorium, with full audiovisual capabilities, for special projects and public events. An inventory of specialized audio and video equipment, from the basics (microphones and camcorders) to more advanced items, such as a Glidecam and Firewire interfaces for audio field production and 3G cell phones for software design projects, is kept available to sign out for field and studio work. The institute's IT services include individual Web site space, RAID access for postproduction and storage, group mail services, and Web streaming. Full access and support are provided for students, faculty members, and guest scholars in the digital media programs. By special arrangement, students in the digital media programs may also gain access to faculty members and facilities in the computer science and electrical engineering departments. The development of facilities and equipment is ongoing and changes rapidly, so it is best for interested students to inquire directly or arrange a campus visit for current details.

More broadly, the Dibner Library contains a variety of in-house materials, including circulating books, reference material, videos, CD-ROMs, journals, indexes, abstracts, and course reserves in a range of disciplines. The library also offers workshops to train students as well as faculty and staff members in making effective use of information technology.

Financial Aid Financial aid includes full-tuition remission and monthly stipends for research and University fellowships. Also available are partial-tuition remission for graduate assistantships and graduate traineeships. Stipends were approximately $1573 per month for the 2006–07 academic year. Additional funding is available to graduate students who work in department offices, assist faculty members at the research labs, and tutor undergraduate students.

Cost of Study In the 2008–09 academic year, tuition is $1081 per credit. Fees per semester are $186, $352, or $528 for students enrolled for 3, 6, or 9 or more credits, respectively.

Living and Housing Costs Each year, graduate students can expect to pay $10,000 in living expenses, $1500 in books and supplies, and $750 in medical insurance fees. An apartment in the Othmer Residence Hall costs $8500 per year for a suite or $10,500 per year for an apartment, including meal plans. Off-campus housing is also available throughout the New York City area.

Student Group Of the University's graduate students, 4.4 percent are African American, 1.6 percent are Hispanic, 10.3 percent are Asian American, and 24 percent are women. Around 42.8 percent are international students who come from more than forty countries.

Location The Brooklyn campus is located at MetroTech Center, one of the most successful joint university–industry–public ventures in the nation, with a new library and student center and new homes for the engineering and computer science programs. MetroTech also offers the opportunity to interact with major information industries. Students can enjoy numerous cultural and recreational activities either in Brooklyn or nearby Manhattan, including museums, parks, and theaters.

The University and The Department Polytechnic Institute of NYU's world-class graduate programs are built on a proud history of discovery and innovation. Intellectual energy is the fuel that drives its people and the content of its challenging academic programs.

The University is diverse, with programs ranging from biomedical engineering to management. Students come from the New York metropolitan area and from all corners of the globe. Despite the diversity, a common thread of technological innovation weaves throughout every department and every member of the faculty. Students become part of a community dedicated to delivering knowledge that can be immediately applied in research, technology, and business.

NYU-Poly's programs suit a wide variety of people. In particular, working professionals value the convenience of evening classes and a campus close to where they live or work. Recent college graduates enjoy the opportunity to increase their credentials at a top university in a concentrated period of time. All graduate students value the technological resources at the four locations, including a multicampus wireless LAN and a wealth of online research databases.

Applying Students must submit the completed application, the $50 application fee, official transcripts, and two letters of recommendation. The deadlines are May 1 for the fall and October 15 for the spring.

Correspondence and Information

Graduate Admissions Office
Polytechnic Institute of NYU
Six MetroTech Center RH 102
Brooklyn, New York 11201

Phone: 718-260-3182
Fax: 718-260-3624
E-mail: gradinfo@poly.edu
Web site: http://www.poly.edu/admissions/graduate
http://www.poly.edu/humanities/graduate/menu.php

Polytechnic Institute of NYU

THE FACULTY AND THEIR RESEARCH

Faculty

Jonathan Bain, Associate Professor of Philosophy of Science; Ph.D., Pittsburgh. Quantum theory, philosophy of space and time.
Teresa Feroli, Assistant Professor of English; Ph.D., Cornell. Renaissance literature, Shakespeare, women's studies.
Jean Gallagher, Associate Professor of English; Ph.D., CUNY Graduate Center. Feminist theory, nineteenth- and twentieth-century American literature, composition and rhetoric.
Jerry M. Hultin, Industry Professor of Management, Law, and Public Policy and University President; J.D., Yale.
Myles Jackson, Bern Dibner Professor of History of Science and Technology; Ph.D., Cambridge. History of physics, music, and biology.
Noel N. Kriftcher, Industry Professor of Humanities and Executive Director, David Packard Center for Technology and Educational Alliances; Ed.D., Hofstra. Educational theory, high school outreach.
Nancy Kwak, Assistant Professor of History; Ph.D., Columbia. Housing policy, urban development post-1945.
Ann Lubrano, Industry Associate Professor of Sociology and Associate Provost; Ph.D., CUNY. Technology and social change, organizations.
Sylvia Kasey Marks, Associate Professor of English; Ph.D., Princeton. Shakespeare, Samuel Richardson, the eighteenth- and nineteenth-century British novel, public speaking, expository writing.
Francis David Mulcahy, Associate Professor of Anthropology; Ph.D., Massachusetts. Language and culture of China and Spain.
Tara Pauliny, Assistant Professor of English and Director of Writing Program; Ph.D., Ohio State. Rhetoric and composition, queer theory.
Lowell L. Scheiner, Associate Professor of Humanities and Communications; M.S., M.A., Columbia. Technical writing, journalism.
Harold P. Sjursen, Industry Professor of Philosophy and Associate Provost for International Studies; Ph.D., New School. History of philosophy, ethics, philosophy of science and technology.
Jonathan Soffer, Associate Professor of History; Ph.D., Columbia; J.D., Denver. Twentieth-century American political and international relations history, urban history with a specialization in the history of New York City since 1945.
Romualdas Sviedrys, Associate Professor of History of Technology; Ph.D., Johns Hopkins. Technology forecasting and technology assessment, history of technology and science.
Richard E. Wener, Associate Professor of Psychology and Department Head; Ph.D., Illinois at Chicago. Environmental psychology.

Lecturers

Sadrul A. Khan, Lecturer of History; Ph.D., Ludwig Maximillian (Germany). World history, Asian history, political science.
Donald S. Phillips, Lecturer of Psychology; B.S., Polytechnic. Experimental and physiological psychology, physical anthropology, paleontology.
Carl Skelton, Lecturer of Digital Media and Director, Integrated Digital Media Institute; M.V.A., Alberta. Digital media.

Instructors

Alph Edwards, Instructor of English; M.A., Hunter. Developmental writing.
Alan B. Goldstein, Instructor of English; B.A., Denver. Political science, philosophy.
Christopher Leslie, Instructor of Technical Communication; Ph.D., CUNY Graduate Center. Humanities computing, hypertext and new media, science fiction and utopian literature, American literature, writing assessment.
James P. Lewis, Instructor of Psychology; M.A., SUNY at Stony Brook. Humanistic psychology.
Elisa Linsky, Instructor of Technical Communication; B.A., Wittenberg. Technical writing, technical presentations, writing across the curriculum.
Alan M. Nadler, Instructor of English; M.F.A., Columbia. Contemporary poetry, the European novel.
Meredith D. Schuman, Instructor of English; M.F.A., CUNY, Brooklyn. Poetry.

QUINNIPIAC UNIVERSITY

School of Communications

Programs of Study

The Quinnipiac University School of Communications offers 36-credit Master of Science degree programs in journalism and in interactive communications. The Graduate Journalism Program prepares students for careers as reporters and editors in print, broadcast, and interactive journalism. Through a balance of courses in both beginning and advanced reportorial skills and analysis of the role of the media, students learn how to report, produce, and analyze news. The program welcomes both qualified students who do not have journalism experience and working journalists who want to upgrade or polish existing skills.

The Graduate Program in Interactive Communications is based on the study of interactivity and the practical techniques of creating, distributing, and managing information and ideas for interactive news, strategic communications, entertainment, and information services. Through a balance of courses in digital media, content development, and analysis, students learn how to plan and create content and to think strategically across media platforms. Students who successfully complete the program are positioned to find career enhancement and fulfillment as content producers and content managers in the interactive space for companies and institutions.

To receive the M.S. degree, students must complete 36 credits with at least a 3.0 average. A 3-credit capstone masterwork experience is required. Students can meet this requirement in the form of a master's project—such as an investigative magazine piece or an interactive narrative presentation—or a thesis that advances knowledge of the field. In addition to traditional course work, students can enroll in an internship. Graduate students have held internships at global, regional, and local media companies, including Fox News, Subway, ESPN, and the Tribune Company.

Research Facilities

The Ed McMahon Mass Communications Center houses the media production facilities for the School of Communications. Exceeding even the current capability of many broadcast stations in the world, the School of Communications' fully digital, high-definition studio offers students training in state-of-the-art production. Not since the introduction of color television in the early 1960s has there been such a monumental change in the quality of television images. Quinnipiac stands at the leading edge of this development, as it is among the first schools in the United States to provide high-definition production capabilities for its students. Sony HDC 910 12-bit HD multiformat studio cameras output 1080i for dazzling resolution and detail. Standard definition is available when required. The fully digital signal path through a Sony MVS 8000A HD/SD production switcher featuring multiple channels of digital video effects preserves pristine picture quality. All video is recorded digitally; video and audio are recorded directly to high-capacity Grass Valley Group HD/SD video servers or, for those productions requiring tape, a new Sony HDWS-2000 HDCAM studio recorder. The studio floor is large (30 feet by 40 feet, with a 16-foot-high grid) and equipped with industry-standard Mole-Richardson lighting units, grip equipment, and ample accessories for any style production. In the field, students shoot digital video with a variety of cameras, including three-chip professional-grade units. A remote equipment room provides students with all the accessories, lighting equipment, and tools needed to produce broadcast-quality audio and video on remote. The center's digital postproduction facilities feature Apple's Final Cut Pro HD. For graphics and animation, a number of high-end applications such as Adobe After Effects, Photoshop, and Discreet Combustion, are available. The McMahon Center also offers an audio production studio loaded with Digidesign's industry-standard Pro Tools software. A wide range of tools for radio production and soundtrack design are available. In addition, a comfortable, twenty-six-seat theater-style screening room with high-quality video projection and five-channel surround sound is available for classes and workshops. Students also have access to a fully equipped computer lab for interactive media production for work both in and out of class. The News Technology Center features the Associated Press ENPS newsroom automation software.

Financial Aid

Several avenues are available to help both full- and part-time students fund their education. Students may be eligible for Federal Stafford Student Loans. Several students each year are awarded graduate assistantships that partially cover tuition. Graduate assistantships are available for full- and part-time students and are renewable.

Cost of Study

Tuition in 2007–08 was $675 per credit hour. In addition, part-time students paid a $30-per-credit student fee, and full-time students paid $275 per semester in student fees.

Living and Housing Costs

On-campus housing is available during the summer. Privately owned housing is available near the campus. Students can contact the Office of Residential Life or visit the University's Web site for information about off-campus housing.

Student Group

The Graduate Journalism Program has an active enrollment of 60 full- and part-time students. Some have extensive work experience; others are entering the workforce. The Graduate Program in Interactive Communications has an active enrollment of 50 full- and part-time students. Applicants come from every region in the United States as well as from Canada, Mexico, and other countries.

Location

Quinnipiac University is located on a beautiful campus in Hamden, Connecticut, a suburb of New Haven. It is approximately 30 minutes from Hartford, 1½ hours from New York City, and 2 hours from Boston.

The University and The School

Quinnipiac University is nationally recognized as one of the leading centers for higher learning in the Northeast and is consistently ranked among the best master's-level universities in the North in *U.S. News & World Report's Guide to America's Best Colleges.* All programs have integrated computer technology into academic and campus life, and Quinnipiac has been recognized in *Yahoo! Internet Life* for its achievements in technology. In 2006, Quinnipiac was ranked ninth in *PC Magazine*'s 2007 Top Wired Colleges. The University enrolls about 6,800 students and offers a full range of undergraduate and graduate programs through the School of Health Sciences, the School of Communications, the School of Business, the College of Liberal Arts, and the School of Law.

Quinnipiac University's School of Communications is one of the most highly regarded centers in the Northeast for superior education in journalism and the diverse fields of communication. By closely integrating professional experiences with a faculty of experts and an outstanding facility, the School thoroughly prepares professionals for rewarding careers in communications.

Applying

Admission to the Graduate Journalism Program is competitive and based on undergraduate performance, experience in the field (either as a student or professional), and professional recommendations. Individuals who hold undergraduate degrees in communications, the liberal arts and humanities, computer sciences, graphic design, and other interdisciplinary and professional disciplines are welcome to apply to the Graduate Program in Interactive Communications. Students must submit the required application form, the application fee, all college/university transcripts, a resume, and two recommendations. Applicants to each program must submit a portfolio sample, such as an article, videotapes, or an undergraduate paper, and a personal statement.

Correspondence and Information

Office of Graduate Admissions
Quinnipiac University
275 Mount Carmel Avenue
Hamden, Connecticut 06518

Phone: 203-582-8672
800-462-1944 (toll-free)
Fax: 203-582-3443
E-mail: graduate@quinnipiac.edu
Web site: http://www.quinnipiac.edu

Quinnipiac University

THE FULL-TIME FACULTY

Lou Adler (M.S., Purdue; J.D., Quinnipiac) is an Associate Professor of Communications. He is a veteran radio and television broadcaster with many years in both on-air and administrative positions with CBS, WOR, and WINS Radio. He joined the staff of WCBS radio when it became an all-news operation and later was elevated to Director of News Operations and Programs for Newsradio-880. He specializes in teaching the techniques of broadcast radio/TV news writing. His publications include articles in *Mass Media and Society and the Communicator,* the journal of the Radio-Television News Directors Association.

Edward Alwood (Ph.D., North Carolina) is an Associate Professor of Journalism. His research specialty concentrates on journalism history, particularly the early Cold War era of the 1940s and 1950s, and news coverage of minorities. His Ph.D. dissertation focused on communists in the press and received the prestigious Nafziger-White Dissertation Award from the Association of Educators in Journalism and Mass Communication. He is the author of the 1996 book *Straight News: Gays, Lesbians, and the News Media.* He worked for fourteen years as a news reporter at several television outlets, including the Washington bureau of CNN.

Lisa M. Burns (M.A., Duquesne) is an Assistant Professor of Media Studies. Her research interests include political communication, gender and the media, and journalism history with a focus on First Ladies and the media. Most recently, she contributed a chapter titled "A Forgotten First Lady: A Rhetorical Reassessment of Ellen Axson Wilson" to *Inventing Their Voices: The Rhetoric of American First Ladies of the Twentieth Century.* A former journalist, Lisa worked as a reporter, producer, and anchor at WDUQ FM 90.5, an NPR affiliate, and KQV 1410 AM, an all-news station, both of which are located in Pittsburgh, Pennsylvania. She covered news and sports, winning several state Associated Press awards.

Margarita Diaz (M.A., New School) is an Assistant Professor of Journalism. She was one of the founding editors of *El Daily News,* the first fully bilingual English-Spanish daily newspaper in the United States. In the 1990s she was an entertainment editor and writer at the *New York Daily News,* where she focused on film, television, and popular music coverage. Diaz has taught journalism at Hunter College and film studies at Barnard College.

David F. Donnelly (Ph.D., Massachusetts) is the Dean of the School of Communications. He has contributed to seven books on the media and has published in numerous journals, including *Communication Research, Telematics and Informatics, New Telecomm Quarterly,* and *The Historical Journal of Film Radio and Television.* He has also written for the *Houston Chronicle* and other print publications and served as a media consultant for many national clients. His video productions have aired on public and commercial stations around the nation, and his three Web sites, the Media Futures Archive, Media Ethicopoly, and the Media Libel Project, are widely used as educational resources by media students and professionals.

Alexander M. C. Halavais (Ph.D., Washington, Seattle), Assistant Professor of Communications, is a social architect interested in ways of helping form a culture of creativity, freedom, and justice. He formerly directed a master's program in informatics at the University at Buffalo (SUNY) and was Research Director for the New Media Research Lab at the University of Washington. He has worked in marketing for a large financial services firm, designed simulations for NASA, and worked as a public school teacher in Japan and as a budget analyst and planner in city government. Alex has published articles and book chapters on the role of computing in social change, particularly in journalism, politics, education, and geography. He has also edited an anthology of writings on cyberpornography and society.

Rich Hanley (M.A., Wesleyan) is an Assistant Professor of Journalism and the Graduate Program Director of Journalism and Interactive Communications. A journalist and producer, writer, and director of documentaries and Web sites, Hanley has worked for more than twenty-five years in the media profession, including a stint at *Time* magazine. His views on current events, the Internet, and pop culture are frequently sought by global and national media. Hanley teaches primarily in the Interactive Communications Graduate Program.

Paul Janensch (M.S., Columbia) an Associate Professor of Communications, spent thirty years as a news professional before joining the Quinnipiac faculty. A top editor of several newspapers, he was president of the Associated Press Managing Editors and served as a Pulitzer Prize competition juror. He has covered crime in Chicago, civil-rights marches in the South, and the Congressional debate over Vietnam in Washington. He has also traveled to Russia and China as a newspaper consultant and media expert. He writes the weekly Professor News column about news media issues for the *Hartford Courant* and records a weekly commentary for the five stations of WNPR Connecticut Public Radio.

Sharon Kleinman (Ph.D., Cornell) is an Associate Professor of Communications and Chair of the Department of Media Studies and Public Relations. She studies the history and social implications of communication technologies, popular culture, and issues concerning online and real-life communities. Her publications include articles in the *Journal of American and Comparative Cultures, Science Communication,* the *Journal of Women and Minorities in Science and Engineering,* and the *Journal of Technology in Human Services* as well as numerous essays in edited books, including biographies of notable scientists and historical essays on communication technologies.

Sean Patrick Lyons (M.S., Columbia) is an Assistant Professor of Communications and a member of the Department of Journalism and Media Production. He has worked as a reporter for the *Boston Globe,* the *Waterbury* (Connecticut) *Republican-American,* the *Palm Beach Post,* and the *Providence Journal.* He has won a Society of Professional Journalists national public service medal and the Livingston Award, among other national awards.

RENSSELAER POLYTECHNIC INSTITUTE

Department of Language, Literature, and Communication

Programs of Study

The Department of Language, Literature, and Communication (LL&C) at Rensselaer is an internationally recognized center for interdisciplinary education, research, and theory development. The study of human communication deals with the processes by which humans create and share meaning. It is an interdisciplinary field embracing speech communication, composition and rhetoric, media studies, visual design, human-computer interaction, and technical communication. LL&C emphasizes those communication processes involved in the creation of meaning in all media, including the new electronic media.

The Department offers M.S. degree programs in human-computer interaction, technical communication, and communication and rhetoric and a Ph.D. in communication and rhetoric. The M.S. degrees can lead to careers in usability engineering, information architecture, interface and Web design, technical communication, or applied communication research or provide a foundation for doctoral study. Graduates of the Ph.D. in Communication and Rhetoric program find careers in business, government, and academia.

The M.S. in Human-Computer Interaction (HCI) program combines course work in human-computer interaction with theory in allied areas such as technical communication, human factors, information design, cognitive science, and computer science. Students gain a complement of theory in these areas and applied work in design and software implementation. The program emphasizes knowledge of computer usability research and interface design over implementation skills. Rensselaer's approach to human-computer interaction differs from other HCI programs by being centered in communication rather than computer science. Graduates are prepared to work as information architects, usability engineers, interface designers, or webmasters, depending on their individual course selections.

The M.S. in Technical Communication program combines work in theory, writing, information design, and content production. This program enables students to gain design skills that resist obsolescence and the capacity to generate content for several electronically based communication media. Students acquire knowledge of information and product usability, product design, and rapid learning of electronic tools, and they gain practice with the information production skills needed to advance in a career as a technical communicator. Graduates are equipped to keep up with rapid changes in information technology and in information design.

The M.S. in Communication and Rhetoric program enables students to study the knowledge base of communication research, to gain research skills used in adding to that base, and to gain experience in applying research to practice. As part of their program students are able to study Web interaction, computer-mediated communication, communication marketing, and other modes of electronically supported discourse. Rensselaer's M.S. in Communication and Rhetoric draws on the core M.S. courses and goes on to give students a grounding in analytical methods and in the research literature of a specific theoretical area. This program emphasizes new areas of theory and research and enables students to conduct applied research in industry or to move on to doctoral study. The program accepts students from discourse-related fields such as English, communication arts, or journalism and students with research experience in the social sciences, physical sciences, or engineering.

The M.S. programs require 30 credit hours of core course work, electives, and a capstone or directed-research independent study project.

The mission of the Ph.D. in Communication and Rhetoric program at Rensselaer is to enable students to make a contribution with rigor, depth, and creativity on issues related to communication in technologically mediated contexts. The program's approach draws on the insights of rhetoric, technical communication, composition, communication studies, human-computer interaction, game studies, and graphic design. Combining the resources of a premier technological university with a faculty strongly grounded in theory and research as well as technology and media, the Department is uniquely positioned to provide an environment for graduate study in communication and technology.

The Ph.D. degree requires satisfactory completion of 90 credit hours beyond the bachelor's degree or 60 hours beyond a related master's degree. While specific plans of study vary to meet individual needs and interests, all students must meet the core program requirements.

Research Facilities

Research is supported by state-of-the-art facilities and equipment including the Rensselaer Libraries, whose electronic information system provides access to collections, databases, and the Internet from campus and remote terminals; the Rensselaer Computing System, which permeates the campus with a coherent array of more than 7,000 nodes of distributed laptops, desktops, advanced workstations, and servers; a shared toolkit of applications for interactive learning and research and high-speed Internet connectivity; one of the country's largest academically based, class 100 clean room facilities; high-performance campuswide computing facilities that allow for serial or parallel computation; and five core laboratories for molecular biology, proteomics, bio-imaging, and tissue engineering.

Rensselaer's research capabilities have been enhanced with the addition of the Computational Center for Nanotechnology Innovations (CCNI). The result of a $100-million collaboration with IBM and New York State, the CCNI is the world's most powerful university-based supercomputing center and a top ten supercomputing center of any kind in the world. The CCNI is made up of massively parallel Blue Gene supercomputers, POWER-based Linux clusters, and Opteron-based clusters, providing more than 100 teraflops of computational muscle and approximately a petabyte of shared online storage.

Other facilities and research centers include the Center for Biotechnology and Interdisciplinary Studies; the George M. Low Center for Industrial Innovation; research centers for integrated electronics, terahertz science, nanotechnology, fuel cell and hydrogen research, lighting research, science and technology policy, and infrastructure and transportation studies; the Geotechnical Centrifuge Research Center; the Darrin Fresh Water Institute; and the Scientific Computation Research Center. In addition, academic departments and faculty laboratories have extensive discipline-specific research capabilities and equipment.

The Department of Language, Literature, and Communication offers superb facilities for computer-mediated communication studies, multimedia development, and new educational environments. These include state-of-the-art computer labs; the digital imaging studio, which is a graduate space set up for computer graphics, computer video, animation, layout, and Web development; the Design Conference Room™, a media-enhanced conference facility and laboratory supporting multidisciplinary collaborative design; specially designed collaborative classrooms; and a writing center that offers one-on-one support for preparing written, oral, and electronic communication projects.

LL&C faculty members and graduate students and their colleagues from the Departments of Cognitive Science, Computer Science, Electronic Arts, Management, and Science and Technology Studies conduct cross-disciplinary studies in the social and behavioral impact of information technologies at the Social and Behavioral Research Laboratory (SBRL), a facility that houses applied and basic research in computer-mediated communication (CMC), human-computer interaction (HCI), psychology, cognitive science, community informatics, and technology studies. The 10,000-square-foot lab contains HCI and human factors research suites with eye-tracking and observational video systems, focus group rooms with both direct and video observation and recording facilities, small CMC research rooms with computer and video systems, an immersive Virtual Reality studio, a computer-aided telephone and Web survey research lab, and a large-group research room. The facility provides research teams with physical space for research projects; laboratory equipment for a broad range of projects; technical support services such as computer programming, networking, and equipment construction; administrative support for conducting funded research; and space for housing postdoctoral associates and graduate research assistants. It promotes cross-disciplinary research efforts by providing a space for interaction among researchers of differing backgrounds and training.

Financial Aid

Financial aid is available in the forms of teaching and research assistantships and fellowships, which include tuition scholarships and stipends. Rensselaer assistantships cover the academic year, with summer support available in many departments. University, corporate, or national fellowships fund many of Rensselaer's full-time graduate students. Outstanding students may qualify for university-sponsored Rensselaer Graduate Fellowship Awards, which carry a minimum stipend of $22,000 and a full tuition and fees scholarship. All fellowship awards are calendar-year awards for full-time graduate students. Low-interest, deferred-repayment graduate loans are available to U.S. citizens with demonstrated need.

Cost of Study

Full-time graduate tuition for the 2008–09 academic year is $36,950. Other costs (estimated living expenses, insurance, etc.) are projected to be about $13,680. Therefore, the cost of attendance for full-time graduate study is approximately $50,630. Part-time study and cohort programs are priced differently. Students should contact Rensselaer for specific cost information related to the programs they wish to study.

Living and Housing Costs

Graduate students at Rensselaer may choose from a variety of housing options. On campus, students can select one of the many residence halls and immerse themselves in campus life or choose from a select number of apartments designed for graduate students only. There are abundant, affordable options off campus as well, many within easy walking distance.

Student Group

Of the 1,176 graduate students, 29 percent are women and 92 percent are full-time, with 75 percent of full-time graduate students studying at the doctoral level.

Student Outcomes

Rensselaer's graduate students are hired in a variety of industries and sectors of the economy and by private and public organizations, the government, and institutions of higher education. Their starting salaries average $74,807 for master's degree recipients and $82,750 for Ph.D. recipients.

Location

Located just 10 miles northeast of Albany, New York State's capital city, Rensselaer's historic 275-acre campus sits on a hill overlooking the city of Troy, New York, and the Hudson River. The area offers a relaxed lifestyle with many cultural and recreational opportunities, with easy access to both the high-energy metropolitan centers of the Northeast—such as Boston, New York City, and Montreal, Canada—and the quiet beauty of the neighboring Adirondack Mountains.

The Institute

Recognized as a leader in interactive learning and interdisciplinary research, Rensselaer continues a tradition of excellence and technological innovation dating back to 1824. Rensselaer has five schools—Architecture, Engineering, Management, Science, and Humanities and Social Sciences—that offer more than 100 graduate programs in over forty-eight disciplines that attract top students, researchers, and professors. The discovery of new scientific concepts and technologies, especially in emerging interdisciplinary fields, is the lifeblood of Rensselaer's culture and a core goal for the faculty, staff, and students. Fueled by significant support from government, industry, and private donors, Rensselaer provides a world-class education in an environment tailored to the individual.

Applying

The admission deadline for the fall semester is January 1. Basic admission requirements are the submission of a completed application form (available online), the required application fee ($75), a statement of background and goals, official transcripts, official scores on the GRE General Test, TOEFL or IELTS scores (if applicable), and two recommendations. A scholarly writing sample is required for Ph.D. applicants.

Correspondence and Information

Department of Language, Literature, and Communication
Russell Sage Laboratory, 4508
Rensselaer Polytechnic Institute
110 8th Street
Troy, New York 12180-3590

Phone: 518 276-6469
E-mail: colmak@rpi.edu
Web site: http://www.llc.rpi.edu/

Rensselaer Polytechnic Institute

THE FACULTY AND THEIR RESEARCH

There are more than 20 LL&C faculty members involved in graduate education. They comprise a large, diverse, yet integrated community dedicated to teaching and mentoring graduate students. LL&C faculty members make an exceptionally strong contribution to research in communication in technologically mediated contexts through an active program of publication in a variety of fields and in the production of artistic media. They are also successful in securing external funding for their work. Recent research has been supported by the National Science Foundation, the Society for Technical Communication, and the Fund for the Improvement of Post-Secondary Education. LL&C faculty members also receive professional recognition and honors for their work. At last count, they had won more than thirty awards, including numerous fellowships, awards for best articles, visiting professorships, teaching awards, and professional society awards. They come from such organizations as the College Art Association, the Fulbright Program, the Game Developer's Conference, the IEEE Professional Communication Society, the International Visual Literacy Association, the National Communication Association, the Popular Culture Association, the Rhetoric Society of America, and the Society for Technical Communication.

Cheryl Geisler, Professor and Department Head; Ph.D., Carnegie Mellon. Cheryl Geisler is a joint Professor of Rhetoric and Composition and Information Technology. Her research focuses on writing in the disciplines and professions and at the work-life interface, especially in the context of emerging communication technologies; the intersection of text, technology, and design; methods of the analysis of verbal data; genre theory; and academic literacy. A body of recent work carried out with colleagues across the university has focused on the advancement of women to the rank of full professor. Geisler is currently serving as Principle Investigator on two major projects: RAMP-Up, a project for Institutional Transformation (http://www.rampup.rpi.edu) funded by the NSF ADVANCE Program to improve the advancement process at Rensselaer, and Tech-Mediated Communication (TMC), a project funded by a major grant from the Society for Technical Communication aimed at developing a set of useful paradigms for the analysis, design, and testing of technical communications in a mediated world (http://www.rpi.edu/~geislc/TMC/). In 2006, Geisler was the recipient of the Kneupper Award for best article in the *Rhetoric Society Quarterly*, and authored a paper recognized as one of the top three papers by the Division of Organization Communication at the National Communication Association. (geislc@rpi.edu)

Audrey Bennett, Associate Professor; M.F.A., Yale. Audrey Bennett teaches and conducts research in graphics. Her research is on the development of an interactive aesthetics (IA) theory in graphics that explains the phenomenon of collaborative visual design. The underpinning of her hypothesis is that the use of interactive techniques, strategies, or technologies that facilitate collaboration from participants at various stages of the design process brings about appropriate cross-cultural aesthetics. Over the past three years she has been testing IA on interdisciplinary design research projects on social robotics, dyslexia, ethnomathematics, and AIDS awareness and prevention. She is editor of *Design Studies: Theory and Research in Graphic Design*, published by Princeton Architectural Press, that chronicles historical and contemporary efforts of designers to broaden the scope of the profession of graphic design to include research. Her work is published in the *Journal of Design Research, Visible Language, Design Issues, The Journal of Graphic Design, The Education of a Graphic Designer, The Education of a Typographer*, and various international design research conference proceedings. From 2002–04, she served as communications director for the board of directors of the Upstate New York Chapter of the AIGA. Currently, she is sponsorship chair. (bennett@rpi.edu)

June Deery, Associate Professor; D.Phil., Oxford. June Deery has published a book on Aldous Huxley and Huxley and the Mysticism of Science and several articles, one of which received a national award. She teaches courses in Advertising and Culture, Media and Popular Culture, Women Writers, Utopian Literature, and Science and Fiction in the Twentieth Century. Her research interests include media studies, television and new media, advertising and culture, popular culture, utopian literature, and literature and science. (deeryj@rpi.edu)

Misa Dubrawski, Clinical Assistant Professor. Misa Dubrawski's research interests include Japanese pedagogy, instructional technology, and computer-assisted language learning. (dubram@rpi.edu)

Ellen Esrock, Associate Professor of Literature; Ph.D., NYU. Drawing on cognitive psychology and neuroscience, Ellen Esrock has focused her research on the role of visual (mental) images in reading and literature and the function of the somato-sensory system in viewing art. In 1994 she published *The Reader's Eye: Visual Imaging as Reader Response* (Baltimore: Johns Hopkins University Press, 1994), which was supported by a Harvard Mellon Faculty Fellowship award. Currently she is working on *Touching Art: Empathy and the Somato-Sensory System*, for which she received a grant from the Italian Academy of Columbia University. Professor Esrock teaches courses in twentieth-century literature and visual art, psychology and literature, and theory/history of photography. She has completed several community service documentary photography projects with graduate and undergraduate RPI students. (esroce@rpi.edu)

Janice Fernheimer, Assistant Professor of Rhetoric; Ph.D., Texas at Austin. Research focuses on rhetorical theory; history of rhetoric; Jewish rhetorical theory and history; nineteenth-century African-American rhetoric; Holocaust representation; rhetoric of the Palestinian-Israeli Conflict; literacy, technology, and writing pedagogy; archival research methods; nineteenth- and twentieth-century African-American and Jewish literature. Her dissertation, "The Rhetoric of Black Jewish Identity Construction in America and Israel: 1964-1972," was supported by the National Foundation for Research in Jewish Culture's Maurice and Marilyn Cohen Doctoral Dissertation Fellowship in Jewish Studies. Professor Fernheimer is revising the manuscript for publication. She is also the author of "Breaking the Commandments of Holocaust Representation? Conflicting Genre Expectations in Audience Responses to *Schindler's List* and *Life is Beautiful*" published in *Beyond Life is Beautiful: Comedy and Tragedy in the Cinema of Roberto Benigni* (Troubadour Publishing, 2005); "Bridging the Divide: Blogs in the Composition Classroom," co-authored with Tom Nelson in *Currents in Electronic Literacy* (December 2005); and "Arguing from Difference: Cooper, Emerson, Guizot, and a More Harmonious America," forthcoming in *Speaking Our Minds: Black Women's Thought in the Nineteenth Century* (University Press of New England 2007). (fernhj@rpi.edu)

Nathan Freier, Assistant Professor of Human-Computer Interaction; Ph.D., Washington (Seattle). Nathan conducts research on children's social and moral development in the context of interactions with personified technologies such as virtual characters and social robots; value-sensitive design of information and communication technologies; and the cross-cultural impact of technology. Amongst other research experiences in human-computer and human-robot interaction, Nathan has investigated children's social and moral judgments about interactions with a personified agent, children's interactions with and conceptions of a robotic dog, young researchers' views on the future of the field of human-robot interaction, the impact on psychological well-being of a large-screen display of natural information in windowless offices, privacy in location-enhanced ubiquitous computing, and the development of an interactive tool for teaching information retrieval and search engine design. (freien@rpi.edu)

Lucien Gerber, Clinical Associate Professor of French; Ph.D., SUNY at Albany. Lucien Gerber teaches all the French courses listed in the Rensselaer Catalog, including independent study courses. He has also taught Seventeenth Century French Drama, Twentieth Century French Drama, Nineteenth Century French Poetry, and Advanced Grammar and Composition. Gerber is the adviser for the student exchange program with fourteen French technical universities. Gerber's research focuses on computer-mediated communication in France. He investigates the French society and its relationship with the communication media, the current state of the Minitel system in France, the extent to which it is being used by the French, the role it plays in education and other aspects of French culture or social or business life, and the tug-of-war between the Minitel and the World Wide Web. (gerbel@rpi.edu)

Carlos Godoy, Assistant Professor; Ph.D., USC; J.D., Berkeley. Professor Godoy's research interests include the socio-psychological consequences of human interaction with media, health communication, message framing, developmental factors in risk-taking, modeling realistic personality in virtual agents, pedagogical agents, interactive media as an unobtrusive behavioral measure, and socially optimized learning in virtual environments. (godoyc@rpi.edu)

Tamar Gordon, Associate Professor of Anthropology; Ph.D., Berkeley. Tamar Gordon's work focuses on the cultural analysis of contemporary religions and their intersections with local and global modernities, themed environments, and Polynesian and American societies. Her graduate courses include Ethnography and Cultural Analysis. She is the author of a book in press, *Mormons and Modernity in Tonga*, and the editor of a collection of articles on ethnic theme parks, also forthcoming, and the director of a documentary film on ethnic theme parks entitled "Global Villages: The Globalization of Ethnic Display." (gordot@rpi.edu)

Roger Grice, Clinical Professor of Technical Communication and Interface Design and Acting Chair, HCI Committee; Ph.D., Rensselaer. Roger Grice is a Fellow of the Society for Technical Communication (STC) and Assistant to the STC President for Membership. He is a senior member of IEEE and serves on IEEE's Publication Services and Products Board. He has received STC's Jay R. Gould Award for Excellence in Teaching Technical Communication and IEEE Professional Communication Society's Alfred N. Goldsmith Award for Contributions to Engineering Communication. Dr. Grice is retired from IBM and now conducts HCI research as a member of the Rensselaer faculty as well as teaching on-campus and distance-education courses on human-computer interaction, communication design for the World Wide Web, information usability, and technical communication. Current research interests include information usability, human-computer interaction, communicating on the World Wide Web, usability testing and evaluation, analysis of computer-games interfaces, effective teaching and learning in the virtual classroom, and designing the total user experience. (gricer@rpi.edu)

Julie Gutmann, Clinical Assistant Professor; D.A., SUNY at Albany. Julie Gutmann's research interests include creative writing (poetry and poetics, creative nonfiction), myth and literature, American poetry, Asian philosophies and religions, and first-year college teaching excellence. (gutmaj@rpi.edu)

Ekaterina Haskins, Associate Professor of Rhetoric; Ph.D., Iowa. Ekaterina Haskins is the author of *Logos and Power in Isocrates and Aristotle* (University of South Carolina Press, 2004). Her research on classical and contemporary rhetoric has been published in the *Quarterly Journal of Speech, Rhetoric Society Quarterly, Philosophy and Rhetoric, Space and Culture, Journal of Communication Inquiry*, and *American Communication Journal* as well as in a number of edited collections. Haskins is Book Review Editor for the *Rhetoric Society Quarterly*. She also serves on editorial boards of the *Quarterly Journal of Speech, Advances in the History of Rhetoric, Controversia*, and the *New Antigone*. In 2007, she served as local arrangements chair for the Rhetoric Society of America Summer Institute, held at Rensselaer Polytechnic Institute. Her research interests include rhetorical theory and history, visual rhetoric, and rhetorics of public memory and national identity. (haskie@rpi.edu)

Robert Krull, Professor of Communication; Ph.D., Wisconsin–Madison. Robert Krull has conducted research on electronic performance support systems such as Web-based documentation and online tutorials and on user interfaces and print-based documentation. He has also studied educational television programs and has taught graduate-level distance courses in HCI for nearly ten years. Krull has won awards for his research from the IEEE Professional Communication Society and the Society for Technical Communication. He has also won the Jay R. Gould Award for instruction in technical communication and the Goldsmith award for his contributions to engineering communication. He has conducted studies of color and highlighting in online interfaces, user access of online help systems in three releases of a visual programming language, and online tutorials and wizards for integrated office software. (krullr@rpi.edu)

Barbara Lewis, Clinical Associate Professor and Director, Center for Communication Practices; Ph.D., Rensselaer. Research interests include composition theory and research, writing center theory and research, theory and practice of peer tutoring, and the function of writing in specific disciplines, especially in engineering design. (lewisb2@rpi.edu)

Michael Lynch, Clinical Assistant Professor; Ph.D., Connecticut. Michael Lynch's research interests include human-computer interaction, analysis of computer game interfaces, design of AI within computer games in support of social interaction and communication, cognitive processes for modeling computer game AI, and speech act theory. (lynchm2@rpi.edu)

Paul Miyamoto, Clinical Associate Professor; M.F.A., Otis Art Institute. Paul Miyamoto's research interests include visual design theory, publication design theory and practice, and exploration of paint-based medium as an expressive art form. (pmiyamot@nycap.rr.com)

Lee Odell, Professor of Composition Theory and Research; Chair, Writing and Institute Core Curriculum Committee; and Associate Dean for Undergraduate Programs, School of Humanities, Arts, and Social Sciences; Ph.D., Michigan. Lee Odell's recent publications discuss ways visual and textual information interact, both in print and online. Other publications include *Evaluating Writing, Research on Composing* (both with Charles Cooper), *Writing in Non-Academic Settings* (with Dixie Goswami), and *Theory and Practice in the Teaching of Writing*. He serves on a number of editorial boards of scholarly journals, including the *Journal of Business and Technical Communication* and the *Journal of Advanced Composition*. Research interests include composition theory and research, integrating visual and verbal information, writing in nonacademic settings, writing in engineering, rethinking literacy, and education reform. (odellc@rpi.edu)

Patricia Search, Professor; M.A., Goddard. Patricia Search teaches courses in visual design theory and user-interface design for interactive multimedia computing. In her current art work and multimedia research, she is designing multimedia installations that explore the aesthetics of space, time, and action in computer interface design. She has had eighteen solo exhibitions of her art, six of which took place in New York City. She has participated in more than 150 juried exhibitions throughout the world, including several SIGGRAPH Art Shows, ISEA (International Symposium on Electronic Art) symposia, and the first United Nations Conference on Women in Beijing, China. She has also served on the Executive Board of the Inter-Society for the Electronic Arts. Her research interests include visual design theory and practice, interaction design and multimedia art, computer animation and hypermedia interface design, indigenous knowledge and interaction design, and multiliteracy models for intercultural communication. (searcp@rpi.edu)

Tong Shen, Clinical Assistant Professor of Chinese; M.A., Chinese Academy of Social Sciences; M.A., Massachusetts Amherst. Chinese linguistics, dialectology, phonology, and general linguistics. (shen3t@rpi.edu)

James Watt, Professor of Communication and Information Technologies and Director, Rensselaer Social and Behavioral Research Laboratory; Ph.D., Wisconsin–Madison. James H. Watt is the co-author of two books (Watt and Vandenberg, *Research Methods for Communication Sciences*; Watt and VanLear, *Dynamic Patterns in Communication Processes*) and more than seventy research articles, book chapters, technical reports, and papers. He is a founding partner in Swift Interactive Technologies (Hopkinton, MA), which provides Web survey research services and specialized computer software for survey research data collection, analysis, and modeling. Watt has recently completed studies of the credibility of Web and television news in wartime; a uses and gratifications analysis of Web use in three countries; and studies of the effect of synchrony and cue richness in online collaboration. Other recently completed projects are a collaboration with Baruch College on a FIPSE grant to evaluate an audio-tactile interface for teaching statistics to blind students and an NSF grant (with TouchGraphics, Inc.) to develop an auditory way-finding system to guide the visually impaired in public spaces. He is currently directing a major national survey research project in SBRL, funded by the Patricia Wieler Memorial ALS Project, to uncover possible environmental factors in the development of ALS (Lou Gherig's disease). (wattj@rpi.edu)

Merrill D. Whitburn, Louis Ellsworth Laflin Professor of English; Ph.D., Iowa. Merrill D. Whitburn teaches courses in the history of rhetoric, technical communication, speech, and the novel. He was awarded the Jay R. Gould Award for Excellence in Teaching Technical Communication by the Society for Technical Communication and the Faculty Distinguished Teaching Award from Texas A&M University. He is currently completing a book entitled *Rhetorical Scope and Performance: The Example of Technical Communication*, which was funded by a Mina Shaughnessy Scholars Award from the Fund for the Improvement of Postsecondary Education and the Carnegie Corporation. Prior to his academic career, Whitburn held positions in communication with Western Electric and the Gelman Instrument Company, and throughout his career he has served as a consultant to industry and other academic institutions. (whitbm@rpi.edu)

James P. Zappen, Professor; Ph.D., Missouri. Jim Zappen has research interests in contemporary rhetorical theory, digital rhetoric, community networking, and information-design processes. He has recently published a book titled *The Rebirth of Dialogue*, which includes an epilogue on dialogue in print and digital media. He is currently working on a new book tentatively titled *Rhetorics of Diversity and Community: Mikhail M. Bakhtin and Kenneth Burke*, based in part upon his research at the Burke archives in Andover, New Jersey. His recent publications include: "Digital Rhetoric," http://www.rpi.edu/~zappenj/Vita/DigitalRhetoric2005.pdf; "Developing a Youth-Services Information System," http://www.rpi.edu/~zappenj/Vita/UserDesignerCollaboration2006.pdf; and "On Persuasion, Icdentification, and Dialectical Symmetry," http://www.rpi.edu/~zappenj/Vita/OnPersuasion2007.pdf. (zappenj@rpi.edu)

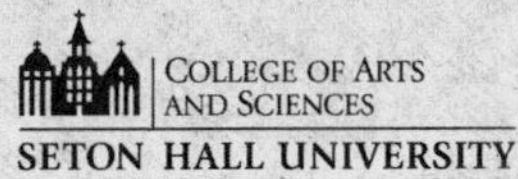

SETON HALL UNIVERSITY

Department of Communication

Programs of Study

The Department of Communication offers three Master of Arts degrees—an onsite program in strategic communication, an online program in strategic communication and leadership, and another online program in corporate and professional communication. These programs of study are designed to serve the needs of the manager, executive, or professional communicator working in the public or private sector. Further details about the programs can be found at http://www.shu.edu/academics/artsci/ma-communication/index.cfm.

The **Master of Arts in Strategic Communication** (MASC) program offers students academically challenging courses that provide insight and practical strategies to help them succeed in the rapidly changing world. The program uniquely develops the critical skills of communication and leadership in ways that can be immediately applied in practice. Faculty members are experienced practitioners who bring extensive and diverse leadership experience to the classroom. Students are challenged to think creatively, apply state-of-the-art technology, and sharpen their leadership skills in a dynamic, small-classroom environment. The 36-credit program is designed to meet the professional needs of each student and can be completed in fifteen to twenty months. Courses are offered on a flexible evening, online, or weekend class schedule. The multidisciplinary program includes such topics as organizational communication, change management/management strategies, strategic communication and leadership, effective presentation skills, communication research, crisis management, group communication, cross-cultural communication, media relations, and public relations.

The **Master of Arts in Strategic Communication and Leadership** (MASCL) program has been designed to meet the needs of today's busy professional. Through a highly interactive online curriculum that allows for significant discussion of strategies and solutions to current issues in effective leadership and communication, the program provides an opportunity to network and study with colleagues and experts in specialized disciplines. Using state-of-the-art online learning technologies, this rigorous program is aimed at providing the high-potential individual with an opportunity to earn a Seton Hall University degree in a convenient cohort-based format. The MASCL requires 36 credits and takes twenty months to complete.

The **Master of Arts in Corporate and Professional Communication** (MACPC) has been designed for those students who want to improve their professional communication skills as well as those who want to improve their personal communication, leadership, critical thinking, and teaming skills. The program attracts a diverse group of students whose backgrounds in corporate, government, and nonprofit sectors in the United States and abroad contribute to the overall learning experience. Telecommunications, health care, entertainment, and pharmaceuticals are some of the many industries that are represented by students within the program. The 33-credit program is designed to meet the professional needs of each student. Courses are offered using an online modality, which allows students to pursue an advanced degree while working. The program can be completed in fifteen to twenty months.

Research Facilities

The Walsh Library, a state-of-the-art 155,000-square-foot building, houses 500,000 titles, 1,875 current periodicals, and an extensive collection of microform and other nonprint items that include videotapes, CD-ROM music, and other electronic media. Fahy Hall has twenty-eight classrooms, two TV studios, a Macintosh and IBM graphics lab, two classroom amphitheaters, and language and statistics labs. McNulty Hall has well-equipped science labs. The College of Nursing Building contains a multipurpose practice-demonstration room with twelve hospital beds, an amphitheater, an independent study area, and a computer laboratory. Completed in 1997, Jubilee Hall, a six-story facility with 126,000 square feet of academic space, features high-tech classrooms with computer and multimedia capabilities.

Financial Aid

Federal aid is available through fellowships, traineeships, and loans. The Office of Financial Aid, through the Educational Opportunity Office, offers Educational Opportunity Fund (EOF) grants to those who document eligibility. Direct federal student loans are also available through the Office of Financial Aid to students enrolled at least half-time.

A limited number of competitive graduate assistantships are available through the Department and through the University. Further details about financial aid and graduate assistantships are available at http://www.shu.edu/applying/graduate/grad-finaid.cfm.

Cost of Study

In 2008–09, tuition is $875 per credit. Full-time students pay $305 per semester in University and technology fees; part-time students pay $185.

Living and Housing Costs

Housing and living costs in South Orange and surrounding towns are comparable to most suburban cities, with studio and one-bedroom apartments renting for $750 to $1000 per month.

Student Group

Seton Hall University has about 4,500 graduate students. The Communication graduate programs attract a diverse group of students whose backgrounds in corporate, government, and nonprofit sectors in the United States and abroad contribute to the overall learning experience. Telecommunications, health care, entertainment, and pharmaceuticals are some of the many industries that are represented by students within the program.

Location

Seton Hall is located on 58 acres in the village of South Orange, New Jersey, a suburban residential area 14 miles southwest of New York City. The town center is a 10-minute walk from the campus and features bookstores, coffee shops, and restaurants. The heart of midtown Manhattan is just 30 minutes away by train. Known as the capital of finance, fashion, art, and entertainment, New York City offers the best of everything.

The University and The College

Founded in 1856, Seton Hall is a private coeducational Catholic institution—the nation's oldest diocesan institution of higher education in the United States. With a total enrollment of about 10,000, the University comprises nine colleges and schools. Seton Hall is accredited by the Middle States Association of Colleges and Schools. Through the incorporation of technology into the curriculum, the College of Arts and Sciences seeks to enhance and enliven the learning environment. Rooted in tradition yet looking to the future, the College offers a rich set of opportunities for intellectual discovery. Graduate students are guided by scholars and specialists toward the mastery of academic and professional areas.

Applying

Students must submit the completed application (available online at http://www.shu.edu/academics/artsci/apply-graduate.cfm), a $50 application fee, transcripts from all previously attended universities and colleges, GRE or MAT scores, three letters of recommendation, and a career goals essay/personal statement. Professionals with five or more years of work experience do not need to provide standardized test scores. The deadlines for fall and spring admission are July 1 and November 1, respectively. Applications are processed on a rolling basis.

Correspondence and Information

Dr. Richard Dool, Director
Graduate Communication Program
Fahy Hall, B45
Seton Hall University
400 South Orange Avenue
South Orange, New Jersey 07079
Phone: 973-761-9490
Fax: 973-761-9234
E-mail: communication@shu.edu
doolrich@shu.edu
Web site: http://www.shu.edu/academics/artsci/ma-communication/

Seton Hall University

THE FACULTY AND THEIR RESEARCH

Communication faculty members combine practical media experience with academic preparation. Each curricular area combines faculty members with impressive professional records and those with doctoral degrees for a blend of the academic and practical. With faculty members concentrating on specialized areas within the Department, students have the opportunity to work closely with their professors in laboratories and extracurricular programs and projects. This fosters one-to-one student-instructor contact, which is a hallmark of a communication education at Seton Hall.

Richard Dool, Assistant Professor; D.Mgt., Maryland. Dr. Dool has eighteen-years' experience as a CEO of both public and private software firms and has managed companies in the United Kingdom, India, Australia, France, and Hong Kong. He is the author of *Enervative Change: The Impact of Change Management Initiatives on Job Satisfaction.* He has also authored articles related to online learning.

Patricia P. Kuchon, Professor; Ph.D., CUNY. For the past thirty-eight years, Dr. Kuchon has successfully served as a communication resource to students, corporate, and nonprofit agencies in the areas of gender communication, effective presentation skills, and the language of leadership. Her background in communication and psychology position her as an expert in personal and interpersonal communication effectiveness and diversity training. Dr. Kuchon is a licensed speech-language pathologist, holds a doctorate in communication sciences, and has been interviewed on a number of television and radio programs. Her professional experience includes working with Fortune 500 businesses, hospital and health-care systems, public and private schools, and hundreds of individuals including CEOs, physicians, politicians, sales persons, teachers, and television personalities who wish to become more effective speakers, leaders, and promoters of diversity in their workplaces.

Monsignor Dennis Mahon, Associate Professor; Ph.D., Syracuse. Msgr. Mahon served as Vice-Chancellor for Planning at Seton Hall from 1986 to 1995 and was the Vice President for Development at Catholic University of America from 1995 to 1997. In addition, Msgr. Mahon was the Executive Director of Catholic Community Services from 1997 to 2001 at Seton Hall.

Peter Reader, Associate Professor and Chair; M.F.A., Wisconsin–Madison. Theatrical design. Reader directs and designs plays for the Theatre-in-the-Round and is creative director for the Summer Theatre-in-the-Round. He has taught at Seton Hall since 1985.

Catherine Zizik, Associate Professor; M.F.A., George Washington. Speech and interpersonal communication. Zizik directs Seton Hall's award-winning forensics team.

Laura Iandiorio, Adjunct Professor; M.A., Rutgers. Professor Iandiorio is a copywriter and communications consultant, with close to twenty years of business writing experience that spans corporate, agency, nonprofit, and consultancy fields. Before starting Iandiorio Consulting, she worked in the communications departments for Dun & Bradstreet and the New Jersey State Bar Association. She specializes in business-to-business writing and serves as an adjunct professor for Seton Hall University and previously for Rutgers University.

Kenneth Mizrach, Adjunct Professor; M.A., Michigan. Professor Mizrach is a seasoned chief executive officer of the VA New Jersey Health Care System and has an impeccable track record as an organizational builder with strong leadership, strategic, and analytical skills.

SOUTHERN ILLINOIS UNIVERSITY CARBONDALE

College of Mass Communication and Media Arts M.F.A. Program

Program of Study

The interdisciplinary Master of Fine Arts (M.F.A.) degree provides substantial advanced study for a small number of highly talented individuals. The program emphasizes the artistic development of the individual student and the creation of high-quality artistic works in photography, film, video, sound, new media, and interdisciplinary media. Course work in production, criticism, theory, history, and combined media studies emphasizes the interwoven character of traditional and contemporary approaches and technologies in the twenty-first-century.

Research Facilities

Southern Illinois University Carbondale has been designated as a New Media Center. State-of-the-art interactive multimedia labs, extensive facilities for audio, film, new media, photography, graphics, and video production, are available. Students have the opportunity to plan and organize the annual international Big Muddy Film Festival or Visiting Arts program. There are opportunities to work with WSIU Public Broadcasting, which operates two PBS-affiliated television stations and two NPR-affiliated FM radio stations. Students may also choose to become involved with the off-campus Big Muddy Independent Media Center, Carbondale's community radio station, and the town's emerging public access TV channel. The College also houses the Global Media Research Center, which brings together communication with other disciplines and draws in academic colleagues nationally and internationally, to study and evaluate global media operations and trends. The extensive holdings and wide array of bibliographic and instructional support services offered by Southern Illinois University Carbondale's Morris Library place it among the foremost research institutions. The library holds memberships in the Association of Research Libraries and the Center of Research Libraries in Chicago.

Financial Aid

Financial support that includes a stipend and a tuition waiver is available. The College provides three years of assistantship funding. A number of fellowship, assistantship, and scholarship opportunities, including those for traditionally underserved populations, are also available at the University level.

Cost of Study

In-state graduate tuition is $313.90 per credit hour in 2008–09. Out-of-state tuition is 2.5 times the in-state tuition rate ($784.75 per credit hour). Graduate students with at least a 25 percent appointment as a graduate assistant receive a tuition scholarship. Fees vary from $511.26 (1 credit hour) to $1416.05 (12 credit hours). Students with a graduate assistantship receive a 25 percent reduction in the Primary Care Medical Fee.

Living and Housing Costs

For married couples, students with families, and single graduate students, the University has 690 efficiency and one-, two-, three-, and four-bedroom apartments that rent for $484 to $686 per month in 2008–09. Residence halls for single graduate students are also available, as are accessible residence hall rooms and apartments for students with disabilities.

Student Group

In 2006–07, there were 25 graduate students in the College's M.F.A. program. The Graduate School has more than 3,644 students and 526 registered professional students.

Location

Carbondale is approximately 100 miles southeast of St. Louis, Missouri. Immediately south of Carbondale begins some of the most rugged and picturesque terrain in Illinois. Within 20 miles of the campus are two state parks and four recreational lakes, and much of the area is a part of the 240,000-acre Shawnee National Forest.

The University

Southern Illinois University Carbondale is a state-funded university founded in 1869. The Department of Cinema and Photography, the School of Journalism, and the Department of Radio-Television are in the College of Mass Communication and Media Arts, located in the Communications Building on the west side of the campus. WSIU Public Broadcasting provides hands-on experience for students.

Applying

Prospective students must present evidence of exceptional talent and/or potential in one or two media pursuits in the degree program and have a minimum GPA of 3.0. This evidence ordinarily consists of a portfolio of photographs or digitally generated art works, one or more films, videos, sound works, multimedia productions, Web art projects, or other evidence of artistic potential as well as a supporting letter of intent. A campus visit and interviews with faculty members are recommended, particularly for applicants with minimal course work in the field. Applications should be received at the Mass Communication and Media Arts graduate office by January 2 for admission consideration.

Correspondence and Information

Director of Graduate Studies
College of Mass Communication and Media Arts
Southern Illinois University Carbondale
Carbondale, Illinois 62901-6606
Phone: 618-452-5120
Fax: 618-453-7714
E-mail: mcmagrad@siu.edu
Web site: http://mcma.siu.edu

Southern Illinois University Carbondale

THE FACULTY AND THEIR INTERESTS

Department of Cinema and Photography

Lilly A. Boruszkowski, Associate Professor; M.F.A., Northwestern, 1979. Cinema production, postproduction sound, editing, documentary and experimental film.

Cade Bursell, Assistant Professor; M.F.A., San Francisco State, 2002. Cinema.

Susan Felleman, Associate Professor; Ph.D., CUNY Graduate Center, 1993. History and theory of film in relation to art, classical and contemporary Hollywood cinema, European "art" film, surrealism, psychoanalytic and feminist theory.

Sarah Kanouse, Assistant Professor; M.F.A., Illinois at Urbana-Champaign, 2004. Public space, media art, cultural geography, labor history, urban and rural relationships, art and activism.

Jyotsna Kapur, Associate Professor; Ph.D., Northwestern, 1998. Feminist and Marxist analysis of media, globalization, children's film and consumer culture, documentary and ethnographic film, the German and Japanese new wave and Indian cinema.

Gary P. Kolb, Professor and Interim Dean; M.F.A., Ohio, 1977. Photography and digital arts.

Fern Logan, Associate Professor; M.F.A., Art Institute of Chicago, 1993. Photography, digital applications and alternative processes.

Antonio Martinez, Assistant Professor; M.F.A., East Carolina, 2005. Digital imaging, alternative printing processes, multimedia installation, class and racial identity.

Daniel Overturf, Associate Professor; M.F.A., Southern Illinois Carbondale, 1983. Photography.

Jan Peterson Roddy, Associate Professor; M.F.A., Illinois, 1987. Photo/digital production, media arts, image and word, art/politics/spirituality, race, class, gender, sexuality in media, rural U.S. culture.

R. William Rowley, Associate Professor; M.F.A., Iowa, 1974. Digital and analog film production and postproduction techniques, experimental filmmaking, observational documentary, intermedia arts.

Deborah Tudor, Associate Professor and Chair; Ph.D., Northwestern, 1992. British cinema, Australian cinema, war and cinema, digital cinema, sports, the documentary.

Dru Vratil, Associate Professor; M.F.A., Iowa, 1998; Screenwriting.

Department of Radio-Television

Lisa Brooten, Assistant Professor; Ph.D., Ohio, 2002. Media and globalization, gender, social movements, political communication, interpretive/critical research methods, ethnography.

David Burns, Assistant Professor; M.F.A., Parsons, 2001. 2-D and 3-D digital imaging and animation.

John Downing, Professor and Director, Global Media Research Center; Ph.D., London School of Economics, 1974. International communication; alternative media and social movements; racism, ethnicity, and media; media and cultural history.

John Hocheimer, Professor and Chair; Ph.D., Stanford, 1986. Community radio, global media, media studies pedagogy, media history, spirituality and education, popular music.

Phylis Johnson, Associate Professor; Ph.D., Southern Illinois Carbondale, 2003. Sound production and performance acoustic ecology and sound culture, radio drama, oral literacy, media education.

Wago Kreider, Assistant Professor; M.F.A., Rutgers, 2006. Independent filmmaking, broadcast television production, media studies.

Novotny Lawrence, Assistant Professor; Ph.D., Kansas, 2004. African American representations in film and television, Japanese animation, Hindi cinema, film history, genre theory.

Sarah Lewison, Assistant Professor; M.F.A., California, San Diego, 2007. Video, media studies.

Eileen Meehan, Professor; Ph.D., Illinois at Urbana-Champaign, 1983. Political economy of the media, cultural studies, mass communications history, critical communications research.

Howard Motyl, Assistant Professor; Film and video production, the documentary.

Jay Needham, Assistant Professor; California Institute of the Arts, 1989. Video, film, digital audio production, electroacoustic music.

Manjunath Pendakur, Professor; Ph.D., Simon Fraser, 1980. Cultural imperialism, U.S. and Canadian film industries, India's film and television industries, media and public policy issues, the New World Information Order debate, globalization issues.

Jake Podber, Assistant Professor; Ph.D., Ohio, 2001. Media studies, oral history, cultural studies, Appalachian studies, media history.

Jan Thompson, Associate Professor; M.G.S., Roosevelt, 1988. Video production, documentary and sports production.

Paul Torre, Assistant Professor; Ph.D., South Carolina, 2006. Electronic media management, TV, film, critical studies, media management, international media market, relationships between Hollywood studios and German media companies.

School of Journalism

Linda Correll, Assistant Professor; M.A., CUNY, Hunter, 2007. Advertising, creativity in advertising.

Shahira Fahmy, Assistant Professor; Ph.D., Missouri–Columbia, 2003. New media, international communication, visual analysis.

William Freivogel, Associate Professor and Director; J.D., Washington (St. Louis), 2001. Journalism, law.

Katherine Frith, Associate Professor; Ed.D. candidate, Amherst. International advertising, copywriting, advertising and society.

Laura Hlavach, Assistant Professor; J.D., Texas, 1985. Libel, open meetings/open records acts, copyrights, twenty-first-century news writing and reporting, pedagogical constructivism.

Walter B. Jaehnig, Associate Professor and Director; Ph.D., Essex (England), 1974. Media ethics, media theory and philosophy, political violence reporting.

Michael Lawrence, University Professor of Journalism; B.A., Knox (Illinois), 1964. Former press secretary to the governor of Illinois, public policy.

Xigen Li, Assistant Professor; Ph.D., Michigan, 1999. News media and the Internet, impact of technology on mass media, theory of influence on news content, international news and media systems, news media and U.S.-China relations, China's news media.

Dennis Lowry, Professor; Ph.D., Iowa, 1972. Social issues in advertising, communication research methods, content analysis.

Cinzia Padovani, Assistant Professor; Ph.D., Colorado at Boulder, 1999. Historical approaches to political economy, public service broadcasting, international communication, social movements and the media.

Jyotika Ramaprasad, Associate Professor; Ph.D., Southern Illinois Carbondale, 1984. Communication and social change, global journalists, international communication, international advertising/consumer behavior.

SOUTHERN ILLINOIS UNIVERSITY CARBONDALE

College of Mass Communication and Media Arts Ph.D. Program

Program of Study The College-wide Ph.D. program engages students in the analysis of the fundamentals of media and communication, whether social, economic, political, cultural, historical, legal/regulatory, or international. Its firm grounding in conceptual and methodological debates is designed to educate researchers and instructors who make significant contributions to the field of media analysis, policies, and practices.

Research Facilities The extensive holdings and wide array of bibliographic and instructional support services offered by Southern Illinois University Carbondale's Morris Library place it among the foremost research institutions. The library holds memberships in the Association of Research Libraries and the Center of Research Libraries in Chicago. The College is home to the Global Media Research Center, which brings together communication with other disciplines and draws in academic colleagues nationally and internationally, to study and evaluate global media operations and trends. The College also houses the New Media Center, extensive labs and studios for interactive multimedia development, film, audio, video, graphics, photography production, and the Communication Resource Center. Students committed to combining media analysis with practice have further opportunities to work with WSIU Public Broadcasting, which operates two PBS-affiliated television stations and two NPR-affiliated FM radio stations. They may also choose to become involved with the College's Big Muddy International Independent Film Festival, Visiting Artists Series, the off-campus Big Muddy Independent Media Center, Carbondale's community radio station, and the town's emerging public access TV channel.

Financial Aid Financial support that includes a stipend and a tuition waiver is available. The College provides four years of assistantship funding. A number of fellowship, assistantship, and scholarship opportunities, including those for traditionally underserved populations, are also available at the University level.

Cost of Study In-state graduate tuition is $313.90 per credit hour in 2008–09. Out-of-state tuition is 2.5 times the in-state tuition rate ($784.75 per credit hour). Graduate students with at least a 25 percent appointment as a graduate assistant receive a tuition scholarship. Fees vary from $511.26 (1 credit hour) to $1416.05 (12 credit hours). Students with a graduate assistantship receive a 25 percent reduction in the Primary Care Medical Fee.

Living and Housing Costs For married couples, students with families, and single graduate students, the University has 690 efficiency and one-, two-, three-, and four-bedroom apartments that rent for $484 to $686 per month in 2008–09. Residence halls for single graduate students are also available, as are accessible residence hall rooms and apartments for students with disabilities.

Student Group In 2006–07, there were 37 graduate students in the College's Ph.D. program. The graduate school has more than 3,644 students and 526 registered professional students.

Location Carbondale is approximately 100 miles southeast of St. Louis, Missouri. Immediately south of Carbondale begins some of the most rugged and picturesque terrain in Illinois. Within 20 miles of the campus are two state parks and four recreational lakes, and much of the area is a part of the 240,000-acre Shawnee National Forest.

The University and the College Southern Illinois University Carbondale is a state-funded university founded in 1869. The Department of Cinema and Photography, the Department of Radio-Television, and the School of Journalism are in the College of Mass Communication and Media Arts, located in the Communications Building on the west side of the campus. WSIU Public Broadcasting, also located in the Communications Building, provides hands-on experience for students.

Applying Students applying to the Ph.D. program are required to have a 3.25 GPA and submit three letters of recommendation and GRE scores. Typically, those admitted score a minimum of 550 verbal and 450 quantitative on the GRE. International students are required to take the TOEFL exam and score 600 or above. Applications should be received in the MCMA graduate office by December 1.

Correspondence and Information

Director of Graduate Studies
College of Mass Communication and Media Arts
Southern Illinois University Carbondale
Carbondale, Illinois 62901-6606
Phone: 618-453-5120
Fax: 618-453-7714
Web site: http://mcmagrad.siu.edu

Southern Illinois University Carbondale

THE FACULTY

Department of Cinema and Photography

Lilly A. Boruszkowski, Associate Professor; M.F.A., Northwestern, 1979. Cinema production, post-production sound, editing, documentary and experimental film.
Cade Bursell, Assistant Professor; M.F.A., San Francisco State, 2002. Cinema.
Susan Felleman, Associate Professor; Ph.D., CUNY, 1993. History and theory of film in relation to art, classical and contemporary Hollywood cinema, European "art" film, surrealism, psychoanalytic and feminist theory.
Sarah Kanouse, Assistant Professor; M.F.A., Illinois at Urbana-Champaign, 2004. Public space, media art, cultural geography, labor history, urban and rural relationships, art and activism.
Jyotsna Kapur, Associate Professor; Ph.D., Northwestern, 1998. Feminist and Marxist analysis of media, globalization, children's film and consumer culture, documentary and ethnographic film, the German and Japanese new wave and Indian cinema.
Gary Kolb, Professor and Interim Dean; M.F.A., Ohio, 1977. Photography and digital arts.
Fern Logan, Associate Professor; M.F.A., Art Institute of Chicago, 1993. Photographer with special interest in digital applications and alternative processes.
Antonio Martinez, Assistant Professor; M.F.A., East Carolina, 2005. Digital imaging, alternative printing processes, multimedia installation, class and racial identity.
Daniel Overturf, Associate Professor; M.F.A., Southern Illinois at Carbondale, 1983. Photography.
Jan Peterson Roddy, Associate Professor; M.F.A., Illinois, 1987. Photo/digital production, media arts, image and word, art/politics/spirituality, race, class, gender, sexuality in media, rural U.S. culture.
R. William Rowley, Associate Professor and Chair; M.F.A., Iowa, 1974. Digital and analog film production and postproduction techniques, experimental filmmaking, observational documentary, intermedia arts.
Deborah Tudor, Associate Professor and Chair; Ph.D., Northwestern, 1992. British cinema, Australian cinema, war and cinema, digital cinema, sports, the documentary.
Dru Vratil, Associate Professor; M.F.A., Iowa, 1998. Screenwriting.

Department of Radio-Television

Lisa Brooten, Assistant Professor; Ph.D., Ohio, 2002. Media and globalization, gender, social movements, political communication, interpretive/critical research methods, ethnography.
David Burns, Assistant Professor; M.F.A., Parsons, 2001. 2-D and 3-D digital imaging and animation.
John Downing, Professor and Director, Global Media Research Center; Ph.D., London School of Economics, 1974. International communication; alternative media and social movements; racism, ethnicity, and media; media and cultural history.
John Hocheimer, Professor and Chair; Ph.D., Stanford, 1986. Community radio, global media, media studies pedagogy, media history, spirituality and education, popular music.
Phylis Johnson, Associate Professor; Ph.D., Southern Illinois Carbondale, 2003. Sound production and performance, acoustic ecology and sound culture, radio drama, oral literacy, media education.
Wago Kreider, Assistant Professor; M.F.A., Rutgers, 2006. Independent filmmaking, broadcast television production, media studies.
Novotny Lawrence, Assistant Professor; Ph.D., Kansas, 2004. African American representations in film and television, Japanese animation, Hindi cinema, film history, genre theory.
Sarah Lewison, Assistant Professor; M.F.A., California, San Diego, 2007. Video, media studies.
Eileen Meehan, Professor; Ph.D., Illinois at Urbana-Champaign, 1983. Political economy of the media, cultural studies, mass communications history, critical communications research.
Howard Motyl, Assistant Professor; Film and video production, the documentary.
Jay Needham, Assistant Professor; M.F.A., California Institute of the Arts, 1989. Video, film, digital audio production, electroacoustic music.
Manjunath Pendakur, Professor; Ph.D., Simon Fraser, 1980. Cultural imperialism, U.S. and Canadian film industries, India's film and television industries, media and public policy issues, the New World Information Order debate, globalization issues.
Jake Podber, Assistant Professor; Ph.D., Ohio, 2001. Media studies, oral history, cultural studies, Appalachian studies, media history.
Jan Thompson, Associate Professor; M.G.S., Roosevelt, 1988. Video production, documentary, sports production.
Paul Torre, Assistant Professor; Ph.D., South Carolina, 2006. Electronic media management, TV, film, critical studies, media management, international media market, relationships between Hollywood studios and German media companies.

School of Journalism

Linda Correll, Assistant Professor; M.A., CUNY, Hunter, 2007. Advertising, creativity in advertising.
Shahira Fahmy, Assistant Professor; Ph.D., Missouri–Columbia, 2003. New media, international communication, visual analysis.
William Freivogel, Associate Professor and Director; J.D., Washington (St. Louis), 2001. Journalism, law.
Katherine Frith, Associate Professor; Ed.D. candidate, Amherst. International advertising, copywriting, advertising and society.
Laura Hlavach, Assistant Professor; J.D., Texas, 1985. Libel, open meetings/open records acts, copyrights, twenty-first-century news writing and reporting, pedagogical constructivism.
Walter B. Jaehnig, Associate Professor and Director; Ph.D., Essex (England), 1974. Media ethics, media theory and philosophy, political violence reporting.
Michael Lawrence, University Professor of Journalism; B.A., Knox (Illinois), 1964. Public policy, former press secretary to the governor of Illinois.
Xigen Li, Assistant Professor; Ph.D., Michigan, 1999. News media and the Internet, impact of technology on mass media, theory of influence on news content, international news and media systems, news media and U.S.-China relations, China's news media.
Dennis Lowry, Professor; Ph.D., Iowa, 1972. Social issues in advertising, communication research methods, content analysis.
Cinzia Padovani, Assistant Professor; Ph.D., Colorado at Boulder, 1999. Historical approaches to political economy, public service broadcasting, international communication, social movements and the media.
Jyotika Ramaprasad, Associate Professor; Ph.D., Southern Illinois Carbondale, 1984. Communication and social change, global journalists, international communication, international advertising/consumer behavior.

SOUTHERN ILLINOIS UNIVERSITY CARBONDALE

Department of Speech Communication Ph.D. Program

Program of Study

Doctoral graduate students elect to specialize in one of six concentrations: communication pedagogy; intercultural communication; interpersonal communication; performance studies; gender, sexuality, and communication; and rhetoric and philosophy of communication. Additional course work is also available in communication and gender, cultural studies, language and social interaction, organizational communication, public address, public relations, and semiotics. The Department of Speech Communication at Southern Illinois University Carbondale (SIUC) offers programs of study leading to the Master of Science and Doctor of Philosophy degrees.

Graduate study in communication pedagogy focuses on teaching communication within the discipline and communication principles in a variety of instructional contexts. Communication pedagogy reflects interests in intercultural communication, multicultural pedagogy, feminist pedagogy, critical pedagogy, teaching methods, at-risk students, special populations, and learning styles.

Graduate study in intercultural communication emphasizes theory and praxis, examining both U.S. national and international cultures with a focus on intercultural and intracultural communication. Courses are taught emphasizing intercultural communication in the classroom as well as in business and training settings.

Interpersonal communication focuses on descriptive, naturalistic approaches to studying everyday interaction. Two primary approaches to interpersonal communication within the Department are conversation analysis and ethnography of communication. Related topics include language behavior, performance in everyday life, ethnographic fieldwork, interpersonal conflict, narrative, and social construction of gender and identity.

Graduate study in performance studies combines an interest in theory and praxis. Performance studies reflects interests in performance as a way of knowing, including historical and theoretical approaches to performance, literary criticism, performance criticism, and gender and performance, as well as interest in performing literature, performance art, and performance composition.

Graduate study in rhetoric and philosophy of communication focuses on phenomenology of composition, reflecting interest in hermeneutic and semiotic phenomenological orientations; philosophy of rhetoric, reflecting interests in argumentation theory, gender studies, philosophy of rhetoric, and cultural studies; and rhetorical studies, reflecting interests in classical and contemporary rhetorical theory.

Research Facilities

The Department offers extensive production opportunities in its performance laboratory, the Marion Kleinau Theatre, a listening laboratory for work in conversation analysis, and a computer laboratory.

Financial Aid

Most students hold graduate assistantships that provide competitive monthly stipends for the academic year as well as tuition waivers throughout the calendar year. As assistants, most students teach two sections of the Introduction to Oral Communication course each semester. Others work with the debate program, the Marion Kleinau Theatre, or the Public Relations Student Society of America or as research assistants. The University also offers a number of highly competitive fellowships, based upon academic accomplishments, letters of recommendation, GRE scores, and potential for success in graduate study. The deadline for applying for financial aid is February 1.

Cost of Study

In-state graduate tuition is $313.90 per credit hour in 2008–09. Out-of-state tuition is 2.5 times the in-state tuition rate ($784.75 per credit hour). Graduate students with at least a 25 percent appointment as a graduate assistant receive a tuition scholarship. Fees vary from $511.26 (1 credit hour) to $1416.05 (12 credit hours). Students with a graduate assistantship receive a 25 percent reduction in the Primary Care Medical Fee.

Living and Housing Costs

For married couples, students with families, and single graduate students, the University has 690 efficiency and one-, two-, three-, and four-bedroom apartments that rent for $484 to $686 per month in 2008–09. Residence halls for single graduate students are also available, as are accessible residence hall rooms and apartments for students with disabilities.

Student Group

The Department sponsors the Speech Communication Organization (SCO). This organization is made up of graduate student members whose purpose is to enhance professional development. In addition, SCO sponsors and plans various social events that include the sharing of peer scholarship and a brown bag discussion series.

Location

SIUC is 350 miles south of Chicago and 100 miles southeast of St. Louis. Nestled in rolling hills bordered by the Ohio and Mississippi Rivers and enhanced by a mild climate, the area has state parks, national forests and wildlife refuges, and large lakes for outdoor recreation. Cultural offerings include theater, opera, concerts, art exhibits, and cinema. Educational facilities for the families of students are excellent.

The University

Southern Illinois University Carbondale is a comprehensive public university with a variety of general and professional education programs. The University offers bachelor's and associate degrees, master's and doctoral degrees, the J.D. degree, and the M.D. degree. The University is fully accredited by the North Central Association of Colleges and Schools. The Graduate School has an essential role in the development and coordination of graduate instruction and research programs. The Graduate Council has academic responsibility for determining graduate standards, recommending new graduate programs and research centers, and establishing policies to facilitate the research effort.

Applying

Applications should be requested from the address given below. Each application must include a completed Departmental and Graduate School application form, three letters of recommendation, official transcripts from all colleges and universities previously attended, a personal statement of career goals, and GRE scores. The deadline for application is February 1 for the following fall. All materials should be sent directly to the Department of Speech Communication.

Correspondence and Information

Ronald J. Pelias
Director of Graduate Studies
Department of Speech Communication
Southern Illinois University
Carbondale, Illinois 62901-6605

Phone: 618-453-2291
Fax: 618-453-2812
E-mail: rpelias@siu.edu
Web site: http://www.siu.edu/departments/cola/spcm

Southern Illinois University Carbondale

THE FACULTY AND THEIR RESEARCH

Residing in the College of Liberal Arts, the Department of Speech Communication has a faculty that is active in regional, national, and international professional communication organizations. As a community of scholars, the faculty sustains a rich diversity of methodological, theoretical, and philosophical interest. The faculty members believe that their mission is to excel in teaching, research, and service. Working with approximately 200 undergraduate majors and more than 65 in-residence graduate students, the faculty members create an environment that fosters opportunity, possibility, and creativity.

Nilanjana R. Bardhan, Associate Professor; Ph.D., Ohio, 1998. Public relations, organizational communication, intercultural/international communication, media criticism, health communication.

Bryan Crow, Associate Professor; Ph.D., Iowa, 1982. Interpersonal communication, conversation analysis, relational pragmatics, language acquisition.

Suzanne Daughton, Associate Professor; Ph.D., Texas, 1991. Rhetorical theory and criticism, political communication, communication and gender, metaphor and narrative in rhetorical discourse.

Craig Gingrich-Philbrook, Associate Professor; Ph.D., Southern Illinois, 1994. Performance studies, performance art, queer theory, Continental philosophy, psychoanalysis, literary theory.

Todd Graham, Director of Debate; Ph.D., Arizona State, 2000. Interpersonal communication, humor studies, qualitative research methods, argumentation theory and practice.

Jonathan M. Gray, Associate Professor; Ph.D., LSU, 1999. Rhetorical theory and criticism, popular culture, communication pedagogy, folklore, cultural studies, performance.

Lenore Langsdorf, Professor; Ph.D., SUNY at Stony Brook, 1977. Argumentation, cultural and rhetorical theory, hermeneutic phenomenology, ethnomethodology, philosophy of communication.

Richard Lanigan, Professor; Ph.D., Southern Illinois, 1969. Philosophy of communication, rhetoric, semiotics, phenomenology, intercultural communication, theory construction and research methods.

Ronald J. Pelias, Professor; Ph.D., Illinois, 1979. Performance studies, performance methodologies and criticism, performance composition, performative writing, performance art.

Elyse L. Pineau, Associate Professor; Ph.D., Northwestern, 1990. Performance studies, autobiography, performance methodologies, performance and gender, communication pedagogy.

Nathan Stucky, Associate Professor; Ph.D., Texas, 1988. Performance studies, narrative theory, conversation analysis, ethnographic performance, performance criticism.

Naida Zukic, Assistant Professor; Ph.D., Minnesota, 2005. Intercultural communication, cultural studies, cyber studies, postcolonial feminist theories, critical communication studies, queer theory.

SYRACUSE UNIVERSITY

S. I. Newhouse School of Public Communications

Programs of Study

The Newhouse School offers programs leading to three graduate degrees: Master of Arts (M.A.), Master of Science (M.S.), and Doctor of Philosophy (Ph.D.). Candidates for the M.A. and M.S. degrees can major in advertising; arts journalism; broadcast journalism; documentary film and history; magazine, newspaper, and online journalism; photography; media studies; new media; public relations; or television-radio-film. A master's program in media management leading to an M.S. degree is offered jointly by the Newhouse School and the Whitman School of Management. A course of study in public diplomacy leading to an M.S. degree in public relations and an M.A. degree in international relations is offered jointly by the Newhouse School and the Maxwell School of Citizenship and Public Affairs. Candidates for the Ph.D. degree receive a Doctor of Philosophy in mass communications. The Newhouse School offers North America's only distance learning program, an interdisciplinary degree program for experienced public relations practitioners, leading to a Master of Science in communications management.

Generally, 36 credits are required for the master's degree. However, 36 to 42 credits are required for the master's degree in media management, 40 credits for broadcast journalism, 39 credits for documentary film and history, 33 credits for photography, and a total of 58 credits for the public diplomacy course of study. Most students complete their studies by taking capstone courses. Television-radio-film students take comprehensive examinations, media studies students write theses, and photography students either write theses or complete special projects. In public relations, students either take a capstone course with a comprehensive examination or write theses.

The Ph.D. program in mass communications involves three years of academic work beyond the master's degree. Students must take a minimum of 60 credits beyond the master's level. A research dissertation is required of all doctoral candidates. The Newhouse School accepts 5 new students each year and provides them with a full-tuition scholarship and a stipend for work in teaching or research.

Research Facilities

Opportunities are available for Newhouse students to assist members of the faculty with research projects. The School has several research areas, including the Bleier Center for Television and Popular Culture and the Knight Chair in Political Reporting. In addition, students have access to the Transactional Records Access Clearinghouse (TRAC), a center devoted to assisting the news media in analyzing government documents through the use of computers. TRAC, which has an office complex at the School, is the leading research center for investigating and implementing new computer-assisted reporting techniques.

Financial Aid

A few general merit-based University fellowships and scholarships are available to Newhouse students. In addition, the School has a number of partial research and teaching graduate assistantships. In 2007–08, assistantships required 15 hours per week of work and provided a stipend of $8250 per year. In addition, graduate assistants may also receive 6 to 24 hours of tuition scholarship per year. Need-based financial aid is also available. More information is available from the University's Office of Financial Aid (http://financialaid.syr.edu/; 315-443-1513).

Cost of Study

Tuition for graduate students was $1012 per credit for the 2007–08 academic year. A student taking 9 credits during both the fall and spring terms is considered to be full-time.

Living and Housing Costs

In 2007–08, one-bedroom apartments were available for single graduate students at the rate of $5140 per semester. Apartments for single graduate students (furnished, with utilities) were $3715 per semester for two-bedroom units. Nonuniversity-operated off-campus apartments cost from approximately $400 per month to $1000 per month.

Student Group

Each year, students with a variety of undergraduate majors are considered for admission to the graduate programs. An undergraduate communications degree is not required. Programs are competitive, and admitted students typically have academic records and Graduate Record Examinations scores well above average. The Newhouse School has a wide and varied alumni base. Many graduates are recognized as leaders in the various fields of public communications.

Student Outcomes

The School operates a Career Development and Alumni Relations office to assist students and alumni with career opportunities. A computerized Career Advisory Network has been established to provide an online database of alumni contacts in businesses throughout the world. Recruiters frequently conduct interviews at the Newhouse School, and current job listings are circulated in a regular e-mail publication produced by the Career Development office.

Location

Syracuse is the crossroads and central distribution point of New York State. A hub of industrial and commercial activity, Syracuse has a metropolitan population of more than half a million. The city offers students many opportunities to gain practical experience in the various fields of communications. Furthermore, many scenic and recreation areas are nearby.

The University and The School

Syracuse University was founded in 1870 by the United Methodist Church, with assistance from the city of Syracuse. Privately endowed, coeducational, and nonsectarian, the University has grown from an original enrollment of 41 students to an overall enrollment of 19,082, which includes 5,926 graduate students. A member of both the Association of American Universities and the Council of Graduate Schools, Syracuse University is considered one of the nation's major institutions of higher learning. The Newhouse School is fully accredited by the Accrediting Council on Education in Journalism and Mass Communications and has an enrollment of approximately 1,800 undergraduate and 250 graduate students.

Applying

Application materials can be obtained by using the information listed in this description or by using the online application on the School's Web site. All applicants must take the GRE General Test. International students who do not hold a U.S. degree or for whom English is not a native language must supply TOEFL scores. Applicants for the media management program may take either the GRE General Test or the GMAT. Applicants for the master's programs must hold a bachelor's degree from an accredited four-year institution and submit official transcripts from their undergraduate institutions. A complete application includes GRE scores, transcripts, letters of recommendation, and an application form. Except for media studies, Newhouse master's programs are designed for students to begin study in midsummer. Fall and spring admission are rarely granted. To apply for fellowships, scholarships, and assistantships, students need only check the appropriate boxes on the admission application form. The deadline for admission applications and merit-based financial aid applications is February 1.

Correspondence and Information

Graduate Records Office
S. I. Newhouse School of Public Communications
215 University Place
Syracuse, New York 13244-2100

Phone: 315-443-4039
Fax: 315-443-1834
E-mail: pcgrad@syr.edu
Web site: http://newhousemasters.syr.edu/

Syracuse University

THE FACULTY

Administration
David M. Rubin, Dean.
Amy Falkner, Associate Dean for Academic Affairs.
Dona Hayes, Associate Dean for Special Projects.
Carla V. Lloyd, Associate Dean of Scholarly and Creative Activity.
Rosanna Grassi, Associate Dean for Student Affairs.
Joel Kaplan, Associate Dean for Professional Graduate Studies.
Carol M. Liebler, Director of the Doctoral Program.
Lynn M. Vanderhoek, Assistant Dean for Advancement.
Karen McGee, Assistant Dean for Student Affairs.

Advertising
James Tsao, Professor and Chair; Ph.D., Temple. Advertising strategy, international advertising, Internet advertising.
Sue Westcott Alessandri, Assistant Professor; Ph.D., North Carolina at Chapel Hill. Advertising research, advertising strategies.
Amy Falkner, Associate Professor; M.A., Syracuse. Media planning, advertising to gay and lesbian markets.
John Philip Jones, Professor; M.A., Cambridge. Advertising research, marketing.
Carla V. Lloyd, Associate Professor; Ph.D., Syracuse. Advertising media, copywriting.
Jennifer Mitchell, Assistant Professor; M.B.A., Notre Dame. Advertising research, strategies.
Ed Russell, Assistant Professor; M.S., Northwestern. Advertising strategies, campaigns.

Broadcast Journalism
Dona Hayes, Associate Professor and Chair; M.S., Syracuse. Broadcast news writing, reporting, production.
Hubert Brown, Associate Professor; M.A., Nebraska–Lincoln. Political reporting, writing.
Michael E. Cremedas, Associate Professor; Ph.D., Florida. Writing, reporting, production management.
Frank Currier, Professor of Practice; M.A., Missouri–Columbia. Radio news reporting, producing.
Barbara Croll Fought, Associate Professor; J.D., Detroit. Broadcast news writing, reporting.
E. Robert Lissit, Associate Professor; M.S., Northwestern. Broadcast news writing, producing.
John Nicholson, Professor of Practice; B.S., Syracuse. Broadcast reporting.
Dow Smith, Associate Professor; M.A., Missouri–Columbia. Broadcast management, news direction, production.
Donald C. Torrance, Associate Professor; B.A., Alfred. Broadcast news writing, production.
Chris Tuohey, Assistant Professor; M.A., Ohio State. Broadcast news reporting.

Communications
Hubert Brown, Associate Professor and Chair; M.A., Nebraska–Lincoln. Political reporting, writing.
Makana Chock, Assistant Professor; Ph.D., Cornell. Communications theory.
Bradley W. Gorham, Associate Professor; Ph.D., Wisconsin–Madison. Media and society, media effects.
Carol M. Liebler, Associate Professor; Ph.D., Wisconsin–Madison. Communications theory, methodology.
David M. Rubin, Professor; Ph.D., Stanford. Communications law, media ethics, mass media and government.
Jay B. Wright, Professor; Ph.D., Syracuse. Communications law, ethics.

Magazine
Melissa Chessher, Associate Professor and Chair; M.A., Baylor. Magazine writing, editing.
William A. Glavin Jr., Professor; M.S., Columbia. Magazine writing, editing.
Robert E. Lloyd, Associate Professor; M.A., Syracuse. Newswriting and reporting, media and society.
Mark J. Obbie, Assistant Professor; M.A., Missouri–Columbia. Magazine article writing and editing.

Newspaper
Steve Davis, Associate Professor and Chair; B.J., Missouri–Columbia. Newswriting, reporting, impact of the Internet on politics.
Joan A. Deppa, Associate Professor; Ph.D., Michigan State. Newswriting, reporting, computer graphics.
Elizabeth Lynne Flocke, Professor; Ph.D., Missouri–Columbia. Newswriting, communications law.
Joel Kaplan, Associate Professor; M.S., Illinois; M.S.L., Yale. Newswriting, investigative reporting, communications law.
Johanna Keller, Director, Goldring Program; M.A., Antioch. Cultural journalism, arts criticism.
C. Marshall Matlock, Associate Professor; M.A., Central Michigan. Newswriting, newspaper design.
Gustav Niebuhr, Professor of Practice; M.A., Oxford. Religious journalism.
Nancy W. Sharp, Professor; M.S.Sc., Syracuse. Newswriting, reporting.
Jo Thomas, Associate Chancellor; M.A., North Carolina at Chapel Hill. Newswriting, reporting.
Francis Ward, Associate Professor; M.A., Syracuse. Newswriting, reporting.

Public Relations
Maria P. Russell, Professor and Chair; M.A., Syracuse. Public relations management.
Dennis F. Kinsey, Associate Professor; Ph.D., Stanford. Public relations theory, research.
Robert M. Kucharavy, Professor of Practice; M.A.L.A., Clark. Public relations management.
Kathryn E. Lee, Adjunct Professor; M.S., Syracuse. Public relations writing.
F. William Smullen III, Adjunct Professor; M.A., Syracuse. Government public relations, national security issues.
Brenda J. Wrigley, Associate Professor; Ph.D., Syracuse. Gender and public relations, diversity issues.
Sean (Sung-Un) Yang, Assistant Professor; Ph.D., Maryland. Public relations research, organization-public relationships.

Television-Radio-Film
Michael Schoonmaker, Chair; Ph.D., Syracuse. Television production, writing, media education.
Stanley R. Alten, Professor; Ph.D., Syracuse. Audio, music recording, writing.
Richard Breyer, Professor; M.A., NYU. Television production, documentary writing, production.
Bud Carey, Associate Professor; B.S., San Diego. Television industry, broadcast sales and promotion.
Fiona Chew, Associate Professor; Ph.D., Washington (Seattle). Television research.
Richard Dubin, Professor of Practice. Television writing, producing, and directing.
Larry Elin, Associate Professor; B.S., Syracuse. Television production, interactive media.
Tula Goenka, Assistant Professor; M.S., Syracuse. Television production, writing.
Sharon R. Hollenback, Professor; Ph.D., Texas at Austin. Television writing, media and society.
Patricia H. Longstaff, Associate Professor; M.P.A., Harvard; J.D., Iowa. Communications law, new technologies.
Peter K. Moller, Professor; M.A., Pennsylvania. Television production, writing.
Evan S. Smith, Associate Professor; M.S., Syracuse. Film business, scriptwriting.
Robert J. Thompson, Professor; Ph.D., Northwestern. Television criticism, production.
Roosevelt R. Wright Jr., Associate Professor; Ph.D., Syracuse. Radio programming, management.

Visual and Interactive Communications
Anthony R. Golden, Associate Professor and Chair; Ph.D., Syracuse. Advertising and illustration photography.
Stephen M. Masiclat, Associate Professor; M.P.S., Cornell. Graphics, multimedia, Web design.
Lawrence Mason Jr., Professor; Ph.D., Syracuse. Communications and society, photojournalism, multimedia.
R. Sean McNaughton, Assistant Professor; B.A., Syracuse. Information graphics.
Bruce Strong, Associate Professor; M.A., Ohio. Photojournalism, multimedia storytelling.
David C. Sutherland, Associate Professor; M.A., Western Kentucky. Photojournalism, graphics.
Sherri A. Taylor, Coordinator, Scholastic Journalism Program; B.A., Baylor. Graphics.

Endowed Research Chairs
George A. Comstock, S. I. Newhouse Professor of Public Communications; Ph.D., Stanford. Mass communication, psychology of the behavioral effects of entertainment, communications theory.
Charlotte Grimes, Knight Chair in Political Reporting; B.S., East Carolina. Media and politics, political reporting, journalism ethics.
Pamela J. Shoemaker, John Ben Snow Professor of Public Communications; Ph.D., Wisconsin–Madison. Communications theory and research, gatekeeping, news content.

UNIVERSITY OF BALTIMORE

Yale Gordon College of Liberal Arts
School of Communications Design

Program of Study

The School of Communications Design's mission is to guide students in the creative endeavors that define their professional lives. In a highly imaginative and supportive atmosphere, students come together from diverse backgrounds to pursue their career interests in creative writing, professional writing, publishing, graphic design, and multimedia. The School offers three highly distinctive degree programs: a Master of Fine Arts (M.F.A.) in Creative Writing & Publishing Arts, an M.F.A. in Integrated Design, and a Master of Arts (M.A.) in Publications Design.

The M.F.A. in Creative Writing & Publishing Arts program (48 credits) is unique in its combined emphasis on writing and publishing; students not only write poetry, fiction, and/or literary nonfiction but also create a variety of innovative publications—from the outrageously experimental to the elegantly traditional—to make their writing public.

The M.F.A. in Integrated Design program (48 credits) is built on the premise that designers of the twenty-first century must be fluent in the language and concepts of multiple media, including print, motion/video, hypermedia, and Web-based technologies. Students develop skills in creative problem solving, design, and production at a level that allows them to make a difference in the highly competitive world of communications.

The M.A. in Publications Design program (36 credits) integrates professional writing and graphic design for students who are pursuing careers in public relations, advertising, and print and electronic publishing. The program's goal is to instill and enhance the habits of analysis and imagination that lead to the effective translation of ideas into print and other media. Classes are held evenings and weekends at the Baltimore campus and during weekends at the Universities at Shady Grove in Rockville, Maryland.

Faculty members include a rich array of accomplished professional writers, poets, graphic designers, and multimedia producers who are also dedicated teachers, passionate about the challenges that arise in verbal and visual communication. Faculty members work closely with students to ensure that all who are motivated can succeed. Applicants often have undergraduate majors in English, journalism, graphic design, studio art, or mass communications, but the programs also enroll students with majors as diverse as biology, geography, business administration, and political science. What they share is a strong interest in how words and images work together.

Research Facilities

The School of Communications Design maintains state-of-the-art facilities to support its students and programs. The Graphics Lab provides access to dozens of high-end workstations, including a variety of scanners and the latest versions of popular publication software, like Adobe Creative Suite and Apple's Final Cut Studio, for graphic design, digital photography, video editing, Web design, and animation. Students can also access high-tech printers and a vast, searchable library of royalty-free photos and clip art.

The Media Lab supports audio and video work with a wide spectrum of equipment: Final Cut Studio editing systems, Digidesign Pro Tools audio systems, multichannel digital and analog mixing consoles, digital still and video cameras, multitrack digital audio decks, and microphone and lighting systems.

The Ampersand Institute for Words & Images offers workshops, short courses, lectures, seminars, and other public events. The institute's mission involves promoting dialogue about the present and future of publishing. These events bring together students, scholars, and entrepreneurs from across the United States.

Financial Aid

The UB Office of Financial Aid assists graduate students in obtaining loans, scholarships, and other means of assistance. Many students participate in internships or work on independent or contractual projects. A limited number of graduate assistantships, which provide tuition remission and a stipend, are available.

Cost of Study

In 2007–08, tuition for liberal arts graduate students who are Maryland residents was $498 per credit hour. Nonresident graduate students paid $751 per credit hour. All students pay a University flat fee ($70 for students taking 1–11 credits; $422.50 for students taking 12 or more credits), a University per-credit fee of $56 (not to exceed $309.50), and a technology fee ($6 per credit from 1–11; $72.50 for 12 credits or more). Web-based classes are an additional $88 per credit for in-state students and $86 per credit for students from out-of-state. Students may pay tuition and fees with cash, check, Visa, MasterCard, or Discover.

Living and Housing Costs

UB is a commuter campus and does not presently offer student housing on campus; however, University-affiliated housing is located within walking distance, and assistance in locating affordable housing is provided by the Center for Student Involvement. UB is located in midtown Baltimore's cultural district, off the Jones Falls Expressway (I-83) and across the street from Pennsylvania Station, which provides MARC commuter and Amtrak service. The University is accessible by major bus routes and its own light rail stop, making the campus an easy commute from a variety of neighborhoods within the Baltimore area.

Student Group

The School of Communications Design's programs are designed to accommodate both full-time and part-time students, many of whom work in publications, public relations, or marketing. Mature and motivated, the School's students want to extend their creative skills, particularly as they relate to print and electronic media. About 180 students from throughout the country are enrolled in the M.A. in Publications Design program. The selective M.F.A. programs were initiated in the 2003–04 academic year; 40 students are enrolled in the Creative Writing & Publishing Arts program, while about 20 are enrolled in the Integrated Design program.

Location

Baltimore is both a big city and a small town. UB is nestled in the Mount Vernon Cultural District—home to art galleries, theaters, the symphony and opera, and historic architecture. The neighborhood serves as the backdrop for First Thursdays, a monthly event that includes the likes of outdoor concerts and wine tasting in nearby art galleries. Within 2 miles of campus is the bustling Inner Harbor, with its shops and waterfront activities, including the National Aquarium, Maryland Science Center, Oriole Park at Camden Yards, and the Ravens' M&T Bank Stadium. The city also offers a museum for nearly every interest and specialty—from the legendary histories told at the Babe Ruth Birthplace and Museum, Edgar Allan Poe House Museum, Eubie Blake Museum, and Great Blacks in Wax Museum to the world-class art found at the Walters Art Museum, Baltimore Museum of Art, and the American Visionary Art Museum. Baltimore is also full of friendly neighborhoods, including Little Italy, Fells Point, Canton, and Hampden. Nighttime pub crawls, vintage shops, steamed crabs, and bocce ball along with street fairs, ethnic festivals, and unique markets make Baltimore a city like few others for those of all ages.

The University

UB offers undergraduate and graduate education in three unique schools: the Yale Gordon College of Liberal Arts, the Merrick School of Business, and the School of Law. The University of Baltimore was founded as a private institution in 1925 and is now part of the University System of Maryland. Total student enrollment is approximately 5,400, and the student-faculty ratio is 16:1.

Applying

A strong undergraduate background or professional experience in communications is required for all programs. Both M.F.A. programs require a bachelor's degree from a regionally accredited institution with an overall grade point average of 3.0 or higher. Applicants must submit a portfolio of work directly to the program director. They are also required to submit two letters of recommendation, a statement of personal interest in the program of study, an official transcript from each higher-education institution attended, the application, and the appropriate application fee to the Office of Graduate Admissions. Admission is for the fall semester only, and applications must be submitted by February 1. The M.A. in Publications Design program requires an undergraduate GPA of 3.0 or higher, but applicants with at least a 2.8 GPA and a strong portfolio in writing or design are given serious consideration. Applicants must submit at least one writing sample, a resume, and a statement of personal interest in the program of study directly to the program director. An official transcript from each higher education institution attended and the application and fee must be submitted to the Office of Graduate Admissions. A personal or telephone interview with the program director is also required.

Correspondence and Information

Office of Graduate Admissions
University of Baltimore
1420 North Charles Street
Baltimore, Maryland 21201-5779

Phone: 410-837-6565
Fax: 410-837-4774
E-mail: gradadmissions@ubalt.edu
Web site: http://www.ubalt.edu/cla

Dr. Stephanie Gibson
Program Director, M.A. in Publications Design
Phone: 410-837-6050
Web site: http://www.ubalt.edu/pubdesign

Professor Kendra Kopelke
Program Director, M.F.A. in Creative Writing & Publishing Arts
Web site: http://www.ubalt.edu/creativewriting

Professor Ed Gold
Program Director, M.F.A. in Integrated Design
Web site: http://www.ubalt.edu/integrateddesign

Contact for either M.F.A. program:

Jaye Crooks
Phone: 410-837-6022
E-mail: gradadmissions@ubalt.edu (for all)

University of Baltimore

THE FACULTY AND THEIR RESEARCH

Virginia Kirby-Smith Carruthers, Associate Professor; Ph.D., Duke. Shakespeare, Australian literature, scholarly editing. Carruthers is editor of *CEAMAGazine* and associate editor of *Deus Loci: The Lawrence Durrell Journal.*

Jane D. Delury, Visiting Assistant Professor; M.A., Johns Hopkins. Creative writing and literary publishing. Delury's work appears in literary journals, including *StoryQuarterly,* the *Sun Magazine,* and *The Iconoclast,* and she has been nominated for Best New American Voices and the Pushcart Prize.

Peter M. Fitz, Assistant Professor; M.A., Johns Hopkins. Computer technology, software design, eighteenth-century literature and art.

Roger W. Friskey, Visiting Assistant Professor; M.S., Northwestern. Professional writing and editing, persuasion. Friskey, formerly a television reporter and corporate spokesperson, is a corporate communications consultant.

Stephanie Gibson, Associate Professor; Ph.D., NYU. Media ecology and communications theory. Gibson is coeditor of *The Emerging CyberCulture* and *Communications in Cyberspace.* She is a recipient of the Jacques Ellul award for Media Ecology Activism for her communications work with the Maryland Coalition Against State Executions.

Edwin Gold, Professor; B.A., Maryland Institute College of Art. Graphic design. Gold is the author of *The Business of Graphic Design* and a columnist for *Step-by-Step Graphics* and the winner of hundreds of awards and citations for excellence.

Kendra Kopelke, Associate Professor; M.A., Johns Hopkins. Creative writing. Kopelke's work has been published in many journals, including the *Georgia Review, The Antioch Review,* and *Partisan Review.* She is the author of two books of poetry, *Eager Street* and *Carpe Diem, Ants,* and the editor of *Passager,* a literary journal.

Arthur J. Magida, Writer in Residence; M.A., Georgetown; M.A., California School of Professional Psychology. Nonfiction, long and short form; specialty writing. Magida regularly writes for a number of national magazines, is an award-winning author of five books (including *Prophet of Rage, The Rabbi and the Hit Man,* and *Opening the Doors of Wonder*) and is a columnist for an online religion magazine.

Stephen H. Matanle, Associate Professor; Ph.D., American. Creative writing, narrative theory, modern and contemporary fiction, film studies. Matanle's work has been published in many journals, including the *Georgia Review, Chicago Review,* and *Poetry.*

Amy Pointer, Instructor; M.F.A., Towson. Designing for print and new media. Pointer is a design consultant with an international client base.

Jonathan L. Shorr, Associate Professor, Chair, and Executive Director; Ph.D., Cincinnati. Corporate communication, script writing, media design, media literacy. Shorr is a media consultant and president of the Baltimore City Cable Commission.

Julie B. Simon, Associate Professor; M.F.A., North Carolina at Greensboro. Video and multimedia production. Simon is a CINE Award–winning director/producer for nontheatrical video production and an accomplished photographer and videographer.

Bert P. Smith, Associate Professor; M.A., Baltimore. History of graphic design, book design, poster design. Smith is the recipient of a number of national awards for book and poster design and is the author and designer of *Greetings from Baltimore* and *Down the Ocean.*

Sarah Jay Verville, Assistant Professor; M.F.A., Maryland Institute College of Art. Digital design. Verville is the recipient of multiple Addy awards and has been featured in *Print* magazine.

Marion Winik, Assistant Professor; M.F.A., CUNY, Brooklyn. Memoir, magazine writing. Winik is the author of six books, the most famous of which is the memoir *First Comes Love.* She has written and continues to write for a wide variety of magazines from *Reader's Digest* to *Playgirl;* her commentary can be heard on National Public Radio's *Morning Edition* and *All Things Considered.*

Betsy Greenleaf Yarrison, Assistant Professor; Ph.D., Wisconsin. Dramatic theory, language behavior, professional writing. Yarrison is the author of an undergraduate technical writing text and is a professional writing consultant.

UNIVERSITY OF DENVER

School of Communication

Programs of Study

The University of Denver offers several graduate degrees in the School of Communication. The Department of Human Communication Studies offers the Doctor of Philosophy and Master of Arts degrees in human communication. The Department of Mass Communications and Journalism Studies offers the Master of Arts in mass communications, with either a video production or a student-designed emphasis, and the Master of Science in public relations or advertising management. The School of Communication offers the Master of Arts in international and intercultural communication, a joint degree with the Graduate School of International Studies. The School of Communication and the Daniels College of Business offer a joint-degree program, the Master of Science in management and communication. The Master of Arts in digital media studies is a joint degree between the School of Communication, the School of Art and Art History, and the Department of Math and Computer Science. Other joint degrees include the Master of Arts in human communication/Master of Science in social work with the Graduate School of Social Work, Master of Arts in mass communications/Doctor of Jurisprudence in the College of Law, and Doctor of Philosophy in human communication/Doctor of Jurisprudence in the College of Law. A policy exists at the University of Denver to promote student-designed dual-degree programs.

Research Facilities

On-campus facilities include a state-of-the-art video production studio; Digital DV, HI-8, and nonlinear computer video editing suites; and extensive field production equipment. The School of Communication provides the latest technology in its computer labs. Students also have access to the research network housed in Penrose Library and Westminster Law Library. In addition, study rooms, computer labs, carrels, and duplication facilities are also available. Students also have access to other nearby major university libraries in the Rocky Mountain Front Range area.

Financial Aid

Financial aid opportunities include both merit-based and need-based options. Merit-based opportunities consist of fellowships, grants, teaching and research assistantships, and Dean's Tuition Scholarship credits. A special minority fellowship is available for the Ph.D. program. Need-based options include work-study positions and loans. Teaching assistantships include a monetary stipend and tuition waivers. Financial aid requests should be completed as close to the application deadline as possible.

Cost of Study

The cost of tuition for the 2007–08 academic year was $873 per quarter credit. Full-time student status is a minimum of 8 hours per quarter. Tuition for students carrying 12 to 18 hours per quarter is $10,476. The cost of books is approximately $1300 per year. Health fees are $360 per year.

Living and Housing Costs

Room and board range between $6000 and $9600 for on- and off-campus housing. Personal costs are approximately $2200.

Student Group

For the 2007–08 academic year, the number of graduate students enrolled in the School of Communication was 136. Graduate students in the School of Communication span a wide range of demographic characteristics, backgrounds, and goals. More than half of the students receive some form of financial aid.

Location

Denver is the cultural and commercial center of the Rocky Mountain area. The area is a leading center for new communication technologies and methodologies worldwide, with a wide variety of communication industries and institutions. Students can continue their graduate education surrounded by the breathtaking beauty of the Rocky Mountains.

The University and The School

The School of Communication at the University of Denver was founded in 1991 and is composed of two well-established academic departments. The Department of Human Communication Studies originated in 1894 and the Department of Mass Communications originated in 1933. There are currently 27 full-time faculty members in the School of Communication. The School has an outstanding teaching faculty, which is committed to ensuring that students get the best education possible. In addition, the School has some of the finest communication scholars in the world. Overall, the faculty's dedication, creativity, and openness to change and innovation have been responsible for the development of one of the most dynamic schools at the University of Denver.

Applying

All individuals applying to the graduate programs in the School of Communication need to supply the following specific information and data: official transcripts from each institution from which the applicant received academic credit and the GRE, which is required for both Ph.D. and master's degree applicants and for both domestic and international students. Applicants must also submit a one-page statement of purpose and three letters of recommendation. International students are required to take the Test of English as a Foreign Language (TOEFL) or the International English Language Testing System (IELTS) test for all programs. Some programs require international students to take the Test of Written English (TWE). International students applying for teaching assistantships must also take the Test of Spoken English (TSE). Students are not admitted to a degree program without having demonstrated competency in the English language.

Application deadlines for School of Communication programs vary. For more details, students should check the School of Communication Web site. Students are encouraged to apply for fall entrance, though occasionally they are admitted during winter or spring quarters.

Correspondence and Information

For more information, students should contact the following at the University of Denver, Denver, Colorado 80208 or visit the Web site at http://soc.du.edu.

For the Ph.D. and M.A. in human communications:

Mary Claire Morr Serewicz, Director of Graduate Admissions
Department of Human Communication
E-mail: mserewic@du.edu

For the M.A. in mass communications or the M.S. in public relations or advertising management:

Renee A. Botta, Director of Graduate Studies
Department of Mass Communications and Journalism
E-mail: mcomadm@du.edu

For the M.A. in international and intercultural communication:

Margaret Thompson, Director
International and Intercultural Communication Program
E-mail: iic@du.edu

For the M.A. in digital media studies:

Trace Reddell, Director
Digital Media Studies
E-mail: treddell@du.edu

University of Denver

THE FACULTY AND THEIR RESEARCH

Renee Botta, Associate Professor; Ph.D., Wisconsin–Madison, 1998. Media effects, audience behavior, quantitative research methods, social and health communication.
Rodney Buxton, Associate Professor; Ph.D., Texas at Austin, 1992. Critical/qualitative analysis, scriptwriting, and directing for television and film.
Lynn Clark, Associate Professor; Ph.D., Colorado at Boulder, 2005. Journalism, new media, religion and media, popular culture.
Christopher D. Coleman, Assistant Professor; M.F.A., Buffalo, SUNY. Digital media technology, digital foundations, combined media, digital animation.
Christof Demont-Heinrich, Assistant Professor; Ph.D., Colorado at Boulder, 2005. Newswriting and reporting, transnational and national identity, media discourse, linguistic and cultural dimensions of globalization, Web design.
Bill Depper, Assistant Professor; M.F.A., Iowa, 1988. Digital media studies.
Fran Dickson, Associate Professor and Chair of the Department of Human Communication Studies; Ph.D., Bowling Green State, 1982. Interpersonal communication, marriage and family communication.
Tony Gault, Associate Professor; M.F.A., Iowa, 1994. Scriptwriting, media production, media analysis.
Cathy A. Grieve, Assistant Professor and Director of Internships; Ph.D., Denver, 1979. Public relations, media effects.
Elizabeth Henry, Lecturer; Ph.D., Iowa, 2000. Film criticism, media history, public relations, literary journalism.
Darrin Hicks, Associate Professor; Ph.D., Southern Illinois, 1995. Rhetorical theory, philosophy of communication.
Nadia Kaneva, Assistant Professor; Ph.D., Colorado at Boulder, 2007. Culture and communication, public relations, globalization, online learning.
Lily Mendoza, Assistant Professor; Ph.D., Arizona State, 2000. International and intercultural communication, communication theory.
Trace Reddell, Assistant Professor; Ph.D., Colorado at Boulder, 1997. Web development, media theory, digital audio production.
Adrienne Russell, Assistant Professor; Ph.D., Indiana Bloomington, 2001. Digital media theory, new media, media controversies, journalism.
Ania Savage, Lecturer; M.S., Columbia, 1964. Domestic and international journalism, public relations.
Sheila Schroeder, Assistant Professor; Ph.D., Indiana, 1999. Qualitative research, video production, television criticism, sports and media.
Steven Scully, Amos B. Hostetter Chair; M.S., Northwestern, 1985. Political communication, television and the U.S. presidency, political advertising.
Mary Claire Morr Serewicz, Assistant Professor; Ph.D., Arizona State, 2002. Interpersonal communication, group facilitation, dating relationships, family communication, gender and communication.
Margaret Thompson, Associate Professor; Ph.D., Wisconsin–Madison, 1989. International communication, media effects, audience behavior, quantitative research methods.
Diane Waldman, Associate Professor; Ph.D., Wisconsin–Madison, 1981. Communication theory, qualitative research methods, film history and criticism.
Roy V. Wood, Professor; Ph.D., Denver, 1965. Organizational communication, research methods, public deliberation and ethics.

UNIVERSITY OF MARYLAND, COLLEGE PARK

Philip Merrill College of Journalism

Programs of Study

The Philip Merrill College of Journalism's programs combine theoretical study with practical, skills-oriented courses. The College's proximity to the nation's capital provides students with the ultimate journalism laboratory, while the graduate program's small size enables faculty members to give students one-on-one academic advising and career counseling. The College offers a Master of Journalism (nonthesis), a Master of Arts in Journalism (thesis), and a doctorate in journalism and public communication.

There are four master's specializations: Public Affairs Reporting (PAR) for those interested in print journalism; Broadcast News for students preparing for careers as TV news correspondents, anchors, or producers; Online News for students preparing for careers in Web journalism; and the Returning Journalist track for mid-career journalists who enroll in a highly individualized course of study. The programs can be completed in as little as twelve months. Master's students may choose to do a thesis.

All master's students, except the returning journalists, spend a capstone semester reporting from one of the College's news operations. PAR students spend a semester in Washington, D.C., or Maryland's state capital, Annapolis, participating in Capital News Service (CNS). Working with faculty editors, students report and write stories each day. Bylined CNS stories are published in virtually every daily newspaper in Maryland and Washington, D.C., including the *Washington Post* and the *Baltimore Sun.*

Broadcast students learn at UMTV, the College's cable TV station. In their last semester, students enroll in Capital News Service and serve as field reporters, producers, writers, and anchors for *Maryland Newsline*, a nightly news show airing on UMTV and carried on cable to more than 600,000 homes in Maryland.

Students interested in online journalism work at the Maryland Newsline Web site in the Capital News Service Online Bureau (http://www.newsline.umd.edu). They divide their time between original reporting for the site and editing and producing packages from the broadcast and print bureaus.

The three-year Ph.D. program produces scholars in journalism and media studies.

Research Facilities

McKeldin Library has 1.6 million volumes and more than 2.3 million microfiche and microfilm units available. The library's online researching system can be accessed 24 hours a day, seven days a week. Hornbake Library houses the nonprint media division, which includes a wide array of documentaries and news programs, including the Library of American Broadcasting and the National Public Broadcasting Archives. In the Journalism Building, students have access to LexisNexis, the Associated Press and McClatchy-Tribune news wires, e-mail, and the Internet. The College houses three computer laboratories for newswriting classes, a new media lab, and computer-assisted journalism and research facilities. Newsrooms in the National Press Building in Washington, D.C., and near the State House in Annapolis are available as part of Capital News Service. The College also offers students a broadcast newsroom at UMTV, the University's cable television station, which includes state-of-the-art television control rooms, studios, editing booths, and field cameras.

Financial Aid

Seventy percent of all full-time Maryland graduate students receive financial support, which may include remission of tuition, graduate assistantships, work-study, and fellowships. University fellowships are awarded to incoming master's and doctoral students on the basis of academic excellence. Fellows receive tuition remission up to 12 credits per semester and annual stipends starting at $14,000. Teaching, research, and administrative assistantships include tuition remission of up to 10 credits per semester and stipends starting at $13,000 per year. Financial support is also available through the College.

The *Washington Post* funds the Howard Simons Fellowship for a master's student who is a member of a minority group and is interested in a newspaper career. The Reuters Fellowship, funded by the international news service, is for a master's student who is a person of color or who has a disability and is interested in a business journalism career. The UCG Graduate Fellowship is for master's students with a background or interest in business reporting. The Eleanor Merrill Fellowships offer various amounts of funding to incoming master's students. The Scripps Howard Foundation Fellowship is offered to an outstanding professional journalist to study in the Ph.D. program. The Gridiron Fellowship is awarded to an incoming master's student, with preference given to students from populations underrepresented in the journalism profession.

Cost of Study

In-state tuition for the 2008–09 academic year is $444 per credit. Out-of-state tuition is $958 per credit. Mandatory fees are about $570 per semester.

Living and Housing Costs

There is limited on-campus graduate housing available; more information can be found at http://www.graduatehills.com/. There is also plenty of off-campus housing nearby in Washington, D.C., and its suburbs. Additional information is available from the Graduate Student Union at http://www.union.umd.edu/GH/basic_needs/graduate_housing.html.

Student Group

There were 78 graduate students in the College last year: 49 master's students and 29 Ph.D. students. Of those, 54 percent were women and 27 percent were members of minority groups.

Location

The University of Maryland is located 8 miles from Washington, D.C., a news center of the world. The city is easily accessible by the Metro subway system, which stops at the campus.

The College

The University established a journalism department in 1947 and in 1972 opened the College of Journalism, which was renamed in honor of media executive Philip Merrill in 2001. The College has gained distinction by blending prize-winning journalists, world-class media scholars, and nationally recognized professional programs. The College publishes *American Journalism Review* and is home to three programs designed to help visiting professionals improve journalism: the Knight Center for Specialized Journalism, the Hubert H. Humphrey Journalism Fellowship program for international journalists, and the Journalism Center on Children and Families. The College is also home to the American Association of Sunday and Feature Editors. The College's Board of Visitors includes former CBS News anchor Walter Cronkite, *Washington Week* moderator Gwen Ifill, *Los Angeles Times* Washington bureau chief Doyle McManus, Pulitzer Prize–winning columnist William Raspberry, NPR vice president Jay Kernis, CBS-TV sports reporter Bonnie Bernstein, and *Washington Post* publisher Bo Jones.

Applying

All applicants must submit GRE scores and international applicants must submit TOEFL results. Most successful applicants have an undergraduate GPA of at least 3.0 and competitive GRE scores. The College admits one master's and one doctoral cohort per year. Doctoral students begin their studies in the fall; master's students have the option of beginning in the summer or fall. There is no spring class admitted to the College. The deadline for international students to apply is January 30. The deadline to be considered for financial aid is February 1. For U.S. citizens not applying for financial aid, the deadline is March 1.

Correspondence and Information

Graduate Office
Philip Merrill College of Journalism
1117 Journalism Building
University of Maryland
College Park, Maryland 20742-7111

Phone: 301-405-2380
Fax: 301-314-9166
E-mail: jourgrad@deans.umd.edu
Web site: http://www.journalism.umd.edu

University of Maryland, College Park

THE FACULTY AND THEIR TEACHING AND RESEARCH INTERESTS

Sandy Banisky, Abell Professor in Baltimore Journalism; J.D., Baltimore. Former city, statehouse, and national reporter; former deputy managing editor at the *(Baltimore) Sun*.
Maurine Hoffman Beasley, Professor; Ph.D., George Washington. Former reporter and editor with the *Kansas City Star* and the *Washington Post*; author and editor of several books, including *The Eleanor Roosevelt Encyclopedia* and *Taking Their Place: A Documentary History of Women and Journalism*. Mass media reporting, history of journalism, women in journalism.
Kevin Blackistone, Shirley Povich Chair in Sports Journalism; M.A., Boston University. Former columnist, the *Dallas Morning News*; commentator, AOLSports, ESPN, NPR, and the *Politico*. Journalism history, press integration, news coverage of societal disparities.
Alice Bonner, Lecturer; Ph.D., North Carolina. Former director of journalism education for the *Freedom Forum*, former reporter and editor for the *Washington Post* and *USA Today*. Journalism history, press integration, news coverage of societal disparities.
David S. Broder, Professor; M.A., Chicago. Reporter and syndicated columnist for the *Washington Post*. Pulitzer Prize winner. Author of seven books, including *Democracy Derailed: Initiative Campaigns and the Power of Money*. Political reporting and press-government relationship.
Ira Chinoy, Associate Professor; A.B., Harvard. Pulitzer Prize winner. Former director of computer-assisted reporting at the *Washington Post*, former reporter for the *Providence Journal* (Rhode Island). Media and technology, computer-assisted reporting.
Cassandra Clayton, Lecturer and Director of Capital News Service broadcast bureau; B.A., Spelman. Former correspondent for NBC News and ABC News/Lifetime; substitute anchor of *NBC Nightly News, Sunrise*, and *Today*. Former anchor, CNBC's *The Real Story* and contributor to BET and MSNBC.
Reese Cleghorn, Professor; M.A., Columbia. Former associate editor of the *Detroit Free Press* and the *Atlanta Journal* and editorial page editor of the *Charlotte Observer*. Editorial writing, coverage of civil rights.
Adrianne Flynn, Lecturer and Director of Washington, D.C., Reporting Program; B.A., Arizona State. Former Capitol Hill reporter for the *Arizona Republic;* reporter for the *Washington Times*, the *Mesa Tribune* (Arizona), and the *Dayton Daily News* (Ohio).
Jon Franklin, Professor and Merrill Chair; B.S., Maryland. Two-time Pulitzer Prize winner. Former reporter for the *(Baltimore) Evening Sun*. Author of five books, including *Writing for Story*. Literary nonfiction writing, science writing, writing complex stories.
Douglas Gomery, Professor Emeritus; Ph.D., Wisconsin. Resident scholar, Library of American Broadcasting; contributor to national publications *(Modern Maturity, Village Voice);* former senior scholar at Woodrow Wilson International Center for Scholars; author of ten books and more than 400 articles. Media economics and media history.
Christopher Hanson, Associate Professor; Ph.D., North Carolina. Former Washington correspondent for Reuters and the *Seattle Post-Intelligencer*, where he was a Pulitzer Prize nominee in 1990. Media ethics, journalism history, public affairs reporting.
Christine Harvey, Lecturer and editor of *Maryland Newsline*, the College's online newsmagazine; B.S., Maryland. Former managing editor for *American Journalism Review;* former associate Metro editor at *washingtonpost.com;* former reporter and editor for the *Washington Times*.
Ray E. Hiebert, Professor Emeritus; Ph.D., Maryland. Founding Dean of College, former director of the American Journalism Center in Budapest, editor of *Public Relations Review*, author of a number of books on journalism and mass media. International communication, media developments in Hungary and Eastern Europe, government-media relations, mass media in society, public relations.
Diana Huffman, *Baltimore Sun* Distinguished Lecturer; J.D., Georgetown. Former managing editor of the *National Journal*, former editor of the *Legal Times*, former press/outreach coordinator for the President's Commission on White House Fellowships. Editing, press law.
Haynes Johnson, Professor and Knight Chair; M.A., Wisconsin. Former reporter, editor, and columnist for the *Washington Star* and the *Washington Post;* Pulitzer Prize winner; author of thirteen books; commentator for the *NewsHour with Jim Lehrer*. Political journalism, history of mass communication in America.
Susan Kopen Katcef, Lecturer; B.A., Maryland. Former news anchor and reporter for WBAL Radio, Baltimore; former general assignment reporter for WJZ Television, Baltimore; former statehouse reporter and producer for Maryland Public Television. Broadcast news.
Rafael Lorente, Lecturer and Director, Capital News Service Annapolis Bureau; M.A., Maryland. Former reporter, the *Miami Herald;* former Washington correspondent, *South Florida Sun-Sentinel*.
Katherine C. McAdams, Associate Professor; Ph.D., North Carolina. Former public information director and research associate, staff writer for the *Durham Morning Herald* (North Carolina), coauthor of *Reaching Audiences: A Guide to Media Writing*. Women in journalism, language effects of journalism.
Susan Moeller, Associate Professor; Ph.D., Harvard. Author of *Compassion Fatigue: How the Media Sell Disease, Famine, War and Death* and *Shooting War: Photography and the American Experience of Combat*. U.S. and global media affairs, visual communications, online news.
Deborah Nelson, Carnegie Visiting Professor; J.D., DePaul. Pulitzer Prize winner at the *Seattle Times;* former investigative editor at the *Washington Post* and the *Los Angeles Times;* former president, Investigative Reporters and Editors. Leads the College's Carnegie University Seminar.
John Newhagen, Associate Professor; Ph.D., Stanford. Former UPI bureau chief, El Salvador; UPI Latin American Bureau, Miami; Foreign Desk, Washington. Research methods; effects of emotion-laden media messages, especially in television news and on the Internet.
Leonard Pitts Jr., Visiting Professor; B.A., USC. Nationally syndicated columnist, Pulitzer Prize winner for commentary in the *Miami Herald;* author of *Becoming Dad: Black Men and the Journey to Fatherhood*. Commentary and cultural criticism.
Eugene L. Roberts Jr., Professor; B.A., North Carolina. Pulitzer Prize winner for *The Race Beat*, former civil rights and war correspondent and managing editor for the *New York Times*, former executive editor for the *Philadelphia Inquirer*. The press and the civil rights movement, narrative writing, newsroom management, journalism ethics.
Carol L. Rogers, Lecturer and Director of Doctoral and Research Studies; Ph.D., Maryland. Former head of Office of Communications, American Association for the Advancement of Science; editor for the journal *Science Communication*. Mass communication, science communication.
George Solomon, Shirley Povich Professor of Sports Journalism; B.S., Florida. Current columnist and former sports editor, the *Washington Post;* ombudsman for ESPN; coeditor, *All those Mornings At The Post: The Twentieth Century in Sports*. Sports journalism.
Linda Steiner, Professor; Ph.D. Illinois. Author of *Conceptions of Gender in Reporting Textbooks, 1890-1990;* coauthor of *And Baby Makes Two* and *Women and Journalism*. Published twenty book chapters and numerous refereed articles. Editor of *Critical Studies Media Communication;* coeditor, *Critical Readings: Gender and Media*. Media ethics, history, public journalism, gender and media.
Carl Sessions Stepp, Professor; M.A., South Carolina. Contributor to many national magazines and newspapers; former national editor and cover story editor for *USA Today*; senior editor, *American Journalism Review*. Reporting, editing, analysis of newspaper performance, mass media and society.
Lee Thornton, Professor, Richard Eaton Chair in Broadcast Journalism, Interim Dean, and President, *American Journalism Review;* Ph.D., Northwestern. Former CBS News White House correspondent, National Public Radio program host, and CNN producer. Broadcast journalism.
Leslie Walker, Knight Visiting Professor in Digital Innovation; M.A., Virginia. Former reporter, the *Baltimore Evening Sun*; former vice president and editor, *washingtonpost.com*; former columnist, the *Washington Post*.
Ron Yaros, Assistant Professor; Ph.D., Wisconsin–Madison. Director, Lab for Communicating Complexity Online; author, *Communicating Complex News*; senior editor, *American Journalism Review*. Broadcast journalism, selection and reception of content in Web and mobile media, processing complex news messages.
Eric J. Zanot, Associate Professor; Ph.D., Illinois. Formerly with Doyle Dane Bernbach advertising agency and consultant to other agencies. Advertising, with special interests in advertising regulation and ethics.

Adjunct Faculty
Myron Beckenstein, former foreign desk editor, *Baltimore Sun*.
Patrick Boyle, editor, *Youth Today* magazine.
Denise Cabrera, former AP Maryland bureau chief.
Albert Calogero, producer/editor, WUSA-TV.
Marlene Cimons, former Washington correspondent, the *Los Angeles Times*.
Merrilee Cox, former Washington bureau chief, *ABC Radio News*.
John Davidson, consultant, former photo editor, the *Dallas Morning News*.
Crystal Davis, copy editor, *McClatchy-Tribune*.
Karen Dinsenbacher, features editor, *McClatchy-Tribune*.
Lucinda Fleeson, curator of the Hubert Humphrey Fellows Journalism Program and former investigative reporter, *Philadelphia Inquirer*.
Michael Flynn, reporter, WRC-TV.
Tom Frank, Washington correspondent, *Newsday*.
Jay Goldman, editor, the *School Administrator*.
Frank Greve, editor, *McClatchy-Tribune*.
Scott Higham, Pulitzer Prize–winning investigative reporter, *Washington Post*.
Tim Jacobsen, freelance photographer.
Glen Justice, former reporter, *New York Times*.
George Lanum, news editor, *Washington Times*.
Jeff Lemberg, former managing editor, *Presstime* magazine.
David Lightman, Washington Bureau Chief, *Hartford Courant*.
Robert Guy Matthews, reporter, *Wall Street Journal*.
Robbie Morganfield, former executive director, *Freedom Forum Diversity Institute*.
Blake Morrison, reporter, *USA Today*.
Alexandra Newman, multimedia producer, *USA Today*.
Sharon O'Malley, freelance writer.
January Payne, editor, *U.S. News & World Report*.
Christina Pino-Marina, reporter and videojournalist, *washingtonpost.com*.
Chris Rukan, layout editor, sports, the *Washington Post*.
Mary Shaffrey, Washington correspondent, *Winston-Salem Journal* (North Carolina).
David Silverstein, former news director, WMAR-TV.
Joseph Weber, metro editor, *Washington Times*.
Cindy Wright, freelance writer and former group news director, Sinclair Broadcast Group.
Jon Wile, news editor, the *Washington Post*.
Corinna Zarek, Freedom of Information Director, the Reporter's Committee for Freedom of the Press.

UNIVERSITY OF MIAMI

School of Communication

Programs of Study

The School of Communication offers both master's- and doctoral-level graduate programs. The Ph.D. in communication is based on advanced research in a variety of academic specializations, all of which allow for individualized degree programs. Thesis and nonthesis M.A. programs are available in communication studies, public relations, broadcast journalism, print journalism, and film studies; M.F.A. programs are offered in motion picture production, producing, and screenwriting. In addition, the School offers a uniquely designed, nonthesis M.A. program in journalism taught entirely in Spanish. The graduate programs in journalism (including the Spanish program) and broadcast journalism can be completed in a twelve-month time frame.

Research Facilities

With the spring 2007 opening of the International Building, the School has more than 85,000 square feet of digital "smart" learning space and resources. The complex includes two teleconference facilities with simultaneous translation capability. The School also operates a news bureau, two television studios, and a sound stage. The School manages UMTV (a cable television station) and a converged multimedia news bureau (in which students write for regional and national newspapers and magazines) as well as the Bill Cosford Cinema, which regularly exhibits the School's archival collection of more than 3,000 35-mm and 70-mm classic and contemporary films. In addition, the campus supports WVUM-FM and the *Miami Hurricane* (a twice-weekly newspaper that is distributed campuswide). As Miami is a major media center, opportunities for graduate-level practicum experience are available. The University houses ample research-support resources.

The Knight Center for International Media is a newly established research-and-development program that houses the Knight Chairs in Visual Journalism and Cross Cultural Communication. The center provides numerous research opportunities and access to a network of international scholars who participate in the center's programs and activities.

Financial Aid

The School offers a limited number of scholarships and assistantships; the latter provide tuition remission as well as a stipend, which is considered earned income for tax purposes. A full range of loans and work-study opportunities are available. On- and off-campus employment opportunities exist for students and their spouses. The majority of graduate students receive some form of financial aid. International students are eligible for assistantships.

Cost of Study

Tuition for all programs is $1424 per credit. The cost of materials varies by program. Students choosing the M.F.A. degree with the production emphasis may receive free film and processing for their projects.

Living and Housing Costs

Graduate students find apartments off campus for approximately $650 to $800 per month. Public transportation to and from the campus is convenient and affordable.

Student Group

The University enrolls approximately 15,000 students (undergraduates and graduates). The School of Communication enrolls approximately 1,300 undergraduate and 150 graduate students. This number includes students from all fifty states and from more than 100 countries.

Student Outcomes

School of Communication alumni include producers, writers, directors, and cinematographers for *Nip/Tuck, The Closer, Millennium, The Pretender, NYPD Blue,* and *Frasier;* editors for *Biography,* CNN, and WAMI; CEOs for MGM networks and WFLD-TV Chicago; anchors for ESPN and WTVJ-TV; and editors/columnists for newspapers across the country that include the *Miami Herald,* the *Washington Post,* and the *Los Angeles Times.*

Location

The University of Miami is located in the heart of Coral Gables, a historic suburb of Miami. Built in the 1920s as one of the first planned communities in the United States, Coral Gables is a striking blend of Mediterranean architecture and tropical beauty. Ten minutes north of the campus by Metrorail is Miami—a world center for international commerce and finance. Cultural activities in Miami, Miami Beach, Coconut Grove, and Coral Gables abound; ballet, opera, art exhibitions, theater productions, and concerts are available throughout the year. The Miami Film Festival presents an array of international films. Greater Miami is also home to Division I intercollegiate athletics as well as NHL, major-league baseball, NFL, and NBA sports. The year-round warm, sunny, tropical climate and the proximity to beaches, the Everglades, and the Florida Keys allow for numerous outdoor activities.

The University and The School

Since its founding in 1926, the University of Miami has become the largest, most comprehensive private institution of higher learning in the Southeast. Among such institutions in the United States, it ranks fifty-second in federally funded research. The 260-acre Coral Gables campus is home to most undergraduate study and serves as the University's administrative center. Graduate studies in education, engineering, the humanities, international studies, law, music, the social sciences, and the natural sciences are also based at this campus, as are a number of highly specialized research centers.

The School's 55 full-time and 21 part-time faculty members are an ideal mix of scholars and professionals in their fields. During their tenure, they have received several distinguished awards, including the Pulitzer Prize, Oscars, and Emmys. Several have been cited as "Educator of the Year" by their respective professional groups; others have been named Fulbright Scholars. They have authored scholarly books and articles as well as book and film reviews. Many have produced and directed feature films and documentaries and authored screenplays for television and film.

Applying

To obtain application materials and information, students should contact the School. The Ph.D. application deadline is December 1. The application deadline for the communication studies, public relations, print journalism, television broadcast journalism, film studies, and motion pictures M.F.A. programs is December 1. The financial aid deadline is March 1. The assistantship application deadline is December 1.

Correspondence and Information

Graduate Studies Office
School of Communication
University of Miami
P.O. Box 248127
Coral Gables, Florida 33124-2105

Phone: 305-284-5236
Fax: 305-284-8701
E-mail: socgrad@miami.edu
Web site: http://com.miami.edu

University of Miami

THE FACULTY AND THEIR TEACHING AREAS

Anthony T. Allegro, Professor of Motion Pictures; Ph.D. (Hispanic studies, specializing in twentieth century fiction and theater); Massachusetts.
Grace Barnes, Associate Professor of Motion Pictures; M.F.A. (film and television production), UCLA.
Andrew Barton, Lecturer in Broadcast Journalism and Media Management; M.A. (journalism), Ohio State.
Michael J. Beatty, Assistant Professor of Communication Studies; Ph.D. (speech education), Ohio State.
Rich Beckman, Professor of Visual Journalism and John S. and James L. Knight Chair in Visual Journalism; M.A., Minnesota.
Terry Adams Bloom, Assistant Professor of Electronic Media, Broadcast Journalism, and Media Management; Ph.D. (television production), North Carolina.
Stephen Bowles, Professor of Motion Pictures; Ph.D. (film history and theory), Northwestern.
Shannon B. Campbell, Assistant Professor of Public Relations; Ph.D. (journalism studies), Texas at Austin.
Sanjeev Chatterjee, Vice Dean, Associate Professor, and Executive Director of Knight Center for International Media; M.F.A. (television production), CUNY, Brooklyn.
Paul Driscoll, Program Director of Electronic Media, Broadcast Journalism, and Media Management; Ph.D. (mass communication), Indiana.
Darlene Drummond, Assistant Professor of Communication Studies; Ph.D. (health communication), Ohio State.
Michel Dupagne, Associate Professor of Electronic Media, Broadcast Journalism, and Media Management; Ph.D. (mass communication), Indiana.
Leonardo Ferreira, Associate Dean, Director of Graduate Studies, and Associate Professor of Electronic Media, Broadcast Journalism, and Media Management; Ph.D. (mass media), Michigan State.
Bruce Garrison, Professor of Journalism; Ph.D. (journalism), Southern Illinois Carbondale.
Valerie Giroux, Lecturer in Communication Studies; Ph.D. (educational leadership/administration), Miami (Florida).
Lisa Gottlieb, Assistant Professor of Motion Pictures; M.F.A. (creative writing), Antioch.
Kim Grinfeder, Assistant Professor of Visual Journalism; M.F.A. (interactive telecommunications), NYU.
Sam Grogg, Dean and Professor of Motion Pictures; Ph.D. (popular culture and film), Bowling Green State.
S. L. Harrison, Associate Professor of Advertising and Public Relations; Ph.D. (advertising and public relations), American.
Robert Hosmon, Vice Dean of Advancement and External Affairs; Ph.D. (English), Arizona State.
Sallie Hughes, Assistant Professor of Journalism and Photography; Ph.D. (Latin American studies),Tulane.
Konstantina Kontaxis, Assistant Professor of Motion Pictures; M.F.A. (film production), Ohio.
Alyse Lancaster, Program Director and Associate Professor of Advertising; Ph.D. (mass communication), Florida.
Christina Lane, Assistant Professor of Motion Pictures; Ph.D. (radio, TV, and film), Texas.
Loup Langton, Associate Professor of Visual Journalism; Ph.D., Texas.
Paul N. Lazarus III, Professor of Motion Pictures; J.D., Yale.
Rafael Lima, Lecturer in Motion Pictures; B.F.A. (screenwriting), El Prado (Spain).
Ronald Mangravite, Assistant Professor of Motion Pictures; M.F.A. (screenwriting), UCLA.
Walter McDowell, Associate Professor of Media Management; Ph.D. (broadcasting), Florida.
Diane Millette, Program Director and Associate Professor of Communication Studies; Ed.D. (instructional communication), West Virginia.
Ileana Oroza, Lecturer in Journalism; M.A. (English literature), North Carolina.
Victoria Orrego-Dunleavy, Assistant Professor of Communication Studies; Ph.D., Michigan State.
Edward J. Pfister, Professor Emeritus of Electronic Media, Broadcast Journalism, and Media Management; M.A. (broadcast management and public communication), Seton Hall.
William D. Rothman, Professor of Motion Pictures; Ph.D. (philosophy), Harvard.
Michelle Seelig, Assistant Professor of Journalism and Photography; Ph.D. (mass communication), Florida State.
Mitchell Shapiro, Professor and Director of Honors Programs, Electronic Media, Broadcast Journalism, and Media Management; Ph.D. (mass communication), Florida State.
John Chase Soliday, Associate Professor of Motion Pictures; Ph.D. (theater), Minnesota.
Gonzalo Soruco, Associate Professor of Advertising and Public Relations; Ph.D. (mass communication), Indiana.
Cornelia Splichal, Lecturer in Advertising and Public Relations; Ph.D. candidate, Miami (Florida).
Sigman Splichal, Program Director and Associate Professor of Journalism and Photography; Ph.D. (communication), Florida.
Don Stacks, Program Director and Professor of Public Relations; Ph.D. (communication studies), Florida.
Randy Stano, Professor of Visual Journalism; M.A. (visual journalism), Syracuse.
David Steinberg, Lecturer in Communication Studies; M.A. (speech communication and debate), Tennessee.
Thomas Steinfatt, Professor of Communication Studies; Ph.D. (communication theory), Michigan State.
Jeffrey Stern, Lecturer in Motion Pictures; B.F.A. (film production and postproduction), Philadelphia.
Edmund Talavera, Associate Professor of Motion Pictures; M.F.A. (film production, cinematography), NYU.
Sam Terilli, Assistant Professor of Journalism; J.D. (journalism and law), Michigan.
Donn Tilson, Associate Professor of Advertising and Public Relations; Ph.D. (public relations), Stirling.
Joseph Treaster, Professor of Journalism and John S. and James L. Knight Chair in Cross Cultural Communication; M.S., Columbia.
Wan-Hsiu "Sunny" Tsai, Assistant Professor of Advertising; Ph.D. (advertising), Texas at Austin.
Jim Virga, Lecturer in Visual Journalism; M.A. (visual arts and communication), Syracuse.
Tsitsi Wakhisi, Associate Professor of Professional Practice and Journalism; M.S.J. (journalism), Northwestern.
Phil Wilett, Lecturer in Advertising; M.A. (advertising), Florida.

On the campus of the University of Miami.

UNIVERSITY OF SOUTHERN CALIFORNIA

Annenberg School for Communication
School of Journalism
School of Communication

Programs In Communication, Journalism, Public Diplomacy, and Public Relations

Programs of Study

Through the School of Journalism and the School of Communication, the USC Annenberg School for Communication offers master's degrees in communication, communication management, global communication, journalism, public diplomacy, and strategic public relations and a Ph.D. in communication.

The School of Journalism, accredited by the Accrediting Council on Education of Journalism and Mass Communication (ACEJMC), offers traditional two-year M.A. programs in print journalism, broadcast journalism, online journalism, and strategic public relations and nine-month M.A. programs in specialized journalism and specialized journalism with an arts journalism emphasis. The School emphasizes hands-on training, ethics, and professional practice. In the traditional two-year journalism programs, an innovative core curriculum teaches newswriting, reporting, and production across three media platforms. After completing the core curriculum, students concentrate on advanced course work in print, broadcast, or online journalism. Student involvement is found in *Annenberg TV News*, for day-of-air broadcasting; *Impact*, for long-form storytelling; and *Annenberg Radio News*, for day-of-air radio broadcasting. The strategic public relations program equips students with the skills to succeed in agency, corporate, and nonprofit work. In the summer after the first year, students in journalism and strategic public relations may study and intern in Cape Town, Hong Kong, or London. In the nine-month specialized journalism programs, students focus on journalism leadership and decision making while completing course work in academic disciplines outside of journalism. In the specialized journalism (the arts) program, art practitioners and artists learn how to write for publications while advancing their academic exposure to the arts.

The School of Communication offers five master's degrees. Communication management students concentrate their studies in one of six tracks: entertainment, global health and social change, marketing, new communication technologies, corporate and strategic corporate communication, and politics, law, and policy communication. Course work is taught in the evening to accommodate students employed full-time during the day. Full-time graduate students complement their learning with internships or relevant work experience. Through the Charles Annenberg Weingarten Program on Online Communities (APOC), students learn to understand and manage the role of social networking. Global communication students complete the first year at the London School of Economics and Political Science and the second year at USC Annenberg. Public diplomacy students take course work from USC Annenberg and the USC School of International Relations. Students complete a summer field experience in the United States or abroad after completing their first year. Students in the M.A. and Ph.D. programs in communication focus their study in one of five areas: information and society; interpersonal and health communication; media, culture, and community; organizational communication; or rhetoric and political communication. Students acquire and demonstrate humanistic and behavioral knowledge of communication while acquiring the skills requisite to scholarly research in the discipline.

Research Facilities

The School is home to the Norman Lear Center for Entertainment Research, the Center for the Digital Future, and the Annenberg Center for Online Communities. It is also a partner with the Annenberg Center and the Schools of Cinema/Television and Engineering in USC's Integrated Media Systems Center, the nation's only university-based multimedia research center, which is funded by the National Science Foundation and the USC Center on Public Diplomacy (in partnership with the College of Letters, Arts, and Sciences).

The Strategic Public Relations Center plays a leading role in the continuing evolution and expansion of the public relations profession, bridging the substantial gap between the public relations profession and the academic community that studies it. A host of centers affiliated with the School of Journalism may be explored on the USC Annenberg Web site.

Financial Aid

Merit scholarships for master's degree students in communication management, journalism, public diplomacy, and strategic public relations are awarded competitively based on the graduate admission application. Global communication students apply for first-year financial support through the London School of Economics and Political Science. Ph.D. students receive full support for five years with University fellowships, graduate teaching assistantships, and research assistantships. Students should visit the USC Financial Aid Web site at http://www.usc.edu/admission/fa/applying_receiving/graduate/costs.html for details about applying for need-based federal financial aid.

Cost of Study

For the 2008–09 academic year, the estimated cost for full-time graduate student tuition and fees is $37,634. The costs of housing, board, books, supplies, and personal expenses vary. Additional expenses include health-center fees, and, for international students, health insurance coverage for each semester. Students should refer to the USC Financial Aid Web site for part-time graduate student estimated budgets.

Living and Housing Costs

USC maintains a number of apartment buildings for graduate students only. Housing applications are sent to admitted students only. Rates for privately owned apartments near USC and elsewhere in greater Los Angeles are comparable to those in other large metropolitan areas. For more information on University housing options and rates, prospective students should visit http://www.housing.usc.edu.

Student Group

USC Annenberg enrolls approximately 550 graduate students. Seventy percent of the students come from the United States, and 30 percent are international students. Some students enter the programs directly after earning the bachelor's degree; however, the majority of students have had some professional experience. The majority of Ph.D. students have completed a master's degree before enrolling at USC Annenberg. Most communication management students work or intern during the day, and many attend school part-time. Master's degree and Ph.D. students attend daytime and evening classes. Graduate student organizations are active in the community.

Student Outcomes

School of Journalism graduates work at many of the nation's leading media and public relations organizations, such as ABC, CBS, NBC, CNN, Ketchum Public Relations, Manning Selvage & Lee, Weber Shandwick Worldwide, Ogilvy & Mather, EXPN, C-SPAN, CNBC, KMEX, Telemundo, KWHY, AOL, varity.com, LATimes.com, eCompanies, WashingtonPost.com, and the Associated Press. Communication management and global communication program graduates pursue careers in marketing communications and public relations, mass media, multimedia and interactive media management, media research and analysis, entertainment management, telecommunications, law and public policy, corporate communications, nonprofit management, and consulting. Graduates work at firms such as Warner Bros., FOXSports.com, GameSpot.com, AOL, McKinsey, KPMG, Nestlé USA, DIRECTV, MGM, Pacific Bell, and ABC TV.

The majority of Ph.D. graduates pursue careers in academia at such institutions as Georgetown University, Johns Hopkins University, Michigan State University, North Carolina State University, Northwestern University, City University of Hong Kong, Tokyo University, and the Universities of Illinois, Indiana, Texas at Austin, and Wisconsin. Ph.D. graduates also work in research, strategic analysis, and consulting with firms such as NuStats, the Pacific Telesis Group, Jet Propulsion Laboratory, and Frank Magid Associates.

Location

USC is located in Los Angeles, California, one of the world's media and entertainment capitals. Proximity to leading newspapers, magazines, television stations, new media companies, and public relations organizations enables the School to have a large number of outstanding professionals on its faculty and to secure internships for students in a multiplicity of fields. Many opportunities exist to contact and interact with alumni and other professionals and senior management, and for research in such areas as interactive media, radio/television/film, telecommunications, information systems, public and government policy, corporate communication, and marketing.

The School

Home to approximately 1,900 graduate and undergraduate students and more than 73 full-time faculty members, the USC Annenberg School offers student career planning services, academic advising, international programs, and a host of speaking series to supplement classroom instruction.

Applying

All applicants must complete the online USC Graduate Admission Application with required supplemental materials, including a professional resume, a statement of purpose, writing samples, and letters of recommendation. Graduate Record Examinations (GRE) General Test scores are required for admission to all graduate degree programs, with the following exceptions: the GRE is not required for admissions to the global communication degree program, and the GMAT is accepted in lieu of the GRE for admission to the communication management degree program. Proof of English language proficiency is required if the student's native language is not English. Students should refer to the USC Annenberg Web site for graduate admission application guidelines for instructions.

Applicants to the M.A./M.Sc. in global communication program must complete the online USC Graduate Admission Application and the online London School of Economics and Political Science application.

Correspondence and Information

Admissions Office
Annenberg School for Communication
University of Southern California
3502 Watt Way, Suite 140
Los Angeles, California 90089-0281
Phone: 213-821-0770
Web site: http://www.annenberg.usc.edu/admission

University of Southern California

THE FACULTY AND THEIR RESEARCH

School of Journalism

Daniel H. Birman, M.A., Lecturer. Nonfiction/documentary producer, executive producer for USC Annenberg's *Impact.*

Laura Castañeda, M.A., Associate Professor of Professional Practice. Former AP reporter, business reporter, coeditor, coauthor.

William Celis, M.S., Associate Professor. Author of *Battle Rock: The Struggle Over a One-Room School in America's Vanishing West.* Former education correspondent, reporter, columnist.

Serena Cha, M.S., Director and Faculty Adviser, Annenberg TV News. Former TV producer.

Dana Chinn, M.B.A., Lecturer. Senior consultant, Media Insight Group.

Mike Chinoy, M.S., Visiting Professor. CNN's former senior Asia correspondent and bureau chief in Hong Kong and Beijing. Received duPont-Columbia, Peabody, and Emmy Awards for coverage of 1989 Tiananmen Square protests in China.

K. C. Cole, B.A., Professor. Science writer, columnist, editor, writer, author of seven books, including *The Universe and the Teacup: The Mathematics of Truth and Beauty.*

Marc Cooper, Lecturer and Associate Director, USC Annenberg Institute for Justice and Journalism. Senior editor, contributing editor, contributing writer, author of three nonfiction books, codirector of the News21 project.

Norman Corwin, B.A., Visiting Professor and Writer-in-Residence. Radio/television dramatist and writer of five stage plays and nineteen books.

Geoffrey Cowan, L.L.B., University Professor and Annenberg Family Chair in Communication Leadership. Communication law attorney, Emmy Award–winning producer, playwright, newspaper columnist.

Ed Cray, B.A., Professor. Journalist, author of eighteen books.

Patricia Dean, M.S., Professor of Professional Practice and Associate Director, School of Journalism. Former senior executive producer and television program director, consumer investigative news producer, and news show and investigative unit producer. Codirects the News21 project.

Jennifer Floto, M.A., Associate Professor of Professional Practice. Former vice president/creative director of Ketchum Public Relations, former vice president/group manager for Manning Selvage & Lee, Los Angeles.

Félix Gutiérrez, Ph.D., Professor. Former senior vice president of Freedom Forum and Newseum, author/coauthor of five books and more than fifty scholarly articles and book chapters on Latinos and other racial/ethnic groups.

Jay T. Harris, B.A., Professor and Wallis Annenberg Chair in Journalism and Democracy. Formerly chairman and publisher of the *San Jose Mercury News;* vice president of operations for Knight-Ridder Inc.; executive editor, *Philadelphia Daily News;* national correspondent and columnist.

Jonathan Kotler, J.D., Associate Professor. Attorney, coauthor, former dean of USC Graduate School.

Josh Kun, Ph.D., Berkeley, Associate Professor. Author, director of the Popular Music Project at Norman Lear Center. Research: music, popular culture, U.S.-Mexico border, race.

Judy Muller, B.A., Associate Professor. Commentator, author, former *ABC News* correspondent and *CBS News* correspondent and radio anchor.

Bryce Nelson, M. Phil., Professor. Former reporter, spokesman for Christopher Commission, and Director of School of Journalism.

Geneva Overholser, M.S., Director, School of Journalism. Award-winning journalist and media scholar, former editor, syndicated columnist, coeditor.

Tim Page, B.A., Visiting Professor. Chief music critic and culture writer for the *Washington Post,* Grammy Award nominee, author, winner of Pulitzer Prize in Criticism (1997).

Michael Parks, B.A., Professor and Director, School of Journalism. Former editor, executive vice president, vice president of Times Mirror Co., bureau chief, winner of Pulitzer Prize in International Reporting (1987).

Larry Pryor, M.S., Associate Professor. Founding editor of *Online Journalism Review;* former *Los Angeles Times* Web-site editor and newspaper writer, editor, and reporter. Research: New media topics.

Richard Reeves, M.E., Lecturer. Author of eleven books, syndicated columnist, former chief correspondent, national editor, magazine columnist, chief political correspondent.

Joe Saltzman, M.S., Professor. News and documentary writer/reporter/producer, author, director of the Image of the Journalist in Popular Culture project.

Stacy Scholder, B.A. Associate Director, *Annenberg TV News.* Former television producer, executive producer, news producer.

Philip Seib, J.D., Professor. Author of numerous books, coeditor. Research: international communication issues related to new media technologies, democratization, war, terrorism.

Willa Seidenberg, B.A., Lecturer and Director, *Annenberg Radio News.* Former radio reporter, anchor, producer, TV news writer, coauthor.

Erna Smith, B.A. Author of several studies on race and the media, former reporter, editor, and copy editor at several newspapers. Research: diversity issues in journalism, journalism education.

Roberto Suro, M.S., Professor and Director, Master of Arts in Specialized Journalism Program. Newspaper print journalist in foreign, domestic, and Washington coverage; author; founding director, Pew Hispanic Center. Research: Hispanic population.

Jerry Swerling, M.S., Professor of Professional Practice and Director, Strategic Public Relations Center. Principal of Swerling & Associates, Communications Management and Organizational Consulting.

Sandy Tolan, Associate Professor. Radio and print journalist, author, producer of radio documentaries and features.

Diane Winston, Ph.D., Associate Professor and Knight Chair in Media and Religion. Author, columnist, coeditor. Former newspaper reporter, television news writer, independent documentary filmmaker.

School of Communication

Jonathan D. Aronson, Ph.D., Professor. Cofounded Annenberg Research Network on International Communication. Research: communications policy, globalization, and international trade and trade negotiations. Former director, USC School of International Relations.

Sandra Ball-Rokeach, Ph.D., Associate Professor and Associate Dean for Faculty Affairs. Rockefeller and Fulbright Fellow. On editorial boards of a number of journals, coeditor of *Communication Research.* Research: transformation of urban communities.

Sarah Banet-Weiser, Ph.D., Associate Professor. Author and coeditor. Research: popular culture, media and consumer culture, with a focus on race, gender, and citizenship.

François Bar, Ph.D., Associate Professor and Director, Annenberg Research Network on International Communication. Research: continuing evolution of communication networks, including their deployment, regulation, and business use.

Daniela Baroffio-Bota, Ph.D., Senior Lecturer. Research: how feminism, U.S. militarism, and race in post-9/11 portrayals of female soldiers both consolidate traditional national ideologies and offer potential for resistance against patriarchal systems.

Manuel Castells, Ph.D., Professor and Wallis Annenberg Chair in Communication Technology and Society. Research: relationship between mass media, communication networks, and political power.

Peter Clarke, Ph.D., Professor. Author and former dean. Research: communication and health behavior; programs to improve the public's well-being, especially among underserved groups.

Michael J. Cody, Ph.D., Professor. Author and editor. Research: interpersonal communication and persuasion.

Jeffrey Cole, Ph.D., Research Professor and Director, Annenberg Center for the Digital Future. Research: effects of media policy, violence, and computer and Internet technology on all aspects of society. Founder/director of the twenty-country World Internet Project.

Geoffrey Cowan, L.L.B., University Professor and Annenberg Family Chair in Communication Leadership. Former director, *Voice of America;* communication law attorney; Emmy Award–winning producer, playwright, and newspaper columnist.

Nicholas Cull, Ph.D., Professor and Director, Master of Public Diplomacy Program. Author of numerous articles, including *Selling War,* one of *Choice* magazine's 10-best academic books of 1995.

Daniel Durbin, Ph.D., Senior Lecturer. Research: rhetoric of sports, health, fitness, nutrition, and medicine; promotion of health, fitness, and medicine in popular-press advertising.

Janet Fulk, Ph.D., Professor. Author. Research: impact of communication systems on collaboration and knowledge distribution across boundaries of space, time, team, organization, and nation.

G. Thomas Goodnight, Ph.D., Professor and Director, Doctoral Studies. Deliberation and postwar society, science communication, argument and aesthetics, public discourse.

Jerrold Green, Ph.D., Research Professor. Formerly with the RAND Corporation, a partner in Best-Associates, a merchant banking firm.

Larry Gross, Ph.D., Professor and Director, School of Communication. Author and editor. Research: media and culture, art and communication, visual communication, media portrayals of minorities.

Thomas A. Hollihan, Ph.D., Professor. Research: arguments that shape public policy and political discourse; including issues of citizenship and community in the postmodern age.

Andrea B. Hollingshead, Ph.D., Associate Professor. Research: strategic communication, knowledge sharing, social influence, decision making in teams and online communities.

Colleen Keough, Ph.D., Clinical Associate Professor. Strategic planning and financial management workshops in Central and Eastern Europe. Research: role of communications in conflict management.

Josh Kun, Ph.D., Associate Professor. Author of *Audiotopia;* directs the Popular Music Project at the Norman Lear Center. Research: music, popular culture, U.S.-Mexico border, race.

Randall Lake, Ph.D., Associate Professor. Writer. Research: contemporary rhetorical theory and practice, particularly political and public argumentation.

Ben Lee, Ph.D., Senior Lecturer. Sociologist and statistician. Research: human behavior in financial markets.

Kwan Min Lee, Ph.D., Assistant Professor. Author of "hot paper" in social sciences. Research: sociopsychological effects of new information and communication technologies, including human-computer and human-robot interaction.

Doe Mayer, Professor and Mary Pickford Chair, School of Cinematic Arts. Coauthor of *Creative Filmmaking From the Inside Out.* Research: practical international application of communication campaign strategies and designs for social issues and health-defined organizations.

Margaret McLaughlin, Ph.D., Professor. Key investigator at Integrated Media Systems Center. Research: use of virtual environments in delivery of health and social services.

Lynn C. Miller, Ph.D., Professor. Research: use of multidisciplinary approaches to create intelligent agents and virtual worlds for testing communication theory and enhancing health and educational outcomes.

Peter R. Monge, Ph.D., Professor. Coauthor and editor. Research: communication networks in a variety of social contexts, ecology of communication processes within organizational communities.

Sheila T. Murphy, Ph.D., Associate Professor. Research: relationship between emotion and cognition and their relative influence on judgments and beliefs, decision making, information processing, agenda setting, politics.

Stephen O'Leary, Ph.D., Associate Professor. Author. Research: religious communication, rhetorical theory, criticism.

Patricia Riley, Ph.D., Associate Professor and Director, M.A./M.Sc. in Global Communication Program. Author and consultant. Research: organizational communication, organizational politics, culture change, knowledge management.

Robert Scheer, Clinical Professor. Journalist and nationally syndicated columnist, author, editor, radio host.

Kenneth K. Sereno, Ph.D., Associate Professor. Research: communication theory, persuasion, interpersonal and family communication, humor's role in intimate relationships, effect of "clicker" technology in the classroom.

Christopher Smith, Ph.D., Senior Lecturer and Director, Johnson Communication Leadership Center. Research: modern financial markets and their impact on everyday culture, pop culture, entertainment's role in public diplomacy, convergence trends in media industries.

Stacy Smith, Ph.D., Associate Professor. Research: children's reactions to mass media, including developmental differences in emotional and cognitive processing; content patterns and effects of the media on youth.

Gordon Stables, Ph.D., Clinical Professor. Research: rhetoric and argumentation, policy debate and forensics, public debate surrounding the global war on terrorism.

Susan Resnick West, Ph.D. Author on performance appraisal, management of professional employees, and evaluation of strategic change efforts. Research: leadership, employee development, and evaluation to enable strategic change;

Dmitri Williams, Ph.D., Assistant Professor. Research: social and economic impacts of new media, with particular emphasis on video games and the Internet.

Ernest J. Wilson III, Ph.D., Professor and Walter Annenberg Chair in Communication. Research: politics of global sustainable innovation in high-tech industries, network inequality, China-Africa relations, and the role of culture in U.S. national security policy.

Section 17
Conflict Resolution and Mediation/Peace Studies

This section contains a directory of institutions offering graduate work in conflict resolution and mediation/peace studies, followed by in-depth entries submitted by institutions that chose to prepare detailed program descriptions. Additional information about programs listed in the directory but not augmented by an in-depth entry may be obtained by writing directly to the dean of a graduate school or chair of a department at the address given in the directory.

For programs offering related work, see also in this book *Political Science and International Affairs* and *Public, Regional, and Industrial Affairs.* In another guide in this series:

Graduate Programs in Business, Education, Health, Information Studies, Law & Social Work

See *Business Administration and Management* and *Law*

CONTENTS

Program Directory

Close-Ups

See also:

Conflict Resolution and Mediation/Peace Studies

Abilene Christian University, Graduate School, College of Arts and Sciences, Department of Conflict Resolution, Abilene, TX 79699-9100. Offers conflict resolution and reconciliation (MA, Certificate). *Faculty:* 6 part-time/adjunct (2 women). *Students:* 2 full-time (1 woman), 50 part-time (33 women); includes 3 minority (1 African American, 2 Hispanic Americans), 1 international. 69 applicants, 59% accepted, 39 enrolled. In 2007, 26 degrees awarded. *Application deadline:* Applications are processed on a rolling basis. Application fee: $40 ($45 for international students). Electronic applications accepted. *Expenses:* Tuition: Full-time $13,368; part-time $557 per hour. Required fees: $700; $34 per hour. $10 per semester. Tuition and fees vary according to degree level and campus/location. *Unit head:* Dr. Joe L. Cope, Graduate Adviser, 325-674-2015, Fax: 325-674-6966, E-mail: copej@acu.edu. *Application contact:* William Horn, Graduate Admissions Counselor, 325-674-2656, Fax: 325-674-6717, E-mail: gradinfo@acu.edu.

American Public University System, AMU/APU Graduate Programs, Charles Town, WV 25414. Offers air warfare (MA Military Studies); American Revolution (MA Military Studies); business administration (MBA); Civil War (MA Military Studies); criminal justice (MA); defense management (MA Military Studies); emergency and disaster management (MA); environmental policy and management (MS); fire science management (MA); global engagement (MA); history (MA); homeland security (MA); humanities (MA); intelligence (MA Military Studies, MA Strategic Intelligence); international peace and conflict resolution (MA); international relations and conflict resolution (MA); joint warfare (MA Military Studies); land warfare international perspective (MA Military Studies); management (MA); military history (MA); military leadership (MA Military Studies); national security studies (MA); naval warfare international (MA Military Studies); naval warfare US (MA Military Studies); political science (MA); public administration (MA); public health (MA); security management (MA); space studies (MS); special ops/LIC (MA Military Studies); sports management (MA); transportation and logistics management (MA); transportation management (MA); unconventional warfare (MA Military Studies); World War II (MA Military Studies). Programs offered via distance learning only. Part-time and evening/weekend programs available. Postbaccalaureate distance learning degree programs offered (no on-campus study). *Faculty:* 10 full-time (3 women), 188 part-time/adjunct (57 women). *Students:* 340 full-time (98 women), 3,567 part-time (790 women); includes 615 minority (317 African Americans, 28 American Indian/Alaska Native, 85 Asian Americans or Pacific Islanders, 185 Hispanic Americans), 20 international. Average age 36. 2,123 applicants, 100% accepted, 893 enrolled. In 2007, 829 degrees awarded. *Degree requirements:* For master's, comprehensive exam. *Entrance requirements:* For master's, bachelor's degree or equivalent, minimum GPA of 2.7 in last 60 hours of course work. *Application deadline:* Applications are processed on a rolling basis. Application fee: $0. Electronic applications accepted. *Expenses:* Tuition: Part-time $275 per semester hour. *Financial support:* Applicants required to submit FAFSA. *Faculty research:* Military history, criminal justice, management performance, national security. *Unit head:* Dr. Frank McCluskey, Provost, 877-468-6268, Fax: 304-724-3780. *Application contact:* Terry Grant, Director of Enrollment Management, 877-468-6268, Fax: 304-724-3780, E-mail: info@apus.edu.

American University, School of International Service, Washington, DC 20016-8001. Offers comparative and regional studies (MA); cross-cultural communication (Certificate); development management (MS); environmental policy (MA); ethics, peace, and global affairs (MA); global environmental policy (MA); international communication (MA); international development (MA); international development management (Certificate); international economic policy (MA); international economic relations (Certificate); international peace and conflict resolution (MA); international politics (MA); international relations (PhD); international service (MIS); the Americas (Certificate); U.S. foreign policy (MA); JD/MA; MBA/MA. Part-time and evening/weekend programs available. *Faculty:* 73 full-time (27 women), 34 part-time/adjunct (15 women). *Students:* 528 full-time (339 women), 355 part-time (218 women); includes 137 minority (39 African Americans, 2 American Indian/Alaska Native, 45 Asian Americans or Pacific Islanders, 51 Hispanic Americans), 119 international. Average age 27. 1,840 applicants, 66% accepted, 321 enrolled. In 2007, 347 master's, 5 doctorates, 12 other advanced degrees awarded. Terminal master's awarded for partial completion of doctoral program. *Degree requirements:* For master's, one foreign language, comprehensive exam, thesis or alternative; for doctorate, one foreign language, comprehensive exam, thesis/dissertation, research practicum; for Certificate, minimum 15 credit hours related course work. *Entrance requirements:* For master's, GRE General Test, 24 credits of course work in related social sciences, minimum GPA of 3.5, 2 letters of recommendation, bachelor's Degree, resumé, statement of purpose; for doctorate, GRE General Test, 2 letters of recommendation, 24 credits in related social sciences. Additional exam requirements/recommendations for international students: Required—TOEFL (minimum score 550 paper-based; 213 computer-based). *Application deadline:* For fall admission, 1/15 priority date for domestic students; for spring admission, 10/1 priority date for domestic students. Applications are processed on a rolling basis. Application fee: $50. *Expenses:* Tuition: Full-time $19,998; part-time $1,111 per credit hour. Required fees: $380. Tuition and fees vary according to program. *Financial support:* Career-related internships or fieldwork, Federal Work-Study, and institutionally sponsored loans available. Financial award application deadline: 1/15. *Faculty research:* International intellectual property, international environmental issues, international law and legal order, international telecommunications/technology, international sustainable development. *Unit head:* Dr. Louis W. Goodman, Dean, 202-885-1600, Fax: 202-885-2494. *Application contact:* Amanda Taylor, Director of Graduate Admissions and Financial Aid, 202-885-1599, Fax: 202-885-2494.

See Close-Up on page 1139.

The American University of Paris, Graduate Programs, Paris, France. Offers finance (MSF); global communications (MAGC); international affairs, conflict resolution and civil society development (MA); Middle Eastern and Islamic studies (MA); public administration (MPA). *Degree requirements:* For master's, thesis. *Entrance requirements:* For master's, minimum undergraduate GPA of 3.0.

Antioch University McGregor, Graduate Programs, Program in Conflict Resolution, Yellow Springs, OH 45387-1609. Offers MA. Part-time and evening/weekend programs available. Postbaccalaureate distance learning degree programs offered (minimal on-campus study). *Faculty:* 1 (woman) full-time, 4 part-time/adjunct (2 women). *Students:* 3 full-time (2 women), 32 part-time (22 women); includes 10 minority (8 African Americans, 2 Asian Americans or Pacific Islanders). Average age 43. 22 applicants, 86% accepted, 16 enrolled. In 2007, 20 degrees awarded. *Degree requirements:* For master's, thesis or alternative. *Entrance requirements:* For master's, resumé, 2 letters of reference. *Application deadline:* For fall admission, 8/15 for domestic and international students; for winter admission, 12/10 for domestic and international students; for spring admission, 3/8 for domestic and international students. Applications are processed on a rolling basis. Application fee: $50. Electronic applications accepted. *Expenses:* Contact institution. *Financial support:* Federal Work-Study available. Financial award applicants required to submit FAFSA. *Unit head:* Iris Weisman, Acting Chair, 937-769-1890, Fax: 937-769-1807, E-mail: iweisman@mcgregor.edu. *Application contact:* Rob McLaughlin, Enrollment Services Manager, 937-769-1816, Fax: 937-769-1804, E-mail: rmclaughlin@mcgregor.edu.

Arcadia University, Graduate Studies, Program in International Peace and Conflict Management, Glenside, PA 19038-3295. Offers MAIPCR. Part-time and evening/weekend programs available. *Degree requirements:* For master's, one foreign language. *Entrance requirements:* For master's, GRE. Additional exam requirements/recommendations for international students: Required—TOEFL. Expenses: Contact institution.

Associated Mennonite Biblical Seminary, Graduate and Professional Programs, Elkhart, IN 46517-1999. Offers Christian formation (MA); divinity (M Div); mission and evangelism (MA); peace studies (MA); theological studies (MA, Certificate). *Accreditation:* ACIPE; ATS. Part-time programs available. *Degree requirements:* For master's, comprehensive exam, thesis optional; for M Div, integration paper. *Entrance requirements:* For M Div, master's, and Certificate, 3 letters of reference. Additional exam requirements/recommendations for international students: Required—TOEFL (minimum score 550 paper-based; 213 computer-based). Electronic applications accepted. *Faculty research:* Biblical studies, theology, church history, church leadership.

Baker University, School of Professional and Graduate Studies, Program in Conflict Management and Dispute Resolution, Baldwin City, KS 66006-0065. Offers MA. Part-time and evening/weekend programs available. *Students:* 1 (woman) full-time, 5 part-time (4 women); includes 1 minority (African American) Average age 45. *Entrance requirements:* Additional exam requirements/recommendations for international students: Required—TOEFL (minimum score 600 paper-based; 250 computer-based). Application fee: $20. *Expenses:* Tuition: Full-time $10,800; part-time $100 per credit hour. Required fees: $130; $130 per year. Tuition and fees vary according to program. *Financial support:* Applicants required to submit FAFSA. *Application contact:* Dr. Cindy Hoss, Assistant Dean for Instruction and Curriculum, 913-491-4432, Fax: 913-491-0470, E-mail: choss@bakeru.edu.

Bethany Theological Seminary, Graduate and Professional Programs, Richmond, IN 47374-4019. Offers biblical studies (MA Th); ministry studies (M Div); peace studies (M Div, MA Th); theological studies (MA Th, CATS); youth ministry (M Div). *Accreditation:* ACIPE; ATS. Part-time programs available. Postbaccalaureate distance learning degree programs offered (minimal on-campus study). *Degree requirements:* For master's, thesis. *Entrance requirements:* For M Div, letters of reference, minimum GPA of 2.75; for master's, letters of reference, minimum GPA of 3.0. Additional exam requirements/recommendations for international students: Required—TOEFL (minimum score 550 paper-based; 218 computer-based).

Brandeis University, Graduate School of Arts and Sciences, Program in Coexistence and Conflict, Waltham, MA 02454-9110. Offers MA, MA/MA. *Faculty:* 3 full-time (1 woman), 2 part-time/adjunct (1 woman). *Students:* 26 full-time (15 women); includes 3 minority (1 African American, 2 Asian Americans or Pacific Islanders), 17 international. 81 applicants, 69% accepted, 13 enrolled. In 2007, 12 degrees awarded. *Degree requirements:* For master's, thesis, internship. *Entrance requirements:* For master's, 3 letters of recommendation, curriculum vitae, resumé. Additional exam requirements/recommendations for international students: Required—TOEFL (minimum score 600 paper-based; 250 computer-based; 100 iBT); Recommended—IELTS (minimum score 7). *Application deadline:* For winter admission, 1/31 priority date for domestic and international students. Applications are processed on a rolling basis. Application fee: $55. Electronic applications accepted. *Financial support:* In 2007–08, 16 students received support. Tuition waivers (partial) available. Financial award application deadline: 4/15; financial award applicants required to submit CSS PROFILE. *Unit head:* Dr. Mari Fitzduff, Director, 781-736-5001, Fax: 781-736-8561, E-mail: mfitzd@brandeis.edu. *Application contact:* Anne Gudaitis, Program Administrator, 781-736-8575, Fax: 781-736-8561, E-mail: gudaitis@brandeis.edu.

Brandeis University, Graduate School of Arts and Sciences, Program in Coexistence and Conflict and Sustainable International Development, Waltham, MA 02454-9110. Offers MA/MA. *Application contact:* David F. Cotter, Graduate School of Arts and Sciences, 781-736-3406, Fax: 781-736-3412, E-mail: cotter@brandeis.edu.

California State University, Dominguez Hills, College of Arts and Humanities, Program in Negotiation, Conflict Resolution and Peacebuilding, Carson, CA 90747-0001. Offers MA. Part-time and evening/weekend programs available. Postbaccalaureate distance learning degree programs offered (no on-campus study). *Faculty:* 5 full-time (3 women), 1 (woman) part-time/adjunct. *Students:* 30 full-time (20 women), 157 part-time (102 women); includes 58 minority (32 African Americans, 8 Asian Americans or Pacific Islanders, 18 Hispanic Americans), 4 international. 148 applicants, 82% accepted, 55 enrolled. In 2007, 31 degrees awarded. *Degree requirements:* For master's, portfolio. *Entrance requirements:* For master's, minimum GPA of 3.2, 3 letters of recommendation. *Application deadline:* For fall admission, 5/1 for domestic and international students; for spring admission, 12/1 for domestic and international students. Application fee: $55. Electronic applications accepted. *Faculty research:* Ethnic conflict, mediator ethics, teacher training, global conflict resolution (including role of ombuds), optimal multicultural process. *Unit head:* Dr. A. Marco Turk, Professor and Director, 310-243-3237, Fax: 310-516-4268, E-mail: amturk@csudh.edu. *Application contact:* Penny Ann LaBaun, Administrative Coordinator, 310-243-3237, Fax: 310-516-4268, E-mail: plabaun@csudh.edu.

Carleton University, Faculty of Graduate Studies, Faculty of Public Affairs and Management, Department of Law, Ottawa, ON K1S 5B6, Canada. Offers conflict resolution (Certificate); legal studies (MA). *Degree requirements:* For master's, thesis. *Entrance requirements:* For master's, honors degree. Additional exam requirements/recommendations for international students: Required—TOEFL. *Application deadline:* Applications are processed on a rolling basis. Application fee: $77 Canadian dollars. *Financial support:* Fellowships, teaching assistantships, institutionally sponsored loans, scholarships/grants, and unspecified assistantships available. *Faculty research:* Legal and social theory; women, law, and gender relations; law, crime, and social order; political economy of law; international law. *Unit head:* Peter Swan, Chair, 613-520-2600 Ext. 3690, Fax: 613-520-4467, E-mail: law@ccs.carleton.ca. *Application contact:* Ron Saunders, Graduate Supervisor, 613-520-2600 Ext. 3690, Fax: 613-520-4467, E-mail: law@cs.carleton.ca.

Chaminade University of Honolulu, Graduate Services, Program in Education, Honolulu, HI 96816-1578. Offers social science via peace education (M Ed). Part-time and evening/weekend programs available. Postbaccalaureate distance learning degree programs offered (minimal on-campus study). *Faculty:* 9 full-time (6 women), 19 part-time/adjunct (17 women). *Students:* 197 full-time (148 women), 127 part-time (97 women); includes 225 minority (19 African Americans, 1 American Indian/Alaska Native, 191 Asian Americans or Pacific Islanders, 14 Hispanic Americans), 2 international. Average age 35. 236 applicants, 81% accepted. In 2007, 102 degrees awarded. *Degree requirements:* For master's, thesis or alternative. *Entrance requirements:* For master's, minimum GPA of 2.75, 3 letters of recommendation. Additional exam requirements/recommendations for international students: Required—TOEFL (minimum score 550 paper-based). *Application deadline:* For fall admission, 9/15 priority date for domestic students; for winter admission, 12/15 priority date for domestic students; for spring admission, 3/1 priority date for domestic students. Applications are processed on a rolling basis. Application fee: $50. *Expenses:* Tuition: Part-time $490 per credit hour. *Financial support:* In 2007–08, 172 students received support. Career-related internships or fieldwork, Federal Work-Study, institutionally sponsored loans, scholarships/grants, and tuition waivers (partial) available. Support available to part-time students. Financial award application deadline: 3/1; financial award applicants required to submit FAFSA. *Faculty research:* Peace and curriculum education. *Unit head:* Dr. David Jelinek, Dean, 808-440-4251, Fax: 808-739-4607. *Application contact:* Gwen Samson, Secretary, Education Department, 808-739-4652, Fax: 808-739-4607, E-mail: med@chaminade.edu.

Columbia College, Graduate Programs, Department of Human Relations, Columbia, SC 29203-5998. Offers human behavior and conflict management (MA); interpersonal relations/conflict management (Certificate); organizational behavior/conflict management (Certificate). Part-time and evening/weekend programs available. Postbaccalaureate distance learning degree programs offered (minimal on-campus study). *Degree requirements:* For master's, thesis, practicum.

Conflict Resolution and Mediation/Peace Studies

Entrance requirements: For master's, GRE General Test, MAT, 2 letters of recommendation, valid teaching certificate, minimum GPA of 3.2. Additional exam requirements/recommendations for international students: Required—TOEFL. Electronic applications accepted. Expenses: Contact institution. *Faculty research:* Envisioning and the resolution of conflict, environmental conflict resolution, crisis negotiation.

Columbia University, School of Continuing Education, Program in Negotiation and Conflict Resolution, New York, NY 10027. Offers MS. Part-time programs available. *Entrance requirements:* For master's, 2 letters of recommendation, professional resum[00e9]. *Application deadline:* For fall admission, 6/16 for domestic students; for spring admission, 11/7 for domestic students. Application fee: $50. Electronic applications accepted. *Expenses:* Tuition: Part-time $1,452 per credit. Required fees: $152 per term. One-time fee: $75 part-time. Full-time tuition and fees vary according to course level, course load, degree level and program.

Cornell University, Graduate School, Graduate Fields of Architecture, Art and Planning, Field of Regional Science, Ithaca, NY 14853-0001. Offers environmental studies (MA, MS, PhD); international spatial problems (MA, MS, PhD); location theory (MA, MS, PhD); multiregional economic analysis (MA, MS, PhD); peace science (MA, MS, PhD); planning methods (MA, MS, PhD); urban and regional economics (MA, MS, PhD). *Faculty:* 20 full-time (3 women). *Students:* 22 full-time (10 women); includes 2 minority (1 African American, 1 Asian American or Pacific Islander), 20 international. Average age 31. 12 applicants, 83% accepted, 5 enrolled. In 2007, 2 master's, 1 doctorate awarded. Terminal master's awarded for partial completion of doctoral program. *Degree requirements:* For master's, thesis; for doctorate, comprehensive exam, thesis/dissertation. *Entrance requirements:* For master's and doctorate, GRE General Test, 2 letters of recommendation. Additional exam requirements/recommendations for international students: Required—TOEFL (minimum score 600 paper-based; 250 computer-based; 77 iBT). *Application deadline:* For fall admission, 1/15 priority date for domestic students. Application fee: $70. Electronic applications accepted. *Financial support:* In 2007–08, 5 students received support, including 1 fellowship with full tuition reimbursement available, 2 research assistantships with full tuition reimbursements available, 2 teaching assistantships with full tuition reimbursements available; institutionally sponsored loans, scholarships/grants, health care benefits, tuition waivers (full and partial), and unspecified assistantships also available. Financial award applicants required to submit FAFSA. *Faculty research:* Urban and regional growth, spatial economics, formation of spatial patterns by socioeconomic systems, non-linear dynamics and complex systems, environmental-economic systems. *Unit head:* Director of Graduate Studies, 607-255-6848, Fax: 607-255-1971. *Application contact:* Graduate Field Assistant, 607-255-6848, Fax: 607-255-1971, E-mail: regsci@cornell.edu.

Creighton University, School of Law, Program in Negotiation and Dispute Resolution, Omaha, NE 68178-0001. Offers MS, Certificate. Part-time and evening/weekend programs available. Postbaccalaureate distance learning degree programs offered (minimal on-campus study). *Students:* 22 full-time (11 women), 44 part-time (30 women). In 2007, 8 degrees awarded. *Degree requirements:* For master's, thesis or alternative, practicum. *Entrance requirements:* Additional exam requirements/recommendations for international students: Required—TOEFL. *Application deadline:* Applications are processed on a rolling basis. Application fee: $40. Electronic applications accepted. *Faculty research:* Nationalism/identity and conflict; health care collaboration; complex adaptive items and conflict engagement; history, memory and conflict; culture and conflict. *Unit head:* Prof. Arthur Pearlstein, Director and Professor of Law, 402-280-3853. *Application contact:* Prof. Jacquenline Font, Associate Director and Assistant Professor, 402-280-3883, E-mail: jnfont@creighton.edu.

Dallas Baptist University, College of Business, Business Administration Program, Dallas, TX 75211-9299. Offers accounting (MBA); business communication (MBA); conflict resolution management (MBA); e-business (MBA); entrepreneurship (MBA); finance (MBA); health care management (MBA); international business (MBA); management (MBA); management information systems (MBA); marketing (MBA); project management (MBA); technology and engineering management (MBA). *Accreditation:* ACBSP. Part-time and evening/weekend programs available. *Faculty:* 55 full-time (22 women), 114 part-time/adjunct (44 women). *Students:* 134 full-time, 335 part-time. 285 applicants, 59% accepted, 115 enrolled. In 2007, 148 degrees awarded. *Entrance requirements:* For master's, GMAT, minimum GPA of 3.0. Additional exam requirements/recommendations for international students: Required—TOEFL, IELTS. *Application deadline:* Applications are processed on a rolling basis. Application fee: $25. Electronic applications accepted. *Expenses:* Tuition: Full-time $9,144; part-time $508 per credit hour. *Financial support:* Federal Work-Study, institutionally sponsored loans, scholarships/grants, and tuition waivers (full and partial) available. Support available to part-time students. Financial award applicants required to submit FAFSA. *Faculty research:* Sports management, services marketing, retailing, strategic management, financial planning/investments. *Unit head:* Dr. Sandra S. Reid, Director, 214-333-5280, Fax: 214-333-5293, E-mail: graduate@dbu.edu. *Application contact:* Kit P. Montgomery, Director of Graduate Programs, 214-333-5242, Fax: 214-333-5579, E-mail: graduate@dbu.edu.

Dallas Baptist University, College of Business, Management Program, Dallas, TX 75211-9299. Offers business communication (MA); conflict resolution management (MA); general management (MA); health care management (MA); human resource management (MA). Part-time and evening/weekend programs available. *Faculty:* 55 full-time (22 women), 114 part-time/adjunct (44 women). *Students:* 20 full-time, 157 part-time. 61 applicants, 62% accepted, 28 enrolled. In 2007, 76 degrees awarded. *Entrance requirements:* For master's, GRE General Test, minimum GPA of 3.0. Additional exam requirements/recommendations for international students: Required—TOEFL, IELTS. *Application deadline:* Applications are processed on a rolling basis. Application fee: $25. Electronic applications accepted. *Expenses:* Tuition: Full-time $9,144; part-time $508 per credit hour. *Financial support:* Federal Work-Study, institutionally sponsored loans, scholarships/grants, and tuition waivers (full and partial) available. Support available to part-time students. Financial award applicants required to submit FAFSA. *Faculty research:* Organizational behavior, conflict personalities. *Unit head:* Candice L Armstrong, Director of Management Program, 214-333-5280, Fax: 214-333-5293, E-mail: graduate@dbu.edu. *Application contact:* Kit P. Montgomery, Director of Graduate Programs, 214-333-5242, Fax: 214-333-5579, E-mail: graduate@dbu.edu.

Duquesne University, Graduate School of Liberal Arts, Graduate Center for Social and Public Policy, Pittsburgh, PA 15282-1750. Offers conflict resolution and peace studies (Certificate); social and public policy (MA, Certificate). Programs are a collaboration between the Departments of Political Science and Sociology. Part-time and evening/weekend programs available. *Faculty:* 15 full-time (3 women), 1 (woman) part-time/adjunct. *Students:* 25 full-time (13 women), 17 part-time (12 women). Average age 27. In 2007, 11 degrees awarded. *Degree requirements:* For master's, thesis. *Entrance requirements:* For master's, GRE General Test. Additional exam requirements/recommendations for international students: Required—TOEFL. *Application deadline:* For fall admission, 4/30 priority date for domestic and international students; for spring admission, 10/31 priority date for domestic and international students. Applications are processed on a rolling basis. Application fee: $50. *Expenses:* Tuition: Part-time $774 per credit. Required fees: $74 per credit. Tuition and fees vary according to program. *Financial support:* In 2007–08, 20 students received support, including 12 research assistantships with full and partial tuition reimbursements available (averaging $9,000 per year), 4 teaching assistantships with full and partial tuition reimbursements available (averaging $9,000 per year); career-related internships or fieldwork, institutionally sponsored loans, scholarships/grants, tuition waivers (full and partial), and unspecified assistantships also available. Support available to part-time students. Financial award application deadline: 5/1. *Faculty research:* Program evaluation, environmental policy, criminal justice policy, health care policy. Total annual research expenditures: $30,000. *Unit head:* Dr. Joseph Yenerall, Director, 412-396-6485, Fax: 412-396-5265, E-mail: socialpolicy@duq.edu.

Eastern Mennonite University, Program in Conflict Transformation, Harrisonburg, VA 22802-2462. Offers MA, Graduate Certificate. Part-time programs available. *Faculty:* 4 full-time (2 women), 6 part-time/adjunct (3 women). *Students:* 39 full-time (19 women), 11 part-time (7 women); includes 2 minority (1 African American, 1 American Indian/Alaska Native), 23 international. Average age 35. 40 applicants, 100% accepted, 25 enrolled. In 2007, 35 master's, 7 other advanced degrees awarded. *Degree requirements:* For master's, practicum. *Entrance requirements:* For master's, minimum undergraduate GPA of 2.75. Additional exam requirements/recommendations for international students: Required—TOEFL (minimum score 550 paper-based; 213 computer-based). *Application deadline:* For fall admission, 2/15 priority date for domestic and international students. Applications are processed on a rolling basis. Application fee: $25. Electronic applications accepted. *Expenses: Contact institution.* Tuition and fees vary according to program. *Financial support:* In 2007–08, 4 students received support. Scholarships/grants available. Financial award application deadline: 6/30; financial award applicants required to submit FAFSA. *Faculty research:* Restorative justice, negotiation, security in an age of terror, trauma recovery, development, peace building. Total annual research expenditures: $30,000. *Unit head:* Dr. David Brubaker, Academic Director, 540-432-4423, Fax: 540-432-4449, E-mail: david.brubaker@emu.edu. *Application contact:* Janelle Myers-Benner, Administrative Assistant, 540-432-4986, Fax: 540-432-4449, E-mail: bennerj@emu.edu.

Florida International University, College of Education, Department of Educational Leadership and Policy Studies, Program in Conflict Resolution and Consensus Building, Miami, FL 33199. Offers Certificate. Part-time and evening/weekend programs available. *Entrance requirements:* Additional exam requirements/recommendations for international students: Required—TOEFL (minimum score 550 paper-based; 213 computer-based; 80 iBT), IELTS (minimum score 6). Electronic applications accepted. *Expenses:* Tuition, state resident: full-time $6,106. Tuition, nonresident: full-time $15,528. Required fees: $284. *Faculty research:* Workforce housing, labor conditions, labor organizations, workforce development.

Fresno Pacific University, Graduate Programs, Program in Peacemaking and Conflict Studies, Fresno, CA 93702-4709. Offers MA. Part-time and evening/weekend programs available. *Faculty:* 3 full-time (0 women). *Students:* Average age 41. 6 applicants, 67% accepted, 0 enrolled. In 2007, 1 degree awarded. *Degree requirements:* For master's, thesis. *Entrance requirements:* For master's, GMAT, MAT, GRE, interview, 2 writing samples. Additional exam requirements/recommendations for international students: Required—TOEFL (minimum score 550 paper-based; 213 computer-based). *Application deadline:* For fall admission, 7/15 for domestic and international students; for spring admission, 11/15 for domestic and international students. Applications are processed on a rolling basis. Application fee: $90. Electronic applications accepted. *Expenses:* Tuition: Full-time $7,470; part-time $415 per unit. *Financial support:* In 2007–08, 26 students received support. Career-related internships or fieldwork, scholarships/grants, and tuition waivers (full and partial) available. Support available to part-time students. Financial award applicants required to submit FAFSA. *Unit head:* Duane Ruth-Heffelbower, Director, 559-253-7202, Fax: 559-252-4800, E-mail: duane.ruth-heffelbower@fresno.edu.

George Mason University, Institute for Conflict Analysis and Resolution, Fairfax, VA 22030. Offers MS, PhD. Part-time and evening/weekend programs available. *Faculty:* 19 full-time (7 women), 14 part-time/adjunct (7 women). *Students:* 72 full-time (46 women), 138 part-time (92 women); includes 30 minority (15 African Americans, 6 Asian Americans or Pacific Islanders, 9 Hispanic Americans), 46 international. Average age 34. 390 applicants, 46% accepted, 93 enrolled. In 2007, 49 master's, 15 doctorates awarded. *Degree requirements:* For master's, thesis optional; for doctorate, one foreign language, comprehensive exam, thesis/dissertation, oral defense of dissertation. *Entrance requirements:* For master's, 3 recommendation letters; for doctorate, sample of written work, 2 recommendation letters. Additional exam requirements/recommendations for international students: Required—TOEFL (minimum score 575 paper-based; 230 computer-based; 88 iBT). *Application deadline:* For fall admission, 4/1 for domestic students, 1/15 for international students; for spring admission, 11/1 for domestic students. Application fee: $60. Electronic applications accepted. *Financial support:* In 2007–08, 29 students received support, including 3 fellowships, 15 research assistantships with partial tuition reimbursements available (averaging $11,500 per year), 1 teaching assistantship (averaging $10,500 per year); career-related internships or fieldwork, Federal Work-Study, scholarships/grants, and unspecified assistantships also available. Support available to part-time students. Financial award application deadline: 3/1; financial award applicants required to submit FAFSA. *Faculty research:* Preventive diplomacy, conflict/dispute resolution, peace/security, political violence, international terrorism. Total annual research expenditures: $90,000. *Unit head:* Dr. Sara Cobb, Director, 703-993-4453, Fax: 703-993-1302, E-mail: icarinfo@gmu.edu.

George Mason University, School of Public Policy, Program in Peace Operations, Fairfax, VA 22030. Offers MNPS. Part-time programs available. *Faculty:* 48 full-time (8 women), 41 part-time/adjunct (6 women). *Students:* 66. 44 applicants, 70% accepted, 22 enrolled. In 2007, 15 degrees awarded. *Degree requirements:* For master's, thesis or alternative. *Entrance requirements:* For master's, minimum undergraduate GPA of 3.0, 2 letters of recommendation, resumé, goals statement. Additional exam requirements/recommendations for international students: Required—TOEFL. *Application deadline:* For fall admission, 6/1 priority date for domestic students, 5/1 priority date for international students; for spring admission, 12/1 priority date for domestic students, 11/1 priority date for international students. Applications are processed on a rolling basis. Application fee: $60. Electronic applications accepted. *Expenses: Contact institution. Financial support:* Career-related internships or fieldwork, Federal Work-Study, scholarships/grants, and tuition waivers (partial) available. Support available to part-time students. Financial award application deadline: 3/1; financial award applicants required to submit FAFSA. *Unit head:* Dr. Allison Frendak-Blume, Director, 703-993-8099, E-mail: spp@gmu.edu. *Application contact:* Leslie Metzger Levin, Director of Graduate Admissions, 703-993-8099, Fax: 703-993-4876, E-mail: lmetzger@gmu.edu.

Georgetown University, Graduate School of Arts and Sciences, Department of Government, Program in Conflict Resolution, Washington, DC 20057. Offers MA. *Students:* 30 full-time (21 women), 6 part-time (3 women); includes 9 minority (1 African American, 7 Asian Americans or Pacific Islanders, 1 Hispanic American), 8 international. *Application contact:* Jennifer Counts, Program Coordinator, 202-687-0513, Fax: 202-687-0597, E-mail: jac252@georgetown.edu.

Huron University USA in London, Graduate Programs, Program in International Relations, London, United Kingdom. Offers conflict resolution (MA); diplomacy (MA); international public law (MA); international relations (MA); Middle East international security (MA); politics (MA); security studies (MA); terrorism (MA); U.S. foreign policy (MA). Part-time programs available. *Entrance requirements:* Additional exam requirements/recommendations for international students: Required—TOEFL (minimum score 580 paper-based; 237 computer-based), TWE (minimum score 5). Electronic applications accepted. *Faculty research:* American foreign politics, Middle East, security studies.

The Johns Hopkins University, Paul H. Nitze School of Advanced International Studies, Washington, DC 20036. Offers international development (Certificate); international public policy (MIPP); international relations (MA, PhD), including African studies (MA), American foreign policy (MA), Asian studies (MA), Canadian studies (MA), conflict management (MA), European studies (MA), global theory and history (MA), international development (MA), international law, and organizations (MA), international policy (MA), international relations (general) (MA), Latin American studies (MA), Middle East studies (MA), Russian and Eurasian studies (MA), strategic studies (MA); international studies (Certificate); JD/MA; MBA/MA; MHS/MA. *Faculty:* 66 full-time (22 women), 158 part-time/adjunct (54 women). *Students:* 578 full-time (256 women), 46 part-time (16 women); includes 85 minority (18 African Americans, 1 American Indian/Alaska Native, 51 Asian Americans or Pacific Islanders, 15 Hispanic Americans), 193 international. Average age 27. In 2007, 359 master's, 13 doctorates awarded. Terminal master's awarded for partial completion of doctoral program. *Degree requirements:* For master's, one foreign language, 16 non-language courses (8 for MIPP), 2 core examinations, comprehensive oral exam, paper (for some programs); for doctorate, 2 foreign languages, thesis/dissertation, 3 comprehensive exams, defense. *Entrance requirements:* For master's, GMAT or GRE General Test, previous course work in economics, foreign language, undergraduate degree; for doctorate, GRE General Test, master's degree. Additional exam

Conflict Resolution and Mediation/Peace Studies

The Johns Hopkins University (continued)
requirements/recommendations for international students: Required—TOEFL (minimum paper-based score of 600, computer-based 250, iBT 100) or IELTS (minimum 7.0). *Application deadline:* For fall admission, 1/7 for domestic students. Application fee: $80. Electronic applications accepted. *Expenses: Contact institution. Financial support:* In 2007–08, 350 students received support, including fellowships (averaging $7,500 per year); career-related internships or fieldwork, Federal Work-Study, and scholarships/grants also available. Financial award application deadline: 2/15; financial award applicants required to submit FAFSA. *Faculty research:* Regional studies and functional fields of international relations, international economics, conflict management, global theory and history, international law and organizations, international policy, strategic studies. *Unit head:* Tara Campbell, Associate Director of Admissions, 202-663-5700, Fax: 202-663-7788. *Application contact:* Dr. Belinda A. Yeomans, Director of Admissions, 202-663-5700, Fax: 202-663-7788, E-mail: admissions.sais@jhu.edu.

Jones International University, Graduate School of Business Administration, Centennial, CO 80112. Offers accounting (MBA); business communication (MABC); entrepreneurship (MABC, MBA); finance (MBA); global enterprise management (MBA); health care management (MBA); information security management (MBA); information technology management (MBA); leadership and influence (MABC); leading the customer-driven organization (MABC); negotiation and conflict management (MBA); project management (MABC, MBA). Program only offered online. Part-time and evening/weekend programs available. Postbaccalaureate distance learning degree programs offered (no on-campus study). *Degree requirements:* For master's, capstone project. *Entrance requirements:* For master's, minimum cumulative GPA of 2.5. Additional exam requirements/recommendations for international students: Recommended—TOEFL (minimum score 550 paper-based; 213 computer-based). Electronic applications accepted.

Kennesaw State University, College of Humanities and Social Sciences, Program in Conflict Management, Kennesaw, GA 30144-5591. Offers MSCM. *Faculty:* 6 full-time (3 women). *Students:* 54 full-time (39 women); includes 20 minority (17 African Americans, 1 American Indian/Alaska Native, 2 Asian Americans or Pacific Islanders), 4 international. Average age 36. 34 applicants, 100% accepted, 26 enrolled. In 2007, 26 degrees awarded. *Entrance requirements:* For master's, GMAT, GRE, LSAT. Additional exam requirements/recommendations for international students: Required—TOEFL (minimum score 550 paper-based; 213 computer-based; 80 iBT), IELTS (minimum score 6). *Application deadline:* For fall admission, 7/1 for domestic and international students. Applications are processed on a rolling basis. Application fee: $50. Electronic applications accepted. *Financial support:* In 2007–08, 1 research assistantship with full tuition reimbursement (averaging $15,000 per year) was awarded; Federal Work-Study and unspecified assistantships also available. Support available to part-time students. Financial award application deadline: 6/15; financial award applicants required to submit FAFSA. *Unit head:* Dr. Linda Johnston, Director, 770-423-6299, Fax: 770-423-6312, E-mail: ljohnsto@kennesaw.edu. *Application contact:* Vilma Marquez, Admissions Counselor, 770-420-4377, Fax: 770-423-6885, E-mail: ksugrad@kennesaw.edu.

Lipscomb University, Institute for Conflict Management, Nashville, TN 37204-3951. Offers MA, Certificate. Part-time and evening/weekend programs available. *Faculty:* 4 part-time/adjunct (1 woman). *Students:* 9 full-time (6 women), 13 part-time (6 women); includes 1 minority (African American) Average age 40. *Degree requirements:* For master's, completion of externship. *Entrance requirements:* For master's, GRE, GMAT, LSAT or equivalent, 3 years work experience. *Expenses: Contact institution. Financial support:* In 2007–08, 1 student received support. Application deadline: 11/8. *Unit head:* Dr. Larry Bridgesmith, Executive Director, 615-966-7145, Fax: 615-966-7143, E-mail: larry.bridgesmith@lipscomb.edu. *Application contact:* Sherri Guenther, Administrative Assistant, 615-966-7140, Fax: 615-966-7143, E-mail: sherri.guenther@lipscomb.edu.

Lipscomb University, MBA Program, Nashville, TN 37204-3951. Offers accounting (MBA); business administration (general) (MBA); conflict management (MBA); financial services (MBA); healthcare management (MBA); leadership (MBA); nonprofit management (MBA); sustainable practice (MBA). *Accreditation:* ACBSP. Part-time and evening/weekend programs available. *Faculty:* 10 full-time (2 women), 6 part-time/adjunct (1 woman). *Students:* 16 full-time (7 women), 63 part-time (25 women); includes 10 minority (8 African Americans, 1 American Indian/Alaska Native, 1 Hispanic American), 1 international. Average age 33. 48 applicants, 73% accepted, 27 enrolled. In 2007, 36 degrees awarded. *Entrance requirements:* For master's, GMAT, interview, 2 references, resumé. Additional exam requirements/recommendations for international students: Required—TOEFL (minimum score 570 paper-based; 230 computer-based). *Application deadline:* For fall admission, 7/1 for domestic students, 2/1 for international students; for winter admission, 12/1 for domestic students, 6/1 for international students. Applications are processed on a rolling basis. Application fee: $50 ($75 for international students). Electronic applications accepted. *Expenses: Contact institution. Financial support:* In 2007–08, 25 students received support. Career-related internships or fieldwork, Federal Work-Study, scholarships/grants, tuition waivers (partial), and unspecified assistantships available. Support available to part-time students. Financial award application deadline: 7/1; financial award applicants required to submit FAFSA. *Faculty research:* Impact of spirituality on organization commitment; leadership; psychological empowerment; training. *Unit head:* Dr. Mike Kendrick, Interim Chair of Graduate Business Studies, 615-966-1833, Fax: 615-966-1818, E-mail: mikekendrick@lipscomb.edu. *Application contact:* Jackie Cash, MBA Assistant, 615-966-1833, Fax: 615-966-1818, E-mail: jackie.cash@lipscomb.edu.

Montclair State University, The Office of Graduate Admissions and Support Services, College of Humanities and Social Sciences, Department of Justice Studies, Montclair, NJ 07043-1624. Offers conflict management in the workplace (Certificate); dispute resolution (MA); governance, compliance and regulation (MA); intellectual property (MA); law and governance (MA); legal management, information and technology (MA); paralegal studies (Certificate). Part-time and evening/weekend programs available. *Faculty:* 7 full-time (6 women), 17 part-time/adjunct (7 women). *Students:* 4 full-time (all women), 47 part-time (37 women); includes 16 minority (7 African Americans, 3 Asian Americans or Pacific Islanders, 6 Hispanic Americans), 3 international. 18 applicants, 50% accepted, 8 enrolled. In 2007, 16 master's, 14 other advanced degrees awarded. *Degree requirements:* For master's, comprehensive exam, thesis or alternative. *Entrance requirements:* For master's, GRE General Test, minimum undergraduate GPA of 2.75, 2 letters of recommendation; for Certificate, 2 letters of recommendation. Additional exam requirements/recommendations for international students: Required—TOEFL (minimum score 83 computer-based). *Application deadline:* For fall admission, 6/1 for international students; for spring admission, 10/1 for international students. Applications are processed on a rolling basis. Application fee: $60. Electronic applications accepted. *Financial support:* Research assistantships with full tuition reimbursements, Federal Work-Study, scholarships/grants, and unspecified assistantships available. Support available to part-time students. Financial award application deadline: 3/1. *Unit head:* Dr. Norma Connolly, Chairperson, 973-655-4152, E-mail: connolyn@mail.montclair.edu. *Application contact:* Prof. Jack Baldwin-LeClair, Adviser, E-mail: leclairj@mail.montclair.edu.

Norwich University, School of Graduate Studies, Program in Diplomacy, Northfield, VT 05663. Offers international commerce (MA); international conflict management (MA); international terrorism (MA). Evening/weekend programs available. *Faculty:* 1 full-time (0 women), 28 part-time/adjunct (3 women). *Students:* 366 full-time (122 women), 9 part-time (1 woman); includes 61 minority (19 African Americans, 1 American Indian/Alaska Native, 18 Asian Americans or Pacific Islanders, 23 Hispanic Americans), 1 international. Average age 33. 151 applicants, 97% accepted, 107 enrolled. In 2007, 145 degrees awarded. *Degree requirements:* For master's, comprehensive exam, thesis optional. *Entrance requirements:* For master's, minimum undergraduate GPA of 2.75. Additional exam requirements/recommendations for international students: Required—TOEFL. *Application deadline:* For fall admission, 8/10 for domestic and international students; for winter admission; 11/7 for domestic and international students; for spring admission, 2/6 for domestic and international students. Application fee: $50. Electronic applications accepted. *Expenses:* Tuition: Full-time $15,768; part-time $657 per credit. Tuition and fees vary according to program. *Financial support:* Scholarships/grants available. Financial award applicants required to submit FAFSA. *Unit head:* Dr. Hal Kearsley, Program Director, 802-485-2730, E-mail: hkearsley@norwich.edu. *Application contact:* Fianna Verret, Administrative Director, 802-485-2783, Fax: 802-485-2533, E-mail: fverret@norwich.edu.

Nova Southeastern University, Graduate School of Humanities and Social Sciences, Department of Conflict Analysis and Resolution, Doctor of Conflict Analysis and Resolution Program, Fort Lauderdale, FL 33314-7796. Offers PhD, PhD/JD. Part-time and evening/weekend programs available. Postbaccalaureate distance learning degree programs offered (minimal on-campus study). *Faculty:* 11 full-time (7 women), 10 part-time/adjunct (4 women). *Students:* 74 full-time (44 women), 103 part-time (65 women); includes 83 minority (61 African Americans, 3 American Indian/Alaska Native, 1 Asian American or Pacific Islander, 18 Hispanic Americans), 17 international. 75 applicants, 92% accepted, 38 enrolled. In 2007, 7 degrees awarded. *Degree requirements:* For doctorate, comprehensive exam, thesis/dissertation, qualifying exam. *Entrance requirements:* For doctorate, interview, minimum GPA of 3.0. Additional exam requirements/recommendations for international students: Required—TOEFL. *Application deadline:* For fall admission, 7/1 priority date for domestic and international students; for winter admission, 11/1 priority date for domestic and international students; for spring admission, 5/1 priority date for domestic students, 3/1 priority date for international students. Applications are processed on a rolling basis. Application fee: $50. Electronic applications accepted. *Financial support:* In 2007–08, 144 students received support, including 12 research assistantships with partial tuition reimbursements available (averaging $10,000 per year), 3 teaching assistantships; career-related internships or fieldwork, Federal Work-Study, scholarships/grants, and unspecified assistantships also available. Financial award application deadline: 4/1; financial award applicants required to submit CSS PROFILE. *Faculty research:* International conflict, violence prevention, facilitation and mediation, communication and conflict. *Application contact:* Marcia Arango, Student Recruitment Coordinator, 954-262-3006, Fax: 954-262-3968, E-mail: marango@nsu.nova.edu.

See Close-Up on page 953.

Nova Southeastern University, Graduate School of Humanities and Social Sciences, Department of Conflict Analysis and Resolution, Master's Program in Conflict Analysis and Resolution, Fort Lauderdale, FL 33314-7796. Offers MS, JD/MS. *Faculty:* 11 full-time (7 women), 10 part-time/adjunct (4 women). *Students:* 28 full-time (24 women), 50 part-time (40 women); includes 42 minority (24 African Americans, 3 Asian Americans or Pacific Islanders, 15 Hispanic Americans), 6 international. 67 applicants, 63% accepted, 40 enrolled. In 2007, 17 degrees awarded. *Degree requirements:* For master's, comprehensive exam, thesis optional. *Entrance requirements:* For master's, interview, minimum GPA of 3.0, writing sample. Application fee: $50. *Faculty research:* International conflict, violence prevention, communication and conflict facilitation, mediation. *Application contact:* Marcia Arango, Student Recruitment Coordinator, 954-262-3006, Fax: 954-262-3968, E-mail: marango@nsu.nova.edu.

See Close-Up on page 953.

Pepperdine University, School of Law, Program in Dispute Resolution, Malibu, CA 90263. Offers LL M, MDR. *Degree requirements:* For master's, thesis. *Entrance requirements:* For master's, GRE General Test or LSAT. Expenses: Contact institution.

Portland State University, Graduate Studies, College of Liberal Arts and Sciences, Program in Conflict Resolution, Portland, OR 97207-0751. Offers MA, MS. *Faculty:* 6 full-time (2 women), 5 part-time/adjunct (4 women). *Students:* 49 full-time (29 women), 63 part-time (45 women); includes 16 minority (9 African Americans, 1 American Indian/Alaska Native, 2 Asian Americans or Pacific Islanders, 4 Hispanic Americans), 8 international. Average age 37. 54 applicants, 98% accepted, 36 enrolled. In 2007, 15 degrees awarded. *Degree requirements:* For master's, thesis or alternative, practicum. *Entrance requirements:* For master's, 3 letters of recommendation. Additional exam requirements/recommendations for international students: Required—TOEFL (minimum score 550 paper-based; 213 computer-based). *Application deadline:* For fall admission, 4/1 for domestic students, 3/1 for international students; for winter admission, 9/1 for domestic students, 8/1 for international students; for spring admission, 11/1 for domestic and international students. *Expenses:* Tuition, state resident: full-time $7,047. Tuition, nonresident: full-time $11,178. *Financial support:* In 2007–08, teaching assistantships with full tuition reimbursements (averaging $5,508 per year); Federal Work-Study also available. *Unit head:* Dr. Robert Gould, Director, 503-725-9175, E-mail: gouldr@pdx.edu. *Application contact:* Stephen Jahnke, Program Administrator, 503-725-9175, E-mail: jahnkes@pdx.edu.

Regis University, College for Professional Studies, MA Program, Denver, CO 80221-1099. Offers criminology (MA); fine arts administration (Certificate); language and communication (MA); mediation (Certificate); psychology (MA); self-designed major (MA); social justice, peace, and reconciliation (Certificate); social science (MA); technical communication (Certificate). Program also offered in Henderson and Las Vegas (Summerlin), NV. Part-time and evening/weekend programs available. Postbaccalaureate distance learning degree programs offered (minimal on-campus study). *Faculty:* 84. *Students:* 218 (167 women). Average age 41. In 2007, 52 degrees awarded. *Degree requirements:* For master's, thesis, research project. *Entrance requirements:* For master's, resumé, recommendations, essays. Additional exam requirements/recommendations for international students: Required—TOEFL (minimum score 213 computer-based), TWE (minimum score 5). *Application deadline:* For fall admission, 8/13 priority date for domestic students, 7/13 priority date for international students; for winter admission, 10/8 priority date for domestic students, 9/8 priority date for international students; for spring admission, 12/17 priority date for domestic students, 11/17 for international students. Applications are processed on a rolling basis. Application fee: $75. Electronic applications accepted. *Expenses: Contact institution. Financial support:* Federal Work-Study available. Support available to part-time students. Financial award application deadline: 3/15; financial award applicants required to submit FAFSA. *Faculty research:* Independent/nonresidential graduate study: new methods and models, adult learning and the capstone experience, Goal Setting, behavior of Adult students, Innovative Studies for Community Colleges. *Unit head:* Dr. Robert Collins, Chair, 303-458-4302, Fax: 303-964-5538. *Application contact:* Graduate Admissions, 800-677-9270 Ext. 4080, Fax: 303-964-5538, E-mail: masters@regis.edu.

Royal Roads University, Graduate Studies, Peace and Conflict Studies Program, Victoria, BC V9B 5Y2, Canada. Offers conflict analysis and management (MA). Postbaccalaureate distance learning degree programs offered (minimal on-campus study). *Degree requirements:* For master's, thesis. *Entrance requirements:* For master's, 5-7 years of related work experience. Additional exam requirements/recommendations for international students: Required—TOEFL (paper-based 570; computer-based 233) or IELTS (paper-based 7) (recommended). Electronic applications accepted. *Faculty research:* Conflict analysis, ethno-political conflict reconciliation, international relations, displaced persons.

St. Edward's University, School of Management and Business, Program in Human Services, Austin, TX 78704. Offers conflict resolution (Certificate); human services (MA), including administration, conflict resolution, human resource management. Part-time and evening/weekend programs available. *Faculty:* 1 (woman) full-time, 8 part-time/adjunct (2 women). *Students:* 8 full-time (7 women), 59 part-time (46 women); includes 35 minority (11 African Americans, 2 Asian Americans or Pacific Islanders, 22 Hispanic Americans). Average age 32. 30 applicants, 83% accepted, 20 enrolled. In 2007, 27 degrees awarded. *Degree requirements:* For master's, minimum 24 resident hours. *Entrance requirements:* For master's, GRE General Test, GMAT, minimum GPA of 2.75 in last 60 hours of course work. Additional exam requirements/recommendations for international students: Required—TOEFL (minimum score 550 paper-based; 213 computer-based; 79 iBT). *Application deadline:* For fall admission, 8/1 for domestic students, 7/1 for international students; for spring admission, 12/1 for domestic students, 11/1 for international students. Applications are processed on a rolling basis. Application fee: $45 ($50 for international students). Electronic applications accepted. *Expenses:* Tuition: Full-time $12,672; part-time $704 per credit hour. Full-time tuition and fees vary according to program. Part-time tuition and fees vary according to course load. *Financial support:* In 2007–08, 3 students received support. Scholarships/grants available. *Faculty research:* Leadership development, organizational management, public policy, emotional intelligence. *Unit head:* Dr. Constance D Porter, Director, 512-416-5827, Fax: 512-448-8492, E-mail: constanp@stedwards.edu. *Application contact:* Kay L. Arnold, Graduate Admissions Coordinator, 512-233-1636, Fax: 512-428-1032, E-mail: kayla@stedwards.edu.

Saint Paul University, Faculty of Human Sciences, Program in Conflict Studies, Ottawa, ON K1S 1C4, Canada. Offers MA. Part-time programs available. *Students:* 119 applicants, 55% accepted, 50 enrolled. In 2007, 25 degrees awarded. *Entrance requirements:* For master's, H=honors BA, B average. *Application deadline:* For fall admission, 3/31 priority date for domestic and international students; for spring admission, 5/1 priority date for domestic students. Applications are processed on a rolling basis. Application fee: $60. *Unit head:* Paul Rigby, Unit Head, 613-236-1393 Ext. 2233. *Application contact:* Diane Boudroault, Head, 613-236-1393 Ext. 2292, E-mail: dboudreault@ustpaul.ca.

SIT Graduate Institute, Graduate Programs, Master's Programs in Intercultural Service, Leadership, and Management, Program in Conflict Transformation, Brattleboro, VT 05302-0676. Offers MA. *Application contact:* Information Contact, 800-336-1616, Fax: 802-258-3500, E-mail: admissions@sit.edu.

Southern Methodist University, School of Education and Human Development, Department of Dispute Resolution and Counseling, Dallas, TX 75275. Offers counseling (MS); dispute resolution (MA). *Faculty:* 5 full-time (1 woman), 34 part-time/adjunct (13 women). *Students:* 3 full-time (all women), 150 part-time (104 women); includes 48 minority (28 African Americans, 6 Asian Americans or Pacific Islanders, 14 Hispanic Americans), 1 international. Average age 35. *Unit head:* Dr. Tony Picchioni, Ph.D, Department Chair, 972-473-3408, Fax: 972-473-3425. *Application contact:* Cynthia McIntyre, Program Manager, 972-473-3431, Fax: 972-473-3425, E-mail: adr@smu.edu or counselingmaster@smu.edu.

Sullivan University, School of Business, Louisville, KY 40205. Offers business (EMBA, MBA); dispute resolution (MSDR); management of information technology (MSMIT). *Entrance requirements:* Additional exam requirements/recommendations for international students: Required—TOEFL.

Tufts University, Fletcher School of Law and Diplomacy, Medford, MA 02155. Offers LL M, MA, MAHA, MALD, MIB, PhD, DVM/MA, JD/MALD, MALD/MA, MALD/MBA, MALD/MS, MD/MA. Postbaccalaureate distance learning degree programs offered (minimal on-campus study). *Faculty:* 34 full-time (7 women), 31 part-time/adjunct (8 women). *Students:* 443 full-time (224 women), 7 part-time (4 women); includes 51 minority (6 African Americans, 1 American Indian/Alaska Native, 26 Asian Americans or Pacific Islanders, 18 Hispanic Americans), 165 international. Average age 31. 1,636 applicants, 34% accepted, 183 enrolled. In 2007, 364 master's, 12 doctorates awarded. *Median time to degree:* Of those who began their doctoral program in fall 1999, 75% received their degree in 8 years or less. *Degree requirements:* For master's, one foreign language, thesis; for doctorate, one foreign language, comprehensive exam, thesis/dissertation, dissertation defense. *Entrance requirements:* For master's and doctorate, GMAT or GRE General Test. Additional exam requirements/recommendations for international students: Required—TOEFL (minimum score 600 paper-based; 250 computer-based; 100 iBT), IELTS (minimum score 7). *Application deadline:* For fall admission, 1/15 for domestic and international students; for spring admission, 10/15 for domestic and international students. Application fee: $70. Electronic applications accepted. *Expenses: Contact institution. Financial support:* Federal Work-Study, institutionally sponsored loans, scholarships/grants, and tuition waivers (partial) available. Financial award application deadline: 1/15; financial award applicants required to submit FAFSA. *Faculty research:* Negotiation and conflict resolution, international organizations, international business and economic law, security studies, development economics. *Unit head:* Stephen W. Bosworth, Dean, 617-627-3050, Fax: 617-627-3712. *Application contact:* Laurie A. Hurley, Director of Admissions and Financial Aid, 617-627-2410, Fax: 617-627-3712, E-mail: fletcheradmissions@tufts.edu.

See Close-Up on page 1169.

TUI University, College of Business Administration, Program in Business Administration, Cypress, CA 90630. Offers business administration (PhD); conflict and negotiation management (MBA); criminal justice administration (MBA); entrepreneurship (MBA); finance (MBA); general management (MBA); human resource management (MBA); information technology management (MBA); international business (MBA); logistics management (MBA); public management (MBA); strategic leadership (MBA). Part-time and evening/weekend programs available. Postbaccalaureate distance learning degree programs offered (no on-campus study). In 2007, 752 master's, 28 doctorates awarded. *Degree requirements:* For doctorate, comprehensive exam, thesis/dissertation, defense of dissertation. *Entrance requirements:* For master's, minimum GPA of 2.5 (students with GPA 3.0 or greater may transfer up to 30% of graduate level credits); for doctorate, minimum GPA of 3.4, curriculum vitae, course work in research methods or statistics. Additional exam requirements/recommendations for international students: Required—TOEFL. *Application deadline:* Applications are processed on a rolling basis. Electronic applications accepted.

Université de Sherbrooke, Faculty of Law, Sherbrooke, QC J1K 2R1, Canada. Offers alternative dispute resolution (LL M, Diploma); biotechnology (LL B); business administration (LL B); business law (Diploma); health law (LL M, Diploma); law (LL B, LL D); legal management (Diploma); notarial law (DDN); transnational law (Diploma). Part-time and evening/weekend programs available. *Degree requirements:* For master's, thesis; for other advanced degree, one foreign language. *Entrance requirements:* For master's and other advanced degree, LL B. Electronic applications accepted.

University of Arkansas at Little Rock, Graduate School, College of Professional Studies, Program in Conflict Mediation, Little Rock, AR 72204-1099. Offers Graduate Certificate. *Unit head:* Dr. Angela L. Brenton, Dean, College of Professional Studies, 501-569-3244, E-mail: albrenton@ualr.edu.

University of Baltimore, Graduate School, The Yale Gordon College of Liberal Arts, Division of Legal, Ethical and Historical Studies, Baltimore, MD 21201-5779. Offers legal and ethical studies (MA); negotiations and conflict management (MS). Part-time and evening/weekend programs available. *Faculty:* 4 full-time (2 women), 2 part-time/adjunct (1 woman). *Students:* 15 full-time (11 women), 59 part-time (47 women); includes 37 minority (32 African Americans, 2 Asian Americans or Pacific Islanders, 3 Hispanic Americans), 3 international. Average age 33. 54 applicants, 93% accepted, 32 enrolled. In 2007, 15 degrees awarded. *Degree requirements:* For master's, thesis optional, internship. *Entrance requirements:* For master's, minimum GPA of 3.0. Additional exam requirements/recommendations for international students: Required—TOEFL (minimum score 550 paper-based; 213 computer-based). *Application deadline:* For fall admission, 8/1 for domestic students, 6/1 for international students; for spring admission, 12/1 for domestic students, 11/1 for international students. Application fee: $45. Electronic applications accepted. *Expenses:* Tuition, state resident: part-time $518 per credit. Tuition, nonresident: part-time $751 per credit. Tuition and fees vary according to program. *Financial support:* In 2007–08, 1 research assistantship with full and partial tuition reimbursement was awarded. Financial award application deadline: 4/1; financial award applicants required to submit FAFSA. *Faculty research:* Communication and conflict, conflict management systems theory. Total annual research expenditures: $38,500. *Unit head:* Dr. Johannes Botes, Director, MS in Negotiations and Conflict Management Program, 410-837-5326, E-mail: jbotes@ubalt.edu. *Application contact:* Wendy Bolyard.

See Close-Up on page 955.

University of Bridgeport, International College, Bridgeport, CT 06604. Offers global development and peace (MA). *Expenses:* Tuition: Part-time $635 per credit. Tuition and fees vary according to course load, degree level and program. *Unit head:* Dr. Thomas Ward, Dean, 203-576-4966, E-mail: ward@bridgeport.edu.

University of Denver, Graduate Studies, Conflict Resolution Institute, Denver, CO 80208. Offers MA. Part-time programs available. *Faculty:* 2 full-time, 13 part-time/adjunct. *Students:* 20 full-time (15 women), 5 part-time (2 women); includes 1 minority (Asian American or Pacific Islander) Average age 30. In 2007, 5 degrees awarded. *Degree requirements:* For master's, thesis, internship. *Entrance requirements:* For master's, GRE, GMAT, or LSAT, 3 letters of recommendation, personal statement. Additional exam requirements/recommendations for international students: Required—TOEFL. *Application deadline:* For fall admission, 2/15 priority date for domestic students; for winter admission, 11/1 priority date for domestic students; for spring admission, 1/15 priority date for domestic students. Applications are processed on a rolling basis. Application fee: $50. Electronic applications accepted. *Financial support:* Career-related internships or fieldwork, Federal Work-Study, scholarships/grants, and tuition waivers (partial) available. Financial award application deadline: 2/15; financial award applicants required to submit FAFSA. *Unit head:* Dr. Karen Feste, Director, 303-871-6477, E-mail: kfeste@du.edu. *Application contact:* Information Contact, 303-871-6477, E-mail: cri@du.edu.

University of Hawaii at Manoa, Graduate Division, Colleges of Arts and Sciences, College of Social Sciences, Spark M. Matsunaga Institute for Peace, Honolulu, HI 96822. Offers conflict resolution (Graduate Certificate). Part-time programs available. *Faculty:* 16 full-time (4 women). *Students:* 9 full-time (7 women), 11 part-time (7 women); includes 2 minority (both Asian Americans or Pacific Islanders), 6 international. 14 applicants, 36% accepted, 5 enrolled. *Entrance requirements:* For degree, GRE General Test. Additional exam requirements/recommendations for international students: Required—TOEFL (minimum score 540 paper-based; 207 computer-based; 76 iBT), IELTS (minimum score 5). *Application deadline:* For fall admission, 2/15 for domestic and international students; for spring admission, 9/30 for domestic and international students. Application fee: $50. *Financial support:* In 2007–08, 2 research assistantships (averaging $15,864 per year) were awarded. *Application contact:* Delores Foley, Chairperson, 808-956-6433, Fax: 808-956-9121.

University of Massachusetts Boston, Office of Graduate Studies, College of Public and Community Service, Program in Dispute Resolution, Boston, MA 02125-3393. Offers MA, Certificate. MA program accepts applications for fall admission only; Certificate program accepts applications for spring admission only. *Degree requirements:* For master's, practicum, final project. *Entrance requirements:* For master's, MAT or GRE, minimum GPA of 2.75; for Certificate, minimum GPA of 2.75. *Faculty research:* Mediation and negotiation, justice and conflict, cross-cultural mediation, environmental fairness, dispute resolution theory and ethics.

University of Missouri–Columbia, Graduate School and School of Law, Program in Dispute Resolution, Columbia, MO 65211. Offers LL M. *Entrance requirements:* Additional exam requirements/recommendations for international students: Required—TOEFL (minimum score 600 paper-based; 250 computer-based).

University of Missouri–St. Louis, College of Arts and Sciences, Department of Sociology, St. Louis, MO 63121. Offers advanced social perspective (MA); community conflict intervention (MA); program design and evaluation research (MA); social policy planning and administration (MA). Part-time and evening/weekend programs available. *Faculty:* 3 full-time (all women), 1 part-time/adjunct (0 women). *Students:* 5 full-time (2 women), 7 part-time (3 women); includes 1 minority (African American) Average age 31. In 2007, 7 degrees awarded. *Degree requirements:* For master's, thesis optional. *Entrance requirements:* For master's, 2 letters of recommendation. Additional exam requirements/recommendations for international students: Required—TOEFL (minimum score 550 paper-based; 213 computer-based). *Application deadline:* For fall admission, 7/15 priority date for domestic students; for spring admission, 12/15 priority date for domestic students. Applications are processed on a rolling basis. Application fee: $35 ($40 for international students). Electronic applications accepted. *Financial support:* In 2007–08, 3 teaching assistantships with full and partial tuition reimbursements (averaging $7,870 per year) were awarded; research assistantships, career-related internships or fieldwork also available. Support available to part-time students. *Faculty research:* Deviance, conflict intervention, minority groups, stratification, social psychology. *Unit head:* Dr. Chicako Usui, Chairperson, 314-516-6366. *Application contact:* 314-516-5458, Fax: 314-516-6996, E-mail: gradadm@umsl.edu.

University of New Brunswick Fredericton, School of Graduate Studies, Policy Studies Program, Fredericton, NB E3B 5A3, Canada. Offers people, property and alternative dispute resolution (M Phil); philosophy politics and economics (M Phil); sustainable development (M Phil). *Faculty:* 6 full-time (2 women), 13 part-time/adjunct (2 women). *Students:* 13 full-time (8 women), 3 part-time (2 women). In 2007, 6 degrees awarded. *Entrance requirements:* For master's, minimum GPA of 3.5, BA. Additional exam requirements/recommendations for international students: Required—TOEFL (minimum score 600 paper-based), TWE (minimum score 5). Application fee: $50 Canadian dollars. *Financial support:* In 2007–08, 5 research assistantships, 2 teaching assistantships (averaging $4,400 per year) were awarded. *Unit head:* Dr. Gwen Davies, Dean of Graduate Studies, 506-458-7150, Fax: 506-453-4817, E-mail: daviesg@unb.ca. *Application contact:* Janet Amurault, Graduate Secretary, 506-458-7558, Fax: 506-453-4817, E-mail: jamiraul@unb.ca.

The University of North Carolina at Greensboro, Graduate School, Program in Conflict Resolution, Greensboro, NC 27412-5001. Offers MA, Certificate. *Students:* 17 full-time (10 women), 36 part-time (34 women); all minorities (14 African Americans, 39 Hispanic Americans). 24 applicants, 46% accepted. *Application deadline:* For fall admission, 7/1 for domestic students. Applications are processed on a rolling basis. Application fee: $45. Electronic applications accepted. *Unit head:* Dr. Cathie Witty, Director/Director of Graduate Studies, 336-334-5295, Fax: 336-334-5283, E-mail: cjwitty@uncg.edu. *Application contact:* Michelle Harkleroad, Director of Graduate Admissions, 336-334-4884, Fax: 336-334-4424, E-mail: mbharkle@uncg.edu.

University of Notre Dame, Graduate School, College of Arts and Letters, Division of Social Science, Joan B. Kroc Institute for International Peace Studies, Notre Dame, IN 46556. Offers MA. *Faculty:* 38 full-time (11 women). *Students:* 39 full-time (25 women); includes 2 minority (both Asian Americans or Pacific Islanders), 30 international. 173 applicants, 13% accepted, 20 enrolled. In 2007, 17 degrees awarded. *Degree requirements:* For master's, one foreign language, comprehensive exam, thesis optional. *Entrance requirements:* For master's, GRE General Test. Additional exam requirements/recommendations for international students: Required—TOEFL (minimum score 600 paper-based; 250 computer-based; 80 iBT). *Application deadline:* For fall admission, 1/5 for domestic and international students. Application fee: $50. Electronic applications accepted. *Financial support:* In 2007–08, 1 fellowship with full tuition reimbursement (averaging $12,000 per year), 1 research assistantship, 17 teaching assistantships (averaging $9,000 per year) were awarded; career-related internships or fieldwork, scholarships/grants, health care benefits, and tuition waivers (full) also available. Financial award application deadline: 1/5. *Faculty research:* The role of international norms and institutions in peacemaking; the impact of religious, philosophical, and cultural influences on peace; the dynamics of intergroup conflict and conflict transformation; the promotion of social, economic, and environmental justice. *Unit head:* Dr. Jaleh Dashti-Gibson, Director of Graduate Studies, 574-631-6970, Fax: 574-631-6973, E-mail: kroc-admissions@nd.edu. *Application contact:* Rosemarie Green, Admissions Coordinator, 574-631-8535, Fax: 574-631-6973, E-mail: green.2@nd.edu.

University of Pittsburgh, Graduate School of Public and International Affairs, International Affairs Division, Program in Human Security, Pittsburgh, PA 15260. Offers MPIA. Part-time and evening/weekend programs available. *Faculty:* 34 full-time (10 women), 18 part-time/adjunct (6 women). *Students:* 20 full-time (14 women), 3 part-time (all women); includes 4 minority (3 African Americans, 1 Asian American or Pacific Islander), 1 international. Average age 25. 48 applicants, 90% accepted, 18 enrolled. In 2007, 63 degrees awarded. *Degree requirements:* For master's, thesis optional, internship, capstone seminar. *Entrance requirements:* For master's, GRE General Test, 3 letters of recommendation, resumé, minimum GPA of 3.2. Additional exam requirements/recommendations for international students: Required—TOEFL (minimum score 550 paper-based; 213 computer-based; 80 iBT), TWE (minimum score 4); Recommended—IELTS (minimum score 7). *Application deadline:* For fall admission, 2/1 for domestic students,

Conflict Resolution and Mediation/Peace Studies

University of Pittsburgh (continued)

1/15 for international students; for spring admission, 11/1 for domestic students, 8/1 for international students. Application fee: $50. *Financial support:* In 2007–08, 41 students received support, including 41 fellowships (averaging $8,280 per year); scholarships/grants and unspecified assistantships also available. Financial award application deadline: 2/1. *Faculty research:* Human rights, human trafficking, threats to civilian populations, child soldiers. Total annual research expenditures: $845,025. *Application contact:* Jessica L. Hatherill, Associate Director of Student Services, 412-648-7640, Fax: 412-648-7641, E-mail: hatherill@gspia.pitt.edu.

University of San Diego, Joan B. Kroc School of Peace Studies, San Diego, CA 92110-2492. Offers MA. *Faculty:* 3 full-time (1 woman), 1 (woman) part-time/adjunct. *Students:* 13 full-time (10 women), 5 international. Average age 30. 34 applicants, 62% accepted, 13 enrolled. In 2007, 9 degrees awarded. *Entrance requirements:* For master's, GRE General Test, minimum GPA of 3.0. Additional exam requirements/recommendations for international students: Required—TOEFL (minimum score 580 paper-based; 237 computer-based), TWE. *Application deadline:* For fall admission, 4/1 for domestic and international students. Applications are processed on a rolling basis. Application fee: $45. Electronic applications accepted. *Expenses:* Tuition: Part-time $1,095 per unit. Tuition and fees vary according to degree level and program. *Financial support:* In 2007–08, 10 fellowships were awarded; career-related internships or fieldwork, Federal Work-Study, institutionally sponsored loans, scholarships/grants, tuition waivers (partial), and unspecified assistantships also available. Support available to part-time students. Financial award application deadline: 5/1; financial award applicants required to submit FAFSA. *Unit head:* Fr. William Headley, Dean, E-mail: wheadley@sandiego.edu. *Application contact:* Stephen Pultz, Director of Admissions, 619-260-4524, Fax: 619-260-4158, E-mail: grads@sandiego.edu.

University of the Sacred Heart, Graduate Programs, Program in Systems of Justice, San Juan, PR 00914-0383. Offers human rights and anti-discriminatory processes (MASJ); mediation and transformation of conflicts (MASJ).

University of Victoria, Faculty of Graduate Studies, Faculty of Human and Social Development, School of Public Administration, Victoria, BC V8W 2Y2, Canada. Offers dispute resolution (MADR); public administration (MPA, PhD); MPA/LL B. Part-time and evening/weekend programs available. Postbaccalaureate distance learning degree programs offered. *Faculty:* 11 full-time (2 women), 22 part-time/adjunct (4 women). *Students:* 154, 4 international. Average age 28. 205 applicants, 38% accepted, 53 enrolled. In 2007, 27 degrees awarded. *Degree requirements:* For master's, thesis (for some programs), report; for doctorate, thesis/dissertation, candidacy exam. *Entrance requirements:* For master's, GMAT or GRE General Test, professional resumé; for doctorate, GMAT or GRE General Test. Additional exam requirements/recommendations for international students: Required—TOEFL (minimum score 610 paper-based; 255 computer-based). *Application deadline:* For fall admission, 3/15 for domestic students, 12/15 for international students. Applications are processed on a rolling basis. Application fee: $75 ($125 for international students). Electronic applications accepted. *Expenses:* Tuition, state resident: full-time $3,110. International tuition: $3,700 full-time. Tuition and fees vary according to program. *Financial support:* In 2007–08, 3 fellowships (averaging $8,266 per year), 4 teaching assistantships were awarded; research assistantships, career-related internships or fieldwork and institutionally sponsored loans also available. Financial award application deadline: 2/15. *Faculty research:* Policy analysis, local government, performance management, energy markets, labor markets. *Unit head:* Dr. Evert A. Lindquist, Director, 250-721-8084, Fax: 250-721-8849, E-mail: padirect@uvic.ca. *Application contact:* Dr. John Langford, Graduate Adviser, 250-721-8057, Fax: 250-721-8849, E-mail: jlangfor@uvic.ca.

Wayne State University, College of Fine, Performing and Communication Arts, Interdisciplinary Program in Dispute Resolution, Detroit, MI 48202. Offers MADR, Certificate, JD/MADR. *Students:* 4 full-time (1 woman), 21 part-time (14 women); includes 9 minority (8 African Americans, 1 Asian American or Pacific Islander). Average age 38. 10 applicants, 60% accepted, 4 enrolled. In 2007, 12 master's, 4 Certificates awarded. *Entrance requirements:* For master's, GMAT, GRE General Test, or LSAT. Additional exam requirements/recommendations for international students: Required—TOEFL (minimum score 550 paper-based; 213 computer-based); Recommended—TWE (minimum score 6). *Application deadline:* For fall admission, 7/1 for domestic students, 6/1 for international students; for winter admission, 10/1 for international students; for spring admission, 2/1 for international students. Applications are processed on a rolling basis. Application fee: $30 ($50 for international students). Electronic applications accepted. *Expenses:* Tuition, state resident: part-time $403 per credit hour. Tuition, nonresident: part-time $890 per credit hour. *Faculty research:* Conflict resolution in higher education; workplace conflict and aggression; cultural diversity; domestic violence; intervention policies of major powers and small states. *Unit head:* Dr. Loraleigh Keashly, Academic Director, 313-577-3221, Fax: 313-577-8800, E-mail: l.keashly@wayne.edu.

NOVA SOUTHEASTERN UNIVERSITY

Graduate School of Humanities and Social Sciences

Program of Study

The Graduate School of Humanities and Social Sciences at Nova Southeastern University (NSU) has distinguished itself nationally and internationally by exploring the theory and practice of addressing human problems and social issues as a dynamic learning community. The School uses an interdisciplinary approach, informed by top-level instructional technologies, to build a bridge between theory, practice, and research drawn from different social sciences, humanities, and helping professions.

The Ph.D. in conflict analysis and resolution advances the study and practice of conflict analysis and resolution by focusing on research, practice, and teaching. Professors mentor and train students in the design and evaluation of models of conflict resolution. Concentrations are available in conflict and crisis management, health-care conflict resolution, culture and ethnic conflict, international peace and conflict, and organizations and schools conflict. The Ph.D. in family therapy is designed for individuals who wish to fully grasp both the historical aspects and cutting-edge theory informing the current practice of family therapy. The doctorate of marriage and family therapy expands and enhances students' existing clinical skills in order to make them top-level practitioners.

Students earning the M.S. in conflict analysis and resolution are exposed to techniques and strategies to help people achieve nonviolent, nonlitigious solutions for conflicts that arise in personal, professional, organizational, and social environments. Concentrations are available in conflict and crisis management, culture and ethnic conflict, health-care conflict resolution, international peace and conflict, and organization and school conflict. Students with a variety of educational and professional backgrounds are encouraged to apply. The M.S. in family therapy trains students to help individuals, couples, and families create positive change in their relationships. Extensive clinical practice and live supervision are an integral part of the program. The M.S. in college student affairs prepares students for the expanded roles and responsibilities of student affairs professionals in today's diverse college and university environments. The M.A. in cross-disciplinary studies enables students to design their own graduate curriculum around their own academic backgrounds, professional goals, and personal interests. Dual-degree M.S./Ph.D., M.S./J.D., and Ph.D./J.D. programs are also available.

In addition to its degree programs, the School also offers graduate certificate programs in advanced family systems, college student personnel administration, conflict analysis and resolution, family ministry, family studies, family systems health care, health-care conflict resolution, and peace studies.

Research Facilities

The 325,000-square-foot Alvin Sherman Library, Research, and Information Technology Center is a joint-use facility with the Broward County Board of County Commissioners. It currently houses approximately 690,000 volumes but has a book capacity of 1.4 million volumes. Agreements have been signed with several libraries throughout the world to provide library support for NSU programs offered in specific geographical areas. Online databases complement the paper-based holdings and provide full-text resources. Interlibrary agreements through organizations such as the Online Computer Library Center and the Southeast Florida Library Information Network provide broad access to a wide range of materials. Community Resolution Services offers training and workshops as well as mediation and facilitation services to individuals, families, groups, and agencies to resolve conflicts on campus and in the broader community. The center supports students who intend to enhance their skills and who want to participate in projects and activities that are rich with prospects for professional development.

Financial Aid

Graduate assistantships for doctoral students are offered for one academic year, depending on the availability of funds. These positions are for a maximum of 20 hours per week. A number of grants and scholarships are available from both the University and other sources. Students may borrow funds under the Federal Stafford Student Loan program or the Federal Perkins Loan program as well as from private lenders. Part-time employment is also available through the Federal Work-Study Program, in which students work up to 20 hours per week.

Cost of Study

In 2008–09, tuition is $765 per academic credit for doctoral students and $525 per credit for master's students. The registration fee is $25 per term, and the student service fee is $250 per term for full-time students and $125 per term for part-time students.

Living and Housing Costs

The University offers graduate on-campus housing in Fort Lauderdale. Graduate apartments and rooms in shared apartments are available. Costs range from $7344 to $13,300 per academic year. For more information, students should contact the Office of Residential Life and Housing at 954-262-7052 or visit http://www.nova.edu/reslife.

Student Group

Approximately 500 students are enrolled in the School each year, comprising a diverse mix of social backgrounds.

Student Outcomes

Graduates of the School are prepared to establish careers in the social science fields as practitioners, researchers, and educators.

Location

Centrally located between Miami and Palm Beach, Fort Lauderdale's 23 miles of beaches make it a popular vacation spot, but its thriving economy has made it one of the most desirable business locations as well. Las Olas Boulevard serves as Fort Lauderdale's centerpiece of fashion, fine dining, and entertainment, while the Riverwalk features the city's arts, science, cultural, and historic district.

The University

Founded in 1964 as Nova University of Advanced Technology, Nova Southeastern University is the largest independent institution of higher education in Florida and the sixth-largest independent institution nationally. It offers associate, bachelor's, master's, educational specialist, doctoral, and first-professional degrees in a wide range of fields and enrolls more than 25,000 students annually. In addition to its main campus in Fort Lauderdale, NSU has locations throughout Florida and across the nation and international sites in the Caribbean, Canada, and the UK.

Applying

Prospective students are required to submit an application for admission, official transcripts from all colleges previously attended, three reference forms, a two- to four-page essay describing academic and professional goals, a current resume, and a $50 application fee. The preferred deadline to apply is July 1 for fall admission, November 1 for winter admission, and March 1 for summer admission. Applications should be mailed to the Graduate School's admissions office.

Correspondence and Information

Carlos Perez, Senior Manager of Recruitment and Community Outreach
Graduate School of Humanities and Social Sciences
Maltz Building
Nova Southeastern University
3301 College Avenue
Fort Lauderdale, Florida 33314-7796

Phone: 954-262-5702
800-541-6682 Ext. 5702 (toll-free)
Fax: 954-262-3893
E-mail: perez@nova.edu
Web site: http://shss.nova.edu/

Nova Southeastern University

THE FACULTY AND THEIR RESEARCH

Elena Bastidas, Assistant Professor of Conflict Resolution and Environmental Studies; Ph.D. (food and resource economics), Florida. Conflict analysis and resolution, economics, conservation and development, gender and development, development of appropriate technology for small farmers, livelihood systems, quantitative methods.

Tommie V. Boyd, Assistant Professor and Chair, Department of Family Therapy; Ph.D. (family therapy), Nova Southeastern, 2000. Family system health care, relationship difficulties, family business counseling, clinical supervision, client-therapist collaborations, narrative therapy.

Christopher F. Burnett, Assistant Professor of Family Therapy; Psy.D. (clinical psychology), Indiana of Pennsylvania, 1992. Application of systems thinking in organizational and social systems, human systems consulting, Bowen family systems theory, systemic approaches to quantitative and qualitative research methodologies.

Ronald J. Chenail, Professor of Family Therapy; Ph.D. (family therapy), Nova, 1989. Discourse in therapy and mediation, qualitative inquiry.

Patricia Cole, Associate Professor of Family Therapy and Family Business; Ph.D. (family therapy), Nova Southeastern, 1993. Family relationships in family business and in other work contexts, gender concerns in the workplace, qualitative research.

Mark Davidheiser, Assistant Professor of Conflict Resolution and Anthropology; Ph.D. (anthropology), Florida, 2004. Culture and conflict, interpersonal conflict analysis and resolution, race and ethnicity, development and assistance, farmer-herder conflict, rural societies, legal reform, Africa, Islam, multiculturalism, community relations, research design and methodology.

Jean-Mathieu Essoh Essis, Assistant Professor of Conflict Resolution and Public Policy; Ph.D. (public policy), George Mason. International negotiation processes and issues, multilateral decision making in the global nuclear weapons nonproliferation treaty regime, conflict resolution and public policy, democratization and public-sector reform in Africa.

Douglas Flemons, Professor of Family Therapy; Ph.D. (family therapy), Nova, 1989. Relational means of creating and understanding contextual phenomena such as therapy, hypnosis, and learning; writing as inquiry; therapeutic imagination.

Paul Gallant, Associate Professor of Family Therapy; Ph.D. (family therapy), Florida State, 1988. Narrative therapy.

Alexia Georgakopoulos, Assistant Professor of Conflict Resolution and Communication; Ph.D. (communication), Arizona State, 2003. Conflict, intercultural communication, organizational communication, pedagogy communication, nonverbal communication, interpersonal communication.

Shelley K. Green, Associate Professor of Family Therapy; Ph.D. (home economics), Texas Tech, 1989. Supervision and training in systemic therapies, the role of gender in team development, therapist learning styles and personal competence, systemic approaches to sexual issues in therapy, brief therapy with persons with AIDS.

James Hibel, Assistant Professor of Family Therapy; Ph.D. (child and family studies), Syracuse, 1981. Teaching and supervision of narrative systemic therapy, theoretical and practical applications of postmodern systemic therapies, application of less-hierarchical models to supervision and training issues.

J. P. Linstroth, Assistant Professor of Conflict Resolution and Anthropology; D.Phil. (social anthropology), Oxford, 2002. Fisheries and maritime disputes, gender theory, European traditions, ritual and performance, material culture and media, ethnonationalist conflict, locality and discord, nationalist politics, kinship, social change, separatist movements, globalization.

Judith McKay, Assistant Professor of Conflict Resolution and Community Studies; Ph.D. (conflict analysis and resolution), Nova Southeastern. Violence prevention and intervention; family, civil, and community mediation; poverty law; gender conflict; communication; comparative law; environmental and public disputes; public policy.

Debra Nixon, Assistant Professor and Associate Chair, Department of Family Therapy; Ph.D. (family therapy), Nova Southeastern, 2000. The person of the therapist in practice, isomorphism of therapeutic approach to classroom instruction, using narrative and relational therapeutic approaches in diversity training, faith-based multicultural diversity training.

Anne Hearon Rambo, Associate Professor of Family Therapy; Ph.D. (family therapy), Nova, 1979. Supervision and training in systemic therapies, therapy as play and play as therapy, development of the therapist's unique personal style, rhetoric and language skills training, family therapy history.

Clare Michele Rice, Assistant Professor of Conflict Resolution and Community Relations; Ph.D. (sociology), Florida International, 2001.

Lee Shilts, Professor of Family Therapy; Ph.D. (family and child development), Virginia Tech, 1988. Brief solution-focused theory and therapy, supervision and training in systemic therapies, use of solution-focused therapy in nontraditional settings, use of letter writing in therapeutic settings.

Marcia Sweedler, Assistant Professor and Interim Chair, Department of Conflict Analysis and Resolution; Ph.D. (education policy, planning, and administration), Maryland. Developing a systemic approach to conflict resolution through training, ADR, and workplace/school climate.

Hamdesa Tuso, Associate Professor of Conflict Resolution and Sociology; Ph.D. (sociology), Michigan State, 1981. Cultural issues of conflict resolution, peacemaking practices, immigrant communities, refugee communities, challenges of sustainable development.

Honggang Yang, Professor of Interdisciplinary Studies and Dean; Ph.D. (applied anthropology), South Florida, 1991. Political anthropology, comparative conflict/peace research, ethnographic/qualitative research methods, graduate distance learning.

UNIVERSITY OF BALTIMORE

Yale Gordon College of Liberal Arts
Division of Legal, Ethical and Historical Studies

Programs of Study The Division of Legal, Ethical and Historical Studies offers two master's degree programs: the Master of Science (M.S.) in Negotiations and Conflict Management and the Master of Arts (M.A.) in Legal and Ethical Studies.

The master's program in Negotiations and Conflict Management is intensely interdisciplinary. The 42-credit program is infused with business, legal, and humanities perspectives and includes both theoretical and practical aspects of the social science of understanding and transforming conflict. This degree is designed to equip students with the skills to manage and resolve conflict and the tools (such as negotiation, mediation, and arbitration) to enhance their existing careers or lead them to professional opportunities in the rapidly growing field of conflict management. The program includes core courses; advanced perspective courses focusing on individual/interpersonal, managerial/governmental, and cultural/ethical/policy perspectives; an internship experience; and a comprehensive capstone course designed to integrate theory and practice and to examine students' broad understanding of and future focus in the field.

The master's program in Legal and Ethical Studies is designed for students who are interested in graduate-level study of law and ethics in a liberal arts setting. In this 36-credit program, students explore a wide range of topics related to the study of law, applied ethics, and legal history, with a particular focus on the American legal system as a whole, the interaction of law and ethics, and the legal history of the mid-Atlantic region. The program's students are motivated by intellectual interest in the liberal arts as well as career goals. This is not a law school program or certification program for the legal field; however, it does help students become more competitive for law school admission.

Research Facilities The Center for Negotiations and Conflict Management, established in 1997, serves as a neutral and impartial forum for the consideration of policy issues associated with dispute resolution and the provision of training and technical assistance in the broad field of conflict management.

Langsdale Library, on the University of Baltimore (UB) campus, provides students with full access to several million volumes and thousands of journals throughout the University System of Maryland. Langsdale Library subscribes to more than 70 online databases that provide on- and off-campus access to full-text journal articles from almost 12,000 titles.

Financial Aid The UB Office of Financial Aid assists graduate students in obtaining loans, scholarships, and other means of assistance. Many students participate in internships or work on independent or contractual projects. A limited number of graduate assistantships, which provide tuition remission and a stipend, are available.

Cost of Study In 2007–08, tuition for liberal arts graduate students who are Maryland residents was $498 per credit hour. Nonresident graduate students paid $751 per credit hour. All students pay a University flat fee ($70 for students taking 1–11 credits; $422.50 for students taking 12 or more credits), a University per-credit fee of $56 (not to exceed $309.50), and a technology fee ($6 per credit from 1–11; $72.50 for 12 credits or more). Web-based classes are an additional $88 per credit for in-state students and $86 per credit for students from out-of-state. Students may pay tuition and fees with cash, check, Visa, MasterCard, or Discover.

Living and Housing Costs UB is a commuter campus and does not presently offer student housing on campus; however, University-affiliated housing is located within walking distance, and assistance in locating affordable housing is provided by the Center for Student Involvement. UB is located in midtown Baltimore's cultural district, off the Jones Falls Expressway (I-83) and across the street from Pennsylvania Station, which provides MARC commuter and Amtrak service. The University is accessible by major bus routes and its own light rail stop, making the campus an easy commute from a variety of neighborhoods within the Baltimore area.

Student Group More than 70 students are enrolled in the M.S. in Negotiations and Conflict Management program, and about 80 are enrolled in the M.A. in Legal and Ethical Studies program. Full- and part-time students, many of whom work while attending school, come from all over the region and from varied academic and professional backgrounds. Some come directly from undergraduate study, while others are seeking career changes.

Location Baltimore is both a big city and a small town. UB is nestled in the Mount Vernon Cultural District—home to art galleries, theaters, the symphony and opera, and historic architecture. The neighborhood serves as the backdrop for First Thursdays, a monthly event that includes the likes of outdoor concerts and wine tasting in nearby art galleries. Within 2 miles of campus is the bustling Inner Harbor, with its shops and waterfront activities, including the National Aquarium, Maryland Science Center, Oriole Park at Camden Yards, and the Ravens' M&T Bank Stadium. The city also offers a museum for nearly every interest and specialty—from the legendary histories told at the Babe Ruth Birthplace and Museum, Edgar Allan Poe House Museum, Eubie Blake Museum, and Great Blacks in Wax Museum to the world-class art found at the Walters Art Museum, Baltimore Museum of Art, and the American Visionary Art Museum. Baltimore is also full of friendly neighborhoods, including Little Italy, Fells Point, Canton, and Hampden. Nighttime pub crawls, vintage shops, steamed crabs, and bocce ball along with street fairs, ethnic festivals, and unique markets make Baltimore a city like few others for those of all ages.

The University UB offers undergraduate and graduate education in three unique schools: the Yale Gordon College of Liberal Arts, the Merrick School of Business, and the School of Law. The University of Baltimore was founded as a private institution in 1925 and is now part of the University System of Maryland. Total student enrollment is approximately 5,400, and the student-faculty ratio is 16:1.

Applying For admission to either program, applicants must have a bachelor's degree from a regionally accredited institution with a minimum grade point average of 3.0. Applicants must submit an official transcript from each higher-education institution attended, an application, and the appropriate application fee. For the M.S. in Negotiations and Conflict Management, a statement of personal interest in the program of study is also required; letters of recommendation, a resume, and/or an interview with the program director may be requested. For the M.A. in Legal and Ethical Studies, a writing sample and/or a statement of personal interest may be requested.

Correspondence and Information

Office of Graduate Admissions
University of Baltimore
1420 North Charles Street
Baltimore, Maryland 21201-5779
Phone: 410-837-6565
Fax: 410-837-4774
E-mail: gradadmissions@ubalt.edu
Web site: http://www.ubalt.edu/cla

Dr. Johannes Botes
Program Director
M.S. in Negotiations and Conflict Management
Phone: 410-837-5323
E-mail: gradadmissions@ubalt.edu
Web site: http://www.ubalt.edu/negotiations

Dr. Jeffrey Sawyer
Program Director
M.A. in Legal and Ethical Studies
Phone: 410-837-5323
E-mail: gradadmissions@ubalt.edu
Web site: http://www.ubalt.edu/legalethicalstudies

University of Baltimore

THE FACULTY AND THEIR RESEARCH

Johannes M. Botes, Associate Professor; Ph.D., George Mason. Conflict transformation, mediation, and media and conflict.
Thomas E. Carney, Associate Professor and Chair; Ph.D., West Virginia; J.D., Toledo. American constitutional and legal history, American religious history and the history of colonial and early America, Central West Africa and South America.
Alfred H. Guy Jr., Associate Professor; Ph.D., Georgia. Applied and professional ethics.
Michael Hayes, Associate Professor; J.D., Virginia. Employment discrimination, labor and employment law, negotiating and counseling.
Joshua J. Kassner, Visiting Assistant Professor; Ph.D., Maryland. Philosophy of law, human rights.
Jeffrey K. Sawyer, Professor; Ph.D., Berkeley. Legal and constitutional history.
Ellen Kabcenell Wayne, Assistant Professor; J.D., North Carolina. Organizational conflict, conflict management systems design, intergroup dialogue, employment discrimination.
John M. Windmueller, Visiting Assistant Professor; Ph.D., George Mason. Community and intercultural conflict resolution, peace studies, evaluation research.

Section 18
Criminology and Forensics

This section contains a directory of institutions offering graduate work in criminology and forensics, followed by in-depth entries submitted by institutions that chose to prepare detailed program descriptions. Additional information about programs listed in the directory but not augmented by an in-depth entry may be obtained by writing directly to the dean of a graduate school or chair of a department at the address given in the directory.

For programs offering related work, see also in this book *Political Science and International Affairs, Psychology and Counseling,* and *Sociology, Anthropology, and Archaeology.* In another guide in this series:

Graduate Programs in Business, Education, Health, Information Studies, Law & Social Work

See *Law* and *Social Work*

CONTENTS

Program Directories

Announcements

Close-Ups

See also:

Criminal Justice and Criminology

Albany State University, College of Arts and Sciences, Department of Criminal Justice, Albany, GA 31705-2717. Offers criminal justice (MS). Part-time programs available. *Degree requirements:* For master's, comprehensive exam. *Entrance requirements:* For master's, GRE General Test, minimum GPA of 2.5. Electronic applications accepted. *Faculty research:* Criminal alcoholic program, prevention of juvenile delinquency, police selection, constitutional issues.

Albany State University, College of Arts and Sciences, Department of History, Political Science and Public Administration, Albany, GA 31705-2717. Offers community and economic development (MPA); criminal justice (MPA); fiscal management (MPA); general management (MPA); health administration and policy (MPA); human resources management (MPA); public policy (MPA); water resource management and policy (MPA). *Accreditation:* NASPAA. Part-time programs available. *Degree requirements:* For master's, comprehensive exam, thesis. *Entrance requirements:* For master's, GRE General Test, minimum GPA of 2.5. Electronic applications accepted. *Faculty research:* Transportation, urban affairs, political economy.

American Public University System, AMU/APU Graduate Programs, Charles Town, WV 25414. Offers air warfare (MA Military Studies); American Revolution (MA Military Studies); business administration (MBA); Civil War (MA Military Studies); criminal justice (MA); defense management (MA Military Studies); emergency and disaster management (MA); environmental policy and management (MS); fire science management (MA); global engagement (MA); history (MA); homeland security (MA); humanities (MA); intelligence (MA Military Studies, MA Strategic Intelligence); international peace and conflict resolution (MA); international relations and conflict resolution (MA); joint warfare (MA Military Studies); land warfare international perspective (MA Military Studies); management (MA); military history (MA); military leadership (MA Military Studies); national security studies (MA); naval warfare international (MA Military Studies); naval warfare US (MA Military Studies); political science (MA); public administration (MA); public health (MA); security management (MA); space studies (MS); special ops/LIC (MA Military Studies); sports management (MA); transportation and logistics management (MA); transportation management (MA); unconventional warfare (MA Military Studies); World War II (MA Military Studies). Programs offered via distance learning only. Part-time and evening/weekend programs available. Postbaccalaureate distance learning degree programs offered (no on-campus study). *Faculty:* 10 full-time (3 women), 188 part-time/adjunct (57 women). *Students:* 340 full-time (98 women), 3,567 part-time (790 women); includes 615 minority (317 African Americans, 28 American Indian/Alaska Native, 85 Asian Americans or Pacific Islanders, 185 Hispanic Americans), 20 international. Average age 36. 2,123 applicants, 100% accepted, 893 enrolled. In 2007, 829 degrees awarded. *Degree requirements:* For master's, comprehensive exam. *Entrance requirements:* For master's, bachelor's degree or equivalent, minimum GPA of 2.7 in last 60 hours of course work. *Application deadline:* Applications are processed on a rolling basis. Application fee: $0. Electronic applications accepted. *Expenses:* Tuition: Part-time $275 per semester hour. *Financial support:* Applicants required to submit FAFSA. *Faculty research:* Military history, criminal justice, management performance, national security. *Unit head:* Dr. Frank McCluskey, Provost, 877-468-6268, Fax: 304-724-3780. *Application contact:* Terry Grant, Director of Enrollment Management, 877-468-6268, Fax: 304-724-3780, E-mail: info@apus.edu.

American University, School of Public Affairs, Department of Justice, Law and Society, Washington, DC 20016-8001. Offers MS, PhD, JD/MS. Part-time and evening/weekend programs available. *Faculty:* 23 full-time (12 women), 9 part-time/adjunct (3 women). *Students:* 43 full-time (28 women), 38 part-time (31 women); includes 13 minority (8 African Americans, 2 Asian Americans or Pacific Islanders, 3 Hispanic Americans), 3 international. Average age 27. 93 applicants, 73% accepted, 24 enrolled. In 2007, 30 master's, 2 doctorates awarded. *Degree requirements:* For master's, comprehensive exam, research requirement; for doctorate, comprehensive exam, thesis/dissertation. *Entrance requirements:* For master's, GRE General Test, statement of purpose; 2 recommendations; for doctorate, GRE, 3.2 gpa. Additional exam requirements/recommendations for international students: Required—TOEFL (minimum score 550 paper-based; 213 computer-based). *Application deadline:* For fall admission, 2/1 for domestic students; for spring admission, 11/1 for domestic students. Application fee: $50. *Expenses:* Tuition: Full-time $19,998; part-time $1,111 per credit hour. Required fees: $380. Tuition and fees vary according to program. *Financial support:* Fellowships, research assistantships, teaching assistantships, career-related internships or fieldwork, Federal Work-Study, institutionally sponsored loans, and tuition waivers (full and partial) available. Financial award application deadline: 2/1. *Faculty research:* Mental health, court management. *Unit head:* Dr. Diedre Golash, Chair, 202-885-2955.

American University of Puerto Rico, Program in Criminal Justice, Bayamón, PR 00960-2037. Offers MA.

Andrew Jackson University, Jeffrey D. Rubenstein College of Criminal Justice, Program in Criminal Justice, Birmingham, AL 35244. Offers MS. Part-time and evening/weekend programs available. Postbaccalaureate distance learning degree programs offered (no on-campus study). *Faculty:* 10 part-time/adjunct (0 women). *Students:* Average age 35. In 2007, 5 degrees awarded. *Entrance requirements:* For master's, course work in calculus, statistics. Additional exam requirements/recommendations for international students: Required—TOEFL (minimum score 550 paper-based; 213 computer-based). *Application deadline:* Applications are processed on a rolling basis. Application fee: $75. *Financial support:* Scholarships/grants available. *Application contact:* Tammy Kassner, Senior Admissions Coordinator, 205-271-9288 Ext. 107, Fax: 205-871-9294, E-mail: tkassner@aju.edu.

Anna Maria College, Graduate Division, Program in Criminal Justice, Paxton, MA 01612. Offers criminal justice (MS). Part-time and evening/weekend programs available. *Faculty:* 6 full-time (1 woman), 3 part-time/adjunct (2 women). *Students:* 25 full-time (12 women), 33 part-time (5 women); includes 4 minority (1 African American, 3 Hispanic Americans). Average age 32. In 2007, 16 degrees awarded. *Degree requirements:* For master's, capstone project or thesis. *Entrance requirements:* For master's, bachelor's degree in related field, minimum GPA of 2.7. Additional exam requirements/recommendations for international students: Required—TOEFL (minimum score 500 paper-based). *Application deadline:* For fall admission, 3/1 priority date for domestic and international students; for spring admission, 11/1 priority date for domestic and international students. Applications are processed on a rolling basis. Application fee: $40. Electronic applications accepted. *Expenses:* Tuition: Part-time $1,272 per course. *Financial support:* Applicants required to submit FAFSA. *Unit head:* Patricia Gavin, Director, 508-849-3377, Fax: 508-849-3343, E-mail: pgavin@annamaria.edu. *Application contact:* Dennis Braun, Director, Graduate and Continuing Education Recruitment, 508-849-3293, Fax: 508-819-3362, E-mail: dbraun@annamaria.edu.

Anna Maria College, Graduate Division, Program in Justice Administration, Paxton, MA 01612. Offers MS. Part-time and evening/weekend programs available. *Faculty:* 5 part-time/adjunct (0 women). *Students:* Average age 35. In 2007, 14 degrees awarded. *Degree requirements:* For master's, capstone project. *Entrance requirements:* Additional exam requirements/recommendations for international students: Required—TOEFL (minimum score 500 paper-based). *Application deadline:* For fall admission, 3/1 for domestic students; for spring admission, 11/1 for domestic students. Applications are processed on a rolling basis. Application fee: $40. Electronic applications accepted. *Expenses:* Tuition: Part-time $1,272 per course. *Unit head:* Patricia Gavin, Director, 508-849-3377, Fax: 508-849-3343, E-mail: pgavin@annamaria.edu. *Application contact:* Dennis Braun, Director, Graduate and Continuing Education Recruitment, 508-849-3293, Fax: 508-819-3362, E-mail: dbraun@annamaria.edu.

Appalachian State University, Cratis D. Williams Graduate School, Department of Government and Justice Studies, Boone, NC 28608. Offers criminal justice (MS); political science (MA); public administration (MPA). Part-time programs available. *Faculty:* 26 full-time (5 women). *Students:* 51 full-time (20 women), 71 part-time (30 women); includes 11 minority (8 African Americans, 1 American Indian/Alaska Native, 2 Asian Americans or Pacific Islanders), 4 international. 77 applicants, 77% accepted, 47 enrolled. In 2007, 45 degrees awarded. *Degree requirements:* For master's, variable foreign language requirement, comprehensive exam, thesis optional. *Entrance requirements:* For master's, GRE General Test. Additional exam requirements/recommendations for international students: Required—TOEFL (minimum score 570 paper-based; 230 computer-based; 79 iBT), IELTS (minimum score 7), TOEFL or IELTS. *Application deadline:* For fall admission, 7/1 for domestic students, 1/1 for international students; for spring admission, 11/1 for domestic students, 6/1 for international students. Applications are processed on a rolling basis. Application fee: $50. Electronic applications accepted. *Expenses:* Tuition, state resident: part-time $127 per semester hour. Tuition, nonresident: part-time $597 per semester hour. Required fees: $18 per semester. *Financial support:* In 2007–08, 35 research assistantships (averaging $7,000 per year) were awarded; fellowships, teaching assistantships, career-related internships or fieldwork, Federal Work-Study, scholarships/grants, and unspecified assistantships also available. Financial award application deadline: 4/1. *Faculty research:* Campaign finance, emerging democracies, bureaucratic politics, judicial behavior, administration of justice. Total annual research expenditures: $43,054. *Unit head:* Dr. Brian Ellison, Chairperson, 828-262-3085, E-mail: ellisonba@appstate.edu.

Arizona State University at the West campus, College of Human Services, School of Criminology and Criminal Justice, Phoenix, AZ 85069-7100. Offers criminal justice (MA); criminology and criminal justice (MS, PhD). Part-time and evening/weekend programs available. *Faculty:* 8 full-time (4 women). *Students:* 16 full-time (12 women), 36 part-time (25 women); includes 11 minority (3 African Americans, 4 Asian Americans or Pacific Islanders, 4 Hispanic Americans). Average age 30. In 2007, 14 degrees awarded. *Degree requirements:* For master's, policy analysis project; for doctorate, thesis/dissertation. *Entrance requirements:* For master's, GRE (MS), 2 letters of recommendation, minimum 3.0 GPA, personal statement; for doctorate, GRE, 2 letters of recommendation, personal statement, resumé. Additional exam requirements/recommendations for international students: Required—TOEFL (minimum score 550 paper-based; 213 computer-based; 83 iBT). *Application deadline:* Applications are processed on a rolling basis. Application fee: $65 ($80 for international students). Electronic applications accepted. *Expenses:* Tuition, state resident: full-time $6,227. Tuition, nonresident: full-time $17,920. Required fees: $146. *Financial support:* In 2007–08, 8 research assistantships with partial tuition reimbursements (averaging $7,255 per year) were awarded; scholarships/grants, tuition waivers (full and partial), and unspecified assistantships also available. Financial award applicants required to submit FAFSA. *Unit head:* Dr. Scott Decker, Director, 602-543-8067, Fax: 602-543-6658, E-mail: scott.decker@asu.edu. *Application contact:* Kathleen Reitdorf, Administrative Assistant, 602-543-6225, Fax: 602-543-6658, E-mail: kathleen.reitdorf@asu.edu.

Arkansas State University, Graduate School, College of Humanities and Social Sciences, Department of Criminology, Sociology, and Geography, Jonesboro, State University, AR 72467. Offers criminal justice (MA, Certificate); sociology (MA); sociology education (SCCT). Part-time programs available. *Faculty:* 7 full-time (4 women). *Students:* 16 full-time (11 women), 19 part-time (11 women); includes 14 minority (all African Americans) Average age 31. 16 applicants, 75% accepted, 12 enrolled. In 2007, 9 degrees awarded. *Degree requirements:* For master's, one foreign language, comprehensive exam, thesis or alternative; for other advanced degree, comprehensive exam. *Entrance requirements:* For master's, GRE General Test or MAT, appropriate bachelor's degree, official transcript; for other advanced degree, GRE General Test or MAT, interview, master's degree, official transcript. Additional exam requirements/recommendations for international students: Required—TOEFL (minimum score 213 computer-based). *Application deadline:* Applications are processed on a rolling basis. Application fee: $30 ($40 for international students). Electronic applications accepted. *Expenses:* Tuition, state resident: full-time $3,528; part-time $196 per hour. Tuition, nonresident: full-time $8,928; part-time $496 per hour. Required fees: $842; $44 per hour. $25 per term. Tuition and fees vary according to course load and program. *Financial support:* Career-related internships or fieldwork, scholarships/grants, and unspecified assistantships available. Financial award application deadline: 7/1; financial award applicants required to submit FAFSA. *Faculty research:* Land use—rural and recreational, resource management, climate change, peopling of the New World, gender, family, sexuality issues. *Unit head:* Dr. Anthony Troy Adams, Chair, 870-972-3705, Fax: 870-972-3694, E-mail: aadams@astate.edu.

Armstrong Atlantic State University, School of Graduate Studies, Program in Criminal Justice, Savannah, GA 31419-1997. Offers MS. Part-time and evening/weekend programs available. *Faculty:* 14 full-time (5 women). *Students:* 3 full-time (1 woman), 7 part-time (5 women); includes 1 African American, 1 Asian American or Pacific Islander. Average age 43. In 2007, 6 degrees awarded. *Degree requirements:* For master's, comprehensive exam, thesis optional. *Entrance requirements:* For master's, GRE General Test or MAT, minimum GPA of 2.5, 2 letters of recommendation. Additional exam requirements/recommendations for international students: Required—TOEFL (minimum score 523 paper-based; 193 computer-based). *Application deadline:* For fall admission, 7/1 priority date for domestic and international students; for spring admission, 11/15 priority date for domestic and international students. Applications are processed on a rolling basis. Application fee: $30. Electronic applications accepted. *Expenses:* Tuition, state resident: full-time $3,228; part-time $135 per hour. Tuition, nonresident: full-time $12,904; part-time $538 per hour. Required fees: $278 per term. *Financial support:* In 2007–08, research assistantships with partial tuition reimbursements (averaging $2,500 per year); career-related internships or fieldwork, Federal Work-Study, scholarships/grants, and unspecified assistantships also available. Support available to part-time students. Financial award applicants required to submit FAFSA. *Unit head:* Dr. Zaphon Wilson, Department Head, 912-927-5296, Fax: 912-921-5876, E-mail: zaphon.wilson@armstrong.edu.

Auburn University Montgomery, School of Sciences, Department of Justice and Public Safety, Montgomery, AL 36124-4023. Offers MSJPS. Part-time and evening/weekend programs available. *Faculty:* 4 full-time (0 women), 3 part-time/adjunct (0 women). *Students:* 17 full-time (10 women), 52 part-time (33 women); includes 42 minority (41 African Americans, 1 American Indian/Alaska Native). Average age 31. In 2007, 26 degrees awarded. *Degree requirements:* For master's, comprehensive exam, thesis optional. *Entrance requirements:* For master's, GRE General Test or MAT. *Application deadline:* Applications are processed on a rolling basis. Application fee: $25. Electronic applications accepted. *Expenses:* Tuition, state resident: full-time $4,536; part-time $189 per credit hour. Tuition, nonresident: full-time $13,608; part-time $567 per credit hour. Required fees: $234. *Financial support:* Career-related internships or fieldwork and scholarships/grants available. Support available to part-time students. Financial award application deadline: 3/1; financial award applicants required to submit FAFSA. *Faculty research:* Law enforcement, corrections, juvenile justice. *Unit head:* Dr. Gloria McPherson, Head, 334-244-3692, Fax: 334-244-3244, E-mail: gmcphers@mail.aum.edu.

Bayamón Central University, Graduate Programs, Program in Business Administration, Bayamón, PR 00960-1725. Offers accounting (MBA); finance (MBA); general business (MBA); management (MBA); management of security and protection (MBA); marketing (MBA). Part-time and evening/weekend programs available. *Degree requirements:* For master's, comprehensive exam (for some programs). *Entrance requirements:* For master's, EXADEP, bachelor's degree in business or related field.

Bellevue University, Graduate School, Bellevue, NE 68005-3098. Offers business (MBA); communications studies (MA, MS); computer information systems (MS); health care administration (MS); human services (MS); leadership (MA); management (MA); security management (MS). MA is delivered in an accelerated executive format. Part-time and evening/weekend programs available. Postbaccalaureate distance learning degree programs offered (no on-campus study). *Degree requirements:* For master's, thesis or project. *Entrance requirements:* For master's, minimum GPA of 2.5 in last 60 hours. Additional exam requirements/recommendations for international students: Required—TOEFL (minimum score 538 paper-based; 200 computer-based).

Boise State University, Graduate College, College of Social Sciences and Public Affairs, Program in Criminal Justice Administration, Boise, ID 83725-0399. Offers MA. *Degree requirements:* For master's, thesis. *Entrance requirements:* For master's, minimum GPA of 3.0. Electronic applications accepted.

Boston University, Metropolitan College (Continuing Education), Department of Applied Social Sciences, Program in Criminal Justice, Boston, MA 02215. Offers MCJ. Part-time and evening/weekend programs available. Postbaccalaureate distance learning degree programs offered (no on-campus study). *Faculty:* 4 full-time (1 woman), 9 part-time/adjunct (2 women). *Students:* 5 full-time (4 women), 490 part-time (269 women); includes 52 minority (20 African Americans, 2 American Indian/Alaska Native, 11 Asian Americans or Pacific Islanders, 19 Hispanic Americans), 13 international. Average age 34. 440 applicants, 57% accepted, 201 enrolled. In 2007, 265 degrees awarded. *Degree requirements:* For master's, comprehensive exam. *Entrance requirements:* Additional exam requirements/recommendations for international students: Required—TOEFL; Recommended—IELTS. *Application deadline:* For fall admission, 7/15 priority date for domestic and international students; for spring admission, 12/15 priority date for domestic students, 11/15 priority date for international students. Applications are processed on a rolling basis. Application fee: $70. Electronic applications accepted. *Expenses:* Tuition: Full-time $34,930; part-time $1,092 per credit. Tuition and fees vary according to class time, course level and program. *Financial support:* In 2007–08, 5 students received support, including 5 research assistantships with full and partial tuition reimbursements available; career-related internships or fieldwork, Federal Work-Study, institutionally sponsored loans, tuition waivers (partial), and unspecified assistantships also available. Support available to part-time students. Financial award application deadline: 6/15; financial award applicants required to submit FAFSA. *Faculty research:* Criminal justice administration and planning, criminology, police, corrections, collective violence, juvenile issues. *Unit head:* Dr. Daniel P. LeClair, Chair, 617-353-3025, Fax: 617-358-3595, E-mail: dleclair@bu.edu.

Bowling Green State University, Graduate College, College of Health and Human Services, Program in Criminal Justice, Bowling Green, OH 43403. Offers MSCJ. Part-time and evening/weekend programs available. Postbaccalaureate distance learning degree programs offered (no on-campus study). *Faculty:* 8 full-time (3 women), 1 (woman) part-time/adjunct. *Students:* 10 full-time (5 women), 10 part-time (7 women); includes 5 minority (2 African Americans, 1 American Indian/Alaska Native, 2 Hispanic Americans), 1 international. Average age 28. 27 applicants, 70% accepted, 10 enrolled. In 2007, 5 degrees awarded. *Degree requirements:* For master's, thesis or alternative. *Entrance requirements:* For master's, GRE General Test. Additional exam requirements/recommendations for international students: Required—TOEFL. *Application deadline:* Applications are processed on a rolling basis. Application fee: $30. Electronic applications accepted. *Financial support:* In 2007–08, 7 research assistantships with full tuition reimbursements (averaging $7,660 per year) were awarded; teaching assistantships, unspecified assistantships also available. *Unit head:* Dr. Steven Lab, Head, 419-372-2326. *Application contact:* Dr. William King, Graduate Coordinator, 419-372-2326.

Bridgewater State College, School of Graduate Studies, School of Arts and Sciences, Department of Sociology, Program in Criminal Justice, Bridgewater, MA 02325-0001. Offers MS. *Entrance requirements:* For master's, GRE General Test. *Application deadline:* For fall admission, 4/1 priority date for domestic students; for spring admission, 10/1 priority date for domestic students. Application fee: $50. *Financial support:* Career-related internships or fieldwork, health care benefits, and unspecified assistantships available. Support available to part-time students.

Buffalo State College, State University of New York, Graduate Studies and Research, Faculty of Applied Science and Education, Department of Criminal Justice, Buffalo, NY 14222-1095. Offers MS. Part-time and evening/weekend programs available. *Degree requirements:* For master's, comprehensive exam, project. *Entrance requirements:* For master's, minimum GPA of 3.0. Additional exam requirements/recommendations for international students: Required—TOEFL (minimum score 550 paper-based; 213 computer-based).

California State University, Fresno, Division of Graduate Studies, College of Social Sciences, Department of Criminology, Fresno, CA 93740-8027. Offers MS. Part-time and evening/weekend programs available. *Faculty:* 12 full-time (4 women). *Students:* 29; includes 13 minority (2 African Americans, 1 American Indian/Alaska Native, 1 Asian American or Pacific Islander, 9 Hispanic Americans), 1 international. Average age 28. 7 applicants. In 2007, 12 degrees awarded. *Degree requirements:* For master's, thesis or alternative. *Entrance requirements:* For master's, GRE General Test, minimum GPA of 3.0. Additional exam requirements/recommendations for international students: Required—TOEFL. *Application deadline:* For fall admission, 5/1 for domestic and international students; for spring admission, 10/1 for domestic and international students. Applications are processed on a rolling basis. Application fee: $55. Electronic applications accepted. *Financial support:* Career-related internships or fieldwork, Federal Work-Study, scholarships/grants, and unspecified assistantships available. Support available to part-time students. Financial award application deadline: 3/1; financial award applicants required to submit FAFSA. *Faculty research:* Substance abuse, gangs vs. law enforcement, needs of female offenders, battered women, crime victims. *Unit head:* Prof. Ruth Masters, Chair, 559-278-2305, Fax: 559-278-7265, E-mail: ruthm@csufresno.edu. *Application contact:* Dr. Peter English, Graduate Program Coordinator, 559-278-2305, Fax: 559-278-7265, E-mail: penglish@csufresno.edu.

California State University, Long Beach, Graduate Studies, College of Health and Human Services, Department of Criminal Justice, Long Beach, CA 90840. Offers MS. Part-time programs available. *Faculty:* 11 full-time (5 women), 21 part-time/adjunct (8 women). *Students:* 19 full-time (13 women), 82 part-time (55 women); includes 12 African Americans, 11 Asian Americans or Pacific Islanders, 43 Hispanic Americans. Average age 29. *Degree requirements:* For master's, comprehensive course or thesis. *Entrance requirements:* For master's, minimum GPA of 3.0. *Application deadline:* For fall admission, 7/1 for domestic students; for spring admission, 12/1 for domestic students. Applications are processed on a rolling basis. Application fee: $55. Electronic applications accepted. *Financial support:* Federal Work-Study, institutionally sponsored loans, and scholarships/grants available. Financial award application deadline: 3/2. *Unit head:* Dr. Judy Hails, Chair, 562-985-4738, Fax: 562-985-8086. *Application contact:* Dr. Elizabeth Deschenes, Graduate Advisor, 562-985-8567, Fax: 562-985-8086, E-mail: libby@csulb.edu.

California State University, Los Angeles, Graduate Studies, College of Health and Human Services, Department of Criminal Justice and Criminalistics, Major in Criminalistics, Los Angeles, CA 90032-8530. Offers MS. *Students:* 16 full-time (12 women), 20 part-time (15 women); includes 16 minority (9 Asian Americans or Pacific Islanders, 7 Hispanic Americans), 4 international. Average age 27. In 2007, 4 degrees awarded. *Degree requirements:* For master's, thesis. *Entrance requirements:* For master's, minimum GPA of 2.75. Additional exam requirements/recommendations for international students: Required—TOEFL. *Application deadline:* For fall admission, 6/30 for domestic students; for spring admission, 2/1 for domestic students. Applications are processed on a rolling basis. Application fee: $55. *Financial support:* Application deadline: 3/1. *Unit head:* Dr. Katherine Roberts, Head, 323-343-4610 Ext. 36231, Fax: 323-343-4646, E-mail: krobert2@calstatela.edu.

California State University, Los Angeles, Graduate Studies, College of Health and Human Services, Department of Criminal Justice and Criminalistics, Major in Criminal Justice, Los Angeles, CA 90032-8530. Offers MS. *Students:* 7 full-time (all women), 18 part-time (17 women); includes 17 minority (3 African Americans, 3 Asian Americans or Pacific Islanders, 11 Hispanic Americans), 3 international. Average age 27. In 2007, 12 degrees awarded. *Degree requirements:* For master's, thesis. *Entrance requirements:* For master's, minimum GPA of 2.75. Additional exam requirements/recommendations for international students: Required—TOEFL. *Application deadline:* For fall admission, 6/30 for domestic students; for spring admission, 2/1 for domestic students. Applications are processed on a rolling basis. Application fee: $55. *Financial support:* Application deadline: 3/1. *Unit head:* Dr. Joseph L. Peterson, Head, 323-343-4610 Ext. 34613, Fax: 323-343-4646, E-mail: joseph.peterson@calstatela.edu.

California State University, Sacramento, Graduate Studies, College of Health and Human Services, Division of Criminal Justice, Sacramento, CA 95819-6048. Offers MS. Part-time programs available. *Students:* 12 full-time (7 women), 30 part-time (17 women); includes 15 minority (2 African Americans, 6 Asian Americans or Pacific Islanders, 7 Hispanic Americans). Average age 28. 39 applicants, 74% accepted, 21 enrolled. *Degree requirements:* For master's, thesis or alternative, writing proficiency exam. *Entrance requirements:* For master's, BA in criminal justice or equivalent, minimum GPA of 2.5 during previous 2 years of course work. Additional exam requirements/recommendations for international students: Required—TOEFL. *Application deadline:* Applications are processed on a rolling basis. Application fee: $55. Electronic applications accepted. *Expenses:* Tuition, state resident: full-time $3,414. Tuition, nonresident: full-time $13,584; part-time $339 per unit. Required fees: $786; $393 per semester. *Financial support:* Career-related internships or fieldwork and Federal Work-Study available. Support available to part-time students. Financial award application deadline: 3/1. *Unit head:* Dr. William Vizzard, Chair, 916-278-6487, Fax: 916-278-7692.

California State University, San Bernardino, Graduate Studies, College of Social and Behavioral Sciences, Department of Criminal Justice, San Bernardino, CA 92407-2397. Offers MA. Part-time programs available. *Faculty:* 10 full-time, 4 part-time/adjunct. *Students:* 11 full-time (4 women), 35 part-time (28 women); includes 23 minority (6 African Americans, 17 Hispanic Americans), 1 international. Average age 25. 36 applicants, 42% accepted, 7 enrolled. In 2007, 7 degrees awarded. *Degree requirements:* For master's, comprehensive exam or thesis. *Entrance requirements:* For master's, GRE General Test, minimum GPA of 3.0. *Application deadline:* For fall admission, 9/1 priority date for domestic students. Applications are processed on a rolling basis. Application fee: $55. *Financial support:* Research assistantships, career-related internships or fieldwork, Federal Work-Study, and institutionally sponsored loans available. Support available to part-time students. *Faculty research:* Crime seriousness, fear of crime, victimization, corrections management, crime correlates. *Unit head:* Dr. Larry Gaines, Chair, 909-537-5506, Fax: 909-537-7025, E-mail: lgaines@csusb.edu.

California State University, Stanislaus, College of Humanities and Social Sciences, Department of Criminal Justice, Turlock, CA 95382. Offers MA. Part-time programs available. *Faculty:* 10. *Students:* 9 full-time (all women), 15 part-time (9 women); includes 12 minority (4 African Americans, 2 Asian Americans or Pacific Islanders, 6 Hispanic Americans), 1 international. Average age 30. In 2007, 5 degrees awarded. *Degree requirements:* For master's, thesis optional. *Entrance requirements:* For master's, 3.0 minimum GPA, 3 letters of reference, personal statement. *Expenses:* Tuition, nonresident: full-time $10,170; part-time $339 per unit. Required fees: $3,972; $2,538 per term. $1,165 per semester. *Financial support:* Fellowships available. Financial award application deadline: 3/2; financial award applicants required to submit FAFSA. *Faculty research:* Police gerontology services, hate crimes, juvenile justice, masculinities and modern society, nutrition and criminal behavior. *Application contact:* Dr. Phyllis Gerstenfeld, Chair, 209-667-3408, Fax: 209-664-7034, E-mail: phyllisg@toto.csustan.edu.

California University of Pennsylvania, School of Graduate Studies and Research, College of Liberal Arts, Department of Sociology/Criminal Justice, California, PA 15419-1394. Offers social science—criminal justice (MA). Part-time and evening/weekend programs available. *Degree requirements:* For master's, comprehensive exam, thesis optional. *Entrance requirements:* For master's, MAT, minimum GPA of 3.0. Additional exam requirements/recommendations for international students: Required—TOEFL (minimum score 550 paper-based; 213 computer-based; 80 iBT). Electronic applications accepted. *Faculty research:* Ethics and law, ethics in police practice, law and morality, police policy, St. Thomas Aquinas and crime.

Capella University, School of Human Services, Minneapolis, MN 55402. Offers addictions counseling (Certificate); counseling studies (MS, PhD); criminal justice (MS, PhD, Certificate); diversity studies (Certificate); general human services (MS, PhD); health care administration (MS, PhD, Certificate); management of nonprofit agencies (MS, PhD, Certificate); marital, couple and family counseling/therapy (MS); marriage and family services (Certificate); mental health counseling (MS); professional counseling (Certificate); social and community services (MS, PhD, Certificate). Part-time and evening/weekend programs available. Postbaccalaureate distance learning degree programs offered (minimal on-campus study). Terminal master's awarded for partial completion of doctoral program. *Degree requirements:* For master's, thesis optional, integrative project; for doctorate, comprehensive exam, thesis/dissertation. *Entrance requirements:* Additional exam requirements/recommendations for international students: Required—TOEFL (minimum score 550 paper-based; 213 computer-based), TWE (minimum score 4). Electronic applications accepted. *Faculty research:* Compulsive and addictive behaviors, substance abuse, assessment of psychopathology and neuropsychology.

Caribbean University, Graduate School, Bayamón, PR 00960-0493. Offers accounting (MBA); administration and supervision (MA Ed); criminal justice (MA); curriculum and instruction (MA Ed); education (PhD); gerontology (MSN); human resources (MBA); museology, archiving and art history (MA Ed); neonatal pediatrics (MSN); physical education (MA Ed); special education (MA Ed). *Entrance requirements:* For master's, interview, minimum GPA of 2.5.

Carnegie Mellon University, H. John Heinz III School of Public Policy and Management, Program in Information Security Policy and Management, Pittsburgh, PA 15213-3891. Offers MSISPM.

Central Connecticut State University, School of Graduate Studies, School of Arts and Sciences, Department of Criminology and Criminal Justice, New Britain, CT 06050-4010. Offers criminal justice (MS). *Faculty:* 10 full-time (3 women), 16 part-time/adjunct (2 women). *Students:* 8 full-time (6 women), 32 part-time (16 women); includes 9 minority (6 African Americans, 3 Hispanic Americans). Average age 32. 16 applicants, 75% accepted, 9 enrolled. In 2007, 4 degrees awarded. *Entrance requirements:* For master's, minimum GPA of 3.0. Additional exam requirements/recommendations for international students: Required—TOEFL. *Application deadline:* For fall admission, 5/1 for domestic students; for spring admission, 12/1 for domestic students. Applications are processed on a rolling basis. Application fee: $50. Electronic applications accepted. *Expenses:* Tuition, area resident: Full-time $4,169. Tuition, state resident: full-time $6,253. Tuition, nonresident: full-time $11,614; part-time $400 per credit. Required fees: $3,322. One-time fee: $62 part-time. Tuition and fees vary according to degree level and program. *Financial support:* In 2007–08, 1 student received support, including 1 research assistantship; career-related internships or fieldwork, Federal Work-Study, scholarships/grants, and unspecified assistantships also available. Support available to part-time students. Financial award application deadline: 3/1; financial award applicants required to submit FAFSA. *Unit head:* Dr. Stephen Cox, Chair, 860-832-3005.

Central Michigan University, College of Graduate Studies, College of Humanities and Social and Behavioral Sciences, Department of Sociology, Anthropology and Social Work, Mount Pleasant, MI 48859. Offers social and criminal justice (MA); sociology (MA). *Degree requirements:* For master's, thesis or alternative. *Entrance requirements:* For master's, 20 hours of course work in sociology, minimum GPA of 3.0. *Faculty research:* Sociological theory, race concept, environmental justice, cultural anthropology.

Chaminade University of Honolulu, Graduate Services, Program in Criminal Justice Administration, Honolulu, HI 96816-1578. Offers criminal justice administration (MSCJA); homeland security (Certificate). Part-time and evening/weekend programs available. Postbaccalaureate distance learning degree programs offered (no on-campus study). *Faculty:* 3 full-time (1 woman), 12 part-time/adjunct (6 women). *Students:* 41 full-time (25 women), 10 part-time (6 women); includes 39 minority (7 African Americans, 30 Asian Americans or Pacific Islanders, 2 Hispanic Americans), 1 international. Average age 29. 36 applicants, 81% accepted, 14 enrolled. In 2007, 28 degrees awarded. *Degree requirements:* For master's, thesis optional. *Entrance requirements:* For master's, minimum undergraduate GPA of 3.0, 3 letters of recommendation. Additional exam requirements/recommendations for international students: Required—TOEFL (minimum score 550 paper-based). *Application deadline:* For fall admission, 9/1 priority date for domestic students; for winter admission, 12/1 for domestic students; for spring admission, 3/1 for domestic students. Applications are processed on a rolling basis.

Criminal Justice and Criminology

Chaminade University of Honolulu (continued)

Application fee: $50. Electronic applications accepted. *Expenses:* Tuition: Part-time $490 per credit hour. *Financial support:* In 2007–08, 36 students received support. Career-related internships or fieldwork, Federal Work-Study, and scholarships/grants available. Financial award application deadline: 3/1; financial award applicants required to submit FAFSA. *Faculty research:* Penology, juvenile delinquency, multicultural and ethnic diversity in criminology, law enforcement administration and training, homeland security. *Unit head:* Ronald Becker, Director, 808-735-4873, Fax: 808-739-4614, E-mail: rbecker@chaminade.edu. *Application contact:* Melissa Hangai, Assistant to the Director, 808-735-4703, Fax: 808-739-4614, E-mail: mscja@chaminade.edu.

Charleston Southern University, Program in Criminal Justice, Charleston, SC 29423-8087. Offers MSCJ. Part-time and evening/weekend programs available. *Degree requirements:* For master's, comprehensive exam, thesis optional. *Entrance requirements:* For master's, GRE or MAT, bachelor's degree in criminal justice. *Faculty research:* Law enforcement, corrections, legal issues.

Chicago State University, School of Graduate and Professional Studies, College of Arts and Sciences, Department of Criminal Justice, Chicago, IL 60628. Offers MS. Part-time and evening/weekend programs available. *Entrance requirements:* For master's, minimum GPA of 2.75. *Faculty research:* Gang crime.

Clark Atlanta University, School of Arts and Sciences, Department of Criminal Justice, Atlanta, GA 30314. Offers MA. Part-time programs available. *Faculty:* 1 full-time (0 women), 2 part-time/adjunct (0 women). *Students:* 7 full-time (5 women), 4 part-time (2 women); includes 10 minority (all African Americans) Average age 26. 4 applicants, 75% accepted, 1 enrolled. In 2007, 4 degrees awarded. *Degree requirements:* For master's, one foreign language, thesis. *Entrance requirements:* For master's, GRE General Test, minimum GPA of 2.5. Additional exam requirements/recommendations for international students: Required—TOEFL (minimum score 500 paper-based; 173 computer-based). *Application deadline:* For fall admission, 4/1 for domestic and international students; for spring admission, 11/1 for domestic and international students. Applications are processed on a rolling basis. Application fee: $40 ($55 for international students). *Expenses:* Tuition: Full-time $11,664; part-time $648 per credit hour. Required fees: $550; $275 per semester. *Financial support:* Fellowships, research assistantships, career-related internships or fieldwork, Federal Work-Study, scholarships/grants, and unspecified assistantships available. Support available to part-time students. Financial award application deadline: 4/30; financial award applicants required to submit FAFSA. *Faculty research:* Race and crime, black ex-offenders in the labor market. *Unit head:* Dr. Komenduri Murty, Chairperson, 404-880-6657, E-mail: kmurty@cau.edu. *Application contact:* Michelle Clark-Davis, Graduate Program Admissions, 404-880-8709, E-mail: mdowis@cau.edu.

Colorado Technical University Colorado Springs, Graduate Studies, Program in Criminal Justice, Colorado Springs, CO 80907-3896. Offers MSM. Postbaccalaureate distance learning degree programs offered.

Colorado Technical University Denver, Program in Computer Science, Greenwood Village, CO 80111. Offers computer systems security (MSCS); software engineering (MSCS); software project management (MSCS). Part-time and evening/weekend programs available. *Degree requirements:* For master's, thesis or alternative. *Entrance requirements:* For master's, minimum undergraduate GPA of 3.0, resumé.

Colorado Technical University Sioux Falls, Program in Criminal Justice, Sioux Falls, SD 57108. Offers MSM.

Columbia College, Program in Criminal Justice, Columbia, MO 65216-0002. Offers MSCJ. Part-time and evening/weekend programs available. *Degree requirements:* For master's, final exams, culminating experience (intensive writing seminar). *Entrance requirements:* For master's, bachelor's degree in criminal justice, minimum GPA of 3.0, 3 recommendations. Additional exam requirements/recommendations for international students: Required—TOEFL (minimum score 550 paper-based; 213 computer-based). *Faculty research:* Organized crime, policing in America.

Columbia Southern University, College of Safety and Emergency Services, Orange Beach, AL 36561. Offers criminal justice (MS); environmental management (MS); occupational safety and health (MS); occupational safety and health/environmental management (MS). Part-time and evening/weekend programs available. Postbaccalaureate distance learning degree programs offered (no on-campus study). *Faculty:* 2 full-time (1 woman), 7 part-time/adjunct (2 women). *Students:* Average age 30. 402 applicants, 49% accepted. In 2007, 83 degrees awarded. *Entrance requirements:* For master's, Bachelor's Degree from accredited/approved institution. Additional exam requirements/recommendations for international students: Required—TOEFL. *Application deadline:* Applications are processed on a rolling basis. Application fee: $25 ($50 for international students). Electronic applications accepted. *Expenses:* Tuition: Part-time $250 per credit hour. One-time fee: $75 part-time. *Unit head:* Dr. Michael Findley, Dean of College of Safety and Emergency Services, 800-977-8449 Ext. 323, Fax: 251-968-2493, E-mail: michael.findley@columbiasouthern.edu. *Application contact:* Admissions Office, 800-977-8449 Ext. 52, Fax: 251-224-0540, E-mail: admissions@columbiasouthern.edu.

Columbus State University, Graduate Studies, College of Arts and Letters, Program in Public Administration, Columbus, GA 31907-5645. Offers justice administration (MPA). Part-time and evening/weekend programs available. *Faculty:* 7 full-time (3 women), 10 part-time/adjunct (0 women). *Students:* 110 full-time (38 women), 230 part-time (88 women); includes 117 minority (111 African Americans, 1 Asian American or Pacific Islander, 5 Hispanic Americans), 3 international. Average age 36. 102 applicants, 81% accepted, 69 enrolled. In 2007, 114 degrees awarded. *Degree requirements:* For master's, comprehensive exam. *Entrance requirements:* For master's, GRE General Test, GMAT, MAT. Additional exam requirements/recommendations for international students: Required—TOEFL (minimum score 550 paper-based; 213 computer-based). *Application deadline:* For fall admission, 5/1 priority date for domestic students, 5/1 for international students; for spring admission, 11/1 for domestic and international students. Applications are processed on a rolling basis. Application fee: $25. Electronic applications accepted. *Expenses:* Tuition, state resident: part-time $143 per semester hour. Tuition, nonresident: part-time $569 per semester hour. Required fees: $273 per term. Tuition and fees vary according to course load. *Financial support:* In 2007–08, 78 students received support, including 7 research assistantships with partial tuition reimbursements available (averaging $3,000 per year); career-related internships or fieldwork, Federal Work-Study, institutionally sponsored loans, scholarships/grants, tuition waivers (full), and unspecified assistantships also available. Support available to part-time students. Financial award application deadline: 5/1; financial award applicants required to submit FAFSA. *Unit head:* Dr. William Chappell, Program Director, 706-568-2055, E-mail: chappell_william@colstate.edu. *Application contact:* Katie Thornton, Graduate Admissions Specialist, 706-568-2035, Fax: 706-568-2462, E-mail: thornton_katie@colstate.edu.

Concordia University, St. Paul, College of Business and Organizational Leadership, St. Paul, MN 55104-5494. Offers business and organizational leadership (MBA); criminal justice (MAHS); human resources (MAOM); organizational management (MAOM); sports management (MAOM). *Accreditation:* ACBSP. Evening/weekend programs available. Postbaccalaureate distance learning degree programs offered (minimal on-campus study). *Faculty:* 12 full-time (5 women), 16 part-time/adjunct (7 women). *Students:* 231 full-time (137 women), 2 part-time (1 women); includes 33 minority (23 African Americans, 9 Asian Americans or Pacific Islanders, 1 Hispanic American), 2 international. Average age 32. In 2007, 63 degrees awarded. *Entrance requirements:* Additional exam requirements/recommendations for international students: Required—TOEFL. *Application deadline:* Applications are processed on a rolling basis. Application fee: $50. Electronic applications accepted. *Financial support:* Federal Work-Study and scholarships/grants available. Financial award applicants required to submit FAFSA. *Unit head:* Dr. Robert DeGregorio, Dean, 651-641-8845, Fax: 651-641-8807, E-mail: degregorio@csp.edu. *Application contact:* Kimberly Craig, Director of Graduate and Cohort Admission, 651-603-6223, Fax: 651-603-6320, E-mail: craig@csp.edu.

Coppin State University, Division of Graduate Studies, Division of Arts and Sciences, Department of Criminal Justice and Law Enforcement, Baltimore, MD 21216-3698. Offers criminal justice (MS). Part-time and evening/weekend programs available. *Faculty:* 6 full-time (1 woman), 5 part-time/adjunct (4 women). *Students:* 13 full-time (10 women), 13 part-time (6 women); includes 22 minority (all African Americans), 1 international. Average age 34. 31 applicants, 35% accepted, 7 enrolled. In 2007, 16 degrees awarded. *Degree requirements:* For master's, thesis optional. *Entrance requirements:* For master's, GRE, minimum GPA of 3.0. *Application deadline:* For fall admission, 8/15 priority date for domestic students; for spring admission, 12/15 priority date for domestic students. Applications are processed on a rolling basis. Application fee: $45. *Expenses:* Tuition, state resident: part-time $217 per credit. Tuition, nonresident: part-time $400 per credit. *Financial support:* Career-related internships or fieldwork, Federal Work-Study, institutionally sponsored loans, and scholarships/grants available. Support available to part-time students. Financial award application deadline: 6/30; financial award applicants required to submit FAFSA. *Unit head:* Dr. Ralph Hughes, Chair, 410-951-3048, E-mail: khughes@coppin.edu.

Curry College, Division of Continuing Education and Graduate Studies, Program in Criminal Justice, Milton, MA 02186-9984. Offers MA. Part-time and evening/weekend programs available. *Faculty:* 5 full-time (1 woman), 5 part-time/adjunct (2 women). *Students:* Average age 32. 32 applicants, 91% accepted, 29 enrolled. In 2007, 59 degrees awarded. *Degree requirements:* For master's, thesis. *Entrance requirements:* For master's, MAT or GRE, resumé, recommendations, interview, written statement. Additional exam requirements/recommendations for international students: Required—TOEFL (minimum score 550 paper-based; 213 computer-based; 80 iBT). *Application deadline:* For fall admission, 8/1 priority date for domestic students, 6/1 for international students; for winter admission, 10/1 for international students; for spring admission, 1/1 priority date for domestic students, 1/28 for international students. Applications are processed on a rolling basis. Application fee: $50. *Expenses: Contact institution.* Part-time tuition and fees vary according to program. *Unit head:* Dr. Rebecca Paynich, Director and Associate Professor, 617-333-2084, Fax: 617-979-3535. *Application contact:* John Bresnahan, Director of Graduate Enrollment and Student Services, 617-333-2243, Fax: 617-979-3535, E-mail: jbresnah0104@curry.edu.

Dallas Baptist University, College of Adult Education, Professional Development Program, Dallas, TX 75211-9299. Offers accounting (MA); business (MA); church leadership (MA); corporate management (MA); counseling (MA); criminal justice (MA); English as a second language (MA); finance (MA); higher education (MA); leadership studies (MA); management (MA); management information systems (MA); marketing (MA); missions (MA). Part-time and evening/weekend programs available. *Faculty:* 55 full-time (22 women), 114 part-time/adjunct (44 women). *Students:* 19 full-time, 72 part-time. 35 applicants, 46% accepted, 12 enrolled. In 2007, 37 degrees awarded. *Entrance requirements:* For master's, minimum GPA of 3.0. Additional exam requirements/recommendations for international students: Required—TOEFL, IELTS. Application fee: $25. *Expenses:* Tuition: Full-time $9,144; part-time $508 per credit hour. *Financial support:* Federal Work-Study, institutionally sponsored loans, scholarships/grants, and tuition waivers (full and partial) available. Support available to part-time students. Financial award applicants required to submit FAFSA. *Unit head:* Dr. David Stricklin, Acting Director, 214-333-5496, Fax: 214-333-5558, E-mail: graduate@dbu.edu. *Application contact:* Kit P. Montgomery, Director of Graduate Programs, 214-333-5242, Fax: 214-333-5579, E-mail: graduate@dbu.edu.

Delta State University, Graduate Programs, College of Arts and Sciences, Division of Social Sciences, Program in Criminal Justice, Cleveland, MS 38733-0001. Offers MSCJ. Part-time programs available. Postbaccalaureate distance learning degree programs offered. *Degree requirements:* For master's, thesis or alternative. *Application deadline:* For fall admission, 8/1 priority date for domestic students; for spring admission, 12/1 priority date for domestic students. Applications are processed on a rolling basis. Application fee: $0. *Expenses:* Tuition, state resident: full-time $4,248. Tuition, nonresident: full-time $10,258. *Financial support:* Research assistantships, career-related internships or fieldwork, Federal Work-Study, and institutionally sponsored loans available. Support available to part-time students. Financial award application deadline: 6/1.

DeSales University, Graduate Division, Program in Criminal Justice, Center Valley, PA 18034-9568. Offers MACJ. *Students:* 29. In 2007, 11 degrees awarded. *Unit head:* Dr. Patrick McGrain, Director, 610-282-1100 Ext. 1584, E-mail: patrick.mcgrain@desales.edu. *Application contact:* Colleen Petrick, Secretary, Social Science Department, 610-212-1100 Ext. 1466, Fax: 610-282-0787, E-mail: colleen.petrick@desales.edu.

Drury University, Program in Criminology/Criminal Justice, Springfield, MO 65802. Offers criminal justice (MS); criminology (MA). Part-time and evening/weekend programs available. *Students:* Average age 33. *Degree requirements:* For master's, thesis (for some programs). *Entrance requirements:* For master's, GMAT or MAT. Additional exam requirements/recommendations for international students: Required—TOEFL. *Application deadline:* For fall admission, 8/25 priority date for domestic students; for spring admission, 1/15 priority date for domestic students. Applications are processed on a rolling basis. Application fee: $25. Electronic applications accepted. *Expenses: Contact institution. Financial support:* Application deadline: 10/15; *Faculty research:* Gangs, fear of crime, social justice, social change and law, drug laws in Iran. *Unit head:* Dr. Jana Bufkin, Director, 417-873-6948, Fax: 417-873-6681, E-mail: grad@drury.edu. *Application contact:* Kay Lowder, Graduate Programs Office Coordinator, 417-873-6948, Fax: 417-873-6681, E-mail: grad@drury.edu.

East Carolina University, Graduate School, College of Human Ecology, Department of Criminal Justice, Greenville, NC 27858-4353. Offers MS. Part-time and evening/weekend programs available. Postbaccalaureate distance learning degree programs offered (no on-campus study). *Students:* 14 full-time (6 women), 30 part-time (12 women); includes 8 minority (all African Americans) Average age 31. 28 applicants, 7% accepted, 1 enrolled. In 2007, 10 degrees awarded. *Degree requirements:* For master's, thesis, internship. *Entrance requirements:* For master's, GRE or MAT, bachelor's degree in criminal justice or related field. Additional exam requirements/recommendations for international students: Required—TOEFL. *Application deadline:* For fall admission, 1/15 priority date for domestic students. Application fee: $50. *Financial support:* In 2007–08, 5 students received support, including 2 research assistantships with tuition reimbursements available (averaging $7,500 per year); career-related internships or fieldwork, Federal Work-Study, institutionally sponsored loans, scholarships/grants, tuition waivers (full), and unspecified assistantships also available. Financial award application deadline: 6/1. *Faculty research:* Corrections, policing, international criminal justice, terrorism. *Unit head:* Dr. James F Anderson, Chair, 252-328-4192, Fax: 252-328-4196, E-mail: andersonjf@ecu.edu.

East Central University, School of Graduate Studies, Department of Human Resources, Ada, OK 74820-6899. Offers administration (MSHR); counseling (MSHR); criminal justice (MSHR); rehabilitation counseling (MSHR). *Accreditation:* CORE. Part-time and evening/weekend programs available. *Faculty:* 7 part-time/adjunct (3 women). *Students:* 83 full-time (71 women), 103 part-time (73 women); includes 54 minority (11 African Americans, 38 American Indian/Alaska Native, 1 Asian American or Pacific Islander, 4 Hispanic Americans). Average age 37. 125 applicants, 90% accepted. In 2007, 60 degrees awarded. *Degree requirements:* For master's, thesis optional. *Entrance requirements:* For master's, GRE General Test, MAT, minimum GPA of 2.5. *Application deadline:* Applications are processed on a rolling basis. Application fee: $0 ($50 for international students). Electronic applications accepted. *Expenses:* Tuition, state resident: full-time $2,784. Required fees: $53. *Financial support:* In 2007–08, 1 teaching assistantship was awarded. *Unit head:* Dr. James Burke, Chairman, 580-332-8000 Ext. 481, E-mail: jburke@ecok.edu. *Application contact:* Juanita L. Pratt, Secretary, 580-310-5708, Fax: 580-282-8691, E-mail: jpratt@ecok.edu.

Eastern Kentucky University, The Graduate School, College of Justice and Safety, Program in Correctional and Juvenile Justice Studies, Richmond, KY 40475-3102. Offers MS. *Faculty:* 4 full-time (1 woman), 1 part-time/adjunct (0 women). *Students:* 8 full-time (6 women), 14 part-time (9 women); includes 4 minority (all African Americans) Average age 33. 24 applicants, 100% accepted. In 2007, 4 degrees awarded. *Degree requirements:* For master's, comprehensive exam (for some programs), thesis (for some programs). *Entrance requirements:* For master's, GRE. Application fee: $35. *Financial support:* In 2007–08, 6 research assistantships (averaging $13,000 per year) were awarded. *Unit head:* Dr. Rick Ruddell, Graduate Program Coordinator, 859-622-1155, Fax: 859-622-6650. *Application contact:* Amy Eades, Assistant to the Coordinator, 859-622-5086, Fax: 859-622-6650, E-mail: amy.eades@eku.edu.

Eastern Kentucky University, The Graduate School, College of Justice and Safety, Program in Criminal Justice and Police Studies, Richmond, KY 40475-3102. Offers criminal justice (MS); criminal justice education (MS); police studies (MS). Part-time programs available. *Faculty:* 9 full-time (2 women). *Students:* 35 full-time (26 women), 31 part-time (10 women); includes 4 minority (all African Americans) Average age 30. 97 applicants, 2% accepted. In 2007, 28 degrees awarded. *Degree requirements:* For master's, thesis optional. *Entrance requirements:* For master's, GRE General Test, minimum GPA of 3.0. Application fee: $35. *Financial support:* Research assistantships, teaching assistantships, career-related internships or fieldwork and Federal Work-Study available. Support available to part-time students. Total annual research expenditures: $37.5 million. *Unit head:* Dr. Carole Garrison, Chair, 859-622-8077, Fax: 859-622-1549.

Eastern Kentucky University, The Graduate School, College of Justice and Safety, Program in Loss Prevention and Safety, Richmond, KY 40475-3102. Offers MS. *Faculty:* 5 full-time (0 women), 1 (woman) part-time/adjunct. *Students:* 14 full-time (3 women), 61 part-time (11 women); includes 3 minority (all African Americans), 2 international. Average age 33. 79 applicants, 20% accepted, 15 enrolled. In 2007, 11 degrees awarded. *Entrance requirements:* For master's, GRE. Application fee: $35. *Unit head:* Dr. Larry Collins, Chair, 859-622-1009, Fax: 859-622-6548.

Eastern Michigan University, Graduate School, College of Arts and Sciences, Department of Sociology, Anthropology and Criminology, Program in Criminology and Criminal Justice, Ypsilanti, MI 48197. Offers MA. *Students:* 6 full-time (3 women), 23 part-time (16 women); includes 7 African Americans, 1 American Indian/Alaska Native, 1 Hispanic American, 1 international. Average age 33. In 2007, 9 degrees awarded. Application fee: $35. *Expenses:* Tuition, state resident: full-time $8,952; part-time $373 per credit hour. Tuition, nonresident: full-time $17,634; part-time $735 per credit hour. Required fees: $896; $34 per credit hour. Tuition and fees vary according to course level, degree level and program. *Application contact:* Dr. Donna Killingbeck, Advisor, 734-487-0012, Fax: 734-487-9666, E-mail: dkillingb@emich.edu.

Eastern Michigan University, Graduate School, College of Technology, School of Technology Studies, Ypsilanti, MI 48197. Offers apparel, textile merchandising (MS); career, technical and workforce education (MS); hotel and restaurant management (MS, Graduate Certificate); information security (MLS, Graduate Certificate); legal administration (Graduate Certificate); technology studies (MLS, MS), including interdisciplinary technology (MLS), technology studies (MS). Part-time and evening/weekend programs available. Postbaccalaureate distance learning degree programs offered (minimal on-campus study). *Faculty:* 30 full-time (13 women). *Students:* 20 full-time (13 women), 82 part-time (43 women); includes 33 minority (26 African Americans, 3 American Indian/Alaska Native, 4 Asian Americans or Pacific Islanders), 15 international. Average age 37. In 2007, 83 master's, 13 other advanced degrees awarded. *Degree requirements:* For master's, thesis optional. *Entrance requirements:* For master's, GRE General Test. Additional exam requirements/recommendations for international students: Required—TOEFL. *Application deadline:* Applications are processed on a rolling basis. Application fee: $35. *Expenses:* Tuition, state resident: full-time $8,952; part-time $373 per credit hour. Tuition, nonresident: full-time $17,634; part-time $735 per credit hour. Required fees: $896; $34 per credit hour. Tuition and fees vary according to course level, degree level and program. *Financial support:* Fellowships, research assistantships with full tuition reimbursements, teaching assistantships with full tuition reimbursements, career-related internships or fieldwork, Federal Work-Study, institutionally sponsored loans, scholarships/grants, tuition waivers (partial), and unspecified assistantships available. Support available to part-time students. Financial award applicants required to submit FAFSA. *Unit head:* Dr. John Boyless, Interim Director, 734-487-1161, Fax: 734-487-7690, E-mail: john.boyless@emich.edu.

East Tennessee State University, School of Graduate Studies, College of Arts and Sciences, Department of Criminal Justice and Criminology, Johnson City, TN 37614. Offers MA. Part-time and evening/weekend programs available. *Degree requirements:* For master's, thesis or alternative. *Entrance requirements:* For master's, GRE General Test, minimum GPA of 3.0. Additional exam requirements/recommendations for international students: Required—TOEFL (minimum score 550 paper-based; 213 computer-based). *Faculty research:* Prisonization, peacemaking, sentencing decisions, family violence and sexual violence, juvenile justice.

Everest University, Graduate Programs, Jacksonville, FL 32256. Offers business (MBA); criminal justice (MS).

Everest University, Program in Criminal Justice, Tampa, FL 33619. Offers MS. Part-time and evening/weekend programs available. Postbaccalaureate distance learning degree programs offered (minimal on-campus study). *Faculty:* 2 part-time/adjunct (0 women). *Students:* 2 full-time (both women), 11 part-time (6 women); includes 12 minority (8 African Americans, 2 Asian Americans or Pacific Islanders, 2 Hispanic Americans). Average age 48. In 2007, 11 degrees awarded. *Degree requirements:* For master's, thesis optional, externship, research practicum. *Entrance requirements:* Additional exam requirements/recommendations for international students: Required—TOEFL (minimum score 550 paper-based; 213 computer-based). *Application deadline:* Applications are processed on a rolling basis. Application fee: $25. *Expenses:* Tuition: Full-time $14,720; part-time $460 per credit hour. Required fees: $60 per quarter. *Financial support:* Federal Work-Study, institutionally sponsored loans, and scholarships/grants available. *Unit head:* Jim Pingel, Chair, 813-621-0041 Ext. 148, Fax: 813-623-5769. *Application contact:* Shandretta Pointer, Admissions Office, 813-621-0041 Ext. 106, Fax: 813-628-0919, E-mail: spointer@cci.edu.

Everest University, Program in Criminal Justice, Lakeland, FL 33801. Offers MS.

Everest University, Program in Criminal Justice, Pompano Beach, FL 33062. Offers MS.

Fairmont State University, Graduate Studies, Program in Criminal Justice, Fairmont, WV 26554. Offers MS. *Degree requirements:* For master's, thesis or comprehensive exam. *Entrance requirements:* For master's, GRE, minimum GPA of 3.0.

Fayetteville State University, Graduate School, Program in Criminal Justice, Fayetteville, NC 28301-4298. Offers MA. *Faculty:* 8 full-time (4 women). *Students:* 4 full-time (3 women), 18 part-time (9 women); includes 15 minority (14 African Americans, 1 Hispanic American). Average age 35. 8 applicants, 100% accepted, 8 enrolled. *Expenses:* Tuition, state resident: full-time $2,118; part-time $265 per credit hour. Tuition, nonresident: full-time $11,708; part-time $1,464 per credit hour. Required fees: $1,218; $152 per credit hour. *Unit head:* Dr. Melissa Barlow, Interim Chair, 910-672-1972, Fax: 910-672-1908, E-mail: mbarlow@uncfsu.edu.

Ferris State University, College of Education and Human Services, School of Criminal Justice, Big Rapids, MI 49307. Offers criminal justice administration (MS). Part-time programs available. *Faculty:* 6 full-time (1 woman), 1 (woman) part-time/adjunct. *Students:* 19 full-time (10 women), 50 part-time (31 women); includes 25 minority (23 African Americans, 1 American Indian/Alaska Native, 1 Hispanic American). Average age 33. 25 applicants, 100% accepted, 24 enrolled. In 2007, 28 degrees awarded. *Degree requirements:* For master's, comprehensive exam, thesis optional. *Entrance requirements:* For master's, bachelor's degree in criminal justice or related field, minimum GPA of 3.0. Additional exam requirements/recommendations for international students: Required—TOEFL. *Application deadline:* For fall admission, 8/23 priority date for domestic students; for winter admission, 12/10 priority date for domestic students. Applications are processed on a rolling basis. Application fee: $30. Electronic applications accepted. *Expenses:* Tuition, state resident: part-time $389 per credit. Tuition, nonresident: part-time $753 per credit. *Financial support:* In 2007–08, 4 students received support, including 2 research assistantships (averaging $4,200 per year); career-related internships or fieldwork also available. *Faculty research:* Policy enactment, health and safety issues, criminological theory, juvenile justice, policy techniques, problem based learning. *Unit head:* Dr. Frank Crowe, Director, 231-591-2840, Fax: 231-591-3792, E-mail: crowef@ferris.edu. *Application contact:* Dr. Nancy L. Hogan, Assistant Professor, 231-591-2664, Fax: 231-591-3792, E-mail: nancy_hogan@ferris.edu.

Fitchburg State College, Division of Graduate and Continuing Education, Program in Criminal Justice, Fitchburg, MA 01420-2697. Offers MS. Part-time and evening/weekend programs available. *Entrance requirements:* For master's, GRE General Test or MAT, letters of recommendation, resumé. Additional exam requirements/recommendations for international students: Required—TOEFL (minimum score 550 paper-based; 213 computer-based; 79 iBT). *Application deadline:* Applications are processed on a rolling basis. Application fee: $25 ($50 for international students). *Expenses:* Tuition, nonresident: part-time $150 per credit. Required fees: $109 per credit. *Financial support:* In 2007–08, research assistantships with partial tuition reimbursements (averaging $5,500 per year); Federal Work-Study, scholarships/grants, and unspecified assistantships also available. Support available to part-time students. Financial award application deadline: 3/1; financial award applicants required to submit FAFSA. *Unit head:* Dr. Richard Wiebe, Chair, 978-665-3356, Fax: 978-554-3658, E-mail: gce@fsc.edu. *Application contact:* Director of Admissions, 978-665-3144, Fax: 978-665-4540, E-mail: admissions@fsc.edu.

Florida Agricultural and Mechanical University, Division of Graduate Studies, Research, and Continuing Education, College of Arts and Sciences, Division of History and Political Sciences, Program in Applied Social Science, Tallahassee, FL 32307-3200. Offers African American history (MASS); criminal justice (MASS); economics (MASS); history (MASS); political science (MASS); public administration (MASS); public management (MASS); social work (MASS); sociology (MASS). Part-time programs available. *Degree requirements:* For master's, thesis optional. *Entrance requirements:* For master's, GRE General Test, minimum GPA of 3.0. *Faculty research:* Southern history, black history, election trends, presidential history.

Florida Atlantic University, College of Architecture, Urban and Public Affairs, Department of Criminology and Criminal Justice, Boca Raton, FL 33431-0991. Offers MCJ. Part-time and evening/weekend programs available. Postbaccalaureate distance learning degree programs offered. *Degree requirements:* For master's, thesis optional. *Entrance requirements:* For master's, GRE General Test, minimum GPA of 3.0, undergraduate course work in statistics and criminology. Additional exam requirements/recommendations for international students: Required—TOEFL. Electronic applications accepted. *Faculty research:* Restorative, justice corrections, logic modeling, criminal justice management, crime causation.

Florida Gulf Coast University, College of Professional Studies, Program in Criminal Justice Studies, Fort Myers, FL 33965-6565. Offers MS. *Faculty:* 30 full-time (12 women), 24 part-time/adjunct (8 women). *Students:* Average age 23. 2 applicants, 100% accepted, 1 enrolled. *Entrance requirements:* For master's, GRE General Test, Minimum GPA of 3.0. Additional exam requirements/recommendations for international students: Required—TOEFL (minimum score 550 paper-based; 213 computer-based). *Application deadline:* For fall admission, 3/1 for domestic students; for spring admission, 11/1 for domestic students. Applications are processed on a rolling basis. Application fee: $30. Electronic applications accepted. *Expenses:* Tuition, state resident: full-time $4,542. Tuition, nonresident: full-time $19,449. Required fees: $1,297. *Unit head:* Tony Barringer, Chair, 239-590-7849, E-mail: tbarring@fgcu.edu.

Florida Gulf Coast University, College of Professional Studies, Program in Public Administration, Fort Myers, FL 33965-6565. Offers criminal justice (MPA); environmental policy (MPA); general public administration (MPA); management (MPA). Part-time programs available. *Faculty:* 30 full-time (12 women), 24 part-time/adjunct (8 women). *Students:* 40 full-time (27 women), 16 part-time (11 women); includes 9 minority (2 African Americans, 2 American Indian/Alaska Native, 2 Asian Americans or Pacific Islanders, 3 Hispanic Americans). Average age 35. 26 applicants, 88% accepted, 17 enrolled. In 2007, 8 degrees awarded. *Entrance requirements:* For master's, GRE General Test, MAT, minimum GPA of 3.0. Additional exam requirements/recommendations for international students: Required—TOEFL (minimum score 550 paper-based; 213 computer-based). *Application deadline:* For fall admission, 7/1 priority date for domestic students; for spring admission, 11/15 for domestic students. Applications are processed on a rolling basis. Application fee: $30. Electronic applications accepted. *Expenses:* Tuition, state resident: full-time $4,542. Tuition, nonresident: full-time $19,449. Required fees: $1,297. *Financial support:* In 2007–08, 5 research assistantships were awarded; career-related internships or fieldwork and tuition waivers (full and partial) also available. Support available to part-time students. *Faculty research:* Personnel, public policy, public finance, housing policy. *Unit head:* Terry Busson, Chair, 239-590-7704, E-mail: tbusson@fgcu.edu. *Application contact:* Roger Green, Information Contact, 239-590-7838, Fax: 239-590-7846.

Florida International University, College of Social Work, Justice and Public Affairs, School of Criminal Justice, Miami, FL 33199. Offers MS. Part-time and evening/weekend programs available. *Faculty:* 13 full-time (5 women). *Students:* 34 full-time (19 women), 43 part-time (31 women); includes 64 minority (27 African Americans, 3 Asian Americans or Pacific Islanders, 34 Hispanic Americans), 1 international. Average age 29. 60 applicants, 62% accepted, 33 enrolled. In 2007, 32 degrees awarded. *Degree requirements:* For master's, thesis optional. *Entrance requirements:* For master's, minimum GPA of 3.0, letters of recommendation. Additional exam requirements/recommendations for international students: Required—TOEFL (minimum score 550 paper-based; 213 computer-based). *Application deadline:* For fall admission, 6/1 for domestic students, 4/1 for international students; for spring admission, 10/1 for domestic students, 9/1 for international students. Applications are processed on a rolling basis. Application fee: $30. Electronic applications accepted. *Expenses:* Tuition, state resident: full-time $6,106. Tuition, nonresident: full-time $15,528. Required fees: $284. *Financial support:* Scholarships/grants available. *Unit head:* Dr. Lisa Stolzenberg, Director, 305-348-5890, Fax: 305-348-2503, E-mail: lisa.stolzenberg@fiu.edu.

Florida State University, Graduate Studies, College of Criminology and Criminal Justice, Tallahassee, FL 32306. Offers MA, MSC, PhD, MPA/MSC, MS/MSW. Part-time and evening/weekend programs available. Postbaccalaureate distance learning degree programs offered (no on-campus study). *Faculty:* 20 full-time (4 women). *Students:* 79 full-time (46 women), 69 part-time (40 women); includes 25 minority (16 African Americans, 1 American Indian/Alaska Native, 4 Asian Americans or Pacific Islanders, 4 Hispanic Americans), 2 international. 118 applicants, 73% accepted, 44 enrolled. In 2007, 33 master's, 3 doctorates awarded. *Degree requirements:* For master's, thesis optional; for doctorate, comprehensive exam, thesis/dissertation. *Entrance requirements:* For master's, GRE General Test; for doctorate, GRE General Test, area paper or thesis. Additional exam requirements/recommendations for international students: Required—TOEFL (minimum score 600 paper-based; 260 computer-based; 100 iBT). *Application deadline:* For fall admission, 7/1 for domestic students, 3/1 for international students. Applications are processed on a rolling basis. Application fee: $30. Electronic applications accepted. *Expenses:* Tuition, state resident: part-time $248 per credit hour. Tuition, nonresident: part-time $880 per credit hour. Tuition and fees vary according to program. *Financial support:* In 2007–08, fellowships with full tuition reimbursements (averaging $16,500 per year), 23 research assistantships with full tuition reimbursements (averaging $11,000 per year), 2 teaching assistantships with full tuition reimbursements (averaging $11,000 per year) were awarded; institutionally sponsored loans, scholarships/grants, tuition waivers (partial), and unspecified assistantships also available. Financial award application deadline: 2/15; financial award applicants required to submit FAFSA. *Faculty research:* Criminological theory, criminal justice administration and planning, criminal justice evaluation, law and social control. *Unit head:* Dr. Thomas Blomberg, Dean, 850-644-7365, Fax: 850-644-9614. *Application contact:*

Criminal Justice and Criminology

Florida State University (continued)
Margarita Frankeberger, Graduate Student Coordinator, 850-644-7373, Fax: 850-644-9614, E-mail: mfrankeberger@fsu.edu.

The George Washington University, Columbian College of Arts and Sciences, Department of Forensic Sciences, Washington, DC 20052. Offers crime scene investigation (MFS); forensic chemistry (MFS, MSFS); forensic molecular biology (MFS, MSFS); forensic sciences (MFS, MSFS); forensic toxicology (MFS, MSFS); high-technology crime investigation (MFS); security management (MFS). High-technology crime investigation and security management programs offered in Arlington, VA. Part-time and evening/weekend programs available. *Degree requirements:* For master's, comprehensive exam. *Entrance requirements:* For master's, GRE General Test, minimum GPA of 3.0. Additional exam requirements/recommendations for international students: Required—TOEFL (minimum score 550 paper-based; 213 computer-based). Electronic applications accepted.

The George Washington University, Columbian College of Arts and Sciences, Department of Sociology, Program in Criminal Justice, Washington, DC 20052. Offers MA. *Degree requirements:* For master's, comprehensive exam. *Entrance requirements:* For master's, GRE General Test, minimum GPA of 3.0. Additional exam requirements/recommendations for international students: Required—TOEFL (minimum score 550 paper-based; 213 computer-based). Electronic applications accepted.

Georgia College & State University, Graduate School, School of Liberal Arts and Sciences, Department of Government and Sociology, Program in Criminal Justice, Milledgeville, GA 31061. Offers MS. *Students:* 6 full-time (5 women), 3 part-time (2 women); includes 3 minority (all African Americans) Average age 27. 10 applicants, 40% accepted, 2 enrolled. In 2007, 4 degrees awarded. *Degree requirements:* For master's, thesis optional, capstone project. *Entrance requirements:* For master's, GRE, 3 letters of recommendation. Additional exam requirements/recommendations for international students: Required—TOEFL. *Expenses:* Tuition, state resident: full-time $3,726. Tuition, nonresident: full-time $14,868. Required fees: $858. Tuition and fees vary according to campus/location. *Financial support:* In 2007–08, 3 research assistantships were awarded. *Unit head:* Dr. Gerald Fisher, Coordinator, Criminal Justice Program, 478-445-0940, E-mail: gerald.fisher@gcsu.edu.

Georgia State University, College of Health and Human Sciences, Department of Criminal Justice, Atlanta, GA 30303-3083. Offers MS. Part-time and evening/weekend programs available. *Faculty:* 12 full-time (5 women), 11 part-time/adjunct (5 women). *Students:* 14 full-time (9 women), 10 part-time (8 women); includes 10 minority (all African Americans) Average age 30. 31 applicants, 29% accepted, 6 enrolled. In 2007, 16 degrees awarded. *Degree requirements:* For master's, thesis optional, capstone seminar (optional). *Entrance requirements:* For master's, GRE General Test. Additional exam requirements/recommendations for international students: Required—TOEFL (minimum score 550 paper-based; 213 computer-based). *Application deadline:* For fall admission, 5/15 priority date for domestic students; for spring admission, 9/15 priority date for domestic students. Applications are processed on a rolling basis. Application fee: $50. Electronic applications accepted. *Expenses:* Tuition, state resident: part-time $221 per credit hour. *Financial support:* In 2007–08, 17 research assistantships with full and partial tuition reimbursements (averaging $2,658 per year), 3 teaching assistantships (averaging $1,000 per year) were awarded; Federal Work-Study, institutionally sponsored loans, scholarships/grants, tuition waivers (partial), and unspecified assistantships also available. Support available to part-time students. Financial award application deadline: 4/1; financial award applicants required to submit FAFSA. *Faculty research:* Violence against women, social support and adolescent crime, agencies and assault victims, minority trust of police, active offender crime and minority status. Total annual research expenditures: $1.1 million. *Unit head:* Dr. Brian K. Payne, Chairman, 404-413-1020, E-mail: bpayne@gsu.edu. *Application contact:* Grace Gipson, Academic Advisor, 404-413-1011, Fax: 404-413-1001, E-mail: chhs-oaa@gsu.edu.

Graduate School and University Center of the City University of New York, Graduate Studies, Program in Criminal Justice, New York, NY 10016-4039. Offers PhD. *Faculty:* 28 full-time (6 women). *Students:* 107 full-time (72 women), 8 part-time (1 woman); includes 26 minority (13 African Americans, 4 Asian Americans or Pacific Islanders, 9 Hispanic Americans), 14 international. Average age 37. 70 applicants, 27% accepted, 17 enrolled. In 2007, 12 degrees awarded. *Degree requirements:* For doctorate, one foreign language, thesis/dissertation. *Entrance requirements:* For doctorate, GRE General Test, writing sample. Additional exam requirements/recommendations for international students: Required—TOEFL. *Application deadline:* For fall admission, 1/15 for domestic students. Application fee: $125. Electronic applications accepted. *Financial support:* In 2007–08, 70 students received support, including 60 fellowships, 5 teaching assistantships; research assistantships, career-related internships or fieldwork, Federal Work-Study, institutionally sponsored loans, and tuition waivers (full and partial) also available. Financial award application deadline: 2/1; financial award applicants required to submit FAFSA. *Unit head:* Dr. Karen Terry, Executive Officer, 212-237-8040, Fax: 212-237-8940, E-mail: kterry@jjay.cuny.edu.

Grambling State University, School of Graduate Studies and Research, College of Professional Studies, Program in Criminal Justice, Grambling, LA 71245. Offers MS. Part-time programs available. *Faculty:* 6 full-time (3 women), 2 part-time/adjunct (0 women). *Students:* 40 full-time (31 women), 22 part-time (17 women); includes 60 minority (all African Americans) Average age 31. In 2007, 11 master's awarded. *Entrance requirements:* For master's, GRE, minimum GPA of 2.5 on last degree, 'A' in four core courses. Additional exam requirements/recommendations for international students: Required—TOEFL. *Application deadline:* For fall admission, 7/1 for domestic students; for spring admission, 12/1 for domestic students. Applications are processed on a rolling basis. Application fee: $20 ($30 for international students). *Expenses:* Tuition, state resident: full-time $1,729. Tuition, nonresident: full-time $3,736. *Financial support:* In 2007–08, 13 research assistantships (averaging $2,750 per year) were awarded; institutionally sponsored loans and unspecified assistantships also available. Financial award application deadline: 5/31; financial award applicants required to submit FAFSA. *Faculty research:* Corrections, terrorism, delinquency, complex organizations, postmodern theory. *Unit head:* Dr. Dilip Das, Director, 318-274-2520, E-mail: dilipd@gram.edu. *Application contact:* Dr. Joyce Montgomery, Coordinator, 318-274-2876, Fax: 318-274-3101, E-mail: montgomeryj@gram.edu.

Grand Valley State University, College of Community and Public Service, School of Criminal Justice, Allendale, MI 49401-9403. Offers MS. Part-time and evening/weekend programs available. *Faculty:* 10 full-time (4 women). *Students:* 16 full-time (10 women), 13 part-time (9 women); includes 3 minority (2 African Americans, 1 Hispanic American), 1 international. Average age 25. 19 applicants, 74% accepted, 10 enrolled. In 2007, 3 degrees awarded. *Degree requirements:* For master's, thesis or alternative. *Entrance requirements:* For master's, minimum GPA of 3.0. Additional exam requirements/recommendations for international students: Required—TOEFL. *Application deadline:* For fall admission, 7/30 priority date for domestic students; for winter admission, 12/10 priority date for domestic students; for spring admission, 4/10 priority date for domestic students. Application fee: $30. *Financial support:* In 2007–08, 12 students received support, including 1 research assistantship with full tuition reimbursement available (averaging $8,000 per year); career-related internships or fieldwork, Federal Work-Study, scholarships/grants, and unspecified assistantships also available. Support available to part-time students. Financial award application deadline: 5/1. *Faculty research:* Correctional administration, juvenile justice issues/gangs, women's issues, leadership, program/policy evaluation. *Unit head:* Dr. William Crawley, Director, 616-331-7143, Fax: 616-331-7155, E-mail: crawleyw@gvsu.edu. *Application contact:* Dr. Debra Ross, Information Contact, 616-331-7150, Fax: 616-331-7155, E-mail: rossd@gvsu.edu.

Hodges University, Graduate Programs, Naples, FL 34119. Offers business administration (MBA); computer information technology (MS); criminal justice (MCJ); education (MPS); information systems management (MIS); interdisciplinary (MPS); law (MPS); management (MSM); professional studies (MPS); psychology (MPS); public administration (MPA). Part-time and evening/weekend programs available. Postbaccalaureate distance learning degree programs offered (no on-campus study). *Faculty:* 16 full-time (4 women), 2 part-time/adjunct (1 woman). *Students:* 37 full-time (25 women), 175 part-time (104 women); includes 64 minority (29 African Americans, 2 Asian Americans or Pacific Islanders, 33 Hispanic Americans). Average age 36. In 2007, 75 degrees awarded. *Degree requirements:* For master's, comprehensive exam (for some programs). *Entrance requirements:* For master's, in-house entrance exam. *Application deadline:* Applications are processed on a rolling basis. Application fee: $50. Electronic applications accepted. *Expenses:* Tuition: Full-time $10,260; part-time $570 per credit hour. Required fees: $190 per trimester. *Financial support:* In 2007–08, 181 students received support. Federal Work-Study and scholarships/grants available. Financial award application deadline: 7/8; financial award applicants required to submit FAFSA. *Unit head:* Terry McMahan, President, 239-513-1122, Fax: 239-598-6253, E-mail: tmcmahan@hodges.edu. *Application contact:* Rita Lampus, Vice President of Student Enrollment Management, 239-513-1122, Fax: 239-598-6253, E-mail: rlampus@internationalcollege.edu.

Illinois State University, Graduate School, College of Applied Science and Technology, Department of Criminal Justice Sciences, Normal, IL 61790-2200. Offers MA, MS. *Faculty:* 10 full-time (5 women). *Students:* 14 full-time (7 women), 22 part-time (16 women); includes 2 minority (1 African American, 1 Hispanic American). 20 applicants, 65% accepted. In 2007, 12 degrees awarded. *Degree requirements:* For master's, thesis or alternative. *Entrance requirements:* For master's, GRE General Test, minimum GPA of 2.6 in last 60 hours of course work. *Application deadline:* Applications are processed on a rolling basis. Application fee: $40. *Expenses:* Tuition, state resident: full-time $3,492; part-time $194 per credit hour. Tuition, nonresident: full-time $7,272; part-time $404 per credit hour. Required fees: $1,024; $57 per credit hour. *Financial support:* In 2007–08, 9 research assistantships (averaging $7,695 per year) were awarded; career-related internships or fieldwork, tuition waivers (full and partial), and unspecified assistantships also available. Financial award application deadline: 4/1. *Faculty research:* Graduate practicum for victim assistance and advocacy, graduate practicum in adult probation cases, graduate practicum in youth intervention program. Total annual research expenditures: $38,078. *Unit head:* Dr. David Folcone, Chairperson, 309-438-7626.

Indiana State University, School of Graduate Studies, College of Arts and Sciences, Department of Criminology and Criminal Justice, Terre Haute, IN 47809-1401. Offers MA, MS. Part-time programs available. Postbaccalaureate distance learning degree programs offered (no on-campus study). *Faculty:* 8 full-time (2 women), 4 part-time/adjunct (2 women). *Students:* 45 full-time (27 women), 102 part-time (47 women); includes 29 minority (24 African Americans, 1 Asian American or Pacific Islander, 4 Hispanic Americans), 4 international. Average age 33. 97 applicants, 80% accepted, 45 enrolled. In 2007, 38 degrees awarded. *Degree requirements:* For master's, thesis (for some programs). *Entrance requirements:* For master's, minimum GPA of 2.75 in undergraduate work, 3.0 in previous graduate work. Additional exam requirements/recommendations for international students: Required—TOEFL (minimum score 550 paper-based). *Application deadline:* For fall admission, 7/1 priority date for domestic students; for spring admission, 11/1 priority date for domestic students. Applications are processed on a rolling basis. Application fee: $35. Electronic applications accepted. *Expenses:* Tuition, state resident: full-time $7,056; part-time $294 per semester hour. Tuition, nonresident: full-time $14,016; part-time $584 per semester hour. Required fees: $175 per semester. *Financial support:* In 2007–08, 7 teaching assistantships with partial tuition reimbursements (averaging $6,300 per year) were awarded; research assistantships with partial tuition reimbursements, career-related internships or fieldwork, tuition waivers (partial), and unspecified assistantships also available. Financial award application deadline: 3/1; financial award applicants required to submit FAFSA. *Faculty research:* Violent crime, rape attitudes, classification of offenders, substance abuse, domestic violence. *Unit head:* Dr. David Skelton, Interim Chairperson, 812-237-2190.

Indiana University Bloomington, University Graduate School, College of Arts and Sciences, Department of Criminal Justice, Bloomington, IN 47405-7000. Offers crime (MA, PhD); criminal justice (MA, PhD); cross-cultural perspectives of crime and justice (MA, PhD); law and society (MA, PhD). Part-time programs available. *Faculty:* 13 full-time (4 women). *Students:* 27 full-time (17 women), 13 part-time (8 women); includes 4 minority (1 African American, 2 American Indian/Alaska Native, 1 Hispanic American), 7 international. Average age 31. 27 applicants, 22% accepted, 6 enrolled. In 2007, 3 master's, 1 doctorate awarded. Terminal master's awarded for partial completion of doctoral program. *Median time to degree:* Of those who began their doctoral program in fall 1999, 20% received their degree in 8 years or less. *Degree requirements:* For master's, thesis optional; for doctorate, thesis/dissertation, foreign language or research practicum. *Entrance requirements:* For master's and doctorate, GRE General Test. Additional exam requirements/recommendations for international students: Required—TOEFL. *Application deadline:* For fall admission, 1/15 for domestic students, 12/15 for international students; for spring admission, 9/1 for domestic and international students. Application fee: $50 ($60 for international students). Electronic applications accepted. *Expenses:* Contact institution. *Financial support:* Fellowships with full tuition reimbursements, teaching assistantships with full tuition reimbursements available. Financial award application deadline: 1/15. *Unit head:* Marla Sandys, Chair, 812-855-5892. *Application contact:* Judy Kelley, Administrative Assistant, 812-855-9880, Fax: 812-855-5522, E-mail: kelleyj@indiana.edu.

Announcement: Indiana University Bloomington provides outstanding opportunities for advanced study in criminal justice. Both the master's and doctoral programs emphasize multidisciplinary study of crime, criminal justice, law and society, and cross-cultural perspectives. The department faculty is among the most interdisciplinary in the country in the area of criminal justice, with members holding degrees in anthropology, criminal justice and criminology, geography, history, law, political science, psychology, and sociology. There are also strong ties to other departments and faculty members within this well-respected Big 10 research university. Students are encouraged to work with faculty members on extensive and varied research projects.

Indiana University Northwest, School of Public and Environmental Affairs, Gary, IN 46408-1197. Offers criminal justice (MPA); environmental affairs (Graduate Certificate); health services administration (MPA); human services administration (MPA); nonprofit management (Graduate Certificate); public management (MPA, Graduate Certificate). *Accreditation:* NASPAA (one or more programs are accredited). Part-time programs available. *Faculty:* 5 full-time (3 women). *Students:* 28 full-time (21 women), 98 part-time (78 women); includes 82 minority (71 African Americans, 1 American Indian/Alaska Native, 1 Asian American or Pacific Islander, 9 Hispanic Americans). Average age 38. In 2007, 29 master's, 27 other advanced degrees awarded. *Entrance requirements:* For master's, GRE General Test or GMAT, letters of recommendation. *Application deadline:* For fall admission, 8/15 priority date for domestic students. Applications are processed on a rolling basis. Application fee: $25. *Expenses:* Tuition, state resident: full-time $4,636; part-time $193 per credit hour. Tuition, nonresident: full-time $10,787; part-time $449 per credit hour. Required fees: $436; $436 per year. Full-time tuition and fees vary according to course load, campus/location and program. *Financial support:* Career-related internships or fieldwork, Federal Work-Study, and tuition waivers (partial) available. Support available to part-time students. Financial award application deadline: 3/1. *Faculty research:* Employment in income security policies, evidence in criminal justice, equal employment law, social welfare policy and welfare reform, public finance in developing countries. *Unit head:* George Assibey-Mensah, Interim Dean/Division Director, 219-980-6695, Fax: 219-980-6737. *Application contact:* Sandra Hall Smith, Secretary, 219-980-6695, Fax: 219-980-6737, E-mail: shsmith@iun.edu.

Indiana University of Pennsylvania, School of Graduate Studies and Research, College of Health and Human Services, Department of Criminology, Doctoral Program in Criminology, Indiana, PA 15705-1087. Offers PhD. Part-time programs available. *Faculty:* 14 full-time (8 women). *Students:* 17 full-time (10 women), 39 part-time (19 women); includes 6 minority (5 African Americans, 1 Asian American or Pacific Islander), 7 international. Average age 33. 24

applicants, 54% accepted, 9 enrolled. In 2007, 1 degree awarded. *Degree requirements:* For doctorate, one foreign language, comprehensive exam, thesis/dissertation. *Entrance requirements:* For doctorate, GRE, 3 letters of recommendation, writing sample, interview. Additional exam requirements/recommendations for international students: Required—TOEFL. *Application deadline:* For fall admission, 7/1 priority date for domestic students; for spring admission, 11/1 for domestic students. Applications are processed on a rolling basis. Application fee: $30. *Expenses:* Tuition, state resident: full-time $6,214; part-time $345 per credit. Tuition, nonresident: full-time $9,944; part-time $552 per credit. Required fees: $43 per credit. One-time fee: $140 part-time. Tuition and fees vary according to course load. *Financial support:* In 2007–08, 4 fellowships (averaging $500 per year), 15 research assistantships with full and partial tuition reimbursements (averaging $6,180 per year), 4 teaching assistantships with partial tuition reimbursements (averaging $17,001 per year) were awarded; Federal Work-Study also available. Support available to part-time students. Financial award application deadline: 3/15; financial award applicants required to submit FAFSA. *Unit head:* Dr. David Myers, Graduate Coordinator, 724-357-5933, E-mail: david@iup.edu.

Indiana University of Pennsylvania, School of Graduate Studies and Research, College of Health and Human Services, Department of Criminology, Master's Program in Criminology, Indiana, PA 15705-1087. Offers MA. Part-time and evening/weekend programs available. *Faculty:* 14 full-time (8 women). *Students:* 39 full-time (28 women), 32 part-time (23 women); includes 6 minority (5 African Americans, 1 Asian American or Pacific Islander), 2 international. Average age 27. 81 applicants, 64% accepted, 39 enrolled. In 2007, 35 degrees awarded. *Degree requirements:* For master's, thesis optional. *Entrance requirements:* For master's, 2 letters of recommendation. Additional exam requirements/recommendations for international students: Required—TOEFL. *Application deadline:* For fall admission, 7/1 priority date for domestic students; for spring admission, 11/1 for domestic students. Applications are processed on a rolling basis. Application fee: $30. *Expenses:* Tuition, state resident: full-time $6,214; part-time $345 per credit. Tuition, nonresident: full-time $9,944; part-time $552 per credit. Required fees: $43 per credit. One-time fee: $140 part-time. Tuition and fees vary according to course load. *Financial support:* In 2007–08, 11 research assistantships with full and partial tuition reimbursements (averaging $2,645 per year) were awarded; fellowships, Federal Work-Study also available. Support available to part-time students. Financial award application deadline: 3/15; financial award applicants required to submit FAFSA. *Unit head:* Dr. Daniel Lee, Graduate Coordinator, 724-357-5977, E-mail: danlee@iup.edu.

Indiana University–Purdue University Indianapolis, School of Public and Environmental Affairs, Indianapolis, IN 46202-2896. Offers health administration (MHA); public affairs (MPA), including criminal justice, environmental management, nonprofit management, policy analysis, public management; JD/MHA; MBA/MHA; MLS/NMC; MLS/PMC; MSN/MHA. *Accreditation:* CAHME (one or more programs are accredited). Part-time and evening/weekend programs available. *Faculty:* 17 full-time (6 women). *Students:* 108 full-time (67 women), 291 part-time (159 women); includes 74 minority (43 African Americans, 1 American Indian/Alaska Native, 25 Asian Americans or Pacific Islanders, 5 Hispanic Americans), 10 international. Average age 35. In 2007, 77 degrees awarded. *Entrance requirements:* For master's, GRE General Test, minimum GPA of 3.0 (preferred). Additional exam requirements/recommendations for international students: Required—TOEFL. *Application deadline:* For fall admission, 7/15 priority date for domestic students; for spring admission, 11/15 for domestic students. Applications are processed on a rolling basis. Application fee: $50 ($60 for international students). *Expenses:* Tuition, state resident: full-time $5,818; part-time $242 per credit hour. Tuition, nonresident: full-time $17,106; part-time $713 per credit hour. Required fees: $629. Tuition and fees vary according to course load, campus/location and program. *Financial support:* In 2007–08, 11 fellowships with full and partial tuition reimbursements (averaging $5,890 per year), 10 teaching assistantships (averaging $9,900 per year) were awarded; research assistantships with full and partial tuition reimbursements, career-related internships or fieldwork, Federal Work-Study, institutionally sponsored loans, and scholarships/grants also available. Support available to part-time students. Financial award application deadline: 3/1. *Faculty research:* Economic development, water and air quality, ethics, financing, organization design and structure. Total annual research expenditures: $1.9 million. *Unit head:* Dr. Greg Lindsey, Associate Dean, 317-274-4656, Fax: 317-274-5153. *Application contact:* 317-274-4656, Fax: 317-274-5153, E-mail: speainfo@speanet.iupui.edu.

See Close-Up on page 1599.

Inter American University of Puerto Rico, Aguadilla Campus, Graduate School, Aguadilla, PR 00605. Offers counseling psychology with an emphasis in family (MS); criminal justice (MA); educative management and leadership (MA); elementary education (MA); industrial mangement (MBA); marketing (MBA). Part-time and evening/weekend programs available. *Degree requirements:* For master's, comprehensive exam. *Entrance requirements:* For master's, EXADEP, 2 letters of recommendation, minimum GPA of 2.5. Electronic applications accepted.

Inter American University of Puerto Rico, Metropolitan Campus, School of Criminal Justice, San Juan, PR 00919-1293. Offers MA. Part-time and evening/weekend programs available. *Degree requirements:* For master's, comprehensive exam. *Entrance requirements:* For master's, GRE or EXADEP, interview. Electronic applications accepted.

Inter American University of Puerto Rico, Ponce Campus, Graduate School, Mercedita, PR 00715-1602. Offers accounting (MBA); biology (M Ed); chemistry (M Ed); criminal justice (MA); elementary education (M Ed); English as a Second Language (M Ed); finance (MBA); history (M Ed); human resources (MBA); marketing (MBA); mathematics (M Ed); Spanish (M Ed). *Entrance requirements:* For master's, minimum GPA of 2.5.

Iona College, School of Arts and Science, Program in Criminal Justice, New Rochelle, NY 10801-1890. Offers MS. Part-time and evening/weekend programs available. *Faculty:* 5 full-time (1 woman), 2 part-time/adjunct (0 women). *Students:* 5 full-time (4 women), 25 part-time (13 women); includes 7 minority (5 African Americans, 2 Hispanic Americans). Average age 32. 23 applicants, 57% accepted, 11 enrolled. In 2007, 9 degrees awarded. *Degree requirements:* For master's, thesis. *Entrance requirements:* For master's, minimum GPA of 2.75. Additional exam requirements/recommendations for international students: Required—TOEFL (minimum score 550 paper-based; 213 computer-based). *Application deadline:* Applications are processed on a rolling basis. Application fee: $50. Electronic applications accepted. *Expenses:* Tuition: Part-time $712 per credit. Required fees: $150 per term. *Financial support:* Unspecified assistantships available. *Faculty research:* Police administration, victimology and criminal justice program evaluation. *Unit head:* Prof. Robert Castelli, Chair, 914-633-2084, E-mail: rcastelli@iona.edu. *Application contact:* Veronica Jarek-Prinz, Director of Graduate Admissions, 914-633-2420, Fax: 914-633-2277, E-mail: vjarekprinz@iona.edu.

Jackson State University, Graduate School, School of Liberal Arts, Center for Urban Affairs/Criminology and Justice Services, Jackson, MS 39217. Offers criminology and justice service (MA). Part-time and evening/weekend programs available. *Degree requirements:* For master's, comprehensive exam, thesis optional. *Entrance requirements:* For master's, GRE General Test. Additional exam requirements/recommendations for international students: Required—TOEFL.

Jacksonville State University, College of Graduate Studies and Continuing Education, College of Arts and Sciences, Department of Criminal Justice, Jacksonville, AL 36265-1602. Offers MS. Part-time and evening/weekend programs available. *Faculty:* 5 full-time (1 woman), 1 part-time/adjunct (0 women). *Students:* 9 full-time (6 women), 21 part-time (16 women); includes 15 minority (all African Americans), 2 international. *Degree requirements:* For master's, thesis optional. *Entrance requirements:* For master's, GRE General Test or MAT. *Application deadline:* Applications are processed on a rolling basis. Application fee: $20. *Financial support:* In 2007–08, 2 research assistantships were awarded. Support available to part-time students. Financial award application deadline: 4/1. *Unit head:* Richard Kenia, Head, 256-782-5339. *Application contact:* 256-782-5329, Fax: 256-782-5321, E-mail: graduate@jsu.edu.

John Jay College of Criminal Justice of the City University of New York, Graduate Studies, Program in Protection Management, New York, NY 10019-1093. Offers MS. Part-time and evening/weekend programs available. *Degree requirements:* For master's, thesis or alternative. *Entrance requirements:* For master's, minimum B average. Additional exam requirements/recommendations for international students: Required—TOEFL (minimum score 500 paper-based; 173 computer-based).

John Jay College of Criminal Justice of the City University of New York, Graduate Studies, Programs in Criminal Justice, New York, NY 10019-1093. Offers criminal justice (MA, PhD); criminology and deviance (PhD); forensic psychology (PhD); forensic science (PhD); law and philosophy (PhD); organizational behavior (PhD); public policy (PhD). Part-time and evening/weekend programs available. Terminal master's awarded for partial completion of doctoral program. *Degree requirements:* For master's, thesis or alternative; for doctorate, one foreign language, thesis/dissertation. *Entrance requirements:* For master's, GRE General Test, minimum B average; for doctorate, GRE General Test. Additional exam requirements/recommendations for international students: Required—TOEFL (minimum score 500 paper-based; 173 computer-based).

The Johns Hopkins University, School of Education, Division of Public Safety Leadership, Baltimore, MD 21218-2699. Offers homeland security (MS); intelligence analysis (MS); management (MS). Part-time and evening/weekend programs available. *Students:* 133 full-time (36 women), 12 part-time (5 women); includes 55 minority (48 African Americans, 5 Asian Americans or Pacific Islanders, 2 Hispanic Americans). Average age 37. 70 applicants, 90% accepted, 60 enrolled. In 2007, 96 degrees awarded. *Entrance requirements:* For master's, minimum GPA of 3.0, interview, resumé, letters of recommendation. Additional exam requirements/recommendations for international students: Required—TOEFL (minimum score 600 paper-based; 250 computer-based; 100 iBT). *Application deadline:* For fall admission, 5/1 for international students; for spring admission, 10/15 for international students. Applications are processed on a rolling basis. Application fee: $60. *Financial support:* Scholarships/grants available. Support available to part-time students. Financial award application deadline: 6/1; financial award applicants required to submit FAFSA. *Faculty research:* Ethics and integrity, counter terrorism, school safety, Homeland Security, identity theft. *Unit head:* Dr. Sheldon Greenberg, Associate Dean, 410-312-4401, Fax: 410-290-1061, E-mail: greenberg@jhu.edu. *Application contact:* Kelly Williams, Academic Administrator, 410-312-4409, Fax: 410-290-1061, E-mail: kelly.williams@jhu.edu.

Kaplan University–Davenport, School of Criminal Justice, Davenport, IA 52807-2095. Offers corrections (MSCJ); global issues in criminal justice (MSCJ); law (MSCJ); leadership and executive management (MSCJ); policing (MSCJ). Part-time and evening/weekend programs available. Postbaccalaureate distance learning degree programs offered (no on-campus study). *Students:* 82 full-time (59 women), 325 part-time (233 women); includes 1 Asian American or Pacific Islander. Average age 37. In 2007, 8 degrees awarded. *Entrance requirements:* Additional exam requirements/recommendations for international students: Required—TOEFL (minimum score 550 paper-based; 218 computer-based; 80 iBT). *Application deadline:* Applications are processed on a rolling basis. Electronic applications accepted. *Expenses:* Tuition: Full-time $12,972; part-time $395 per credit. Required fees: $100 per term. Tuition and fees vary according to course load and program. *Unit head:* Frank J. DiMarino, Head, 866-527-5268.

Kean University, College of Business and Public Administration, Program in Public Administration, Union, NJ 07083. Offers criminal justice (MPA); environmental management (MPA); health services administration (MPA); non-profit management (MPA); public administration (MPA). *Accreditation:* NASPAA. Part-time and evening/weekend programs available. *Faculty:* 7 full-time (4 women). *Students:* 63 full-time (37 women), 82 part-time (52 women); includes 68 African Americans, 6 Asian Americans or Pacific Islanders, 17 Hispanic Americans, 14 international. Average age 32. 64 applicants, 73% accepted, 25 enrolled. In 2007, 58 degrees awarded. *Degree requirements:* For master's, thesis, internship, research seminar. *Entrance requirements:* For master's, 2 letters of recommendation, interview, essay. *Application deadline:* For fall admission, 5/1 for domestic students; for spring admission, 11/1 for domestic students. Application fee: $60 ($150 for international students). Electronic applications accepted. *Expenses:* Tuition, state resident: full-time $9,384; part-time $391 per credit. Tuition, nonresident: full-time $12,720; part-time $530 per credit. Required fees: $2,382; $99 per credit. Part-time tuition and fees vary according to course load. *Financial support:* In 2007–08, 15 research assistantships with full tuition reimbursements (averaging $3,217 per year) were awarded; unspecified assistantships also available. *Faculty research:* Fiscal impact of New Federalism, New Jersey state and local government, computer application in public management. *Unit head:* Dr. Craig P. Donovan, Program Coordinator, 908-737-4307, E-mail: cpdonova@kean.edu. *Application contact:* Joanne Morris, Director of Graduate Admissions, 908-737-3355, Fax: 908-737-3354, E-mail: grad-adm@kean.edu.

Keiser University, Program in Criminal Justice, Fort Lauderdale, FL 33309. Offers MA.

Kent State University, College of Arts and Sciences, Department of Justice Studies, Kent, OH 44242-0001. Offers MA. Part-time and evening/weekend programs available. *Faculty:* 14 full-time (6 women), 2 part-time/adjunct (0 women). *Students:* 14 full-time (4 women), 34 part-time (24 women); includes 6 minority (all African Americans), 5 international. 31 applicants, 77% accepted, 16 enrolled. In 2007, 9 degrees awarded. *Degree requirements:* For master's, comprehensive exam, thesis optional. *Entrance requirements:* For master's, minimum GPA of 2.75. Additional exam requirements/recommendations for international students: Required—TOEFL. *Application deadline:* For fall admission, 7/12 for domestic and international students; for spring admission, 11/29 for domestic and international students. Applications are processed on a rolling basis. Application fee: $30. Electronic applications accepted. *Financial support:* In 2007–08, 4 students received support, including 4 research assistantships with full tuition reimbursements available (averaging $3,150 per year); teaching assistantships, career-related internships or fieldwork, Federal Work-Study, institutionally sponsored loans, and tuition waivers (full) also available. Financial award application deadline: 2/1. *Faculty research:* School violence, community policing. *Unit head:* Dr. Mark Colvin, Chair, 330-672-2775, E-mail: mcolvin1@kent.edu. *Application contact:* Dr. Shelley Listwan, Graduate Coordinator, 330-672-7880, Fax: 330-672-5394, E-mail: slistwan@kent.edu.

Keuka College, Program in Criminal Justice Administration, Keuka Park, NY 14478-0098. Offers MS. Part-time and evening/weekend programs available. *Faculty:* 6 part-time/adjunct (2 women). *Students:* 11 full-time (8 women), 35 part-time (19 women); includes 15 minority (11 African Americans, 1 Asian American or Pacific Islander, 3 Hispanic Americans). 102 applicants, 100% accepted. In 2007, 9 degrees awarded. *Application deadline:* For fall admission, 8/15 for domestic students; for winter admission, 12/15 for domestic students; for spring admission, 4/15 for domestic students. Application fee: $30. *Expenses: Contact institution.* Tuition and fees vary according to program. *Unit head:* Dr. Tom Tremer, Program Director, 315-279-5672, E-mail: ttremer@mail.keuka.edu.

Lamar University, College of Graduate Studies, College of Arts and Sciences, Department of Sociology, Social Work, and Criminal Justice, Beaumont, TX 77710. Offers applied criminology (MS). Part-time programs available. *Faculty:* 3 full-time (1 woman), 1 part-time/adjunct (0 women). *Students:* 2 full-time (both women), 1 (woman) part-time. Average age 27. 16 applicants, 31% accepted, 0 enrolled. In 2007, 4 degrees awarded. *Degree requirements:* For master's, thesis or alternative, applied projects. *Entrance requirements:* For master's, GRE General Test. Additional exam requirements/recommendations for international students: Required—TOEFL. *Application deadline:* For fall admission, 8/1 priority date for domestic students; for spring admission, 12/1 priority date for domestic students. Applications are processed on a rolling basis. Application fee: $25 ($50 for international students). *Expenses:* Tuition, state resident: part-time $348 per semester hour. Tuition, nonresident: part-time $626 per semester hour. Tuition and fees vary according to course load. *Financial support:* In 2007–08, 9 students received support, including 3 fellowships with partial tuition reimbursements available (averaging $1,000 per year); career-related internships or fieldwork, Federal Work-Study, and scholarships/

Criminal Justice and Criminology

Lamar University (continued)
grants also available. Support available to part-time students. Financial award application deadline: 4/1; financial award applicants required to submit FAFSA. *Faculty research:* Corrections, planning and evaluations, juveniles, terrorism, Mexican criminal justice. *Unit head:* Dr. Li-Chen J. Ma, Chair, 409-880-8545, Fax: 409-880-2324, E-mail: lma@lamar.edu. *Application contact:* Dr. J. Rick Altemose, Graduate Program Director, 409-880-8549, Fax: 409-880-2324, E-mail: altemosejr@hal.lamar.edu.

Lewis University, College of Arts and Sciences, Program in Criminal/Social Justice, Romeoville, IL 60446. Offers criminal/social justice (MS). Part-time and evening/weekend programs available. *Faculty:* 4 full-time (1 woman), 11 part-time/adjunct (3 women). *Students:* 12 full-time (10 women), 102 part-time (39 women); includes 39 minority (22 African Americans, 2 Asian Americans or Pacific Islanders, 15 Hispanic Americans). Average age 36. 46 applicants, 61% accepted, 28 enrolled. *Entrance requirements:* For master's, bachelor's degree or a minimum of 12 related hours in criminal/social justice, 2 letters of recommendation, minimum GPA of 3.0, interview. Additional exam requirements/recommendations for international students: Required—TOEFL (minimum score 550 paper-based; 213 computer-based). *Application deadline:* For fall admission, 5/1 priority date for international students; for spring admission, 11/15 priority date for international students. Applications are processed on a rolling basis. Application fee: $40. Electronic applications accepted. *Financial support:* Federal Work-Study, scholarships/grants, tuition waivers (full and partial), and unspecified assistantships available. Financial award application deadline: 5/1; financial award applicants required to submit FAFSA. *Faculty research:* Community policing, management, terrorism, biological warfare, drugs. *Unit head:* Dr. Calvin Edwards, Chair of Justice, Law and Public Safety Studies, 815-838-0500, Fax: 815-836-5870, E-mail: koloshsa@lewisu.edu. *Application contact:* Sarah Kolosh, Coordinator, 815-838-0500 Ext. 5686, Fax: 815-836-5870, E-mail: koloshsa@lewisu.edu.

Lincoln University, School of Graduate Studies and Continuing Education, College of Liberal Arts, Education and Journalism, Department of Social and Behavioral Sciences, Jefferson City, MO 65102. Offers history (MA); social science (MA), including history, political science, sociology; sociology (MA); sociology/criminal justice (MA). Part-time and evening/weekend programs available. *Faculty:* 12 part-time/adjunct (4 women). *Students:* 13 full-time (9 women), 17 part-time (7 women); includes 16 minority (13 African Americans, 1 American Indian/Alaska Native, 2 Hispanic Americans), 3 international. Average age 33. 9 applicants, 89% accepted, 5 enrolled. In 2007, 6 degrees awarded. *Degree requirements:* For master's, comprehensive exam, thesis optional. *Entrance requirements:* For master's, GRE General Test or MAT, 15 undergraduate hours of course work in social science including 6 hours upper-division, with 9 hours in the area of concentration; see parent units for general requirements. Additional exam requirements/recommendations for international students: Required—TOEFL (minimum score 500 paper-based; 173 computer-based; 61 iBT). *Application deadline:* For fall admission, 7/1 priority date for domestic and international students; for spring admission, 12/1 priority date for domestic and international students. Applications are processed on a rolling basis. Application fee: $20. *Expenses:* Tuition, state resident: full-time $5,400; part-time $225 per credit hour. Tuition, nonresident: full-time $10,020; part-time $417 per credit hour. Required fees: $360; $15 per credit hour. $20 per semester. *Financial support:* Federal Work-Study and scholarships/grants available. Financial award application deadline: 4/1; financial award applicants required to submit FAFSA. *Faculty research:* Suicide prevention. *Unit head:* Dr. Antonio Holland, Department Head, 573-681-5145, Fax: 573-681-5150, E-mail: hollanda@lincolnu.edu.

Lindenwood University, Graduate Programs, Programs in Individualized Education, St. Charles, MO 63301-1695. Offers administration (MSA); business administration (MBA); communication (MS); communications (MA); criminal justice and administration (MS); gerontology (MA); health management (MS); human resource management (MS); information technology (MBA, Certificate); management (MSA); managing information technology (MS); marketing (MSA); writing (MFA). Part-time and evening/weekend programs available. *Faculty:* 13 full-time (7 women), 54 part-time/adjunct (32 women). *Students:* 774 full-time (495 women), 55 part-time (32 women); includes 226 minority (213 African Americans, 9 Asian Americans or Pacific Islanders, 4 Hispanic Americans), 17 international. Average age 35. In 2007, 299 degrees awarded. *Degree requirements:* For master's, thesis (for some programs), minimum GPA of 3.0, 1 colloquium per term. *Entrance requirements:* For master's, interview, minimum GPA of 3.0. Additional exam requirements/recommendations for international students: Required—TOEFL (minimum score 550 paper-based; 213 computer-based; 80 iBT). *Application deadline:* For fall admission, 9/30 priority date for domestic and international students; for winter admission, 12/30 priority date for domestic and international students; for spring admission, 3/30 priority date for domestic and international students. Applications are processed on a rolling basis. Application fee: $30 ($100 for international students). *Expenses:* Tuition: Full-time $12,400; part-time $350 per hour. Full-time tuition and fees vary according to degree level and program. *Financial support:* Career-related internships or fieldwork, institutionally sponsored loans, tuition waivers (partial), and unspecified assistantships available. Financial award application deadline: 6/30; financial award applicants required to submit FAFSA. *Unit head:* Dan Kemper, Dean of Lindenwood College for Individual Education, 636-949-4501, Fax: 636-949-4505, E-mail: dkemper@lindenwood.edu. *Application contact:* Brett Barger, Dean of Evening Admissions and Extension Campuses, 636-949-4934, Fax: 636-949-4109, E-mail: adultadmissions@lindenwood.edu.

Long Island University, Brentwood Campus, School of Public Service, Brentwood, NY 11717. Offers criminal justice (MS). Part-time and evening/weekend programs available. *Faculty:* 3 full-time (2 women). *Students:* 15 full-time (7 women). Average age 39. 20 applicants, 85% accepted, 15 enrolled. In 2007, 10 degrees awarded. *Application deadline:* Applications are processed on a rolling basis. Application fee: $0. *Expenses:* Tuition: Full-time $15,030; part-time $835 per credit. Required fees: $460; $230 per term. Full-time tuition and fees vary according to program. *Financial support:* Scholarships/grants and unspecified assistantships available. Support available to part-time students. *Unit head:* Dr. Robert Sanatore, Head, 516-299-3017.

Long Island University, C.W. Post Campus, College of Management, Department of Criminal Justice, Brookville, NY 11548-1300. Offers criminal justice (MS); fraud examination (MS); security administration (MS). Part-time and evening/weekend programs available. *Faculty:* 1 full-time (0 women), 11 part-time/adjunct (1 woman). *Students:* 31 full-time (22 women), 11 part-time (6 women); includes 11 minority (7 African Americans, 1 Asian American or Pacific Islander, 3 Hispanic Americans), 1 international. Average age 28. 17 applicants, 100% accepted, 14 enrolled. In 2007, 28 degrees awarded. *Degree requirements:* For master's, thesis. *Entrance requirements:* For master's, minimum GPA of 3.0, background in criminal justice. *Application deadline:* Applications are processed on a rolling basis. Application fee: $30. Electronic applications accepted. *Expenses:* Tuition: Part-time $825 per credit. Tuition and fees vary according to course load. *Financial support:* In 2007–08, 1 student received support, including research assistantships (averaging $6,000 per year); career-related internships or fieldwork, Federal Work-Study, institutionally sponsored loans, and unspecified assistantships also available. Support available to part-time students. Financial award application deadline: 5/15; financial award applicants required to submit CSS PROFILE or FAFSA. *Faculty research:* Crime statistics, terrorism, women and law, policing. *Unit head:* Dr. Harvey Kushner, Chair, 516-299-2468, Fax: 516-299-2587, E-mail: harvey.kushner@liu.edu. *Application contact:* Laura Tojo, Advisor, 516-299-2986, E-mail: laura.tojo@liu.edu.

Longwood University, Office of Graduate Studies, Department of Sociology, Anthropology, and Criminal Justice Studies, Farmville, VA 23909. Offers criminal justice (MS). Part-time and evening/weekend programs available. *Degree requirements:* For master's, comprehensive exam (for some programs), thesis (for some programs). *Entrance requirements:* For master's, minimum GPA of 2.75. Additional exam requirements/recommendations for international students: Required—TOEFL (minimum score 550 paper-based; 213 computer-based).

Loyola University Chicago, Graduate School, Department of Criminal Justice, Chicago, IL 60611-2196. Offers MA. Part-time and evening/weekend programs available. *Faculty:* 8 full-time (1 woman), 12 part-time/adjunct (1 woman). *Students:* 18 full-time (9 women), 21 part-time (13 women); includes 10 minority (5 African Americans, 1 Asian American or Pacific Islander, 4 Hispanic Americans). Average age 26. 19 applicants, 84% accepted, 11 enrolled. In 2007, 21 degrees awarded. *Degree requirements:* For master's, comprehensive exam, thesis or alternative, field practicum. *Entrance requirements:* For master's, GRE, minimum GPA of 3.0. Additional exam requirements/recommendations for international students: Required—TOEFL (minimum score 550 paper-based; 213 computer-based). *Application deadline:* For fall admission, 6/15 priority date for domestic students; for spring admission, 12/1 for domestic students. Applications are processed on a rolling basis. Application fee: $50. Electronic applications accepted. *Expenses:* Tuition: Full-time $12,780; part-time $710 per credit hour. Required fees: $55 per semester. Full-time tuition and fees vary according to program. *Financial support:* In 2007–08, 3 students received support, including research assistantships with partial tuition reimbursements available (averaging $7,800 per year); career-related internships or fieldwork, scholarships/grants, and tuition waivers (full and partial) also available. Financial award application deadline: 2/1; financial award applicants required to submit FAFSA. *Faculty research:* Crime and delinquency causation, effectiveness and efficiency of criminal justice system. Total annual research expenditures: $120,000. *Unit head:* Dr. David Olson, Chair, 312-915-7563, Fax: 312-915-7650, E-mail: dolson1@luc.edu. *Application contact:* Dr. Gad Bensinger, Graduate Program Director, 312-915-7568, Fax: 312-915-8593, E-mail: gbesin@luc.edu.

Loyola University New Orleans, College of Social Sciences, Program in Criminal Justice, New Orleans, LA 70118-6195. Offers MCJ. Part-time and evening/weekend programs available. *Students:* 6 full-time (4 women), 21 part-time (16 women); includes 9 minority (8 African Americans, 1 Hispanic American). Average age 29. 15 applicants, 100% accepted, 21 enrolled. In 2007, 19 degrees awarded. *Degree requirements:* For master's, comprehensive exam, research and practicum. *Entrance requirements:* For master's, GRE, resumé, interview, letters of recommendation, transcript, essay, work experience. Additional exam requirements/recommendations for international students: Required—TOEFL (minimum score 550 paper-based; 213 computer-based). *Application deadline:* For fall admission, 8/1 priority date for domestic and international students; for spring admission, 1/5 priority date for domestic and international students. Applications are processed on a rolling basis. Application fee: $20. Electronic applications accepted. *Expenses: Contact institution. Financial support:* In 2007–08, 4 research assistantships (averaging $4,000 per year) were awarded; scholarships/grants and unspecified assistantships also available. Financial award application deadline: 5/1; financial award applicants required to submit FAFSA. *Unit head:* Dr. William E. Thornton, Director, 504-865-2134, Fax: 504-865-3883, E-mail: thornton@loyno.edu. *Application contact:* David Aplin, Assistant to the Director, 504-865-3323, Fax: 504-865-3883, E-mail: daplin@loyno.edu.

Lynn University, College of Arts and Sciences, Boca Raton, FL 33431-5598. Offers applied psychology (MS); criminal justice administration (MS); emergency planning and administration (MS, Certificate). Part-time and evening/weekend programs available. Postbaccalaureate distance learning degree programs offered. *Entrance requirements:* For master's, GRE, resumé, 2 letters of recommendation, minimum undergraduate GPA of 3.0. Additional exam requirements/recommendations for international students: Required—TOEFL (minimum score 550 paper-based; 213 computer-based). *Faculty research:* Terrorism, criminological theory, corrections, emergency planning.

Madonna University, School of Business, Livonia, MI 48150-1173. Offers business administration (MBA); international business (MSBA); leadership studies (MSBA); leadership studies in criminal justice (MSBA); quality and operations management (MSBA). Part-time and evening/weekend programs available. Postbaccalaureate distance learning degree programs offered (minimal on-campus study). *Degree requirements:* For master's, thesis (for some programs), foreign language proficiency (international business). *Entrance requirements:* For master's, GMAT, GRE General Test, minimum GPA of 3.0. Electronic applications accepted. *Faculty research:* Management, women in management, future studies.

Marshall University, Academic Affairs Division, College of Liberal Arts, Department of Criminal Justice, Huntington, WV 25755. Offers MS. Evening/weekend programs available. *Faculty:* 4 full-time (2 women), 6 part-time/adjunct (1 woman). *Students:* 17 full-time (13 women), 10 part-time (7 women); includes 1 minority (African American), 1 international. Average age 26. In 2007, 8 degrees awarded. *Degree requirements:* For master's, thesis optional. *Entrance requirements:* For master's, GRE General Test. Application fee: $40. *Unit head:* Dr. Margaret Phipps Brown, Chairperson, 304-696-3086, E-mail: brownmp@marshall.edu. *Application contact:* Information Contact, 304-746-1900, Fax: 304-746-1902, E-mail: services@marshall.edu.

Marywood University, Academic Affairs, College of Health and Human Services, Department of Nursing and Public Administration, Program in Public Administration, Scranton, PA 18509-1598. Offers criminal justice (MPA); public administration (MPA); MPA/MSW. *Students:* 4 full-time (all women), 11 part-time (5 women); includes 2 minority (both African Americans) Average age 30. In 2007, 8 degrees awarded. *Degree requirements:* For master's, thesis or alternative, internship/practicum. *Entrance requirements:* Additional exam requirements/recommendations for international students: Required—TOEFL (minimum score 550 paper-based; 213 computer-based). *Application deadline:* For fall admission, 4/15 priority date for domestic and international students; for spring admission, 11/15 priority date for domestic and international students. Applications are processed on a rolling basis. Application fee: $30. Electronic applications accepted. *Expenses:* Tuition: Full-time $15,290; part-time $695 per credit. Required fees: $990; $370 per term. Tuition and fees vary according to degree level. *Financial support:* Research assistantships with tuition reimbursements, career-related internships or fieldwork, scholarships/grants, tuition waivers (partial), and unspecified assistantships available. Support available to part-time students. Financial award application deadline: 2/15; financial award applicants required to submit FAFSA. *Application contact:* Tammy Manka, Assistant Director of Graduate Admissions, 570-340-6002, E-mail: tmanka@marywood.edu.

Marywood University, Academic Affairs, College of Liberal Arts and Sciences, Department of Social Sciences, Program in Criminal Justice, Scranton, PA 18509-1598. Offers MS. *Students:* 4 full-time (1 woman), 16 part-time (12 women), 1 international. Average age 29. In 2007, 3 degrees awarded. Application fee: $30. *Expenses:* Tuition: Full-time $15,290; part-time $695 per credit. Required fees: $990; $370 per term. Tuition and fees vary according to degree level. *Unit head:* Dr. Walter Broughton, Head, 570-348-6211 Ext. 2400.

Mercyhurst College, Graduate Program, Program in Administration of Justice, Erie, PA 16546. Offers administration of justice (MS). Part-time and evening/weekend programs available. *Faculty:* 1 full-time (0 women), 8 part-time/adjunct (0 women). *Students:* 31 full-time (16 women), 3 part-time (2 women); includes 2 minority (1 African American, 1 Asian American or Pacific Islander), 2 international. Average age 29. 19 applicants, 79% accepted, 12 enrolled. In 2007, 9 degrees awarded. *Degree requirements:* For master's, thesis optional. *Entrance requirements:* For master's, GRE General Test, MAT, or minimum GPA of 3.0. Additional exam requirements/recommendations for international students: Required—TOEFL. *Application deadline:* For fall admission, 8/1 priority date for domestic students; for spring admission, 1/1 for domestic students. Applications are processed on a rolling basis. Application fee: $35. Electronic applications accepted. *Financial support:* In 2007–08, 23 students received support, including 1 fellowship with tuition reimbursement available (averaging $7,600 per year), 21 research assistantships with tuition reimbursements available (averaging $6,000 per year); career-related internships or fieldwork, institutionally sponsored loans, scholarships/grants, and unspecified assistantships also available. Support available to part-time students. Financial award application deadline: 5/15; financial award applicants required to submit FAFSA. *Faculty research:* Research methods, criminal justice administration, juvenile justice. Total annual research expenditures: $300,000. *Unit head:* Dr. Frank E. Hagan, Director, 814-824-2265, Fax: 814-824-2438. *Application contact:* Justin Ross, Academic Coordinator, 814-824-2985, Fax: 814-824-2055, E-mail: jross@mercyhurst.edu.

Mercyhurst College, Graduate Program, Program in Applied Intelligence, Erie, PA 16546. Offers MS, Certificate. *Faculty:* 2 full-time (0 women), 4 part-time/adjunct (2 women). *Students:* 45 full-time (19 women), 62 part-time (25 women); includes 3 minority (1 African American, 2

Hispanic Americans), 1 international. Average age 30. 103 applicants, 63% accepted, 60 enrolled. In 2007, 13 master's, 78 other advanced degrees awarded. *Entrance requirements:* For master's, GRE or MAT, interview. Additional exam requirements/recommendations for international students: Required—TOEFL. *Application deadline:* For fall admission, 8/1 for domestic students; for winter admission, 11/1 for domestic students; for spring admission, 2/1 for domestic students. Applications are processed on a rolling basis. Application fee: $35. Electronic applications accepted. *Financial support:* In 2007–08, 15 research assistantships with full and partial tuition reimbursements (averaging $6,500 per year) were awarded. Total annual research expenditures: $334,000. *Unit head:* James Breckenridge, Director, Graduate Program in Applied Intelligence, 814-824-2458. *Application contact:* Justin Ross, Academic Coordinator, 814-824-2985, Fax: 814-824-2055, E-mail: jross@mercyhurst.edu.

Methodist University, School of Graduate Studies, Fayetteville, NC 28311-1498. Offers business administration (MBA); justice administration (MJA); physician assistant studies (MPA).

Michigan State University, The Graduate School, College of Social Science, School of Criminal Justice, East Lansing, MI 48824. Offers criminal justice (MS, PhD); forensic science (MS). Postbaccalaureate distance learning degree programs offered. *Entrance requirements:* Additional exam requirements/recommendations for international students: Required—TOEFL. Electronic applications accepted. *Expenses:* Tuition, state resident: part-time $379 per credit hour. Tuition, nonresident: part-time $800 per credit hour. Tuition and fees vary according to program.

See Close-Up on page 981.

Middle Tennessee State University, College of Graduate Studies, College of Education and Behavioral Science, Department of Criminal Justice Administration, Murfreesboro, TN 37132. Offers MCJ. Part-time and evening/weekend programs available. Postbaccalaureate distance learning degree programs offered. *Faculty:* 6 full-time (2 women). *Students:* 3 full-time (2 women), 45 part-time (26 women); includes 22 minority (21 African Americans, 1 Hispanic American). Average age 28. 60 applicants, 92% accepted. In 2007, 3 degrees awarded. *Degree requirements:* For master's, one foreign language, comprehensive exam, thesis. *Entrance requirements:* For master's, GRE or MAT. Additional exam requirements/recommendations for international students: Required—TOEFL (paper-based 525; computer-based 195; IBT 71) or IELTS (6.0). *Application deadline:* For fall admission, 8/1 priority date for domestic students. Applications are processed on a rolling basis. Application fee: $25. Electronic applications accepted. *Financial support:* In 2007–08, 1 student received support. Institutionally sponsored loans available. Support available to part-time students. Financial award application deadline: 5/1; financial award applicants required to submit FAFSA. *Unit head:* Dr. Deborah Newman, Chair, 615-898-2630, Fax: 615-898-5614, E-mail: dnewman@mtsu.edu.

Midwestern State University, Graduate Studies, College of Health Sciences and Human Services, Program in Health Services and Public Administration, Wichita Falls, TX 76308. Offers health services administration (MHA); public administration (MPA); public administration (administrative justice) (MPA); public administration (health services administration) with certificate (MPA); public administration (health services) (MPA). Part-time and evening/weekend programs available. *Degree requirements:* For master's, comprehensive exam, thesis. *Entrance requirements:* For master's, GRE. Additional exam requirements/recommendations for international students: Required—TOEFL (minimum score 550 paper-based; 213 computer-based). Electronic applications accepted.

Minot State University, Graduate School, Program in Criminal Justice, Minot, ND 58707-0002. Offers MS. *Faculty:* 5 full-time (1 woman). *Students:* 7 applicants, 71% accepted. In 2007, 3 degrees awarded. *Degree requirements:* For master's, comprehensive exam, thesis. *Entrance requirements:* For master's, GRE General Test, bachelor's degree minor in criminal justice or related field, minimum GPA of 3.0. Additional exam requirements/recommendations for international students: Required—TOEFL. *Application deadline:* Applications are processed on a rolling basis. Application fee: $35. *Expenses:* Tuition, state resident: full-time $5,264. Tuition, nonresident: full-time $14,053. Required fees: $700. *Financial support:* In 2007–08, 10 research assistantships with partial tuition reimbursements (averaging $2,500 per year) were awarded; teaching assistantships with partial tuition reimbursements, career-related internships or fieldwork, institutionally sponsored loans, scholarships/grants, traineeships, tuition waivers (partial), and unspecified assistantships also available. Support available to part-time students. Financial award application deadline: 4/1. *Faculty research:* Sentencing, white-collar/organizational crime, juveniles, gender issues, policy analysis. Total annual research expenditures: $1.5 million. *Unit head:* Dr. Harry Hoffman, Graduate Program Coordinator, 701-858-3284. *Application contact:* Brenda Anderson, Administrative Assistant, 701-858-3250, Fax: 701-858-4286, E-mail: brenda.anderson@minotstateu.edu.

Mississippi College, Graduate School, College of Arts and Sciences, School of Humanities and Social Sciences, Department of History and Political Science, Clinton, MS 39058. Offers administration of justice (MSS); history (M Ed, MA, MSS); paralegal studies (Certificate); political science (MSS); social sciences (M Ed, MSS). Part-time programs available. *Faculty:* 5 full-time (1 woman), 2 part-time/adjunct (0 women). *Students:* 12 full-time (7 women), 17 part-time (14 women); includes 7 minority (6 African Americans, 1 American Indian/Alaska Native), 1 international. Average age 27. In 2007, 5 master's, 2 other advanced degrees awarded. *Degree requirements:* For master's, one foreign language, comprehensive exam, thesis (for some programs). *Entrance requirements:* For master's, GRE or NTE, minimum GPA of 2.5. Additional exam requirements/recommendations for international students: Recommended—IELTS. *Application deadline:* For fall admission, 8/15 priority date for domestic students. Applications are processed on a rolling basis. Application fee: $25. Electronic applications accepted. *Expenses:* Tuition: Full-time $7,470; part-time $415 per hour. Required fees: $1,160 per term. Part-time tuition and fees vary according to course load and degree level. *Financial support:* Teaching assistantships, Federal Work-Study, scholarships/grants, and unspecified assistantships available. Support available to part-time students. Financial award application deadline: 4/1; financial award applicants required to submit FAFSA. *Unit head:* Dr. Kirk Ford, Chair, 601-925-3326, E-mail: ford@mc.edu.

Mississippi Valley State University, Department of Criminal Justice and Social Work, Itta Bena, MS 38941-1400. Offers criminal justice (MS). Part-time and evening/weekend programs available. *Degree requirements:* For master's, thesis optional. *Entrance requirements:* For master's, minimum GPA of 2.5. Electronic applications accepted. *Faculty research:* Police in the criminal justice system, the United States and international terrorism.

Missouri State University, Graduate College, College of Humanities and Public Affairs, Department of Sociology, Anthropology, and Criminology, Springfield, MO 65804-0094. Offers criminology (MS). *Faculty:* 11 full-time (2 women). *Students:* 13 full-time (10 women); includes 2 minority (1 African American, 1 Asian American or Pacific Islander). Average age 27. 17 applicants, 82% accepted, 12 enrolled. *Entrance requirements:* For master's, minimum GPA of 3.0. Additional exam requirements/recommendations for international students: Required—TOEFL (minimum score 550 paper-based; 213 computer-based; 79 iBT). *Application deadline:* For fall admission, 7/20 priority date for domestic students; for spring admission, 12/20 priority date for domestic students. Application fee: $35. *Expenses:* Tuition, state resident: full-time $3,708; part-time $206 per credit hour. Tuition, nonresident: full-time $7,236; part-time $206 per credit hour. Required fees: $622. Full-time tuition and fees vary according to course level, course load, program and reciprocity agreements. *Financial support:* In 2007–08, 1 research assistantship with full tuition reimbursement (averaging $7,050 per year) was awarded; teaching assistantships with full tuition reimbursements, Federal Work-Study and unspecified assistantships also available. Financial award application deadline: 3/31; financial award applicants required to submit FAFSA. *Unit head:* Dr. Karl Kunkel, Head, 417-836-5640, Fax: 417-836-6416, E-mail: karlkunkel@missouristate.edu.

Missouri State University, Graduate College, Interdisciplinary Program in Administrative Studies, Springfield, MO 65804-0094. Offers applied communication (MSAS); criminal justice (MSAS); environmental management (MSAS); project management (MSAS); sports management (MSAS). Part-time programs available. Postbaccalaureate distance learning degree programs offered (no on-campus study). *Students:* 21 full-time (10 women), 64 part-time (35 women); includes 5 minority (4 African Americans, 1 Hispanic American), 1 international. Average age 35. 17 applicants, 94% accepted, 13 enrolled. In 2007, 21 degrees awarded. *Degree requirements:* For master's, comprehensive exam, thesis or alternative. *Entrance requirements:* For master's, GRE, GMAT, 3 years of work experience. Additional exam requirements/recommendations for international students: Required—TOEFL (minimum score 550 paper-based; 213 computer-based; 79 iBT). *Application deadline:* For fall admission, 7/20 priority date for domestic students; for spring admission, 12/20 priority date for domestic students. Applications are processed on a rolling basis. Application fee: $35. Electronic applications accepted. *Expenses:* Tuition, state resident: full-time $3,708; part-time $206 per credit hour. Tuition, nonresident: full-time $7,236; part-time $206 per credit hour. Required fees: $622. Full-time tuition and fees vary according to course level, course load, program and reciprocity agreements. *Financial support:* In 2007–08, 4 teaching assistantships (averaging $7,050 per year) were awarded; research assistantships, career-related internships or fieldwork, Federal Work-Study, institutionally sponsored loans, scholarships/grants, and unspecified assistantships also available. Support available to part-time students. Financial award application deadline: 3/31; financial award applicants required to submit FAFSA. *Unit head:* John Bourhis, Director, 417-836-6390, E-mail: johnbourhis@missouristate.edu.

Monmouth University, Graduate School, Department of Criminal Justice, West Long Branch, NJ 07764-1898. Offers criminal justice administration (MA, Certificate). Part-time and evening/weekend programs available. *Faculty:* 7 full-time (0 women), 2 part-time/adjunct (1 woman). *Students:* 9 full-time (6 women), 26 part-time (14 women); includes 7 minority (5 African Americans, 2 Hispanic Americans). Average age 30. 21 applicants, 100% accepted, 10 enrolled. In 2007, 17 degrees awarded. *Degree requirements:* For master's, comprehensive exam, thesis or alternative. *Entrance requirements:* For master's, minimum GPA of 3.0 in major, 2.5 overall. Additional exam requirements/recommendations for international students: Required—TOEFL (minimum score 550 paper-based; 213 computer-based; 79 iBT), IELTS (minimum score 5), MELAB 77, Cambridge A, B, C. *Application deadline:* For fall admission, 7/15 priority date for domestic students, 6/1 for international students; for spring admission, 11/15 priority date for domestic students, 11/1 for international students. Applications are processed on a rolling basis. Application fee: $50. Electronic applications accepted. *Financial support:* In 2007–08, 20 students received support, including 20 fellowships (averaging $1,913 per year), 2 research assistantships (averaging $2,451 per year); career-related internships or fieldwork, scholarships/grants, tuition waivers (full and partial), and unspecified assistantships also available. Support available to part-time students. Financial award application deadline: 3/1; financial award applicants required to submit FAFSA. *Faculty research:* Violent crimes, criminal pathology, terrorism, computer crime, comparative CJ systems. *Unit head:* Dr. Gregory Coram, Director, 732-571-3448, Fax: 732-263-5148, E-mail: coram@monmouth.edu. *Application contact:* Kevin Roane, Director, Office of Graduate Admission, 732-571-3452, Fax: 732-263-5123, E-mail: gradadm@monmouth.edu.

Morehead State University, Graduate Programs, Caudill College of Humanities, Department of Sociology, Social Work and Criminology, Morehead, KY 40351. Offers criminology (MA); general sociology (MA); gerontology (MA). Part-time and evening/weekend programs available. *Faculty:* 8 full-time (3 women), 2 part-time/adjunct (1 woman). *Students:* 14 full-time (8 women), 7 part-time (3 women). Average age 28. In 2007, 3 degrees awarded. *Degree requirements:* For master's, comprehensive exam, thesis optional. *Entrance requirements:* For master's, GRE General Test, minimum GPA of 3.0 in sociology, 2.5 overall; 18 hours of course work in sociology, writing sample. Additional exam requirements/recommendations for international students: Required—TOEFL (minimum score 500 paper-based; 173 computer-based). *Application deadline:* For fall admission, 8/1 priority date for domestic and international students; for spring admission, 12/1 priority date for domestic and international students. Applications are processed on a rolling basis. Application fee: $0 ($55 for international students). Electronic applications accepted. *Financial support:* In 2007–08, 5 teaching assistantships (averaging $6,000 per year) were awarded; career-related internships or fieldwork, Federal Work-Study, and unspecified assistantships also available. Financial award application deadline: 4/1; financial award applicants required to submit FAFSA. *Faculty research:* Death and dying; aging, drinking, and drugs; economic development; adult children of alcoholics. *Unit head:* Dr. Robert Bylund, Chair, 606-783-2656, Fax: 606-783-5027, E-mail: r.bylund@moreheadstate.edu. *Application contact:* Michelle Barber, Graduate Admissions Counselor, 606-783-2039, Fax: 606-783-5061, E-mail: m.barber@moreheadstate.edu.

Mountain State University, Graduate Studies, Program in Criminal Justice Administration, Beckley, WV 25802-9003. Offers MCJA. Part-time and evening/weekend programs available. Postbaccalaureate distance learning degree programs offered (no on-campus study). *Faculty:* 8 full-time (2 women), 6 part-time/adjunct (3 women). *Students:* 19 full-time (7 women), 5 part-time (2 women); includes 4 minority (all African Americans) Average age 35. 35 applicants, 66% accepted, 23 enrolled. In 2007, 2 degrees awarded. *Degree requirements:* For master's, thesis or alternative. *Entrance requirements:* Additional exam requirements/recommendations for international students: Required—TOEFL (minimum score 550 paper-based; 213 computer-based); Recommended—IELTS (minimum score 7). *Application deadline:* For fall admission, 5/31 priority date for domestic and international students. Applications are processed on a rolling basis. Application fee: $25 ($50 for international students). Electronic applications accepted. *Financial support:* Federal Work-Study, scholarships/grants, and unspecified assistantships available. Support available to part-time students. Financial award applicants required to submit FAFSA. *Unit head:* Dr. Brian Holloway, Dean of Graduate Studies, 304-929-1438, Fax: 304-929-1637, E-mail: holloway@mountainstate.edu. *Application contact:* Dinah Rock, Coordinator of Graduate Academic Services, 304-929-1588, Fax: 304-929-1637, E-mail: drock@mountainstate.edu.

Mount Aloysius College, Program in Correctional Administration, Cresson, PA 16630-1999. Offers MA. *Entrance requirements:* For master's, GRE General Test.

New Jersey City University, Graduate Studies and Continuing Education, College of Professional Studies, Department of Criminal Justice, Jersey City, NJ 07305-1597. Offers criminal justice (MS); law enforcement (MS). Part-time and evening/weekend programs available. *Faculty:* 7. *Students:* 2 full-time (1 woman), 18 part-time (12 women); includes 11 minority (3 African Americans, 1 Asian American or Pacific Islander, 7 Hispanic Americans). Average age 30. In 2007, 6 degrees awarded. *Degree requirements:* For master's, thesis or alternative. *Entrance requirements:* For master's, GRE General Test or MAT. Additional exam requirements/recommendations for international students: Required—TOEFL. *Application deadline:* For fall admission, 8/1 priority date for domestic students; for spring admission, 12/1 for domestic students. Applications are processed on a rolling basis. Application fee: $0. *Expenses:* Tuition, state resident: full-time $7,462. Tuition, nonresident: full-time $13,762. Required fees: $1,296. *Financial support:* Unspecified assistantships available. *Unit head:* Dr. Shirely Williams, Chairperson, 201-200-3492, E-mail: swilliams@njcu.edu.

New Mexico State University, Graduate School, College of Arts and Sciences, Department of Criminal Justice, Las Cruces, NM 88003-8001. Offers MCJ. Part-time and evening/weekend programs available. Postbaccalaureate distance learning degree programs offered (no on-campus study). *Faculty:* 9 full-time (3 women). *Students:* 33 full-time (26 women), 65 part-time (35 women); includes 41 minority (3 African Americans, 4 American Indian/Alaska Native, 1 Asian American or Pacific Islander, 33 Hispanic Americans). Average age 32. 29 applicants, 86% accepted, 20 enrolled. In 2007, 34 degrees awarded. *Degree requirements:* For master's, comprehensive exam, thesis optional, oral and written exams. *Entrance requirements:* For master's, minimum GPA of 3.0. *Application deadline:* For fall admission, 4/1 priority date for domestic students; for spring admission, 11/1 priority date for domestic students. Applications are processed on a rolling basis. Application fee: $30 ($50 for international students). Electronic applications accepted. *Expenses:* Tuition, state resident: full-time $3,602; part-time $199 per credit. Tuition, nonresident: full-time $13,380; part-time $607 per

Criminal Justice and Criminology

New Mexico State University (continued)

credit. Required fees: $1,178. *Financial support:* In 2007–08, 14 teaching assistantships with partial tuition reimbursements were awarded; fellowships with partial tuition reimbursements, research assistantships with partial tuition reimbursements, career-related internships or fieldwork, health care benefits, and unspecified assistantships also available. Financial award application deadline: 4/1. *Faculty research:* Juvenile justice, jails and prison administration, courts and legal decision making, victim studies, policy and evaluation research. *Unit head:* Dr. James R. Maupin, Head, 575-646-3316, Fax: 575-646-2827, E-mail: jmaupin@nmsu.edu. *Application contact:* Thomas Winfree, Professor, 575-646-1592, Fax: 575-646-2827, E-mail: twinfree@nmsu.edu.

Niagara University, Graduate Division of Arts and Sciences, Department of Criminal Justice, Niagara Falls, Niagara University, NY 14109. Offers criminal justice administration (MS). *Faculty:* 5 full-time (1 woman). *Students:* 23 full-time (17 women), 15 part-time (5 women); includes 3 minority (2 African Americans, 1 Hispanic American), 2 international. In 2007, 26 degrees awarded. *Entrance requirements:* For master's, GRE. Additional exam requirements/recommendations for international students: Required—TOEFL. *Application deadline:* For fall admission, 8/1 for domestic students. Applications are processed on a rolling basis. Application fee: $30. *Expenses:* Tuition: Full-time $11,790; part-time $655 per credit. Required fees: $50; $25 per term. *Financial support:* Fellowships, career-related internships or fieldwork and Federal Work-Study available. Support available to part-time students. *Unit head:* Dr. Talia Harmon, Director, 716-286-8093, Fax: 716-286-8061, E-mail: tharmon@niagara.edu.

Norfolk State University, School of Graduate Studies, School of Liberal Arts, Department of Sociology, Program in Criminal Justice, Norfolk, VA 23504. Offers MA.

North Carolina Central University, Division of Academic Affairs, College of Arts and Sciences, Department of Criminal Justice, Durham, NC 27707-3129. Offers MS. Part-time and evening/weekend programs available. *Degree requirements:* For master's, one foreign language, comprehensive exam, thesis or alternative. *Entrance requirements:* For master's, GRE, minimum GPA of 3.0 in major, 2.5 overall. Additional exam requirements/recommendations for international students: Required—TOEFL.

North Dakota State University, College of Graduate and Interdisciplinary Studies, College of Arts, Humanities and Social Sciences, Department of Criminal Justice and Political Science, Fargo, ND 58105. Offers criminal justice (MS, PhD). Part-time programs available. *Faculty:* 3 full-time (1 woman). *Students:* 5 full-time (4 women), 4 part-time (1 woman). Average age 25. 6 applicants, 67% accepted, 2 enrolled. In 2007, 4 master's, 1 doctorate awarded. Terminal master's awarded for partial completion of doctoral program. *Median time to degree:* Of those who began their doctoral program in fall 1999, 1% received their degree in 8 years or less. *Degree requirements:* For master's, thesis (for some programs); for doctorate, comprehensive exam, thesis/dissertation. *Entrance requirements:* For master's, minimum GPA of 3.0 in last 60 credit hours, approved bachelor's degree, course work in research methods and statistics; for doctorate, GRE General Test, minimum GPA of 3.0 over last 60 credit hours, 3 letters of recommendation. Additional exam requirements/recommendations for international students: Required—TOEFL (minimum score 525 paper-based; 197 computer-based; 71 iBT). *Application deadline:* For spring admission, 4/1 priority date for domestic students, 4/1 for international students. Applications are processed on a rolling basis. Application fee: $45 ($60 for international students). *Expenses:* Tuition, state resident: full-time $5,376; part-time $224 per credit. Tuition, nonresident: full-time $14,354; part-time $598 per credit. Required fees: $962; $40 per credit. Part-time tuition and fees vary according to course load and reciprocity agreements. *Financial support:* In 2007–08, 6 research assistantships with tuition reimbursements (averaging $12,000 per year), 3 teaching assistantships with tuition reimbursements (averaging $6,000 per year) were awarded; career-related internships or fieldwork, institutionally sponsored loans, tuition waivers (full), and unspecified assistantships also available. Financial award application deadline: 4/1. *Faculty research:* Corrections, policing, drugs and crime, gender and crime, criminology. Total annual research expenditures: $150,000. *Unit head:* Dr. Kevin Thompson, Chair, 701-231-8938, Fax: 701-231-5877, E-mail: kevin.thompson@ndsu.edu.

Northeastern State University, Graduate College, College of Liberal Arts, Program in Criminal Justice and Legal Studies, Tahlequah, OK 74464-2399. Offers criminal justice (MS). Part-time and evening/weekend programs available. *Students:* 11 full-time (7 women), 26 part-time (20 women); includes 12 minority (3 African Americans, 9 American Indian/Alaska Native). In 2007, 6 degrees awarded. *Degree requirements:* For master's, thesis optional, oral exam. *Entrance requirements:* For master's, MAT or GRE, minimum GPA of 2.5. Additional exam requirements/recommendations for international students: Required—TOEFL (minimum score 213 computer-based). *Application deadline:* For fall admission, 6/1 priority date for domestic students. Applications are processed on a rolling basis. Application fee: $0 ($25 for international students). Electronic applications accepted. *Financial support:* Teaching assistantships, Federal Work-Study available. Financial award application deadline: 3/1. *Unit head:* Dr. Bill Heck, Chair, 918-456-5511 Ext. 3527, E-mail: heck@nsuok.edu.

Northeastern University, College of Criminal Justice, Boston, MA 02115-5096. Offers MS, PhD. Part-time and evening/weekend programs available. *Faculty:* 18 full-time (4 women), 5 part-time/adjunct. *Students:* 71 full-time (46 women), 18 part-time (8 women). 129 applicants, 62% accepted. In 2007, 21 degrees awarded. *Degree requirements:* For master's, comprehensive exam, thesis optional. *Entrance requirements:* For master's and doctorate, GRE General Test. Additional exam requirements/recommendations for international students: Required—TOEFL. *Application deadline:* For fall admission, 3/1 for domestic students; for spring admission, 10/1 for domestic students. Applications are processed on a rolling basis. Application fee: $50. Electronic applications accepted. *Financial support:* In 2007–08, 12 teaching assistantships with full tuition reimbursements (averaging $13,654 per year) were awarded; research assistantships with full and partial tuition reimbursements, career-related internships or fieldwork, Federal Work-Study, and institutionally sponsored loans also available. Support available to part-time students. Financial award application deadline: 3/31; financial award applicants required to submit FAFSA. *Faculty research:* Juvenile justice, victimology, serial and mass murder, private security, criminology corrections, race and crime. *Unit head:* Jack McDevitt, Associate Dean, 617-373-2813, Fax: 617-373-8723. *Application contact:* Laurie A. Mastone, Assistant to the Director, 617-373-2813, Fax: 617-373-8723, E-mail: l.mastone@neu.edu.

Northern Arizona University, Graduate College, College of Social and Behavioral Sciences, Department of Criminal Justice, Flagstaff, AZ 86011. Offers criminal justice (MS); criminal justice policy and planning (Certificate). *Degree requirements:* For master's, thesis.

Northern Michigan University, College of Graduate Studies, College of Professional Studies, Department of Criminal Justice, Marquette, MI 49855-5301. Offers MS. Part-time and evening/weekend programs available. *Entrance requirements:* For master's, minimum GPA of 3.0.

Norwich University, School of Graduate Studies, Program in Justice Administration, Northfield, VT 05663. Offers MJA. Evening/weekend programs available. *Faculty:* 8 part-time/adjunct (3 women). *Students:* 81 full-time (33 women), 2 part-time; includes 8 minority (4 African Americans, 1 American Indian/Alaska Native, 3 Hispanic Americans). Average age 36. 24 applicants, 88% accepted, 18 enrolled. In 2007, 69 degrees awarded. *Entrance requirements:* For master's, minimum GPA of 2.75. Additional exam requirements/recommendations for international students: Required—TOEFL. *Application deadline:* For fall admission, 8/10 for domestic and international students; for winter admission, 11/7 for domestic and international students; for spring admission, 2/6 for domestic and international students. Application fee: $50. Electronic applications accepted. *Expenses:* Tuition: Full-time $15,768; part-time $657 per credit. Tuition and fees vary according to program. *Financial support:* Scholarships/grants available. Financial award applicants required to submit FAFSA. *Unit head:* Donal Hartman, Program Director, 802-485-2730, E-mail: dhartman@norwich.edu. *Application contact:* Chris Ormsby, Administrative Director, 802-485-2730, Fax: 802-485-2533, E-mail: cormsby@norwich.edu.

Nova Southeastern University, Criminal Justice Institute, Program in Criminal Justice, Fort Lauderdale, FL 33314-7796. Offers MS. *Faculty:* 41 part-time/adjunct (7 women). *Students:* 10 full-time (7 women), 131 part-time (91 women); includes 90 minority (67 African Americans, 23 Hispanic Americans). 41 applicants, 73% accepted, 30 enrolled. In 2007, 35 degrees awarded. *Degree requirements:* For master's, comprehensive exam (for some programs), thesis optional. *Entrance requirements:* For master's, 3 letters of recommendation, minimum GPA of 2.5. *Application deadline:* For fall admission, 7/8 for domestic students; for winter admission, 1/8 for domestic students; for spring admission, 3/8 for domestic students. Application fee: $50. *Financial support:* Applicants required to submit FAFSA. *Unit head:* Dr. Tammy Kushner, Director, 954-262-7001, Fax: 954-937-7005, E-mail: kushner@nova.edu. *Application contact:* Russell Garner, Information Contact/Administrative Assistant, 954-262-7001, E-mail: cji@nova.edu.

See Close-Up on page 983.

Oklahoma City University, Petree College of Arts and Sciences, Division of Sociology and Justice Studies, Oklahoma City, OK 73106-1402. Offers criminal justice (MCJ). Part-time and evening/weekend programs available. *Faculty:* 4 full-time (1 woman), 3 part-time/adjunct (2 women). *Students:* 11 full-time (8 women), 4 part-time (3 women); includes 3 minority (all African Americans), 1 international. Average age 31. 9 applicants, 89% accepted. In 2007, 5 degrees awarded. *Degree requirements:* For master's, thesis optional. *Entrance requirements:* For master's, minimum GPA of 3.0. Additional exam requirements/recommendations for international students: Required—TOEFL. *Application deadline:* For fall admission, 8/22 for domestic students; for spring admission, 1/15 for domestic students. Applications are processed on a rolling basis. Application fee: $30 ($70 for international students). *Expenses:* Contact institution. *Financial support:* Fellowships with partial tuition reimbursements, career-related internships or fieldwork available. Financial award application deadline: 8/1; financial award applicants required to submit FAFSA. *Faculty research:* Victims, police, corrections, security, women and crime. *Unit head:* Dr. Jody Horn, Director, 405-208-5247, Fax: 405-208-5447, E-mail: jhorn@okcu.edu. *Application contact:* Leslie McKenzie, Director, Graduate Admissions, 800-633-7242, Fax: 405-208-5356, E-mail: gadmissions@okcu.edu.

Oklahoma State University, College of Arts and Sciences, Department of Sociology, Stillwater, OK 74078. Offers corrections (MS); sociology (MS, PhD). *Faculty:* 16 full-time (4 women), 1 (woman) part-time/adjunct. *Students:* 15 full-time (9 women), 23 part-time (16 women); includes 5 minority (3 African Americans, 1 American Indian/Alaska Native, 1 Hispanic American), 6 international. Average age 36. 46 applicants, 33% accepted, 11 enrolled. In 2007, 4 degrees awarded. *Degree requirements:* For master's, thesis; for doctorate, 2 foreign languages, thesis/dissertation. *Entrance requirements:* For master's and doctorate, GRE General Test or GMAT. Additional exam requirements/recommendations for international students: Required—TOEFL. *Application deadline:* For fall admission, 3/1 priority date for international students; for spring admission, 8/1 priority date for international students. Applications are processed on a rolling basis. Application fee: $40 ($75 for international students). Electronic applications accepted. *Expenses:* Tuition, state resident: full-time $4,993; part-time $148 per credit hour. Tuition, nonresident: full-time $14,755; part-time $555 per credit hour. Tuition and fees vary according to program. *Financial support:* In 2007–08, 4 research assistantships (averaging $12,515 per year), 19 teaching assistantships (averaging $14,478 per year) were awarded; career-related internships or fieldwork, Federal Work-Study, scholarships/grants, health care benefits, tuition waivers (partial), and unspecified assistantships also available. Support available to part-time students. Financial award application deadline: 3/1. *Faculty research:* Criminology/correction/legal issues; race, ethnicity, and gender in American society; environmental conflict and population problems; international comparative research; social change and social movement in American culture. *Unit head:* Dr. Patricia Bell, Head, 405-744-6105.

Old Dominion University, College of Arts and Letters, Program in Criminology and Criminal Justice, Norfolk, VA 23529. Offers PhD. Part-time and evening/weekend programs available. *Faculty:* 15 full-time (10 women). *Students:* 6 full-time (2 women), 2 part-time (1 woman); includes 1 minority (Asian American or Pacific Islander) Average age 37. 14 applicants, 79% accepted, 8 enrolled. *Degree requirements:* For doctorate, comprehensive exam, thesis/dissertation, 48 credit hours. *Entrance requirements:* For doctorate, GRE General Test, MA degree; grad GPA 3.25; theory, methods, stats grad coursework; letters of reference, writing sample. Additional exam requirements/recommendations for international students: Required—TOEFL. *Application deadline:* For fall admission, 2/15 for domestic and international students. Application fee: $40. Electronic applications accepted. *Expenses:* Tuition, state resident: part-time $304 per credit hour. Tuition, nonresident: part-time $761 per credit hour. *Financial support:* In 2007–08, 5 students received support, including 3 fellowships with full tuition reimbursements available (averaging $15,000 per year), 2 teaching assistantships with full tuition reimbursements available (averaging $15,000 per year). Financial award application deadline: 2/15. *Faculty research:* Inequality, crime and justice; domestic violence; community justice; criminological theory; methods; policing; courts and corrections. *Unit head:* Dr. Mona Danner, Graduate Program Director, 757-683-5931, Fax: 757-683-5634, E-mail: mdanner@odu.edu.

Penn State Harrisburg, Graduate School, School of Public Affairs, Middletown, PA 17057-4898. Offers criminal justice (MA); health administration (MHA); public administration (MPA); public affairs (PhD); MPA/JD. *Unit head:* Dr. Steven A. Peterson, Director, 717-948-6154, E-mail: sap12@psu.edu.

Penn State University Park, Graduate School, College of the Liberal Arts, Department of Sociology, State College, University Park, PA 16802-1503. Offers crime, law, and justice (MA, PhD); sociology (MA, PhD). *Expenses:* Tuition, state resident: full-time $14,738; part-time $614 per credit. Tuition, nonresident: full-time $26,050; part-time $1,085 per credit. Tuition and fees vary according to course load, program and student level. *Unit head:* Dr. John D. McCarthy, Head, 814-863-8260, Fax: 814-863-7216, E-mail: jxm516@psu.edu.

Point Park University, School of Arts and Sciences, Department of Criminal Justice and Intelligence Studies, Pittsburgh, PA 15222-1984. Offers criminal justice administration (MS). Evening/weekend programs available. *Faculty:* 4 full-time, 1 part-time/adjunct. *Students:* 23 full-time (16 women), 1 part-time; includes 11 minority (all African Americans) Average age 34. 43 applicants, 42% accepted, 16 enrolled. In 2007, 23 degrees awarded. *Entrance requirements:* For master's, minimum GPA of 2.75, resumé, 2 letters of recommendation. Additional exam requirements/recommendations for international students: Required—TOEFL. *Application deadline:* Applications are processed on a rolling basis. Electronic applications accepted. *Expenses:* Tuition: Full-time $10,566; part-time $587 per credit. Required fees: $360; $20 per credit. *Financial support:* In 2007–08, 12 students received support. Scholarships/grants and unspecified assistantships available. Financial award application deadline: 5/1; financial award applicants required to submit FAFSA. *Unit head:* Gregory Rogers, Acting Chair, 412-392-3830, Fax: 412-392-3925, E-mail: grogers@pointpark.edu. *Application contact:* Lynn Ribar, Assistant Director of Adult Enrollment, 412-392-3908, Fax: 412-392-6164, E-mail: lribar@pointpark.edu.

Polytechnic Institute of NYU, Department of Computer and Information Science, Brooklyn, NY 11201-2990. Offers computer science (MS, PhD); cyber security (Graduate Certificate); software engineering (Graduate Certificate). Part-time and evening/weekend programs available. *Faculty:* 20 full-time (2 women), 12 part-time/adjunct (0 women). *Students:* 146 full-time (29 women), 64 part-time (12 women); includes 14 minority (1 African American, 9 Asian Americans or Pacific Islanders, 4 Hispanic Americans), 153 international. Average age 32. 533 applicants, 65% accepted, 94 enrolled. In 2007, 64 master's, 6 doctorates awarded. *Degree requirements:* For master's, comprehensive exam (for some programs), thesis (for some programs); for doctorate, comprehensive exam, thesis/dissertation. *Entrance requirements:* For master's, BA or BS in computer science, mathematics, science, or engineering; working knowledge of a high-level program; for doctorate, GRE General Test, GRE Subject Test, qualifying exam, BA or BS in science, engineering, or management; MS or 1 year of graduate course work. Additional exam requirements/recommendations for international students: Required—TOEFL (minimum score 550 paper-based; 213 computer-based); Recommended—IELTS (minimum score 7). *Application deadline:* For fall admission, 7/15 priority date for domestic students, 4/1 priority date for international students; for spring admission, 12/15 priority date for domestic students, 10/1 priority date for international students. Applications are processed on a rolling basis. Application fee: $55. Electronic applications accepted. *Expenses:* Tuition: Full-time $18,486; part-time $1,027 per credit. Required fees: $352 per semester. *Financial support:* In 2007–08, 36 fellowships with partial tuition reimbursements (averaging $2,037 per year) were awarded; research assistantships, teaching assistantships, institutionally sponsored loans also available. Support available to part-time students. Financial award applicants required to submit FAFSA. Total annual research expenditures: $561,018. *Unit head:* Dr. Stuart Steele, Head, 718-260-3357, Fax: 718-260-3609, E-mail: ssteele@rama.poly.edu. *Application contact:* Anthea Jeffrey, Graduate Admissions, 718-260-3200, Fax: 718-260-3624, E-mail: gradinfo@poly.edu.

Pontifical Catholic University of Puerto Rico, Institute of Graduate Studies in Behavioral Science and Community Affairs, Program in Criminology, Ponce, PR 00717-0777. Offers MA. Part-time and evening/weekend programs available. *Degree requirements:* For master's, thesis. *Entrance requirements:* For master's, EXADEP, 3 letters of recommendation, interview, minimum GPA of 2.75.

Pontificia Universidad Catolica Madre y Maestra, Graduate School, Santiago, Dominican Republic. Offers administration (M Adm, M Ed); architecture of interiors (M Arch); architecture of tourist lodgings (M Arch); construction administration (ME); convergent networks (ME); corporate business law (LL M); criminal procedure law (LL M); earthquake-resistant engineering (ME); environmental engineering (MEE); finance (M Mgmt); human resources (EMBA); international business (M Mgmt); international relations (LL M); labor law and Social Security (M Mgmt); logistics management (ME); marketing (M Mgmt); urban planning (M Urb). *Entrance requirements:* For master's, curriculum vitae, interview.

Portland State University, Graduate Studies, College of Urban and Public Affairs, Hatfield School of Government, Division of Criminology and Criminal Justice, Portland, OR 97207-0751. Offers MS, PhD. Part-time programs available. *Faculty:* 10 full-time (6 women), 11 part-time/adjunct (2 women). *Students:* 22 full-time (18 women), 11 part-time (7 women); includes 8 minority (4 African Americans, 2 American Indian/Alaska Native, 1 Asian American or Pacific Islander, 1 Hispanic American). Average age 29. 14 applicants, 100% accepted, 12 enrolled. In 2007, 12 degrees awarded. *Degree requirements:* For master's, thesis or alternative, comprehensive oral exam; for doctorate, comprehensive exam, thesis/dissertation, residency. *Entrance requirements:* For master's, minimum GPA of 3.0 in upper-division course work or 2.75 overall; for doctorate, GRE General Test. Additional exam requirements/recommendations for international students: Required—TOEFL (minimum score 550 paper-based; 213 computer-based). *Application deadline:* For fall admission, 3/15 priority date for domestic students, 3/1 priority date for international students. Application fee: $50. *Expenses:* Tuition, state resident: full-time $7,047. Tuition, nonresident: full-time $11,178. *Financial support:* In 2007–08, 2 research assistantships with full tuition reimbursements (averaging $5,508 per year), 3 teaching assistantships with full tuition reimbursements (averaging $8,262 per year) were awarded; fellowships, career-related internships or fieldwork, Federal Work-Study, scholarships/grants, and unspecified assistantships also available. Support available to part-time students. Financial award application deadline: 3/1; financial award applicants required to submit FAFSA. *Faculty research:* History of criminal justice, mental health issues, international terrorism, offender assessment, domestic violence. Total annual research expenditures: $558,575. *Unit head:* Dr. Annette Jolin, Chair, 503-725-4014, Fax: 503-725-5199.

Radford University, Graduate College, College of Humanities and Behavioral Sciences, Department of Criminal Justice, Radford, VA 24142. Offers MA, MS. Part-time programs available. Postbaccalaureate distance learning degree programs offered (minimal on-campus study). *Faculty:* 9 full-time (4 women). *Students:* Average age 27. 13 applicants, 100% accepted, 9 enrolled. In 2007, 23 degrees awarded. *Degree requirements:* For master's, comprehensive exam, thesis optional. *Entrance requirements:* For master's, minimum GPA 2.9. *Application deadline:* For fall admission, 3/1 priority date for domestic students, 12/1 for international students; for spring admission, 10/1 for domestic students, 7/1 for international students. Applications are processed on a rolling basis. Application fee: $40. Electronic applications accepted. *Financial support:* In 2007–08, 16 students received support, including 13 research assistantships with partial tuition reimbursements available (averaging $8,000 per year), 1 teaching assistantship with partial tuition reimbursement available (averaging $8,700 per year); career-related internships or fieldwork, Federal Work-Study, institutionally sponsored loans, scholarships/grants, and unspecified assistantships also available. Financial award application deadline: 3/1; financial award applicants required to submit FAFSA. *Unit head:* Dr. Isaac Van Patten, Chair, 540-831-6737, Fax: 540-831-6075, E-mail: ivanpatt@radford.edu. *Application contact:* Dr. Stephen Owen, Interim Graduate Coordinator, 540-831-6339.

Regis University, College for Professional Studies, MA Program, Denver, CO 80221-1099. Offers criminology (MA); fine arts administration (Certificate); language and communication (MA); mediation (Certificate); psychology (MA); self-designed major (MA); social justice, peace, and reconciliation (Certificate); social science (MA); technical communication (Certificate). Program also offered in Henderson and Las Vegas (Summerlin), NV. Part-time and evening/weekend programs available. Postbaccalaureate distance learning degree programs offered (minimal on-campus study). *Faculty:* 84. *Students:* 218 (167 women). Average age 41. In 2007, 52 degrees awarded. *Degree requirements:* For master's, thesis, research project. *Entrance requirements:* For master's, resumé, recommendations, essays. Additional exam requirements/recommendations for international students: Required—TOEFL (minimum score 213 computer-based), TWE (minimum score 5). *Application deadline:* For fall admission, 8/13 priority date for domestic students, 7/13 priority date for international students; for winter admission, 10/8 priority date for domestic students, 9/8 priority date for international students; for spring admission, 12/17 priority date for domestic students, 11/17 for international students. Applications are processed on a rolling basis. Application fee: $75. Electronic applications accepted. *Expenses:* Contact institution. *Financial support:* Federal Work-Study available. Support available to part-time students. Financial award application deadline: 3/15; financial award applicants required to submit FAFSA. *Faculty research:* Independent/nonresidential graduate study: new methods and models, adult learning and the capstone experience, Goal Setting, behavior of Adult students, Innovative Studies for Community Colleges. *Unit head:* Dr. Robert Collins, Chair, 303-458-4302, Fax: 303-964-5538. *Application contact:* Graduate Admissions, 800-677-9270 Ext. 4080, Fax: 303-964-5538, E-mail: masters@regis.edu.

The Richard Stockton College of New Jersey, School of Graduate and Continuing Education, Program in Criminal Justice, Pomona, NJ 08240-0195. Offers MA. Part-time and evening/weekend programs available. *Faculty:* 6 full-time (3 women). *Students:* 12 full-time (4 women), 17 part-time (12 women); includes 1 African American, 1 Asian American or Pacific Islander. Average age 25. 26 applicants, 62% accepted, 13 enrolled. *Degree requirements:* For master's, comprehensive exam (for some programs), thesis. *Entrance requirements:* For master's, GRE General Test, minimum GPA of 3.0. Additional exam requirements/recommendations for international students: Required—TOEFL. *Application deadline:* For fall admission, 8/15 for domestic and international students; for spring admission, 1/5 for domestic and international students. Application fee: $50. *Expenses:* Tuition, state resident: part-time $439 per credit. Required fees: $105 per credit. Tuition and fees vary according to course load and degree level. *Financial support:* Fellowships, research assistantships, career-related internships or fieldwork, scholarships/grants, and unspecified assistantships available. Financial award application deadline: 3/1; financial award applicants required to submit FAFSA. *Faculty research:* Homeland security, forensic psychology, corrections, sex crimes, violent crimes. *Unit head:* Dr. Christine Tartaro, Director, 609-626-6035, E-mail: christine.tartaro@stockton.edu.

Roger Williams University, School of Justice Studies, Bristol, RI 02809. Offers criminal justice (MS). Part-time and evening/weekend programs available. *Faculty:* 6 full-time (3 women). *Students:* 3 full-time (0 women), 48 part-time (13 women); includes 2 minority (1 Asian American or Pacific Islander, 1 Hispanic American). Average age 31. 17 applicants, 76% accepted, 5 enrolled. In 2007, 15 degrees awarded. *Degree requirements:* For master's, comprehensive exam, thesis. *Entrance requirements:* For master's, GRE or MAT. *Application deadline:* For fall admission, 8/1 priority date for domestic students; for spring admission, 12/1 priority date for domestic students. Applications are processed on a rolling basis. Application fee: $50. Electronic applications accepted. *Expenses:* Contact institution. *Financial support:* In 2007–08, 7 students received support; research assistantships with partial tuition reimbursements available, career-related internships or fieldwork and health care benefits available. Financial award applicants required to submit FAFSA. *Unit head:* Stephanie Manzi, Dean, 401-254-3715, Fax: 401-254-3431, E-mail: smanzi@rwu.edu. *Application contact:* Suzanne Faubl, Director of Graduate Admissions, 401-254-3809, Fax: 401-254-3557, E-mail: sfaubl@rwu.edu.

Announcement: Roger Williams University's School of Justice Studies offers the Master of Science in Criminal Justice and the Joint Master of Science/Juris Doctor (in conjunction with the Roger Williams School of Law). Applicants to the joint-degree program must apply to both schools separately. Both programs are dedicated to providing a top-quality education that will prepare students to successfully meet the challenges facing modern justice system professionals.

See Close-Up on page 987.

Rowan University, Graduate School, College of Liberal Arts and Sciences, Program in Criminal Justice, Glassboro, NJ 08028-1701. Offers MA. *Faculty:* 4 full-time (2 women). *Students:* 5 full-time (2 women); includes 1 minority (African American) Average age 25. 10 applicants, 60% accepted, 3 enrolled. *Application deadline:* Applications are processed on a rolling basis. Application fee: $50. Electronic applications accepted. *Expenses:* Tuition, nonresident: full-time $9,882; part-time $549 per credit. Required fees: $104,385 per credit. *Unit head:* Dr. Wanda Folgia, Advisor, 856-256-4500 Ext. 3535.

Rutgers, The State University of New Jersey, Camden, Graduate School of Arts and Sciences, Program in Criminal Justice, Camden, NJ 08102-1401. Offers MA. Part-time and evening/weekend programs available. *Degree requirements:* For master's, comprehensive exam, thesis optional. Electronic applications accepted. *Faculty research:* Criminal justice policy, public management, children in criminal justice system, violence, gender and crime.

Rutgers, The State University of New Jersey, Newark, Graduate School, School of Criminal Justice, Newark, NJ 07102. Offers MA, PhD. *Degree requirements:* For master's, thesis optional. *Entrance requirements:* For master's and doctorate, GRE, minimum GPA of 3.0.

Sacred Heart University, Graduate Programs, College of Arts and Sciences, Department of Criminal Justice, Fairfield, CT 06825-1000. Offers MA. Part-time programs available. *Faculty:* 4 full-time (1 woman). *Students:* 9 full-time (5 women), 9 part-time (5 women); includes 5 minority (2 African Americans, 3 Hispanic Americans), 1 international. 28 applicants, 93% accepted, 14 enrolled. *Degree requirements:* For master's, thesis optional. *Entrance requirements:* Additional exam requirements/recommendations for international students: Required—TOEFL (minimum score 550 paper-based; 213 computer-based). *Application deadline:* Applications are processed on a rolling basis. Application fee: $50 ($100 for international students). Electronic applications accepted. *Expenses:* Tuition: Part-time $510 per credit. Tuition and fees vary according to program. *Financial support:* Career-related internships or fieldwork, institutionally sponsored loans, and unspecified assistantships available. Support available to part-time students. Financial award applicants required to submit FAFSA. *Unit head:* Dr. Pearl Jacobs, Chair, 203-365-7764, E-mail: jacobsp@sacredheart.edu. *Application contact:* Alexis Haakonsen, Dean of Graduate Admissions, 203-365-7619, Fax: 203-365-4732, E-mail: haakonsena@sacredheart.edu.

Sage Graduate School, Graduate School, Department of Sociology and Criminal Justice, Troy, NY 12180-4115. Offers forensic mental health (MS, Certificate). *Expenses:* Tuition: Full-time $9,720; part-time $540 per credit hour. *Application contact:* Shannon K. Easton.

St. Ambrose University, College of Arts and Sciences, Program in Criminal Justice, Davenport, IA 52803-2898. Offers criminal justice (MCJ); juvenile justice education (MCJ). Part-time and evening/weekend programs available. *Faculty:* 2 full-time (0 women), 3 part-time/adjunct (0 women). *Students:* 8 full-time (4 women), 25 part-time (13 women); includes 4 minority (3 African Americans, 1 Hispanic American). Average age 33. 10 applicants, 80% accepted, 7 enrolled. In 2007, 13 degrees awarded. *Degree requirements:* For master's, thesis (for some programs), practicum or project. *Entrance requirements:* For master's, 2 years of work experience, 2 letters of recommendation, personal interview. Additional exam requirements/recommendations for international students: Required—TOEFL. *Application deadline:* For fall admission, 8/15 priority date for domestic students, 8/15 for international students; for spring admission, 11/1 for domestic and international students. Applications are processed on a rolling basis. Application fee: $25. Electronic applications accepted. *Expenses:* Tuition: Full-time $6,048; part-time $672 per hour. Tuition and fees vary according to course load, degree level, campus/location, program and reciprocity agreements. *Financial support:* In 2007–08, 23 students received support, including 4 research assistantships with partial tuition reimbursements available (averaging $3,135 per year); career-related internships or fieldwork and unspecified assistantships also available. Support available to part-time students. Financial award application deadline: 3/15; financial award applicants required to submit FAFSA. *Faculty research:* Community policing. *Unit head:* Waylon McCulloh, Acting Head, 563-333-6078, Fax: 563-333-6243, E-mail: mccullohwaynec@sau.edu. *Application contact:* Elizabeth Berridge, Director of Graduate Student Recruitment, 563-333-6271, Fax: 563-333-6268, E-mail: berridgeelizabethb@sau.edu.

St. Cloud State University, School of Graduate Studies, College of Social Sciences, Department of Criminal Justice, St. Cloud, MN 56301-4498. Offers criminal justice administration (MS); criminal justice counseling (MS); public safety executive leadership (MS). Part-time programs available. Postbaccalaureate distance learning degree programs offered (minimal on-campus study). *Faculty:* 10 full-time (2 women), 15 part-time/adjunct (2 women). *Students:* 46 full-time (22 women), 40 part-time (27 women); includes 3 minority (1 African American, 2 Hispanic Americans), 8 international. 17 applicants, 100% accepted. In 2007, 28 degrees awarded. *Degree requirements:* For master's, thesis or alternative. *Entrance requirements:* For master's, GRE General Test, minimum GPA of 2.75. Additional exam requirements/recommendations for international students: Required—MELAB; Recommended—TOEFL (minimum score 550 paper-based; 213 computer-based), IELTS (minimum score 7). *Application deadline:* For fall admission, 6/1 priority date for domestic students, 4/1 for international students; for spring admission, 10/1 priority date for domestic students, 8/1 for international students. Applications are processed on a rolling basis. Application fee: $35. Electronic applications accepted. *Expenses:* Tuition, state resident: part-time $267 per credit. Tuition, nonresident: part-time $418 per credit. Required fees: $28 per credit. *Financial support:* Federal Work-Study and unspecified assistantships available. Financial award application deadline: 3/1. *Unit head:* Dr. Robert Prout, Chairperson, 320-308-4101, Fax: 320-308-2993, E-mail: crimjustice@stcloudstate.edu. *Application contact:* Linda Lou Krueger, School of Graduate Studies, 320-308-2113, Fax: 320-308-5371, E-mail: lekrueger@stcloudstate.edu.

St. John's University, St. John's College of Liberal Arts and Sciences, Department of Sociology and Anthropology, Queens, NY 11439. Offers criminology and justice (MA); sociology (MA). Part-time and evening/weekend programs available. *Faculty:* 13 full-time (6 women), 15 part-time/adjunct (6 women). *Students:* 28 full-time (17 women), 49 part-time (28 women); includes 37 minority (21 African Americans, 4 Asian Americans or Pacific Islanders, 12 Hispanic Americans), 5 international. Average age 28. 59 applicants, 78% accepted, 36 enrolled. In 2007, 22 degrees awarded. *Degree requirements:* For master's, comprehensive exam, thesis optional. *Entrance requirements:* For master's, 18 undergraduate credits in social services, minimum GPA of 3.0. Additional exam requirements/recommendations for international students: Required—TOEFL (minimum score 500 paper-based; 173 computer-based; 61 iBT), IELTS (minimum score 6). *Application deadline:* For fall admission, 5/1 priority date for

Criminal Justice and Criminology

St. John's University (continued)
domestic and international students; for spring admission, 11/1 priority date for domestic and international students. Applications are processed on a rolling basis. Application fee: $40. Electronic applications accepted. *Financial support:* Research assistantships, career-related internships or fieldwork and scholarships/grants available. Support available to part-time students. Financial award application deadline: 3/1; financial award applicants required to submit FAFSA. *Faculty research:* Global black power movement, poverty, domestic violence and human trafficking, female juvenile violence, media and race. *Unit head:* Dr. Dawn Esposito, Chair, 718-990-5667, E-mail: espositd@stjohns.edu. *Application contact:* Beth Evans, Associate Vice President and Executive Director, Enrollment Management, 718-990-6999, Fax: 718-990-5686, E-mail: gradhelp@stjohns.edu.

Saint Joseph's University, College of Arts and Sciences, Department of Criminal Justice, Philadelphia, PA 19131-1395. Offers administration/police executive (MS); behavior analysis (MS, Post-Master's Certificate); criminal justice (MS, Post-Master's Certificate); criminology (MS); federal law (MS); intelligence and crime (MS); probation, parole, and corrections (MS). Evening/weekend programs available. *Students:* 2 full-time (1 woman), 178 part-time (107 women); includes 56 minority (49 African Americans, 1 Asian American or Pacific Islander, 6 Hispanic Americans), 2 international. Average age 33. In 2007, 118 degrees awarded. *Degree requirements:* For master's, thesis. *Entrance requirements:* For master's, GRE General Test or minimum GPA of 3.0, 2 letters of recommendation, personal statement, application, official transcripts. Additional exam requirements/recommendations for international students: Required—TOEFL (minimum score 550 paper-based; 213 computer-based; 79 iBT). *Application deadline:* For fall admission, 7/15 priority date for domestic students, 4/15 for international students; for winter admission, 1/15 for international students; for spring admission, 11/15 priority date for domestic students, 10/15 for international students. Applications are processed on a rolling basis. Application fee: $35. Electronic applications accepted. *Expenses:* Tuition: Part-time $738 per credit. Tuition and fees vary according to degree level and program. *Financial support:* Career-related internships or fieldwork and unspecified assistantships available. *Unit head:* Patricia Griffin, Director, 610-660-1294.

Saint Leo University, Graduate Business Studies, Saint Leo, FL 33574-6665. Offers accounting (MBA); business (MBA); criminal justice (MBA); health services management (MBA); human resource administration (MBA); information security management (MBA); sport business (MBA). Part-time and evening/weekend programs available. Postbaccalaureate distance learning degree programs offered (no on-campus study). *Faculty:* 16 full-time (5 women), 34 part-time/adjunct (9 women). *Students:* 320 full-time (203 women), 534 part-time (315 women); includes 281 minority (217 African Americans, 5 American Indian/Alaska Native, 12 Asian Americans or Pacific Islanders, 47 Hispanic Americans), 9 international. Average age 36. In 2007, 255 degrees awarded. *Degree requirements:* For master's, thesis. *Entrance requirements:* For master's, GMAT, 5 years of professional work experience, resumé, 2 letters of recommendation. Additional exam requirements/recommendations for international students: Required—TOEFL (minimum score 550 paper-based; 213 computer-based). *Application deadline:* For fall admission, 7/1 priority date for domestic students; for spring admission, 11/12 priority date for domestic students. Applications are processed on a rolling basis. Application fee: $45. Electronic applications accepted. *Expenses: Contact institution.* Tuition and fees vary according to campus/location and program. *Financial support:* In 2007–08, 39 students received support. Career-related internships or fieldwork, Federal Work-Study, and scholarships/grants available. Support available to part-time students. Financial award application deadline: 3/1; financial award applicants required to submit FAFSA. *Unit head:* Dr. Robert Robertson, Director, 352-588-8758, Fax: 352-588-8912, E-mail: mba@saintleo.edu. *Application contact:* Jared Welling, Director, Graduate/Weekend and Evening Admission, 800-707-8846, Fax: 352-588-7873, E-mail: grad.admissions@saintleo.edu.

Saint Leo University, Graduate Studies in Criminal Justice, Saint Leo, FL 33574-6665. Offers criminal justice (MS); critical incident management (MS). Part-time and evening/weekend programs available. Postbaccalaureate distance learning degree programs offered (no on-campus study). *Faculty:* 7 full-time (1 woman), 8 part-time/adjunct (0 women). *Students:* 61 full-time (31 women), 143 part-time (81 women); includes 75 minority (57 African Americans, 2 Asian Americans or Pacific Islanders, 16 Hispanic Americans), 1 international. Average age 37. In 2007, 35 degrees awarded. *Entrance requirements:* For master's, minimum GPA of 3.0. Additional exam requirements/recommendations for international students: Required—TOEFL (minimum score 550 paper-based; 213 computer-based). *Application deadline:* For fall admission, 7/1 priority date for domestic and international students; for spring admission, 11/1 priority date for domestic and international students. Applications are processed on a rolling basis. Application fee: $45. Electronic applications accepted. *Expenses:* Tuition: Full-time $9,900; part-time $550 per semester hour. Required fees: $660; $110 per course. Tuition and fees vary according to campus/location and program. *Financial support:* In 2007–08, 11 students received support. Federal Work-Study and scholarships/grants available. Support available to part-time students. *Unit head:* Dr. Robert Diemer, Director, 352-588-8974, Fax: 352-588-8289, E-mail: robert.diemer@saintleo.edu. *Application contact:* Jared Welling, Director, Graduate/Weekend and Evening Admission, 800-707-8846, Fax: 352-588-7873, E-mail: grad.admissions@saintleo.edu.

Saint Mary's University, Faculty of Arts, Program in Criminology, Halifax, NS B3H 3C3, Canada. Offers MA. Part-time programs available. *Degree requirements:* For master's, thesis. *Entrance requirements:* For master's, honors degree, minimum QPA of 3.33. Expenses: Contact institution.

St. Thomas University, School of Business, Department of Management, Miami Gardens, FL 33054-6459. Offers accounting (MBA); general management (MSM, Certificate); health management (MBA, MSM, Certificate); human resource management (MBA, MSM, Certificate); international business (MBA, MIB, MSM, Certificate); justice administration (MSM, Certificate); management accounting (MSM, Certificate); public management (MSM, Certificate); sports administration (MS). Part-time and evening/weekend programs available. *Students:* 35 full-time (24 women), 78 part-time (53 women); includes 89 minority (64 African Americans, 25 Hispanic Americans), 5 international. Average age 37. In 2007, 57 degrees awarded. *Degree requirements:* For master's, comprehensive exam. *Entrance requirements:* For master's, interview, minimum GPA of 3.0 or GMAT. Additional exam requirements/recommendations for international students: Required—TOEFL (minimum score 550 paper-based; 213 computer-based; 79 iBT). *Application deadline:* Applications are processed on a rolling basis. Application fee: $40. Electronic applications accepted. *Financial support:* Career-related internships or fieldwork and unspecified assistantships available. Support available to part-time students. Financial award application deadline: 4/15; financial award applicants required to submit FAFSA. *Unit head:* Dr. Seok-Ho Song, Program Director, 305-474-6909, Fax: 305-628-6510, E-mail: ssong@stu.edu. *Application contact:* Margarette Fleuricourt, Graduate Admissions Officer, 305-628-6546, Fax: 305-628-6591, E-mail: graduate@stu.edu.

Salem State College, Graduate School, Program in Criminal Justice, Salem, MA 01970-5353. Offers MS. Part-time and evening/weekend programs available. *Students:* 1 (woman) full-time, 13 part-time (5 women); includes 1 Hispanic American. Average age 30.Application fee: $35. *Unit head:* Ann Sullivan, Coordinator, 978-542-6321, E-mail: asullivan@salemstate.edu.

Salve Regina University, Graduate Studies, Programs in Administration of Justice, Newport, RI 02840-4192. Offers justice and homeland security (MS); law enforcement leadership (MS, MSM).

Sam Houston State University, College of Criminal Justice, Huntsville, TX 77341. Offers criminal justice (MS, PhD); criminal justice and criminology (MA); criminal justice management (MS); forensic science (MS). *Faculty:* 30 full-time (10 women). *Students:* 77 full-time (44 women), 114 part-time (45 women); includes 25 minority (7 African Americans, 1 American Indian/Alaska Native, 3 Asian Americans or Pacific Islanders, 14 Hispanic Americans), 40 international. Average age 32. In 2007, 53 master's, 16 doctorates awarded. *Degree requirements:* For master's, thesis (for some programs); for doctorate, comprehensive exam, thesis/dissertation. *Entrance requirements:* For master's, GRE General Test; for doctorate, GRE General Test, master's degree. *Application deadline:* For fall admission, 8/1 for domestic students; for spring admission, 12/1 for domestic students. Applications are processed on a rolling basis. Application fee: $20. *Expenses:* Tuition, state resident: full-time $5,026; part-time $184 per semester hour. Tuition, nonresident: full-time $10,586; part-time $462 per semester hour. Required fees: $494 per semester. *Financial support:* Fellowships, research assistantships, teaching assistantships, career-related internships or fieldwork, Federal Work-Study, institutionally sponsored loans, and unspecified assistantships available. Support available to part-time students. Financial award application deadline: 5/31; financial award applicants required to submit FAFSA. *Unit head:* Dr. Vincent Webb, Dean, 936-294-1632, Fax: 936-294-1653, E-mail: vwebb@shsu.edu. *Application contact:* Doris Powell, Advisor, 936-294-3637.

San Diego State University, Graduate and Research Affairs, College of Professional Studies and Fine Arts, School of Public Affairs, Program in Criminal Justice Administration, San Diego, CA 92182. Offers MPA. Part-time programs available. *Students:* 9 full-time (5 women), 7 part-time (3 women); includes 9 minority (5 Asian Americans or Pacific Islanders, 4 Hispanic Americans). Average age 29. 11 applicants, 73% accepted, 5 enrolled. In 2007, 2 degrees awarded. *Entrance requirements:* For master's, GRE General Test, 2 letters of reference. Additional exam requirements/recommendations for international students: Required—TOEFL. *Application deadline:* For fall admission, 5/1 for domestic and international students; for spring admission, 11/1 for domestic students, 10/1 for international students. Applications are processed on a rolling basis. Application fee: $55. Electronic applications accepted. *Financial support:* Career-related internships or fieldwork available. Financial award applicants required to submit FAFSA. *Unit head:* Jeffrey McIlwain, Graduate Advisor, 619-594-3876, Fax: 619-594-1165. *Application contact:* Natalie Pearl, Graduate Advisor, 619-594-1948, Fax: 619-594-1165, E-mail: pearl@mail.sdsu.edu.

San Diego State University, Graduate and Research Affairs, College of Professional Studies and Fine Arts, School of Public Affairs, Program in Criminal Justice and Criminology, San Diego, CA 92182. Offers MS. *Students:* 12 full-time (11 women), 5 part-time (3 women); includes 9 minority (1 African American, 1 Asian American or Pacific Islander, 7 Hispanic Americans). 37 applicants, 59% accepted, 13 enrolled. In 2007, 20 degrees awarded. *Entrance requirements:* For master's, GRE General Test, 2 letters of reference. Additional exam requirements/recommendations for international students: Required—TOEFL. *Application deadline:* For fall admission, 5/1 for domestic and international students; for spring admission, 11/1 for domestic students, 10/1 for international students. Applications are processed on a rolling basis. Application fee: $55. Electronic applications accepted. *Financial support:* Applicants required to submit FAFSA. *Unit head:* Jeffrey McIlwain, Graduate Advisor, 619-594-3876, Fax: 619-594-1165. *Application contact:* Natalie Pearl, Graduate Advisor, 619-594-1948, Fax: 619-594-1165, E-mail: pearl@mail.sdsu.edu.

San Jose State University, Graduate Studies and Research, College of Applied Sciences and Arts, Department of Justice Studies, San Jose, CA 95192-0001. Offers MS. Part-time programs available. *Students:* 14 full-time (10 women), 14 part-time (11 women); includes 13 minority (2 African Americans, 1 American Indian/Alaska Native, 2 Asian Americans or Pacific Islanders, 8 Hispanic Americans), 1 international. Average age 29. 29 applicants, 48% accepted, 8 enrolled. In 2007, 11 degrees awarded. *Degree requirements:* For master's, thesis or alternative. *Entrance requirements:* For master's, GRE or LSAT, minimum GPA of 3.0. Additional exam requirements/recommendations for international students: Required—TOEFL. *Application deadline:* For fall admission, 6/29 for domestic students; for spring admission, 11/30 for domestic students. Applications are processed on a rolling basis. Application fee: $59. Electronic applications accepted. *Financial support:* Career-related internships or fieldwork and institutionally sponsored loans available. Support available to part-time students. Financial award application deadline: 7/1; financial award applicants required to submit FAFSA. *Faculty research:* Employee stress, interagency cooperation, prison industries, application of death penalty sentences, sucrose ingestion and delinquency. *Unit head:* Mona Lynch, Chair, 408-924-2940, Fax: 408-924-2953.

Seattle University, College of Arts and Sciences, Department of Criminal Justice, Seattle, WA 98122-1090. Offers MACJ.

Shippensburg University of Pennsylvania, School of Graduate Studies, College of Education and Human Services, Department of Criminal Justice, Shippensburg, PA 17257-2299. Offers administration of justice (MS). Part-time and evening/weekend programs available. *Faculty:* 7 full-time (1 woman). *Students:* 8 full-time (4 women), 49 part-time (30 women); includes 9 minority (7 African Americans, 1 American Indian/Alaska Native, 1 Hispanic American). Average age 30. 41 applicants, 85% accepted, 24 enrolled. In 2007, 34 degrees awarded. *Degree requirements:* For master's, thesis optional, internship or practicum. *Entrance requirements:* For master's, GRE or MAT (if GPA is below 2.75). Additional exam requirements/recommendations for international students: Required—TOEFL (minimum score 560 paper-based; 220 computer-based). *Application deadline:* For fall admission, 3/1 for international students; for spring admission, 7/1 for international students. Applications are processed on a rolling basis. Application fee: $30. Electronic applications accepted. *Expenses:* Tuition, state resident: part-time $345 per credit. Tuition, nonresident: part-time $552 per credit. Required fees: $28 per credit. Tuition and fees vary according to course load. *Financial support:* In 2007–08, 3 research assistantships with full tuition reimbursements (averaging $3,575 per year) were awarded; career-related internships or fieldwork, scholarships/grants, and unspecified assistantships also available. Support available to part-time students. Financial award application deadline: 3/1; financial award applicants required to submit FAFSA. *Unit head:* Dr. Robert Freeman, Chairperson, 717-477-1558, Fax: 717-477-4087, E-mail: rmfree@ship.edu. *Application contact:* Renee Payne, Associate Dean of Graduate Admissions, 717-477-1231, Fax: 717-477-4016, E-mail: rmpayn@ship.edu.

Simon Fraser University, Graduate Studies, Faculty of Arts and Social Sciences, School of Criminology, Burnaby, BC V5A 1S6, Canada. Offers MA, PhD. *Degree requirements:* For master's, thesis; for doctorate, thesis/dissertation. *Entrance requirements:* For master's, minimum GPA of 3.0; for doctorate, minimum GPA of 3.5. Additional exam requirements/recommendations for international students: Required—TOEFL or IELTS. *Faculty research:* Media and crime, feminist jurisprudence, policy evaluation, penology, terrorism.

Southeast Missouri State University, School of Graduate Studies, Department of Criminal Justice, Cape Girardeau, MO 63701-4799. Offers MS. Part-time and evening/weekend programs available. *Faculty:* 6 full-time (1 woman). *Students:* 4 full-time (2 women), 31 part-time (18 women); includes 7 minority (6 African Americans, 1 Asian American or Pacific Islander). Average age 30. 19 applicants, 100% accepted. In 2007, 4 degrees awarded. *Degree requirements:* For master's, comprehensive exam (for some programs), thesis or alternative. *Entrance requirements:* For master's, minimum GPA of 2.5. Additional exam requirements/recommendations for international students: Required—TOEFL (minimum score 550 paper-based; 213 computer-based). *Application deadline:* For fall admission, 8/1 for domestic students, 6/1 for international students; for spring admission, 11/21 for domestic students, 10/1 for international students. Applications are processed on a rolling basis. Application fee: $25 ($100 for international students). Electronic applications accepted. *Expenses:* Tuition, state resident: part-time $224 per credit hour. Tuition, nonresident: part-time $395 per credit hour. Tuition and fees vary according to course load and program. *Financial support:* In 2007–08, 18 students received support, including 5 research assistantships with full tuition reimbursements available (averaging $7,600 per year); career-related internships or fieldwork and unspecified assistantships also available. Financial award applicants required to submit FAFSA. *Unit head:* Dr. John Wade, Chairperson, 573-651-2685, E-mail: jwade@semo.edu. *Application contact:* Marsha L. Arant, Senior Administrative Assistant, Office of Graduate Studies, 573-651-2192, Fax: 573-651-2001, E-mail: marant@semo.edu.

Southern Illinois University Carbondale, Graduate School, College of Liberal Arts, Administration of Justice Program, Carbondale, IL 62901-4701. Offers MA. *Faculty:* 10 full-time (3 women). *Students:* 5 full-time (3 women), 21 part-time (10 women); includes 2 minority

(1 African American, 1 Hispanic American), 3 international. 15 applicants, 47% accepted, 3 enrolled. In 2007, 2 degrees awarded. *Degree requirements:* For master's, thesis optional. *Entrance requirements:* For master's, GRE General Test, minimum GPA of 2.7. Additional exam requirements/recommendations for international students: Required—TOEFL. *Application deadline:* Applications are processed on a rolling basis. Application fee: $20. *Financial support:* In 2007–08, 2 fellowships with full tuition reimbursements, 5 research assistantships with full tuition reimbursements, 13 teaching assistantships with full tuition reimbursements were awarded; career-related internships or fieldwork, Federal Work-Study, and institutionally sponsored loans also available. Support available to part-time students. *Faculty research:* Corrections, criminology, law enforcement, crime prevention, victims of crime. Total annual research expenditures: $300,000. *Unit head:* Kimberly Leonard, Director, 618-453-6362, Fax: 618-453-6377. *Application contact:* Monica Russell, Graduate Secretary, 618-453-6372, Fax: 618-453-6377, E-mail: mccalla@siu.edu.

Southern University and Agricultural and Mechanical College, Graduate School, Nelson Mandela School of Public Policy and Urban Affairs, Department of Criminal Justice, Baton Rouge, LA 70813. Offers MS. *Faculty:* 3 full-time (0 women). *Students:* 31 full-time (23 women), 34 part-time (23 women); includes 44 minority (all African Americans) 24 applicants, 79% accepted, 15 enrolled. In 2007, 13 degrees awarded. *Entrance requirements:* Additional exam requirements/recommendations for international students: Required—TOEFL (minimum score 525 paper-based; 193 computer-based). *Application deadline:* For fall admission, 4/15 priority date for domestic and international students; for spring admission, 11/1 priority date for domestic and international students. Application fee: $25. *Unit head:* Dr. Russell Dawkins, Chair, 225-771-2095, Fax: 225-771-2918, E-mail: russell_dawkins@subr.edu.

Southwestern College, Professional Studies Programs, Wichita, KS 67207. Offers business administration (MBA); leadership (MS); management (MS); security administration (MS); specialized ministries (MA). Part-time and evening/weekend programs available. Postbaccalaureate distance learning degree programs offered (minimal on-campus study). *Faculty:* 30 part-time/adjunct (12 women). *Students:* 77 full-time (34 women), 80 part-time (39 women); includes 20 minority (12 African Americans, 1 Asian American or Pacific Islander, 7 Hispanic Americans). Average age 36. 46 applicants, 96% accepted, 44 enrolled. In 2007, 74 degrees awarded. *Degree requirements:* For master's, practicum/capstone project. *Entrance requirements:* For master's, baccalaureate degree; minimum GPA of 2.5, 3.0 for MBA. Application fee: $0. *Expenses:* Tuition: Part-time $435 per credit hour. *Financial support:* In 2007–08, 89 students received support. Tuition waivers (partial) and unspecified assistantships available. Financial award application deadline: 4/1. *Unit head:* Dr. Jeni McRay, Director of Academic Affairs, 888-684-5335 Ext. 203, Fax: 316-688-5218, E-mail: jeni.mcray@sckans.edu.

Suffolk University, College of Arts and Sciences, Department of Criminal Justice, Boston, MA 02108-2770. Offers MSCJ, JD/MSCJ. Part-time programs available. *Faculty:* 14 full-time (8 women), 3 part-time/adjunct (2 women). *Students:* 24 full-time (22 women), 49 part-time (39 women); includes 14 minority (11 African Americans, 1 Asian American or Pacific Islander, 2 Hispanic Americans), 1 international. Average age 26. 63 applicants, 87% accepted, 35 enrolled. In 2007, 39 degrees awarded. *Entrance requirements:* For master's, GMAT or GRE. Additional exam requirements/recommendations for international students: Required—TOEFL (minimum score 550 paper-based; 213 computer-based; 80 iBT). *Application deadline:* For fall admission, 6/15 priority date for domestic students, 6/15 for international students; for spring admission, 11/1 priority date for domestic students, 11/1 for international students. Applications are processed on a rolling basis. Application fee: $50. Electronic applications accepted. *Expenses: Contact institution. Financial support:* In 2007–08, 46 fellowships with partial tuition reimbursements (averaging $3,783 per year) were awarded; career-related internships or fieldwork, Federal Work-Study, and institutionally sponsored loans also available. Support available to part-time students. Financial award application deadline: 4/1; financial award applicants required to submit FAFSA. *Faculty research:* Restorative justice, anti-gang initiative, healthcare for female ex-offenders, violence against women, juvenile justice and the courts. *Unit head:* Dr. Donald R. Morton, Director, 617-305-1990, Fax: 617-720-0490, E-mail: dmorton@suffolk.edu. *Application contact:* Judith Reynolds, Director of Graduate Admissions, 617-573-8302, Fax: 617-523-0116, E-mail: grad.admission@suffolk.edu.

Sul Ross State University, School of Professional Studies, Department of Criminal Justice, Alpine, TX 79832. Offers MS. *Entrance requirements:* For master's, GRE General Test, minimum GPA of 2.5 in last 60 hours of undergraduate work.

Tarleton State University, College of Graduate Studies, College of Liberal and Fine Arts, Department of Social Work, Sociology, and Criminal Justice, Stephenville, TX 76402. Offers criminal justice (MCJ). Part-time and evening/weekend programs available. *Faculty:* 3 full-time (1 woman), 2 part-time/adjunct (1 woman). *Students:* 16 full-time (4 women), 12 part-time (8 women); includes 8 minority (6 African Americans, 1 Asian American or Pacific Islander, 1 Hispanic American). Average age 37. 11 applicants, 82% accepted, 8 enrolled. In 2007, 4 degrees awarded. *Degree requirements:* For master's, comprehensive exam (for some programs), thesis optional. *Entrance requirements:* For master's, GRE General Test, minimum GPA of 3.0. Additional exam requirements/recommendations for international students: Required—TOEFL (minimum score 550 paper-based; 213 computer-based). *Application deadline:* For fall admission, 8/5 priority date for domestic students; for spring admission, 12/1 for domestic students. Applications are processed on a rolling basis. Application fee: $25 ($125 for international students). Electronic applications accepted. *Expenses:* Tuition, state resident: full-time $2,520; part-time $140 per credit hour. Tuition, nonresident: full-time $7,344; part-time $408 per credit hour. Required fees: $948; $39 per credit hour. *Financial support:* Career-related internships or fieldwork and Federal Work-Study available. Support available to part-time students. Financial award application deadline: 5/1; financial award applicants required to submit FAFSA. *Unit head:* Dr. Lori Anderson, Department Head, 254-968-9024, Fax: 254-968-9288, E-mail: ljanderson@tarleton.edu.

Temple University, Graduate School, College of Liberal Arts, Department of Criminal Justice, Philadelphia, PA 19122-6096. Offers MA, PhD. Part-time programs available. Terminal master's awarded for partial completion of doctoral program. *Degree requirements:* For master's, thesis optional; for doctorate, thesis/dissertation, qualifying exams. *Entrance requirements:* For master's, GRE General Test, minimum GPA of 3.0; for doctorate, GRE General Test. Additional exam requirements/recommendations for international students: Required—TOEFL (minimum score 550 paper-based; 213 computer-based; 79 iBT). Electronic applications accepted. *Faculty research:* Criminal justice policy formulation, courts, correctional alternatives, community crime prevention, juvenile justice.

Tennessee State University, The School of Graduate Studies and Research, College of Arts and Sciences, Department of Criminal Justice, Nashville, TN 37209-1561. Offers MCJ. *Faculty:* 3 full-time (1 woman), 3 part-time/adjunct (2 women). *Students:* 1 (woman) full-time, 39 part-time (25 women); includes 29 minority (all African Americans) Average age 32. 25 applicants, 52% accepted, 3 enrolled. In 2007, 1 degree awarded. *Degree requirements:* For master's, thesis. *Entrance requirements:* For master's, GRE General Test or MAT. Application fee: $25. *Expenses:* Tuition, state resident: full-time $6,271; part-time $490 per hour. Tuition, nonresident: full-time $16,550; part-time $936 per hour. *Financial support:* Unspecified assistantships available. *Unit head:* Dr. Deborah Burris-Kitchen, Head, 615-963-5571, E-mail: dburrisp-kitchen@tnstate.edu.

Texas A&M International University, Office of Graduate Studies and Research, College of Arts and Sciences, Department of Behavioral, Applied Sciences, and Criminal Justice, Laredo, TX 78041-1900. Offers counseling psychology (MACP); criminal justice (MS); psychology (MS); sociology (MA). *Faculty:* 10 full-time (5 women), 1 (woman) part-time/adjunct. *Students:* 14 full-time (11 women), 68 part-time (40 women); includes 76 minority (1 Asian American or Pacific Islander, 75 Hispanic Americans), 2 international. Average age 30. 40 applicants, 88% accepted, 21 enrolled. In 2007, 24 degrees awarded. *Degree requirements:* For master's, thesis (for some programs). *Entrance requirements:* For master's, GRE General Test. Additional exam requirements/recommendations for international students: Required—TOEFL (minimum score 550 paper-based; 213 computer-based). *Application deadline:* For fall admission, 7/15 priority date for domestic students; for spring admission, 11/12 for domestic students. Applications are processed on a rolling basis. Application fee: $25. *Financial support:* In 2007–08, 44 students received support. Application deadline: 11/1. *Unit head:* Dr. John Kilburn, Chair, 956-326-2667, Fax: 956-326-2459, E-mail: jkilburn@tamiu.edu. *Application contact:* Rosie Espinoza-Dickinson, Director of Admissions, 956-326-2200, Fax: 956-326-2199, E-mail: enroll@tamiu.edu.

Texas Southern University, Graduate School, School of Public Affairs, Program in Administration of Justice, Houston, TX 77004-4584. Offers MS, PhD. *Faculty:* 4 full-time (1 woman). *Students:* 2 full-time (1 woman), 5 part-time (2 women); includes 6 minority (all African Americans) Average age 35. 11 applicants, 91% accepted, 7 enrolled.Application fee: $50 ($75 for international students). *Unit head:* Dr. Daniel Abeyie, Chair, 713-313-4808, E-mail: georgesabeyide@tsu.edu.

Texas State University–San Marcos, Graduate School, College of Applied Arts, Department of Criminal Justice, San Marcos, TX 78666. Offers MSCJ. Part-time and evening/weekend programs available. *Faculty:* 8 full-time (2 women). *Students:* 36 full-time (24 women), 38 part-time (14 women); includes 27 minority (6 African Americans, 1 American Indian/Alaska Native, 1 Asian American or Pacific Islander, 19 Hispanic Americans). Average age 30. 48 applicants, 100% accepted, 32 enrolled. In 2007, 30 degrees awarded. *Degree requirements:* For master's, comprehensive exam. *Entrance requirements:* For master's, minimum GPA of 2.75 in last 60 hours of course work. Additional exam requirements/recommendations for international students: Required—TOEFL (minimum score 550 paper-based; 213 computer-based). *Application deadline:* For fall admission, 6/15 priority date for domestic students; for spring admission, 10/15 priority date for domestic students. Applications are processed on a rolling basis. Application fee: $40 ($90 for international students). Electronic applications accepted. *Expenses:* Tuition, state resident: full-time $3,780; part-time $210 per credit hour. Tuition, nonresident: full-time $8,784; part-time $488 per credit hour. Required fees: $493 per semester. Full-time tuition and fees vary according to course load. *Financial support:* In 2007–08, 54 students received support, including 7 research assistantships (averaging $4,970 per year), 16 teaching assistantships (averaging $5,076 per year); Federal Work-Study and institutionally sponsored loans also available. Support available to part-time students. Financial award application deadline: 4/1; financial award applicants required to submit FAFSA. *Faculty research:* Workplace violence, ethics, psychological profiling, tactical law enforcement, comparative justice systems. Total annual research expenditures: $4.4 million. *Unit head:* Dr. Quint C. Thurman, Chair, 512-245-2174, Fax: 512-245-8063, E-mail: qt10@txstate.edu. *Application contact:* Dr. Joy Pollock, Advisor, 512-245-7706, Fax: 512-245-8063, E-mail: jp12@txstate.edu.

Texas State University–San Marcos, Graduate School, Interdisciplinary Studies Program in Criminal Justice, San Marcos, TX 78666. Offers MSIS. Part-time and evening/weekend programs available. *Degree requirements:* For master's, comprehensive exam. *Application deadline:* For fall admission, 6/15 priority date for domestic students; for spring admission, 10/15 priority date for domestic students. Applications are processed on a rolling basis. Application fee: $40 ($90 for international students). *Expenses:* Tuition, state resident: full-time $3,780; part-time $210 per credit hour. Tuition, nonresident: full-time $8,784; part-time $488 per credit hour. Required fees: $493 per semester. Full-time tuition and fees vary according to course load. *Financial support:* Application deadline: 4/1; *Unit head:* Dr. Gini Deibert, Advisor, 512-245-2174, Fax: 512-245-8063, E-mail: gd11@txstate.edu.

Tiffin University, Program in Business Administration, Tiffin, OH 44883-2161. Offers general management (MBA); leadership (MBA); safety and security management (MBA); sports management (MBA). *Accreditation:* ACBSP. Part-time and evening/weekend programs available. Postbaccalaureate distance learning degree programs offered (no on-campus study). *Entrance requirements:* For master's, minimum undergraduate GPA of 2.5, work experience. Additional exam requirements/recommendations for international students: Required—TOEFL (minimum score 550 paper-based; 213 computer-based). Electronic applications accepted. *Faculty research:* Small business, executive development operations, research and statistical analysis, market research, management information systems.

Tiffin University, Program in Criminal Justice, Tiffin, OH 44883-2161. Offers crime analysis (MSCJ); criminal behavior (MSCJ); forensic psychology (MSCJ); homeland security administration (MSCJ); justice administration (MSCJ). Part-time and evening/weekend programs available. Postbaccalaureate distance learning degree programs offered (no on-campus study). *Degree requirements:* For master's, thesis optional. *Entrance requirements:* For master's, minimum undergraduate GPA of 2.5, work experience. Additional exam requirements/recommendations for international students: Required—TOEFL (minimum score 550 paper-based; 213 computer-based). Electronic applications accepted. *Faculty research:* Terrorism, intelligence, homeland security, guns and crime.

Troy University, Graduate School, College of Arts and Sciences, Program in Criminal Justice, Troy, AL 36082. Offers administration of criminal justice (MS). Part-time and evening/weekend programs available. *Students:* 99 full-time (52 women), 230 part-time (99 women); includes 188 minority (169 African Americans, 2 American Indian/Alaska Native, 7 Asian Americans or Pacific Islanders, 10 Hispanic Americans). Average age 35. In 2007, 65 degrees awarded. *Degree requirements:* For master's, comprehensive exam, thesis optional. *Entrance requirements:* For master's, GRE General Test, MAT, minimum GPA of 2.5. Additional exam requirements/recommendations for international students: Required—TOEFL (minimum score 523 paper-based; 200 computer-based). *Application deadline:* For fall admission, 6/1 for international students; for spring admission, 10/15 for international students. Applications are processed on a rolling basis. Application fee: $50. Electronic applications accepted. *Financial support:* Available to part-time students. Applicants required to submit FAFSA. *Faculty research:* Crime victims, criminal justice personnel issues, disability issues in criminal justice. *Unit head:* Dr. Bill Grantham, Chairman, 334-670-3637, Fax: 334-670-3723, E-mail: bgranth@troy.edu. *Application contact:* Brenda K. Campbell, Director of Graduate Admissions, 334-670-3178, Fax: 334-670-3733, E-mail: bcamp@troy.edu.

TUI University, College of Business Administration, Program in Business Administration, Cypress, CA 90630. Offers business administration (PhD); conflict and negotiation management (MBA); criminal justice administration (MBA); entrepreneurship (MBA); finance (MBA); general management (MBA); human resource management (MBA); information technology management (MBA); international business (MBA); logistics management (MBA); public management (MBA); strategic leadership (MBA). Part-time and evening/weekend programs available. Postbaccalaureate distance learning degree programs offered (no on-campus study). In 2007, 752 master's, 28 doctorates awarded. *Degree requirements:* For doctorate, comprehensive exam, thesis/dissertation, defense of dissertation. *Entrance requirements:* For master's, minimum GPA of 2.5 (students with GPA 3.0 or greater may transfer up to 30% of graduate level credits); for doctorate, minimum GPA of 3.4, curriculum vitae, course work in research methods or statistics. Additional exam requirements/recommendations for international students: Required—TOEFL. *Application deadline:* Applications are processed on a rolling basis. Electronic applications accepted.

Universidad Autonoma de Guadalajara, Graduate Programs, Guadalajara, Mexico. Offers advertising and corporate communications (MA); architecture (M Arch); business (MBA); computational science (MCC); education (Ed M, Ed D); international business (MIB); international corporate law (LL M); manufacturing systems (MMS); philosophy (MA, PhD); prosecution law (LL M); quality systems (MQS); renewable energy (MS); teaching mathematics (MA).

Universidad del Este, Graduate School, Carolina, PR 00983. Offers accounting (MBA); administration (M Ed); criminal justice and criminology (MA); education (M Ed); elementary education (M Ed); human resources (MBA); management (MBA); post-secondary administration

Criminal Justice and Criminology

Universidad del Este (continued)
(M Ed); social work (MA), including administrative social work, clinical social work, social politics; teaching chemistry (M Ed); teaching English (M Ed); teaching Spanish (M Ed).

Universidad del Turabo, Graduate Programs, School of Social Sciences and Humanities, Programs in Public Affairs, Program in Criminal Justice Studies, Gurabo, PR 00778-3030. Offers MPA. *Faculty:* 2 full-time (1 woman), 8 part-time/adjunct (3 women). *Students:* 35 full-time (19 women), 12 part-time (7 women); all Hispanic Americans Average age 32. In 2007, 25 degrees awarded. *Entrance requirements:* For master's, GRE, EXADEP, interview. *Application deadline:* For fall admission, 8/5 for domestic students. Application fee: $25. *Expenses:* Tuition: Full-time $5,560. *Financial support:* Institutionally sponsored loans available. *Application contact:* Virginia González, Admissions Officer, 787-746-3009.

Université de Montréal, Faculty of Arts and Sciences, School of Criminology, Montréal, QC H3C 3J7, Canada. Offers M Sc, PhD. *Faculty:* 24 full-time (6 women). *Students:* 158 full-time (123 women), 28 part-time (21 women). 142 applicants, 48% accepted, 61 enrolled. In 2007, 30 master's, 7 doctorates awarded. Terminal master's awarded for partial completion of doctoral program. *Degree requirements:* For master's, thesis; for doctorate, thesis/dissertation, general exam. *Entrance requirements:* For master's, B Sc in criminology or the equivalent; for doctorate, M Sc in criminology or equivalent. *Application deadline:* For fall admission, 2/1 for domestic students. Applications are processed on a rolling basis. Application fee: $100. Electronic applications accepted. *Financial support:* Fellowships, research assistantships, teaching assistantships, career-related internships or fieldwork available. Financial award application deadline: 3/15. *Faculty research:* Criminal behavior, criminality, prison population, victims of crime, female offender. *Unit head:* Jean Proulx, Chairman, 514-343-6387, Fax: 514-343-5650, E-mail: jean-proulx@umontreal.ca. *Application contact:* Marie-Marthe Cousineau, Graduate Student Affairs for the M Sc, 514-343-7322, Fax: 514-343-5650, E-mail: mm.cousineau@umontreal.ca.

University at Albany, State University of New York, School of Criminal Justice, Albany, NY 12222-0001. Offers MA, PhD, MSW/MA. Part-time programs available. *Students:* 67 full-time (39 women), 53 part-time (35 women); includes 12 African Americans, 5 Asian Americans or Pacific Islanders, 7 Hispanic Americans, 13 international. Average age 32. In 2007, 36 master's, 11 doctorates awarded. *Degree requirements:* For doctorate, thesis/dissertation. *Entrance requirements:* For master's and doctorate, GRE General Test. Additional exam requirements/recommendations for international students: Required—TOEFL (minimum score 550 paper-based; 213 computer-based). *Application deadline:* For fall admission, 7/1 for domestic students, 5/1 for international students. Applications are processed on a rolling basis. Application fee: $75. Electronic applications accepted. *Expenses:* Tuition, state resident: part-time $576 per credit. Tuition, nonresident: part-time $910 per credit. Tuition and fees vary according to program. *Financial support:* Fellowships, research assistantships, teaching assistantships, career-related internships or fieldwork, Federal Work-Study, and institutionally sponsored loans available. Financial award application deadline: 4/1. *Faculty research:* Causes of delinquency, comparative policing, world crime data, correctional policy, family violence. *Unit head:* Julie Horney, Dean, 518-442-5214.

University College of the Fraser Valley, Graduate Studies, Abbotsford, BC V2S 7M8, Canada. Offers criminal justice (MA). Evening/weekend programs available. *Faculty:* 5 full-time (1 woman), 2 part-time/adjunct (0 women). *Students:* 35 full-time (17 women), 12 part-time (9 women); includes 5 Asian Americans or Pacific Islanders. 23 applicants, 65% accepted, 13 enrolled. In 2007, 4 degrees awarded. *Degree requirements:* For master's, thesis optional, major research paper. *Entrance requirements:* For master's, bachelor's degree and work experience in related field. Additional exam requirements/recommendations for international students: Required—LPI exam; Recommended—TOEFL (minimum score 88 iBT), IELTS (minimum score 7), TWE. *Application deadline:* For fall admission, 1/31 priority date for domestic students, 4/1 priority date for international students; for winter admission, 9/30 priority date for domestic students, 10/1 priority date for international students; for spring admission, 12/31 priority date for domestic students, 2/1 priority date for international students. Application fee: $45 ($150 for international students). Electronic applications accepted. *Expenses:* Contact institution. *Financial support:* Research assistantships, health care benefits and employer sponsorship available. Financial award application deadline: 5/10. *Faculty research:* Human trafficking, illegal drug trade, criminal justice, criminology, safe schools. *Unit head:* Yvon Dandurand, Graduate Studies Committee Chair, 604-864-4654, Fax: 778-880-0356, E-mail: yvon_dandurand@ucfv.ca. *Application contact:* Educational Advisors, 604-854-4528, Fax: 604-855-7614, E-mail: advising@ucfv.ca.

The University of Alabama, Graduate School, College of Arts and Sciences, Department of Criminal Justice, Tuscaloosa, AL 35487. Offers MS. Part-time programs available. *Faculty:* 6 full-time (3 women). *Students:* 14 full-time (8 women), 6 part-time (4 women); includes 4 minority (3 African Americans, 1 American Indian/Alaska Native). Average age 25. 15 applicants, 47% accepted, 5 enrolled. In 2007, 9 degrees awarded. *Degree requirements:* For master's, comprehensive exam, thesis optional, thesis or policy and practice course. *Entrance requirements:* For master's, GRE. Additional exam requirements/recommendations for international students: Required—TOEFL. *Application deadline:* For fall admission, 3/1 priority date for domestic and international students; for winter admission, 11/1 priority date for domestic and international students. Applications are processed on a rolling basis. Application fee: $30. Electronic applications accepted. *Expenses:* Tuition, state resident: full-time $5,700. Tuition, nonresident: full-time $16,518. *Financial support:* In 2007–08, 1 fellowship (averaging $1,500 per year), 11 teaching assistantships with partial tuition reimbursements (averaging $5,145 per year) were awarded; institutionally sponsored loans, health care benefits, and unspecified assistantships also available. Financial award application deadline: 3/15. *Faculty research:* Domestic violence, AIDS research, youth and violence, gender crime, drugs and alcohol abuse, crime prevention. Total annual research expenditures: $20,256. *Unit head:* Dr. Celia C. Lo, Chair and Professor, 205-348-7795, Fax: 205-348-7178, E-mail: clo@ua.edu. *Application contact:* Dr. David R. Forde, Professor, 205-348-7795, Fax: 205-348-7178, E-mail: drforde@ua.edu.

The University of Alabama at Birmingham, School of Social and Behavioral Sciences, Department of Justice Sciences, Birmingham, AL 35294. Offers criminal justice (MSCJ); forensic science (MSFS). Evening/weekend programs available. *Students:* 25 full-time (19 women), 5 part-time (4 women); includes 4 minority (3 African Americans, 1 Asian American or Pacific Islander), 2 international. Average age 27. In 2007, 7 degrees awarded. *Degree requirements:* For master's, thesis or alternative. *Entrance requirements:* For master's, GRE General Test or MAT. *Application deadline:* Applications are processed on a rolling basis. Application fee: $35 ($60 for international students). Electronic applications accepted. *Financial support:* Career-related internships or fieldwork available. *Unit head:* Dr. John J. Sloan, Chair, 205-934-2069.

University of Alaska Fairbanks, College of Liberal Arts, Department of Justice, Fairbanks, AK 99775-7520. Offers criminal justice management and administration (MA). Part-time programs available. Postbaccalaureate distance learning degree programs offered. *Degree requirements:* For master's, comprehensive exam, thesis or alternative, oral defense. *Entrance requirements:* For master's, GRE General Test. Additional exam requirements/recommendations for international students: Required—TOEFL (minimum score 550 paper-based; 213 computer-based). Electronic applications accepted. *Faculty research:* Substative and procedural law, native Alaskans imprisoned in the Alaska State Department of Corrections, school violence, substance abuse in juveniles, community justice.

University of Alberta, Faculty of Graduate Studies and Research, Department of Sociology, Edmonton, AB T6G 2E1, Canada. Offers criminal justice (MA); demography (MA, PhD); sociology (MA, PhD). Part-time programs available. *Degree requirements:* For master's, thesis (for some programs); for doctorate, thesis/dissertation. *Faculty research:* Criminology, knowledge and culture, methods and theory, population studies, stratification.

University of Arkansas at Little Rock, Graduate School, College of Professional Studies, Department of Criminal Justice, Little Rock, AR 72204-1099. Offers MA, MS. MS program is by distance education. Part-time and evening/weekend programs available. *Students:* Average age 31. *Degree requirements:* For master's, thesis defense or written comprehensive exam. *Entrance requirements:* For master's, GRE General Test or MAT, interview, minimum GPA of 2.75. *Application deadline:* Applications are processed on a rolling basis. *Financial support:* Research assistantships with tuition reimbursements, teaching assistantships with tuition reimbursements, career-related internships or fieldwork, Federal Work-Study, institutionally sponsored loans, and unspecified assistantships available. Support available to part-time students. *Faculty research:* Dissemination and analysis of behavioral science knowledge, leadership and managerial skills, philosophy of individual rights and humane treatment. *Unit head:* Dr. Mary L. Parker, Chairperson, 501-569-3195, E-mail: mlparker@ualr.edu. *Application contact:* Dr. Jeff Walker, Coordinator, 501-569-3195, E-mail: jbwalker@ualr.edu.

University of Baltimore, Graduate School, The Yale Gordon College of Liberal Arts, Division of Criminology, Criminal Justice, and Social Policy, Baltimore, MD 21201-5779. Offers criminal justice (MS); JD/MS. Part-time and evening/weekend programs available. *Faculty:* 5 full-time (1 woman), 7 part-time/adjunct (1 woman). *Students:* 14 full-time (11 women), 61 part-time (49 women); includes 41 minority (39 African Americans, 2 Hispanic Americans), 3 international. Average age 28. 46 applicants, 76% accepted, 21 enrolled. In 2007, 21 degrees awarded. *Degree requirements:* For master's, thesis or alternative. *Entrance requirements:* For master's, interview, minimum GPA of 2.8. Additional exam requirements/recommendations for international students: Required—TOEFL (minimum score 550 paper-based; 213 computer-based). *Application deadline:* For fall admission, 8/1 priority date for domestic students, 6/1 for international students; for spring admission, 12/1 for domestic students, 11/1 for international students. Applications are processed on a rolling basis. Application fee: $45. Electronic applications accepted. *Expenses:* Tuition, state resident: part-time $518 per credit. Tuition, nonresident: part-time $751 per credit. Tuition and fees vary according to program. *Financial support:* In 2007–08, 8 research assistantships were awarded; fellowships, career-related internships or fieldwork and Federal Work-Study also available. Support available to part-time students. Financial award application deadline: 4/1; financial award applicants required to submit FAFSA. *Faculty research:* Drugs and violence, police and community policing, women and crime, victimization, correction in community. Total annual research expenditures: $2 million. *Unit head:* Dr. Heather Pfeifer, Program Director, 410-837-5292, E-mail: hpfeifer@ubalt.edu. *Application contact:* Wendy Bolyard.

See Close-Up on page 989.

University of California, Irvine, Office of Graduate Studies, School of Social Ecology, Department of Criminology, Law and Society, Irvine, CA 92697. Offers MAS, PhD. *Students:* 89 full-time (56 women); includes 28 minority (5 African Americans, 15 Asian Americans or Pacific Islanders, 8 Hispanic Americans), 2 international. In 2007, 23 master's, 3 doctorates awarded. *Degree requirements:* For doctorate, thesis/dissertation, research project. *Entrance requirements:* For master's and doctorate, GRE General Test, minimum GPA of 3.0. Additional exam requirements/recommendations for international students: Required—TOEFL (minimum score 550 paper-based; 213 computer-based). *Application deadline:* For fall admission, 1/15 priority date for domestic students; for winter admission, 10/15 priority date for domestic students. Application fee: $60. Electronic applications accepted. *Financial support:* Fellowships, research assistantships with full tuition reimbursements, teaching assistantships, institutionally sponsored loans, traineeships, health care benefits, and unspecified assistantships available. Financial award application deadline: 3/1; financial award applicants required to submit FAFSA. *Faculty research:* White-collar and corporate crime; immigration, the poor, homelessness, and governmental regulation; sentencing, community corrections, and diversion; mathematical and scientific evidence in jury trials; legal and criminological theory development. *Unit head:* Valerie Jenness, Chair, 949-824-5575, E-mail: jenness@uci.edu. *Application contact:* Jill Vidas, Academic Counselor, 949-824-5918, Fax: 949-824-2056, E-mail: jjvidas@uci.edu.

University of Central Florida, College of Health and Public Affairs, Department of Criminal Justice and Legal Studies, Orlando, FL 32816. Offers corrections leadership (Certificate); crime analysis (Certificate); criminal justice (MS); juvenile justice leadership (Certificate); police leadership (Certificate); victims assistance (Certificate). Part-time and evening/weekend programs available. *Faculty:* 34 full-time (11 women), 38 part-time/adjunct (7 women). *Degree requirements:* For master's, thesis or alternative. *Entrance requirements:* For master's, GRE General Test, minimum GPA of 3.0. Additional exam requirements/recommendations for international students: Required—TOEFL. *Application deadline:* For fall admission, 7/15 for domestic students; for spring admission, 4/15 for domestic students. Electronic applications accepted. *Expenses:* Tuition, state resident: full-time $6,484. Tuition, nonresident: full-time $23,938. Tuition and fees vary according to program. *Financial support:* Fellowships with partial tuition reimbursements, research assistantships with partial tuition reimbursements, teaching assistantships with partial tuition reimbursements, career-related internships or fieldwork, Federal Work-Study, institutionally sponsored loans, tuition waivers (partial), and unspecified assistantships available. Financial award application deadline: 3/1; financial award applicants required to submit FAFSA. *Unit head:* Dr. Robert Langworthy, Interim Chair, 407-823-6486, E-mail: rlangwor@mail.ucf.edu.

University of Central Missouri, The Graduate School, College of Health and Human Services, Department of Criminal Justice, Warrensburg, MO 64093. Offers criminal justice (MS), including administration of justice, administration/corrections, administrative/juvenile justices, corrections. Part-time programs available. *Faculty:* 18 full-time (4 women). *Students:* 38 full-time (24 women), 89 part-time (44 women); includes 11 minority (8 African Americans, 1 Asian American or Pacific Islander, 2 Hispanic Americans). Average age 31. 45 applicants, 87% accepted, 26 enrolled. In 2007, 25 degrees awarded. *Degree requirements:* For master's, thesis or comprehensive exam. *Entrance requirements:* For master's, GRE General Test, minimum GPA of 2.75, 15 hours of course work in criminal justice. Additional exam requirements/recommendations for international students: Required—TOEFL (minimum score 500 paper-based; 173 computer-based). *Application deadline:* For fall admission, 6/1 priority date for domestic students, 5/1 priority date for international students; for spring admission, 10/1 priority date for domestic students, 10/1 for international students. Applications are processed on a rolling basis. Application fee: $30 ($50 for international students). *Expenses:* Tuition, state resident: full-time $6,259; part-time $256 per credit hour. Tuition, nonresident: full-time $11,915; part-time $491 per credit hour. Required fees: $604; $20 per credit hour. *Financial support:* In 2007–08, 6 students received support. Federal Work-Study, scholarships/grants, unspecified assistantships, and 2 administrative assistantships available. Support available to part-time students. Financial award application deadline: 3/1; financial award applicants required to submit FAFSA. *Faculty research:* Restorative justice, sexual assault and the criminal justice system, police accountability, evaluation and court house shootings, juvenile justice, correctional reentry initiative, crime. Total annual research expenditures: $5,000. *Unit head:* Dr. Betsy Kreisel, Interim Chair, 660-543-4950, Fax: 660-543-8306, E-mail: kreisel@ucmo.edu.

University of Central Missouri, The Graduate School, College of Health and Human Services, Department of Safety Sciences, Warrensburg, MO 64093. Offers fire science (MS); human services/public services (Ed S); industrial hygiene (MS); industrial safety management (MS); loss control (MS); occupational safety management (MS); public safety (MS); security (MS); transportation safety (MS). *Accreditation:* ABET (one or more programs are accredited). Part-time programs available. *Faculty:* 10 full-time (2 women). *Students:* 21 full-time (8 women), 17 part-time (5 women); includes 10 minority (4 African Americans, 2 American Indian/Alaska Native, 2 Asian Americans or Pacific Islanders, 2 Hispanic Americans), 6 international. Average age 34. 16 applicants, 44% accepted, 7 enrolled. In 2007, 20 master's, 1 other advanced degree awarded. *Degree requirements:* For master's, comprehensive exam. *Entrance requirements:* For master's, GRE General Test, minimum GPA of 2.5, 15 hours of course work in related area; for Ed S, master's degree in related field. Additional exam requirements/recommendations for international students: Required—TOEFL (minimum score 500 paper-based; 173 computer-based). *Application deadline:* For fall admission, 6/1 priority date for domestic students, 5/1 priority date for international students; for spring admission, 10/1 priority date for domestic students, 10/1 for international students. Applications are processed on a rolling basis. Application fee: $30 ($50 for international students). *Expenses:* Tuition, state resident: full-time $6,259; part-time $256 per credit hour. Tuition, nonresident: full-time $11,915; part-time $491 per credit hour. Required fees: $604; $20 per credit hour. *Financial support:* In 2007–08, 5 students received support. Federal Work-Study, scholarships/grants, unspecified assistantships, and administrative and laboratory assistantships available. Support available to part-time students. Financial award application deadline: 3/1; financial award applicants required to submit FAFSA. *Unit head:* Larry Womble, Interim Chair, 660-543-4017, E-mail: womble@ucmo.edu.

University of Central Oklahoma, College of Graduate Studies and Research, College of Liberal Arts, Department of Sociology, Criminal Justice and Substance Abuse Studies, Edmond, OK 73034-5209. Offers criminal justice management and administration (MA). Part-time programs available. *Faculty:* 10 full-time (5 women), 6 part-time/adjunct (4 women). *Students:* 9 full-time (4 women), 18 part-time (11 women); includes 7 minority (5 African Americans, 1 American Indian/Alaska Native, 1 Hispanic American). Average age 32. 26 applicants, 100% accepted. In 2007, 4 degrees awarded. *Entrance requirements:* Additional exam requirements/recommendations for international students: Required—TOEFL (minimum score 550 paper-based; 213 computer-based). *Application deadline:* For fall admission, 7/1 for international students; for spring admission, 11/1 for international students. Applications are processed on a rolling basis. Application fee: $25. Electronic applications accepted. *Expenses:* Tuition, state resident: full-time $3,516; part-time $147 per hour. Tuition, nonresident: full-time $9,054; part-time $377 per hour. Required fees: $433; $18 per hour. *Financial support:* Unspecified assistantships available. Financial award application deadline: 3/31; financial award applicants required to submit FAFSA. *Faculty research:* Gender issues, violent offenders. *Unit head:* Dr. David Ford, Chairperson, 405-974-5622. *Application contact:* Dr. Sid Brown, Director, Program in Criminal Justice Management, 405-974-5271, Fax: 405-974-3823, E-mail: sbrown@ucok.edu.

University of Cincinnati, Graduate School, College of Education, Criminal Justice, and Human Services, Division of Criminal Justice, Cincinnati, OH 45221. Offers MS, PhD. Part-time programs available. Postbaccalaureate distance learning degree programs offered (no on-campus study). *Students:* 119 full-time (67 women), 566 part-time (316 women); includes 166 minority (121 African Americans, 2 American Indian/Alaska Native, 10 Asian Americans or Pacific Islanders, 33 Hispanic Americans), 22 international. In 2007, 233 master's, 4 doctorates awarded. *Degree requirements:* For master's, thesis or alternative; for doctorate, thesis/dissertation. *Entrance requirements:* For master's, GRE or MAT, minimum GPA of 3.0; for doctorate, minimum GPA of 3.5. Additional exam requirements/recommendations for international students: Required—TOEFL (minimum score 550 paper-based), OEPT 3. *Application deadline:* For fall admission, 2/1 for domestic students. Application fee: $40. Electronic applications accepted. *Financial support:* Fellowships, tuition waivers (partial) and unspecified assistantships available. Support available to part-time students. Total annual research expenditures: $903,893. *Unit head:* Dr. Edward J. Latessa, Head, 513-556-5836, Fax: 513-556-3303, E-mail: edward.latessa@uc.edu. *Application contact:* John Wright, Director, Graduate Programs, 513-556-5829, E-mail: john.wright@uc.edu.

University of Colorado at Colorado Springs, Graduate School, Graduate School of Public Affairs, Colorado Springs, CO 80933-7150. Offers criminal justice (MCJ); public administration (MPA). Part-time and evening/weekend programs available. *Faculty:* 8 full-time (2 women), 25 part-time/adjunct (15 women). *Students:* 84 full-time (52 women), 66 part-time (40 women); includes 34 minority (8 African Americans, 8 Asian Americans or Pacific Islanders, 18 Hispanic Americans). Average age 35. 32 applicants, 78% accepted, 19 enrolled. In 2007, 24 degrees awarded. *Degree requirements:* For master's, internship (if no experience), capstone project. *Entrance requirements:* For master's, GRE General Test, GMAT, LSAT, minimum GPA of 3.0. *Application deadline:* For fall admission, 6/1 priority date for domestic students; for spring admission, 11/1 for domestic students. Applications are processed on a rolling basis. Application fee: $60 ($75 for international students). *Expenses:* Contact institution. *Financial support:* Career-related internships or fieldwork and Federal Work-Study available. Support available to part-time students. *Unit head:* Dr. Kathleen Beatty, Dean, 719-262-4182, Fax: 719-262-4183, E-mail: kbeatty@uccs.edu. *Application contact:* Mary Lou Kartis, Program Assistant, 719-262-4182, Fax: 719-262-4183, E-mail: mkartis@uccs.edu.

University of Colorado Denver, Graduate School of Public Affairs, Program in Criminal Justice, Denver, CO 80217-3364. Offers MCJ. Part-time and evening/weekend programs available. *Faculty:* 5 full-time (3 women). *Students:* 9 full-time (6 women), 33 part-time (24 women); includes 11 minority (4 African Americans, 1 American Indian/Alaska Native, 1 Asian American or Pacific Islander, 5 Hispanic Americans). Average age 32. 31 applicants, 84% accepted, 7 enrolled. In 2007, 20 degrees awarded. *Degree requirements:* For master's, comprehensive exam, thesis optional. *Entrance requirements:* For master's, GRE General Test, minimum GPA of 3.0. Additional exam requirements/recommendations for international students: Required—TOEFL (minimum score 500 paper-based). *Application deadline:* For fall admission, 6/1 priority date for domestic students, 1/1 priority date for international students; for spring admission, 11/1 for domestic students, 5/1 for international students. Applications are processed on a rolling basis. Application fee: $50 ($60 for international students). *Financial support:* In 2007–08, 6 fellowships were awarded; research assistantships, teaching assistantships, career-related internships or fieldwork, Federal Work-Study, and institutionally sponsored loans also available. Support available to part-time students. Financial award application deadline: 4/1; financial award applicants required to submit FAFSA. *Unit head:* Dr. Mary Dodge, Director, 303-315-2086, Fax: 303-556-5971, E-mail: mary.dodge@cudenver.edu. *Application contact:* Antoinette Sandoval, Student Service Specialist, 303-556-5972, Fax: 303-556-5971, E-mail: antoinette.sandoval@cudenver.edu.

Announcement: The Master in Criminal Justice (MCJ) program focuses on law enforcement, the judiciary, correctional systems, juvenile justice, and the formulation of laws and codes. The program requires 36 graduate semester hours, including a thesis or a final comprehensive exam. Courses are typically delivered on campus in a late afternoon/evening format. The MCJ is offered in Denver and Colorado Springs, with an Executive Option held in an intensive weekend format. Many students use the criminal justice program as a stepping stone to executive positions in police administration, probation, parole, counseling, juvenile crime, domestic violence, or drug rehabilitation or governmental agency positions at the local, state, or federal levels. A new concentration is offered in domestic violence. Some prelaw students enroll to augment their knowledge of criminal justice before beginning training in criminal law. Applications are processed on a continuing basis. The MCJ program accepts GRE General Test, GMAT, or LSAT scores that are no more than five years old. Contact: Brendan Hardy, 303-315-2227, e-mail: cj@cudenver.edu or visit the Web site: http://spa.cudenver.edu.

See Close-Up on page 1631.

University of Delaware, College of Arts and Sciences, Department of Sociology and Criminology, Newark, DE 19716. Offers criminology (MA, PhD); sociology (MA, PhD). *Faculty:* 23 full-time (13 women), 1 part-time/adjunct (0 women). *Students:* 52 full-time (31 women), 4 part-time (3 women); includes 11 minority (6 African Americans, 5 Hispanic Americans), 3 international. Average age 26. 83 applicants, 43% accepted, 14 enrolled. In 2007, 7 master's, 6 doctorates awarded. *Degree requirements:* For master's, thesis; for doctorate, comprehensive exam, thesis/dissertation. *Entrance requirements:* For master's and doctorate, GRE, 3 letters of recommendation. Additional exam requirements/recommendations for international students: Required—TOEFL. *Application deadline:* For fall admission, 2/1 for domestic students. Application fee: $60. Electronic applications accepted. *Financial support:* In 2007–08, 38 students received support, including 2 fellowships with full tuition reimbursements available (averaging $14,600 per year), 15 research assistantships with full tuition reimbursements available (averaging $14,600 per year), 21 teaching assistantships with full tuition reimbursements available (averaging $14,600 per year). Financial award application deadline: 2/1. *Faculty research:* Sex and gender, criminology/deviance, theory, methods, collective behavior. Total annual research expenditures: $5.5 million. *Unit head:* Dr. Ronet D. Bachman, Chair, 302-831-2581, Fax: 302-831-2607. *Application contact:* Dr. Anne Bowler, Director of Graduate Studies, 302-831-2581, Fax: 302-831-2607, E-mail: abowler@udel.edu.

University of Denver, University College, Denver, CO 80208. Offers applied communication (MAS, MPS, Certificate); computer information systems (MAS, Certificate); environmental policy and management (MAS, Certificate); geographic information systems (MAS, Certificate); human resource administration (MPS, Certificate); knowledge and information technologies (MAS); liberal studies (MLS, Certificate); modern languages (MLS, Certificate); organizational leadership (MPS, Certificate); security management (Certificate); technology management (MAS, Certificate), including 21st century strategic management (MAS), international markets (MAS), project management (MAS), research and development management (MAS); telecommunications (MAS, Certificate), including broadband (MAS), telecommunications management and policy (MAS), telecommunications technology (MAS), wireless networks (MAS). Part-time and evening/weekend programs available. Postbaccalaureate distance learning degree programs offered (no on-campus study). *Students:* 29 full-time (15 women), 524 part-time (304 women); includes 92 minority (37 African Americans, 3 American Indian/Alaska Native, 17 Asian Americans or Pacific Islanders, 35 Hispanic Americans), 53 international. Average age 36. 625 applicants, 97% accepted, 359 enrolled. In 2007, 151 master's, 2 Certificates awarded. *Entrance requirements:* Additional exam requirements/recommendations for international students: Required—TOEFL (minimum score 550 paper-based; 213 computer-based). *Application deadline:* Applications are processed on a rolling basis. Application fee: $75. Electronic applications accepted. *Expenses:* Contact institution. *Financial support:* Applicants required to submit FAFSA. *Unit head:* Dr. James Davis, Dean, 303-871-2291, Fax: 303-871-4047, E-mail: jdavis@du.edu. *Application contact:* Information Contact, 303-871-3069.

University of Detroit Mercy, College of Liberal Arts and Education, Department of Criminal Justice and Human Services, Program in Criminal Justice Studies, Detroit, MI 48221. Offers MA. Part-time and evening/weekend programs available. *Degree requirements:* For master's, thesis or alternative. *Entrance requirements:* For master's, minimum GPA of 2.75. *Faculty research:* Socialization and social control, law and correction practices.

University of Detroit Mercy, College of Liberal Arts and Education, Department of Criminal Justice and Human Services, Program in Security Administration, Detroit, MI 48221. Offers MS. Part-time and evening/weekend programs available. *Degree requirements:* For master's, thesis or alternative. *Entrance requirements:* For master's, minimum GPA of 2.75. *Faculty research:* Physical information and personnel security.

University of Florida, Graduate School, College of Liberal Arts and Sciences, Department of Criminology, Law and Society, Gainesville, FL 32611. Offers criminology and law (MA, PhD); MA/JD; MA/PhD. *Faculty:* 7 full-time (2 women), 1 part-time/adjunct (0 women). *Students:* 39 (23 women); includes 6 minority (1 African American, 5 Hispanic Americans) 3 international. In 2007, 3 master's, 1 doctorate awarded. *Expenses:* Tuition, state resident: full-time $7,478. Tuition, nonresident: full-time $22,603. *Financial support:* In 2007–08, 28 teaching assistantships (averaging $9,903 per year) were awarded; research assistantships. *Unit head:* Lonn Lanza-Kaduce, Chair, 352-392-1025 Ext. 222, Fax: 352-392-5065, E-mail: llkkll@crim.ufl.edu. *Application contact:* Karen F. Parker, Graduate Coordinator, 352-392-1025, Fax: 352-392-5065, E-mail: grad.coord@crim.ufl.edu.

University of Great Falls, Graduate Studies, Program in Criminal Justice, Great Falls, MT 59405. Offers MSM. Part-time and evening/weekend programs available. *Faculty:* 3 full-time (1 woman), 1 part-time/adjunct (0 women). *Students:* 1 (woman) full-time, 5 part-time (2 women); includes 1 minority (American Indian/Alaska Native). Average age 35. 4 applicants, 100% accepted, 4 enrolled. In 2007, 2 degrees awarded. *Degree requirements:* For master's, thesis optional. *Entrance requirements:* For master's, GRE General Test or MAT, 3 letters of recommendation. Additional exam requirements/recommendations for international students: Required—TOEFL (minimum score 500 paper-based; 205 computer-based). *Application deadline:* For fall admission, 8/15 priority date for domestic students, 6/15 priority date for international students; for spring admission, 12/15 priority date for domestic students, 10/15 priority date for international students. Applications are processed on a rolling basis. Application fee: $50. Electronic applications accepted. *Expenses:* Tuition: Part-time $520 per credit. Required fees: $60 per semester. Tuition and fees vary according to course load. *Financial support:* In 2007–08, 3 students received support. Career-related internships or fieldwork, Federal Work-Study, and institutionally sponsored loans available. Support available to part-time students. Financial award application deadline: 6/1; financial award applicants required to submit FAFSA. *Faculty research:* Delinquency, domestic violence law. *Unit head:* Dr. Craig A. Ganster, Director, 406-791-5363, E-mail: cganster01@ugf.edu.

University of Guelph, Graduate Program Services, College of Social and Applied Human Sciences, Department of Criminology and Criminal Justice Policy, Guelph, ON N1G 2W1, Canada. Offers MA. *Faculty:* 10 full-time (3 women). *Students:* 12 full-time (8 women). 30 applicants, 53% accepted, 10 enrolled. *Degree requirements:* For master's, thesis or major paper. *Entrance requirements:* For master's, minimum B+ average during previous 2 years of coursework. *Application deadline:* For fall admission, 2/1 for domestic and international students. Application fee: $85. Electronic applications accepted. *Financial support:* In 2007–08, 20 teaching assistantships (averaging $5,106 per year) were awarded; scholarships/grants also available. *Unit head:* Dr. B. Sheldrick, Chair, 519-824-4120 Ext. 56503, Fax: 519-822-7703, E-mail: sheldric@uoguelph.ca. *Application contact:* Dr. W. O'Grady, Coordinator, 519-824-4120 Ext. 58943, Fax: 519-822-7703, E-mail: wogrady@uoguelph.ca.

University of Guelph, Graduate Program Services, College of Social and Applied Human Sciences, Department of Sociology and Anthropology, Guelph, ON N1G 2W1, Canada. Offers anthropology (MA); crime and criminal justice policy (MA); sociology (MA, PhD). *Faculty:* 24 full-time (13 women). *Students:* 34 full-time (31 women). Average age 25. 119 applicants, 31% accepted, 17 enrolled. In 2007, 14 degrees awarded. *Degree requirements:* For master's, thesis or major paper; for doctorate, comprehensive exam, thesis/dissertation. *Entrance requirements:* For master's, minimum B+ average during previous 2 years of course work, honors BA or equivalent; for doctorate, must have an MA in Sociology, must have 80% or higher in graduate level studies. Additional exam requirements/recommendations for international students: Required—TOEFL (minimum score 550 paper-based; 213 computer-based; 89 iBT), IELTS (minimum score 7), TOEFL or IELTS. *Application deadline:* For fall admission, 2/1 for domestic and international students. Application fee: $85. Electronic applications accepted. *Financial support:* In 2007–08, 103 teaching assistantships (averaging $5,106 per year) were awarded; research assistantships, scholarships/grants also available. *Faculty research:* Rural and development sociology; education, employment, and the workplace; race, ethnicity, and native studies; criminology and deviance; social psychology. *Unit head:* Dr. F. J. Schryer, Chair, 519-824-4120 Ext. 56527, Fax: 519-837-9561, E-mail: fschryer@uoguelph.ca. *Application contact:* Dr. M. Dawson, Graduate Coordinator, 519-824-4120 Ext. 56078, Fax: 519-837-9561, E-mail: mdawson@uoguelph.ca.

University of Houston–Clear Lake, School of Human Sciences and Humanities, Programs in Human Sciences, Houston, TX 77058-1098. Offers behavioral sciences (MA), including behavioral sciences-general, behavioral sciences-psychology, behavioral sciences-sociology; clinical psychology (MA); criminology (MA); cross-cultural studies (MA); family therapy (MA); fitness and human performance (MA); school psychology (MA). *Accreditation:* AAMFT/COAMFTE. Part-time and evening/weekend programs available. Postbaccalaureate distance learning degree programs offered (minimal on-campus study). *Degree requirements:* For master's, thesis or alternative. *Entrance requirements:* For master's, GRE General Test. Additional exam requirements/recommendations for international students: Required—TOEFL (minimum score 550 paper-based; 213 computer-based). Electronic applications accepted. *Faculty research:* Smoking cessation, adolescent sexuality, white collar crime, serial murder, human factors/human computer interaction.

Criminal Justice and Criminology

University of Houston–Downtown, Graduate Programs, College of Public Service, Department of Criminal Justice, Houston, TX 77002-1001. Offers MS. Part-time and evening/weekend programs available. *Faculty:* 5 full-time (3 women), 1 part-time/adjunct (0 women). *Students:* 13 full-time (5 women), 31 part-time (13 women); includes 23 minority (8 African Americans, 2 Asian Americans or Pacific Islanders, 13 Hispanic Americans), 3 international. Average age 36. In 2007, 8 degrees awarded. *Degree requirements:* For master's, comprehensive exam, thesis optional. *Entrance requirements:* For master's, GRE, MAT or GMAT, personal statement, 3 letters of reference. Additional exam requirements/recommendations for international students: Required—TOEFL (minimum score 550 paper-based; 213 computer-based; 80 iBT). *Application deadline:* For fall admission, 8/1 for domestic students, 5/1 for international students; for spring admission, 11/15 for domestic students, 10/15 for international students. Applications are processed on a rolling basis. Application fee: $35 ($60 for international students). Electronic applications accepted. *Expenses:* Tuition, state resident: full-time $3,060; part-time $170 per credit. Tuition, nonresident: full-time $7,434; part-time $413 per credit. Required fees: $704. *Financial support:* Scholarships/grants available. Financial award application deadline: 4/1; financial award applicants required to submit FAFSA. *Unit head:* Dr. Elizabeth McConnell, Chair, 713-221-8943, Fax: 713-221-2726, E-mail: mcconnelle@uhd.edu. *Application contact:* Traneshia Parker, Assistant Director of Admissions, Graduate and International Admissions, 713-221-8910, Fax: 713-223-7984, E-mail: parkert@uhd.edu.

University of Houston–Downtown, Graduate Programs, College of Public Service, Security Management for Executives Program, Houston, TX 77002-1001. Offers MSM. Part-time and evening/weekend programs available. *Faculty:* 1 full-time (0 women), 1 part-time/adjunct (0 women). *Students:* 2 full-time (0 women), 17 part-time (2 women); includes 3 minority (1 African American, 1 Asian American or Pacific Islander, 1 Hispanic American), 4 international. Average age 36. In 2007, 6 degrees awarded. *Entrance requirements:* For master's, GRE, GMAT or MAT, 3 years work experience, letter from applicant, 3 letters of reference. Additional exam requirements/recommendations for international students: Required—TOEFL (minimum score 550 paper-based; 213 computer-based; 80 iBT). *Application deadline:* For fall admission, 8/1 for domestic students, 5/1 for international students. Applications are processed on a rolling basis. Application fee: $35 ($60 for international students). Electronic applications accepted. *Expenses:* Tuition, state resident: full-time $3,060; part-time $170 per credit. Tuition, nonresident: full-time $7,434; part-time $413 per credit. Required fees: $704. *Financial support:* Application deadline: 4/1; *Unit head:* Dr. Beth Pelz, Dean, 713-221-8197, E-mail: pelzb@uhd.edu. *Application contact:* Traneshia Parker, Assistant Director of Admissions, Graduate and International Admissions, 713-221-8910, Fax: 713-223-7984, E-mail: parkert@uhd.edu.

University of Illinois at Chicago, Graduate College, College of Liberal Arts and Sciences, Department of Criminal Justice, Chicago, IL 60607-7128. Offers MA. Evening/weekend programs available. *Degree requirements:* For master's, thesis. *Entrance requirements:* For master's, GRE General Test, minimum GPA of 3.0. Additional exam requirements/recommendations for international students: Required—TOEFL. Electronic applications accepted. *Faculty research:* Sentencing probation, police and court use of scientific evidence, community mediation and conflict resolution.

University of Louisiana at Monroe, Graduate Studies and Research, College of Arts and Sciences, Program in Criminal Justice, Monroe, LA 71209-0001. Offers MA. Part-time and evening/weekend programs available. *Faculty:* 6 full-time (0 women). *Students:* 19 full-time (13 women), 15 part-time (11 women); includes 15 African Americans, 1 American Indian/Alaska Native. Average age 28. In 2007, 23 degrees awarded. *Degree requirements:* For master's, thesis optional. *Entrance requirements:* For master's, GRE General Test, minimum GPA of 2.5. Additional exam requirements/recommendations for international students: Required—TOEFL (minimum score 500 paper-based; 173 computer-based; 61 iBT). *Application deadline:* For fall admission, 8/22 priority date for domestic students, 7/1 for international students; for winter admission, 12/12 priority date for domestic students; for spring admission, 1/17 for domestic students, 11/1 for international students. Applications are processed on a rolling basis. Application fee: $20 ($30 for international students). Electronic applications accepted. *Expenses:* Tuition, state resident: full-time $2,220. Tuition, nonresident: full-time $8,172. *Financial support:* In 2007–08, 1 research assistantship with full tuition reimbursement (averaging $2,500 per year), 2 teaching assistantships with full tuition reimbursements (averaging $2,500 per year) were awarded; career-related internships or fieldwork, Federal Work-Study, and unspecified assistantships also available. Financial award application deadline: 4/1; financial award applicants required to submit FAFSA. *Unit head:* Dr. Harold Williamson, Head, 318-342-1440, Fax: 318-342-1431, E-mail: hwilliamson@ulm.edu.

University of Louisville, Graduate School, College of Arts and Sciences, Department of Justice Administration, Louisville, KY 40292-0001. Offers MS. *Students:* 16 full-time (12 women), 46 part-time (31 women); includes 9 minority (8 African Americans, 1 Asian American or Pacific Islander), 1 international. Average age 31. In 2007, 36 degrees awarded. *Degree requirements:* For master's, comprehensive exam (for some programs), thesis (for some programs), professional paper. *Entrance requirements:* For master's, GRE General Test, letters of recommendation. *Application deadline:* For fall admission, 7/1 priority date for domestic students. Application fee: $50. Electronic applications accepted. *Financial support:* In 2007–08, 3 research assistantships (averaging $12,000 per year) were awarded. *Unit head:* Dr. Deborah G. Wilson, Chair, 502-852-6567, Fax: 502-852-0065, E-mail: dgwilson@louisville.edu.

University of Management and Technology, Program in Criminal Justice, Arlington, VA 22209. Offers MS.

University of Maryland, College Park, Graduate Studies, College of Behavioral and Social Sciences, Department of Criminology and Criminal Justice, College Park, MD 20742. Offers MA, PhD, JD/MA. Part-time and evening/weekend programs available. *Faculty:* 23 full-time (12 women), 22 part-time/adjunct (8 women). *Students:* 91 full-time (67 women), 32 part-time (21 women); includes 18 minority (9 African Americans, 3 Asian Americans or Pacific Islanders, 6 Hispanic Americans), 14 international. 204 applicants, 45% accepted, 32 enrolled. In 2007, 47 master's, 7 doctorates awarded. Terminal master's awarded for partial completion of doctoral program. *Median time to degree:* Of those who began their doctoral program in fall 1999, 44% received their degree in 8 years or less. *Degree requirements:* For master's, comprehensive exam, thesis optional; for doctorate, comprehensive exam, thesis/dissertation. *Entrance requirements:* For master's, GRE General Test, minimum GPA of 3.0, 3 letters of recommendation; for doctorate, GRE General Test. Additional exam requirements/recommendations for international students: Required—TOEFL. *Application deadline:* For fall admission, 12/1 for domestic students, 2/1 for international students; for spring admission, 9/1 for domestic students, 6/1 for international students. Applications are processed on a rolling basis. Application fee: $60. Electronic applications accepted. *Financial support:* In 2007–08, 4 fellowships with full tuition reimbursements (averaging $13,847 per year), 22 research assistantships with tuition reimbursements (averaging $14,862 per year), 26 teaching assistantships with tuition reimbursements (averaging $14,809 per year) were awarded; Federal Work-Study and scholarships/grants also available. Support available to part-time students. Financial award applicants required to submit FAFSA. *Faculty research:* Theory, crime prevention, death penalty, criminal justice technology, policy. Total annual research expenditures: $888,078. *Unit head:* Dr. Sally Simpson, Chair, 301-405-6838, Fax: 301-405-4733, E-mail: ssimpson@umd.edu. *Application contact:* Dean of Graduate School, 301-405-4190, Fax: 301-314-9305.

University of Maryland Eastern Shore, Graduate Programs, Department of Criminal Justice, Princess Anne, MD 21853-1299. Offers criminology and criminal justice (MS). Part-time and evening/weekend programs available. *Faculty:* 6 full-time (4 women). *Students:* 18 full-time (15 women), 12 part-time (9 women); includes 22 minority (21 African Americans, 1 Hispanic American). Average age 25. 9 applicants, 100% accepted, 9 enrolled. In 2007, 10 degrees awarded. *Degree requirements:* For master's, comprehensive exam, thesis optional. *Entrance requirements:* For master's, GRE General Test, interview. Additional exam requirements/recommendations for international students: Required—TOEFL (minimum score 213 computer-based; 80 iBT). *Application deadline:* For fall admission, 4/15 priority date for domestic and international students; for spring admission, 10/30 priority date for domestic and international students. Applications are processed on a rolling basis. Application fee: $30. *Financial support:* In 2007–08, 2 students received support, including 2 research assistantships (averaging $5,074 per year); scholarships/grants and unspecified assistantships also available. Financial award application deadline: 3/1; financial award applicants required to submit FAFSA. *Unit head:* Dr. Robert Harleston, Chair, 410-651-6578, Fax: 410-651-8919, E-mail: raharleston@umes.edu.

University of Massachusetts Lowell, College of Arts and Sciences, Department of Criminal Justice and Criminology, Lowell, MA 01854-2881. Offers MA. Part-time and evening/weekend programs available. *Faculty:* 12 full-time (5 women), 7 part-time/adjunct (1 woman). *Degree requirements:* For master's, thesis optional. *Entrance requirements:* For master's, GRE General Test or MAT. *Application deadline:* For fall admission, 4/1 priority date for domestic students; for spring admission, 10/1 for domestic students. Applications are processed on a rolling basis. Application fee: $20 ($35 for international students). Electronic applications accepted. *Financial support:* Research assistantships with full tuition reimbursements, teaching assistantships with full tuition reimbursements, career-related internships or fieldwork, Federal Work-Study, institutionally sponsored loans, scholarships/grants, and traineeships available. Support available to part-time students. Financial award application deadline: 4/1. *Faculty research:* Family violence, criminal justice management, corrections, policing, delinquency. *Unit head:* Dr. Eva Buzawa, Chair, 978-934-4262, E-mail: eva_buzawa@uml.edu. *Application contact:* Dr. Alan Jay Lincoln, Coordinator, 978-934-2383, Fax: 978-934-3010, E-mail: alan_lincoln@uml.edu.

University of Memphis, Graduate School, College of Arts and Sciences, School of Urban Affairs and Public Policy, Department of Criminology and Criminal Justice, Memphis, TN 38152. Offers MA. Part-time programs available. *Faculty:* 3 full-time (1 woman), 3 part-time/adjunct (0 women). *Students:* 9 full-time (5 women), 1 (woman) part-time; includes 2 minority (1 African American, 1 Hispanic American). Average age 24. 13 applicants, 31% accepted, 2 enrolled. In 2007, 4 degrees awarded. *Degree requirements:* For master's, comprehensive exam, thesis optional. *Entrance requirements:* For master's, GRE General Test, minimum GPA of 3.0. *Application deadline:* For fall admission, 6/1 for domestic students; for spring admission, 11/1 for domestic students. Application fee: $35 ($60 for international students). *Expenses:* Tuition, state resident: full-time $6,990; part-time $377 per hour. Tuition, nonresident: full-time $17,818; part-time $830 per hour. Tuition and fees vary according to course load and program. *Financial support:* In 2007–08, 7 research assistantships with full tuition reimbursements (averaging $3,350 per year), 1 teaching assistantship with full tuition reimbursement (averaging $3,000 per year) were awarded; career-related internships or fieldwork, institutionally sponsored loans, and tuition waivers (partial) also available. *Faculty research:* Violence, crime prevention, crime analysis, survey research, crisis intervention. *Application contact:* Dr. Margaret Vandiver, Coordinator of Graduate Studies, 901-678-2737, Fax: 901-678-5279, E-mail: vandiver@memphis.edu.

University of Minnesota, Duluth, Graduate School, College of Liberal Arts, Department of Sociology/Anthropology, Program in Criminology, Duluth, MN 55812-2496. Offers MA. Part-time and evening/weekend programs available. *Faculty:* 12 full-time (5 women). *Students:* 11 full-time (9 women). Average age 20. 13 applicants, 46% accepted, 6 enrolled. *Degree requirements:* For master's, thesis or alternative. *Entrance requirements:* For master's, minimum GPA of 3.0, letter of recommendation, personal statement. Additional exam requirements/recommendations for international students: Required—TOEFL. *Application deadline:* For fall admission, 7/15 for domestic students; for spring admission, 11/1 for domestic students. Applications are processed on a rolling basis. Application fee: $55 ($75 for international students). *Expenses:* Tuition, state resident: part-time $812 per credit. Tuition, nonresident: part-time $1,403 per credit. Tuition and fees vary according to program. *Financial support:* In 2007–08, 1 student received support, including 1 teaching assistantship with full tuition reimbursement available (averaging $13,065 per year); research assistantships, tuition waivers (partial) also available. Financial award application deadline: 7/31. *Faculty research:* Restorative justice, juvenile delinquency, social justice, program evaluation. *Unit head:* Dr. John Hamlin, Director of Graduate Studies, 218-726-6387, Fax: 218-726-7759, E-mail: jhamlin@d.umn.edu. *Application contact:* Tami Vatalaro, Executive Administrative Specialist, 218-726-7801, Fax: 218-726-7759, E-mail: tvatalar@d.umn.edu.

University of Missouri–Kansas City, College of Arts and Sciences, Program in Criminal Justice and Criminology/Sociology, Kansas City, MO 64110-2499. Offers criminal justice and criminology (MS); sociology (MA, PhD). Part-time and evening/weekend programs available. *Faculty:* 19 full-time (12 women), 4 part-time/adjunct (2 women). *Students:* 8 full-time (7 women), 41 part-time (30 women); includes 7 minority (5 African Americans, 2 Asian Americans or Pacific Islanders). Average age 31. 23 applicants, 61% accepted, 12 enrolled. In 2007, 10 degrees awarded. *Degree requirements:* For master's, thesis optional. *Entrance requirements:* For master's, GRE, minimum GPA of 3.0 in major, 2.7 overall. Additional exam requirements/recommendations for international students: Required—TOEFL. *Application deadline:* For fall admission, 3/1 for domestic and international students; for spring admission, 11/1 for domestic and international students. Applications are processed on a rolling basis. Application fee: $35 ($50 for international students). Electronic applications accepted. *Expenses:* Tuition, state resident: part-time $287 per hour. Tuition, nonresident: part-time $741 per hour. Required fees: $31 per hour. Tuition and fees vary according to program. *Financial support:* In 2007–08, 1 research assistantship with full tuition reimbursement (averaging $12,000 per year), 7 teaching assistantships with full and partial tuition reimbursements (averaging $12,000 per year) were awarded; career-related internships or fieldwork, Federal Work-Study, institutionally sponsored loans, and tuition waivers (partial) also available. Support available to part-time students. Financial award application deadline: 3/1; financial award applicants required to submit FAFSA. *Faculty research:* Death penalty, community corrections, gerontology, religious movements, urban community and neighborhoods. Total annual research expenditures: $250,036. *Unit head:* Dr. Linda Breytspraak, Chairperson, 816-235-2514, Fax: 816-235-1117. *Application contact:* Dr. Wayne L. Lucas, Graduate Adviser, 816-235-1598, Fax: 816-235-1117, E-mail: lucasw@umkc.edu.

University of Missouri–St. Louis, College of Arts and Sciences, Department of Criminology and Criminal Justice, St. Louis, MO 63121. Offers MA, PhD. *Faculty:* 15 full-time (7 women), 1 part-time/adjunct (0 women). *Students:* 28 full-time (20 women), 29 part-time (18 women); includes 6 minority (5 African Americans, 1 Hispanic American), 2 international. Average age 28. In 2007, 9 master's, 3 doctorates awarded. *Degree requirements:* For doctorate, thesis/dissertation. *Entrance requirements:* For doctorate, GRE General Test, writing sample, 3 letters of recommendation. Additional exam requirements/recommendations for international students: Required—TOEFL (minimum score 550 paper-based; 213 computer-based). *Application deadline:* For fall admission, 4/1 for domestic students. Applications are processed on a rolling basis. Application fee: $35 ($40 for international students). Electronic applications accepted. *Financial support:* In 2007–08, 17 research assistantships with full and partial tuition reimbursements (averaging $12,600 per year), 3 teaching assistantships with full and partial tuition reimbursements (averaging $14,100 per year) were awarded; fellowships with full tuition reimbursements, career-related internships or fieldwork also available. *Faculty research:* Crime control, criminological theory, juvenile delinquency, violence, drugs. *Unit head:* Dr. Richard Rosenfeld, Director of Graduate Studies, 314-516-5031, Fax: 314-516-5048, E-mail: richard_rosenfeld@umsl.edu. *Application contact:* 314-516-5458, Fax: 314-516-6996, E-mail: gradadm@umsl.edu.

The University of Montana, Graduate School, College of Arts and Sciences, Department of Sociology, Missoula, MT 59812-0002. Offers criminology (MA); rural and environmental change (MA); sociology (MA). *Entrance requirements:* For master's, GRE General Test. Additional exam requirements/recommendations for international students: Required—TOEFL. *Faculty research:* Housing, homelessness, hunger, infant mortality, work safety.

University of Nebraska at Omaha, Graduate Studies and Research, College of Public Affairs and Community Service, Department of Criminal Justice, Omaha, NE 68182. Offers MA, MS,

PhD. Part-time and evening/weekend programs available. *Faculty:* 13 full-time (7 women). *Students:* 29 full-time (21 women), 38 part-time (18 women); includes 6 minority (1 African American, 2 Asian Americans or Pacific Islanders, 3 Hispanic Americans), 9 international. Average age 31. 55 applicants, 53% accepted, 15 enrolled. In 2007, 2 master's, 2 doctorates awarded. Terminal master's awarded for partial completion of doctoral program. *Degree requirements:* For master's, comprehensive exam, thesis (for some programs); for doctorate, comprehensive exam, thesis/dissertation. *Entrance requirements:* For master's, GRE General Test or MAT, previous course work in criminal justice, statistics, and research methods; minimum GPA of 3.0; for doctorate, GRE General Test, letters of recommendation, statement of intent. Additional exam requirements/recommendations for international students: Required—TOEFL (minimum score 550 paper-based; 213 computer-based; 80 iBT). *Application deadline:* For fall admission, 2/15 for domestic students; for spring admission, 12/1 priority date for domestic students. Applications are processed on a rolling basis. Application fee: $45. Electronic applications accepted. *Financial support:* In 2007–08, 45 students received support; research assistantships with tuition reimbursements available, teaching assistantships with tuition reimbursements available, career-related internships or fieldwork, Federal Work-Study, institutionally sponsored loans, scholarships/grants, tuition waivers (partial), and unspecified assistantships available. Support available to part-time students. Financial award application deadline: 3/1; financial award applicants required to submit FAFSA. *Unit head:* Dr. Candice Batten, Head, 402-554-2610. *Application contact:* Dr. William Wakefield, Student Contact, 402-554-2610.

University of Nevada, Las Vegas, Graduate College, Greenspun College of Urban Affairs, Department of Criminal Justice, Las Vegas, NV 89154-9900. Offers MA. Part-time programs available. *Faculty:* 11 full-time (4 women), 2 part-time/adjunct (both women). *Students:* 16 full-time (15 women), 22 part-time (9 women); includes 10 minority (2 African Americans, 1 American Indian/Alaska Native, 4 Asian Americans or Pacific Islanders, 3 Hispanic Americans). 46 applicants, 50% accepted, 19 enrolled. In 2007, 5 degrees awarded. *Degree requirements:* For master's, comprehensive exam (for some programs), thesis (for some programs). *Entrance requirements:* For master's, minimum GPA of 3.0 during previous 2 years, 2.75 overall. Additional exam requirements/recommendations for international students: Required—TOEFL (minimum score 550 paper-based; 213 computer-based; 80 iBT). *Application deadline:* For fall admission, 3/1 for domestic and international students. Application fee: $60 ($75 for international students). Electronic applications accepted. *Expenses:* Tuition, state resident: part-time $198 per credit. Tuition, nonresident: part-time $416 per credit. Required fees: $256 per semester. Tuition and fees vary according to course load and reciprocity agreements. *Financial support:* In 2007–08, 3 research assistantships with partial tuition reimbursements (averaging $10,000 per year), 6 teaching assistantships with partial tuition reimbursements (averaging $10,000 per year) were awarded; career-related internships or fieldwork, Federal Work-Study, institutionally sponsored loans, scholarships/grants, health care benefits, and unspecified assistantships also available. Support available to part-time students. Financial award application deadline: 3/1. *Unit head:* Dr. Joel Liberman, Chair, 702-895-3731. *Application contact:* Graduate College Admissions Evaluator, 702-895-3320, Fax: 702-895-4180, E-mail: gradcollege@unlv.edu.

University of Nevada, Reno, Graduate School, College of Liberal Arts, School of Social Research and Justice Studies, Department of Criminal Justice, Reno, NV 89557. Offers MA. *Faculty:* 4. *Students:* 4 full-time (1 woman), 11 part-time (10 women); includes 3 minority (1 African American, 1 Asian American or Pacific Islander, 1 Hispanic American). Average age 32. 9 applicants, 56% accepted. In 2007, 5 degrees awarded. *Degree requirements:* For master's, comprehensive exam, thesis optional. *Entrance requirements:* For master's, GRE or LSAT, undergraduate degree in criminal justice with minimum GPA of 3.0. Additional exam requirements/recommendations for international students: Required—TOEFL. *Application deadline:* For fall admission, 3/31 for domestic students. Applications are processed on a rolling basis. Application fee: $60 ($95 for international students). Electronic applications accepted. *Expenses:* Tuition, state resident: full-time $2,774; part-time $154 per credit. Tuition, nonresident: full-time $13,578; part-time $330 per credit. Required fees: $49 per semester. *Unit head:* Dr. Matt Leone, Graduate Program Director, 775-784-4681, E-mail: mleone@unr.edu.

University of Nevada, Reno, Graduate School, College of Liberal Arts, School of Social Research and Justice Studies, Department of Judicial Studies, Program in Justice Management, Reno, NV 89557. Offers MJ. In 2007, 1 degree awarded. *Expenses:* Tuition, state resident: full-time $2,774; part-time $154 per credit. Tuition, nonresident: full-time $13,578; part-time $330 per credit. Required fees: $49 per semester. *Unit head:* Jane Robinson, Graduate Director, 775-784-6270.

University of New Haven, Graduate School, Henry C. Lee College of Criminal Justice and Forensic Sciences, Program in Criminal Justice, West Haven, CT 06516-1916. Offers correctional counseling (MS); criminal justice management (MS); security management (MS). Part-time and evening/weekend programs available. *Students:* 26 full-time (18 women), 58 part-time (35 women); includes 27 minority (14 African Americans, 1 American Indian/Alaska Native, 2 Asian Americans or Pacific Islanders, 10 Hispanic Americans), 2 international. In 2007, 28 degrees awarded. *Degree requirements:* For master's, thesis or alternative. *Application deadline:* Applications are processed on a rolling basis. Application fee: $50. *Expenses:* Tuition: Part-time $630 per credit. Required fees: $40 per term. *Financial support:* Career-related internships or fieldwork and Federal Work-Study available. Support available to part-time students. Financial award application deadline: 5/1. *Unit head:* Dr. James Cassidy, Coordinator, 203-932-7374.

See Close-Up on page 991.

University of New Mexico, Robert O. Anderson Graduate School of Management, Albuquerque, NM 87131-2039. Offers accounting (M Acc, MBA), including accounting, tax accounting (MBA); financial, international and technology management (MBA), including financial management, international management, international management in Latin America, management of technology; marketing, information and decision sciences (MBA), including information assurance, management information systems, marketing management, operations management; organizational studies (MBA), including human resources management, policy and planning; JD/MBA; MBA/MA; MBA/MEME. *Accreditation:* AACSB. Part-time and evening/weekend programs available. *Faculty:* 59 full-time (17 women), 39 part-time/adjunct (13 women). *Students:* Average age 32. In 2007, 247 degrees awarded. *Entrance requirements:* For master's, GMAT. Additional exam requirements/recommendations for international students: Required—TOEFL (minimum score 550 paper-based; 213 computer-based). *Application deadline:* For fall admission, 6/1 priority date for domestic students, 3/1 for international students; for spring admission, 11/1 priority date for domestic students, 8/1 for international students. Applications are processed on a rolling basis. Application fee: $50. *Financial support:* In 2007–08, 20 fellowships (averaging $2,000 per year), 50 research assistantships with partial tuition reimbursements (averaging $5,000 per year), 2 teaching assistantships with partial tuition reimbursements (averaging $5,000 per year) were awarded; career-related internships or fieldwork, Federal Work-Study, scholarships/grants, and unspecified assistantships also available. *Faculty research:* Organizational and social aspects of accounting, entrepreneurial learning, information requirements analysis, product disposition and replacement. *Unit head:* Dr. Amy Wohlert, Interim Dean, 505-277-6148, Fax: 505-277-7108, E-mail: awohlert@unm.edu. *Application contact:* Mary Berger, Programs Manager, 505-277-3147, Fax: 505-277-9356, E-mail: berger@mgt.unm.edu.

University of North Alabama, College of Arts and Sciences, Department of Social Work and Criminal Justice, Florence, AL 35632-0001. Offers criminal justice (MSCJ). Part-time and evening/weekend programs available. *Faculty:* 3 part-time/adjunct (0 women). *Students:* 10 full-time (9 women), 11 part-time (9 women); includes 7 minority (all African Americans) Average age 33. In 2007, 6 degrees awarded. *Entrance requirements:* For master's, GRE General Test, MAT. *Application deadline:* For fall admission, 7/1 priority date for domestic students; for spring admission, 12/1 for domestic students. Applications are processed on a rolling basis. Application fee: $25. Electronic applications accepted. *Expenses:* Tuition, state resident: part-time $170 per credit hour. Tuition, nonresident: part-time $340 per credit hour. *Unit head:* Dr. Joy Borah, Chair, 256-765-4531. *Application contact:* Dr. Sue Wilson, Dean of Enrollment Management, 256-765-4316, Fax: 256-765-4349, E-mail: sjwilson@una.edu.

The University of North Carolina at Charlotte, Graduate School, College of Arts and Sciences, Department of Criminal Justice, Charlotte, NC 28223-0001. Offers MS. Part-time and evening/weekend programs available. *Faculty:* 12 full-time (6 women). *Students:* 14 full-time (10 women), 15 part-time (10 women); includes 1 minority (Asian American or Pacific Islander), 1 international. Average age 27. 18 applicants, 72% accepted, 7 enrolled. In 2007, 14 degrees awarded. *Degree requirements:* For master's, thesis or comprehensive exam. *Entrance requirements:* For master's, GRE General Test or MAT, minimum GPA of 3.0 in undergraduate major, 2.75 overall. Additional exam requirements/recommendations for international students: Required—TOEFL (minimum score 557 paper-based; 220 computer-based). *Application deadline:* For fall admission, 7/1 for domestic students, 5/1 for international students; for spring admission, 11/1 for domestic students, 10/1 for international students. Applications are processed on a rolling basis. Application fee: $55. Electronic applications accepted. *Expenses:* Tuition, state resident: full-time $2,855. Tuition, nonresident: full-time $13,062. Required fees: $1,692. *Financial support:* In 2007–08, 4 research assistantships (averaging $12,006 per year), 5 teaching assistantships (averaging $8,000 per year) were awarded; fellowships, career-related internships or fieldwork, Federal Work-Study, institutionally sponsored loans, scholarships/grants, and unspecified assistantships also available. Support available to part-time students. Financial award application deadline: 4/1; financial award applicants required to submit FAFSA. *Faculty research:* Social psychology, terrorism, and identity; diminished capacity mitigation in death penalty proceedings; effects of prenatal problems, family functioning, and neighborhood disadvantage in predicting violent offending; dynamic nature of the drug use/serious violence relationship; Chinese birth cohort: criminological implications. *Unit head:* Dr. Vivian B. Lord, Chair, 704-687-2562, Fax: 704-687-3349, E-mail: vblord@email.uncc.edu. *Application contact:* Kathy B. Giddings, Director of Graduate Admissions, 704-687-3366, Fax: 704-687-3279, E-mail: agidding@uncc.edu.

The University of North Carolina at Greensboro, Graduate School, College of Arts and Sciences, Department of Sociology, Greensboro, NC 27412-5001. Offers criminology (MA); sociology (MA). Part-time programs available. *Faculty:* 15 full-time (7 women), 1 part-time/adjunct (0 women). *Students:* 23 full-time (17 women), 21 part-time (11 women); includes 7 minority (5 African Americans, 1 American Indian/Alaska Native, 1 Hispanic American). 30 applicants, 30% accepted. *Degree requirements:* For master's, comprehensive exam, thesis. *Entrance requirements:* For master's, GRE General Test. Additional exam requirements/recommendations for international students: Required—TOEFL. *Application deadline:* For fall admission, 3/15 priority date for domestic students; for spring admission, 11/1 for domestic students. Applications are processed on a rolling basis. Application fee: $45. Electronic applications accepted. *Financial support:* In 2007–08, 13 students received support, including 5 research assistantships with full tuition reimbursements available; fellowships with full tuition reimbursements available, teaching assistantships with full tuition reimbursements available, career-related internships or fieldwork, Federal Work-Study, scholarships/grants, and traineeships also available. Support available to part-time students. *Unit head:* Dr. Julie V. Brown, Head, 336-334-5295, Fax: 336-334-5283. *Application contact:* Michelle Harkleroad, Director of Graduate Admissions, 336-334-4884, Fax: 336-334-4424, E-mail: mbharkle@uncg.edu.

The University of North Carolina Wilmington, College of Arts and Sciences, Department of Sociology and Criminology, Wilmington, NC 28403-3297. Offers criminology (MA); public sociology (MA). *Students:* 9 full-time (all women), 2 part-time (1 woman). Average age 29. 18 applicants, 67% accepted, 11 enrolled. *Degree requirements:* For master's, thesis or internship. *Application deadline:* For fall admission, 6/15 for domestic students. Application fee: $45. Electronic applications accepted. *Expenses:* Tuition, state resident: full-time $2,714. Tuition, nonresident: full-time $12,579. Required fees: $1,985. *Financial support:* In 2007–08, 5 teaching assistantships were awarded; unspecified assistantships also available. *Unit head:* Kimberly J. Cook, Chair, 910-962-3785, E-mail: cookk@uncw.edu.

See Close-Up on page 1719.

University of North Dakota, Graduate School, College of Arts and Sciences, Program in Criminal Justice, Grand Forks, ND 58202. Offers PhD. Part-time programs available. *Faculty:* 5 full-time (2 women). *Students:* 1 full-time (0 women), 6 part-time (2 women); includes 1 American Indian/Alaska Native, 1 international. 4 applicants, 25% accepted, 1 enrolled. *Entrance requirements:* For doctorate, GRE General Test. Additional exam requirements/recommendations for international students: Required—TOEFL (minimum score 550 paper-based; 213 computer-based; 79 iBT), IELTS (minimum score 7). *Application deadline:* For fall admission, 3/31 for domestic and international students; for spring admission, 10/15 for domestic and international students. Applications are processed on a rolling basis. Application fee: $35. Electronic applications accepted. *Expenses:* Tuition, state resident: full-time $4,050; part-time $225 per credit. Tuition, nonresident: full-time $10,818; part-time $601 per credit. Required fees: $110 per semester. Tuition and fees vary according to class time, campus/location, program and reciprocity agreements. *Financial support:* In 2007–08, research assistantships with full and partial tuition reimbursements (averaging $10,413 per year), 3 teaching assistantships with full and partial tuition reimbursements (averaging $10,413 per year) were awarded; fellowships with partial tuition reimbursements, Federal Work-Study, scholarships/grants, health care benefits, and unspecified assistantships also available. Support available to part-time students. Financial award applicants required to submit FAFSA. *Unit head:* Dr. Michael Meyer, Graduate Director, 701-777-4181, E-mail: michael_meyer2@und.nodak.edu. *Application contact:* Brenda Halle, Admissions Specialist, 701-777-2947, Fax: 701-777-3619, E-mail: brendahalle@mail.und.edu.

University of Northern Iowa, Graduate College, College of Social and Behavioral Sciences, Department of Sociology, Anthropology and Criminology, Cedar Falls, IA 50614. Offers criminology (MA); sociology (MA). Part-time and evening/weekend programs available. *Students:* 10 full-time (5 women), 4 part-time (3 women), 3 international. 18 applicants, 56% accepted, 8 enrolled. In 2007, 1 degree awarded. *Degree requirements:* For master's, thesis. *Entrance requirements:* For master's, minimum GPA of 3.0. Additional exam requirements/recommendations for international students: Required—TOEFL (minimum score 500 paper-based; 180 computer-based; 61 iBT). *Application deadline:* For fall admission, 8/1 priority date for domestic students. Applications are processed on a rolling basis. Application fee: $30 ($50 for international students). Electronic applications accepted. *Expenses:* Tuition, state resident: full-time $6,246; part-time $694 per credit hour. Tuition, nonresident: full-time $14,554; part-time $694 per credit hour. Required fees: $838; $119 per semester. *Financial support:* Career-related internships or fieldwork, Federal Work-Study, scholarships/grants, and tuition waivers (full and partial) available. Support available to part-time students. Financial award application deadline: 2/1. *Unit head:* Dr. Kent Sandstrom, Head, 319-273-2786, Fax: 319-273-7104, E-mail: kent.sandstrom@uni.edu.

University of North Florida, College of Arts and Sciences, Department of Criminology and Criminal Justice, Jacksonville, FL 32224-2645. Offers criminal justice (MSCJ). *Faculty:* 6 full-time (3 women). *Students:* 7 full-time (5 women), 15 part-time (9 women); includes 3 minority (1 African American, 2 Hispanic Americans), 2 international. Average age 30. 28 applicants, 39% accepted, 10 enrolled. In 2007, 10 degrees awarded. *Degree requirements:* For master's, comprehensive exam, thesis optional. *Entrance requirements:* For master's, GRE General Test, minimum GPA of 3.0 in last 60 hours, letters of recommendation. Additional exam requirements/recommendations for international students: Required—TOEFL (minimum score 500 paper-based; 173 computer-based). *Application deadline:* For fall admission, 7/1 priority date for domestic students, 5/1 for international students; for spring admission, 11/1 priority date for domestic students, 10/1 for international students. Applications are processed on a rolling basis. Application fee: $30. Electronic applications accepted. *Expenses:* Tuition, state resident: part-time $266 per credit hour. Tuition, nonresident: part-time $858 per credit hour. One-time fee: $35 part-time. Tuition and fees vary according to program. *Financial support:* In 2007–08, 8 students received support, including 2 teaching assistantships (averaging $6,000

Criminal Justice and Criminology

University of North Florida (continued)
per year). Financial award application deadline: 4/1; financial award applicants required to submit FAFSA. *Unit head:* Dr. Michael Hallett, Chair, 904-620-2850, E-mail: mhallett@unf.edu.

University of North Texas, Robert B. Toulouse School of Graduate Studies, College of Public Affairs and Community Service, Department of Criminal Justice, Denton, TX 76203. Offers MS. Part-time and evening/weekend programs available. *Faculty:* 11 full-time (4 women). *Students:* 16 full-time (8 women), 41 part-time (27 women); includes 21 minority (12 African Americans, 1 American Indian/Alaska Native, 3 Asian Americans or Pacific Islanders, 5 Hispanic Americans), 1 international. Average age 31. 45 applicants, 44% accepted, 13 enrolled. In 2007, 9 degrees awarded. *Degree requirements:* For master's, comprehensive exam, thesis optional, students can choose either option. *Entrance requirements:* For master's, GRE General Test, personal statement. Additional exam requirements/recommendations for international students: Required—proof of English language proficiency required for non-native English speakers; Recommended—TOEFL (minimum score 550 paper-based; 213 computer-based). *Application deadline:* For fall admission, 7/15 priority date for domestic students; for spring admission, 11/15 priority date for domestic students. Application fee: $50 ($75 for international students). *Financial support:* Fellowships, research assistantships, teaching assistantships available. *Faculty research:* Law enforcement administration/strategy, juvenile justice/delinquency, violent crime/victimization, terrorism correction administration/issues, capital punishment, criminalistics. *Unit head:* Dr. Peggy Tobolwsky, Chair, 940-565-2562, Fax: 940-565-2548, E-mail: peggy@pacs.unt.edu. *Application contact:* Dr. Eric Fritsch, Graduate Adviser, 940-565-4954, Fax: 940-565-2548, E-mail: efritsch@scs.unt.edu.

University of Ottawa, Faculty of Graduate and Postdoctoral Studies, Faculty of Social Sciences, Department of Criminology, Ottawa, ON K1N 6N5, Canada. Offers MA, MCA, PhD. *Degree requirements:* For master's, thesis or alternative. *Entrance requirements:* For master's, honors bachelor's degree or equivalent, minimum B average. Electronic applications accepted. *Faculty research:* Creation and reform of criminal policies in Canada.

University of Pennsylvania, School of Arts and Sciences, Graduate Group in Criminology, Philadelphia, PA 19104. Offers MA, MS, PhD.

University of Phoenix, The Artemis School, College of Health and Human Services, Phoenix, AZ 85034-7209. Offers administration of justice and security (MS); health care administration (MHA); health care management (MBA, MSN); nurse practitioner (MSN); nursing (MSN); nursing education (MSN); psychology (MS); MSN/MBA-HCM; MSN/MHA. *Accreditation:* AACN. Evening/weekend programs available. *Degree requirements:* For master's, thesis (for some programs). *Entrance requirements:* For master's, 3 years of work experience, minimum undergraduate GPA of 2.5, RN license. Additional exam requirements/recommendations for international students: Required—TOEFL (minimum score 550 paper-based; 213 computer-based; 79 iBT). Electronic applications accepted.

University of Phoenix–Augusta Campus, College of Social and Behavioral Science, Augusta, GA 30909-4583. Offers administration of justice and security (MS).

University of Phoenix–Austin Campus, College of Social and Behavioral Science, Austin, TX 78759. Offers administration of justice and security (MS); psychology (MS).

University of Phoenix–Bay Area Campus, The Artemis School, College of Health and Human Services, Pleasanton, CA 94588-3677. Offers administration of justice and security (MS); family nurse practitioner (MSN); health care management (MBA); marriage, family and child therapy (MSC). Evening/weekend programs available. *Degree requirements:* For master's, thesis (for some programs). *Entrance requirements:* For master's, minimum undergraduate GPA of 2.5, 3 years of work experience, RN license. Additional exam requirements/recommendations for international students: Required—TOEFL (minimum score 550 paper-based; 213 computer-based; 79 iBT). Electronic applications accepted.

University of Phoenix–Chattanooga Campus, College of Social and Behavioral Science, Chattanooga, TN 37421-3707. Offers administration of justice and security (MS).

University of Phoenix–Cheyenne Campus, College of Social and Behavioral Science, Cheyenne, WY 82009. Offers administration of justice and security (MS); psychology (MS).

University of Phoenix–Cleveland Campus, The Artemis School, College of Health and Human Services, Independence, OH 44131-2194. Offers administration of justice and security (MS); health care management (MBA); nursing (MSN); psychology (MS). Evening/weekend programs available. *Degree requirements:* For master's, thesis (for some programs). *Entrance requirements:* For master's, minimum undergraduate GPA of 2.5, 3 years of work experience. Additional exam requirements/recommendations for international students: Required—TOEFL (minimum score 550 paper-based; 213 computer-based; 79 iBT). Electronic applications accepted.

University of Phoenix–Des Moines Campus, College of Social and Behavioral Science, Des Moines, IA 50266. Offers administration of justice and security (MS).

University of Phoenix–Harrisburg Campus, College of Social and Behavioral Science, Harrisburg, PA 17112. Offers administration of justice and security (MS); psychology (MS).

University of Phoenix–Hawaii Campus, The Artemis School, College of Health and Human Services, Honolulu, HI 96813-4317. Offers administration of justice and security (MS); community counseling (MSC); family nurse practitioner (MSN); health administration (MHA); health care management (MBA); marriage, family and child therapy (MSC); nursing (MSN); psychology (MS). Evening/weekend programs available. *Degree requirements:* For master's, thesis (for some programs). *Entrance requirements:* For master's, minimum undergraduate GPA of 2.5, 3 years of work experience, RN license. Additional exam requirements/recommendations for international students: Required—TOEFL (minimum score 550 paper-based; 213 computer-based; 79 iBT). Electronic applications accepted.

University of Phoenix–Indianapolis Campus, The Artemis School, College of Health and Human Services, Indianapolis, IN 46250-932. Offers administration of justice and security (MS); health administration (MHA); health care management (MBA); nursing (MSN); psychology (MS). Evening/weekend programs available. *Degree requirements:* For master's, thesis. *Entrance requirements:* For master's, 3 years work experience, minimum undergraduate GPA of 2.5. Additional exam requirements/recommendations for international students: Required—TOEFL (minimum score 500 paper-based; 213 computer-based). Electronic applications accepted.

University of Phoenix–Jersey City Campus, College of Social and Behavioral Science, Jersey City, NJ 07310. Offers administration of justice and security (MS); psychology (MS).

University of Phoenix–Kansas City Campus, The Artemis School, College of Health and Human Services, Kansas City, MO 64131-4517. Offers administration of justice and security (MS); community counseling (MSC); health administration (MHA); health care management (MBA); nursing (MSN). Evening/weekend programs available. *Degree requirements:* For master's, thesis (for some programs). *Entrance requirements:* For master's, 3 years work experience, minimum undergraduate GPA or 2.5. Additional exam requirements/recommendations for international students: Required—TOEFL (minimum score 550 paper-based; 213 computer-based).

University of Phoenix–Louisiana Campus, The Artemis School, College of Health and Human Services, Metairie, LA 70001-2082. Offers administration of justice and security (MS); health care management (MBA); nursing (MSN); psychology (MS); MSN/MBA. Evening/weekend programs available. *Degree requirements:* For master's, thesis (for some programs). *Entrance requirements:* For master's, minimum undergraduate GPA of 2.5, 3 years experience, RN license. Additional exam requirements/recommendations for international students: Required—TOEFL (minimum score 550 paper-based; 213 computer-based; 79 iBT). Electronic applications accepted.

University of Phoenix–Maryland Campus, The Artemis School, College of Health and Human Services, Columbia, MD 21045-5424. Offers administration of justice and security (MS); nursing (MSN); nursing education (MSN); psychology (MS); MSN/MBA; MSN/MHA. Evening/weekend programs available. *Degree requirements:* For master's, thesis (for some programs). *Entrance requirements:* For master's, minimum undergraduate GPA of 2.5, 3 years work experience. Additional exam requirements/recommendations for international students: Required—TOEFL (minimum score 550 paper-based; 213 computer-based; 79 iBT). Electronic applications accepted.

University of Phoenix–Memphis Campus, College of Social and Behavioral Science, Cordova, TN 38018. Offers administration of justice and security (MS).

University of Phoenix–Northern Nevada Campus, College of Social and Behavioral Science, Reno, NV 89511. Offers administration of justice and security (MS); marriage, family and child therapy (MSC); psychology (MS); school counseling (MSC).

University of Phoenix–Northern Virginia Campus, College of Social and Behavioral Science, Reston, VA 20190. Offers administration of justice and security (MS).

University of Phoenix–Northwest Arkansas Campus, College of Social and Behavioral Science, Rogers, AR 72756-9615. Offers administration of justice and security (MS).

University of Phoenix–Omaha Campus, College of Social and Behavioral Science, Omaha, NE 68154-5240. Offers administration of justice and security (MS).

University of Phoenix–Oregon Campus, The Artemis School, College of Health and Human Services, Tigard, OR 97223. Offers administration of justice and security (MS); health administration (MHA); health care management (MBA); nursing (MSN); psychology (MS); MSN/MBA. Evening/weekend programs available. *Degree requirements:* For master's, thesis (for some programs). *Entrance requirements:* For master's, minimum undergraduate GPA of 2.5, 3 years of work experience, current RN license (nursing). Additional exam requirements/recommendations for international students: Required—TOEFL (minimum score 550 paper-based; 213 computer-based; 79 iBT). Electronic applications accepted.

University of Phoenix–Pittsburgh Campus, The Artemis School, College of Health and Human Services, Pittsburgh, PA 15276. Offers administration of justice and security (MS); health administration (MHA); health care management (MBA); nursing (MSN); nursing education (MSN); psychology (MS); MSN/MBA; MSN/MHA. Evening/weekend programs available. *Degree requirements:* For master's, thesis (for some programs). *Entrance requirements:* For master's, minimum undergraduate GPA of 2.5, 3 years work experience, current RN license (nursing). Additional exam requirements/recommendations for international students: Required—TOEFL (minimum score 550 paper-based; 213 computer-based; 79 iBT). Electronic applications accepted.

University of Phoenix–Renton Learning Center, College of Social and Behavioral Science, Renton, WA 98005. Offers administration of justice and security (MS).

University of Phoenix–Richmond Campus, The Artemis School, College of Health and Human Services, Richmond, VA 23230. Offers administration of justice and security (MS); health administration (MHA); health care management (MBA); nursing (MSN); psychology (MS). Evening/weekend programs available. *Degree requirements:* For master's, thesis (for some programs). *Entrance requirements:* For master's, minimum undergraduate GPA of 2.5, 3 years work experience, current RN license for nursing programs. Additional exam requirements/recommendations for international students: Required—TOEFL (minimum score 500 paper-based; 213 computer-based; 79 iBT). Electronic applications accepted.

University of Phoenix–Sacramento Valley Campus, The Artemis School, College of Health and Human Services, Sacramento, CA 95833-3632. Offers administration of justice and security (MS); family nurse practitioner (MSN); health care management (MBA); marriage, family and child counseling (MSC); nursing (MSN); nursing education (MSN). Evening/weekend programs available. *Degree requirements:* For master's, thesis (for some programs). *Entrance requirements:* For master's, RN license, minimum undergraduate GPA of 2.5, 3 years work experience. Additional exam requirements/recommendations for international students: Required—TOEFL (minimum score 550 paper-based; 213 computer-based; 79 iBT). Electronic applications accepted.

University of Phoenix–San Antonio Campus, College of Social and Behavioral Science, San Antonio, TX 78230. Offers administration of justice and security (MS); psychology (MS).

University of Phoenix–San Diego Campus, The Artemis School, College of Health and Human Services, San Diego, CA 92123. Offers administration of justice and security (MS); marriage, family and child counseling (MSC); marriage, family and child therapy (MSC); nursing (MSN); MSN/MBA. Evening/weekend programs available. *Degree requirements:* For master's, thesis (for some programs). *Entrance requirements:* For master's, minimum undergraduate GPA of 2.5, 3 years work experience, RN license. Additional exam requirements/recommendations for international students: Required—TOEFL (minimum score 550 paper-based; 213 computer-based; 79 iBT). Electronic applications accepted.

University of Phoenix–Savannah Campus, College of Social and Behavioral Science, Savannah, GA 31405-7400. Offers administration of justice and security (MS).

University of Phoenix–Southern Arizona Campus, The Artemis School, College of Health and Human Services, Tucson, AZ 85711. Offers administration of justice and security (MS); family nurse practitioner (Certificate); health administration (MHA); marriage, family and child therapy (MSC); nursing (MSN). Evening/weekend programs available. *Degree requirements:* For master's, thesis (for some programs). *Entrance requirements:* For master's, minimum undergraduate GPA of 2.5, 3 years of work experience, RN license. Additional exam requirements/recommendations for international students: Required—TOEFL (minimum score 550 paper-based; 213 computer-based; 79 iBT). Electronic applications accepted.

University of Phoenix–Springfield Campus, College of Social and Behavioral Science, Springfield, MO 65804-7211. Offers administration of justice and security (MS).

University of Pittsburgh, Graduate School of Public and International Affairs, Doctoral Program in Public and International Affairs, Pittsburgh, PA 15260. Offers development policy (PhD); foreign and security policy (PhD); international political economy (PhD); public administration (PhD); public policy (PhD). *Accreditation:* NASPAA. Part-time programs available. *Faculty:* 34 full-time (10 women), 18 part-time/adjunct (6 women). *Students:* 39 full-time (15 women), 8 part-time (6 women); includes 6 minority (2 African Americans, 3 Asian Americans or Pacific Islanders, 1 Hispanic American), 10 international. Average age 30. 61 applicants, 30% accepted, 11 enrolled. In 2007, 8 degrees awarded. *Degree requirements:* For doctorate, comprehensive exam, thesis/dissertation. *Entrance requirements:* For doctorate, GRE, 3 letters of recommendation, resumé, minimum GPA of 3.0, writing sample. Additional exam requirements/recommendations for international students: Required—TOEFL (minimum score 600 paper-based; 250 computer-based; 100 iBT), TWE (minimum score 4); Recommended—IELTS (minimum score 7). *Application deadline:* For fall admission, 2/1 for domestic students, 1/15 for international students. Application fee: $50. Electronic applications accepted. *Financial support:* In 2007–08, 13 students received support, including 13 fellowships (averaging $28,580 per year); scholarships/grants and unspecified assistantships also available. Financial award application deadline: 2/1. *Faculty research:* International political economy, international development, public administration, public policy, foreign policy, international security policy. Total annual research expenditures: $845,025. *Unit head:* Dr. Phyllis Coontz, Doctoral Program Coordinator, 412-648-2654, Fax: 412-648-2605, E-mail: pcoontz@gspia.pitt.edu. *Application* *contact:* Jessica L. Hatherill, Associate Director of Student Services, 412-648-7640, Fax: 412-648-7641, E-mail: hatherill@gspia.pitt.edu.

See Close-Up on page 1645.

University of Regina, Faculty of Graduate Studies and Research, Faculty of Arts, Department of Justice Studies, Regina, SK S4S 0A2, Canada. Offers human justice (MA); justice studies (MA); police studies (MA). *Faculty:* 3 full-time (1 woman), 3 part-time/adjunct (1 woman). *Students:* 10 full-time (6 women), 12 part-time (6 women). 14 applicants, 43% accepted, 5 enrolled. In 2007, 1 degree awarded. *Degree requirements:* For master's, thesis. *Entrance requirements:* Additional exam requirements/recommendations for international students: Required—TOEFL (minimum score 580 paper-based; 237 computer-based; 88 iBT). *Application deadline:* For fall admission, 3/31 for domestic students. Application fee: $85 ($100 for international students). Electronic applications accepted. *Financial support:* In 2007–08, 3 fellowships (averaging $15,750 per year), research assistantships (averaging $13,875 per year), 1 teaching assistantship (averaging $13,060 per year) were awarded. *Unit head:* Dr. Jim Mulvale, Head, 306-585-4237, E-mail: jim.mulvale@uregina.ca. *Application contact:* Dr. Annette Desmerais, Program Coordinator, 306-585-5066, E-mail: annette.desamarais@uregina.ca.

University of South Africa, College of Law, Pretoria, South Africa. Offers correctional services management (M Tech); criminology (MA, PhD); law (LL M, LL D); penology (MA, PhD); police science (MA, PhD); policing (M Tech); security risk management (M Tech); social science in criminology (MA).

University of South Carolina, The Graduate School, College of Arts and Sciences, Department of Criminology and Criminal Justice, Columbia, SC 29208. Offers MA, PhD, JD/MA. Part-time and evening/weekend programs available. *Faculty:* 8 full-time (2 women), 3 part-time/adjunct (0 women). *Students:* 12 full-time (4 women), 14 part-time (9 women); includes 2 minority (1 African American, 1 Asian American or Pacific Islander). Average age 26. 31 applicants, 39% accepted, 5 enrolled. In 2007, 13 degrees awarded. *Degree requirements:* For master's, comprehensive exam, thesis; for doctorate, comprehensive exam, thesis/dissertation. *Entrance requirements:* For master's and doctorate, GRE. Additional exam requirements/recommendations for international students: Required—TOEFL. *Application deadline:* For fall admission, 7/1 for domestic and international students; for spring admission, 11/15 for domestic and international students. Applications are processed on a rolling basis. Application fee: $40. Electronic applications accepted. *Expenses:* Tuition, state resident: part-time $440 per hour. Tuition, nonresident: part-time $936 per hour. Required fees: $17 per hour. Tuition and fees vary according to program. *Financial support:* In 2007–08, 7 students received support, including 7 research assistantships with tuition reimbursements available (averaging $12,250 per year); fellowships with tuition reimbursements available, career-related internships or fieldwork and unspecified assistantships also available. Financial award application deadline: 3/1. *Faculty research:* Juvenile delinquency, substance abuse, policy development, minority issues, law enforcement services. *Unit head:* Michael R. Smith, Chair, 803-777-7097, Fax: 803-777-9600. *Application contact:* Barbara A. Koons-Witt, Information Contact, 803-777-0107, Fax: 803-777-9600, E-mail: bakoons@gwm.sc.edu.

University of Southern Mississippi, Graduate School, College of Science and Technology, Department of Administration of Justice, Hattiesburg, MS 39406-0001. Offers administration of justice (PhD); corrections (MA, MS); juvenile justice (MA, MS); law enforcement (MA, MS). Part-time programs available. *Faculty:* 7 full-time (2 women). *Students:* 22 full-time (15 women), 25 part-time (13 women); includes 11 minority (9 African Americans, 2 Hispanic Americans), 2 international. Average age 33. 18 applicants, 56% accepted, 10 enrolled. In 2007, 4 master's, 2 doctorates awarded. *Degree requirements:* For master's, comprehensive exam, thesis; for doctorate, comprehensive exam, thesis/dissertation. *Entrance requirements:* For master's, GRE General Test, minimum GPA of 2.75 in last 2 years, 3.0 in field of study; for doctorate, GRE General Test, minimum GPA of 3.5. Additional exam requirements/recommendations for international students: Required—TOEFL. *Application deadline:* For fall admission, 3/15 priority date for domestic students, 3/15 for international students. Applications are processed on a rolling basis. Application fee: $30. *Financial support:* In 2007–08, 3 research assistantships with full tuition reimbursements (averaging $11,136 per year), 8 teaching assistantships with full tuition reimbursements (averaging $11,136 per year) were awarded; career-related internships or fieldwork, Federal Work-Study, and institutionally sponsored loans also available. Financial award application deadline: 3/15. *Faculty research:* Crime in the family, police training models, humanities and criminal justice. *Unit head:* Lisa Nored, Chair, 601-266-4509, Fax: 601-266-4391.

University of South Florida, Graduate School, College of Arts and Sciences, Department of Criminology, Tampa, FL 33620-9951. Offers criminal justice administration (MA); criminology (MA, PhD). *Faculty:* 14 full-time (4 women). *Students:* 40 full-time (25 women), 99 part-time (59 women); includes 22 minority (15 African Americans, 1 American Indian/Alaska Native, 2 Asian Americans or Pacific Islanders, 4 Hispanic Americans), 7 international. 108 applicants, 63% accepted, 45 enrolled. In 2007, 5 master's, 1 doctorate awarded. *Degree requirements:* For master's, thesis optional; for doctorate, comprehensive exam, thesis/dissertation. *Entrance requirements:* For master's, GRE General Test (criminology), 3 letters of recommendation, statement of purpose, writing sample; for doctorate, GRE General Test, 3 letters of recommendation, statement of purpose, writing sample. Application fee: $30. Electronic applications accepted. *Financial support:* In 2007–08, 10 students received support, including 1 fellowship with full tuition reimbursement available (averaging $20,000 per year), 2 research assistantships with partial tuition reimbursements available (averaging $10,000 per year), 8 teaching assistantships with partial tuition reimbursements available (averaging $10,000 per year); scholarships/grants also available. *Faculty research:* Criminal theory, drug abuse, violence, policing. Total annual research expenditures: $188,096. *Unit head:* Dr. Thomas Mieczkowski, Chairperson, 813-974-8281, Fax: 813-974-2803, E-mail: mieczkow@cas.usf.edu. *Application contact:* Dr. Christine S. Sellers, Graduate Program Director, 813-974-9547, Fax: 813-974-2803, E-mail: csellers@cas.usf.edu.

The University of Tennessee, Graduate School, College of Arts and Sciences, Department of Sociology, Knoxville, TN 37996. Offers criminology (MA, PhD); energy, environment, and resource policy (MA, PhD); political economy (MA, PhD). Part-time programs available. *Degree requirements:* For master's, thesis or alternative; for doctorate, thesis/dissertation. *Entrance requirements:* For master's, GRE General Test, minimum GPA of 3.0; for doctorate, GRE General Test, minimum GPA of 3.5. Additional exam requirements/recommendations for international students: Required—TOEFL. Electronic applications accepted.

The University of Tennessee at Chattanooga, Graduate School, College of Arts and Sciences, Department of Criminal Justice, Chattanooga, TN 37403-2598. Offers MSCJ. Part-time and evening/weekend programs available. *Faculty:* 5 full-time (2 women). *Students:* 14 full-time (9 women), 19 part-time (9 women); includes 7 minority (all African Americans) Average age 30. 19 applicants, 95% accepted, 9 enrolled. In 2007, 8 degrees awarded. *Degree requirements:* For master's, thesis (for some programs), qualifying exams, internship. *Entrance requirements:* For master's, GRE General Test or MAT. Additional exam requirements/recommendations for international students: Required—TOEFL (minimum score 550 paper-based; 213 computer-based; 79 iBT); Recommended—IELTS (minimum score 6). *Application deadline:* For fall admission, 8/1 priority date for domestic students, 6/1 for international students; for spring admission, 12/1 priority date for domestic students, 10/1 for international students. Applications are processed on a rolling basis. Application fee: $30 ($35 for international students). Electronic applications accepted. *Expenses:* Tuition, state resident: full-time $5,854; part-time $393 per hour. Tuition, nonresident: full-time $15,816; part-time $946 per hour. Required fees: $1,090; $256 per hour. *Financial support:* In 2007–08, 5 fellowships with full and partial tuition reimbursements (averaging $4,950 per year) were awarded; career-related internships or fieldwork, Federal Work-Study, institutionally sponsored loans, scholarships/grants, tuition waivers (partial), and unspecified assistantships also available. Support available to part-time students. Financial award application deadline: 4/1; financial award applicants required to submit FAFSA. *Faculty research:* Violence against women; crime prevention; police accountability; criminal justice privatization; public policy. *Unit head:* Dr. Helen M. Eigenberg, Chair, 423-425-4135, Fax: 423-425-2228, E-mail: helen-eigenberg@utc.edu. *Application contact:* Dr. Deborah E. Arfken, Dean of Graduate Studies, 423-425-4666, Fax: 423-425-5223, E-mail: deborah-arfken@utc.edu.

The University of Texas at Arlington, Graduate School, College of Liberal Arts, Department of Criminology and Criminal Justice, Arlington, TX 76019. Offers MA. Part-time and evening/weekend programs available. *Faculty:* 4 full-time (0 women). *Students:* 9 full-time (all women), 37 part-time (22 women); includes 16 minority (7 African Americans, 1 American Indian/Alaska Native, 1 Asian American or Pacific Islander, 7 Hispanic Americans). 26 applicants, 65% accepted, 14 enrolled. In 2007, 24 degrees awarded. *Degree requirements:* For master's, thesis or alternative. *Entrance requirements:* For master's, GRE General Test, minimum GPA of 3.0 in last 60 hours of undergraduate course work, 3 letters of recommendation. Additional exam requirements/recommendations for international students: Required—TOEFL (minimum score 550 paper-based; 213 computer-based). *Application deadline:* For fall admission, 6/16 for domestic students. Applications are processed on a rolling basis. Application fee: $35 ($50 for international students). *Expenses:* Tuition, state resident: full-time $5,934. Tuition, nonresident: full-time $10,938. *Financial support:* In 2007–08, 1 fellowship (averaging $1,000 per year), 1 research assistantship, 1 teaching assistantship were awarded; career-related internships or fieldwork also available. Financial award application deadline: 6/1; financial award applicants required to submit FAFSA. *Unit head:* Dr. Alejandro del Carmen, Chair, 817-272-3318, Fax: 817-272-5673, E-mail: adelcarmen@uta.edu.

The University of Texas at Dallas, School of Economic, Political and Policy Sciences, Program in Criminology, Richardson, TX 75083-0688. Offers MS, PhD. Part-time and evening/weekend programs available. *Faculty:* 5 full-time (3 women), 1 (woman) part-time/adjunct. *Students:* 19 full-time (13 women), 12 part-time (5 women); includes 10 minority (8 African Americans, 1 Asian American or Pacific Islander, 1 Hispanic American). Average age 32. 37 applicants, 95% accepted, 25 enrolled. In 2007, 1 master's, 2 doctorates awarded. *Degree requirements:* For master's, thesis; for doctorate, thesis/dissertation. *Entrance requirements:* For master's, GRE General Test, minimum GPA of 3.0 in upper-level course work in field. Additional exam requirements/recommendations for international students: Required—TOEFL (minimum score 550 paper-based; 213 computer-based). *Application deadline:* For fall admission, 7/15 for domestic students; for spring admission, 11/15 for domestic students. Applications are processed on a rolling basis. Application fee: $50 ($100 for international students). Electronic applications accepted. *Expenses:* Tuition, state resident: full-time $7,052. Tuition, nonresident: full-time $12,632. Tuition and fees vary according to course load. *Financial support:* In 2007–08, 4 teaching assistantships (averaging $12,460 per year) were awarded; research assistantships, career-related internships or fieldwork, Federal Work-Study, institutionally sponsored loans, scholarships/grants, and unspecified assistantships also available. Support available to part-time students. Financial award application deadline: 4/30; financial award applicants required to submit FAFSA. *Unit head:* Dr. James Marquart, Head, 972-883-4982, E-mail: marquart@utdallas.edu. *Application contact:* Remona McLain, Program Assistant, 972-883-4982, Fax: 972-883-2735, E-mail: mclain@utdallas.edu.

The University of Texas at San Antonio, College of Public Policy, Department of Criminal Justice, San Antonio, TX 78249-0617. Offers justice policy (MS). Part-time and evening/weekend programs available. *Faculty:* 9 full-time (5 women). *Students:* 12 full-time (4 women), 42 part-time (21 women); includes 36 minority (2 African Americans, 2 Asian Americans or Pacific Islanders, 32 Hispanic Americans), 1 international. Average age 32. 21 applicants, 86% accepted, 18 enrolled. In 2007, 10 degrees awarded. *Degree requirements:* For master's, comprehensive exam, thesis optional. *Entrance requirements:* For master's, GRE General Test, minimum GPA of 3.0 on last 60 hours. Additional exam requirements/recommendations for international students: Required—TOEFL (minimum score 500 paper-based; 173 computer-based). *Application deadline:* For fall admission, 7/1 for domestic students, 4/1 for international students; for spring admission, 11/1 for domestic students, 9/1 for international students. Applications are processed on a rolling basis. Application fee: $45 ($80 for international students). Electronic applications accepted. *Financial support:* In 2007–08, 7 research assistantships (averaging $3,552 per year) were awarded; career-related internships or fieldwork, Federal Work-Study, and unspecified assistantships also available. Total annual research expenditures: $714. *Unit head:* Dr. James M. Miller, Chair, 210-458-2537, Fax: 210-458-2680, E-mail: jm.miller@utsa.edu.

The University of Texas at Tyler, College of Arts and Sciences, Department of Social Sciences, Tyler, TX 75799-0001. Offers criminal justice (MS); public administration (MPA); sociology (MS). Part-time and evening/weekend programs available. Postbaccalaureate distance learning degree programs offered. *Faculty:* 15 full-time (2 women). *Students:* 3 full-time (2 women), 25 part-time (18 women); includes 5 minority (4 African Americans, 1 Hispanic American), 14 international. Average age 31. 18 applicants, 100% accepted, 11 enrolled. In 2007, 6 degrees awarded. *Degree requirements:* For master's, comprehensive exam. *Entrance requirements:* For master's, GRE General Test, minimum GPA of 3.0. *Application deadline:* Applications are processed on a rolling basis. Application fee: $0. *Expenses:* Tuition, state resident: part-time $627 per semester hour. Tuition, nonresident: part-time $908 per semester hour. Required fees: $107 per semester hour. Tuition and fees vary according to course load. *Financial support:* In 2007–08, 1 fellowship (averaging $1,000 per year), 2 research assistantships, 2 teaching assistantships were awarded; career-related internships or fieldwork, Federal Work-Study, and scholarships/grants also available. Support available to part-time students. Financial award application deadline: 7/1; financial award applicants required to submit FAFSA. *Faculty research:* Urban segregation, minority business, violent crime, gender discrimination. *Unit head:* Dr. Ken Wink, Chair, 903-566-7434, Fax: 903-565-5537, E-mail: kwink@mail.uttyl.edu. *Application contact:* Pam Morrow, Assistant to Dean for Enrollment Management, 903-566-7205, Fax: 903-566-7068, E-mail: pmorrow@uttyler.edu.

The University of Texas of the Permian Basin, Office of Graduate Studies, College of Arts and Sciences, Department of Behavioral Science, Program in Criminal Justice Administration, Odessa, TX 79762-0001. Offers MS. Part-time and evening/weekend programs available. *Degree requirements:* For master's, comprehensive exam (for some programs), thesis (for some programs). *Entrance requirements:* For master's, GRE General Test, 3 letters of recommendation. Additional exam requirements/recommendations for international students: Required—TOEFL (minimum score 550 paper-based; 213 computer-based).

The University of Texas–Pan American, College of Social and Behavioral Sciences, Department of Criminal Justice, Edinburg, TX 78541-2999. Offers MS. Part-time and evening/weekend programs available. Postbaccalaureate distance learning degree programs offered (no on-campus study). *Faculty:* 7 full-time (2 women). *Students:* 4 full-time (all women), 36 part-time (10 women); includes 36 minority (1 African American, 35 Hispanic Americans). Average age 26. 12 applicants, 42% accepted, 5 enrolled. In 2007, 2 degrees awarded. *Degree requirements:* For master's, comprehensive exam, thesis optional, applied project or thesis. *Entrance requirements:* For master's, minimum GPA of 2.75. *Application deadline:* For fall admission, 7/15 priority date for domestic students; for spring admission, 12/15 priority date for domestic students. Applications are processed on a rolling basis. Application fee: $0. *Financial support:* Institutionally sponsored loans available. Financial award application deadline: 4/15; financial award applicants required to submit CSS PROFILE or FAFSA. *Faculty research:* Comparative criminal justice systems, death penalty, community policing, Hispanic women. *Unit head:* Dr. S. George Vincentnathon, Chair, 956-381-3566 Ext. 3568, Fax: 956-381-2490, E-mail: gvincent@panam.edu. *Application contact:* Dr. Joseph A-Gyamfi, Graduate Director, 956-316-7061, Fax: 956-381-3680, E-mail: appiahen@panam.edu.

The University of Toledo, College of Graduate Studies, College of Health Science and Human Service, Division of Human Services, Department of Criminal Justice, Toledo, OH 43606-3390. Offers criminal justice (MA); juvenile justice (Certificate); severe behavioral spectrum (Certificate). *Faculty:* 10. *Students:* 28 full-time (21 women), 13 part-time (8 women); includes 16 minority (all African Americans) Average age 31. 21 applicants, 95% accepted, 12 enrolled.

Criminal Justice and Criminology

The University of Toledo (continued)
In 2007, 26 master's, 3 other advanced degrees awarded. *Application deadline:* For fall admission, 1/15 priority date for domestic students. Application fee: $45. *Financial support:* In 2007–08, 6 teaching assistantships with full tuition reimbursements (averaging $7,600 per year) were awarded; research assistantships with full tuition reimbursements, Federal Work-Study, scholarships/grants, tuition waivers (full and partial), and unspecified assistantships also available. *Unit head:* Dr. Eric Lambert, Head, 419-530-2231.

University of Toronto, School of Graduate Studies, Social Sciences Division, Centre for Criminology, Toronto, ON M5S 1A1, Canada. Offers MA, PhD. Part-time programs available. *Faculty:* 12 full-time, 4 part-time/adjunct. *Students:* 45 full-time (33 women), 4 part-time, 2 international. 184 applicants, 25% accepted. In 2007, 26 degrees awarded. *Degree requirements:* For master's, research paper (optional); for doctorate, comprehensive exam, thesis/dissertation. *Entrance requirements:* For master's, 2 letters of reference, bachelor's degree in social science or humanities, minimum B+ average in last 2 years of undergraduate study; for doctorate, 2 letters of reference, MA in criminology or equivalent, minimum A– average. Additional exam requirements/recommendations for international students: Required—TOEFL (minimum score 580 paper-based; 237 computer-based), TWE (minimum score 5). *Application deadline:* For fall admission, 2/1 for domestic students; for winter admission, 10/1 for domestic students, 9/1 for international students. Application fee: $100 Canadian dollars. *Unit head:* R. I. Gartner, Director, 416-978-7124 Ext. 235, Fax: 416-978-4195. *Application contact:* Monica Bristol, Graduate Administrator, 416-978-7124 Ext. 225, Fax: 416-978-4195, E-mail: crim.grad@utoronto.ca.

University of West Florida, College of Professional Studies, Program in Administration, Pensacola, FL 32514-5750. Offers acquisition and contract administration (MSA); biomedical/pharmaceutical (MSA); criminal justice administration (MSA); education leadership (MSA); healthcare administration (MSA); nursing administration (MSA); public administration (MSA). Part-time and evening/weekend programs available. Postbaccalaureate distance learning degree programs offered (no on-campus study). *Faculty:* 8 full-time (4 women), 2 part-time/adjunct (both women). *Students:* 15 full-time (12 women), 110 part-time (67 women); includes 33 minority (20 African Americans, 3 American Indian/Alaska Native, 4 Asian Americans or Pacific Islanders, 6 Hispanic Americans). Average age 29. 71 applicants, 56% accepted, 32 enrolled. In 2007, 35 degrees awarded. *Entrance requirements:* For master's, GRE General Test, minimum GPA of 3.0. Additional exam requirements/recommendations for international students: Required—TOEFL (minimum score 550 paper-based; 213 computer-based). *Application deadline:* For fall admission, 6/1 for domestic students, 5/15 for international students; for spring admission, 11/1 for domestic students, 10/1 for international students. Applications are processed on a rolling basis. Application fee: $30. *Expenses:* Tuition, state resident: full-time $6,054; part-time $252 per credit. Tuition, nonresident: full-time $21,886; part-time $912 per credit. *Financial support:* Fellowships, career-related internships or fieldwork, scholarships/grants, and unspecified assistantships available. Support available to part-time students. Financial award application deadline: 4/15; financial award applicants required to submit FAFSA. *Unit head:* Dr. Bill Tankersley, MSA Acquisition and Contract Administration Coordinator, 850-474-2338.

University of West Georgia, Graduate School, College of Arts and Sciences, Department of Sociology and Criminology, Program in Criminology, Carrollton, GA 30118. Offers MA. *Expenses:* Tuition, state resident: full-time $2,448; part-time $136 per semester hour. Tuition, nonresident: full-time $9,774; part-time $543 per semester hour. Required fees: $26 per semester hour. $173 per semester. *Application contact:* Dr. Charles W. Clark, Interim Dean, 678-839-6508, E-mail: cclark@westga.edu.

University of Windsor, Faculty of Graduate Studies, Faculty of Arts and Social Sciences, Department of Sociology and Anthropology, Windsor, ON N9B 3P4, Canada. Offers criminology (MA); sociology (MA); sociology-social justice (PhD). Part-time programs available. *Faculty:* 27 full-time (13 women). *Students:* 48 full-time (31 women), 3 part-time (all women). 99 applicants, 38% accepted. In 2007, 12 degrees awarded. *Degree requirements:* For master's, thesis; for doctorate, comprehensive exam, thesis/dissertation. *Entrance requirements:* For master's, minimum B+ average; for doctorate, writing sample, minimum B+ average. Additional exam requirements/recommendations for international students: Required—TOEFL (minimum score 560 paper-based; 220 computer-based). *Application deadline:* For fall admission, 7/1 priority date for domestic students. Applications are processed on a rolling basis. Application fee: $55. Electronic applications accepted. *Financial support:* In 2007–08, 33 teaching assistantships (averaging $9,409 per year) were awarded; Federal Work-Study, scholarships/grants, unspecified assistantships, and bursaries also available. Financial award application deadline: 2/15. *Faculty research:* Power and social change; criminology/deviance; social psychology; comparative development; race and ethnic relations; family, sex, and gender, social justice. *Unit head:* Dr. William deLint, Head, 519-253-3000 Ext. 3498, Fax: 519-971-3621, E-mail: delint@uwindsor.ca. *Application contact:* Applicant Services, 519-253-3000 Ext. 6459, Fax: 519-971-3653, E-mail: gradadmit@uwindsor.ca.

University of Wisconsin–Milwaukee, Graduate School, School of Social Welfare, Department of Criminal Justice, Milwaukee, WI 53201-0413. Offers MS. Part-time programs available. *Faculty:* 8 full-time (1 woman). *Students:* 13 full-time (7 women), 17 part-time (7 women); includes 6 minority (4 African Americans, 1 American Indian/Alaska Native, 1 Hispanic American). 39 applicants, 38% accepted, 10 enrolled. In 2007, 12 degrees awarded. *Degree requirements:* For master's, thesis or alternative. *Entrance requirements:* For master's, GRE General Test, MAT. *Application deadline:* For fall admission, 1/1 priority date for domestic students; for spring admission, 9/1 for domestic students. Applications are processed on a rolling basis. Application fee: $45 ($75 for international students). *Expenses:* Tuition, state resident: part-time $530 per credit. Tuition, nonresident: part-time $1,428 per credit. Required fees: $19 per credit. $229 per term. Tuition and fees vary according to course load and program. *Financial support:* In 2007–08, 4 teaching assistantships were awarded; fellowships, research assistantships, career-related internships or fieldwork and unspecified assistantships also available. Support available to part-time students. Financial award application deadline: 4/15. *Unit head:* Steven Brandl, Representative, 414-229-5443, Fax: 414-229-5311, E-mail: sgb@uwm.edu.

University of Wisconsin–Platteville, School of Graduate Studies, Distance Learning Center, Online Master of Science in Criminal Justice, Platteville, WI 53818-3099. Offers MS. Part-time and evening/weekend programs available. Postbaccalaureate distance learning degree programs offered (no on-campus study). *Students:* 2 full-time (both women), 64 part-time (26 women); includes 5 minority (3 African Americans, 2 Hispanic Americans). 28 applicants, 61% accepted. In 2007, 18 degrees awarded. *Degree requirements:* For master's, thesis or alternative. *Entrance requirements:* Additional exam requirements/recommendations for international students: Required—TOEFL (minimum score 500 paper-based; 173 computer-based). *Application deadline:* For fall admission, 7/1 priority date for domestic students; for spring admission, 11/1 priority date for domestic students. Applications are processed on a rolling basis. Application fee: $56. Electronic applications accepted. *Expenses:* Contact institution. *Financial support:* Scholarships/grants available. Support available to part-time students. *Unit head:* Dr. Cheryl Banachowski-Fuller, Coordinator, 608-342-1652, Fax: 608-342-1986, E-mail: banachoc@uwplatt.edu. *Application contact:* 608-342-1652, Fax: 608-342-1986, E-mail: criminaljstc@uwplatt.edu.

Upper Iowa University, Online Master's Programs, Fayette, IA 52142-1857. Offers accounting (MBA); corporate financial management (MBA); global business (MBA); health and human services (MPA); homeland security (MPA); human resources management (MBA); justice administration (MPA); organizational development (MBA); public personnel management (MPA); quality management (MBA). MBA also available at Madison, Wisconsin campus. Part-time programs available. Postbaccalaureate distance learning degree programs offered (no on-campus study). *Faculty:* 1 full-time (0 women), 25 part-time/adjunct (12 women). *Students:* 255 full-time (170 women); includes 58 minority (44 African Americans, 1 American Indian/Alaska Native, 7 Asian Americans or Pacific Islanders, 6 Hispanic Americans), 3 international. 127 applicants, 85% accepted, 64 enrolled. In 2007, 72 degrees awarded. *Degree requirements:* For master's, research project. *Entrance requirements:* For master's, GMAT, GRE, or minimum GPA of 2.7 during last 60 hours. Additional exam requirements/recommendations for international students: Required—TOEFL (minimum score 570 paper-based; 230 computer-based). *Application deadline:* Applications are processed on a rolling basis. Application fee: $50. Electronic applications accepted. *Financial support:* In 2007–08, 153 students received support. Available to part-time students. Applicants required to submit FAFSA. *Faculty research:* Total quality management, CQI, teams, organization culture and climate, management. *Application contact:* David Hannum, Online Program Recruiter/Advisor, 866-225-2208, E-mail: hannumd@uiu.edu.

Utica College, Program in Economic Crime and Fraud Management, Utica, NY 13502-4892. Offers MBA. Part-time and evening/weekend programs available. Postbaccalaureate distance learning degree programs offered (minimal on-campus study). *Faculty:* 7 full-time (0 women). *Students:* 8 full-time (7 women), 123 part-time (80 women); includes 19 minority (9 African Americans, 1 American Indian/Alaska Native, 2 Asian Americans or Pacific Islanders, 7 Hispanic Americans), 5 international. Average age 33. 70 applicants, 94% accepted, 55 enrolled. In 2007, 29 degrees awarded. *Entrance requirements:* For master's, BS, minimum GPA of 3.0. Additional exam requirements/recommendations for international students: Required—TOEFL (minimum score 525 paper-based; 195 computer-based). *Application deadline:* Applications are processed on a rolling basis. Application fee: $50. Electronic applications accepted. *Expenses:* Contact institution. *Financial support:* In 2007–08, 86 students received support. Career-related internships or fieldwork, scholarships/grants, tuition waivers (partial), and unspecified assistantships available. Support available to part-time students. Financial award application deadline: 3/15; financial award applicants required to submit FAFSA. *Unit head:* Dr. R. Bruce McBride, Director of Economic Crime Graduate Programs, 315-792-3808, E-mail: rmcbride@utica.edu. *Application contact:* John D. Rowe, Director of Graduate Admissions, 315-792-3824, Fax: 315-792-3003, E-mail: jrowe@utica.edu.

Utica College, Program in Economic Crime Management, Utica, NY 13502-4892. Offers MS. Part-time programs available. Postbaccalaureate distance learning degree programs offered (minimal on-campus study). *Faculty:* 4 full-time (0 women). *Students:* Average age 37. 34 applicants, 97% accepted, 30 enrolled. In 2007, 16 degrees awarded. *Degree requirements:* For master's, thesis. *Entrance requirements:* For master's, BS, minimum GPA of 3.0. Additional exam requirements/recommendations for international students: Required—TOEFL (minimum score 525 paper-based; 195 computer-based). *Application deadline:* Applications are processed on a rolling basis. Application fee: $50. Electronic applications accepted. *Expenses:* Contact institution. *Financial support:* In 2007–08, 38 students received support. Career-related internships or fieldwork, scholarships/grants, tuition waivers (partial), and unspecified assistantships available. Support available to part-time students. Financial award applicants required to submit FAFSA. *Unit head:* Dr. R. Bruce McBride, Director of Economic Crime Graduate Programs, 315-792-3808, E-mail: rmcbride@utica.edu. *Application contact:* John D. Rowe, Director of Graduate Admissions, 315-792-3824, Fax: 315-792-3003, E-mail: jrowe@utica.edu.

Valdosta State University, Graduate School, College of Arts and Sciences, Department of Sociology, Anthropology, and Criminal Justice, Program in Criminal Justice, Valdosta, GA 31698. Offers MS. Part-time and evening/weekend programs available. *Faculty:* 4 full-time (1 woman). *Students:* 10 full-time (6 women), 6 part-time (2 women); includes 6 minority (3 African Americans, 2 Asian Americans or Pacific Islanders, 1 Hispanic American). Average age 29. 5 applicants, 60% accepted, 3 enrolled. In 2007, 4 degrees awarded. *Degree requirements:* For master's, thesis or alternative, comprehensive written and/or oral exams. *Entrance requirements:* For master's, GRE General Test, minimum GPA of 2.5. Additional exam requirements/recommendations for international students: Required—TOEFL (minimum score 523 paper-based; 193 computer-based). *Application deadline:* For fall admission, 7/1 for domestic and international students; for spring admission, 11/15 for domestic and international students. Applications are processed on a rolling basis. Application fee: $40. Electronic applications accepted. *Expenses:* Tuition, state resident: part-time $147 per hour. Tuition, nonresident: part-time $586 per hour. Required fees: $520 per semester. Tuition and fees vary according to course level, course load, campus/location and program. *Financial support:* In 2007–08, 2 students received support, including 2 research assistantships with full tuition reimbursements available (averaging $2,452 per year); institutionally sponsored loans, scholarships/grants, and unspecified assistantships also available. Support available to part-time students. Financial award application deadline: 7/1; financial award applicants required to submit FAFSA. *Application contact:* Dr. Fred Knowles, Coordinator, 229-333-5943, Fax: 229-333-5492.

Villanova University, Graduate School of Liberal Arts and Sciences, Criminal Justice Program, Villanova, PA 19085-1699. Offers MA. Part-time and evening/weekend programs available. *Faculty:* 4 full-time (1 woman). *Students:* 14 full-time (9 women), 1 (woman) part-time; includes 4 minority (3 African Americans, 1 Hispanic American). Average age 25. 22 applicants, 82% accepted. In 2007, 9 degrees awarded. *Degree requirements:* For master's, comprehensive exam, thesis optional. *Entrance requirements:* For master's, GRE General Test, minimum GPA of 3.0. Additional exam requirements/recommendations for international students: Required—TOEFL. *Application deadline:* For fall admission, 8/1 for domestic and international students; for spring admission, 12/1 for domestic and international students. Applications are processed on a rolling basis. Application fee: $50. Electronic applications accepted. *Financial support:* Research assistantships, career-related internships or fieldwork, Federal Work-Study, scholarships/grants, and unspecified assistantships available. Financial award applicants required to submit FAFSA. *Unit head:* Dr. Thomas Arvanites, Director, 610-519-4774.

Virginia College at Birmingham, Virginia College Online, Birmingham, AL 35209. Offers business administration (MBA); criminal justice (MCJ); cybersecurity (MC). Part-time and evening/weekend programs available. Postbaccalaureate distance learning degree programs offered (no on-campus study). *Unit head:* Stan Banks, President, Virginia College Online, 888-827-7770, E-mail: vcadm@vc.edu. *Application contact:* Darrel Hanbury, Director of Admissions, 888-827-7770, E-mail: vcoadm@vc.edu.

Virginia Commonwealth University, Graduate School, College of Humanities and Sciences, Wilder School of Government and Public Affairs, Department of Criminal Justice, Richmond, VA 23284-9005. Offers MS, CCJA. Part-time and evening/weekend programs available. *Faculty:* 6 full-time (2 women). *Students:* 35 full-time (29 women), 31 part-time (15 women); includes 20 minority (18 African Americans, 1 American Indian/Alaska Native, 1 Asian American or Pacific Islander), 2 international. 46 applicants, 59% accepted, 13 enrolled. In 2007, 41 master's, 3 other advanced degrees awarded. *Degree requirements:* For master's, thesis or comprehensive exam. *Entrance requirements:* For master's, GRE General Test, minimum GPA of 2.7. *Application deadline:* For fall admission, 4/1 for domestic students; for spring admission, 11/1 for domestic students. Applications are processed on a rolling basis. Application fee: $50. *Expenses:* Tuition, state resident: full-time $7,224; part-time $401 per credit. Tuition, nonresident: full-time $16,072; part-time $891 per credit. Required fees: $1,679; $63 per credit. Tuition and fees vary according to campus/location. *Financial support:* Federal Work-Study, institutionally sponsored loans, and tuition waivers (full and partial) available. Support available to part-time students. Financial award application deadline: 3/1. *Unit head:* Dr. Jay Albanese, Chair, 804-827-0525, E-mail: jsalbane@vcu.edu. *Application contact:* Dr. James L. Hague, Graduate Program Director, 804-828-2292, Fax: 804-828-1253, E-mail: jlhague@vcu.edu.

Walden University, Graduate Programs, School of Counseling and Social Science, Minneapolis, MN 55401. Offers human services (PhD), including clinical social work, counseling, criminal justice, family studies and intervention strategies, general program in human services, human services administration, self-designed program in human services, social policy analysis and planning; mental health counseling (MS). Part-time and evening/weekend programs available. *Students:* 586 full-time (496 women), 505 part-time (410 women); includes 413 minority (351 African Americans, 14 American Indian/Alaska Native, 11 Asian Americans or Pacific Islanders, 37 Hispanic Americans), 10 international. Average age 39. 538 applicants, 72% accepted, 207 enrolled. In 2007, 4 degrees awarded. *Degree requirements:* For master's, residency requirements; for doctorate, thesis/dissertation, residency requirements. *Entrance requirements:* For master's, BS in related field; for doctorate, 3 years of professional experience (preferred), minimum GPA of 3.0, master's degree. Additional exam requirements/recommendations for international students: Required—TOEFL (minimum score 550 paper-based; 213 computer-based), IELTS (minimum score 7). *Application deadline:* For fall admission, 8/15 priority date for domestic and international students; for winter admission, 11/15 priority date for domestic and international students; for spring admission, 12/15 priority date for domestic and international students. Applications are processed on a rolling basis. Application fee: $50. Electronic applications accepted. *Financial support:* Fellowships, Federal Work-Study, institutionally sponsored loans, scholarships/grants, and unspecified assistantships available. Financial award applicants required to submit FAFSA. *Unit head:* Savitri Dixon-Saxon, Associate Dean, 800-925-3368, Fax: 612-338-5092. *Application contact:* Office of Student Enrollment, 866-4-WALDEN, Fax: 410-843-8780.

Walden University, Graduate Programs, School of Public Policy and Administration, Minneapolis, MN 55401. Offers criminal justice (MPA, PhD); health services (MPA, PhD); homeland security policy and coordination (MPA, PhD); international nongovernmental organizations (MPA, PhD); knowledge management (MPA, PhD); nonprofit management and leadership (MPA, PhD); public management and leadership (MPA, PhD); public policy (MPA, PhD); public safety management (MPA, PhD). Part-time and evening/weekend programs available. Postbaccalaureate distance learning degree programs offered (minimal on-campus study). *Students:* 433 full-time (228 women), 148 part-time (79 women); includes 265 minority (234 African Americans, 6 American Indian/Alaska Native, 11 Asian Americans or Pacific Islanders, 14 Hispanic Americans), 4 international. Average age 42. 475 applicants, 76% accepted, 220 enrolled. In 2007, 71 master's, 7 doctorates awarded. *Degree requirements:* For doctorate, thesis/dissertation. *Entrance requirements:* For master's, minimum GPA of 3.0; for doctorate, 3 years of professional experience, master's degree. Additional exam requirements/recommendations for international students: Required—TOEFL (minimum score 550 paper-based; 213 computer-based), IELTS (minimum score 7). *Application deadline:* For fall admission, 8/15 priority date for domestic and international students; for winter admission, 11/15 priority date for domestic and international students; for spring admission, 12/15 priority date for domestic and international students. Applications are processed on a rolling basis. Application fee: $50. Electronic applications accepted. *Financial support:* Fellowships with partial tuition reimbursements, Federal Work-Study, institutionally sponsored loans, scholarships/grants, and unspecified assistantships available. Financial award application deadline: 6/1; financial award applicants required to submit FAFSA. *Unit head:* Gary Kelsey, Associate Dean, 800-925-3368, Fax: 612-338-5092. *Application contact:* 866-4-WALDEN, Fax: 410-843-8780, E-mail: request@waldenu.edu.

Washburn University, School of Applied Studies, Department of Criminal Justice, Topeka, KS 66621. Offers MCJ. Part-time and evening/weekend programs available. Postbaccalaureate distance learning degree programs offered (minimal on-campus study). *Faculty:* 6 full-time (2 women), 2 part-time/adjunct (1 woman). *Students:* 17 full-time (9 women), 17 part-time (9 women); includes 7 minority (3 African Americans, 2 American Indian/Alaska Native, 2 Hispanic Americans), 1 international. In 2007, 18 degrees awarded. *Degree requirements:* For master's, thesis. *Entrance requirements:* For master's, GRE, 3 letters of reference. *Application deadline:* For fall admission, 4/1 priority date for domestic and international students; for spring admission, 11/1 priority date for domestic and international students. Applications are processed on a rolling basis. Application fee: $35. Electronic applications accepted. *Expenses:* Tuition, state resident: full-time $4,590; part-time $255 per credit hour. Tuition, nonresident: full-time $9,360; part-time $520 per credit hour. Required fees: $86; $43 per semester. Tuition and fees vary according to program. *Financial support:* Institutionally sponsored loans and scholarships/grants available. Support available to part-time students. Financial award application deadline: 3/1; financial award applicants required to submit FAFSA. *Faculty research:* Practitioner behavior, police management and training, field and institutional correction administration, terrorism, police training, sex slaves. *Unit head:* Dr. Gerald Bayens, Department Chair, 785-670-1411, Fax: 785-670-1027, E-mail: gerald.bayens@washburn.edu. *Application contact:* Dr. Phyllis Berry, Graduate Coordinator, 785-670-2057, Fax: 785-670-1027, E-mail: phyllis.berry@washburn.edu.

Washington State University, Graduate School, College of Liberal Arts, Department of Political Science, Program in Criminal Justice, Pullman, WA 99164. Offers MA, PhD. *Faculty:* 27. *Students:* 28 full-time (14 women), 8 part-time (5 women); includes 4 minority (3 African Americans, 1 American Indian/Alaska Native), 3 international. Average age 32. 36 applicants, 50% accepted, 6 enrolled. In 2007, 5 master's, 2 doctorates awarded. *Degree requirements:* For master's, comprehensive exam (for some programs), thesis, oral exam; for doctorate, comprehensive exam, thesis/dissertation, oral or written exam. *Entrance requirements:* For master's, GRE General Test, minimum GPA of 3.0; for doctorate, GRE General Test, minimum GPA of 3.5. *Application deadline:* For fall admission, 2/1 for domestic and international students; for spring admission, 11/1 for domestic students, 7/1 for international students. Application fee: $50. Electronic applications accepted. *Financial support:* In 2007–08, 26 students received support, including 6 research assistantships with full and partial tuition reimbursements available (averaging $13,917 per year), 7 teaching assistantships with full and partial tuition reimbursements available (averaging $13,056 per year); career-related internships or fieldwork, Federal Work-Study, institutionally sponsored loans, tuition waivers (partial), and teaching associateships also available. Financial award application deadline: 2/1; financial award applicants required to submit FAFSA. *Faculty research:* Community policing, community justice, corrections policy, crime prevention policy, criminal justice management. *Unit head:* Dr. Travis Pratt, Director, 509-335-4075, Fax: 509-335-7990, E-mail: tcpratt@wsu.edu. *Application contact:* Graduate School Admissions, 800-GRADWSU, Fax: 509-335-1949, E-mail: gradsch@wsu.edu.

Washington State University Spokane, Graduate Programs, Program in Criminal Justice, Spokane, WA 99210-1495. Offers MA, PhD. *Faculty:* 11. *Students:* 14 full-time (6 women), 9 part-time (6 women); includes 2 minority (1 African American, 1 American Indian/Alaska Native). Average age 42. 12 applicants, 67% accepted, 6 enrolled. *Degree requirements:* For master's, comprehensive exam, thesis (for some programs); for doctorate, comprehensive exam, thesis/dissertation. *Entrance requirements:* For master's, GRE, minimum GPA of 3.0. Additional exam requirements/recommendations for international students: Required—TOEFL (minimum score 550 paper-based). *Application deadline:* For fall admission, 7/15 priority date for domestic students, 3/1 for international students; for spring admission, 10/15 priority date for domestic students, 7/1 for international students. Application fee: $50. *Financial support:* In 2007–08, 13 students received support, including 1 fellowship (averaging $3,000 per year), 2 research assistantships (averaging $13,917 per year), 2 teaching assistantships (averaging $13,056 per year). *Faculty research:* Community oriented policing, crime, criminology theory, jury system, judicial evaluations, police performance. Total annual research expenditures: $443,591. *Unit head:* Dr. David Brody, Director, 509-358-7952, Fax: 509-358-7900, E-mail: brody@wsu.edu. *Application contact:* Graduate School Admissions, 800-GRADWSU, Fax: 509-335-1949, E-mail: gradsch@wsu.edu.

Wayland Baptist University, Graduate Programs, Program in Counseling, Plainview, TX 79072-6998. Offers counseling (MA); government administration (MPA); justice administration (MPA). Part-time and evening/weekend programs available. Postbaccalaureate distance learning degree programs offered. *Faculty:* 2 full-time (1 woman), 2 part-time/adjunct (1 woman). *Students:* 2 full-time (both women), 78 part-time (64 women); includes 16 minority (1 African American, 15 Hispanic Americans). Average age 33. 42 applicants, 100% accepted. *Degree requirements:* For master's, comprehensive exam. *Entrance requirements:* For master's, GRE, MAT. Application fee: $35. *Expenses:* Tuition: Full-time $6,390; part-time $355 per credit hour. Required fees: $600; $50 per term. Full-time tuition and fees vary according to course load. *Financial support:* Federal Work-Study, institutionally sponsored loans, and scholarships/grants available. Support available to part-time students. Financial award application deadline: 5/1; financial award applicants required to submit FAFSA. *Unit head:* Dr. Estelle Owens, Chairman, 806-291-1171, Fax: 806-291-1972, E-mail: owensest@wbu.edu.

Wayne State University, College of Liberal Arts and Sciences, Department of Criminal Justice, Detroit, MI 48202. Offers MS. *Students:* 10 full-time (7 women), 25 part-time (19 women); includes 8 minority (6 African Americans, 2 Hispanic Americans), 3 international. Average age 28. 27 applicants, 56% accepted, 12 enrolled. In 2007, 8 degrees awarded. *Degree requirements:* For master's, comprehensive exam, essay. *Entrance requirements:* For master's, GRE if GPA is between 2.75 and 2.99, minimum GPA of 3.0 (resumé and writing sample if less than 3.0), 2 letters of recommendation, personal statement. Additional exam requirements/recommendations for international students: Required—TOEFL (minimum score 550 paper-based; 213 computer-based); Recommended—TWE (minimum score 6). *Application deadline:* For fall admission, 7/1 for domestic students, 5/1 for international students; for winter admission, 11/1 for domestic students, 9/1 for international students. Applications are processed on a rolling basis. Application fee: $50. Electronic applications accepted. *Expenses:* Tuition, state resident: part-time $403 per credit hour. Tuition, nonresident: part-time $890 per credit hour. *Financial support:* In 2007–08, 2 students received support, including 1 teaching assistantship with tuition reimbursement available (averaging $13,672 per year); scholarships/grants also available. *Faculty research:* Criminology, juvenile delinquency & justice, law, policing, corrections, social deviance. *Unit head:* Marvin Zalman, Chair, 313-577-2705, Fax: 313-577-9977, E-mail: aa1887@wayne.edu.

Wayne State University, College of Liberal Arts and Sciences, Department of Political Science, Program in Public Administration, Detroit, MI 48202. Offers criminal justice (MPA); public administration (MPA). *Accreditation:* NASPAA. Evening/weekend programs available. *Students:* 17 full-time (12 women), 63 part-time (42 women); includes 34 minority (30 African Americans, 1 American Indian/Alaska Native, 1 Asian American or Pacific Islander, 2 Hispanic Americans), 4 international. Average age 29. 57 applicants, 60% accepted, 26 enrolled. In 2007, 18 degrees awarded. *Entrance requirements:* For master's, GRE General Test. Additional exam requirements/recommendations for international students: Required—TOEFL (minimum score 550 paper-based; 213 computer-based); Recommended—TWE (minimum score 6). *Application deadline:* For fall admission, 7/1 for domestic students, 6/1 for international students; for winter admission, 10/1 for international students; for spring admission, 2/1 for international students. Applications are processed on a rolling basis. Application fee: $30 ($50 for international students). Electronic applications accepted. *Expenses:* Tuition, state resident: part-time $403 per credit hour. Tuition, nonresident: part-time $890 per credit hour. *Faculty research:* Urban politics, urban education, state administration. *Unit head:* John Strate, Director, 313-577-2639, E-mail: jstrate@wayne.edu.

Webster University, School of Business and Technology, Department of Business, St. Louis, MO 63119-3194. Offers business (MA); business and organizational security management (MBA); computer resources and information management (MBA); environmental management (MBA); finance (MA, MBA); health services management (MBA); human resources development (MBA); human resources management (MBA); international business (MA, MBA); management and leadership (MBA); marketing (MBA); procurement and acquisitions management (MBA); telecommunications management (MBA). Part-time and evening/weekend programs available. Postbaccalaureate distance learning degree programs offered (no on-campus study). *Students:* 1,226 full-time (605 women), 4,315 part-time (2,191 women); includes 2,006 minority (1,431 African Americans, 24 American Indian/Alaska Native, 238 Asian Americans or Pacific Islanders, 313 Hispanic Americans), 519 international. Average age 33. *Application deadline:* Applications are processed on a rolling basis. Application fee: $35 ($50 for international students). *Expenses:* Tuition: Full-time $9,360; part-time $520 per credit. *Financial support:* Federal Work-Study available. Support available to part-time students. Financial award application deadline: 4/1; financial award applicants required to submit FAFSA. *Unit head:* Bradford Scott, Chair, 314-961-2260 Ext. 7574, Fax: 314-968-7077, E-mail: buschair@webster.edu. *Application contact:* Director of Graduate and Evening Student Admissions, Fax: 314-968-7116, E-mail: gadmit@webster.edu.

Webster University, School of Business and Technology, Department of Management, St. Louis, MO 63119-3194. Offers business and organizational security management (MA); computer resources and information management (MA); environmental management (MS); health care management (MA); health services management (MA); human resources development (MA); human resources management (MA); management (DM); management and leadership (MA); marketing (MA); procurement and acquisitions management (MA); public administration (MA); quality management (MA); space systems operations management (MS); telecommunications management (MA). Part-time and evening/weekend programs available. Postbaccalaureate distance learning degree programs offered (no on-campus study). *Students:* 1,368 full-time (657 women), 4,911 part-time (2,697 women); includes 3,131 minority (2,475 African Americans, 40 American Indian/Alaska Native, 169 Asian Americans or Pacific Islanders, 447 Hispanic Americans), 120 international. Average age 37. In 2007, 9 degrees awarded. *Degree requirements:* For doctorate, thesis/dissertation, written exam. *Entrance requirements:* For doctorate, GMAT, 3 years of work experience, MBA. *Application deadline:* Applications are processed on a rolling basis. Application fee: $25 ($50 for international students). *Expenses:* Tuition: Full-time $9,360; part-time $520 per credit. *Financial support:* Federal Work-Study available. Support available to part-time students. Financial award application deadline: 4/1; financial award applicants required to submit FAFSA. *Unit head:* Jeffrey Haldeman, Chair, 314-961-2660 Ext. 7552, Fax: 314-968-7077, E-mail: mgtchair@webster.edu. *Application contact:* Director of Graduate and Evening Student Admissions, Fax: 314-968-7116, E-mail: gadmit@webster.edu.

West Chester University of Pennsylvania, Office of Graduate Studies and Extended Education, College of Business and Public Affairs, Department of Criminal Justice, West Chester, PA 19383. Offers criminal justice (MS); criminal justice—thesis (MS). Part-time and evening/weekend programs available. *Students:* 7 full-time (5 women), 15 part-time (10 women); includes 2 minority (1 African American, 1 Hispanic American). Average age 27. 11 applicants, 100% accepted, 6 enrolled. In 2007, 11 degrees awarded. *Degree requirements:* For master's, comprehensive exam, thesis optional. *Entrance requirements:* For master's, MAT, interview, minimum GPA of 3.0. Additional exam requirements/recommendations for international students: Required—TOEFL (minimum score 550 paper-based; 213 computer-based; 80 iBT). *Application deadline:* For fall admission, 4/15 priority date for domestic students; for spring admission, 10/15 for domestic students. Applications are processed on a rolling basis. Application fee: $35. *Expenses:* Tuition, state resident: part-time $345 per credit. Tuition, nonresident: part-time $552 per credit. Tuition and fees vary according to course load. *Financial support:* In 2007–08, research assistantships with full and partial tuition reimbursements (averaging $5,000 per year); unspecified assistantships also available. Support available to part-time students. Financial award application deadline: 2/15; financial award applicants required to submit FAFSA. *Faculty research:* Criminal law, criminal procedure, constitutional interpretation. *Unit head:* Dr. Jana Nestlerode, Chair, 610-436-2647. *Application contact:* Dr. Mary P. Brewster, Graduate Coordinator, 610-436-2630, E-mail: mbrewster@wcupa.edu.

Western Connecticut State University, Division of Graduate Studies, Ancell School of Business, Program in Justice Administration, Danbury, CT 06810-6885. Offers MS. Part-time and evening/weekend programs available. *Faculty:* 4 full-time (1 woman). *Students:* 2 full-time (0 women), 9 part-time (4 women); includes 1 minority (African American), 1 international. Average age 30. 3 applicants, 67% accepted, 1 enrolled. In 2007, 7 degrees awarded. *Degree requirements:* For master's, comprehensive exam or research project. *Entrance requirements:* For master's, GMAT, GRE, LSAT, or MAT. *Application deadline:* For fall admission, 8/5 priority date for domestic students; for spring admission, 1/5 priority date for domestic students. Applications are processed on a rolling basis. Application fee: $50. *Expenses:* Tuition, state resident: full-time $4,169. Tuition, nonresident: full-time $11,614. Required fees: $3,278. *Financial support:* Fellowships, career-related internships or fieldwork available. Support available to part-time students. Financial award application deadline: 5/1; financial award applicants required to submit FAFSA. *Unit head:* Dr. Anthony G. Markert, Assistant Professor, 203-837-8469. *Application contact:* Chris Shankle, Associate Director of Graduate Admissions, 203-837-8244, Fax: 203-837-8338, E-mail: shanklec@wcsu.edu.

Criminal Justice and Criminology

Western Illinois University, School of Graduate Studies, College of Education and Human Services, Department of Law Enforcement and Justice Administration, Macomb, IL 61455-1390. Offers law enforcement and justice administration (MA); police executive administration (Certificate). Part-time programs available. *Students:* 38 full-time (13 women), 63 part-time (21 women); includes 10 minority (7 African Americans, 3 Hispanic Americans), 1 international. Average age 31. 38 applicants, 82% accepted. In 2007, 39 master's, 6 other advanced degrees awarded. *Degree requirements:* For master's, thesis or alternative. *Entrance requirements:* For master's, GRE or MAT, minimum GPA of 3.0. Additional exam requirements/recommendations for international students: Required—TOEFL (minimum score 520 paper-based; 190 computer-based; 68 iBT). *Application deadline:* Applications are processed on a rolling basis. Application fee: $30. Electronic applications accepted. *Expenses:* Tuition, state resident: part-time $217 per credit hour. Tuition, nonresident: part-time $433 per credit hour. Required fees: $54 per credit hour. *Financial support:* In 2007–08, 11 students received support, including 11 research assistantships with full tuition reimbursements available (averaging $6,800 per year). Financial award applicants required to submit FAFSA. *Unit head:* Dr. Darrell Ross, Chairperson, 309-298-1038. *Application contact:* Dr. Barbara Baily, Director of Graduate Studies/Associate Provost, 309-298-1806, Fax: 309-298-2345, E-mail: grad-office@wiu.edu.

Western Oregon University, Graduate Programs, College of Liberal Arts and Sciences, Division of Social Science, Monmouth, OR 97361-1394. Offers criminal justice (MA, MS). Part-time and evening/weekend programs available. *Faculty:* 3 full-time (1 woman), 8 part-time/adjunct (3 women). *Students:* 7 full-time (3 women), 4 part-time (1 woman); includes 1 minority (American Indian/Alaska Native). Average age 35. 10 applicants, 60% accepted, 6 enrolled. In 2007, 5 degrees awarded. *Degree requirements:* For master's, thesis optional, written exams. *Entrance requirements:* For master's, minimum GPA of 3.0. Additional exam requirements/recommendations for international students: Required—TOEFL (minimum score 550 paper-based; 213 computer-based; 79 iBT), IELTS (minimum score 7). *Application deadline:* Applications are processed on a rolling basis. Application fee: $50. *Expenses:* Tuition, state resident: full-time $9,648; part-time $346 per quarter. Tuition, nonresident: full-time $15,588; part-time $526 per quarter. Required fees: $374 per quarter. Tuition and fees vary according to course level and course load. *Financial support:* In 2007–08, 2 teaching assistantships with full tuition reimbursements (averaging $676 per year) were awarded; research assistantships with full tuition reimbursements, career-related internships or fieldwork, Federal Work-Study, and tuition waivers (full and partial) also available. Support available to part-time students. Financial award application deadline: 3/1; financial award applicants required to submit FAFSA. *Faculty research:* Prison to community transition of adult felons, community justice, restorative justice, parole and probation. *Unit head:* Dr. Stephen Gibbons, Coordinator, 503-838-8317, Fax: 503-838-8034, E-mail: gibbons@wou.edu. *Application contact:* Dr. David McDonald, Associate Provost for Retention and Enrollment Management, 503-838-8919, Fax: 503-838-8067, E-mail: mcdonald@wou.edu.

Westfield State College, Division of Graduate and Continuing Education, Department of Criminal Justice, Westfield, MA 01086. Offers MS. Part-time and evening/weekend programs available. *Degree requirements:* For master's, comprehensive exam, thesis (for some programs). *Entrance requirements:* For master's, GRE General Test or MAT, minimum undergraduate GPA of 2.7.

West Texas A&M University, College of Education and Social Sciences, Department of History and Political Science, Program in Criminal Justice, Canyon, TX 79016-0001. Offers MA. Part-time and evening/weekend programs available. *Degree requirements:* For master's, comprehensive exam, thesis optional. *Entrance requirements:* For master's, GRE General Test. Additional exam requirements/recommendations for international students: Required—TOEFL (minimum score 550 paper-based). Electronic applications accepted. *Faculty research:* Racial profiling, changing nature of prisons, campus police and parking services.

Wichita State University, Graduate School, Fairmount College of Liberal Arts and Sciences, School of Community Affairs, Wichita, KS 67260. Offers criminal justice (MA); gerontology (MA). Part-time programs available. Electronic applications accepted.

Widener University, College of Arts and Sciences, Program in Criminal Justice, Chester, PA 19013-5792. Offers MA, Psy D/MA. Part-time and evening/weekend programs available. *Faculty:* 1 full-time (0 women), 2 part-time/adjunct (0 women). *Students:* 4 full-time (0 women), 5 part-time (4 women); includes 1 minority (African American), 1 international. Average age 27. 21 applicants, 90% accepted. In 2007, 10 degrees awarded. *Degree requirements:* For master's, project. *Entrance requirements:* For master's, interview, minimum undergraduate GPA of 3.0. *Application deadline:* For fall admission, 3/1 priority date for domestic students. Applications are processed on a rolling basis. Application fee: $25 ($300 for international students). *Expenses:* Contact institution. Tuition and fees vary according to course load and program. *Financial support:* Career-related internships or fieldwork and institutionally sponsored loans available. Support available to part-time students. Financial award application deadline: 5/1. *Faculty research:* Criminal law and procedure, corrections, domestic violence. *Unit head:* Dr. William E. Harver, Director, 610-499-4554, Fax: 510-499-4605, E-mail: william.e.harver@widener.edu.

Wilmington University, Division of Behavioral Science, New Castle, DE 19720-6491. Offers administration of human services (MS); administration of justice (MS); community counseling (MS). *Accreditation:* ACA. Part-time and evening/weekend programs available. *Faculty:* 3 full-time (1 woman). *Students:* 68 full-time (48 women), 196 part-time (148 women); includes 41 minority (35 African Americans, 1 American Indian/Alaska Native, 1 Asian American or Pacific Islander, 4 Hispanic Americans). Average age 35. 146 applicants, 88% accepted, 99 enrolled. In 2007, 64 degrees awarded. *Entrance requirements:* Additional exam requirements/recommendations for international students: Required—TOEFL (minimum score 500 paper-based; 173 computer-based). *Application deadline:* Applications are processed on a rolling basis. Application fee: $25. Electronic applications accepted. *Expenses:* Tuition: Full-time $6,246; part-time $1,041 per course. Tuition and fees vary according to degree level and campus/location. *Financial support:* Applicants required to submit FAFSA. *Unit head:* Christian Trowbridge, Chair, 302-295-1151, Fax: 302-328-5164. *Application contact:* Chris Ferguson, Director of Admissions, 302-356-4636 Ext. 256, Fax: 302-328-5164, E-mail: inquire@wilmcoll.edu.

Wright State University, School of Graduate Studies, College of Liberal Arts, Program in Applied Behavioral Science, Dayton, OH 45435. Offers criminal justice and social problems (MA); international and comparative politics (MA). *Degree requirements:* For master's, thesis optional. *Entrance requirements:* Additional exam requirements/recommendations for international students: Required—TOEFL. *Faculty research:* Training and development, criminal justice and social problems, community systems, human factors, industrial/organizational psychology.

Xavier University, College of Social Sciences, Health and Education, Department of Criminal Justice, Cincinnati, OH 45207. Offers MS. Part-time and evening/weekend programs available. *Faculty:* 4 full-time (1 woman), 1 part-time/adjunct (0 women). *Students:* 5 full-time (2 women), 22 part-time (14 women); includes 9 minority (8 African Americans, 1 Hispanic American), 1 international. Average age 29. In 2007, 13 degrees awarded. *Degree requirements:* For master's, comprehensive exam, thesis or alternative. *Entrance requirements:* For master's, MAT, GRE, or LSAT, minimum GPA of 2.7. Additional exam requirements/recommendations for international students: Required—TOEFL (minimum score 550 paper-based; 213 computer-based). *Application deadline:* For fall admission, 8/15 priority date for domestic students. Applications are processed on a rolling basis. Application fee: $35. Electronic applications accepted. *Financial support:* Career-related internships or fieldwork, scholarships/grants, and unspecified assistantships available. Support available to part-time students. Financial award applicants required to submit FAFSA. *Faculty research:* Women and crime, gun violence, homicide, crime policy, policing. *Unit head:* Dr. Kam Wong, Chair, 513-745-2098, Fax: 513-745-3220, E-mail: wong1@xavier.edu. *Application contact:* Roger Bosse, Interim Director of Graduate Studies, 513-745-3357, Fax: 513-745-1048, E-mail: bosse@xavier.edu.

Youngstown State University, Graduate School, College of Health and Human Services, Department of Criminal Justice, Youngstown, OH 44555-0001. Offers MS. Part-time and evening/weekend programs available. *Degree requirements:* For master's, thesis optional. *Entrance requirements:* For master's, minimum GPA of 2.7. Additional exam requirements/recommendations for international students: Required—TOEFL. *Faculty research:* Police human resource allocation, police administration, computerized test development, criminal law.

Forensic Sciences

Alliant International University–Irvine, Center for Forensic Studies, Irvine, CA 92612. Offers Psy D.

See Close-Up on page 1371.

Arcadia University, Graduate Studies, Program in Forensic Science, Glenside, PA 19038-3295. Offers MSFS.

Argosy University, Chicago, College of Psychology and Behavioral Sciences, Chicago, IL 60654. Offers clinical psychology (MA, Psy D), including child and adolescent psychology (Psy D), client-centered and experiential psychotherapies (Psy D), diversity and multicultural psychology (Psy D), family psychology (Psy D), forensic psychology (Psy D), health psychology (Psy D), psychoanalytic psychology (Psy D), psychology and spirituality (Psy D); community counseling (MA); counseling psychology (Ed D), including counselor education and supervision; counselor education and supervision (Ed D); organizational leadership (Ed D). *Accreditation:* APA (one or more programs are accredited). Postbaccalaureate distance learning degree programs offered (minimal on-campus study).

See Close-Up on page 1379.

Boston University, School of Medicine, Program in Biomedical Forensics, Boston, MA 02215. Offers MS. Part-time and evening/weekend programs available. Postbaccalaureate distance learning degree programs offered (minimal on-campus study). *Faculty:* 3 full-time (all women), 5 part-time/adjunct (2 women). *Degree requirements:* For master's, thesis. *Entrance requirements:* For master's, GRE. Additional exam requirements/recommendations for international students: Required—TOEFL. *Application deadline:* For fall admission, 7/1 priority date for domestic and international students. Applications are processed on a rolling basis. Application fee: $50. Electronic applications accepted. *Expenses:* Tuition: Full-time $34,930; part-time $1,092 per credit. Tuition and fees vary according to class time, course level and program. *Unit head:* Dr. Tara L. Moore, Co-Director, 617-638-4054, Fax: 617-638-4922, E-mail: tlmoore@bu.edu.

Cedar Crest College, Program in Forensic Science, Allentown, PA 18104-6196. Offers MS. *Faculty:* 5 full-time (2 women), 1 (woman) part-time/adjunct. *Students:* 11 full-time (all women). Average age 22. 12 applicants, 100% accepted, 11 enrolled. *Degree requirements:* For master's, thesis, completion of coursework with a minimum GPA of 3.0. *Entrance requirements:* For master's, GRE. *Application deadline:* For fall admission, 1/2 priority date for domestic students. Applications are processed on a rolling basis. Application fee: $50. Electronic applications accepted. *Expenses:* Contact institution. *Financial support:* In 2007–08, 4 students received support. Unspecified assistantships available. *Faculty research:* Geotyping of low copy number DNA, presumptive and conformatory testing of GHB and GBL. *Unit head:* Dr. Lawrence A. Quarino, Director and Associate Professor, 610-606-4666 Ext. 3507, Fax: 610-740-3787, E-mail: laquarin@cedarcrest.edu. *Application contact:* Nancy Hollinger, Director of Lifelong Learning, 610-606-4666 Ext. 3362, E-mail: nlhollin@cedarcrest.edu.

Chaminade University of Honolulu, Graduate Services, Program in Forensic Science, Honolulu, HI 96816-1578. Offers MSFS. Part-time programs available. *Faculty:* 2 full-time (0 women), 1 (woman) part-time/adjunct. *Students:* 12 full-time (10 women); includes 9 minority (1 African American, 8 Asian Americans or Pacific Islanders). Average age 27. 10 applicants, 40% accepted, 3 enrolled. *Degree requirements:* For master's, comprehensive exam, thesis or alternative. *Entrance requirements:* For master's, GRE, 2 letters of recommendation. Additional exam requirements/recommendations for international students: Required—TOEFL (minimum score 550 paper-based; 250 computer-based). *Application deadline:* For fall admission, 7/1 for domestic students; for spring admission, 12/1 for domestic students. Applications are processed on a rolling basis. Application fee: $50. *Expenses:* Tuition: Part-time $490 per credit hour. *Financial support:* In 2007–08, 1 teaching assistantship with full tuition reimbursement was awarded. *Unit head:* Dr. Lee Goff, Director, Forensic Sciences, 808-440-4209, Fax: 808-440-4278, E-mail: lgoff@chaminade.edu. *Application contact:* Heidi Harakuni, Information Contact, 808-440-4204, Fax: 808-440-4278, E-mail: msfs@chaminade.edu.

Duquesne University, Bayer School of Natural and Environmental Sciences, Program in Forensic Science and Law, Pittsburgh, PA 15282-0001. Offers MS. *Faculty:* 1 full-time (0 women), 21 part-time/adjunct (7 women). *Students:* 30 full-time (24 women); includes 1 minority (African American) Average age 23. 30 applicants, 100% accepted, 30 enrolled. In 2007, 42 degrees awarded. *Financial support:* Fellowships, research assistantships, teaching assistantships available. Financial award application deadline: 5/1. *Faculty research:* Extraction protocols, mass spectrometry, synthetic fiber analysis, synthetic polymer characterization, trace analysis. *Unit head:* Dr. Federick W. Fochtman, Director, 412-396-6373, E-mail: fochtman@duq.edu. *Application contact:* Val Lijewski, Academic Advisor, 412-396-1084, Fax: 412-396-1402, E-mail: lijewskski@duq.edu.

Florida Gulf Coast University, College of Professional Studies, Program in Criminal Forensic Studies, Fort Myers, FL 33965-6565. Offers MS. *Faculty:* 30 full-time (12 women), 24 part-time/adjunct (8 women). *Students:* 15 full-time (11 women), 21 part-time (16 women); includes 3 minority (1 African American, 2 Hispanic Americans), 1 international. Average age 26. 31 applicants, 94% accepted, 23 enrolled. *Entrance requirements:* For master's, GRE General Test, minimum GPA 3.0. Additional exam requirements/recommendations for international students: Required—TOEFL (minimum score 550 paper-based; 213 computer-based). *Application deadline:* For fall admission, 4/1 for domestic students; for spring admission, 11/15 for domestic students. Applications are processed on a rolling basis. Application fee: $30. Electronic applications accepted. *Expenses:* Tuition, state resident: full-time $4,542. Tuition, nonresident: full-time $19,449. Required fees: $1,297. *Financial support:* Research assistantships, career-related internships or fieldwork and tuition waivers (full and partial) available. Support available to part-time students.

Florida International University, College of Arts and Sciences, Department of Chemistry, Miami, FL 33199. Offers chemistry (MS, PhD); forensic science (MS). Part-time and evening/weekend programs available. *Faculty:* 25 full-time (4 women). *Students:* 77 full-time (48 women), 24 part-time (15 women); includes 38 minority (9 African Americans, 6 Asian Americans or Pacific Islanders, 23 Hispanic Americans), 41 international. Average age 28. 121 applicants, 26% accepted, 9 enrolled. In 2007, 7 master's, 4 doctorates awarded. *Degree requirements:* For master's, thesis; for doctorate, comprehensive exam, thesis/dissertation. *Entrance requirements:* For master's and doctorate, GRE General Test, minimum GPA of 3.0. Additional exam requirements/recommendations for international students: Required—TOEFL (minimum score 550 paper-based; 213 computer-based). *Application deadline:* For fall admission, 6/1 for domestic students, 4/1 for international students; for spring admission, 10/1 for domestic students, 9/1 for international students. Applications are processed on a rolling basis. Application fee: $30. Electronic applications accepted. *Expenses:* Tuition, state resident: full-time $6,106. Tuition, nonresident: full-time $15,528. Required fees: $284. *Financial support:* Fellowships, research assistantships, teaching assistantships, Federal Work-Study, institutionally sponsored loans, and scholarships/grants available. Support available to part-time students. *Faculty research:* Organic synthesis and reaction catalysis, environmental chemistry, molecular beam studies, organic geochemistry, bioinorganic and organometallic chemistry. *Unit head:* Dr. Stanislaw Wnuk, Chairperson, 305-348-2606, Fax: 305-348-3772, E-mail: stanislaw.wnuk@fiu.edu.

Florida International University, College of Arts and Sciences, Program in Forensic Science, Miami, FL 33199. Offers MS. *Students:* 8 full-time (5 women), 14 part-time (11 women); includes 11 minority (1 African American, 1 Asian American or Pacific Islander, 9 Hispanic Americans). Average age 26. 44 applicants, 20% accepted, 5 enrolled. In 2007, 4 degrees awarded. *Entrance requirements:* For master's, GRE, minimum GPA of 3.0, 3 letters of recommendation. Additional exam requirements/recommendations for international students: Required—TOEFL (minimum score 550 paper-based; 213 computer-based). *Application deadline:* For fall admission, 6/1 for domestic students, 4/1 for international students; for spring admission, 10/1 for domestic students, 9/1 for international students. Applications are processed on a rolling basis. Application fee: $30. Electronic applications accepted. *Expenses:* Tuition, state resident: full-time $6,106. Tuition, nonresident: full-time $15,528. Required fees: $284. *Financial support:* Research assistantships, teaching assistantships available. *Unit head:* Dr. Kenneth Furton, Dean, College of Arts and Sciences, 305-348-2864, Fax: 305-348-4172, E-mail: furtonk@fiu.edu.

The George Washington University, Columbian College of Arts and Sciences, Department of Forensic Sciences, Washington, DC 20052. Offers crime scene investigation (MFS); forensic chemistry (MFS, MSFS); forensic molecular biology (MFS, MSFS); forensic sciences (MFS, MSFS); forensic toxicology (MFS, MSFS); high-technology crime investigation (MFS); security management (MFS). High-technology crime investigation and security management programs offered in Arlington, VA. Part-time and evening/weekend programs available. *Degree requirements:* For master's, comprehensive exam. *Entrance requirements:* For master's, GRE General Test, minimum GPA of 3.0. Additional exam requirements/recommendations for international students: Required—TOEFL (minimum score 550 paper-based; 213 computer-based). Electronic applications accepted.

John Jay College of Criminal Justice of the City University of New York, Graduate Studies, Program in Forensic Computing, New York, NY 10019-1093. Offers MS. Part-time and evening/weekend programs available. *Degree requirements:* For master's, thesis or alternative. *Entrance requirements:* For master's, GRE General Test, minimum B average. Additional exam requirements/recommendations for international students: Required—TOEFL (minimum score 500 paper-based; 173 computer-based).

John Jay College of Criminal Justice of the City University of New York, Graduate Studies, Program in Forensic Science, New York, NY 10019-1093. Offers MS. Part-time and evening/weekend programs available. *Degree requirements:* For master's, thesis. *Entrance requirements:* For master's, GRE, minimum B average. Additional exam requirements/recommendations for international students: Required—TOEFL (minimum score 500 paper-based; 173 computer-based).

John Jay College of Criminal Justice of the City University of New York, Graduate Studies, Programs in Criminal Justice, New York, NY 10019-1093. Offers criminal justice (MA, PhD); criminology and deviance (PhD); forensic psychology (PhD); forensic science (PhD); law and philosophy (PhD); organizational behavior (PhD); public policy (PhD). Part-time and evening/weekend programs available. Terminal master's awarded for partial completion of doctoral program. *Degree requirements:* For master's, thesis or alternative; for doctorate, one foreign language, thesis/dissertation. *Entrance requirements:* For master's, GRE General Test, minimum B average; for doctorate, GRE General Test. Additional exam requirements/recommendations for international students: Required—TOEFL (minimum score 500 paper-based; 173 computer-based).

McGill University, Faculty of Graduate and Postdoctoral Studies, Faculty of Dentistry, Montréal, QC H3A 2T5, Canada. Offers forensic dentistry (Certificate); oral and maxillofacial surgery (M Sc, PhD). *Faculty:* 24 full-time (10 women), 229 part-time/adjunct (69 women). *Students:* 28 full-time (14 women). 24 applicants, 50% accepted, 7 enrolled. In 2007, 6 degrees awarded.

Mercyhurst College, Graduate Program, Program in Forensic and Biological Anthropology, Erie, PA 16546. Offers MS. *Faculty:* 2 full-time (0 women), 4 part-time/adjunct (1 woman). *Students:* 12 full-time (10 women); includes 4 minority (1 African American, 1 American Indian/Alaska Native, 2 Hispanic Americans). Average age 27. 78 applicants, 10% accepted, 5 enrolled. In 2007, 7 degrees awarded. *Entrance requirements:* For master's, GRE or MAT, undergraduate degree in related field, interview. Additional exam requirements/recommendations for international students: Required—TOEFL. *Application deadline:* For fall admission, 8/1 for domestic students; for winter admission, 11/1 for domestic students; for spring admission, 2/1 for domestic students. Application fee: $35. *Financial support:* In 2007–08, 5 research assistantships with full and partial tuition reimbursements (averaging $6,500 per year) were awarded. Financial award applicants required to submit FAFSA. Total annual research expenditures: $575,000. *Unit head:* Dr. Dennis Dirkmaat, Director, Graduate Program in Biological and Forensic Anthropology, 814-824-2105, E-mail: ddirkmaat@mercyhurst.edu. *Application contact:* Justin Ross, Academic Coordinator, 814-824-2985, Fax: 814-824-2055, E-mail: jross@mercyhurst.edu.

Michigan State University, The Graduate School, College of Social Science, School of Criminal Justice, East Lansing, MI 48824. Offers criminal justice (MS, PhD); forensic science (MS). Postbaccalaureate distance learning degree programs offered. *Entrance requirements:* Additional exam requirements/recommendations for international students: Required—TOEFL. Electronic applications accepted. *Expenses:* Tuition, state resident: part-time $379 per credit hour. Tuition, nonresident: part-time $800 per credit hour. Tuition and fees vary according to program.

See Close-Up on page 981.

National University, Academic Affairs, College of Letters and Sciences, Department of Professional Studies, La Jolla, CA 92037-1011. Offers forensic science (MFS); public administration (MPA). Part-time and evening/weekend programs available. Postbaccalaureate distance learning degree programs offered (no on-campus study). *Faculty:* 8 full-time (2 women), 147 part-time/adjunct (42 women). *Students:* 128 full-time (61 women), 176 part-time (86 women); includes 123 minority (48 African Americans, 21 Asian Americans or Pacific Islanders, 54 Hispanic Americans), 2 international. Average age 37. 540 applicants. In 2007, 272 degrees awarded. *Degree requirements:* For master's, thesis. *Entrance requirements:* For master's, interview, minimum GPA of 2.5. Additional exam requirements/recommendations for international students: Required—TOEFL (minimum score 550 paper-based; 213 computer-based; 80 iBT), IELTS (minimum score 6). *Application deadline:* Applications are processed on a rolling basis. Application fee: $60 ($65 for international students). Electronic applications accepted. *Expenses:* Tuition: Full-time $8,262; part-time $306 per unit. One-time fee: $60. *Financial support:* Career-related internships or fieldwork, institutionally sponsored loans, scholarships/grants, and tuition waivers (partial) available. Support available to part-time students. Financial award application deadline: 6/30; financial award applicants required to submit FAFSA. *Unit head:* Chandrika M. Kelso, Associate Professor and Chair, 858-642-8433, Fax: 858-642-8715, E-mail: ckelso@nu.edu. *Application contact:* Dominick Giovanniello, Associate Regional Dean—San Diego, 800-NAT-UNIV, Fax: 858-642-8709, E-mail: dgiovann@nu.edu.

Nebraska Wesleyan University, University College, Program in Forensic Science, Lincoln, NE 68504-2796. Offers MFS. Part-time and evening/weekend programs available. *Faculty:* 3 full-time (2 women), 9 part-time/adjunct (3 women). *Students:* 40 full-time (30 women), 68 part-time (52 women); includes 1 minority (Hispanic American), 1 international. Average age 29. In 2007, 25 degrees awarded. Application fee: $50. *Expenses:* Tuition: Part-time $305 per credit hour. *Unit head:* Dr. Melissa Connor, Director, 402-465-2550, E-mail: mconnor@nebrwesleyan.edu.

Oklahoma State University Center for Health Sciences, Graduate Program in Forensic Sciences, Tulsa, OK 74107-1898. Offers forensic DNA/molecular biology (MS); forensic examination of questioned documents (MFSA, Certificate); forensic pathology (MS); forensic psychology (MS); forensic sciences (MFSA); forensic toxicology (MS). Part-time and evening/weekend programs available. Postbaccalaureate distance learning degree programs offered (no on-campus study). *Faculty:* 2 full-time (0 women), 14 part-time/adjunct (5 women). *Students:* 3 full-time (1 woman), 21 part-time (14 women); includes 6 minority (4 African Americans, 1 Asian American or Pacific Islander, 1 Hispanic American), 1 international. Average age 34. 27 applicants, 63% accepted, 8 enrolled. In 2007, 12 master's, 1 other advanced degree awarded. *Degree requirements:* For master's, comprehensive exam (for some programs), thesis (for some programs). *Entrance requirements:* For master's, MAT (MFSA) or GRE General Test, professional experience (MFSA). Additional exam requirements/recommendations for international students: Required—TOEFL (minimum score 600 paper-based; 250 computer-based), TWE (minimum score 5). *Application deadline:* For fall admission, 3/1 for domestic and international students; for spring admission, 10/1 for domestic and international students. Application fee: $40 ($75 for international students). *Financial support:* In 2007–08, 10 students received support, including 10 research assistantships (averaging $29,000 per year); career-related internships or fieldwork, Federal Work-Study, and tuition waivers (partial) also available. Support available to part-time students. *Faculty research:* DNA typing, DNA polymorphism, identification through DNA, disease transmission, forensic dentistry, neurotoxicity of HIV, forensic toxicology method development, toxin detection and characterization. Total annual research expenditures: $58,000. *Unit head:* Dr. Robert T. Allen, Director, 918-561-1108, Fax: 918-561-8414. *Application contact:* Cathy Newsome, Coordinator, 918-699-8608, Fax: 918-561-8414, E-mail: cathy.newsome@okstate.edu.

Pace University, Dyson College of Arts and Sciences, Program in Forensic Science, New York, NY 10038. Offers MS. *Students:* 31 full-time (27 women), 17 part-time (15 women); includes 17 minority (6 African Americans, 8 Asian Americans or Pacific Islanders, 3 Hispanic Americans). Average age 25. 102 applicants, 67% accepted, 15 enrolled. In 2007, 28 degrees awarded. *Entrance requirements:* Additional exam requirements/recommendations for international students: Required—TOEFL. *Application deadline:* For fall admission, 8/1 priority date for domestic students; for spring admission, 12/1 priority date for domestic students. Application fee: $65. Electronic applications accepted. *Expenses:* Tuition: Part-time $856 per credit. Tuition and fees vary according to degree level and program. *Financial support:* Application deadline: 2/15; *Unit head:* Dr. Ellen Weiser, Department Chair, 212-346-1502. *Application contact:* Joanna Broda, Director of Admissions, 212-346-1652, Fax: 212-346-1585, E-mail: gradnyc@pace.edu.

See Close-Up on page 985.

Philadelphia College of Osteopathic Medicine, Graduate and Professional Programs, Program in Forensic Medicine, Philadelphia, PA 19131-1694. Offers MS. *Entrance requirements:* For master's, minimum GPA of 3.0; coursework in biology, chemistry, anatomy and physiology .

Sam Houston State University, College of Criminal Justice, Huntsville, TX 77341. Offers criminal justice (MS, PhD); criminal justice and criminology (MA); criminal justice management (MS); forensic science (MS). *Faculty:* 30 full-time (10 women). *Students:* 77 full-time (44 women), 114 part-time (45 women); includes 25 minority (7 African Americans, 1 American Indian/Alaska Native, 3 Asian Americans or Pacific Islanders, 14 Hispanic Americans), 40 international. Average age 32. In 2007, 53 master's, 16 doctorates awarded. *Degree requirements:* For master's, thesis (for some programs); for doctorate, comprehensive exam, thesis/dissertation. *Entrance requirements:* For master's, GRE General Test; for doctorate, GRE General Test, master's degree. *Application deadline:* For fall admission, 8/1 for domestic students; for spring admission, 12/1 for domestic students. Applications are processed on a rolling basis. Application fee: $20. *Expenses:* Tuition, state resident: full-time $5,026; part-time $184 per semester hour. Tuition, nonresident: full-time $10,586; part-time $462 per semester hour. Required fees: $494 per semester. *Financial support:* Fellowships, research assistantships, teaching assistantships, career-related internships or fieldwork, Federal Work-Study, institutionally sponsored loans, and unspecified assistantships available. Support available to part-time students. Financial award application deadline: 5/31; financial award applicants required to submit FAFSA. *Unit head:* Dr. Vincent Webb, Dean, 936-294-1632, Fax: 936-294-1653, E-mail: vwebb@shsu.edu. *Application contact:* Doris Powell, Advisor, 936-294-3637.

Southern Utah University, College of Science, Program in Forensic Science, Cedar City, UT 84720-2498. Offers MS. *Faculty:* 10 full-time (3 women), 4 part-time/adjunct (0 women). *Students:* 25 full-time (16 women), 15 part-time (7 women); includes 2 minority (both Asian Americans or Pacific Islanders) 24 applicants, 83% accepted, 19 enrolled. *Application deadline:* Applications are processed on a rolling basis. Application fee: $50 ($65 for international students). Electronic applications accepted. *Unit head:* Dr. Harold Ornes, Dean, College of Science, 435-586-7920, Fax: 435-865-8550, E-mail: ornes@suu.edu.

Stevenson University, Graduate and Professional Studies Programs, Program in Forensic Science, Stevenson, MD 21153. Offers MS. Partnership program with Maryland State Police Forensic Sciences Division. *Students:* 15 full-time, 4 part-time. In 2007, 4 degrees awarded. *Entrance requirements:* For master's, bachelor's degree in chemistry, biology, physics, or a related science with a minimum cumulative and science/math GPA of 3.2; course/lab work in general biology, general chemistry, organic chemistry, physics, cell biology, molecular genetics, analytical chemistry, instrumental analysis, human anatomy and physiology, biotechniques, and biochemistry. *Expenses:* Tuition: Full-time $16,020; part-time $450 per credit. Required fees: $1,000; $75 per term.

Stevenson University, Graduate and Professional Studies Programs, Program in Forensic Studies, Stevenson, MD 21153. Offers forensic accounting (MS); forensic legal professional (MS); information technology (MS); interdisciplinary track (MS); investigations (MS). Postbaccalaureate distance learning degree programs offered (minimal on-campus study). *Students:* 40 full-time, 121 part-time. In 2007, 24 degrees awarded. *Degree requirements:* For master's, capstone course. *Expenses:* Tuition: Full-time $16,020; part-time $450 per credit. Required fees: $1,000; $75 per term.

Towson University, College of Graduate Studies and Research, Program in Forensic Science, Towson, MD 21252-0001. Offers MS. *Students:* 15 full-time (11 women), 3 part-time (2 women); includes 4 minority (all African Americans), 2 international. Average age 26. 10 applicants, 90% accepted, 7 enrolled. *Entrance requirements:* For master's, minimum GPA 3.0 for full admission, Bachelor's in chemistry or forensic chemistry or related field. *Expenses:* Tuition, state resident: part-time $286 per credit. Tuition, nonresident: part-time $600 per credit. Required fees: $75 per credit. *Unit head:* Mark Profili, Graduate Program Director, 410-704-2668, E-mail: mprofili@towson.edu.

Universidad del Turabo, Graduate Programs, School of Social Sciences and Humanities, Programs in Public Affairs, Program in Forensic Science, Gurabo, PR 00778-3030. Offers MSS. *Students:* 86 full-time (64 women), 27 part-time (18 women); all Hispanic Americans Average

Forensic Sciences

Universidad del Turabo (continued)
age 29. In 2007, 23 degrees awarded. *Expenses:* Tuition: Full-time $5,560. *Application contact:* Virginia González, Admissions Officer, 787-746-3009.

University at Albany, State University of New York, College of Arts and Sciences, Department of Biological Sciences, Albany, NY 12222-0001. Offers biodiversity, conservation, and policy (MS); ecology, evolution, and behavior (MS, PhD); forensic molecular biology (MS); molecular, cellular, developmental, and neural biology (MS, PhD). *Students:* 47 full-time (28 women), 23 part-time (12 women). Average age 28. 135 applicants, 27% accepted, 21 enrolled. In 2007, 15 master's, 4 doctorates awarded. *Degree requirements:* For master's, one foreign language; for doctorate, one foreign language, thesis/dissertation. *Entrance requirements:* For master's and doctorate, GRE General Test. Additional exam requirements/recommendations for international students: Required—TOEFL (minimum score 550 paper-based; 213 computer-based). *Application deadline:* For fall admission, 2/15 priority date for domestic students, 5/1 for international students; for spring admission, 11/1 for domestic and international students. Applications are processed on a rolling basis. Application fee: $75. Electronic applications accepted. *Expenses:* Tuition, state resident: part-time $576 per credit. Tuition, nonresident: part-time $910 per credit. Tuition and fees vary according to program. *Financial support:* Fellowships, research assistantships, teaching assistantships, unspecified assistantships and minority assistantships available. Financial award application deadline: 5/1. *Faculty research:* Interferon, neural development, RNA self-splicing, behavioral ecology, DNA repair enzymes. *Unit head:* Dr. Albert Millis, Chair, 518-442-4300.

The University of Alabama at Birmingham, School of Social and Behavioral Sciences, Department of Justice Sciences, Birmingham, AL 35294. Offers criminal justice (MSCJ); forensic science (MSFS). Evening/weekend programs available. *Students:* 25 full-time (19 women), 5 part-time (4 women); includes 4 minority (3 African Americans, 1 Asian American or Pacific Islander), 2 international. Average age 27. In 2007, 7 degrees awarded. *Degree requirements:* For master's, thesis or alternative. *Entrance requirements:* For master's, GRE General Test or MAT. *Application deadline:* Applications are processed on a rolling basis. Application fee: $35 ($60 for international students). Electronic applications accepted. *Financial support:* Career-related internships or fieldwork available. *Unit head:* Dr. John J. Sloan, Chair, 205-934-2069.

University of California, Davis, Graduate Studies, Graduate Group in Forensic Science, Davis, CA 95616. Offers MS. *Degree requirements:* For master's, thesis. *Entrance requirements:* Additional exam requirements/recommendations for international students: Required—TOEFL (minimum score 550 paper-based; 213 computer-based), IELTS (minimum score 7). Electronic applications accepted.

University of Central Florida, College of Health and Public Affairs, Department of Criminal Justice and Legal Studies, Orlando, FL 32816. Offers corrections leadership (Certificate); crime analysis (Certificate); criminal justice (MS); juvenile justice leadership (Certificate); police leadership (Certificate); victims assistance (Certificate). Part-time and evening/weekend programs available. *Faculty:* 34 full-time (11 women), 38 part-time/adjunct (7 women). *Degree requirements:* For master's, thesis or alternative. *Entrance requirements:* For master's, GRE General Test, minimum GPA of 3.0. Additional exam requirements/recommendations for international students: Required—TOEFL. *Application deadline:* For fall admission, 7/15 for domestic students; for spring admission, 4/15 for domestic students. Electronic applications accepted. *Expenses:* Tuition, state resident: full-time $6,484. Tuition, nonresident: full-time $23,938. Tuition and fees vary according to program. *Financial support:* Fellowships with partial tuition reimbursements, research assistantships with partial tuition reimbursements, teaching assistantships with partial tuition reimbursements, career-related internships or fieldwork, Federal Work-Study, institutionally sponsored loans, tuition waivers (partial), and unspecified assistantships available. Financial award application deadline: 3/1; financial award applicants required to submit FAFSA. *Unit head:* Dr. Robert Langworthy, Interim Chair, 407-823-6486, E-mail: rlangwor@mail.ucf.edu.

University of Central Florida, College of Sciences, Department of Chemistry, Orlando, FL 32816. Offers chemistry (MS, PhD); computer forensics (Certificate); forensic analysis (MS); forensic biochemistry (MS); industrial chemistry (MS). Part-time and evening/weekend programs available. *Faculty:* 27 full-time (3 women), 3 part-time/adjunct (0 women). *Degree requirements:* For master's, thesis, final exam. *Entrance requirements:* For master's, GRE General Test, minimum GPA of 3.0 in last 60 hours. Additional exam requirements/recommendations for international students: Required—TOEFL. *Application deadline:* For fall admission, 7/15 for domestic students; for spring admission, 12/1 for domestic students. Application fee: $30. Electronic applications accepted. *Expenses:* Tuition, state resident: full-time $6,484. Tuition, nonresident: full-time $23,938. Tuition and fees vary according to program. *Financial support:* Fellowships with partial tuition reimbursements, research assistantships with partial tuition reimbursements, teaching assistantships with partial tuition reimbursements, career-related internships or fieldwork, Federal Work-Study, institutionally sponsored loans, tuition waivers (partial), and unspecified assistantships available. Financial award application deadline: 3/1; financial award applicants required to submit FAFSA. *Faculty research:* Physical and synthetic organic chemistry, lasers, polymers, biochemical action of pesticides, environmental analysis. Total annual research expenditures: $645,000. *Unit head:* Dr. Kevin D. Belfield, Chair, 407-823-2246, Fax: 407-823-2252, E-mail: kbelfield@mail.ucf.edu.

University of Florida, College of Pharmacy, Programs in Forensic Science, Gainesville, FL 32611. Offers forensic DNA and serology (MS, Certificate); forensic drug chemistry (MS, Certificate); forensic toxicology (MS, Certificate). *Faculty:* 7. *Expenses:* Tuition, state resident: full-time $7,478. Tuition, nonresident: full-time $22,603. *Application contact:* Dr. William J. Millard, Executive Associate Dean, 352-273-6311, Fax: 352-273-6306, E-mail: millard@cop.ufl.edu.

University of Illinois at Chicago, College of Pharmacy and Graduate College, Research and Graduate Studies, College of Pharmacy, Program in Forensic Science, Chicago, IL 60607-7128. Offers MS. *Degree requirements:* For master's, thesis. *Entrance requirements:* For master's, GRE General Test. Additional exam requirements/recommendations for international students: Required—TOEFL. *Faculty research:* Interpretation of physical evidence, utilization of physical evidence, analytical toxicology of controlled substances, automated fingerprint systems, dye and ink characterizations.

University of New Haven, Graduate School, Henry C. Lee College of Criminal Justice and Forensic Sciences, Program in Forensic Science, West Haven, CT 06516-1916. Offers advanced investigation (MS); criminalistics (MS); forensic science (MS). Part-time and evening/weekend programs available. *Students:* 79 full-time (68 women), 46 part-time (36 women); includes 9 minority (3 African Americans, 2 American Indian/Alaska Native, 2 Asian Americans or Pacific Islanders, 2 Hispanic Americans), 2 international. In 2007, 48 degrees awarded. *Degree requirements:* For master's, thesis or alternative. *Entrance requirements:* For master's, GRE Subject Test. *Application deadline:* Applications are processed on a rolling basis. Application fee: $50. *Expenses:* Tuition: Part-time $630 per credit. Required fees: $40 per term. *Financial support:* Career-related internships or fieldwork and Federal Work-Study available. Support available to part-time students. Financial award application deadline: 5/1; financial award applicants required to submit FAFSA. *Unit head:* Dr. Timothy Palmbach, Coordinator, 203-932-7116.

See Close-Up on page 991.

University of North Texas Health Science Center at Fort Worth, Graduate School of Biomedical Sciences, Fort Worth, TX 76107-2699. Offers anatomy and cell biology (MS, PhD); biochemistry and molecular biology (MS, PhD); biomedical sciences (MS, PhD); biotechnology (MS); forensic genetics (MS); integrative physiology (MS, PhD); medical science (MS); microbiology and immunology (MS, PhD); pharmacology (MS, PhD); science education (MS); DO/MS; DO/PhD. Terminal master's awarded for partial completion of doctoral program. *Degree requirements:* For master's, thesis; for doctorate, thesis/dissertation. *Entrance requirements:* For master's and doctorate, GRE General Test. Additional exam requirements/recommendations for international students: Required—TOEFL. Expenses: Contact institution. *Faculty research:* Alzheimer's disease, aging, eye diseases, cancer, cardiovascular disease.

University of Rhode Island, Graduate School, College of Arts and Sciences, Department of Computer Science and Statistics, Kingston, RI 02881. Offers applied mathematics (PhD), including computer science, statistics; computer science (MS, PhD); digital forensics (Graduate Certificate); statistics (MS). In 2007, 4 degrees awarded. *Degree requirements:* For master's, thesis optional; for doctorate, one foreign language, thesis/dissertation. *Entrance requirements:* For master's, GRE Subject Test. *Application deadline:* For fall admission, 4/15 priority date for domestic students. Applications are processed on a rolling basis. Application fee: $35. *Expenses:* Tuition, state resident: full-time $6,936; part-time $385 per credit. Tuition, nonresident: full-time $19,044; part-time $1,058 per credit. Required fees: $1,508; $48 per credit. $30 per semester. One-time fee: $80 part-time. *Financial support:* Unspecified assistantships available. *Unit head:* Dr. James Kowalski, Chair, 401-874-2701.

Virginia Commonwealth University, Graduate School, College of Humanities and Sciences, Department of Forensic Science, Richmond, VA 23284-9005. Offers MS. *Students:* 47 full-time (42 women), 1 (woman) part-time; includes 5 minority (2 African Americans, 1 American Indian/Alaska Native, 2 Hispanic Americans), 3 international. 152 applicants, 32% accepted, 25 enrolled. *Expenses:* Tuition, state resident: full-time $7,224; part-time $401 per credit. Tuition, nonresident: full-time $16,072; part-time $891 per credit. Required fees: $1,679; $63 per credit. Tuition and fees vary according to campus/location. *Unit head:* Dr. William B. Eggleston, Chair, 804-828-0799, E-mail: wbeggles@vcu.edu. *Application contact:* Tracey D. Cruz, Program Director, 804-828-0642, E-mail: tcdawson@vcu.edu.

See Close-Up on page 457.

West Virginia University, Eberly College of Arts and Sciences, Department of Biology, Morgantown, WV 26506. Offers cell and molecular biology (MS, PhD); environmental and evolutionary biology (MS, PhD); forensic biology (MS, PhD); genomic biology (MS, PhD); neurobiology (MS, PhD). *Faculty:* 19 full-time (7 women), 7 part-time/adjunct (6 women). *Students:* 38 full-time (21 women), 6 part-time (4 women), 19 international. Average age 27. 45 applicants, 20% accepted, 7 enrolled. In 2007, 5 master's, 2 doctorates awarded. Terminal master's awarded for partial completion of doctoral program. *Degree requirements:* For master's, thesis, final exam; for doctorate, thesis/dissertation, preliminary and final exams. *Entrance requirements:* For master's, GRE General Test, GRE Subject Test, minimum GPA of 3.0; for doctorate, GRE General Test, minimum GPA of 3.0. Additional exam requirements/recommendations for international students: Required—TOEFL. *Application deadline:* For fall admission, 1/1 priority date for domestic and international students. Applications are processed on a rolling basis. Application fee: $45. *Expenses:* Tuition, state resident: full-time $5,196; part-time $292 per credit hour. Tuition, nonresident: full-time $15,064; part-time $840 per credit hour. Tuition and fees vary according to program. *Financial support:* In 2007–08, 43 students received support, including fellowships with full tuition reimbursements available (averaging $20,000 per year), 1 research assistantship with full and partial tuition reimbursement available (averaging $17,000 per year), 32 teaching assistantships with full and partial tuition reimbursements available (averaging $15,000 per year); Federal Work-Study and institutionally sponsored loans also available. Financial award application deadline: 4/1; financial award applicants required to submit FAFSA. *Faculty research:* Environmental biology, genetic engineering, developmental biology, global change, biodiversity. Total annual research expenditures: $1.5 million. *Unit head:* Dr. Jeffrey D. Wells, Chair, 304-293-5201, Fax: 304-293-6363, E-mail: jdwells@mail.wvu.edu. *Application contact:* Dr. William T. Peterjohn, Associate Chair for Graduate Studies, 304-293-5201 Ext. 31510, Fax: 304-293-6363, E-mail: william.peterjohn@mail.wvu.edu.

MICHIGAN STATE UNIVERSITY

School of Criminal Justice

Programs of Study

The School of Criminal Justice at Michigan State University (MSU) offers the Master of Science and Doctor of Philosophy in criminal justice.

The master's degree requires a minimum of 30 semester hours. Students may elect to complete a thesis or a policy paper. The program is designed for those wishing to strengthen leadership and management skills in law enforcement, corrections, and delinquency prevention and for those applying to a research-oriented Ph.D. program in criminal justice. A specialization in security management, which provides a multidisciplinary educational experience for students interested in private and government security, is offered. A forensic science master's degree, combining science and criminal justice, is available for individuals with a bachelor's degree in natural science. The forensic program has a 38-credit requirement and students must complete a thesis.

The School of Criminal Justice also offers the Master of Science in criminal justice through the Internet. This program, geared towards professionals, includes specializations in security management and judicial administration. The School also offers Internet-based Homeland Security, Intelligence Analysis, Security Management, and International Focus Graduate Certificate Programs.

The Ph.D. program provides a strong foundation for students who wish to pursue careers in research and teaching. The program consists of core courses and electives in criminal justice and a cognate area, which may be in social science or a focus area that reflects individual interests such as race and ethnicity, gender, organizational theory, labor and industrial relations, urban studies, or Latino studies. A quantitative research component is required. A guidance committee assists students individually with the development of their program, based on individual educational backgrounds and career objectives.

Research Facilities

A computer laboratory is available to students, with IBM workstations and relevant databases for research and management issues. The available software and training include those associated with several statistical packages, such as SPSS for Windows and SAS, and alternative software systems for databases, graphics, spreadsheets, word processing, and desktop publishing. The University library is among the nation's largest, with more than 4 million volumes, 5 million items on microfilm and microfiche, and approximately 28,000 serial subscriptions.

Computing facilities at MSU include more than fifty microcomputer laboratories across the campus, several of which are available 24 hours a day during the week. Multiple services for the University community are available, including statistical consulting and a computer store that sells equipment at an academic discount. E-mail accounts are free for all students and faculty and staff members.

The School formally collaborates with the National Criminal Justice Data Archive, which provides numerous opportunities for research and advanced methodological courses. In addition, the School and MSU have established many international partnerships offering unique opportunities for global scholarship.

Financial Aid

Graduate assistantships at the master's and doctoral levels are available on a competitive basis. To be considered for an assistantship, students must be admitted to the criminal justice program with regular status. Stipends for 2007–08 ranged from $629 to $2078 per month. The assistantships require that the student work 10 to 30 hours per week on research projects and teaching. In addition, all assistantships provide a tuition award of 18 credits per academic year, a waiver of out-of-state tuition, and health insurance.

Cost of Study

Tuition for the 2007–08 academic year was $378.75 per credit hour for in-state students and $800 per credit hour for out-of-state students. Fees, including registration and technology support fees, totaled $466.

Living and Housing Costs

Housing for graduate students is available both on and off campus and varies in cost. The area market average for room and board is $6000 per academic year. Health insurance is available through the University.

Student Group

The School has an enrollment of approximately 850 undergraduates, 75 master's students, and 35 doctoral students. In fall 2005, 43 percent of master's students were women, 12 percent were members of minority groups, and 9 percent were international students; 43 percent of the doctoral candidates were women, 16 percent were members of minority groups, and 22 percent were international students.

Location

Located on the banks of the Red Cedar River, the nation's first land-grant university is situated on one of the most beautiful campuses in the country. The 5,198-acre East Lansing campus, an arboretum park with four designated natural areas, has received many national awards for its beauty and wealth of plant life. Lansing, the state capital, is only 2 miles from the campus and provides ready access to public agencies and businesses for students who seek research and practicum sites. With a population of 400,000, the metropolitan Lansing area offers diverse cultural and recreational activities. The Great Lakes, Detroit, and Ontario are all within 90 miles, and housing is attractive and affordable.

The University

Founded in 1855, MSU is one of the leading institutions of higher education in the United States. The University ranks among the fifteen largest in the nation, and has a total enrollment of approximately 43,366 students. More than 7,900 students are enrolled in graduate programs.

Academic programs are directed by faculty members with national and international reputations. Faculty members at MSU work closely with graduate students and take pride in meeting the academic needs of individual students.

Applying

Applications for admission that are not submitted online must be accompanied by the application fee. Prospective doctoral students' applications are reviewed once each year. To ensure full consideration for the Ph.D. program, application materials, including scores from the GRE General Test, must be received by January 10. For master's degree applicants, all application materials, including scores from the GRE General Test, must be received by February 1 for the fall semester and September 1 for the spring semester. All application materials should be sent to the School of Criminal Justice.

Correspondence and Information

School of Criminal Justice
560 Baker Hall
Michigan State University
East Lansing, Michigan 48824-1118

Phone: 517-353-7133
E-mail: burrier@msu.edu
Web site: http://www.criminaljustice.msu.edu

Michigan State University

THE FACULTY

Timothy Bynum, Professor; Ph.D., Florida State. Evaluation, research design, law enforcement, corrections policy analysis.
David Carter, Professor; Ph.D., Sam Houston State. Police management/policy, computer crime, law enforcement intelligence.
Steve Chermak, Associate Professor; Ph.D., SUNY at Albany. Presentation of crime in media, terrorism, evaluating criminal justice interventions.
Charles Corley, Associate Professor; Ph.D., Bowling Green State. Delinquency causation and control, management of correctional programs.
Christina DeJong, Associate Professor; Ph.D., Maryland College Park. Gender, race, and crime; research methodology; sentencing.
Steven Dow, Associate Professor; Ph.D., Michigan; J.D., Ohio State. Law and politics.
David Foran, Associate Professor; Ph.D., Michigan. Forensic biology.
Carole Gibbs, Assistant Professor; Ph.D., Maryland, College Park. Criminological theory, corporate crime, gender/race/class and crime, environmental justice.
Homer Hawkins, Associate Professor; Ph.D., Michigan State. Adult and juvenile corrections, delinquency causation and control.
Vincent Hoffman, Associate Professor; Ph.D., Michigan State. Adult and juvenile corrections.
John Hudzik, Professor; Ph.D., Michigan State. Planning and budgeting, courts, manpower.
Sanja Kutnjak Ivkovich, Associate Professor; Ph.D., Delaware; J.D., Harvard. Police deviance, judicial behavior and issues in global crime.
Christopher Maxwell, Assistant Professor; Ph.D., Rutgers. Crime prevention programs, criminal justice processing of intimate violence and hate-motivated crimes.
Sheila Royo Maxwell, Associate Professor; Ph.D., Rutgers. Drug treatment and control, community corrections, juvenile crime.
Edmund McGarrell, Professor and Director; Ph.D., SUNY at Albany. Communities and crime, strategic responses, restorative justice.
Christopher Melde, Assistant Professor; Ph.D., Missouri. Evaluation research, perceptions of crime, juvenile delinquency/victimization, corrections, criminological theory, research methods.
Merry Morash, Professor; Ph.D., Maryland College Park. Gender and crime, criminological theory and methods.
Mahesh Nalla, Professor; Ph.D., SUNY at Albany. Traditional/nontraditional policing, security management, comparative criminal justice.
Christopher Smith, Professor; Ph.D., Connecticut; J.D., Tennessee. Courts, criminal procedure, corrections law.
Jesenia Pizarro Terrill, Assistant Professor; Ph.D., Rutgers. Social ecology of violent crime, homicide victimization and perpetration, corrections policy, international and transnational crime.
William Terrill, Associate Professor; Ph.D., Rutgers. Policing, use of force.
Ruth Waddell, Assistant Professor; Ph.D., Strathclyde. Forensic chemistry.
Carol Zimmermann, Visiting Professor; Ph.D., Michigan State. Juvenile justice, risk analysis, public policies and organizations.

NOVA SOUTHEASTERN UNIVERSITY

Criminal Justice Institute
Master of Science Degree in Criminal Justice

Program of Study

The Master of Science degree in criminal justice is offered online through the Criminal Justice Institute at Nova Southeastern University (NSU). Graduate students participate in a program that challenges them to examine and understand complex theory and issues surrounding criminal behavior, prevention, and intervention at the local, state, and federal levels. The program design begins with core courses that establish a foundation of knowledge, which is then augmented by several specialty tracks. These concentrations allow students to focus their studies in a particular area of interest and develop the advanced analytical skills necessary to become effective researchers and criminal justice professionals.

Courses are offered during four terms: fall, winter, spring, and summer. The total number of credits required to successfully complete the master's program is 36, including five core courses, ten specialization courses, and two elective courses. A typical student's time commitment is approximately 1½ years, averaging two courses per semester.

Through online technology, students from agencies and professional environments all over the world share the classroom. For the past forty years, Nova Southeastern University has been a leader in innovative educational delivery. Online learning is immediate and intensely interactive. It allows learning to reach beyond traditional boundaries and promotes a spirited exchange of knowledge, experience, and perspective. Students are able to collaborate with professionals who are actively involved in criminal justice agencies and form close bonds with their peers as well as with their professors, who serve as valued guides and mentors. The instructors are experts in their respective fields and guide their students in developing the skills necessary to reach their goals, including teaching, research, and professional employment in the criminal justice field.

Research Facilities

Nova Southeastern University has a complete library located on the main campus. It is accessible to all students in the master's degree program. The online format of the program enables students to conduct online research through the Internet and research service providers. The library has the capacity to house 1.4 million volumes of reference materials, making it the largest in Florida. The University Computing Center provides data processing facilities and services to meet the instructional, research, and administrative needs of the University and is available to qualified students for computer-oriented course work.

Financial Aid

Nova Southeastern University's Office of Student Financial Assistance administers comprehensive federal, state, institutional, and private financial aid programs. Students interested in receiving a financial aid packet should contact the Office of Student Financial Assistance at 954-262-3380 or 800-806-3680 (toll-free) or via the Internet at http://www.nova.edu/cwis/finaid. Because normal application processing takes six to eight weeks, and sometimes as many as twelve weeks, it is recommended that students apply for financial aid well in advance of the date funds will be needed. Awards are made only for the academic year. Applications are generally available each January for the following academic year. Nova Southeastern University offers scholarships, Federal Stafford Student Loans, Federal Perkins Loans, and Federal Work-Study Program positions for students who meet eligibility requirements.

Cost of Study

Tuition is $520 per credit hour. There is a registration fee of $50 per semester, and books and supplies cost $80–$200 per course. The application for degree fee is $75. Fees are subject to change without notice.

Living and Housing Costs

Students enrolled in the Master of Science degree program in criminal justice are enrolled online from around the world.

Student Group

While some students have an interest in pursuing a master's degree in this field without prior experience, most students enrolled in the program are employed in some capacity in the criminal justice field.

Location

The main campus of Nova Southeastern University is located on a 300-acre site in Fort Lauderdale, Florida. Fort Lauderdale is part of Broward County, a principal coastal area in south Florida and a rapidly growing community for business, industrial, electronics, and computer opportunities. NSU is 10 miles inland from the Atlantic Ocean and is easily accessible from major highways, including I-75, I-95, I-595, the Sawgrass Expressway, and Florida's Turnpike. The climate is subtropical and has an average year-round temperature of 75 degrees. Natural areas for outdoor activities such as sailing, fishing, golf, tennis, and swimming are easily and quickly accessible from the University. With tourism as a major industry, Fort Lauderdale provides some of the best in shopping, dining, and cultural offerings, which include concerts, opera, ballet, museums, theater, and professional sporting events.

The University and The Institute

Nova Southeastern University is an independent, nonsectarian, fully accredited, coeducational university chartered by the state of Florida in 1964. As an acknowledged leader in field-based degree programs, NSU offers courses of study leading to bachelor's, master's, educational specialist, and doctoral degrees. Undergraduate and graduate programs are offered in allied health (physical therapy, physician assistant studies, and occupational therapy), business, computer sciences, criminal justice, dental medicine, education, law, marine medicine, medical education, optometry, osteopathic medicine, pharmacy, psychology, public administration, and social sciences. NSU has a total enrollment of more than 23,520 students, including over 5,220 undergraduates.

The Institute was established in 2001 to provide a supportive academic and professional environment for faculty members and students studying criminal justice.

Applying

To be admitted to the program, applicants must complete all parts of the admissions application form; submit an official transcript for each postsecondary school attended; provide a personal statement 150 to 300 words in length, indicating their goals in pursing a criminal justice degree at the graduate level; provide three letters of recommendation; and include a nonrefundable $50 application fee.

Correspondence and Information

Enrollment Processing Services (EPS)
Attention: Criminal Justice Institute
Nova Southeastern University
3301 College Avenue
P.O. Box 299000
Fort Lauderdale, Florida 33329-9905
Phone: 954-262-7001
800-541-NOVA (6682; toll-free)
E-mail: cji@nova.edu
Web site: http://www.cji.nova.edu

Nova Southeastern University

THE FACULTY AND THEIR RESEARCH

Catherine Arcabascio, Professor and CJI Course Director; J.D., Boston College, 1987. Co-Founder and Director of the Florida Innocence Project.
Richard Beauchamp, Adjunct Professor; J.D., Stetson, 1984. Practices in the areas of insurance, real estate, commercial, and construction litigation and nursing home/health-care litigation.
Warren Brown, Adjunct Assistant Professor and Detective; Ph.D., Nova Southeastern, 2000; certified law enforcement officer. Conflict resolution, cultural diversity, defense tactics, hostage negotiation, drug abuse resistance education, gang resistance, investigation and interrogations.
Johnny Burris, Law School Professor and CJI Course Director; LL.M., Columbia, 1984. Criminal procedure, constitutional law, administrative law.
Frank De Piano, University Professor, Vice President of Academic Affairs, Chair, and CJI Course Director; Ph.D., South Carolina, 1980. Clinical psychology.
James Nardozzi, Adjunct Assistant Professor and Deputy Chief of Police; D.P.A., Nova Southeastern, 2003; certified law enforcement officer. Police administration and management, criminal investigation, white-collar crime, criminal justice.
Irving Rosenbaum, Vice Chancellor and Provost, Health Professions, and CJI Course Director; D.P.A., Nova Southeastern, 1984. Town administrator, city manager, consultant, research analyst, management analyst.
Rae Shearn, Esq., Adjunct Professor; former division chief prosecutor for Janet Reno. Currently, Shearn practices criminal defense in state and federal courts in the area of white-collar crime, complex RICO prosecutions, narcotic offenses, death-penalty litigation, and criminal defense for all other criminal prosecution.
Vincent Van Hasselt, Professor, CJI Course Director, and Interim Associate Dean, Center for Psychological Studies; Ph.D., Pittsburgh, 1979; certified law enforcement officer. Interpersonal violence, police psychology, criminal investigative analysis (psychological profiling), apprehension, interviewing and interrogation techniques, behavioral criminology.
George Yacoubian, Adjunct Assistant Professor and Director of Research; Ph.D., Madison, 2001. Drug treatment, drug prevention, drug-testing technology, genocide.

PACE UNIVERSITY

Program in Forensic Science

Program of Study

Pace University has established its Master of Science (M.S.) Program in Forensic Science to meet society's growing need to have competent scientists in crime scene investigations who are capable of utilizing the most modern analytical equipment and procedures for solving crimes. All students admitted to the program are required to have a strong scientific background in biology, chemistry, and physics as well as basic forensic courses. After a 4-credit summer internship at a forensic laboratory, all students take a 36-credit program that includes a thesis mentored by experts in forensic science. Pace University has created close relationships with medical examiners and forensic laboratories in the New York City area. Many of its adjunct faculty members are specialists who work in these centers of forensic investigations and serve as mentors to the graduate students.

Research Facilities

The Pace University Library is a comprehensive teaching library and student learning center, a virtual library that combines strong core collections with ubiquitous access to global Internet resources to support broad and diversified curricula. Reciprocal borrowing and access accords, traditional interlibrary loan services, and commercial document delivery options supplement the aggregate library. Pace offers Instructional Services Librarians, a state-of-the-art electronic classroom, digital reference services, and multimedia applications. Pace's computer resource centers are linked to high-speed data networks and feature sophisticated hardware and software to facilitate active learning. Recognized as one of America's most wired universities, Pace supports high-speed Internet and Internet2 access on every campus. Residence facilities are wired, and most public areas are enabled for wireless connectivity. Full-motion videoconference facilities enable remote delivery of instruction between campus sites for synchronous learning applications. Many courses are Web assisted with state-of-the-art software, and some courses and programs are completely Web based.

Financial Aid

Pace's comprehensive student financial aid assistance program includes scholarships, graduate assistantships, student loans, and tuition payment plans. Scholarships are awarded to students in recognition of academic achievement and are available for full- and part-time study. Highly qualified students may be eligible for assistantships awarded by departments, which paid stipends of up to $5100 and provided tuition remission up to 24 credits during the 2007–08 academic year. Pace participates in all major federal and state financial aid programs, such as Direct Loans, New York State Tuition Assistance Program (TAP), and Federal Perkins Loans. All students are encouraged to apply for these programs by filing the Free Application for Federal Student Aid (FAFSA).

Cost of Study

Tuition for graduate courses is $890 per credit in 2008–09.

Living and Housing Costs

Residence facilities are available on campus in both New York City and Westchester. Double-occupancy rooms ranged from approximately $8500 to $12,000 for the 2007–08 academic year. University-operated off-campus housing is available in proximity to the New York City campus.

Student Group

Pace students represent diversified personal, cultural, and educational backgrounds. Many students are employed and pursue graduate study for personal growth and career advancement; 27 percent are enrolled part-time in evening classes. Current enrollment in the graduate forensic science program is approximately 10 students.

Location

Pace University is a multicampus institution with campuses in both New York City and Westchester County, New York. All locations are within reach of cultural, business, and social resources and opportunities. The downtown Manhattan campus is adjacent to Wall Street and City Hall. Pace's Midtown Center is a short distance from Times Square, theaters, and Grand Central Station. The Pleasantville/Briarcliff campus is in a suburban setting, surrounded by towns offering various forms of recreation. The Graduate Center and the School of Law are located in White Plains among major retail districts and many corporate headquarters. All locations are accessible by public transportation. The graduate forensic science program is available at the New York City campus.

The University

Founded in 1906, Pace University is a private, nonsectarian, coeducational institution. Originally founded as a school of accounting, Pace Institute was designated Pace College in 1973. Through growth and various successes, it was renamed Pace University, as approved by the New York State Board of Regents. Today, Pace offers comprehensive undergraduate, graduate, doctoral, and professional programs through six schools and colleges at several campus locations.

Applying

Admission to Pace University requires successful completion of a U.S. baccalaureate degree or its equivalent from an accredited institution. Students must submit a completed application, the application fee, official transcripts from all postsecondary institutions, a personal statement, a resume, and two letters of recommendation. International students must submit official TOEFL scores and official transcripts in the native language with a professional English translation. Applications should be submitted by August 1 for the fall semester, December 1 for the spring semester, and May 1 for summer sessions. International applications should be submitted five months prior to these dates.

Correspondence and Information

Office of Graduate Admission
Pace University
1 Pace Plaza
New York, New York 10038
Phone: 212-346-1531
Fax: 212-346-1585
E-mail: gradnyc@pace.edu
Web site: http://www.pace.edu

Office of Graduate Admission
Pace University
1 Martine Avenue
White Plains, New York 10606
Phone: 914-422-4283
Fax: 914-422-4287
E-mail: gradwp@pace.edu
Web site: http://www.pace.edu

Pace University

THE FACULTY AND THEIR RESEARCH

Sheila Estacio, M.S. (forensic science), New Haven. Forensic investigations.
Regina Healy, M.S. (forensic science), CUNY, John Jay. Forensic medical examination.
Robin Helburn, Ph.D. (chemistry), Colorado School of Mines. Separations chemistry.
Raifah Kabbani, Ph.D. (chemistry), Fordham. Analytical spectroscopy.
Kyra Keblish, M.S. (biology), CUNY, Hunter. Forensic biology.
Scott Kovar, B.S. (forensic science), CUNY, John Jay. Crime scene investigation and forensic microscopy.
Peter Pizzola, Ph.D. (criminal justice with forensic science concentration), CUNY. Crime scene reconstruction.

ROGER WILLIAMS UNIVERSITY

School of Justice Studies

Programs of Study

Today's criminal justice system professional faces an increasingly complex society. The School of Justice Studies at Roger Williams University (RWU) is aware of the growing need for competent, well-rounded individuals who can rise to these challenges. Because of this, the School offers two graduate degree programs: the Master of Science degree program in criminal justice and the joint Master of Science/Juris Doctor (M.S./J.D.) degree. These degree programs prepare graduates to formulate justice system policy and serve effectively as administrators of U.S. justice system agencies.

The master's programs permit students to explore the fields of criminology, examining the nature and causes of crime, and justice system management, which focuses on modern administrative theory, legal issues in personnel administration, and the management of criminal justice agencies).

Drawing on the strengths of the School of Law as well as the Roger Williams University School of Justice Studies, RWU offers a concentrated joint-degree program for students interested in criminal justice. The dual-degree program allows students to complete the Juris Doctor (J.D.) and the Master of Science (M.S.) in criminal justice in an accelerated period of study.

Research Facilities

A wide array of instructional resources is available to students. The University's state-of-the-art computer laboratories allow student access to the latest word and statistical processing software packages available, including full Internet access. The University's expansive library houses approximately 2,000 volumes and 150 films and other nonprint materials related to the U.S. justice system. Master's degree candidates also have access to the Lexis/Nexis network and Westlaw as well as the RWU Law School libraries. In addition, the University is a member of the Helin consortium, which gives students access to more than 1 million volumes of printed material.

The Roger Williams University libraries' mission is to provide leadership for the development, organization, and sharing of resource collections, ensuring optimal access to information (from any reputable source), instruction of users, and services responsive to the users' needs. The libraries also strive to promote the values and capacities associated with intellectual inquiry, lifelong learning, and knowledge management.

Financial Aid

Roger Williams University recognizes the need on the part of some students for financial assistance to meet the cost of higher education. Students with financial need may be able to receive funds available through federal loan programs. Students with fully accepted status who maintain a minimum of 6 credits are eligible to receive loans that cover the cost of graduate education. In order to be considered for the federal loan programs, students must submit the Free Application for Federal Student Aid (FAFSA), which is available from the Office of Financial Aid or at http://www.fafsa.gov.

Cost of Study

The 2007–08 graduate tuition was $600 per credit. Each 3-credit course cost $1800. A slight increase is expected for the 2008–09 academic year. Some additional fees may apply.

Living and Housing Costs

The Department of Housing has designated a select group of University apartments as graduate housing. However, University housing is not guaranteed for graduate students, and the majority of graduate students seek a variety of off-campus housing options. In 2006–07, the average cost for graduate housing was $7150 per academic year. Off-campus housing costs vary depending on the size and location of the unit.

Student Group

Each entering class has approximately 15 students. Many students have already begun their careers as justice system professionals, while others are looking to further their undergraduate studies in the field of criminal justice. The small class size makes cultivating working relationships with members of the faculty an easy task.

Location

The University is located on 140 beautiful acres of waterfront campus in historic Bristol, Rhode Island. This location offers the comfort of a small, local community and is only 20 minutes from scenic Newport. It is also only an hour from Boston and approximately 3 hours from New York City.

The University and The School

Roger Williams, founder of Rhode Island and namesake of the University, is remembered as a leading champion of freedom in the American colonies. His quest for knowledge and truth is preserved at Roger Williams University. The University is progressive, innovative, dedicated to diversity, and committed to individualism.

In addition to offering undergraduate and graduate degrees, the School of Justice Studies also includes the Justice System Training and Research Institute. The institute serves as a national model for integrating current research methodologies and state-of-the-art technology with the programmatic needs of the justice system. This makes additional learning and training opportunities available to students as well as outside criminal justice professionals.

The School of Justice Studies is staffed by a regionally, nationally, and internationally known faculty. The majority of the faculty members hold Ph.D. degrees in criminal justice, sociology, psychology, or a closely related field. Many hold the Juris Doctor as well as their other doctoral degrees.

Applying

Admission requirements include a bachelor's degree from an accredited institution, official transcripts of all previous undergraduate and graduate course work, a personal statement discussing relevant past experiences and career goals, two letters of recommendation attesting to the candidate's potential to complete graduate work, and a completed application form signed and accompanied by the $50 application fee. Entrance exams are not required, but applicants with an overall undergraduate grade point average below 3.0 are strongly encouraged to take either the GRE or MAT. Students interested in the Master of Science in Criminal Justice/Juris Doctor degree must apply separately to both the graduate program in the School of Justice Studies and the Juris Doctor program in the School of Law and may submit their LSAT scores with both applications.

Applications are accepted in both paper and electronic form.

Correspondence and Information

Suzanne Faubl
Director of Graduate Admission
Roger Williams University
One Old Ferry Road
Bristol, Rhode Island 02809

Phone: 888-674-8479 (toll-free)
E-mail: gradadmit@rwu.edu
Web site: http://www.rwu.edu

Roger Williams University

THE FACULTY

Stephanie P. Manzi, Dean; Ph.D., Maryland.
Kathleen M. Dunn, Associate Professor of Criminal Justice; J.D., Boston University; Ph.D., Brown.
Robert P. Engvall, Associate Professor of Criminal Justice; J.D., Ph.D., Iowa.
Jeffrey A. Jenkins, Associate Professor of Criminal Justice; J.D., New Mexico; Ed.D., Rutgers.
Christopher Menton, Associate Professor of Criminal Justice; Ed.D., Boston University.
Melissa Russano, Assistant Professor of Criminal Justice; Ph.D., Florida International.
Yolanda M. Scott, Associate Professor of Criminal Justice; Ph.D., Kentucky.

UNIVERSITY OF BALTIMORE

Yale Gordon College of Liberal Arts
Division of Criminal Justice, Criminology and Social Policy

Programs of Study

The Division of Criminal Justice, Criminology and Social Policy offers the Master of Science (M.S.) in Criminal Justice program. The program combines solutions to real-life criminal justice issues with theoretical study in criminology and justice; students learn current research practices and graduate with an ability to evaluate programs and participate in the development of criminal justice policy. Faculty members often include students in their research projects, which are frequently designed to benefit the Baltimore community.

The 36-credit program has two options: 30 credits of course work and a 6-credit thesis or 36 credits of course work and two written comprehensive examinations. The core curriculum includes an exploration of concepts in justice and various theories of criminal behavior, research, and statistical techniques coupled with program planning and systems applications. Students have the option to specialize in one of four areas: law enforcement, courts and law, corrections, or juvenile justice. Graduates are prepared for positions in mid-level administration and to advance their careers in criminal justice. Alumni are employed in government and private security organizations; in city, county, and state police departments or corrections agencies; and in private companies. Other graduates have advanced to doctoral study and are college or academy professors.

Research Facilities

Langsdale Library, on the University of Baltimore (UB) campus, houses many books and periodicals focusing on criminal justice, criminology, and social policy. The library also provides students with full access to several million volumes and thousands of journals throughout the University System of Maryland. It subscribes to more than 70 online databases that provide on- and off-campus access to full-text journal articles from almost 12,000 titles.

The University's computing facilities support the statistics and research course work that the program requires.

Financial Aid

The UB Office of Financial Aid assists graduate students in obtaining loans, scholarships, and other means of assistance. Many students participate in internships or work on independent or contractual projects. A limited number of graduate assistantships, which provide tuition remission and a stipend, are available.

Cost of Study

In 2007–08, tuition for liberal arts graduate students who are Maryland residents was $498 per credit hour. Nonresident graduate students paid $751 per credit hour. All students pay a University flat fee ($70 for students taking 1–11 credits; $422.50 for students taking 12 or more credits), a University per-credit fee of $56 (not to exceed $309.50), and a technology fee ($6 per credit from 1–11; $72.50 for 12 credits or more). Web-based classes are an additional $88 per credit for in-state students and $86 per credit for students from out-of-state. Students may pay tuition and fees with cash, check, Visa, MasterCard, or Discover.

Living and Housing Costs

UB is a commuter campus and does not presently offer student housing on campus; however, University-affiliated housing is located within walking distance, and assistance in locating affordable housing is provided by the Center for Student Involvement. UB is located in midtown Baltimore's cultural district, off the Jones Falls Expressway (I-83) and across the street from Pennsylvania Station, which provides MARC commuter and Amtrak service. The University is accessible by major bus routes and its own light rail stop, making the campus an easy commute from a variety of neighborhoods within the Baltimore area.

Student Group

Approximately 75 graduate students are enrolled in this program, and many are residents of the Baltimore–Washington, D.C., metropolitan region. Typical students work full-time and attend classes part-time in the evenings. Students are often dedicated professionals, interested in career advancement and intent on applying what is learned in the classroom to what is happening in the workplace. Student-faculty interaction includes mentoring and shared research projects.

Location

Baltimore is both a big city and a small town. UB is nestled in the Mount Vernon Cultural District—home to art galleries, theaters, the symphony and opera, and historic architecture. The neighborhood serves as the backdrop for First Thursdays, a monthly event that includes the likes of outdoor concerts and wine tasting in nearby art galleries. Within 2 miles of campus is the bustling Inner Harbor, with its shops and waterfront activities, including the National Aquarium, Maryland Science Center, Oriole Park at Camden Yards, and the Ravens' M&T Bank Stadium. The city also offers a museum for nearly every interest and specialty—from the legendary histories told at the Babe Ruth Birthplace and Museum, Edgar Allan Poe House Museum, Eubie Blake Museum, and Great Blacks in Wax Museum to the world-class art found at the Walters Art Museum, Baltimore Museum of Art, and the American Visionary Art Museum. Baltimore is also full of friendly neighborhoods, including Little Italy, Fells Point, Canton, and Hampden. Nighttime pub crawls, vintage shops, steamed crabs, and bocce ball along with street fairs, ethnic festivals, and unique markets make Baltimore a city like few others for those of all ages.

The University

UB offers undergraduate and graduate education in three unique schools: the Yale Gordon College of Liberal Arts, the Merrick School of Business, and the School of Law. The University of Baltimore was founded as a private institution in 1925 and is now part of the University System of Maryland. Total student enrollment is approximately 5,400, and the student-faculty ratio is 16:1.

Applying

Ideal applicants to this program have an undergraduate degree from a regionally accredited college or university with a minimum cumulative grade point average of at least 2.8. An academic background in a field related to criminal justice and successful completion of undergraduate courses in statistics and criminological theory are required for unconditional admission. Applicants must also submit an official transcript from each higher-education institution attended, a statement of personal interest in the program of study, an application, and the appropriate application fee. Applicants may also be asked to submit letters of recommendation and/or a resume.

Correspondence and Information

Office of Graduate Admissions
University of Baltimore
1420 North Charles Street
Baltimore, Maryland 21201-5779
Phone: 410-837-6565
Fax: 410-837-4774
E-mail: gradadmissions@ubalt.edu
Web site: http://www.ubalt.edu/cla

Dr. Heather Pfeifer
Program Director, M.S. in Criminal Justice
Phone: 410-837-5292
E-mail: gradadmissions@ubalt.edu
Web site: http://www.ubalt.edu/criminaljustice

University of Baltimore

THE FACULTY AND THEIR RESEARCH

Kathleen J. Block, Associate Professor; Ph.D., Maryland. Juvenile delinquency, juvenile justice, age and crime, criminal courts.

Mengyan Dai, Assistant Professor; Ph.D., Cincinnati. Policing, international comparative perspectives in criminal justice, quantitative research skills.

Jami Grant, Assistant Professor; Ph.D., Maryland. Crime mapping, hot-spot analysis, gun violence and forensic studies.

Heather Pfeifer, Associate Professor; Ph.D., Maryland. Juvenile delinquency and victimization, juvenile justice, drug trends and policy, victimology, criminological theory.

Jeffrey Ian Ross, Associate Professor; Ph.D., Colorado. Policing, political crime, terrorism, corrections, violent crime, international and comparative perspectives.

Cindy J. Smith, Associate Professor; Ph.D., California, Irvine. Program and policy evaluation, prison work programs, juvenile sex offenders, human trafficking, comparative research methods.

Debra L. Stanley, Professor and Chair; Ph.D., Maryland. Child homicide, domestic violence, substance abuse, victimology, evaluation research.

Benjamin S. Wright, Associate Professor; Ph.D., Florida State. Law enforcement, courts, and the law.

UNIVERSITY OF NEW HAVEN

Henry C. Lee College of Criminal Justice and Forensic Sciences

Programs of Study

The Henry C. Lee College of Criminal Justice and Forensic Sciences provides graduate programs in criminal justice, fire science, forensic science, and national security. These core degree programs also have available specialized areas of study, such as criminalistics, advanced investigations, arson investigation, forensic computer investigation, forensic psychology, victimology, crime analysis, information protection and security, criminal justice management, public safety management, and industrial hygiene. The College provides a broad professional education that incorporates classroom learning with laboratory and field experience. The College attracts students of varied levels of experience, from recent college graduates to seasoned professionals. It also serves professionals seeking programs designed to meet requirements of national and/or regional accreditations and licensures. The Master of Science (M.S.) in national security and public safety and the M.S. in national security with a concentration in information protection and security are offered at the main campus in Connecticut as well as at Crystal City in Arlington, Virginia.

Research Facilities

The Henry C. Lee College of Criminal Justice and Forensic Sciences maintains state-of-the-art laboratories with all the necessary equipment to teach both criminalistics and advanced investigation aspects of forensic science. The University makes highly sophisticated crime and arson software available to its students for crime mapping and analysis, investigations, and computer forensic applications, as well as other tools and standard software packages. Students also have access to high-quality labs and specialized research as well as access to the National Crime Scene Training Center at the Henry C. Lee Institute of Forensic Science and its faculty, collection of papers, and Forensic Science Museum. The University supports LexisNexis on its network, and a wide variety of electronic data systems and research databases are available through the Peterson Library on the campus network.

Financial Aid

Financial aid is available for graduate students through assistantships and loans. The University participates in the Federal Stafford Loan programs.

Cost of Study

Tuition for master's degree students for the 2007–08 academic year was $630 per graduate credit or $1890 for most graduate courses. The one-time-only application fee is $50, and there is a Graduate Student Council fee of $60 each year as well as a technology fee of $20 per term. Laboratory fees vary, depending on course content. All charges and fees are subject to change.

Living and Housing Costs

There is no campus housing for graduate students; however, the Office of Residential Life maintains a partial listing of apartments in the local area at a variety of costs. The greater New Haven area is rich in housing availability because there are so many colleges and universities clustered nearby.

Student Group

There are approximately 310 enrolled graduate students throughout the Henry C. Lee College of Criminal Justice and Forensic Sciences. Many actively participate in a range of professional and social organizations. Students are drawn from across the United States and more than fifty other countries.

Location

The main campus rests on a hilltop in West Haven, less than 3 miles from the heart of New Haven and near the junction of Interstates 95 and 91. West Haven is a shoreline town with convenient access to New York, Boston, and Providence. Rail, bus, and air transportation are all within easy reach.

The University

Founded in 1920, the University of New Haven (UNH) is accredited as a general-purpose institution by the New England Association of Schools and Colleges. Individual programs and departments also take pride in various professional accreditations specific to their disciplines. In order to accommodate working adults, many classes are offered in the evening and typically meet once a week. Some classes also meet in the daytime and on weekends and are delivered using online formats.

The graduate school operates on a trimester schedule, with three courses per term considered full-time enrollment. The entire graduate population comprises approximately 1,760 students matriculated in just under thirty different master's-level programs. A portion of the student body is composed of recent graduates attending UNH on a full-time basis, and some are working professionals with a number of years of experience who attend graduate school on a part-time basis. The University of New Haven encourages and enjoys a diverse population among its entire student body.

Applying

Applicants must hold a baccalaureate degree from an accredited college or university. All applicants must submit the following: a formal application, the nonrefundable $50 application fee, two letters of recommendation, and final, official undergraduate transcripts of all previous college work, sent directly from the issuing institution. International transcripts should be accompanied by an equivalency evaluation from a recognized agency. For students whose native language is not English, a TOEFL score is required (190 on the computer-generated test, 70 on the Internet-based test, or 520 on the paper-based test). GRE scores are required of all applicants to the forensic science criminalistics program. The deadline for application to the M.S. in forensic science program is February 15 for the following September. All other program applications are accepted on a rolling basis. Entrance to the M.S. in forensic science and M.S. in criminal justice degree programs is in September only.

Correspondence and Information

Eloise Gormley
Director of Graduate Admissions
University of New Haven
300 Boston Post Road
West Haven, Connecticut 06516

Phone: 203-932-7133
800-DIAL-UNH Ext. 7133 (toll-free)
Fax: 203-932-7137
E-mail: gradinfo@newhaven.edu
Web site: http://www.newhaven.edu

University of New Haven

THE FACULTY

The University faculty consists of approximately 470 full- and part-time professors. Faculty members teaching in the Henry C. Lee College of Criminal Justice and Forensic Sciences are listed.

James Adcock, Ph.D., South Carolina.
James Cassidy, Ph.D., Hahnemann; J.D., Villanova.
Howard Cohen, Ph.D., Michigan.
Heather Coyle, Ph.D., New Hampshire.
Ernie Dorling, M.P.A., Troy State.
Nelson Dunston, M.S., Maryland.
Mario Gaboury, Ph.D., Penn State; J.D., Georgetown.
Azriel Gorski, Ph.D., Hebrew (Jerusalem).
Howard Harris, Ph.D., Yale; J.D., St. Louis.
Sorin Iliescu, M.S., New Haven.
Thomas Johnson, D.Crim., Berkeley.
Michael Lawlor, J.D., George Washington.
Henry C. Lee, Ph.D., NYU.
Robert Massicotte, M.S., New Haven.
Jim Matschulat, M.B.A., St. John's (New York).
James Monahan, Ph.D., Florida State.
Lynn Monahan, Ph.D., Oregon.
Donna Morris, J.D., Yale.
Fadia Narchet, Ph.D., Florida International.
William Norton, Ph.D., Florida State; J.D., Connecticut.
Martin O'Connor, J.D., Connecticut.
Timothy Palmbach, J.D., Connecticut.
Gerald Robin, Ph.D., Pennsylvania.
Christopher Sedelmaier, Ph.D., Rutgers.
Frederick Smith, Ph.D., Pittsburgh.
William Tafoya, Ph.D., Maryland.
Tracy Tambora, M.S., New Haven.
Michael York, Ph.D., Maryland.

Emeritus Faculty
Brad Garber, Ph.D., Berkeley.
David Maxwell, J.D., Miami (Florida).
L. Craig Parker, Ph.D., SUNY at Buffalo.

Section 19
Economics

This section contains a directory of institutions offering graduate work in economics, followed by in-depth entries submitted by institutions that chose to prepare detailed program descriptions. Additional information about programs listed in the directory but not augmented by an in-depth entry may be obtained by writing directly to the dean of a graduate school or chair of a department at the address given in the directory.

For programs offering related work, see also in this book *Family and Consumer Sciences, Political Science and International Affairs,* and *Public, Regional, and Industrial Affairs.* In the other guides in this series:

Graduate Programs in the Physical Sciences, Mathematics, Agricultural Sciences, the Environment & Natural Resources

See *Agricultural and Food Sciences* and *Mathematical Sciences*

Graduate Programs in Engineering & Applied Sciences

See *Computer Science and Information Technology; Geological, Mineral/Mining, and Petroleum Engineering;* and *Industrial Engineering*

Graduate Programs in Business, Education, Health, Information Studies, Law & Social Work

See *Business Administration and Management*

CONTENTS

Program Directories

Announcements

Close-Ups

See also:

Agricultural Economics and Agribusiness

Alabama Agricultural and Mechanical University, School of Graduate Studies, School of Agricultural and Environmental Sciences, Department of Agribusiness, Huntsville, AL 35811. Offers MS. Part-time programs available. *Faculty:* 1 part-time/adjunct (0 women). *Students:* 4 full-time (1 woman), 4 part-time (3 women); includes 6 minority (all African Americans), 2 international. In 2007, 1 degree awarded. *Degree requirements:* For master's, thesis (for some programs). *Entrance requirements:* For master's, GRE General Test. *Application deadline:* For fall admission, 5/1 priority date for domestic students. Applications are processed on a rolling basis. Application fee: $25. Electronic applications accepted. *Financial support:* In 2007–08, fellowships with tuition reimbursements (averaging $15,000 per year), research assistantships with tuition reimbursements (averaging $10,000 per year) were awarded. Financial award application deadline: 4/1. *Faculty research:* Farm economics. *Unit head:* Dr. Willie J. Cheatham, Chair, 256-372-5410.

Alcorn State University, School of Graduate Studies, School of Agriculture and Applied Science, Alcorn State, MS 39096-7500. Offers agricultural economics (MS Ag); agronomy (MS Ag); animal science (MS Ag). *Degree requirements:* For master's, thesis optional. *Faculty research:* Aquatic systems, dairy herd improvement, fruit production, alternative farming practices.

American University of Beirut, Graduate Programs, Faculty of Agricultural and Food Sciences, Beirut, Lebanon. Offers agricultural economics (MS); animal sciences (MS); ecosystem management (MSES); food technology (MS); irrigation (MS); mechanization (MS); nutrition (MS); plant protection (MS); plant science (MS); poultry science (MS); soils (MS). Part-time programs available. *Faculty:* 21 full-time (5 women), 2 part-time/adjunct (1 woman). *Students:* 15 full-time (12 women), 67 part-time (54 women). Average age 23. 85 applicants, 78% accepted, 22 enrolled. In 2007, 35 degrees awarded. *Degree requirements:* For master's, one foreign language, comprehensive exam, thesis (for some programs). *Entrance requirements:* For master's, letter of recommendation. Additional exam requirements/recommendations for international students: Required—TOEFL (minimum score 600 paper-based; 250 computer-based; 100 iBT), IELTS (minimum score 8). *Application deadline:* For fall admission, 4/30 for domestic and international students; for spring admission, 11/1 for domestic and international students. Application fee: $50. *Expenses:* Tuition: Full-time $9,954; part-time $553 per credit. Tuition and fees vary according to course load and program. *Financial support:* In 2007–08, 39 research assistantships, 32 teaching assistantships with full and partial tuition reimbursements were awarded; career-related internships or fieldwork, institutionally sponsored loans, scholarships/grants, health care benefits, and unspecified assistantships also available. Financial award application deadline: 2/2. *Faculty research:* Sustainable animal systems/agriculture; natural resource management; community nutrition, obesity and food safety; integrated pest management; ecosystem management. Total annual research expenditures: $260,000. *Unit head:* Prof. Nahla Hwalla, Dean, 961-1343002 Ext. 4400, Fax: 961-1744460, E-mail: nahla@aub.edu.lb. *Application contact:* Dr. Salim Kanaan, Director, Admissions Office, 961-1350000 Ext. 2594, Fax: 961-1750775, E-mail: sk00@aub.edu.lb.

Arizona State University at the Polytechnic Campus, Morrison School of Management and Agribusiness, Mesa, AZ 85212. Offers agribusiness (MS). Part-time and evening/weekend programs available. *Faculty:* 20 full-time (2 women). *Students:* 20 full-time (10 women), 17 part-time (6 women); includes 4 minority (2 African Americans, 1 Asian American or Pacific Islander, 1 Hispanic American), 8 international. Average age 34. In 2007, 1 degree awarded. *Degree requirements:* For master's, thesis, oral defense. *Entrance requirements:* For master's, GMAT, GRE General Test, MAT, minimum GPA of 3.0, 3 letters of recommendation, resumé. Additional exam requirements/recommendations for international students: Required—TOEFL (minimum score 550 paper-based; 213 computer-based); Recommended—TWE. *Application deadline:* Applications are processed on a rolling basis. Application fee: $50. Electronic applications accepted. *Expenses:* Tuition, state resident: full-time $4,620. Tuition, nonresident: full-time $16,853. Tuition and fees vary according to course level, course load and program. *Financial support:* In 2007–08, 3 fellowships with partial tuition reimbursements (averaging $18,000 per year), 12 research assistantships with full and partial tuition reimbursements (averaging $7,457 per year) were awarded; teaching assistantships with partial tuition reimbursements, career-related internships or fieldwork, Federal Work-Study, institutionally sponsored loans, scholarships/grants, health care benefits, and tuition waivers (full and partial) also available. Support available to part-time students. Financial award application deadline: 3/1; financial award applicants required to submit CSS PROFILE or FAFSA. *Faculty research:* Agribusiness marketing, management and financial structuring. Total annual research expenditures: $593,727. *Unit head:* Dr. Paul Patterson, Dean, 480-727-1124, Fax: 480-727-1961, E-mail: paul.patterson@asu.edu. *Application contact:* Dr. Troy Schmitz, Associate Professor of Agribusiness, 480-727-1566, Fax: 480-727-1946, E-mail: troy.schmitz@asu.edu.

Auburn University, Graduate School, College of Agriculture, Department of Agricultural Economics and Rural Sociology, Auburn University, AL 36849. Offers agricultural economics (M Ag, MS); applied economics (PhD). Part-time programs available. *Faculty:* 16 full-time (3 women). *Students:* 14 full-time (7 women), 12 part-time (5 women); includes 4 minority (3 African Americans, 1 Asian American or Pacific Islander), 14 international. Average age 31. 13 applicants, 92% accepted, 5 enrolled. In 2007, 8 master's, 4 doctorates awarded. *Degree requirements:* For master's, thesis (for some programs); for doctorate, thesis/dissertation. *Entrance requirements:* For master's and doctorate, GRE General Test. *Application deadline:* For fall admission, 7/7 for domestic students; for spring admission, 11/24 for domestic students. Applications are processed on a rolling basis. Application fee: $25 ($50 for international students). Electronic applications accepted. *Financial support:* Research assistantships, teaching assistantships, Federal Work-Study available. Support available to part-time students. Financial award application deadline: 3/15. *Faculty research:* Farm management, agricultural marketing, production economics, resource economics, agricultural finance. *Unit head:* Dr. Curtis M. Jolly, Chair, 334-844-4800. *Application contact:* Dr. Joe Pittman, Interim Dean of the Graduate School, 334-844-4700.

California Polytechnic State University, San Luis Obispo, College of Agriculture, Food and Environmental Sciences, Department of Agribusiness, San Luis Obispo, CA 93407. Offers MS. Part-time programs available. *Faculty:* 5 full-time (0 women), 3 part-time/adjunct (1 woman). *Students:* 5 full-time (4 women), 1 (woman) part-time; includes 2 minority (1 African American, 1 Hispanic American). 3 applicants, 100% accepted, 2 enrolled. In 2007, 2 degrees awarded. *Degree requirements:* For master's, comprehensive exam, thesis. *Entrance requirements:* For master's, GRE General Test, minimum GPA of 2.75 in last 90 quarter units of course work. Additional exam requirements/recommendations for international students: Required—TOEFL (minimum score 550 paper-based; 213 computer-based), TWE (minimum score 4.5). *Application deadline:* For fall admission, 7/1 for domestic students, 11/30 for international students; for winter admission, 11/1 for domestic students, 6/30 for international students; for spring admission, 2/1 for domestic students. Application fee: $55. *Expenses:* Tuition, nonresident: part-time $226 per unit. Required fees: $1,777 per quarter. *Financial support:* Application deadline: 3/2; *Unit head:* Dr. James Ahern, Graduate Coordinator, 805-756-5030, Fax: 805-756-5040, E-mail: jahern@calpoly.edu.

Colorado State University, Graduate School, College of Agricultural Sciences, Department of Agricultural and Resource Economics, Fort Collins, CO 80523-0015. Offers MS, PhD. *Faculty:* 15 full-time (1 woman), 1 part-time/adjunct (0 women). *Students:* 20 full-time (10 women), 11 part-time (5 women); includes 3 minority (1 American Indian/Alaska Native, 2 Hispanic Americans), 8 international. Average age 29. 38 applicants, 76% accepted, 9 enrolled. In 2007, 2 master's, 2 doctorates awarded. *Degree requirements:* For master's, thesis optional; for doctorate, thesis/dissertation, exams. *Entrance requirements:* For master's and doctorate, GRE General Test, minimum GPA of 3.0. Additional exam requirements/recommendations for international students: Required—TOEFL. *Application deadline:* For fall admission, 2/1 priority date for domestic and international students; for spring admission, 11/1 priority date for domestic and international students. Applications are processed on a rolling basis. Application fee: $50. Electronic applications accepted. *Expenses:* Tuition, state resident: full-time $4,887; part-time $272 per credit. Tuition, nonresident: full-time $16,425; part-time $913 per credit. Required fees: $1,379; $75 per credit. *Financial support:* In 2007–08, 1 fellowship (averaging $51,136 per year), 17 research assistantships with full tuition reimbursements (averaging $11,031 per year), 6 teaching assistantships with full tuition reimbursements (averaging $7,436 per year) were awarded; career-related internships or fieldwork, Federal Work-Study, scholarships/grants, traineeships, and unspecified assistantships also available. Financial award application deadline: 2/15; financial award applicants required to submit FAFSA. *Faculty research:* Agricultural production economics, marketing and agribusiness economics, international development, natural resource economics, environmental economics. Total annual research expenditures: $1.3 million. *Unit head:* Stephen P. Davies, Chair, 970-491-6955, Fax: 970-491-2067, E-mail: stephen.davies@colostate.edu. *Application contact:* Barbara A. Brown, Program Assistant, 970-491-6955, Fax: 970-491-2067, E-mail: barbara.brown@colostate.edu.

Cornell University, Graduate School, Graduate Fields of Agriculture and Life Sciences, Field of Applied Economics and Management, Ithaca, NY 14853-0001. Offers agricultural economics (MPS, MS, PhD), including agricultural finance, applied econometrics and quantitative analysis, economics of development, farm management and production economics (MPS), marketing and food distribution (MPS), public policy analysis (MPS); resource economics (MPS, MS, PhD), including environmental economics, environmental management (MPS), resource economics. *Faculty:* 51 full-time (7 women). *Students:* 76 full-time (30 women); includes 2 minority (both Asian Americans or Pacific Islanders), 53 international. Average age 29. 228 applicants, 34% accepted, 22 enrolled. In 2007, 11 master's, 7 doctorates awarded. Terminal master's awarded for partial completion of doctoral program. *Degree requirements:* For master's, thesis (MS); for doctorate, comprehensive exam, thesis/dissertation. *Entrance requirements:* For master's and doctorate, GRE General Test, 2 letters of recommendation. Additional exam requirements/recommendations for international students: Required—TOEFL (minimum score 550 paper-based; 213 computer-based; 77 iBT). *Application deadline:* For fall admission, 1/15 priority date for domestic students. Application fee: $70. Electronic applications accepted. *Financial support:* In 2007–08, 50 students received support, including 16 fellowships with full tuition reimbursements available, 21 research assistantships with full tuition reimbursements available, 13 teaching assistantships with full tuition reimbursements available; institutionally sponsored loans, scholarships/grants, health care benefits, tuition waivers (full and partial), and unspecified assistantships also available. Financial award applicants required to submit FAFSA. *Faculty research:* Production economics, international economic development and trade, farm management and finance, resource and environmental economics, agricultural marketing and policy. *Unit head:* Director of Graduate Studies, 607-255-8048, Fax: 607-255-9984, E-mail: aegrad@cornell.edu. *Application contact:* Graduate Field Assistant, 607-255-8048, Fax: 607-255-9984, E-mail: aegrad@cornell.edu.

Cornell University, Graduate School, Graduate Fields of Agriculture and Life Sciences, Field of International Agriculture and Rural Development, Ithaca, NY 14853-0001. Offers international agriculture and development (MPS). *Faculty:* 52 full-time (12 women). *Students:* 18 full-time (10 women); includes 3 minority (1 American Indian/Alaska Native, 2 Asian Americans or Pacific Islanders), 6 international. Average age 32. 38 applicants, 84% accepted, 8 enrolled. In 2007, 4 degrees awarded. *Degree requirements:* For master's, project paper. *Entrance requirements:* For master's, GRE General Test (recommended), 2 years of development experience, 2 letters of recommendation. Additional exam requirements/recommendations for international students: Required—TOEFL (minimum score 550 paper-based; 213 computer-based; 77 iBT). *Application deadline:* For fall admission, 3/1 for domestic students. Application fee: $70. Electronic applications accepted. *Financial support:* In 2007–08, 4 students received support, including 3 fellowships with full tuition reimbursements available, 1 teaching assistantship with full tuition reimbursement available; research assistantships with full tuition reimbursements available, institutionally sponsored loans, scholarships/grants, health care benefits, tuition waivers (full and partial), and unspecified assistantships also available. Financial award applicants required to submit FAFSA. *Unit head:* Director of Graduate Studies, 607-255-3037, Fax: 607-255-1005. *Application contact:* Graduate Field Assistant, 607-255-3035, Fax: 607-255-1005, E-mail: mpsiard@cornell.edu.

Delaware Valley College, Program in Food and Agribusiness, Doylestown, PA 18901-2697. Offers MBA. *Faculty:* 2 part-time/adjunct (0 women). *Students:* 4 full-time (2 women), 22 part-time (11 women); includes 1 African American, 1 Asian American or Pacific Islander. 4 applicants, 100% accepted, 4 enrolled. In 2007, 4 degrees awarded. *Entrance requirements:* For master's, GMAT or undergraduate GPA greater than 3.0. Application fee: $50. *Expenses:* Contact institution. *Unit head:* Tom Kennedy, Director, 215-489-2322, E-mail: thomas.kennedy@delval.edu.

Florida Agricultural and Mechanical University, Division of Graduate Studies, Research, and Continuing Education, College of Engineering Science, Technology, and Agriculture, Division of Agricultural Sciences, Tallahassee, FL 32307-3200. Offers agribusiness (MS); animal science (MS); engineering technology (MS); entomology (MS); food science (MS); international programs (MS); plant science (MS). *Degree requirements:* For master's, thesis. *Entrance requirements:* For master's, GRE General Test, minimum GPA of 3.0. Additional exam requirements/recommendations for international students: Required—TOEFL (minimum score 500 paper-based).

Illinois State University, Graduate School, College of Applied Science and Technology, Department of Agriculture, Normal, IL 61790-2200. Offers agribusiness (MS). *Faculty:* 11 full-time (1 woman). *Students:* 12 full-time (7 women), 3 international. 11 applicants, 82% accepted. In 2007, 5 master's awarded. *Degree requirements:* For master's, thesis optional. *Entrance requirements:* For master's, GRE General Test, minimum GPA of 3.0 in last 60 hours. *Application deadline:* Applications are processed on a rolling basis. Application fee: $40. *Expenses:* Tuition, state resident: full-time $3,492; part-time $194 per credit hour. Tuition, nonresident: full-time $7,272; part-time $404 per credit hour. Required fees: $1,024; $57 per credit hour. *Financial support:* In 2007–08, 7 research assistantships (averaging $7,560 per year), 1 teaching assistantship (averaging $13,500 per year) were awarded; tuition waivers (full) and unspecified assistantships also available. Financial award application deadline: 4/1. *Faculty research:* Engineering-economic system models for rural ethanol production facilities, development and evaluation of a propane-fueled, production scale, on-site thermal destruction system C-FAR 2007; field scale evaluation and technology transfer of economically, ecologically systems; sound liquid swine manure treatment and application. Total annual research expenditures: $1.1 million. *Unit head:* Dr. Robert Rhykerd, Chairperson, 309-438-5654.

Instituto Centroamericano de Administración de Empresas, Graduate Programs, La Garita, Costa Rica. Offers agribusiness (MIAM); business administration (EMBA); entrepreneurial economics (MBA); industry and technology (MBA); sustainable development (MBA). *Degree requirements:* For master's, comprehensive exam, essay. *Entrance requirements:* For master's, GMAT or GRE, fluency in Spanish, interview, letters of recommendation, minimum 1 year of work experience. Electronic applications accepted. *Faculty research:* Competitiveness, production.

Iowa State University of Science and Technology, Graduate College, College of Liberal Arts and Sciences, Department of Economics and College of Agriculture, Program in Agricultural Economics, Ames, IA 50011. Offers MS, PhD. *Faculty:* 26 full-time (2 women), 3 part-time/adjunct (all women). *Students:* 44 full-time (12 women), 3 part-time (2 women); includes 1 minority (Asian American or Pacific Islander), 37 international. 65 applicants, 34% accepted, 13 enrolled. In 2007, 3 master's, 2 doctorates awarded. *Degree requirements:* For master's, thesis or alternative; for doctorate, thesis/dissertation. *Entrance requirements:* For master's and doctorate, GRE General Test. Additional exam requirements/recommendations for international students: Required—TOEFL (paper-based 570; computer-based 230; iBT 79) or

IELTS (6.5). *Application deadline:* For fall admission, 1/20 priority date for domestic and international students. Application fee: $30 ($70 for international students). Electronic applications accepted. *Financial support:* In 2007–08, 10 research assistantships with full and partial tuition reimbursements (averaging $21,797 per year), 33 teaching assistantships with full and partial tuition reimbursements (averaging $20,641 per year) were awarded; fellowships, scholarships/grants, health care benefits, and unspecified assistantships also available. *Unit head:* Section Leader, 515-294-2702.

Kansas State University, Graduate School, College of Agriculture, Department of Agricultural Economics, Manhattan, KS 66506. Offers MAB, MS, PhD. Part-time programs available. Postbaccalaureate distance learning degree programs offered (minimal on-campus study). *Faculty:* 23 full-time (1 woman), 2 part-time/adjunct (0 women). *Students:* 44 full-time (20 women), 2 part-time; includes 1 minority (African American), 9 international. Average age 27. 41 applicants, 83% accepted, 9 enrolled. In 2007, 16 master's, 9 doctorates awarded. Terminal master's awarded for partial completion of doctoral program. *Degree requirements:* For master's, thesis or alternative, oral exam; for doctorate, thesis/dissertation, preliminary exams. *Entrance requirements:* For master's and doctorate, GRE General Test. Additional exam requirements/recommendations for international students: Required—TOEFL (minimum score 550 paper-based; 213 computer-based). *Application deadline:* For fall admission, 2/1 priority date for domestic students; for spring admission, 10/1 for domestic students. Applications are processed on a rolling basis. Application fee: $30 ($55 for international students). Electronic applications accepted. *Financial support:* In 2007–08, 25 research assistantships (averaging $14,288 per year), 8 teaching assistantships with partial tuition reimbursements (averaging $8,966 per year) were awarded; Federal Work-Study, institutionally sponsored loans, and scholarships/grants also available. Support available to part-time students. Financial award application deadline: 3/1; financial award applicants required to submit FAFSA. *Faculty research:* Farm management and policy, livestock and grain marketing, agribusiness and cooperative issues, natural resource issues, industrial organization issues. Total annual research expenditures: $1.7 million. *Unit head:* Bryan Schurle, Head, 785-532-4489, Fax: 785-532-6925, E-mail: bschurle@ksu.edu. *Application contact:* Dr. Sean Fox, Director, 785-532-4446, Fax: 785-532-6925, E-mail: seanfox@ksu.edu.

Louisiana State University and Agricultural and Mechanical College, Graduate School, College of Agriculture, Department of Agricultural Economics and Agribusiness, Baton Rouge, LA 70803. Offers MS, PhD. *Faculty:* 19 full-time (0 women). *Students:* 31 full-time (10 women), 4 part-time (3 women); includes 1 Hispanic American, 25 international. Average age 33. 30 applicants, 37% accepted, 4 enrolled. In 2007, 11 degrees awarded. *Degree requirements:* For master's, thesis (for some programs); for doctorate, thesis/dissertation. *Entrance requirements:* For master's and doctorate, GRE General Test, minimum GPA of 3.0. Additional exam requirements/recommendations for international students: Required—TOEFL (minimum score 550 paper-based; 213 computer-based; 79 iBT). *Application deadline:* For fall admission, 1/25 priority date for domestic students, 5/15 for international students; for spring admission, 10/15 for international students. Applications are processed on a rolling basis. Application fee: $25. Electronic applications accepted. *Financial support:* In 2007–08, 32 students received support, including 1 fellowship (averaging $11,804 per year), 28 research assistantships with partial tuition reimbursements available (averaging $14,310 per year); teaching assistantships with partial tuition reimbursements available, Federal Work-Study, institutionally sponsored loans, scholarships/grants, health care benefits, tuition waivers (full and partial), and unspecified assistantships also available. Financial award applicants required to submit FAFSA. *Faculty research:* Natural and environmental economics, agribusiness, marketing, production economics, community economics, rural development. Total annual research expenditures: $4,750. *Unit head:* Dr. Gail L. Cramer, Head, 225-578-3282, Fax: 225-578-2716, E-mail: gcramer@agctr.lsu.edu. *Application contact:* Dr. Richard Kaemierczak, Graduate Coordinator, 225-578-2712, Fax: 225-578-2716, E-mail: rkazmierczak@agcenter.lsu.edu.

McGill University, Faculty of Graduate and Postdoctoral Studies, Faculty of Agricultural and Environmental Sciences, Department of Agricultural Economics, Montréal, QC H3A 2T5, Canada. Offers M Sc. *Students:* 16 full-time (10 women), 1 (woman) part-time. 11 applicants, 64% accepted, 3 enrolled. In 2007, 6 degrees awarded.

Michigan State University, The Graduate School, College of Agriculture and Natural Resources, Department of Agricultural, Food, and Resource Economics, East Lansing, MI 48824. Offers agricultural economics (MS, PhD). *Entrance requirements:* Additional exam requirements/recommendations for international students: Required—TOEFL (minimum score 550 paper-based; 213 computer-based), Michigan State University ELT (85), Michigan ELAB (83). Electronic applications accepted. *Expenses:* Tuition, state resident: part-time $379 per credit hour. Tuition, nonresident: part-time $800 per credit hour. Tuition and fees vary according to program.

Mississippi State University, College of Agriculture and Life Sciences, Department of Agricultural Economics, Mississippi State, MS 39762. Offers agribusiness management (MABM); agricultural economics (PhD). Part-time programs available. *Faculty:* 18 full-time (1 woman), 1 part-time/adjunct (0 women). *Students:* 15 full-time (4 women), 1 (woman) part-time; includes 1 minority (African American) Average age 23. 8 applicants, 50% accepted, 4 enrolled. In 2007, 7 degrees awarded. *Degree requirements:* For master's, thesis (for some programs), comprehensive oral or written exam, thesis defense; for doctorate, thesis/dissertation, qualifying written exam, research exam. *Entrance requirements:* For master's, GRE, GMAT, minimum GPA of 3.0; for doctorate, GRE, minimum GPA of 3.0. Additional exam requirements/recommendations for international students: Required—TOEFL. *Application deadline:* For fall admission, 7/1 for domestic students; for spring admission, 11/1 for domestic students. Applications are processed on a rolling basis. Application fee: $30. Electronic applications accepted. *Expenses:* Tuition, state resident: full-time $4,978; part-time $274 per hour. Tuition, nonresident: full-time $11,469; part-time $635 per hour. *Financial support:* Research assistantships with full tuition reimbursements, teaching assistantships with full tuition reimbursements, career-related internships or fieldwork, Federal Work-Study, institutionally sponsored loans, and unspecified assistantships available. Financial award application deadline: 4/1; financial award applicants required to submit FAFSA. *Faculty research:* Production economics, policy, resource economics, international trade, agribusiness management. *Unit head:* Dr. Steven C. Turner, Head, 662-325-2049, Fax: 662-325-8777, E-mail: turner@aegcon.msstate.edu. *Application contact:* Dr. William A. Person, Interim Associate Vice President for Academic Affairs/Interim Dean of Graduate Studies, 662-325-7400, Fax: 662-325-1967, E-mail: grad@grad.msstate.edu.

Montana State University, College of Graduate Studies, College of Agriculture, Department of Agricultural Economics and Economics, Bozeman, MT 59717. Offers applied economics (MS). Part-time programs available. *Faculty:* 17 full-time (2 women), 6 part-time/adjunct (2 women). *Students:* 13 full-time (5 women), 8 part-time (1 woman), 1 international. Average age 24. 20 applicants, 65% accepted, 7 enrolled. In 2007, 3 degrees awarded. *Degree requirements:* For master's, comprehensive exam. *Entrance requirements:* For master's, GRE General Test. Additional exam requirements/recommendations for international students: Required—TOEFL (minimum score 550 paper-based; 213 computer-based). *Application deadline:* For fall admission, 7/15 priority date for domestic students, 5/15 priority date for international students; for spring admission, 12/1 priority date for domestic students, 10/1 priority date for international students. Applications are processed on a rolling basis. Application fee: $30. Electronic applications accepted. *Expenses:* Tuition, state resident: full-time $5,176. Tuition, nonresident: full-time $13,070. *Financial support:* In 2007–08, 4 research assistantships with partial tuition reimbursements were awarded; teaching assistantships with partial tuition reimbursements, unspecified assistantships also available. Financial award application deadline: 3/1; financial award applicants required to submit FAFSA. *Faculty research:* Agricultural production, agricultural marketing/finance, governance (private and public), natural resource management. Total annual research expenditures: $1.3 million. *Unit head:* Myles Watts, Co-Interim Head, 406-994-3701, Fax: 406-994-4838, E-mail: agecon@montana.edu.

New Mexico State University, Graduate School, College of Agriculture and Home Economics, Department of Agricultural Economics and Agricultural Business, Las Cruces, NM 88003-8001. Offers agribusiness (M Ag, MBA); agricultural economics (MS); economics (MA). Part-time programs available. *Faculty:* 10 full-time (3 women), 1 part-time/adjunct (0 women). *Students:* 19 full-time (8 women), 4 part-time (2 women); includes 1 African American, 13 international. Average age 27. 10 applicants, 90% accepted, 4 enrolled. In 2007, 13 degrees awarded. *Degree requirements:* For master's, thesis (for some programs). *Entrance requirements:* For master's, previous course work in intermediate microeconomics, intermediate macroeconomics, college-level calculus, statistics. Additional exam requirements/recommendations for international students: Required—TOEFL. *Application deadline:* For fall admission, 7/1 priority date for domestic and international students; for spring admission, 11/1 priority date for domestic and international students. Applications are processed on a rolling basis. Application fee: $30 ($50 for international students). Electronic applications accepted. *Expenses:* Tuition, state resident: full-time $3,602; part-time $199 per credit. Tuition, nonresident: full-time $13,380; part-time $607 per credit. Required fees: $1,178. *Financial support:* In 2007–08, 3 fellowships, 15 research assistantships, 2 teaching assistantships were awarded; career-related internships or fieldwork and health care benefits also available. Financial award application deadline: 3/1. *Faculty research:* Natural resource policy, production economics and farm/ranch management, agribusiness and marketing, international marketing and trade, agricultural risk management. *Unit head:* Dr. Octavio A. Ramirez, Head, 575-646-3215, Fax: 575-646-3808, E-mail: oramirez@nmsu.edu. *Application contact:* Dr. Allen Torell, Professor, 575-646-4732, Fax: 575-646-3808, E-mail: atorell@nmsu.edu.

North Carolina Agricultural and Technical State University, Graduate School, School of Agriculture and Environmental and Allied Sciences, Department of Agribusiness, Applied Economics, and Agriscience Education, Greensboro, NC 27411. Offers agricultural economics (MS); agricultural education (MS). *Accreditation:* NCATE. Part-time and evening/weekend programs available. *Degree requirements:* For master's, comprehensive exam, thesis or alternative, qualifying exam. *Entrance requirements:* For master's, GRE General Test, minimum GPA of 3.0. *Faculty research:* Aid for small farmers, agricultural technology resources, labor force mobility, agrology.

North Carolina State University, Graduate School, College of Agriculture and Life Sciences, Program in Agricultural and Resource Economics, Raleigh, NC 27695. Offers MS. Part-time programs available. *Degree requirements:* For master's, thesis. *Entrance requirements:* For master's, GRE General Test (financial award applicants). Additional exam requirements/recommendations for international students: Required—TOEFL. Electronic applications accepted. *Faculty research:* Resource economics, international economics, labor economics, econometrics, environmental economics.

North Dakota State University, College of Graduate and Interdisciplinary Studies, College of Agriculture, Food Systems, and Natural Resources, Department of Agribusiness and Applied Economics, Fargo, ND 58105. Offers agribusiness and applied economics (MS); international agribusiness (MS); natural resource management (MS). Part-time programs available. *Faculty:* 16 full-time (3 women), 5 part-time/adjunct (1 woman). *Students:* 25 full-time (7 women), 2 part-time (1 woman). Average age 24. 28 applicants, 68% accepted, 12 enrolled. In 2007, 13 degrees awarded. *Degree requirements:* For master's, thesis. *Entrance requirements:* For master's, minimum GPA of 3.0. Additional exam requirements/recommendations for international students: Required—TOEFL (minimum score 525 paper-based; 225 computer-based; 71 iBT). *Application deadline:* For fall admission, 2/1 priority date for domestic students, 3/1 priority date for international students. Applications are processed on a rolling basis. Application fee: $45 ($60 for international students). Electronic applications accepted. *Expenses:* Tuition, state resident: full-time $5,376; part-time $224 per credit. Tuition, nonresident: full-time $14,354; part-time $598 per credit. Required fees: $962; $40 per credit. Part-time tuition and fees vary according to course load and reciprocity agreements. *Financial support:* In 2007–08, 8 research assistantships with tuition reimbursements (averaging $14,520 per year) were awarded; Federal Work-Study and institutionally sponsored loans also available. Financial award application deadline: 4/15. *Faculty research:* Agribusiness, transportation, marketing, microeconomics, trade. Total annual research expenditures: $1 million. *Unit head:* Dr. Thomas I. Wahl, Chair, 701-231-7470, Fax: 701-231-7400.

Northwest Missouri State University, Graduate School, Melvin and Valorie Booth College of Business and Professional Studies, Department of Agriculture, Program in Agricultural Economics, Maryville, MO 64468-6001. Offers MBA. *Faculty:* 6 full-time (1 woman). *Students:* 2 full-time (1 woman). 3 applicants, 67% accepted, 1 enrolled. In 2007, 1 degree awarded. *Degree requirements:* For master's, comprehensive exam. *Entrance requirements:* For master's, GMAT, minimum GPA of 2.5. Additional exam requirements/recommendations for international students: Required—TOEFL (minimum score 550 paper-based; 213 computer-based). *Application deadline:* For fall admission, 7/1 for domestic and international students; for spring admission, 12/1 for domestic students, 11/15 for international students. Applications are processed on a rolling basis. Application fee: $0 ($50 for international students). *Financial support:* In 2007–08, research assistantships with full tuition reimbursements (averaging $6,000 per year), teaching assistantships with full tuition reimbursements (averaging $6,000 per year) were awarded. Financial award application deadline: 3/1; financial award applicants required to submit FAFSA. *Application contact:* Dr. Frances Shipley, Dean of Graduate School, 660-562-1145, Fax: 660-562-1096, E-mail: gradsch@nwmissouri.edu.

The Ohio State University, Graduate School, College of Food, Agricultural, and Environmental Sciences, Department of Agricultural, Environmental, and Development Economics, Columbus, OH 43210. Offers agricultural economics and rural sociology (MS, PhD). *Faculty:* 32. *Students:* 67 full-time (32 women), 5 part-time (1 woman); includes 3 minority (1 African American, 2 Asian Americans or Pacific Islanders), 39 international. Average age 28. In 2007, 12 master's, 9 doctorates awarded. *Degree requirements:* For master's, thesis optional; for doctorate, thesis/dissertation. *Entrance requirements:* For master's and doctorate, GRE General Test. Additional exam requirements/recommendations for international students: Required—TOEFL (paper-based 550; computer-based 213) or IELTS (7) or Michigan English Language Assessment Battery (92). *Application deadline:* For fall admission, 8/15 priority date for domestic students, 7/1 priority date for international students; for winter admission, 12/1 priority date for domestic students, 11/1 priority date for international students; for spring admission, 3/1 priority date for domestic students, 2/1 priority date for international students. Applications are processed on a rolling basis. Application fee: $40 ($50 for international students). Electronic applications accepted. *Financial support:* Fellowships, research assistantships, teaching assistantships, Federal Work-Study and institutionally sponsored loans available. Support available to part-time students. *Unit head:* Stan Thompson, Graduate Studies Committee Chair, 614-292-7911, Fax: 614-292-4749, E-mail: thompson.51@osu.edu. *Application contact:* Graduate Admissions, 614-292-9444, Fax: 614-292-3895, E-mail: domestic.grad@osu.edu.

Oklahoma State University, College of Agricultural Science and Natural Resources, Department of Agricultural Economics, Stillwater, OK 74078. Offers M Ag, MS, PhD. *Faculty:* 32 full-time (7 women), 1 part-time/adjunct (0 women). *Students:* 51 full-time (19 women), 16 part-time (4 women); includes 7 minority (1 African American, 3 American Indian/Alaska Native, 1 Asian American or Pacific Islander, 2 Hispanic Americans), 34 international. Average age 29. 61 applicants, 66% accepted, 19 enrolled. In 2007, 11 master's, 6 doctorates awarded. *Degree requirements:* For master's, thesis, thesis or report, oral exam; for doctorate, comprehensive exam, thesis/dissertation. *Entrance requirements:* For master's and doctorate, GRE or GMAT. Additional exam requirements/recommendations for international students: Required—TOEFL. *Application deadline:* For fall admission, 3/1 priority date for international students; for spring admission, 8/1 priority date for international students. Applications are processed on a rolling basis. Application fee: $40 ($75 for international students). Electronic applications accepted. *Expenses:* Tuition, state resident: full-time $4,993; part-time $148 per credit hour. Tuition, nonresident: full-time $14,755; part-time $555 per credit hour. Tuition and fees vary according to program. *Financial support:* In 2007–08, 36 research assistantships (averaging $14,614 per year), 7 teaching assistantships (averaging $18,007 per year) were awarded; career-related internships or fieldwork, Federal Work-Study, scholarships/grants, health care benefits, tuition waivers (partial), and unspecified assistantships also available. Support available to part-time

Agricultural Economics and Agribusiness

Oklahoma State University (continued)
students. Financial award application deadline: 3/1; financial award applicants required to submit FAFSA. *Faculty research:* Marketing and agribusiness, production and farm management, policy and natural resources, community and rural development, international trade and development. *Unit head:* Dr. Mike Woods, Head, 405-744-6161, Fax: 405-744-8210.

Oregon State University, Graduate School, College of Agricultural Sciences, Department of Agricultural and Resource Economics, Corvallis, OR 97331. Offers agricultural and resource economics (M Agr, MAIS, MS, PhD); economics (MS, PhD). MS and PhD in economics offered through the University Graduate Faculty of Economics. Part-time programs available. *Faculty:* 11 full-time (2 women), 2 part-time/adjunct (both women). *Students:* 31 full-time (12 women), 2 part-time (1 woman); includes 1 minority (American Indian/Alaska Native), 16 international. Average age 29. In 2007, 3 master's, 8 doctorates awarded. Terminal master's awarded for partial completion of doctoral program. *Degree requirements:* For master's, thesis (for some programs); for doctorate, thesis/dissertation. *Entrance requirements:* For master's and doctorate, GRE General Test, minimum GPA of 3.0 in last 90 hours. Additional exam requirements/recommendations for international students: Required—TOEFL. *Application deadline:* For fall admission, 3/1 for domestic students. Applications are processed on a rolling basis. Application fee: $50. *Expenses:* Tuition, state resident: full-time $9,126; part-time $338 per credit. Tuition, nonresident: full-time $14,796; part-time $548 per credit. Required fees: $1,447. *Financial support:* Fellowships, research assistantships, teaching assistantships, career-related internships or fieldwork, Federal Work-Study, and institutionally sponsored loans available. Support available to part-time students. Financial award application deadline: 2/1. *Faculty research:* Marine economics, environmental economics, effects of global climate change on agriculture, efficiency of agricultural markets, analysis of aquaculture development. *Unit head:* Dr. Gregory M. Perry, Department Head, 541-737-2942, Fax: 541-737-2563. *Application contact:* Kathy Carpenter, Administrative Assistant, 541-737-1398, Fax: 541-737-1441, E-mail: kathy.carpenter@orst.edu.

Penn State University Park, Graduate School, College of Agricultural Sciences, Department of Agricultural Economics and Rural Sociology, State College, University Park, PA 16802-1503. Offers agricultural, environmental and regional economics (M Agr, MS, PhD); rural sociology (M Agr, MS, PhD). *Expenses:* Tuition, state resident: full-time $14,738; part-time $614 per credit. Tuition, nonresident: full-time $26,050; part-time $1,085 per credit. Tuition and fees vary according to course load, program and student level. *Unit head:* Dr. Stephen M. Smith, Head, 814-865-5461, Fax: 814-865-3746, E-mail: smsmith@psu.edu.

Prairie View A&M University, College of Agriculture and Human Sciences, Prairie View, TX 77446-0519. Offers agricultural economics (MS); animal sciences (MS); interdisciplinary human sciences (MS); soil science (MS). Part-time and evening/weekend programs available. *Faculty:* 8 full-time (4 women), 9 part-time/adjunct (3 women). *Students:* 36 full-time (29 women), 62 part-time (51 women); includes 89 minority (86 African Americans, 1 American Indian/Alaska Native, 2 Hispanic Americans). Average age 33. 147 applicants, 100% accepted. In 2007, 30 degrees awarded. *Degree requirements:* For master's, comprehensive exam, thesis (for some programs), field placement. *Entrance requirements:* For master's, GRE General Test, minimum GPA of 2.45. Additional exam requirements/recommendations for international students: Required—TOEFL (minimum score 550 paper-based). *Application deadline:* For fall admission, 6/1 for domestic and international students; for spring admission, 10/1 for domestic and international students. Applications are processed on a rolling basis. Application fee: $50. *Financial support:* In 2007–08, 57 students received support, including 8 fellowships with tuition reimbursements available (averaging $12,000 per year), 10 research assistantships with tuition reimbursements available (averaging $15,000 per year); career-related internships or fieldwork, Federal Work-Study, institutionally sponsored loans, scholarships/grants, tuition waivers (partial), and unspecified assistantships also available. Support available to part-time students. Financial award application deadline: 4/1; financial award applicants required to submit FAFSA. *Faculty research:* Domestic violence prevention, water quality, food growth regulators, wetland dynamics, biochemistry, poultry disaster, obesity and nutrition, family therapy. Total annual research expenditures: $4 million. *Application contact:* Dr. Richard W. Griffin, Interim Department Head, 936-261-2520, Fax: 936-261-5148, E-mail: rwgriffin@pvanu.edu.

Purdue University, Graduate School, College of Agriculture, Department of Agricultural Economics, West Lafayette, IN 47907. Offers agricultural economics (MS, PhD); food and agricultural business (EMBA). Part-time programs available. Terminal master's awarded for partial completion of doctoral program. *Degree requirements:* For master's, thesis (for some programs); for doctorate, thesis/dissertation. *Entrance requirements:* For master's and doctorate, GRE General Test. Additional exam requirements/recommendations for international students: Required—TOEFL, TWE (minimum score 4). Electronic applications accepted. *Faculty research:* Marketing, international trade, policy and development, production, resources.

Rutgers, The State University of New Jersey, New Brunswick, Graduate School, Program in Food and Business Economics, New Brunswick, NJ 08901-1281. Offers MS. Part-time programs available. *Degree requirements:* For master's, comprehensive exam, thesis or alternative. *Entrance requirements:* Additional exam requirements/recommendations for international students: Required—TOEFL. Electronic applications accepted. *Faculty research:* Science policy, land use, nutrition policy, food industry, international development.

South Carolina State University, School of Graduate Studies, Department of Accounting, Agribusiness and Economics, Orangeburg, SC 29117-0001. Offers agribusiness (MS); agribusiness and entrepreneurship (MBA). Part-time and evening/weekend programs available. *Faculty:* 3 full-time (1 woman). *Students:* 3 full-time (all women), 3 part-time (1 woman); includes 5 minority (all African Americans) Average age 27. 9 applicants, 33% accepted, 1 enrolled. In 2007, 1 degree awarded. *Degree requirements:* For master's, thesis optional, departmental qualifying exam. *Entrance requirements:* For master's, GMAT or GRE, minimum GPA of 2.8. *Application deadline:* For fall admission, 6/15 for domestic and international students; for spring admission, 11/1 for domestic and international students. Applications are processed on a rolling basis. Application fee: $25. Electronic applications accepted. *Financial support:* Fellowships, research assistantships, career-related internships or fieldwork, Federal Work-Study, and institutionally sponsored loans available. Financial award application deadline: 6/1. *Faculty research:* Small farm income and profitability, agricultural credit, aquaculture, low-input sustainable agriculture, rural development. *Unit head:* Dr. Haile M. Gebre-Selassie, Interim Chair, 803-536-8070, Fax: 803-533-3639, E-mail: selassie@scsu.edu. *Application contact:* Annette Hazzard-Jones, Program Coordinator II, 803-536-8809, Fax: 803-536-8812, E-mail: zs_ahazzard@scsu.edu.

Southern Illinois University Carbondale, Graduate School, College of Agriculture, Department of Agribusiness Economics, Carbondale, IL 62901-4701. Offers MS, MBA/MS. Part-time programs available. *Faculty:* 6 full-time (0 women). *Students:* 10 full-time (5 women), 2 part-time; includes 2 minority (both African Americans), 3 international. 6 applicants, 67% accepted, 2 enrolled. In 2007, 5 degrees awarded. *Degree requirements:* For master's, thesis. *Entrance requirements:* For master's, minimum GPA of 2.7. Additional exam requirements/recommendations for international students: Required—TOEFL. *Application deadline:* For fall admission, 7/1 priority date for domestic students. Applications are processed on a rolling basis. Application fee: $0. *Financial support:* In 2007–08, 12 research assistantships with tuition reimbursements, 5 teaching assistantships with tuition reimbursements were awarded; fellowships with tuition reimbursements, Federal Work-Study, institutionally sponsored loans, and tuition waivers (full) also available. Support available to part-time students. Financial award application deadline: 3/15. *Faculty research:* Agricultural finance and credit, agribusiness management, resource use, rural area economic development, marketing and price analysis. *Unit head:* Steven Kraft, Chairperson, 618-453-2421, E-mail: sekraft@siu.edu. *Application contact:* Nancy McCalla, Administrative Clerk, 618-453-2421, Fax: 618-453-1708, E-mail: monicar@siu.edu.

Texas A&M University, College of Agriculture and Life Sciences, Department of Agricultural Economics, College Station, TX 77843. Offers MAB, MS, PhD. Part-time programs available. *Faculty:* 25. *Students:* 99 full-time (34 women), 18 part-time (3 women); includes 6 minority (2 African Americans, 4 Hispanic Americans), 67 international. Average age 29. 76 applicants, 86% accepted, 30 enrolled. In 2007, 16 master's, 7 doctorates awarded. Terminal master's awarded for partial completion of doctoral program. *Median time to degree:* Of those who began their doctoral program in fall 1999, 100% received their degree in 8 years or less. *Degree requirements:* For master's, comprehensive exam (for some programs), thesis (for some programs); for doctorate, comprehensive exam, thesis/dissertation. *Entrance requirements:* For master's and doctorate, GRE General Test. Additional exam requirements/recommendations for international students: Required—TOEFL. *Application deadline:* For fall admission, 3/1 for domestic students; for spring admission, 8/1 for domestic students. Applications are processed on a rolling basis. Application fee: $50 ($75 for international students). Electronic applications accepted. *Expenses:* Tuition, state resident: full-time $6,129. Tuition, nonresident: full-time $11,689. Tuition and fees vary according to course load. *Financial support:* Fellowships, research assistantships, teaching assistantships, career-related internships or fieldwork, Federal Work-Study, institutionally sponsored loans, and unspecified assistantships available. Financial award application deadline: 3/1; financial award applicants required to submit FAFSA. *Faculty research:* Production economics, agricultural finance, resources, marketing and policy, agribusiness. *Unit head:* A. Gene Nelson, Head, 979-845-2116, Fax: 979-862-1563. *Application contact:* Vicki L. Heard, Graduate Admissions Supervisor, 979-845-5222, Fax: 979-862-1563, E-mail: vheard@tamu.edu.

Texas A&M University–Kingsville, College of Graduate Studies, College of Agriculture and Home Economics, Program in Agribusiness, Kingsville, TX 78363. Offers MS. *Degree requirements:* For master's, comprehensive exam, thesis or alternative. *Entrance requirements:* For master's, GRE General Test, minimum GPA of 3.0. Additional exam requirements/recommendations for international students: Required—TOEFL.

Texas Tech University, Graduate School, College of Agricultural Sciences and Natural Resources, Department of Agricultural and Applied Economics, Lubbock, TX 79409. Offers agribusiness (MAB); agricultural and applied economics (MS, PhD); JD/MS. Part-time programs available. *Faculty:* 11 full-time (0 women). *Students:* 24 full-time (11 women), 3 part-time; includes 5 minority (1 African American, 2 Asian Americans or Pacific Islanders, 2 Hispanic Americans), 9 international. Average age 30. 20 applicants, 75% accepted, 8 enrolled. In 2007, 5 master's, 2 doctorates awarded. *Degree requirements:* For master's, thesis or alternative; for doctorate, thesis/dissertation. *Entrance requirements:* For master's and doctorate, GRE General Test. Additional exam requirements/recommendations for international students: Required—TOEFL (minimum score 550 paper-based; 213 computer-based). *Application deadline:* For fall admission, 3/1 priority date for international students; for spring admission, 11/1 priority date for international students. Applications are processed on a rolling basis. Application fee: $50 ($60 for international students). Electronic applications accepted. *Expenses:* Tuition, state resident: part-time $373 per credit hour. Tuition, nonresident: part-time $651 per credit hour. Tuition and fees vary according to program. *Financial support:* In 2007–08, 24 students received support, including 19 research assistantships with partial tuition reimbursements available (averaging $13,275 per year), 1 teaching assistantship with partial tuition reimbursement available (averaging $12,000 per year); Federal Work-Study and institutionally sponsored loans also available. Support available to part-time students. Financial award application deadline: 4/15; financial award applicants required to submit FAFSA. *Faculty research:* Economics of the U.S. cotton and textile industries, natural resource management in semi-arid climates, commodity policy analysis, international trade in agricultural products, agribusiness analysis. Total annual research expenditures: $1.3 million. *Unit head:* Dr. Eduardo Segarra, Chair, 806-742-2821, Fax: 806-742-1099, E-mail: eduardo.segarra@ttu.edu. *Application contact:* Dr. Tom Knight, Graduate Adviser, 806-742-2821, Fax: 806-742-1099, E-mail: tom.knight@ttu.edu.

Texas Tech University, Jerry S. Rawls College of Business Administration, Programs in Business Administration, Lubbock, TX 79409. Offers agricultural business (MBA); entrepreneurship (MBA); finance (MBA); general business (MBA); health organization management (MBA); international business (MBA); management and leadership skills (MBA); management information systems (MBA); marketing (MBA); statistics (MBA); JD/MBA; MBA/M Arch; MBA/MA; MBA/MD; MBA/MS. Part-time and evening/weekend programs available. *Faculty:* 4 full-time (0 women), 1 part-time/adjunct (0 women). *Students:* 68 full-time (20 women), 367 part-time (128 women); includes 73 minority (9 African Americans, 5 American Indian/Alaska Native, 17 Asian Americans or Pacific Islanders, 42 Hispanic Americans), 36 international. Average age 25. 363 applicants, 74% accepted, 225 enrolled. In 2007, 216 degrees awarded. *Degree requirements:* For master's, capstone course. *Entrance requirements:* For master's, GMAT, holistic review of academic credentials. Additional exam requirements/recommendations for international students: Required—TOEFL (minimum score 550 paper-based; 213 computer-based; 79 iBT). *Application deadline:* For fall admission, 7/1 priority date for domestic students, 3/1 priority date for international students; for spring admission, 11/1 priority date for domestic students, 9/1 priority date for international students. Applications are processed on a rolling basis. Application fee: $50 ($60 for international students). Electronic applications accepted. *Expenses:* Tuition, state resident: part-time $373 per credit hour. Tuition, nonresident: part-time $651 per credit hour. Tuition and fees vary according to program. *Financial support:* In 2007–08, 10 research assistantships (averaging $8,000 per year) were awarded; teaching assistantships, career-related internships or fieldwork, Federal Work-Study, scholarships/grants, health care benefits, and unspecified assistantships also available. Support available to part-time students. Financial award applicants required to submit FAFSA. *Unit head:* Dr. W. Jay Conover, Director, 806-742-1546, Fax: 806-742-3958, E-mail: jay.conover@ttu.edu. *Application contact:* Cynthia D. Barnes, Director, Graduate Services Center, 806-742-3184, Fax: 806-742-3958, E-mail: ba_grad@ttu.edu.

Tropical Agriculture Research and Higher Education Center, Graduate School, Turrialba, Costa Rica. Offers agribusiness (MS); agroforestry systems (PhD); environmental socioeconomics (MS); forestry in tropical and subtropical zones (PhD); integrated watershed management (MS); management and conservation of tropical rainforests and biodiversity (MS); organic farming (MS); tropical agriculture (PhD); tropical agroforestry (MS). *Entrance requirements:* For master's, GRE, 2 years of related professional experience, letters of recommendation; for doctorate, GRE, 4 letters of recommendation, letter of support from employing organization, master's degree in agronomy, biological sciences, forestry, natural resources or related field. Additional exam requirements/recommendations for international students: Required—TOEFL (minimum score 550 paper-based; 213 computer-based). Electronic applications accepted. *Faculty research:* Biodiversity in fragmented landscapes, ecosystem management, integrated pest management, environmental livestock production, biotechnology carbon balances in diverse land uses.

Tuskegee University, Graduate Programs, College of Agricultural, Environmental and Natural Sciences, Department of Agricultural Sciences, Program in Agricultural and Resource Economics, Tuskegee, AL 36088. Offers MS. *Faculty:* 13 full-time (1 woman), 2 part-time/adjunct (1 woman). *Students:* 9 full-time (6 women), 3 part-time (1 woman); includes 8 minority (all African Americans), 4 international. Average age 32. In 2007, 3 degrees awarded. *Degree requirements:* For master's, thesis. *Entrance requirements:* For master's, GRE General Test. Additional exam requirements/recommendations for international students: Required—TOEFL (minimum score 500 paper-based; 173 computer-based). *Application deadline:* For fall admission, 7/15 for domestic students. Applications are processed on a rolling basis. Application fee: $25 ($35 for international students). *Expenses:* Tuition: Full-time $13,520; part-time $810 per credit. Required fees: $720; $460 per term. *Financial support:* Application deadline: 4/15. *Unit head:* Dr. P. K. Biswas, Head, Department of Agricultural Sciences, 334-727-8446.

Université Laval, Faculty of Agricultural and Food Sciences, Department of Agricultural Economics and Consumer Sciences, Program in Agricultural Economics, Québec, QC G1K 7P4, Canada. Offers M Sc. Part-time programs available. *Degree requirements:* For master's, thesis (for some programs). *Entrance requirements:* For master's, knowledge of French. Electronic applications accepted.

University of Alberta, Faculty of Graduate Studies and Research, Department of Rural Economy, Edmonton, AB T6G 2E1, Canada. Offers agricultural economics (M Ag, M Sc, PhD); forest economics (M Ag, M Sc, PhD); rural sociology (M Ag, M Sc); MBA/M Ag. Part-time programs available. *Degree requirements:* For doctorate, thesis/dissertation. *Entrance requirements:* Additional exam requirements/recommendations for international students: Required—TOEFL. *Faculty research:* Agroforestry, development, extension education, marketing and trade, natural resources and environment, policy, production economics.

The University of Arizona, Graduate College, College of Agriculture and Life Sciences, Department of Agricultural and Resource Economics, Tucson, AZ 85721. Offers MS. *Faculty:* 11. *Students:* Average age 27. 24 applicants, 54% accepted, 11 enrolled. In 2007, 9 degrees awarded. *Degree requirements:* For master's, thesis or alternative. *Entrance requirements:* For master's, GRE General Test, 3 letters of recommendation, minimum GPA of 3.0, statement of purpose. Additional exam requirements/recommendations for international students: Required—TOEFL. *Application deadline:* For fall admission, 2/1 for domestic and international students; for spring admission, 10/1 for domestic students, 6/1 for international students. Applications are processed on a rolling basis. Application fee: $50. *Financial support:* Research assistantships, teaching assistantships, institutionally sponsored loans and tuition waivers (partial) available. Financial award application deadline: 3/1. *Faculty research:* Natural resources, international development trade, production and marketing, agricultural policy, rural development. Total annual research expenditures: $429,155. *Unit head:* Dr. Gary D. Thompson, Head, 520-621-6249, E-mail: garyt@ag.arizona.edu. *Application contact:* Nancy Smith, Graduate Coordinator, 520-621-2421, E-mail: garec@ag.arizona.edu.

University of Arkansas, Graduate School, Dale Bumpers College of Agricultural, Food and Life Sciences, Department of Agricultural Economics, Fayetteville, AR 72701-1201. Offers MS. *Students:* 15 full-time (9 women), 9 part-time (3 women); includes 8 minority (7 African Americans, 1 Hispanic American), 8 international. In 2007, 13 degrees awarded. *Degree requirements:* For master's, thesis optional. Application fee: $40 ($50 for international students). *Financial support:* In 2007–08, 2 fellowships with tuition reimbursements, 6 research assistantships, 1 teaching assistantship were awarded; career-related internships or fieldwork and Federal Work-Study also available. Support available to part-time students. Financial award application deadline: 4/1; financial award applicants required to submit FAFSA. *Unit head:* Dr. Bruce Ahrendsen, Chair, 479-575-2323, E-mail: ahrend@uark.edu. *Application contact:* Dr. Lucas Parsch, Graduate Coordinator, 479-575-2323, E-mail: lparsch@uark.edu.

The University of British Columbia, Faculty of Graduate Studies, Faculty of Land and Food Systems, Agricultural Economics Program, Vancouver, BC V6T 1Z1, Canada. Offers M Sc. Part-time programs available. *Faculty:* 4 full-time (0 women), 3 part-time/adjunct (1 woman). *Students:* 15 full-time (8 women); includes 2 African Americans, 7 Asian Americans or Pacific Islanders, 1 Hispanic American. Average age 31. 8 applicants, 75% accepted, 3 enrolled. In 2007, 3 degrees awarded. *Degree requirements:* For master's, thesis. *Entrance requirements:* Additional exam requirements/recommendations for international students: Required—TOEFL (minimum score 577 paper-based; 233 computer-based; 90 iBT), IELTS (minimum score 7). *Application deadline:* For fall admission, 1/3 for domestic and international students; for winter admission, 6/1 for domestic and international students; for spring admission, 9/1 for domestic and international students. Applications are processed on a rolling basis. Application fee: $90 Canadian dollars ($150 Canadian dollars for international students). Electronic applications accepted. *Financial support:* In 2007–08, 5 students received support, including 1 fellowship (averaging $20,000 per year), 2 research assistantships (averaging $12,000 per year), 2 teaching assistantships (averaging $8,000 per year); Federal Work-Study, institutionally sponsored loans, scholarships/grants, and tuition waivers (partial) also available. *Faculty research:* International development, natural resources and environmental economics, marketing and trade, agribusiness, food market analysis, applied econometrics. *Unit head:* Dr. Sumeet Gulati, Graduate Advisor, 604-822-2144, Fax: 604-822-4400, E-mail: sumeet.gulati@ubc.ca. *Application contact:* Lia Maria Dragan, Graduate Programs Assistant, 604-822-8373, Fax: 604-822-4400, E-mail: gradapp@interchange.ubc.ca.

University of California, Berkeley, Graduate Division, College of Natural Resources, Department of Agricultural and Resource Economics, Berkeley, CA 94720-1500. Offers PhD. *Degree requirements:* For doctorate, thesis/dissertation, qualifying exam. *Entrance requirements:* For doctorate, GRE General Test, minimum GPA of 3.0, 3 letters of recommendation. *Application deadline:* For fall admission, 2/10 for domestic students. Application fee: $70 ($90 for international students). *Financial support:* Fellowships, research assistantships, teaching assistantships, institutionally sponsored loans, scholarships/grants, tuition waivers (full and partial), and unspecified assistantships available. Financial award applicants required to submit FAFSA. *Faculty research:* Agricultural economics and policy, environmental and resource economics and policy, international agricultural development and trade. *Unit head:* Jeffrey Perloff, Chair, 510-642-9574, E-mail: perloff@are.berkeley.edu. *Application contact:* Gail T. Vawter, Student Affairs Officer, 510-642-3347, Fax: 510-643-8911, E-mail: gradadm@are.berkeley.edu.

University of California, Davis, Graduate Studies, Program in Agricultural and Resource Economics, Davis, CA 95616. Offers MS, PhD, MBA/MS. Terminal master's awarded for partial completion of doctoral program. *Degree requirements:* For master's, thesis optional; for doctorate, thesis/dissertation. *Entrance requirements:* For master's, GRE General Test, minimum GPA of 3.0; for doctorate, GRE General Test, minimum GPA of 3.3. Additional exam requirements/recommendations for international students: Required—TOEFL (minimum score 550 paper-based; 213 computer-based). Electronic applications accepted. *Faculty research:* Applied microeconomics, international trade, development, econometrics, environmental economics.

University of California, Santa Barbara, Graduate Division, Donald Bren School of Environmental Science and Management, Santa Barbara, CA 93106. Offers economics and environmental science (PhD); environmental science and management (MESM, PhD). *Faculty:* 19 full-time (5 women), 4 part-time/adjunct (0 women). *Students:* 167 full-time (96 women); includes 17 minority (1 African American, 1 American Indian/Alaska Native, 11 Asian Americans or Pacific Islanders, 4 Hispanic Americans), 9 international. Average age 27. 297 applicants, 61% accepted, 73 enrolled. In 2007, 58 master's, 5 doctorates awarded. *Median time to degree:* Of those who began their doctoral program in fall 1999, 60% received their degree in 8 years or less. *Degree requirements:* For master's, thesis optional, group project as student thesis; for doctorate, comprehensive exam, thesis/dissertation. *Entrance requirements:* For master's and doctorate, GRE. Additional exam requirements/recommendations for international students: Required—TOEFL (minimum score 550 paper-based; 213 computer-based; 80 iBT). *Application deadline:* For fall admission, 1/10 for domestic and international students. Application fee: $60. Electronic applications accepted. *Expenses:* Tuition, nonresident: full-time $14,888. Required fees: $10,108. *Financial support:* In 2007–08, 124 students received support, including 37 fellowships with full and partial tuition reimbursements available (averaging $9,800 per year), 14 research assistantships with full tuition reimbursements available (averaging $11,140 per year), 18 teaching assistantships with partial tuition reimbursements available (averaging $4,531 per year); career-related internships or fieldwork, Federal Work-Study, institutionally sponsored loans, scholarships/grants, traineeships, health care benefits, and unspecified assistantships also available. Financial award application deadline: 2/15; financial award applicants required to submit FAFSA. *Faculty research:* Resource economics, renewable resources, biogeography terrestrial ecology, business strategy and the environment, snow hydrology, earth system science, geomorphology, hydrology. *Unit head:* Dr. Ernst Von Weizsacker, Dean, 805-893-7577, E-mail: ernst@bren.ucsb.edu. *Application contact:* Chelsea Houdyshell, Graduate Advisor, 805-893-7611, Fax: 805-893-7612, E-mail: chelsea@bren.ucsb.edu.

University of Connecticut, Graduate School, College of Agriculture and Natural Resources, Department of Agricultural and Resource Economics, Field of Agricultural and Resource Economics, Storrs, CT 06269. Offers MS, PhD. *Faculty:* 16 full-time (4 women). *Students:* 27 full-time (16 women), 9 part-time (5 women); includes 1 minority (Hispanic American), 19 international. Average age 31. 53 applicants, 17% accepted, 8 enrolled. In 2007, 8 master's, 2 doctorates awarded. Terminal master's awarded for partial completion of doctoral program. *Degree requirements:* For master's, comprehensive exam; for doctorate, thesis/dissertation. *Entrance requirements:* For master's and doctorate, GRE General Test. Additional exam requirements/recommendations for international students: Required—TOEFL (minimum score 550 paper-based; 213 computer-based). *Application deadline:* For fall admission, 2/1 priority date for domestic and international students; for spring admission, 11/1 for domestic students, 10/1 for international students. Applications are processed on a rolling basis. Application fee: $55. Electronic applications accepted. *Expenses:* Tuition, state resident: part-time $469 per credit hour. Tuition, nonresident: part-time $1,218 per credit hour. *Financial support:* In 2007–08, 19 research assistantships with full tuition reimbursements, 3 teaching assistantships with full tuition reimbursements were awarded; Federal Work-Study, scholarships/grants, health care benefits, and unspecified assistantships also available. Financial award application deadline: 2/1; financial award applicants required to submit FAFSA. *Application contact:* Farhed Shah, Chairperson, 860-486-4467, Fax: 860-486-1932, E-mail: farhed.shah@uconn.edu.

University of Delaware, College of Agriculture and Natural Resources, Department of Food and Resource Economics, Newark, DE 19716. Offers agricultural economics (MS); agriculture and technical education (MA); bioresources engineering (MS). Part-time programs available. *Faculty:* 10 full-time (1 woman), 2 part-time/adjunct (0 women). *Students:* 16 full-time (13 women), 1 part-time, 8 international. Average age 25. 9 applicants, 67% accepted, 4 enrolled. In 2007, 5 degrees awarded. *Degree requirements:* For master's, thesis. *Entrance requirements:* For master's, GRE General Test, 3 letters of recommendation. Additional exam requirements/recommendations for international students: Required—TOEFL (minimum score 550 paper-based; 213 computer-based). *Application deadline:* For fall admission, 2/1 priority date for domestic students; for spring admission, 12/1 for domestic students. Application fee: $60. Electronic applications accepted. *Financial support:* In 2007–08, 10 students received support, including 8 research assistantships with full tuition reimbursements available (averaging $13,556 per year), 1 teaching assistantship with full tuition reimbursement available (averaging $14,916 per year); fellowships, scholarships/grants, tuition waivers (full), and unspecified assistantships also available. Financial award application deadline: 3/1. *Faculty research:* Experimental economics, environmental and resource economics, land use, law and economics. Total annual research expenditures: $54,224. *Unit head:* Dr. Thomas W. Ilvento, Chair, 302-831-6773, Fax: 302-831-6243, E-mail: ilvento@udel.edu. *Application contact:* Judy Gibbons, Office Coordinator, 302-831-2511, Fax: 302-831-6243, E-mail: judy@udel.edu.

University of Florida, Graduate School, College of Agricultural and Life Sciences, Department of Food and Resource Economics, Gainesville, FL 32611. Offers MAB, MS, PhD. *Faculty:* 29 full-time (6 women). *Students:* 79 (37 women); includes 12 minority (6 African Americans, 1 American Indian/Alaska Native, 3 Asian Americans or Pacific Islanders, 2 Hispanic Americans) 20 international. In 2007, 28 master's, 5 doctorates awarded. *Degree requirements:* For master's, thesis optional; for doctorate, thesis/dissertation. *Entrance requirements:* For master's and doctorate, GRE General Test, minimum GPA of 3.0. Additional exam requirements/recommendations for international students: Required—TOEFL. *Application deadline:* For fall admission, 6/1 priority date for domestic students. Applications are processed on a rolling basis. Application fee: $20. Electronic applications accepted. *Expenses:* Tuition, state resident: full-time $7,478. Tuition, nonresident: full-time $22,603. *Financial support:* In 2007–08, 32 research assistantships (averaging $11,711 per year), 2 teaching assistantships (averaging $10,425 per year) were awarded; fellowships, unspecified assistantships also available. Financial award application deadline: 2/1. *Faculty research:* Agribusiness management, production, environmental economics, international trade, economic development. *Unit head:* Dr. Thomas H. Spreen, Chair, 352-392-1826 Ext. 209, Fax: 352-846-0988, E-mail: thspreen@ifas.ufl.edu. *Application contact:* Dr. Jeff Burkhardt, Coordinator, 352-392-1826 Ext. 314, Fax: 352-846-0988, E-mail: rburkhardt@ifas.ufl.edu.

University of Georgia, Graduate School, College of Agricultural and Environmental Sciences, Department of Agricultural and Applied Economics, Athens, GA 30602. Offers agricultural economics (MAE, MS, PhD); environmental economics (MS). *Faculty:* 18 full-time (1 woman). *Students:* 35 full-time (12 women), 2 part-time; includes 4 minority (2 African Americans, 2 Asian Americans or Pacific Islanders), 16 international. 45 applicants, 22% accepted, 4 enrolled. In 2007, 10 master's, 2 doctorates awarded. *Degree requirements:* For master's, thesis (MS); for doctorate, thesis/dissertation. *Entrance requirements:* For master's and doctorate, GRE General Test. *Application deadline:* For fall admission, 7/1 priority date for domestic students; for spring admission, 11/15 for domestic students. Application fee: $50. Electronic applications accepted. *Financial support:* Fellowships, research assistantships, teaching assistantships, career-related internships or fieldwork and unspecified assistantships available. *Unit head:* Dr. Jeffrey H. Dorfman, Interim Head, 706-542-0754, Fax: 706-542-0739, E-mail: jdorfman@agecon.uga.edu. *Application contact:* Dr. James Epperson, Graduate Coordinator, 706-543-0766, Fax: 706-542-0739, E-mail: jepperson@agecon.uga.edu.

University of Guelph, Graduate Program Services, College of Management and Economics, MBA Program, Guelph, ON N1G 2W1, Canada. Offers food and agribusiness management (MBA); hospitality and tourism management (MBA). Part-time and evening/weekend programs available. Postbaccalaureate distance learning degree programs offered (minimal on-campus study). *Faculty:* 37 full-time (10 women), 7 part-time/adjunct (0 women). *Students:* 80 full-time (29 women); includes 18 minority (3 African Americans, 15 Asian Americans or Pacific Islanders). Average age 35. 78 applicants, 55% accepted, 33 enrolled. In 2007, 23 degrees awarded. *Entrance requirements:* For master's, minimum B-average, minimum of 3 years of relevant work experience. Additional exam requirements/recommendations for international students: Required—TOEFL (minimum score 550 paper-based; 213 computer-based). *Application deadline:* For spring admission, 4/30 priority date for domestic and international students. Applications are processed on a rolling basis. Application fee: $150. Electronic applications accepted. *Financial support:* In 2007–08, 24 students received support, including 12 teaching assistantships (averaging $5,100 per year); scholarships/grants also available. *Faculty research:* Marketing, operations management, business policy, financial management, organizational behavior. *Unit head:* Prof. Geoff Smith, Assistant Dean, Executive Programs, 519-824-4120 Ext. 58855, Fax: 519-8838-0661, E-mail: gwsmith@uoguelph.ca. *Application contact:* Patti Lago, Manager, Graduate Programs (FOM), 519-824-4120 Ext. 56617, Fax: 519-836-0661, E-mail: plago@uoguelph.ca.

University of Guelph, Graduate Program Services, Ontario Agricultural College, Department of Food, Agricultural and Resource Economics, Guelph, ON N1G 2W1, Canada. Offers agricultural economics (M Sc, PhD); collaborative international development studies (MA/M Sc); MA/M Sc. Part-time programs available. *Faculty:* 11 full-time (0 women), 2 part-time/adjunct (0 women). *Students:* 30 full-time (9 women), 3 part-time (1 woman); includes 12 minority (4 African Americans, 6 Asian Americans or Pacific Islanders, 2 Hispanic Americans). Average age 28. 57 applicants, 40% accepted, 18 enrolled. In 2007, 16 master's, 8 doctorates awarded. *Degree requirements:* For master's, thesis; for doctorate, comprehensive exam, thesis/dissertation. *Entrance requirements:* For master's, minimum B- average during previous 2 years of course work; for doctorate, minimum B standing in recognized master's degree. Additional exam requirements/recommendations for international students: Required—TOEFL (minimum score 550 paper-based; 213 computer-based), IELTS (minimum score 7). *Application deadline:* For winter admission, 1/31 for domestic and international students. Application fee: $85. Electronic applications accepted. *Financial support:* In 2007–08, 1 fellowship with tuition reimbursement (averaging $10,000 per year), 15 research assistantships with tuition reimbursements (averaging $18,000 per year), 8 teaching assistantships with tuition reimbursements (averaging $18,000 per year) were awarded; scholarships/grants and unspecified assistantships also available. Financial award application deadline: 5/1. *Faculty research:* Agricultural policy, agribusiness, environmental economics, agricultural marketing, production economics. Total annual research expenditures: $1.3 million. *Unit head:* Dr. Alfons Weersink, Acting Chair, 519-824-4120 Ext. 52766, Fax: 519-767-1510, E-mail: aqeersin@

Agricultural Economics and Agribusiness

University of Guelph (continued)
uoguelph.ca. *Application contact:* Dr. Glenn Fox, Graduate Coordinator, 519-824-4120 Ext. 52768, Fax: 519-767-1510, E-mail: gfox@uoguelph.ca.

University of Idaho, College of Graduate Studies, College of Agricultural and Life Sciences, Department of Agricultural Economics and Rural Sociology, Moscow, ID 83844-2282. Offers agricultural economics (MS). *Students:* 12. Average age 27. In 2007, 7 master's awarded. *Entrance requirements:* For master's, minimum GPA of 2.8. *Application deadline:* For fall admission, 8/1 for domestic students; for spring admission, 12/15 for domestic students. Application fee: $55 ($60 for international students). *Financial support:* Research assistantships, teaching assistantships available. Financial award application deadline: 2/15. *Unit head:* Dr. Larry W Van Tassell, Head, 208-885-7869, Fax: 208-885-5759.

University of Illinois at Urbana–Champaign, Graduate College, College of Agricultural, Consumer and Environmental Sciences, Department of Agricultural and Consumer Economics, Champaign, IL 61820. Offers MS, PhD. *Faculty:* 35 full-time (10 women), 1 (woman) part-time/adjunct. *Students:* 49 full-time (22 women), 18 part-time (6 women); includes 6 minority (2 African Americans, 2 Asian Americans or Pacific Islanders, 2 Hispanic Americans), 38 international. 83 applicants, 28% accepted, 12 enrolled. In 2007, 5 master's, 8 doctorates awarded. *Degree requirements:* For master's, thesis; for doctorate, thesis/dissertation. *Entrance requirements:* For master's, minimum GPA of 3.0. *Application deadline:* Applications are processed on a rolling basis. Application fee: $60 ($75 for international students). Electronic applications accepted. *Financial support:* In 2007–08, 10 fellowships, 48 research assistantships, 26 teaching assistantships were awarded; tuition waivers (full and partial) also available. Financial award application deadline: 2/15. *Unit head:* Robert J. Hauser, Head, 217-333-8859, Fax: 217-333-5538, E-mail: r-hauser@uiuc.edu. *Application contact:* Linda Foste, Administrative Assistant, 217-333-1830, Fax: 217-244-7088, E-mail: l-foste@uiuc.edu.

University of Kentucky, Graduate School, College of Agriculture, Program in Agricultural Economics, Lexington, KY 40546-0276. Offers MS, PhD. *Faculty:* 21 full-time (2 women), 2 part-time/adjunct (1 woman). *Students:* 34 full-time (13 women), 8 part-time (1 woman), 21 international. Average age 30. 39 applicants, 41% accepted, 10 enrolled. In 2007, 3 master's, 3 doctorates awarded. *Median time to degree:* Of those who began their doctoral program in fall 1999, 64% received their degree in 8 years or less. *Degree requirements:* For master's, comprehensive exam, thesis optional; for doctorate, comprehensive exam, thesis/dissertation. *Entrance requirements:* For master's, GRE General Test, minimum undergraduate GPA of 2.75; for doctorate, GRE General Test, minimum graduate GPA of 3.0. Additional exam requirements/recommendations for international students: Required—TOEFL (minimum score 550 paper-based; 213 computer-based). *Application deadline:* For fall admission, 7/17 priority date for domestic students, 2/1 priority date for international students; for spring admission, 12/13 priority date for domestic students, 6/15 priority date for international students. Application fee: $50 ($65 for international students). Electronic applications accepted. *Expenses:* Tuition, state resident: part-time $437 per credit hour. Tuition, nonresident: part-time $931 per credit hour. *Financial support:* In 2007–08, 33 students received support, including 1 fellowship with full tuition reimbursement available, 32 research assistantships with full tuition reimbursements available (averaging $12,700 per year); teaching assistantships with full tuition reimbursements available, Federal Work-Study, institutionally sponsored loans, scholarships/grants, traineeships, and health care benefits also available. Support available to part-time students. Financial award application deadline: 3/15. *Faculty research:* Food and agricultural marketing, agricultural and food policy, natural resources and environment, rural economic development. *Unit head:* Dr. David Freshwake, Director of Graduate Studies, 859-257-1872, Fax: 859-323-1913, E-mail: dfresh@uky.edu. *Application contact:* Dr. Brian Jackson, Senior Associate Dean, 859-257-4667, Fax: 859-257-4676, E-mail: brian.jackson@uky.edu.

University of Maine, Graduate School, College of Natural Sciences, Forestry, and Agriculture, Department of Resource Economics and Policy, Orono, ME 04469. Offers resource economics and policy (MS); resource utilization (MS). Part-time programs available. *Faculty:* 13. *Students:* 14 full-time (9 women), 2 part-time (both women); includes 1 minority (Hispanic American), 4 international. Average age 32. 9 applicants, 78% accepted, 5 enrolled. In 2007, 6 master's awarded. *Degree requirements:* For master's, thesis (for some programs). *Entrance requirements:* For master's, GRE General Test. Additional exam requirements/recommendations for international students: Required—TOEFL. *Application deadline:* For fall admission, 2/1 priority date for domestic students. Applications are processed on a rolling basis. Application fee: $60. Electronic applications accepted. *Financial support:* In 2007–08, 10 research assistantships with tuition reimbursements (averaging $14,000 per year), 3 teaching assistantships with tuition reimbursements (averaging $10,190 per year) were awarded; career-related internships or fieldwork, Federal Work-Study, institutionally sponsored loans, scholarships/grants, and tuition waivers (full and partial) also available. Support available to part-time students. Financial award application deadline: 3/1. *Faculty research:* International trade, agricultural marketing, nonmarketing valuation, livestock health economics. *Unit head:* Dr. George Criner, Chair, 207-581-3151, Fax: 207-581-4278. *Application contact:* Scott G. Delcourt, Associate Dean of the Graduate School, 207-581-3219, Fax: 207-581-3232, E-mail: graduate@maine.edu.

University of Manitoba, Faculty of Graduate Studies, Faculty of Agriculture, Department of Agribusiness and Agricultural Economics, Winnipeg, MB R3T 2N2, Canada. Offers M Sc, PhD. *Degree requirements:* For master's, thesis or alternative; for doctorate, thesis/dissertation.

University of Maryland, College Park, Graduate Studies, College of Agriculture and Natural Resources, Department of Agricultural and Resource Economics, College Park, MD 20742. Offers agriculture economics (MS, PhD); resource economics (MS, PhD). Part-time and evening/weekend programs available. *Faculty:* 21 full-time (4 women), 2 part-time/adjunct (1 woman). *Students:* 70 full-time (25 women), 4 part-time (2 women); includes 2 minority (both Asian Americans or Pacific Islanders), 44 international. 140 applicants, 21% accepted, 16 enrolled. In 2007, 6 master's, 6 doctorates awarded. *Median time to degree:* Of those who began their doctoral program in fall 1999, 13% received their degree in 8 years or less. *Degree requirements:* For master's, variable foreign language requirement, thesis optional, oral exam; for doctorate, variable foreign language requirement, oral dissertation defense. *Entrance requirements:* For master's, GRE General Test, minimum GPA of 3.0, course work in microeconomics and calculus, 3 letters of recommendation; for doctorate, GRE General Test. Additional exam requirements/recommendations for international students: Required—TOEFL. *Application deadline:* For fall admission, 2/1 for domestic and international students; for spring admission, 10/1 for domestic students, 6/1 for international students. Applications are processed on a rolling basis. Application fee: $60 ($70 for international students). Electronic applications accepted. *Financial support:* In 2007–08, 1 fellowship with full tuition reimbursement (averaging $10,800 per year), 44 research assistantships with tuition reimbursements (averaging $17,021 per year), 1 teaching assistantship with tuition reimbursement (averaging $16,672 per year) were awarded; Federal Work-Study and scholarships/grants also available. Support available to part-time students. Financial award applicants required to submit FAFSA. *Faculty research:* Agricultural development, international trade, agricultural marketing, econometrics, farm management and production economics. Total annual research expenditures: $1.2 million. *Application contact:* Dean of Graduate School, 301-405-0358, Fax: 301-314-9305.

University of Massachusetts Amherst, Graduate School, College of Natural Resources and the Environment, Department of Resource Economics, Amherst, MA 01003. Offers MS, PhD. Part-time programs available. *Faculty:* 14 full-time (3 women). *Students:* 20 full-time (9 women), 2 part-time (both women); includes 2 minority (both Asian Americans or Pacific Islanders), 10 international. Average age 28. 30 applicants, 43% accepted, 8 enrolled. In 2007, 8 master's, 2 doctorates awarded. Terminal master's awarded for partial completion of doctoral program. *Degree requirements:* For master's, thesis or alternative; for doctorate, thesis/dissertation. *Entrance requirements:* For master's and doctorate, GRE General Test. Additional exam requirements/recommendations for international students: Required—TOEFL (minimum score 530 paper-based; 197 computer-based). *Application deadline:* For fall admission, 2/1 priority date for domestic and international students. Applications are processed on a rolling basis. Application fee: $50 ($65 for international students). Electronic applications accepted. *Expenses:* Tuition, state resident: full-time $2,640; part-time $110 per credit. Tuition, nonresident: full-time $9,936; part-time $414 per credit. Required fees: $7,455. One-time fee: $332. Tuition and fees vary according to course load, campus/location, program and reciprocity agreements. *Financial support:* In 2007–08, 2 fellowships with full tuition reimbursements (averaging $8,422 per year), 19 research assistantships with full tuition reimbursements (averaging $6,874 per year), 14 teaching assistantships with full tuition reimbursements (averaging $9,586 per year) were awarded; career-related internships or fieldwork, Federal Work-Study, scholarships/grants, traineeships, and unspecified assistantships also available. Support available to part-time students. Financial award application deadline: 2/1. *Unit head:* Dr. Julie Caswell, Director, 413-545-2490, Fax: 413-545-5853, E-mail: caswell@resecon.umass.edu.

University of Missouri–Columbia, Graduate School, College of Agriculture, Food and Natural Resources, Department of Agricultural Economics, Columbia, MO 65211. Offers MS, PhD. *Degree requirements:* For doctorate, thesis/dissertation. *Entrance requirements:* For master's and doctorate, GRE General Test, minimum GPA of 3.0. Additional exam requirements/recommendations for international students: Required—TOEFL (minimum score 600 paper-based; 205 computer-based).

University of Nebraska–Lincoln, Graduate College, College of Agricultural Sciences and Natural Resources, Department of Agricultural Economics, Lincoln, NE 68588. Offers MS, PhD. *Degree requirements:* For master's, thesis optional; for doctorate, comprehensive exam, thesis/dissertation. *Entrance requirements:* For master's and doctorate, GRE General Test. Additional exam requirements/recommendations for international students: Required—TOEFL (minimum score 550 paper-based; 213 computer-based). Electronic applications accepted. *Faculty research:* Marketing and agribusiness, production economics, resource law, international trade and development, rural policy and revitalization.

University of Nevada, Reno, Graduate School, College of Agriculture, Biotechnology and Natural Resources, Department of Resource Economics, Reno, NV 89557. Offers MS, PhD. *Faculty:* 15. *Students:* 15 full-time (10 women), 6 part-time (4 women), 10 international. Average age 33. 20 applicants, 85% accepted, 9 enrolled. In 2007, 2 degrees awarded. *Degree requirements:* For master's, thesis optional. *Entrance requirements:* For master's, GRE General Test, minimum GPA of 2.75; for doctorate, GRE General Test. Additional exam requirements/recommendations for international students: Required—TOEFL. *Application deadline:* For fall admission, 3/1 priority date for domestic students; for spring admission, 11/1 for domestic students. Applications are processed on a rolling basis. Application fee: $60 ($95 for international students). *Expenses:* Tuition, state resident: full-time $2,774; part-time $154 per credit. Tuition, nonresident: full-time $13,578; part-time $330 per credit. Required fees: $49 per semester. *Financial support:* In 2007–08, 12 research assistantships were awarded. Financial award application deadline: 3/1. *Unit head:* Dr. Kim Rollins, Graduate Program Director, 775-784-1677.

University of Puerto Rico, Mayagüez Campus, Graduate Studies, College of Agricultural Sciences, Department of Agricultural Economics, Mayagüez, PR 00681-9000. Offers MS. Part-time programs available. *Faculty:* 11 full-time (6 women). *Students:* 6 full-time (5 women), 6 part-time (2 women); includes 9 minority (all Hispanic Americans), 3 international. 3 applicants, 100% accepted, 0 enrolled. In 2007, 2 degrees awarded. *Degree requirements:* For master's, comprehensive exam, thesis. *Entrance requirements:* For master's, bachelor's degree in agricultural economics or its equivalent. *Application deadline:* For fall admission, 2/15 for domestic and international students; for spring admission, 9/15 for domestic and international students. Applications are processed on a rolling basis. Application fee: $25. *Financial support:* In 2007–08, 8 students received support, including fellowships (averaging $12,000 per year), 2 research assistantships with tuition reimbursements available (averaging $15,000 per year), 5 teaching assistantships with tuition reimbursements available (averaging $8,500 per year); Federal Work-Study and institutionally sponsored loans also available. *Faculty research:* Farm management, agricultural development, agrimarketing, natural resource economics. *Unit head:* Dr. Jorge González, Director, 787-265-3860 Ext. 2471, Fax: 787-265-3860. *Application contact:* Margarita Olivencia, Secretary, 787-832-4040 Ext. 2471, Fax: 787-265-3860, E-mail: molivencia@uprm.edu.

University of Saskatchewan, College of Graduate Studies and Research, College of Agriculture, Department of Agricultural Economics, Saskatoon, SK S7N 5A2, Canada. Offers M Ag, M Sc, MA, PhD. *Degree requirements:* For master's, thesis; for doctorate, thesis/dissertation. *Entrance requirements:* Additional exam requirements/recommendations for international students: Required—TOEFL.

University of Saskatchewan, College of Graduate Studies and Research, Edwards School of Business, Program in Business Administration, Saskatoon, SK S7N 5A2, Canada. Offers agribusiness management (MBA); biotechnology management (MBA); health services management (MBA); indigenous management (MBA); international business management (MBA).

University of Vermont, Graduate College, College of Agriculture and Life Sciences, Department of Community Development and Applied Economics, Burlington, VT 05405. Offers community development and applied economics (MS); public administration (MPA). *Students:* 20 (10 women); includes 1 minority (Asian American or Pacific Islander) 22 applicants, 73% accepted, 6 enrolled. In 2007, 7 degrees awarded. *Degree requirements:* For master's, thesis. *Entrance requirements:* For master's, GRE General Test. Additional exam requirements/recommendations for international students: Required—TOEFL (minimum score 550 paper-based; 213 computer-based; 80 iBT). *Application deadline:* For fall admission, 4/1 priority date for domestic students; for spring admission, 11/15 for domestic students. Applications are processed on a rolling basis. Application fee: $40. Electronic applications accepted. *Financial support:* Fellowships, research assistantships, teaching assistantships, career-related internships or fieldwork available. Financial award application deadline: 3/1. *Faculty research:* Agricultural production and marketing. *Unit head:* Dr. J. Kolodinsky, Chairperson, 802-656-2001.

University of Wisconsin–Madison, Graduate School, College of Agricultural and Life Sciences, Department of Agricultural and Applied Economics, Madison, WI 53706-1380. Offers MA, MS, PhD. Part-time programs available. *Degree requirements:* For doctorate, thesis/dissertation, preliminary exams. *Entrance requirements:* For master's and doctorate, GRE General Test. Additional exam requirements/recommendations for international students: Required—TOEFL. Electronic applications accepted. *Faculty research:* Environmental and resource economics, international development, state and local economics, food systems, markets and trade.

University of Wyoming, Graduate School, College of Agriculture, Department of Agricultural and Applied Economics, Laramie, WY 82070. Offers MS. Part-time programs available. *Faculty:* 12 full-time (2 women), 1 part-time/adjunct (0 women). *Students:* 8 full-time (3 women), 2 part-time (1 woman), 1 international. Average age 27. 11 applicants, 45% accepted. In 2007, 2 degrees awarded. *Degree requirements:* For master's, thesis (for some programs). *Entrance requirements:* For master's, GRE General Test, minimum GPA of 3.0. Additional exam requirements/recommendations for international students: Required—TOEFL. *Application deadline:* For fall admission, 2/15 priority date for domestic students, 2/1 for international students; for spring admission, 10/1 priority date for domestic students. Applications are processed on a rolling basis. Application fee: $50. Electronic applications accepted. *Financial support:* In 2007–08, 5 research assistantships with tuition reimbursements (averaging $10,062 per year) were awarded; career-related internships or fieldwork, Federal Work-Study, and institutionally sponsored loans also available. Financial award application deadline: 2/1; financial award applicants required to submit FAFSA. *Faculty research:* Farm management, agricultural markets, water economics, community development, agricultural business. Total annual research expenditures: $250,000. *Unit head:* Dr. Roger H. Coupal, Interim Department Head, 307-766-2386, Fax: 307-766-5544, E-mail: coupal@uwyo.edu.

Virginia Polytechnic Institute and State University, Graduate School, College of Agriculture and Life Sciences, Department of Agricultural and Applied Economics, Blacksburg, VA 24061. Offers agribusiness (MS); agricultural economics (MS); applied economics (MS); developmental and international economics (PhD); econometrics (PhD); macro and micro economics (PhD); markets and industrial organizations (PhD); public and regional/urban economics (PhD); resource and environmental economics (PhD). *Entrance requirements:* For master's and doctorate, GRE General Test. Additional exam requirements/recommendations for international students: Required—TOEFL (minimum score 575 paper-based; 231 computer-based). Electronic applications accepted. *Faculty research:* Rural development.

Washington State University, Graduate School, College of Agricultural, Human, and Natural Resource Sciences, School of Economic Sciences, Pullman, WA 99164. Offers agribusiness (MA, Certificate); agricultural economics (MA, PhD); applied economics (MA); economics (MA, PhD, Certificate), including applied economics (MA), economics (MA, PhD), international business economics (Certificate). *Faculty:* 32. *Students:* 68 full-time (20 women), 9 part-time (5 women); includes 2 minority (1 Asian American or Pacific Islander, 1 Hispanic American), 43 international. Average age 28. 179 applicants, 23% accepted, 26 enrolled. In 2007, 7 master's, 1 doctorate awarded. Terminal master's awarded for partial completion of doctoral program. *Degree requirements:* For master's, comprehensive exam (for some programs), thesis (for some programs), oral exam; for doctorate, comprehensive exam, thesis/dissertation, oral exam, written exam, qualifying exams. *Entrance requirements:* For master's and doctorate, minimum GPA of 3.0, 3 letters of recommendation. Additional exam requirements/recommendations for international students: Required—TOEFL (minimum score 550 paper-based; 213 computer-based). *Application deadline:* For fall admission, 2/15 priority date for domestic students, 2/1 priority date for international students. Applications are processed on a rolling basis. Application fee: $50. Electronic applications accepted. *Financial support:* In 2007–08, 59 students received support, including 3 fellowships (averaging $2,833 per year), 36 research assistantships with full and partial tuition reimbursements available (averaging $13,917 per year), 15 teaching assistantships with full and partial tuition reimbursements available (averaging $13,056 per year); career-related internships or fieldwork, Federal Work-Study, institutionally sponsored loans, tuition waivers (partial), and teaching associateships also available. Financial award application deadline: 4/1; financial award applicants required to submit FAFSA. *Faculty research:* Marketing, natural resources, production economics. Total annual research expenditures: $1.1 million. *Unit head:* Dr. Ron Mittelhammer, Director, 509-335-5555, E-mail: mittleha@wsu.edu. *Application contact:* Graduate School Admissions, 800-GRADWSU, Fax: 509-335-1949, E-mail: gradsch@wsu.edu.

West Texas A&M University, College of Agriculture, Nursing, and Natural Sciences, Division of Agriculture, Emphasis in Agricultural Business and Economics, Canyon, TX 79016-0001. Offers MS. Part-time programs available. *Degree requirements:* For master's, comprehensive exam, thesis optional. *Entrance requirements:* For master's, GRE General Test. Additional exam requirements/recommendations for international students: Required—TOEFL (minimum score 550 paper-based). Electronic applications accepted. *Faculty research:* Utilizing expected revenue in selecting optimal marketing alternatives for fixed resource cow/calf operators in the Texas panhandle.

West Virginia University, Davis College of Agriculture, Forestry and Consumer Sciences, Division of Resource Management and Sustainable Development, Program in Agricultural and Resource Economics, Morgantown, WV 26506. Offers MS. Part-time programs available. *Students:* 6 full-time (1 woman); includes 1 minority (African American), 3 international. Average age 26. 8 applicants, 100% accepted, 1 enrolled. In 2007, 3 degrees awarded. *Degree requirements:* For master's, thesis optional. *Entrance requirements:* For master's, GRE General Test, minimum GPA of 2.5, 1 calculus course. Additional exam requirements/recommendations for international students: Required—TOEFL. *Application deadline:* Applications are processed on a rolling basis. Application fee: $45. *Expenses:* Tuition, state resident: full-time $5,196; part-time $292 per credit hour. Tuition, nonresident: full-time $15,064; part-time $840 per credit hour. Tuition and fees vary according to program. *Financial support:* In 2007–08, 9 research assistantships (averaging $11,700 per year) were awarded; teaching assistantships, Federal Work-Study, institutionally sponsored loans, and tuition waivers (full and partial) also available. Financial award application deadline: 2/1; financial award applicants required to submit FAFSA. *Faculty research:* Agricultural production and marketing, rural development, mineral and energy economics, economic development. *Unit head:* Dr. Alan R. Collins, Chair, 304-293-4832 Ext. 4473, Fax: 304-293-3752, E-mail: alan.collins@mail.wvu.edu.

William Woods University, Graduate and Adult Studies, Fulton, MO 65251-1098. Offers administration (Ed S); agriculture (MBA); athletic/activities administration (M Ed); curriculum and instruction (M Ed); curriculum leadership (Ed S); elementary administration (M Ed); health management (MBA); human resources (MBA); principalship (Ed S); secondary administration (M Ed); special education director (M Ed). Evening/weekend programs available. *Degree requirements:* For master's, capstone course (MBA), action research (M Ed); for Ed S, field experience. *Entrance requirements:* For master's, 2 recommendations, resumé, BA/BS; teaching certification (M Ed); course work in economics and accounting (MBA); for Ed S, M Ed, 2 letters of recommendation, resumé, teaching certification. Additional exam requirements/recommendations for international students: Required—TOEFL (minimum score 550 paper-based). *Application deadline:* Applications are processed on a rolling basis. Application fee: $25. Electronic applications accepted. *Financial support:* Institutionally sponsored loans available. Financial award applicants required to submit FAFSA. *Unit head:* Sean Siebert, Dean of Graduate and Adult Studies Enrollment Services, 573-592-4383, Fax: 573-592-1164. *Application contact:* Linda Rembish, Administrative Assistant, 800-995-3199, Fax: 573-592-1164, E-mail: adulted@williamwoods.edu.

Applied Economics

American University, College of Arts and Sciences, Department of Economics, Washington, DC 20016-8001. Offers applied microeconomics (Certificate); economics (MA, PhD); international economic relations (Certificate). Part-time and evening/weekend programs available. *Faculty:* 25 full-time (11 women), 1 part-time/adjunct (0 women). *Students:* 59 full-time (22 women), 71 part-time (32 women); includes 14 minority (7 African Americans, 3 Asian Americans or Pacific Islanders, 4 Hispanic Americans), 55 international. Average age 29. 181 applicants, 71% accepted, 38 enrolled. In 2007, 29 master's, 5 doctorates, 1 other advanced degree awarded. Terminal master's awarded for partial completion of doctoral program. *Degree requirements:* For master's, comprehensive exam, thesis or alternative; for doctorate, comprehensive exam, thesis/dissertation, 2 research seminars, field requirement. *Entrance requirements:* For master's, GRE; for doctorate, GRE General Test; for Certificate, Bachelor's Degree. Additional exam requirements/recommendations for international students: Required—TOEFL (minimum score 550 paper-based; 213 computer-based). *Application deadline:* For spring admission, 10/1 for domestic students. Applications are processed on a rolling basis. Application fee: $50. *Expenses:* Tuition: Full-time $19,998; part-time $1,111 per credit hour. Required fees: $380. Tuition and fees vary according to program. *Financial support:* Fellowships with full tuition reimbursements, research assistantships, teaching assistantships with full tuition reimbursements, career-related internships or fieldwork, Federal Work-Study, institutionally sponsored loans, and tuition waivers (full and partial) available. Financial award application deadline: 2/1. *Faculty research:* Political economy, development, labor, gender. *Unit head:* Dr. John Willoughby, Chair, 202-885-3759, Fax: 202-885-3790.

Auburn University, Graduate School, College of Agriculture, Department of Agricultural Economics and Rural Sociology, Auburn University, AL 36849. Offers agricultural economics (M Ag, MS); applied economics (PhD). Part-time programs available. *Faculty:* 16 full-time (3 women). *Students:* 14 full-time (7 women), 12 part-time (5 women); includes 4 minority (3 African Americans, 1 Asian American or Pacific Islander), 14 international. Average age 31. 13 applicants, 92% accepted, 5 enrolled. In 2007, 8 master's, 4 doctorates awarded. *Degree requirements:* For master's, thesis (for some programs); for doctorate, thesis/dissertation. *Entrance requirements:* For master's and doctorate, GRE General Test. *Application deadline:* For fall admission, 7/7 for domestic students; for spring admission, 11/24 for domestic students. Applications are processed on a rolling basis. Application fee: $25 ($50 for international students). Electronic applications accepted. *Financial support:* Research assistantships, teaching assistantships, Federal Work-Study available. Support available to part-time students. Financial award application deadline: 3/15. *Faculty research:* Farm management, agricultural marketing, production economics, resource economics, agricultural finance. *Unit head:* Dr. Curtis M. Jolly, Chair, 334-844-4800. *Application contact:* Dr. Joe Pittman, Interim Dean of the Graduate School, 334-844-4700.

Buffalo State College, State University of New York, Graduate Studies and Research, Faculty of Natural and Social Sciences, Department of Economics and Finance, Buffalo, NY 14222-1095. Offers applied economics (MA). *Degree requirements:* For master's, project. *Entrance requirements:* Additional exam requirements/recommendations for international students: Required—TOEFL (minimum score 550 paper-based; 213 computer-based).

Clemson University, Graduate School, College of Agriculture, Forestry and Life Sciences, Department of Applied Economics and Statistics, Program in Applied Economics and Statistics, Clemson, SC 29634. Offers MS. *Students:* 10 full-time (5 women), 8 international. Average age 24. 29 applicants, 48% accepted, 6 enrolled. In 2007, 6 degrees awarded. *Degree requirements:* For master's, thesis optional. *Entrance requirements:* For master's, GRE General Test, minimum GPA of 3.0. Additional exam requirements/recommendations for international students: Required—TOEFL. *Application deadline:* For fall admission, 5/1 for domestic students, 4/15 for international students; for spring admission, 10/1 for domestic students, 9/15 for international students. Applications are processed on a rolling basis. Application fee: $55. *Financial support:* Application deadline: 3/1; *Unit head:* Dr. William Bridges, Program Coordinator, 864-656-3012, Fax: 864-656-5776. *Application contact:* Ellen Reneke, Staff Assistant for Graduate Programs, 864-656-5741, Fax: 864-656-5776, E-mail: ereneke@clemson.edu.

Clemson University, Graduate School, College of Business and Behavioral Science, Department of Economics, Program in Applied Economics, Clemson, SC 29634. Offers PhD. *Students:* 66 full-time (33 women), 5 part-time (1 woman); includes 4 minority (1 African American, 1 Asian American or Pacific Islander, 2 Hispanic Americans), 39 international. Average age 26. 108 applicants, 47% accepted, 22 enrolled. In 2007, 10 degrees awarded. *Degree requirements:* For doctorate, thesis/dissertation. *Entrance requirements:* For doctorate, GRE General Test, minimum GPA of 3.0, MS. Additional exam requirements/recommendations for international students: Required—TOEFL. *Application deadline:* For fall admission, 5/1 for domestic students, 4/15 for international students; for spring admission, 10/1 for domestic students, 9/15 for international students. Applications are processed on a rolling basis. Application fee: $55. *Financial support:* In 2007–08, 11 fellowships (averaging $5,200 per year), 27 research assistantships (averaging $13,400 per year), 44 teaching assistantships (averaging $14,900 per year) were awarded. Financial award application deadline: 3/1; financial award applicants required to submit FAFSA. *Faculty research:* Policy production, marketing, natural resources, regional development, industrial organization. *Unit head:* Dr. Hoke Hill, Chair, 864-656-3225.

Cornell University, Graduate School, Graduate Fields of Arts and Sciences, Field of Economics, Ithaca, NY 14853-0001. Offers applied economics (PhD); basic analytical economics (PhD); econometrics and economic statistics (PhD); economic development and planning (PhD); economic theory (PhD); industrial organization and control (PhD); international economics (PhD); labor economics (PhD); monetary and macroeconomics (PhD); public finance (PhD). *Faculty:* 74 full-time (10 women). *Students:* 102 full-time (37 women); includes 6 minority (2 African Americans, 3 Asian Americans or Pacific Islanders, 1 Hispanic American), 63 international. Average age 28. 538 applicants, 14% accepted, 25 enrolled. In 2007, 23 doctorates awarded. *Degree requirements:* For doctorate, comprehensive exam, thesis/dissertation. *Entrance requirements:* For doctorate, GRE General Test, 3 letters of recommendation. Additional exam requirements/recommendations for international students: Required—TOEFL (minimum score 550 paper-based; 213 computer-based; 77 iBT). *Application deadline:* For fall admission, 1/15 priority date for domestic students. Application fee: $70. Electronic applications accepted. *Financial support:* In 2007–08, 88 students received support, including 24 fellowships with full tuition reimbursements available, 13 research assistantships with full tuition reimbursements available, 51 teaching assistantships with full tuition reimbursements available; institutionally sponsored loans, scholarships/grants, health care benefits, tuition waivers (full and partial), and unspecified assistantships also available. Financial award applicants required to submit FAFSA. *Faculty research:* Learning and games, economics of education, political economy, transfer payments, time series and nonparametrics. *Unit head:* Director of Graduate Studies, 607-255-4893, Fax: 607-255-2818. *Application contact:* Graduate Field Assistant, 607-255-4893, Fax: 607-255-2818, E-mail: econ_phd@cornell.edu.

Eastern Michigan University, Graduate School, College of Arts and Sciences, Department of Economics, Ypsilanti, MI 48197. Offers applied economics (MA); economics (MA); health economics (MA); international economics and development (MA); trade and development (MA). Part-time and evening/weekend programs available. Postbaccalaureate distance learning degree programs offered (minimal on-campus study). *Faculty:* 11 full-time (2 women). *Students:* 18 full-time (10 women), 34 part-time (11 women); includes 13 minority (11 African Americans, 1 Asian American or Pacific Islander, 1 Hispanic American), 14 international. Average age 29. In 2007, 27 degrees awarded. *Degree requirements:* For master's, thesis or alternative. *Entrance requirements:* Additional exam requirements/recommendations for international students: Required—TOEFL. *Application deadline:* Applications are processed on a rolling basis. Application fee: $35. *Expenses:* Tuition, state resident: full-time $8,952; part-time $373 per credit hour. Tuition, nonresident: full-time $17,634; part-time $735 per credit hour. Required fees: $896; $34 per credit hour. Tuition and fees vary according to course level, degree level and program. *Financial support:* Fellowships, research assistantships with full tuition reimbursements, teaching assistantships with full tuition reimbursements, career-related internships or fieldwork, Federal Work-Study, institutionally sponsored loans, scholarships/grants, tuition waivers (partial), and unspecified assistantships available. Support available to part-time students. Financial award applicants required to submit FAFSA. *Unit head:* Dr. Raouf S. Hanna, Head, 734-487-3395, Fax: 734-487-9666, E-mail: rhanna@emich.edu. *Application contact:* Dr. David Crary, Advisor, 734-487-0001, Fax: 734-487-9666, E-mail: dcrary@emich.edu.

Georgia Southern University, Jack N. Averitt College of Graduate Studies, College of Business Administration, Program in Applied Economics, Statesboro, GA 30460. Offers MS. Program is held online. *Expenses:* Tuition, state resident: full-time $3,516; part-time $147 per semester hour. Tuition, nonresident: full-time $14,060; part-time $586 per semester hour.

Applied Economics

Georgia Southern University (continued)

Required fees: $562 per term. *Application contact:* 912-478-5384, Fax: 912-478-0740, E-mail: gradadmissions@georgiasouthern.edu.

HEC Montreal, School of Business Administration, Master of Science Programs in Administration, Program in Applied Economics, Montréal, QC H3T 2A7, Canada. Offers M Sc. All courses are given in French. Part-time programs available. *Degree requirements:* For master's, one foreign language, thesis. Electronic applications accepted. Tuition charges are reported in Canadian dollars. *Expenses:* Tuition, state resident: full-time $5,800 Canadian dollars. Tuition, nonresident: full-time $12,200 Canadian dollars. International tuition: $23,300 Canadian dollars full-time. *Financial support:* Fellowships, research assistantships, teaching assistantships, scholarships/grants available. *Application contact:* Francine Blais, Administrative Director, 514-340-6112, Fax: 514-340-6411, E-mail: francine.blais@hec.ca.

The Johns Hopkins University, Zanvyl Krieger School of Arts and Sciences, Advanced Academic Programs, Program in Applied Economics, Washington, DC 20036. Offers MA. Part-time and evening/weekend programs available. *Faculty:* 1 full-time, 16 part-time/adjunct. *Students:* 97 applicants, 79% accepted, 73 enrolled. *Degree requirements:* For master's, thesis (for some programs). *Entrance requirements:* For master's, minimum 3.0 GPA, coursework in microeconomics and macroeconomics. Additional exam requirements/recommendations for international students: Required—TOEFL (minimum score 250 computer-based; 100 iBT). *Application deadline:* For fall admission, 5/31 priority date for domestic students, 4/31 priority date for international students; for spring admission, 10/31 priority date for domestic and international students. Applications are processed on a rolling basis. Application fee: $70. Electronic applications accepted. *Financial support:* Applicants required to submit FAFSA. *Unit head:* Dr. Frank Weiss, Associate Program Chair, 202-452-0769, E-mail: fdweiss@jhu.edu. *Application contact:* Rachel C. Jenkins, Admissions Manager, 202-452-1941, Fax: 202-452-1970, E-mail: aapadmissions@jhu.edu.

See Close-Up on page 1027.

Mississippi State University, College of Business and Industry, Department of Finance and Economics, Mississippi State, MS 39762. Offers applied economics (PhD); economics (MA); finance (MSBA). Part-time programs available. *Faculty:* 18 full-time (4 women), 6 part-time/adjunct (2 women). *Students:* 1 full-time (0 women), 1 (woman) part-time, 1 international. Average age 28. 61 applicants, 21% accepted. In 2007, 8 master's, 1 doctorate awarded. Terminal master's awarded for partial completion of doctoral program. *Degree requirements:* For master's, comprehensive exam, thesis optional; for doctorate, comprehensive exam, thesis/dissertation. *Entrance requirements:* For master's and doctorate, GMAT, GRE General Test. *Application deadline:* For fall admission, 7/1 for domestic students; for spring admission, 11/1 for domestic students. Applications are processed on a rolling basis. Application fee: $30. *Expenses:* Tuition, state resident: full-time $4,978; part-time $274 per hour. Tuition, nonresident: full-time $11,469; part-time $635 per hour. *Financial support:* In 2007–08, 1 teaching assistantship with tuition reimbursement (averaging $19,220 per year) was awarded; research assistantships with tuition reimbursements, Federal Work-Study, scholarships/grants, health care benefits, and unspecified assistantships also available. Financial award applicants required to submit FAFSA. *Faculty research:* Economics development, mergers, event studies, economic education, bank performance. Total annual research expenditures: $421,000. *Unit head:* Dr. Paul W. Grimes, Head, 662-325-2341, Fax: 662-325-1977, E-mail: pgrimes@cobilan.msstate.edu. *Application contact:* Dr. William A. Person, Interim Associate Vice President for Academic Affairs/Interim Dean of Graduate Studies, 662-325-7400, Fax: 662-325-1967, E-mail: grad@grad.msstate.edu.

Montana State University, College of Graduate Studies, College of Agriculture, Department of Agricultural Economics and Economics, Bozeman, MT 59717. Offers applied economics (MS). Part-time programs available. *Faculty:* 17 full-time (2 women), 6 part-time/adjunct (2 women). *Students:* 13 full-time (5 women), 8 part-time (1 woman), 1 international. Average age 24. 20 applicants, 65% accepted, 7 enrolled. In 2007, 3 degrees awarded. *Degree requirements:* For master's, comprehensive exam. *Entrance requirements:* For master's, GRE General Test. Additional exam requirements/recommendations for international students: Required—TOEFL (minimum score 550 paper-based; 213 computer-based). *Application deadline:* For fall admission, 7/15 priority date for domestic students, 5/15 priority date for international students; for spring admission, 12/1 priority date for domestic students, 10/1 priority date for international students. Applications are processed on a rolling basis. Application fee: $30. Electronic applications accepted. *Expenses:* Tuition, state resident: full-time $5,176. Tuition, nonresident: full-time $13,070. *Financial support:* In 2007–08, 4 research assistantships with partial tuition reimbursements were awarded; teaching assistantships with partial tuition reimbursements, unspecified assistantships also available. Financial award application deadline: 3/1; financial award applicants required to submit FAFSA. *Faculty research:* Agricultural production, agricultural marketing/finance, governance (private and public), natural resource management. Total annual research expenditures: $1.3 million. *Unit head:* Myles Watts, Co-Interim Head, 406-994-3701, Fax: 406-994-4838, E-mail: agecon@montana.edu.

New York University, Graduate School of Arts and Science, Department of Economics, New York, NY 10012-1019. Offers applied economic analysis (Advanced Certificate); economics (MA, PhD); JD/MA; MD/PhD. Part-time and evening/weekend programs available. *Faculty:* 35 full-time (2 women), 29 part-time/adjunct. *Students:* 240 full-time (82 women), 39 part-time (15 women); includes 18 minority (1 African American, 14 Asian Americans or Pacific Islanders, 3 Hispanic Americans), 199 international. Average age 27. 1,056 applicants, 21% accepted, 91 enrolled. In 2007, 66 master's, 9 doctorates awarded. Terminal master's awarded for partial completion of doctoral program. *Degree requirements:* For master's, thesis; for doctorate, one foreign language, thesis/dissertation, 4 qualifying exams. *Entrance requirements:* For master's and doctorate, GRE General Test; for Advanced Certificate, master's degree. Additional exam requirements/recommendations for international students: Required—TOEFL. *Application deadline:* For fall admission, 1/4 priority date for domestic students. Application fee: $85. *Financial support:* Fellowships with tuition reimbursements, research assistantships with tuition reimbursements, teaching assistantships with tuition reimbursements, Federal Work-Study, institutionally sponsored loans, scholarships/grants, health care benefits, and unspecified assistantships available. Financial award application deadline: 1/4; financial award applicants required to submit FAFSA. *Faculty research:* Economic theory, experimental economics, growth and development, macroeconomics and finance, international trade and international finance. *Unit head:* David Pearce, Chair, 212-998-8900, Fax: 212-995-4186, E-mail: admissions@econ.nyu.edu. *Application contact:* Debraj Ray, Director of Graduate Studies, 212-998-8900, Fax: 212-995-4186, E-mail: gsas.admissions@nyu.edu.

North Carolina Agricultural and Technical State University, Graduate School, School of Agriculture and Environmental and Allied Sciences, Department of Agribusiness, Applied Economics, and Agriscience Education, Greensboro, NC 27411. Offers agricultural economics (MS); agricultural education (MS). *Accreditation:* NCATE. Part-time and evening/weekend programs available. *Degree requirements:* For master's, comprehensive exam, thesis or alternative, qualifying exam. *Entrance requirements:* For master's, GRE General Test, minimum GPA of 3.0. *Faculty research:* Aid for small farmers, agricultural technology resources, labor force mobility, agrology.

Northeastern University, College of Arts and Sciences, Department of Economics, Boston, MA 02115-5096. Offers MA, PhD. Part-time and evening/weekend programs available. *Faculty:* 15 full-time (2 women). *Students:* 43 full-time (24 women), 9 part-time (3 women). 121 applicants, 46% accepted. In 2007, 7 degrees awarded. *Degree requirements:* For master's and doctorate, comprehensive exam. *Entrance requirements:* For master's, GRE. Additional exam requirements/recommendations for international students: Required—TOEFL. *Application deadline:* For fall admission, 8/1 for domestic students, 5/1 priority date for international students; for spring admission, 12/1 for domestic and international students. Applications are processed on a rolling basis. Application fee: $50. *Financial support:* In 2007–08, 12 teaching assistantships (averaging $15,667 per year) were awarded; Federal Work-Study, institutionally sponsored loans, tuition waivers (full and partial), and unspecified assistantships also available. Financial award application deadline: 2/1; financial award applicants required to submit FAFSA. *Faculty research:* U.S. labor markets, applied economics, microeconomic theory, macroeconomic theory, econometrics. *Unit head:* Dr. Steven Morrison, Chair, 617-373-2872, Fax: 617-373-3640, E-mail: econ@neu.edu. *Application contact:* Dr. Gregory Wassall, Graduate Coordinator, 617-373-2882, Fax: 617-373-3640, E-mail: econ@neu.edu.

See Close-Up on page 1029.

Ohio University, Graduate College, College of Arts and Sciences, Department of Economics, Athens, OH 45701-2979. Offers applied economics (MA); financial economics (MFE). Evening/weekend programs available. *Faculty:* 15 full-time (3 women). *Students:* 31 full-time (16 women), 9 part-time (3 women); includes 2 minority (both American Indian/Alaska Native), 34 international. 94 applicants, 70% accepted, 21 enrolled. In 2007, 19 degrees awarded. *Degree requirements:* For master's, thesis or alternative. *Entrance requirements:* For master's, GRE or GMAT, minimum GPA of 3.0. Additional exam requirements/recommendations for international students: Required—TOEFL (minimum score 550 paper-based). *Application deadline:* For fall admission, 3/15 priority date for domestic students, 2/15 priority date for international students. Applications are processed on a rolling basis. Application fee: $50 ($55 for international students). *Financial support:* In 2007–08, 15 research assistantships with tuition reimbursements were awarded; Federal Work-Study, institutionally sponsored loans, scholarships/grants, and unspecified assistantships also available. Financial award application deadline: 3/15. *Faculty research:* Macroeconomics, public finance, international economics and finance, monetary theory, healthcare economics. *Unit head:* Dr. Roy Boyd, Chair, 740-593-2040, E-mail: boydr1@ohio.edu. *Application contact:* Dr. K. Doroodian, Graduate Chair, 740-593-2046, E-mail: doroodia@ohio.edu.

Old Dominion University, College of Business and Public Administration, Master's Program in Business Administration, Norfolk, VA 23529. Offers business and economic forecasting (MBA); financial analysis and valuation (MBA); information technology and enterprise integration (MBA); international business (MBA); maritime and port management (MBA); public administration (MBA). *Accreditation:* AACSB. Part-time and evening/weekend programs available. *Faculty:* 66 full-time (15 women), 6 part-time/adjunct (1 woman). *Students:* 86 full-time (38 women), 201 part-time (86 women); includes 53 minority (33 African Americans, 1 American Indian/Alaska Native, 16 Asian Americans or Pacific Islanders, 3 Hispanic Americans), 36 international. Average age 31. 235 applicants, 71% accepted, 114 enrolled. In 2007, 83 degrees awarded. *Entrance requirements:* For master's, GMAT, letters of reference, resumé, essay, transcripts, calculus. Additional exam requirements/recommendations for international students: Required—TOEFL (minimum score 550 paper-based; 213 computer-based; 80 iBT). *Application deadline:* For fall admission, 6/1 priority date for domestic students, 4/15 priority date for international students; for spring admission, 11/1 priority date for domestic students, 10/1 priority date for international students. Applications are processed on a rolling basis. Application fee: $40. Electronic applications accepted. *Expenses:* Tuition, state resident: part-time $304 per credit hour. Tuition, nonresident: part-time $761 per credit hour. *Financial support:* In 2007–08, 46 students received support, including 31 research assistantships with partial tuition reimbursements available (averaging $7,000 per year), 3 teaching assistantships with partial tuition reimbursements available (averaging $6,300 per year); career-related internships or fieldwork, scholarships/grants, and unspecified assistantships also available. Support available to part-time students. Financial award application deadline: 2/15; financial award applicants required to submit FAFSA. *Faculty research:* International business, buyer behavior, financial markets, strategy, operations research. *Unit head:* Dr. Bruce Rubin, Graduate Program Director, 757-683-3585, E-mail: mbainfo@odu.edu. *Application contact:* Shanna Wood, MBA Program Manager, 757-683-3585, Fax: 757-683-5750, E-mail: mbainfo@odu.edu.

Portland State University, Graduate Studies, College of Liberal Arts and Sciences, Department of Economics, Portland, OR 97207-0751. Offers applied economics (MA, MS); economics (PhD); general economics (MA, MS). Part-time programs available. *Faculty:* 14 full-time (4 women), 6 part-time/adjunct (1 woman). *Students:* 13 full-time (4 women), 5 part-time (4 women); includes 3 minority (2 Asian Americans or Pacific Islanders, 1 Hispanic American), 4 international. Average age 29. 19 applicants, 68% accepted, 7 enrolled. In 2007, 10 degrees awarded. *Degree requirements:* For master's, thesis optional; for doctorate, one foreign language, thesis/dissertation. *Entrance requirements:* For master's, minimum GPA of 3.0 in upper-division course work or 2.75 overall, course work in calculus. Additional exam requirements/recommendations for international students: Required—TOEFL (minimum score 550 paper-based; 213 computer-based). *Application deadline:* For fall admission, 4/1 for domestic students, 3/1 for international students; for spring admission, 11/1 for domestic and international students. Applications are processed on a rolling basis. Application fee: $50. *Expenses:* Tuition, state resident: full-time $7,047. Tuition, nonresident: full-time $11,178. *Financial support:* In 2007–08, 2 research assistantships with full tuition reimbursements (averaging $6,120 per year) were awarded; teaching assistantships, career-related internships or fieldwork, Federal Work-Study, and unspecified assistantships also available. Support available to part-time students. Financial award application deadline: 3/1; financial award applicants required to submit FAFSA. *Faculty research:* NAFTA, economies of transition, economics of Eastern Europe, artificial intelligence, comparative economic systems. Total annual research expenditures: $275,425. *Unit head:* Dr. John Walker, Chair, 503-725-3915, Fax: 503-725-3945. *Application contact:* Rita Spears, Office Specialist, 503-725-3941, Fax: 503-725-3945, E-mail: spearsr@pdx.edu.

Roosevelt University, Graduate Division, College of Arts and Sciences, Department of Economics, Chicago, IL 60605-1394. Offers applied economics (MA); economics (MA). Part-time and evening/weekend programs available. *Students:* 6 full-time (2 women), 8 part-time (4 women); includes 6 minority (all African Americans), 4 international. Average age 29. 20 applicants, 20% accepted, 3 enrolled. *Degree requirements:* For master's, thesis or alternative. *Entrance requirements:* For master's, minimum GPA of 2.7. *Application deadline:* For fall admission, 6/1 priority date for domestic students. Applications are processed on a rolling basis. Application fee: $25 ($35 for international students). *Financial support:* In 2007–08, 4 students received support, including 1 teaching assistantship; career-related internships or fieldwork, Federal Work-Study, scholarships/grants, and tuition waivers (full and partial) also available. Financial award application deadline: 2/15. *Faculty research:* Labor, gender issues, international trade and development, entrepreneurship, political economy and money. Total annual research expenditures: $5,000. *Unit head:* June Lapidus, Head, 312-341-3670. *Application contact:* Joanne Canyon-Heller, Coordinator of Graduate Admission, 877-APPLY RU, Fax: 312-281-3356, E-mail: applyru@roosevelt.edu.

St. Cloud State University, School of Graduate Studies, College of Social Sciences, Department of Economics, St. Cloud, MN 56301-4498. Offers applied economics (MS); public and nonprofit institutions (MS). Part-time programs available. *Faculty:* 20 full-time (5 women), 1 part-time/adjunct (0 women). *Students:* 17 full-time (7 women), 8 part-time (4 women); includes 3 minority (all African Americans), 13 international. 8 applicants, 75% accepted, 5 enrolled. In 2007, 2 degrees awarded. *Degree requirements:* For master's, thesis or alternative. *Entrance requirements:* For master's, GRE General Test, minimum GPA of 2.75. Additional exam requirements/recommendations for international students: Recommended—TOEFL (minimum score 550 paper-based; 213 computer-based), IELTS (minimum score 7). *Application deadline:* For fall admission, 6/1 priority date for domestic students, 4/1 for international students; for spring admission, 10/1 priority date for domestic students, 8/1 for international students. Applications are processed on a rolling basis. Application fee: $35. Electronic applications accepted. *Expenses:* Tuition, state resident: part-time $267 per credit. Tuition, nonresident: part-time $418 per credit. Required fees: $28 per credit. *Financial support:* Federal Work-Study, scholarships/grants, and unspecified assistantships available. *Unit head:* Dr. King Bahaian, Chairperson, 320-308-2968, E-mail: kbahaian@stcloudstate.edu. *Application contact:* Linda Lou Krueger, School of Graduate Studies, 320-308-2113, Fax: 320-308-5371, E-mail: lekrueger@stcloudstate.edu.

San Jose State University, Graduate Studies and Research, College of Social Sciences, Department of Economics, San Jose, CA 95192-0001. Offers applied economics (MA); economics (MA). Part-time programs available. *Students:* 40 full-time (18 women), 33 part-time (15 women); includes 22 minority (16 Asian Americans or Pacific Islanders, 6 Hispanic Americans), 22 international. Average age 30. 66 applicants, 68% accepted, 22 enrolled. In 2007, 31 degrees awarded. *Degree requirements:* For master's, comprehensive exam, thesis optional. *Entrance requirements:* For master's, GRE, minimum GPA of 3.0. *Application deadline:* For fall admission, 6/29 for domestic students; for spring admission, 11/30 for domestic students. Applications are processed on a rolling basis. Application fee: $59. Electronic applications accepted. *Financial support:* In 2007–08, 2 teaching assistantships were awarded. Financial award applicants required to submit FAFSA. *Unit head:* Dr. Lydia Ortega, Chair, 408-924-5400, Fax: 408-924-5406.

Southern Methodist University, Dedman College, Department of Economics, Dallas, TX 75275. Offers applied economics (MA); economics (MA, PhD); JD/MA. Part-time and evening/weekend programs available. *Faculty:* 17 full-time (1 woman), 1 part-time/adjunct (0 women). *Students:* 49 full-time (22 women), 15 part-time (4 women); includes 7 minority (1 African American, 1 American Indian/Alaska Native, 4 Asian Americans or Pacific Islanders, 1 Hispanic American), 38 international. Average age 27. 85 applicants, 89% accepted, 16 enrolled. In 2007, 20 master's, 4 doctorates awarded. Terminal master's awarded for partial completion of doctoral program. *Median time to degree:* Of those who began their doctoral program in fall 1999, 100% received their degree in 8 years or less. *Degree requirements:* For master's, thesis optional, oral qualifying exam; for doctorate, thesis/dissertation, written exams. *Entrance requirements:* For master's, GRE General Test or GMAT, 12 hours course work in economics, minimum GPA of 3.0, previous course work in calculus and statistics; for doctorate, GRE General Test, minimum GPA of 3.0, 3 semesters of course work in calculus, 1 semester of course work in statistics, 1 semester of course work in linear algebra. Additional exam requirements/recommendations for international students: Required—TOEFL (minimum score 550 paper-based; 213 computer-based). *Application deadline:* For fall admission, 2/1 priority date for domestic students; for spring admission, 11/30 priority date for domestic students. Applications are processed on a rolling basis. Application fee: $75. Electronic applications accepted. *Financial support:* In 2007–08, 1 fellowship with full tuition reimbursement (averaging $16,000 per year), 2 research assistantships with full tuition reimbursements (averaging $16,000 per year), 20 teaching assistantships with full tuition reimbursements (averaging $16,000 per year) were awarded; tuition waivers (partial) also available. Financial award application deadline: 2/1; financial award applicants required to submit FAFSA. *Faculty research:* Economic theory, game theory, econometrics, international trade, labor. *Unit head:* Dr. Kamal Saggi, Chair, 214-768-3274, Fax: 214-768-1821, E-mail: ksaggi@mail.smu.edu. *Application contact:* Information Contact, 214-768-4337.

Texas Tech University, Graduate School, College of Agricultural Sciences and Natural Resources, Department of Agricultural and Applied Economics, Lubbock, TX 79409. Offers agribusiness (MAB); agricultural and applied economics (MS, PhD); JD/MS. Part-time programs available. *Faculty:* 11 full-time (0 women). *Students:* 24 full-time (11 women), 3 part-time; includes 5 minority (1 African American, 2 Asian Americans or Pacific Islanders, 2 Hispanic Americans), 9 international. Average age 30. 20 applicants, 75% accepted, 8 enrolled. In 2007, 5 master's, 2 doctorates awarded. *Degree requirements:* For master's, thesis or alternative; for doctorate, thesis/dissertation. *Entrance requirements:* For master's and doctorate, GRE General Test. Additional exam requirements/recommendations for international students: Required—TOEFL (minimum score 550 paper-based; 213 computer-based). *Application deadline:* For fall admission, 3/1 priority date for international students; for spring admission, 11/1 priority date for international students. Applications are processed on a rolling basis. Application fee: $50 ($60 for international students). Electronic applications accepted. *Expenses:* Tuition, state resident: part-time $373 per credit hour. Tuition, nonresident: part-time $651 per credit hour. Tuition and fees vary according to program. *Financial support:* In 2007–08, 24 students received support, including 19 research assistantships with partial tuition reimbursements available (averaging $13,275 per year), 1 teaching assistantship with partial tuition reimbursement available (averaging $12,000 per year); Federal Work-Study and institutionally sponsored loans also available. Support available to part-time students. Financial award application deadline: 4/15; financial award applicants required to submit FAFSA. *Faculty research:* Economics of the U.S. cotton and textile industries, natural resource management in semi-arid climates, commodity policy analysis, international trade in agricultural products, agribusiness analysis. Total annual research expenditures: $1.3 million. *Unit head:* Dr. Eduardo Segarra, Chair, 806-742-2821, Fax: 806-742-1099, E-mail: eduardo.segarra@ttu.edu. *Application contact:* Dr. Tom Knight, Graduate Adviser, 806-742-2821, Fax: 806-742-1099, E-mail: tom.knight@ttu.edu.

University of California, Santa Cruz, Division of Graduate Studies, Division of Social Sciences, Program in Applied Economics and Finance, Santa Cruz, CA 95064. Offers MS. *Faculty:* 22 full-time (3 women). *Students:* 24 full-time (12 women), 1 (woman) part-time; includes 4 minority (all Asian Americans or Pacific Islanders), 11 international. 52 applicants, 69% accepted, 9 enrolled. In 2007, 18 degrees awarded. *Degree requirements:* For master's, thesis or alternative, project. *Entrance requirements:* For master's, GRE General Test, GRE Subject Test. *Application deadline:* For fall admission, 2/1 for domestic students. Application fee: $60. *Expenses:* Tuition, nonresident: full-time $14,694. Required fees: $11,360. *Financial support:* Research assistantships, teaching assistantships, career-related internships or fieldwork, Federal Work-Study, and institutionally sponsored loans available. Financial award application deadline: 2/1. *Faculty research:* Economic decision-making skills for the design and operation of complex institutional systems. *Unit head:* Robert Fairlie, Director, 831-459-3332, E-mail: rfairlie@ucsc.edu. *Application contact:* Cristina M. Intintoli, Graduate Coordinator, 831-427-6600, E-mail: cmintint@ucsc.edu.

University of Georgia, Graduate School, College of Agricultural and Environmental Sciences, Department of Agricultural and Applied Economics, Athens, GA 30602. Offers agricultural economics (MAE, MS, PhD); environmental economics (MS). *Faculty:* 18 full-time (1 woman). *Students:* 35 full-time (12 women), 2 part-time; includes 4 minority (2 African Americans, 2 Asian Americans or Pacific Islanders), 16 international. 45 applicants, 22% accepted, 4 enrolled. In 2007, 10 master's, 2 doctorates awarded. *Degree requirements:* For master's, thesis (MS); for doctorate, thesis/dissertation. *Entrance requirements:* For master's and doctorate, GRE General Test. *Application deadline:* For fall admission, 7/1 priority date for domestic students; for spring admission, 11/15 for domestic students. Application fee: $50. Electronic applications accepted. *Financial support:* Fellowships, research assistantships, teaching assistantships, career-related internships or fieldwork and unspecified assistantships available. *Unit head:* Dr. Jeffrey H. Dorfman, Interim Head, 706-542-0754, Fax: 706-542-0739, E-mail: jdorfman@agecon.uga.edu. *Application contact:* Dr. James Epperson, Graduate Coordinator, 706-543-0766, Fax: 706-542-0739, E-mail: jepperson@agecon.uga.edu.

University of Michigan, Horace H. Rackham School of Graduate Studies, College of Literature, Science, and the Arts, Department of Economics, Program in Applied Economics, Ann Arbor, MI 48109. Offers AM. Part-time programs available. *Faculty:* 49 full-time (6 women). *Students:* 49 full-time (18 women). 123 applicants, 71% accepted, 31 enrolled. In 2007, 47 degrees awarded. *Entrance requirements:* For master's, GRE General Test. Additional exam requirements/recommendations for international students: Required—TOEFL (minimum score 600 paper-based; 250 computer-based). *Application deadline:* For fall admission, 2/5 for domestic and international students. Application fee: $60 ($75 for international students). *Faculty research:* Econometric analysis transition, macro. *Unit head:* John Laitner, Director, 734-763-5316, Fax: 734-764-2769. *Application contact:* Larue Cochran, Student Services Assistant, 734-763-5316, Fax: 734-764-2769, E-mail: larue@umich.edu.

University of Minnesota, Twin Cities Campus, Graduate School, College of Food, Agricultural and Natural Resource Sciences, Program in Applied Economics, Minneapolis, MN 55455-0213. Offers MS, PhD. *Faculty:* 56 full-time (16 women), 2 part-time/adjunct (0 women). *Students:* 114 full-time (46 women); includes 31 minority (6 African Americans, 17 Asian Americans or Pacific Islanders, 8 Hispanic Americans), 65 international. 148 applicants, 22% accepted, 28 enrolled. In 2007, 4 master's, 6 doctorates awarded. *Median time to degree:* Of those who began their doctoral program in fall 1999, 78% received their degree in 8 years or less. *Degree requirements:* For master's, comprehensive exam, thesis; for doctorate, comprehensive exam, thesis/dissertation. *Entrance requirements:* For master's and doctorate, GRE, minimum GPA of 3.0 preferred. Additional exam requirements/recommendations for international students: Required—TOEFL (minimum score 550 paper-based; 213 computer-based; 79 iBT). *Application deadline:* For fall admission, 12/15 for domestic students; for spring admission, 10/15 for domestic students. Applications are processed on a rolling basis. Application fee: $55 ($75 for international students). Electronic applications accepted. *Financial support:* In 2007–08, 44 students received support, including 1 fellowship with full tuition reimbursement available (averaging $20,000 per year), 32 research assistantships with full tuition reimbursements available (averaging $19,000 per year), 11 teaching assistantships with full tuition reimbursements available (averaging $19,000 per year); health care benefits, tuition waivers (full and partial), unspecified assistantships, and stipends also available. Financial award application deadline: 12/15. *Faculty research:* Consumer behavior, household and labor, policy analysis and health, production and marketing, resource and environmental, trade and development. Total annual research expenditures: $1.7 million. *Unit head:* Dr. Terry Hurley, Director of Graduate Studies, 612-625-7028, Fax: 612-625-6245, E-mail: tmh@umn.edu. *Application contact:* Linda Schwartz, Program Coordinator, 612-625-3777, Fax: 612-625-6245, E-mail: lschwart@umn.edu.

University of Nevada, Reno, Graduate School, College of Agriculture, Biotechnology and Natural Resources, Department of Resource Economics, Reno, NV 89557. Offers MS, PhD. *Faculty:* 15. *Students:* 15 full-time (10 women), 6 part-time (4 women), 10 international. Average age 33. 20 applicants, 85% accepted, 9 enrolled. In 2007, 2 degrees awarded. *Degree requirements:* For master's, thesis optional. *Entrance requirements:* For master's, GRE General Test, minimum GPA of 2.75; for doctorate, GRE General Test. Additional exam requirements/recommendations for international students: Required—TOEFL. *Application deadline:* For fall admission, 3/1 priority date for domestic students; for spring admission, 11/1 for domestic students. Applications are processed on a rolling basis. Application fee: $60 ($95 for international students). *Expenses:* Tuition, state resident: full-time $2,774; part-time $154 per credit. Tuition, nonresident: full-time $13,578; part-time $330 per credit. Required fees: $49 per semester. *Financial support:* In 2007–08, 12 research assistantships were awarded. Financial award application deadline: 3/1. *Unit head:* Dr. Kim Rollins, Graduate Program Director, 775-784-1677.

University of New Brunswick Fredericton, School of Graduate Studies, Faculty of Arts, Department of Economics, Fredericton, NB E3B 5A3, Canada. Offers applied economics and finance (M Sc); economics (MA). Program in applied economics and finance offered at UNB Saint John Campus. Part-time programs available. *Faculty:* 14 full-time (1 woman). *Students:* 10 full-time (4 women), 1 (woman) part-time. Average age 23. 40 applicants, 65% accepted. In 2007, 4 degrees awarded. *Entrance requirements:* For master's, GRE, minimum GPA of 3.0. Additional exam requirements/recommendations for international students: Required—TWE, TOEFL (minimum paper-based score of 550) or IELTS. *Application deadline:* 1/31 for domestic and international students. Applications are processed on a rolling basis. Application fee: $50 Canadian dollars. *Financial support:* In 2007–08, 2 research assistantships, 2 teaching assistantships were awarded; fellowships, scholarships/grants, health care benefits, and unspecified assistantships also available. Financial award application deadline: 1/31. *Faculty research:* Epidemiology and Population Health, Micro/Macro Economics, Economics of Transportation, Regional Development. *Unit head:* Dr. Yuri Yevdokimov, Director of Graduate Studies, 506-447-3221, Fax: 506-453-4514, E-mail: yuri@unb.ca. *Application contact:* Melanie Lawson, Graduate Secretary, 506-458-7420, Fax: 506-453-4514, E-mail: melanie@unb.ca.

The University of North Carolina at Greensboro, Graduate School, Bryan School of Business and Economics, Department of Economics, Program in Applied Economics, Greensboro, NC 27412-5001. Offers MA, MA/PhD. *Students:* 36 full-time (11 women), 3 part-time (all women); includes 5 minority (1 African American, 3 Asian Americans or Pacific Islanders, 1 Hispanic American). *Degree requirements:* For master's, comprehensive exam, thesis or alternative. *Entrance requirements:* For master's, GRE. Additional exam requirements/recommendations for international students: Required—TOEFL. *Application deadline:* For fall admission, 3/1 for domestic and international students; for spring admission, 11/1 for domestic students, 10/1 for international students. Applications are processed on a rolling basis. Application fee: $45. Electronic applications accepted. *Financial support:* Fellowships with partial tuition reimbursements, research assistantships available. Financial award application deadline: 3/1. *Application contact:* Michelle Harkleroad, Director of Graduate Admissions, 336-334-4884, Fax: 336-334-4424, E-mail: mbharkle@uncg.edu.

University of North Dakota, Graduate School, College of Business and Public Administration, Applied Economics Program, Grand Forks, ND 58202. Offers MSAE. *Faculty:* 9 full-time (1 woman). *Students:* 4 full-time (1 woman), 6 part-time; includes 2 American Indian/Alaska Native, 3 international. 8 applicants, 63% accepted, 5 enrolled. In 2007, 3 degrees awarded. *Degree requirements:* For master's, comprehensive exam, thesis or alternative. *Entrance requirements:* For master's, GRE General Test. Additional exam requirements/recommendations for international students: Required—TOEFL (minimum score 550 paper-based; 213 computer-based; 79 iBT), IELTS (minimum score 7). *Application deadline:* For fall admission, 2/15 priority date for domestic and international students; for spring admission, 10/15 priority date for domestic and international students. Application fee: $35. *Expenses:* Tuition, state resident: full-time $4,050; part-time $225 per credit. Tuition, nonresident: full-time $10,818; part-time $601 per credit. Required fees: $110 per semester. Tuition and fees vary according to class time, campus/location, program and reciprocity agreements. *Financial support:* In 2007–08, 1 research assistantship with full and partial tuition reimbursement, 2 teaching assistantships with full and partial tuition reimbursements were awarded; fellowships with full and partial tuition reimbursements, Federal Work-Study, scholarships/grants, health care benefits, tuition waivers (full and partial), and unspecified assistantships also available. Support available to part-time students. Financial award applicants required to submit FAFSA. *Unit head:* Dr. Daniel Biedermann, Graduate Director, 701-777-2637, E-mail: daniel_biedermann@und.edu. *Application contact:* Brenda Halle, Admissions Specialist, 701-777-2947, Fax: 701-777-3619, E-mail: brendahalle@mail.und.edu.

University of North Texas, Robert B. Toulouse School of Graduate Studies, College of Public Affairs and Community Service, Institute of Applied Economics, Denton, TX 76203. Offers MS. Part-time programs available. *Faculty:* 3 full-time (0 women). *Students:* 6 full-time (1 woman), 4 part-time (2 women); includes 2 minority (both African Americans), 4 international. Average age 31. 13 applicants, 38% accepted, 4 enrolled. *Degree requirements:* For master's, comprehensive exam, thesis or alternative. *Entrance requirements:* For master's, GRE General Test or GMAT, minimum B average in last 60 hours of course work. Additional exam requirements/recommendations for international students: Required—proof of English language proficiency required for non-native English speakers; Recommended—TOEFL (minimum score 550 paper-based; 213 computer-based). *Application deadline:* For fall admission, 7/15 for domestic students; for spring admission, 11/15 for domestic students. Application fee: $50 ($75 for international students). *Financial support:* In 2007–08, research assistantships (averaging $10,000 per year); career-related internships or fieldwork, Federal Work-Study, and tuition waivers (partial) also available. *Faculty research:* Economic/fiscal impact of sports and entertainment venues, economic development potential of stem cell research, state and local incentive programs, city and metropolitan area industrial targeting dispute resolution. Total annual research expenditures: $125,000. *Unit head:* Dr. Bernard Weinstein, Director, 940-565-3437, Fax: 940-565-4658. *Application contact:* Dr. Terry Clower, Graduate Adviser, 940-565-3437, Fax: 940-565-4658, E-mail: tclower@unt.edu.

University of Vermont, Graduate College, College of Agriculture and Life Sciences, Department of Community Development and Applied Economics, Burlington, VT 05405. Offers community development and applied economics (MS); public administration (MPA). *Students:* 20 (10

Applied Economics

University of Vermont (continued)
women); includes 1 minority (Asian American or Pacific Islander) 22 applicants, 73% accepted, 6 enrolled. In 2007, 7 degrees awarded. *Degree requirements:* For master's, thesis. *Entrance requirements:* For master's, GRE General Test. Additional exam requirements/recommendations for international students: Required—TOEFL (minimum score 550 paper-based; 213 computer-based; 80 iBT). *Application deadline:* For fall admission, 4/1 priority date for domestic students; for spring admission, 11/15 for domestic students. Applications are processed on a rolling basis. Application fee: $40. Electronic applications accepted. *Financial support:* Fellowships, research assistantships, teaching assistantships, career-related internships or fieldwork available. Financial award application deadline: 3/1. *Faculty research:* Agricultural production and marketing. *Unit head:* Dr. J. Kolodinsky, Chairperson, 802-656-2001.

University of Wisconsin–Madison, Graduate School, College of Agricultural and Life Sciences, Department of Agricultural and Applied Economics, Madison, WI 53706-1380. Offers MA, MS, PhD. Part-time programs available. *Degree requirements:* For doctorate, thesis/dissertation, preliminary exams. *Entrance requirements:* For master's and doctorate, GRE General Test. Additional exam requirements/recommendations for international students: Required—TOEFL. Electronic applications accepted. *Faculty research:* Environmental and resource economics, international development, state and local economics, food systems, markets and trade.

University of Wyoming, Graduate School, College of Agriculture, Department of Agricultural and Applied Economics, Laramie, WY 82070. Offers MS. Part-time programs available. *Faculty:* 12 full-time (2 women), 1 part-time/adjunct (0 women). *Students:* 8 full-time (3 women), 2 part-time (1 woman), 1 international. Average age 27. 11 applicants, 45% accepted. In 2007, 2 degrees awarded. *Degree requirements:* For master's, thesis (for some programs). *Entrance requirements:* For master's, GRE General Test, minimum GPA of 3.0. Additional exam requirements/recommendations for international students: Required—TOEFL. *Application deadline:* For fall admission, 2/15 priority date for domestic students, 2/1 for international students; for spring admission, 10/1 priority date for domestic students. Applications are processed on a rolling basis. Application fee: $50. Electronic applications accepted. *Financial support:* In 2007–08, 5 research assistantships with tuition reimbursements (averaging $10,062 per year) were awarded; career-related internships or fieldwork, Federal Work-Study, and institutionally sponsored loans also available. Financial award application deadline: 2/1; financial award applicants required to submit FAFSA. *Faculty research:* Farm management, agricultural markets, water economics, community development, agricultural business. Total annual research expenditures: $250,000. *Unit head:* Dr. Roger H. Coupal, Interim Department Head, 307-766-2386, Fax: 307-766-5544, E-mail: coupal@uwyo.edu.

Utah State University, School of Graduate Studies, College of Business and College of Agriculture, Department of Economics, Program in Applied Economics, Logan, UT 84322. Offers MS. Part-time programs available. *Degree requirements:* For master's, thesis optional. *Entrance requirements:* For master's, GRE General Test, minimum GPA of 3.0.

Virginia Polytechnic Institute and State University, Graduate School, College of Agriculture and Life Sciences, Department of Agricultural and Applied Economics, Blacksburg, VA 24061. Offers agribusiness (MS); agricultural economics (MS); applied economics (MS); developmental and international economics (PhD); econometrics (PhD); macro and micro economics (PhD); markets and industrial organizations (PhD); public and regional/urban economics (PhD); resource and environmental economics (PhD). *Entrance requirements:* For master's and doctorate, GRE General Test. Additional exam requirements/recommendations for international students: Required—TOEFL (minimum score 575 paper-based; 231 computer-based). Electronic applications accepted. *Faculty research:* Rural development.

Washington State University, Graduate School, College of Agricultural, Human, and Natural Resource Sciences, School of Economic Sciences, Department of Economics, Pullman, WA 99164. Offers applied economics (MA); economics (MA, PhD); international business economics (Certificate). *Faculty:* 16 full-time (1 woman). *Students:* 45 full-time (15 women), 8 part-time (5 women), 24 international. Average age 30. 135 applicants, 21% accepted, 16 enrolled. In 2007, 7 master's, 8 doctorates awarded. *Degree requirements:* For master's, comprehensive exam (for some programs), thesis (for some programs), oral exam; for doctorate, comprehensive exam, thesis/dissertation, oral exam, written exam, field exams. *Entrance requirements:* For master's, GRE General Test, minimum GPA of 3.0; for doctorate, GRE General Test or GMAT, minimum GPA of 3.0. Additional exam requirements/recommendations for international students: Required—TOEFL. *Application deadline:* For fall admission, 3/1 priority date for domestic students. Applications are processed on a rolling basis. Application fee: $50. *Financial support:* In 2007–08, research assistantships (averaging $13,917 per year), 13 teaching assistantships (averaging $13,506 per year) were awarded; career-related internships or fieldwork, Federal Work-Study, institutionally sponsored loans, tuition waivers (partial), and teaching associateships also available. Financial award application deadline: 4/1; financial award applicants required to submit FAFSA. *Faculty research:* Economic theory and quantitative methods, applied microeconomics. Total annual research expenditures: $80,141. *Application contact:* Graduate School Admissions, 800-GRADWSU, Fax: 509-335-1949, E-mail: gradsch@wsu.edu.

Western Michigan University, Graduate College, College of Arts and Sciences, Department of Economics, Kalamazoo, MI 49008-5202. Offers applied economics (PhD); economics (MA). *Degree requirements:* For master's, thesis, oral or written exams; for doctorate, thesis/dissertation, oral exam, internship. *Entrance requirements:* For doctorate, GRE General Test.

Wright State University, School of Graduate Studies, Raj Soin College of Business, Department of Economics, Program in Social and Applied Economics, Dayton, OH 45435. Offers MS.

Economics

Alabama Agricultural and Mechanical University, School of Graduate Studies, School of Business, Department of Economics and Finance, Huntsville, AL 35811. Offers MS. Evening/weekend programs available. In 2007, 2 degrees awarded. *Degree requirements:* For master's, comprehensive exam. *Entrance requirements:* For master's, GRE General Test, minimum undergraduate GPA of 2.5. Additional exam requirements/recommendations for international students: Required—TOEFL. *Application deadline:* For fall admission, 5/1 for domestic students. Applications are processed on a rolling basis. Application fee: $25. Electronic applications accepted. *Financial support:* In 2007–08, 1 teaching assistantship with tuition reimbursement (averaging $9,000 per year) was awarded; career-related internships or fieldwork also available. Financial award application deadline: 4/1. *Faculty research:* Energy, banking, financial management, agricultural economics, sports economics. *Unit head:* Dr. Mohammad Robbani, Chair, 256-372-5095, Fax: 256-372-5874.

Albany State University, College of Arts and Sciences, Department of History, Political Science and Public Administration, Albany, GA 31705-2717. Offers community and economic development (MPA); criminal justice (MPA); fiscal management (MPA); general management (MPA); health administration and policy (MPA); human resources management (MPA); public policy (MPA); water resource management and policy (MPA). *Accreditation:* NASPAA. Part-time programs available. *Degree requirements:* For master's, comprehensive exam, thesis. *Entrance requirements:* For master's, GRE General Test, minimum GPA of 2.5. Electronic applications accepted. *Faculty research:* Transportation, urban affairs, political economy.

American University, College of Arts and Sciences, Department of Economics, Washington, DC 20016-8001. Offers applied microeconomics (Certificate); economics (MA, PhD); international economic relations (Certificate). Part-time and evening/weekend programs available. *Faculty:* 25 full-time (11 women), 1 part-time/adjunct (0 women). *Students:* 59 full-time (22 women), 71 part-time (32 women); includes 14 minority (7 African Americans, 3 Asian Americans or Pacific Islanders, 4 Hispanic Americans), 55 international. Average age 29. 181 applicants, 71% accepted, 38 enrolled. In 2007, 29 master's, 5 doctorates, 1 other advanced degree awarded. Terminal master's awarded for partial completion of doctoral program. *Degree requirements:* For master's, comprehensive exam, thesis or alternative; for doctorate, comprehensive exam, thesis/dissertation, 2 research seminars, field requirement. *Entrance requirements:* For master's, GRE; for doctorate, GRE General Test; for Certificate, Bachelor's Degree. Additional exam requirements/recommendations for international students: Required—TOEFL (minimum score 550 paper-based; 213 computer-based). *Application deadline:* For spring admission, 10/1 for domestic students. Applications are processed on a rolling basis. Application fee: $50. *Expenses:* Tuition: Full-time $19,998; part-time $1,111 per credit hour. Required fees: $380. Tuition and fees vary according to program. *Financial support:* Fellowships with full tuition reimbursements, research assistantships, teaching assistantships with full tuition reimbursements, career-related internships or fieldwork, Federal Work-Study, institutionally sponsored loans, and tuition waivers (full and partial) available. Financial award application deadline: 2/1. *Faculty research:* Political economy, development, labor, gender. *Unit head:* Dr. John Willoughby, Chair, 202-885-3759, Fax: 202-885-3790.

The American University in Cairo, Graduate Studies and Research, School of Business, Economics and Communication, Department of Economics, Cairo, Egypt. Offers MA. Part-time programs available. *Degree requirements:* For master's, thesis or alternative. *Entrance requirements:* For master's, GMAT. Additional exam requirements/recommendations for international students: Required—English entrance exam. Electronic applications accepted. *Faculty research:* Macro-economic policies, agricultural growth and rural credit markets, alleviation of poverty in Egypt.

American University of Beirut, Graduate Programs, Faculty of Arts and Sciences, Beirut, Lebanon. Offers anthropology (MA); Arabic language and literature (MA); archaeology (MA); biology (MS); chemistry (MS); computer science (MS); economics (MA); education (MA); English language (MA); English literature (MA); environmental policy planning (MSES); financial economics (MAFE); geology (MS); history (MA); mathematics (MA, MS); Middle Eastern studies (MA); philosophy (MA); physics (MS); political studies (MA); psychology (MA); public administration (MA); sociology (MA); statistics (MA, MS). Part-time programs available. *Faculty:* 108 full-time (29 women), 5 part-time/adjunct (3 women). *Students:* 134 full-time (92 women), 228 part-time (167 women). Average age 25. 319 applicants, 67% accepted, 91 enrolled. In 2007, 144 degrees awarded. *Degree requirements:* For master's, one foreign language, comprehensive exam, thesis (for some programs). *Entrance requirements:* For master's, GRE, letter of recommendation. Additional exam requirements/recommendations for international students: Required—TOEFL (minimum score 600 paper-based; 250 computer-based; 100 iBT), IELTS (minimum score 8). *Application deadline:* For fall admission, 4/30 for domestic and international students; for spring admission, 11/1 for domestic and international students. Application fee: $50. *Expenses:* Tuition: Full-time $9,954; part-time $553 per credit. Tuition and fees vary according to course load and program. *Financial support:* In 2007–08, 28 students received support. Career-related internships or fieldwork, institutionally sponsored loans, scholarships/grants, health care benefits, and unspecified assistantships available. Financial award application deadline: 2/4; financial award applicants required to submit FAFSA. *Faculty research:* String theory and supergravity; computer graphics; algebra and number theory; popular Arabic literature; marine and freshwater biology; integrating science, math and technology. Total annual research expenditures: $132,270. *Unit head:* Khalil Bitar, Dean, 961-1374374 Ext. 3800, Fax: 961-1744461, E-mail: kmb@aub.edu.lb. *Application contact:* Dr. Salim Kanaan, Director, Admissions Office, 961-1350000 Ext. 2594, Fax: 961-1750775, E-mail: sk00@aub.edu.lb.

Andrews University, School of Graduate Studies, School of Business, Department of Accounting, Economics and Finance, Berrien Springs, MI 49104. Offers MBA, MSA.

Arizona State University, Graduate College, W.P. Carey School of Business, Department of Economics, Tempe, AZ 85287. Offers MS, PhD, JD/MS, MBA/MS. *Degree requirements:* For master's, thesis or alternative; for doctorate, thesis/dissertation. *Entrance requirements:* For master's and doctorate, GRE.

Auburn University, Graduate School, College of Business, Department of Economics, Auburn University, AL 36849. Offers MS. Part-time programs available. *Faculty:* 12 full-time (1 woman). *Students:* 13 full-time (2 women), 4 part-time (1 woman); includes 2 minority (1 African American, 1 Asian American or Pacific Islander), 2 international. Average age 25. 33 applicants, 79% accepted, 13 enrolled. In 2007, 4 degrees awarded. *Degree requirements:* For master's, thesis. *Entrance requirements:* For master's, GMAT, GRE General Test. Additional exam requirements/recommendations for international students: Required—TOEFL. *Application deadline:* For fall admission, 7/7 for domestic students; for spring admission, 11/24 for domestic students. Applications are processed on a rolling basis. Application fee: $25 ($50 for international students). Electronic applications accepted. *Financial support:* Teaching assistantships, career-related internships or fieldwork and Federal Work-Study available. Support available to part-time students. Financial award application deadline: 3/15. *Unit head:* Dr. Steven B. Caudill, Interim Chair, 334-844-2907. *Application contact:* Dr. Joe Pittman, Interim Dean of the Graduate School, 334-844-4700.

Baylor University, Graduate School, Hankamer School of Business, Department of Economics, Waco, TX 76798. Offers economics (MS Eco); international economics (MA, MS). *Students:* 15 full-time (7 women), 1 part-time; includes 1 minority (Asian American or Pacific Islander), 10 international. In 2007, 7 degrees awarded. *Entrance requirements:* For master's, GMAT or GRE General Test. *Application deadline:* For fall admission, 8/1 for domestic students; for spring admission, 12/1 for domestic students. Applications are processed on a rolling basis. Application fee: $25. *Financial support:* Research assistantships, Federal Work-Study and institutionally sponsored loans available. Financial award application deadline: 4/1. *Faculty research:* Econometrics, international economics, private enterprise, comparative economic systems. *Unit head:* Dr. Steve Green, Chair, 254-710-2263, Fax: 254-710-3265, E-mail: steve_green@baylor.edu. *Application contact:* Vicky Todd, Administrative Assistant, 254-710-3718, Fax: 254-710-1066, E-mail: mba@hsb.baylor.edu.

Bernard M. Baruch College of the City University of New York, Zicklin School of Business, Department of Economics and Finance, Program in Economics, New York, NY 10010-5585. Offers MBA. Part-time and evening/weekend programs available. *Entrance requirements:* For master's, GMAT, 2 letters of recommendation, resumé, 2 years of work experience. Additional exam requirements/recommendations for international students: Required—TOEFL (minimum score 590 paper-based; 243 computer-based), TWE (minimum score 5).

Boston College, Graduate School of Arts and Sciences, Department of Economics, Chestnut Hill, MA 02467-3800. Offers PhD. *Students:* 78 full-time (29 women); includes 5 minority (2

African Americans, 2 Asian Americans or Pacific Islanders, 1 Hispanic American), 57 international. 312 applicants, 14% accepted, 17 enrolled. In 2007, 4 doctorates awarded. *Degree requirements:* For doctorate, comprehensive exam, thesis/dissertation. *Entrance requirements:* For doctorate, GRE General Test, GRE Subject Test. Additional exam requirements/recommendations for international students: Required—TOEFL (minimum score 590 paper-based; 250 computer-based; 91 iBT). *Application deadline:* For fall admission, 1/15 for domestic students. Application fee: $70. Electronic applications accepted. *Financial support:* Fellowships, research assistantships, teaching assistantships, Federal Work-Study, scholarships/grants, and tuition waivers (full) available. Support available to part-time students. Financial award application deadline: 3/1; financial award applicants required to submit FAFSA. *Faculty research:* Econometrics, international economics, public sector economics, monetary economics, urban economics. *Unit head:* Dr. Marvin Kraus, Chairperson, 617-552-3683. *Application contact:* Dr. Dick Trusch, Graduate Program Director, 617-552-3683, E-mail: richard.trusch@bc.edu.

Boston University, Graduate School of Arts and Sciences, Department of Economics, Boston, MA 02215. Offers economic policy (MAEP); economics (MA, PhD); political economy (MAPE); MBA/MA. *Students:* 240 full-time (93 women), 9 part-time (5 women); includes 9 minority (1 African American, 5 Asian Americans or Pacific Islanders, 3 Hispanic Americans), 198 international. Average age 28. 946 applicants, 34% accepted, 112 enrolled. In 2007, 86 master's, 12 doctorates awarded. Terminal master's awarded for partial completion of doctoral program. *Degree requirements:* For master's, one foreign language, comprehensive exam; for doctorate, one foreign language, comprehensive exam, thesis/dissertation, qualifying exam. *Entrance requirements:* For master's and doctorate, GRE General Test, 3 letters of recommendation. Additional exam requirements/recommendations for international students: Required—TOEFL (minimum score 550 paper-based; 213 computer-based). *Application deadline:* For fall admission, 3/1 for domestic and international students. Application fee: $70. *Expenses:* Tuition: Full-time $34,930; part-time $1,092 per credit. Tuition and fees vary according to class time, course level and program. *Financial support:* In 2007–08, 91 students received support, including 5 fellowships with full tuition reimbursements available (averaging $18,000 per year), 17 research assistantships with full and partial tuition reimbursements available (averaging $17,500 per year), 25 teaching assistantships with full tuition reimbursements available (averaging $17,500 per year); Federal Work-Study and scholarships/grants also available. Support available to part-time students. Financial award application deadline: 1/15; financial award applicants required to submit FAFSA. *Unit head:* Kevin Lang, Chairman, 617-353-5694, Fax: 617-353-4449, E-mail: lang@bu.edu. *Application contact:* Andrew Campolieto, Graduate Program Administrator, 617-353-4454, Fax: 617-353-4449, E-mail: acamp@bu.edu.

Boston University, Metropolitan College (Continuing Education), Department of Administrative Sciences, Boston, MA 02215. Offers banking and financial management (MSM); business continuity in emergency management (MSM); economics development and tourism management (MSAS); electronic commerce, systems, and technology (MSAS); financial economics (MSAS); human resource management (MSM); innovation and technology (MSAS); insurance management (MSM); international market management (MSM); multinational commerce (MSAS); project management (MSM). *Accreditation:* AACSB. Part-time and evening/weekend programs available. Postbaccalaureate distance learning degree programs offered (no on-campus study). *Faculty:* 12 full-time (1 woman), 40 part-time/adjunct (8 women). *Students:* 550 full-time (240 women), 430 part-time (230 women); includes 48 minority (all Hispanic Americans), 220 international. Average age 30. 500 applicants, 60% accepted, 290 enrolled. In 2007, 260 degrees awarded. *Degree requirements:* For master's, thesis optional. *Entrance requirements:* For master's, 1 year of work experience, minimum GPA of 3.0. Additional exam requirements/recommendations for international students: Required—TOEFL (minimum score 560 paper-based; 220 computer-based; 84 iBT). *Application deadline:* Applications are processed on a rolling basis. Application fee: $70. Electronic applications accepted. *Expenses:* Tuition: Full-time $34,930; part-time $1,092 per credit. Tuition and fees vary according to class time, course level and program. *Financial support:* In 2007–08, 15 students received support, including 8 research assistantships (averaging $10,000 per year); career-related internships or fieldwork and Federal Work-Study also available. *Faculty research:* International business, innovative process. *Unit head:* Dr. Kip Becker, Chairman, 617-353-3016, E-mail: adminsc@bu.edu. *Application contact:* Lucille Dicker, Administrative Sciences Department, 617-353-3016, E-mail: adminsc@bu.edu.

Bowling Green State University, Graduate College, College of Business Administration, Department of Economics, Bowling Green, OH 43403. Offers MA. Part-time programs available. *Faculty:* 11 full-time (2 women), 1 part-time/adjunct (0 women). *Students:* 18 full-time (9 women); includes 1 minority (African American), 13 international. Average age 27. 34 applicants, 76% accepted, 10 enrolled. In 2007, 14 degrees awarded. *Degree requirements:* For master's, thesis or alternative. *Entrance requirements:* For master's, GRE General Test. Additional exam requirements/recommendations for international students: Required—TOEFL. *Application deadline:* Applications are processed on a rolling basis. Application fee: $30. Electronic applications accepted. *Financial support:* In 2007–08, 1 research assistantship with full tuition reimbursement (averaging $4,202 per year) was awarded; teaching assistantships with full tuition reimbursements, career-related internships or fieldwork, institutionally sponsored loans, and unspecified assistantships also available. Financial award applicants required to submit FAFSA. *Faculty research:* Labor economics, monetary economics, economic education, mathematical economics. *Unit head:* Dr. John Hoag, Chair, 419-372-8231. *Application contact:* Dr. Peter VanderHart, Graduate Coordinator, 419-372-8070.

Brandeis University, International Business School, Waltham, MA 02454-9110. Offers finance (MSF); international business (MBAi); international economics and finance (MA, PhD); international finance/international economics (MBAi). Part-time and evening/weekend programs available. Terminal master's awarded for partial completion of doctoral program. *Degree requirements:* For master's, one foreign language, semester abroad; for doctorate, thesis/dissertation. *Entrance requirements:* For master's, GMAT or GRE General Test (MA), GMAT (MBAi and MSF); for doctorate, GRE General Test. Additional exam requirements/recommendations for international students: Required—TOEFL (minimum score 600 paper-based; 250 computer-based), IELTS (minimum score 7). Electronic applications accepted. *Faculty research:* International finance and business, trade policy, macroeconomics, Asian economic issues, developmental economics.

See Close-Up on page 1025.

Brock University, Faculty of Graduate Studies, Faculty of Social Sciences, Program in Business Economics, St. Catharines, ON L2S 3A1, Canada. Offers MBE. *Degree requirements:* For master's, thesis or alternative. *Entrance requirements:* For master's, honours degree. Additional exam requirements/recommendations for international students: Required—TOEFL (minimum score 550 paper-based; 213 computer-based; 80 iBT), IELTS (minimum score 7), TWE (minimum score 4). Electronic applications accepted. *Faculty research:* Microeconomic theory, macroeconomics, econometrics, applied econometrics, economic development.

Brooklyn College of the City University of New York, Division of Graduate Studies, Department of Economics, Brooklyn, NY 11210-2889. Offers accounting (MS); economics (MA). Part-time and evening/weekend programs available. *Students:* 12 full-time (5 women), 95 part-time (57 women); includes 44 minority (34 African Americans, 8 Asian Americans or Pacific Islanders, 2 Hispanic Americans), 29 international. 90 applicants, 61% accepted, 34 enrolled. In 2007, 39 degrees awarded. *Degree requirements:* For master's, comprehensive exam, thesis or alternative. *Entrance requirements:* For master's, 2 letters of recommendation. Additional exam requirements/recommendations for international students: Required—TOEFL. *Application deadline:* For fall admission, 3/1 priority date for domestic students, 2/1 priority date for international students; for spring admission, 11/1 priority date for domestic students, 10/1 priority date for international students. Applications are processed on a rolling basis. Application fee: $125. Electronic applications accepted. *Financial support:* Career-related internships or fieldwork, Federal Work-Study, institutionally sponsored loans, and scholarships/grants available. Support available to part-time students. Financial award application deadline: 5/1; financial award applicants required to submit FAFSA. *Faculty research:* Econometrics, environmental economics, microeconomics, macroeconomics, taxation. *Unit head:* Dr. Robert Bell, Chairperson, 718-951-5317, E-mail: rbell brooklyn.cuny.edu. *Application contact:* Hernan Sierra, Graduate Admissions Coordinator, 718-951-4536, Fax: 718-951-4506, E-mail: grads@brooklyn.cuny.edu.

Brown University, Graduate School, Department of Economics, Providence, RI 02912. Offers AM, PhD. Terminal master's awarded for partial completion of doctoral program. *Degree requirements:* For master's, core exam; for doctorate, thesis/dissertation. *Entrance requirements:* For master's and doctorate, GRE General Test.

Buffalo State College, State University of New York, Graduate Studies and Research, Faculty of Natural and Social Sciences, Department of Economics and Finance, Buffalo, NY 14222-1095. Offers applied economics (MA). *Degree requirements:* For master's, project. *Entrance requirements:* Additional exam requirements/recommendations for international students: Required—TOEFL (minimum score 550 paper-based; 213 computer-based).

California Institute of Technology, Division of the Humanities and Social Sciences, Social Science Program, Pasadena, CA 91125-0001. Offers economics (PhD); political science (PhD); social science (MS). *Faculty:* 29 full-time (3 women). *Students:* 37 full-time (10 women); includes 9 minority (7 Asian Americans or Pacific Islanders, 2 Hispanic Americans), 14 international. Average age 26. 186 applicants, 10% accepted, 11 enrolled. In 2007, 5 master's, 7 doctorates awarded. Terminal master's awarded for partial completion of doctoral program. *Degree requirements:* For doctorate, thesis/dissertation. *Entrance requirements:* For doctorate, GRE General Test. *Application deadline:* For fall admission, 1/1 for domestic students. Application fee: $80. Electronic applications accepted. *Financial support:* In 2007–08, 34 students received support, including 12 fellowships (averaging $25,000 per year), 16 research assistantships (averaging $25,000 per year), 10 teaching assistantships (averaging $25,000 per year); Federal Work-Study, institutionally sponsored loans, scholarships/grants, and unspecified assistantships also available. *Faculty research:* Individual and group decision making, design of political and economic institutions, experimental social science, public policy, quantitative history. *Application contact:* Laurel Auchampaugh, Graduate Secretary, 626-395-4206, Fax: 626-405-9841, E-mail: gradsec@hss.caltech.edu.

California State Polytechnic University, Pomona, Academic Affairs, College of Letters, Arts, and Social Sciences, Program in Economics, Pomona, CA 91768-2557. Offers MS. Part-time programs available. *Students:* 10 full-time (5 women), 37 part-time (13 women); includes 22 minority (3 African Americans, 9 Asian Americans or Pacific Islanders, 10 Hispanic Americans), 12 international. Average age 31. 29 applicants, 86% accepted, 20 enrolled. In 2007, 9 degrees awarded. *Degree requirements:* For master's, thesis or alternative. *Entrance requirements:* For master's, GRE General Test. *Application deadline:* For fall admission, 5/1 priority date for domestic students; for winter admission, 10/15 priority date for domestic students; for spring admission, 1/20 priority date for domestic students. Applications are processed on a rolling basis. Application fee: $55. Electronic applications accepted. *Expenses:* Tuition, nonresident: full-time $7,232; part-time $226 per unit. Required fees: $3,920. One-time fee: $2,486 part-time. *Financial support:* In 2007–08, 9 students received support. Federal Work-Study and institutionally sponsored loans available. Support available to part-time students. Financial award application deadline: 3/2; financial award applicants required to submit FAFSA. *Unit head:* Dr. Maureen Burton, Coordinator, 909-869-3853, E-mail: mburton@csupomona.edu.

California State University, East Bay, Academic Programs and Graduate Studies, College of Business and Economics, Department of Economics, Hayward, CA 94542-3000. Offers business economics (MBA); economics (MA, MBA); economics for teachers (MBA). Part-time and evening/weekend programs available. *Faculty:* 5 full-time (0 women), 1 part-time/adjunct (0 women). *Students:* 10 full-time (5 women), 34 part-time (18 women); includes 17 minority (5 African Americans, 10 Asian Americans or Pacific Islanders, 2 Hispanic Americans), 7 international. Average age 33. 35 applicants, 69% accepted, 10 enrolled. In 2007, 5 degrees awarded. *Degree requirements:* For master's, comprehensive exam, thesis optional, project or thesis. *Entrance requirements:* For master's, GMAT, minimum GPA of 2.75 during previous 2 years of course work. Additional exam requirements/recommendations for international students: Required—TOEFL (minimum score 550 paper-based; 213 computer-based). *Application deadline:* For fall admission, 5/31 for domestic students, 4/30 for international students; for winter admission, 9/30 for domestic and international students; for spring admission, 12/31 for domestic students, 11/30 for international students. Applications are processed on a rolling basis. Application fee: $55. Electronic applications accepted. *Expenses:* Required fees: $3,987; $851 per quarter. *Financial support:* Career-related internships or fieldwork, Federal Work-Study, and institutionally sponsored loans available. Support available to part-time students. Financial award application deadline: 3/2. *Unit head:* Dr. Nan Maxwell, Chair, 510-885-3265, Fax: 510-885-4699, E-mail: nan.maxwell@csueastbay.edu. *Application contact:* Doris Duncan, Director of Graduate Programs, 510-885-3364, Fax: 510-885-2176, E-mail: doris.duncan@csueastbay.edu.

California State University, Fullerton, Graduate Studies, College of Business and Economics, Department of Economics, Fullerton, CA 92834-9480. Offers business economics (MBA); economics (MA). Part-time and evening/weekend programs available. *Students:* 17 full-time (3 women), 19 part-time (9 women); includes 14 minority (1 African American, 10 Asian Americans or Pacific Islanders, 3 Hispanic Americans), 8 international. Average age 29. 42 applicants, 45% accepted, 9 enrolled. In 2007, 12 degrees awarded. *Degree requirements:* For master's, thesis. *Entrance requirements:* For master's, GMAT, GRE General Test. Application fee: $55. *Financial support:* Teaching assistantships, Federal Work-Study, institutionally sponsored loans, and scholarships/grants available. Support available to part-time students. Financial award application deadline: 3/1. *Faculty research:* Environmental and natural resource issues. *Unit head:* Dr. James Dietz, Chair, 714-278-2228. *Application contact:* Dr. Jane Hall, Adviser, 714-278-2236.

California State University, Long Beach, Graduate Studies, College of Liberal Arts, Department of Economics, Long Beach, CA 90840. Offers economics (MA). Part-time programs available. *Faculty:* 14 full-time (4 women), 20 part-time/adjunct (6 women). *Students:* 17 full-time (10 women), 49 part-time (25 women); includes 39 minority (1 African American, 29 Asian Americans or Pacific Islanders, 9 Hispanic Americans). Average age 31. *Degree requirements:* For master's, comprehensive exam or thesis. *Entrance requirements:* For master's, GRE General Test, GRE Subject Test, minimum GPA of 3.0. *Application deadline:* For fall admission, 7/1 for domestic students; for spring admission, 12/1 for domestic students. Applications are processed on a rolling basis. Application fee: $55. Electronic applications accepted. *Financial support:* Federal Work-Study, institutionally sponsored loans, and scholarships/grants available. Financial award application deadline: 3/2. *Faculty research:* Trade and development, economic forecasting, resource economics. *Unit head:* Dr. Joseph P. Magaddino, Chair, 562-985-5061, Fax: 562-985-5804, E-mail: magaddin@csulb.edu. *Application contact:* Dr. Alejandra C Edwards, Graduate Coordinator, 562-985-5969, Fax: 562-985-5804, E-mail: acoxedwa@csulb.edu.

California State University, Los Angeles, Graduate Studies, College of Business and Economics, Department of Economics and Statistics, Los Angeles, CA 90032-8530. Offers analytical quantitative economics (MA); business economics (MA, MBA, MS); economics (MA). Part-time and evening/weekend programs available. *Faculty:* 3 full-time (0 women), 1 part-time/adjunct (0 women). *Students:* 5 full-time (3 women), 11 part-time (3 women); includes 5 minority (1 American Indian/Alaska Native, 1 Asian American or Pacific Islander, 3 Hispanic Americans), 7 international. Average age 30. In 2007, 4 degrees awarded. *Degree requirements:* For master's, comprehensive exam or thesis. *Entrance requirements:* For master's, GMAT, minimum GPA of 2.5 during previous 2 years of course work. Additional exam requirements/recommendations for international students: Required—TOEFL. *Application deadline:* For fall admission, 6/30 for domestic students; for spring admission, 11/30 for domestic students. Applications are processed on a rolling basis. Application fee: $55. *Financial support:* Career-related internships or fieldwork and Federal Work-Study available. Support available to part-time

Economics

California State University, Los Angeles (continued)

students. Financial award application deadline: 3/1. *Unit head:* Dr. Edward Hsieh, Chair, 323-343-2930 Ext. 32939, Fax: 323-343-5462, E-mail: ehsieh@calstatela.edu.

Carleton University, Faculty of Graduate Studies, Faculty of Public Affairs and Management, Department of Economics, Ottawa, ON K1S 5B6, Canada. Offers MA, PhD. *Degree requirements:* For master's, thesis optional; for doctorate, comprehensive exam, thesis/dissertation. *Entrance requirements:* For master's, honors degree; for doctorate, master's degree. Additional exam requirements/recommendations for international students: Required—TOEFL. *Application deadline:* Applications are processed on a rolling basis. Application fee: $77 Canadian dollars. *Financial support:* Fellowships, research assistantships, teaching assistantships, institutionally sponsored loans, scholarships/grants, and unspecified assistantships available. *Faculty research:* Monetary economics, economic development, public economics, industrial organization, international trade. *Unit head:* Keir Armstrong, Chair, 613-520-2600 Ext. 3744, Fax: 613-520-3906, E-mail: economics@carleton.ca. *Application contact:* Marge Brooks, Graduate Administrator, 613-520-2600 Ext. 3743, Fax: 613-520-3906, E-mail: economics@carleton.ca.

Carleton University, Faculty of Graduate Studies, Faculty of Public Affairs and Management, Institute of Political Economy, Ottawa, ON K1S 5B6, Canada. Offers MA, PhD. *Degree requirements:* For master's, thesis optional. *Entrance requirements:* For master's, honors degree. Additional exam requirements/recommendations for international students: Required—TOEFL. *Application deadline:* Applications are processed on a rolling basis. Application fee: $77 Canadian dollars. *Financial support:* Fellowships, research assistantships, teaching assistantships, institutionally sponsored loans, scholarships/grants, and unspecified assistantships available. *Faculty research:* Relationships between economy and politics as they affect the political, social and cultural life of societies; historical processes whereby social change is located in the interaction of the economic, political and cultural, and ideological moments of social life. *Unit head:* Rianne Mahon, Director, 613-520-2600 Ext. 7414, Fax: 613-260-2154. *Application contact:* Donna Coghill, Institute Administrator, 613-520-2600 Ext. 7414, Fax: 613-520-2154, E-mail: donna_coghill@carleton.ca.

Carnegie Mellon University, Tepper School of Business, Program in Economics, Pittsburgh, PA 15213-3891. Offers MS, PhD. *Degree requirements:* For doctorate, thesis/dissertation. *Entrance requirements:* For master's, GMAT; for doctorate, GMAT, GRE General Test. *Faculty research:* Research allocation under asymmetric information, monetary theory, estimation of rational expectations models.

Carnegie Mellon University, Tepper School of Business, Program in Political Economy, Pittsburgh, PA 15213-3891. Offers PhD. *Degree requirements:* For doctorate, thesis/dissertation.

Case Western Reserve University, Weatherhead School of Management, Department of Economics, Cleveland, OH 44106. Offers MBA. Part-time and evening/weekend programs available. *Entrance requirements:* For master's, GMAT. *Application deadline:* For fall admission, 4/15 priority date for domestic students. Applications are processed on a rolling basis. Application fee: $50. *Financial support:* Career-related internships or fieldwork, Federal Work-Study, institutionally sponsored loans, and tuition waivers (full and partial) available. Financial award application deadline: 5/1. *Faculty research:* Public finance and public choice, direct foreign investment, employment relationships, technical and institutional change, regional economics. *Unit head:* James B. Rebitzer, Chairman, 216-368-4110, Fax: 216-368-5039, E-mail: jbr@po.cwru.edu.

The Catholic University of America, School of Arts and Sciences, Department of Business and Economics, Washington, DC 20064. Offers international political economics (MA). Part-time and evening/weekend programs available. *Faculty:* 8 full-time (3 women), 9 part-time/adjunct (6 women). *Students:* 3 full-time (all women), 29 part-time (20 women); includes 16 minority (11 African Americans, 2 Asian Americans or Pacific Islanders, 3 Hispanic Americans). Average age 34. 28 applicants, 14% accepted, 0 enrolled. In 2007, 1 degree awarded. *Degree requirements:* For master's, comprehensive exam. *Entrance requirements:* For master's, GRE General Test, 3 letters of recommendation. Additional exam requirements/recommendations for international students: Required—TOEFL (minimum score 580 paper-based; 237 computer-based). *Application deadline:* For fall admission, 2/1 priority date for domestic students; for spring admission, 11/15 priority date for domestic students. Applications are processed on a rolling basis. Application fee: $55. Electronic applications accepted. *Financial support:* Teaching assistantships, career-related internships or fieldwork, Federal Work-Study, scholarships/grants, tuition waivers (full and partial), and unspecified assistantships available. Support available to part-time students. Financial award application deadline: 2/1; financial award applicants required to submit FAFSA. *Unit head:* Dr. Kevin F. Forbes, Chair, 202-319-5236, Fax: 202-319-4426, E-mail: forbes@cua.edu.

Central European University, Graduate Studies, Department of Legal Studies, Budapest, Hungary. Offers comparative constitutional law (LL M); economic and legal studies (LL M, MA); human rights (LL M, MA); international business law (LL M); legal studies (SJD). *Faculty:* 7 full-time (2 women), 3 part-time/adjunct (1 woman). *Students:* 109 full-time (61 women). Average age 26. 579 applicants, 21% accepted, 85 enrolled. In 2007, 42 master's, 4 doctorates awarded. Terminal master's awarded for partial completion of doctoral program. *Median time to degree:* Of those who began their doctoral program in fall 1999, 75% received their degree in 8 years or less. *Degree requirements:* For master's, one foreign language, thesis; for doctorate, one foreign language, comprehensive exam, thesis/dissertation. *Entrance requirements:* For master's and doctorate, LSAT, CEU admissions exams. Additional exam requirements/recommendations for international students: Required—TOEFL (minimum score 570 paper-based; 230 computer-based). *Application deadline:* For fall admission, 1/5 for domestic and international students. Application fee: $0. Electronic applications accepted. *Expenses:* Contact institution. Tuition charges are reported in euros. *Financial support:* In 2007–08, 84 students received support, including 65 fellowships with full and partial tuition reimbursements available (averaging $5,000 per year); career-related internships or fieldwork, institutionally sponsored loans, scholarships/grants, and tuition waivers (full and partial) also available. Financial award application deadline: 1/5. *Faculty research:* Institutional, constitutional and human rights in European Union law, biomedical law and reproductive rights, data protection law, Islamic banking and finance. *Unit head:* Dr. Stefan Messmann, Head, 361-327-3274, Fax: 361-327-3198, E-mail: legalst@ceu.hu. *Application contact:* Maria Balla, Coordinator, 361-327-3204, Fax: 361-327-3198, E-mail: ballam@ceu.hu.

Central European University, Graduate Studies, School of Social Sciences and Humanities, Budapest, Hungary. Offers economics (MA, PhD); gender studies (MA, PhD); international relations and European studies (MA, PhD); mathematics and its applications (MS, PhD); medieval studies (MA, PhD); nationalism studies (MA, PhD); philosophy (MA, PhD); political science (MA, PhD); public policy (MA, PhD); sociology and social anthropology (MA, PhD). *Faculty:* 75 full-time (25 women), 46 part-time/adjunct (10 women). *Students:* 625 full-time (355 women). Average age 26. 2,500 applicants, 31% accepted, 540 enrolled. In 2007, 325 master's, 20 doctorates awarded. Terminal master's awarded for partial completion of doctoral program. *Degree requirements:* For master's, one foreign language, thesis; for doctorate, one foreign language, comprehensive exam, thesis/dissertation. *Entrance requirements:* For master's, CEU subject tests, interview; for doctorate, GRE, CEU subject test, interview. Additional exam requirements/recommendations for international students: Required—TOEFL (minimum score 570 paper-based; 230 computer-based). *Application deadline:* For fall admission, 1/15 priority date for domestic and international students. Application fee: $0. Electronic applications accepted. Tuition charges are reported in euros. *Expenses:* Tuition: Full-time 10,000 euros; part-time 315 euros per credit. *Financial support:* In 2007–08, 402 students received support, including 350 fellowships with full and partial tuition reimbursements available (averaging $5,000 per year); career-related internships or fieldwork, institutionally sponsored loans, and scholarships/grants also available. Financial award application deadline: 1/5. *Faculty research:* Civil society, fiscal decentralization, party politics, political philosophy (especially Liberalism, theory of Democracy). Total annual research expenditures: $35,000. *Unit head:* Dr. Howard Michael Robinson, Provost, 361-327-3003, Fax: 361-327-3211, E-mail: robinson@ceu.hu. *Application contact:* Zsuzsanna Jaszberenyi, Admissions Officer, 361-327-3009, Fax: 361-327-3211, E-mail: admissions@ceu.hu.

See Close-Up on page 447.

Central Michigan University, College of Graduate Studies, College of Business Administration, Department of Economics, Mount Pleasant, MI 48859. Offers MA. *Degree requirements:* For master's, thesis or alternative. *Entrance requirements:* For master's, GMAT. *Faculty research:* International trade, public choice/labor, economic development.

City College of the City University of New York, Graduate School, College of Liberal Arts and Science, Division of Social Science, Department of Economics, New York, NY 10031-9198. Offers MA. Part-time programs available. *Students:* 5 full-time (3 women), 55 part-time (16 women); includes 30 minority (10 African Americans, 12 Asian Americans or Pacific Islanders, 8 Hispanic Americans), 27 international. 36 applicants, 78% accepted, 13 enrolled. In 2007, 34 degrees awarded. *Degree requirements:* For master's, comprehensive exam, proficiency in a foreign language or advanced statistics. *Entrance requirements:* For master's, GRE. Additional exam requirements/recommendations for international students: Required—TOEFL (minimum score 550 paper-based; 213 computer-based). *Application deadline:* For fall admission, 5/1 for domestic students; for spring admission, 11/15 for domestic students. Application fee: $125. *Financial support:* Fellowships, Federal Work-Study and tuition waivers (full and partial) available. Support available to part-time students. Financial award application deadline: 5/1. *Faculty research:* International economics, health, banking. *Unit head:* Joseph Berechman, Chair, 212-650-6208, Fax: 212-650-6341. *Application contact:* Mitchell Kellman, Adviser, 212-650-6203, Fax: 212-650-6341, E-mail: tiger998@hotmail.com.

Claremont Graduate University, Graduate Programs, School of Politics and Economics, Department of Economics, Claremont, CA 91711-6160. Offers business and financial economics (MA, PhD); economic development (Certificate); economics (PhD); industrial organization (PhD); international and development economics (PhD); international economics policy and development (MA); international money and finance (PhD); neuroeconomics (PhD); political economy and public policy (MA); public choice and public economics (PhD); MBA/PhD. Part-time programs available. *Faculty:* 6 full-time (0 women), 3 part-time/adjunct (1 woman). *Students:* 92 full-time (25 women), 5 part-time (1 woman); includes 12 minority (2 African Americans, 5 Asian Americans or Pacific Islanders, 5 Hispanic Americans), 59 international. Average age 33. In 2007, 10 master's, 13 doctorates awarded. *Degree requirements:* For doctorate, 2 foreign languages, comprehensive exam, thesis/dissertation. *Entrance requirements:* For master's and doctorate, GRE General Test. *Application deadline:* For fall admission, 2/15 priority date for domestic students. Applications are processed on a rolling basis. Electronic applications accepted. *Expenses:* Tuition: Full-time $31,640; part-time $1,376 per unit. Required fees: $145 per semester. Tuition and fees vary according to course load, degree level and program. *Financial support:* Fellowships, research assistantships, teaching assistantships, Federal Work-Study and institutionally sponsored loans available. Support available to part-time students. Financial award application deadline: 2/15; financial award applicants required to submit FAFSA. *Faculty research:* International and financial economics, law and economics, regulation, public choice economics. *Unit head:* Arthur Denzau, Chair, 909-621-8782, Fax: 909-621-8545, E-mail: arthur.denzau@cgu.edu.

Claremont Graduate University, Graduate Programs, School of Politics and Economics, Department of Politics and Policy, Claremont, CA 91711-6160. Offers American politics (MA, PhD); comparative politics (PhD); international political economy (MA); international studies (MA); political philosophy (PhD); political science (PhD); politics, economics and business (MA); public policy (MA, PhD); world politics (PhD); MBA/PhD. Part-time programs available. *Faculty:* 7 full-time (3 women), 9 part-time/adjunct (1 woman). *Students:* 181 full-time (69 women), 19 part-time (8 women); includes 35 minority (8 African Americans, 10 Asian Americans or Pacific Islanders, 17 Hispanic Americans), 45 international. Average age 34. In 2007, 27 master's, 19 doctorates awarded. Terminal master's awarded for partial completion of doctoral program. *Degree requirements:* For master's, thesis; for doctorate, one foreign language, thesis/dissertation. *Entrance requirements:* For master's and doctorate, GRE General Test. *Application deadline:* For fall admission, 2/15 priority date for domestic students. Applications are processed on a rolling basis. Electronic applications accepted. *Expenses:* Tuition: Full-time $31,640; part-time $1,376 per unit. Required fees: $145 per semester. Tuition and fees vary according to course load, degree level and program. *Financial support:* Fellowships, research assistantships, teaching assistantships, career-related internships or fieldwork, Federal Work-Study, and institutionally sponsored loans available. Support available to part-time students. Financial award application deadline: 2/15; financial award applicants required to submit FAFSA. *Faculty research:* Environmental policy, international debt, global democratization, Third World development, public sector discrimination. *Unit head:* Jean Schroedel, Chair, 909-621-8696, Fax: 909-621-8545, E-mail: jean.schroedel@cgu.edu.

Clark Atlanta University, School of Business Administration, Department of Economics, Atlanta, GA 30314. Offers MA. Part-time programs available. *Faculty:* 1 part-time/adjunct (0 women). *Students:* 1 applicant, 100% accepted, 0 enrolled. *Degree requirements:* For master's, one foreign language, thesis. *Entrance requirements:* For master's, GRE General Test, minimum GPA of 2.5. Additional exam requirements/recommendations for international students: Required—TOEFL (minimum score 500 paper-based; 173 computer-based). *Application deadline:* For fall admission, 4/1 for domestic and international students; for spring admission, 11/1 for domestic and international students. Applications are processed on a rolling basis. Application fee: $40 ($55 for international students). Electronic applications accepted. *Expenses:* Tuition: Full-time $11,664; part-time $648 per credit hour. Required fees: $550; $275 per semester. *Financial support:* Career-related internships or fieldwork, Federal Work-Study, scholarships/grants, and unspecified assistantships available. Support available to part-time students. Financial award application deadline: 4/30; financial award applicants required to submit FAFSA. *Faculty research:* Minority energy demand. *Unit head:* Dr. Ajamu Nyomba, Chairperson, 404-880-6286, E-mail: anyomba@cau.edu. *Application contact:* Michelle Clark-Davis, Graduate Program Admissions, 404-880-8709, E-mail: mdowis@cau.edu.

Clark University, Graduate School, Department of Economics, Worcester, MA 01610-1477. Offers PhD. *Faculty:* 9 full-time (3 women), 2 part-time/adjunct (0 women). *Students:* 40 full-time (17 women), 30 international. Average age 29. 47 applicants, 70% accepted, 12 enrolled. In 2007, 2 doctorates awarded. *Degree requirements:* For doctorate, thesis/dissertation. *Entrance requirements:* For doctorate, GRE General Test. Additional exam requirements/recommendations for international students: Required—TOEFL. *Application deadline:* For fall admission, 2/15 priority date for domestic students. Applications are processed on a rolling basis. Application fee: $50. *Expenses:* Tuition: Full-time $32,600; part-time $1,019 per credit. Required fees: $30. Tuition and fees vary according to program. *Financial support:* In 2007–08, fellowships with full and partial tuition reimbursements (averaging $12,000 per year), 2 research assistantships with full and partial tuition reimbursements (averaging $12,000 per year), 9 teaching assistantships with full and partial tuition reimbursements (averaging $12,000 per year) were awarded; career-related internships or fieldwork, institutionally sponsored loans, and tuition waivers (full and partial) also available. *Faculty research:* Public finance, economic development, industrial organization, international finance and trade, environmental regulation. Total annual research expenditures: $226,000. *Unit head:* Dr. Wayne Gray, Chair, 508-793-7226. *Application contact:* Cindy Rice, Department Secretary, 508-793-7226, Fax: 508-793-8849, E-mail: economics@clarku.edu.

Clemson University, Graduate School, College of Business and Behavioral Science, Department of Economics, Program in Economics, Clemson, SC 29634. Offers MA. *Students:* 15 full-time (1 woman), 2 part-time; includes 1 Asian American or Pacific Islander, 4 international. 32 applicants, 78% accepted, 10 enrolled. In 2007, 16 degrees awarded. *Entrance requirements:* Additional exam requirements/recommendations for international students: Required—TOEFL. *Application deadline:* For fall admission, 6/1 for domestic students, 4/15 for international students; for spring admission, 9/15 for international students. *Financial support:* In 2007–08,

1 research assistantship (averaging $8,000 per year), 7 teaching assistantships (averaging $12,000 per year) were awarded. *Application contact:* Dr. C. Matt Lindsay, Director of Graduate Programs, 864-656-3955, Fax: 864-656-4192, E-mail: lindsay@clemson.edu.

Cleveland State University, College of Graduate Studies, College of Liberal Arts and Social Sciences, Department of Economics, Cleveland, OH 44115. Offers MA. Part-time and evening/weekend programs available. *Faculty:* 7 full-time (1 woman). *Students:* 8 full-time (2 women), 16 part-time (7 women); includes 5 minority (3 African Americans, 2 Asian Americans or Pacific Islanders), 1 international. Average age 28. 35 applicants, 69% accepted, 10 enrolled. In 2007, 7 degrees awarded. *Entrance requirements:* For master's, minimum GPA of 2.75; coursework in micro theory, macro theory, statistics, and calculus. Additional exam requirements/recommendations for international students: Required—TOEFL (minimum score 515 paper-based; 197 computer-based). *Application deadline:* For fall admission, 8/20 priority date for domestic students, 5/20 priority date for international students. Applications are processed on a rolling basis. Application fee: $30. Electronic applications accepted. *Financial support:* In 2007–08, 2 students received support, including 4 research assistantships with full tuition reimbursements available (averaging $3,780 per year); teaching assistantships with full tuition reimbursements available, scholarships/grants and unspecified assistantships also available. *Faculty research:* Labor economics, health economics, energy, environment, economics of law, organization theory, industrial organization. *Unit head:* Dr. Myong-Hun Chang, Chairperson, 216-687-4523, Fax: 216-687-9206, E-mail: m.chang@csuohio.edu. *Application contact:* Glenda Carbaugh, Administrative Secretary, 216-687-4520, Fax: 216-687-9206, E-mail: g.carbaugh@csuohio.edu.

Cleveland State University, College of Graduate Studies, Maxine Goodman Levin College of Urban Affairs, Department of Urban Studies, Cleveland, OH 44115. Offers geographic information systems (Certificate); local and urban management (Certificate); nonprofit management (Certificate); research administration (Certificate); urban economic development (Certificate); urban real estate development and finance (Certificate); urban studies (MS); urban studies and public affairs (PhD). Part-time and evening/weekend programs available. *Faculty:* 26 full-time (10 women), 20 part-time/adjunct (11 women). *Students:* 92 full-time (45 women), 180 part-time (98 women); includes 28 minority (24 African Americans, 1 Asian American or Pacific Islander, 3 Hispanic Americans). Average age 39. 185 applicants, 76% accepted, 86 enrolled. In 2007, 92 master's, 5 doctorates awarded. *Median time to degree:* Of those who began their doctoral program in fall 1999, 40% received their degree in 8 years or less. *Degree requirements:* For master's, thesis or alternative, exit project, capstone course; for doctorate, comprehensive exam, thesis/dissertation. *Entrance requirements:* For master's, GRE General Test, minimum GPA of 3.0; for doctorate, GRE General Test, minimum GPA of 3.5. Additional exam requirements/recommendations for international students: Required—TOEFL (minimum score 525 paper-based; 197 computer-based). *Application deadline:* For fall admission, 7/15 priority date for domestic students, 5/15 for international students; for spring admission, 11/1 for international students. Applications are processed on a rolling basis. Application fee: $30. Electronic applications accepted. *Financial support:* In 2007–08, 60 students received support, including 40 research assistantships with full and partial tuition reimbursements available (averaging $7,632 per year), 1 teaching assistantship with full and partial tuition reimbursement available (averaging $7,800 per year); career-related internships or fieldwork, Federal Work-Study, institutionally sponsored loans, scholarships/grants, tuition waivers (full and partial), and unspecified assistantships also available. Support available to part-time students. Financial award application deadline: 3/1. *Faculty research:* Environmental issues, economic development, urban and public policy, public management. *Unit head:* Dr. Wendy Kellogg, Director, 216-687-5265, Fax: 216-687-9342, E-mail: w.kellogg@csuohio.edu. *Application contact:* Graduate Advisor, 216-523-7522, Fax: 216-687-5398, E-mail: urbanprograms@csuohio.edu.

Cleveland State University, College of Graduate Studies, Maxine Goodman Levin College of Urban Affairs, Program in Urban Planning, Design, and Development, Cleveland, OH 44115. Offers geographic information systems (Certificate); local and urban management (Certificate); urban economic development (Certificate); urban planning, design, and development (MUPDD); urban real estate development and finance (Certificate); JD/MUPDD. *Accreditation:* ACSP. Part-time and evening/weekend programs available. *Faculty:* 26 full-time (10 women), 12 part-time/adjunct (5 women). *Students:* 25 full-time (10 women), 46 part-time (23 women); includes 13 minority (12 African Americans, 1 Asian American or Pacific Islander), 7 international. Average age 30. 55 applicants, 82% accepted, 23 enrolled. In 2007, 7 degrees awarded. *Degree requirements:* For master's, project or thesis. *Entrance requirements:* For master's, GRE General Test (minimum score: verbal and quantitative 50th percentile, analytical writing 4.0), minimum GPA of 3.0. Additional exam requirements/recommendations for international students: Required—TOEFL (minimum score 525 paper-based; 197 computer-based). *Application deadline:* For fall admission, 7/15 priority date for domestic students, 5/15 for international students; for spring admission, 11/1 for international students. Applications are processed on a rolling basis. Application fee: $30. Electronic applications accepted. *Financial support:* In 2007–08, 21 students received support, including 13 research assistantships with full and partial tuition reimbursements available (averaging $6,960 per year); teaching assistantships with full and partial tuition reimbursements available, career-related internships or fieldwork, Federal Work-Study, tuition waivers (full and partial), and unspecified assistantships also available. Support available to part-time students. Financial award application deadline: 3/1. *Faculty research:* Housing and neighborhood development, urban housing policy, environmental sustainability, economic development. *Unit head:* Dr. W. Dennis Keating, Director, 216-687-2298, Fax: 216-687-2013, E-mail: w.keating@csuohio.edu. *Application contact:* Graduate Advisor, 216-523-7522, Fax: 216-687-5398, E-mail: urbanprograms@csuohio.edu.

Colorado State University, Graduate School, College of Liberal Arts, Department of Economics, Fort Collins, CO 80523-0015. Offers MA, PhD. Part-time programs available. *Faculty:* 12 full-time (4 women), 3 part-time/adjunct (1 woman). *Students:* 32 full-time (7 women), 32 part-time (13 women); includes 3 minority (1 Asian American or Pacific Islander, 2 Hispanic Americans), 26 international. Average age 33. 72 applicants, 75% accepted, 13 enrolled. In 2007, 9 master's, 7 doctorates awarded. Terminal master's awarded for partial completion of doctoral program. *Degree requirements:* For master's, thesis optional; for doctorate, comprehensive exam, thesis/dissertation. *Entrance requirements:* For master's and doctorate, GRE General Test, minimum GPA of 3.0. Additional exam requirements/recommendations for international students: Required—TOEFL. *Application deadline:* For fall admission, 2/1 priority date for domestic students, 2/1 for international students. Applications are processed on a rolling basis. Application fee: $50. Electronic applications accepted. *Expenses:* Tuition, state resident: full-time $4,887; part-time $272 per credit. Tuition, nonresident: full-time $16,425; part-time $913 per credit. Required fees: $1,379; $75 per credit. *Financial support:* In 2007–08, 20 teaching assistantships with full tuition reimbursements (averaging $11,496 per year) were awarded; fellowships, research assistantships, career-related internships or fieldwork, Federal Work-Study, institutionally sponsored loans, scholarships/grants, traineeships, and unspecified assistantships also available. Financial award application deadline: 3/1; financial award applicants required to submit FAFSA. *Faculty research:* Regional and development economics, political economy, international trade and investment, public finance. Total annual research expenditures: $211,660. *Unit head:* Dr. Steven J. Shulman, Chair, 970-491-6566, Fax: 970-491-2925. *Application contact:* Dr. Robert W. Kling, Coordinator of Graduate Studies, 970-491-5598, Fax: 970-491-2925.

Columbia University, Graduate School of Arts and Sciences, Division of Social Sciences, Department of Economics, New York, NY 10027. Offers M Phil, MA, PhD, JD/MA, JD/PhD. *Faculty:* 36 full-time, 1 part-time/adjunct. *Students:* 118 full-time (38 women), 5 part-time (2 women). Average age 29. 715 applicants, 10% accepted. In 2007, 16 master's, 15 doctorates awarded. *Degree requirements:* For master's, thesis or alternative; for doctorate, thesis/dissertation. *Entrance requirements:* For master's and doctorate, GRE General Test, GRE Subject Test, previous course work in mathematics. Additional exam requirements/recommendations for international students: Required—TOEFL. Application fee: $90. *Expenses:* Tuition: Part-time $1,452 per credit. Required fees: $152 per term. One-time fee: $75 part-time. Full-time tuition and fees vary according to course level, course load, degree level and program. *Financial support:* Fellowships, teaching assistantships, Federal Work-Study and institutionally sponsored loans available. Support available to part-time students. Financial award application deadline: 1/5; financial award applicants required to submit FAFSA. *Faculty research:* International trade. *Unit head:* Janet Currie, Chair, 212-854-4520, Fax: 212-854-8059, E-mail: jc2663@columbia.edu.

Columbia University, Graduate School of Business, Doctoral Program in Business, New York, NY 10027. Offers business (PhD), including accounting, decision, risk, and operations, finance and economics, management, marketing. *Accreditation:* AACSB. *Faculty:* 117 full-time (14 women), 124 part-time/adjunct (18 women). *Students:* 114 full-time (38 women); includes 6 minority (5 Asian Americans or Pacific Islanders, 1 Hispanic American), 87 international. Average age 27. 603 applicants, 6% accepted, 7 enrolled. In 2007, 16 degrees awarded. *Median time to degree:* Of those who began their doctoral program in fall 1999, 76% received their degree in 8 years or less. *Degree requirements:* For doctorate, comprehensive exam, thesis/dissertation, major field exam, research paper, thesis proposal. *Entrance requirements:* For doctorate, GMAT or GRE (finance), 2 letters of reference, resumé. Additional exam requirements/recommendations for international students: Required—TOEFL. *Application deadline:* For fall admission, 1/1 for domestic and international students. Application fee: $75. Electronic applications accepted. *Expenses:* Contact institution. One-time fee: $75 part-time. Full-time tuition and fees vary according to course level, course load, degree level and program. *Financial support:* In 2007–08, 90 students received support, including fellowships with full tuition reimbursements available (averaging $22,000 per year), research assistantships (averaging $4,000 per year); teaching assistantships, career-related internships or fieldwork, institutionally sponsored loans, health care benefits, tuition waivers (full), and unspecified assistantships also available. *Unit head:* Elizabeth Elam Chang, Administrative Director, 212-854-2836, Fax: 212-932-2359, E-mail: phdinfo@gsb.columbia.edu.

Columbia University, Graduate School of Business, MBA Program, New York, NY 10027. Offers accounting (MBA); decision, risk, and operations (MBA); entrepreneurship (MBA); finance and economics (MBA); human resource management (MBA); international business (MBA); management/leadership (MBA); marketing (MBA); media (MBA); real estate (MBA); social enterprise (MBA); DDS/MBA; JD/MBA; MBA/MIA; MBA/MPH; MBA/MS; MD/MBA. *Faculty:* 117 full-time (14 women), 124 part-time/adjunct (18 women). *Students:* 1,226 full-time (420 women); includes 274 minority (75 African Americans, 4 American Indian/Alaska Native, 162 Asian Americans or Pacific Islanders, 33 Hispanic Americans), 409 international. Average age 28. 5,623 applicants, 16% accepted, 711 enrolled. In 2007, 711 degrees awarded. *Entrance requirements:* For master's, GMAT, 2 letters of recommendation, official transcripts, essay, personal statement, completed application. Additional exam requirements/recommendations for international students: Required—TOEFL. *Application deadline:* For fall admission, 4/15 for domestic students, 3/4 for international students; for spring admission, 10/8 for domestic and international students. Applications are processed on a rolling basis. Application fee: $250. Electronic applications accepted. *Expenses:* Tuition: Part-time $1,452 per credit. Required fees: $152 per term. One-time fee: $75 part-time. Full-time tuition and fees vary according to course level, course load, degree level and program. *Financial support:* Fellowships, research assistantships, teaching assistantships, career-related internships or fieldwork, institutionally sponsored loans, scholarships/grants, and unspecified assistantships available. Financial award applicants required to submit FAFSA. *Unit head:* Prof. Amir Ziv, Vice Dean of Students and the MBA Program, 212-854-3485, Fax: 212-932-0545, E-mail: az50@columbia.edu. *Application contact:* Linda B. Meehan, Assistant Dean of Admissions, 212-854-1961, Fax: 212-662-6754, E-mail: apply@gsb.columbia.edu.

Concordia University, School of Graduate Studies, Faculty of Arts and Science, Department of Economics, Montréal, QC H3G 1M8, Canada. Offers MA, PhD, Diploma. *Degree requirements:* For master's, thesis or alternative, research paper; for doctorate, one foreign language, comprehensive exam, thesis/dissertation, research seminar. *Entrance requirements:* For master's and doctorate, honors degree in economics or equivalent. *Faculty research:* Trade and industrial adjustment, tax policy and reform, environmental policy, economics of migration, economics of telecommunications.

Cornell University, Graduate School, Graduate Fields of Architecture, Art and Planning, Field of Regional Science, Ithaca, NY 14853-0001. Offers environmental studies (MA, MS, PhD); international spatial problems (MA, MS, PhD); location theory (MA, MS, PhD); multiregional economic analysis (MA, MS, PhD); peace science (MA, MS, PhD); planning methods (MA, MS, PhD); urban and regional economics (MA, MS, PhD). *Faculty:* 20 full-time (3 women). *Students:* 22 full-time (10 women); includes 2 minority (1 African American, 1 Asian American or Pacific Islander), 20 international. Average age 31. 12 applicants, 83% accepted, 5 enrolled. In 2007, 2 master's, 1 doctorate awarded. Terminal master's awarded for partial completion of doctoral program. *Degree requirements:* For master's, thesis; for doctorate, comprehensive exam, thesis/dissertation. *Entrance requirements:* For master's and doctorate, GRE General Test, 2 letters of recommendation. Additional exam requirements/recommendations for international students: Required—TOEFL (minimum score 600 paper-based; 250 computer-based; 77 iBT). *Application deadline:* For fall admission, 1/15 priority date for domestic students. Application fee: $70. Electronic applications accepted. *Financial support:* In 2007–08, 5 students received support, including 1 fellowship with full tuition reimbursement available, 2 research assistantships with full tuition reimbursements available, 2 teaching assistantships with full tuition reimbursements available; institutionally sponsored loans, scholarships/grants, health care benefits, tuition waivers (full and partial), and unspecified assistantships also available. Financial award applicants required to submit FAFSA. *Faculty research:* Urban and regional growth, spatial economics, formation of spatial patterns by socioeconomic systems, non-linear dynamics and complex systems, environmental-economic systems. *Unit head:* Director of Graduate Studies, 607-255-6848, Fax: 607-255-1971. *Application contact:* Graduate Field Assistant, 607-255-6848, Fax: 607-255-1971, E-mail: regsci@cornell.edu.

Cornell University, Graduate School, Graduate Fields of Arts and Sciences, Field of Economics, Ithaca, NY 14853-0001. Offers applied economics (PhD); basic analytical economics (PhD); econometrics and economic statistics (PhD); economic development and planning (PhD); economic theory (PhD); industrial organization and control (PhD); international economics (PhD); labor economics (PhD); monetary and macroeconomics (PhD); public finance (PhD). *Faculty:* 74 full-time (10 women). *Students:* 102 full-time (37 women); includes 6 minority (2 African Americans, 3 Asian Americans or Pacific Islanders, 1 Hispanic American), 63 international. Average age 28. 538 applicants, 14% accepted, 25 enrolled. In 2007, 23 doctorates awarded. *Degree requirements:* For doctorate, comprehensive exam, thesis/dissertation. *Entrance requirements:* For doctorate, GRE General Test, 3 letters of recommendation. Additional exam requirements/recommendations for international students: Required—TOEFL (minimum score 550 paper-based; 213 computer-based; 77 iBT). *Application deadline:* For fall admission, 1/15 priority date for domestic students. Application fee: $70. Electronic applications accepted. *Financial support:* In 2007–08, 88 students received support, including 24 fellowships with full tuition reimbursements available, 13 research assistantships with full tuition reimbursements available, 51 teaching assistantships with full tuition reimbursements available; institutionally sponsored loans, scholarships/grants, health care benefits, tuition waivers (full and partial), and unspecified assistantships also available. Financial award applicants required to submit FAFSA. *Faculty research:* Learning and games, economics of education, political economy, transfer payments, time series and nonparametrics. *Unit head:* Director of Graduate Studies, 607-255-4893, Fax: 607-255-2818. *Application contact:* Graduate Field Assistant, 607-255-4893, Fax: 607-255-2818, E-mail: econ_phd@cornell.edu.

Dalhousie University, Faculty of Science, Department of Economics, Halifax, NS B3H 4R2, Canada. Offers MA, MDE, PhD. *Faculty:* 14 full-time, 1 part-time/adjunct. *Students:* 29 full-time (16 women), 12 part-time (5 women). 61 applicants, 49% accepted. In 2007, 5 master's, 1 doctorate awarded. *Degree requirements:* For master's, thesis; for doctorate, thesis/dissertation. *Entrance requirements:* For master's and doctorate, GRE (recommended). Additional exam requirements/recommendations for international students: Required—TOEFL. *Application deadline:* For fall admission, 6/1 for domestic students. Applications are processed

Economics

Dalhousie University (continued)

on a rolling basis. Application fee: $60. *Financial support:* In 2007–08, 8 fellowships (averaging $9,500 per year), 1 research assistantship (averaging $1,830 per year), 11 teaching assistantships (averaging $3,705 per year) were awarded. *Faculty research:* Applied econometrics, industrial organization, labor and income distribution, economic theory (micro and macro), resource economics (fishing, forestry). Total annual research expenditures: $98,500. *Unit head:* Dr. Lars Osberg, Chair, 902-494-2026, Fax: 902-494-6917, E-mail: economics@dal.ca. *Application contact:* Dr. Barry Lesser, Chair, 902-494-1682, Fax: 902-494-6917, E-mail: barry.lesser@dal.ca.

DePaul University, Charles H. Kellstadt Graduate School of Business and College of Liberal Arts and Sciences, Department of Economics, Chicago, IL 60604-2287. Offers applied economics (MBA); economics (MA); international business (MBA). Part-time and evening/weekend programs available. *Faculty:* 21 full-time (5 women), 8 part-time/adjunct (1 woman). *Students:* 48 full-time (17 women), 32 part-time (13 women); includes 16 minority (3 African Americans, 8 Asian Americans or Pacific Islanders, 5 Hispanic Americans), 14 international. Average age 29. 23 applicants, 83% accepted. In 2007, 7 master's awarded. *Degree requirements:* For master's, thesis optional. *Entrance requirements:* For master's, GMAT (MBA). Additional exam requirements/recommendations for international students: Required—TOEFL, GRE. *Application deadline:* For fall admission, 7/1 for domestic students; for winter admission, 10/1 for domestic students; for spring admission, 2/1 for domestic students. Applications are processed on a rolling basis. Application fee: $40. Electronic applications accepted. *Financial support:* In 2007–08, 3 students received support, including 2 research assistantships with partial tuition reimbursements available (averaging $9,999 per year). Support available to part-time students. *Faculty research:* Forensic economics, game theory sports, economics of education, banking in Poland and Thailand. *Unit head:* Dr. Michael S. Miller, Chairperson, 312-362-8477, Fax: 312-362-5452, E-mail: mmiller@depaul.edu. *Application contact:* Kavitha Chinthada, Director of Graduate Admissions, 773-325-7885, Fax: 773-325-7311, E-mail: kchintha@depaul.edu.

Drexel University, LeBow College of Business, Program in Business Administration, Philadelphia, PA 19104-2875. Offers business administration (MBA, PhD, APC), including accounting (MBA, PhD), decision sciences (PhD), economics (MBA, PhD), finance (MBA, PhD), legal studies (MBA), management (MBA), marketing (MBA, PhD), organizational sciences (PhD), quantitative methods (MBA), strategic management (PhD). *Accreditation:* AACSB. Part-time and evening/weekend programs available. Postbaccalaureate distance learning degree programs offered (minimal on-campus study). Terminal master's awarded for partial completion of doctoral program. *Entrance requirements:* For master's, GMAT, minimum GPA of 2.75; for doctorate, GMAT. Additional exam requirements/recommendations for international students: Required—TOEFL. Electronic applications accepted. *Faculty research:* Decision support systems, individual and group behavior, operations research, techniques and strategy.

Duke University, Graduate School, Department of Economics, Durham, NC 27708. Offers AM, PhD, JD/AM. *Faculty:* 41 full-time. *Students:* 150 full-time (58 women); includes 11 minority (3 African Americans, 1 American Indian/Alaska Native, 4 Asian Americans or Pacific Islanders, 3 Hispanic Americans), 96 international. 555 applicants, 26% accepted, 64 enrolled. In 2007, 26 master's, 12 doctorates awarded. *Degree requirements:* For doctorate, thesis/dissertation. *Entrance requirements:* For master's and doctorate, GRE General Test. Additional exam requirements/recommendations for international students: Required—TOEFL (minimum score 550 paper-based; 213 computer-based; 83 iBT), IELTS (minimum score 7). *Application deadline:* For fall admission, 12/15 priority date for domestic and international students. Application fee: $75. Electronic applications accepted. *Financial support:* Fellowships, research assistantships, teaching assistantships, Federal Work-Study available. Financial award application deadline: 12/31. *Unit head:* Peter Arcidiacono, Director of Graduate Studies, 919-660-1884, Fax: 919-660-1879, E-mail: can6@duke.edu.

East Carolina University, Graduate School, Thomas Harriot College of Arts and Sciences, Department of Economics, Greenville, NC 27858-4353. Offers applied resource economics (MS). Part-time programs available. *Faculty:* 13 full-time (1 woman). *Students:* 10 full-time (3 women); includes 2 minority (both African Americans), 4 international. Average age 26. 15 applicants, 27% accepted, 2 enrolled. In 2007, 20 degrees awarded. *Degree requirements:* For master's, one foreign language, comprehensive exam. *Entrance requirements:* For master's, GRE General Test. Additional exam requirements/recommendations for international students: Required—TOEFL. *Application deadline:* For fall admission, 6/1 priority date for domestic students. Applications are processed on a rolling basis. Application fee: $50. *Financial support:* Research assistantships with partial tuition reimbursements, teaching assistantships with partial tuition reimbursements available. Financial award application deadline: 6/1. *Unit head:* Dr. Richard Ericson, Chair, 252-328-6006, Fax: 252-328-6743, E-mail: ericsonr@ecu.edu. *Application contact:* Dean of Graduate School, 252-328-6012, Fax: 252-328-6071, E-mail: gradschool@ecu.edu.

Eastern Illinois University, Graduate School, College of Sciences, Department of Economics, Charleston, IL 61920-3099. Offers MA. *Faculty:* 15 full-time (0 women). In 2007, 10 degrees awarded. *Application deadline:* For fall admission, 7/31 priority date for domestic students. Applications are processed on a rolling basis. Application fee: $30. *Expenses:* Tuition, state resident: part-time $218 per hour. Tuition, nonresident: part-time $654 per hour. *Financial support:* In 2007–08, research assistantships with tuition reimbursements (averaging $7,200 per year), 5 teaching assistantships with tuition reimbursements (averaging $7,200 per year) were awarded. *Unit head:* Dr. Ebrahim Karbassioon, Chairperson, 217-581-5429, Fax: 217-581-5997, E-mail: ekarbassioon@eiu.edu. *Application contact:* Dr. Mukti Upadhyay, Coordinator, 217-581-3812, Fax: 217-581-5997, E-mail: mpupadhyay@eiu.edu.

Eastern Michigan University, Graduate School, College of Arts and Sciences, Department of Economics, Ypsilanti, MI 48197. Offers applied economics (MA); economics (MA); health economics (MA); international economics and development (MA); trade and development (MA). Part-time and evening/weekend programs available. Postbaccalaureate distance learning degree programs offered (minimal on-campus study). *Faculty:* 11 full-time (2 women). *Students:* 18 full-time (10 women), 34 part-time (11 women); includes 13 minority (11 African Americans, 1 Asian American or Pacific Islander, 1 Hispanic American), 14 international. Average age 29. In 2007, 27 degrees awarded. *Degree requirements:* For master's, thesis or alternative. *Entrance requirements:* Additional exam requirements/recommendations for international students: Required—TOEFL. *Application deadline:* Applications are processed on a rolling basis. Application fee: $35. *Expenses:* Tuition, state resident: full-time $8,952; part-time $373 per credit hour. Tuition, nonresident: full-time $17,634; part-time $735 per credit hour. Required fees: $896; $34 per credit hour. Tuition and fees vary according to course level, degree level and program. *Financial support:* Fellowships, research assistantships with full tuition reimbursements, teaching assistantships with full tuition reimbursements, career-related internships or fieldwork, Federal Work-Study, institutionally sponsored loans, scholarships/grants, tuition waivers (partial), and unspecified assistantships available. Support available to part-time students. Financial award applicants required to submit FAFSA. *Unit head:* Dr. Raouf S. Hanna, Head, 734-487-3395, Fax: 734-487-9666, E-mail: rhanna@emich.edu. *Application contact:* Dr. David Crary, Advisor, 734-487-0001, Fax: 734-487-9666, E-mail: dcrary@emich.edu.

Eastern University, Graduate Business Programs, St. Davids, PA 19087-3696. Offers business administration (MBA), including accounting, economics, finance, management, marketing; economic development (MBA, MS); nonprofit management (MBA, MS); M Div/MBA; M Div/MS. Part-time and evening/weekend programs available. *Degree requirements:* For master's, thesis (for some programs). *Entrance requirements:* For master's, GMAT (MBA), minimum GPA of 2.5. Expenses: Contact institution. *Faculty research:* Micro-level economic development, China welfare and economic development, macroethics, micro- and macro-level economic development in transitional economics, organizational effectiveness.

East Tennessee State University, School of Graduate Studies, College of Business and Technology, Department of Economics, Finance, and Urban Studies, Johnson City, TN 37614. Offers city management (MCM); community development (MPM); general administration (MPM); municipal service management (MPM); urban and regional economic development (MPM); urban and regional planning (MPM). *Degree requirements:* For master's, internship, oral defense of thesis, research report. *Entrance requirements:* For master's, GRE General Test, minimum GPA of 3.0. Additional exam requirements/recommendations for international students: Required—TOEFL (minimum score 550 paper-based; 213 computer-based).

Emory University, Graduate School of Arts and Sciences, Department of Economics, Atlanta, GA 30322-1100. Offers PhD. *Degree requirements:* For doctorate, comprehensive exam, thesis/dissertation. *Entrance requirements:* For doctorate, GRE General Test. Electronic applications accepted. *Faculty research:* Applied microeconomics, econometrics, public choice, macroeconomics, law and economics.

Florida Agricultural and Mechanical University, Division of Graduate Studies, Research, and Continuing Education, College of Arts and Sciences, Division of History and Political Sciences, Program in Applied Social Science, Tallahassee, FL 32307-3200. Offers African American history (MASS); criminal justice (MASS); economics (MASS); history (MASS); political science (MASS); public administration (MASS); public management (MASS); social work (MASS); sociology (MASS). Part-time programs available. *Degree requirements:* For master's, thesis optional. *Entrance requirements:* For master's, GRE General Test, minimum GPA of 3.0. *Faculty research:* Southern history, black history, election trends, presidential history.

Florida Atlantic University, College of Business, Department of Economics, Boca Raton, FL 33431-0991. Offers MS, MST. Part-time and evening/weekend programs available. *Degree requirements:* For master's, thesis optional. *Entrance requirements:* For master's, GMAT, GRE General Test, minimum GPA of 3.0. Additional exam requirements/recommendations for international students: Required—TOEFL (minimum score 600 paper-based; 250 computer-based). *Faculty research:* International trade and finance, decision making, monetary conditions, economic fluctuations and growth.

Florida International University, College of Arts and Sciences, Department of Economics, Miami, FL 33199. Offers MA, PhD. Part-time and evening/weekend programs available. *Faculty:* 15 full-time (4 women), 1 part-time/adjunct (0 women). *Students:* 31 full-time (9 women), 6 part-time (2 women); includes 8 minority (2 African Americans, 6 Hispanic Americans), 25 international. Average age 30. 64 applicants, 36% accepted, 13 enrolled. In 2007, 3 master's, 4 doctorates awarded. *Degree requirements:* For master's, thesis or alternative; for doctorate, comprehensive exam, thesis/dissertation. *Entrance requirements:* For master's, GRE, minimum GPA of 3.0, letters of recommendation; for doctorate, GRE General Test, 3 letters of recommendation, minimum GPA of 3.0. Additional exam requirements/recommendations for international students: Required—TOEFL (minimum score 550 paper-based; 213 computer-based). *Application deadline:* For fall admission, 6/1 for domestic students, 4/1 for international students; for spring admission, 10/1 for domestic students, 9/1 for international students. Applications are processed on a rolling basis. Application fee: $30. Electronic applications accepted. *Expenses:* Tuition, state resident: full-time $6,106. Tuition, nonresident: full-time $15,528. Required fees: $284. *Financial support:* In 2007–08, 2 fellowships, 4 research assistantships, 1 teaching assistantship were awarded; Federal Work-Study, scholarships/grants, and tuition waivers (partial) also available. *Faculty research:* Economic development, international economics, urban/regional economics, Latin American economics. *Unit head:* Dr. John H. Boyd, Chairperson, 305-348-2316, Fax: 305-348-1524, E-mail: boydj@fiu.edu.

Florida State University, Graduate Studies, College of Social Sciences, Department of Economics, Tallahassee, FL 32306. Offers MS, PhD, JD/MS. Part-time programs available. *Faculty:* 28 full-time (3 women), 9 part-time/adjunct (5 women). *Students:* 59 full-time (17 women), 9 part-time (1 woman); includes 6 minority (1 African American, 1 Asian American or Pacific Islander, 4 Hispanic Americans), 19 international. Average age 26. 121 applicants, 44% accepted, 34 enrolled. In 2007, 16 master's, 5 doctorates awarded. Terminal master's awarded for partial completion of doctoral program. *Median time to degree:* Of those who began their doctoral program in fall 1999, 11% received their degree in 8 years or less. *Degree requirements:* For master's, thesis or alternative; for doctorate, thesis/dissertation, 2 comprehensive exams, workshops. *Entrance requirements:* For master's, GRE General Test, minimum GPA of 3.0, minimum GPA of 3.4 on graduate work, minimum 1 course each in statistics and calculus; for doctorate, GRE General Test, minimum graduate GPA of 3.4, minimum 1 course in statistics, 2 in calculus, and 1 in linear algebra. Additional exam requirements/recommendations for international students: Required—TOEFL (minimum score 550 paper-based; 213 computer-based; 80 iBT). *Application deadline:* For fall admission, 7/1 priority date for domestic students, 5/1 priority date for international students; for spring admission, 11/1 priority date for domestic students, 9/1 priority date for international students. Applications are processed on a rolling basis. Application fee: $30. Electronic applications accepted. *Expenses:* Tuition, state resident: part-time $248 per credit hour. Tuition, nonresident: part-time $880 per credit hour. Tuition and fees vary according to program. *Financial support:* In 2007–08, 38 students received support, including fellowships with full tuition reimbursements available (averaging $20,000 per year), 5 research assistantships with full tuition reimbursements available (averaging $13,500 per year), 22 teaching assistantships with full tuition reimbursements available (averaging $13,500 per year). Financial award application deadline: 1/31; financial award applicants required to submit FAFSA. *Faculty research:* Lbor, industrial organization, international, experimental/behavioral. Total annual research expenditures: $315,000. *Unit head:* Dr. Bruce L. Benson, Chairman, 850-644-5001, Fax: 850-644-4535, E-mail: bbenson@fsu.edu. *Application contact:* Dr. Thomas W. Zuehlke, Graduate Director, 850-644-7206, Fax: 850-644-4535, E-mail: tzuehlke@fsu.edu.

Fordham University, Graduate School of Arts and Sciences, Department of Economics, New York, NY 10458. Offers MA, PhD. Part-time and evening/weekend programs available. *Faculty:* 22 full-time (4 women). *Students:* 28 full-time (18 women), 57 part-time (18 women); includes 4 minority (2 Asian Americans or Pacific Islanders, 2 Hispanic Americans), 43 international. Average age 30. 109 applicants, 45% accepted, 14 enrolled. In 2007, 24 master's, 7 doctorates awarded. Terminal master's awarded for partial completion of doctoral program. *Median time to degree:* Of those who began their doctoral program in fall 1999, 50% received their degree in 8 years or less. *Degree requirements:* For master's, comprehensive exam; for doctorate, comprehensive exam, thesis/dissertation. *Entrance requirements:* For master's and doctorate, GRE General Test. Additional exam requirements/recommendations for international students: Required—TOEFL (minimum score 600 paper-based; 250 computer-based). *Application deadline:* For fall admission, 1/4 priority date for domestic students; for spring admission, 11/1 for domestic students. Application fee: $70. Electronic applications accepted. *Expenses:* Tuition: Full-time $23,880; part-time $995 per credit. *Financial support:* In 2007–08, 29 students received support, including 2 fellowships with tuition reimbursements available (averaging $22,225 per year), 10 research assistantships with tuition reimbursements available (averaging $16,290 per year), 17 teaching assistantships with tuition reimbursements available (averaging $12,593 per year); career-related internships or fieldwork, institutionally sponsored loans, tuition waivers (full and partial), and unspecified assistantships also available. Financial award application deadline: 1/4; financial award applicants required to submit FAFSA. *Faculty research:* Developmental economics, econometrics. Total annual research expenditures: $25,000. *Unit head:* Dr. Henry Schwalbenberg, Chair, 718-817-3866, Fax: 718-817-3518. *Application contact:* Charlene Dundie, Director of Graduate Admissions, 718-817-4420, Fax: 718-817-3566, E-mail: dundie@fordham.edu.

Fordham University, Graduate School of Arts and Sciences, Program in International Political Economy and Development, New York, NY 10458. Offers MA, Certificate. Part-time and evening/weekend programs available. *Faculty:* 23. *Students:* 36 full-time (12 women), 20 part-time (9 women); includes 7 minority (1 American Indian/Alaska Native, 4 Asian Americans or Pacific Islanders, 2 Hispanic Americans), 12 international. Average age 28. 202 applicants, 39% accepted, 26 enrolled. In 2007, 37 degrees awarded. *Degree requirements:* For master's, comprehensive exam. *Entrance requirements:* For master's, GRE General Test. Additional exam requirements/recommendations for international students: Required—TOEFL (minimum score 600 paper-based; 250 computer-based). *Application deadline:* For fall admission, 1/4 priority date for domestic students; for spring admission, 11/1 for domestic students. Application fee: $70. Electronic applications accepted. *Expenses:* Tuition: Full-time $23,880; part-time $995 per credit. *Financial support:* In 2007–08, 14 students received support, including 1 fellowship with tuition reimbursement available (averaging $21,100 per year), 13 research assistantships with tuition reimbursements available (averaging $13,769 per year); career-related internships or fieldwork, institutionally sponsored loans, tuition waivers (full and partial), and unspecified assistantships also available. Financial award application deadline: 1/4; financial award applicants required to submit FAFSA. *Faculty research:* International economics, comparative international politics, international banking and finance, international development, emerging markets and country risk analysis. *Unit head:* Dr. Henry Schwalbenberg, Chair, 718-817-3866, Fax: 718-817-3518. *Application contact:* Charlene Dundie, Director of Graduate Admissions, 718-817-4420, Fax: 718-817-3566, E-mail: dundie@fordham.edu.

See Close-Up on page 1147.

George Mason University, College of Humanities and Social Sciences, Department of Economics, Fairfax, VA 22030. Offers economic systems design (Graduate Certificate); economics (MA, PhD). *Faculty:* 36 full-time (1 woman), 9 part-time/adjunct (1 woman). *Students:* 85 full-time (23 women), 119 part-time (30 women); includes 17 minority (2 African Americans, 10 Asian Americans or Pacific Islanders, 5 Hispanic Americans), 44 international. Average age 29. 260 applicants, 50% accepted, 76 enrolled. In 2007, 41 master's, 15 doctorates awarded. *Degree requirements:* For master's, thesis optional, 2 comprehensive exams; for doctorate, thesis/dissertation, 2 preliminary exams, field exams. *Entrance requirements:* For master's, GRE General Test, GRE Subject Test, introductory and intermediate course work in macro and microeconomics, undergraduate course work in calculus; for doctorate, GRE General Test, GRE Subject Test, course work in analytic geometry, 1 year of course work in statistics, introductory and intermediate course work in macro and microeconomics. *Application deadline:* For fall admission, 5/1 for domestic students; for spring admission, 11/1 for domestic students. Application fee: $60 ($75 for international students). Electronic applications accepted. *Financial support:* Fellowships, research assistantships, teaching assistantships available. Support available to part-time students. Financial award application deadline: 3/1; financial award applicants required to submit FAFSA. *Unit head:* Dr. Donald Boudreaux, Chairman, 703-993-1157, Fax: 703-993-1133, E-mail: dboudrea@gmu.edu.

Georgetown University, Graduate School of Arts and Sciences, Department of Economics, Washington, DC 20057. Offers PhD, MA/PhD, MS/MA. *Degree requirements:* For doctorate, comprehensive exam, thesis/dissertation. *Entrance requirements:* For doctorate, GRE General Test. Additional exam requirements/recommendations for international students: Required—TOEFL. *Faculty research:* International economics, economic development.

The George Washington University, Columbian College of Arts and Sciences, Department of Economics, Washington, DC 20052. Offers MA, PhD. Part-time and evening/weekend programs available. Terminal master's awarded for partial completion of doctoral program. *Degree requirements:* For master's, comprehensive exam, thesis or alternative; for doctorate, thesis/dissertation, general exam. *Entrance requirements:* For master's and doctorate, GRE General Test, minimum GPA of 3.0. Additional exam requirements/recommendations for international students: Required—TOEFL (minimum score 550 paper-based; 213 computer-based). Electronic applications accepted.

Georgia Institute of Technology, Graduate Studies and Research, Ivan Allen College of Policy and International Affairs, School of Economics, Atlanta, GA 30332-0001. Offers MS. *Degree requirements:* For master's, thesis. *Entrance requirements:* For master's, GRE. Additional exam requirements/recommendations for international students: Required—TOEFL. *Faculty research:* Land use patterns in developing countries, office automation and productivity, dynamic modeling of financial markets.

Georgia State University, Andrew Young School of Policy Studies, Department of Economics, Atlanta, GA 30303-3083. Offers MA, PhD. MA offered through the College of Arts and Sciences. Part-time and evening/weekend programs available. *Faculty:* 27 full-time (8 women). *Students:* 91 full-time (32 women), 13 part-time (3 women); includes 14 minority (8 African Americans, 1 American Indian/Alaska Native, 2 Asian Americans or Pacific Islanders, 3 Hispanic Americans), 49 international. Average age 30. 143 applicants, 37% accepted, 24 enrolled. In 2007, 24 master's, 22 doctorates awarded. Terminal master's awarded for partial completion of doctoral program. *Degree requirements:* For master's, thesis optional; for doctorate, comprehensive exam, thesis/dissertation. *Entrance requirements:* For master's, GRE; for doctorate, GRE General Test. Additional exam requirements/recommendations for international students: Required—TOEFL. *Application deadline:* For fall admission, 4/1 for domestic and international students; for spring admission, 10/1 for domestic and international students. Applications are processed on a rolling basis. Application fee: $50. Electronic applications accepted. *Expenses:* Tuition, state resident: part-time $221 per credit hour. *Financial support:* In 2007–08, fellowships with tuition reimbursements (averaging $7,000 per year), 42 research assistantships with full tuition reimbursements (averaging $17,000 per year), 30 teaching assistantships with full tuition reimbursements (averaging $17,000 per year) were awarded; career-related internships or fieldwork and tuition waivers (partial) also available. Support available to part-time students. Financial award applicants required to submit FAFSA. *Faculty research:* Tax policy, economic growth and development, environmental economics, urban and regional economics, economics of science. *Unit head:* Dr. James Alm, Chair, 404-413-0093, E-mail: jalm@gsu.edu. *Application contact:* Sue Fagan, Office of Academic Assistance Director, 404-413-0021, Fax: 404-413-0023, E-mail: suefagan@gsu.edu.

Georgia State University, Andrew Young School of Policy Studies, Department of Public Administration and Urban Studies, Atlanta, GA 30303-3083. Offers disaster management (Certificate); non-profit management (Certificate); planning and economic development (Certificate); public administration (MPA); public policy (PhD); urban policy studies (MS); JD/MPA. *Accreditation:* NASPAA (one or more programs are accredited). Part-time and evening/weekend programs available. *Faculty:* 15 full-time (5 women). *Students:* 131 full-time (82 women), 91 part-time (58 women); includes 83 minority (73 African Americans, 7 Asian Americans or Pacific Islanders, 3 Hispanic Americans), 32 international. Average age 32. 250 applicants, 49% accepted, 74 enrolled. In 2007, 51 master's, 1 doctorate, 7 other advanced degrees awarded. Terminal master's awarded for partial completion of doctoral program. *Degree requirements:* For master's, thesis optional; for doctorate, comprehensive exam, thesis/dissertation. *Entrance requirements:* For master's and doctorate, GRE General Test. Additional exam requirements/recommendations for international students: Required—TOEFL. *Application deadline:* For fall admission, 4/1 for domestic students; for spring admission, 10/1 for domestic students. Applications are processed on a rolling basis. Application fee: $50. Electronic applications accepted. *Expenses:* Tuition, state resident: part-time $221 per credit hour. *Financial support:* In 2007–08, 34 research assistantships with full tuition reimbursements were awarded; fellowships, teaching assistantships with full tuition reimbursements, career-related internships or fieldwork, Federal Work-Study, institutionally sponsored loans, scholarships/grants, and tuition waivers (partial) also available. Support available to part-time students. Financial award applicants required to submit FAFSA. *Faculty research:* Public management, urban policy, policy analysis, public finance, public involvement. *Unit head:* Dr. Greg Streib, Chair, 404-413-0116, E-mail: gstreib@gsu.edu. *Application contact:* Sue Fagan, Office of Academic Assistance Director, 404-413-0021, Fax: 404-413-0023, E-mail: suefagan@gsu.edu.

Georgia State University, J. Mack Robinson College of Business, Program in General Business Administration, Atlanta, GA 30303-3083. Offers accounting/information systems (MBA); economics (MBA, MS); enterprise risk management (MBA); general business (MBA); general business administration (EMBA, PMBA); information systems consulting (MBA); information systems risk management (MBA); international business and information technology (MBA); international entrepreneurship (MBA); MBA/JD. *Accreditation:* AACSB. Part-time and evening/weekend programs available. *Faculty:* 153 full-time (40 women), 4 part-time/adjunct (1 woman). *Students:* 264 full-time (100 women), 162 part-time (46 women); includes 114 minority (68 African Americans, 2 American Indian/Alaska Native, 29 Asian Americans or Pacific Islanders, 15 Hispanic Americans), 38 international. 150 applicants, 73% accepted, 45 enrolled. In 2007, 130 degrees awarded. *Entrance requirements:* For master's, GMAT. Additional exam requirements/recommendations for international students: Required—TOEFL (minimum score 610 paper-based; 255 computer-based; 101 iBT). *Application deadline:* For fall admission, 4/1 for domestic students, 2/1 for international students; for spring admission, 10/15 for domestic students, 5/1 for international students. Applications are processed on a rolling basis. Application fee: $50. Electronic applications accepted. *Expenses:* Tuition, state resident: part-time $221 per credit hour. *Financial support:* Research assistantships, tuition waivers (partial) available. Support available to part-time students. Financial award application deadline: 5/1; financial award applicants required to submit FAFSA. *Unit head:* Dr. Jane F. Mutchler, Associate Dean, 404-413-7000. *Application contact:* Dr. Diane M. Fennig, Director of Master's Admissions and Advisement, 404-413-7130, E-mail: mastersadmissions@gsu.edu.

Graduate School and University Center of the City University of New York, Graduate Studies, Program in Economics, New York, NY 10016-4039. Offers PhD. *Faculty:* 53 full-time (10 women). *Students:* 96 full-time (48 women), 1 part-time; includes 6 minority (1 African American, 4 Asian Americans or Pacific Islanders, 1 Hispanic American), 65 international. Average age 33. 66 applicants, 55% accepted, 75 enrolled. In 2007, 8 degrees awarded. *Degree requirements:* For doctorate, thesis/dissertation. *Entrance requirements:* For doctorate, GRE General Test. Additional exam requirements/recommendations for international students: Required—TOEFL. *Application deadline:* For fall admission, 4/15 for domestic students; for spring admission, 11/15 for domestic students. Application fee: $125. Electronic applications accepted. *Financial support:* In 2007–08, 63 students received support, including 60 fellowships, 10 teaching assistantships; research assistantships, career-related internships or fieldwork, Federal Work-Study, institutionally sponsored loans, and tuition waivers (full and partial) also available. Financial award application deadline: 2/1; financial award applicants required to submit FAFSA. *Unit head:* Dr. Thom Thurston, Executive Officer, 212-817-8256, Fax: 212-817-1514, E-mail: tthurston@gc.cuny.edu.

Harvard University, Graduate School of Arts and Sciences, Committee on Business Economics, Cambridge, MA 02138. Offers PhD. *Degree requirements:* For doctorate, thesis/dissertation. *Entrance requirements:* For doctorate, GMAT or GRE General Test. Additional exam requirements/recommendations for international students: Required—TOEFL. *Expenses:* Tuition: Full-time $31,456. Full-time tuition and fees vary according to program and student level.

Harvard University, Graduate School of Arts and Sciences, Department of Economics, Cambridge, MA 02138. Offers PhD. *Degree requirements:* For doctorate, thesis/dissertation, oral exam. *Entrance requirements:* For doctorate, GRE General Test, GRE Subject Test. Additional exam requirements/recommendations for international students: Required—TOEFL. *Expenses:* Tuition: Full-time $31,456. Full-time tuition and fees vary according to program and student level. *Faculty research:* Industrial organization, macromonetary issues, international economics.

Hawai'i Pacific University, College of Business Administration, Honolulu, HI 96813. Offers accounting/CPA (MBA); communication (MBA); e-business (MBA); economics (MBA); finance (MBA); human resource management (MBA); information systems (MBA); international business (MBA); management (MBA); marketing (MBA); organizational change (MBA); travel industry management (MBA). Part-time and evening/weekend programs available. *Faculty:* 40 full-time (16 women), 30 part-time/adjunct (10 women). *Students:* 280 full-time (132 women), 193 part-time (91 women); includes 144 minority (11 African Americans, 7 American Indian/Alaska Native, 119 Asian Americans or Pacific Islanders, 7 Hispanic Americans), 219 international. Average age 29. 204 applicants, 95% accepted, 110 enrolled. In 2007, 150 degrees awarded. *Degree requirements:* For master's, thesis. *Entrance requirements:* For master's, GMAT. Additional exam requirements/recommendations for international students: Recommended—TOEFL (minimum score 550 paper-based; 213 computer-based; 80 iBT), TWE (minimum score 5). *Application deadline:* For fall admission, 2/15 priority date for domestic students; for spring admission, 10/15 priority date for domestic students. Applications are processed on a rolling basis. Application fee: $50. Electronic applications accepted. *Expenses:* Tuition: Full-time $14,400. Required fees: $1,885. Tuition and fees vary according to course load and program. *Financial support:* In 2007–08, 107 students received support; research assistantships, career-related internships or fieldwork, Federal Work-Study, scholarships/grants, and unspecified assistantships available. Support available to part-time students. Financial award application deadline: 3/1; financial award applicants required to submit FAFSA. *Faculty research:* Statistical control process as used by management, studies in comparative cross-cultural management styles, not-for-profit management. *Unit head:* Dr. Charles Steilen, Dean, 808-544-9301, Fax: 808-544-0283, E-mail: csteilen@hpu.edu. *Application contact:* Danny Lam, Assistant Director of Graduate Admissions, 808-544-1135, Fax: 808-544-0280, E-mail: graduate@hpu.edu.

Howard University, Graduate School, Department of Economics, Washington, DC 20059-0002. Offers MA, PhD. Part-time programs available. *Degree requirements:* For master's, comprehensive exam, thesis optional; for doctorate, one foreign language, comprehensive exam, thesis/dissertation. *Entrance requirements:* For master's, GRE General Test, minimum GPA of 3.0; for doctorate, GRE General Test, master's degree in economics or related field, minimum GPA of 3.0. Electronic applications accepted. *Expenses:* Tuition: Full-time $16,175; part-time $899 per credit hour. Required fees: $805. *Faculty research:* Economic development, international trade, urban rentalization.

Hunter College of the City University of New York, Graduate School, School of Arts and Sciences, Department of Economics, New York, NY 10021-5085. Offers accounting (MS); economics (MA). Part-time and evening/weekend programs available. *Faculty:* 5 full-time (1 woman), 7 part-time/adjunct (0 women). *Students:* 8 full-time (3 women), 27 part-time (12 women); includes 11 minority (3 African Americans, 7 Asian Americans or Pacific Islanders, 1 Hispanic American). Average age 29. 24 applicants, 42% accepted, 6 enrolled. In 2007, 15 degrees awarded. *Degree requirements:* For master's, research paper or thesis. *Entrance requirements:* For master's, GMAT or GRE General Test, minimum GPA of 3.0, 18 credits of undergraduate course work in economics (9 in mathematics), 2 letters of recommendation (1 from a member of economics department). Additional exam requirements/recommendations for international students: Required—TOEFL. *Application deadline:* For fall admission, 4/1 for domestic students, 2/1 for international students; for spring admission, 11/1 for domestic students, 9/1 for international students. Application fee: $125. *Expenses:* Tuition, state resident: full-time $6,400; part-time $270 per credit. Tuition, nonresident: part-time $500 per credit. One-time fee: $125 full-time. Tuition and fees vary according to program. *Financial support:* Fellowships, research assistantships, teaching assistantships, career-related internships or fieldwork, Federal Work-Study, institutionally sponsored loans, and tuition waivers (partial) available. Support available to part-time students. *Faculty research:* Earnings of immigrants and minority groups, taxation and the regional economy. *Unit head:* Dr. Marjorie P. Honig, Chairperson, 212-772-5400, Fax: 212-772-5398, E-mail: mhonig@hunter.cuny.edu. *Application contact:* Randall Filer, Professor of Economics, Graduate Advisor, 212-772-5399, Fax: 212-772-5398, E-mail: grad.econadvisor@hunter.cuny.edu.

Illinois State University, Graduate School, College of Arts and Sciences, Department of Economics, Normal, IL 61790-2200. Offers MA, MS. *Faculty:* 13 full-time (1 woman). *Students:* 28 full-time (9 women), 5 part-time (4 women); includes 2 minority (1 African American, 1 Hispanic American), 16 international. 31 applicants, 87% accepted. In 2007, 9 degrees awarded. *Degree requirements:* For master's, thesis or alternative. *Entrance requirements:* For master's, GRE General Test, minimum GPA of 2.6 in last 60 hours of course work. *Application deadline:* Applications are processed on a rolling basis. Application fee: $40. *Expenses:* Tuition, state resident: full-time $3,492; part-time $194 per credit hour. Tuition, nonresident: full-time $7,272; part-time $404 per credit hour. Required fees: $1,024; $57 per credit hour. *Financial support:* In 2007–08, 21 research assistantships (averaging $6,482 per year), 1 teaching assistantship

Economics

Illinois State University (continued)
(averaging $3,627 per year) were awarded; tuition waivers (full) and unspecified assistantships also available. Financial award application deadline: 4/1. *Faculty research:* Stevenson Center Graduate Assistantship in Community/Economic Development; the social, economic and educational correlates of rural school closure; Stevenson Center Americorps project. Total annual research expenditures: $725,648. *Unit head:* Dr. James Payne, Chairperson, 309-438-8625.

Indiana University Bloomington, Kelley School of Business, Department of Business Economics and Public Policy, Bloomington, IN 47405-7000. Offers PhD. *Faculty:* 8 full-time (1 woman), 1 part-time/adjunct (0 women). *Students:* 20 applicants, 10% accepted, 2 enrolled. In 2007, 2 degrees awarded. *Median time to degree:* Of those who began their doctoral program in fall 1999, 95% received their degree in 8 years or less. *Degree requirements:* For doctorate, comprehensive exam, thesis/dissertation. *Entrance requirements:* For doctorate, GRE or GMAT, bachelors degree. Additional exam requirements/recommendations for international students: Required—TOEFL (minimum score 630 paper-based; 267 computer-based; 80 iBT). *Financial support:* Fellowships with full tuition reimbursements available. *Faculty research:* Industrial organization, pricing, environmental regulation and policy, information economics, economics of law and organization. *Unit head:* Dr. John W. Maxwell, Professor of Business Economics and Public Policy, 812-855-9219, Fax: 812-855-3354, E-mail: jwmax@indiana.edu. *Application contact:* Dr. Michael R. Baye, Bert Elwert Professor of Business Economics, 812-855-9219, Fax: 812-855-3354, E-mail: mbaye@indiana.edu.

Indiana University Bloomington, University Graduate School, College of Arts and Sciences, Department of Economics, Bloomington, IN 47405-7000. Offers MA, PhD. *Faculty:* 30 full-time (3 women). *Students:* 93 full-time (29 women), 7 part-time (1 woman); includes 2 minority (both Asian Americans or Pacific Islanders), 78 international. Average age 30. 169 applicants, 38% accepted, 20 enrolled. In 2007, 9 master's, 7 doctorates awarded. Terminal master's awarded for partial completion of doctoral program. *Median time to degree:* Of those who began their doctoral program in fall 1999, 56% received their degree in 8 years or less. *Degree requirements:* For master's, one foreign language, thesis optional; for doctorate, one foreign language, comprehensive exam, thesis/dissertation, field exams. *Entrance requirements:* For master's and doctorate, GRE General Test, minimum 3 intermediate-level mathematics courses. Additional exam requirements/recommendations for international students: Required—TOEFL. *Application deadline:* For fall admission, 1/15 priority date for domestic students, 12/15 for international students; for spring admission, 9/1 for domestic and international students. Applications are processed on a rolling basis. Application fee: $50 ($60 for international students). *Financial support:* Fellowships with full tuition reimbursements, research assistantships with full tuition reimbursements, teaching assistantships with full tuition reimbursements, institutionally sponsored loans available. Financial award application deadline: 1/15. *Faculty research:* Games, experiments and organization, transition economics, growth and development, macroeconomics, econometrics. *Unit head:* Gerhard Glomm, Chair, 812-855-6160. *Application contact:* Chris Cunningham, Graduate Services Assistant, 812-855-8453, Fax: 812-855-3736, E-mail: rcunning@indiana.edu.

Indiana University–Purdue University Indianapolis, Department of Economics, Indianapolis, IN 46202-2896. Offers MA, MA/MA. *Faculty:* 16 full-time (3 women). *Students:* 5 full-time (2 women), 18 part-time (5 women); includes 1 minority (Asian American or Pacific Islander), 9 international. Average age 29. 35 applicants, 37% accepted, 13 enrolled. In 2007, 7 degrees awarded. *Entrance requirements:* For master's, GRE, minimum GPA of 3.0; courses in economic theory, statistics, calculus. Additional exam requirements/recommendations for international students: Required—TOEFL (minimum score 600 paper-based). *Application deadline:* For fall admission, 2/1 priority date for domestic and international students. Application fee: $50 ($60 for international students). *Expenses:* Tuition, state resident: full-time $5,818; part-time $242 per credit hour. Tuition, nonresident: full-time $17,106; part-time $713 per credit hour. Required fees: $629. Tuition and fees vary according to course load, campus/location and program. *Financial support:* In 2007–08, 1 fellowship with partial tuition reimbursement (averaging $10,000 per year), 7 teaching assistantships (averaging $9,586 per year) were awarded; research assistantships with partial tuition reimbursements, career-related internships or fieldwork and health care benefits also available. *Faculty research:* Charitable giving. *Unit head:* Paul Carlin, Chair, 317-278-9236, E-mail: pcarlin@iupui.edu. *Application contact:* Natalie Harvey, Information Contact, 317-274-4756, Fax: 317-274-0097.

Instituto Centroamericano de Administración de Empresas, Graduate Programs, La Garita, Costa Rica. Offers agribusiness (MIAM); business administration (EMBA); entrepreneurial economics (MBA); industry and technology (MBA); sustainable development (MBA). *Degree requirements:* For master's, comprehensive exam, essay. *Entrance requirements:* For master's, GMAT or GRE, fluency in Spanish, interview, letters of recommendation, minimum 1 year of work experience. Electronic applications accepted. *Faculty research:* Competitiveness, production.

Instituto Tecnológico y de Estudios Superiores de Monterrey, Campus Ciudad de México, Division of Business, Ciudad de Mexico, Mexico. Offers business administration (EMBA, MBA, PhD); economy (MBA); finance (MBA). Part-time and evening/weekend programs available. Postbaccalaureate distance learning degree programs offered (minimal on-campus study). *Entrance requirements:* For master's and doctorate, Instituto entrance exam. Additional exam requirements/recommendations for international students: Required—TOEFL.

Inter American University of Puerto Rico, Metropolitan Campus, Faculty of Economics and Administrative Sciences, School of Economics, San Juan, PR 00919-1293. Offers accounting (MBA); finance (MBA); international business (MIB, PhD).

Iowa State University of Science and Technology, Graduate College, College of Liberal Arts and Sciences, Department of Economics, Ames, IA 50011. Offers agricultural economics (MS, PhD); economics (MS, PhD); JD/MS; JD/PhD. *Faculty:* 43 full-time (5 women), 5 part-time/adjunct (4 women). *Students:* 89 full-time (32 women), 14 part-time (8 women); includes 2 minority (1 Asian American or Pacific Islander, 1 Hispanic American), 81 international. 279 applicants, 18% accepted, 29 enrolled. In 2007, 16 master's, 7 doctorates awarded. *Degree requirements:* For master's, thesis or alternative; for doctorate, thesis/dissertation. *Entrance requirements:* For master's and doctorate, GRE General Test. Additional exam requirements/recommendations for international students: Required—TOEFL (paper-based 570; computer-based 230; iBT 88) or IELTS (6.5). *Application deadline:* For fall admission, 1/20 priority date for domestic and international students. Application fee: $30 ($70 for international students). Electronic applications accepted. *Financial support:* In 2007–08, 22 research assistantships with full and partial tuition reimbursements (averaging $20,813 per year), 65 teaching assistantships with full and partial tuition reimbursements (averaging $21,042 per year) were awarded; fellowships, scholarships/grants, health care benefits, and unspecified assistantships also available. *Unit head:* Dr. J. Arne Hallam, Chair, 515-294-2712, Fax: 515-294-7755, E-mail: grad@econ.iastate.edu. *Application contact:* Dr. John Schroeter, Information Contact, 515-294-2702, E-mail: grad@econ.iastate.edu.

The Johns Hopkins University, Zanvyl Krieger School of Arts and Sciences, Department of Economics, Baltimore, MD 21218-2699. Offers PhD. *Faculty:* 14 full-time (1 woman), 4 part-time/adjunct (1 woman). *Students:* 41 full-time (15 women), 15 international. Average age 24. 378 applicants, 3% accepted, 10 enrolled. In 2007, 14 doctorates awarded. *Median time to degree:* Of those who began their doctoral program in fall 1999, 99% received their degree in 8 years or less. *Degree requirements:* For doctorate, comprehensive exam, thesis/dissertation. *Entrance requirements:* For doctorate, GRE General Test. Additional exam requirements/recommendations for international students: Required—TOEFL (minimum score 600 paper-based; 250 computer-based). *Application deadline:* For fall admission, 1/1 priority date for domestic and international students. Applications are processed on a rolling basis. Application fee: $65. Electronic applications accepted. *Financial support:* In 2007–08, 5 fellowships with full tuition reimbursements (averaging $14,000 per year), 5 research assistantships with full tuition reimbursements (averaging $14,000 per year), 39 teaching assistantships with full tuition reimbursements (averaging $15,000 per year) were awarded; Federal Work-Study and institutionally sponsored loans also available. Financial award application deadline: 4/15; financial award applicants required to submit FAFSA. *Faculty research:* General economic theory, econometrics and mathematical economics, trade and development, game theory, urban economics. *Unit head:* Prof. Joseph Harrington, Chair, 410-516-7615, Fax: 410-516-7600, E-mail: joe.harrington@jhu.edu. *Application contact:* Julia Ross, Graduate Admissions Coordinator, 410-516-7570, Fax: 410-516-7600, E-mail: econadmissions@jhu.edu.

Kansas State University, Graduate School, College of Arts and Sciences, Department of Economics, Manhattan, KS 66506. Offers MA, PhD. Part-time programs available. *Faculty:* 11 full-time (1 woman), 5 part-time/adjunct (2 women). *Students:* 50 full-time (14 women), 11 part-time (5 women); includes 5 minority (1 African American, 3 Asian Americans or Pacific Islanders, 1 Hispanic American), 37 international. 50 applicants, 24% accepted, 7 enrolled. In 2007, 5 master's, 7 doctorates awarded. Terminal master's awarded for partial completion of doctoral program. *Degree requirements:* For master's, thesis optional; for doctorate, comprehensive exam, thesis/dissertation. *Entrance requirements:* For master's, GRE (highly recommended), minimum GPA of 3.0; course work in microeconomics, macroeconomics, calculus and statistics; for doctorate, GRE (highly recommended), course work in microeconomics, macroeconomics, and calculus. Additional exam requirements/recommendations for international students: Required—TOEFL (minimum score 550 paper-based; 213 computer-based). *Application deadline:* For fall admission, 2/1 priority date for domestic and international students; for spring admission, 10/1 for domestic students, 8/1 priority date for international students. Applications are processed on a rolling basis. Application fee: $30 ($55 for international students). Electronic applications accepted. *Financial support:* In 2007–08, 16 teaching assistantships with full tuition reimbursements (averaging $12,384 per year) were awarded; fellowships, research assistantships, career-related internships or fieldwork, institutionally sponsored loans, and scholarships/grants also available. Support available to part-time students. Financial award application deadline: 3/1; financial award applicants required to submit FAFSA. *Faculty research:* Macroeconomics; microeconomics and labor economics; development and growth; international economics; industrial organization. Total annual research expenditures: $6,179. *Unit head:* Dr. Lloyd Thomas, Head, 785-532-7357, Fax: 785-532-6919, E-mail: lbt@ksu.edu. *Application contact:* Dr. William Blankenau, Director, 785-532-6340, Fax: 785-532-6919, E-mail: blankenw@ksu.edu.

Kent State University, Graduate School of Management, Master's Program in Economics, Kent, OH 44242-0001. Offers MA. Part-time programs available. *Faculty:* 10 full-time (2 women), 2 part-time/adjunct (both women). *Students:* 16 full-time (9 women), 3 part-time (2 women), 10 international. Average age 25. 21 applicants, 90% accepted, 6 enrolled. In 2007, 17 degrees awarded. *Entrance requirements:* For master's, GMAT or GRE General Test, minimum GPA of 2.75. Additional exam requirements/recommendations for international students: Required—TOEFL (minimum score 550 paper-based; 213 computer-based). *Application deadline:* For fall admission, 4/1 priority date for domestic students, 3/1 for international students; for spring admission, 12/15 for domestic students. Applications are processed on a rolling basis. Application fee: $30. Electronic applications accepted. *Financial support:* In 2007–08, 11 students received support, including 11 research assistantships with full tuition reimbursements available (averaging $5,025 per year); fellowships, Federal Work-Study also available. Financial award application deadline: 4/1; financial award applicants required to submit FAFSA. *Faculty research:* Macro- and microeconomic theory, labor economics, international economics, quantitative methods. *Unit head:* Dr. Richard J. Kent, Chair, 330-672-2366, Fax: 330-672-9808, E-mail: rkent@kent.edu. *Application contact:* Louise M. Ditchey, Director, 330-672-2282, Fax: 330-672-7303, E-mail: gradbus@kent.edu.

Lakehead University, Graduate Studies, Faculty of Social Sciences and Humanities, Department of Economics, Thunder Bay, ON P7B 5E1, Canada. Offers MA. Part-time and evening/weekend programs available. *Degree requirements:* For master's, thesis or comprehensive exams, research papers. *Entrance requirements:* For master's, minimum B average. Additional exam requirements/recommendations for international students: Required—TOEFL. *Faculty research:* Public finance, economic history, mathematical economics, quantitative economics.

Lehigh University, College of Business and Economics, Department of Economics, Bethlehem, PA 18015-3094. Offers economics (MS, PhD); health and bio-pharmaceutical economics (MS). Part-time and evening/weekend programs available. *Faculty:* 11 full-time (3 women), 1 part-time/adjunct (0 women). *Students:* 22 full-time (10 women), 6 part-time (2 women), 16 international. Average age 26. 58 applicants, 66% accepted, 9 enrolled. In 2007, 14 master's, 1 doctorate awarded. Terminal master's awarded for partial completion of doctoral program. *Degree requirements:* For master's, thesis optional; for doctorate, comprehensive exam, thesis/dissertation, proposal defense. *Entrance requirements:* For master's and doctorate, GMAT or GRE General Test. Additional exam requirements/recommendations for international students: Required—TOEFL (minimum score 600 paper-based; 250 computer-based; 94 iBT). *Application deadline:* For fall admission, 7/15 for domestic students; for spring admission, 12/1 for domestic students. Applications are processed on a rolling basis. Application fee: $65. Electronic applications accepted. *Expenses:* Contact institution. *Financial support:* In 2007–08, 3 fellowships with full tuition reimbursements (averaging $13,200 per year), 10 teaching assistantships with full tuition reimbursements (averaging $13,200 per year) were awarded; research assistantships with tuition reimbursements, health care benefits, tuition waivers (full and partial), and unspecified assistantships also available. Financial award application deadline: 1/15. *Faculty research:* Public finance, investments, applied econometrics, labor economics. Total annual research expenditures: $118,217. *Unit head:* Dr. Robert Thornton, Director of MS Programs, 610-758-3460, Fax: 610-758-4677, E-mail: rjt1@lehigh.edu. *Application contact:* Corinn McBride, Director of Recruitment and Admissions, 610-758-3418, Fax: 610-758-5283, E-mail: com207@lehigh.edu.

Long Island University, Brooklyn Campus, Richard L. Conolly College of Liberal Arts and Sciences, Department of Economics, Brooklyn, NY 11201-8423. Offers MA. Part-time and evening/weekend programs available. *Degree requirements:* For master's, thesis or alternative. *Entrance requirements:* For master's, 2 letters of recommendation. Additional exam requirements/recommendations for international students: Required—TOEFL (minimum score 550 paper-based; 173 computer-based). Electronic applications accepted.

Louisiana State University and Agricultural and Mechanical College, Graduate School, E. J. Ourso College of Business, Department of Economics, Baton Rouge, LA 70803. Offers MS, PhD. *Faculty:* 12 full-time (0 women). *Students:* 27 full-time (10 women), 2 part-time (1 woman); includes 1 Asian American or Pacific Islander, 20 international. Average age 29. 63 applicants, 29% accepted, 8 enrolled. In 2007, 4 master's, 3 doctorates awarded. Terminal master's awarded for partial completion of doctoral program. *Degree requirements:* For doctorate, thesis/dissertation. *Entrance requirements:* For master's and doctorate, GRE General Test, minimum GPA of 3.0. Additional exam requirements/recommendations for international students: Required—TOEFL (minimum score 550 paper-based; 213 computer-based; 79 iBT). *Application deadline:* For fall admission, 1/25 priority date for domestic students, 5/15 for international students; for spring admission, 10/15 for international students. Applications are processed on a rolling basis. Application fee: $25. *Financial support:* In 2007–08, 26 students received support, including 2 fellowships (averaging $31,420 per year), 10 research assistantships with full and partial tuition reimbursements available (averaging $14,000 per year), 12 teaching assistantships with full and partial tuition reimbursements available (averaging $12,958 per year); Federal Work-Study, scholarships/grants, health care benefits, and unspecified assistantships also available. Support available to part-time students. Financial award application deadline: 6/15; financial award applicants required to submit FAFSA. *Faculty research:* Microeconomics, macroeconomics, econometrics, industrial organization, public finance, labor. Total annual research expenditures: $493,896. *Unit head:* Dr. Robert Newman, Chair, 225-578-3794, Fax: 225-578-3807, E-mail: eonewm@lsu.edu. *Application contact:* Dr. Sudipta Sarangi, Graduate Director, 225-578-7193, Fax: 225-578-3807, E-mail: sarangi@lsu.edu.

Louisiana Tech University, Graduate School, College of Business, Department of Finance and Economics, Ruston, LA 71272. Offers business economics (MBA, DBA); finance (MBA, DBA). Part-time programs available. *Degree requirements:* For doctorate, thesis/dissertation. *Entrance requirements:* For master's and doctorate, GMAT. *Application deadline:* For fall admission, 7/29 for domestic students; for spring admission, 2/3 for domestic students. Application fee: $20 ($30 for international students). *Financial support:* Fellowships, research assistantships, teaching assistantships available. Financial award application deadline: 2/1. *Unit head:* Dr. Dwight Anderson, Head, 318-257-4149, Fax: 318-257-4253, E-mail: dwight@latech.edu.

Loyola College in Maryland, Graduate Programs, Sellinger School of Business and Management, Program in Business Administration, Baltimore, MD 21210-2699. Offers decision sciences (MBA); economics (MBA); finance (MBA); marketing/management (MBA). *Accreditation:* AACSB. Part-time and evening/weekend programs available. *Entrance requirements:* For master's, GMAT. Additional exam requirements/recommendations for international students: Required—TOEFL (minimum score 550 paper-based; 213 computer-based).

Marquette University, Graduate School of Management, Department of Economics, Milwaukee, WI 53201-1881. Offers business economics (MSAE); financial economics (MSAE); international economics (MSAE). Part-time and evening/weekend programs available. *Faculty:* 12 full-time (4 women), 5 part-time/adjunct (1 woman). *Students:* 21 full-time (8 women), 15 part-time (3 women); includes 2 minority (1 African American, 1 Hispanic American), 15 international. Average age 27. 42 applicants, 90% accepted, 16 enrolled. In 2007, 17 degrees awarded. *Degree requirements:* For master's, comprehensive exam, thesis or alternative, essay. *Entrance requirements:* For master's, GMAT or GRE General Test. Additional exam requirements/recommendations for international students: Required—TOEFL. Application fee: $40. *Financial support:* In 2007–08, 6 teaching assistantships were awarded; research assistantships, Federal Work-Study, institutionally sponsored loans, scholarships/grants, and tuition waivers (full and partial) also available. Support available to part-time students. Financial award application deadline: 2/15. *Faculty research:* Monetary and fiscal policy in open economy, housing and regional migration, political economy of taxation and state/local government. *Unit head:* Dr. David Clark, Chair, 414-288-3339, Fax: 414-288-5757. *Application contact:* Farrokh Nourzad, Information Contact, 414-288-3570.

Massachusetts Institute of Technology, School of Humanities, Arts, and Social Sciences, Department of Economics, Cambridge, MA 02139-4307. Offers SM, PhD. *Faculty:* 33 full-time (6 women). *Students:* 116 full-time (37 women); includes 13 minority (1 African American, 10 Asian Americans or Pacific Islanders, 2 Hispanic Americans), 62 international. Average age 26. 621 applicants, 7% accepted, 21 enrolled. In 2007, 26 degrees awarded. Terminal master's awarded for partial completion of doctoral program. *Degree requirements:* For master's, thesis; for doctorate, comprehensive exam, thesis/dissertation. *Entrance requirements:* For doctorate, GRE General Test. Additional exam requirements/recommendations for international students: Required—TOEFL (minimum score 600 paper-based; 250 computer-based). *Application deadline:* For fall admission, 1/2 for domestic and international students. Application fee: $70. Electronic applications accepted. *Expenses:* Tuition: Full-time $34,760; part-time $545 per unit. Required fees: $236. *Financial support:* In 2007–08, 101 students received support, including 46 fellowships with tuition reimbursements available (averaging $29,868 per year), 1 research assistantship with tuition reimbursement available (averaging $32,000 per year), 41 teaching assistantships with tuition reimbursements available (averaging $32,918 per year); Federal Work-Study, institutionally sponsored loans, scholarships/grants, health care benefits, and unspecified assistantships also available. *Faculty research:* Theoretical and Applied Macroeconomics; Development Economics and Economic Growth; Public Economics and Political Economy; Labor Economics and Industrial Organization; Econometrics and Economic Theory. Total annual research expenditures: $974,000. *Unit head:* Prof. James Poterba, Head, 617-253-3361, Fax: 617-253-1330. *Application contact:* Student Contact, 617-253-8787, Fax: 617-253-1330, E-mail: econ-admit@mit.edu.

McGill University, Faculty of Graduate and Postdoctoral Studies, Faculty of Arts, Department of Economics, Montréal, QC H3A 2T5, Canada. Offers economics (MA, PhD); social statistics (MA). *Faculty:* 37 full-time (6 women), 6 part-time/adjunct (3 women). *Students:* 70 full-time (26 women), 10 part-time (6 women). 345 applicants, 31% accepted, 43 enrolled. In 2007, 30 master's, 2 doctorates awarded.

McMaster University, School of Graduate Studies, Faculty of Social Sciences, Department of Economics, Hamilton, ON L8S 4M2, Canada. Offers MA, PhD. Part-time programs available. *Faculty:* 27 full-time, 2 part-time/adjunct. *Students:* 37 full-time, 1 part-time. 75 applicants, 48% accepted. *Degree requirements:* For doctorate, comprehensive exam, thesis/dissertation. *Entrance requirements:* For master's, GRE (recommended), honors BA in economics; for doctorate, GRE (recommended), B+ average in a master's degree. Additional exam requirements/recommendations for international students: Required—TOEFL (minimum score 580 paper-based; 237 computer-based). *Application deadline:* For fall admission, 2/1 priority date for domestic students. Application fee: $90. *Financial support:* In 2007–08, fellowships (averaging $4,500 per year), 12 research assistantships (averaging $3,800 per year), 25 teaching assistantships (averaging $8,440 per year) were awarded; scholarships/grants also available. *Faculty research:* Applied microeconomics, econometrics, health economics, labor economics, public finance. Total annual research expenditures: $400,000. *Unit head:* Dr. Mike Veall, Chair, 905-525-9140 Ext. 24591, Fax: 905-521-8232, E-mail: veall@mcmaster.ca. *Application contact:* Jan Martens, Graduate Secretary, 905-525-9140 Ext. 24731, Fax: 905-521-8232, E-mail: martens@mcmaster.ca.

Memorial University of Newfoundland, School of Graduate Studies, Department of Economics, St. John's, NL A1C 5S7, Canada. Offers MA. *Degree requirements:* For master's, thesis optional, essay course. *Entrance requirements:* For master's, honors degree (minimum 2nd class standing). *Faculty research:* Public sector economics, natural resource economics.

Miami University, Graduate School, Farmer School of Business, Department of Economics, Oxford, OH 45056. Offers MA. Part-time programs available. *Degree requirements:* For master's, thesis or alternative, final exam. *Entrance requirements:* For master's, GMAT, minimum undergraduate GPA of 3.0 during previous 2 years or 2.75 overall. Additional exam requirements/recommendations for international students: Required—TOEFL (minimum score 550 paper-based; 213 computer-based), TWE (minimum score 4).

Michigan State University, The Graduate School, College of Social Science, Department of Economics, East Lansing, MI 48824. Offers MA, PhD. *Entrance requirements:* Additional exam requirements/recommendations for international students: Required—TOEFL. Electronic applications accepted. *Expenses:* Tuition, state resident: part-time $379 per credit hour. Tuition, nonresident: part-time $800 per credit hour. Tuition and fees vary according to program.

Middle Tennessee State University, College of Graduate Studies, College of Business, Department of Economics and Finance, Murfreesboro, TN 37132. Offers MA, PhD. Part-time and evening/weekend programs available. Postbaccalaureate distance learning degree programs offered. *Faculty:* 20 full-time (3 women). *Students:* 12 full-time (3 women), 26 part-time (12 women); includes 15 minority (4 African Americans, 11 Asian Americans or Pacific Islanders). Average age 30. 30 applicants, 50% accepted. In 2007, 9 master's, 2 doctorates awarded. *Degree requirements:* For master's, thesis optional; for doctorate, comprehensive exam, thesis/dissertation. *Entrance requirements:* For master's and doctorate, GRE or MAT. Additional exam requirements/recommendations for international students: Required—TOEFL (paper-based 525; computer-based 195; IBT 71) or IELTS (6.0). *Application deadline:* For fall admission, 8/1 priority date for domestic students. Applications are processed on a rolling basis. Application fee: $25. Electronic applications accepted. *Financial support:* In 2007–08, 21 students received support. Institutionally sponsored loans available. Support available to part-time students. Financial award application deadline: 5/1; financial award applicants required to submit FAFSA. *Unit head:* Dr. Charles Baum, Chair, 615-898-2520, Fax: 615-898-5596, E-mail: cbaum@mtsu.edu.

Announcement: The department offers the MA and PhD degrees in economics. The PhD is an applied program with specializations in financial economics, labor economics, and economics of education. Assistantships with tuition waivers are available in both the MA and PhD programs. There is no foreign language requirement.

Mississippi State University, College of Business and Industry, Department of Finance and Economics, Mississippi State, MS 39762. Offers applied economics (PhD); economics (MA); finance (MSBA). Part-time programs available. *Faculty:* 18 full-time (4 women), 6 part-time/adjunct (2 women). *Students:* 1 full-time (0 women), 1 (woman) part-time, 1 international. Average age 28. 61 applicants, 21% accepted. In 2007, 8 master's, 1 doctorate awarded. Terminal master's awarded for partial completion of doctoral program. *Degree requirements:* For master's, comprehensive exam, thesis optional; for doctorate, comprehensive exam, thesis/dissertation. *Entrance requirements:* For master's and doctorate, GMAT, GRE General Test. *Application deadline:* For fall admission, 7/1 for domestic students; for spring admission, 11/1 for domestic students. Applications are processed on a rolling basis. Application fee: $30. *Expenses:* Tuition, state resident: full-time $4,978; part-time $274 per hour. Tuition, nonresident: full-time $11,469; part-time $635 per hour. *Financial support:* In 2007–08, 1 teaching assistantship with tuition reimbursement (averaging $19,220 per year) was awarded; research assistantships with tuition reimbursements, Federal Work-Study, scholarships/grants, health care benefits, and unspecified assistantships also available. Financial award applicants required to submit FAFSA. *Faculty research:* Economics development, mergers, event studies, economic education, bank performance. Total annual research expenditures: $421,000. *Unit head:* Dr. Paul W. Grimes, Head, 662-325-2341, Fax: 662-325-1977, E-mail: pgrimes@cobilan.msstate.edu. *Application contact:* Dr. William A. Person, Interim Associate Vice President for Academic Affairs/Interim Dean of Graduate Studies, 662-325-7400, Fax: 662-325-1967, E-mail: grad@grad.msstate.edu.

Montclair State University, The Office of Graduate Admissions and Support Services, School of Business, Department of Economics and Finance, Montclair, NJ 07043-1624. Offers business economics (MBA); finance (MBA). Part-time and evening/weekend programs available. *Faculty:* 16 full-time (4 women). *Students:* 23 full-time (11 women), 76 part-time (24 women); includes 19 minority (5 African Americans, 9 Asian Americans or Pacific Islanders, 5 Hispanic Americans), 13 international. 68 applicants, 31% accepted, 20 enrolled. In 2007, 32 degrees awarded. *Entrance requirements:* For master's, GRE General Test, 2 letters of recommendation, resumé. Additional exam requirements/recommendations for international students: Required—TOEFL (minimum score 83 computer-based). *Application deadline:* For fall admission, 6/1 for international students; for spring admission, 10/1 for international students. Applications are processed on a rolling basis. Application fee: $60. Electronic applications accepted. *Financial support:* In 2007–08, 2 research assistantships with full tuition reimbursements (averaging $7,000 per year) were awarded; Federal Work-Study, scholarships/grants, and unspecified assistantships also available. Support available to part-time students. Financial award application deadline: 3/1; financial award applicants required to submit FAFSA. *Unit head:* Dr. Richard Lord, Chair, 973-655-5255.

Morgan State University, School of Graduate Studies, College of Liberal Arts, Department of Economics, Baltimore, MD 21251. Offers MA. *Faculty:* 5 full-time. *Degree requirements:* For master's, comprehensive exam. *Entrance requirements:* For master's, GRE. Additional exam requirements/recommendations for international students: Required—TOEFL (minimum score 550 paper-based; 213 computer-based). *Application deadline:* For fall admission, 2/1 priority date for domestic students; for spring admission, 10/1 priority date for domestic students. Applications are processed on a rolling basis. Application fee: $0. *Financial support:* Fellowships with full tuition reimbursements, research assistantships with full tuition reimbursements, career-related internships or fieldwork, Federal Work-Study, institutionally sponsored loans, scholarships/grants, health care benefits, tuition waivers (full and partial), and unspecified assistantships available. Support available to part-time students. Financial award application deadline: 2/1. *Unit head:* Dr. Tekie Fessehatzion, Chair, 443-885-3662. *Application contact:* Dr. Mark Garrison, Associate Dean, 443-885-3185, Fax: 443-885-8226, E-mail: mark.garrison@morgan.edu.

Murray State University, College of Business and Public Affairs, Program in Economics, Murray, KY 42071. Offers MS. Part-time programs available. *Entrance requirements:* For master's, GRE General Test or GMAT, economics minor or equivalent, students may be conditionally admitted and fulfill undergraduate requirements. Additional exam requirements/recommendations for international students: Required—TOEFL. *Faculty research:* Economic education, public finance, economic development, banking, telecommunications systems management.

National University, Academic Affairs, School of Business and Management, Department of Accounting and Finance, La Jolla, CA 92037-1011. Offers EMBA, MBA. Part-time and evening/weekend programs available. Postbaccalaureate distance learning degree programs offered (no on-campus study). *Faculty:* 10 full-time (1 woman). *Students:* 21 full-time (11 women), 24 part-time (9 women); includes 16 minority (4 African Americans, 4 Asian Americans or Pacific Islanders, 8 Hispanic Americans), 5 international. Average age 33. 676 applicants. In 2007, 10 degrees awarded. *Degree requirements:* For master's, thesis. *Entrance requirements:* For master's, interview, minimum GPA of 2.5. Additional exam requirements/recommendations for international students: Required—TOEFL (minimum score 550 paper-based; 213 computer-based; 80 iBT), IELTS (minimum score 6). *Application deadline:* Applications are processed on a rolling basis. Application fee: $60 ($65 for international students). Electronic applications accepted. *Expenses:* Tuition: Full-time $8,262; part-time $306 per unit. One-time fee: $60. *Financial support:* Career-related internships or fieldwork, institutionally sponsored loans, scholarships/grants, and tuition waivers (partial) available. Support available to part-time students. Financial award application deadline: 6/30; financial award applicants required to submit FAFSA. *Unit head:* Donald A. Schwartz, Chair and Associate Professor, 858-642-8420, E-mail: dschwartz@nu.edu. *Application contact:* Dominick Giovanniello, Associate Regional Dean—San Diego, 800-NAT-UNIV, Fax: 858-642-8709, E-mail: dgiovann@nu.edu.

New Mexico State University, Graduate School, College of Agriculture and Home Economics, Department of Agricultural Economics and Agricultural Business, Las Cruces, NM 88003-8001. Offers agribusiness (M Ag, MBA); agricultural economics (MS); economics (MA). Part-time programs available. *Faculty:* 10 full-time (3 women), 1 part-time/adjunct (0 women). *Students:* 19 full-time (8 women), 4 part-time (2 women); includes 1 African American, 13 international. Average age 27. 10 applicants, 90% accepted, 4 enrolled. In 2007, 13 degrees awarded. *Degree requirements:* For master's, thesis (for some programs). *Entrance requirements:* For master's, previous course work in intermediate microeconomics, intermediate macroeconomics, college-level calculus, statistics. Additional exam requirements/recommendations for international students: Required—TOEFL. *Application deadline:* For fall admission, 7/1 priority date for domestic and international students; for spring admission, 11/1 priority date for domestic and international students. Applications are processed on a rolling basis. Application fee: $30 ($50 for international students). Electronic applications accepted. *Expenses:* Tuition, state resident: full-time $3,602; part-time $199 per credit. Tuition, nonresident: full-time $13,380; part-time $607 per credit. Required fees: $1,178. *Financial support:* In 2007–08, 3 fellowships, 15 research assistantships, 2 teaching assistantships were awarded; career-related internships or fieldwork and health care benefits also available. Financial award application deadline: 3/1. *Faculty research:* Natural resource policy, production economics and farm/ranch management, agribusiness and marketing, international marketing and trade, agricultural risk management. *Unit head:* Dr. Octavio A. Ramirez, Head, 575-646-3215, Fax: 575-646-3808, E-mail: oramirez@nmsu.edu. *Application contact:* Dr. Allen Torell, Professor, 575-646-4732, Fax: 575-646-3808, E-mail: atorell@nmsu.edu.

New Mexico State University, Graduate School, College of Business, Department of Economics and International Business, Las Cruces, NM 88003-8001. Offers economics (MA); experimental

Economics

New Mexico State University (continued)
statistics (MS). Part-time programs available. *Faculty:* 19 full-time (2 women). *Students:* 34 full-time (12 women), 8 part-time (3 women); includes 9 minority (1 African American, 1 Asian American or Pacific Islander, 7 Hispanic Americans), 24 international. Average age 30. 10 applicants, 100% accepted, 6 enrolled. In 2007, 20 degrees awarded. *Degree requirements:* For master's, thesis or alternative. *Entrance requirements:* For master's, minimum GPA of 3.0. Additional exam requirements/recommendations for international students: Required—TOEFL. *Application deadline:* Applications are processed on a rolling basis. Application fee: $30 ($50 for international students). Electronic applications accepted. *Expenses:* Tuition, state resident: full-time $3,602; part-time $199 per credit. Tuition, nonresident: full-time $13,380; part-time $607 per credit. Required fees: $1,178. *Financial support:* In 2007–08, 1 fellowship, 10 research assistantships, 15 teaching assistantships were awarded; career-related internships or fieldwork, Federal Work-Study, and health care benefits also available. Support available to part-time students. Financial award application deadline: 3/1. *Faculty research:* Public utilities, environment, linear models, biological sampling, public policy. *Unit head:* Dr. Anthony Popp, Graduate Adviser, 575-646-5198, Fax: 575-646-1915, E-mail: apopp@nmsu.edu. *Application contact:* Dr. Anthony Popp, Graduate Adviser, 575-646-5198, Fax: 575-646-1915, E-mail: apopp@nmsu.edu.

The New School: A University, The New School for Social Research, Department of Economics, New York, NY 10011. Offers MA, DS Sc, PhD. Part-time and evening/weekend programs available. *Faculty:* 7 full-time (1 woman), 2 part-time/adjunct (0 women). *Students:* 84 full-time (24 women), 47 part-time (11 women); includes 20 minority (7 African Americans, 5 Asian Americans or Pacific Islanders, 8 Hispanic Americans), 63 international. Average age 34. In 2007, 32 master's, 8 doctorates awarded. Terminal master's awarded for partial completion of doctoral program. *Degree requirements:* For master's, exam; for doctorate, one foreign language, thesis/dissertation, qualifying exam. *Entrance requirements:* For master's, GRE General Test; for doctorate, GRE General Test, MA. Additional exam requirements/recommendations for international students: Required—TOEFL (minimum score 600 paper-based; 250 computer-based; 100 iBT). *Application deadline:* For fall admission, 1/15 priority date for domestic students. Applications are processed on a rolling basis. Application fee: $50. *Financial support:* Fellowships, research assistantships, teaching assistantships, career-related internships or fieldwork, Federal Work-Study, scholarships/grants, and tuition waivers (full and partial) available. Financial award application deadline: 3/1; financial award applicants required to submit FAFSA. *Faculty research:* Heterodox, history of economic thought, post-Keynesian, global political economy and finance. *Unit head:* Dr. Willi Semmler, Chair, 212-229-5717 Ext. 3050, E-mail: semmlerw@newschool.edu. *Application contact:* Robert MacDonald, Director of Admissions, 800-523-5710 Ext. 3007, Fax: 212-989-7102, E-mail: macdonar@newschool.edu.

See Close-Up on page 1653.

New York University, Graduate School of Arts and Science, Department of Economics, New York, NY 10012-1019. Offers applied economic analysis (Advanced Certificate); economics (MA, PhD); JD/MA; MD/PhD. Part-time and evening/weekend programs available. *Faculty:* 35 full-time (2 women), 29 part-time/adjunct. *Students:* 240 full-time (82 women), 39 part-time (15 women); includes 18 minority (1 African American, 14 Asian Americans or Pacific Islanders, 3 Hispanic Americans), 199 international. Average age 27. 1,056 applicants, 21% accepted, 91 enrolled. In 2007, 66 master's, 9 doctorates awarded. Terminal master's awarded for partial completion of doctoral program. *Degree requirements:* For master's, thesis; for doctorate, one foreign language, thesis/dissertation, 4 qualifying exams. *Entrance requirements:* For master's and doctorate, GRE General Test; for Advanced Certificate, master's degree. Additional exam requirements/recommendations for international students: Required—TOEFL. *Application deadline:* For fall admission, 1/4 priority date for domestic students. Application fee: $85. *Financial support:* Fellowships with tuition reimbursements, research assistantships with tuition reimbursements, teaching assistantships with tuition reimbursements, Federal Work-Study, institutionally sponsored loans, scholarships/grants, health care benefits, and unspecified assistantships available. Financial award application deadline: 1/4; financial award applicants required to submit FAFSA. *Faculty research:* Economic theory, experimental economics, growth and development, macroeconomics and finance, international trade and international finance. *Unit head:* David Pearce, Chair, 212-998-8900, Fax: 212-995-4186, E-mail: admissions@econ.nyu.edu. *Application contact:* Debraj Ray, Director of Graduate Studies, 212-998-8900, Fax: 212-995-4186, E-mail: gsas.admissions@nyu.edu.

New York University, Leonard N. Stern School of Business, Department of Economics, New York, NY 10012-1019. Offers MBA, PhD. *Faculty research:* Applied macroeconomics, macroeconomics and macroeconomic policy, international financial markets, international trade and business, game theory.

North Carolina State University, Graduate School, College of Management, Raleigh, NC 27695. Offers accounting (MAC); business administration (MBA), including financial management, information technology management, marketing management, product innovation management, supply chain management, technology commercialization; economics (M Econ, MA, PhD). Part-time programs available. Terminal master's awarded for partial completion of doctoral program. *Degree requirements:* For doctorate, thesis/dissertation. *Entrance requirements:* For master's and doctorate, GRE General Test (financial award applicants). Additional exam requirements/recommendations for international students: Required—TOEFL. Electronic applications accepted.

North Carolina State University, Graduate School, College of Management, Department of Economics and College of Agriculture and Life Sciences, Program in Economics, Raleigh, NC 27695. Offers M Econ, MA, PhD. Part-time programs available. Terminal master's awarded for partial completion of doctoral program. *Degree requirements:* For master's, thesis (for some programs); for doctorate, thesis/dissertation. *Entrance requirements:* For master's and doctorate, GRE General Test. Additional exam requirements/recommendations for international students: Required—TOEFL. Electronic applications accepted. *Faculty research:* Endogenous growth modeling, generalized methods of moments estimation, integration and trade, agricultural policy, path dependence and network externalities.

Northeastern University, College of Arts and Sciences, Department of Economics, Boston, MA 02115-5096. Offers MA, PhD. Part-time and evening/weekend programs available. *Faculty:* 15 full-time (2 women). *Students:* 43 full-time (24 women), 9 part-time (3 women). 121 applicants, 46% accepted. In 2007, 7 degrees awarded. *Degree requirements:* For master's and doctorate, comprehensive exam. *Entrance requirements:* For master's, GRE. Additional exam requirements/recommendations for international students: Required—TOEFL. *Application deadline:* For fall admission, 8/1 for domestic students, 5/1 priority date for international students; for spring admission, 12/1 for domestic and international students. Applications are processed on a rolling basis. Application fee: $50. *Financial support:* In 2007–08, 12 teaching assistantships (averaging $15,667 per year) were awarded; Federal Work-Study, institutionally sponsored loans, tuition waivers (full and partial), and unspecified assistantships also available. Financial award application deadline: 2/1; financial award applicants required to submit FAFSA. *Faculty research:* U.S. labor markets, applied economics, microeconomic theory, macroeconomic theory, econometrics. *Unit head:* Dr. Steven Morrison, Chair, 617-373-2872, Fax: 617-373-3640, E-mail: econ@neu.edu. *Application contact:* Dr. Gregory Wassall, Graduate Coordinator, 617-373-2882, Fax: 617-373-3640, E-mail: econ@neu.edu.

See Close-Up on page 1029.

Northern Illinois University, Graduate School, College of Liberal Arts and Sciences, Department of Economics, De Kalb, IL 60115-2854. Offers MA, PhD. Part-time programs available. *Faculty:* 15 full-time (3 women). *Students:* 25 full-time (9 women), 7 part-time (3 women); includes 4 minority (1 African American, 2 Asian Americans or Pacific Islanders, 1 Hispanic American), 21 international. Average age 29. 86 applicants, 45% accepted, 11 enrolled. In 2007, 6 master's, 3 doctorates awarded. Terminal master's awarded for partial completion of doctoral program. *Degree requirements:* For master's, comprehensive exam, thesis or alternative; for doctorate, thesis/dissertation, candidacy exam, dissertation defense, research seminar. *Entrance requirements:* For master's, GRE General Test, minimum GPA of 2.75; for doctorate, GRE General Test, minimum GPA of 2.75 (undergraduate), 3.2 (graduate). Additional exam requirements/recommendations for international students: Required—TOEFL (minimum score 550 paper-based; 213 computer-based). *Application deadline:* For fall admission, 6/1 for domestic students, 5/1 for international students; for spring admission, 11/1 for domestic students, 10/1 for international students. Applications are processed on a rolling basis. Application fee: $30. Electronic applications accepted. *Expenses:* Tuition, area resident: Part-time $226 per credit hour. Tuition, state resident: full-time $5,424; part-time $225 per credit hour. Tuition, nonresident: full-time $10,848. Required fees: $2,416; $64 per credit hour. *Financial support:* In 2007–08, 11 research assistantships with full tuition reimbursements, 19 teaching assistantships with full tuition reimbursements were awarded; fellowships with full tuition reimbursements, career-related internships or fieldwork, Federal Work-Study, scholarships/grants, tuition waivers (full), and unspecified assistantships also available. Support available to part-time students. Financial award applicants required to submit FAFSA. *Faculty research:* Unemployment, behavior under uncertainty, effect of debt on compensation and capital utilization, racial inequality of earnings. *Unit head:* Dr. Eliakim Katz, Chair, 815-753-6970, Fax: 815-753-6302, E-mail: ekatz@niu.edu. *Application contact:* Dr. Ardeshir Dalal, Director, Graduate Studies, 815-753-6966.

Northwestern University, The Graduate School, Judd A. and Marjorie Weinberg College of Arts and Sciences, Department of Economics, Evanston, IL 60208. Offers MA, PhD, JD/PhD. Admissions and degrees offered through The Graduate School. *Degree requirements:* For doctorate, thesis/dissertation, preliminary written exam. *Entrance requirements:* For doctorate, GRE General Test. Additional exam requirements/recommendations for international students: Required—TOEFL. *Faculty research:* Organization of industry, behavior of labor markets, effects of monetary policy, theory of markets.

Northwestern University, The Graduate School, Kellogg School of Management, Program in Managerial Economics and Strategy, Evanston, IL 60208. Offers PhD. Admissions and degree offered through The Graduate School. *Degree requirements:* For doctorate, comprehensive exam, thesis/dissertation. *Entrance requirements:* For doctorate, GMAT or GRE General Test. Additional exam requirements/recommendations for international students: Required—TOEFL. Electronic applications accepted. *Faculty research:* Competitive strategy and organization, managerial economics, decision sciences, game theory, operations management.

Oakland University, Graduate Study and Lifelong Learning, School of Business Administration, Department of Economics, Rochester, MI 48309-4401. Offers Certificate. *Faculty:* 3 full-time (1 woman). Application fee: $35. *Expenses:* Tuition, state resident: full-time $9,936; part-time $414 per credit. Tuition, nonresident: full-time $17,202; part-time $716 per credit. *Unit head:* Dr. Addington Coppin, Chair, 248-370-3283, Fax: 248-370-4604, E-mail: coppin@oakland.edu.

The Ohio State University, Graduate School, College of Social and Behavioral Sciences, School of Social and Behavioral Science, Department of Economics, Columbus, OH 43210. Offers MA, PhD. *Faculty:* 38. *Students:* 98 full-time (29 women); includes 7 minority (6 Asian Americans or Pacific Islanders, 1 Hispanic American), 71 international. Average age 27. In 2007, 39 master's, 15 doctorates awarded. *Degree requirements:* For doctorate, thesis/dissertation. *Entrance requirements:* Additional exam requirements/recommendations for international students: Required—TOEFL (minimum score 600 paper-based; 250 computer-based). *Application deadline:* For fall admission, 8/15 priority date for domestic students, 7/1 priority date for international students; for winter admission, 12/1 priority date for domestic students, 11/1 priority date for international students; for spring admission, 3/1 priority date for domestic students, 2/1 priority date for international students. Applications are processed on a rolling basis. Application fee: $40 ($50 for international students). Electronic applications accepted. *Financial support:* Fellowships, research assistantships, teaching assistantships, Federal Work-Study and institutionally sponsored loans available. Support available to part-time students. *Unit head:* Hajime Miyazaki, Graduate Studies Committee Chair, 614-292-6701, Fax: 614-292-3906, E-mail: miyazaki.1@osu.edu. *Application contact:* 614-292-9444, Fax: 614-292-3895, E-mail: domestic.grad@osu.edu.

Ohio University, Graduate College, College of Arts and Sciences, Department of Economics, Athens, OH 45701-2979. Offers applied economics (MA); financial economics (MFE). Evening/weekend programs available. *Faculty:* 15 full-time (3 women). *Students:* 31 full-time (16 women), 9 part-time (3 women); includes 2 minority (both American Indian/Alaska Native), 34 international. 94 applicants, 70% accepted, 21 enrolled. In 2007, 19 degrees awarded. *Degree requirements:* For master's, thesis or alternative. *Entrance requirements:* For master's, GRE or GMAT, minimum GPA of 3.0. Additional exam requirements/recommendations for international students: Required—TOEFL (minimum score 550 paper-based). *Application deadline:* For fall admission, 3/15 priority date for domestic students, 2/15 priority date for international students. Applications are processed on a rolling basis. Application fee: $50 ($55 for international students). *Financial support:* In 2007–08, 15 research assistantships with tuition reimbursements were awarded; Federal Work-Study, institutionally sponsored loans, scholarships/grants, and unspecified assistantships also available. Financial award application deadline: 3/15. *Faculty research:* Macroeconomics, public finance, international economics and finance, monetary theory, healthcare economics. *Unit head:* Dr. Roy Boyd, Chair, 740-593-2040, E-mail: boydr1@ohio.edu. *Application contact:* Dr. K. Doroodian, Graduate Chair, 740-593-2046, E-mail: doroodia@ohio.edu.

Oklahoma State University, William S. Spears School of Business, Department of Economics and Legal Studies in Business, Stillwater, OK 74078. Offers MS, PhD. *Faculty:* 23 full-time (6 women), 5 part-time/adjunct (2 women). *Students:* 21 full-time (7 women), 16 part-time (6 women); includes 2 minority (1 American Indian/Alaska Native, 1 Hispanic American), 22 international. Average age 31. 61 applicants, 44% accepted, 11 enrolled. In 2007, 6 degrees awarded. *Degree requirements:* For doctorate, thesis/dissertation. *Entrance requirements:* For master's and doctorate, GRE General Test or GMAT. Additional exam requirements/recommendations for international students: Required—TOEFL. *Application deadline:* For fall admission, 3/1 priority date for international students; for spring admission, 8/1 priority date for international students. Applications are processed on a rolling basis. Application fee: $40 ($75 for international students). Electronic applications accepted. *Expenses:* Tuition, state resident: full-time $4,993; part-time $148 per credit hour. Tuition, nonresident: full-time $14,755; part-time $555 per credit hour. Tuition and fees vary according to program. *Financial support:* In 2007–08, 20 teaching assistantships (averaging $13,302 per year) were awarded; career-related internships or fieldwork, Federal Work-Study, scholarships/grants, health care benefits, tuition waivers (partial), and unspecified assistantships also available. Support available to part-time students. Financial award application deadline: 3/1. *Faculty research:* Economics and legal studies in business regional economic modeling/econometrics, urban/regional economics, monetary economics, international trade/finance/development, environmental economics. *Unit head:* Dr. Ronald Moomaw, Head, 405-744-5195, E-mail: moomaw@okstate.edu.

Old Dominion University, College of Business and Public Administration, Program in Economics, Norfolk, VA 23529. Offers MA. Part-time and evening/weekend programs available. *Faculty:* 11 full-time (1 woman). *Students:* 16 full-time (6 women), 15 part-time (7 women); includes 8 minority (4 African Americans, 3 Asian Americans or Pacific Islanders, 1 Hispanic American), 9 international. Average age 28. 25 applicants, 84% accepted, 11 enrolled. In 2007, 6 degrees awarded. *Degree requirements:* For master's, comprehensive exam, thesis optional, independent research. *Entrance requirements:* For master's, GMAT or GRE General Test, minimum GPA of 2.5. Additional exam requirements/recommendations for international students: Required—TOEFL (minimum score 520 paper-based; 213 computer-based; 79 iBT). *Application deadline:* For fall admission, 8/1 priority date for domestic students; for spring admission, 10/1 priority date for domestic students. Applications are processed on a rolling basis. Application fee: $40. Electronic applications accepted. *Expenses:* Tuition, state resident: part-time $304 per credit hour. Tuition, nonresident: part-time $761 per credit hour. *Financial* *support:* In 2007–08, 4 students received support, including 4 teaching assistantships with tuition reimbursements available (averaging $5,000 per year); research assistantships with tuition reimbursements available, career-related internships or fieldwork, scholarships/grants, tuition waivers (partial), and unspecified assistantships also available. Financial award application deadline: 8/1; financial award applicants required to submit FAFSA. *Faculty research:* International economics, transportation, monetary economics, immigration, econometrics. *Unit head:* Dr. David Duden Selover, Graduate Program Director, 757-683-3541, Fax: 757-638-5639, E-mail: dselover@odu.edu.

Oregon State University, Graduate School, College of Agricultural Sciences, Department of Agricultural and Resource Economics, Corvallis, OR 97331. Offers agricultural and resource economics (M Agr, MAIS, MS, PhD); economics (MS, PhD). MS and PhD in economics offered through the University Graduate Faculty of Economics. Part-time programs available. *Faculty:* 11 full-time (2 women), 2 part-time/adjunct (both women). *Students:* 31 full-time (12 women), 2 part-time (1 woman); includes 1 minority (American Indian/Alaska Native), 16 international. Average age 29. In 2007, 3 master's, 8 doctorates awarded. Terminal master's awarded for partial completion of doctoral program. *Degree requirements:* For master's, thesis (for some programs); for doctorate, thesis/dissertation. *Entrance requirements:* For master's and doctorate, GRE General Test, minimum GPA of 3.0 in last 90 hours. Additional exam requirements/recommendations for international students: Required—TOEFL. *Application deadline:* For fall admission, 3/1 for domestic students. Applications are processed on a rolling basis. Application fee: $50. *Expenses:* Tuition, state resident: full-time $9,126; part-time $338 per credit. Tuition, nonresident: full-time $14,796; part-time $548 per credit. Required fees: $1,447. *Financial support:* Fellowships, research assistantships, teaching assistantships, career-related internships or fieldwork, Federal Work-Study, and institutionally sponsored loans available. Support available to part-time students. Financial award application deadline: 2/1. *Faculty research:* Marine economics, environmental economics, effects of global climate change on agriculture, efficiency of agricultural markets, analysis of aquaculture development. *Unit head:* Dr. Gregory M. Perry, Department Head, 541-737-2942, Fax: 541-737-2563. *Application contact:* Kathy Carpenter, Administrative Assistant, 541-737-1398, Fax: 541-737-1441, E-mail: kathy.carpenter@orst.edu.

Oregon State University, Graduate School, College of Forestry, Department of Forest Resources, Corvallis, OR 97331. Offers economics (MS, PhD); forest resources (MAIS, MF, MS, PhD). MS and PhD programs in economics offered through the University Graduate Faculty of Economics. *Accreditation:* SAF (one or more programs are accredited). Part-time programs available. *Faculty:* 14 full-time (3 women), 3 part-time/adjunct (1 woman). *Students:* 34 full-time (18 women), 6 part-time (5 women); includes 3 minority (1 Asian American or Pacific Islander, 2 Hispanic Americans), 5 international. Average age 31. In 2007, 5 master's, 6 doctorates awarded. Terminal master's awarded for partial completion of doctoral program. *Degree requirements:* For master's, thesis (for some programs); for doctorate, thesis/dissertation. *Entrance requirements:* For master's and doctorate, GRE General Test, minimum GPA of 3.0 in last 90 hours. Additional exam requirements/recommendations for international students: Required—TOEFL. *Application deadline:* For fall admission, 2/1 priority date for domestic students. Applications are processed on a rolling basis. Application fee: $50. *Expenses:* Tuition, state resident: full-time $9,126; part-time $338 per credit. Tuition, nonresident: full-time $14,796; part-time $548 per credit. Required fees: $1,447. *Financial support:* Fellowships, research assistantships, teaching assistantships, career-related internships or fieldwork, Federal Work-Study, and institutionally sponsored loans available. Support available to part-time students. Financial award application deadline: 2/1. *Faculty research:* Geographic information systems, long-term productivity, recreation, silviculture, biometrics, policy. *Unit head:* Dr. Darius M. Adams, Interim Head, 541-737-5504, Fax: 541-737-3049, E-mail: darius.adams@oregonstate.edu. *Application contact:* Marty A. Roberts, Coordinator, 541-737-1485, Fax: 541-737-3049, E-mail: marty.roberts@oregonstate.edu.

Oregon State University, Graduate School, College of Liberal Arts, Department of Economics, Corvallis, OR 97331. Offers MA, MS, PhD. Part-time programs available. *Faculty:* 10 full-time (4 women), 1 part-time/adjunct (0 women). *Students:* 13 full-time (4 women), 3 part-time (all women), 10 international. Average age 28. In 2007, 3 master's, 1 doctorate awarded. Terminal master's awarded for partial completion of doctoral program. *Degree requirements:* For master's, thesis or alternative; for doctorate, thesis/dissertation. *Entrance requirements:* For master's and doctorate, GRE General Test, minimum GPA of 3.0 in last 90 hours. Additional exam requirements/recommendations for international students: Required—TOEFL. *Application deadline:* For fall admission, 3/1 priority date for domestic students. Applications are processed on a rolling basis. Application fee: $50. *Expenses:* Tuition, state resident: full-time $9,126; part-time $338 per credit. Tuition, nonresident: full-time $14,796; part-time $548 per credit. Required fees: $1,447. *Financial support:* Research assistantships, teaching assistantships, career-related internships or fieldwork, Federal Work-Study, and institutionally sponsored loans available. Support available to part-time students. Financial award application deadline: 3/1. *Faculty research:* Applied microeconomics, applied econometrics. *Unit head:* Dr. Carlos Martins-Filho, Chair, 541-737-1476, Fax: 541-737-5917, E-mail: carlos.martins@oregonstate.edu.

Pace University, Lubin School of Business, Program in Business Economics, New York, NY 10038. Offers corporate economic planning (MBA); financial economics (MBA); international economics (MBA). Part-time and evening/weekend programs available. *Students:* 3 full-time (1 woman), 4 part-time; includes 1 minority (Asian American or Pacific Islander), 3 international. Average age 29. 7 applicants, 14% accepted, 0 enrolled. In 2007, 4 degrees awarded. *Entrance requirements:* For master's, GMAT. *Application deadline:* For fall admission, 7/31 priority date for domestic students; for spring admission, 11/30 for domestic students. Applications are processed on a rolling basis. Application fee: $65. Electronic applications accepted. *Expenses:* Tuition: Part-time $856 per credit. Tuition and fees vary according to degree level and program. *Financial support:* Research assistantships, career-related internships or fieldwork and Federal Work-Study available. Support available to part-time students. Financial award applicants required to submit FAFSA. *Unit head:* Dr. Richard Lynn, Chairperson, 212-346-1817. *Application contact:* Joanna Broda, Director of Admissions, 212-346-1652, Fax: 212-346-1585, E-mail: gradnyc@pace.edu.

Penn State University Park, Graduate School, College of the Liberal Arts, Department of Economics, State College, University Park, PA 16802-1503. Offers MA, PhD. *Expenses:* Tuition, state resident: full-time $14,738; part-time $614 per credit. Tuition, nonresident: full-time $26,050; part-time $1,085 per credit. Tuition and fees vary according to course load, program and student level. *Unit head:* Dr. Robert C. Marshall, Head, 814-865-0277, E-mail: rmarshall@psu.edu. *Application contact:* Dr. Neil Wallace, Director of Graduate Studies, E-mail: neilw@psu.edu.

Pepperdine University, School of Public Policy, Malibu, CA 90263. Offers American politics (MPP); economics (MPP); international relations (MPP); public policy (MPP); state and local policy (MPP). *Entrance requirements:* For master's, GRE, 2 letters of recommendation, resumé. Additional exam requirements/recommendations for international students: Required—TOEFL. Electronic applications accepted.

See Close-Up on page 1619.

Peru State College, Graduate Programs, Program in Organizational Management, Peru, NE 68421. Offers MS. Program offered online only. Part-time programs available. *Faculty:* 6. *Students:* Average age 34. 38 applicants, 95% accepted, 25 enrolled. *Degree requirements:* For master's, thesis (for some programs). *Application deadline:* For fall admission, 8/6 priority date for domestic students; for spring admission, 1/5 priority date for domestic students. Application fee: $0. *Expenses:* Contact institution. *Faculty research:* Emotional intelligence. *Unit head:* Dr. Bruce Batterson, Dean of Professional Studies, 402-872-2427, Fax: 402-872-2422, E-mail: bbatterson@oakmail.peru.edu. *Application contact:* Linda Staples, Administrative Assistant, 402-872-2314, Fax: 402-872-2422, E-mail: lstaples@oakmail.peru.edu.

Portland State University, Graduate Studies, College of Liberal Arts and Sciences, Department of Economics, Portland, OR 97207-0751. Offers applied economics (MA, MS); economics (PhD); general economics (MA, MS). Part-time programs available. *Faculty:* 14 full-time (4 women), 6 part-time/adjunct (1 woman). *Students:* 13 full-time (4 women), 5 part-time (4 women); includes 3 minority (2 Asian Americans or Pacific Islanders, 1 Hispanic American), 4 international. Average age 29. 19 applicants, 68% accepted, 7 enrolled. In 2007, 10 degrees awarded. *Degree requirements:* For master's, thesis optional; for doctorate, one foreign language, thesis/dissertation. *Entrance requirements:* For master's, minimum GPA of 3.0 in upper-division course work or 2.75 overall, course work in calculus. Additional exam requirements/recommendations for international students: Required—TOEFL (minimum score 550 paper-based; 213 computer-based). *Application deadline:* For fall admission, 4/1 for domestic students, 3/1 for international students; for spring admission, 11/1 for domestic and international students. Applications are processed on a rolling basis. Application fee: $50. *Expenses:* Tuition, state resident: full-time $7,047. Tuition, nonresident: full-time $11,178. *Financial support:* In 2007–08, 2 research assistantships with full tuition reimbursements (averaging $6,120 per year) were awarded; teaching assistantships, career-related internships or fieldwork, Federal Work-Study, and unspecified assistantships also available. Support available to part-time students. Financial award application deadline: 3/1; financial award applicants required to submit FAFSA. *Faculty research:* NAFTA, economies of transition, economics of Eastern Europe, artificial intelligence, comparative economic systems. Total annual research expenditures: $275,425. *Unit head:* Dr. John Walker, Chair, 503-725-3915, Fax: 503-725-3945. *Application contact:* Rita Spears, Office Specialist, 503-725-3941, Fax: 503-725-3945, E-mail: spearsr@pdx.edu.

Portland State University, Graduate Studies, Systems Science Program, Portland, OR 97207-0751. Offers computational intelligence (Certificate); computer modeling and simulation (Certificate); systems science (MS); systems science/anthropology (PhD); systems science/business administration (PhD); systems science/civil engineering (PhD); systems science/economics (PhD); systems science/engineering management (PhD); systems science/general (PhD); systems science/mathematical sciences (PhD); systems science/mechanical engineering (PhD); systems science/psychology (PhD); systems science/sociology (PhD). *Faculty:* 3 full-time (0 women). *Students:* 9 full-time (2 women), 11 part-time (2 women); includes 6 minority (3 Asian Americans or Pacific Islanders, 3 Hispanic Americans), 13 international. Average age 38. 8 applicants, 100% accepted, 6 enrolled. In 2007, 4 master's, 6 doctorates awarded. *Degree requirements:* For doctorate, variable foreign language requirement, thesis/dissertation. *Entrance requirements:* For master's, 2 letters of recommendation; for doctorate, GMAT, GRE General Test, minimum undergraduate GPA of 3.0. Additional exam requirements/recommendations for international students: Required—TOEFL. *Application deadline:* For fall admission, 2/1 for domestic students; for spring admission, 11/1 for domestic students. Application fee: $50. *Expenses:* Tuition, state resident: full-time $7,047. Tuition, nonresident: full-time $11,178. *Financial support:* In 2007–08, 1 research assistantship with full tuition reimbursement (averaging $5,980 per year) was awarded; teaching assistantships with full tuition reimbursements, career-related internships or fieldwork, Federal Work-Study, scholarships/grants, and unspecified assistantships also available. Support available to part-time students. Financial award application deadline: 3/1; financial award applicants required to submit FAFSA. *Faculty research:* Systems theory and methodology, artificial intelligence neural networks, information theory, nonlinear dynamics/chaos, modeling and simulation. Total annual research expenditures: $5,370. *Unit head:* George Lendaris, Acting Director, 503-725-4960. *Application contact:* Dawn Sharafi, Administrative Assistant, 503-725-4960, E-mail: dawn@sysc.pdx.edu.

Princeton University, Graduate School, Department of Economics, Princeton, NJ 08544-1019. Offers economics (PhD); economics and demography (PhD). *Degree requirements:* For doctorate, thesis/dissertation. *Entrance requirements:* For doctorate, GRE General Test, GRE Subject Test (recommended), working knowledge of multivariate calculus and matrix algebra. Additional exam requirements/recommendations for international students: Required—TOEFL (minimum score 600 paper-based; 250 computer-based). Electronic applications accepted.

Princeton University, Graduate School, Program in Population Studies, Princeton, NJ 08544-1019. Offers demography (PhD, Certificate); demography and public affairs (PhD); economics and demography (PhD); sociology and demography (PhD). *Degree requirements:* For doctorate, thesis/dissertation. *Entrance requirements:* For doctorate, GRE General Test. Additional exam requirements/recommendations for international students: Required—TOEFL (minimum score 600 paper-based; 250 computer-based). Electronic applications accepted. *Faculty research:* Models, fertility, infant and child mortality, migration.

Purdue University, Graduate School, Krannert School of Management, Department of Economics, West Lafayette, IN 47907. Offers PhD. *Degree requirements:* For doctorate, comprehensive exam, thesis/dissertation. *Entrance requirements:* For doctorate, GRE General Test, GMAT. Additional exam requirements/recommendations for international students: Required—TOEFL (minimum score 575 paper-based; 233 computer-based; 77 iBT), IELTS (minimum score 7). Electronic applications accepted. *Faculty research:* Experimental economics, monetary economics, transportation, industrial organization.

Quinnipiac University, School of Business, Program in Business Administration, Hamden, CT 06518-1940. Offers accounting (MBA); chartered financial analyst (MBA); economics (MBA); finance (MBA); healthcare management (MBA); information systems management (MBA); international business (MBA); management (MBA); marketing (MBA); JD/MBA. *Accreditation:* AACSB. Part-time and evening/weekend programs available. *Faculty:* 13 full-time (3 women), 3 part-time/adjunct (2 women). *Students:* 37 full-time (14 women), 92 part-time (31 women); includes 8 minority (3 African Americans, 5 Hispanic Americans), 8 international. Average age 29. 113 applicants, 65% accepted, 38 enrolled. In 2007, 75 degrees awarded. *Entrance requirements:* For master's, GMAT, minimum GPA of 3.0. Additional exam requirements/recommendations for international students: Required—TOEFL (minimum score 575 paper-based; 233 computer-based; 90 iBT), IELTS (minimum score 7). *Application deadline:* For fall admission, 7/30 priority date for domestic students, 4/30 priority date for international students; for spring admission, 12/15 priority date for domestic students, 9/15 priority date for international students. Applications are processed on a rolling basis. Application fee: $45. Electronic applications accepted. *Expenses:* Tuition: Part-time $675 per credit. Required fees: $30 per credit. Tuition and fees vary according to course load. *Financial support:* Tuition waivers (partial) and unspecified assistantships available. Support available to part-time students. Financial award application deadline: 4/15; financial award applicants required to submit FAFSA. *Faculty research:* Equity compensation, marketing relationships and public policy, corporate governance, international business. *Unit head:* Jennifer Boutin, Assistant Director of Graduate Admissions, 203-582-3721, Fax: 203-582-3443, E-mail: jennifer.boutin@quinnipiac.edu. *Application contact:* 800-462-1944, Fax: 203-582-3443, E-mail: graduate@quinnipiac.edu.

Regent University, Graduate School, Robertson School of Government, Virginia Beach, VA 23464-9800. Offers health care policy and administration (MA); international politics (MA); law and public policy (MA); political leadership and management (MA); political management (MA); public administration (MA); public policy (MA); terrorism and homeland defense (MA); world economies and political development (MA); JD/MA; M Div/MA; M Ed/MA; MBA/MA. Part-time programs available. *Faculty:* 6 full-time (2 women), 11 part-time/adjunct (1 woman). *Students:* 50 full-time (31 women), 67 part-time (32 women); includes 31 minority (20 African Americans, 1 American Indian/Alaska Native, 2 Asian Americans or Pacific Islanders, 8 Hispanic Americans), 2 international. Average age 31. 147 applicants, 50% accepted, 28 enrolled. In 2007, 47 degrees awarded. *Degree requirements:* For master's, thesis optional, internship. *Entrance requirements:* For master's, GRE General Test or LSAT, minimum undergraduate GPA of 3.0, writing sample, resumé, interview, references, transcripts. Additional exam requirements/recommendations for international students: Required—TOEFL (minimum score 577 paper-based; 233 computer-based). *Application deadline:* For fall admission, 5/1 priority date for domestic students; for spring admission, 11/1 priority date for domestic students. Applications are processed on a rolling basis. Application fee: $50. Electronic applications accepted. *Expenses:* Contact institution. *Financial support:* In 2007–08, 123 students

Economics

Regent University (continued)
received support. Career-related internships or fieldwork, scholarships/grants, tuition waivers (full and partial), and unspecified assistantships available. Support available to part-time students. Financial award application deadline: 9/1; financial award applicants required to submit FAFSA. *Faculty research:* Education reform, political character issues, social capital concerns, administrative ethics, biblical law and public policy. *Unit head:* Dr. Charles W. Dunn, Dean, 757-226-4322, Fax: 757-226-4643, E-mail: cwdunn@regent.edu. *Application contact:* Althea Bishard, Registrar and Executive Director of Enrollment and Academic Services, 800-373-5504, Fax: 757-226-4381, E-mail: admissions@regent.edu.

Rensselaer Polytechnic Institute, Graduate School, School of Humanities and Social Sciences, Department of Economics, Program in Economics, Troy, NY 12180-3590. Offers MS. Part-time programs available. *Faculty:* 7 full-time (1 woman). In 2007, 1 degree awarded. *Degree requirements:* For master's, thesis. *Entrance requirements:* For master's, GRE General Test. Additional exam requirements/recommendations for international students: Required—TOEFL (minimum score 570 paper-based; 230 computer-based), TWE. *Application deadline:* For fall admission, 1/15 priority date for domestic and international students. Applications are processed on a rolling basis. Application fee: $75. Electronic applications accepted. *Expenses:* Tuition: Full-time $34,900; part-time $1,454 per credit. Required fees: $1,802. *Financial support:* Application deadline: 2/1. *Faculty research:* Economic development, cost-benefit analysis, productivity and technological change, international economics. *Application contact:* Betty Jean Kaufman, Administrative Assistant, 518-276-6387, Fax: 518-276-2235, E-mail: kaufmb@rpi.edu.

See Close-Up on page 1031.

Rensselaer Polytechnic Institute, Graduate School, School of Humanities and Social Sciences, Program in Ecological Economics, Values, and Policy, Troy, NY 12180-3590. Offers MS. Part-time programs available. *Faculty:* 9 full-time (3 women). *Students:* 6 applicants, 83% accepted, 3 enrolled. *Degree requirements:* For master's, professional project. *Entrance requirements:* For master's, GRE General Test. Additional exam requirements/recommendations for international students: Required—TOEFL (minimum score 600 paper-based; 250 computer-based). *Application deadline:* For fall admission, 1/15 priority date for domestic students, 1/15 for international students. Applications are processed on a rolling basis. Application fee: $75. Electronic applications accepted. *Expenses:* Tuition: Full-time $34,900; part-time $1,454 per credit. Required fees: $1,802. *Financial support:* Fellowships, research assistantships, teaching assistantships, career-related internships or fieldwork and institutionally sponsored loans available. Financial award application deadline: 1/15. *Faculty research:* Environmental politics and policy, environmentalism, political economy, third world politics, environmental health. *Unit head:* Dr. David Hess, Director of Graduate Studies, 518-276-8509, Fax: 518-276-2659, E-mail: hessd@rpi.edu.

Rice University, Graduate Programs, School of Social Sciences, Department of Economics, Houston, TX 77251-1892. Offers MA, PhD. *Degree requirements:* For master's, thesis; for doctorate, thesis/dissertation. *Entrance requirements:* For master's and doctorate, GRE General Test, minimum GPA of 3.0. Additional exam requirements/recommendations for international students: Required—TOEFL (minimum score 600 paper-based; 250 computer-based; 90 iBT). Electronic applications accepted. *Faculty research:* Income distribution and small-scale industry in less developed countries, international commodity markets, microeconomic foundations, urban development, optimal taxation.

Roosevelt University, Graduate Division, College of Arts and Sciences, Department of Economics, Chicago, IL 60605-1394. Offers applied economics (MA); economics (MA). Part-time and evening/weekend programs available. *Students:* 6 full-time (2 women), 8 part-time (4 women); includes 6 minority (all African Americans), 4 international. Average age 29. 20 applicants, 20% accepted, 3 enrolled. *Degree requirements:* For master's, thesis or alternative. *Entrance requirements:* For master's, minimum GPA of 2.7. *Application deadline:* For fall admission, 6/1 priority date for domestic students. Applications are processed on a rolling basis. Application fee: $25 ($35 for international students). *Financial support:* In 2007–08, 4 students received support, including 1 teaching assistantship; career-related internships or fieldwork, Federal Work-Study, scholarships/grants, and tuition waivers (full and partial) also available. Financial award application deadline: 2/15. *Faculty research:* Labor, gender issues, international trade and development, entrepreneurship, political economy and money. Total annual research expenditures: $5,000. *Unit head:* June Lapidus, Head, 312-341-3670. *Application contact:* Joanne Canyon-Heller, Coordinator of Graduate Admission, 877-APPLY RU, Fax: 312-281-3356, E-mail: applyru@roosevelt.edu.

Rutgers, The State University of New Jersey, Newark, Graduate School, Program in Economics, Newark, NJ 07102. Offers MA.

Rutgers, The State University of New Jersey, Newark, Rutgers Business SchoolûNewark and New Brunswick, Department of Finance and Economics, Newark, NJ 07102. Offers MBA, MQF. *Entrance requirements:* For master's, GMAT (MBA), GRE (MQF). Additional exam requirements/recommendations for international students: Required—TOEFL.

Rutgers, The State University of New Jersey, New Brunswick, Graduate School, Program in Economics, New Brunswick, NJ 08901-1281. Offers MA, PhD. Terminal master's awarded for partial completion of doctoral program. *Degree requirements:* For master's, comprehensive exam (for some programs), thesis or alternative; for doctorate, comprehensive exam, thesis/dissertation. *Entrance requirements:* For master's and doctorate, GRE General Test. Additional exam requirements/recommendations for international students: Required—TOEFL. Electronic applications accepted. *Faculty research:* Econometrics, microeconomics, macroeconomics, economichistory.

St. Cloud State University, School of Graduate Studies, College of Social Sciences, Department of Economics, St. Cloud, MN 56301-4498. Offers applied economics (MS); public and nonprofit institutions (MS). Part-time programs available. *Faculty:* 20 full-time (5 women), 1 part-time/adjunct (0 women). *Students:* 17 full-time (7 women), 8 part-time (4 women); includes 3 minority (all African Americans), 13 international. 8 applicants, 75% accepted, 5 enrolled. In 2007, 2 degrees awarded. *Degree requirements:* For master's, thesis or alternative. *Entrance requirements:* For master's, GRE General Test, minimum GPA of 2.75. Additional exam requirements/recommendations for international students: Recommended—TOEFL (minimum score 550 paper-based; 213 computer-based), IELTS (minimum score 7). *Application deadline:* For fall admission, 6/1 priority date for domestic students, 4/1 for international students; for spring admission, 10/1 priority date for domestic students, 8/1 for international students. Applications are processed on a rolling basis. Application fee: $35. Electronic applications accepted. *Expenses:* Tuition, state resident: part-time $267 per credit. Tuition, nonresident: part-time $418 per credit. Required fees: $28 per credit. *Financial support:* Federal Work-Study, scholarships/grants, and unspecified assistantships available. *Unit head:* Dr. King Bahaian, Chairperson, 320-308-2968, E-mail: kbahaian@stcloudstate.edu. *Application contact:* Linda Lou Krueger, School of Graduate Studies, 320-308-2113, Fax: 320-308-5371, E-mail: lekrueger@stcloudstate.edu.

San Diego State University, Graduate and Research Affairs, College of Arts and Letters, Department of Economics, San Diego, CA 92182. Offers MA. *Students:* 33 full-time (12 women), 22 part-time (10 women); includes 12 minority (3 African Americans, 1 American Indian/Alaska Native, 7 Asian Americans or Pacific Islanders, 1 Hispanic American), 16 international. Average age 29. 77 applicants, 78% accepted, 27 enrolled. In 2007, 21 degrees awarded. *Entrance requirements:* For master's, GRE General Test, 2 letters of recommendation. Additional exam requirements/recommendations for international students: Required—TOEFL. *Application deadline:* For fall admission, 5/1 for domestic and international students; for spring admission, 11/1 for domestic students, 10/1 for international students. Applications are processed on a rolling basis. Application fee: $55. Electronic applications accepted. *Financial support:* In 2007–08, 19 teaching assistantships were awarded; career-related internships or fieldwork also available. *Faculty research:* Financing public education, demand for alternative fuel vehicles, economics of the Gold Rush, interdependence of equity and economic efficiency, economics of welfare. Total annual research expenditures: $174,000. *Unit head:* Mark Thayer, Chair, 619-594-5530, Fax: 619-594-5062. *Application contact:* Dean Popp, Graduate Coordinator, 619-594-5502, Fax: 619-594-5062, E-mail: dpopp@mail.sdsu.edu.

San Francisco State University, Division of Graduate Studies, College of Behavioral and Social Sciences, Department of Economics, San Francisco, CA 94132-1722. Offers MA. *Unit head:* Dr. Don Mar, Chair, 415-338-1839. *Application contact:* Dr. Sudip Chattopadhyay, Graduate Coordinator, 415-338-1839, E-mail: sudip@sfsu.edu.

San Jose State University, Graduate Studies and Research, College of Social Sciences, Department of Economics, San Jose, CA 95192-0001. Offers applied economics (MA); economics (MA). Part-time programs available. *Students:* 40 full-time (18 women), 33 part-time (15 women); includes 22 minority (16 Asian Americans or Pacific Islanders, 6 Hispanic Americans), 22 international. Average age 30. 66 applicants, 68% accepted, 22 enrolled. In 2007, 31 degrees awarded. *Degree requirements:* For master's, comprehensive exam, thesis optional. *Entrance requirements:* For master's, GRE, minimum GPA of 3.0. *Application deadline:* For fall admission, 6/29 for domestic students; for spring admission, 11/30 for domestic students. Applications are processed on a rolling basis. Application fee: $59. Electronic applications accepted. *Financial support:* In 2007–08, 2 teaching assistantships were awarded. Financial award applicants required to submit FAFSA. *Unit head:* Dr. Lydia Ortega, Chair, 408-924-5400, Fax: 408-924-5406.

Seattle Pacific University, Graduate School, School of Business and Economics, Seattle, WA 98119-1997. Offers MBA, MS. Part-time and evening/weekend programs available. *Faculty:* 1 full-time (0 women). *Students:* 14 full-time (7 women), 91 part-time (31 women); includes 18 minority (7 African Americans, 9 Asian Americans or Pacific Islanders, 2 Hispanic Americans), 9 international. 92 applicants, 49% accepted, 42 enrolled. In 2007, 38 degrees awarded. *Entrance requirements:* For master's, GMAT, minimum AACSB index of 1060. *Application deadline:* For fall admission, 8/1 priority date for domestic students; for winter admission, 11/1 for domestic students; for spring admission, 2/1 for domestic students. Applications are processed on a rolling basis. *Expenses:* Tuition: Part-time $522 per credit hour. Tuition and fees vary according to program. *Financial support:* In 2007–08, 5 students received support, including 2 research assistantships; career-related internships or fieldwork also available. Financial award applicants required to submit FAFSA. *Unit head:* Gary Karns, Graduate Director, 206-281-2948, Fax: 206-281-2733. *Application contact:* Debbie Wysomierski, Assistant Graduate Director, 206-281-2753, Fax: 206-281-2733, E-mail: mba@spu.edu.

Simon Fraser University, Graduate Studies, Faculty of Arts and Social Sciences, Department of Economics, Burnaby, BC V5A 1S6, Canada. Offers MA, PhD. Evening/weekend programs available. *Degree requirements:* For doctorate, comprehensive exam, thesis/dissertation. *Entrance requirements:* For master's, GRE, minimum GPA of 3.0; for doctorate, GRE, minimum GPA of 3.5. Additional exam requirements/recommendations for international students: Required—TWE or IELTS. *Faculty research:* Industrial organization, public economics, econometrics, labor, macroeconomics.

South Dakota State University, Graduate School, College of Agriculture and Biological Sciences, Department of Economics, Brookings, SD 57007. Offers MS. *Degree requirements:* For master's, comprehensive exam, thesis (for some programs), oral exam. *Entrance requirements:* For master's, minimum GPA of 2.75. Additional exam requirements/recommendations for international students: Required—TOEFL (minimum score 550 paper-based; 213 computer-based; 79 iBT). *Faculty research:* Sustainable agriculture, rural finance, grain and livestock marketing, agricultural policy, applied economics.

Southern Illinois University Carbondale, Graduate School, College of Liberal Arts, Department of Economics, Carbondale, IL 62901-4701. Offers MA, MS, PhD. *Faculty:* 9 full-time (0 women). *Students:* 30 full-time (10 women), 8 part-time (4 women); includes 5 minority (2 African Americans, 2 Asian Americans or Pacific Islanders, 1 Hispanic American), 27 international. 95 applicants, 22% accepted, 5 enrolled. In 2007, 1 master's, 7 doctorates awarded. *Degree requirements:* For master's, thesis; for doctorate, thesis/dissertation. *Entrance requirements:* For master's, GRE General Test, minimum GPA of 2.7; for doctorate, GRE General Test, minimum GPA of 3.25. Additional exam requirements/recommendations for international students: Required—TOEFL. *Application deadline:* Applications are processed on a rolling basis. Application fee: $20. *Financial support:* In 2007–08, 23 students received support, including 2 fellowships with full tuition reimbursements available, 2 research assistantships with full tuition reimbursements available, 17 teaching assistantships with full tuition reimbursements available; Federal Work-Study, institutionally sponsored loans, and tuition waivers (full) also available. Support available to part-time students. *Faculty research:* Advanced economic theory, applied microeconomics, economic development, finance, international economics, monetary theory and policy. *Unit head:* Dr. Richard Grabowski, Chairperson, 618-453-2713, E-mail: ricardo@siu.edu. *Application contact:* Sandy McRoy, Administrative Clerk, 618-453-5084, E-mail: smac59@siu.edu.

Announcement: The Department of Economics at Southern Illinois University Carbondale has the only endowed chair in the University, the Vandeveer Chair in Economics. It is currently held by Professor Sajal Lahiri, who is an internationally known and respected scholar in international and development economics. The Department is ranked 83rd in the world in terms of research in trade and economic development. It is ranked 48th in the world in terms of research on international trade/factor movements.

See Close-Up on page 1033.

Southern Illinois University Edwardsville, Graduate Studies and Research, School of Business, Department of Economics and Finance, Edwardsville, IL 62026-0001. Offers MA, MS. Part-time and evening/weekend programs available. *Faculty:* 13 full-time (1 woman). *Students:* 25 full-time (11 women), 18 part-time (6 women); includes 4 minority (3 African Americans, 1 Asian American or Pacific Islander), 20 international. Average age 33. 43 applicants, 56% accepted. In 2007, 20 degrees awarded. *Degree requirements:* For master's, thesis or alternative, final exam, portfolio. *Entrance requirements:* For master's, GMAT or GRE. Additional exam requirements/recommendations for international students: Required—TOEFL. *Application deadline:* For fall admission, 7/20 for domestic students, 6/1 for international students; for spring admission, 12/14 for domestic students, 10/1 for international students. Application fee: $30. Electronic applications accepted. *Financial support:* In 2007–08, 3 fellowships with full tuition reimbursements, 6 research assistantships with full tuition reimbursements were awarded; teaching assistantships with full tuition reimbursements, career-related internships or fieldwork, Federal Work-Study, institutionally sponsored loans, traineeships, and unspecified assistantships also available. Support available to part-time students. Financial award application deadline: 3/1; financial award applicants required to submit FAFSA. *Unit head:* Dr. Rik Hafer, Chair, 618-650-2542, E-mail: rhafer@siue.edu. *Application contact:* Dr. Ali Kutan, Director, 618-650-3473, E-mail: akutan@siue.edu.

Southern Methodist University, Dedman College, Department of Economics, Dallas, TX 75275. Offers applied economics (MA); economics (MA, PhD); JD/MA. Part-time and evening/weekend programs available. *Faculty:* 17 full-time (1 woman), 1 part-time/adjunct (0 women). *Students:* 49 full-time (22 women), 15 part-time (4 women); includes 7 minority (1 African American, 1 American Indian/Alaska Native, 4 Asian Americans or Pacific Islanders, 1 Hispanic American), 38 international. Average age 27. 85 applicants, 89% accepted, 16 enrolled. In 2007, 20 master's, 4 doctorates awarded. Terminal master's awarded for partial completion of doctoral program. *Median time to degree:* Of those who began their doctoral program in fall 1999, 100% received their degree in 8 years or less. *Degree requirements:* For master's, thesis optional, oral qualifying exam; for doctorate, thesis/dissertation, written exams. *Entrance requirements:* For master's, GRE General Test or GMAT, 12 hours course work in economics, minimum GPA of 3.0, previous course work in calculus and statistics; for doctorate, GRE General Test, minimum GPA of 3.0, 3 semesters of course work in calculus, 1 semester of course work in statistics, 1 semester of course work in linear algebra. Additional exam requirements/recommendations for international students: Required—TOEFL (minimum score 550 paper-based; 213 computer-based). *Application deadline:* For fall admission, 2/1 priority date for domestic students; for spring admission, 11/30 priority date for domestic students. Applications are processed on a rolling basis. Application fee: $75. Electronic applications accepted. *Financial support:* In 2007–08, 1 fellowship with full tuition reimbursement (averaging $16,000 per year), 2 research assistantships with full tuition reimbursements (averaging $16,000 per year), 20 teaching assistantships with full tuition reimbursements (averaging $16,000 per year) were awarded; tuition waivers (partial) also available. Financial award application deadline: 2/1; financial award applicants required to submit FAFSA. *Faculty research:* Economic theory, game theory, econometrics, international trade, labor. *Unit head:* Dr. Kamal Saggi, Chair, 214-768-3274, Fax: 214-768-1821, E-mail: ksaggi@mail.smu.edu. *Application contact:* Information Contact, 214-768-4337.

Stanford University, School of Humanities and Sciences, Department of Economics, Stanford, CA 94305-9991. Offers PhD. *Degree requirements:* For doctorate, thesis/dissertation, oral exam. *Entrance requirements:* For doctorate, GRE General Test. Additional exam requirements/recommendations for international students: Required—TOEFL. Electronic applications accepted.

State University of New York at Binghamton, Graduate School, School of Arts and Sciences, Department of Economics, Binghamton, NY 13902-6000. Offers economics (MA, PhD); economics and finance (MA, PhD). *Faculty:* 23 full-time (4 women), 4 part-time/adjunct (0 women). *Students:* 61 full-time (28 women), 9 part-time (3 women); includes 4 minority (1 African American, 2 Asian Americans or Pacific Islanders, 1 Hispanic American), 54 international. Average age 28. 131 applicants, 44% accepted, 22 enrolled. In 2007, 15 master's, 10 doctorates awarded. Terminal master's awarded for partial completion of doctoral program. *Degree requirements:* For doctorate, thesis/dissertation. *Entrance requirements:* For master's and doctorate, GRE General Test. Additional exam requirements/recommendations for international students: Required—TOEFL. *Application deadline:* For fall admission, 8/15 priority date for domestic students, 1/15 priority date for international students; for spring admission, 11/1 for domestic students, 10/1 priority date for international students. Applications are processed on a rolling basis. Application fee: $60. Electronic applications accepted. *Financial support:* In 2007–08, 2 fellowships with full tuition reimbursements (averaging $12,000 per year), 3 research assistantships (averaging $15,000 per year), 22 teaching assistantships with full tuition reimbursements (averaging $15,000 per year) were awarded; Federal Work-Study, institutionally sponsored loans, scholarships/grants, tuition waivers (full and partial), and unspecified assistantships also available. Financial award application deadline: 2/15. *Unit head:* Dr. Clifford Kern, Chairperson, 607-777-2228, E-mail: ckern@binghamton.edu.

Stony Brook University, State University of New York, Graduate School, College of Arts and Sciences, Department of Economics, Stony Brook, NY 11794. Offers MA, PhD. *Faculty:* 10 full-time (1 woman), 5 part-time/adjunct (0 women). *Students:* 51 full-time (31 women), 2 part-time (both women); includes 5 minority (1 African American, 3 Asian Americans or Pacific Islanders, 1 Hispanic American), 42 international. Average age 28. 124 applicants, 23% accepted. In 2007, 9 master's, 4 doctorates awarded. *Degree requirements:* For doctorate, comprehensive exam, thesis/dissertation. *Entrance requirements:* For master's and doctorate, GRE General Test. Additional exam requirements/recommendations for international students: Required—TOEFL. *Application deadline:* For fall admission, 1/15 for domestic students. Application fee: $60. *Financial support:* In 2007–08, 2 research assistantships, 35 teaching assistantships were awarded; fellowships also available. *Faculty research:* Economic theory, game theory, econometrics, macroeconomics, applied microeconomics. Total annual research expenditures: $123,231. *Unit head:* Dr. William Dawes, Co-Chair, 631-632-7530. *Application contact:* Dr. Sandro Brusco, Director of Graduate Studies, 631-632-7548, E-mail: sbrusco@notes.cc.sunysb.edu.

Announcement: The Center for Game Theory in Economics holds an annual Game Theory Festival, which is attended by internationally prominent researchers in game theory and economics and open to graduate students. The Festival consists of an International Conference on Game Theory and several workshops. For more information, visit http://www.gtcenter.org/.

See Close-Up on page 1035.

Suffolk University, College of Arts and Sciences, Department of Economics, Boston, MA 02108-2770. Offers economic policy (MSEP); economics (PhD); international economics (MSIE); JD/MSIE. Part-time and evening/weekend programs available. *Faculty:* 12 full-time (4 women). *Students:* 14 full-time (3 women), 13 part-time (4 women); includes 1 African American, 1 Hispanic American, 15 international. Average age 29. 72 applicants, 58% accepted, 9 enrolled. In 2007, 4 master's, 4 doctorates awarded. *Degree requirements:* For doctorate, comprehensive exam, thesis/dissertation. *Entrance requirements:* For master's, GRE General Test or GMAT; for doctorate, GRE, letters of recommendation. Additional exam requirements/recommendations for international students: Required—TOEFL (minimum score 550 paper-based; 213 computer-based; 80 iBT). *Application deadline:* For fall admission, 6/15 priority date for domestic students, 6/15 for international students; for spring admission, 11/1 priority date for domestic students, 11/1 for international students. Applications are processed on a rolling basis. Application fee: $50. Electronic applications accepted. *Expenses:* Contact institution. *Financial support:* In 2007–08, 18 students received support, including 14 fellowships with full and partial tuition reimbursements available (averaging $16,285 per year); career-related internships or fieldwork, Federal Work-Study, and institutionally sponsored loans also available. Support available to part-time students. Financial award application deadline: 4/1; financial award applicants required to submit FAFSA. *Faculty research:* Trade demands, fair tax, smoking, multinational firms, charitable giving, fair tax. *Unit head:* Dr. David Tuerch, Director, 617-573-8670, Fax: 617-720-4272, E-mail: dtuerch@suffolk.edu. *Application contact:* Judith Reynolds, Director of Graduate Admissions, 617-573-8302, Fax: 617-523-0116, E-mail: grad.admission@suffolk.edu.

See Close-Up on page 1037.

Syracuse University, Graduate School, Maxwell School of Citizenship and Public Affairs, Department of Economics, Syracuse, NY 13244. Offers MA, PhD. *Students:* 44 full-time (19 women), 5 part-time (1 woman); includes 5 minority (1 African American, 3 Asian Americans or Pacific Islanders, 1 Hispanic American), 24 international. 68 applicants, 50% accepted, 15 enrolled. In 2007, 32 master's, 6 doctorates awarded. *Degree requirements:* For doctorate, comprehensive exam, thesis/dissertation. *Entrance requirements:* For master's and doctorate, GRE General Test. Additional exam requirements/recommendations for international students: Required—TOEFL. *Application deadline:* For fall admission, 2/1 priority date for domestic students. Applications are processed on a rolling basis. Application fee: $75. Electronic applications accepted. *Expenses:* Tuition: Full-time $18,216; part-time $1,012 per credit. Required fees: $980. Tuition and fees vary according to program. *Financial support:* Fellowships with full tuition reimbursements, research assistantships with full tuition reimbursements, teaching assistantships with full and partial tuition reimbursements, tuition waivers (partial) available. *Faculty research:* International economics, labor economics, public finance, urban economics. *Unit head:* Dr. Devashish Mitra, Chair, 315-443-3612, Fax: 315-443-3717. *Application contact:* Laura Sauta, Recruiting Contact, 315-443-2414.

Tarleton State University, College of Graduate Studies, College of Business Administration, Department of Accounting, Finance and Economics, Stephenville, TX 76402. Offers business administration (MBA). Part-time and evening/weekend programs available. *Faculty:* 9 full-time (1 woman). *Students:* 43 full-time (21 women), 160 part-time (85 women); includes 49 minority (28 African Americans, 6 Asian Americans or Pacific Islanders, 15 Hispanic Americans), 10 international. Average age 34. 98 applicants, 85% accepted, 66 enrolled. In 2007, 51 degrees awarded. *Entrance requirements:* For master's, GRE or GMAT, minimum GPA of 3.0. Additional exam requirements/recommendations for international students: Required—TOEFL (minimum score 550 paper-based; 213 computer-based). *Application deadline:* For fall admission, 8/5 priority date for domestic students; for spring admission, 12/1 for domestic students. Applications are processed on a rolling basis. Application fee: $25 ($125 for international students). Electronic applications accepted. *Expenses:* Tuition, state resident: full-time $2,520; part-time $140 per credit hour. Tuition, nonresident: full-time $7,344; part-time $408 per credit hour. Required fees: $948; $39 per credit hour. *Financial support:* Research assistantships, teaching assistantships available. Financial award application deadline: 5/1; financial award applicants required to submit FAFSA. *Unit head:* Dr. Sankar Sundarrajan, Department Head, 254-968-9913, Fax: 254-968-9665, E-mail: sundar@tarleton.edu.

Teachers College, Columbia University, Graduate Faculty of Education, Department of International and Transcultural Studies, Program in Economics and Education, New York, NY 10027-6696. Offers Ed M, MA, Ed D, PhD. *Faculty:* 3 full-time (0 women). *Students:* 29 full-time (17 women), 29 part-time (15 women); includes 20 minority (2 African Americans, 12 Asian Americans or Pacific Islanders, 6 Hispanic Americans), 21 international. Average age 29. 55 applicants, 84% accepted, 18 enrolled. In 2007, 8 master's, 2 doctorates awarded. *Degree requirements:* For doctorate, variable foreign language requirement, thesis/dissertation. *Entrance requirements:* For master's and doctorate, GRE. *Application deadline:* For fall admission, 5/15 for domestic students; for spring admission, 12/1 for domestic students. Application fee: $70. *Financial support:* Career-related internships or fieldwork, Federal Work-Study, institutionally sponsored loans, and tuition waivers (full and partial) available. Support available to part-time students. Financial award application deadline: 2/1. *Faculty research:* Education and economic growth, efficiency in education, training in education, labor and education policy, economic status of immigrant groups. *Application contact:* Deanna Ghozati, Assistant Director of Admission, 212-678-4018, Fax: 212-678-4171, E-mail: ghozati@tc.edu.

See Close-Up on page 1715.

Temple University, Graduate School, Fox School of Business and Management, Doctoral Programs in Business, Philadelphia, PA 19122-6096. Offers accounting (PhD); economics (PhD); finance (PhD); general and strategic management (PhD); healthcare management (PhD); human resource administration (PhD); international business administration (PhD); management information systems (PhD); management science/operations research (PhD); marketing (PhD); risk, insurance, and health-care management (PhD); statistics (PhD); tourism (PhD). *Accreditation:* AACSB. *Students:* 156 full-time (78 women); includes 15 minority (5 African Americans, 10 Asian Americans or Pacific Islanders), 91 international. Average age 35. 109 applicants, 55% accepted, 25 enrolled. In 2007, 1 degree awarded. *Degree requirements:* For doctorate, thesis/dissertation. *Entrance requirements:* For doctorate, GRE General Test, GMAT, minimum GPA of 3.0, master's degree. Additional exam requirements/recommendations for international students: Required—TOEFL (minimum score 575 paper-based; 230 computer-based; 88 iBT), IELTS (minimum score 7). *Application deadline:* For fall admission, 1/15 for domestic students, 12/15 for international students. Applications are processed on a rolling basis. Application fee: $50. Electronic applications accepted. *Financial support:* Fellowships with full and partial tuition reimbursements, research assistantships with full and partial tuition reimbursements, teaching assistantships with full and partial tuition reimbursements available. Financial award applicants required to submit FAFSA. *Unit head:* William E. Aaronson, Head, 215-204-8128, E-mail: william.aaronson@temple.edu. *Application contact:* Stefanie Visheb, Associate Director, E-mail: stefanie.vishab@temple.edu.

Temple University, Graduate School, Fox School of Business and Management, Master's Programs in Business, MA Programs, Philadelphia, PA 19122-6096. Offers economics (MA). *Students:* 8 full-time (3 women), 4 part-time (1 woman), 5 international. Average age 28. 11 applicants, 82% accepted, 2 enrolled. In 2007, 3 degrees awarded. *Entrance requirements:* For master's, GRE General Test, minimum undergraduate GPA of 3.0. Additional exam requirements/recommendations for international students: Required—TOEFL (minimum score 575 paper-based; 230 computer-based; 88 iBT). *Application deadline:* For fall admission, 4/15 for domestic students, 1/15 for international students; for spring admission, 9/30 for domestic students, 9/1 for international students. Application fee: $50. *Financial support:* Applicants required to submit FAFSA. *Application contact:* William McDonald, Director of Enrollment Management, 215-204-1184, Fax: 215-204-1632, E-mail: william.mcdonald@temple.edu.

Texas A&M University, College of Liberal Arts, Department of Economics, College Station, TX 77843. Offers MS, PhD. Part-time programs available. *Faculty:* 23. *Students:* 102 full-time (29 women), 8 part-time (2 women); includes 7 minority (3 Asian Americans or Pacific Islanders, 4 Hispanic Americans), 84 international. Average age 31. 244 applicants, 46% accepted, 32 enrolled. In 2007, 18 master's, 13 doctorates awarded. Terminal master's awarded for partial completion of doctoral program. *Degree requirements:* For master's, comprehensive exam, thesis optional; for doctorate, comprehensive exam, thesis/dissertation. *Entrance requirements:* For master's and doctorate, GRE General Test. Additional exam requirements/recommendations for international students: Required—TOEFL. *Application deadline:* For fall admission, 3/1 priority date for domestic students; for winter admission, 8/1 priority date for domestic students; for spring admission, 11/1 priority date for domestic students. Applications are processed on a rolling basis. Application fee: $50 ($75 for international students). Electronic applications accepted. *Expenses:* Tuition, state resident: full-time $6,129. Tuition, nonresident: full-time $11,689. Tuition and fees vary according to course load. *Financial support:* In 2007–08, fellowships (averaging $14,850 per year), research assistantships (averaging $12,380 per year), teaching assistantships (averaging $10,062 per year) were awarded; scholarships/grants, tuition waivers, and unspecified assistantships also available. Financial award application deadline: 2/1; financial award applicants required to submit FAFSA. *Faculty research:* Tax policy, state tax, labor, international economics, macroeconomics. *Unit head:* Dr. Leonardo Avernheimer, Head, 979-845-7358, Fax: 979-847-8757, E-mail: leonardo@econ.tamu.edu. *Application contact:* Christi Essix, Graduate Admissions Supervisor, 979-845-7376, Fax: 979-847-8557, E-mail: christi@econ.tamu.edu.

Texas A&M University–Commerce, Graduate School, College of Business and Technology, Department of Economics and Finance, Commerce, TX 75429-3011. Offers economics (MA, MS). Part-time programs available. *Faculty:* 5 full-time (1 woman). *Students:* 14 full-time (5 women), 17 part-time (8 women); includes 9 minority (5 African Americans, 1 Asian American or Pacific Islander, 3 Hispanic Americans), 13 international. Average age 36. In 2007, 12 degrees awarded. *Degree requirements:* For master's, comprehensive exam, thesis (for some programs). *Entrance requirements:* For master's, GMAT or GRE General Test. *Application deadline:* For fall admission, 6/1 priority date for domestic students; for spring admission, 11/1 priority date for domestic students. Applications are processed on a rolling basis. Application fee: $0 ($25 for international students). Electronic applications accepted. *Financial support:* In 2007–08, research assistantships (averaging $7,875 per year), teaching assistantships (averaging $7,875 per year) were awarded; Federal Work-Study, institutionally sponsored loans, and scholarships/grants also available. Financial award application deadline: 5/1; financial award applicants required to submit FAFSA. *Faculty research:* Economic activity, forensic economics, volatility and finance, international economics. *Unit head:* Stephen L. Avard, Interim Head, 903-886-5681, E-mail: steve_avard@tamu-commerce.edu. *Application contact:* Tammi Thompson, Graduate Admissions Adviser, 843-886-5167, Fax: 843-886-5165, E-mail: tammi_thompson@tamu-commerce.edu.

Texas Tech University, Graduate School, College of Arts and Sciences, Department of Economics and Geography, Lubbock, TX 79409. Offers economics (MA, PhD). Part-time programs available. *Faculty:* 11 full-time (2 women), 1 part-time/adjunct (0 women). *Students:* 24 full-time (10 women), 10 part-time (3 women); includes 5 minority (1 African American, 3 Asian Americans or Pacific Islanders, 1 Hispanic American), 21 international. Average age 30. 37 applicants, 76% accepted, 8 enrolled. In 2007, 6 master's, 3 doctorates awarded. *Degree requirements:* For master's, thesis (for some programs); for doctorate, thesis/dissertation. *Entrance requirements:* For master's and doctorate, GRE General Test. Additional exam requirements/recommendations for international students: Required—TOEFL (minimum score 550 paper-based; 213 computer-based). *Application deadline:* For fall admission, 3/1 priority

Economics

Texas Tech University (continued)
date for international students; for spring admission, 11/1 priority date for international students. Applications are processed on a rolling basis. Application fee: $50 ($60 for international students). Electronic applications accepted. *Expenses:* Tuition, state resident: part-time $373 per credit hour. Tuition, nonresident: part-time $651 per credit hour. Tuition and fees vary according to program. *Financial support:* In 2007–08, 12 students received support, including 30 teaching assistantships with partial tuition reimbursements available (averaging $11,859 per year); research assistantships with partial tuition reimbursements available, Federal Work-Study and institutionally sponsored loans also available. Support available to part-time students. Financial award application deadline: 4/15; financial award applicants required to submit FAFSA. *Faculty research:* Pensions and retirement, economics of natural disasters, water, monetary and international economics, transportation economics. Total annual research expenditures:$79,568. *Unit head:* Dr. Joseph E. King, Chair, 806-742-2201, Fax: 806-742-1137, E-mail: joseph.king@ttu.edu. *Application contact:* Dr. Thomas E. Steinmeier, Graduate Adviser, 806-742-2201, Fax: 806-742-1137, E-mail: thomas.steinmeier@ttu.edu.

Trinity College, Graduate Programs, Department of Economics, Hartford, CT 06106-3100. Offers MA. Part-time and evening/weekend programs available. *Degree requirements:* For master's, thesis optional, qualifying exam. *Entrance requirements:* For master's, minimum GPA of 3.0.

Tufts University, Graduate School of Arts and Sciences, Department of Economics, Medford, MA 02155. Offers MA. *Faculty:* 22 full-time, 10 part-time/adjunct. *Students:* 22 (9 women); includes 5 minority (1 African American, 3 Asian Americans or Pacific Islanders, 1 Hispanic American) 9 international. 97 applicants, 53% accepted, 12 enrolled. In 2007, 17 degrees awarded. *Degree requirements:* For master's, thesis optional. *Entrance requirements:* For master's, GRE General Test. Additional exam requirements/recommendations for international students: Required—TOEFL (minimum score 550 paper-based; 213 computer-based; 80 iBT). *Application deadline:* For fall admission, 2/15 for domestic students, 12/30 for international students. Applications are processed on a rolling basis. Application fee: $70. Electronic applications accepted. *Expenses:* Tuition: Full-time $35,052. *Financial support:* Teaching assistantships with full and partial tuition reimbursements, Federal Work-Study, scholarships/grants, and tuition waivers (partial) available. Support available to part-time students. Financial award application deadline: 2/15; financial award applicants required to submit FAFSA. *Unit head:* Enrico Spolaore, Chair, 617-627-3560, Fax: 617-627-3917.

Tulane University, School of Liberal Arts, Department of Economics, New Orleans, LA 70118-5669. Offers MA, PhD. *Degree requirements:* For master's, thesis or alternative; for doctorate, one foreign language, thesis/dissertation. *Entrance requirements:* For master's, GRE General Test, minimum B average in undergraduate course work; for doctorate, GRE General Test. Additional exam requirements/recommendations for international students: Required—TOEFL. Electronic applications accepted. *Faculty research:* Economic development, public finance, labor economics, international and regional economics, industrial organization.

Universidad de las Américas–Puebla, Division of Graduate Studies, School of Social Sciences, Program in Economics, Puebla, Mexico. Offers economics (MA); finance (M Adm). Part-time and evening/weekend programs available. *Degree requirements:* For master's, one foreign language, thesis. *Faculty research:* Economic models (mathematics), industrial organization, assets and values market.

Universidad Nacional Pedro Henriquez Urena, Graduate School, Santo Domingo, Dominican Republic. Offers accounting and auditing (M Acct); animal production (M Agr); business administration (MBA, PhD); Caribbean tropical architecture (M Arch); conservation of monuments and cultural goods (M Arch); economics (M Econ); education (PhD); environmental engineering (MEE); horticulture (M Agr); hospital administration (PhD); humanities (PhD); international relations (MPS); management of natural resources (MNRM); project management (M Man, MPM); public administration (MPS); sanitary engineering (ME); social science (PhD); veterinary medicine (DVM).

Université de Moncton, Faculty of Arts and Social Sciences, Department of Economics, Moncton, NB E1A 3E9, Canada. Offers MA. *Degree requirements:* For master's, one foreign language, thesis. *Entrance requirements:* For master's, minimum GPA of 3.0. *Faculty research:* Free trade, public finance, small and medium size businesses, regional development, demography and development.

Université de Montréal, Faculty of Arts and Sciences, Department of Economic Sciences, Montréal, QC H3C 3J7, Canada. Offers M Sc, PhD. *Faculty:* 31 full-time (3 women). *Students:* 172 full-time (57 women), 11 part-time (1 woman). 316 applicants, 22% accepted, 49 enrolled. In 2007, 39 master's, 3 doctorates awarded. *Degree requirements:* For master's, one foreign language, thesis; for doctorate, one foreign language, thesis/dissertation, general exam. *Application deadline:* For fall admission, 2/1 priority date for domestic students; for winter admission, 11/1 priority date for domestic students; for spring admission, 2/1 priority date for domestic students. Application fee: $100. Electronic applications accepted. *Financial support:* Fellowships, research assistantships, teaching assistantships available. Financial award application deadline: 2/1. *Faculty research:* Applied and economic theory, public choice, international trade, labor economics, industrial organization. *Unit head:* Michel Poitevin, Chair, 514-343-6539, Fax: 514-343-7221. *Application contact:* Lyne Racine, Student Files Management Technician, 514-343-7213, Fax: 514-343-7221.

Université de Sherbrooke, Faculty of Letters and Human Sciences, Department of Economics, Sherbrooke, QC J1K 2R1, Canada. Offers MA. *Degree requirements:* For master's, thesis. *Faculty research:* Economic development, public finance, macroeconomics.

Université du Québec à Montréal, Graduate Programs, Program in Economics, Montréal, QC H3C 3P8, Canada. Offers M Sc, PhD. Part-time programs available. *Degree requirements:* For master's, thesis; for doctorate, thesis/dissertation. *Entrance requirements:* For master's, appropriate bachelor's degree or equivalent, proficiency in French; for doctorate, appropriate master's degree or equivalent, proficiency in French.

Université Laval, Faculty of Social Sciences, Department of Economics, Programs in Economics, Québec, QC G1K 7P4, Canada. Offers MA, PhD. Terminal master's awarded for partial completion of doctoral program. *Degree requirements:* For master's, thesis (for some programs); for doctorate, comprehensive exam, thesis/dissertation. *Entrance requirements:* For master's and doctorate, knowledge of French. Electronic applications accepted.

University at Albany, State University of New York, College of Arts and Sciences, Department of Economics, Albany, NY 12222-0001. Offers economics (MA, PhD); regulatory economics (Certificate). Part-time programs available. *Students:* 67 full-time (29 women), 40 part-time (14 women). Average age 29. In 2007, 28 master's, 3 other advanced degrees awarded. Terminal master's awarded for partial completion of doctoral program. *Degree requirements:* For doctorate, one foreign language, thesis/dissertation. *Entrance requirements:* For doctorate, GRE General Test, GRE Subject Test. Additional exam requirements/recommendations for international students: Required—TOEFL (minimum score 550 paper-based; 213 computer-based). *Application deadline:* For fall admission, 2/15 for domestic students, 5/1 for international students. Applications are processed on a rolling basis. Application fee: $75. Electronic applications accepted. *Expenses:* Tuition, state resident: part-time $576 per credit. Tuition, nonresident: part-time $910 per credit. Tuition and fees vary according to program. *Financial support:* Fellowships, research assistantships, teaching assistantships, career-related internships or fieldwork, institutionally sponsored loans, and lectureships available. Financial award application deadline: 2/15. *Faculty research:* Expectations of inflation and interest rates, diffusion of new technology, labor markets in developing countries, government deficits and international exchange markets. *Unit head:* Dr. Michael J. Sattinger, Chair, 518-442-4735.

University at Buffalo, the State University of New York, Graduate School, College of Arts and Sciences, Department of Economics, Buffalo, NY 14260. Offers economics (MA, MS, PhD); financial economics (Certificate); health services (Certificate); information and Internet economics (Certificate); international economics (Certificate); law and regulation (Certificate); urban and regional economics (Certificate). Terminal master's awarded for partial completion of doctoral program. *Degree requirements:* For master's, comprehensive exam, thesis optional, theory exam; for doctorate, thesis/dissertation, field and theory exams. *Entrance requirements:* For master's and doctorate, GRE General Test. Additional exam requirements/recommendations for international students: Required—TOEFL (minimum score 550 paper-based; 213 computer-based). Electronic applications accepted. *Faculty research:* International economics, econometrics, applied economics, urban economics, economic growth and development.

The University of Akron, Graduate School, Buchtel College of Arts and Sciences, Department of Economics, Akron, OH 44325. Offers economics (MA). Part-time programs available. *Faculty:* 5 full-time (0 women), 2 part-time/adjunct (1 woman). *Students:* 18 full-time (9 women), 1 part-time; includes 1 minority (Asian American or Pacific Islander), 9 international. Average age 24. 22 applicants, 86% accepted, 9 enrolled. In 2007, 6 degrees awarded. *Degree requirements:* For master's, thesis optional. *Entrance requirements:* For master's, minimum GPA of 2.75, letters of recommendation. Additional exam requirements/recommendations for international students: Required—TOEFL (minimum score 550 paper-based; 213 computer-based; 79 iBT). *Application deadline:* For fall admission, 2/15 for domestic students. Applications are processed on a rolling basis. Application fee: $30 ($40 for international students). Electronic applications accepted. *Expenses:* Tuition, state resident: full-time $6,164; part-time $342 per credit. Tuition, nonresident: full-time $10,575; part-time $588 per credit. Required fees: $806; $43 per credit. $12 per term. Tuition and fees vary according to course load, degree level and program. *Financial support:* In 2007–08, 16 teaching assistantships with full tuition reimbursements were awarded; research assistantships with full tuition reimbursements, institutionally sponsored loans and tuition waivers (full) also available. *Faculty research:* Regional economic performance, effects of addiction on labor market outcomes, programmatic assessment, regional trading arrangements, agriculture production in early twentieth-century South. *Unit head:* Dr. Michael Nelson, Chair, 330-972-7939, E-mail: nelson2@uakron.edu. *Application contact:* Dr. Gary Garofalo, Director of Graduate Studies, 330-972-7974, E-mail: ggarofalo@uakron.edu.

The University of Alabama, Graduate School, Manderson Graduate School of Business, Economics, Finance and Legal Studies Department, Tuscaloosa, AL 35487. Offers economics (MA, PhD); finance (MS, PhD). *Faculty:* 23 full-time (2 women). *Students:* 47 full-time (15 women), 10 part-time (5 women); includes 5 minority (2 African Americans, 3 Asian Americans or Pacific Islanders), 19 international. Average age 29. 119 applicants, 34% accepted, 16 enrolled. In 2007, 27 master's, 12 doctorates awarded. Terminal master's awarded for partial completion of doctoral program. *Median time to degree:* Of those who began their doctoral program in fall 1999, 99% received their degree in 8 years or less. *Degree requirements:* For master's, comprehensive exam, thesis, comprehensive exam (MA), thesis (MSC); for doctorate, comprehensive exam, thesis/dissertation. *Entrance requirements:* For master's, GMAT, GRE; for doctorate, GRE or GMAT. Additional exam requirements/recommendations for international students: Required—TOEFL (minimum score 550 paper-based; 213 computer-based). *Application deadline:* For fall admission, 7/1 priority date for domestic students, 1/15 for international students; for spring admission, 11/1 priority date for domestic students, 6/1 for international students. Applications are processed on a rolling basis. Application fee: $30. Electronic applications accepted. *Financial support:* In 2007–08, 10 fellowships (averaging $10,000 per year), 21 research assistantships with full and partial tuition reimbursements (averaging $12,000 per year), 15 teaching assistantships with full and partial tuition reimbursements (averaging $12,000 per year) were awarded; Federal Work-Study, institutionally sponsored loans, and unspecified assistantships also available. *Faculty research:* Taxation, futures market, monetary theory and policy, income distribution. *Unit head:* Prof. Billy P. Helms, Head, 205-348-8067, E-mail: bhelms@cba.ua.edu.

University of Alaska Fairbanks, School of Management, Department of Economics, Fairbanks, AK 99775-7520. Offers resource economics and applied economics (MS). Part-time programs available. *Degree requirements:* For master's, comprehensive exam, thesis or alternative. *Entrance requirements:* For master's, GRE General Test. Additional exam requirements/recommendations for international students: Required—TOEFL (minimum score 550 paper-based; 213 computer-based). Electronic applications accepted. *Faculty research:* Statistics; resource and agriculture economics; oil, gas, and energy.

University of Alberta, Faculty of Graduate Studies and Research, Department of Economics, Edmonton, AB T6G 2E1, Canada. Offers economics (MA, PhD); economics and finance (MA); environmental and natural resource economics (PhD). Part-time programs available. *Degree requirements:* For doctorate, thesis/dissertation. *Entrance requirements:* For master's and doctorate, GRE. Additional exam requirements/recommendations for international students: Required—TOEFL. *Faculty research:* Public finance, international trade, industrial organization, Pacific Rim economics, monetary economics.

The University of Arizona, Graduate College, Eller College of Management, Department of Economics, Tucson, AZ 85721. Offers MA, PhD, JD/MA, JD/PhD. *Faculty:* 27. *Students:* 42 full-time (14 women), 2 part-time; includes 2 minority (1 African American, 1 Hispanic American), 22 international. Average age 29. 154 applicants, 18% accepted, 14 enrolled. In 2007, 9 master's, 6 doctorates awarded. Terminal master's awarded for partial completion of doctoral program. *Degree requirements:* For master's, comprehensive exam; for doctorate, thesis/dissertation. *Entrance requirements:* For master's, GRE General Test, 3 letters of recommendation, statement of purpose; for doctorate, GRE General Test, minimum GPA of 3.0, 3 letters of recommendation, statement of purpose. Additional exam requirements/recommendations for international students: Required—TOEFL (minimum score 550 paper-based). *Application deadline:* For fall admission, 2/1 for domestic and international students. Applications are processed on a rolling basis. Application fee: $50. Electronic applications accepted. *Financial support:* In 2007–08, 30 students received support; fellowships with tuition reimbursements available, research assistantships with tuition reimbursements available, teaching assistantships with tuition reimbursements available, Federal Work-Study, scholarships/grants, tuition waivers (partial), and unspecified assistantships available. Financial award application deadline: 2/1. *Faculty research:* Applied microeconomics, experimental economics, economic history, microeconomic theory, property rights, industrial organization. Total annual research expenditures: $437,709. *Unit head:* Dr. Mark Walker, Head, 520-621-2821, Fax: 520-621-8450, E-mail: mwalker@eller.arizona.edu. *Application contact:* Lana Sooter, Information Contact, 520-621-2821, Fax: 520-621-8450, E-mail: lsooter@email.arizona.edu.

University of Arkansas, Graduate School, Sam M. Walton College of Business Administration, Department of Economics, Fayetteville, AR 72701-1201. Offers MA, PhD. *Students:* 7 full-time (3 women), 3 international. In 2007, 5 degrees awarded. *Degree requirements:* For doctorate, variable foreign language requirement, thesis/dissertation. *Entrance requirements:* For master's and doctorate, GRE General Test. Application fee: $40 ($50 for international students). *Financial support:* In 2007–08, 1 fellowship with tuition reimbursement, 4 research assistantships, 1 teaching assistantship were awarded; career-related internships or fieldwork and Federal Work-Study also available. Support available to part-time students. Financial award application deadline: 4/1; financial award applicants required to submit FAFSA. *Unit head:* Dr. Joseph Ziegler, Chair, 479-575-3266, E-mail: jziegler@uark.edu. *Application contact:* Raja Kali, Graduate Coordinator, 479-575-6219, E-mail: kali@uark.edu.

The University of British Columbia, Faculty of Arts and Faculty of Graduate Studies, Department of Economics, Vancouver, BC V6T 1Z1, Canada. Offers MA, PhD. *Faculty:* 37 full-time (2 women). *Students:* 76 full-time (19 women). 585 applicants, 34% accepted, 68 enrolled. In 2007, 30 master's, 11 doctorates awarded. *Median time to degree:* Of those who began their doctoral program in fall 1999, 100% received their degree in 8 years or less. *Degree requirements:* For master's, thesis (for some programs); for doctorate, comprehensive exam, thesis/dissertation. *Entrance requirements:* For master's and doctorate, GRE General Test. Additional exam requirements/recommendations for international students: Required—TOEFL (minimum score 550 paper-based; 213 computer-based; 80 iBT). *Application deadline:* For fall admission, 3/1 for domestic and international students. Applications are processed on a rolling basis. Application fee: $90 Canadian dollars ($150 Canadian dollars for international students). Electronic applications accepted. *Financial support:* In 2007–08, 48 students received support, including fellowships with tuition reimbursements available (averaging $15,000 per year), research assistantships with tuition reimbursements available (averaging $6,000 per year), teaching assistantships with tuition reimbursements available (averaging $10,000 per year); tuition waivers (partial) also available. Financial award application deadline: 1/31. *Faculty research:* Economic theory, international economics, labor economics, public finance, economic development. *Unit head:* Dr. Brian Copeland, Head, 604-822-8215, Fax: 604-822-9239, E-mail: copeland@econ.ubc.ca. *Application contact:* Maureen Chin, Graduate Admissions, 604-822-4616, Fax: 604-822-5915, E-mail: econgrad@econ.ubc.ca.

University of Calgary, Faculty of Graduate Studies, Faculty of Social Sciences, Department of Economics, Calgary, AB T2N 1N4, Canada. Offers M Ec, MA, PhD. Part-time and evening/weekend programs available. *Degree requirements:* For master's, thesis (for some programs); for doctorate, thesis/dissertation, candidacy exam. *Entrance requirements:* Additional exam requirements/recommendations for international students: Required—TOEFL. *Faculty research:* Energy economics, public finance/public choice, resource economics, international trade, monetary economics.

University of California, Berkeley, Graduate Division, College of Letters and Science, Department of Economics, Berkeley, CA 94720-1500. Offers PhD, JD/MA. *Degree requirements:* For doctorate, thesis/dissertation, field exams, oral qualifying exam. *Entrance requirements:* For doctorate, GRE General Test, minimum GPA of 3.0, 3 letters of recommendation. Additional exam requirements/recommendations for international students: Required—TOEFL. *Application deadline:* For fall admission, 12/12 for domestic students. Application fee: $70 ($90 for international students). *Financial support:* Fellowships, research assistantships, teaching assistantships, unspecified assistantships available. *Unit head:* Ben Hermalin, Chair, 510-642-3581, E-mail: hermalin@econ.berkeley.edu. *Application contact:* Patrick G. Allen, Graduate Advisor, 510-642-0824, Fax: 510-642-6615, E-mail: gradofc@econ.berkeley.edu.

University of California, Davis, Graduate Studies, Program in Economics, Davis, CA 95616. Offers MA, PhD. Terminal master's awarded for partial completion of doctoral program. *Degree requirements:* For master's, comprehensive exam (for some programs), thesis (for some programs); for doctorate, thesis/dissertation. *Entrance requirements:* For master's, GRE General Test, minimum GPA of 3.0; for doctorate, GRE General Test, minimum GPA of 3.25. Additional exam requirements/recommendations for international students: Required—TOEFL (minimum score 550 paper-based; 213 computer-based). Electronic applications accepted. *Faculty research:* Applied microeconomics, macroeconomics, international studies, economic theory, economic history.

University of California, Irvine, Office of Graduate Studies, School of Social Sciences, Department of Economics, Irvine, CA 92697. Offers economics (MA, PhD); public choice (MA, PhD); transportation economics (MA, PhD). *Students:* 72 full-time (28 women); includes 11 minority (8 Asian Americans or Pacific Islanders, 3 Hispanic Americans), 40 international. In 2007, 8 master's, 7 doctorates awarded. *Degree requirements:* For doctorate, thesis/dissertation. *Entrance requirements:* For master's, GRE, minimum GPA of 3.0; for doctorate, GRE General Test, minimum GPA of 3.0. Additional exam requirements/recommendations for international students: Required—TOEFL (minimum score 550 paper-based; 213 computer-based). *Application deadline:* For fall admission, 1/15 priority date for domestic students; for winter admission, 10/15 priority date for domestic students. Applications are processed on a rolling basis. Application fee: $40. Electronic applications accepted. *Financial support:* Fellowships, research assistantships with full tuition reimbursements, teaching assistantships, institutionally sponsored loans, traineeships, health care benefits, and unspecified assistantships available. Financial award application deadline: 3/1; financial award applicants required to submit FAFSA. *Faculty research:* Econometrics, urban economics, applied microeconomics. *Unit head:* Michelle Garfinkel, Chair, 949-824-3190, E-mail: mrgarfin@uci.edu. *Application contact:* Diane Enriquez, Graduate Counselor, 949-824-5924, Fax: 949-824-3548, E-mail: dmvargas@uci.edu.

University of California, Los Angeles, Graduate Division, College of Letters and Science, Department of Economics, Los Angeles, CA 90095. Offers MA, PhD. *Students:* 104 full-time (33 women); includes 9 minority (8 Asian Americans or Pacific Islanders, 1 Hispanic American), 62 international. Average age 28. 453 applicants, 24% accepted, 20 enrolled. In 2007, 21 master's, 23 doctorates awarded. Terminal master's awarded for partial completion of doctoral program. *Median time to degree:* Of those who began their doctoral program in fall 1999, 82% received their degree in 8 years or less. *Degree requirements:* For master's, comprehensive exam; for doctorate, thesis/dissertation, oral and written qualifying exams. *Entrance requirements:* For master's, GRE General Test, degree objective must be Ph.D; for doctorate, GRE General Test, minimum undergraduate GPA of 3.0. *Application deadline:* For fall admission, 12/15 for domestic students. Application fee: $60. Electronic applications accepted. *Expenses:* Tuition, nonresident: full-time $5,728. Required fees: $8,966. Full-time tuition and fees vary according to program and student level. *Financial support:* In 2007–08, 103 fellowships with full and partial tuition reimbursements, 18 research assistantships with full and partial tuition reimbursements, 75 teaching assistantships with full and partial tuition reimbursements were awarded; Federal Work-Study, institutionally sponsored loans, scholarships/grants, and tuition waivers (full and partial) also available. Financial award application deadline: 3/1; financial award applicants required to submit FAFSA. *Unit head:* Dr. Gary Hansen, Chair, 310-206-1413. *Application contact:* Departmental Office, 310-206-1413, E-mail: bgalcia@econ.ucla.edu.

University of California, Riverside, Graduate Division, Department of Economics, Riverside, CA 92521-0102. Offers MA, PhD. *Faculty:* 24 full-time (6 women). *Students:* 57 full-time (24 women); includes 8 minority (1 African American, 5 Asian Americans or Pacific Islanders, 2 Hispanic Americans), 39 international. Average age 30. 145 applicants, 35% accepted, 18 enrolled. In 2007, 3 master's, 6 doctorates awarded. Terminal master's awarded for partial completion of doctoral program. *Degree requirements:* For master's, comprehensive exam; for doctorate, thesis/dissertation, qualifying exams. *Entrance requirements:* For master's and doctorate, GRE General Test, minimum GPA of 3.2. Additional exam requirements/recommendations for international students: Required—TOEFL (minimum score 550 paper-based; 213 computer-based; 80 iBT). *Application deadline:* For fall admission, 5/1 for domestic students, 2/1 for international students. Applications are processed on a rolling basis. Application fee: $60 ($75 for international students). Electronic applications accepted. *Financial support:* In 2007–08, fellowships with partial tuition reimbursements (averaging $12,000 per year), teaching assistantships with partial tuition reimbursements (averaging $16,500 per year) were awarded; research assistantships, career-related internships or fieldwork, institutionally sponsored loans, and tuition waivers (full and partial) also available. Financial award application deadline: 2/1; financial award applicants required to submit FAFSA. *Faculty research:* Advanced political economy; resource and environmental economics; advanced econometrics; labor economics; advanced microeconomics theory; advanced macroeconomics theory; development economics; economic history; international trade theory; money, credit and business cycles; public economics. *Unit head:* Dr. Gloria Gonzalez-Rivera, Chair, 951-827-1474, Fax: 951-827-5685, E-mail: econgrad@pop.ucr.edu. *Application contact:* Amanda Labagnara, Graduate Program Assistant, 951-827-1474, Fax: 951-827-5685, E-mail: econgrad@ucr.edu.

Announcement: The University of California, Riverside, 60 miles east of Los Angeles, offers undergraduate and graduate degree programs in economics. The graduate program offers PhD and MA degrees in preparation for research and teaching as well as for positions in government and the private sector. Application contact: Graduate Student Affairs, phone: 951-827-1474.

University of California, San Diego, Office of Graduate Studies, Department of Economics, La Jolla, CA 92093. Offers economics (PhD); economics and international affairs (PhD). *Degree requirements:* For doctorate, thesis/dissertation. *Entrance requirements:* For doctorate, GRE General Test. Electronic applications accepted. *Faculty research:* Microfoundations of macroeconomics, econometric model specification and testing, industrial organization.

University of California, San Diego, Office of Graduate Studies, Graduate School of International Relations and Pacific Studies, La Jolla, CA 92093-0520. Offers economics and international affairs (PhD); Pacific international affairs (MPIA); political science and international affairs (PhD). *Degree requirements:* For master's, one foreign language; for doctorate, thesis/dissertation. *Entrance requirements:* For master's, GMAT or GRE General Test; for doctorate, GRE General Test. Additional exam requirements/recommendations for international students: Required—TOEFL (minimum score 550 paper-based; 213 computer-based). Electronic applications accepted. *Faculty research:* Pacific Rim as system and placement in global relations; studies in international economics, management and finance; analysis of patterns of policymaking in countries of the Pacific.

See Close-Up on page 1171.

University of California, Santa Barbara, Graduate Division, College of Letters and Sciences, Division of Social Sciences, Department of Economics, Santa Barbara, CA 93106. Offers economics (MA, PhD), including business economics (MA); MA/PhD. *Faculty:* 27 full-time (2 women), 19 part-time/adjunct (4 women). *Students:* 75 full-time (27 women); includes 10 minority (6 Asian Americans or Pacific Islanders, 4 Hispanic Americans), 16 international. Average age 26. 234 applicants, 43% accepted, 30 enrolled. In 2007, 33 master's, 12 doctorates awarded. Terminal master's awarded for partial completion of doctoral program. *Median time to degree:* Of those who began their doctoral program in fall 1999, 38% received their degree in 8 years or less. *Degree requirements:* For master's, comprehensive exam, thesis, pass all courses with B or better; for doctorate, comprehensive exam, thesis/dissertation, pass all courses with B+ or better, completion of 2 fields and field electives. *Entrance requirements:* For master's and doctorate, GRE General Test. Additional exam requirements/recommendations for international students: Required—TOEFL (minimum score 550 paper-based; 213 computer-based; 80 iBT). *Application deadline:* For fall admission, 12/1 for domestic and international students. Application fee: $60. Electronic applications accepted. *Expenses:* Tuition, nonresident: full-time $14,888. Required fees: $10,108. *Financial support:* In 2007–08, 30 students received support, including 28 fellowships with full and partial tuition reimbursements available (averaging $9,558 per year), 108 teaching assistantships with full and partial tuition reimbursements available (averaging $15,000 per year); Federal Work-Study, institutionally sponsored loans, scholarships/grants, health care benefits, tuition waivers (full and partial), and unspecified assistantships also available. Support available to part-time students. Financial award application deadline: 12/1; financial award applicants required to submit FAFSA. *Faculty research:* Labor economics, econometrics, macroeconomics, environmental and natural resources economics (EES), public finance/finance. *Unit head:* Peter Khun, Chair, 805-893-3666, Fax: 805-893-8830. *Application contact:* Mark Patterson, Staff Graduate Advisor, 805-893-2205, Fax: 805-893-8830, E-mail: mark@econ.ucsb.edu.

University of California, Santa Barbara, Graduate Division, Donald Bren School of Environmental Science and Management, Santa Barbara, CA 93106. Offers economics and environmental science (PhD); environmental science and management (MESM, PhD). *Faculty:* 19 full-time (5 women), 4 part-time/adjunct (0 women). *Students:* 167 full-time (96 women); includes 17 minority (1 African American, 1 American Indian/Alaska Native, 11 Asian Americans or Pacific Islanders, 4 Hispanic Americans), 9 international. Average age 27. 297 applicants, 61% accepted, 73 enrolled. In 2007, 58 master's, 5 doctorates awarded. *Median time to degree:* Of those who began their doctoral program in fall 1999, 60% received their degree in 8 years or less. *Degree requirements:* For master's, thesis optional, group project as student thesis; for doctorate, comprehensive exam, thesis/dissertation. *Entrance requirements:* For master's and doctorate, GRE. Additional exam requirements/recommendations for international students: Required—TOEFL (minimum score 550 paper-based; 213 computer-based; 80 iBT). *Application deadline:* For fall admission, 1/10 for domestic and international students. Application fee: $60. Electronic applications accepted. *Expenses:* Tuition, nonresident: full-time $14,888. Required fees: $10,108. *Financial support:* In 2007–08, 124 students received support, including 37 fellowships with full and partial tuition reimbursements available (averaging $9,800 per year), 14 research assistantships with full tuition reimbursements available (averaging $11,140 per year), 18 teaching assistantships with partial tuition reimbursements available (averaging $4,531 per year); career-related internships or fieldwork, Federal Work-Study, institutionally sponsored loans, scholarships/grants, traineeships, health care benefits, and unspecified assistantships also available. Financial award application deadline: 2/15; financial award applicants required to submit FAFSA. *Faculty research:* Resource economics, renewable resources, biogeography terrestrial ecology, business strategy and the environment, snow hydrology, earth system science, geomorphology, hydrology. *Unit head:* Dr. Ernst Von Weizsacker, Dean, 805-893-7577, E-mail: ernst@bren.ucsb.edu. *Application contact:* Chelsea Houdyshell, Graduate Advisor, 805-893-7611, Fax: 805-893-7612, E-mail: chelsea@bren.ucsb.edu.

University of California, Santa Cruz, Division of Graduate Studies, Division of Social Sciences, Program in International Economics, Santa Cruz, CA 95064. Offers PhD. *Faculty:* 22 full-time (3 women). *Students:* 40 full-time (18 women), 1 (woman) part-time; includes 2 minority (both Hispanic Americans), 28 international. 121 applicants, 26% accepted, 11 enrolled. In 2007, 6 doctorates awarded. *Degree requirements:* For doctorate, thesis/dissertation, 4 field exams, econometrics project. *Entrance requirements:* For doctorate, GRE General Test. *Application deadline:* For fall admission, 1/15 for domestic students. Application fee: $60. *Expenses:* Tuition, nonresident: full-time $14,694. Required fees: $11,360. *Financial support:* Research assistantships, teaching assistantships, career-related internships or fieldwork, Federal Work-Study, institutionally sponsored loans, and tuition waivers (partial) available. Financial award application deadline: 2/1. *Faculty research:* Current and emerging issues in taxation, industrial policy, environmental regulation, market structure. *Unit head:* Phillip McCalman, Director, 831-59-4381, E-mail: mccalman@ucsc.edu. *Application contact:* Cristina M. Intintoli, Graduate Assistant, 831-459-2219, E-mail: cmintint@cats.ucsc.edu.

University of Central Arkansas, Graduate School, College of Business Administration, Program in Community and Economic Development, Conway, AR 72035-0001. Offers MS. *Students:* 15 full-time (4 women), 16 part-time (9 women); includes 3 minority (2 African Americans, 1 Hispanic American), 7 international. 17 applicants, 94% accepted, 16 enrolled. In 2007, 6 degrees awarded. *Degree requirements:* For master's, comprehensive exam, thesis. *Entrance requirements:* For master's, GRE General Test, minimum GPA of 2.7. Additional exam requirements/recommendations for international students: Required—TOEFL (minimum score 550 paper-based; 213 computer-based). *Application deadline:* For fall admission, 3/1 priority date for domestic students; for spring admission, 10/1 priority date for domestic students. Applications are processed on a rolling basis. Application fee: $25 ($40 for international students). *Expenses:* Contact institution. *Financial support:* Career-related internships or fieldwork, Federal Work-Study, and unspecified assistantships available. Financial award applicants required to submit FAFSA. *Unit head:* Dr. Lauren Maxwell, Coordinator, 501-450-5349. *Application contact:* Brenda Herring, Admissions Assistant, 501-450-5065, Fax: 501-450-5678, E-mail: bherring@uca.edu.

University of Central Florida, College of Business Administration, Department of Economics, Orlando, FL 32816. Offers MS, PhD. Part-time and evening/weekend programs available. *Faculty:* 23 full-time (4 women), 2 part-time/adjunct (0 women). *Degree requirements:* For master's, comprehensive exam, thesis or alternative. *Entrance requirements:* For master's, GMAT, minimum GPA of 3.0 in last 60 hours. Additional exam requirements/recommendations for international students: Required—TOEFL. *Application deadline:* For fall admission, 6/15 priority date for domestic students; for spring admission, 11/1 priority date for domestic students. Application fee: $30. Electronic applications accepted. *Expenses:* Tuition, state

Economics

University of Central Florida (continued)
resident: full-time $6,484. Tuition, nonresident: full-time $23,938. Tuition and fees vary according to program. *Financial support:* Fellowships with partial tuition reimbursements, research assistantships with partial tuition reimbursements, teaching assistantships with partial tuition reimbursements, career-related internships or fieldwork, Federal Work-Study, institutionally sponsored loans, tuition waivers (partial), and unspecified assistantships available. Financial award application deadline: 3/1; financial award applicants required to submit FAFSA. *Unit head:* Dr. J. Wally Milon, Chair, 407-823-4429, E-mail: wally.milon@bus.ucf.edu.

University of Chicago, Division of Social Sciences, Department of Economics, Chicago, IL 60637-1513. Offers PhD. *Students:* 166. In 2007, 30 degrees awarded. *Degree requirements:* For doctorate, one foreign language, thesis/dissertation, written exams in 2 fields. *Entrance requirements:* For doctorate, GRE General Test. Additional exam requirements/recommendations for international students: Required—TOEFL, IELTS (minimum score 7). *Application deadline:* For fall admission, 12/28 for domestic and international students. Application fee: $100. Electronic applications accepted. *Financial support:* Fellowships, research assistantships, teaching assistantships, Federal Work-Study, institutionally sponsored loans, scholarships/grants, traineeships, health care benefits, and unspecified assistantships available. Financial award application deadline: 12/28; financial award applicants required to submit FAFSA. *Unit head:* Prof. Phil Reny, Chair, 773-702-9106. *Application contact:* Office of the Dean of Students, 773-702-8415.

University of Cincinnati, Graduate School, McMicken College of Arts and Sciences, Department of Economics, Program in Applied Economics, Cincinnati, OH 45221. Offers MA. Part-time and evening/weekend programs available. *Faculty:* 12 full-time (3 women), 5 part-time/adjunct (0 women). *Students:* 26 full-time (11 women), 1 part-time; includes 2 minority (1 African American, 1 Asian American or Pacific Islander), 15 international. Average age 23. 47 applicants. In 2007, 14 degrees awarded. *Degree requirements:* For master's, thesis optional. *Entrance requirements:* For master's, GRE General Test or GMAT, intermediate micro, macro theory, statistics, calculus. Additional exam requirements/recommendations for international students: Required—TOEFL. *Application deadline:* For fall admission, 4/1 priority date for domestic and international students. Applications are processed on a rolling basis. Application fee: $30. Electronic applications accepted. *Financial support:* In 2007–08, 20 students received support, including fellowships with full tuition reimbursements available (averaging $10,289 per year), research assistantships with full tuition reimbursements available (averaging $10,289 per year), teaching assistantships with full tuition reimbursements available (averaging $10,289 per year); career-related internships or fieldwork, scholarships/grants, tuition waivers (partial), and unspecified assistantships also available. Financial award application deadline: 4/1. *Faculty research:* Econometrics, labor markets, pollution markets, transportation. *Application contact:* Dr. Haynes C. Goddard, Graduate Program Director, 513-556-2621, Fax: 513-556-2669, E-mail: haynes.goddard@uc.edu.

University of Colorado at Boulder, Graduate School, College of Arts and Sciences, Department of Economics, Boulder, CO 80309. Offers MA, PhD. *Faculty:* 29. *Students:* 61 full-time (25 women), 16 part-time (4 women); includes 2 minority (both Hispanic Americans), 40 international. Average age 30. 72 applicants, 58% accepted. In 2007, 11 master's, 12 doctorates awarded. Terminal master's awarded for partial completion of doctoral program. *Degree requirements:* For master's, comprehensive exam, thesis or alternative; for doctorate, comprehensive exam, thesis/dissertation, preliminary exam. *Entrance requirements:* For master's, GRE General Test, minimum undergraduate GPA of 2.75; for doctorate, GRE General Test. Additional exam requirements/recommendations for international students: Required—TOEFL. *Application deadline:* For fall admission, 2/1 priority date for domestic students, 12/1 for international students. Applications are processed on a rolling basis. Application fee: $50 ($60 for international students). *Financial support:* In 2007–08, 15 fellowships with full tuition reimbursements (averaging $3,933 per year), 3 research assistantships with full tuition reimbursements (averaging $15,048 per year) were awarded; tuition waivers (full) also available. Financial award application deadline: 2/1; financial award applicants required to submit FAFSA. *Faculty research:* Public economics and natural resources and environmental economics, international, econometrics, urban and regional economics, development economics, economic history. Total annual research expenditures: $508,605. *Unit head:* Keith E. Maskus, Chair, 303-492-7588, Fax: 303-492-8960, E-mail: keith.maskus@colorado.edu. *Application contact:* Graduate Assistant, 303-492-6396, Fax: 303-492-8960, E-mail: econ@colorado.edu.

University of Colorado Denver, College of Liberal Arts and Sciences, Department of Economics, Denver, CO 80217-3364. Offers MA. Part-time and evening/weekend programs available. *Faculty:* 11 full-time (2 women). *Students:* 22 full-time (4 women), 29 part-time (6 women); includes 6 minority (3 African Americans, 1 Asian American or Pacific Islander, 2 Hispanic Americans), 16 international. Average age 31. 35 applicants, 46% accepted, 11 enrolled. In 2007, 15 degrees awarded. *Degree requirements:* For master's, thesis or alternative. *Entrance requirements:* For master's, GRE General Test, 15 hours of course work in economics, minimum GPA of 2.5. Additional exam requirements/recommendations for international students: Required—TOEFL (minimum score 525 paper-based; 197 computer-based). *Application deadline:* For fall admission, 6/1 for domestic students; for spring admission, 11/1 for domestic students. Applications are processed on a rolling basis. Application fee: $50 ($75 for international students). Electronic applications accepted. *Financial support:* Research assistantships, teaching assistantships, Federal Work-Study available. Financial award application deadline: 4/1; financial award applicants required to submit FAFSA. Total annual research expenditures: $85,986. *Unit head:* Dr. Laura Argys, Chair, 303-556-3949, Fax: 303-556-3547, E-mail: laura.argys@cudenver.edu. *Application contact:* Christine Lukvec, Program Assistant, 303-556-4413, Fax: 303-556-3547, E-mail: christine.lukvec@cudenver.edu.

University of Connecticut, Graduate School, College of Liberal Arts and Sciences, Department of Economics, Field of Economics, Storrs, CT 06269. Offers MA, PhD. *Faculty:* 32 full-time (4 women). *Students:* 59 full-time (28 women), 13 part-time (5 women); includes 8 minority (4 African Americans, 4 Asian Americans or Pacific Islanders), 38 international. Average age 30. 194 applicants, 16% accepted, 23 enrolled. In 2007, 11 master's, 7 doctorates awarded. *Degree requirements:* For master's, comprehensive exam; for doctorate, thesis/dissertation. *Entrance requirements:* For master's and doctorate, GRE General Test, GRE Subject Test. Additional exam requirements/recommendations for international students: Required—TOEFL (minimum score 550 paper-based; 213 computer-based). *Application deadline:* For fall admission, 2/1 priority date for domestic and international students; for spring admission, 11/1 for domestic students, 10/1 for international students. Applications are processed on a rolling basis. Application fee: $55. Electronic applications accepted. *Expenses:* Tuition, state resident: part-time $469 per credit hour. Tuition, nonresident: part-time $1,218 per credit hour. *Financial support:* In 2007–08, 8 research assistantships with full tuition reimbursements, 38 teaching assistantships with full tuition reimbursements were awarded; fellowships, Federal Work-Study, scholarships/grants, health care benefits, and unspecified assistantships also available. Financial award application deadline: 2/1; financial award applicants required to submit FAFSA. *Application contact:* Rosanne Fitzgerald, Graduate Program Coordinator, 860-486-4633, Fax: 860-486-4463, E-mail: rosanne.fitzgerald@uconn.edu.

University of Delaware, Alfred Lerner College of Business and Economics, Department of Economics, Newark, DE 19716. Offers economics (MA, MS, PhD); economics for entrepreneurship and educators (MA); MA/MBA. Part-time programs available. *Faculty:* 25 full-time (3 women). *Students:* 82 full-time (32 women), 2 part-time (1 woman); includes 7 minority (3 African Americans, 2 American Indian/Alaska Native, 2 Asian Americans or Pacific Islanders), 42 international. Average age 29. 115 applicants, 61% accepted, 20 enrolled. In 2007, 45 master's, 4 doctorates awarded. *Degree requirements:* For master's, comprehensive exam, thesis (for some programs), mathematics review exam, research project; for doctorate, comprehensive exam, thesis/dissertation, field exam. *Entrance requirements:* For master's, GMAT or GRE General Test, minimum GPA of 2.5; for doctorate, GRE General Test, minimum GPA of 3.5 in graduate economics course work. Additional exam requirements/recommendations for international students: Required—TOEFL (minimum score 550 paper-based; 225 computer-based). *Application deadline:* For fall admission, 5/1 for domestic students, 2/1 priority date for international students; for spring admission, 11/1 for domestic students, 10/1 for international students. Application fee: $60. Electronic applications accepted. *Financial support:* In 2007–08, 40 students received support, including 2 fellowships with full tuition reimbursements available (averaging $14,600 per year), 16 research assistantships with full and partial tuition reimbursements available (averaging $14,600 per year), 14 teaching assistantships with full and partial tuition reimbursements available (averaging $14,600 per year); career-related internships or fieldwork, scholarships/grants, health care benefits, tuition waivers (partial), and unspecified assistantships also available. Financial award application deadline: 2/15. *Faculty research:* Applied quantitative economics, industrial organization, resource economics, monetary economics, labor economics. Total annual research expenditures: $75,000. *Unit head:* Dr. Saul D. Hoffman, Chair, 302-831-1907, Fax: 302-831-6968, E-mail: hoffmans@lerner.udel.edu. *Application contact:* Dr. Kenneth Lewis, Associate Chairman, 302-831-1912, Fax: 302-831-6968, E-mail: lewisk@udel.edu.

University of Denver, Faculty of Arts and Humanities/Social Sciences, Department of Economics, Denver, CO 80208. Offers MA. Part-time programs available. *Faculty:* 7 full-time (2 women). *Students:* 9 full-time (1 woman), 3 part-time (1 woman); includes 3 minority (1 African American, 1 Asian American or Pacific Islander, 1 Hispanic American), 6 international. Average age 26. In 2007, 6 degrees awarded. *Degree requirements:* For master's, thesis. *Entrance requirements:* For master's, GRE. Additional exam requirements/recommendations for international students: Required—TOEFL. *Application deadline:* Applications are processed on a rolling basis. Application fee: $50. Electronic applications accepted. *Financial support:* In 2007–08, 5 teaching assistantships with full and partial tuition reimbursements (averaging $4,000 per year) were awarded; career-related internships or fieldwork, Federal Work-Study, and scholarships/grants also available. Support available to part-time students. Financial award application deadline: 3/1; financial award applicants required to submit FAFSA. *Unit head:* Dr. Peter Ho, Chairperson, 303-871-2685. *Application contact:* Information Contact, 303-871-2685, E-mail: econ04@denver.du.edu.

University of Florida, Graduate School, Warrington College of Business Administration, Hough Graduate School of Business, Department of Economics, Gainesville, FL 32611. Offers MA, PhD. *Faculty:* 17 full-time (2 women). *Students:* 26 (15 women); includes 2 minority (both Hispanic Americans) 12 international. In 2007, 1 master's, 7 doctorates awarded. Terminal master's awarded for partial completion of doctoral program. *Degree requirements:* For master's, thesis optional; for doctorate, thesis/dissertation. *Entrance requirements:* Additional exam requirements/recommendations for international students: Required—TOEFL (minimum score 550 paper-based; 213 computer-based). *Application deadline:* For fall admission, 2/16 for domestic students. Applications are processed on a rolling basis. Application fee: $30. Electronic applications accepted. *Expenses:* Tuition, state resident: full-time $7,478. Tuition, nonresident: full-time $22,603. *Financial support:* In 2007–08, 4 teaching assistantships (averaging $26,640 per year) were awarded; fellowships, research assistantships, unspecified assistantships also available. *Faculty research:* Econometrics, international economics, industrial organization, public finance, economic theory. *Unit head:* Dr. Jonathan H. Hamilton, Chair, 352-392-2999, Fax: 352-392-7860, E-mail: hamilton@ufl.edu. *Application contact:* Dr. Steven Slutsky, Coordinator, 352-392-8106, Fax: 352-392-7860, E-mail: steven.slutsky@cba.ufl.edu.

University of Georgia, Graduate School, Terry College of Business, Department of Economics, Athens, GA 30602. Offers MA, PhD. *Faculty:* 15 full-time (1 woman). *Students:* 28 full-time (9 women), 1 part-time; includes 3 minority (2 Asian Americans or Pacific Islanders, 1 Hispanic American), 15 international. 80 applicants, 28% accepted, 5 enrolled. In 2007, 2 master's, 3 doctorates awarded. *Degree requirements:* For master's, thesis; for doctorate, thesis/dissertation. *Entrance requirements:* For master's and doctorate, GRE General Test. *Application deadline:* For fall admission, 7/1 priority date for domestic students; for spring admission, 11/15 for domestic students. Application fee: $50. Electronic applications accepted. *Financial support:* Fellowships, research assistantships, teaching assistantships available. *Unit head:* Dr. William D. Lastrapes, Head, 706-542-3569, Fax: 706-542-3376, E-mail: last@terry.uga.edu. *Application contact:* Dr. David B. Mustard, Graduate Coordinator, 706-542-3624, Fax: 706-542-3376, E-mail: econge@terry.uga.edu.

University of Guelph, Graduate Program Services, College of Management and Economics, Department of Economics, Guelph, ON N1G 2W1, Canada. Offers MA, PhD. Part-time programs available. *Faculty:* 24 full-time (6 women). *Students:* 40 full-time (20 women). Average age 25. 152 applicants, 37% accepted, 21 enrolled. In 2007, 15 master's, 4 doctorates awarded. *Degree requirements:* For master's, thesis or alternative; for doctorate, comprehensive exam, thesis/dissertation. *Entrance requirements:* For master's, minimum B+ average during previous 2 years of course work; for doctorate, minimum A- average, MA in economics. Additional exam requirements/recommendations for international students: Required—TOEFL (minimum score 550 paper-based; 213 computer-based; 89 iBT), IELTS (minimum score 7). *Application deadline:* For fall admission, 1/31 priority date for domestic and international students. Applications are processed on a rolling basis. Application fee: $85. Electronic applications accepted. *Financial support:* In 2007–08, 9 research assistantships (averaging $2,759 per year), 72 teaching assistantships (averaging $15,321 per year) were awarded; scholarships/grants, unspecified assistantships, and bursaries also available. *Faculty research:* Resource and environmental economics, econometrics, labor economics, micro and macro economics. Total annual research expenditures: $75,000. *Unit head:* Dr. J. Livernois, Chair, 519-824-4120 Ext. 56339, Fax: 519-763-8497, E-mail: live@uoguelph.ca. *Application contact:* Dr. R. McKitrick, Associate Professor and Graduate Coordinator, 519-824-4120 Ext. 52532, Fax: 519-763-8497, E-mail: rmckitri@uoguelph.ca.

University of Hawaii at Manoa, Graduate Division, Colleges of Arts and Sciences, College of Social Sciences, Department of Economics, Honolulu, HI 96822. Offers MA, PhD. Part-time programs available. *Faculty:* 24 full-time (4 women), 8 part-time/adjunct (1 woman). *Students:* 43 full-time (22 women), 10 part-time (5 women); includes 10 minority (all Asian Americans or Pacific Islanders), 36 international. Average age 31. 62 applicants, 60% accepted, 15 enrolled. Terminal master's awarded for partial completion of doctoral program. *Median time to degree:* Of those who began their doctoral program in fall 1999, 36% received their degree in 8 years or less. *Degree requirements:* For master's, thesis optional; for doctorate, comprehensive exam, thesis/dissertation. *Entrance requirements:* For master's and doctorate, GRE General Test. Additional exam requirements/recommendations for international students: Required—TOEFL (minimum score 500 paper-based; 173 computer-based; 61 iBT), IELTS (minimum score 5). *Application deadline:* For fall admission, 1/15 for domestic and international students; for spring admission, 8/1 for domestic and international students. Application fee: $50. *Financial support:* In 2007–08, 8 research assistantships (averaging $17,442 per year), 9 teaching assistantships (averaging $14,331 per year) were awarded; fellowships also available. *Faculty research:* Trade, development, demography, labor, resource economics. *Application contact:* Theresa Greaney, Graduate Chair, 808-956-2321, Fax: 808-956-4347, E-mail: greaney@hawaii.edu.

University of Houston, College of Liberal Arts and Social Sciences, Department of Economics, Houston, TX 77204. Offers MA, PhD. Part-time programs available. *Faculty:* 13 full-time (4 women), 1 part-time/adjunct (0 women). *Students:* 49 full-time (16 women), 5 part-time (3 women); includes 8 minority (1 American Indian/Alaska Native, 4 Asian Americans or Pacific Islanders, 3 Hispanic Americans), 36 international. Average age 28. 43 applicants, 95% accepted, 15 enrolled. In 2007, 7 master's, 5 doctorates awarded. Terminal master's awarded for partial completion of doctoral program. *Degree requirements:* For doctorate, thesis/dissertation. *Entrance requirements:* For master's, GRE General Test, minimum GPA of 3.0; for doctorate, GRE General Test, master's degree, minimum GPA of 3.0. *Application deadline:* For fall admission, 5/2 for domestic students. Application fee: $0 ($75 for international students). *Expenses:* Tuition, state resident: full-time $6,297; part-time $262 per credit. Tuition, nonresident: full-time $12,969; part-time $540 per credit. Required fees: $2,696. *Financial support:* In 2007–08, 40 teaching assistantships with full tuition reimbursements (averaging $12,300 per year) were awarded; fellowships with full tuition reimbursements, research assistantships with full tuition reimbursements, career-related internships or fieldwork, Federal Work-Study, institutionally sponsored loans, scholarships/grants, health care benefits, and unspecified assistantships also available. Support available to part-time students. Financial award application deadline: 2/1. *Faculty research:* Econometrics, labor economics, international economics, public finance. *Unit head:* Dr. David Papell, Graduate Director, 713-743-3800, Fax: 713-743-3798, E-mail: dpapell@uh.edu.

University of Houston–Victoria, School of Business Administration, Victoria, TX 77901-4450. Offers accounting (MBA); economic development and entrepreneurship (MS); finance (GMBA, MBA); general business (MBA); international business (MBA); management (GMBA, MBA); marketing (MBA). *Accreditation:* AACSB. Part-time and evening/weekend programs available. Postbaccalaureate distance learning degree programs offered (no on-campus study). *Faculty:* 28 full-time (7 women). *Students:* 143 full-time (76 women), 566 part-time (276 women); includes 353 minority (138 African Americans, 1 American Indian/Alaska Native, 140 Asian Americans or Pacific Islanders, 74 Hispanic Americans), 63 international. In 2007, 123 degrees awarded. *Entrance requirements:* For master's, GMAT. Additional exam requirements/recommendations for international students: Required—TOEFL (minimum score 550 paper-based; 213 computer-based). *Application deadline:* For fall admission, 6/1 for international students; for spring admission, 10/1 for international students. Applications are processed on a rolling basis. Application fee: $0. Electronic applications accepted. *Expenses:* Tuition, state resident: full-time $3,492; part-time $194 per semester hour. Tuition, nonresident: full-time $7,596; part-time $422 per semester hour. Required fees: $774; $43 per semester hour. Tuition and fees vary according to course load. *Financial support:* In 2007–08, research assistantships with partial tuition reimbursements (averaging $2,000 per year), teaching assistantships with partial tuition reimbursements (averaging $2,000 per year) were awarded; career-related internships or fieldwork, Federal Work-Study, scholarships/grants, and unspecified assistantships also available. Support available to part-time students. Financial award application deadline: 4/15. *Faculty research:* Economic development, marketing, finance. *Unit head:* Charles Bullock, Dean, 361-570-4230, Fax: 361-570-4229, E-mail: bullockc@uhv.edu. *Application contact:* Jane Mims, Director of Student Services, 361-370-0239, E-mail: mims@uhv.edu.

University of Illinois at Chicago, Graduate College, Liautaud Graduate School of Business, Department of Economics, Chicago, IL 60607-7128. Offers economics (MA, PhD); public policy analysis (PhD); MBA/MA. Terminal master's awarded for partial completion of doctoral program. *Degree requirements:* For master's, comprehensive exam; for doctorate, thesis/dissertation. *Entrance requirements:* For master's and doctorate, GRE General Test, minimum GPA of 2.75. Additional exam requirements/recommendations for international students: Required—TOEFL. Electronic applications accepted. *Faculty research:* International, labor, and urban economics.

University of Illinois at Urbana–Champaign, Graduate College, College of Liberal Arts and Sciences, Department of Economics, Champaign, IL 61820. Offers MS, PhD. *Faculty:* 25 full-time (3 women), 3 part-time/adjunct (0 women). *Students:* 154 full-time (54 women), 14 part-time (4 women); includes 3 minority (1 African American, 2 Asian Americans or Pacific Islanders), 141 international. 469 applicants, 17% accepted, 62 enrolled. In 2007, 60 master's, 14 doctorates awarded. Terminal master's awarded for partial completion of doctoral program. *Degree requirements:* For doctorate, thesis/dissertation. *Entrance requirements:* For master's, GRE General Test, minimum GPA of 3.0; for doctorate, GRE General Test, minimum GPA of 3.3. *Application deadline:* Applications are processed on a rolling basis. Application fee: $60 ($75 for international students). Electronic applications accepted. *Financial support:* In 2007–08, 16 fellowships, 8 research assistantships, 61 teaching assistantships were awarded. Financial award application deadline: 2/15. *Unit head:* Dr. J. Fred Giertz, Head, 217-333-0120, Fax: 217-244-6678, E-mail: jgiertz@uiuc.edu. *Application contact:* Toni Wendler, Graduate Administrative Secretary, 217-333-0120, Fax: 217-244-6678, E-mail: twendler@uiuc.edu.

See Close-Up on page 1039.

The University of Iowa, Henry B. Tippie College of Business, Department of Economics, Iowa City, IA 52242-1316. Offers PhD. *Faculty:* 18 full-time (4 women), 10 part-time/adjunct (2 women). *Students:* 34 full-time (8 women), 2 part-time (1 woman), 27 international. Average age 28. 178 applicants, 13% accepted, 12 enrolled. In 2007, 5 degrees awarded. *Degree requirements:* For doctorate, comprehensive exam, thesis/dissertation, thesis defense. *Entrance requirements:* For doctorate, GRE General Test. Additional exam requirements/recommendations for international students: Required—TOEFL (minimum score 600 paper-based; 250 computer-based; 100 iBT); Recommended—IELTS (minimum score 7). *Application deadline:* For fall admission, 1/15 priority date for domestic and international students. Applications are processed on a rolling basis. Application fee: $60 ($85 for international students). Electronic applications accepted. *Expenses:* Tuition, state resident: part-time $349 per hour. Tuition, nonresident: part-time $349 per hour. Tuition and fees vary according to course load and program. *Financial support:* In 2007–08, 34 students received support, including 2 fellowships with full tuition reimbursements available (averaging $18,000 per year), 5 research assistantships with full tuition reimbursements available (averaging $16,300 per year), 27 teaching assistantships with full tuition reimbursements available (averaging $16,300 per year); institutionally sponsored loans, scholarships/grants, health care benefits, and unspecified assistantships also available. Financial award application deadline: 1/15. *Faculty research:* Political economy, macroeconomics, econometrics, game theory, economic development. *Unit head:* Prof. B. Ravikumar, Director/Executive Officer, 319-335-0829, Fax: 319-335-1956, E-mail: ravikumar@uiowa.edu. *Application contact:* Renea L. Jay, PhD Program Coordinator, 319-335-0830, Fax: 319-335-1956, E-mail: renea-jay@uiowa.edu.

University of Kansas, Research and Graduate Studies, College of Liberal Arts and Sciences, Department of Economics, Lawrence, KS 66045. Offers MA, PhD, JD/MA. Part-time programs available. *Faculty:* 19. *Students:* 64 full-time (21 women), 5 part-time (2 women); includes 4 minority (1 African American, 3 Asian Americans or Pacific Islanders), 46 international. Average age 29. 92 applicants, 63% accepted, 19 enrolled. In 2007, 12 master's, 5 doctorates awarded. Terminal master's awarded for partial completion of doctoral program. *Degree requirements:* For master's, comprehensive exam, thesis or alternative; for doctorate, thesis/dissertation. *Entrance requirements:* For doctorate, GRE. Additional exam requirements/recommendations for international students: Required—TOEFL. *Application deadline:* For fall admission, 2/1 priority date for domestic and international students; for winter admission, 5/1 priority date for domestic and international students; for spring admission, 11/1 priority date for domestic and international students. Applications are processed on a rolling basis. Application fee: $55 ($60 for international students). Electronic applications accepted. *Expenses:* Tuition, state resident: full-time $5,838. Tuition, nonresident: full-time $13,409. Tuition and fees vary according to program. *Financial support:* In 2007–08, 1 fellowship with full tuition reimbursement, 5 research assistantships with full tuition reimbursements, 22 teaching assistantships with full and partial tuition reimbursements were awarded; institutionally sponsored loans, scholarships/grants, health care benefits, and unspecified assistantships also available. Financial award application deadline: 2/1. *Faculty research:* Macroeconomics, econometrics, organization, microeconomics, development, international economics. *Unit head:* Joseph Sicilian, Chair, 785-864-3501, Fax: 785-864-5270, E-mail: jsic@ku.edu. *Application contact:* Elizabeth Asiedu, Graduate Director, 785-864-3501, Fax: 785-864-5270, E-mail: asiedu@ku.edu.

University of Kentucky, Graduate School, Gatton College of Business and Economics, Program in Economics, Lexington, KY 40506-0032. Offers MS, PhD. *Faculty:* 54 full-time (8 women), 2 part-time/adjunct (1 woman). *Students:* 39 full-time (14 women), 3 part-time; includes 5 minority (4 African Americans, 1 Hispanic American), 19 international. Average age 29. 114 applicants, 23% accepted, 7 enrolled. In 2007, 12 master's, 10 doctorates awarded. *Median time to degree:* Of those who began their doctoral program in fall 1999, 64% received their degree in 8 years or less. *Degree requirements:* For master's, comprehensive exam; for doctorate, comprehensive exam, thesis/dissertation. *Entrance requirements:* For master's, GMAT, minimum undergraduate GPA of 2.75; for doctorate, GMAT, minimum undergraduate GPA of 3.0. Additional exam requirements/recommendations for international students: Required—TOEFL (minimum score 550 paper-based; 213 computer-based). *Application deadline:* For fall admission, 7/17 priority date for domestic students, 2/1 priority date for international students; for spring admission, 12/13 priority date for domestic students, 6/15 priority date for international students. Application fee: $50 ($65 for international students). Electronic applications accepted. *Expenses:* Tuition, state resident: part-time $437 per credit hour. Tuition, nonresident: part-time $931 per credit hour. *Financial support:* In 2007–08, 31 students received support, including 7 fellowships with full tuition reimbursements available (averaging $2,698 per year), 7 research assistantships with full tuition reimbursements available (averaging $12,450 per year), 21 teaching assistantships with full tuition reimbursements available (averaging $11,688 per year); Federal Work-Study, institutionally sponsored loans, scholarships/grants, traineeships, health care benefits, tuition waivers (partial), and unspecified assistantships also available. Support available to part-time students. Financial award application deadline: 3/15. *Faculty research:* Public economics, international economics and economic development, labor economics, environmental economics, industrial economics. *Unit head:* Dr. William Hoyt, Director of Graduate Studies, 859-257-2518, Fax: 859-323-1920, E-mail: william.hoyt@uky.edu. *Application contact:* Dr. Brian Jackson, Senior Associate Dean, 859-257-4667, Fax: 859-257-4676, E-mail: brian.jackson@uky.edu.

University of Lethbridge, School of Graduate Studies, Lethbridge, AB T1K 3M4, Canada. Offers accounting (MScM); addictions counseling (M Sc); agricultural biotechnology (M Sc); agricultural studies (M Sc, MA); anthropology (MA); archaeology (MA); art (MA); biochemistry (M Sc); biological sciences (M Sc); biomolecular science (PhD); biosystems and biodiversity (PhD); Canadian studies (MA); chemistry (M Sc); computer science (M Sc); computer science and geographical information science (M Sc); counseling psychology (M Ed); dramatic arts (MA); earth, space, and physical science (PhD); economics (MA); educational leadership (M Ed); English (MA); environmental science (M Sc); evolution and behavior (PhD); exercise science (M Sc); finance (MScM); French (MA); French/German (MA); French/Spanish (MA); general education (M Ed); general management (MScM); geography (M Sc, MA); German (MA); health sciences (M Sc, MA); history (MA); human resource management and labour relations (MScM); individualized multidisciplinary (M Sc, MA); information systems (MScM); international management (MScM); kinesiology (M Sc, MA); management (M Sc, MA); marketing (MScM); mathematics (M Sc); music (MA); Native American studies (MA); neuroscience (M Sc, PhD); new media (MA); nursing (M Sc); philosophy (MA); physics (M Sc); policy and strategy (MScM); political science (MA); psychology (M Sc, MA); religious studies (MA); sociology (MA); theoretical and computational science (PhD); urban and regional studies (MA). Part-time and evening/weekend programs available. *Students:* 215 full-time, 98 part-time. In 2007, 87 master's, 1 doctorate awarded. *Degree requirements:* For doctorate, comprehensive exam, thesis/dissertation. *Entrance requirements:* For master's, GMAT (M Sc in management), bachelor's degree in related field, minimum GPA of 3.0 during previous 20 graded semester courses, 2 years teaching or related experience (M Ed); for doctorate, master's degree, minimum graduate GPA of 3.5. Additional exam requirements/recommendations for international students: Required—TOEFL. Application fee: $60 Canadian dollars. *Financial support:* Fellowships, research assistantships, teaching assistantships, scholarships/grants, health care benefits, and unspecified assistantships available. *Faculty research:* Movement and brain plasticity, gibberellin physiology, photosynthesis, carbon cycling, molecular properties of main-group ring components. *Unit head:* Dr. Jo-Anne Fiske, Interim Dean, 403-329-2121, Fax: 403-329-2097. *Application contact:* Jennifer Geddes, Graduate Liaison Officer, 403-329-2762, Fax: 403-329-5159, E-mail: jennifer.geddes@uleth.ca.

University of Maine, Graduate School, College of Business, Public Policy and Health, Department of Economics, Orono, ME 04469. Offers economics (MA); financial economics (MA). Part-time programs available. *Faculty:* 7. *Students:* 10 full-time (6 women), 1 part-time, 7 international. Average age 27. 17 applicants, 88% accepted, 9 enrolled. In 2007, 5 master's awarded. *Degree requirements:* For master's, thesis optional. *Entrance requirements:* For master's, GRE General Test. Additional exam requirements/recommendations for international students: Required—TOEFL. *Application deadline:* For fall admission, 2/1 priority date for domestic students. Applications are processed on a rolling basis. Application fee: $60. Electronic applications accepted. *Financial support:* In 2007–08, 3 teaching assistantships with full tuition reimbursements (averaging $9,010 per year) were awarded; fellowships with full tuition reimbursements, career-related internships or fieldwork, Federal Work-Study, institutionally sponsored loans, and tuition waivers (full and partial) also available. Support available to part-time students. Financial award application deadline: 3/1. *Faculty research:* Health and marine resource economics, alternative political economy. *Unit head:* Ralph Townsend, Chair, 207-881-1850, Fax: 207-581-1953. *Application contact:* Scott G. Delcourt, Associate Dean of the Graduate School, 207-581-3219, Fax: 207-581-3232, E-mail: graduate@maine.edu.

University of Manitoba, Faculty of Graduate Studies, Faculty of Arts, Department of Economics, Winnipeg, MB R3T 2N2, Canada. Offers MA, PhD. *Degree requirements:* For master's, thesis or alternative; for doctorate, one foreign language, thesis/dissertation.

University of Maryland, Baltimore County, Graduate School, College of Arts, Humanities and Social Sciences, Department of Economics, Program in Economic Policy Analysis, Baltimore, MD 21250. Offers MA. Part-time and evening/weekend programs available. *Faculty:* 25 full-time (8 women), 1 part-time/adjunct (0 women). *Students:* 9 full-time (6 women), 12 part-time (6 women); includes 7 minority (3 African Americans, 3 Asian Americans or Pacific Islanders, 1 Hispanic American), 3 international. Average age 29. 33 applicants, 61% accepted, 9 enrolled. In 2007, 6 degrees awarded. *Degree requirements:* For master's, comprehensive exam. *Entrance requirements:* For master's, GRE General Test, undergraduate coursework in economic theory, econometrics, calculus. Additional exam requirements/recommendations for international students: Required—TOEFL. *Application deadline:* For fall admission, 7/1 for domestic students, 1/1 priority date for international students. Applications are processed on a rolling basis. Application fee: $45. Electronic applications accepted. *Financial support:* In 2007–08, 5 students received support, including 4 research assistantships with full and partial tuition reimbursements available (averaging $11,324 per year), 1 teaching assistantship with full tuition reimbursement available (averaging $11,324 per year); Federal Work-Study, health care benefits, tuition waivers (full and partial), and unspecified assistantships also available. Support available to part-time students. Financial award application deadline: 2/15; financial award applicants required to submit FAFSA. *Faculty research:* International trade policy analysis, health and hospital policy evaluation, environmental policy analysis, economics of education, economic growth and development. Total annual research expenditures: $25,000. *Unit head:* Dr. David F. Mitch, Professor of Economics and Graduate Director, 410-455-2157, Fax: 410-455-1054, E-mail: mitch@umbc.edu.

University of Maryland, College Park, Graduate Studies, College of Behavioral and Social Sciences, Department of Economics, College Park, MD 20742. Offers MA, PhD. Part-time and evening/weekend programs available. *Faculty:* 42 full-time (12 women), 21 part-time/adjunct (5 women). *Students:* 133 full-time (51 women), 1 part-time; includes 10 minority (2 African Americans, 5 Asian Americans or Pacific Islanders, 3 Hispanic Americans), 88 international. 632 applicants, 12% accepted, 24 enrolled. In 2007, 14 master's, 24 doctorates awarded. Terminal master's awarded for partial completion of doctoral program. *Median time to degree:* Of those who began their doctoral program in fall 1999, 56% received their degree in 8 years or less. *Degree requirements:* For master's, comprehensive exam, thesis optional; for doctorate, comprehensive exam, thesis/dissertation, exams. *Entrance requirements:* For master's, GRE General Test, minimum GPA of 3.0, course work in calculus and mathematics, 3 letters of recommendation; for doctorate, GRE General Test, calculus background. Additional exam requirements/recommendations for international students: Required—TOEFL. *Application deadline:* For fall admission, 1/7 for domestic and international students. Applications are processed on a rolling basis. Application fee: $60. Electronic applications accepted. *Financial support:* In 2007–08, 5 fellowships with full tuition reimbursements (averaging $14,744 per year), 7 research assistantships with tuition reimbursements (averaging $16,128 per year), 89

Economics

University of Maryland, College Park (continued)
teaching assistantships with tuition reimbursements (averaging $15,964 per year) were awarded; Federal Work-Study and scholarships/grants also available. Support available to part-time students. Financial award applicants required to submit FAFSA. *Faculty research:* International economics, natural resource and environmental economics, forecasting and policy analysis, economic growth, demography of inequality. Total annual research expenditures: $2.2 million. *Unit head:* Dr. Peter Murrell, Chairman, 301-405-3506, Fax: 301-405-4733, E-mail: pmurrell@umd.edu. *Application contact:* Dean of Graduate School, 301-405-0358, Fax: 301-314-9305.

University of Maryland, College Park, Graduate Studies, College of Behavioral and Social Sciences, Department of Government and Politics, College Park, MD 20742. Offers American politics (PhD); comparative politics (PhD); international relations (PhD); political economy (PhD); political theory (PhD). Part-time and evening/weekend programs available. *Faculty:* 47 full-time (11 women), 11 part-time/adjunct (3 women). *Students:* 132 full-time (59 women), 22 part-time (9 women); includes 29 minority (8 African Americans, 15 Asian Americans or Pacific Islanders, 6 Hispanic Americans), 24 international. 277 applicants, 18% accepted, 16 enrolled. In 2007, 9 doctorates awarded. *Median time to degree:* Of those who began their doctoral program in fall 1999, 41% received their degree in 8 years or less. *Degree requirements:* For doctorate, comprehensive exam, thesis/dissertation, written exams in 2 fields. *Entrance requirements:* For doctorate, GRE General Test, minimum GPA of 3.5, writing sample. Additional exam requirements/recommendations for international students: Required—TOEFL. *Application deadline:* For fall admission, 2/1 for domestic and international students. Applications are processed on a rolling basis. Application fee: $60. Electronic applications accepted. *Financial support:* In 2007–08, 10 fellowships with full tuition reimbursements (averaging $17,695 per year), 3 research assistantships with tuition reimbursements (averaging $15,383 per year), 66 teaching assistantships with tuition reimbursements (averaging $14,997 per year) were awarded; career-related internships or fieldwork, Federal Work-Study, scholarships/grants, and unspecified assistantships also available. Support available to part-time students. Financial award applicants required to submit FAFSA. *Faculty research:* International development/conflict, international security, post-communist society, public service, dynamics of conflict and conflict resolution. Total annual research expenditures: $2.3 million. *Unit head:* Dr. Mark Lichbach, Chairman, 301-405-4160, Fax: 301-314-9690, E-mail: mlichbac@umd.edu. *Application contact:* Dean of Graduate School, 301-405-0358, Fax: 301-314-9305.

University of Massachusetts Amherst, Graduate School, College of Social and Behavioral Sciences, Department of Economics, Amherst, MA 01003. Offers MA, PhD. Part-time programs available. *Faculty:* 22 full-time (5 women). *Students:* 72 full-time (30 women), 13 part-time (7 women); includes 7 minority (1 African American, 1 Asian American or Pacific Islander, 5 Hispanic Americans), 44 international. Average age 32. 168 applicants, 16% accepted, 11 enrolled. In 2007, 7 master's, 5 doctorates awarded. Terminal master's awarded for partial completion of doctoral program. *Degree requirements:* For master's, thesis or alternative; for doctorate, thesis/dissertation. *Entrance requirements:* For master's and doctorate, GRE General Test. Additional exam requirements/recommendations for international students: Required—TOEFL (minimum score 530 paper-based; 197 computer-based). *Application deadline:* For fall admission, 1/15 priority date for domestic and international students. Applications are processed on a rolling basis. Application fee: $50 ($65 for international students). Electronic applications accepted. *Expenses:* Tuition, state resident: full-time $2,640; part-time $110 per credit. Tuition, nonresident: full-time $9,936; part-time $414 per credit. Required fees: $7,455. One-time fee: $332. Tuition and fees vary according to course load, campus/location, program and reciprocity agreements. *Financial support:* In 2007–08, 4 fellowships with full tuition reimbursements (averaging $7,237 per year), 3 research assistantships with full tuition reimbursements (averaging $3,250 per year), 60 teaching assistantships with full tuition reimbursements (averaging $8,471 per year) were awarded; career-related internships or fieldwork, Federal Work-Study, scholarships/grants, traineeships, and unspecified assistantships also available. Support available to part-time students. Financial award application deadline: 1/15. *Unit head:* Dr. Diane Flaherty, Chair, 413-545-3815, Fax: 413-545-2921, E-mail: chair@econs.umass.edu.

University of Massachusetts Lowell, College of Arts and Sciences, Department of Regional Economic and Social Development, Lowell, MA 01854-2881. Offers MA, Graduate Certificate. Part-time programs available. *Faculty:* 14 full-time (5 women). *Entrance requirements:* For master's, GRE. *Application deadline:* For fall admission, 4/1 priority date for domestic students; for spring admission, 10/1 priority date for domestic students. Applications are processed on a rolling basis. Application fee: $20 ($35 for international students). Electronic applications accepted. *Financial support:* Research assistantships with full tuition reimbursements, teaching assistantships with full tuition reimbursements, career-related internships or fieldwork, Federal Work-Study, institutionally sponsored loans, scholarships/grants, and traineeships available. Support available to part-time students. *Unit head:* Philip Moss, Chair, 978-934-2787, E-mail: philip_moss@uml.edu.

University of Memphis, Graduate School, Fogelman College of Business and Economics, Department of Economics, Memphis, TN 38152. Offers MA, PhD. Part-time programs available. *Faculty:* 8 full-time (0 women), 1 part-time/adjunct (0 women). *Students:* 4 full-time (1 woman), 3 part-time; includes 1 minority (African American), 3 international. Average age 27. 9 applicants, 56% accepted, 1 enrolled. In 2007, 16 degrees awarded. *Degree requirements:* For master's, comprehensive exam, thesis or alternative; for doctorate, comprehensive exam, thesis/dissertation. *Entrance requirements:* For master's, GMAT or GRE General Test, previous course work in statistics, intermediate micro and macro theory; for doctorate, GMAT, interview, minimum GPA of 3.4. *Application deadline:* For fall admission, 8/1 for domestic students; for spring admission, 12/1 for domestic students. Application fee: $35 ($60 for international students). *Expenses:* Tuition, state resident: full-time $6,990; part-time $377 per hour. Tuition, nonresident: full-time $17,818; part-time $830 per hour. Tuition and fees vary according to course load and program. *Financial support:* In 2007–08, 12 research assistantships with full tuition reimbursements (averaging $5,800 per year), 3 teaching assistantships with full tuition reimbursements (averaging $3,000 per year) were awarded; scholarships/grants also available. Financial award application deadline: 3/1. *Faculty research:* Tax research, medical economics, law and economics, labor economics, U.S. and Japanese economic relations. *Unit head:* Dr. Julia A. Heath, Chair, 901-678-2785, Fax: 901-678-8397, E-mail: jheath@cc.memphis.edu. *Application contact:* Dr. Pinaki Bose, Director of MBA Programs, 901-678-5528, Fax: 901-678-4705, E-mail: psbose@memphis.edu.

University of Memphis, Graduate School, Fogelman College of Business and Economics, Program in Business Administration, Memphis, TN 38152. Offers accounting (MBA, PhD); economics (MBA, PhD); executive business administration (MBA); finance (PhD); finance, insurance, and real estate (MBA, MS); international business administration (IMBA); management (MBA, MS, PhD); management information systems (MBA, MS, PhD); management science (MBA); marketing (MBA, MS); marketing and supply chain management (PhD); real estate development (MS); JD/MBA. *Accreditation:* AACSB. *Faculty:* 62 full-time (6 women), 69 part-time/adjunct (64 women). *Students:* 179 full-time (65 women), 175 part-time (58 women); includes 53 minority (35 African Americans, 14 Asian Americans or Pacific Islanders, 4 Hispanic Americans), 103 international. Average age 31. 346 applicants, 53% accepted, 111 enrolled. In 2007, 127 master's, 11 doctorates awarded. *Degree requirements:* For master's, comprehensive exam; for doctorate, comprehensive exam, thesis/dissertation. *Entrance requirements:* For master's, GMAT, resumé; for doctorate, GMAT, interview, minimum GPA of 3.4, resumé, letter of recommendation. Additional exam requirements/recommendations for international students: Required—TOEFL (minimum score 550 paper-based; 220 computer-based). *Application deadline:* For fall admission, 8/1 for domestic students; for spring admission, 12/1 for domestic students. Application fee: $35 ($60 for international students). *Expenses:* Tuition, state resident: full-time $6,990; part-time $377 per hour. Tuition, nonresident: full-time $17,818; part-time $830 per hour. Tuition and fees vary according to course load and program. *Financial support:* Research assistantships with full tuition reimbursements, teaching assistantships, career-related internships or fieldwork, scholarships/grants, and unspecified assistantships available. Financial award application deadline: 3/1. *Faculty research:* Competitive business strategy, finance microstructures, supply chain management innovations, health care economics, litigation risks and corporate audits. *Application contact:* Dr. Carol V. Danehower, Associate Dean for Programs, 901-678-5402, Fax: 901-678-3579, E-mail: fcbegp@memphis.edu.

University of Miami, Graduate School, School of Business Administration, Department of Economics, Coral Gables, FL 33124. Offers economic development (MA, PhD); environmental economics (PhD); human resource economics (MA, PhD); international economics (MA, PhD); macroeconomics (PhD). Students admitted every two years in the fall semester. *Faculty:* 13 full-time (7 women). *Students:* 10 full-time (4 women); includes 1 minority (African American), 7 international. Average age 32. 95 applicants, 14% accepted, 7 enrolled. In 2007, 1 master's, 4 doctorates awarded. Terminal master's awarded for partial completion of doctoral program. *Median time to degree:* Of those who began their doctoral program in fall 1999, 90% received their degree in 8 years or less. *Degree requirements:* For master's, comprehensive exam; for doctorate, comprehensive exam, thesis/dissertation. *Entrance requirements:* For master's and doctorate, GRE General Test, minimum GPA of 3.0. Additional exam requirements/recommendations for international students: Required—TOEFL (minimum score 550 paper-based). *Application deadline:* For fall admission, 3/1 for domestic and international students. Application fee: $50. *Financial support:* In 2007–08, 10 students received support, including fellowships with full tuition reimbursements available (averaging $20,000 per year), 4 research assistantships, 5 teaching assistantships with full tuition reimbursements available (averaging $3,500 per year); tuition waivers (partial) and unspecified assistantships also available. Financial award application deadline: 3/15. *Faculty research:* International economics/trade, applied microeconomics, development. Total annual research expenditures: $426,180. *Unit head:* Dr. David Kelly, Chairman, 305-284-3725, Fax: 305-284-2985, E-mail: dkelly@miami.edu.

University of Michigan, Horace H. Rackham School of Graduate Studies, College of Literature, Science, and the Arts, Department of Economics, Ann Arbor, MI 48109. Offers applied economics (AM); economics (AM, PhD); public policy and economics (PhD); social work and economics (PhD); JD/PhD; MPP/AM. *Faculty:* 56 full-time (9 women). *Students:* 147 full-time (50 women); includes 13 minority (4 African Americans, 6 Asian Americans or Pacific Islanders, 3 Hispanic Americans), 55 international. Average age 27. 519 applicants, 29% accepted, 30 enrolled. In 2007, 42 master's, 26 doctorates awarded. Terminal master's awarded for partial completion of doctoral program. *Median time to degree:* Of those who began their doctoral program in fall 1999, 38% received their degree in 8 years or less. *Degree requirements:* For doctorate, oral defense of dissertation, preliminary exam. *Entrance requirements:* For master's and doctorate, GRE General Test. Additional exam requirements/recommendations for international students: Required—TOEFL (minimum score 600 paper-based; 250 computer-based). *Application deadline:* For fall admission, 12/15 for domestic and international students. Application fee: $60 ($75 for international students). Electronic applications accepted. *Financial support:* In 2007–08, 114 students received support, including 46 fellowships with tuition reimbursements available (averaging $16,000 per year), 6 research assistantships with tuition reimbursements available (averaging $15,200 per year), 59 teaching assistantships with tuition reimbursements available (averaging $15,200 per year); career-related internships or fieldwork and traineeships also available. Financial award application deadline: 12/15. *Faculty research:* Economic and econometrical analysis, industrial organization, international trade, public finance, development, health, labor, population standard, macro, theory. *Unit head:* Prof. Linda Tesar, Chair, 734-763-2254, Fax: 734-764-2769, E-mail: ltesar@umich.edu. *Application contact:* Prof. David Lam, Director of Graduate Studies, 734-763-9237, Fax: 734-764-2769, E-mail: davidl@umich.edu.

University of Minnesota, Twin Cities Campus, Graduate School, College of Liberal Arts, Department of Economics, Minneapolis, MN 55455-0213. Offers PhD. *Faculty:* 27 full-time (4 women), 8 part-time/adjunct (1 woman). *Students:* 133 full-time (37 women); includes 2 minority (1 Asian American or Pacific Islander, 1 Hispanic American), 107 international. Average age 29. 372 applicants, 14% accepted, 24 enrolled. In 2007, 11 degrees awarded. *Degree requirements:* For doctorate, thesis/dissertation, preliminary exams. *Entrance requirements:* For doctorate, GRE General Test. Additional exam requirements/recommendations for international students: Required—TOEFL (minimum score 600 paper-based; 250 computer-based; 100 iBT), IELTS (minimum score 7). *Application deadline:* For fall admission, 12/31 priority date for domestic and international students. Application fee: $55 ($75 for international students). Electronic applications accepted. *Financial support:* In 2007–08, 98 students received support, including fellowships with full tuition reimbursements available (averaging $19,000 per year), research assistantships with full tuition reimbursements available (averaging $14,300 per year), teaching assistantships with full tuition reimbursements available (averaging $13,800 per year). Financial award application deadline: 12/31. *Faculty research:* Econometrics, macro- and monetary economics, mathematical economics, industrial organization, applied micro theory. *Unit head:* Larry Jones, Chair, 612-625-6353, Fax: 612-624-0209. *Application contact:* Timothy J. Kehoe, Director of Graduate Studies, 612-625-6833, Fax: 612-624-0209, E-mail: econdgs@econ.umn.edu.

University of Mississippi, Graduate School, College of Liberal Arts, Department of Economics, Oxford, University, MS 38677. Offers MA, PhD. *Faculty:* 12 full-time (2 women), 1 part-time/adjunct (0 women). *Students:* 19 full-time (9 women), 3 part-time (1 woman); includes 3 minority (all African Americans), 13 international. In 2007, 4 master's, 2 doctorates awarded. *Application deadline:* For fall admission, 4/1 for domestic students; for spring admission, 10/1 for domestic students. Applications are processed on a rolling basis. Electronic applications accepted. *Expenses:* Tuition, state resident: full-time $4,932. Tuition, nonresident: full-time $11,436. *Financial support:* Scholarships/grants available. Financial award applicants required to submit FAFSA. *Unit head:* Dr. Mark V. Van Boening, Interim Chair, 662-915-6942, Fax: 662-915-6943, E-mail: bmvan@olemiss.edu.

University of Missouri–Columbia, Graduate School, College of Arts and Sciences, Department of Economics, Columbia, MO 65211. Offers MA, PhD, JD/MA. Terminal master's awarded for partial completion of doctoral program. *Degree requirements:* For doctorate, thesis/dissertation. *Entrance requirements:* For master's and doctorate, GRE General Test, minimum GPA of 3.0.

University of Missouri–Kansas City, College of Arts and Sciences, Department of Economics, Kansas City, MO 64110-2499. Offers MA, PhD. PhD offered through the School of Graduate Studies. Part-time and evening/weekend programs available. *Faculty:* 11 full-time (1 woman), 4 part-time/adjunct (0 women). *Students:* 15 full-time (4 women), 12 part-time (3 women); includes 6 minority (4 African Americans, 2 Asian Americans or Pacific Islanders), 11 international. Average age 29. 30 applicants, 67% accepted, 7 enrolled. In 2007, 8 degrees awarded. *Degree requirements:* For doctorate, comprehensive exam, thesis/dissertation. *Entrance requirements:* For master's, GRE or minimum undergraduate GPA of 2.5; for doctorate, GRE, master's degree in economics or equivalent. Additional exam requirements/recommendations for international students: Required—TOEFL. *Application deadline:* For fall admission, 2/1 priority date for domestic and international students; for spring admission, 9/1 priority date for domestic and international students. Applications are processed on a rolling basis. Application fee: $35 ($50 for international students). Electronic applications accepted. *Expenses:* Tuition, state resident: part-time $287 per hour. Tuition, nonresident: part-time $741 per hour. Required fees: $31 per hour. Tuition and fees vary according to program. *Financial support:* In 2007–08, 19 teaching assistantships with tuition reimbursements (averaging $12,916 per year) were awarded; fellowships with tuition reimbursements, research assistantships with tuition reimbursements, career-related internships or fieldwork, Federal Work-Study, institutionally sponsored loans, and tuition waivers (full and partial) also available. Support available to part-time students. Financial award application deadline: 3/1; financial award applicants required to submit FAFSA. *Faculty research:* International trade, general theory, institutions/utilities, forensic economics, human resources. Total annual research expenditures: $240,338. *Unit head:* James Sturgeon, Chair, 816-235-2837, Fax: 816-238-2836, E-mail: sturgeonj@umkc.edu. *Application contact:* Fred Lee, Graduate Adviser, 816-235-2543, Fax: 816-238-2836, E-mail: leefs@umkc.edu.

University of Missouri–St. Louis, College of Arts and Sciences, Department of Economics, St. Louis, MO 63121. Offers general economics (MA), including business economics; managerial economics (Certificate). Part-time and evening/weekend programs available. *Faculty:* 10 full-time (3 women), 2 part-time/adjunct (1 woman). *Students:* 12 full-time (3 women), 7 part-time (5 women); includes 3 minority (1 African American, 1 Asian American or Pacific Islander, 1 Hispanic American), 6 international. Average age 27. In 2007, 6 degrees awarded. *Entrance requirements:* For master's, GRE General Test, 2 letters of recommendation. Additional exam requirements/recommendations for international students: Required—TOEFL (minimum score 550 paper-based; 213 computer-based). *Application deadline:* For fall admission, 7/1 priority date for domestic students; for spring admission, 12/1 priority date for domestic students. Applications are processed on a rolling basis. Application fee: $35 ($40 for international students). Electronic applications accepted. *Financial support:* In 2007–08, 7 research assistantships with full and partial tuition reimbursements (averaging $5,000 per year) were awarded; fellowships with full tuition reimbursements, teaching assistantships with full and partial tuition reimbursements also available. *Faculty research:* Health economics, public policy analysis, econometrics, public choice, telecommunications and forensic economics. *Unit head:* Dr. Donald Kridel, Director of Graduate Studies, 314-516-5351, Fax: 314-516-5562, E-mail: kridel@umsl.edu. *Application contact:* 314-516-5458, Fax: 314-516-6996, E-mail: gradadm@umsl.edu.

The University of Montana, Graduate School, College of Arts and Sciences, Department of Economics, Missoula, MT 59812-0002. Offers MA. *Degree requirements:* For master's, thesis. *Entrance requirements:* For master's, GRE General Test. Additional exam requirements/recommendations for international students: Required—TOEFL (minimum score 525 paper-based; 197 computer-based). *Faculty research:* Resource economics, public policy, environmental economics, economic development, regional economics.

University of Nebraska at Omaha, Graduate Studies and Research, College of Business Administration, Department of Economics, Omaha, NE 68182. Offers MA, MS. Part-time and evening/weekend programs available. *Faculty:* 10 full-time (2 women). *Students:* 38 full-time (18 women), 36 part-time (11 women); includes 4 minority (all African Americans), 39 international. Average age 32. 52 applicants, 54% accepted, 17 enrolled. In 2007, 13 degrees awarded. *Degree requirements:* For master's, comprehensive exam, thesis (for some programs). *Entrance requirements:* For master's, minimum GPA of 3.0. Additional exam requirements/recommendations for international students: Required—TOEFL (minimum score 530 paper-based; 197 computer-based; 71 iBT). *Application deadline:* For fall admission, 7/1 priority date for domestic students; for spring admission, 12/15 priority date for domestic students. Applications are processed on a rolling basis. Application fee: $45. Electronic applications accepted. *Financial support:* In 2007–08, 48 students received support; research assistantships with tuition reimbursements available, Federal Work-Study, institutionally sponsored loans, scholarships/grants, and unspecified assistantships available. Support available to part-time students. Financial award application deadline: 3/1; financial award applicants required to submit FAFSA. *Faculty research:* Labor, economics of science, international development, monetary economics, econometrics. *Unit head:* Dr. Donald Baum, Graduate Chair, 402-554-2570.

University of Nebraska–Lincoln, Graduate College, College of Business Administration, Department of Economics, Lincoln, NE 68588. Offers MA, PhD, JD/MA. *Degree requirements:* For master's, thesis optional; for doctorate, comprehensive exam, thesis/dissertation. *Entrance requirements:* For master's and doctorate, GRE General Test. Additional exam requirements/recommendations for international students: Required—TOEFL (minimum score 550 paper-based; 213 computer-based). Electronic applications accepted. *Faculty research:* Applied microeconomics, economic education, international trade and finance, public finance, regional and institutional economics.

University of Nevada, Las Vegas, Graduate College, College of Business, Department of Economics, Las Vegas, NV 89154-9900. Offers MA. Part-time and evening/weekend programs available. *Faculty:* 16 full-time (1 woman), 1 part-time/adjunct (0 women). *Students:* 14 full-time (4 women), 12 part-time (2 women); includes 6 minority (2 African Americans, 2 Asian Americans or Pacific Islanders, 2 Hispanic Americans), 3 international. 25 applicants, 64% accepted, 12 enrolled. In 2007, 6 degrees awarded. *Degree requirements:* For master's, thesis. *Entrance requirements:* For master's, GRE General Test or GMAT, minimum GPA of 3.0. Additional exam requirements/recommendations for international students: Required—TOEFL (minimum score 550 paper-based; 213 computer-based; 80 iBT). *Application deadline:* For fall admission, 6/15 for domestic students, 5/1 for international students; for spring admission, 11/15 for domestic students, 10/1 for international students. Application fee: $60 ($75 for international students). Electronic applications accepted. *Expenses:* Tuition, state resident: part-time $198 per credit. Tuition, nonresident: part-time $416 per credit. Required fees: $256 per semester. Tuition and fees vary according to course load and reciprocity agreements. *Financial support:* In 2007–08, 6 research assistantships with partial tuition reimbursements (averaging $10,000 per year), teaching assistantships with partial tuition reimbursements (averaging $10,000 per year) were awarded; career-related internships or fieldwork, Federal Work-Study, institutionally sponsored loans, scholarships/grants, health care benefits, and unspecified assistantships also available. Support available to part-time students. Financial award application deadline: 3/1. *Unit head:* Dr. Steve Miller, Chair, 702-895-3194. *Application contact:* Graduate College Admissions Evaluator, 702-895-3320, Fax: 702-895-4180, E-mail: gradcollege@unlv.edu.

University of Nevada, Reno, Graduate School, College of Business Administration, Department of Economics, Reno, NV 89557. Offers MA, MS. *Faculty:* 15. *Students:* 7 full-time (0 women), 18 part-time (14 women); includes 7 minority (1 American Indian/Alaska Native, 4 Asian Americans or Pacific Islanders, 2 Hispanic Americans), 4 international. Average age 29. 32 applicants, 50% accepted, 8 enrolled. In 2007, 13 degrees awarded. *Degree requirements:* For master's, thesis. *Entrance requirements:* For master's, GMAT or GRE, minimum GPA of 2.75. Additional exam requirements/recommendations for international students: Required—TOEFL. *Application deadline:* For fall admission, 4/15 priority date for domestic students; for spring admission, 10/15 for domestic students. Applications are processed on a rolling basis. Application fee: $60 ($95 for international students). *Expenses:* Tuition, state resident: full-time $2,774; part-time $154 per credit. Tuition, nonresident: full-time $13,578; part-time $330 per credit. Required fees: $49 per semester. *Financial support:* In 2007–08, 4 research assistantships, 1 teaching assistantship were awarded; Federal Work-Study and institutionally sponsored loans also available. Financial award application deadline: 3/1. *Faculty research:* Applied microeconomics, public finance, development, labor. *Unit head:* Dr. Frederico Guerro, Graduate Program Director, 775-784-6864.

University of New Brunswick Fredericton, School of Graduate Studies, Faculty of Arts, Department of Economics, Fredericton, NB E3B 5A3, Canada. Offers applied economics and finance (M Sc); economics (MA). Program in applied economics and finance offered at UNB Saint John Campus. Part-time programs available. *Faculty:* 14 full-time (1 woman). *Students:* 10 full-time (4 women), 1 (woman) part-time. Average age 23. 40 applicants, 65% accepted. In 2007, 4 degrees awarded. *Entrance requirements:* For master's, GRE, minimum GPA of 3.0. Additional exam requirements/recommendations for international students: Required—TWE, TOEFL (minimum paper-based score of 550) or IELTS. *Application deadline:* 1/31 for domestic and international students. Applications are processed on a rolling basis. Application fee: $50 Canadian dollars. *Financial support:* In 2007–08, 2 research assistantships, 2 teaching assistantships were awarded; fellowships, scholarships/grants, health care benefits, and unspecified assistantships also available. Financial award application deadline: 1/31. *Faculty research:* Epidemiology and Population Health, Micro/Macro Economics, Economics of Transportation, Regional Development. *Unit head:* Dr. Yuri Yevdokimov, Director of Graduate Studies, 506-447-3221, Fax: 506-453-4514, E-mail: yuri@unb.ca. *Application contact:* Melanie Lawson, Graduate Secretary, 506-458-7420, Fax: 506-453-4514, E-mail: melanie@unb.ca.

University of New Brunswick Fredericton, School of Graduate Studies, Policy Studies Program, Fredericton, NB E3B 5A3, Canada. Offers people, property and alternative dispute resolution (M Phil); philosophy politics and economics (M Phil); sustainable development (M Phil). *Faculty:* 6 full-time (2 women), 13 part-time/adjunct (2 women). *Students:* 13 full-time (8 women), 3 part-time (2 women). In 2007, 6 degrees awarded. *Entrance requirements:* For master's, minimum GPA of 3.5, BA. Additional exam requirements/recommendations for international students: Required—TOEFL (minimum score 600 paper-based), TWE (minimum score 5). Application fee: $50 Canadian dollars. *Financial support:* In 2007–08, 5 research assistantships, 2 teaching assistantships (averaging $4,400 per year) were awarded. *Unit head:* Dr. Gwen Davies, Dean of Graduate Studies, 506-458-7150, Fax: 506-453-4817, E-mail: daviesg@unb.ca. *Application contact:* Janet Amurault, Graduate Secretary, 506-458-7558, Fax: 506-453-4817, E-mail: jamiraul@unb.ca.

University of New Hampshire, Graduate School, Whittemore School of Business and Economics, Department of Economics, Durham, NH 03824. Offers MA, PhD. Part-time programs available. *Faculty:* 13 full-time. *Students:* 27 full-time (13 women), 4 part-time (1 woman), 12 international. Average age 35. 48 applicants, 90% accepted, 20 enrolled. In 2007, 7 master's, 2 doctorates awarded. Terminal master's awarded for partial completion of doctoral program. *Degree requirements:* For master's, thesis or alternative; for doctorate, one foreign language, thesis/dissertation. *Entrance requirements:* For master's and doctorate, GRE General Test. Additional exam requirements/recommendations for international students: Required—TOEFL (minimum score 550 paper-based; 213 computer-based; 80 iBT). *Application deadline:* For fall admission, 4/1 priority date for domestic students, 4/1 for international students. Applications are processed on a rolling basis. Application fee: $60. Electronic applications accepted. *Financial support:* In 2007–08, 4 research assistantships, 19 teaching assistantships were awarded; fellowships, career-related internships or fieldwork, Federal Work-Study, scholarships/grants, and tuition waivers (full and partial) also available. Support available to part-time students. Financial award application deadline: 2/15. *Faculty research:* Labor economics, international development, econometrics, finance, political economy. *Unit head:* Dr. Bruce Elmslie, Chair, 603-862-3347. *Application contact:* Sinthy Kounlasa, Administrative Assistant, 603-862-3457, E-mail: wsbe.grad@unh.edu.

See Close-Up on page 1041.

University of New Mexico, Graduate School, College of Arts and Sciences, Department of Economics, Albuquerque, NM 87131-2039. Offers MA, PhD. Part-time programs available. *Faculty:* 13 full-time (6 women), 6 part-time/adjunct (1 woman). *Students:* 45 full-time (13 women), 15 part-time (6 women); includes 15 minority (1 African American, 2 American Indian/Alaska Native, 2 Asian Americans or Pacific Islanders, 10 Hispanic Americans), 13 international. Average age 33. 68 applicants, 37% accepted, 16 enrolled. In 2007, 15 master's, 3 doctorates awarded. Terminal master's awarded for partial completion of doctoral program. *Degree requirements:* For master's, comprehensive exam, thesis or alternative; for doctorate, comprehensive exam, thesis/dissertation. *Entrance requirements:* For master's and doctorate, GRE General Test, 3 letters of recommendation, letter of intent. Additional exam requirements/recommendations for international students: Required—TOEFL (minimum score 550 paper-based; 213 computer-based). *Application deadline:* For fall admission, 3/7 priority date for domestic students; for spring admission, 8/1 for domestic students. Applications are processed on a rolling basis. Application fee: $50. Electronic applications accepted. *Financial support:* In 2007–08, 18 students received support, including 7 research assistantships with tuition reimbursements available (averaging $6,722 per year), 6 teaching assistantships (averaging $6,722 per year); fellowships with tuition reimbursements available, Federal Work-Study, scholarships/grants, health care benefits, and unspecified assistantships also available. Support available to part-time students. Financial award application deadline: 3/1; financial award applicants required to submit FAFSA. *Faculty research:* Public finance, international/development economics, labor/human resource economics, econometrics, core theory, environmental/natural resource economics. Total annual research expenditures: $468,596. *Unit head:* Dr. Philip Gandertah, Chair, 505-277-1962, Fax: 505-277-9445, E-mail: gandini@unm.edu. *Application contact:* Catherine Hart, Academic Advisor, 505-277-5304, Fax: 505-277-9445, E-mail: chart1@unm.edu.

University of New Orleans, Graduate School, College of Business Administration, Department of Economics and Finance, Program in Financial Economics, New Orleans, LA 70148. Offers PhD. *Faculty:* 12 full-time (2 women). *Students:* 32 full-time (6 women), 8 part-time (4 women); includes 6 minority (4 African Americans, 2 Asian Americans or Pacific Islanders), 21 international. Average age 33. 69 applicants, 78% accepted, 6 enrolled. In 2007, 4 degrees awarded. Terminal master's awarded for partial completion of doctoral program. *Degree requirements:* For doctorate, one foreign language, comprehensive exam, thesis/dissertation, general exams. *Entrance requirements:* For doctorate, GRE General Test, minimum GPA of 3.0. Additional exam requirements/recommendations for international students: Required—TOEFL (minimum score 550 paper-based; 213 computer-based; 79 iBT). *Application deadline:* For fall admission, 7/1 priority date for domestic students, 6/1 for international students; for spring admission, 11/15 priority date for domestic students, 10/1 for international students. Applications are processed on a rolling basis. Application fee: $20. Electronic applications accepted. *Financial support:* Fellowships, research assistantships, teaching assistantships, Federal Work-Study available. Financial award application deadline: 5/15; financial award applicants required to submit FAFSA. *Faculty research:* Urban and regional economics, economic development, monetary theory and policy, international finance. *Application contact:* Dr. Atsuyuki Naka, Graduate Coordinator, 504-280-6896, Fax: 504-280-6397, E-mail: anaka@uno.edu.

The University of North Carolina at Chapel Hill, Graduate School, College of Arts and Sciences, Department of Economics, Chapel Hill, NC 27599. Offers MS, PhD. Terminal master's awarded for partial completion of doctoral program. *Degree requirements:* For master's, comprehensive exam, thesis or alternative; for doctorate, comprehensive exam, thesis/dissertation. *Entrance requirements:* For master's, GRE General Test, minimum GPA of 3.0; for doctorate, GRE General Test, minimum GPA of 3.5. Additional exam requirements/recommendations for international students: Required—TOEFL (minimum score 550 paper-based; 213 computer-based). Electronic applications accepted. *Faculty research:* Health economics, micro theory/IO, labor economics, economic history, financial econometrics.

The University of North Carolina at Charlotte, Graduate School, Belk College of Business Administration, Department of Economics, Charlotte, NC 28223-0001. Offers MS. Part-time and evening/weekend programs available. *Faculty:* 17 full-time (4 women), 1 part-time/adjunct (0 women). *Students:* 19 full-time (9 women), 14 part-time (7 women); includes 7 minority (1 African American, 4 Asian Americans or Pacific Islanders, 2 Hispanic Americans), 12 international. Average age 27. 36 applicants, 92% accepted, 23 enrolled. In 2007, 11 degrees awarded. *Degree requirements:* For master's, thesis or project. *Entrance requirements:* For master's, GRE General Test, minimum undergraduate GPA of 3.0 in major, 2.8 overall. Additional exam requirements/recommendations for international students: Required—TOEFL (minimum score 557 paper-based; 220 computer-based). *Application deadline:* For fall admission, 7/15 for domestic students, 5/1 for international students; for spring admission, 11/15 for domestic students, 10/1 for international students. Applications are processed on a rolling basis. Application fee: $55. Electronic applications accepted. *Expenses:* Tuition, state resident: full-time $2,855. Tuition, nonresident: full-time $13,062. Required fees: $1,692. *Financial support:* In 2007–08, 1 fellowship (averaging $10,000 per year), 18 teaching assistantships (averaging $8,000 per year) were awarded; research assistantships, career-related internships or fieldwork, Federal Work-Study, institutionally sponsored loans, scholarships/grants, and unspecified assistantships also available. Support available to part-time students. Financial award application deadline: 4/1; financial award applicants required to submit FAFSA. *Faculty research:* Health care, taxation, energy, economic growth, monetary policy. *Unit head:* Dr. Richard A. Zuber, Chair, 704-687-2185, Fax: 704-687-6442, E-mail: razuber@emial.uncc.edu. *Application contact:* Kathy B. Giddings, Director of Graduate Admissions, 704-687-3366, Fax: 704-687-3279, E-mail: agidding@uncc.edu.

The University of North Carolina at Greensboro, Graduate School, Bryan School of Business and Economics, Department of Economics, Program in Economics, Greensboro, NC 27412-

Economics

The University of North Carolina at Greensboro (continued)

5001. Offers PhD. *Students:* 7 full-time (0 women), 2 part-time. Average age 40. *Degree requirements:* For doctorate, comprehensive exam, thesis/dissertation. *Entrance requirements:* Additional exam requirements/recommendations for international students: Required—TOEFL. *Application deadline:* For fall admission, 3/1 priority date for domestic and international students; for spring admission, 11/1 for domestic students, 10/1 priority date for international students. Applications are processed on a rolling basis. Application fee: $45. Electronic applications accepted. *Financial support:* In 2007–08, 4 students received support; fellowships with partial tuition reimbursements available, research assistantships with partial tuition reimbursements available available. Financial award application deadline: 3/1. *Application contact:* Michelle Harkleroad, Director of Graduate Admissions, 336-334-4884, Fax: 336-334-4424, E-mail: mbharkle@uncg.edu.

University of North Texas, Robert B. Toulouse School of Graduate Studies, College of Arts and Sciences, Department of Economics, Denton, TX 76203. Offers economic research (MS); economics (MA, MS); labor and industrial relations (MS). Part-time programs available. *Faculty:* 16 full-time (7 women). *Students:* 32 full-time (11 women), 11 part-time (3 women); includes 6 minority (2 African Americans, 1 Asian American or Pacific Islander, 3 Hispanic Americans), 19 international. Average age 28. 26 applicants, 73% accepted, 9 enrolled. In 2007, 4 degrees awarded. *Degree requirements:* For master's, comprehensive exam, thesis (for some programs). *Entrance requirements:* For master's, GMAT, GRE General Test, 3.0 GPA, 2 letters of recommendation, 500 word essay. Additional exam requirements/recommendations for international students: Required—proof of English language proficiency required for non-native English speakers; Recommended—TOEFL (minimum score 550 paper-based; 213 computer-based). *Application deadline:* For fall admission, 7/15 for domestic students; for spring admission, 11/15 for domestic students. Application fee: $50 ($75 for international students). *Financial support:* In 2007–08, 3 fellowships with partial tuition reimbursements (averaging $10,740 per year), 9 research assistantships with partial tuition reimbursements (averaging $9,060 per year), 5 teaching assistantships with partial tuition reimbursements (averaging $9,060 per year) were awarded; career-related internships or fieldwork, Federal Work-Study, and institutionally sponsored loans also available. Support available to part-time students. Financial award application deadline: 4/1. *Faculty research:* Resource economics, international trade and development, immigration, telecommunications, micro enterprise development. Total annual research expenditures: $150,000. *Unit head:* Dr. Steven L. Cobb, Chair, 940-565-2573, Fax: 940-565-4426, E-mail: cobb@econ.unt.edu. *Application contact:* Dr. Margie A. Tieslau, Graduate Adviser, 940-565-3442, Fax: 940-565-4426, E-mail: tieslau@unt.edu.

University of Notre Dame, Graduate School, College of Arts and Letters, Division of Social Science, Department of Economics and Econometrics, Notre Dame, IN 46556. Offers MA, PhD. *Students:* 21 full-time (6 women); includes 2 minority (1 African American, 1 Asian American or Pacific Islander), 8 international. 107 applicants, 13% accepted, 7 enrolled. In 2007, 4 degrees awarded. Terminal master's awarded for partial completion of doctoral program. *Degree requirements:* For master's, comprehensive exam (for some programs), thesis optional; for doctorate, thesis/dissertation, candidacy exam. *Entrance requirements:* For doctorate, GRE General Test. Additional exam requirements/recommendations for international students: Required—TOEFL (minimum score 600 paper-based; 250 computer-based; 80 iBT). *Application deadline:* For fall admission, 1/15 priority date for domestic and international students. Application fee: $50. Electronic applications accepted. *Financial support:* In 2007–08, fellowships (averaging $22,000 per year), 16 teaching assistantships (averaging $16,000 per year) were awarded. Financial award application deadline: 1/15. *Unit head:* Dr. Kali Rath, Director of Graduate Studies, 574-631-7698, Fax: 574-631-4783, E-mail: ecoe@nd.edu. *Application contact:* Dr. Jarren Gonzales, Director of Graduate Admissions, 574-631-7706, Fax: 574-631-4183.

University of Oklahoma, Graduate College, College of Arts and Sciences, Department of Economics, Norman, OK 73019-0390. Offers MA, PhD. Part-time programs available. Postbaccalaureate distance learning degree programs offered (no on-campus study). *Faculty:* 17 full-time (4 women), 5 part-time/adjunct (2 women). *Students:* 36 full-time (9 women), 72 part-time (12 women); includes 22 minority (8 African Americans, 1 American Indian/Alaska Native, 8 Asian Americans or Pacific Islanders, 5 Hispanic Americans), 18 international. 52 applicants, 88% accepted, 25 enrolled. In 2007, 38 master's, 4 doctorates awarded. Terminal master's awarded for partial completion of doctoral program. *Degree requirements:* For doctorate, 2 foreign languages, thesis/dissertation, general exams. *Entrance requirements:* For master's, GRE General Test, minimum GPA of 3.0 in last 60 hours of course work; for doctorate, GRE General Test. Additional exam requirements/recommendations for international students: Required—TOEFL (minimum score 550 paper-based; 213 computer-based). *Application deadline:* For fall admission, 4/1 for domestic and international students; for spring admission, 9/1 for domestic and international students. Applications are processed on a rolling basis. Application fee: $40 ($90 for international students). Electronic applications accepted. *Expenses:* Tuition, state resident: full-time $3,451; part-time $144 per credit hour. Tuition, nonresident: full-time $12,432; part-time $518 per credit hour. Required fees: $1,925; $70 per credit hour. $122 per semester. *Financial support:* In 2007–08, 20 teaching assistantships with partial tuition reimbursements (averaging $13,144 per year) were awarded; research assistantships, scholarships/grants, health care benefits, tuition waivers (partial), unspecified assistantships, and opportunities for extra teaching to earn money also available. Financial award applicants required to submit FAFSA. *Faculty research:* Industrial organization, international/macro economics; growth and development; public finance. Total annual research expenditures: $29,995. *Unit head:* Dr. Lex Holmes, Chair, 405-325-2861, Fax: 405-325-5842, E-mail: aholmes@ou.edu. *Application contact:* Cynthia Rogers, Graduate Liaison, 405-235-5843, Fax: 405-325-5842, E-mail: crogers@ou.edu.

University of Oregon, Graduate School, College of Arts and Sciences, Department of Economics, Eugene, OR 97403. Offers MA, MS, PhD. *Faculty:* 14 full-time (2 women), 2 part-time/adjunct (0 women). *Students:* 41 full-time (10 women), 3 part-time; includes 1 minority (Hispanic American), 16 international. 84 applicants, 56% accepted. In 2007, 22 master's, 5 doctorates awarded. Terminal master's awarded for partial completion of doctoral program. *Degree requirements:* For master's, thesis or alternative; for doctorate, thesis/dissertation, qualifying exam. *Entrance requirements:* For master's and doctorate, GRE General Test, minimum GPA of 3.0. Additional exam requirements/recommendations for international students: Required—TOEFL. *Application deadline:* For fall admission, 7/15 for domestic students; for winter admission, 10/15 for domestic students; for spring admission, 1/15 for domestic students. Application fee: $50. *Financial support:* In 2007–08, 24 teaching assistantships were awarded. Financial award application deadline: 3/15. *Faculty research:* Labor economics, macroeconomics, international economics, industrial organization, public finance. *Unit head:* Larry Singell, Head, 541-346-4672. *Application contact:* Georgette Winther, Admissions Contact, 541-346-1261, Fax: 541-346-1243, E-mail: gwinther@uoregon.edu.

University of Ottawa, Faculty of Graduate and Postdoctoral Studies, Faculty of Social Sciences, Department of Economics, Ottawa, ON K1N 6N5, Canada. Offers MA, PhD. Part-time programs available. *Degree requirements:* For master's, thesis or alternative; for doctorate, comprehensive exam, thesis/dissertation. *Entrance requirements:* For master's, honors bachelor's degree or equivalent, minimum B average; for doctorate, master's degree, minimum B+ average. Electronic applications accepted. *Faculty research:* Public economics, industrial organizations, monetary economics, international economics, economic development.

University of Pennsylvania, School of Arts and Sciences, Graduate Group in Economics, Philadelphia, PA 19104. Offers AM, PhD, JD/AM, JD/PhD. *Degree requirements:* For doctorate, thesis/dissertation. *Entrance requirements:* For doctorate, GRE General Test. Additional exam requirements/recommendations for international students: Required—TOEFL. Electronic applications accepted. *Faculty research:* Economic theory, econometrics, international economics, monetary/macroeconomics, applied microeconomics, empirical microeconomics.

University of Pittsburgh, Graduate School of Public and International Affairs, Doctoral Program in Public and International Affairs, Pittsburgh, PA 15260. Offers development policy (PhD); foreign and security policy (PhD); international political economy (PhD); public administration (PhD); public policy (PhD). *Accreditation:* NASPAA. Part-time programs available. *Faculty:* 34 full-time (10 women), 18 part-time/adjunct (6 women). *Students:* 39 full-time (15 women), 8 part-time (6 women); includes 6 minority (2 African Americans, 3 Asian Americans or Pacific Islanders, 1 Hispanic American), 10 international. Average age 30. 61 applicants, 30% accepted, 11 enrolled. In 2007, 8 degrees awarded. *Degree requirements:* For doctorate, comprehensive exam, thesis/dissertation. *Entrance requirements:* For doctorate, GRE, 3 letters of recommendation, resumé, minimum GPA of 3.0, writing sample. Additional exam requirements/recommendations for international students: Required—TOEFL (minimum score 600 paper-based; 250 computer-based; 100 iBT), TWE (minimum score 4); Recommended—IELTS (minimum score 7). *Application deadline:* For fall admission, 2/1 for domestic students, 1/15 for international students. Application fee: $50. Electronic applications accepted. *Financial support:* In 2007–08, 13 students received support, including 13 fellowships (averaging $28,580 per year); scholarships/grants and unspecified assistantships also available. Financial award application deadline: 2/1. *Faculty research:* International political economy, international development, public administration, public policy, foreign policy, international security policy. Total annual research expenditures: $845,025. *Unit head:* Dr. Phyllis Coontz, Doctoral Program Coordinator, 412-648-2654, Fax: 412-648-2605, E-mail: pcoontz@gspia.pitt.edu. *Application contact:* Jessica L. Hatherill, Associate Director of Student Services, 412-648-7640, Fax: 412-648-7641, E-mail: hatherill@gspia.pitt.edu.

See Close-Up on page 1645.

University of Pittsburgh, Graduate School of Public and International Affairs, International Affairs Division, Program in Global Political Economy, Pittsburgh, PA 15260. Offers MPIA, JD/MPIA, MBA/MPIA, MID/MPIA, MPA/MPIA, MSIS/MPIA. Part-time and evening/weekend programs available. *Faculty:* 34 full-time (10 women), 18 part-time/adjunct (6 women). *Students:* 21 full-time (12 women), 9 part-time (5 women); includes 3 minority (1 African American, 2 Asian Americans or Pacific Islanders), 5 international. Average age 25. 55 applicants, 87% accepted, 15 enrolled. In 2007, 63 degrees awarded. *Degree requirements:* For master's, thesis optional, internship, capstone seminar. *Entrance requirements:* For master's, GRE General Test, 3 letters of recommendation, resumé, minimum GPA of 3.2 . Additional exam requirements/recommendations for international students: Required—TOEFL (minimum score 550 paper-based; 213 computer-based; 80 iBT), TWE (minimum score 4); Recommended—IELTS (minimum score 7). *Application deadline:* For fall admission, 2/1 for domestic students, 1/15 for international students; for spring admission, 11/1 for domestic students, 8/1 for international students. Application fee: $50. Electronic applications accepted. *Financial support:* In 2007–08, 41 students received support, including 41 fellowships (averaging $8,280 per year); career-related internships or fieldwork, scholarships/grants, and unspecified assistantships also available. Financial award application deadline: 2/1. *Faculty research:* Political economy, international security/defense/intelligence, transnational crime, international trade, international finance, terrorism. Total annual research expenditures: $845,025. *Application contact:* Michael Rizzi, Graduate Enrollment Counselor, 412-648-7643, Fax: 412-648-7641, E-mail: rizzim@pitt.edu.

University of Pittsburgh, School of Arts and Sciences, Department of Economics, Pittsburgh, PA 15260. Offers PhD. Part-time programs available. *Faculty:* 22 full-time (3 women), 1 (woman) part-time/adjunct. *Students:* 49 full-time (20 women); includes 30 minority (2 African Americans, 23 Asian Americans or Pacific Islanders, 5 Hispanic Americans). Average age 24. 200 applicants, 15% accepted. In 2007, 9 degrees awarded. Terminal master's awarded for partial completion of doctoral program. *Median time to degree:* Of those who began their doctoral program in fall 1999, 36% received their degree in 8 years or less. *Degree requirements:* For doctorate, comprehensive exam, thesis/dissertation, PhD Comprehensive Research Paper. *Entrance requirements:* For doctorate, GRE, 3 letters of recommendation, transcripts. Additional exam requirements/recommendations for international students: Required—TOEFL (minimum score 550 paper-based; 213 computer-based; 80 iBT), IELTS (minimum score 7). *Application deadline:* For fall admission, 1/15 for domestic and international students. Applications are processed on a rolling basis. Application fee: $50. Electronic applications accepted. *Financial support:* In 2007–08, 41 students received support, including 11 fellowships with full tuition reimbursements available (averaging $17,162 per year), 5 research assistantships with full tuition reimbursements available (averaging $15,070 per year), 25 teaching assistantships with full tuition reimbursements available (averaging $14,485 per year); institutionally sponsored loans, scholarships/grants, traineeships, health care benefits, tuition waivers (full), and unspecified assistantships also available. Financial award application deadline: 1/15. *Faculty research:* Game theory, experimental economics, regional economics, labor, international trade. Total annual research expenditures: $1.5 million. *Unit head:* Dr. David N. De Jong, Department Chair, 412-648-2242, Fax: 41-648-7038, E-mail: dejong@pitt.edu. *Application contact:* Amy M. Linn, Graduate Administrator, 412-648-1399, Fax: 412-648-1793, E-mail: amlinn@pitt.edu.

University of Puerto Rico, Río Piedras, College of Social Sciences, Department of Economics, San Juan, PR 00931-3300. Offers MA. Part-time programs available. *Students:* 27 full-time (15 women), 23 part-time (10 women). Average age 29. In 2007, 7 degrees awarded. *Degree requirements:* For master's, comprehensive exam, thesis. *Entrance requirements:* For master's, GRE, PAEG, interview, minimum GPA of 3.0, letter of recommendation. *Application deadline:* For fall admission, 2/1 for domestic and international students. Application fee: $17. *Expenses:* Tuition, state resident: full-time $1,808; part-time $113 per credit. Tuition, nonresident: full-time $5,248; part-time $328 per credit. Required fees: $72 per term. *Financial support:* Fellowships, research assistantships, teaching assistantships, Federal Work-Study, institutionally sponsored loans, and tuition waivers (partial) available. Financial award application deadline: 5/31. *Unit head:* Dr. Erresho Rodriguez-Rodriguez, Director, 787-764-0000 Ext. 2459. *Application contact:* Administrative Officer, 787-764-0000 Ext. 4167.

University of Regina, Faculty of Graduate Studies and Research, Johnson-Shoyama Graduate School of Public Policy, Regina, SK S4S 0A2, Canada. Offers economic analysis for public policy (Master's Certificate); non-profit management (Master's Certificate); public management (MPA, Master's Certificate); public policy (MPA, PhD, Master's Certificate). Part-time and evening/weekend programs available. *Faculty:* 6 full-time (3 women). *Students:* 60 full-time (30 women), 53 part-time (37 women). 104 applicants, 86% accepted. In 2007, 9 degrees awarded. *Entrance requirements:* Additional exam requirements/recommendations for international students: Required—TOEFL (minimum score 580 paper-based; 237 computer-based; 88 iBT). *Application deadline:* Applications are processed on a rolling basis. Application fee: $85 ($100 for international students). Electronic applications accepted. *Expenses:* Contact institution. *Financial support:* In 2007–08, 13 fellowships (averaging $15,750 per year), 1 research assistantship (averaging $13,875 per year), 7 teaching assistantships (averaging $13,060 per year) were awarded. Financial award application deadline: 6/15. *Faculty research:* Public administration and policy. *Unit head:* Dr. Ken Rasmussen, Associate Dean, 306-585-5463, E-mail: ken.rasmussen@uregina.ca. *Application contact:* Devon Anderson, Information Contact, 306-585-5462, E-mail: devon.anderson@uregina.ca.

University of Rhode Island, Graduate School, College of the Environment and Life Sciences, Department of Environmental and Natural Resource Economics, Kingston, RI 02881. Offers MS, PhD. In 2007, 15 master's, 1 doctorate awarded. *Degree requirements:* For master's, thesis optional; for doctorate, thesis/dissertation. *Entrance requirements:* For master's and doctorate, GRE General Test. Additional exam requirements/recommendations for international students: Required—TOEFL. *Application deadline:* For fall admission, 4/15 priority date for domestic students. Applications are processed on a rolling basis. *Expenses:* Tuition, state resident: full-time $6,936; part-time $385 per credit. Tuition, nonresident: full-time $19,044; part-time $1,058 per credit. Required fees: $1,508; $48 per credit. $30 per semester. One-time fee: $80 part-time. *Unit head:* Dr. James Anderson, Chairperson, 401-874-4568.

Economics

University of Rochester, The College, Arts and Sciences, Department of Economics, Rochester, NY 14627-0250. Offers MA, PhD. *Degree requirements:* For doctorate, thesis/dissertation, qualifying exam. *Entrance requirements:* For doctorate, GRE General Test, GRE Subject Test (strongly recommended). Additional exam requirements/recommendations for international students: Required—TOEFL.

University of San Francisco, College of Arts and Sciences, Department of Economics, San Francisco, CA 94117-1080. Offers economics (MA); financial analysis (MS); international and development economics (MA). Part-time and evening/weekend programs available. *Faculty:* 8 full-time (1 woman), 6 part-time/adjunct (0 women). *Students:* 171 full-time (87 women), 13 part-time (3 women); includes 36 minority (2 African Americans, 27 Asian Americans or Pacific Islanders, 7 Hispanic Americans), 77 international. Average age 28. 499 applicants, 74% accepted, 108 enrolled. In 2007, 73 degrees awarded. *Degree requirements:* For master's, comprehensive exam, thesis or alternative. *Entrance requirements:* For master's, GRE General Test (recommended), BA in economics (preferred). Additional exam requirements/recommendations for international students: Required—TOEFL. *Application deadline:* For fall admission, 7/15 priority date for domestic students; for spring admission, 12/15 for domestic students. Applications are processed on a rolling basis. Application fee: $55 ($65 for international students). *Expenses:* Tuition: Part-time $1,005 per unit. Tuition and fees vary according to degree level, campus/location and program. *Financial support:* In 2007–08, 138 students received support; fellowships, teaching assistantships, career-related internships or fieldwork available. Financial award application deadline: 3/2; financial award applicants required to submit FAFSA. *Faculty research:* Economic development, forecasting and planning, labor markets, Pacific Rim, financial markets. *Unit head:* John Veitch, Chair, 415-422-6784, Fax: 415-422-5784.

University of San Francisco, Masagung Graduate School of Management, Program in Business Administration, San Francisco, CA 94117-1080. Offers business economics (MBA); e-business (MBA); entrepreneurship (MBA); finance (MBA); international business (MBA); management (MBA); marketing (MBA); telecommunications management and policy (MBA); JD/MBA; MSN/MBA. *Accreditation:* AACSB. *Faculty:* 19 full-time (3 women), 16 part-time/adjunct (4 women). *Students:* 236 full-time (103 women), 54 part-time (29 women); includes 63 minority (7 African Americans, 40 Asian Americans or Pacific Islanders, 16 Hispanic Americans), 88 international. Average age 28. 459 applicants, 62% accepted, 128 enrolled. In 2007, 106 degrees awarded. *Entrance requirements:* For master's, GMAT, minimum undergraduate GPA of 3.2. Additional exam requirements/recommendations for international students: Required—TOEFL. *Application deadline:* For fall admission, 7/1 priority date for domestic students; for spring admission, 11/30 for domestic students. Applications are processed on a rolling basis. Application fee: $55 ($65 for international students). *Expenses:* Tuition: Part-time $1,005 per unit. Tuition and fees vary according to degree level, campus/location and program. *Financial support:* In 2007–08, 132 students received support; fellowships available. Financial award application deadline: 3/2; financial award applicants required to submit FAFSA. *Faculty research:* International financial markets, technology transfer licensing, international marketing, strategic planning. Total annual research expenditures: $50,000. *Unit head:* Carol Langlois, Director, 415-422-6314, Fax: 415-422-2502.

University of Saskatchewan, College of Graduate Studies and Research, College of Arts and Sciences, Department of Economics, Saskatoon, SK S7N 5A2, Canada. Offers MA. *Degree requirements:* For master's, thesis (for some programs). *Entrance requirements:* Additional exam requirements/recommendations for international students: Required—TOEFL.

University of South Africa, College of Economic and Management Sciences, Pretoria, South Africa. Offers accounting (D Admin, D Com); accounting science (DA); auditing (D Admin, D Com); business administration (M Tech); business economics (D Admin); business leadership (DBL); business management (D Admin, D Com); economic management analysis (M Tech); economics (D Admin, D Com, PhD); human resource development (M Tech); industrial psychology (D Admin, D Com, PhD); logistics (D Com); marketing (M Tech); public administration (D Admin, D Com, DPA, PhD); public management (M Tech); quantitative management (D Admin, D Com); real estate (M Tech); statistics (D Admin, PhD); tourism management (D Admin, D Com); transport economics (D Admin, D Com).

University of South Carolina, The Graduate School, Moore School of Business, Economics Program, Columbia, SC 29208. Offers MA, PhD, JD/MA. *Faculty:* 94 full-time (18 women), 33 part-time/adjunct (5 women). *Students:* 7 full-time (2 women), 4 part-time (1 woman); includes 2 minority (both African Americans), 3 international. Average age 25. 69 applicants, 38% accepted, 10 enrolled. In 2007, 3 master's awarded. *Degree requirements:* For master's, comprehensive exam (for some programs), thesis; for doctorate, comprehensive exam, thesis/dissertation, qualifying exam. *Entrance requirements:* For master's, GMAT or GRE General Test, minimum GPA of 3.0; for doctorate, GRE General Test. Additional exam requirements/recommendations for international students: Required—TOEFL (minimum score 600 paper-based; 250 computer-based; 100 iBT). *Application deadline:* For fall admission, 1/15 priority date for domestic and international students. Applications are processed on a rolling basis. Application fee: $40. Electronic applications accepted. *Financial support:* In 2007–08, 12 students received support, including 4 fellowships with full tuition reimbursements available (averaging $2,000 per year), 5 research assistantships with full tuition reimbursements available (averaging $15,500 per year), 3 teaching assistantships with full tuition reimbursements available (averaging $15,500 per year); Federal Work-Study, institutionally sponsored loans, tuition waivers (partial), and unspecified assistantships also available. Financial award application deadline: 12/1. *Faculty research:* Monetary theory, labor economics, international economics, industrial organization. *Unit head:* Dr. Randolph C. Martin, Chairperson, 803-777-4356, Fax: 803-777-6876, E-mail: rmartin@moore.sc.edu. *Application contact:* Dr. Melayne M. McInnes, Academic Director, 803-777-6087, Fax: 803-777-3176, E-mail: mcinnes@moore.sc.edu.

University of Southern California, Graduate School, College of Letters, Arts and Sciences, Department of Economics, Program in Economic Development Programming, Los Angeles, CA 90089. Offers MA. Part-time and evening/weekend programs available. *Faculty:* 2 full-time (0 women). *Students:* 1 (woman) full-time, 1 international. 7 applicants, 43% accepted.Terminal master's awarded for partial completion of doctoral program. *Degree requirements:* For master's, thesis. *Entrance requirements:* For master's, GRE General Test. *Application deadline:* For fall admission, 4/15 for domestic students; for spring admission, 11/1 for domestic students. Applications are processed on a rolling basis. Application fee: $85. *Financial support:* Application deadline: 2/15. *Application contact:* Morgan Ponder, Information Contact, 213-740-2311.

University of Southern California, Graduate School, College of Letters, Arts and Sciences, Department of Economics, Programs in Economics, Los Angeles, CA 90089. Offers MA, PhD. *Students:* 85 full-time (34 women), 3 part-time (1 woman); includes 3 minority (2 Asian Americans or Pacific Islanders, 1 Hispanic American), 75 international. 252 applicants, 37% accepted. In 2007, 25 master's, 11 doctorates awarded. *Degree requirements:* For doctorate, thesis/dissertation. *Entrance requirements:* For master's and doctorate, GRE General Test. Application fee: $85. *Financial support:* Application deadline: 2/15. *Faculty research:* Economics organization and law, economic development, econometrics, theory, dynamic. *Application contact:* Morgan Ponder, Information Contact, 213-740-2311.

University of Southern Mississippi, Graduate School, College of Science and Technology, Department of Economic and Workforce Development, Hattiesburg, MS 39406-0001. Offers economic development (MS); human capital development (PhD); workforce training and development (MS). Part-time programs available. *Faculty:* 7 full-time (3 women), 1 (woman) part-time/adjunct. *Students:* 30 full-time (18 women), 23 part-time (10 women); includes 16 minority (all African Americans), 3 international. Average age 36. 32 applicants, 69% accepted, 20 enrolled. In 2007, 9 master's, 3 doctorates awarded. *Degree requirements:* For master's, comprehensive exam, thesis optional, internships; for doctorate, comprehensive exam, thesis/dissertation. *Entrance requirements:* For master's, GMAT, GRE General Test, minimum GPA of 2.75 in last 60 hours; for doctorate, GMAT, GRE General Test, minimum GPA of 3.5. Additional exam requirements/recommendations for international students: Required—TOEFL. *Application deadline:* For fall admission, 8/1 for domestic students, 3/1 for international students; for spring admission, 1/3 for domestic and international students. Application fee: $30. Electronic applications accepted. *Financial support:* In 2007–08, 11 students received support, including 5 research assistantships with full tuition reimbursements available (averaging $10,724 per year), 1 teaching assistantship with full tuition reimbursement available (averaging $10,724 per year); career-related internships or fieldwork and Federal Work-Study also available. Financial award application deadline: 3/1. *Faculty research:* Economic development, international studies, geography. *Unit head:* Dr. Kenneth Malone, Chair, 601-266-4736, Fax: 601-266-6071, E-mail: ken.malone@usm.edu. *Application contact:* Dr. Cyndi Gaudet, Graduate Coordinator, 601-266-6519, Fax: 601-266-6071.

University of South Florida, Graduate School, College of Business Administration, Department of Economics, Tampa, FL 33620-9951. Offers MA, PhD. Part-time and evening/weekend programs available. *Faculty:* 12 full-time (1 woman), 2 part-time/adjunct (0 women). *Students:* 13 full-time (4 women), 18 part-time (7 women); includes 6 minority (all Hispanic Americans), 3 international. Average age 30. 30 applicants, 63% accepted, 11 enrolled. In 2007, 12 degrees awarded. *Degree requirements:* For master's, comprehensive exam; for doctorate, comprehensive exam, thesis/dissertation. *Entrance requirements:* For master's, GMAT, minimum GPA of 3.0 in last 60 hours of course work. Additional exam requirements/recommendations for international students: Required—TOEFL (minimum score 550 paper-based; 213 computer-based). *Application deadline:* For fall admission, 12/1 for domestic students. Applications are processed on a rolling basis. Application fee: $30. *Financial support:* Unspecified assistantships available. Support available to part-time students. Financial award application deadline: 2/1; financial award applicants required to submit FAFSA. Total annual research expenditures: $145,178. *Unit head:* Dr. Kwabena Gyimah-Brempong, Chairperson, 813-974-4252, Fax: 813-974-6510, E-mail: kgyimah@coba.usf.edu. *Application contact:* Lisa Gibert, Graduate Programs Secretary, 813-974-4252, Fax: 813-974-6510, E-mail: econgrad@coba.usf.edu.

The University of Tampa, John H. Sykes College of Business, Tampa, FL 33606-1490. Offers accounting (MBA, MS); economics (MBA); entrepreneurship (MBA); finance (MBA, MS); information systems management (MBA); innovation management (MS); international business (MBA); management (MBA); marketing (MBA, MS). *Accreditation:* AACSB. Part-time and evening/weekend programs available. *Faculty:* 42 full-time (11 women), 6 part-time/adjunct (2 women). *Students:* 158 full-time (63 women), 400 part-time (158 women); includes 80 minority (16 African Americans, 1 American Indian/Alaska Native, 18 Asian Americans or Pacific Islanders, 45 Hispanic Americans), 86 international. Average age 31. 392 applicants, 74% accepted, 201 enrolled. In 2007, 176 degrees awarded. *Entrance requirements:* For master's, GMAT. Additional exam requirements/recommendations for international students: Required—TOEFL (minimum score 577 paper-based; 230 computer-based; 90 iBT). *Application deadline:* For fall admission, 7/15 for domestic students, 6/1 for international students; for spring admission, 12/15 for domestic students, 11/1 for international students. Applications are processed on a rolling basis. Application fee: $40. Electronic applications accepted. *Expenses:* Tuition: Part-time $450 per credit hour. Required fees: $35 per semester. *Financial support:* In 2007–08, 50 students received support, including 50 research assistantships with tuition reimbursements available (averaging $3,000 per year); career-related internships or fieldwork and unspecified assistantships also available. Support available to part-time students. Financial award applicants required to submit FAFSA. *Faculty research:* Industrial organization and antitrust, artificial intelligence, corporate quality, leadership, ethics, quality. *Unit head:* Dr. William L. Rhey, Dean Graduate Studies, 813-258-7409, Fax: 813-259-5403, E-mail: wrhey@ut.edu. *Application contact:* Fernando Nolasco, Director of Graduate Studies, 813-258-7409, Fax: 813-259-5403, E-mail: fnolasco@ut.edu.

The University of Tennessee, Graduate School, College of Arts and Sciences, Department of Sociology, Knoxville, TN 37996. Offers criminology (MA, PhD); energy, environment, and resource policy (MA, PhD); political economy (MA, PhD). Part-time programs available. *Degree requirements:* For master's, thesis or alternative; for doctorate, thesis/dissertation. *Entrance requirements:* For master's, GRE General Test, minimum GPA of 3.0; for doctorate, GRE General Test, minimum GPA of 3.5. Additional exam requirements/recommendations for international students: Required—TOEFL. Electronic applications accepted.

The University of Tennessee, Graduate School, College of Business Administration, Department of Economics, Knoxville, TN 37996. Offers MA, PhD. *Degree requirements:* For master's, thesis or alternative; for doctorate, thesis/dissertation. *Entrance requirements:* For master's and doctorate, GRE General Test or GMAT, minimum GPA of 2.7. Additional exam requirements/recommendations for international students: Required—TOEFL. Electronic applications accepted.

The University of Texas at Arlington, Graduate School, College of Business Administration, Department of Economics, Arlington, TX 76019. Offers MA. Part-time and evening/weekend programs available. *Faculty:* 6 full-time (0 women). *Students:* 12 full-time (5 women), 16 part-time (4 women); includes 6 minority (4 African Americans, 1 Asian American or Pacific Islander, 1 Hispanic American), 1 international. 24 applicants, 50% accepted, 11 enrolled. In 2007, 7 degrees awarded. *Degree requirements:* For master's, thesis optional. *Entrance requirements:* For master's, GMAT or GRE General Test. Additional exam requirements/recommendations for international students: Required—TOEFL (minimum score 550 paper-based; 213 computer-based; 79 iBT). *Application deadline:* For fall admission, 6/15 for domestic students. Applications are processed on a rolling basis. Application fee: $35 ($50 for international students). *Expenses:* Tuition, state resident: full-time $5,934. Tuition, nonresident: full-time $10,938. *Financial support:* In 2007–08, 1 fellowship (averaging $1,000 per year), research assistantships (averaging $6,000 per year), 14 teaching assistantships (averaging $13,000 per year) were awarded; career-related internships or fieldwork, scholarships/grants, and unspecified assistantships also available. Support available to part-time students. Financial award application deadline: 6/1; financial award applicants required to submit FAFSA. *Application contact:* Roger Wehr, Graduate Advisor, 817-272-3287, Fax: 817-272-3145, E-mail: wehr@uta.edu.

The University of Texas at Austin, Graduate School, College of Liberal Arts, Department of Economics, Austin, TX 78712-1111. Offers MA, MS Econ, PhD. Part-time programs available. *Degree requirements:* For master's, thesis; for doctorate, comprehensive exam, thesis/dissertation. *Entrance requirements:* For master's and doctorate, GRE General Test, minimum GPA of 3.5 (based on upper-division undergraduate and graduate course work). Additional exam requirements/recommendations for international students: Required—TOEFL. Electronic applications accepted. *Faculty research:* Industrial organization, game theory, monetary economics, labor economics, public economics.

The University of Texas at Dallas, School of Economic, Political and Policy Sciences, Program in Economics, Richardson, TX 75083-0688. Offers MS, PhD. Part-time and evening/weekend programs available. *Faculty:* 18 full-time (5 women). *Students:* 34 full-time (15 women), 13 part-time (5 women); includes 9 minority (8 Asian Americans or Pacific Islanders, 1 Hispanic American), 22 international. Average age 30. 65 applicants, 69% accepted, 11 enrolled. In 2007, 18 master's, 1 doctorate awarded. *Degree requirements:* For master's, internship; for doctorate, thesis/dissertation. *Entrance requirements:* For master's and doctorate, GRE General Test, minimum GPA of 3.0 in upper-level course work in field. Additional exam requirements/recommendations for international students: Required—TOEFL (minimum score 550 paper-based; 213 computer-based). *Application deadline:* For fall admission, 7/15 for domestic students; for spring admission, 11/15 for domestic students. Applications are processed on a rolling basis. Application fee: $50 ($100 for international students). Electronic applications accepted. *Expenses:* Tuition, state resident: full-time $7,052. Tuition, nonresident: full-time $12,632. Tuition and fees vary according to course load. *Financial support:* In 2007–08, 7 research assistantships with tuition reimbursements (averaging $12,161 per year), 17 teaching assistantships with tuition reimbursements (averaging $11,756 per year) were awarded; fellowships, career-related internships or fieldwork, Federal Work-Study, institutionally sponsored loans, scholarships/grants, and unspecified assistantships also available. Support available to

Economics

The University of Texas at Dallas (continued)
part-time students. Financial award application deadline: 4/30; financial award applicants required to submit FAFSA. *Faculty research:* Economic base of distressed counties, analysis of nonprofits and their for-profit counterparts. *Unit head:* Dr. James Murdoch, Program Head, 972-883-4964, Fax: 972-883-2735, E-mail: murdoch@utdallas.edu. *Application contact:* Judy Du, Program Assistant, 972-883-4964, E-mail: judy.du@utdallas.edu.

See Close-Up on page 1043.

The University of Texas at Dallas, School of Economic, Political and Policy Sciences, Program in Public Policy and Political Economy, Richardson, TX 75083-0688. Offers MPP, MS, PhD. Part-time and evening/weekend programs available. *Faculty:* 25 full-time (7 women), 2 part-time/adjunct (0 women). *Students:* 31 full-time (11 women), 36 part-time (17 women); includes 17 minority (10 African Americans, 4 Asian Americans or Pacific Islanders, 3 Hispanic Americans), 19 international. Average age 40. 30 applicants, 83% accepted, 11 enrolled. In 2007, 10 degrees awarded. *Degree requirements:* For doctorate, thesis/dissertation. *Entrance requirements:* For doctorate, GRE General Test, minimum GPA of 3.0 in upper-level course work in field. Additional exam requirements/recommendations for international students: Required—TOEFL (minimum score 550 paper-based; 213 computer-based). *Application deadline:* For fall admission, 7/15 for domestic students; for spring admission, 11/15 for domestic students. Applications are processed on a rolling basis. Application fee: $50 ($100 for international students). Electronic applications accepted. *Expenses:* Tuition, state resident: full-time $7,052. Tuition, nonresident: full-time $12,632. Tuition and fees vary according to course load. *Financial support:* In 2007–08, 3 research assistantships with tuition reimbursements (averaging $15,300 per year), 17 teaching assistantships with tuition reimbursements (averaging $10,487 per year) were awarded; fellowships, career-related internships or fieldwork, Federal Work-Study, institutionally sponsored loans, and scholarships/grants also available. Support available to part-time students. Financial award application deadline: 4/30; financial award applicants required to submit FAFSA. *Faculty research:* New leadership development, gender and leadership, globalization and leadership opportunities in democracy. *Unit head:* Dr. Euel Elliot, Program Head, 972-883-6406, Fax: 972-883-2735, E-mail: eelliott@utdallas.edu. *Application contact:* Judy C. Robertson, Program Assistant, 972-883-6406, E-mail: judy.robertson@utdallas.edu.

See Close-Up on page 1043.

The University of Texas at El Paso, Graduate School, College of Business Administration, Department of Economics and Finance, El Paso, TX 79968-0001. Offers MS. Part-time and evening/weekend programs available. *Degree requirements:* For master's, thesis optional. *Entrance requirements:* For master's, GMAT, minimum GPA of 2.7. Additional exam requirements/recommendations for international students: Required—TOEFL. Electronic applications accepted.

The University of Texas at San Antonio, College of Business, Department of Economics, San Antonio, TX 78249-0617. Offers business economics (MBA); economics (MA). Part-time and evening/weekend programs available. *Faculty:* 8 full-time (4 women), 1 part-time/adjunct (0 women). *Students:* 8 full-time (4 women), 15 part-time (5 women); includes 5 minority (4 Asian Americans or Pacific Islanders, 1 Hispanic American), 2 international. Average age 30. 12 applicants, 50% accepted, 3 enrolled. In 2007, 6 degrees awarded. *Degree requirements:* For master's, comprehensive exam, thesis optional. *Entrance requirements:* For master's, GMAT or GRE, minimum GPA of 3.0. Additional exam requirements/recommendations for international students: Required—TOEFL (minimum score 500 paper-based; 173 computer-based). *Application deadline:* For fall admission, 7/1 for domestic students, 4/1 for international students; for spring admission, 11/1 for domestic students, 9/1 for international students. Application fee: $45 ($80 for international students). *Financial support:* In 2007–08, 6 teaching assistantships (averaging $6,628 per year) were awarded; career-related internships or fieldwork, Federal Work-Study, scholarships/grants, and unspecified assistantships also available. Support available to part-time students. Total annual research expenditures: $31,436. *Unit head:* Dr. Kenneth E. Weiher, Chair, 210-458-5315, Fax: 210-458-5837, E-mail: kweiher@utsa.edu.

The University of Texas–Pan American, College of Business Administration, Program in International Business, Edinburg, TX 78541-2999. Offers computer information systems (PhD); economics (PhD); finance (PhD); management (PhD); marketing (PhD). *Faculty:* 30 full-time (8 women). *Students:* 67 full-time (28 women), 2 part-time (1 woman); includes 39 minority (7 African Americans, 12 Asian Americans or Pacific Islanders, 20 Hispanic Americans). Average age 30. 70 applicants, 29% accepted, 17 enrolled. In 2007, 4 degrees awarded. *Median time to degree:* Of those who began their doctoral program in fall 1999, 85% received their degree in 8 years or less. *Degree requirements:* For doctorate, comprehensive exam, thesis/dissertation. *Entrance requirements:* For doctorate, GMAT or GRE. Additional exam requirements/recommendations for international students: Required—TOEFL, IELTS. *Application deadline:* For fall admission, 3/31 for domestic and international students. Applications are processed on a rolling basis. Application fee: $35. Electronic applications accepted. *Expenses:* Contact institution. *Financial support:* In 2007–08, 40 research assistantships (averaging $18,000 per year), 13 teaching assistantships (averaging $18,000 per year) were awarded; health care benefits and unspecified assistantships also available. *Unit head:* Dr. Marc W. Simpson, PhD Program Director, 956-384-5225, Fax: 956-381-2867.

The University of Toledo, College of Graduate Studies, College of Arts and Sciences, Department of Economics, Toledo, OH 43606-3390. Offers MA. *Faculty:* 10. *Students:* 8 full-time (1 woman), 1 part-time; includes 2 minority (both African Americans), 3 international. Average age 25. 32 applicants, 53% accepted, 8 enrolled. In 2007, 6 degrees awarded. *Degree requirements:* For master's, comprehensive exam, paper or thesis. *Entrance requirements:* For master's, GRE General Test, minimum GPA of 2.75. *Application deadline:* For fall admission, 8/1 priority date for domestic students. Application fee: $45. Electronic applications accepted. *Financial support:* In 2007–08, 6 teaching assistantships with full tuition reimbursements (averaging $8,200 per year) were awarded; research assistantships, career-related internships or fieldwork, Federal Work-Study, institutionally sponsored loans, scholarships/grants, tuition waivers (full), and unspecified assistantships also available. Support available to part-time students. Financial award application deadline: 4/1; financial award applicants required to submit FAFSA. *Faculty research:* Economic development. *Unit head:* Dr. Michael Dowd, Chair, 419-530-4603, Fax: 419-530-7844, E-mail: mdowd@utoledo.edu.

The University of Toledo, College of Graduate Studies, College of Business Administration, Department of Finance and Business Economics, Toledo, OH 43606-3390. Offers MBA. Evening/weekend programs available. *Faculty:* 3. *Students:* 33 full-time (9 women), 24 part-time (6 women); includes 3 minority (2 African Americans, 1 Hispanic American), 19 international. Average age 27. 65 applicants, 46% accepted, 24 enrolled. In 2007, 34 degrees awarded. *Degree requirements:* For master's, thesis or alternative. *Entrance requirements:* For master's, GMAT. Additional exam requirements/recommendations for international students: Required—TOEFL. *Application deadline:* For fall admission, 1/15 priority date for domestic students. Applications are processed on a rolling basis. Application fee: $45. *Financial support:* Research assistantships, career-related internships or fieldwork, Federal Work-Study, institutionally sponsored loans, scholarships/grants, tuition waivers (full), unspecified assistantships, and administrative assistantships available. Support available to part-time students. Financial award application deadline: 4/1; financial award applicants required to submit FAFSA. *Faculty research:* Financial management, banking, international finance, investments. *Unit head:* Dr. Andrew Solocha, Chair, 419-530-2564.

The University of Toledo, College of Graduate Studies, College of Education, Department of Curriculum and Instruction, Program in Education and Economics, Toledo, OH 43606-3390. Offers MAE. *Application deadline:* For fall admission, 1/15 priority date for domestic students. Application fee: $45. *Financial support:* Federal Work-Study, scholarships/grants, tuition waivers, and unspecified assistantships available.

University of Toronto, School of Graduate Studies, Social Sciences Division, Department of Economics, Toronto, ON M5S 1A1, Canada. Offers MA, MFE, PhD. Part-time programs available. *Faculty:* 46 full-time, 16 part-time/adjunct. *Students:* 169 full-time (65 women), 10 part-time, 38 international. 763 applicants, 24% accepted. In 2007, 2 master's, 9 doctorates awarded. *Degree requirements:* For doctorate, comprehensive exam, thesis/dissertation. *Entrance requirements:* For master's, GRE (for applicants without a degree from a Canadian university), minimum B average in final year, 2 letters of reference; for doctorate, GRE (for applicants without a degree from a Canadian university), master's degree in economics, minimum B+ average, 3 letters of reference. Additional exam requirements/recommendations for international students: Required—TOEFL (minimum score 580 paper-based; 237 computer-based), TWE (minimum score 5), IELTS (minimum score: 7) or MELAB (minimum score: 85). *Application deadline:* For fall admission, 2/1 for domestic students. Application fee: $100 Canadian dollars. *Financial support:* Fellowships, research assistantships, teaching assistantships, career-related internships or fieldwork available. *Unit head:* Prof. Arthur Hosios, Chair, 416-978-4724, Fax: 416-946-3275. *Application contact:* Margaret Abou Haidar, Business Officer, 416-978-4615, Fax: 416-978-6713, E-mail: abouhaid@chass.utoronto.ca.

University of Utah, The Graduate School, College of Social and Behavioral Science, Department of Economics, Salt Lake City, UT 84112-1107. Offers econometrics (M Stat, MA, MS, PhD); economics (M Phil). Part-time programs available. *Faculty:* 22 full-time (4 women), 1 part-time/adjunct (0 women). *Students:* 65 full-time (20 women), 42 part-time (11 women); includes 13 minority (5 Asian Americans or Pacific Islanders, 8 Hispanic Americans), 36 international. Average age 32. 113 applicants, 61% accepted, 28 enrolled. In 2007, 19 master's, 9 doctorates awarded. Terminal master's awarded for partial completion of doctoral program. *Degree requirements:* For master's, thesis or alternative, exam, oral presentation, research project; for doctorate, comprehensive exam, thesis/dissertation. *Entrance requirements:* For master's, GRE General Test, undergraduate course work in economics; for doctorate, GRE General Test, GRE Subject Test, minimum GPA of 3.0, course work in calculus and statistics. Additional exam requirements/recommendations for international students: Required—TOEFL (minimum score 500 paper-based; 173 computer-based). *Application deadline:* For fall admission, 7/1 for domestic students. Application fee: $45 ($65 for international students). *Financial support:* In 2007–08, 45 students received support, including 1 fellowship with full tuition reimbursement available (averaging $10,000 per year), 1 research assistantship (averaging $10,000 per year), 43 teaching assistantships (averaging $10,500 per year); career-related internships or fieldwork, Federal Work-Study, institutionally sponsored loans, and health care benefits also available. Financial award application deadline: 2/1. *Faculty research:* History of economic thought, political economy, monetary economy, labor. Total annual research expenditures: $54,114. *Unit head:* Korkut Erturk, Chair, 801-581-7481, Fax: 801-585-5649.

University of Utah, The Graduate School, Interdepartmental Program in Statistics, Salt Lake City, UT 84112-1107. Offers biostatistics (MST); business (MST); economics (MST); educational psychology (MST); mathematics (MST); sociology (MST); statistics (M Stat). Part-time programs available. *Students:* 10 full-time (6 women), 21 part-time (6 women); includes 4 minority (all Asian Americans or Pacific Islanders) Average age 32. 59 applicants, 44% accepted. In 2007, 12 degrees awarded. *Degree requirements:* For master's, comprehensive exam, projects. *Entrance requirements:* For master's, minimum GPA of 3.0; course work in calculus, matrix theory, statistics. Additional exam requirements/recommendations for international students: Required—TOEFL (minimum score 500 paper-based; 173 computer-based). *Application deadline:* For fall admission, 7/1 for domestic students. Applications are processed on a rolling basis. Application fee: $45 ($65 for international students). *Financial support:* Career-related internships or fieldwork available. *Faculty research:* Biostatistics, management, economics, educational psychology, mathematics. *Unit head:* Tariq Mughal, Chair, University Statistics Committee, 801-585-9547, E-mail: tariq.mughal@business.utah.edu. *Application contact:* Glenda Pruemper, Administrative Assistant, 801-581-7148, Fax: 801-581-5566, E-mail: pruemper@ed.utah.edu.

University of Victoria, Faculty of Graduate Studies, Faculty of Social Sciences, Department of Economics, Victoria, BC V8W 2Y2, Canada. Offers MA, PhD. Part-time programs available. *Faculty:* 18 full-time (3 women). *Students:* 51 full-time, 14 international. Average age 24. 147 applicants, 14% accepted, 15 enrolled. In 2007, 15 degrees awarded. *Degree requirements:* For master's, comprehensive exam (for some programs), thesis optional; for doctorate, comprehensive exam, thesis/dissertation, candidacy exam. *Entrance requirements:* For master's and doctorate, GRE. Additional exam requirements/recommendations for international students: Required—TOEFL (minimum score 575 paper-based; 233 computer-based), IELTS (minimum score 7). *Application deadline:* For fall admission, 2/15 priority date for domestic students, 9/15 priority date for international students. Applications are processed on a rolling basis. Application fee: $75 ($125 for international students). Electronic applications accepted. *Expenses:* Tuition, state resident: full-time $3,110. International tuition: $3,700 full-time. Tuition and fees vary according to program. *Financial support:* In 2007–08, 27 fellowships, 1 research assistantship (averaging $6,000 per year), 27 teaching assistantships (averaging $5,500 per year) were awarded; career-related internships or fieldwork and institutionally sponsored loans also available. Financial award application deadline: 2/15. *Faculty research:* Industrial organization, cost/benefit, applied economics, econometrics, airline economics, health economics. *Unit head:* Dr. Donald G. Ferguson, Chair, 250-721-8531, Fax: 250-721-6214, E-mail: dferg@uvic.ca. *Application contact:* Dr. Graham M. Voss, Graduate Adviser, 250-721-8545, Fax: 250-721-6214, E-mail: gvoss@uvic.ca.

University of Virginia, College and Graduate School of Arts and Sciences, Department of Economics, Charlottesville, VA 22903. Offers MA, PhD, JD/MA. *Faculty:* 24 full-time (1 woman), 2 part-time/adjunct (0 women). *Students:* 101 full-time (40 women), 1 part-time; includes 5 minority (all Asian Americans or Pacific Islanders), 55 international. Average age 27. 353 applicants, 46% accepted, 23 enrolled. In 2007, 24 master's, 10 doctorates awarded. *Degree requirements:* For master's, comprehensive exam, thesis; for doctorate, comprehensive exam, thesis/dissertation. *Entrance requirements:* For master's and doctorate, GRE General Test. *Application deadline:* Applications are processed on a rolling basis. Application fee: $60. Electronic applications accepted. *Financial support:* Fellowships, research assistantships, teaching assistantships, tuition waivers (full and partial) available. Financial award applicants required to submit FAFSA. *Faculty research:* Macroeconomics, public economics, labor, industrial organization, economic history. *Unit head:* William Johnson, Chair, 434-924-3177, Fax: 434-982-2904, E-mail: econ-dgs@virginia.edu.

University of Washington, Graduate School, College of Arts and Sciences, Department of Economics, Seattle, WA 98195. Offers MA, PhD. Terminal master's awarded for partial completion of doctoral program. *Degree requirements:* For master's, internship; for doctorate, comprehensive exam, thesis/dissertation. *Entrance requirements:* For master's and doctorate, GRE General Test, minimum GPA of 3.0. Additional exam requirements/recommendations for international students: Required—TOEFL. Electronic applications accepted. *Faculty research:* Microeconomic theory; macroeconomic theory; econometrics; natural resource economics; international, development, and industrial organization.

University of Waterloo, Graduate Studies, Faculty of Arts, Department of Economics, Waterloo, ON N2L 3G1, Canada. Offers MA, PhD. Part-time programs available. *Faculty:* 21 full-time (3 women), 9 part-time/adjunct (2 women). *Students:* 64. 293 applicants, 17% accepted, 22 enrolled. In 2007, 23 degrees awarded. *Entrance requirements:* For master's, honors degree, minimum B average. Additional exam requirements/recommendations for international students: Required—TOEFL, TWE. *Application deadline:* For fall admission, 2/1 for domestic and international students. Applications are processed on a rolling basis. Application fee: $75 Canadian dollars. Electronic applications accepted. *Financial support:* In 2007–08, 9 teaching assistantships (averaging $12,080 Canadian dollars per year) were awarded; career-related internships or fieldwork also available. Financial award application deadline: 2/1. *Faculty research:* Applied microeconomics, applied macroeconomics, public finance, international trade and finance, wage inflation and consumer problems. *Unit head:* Dr. J. Brox, Chair,

519-888-4567 Ext. 32463, E-mail: jbrox@uwaterloo.ca. *Application contact:* Pat Shaw, Graduate Coordinator, 519-888-4567 Ext. 36556, Fax: 519-725-0530, E-mail: pshaw@watarts.uwaterloo.ca.

The University of Western Ontario, Faculty of Graduate Studies, Social Sciences Division, Department of Economics, London, ON N6A 5B8, Canada. Offers MA, PhD. *Faculty:* 28 full-time (3 women). *Students:* 44 full-time (11 women), 2 part-time; includes 21 minority (2 African Americans, 19 Asian Americans or Pacific Islanders), 2 international. 197 applicants. In 2007, 11 master's, 4 doctorates awarded. *Degree requirements:* For doctorate, thesis/dissertation. *Entrance requirements:* For master's, GRE, honours BA with B+ average. Additional exam requirements/recommendations for international students: Required—TOEFL. *Application deadline:* For fall admission, 2/1 priority date for domestic students. Application fee: $60. *Financial support:* In 2007–08, 36 teaching assistantships with partial tuition reimbursements (averaging $8,200 per year) were awarded. Financial award application deadline: 2/1. *Unit head:* Dr. Chris Robinson, Acting Chair, 519-661-2111 Ext. 85294, E-mail: robinson@uwo.ca. *Application contact:* Yvonne Adams, Graduate Assistant, 519-661-3505, Fax: 519-661-3666, E-mail: yadams@uwo.ca.

University of Windsor, Faculty of Graduate Studies, Faculty of Science, Department of Economics, Windsor, ON N9B 3P4, Canada. Offers MA. Part-time programs available. *Faculty:* 8 full-time (1 woman). *Students:* 19 full-time (11 women), 1 part-time. 156 applicants, 33% accepted. In 2007, 18 degrees awarded. *Degree requirements:* For master's, thesis or alternative. *Entrance requirements:* For master's, minimum B average. Additional exam requirements/recommendations for international students: Required—TOEFL (minimum score 560 paper-based; 220 computer-based). *Application deadline:* For fall admission, 7/1 priority date for domestic students; for winter admission, 11/1 for domestic students; for spring admission, 3/1 for domestic students. Applications are processed on a rolling basis. Application fee: $55. Electronic applications accepted. *Financial support:* In 2007–08, 14 teaching assistantships (averaging $8,901 per year) were awarded; Federal Work-Study, scholarships/grants, tuition waivers (full and partial), unspecified assistantships, and bursaries also available. Financial award application deadline: 2/15. *Faculty research:* International trade, economic growth, microeconomic theory. *Unit head:* Dr. Peter Townley, Head, 519-253-3000 Ext. 2368, Fax: 519-973-7096, E-mail: ptownley@uwindsor.ca. *Application contact:* Applicant Services, 519-253-3000 Ext. 6459, Fax: 519-971-3653, E-mail: gradadmit@uwindsor.ca.

University of Wisconsin–Madison, Graduate School, College of Letters and Science, Department of Economics, Madison, WI 53706-1380. Offers PhD. *Degree requirements:* For doctorate, thesis/dissertation. *Entrance requirements:* For doctorate, GRE General Test, 3 semesters of course work in calculus, 1 semester of course work in algebra and mathematics/statistics. Electronic applications accepted.

University of Wisconsin–Milwaukee, Graduate School, College of Letters and Sciences, Department of Economics, Milwaukee, WI 53201-0413. Offers MA, PhD. *Faculty:* 22 full-time (3 women). *Students:* 71 full-time (25 women), 14 part-time (4 women); includes 3 minority (1 African American, 1 Asian American or Pacific Islander, 1 Hispanic American), 52 international. 113 applicants, 64% accepted, 37 enrolled. In 2007, 24 master's, 5 doctorates awarded. *Degree requirements:* For doctorate, thesis/dissertation. *Entrance requirements:* For master's, GRE General Test; for doctorate, GRE General Test, GRE Subject Test. *Application deadline:* For fall admission, 1/1 priority date for domestic students; for spring admission, 9/1 for domestic students. Applications are processed on a rolling basis. Application fee: $45 ($75 for international students). *Expenses:* Tuition, state resident: part-time $530 per credit. Tuition, nonresident: part-time $1,428 per credit. Required fees: $19 per credit. $229 per term. Tuition and fees vary according to course load and program. *Financial support:* In 2007–08, 34 teaching assistantships were awarded; fellowships, research assistantships, career-related internships or fieldwork and unspecified assistantships also available. Support available to part-time students. Financial award application deadline: 4/15. *Unit head:* M. Bahmani-Oskooee, Representative, 414-229-4334, Fax: 414-229-3860, E-mail: bahmani@uwm.edu.

University of Wyoming, Graduate School, College of Business, Department of Economics and Finance, Program in Economics, Laramie, WY 82070. Offers MS, PhD. Part-time programs available. *Faculty:* 10 full-time (0 women), 3 part-time/adjunct (1 woman). *Students:* 28 full-time (3 women), 17 part-time (7 women); includes 1 minority (African American), 19 international. Average age 31. 8 applicants, 25% accepted, 2 enrolled. In 2007, 2 doctorates awarded. *Degree requirements:* For master's, thesis; for doctorate, comprehensive exam, thesis/dissertation. *Entrance requirements:* For master's, GRE General Test or GMAT, minimum GPA of 3.0; for doctorate, GRE General Test, minimum GPA of 3.0. Additional exam requirements/recommendations for international students: Required—TOEFL (minimum score 525 paper-based; 197 computer-based). *Application deadline:* For fall admission, 3/1 for domestic students; for spring admission, 10/1 for domestic students. Applications are processed on a rolling basis. Application fee: $50. *Financial support:* In 2007–08, 10 research assistantships with full tuition reimbursements (averaging $14,886 per year), 10 teaching assistantships with full tuition reimbursements (averaging $14,886 per year) were awarded. Financial award application deadline: 3/1. *Faculty research:* Resource and environmental economics, industrial organization, regulation. *Application contact:* Carrie Miller, Office Associate, 307-766-2175, Fax: 307-766-5090, E-mail: carriem@uwyo.edu.

University of Wyoming, Graduate School, College of Business, Department of Economics and Finance, Program in Economics and Finance, Laramie, WY 82070. Offers MS. *Students:* 3 applicants, 33% accepted, 1 enrolled. *Degree requirements:* For master's, thesis. *Entrance requirements:* For master's, GRE, minimum GPA of 3.0. Additional exam requirements/recommendations for international students: Required—TOEFL (minimum score 540 paper-based; 207 computer-based; 76 iBT). *Application deadline:* For fall admission, 3/1 for domestic and international students; for spring admission, 11/1 for domestic and international students. Application fee: $50. *Financial support:* In 2007–08, research assistantships with partial tuition reimbursements (averaging $5,348 per year), teaching assistantships with partial tuition reimbursements (averaging $5,348 per year) were awarded. Financial award application deadline: 3/1. *Faculty research:* Financial economics. *Application contact:* Abby Derr, Graduate Coordinator, 307-766-2175, Fax: 307-766-5090, E-mail: derra7@uwyo.edu.

Utah State University, School of Graduate Studies, College of Business and College of Agriculture, Department of Economics, Logan, UT 84322. Offers applied economics (MS); economics (MA, MS, PhD). Terminal master's awarded for partial completion of doctoral program. *Degree requirements:* For master's, thesis (for some programs); for doctorate, comprehensive exam, thesis/dissertation. *Entrance requirements:* For master's, GRE General Test, GMAT, minimum GPA of 3.0, TOEFL for international; for doctorate, GRE General Test, minimum GPA of 3.0, TOEFL. Additional exam requirements/recommendations for international students: Required—TOEFL. Electronic applications accepted. *Faculty research:* Resource economics, economic theory, international trade, industrial organization, development.

Vanderbilt University, Graduate School, Department of Economics, Nashville, TN 37240-1001. Offers economic development (MA); economics (MA, MAT, PhD); JD/PhD. *Faculty:* 42 full-time (11 women). *Students:* 100 full-time (31 women), 2 part-time; includes 4 minority (3 African Americans, 1 Hispanic American), 71 international. Average age 28. 389 applicants, 28% accepted, 32 enrolled. In 2007, 29 master's, 2 doctorates awarded. *Degree requirements:* For master's, thesis or alternative; for doctorate, thesis/dissertation, final and qualifying exams. *Entrance requirements:* For master's and doctorate, GRE General Test, GRE Subject Test (recommended). *Application deadline:* For fall admission, 1/15 for domestic and international students; for spring admission, 11/1 for domestic students. Applications are processed on a rolling basis. Application fee: $0. Electronic applications accepted. *Financial support:* Fellowships with full and partial tuition reimbursements, teaching assistantships with full and partial tuition reimbursements, career-related internships or fieldwork, Federal Work-Study, institutionally sponsored loans, and health care benefits available. Financial award application deadline: 1/15; financial award applicants required to submit CSS PROFILE or FAFSA. *Faculty research:* Economic theory, applied fields, developmental economics, environmental economics, health economics and policy. *Unit head:* Eric Bond, Chair, 615-322-2871, Fax: 615-343-8495. *Application contact:* Jeremy Atack, Director of Graduate Studies, 615-322-2871, Fax: 615-343-8495, E-mail: jeremy.atack@vanderbilt.edu.

Vanderbilt University, Law School, Nashville, TN 37203. Offers law (JD, LL M); law and economics (PhD); JD/M Div; JD/MA; JD/MBA; JD/MD; JD/MPP; JD/MTS; JD/PhD; LL M/MA. *Accreditation:* ABA. *Faculty:* 53 full-time (21 women), 63 part-time/adjunct (21 women). *Students:* 629 full-time (291 women); includes 99 minority (50 African Americans, 5 American Indian/Alaska Native, 28 Asian Americans or Pacific Islanders, 16 Hispanic Americans), 40 international. Average age 25. 3,985 applicants, 25% accepted, 193 enrolled. In 2007, 223 first professional degrees, 16 master's awarded. *Entrance requirements:* LSAT. Additional exam requirements/recommendations for international students: Required—TOEFL. *Application deadline:* For fall admission, 3/15 for domestic students. Applications are processed on a rolling basis. Application fee: $50. Electronic applications accepted. *Expenses: Contact institution. Financial support:* In 2007–08, 90 students received support. Career-related internships or fieldwork, Federal Work-Study, institutionally sponsored loans, and scholarships/grants available. Financial award application deadline: 2/15; financial award applicants required to submit FAFSA. *Unit head:* Edward L Rubin, Dean, 615-322-2615. *Application contact:* G. Todd Morton, Assistant Dean for Admissions, 615-322-6452, Fax: 615-322-1531.

Virginia Commonwealth University, Graduate School, School of Business, Program in Economics, Richmond, VA 23284-9005. Offers MA, MBA, MS. *Faculty:* 12 full-time (3 women). *Students:* 12 full-time (5 women), 10 part-time (4 women); includes 6 minority (1 African American, 2 American Indian/Alaska Native, 1 Asian American or Pacific Islander, 2 Hispanic Americans), 4 international. 34 applicants, 59% accepted. In 2007, 3 degrees awarded. *Degree requirements:* For master's, thesis optional. *Entrance requirements:* For master's, GRE General Test. *Application deadline:* For fall admission, 7/15 for domestic students; for spring admission, 3/15 for domestic students. Applications are processed on a rolling basis. Application fee: $50. *Expenses:* Tuition, state resident: full-time $7,224; part-time $401 per credit. Tuition, nonresident: full-time $16,072; part-time $891 per credit. Required fees: $1,679; $63 per credit. Tuition and fees vary according to campus/location. *Financial support:* Fellowships, research assistantships, teaching assistantships, Federal Work-Study, institutionally sponsored loans, and tuition waivers (full and partial) available. Financial award application deadline: 3/15. *Unit head:* Dr. Edward L. Millner, Chair, 804-828-1717, Fax: 804-828-1719, E-mail: elmillne@vcu.edu. *Application contact:* Jana McQuaid, Graduate Program Director, 804-828-1741, Fax: 804-828-7174, E-mail: jpmcquaid@vcu.edu.

Virginia Polytechnic Institute and State University, Graduate School, College of Agriculture and Life Sciences, Department of Agricultural and Applied Economics, Blacksburg, VA 24061. Offers agribusiness (MS); agricultural economics (MS); applied economics (MS); developmental and international economics (PhD); econometrics (PhD); macro and micro economics (PhD); markets and industrial organizations (PhD); public and regional/urban economics (PhD); resource and environmental economics (PhD). *Entrance requirements:* For master's and doctorate, GRE General Test. Additional exam requirements/recommendations for international students: Required—TOEFL (minimum score 575 paper-based; 231 computer-based). Electronic applications accepted. *Faculty research:* Rural development.

Virginia Polytechnic Institute and State University, Graduate School, College of Science, Department of Economics, Blacksburg, VA 24061. Offers MA, PhD. *Entrance requirements:* For master's and doctorate, GRE. Additional exam requirements/recommendations for international students: Required—TOEFL (minimum score 500 paper-based; 213 computer-based). Electronic applications accepted.

Virginia State University, School of Graduate Studies, Research, and Outreach, School of Liberal Arts and Education, Department of Economics, Petersburg, VA 23806-0001. Offers MA. *Degree requirements:* For master's, thesis optional. *Entrance requirements:* For master's, GRE General Test.

Walsh College of Accountancy and Business Administration, Graduate Programs, Program in Economics, Troy, MI 48007-7006. Offers MAE.

Washington State University, Graduate School, College of Agricultural, Human, and Natural Resource Sciences, School of Economic Sciences, Department of Economics, Pullman, WA 99164. Offers applied economics (MA); economics (MA, PhD); international business economics (Certificate). *Faculty:* 16 full-time (1 woman). *Students:* 45 full-time (15 women), 8 part-time (5 women), 24 international. Average age 30. 135 applicants, 21% accepted, 16 enrolled. In 2007, 7 master's, 8 doctorates awarded. *Degree requirements:* For master's, comprehensive exam (for some programs), thesis (for some programs), oral exam; for doctorate, comprehensive exam, thesis/dissertation, oral exam, written exam, field exams. *Entrance requirements:* For master's, GRE General Test, minimum GPA of 3.0; for doctorate, GRE General Test or GMAT, minimum GPA of 3.0. Additional exam requirements/recommendations for international students: Required—TOEFL. *Application deadline:* For fall admission, 3/1 priority date for domestic students. Applications are processed on a rolling basis. Application fee: $50. *Financial support:* In 2007–08, research assistantships (averaging $13,917 per year), 13 teaching assistantships (averaging $13,506 per year) were awarded; career-related internships or fieldwork, Federal Work-Study, institutionally sponsored loans, tuition waivers (partial), and teaching associateships also available. Financial award application deadline: 4/1; financial award applicants required to submit FAFSA. *Faculty research:* Economic theory and quantitative methods, applied microeconomics. Total annual research expenditures: $80,141. *Application contact:* Graduate School Admissions, 800-GRADWSU, Fax: 509-335-1949, E-mail: gradsch@wsu.edu.

Washington University in St. Louis, Graduate School of Arts and Sciences, Department of Economics, St. Louis, MO 63130-4899. Offers MA, PhD, JD/MA, JD/PhD. Terminal master's awarded for partial completion of doctoral program. *Degree requirements:* For master's, thesis or alternative; for doctorate, one foreign language, thesis/dissertation. *Entrance requirements:* For master's and doctorate, GRE General Test, GRE Subject Test. Electronic applications accepted.

Announcement: Washington University's PhD program prepares students for careers in academics, business, and government. Generous financial support is provided throughout the degree program. Students work closely with eminent research faculty in econometrics, economic history, economic theory, labor economics, industrial organization, institutional economics, macroeconomics, and public economics. See http://economics.wustl.edu for more information.

Wayne State University, College of Liberal Arts and Sciences, Department of Economics, Detroit, MI 48202. Offers MA, PhD, JD/MA. *Students:* 64 full-time (30 women), 12 part-time (4 women); includes 11 minority (6 African Americans, 4 Asian Americans or Pacific Islanders, 1 Hispanic American), 33 international. Average age 31. 73 applicants, 51% accepted, 18 enrolled. In 2007, 21 master's, 1 doctorate awarded. *Degree requirements:* For master's, thesis optional; for doctorate, thesis/dissertation. *Entrance requirements:* For master's, minimum GPA of 3.0; for doctorate, GRE, minimum GPA of 3.0. Additional exam requirements/recommendations for international students: Required—TOEFL (minimum score 550 paper-based; 213 computer-based); Recommended—TWE (minimum score 6). *Application deadline:* For fall admission, 7/1 for domestic students, 6/1 for international students; for winter admission, 10/1 for international students; for spring admission, 2/1 for international students. Applications are processed on a rolling basis. Application fee: $30 ($50 for international students). Electronic applications accepted. *Expenses:* Tuition, state resident: part-time $403 per credit hour. Tuition, nonresident: part-time $890 per credit hour. *Financial support:* In 2007–08, 2 fellowships with tuition reimbursements (averaging $13,001 per year), 21 teaching assistantships with tuition reimbursements (averaging $13,672 per year) were awarded; research assistantships, institutionally sponsored loans and tuition waivers (full and partial) also available. Support available to part-time students. Financial award application deadline: 3/1. *Faculty research:* Health economics, international economics, macro economics, urban and labor economics,

Economics

Wayne State University (continued)

econometrics. *Unit head:* Li Way Lee, Chair, 313-577-3345, Fax: 313-577-0149, E-mail: aa1313@wayne.edu. *Application contact:* Allen Goodman, Director, 313-577-3235, E-mail: allen.goodman@wayne.edu.

Wayne State University, College of Liberal Arts and Sciences, Interdisciplinary Program in Economic Development, Detroit, MI 48202. Offers Certificate. *Students:* Average age 28. 2 applicants, 0% accepted. In 2007, 1 degree awarded. *Entrance requirements:* Additional exam requirements/recommendations for international students: Required—TOEFL (minimum score 550 paper-based; 213 computer-based); Recommended—TWE (minimum score 6). *Application deadline:* For fall admission, 7/1 for domestic students, 6/1 for international students; for winter admission, 10/1 for international students; for spring admission, 2/1 for international students. Applications are processed on a rolling basis. Application fee: $30 ($50 for international students). Electronic applications accepted. *Expenses:* Tuition, state resident: part-time $403 per credit hour. Tuition, nonresident: part-time $890 per credit hour. *Application contact:* Linda Johnson, Academic Services Officer, 313-577-5071, Fax: 313-577-8800.

West Chester University of Pennsylvania, Office of Graduate Studies and Extended Education, College of Business and Public Affairs, Program in Business Administration, West Chester, PA 19383. Offers business (Certificate); economics/finance (MBA); executive business administration (MBA); general business (MBA); management (MBA); technology and electronic commerce (MBA). *Accreditation:* AACSB. Part-time and evening/weekend programs available. *Students:* 2 full-time (1 woman), 66 part-time (24 women); includes 16 minority (4 African Americans, 10 Asian Americans or Pacific Islanders, 2 Hispanic Americans), 3 international. Average age 33. 49 applicants, 86% accepted, 17 enrolled. In 2007, 32 degrees awarded. *Degree requirements:* For master's, comprehensive exam, thesis optional. *Entrance requirements:* For master's, GMAT, interview, minimum GPA of 3.0. Additional exam requirements/recommendations for international students: Required—TOEFL (minimum score 550 paper-based; 213 computer-based; 80 iBT). *Application deadline:* For fall admission, 4/15 priority date for domestic students; for spring admission, 10/15 for domestic students. Applications are processed on a rolling basis. Application fee: $35. *Expenses:* Tuition, state resident: part-time $345 per credit. Tuition, nonresident: part-time $552 per credit. Tuition and fees vary according to course load. *Financial support:* In 2007–08, 4 research assistantships with full and partial tuition reimbursements (averaging $5,000 per year) were awarded; unspecified assistantships also available. Support available to part-time students. Financial award application deadline: 2/15; financial award applicants required to submit FAFSA. *Unit head:* Dr. Paul Christ, Director, 610-436-2608, E-mail: pchrist@wcupa.edu. *Application contact:* Dr. Paul Christ, Graduate Coordinator, 610-436-2608, E-mail: mba@wcupa.edu.

Western Illinois University, School of Graduate Studies, College of Business and Technology, Department of Economics, Macomb, IL 61455-1390. Offers MA. Part-time programs available. *Students:* 23 full-time (2 women), 3 part-time; includes 6 minority (5 African Americans, 1 Hispanic American), 14 international. Average age 30. 20 applicants, 90% accepted. In 2007, 13 degrees awarded. *Degree requirements:* For master's, thesis or alternative. *Entrance requirements:* Additional exam requirements/recommendations for international students: Required—TOEFL (minimum score 550 paper-based; 213 computer-based; 80 iBT). *Application deadline:* Applications are processed on a rolling basis. Application fee: $30. Electronic applications accepted. *Expenses:* Tuition, state resident: part-time $217 per credit hour. Tuition, nonresident: part-time $433 per credit hour. Required fees: $54 per credit hour. *Financial support:* In 2007–08, 7 students received support, including 7 research assistantships with full tuition reimbursements available (averaging $6,800 per year). Financial award applicants required to submit FAFSA. *Unit head:* Dr. Warren Jones, Chairperson, 309-298-1153. *Application contact:* Dr. Barbara Baily, Director of Graduate Studies/Associate Provost, 309-298-1806, Fax: 309-298-2345, E-mail: grad-office@wiu.edu.

Western Michigan University, Graduate College, College of Arts and Sciences, Department of Economics, Kalamazoo, MI 49008-5202. Offers applied economics (PhD); economics (MA). *Degree requirements:* For master's, thesis, oral or written exams; for doctorate, thesis/dissertation, oral exam, internship. *Entrance requirements:* For doctorate, GRE General Test.

West Texas A&M University, College of Business, Department of Accounting, Economics, and Finance, Program in Finance and Economics, Canyon, TX 79016-0001. Offers MS. Part-time and evening/weekend programs available. Postbaccalaureate distance learning degree programs offered (minimal on-campus study). *Degree requirements:* For master's, comprehensive exam, thesis optional. *Entrance requirements:* For master's, GMAT. Additional exam requirements/recommendations for international students: Required—TOEFL (minimum score 550 paper-based). Electronic applications accepted. *Faculty research:* International trade composition, cycle of poverty, trade effects in Asian countries, structural problems in Japanese economy, reform and the US sugar program-Nebraska.

West Virginia University, College of Business and Economics, Division of Economics and Finance, Morgantown, WV 26506. Offers business analysis (MA); developmental financial economics (PhD); environmental and resource economics (PhD); international economics (PhD); mathematical economics (MA); monetary economics (PhD); public finance (PhD); public policy (MA); regional and urban economics (PhD); statistics and economics (MA). *Faculty:* 19 full-time (1 woman), 4 part-time/adjunct (1 woman). *Students:* 49 full-time (19 women), 7 part-time (3 women); includes 2 minority (1 African American, 1 Asian American or Pacific Islander), 26 international. Average age 29. 100 applicants, 25% accepted, 14 enrolled. In 2007, 5 master's, 5 doctorates awarded. Terminal master's awarded for partial completion of doctoral program. *Median time to degree:* Of those who began their doctoral program in fall 1999, 73% received their degree in 8 years or less. *Degree requirements:* For master's, thesis optional; for doctorate, comprehensive exam, thesis/dissertation. *Entrance requirements:* For master's and doctorate, GRE General Test, minimum GPA of 3.0; course work in intermediate microeconomics, intermediate macroeconomics, calculus, and statistics. Additional exam requirements/recommendations for international students: Required—TOEFL. *Application deadline:* For fall admission, 3/1 priority date for domestic and international students. Applications are processed on a rolling basis. Application fee: $50. Electronic applications accepted. *Expenses:* Tuition, state resident: full-time $5,196; part-time $292 per credit hour. Tuition, nonresident: full-time $15,064; part-time $840 per credit hour. Tuition and fees vary according to program. *Financial support:* In 2007–08, 55 students received support, including 4 fellowships with full tuition reimbursements available (averaging $23,750 per year), 7 research assistantships with full tuition reimbursements available (averaging $9,300 per year), 25 teaching assistantships with full tuition reimbursements available (averaging $9,300 per year); Federal Work-Study, institutionally sponsored loans, and tuition waivers (full and partial) also available. Financial award application deadline: 3/1; financial award applicants required to submit FAFSA. *Faculty research:* Financial economics, regional/urban development, public economics, international trade/international finance/development economics, monetary economics. Total annual research expenditures: $188,762. *Unit head:* Dr. William N. Trumbull, Director, 304-293-7860, Fax: 304-293-2233, E-mail: william.trumbull@mail.wvu.edu. *Application contact:* Nicki Metts, Program Assistant II, 304-293-7859, Fax: 304-293-5652, E-mail: nicki.metts@mail.wvu.edu.

Wichita State University, Graduate School, W. Frank Barton School of Business, Department of Economics, Wichita, KS 67260. Offers business economics (MA); economic analysis (MA). Part-time and evening/weekend programs available. *Degree requirements:* For master's, thesis or written comprehensive exam. *Entrance requirements:* For master's, GRE General Test, minimum GPA of 2.75. Additional exam requirements/recommendations for international students: Required—TOEFL. Electronic applications accepted. *Faculty research:* Law economics, general aviation industry, public choice, financial and monetary economics, labor and human resources.

Wilfrid Laurier University, Faculty of Graduate Studies, School of Business and Economics, Department of Economics, Waterloo, ON N2L 3C5, Canada. Offers MA. *Faculty:* 21 full-time. *Students:* 17 full-time, 1 part-time. 84 applicants, 38% accepted, 15 enrolled. In 2007, 14 degrees awarded. *Entrance requirements:* For master's, honors BA or the equivalent in economics, minimum B average in undergraduate course work. Additional exam requirements/recommendations for international students: Required—TOEFL (minimum score 230 computer-based; 89 iBT). *Application deadline:* For fall admission, 2/1 priority date for domestic students. Application fee: $75. Electronic applications accepted. *Financial support:* Fellowships, research assistantships, teaching assistantships, career-related internships or fieldwork available. *Faculty research:* Economic forecasting, economic policy analysis, industry and market studies, financial economics, strategic planning, public policy and business. *Unit head:* Dr. Terrance Levesque, Chairperson, 519-884-1970 Ext. 2945. *Application contact:* Jennifer Poppe, Student Contact, 519-884-0710 Ext. 3536, Fax: 519-884-1020, E-mail: gradstudies@wlu.ca.

Wright State University, School of Graduate Studies, Raj Soin College of Business, Department of Economics, Dayton, OH 45435. Offers business economics (MBA); social and applied economics (MS); MBA/MS. *Entrance requirements:* For master's, GRE General Test. Additional exam requirements/recommendations for international students: Required—TOEFL.

Yale University, Graduate School of Arts and Sciences, Department of Economics, New Haven, CT 06520. Offers economics (PhD); international and development economics (MA). *Degree requirements:* For doctorate, thesis/dissertation. *Entrance requirements:* For master's, GRE General Test; for doctorate, GRE General Test, GRE Subject Test. *Faculty research:* Economic history of Western Europe, environmental economics, economic growth and development.

York University, Faculty of Graduate Studies, Faculty of Arts, Program in Economics, Toronto, ON M3J 1P3, Canada. Offers MA, PhD. Part-time programs available. *Degree requirements:* For doctorate, comprehensive exam, thesis/dissertation. Electronic applications accepted.

Youngstown State University, Graduate School, College of Arts and Sciences, Department of Economics, Youngstown, OH 44555-0001. Offers MA. Part-time programs available. *Degree requirements:* For master's, comprehensive exam, thesis optional. *Entrance requirements:* For master's, minimum GPA of 2.7, 21 hours in economics. Additional exam requirements/recommendations for international students: Required—TOEFL. *Faculty research:* Forecasting, applied econometrics, labor economics, applied macroeconomics, industrial organization.

Mineral Economics

Colorado School of Mines, Graduate School, Division of Economics and Business, Golden, CO 80401-1887. Offers engineering and technology management (MS); mineral economics (MS, PhD). Part-time programs available. *Faculty:* 19 full-time (4 women), 3 part-time/adjunct (1 woman). *Students:* 72 full-time (12 women), 14 part-time (3 women); includes 11 minority (2 African Americans, 2 Asian Americans or Pacific Islanders, 7 Hispanic Americans), 30 international. 115 applicants, 79% accepted, 37 enrolled. In 2007, 43 master's, 2 doctorates awarded. *Degree requirements:* For doctorate, comprehensive exam, thesis/dissertation. *Entrance requirements:* For master's and doctorate, GRE General Test. Additional exam requirements/recommendations for international students: Required—TOEFL (minimum score 550 paper-based; 213 computer-based; 80 iBT). *Application deadline:* For fall admission, 1/15 priority date for domestic and international students; for spring admission, 9/1 priority date for domestic and international students. Application fee: $50 ($70 for international students). Electronic applications accepted. *Expenses:* Tuition, state resident: full-time $8,964; part-time $448 per credit. Tuition, nonresident: full-time $21,744; part-time $1,130 per credit. Required fees: $1,287; $643 per semester. *Financial support:* In 2007–08, 29 students received support, including 1 fellowship with full tuition reimbursement available (averaging $19,968 per year), 5 research assistantships with full tuition reimbursements available (averaging $19,968 per year), 14 teaching assistantships with full tuition reimbursements available (averaging $19,968 per year); scholarships/grants, health care benefits, and unspecified assistantships also available. Financial award applicants required to submit FAFSA. *Faculty research:* International trade, resource and environmental economics, energy economics, operations research. Total annual research expenditures: $36,810. *Unit head:* Dr. Carol Dahl, Acting Head, 303-273-3981, Fax: 303-273-3416. *Application contact:* Kathleen A. Feighny, Program Manager, 303-273-3979, Fax: 303-273-3416, E-mail: kfeighny@mines.edu.

Michigan Technological University, Graduate School, School of Business and Economics, Program in Applied Natural Resource Economics, Houghton, MI 49931-1295. Offers MS. Part-time programs available. *Faculty:* 24 full-time (6 women). *Students:* 8 full-time (3 women), 6 international. Average age 30. 6 applicants, 33% accepted, 0 enrolled. In 2007, 3 degrees awarded. *Degree requirements:* For master's, comprehensive exam, thesis (for some programs). *Entrance requirements:* For master's, GRE. Additional exam requirements/recommendations for international students: Required—TOEFL (minimum score 550 paper-based; 213 computer-based). *Application deadline:* Applications are processed on a rolling basis. Application fee: $40 ($45 for international students). Electronic applications accepted. *Financial support:* In 2007–08, 2 students received support, including 1 fellowship with full tuition reimbursement available (averaging $9,542 per year), research assistantships with full tuition reimbursements available (averaging $9,542 per year), 1 teaching assistantship with full tuition reimbursement available (averaging $9,542 per year); career-related internships or fieldwork, Federal Work-Study, scholarships/grants, health care benefits, tuition waivers (partial), unspecified assistantships, and co-op also available. Financial award applicants required to submit FAFSA. *Application contact:* Dr. Gary A. Campbell, Co-Director, 906-487-2808, Fax: 906-487-2944, E-mail: gacampbe@mtu.edu.

The University of Texas at Austin, Graduate School, Cockrell School of Engineering, Department of Petroleum and Geosystems Engineering, Program in Energy and Mineral Resources, Austin, TX 78712-1111. Offers MA, MS. *Degree requirements:* For master's, thesis, seminar. *Entrance requirements:* For master's, GRE General Test. Additional exam requirements/recommendations for international students: Required—TOEFL. Electronic applications accepted.

BRANDEIS UNIVERSITY

International Business School

Programs of Study The International Business School (IBS) at Brandeis University offers innovative master's and Ph.D. programs for students preparing for careers in international business, finance, and economics. IBS offers full-time programs, including the Master in Business Administration/international (M.B.A.), the Master of Arts in international economics and finance (MAief), and the M.S./Ph.D. in international economics and finance. IBS also offers an innovative Master of Science in Finance (M.S.F.) program that can be completed on a part-time basis or on a full-time basis in one year.

The M.B.A.'s global orientation, multicultural training, and international experience distinguish it from "generic" M.B.A. programs. Although students study all subjects covered in a traditional M.B.A. program, they learn in a global context. The M.B.A. prepares students for business careers in multinational enterprises, smaller firms operating across borders, and consulting firms that serve international enterprises. A unique feature of the M.B.A. is a semester of study with one of eighteen business schools in Europe, Asia, or Latin America. Demonstrated proficiency in a language other than English is required.

IBS also offers the MAief degree, a highly specialized degree that combines aspects of international business and international affairs. Designed for recent college graduates and experienced professionals, this program most benefits students who seek careers in international finance and economic policy.

The M.S.F. consists of ten courses and can be completed on a part-time or full-time basis. An elective may include a one-week field-study course given on location in a major international financial market.

The M.S./Ph.D. program provides advanced training in theory, research, and creative problem solving for students who are interested in careers in research, teaching, and policymaking. The M.S./Ph.D. has alternating-year admission, with the next intake in August 2008.

Research Facilities Both master's and Ph.D. students frequently participate in faculty research and in seminars and discussions with visiting scholars and practitioners. Officially designated as one of thirteen U.S. APEC Study Centers, the School provides special opportunities for those interested in Asian economics and business. There is also a strong faculty group specializing in Latin American economies. IBS operates its own IBM-compatible computer network and maintains major databases of U.S. and international statistics. The network is connected to several Brandeis mainframe computers and the Internet. Brandeis libraries hold a basic collection in the School's fields; specialized material is available from other local libraries through the Boston Library Consortium.

Financial Aid Candidates for the full-time programs may apply for tuition scholarships, assistantships, and loans. Aid is based on merit and need and is open to both U.S. and international students. Special scholarships are also available for U.S. students considering careers in international business and finance. Special funds make possible more generous aid to Ph.D. candidates. U.S. applicants for financial aid must file a Free Application for Federal Student Aid (FAFSA) form.

Cost of Study Tuition for 2007–08 was $34,566 per year for full-time programs, including the one-year M.S.F. program, which was $3200 per course for part-time students. During their semester abroad, master's students continue to pay tuition to Brandeis and are awarded travel grants toward the cost of airfare.

Living and Housing Costs The minimum yearly cost of living is estimated at $12,000. Limited graduate housing is available on campus; rent for a one-bedroom apartment nearby ranges from $500 to $800 per month.

Student Group IBS's graduate programs emphasize close student-faculty interaction in teaching and research; admission is limited to approximately 10 Ph.D. students biannually and 125 master's students each year. The student body is talented and diverse; more than half of the master's candidates are international, and nearly half are women. Social and extracurricular activities are organized by the Student Association and the Alumni Association.

Student Outcomes Virtually all graduates of the program are employed in positions utilizing their economic, financial, and international training. Leading employers include Citibank, PricewaterhouseCoopers, JP Morgan/Chase, Goldman Sachs, Standard and Poor's, and the U.S. Federal Reserve Banks. Graduates from recent classes have received offers from consulting firms such as the Boston Consulting Group, McKinsey and Co., and Accenture and from corporations such as Lycos and Corning International. Students work closely with the Office of Career Services to learn about career alternatives and to implement effective career development strategy during their time at Brandeis.

Location Brandeis is located 10 miles west of Boston and Cambridge on a parklike, 250-acre campus. The School is located in a wooded corner of the campus in the Sachar International Center. The urban and educational amenities of Boston and Cambridge are easily reached by public transportation.

The University Founded in 1948, Brandeis is one of the leading private research universities in the United States, with approximately 3,000 undergraduates and 1,200 graduate students. The University has excellent sports facilities and frequently brings distinguished lecturers, artists, and musical and theatrical performances to the campus.

Applying Master's program applications are reviewed three times each year—November 15, February 15, and April 15. The next Ph.D. application deadline is January 15, 2008. (Ph.D. applications are accepted biannually.) To maximize chances for admission and financial aid, students are urged to apply by February 15. An interview is recommended but not required. All applications must include official transcripts, test scores, three letters of recommendation, a resume, and a goal statement. The M.A. program accepts either GRE or GMAT testing. The M.B.A. and M.S.F. require the GMAT. Ph.D. students are required to take the General Test of the GRE. All international applicants must submit TOEFL scores.

Prior preparation for the MAief programs should include at least two undergraduate semester courses in economics and some background in a major modern foreign language. Some prior work experience is recommended for applicants to the M.B.A. program, and two to three years of experience are required for the M.S.F. program. Prior preparation for the Ph.D. program should include courses in statistics, intermediate microeconomics and macroeconomics, and some exposure to differential, integral, and multivariate calculus and linear algebra.

Correspondence and Information

Holly L. Chase
Assistant Dean for Admissions
International Business School
Brandeis University, MS 032
Waltham, Massachusetts 02454-9110
Phone: 781-736-2252
800-878-8866 (toll-free, United States only, for catalog and application)
Fax: 781-736-2263
E-mail: admission@lemberg.brandeis.edu
Web site: http://www.brandeis.edu/global

Brandeis University

THE FACULTY AND THEIR TEACHING AND RESEARCH AREAS

Full-Time Faculty

Chad P. Bown, Ph.D., Wisconsin–Madison. International trade, trade policy, GATT/WTO.
Linda Bui, Ph.D., MIT. Environmental economics, industrial organization, public economics.
Laarni Bulan, Ph.D., Columbia. Empirical corporate finance and real options.
Anne P. Carter, Ph.D., Harvard. Technical progress, input-output.
Stephen Cecchetti, Ph.D., Berkeley. Macroeconomics, monetary theory.
F. Trenery Dolbear Jr., Ph.D., Yale. Macroeconomics, computer simulation, uncertainty.
Can Erbil, Ph.D., Boston College. Economic modeling, political economy and development economics, international trade.
Benjamin Gomes-Casseres, D.B.A., Harvard. International business, corporate alliances.
Adam B. Jaffe, Ph.D., Harvard. Technology, economic growth, industrial organization.
Gary H. Jefferson, Ph.D., Yale. China, development, transition, industrial organization.
Blake D. LeBaron, Ph.D., Chicago. International finance, exchange rates, artificial stock markets.
Rachel McCulloch, Ph.D., Chicago. International economics, development, foreign investment.
Nidhiya Menon, Ph.D., Brown. Econometric analysis of micro credit, empirical microeconomics, econometrics, development economics, labor economics.
Andrew Molinsky, Ph.D., Harvard. Organizational behavior, cross-cultural interaction.
Carol Osler, Ph.D., Princeton. Asset pricing, currency market microstructure, exchange rate dynamics, finance.
Peter A. Petri, Ph.D., Harvard. International trade, development, East Asia.
Charles Reed, M.B.A., Harvard. Entrepreneurship, venture business plans.
Paroma Sanyal, Ph.D., California, Irvine. R&D and technology, industrial organization, environmental economics, electricity deregulation.
Rashmi Shankar, Ph.D., California, Santa Cruz. Currency crises, econometrics, international finance, macroeconomics.
Narayanan Subramanian, Ph.D., Brown. International finance.

Adjunct Faculty

Alexander Aikens III, J.D., Northeastern. Corporate finance, credit analysis, bankruptcy, debt and equity valuations.
Christopher Alt, Ph.D., MIT. Finance, applied economics, strategic planning.
Michael Appell, M.A., Brandeis. Corporate ethics, social responsibility.
Serkan Bahceci, M.A., Brown. Econometrics, microeconomics.
John W. Ballantine, Ph.D., NYU. Corporate finance, labor economics, strategic management.
Edward J. Bayone, M.I.A., Columbia. Risk analysis, global banking.
Alfonso Canella, M.B.A., Boston University. Financial modeling, equity valuation, capital budgeting.
Atreya Chakraborty, Ph.D., Boston College. Industrial organization, corporate finance, regulation.
Jennifer Chu, M.S., Brandeis. Asset pricing, equity markets, financial economics, investor behavior, portfolio management.
Steven Cohen, LL.D., Columbia. Executive mentoring, mediation, negotiations.
Michael H. Coiner, Ph.D., Yale. Economics of higher education, international economics, macroeconomics.
Hugh Lagan Crowther, M.B.A., M.S., Bridgeport. Investment research, strategy and analytics marketing, investment technology, portfolio manufacturing, quantitative equity, research, management and trading.
Egidio Diodati, M.B.A., Suffolk. Advertising, Asian business practices, business policy, European business practices, international marketing.
Ron D'Vari, Ph.D., UCLA. Fixed-income securities, international portfolio management, risk management.
Ellen Gates, M.S., Brandeis. Statistical data, retrieval and manipulation, statistical analysis, statistical related process design.
Gautam George, M.S., Brandeis. Agent-based experiments, commons economy, currency crises, development, sovereign debt.
Martin J. Gross, LL.M., NYU; J.D., Chicago. Asset management, hedge funds.
Richard Keith, D.B.A., Florida State. Managerial accounting, finance, planning and control.
Danny M. Leipziger, Ph.D., Brown. International institutions in the global economy.
Michael L. Oshins, M.P.S., Cornell. Service management.
Alisa Peled, Ph.D., Harvard. Political economy of the Middle East.
Cynthia Phillips, M.S., Lesley. Electronic commerce.
Ayako Saiki, Ph.D., Brandeis. Exchange rate regimes.
Ferhan Salman, M.S., Middle East Technical (Turkey). Applied finance, growth, public finance.
Shahbaz Sheikh, M.S., Brandeis. Asset ownership, executive compensation, foreign debt, Pakistan economy.
William Sherden, M.B.A., Stanford. Competitive strategy.
Simon Sherrington, M.A., Oxford. Foreign direct investment, government-business relations, political economy.
Thomas A. Shively, M.B.A., Chicago. Fixed income securities.
Lloyd J. Tanlu, M.A., Brandeis. Accounting principles, budget analysis.
Grace Zimmerman, M.B.A., Harvard. Business planning, entrepreneurship, marketing, sales.

BOARD OF OVERSEERS

Ronald M. Ansin.
Roger Berkowitz, President and Chief Executive Officer, Legal Sea Foods.
Steven Bunson '82, Managing Director, Goldman Sachs Group, Inc.
Julian Cohen, Senior Partner, Leatherbee and Company.
Donald G. Drapkin '68, Vice Chairman and Director, MacAndrews & Forbes Holdings Inc.
Alan S. Elkin, Chairman and Chief Executive Officer, Active International.
Paul Fruitt, Vice President, Corporate Planning (retired), The Gillette Company.
Richard E. Goldman, Executive Vice President (retired), Men's Wearhouse.
Martin J. Gross, Esq., President, Sandalwood Securities, Inc.
Charles B. Housen, Chairman, Erving Industries, Inc.
Gary N. Jacobs, Esq., '66, Executive Vice President and General Counsel, MGM-Mirage-Bellagio.
Larry S. Kanarek '76, Director, McKinsey & Company, Inc.
Barry Kaplan '77, Managing Director, Goldman, Sachs.
Amy Kessler '90, Associate Director, Bear Stearns and Company.
Suk Won Kim '70, Chairman, Ssangyong Cement Industrial Co., Ltd.
George T. Lowy, Esq., Partner, Cravath, Swaine & Moore.
Dr. John H. McArthur, Dean Emeritus, Harvard Business School.
Shari Redstone, Esq., President, National Amusements, Inc.
Theodor Schmidt-Scheuber, Chairman, North Hampton Partners, LP.
Dr. Michael P. Schulhof '70.
Ambassador Ira S. Shapiro, Esq., '69, Greenberg Traurig.
Malcolm L. Sherman, Chairman of the Board, Gordon Brothers, Inc.
Sheldon I. Stein '74, Senior Managing Director, Bear Stearns and Company.
Shinichiro Torii, President, Suntory Limited.
Stanley B. Tulin, Vice Chairman and Chief Financial Officer, AXA Financial and The Equitable Life Assurance Society of the U.S.
Adam Usdan, General Partner, Trellus Management Company, LLC.
John Usdan, President, Midwood Management Corporation.
The Honorable Milton A. Wolf, Former U.S. Ambassador to Austria, Milton A. Wolf Investors.

AFFILIATED FOREIGN UNIVERSITIES

American University in Bulgaria.
Copenhagen School of Economics and Business Administration, Denmark.
École Supérieure des Sciences Economiques et Commerciales (ESSEC), France.
Erasmus University, The Netherlands.
ESADE International Management Program, Spain.
Fundaçao Getulio Vargas, Brazil.
Instituto Tecnológico Autónomo de México, Mexico.
International University, Japan.
Keio University, Japan.
Koblenz School of Corporate Management, Germany.
Luigi Bocconi University, Italy.
National University of Singapore.
Tel Aviv University, Israel.
Universiteit Maastricht, The Netherlands.
University of International Business and Economics, Beijing, China.
University of Paris IX (Dauphine), France.
Waseda University, Japan.
Yonsei University, Korea.

THE JOHNS HOPKINS UNIVERSITY

Zanvyl Krieger School of Arts and Sciences
Advanced Academic Programs
Master of Arts in Applied Economics

Programs of Study

The Johns Hopkins University M.A. in Applied Economics program is a ten-course evening program geared toward working adults. This part-time program can be completed in as little as two years. While emphasizing quantitative techniques, the program's substantive scope is wide. Students choose from more than twenty electives spanning the subfields of economics, enabling students to build their own curricula. Students can concentrate their studies in public policy, for example, for contributing to any level of government policy formulation and policymaking. Business economics is available for those who plan to work as economists in the private sector. Breadth of training is highly desirable in this subfield, and this program provides it. Students can concentrate in finance and macroeconomics to exploit the increasing complementarity between these fields. Others have built programs around international economics and development in order to gain an analytical and quantitative perspective on global issues. Other examples of available subfields around which students have customized their programs are environmental economics and health economics.

Together with the Carey Business School of Johns Hopkins University, a dual M.A. in Applied Economics/Graduate Certificate in Financial Management and a dual M.A. in Applied Economics/Graduate Certificate in Investments are also offered. Each of these dual diplomas comprise fourteen courses, eight through the Applied Economics program and six at Carey.

Research Facilities

Students in Washington use the Library Resource Center at 1717 Massachusetts Avenue, NW. The center's staff arranges interlibrary loans and offers reserve services and a collection of program-specific reference materials. The Library Resource Center has eleven workstations in the electronic research room connecting to the Eisenhower Library's Horizon WebPac, the Hopkins online catalog search tool, and a vast array of electronic databases, journals, and periodicals. A twenty-four-station student computer lab is filled with state-of-the-art econometric software.

Financial Aid

Federal financial aid in the form of student loans is available on a limited basis to degree candidates who are enrolled in two or more courses per semester. Applicants must be U.S. citizens or permanent residents.

Cost of Study

Tuition is $2560 per course in 2008–09. Ten courses are required to complete the degree.

Living and Housing Costs

Students make their own arrangements for housing.

Student Group

There are 280 active students in the Applied Economics program as of spring 2008. Almost all have jobs in the government, private, or nonprofit sectors. The average student age is 26. Some students come directly from college; others have work experience. Not nearly all of the students have been undergraduate economics majors. Some wish to complement their existing undergraduate or professional skills—in business, engineering, law, or natural science—with quantitative economics skills. The students are motivated to advance or broaden their careers and, occasionally, change direction. For all that, the classroom atmosphere is characterized by an exceptionally high degree of intellectual curiosity.

Location

The Johns Hopkins University Washington D.C. Center is located at 1717 Massachusetts Ave, NW, close to the Carey Business School and the School of Advanced International Studies, two other Johns Hopkins Divisions. The center is located in Washington's vibrant Dupont Circle neighborhood, a block from the Dupont Circle Metro station.

The University and The School

Johns Hopkins University is America's oldest research university. The Applied Economics program is part of Advanced Academic Programs, the part-time graduate and noncredit programs of the Zanvyl Krieger School of Arts and Sciences.

Applying

Admission requirements are a bachelor's degree or higher with a GPA of 3.0 on a 4.0 scale in the latter half of an applicant's studies or a graduate degree in an appropriate field (relevant work experience also can be considered), one semester of introductory microeconomics, one semester of introductory macroeconomics, and one semester of undergraduate calculus or equivalent (those without calculus can be admitted as provisional students and take Mathematical Methods for Economics as an eleventh program course).

To apply, students should submit a completed application, the application fee of $70, a resume or statement of purpose not to exceed 500 words (only one is needed), two letters of recommendation, official undergraduate transcripts, and graduate transcripts (if applicable). International students must also submit TOEFL scores, a course-by-course credential evaluation performed by an independent evaluation service, and a vaccination form if they are under 26 years of age.

Online applications are encouraged.

Correspondence and Information

Advanced Academic Programs
The Johns Hopkins University
1717 Massachusetts Ave NW, Suite 101
Washington, D.C. 20036

Phone: 202-452-1940
Fax: 202-452-1970
E-mail: aapadmissions@jhu.edu
Web site: http://advanced.jhu.edu/academic/applied-economics/

The Johns Hopkins University

THE FACULTY

The faculty, who all hold Ph.D.'s, are accomplished practitioners who work in policy positions at the Federal Reserve Board; at federal agencies such as the Department of Justice, the Department of the Treasury, and the Bureau of Labor Statistics; at the IMF; and at private consulting firms. They are ideal for this program because they use the science of economics to understand real-world problems, including policy problems, in their day-to-day work, and they bring their outlook into the classroom. They have, in part, held academic positions; many publish; and they are, in various ways, on top of their fields. They are in the classroom because they wish to teach.

Joe Aldy, Ph.D., Harvard University, is a Fellow at Resources for the Future. He served on the staff to the President's Council of Economic Advisers from 1997–2000.
David Arseneau, Ph.D., University of Virginia, is an economist in the Division of International Finance at the Federal Reserve Board.
Ron Borzekowski, Ph.D., Stanford University, is an economist in the Financial Studies Section at the Federal Reserve Board.
Allan Brunner, Ph.D., Duke University, is in the European Department at the International Monetary Fund.
Cory Capps, Ph.D., Northwestern University, is a principal in the Antitrust Practice Group at Bates White.
Curtis Carlson, Ph.D., University of Maryland, is a Tax Policy Analyst at the Department of the Treasury. He has worked as a Senior Economist for the Council of Economic Advisors.
Sanjay Chugh, Ph.D., University of Pennsylvania, is Assistant Professor of Economics at the University of Maryland. Prior to his appointment there, he spent three years as a staff economist at the Federal Reserve Board.
James Cooper, Ph.D., Emory University, and J.D., George Mason University, is the Deputy Director for Policy Planning at the Federal Trade Commission.
Paul Dockins, Ph.D., Duke University, manages the Science Policy and Analysis Division at the Environmental Protection Agency's National Center for Environmental Economics.
Elaine Fortowsky, Ph.D., Rice University, is an economist at Fannie Mae.
Anna Fruttero, Ph.D., New York University, is an economist at the World Bank.
Ed Gamber, Ph.D., Virginia Tech, is Professor of Economics at Lafayette College.
Christopher Garmon, Ph.D., University of Florida, is an economist with the Federal Trade Commission. He won the 2007 Applied Economics' Excellence in Teaching Award.
Nate Goldstein, Ph.D., Stanford University, is a Research Economist with the U.S. Department of Justice, Antitrust Division.
Elise Gould, Ph.D., University of Wisconsin, is an economist at the Economic Policy Institute.
Patrick Greenlee, Ph.D., Northwestern University, is a Research Economist in the Antitrust Division of the U.S. Department of Justice.
Charles Griffiths, Ph.D., University of Maryland, is an Economist at the Environmental Protection Agency's National Center for Environmental Economics. He recently worked as a Senior Economist at the Council of Economic Advisers.
Joseph Gruber, Ph.D., Johns Hopkins University, is at the International Finance Division of the Federal Reserve Board.
Rene Kamita, Ph.D., University of California, Berkeley, is an economist with the Antitrust Division at the U.S. Department of Justice.
Robert Kneuper, Ph.D., Clemson University, is a Senior Managing Economist with LECG, a consulting firm.
Sang-Sub Lee, Ph.D., University of North Carolina, Chapel Hill, is Risk Modeling Director at Freddie Mac.
Michael Lettau, Ph.D., University of Wisconsin, is a research economist at the U.S. Bureau of Labor Statistics. He won Applied Economics' Excellence in Teaching award for 2008.
John McClelland, Ph.D., University of Maryland, is in the Office of Tax Analysis at the Department of the Treasury. He is the recipient of the program's 2005 Excellence in Teaching award.
Robert McClelland, Ph.D., University of California, Davis, is Chief of the Price Index Research Division at the Bureau of Labor Statistics. He received the program's Excellence in Teaching award in 2006.
Alexandra Minicozzi, Ph.D., University of Wisconsin, works for the Congressional Budget Office as a health policy analyst.
Fabio Natalucci, Ph.D., New York University, is a Senior Economist in the Monetary & Financial Stability section of the Federal Reserve Board.
Pär Österholm, Ph.D., from Uppsala University, works as an economist at Sveriges Riksbank, and is presently a visiting researcher at the International Monetary Fund.
Joshua Pinkston, Ph.D., Northwestern University, is an economist at the Bureau of Labor Statistics.
Jeremy Rudd, Ph.D., Princeton University, is a Senior Economist in the Macroeconomic Analysis section of the Federal Reserve Board.
John Schindler, Ph.D., University of Pennsylvania, is a Senior Economist at the Federal Reserve Board.
Edward Seiler, Ph.D., University of Chicago, is Senior Economist at Fannie Mae.
Michael Shelby, Ph.D., Boston University, is Chief of the Economic Analysis Branch in the Office of Atmospheric Programs at the Environmental Protection Agency.
Loren Smith, Ph.D., University of Virginia, is a staff economist in the Bureau of Economics at the U.S. Federal Trade Commission.
Kathleen Toma, Ph.D., University of Kentucky, works for the Department of Treasury in the Office of Tax Analysis.
Jonathan Veum, Ph.D., University of North Carolina at Chapel Hill, is Market/Credit Risk and Strategy Director at Freddie Mac.
David Weiskopf, Ph.D., Vanderbilt University, is Senior Managing Economist at LECG, an international consulting firm.
Elliot Williams, Ph.D., University of California, San Diego, is an economist at the Bureau of Labor Statistics.
Dean Williamson, Ph.D., Caltech, is Research Economist at the Antitrust Division of the U.S. Department of Justice. In the 2007–08 academic year he was the Victor H. Kramer Fellow at Harvard Law School.

NORTHEASTERN UNIVERSITY

Graduate School of Arts and Sciences
Department of Economics

Programs of Study

The Department of Economics offers a Master of Arts (M.A.) program and a Ph.D. program in applied economics. Both programs permit full- and part-time study.

The M.A. program is designed to serve the need for a terminal graduate degree for professional economists, government officials, and economic consultants, and to lay the groundwork for students who wish to pursue the Ph.D. degree. The M.A. degree is designed to provide a solid foundation in economic theory and quantitative methods (core courses), while providing an opportunity for students to apply the tools of economic analysis to particular policy areas. The focus of the program is on application and practice. Development of presentation skills and ability to produce project-oriented writing assignments are essential to the program and are emphasized in the elective (application) courses. Even the core courses incorporate application of theory and/or methods. The ability to incorporate co-op (paid work) into the program enhances the practice orientation of the degree. The program can be completed in one to two years. Students are required to complete 32 semester hours of academic work, of which 16 semester hours constitute core courses.

The Ph.D. program in applied economics is small and focused. After taking courses in microeconomic and macroeconomic theory and applied econometrics, students specialize in either industrial organization or labor economics. An optional subfield in transportation economics is available to students specializing in industrial organization. The primary purpose is to prepare students for research positions in government, consulting firms, and industry. The program consists of 24 semester hours of work for those entering with a master's degree and 48 semester hours for those entering with a bachelor's degree. At the doctoral level, 16 semester hours are focused on developing an advanced theoretical and quantitative foundation. The remainder of the course work involves sophisticated application of analytical tools in the chosen fields. A capstone course is included in this curriculum.

Research Facilities

Research facilities available to Northeastern students include the University's Snell Library, the world-renowned Boston Public Library, and, through an interlibrary consortium, the libraries of other major universities in the region. Computing facilities include access to personal computers in the Economics Student Resource Center and a wireless network that links to University and department software.

The Department houses the Center for Labor Market Studies, which provides access to facilities, libraries, information resources, and research opportunities. The Department is also associated with the Center for Urban and Regional Policy and is the home of the *Journal of Transport Economics and Policy.*

Financial Aid

Full-time students are eligible for financial aid consideration. Teaching assistantships provide a stipend of $16,225 (2008–09 rates), plus tuition remission, for 20 hours of work per week. Graduate Student Scholarships provide tuition remission only. Paid full-time work for three to six months as a practicing economist is also available to qualified students within the context of the M.A. degree program.

Cost of Study

Graduate tuition for 2008–09 is $1035 per semester hour. Fees include the health services fee (per academic year), $1975; international student fee (one time only), $250; student center fee (per term), $70 (full-time), $10 part-time); student recreation fee (per term), $46 (full-time), $15 (part-time); and student activities fee (per term), $12.

Living and Housing Costs

On-campus housing is fully furnished, and apartments are available to full-time graduate students on a first-come, first-served basis. Students should contact housing@neu.edu for current information about on- and off-campus housing options.

Student Group

Currently, there are about 40 graduate students in the Department, of whom approximately half are women and 75 percent are international students. Most students study full-time. It is estimated that the Ph.D. program represents about one third of the graduate student body.

Location

Northeastern University is located in Boston. The city is a hub of cultural, educational, and social activity. More than 300,000 college students from around the country and the world call Boston home. In addition to Northeastern's offerings, many neighboring colleges and universities offer seminars and workshops open to Northeastern students. Among the hundreds of cultural attractions are the Museum of Fine Arts and Symphony Hall, both of which are adjacent to Northeastern. Boston is also the regional headquarters of several federal agencies, including the Departments of Labor, Health and Human Services, Education, Commerce, and Housing and Urban Development. In addition, the region's Federal Reserve Bank is located in Boston.

The University

Founded in 1898, Northeastern is an independent urban university with nine graduate and professional schools that offer more than 100 graduate and postgraduate degree programs. The University is the world leader in cooperative education, a program that enables students to combine paid off-campus work experience with traditional course work in obtaining a degree. The University has a distinguished faculty of dedicated teachers and scholars.

Applying

Application materials are to include the following: a completed application form, a $50 nonrefundable application fee, official copies of all undergraduate and graduate transcripts, GRE aptitude scores, and three letters of recommendation, preferably from academic sources. Applicants requesting financial aid must submit an application by February 1. International students are required to submit a completed Declaration and Certification of Finances (DCF) form for the University to issue visa application forms (I-20 or DS-2019). International students must provide evidence of English proficiency.

Correspondence and Information

Department of Economics
301 Lake Hall
Northeastern University
360 Huntington Avenue
Boston, Massachusetts 02115

Phone: 617-373-2871
E-mail: econ@neu.edu
Web site: http://www.economics.neu.edu

Northeastern University

THE FACULTY AND THEIR RESEARCH

M. Shahid Alam, Professor; Ph.D., Western Ontario. Development economics, international trade.
Neil O. Alper, Associate Professor; Ph.D., Pittsburgh. Labor economics, economics of crime, cultural economics.
Oscar T. Brookins, Associate Professor; Ph.D., SUNY at Buffalo. Economic theory, policy.
Kamran M. Dadkhah, Associate Professor; Ph.D., Indiana. Econometrics, macroeconomics.
James R. Dana, Professor; Ph.D., MIT. Industrial organization, competitive strategy, operations management.
Alan W. Dyer, Associate Professor; Ph.D., Maryland College Park. History of economic thought, institutionalist theory.
Sungwoo Kim, Professor; Ph.D., Berkeley. Microeconomic theory, econometrics, regional economics.
John E. Kwoka Jr., Finnegan Distinguished Professor; Ph.D., Pennsylvania. Industrial organization.
Maria José Luengo-Prado, Assistant Professor; Ph.D., Brown. Macroeconomics, consumption, computational economics.
Steven A. Morrison, Professor and Chair; Ph.D., Berkeley. Transportation economics.
Andrew M. Sum, Professor; B.A., MIT. Labor economics, human resource policies and programs, economic policy and planning, urban economics.
Zhongmin Wang, Assistant Professor; Ph.D., Georgetown. Industrial organization, regulatory economics, competition law, energy economics.
Gregory H. Wassall, Associate Professor and Graduate Coordinator; Ph.D., Rutgers. Cultural economics, public economics, microeconomics.

RENSSELAER POLYTECHNIC INSTITUTE

Department of Economics

Programs of Study Rensselaer's Department of Economics offers Ph.D. and M.S. degrees with emphasis on its focal areas of ecological economics and the economics of technological change. As part of a leading technological university, the Department is uniquely positioned to offer graduate training in ecological economics, and this fast-growing field offers unparalleled opportunities for linking economics to new developments in the natural sciences and in the other social sciences. The Department's courses in economics impart both general knowledge—of microeconomic and macroeconomic processes and of tools for economic analysis—and specific knowledge relevant to informed decision-making about the environment and R&D processes. Armed with a deeper understanding of economics and the far-reaching consequences of economic policies, graduates are equipped to understand and effectively influence the forces around them.

The Ph.D. requires 90 credits beyond the bachelor's degree and 60 beyond the master's degree. Students are required to take 30 credits of core courses and electives (ten courses) in addition to passing comprehensive exams and proposing, writing, and defending the Ph.D. dissertation. The Department maintains a small Ph.D. in Ecological Economics program in which students have the opportunity to work closely with distinguished faculty members. Students are expected to carry out original research and are provided with the skills and attention to become leaders. The faculty members focus their research in two main areas. In ecological economics, they analyze how the global economy and local economies can and will change in the future, reflecting social values and economic policies for dealing with global environmental change. In the economics of technological change, they probe the forces driving technology creation and diffusion, the transfer of technology from universities to firms, the evolution of industries, and technology evaluation and development—hence the well-being of the world's people. In both areas, close attention is paid to empirical facts, ensuring relevance for the models and analyses. Research assistantships cover diverse topics, including sustainable regional development, climate change policy, renewable energy economics, and sustainable livelihoods. In particular, work in the area of sustainable development involves quantitative models linking economic structure, socioeconomic characteristics, and ecosystem services. Such research covers both global analysis—such as how climate change may impact future quantities and prices of food—and community initiatives, in both the U.S. and abroad, that involve public participation.

The Department of Economics also offers a Master of Science degree in economics, which is designed to meet the needs of traditional students as well as those of returning students who wish to integrate their professional experience with additional training in economics. This degree requires 30 credits beyond the bachelor's degree with a minimum of 24 credit hours in residency. An applied master's thesis can account for 6 of the credit hours. The program is specifically designed for students who wish to tailor an advanced degree to their career goals. In addition to a solid grounding in economic theory, they are able to develop in-depth knowledge in applied economics in a particular area of interest.

Students may also opt for a Professional Master's Degree in Ecological Economics, Values, and Policy (EEVP), a dual major offered with the Department of Science and Technology Studies.

Research Facilities Research is supported by state-of-the-art facilities and equipment including the Rensselaer Libraries, whose electronic information system provides access to collections, databases, and the Internet from campus and remote terminals; the Rensselaer Computing System, which permeates the campus with a coherent array of more than 7,000 nodes of distributed laptops, desktops, advanced workstations, and servers; a shared toolkit of applications for interactive learning and research and high-speed Internet connectivity; one of the country's largest academically based, class 100 clean room facilities; high-performance campuswide computing facilities that allow for serial or parallel computation; and five core laboratories for molecular biology, proteomics, bio-imaging, and tissue engineering.

Rensselaer's research capabilities have been enhanced with the addition of the Computational Center for Nanotechnology Innovations (CCNI). The result of a $100-million collaboration with IBM and New York State, the CCNI is the world's most powerful university-based supercomputing center and a top ten supercomputing center of any kind in the world. The CCNI is made up of massively parallel Blue Gene supercomputers, POWER-based Linux clusters, and Opteron-based clusters, providing more than 100 teraflops of computational muscle and approximately a petabyte of shared online storage.

Other facilities and research centers include the Center for Biotechnology and Interdisciplinary Studies; the George M. Low Center for Industrial Innovation; research centers for integrated electronics, terahertz science, nanotechnology, fuel cell and hydrogen research, lighting research, science and technology policy, and infrastructure and transportation studies; the Geotechnical Centrifuge Research Center; the Darrin Fresh Water Institute; and the Scientific Computation Research Center.

In addition, academic departments and faculty laboratories have extensive discipline-specific research capabilities and equipment.

Financial Aid Financial aid is available in the forms of teaching and research assistantships and fellowships, which include tuition scholarships and stipends. Rensselaer assistantships cover the academic year, with summer support available in many departments. University, corporate, or national fellowships fund many of Rensselaer's full-time graduate students. Outstanding students may qualify for university-sponsored Rensselaer Graduate Fellowship Awards, which carry a minimum stipend of $22,000 and a full tuition and fees scholarship. All fellowship awards are calendar-year awards for full-time graduate students. Low-interest, deferred-repayment graduate loans are available to U.S. citizens with demonstrated need.

Cost of Study Full-time graduate tuition for the 2008–09 academic year is $36,950. Other costs (estimated living expenses, insurance, etc.) are projected to be about $13,680. Therefore, the cost of attendance for full-time graduate study is approximately $50,630. Part-time study and cohort programs are priced differently. Students should contact Rensselaer for specific cost information related to the programs they wish to study.

Living and Housing Costs Graduate students at Rensselaer may choose from a variety of housing options. On campus, students can select one of the many residence halls and immerse themselves in campus life or choose from a select number of apartments designed for graduate students only. There are abundant, affordable options off campus as well, many within easy walking distance.

Student Group Of the 1,176 graduate students, 29 percent are women and 92 percent are full-time, with 75 percent of full-time graduate students studying at the doctoral level.

Student Outcomes Rensselaer's graduate students are hired in a variety of industries and sectors of the economy and by private and public organizations, the government, and institutions of higher education. Their starting salaries average $74,807 for master's degree recipients and $82,750 for Ph.D. recipients.

Location Located just 10 miles northeast of Albany, New York State's capital city, Rensselaer's historic 275-acre campus sits on a hill overlooking the city of Troy, New York, and the Hudson River. The area offers a relaxed lifestyle with many cultural and recreational opportunities, with easy access to both the high-energy metropolitan centers of the Northeast—such as Boston, New York City, and Montreal, Canada—and the quiet beauty of the neighboring Adirondack Mountains.

The Institute Recognized as a leader in interactive learning and interdisciplinary research, Rensselaer continues a tradition of excellence and technological innovation dating back to 1824. Rensselaer has five schools—Architecture, Engineering, Management, Science, and Humanities and Social Sciences—that offer more than 100 graduate programs in over forty-eight disciplines that attract top students, researchers, and professors. The discovery of new scientific concepts and technologies, especially in emerging interdisciplinary fields, is the lifeblood of Rensselaer's culture and a core goal for the faculty, staff, and students. Fueled by significant support from government, industry, and private donors, Rensselaer provides a world-class education in an environment tailored to the individual.

Applying Science and engineering backgrounds, as well as traditional economics backgrounds, are good starting points for work on the economics of technology and industry. Students are considered each year for admission in the fall semester. The admission deadline for the fall semester is January 1. Basic admission requirements are the submission of a completed application form (available online), the required application fee ($75), a statement of background and goals, official transcripts, official scores on the GRE General Test or the GMAT, TOEFL or IELTS scores (if applicable), and two recommendations. A scholarly writing sample is also required for Ph.D. applicants.

Correspondence and Information

Department of Economics
Russell Sage Laboratory
Rensselaer Polytechnic Institute
110 8th Street
Troy, New York 12180
Phone: 518-276-6387
E-mail: kaufmb@rpi.edu
Web site: http://www.economics.rpi.edu/about.html

Rensselaer Polytechnic Institute

THE FACULTY AND THEIR RESEARCH

James Adams, Professor; Ph.D., Chicago. James D. Adams is Professor of Economics at Rensselaer, the former department head (2006–08), and a research associate of the National Bureau of Economic Research in Cambridge, Massachusetts. Prior to joining Rensselaer he was Professor of Economics at the University of Florida. He has held visiting appointments at the U.S. Bureau of Labor Statistics, the U.S. Bureau of the Census, and the George J. Stigler Center for the Study of the Economy and the State at the University of Chicago. He recently served on the Telecommunications R&D Board of the National Academy of Sciences, Washington, D.C., and has advised the Advanced Technology Program of the U.S. National Institute of Standards and Technology on issues of data quality and policy evaluation. Dr. Adams has published numerous articles on the economics of technical change, with emphasis on the causes and consequences of industrial and academic research and development, as well as a range of articles in the fields of labor and public economics. His recent research focuses on the limits of the firm in research and development, the measurement of scientific influence, the identification of alternative channels of knowledge externalities in the economy, the structure and meaning of scientific teams and collaborations, the speed of diffusion of scientific research, the interaction between investment in industrial research and development and investment in physical capital, and the determinants of research and teaching productivity in academia. (adamsj@rpi.edu)

Science and industry: Tracing the flow of basic research through manufacturing and trade. *Econ. Innovat. New Techol.* 2008. (http://www.economics.rpi.edu/workingpapers/rpi0614.pdf)

Learning, internal research, and spillovers: Evidence from a sample of R&D laboratories. *Econ. Innovat. New Techol.* 2006. (http://www.economics.rpi.edu/workingpapers/rpi0409.pdf)

Scientific teams and institutional collaborations: Evidence from U.S. universities, 1991–1999. *Res. Pol.* 34(3):259–85, 2005.

The influence of federal laboratory R&D on industrial research. *Rev. Econ. Statist.* 85:1003–20, 2003.

Faye Duchin, Professor; Ph.D., Berkeley. For many years, Dr. Duchin has been engaged in formulating alternative scenarios about technological change and analyzing their implications for employment and economic well-being as well as for resource use and the environment. The research makes use of mathematical models of individual economies and the world economy implemented with input-output databases. A sustainable development research agenda requires cross-disciplinary collaborations and needs to engage not only the policy community and corporate decision makers but also civil society. This research involves collaborations with colleagues in several countries, and Dr. Duchin is also involved in building scholarly networks through her leadership roles in several international professional societies and scholarly journals. At the present time, she is especially active in the integration of input-output economics and industrial ecology, mainly input-output models of economies and engineering-based life-cycle analysis. (duchin@rpi.edu)

A world trade model based on comparative advantage with m regions, n goods, and k factors. *Econ. Syst. Res.* 17(2):141–62, 2005. (http://econpapers.repec.org/paper/rpirpiwpe/0309.htm)

Sustainable consumption of food. *J. Ind. Ecol.* 9(1–2):99–114, 2005. (http://econpapers.repec.org/paper/rpirpiwpe/0405.htm)

World trade as the adjustment mechanism of agriculture to climate change. *Climatic Change* 82(3–4):393–409, 2007. (http://econpapers.repec.org/paper/rpirpiwpe/0507.htm)

Arturo Estrella, Professor and Department Head; Ph.D., Harvard. Dr. Estrella's research focuses on predictive power of the term structure of interest rates; affine models of the term structure of interest rates; macroeconomic models: theoretical and empirical; use of macro economic models in monetary policy analysis; bank capital regulation; corporate finance, particularly in the financial sector; and financial markets and instruments. (estrea@rpi.edu)

Monetary tightening cycles and the predictability of economic activity. *Econ. Lett.*, in press.

The yield curve as a leading indicator: Some practical issues. *Current Issues in Economics and Finance,* New York: Federal Reserve Bank, July/August, 2006. With Trubin.

Why does the yield curve predict output and inflation? *Econ. J.* July, 2005.

John Gowdy, Professor; Ph.D., West Virginia. Dr. Gowdy's research focuses on ecological economics, including economic valuation of biodiversity and environmental theory and policy; behavioral economics and environmental policy; economic anthropology, including the sustainability of complex societies; evolutionary models of economic change; and biophysical models of sustainability. (gowdyj@rpi.edu)

Microeconomic Theory Old and New: A Student's Guide. Palo Alto: Stanford University Press, in press.

Paradise for Sale: A Parable of Nature. Berkeley: University of California Press, 2000. With McDaniel.

Behavioral economics and climate change policy. *J. Econ. Behav. Organ.*, in press.

Toward a new welfare foundation for sustainability. *Ecolog. Econ.* 53:211–22, 2005.

The approach of ecological economics. *Cambridge J. Econ.* 29(2):207–22, 2005. With Erickson.

The revolution in welfare economics and its implications for environmental valuation. *Land Econ.* 80(2):239–57, 2004.

John Heim, Clinical Professor; M.P.A., Harvard; M.S., Ph.D., SUNY at Albany. Dr. Heim's current research focuses on converting Hick's IS-LM version of Keynesian theory into a system of mechanics by finding stable and unambiguous estimates of the parameters in the IS and LM equations. Work to date on the IS curve is substantially progressed and suggests that with the addition of accelerator, crowd out, and Tobin's q variables, the IS curve predicts most of the variance in the real GDP quite well. Work on the LM curve is in a more preliminary stage. Work on determining the mechanism that brings the system into equilibrium at the intersection of the two curves is well progressed. A second area of research interest is the East Asian economic recovery after the 1997–1998 economic crisis. Preliminary investigation of whether the recovery was generated by the effects classical mechanics or Keynesian mechanics is underway.(heimj@rpi.edu)

Lighting Fixtures With Specular Reflectors Compared To Lighting Fixtures With Ordinary Reflectors: A Cost Benefit Study. Delmar, N.Y.: The Dormitory Authority of the State of New York, 1996.

A/E fee schedules: 1991 comparison of FDC with certain states and other public entities. Albany, N.Y.: The NYS Facilities Development Corporation, 1991.

Robert W. Jones, Clinical Assistant Professor; M.B.A, Rochester; Ph.D., Rensselaer. Dr. Jones' research focuses on regional economics, valuation of closely held businesses, and economics and law. (jonesr2@rpi.edu)

An institutional perception of cooperative behavior. *J. Soc. Econ.* 32:233–48, 2003. With Onyeiwu.

Daniel Shawhan, Assistant Professor; Ph.D., Cornell. Dr. Shawhan's research focuses on environmental regulation of electric power industry, electricity market design, human behavior in decisions involving up-front costs, and delayed benefits. (shawhd@rpi.edu)

Is time inconsistency primarily a male problem? *J. Econ. Behav. Organ.* Feburary, 2008.

Tradable permit markets. In *Experimental Methods, Environmental Economics,* eds. T. Cheery, S. Kroll, and J. Shogren. New York: Routledge, 2007.

Markets for reactive power and reliability: A white paper. Engineering and Economics of Electricity Research Group White Paper, December 5, 2006. Available at http://e3rg.pserc,cornell.edu/node/100.

Kenneth Simons, Assistant Professor; Ph.D., Carnegie Mellon. Professor Simons is an expert in the dynamics of industrial organization and technological change. His work probes industry shakeouts, cross-industry differences in competitive dynamics, firm survival, merger and acquisition, entrepreneurship, technological innovation, and disruptive technological change. The work involves detailed empirical study using state-of-the-art methods for industry dynamics and technology research, complemented with theoretical industrial organization modeling plus simulation and computational methods. Prior to joining RPI, he was on the faculty of the University of London's Royal Holloway College. He has served as chairman of the Network of Industrial Economists and editorial board member of two journals, and has organized several conferences on industrial organization and technological change. Student research opportunities may be available. He has employed several Ph.D. and undergraduate students as research assistants, as well as serving as advisor or committee member for numerous Ph.D. students. (simonk@rpi.edu)

Ownership change, productivity, and human capital: New evidence from matched employer-employee data in Swedish manufacturing. In *Producer Dynamics: New Evidence from Micro Data.* Chicago: University of Chicago Press, for the National Bureau of Economic Research, in press. With Siegel and Lindstrom.

Lighting industry. In *Innovation in Global Industries-U.S. Firms Competing in a New World.* Washington, D.C.: National Academics Press: 163–205, 2008. With Sanderson, Walls, and Lai.

Industry shakeouts and technological change. *Int. J. Ind. Organ.* 23(1–2):23–43, 2005. With Klepper.

Political instability and growth in dictatorships. *Public Choice* 125(3–4):445–70, 2005. With Overland and Spagat.

Donald Vitaliano, Professor; Ph.D., CUNY. Dr. Vitaliano's research agenda focuses on efficiency and productivity measurement, with particular interest in the public sector. Both stochastic frontier regression and data envelopment analysis are employed in these studies. Three new papers dealing with corporate social responsibility have been recently published. In addition, three papers relating to electric utility, gender wage differences based on human capital and corporate social responsibility and land turnover are under review. (vitald@rpi.edu)

An empirical analysis of the strategic use of corporate social responsibility. *J. Econ. Manag. Strat.* 16(3):773–92, 2007. With Siegel.

How increased enforcement can offset statutory deregulation: The case of the community reinvestment act. *J. Financ. Regul. Compl.* 15(3):1358–88, 2007. With Stella.

The cost of corporate social responsibility: The case of the community reinvestment act. *J. Prod. Anal.* 26:235–44, 2006. With Stella.

SOUTHERN ILLINOIS UNIVERSITY CARBONDALE

Department of Economics
Doctoral Program

Program of Study

The Department of Economics at Southern Illinois University Carbondale (SIUC) offers a doctoral degree that is designed to be completed in four years. In the first year, the student takes courses in macroeconomics, microeconomics, and mathematical economics and is required to pass qualifying exams in microeconomics and macroeconomics. In the second year, the student completes one field of specialization, begins econometrics, and takes the field exam (summer of second year). In the third year, the student completes the second field, finishes econometrics, and starts on a research topic for the dissertation. The fourth year is devoted to completion of the dissertation. The fields offered by the Department are international economics, economic development, and monetary theory and policy. The student may, with the permission of the Director of Graduate Studies, pursue a field in finance. All of the courses for this field are taught in the College of Business.

Research Facilities

Research facilities include Morris Library which contains more than 2.6 million volumes and subscribes to more than 12,000 current serials. Library users have access to nearly 900 electronic data files and CD-ROM products via multiple workstations throughout the library. The University maintains an extensive and up-to-date computer system with four instructional laboratories. The Department maintains its own computer lab and its own library of software most used by economists.

Financial Aid

Departmental teaching assistantships are available on a competitive basis. Half-time assistantships with stipends of $1362 per month are available for Ph.D. students. A 15-hour tuition waiver accompanies each assistantship.

Cost of Study

In-state graduate tuition is $313.90 per credit hour in 2008–09. Out-of-state tuition is 2.5 times the in-state tuition rate ($784.75 per credit hour). Graduate students with at least a 25 percent appointment as a graduate assistant receive a tuition scholarship. Fees vary from $511.26 (1 credit hour) to $1416.05 (12 credit hours). Students with a graduate assistantship receive a 25 percent reduction in the Primary Care Medical Fee.

Living and Housing Costs

For married couples, students with families, and single graduate students, the University has 690 efficiency and one-, two-, three-, and four-bedroom apartments that rent for $484 to $686 per month in 2008–09. Residence halls for single graduate students are also available, as are accessible residence hall rooms and apartments for students with disabilities.

Student Group

There were 41 students enrolled in the graduate program in economics in fall 2007. There are more than 4,300 students enrolled in graduate programs in the University, with a total student enrollment of 21,387.

Location

SIUC is 350 miles south of Chicago and 100 miles southeast of St. Louis. Nestled in rolling hills bordered by the Ohio and Mississippi Rivers and enhanced by a mild climate, the area has state parks, national forests and wildlife refuges, and large lakes for outdoor recreation. Cultural offerings include theater, opera, concerts, art exhibits, and cinema. Educational facilities for the families of students are excellent.

The University

Southern Illinois University Carbondale is a comprehensive public university with a variety of general and professional education programs. The University offers associate, bachelor's, master's, Ph.D., J.D., and M.D. degrees. The University is fully accredited by the North Central Association of Colleges and Schools. The Graduate School has an essential role in the development and coordination of graduate instruction and research programs. The Graduate Council has academic responsibility for determining graduate standards, recommending new graduate programs and research centers, and establishing policies to facilitate the research effort.

Applying

A student with a bachelor's degree must have a grade point average of 2.7 (A = 4.0) or above in the last 60 hours of undergraduate work, while those entering with a master's degree must have a grade point average of 3.25 in all graduate course work. All applicants are required to take the Graduate Record Examinations. International applicants must earn a minimum score of 550 on the Test of English as a Foreign Language (TOEFL) exam (220 on the computerized version). Additional information can be found on the Departmental Web site listed below.

Correspondence and Information

Professor Subhash C. Sharma
Director of Graduate Studies
Department of Economics
Southern Illinois University
Carbondale, Illinois 62901-4515

Mrs. Sandra McRoy, Graduate Secretary
Department of Economics
Southern Illinois University
Carbondale, Illinois 62901-4515
Phone: 618-536-7746
Fax: 618-453-2717
Web site: http://www.siu.edu/~econ/

Southern Illinois University Carbondale

THE FACULTY AND THEIR RESEARCH

Zsolt Becsi, Assistant Professor; Ph.D., Wisconsin–Madison, 1991. Public finance, macroeconomics.
Bilateral war in a multilateral world: Carrots and sticks for conflict resolution. *Can. J. Econ.* 2006. With Lahiri.
War technology, war, and welfare. *India Macroeconomics Annual 2004–2005* ed. Sugata Marjit. Calcutta: The Reserve Bank of India Endowment. With Lahiri.
Chifeng Dai, Assistant Professor; Ph.D., Florida, 2003. Industrial organization, contract theory, public economics, health economics, applied econometrics.
Delegating management to experts. *Rand J. Econ.* 2006. With Lopomo and Lewis.
Scott Gilbert, Associate Professor; Ph.D., California, San Diego, 1996. Econometrics, macroeconomics and finance.
The impact of skewness in the hedging decision. *J. Futures Markets,* 26(5):503–20, 2006. With Jones and Hatfield.
Testing for latent factors in models with autocorrelation and heteroskedasticity of unknown form. *Southern Econ. J.* 72:236–52, 2005. With Zemcik.
Richard Grabowski, Professor; Ph.D. Utah, 1977. Economic development.
Economic growth and institutional change. *Int. J. Dev. Issues* 4:39–70, 2005.
Agricultural revolution, political development, and long run growth. *Can. J. Dev. Stud.* 26:393–407, 2005.
Sajal Lahiri, Vandeveer Chair Professor; Ph.D., Indian Statistical Institute, 1976.
On the provision of official and private foreign aid. *J. Dev. Econ.* 80:179–97, 2006. With Schweinberger.
Food for education versus school quality: A comparison of policy options to reduce child labor. *Can. J. Econ.* 38:394–419, 2005. With Jafarey.
Thomas Mitchell, Associate Professor; Ph.D., Brown, 1984. Microeconomic theory, mathematical economics.
Conservation laws for microeconomists!: Comments on economic conservation laws as indices of corporate performance. *Japan World Economy,* 16:269–76, 2004.
Indeterminate output allocations. In *Economic Theory, Dynamics and Markets: Essays in Honor of Ryuzo Sato,* pp. 429–37, eds. T. Negishi, R. V. Ramachandran, and K. Mino. Boston: Kluwer Academy Publishers, 2001.
A. K. M. Morshed, Assistant Professor; Ph.D., Washington (Seattle), 2001. Macroeconomic theory, international finance.
Is there really a "border effect?" *J. Int. Money Finance,* 26(7):1229–38, 2007.
Additional sources of bias in half-life estimation. *Computational Statistics and Data Analysis,* in press. With Seong and Ahn.
Basharat A. Pitafi, Assistant Professor; Ph.D., Hawaii, 2004. Public economics, resource economics.
Prevention, eradication, and containment of invasive species: Illustrations from Hawaii. *Agr. Resource Econ. Rev.,* in press.
The economic value of watershed conservation. *Land management impacts on coastal watershed hydrology,* in press, eds. Fares and Kadi. Southampton: WIT Press.
Daniel Primont, Professor; Ph.D., California, Santa Barbara, 1970. Microeconomic theory, mathematical economics
Directional duality theory. *Econ. Theory,* 29(1):239–47, 2006. With Färe.
Luenberger productivity indicators: Aggregation across firms. *J. Prod. Anal.,* in press. With Färe.
Subhash C. Sharma, Professor; Ph.D., Kentucky, 1983. Econometrics, statistics, time-series analysis, monetary economics, development economics.
An examination of momentum strategies in commodity futures markets. *J. Futures Markets* 2007. With Shen and Szakmary.
Currency substitution in Asian countries. *J. Asian Econ.* 16:489–532, 2005. With Kandil and Chaisrisawatsuk.
Kevin Sylwester, Associate Professor; Ph.D., Wisconsin–Madison, 1997. Macroeconomics, economic growth, and development.
A note on geography, institutions, and income inequality. *Econ. Letters* 85:235–40, 2004.
Income inequality and population density 1500 AD: A connection. *J. Econ. Development* 28(2):61–82, 2003.
Alison Watts, Associate Professor; Ph.D., Duke, 1993. Microeconomics, game theory and law and economics.
Formation of buyer-seller trade networks in a quality-differentiated product market. *Can. J. Econ.* 39:971–1004, 2006. With Wang.
Uniqueness of equilibrium in cost sharing games. *J. Math. Econ.* 37:47–70, 2002.

STONY BROOK UNIVERSITY, STATE UNIVERSITY OF NEW YORK

Department of Economics

Program of Study

The Department offers a Ph.D. degree in economics. All courses are at the Ph.D. level; however, after 30 credits, a student can receive an M.A. degree. The Department offers an integrated program centered on applied microeconomic theory, macroeconomics, mathematical modeling, simulation, and econometrics. The program is based on the view that the various fields in economics have a very large overlap in terms of economic theory and empirical methodology and that they differ mainly in terms of some of the structure that is put on otherwise common models. In line with this view, the courses for the program are divided into eight core courses, six field courses, and a research workshop. The core courses are mostly taken in the first year, with the second year and part of the third year devoted to field courses. The core courses provide the theory and econometric techniques that are a necessary foundation for the field courses. These courses do not require previous knowledge of economics but proceed quickly through the foundations using mathematics through multivariate calculus and linear algebra. The field courses are in the areas of game theory, industrial organization, labor economics, health economics, economic demography and growth, computational economics and dynamic modeling, computational macroeconomics, and applied econometrics. Taking advantage of the overlap in fields, these courses are designed to cover a wide set of theoretical structures and research methodologies used throughout economics, to show how these techniques are transported from field to field, and to let students see in depth some particular applications. As a whole, these courses give students a strong foundation for economic research in a broad variety of fields. Students choose a thesis adviser by the beginning of the third year and pass a thesis proposal defense by the end of the third year. Given the overlap in fields, faculty guidance is available for a wide variety of research topics. Students can expect to work closely with a thesis adviser and a number of other faculty members on their theses. The Department has an active seminar series with both inside and outside faculty speakers and an active graduate student–run seminar series to present and discuss thesis research. Various groups of faculty members also run workshops for their thesis students. The typical student takes about five years to complete the Ph.D. The Ph.D. program prepares students for careers as economics faculty members in research universities and four-year colleges and as researchers on complicated economic questions in the private and government sectors. Two examples of the research topics shared by academic researchers and private and government researchers are pricing for communications networks and effects of government trade policy.

Research Facilities

The Social Science Data Lab is a state-of-the-art microcomputer facility with mathematical modeling and statistical software, along with many other standard software titles. It is connected to the Internet and is available to all social science graduate students. The Smith departmental Sun multiprocessor networked workstation is available to students working on computationally intensive research. Most student offices are now equipped with microcomputers. The University library is highly oriented toward the electronic supply of text and data and subscribes to many electronic journals and electronic working paper series and literature databases.

Financial Aid

The Department offers financial support in the form of teaching assistantships (TAs) paying a stipend of around $15,000 per academic year, along with a full-tuition scholarship, which pays full tuition (but not the fees) to a limited number of applicants. About 12 students are admitted each fall with financial support. It has been the Department's practice to fund for four years those supported students who maintain good progress in their studies and teaching duties. For students who perform well as scholars and teachers, there may be other means of support available in the fifth year. Special Turner Fellowships and a full tuition scholarship are available to qualified citizens or permanent residents who are Native American, African American, or Hispanic American.

Cost of Study

In 2008–09, full-time tuition at 12 credits for entering in-state residents is $3450 per semester, while out-of-state residents and international students pay $5460. Additional fees for each semester, including (but not limited to) the infirmary, activity, technology, and transportation fees, total about $875. International students also pay a service fee of approximately $35 per semester and an orientation fee of $50. Fees for the mandatory Student Health Insurance Plan vary depending on citizenship and employment status.

Living and Housing Costs

For 2008–09, Stony Brook calculates the cost of education excluding tuition, fees, and insurance at $14,228 per year. On-campus apartments range in cost from approximately $336 per month to approximately $1456 per month, depending on the size of the unit and the number of students sharing the space. Off-campus housing options include rooms, houses, and apartments that can be rented from approximately $350 to $2500 per month. Costs including books, food, and transportation may vary depending on academic program and/or personal circumstances.

Student Group

There are generally about 40 to 45 Ph.D. students in residence, with about an equal number of men and women. Most of the students are international. Almost all students receive financial support. The Department seeks students with a strong aptitude and interest in mathematical modeling of economic phenomena. Preparation in linear algebra and multivariate calculus is essential. In addition to undergraduate economics majors with strong mathematical preparation, students with majors in other mathematical modeling disciplines, such as engineering, physics, and mathematics, are invited to apply. In the profession as a whole, a large number of current Ph.D. economists majored in engineering, physics, or mathematics as undergraduates and wanted to use their skills on more people-oriented questions. The Department does give preference to U.S. citizens or permanent residents who satisfy the requirements on interest and preparation.

Student Outcomes

Recent graduates have taken positions in both academia and the private sector. Some recent placements in academia have been as assistant professors at Florida State University at Tallahassee, California State University at Northridge, the University of Pittsburgh, and National Chi-Nan University in Taiwan. Some have taken postdoctoral appointments at institutions such as Yale University. Private-sector placements have been in various economic consulting firms and government policy and research offices. Former graduates who are more advanced in their careers are at institutions such as Rutgers and UCLA in academia and the Office of Tax Analysis, U.S. Treasury, in the public sector.

Location

The University is located on the North Shore of Long Island, about 60 miles east of New York City; Stony Brook offers a direct connection to New York City by train. For more information, students should visit the University's Web site.

The University

Stony Brook is classified by the Carnegie Foundation as a Type I research university, its highest distinction, which is granted to fewer than 2 percent of all colleges and universities nationwide. The University has strong mathematics, applied mathematics, computer science, and engineering departments, which are important resources for doing mathematical modeling.

Applying

Students are admitted to start in the fall semester only. Admission and financial aid applications should be filed by January 15. For information on applying and other general graduate school information, students should visit http://www.grad.sunysb.edu. The information on applying is on the How to Apply link. The application fee of $60 must be paid for the application to be considered. In the personal statement on the application and as information for references, students should remember that the Department seeks students with the interest, the aptitude, and the necessary skills to do mathematical modeling in economic science. As part of the statement, the Department requires a short description of the content and level of the mathematics courses the student has taken. Students should note on the application if they are interested in admission without financial support; otherwise, they will not be offered admission unless the Department can also offer financial aid.

Correspondence and Information

Liza Murphy
Graduate Coordinator
Department of Economics
Stony Brook University
Stony Brook, New York 11794-4384
Phone: 631-632-7530
Fax: 631-632-7516
E-mail: graduate_economics@notes.cc.sunysb.edu

For questions about academic aspects of the Ph.D. program, students should contact:

Professor Hugo Beniztez-Silva
Graduate Program Director
Department of Economics
Stony Brook University
Stony Brook, New York 11794-4384
Phone: 631-632-7551
Fax: 631-632-7516
E-mail: hugo.benitez-silva@sunysb.edu
Web site: http://www.sunysb.edu/economics

Stony Brook University, State University of New York

THE FACULTY AND THEIR RESEARCH

Alexis Anagnostopoulos, Assistant Professor; Ph.D., London Business School, 2005. Macroeconomics, computational economics.
Hugo Benitez-Silva, Associate Professor; Ph.D., Yale, 2000. Labor economics, computational economics.
Sandro Brusco, Associate Professor and Graduate Program Director; Ph.D., Stanford, 1993. Mechanism design, auctions.
Eva Carceles-Poveda, Assistant Professor; Ph.D., Universitat Pompeu Fabra, 2001. Macroeconomics, financial economics, international economics.
William Dawes, Associate Professor and Co-Chair; Ph.D., Purdue, 1972. Econometrics, economic history.
Pradeep Dubey, Professor; Ph.D., Cornell, 1975. Game theory, mathematical economics.
Shanjun Li, Assistant Professor; Ph.D., Duke, 2007. Industrial organization, econometrics, environmental economics, applied econometrics.
Mark Montgomery, Professor; Ph.D., Michigan, 1982. Economic demography, development economics, econometrics.
Thomas J. Muench, Professor; Ph.D., Purdue, 1965. Mathematical economics, macroeconomics, econometrics, urban economics.
Silvio Rendon, Assistant Professor; Ph.D., NYU, 1997. Labor economics, applied econometrics, macroeconomics, industrial organization.
John A. Rizzo, Professor (joint with the Department of Preventive Medicine); Ph.D., Brown. Health economics, public health.
Warren C. Sanderson, Professor and Co-Chair; Ph.D., Stanford, 1974. Economic demography, economic history, labor economics.
Wei Tan, Assistant Professor; Ph.D., Johns Hopkins, 2005. Industrial organization, applied econometrics, health economics.
Yair Tauman, Professor; Ph.D., Hebrew (Jerusalem), 1978. Industrial organization, game theory.
Michael Zweig, Professor; Ph.D., Michigan, 1967. Political economy, labor economics.

SUFFOLK UNIVERSITY

Graduate Programs in Economics

Programs of Study

The economics department offers three graduate programs of study: the Ph.D. in economics, the Master of Science in International Economics (M.S.I.E.), and the Master of Science in Economic Policy (M.S.E.P.). In addition, the department offers a joint program with the Law School (J.D./M.S.I.E.).

The Ph.D. program offers both midcareer professionals and new graduates a program with an applied focus, taught by experienced faculty members, with convenient full-time and part-time program options. As part of the Department of Economics, the program is academically rigorous and theoretically sound. The unique applied focus of the Suffolk Ph.D. program enables graduates not only to seek academic appointments but also to compete for jobs in the business sector and advance in their fields. The core required courses provide a foundation in economics; the electives allow students to tailor their studies to their particular interests in theory and research.

The Master of Science in International Economics meets the needs of today's world, where business and government decisions are made in an increasingly global environment. The M.S.I.E. is a highly focused study of international economics that equips students with sophisticated quantitative skills. It prepares students for professional careers in international business, international finance, and international economic policy as analysts and consultants. M.S.I.E. students are qualified to work for multinational corporations, financial institutions, economic consulting firms, international law firms, and various international organizations.

The Master of Science in Economic Policy prepares students for careers in government, public policy research, or government relations. It provides the knowledge and skills needed for government budgeting, tax-revenue forecasting, the regulation of public utilities, and the litigation of antitrust issues. Students find the program useful preparation for managing a government agency, providing in-house or consulting advice on policy issues, representing clients in government hearings, writing reports on public policy issues, and providing expert testimony.

Research Facilities

Research facilities include the Mildred F. Sawyer Library and the Moakley Law Library. Students also have access, through an interlibrary program, to other major libraries in the region. As Boston residents, all students have access to the world-class Boston Public Library. Computing facilities, which provide access to current databases and software, are available for graduate students in the department. Facilities are also available at several on-campus computer labs. In addition, the Department of Economics houses the nationally recognized Beacon Hill Institute for Public Policy Research. The Beacon Hill Institute applies state-of-the-art statistical, mathematical, and econometric methods to provide economic analyses of today's leading public policy issues. Opportunities exist for graduate students to work and intern with this leading research institution.

Financial Aid

The graduate programs offer various levels of financial support. Outstanding full-time candidates may receive financial awards, including a full tuition waiver for up to three years and teaching or research assistantships. Partial financial awards are offered to qualified full-time students. Excellent candidates for part-time study may be awarded a tuition waiver. Additional opportunities exist for grants and scholarships.

Cost of Study

For the master's programs, full-time tuition is $10,175 per semester (four courses), and part-time tuition is $2775 per course. For the Ph.D. program, tuition is $3531 per course.

Living and Housing Costs

Limited on-campus housing is offered at Suffolk's Residence Hall overlooking the Boston Common. It is a short walk to the main academic and administrative buildings. Accommodations are in single, double, triple, and quad rooms or in suites. Suffolk's Off-Campus Housing Office (OCHO) helps students find housing by gathering information on apartment sublets, rentals, and sharing opportunities. The office maintains a list of students seeking roommates, posts advertisements for roommates, and works with area realtors to better serve students. A complete list of realtors is available upon request.

Student Group

The graduate students in economics include a broad range of U.S. and international students, both recent college graduates and midcareer professionals. Full-time and part-time students are welcomed, resulting in a diverse mix of backgrounds and experiences being shared in the classrooms. Classes are typically small, giving students close working relationships with each other and the faculty members. The favorable faculty-student ratio fosters an environment of personalized mentoring, helping students achieve their individual professional and academic goals.

Location

Suffolk University is located on Boston's renowned Beacon Hill, within easy reach of Boston's governmental, financial, cultural, and historic centers. A city rich in history and culture, Boston has more than fifty of the finest colleges and universities in the nation. Founded in 1630, ten years after the Pilgrims landed at Plymouth, Boston is the capital of the commonwealth of Massachusetts and is the largest city in New England. The city of Boston has a population of more than 600,000 people, including a significant number of college students, whose heritage is worldwide.

The University and The School

Founded in 1906 as Suffolk School of Law by Gleason L. Archer, Suffolk University now offers fifty-six undergraduate and graduate degree and certificate programs. Suffolk was named in *Barron's Best Buys in College Education.* Suffolk also offers programs on the campuses of Cape Cod Community College, Merrimack College, and Dean College and has branch campuses in Madrid, Spain, and Dakar, Senegal.

Applying

Information on admission procedures and requirements is available at the Web site (http://www.suffolk.edu/economics) or by contacting the Office of Graduate Admission (information below). The Ph.D. program enrolls new students only in the fall semester. Applications must be received by February 1. The master's programs enroll new full-time students only in the fall. Applications must be received by June 15 for the fall semester (March 15 for those interested in financial aid) and November 1 for the spring semester.

Correspondence and Information

Office of Graduate Admission
Suffolk University
8 Ashburton Place
Boston, Massachusetts 02108-2701

Phone: 617-573-8302
Fax: 617-523-0116
E-mail: grad.admission@suffolk.edu
Web site: http://www.suffolk.edu

Suffolk University

THE FACULTY

The Department of Economics at Suffolk University consists of a vibrant group of 12 full-time scholars. Faculty members are active in research, policy advising, writing, and consulting. Research interests of the faculty members are diverse but are in the general area of applied economics and finance, with special emphasis on the issues of economic policy and international economics.

Specific research interests of the faculty include economic development, taxation, econometric and CGE tax modeling for states of the U.S., economic reconstruction of war-torn economies, issues in education and education reform, empirical investigation of rent-to-own agreements, welfare reform, economics of regulation, empirical viability of recent developments in contract theory, competitive dynamics, spatial competition, product differentiation in U.S. motion-pictures exhibition markets, productivity growth, international debt problems and currency crisis, foreign direct investment and capital flows to emerging markets, determinants of market-assessed sovereign risk, international trade, economic justice, political economy of international economic relations, optimal investment decisions for the long term, timing issues in the high-tech IPO aftermarket, and financial valuation of knowledge assets of biotechnology firms.

David G. Tuerck, Professor and Chairman; Ph.D., Virginia. Tax policy, public choice, macroeconomic theory.
In-Mee Baek, Professor; Ph.D., Indiana. International investment, currency crisis, foreign capital flows, international debt problems.
Darlene C. Chisholm, Professor; Ph.D., Washington (Seattle). Industrial organization, applied microeconomic theory, empirical contract studies, spatial competition and product differentiation in U.S. motion-picture industry.
A. Tolga Ergun, Assistant Professor; Ph.D., Arizona. Econometrics, financial economics.
Haldun Evrenk, Assistant Professor; Ph.D., Boston University. Political economy, development economics, public finance, industrial organization.
Lou Foglia, Instructor; M.A., Northeastern. Microeconomics, macroeconomics, money, banking.
Jonathan Haughton, Associate Professor; Ph.D., Harvard. Development economics, tax policy, competitiveness, international economics.
Jongbyung Jun, Assistant Professor; Ph.D., Michigan State. Foreign exchange rate determination, applied time-series econometrics, international trade and finance.
Alison Kelly, Professor; Ph.D., Boston College. Productivity growth, issues in education, applied statistical methods.
Shahruz Mohtadi, Associate Professor; Ph.D., LSU. International economics, monetary economics.
Benjamin Powell, Assistant Professor; Ph.D., George Mason. Austrian economics, economic development, public choice, applied microeconomics.
Serge Shikher, Assistant Professor; Ph.D., Boston University. International trade, international finance, macroeconomics, development.

UNIVERSITY OF ILLINOIS AT URBANA–CHAMPAIGN

Department of Economics
Program in Policy Economics

Programs of Study

The Program in Policy Economics, offered by the Department of Economics, is a specially designed, intensive program of study leading to a Master of Science degree in economics from the University of Illinois. It is intended for promising young administrators in government and private institutions, in both developing countries and advanced industrial countries, who need additional training in the areas of economic analysis and quantitative techniques. It is also for young scholars interested in a terminal master's degree.

A complementary mission of the program is to help interested students acquire the necessary background to pursue a doctorate in economics. While earning the master's degree, they learn if the pursuit of a Ph.D. degree is within their reach and suits their purposes.

The program offers more than forty courses in twelve different areas of specialization. These courses are taught by a faculty of more than 30 members.

Students with an excellent background in economics and quantitative methods and a high level of proficiency in English can complete the program in one year. Students with low proficiency in English, limited training in economics, or who completed their university course work several years ago are generally required to take an additional one or two semesters to complete the master's degree. Students who wish to take advantage of the extensive course offerings at the University and study in additional areas or fields may remain up to two years to complete their program of study.

Students select one field from advanced econometrics (this field requires special prerequisites), development economics, economic policy, environment and natural resources, health economics, industrial organization, international economics, labor economics, law and economics, monetary economics, public economics, and urban and regional economics.

Program enrichment offers special training on computers; internationally known guest speakers; field trips to business, financial, and government institutions; and tutorial help for students encountering difficulty in courses.

Research Facilities

The University library has the largest collection of any public university in the world and ranks third among U.S. academic libraries.

Financial Aid

No financial aid is available for students or their spouses.

Cost of Study

Tuition and fees for the first year are $32,900 in 2008–09. Tuition and fees are subject to change for the second year (2009–10). Books and supplies cost approximately $2407 per year.

Living and Housing Costs

Students can reside in University graduate student dormitories, University married student housing, or private apartments or rooms. The estimated living allowance is $1450 per month, or $17,400 per year. The current estimated cost for accompanying dependents is as follows: for one dependent, $6200 per year; for two, $9980 per year; and, for each additional dependent, $1920 per year. The current annual rate for health insurance is $3096 for a spouse and $1542 for children (subject to change).

Student Group

Program alumni come from ninety-five different countries. The 86 students who are currently enrolled are from sixteen countries: Afghanistan, Belgium, Brazil, China, Dominican Republic, Guatemala, Indonesia, Iran, Italy, Korea, Peru, Taiwan, Tanzania, Thailand, Turkey, and the United States. All students are registered full-time, and 39 percent are women.

Student Outcomes

Upon completion of the program, participants usually return to their previous positions or similar ones with enlarged opportunities. Some continue to work on their Ph.D. degrees (at the University of Illinois and elsewhere). Jobs that graduates return to include university instructor and researcher, commercial bank manager, chief executive officer, economic journalist and senior economist at a research institute, central bank economist and manager, securities analyst, chief expert at the Ministry of Trade, associate director at the Ministry of Construction, and manager at the Ministry of Finance. Over the years, some have risen in rank to hold such positions as president, governor, and deputy governor in central banks and top government cabinet positions, including Minister of Finance, Minister of Commerce and Industry, and Minister of Rural Development.

Location

Urbana-Champaign, with its mixture of rural and urban influences, education and culture, and high technology and research, offers the feeling and sophistication of a big city while retaining its Midwestern warmth.

Available athletic facilities include two golf courses, several tennis courts, jogging tracks, basketball courts, soccer fields, handball/racquetball courts, squash courts, five swimming pools, and weightlifting rooms.

The University

Since its founding in 1867, the University of Illinois at Urbana-Champaign has steadily gained in stature and is recognized as one of the leading universities in the world. The University is known primarily for its achievements in research and graduate studies.

Another prime indicator of the campus's excellence is the success of its alumni. Eleven alumni have won Nobel Prizes for the United States and another 18 have won the Pulitzer Prize.

Applying

Required materials are an application and fee, official transcript (translated if not in English) from all universities and colleges attended, three letters of recommendation, and, for students from non-English-speaking countries, scores on the Test of English as a Foreign Language (TOEFL).

Since admission is granted on a continuing basis, students should submit their completed application materials as soon as possible. Although there is no deadline date for applications, the program is usually full by April 1.

Correspondence and Information

M.S. Program
Director, Master's Program
313 David Kinley Hall
1407 West Gregory Drive
Urbana, Illinois 61801
Phone: 217-333-7651
Fax: 217-244-7368
E-mail: mspe@illinois.edu
Web site: http://www.mspe.uiuc.edu

Ph.D. Program:
Graduate Coordinator
410 David Kinley Hall
1407 West Gregory Drive
Urbana, Illinois 61801
Phone: 217-333-0120
Fax: 217-244-6678
E-mail: econ@illinois.edu
Web site: http://www.economics.uiuc.edu

University of Illinois at Urbana-Champaign

THE FACULTY AND THEIR RESEARCH

Professors
Werner Baer, Ph.D., Harvard, 1958. Development, international economics.
Anil K. Bera, Ph.D., Australian National, 1982. Econometrics.
Daniel M. Bernhardt, Ph.D., Carnegie-Mellon, 1986. Economic theory, industrial organization, banking.
In-Koo Cho, Ph.D., Princeton, 1986. Microeconomics, macroeconomics.
*Lawrence DeBrock, Ph.D., Cornell, 1979. Industrial organization, microeconomics.
Hadi S. Esfahani, Ph.D., Berkeley, 1984. Economic development, international trade.
Firouz Gahvari: Ph.D., UCLA, 1981. Public economics.
*J. Fred Giertz, Ph.D., Northwestern, 1970. Public finance and public choice.
Fred M. Gottheil, Ph.D., Duke, 1959. Comparative economic systems, Middle East economics, history of economic thought.
*Geoffrey J. D. Hewings, Ph.D., Washington, 1969. Macroeconomics, urban and regional planning.
*Charles M. Kahn, Ph.D., Harvard, 1981. Economics of information and uncertainty, game theory.
Roger W. Koenker, Ph.D., Michigan, 1974. Econometric theory and applications, industrial organization.
Stefan Krasa, Ph.D., Vienna, 1987. Microeconomics.
*Crain Olson, Ph.D., Wisconsin, 1979. Labor economics.
Salim Rashid, Ph.D., Yale, 1976. Microeconomic theory, history of economic thought, mathematical economics.
Bart Taub, Ph.D., Chicago, 1981. Macroeconomics.
*Thomas S. Ulen, Ph.D., Stanford, 1978. Law and economics.
Anne P. Villamil, Ph.D., Minnesota, 1988. Monetary economics.
Steven R. Williams, Head of Department; Ph.D., Northwestern, 1982. Microeconomic theory, mathematical economics.
Nicholas C. Yannelis, Ph.D., Rochester, 1983. Mathematical economics, game theory.

Associate Professors
George Deltas, Ph.D., Yale, 1995. Microeconomics, industrial organization.
Stephen Parente, Ph.D., Minnesota, 1990. Macroeconomics, development and growth.
*Elizabeth Powers, Ph.D., Pennsylvania, 1994. Labor economics.

Assistant Professors
Richard Akresh, Ph.D., Yale, 2004. Economic development.
Luciano de Castro, Ph.D., Institute of Pure and Applied Mathematics (Brazil), 2004. Mathematical economics, auction theory.
Todd Elder, Ph.D., Northwestern, 2001. Labor.
Seung-Hyun Hong, Ph.D. candidate, Stanford. Industrial organization.
*Darren Lubotsky, Ph.D., Berkeley, 2000. Labor economics.
Makoto Nakajima, Ph.D., Pennsylvania, 2004. Macroeconomics.
Mattias Polborn, Ph.D., Munich, 1998. Public economics.
Daniela Puzzello, Ph.D., Purdue, 2005. Economic and monetary theory.
Leonardo Rezende, Ph.D., Stanford, 2003. Industrial organization.
Juha Seppala, Ph.D., Chicago, 2000. Macroeconomics.
Rui Zhao, Ph.D., Chicago, 2000. Macroeconomics, transition.

Lecturers
Kristine Brown, Ph.D., Berkeley, 2007. Labor economics.
Jose Jazquez, Ph.D., Rensselaer, 2001. Environmental economics.
Joseph Petry, Ph.D., Illinois, 1991. Statistics.
Colleen Schultz, Ph.D., Illinois, 1998. Industrial organization, health, law and economics.
Ali Toossi, Ph.D., Illinois, 2002. Industrial organization, political economy.

**Joint appointment with other departments or institutes in the University.*

UNIVERSITY OF NEW HAMPSHIRE

Whittemore School of Business and Economics
Economics Programs

Programs of Study

The Whittemore School offers programs of study leading to both the M.A. and the Ph.D. degrees in economics. Applicants may enroll in the fall. The M.A. degree can be completed in one calendar year. The Ph.D. program is currently under review.

The principal requirements for the M.A. degree are 30 semester hours of graduate course work, two courses in economic theory, one course in econometrics, a yearlong graduate economics seminar, and a master's research paper. M.A. students may select electives from a variety of areas. The M.A. satisfies the first year of the Ph.D. program.

Currently, the Ph.D. program is based on the following key features: a series of core courses, two fields of specialization, several significant research requirements, comprehensive exams in economic theory, and field exams in the two chosen fields. The core courses consist of two courses in microeconomic theory, macroeconomic theory, and econometrics and one course each in the history of thought and in economic thought and methodology. Separate comprehensive exams are given in microeconomic and macroeconomic theory. Beyond the core, students are required to take two fields of concentration, each consisting of a two-course sequence and a field exam. The department offers fields of concentration in international economics, development and sustainability, environmental and energy economics, public economics, and history of economic thought. Students should refer to the Web site for information on any revisions to the curriculum.

A continuous, integrated approach to research is a highlight of the program. New students enroll in the department's weekly seminar series and are presented research by faculty members, advanced graduate students, and well-known guest speakers. Near the end of the program, Ph.D. students generally develop a research proposal for the dissertation and present it to the workshop.

In addition to the research emphasis of the Ph.D. program, the department encourages students interested in teaching to pursue the optional 12-semester-hour cognate in college teaching. The University of New Hampshire's (UNH) Preparing Future Faculty program is designed to provide graduate students with the necessary tools to become successful faculty members. Students can visit http://www.gradschool.unh.edu/pff for more information about the program.

Research Facilities

The University library houses more than 1.1 million volumes, 6,500 periodical subscriptions, and 1 million government documents that form the core of print materials. Electronic sources include EBSCOhost, which provides indexes to general, academic, and business periodicals; LexisNexis, which accesses a wide variety of full-text news and legal information; and PubMed, which contains 9 million citations of medical materials. The library provides access to a wide variety of materials, from medieval manuscripts to electronic data sets, from nineteenth-century novels to Web-based full-text documents, and from bound periodicals to electronic journals. For more information, students should visit the Web site at http://www.library.unh.edu.

Financial Aid

Applicants with strong academic records may qualify for graduate assistantships. For 20 hours of work per week, graduate assistants receive a stipend of $14,100 (proposed) for the 2008–09 academic year plus a tuition waiver; for 10 hours a week, they receive $7010 (proposed) plus a waiver of half the tuition, of which the remainder is paid at the in-state rate. Tuition scholarships are also available for both full- and part-time students, as are federally funded loans for those who qualify.

Cost of Study

In 2008–09, proposed tuition for full-time students is $14,350 per year for New Hampshire residents and $25,525 per year for nonresidents. Mandatory yearly fees are expected to be $1446 plus a health insurance fee of $1490 if the student does not already have health insurance.

Living and Housing Costs

Babcock Hall, the graduate residence hall, provides single rooms at a proposed cost of $5654 for the 2008–09 academic year. Students may remain in Babcock during the summer at reduced rates. Limited on-campus housing for married students is provided at Forest Park. Proposed prices for 2008–09 for efficiency and one- or two-bedroom apartments range from $706 to $935 per month. Off-campus housing is available in a wide range of prices. For further information, applicants should visit the UNH Housing Web site at http://www.unh.edu/housing.

Student Group

The University has an enrollment of 13,544 students, 2,481 of whom are graduate students; many are from other countries. The economics graduate program typically has between 15 and 20 students enrolled.

Location

Located 65 miles north of Boston, the University of New Hampshire occupies a picturesque 200-acre campus in the attractive New England town of Durham. It is only 10 miles from the Atlantic Ocean and 60 miles from New Hampshire's scenic lakes and mountains.

The University and The School

Founded in 1886, the University of New Hampshire serves as a cultural and scientific center for the area, with the New England Center, Space Science Center, and Paul Arts Center. The Whittemore School of Business and Economics, established in 1962 and one of the University's six schools and colleges, offers undergraduate as well as graduate degrees.

Applying

An applicant for admission must submit the following materials to the Graduate School, Room 109, Thompson Hall, University of New Hampshire: the official Graduate School application forms for admission to graduate study; two official transcripts showing the grades earned in all of the applicant's previous graduate and undergraduate academic work; three letters of recommendation from persons in a position to judge the applicant's preparation for and ability to undertake graduate study (e.g., the applicant's previous instructors or coworkers); GRE scores; and, for all international applicants, TOEFL scores.

Application deadlines are July 1 for the fall session. The fall deadline for applications from international students is April 1. Applicants who wish to be considered for graduate assistantships and tuition scholarships should submit the completed application by February 1.

Correspondence and Information

Whittemore School of Business and Economics
Graduate Programs Office
116 McConnell Hall
University of New Hampshire
15 Academic Way
Durham, New Hampshire 03824-3593

Phone: 603-862-1367
Fax: 603-862-4468
E-mail: wsbe.grad@unh.edu
Web site: http://wsbe.unh.edu/grad/

University of New Hampshire

THE FACULTY AND THEIR RESEARCH

Business Administration

E. Hachemi Aliouche, Associate Professor of Hospitality Management and Senior Research Fellow, Rosenberg International Center of Franchising; Ph.D., New Hampshire. Financial aspects of franchising and financial valuation.

Carole K. Barnett, Associate Professor of Management; Ph.D., Michigan. Organizational leadership and learning, change and transformation, design and development, culture.

Clayton Barrows, Professor of Hospitality Management; Ed.D., Massachusetts. Food and beverage management, private club management.

Brian Bolton, Assistant Professor of Finance; Ph.D., Colorado. Corporate governance and initial public offering, financial markets and infrastructure, capital structure, financial econometrics, investments.

Ludwig Bstieler, Assistant Professor of Marketing; Ph.D., Innsbruck (Austria). Design and marketing of new products, market research methods.

Stephen Ciccone, Associate Professor of Finance; Ph.D., Florida State. Investments, stock return anomalies, international corporate governance, analyst forecast issues.

Eleanne Solorzano Dowd, Associate Professor of Statistics; Ph.D., South Carolina. Nonparametric statistics, multiple comparisons, statistical computing, distribution theory, Bayesian inference.

Vanessa Urch Druskat, Associate Professor of Organizational Behavior and Management; Ph.D., Boston University. Work team and team leader effectiveness, the influence of emotional competence on team effectiveness and on leader effectiveness, effective leadership in public school systems.

Joseph F. Durocher, Associate Professor of Hospitality Management; Ph.D., Cornell. Food service management, restaurant and hotel design, computers in management and training, economic forecasting for the hospitality industry.

Devkamal Dutta, Assistant Professor of Strategic Management and Entrepreneurship; Ph.D., Western Ontario. Intersection of competitive strategies and competitive dynamics, entrepreneurial cognition, opportunity recognition, knowledge exchange in multinationals.

Ahmad Etebari, Chair and Professor of Accounting and Finance; Ph.D., North Texas State. Investments, corporate finance.

Ross Gittell, Professor of Business Administration; Ph.D., Harvard. Business, government and competition, regional and urban development, business and public policy.

Raymond J. Goodman Jr., Chair and Professor of Hospitality Management; Ph.D., Cornell. Human resources management: training and performance evaluation; retirement facilities planning, design, marketing, management and operations; lodging and restaurant industry indexing and forecasting.

Roger Grinde, Associate Dean and Associate Professor of Decision Sciences; Ph.D., Penn State. Operations research, spreadsheet model auditing and control, mathematical modeling.

Charles W. Gross, Professor of Marketing; Ph.D., Colorado. International marketing, marketing planning and strategy, forecasting.

Khole Gwebu, Assistant Professor of Decision Sciences; Ph.D., Kent State. E-commerce, reverse auctions, agent-based simulations, multicultural decision making, IT outsourcing.

Bowe Hansen, Assistant Professor of Accounting; Ph.D., Emory. International accounting, accounting quality and transparency, accounting regulation.

Paul Harvey, Assistant Professor of Organizational Behavior; Ph.D., Florida State. Emotions and perceptions, ethical decision making, stress, entitlement, and abusive supervision.

Daniel E. Innis, Dean and Professor of Marketing; Ph.D., Ohio State. Marketing, consumer behavior, customer service, strategic planning, business-to-business marketing, supply chain.

Afshad J. Irani, Associate Professor of Accounting and Academic Director, M.S. in Accounting; Ph.D., Penn State. Voluntary disclosure, earnings management, insider trading, SEC and FASB regulations.

William Johnson, Assistant Professor of Finance; Ph.D., Michigan State. Initial public offerings, conflicts of interest in investment banking, product market relationships.

Fred R. Kaen, Professor of Finance and Co-Director, International Private Enterprise Center; Ph.D., Michigan. Financial management, international finance, corporate finance, corporate governance.

Peter Lane, Chair of Marketing and Associate Professor of Strategic Management and Technology; Ph.D., Connecticut. Strategy development processes, strategic alliances and joint ventures, technology and innovation management, intellectual capital management.

Jun Li, Assistant Professor of Strategic Management and Entrepreneurship; Ph.D., Texas A&M. Strategic leadership and governance in IPO-stage firms, new-venture strategy and entrepreneurship, multinational corporations in transnational economies.

Yixin Liu, Assistant Professor of Finance; Ph.D., Iowa. Corporate governance, agency issues, capital structure and debt issues, insider trading.

Michael J. Merenda, Chair of Management and Professor of Strategic Management; Ph.D., Massachusetts Amherst. Strategic planning and management, entrepreneurship, international business and SME competitiveness.

Anthony Pescosolido, Assistant Professor of Organizational Behavior and Management; Ph.D., Case Western Reserve. Team dynamics, emotion in organizations, emergent leadership, team leadership.

Catherine Plante, Associate Professor of Accounting; Ph.D., Ohio State. Financial, governmental, and nonprofit accounting.

R. Dan Reid, Associate Professor of Operations Management; Ph.D., Ohio State. Production/operations management, purchasing, business logistics, supply chain management.

Richard Saavedra, Associate Professor of Organizational Behavior; Ph.D., Michigan. Work team design and management, mood and behavior, social influence and comparison processes.

Udo Schlentrich, Associate Professor of Hospitality Management and Director, Rosenberg International Center of Franchising; Ph.D., Strathclyde. Consumer marketing, international hospitality and tourism, franchising, finance and project development, hospitality marketing, international hospitality management.

Christine Shea, Associate Dean of Graduate Programs and Research and Associate Professor of Technology and Operations Management; Ph.D., Western Ontario. Technology and operations management, managing innovation, nanotechnology.

Barry Shore, Professor of Information Systems; Ph.D., Wisconsin. Information systems, international management.

Jeffrey E. Sohl, Professor of Entrepreneurship and Decision Sciences and Director, Center for Venture Research; Ph.D., Maryland. Early-stage equity financing of high-growth ventures, trends in the angel market, time series forecasting, entrepreneurship.

A. R. Venkatachalam, Chair of Decision Sciences, Professor of Information Systems, and Director, Enterprise Integration Research Center; Ph.D., Alabama. MIS, artificial intelligence in business, global information management, electronic commerce, enterprise integration, information technology, outsourcing, emerging technologies, technology management.

Jing Wang, Assistant Professor of Decision Sciences; Ph.D., Kent State. The role of social networks in the success of open source systems, management of information systems, managing across the enterprise.

Craig Wood, Associate Professor of Operations Management; Ph.D., Ohio State. Production and operations management, operations strategy, total quality management, technology management, project management, supply chain management.

Emily Xu, Assistant Professor of Accounting; Ph.D., Massachusetts Amherst. Financial analysis, valuation models, financial reporting.

Goksel Yalcinkaya, Assistant Professor of Marketing; Ph.D., Michigan State. Marketing and diffusion of innovations, both domestically and internationally.

Honggeng Zhou, Assistant Professor of Decision Sciences; Ph.D., Ohio State. Supply chain management, information systems and technology management, production and operations management, operations strategy.

Economics

Reagan Baughman, Assistant Professor of Economics; Ph.D., Syracuse. Labor economics, public finance, health economics and policy.

Karen Smith Conway, Professor of Economics; Ph.D., North Carolina at Chapel Hill. Public economics, applied econometrics, labor supply, health economics.

Bruce T. Elmslie, Chair and Professor of Economics; Ph.D., Utah. International trade, history of economic thought, growth theory.

Richard W. England, Professor of Economics and Natural Resources; Ph.D., Michigan. Environmental policy, ecological economics, environmental management, property taxation, smart growth, land development, local economic development, state and local government finance.

Michael Goldberg, Associate Professor of Economics and Academic Director, Economics Graduate Program; Ph.D., NYU. International finance, macroeconomic theory, financial markets, expectations.

Marc W. Herold, Associate Professor of Economic Development and Women's Studies; Ph.D., Berkeley. Third World economic development, Brazil, women and development, international studies, postmodernism, economic systems, political economy, civilian causalities of war.

Ju-Chin Huang, Associate Professor of Economics; Ph.D., North Carolina State. Applied econometrics, environmental economics.

Robert D. Mohr, Assistant Professor of Economics; Ph.D., Texas at Austin. Environmental and natural resource economics, public finance.

Neil B. Niman, Associate Professor of Economics; Ph.D., Texas at Austin. Evolutionary economics, organizational economics, history of economic thought.

Torsten Schmidt, Associate Professor of Economics; Ph.D., Florida. Industrial organization, econometrics, microeconomic theory, economics of information and uncertainty.

Evangelos O. Simos, Professor of Economics; Ph.D., Northern Illinois. Macroeconomics, international trade and finance, modeling and forecasting, econometrics, economic growth, monetary theory and policy, international affairs.

James R. Wible, Professor of Economics; Ph.D., Penn State. Macroeconomics and monetary theory, economics of science and philosophy of science, law and economics.

Robert Woodward, Forrest D. McKerley Professor of Health Economics; Ph.D., Washington (St. Louis). Economics, health economics, pharmaco-economics, Medicare, health-care reform, transplantation economics.

THE UNIVERSITY OF TEXAS AT DALLAS

School of Economic, Political, and Policy Sciences

Programs of Study

The School of Economic, Political, and Policy Sciences (EPPS) at the University of Texas at Dallas (UT Dallas) offers Ph.D.s in criminology, economics, geospatial information sciences, political science, public affairs, and public policy and political economy (PPPE). It also offers master's degrees in applied sociology, criminology, economics, geospatial information sciences (in conjunction with the School of Natural Sciences), international political economy, public affairs, and public policy. Students receive education through lecture, internships, and workshop courses; a basic knowledge of statistics and computer skills is considered crucial.

EPPS offers a 36-hour M.S. program in applied sociology. This includes 12 hours of core courses in applied sociology, 15 hours of core courses, and 3 hours of internship. The program is designed for students interested in areas such as nonprofit organizations and federal, state, and local government philosophy. For more information, students should contact Judy Robertson (judy@utdallas.edu) or Dr. James Marquart (marquart@utdallas.edu).

The 36-hour Master of Science in criminology provides students with a coherent and intellectually challenging degree that prepares them to conduct interdisciplinary research on various aspects of criminology and/or criminal justice, depending on their specific areas of specialty. Students will be well prepared for analytical and administrative posts in international and domestic research and policy institutions, criminal justice organizations, and the private sector. For more information, students should contact Remona McLain (remona.mclain@utdallas.edu) or Dr. James Marquart (marquart@utdallas.edu).

The 36-hour M.S. in economics is aimed at students seeking to learn advanced economic theory and apply advanced economic tools to real socioeconomic problems. For more information, students should contact Judy Du (judy.du@utdallas.edu) or Dr. James Murdoch (murdoch@utdallas.edu).

In addition, EPPS offers a 30-hour M.S. in geospatial information sciences (GIS). Offered jointly by the School of Economic, Political, and Policy Sciences and the School of Natural Sciences and Mathematics, it focuses on the use of geographic information systems. For more information, students should contact Judy Robertson (judy@utdallas.edu) or Dr. Ron Briggs (briggs@utdallas.edu).

The School also offers a 36-hour Master of Science in international political economy (IPE) that consists of three components, including required course work (18 hours), prescribed electives (12 hours), and free electives (6 hours). Moreover, students must demonstrate a foreign language proficiency equivalent to two years of study in one foreign language before graduation. For more information, students should contact Judy Robertson (judy@utdallas.edu) or Dr. Jennifer Holmes (jholmes@utdallas.edu).

The Master of Public Affairs (M.P.A.) degree is a 42-hour, interdisciplinary program that includes 21 hours of core courses and 18 hours of directed electives as well as an internship or workshop. It explores the interrelationship between economic, political, and social institutions. Students may emphasize course work in management, policy analysis, or applied technology. The curriculum places strong emphasis upon the development of computer and statistical skills that are necessary for successful performance in both the public and private sectors in the twenty-first century. For more information, students should contact Del Prisock (delfina@utdallas.edu) or Dr. Doug Watson (djw034000@utdallas.edu).

The M.S. in public policy is an interdisciplinary 36-hour graduate degree designed to develop those skill sets critical for a career in which a solid understanding of the public policy process and the analysis and evaluation of public policies are essential. Specific skills include knowledge of the policy process and related ethical concerns, rigorous research skills that provide students with an essential grounding in statistical and data analysis and research design, and effective communication skills. Students will be prepared for analytical and administrative positions and responsibilities in a wide array of professional settings in the public, non-profit, and private sectors. For more information, students should contact Judy Robertson (judy@utdallas.edu) or Dr. Marie Chevrier (chevrier@utdallas.edu).

The Ph.D. degree in criminology is an interdisciplinary, research-oriented program that provides students with a coherent and intellectually challenging research degree that prepares them for an academic appointment as a university professor or an administrative appointment with oversight of research and development within criminal justice organizations. Graduates of the program will be competent to teach and conduct interdisciplinary research at both graduate and undergraduate levels in aspects of criminology and/or criminal justice, depending on their specific areas of specialty. They also will be well prepared for analytical and administrative posts in international and domestic research and policy institutions and in the private sector. For more information, students should contact Lynne Boyer (lynne.boyer@utdallas.edu) or Dr. Robert Lawry (Robert.lowry@utdallas.edu).

The Ph.D. program in economics prepares students for careers in academics as well as research-oriented positions in the private and public sector. It provides cutting-edge education in micro and macroeconomic theory, rigorous training in mathematical and econometric techniques, and extensive exposure to various research areas in economics. Students complete a set of core courses, pass comprehensive exams in microeconomic and macroeconomic theory as well as econometrics, are certified in two research areas in economics, and submit and defend a dissertation. For more information, students should contact Judy Du (judy.du@utdallas.edu) or Dr. James Murdoch (murdoch@utdallas.edu).

The Ph.D. program in geospatial information sciences, offered with the Schools of Natural Sciences and Mathematics as well as Engineering and Computer Science, offers advanced training in geographic information sciences and related fields. Students complete core courses and pass a qualifying exam before proceeding to the dissertation. For more information, students should contact Judy Robertson (judy@utdallas.edu) or Dr. Ron Briggs (briggs@utdallas.edu).

The Ph.D. in political science provides a rigorous, student-focused disciplinary program with multidisciplinary links. Students receive state-of-the-science graduate education in political methodology and the fields of democratization, globalization and international relations, institutions and processes, and public management and decision making. Students complete a set of core courses, course work in their designated major and minor fields, and examinations in the core courses and major and minor fields; students also write and defend a dissertation. For more information, students should contact Lynne Boyer (lynne.boyer@utdallas.edu) or Dr. Robert Lowry (robert.lowry@utdallas.edu).

The Ph.D. in public affairs is an interdisciplinary program that prepares graduates to assume positions in academe, research-producing organizations, or positions of administrative authority in public organizations. The degree is nontraditional in that it requires all students to conduct applied, field-based research as the foundation for the production of their dissertations. The Ph.D. program in public affairs is a cohort program, with entering cohorts beginning each fall semester. For more information, students should contact Del Prisock (delfina@utdallas.edu) or Dr. Doug Watson (djw032000@utdallas.edu).

The Ph.D. in public policy and political economy is centered in critical thought and interdisciplinary research that explores the interaction of institutions, markets, and public policies. Students are expected to complete a set of core courses in topics related to public policy, including rigorous training in statistics and research design; students must also complete course work in two fields and a specialization and defend a dissertation. For more information, students should contact Judy Robertson (judy@utdallas.edu) or Dr. Euel Elliott (eelliott@utdallas.edu).

Research Facilities

The University of Texas at Dallas has advanced computing facilities. The School of Economic, Political, and Policy Sciences also houses the Bruton Center for Development Studies and the Center for Educational Studies and is affiliated with the Cecil and Ida Green Center for Science and Society. Students have access to the computing facilities in the School of Economic, Political, and Policy Sciences and the University's Computing Center. The School's two computing laboratories house over 30 computers that are network linked and equipped with major social science software packages, including E-Views, R, RATS, SPSS, and STATA. A computerized geographic information system, the LexisNexis Database, and WestLaw are also available for student use. The University's Computing Center provides personal computers and UNIX workstations. Many important data and reference materials are available online from professional associations or at UT–D via the Library's and School's memberships in the Inter-University Consortium for Political and Social Research (ICPSR), the Roper Center, the University Consortium for Geographic Information Science (UCGIS), and other organizations. The library has a substantial number of social science journals.

Financial Aid

The School of Economic, Political, and Policy Sciences (EPPS) provides teaching assistantships that range from $1100 to $1400, depending on experience. Students who are awarded a full-time, 20-hour assistantship receive in-state tuition waivers. The School also offers tuition waivers that cover all tuition for up to 12 credit hours. Teaching assistantships and graduate studies scholarships are competitive, with GRE scores and grades being important criteria in the selection process.

Cost of Study

Tuition and fees can be expected to be in the range of $7000 to $9000 per year for full-time in-state students taking 9 hours per semester, including summers. Costs might be higher for international and out-of-state students. Students are eligible for teaching assistantships and graduate-studies scholarships, as detailed above.

Living and Housing Costs

On-campus housing is available at Waterview Park Apartments, with rents varying from $600 to $800 per month.

Student Group

There are 6,000 graduate students and more than 8,000 undergraduates studying at UT–Dallas. UT-Dallas also has a varied international student body in both graduate and undergraduate programs of study.

Location

Richardson is located just north of Dallas and south of Plano in a pleasant suburban setting. It is near the high-technology corridor that is home to Ericsson, Nortel, and numerous other telecommunications companies.

The University

UT–Dallas was created in September 1969 by Act of the Sixty-First Texas Legislature, which provided for transfer of the privately funded Southwest Center for Advanced Studies (SCAS) to the state of Texas. Undergraduate and graduate programs grew rapidly. Today, UT–Dallas has a distinguished faculty that includes numerous members of the National Academy of Sciences and National Academy of Engineering.

Applying

Application for admission to the graduate school can be made for fall, spring, or summer. GRE scores are required for degree-seeking students, although applicants may be admitted provisionally as nondegree students. A combined verbal and quantitative GRE score of at least 1100 is recommended for doctoral students, and a combined score of at least 1000 is recommended for master's degree students.

Correspondence and Information

Euel Elliott, Associate Dean for Academic Programs
School of Economic, Political, and Policy Sciences
Box 830688
The University of Texas at Dallas
Richardson, Texas 75083-0688

E-mail: eelliott@utdallas.edu
Web site: http://www.utdallas.edu/epps

The University of Texas at Dallas

THE FACULTY AND THEIR RESEARCH

Bobby C. Alexander, Associate Professor of Sociology; Ph.D. (religious studies/social-scientific study of religion), Columbia, 1985. Religious studies.
Sheila Amin Gutiérrez de Piñeres, Professor of Economics; Ph.D. (economics), Duke, 1992. Latin American development, trade policy.
Philip K. Armour, Associate Professor of Sociology; Ph.D. (sociology), Berkeley, 1979. Sociology of religion, medical sociology.
Donald R. Arbuckle, Clinical Research Professor; Ph.D. (American civilizations), Pennsylvania. Public management, bureaucratic behavior, policymaking.
Daniel Arce, Professor of Economics; Ph.D. (economics), Illinois at Urbana–Champaign, 1992. Economics, defense economics.
Paul Battaglio, Assistant Professor of Public Affairs; Ph.D. (public administration), Georgia, 2005. Comparative policy and administration, public human resource management, comparative political attitudes.
Brian Bearry, Senior Lecturer; Ph.D. (political science), North Texas, 1958. American political institutions, political theory.
Ted Benavides, Senior Lecturer; M.P.A., SMU, 1994. Public management, human resources management.
Nathan Berg, Associate Professor of Economics; Ph.D. (economics), Kansas, 2001. Finance, behavioral economics.
Kurt J. Beron, Professor of Economics and Political Economy; Ph.D. (economics), North Carolina at Chapel Hill, 1985. Education policy, tax compliance, Internet economics.
Brian J. L. Berry, Lloyd Viel Berkner Regental Professor, Professor of Political Economy, and Dean; Ph.D. (geography), Washington (Seattle), 1958. Urban economics and geography, development, cycles of growth and decline.
Denise Paquette Boots, Assistant Professor; Ph.D. (criminology), South Florida, 2006. American correction systems, family and interpersonal violence, juvenile delinquency.
Patrick T. Brandt, Assistant Professor of Political Science; Ph.D. (political science), Indiana, 2001. Presidency, congressional behavior, time series analysis, Bayesian econometrics.
Timothy Bray, Clinical Assistant Professor of Criminology and Sociology; Ph.D. (criminology), Missouri–St. Louis, 2002. Criminology.
Ronald Briggs, Professor of Geospatial Sciences and Program Head for Geospatial Sciences; Ph.D. (geography), Ohio State, 1972. Technological change, urban and regional development.
Thomas Brunell, Associate Professor of Political Science; Ph.D. (political science), California, Irvine, 1997. Congressional behavior, congressional elections.
Anthony Champagne, Professor of Political Science; Ph.D. (political science), Illinois, 1973. Law and public policy, judicial politics.
Marie Isabelle Chevrier, Associate Professor of Public Policy and Political Economy; Ph.D. (public policy), Harvard, 1991. Arms control, international negotiation.
Harold D. Clarke, Professor of Political Science and Program Head for Political Science; Ph.D. (political science), Duke, 1971. Electoral behavior, public opinion and political support.
Rachel Croson, Professor of Economics; Ph.D. (economics), Harvard, 1994. Economics, experimental economics, behavioral economics.
Kruti R. Dholakia, Clinical Assistant Professor of Political Economy and Associate Dean for Undergraduate Programs; Ph.D. (public policy and political economy), Texas at Dallas, 2006. Methodology, global economy, development economics, health policy.
Lloyd J. Dumas, Professor of Public Policy and Political Economy; Ph.D. (economics), Columbia, 1972. International security, economic conversion, human and technical reliability.
Catherine C. Eckel, Professor of Economics; Ph.D. (economics), Virginia, 1983. Experimental economics, risk and decision making, economic education.
Euel Elliott, Professor of Public Policy and Political Economy, Senior Associate Dean, and Director of Graduate Studies; Ph.D. (political science), Duke, 1987. Public policy (general), regulatory policy, electoral behavior, nonlinear dynamics.
Simon Fass, Associate Professor of Public Policy and Political Economy; Ph.D. (urban planning), UCLA, 1978. Economic and political development.
Daniel Griffith, Ashbel Smith Professor of Geography and Geospatial Sciences; Ph.D. (geography), Toronto, 1978. Spatial statistics, quantitative urban-economic geography, applied statistics.
Edward J. Harpham, Professor of Political Science and Political Economy and Director of Collegium V Honors Program; Ph.D. (government), Cornell, 1980. Political theory, public policy.
Wendy L. Hassett, Senior Lecturer; Ph.D. (public administration and public policy), Auburn, 2003. Public management, human resource development.
Karen Hayslett-McCall, Assistant Professor of Sociology; Ph.D. (sociology), Penn State, 2002. Criminology, spatial analysis of crime, crime and neighborhoods.
Donald A. Hicks, Professor of Public Policy and Political Economy and Vice Chairman, Bruton Center for Development Studies; Ph.D. (sociology), North Carolina at Chapel Hill, 1976. Urban and regional policy, technology innovation and diffusion.
Karl Ho, Senior Lecturer; Ph.D. (political science), North Texas, 1996. Electoral behavior, public opinion, political parties.
Irving Hoch, Professor Emeritus of Economics; Ph.D. (economics), Chicago, 1957. Microeconomics, health and environmental policy.
Bruce Jacobs, Professor of Sociology and Criminology; Ph.D. (sociology), USC, 1994. Street offenders, drugs and crime, qualitative methods.
Paul A. Jargowsky, Professor of Sociology and of Public Policy and Political Economy; Ph.D. (public policy), Harvard, 1991. Welfare policy.
Linda Camp Keith, Assistant Professor of Political Science; Ph.D. (political science), North Texas, 1999. Public law/judicial process, human rights.
L. Douglas Kiel, Professor of Public Administration; Ph.D. (political science), Oklahoma, 1986. Public administration, organizational change, productivity improvement, nonlinear dynamics.
Tom Kovandzic, Associate Professor of Criminology; Ph.D. (criminal justice and criminology), Florida State, 1999. Firearms and violence, criminal justice policy, quantitative methods, inequality and crime, and policing, with particular interest in use of econometric methods as a tool to evaluate criminal justice policy initiatives.
Danielle Lavin-Loucks, Clinical Assistant Professor of Sociology; Ph.D. (sociology), Indiana, 2002. Criminology, parole, social psychology, qualitative methods.
Murray Leaf, Professor of Public Policy and Political Economy; Ph.D. (social anthropology), Chicago, 1966. Comparative social and economic development.
Xin Li, Assistant Professor of Economics; Ph.D. (economics), Michigan, 2006. Public economics, labor economics, experimental economics, economics of the Internet.
Robert Lowry, Professor of Political Science and of Public Policy and Political Economy and Program Head for Political Science; Ph.D. (political science), Harvard, 1993. Institutions and organizations, methodology.
James W. Marquart, Professor of Criminology and Program Head for Criminology; Ph.D. (sociology), Texas A&M, 1983. Criminology, legal reform, victimology, health issues in prison populations, community-based corrections.
Susan McElroy, Associate Professor of Economics and Political Economy; Ph.D. (economics of education), Stanford, 1996. Education policy.
Robert Morris, Assistant Professor of Criminology; Ph.D. (criminology) Sam Houston State, 2007. White-collar offending over the life course, computer crime and computer deviance, identity theft, quantitative methods.
James C. Murdoch, Professor of Economics and Program Head for Economics; Ph.D. (economics), Wyoming, 1982. Environmental policy, public goods provision, coalition theory.
Stephanie P. Newbold, Assistant Professor of Public Affairs; Ph.D. (public administration), Virginia Tech, 2006. Ethics, public management, political theory, administrative theory.
Clint W. Peinhardt, Assistant Professor of Political Science; Ph.D. (political science), Michigan, 2004. International political economy, economic development and transition, formal modeling.
Fang Qiu, Associate Professor of Geospatial Sciences and Political Economy; Ph.D. (geography), South Carolina, 2000. Geographic information sciences (GIS), remote sensing.
Lawrence J. Redlinger, Professor of Sociology and of Public Policy and Political Economy and Associate Provost; Ph.D. (sociology), Northwestern, 1969. Cultural and intergroup relations, social control and regulation.
Todd Sandler, Professor of Economics and Political Science; Ph.D. (economics), SUNY at Binghamton, 1971. International relations, public economics, collective action, theories of terrorism.
Alicia C. Schortgen, Assistant Professor of Public Affairs; Ph.D. (public affairs), Texas at Dallas, 2006. Nonprofit organizations, ethics in public administration, leadership in public service.
Richard K. Scotch, Professor of Sociology and of Public Policy and Political Economy; Ph.D. (sociology), Harvard, 1982. Social policy, health policy, disabilities policy.
Barry J. Seldon, Professor of Economics; Ph.D. (economics), Duke, 1985. Microeconomics, industrial organization, advertising.
Kevin Siqueira, Associate Professor of Economics; Ph.D. (economics), Iowa State, 1998. Public economics, environmental economics, microeconomic theory, game theory.
Sheryl Skaggs, Assistant Professor of Sociology; Ph.D. (sociology), North Carolina State, 2001. Work, organizations and industry, social inequality.
Marianne C. Stewart, Professor of Political Science; Ph.D. (political science), Duke, 1986. Comparative politics, Anglo-American voting behavior, political participation.
Gregory S. Thielemann, Associate Professor of Political Economy; Ph.D. (political science), Rice, 1988. Southern politics, gay and lesbian politics.
Michael Tiefelsdorf, Associate Professor of Geography and Geospatial Sciences; Ph.D. (geography), Free University of Berlin, 1988. Spatial processes, spatial statistics, quantitative geography.
Paul E. Tracy, Professor of Sociology and of Public Policy and Political Economy; Ph.D. (sociology and criminology), Pennsylvania, 1978. Criminology, juvenile delinquency.
Lynne Vieraitis, Associate Professor of Criminology; Ph.D. (criminal justice and criminology), Florida State, 2000. Inequality and crime, gender and crime, violence against women, theoretical criminology.
Wim P. M. Vijverberg, Professor of Economics and of Public Policy and Political Economy; Ph.D. (economics), Pittsburgh, 1981. Labor markets, development, econometrics.
Douglas Watson, Professor of Public Administration and Program Head for Public Affairs; Ph.D. (public policy and public administration), Auburn, 1992. State and local government.
Carole J. Wilson, Assistant Professor of Political Science; Ph.D. (political science), North Carolina at Chapel Hill, 2001. Comparative politics, NAFTA, U.S.-Mexico relations.
John L. Worrall, Professor of Criminology; Ph.D. (political science), Washington State, 1999. Crime central policy, legal issues in policing, methodology.

Section 20
Family and Consumer Sciences

This section contains a directory of institutions offering graduate work in family and consumer sciences, followed by in-depth entries submitted by institutions that chose to prepare detailed program descriptions. Additional information about programs listed in the directory but not augmented by an in-depth entry may be obtained by writing directly to the dean of a graduate school or chair of a department at the address given in the directory.

For programs offering related work, see also in this book *Economics, Psychology and Counseling,* and *Sociology, Anthropology, and Archaeology.* In another guide in this series:

Graduate Programs in Business, Education, Health, Information Studies, Law & Social Work

See *Social Work*

CONTENTS

Program Directories

Announcement

Close-Ups

See also:

Family and Consumer Sciences-General

Alabama Agricultural and Mechanical University, School of Graduate Studies, School of Agricultural and Environmental Sciences, Department of Family and Consumer Sciences, Huntsville, AL 35811. Offers family and consumer sciences (MS); food science (MS, PhD). Part-time and evening/weekend programs available. *Faculty:* 8 full-time (6 women), 1 (woman) part-time/adjunct. *Students:* 16 full-time (13 women), 27 part-time (26 women); includes 38 minority (all African Americans), 5 international. In 2007, 11 degrees awarded. *Degree requirements:* For master's, comprehensive exam, thesis optional; for doctorate, one foreign language, thesis/dissertation. *Entrance requirements:* For master's, GRE General Test; for doctorate, GRE General Test, MS. *Application deadline:* For fall admission, 5/1 for domestic students. Applications are processed on a rolling basis. Application fee: $25. Electronic applications accepted. *Financial support:* In 2007–08, 2 research assistantships with tuition reimbursements (averaging $9,000 per year), teaching assistantships with tuition reimbursements (averaging $9,000 per year) were awarded; career-related internships or fieldwork, Federal Work-Study, and traineeships also available. Financial award application deadline: 4/1. *Faculty research:* Food biotechnology, nutrition, food microbiology, food engineering, food chemistry. *Unit head:* Dr. Cynthia Smith, Chair, 256-372-5455, Fax: 256-372-5433.

Appalachian State University, Cratis D. Williams Graduate School, Department of Family and Consumer Sciences, Boone, NC 28608. Offers child development (MA); family and consumer science (MA); family and consumer science education (MA). Part-time programs available. *Faculty:* 9 full-time (8 women). *Students:* 12 full-time (all women), 6 part-time (5 women); includes 2 minority (1 Asian American or Pacific Islander, 1 Hispanic American). 14 applicants, 64% accepted, 8 enrolled. In 2007, 5 master's awarded. *Degree requirements:* For master's, comprehensive exam, thesis optional. *Entrance requirements:* For master's, GRE General Test, 3 letters of recommendation. Additional exam requirements/recommendations for international students: Required—TOEFL (minimum score 550 paper-based; 230 computer-based). *Application deadline:* For fall admission, 7/1 priority date for domestic students, 1/1 for international students; for spring admission, 11/1 for domestic students, 6/1 for international students. Application fee: $50. *Expenses:* Tuition, state resident: part-time $127 per semester hour. Tuition, nonresident: part-time $597 per semester hour. Required fees: $18 per semester. *Financial support:* In 2007–08, 5 teaching assistantships (averaging $7,000 per year) were awarded; fellowships, research assistantships, career-related internships or fieldwork, scholarships/grants, and unspecified assistantships also available. Financial award application deadline: 7/1. *Faculty research:* Food antioxidants, preschool curriculum, children with special needs, family child care, FCS curriculum content. Total annual research expenditures:$78,692. *Unit head:* Dr. Sarah Jordan, Chairperson, 828-262-2661, E-mail: jordansr@appstate.edu. *Application contact:* Dr. Sammie Garner, Graduate Director, 828-262-2698, E-mail: garnersg@appstate.edu.

Ball State University, Graduate School, College of Applied Science and Technology, Department of Family and Consumer Sciences, Muncie, IN 47306-1099. Offers MA, MS. *Faculty:* 23. *Students:* 25 full-time (22 women), 23 part-time (all women); includes 5 minority (1 African American, 1 Asian American or Pacific Islander, 3 Hispanic Americans). Average age 25. 38 applicants, 55% accepted, 19 enrolled. In 2007, 17 degrees awarded. *Entrance requirements:* For master's, resumé. Application fee: $25 ($35 for international students). *Expenses:* Tuition, state resident: full-time $6,864. Tuition, nonresident: full-time $17,932. Required fees: $1,866. *Financial support:* In 2007–08, 22 teaching assistantships with full tuition reimbursements (averaging $8,515 per year) were awarded; research assistantships with full tuition reimbursements, career-related internships or fieldwork also available. Financial award application deadline: 3/1. *Faculty research:* Maternal and infant nutrition, nutrition education. *Unit head:* Dr. Alice Spangler, Head, 765-285-5932, Fax: 765-285-2314, E-mail: aspangler@bsu.edu.

Bowling Green State University, Graduate College, College of Education and Human Development, School of Family and Consumer Sciences, Bowling Green, OH 43403. Offers food and nutrition (MFCS); human development and family studies (MFCS). Part-time programs available. *Faculty:* 20 full-time (15 women), 4 part-time/adjunct (2 women). *Students:* 10 full-time (8 women), 23 part-time (all women); includes 4 minority (all Hispanic Americans), 2 international. Average age 28. 29 applicants, 69% accepted, 20 enrolled. In 2007, 4 degrees awarded. *Degree requirements:* For master's, thesis. *Entrance requirements:* For master's, GRE General Test, minimum GPA of 3.0. Additional exam requirements/recommendations for international students: Required—TOEFL. *Application deadline:* For fall admission, 3/1 priority date for domestic students. Application fee: $30. Electronic applications accepted. *Financial support:* In 2007–08, 1 research assistantship with full tuition reimbursement (averaging $8,404 per year), 9 teaching assistantships with full tuition reimbursements (averaging $7,089 per year) were awarded; career-related internships or fieldwork and unspecified assistantships also available. Financial award applicants required to submit FAFSA. *Faculty research:* Public health, wellness, social issues and policies, ethnic foods, nutrition and aging. *Unit head:* Dr. Deborah Wooldridge, Director, 419-372-7823. *Application contact:* Dr. Dawn Anderson, Graduate Coordinator, 419-372-8090.

California State University, Fresno, Division of Graduate Studies, College of Agricultural Sciences and Technology, Department of Child, Family and Consumer Sciences, Fresno, CA 93740-8027. Offers family and consumer sciences (MS). Currently not accepting applications. Part-time and evening/weekend programs available. *Students:* 1; minority (Hispanic American) *Degree requirements:* For master's, thesis (for some programs). *Entrance requirements:* For master's, GRE General Test, minimum GPA of 3.0 in last 60 hours. Additional exam requirements/recommendations for international students: Required—TOEFL. *Application deadline:* Applications are processed on a rolling basis. Application fee: $55. Electronic applications accepted. *Financial support:* Fellowships, career-related internships or fieldwork, Federal Work-Study, institutionally sponsored loans, and scholarships/grants available. Support available to part-time students. Financial award application deadline: 3/1; financial award applicants required to submit FAFSA. *Unit head:* Dr. Marianne Jones, Chair, 559-278-2283, Fax: 559-278-7824, E-mail: mariannej@csufresno.edu.

California State University, Long Beach, Graduate Studies, College of Health and Human Services, Department of Family and Consumer Sciences, Long Beach, CA 90840. Offers family and consumer sciences (MA); nutritional sciences (MS), including nutritional sciences/dietetics and food administration. Part-time and evening/weekend programs available. *Faculty:* 18 full-time (13 women), 29 part-time/adjunct (25 women). *Students:* 29 full-time (25 women), 44 part-time (37 women); includes 29 minority (1 African American, 17 Asian Americans or Pacific Islanders, 11 Hispanic Americans). Average age 33. *Degree requirements:* For master's, comprehensive exam or thesis. *Entrance requirements:* For master's, GRE (MS), minimum GPA of 3.0. *Application deadline:* For fall admission, 5/1 for domestic students; for spring admission, 11/1 for domestic students. Applications are processed on a rolling basis. Application fee: $55. Electronic applications accepted. *Financial support:* Federal Work-Study, institutionally sponsored loans, and scholarships/grants available. Financial award application deadline: 3/2. *Faculty research:* School uniforms, consumer complaining behavior, nutrition and fitness education and behavior change, curriculum change, teaching experience of interns. *Unit head:* Dr. M Sue Stanley, Chair, 562-985-4484, Fax: 562-985-4414, E-mail: stanleym@csulb.edu. *Application contact:* Dr. Mary Jacob, Graduate Coordinator, 562-985-4484, Fax: 562-985-4414, E-mail: marjacob@csulb.edu.

California State University, Northridge, Graduate Studies, College of Health and Human Development, Department of Family and Consumer Sciences, Northridge, CA 91330. Offers MS. Part-time and evening/weekend programs available. *Faculty:* 18 full-time (13 women), 44 part-time/adjunct (37 women). *Students:* 60 full-time (53 women), 73 part-time (70 women); includes 44 minority (9 African Americans, 13 Asian Americans or Pacific Islanders, 22 Hispanic Americans), 12 international. Average age 32. 132 applicants, 74% accepted, 54 enrolled. In 2007, 35 degrees awarded. *Degree requirements:* For master's, thesis, project, or comprehensive exam. *Entrance requirements:* For master's, GRE General Test or minimum GPA of 3.0. Additional exam requirements/recommendations for international students: Required—TOEFL. *Application deadline:* For fall admission, 11/30 for domestic students. Application fee: $55. *Financial support:* Teaching assistantships, career-related internships or fieldwork, Federal Work-Study, and institutionally sponsored loans available. Financial award application deadline: 3/1. *Unit head:* Dr. Alyce Akers, Chair, 818-677-3051.

Central Michigan University, College of Graduate Studies, College of Education and Human Services, Department of Human Environmental Studies, Mount Pleasant, MI 48859. Offers human development and family studies (MA); nutrition and dietetics (MS). *Degree requirements:* For master's, thesis or alternative. *Entrance requirements:* For master's, GRE (MA), minimum GPA of 3.0 in last 60 hours, 15 credits of course work in human development and family studies or related area (MA). *Faculty research:* Human growth and development, family studies and human sexuality, nutritional food science/food services, apparel and textile retailing, computer-aided design for apparel and interior design.

Central Washington University, Graduate Studies, Research and Continuing Education, College of Education and Professional Studies, Department of Family and Consumer Sciences, Ellensburg, WA 98926. Offers family and consumer sciences education (MS); family studies (MS); nutrition (MS). Part-time programs available. *Faculty:* 11 full-time (7 women). *Students:* 12 full-time (11 women), 2 part-time (both women). 20 applicants, 70% accepted, 13 enrolled. In 2007, 13 degrees awarded. *Degree requirements:* For master's, thesis or alternative. *Entrance requirements:* For master's, GRE General Test (nutrition), minimum GPA of 3.0. Additional exam requirements/recommendations for international students: Required—TOEFL (minimum score 550 paper-based; 213 computer-based; 79 iBT). *Application deadline:* For fall admission, 4/1 priority date for domestic students; for winter admission, 10/1 for domestic students; for spring admission, 1/1 for domestic students. Applications are processed on a rolling basis. Application fee: $50. Electronic applications accepted. *Expenses:* Tuition, state resident: full-time $2,209; part-time $221 per credit. Tuition, nonresident: full-time $4,939; part-time $442 per credit. Required fees: $207 per quarter. Tuition and fees vary according to degree level. *Financial support:* In 2007–08, 1 teaching assistantship with partial tuition reimbursement (averaging $8,100 per year) was awarded; research assistantships, Federal Work-Study, health care benefits, and unspecified assistantships also available. Financial award application deadline: 3/1; financial award applicants required to submit FAFSA. *Unit head:* Dr. Jan Bowers, Chair, 509-963-2766. *Application contact:* Justine Eason, Admissions Program Coordinator, 509-963-3103, Fax: 509-963-1799, E-mail: masters@cwu.edu.

Clemson University, Institute on Family and Neighborhood Life and Interdisciplinary Studies, Program in International Family and Community Studies, Clemson, SC 29634. Offers PhD. *Students:* 10 full-time (9 women), 2 part-time (both women), 5 international. 16 applicants, 63% accepted, 7 enrolled. *Degree requirements:* For doctorate, one foreign language, comprehensive exam, thesis/dissertation (for some programs). *Entrance requirements:* For doctorate, GRE and/or MAT, 3 letters of recommendation from professionals familiar with the applicant's academic work and/or community service. Additional exam requirements/recommendations for international students: Required—TOEFL. *Application deadline:* For fall admission, 3/1 for domestic and international students. Application fee: $55. Electronic applications accepted. *Financial support:* In 2007–08, 5 fellowships with partial tuition reimbursements, 5 research assistantships with partial tuition reimbursements, 5 teaching assistantships with partial tuition reimbursements were awarded; career-related internships or fieldwork, scholarships/grants, health care benefits, and unspecified assistantships also available. *Unit head:* Dr. Bonnie Holaday, Program Coordinator, 864-656-6288, Fax: 864-656-6281, E-mail: holaday@clemson.edu.

Cornell University, Graduate School, Graduate Fields of Human Ecology, Ithaca, NY 14853-0001. Offers MA, MHA, MPS, MS, PhD. *Accreditation:* CAHME (one or more programs are accredited). *Faculty:* 95 full-time (38 women). *Students:* 133 full-time (85 women); includes 27 minority (5 African Americans, 13 Asian Americans or Pacific Islanders, 9 Hispanic Americans), 39 international. Average age 27. 237 applicants, 36% accepted, 51 enrolled. In 2007, 38 master's, 13 doctorates awarded. *Degree requirements:* For doctorate, comprehensive exam, thesis/dissertation. *Entrance requirements:* For master's and doctorate, GRE General Test. Additional exam requirements/recommendations for international students: Required—TOEFL. Application fee: $70. Electronic applications accepted. *Expenses: Contact institution. Financial support:* In 2007–08, 85 students received support, including 13 fellowships with full tuition reimbursements available, 27 research assistantships with full tuition reimbursements available, 45 teaching assistantships with full tuition reimbursements available; institutionally sponsored loans, scholarships/grants, health care benefits, tuition waivers (full and partial), and unspecified assistantships also available. Financial award applicants required to submit FAFSA. *Application contact:* Graduate School Application Requests, Caldwell Hall, 607-255-5820.

Eastern Illinois University, Graduate School, Lumpkin College of Business and Applied Sciences, School of Family and Consumer Sciences, Charleston, IL 61920-3099. Offers dietetics (MS); family and consumer sciences (MS). Part-time programs available. *Faculty:* 12 full-time (10 women). *Students:* 34 full-time (33 women), 29 part-time (all women). In 2007, 40 degrees awarded. *Degree requirements:* For master's, comprehensive exam. *Application deadline:* For fall admission, 7/31 priority date for domestic students. Applications are processed on a rolling basis. Application fee: $30. *Expenses:* Tuition, state resident: part-time $218 per hour. Tuition, nonresident: part-time $654 per hour. *Financial support:* In 2007–08, 2 research assistantships with tuition reimbursements (averaging $7,200 per year), 6 teaching assistantships with tuition reimbursements (averaging $7,200 per year) were awarded; career-related internships or fieldwork also available. *Unit head:* Dr. James Painter, Chairperson, 217-581-6076, Fax: 217-581-6090, E-mail: jepainter@eiu.edu. *Application contact:* Dr. Frances Murphy, Coordinator, 217-581-6997, Fax: 217-581-6090, E-mail: flmurphy@eiu.edu.

Florida State University, Graduate Studies, College of Human Sciences, Tallahassee, FL 32306. Offers MS, PhD. *Accreditation:* AAMFT/COAMFTE. Part-time programs available. *Faculty:* 43 full-time (31 women). *Students:* 137 full-time (100 women), 58 part-time (45 women); includes 54 minority (32 African Americans, 1 American Indian/Alaska Native, 6 Asian Americans or Pacific Islanders, 15 Hispanic Americans), 22 international. 201 applicants, 37% accepted, 48 enrolled. In 2007, 34 master's, 16 doctorates awarded. *Degree requirements:* For master's, comprehensive exam (for some programs), thesis optional; for doctorate, thesis/dissertation. *Entrance requirements:* For master's and doctorate, GRE General Test, minimum GPA of 3.0. Additional exam requirements/recommendations for international students: Required—TOEFL (minimum score 80 iBT). *Application deadline:* For fall admission, 7/1 for domestic students, 5/1 for international students; for spring admission, 11/1 for domestic students, 12/1 for international students. Applications are processed on a rolling basis. Application fee: $30. Electronic applications accepted. *Expenses:* Tuition, state resident: part-time $248 per credit hour. Tuition, nonresident: part-time $880 per credit hour. Tuition and fees vary according to program. *Financial support:* In 2007–08, 94 students received support, including 4 fellowships with partial tuition reimbursements available (averaging $10,000 per year), 14 research assistantships with partial tuition reimbursements available (averaging $8,000 per year), 60 teaching assistantships with partial tuition reimbursements available (averaging $8,000 per year); career-related internships or fieldwork, Federal Work-Study, institutionally sponsored loans, scholarships/grants, and unspecified assistantships also available. Financial award application deadline: 1/15; financial award applicants required to submit FAFSA. *Faculty research:* Child and adolescent development, merchandising, accessible housing, culturally diverse classrooms, motor behavior. *Unit head:* Dr. Billie J. Collier, Dean, 850-644-1281, Fax: 850-644-0700, E-mail: bcollier@fsu.edu. *Application contact:* Jennifer Boyles, Academic Program Specialist, 850-644-7221, Fax: 850-644-0700, E-mail: jaboyles@fsu.edu.

See Close-Up on page 1073.

Family and Consumer Sciences-General

Fontbonne University, Graduate Programs, Department of Human Environmental Sciences, St. Louis, MO 63105-3098. Offers family and consumer sciences (MA). *Degree requirements:* For master's, action paper/presentation portfolio. *Entrance requirements:* For master's, minimum GPA of 2.8. *Faculty research:* Early intervention, public policy: children and families, program designer.

Illinois State University, Graduate School, College of Applied Science and Technology, Department of Family and Consumer Sciences, Normal, IL 61790-2200. Offers MA, MS. *Faculty:* 9 full-time (7 women). *Students:* 24 full-time (23 women), 13 part-time (all women); includes 1 minority (Asian American or Pacific Islander), 2 international. 25 applicants, 76% accepted. In 2007, 17 degrees awarded. *Degree requirements:* For master's, thesis or alternative. *Entrance requirements:* For master's, GRE General Test, minimum GPA of 2.8 in last 60 hours of course work. *Application deadline:* Applications are processed on a rolling basis. Application fee: $40. *Expenses:* Tuition, state resident: full-time $3,492; part-time $194 per credit hour. Tuition, nonresident: full-time $7,272; part-time $404 per credit hour. Required fees: $1,024; $57 per credit hour. *Financial support:* In 2007–08, 16 research assistantships (averaging $4,523 per year), 4 teaching assistantships (averaging $4,388 per year) were awarded; tuition waivers (full) and unspecified assistantships also available. Financial award application deadline: 4/1. *Faculty research:* Graduate practicum assistantships, startup for Jump Start of McLean County grant, providing low-income preschool children with early literacy experiences, generations of Hope-ICI replication. Total annual research expenditures: $146,744. *Unit head:* Dr. Connor Walters, Chairperson, 309-438-2517.

Indiana State University, School of Graduate Studies, College of Arts and Sciences, Department of Family and Consumer Sciences, Terre Haute, IN 47809-1401. Offers dietetics (MS); family and consumer sciences education (MS); inter-area option (MS). *Accreditation:* ADtA. Part-time programs available. *Faculty:* 5 full-time (4 women). *Students:* 12 full-time (all women), 7 part-time (6 women); includes 4 minority (3 African Americans, 1 Asian American or Pacific Islander), 2 international. Average age 33. 13 applicants, 100% accepted, 5 enrolled. In 2007, 9 degrees awarded. *Degree requirements:* For master's, thesis optional. *Application deadline:* For fall admission, 7/1 priority date for domestic students; for spring admission, 11/1 priority date for domestic students. Applications are processed on a rolling basis. Application fee: $35. Electronic applications accepted. *Expenses:* Tuition, state resident: full-time $7,056; part-time $294 per semester hour. Tuition, nonresident: full-time $14,016; part-time $584 per semester hour. Required fees: $175 per semester. *Financial support:* In 2007–08, 2 research assistantships with partial tuition reimbursements (averaging $7,000 per year) were awarded; teaching assistantships, tuition waivers (partial) also available. Financial award application deadline: 3/1; financial award applicants required to submit FAFSA. *Unit head:* Dr. Frederica Kramer, Chairperson, 812-237-3297.

Iowa State University of Science and Technology, Graduate College, College of Human Sciences, Program in Family and Consumer Sciences, Ames, IA 50011. Offers MFCS. *Students:* 3 full-time (all women), 31 part-time (23 women); includes 2 minority (both African Americans) 11 applicants, 64% accepted, 5 enrolled. In 2007, 3 degrees awarded. *Degree requirements:* For master's, thesis or alternative. *Entrance requirements:* For master's, GRE General Test. Additional exam requirements/recommendations for international students: Required—TOEFL (paper-based 550; computer-based 213; iBT 79) or IELTS (6.5). *Application deadline:* For fall admission, 3/15 priority date for domestic and international students; for spring admission, 10/15 priority date for domestic and international students. Application fee: $30 ($70 for international students). Electronic applications accepted. *Financial support:* In 2007–08, 1 research assistantship with full and partial tuition reimbursement (averaging $17,328 per year) was awarded; teaching assistantships with full and partial tuition reimbursements, scholarships/grants, health care benefits, and unspecified assistantships also available. *Unit head:* Dr. Thomas Andre, Supervisory Committee Chair, 515-294-5397, E-mail: mfcsinfo@iastate.edu.

Kansas State University, Graduate School, College of Human Ecology, Manhattan, KS 66506. Offers MS, PhD. Part-time programs available. Postbaccalaureate distance learning degree programs offered. *Faculty:* 46 full-time (33 women), 15 part-time/adjunct (8 women). *Students:* 338 full-time (250 women), 122 part-time (70 women); includes 49 minority (34 African Americans, 5 American Indian/Alaska Native, 5 Asian Americans or Pacific Islanders, 5 Hispanic Americans), 51 international. 239 applicants, 62% accepted, 72 enrolled. In 2007, 58 master's, 18 doctorates awarded. *Degree requirements:* For master's, residency; for doctorate, thesis/dissertation, residency. *Application deadline:* For fall admission, 2/1 priority date for domestic and international students; for spring admission, 9/1 for domestic students, 9/1 priority date for international students. Application fee: $30 ($55 for international students). Electronic applications accepted. *Financial support:* In 2007–08, 27 research assistantships (averaging $13,778 per year), 11 teaching assistantships with full and partial tuition reimbursements (averaging $10,082 per year) were awarded; fellowships with partial tuition reimbursements, career-related internships or fieldwork, Federal Work-Study, institutionally sponsored loans, scholarships/grants, and tuition waivers (full) also available. Support available to part-time students. Financial award application deadline: 3/1; financial award applicants required to submit FAFSA. *Faculty research:* Apparel and textiles, food service and hospitality management, life span human development, family life education and consultation, marriage and family therapy. Total annual research expenditures: $8.7 million. *Unit head:* Virginia Moxley, Dean, 785-532-5500, Fax: 785-532-5504, E-mail: moxley@ksu.edu. *Application contact:* Patricia Haas, Administrative Specialist, 785-532-5500, Fax: 785-532-5504, E-mail: haas@humec.ksu.edu.

Kent State University, Graduate School of Education, Health, and Human Services, School of Family and Consumer Studies, Kent, OH 44242-0001. Offers MA, MS. Part-time programs available. *Faculty:* 21 full-time (14 women). *Students:* 25 full-time (21 women), 13 part-time (12 women); includes 4 minority (2 African Americans, 2 Asian Americans or Pacific Islanders), 4 international. Average age 33. 32 applicants, 50% accepted. In 2007, 11 degrees awarded. *Degree requirements:* For master's, thesis (for some programs). *Entrance requirements:* For master's, GRE, minimum GPA of 3.0, 3 letters of recommendation. Additional exam requirements/recommendations for international students: Required—TOEFL. *Application deadline:* Applications are processed on a rolling basis. Application fee: $30. Electronic applications accepted. *Financial support:* In 2007–08, 4 students received support, including 4 research assistantships with full tuition reimbursements available (averaging $8,313 per year); Federal Work-Study, scholarships/grants, and unspecified assistantships also available. Financial award application deadline: 2/1; financial award applicants required to submit FAFSA. *Faculty research:* Training human service workers, health care services for older adults, early adolescent development, caregiving arrangements with aging families, peace and war. *Unit head:* Dr. Mary Dellmann-Jenkins, Director, 330-672-2197, Fax: 330-672-2194, E-mail: mdellman@kent.edu. *Application contact:* Nancy Miller, Academic Program Coordinator, 330-672-2576, Fax: 330-672-9162, E-mail: ogs@kent.edu.

Lamar University, College of Graduate Studies, College of Education and Human Development, Department of Family and Consumer Sciences, Beaumont, TX 77710. Offers family and consumer science (MS); vocational home economics (Certificate). Part-time and evening/weekend programs available. *Faculty:* 6 full-time (5 women), 2 part-time/adjunct (1 woman). *Students:* 9 full-time (all women), 7 part-time (all women); includes 4 minority (2 African Americans, 1 American Indian/Alaska Native, 1 Asian American or Pacific Islander). Average age 31. 17 applicants, 53% accepted, 1 enrolled. In 2007, 2 degrees awarded. *Degree requirements:* For master's, thesis optional. *Entrance requirements:* For master's, GRE General Test. Additional exam requirements/recommendations for international students: Required—TOEFL. *Application deadline:* For fall admission, 8/1 for domestic students; for spring admission, 12/1 for domestic students. Applications are processed on a rolling basis. Application fee: $25 ($50 for international students). *Expenses:* Tuition, state resident: part-time $348 per semester hour. Tuition, nonresident: part-time $626 per semester hour. Tuition and fees vary according to course load. *Financial support:* In 2007–08, 3 students received support, including 3 teaching assistantships (averaging $5,000 per year); fellowships, research assistantships, career-related internships or fieldwork, Federal Work-Study, and institutionally sponsored loans also available. Support available to part-time students. Financial award application deadline: 4/1. *Faculty research:* Maternal and infant nutrition, eating disorders, sports nutrition, human sexuality, family violence. *Unit head:* Dr. Connie Ruiz, Chair, 409-880-8663, Fax: 409-880-8666. *Application contact:* Sandy Drane, Coordinator of Graduate Admissions, 409-880-8356, Fax: 409-880-8414, E-mail: gradmissions@hal.lamar.edu.

Louisiana State University and Agricultural and Mechanical College, Graduate School, College of Agriculture, School of Human Ecology, Baton Rouge, LA 70803. Offers MS, PhD. Part-time programs available. *Faculty:* 33 full-time (18 women). *Students:* 37 full-time (33 women), 11 part-time (9 women); includes 8 minority (5 African Americans, 2 Asian Americans or Pacific Islanders, 1 Hispanic American), 16 international. Average age 30. 29 applicants, 69% accepted, 10 enrolled. In 2007, 9 master's, 6 doctorates awarded. *Degree requirements:* For master's, thesis; for doctorate, thesis/dissertation. *Entrance requirements:* For master's and doctorate, GRE General Test, minimum GPA of 3.0. Additional exam requirements/recommendations for international students: Required—TOEFL (minimum score 550 paper-based; 213 computer-based; 79 iBT). *Application deadline:* For fall admission, 1/25 priority date for domestic students, 5/15 for international students; for spring admission, 10/15 for international students. Applications are processed on a rolling basis. Application fee: $25. Electronic applications accepted. *Financial support:* In 2007–08, 43 students received support, including 18 research assistantships with full and partial tuition reimbursements available (averaging $15,372 per year), 11 teaching assistantships with full and partial tuition reimbursements available (averaging $9,536 per year); fellowships with full and partial tuition reimbursements available, career-related internships or fieldwork, Federal Work-Study, institutionally sponsored loans, scholarships/grants, health care benefits, and unspecified assistantships also available. Support available to part-time students. Financial award application deadline: 4/15; financial award applicants required to submit FAFSA. *Faculty research:* Nutrition for optimum health, textile and apparel production development, children's relationships with parents and caregivers, contextual influences on families. Total annual research expenditures: $163,775. *Unit head:* Dr. Roy Martin, Director, 225-578-2282, Fax: 225-578-2697, E-mail: rjmartin@lsu.edu. *Application contact:* Dr. Jenna T Kuttruff, Graduate Advisor, 225-578-1600, Fax: 225-578-2697, E-mail: jkutt1@lsu.edu.

Louisiana Tech University, Graduate School, College of Applied and Natural Sciences, School for Human Ecology, Ruston, LA 71272. Offers dietetics (MS); human ecology (MS). Part-time programs available. *Degree requirements:* For master's, thesis or alternative, Registered Dietician Exam eligibility. *Entrance requirements:* For master's, GRE General Test. *Application deadline:* For fall admission, 7/29 priority date for domestic students; for spring admission, 2/3 for domestic students. Applications are processed on a rolling basis. Application fee: $20 ($30 for international students). *Financial support:* Fellowships, research assistantships, career-related internships or fieldwork and Federal Work-Study available. Financial award application deadline: 2/1. *Unit head:* Dr. Amy Yates, Head, 318-257-3727, Fax: 318-257-4014. *Application contact:* Dr. William Campbell, Director of Graduate Studies, 318-257-4287, Fax: 318-257-5060, E-mail: campbell@latech.edu.

Marshall University, Academic Affairs Division, College of Education and Human Services, Division of Human Development and Allied Technology, Department of Family and Consumer Sciences, Huntington, WV 25755. Offers MA. *Faculty:* 7 full-time (4 women), 15 part-time/adjunct (8 women). *Students:* 1 (woman) full-time, 2 part-time (both women). Average age 26. *Degree requirements:* For master's, thesis optional, comprehensive assessment. Application fee: $40. *Unit head:* Prof. Mary Mhango, Program Coordinator, 304-96-3535, E-mail: mhango@marshall.edu. *Application contact:* Information Contact, 304-746-1900, Fax: 304-746-1902, E-mail: services@marshall.edu.

Missouri State University, Graduate College, College of Natural and Applied Sciences, Department of Fashion and Interior Design, Springfield, MO 65804-0094. Offers secondary education (MS Ed), including consumer sciences. *Faculty:* 3 full-time (all women). *Degree requirements:* For master's, comprehensive exam, thesis or alternative. *Entrance requirements:* For master's, GRE (MNAS), 9–12 teaching certification (MS Ed), minimum GPA of 3.0 (MNAS). Additional exam requirements/recommendations for international students: Required—TOEFL (minimum score 550 paper-based; 213 computer-based; 79 iBT). *Application deadline:* For fall admission, 7/20 priority date for domestic students; for spring admission, 12/20 priority date for domestic students. Application fee: $35. *Expenses:* Tuition, state resident: full-time $3,708; part-time $206 per credit hour. Tuition, nonresident: full-time $7,236; part-time $206 per credit hour. Required fees: $622. Full-time tuition and fees vary according to course level, course load, program and reciprocity agreements. *Financial support:* Research assistantships, teaching assistantships with full tuition reimbursements, career-related internships or fieldwork, Federal Work-Study, scholarships/grants, and unspecified assistantships available. Financial award application deadline: 3/31; financial award applicants required to submit FAFSA. *Faculty research:* Clothing design, merchandising, hospitality and restaurant management, interior design. *Unit head:* Dr. Jeannie Ireland, Head, 417-836-5497, Fax: 417-836-4341, E-mail: jeannieireland@missouristate.edu.

New Mexico State University, Graduate School, College of Agriculture and Home Economics, Department of Family and Consumer Sciences, Las Cruces, NM 88003-8001. Offers MS. Part-time programs available. *Faculty:* 10 full-time (8 women), 1 part-time/adjunct (0 women). *Students:* 22 full-time (18 women), 14 part-time (12 women); includes 13 minority (1 African American, 1 American Indian/Alaska Native, 11 Hispanic Americans), 2 international. Average age 35. 14 applicants, 57% accepted, 8 enrolled. In 2007, 15 degrees awarded. *Degree requirements:* For master's, comprehensive exam (for some programs), thesis (for some programs), oral exam. *Entrance requirements:* For master's, GRE, 3 letters of reference, resumé. Additional exam requirements/recommendations for international students: Required—TOEFL. *Application deadline:* For fall admission, 6/30 priority date for domestic students, 3/1 priority date for international students; for spring admission, 11/30 for domestic and international students. Applications are processed on a rolling basis. Application fee: $30 ($50 for international students). Electronic applications accepted. *Expenses:* Tuition, state resident: full-time $3,602; part-time $199 per credit. Tuition, nonresident: full-time $13,380; part-time $607 per credit. Required fees: $1,178. *Financial support:* In 2007–08, 6 research assistantships, 7 teaching assistantships were awarded; career-related internships or fieldwork, Federal Work-Study, scholarships/grants, health care benefits, and unspecified assistantships also available. Support available to part-time students. Financial award application deadline: 3/1. *Faculty research:* Work, stress, and family functioning; youth at risk; food product analysis; diet and health. *Unit head:* Dr. Martha Archuleta, Head, 575-646-3936, Fax: 575-646-1889, E-mail: maarchul@nmsu.edu. *Application contact:* Dr. Wanda A Eastman, Coordinator, 575-646-1180, Fax: 575-646-1889, E-mail: wmorgan@nmsu.edu.

North Carolina Central University, Division of Academic Affairs, College of Arts and Sciences, Department of Human Sciences, Durham, NC 27707-3129. Offers MS. Part-time and evening/weekend programs available. *Degree requirements:* For master's, one foreign language, comprehensive exam, thesis. *Entrance requirements:* For master's, GRE, minimum GPA of 3.0 in major, 2.5 overall. Additional exam requirements/recommendations for international students: Required—TOEFL.

North Dakota State University, College of Graduate and Interdisciplinary Studies, College of Human Development and Education, School of Education, Program in Family and Consumer Sciences Education, Fargo, ND 58105. Offers M Ed, MS. *Accreditation:* NCATE. Part-time programs available. *Faculty:* 1 (woman) full-time. *Students:* Average age 40. 1 applicant, 100% accepted, 1 enrolled. *Degree requirements:* For master's, comprehensive exam, thesis or alternative. *Entrance requirements:* For master's, MAT. Additional exam requirements/recommendations for international students: Required—TOEFL. *Application deadline:* Applications are processed on a rolling basis. Application fee: $45 ($60 for international students). *Expenses:* Tuition, state resident: full-time $5,376; part-time $224 per credit. Tuition, nonresident: full-time $14,354; part-time $598 per credit. Required fees: $962; $40 per credit. Part-time tuition and fees vary according to course load and reciprocity agreements. *Financial support:* Teaching assistantships, career-related internships or fieldwork and institutionally sponsored

Family and Consumer Sciences-General

North Dakota State University (continued)
loans available. Financial award application deadline: 4/15. *Faculty research:* Needs of beginning teachers, learning styles and achievement, school-level variables and curriculum change. *Application contact:* Dr. Mari Borr, Assistant Professor, 701-231-7968, Fax: 701-231-9685, E-mail: mari.borr@ndsu.edu.

The Ohio State University, Graduate School, College of Education and Human Ecology, Program in Family and Consumer Sciences Education, Columbus, OH 43210. Offers M Ed, MS. *Accreditation:* ADtA. *Faculty:* 8. *Students:* Average age 48. *Degree requirements:* For master's, thesis optional. *Entrance requirements:* Additional exam requirements/recommendations for international students: Required—TOEFL (minimum score 577 paper-based; 233 computer-based). *Application deadline:* For fall admission, 8/15 priority date for domestic students, 7/1 priority date for international students; for winter admission, 12/1 priority date for domestic students, 11/1 priority date for international students; for spring admission, 3/1 priority date for domestic students, 2/1 priority date for international students. Applications are processed on a rolling basis. Application fee: $40 ($50 for international students). Electronic applications accepted. *Financial support:* Fellowships, research assistantships, teaching assistantships, Federal Work-Study and institutionally sponsored loans available. Support available to part-time students. *Unit head:* Albert J. Davis, Graduate Studies Committee Chair, 614-292-7705, Fax: 614-292-2581, E-mail: davis.7@osu.edu. *Application contact:* 614-292-9444, Fax: 614-292-3895, E-mail: domestic.grad@osu.edu.

Ohio University, Graduate College, College of Health and Human Services, School of Human and Consumer Sciences, Athens, OH 45701-2979. Offers child development and family life (MS); early childhood education (MS); family studies (MS); food and nutrition (MS). Part-time programs available. *Faculty:* 13 full-time (9 women), 5 part-time/adjunct (all women). *Students:* 11 full-time (9 women), 5 part-time (4 women); includes 5 minority (2 African Americans, 3 Asian Americans or Pacific Islanders). Average age 26. 16 applicants, 69% accepted, 9 enrolled. In 2007, 8 degrees awarded. *Degree requirements:* For master's, thesis. *Entrance requirements:* For master's, GRE. Additional exam requirements/recommendations for international students: Required—TOEFL. *Application deadline:* For fall admission, 3/1 priority date for domestic students. Applications are processed on a rolling basis. Application fee: $50 ($55 for international students). Electronic applications accepted. *Financial support:* In 2007–08, 6 teaching assistantships (averaging $9,815 per year) were awarded; career-related internships or fieldwork, Federal Work-Study, institutionally sponsored loans, and unspecified assistantships also available. Financial award application deadline: 3/15. *Faculty research:* Diversity, developmentally appropriate activities, death and dying, gerontology, sexuality education. *Unit head:* Dr. V. Ann Paulins, Director, 740-593-2880, Fax: 740-593-0289, E-mail: paulins@ohio.edu.

Oklahoma State University, College of Human Environmental Sciences, Programs in Human Environmental Sciences, Stillwater, OK 74078. Offers MS, PhD. *Faculty:* 1 (woman) full-time. *Students:* Average age 35. 74 applicants, 36% accepted, 12 enrolled. In 2007, 1 master's, 9 doctorates awarded. *Entrance requirements:* For master's and doctorate, GRE or GMAT. *Application deadline:* For fall admission, 3/1 priority date for international students; for spring admission, 8/1 priority date for international students. Application fee: $40 ($75 for international students). Electronic applications accepted. *Expenses:* Tuition, state resident: full-time $4,993; part-time $148 per credit hour. Tuition, nonresident: full-time $14,755; part-time $555 per credit hour. Tuition and fees vary according to program. *Financial support:* Research assistantships, teaching assistantships available. *Unit head:* Dr. Stephan Wilson, Dean, College of Human Environmental Sciences, 405-744-5053.

Oregon State University, Graduate School, College of Education, Program in Family and Consumer Sciences Education, Corvallis, OR 97331. Offers MAT, MS. Part-time programs available. In 2007, 3 degrees awarded. *Degree requirements:* For master's, thesis (for some programs). *Entrance requirements:* For master's, NTE, California Basic Educational Skills Test, minimum GPA of 3.0 in last 90 hours of course work. Additional exam requirements/recommendations for international students: Required—TOEFL. *Application deadline:* For fall admission, 1/15 for domestic students. Application fee: $50. *Expenses:* Tuition, state resident: full-time $9,126; part-time $338 per credit. Tuition, nonresident: full-time $14,796; part-time $548 per credit. Required fees: $1,447. *Financial support:* Fellowships, career-related internships or fieldwork, Federal Work-Study, and institutionally sponsored loans available. Support available to part-time students. Financial award application deadline: 2/1. *Faculty research:* Economy of time and methods. *Unit head:* Dr. Chris L. Ward, Coordinator, 541-737-1080, Fax: 541-737-2040, E-mail: chris.ward@oregonstate.edu.

Prairie View A&M University, College of Agriculture and Human Sciences, Prairie View, TX 77446-0519. Offers agricultural economics (MS); animal sciences (MS); interdisciplinary human sciences (MS); soil science (MS). Part-time and evening/weekend programs available. *Faculty:* 8 full-time (4 women), 9 part-time/adjunct (3 women). *Students:* 36 full-time (29 women), 62 part-time (51 women); includes 89 minority (86 African Americans, 1 American Indian/Alaska Native, 2 Hispanic Americans). Average age 33. 147 applicants, 100% accepted. In 2007, 30 degrees awarded. *Degree requirements:* For master's, comprehensive exam, thesis (for some programs), field placement. *Entrance requirements:* For master's, GRE General Test, minimum GPA of 2.45. Additional exam requirements/recommendations for international students: Required—TOEFL (minimum score 550 paper-based). *Application deadline:* For fall admission, 6/1 for domestic and international students; for spring admission, 10/1 for domestic and international students. Applications are processed on a rolling basis. Application fee: $50. *Financial support:* In 2007–08, 57 students received support, including 8 fellowships with tuition reimbursements available (averaging $12,000 per year), 10 research assistantships with tuition reimbursements available (averaging $15,000 per year); career-related internships or fieldwork, Federal Work-Study, institutionally sponsored loans, scholarships/grants, tuition waivers (partial), and unspecified assistantships also available. Support available to part-time students. Financial award application deadline: 4/1; financial award applicants required to submit FAFSA. *Faculty research:* Domestic violence prevention, water quality, food growth regulators, wetland dynamics, biochemistry, poultry disaster, obesity and nutrition, family therapy. Total annual research expenditures: $4 million. *Application contact:* Dr. Richard W. Griffin, Interim Department Head, 936-261-2520, Fax: 936-261-5148, E-mail: rwgriffin@pvamu.edu.

Purdue University, Graduate School, College of Consumer and Family Sciences, West Lafayette, IN 47907. Offers MS, PhD. Part-time programs available. *Degree requirements:* For doctorate, thesis/dissertation. *Entrance requirements:* Additional exam requirements/recommendations for international students: Required—TOEFL. Electronic applications accepted.

Queens College of the City University of New York, Division of Graduate Studies, Mathematics and Natural Sciences Division, Department of Family, Nutrition and Exercise Sciences, Flushing, NY 11367-1597. Offers home economics (MS Ed); physical education and exercise sciences (MS Ed). Part-time and evening/weekend programs available. *Faculty:* 12 full-time (7 women). *Students:* 1 (woman) full-time, 58 part-time (45 women). 49 applicants, 78% accepted, 27 enrolled. In 2007, 2 degrees awarded. *Degree requirements:* For master's, research project. *Entrance requirements:* For master's, minimum GPA of 3.0. Additional exam requirements/recommendations for international students: Required—TOEFL. *Application deadline:* For fall admission, 4/1 for domestic students; for spring admission, 11/1 for domestic students. Applications are processed on a rolling basis. Application fee: $125. *Financial support:* Career-related internships or fieldwork, Federal Work-Study, institutionally sponsored loans, tuition waivers (partial), and adjunct lectureships available. Support available to part-time students. Financial award application deadline: 4/1; financial award applicants required to submit FAFSA. *Faculty research:* Exercise and environmental physiology, interdisciplinary approaches to school curricula using outdoor education, program development in cardiac rehabilitation and adult fitness, nutrition education. *Unit head:* Dr. Elizabeth Lowe, Chairperson, 718-997-4168. *Application contact:* Mario Caruso, Director of Graduate Admissions, 718-997-5200, Fax: 718-997-5193, E-mail: graduate_admissions@qc.edu.

Sam Houston State University, College of Humanities and Social Sciences, Department of Family and Consumer Sciences, Huntsville, TX 77341. Offers MA. Part-time and evening/weekend programs available. *Faculty:* 5 full-time (4 women). *Students:* 18 full-time (all women), 2 part-time (both women); includes 6 minority (1 African American, 3 Asian Americans or Pacific Islanders, 2 Hispanic Americans), 1 international. Average age 27. In 2007, 11 degrees awarded. *Entrance requirements:* For master's, GRE General Test, minimum GPA of 2.5. *Application deadline:* For fall admission, 8/1 for domestic students; for spring admission, 12/1 for domestic students. Application fee: $20. *Expenses:* Tuition, state resident: full-time $5,026; part-time $184 per semester hour. Tuition, nonresident: full-time $10,586; part-time $462 per semester hour. Required fees: $494 per semester. *Financial support:* Teaching assistantships available. Financial award application deadline: 5/31; financial award applicants required to submit FAFSA. *Unit head:* Dr. Janis White, Chair, 936-294-1242, Fax: 936-294-4204, E-mail: jwhite@shsu.edu. *Application contact:* Dr. Claudia Sealey-Potts, Advisor, 936-294-1250, E-mail: clapotts@shsu.edu.

San Francisco State University, Division of Graduate Studies, College of Health and Human Services, Department of Consumer and Family Studies/Dietetics, San Francisco, CA 94132-1722. Offers family and consumer sciences (MA). Part-time programs available. *Application deadline:* Applications are processed on a rolling basis. *Unit head:* Nancy Rabolt, Chair, 415-338-2060, E-mail: nrabolt@sfsu.edu.

South Carolina State University, School of Graduate Studies, Department of Family and Consumer Sciences, Orangeburg, SC 29117-0001. Offers individual and family development (MS); nutritional sciences (MS). Part-time and evening/weekend programs available. *Faculty:* 7 full-time (all women). *Students:* 19 full-time (18 women), 26 part-time (24 women); includes 43 minority (all African Americans) Average age 33. 18 applicants, 89% accepted, 9 enrolled. In 2007, 12 master's awarded. *Degree requirements:* For master's, thesis optional, departmental qualifying exam. *Entrance requirements:* For master's, GRE, MAT, or NTE, minimum GPA of 2.7. *Application deadline:* For fall admission, 6/15 priority date for domestic students, 6/15 for international students; for spring admission, 11/1 for domestic and international students. Applications are processed on a rolling basis. Application fee: $25. Electronic applications accepted. *Financial support:* Fellowships, institutionally sponsored loans available. Financial award application deadline: 6/1. *Faculty research:* Societal competence, relationship of parent-child interaction to adult, quality of well-being of rural elders. *Unit head:* Dr. Ethel Jones, Chair, 803-536-8958, Fax: 803-533-3268, E-mail: egjones@scsu.edu. *Application contact:* Annette Hazzard-Jones, Program Coordinator II, 803-536-8809, Fax: 803-536-8812, E-mail: zs_ahazzard@scsu.edu.

South Dakota State University, Graduate School, College of Family and Consumer Sciences, Department of Human Development, Consumer and Family Sciences, Brookings, SD 57007. Offers MFCS. *Entrance requirements:* For master's, resumé. Additional exam requirements/recommendations for international students: Required—TOEFL (minimum score 525 paper-based).

Southeast Missouri State University, School of Graduate Studies, Department of Human Environmental Studies, Cape Girardeau, MO 63701-4799. Offers home economics (MA); human environmental studies (MA). Part-time programs available. *Faculty:* 11 full-time (9 women). *Students:* 8 full-time (7 women), 16 part-time (all women); includes 5 minority (3 African Americans, 2 Asian Americans or Pacific Islanders). Average age 30. 14 applicants, 100% accepted. In 2007, 4 degrees awarded. *Degree requirements:* For master's, thesis or alternative. *Entrance requirements:* For master's, GRE General Test, MAT, minimum GPA of 2.75. Additional exam requirements/recommendations for international students: Required—TOEFL (minimum score 550 paper-based; 213 computer-based). *Application deadline:* For fall admission, 8/1 for domestic students, 6/1 for international students; for spring admission, 11/21 for domestic students, 10/1 for international students. Applications are processed on a rolling basis. Application fee: $25 ($100 for international students). Electronic applications accepted. *Expenses:* Tuition, state resident: part-time $224 per credit hour. Tuition, nonresident: part-time $395 per credit hour. Tuition and fees vary according to course load and program. *Financial support:* In 2007–08, 14 students received support, including 3 research assistantships with full tuition reimbursements available (averaging $7,600 per year), 8 teaching assistantships with full tuition reimbursements available (averaging $7,600 per year); unspecified assistantships also available. Financial award applicants required to submit FAFSA. *Unit head:* Dr. Paula King, Chairperson, 573-651-2312, E-mail: pking@semo.edu. *Application contact:* Marsha L. Arant, Senior Administrative Assistant, Office of Graduate Studies, 573-651-2192, Fax: 573-651-2001, E-mail: marant@semo.edu.

State University of New York College at Oneonta, Graduate Education, Division of Education, Department of Secondary Education, Oneonta, NY 13820-4015. Offers adolescence education (MS Ed); family and consumer science education (MS Ed). *Accreditation:* NCATE. Part-time and evening/weekend programs available. *Students:* 2 full-time (1 woman), 14 part-time (5 women). 3 applicants, 100% accepted, 3 enrolled. *Entrance requirements:* For master's, GRE General Test. *Application deadline:* For fall admission, 3/25 priority date for domestic students; for spring admission, 10/1 priority date for domestic students. Applications are processed on a rolling basis. Application fee: $50. *Expenses:* Tuition, state resident: full-time $6,900; part-time $288 per credit. Tuition, nonresident: full-time $10,920; part-time $455 per credit. Required fees: $1,120; $35 per credit. *Unit head:* Dr. Dennis Banks, Chair, 607-436-3075, Fax: 607-436-2554, E-mail: banksdn@oneonta.edu.

Stephen F. Austin State University, Graduate School, College of Education, Department of Human Sciences, Nacogdoches, TX 75962. Offers MS. *Degree requirements:* For master's, comprehensive exam, thesis or alternative. *Entrance requirements:* For master's, GRE General Test. Additional exam requirements/recommendations for international students: Required—TOEFL. *Faculty research:* Consumer economics, nutrition education, clothing and textiles, family, interior design.

Tennessee State University, The School of Graduate Studies and Research, School of Agriculture and Consumer Sciences, Nashville, TN 37209-1561. Offers agricultural sciences (MS), including agribusiness, agricultural education, animal science, plant science. Part-time and evening/weekend programs available. *Faculty:* 6 full-time (0 women). *Students:* 5 full-time (4 women), 3 part-time (2 women); includes 6 minority (all African Americans), 1 international. Average age 31. 9 applicants, 56% accepted, 3 enrolled. In 2007, 10 degrees awarded. *Degree requirements:* For master's, thesis. *Entrance requirements:* For master's, GRE General Test, GRE Subject Test, MAT. Application fee: $25. *Expenses:* Tuition, state resident: full-time $6,271; part-time $490 per hour. Tuition, nonresident: full-time $16,550; part-time $936 per hour. *Financial support:* In 2007–08, 2 research assistantships (averaging $6,511 per year), 1 teaching assistantship (averaging $6,511 per year) were awarded. *Faculty research:* Small farm economics, ornamental horticulture, beef cattle production, rural elderly. *Unit head:* Dr. Chandra Reddy, Dean, 615-963-7620, Fax: 615-963-5888.

Texas A&M University–Kingsville, College of Graduate Studies, College of Agriculture and Home Economics, Department of Human Sciences, Kingsville, TX 78363. Offers MS. Part-time and evening/weekend programs available. *Degree requirements:* For master's, comprehensive exam, thesis or alternative. *Entrance requirements:* For master's, GRE General Test, minimum GPA of 3.0. Additional exam requirements/recommendations for international students: Required—TOEFL. *Faculty research:* Mexican-American families, abuse in families, nontraditional students.

Texas Southern University, Graduate School, College of Liberal Arts and Behavioral Sciences, Department of Human Services and Consumer Sciences, Houston, TX 77004-4584. Offers MS. Part-time and evening/weekend programs available. *Faculty:* 2 full-time (both women). *Students:* 9 full-time (8 women), 15 part-time (13 women); includes 25 minority (23 African Americans, 1 American Indian/Alaska Native, 1 Hispanic American). Average age 33. 12 applicants, 100% accepted, 10 enrolled. In 2007, 8 degrees awarded. *Degree requirements:* For master's, comprehensive exam, thesis (for some programs). *Entrance requirements:* For master's, GRE General Test, minimum GPA of 2.5. Additional exam requirements/recommendations for international students: Required—TOEFL. *Application deadline:* For fall admission, 7/15 priority date for domestic students. Applications are processed on a rolling basis. Application fee: $50 ($75 for international students). *Financial support:* Research assistantships, teaching assistantships, career-related internships or fieldwork and institutionally sponsored loans available. Financial award application deadline: 5/1. *Faculty research:* Food radiation/food for space travel, adolescent parenting, gerontology/grandparenting. *Unit head:* Dr. Shirley R. Nealy, Chair, 713-313-7638, Fax: 713-313-7228, E-mail: nealy_sr@tsu.edu.

Texas Tech University, Graduate School, College of Human Sciences, Lubbock, TX 79409. Offers MS, PhD, JD/MS. Part-time and evening/weekend programs available. Postbaccalaureate distance learning degree programs offered (minimal on-campus study). *Faculty:* 48 full-time (33 women), 2 part-time/adjunct (1 woman). *Students:* 194 full-time (116 women), 96 part-time (55 women); includes 39 minority (11 African Americans, 3 American Indian/Alaska Native, 11 Asian Americans or Pacific Islanders, 14 Hispanic Americans), 51 international. Average age 31. 284 applicants, 62% accepted, 71 enrolled. In 2007, 51 master's, 22 doctorates awarded. *Degree requirements:* For doctorate, thesis/dissertation. *Entrance requirements:* For master's, GRE; for doctorate, GRE General Test. Additional exam requirements/recommendations for international students: Required—TOEFL (minimum score 550 paper-based; 213 computer-based). *Application deadline:* For fall admission, 3/1 priority date for domestic students; for spring admission, 11/1 priority date for domestic students. Applications are processed on a rolling basis. Application fee: $50 ($60 for international students). Electronic applications accepted. *Expenses: Contact institution.* Tuition and fees vary according to program. *Financial support:* In 2007–08, 213 students received support, including 37 research assistantships with partial tuition reimbursements available (averaging $12,821 per year), 93 teaching assistantships with partial tuition reimbursements available (averaging $12,401 per year); career-related internships or fieldwork, Federal Work-Study, institutionally sponsored loans, and scholarships/grants also available. Support available to part-time students. Financial award application deadline: 4/15; financial award applicants required to submit FAFSA. *Faculty research:* Substance abuse and recovery; the role of nutrition in the prevention of obesity; cancer and illness; the role of family factors in children's treatment response to cancer and serious illness; financial planning and credit management. Total annual research expenditures: $1.8 million. *Unit head:* Dr. Linda C. Hoover, Dean, 806-742-3031, Fax: 806-742-1849. *Application contact:* Dr. Kitty S. Harris, Associate Dean, 806-742-3031, Fax: 806-742-1849, E-mail: kitty.s.harris@ttu.edu.

Tufts University, Graduate School of Arts and Sciences, Department of Child Development, Medford, MA 02155. Offers applied developmental psychology (PhD); child development (MA, CAGS); early childhood education (MAT). Part-time programs available. *Faculty:* 15 full-time, 8 part-time/adjunct. *Students:* 102 (89 women); includes 17 minority (7 African Americans, 5 Asian Americans or Pacific Islanders, 5 Hispanic Americans) 12 international. 123 applicants, 64% accepted, 35 enrolled. In 2007, 70 master's, 6 doctorates, 2 other advanced degrees awarded. *Degree requirements:* For master's, thesis (for some programs); for doctorate, thesis/dissertation. *Entrance requirements:* For master's and doctorate, GRE General Test. Additional exam requirements/recommendations for international students: Required—TOEFL (minimum score 550 paper-based; 213 computer-based; 80 iBT). *Application deadline:* For fall admission, 1/15 for domestic and international students. Applications are processed on a rolling basis. Application fee: $70. Electronic applications accepted. *Expenses:* Tuition: Full-time $35,052. *Financial support:* Fellowships, research assistantships with full and partial tuition reimbursements, teaching assistantships with full and partial tuition reimbursements, career-related internships or fieldwork, Federal Work-Study, scholarships/grants, and tuition waivers (partial) available. Support available to part-time students. Financial award application deadline: 1/15; financial award applicants required to submit FAFSA. *Unit head:* Ellen Pinderhughes, Chair, 617-628-5000.

The University of Akron, Graduate School, College of Fine and Applied Arts, School of Family and Consumer Sciences, Akron, OH 44325. Offers child and family development (MA), including child development, family development; child life (MA); clothing, textiles and interiors (MA); nutrition and dietetics (MS). Part-time and evening/weekend programs available. *Faculty:* 12 full-time (6 women), 41 part-time/adjunct (32 women). *Students:* 17 full-time (16 women), 6 part-time (all women); includes 3 minority (all African Americans), 1 international. Average age 29. 12 applicants, 50% accepted, 5 enrolled. In 2007, 7 master's awarded. *Degree requirements:* For master's, comprehensive exam, thesis optional, oral exam. *Entrance requirements:* For master's, GRE, minimum GPA of 2.75, letters of recommendation, personal statement of goals, interview. Additional exam requirements/recommendations for international students: Required—TOEFL (minimum score 550 paper-based; 213 computer-based; 79 iBT). *Application deadline:* For fall admission, 3/1 for domestic and international students; for spring admission, 10/1 for domestic and international students. Applications are processed on a rolling basis. Application fee: $30 ($40 for international students). Electronic applications accepted. *Expenses:* Tuition, state resident: full-time $6,164; part-time $342 per credit. Tuition, nonresident: full-time $10,575; part-time $588 per credit. Required fees: $806; $43 per credit. $12 per term. Tuition and fees vary according to course load, degree level and program. *Financial support:* In 2007–08, 1 research assistantship with full tuition reimbursement, 14 teaching assistantships with full tuition reimbursements were awarded; career-related internships or fieldwork, Federal Work-Study, institutionally sponsored loans, tuition waivers (full), and unspecified assistantships also available. *Faculty research:* Nutritional health wellness/sports nutrition; historical/cultural aspects of clothing, textiles, interiors; FCS curriculum development; life span gender roles; families in international and historical perspectives. Total annual research expenditures: $32,517. *Unit head:* Dr. Richard Glotzer, Chair, 330-972-5399, E-mail: glotzer@uakron.edu. *Application contact:* Dr. Susan M. Witt, Graduate Director, 330-972-7729, E-mail: susan8@uakron.edu.

The University of Alabama, Graduate School, College of Human Environmental Sciences, Tuscaloosa, AL 35487. Offers MA, MS, MSHES, PhD. Part-time and evening/weekend programs available. Postbaccalaureate distance learning degree programs offered (no on-campus study). *Faculty:* 23 full-time (16 women). *Students:* 145 full-time (98 women), 203 part-time (143 women); includes 69 minority (59 African Americans, 1 American Indian/Alaska Native, 5 Asian Americans or Pacific Islanders, 4 Hispanic Americans), 5 international. Average age 31. 220 applicants, 84% accepted, 61 enrolled. In 2007, 152 master's, 2 doctorates awarded. *Degree requirements:* For doctorate, thesis/dissertation. *Entrance requirements:* For master's, GRE General Test or MAT (minimum score: 50th percentile), minimum GPA of 3.0; for doctorate, GRE General Test or MAT, minimum GPA of 3.0. *Application deadline:* For fall admission, 7/6 for domestic students. Applications are processed on a rolling basis. Application fee: $30. Electronic applications accepted. *Expenses:* Tuition, state resident: full-time $5,700. Tuition, nonresident: full-time $16,518. *Financial support:* In 2007–08, 2 research assistantships with full tuition reimbursements (averaging $9,000 per year) were awarded; fellowships with tuition reimbursements, teaching assistantships with full tuition reimbursements, career-related internships or fieldwork, Federal Work-Study, institutionally sponsored loans, and scholarships/grants also available. *Faculty research:* Student's use of credit, determinants of income differential: comparing Asians with Blacks and Whites, expenditure patterns of Chinese, racial and ethnic different in the likelihood of charitable contributions; health insurance coverage and precautionary behavior savings. Total annual research expenditures: $43,097. *Unit head:* Dr. Milla D. Boschung, Dean, 205-348-6250, Fax: 205-348-1786, E-mail: mboschun@ches.ua.edu.

University of Alberta, Faculty of Graduate Studies and Research, Department of Human Ecology, Edmonton, AB T6G 2E1, Canada. Offers family ecology and practice (M Sc, PhD); textiles and clothing (M Sc, MA, PhD). Postbaccalaureate distance learning degree programs offered (no on-campus study). *Degree requirements:* For master's, thesis (for some programs); for doctorate, comprehensive exam, thesis/dissertation. *Entrance requirements:* For master's and doctorate, minimum GPA of 7.0 on a 9.0 scale. Additional exam requirements/recommendations for international students: Required—TOEFL (minimum score 580 paper-based; 237 computer-based). *Faculty research:* Families and aging, family and child poverty, paid and unpaid work of families, textiles and clothing, parent-child relationships.

The University of Arizona, Graduate College, College of Agriculture and Life Sciences, School of Family and Consumer Sciences, Tucson, AZ 85721. Offers MS, PhD. Part-time programs available. *Faculty:* 18. *Students:* 37 full-time (28 women), 4 part-time (3 women); includes 8 minority (1 African American, 3 Asian Americans or Pacific Islanders, 4 Hispanic Americans), 11 international. Average age 34. 28 applicants, 29% accepted, 7 enrolled. In 2007, 4 master's, 2 doctorates awarded. *Entrance requirements:* For master's and doctorate, GRE General Test, minimum GPA of 3.0. Additional exam requirements/recommendations for international students: Required—TOEFL. *Application deadline:* Applications are processed on a rolling basis. Application fee: $50. *Financial support:* Fellowships, research assistantships, teaching assistantships, career-related internships or fieldwork, Federal Work-Study, institutionally sponsored loans, and tuition waivers (full) available. Financial award application deadline: 3/1. *Unit head:* Dr. Soyeon Shim, Director, 520-621-1075, Fax: 520-621-9445, E-mail: shim@ag.arizona.edu. *Application contact:* Julie Longstaff, Program Coordinator, 520-621-1075, Fax: 520-621-9445, E-mail: jules@u.arizona.edu.

University of Arkansas, Graduate School, Dale Bumpers College of Agricultural, Food and Life Sciences, School of Human Environmental Sciences, Fayetteville, AR 72701-1201. Offers MS. Part-time programs available. Postbaccalaureate distance learning degree programs offered (minimal on-campus study). *Students:* 8 full-time (all women), 16 part-time (all women); includes 2 minority (1 African American, 1 Hispanic American), 3 international. In 2007, 4 degrees awarded. *Degree requirements:* For master's, comprehensive exam, thesis (for some programs). Application fee: $40 ($50 for international students). *Financial support:* In 2007–08, 4 research assistantships were awarded; fellowships, teaching assistantships, Federal Work-Study also available. Support available to part-time students. Financial award application deadline: 4/1; financial award applicants required to submit FAFSA. *Unit head:* Dr. Mary Warnock, Unit Head, 479-575-4305, E-mail: hesc@uark.edu.

University of Central Arkansas, Graduate School, College of Health and Behavioral Sciences, Department of Family and Consumer Sciences, Conway, AR 72035-0001. Offers MS. *Faculty:* 1 (woman) full-time. *Students:* 33 full-time (31 women), 36 part-time (35 women); includes 11 minority (10 African Americans, 1 Hispanic American). 30 applicants, 100% accepted, 30 enrolled. In 2007, 31 degrees awarded. *Degree requirements:* For master's, comprehensive exam, thesis optional. *Entrance requirements:* For master's, GRE General Test, minimum GPA of 2.7. Additional exam requirements/recommendations for international students: Required—TOEFL (minimum score 550 paper-based; 213 computer-based). *Application deadline:* For fall admission, 3/1 priority date for domestic students; for spring admission, 10/1 for domestic students. Applications are processed on a rolling basis. Application fee: $25 ($40 for international students). *Expenses: Contact institution.* *Financial support:* Career-related internships or fieldwork, scholarships/grants, and unspecified assistantships available. Support available to part-time students. Financial award application deadline: 2/15. *Faculty research:* Neurology, developmental disabilities, diet consequences. *Unit head:* Dr. Mary Harlan, Chairperson, 501-450-5950, Fax: 501-450-5958, E-mail: maryh@uca.edu. *Application contact:* Patti Hornor, Administrative Assistant, 501-450-5063, Fax: 501-450-5678, E-mail: pattih@uca.edu.

University of Central Oklahoma, College of Graduate Studies and Research, College of Education, Department of Human Environmental Sciences, Edmond, OK 73034-5209. Offers family and child studies (MS); family and consumer science education (MS); interior design (MS); nutrition-food management (MS). Part-time programs available. *Faculty:* 5 full-time (all women), 5 part-time/adjunct (3 women). *Students:* 38 full-time (32 women), 57 part-time (54 women); includes 24 minority (13 African Americans, 4 American Indian/Alaska Native, 3 Asian Americans or Pacific Islanders, 4 Hispanic Americans), 4 international. Average age 30. 21 applicants, 95% accepted. In 2007, 20 degrees awarded. *Entrance requirements:* Additional exam requirements/recommendations for international students: Required—TOEFL (minimum score 550 paper-based; 213 computer-based). *Application deadline:* For fall admission, 7/1 for international students; for spring admission, 11/1 for international students. Applications are processed on a rolling basis. Application fee: $25. Electronic applications accepted. *Expenses:* Tuition, state resident: full-time $3,516; part-time $147 per hour. Tuition, nonresident: full-time $9,054; part-time $377 per hour. Required fees: $433; $18 per hour. *Financial support:* Career-related internships or fieldwork and unspecified assistantships available. Financial award application deadline: 3/31; financial award applicants required to submit FAFSA. *Faculty research:* Dietetics and food science. *Unit head:* Dr. Kaye Sears, Chairperson, 405-974-5786.

University of Florida, Graduate School, College of Agricultural and Life Sciences, Department of Family, Youth, and Community Sciences, Gainesville, FL 32611. Offers MFYCS, MS. *Faculty:* 18 full-time (13 women). *Students:* 18 (17 women); includes 6 minority (3 African Americans, 3 Hispanic Americans) 1 international. In 2007, 11 degrees awarded. *Expenses:* Tuition, state resident: full-time $7,478. Tuition, nonresident: full-time $22,603. *Financial support:* In 2007–08, 1 research assistantship (averaging $8,999 per year), 8 teaching assistantships (averaging $9,671 per year) were awarded. *Unit head:* Dr. Nayda I. Torres, Chair, 352-392-1778 Ext. 221, E-mail: nitorres@ifas.ufl.edu. *Application contact:* Dr. Mickie Swisher, Graduate Coordinator, 352-392-2202 Ext. 256, Fax: 352-392-8196, E-mail: meswisher@mail.ifas.ufl.edu.

University of Georgia, Graduate School, College of Family and Consumer Sciences, Athens, GA 30602. Offers MAT, MFCS, MS, PhD. *Faculty:* 58 full-time (37 women). *Students:* 99 full-time (82 women), 18 part-time (14 women); includes 20 minority (14 African Americans, 2 Asian Americans or Pacific Islanders, 4 Hispanic Americans), 19 international. 149 applicants, 47% accepted, 33 enrolled. In 2007, 25 master's, 14 doctorates awarded. *Degree requirements:* For doctorate, thesis/dissertation. *Entrance requirements:* For master's and doctorate, GRE General Test. *Application deadline:* For fall admission, 7/1 priority date for domestic students; for spring admission, 11/15 for domestic students. Application fee: $50. Electronic applications accepted. *Financial support:* Fellowships, research assistantships, teaching assistantships, unspecified assistantships available. *Unit head:* Dr. Laura Dunn Jolly, Dean, 706-542-4879, Fax: 706-542-4862, E-mail: ljolly@fcs.uga.edu.

University of Houston, College of Technology, Department of Human Development and Consumer Science, Houston, TX 77204. Offers MS. *Faculty:* 2 full-time (1 woman), 1 (woman) part-time/adjunct. *Students:* 17 full-time (12 women), 26 part-time (14 women); includes 12 minority (5 African Americans, 2 American Indian/Alaska Native, 4 Asian Americans or Pacific Islanders, 1 Hispanic American), 6 international. Average age 36. 25 applicants, 88% accepted, 15 enrolled. In 2007, 7 degrees awarded. *Expenses:* Tuition, state resident: full-time $6,297; part-time $262 per credit. Tuition, nonresident: full-time $12,969; part-time $540 per credit. Required fees: $2,696. *Unit head:* Carole Goodson, Chairperson, 713-743-4046, Fax: 713-743-4033.

University of Louisiana at Lafayette, Graduate School, School of Human Resources, Lafayette, LA 70504. Offers MS. Part-time programs available. *Degree requirements:* For master's, thesis or alternative. *Entrance requirements:* For master's, GRE General Test, minimum GPA of 2.75. Additional exam requirements/recommendations for international students: Required—TOEFL (minimum score 550 paper-based; 213 computer-based). Electronic applications accepted. *Faculty research:* Nutrition education, crawfish use and nutrients.

University of Manitoba, Faculty of Graduate Studies, Faculty of Human Ecology, Winnipeg, MB R3T 2N2, Canada. Offers M Sc. *Degree requirements:* For master's, thesis.

University of Maryland, College Park, Graduate Studies, School of Public Health, Department of Family Science, College Park, MD 20742. Offers family studies (PhD); marriage and family therapy (MS). *Accreditation:* AAMFT/COAMFTE. Part-time and evening/weekend programs available. *Faculty:* 15 full-time (12 women), 14 part-time/adjunct (11 women). *Students:* 40 full-time (35 women), 1 (woman) part-time; includes 10 minority (8 African Americans, 1 Asian American or Pacific Islander, 1 Hispanic American), 2 international. 91 applicants, 24%

Family and Consumer Sciences-General

University of Maryland, College Park (continued)
accepted, 17 enrolled. In 2007, 17 master's, 9 doctorates awarded. *Degree requirements:* For master's, thesis or alternative; for doctorate, comprehensive exam, thesis/dissertation, oral defense. *Entrance requirements:* For master's, GRE General Test, minimum GPA of 3.0, 3 letters of recommendation; for doctorate, GRE General Test, minimum GPA of 3.0, 3 letters of recommendation, research sample. *Application deadline:* For fall admission, 1/15 for domestic students, 2/1 for international students. Applications are processed on a rolling basis. Application fee: $60. Electronic applications accepted. *Financial support:* In 2007–08, 8 fellowships with full tuition reimbursements (averaging $7,450 per year), 1 research assistantship with tuition reimbursement (averaging $15,126 per year), 28 teaching assistantships with tuition reimbursements (averaging $14,911 per year) were awarded; career-related internships or fieldwork, Federal Work-Study, and scholarships/grants also available. Support available to part-time students. Financial award applicants required to submit FAFSA. *Faculty research:* Family life quality, interracial couples, child support, homeless families, family and child well-being. Total annual research expenditures: $291,811. *Unit head:* Dr. Sally Koblinsky, Chairman, 301-405-1377, Fax: 301-314-9161, E-mail: koblinsk@umd.edu. *Application contact:* Dean of Graduate School, 301-405-0358, Fax: 301-314-9305.

See Close-Up on page 1075.

University of Memphis, Graduate School, University College, Department of Merchandising and Consumer Science, Memphis, TN 38152. Offers consumer science and education (MS). Part-time programs available. *Faculty:* 3 full-time (all women). *Students:* 4 full-time (0 women), 5 part-time (2 women); includes 8 minority (all African Americans) Average age 26. 2 applicants, 100% accepted, 2 enrolled. *Degree requirements:* For master's, comprehensive exam, thesis (for some programs). *Entrance requirements:* For master's, GRE General Test or MAT. Application fee: $35 ($60 for international students). Electronic applications accepted. *Expenses:* Tuition, state resident: full-time $6,990; part-time $377 per hour. Tuition, nonresident: full-time $17,818; part-time $830 per hour. Tuition and fees vary according to course load and program. *Financial support:* Career-related internships or fieldwork and scholarships/grants available. *Faculty research:* Family and consumer studies, merchandising. *Unit head:* Dr. Dixie R. Crase, Coordinator of Graduate Studies, 901-678-2301, Fax: 901-678-5324, E-mail: drcrase@memphis.edu.

University of Missouri–Columbia, Graduate School, College of Human Environmental Science, Columbia, MO 65211. Offers MA, MS, PhD. Part-time programs available. *Degree requirements:* For doctorate, thesis/dissertation. *Entrance requirements:* For master's and doctorate, GRE General Test, minimum GPA of 3.0. Additional exam requirements/recommendations for international students: Required—TOEFL.

University of Nebraska–Lincoln, Graduate College, College of Education and Human Sciences, Interdepartmental Area of Human Resources and Family Sciences, Lincoln, NE 68588. Offers MS, PhD. Postbaccalaureate distance learning degree programs offered. *Degree requirements:* For master's, thesis optional; for doctorate, comprehensive exam, thesis/dissertation. *Entrance requirements:* For master's, GRE General Test; for doctorate, GRE General Test, writing sample. Additional exam requirements/recommendations for international students: Required—TOEFL (minimum score 550 paper-based; 213 computer-based). Electronic applications accepted.

The University of North Carolina at Greensboro, Graduate School, School of Human Environmental Sciences, Greensboro, NC 27412-5001. Offers M Ed, MS, MSW, PhD, Certificate. *Faculty:* 59 full-time (40 women), 11 part-time/adjunct (8 women). *Students:* 221 full-time (199 women), 13 part-time (10 women); includes 78 minority (57 African Americans, 1 American Indian/Alaska Native, 14 Asian Americans or Pacific Islanders, 6 Hispanic Americans). 152 applicants, 39% accepted. *Degree requirements:* For master's, thesis (for some programs); for doctorate, thesis/dissertation. *Entrance requirements:* For master's and doctorate, GRE General Test. Additional exam requirements/recommendations for international students: Required—TOEFL. Application fee: $45. Electronic applications accepted. *Financial support:* Fellowships with full tuition reimbursements, research assistantships with full tuition reimbursements, teaching assistantships with full tuition reimbursements, unspecified assistantships available. *Faculty research:* Impact of phosphate removal, protective clothing for pesticide workers, adolescent mothers, cancer prevention, immuno-stimulant effects. *Unit head:* Laura S. Sims, Dean, 336-334-5980, Fax: 336-334-5089, E-mail: lssims@uncg.edu. *Application contact:* Michelle Harkleroad, Director of Graduate Admissions, 336-334-4884, Fax: 336-334-4424, E-mail: mbharkle@uncg.edu.

University of Puerto Rico, Río Piedras, College of Education, Program in Family Ecology and Nutrition, San Juan, PR 00931-3300. Offers M Ed. Part-time programs available. *Students:* 12 full-time (all women), 5 part-time (all women); all minorities (all Hispanic Americans) Average age 34. 1 applicant, 100% accepted, 1 enrolled. In 2007, 2 degrees awarded. *Degree requirements:* For master's, thesis. *Entrance requirements:* For master's, PAEG or GRE, minimum GPA of 3.0, letter of recommendation. *Application deadline:* For fall admission, 2/1 for domestic and international students. Application fee: $17. *Expenses:* Tuition, state resident: full-time $1,808; part-time $113 per credit. Tuition, nonresident: full-time $5,248; part-time $328 per credit. Required fees: $72 per term. *Financial support:* Fellowships, research assistantships, teaching assistantships, career-related internships or fieldwork, Federal Work-Study, institutionally sponsored loans, and tuition waivers (partial) available. Financial award application deadline: 5/31. *Unit head:* Dr. Loyda Martinez, Coordinator, 787-764-0000 Ext. 4361, Fax: 787-763-4130. *Application contact:* Information Contact, 787-764-0000 Ext. 4368, Fax: 787-763-4130.

University of South Africa, College of Agriculture and Environmental Sciences, Pretoria, South Africa. Offers agriculture (MS); consumer science (MCS); environmental management (MA, MS, PhD); environmental science (MA, MS, PhD); geography (MA, MS, PhD); horticulture (M Tech); human ecology (MHE); life sciences (MS); nature conservation (M Tech).

The University of Tennessee, Graduate School, College of Education, Health and Human Sciences, Program in Human Ecology, Knoxville, TN 37996. Offers child and family studies (PhD); community health (PhD); nutrition science (PhD); retailing and consumer sciences (PhD); textile science (PhD). *Degree requirements:* For doctorate, thesis/dissertation. *Entrance requirements:* For doctorate, GRE General Test, minimum GPA of 2.7. Additional exam requirements/recommendations for international students: Required—TOEFL. Electronic applications accepted.

The University of Tennessee at Martin, Graduate Programs, College of Agriculture and Applied Sciences, Department of Family and Consumer Sciences, Martin, TN 38238-1000. Offers dietetics (MSFCS); general family and consumer sciences (MSFCS). Part-time programs available. *Faculty:* 6. *Students:* 19 (all women) 21 applicants, 90% accepted, 8 enrolled. In 2007, 6 degrees awarded. *Degree requirements:* For master's, comprehensive exam, thesis optional. *Entrance requirements:* For master's, GRE General Test, minimum GPA of 2.5. Additional exam requirements/recommendations for international students: Required—TOEFL (minimum score 525 paper-based; 197 computer-based). *Application deadline:* For fall admission, 8/1 priority date for domestic students, 8/1 for international students; for spring admission, 1/1 for domestic and international students. Applications are processed on a rolling basis. Application fee: $30 ($50 for international students). Electronic applications accepted. *Expenses:* Tuition, state resident: full-time $2,893; part-time $323 per credit hour. Tuition, nonresident: full-time $7,913; part-time $881 per credit hour. Required fees: $220 per credit hour. *Financial support:* In 2007–08, 3 students received support. Scholarships/grants, tuition waivers (partial), and unspecified assistantships available. Financial award application deadline: 3/1. *Faculty research:* Children with developmental disabilities, regional food product development and marketing, parent education. *Unit head:* Dr. Lisa LeBleu, Coordinator, 731-881-7116, E-mail: llebleu@utm.edu. *Application contact:* Linda S. Arant, Student Services Specialist, 731-881-7012, Fax: 731-881-7499, E-mail: larant@utm.edu.

The University of Texas at Austin, Graduate School, College of Natural Sciences, Department of Human Ecology, Austin, TX 78712-1111. Offers child development and family relations (MA, PhD); nutritional sciences (MA, PhD), including nutrition (MA), nutritional sciences (PhD). *Degree requirements:* For master's, thesis; for doctorate, thesis/dissertation. *Entrance requirements:* For master's and doctorate, GRE General Test. Electronic applications accepted.

University of Wisconsin–Madison, Graduate School, School of Human Ecology, Madison, WI 53706-1380. Offers consumer behavior and family economics (MS, PhD); design studies (MFA, MS, PhD); human development and family studies (MS, PhD). *Degree requirements:* For master's, thesis (for some programs); for doctorate, comprehensive exam, thesis/dissertation. *Entrance requirements:* For master's, GRE General Test, portfolio (design studies), 3 letters of recommendation; for doctorate, GRE General Test. Additional exam requirements/recommendations for international students: Required—TOEFL (minimum score 580 paper-based; 237 computer-based). Electronic applications accepted.

University of Wisconsin–Stevens Point, College of Professional Studies, School of Health Promotion and Human Development, Program in Human and Community Resources, Stevens Point, WI 54481-3897. Offers MS. Part-time programs available. *Degree requirements:* For master's, thesis or alternative. *Entrance requirements:* For master's, minimum GPA of 2.75. *Application deadline:* For fall admission, 5/1 priority date for domestic students. Applications are processed on a rolling basis. Application fee: $45. *Expenses:* Tuition, state resident: full-time $6,161. Tuition, nonresident: full-time $16,771. Required fees: $884. Tuition and fees vary according to course load. *Financial support:* Research assistantships, teaching assistantships, Federal Work-Study available. Support available to part-time students. Financial award application deadline: 5/1; financial award applicants required to submit FAFSA. *Application contact:* Dr. Jasia Steinmetz, Information Contact, 715-346-2830, Fax: 715-346-2720, E-mail: jsteinme@uwsp.edu.

Utah State University, School of Graduate Studies, College of Education and Human Services, Department of Family, Consumer, and Human Development, Logan, UT 84322. Offers family and human development (MFHD); family, consumer, and human development (MS, PhD), including adolescence/youth (MS), adult development/aging (MS), consumer science (MS), infancy/childhood (MS), marriage and family relations (MS), marriage and family therapy (MS). *Accreditation:* AAMFT/COAMFTE (one or more programs are accredited). Part-time and evening/weekend programs available. Postbaccalaureate distance learning degree programs offered (minimal on-campus study). *Degree requirements:* For master's, thesis; for doctorate, comprehensive exam, thesis/dissertation, competencies. *Entrance requirements:* For master's, GRE General Test or MAT, minimum GPA of 3.0, 3 letters of recommendation; for doctorate, GRE, minimum GPA of 3.0, 3 letters of recommendation. Additional exam requirements/recommendations for international students: Required—TOEFL. Electronic applications accepted. *Faculty research:* Marriage and family relations, adolescent problem behavior, family financial management, early literacy, mental health in the elderly, parent child attachment.

Western Michigan University, Graduate College, College of Education, Department of Family and Consumer Sciences, Program in Family and Consumer Sciences, Kalamazoo, MI 49008-5202. Offers MA. *Faculty research:* Parenting education, kinship care, entrepreneurship, textiles and dress, nutrition.

Child and Family Studies

Arizona State University, Graduate College, College of Liberal Arts and Sciences, Division of Social Sciences, Department of Family and Human Development, Tempe, AZ 85287. Offers family and human development (MS); family science (PhD). *Degree requirements:* For master's, thesis or alternative; for doctorate, thesis/dissertation. *Entrance requirements:* For master's and doctorate, GRE.

Auburn University, Graduate School, College of Human Sciences, Department of Human Development and Family Studies, Auburn University, AL 36849. Offers MS, PhD. *Accreditation:* AAMFT/COAMFTE (one or more programs are accredited). Part-time programs available. *Faculty:* 12 full-time (7 women). *Students:* 26 full-time (24 women), 20 part-time (18 women); includes 7 minority (4 African Americans, 3 Asian Americans or Pacific Islanders), 11 international. Average age 26. 49 applicants, 59% accepted, 15 enrolled. In 2007, 18 master's, 7 doctorates awarded. *Degree requirements:* For master's, thesis, oral exam; for doctorate, thesis/dissertation. *Entrance requirements:* For master's, GRE General Test; for doctorate, GRE General Test, master's degree. *Application deadline:* For fall admission, 7/7 for domestic students; for spring admission, 11/24 for domestic students. Applications are processed on a rolling basis. Application fee: $25 ($50 for international students). *Financial support:* Research assistantships, teaching assistantships, Federal Work-Study available. Support available to part-time students. Financial award application deadline: 3/15. *Faculty research:* Family influences on personality and social development, parent-child relations, infancy, day care, parent education. *Unit head:* Dr. Leanne K. Lamke, Head, 334-844-4151, E-mail: mbradbar@humsci.auburn.edu. *Application contact:* Dr. Joe Pittman, Interim Dean of the Graduate School, 334-844-4700.

Bank Street College of Education, Graduate School, Program in Child Life, New York, NY 10025. Offers MS. *Students:* 25 full-time (all women), 7 part-time (all women); includes 5 minority (2 African Americans, 2 Asian Americans or Pacific Islanders, 1 Hispanic American). Average age 25. 27 applicants, 70% accepted, 17 enrolled. In 2007, 8 degrees awarded. *Degree requirements:* For master's, thesis. *Entrance requirements:* For master's, interview. Additional exam requirements/recommendations for international students: Required—TOEFL (minimum score 600 paper-based; 250 computer-based). *Application deadline:* For fall admission, 3/1 priority date for domestic students; for spring admission, 11/1 priority date for domestic students. Applications are processed on a rolling basis. Application fee: $50. *Expenses:* Tuition: Part-time $1,010 per credit. *Financial support:* Career-related internships or fieldwork, Federal Work-Study, scholarships/grants, and unspecified assistantships available. Support available to part-time students. Financial award application deadline: 4/15; financial award applicants required to submit FAFSA. *Faculty research:* Therapeutic play in child life setting, child advocacy, psychosocial and educational intervention with care of sick children. *Unit head:* Troy Pinkney-Ragsdale, Director, 212-875-4473, Fax: 212-875-4753, E-mail: tpinkneyragsdale@bankstreet.edu. *Application contact:* Ann Morgan, Director of Graduate Admissions, 212-875-4403, Fax: 212-875-4678, E-mail: amorgan@bankstreet.edu.

Bowling Green State University, Graduate College, College of Education and Human Development, School of Family and Consumer Sciences, Bowling Green, OH 43403. Offers food and nutrition (MFCS); human development and family studies (MFCS). Part-time programs available. *Faculty:* 20 full-time (15 women), 4 part-time/adjunct (2 women). *Students:* 10 full-time (8 women), 23 part-time (all women); includes 4 minority (all Hispanic Americans),

2 international. Average age 28. 29 applicants, 69% accepted, 20 enrolled. In 2007, 4 degrees awarded. *Degree requirements:* For master's, thesis. *Entrance requirements:* For master's, GRE General Test, minimum GPA of 3.0. Additional exam requirements/recommendations for international students: Required—TOEFL. *Application deadline:* For fall admission, 3/1 priority date for domestic students. Application fee: $30. Electronic applications accepted. *Financial support:* In 2007–08, 1 research assistantship with full tuition reimbursement (averaging $8,404 per year), 9 teaching assistantships with full tuition reimbursements (averaging $7,089 per year) were awarded; career-related internships or fieldwork and unspecified assistantships also available. Financial award applicants required to submit FAFSA. *Faculty research:* Public health, wellness, social issues and policies, ethnic foods, nutrition and aging. *Unit head:* Dr. Deborah Wooldridge, Director, 419-372-7823. *Application contact:* Dr. Dawn Anderson, Graduate Coordinator, 419-372-8090.

Brandeis University, The Heller School for Social Policy and Management, Program in Social Policy, Waltham, MA 02454-9110. Offers aging (MPP); assets and inequalities (PhD); behavioral health (MPP); children, youth and families (MPP, PhD); general social policy (MPP); health (MPP); health and behavioral health (PhD); poverty alleviation and development (MPP). Part-time programs available. *Degree requirements:* For doctorate, thesis/dissertation, qualifying paper, 2 year residency. *Entrance requirements:* For doctorate, GRE General Test. Additional exam requirements/recommendations for international students: Required—TOEFL (minimum score 600 paper-based). Electronic applications accepted. *Faculty research:* Health policy, child and family policy, mental health policy, disability policy, aging policy, substance abuse, work, inequality and social change.

See Close-Ups on pages 1581 and 1579.

Brigham Young University, Graduate Studies, College of Family, Home, and Social Sciences, Program in Marriage, Family and Human Development, Provo, UT 84602-1001. Offers MS, PhD. *Accreditation:* AAMFT/COAMFTE. *Faculty:* 24 full-time (5 women). *Students:* 28 full-time (19 women); includes 1 minority (Asian American or Pacific Islander), 2 international. Average age 28. 22 applicants, 36% accepted, 6 enrolled. In 2007, 4 master's awarded. *Degree requirements:* For master's, thesis; for doctorate, comprehensive exam, thesis/dissertation, 2 publishable papers. *Entrance requirements:* For master's and doctorate, GRE General Test, minimum GPA of 3.0 in last 60 semester hours, letters of recommendation. Additional exam requirements/recommendations for international students: Required—TOEFL (minimum score 580 paper-based; 237 computer-based; 85 iBT), IELTS (minimum score 7). *Application deadline:* For fall admission, 1/10 for domestic and international students. Application fee: $50. Electronic applications accepted. *Financial support:* In 2007–08, 20 research assistantships with full and partial tuition reimbursements (averaging $5,096 per year), 5 teaching assistantships with full and partial tuition reimbursements (averaging $5,096 per year) were awarded; scholarships/grants and unspecified assistantships also available. Financial award application deadline: 1/10. *Faculty research:* Early childhood education, family process, family life education. *Unit head:* Dr. Richard Miller, Director, School of Life, 801-422-2069, Fax: 801-422-0230, E-mail: rick_miller@byu.edu.

Brock University, Faculty of Graduate Studies, Faculty of Social Sciences, Program in Child and Youth Studies, St. Catharines, ON L2S 3A1, Canada. Offers MA. Part-time programs available. *Degree requirements:* For master's, thesis. *Entrance requirements:* For master's, honors BA. Additional exam requirements/recommendations for international students: Required—TOEFL (minimum score 550 paper-based; 213 computer-based; 80 iBT), IELTS (minimum score 7), TWE (minimum score 4). Electronic applications accepted. *Faculty research:* Cognitive mechanisms, youth resilience, developmental disabilities, parent-child interactions and communication.

Capella University, School of Human Services, Minneapolis, MN 55402. Offers addictions counseling (Certificate); counseling studies (MS, PhD); criminal justice (MS, PhD, Certificate); diversity studies (Certificate); general human services (MS, PhD); health care administration (MS, PhD, Certificate); management of nonprofit agencies (MS, PhD, Certificate); marital, couple and family counseling/therapy (MS); marriage and family services (Certificate); mental health counseling (MS); professional counseling (Certificate); social and community services (MS, PhD, Certificate). Part-time and evening/weekend programs available. Postbaccalaureate distance learning degree programs offered (minimal on-campus study). Terminal master's awarded for partial completion of doctoral program. *Degree requirements:* For master's, thesis optional, integrative project; for doctorate, comprehensive exam, thesis/dissertation. *Entrance requirements:* Additional exam requirements/recommendations for international students: Required—TOEFL (minimum score 550 paper-based; 213 computer-based), TWE (minimum score 4). Electronic applications accepted. *Faculty research:* Compulsive and addictive behaviors, substance abuse, assessment of psychopathology and neuropsychology.

Central Michigan University, College of Graduate Studies, College of Education and Human Services, Department of Human Environmental Studies, Mount Pleasant, MI 48859. Offers human development and family studies (MA); nutrition and dietetics (MS). *Degree requirements:* For master's, thesis or alternative. *Entrance requirements:* For master's, GRE (MA), minimum GPA of 3.0 in last 60 hours, 15 credits of course work in human development and family studies or related area (MA). *Faculty research:* Human growth and development, family studies and human sexuality, nutritional food science/food services, apparel and textile retailing, computer-aided design for apparel and interior design.

Central Washington University, Graduate Studies, Research and Continuing Education, College of Education and Professional Studies, Department of Family and Consumer Sciences, Ellensburg, WA 98926. Offers family and consumer sciences education (MS); family studies (MS); nutrition (MS). Part-time programs available. *Faculty:* 11 full-time (7 women). *Students:* 12 full-time (11 women), 2 part-time (both women). 20 applicants, 70% accepted, 13 enrolled. In 2007, 13 degrees awarded. *Degree requirements:* For master's, thesis or alternative. *Entrance requirements:* For master's, GRE General Test (nutrition), minimum GPA of 3.0. Additional exam requirements/recommendations for international students: Required—TOEFL (minimum score 550 paper-based; 213 computer-based; 79 iBT). *Application deadline:* For fall admission, 4/1 priority date for domestic students; for winter admission, 10/1 for domestic students; for spring admission, 1/1 for domestic students. Applications are processed on a rolling basis. Application fee: $50. Electronic applications accepted. *Expenses:* Tuition, state resident: full-time $2,209; part-time $221 per credit. Tuition, nonresident: full-time $4,939; part-time $442 per credit. Required fees: $207 per quarter. Tuition and fees vary according to degree level. *Financial support:* In 2007–08, 1 teaching assistantship with partial tuition reimbursement (averaging $8,100 per year) was awarded; research assistantships, Federal Work-Study, health care benefits, and unspecified assistantships also available. Financial award application deadline: 3/1; financial award applicants required to submit FAFSA. *Unit head:* Dr. Jan Bowers, Chair, 509-963-2766. *Application contact:* Justine Eason, Admissions Program Coordinator, 509-963-3103, Fax: 509-963-1799, E-mail: masters@cwu.edu.

Clemson University, Institute on Family and Neighborhood Life and Interdisciplinary Studies, Program in International Family and Community Studies, Clemson, SC 29634. Offers PhD. *Students:* 10 full-time (9 women), 2 part-time (both women), 5 international. 16 applicants, 63% accepted, 7 enrolled. *Degree requirements:* For doctorate, one foreign language, comprehensive exam, thesis/dissertation (for some programs). *Entrance requirements:* For doctorate, GRE and/or MAT, 3 letters of recommendation from professionals familiar with the applicant's academic work and/or community service. Additional exam requirements/recommendations for international students: Required—TOEFL. *Application deadline:* For fall admission, 3/1 for domestic and international students. Application fee: $55. Electronic applications accepted. *Financial support:* In 2007–08, 5 fellowships with partial tuition reimbursements, 5 research assistantships with partial tuition reimbursements, 5 teaching assistantships with partial tuition reimbursements were awarded; career-related internships or fieldwork, scholarships/grants, health care benefits, and unspecified assistantships also available. *Unit head:* Dr. Bonnie Holaday, Program Coordinator, 864-656-6288, Fax: 864-656-6281, E-mail: holaday@clemson.edu.

Colorado State University, Graduate School, College of Applied Human Sciences, Department of Human Development and Family Studies, Fort Collins, CO 80523-0015. Offers MS. *Accreditation:* AAMFT/COAMFTE. Part-time programs available. *Faculty:* 13 full-time (9 women). *Students:* 21 full-time (20 women), 18 part-time (all women); includes 1 minority (Asian American or Pacific Islander), 2 international. Average age 32. 102 applicants, 27% accepted, 15 enrolled. In 2007, 8 degrees awarded. *Degree requirements:* For master's, thesis. *Entrance requirements:* For master's, GRE General Test, minimum GPA of 3.0; course work in human development, family studies, and statistics, letters of recommendation forms, additional departmental application, interview. Additional exam requirements/recommendations for international students: Required—TOEFL (minimum score 550 paper-based; 220 computer-based); Recommended—TWE. *Application deadline:* For fall admission, 1/15 for domestic and international students. Application fee: $50. Electronic applications accepted. *Expenses:* Tuition, state resident: full-time $4,887; part-time $272 per credit. Tuition, nonresident: full-time $16,425; part-time $913 per credit. Required fees: $1,379; $75 per credit. *Financial support:* In 2007–08, 12 students received support, including 2 research assistantships with partial tuition reimbursements available (averaging $8,915 per year), 12 teaching assistantships with partial tuition reimbursements available (averaging $8,420 per year); fellowships, career-related internships or fieldwork, Federal Work-Study, institutionally sponsored loans, scholarships/grants, and unspecified assistantships also available. Financial award application deadline: 1/15; financial award applicants required to submit FAFSA. *Faculty research:* Promoting resiliency and optimal development; gender, culture and diversity; intervention programming and evaluation; gerontology/aging. Total annual research expenditures: $733,061. *Unit head:* Dr. Lise Youngblade, Interim Department Head, 970-491-5558, Fax: 970-491-7975, E-mail: lise.youngblade@colostate.edu. *Application contact:* Dr. Karen C. Barrett, Graduate Chair, 970-491-7382, Fax: 970-491-7975, E-mail: barrett@cahs.colostate.edu.

Concordia University, School of Graduate Studies, Faculty of Arts and Science, Department of Education, Program in Child Study, Montréal, QC H3G 1M8, Canada. Offers MA. *Degree requirements:* For master's, one foreign language, thesis optional. *Entrance requirements:* For master's, minimum B average in undergraduate course work. *Faculty research:* Development and family relations, children and technology, cooperative learning strategies, exceptional children, second language acquisition.

Concordia University, St. Paul, College of Education, St. Paul, MN 55104-5494. Offers curriculum and instruction (MA Ed); differentiated instruction (MA Ed); early childhood (MA Ed); educational leadership (MA Ed); family life education (MAHS); special education (Certificate). *Accreditation:* NCATE. Evening/weekend programs available. Postbaccalaureate distance learning degree programs offered (minimal on-campus study). *Faculty:* 12 full-time (9 women), 34 part-time/adjunct (25 women). *Students:* 376 full-time (327 women), 5 part-time (4 women); includes 47 minority (33 African Americans, 11 Asian Americans or Pacific Islanders, 3 Hispanic Americans), 2 international. Average age 36. In 2007, 47 master's, 4 Certificates awarded. *Entrance requirements:* Additional exam requirements/recommendations for international students: Required—TOEFL. *Application deadline:* Applications are processed on a rolling basis. Application fee: $50. Electronic applications accepted. *Unit head:* Prof. Lonn Maly, Dean, 651-641-8278, Fax: 651-641-8807, E-mail: maly@csp.edu. *Application contact:* Kimberly Craig, Director of Graduate and Cohort Admission, 651-603-6223, Fax: 651-603-6320, E-mail: craig@csp.edu.

Concordia University Wisconsin, Graduate Programs, Department of Education, Program in Family Studies, Mequon, WI 53097-2402. Offers MS Ed. *Degree requirements:* For master's, comprehensive exam, thesis or alternative. *Entrance requirements:* For master's, minimum GPA of 3.0. Additional exam requirements/recommendations for international students: Required—TOEFL.

Cornell University, Graduate School, Graduate Fields of Human Ecology, Field of Human Development, Ithaca, NY 14853-0001. Offers developmental psychology (PhD), including cognitive development, developmental psychopathology, ecology of human development, social and personality development; human development and family studies (PhD), including ecology of human development, family studies and the life course. *Faculty:* 35 full-time (12 women). *Students:* 29 full-time (22 women); includes 4 minority (2 Asian Americans or Pacific Islanders, 2 Hispanic Americans), 10 international. Average age 27. 63 applicants, 19% accepted, 5 enrolled. In 2007, 5 doctorates awarded. *Degree requirements:* For doctorate, comprehensive exam, thesis/dissertation, pre-doctoral research project, teaching experience. *Entrance requirements:* For doctorate, GRE General Test, 2 letters of recommendation. Additional exam requirements/recommendations for international students: Required—TOEFL (minimum score 550 paper-based; 213 computer-based; 77 iBT). *Application deadline:* For fall admission, 1/15 for domestic students. Application fee: $70. Electronic applications accepted. *Financial support:* In 2007–08, 28 students received support, including 6 fellowships with full tuition reimbursements available, 6 research assistantships with full tuition reimbursements available, 16 teaching assistantships with full tuition reimbursements available; institutionally sponsored loans, scholarships/grants, health care benefits, tuition waivers (full and partial), and unspecified assistantships also available. Financial award applicants required to submit FAFSA. *Faculty research:* Cognitive development, developmental psychopathology, ecology of human development, family studies and the life course, social and personality development. *Unit head:* Director of Graduate Studies, 607-255-3181, Fax: 607-255-9856. *Application contact:* Graduate Field Assistant, 607-255-3181, Fax: 607-255-9856, E-mail: hdfs@cornell.edu.

East Carolina University, Graduate School, College of Human Ecology, Department of Child Development and Family Relations, Greenville, NC 27858-4353. Offers child development and family relations (MS); marriage and family therapy (MS). *Accreditation:* AAMFT/COAMFTE. Part-time programs available. *Students:* 45 full-time (38 women), 17 part-time (all women); includes 13 minority (8 African Americans, 1 American Indian/Alaska Native, 1 Asian American or Pacific Islander, 3 Hispanic Americans). Average age 27. 30 applicants, 3% accepted, 1 enrolled. In 2007, 21 degrees awarded. *Degree requirements:* For master's, comprehensive exam, thesis optional. *Application deadline:* For fall admission, 1/15 for domestic students; for spring admission, 10/15 for domestic students. Applications are processed on a rolling basis. Application fee: $50. *Financial support:* In 2007–08, 18 students received support, including 10 research assistantships, 8 teaching assistantships; career-related internships or fieldwork, Federal Work-Study, institutionally sponsored loans, and scholarships/grants also available. Support available to part-time students. Financial award application deadline: 6/1. *Faculty research:* Child care quality, mental health delivery systems for children, family violence. *Unit head:* Dr. Cynthia Johnson, Chairperson, 252-328-4273, E-mail: johnsoncy@ecu.edu.

Eastern Michigan University, Graduate School, College of Health and Human Services, School of Social Work, Ypsilanti, MI 48197. Offers family and children's services (MSW); gerontology (Graduate Certificate); gerontology-dementia (Graduate Certificate); mental health and chemical dependency (MSW); services to the aging (MSW). *Accreditation:* CSWE. Part-time and evening/weekend programs available. Postbaccalaureate distance learning degree programs offered (minimal on-campus study). *Faculty:* 18 full-time (15 women). *Students:* 26 full-time (21 women), 164 part-time (142 women); includes 78 minority (69 African Americans, 3 American Indian/Alaska Native, 4 Asian Americans or Pacific Islanders, 2 Hispanic Americans), 1 international. Average age 35. In 2007, 117 master's, 17 other advanced degrees awarded. *Entrance requirements:* Additional exam requirements/recommendations for international students: Required—TOEFL. *Application deadline:* Applications are processed on a rolling basis. Application fee: $35. *Expenses:* Tuition, state resident: full-time $8,952; part-time $373 per credit hour. Tuition, nonresident: full-time $17,634; part-time $735 per credit hour. Required fees: $896; $34 per credit hour. Tuition and fees vary according to course level, degree level and program. *Financial support:* Fellowships, research assistantships with full tuition reimbursements, teaching assistantships with full tuition reimbursements, career-related internships or fieldwork, Federal Work-Study, institutionally sponsored loans, scholarships/grants, tuition waivers (partial), and unspecified assistantships available. Support available to part-time students. Financial award applicants required to submit FAFSA. *Unit head:* Prof. Marjorie Ziefert, Director, 734-487-0393, Fax: 734-487-6832, E-mail: marjorie.ziefert@emich.edu.

Child and Family Studies

Eastern Michigan University (continued)

Application contact: Julie Harkema, Advisor, 734-487-0393, Fax: 734-487-6832, E-mail: jharkema@emich.edu.

Florida State University, Graduate Studies, College of Human Sciences, Department of Family and Child Sciences, Tallahassee, FL 32306. Offers child development (MS, PhD); family relations (MS, PhD); marriage and family therapy (PhD). *Accreditation:* AAMFT/COAMFTE. Part-time programs available. *Faculty:* 16 full-time (9 women). *Students:* 29 full-time (20 women), 38 part-time (32 women); includes 20 minority (14 African Americans, 2 Asian Americans or Pacific Islanders, 4 Hispanic Americans), 2 international. 47 applicants, 30% accepted, 10 enrolled. In 2007, 4 master's, 10 doctorates awarded. *Degree requirements:* For master's, comprehensive exam, thesis optional; for doctorate, thesis/dissertation. *Entrance requirements:* For master's and doctorate, GRE General Test, minimum GPA of 3.0. Additional exam requirements/recommendations for international students: Required—TOEFL (minimum score 80 iBT). *Application deadline:* For fall admission, 7/1 for domestic students, 5/1 for international students; for spring admission, 11/1 for domestic students, 12/1 for international students. Application fee: $30. Electronic applications accepted. *Expenses:* Tuition, state resident: part-time $248 per credit hour. Tuition, nonresident: part-time $880 per credit hour. Tuition and fees vary according to program. *Financial support:* In 2007–08, 31 students received support, including 1 fellowship (averaging $10,000 per year), research assistantships with partial tuition reimbursements available (averaging $5,000 per year), teaching assistantships with partial tuition reimbursements available (averaging $5,000 per year); career-related internships or fieldwork, Federal Work-Study, institutionally sponsored loans, scholarships/grants, and unspecified assistantships also available. Financial award application deadline: 1/15; financial award applicants required to submit FAFSA. *Faculty research:* Addictions, family therapy, sexuality, parent-child relations, adolescent development. *Unit head:* Dr. Kay Pasley, Chair, 850-644-3217, Fax: 850-644-3439, E-mail: kpasley@admin.fsu.edu. *Application contact:* Suzi Hyacinthe, Academic Support Assistant, 850-644-3217, Fax: 850-644-3439, E-mail: shyacinthe@admin.fsu.edu.

See Close-Up on page 1073.

Indiana University Bloomington, School of Health, Physical Education and Recreation, Department of Applied Health Science, Bloomington, IN 47405-7000. Offers health behavior (PhD); health promotion (MS); human development/family studies (MS); nutrition science (MS); public health (MPH); safety management (MS); school and college health programs (MS). PhD offered through the University Graduate School. *Accreditation:* CEPH (one or more programs are accredited). *Faculty:* 23 full-time (12 women). *Students:* 84 full-time (64 women), 51 part-time (36 women); includes 16 minority (12 African Americans, 1 American Indian/Alaska Native, 2 Asian Americans or Pacific Islanders, 1 Hispanic American), 26 international. Average age 30. 94 applicants, 88% accepted, 54 enrolled. In 2007, 36 master's, 4 doctorates awarded. *Degree requirements:* For master's, thesis optional; for doctorate, thesis/dissertation. *Entrance requirements:* For master's, GRE (MS in nutrition science), 3 recommendations; for doctorate, GRE, 3 recommendations. Additional exam requirements/recommendations for international students: Required—TOEFL (minimum score 550 paper-based; 213 computer-based; 79 iBT). *Application deadline:* For fall admission, 4/30 priority date for domestic students, 12/1 priority date for international students; for spring admission, 11/15 priority date for domestic students, 9/1 priority date for international students. Application fee: $50 ($60 for international students). *Financial support:* In 2007–08, 80 students received support, including 12 fellowships (averaging $2,316 per year), 50 research assistantships (averaging $7,536 per year), 27 teaching assistantships with full and partial tuition reimbursements available (averaging $11,251 per year); career-related internships or fieldwork, Federal Work-Study, institutionally sponsored loans, scholarships/grants, tuition waivers (partial), and fee remissions also available. Financial award application deadline: 3/1. *Faculty research:* Cancer education, HIV/AIDS and drug education, public health, parent-child interactions, safety education. *Unit head:* Dr. Mohammad R. Torabi, Chair, 812-855-4808, Fax: 812-855-3936, E-mail: torabi@indiana.edu.

Indiana University–Purdue University Indianapolis, School of Liberal Arts, Department of Sociology, Indianapolis, IN 46202-2896. Offers family/gender studies (MA); medical sociology (MA); work/occupations (MA). *Faculty:* 17 full-time (8 women). *Students:* 13 full-time (11 women), 7 part-time (4 women); includes 3 minority (all African Americans), 1 international. Average age 27. In 2007, 5 degrees awarded. Application fee: $50 ($60 for international students). *Expenses:* Tuition, state resident: full-time $5,818; part-time $242 per credit hour. Tuition, nonresident: full-time $17,106; part-time $713 per credit hour. Required fees: $629. Tuition and fees vary according to course load, campus/location and program. *Financial support:* In 2007–08, 2 fellowships (averaging $9,500 per year), 2 teaching assistantships (averaging $6,309 per year) were awarded. *Unit head:* Carrie Foote, Director of Graduate Studies, 317-274-8981, E-mail: sociology@iupui.edu.

Iowa State University of Science and Technology, Graduate College, College of Human Sciences, Department of Human Development and Family Studies, Ames, IA 50011. Offers human development and family studies (MFCS, MS, PhD); marriage and family therapy (PhD). *Accreditation:* AAMFT/COAMFTE. *Faculty:* 26 full-time (19 women), 7 part-time/adjunct (5 women). *Students:* 53 full-time (45 women), 17 part-time (15 women); includes 4 minority (2 Asian Americans or Pacific Islanders, 2 Hispanic Americans), 10 international. 50 applicants, 78% accepted, 22 enrolled. In 2007, 14 master's, 7 doctorates awarded. *Degree requirements:* For master's, thesis; for doctorate, thesis/dissertation. *Entrance requirements:* For master's and doctorate, GRE General Test. Additional exam requirements/recommendations for international students: Required—TOEFL (paper-based 550; computer-based 213; iBT 79) or IELTS (6.0). *Application deadline:* For fall admission, 12/1 priority date for domestic students. Application fee: $30 ($70 for international students). Electronic applications accepted. *Financial support:* In 2007–08, 31 research assistantships with full and partial tuition reimbursements (averaging $17,019 per year), 10 teaching assistantships with full and partial tuition reimbursements (averaging $20,457 per year) were awarded; fellowships, scholarships/grants also available. *Faculty research:* Child development, early childhood education, family resource management and housing, life span studies. *Unit head:* Dr. Maurice M. MacDonald, Chair, 515-294-6316, Fax: 515-294-2502, E-mail: hdfs-grad-adm@iastate.edu. *Application contact:* Dr. Dee Draper, Director of Graduate Education, 515-294-4024, Fax: 515-294-2502, E-mail: hdfs-grad-adm@iastate.edu.

Kansas State University, Graduate School, College of Human Ecology, Program in Human Ecology, Manhattan, KS 66506. Offers apparel and textiles (PhD); family life education and consultation (PhD); food service, hospitality management, and administrative dietetics (PhD); institutional management (PhD); lifespan and human development (PhD); marriage and family therapy (PhD). *Students:* 44 full-time (29 women), 23 part-time (12 women); includes 12 minority (9 African Americans, 1 American Indian/Alaska Native, 2 Asian Americans or Pacific Islanders), 14 international. 39 applicants, 54% accepted, 6 enrolled. In 2007, 14 degrees awarded. *Application deadline:* For fall admission, 2/1 priority date for domestic and international students; for spring admission, 8/1 priority date for domestic and international students. Application fee: $30 ($55 for international students). *Unit head:* Elizabeth McCullough, Director, 785-532-2284, Fax: 785-532-3796, E-mail: lizm@ksu.edu.

Kansas State University, Graduate School, College of Human Ecology, School of Family Studies and Human Services, Manhattan, KS 66506. Offers family studies and human services (MS). *Accreditation:* AAMFT/COAMFTE; ASHA. Part-time programs available. *Faculty:* 20 full-time (14 women), 6 part-time/adjunct (3 women). *Students:* 194 full-time (146 women), 61 part-time (31 women); includes 21 minority (14 African Americans, 3 American Indian/Alaska Native, 1 Asian American or Pacific Islander, 3 Hispanic Americans), 5 international. 153 applicants, 61% accepted, 34 enrolled. In 2007, 45 degrees awarded. *Degree requirements:* For master's, thesis or alternative, oral exam, residency. *Entrance requirements:* For master's, GRE, minimum GPA of 3.0 in last 2 years of undergraduate study. Additional exam requirements/recommendations for international students: Required—TOEFL (minimum score 600 paper-based; 250 computer-based). *Application deadline:* For fall admission, 2/1 priority date for domestic students, 1/15 priority date for international students; for spring admission, 10/1 priority date for domestic students, 8/1 for international students. Applications are processed on a rolling basis. Application fee: $30 ($55 for international students). *Financial support:* In 2007–08, 4 research assistantships (averaging $11,050 per year), 6 teaching assistantships with full and partial tuition reimbursements (averaging $10,167 per year) were awarded; Federal Work-Study, institutionally sponsored loans, scholarships/grants, and unspecified assistantships also available. Support available to part-time students. Financial award application deadline: 3/1; financial award applicants required to submit FAFSA. *Faculty research:* Health and security of military families, personal and family risk assessment and evaluation, disorders of communication and swallowing, families and health. Total annual research expenditures: $2.1 million. *Unit head:* Dr. William Meredith, Head, 785-532-1472, Fax: 785-532-5505, E-mail: meredith@ksu.edu. *Application contact:* Esther Maddux, Director, 785-532-1940, Fax: 785-532-5505, E-mail: emaddux@ksu.edu.

Loma Linda University, School of Science and Technology, Department of Counseling and Family Science, Loma Linda, CA 92350. Offers MA, MS, DMFT, PhD, Certificate, MA/Certificate. *Faculty:* 10 full-time (6 women), 4 part-time/adjunct (2 women). *Students:* 124 full-time (100 women), 53 part-time (36 women); includes 65 minority (25 African Americans, 2 American Indian/Alaska Native, 14 Asian Americans or Pacific Islanders, 24 Hispanic Americans), 48 international. *Degree requirements:* For master's, comprehensive exam, thesis optional; for doctorate, comprehensive exam, thesis/dissertation (for some programs). *Entrance requirements:* For master's, minimum 3.0 GPA; for doctorate, GRE. Additional exam requirements/recommendations for international students: Required—TOEFL (minimum score 550 paper-based; 213 computer-based), MTELP. *Application deadline:* For fall admission, 6/15 for domestic and international students. Application fee: $60. Electronic applications accepted.

Miami University, Graduate School, School of Education and Allied Professions, Department of Family Studies and Social Work, Oxford, OH 45056. Offers child and family studies (MS). Part-time programs available. *Degree requirements:* For master's, thesis or alternative, final exam. *Entrance requirements:* For master's, MAT, minimum undergraduate GPA of 3.0 during previous 2 years or 2.75 overall.

Michigan State University, The Graduate School, College of Social Science, Department of Family and Child Ecology, East Lansing, MI 48824. Offers child development (MA); community services (MS); family and child ecology (PhD); family studies (MA); marriage and family therapy (MA); youth development (MA). *Accreditation:* AAMFT/COAMFTE (one or more programs are accredited). *Entrance requirements:* For master's, GRE General Test, minimum GPA of 3.0 in last 2 years of undergraduate course work, 3 letters of recommendation; for doctorate, GRE General Test, minimum GPA of 3.0, 3 letters of recommendation, background in behavioral sciences. Additional exam requirements/recommendations for international students: Required—TOEFL. Electronic applications accepted. *Expenses:* Tuition, state resident: part-time $379 per credit hour. Tuition, nonresident: part-time $800 per credit hour. Tuition and fees vary according to program.

Middle Tennessee State University, College of Graduate Studies, College of Education and Behavioral Science, Department of Human Sciences, Murfreesboro, TN 37132. Offers child development and family studies (MS); nutrition and food science (MS). Part-time and evening/weekend programs available. Postbaccalaureate distance learning degree programs offered. *Faculty:* 7 full-time (all women). *Students:* Average age 27. 24 applicants, 71% accepted. In 2007, 4 degrees awarded. *Degree requirements:* For master's, comprehensive exam, thesis. *Entrance requirements:* For master's, GRE or MAT. Additional exam requirements/recommendations for international students: Required—TOEFL (paper-based 525; computer-based 195; IBT 71) or IELTS (6.0). *Application deadline:* For fall admission, 8/1 priority date for domestic students. Applications are processed on a rolling basis. Application fee: $25. Electronic applications accepted. *Financial support:* In 2007–08, 5 students received support. Application deadline: 5/1. *Faculty research:* Courtship relationships, feminist methodology and epistemology in family studies, school uniforms, body fat in elderly, asynchronous distance education. *Unit head:* Dr. Dellmar Walker, Chair, 615-898-2884.

Missouri State University, Graduate College, College of Education, Department of Childhood Education and Family Studies, Program in Early Childhood and Family Development, Springfield, MO 65804-0094. Offers MS. Part-time programs available. Postbaccalaureate distance learning degree programs offered. *Students:* 2 full-time (both women), 11 part-time (all women). Average age 30. 4 applicants, 100% accepted, 3 enrolled. In 2007, 1 degree awarded. *Entrance requirements:* For master's, GRE, minimum GPA of 3.0. Additional exam requirements/recommendations for international students: Required—TOEFL (minimum score 550 paper-based; 213 computer-based; 79 iBT). *Application deadline:* For fall admission, 7/20 priority date for domestic students; for spring admission, 12/20 priority date for domestic students. Applications are processed on a rolling basis. Application fee: $35. Electronic applications accepted. *Expenses:* Tuition, state resident: full-time $3,708; part-time $206 per credit hour. Tuition, nonresident: full-time $7,236; part-time $206 per credit hour. Required fees: $622. Full-time tuition and fees vary according to course level, course load, program and reciprocity agreements. *Financial support:* In 2007–08, 1 research assistantship with full tuition reimbursement (averaging $7,050 per year) was awarded; teaching assistantships with full tuition reimbursements. *Unit head:* Dr. Sue George, Program Director, 417-836-5984, Fax: 417-836-8900, E-mail: suegeorge@missouristate.edu.

Mount Saint Vincent University, Graduate Programs, Department of Child and Youth Study, Halifax, NS B3M 2J6, Canada. Offers MA. Part-time and evening/weekend programs available. *Degree requirements:* For master's, thesis. *Entrance requirements:* For master's, bachelor's degree in related field, minimum B+ average, professional experience. Electronic applications accepted.

Mount Saint Vincent University, Graduate Programs, Department of Family Studies and Gerontology, Halifax, NS B3M 2J6, Canada. Offers MA. Part-time programs available. Postbaccalaureate distance learning degree programs offered (minimal on-campus study). *Degree requirements:* For master's, thesis. *Entrance requirements:* For master's, minimum GPA of 3.0; course work in statistics, research methods, family and social theories.

North Dakota State University, College of Graduate and Interdisciplinary Studies, College of Human Development and Education, Department of Child Development and Family Science, Fargo, ND 58105. Offers child development and family science (MS); couple and family therapy (MS); family financial planning (MS); gerontology (MS, PhD). *Accreditation:* AAMFT/COAMFTE. Part-time and evening/weekend programs available. Postbaccalaureate distance learning degree programs offered (no on-campus study). *Faculty:* 12 full-time (7 women). *Students:* 39 full-time (35 women), 14 part-time (13 women); includes 5 minority (1 African American, 2 American Indian/Alaska Native, 2 Asian Americans or Pacific Islanders), 1 international. 22 applicants, 64% accepted, 12 enrolled. In 2007, 6 degrees awarded. *Degree requirements:* For master's, thesis or alternative; for doctorate, thesis/dissertation. *Entrance requirements:* Additional exam requirements/recommendations for international students: Required—TOEFL (minimum score 525 paper-based; 197 computer-based; 71 iBT). *Application deadline:* For fall admission, 2/1 for domestic and international students; for spring admission, 10/1 for domestic and international students. Application fee: $45 ($60 for international students). *Expenses:* Tuition, state resident: full-time $5,376; part-time $224 per credit. Tuition, nonresident: full-time $14,354; part-time $598 per credit. Required fees: $962; $40 per credit. Part-time tuition and fees vary according to course load and reciprocity agreements. *Financial support:* In 2007–08, 17 students received support, including research assistantships with full tuition reimbursements available (averaging $3,000 per year), 17 teaching assistantships with full tuition reimbursements available (averaging $3,000 per year); career-related internships or fieldwork, Federal Work-Study, institutionally sponsored loans, and tuition waivers (full) also available. Financial award application deadline: 4/1. *Faculty research:* Family therapy, resilience, parenting, adolescent development, mental health. Total annual research expenditures:$333,582. *Unit head:* Dr. James Deal, Head, 701-231-7568, Fax: 701-231-9645, E-mail: jim_deal@

ndsu.edu. *Application contact:* Theresa Anderson, Administrative Assistant, 701-231-8628, Fax: 701-231-9645, E-mail: theresa.anderson@ndsu.edu.

Northern Illinois University, Graduate School, College of Health and Human Sciences, School of Family, Consumer and Nutrition Sciences, De Kalb, IL 60115-2854. Offers applied family and child studies (MS); nutrition and dietetics (MS). *Accreditation:* AAMFT/COAMFTE. Part-time programs available. *Faculty:* 16 full-time (14 women), 2 part-time/adjunct (1 woman). *Students:* 65 full-time (47 women), 24 part-time (21 women); includes 15 minority (6 African Americans, 1 American Indian/Alaska Native, 6 Asian Americans or Pacific Islanders, 2 Hispanic Americans), 22 international. Average age 28. 9 applicants, 789% accepted, 22 enrolled. In 2007, 22 degrees awarded. *Degree requirements:* For master's, comprehensive exam, internship, thesis (nutrition and dietetics). *Entrance requirements:* For master's, GRE General Test, minimum GPA of 2.75. Additional exam requirements/recommendations for international students: Required—TOEFL (minimum score 550 paper-based; 213 computer-based). *Application deadline:* For fall admission, 6/1 for domestic students, 5/1 for international students; for spring admission, 11/1 for domestic students, 10/1 for international students. Applications are processed on a rolling basis. Application fee: $30. Electronic applications accepted. *Expenses:* Tuition, area resident: Part-time $226 per credit hour. Tuition, state resident: full-time $5,424; part-time $225 per credit hour. Tuition, nonresident: full-time $10,848. Required fees: $2,416; $64 per credit hour. *Financial support:* In 2007–08, 24 research assistantships with full tuition reimbursements, 5 teaching assistantships with full tuition reimbursements were awarded; fellowships with full tuition reimbursements, career-related internships or fieldwork, Federal Work-Study, scholarships/grants, tuition waivers (full), and unspecified assistantships also available. Support available to part-time students. Financial award applicants required to submit FAFSA. *Faculty research:* Preliminary child development, hospitality administration in Asia, sports nutrition, eating disorders. *Unit head:* Dr. Laura Smart, Acting Chair, 815-753-1960, Fax: 815-753-1321, E-mail: lsmart@niu.edu.

Nova Southeastern University, Fischler School of Education and Human Services, Programs in Human Services, Fort Lauderdale, FL 33314-7796. Offers child and youth care administration (MS); child and youth studies (Ed D); child protection (MHS); early childhood education administration (MS); family support studies (MS); health professions education (MS); substance abuse counseling and education (MS). Part-time and evening/weekend programs available. *Faculty:* 3 part-time/adjunct (2 women). *Students:* 192 full-time (163 women), 41 part-time (37 women); includes 141 minority (116 African Americans, 1 Asian American or Pacific Islander, 24 Hispanic Americans), 3 international. Average age 38. 26 applicants, 77% accepted, 20 enrolled. In 2007, 6 master's, 64 doctorates awarded. *Degree requirements:* For master's, thesis, practicum; for doctorate, thesis/dissertation, practicum. *Entrance requirements:* For master's, GRE or MAT, work experience in field, minimum GPA of 2.5; for doctorate, GRE or MAT, master's degree, minimum GPA of 3.0, work experience. Additional exam requirements/recommendations for international students: Recommended—TOEFL (minimum score 550 paper-based; 213 computer-based), IELTS (minimum score 6). *Application deadline:* For fall admission, 8/11 priority date for domestic and international students; for winter admission, 12/28 priority date for domestic and international students; for spring admission, 4/22 priority date for domestic and international students. Applications are processed on a rolling basis. Application fee: $50. Electronic applications accepted. *Expenses: Contact institution. Financial support:* Career-related internships or fieldwork and Federal Work-Study available. Support available to part-time students. Financial award application deadline: 1/7. *Unit head:* Dr. Elda Veloso, Associate Dean, 954-262-8538, Fax: 954-262-2917, E-mail: veloso@nova.edu. *Application contact:* Dr. Jennifer Quiñones Nottingham, Dean of Student Affairs, 800-986-3223 Ext. 8624, Fax: 954-262-3883, E-mail: jlquinon@nova.edu.

The Ohio State University, Graduate School, College of Education and Human Ecology, Department of Human Development and Family Science, Columbus, OH 43210. Offers M Ed, MS, PhD. *Faculty:* 24. *Students:* 18 full-time (16 women), 17 part-time (13 women); includes 3 minority (all African Americans), 10 international. Average age 29. In 2007, 10 master's, 7 doctorates awarded. *Degree requirements:* For master's, thesis optional; for doctorate, thesis/dissertation. *Entrance requirements:* For master's and doctorate, GRE General Test. Additional exam requirements/recommendations for international students: Required—TOEFL (minimum score 577 paper-based; 233 computer-based). *Application deadline:* For fall admission, 8/15 priority date for domestic students, 7/1 priority date for international students; for winter admission, 12/1 priority date for domestic students, 11/1 priority date for international students; for spring admission, 3/1 priority date for domestic students, 2/1 priority date for international students. Applications are processed on a rolling basis. Application fee: $40 ($50 for international students). Electronic applications accepted. *Financial support:* Fellowships, research assistantships, teaching assistantships, Federal Work-Study and institutionally sponsored loans available. Support available to part-time students. *Unit head:* Suzanne Bartle-Haring, Graduate Studies Committee Chair, 614-292-5685, Fax: 614-292-2581, E-mail: haring.19@osu.edu. *Application contact:* 614-292-9444, Fax: 614-292-3895, E-mail: domestic.grad@osu.edu.

Ohio University, Graduate College, College of Health and Human Services, School of Human and Consumer Sciences, Athens, OH 45701-2979. Offers child development and family life (MS); early childhood education (MS); family studies (MS); food and nutrition (MS). Part-time programs available. *Faculty:* 13 full-time (9 women), 5 part-time/adjunct (all women). *Students:* 11 full-time (9 women), 5 part-time (4 women); includes 5 minority (2 African Americans, 3 Asian Americans or Pacific Islanders). Average age 26. 16 applicants, 69% accepted, 9 enrolled. In 2007, 8 degrees awarded. *Degree requirements:* For master's, thesis. *Entrance requirements:* For master's, GRE. Additional exam requirements/recommendations for international students: Required—TOEFL. *Application deadline:* For fall admission, 3/1 priority date for domestic students. Applications are processed on a rolling basis. Application fee: $50 ($55 for international students). Electronic applications accepted. *Financial support:* In 2007–08, 6 teaching assistantships (averaging $9,815 per year) were awarded; career-related internships or fieldwork, Federal Work-Study, institutionally sponsored loans, and unspecified assistantships also available. Financial award application deadline: 3/15. *Faculty research:* Diversity, developmentally appropriate activities, death and dying, gerontology, sexuality education. *Unit head:* Dr. V. Ann Paulins, Director, 740-593-2880, Fax: 740-593-0289, E-mail: paulins@ohio.edu.

Oklahoma State University, College of Human Environmental Sciences, Department of Human Development and Family Science, Stillwater, OK 74078. Offers MS, PhD. *Accreditation:* AAMFT/COAMFTE (one or more programs are accredited). *Faculty:* 28 full-time (19 women), 6 part-time/adjunct (5 women). *Students:* 28 full-time (22 women), 35 part-time (30 women); includes 12 minority (3 African Americans, 6 American Indian/Alaska Native, 3 Hispanic Americans), 5 international. Average age 32. 43 applicants, 35% accepted, 14 enrolled. In 2007, 17 degrees awarded. *Degree requirements:* For master's, thesis; for doctorate, thesis/dissertation. *Entrance requirements:* For master's and doctorate, GRE or GMAT. Additional exam requirements/recommendations for international students: Required—TOEFL. *Application deadline:* For fall admission, 3/1 priority date for international students; for spring admission, 8/1 priority date for international students. Applications are processed on a rolling basis. Application fee: $40 ($75 for international students). Electronic applications accepted. *Expenses:* Tuition, state resident: full-time $4,993; part-time $148 per credit hour. Tuition, nonresident: full-time $14,755; part-time $555 per credit hour. Tuition and fees vary according to program. *Financial support:* In 2007–08, 35 research assistantships (averaging $9,746 per year), 11 teaching assistantships (averaging $8,916 per year) were awarded; career-related internships or fieldwork, Federal Work-Study, and tuition waivers (partial) also available. Support available to part-time students. Financial award application deadline: 3/1. *Faculty research:* Family relations and child development, consequences of adolescent parenting, family stress and coping, impacts of sexual abuse on families, children's social cognition and self-competence, gerontology and health care. *Unit head:* Dr. Sue Williams, Head, 405-744-5057.

Oregon State University, Graduate School, College of Health and Human Sciences, Department of Human Development and Family Sciences, Corvallis, OR 97331. Offers gerontology (MAIS); human development and family studies (MS, PhD). *Faculty:* 17 full-time (11 women), 6 part-time/adjunct (all women). *Students:* 30 full-time (25 women), 4 part-time (all women); includes 4 minority (3 Asian Americans or Pacific Islanders, 1 Hispanic American), 9 international. Average age 37. In 2007, 3 master's, 1 doctorate awarded. *Degree requirements:* For doctorate, thesis/dissertation. *Entrance requirements:* For master's and doctorate, GRE, minimum GPA of 3.0 in last 90 hours. Additional exam requirements/recommendations for international students: Required—TOEFL. *Application deadline:* Applications are processed on a rolling basis. Application fee: $50. *Expenses:* Tuition, state resident: full-time $9,126; part-time $338 per credit. Tuition, nonresident: full-time $14,796; part-time $548 per credit. Required fees: $1,447. *Financial support:* Research assistantships, teaching assistantships, career-related internships or fieldwork, Federal Work-Study, and institutionally sponsored loans available. Support available to part-time students. Financial award application deadline: 2/1. *Unit head:* Dr. Carolyn Aldwin, Chair, 541-737-2024, Fax: 541-737-1076, E-mail: carolyn.aldwin@oregonstate.edu.

Oxford Graduate School, Graduate Programs, Dayton, TN 37321-6736. Offers family life education (M Litt); organizational leadership in nonprofits (M Litt); religion and society (D Phil).

Penn State University Park, Graduate School, College of Health and Human Development, Department of Human Development and Family Studies, State College, University Park, PA 16802-1503. Offers MS, PhD. *Expenses:* Tuition, state resident: full-time $14,738; part-time $614 per credit. Tuition, nonresident: full-time $26,050; part-time $1,085 per credit. Tuition and fees vary according to course load, program and student level. *Unit head:* Dr. Steven H. Zarit, Head, 814-865-5260, Fax: 814-863-7963, E-mail: z67@psu.edu. *Application contact:* Dr. Douglas M. Teti, Professor in Charge of Graduate Program, 814-865-2644, E-mail: dmt16@psu.edu.

Purdue University, Graduate School, College of Consumer and Family Sciences, Department of Child Development and Family Studies, West Lafayette, IN 47907. Offers developmental studies (MS, PhD); family studies (MS, PhD); marriage and family therapy (MS, PhD). *Accreditation:* AAMFT/COAMFTE (one or more programs are accredited). Part-time programs available. Terminal master's awarded for partial completion of doctoral program. *Degree requirements:* For master's, thesis; for doctorate, thesis/dissertation. *Entrance requirements:* For master's and doctorate, GRE General Test. Additional exam requirements/recommendations for international students: Required—TWE. Electronic applications accepted. *Faculty research:* Inclusion of children with special needs, families as learning environments, relationships in child care, work-family relations, AIDS prevention.

Roberts Wesleyan College, Division of Social Work, Rochester, NY 14624-1997. Offers child and family practice (MSW); congregational and community practice (MSW); mental health practice (MSW). *Accreditation:* CSWE. *Entrance requirements:* For master's, minimum GPA of 2.75. *Faculty research:* Religion and social work, family studies, values and ethics.

Sage Graduate School, Graduate School, Department of Psychology, Program in Community Psychology, Troy, NY 12180-4115. Offers child care and children's services (MA); community counseling (MA); community health education (MA); general psychology (MA). Part-time and evening/weekend programs available. *Faculty:* 4 full-time (all women), 4 part-time/adjunct (1 woman). *Students:* 38 full-time (36 women), 65 part-time (60 women); includes 13 minority (8 African Americans, 2 American Indian/Alaska Native, 1 Asian American or Pacific Islander, 2 Hispanic Americans). Average age 29. 66 applicants, 50% accepted, 19 enrolled. In 2007, 33 degrees awarded. *Degree requirements:* For master's, thesis or alternative. *Entrance requirements:* For master's, minimum GPA of 2.75, official transcripts, 2 letters of reference, undergraduate courses in statistics, history and systems of psychology, three other courses in behavioral scince, personel prospectus statement, current resum&e, completed application. Additional exam requirements/recommendations for international students: Required—TOEFL (minimum score 550 paper-based; 213 computer-based). *Application deadline:* Applications are processed on a rolling basis. Application fee: $40. *Expenses:* Tuition: Full-time $9,720; part-time $540 per credit hour. *Financial support:* Fellowships, research assistantships, teaching assistantships, Federal Work-Study, scholarships/grants, and unspecified assistantships available. Support available to part-time students. Financial award application deadline: 3/1; financial award applicants required to submit FAFSA. *Unit head:* Dr. Bronna Romanoff, Director, 518-244-2260, E-mail: romanb@sage.edu. *Application contact:* Shannon K. Easton, Director of Graduate and Adult Admission, 518-244-2443, Fax: 518-244-6880, E-mail: sgsadm@sage.edu.

St. Cloud State University, School of Graduate Studies, College of Education, Department of Child and Family Studies, St. Cloud, MN 56301-4498. Offers MS. *Faculty:* 6 full-time (5 women), 3 part-time/adjunct (all women). *Students:* 10 applicants, 100% accepted. In 2007, 4 degrees awarded. *Degree requirements:* For master's, thesis or alternative. *Entrance requirements:* For master's, GRE General Test, minimum GPA of 2.75. Additional exam requirements/recommendations for international students: Required—MELAB; Recommended—TOEFL (minimum score 550 paper-based; 213 computer-based), IELTS (minimum score 7). *Application deadline:* For fall admission, 6/1 for domestic students, 4/1 for international students; for spring admission, 10/1 for domestic students, 8/1 for international students. Applications are processed on a rolling basis. Application fee: $35. Electronic applications accepted. *Expenses:* Tuition, state resident: part-time $267 per credit. Tuition, nonresident: part-time $418 per credit. Required fees: $28 per credit. *Financial support:* Federal Work-Study, scholarships/grants, and unspecified assistantships available. Financial award application deadline: 3/1. *Unit head:* Dr. Glen Palm, Coordinator, 320-308-3969, E-mail: gfpalm@stcloudstate.edu. *Application contact:* Linda Lou Krueger, School of Graduate Studies, 320-308-2113, Fax: 320-308-5371, E-mail: lekrueger@stcloudstate.edu.

Saint Joseph College, Graduate Division, Department of Counselor Education, West Hartford, CT 06117-2700. Offers community counseling (MA), including child welfare, pastoral counseling, school counseling; spirituality (Certificate). Part-time and evening/weekend programs available. *Degree requirements:* For master's, comprehensive exam, thesis optional, Capstone project. *Entrance requirements:* For master's, PRAXIS I (school counseling), 2 letters of recommendation. Electronic applications accepted.

San Diego State University, Graduate and Research Affairs, College of Education, Department of Child and Family Development, San Diego, CA 92182. Offers child development (MS). Part-time programs available. In 2007, 2 degrees awarded. *Degree requirements:* For master's, thesis. *Entrance requirements:* For master's, GRE General Test, 3 letters of recommendation, interview. Additional exam requirements/recommendations for international students: Required—TOEFL. *Application deadline:* For fall admission, 5/1 for domestic students; for spring admission, 11/1 for domestic students, 10/1 for international students. Applications are processed on a rolling basis. Application fee: $55. Electronic applications accepted. *Financial support:* Unspecified assistantships available. *Unit head:* Thomas W. Roberts, Chair, 619-594-5380, Fax: 619-594-5921, E-mail: troberts@mail.sdsu.edu. *Application contact:* Thomas W. Roberts, Chair, 619-594-5380, Fax: 619-594-5921, E-mail: troberts@mail.sdsu.edu.

San Jose State University, Graduate Studies and Research, College of Education, Department of Child and Adolescent Development, San Jose, CA 95192-0001. Offers MA. *Students:* 5 full-time (all women), 21 part-time (20 women); includes 5 minority (1 African American, 4 Asian Americans or Pacific Islanders), 1 international. Average age 34. 22 applicants, 64% accepted, 13 enrolled. In 2007, 14 degrees awarded. *Application deadline:* For fall admission, 6/29 for domestic students; for spring admission, 11/30 for domestic students. Applications are processed on a rolling basis. Application fee: $59. Electronic applications accepted. *Financial support:* Applicants required to submit FAFSA. *Unit head:* Dr. Toni Campbell, Chair, 408-924-3725, Fax: 408-924-3758.

South Carolina State University, School of Graduate Studies, Department of Family and Consumer Sciences, Orangeburg, SC 29117-0001. Offers individual and family development (MS); nutritional sciences (MS). Part-time and evening/weekend programs available. *Faculty:* 7 full-time (all women). *Students:* 19 full-time (18 women), 26 part-time (24 women); includes

Child and Family Studies

South Carolina State University (continued)
43 minority (all African Americans) Average age 33. 18 applicants, 89% accepted, 9 enrolled. In 2007, 12 master's awarded. *Degree requirements:* For master's, thesis optional, departmental qualifying exam. *Entrance requirements:* For master's, GRE, MAT, or NTE, minimum GPA of 2.7. *Application deadline:* For fall admission, 6/15 priority date for domestic students, 6/15 for international students; for spring admission, 11/1 for domestic and international students. Applications are processed on a rolling basis. Application fee: $25. Electronic applications accepted. *Financial support:* Fellowships, institutionally sponsored loans available. Financial award application deadline: 6/1. *Faculty research:* Societal competence, relationship of parent-child interaction to adult, quality of well-being of rural elders. *Unit head:* Dr. Ethel Jones, Chair, 803-536-8958, Fax: 803-533-3268, E-mail: egjones@scsu.edu. *Application contact:* Annette Hazzard-Jones, Program Coordinator II, 803-536-8809, Fax: 803-536-8812, E-mail: zs_ahazzard@scsu.edu.

Spring Arbor University, School of Adult Studies, Spring Arbor, MI 49283-9799. Offers counseling (MAC); family studies (MAFS); organizational management (MAOM). Part-time and evening/weekend programs available. Postbaccalaureate distance learning degree programs offered (no on-campus study). *Faculty:* 4 full-time (2 women), 155 part-time/adjunct (72 women). *Students:* 691 full-time (557 women), 182 part-time (140 women); includes 210 minority (187 African Americans, 2 American Indian/Alaska Native, 7 Asian Americans or Pacific Islanders, 14 Hispanic Americans), 3 international. In 2007, 249 degrees awarded. *Entrance requirements:* For master's, minimum GPA of 3.0, interview, writing sample, 2 professional references. Additional exam requirements/recommendations for international students: Required—TOEFL (minimum score 550 paper-based; 220 computer-based). *Application deadline:* Applications are processed on a rolling basis. Application fee: $40. Electronic applications accepted. *Expenses:* Tuition: Full-time $4,560; part-time $380 per credit. Required fees: $75 per term. One-time fee: $40 part-time. Tuition and fees vary according to course load and program. *Financial support:* Scholarships/grants available. Support available to part-time students. Financial award applicants required to submit FAFSA. *Unit head:* Natalie Gianetti, Dean of Adult Studies, 517-750-1200 Ext. 1343, Fax: 517-750-6602, E-mail: gianetti@arbor.edu. *Application contact:* Dr. Carl Pavey, Director of Graduate Studies, 517-750-1200 Ext. 1653, Fax: 517-750-6602, E-mail: cpavey@arbor.edu.

Springfield College, Graduate Programs, School of Social Work, Springfield, MA 01109-3797. Offers advanced generalist (weekday and weekend) (MSW); advanced standing (MSW); practice with children and adolescents (PMC); JD/MSW. *Accreditation:* CSWE. Part-time and evening/weekend programs available. *Faculty:* 11 full-time (5 women), 29 part-time/adjunct (20 women). *Students:* 172 full-time, 84 part-time. Average age 34. 283 applicants, 79% accepted, 136 enrolled. In 2007, 97 degrees awarded. *Degree requirements:* For master's, fieldwork. *Entrance requirements:* For master's, minimum GPA of 3.0 during previous 2 years. Additional exam requirements/recommendations for international students: Required—TOEFL (minimum score 550 paper-based; 213 computer-based). *Application deadline:* For fall admission, 3/1 priority date for domestic students. Applications are processed on a rolling basis. Application fee: $50. Electronic applications accepted. *Expenses:* Tuition: Full-time $12,942; part-time $719 per semester hour. Required fees: $25. Tuition and fees vary according to program. *Financial support:* Fellowships with partial tuition reimbursements, teaching assistantships with partial tuition reimbursements, career-related internships or fieldwork, Federal Work-Study, institutionally sponsored loans, scholarships/grants, and unspecified assistantships available. Financial award application deadline: 3/1. *Faculty research:* Child and adolescent practice, health and aging, human rights, mental health. *Unit head:* Dr. Francine Vecchiolla, Dean, 413-748-3060, Fax: 413-748-3069, E-mail: francine_vecchiolla@spfldcol.edu. *Application contact:* Donald James Shaw, Director of Graduate Admissions, 413-748-3060, Fax: 413-748-3069, E-mail: donald_shaw_jr@spfldcol.edu.

Stanford University, School of Education, Program in Psychological Studies in Education, Stanford, CA 94305-9991. Offers child and adolescent development (PhD); counseling psychology (PhD); educational psychology (PhD). *Degree requirements:* For doctorate, thesis/dissertation. *Entrance requirements:* For doctorate, GRE General Test. Electronic applications accepted.

State University of New York at Oswego, Graduate Studies, School of Education, Department of Vocational Teacher Preparation, Oswego, NY 13126. Offers agriculture (MS Ed); business and marketing (MS Ed); family and consumer sciences (MS Ed); health careers (MS Ed); technical education (MS Ed); trade education (MS Ed). *Accreditation:* NCATE. Part-time and evening/weekend programs available. *Faculty:* 5 full-time, 5 part-time/adjunct. *Students:* 23 full-time (10 women), 47 part-time (22 women); includes 6 minority (3 African Americans, 2 Asian Americans or Pacific Islanders, 1 Hispanic American). Average age 40. 33 applicants, 100% accepted. In 2007, 35 degrees awarded. *Degree requirements:* For master's, thesis or alternative. *Entrance requirements:* Additional exam requirements/recommendations for international students: Required—TOEFL (minimum score 560 paper-based; 220 computer-based). *Application deadline:* For fall admission, 4/1 for domestic students; for spring admission, 10/1 for domestic students. Applications are processed on a rolling basis. Application fee: $50. *Expenses:* Tuition, state resident: full-time $6,900; part-time $288 per credit. Tuition, nonresident: full-time $10,920; part-time $455 per credit. Required fees: $607; $32 per credit. $225 per term. Tuition and fees vary according to degree level. *Financial support:* In 2007–08, 4 students received support, including 2 fellowships (averaging $5,100 per year), 2 teaching assistantships (averaging $3,800 per year); career-related internships or fieldwork, Federal Work-Study, institutionally sponsored loans, health care benefits, and unspecified assistantships also available. Support available to part-time students. Financial award application deadline: 4/1; financial award applicants required to submit FAFSA. *Unit head:* Dr. Margaret Martin, Chair, 315-312-2480.

Syracuse University, Graduate School, College of Human Ecology, Department of Child and Family Studies, Syracuse, NY 13244. Offers MA, MS, PhD. *Accreditation:* AAMFT/COAMFTE (one or more programs are accredited). Part-time programs available. *Students:* 28 full-time (25 women), 14 part-time (all women); includes 6 minority (4 African Americans, 1 Asian American or Pacific Islander, 1 Hispanic American), 11 international. 17 applicants, 53% accepted, 6 enrolled. In 2007, 3 master's, 2 doctorates awarded. *Degree requirements:* For master's, comprehensive exam (for some programs); for doctorate, thesis/dissertation. *Entrance requirements:* For master's and doctorate, GRE General Test. Additional exam requirements/recommendations for international students: Required—TOEFL. *Application deadline:* For fall admission, 3/15 for domestic students. Application fee: $75. Electronic applications accepted. *Expenses:* Tuition: Full-time $18,216; part-time $1,012 per credit. Required fees: $980. Tuition and fees vary according to program. *Financial support:* Fellowships with full tuition reimbursements, research assistantships with tuition reimbursements, teaching assistantships with full and partial tuition reimbursements, tuition waivers (partial) available. *Unit head:* Dr. Ambika Krishnakumar, Chair, 315-443-4293, Fax: 315-443-9402. *Application contact:* Amy Pangborn, Information Contact, 315-443-5555, E-mail: inquire@hshp.syr.edu.

Texas State University–San Marcos, Graduate School, College of Applied Arts, Department of Family and Consumer Science, Program in Family and Child Studies, San Marcos, TX 78666. Offers MS. *Faculty:* 3 full-time (all women), 1 (woman) part-time/adjunct. *Students:* 7 full-time (all women), 16 part-time (all women); includes 7 minority (5 African Americans, 2 Hispanic Americans), 1 international. Average age 27. 14 applicants, 93% accepted, 8 enrolled. In 2007, 5 degrees awarded. *Degree requirements:* For master's, thesis (for some programs). *Entrance requirements:* For master's, minimum GPA of 2.75 in last 60 hours of course work. Additional exam requirements/recommendations for international students: Required—TOEFL (minimum score 550 paper-based; 213 computer-based). *Application deadline:* For fall admission, 6/15 priority date for domestic students; for spring admission, 10/15 for domestic students. Applications are processed on a rolling basis. Application fee: $40 ($90 for international students). *Expenses:* Tuition, state resident: full-time $3,780; part-time $210 per credit hour. Tuition, nonresident: full-time $8,784; part-time $488 per credit hour. Required fees: $493 per semester. Full-time tuition and fees vary according to course load. *Financial support:* In 2007–08, 20 students received support, including 1 research assistantship (averaging $5,076 per year), 7 teaching assistantships (averaging $4,424 per year). Financial award application deadline: 4/1. Total annual research expenditures: $3,789. *Unit head:* Dr. Sue Williams, Graduate Adviser, 512-245-2155, Fax: 512-245-3829, E-mail: sw10@txstate.edu.

Texas Tech University, Graduate School, College of Human Sciences, Department of Human Development and Family Studies, Lubbock, TX 79409. Offers gerontology (MS); human development and family studies (MS, PhD). *Accreditation:* AAMFT/COAMFTE (one or more programs are accredited). Part-time programs available. *Faculty:* 20 full-time (16 women). *Students:* 45 full-time (38 women), 16 part-time (12 women); includes 9 minority (1 African American, 1 American Indian/Alaska Native, 3 Asian Americans or Pacific Islanders, 4 Hispanic Americans), 13 international. Average age 34. 44 applicants, 75% accepted, 16 enrolled. In 2007, 2 master's, 2 doctorates awarded. *Degree requirements:* For master's, thesis; for doctorate, thesis/dissertation. *Entrance requirements:* For master's and doctorate, GRE General Test. Additional exam requirements/recommendations for international students: Required—TOEFL (minimum score 550 paper-based; 213 computer-based). *Application deadline:* For fall admission, 3/1 priority date for international students; for spring admission, 11/1 priority date for international students. Applications are processed on a rolling basis. Application fee: $50 ($60 for international students). Electronic applications accepted. *Expenses:* Tuition, state resident: part-time $373 per credit hour. Tuition, nonresident: part-time $651 per credit hour. Tuition and fees vary according to program. *Financial support:* In 2007–08, 50 students received support, including 11 research assistantships with partial tuition reimbursements available (averaging $12,849 per year), 35 teaching assistantships with partial tuition reimbursements available (averaging $12,986 per year); career-related internships or fieldwork, Federal Work-Study, institutionally sponsored loans, and scholarships/grants also available. Support available to part-time students. Financial award application deadline: 4/15; financial award applicants required to submit FAFSA. *Faculty research:* Parenting, marital and premarital relationships, adolescent drug abuse, life span; child development. Total annual research expenditures: $72,657. *Unit head:* Anisa Zvonkovic, Interim Chair, 806-742-3000 Ext. 279, Fax: 806-742-0285, E-mail: anisa.zvonkovic@ttu.edu. *Application contact:* Judy McMurry, Graduate Secretary, 806-742-3000, Fax: 806-742-0285.

Texas Woman's University, Graduate School, College of Professional Education, Department of Family Sciences, Denton, TX 76201. Offers child development (MS, PhD); counseling and development (MS); early childhood education (M Ed, MA, MS, Ed D); family studies (MS, PhD); family therapy (MS, PhD). *Accreditation:* ACA (one or more programs are accredited). Part-time and evening/weekend programs available. *Students:* 100 full-time (93 women), 336 part-time (308 women); includes 134 minority (89 African Americans, 5 American Indian/Alaska Native, 11 Asian Americans or Pacific Islanders, 29 Hispanic Americans), 15 international. Average age 36. In 2007, 79 master's, 11 doctorates awarded. *Median time to degree:* Of those who began their doctoral program in fall 1999, 50% received their degree in 8 years or less. *Degree requirements:* For doctorate, comprehensive exam, thesis/dissertation. *Entrance requirements:* For master's, interview, writing sample, minimum GPA of 3.25 may be required; for doctorate, interview, writing sample may be required, GPA 3.25 last 60 hours of course work. Additional exam requirements/recommendations for international students: Required—TOEFL (minimum score 550 paper-based; 213 computer-based; 79 iBT). *Application deadline:* For fall admission, 2/15 for domestic students, 4/15 for international students; for spring admission, 9/15 for domestic students, 8/1 for international students. Applications are processed on a rolling basis. Application fee: $30 ($50 for international students). Electronic applications accepted. *Expenses:* Tuition, state resident: full-time $3,294; part-time $183 per credit. Tuition, nonresident: full-time $8,298; part-time $461 per credit. Required fees: $985; $55 per credit. Tuition and fees vary according to degree level. *Financial support:* In 2007–08, 3 research assistantships (averaging $10,746 per year), 20 teaching assistantships (averaging $10,746 per year) were awarded; career-related internships or fieldwork, Federal Work-Study, institutionally sponsored loans, scholarships/grants, traineeships, health care benefits, and unspecified assistantships also available. Support available to part-time students. Financial award application deadline: 3/1; financial award applicants required to submit FAFSA. *Faculty research:* Parenting/parent education, distance education, play therapy, family sexuality, diversity. *Unit head:* Dr. Larry LeFlore, Chair, 940-898-2685, Fax: 940-898-2676, E-mail: lleflore@twu.edu. *Application contact:* Samuel Wheeler, Assistant Director of Admissions, 940-898-3188, Fax: 940-898-3081, E-mail: wheelersr@twu.edu.

Towson University, College of Graduate Studies and Research, Program in Family-Professional Collaboration, Towson, MD 21252-0001. Offers Certificate. *Students:* 1 (woman) full-time, 1 (woman) part-time. Average age 25. 1 applicant, 100% accepted, 1 enrolled. In 2007, 5 degrees awarded. Application fee: $50. *Expenses:* Tuition, state resident: part-time $286 per credit. Tuition, nonresident: part-time $600 per credit. Required fees: $75 per credit. *Unit head:* Karen Eskow, Graduate Program Director, 410-704-2849, E-mail: keskow@towson.edu. *Application contact:* The Graduate School, 410-704-2501, Fax: 410-704-4675, E-mail: grads@towson.edu.

Tufts University, Graduate School of Arts and Sciences, Department of Child Development, Medford, MA 02155. Offers applied developmental psychology (PhD); child development (MA, CAGS); early childhood education (MAT). Part-time programs available. *Faculty:* 15 full-time, 8 part-time/adjunct. *Students:* 102 (89 women); includes 17 minority (7 African Americans, 5 Asian Americans or Pacific Islanders, 5 Hispanic Americans) 12 international. 123 applicants, 64% accepted, 35 enrolled. In 2007, 70 master's, 6 doctorates, 2 other advanced degrees awarded. *Degree requirements:* For master's, thesis (for some programs); for doctorate, thesis/dissertation. *Entrance requirements:* For master's and doctorate, GRE General Test. Additional exam requirements/recommendations for international students: Required—TOEFL (minimum score 550 paper-based; 213 computer-based; 80 iBT). *Application deadline:* For fall admission, 1/15 for domestic and international students. Applications are processed on a rolling basis. Application fee: $70. Electronic applications accepted. *Expenses:* Tuition: Full-time $35,052. *Financial support:* Fellowships, research assistantships with full and partial tuition reimbursements, teaching assistantships with full and partial tuition reimbursements, career-related internships or fieldwork, Federal Work-Study, scholarships/grants, and tuition waivers (partial) available. Support available to part-time students. Financial award application deadline: 1/15; financial award applicants required to submit FAFSA. *Unit head:* Ellen Pinderhughes, Chair, 617-628-5000.

The University of Akron, Graduate School, College of Fine and Applied Arts, School of Family and Consumer Sciences, Program in Child and Family Development, Akron, OH 44325. Offers child development (MA); family development (MA). *Students:* 4 full-time (all women), 3 part-time (all women); includes 1 minority (African American), 1 international. Average age 30. 5 applicants, 60% accepted, 2 enrolled. In 2007, 1 degree awarded. *Degree requirements:* For master's, comprehensive exam, thesis optional, project or thesis. *Entrance requirements:* For master's, GRE, minimum GPA of 2.75, letters of recommendation, personal statement of goals; interview. Additional exam requirements/recommendations for international students: Required—TOEFL (minimum score 550 paper-based; 213 computer-based; 79 iBT). *Application deadline:* For fall admission, 3/1 for domestic and international students; for spring admission, 10/1 for domestic and international students. Applications are processed on a rolling basis. Application fee: $30 ($40 for international students). Electronic applications accepted. *Expenses:* Tuition, state resident: full-time $6,164; part-time $342 per credit. Tuition, nonresident: full-time $10,575; part-time $588 per credit. Required fees: $806; $43 per credit. $12 per term. Tuition and fees vary according to course load, degree level and program. *Unit head:* Dr. Susan M. Witt, Graduate Director, 330-972-7729, E-mail: susan8@uakron.edu.

The University of Akron, Graduate School, College of Fine and Applied Arts, School of Family and Consumer Sciences, Program in Child Life, Akron, OH 44325. Offers MA. *Students:* 4 full-time (all women), 1 (woman) part-time. Average age 24. 4 applicants, 0% accepted, 1 enrolled. In 2007, 1 degree awarded. *Degree requirements:* For master's, comprehensive exam, thesis optional, project or thesis. *Entrance requirements:* For master's, GRE, minimum

GPA of 2.75, letters of recommendation, personal statement of goals, interview. Additional exam requirements/recommendations for international students: Required—TOEFL (minimum score 550 paper-based; 213 computer-based; 79 iBT). *Application deadline:* For fall admission, 3/1 for domestic and international students; for spring admission, 10/1 for domestic and international students. Applications are processed on a rolling basis. Application fee: $30 ($40 for international students). Electronic applications accepted. *Expenses:* Tuition, state resident: full-time $6,164; part-time $342 per credit. Tuition, nonresident: full-time $10,575; part-time $588 per credit. Required fees: $806; $43 per credit. $12 per term. Tuition and fees vary according to course load, degree level and program. *Unit head:* Rose Resler, Instructor, 330-972-8040, E-mail: rresler@uakron.edu.

The University of Alabama, Graduate School, College of Human Environmental Sciences, Department of Human Development and Family Studies, Tuscaloosa, AL 35487. Offers MSHES. *Faculty:* 6 full-time (4 women). *Students:* 19 full-time (all women), 9 part-time (all women); includes 4 minority (all African Americans) Average age 29. 25 applicants, 64% accepted, 10 enrolled. In 2007, 6 degrees awarded. *Degree requirements:* For master's, thesis (for some programs). *Entrance requirements:* For master's, GRE General Test or MAT, minimum GPA of 3.0. Additional exam requirements/recommendations for international students: Required—TOEFL. *Application deadline:* For fall admission, 7/6 for domestic students. Applications are processed on a rolling basis. Application fee: $30. Electronic applications accepted. *Expenses:* Tuition, state resident: full-time $5,700. Tuition, nonresident: full-time $16,518. *Financial support:* In 2007–08, 2 students received support, including research assistantships with full tuition reimbursements available (averaging $10,908 per year), teaching assistantships with full tuition reimbursements available (averaging $10,908 per year); career-related internships or fieldwork, Federal Work-Study, scholarships/grants, and health care benefits also available. Financial award application deadline: 3/15. *Faculty research:* Parent/child relationships, psychosocial care of hospitalized children, family strengths and adolescent wildness, depression in mothers and infants. *Unit head:* Dr. Carroll M. Tingle, Chair, 205-348-6158, Fax: 205-348-8153, E-mail: ctingle@ches.ua.edu. *Application contact:* Dr. Mary Elizabeth Curtner-Smith, Associate Professor, 205-348-8151, E-mail: mcurtner@ches.ua.edu.

The University of Arizona, Graduate College, College of Agriculture and Life Sciences, School of Family and Consumer Sciences, Division of Family Studies and Human Development, Tucson, AZ 85721. Offers family and consumer sciences education (MS); family studies and human development (PhD). In 2007, 3 master's, 5 doctorates awarded. Terminal master's awarded for partial completion of doctoral program. *Entrance requirements:* For master's, GRE General Test, minimum undergraduate GPA of 3.0, personal resumè, personal statement, 3 letters of recommendation. Additional exam requirements/recommendations for international students: Required—TOEFL. *Application deadline:* For fall admission, 1/15 for domestic and international students. Applications are processed on a rolling basis. Application fee: $50. *Unit head:* Dr. Angela R. Taylor, Division Chair, 520-621-7129, Fax: 520-621-3401, E-mail: artaylor@u.arizona.edu. *Application contact:* Mary Helen Scott, Administrative Assistant, 520-621-5884, Fax: 520-621-3401, E-mail: mhscott@ag.arizona.edu.

University of California, Santa Barbara, Graduate Division, Gevirtz Graduate School of Education, Santa Barbara, CA 93106. Offers counseling, clinical and school psychology (PhD), including clinical psychology, counseling psychology; education (MA, PhD), including child and adolescent development, cultural perspectives and comparative education, educational leadership and organizations, research methodology, special education disabilities and risk studies (MA), special education, disabilities and risk studies (PhD), teaching and learning; educational leadership (Ed D); school psychology (M Ed); MA/PhD. *Accreditation:* APA (one or more programs are accredited). Postbaccalaureate distance learning degree programs offered (minimal on-campus study). *Faculty:* 36 full-time (18 women), 7 part-time/adjunct (3 women). *Students:* 400 full-time (308 women); includes 119 minority (11 African Americans, 6 American Indian/Alaska Native, 46 Asian Americans or Pacific Islanders, 56 Hispanic Americans), 18 international. Average age 31. 721 applicants, 41% accepted, 189 enrolled. In 2007, 157 master's, 35 doctorates awarded. Terminal master's awarded for partial completion of doctoral program. *Median time to degree:* Of those who began their doctoral program in fall 1999, 60% received their degree in 8 years or less. *Degree requirements:* For master's, comprehensive exam (for some programs), thesis (for some programs); for doctorate, comprehensive exam (for some programs), thesis/dissertation, qualifying exam. *Entrance requirements:* For master's, GRE, MAT (M Ed); for doctorate, GRE. Additional exam requirements/recommendations for international students: Required—TOEFL (minimum score 550 paper-based; 213 computer-based; 80 iBT). *Application deadline:* For fall admission, 12/15 priority date for domestic and international students. Application fee: $60. Electronic applications accepted. *Expenses:* Tuition, nonresident: full-time $14,888. Required fees: $10,108. *Financial support:* In 2007–08, 292 students received support, including 170 fellowships with full and partial tuition reimbursements available (averaging $5,200 per year), 80 research assistantships with full and partial tuition reimbursements available, 124 teaching assistantships with full and partial tuition reimbursements available; career-related internships or fieldwork, Federal Work-Study, institutionally sponsored loans, scholarships/grants, traineeships, health care benefits, and unspecified assistantships also available. Financial award applicants required to submit FAFSA. *Faculty research:* Professional development, early childhood development, school violence, literacy, science/math initiative. Total annual research expenditures: $4.2 million. *Unit head:* Carol Dixon, Associate Dean of Students, 805-893-2137, Fax: 805-893-7264, E-mail: sao@education.ucsb.edu. *Application contact:* Katie Tucciarone, Student Affairs Officer, 805-893-2137, Fax: 805-893-2588, E-mail: katiet@education.ucsb.edu.

University of Central Florida, College of Health and Public Affairs, School of Social Work, Orlando, FL 32816. Offers addictions (Certificate); aging studies (Certificate); children's services (Certificate); school social work (Certificate); social work (MSW); social work administration (Certificate). *Accreditation:* CSWE. Part-time and evening/weekend programs available. *Faculty:* 16 full-time (11 women), 21 part-time/adjunct (16 women). *Degree requirements:* For master's, thesis or alternative, field education. *Entrance requirements:* For master's, resumé. Additional exam requirements/recommendations for international students: Required—TOEFL. *Application deadline:* For fall admission, 3/1 for domestic students. Application fee: $30. Electronic applications accepted. *Expenses:* Tuition, state resident: full-time $6,484. Tuition, nonresident: full-time $23,938. Tuition and fees vary according to program. *Financial support:* Fellowships with partial tuition reimbursements, research assistantships with partial tuition reimbursements, teaching assistantships with partial tuition reimbursements, career-related internships or fieldwork, Federal Work-Study, institutionally sponsored loans, and unspecified assistantships available. Financial award application deadline: 3/1; financial award applicants required to submit FAFSA. *Unit head:* Dr. John Ronnau, Director, 407-823-2208, Fax: 407-823-5697, E-mail: jronnau@mail.ucf.edu.

University of Connecticut, Graduate School, College of Liberal Arts and Sciences, Department of Human Development and Family Studies, Field of Human Development and Family Studies, Storrs, CT 06269. Offers culture, health and human development (Graduate Certificate); human development and family studies (MA, PhD). *Accreditation:* AAMFT/COAMFTE. *Faculty:* 25 full-time (16 women). *Students:* 47 full-time (42 women), 9 part-time (8 women); includes 10 minority (3 African Americans, 3 Asian Americans or Pacific Islanders, 4 Hispanic Americans), 7 international. Average age 33. 79 applicants, 25% accepted, 18 enrolled. In 2007, 11 master's, 2 doctorates awarded. Terminal master's awarded for partial completion of doctoral program. *Degree requirements:* For master's, comprehensive exam; for doctorate, thesis/dissertation. *Entrance requirements:* For master's and doctorate, GRE General Test. Additional exam requirements/recommendations for international students: Required—TOEFL (minimum score 550 paper-based; 213 computer-based). *Application deadline:* For fall admission, 2/1 priority date for domestic and international students; for spring admission, 11/1 for domestic students, 10/1 for international students. Applications are processed on a rolling basis. Application fee: $55. Electronic applications accepted. *Expenses:* Tuition, state resident: part-time $469 per credit hour. Tuition, nonresident: part-time $1,218 per credit hour. *Financial support:* In 2007–08, 6 research assistantships with full tuition reimbursements, 34 teaching assistantships with full tuition reimbursements were awarded; fellowships, career-related internships or fieldwork, Federal Work-Study, scholarships/grants, health care benefits, and unspecified assistantships also available. Financial award application deadline: 2/1; financial award applicants required to submit FAFSA. *Application contact:* Liz Little, Administrative Assistant, 860-486-4721, Fax: 860-486-3452, E-mail: elizabeth.little@uconn.edu.

University of Delaware, College of Human Services, Education and Public Policy, Department of Individual and Family Studies, Newark, DE 19716. Offers human development and family studies (MS, PhD). Part-time programs available. *Faculty:* 21 full-time (15 women). *Students:* 20 full-time (19 women), 3 part-time (2 women); includes 2 minority (both Asian Americans or Pacific Islanders), 4 international. Average age 32. 16 applicants, 19% accepted, 3 enrolled. In 2007, 10 master's, 1 doctorate awarded. Terminal master's awarded for partial completion of doctoral program. *Median time to degree:* Of those who began their doctoral program in fall 1999, 99% received their degree in 8 years or less. *Degree requirements:* For master's, thesis or alternative; for doctorate, comprehensive exam, thesis/dissertation. *Entrance requirements:* For master's and doctorate, GRE General Test, 3 letters of recommendation. Additional exam requirements/recommendations for international students: Required—TOEFL. *Application deadline:* For fall admission, 2/1 for domestic and international students. Application fee: $60. Electronic applications accepted. *Financial support:* In 2007–08, 20 students received support, including 1 fellowship with full tuition reimbursement available (averaging $11,000 per year), 16 research assistantships with full tuition reimbursements available (averaging $11,000 per year), 3 teaching assistantships with full tuition reimbursements available (averaging $11,000 per year); career-related internships or fieldwork and institutionally sponsored loans also available. Financial award application deadline: 2/1. *Faculty research:* Early childhood inclusive education, relationships, family risk and resilience, disability issues, program development and evaluation. Total annual research expenditures: $2.5 million. *Unit head:* Dr. Donald G. Unger, Acting Chair, 302-831-1922, Fax: 302-831-8776. *Application contact:* Dr. John Bishop, Associate Professor, Graduate Coordinator, 302-831-6500, Fax: 302-831-8776, E-mail: jbbishop@udel.edu.

University of Denver, College of Education, Denver, CO 80208. Offers counseling psychology (MA, PhD); curriculum and instruction (MA, PhD, Certificate), including curriculum leadership (MA, PhD); educational administration and policy studies (Certificate); educational psychology (MA, PhD, Ed S), including child and family studies (MA, PhD), quantitative research methods (MA, PhD), school psychology (PhD, Ed S); higher education and adult studies (MA, PhD); library and information science (MLIS); library and information sciences (Certificate); school administration (PhD). *Accreditation:* ALA; APA (one or more programs are accredited). Part-time and evening/weekend programs available. Postbaccalaureate distance learning degree programs offered (no on-campus study). *Faculty:* 26 full-time (18 women). *Students:* 327 full-time (260 women), 438 part-time (343 women); includes 119 minority (31 African Americans, 7 American Indian/Alaska Native, 14 Asian Americans or Pacific Islanders, 67 Hispanic Americans), 15 international. Average age 34. 778 applicants, 76% accepted, 368 enrolled. In 2007, 183 master's, 29 doctorates, 54 other advanced degrees awarded. Terminal master's awarded for partial completion of doctoral program. *Degree requirements:* For master's, comprehensive exam; for doctorate, 2 foreign languages, comprehensive exam, thesis/dissertation. *Entrance requirements:* For master's and doctorate, GRE General Test or MAT. *Application deadline:* Applications are processed on a rolling basis. Application fee: $50. Electronic applications accepted. *Financial support:* In 2007–08, 58 teaching assistantships with full and partial tuition reimbursements (averaging $6,300 per year) were awarded; career-related internships or fieldwork, Federal Work-Study, institutionally sponsored loans, and scholarships/grants also available. Support available to part-time students. Financial award application deadline: 3/1; financial award applicants required to submit FAFSA. *Faculty research:* Parkinson's disease, personnel training, development and assessments, gifted education, service learning, transportation, public schools. Total annual research expenditures: $340,000. *Unit head:* Dr. Virginia Maloney, Dean, 303-871-2509. *Application contact:* Linda McCarthy, Student Services Coordinator, 303-871-2509, E-mail: edinfo@du.edu.

University of Georgia, Graduate School, College of Education, Department of Elementary and Social Studies Education, Athens, GA 30602. Offers early childhood education (M Ed, MAT, PhD, Ed S), including child and family development (MAT); elementary education (PhD); middle school education (M Ed, PhD, Ed S); social studies education (M Ed, Ed D, PhD, Ed S). *Faculty:* 14 full-time (9 women). *Students:* 108 full-time (76 women), 120 part-time (96 women); includes 26 minority (17 African Americans, 5 Asian Americans or Pacific Islanders, 4 Hispanic Americans), 11 international. 168 applicants, 57% accepted, 41 enrolled. In 2007, 86 master's, 6 doctorates, 5 other advanced degrees awarded. *Entrance requirements:* For master's and Ed S, GRE General Test or MAT; for doctorate, GRE General Test. *Application deadline:* For fall admission, 7/1 priority date for domestic students; for spring admission, 11/15 for domestic students. Application fee: $50. Electronic applications accepted. *Financial support:* Fellowships, research assistantships, teaching assistantships, unspecified assistantships available. *Unit head:* Dr. Ronald L. VanSickle, Interim Head, 706-542-6486, E-mail: rvansick@uga.edu. *Application contact:* Dr. John D. Hoge, Graduate Coordinator, 706-542-4416, E-mail: jdhoge@uga.edu.

University of Georgia, Graduate School, College of Family and Consumer Sciences, Department of Child and Family Development, Athens, GA 30602. Offers child and family development (MS, PhD); early childhood education (MAT), including child and family development. *Accreditation:* AAMFT/COAMFTE (one or more programs are accredited). *Faculty:* 16 full-time (11 women). *Students:* 40 full-time (35 women), 9 part-time (8 women); includes 7 minority (5 African Americans, 2 Hispanic Americans), 7 international. 63 applicants, 35% accepted, 10 enrolled. In 2007, 8 master's, 5 doctorates awarded. *Degree requirements:* For master's, thesis (MS); for doctorate, thesis/dissertation. *Entrance requirements:* For master's and doctorate, GRE General Test. *Application deadline:* For fall admission, 7/1 priority date for domestic students; for spring admission, 11/15 for domestic students. Application fee: $50. Electronic applications accepted. *Financial support:* Fellowships, research assistantships, teaching assistantships, unspecified assistantships available. *Unit head:* Dr. Donald W. Bower, Interim Head, 706-542-7566, Fax: 706-542-4389, E-mail: dbower@uga.edu. *Application contact:* Dr. David Wright, Graduate Coordinator, 706-542-4825, E-mail: dwright@fcs.uga.edu.

University of Guelph, Graduate Program Services, College of Social and Applied Human Sciences, Department of Family Relations and Applied Nutrition, Guelph, ON N1G 2W1, Canada. Offers applied nutrition (MAN); family relations and human development (M Sc, PhD), including applied human nutrition, couple and family therapy (M Sc), family relations and human development. *Accreditation:* AAMFT/COAMFTE (one or more programs are accredited). Part-time programs available. *Faculty:* 23 full-time (16 women). *Students:* 56 full-time (51 women), 5 part-time (all women); includes 4 minority (2 African Americans, 1 Asian American or Pacific Islander, 1 Hispanic American), 2 international. Average age 30. 153 applicants, 32% accepted, 33 enrolled. In 2007, 9 master's, 3 doctorates awarded. *Median time to degree:* Of those who began their doctoral program in fall 1999, 100% received their degree in 8 years or less. *Degree requirements:* For master's, thesis (for some programs); for doctorate, comprehensive exam, thesis/dissertation. *Entrance requirements:* For master's, minimum B+ average; for doctorate, master's degree in family relations and human development or related field with a minimum B+ average or master's degree in applied human nutrition. Additional exam requirements/recommendations for international students: Required—TOEFL (minimum score 600 paper-based; 250 computer-based). *Application deadline:* For fall admission, 1/2 priority date for domestic and international students. Application fee: $85. Electronic applications accepted. *Financial support:* In 2007–08, 54 students received support; fellowships, research assistantships, teaching assistantships, career-related internships or fieldwork and health care benefits available. *Faculty research:* Child and adolescent development, social gerontology, family roles and relations, couple and family therapy, applied human nutrition. Total annual research expenditures: $500,000. *Unit head:* Dr. Susan Lollis, Interim Chair, 519-824-4120 Ext. 56326, Fax: 519-766-0691, E-mail: slollis@uoguelph.ca. *Application contact:* Jo Anne Waechter, Graduate Secretary, 519-824-4120 Ext. 53968, Fax: 519-766-0691, E-mail: jwaechte@uoguelph.ca.

Child and Family Studies

University of Illinois at Springfield, Graduate Programs, College of Education and Human Services, Program in Human Services, Springfield, IL 62703-5407. Offers alcoholism and substance abuse (MA); child and family services (MA); gerontology (MA); social services administration (MA). Part-time and evening/weekend programs available. Postbaccalaureate distance learning degree programs offered. *Faculty:* 4 full-time (3 women), 2 part-time/adjunct (both women). *Students:* 36 full-time (30 women), 64 part-time (53 women); includes 23 minority (21 African Americans, 2 American Indian/Alaska Native), 1 international. Average age 36. 52 applicants, 62% accepted, 27 enrolled. In 2007, 10 degrees awarded. *Degree requirements:* For master's, thesis optional, internship. *Entrance requirements:* For master's, 2 letters of reference, minimum undergraduate GPA of 3.0, prerequisite courses in lifespan development and research methods, personal statement. Additional exam requirements/recommendations for international students: Required—TOEFL (minimum score 550 paper-based; 213 computer-based). *Application deadline:* For fall admission, 2/15 priority date for domestic and international students; for spring admission, 9/15 priority date for domestic and international students. Application fee: $50 ($60 for international students). *Expenses:* Tuition, state resident: full-time $5,424; part-time $226 per credit hour. Tuition, nonresident: part-time $553 per credit hour. Required fees: $618 per term. *Financial support:* In 2007–08, research assistantships with full tuition reimbursements (averaging $7,988 per year), teaching assistantships with full tuition reimbursements (averaging $7,988 per year) were awarded; career-related internships or fieldwork, scholarships/grants, health care benefits, and unspecified assistantships also available. Support available to part-time students. Financial award application deadline: 11/15. *Unit head:* Dr. Carolyn Peck, Program Administrator, 217-206-7577, Fax: 217-206-6775, E-mail: peck.carolyn@uis.edu.

University of Kentucky, Graduate School, College of Agriculture, Program in Family Studies, Human Development, and Resource Management, Lexington, KY 40506-0032. Offers MSFAM, PhD. *Accreditation:* AAMFT/COAMFTE. *Faculty:* 12 full-time (7 women), 2 part-time/adjunct (0 women). *Students:* 30 full-time (22 women), 11 part-time (all women); includes 3 minority (all African Americans), 3 international. Average age 33. 42 applicants, 26% accepted, 9 enrolled. In 2007, 14 master's, 2 doctorates awarded. *Degree requirements:* For master's, comprehensive exam, thesis optional. *Entrance requirements:* For master's, GRE General Test, minimum undergraduate GPA of 2.75; for doctorate, GRE General Test, minimum undergraduate GPA of 3.0. Additional exam requirements/recommendations for international students: Required—TOEFL (minimum score 550 paper-based; 213 computer-based). *Application deadline:* For fall admission, 7/17 priority date for domestic students, 2/1 priority date for international students; for spring admission, 12/13 priority date for domestic students, 6/15 priority date for international students. Application fee: $50 ($65 for international students). Electronic applications accepted. *Expenses:* Tuition, state resident: part-time $437 per credit hour. Tuition, nonresident: part-time $931 per credit hour. *Financial support:* In 2007–08, 24 students received support, including 5 fellowships with full tuition reimbursements available (averaging $2,776 per year), 6 research assistantships with full tuition reimbursements available (averaging $4,800 per year), 19 teaching assistantships with full tuition reimbursements available (averaging $4,800 per year); Federal Work-Study, scholarships/grants, traineeships, health care benefits, tuition waivers (partial), and unspecified assistantships also available. Support available to part-time students. Financial award application deadline: 3/15. *Faculty research:* Early childhood education, family therapy, family resource management and consumer studies, human development. *Unit head:* Dr. Raymond Forge, Head, 859-257-7750, Fax: 859-257-4095. *Application contact:* Dr. Brian Jackson, Senior Associate Dean, 859-257-4667, Fax: 859-257-4676, E-mail: brian.jackson@uky.edu.

University of La Verne, College of Education and Organizational Leadership, Department of Education, Programs in Child Development/Child Life, La Verne, CA 91750-4443. Offers child development (MS); child life (MS). Part-time programs available. *Faculty:* 16 full-time (8 women), 14 part-time/adjunct (7 women). *Students:* 40 full-time (39 women), 24 part-time (23 women); includes 34 minority (6 African Americans, 13 Asian Americans or Pacific Islanders, 15 Hispanic Americans), 1 international. Average age 30. In 2007, 26 degrees awarded. *Entrance requirements:* For master's, minimum GPA of 3.0, 3 letters of reference, writing sample. Additional exam requirements/recommendations for international students: Required—TOEFL (minimum score 550 paper-based; 213 computer-based). *Application deadline:* Applications are processed on a rolling basis. Application fee: $50. *Expenses: Contact institution.* Tuition and fees vary according to course load and program. *Financial support:* Institutionally sponsored loans, scholarships/grants, and unspecified assistantships available. Financial award application deadline: 3/2; financial award applicants required to submit FAFSA. *Unit head:* Dr. Barbara Nicoll, Chairperson, 909-593-3511 Ext. 4632, Fax: 909-392-2710, E-mail: nicollb@ulv.edu. *Application contact:* Connie Hamlow, Admissions Information Specialist, 909-593-3511 Ext. 4244, Fax: 909-392-2761, E-mail: gradadmission@ulv.edu.

University of Manitoba, Faculty of Graduate Studies, Faculty of Human Ecology, Department of Family Studies, Winnipeg, MB R3T 2N2, Canada. Offers M Sc. *Degree requirements:* For master's, thesis.

University of Maryland, College Park, Graduate Studies, School of Public Health, Department of Family Science, College Park, MD 20742. Offers family studies (PhD); marriage and family therapy (MS). *Accreditation:* AAMFT/COAMFTE. Part-time and evening/weekend programs available. *Faculty:* 15 full-time (12 women), 14 part-time/adjunct (11 women). *Students:* 40 full-time (35 women), 1 (woman) part-time; includes 10 minority (8 African Americans, 1 Asian American or Pacific Islander, 1 Hispanic American), 2 international. 91 applicants, 24% accepted, 17 enrolled. In 2007, 17 master's, 9 doctorates awarded. *Degree requirements:* For master's, thesis or alternative; for doctorate, comprehensive exam, thesis/dissertation, oral defense. *Entrance requirements:* For master's, GRE General Test, minimum GPA of 3.0, 3 letters of recommendation; for doctorate, GRE General Test, minimum GPA of 3.0, 3 letters of recommendation, research sample. *Application deadline:* For fall admission, 1/15 for domestic students, 2/1 for international students. Applications are processed on a rolling basis. Application fee: $60. Electronic applications accepted. *Financial support:* In 2007–08, 8 fellowships with full tuition reimbursements (averaging $7,450 per year), 1 research assistantship with tuition reimbursement (averaging $15,126 per year), 28 teaching assistantships with tuition reimbursements (averaging $14,911 per year) were awarded; career-related internships or fieldwork, Federal Work-Study, and scholarships/grants also available. Support available to part-time students. Financial award applicants required to submit FAFSA. *Faculty research:* Family life quality, interracial couples, child support, homeless families, family and child well-being. Total annual research expenditures: $291,811. *Unit head:* Dr. Sally Koblinsky, Chairman, 301-405-1377, Fax: 301-314-9161, E-mail: koblinsk@umd.edu. *Application contact:* Dean of Graduate School, 301-405-0358, Fax: 301-314-9305.

See Close-Up on page 1075.

University of Minnesota, Twin Cities Campus, Graduate School, College of Education and Human Development, Department of Family Social Science, Minneapolis, MN 55455-0213. Offers marriage and family therapy (MA, PhD). *Accreditation:* AAMFT/COAMFTE (one or more programs are accredited). *Faculty:* 18 full-time (13 women). *Students:* 52 full-time (42 women), 14 part-time (11 women); includes 11 minority (3 African Americans, 2 American Indian/Alaska Native, 5 Asian Americans or Pacific Islanders, 1 Hispanic American), 15 international. Average age 36. 24 applicants, 67% accepted, 10 enrolled. In 2007, 3 master's, 6 doctorates awarded. *Median time to degree:* Of those who began their doctoral program in fall 1999, 86% received their degree in 8 years or less. *Degree requirements:* For master's, thesis; for doctorate, thesis/dissertation. *Entrance requirements:* For master's and doctorate, GRE General Test, minimum undergraduate GPA of 3.0 (preferred). Additional exam requirements/recommendations for international students: Required—TOEFL. *Application deadline:* For fall admission, 12/15 for domestic students. Application fee: $55 ($75 for international students). *Financial support:* In 2007–08, 41 research assistantships (averaging $25,212 per year), 13 teaching assistantships (averaging $26,543 per year) were awarded; fellowships, career-related internships or fieldwork, Federal Work-Study, institutionally sponsored loans, and tuition waivers (partial) also available. Financial award application deadline: 6/30; financial award applicants required to submit FAFSA. *Faculty research:* Families and diversity, families and health, families and economic well-being, individuals and relationships across the lifespan. Total annual research expenditures: $1.3 million. *Unit head:* Dr. Jan McCulloch, Head, 612-624-1208, Fax: 612-625-4227, E-mail: jmccullo@che.umn.edu. *Application contact:* Roberta Daigle, Information Contact, 612-625-3116, E-mail: rdaigle@che.umn.edu.

University of Missouri–Columbia, Graduate School, College of Human Environmental Science, Department of Human Development and Family Studies, Columbia, MO 65211. Offers MA, MS, PhD. *Entrance requirements:* For master's, GRE General Test, minimum GPA of 3.0. Additional exam requirements/recommendations for international students: Required—TOEFL (minimum score 550 paper-based; 220 computer-based).

University of Nebraska–Lincoln, Graduate College, College of Education and Human Sciences, Department of Family and Consumer Sciences, Lincoln, NE 68588. Offers family and consumer sciences (MS); human resources and family sciences (PhD). *Accreditation:* AAMFT/COAMFTE (one or more programs are accredited). Postbaccalaureate distance learning degree programs offered. *Degree requirements:* For master's, thesis optional. *Entrance requirements:* For master's, GRE. Additional exam requirements/recommendations for international students: Required—TOEFL (minimum score 550 paper-based; 213 computer-based). Electronic applications accepted. *Faculty research:* Marriage and family therapy, child development/early childhood education, family financial management.

University of Nevada, Reno, Graduate School, College of Health and Human Sciences, Department of Human Development and Family Studies, Reno, NV 89557. Offers MS. *Faculty:* 14. *Students:* 6 full-time (all women), 12 part-time (10 women); includes 5 minority (1 African American, 2 Asian Americans or Pacific Islanders, 2 Hispanic Americans), 1 international. Average age 33. 11 applicants, 45% accepted, 4 enrolled. In 2007, 3 degrees awarded. *Degree requirements:* For master's, thesis. *Entrance requirements:* For master's, GRE General Test, minimum GPA of 3.0. Additional exam requirements/recommendations for international students: Required—TOEFL. *Application deadline:* For fall admission, 3/30 for domestic students; for spring admission, 10/1 for domestic students. Application fee: $60 ($95 for international students). *Expenses:* Tuition, state resident: full-time $2,774; part-time $154 per credit. Tuition, nonresident: full-time $13,578; part-time $330 per credit. Required fees: $49 per semester. *Financial support:* In 2007–08, 10 research assistantships, 2 teaching assistantships were awarded; tuition waivers (full) also available. Financial award application deadline: 3/30. *Unit head:* Dr. Karen Kopera–Frye, Graduate Program Director, 775-784-7010, E-mail: kfrye@unr.edu.

University of New Hampshire, Graduate School, School of Health and Human Services, Department of Family Studies, Durham, NH 03824. Offers family studies (MS); marriage and family therapy (MS). *Accreditation:* AAMFT/COAMFTE. Part-time programs available. *Faculty:* 8 full-time. *Students:* 15 full-time (12 women), 7 part-time (6 women); includes 3 minority (2 African Americans, 1 Asian American or Pacific Islander), 1 international. Average age 30. 25 applicants, 48% accepted, 8 enrolled. In 2007, 6 degrees awarded. *Degree requirements:* For master's, thesis or alternative. *Entrance requirements:* For master's, GRE General Test. Additional exam requirements/recommendations for international students: Required—TOEFL (minimum score 550 paper-based; 213 computer-based; 80 iBT). *Application deadline:* For fall admission, 4/1 priority date for domestic students, 4/1 for international students; for winter admission, 12/1 for domestic students. Applications are processed on a rolling basis. Application fee: $60. Electronic applications accepted. *Financial support:* In 2007–08, 1 research assistantship, 5 teaching assistantships were awarded; fellowships, career-related internships or fieldwork, Federal Work-Study, scholarships/grants, and tuition waivers (full and partial) also available. Support available to part-time students. Financial award application deadline: 2/15. *Unit head:* Dr. Elizabeth Dolan, Chairperson, 603-862-2137. *Application contact:* Mary Leighton, Administrative Assistant, 603-862-5021, E-mail: family.studies@unh.edu.

University of New Mexico, Graduate School, College of Education, Department of Individual, Family and Community Education, Program in Family Studies, Albuquerque, NM 87131-2039. Offers MA, PhD. Part-time and evening/weekend programs available. *Students:* 8 full-time (all women), 16 part-time (all women); includes 14 minority (2 African Americans, 3 American Indian/Alaska Native, 1 Asian American or Pacific Islander, 8 Hispanic Americans), 1 international. Average age 42. 9 applicants, 33% accepted, 3 enrolled. In 2007, 5 master's, 3 doctorates awarded. *Degree requirements:* For master's, comprehensive exam, thesis (for some programs); for doctorate, comprehensive exam, thesis/dissertation. *Entrance requirements:* For master's, written paper, 3 letters of recommendation, personal statement, departmental application; for doctorate, GRE General Test, written paper, 3 letters of recommendation, personal statement, departmental application, interview. *Application deadline:* For fall admission, 3/15 priority date for domestic students; for spring admission, 10/15 priority date for domestic students. Applications are processed on a rolling basis. Application fee: $50. Electronic applications accepted. *Financial support:* In 2007–08, 10 students received support, including 1 research assistantship (averaging $1,761 per year), 3 teaching assistantships with full and partial tuition reimbursements available (averaging $6,402 per year). Financial award application deadline: 3/1; financial award applicants required to submit FAFSA. *Faculty research:* Home, community and school relations; multicultural issues; parent-child interactions; grandparents as primary caretakers for grandchildren; fathering, early childhood evaluation. *Unit head:* Dr. Virginia Shipman, Professor, 505-277-4063, Fax: 505-277-8361, E-mail: vshipman@unm.edu. *Application contact:* Cynthia Salas, Department Administrator, 505-277-4535, Fax: 505-277-8361, E-mail: casalas@unm.edu.

The University of North Carolina at Greensboro, Graduate School, School of Human Environmental Sciences, Department of Human Development and Family Studies, Greensboro, NC 27412-5001. Offers M Ed, MS, PhD. *Faculty:* 21 full-time (17 women), 9 part-time/adjunct (7 women). *Students:* 44 full-time (42 women), 9 part-time (7 women); includes 12 minority (5 African Americans, 1 American Indian/Alaska Native, 5 Asian Americans or Pacific Islanders, 1 Hispanic American). 58 applicants, 29% accepted. *Degree requirements:* For master's, one foreign language; for doctorate, one foreign language, thesis/dissertation. *Entrance requirements:* For master's and doctorate, GRE General Test. Additional exam requirements/recommendations for international students: Required—TOEFL. *Application deadline:* For fall admission, 3/15 for domestic students. Application fee: $45. Electronic applications accepted. *Expenses: Contact institution. Financial support:* Fellowships with full tuition reimbursements, research assistantships with full tuition reimbursements, teaching assistantships with full tuition reimbursements, career-related internships or fieldwork, Federal Work-Study, scholarships/grants, traineeships, and unspecified assistantships available. Support available to part-time students. *Faculty research:* Adolescent mothers, multi-handicapped, older adults. *Unit head:* Dr. Dan Perlman, Chair, 336-334-5307, Fax: 336-334-5076, E-mail: d_perlma@uncg.edu. *Application contact:* Michelle Harkleroad, Director of Graduate Admissions, 336-334-4884, Fax: 336-334-4424, E-mail: mbharkle@uncg.edu.

University of North Texas, Robert B. Toulouse School of Graduate Studies, College of Education, Department of Educational Psychology, Program in Development and Family Studies, Denton, TX 76203. Offers MS. Evening/weekend programs available. *Students:* 9 full-time (8 women), 12 part-time (all women); includes 2 minority (1 African American, 1 Hispanic American), 2 international. Average age 29. 12 applicants, 58% accepted, 3 enrolled. In 2007, 5 master's awarded. *Degree requirements:* For master's, comprehensive exam, thesis optional. *Entrance requirements:* For master's, GRE General Test, letter of application, resumè, references. Additional exam requirements/recommendations for international students: Required—proof of English language proficiency required for non-native English speakers; Recommended—TOEFL (minimum score 550 paper-based; 213 computer-based). *Application deadline:* For fall admission, 7/15 for domestic students; for spring admission, 11/15 for domestic students. Application fee: $50 ($75 for international students). *Financial support:* Teaching assistantships, career-related internships or fieldwork, Federal Work-Study, and institutionally sponsored loans available. Financial award application deadline: 4/1. *Faculty* *research:* Parent-child issues, cognitive development, social development. *Application contact:* Dr. Rebecca Glover, Graduate Advisor, 940-565-2000, E-mail: bglover@unt.edu.

University of Rhode Island, Graduate School, College of Human Science and Services, Department of Human Development and Family Studies, Kingston, RI 02881. Offers college student personnel (MS); human development and family studies (MS); marriage and family therapy (MS). *Accreditation:* AAMFT/COAMFTE. Evening/weekend programs available. *Entrance requirements:* For master's, GRE or MAT. *Application deadline:* For fall admission, 4/15 priority date for domestic students; for spring admission, 11/15 for domestic students. Applications are processed on a rolling basis. Application fee: $35. *Expenses:* Tuition, state resident: full-time $6,936; part-time $385 per credit. Tuition, nonresident: full-time $19,044; part-time $1,058 per credit. Required fees: $1,508; $48 per credit. $30 per semester. One-time fee: $80 part-time. *Financial support:* Career-related internships or fieldwork available. *Unit head:* Dr. Jerome Adams, Chair, 401-874-5962.

University of Southern Mississippi, Graduate School, College of Education and Psychology, Department of Child and Family Studies, Hattiesburg, MS 39406-0001. Offers child and family studies (MS); early intervention (MS); marriage and family therapy (MS). *Accreditation:* AAMFT/COAMFTE. Part-time programs available. *Faculty:* 8 full-time (4 women). *Students:* 29 full-time (27 women), 19 part-time (18 women); includes 15 minority (13 African Americans, 1 Asian American or Pacific Islander, 1 Hispanic American), 1 international. Average age 28. 51 applicants, 51% accepted, 22 enrolled. In 2007, 20 master's awarded. *Degree requirements:* For master's, comprehensive exam, thesis optional. *Entrance requirements:* For master's, GRE General Test, minimum GPA of 2.75 in last 60 hours. Additional exam requirements/recommendations for international students: Required—TOEFL. *Application deadline:* For fall admission, 3/1 priority date for domestic students, 3/1 for international students. Applications are processed on a rolling basis. Application fee: $30. Electronic applications accepted. *Financial support:* In 2007–08, 21 students received support, including 1 research assistantship with full tuition reimbursement available (averaging $5,164 per year), teaching assistantships with full tuition reimbursements available (averaging $5,458 per year); fellowships, career-related internships or fieldwork, Federal Work-Study, institutionally sponsored loans, scholarships/grants, and unspecified assistantships also available. Financial award application deadline: 3/15. *Faculty research:* School food service, teen pregnancy, diet and cholesterol metabolism. *Unit head:* Dr. Ann Blackwell, Chair, 601-266-5661, Fax: 601-266-4680.

The University of Tennessee, Graduate School, College of Education, Health and Human Sciences, Department of Child and Family Studies, Knoxville, TN 37996. Offers child and family studies (MS); early childhood education (MS). Part-time programs available. *Degree requirements:* For master's, thesis or alternative. *Entrance requirements:* For master's, GRE General Test, minimum GPA of 2.7. Additional exam requirements/recommendations for international students: Required—TOEFL. Electronic applications accepted.

The University of Tennessee, Graduate School, College of Education, Health and Human Sciences, Program in Human Ecology, Knoxville, TN 37996. Offers child and family studies (PhD); community health (PhD); nutrition science (PhD); retailing and consumer sciences (PhD); textile science (PhD). *Degree requirements:* For doctorate, thesis/dissertation. *Entrance requirements:* For doctorate, GRE General Test, minimum GPA of 2.7. Additional exam requirements/recommendations for international students: Required—TOEFL. Electronic applications accepted.

The University of Tennessee at Martin, Graduate Programs, College of Agriculture and Applied Sciences, Department of Family and Consumer Sciences, Martin, TN 38238-1000. Offers dietetics (MSFCS); general family and consumer sciences (MSFCS). Part-time programs available. *Faculty:* 6. *Students:* 19 (all women) 21 applicants, 90% accepted, 8 enrolled. In 2007, 6 degrees awarded. *Degree requirements:* For master's, comprehensive exam, thesis optional. *Entrance requirements:* For master's, GRE General Test, minimum GPA of 2.5. Additional exam requirements/recommendations for international students: Required—TOEFL (minimum score 525 paper-based; 197 computer-based). *Application deadline:* For fall admission, 8/1 priority date for domestic students, 8/1 for international students; for spring admission, 1/1 for domestic and international students. Applications are processed on a rolling basis. Application fee: $30 ($50 for international students). Electronic applications accepted. *Expenses:* Tuition, state resident: full-time $2,893; part-time $323 per credit hour. Tuition, nonresident: full-time $7,913; part-time $881 per credit hour. Required fees: $220 per credit hour. *Financial support:* In 2007–08, 3 students received support. Scholarships/grants, tuition waivers (partial), and unspecified assistantships available. Financial award application deadline: 3/1. *Faculty research:* Children with developmental disabilities, regional food product development and marketing, parent education. *Unit head:* Dr. Lisa LeBleu, Coordinator, 731-881-7116, E-mail: llebleu@utm.edu. *Application contact:* Linda S. Arant, Student Services Specialist, 731-881-7012, Fax: 731-881-7499, E-mail: larant@utm.edu.

The University of Texas at Austin, Graduate School, College of Natural Sciences, Department of Human Ecology, Program in Human Development and Family Sciences, Austin, TX 78712-1111. Offers MA, PhD. *Degree requirements:* For master's, thesis; for doctorate, thesis/dissertation. *Entrance requirements:* For master's and doctorate, GRE General Test. Additional exam requirements/recommendations for international students: Required—TOEFL. Electronic applications accepted. *Faculty research:* Marriage and family relationships, parenting, impact of television on children, courtship, family policy.

The University of Texas at Dallas, School of Behavioral and Brain Sciences, Program in Psychological Sciences, Richardson, TX 75083-0688. Offers early childhood disorders (MS); psychological sciences (MS, PhD). Part-time and evening/weekend programs available. *Faculty:* 30 full-time (15 women), 1 (woman) part-time/adjunct. *Students:* 30 full-time (27 women), 15 part-time (all women); includes 9 minority (3 African Americans, 4 Asian Americans or Pacific Islanders, 2 Hispanic Americans), 10 international. Average age 30. 51 applicants, 63% accepted, 16 enrolled. In 2007, 16 master's, 2 doctorates awarded. *Degree requirements:* For master's, directed project or internship. *Entrance requirements:* For master's, GRE General Test, minimum GPA of 3.0 in upper-level course work. Additional exam requirements/recommendations for international students: Required—TOEFL (minimum score 550 paper-based; 213 computer-based). *Application deadline:* For fall admission, 7/15 for domestic students; for spring admission, 11/15 for domestic students. Applications are processed on a rolling basis. Application fee: $50 ($100 for international students). Electronic applications accepted. *Expenses:* Tuition, state resident: full-time $7,052. Tuition, nonresident: full-time $12,632. Tuition and fees vary according to course load. *Financial support:* In 2007–08, 13 teaching assistantships with tuition reimbursements (averaging $10,131 per year) were awarded; fellowships, research assistantships with tuition reimbursements, career-related internships or fieldwork, Federal Work-Study, scholarships/grants, and unspecified assistantships also available. Support available to part-time students. Financial award application deadline: 4/30; financial award applicants required to submit FAFSA. *Faculty research:* Social competence in normal and hyperactive youth, preschool number development, social-emotional development, family and peer relationships. *Unit head:* Dr. Melanie J. Spence, Head, PhD Programs, 972-883-2206, Fax: 972-883-2491, E-mail: mspence@utdallas.edu. *Application contact:* Dr. Robert D. Stillman, Head, 972-883-3106, Fax: 972-883-3022, E-mail: stillman@utdallas.edu.

University of Utah, The Graduate School, College of Social and Behavioral Science, Department of Family and Consumer Studies, Salt Lake City, UT 84112-1107. Offers MS. *Faculty:* 18 full-time (10 women), 1 (woman) part-time/adjunct. *Students:* 9 full-time (7 women), 4 part-time (2 women), 2 international. Average age 31. 15 applicants, 33% accepted, 5 enrolled. In 2007, 5 degrees awarded. *Degree requirements:* For master's, thesis optional. *Entrance requirements:* For master's, GRE General Test, minimum undergraduate GPA of 3.0. Additional exam requirements/recommendations for international students: Required—TOEFL (minimum score 500 paper-based; 173 computer-based). *Application deadline:* For spring admission, 3/1 for domestic students. Application fee: $45 ($65 for international students). *Financial support:* Research assistantships with full tuition reimbursements, teaching assistantships with full tuition reimbursements available. Financial award application deadline: 2/15. *Faculty research:* Social, physical and economic contexts of families and communities. Total annual research expenditures: $14,858. *Unit head:* Dr. Cheryl Wright, Chair, 801-581-4431, E-mail: cheryl.wright@fcs.utah.edu. *Application contact:* Barbara Brown, Graduate Director, 801-581-7111, E-mail: barbara.brown@fcs.utah.edu.

University of Victoria, Faculty of Graduate Studies, Faculty of Human and Social Development, School of Child and Youth Care, Victoria, BC V8W 2Y2, Canada. Offers MA, PhD. Part-time programs available. *Students:* 55, 2 international. Average age 33. 56 applicants, 25% accepted, 14 enrolled. In 2007, 6 master's, 3 doctorates awarded. *Degree requirements:* For master's, thesis. *Entrance requirements:* For master's, resumé, professional references, sample of academic writing. Additional exam requirements/recommendations for international students: Required—TOEFL (minimum score 575 paper-based; 233 computer-based), IELTS (minimum score 7). *Application deadline:* For fall admission, 1/31 for domestic students, 12/15 for international students. Applications are processed on a rolling basis. Application fee: $75 ($125 for international students). Electronic applications accepted. *Expenses:* Tuition, state resident: full-time $3,110. International tuition: $3,700 full-time. Tuition and fees vary according to program. *Financial support:* Application deadline: 2/15. *Unit head:* Daniel Scott, Director, 250-492-4770, Fax: 250-721-7218, E-mail: dgscott@uvic.ca. *Application contact:* Katherine Woodhouse, Administrative Officer, 250-721-7980, Fax: 250-721-7218, E-mail: kwoodhou@uvic.ca.

University of Wisconsin–Madison, Graduate School, School of Human Ecology, Program in Human Development and Family Studies, Madison, WI 53706-1380. Offers MS, PhD. Part-time programs available. Terminal master's awarded for partial completion of doctoral program. *Degree requirements:* For master's, thesis; for doctorate, comprehensive exam, thesis/dissertation. *Entrance requirements:* For master's, GRE General Test, 3 letters of recommendation; for doctorate, GRE General Test, MS or MA, 3 letters of recommendation. Additional exam requirements/recommendations for international students: Required—TOEFL. Electronic applications accepted. *Faculty research:* Human development, adolescence, adulthood, prevention, intervention.

University of Wisconsin–Stout, Graduate School, College of Human Development, Program in Family Studies and Human Development, Menomonie, WI 54751. Offers MS. Part-time programs available. *Faculty:* 2 full-time (1 woman). *Students:* 1 (woman) full-time, 15 part-time (14 women); includes 1 minority (African American), 1 international. Average age 35. 4 applicants, 100% accepted, 1 enrolled. In 2007, 4 degrees awarded. *Degree requirements:* For master's, thesis. *Entrance requirements:* For master's, minimum GPA of 2.75. Additional exam requirements/recommendations for international students: Required—TOEFL (minimum score 500 paper-based; 173 computer-based; 61 iBT). *Application deadline:* Applications are processed on a rolling basis. Application fee: $45. Electronic applications accepted. *Expenses:* Tuition, state resident: part-time $332 per credit. Tuition, nonresident: part-time $553 per credit. *Financial support:* In 2007–08, 2 research assistantships with partial tuition reimbursements (averaging $8,712 per year) were awarded; teaching assistantships with partial tuition reimbursements, Federal Work-Study, scholarships/grants, tuition waivers (partial), and unspecified assistantships also available. Support available to part-time students. Financial award application deadline: 4/1; financial award applicants required to submit FAFSA. *Faculty research:* Diversity, work and family medical ethics, family policy, dementia and families. *Unit head:* Dr. Dale Hawley, Director, 715-232-1273, E-mail: hawleyd@uwstout.edu. *Application contact:* Anne E. Johnson, Graduate Student Evaluator, 715-232-1322, Fax: 715-232-2413, E-mail: johnsona@uwstout.edu.

Utah State University, School of Graduate Studies, College of Education and Human Services, Department of Family, Consumer, and Human Development, Logan, UT 84322. Offers family and human development (MFHD); family, consumer, and human development (MS, PhD), including adolescence/youth (MS), adult development/aging (MS), consumer science (MS), infancy/childhood (MS), marriage and family relations (MS), marriage and family therapy (MS). *Accreditation:* AAMFT/COAMFTE (one or more programs are accredited). Part-time and evening/weekend programs available. Postbaccalaureate distance learning degree programs offered (minimal on-campus study). *Degree requirements:* For master's, thesis; for doctorate, comprehensive exam, thesis/dissertation, competencies. *Entrance requirements:* For master's, GRE General Test or MAT, minimum GPA of 3.0, 3 letters of recommendation; for doctorate, GRE, minimum GPA of 3.0, 3 letters of recommendation. Additional exam requirements/recommendations for international students: Required—TOEFL. Electronic applications accepted. *Faculty research:* Marriage and family relations, adolescent problem behavior, family financial management, early literacy, mental health in the elderly, parent child attachment.

Vanderbilt University, Peabody College, Department of Psychology and Human Development, Nashville, TN 37240-1001. Offers child studies (M Ed). *Accreditation:* APA. Part-time programs available. *Faculty:* 25 full-time (13 women), 2 part-time/adjunct (0 women). *Students:* 15 full-time (12 women), 3 part-time (all women); includes 3 minority (1 African American, 1 Asian American or Pacific Islander, 1 Hispanic American). Average age 25. 18 applicants, 89% accepted, 9 enrolled. In 2007, 13 degrees awarded. *Degree requirements:* For master's, comprehensive exam, thesis optional. *Entrance requirements:* For master's, GRE General Test. Additional exam requirements/recommendations for international students: Required—TOEFL (minimum score 550 paper-based; 213 computer-based). *Application deadline:* For fall admission, 12/31 for domestic and international students; for spring admission, 11/1 for domestic and international students. Applications are processed on a rolling basis. Application fee: $0. Electronic applications accepted. *Financial support:* In 2007–08, 12 students received support, including 4 fellowships with full and partial tuition reimbursements available, 8 research assistantships with full and partial tuition reimbursements available; teaching assistantships with full and partial tuition reimbursements available, Federal Work-Study, institutionally sponsored loans, scholarships/grants, and unspecified assistantships also available. Financial award application deadline: 2/1; financial award applicants required to submit FAFSA. *Faculty research:* Cognitive, language and social development; stress, coping and emotion; quantitative methods and evaluation; clinical intervention and prevention; individual differences, disabilities and developmental psychopathology. *Unit head:* John Rieser, Acting Chair, 615-322-8141, Fax: 615-343-9494, E-mail: j.rieser@vanderbilt.edu. *Application contact:* Sharone Hall, Educational Coordinator, 615-343-4963, Fax: 615-343-9494, E-mail: sharone.k.hall@vanderbilt.edu.

Virginia Polytechnic Institute and State University, Graduate School, College of Liberal Arts and Human Sciences, Department of Human Development, Blacksburg, VA 24061. Offers adult development and aging (MS, PhD); adult learning and human resource development (MS, PhD); child development (MS, PhD); family studies (MS, PhD); marriage and family therapy (MS, PhD). *Accreditation:* AAMFT/COAMFTE (one or more programs are accredited). *Entrance requirements:* For master's and doctorate, GRE General Test. Additional exam requirements/recommendations for international students: Required—TOEFL (minimum score 600 paper-based; 250 computer-based). Electronic applications accepted. *Faculty research:* Stress management, children's play, dual-career families, social cognition, relationships of elderly.

Walden University, Graduate Programs, School of Counseling and Social Science, Minneapolis, MN 55401. Offers human services (PhD), including clinical social work, counseling, criminal justice, family studies and intervention strategies, general program in human services, human services administration, self-designed program in human services, social policy analysis and planning; mental health counseling (MS). Part-time and evening/weekend programs available. *Students:* 586 full-time (496 women), 505 part-time (410 women); includes 413 minority (351 African Americans, 14 American Indian/Alaska Native, 11 Asian Americans or Pacific Islanders, 37 Hispanic Americans), 10 international. Average age 39. 538 applicants, 72% accepted, 207 enrolled. In 2007, 4 degrees awarded. *Degree requirements:* For master's, residency requirements; for doctorate, thesis/dissertation, residency requirements. *Entrance requirements:* For master's, BS in related field; for doctorate, 3 years of professional experience (preferred), minimum GPA of 3.0, master's degree. Additional exam requirements/recommendations for

Child and Family Studies

Walden University (continued)
international students: Required—TOEFL (minimum score 550 paper-based; 213 computer-based), IELTS (minimum score 7). *Application deadline:* For fall admission, 8/15 priority date for domestic and international students; for winter admission, 11/15 priority date for domestic and international students; for spring admission, 12/15 priority date for domestic and international students. Applications are processed on a rolling basis. Application fee: $50. Electronic applications accepted. *Financial support:* Fellowships, Federal Work-Study, institutionally sponsored loans, scholarships/grants, and unspecified assistantships available. Financial award applicants required to submit FAFSA. *Unit head:* Savitri Dixon-Saxon, Associate Dean, 800-925-3368, Fax: 612-338-5092. *Application contact:* Office of Student Enrollment, 866-4-WALDEN, Fax: 410-843-8780.

Wayne State University, Graduate School, Interdisciplinary Program in Infant Mental Health, Detroit, MI 48202. Offers Certificate. *Students:* Average age 41. In 2007, 2 degrees awarded. *Entrance requirements:* For degree, concurrent admission to a master's or doctoral program, or master's degree; letters of reference. Additional exam requirements/recommendations for international students: Required—TOEFL (minimum score 550 paper-based; 213 computer-based); Recommended—TWE (minimum score 6). *Application deadline:* For fall admission, 7/1 for domestic students, 6/1 for international students; for winter admission, 10/1 for international students; for spring admission, 2/1 for international students. Applications are processed on a rolling basis. Application fee: $30 ($50 for international students). Electronic applications accepted. *Expenses:* Tuition, state resident: part-time $403 per credit hour. Tuition, nonresident: part-time $890 per credit hour. *Financial support:* Career-related internships or fieldwork, institutionally sponsored loans, scholarships/grants, and tuition waivers (partial) available. *Faculty research:* Infant mental health treatment, early intervention, child abuse and neglect, readiness, attachment. *Unit head:* Dr. Ann Stacks, Director, 313-872-2408, Fax: 313-875-0947. *Application contact:* Gail Brumitt, Graduate Director, 313-872-1790, E-mail: ac8499@wayne.edu.

West Virginia University, College of Human Resources and Education, Department of Technology, Learning and Culture, Program in Child Development and Family Studies, Morgantown, WV 26506. Offers MA. Part-time programs available. *Students:* 12 full-time (all women), 3 part-time (all women); includes 1 minority (Hispanic American) Average age 30. 19 applicants, 58% accepted, 5 enrolled. In 2007, 2 degrees awarded. *Degree requirements:* For master's, thesis. *Entrance requirements:* For master's, GRE General Test, Minimum GPA 3.0, Interview. Additional exam requirements/recommendations for international students: Required—TOEFL. *Application deadline:* For spring admission, 2/15 priority date for international students. Applications are processed on a rolling basis. Application fee: $50. Electronic applications accepted. *Expenses:* Tuition, state resident: full-time $5,196; part-time $292 per credit hour. Tuition, nonresident: full-time $15,064; part-time $840 per credit hour. Tuition and fees vary according to program. *Financial support:* In 2007–08, teaching assistantships with full tuition reimbursements (averaging $8,264 per year); career-related internships or fieldwork, Federal Work-Study, institutionally sponsored loans, scholarships/grants, tuition waivers (full and partial), and unspecified assistantships also available. Financial award application deadline: 2/1; financial award applicants required to submit FAFSA. *Application contact:* Judy Martin, Secretary, 304-293-6875, Fax: 304-293-9424, E-mail: judy.martin@mail.wvu.edu.

Wheelock College, Graduate Programs, Division of Child and Family Studies, Boston, MA 02215-4176. Offers family studies (MS); family support and parent education (MS); family, culture, and society (MS). Part-time programs available. Postbaccalaureate distance learning degree programs offered (minimal on-campus study). *Degree requirements:* For master's, comprehensive exam. Electronic applications accepted. *Faculty research:* Cross-cultural studies of parenting, effects of chronic illness on families, parenting education.

Child Development

American International College, School of Arts, Education and Science, Department of Education, Springfield, MA 01109-3189. Offers administration (M Ed, CAGS); child development (MA, Ed D), including educational psychology; elementary education (M Ed, CAGS); reading (M Ed, CAGS); secondary education (M Ed, CAGS); special education (M Ed, CAGS); teaching (MAT). Part-time and evening/weekend programs available. *Faculty:* 10 full-time (6 women), 135 part-time/adjunct (82 women). *Students:* 43 full-time (33 women), 624 part-time (526 women); includes 46 minority (24 African Americans, 6 Asian Americans or Pacific Islanders, 16 Hispanic Americans), 2 international. Average age 39. In 2007, 54 master's, 2 doctorates, 7 other advanced degrees awarded. Terminal master's awarded for partial completion of doctoral program. *Degree requirements:* For master's, comprehensive exam (for some programs), thesis (for some programs), practicum; for doctorate, comprehensive exam (for some programs), thesis/dissertation; for CAGS, practicum. *Entrance requirements:* For master's, minimum B- average in undergraduate course work, BS or BA; for doctorate, GRE General Test, interview. Additional exam requirements/recommendations for international students: Required—TOEFL. *Application deadline:* For fall admission, 7/1 priority date for domestic and international students; for spring admission, 12/1 priority date for domestic and international students. Applications are processed on a rolling basis. Application fee: $50. Electronic applications accepted. *Expenses:* Tuition: Part-time $615 per credit hour. Full-time tuition and fees vary according to degree level, campus/location and program. *Financial support:* Career-related internships or fieldwork and institutionally sponsored loans available. Financial award applicants required to submit FAFSA. *Unit head:* Dr. Barbara Dautrich, Chair, 413-205-3407, Fax: 413-205-3943, E-mail: barbara.dautrich@aic.edu. *Application contact:* Barbara Z. Benoit, Director of Graduate Admissions, 413-205-3700, Fax: 413-205-3051, E-mail: barbara.benoit@aic.edu.

American International College, School of Arts, Education and Science, Department of Psychology, Springfield, MA 01109-3189. Offers child development (MA, Ed D), including educational psychology; clinical psychology (MA); forensic psychology (MS). Part-time and evening/weekend programs available. *Faculty:* 4 full-time (1 woman), 5 part-time/adjunct (2 women). *Students:* 76 full-time (65 women), 52 part-time (43 women); includes 28 minority (15 African Americans, 1 American Indian/Alaska Native, 4 Asian Americans or Pacific Islanders, 8 Hispanic Americans), 1 international. Average age 35. In 2007, 24 master's, 2 doctorates awarded. *Median time to degree:* Of those who began their doctoral program in fall 1999, 100% received their degree in 8 years or less. *Degree requirements:* For master's, comprehensive exam (for some programs), thesis (for some programs), practicum. *Entrance requirements:* For master's, minimum GPA of 3.0, BS or BA; for doctorate, GRE General Test, interview. Additional exam requirements/recommendations for international students: Required—TOEFL. *Application deadline:* For fall admission, 4/1 for domestic students, 4/15 for international students. Applications are processed on a rolling basis. Application fee: $50. Electronic applications accepted. *Expenses:* Tuition: Part-time $615 per credit hour. Full-time tuition and fees vary according to degree level, campus/location and program. *Financial support:* In 2007–08, 6 fellowships were awarded; career-related internships or fieldwork and institutionally sponsored loans also available. Financial award applicants required to submit FAFSA. *Unit head:* Dr. John DeFrancesco, Director, 413-205-3343, Fax: 413-205-3943, E-mail: john.defrancesco@aic.edu. *Application contact:* Barbara Z. Benoit, Director of Graduate Admissions, 413-205-3700, Fax: 413-205-3051, E-mail: barbara.benoit@aic.edu.

Appalachian State University, Cratis D. Williams Graduate School, Department of Family and Consumer Sciences, Boone, NC 28608. Offers child development (MA); family and consumer science education (MA). Part-time programs available. *Faculty:* 9 full-time (8 women). *Students:* 12 full-time (all women), 6 part-time (5 women); includes 2 minority (1 Asian American or Pacific Islander, 1 Hispanic American). 14 applicants, 64% accepted, 8 enrolled. In 2007, 5 master's awarded. *Degree requirements:* For master's, comprehensive exam, thesis optional. *Entrance requirements:* For master's, GRE General Test, 3 letters of recommendation. Additional exam requirements/recommendations for international students: Required—TOEFL (minimum score 550 paper-based; 230 computer-based). *Application deadline:* For fall admission, 7/1 priority date for domestic students, 1/1 for international students; for spring admission, 11/1 for domestic students, 6/1 for international students. Application fee: $50. *Expenses:* Tuition, state resident: part-time $127 per semester hour. Tuition, nonresident: part-time $597 per semester hour. Required fees: $18 per semester. *Financial support:* In 2007–08, 5 teaching assistantships (averaging $7,000 per year) were awarded; fellowships, research assistantships, career-related internships or fieldwork, scholarships/grants, and unspecified assistantships also available. Financial award application deadline: 7/1. *Faculty research:* Food antioxidants, preschool curriculum, children with special needs, family child care, FCS curriculum content. Total annual research expenditures:$78,692. *Unit head:* Dr. Sarah Jordan, Chairperson, 828-262-2661, E-mail: jordansr@appstate.edu. *Application contact:* Dr. Sammie Garner, Graduate Director, 828-262-2698, E-mail: garnersg@appstate.edu.

Arcadia University, Graduate Studies, Department of Education, Glenside, PA 19038-3295. Offers art education (M Ed, MA Ed); biology education (MA Ed); chemistry education (MA Ed); child development (CAS); computer education (M Ed, CAS); computer education 7–12 (MA Ed); early childhood education (M Ed, CAS), including individualized (M Ed), master teacher (M Ed), research in child development (M Ed); educational leadership (M Ed, CAS); educational psychology (CAS); elementary education (M Ed, CAS); English education (MA Ed); environmental education (MA Ed, CAS); history education (MA Ed); language arts (M Ed, CAS); mathematics education (M Ed, MA Ed, CAS); music education (MA Ed); psychology (MA Ed); pupil personnel services (CAS); reading (M Ed, CAS); school library science (M Ed); science education (M Ed, CAS); secondary education (M Ed, CAS); special education (M Ed, Ed D, CAS); theater arts (MA Ed); written communication (MA Ed). *Accreditation:* NASAD. Part-time and evening/weekend programs available. Postbaccalaureate distance learning degree programs offered (minimal on-campus study). Electronic applications accepted.

California State University, Los Angeles, Graduate Studies, College of Health and Human Services, Department of Child and Family Studies, Program in Child Development, Los Angeles, CA 90032-8530. Offers MA. Part-time and evening/weekend programs available. *Students:* 8 full-time (all women), 24 part-time (all women); includes 22 minority (5 African Americans, 3 Asian Americans or Pacific Islanders, 14 Hispanic Americans), 3 international. Average age 30. In 2007, 7 degrees awarded. *Degree requirements:* For master's, comprehensive exam, project or thesis. *Entrance requirements:* For master's, bachelor's degree in child development or related field. Additional exam requirements/recommendations for international students: Required—TOEFL. *Application deadline:* For fall admission, 6/30 for domestic students; for spring admission, 2/1 for domestic students. Applications are processed on a rolling basis. Application fee: $55. *Financial support:* Career-related internships or fieldwork and Federal Work-Study available. Support available to part-time students. Financial award application deadline: 3/1. *Faculty research:* Parenting, infancy, family life. *Unit head:* Dr. Anupama Joshi, Head, 323-343-5417, E-mail: ajoshi@calstatela.edu.

California State University, San Bernardino, Graduate Studies, College of Social and Behavioral Sciences, Department of Psychology, San Bernardino, CA 92407-2397. Offers child development (MA); clinical/counseling psychology (MS); general/experimental psychology (MA); industrial/organizational psychology (MS). *Faculty:* 29 full-time, 30 part-time/adjunct. *Students:* 97 full-time (74 women), 35 part-time (24 women); includes 40 minority (6 African Americans, 5 Asian Americans or Pacific Islanders, 29 Hispanic Americans), 4 international. Average age 26. 166 applicants, 37% accepted, 43 enrolled. *Entrance requirements:* For master's, minimum GPA of 3.0 in major. *Application deadline:* For fall admission, 8/31 priority date for domestic students. Application fee: $55. *Financial support:* Fellowships, research assistantships, teaching assistantships, career-related internships or fieldwork, Federal Work-Study, institutionally sponsored loans, and unspecified assistantships available. *Faculty research:* Perceptual development, human memory, psychopharmacology, psychology of women, language acquisition. *Unit head:* Dr. Joanna S. Worthley, Chair, 909-537-5570, Fax: 909-537-7003, E-mail: jworthley@csusb.edu. *Application contact:* Stacy Brooks, Graduate Secretary, 909-537-5570, Fax: 909-537-7003, E-mail: sbrooks@csusb.edu.

California State University, Stanislaus, College of Human and Health Sciences, Department of Psychology, Turlock, CA 95382. Offers behavior analysis (MS); child development (Graduate Certificate); counseling (MS); psychology (MA, MS). Part-time programs available. *Faculty:* 18. *Students:* 22 full-time (18 women), 25 part-time (20 women); includes 11 minority (1 African American, 1 Asian American or Pacific Islander, 9 Hispanic Americans). Average age 31. 15 applicants, 100% accepted, 9 enrolled. In 2007, 16 degrees awarded. *Degree requirements:* For master's, thesis. *Entrance requirements:* For master's, GRE General Test, minimum GPA of 3.0, 3 letters of reference, personal statement. Additional exam requirements/recommendations for international students: Required—TOEFL (minimum score 550 paper-based; 213 computer-based). *Application deadline:* For fall admission, 2/1 for domestic and international students. Application fee: $55. Electronic applications accepted. *Expenses:* Tuition, nonresident: full-time $10,170; part-time $339 per unit. Required fees: $3,972; $2,538 per term. $1,165 per semester. *Financial support:* Fellowships, career-related internships or fieldwork and Federal Work-Study available. Financial award application deadline: 3/2; financial award applicants required to submit FAFSA. *Faculty research:* Hedonic tone judgement, syntax and autism, early literacy assessment and native and non-native languages. *Application contact:* Dr. Gina M. Pallotta, Chair, 209-667-3386.

East Carolina University, Graduate School, College of Human Ecology, Department of Child Development and Family Relations, Greenville, NC 27858-4353. Offers child development and family relations (MS); marriage and family therapy (MS). *Accreditation:* AAMFT/COAMFTE. Part-time programs available. *Students:* 45 full-time (38 women), 17 part-time (all women); includes 13 minority (8 African Americans, 1 American Indian/Alaska Native, 1 Asian American or Pacific Islander, 3 Hispanic Americans). Average age 27. 30 applicants, 3% accepted, 1 enrolled. In 2007, 21 degrees awarded. *Degree requirements:* For master's, comprehensive exam, thesis optional. *Application deadline:* For fall admission, 1/15 for domestic students; for spring admission, 10/15 for domestic students. Applications are processed on a rolling basis. Application fee: $50. *Financial support:* In 2007–08, 18 students received support, including 10 research assistantships, 8 teaching assistantships; career-related internships or fieldwork, Federal Work-Study, institutionally sponsored loans, and scholarships/grants also available. Support available to part-time students. Financial award application deadline: 6/1. *Faculty research:* Child care quality, mental health delivery systems for children, family violence. *Unit head:* Dr. Cynthia Johnson, Chairperson, 252-328-4273, E-mail: johnsoncy@ecu.edu.

Erikson Institute, Academic Programs, Program in Child Development, Chicago, IL 60611-5627. Offers MS. *Degree requirements:* For master's, comprehensive exam, internship. *Entrance* *requirements:* For master's, 3 letters of recommendation, minimum GPA of 2.75. Additional exam requirements/recommendations for international students: Required—TOEFL.

Florida State University, Graduate Studies, College of Human Sciences, Department of Family and Child Sciences, Tallahassee, FL 32306. Offers child development (MS, PhD); family relations (MS, PhD); marriage and family therapy (PhD). *Accreditation:* AAMFT/COAMFTE. Part-time programs available. *Faculty:* 16 full-time (9 women). *Students:* 29 full-time (20 women), 38 part-time (32 women); includes 20 minority (14 African Americans, 2 Asian Americans or Pacific Islanders, 4 Hispanic Americans), 2 international. 47 applicants, 30% accepted, 10 enrolled. In 2007, 4 master's, 10 doctorates awarded. *Degree requirements:* For master's, comprehensive exam, thesis optional; for doctorate, thesis/dissertation. *Entrance requirements:* For master's and doctorate, GRE General Test, minimum GPA of 3.0. Additional exam requirements/recommendations for international students: Required—TOEFL (minimum score 80 iBT). *Application deadline:* For fall admission, 7/1 for domestic students, 5/1 for international students; for spring admission, 11/1 for domestic students, 12/1 for international students. Application fee: $30. Electronic applications accepted. *Expenses:* Tuition, state resident: part-time $248 per credit hour. Tuition, nonresident: part-time $880 per credit hour. Tuition and fees vary according to program. *Financial support:* In 2007–08, 31 students received support, including 1 fellowship (averaging $10,000 per year), research assistantships with partial tuition reimbursements available (averaging $5,000 per year), teaching assistantships with partial tuition reimbursements available (averaging $5,000 per year); career-related internships or fieldwork, Federal Work-Study, institutionally sponsored loans, scholarships/grants, and unspecified assistantships also available. Financial award application deadline: 1/15; financial award applicants required to submit FAFSA. *Faculty research:* Addictions, family therapy, sexuality, parent-child relations, adolescent development. *Unit head:* Dr. Kay Pasley, Chair, 850-644-3217, Fax: 850-644-3439, E-mail: kpasley@admin.fsu.edu. *Application contact:* Suzi Hyacinthe, Academic Support Assistant, 850-644-3217, Fax: 850-644-3439, E-mail: shyacinthe@admin.fsu.edu.

See Close-Up on page 1073.

Michigan State University, The Graduate School, College of Social Science, Department of Family and Child Ecology, East Lansing, MI 48824. Offers child development (MA); community services (MS); family and child ecology (PhD); family studies (MA); marriage and family therapy (MA); youth development (MA). *Accreditation:* AAMFT/COAMFTE (one or more programs are accredited). *Entrance requirements:* For master's, GRE General Test, minimum GPA of 3.0 in last 2 years of undergraduate course work, 3 letters of recommendation; for doctorate, GRE General Test, minimum GPA of 3.0, 3 letters of recommendation, background in behavioral sciences. Additional exam requirements/recommendations for international students: Required—TOEFL. Electronic applications accepted. *Expenses:* Tuition, state resident: part-time $379 per credit hour. Tuition, nonresident: part-time $800 per credit hour. Tuition and fees vary according to program.

Middle Tennessee State University, College of Graduate Studies, College of Education and Behavioral Science, Department of Human Sciences, Murfreesboro, TN 37132. Offers child development and family studies (MS); nutrition and food science (MS). Part-time and evening/weekend programs available. Postbaccalaureate distance learning degree programs offered. *Faculty:* 7 full-time (all women). *Students:* Average age 27. 24 applicants, 71% accepted. In 2007, 4 degrees awarded. *Degree requirements:* For master's, comprehensive exam, thesis. *Entrance requirements:* For master's, GRE or MAT. Additional exam requirements/recommendations for international students: Required—TOEFL (paper-based 525; computer-based 195; IBT 71) or IELTS (6.0). *Application deadline:* For fall admission, 8/1 priority date for domestic students. Applications are processed on a rolling basis. Application fee: $25. Electronic applications accepted. *Financial support:* In 2007–08, 5 students received support. Application deadline: 5/1. *Faculty research:* Courtship relationships, feminist methodology and epistemology in family studies, school uniforms, body fat in elderly, asynchronous distance education. *Unit head:* Dr. Dellmar Walker, Chair, 615-898-2884.

North Dakota State University, College of Graduate and Interdisciplinary Studies, College of Human Development and Education, Department of Child Development and Family Science, Fargo, ND 58105. Offers child development and family science (MS); couple and family therapy (MS); family financial planning (MS); gerontology (MS, PhD). *Accreditation:* AAMFT/COAMFTE. Part-time and evening/weekend programs available. Postbaccalaureate distance learning degree programs offered (no on-campus study). *Faculty:* 12 full-time (7 women). *Students:* 39 full-time (35 women), 14 part-time (13 women); includes 5 minority (1 African American, 2 American Indian/Alaska Native, 2 Asian Americans or Pacific Islanders), 1 international. 22 applicants, 64% accepted, 12 enrolled. In 2007, 6 degrees awarded. *Degree requirements:* For master's, thesis or alternative; for doctorate, thesis/dissertation. *Entrance requirements:* Additional exam requirements/recommendations for international students: Required—TOEFL (minimum score 525 paper-based; 197 computer-based; 71 iBT). *Application deadline:* For fall admission, 2/1 for domestic and international students; for spring admission, 10/1 for domestic and international students. Application fee: $45 ($60 for international students). *Expenses:* Tuition, state resident: full-time $5,376; part-time $224 per credit. Tuition, nonresident: full-time $14,354; part-time $598 per credit. Required fees: $962; $40 per credit. Part-time tuition and fees vary according to course load and reciprocity agreements. *Financial support:* In 2007–08, 17 students received support, including research assistantships with full tuition reimbursements available (averaging $3,000 per year), 17 teaching assistantships with full tuition reimbursements available (averaging $3,000 per year); career-related internships or fieldwork, Federal Work-Study, institutionally sponsored loans, and tuition waivers (full) also available. Financial award application deadline: 4/1. *Faculty research:* Family therapy, resilience, parenting, adolescent development, mental health. Total annual research expenditures:$333,582. *Unit head:* Dr. James Deal, Head, 701-231-7568, Fax: 701-231-9645, E-mail: jim_deal@ndsu.edu. *Application contact:* Theresa Anderson, Administrative Assistant, 701-231-8628, Fax: 701-231-9645, E-mail: theresa.anderson@ndsu.edu.

Ohio University, Graduate College, College of Health and Human Services, School of Human and Consumer Sciences, Athens, OH 45701-2979. Offers child development and family life (MS); early childhood education (MS); family studies (MS); food and nutrition (MS). Part-time programs available. *Faculty:* 13 full-time (9 women), 5 part-time/adjunct (all women). *Students:* 11 full-time (9 women), 5 part-time (4 women); includes 5 minority (2 African Americans, 3 Asian Americans or Pacific Islanders). Average age 26. 16 applicants, 69% accepted, 9 enrolled. In 2007, 8 degrees awarded. *Degree requirements:* For master's, thesis. *Entrance requirements:* For master's, GRE. Additional exam requirements/recommendations for international students: Required—TOEFL. *Application deadline:* For fall admission, 3/1 priority date for domestic students. Applications are processed on a rolling basis. Application fee: $50 ($55 for international students). Electronic applications accepted. *Financial support:* In 2007–08, 6 teaching assistantships (averaging $9,815 per year) were awarded; career-related internships or fieldwork, Federal Work-Study, institutionally sponsored loans, and unspecified assistantships also available. Financial award application deadline: 3/15. *Faculty research:* Diversity, developmentally appropriate activities, death and dying, gerontology, sexuality education. *Unit head:* Dr. V. Ann Paulins, Director, 740-593-2880, Fax: 740-593-0289, E-mail: paulins@ohio.edu.

Purdue University, Graduate School, College of Consumer and Family Sciences, Department of Child Development and Family Studies, West Lafayette, IN 47907. Offers developmental studies (MS, PhD); family studies (MS, PhD); marriage and family therapy (MS, PhD). *Accreditation:* AAMFT/COAMFTE (one or more programs are accredited). Part-time programs available. Terminal master's awarded for partial completion of doctoral program. *Degree requirements:* For master's, thesis; for doctorate, thesis/dissertation. *Entrance requirements:* For master's and doctorate, GRE General Test. Additional exam requirements/recommendations for international students: Required—TWE. Electronic applications accepted. *Faculty research:* Inclusion of children with special needs, families as learning environments, relationships in child care, work-family relations, AIDS prevention.

Rutgers, The State University of New Jersey, Camden, Graduate School of Arts and Sciences, Program in Childhood Studies, Camden, NJ 08102-1401. Offers MA, PhD.

San Diego State University, Graduate and Research Affairs, College of Education, Department of Child and Family Development, San Diego, CA 92182. Offers child development (MS). Part-time programs available. In 2007, 2 degrees awarded. *Degree requirements:* For master's, thesis. *Entrance requirements:* For master's, GRE General Test, 3 letters of recommendation, interview. Additional exam requirements/recommendations for international students: Required—TOEFL. *Application deadline:* For fall admission, 5/1 for domestic students; for spring admission, 11/1 for domestic students, 10/1 for international students. Applications are processed on a rolling basis. Application fee: $55. Electronic applications accepted. *Financial support:* Unspecified assistantships available. *Unit head:* Thomas W. Roberts, Chair, 619-594-5380, Fax: 619-594-5921, E-mail: troberts@mail.sdsu.edu. *Application contact:* Thomas W. Roberts, Chair, 619-594-5380, Fax: 619-594-5921, E-mail: troberts@mail.sdsu.edu.

Sarah Lawrence College, Graduate Studies, Program in Child Development, Bronxville, NY 10708-5999. Offers MA. Part-time programs available. *Faculty:* 7 part-time/adjunct (5 women). *Students:* 9 full-time (8 women), 9 part-time (all women); includes 4 minority (2 African Americans, 1 Asian American or Pacific Islander, 1 Hispanic American), 2 international. Average age 30. 60 applicants, 32% accepted, 9 enrolled. In 2007, 2 degrees awarded. *Degree requirements:* For master's, thesis, fieldwork. *Entrance requirements:* For master's, minimum B average in undergraduate coursework. *Application deadline:* For fall admission, 2/1 for domestic and international students. Applications are processed on a rolling basis. Application fee: $60. *Expenses:* Tuition: Part-time $1,034 per credit. Required fees: $430 per year. Tuition and fees vary according to program. *Financial support:* In 2007–08, 9 fellowships (averaging $5,501 per year) were awarded; career-related internships or fieldwork and scholarships/grants also available. Support available to part-time students. Financial award application deadline: 3/1; financial award applicants required to submit FAFSA. *Unit head:* Barbara Schecter, Director, 914-395-2247. *Application contact:* Susan Guma, Dean of Graduate Studies, 914-395-2373, E-mail: sguma@mail.slc.edu.

Southern New Hampshire University, School of Education, Manchester, NH 03106-1045. Offers business education (MS); child development (M Ed); computer technology education (Certificate); curriculum and instruction (M Ed); education (M Ed, CAS); elementary education (M Ed); general special education (Certificate); school business administrator (Certificate); secondary education (M Ed); training and development (Certificate). Part-time and evening/weekend programs available. Postbaccalaureate distance learning degree programs offered (no on-campus study). *Faculty:* 6 full-time (5 women), 16 part-time/adjunct (10 women). *Students:* Average age 35. In 2007, 52 degrees awarded. *Degree requirements:* For master's, comprehensive exam (for some programs), thesis or alternative. *Entrance requirements:* For master's, PRAXIS I, minimum GPA of 2.75. Additional exam requirements/recommendations for international students: Required—TOEFL (minimum score 550 paper-based; 213 computer-based). *Application deadline:* Applications are processed on a rolling basis. Application fee: $25. Electronic applications accepted. *Expenses: Contact institution. Financial support:* Institutionally sponsored loans available. Financial award applicants required to submit FAFSA. *Unit head:* Dr. Ellen J. Kalicki, Associate Dean, 603-668-2211 Ext. 2491, Fax: 603-629-4673, E-mail: e.kalicki@snhu.edu. *Application contact:* Scott Durand, Director of Graduate Enrollment Services, 603-644-3102 Ext. 3338, Fax: 603-644-3144, E-mail: s.durand@snhu.edu.

Texas Woman's University, Graduate School, College of Professional Education, Department of Family Sciences, Denton, TX 76201. Offers child development (MS, PhD); counseling and development (MS); early childhood education (M Ed, MA, MS, Ed D); family studies (MS, PhD); family therapy (MS, PhD). *Accreditation:* ACA (one or more programs are accredited). Part-time and evening/weekend programs available. *Students:* 100 full-time (93 women), 336 part-time (308 women); includes 134 minority (89 African Americans, 5 American Indian/Alaska Native, 11 Asian Americans or Pacific Islanders, 29 Hispanic Americans), 15 international. Average age 36. In 2007, 79 master's, 11 doctorates awarded. *Median time to degree:* Of those who began their doctoral program in fall 1999, 50% received their degree in 8 years or less. *Degree requirements:* For doctorate, comprehensive exam, thesis/dissertation. *Entrance requirements:* For master's, interview, writing sample, minimum GPA of 3.25 may be required; for doctorate, interview, writing sample may be required, GPA 3.25 last 60 hours of course work. Additional exam requirements/recommendations for international students: Required—TOEFL (minimum score 550 paper-based; 213 computer-based; 79 iBT). *Application deadline:* For fall admission, 2/15 for domestic students, 4/15 for international students; for spring admission, 9/15 for domestic students, 8/1 for international students. Applications are processed on a rolling basis. Application fee: $30 ($50 for international students). Electronic applications accepted. *Expenses:* Tuition, state resident: full-time $3,294; part-time $183 per credit. Tuition, nonresident: full-time $8,298; part-time $461 per credit. Required fees: $985; $55 per credit. Tuition and fees vary according to degree level. *Financial support:* In 2007–08, 3 research assistantships (averaging $10,746 per year), 20 teaching assistantships (averaging $10,746 per year) were awarded; career-related internships or fieldwork, Federal Work-Study, institutionally sponsored loans, scholarships/grants, traineeships, health care benefits, and unspecified assistantships also available. Support available to part-time students. Financial award application deadline: 3/1; financial award applicants required to submit FAFSA. *Faculty research:* Parenting/parent education, distance education, play therapy, family sexuality, diversity. *Unit head:* Dr. Larry LeFlore, Chair, 940-898-2685, Fax: 940-898-2676, E-mail: lleflore@twu.edu. *Application contact:* Samuel Wheeler, Assistant Director of Admissions, 940-898-3188, Fax: 940-898-3081, E-mail: wheelersr@twu.edu.

Tufts University, Graduate School of Arts and Sciences, Department of Child Development, Medford, MA 02155. Offers applied developmental psychology (PhD); child development (MA, CAGS); early childhood education (MAT). Part-time programs available. *Faculty:* 15 full-time, 8 part-time/adjunct. *Students:* 102 (89 women); includes 17 minority (7 African Americans, 5 Asian Americans or Pacific Islanders, 5 Hispanic Americans) 12 international. 123 applicants, 64% accepted, 35 enrolled. In 2007, 70 master's, 6 doctorates, 2 other advanced degrees awarded. *Degree requirements:* For master's, thesis (for some programs); for doctorate, thesis/dissertation. *Entrance requirements:* For master's and doctorate, GRE General Test. Additional exam requirements/recommendations for international students: Required—TOEFL (minimum score 550 paper-based; 213 computer-based; 80 iBT). *Application deadline:* For fall admission, 1/15 for domestic and international students. Applications are processed on a rolling basis. Application fee: $70. Electronic applications accepted. *Expenses:* Tuition: Full-time $35,052. *Financial support:* Fellowships, research assistantships with full and partial tuition reimbursements, teaching assistantships with full and partial tuition reimbursements, career-related internships or fieldwork, Federal Work-Study, scholarships/grants, and tuition waivers (partial) available. Support available to part-time students. Financial award application deadline: 1/15; financial award applicants required to submit FAFSA. *Unit head:* Ellen Pinderhughes, Chair, 617-628-5000.

Announcement: The Eliot-Pearson Department of Child Development is one of the country's leading departments serving children, youth, and families through its research, practice, and teaching. Noted for its interdisciplinary work and integration of research and practice, the department prepares students, through its MA, MAT, and PhD programs, to become leaders in a variety of fields, including education, developmental science, early intervention, advocacy, program evaluation, the arts and technology, and a variety of health-related fields. Please consult the department's Web site: http://ase.tufts.edu/epcd.

The University of Akron, Graduate School, College of Fine and Applied Arts, School of Family and Consumer Sciences, Program in Child and Family Development, Akron, OH 44325. Offers child development (MA); family development (MA). *Students:* 4 full-time (all women), 3 part-time (all women); includes 1 minority (African American), 1 international. Average age 30. 5 applicants, 60% accepted, 2 enrolled. In 2007, 1 degree awarded. *Degree requirements:* For master's, comprehensive exam, thesis optional, project or thesis. *Entrance requirements:* For master's, GRE, minimum GPA of 2.75, letters of recommendation, personal

Child Development

The University of Akron (continued)
statement of goals; interview. Additional exam requirements/recommendations for international students: Required—TOEFL (minimum score 550 paper-based; 213 computer-based; 79 iBT). *Application deadline:* For fall admission, 3/1 for domestic and international students; for spring admission, 10/1 for domestic and international students. Applications are processed on a rolling basis. Application fee: $30 ($40 for international students). Electronic applications accepted. *Expenses:* Tuition, state resident: full-time $6,164; part-time $342 per credit. Tuition, nonresident: full-time $10,575; part-time $588 per credit. Required fees: $806; $43 per credit. $12 per term. Tuition and fees vary according to course load, degree level and program. *Unit head:* Dr. Susan M. Witt, Graduate Director, 330-972-7729, E-mail: susan8@uakron.edu.

University of California, Davis, Graduate Studies, Graduate Group in Child Development, Davis, CA 95616. Offers MS. *Degree requirements:* For master's, comprehensive exam (for some programs), thesis (for some programs). *Entrance requirements:* For master's, GRE General Test, minimum GPA of 3.0. Additional exam requirements/recommendations for international students: Required—TOEFL (minimum score 550 paper-based; 213 computer-based). Electronic applications accepted. *Faculty research:* Cognitive development, socio-emotional development, early childhood.

University of La Verne, College of Education and Organizational Leadership, Department of Education, Programs in Child Development/Child Life, La Verne, CA 91750-4443. Offers child development (MS); child life (MS). Part-time programs available. *Faculty:* 16 full-time (8 women), 14 part-time/adjunct (7 women). *Students:* 40 full-time (39 women), 24 part-time (23 women); includes 34 minority (6 African Americans, 13 Asian Americans or Pacific Islanders, 15 Hispanic Americans), 1 international. Average age 30. In 2007, 26 degrees awarded. *Entrance requirements:* For master's, minimum GPA of 3.0, 3 letters of reference, writing sample. Additional exam requirements/recommendations for international students: Required—TOEFL (minimum score 550 paper-based; 213 computer-based). *Application deadline:* Applications are processed on a rolling basis. Application fee: $50. *Expenses: Contact institution.* Tuition and fees vary according to course load and program. *Financial support:* Institutionally sponsored loans, scholarships/grants, and unspecified assistantships available. Financial award application deadline: 3/2; financial award applicants required to submit FAFSA. *Unit head:* Dr. Barbara Nicoll, Chairperson, 909-593-3511 Ext. 4632, Fax: 909-392-2710, E-mail: nicollb@ulv.edu. *Application contact:* Connie Hamlow, Admissions Information Specialist, 909-593-3511 Ext. 4244, Fax: 909-392-2761, E-mail: gradadmission@ulv.edu.

University of Minnesota, Twin Cities Campus, Graduate School, College of Education and Human Development, Institute of Child Development, Minneapolis, MN 55455-0213. Offers child psychology (MA, PhD); early childhood education (M Ed, MA, PhD); school psychology (MA, PhD). *Faculty:* 20 full-time (8 women). *Students:* 85 full-time (76 women), 48 part-time (45 women); includes 12 minority (4 African Americans, 1 American Indian/Alaska Native, 3 Asian Americans or Pacific Islanders, 4 Hispanic Americans), 10 international. Average age 31. 131 applicants, 38% accepted, 38 enrolled. In 2007, 45 master's, 7 doctorates awarded. *Financial support:* In 2007–08, 26 fellowships (averaging $22,938 per year), 25 research assistantships with full tuition reimbursements (averaging $25,212 per year), 27 teaching assistantships with full tuition reimbursements (averaging $26,543 per year) were awarded. *Faculty research:* Developmental affective and cognitive neuroscience; developmental psychopathology; intervention and prevention science; social and emotional development; cognitive, language, and perceptual development. Total annual research expenditures: $2.8 million. *Unit head:* Dr. Nicki Crick, Director, 612-625-8879, Fax: 612-624-6373, E-mail: crick001@umn.edu. *Application contact:* Claudia Johnston, Information Contact, 612-624-2576, Fax: 612-624-6373, E-mail: johnstc@staff.tc.umn.edu.

The University of North Carolina at Charlotte, Graduate School, College of Education, Department of Special Education and Child Development, Charlotte, NC 28223-0001. Offers special education (M Ed, PhD), including academically gifted (M Ed), behavioral—emotional handicaps (M Ed), cross-categorical disabilities (M Ed), learning disabilities (M Ed), mental handicaps (M Ed), severe and profound handicaps (M Ed). Part-time programs available. *Faculty:* 25 full-time (18 women), 8 part-time/adjunct (all women). *Students:* 13 full-time (12 women), 42 part-time (40 women); includes 3 minority (1 African American, 2 American Indian/Alaska Native), 2 international. Average age 35. 15 applicants, 73% accepted, 10 enrolled. In 2007, 11 master's, 4 doctorates awarded. *Degree requirements:* For doctorate, comprehensive exam, dissertation, portfolio, qualifying exam. *Entrance requirements:* For master's, GRE or MAT; for doctorate, GRE or MAT, 3 letters of reference, resumé or curriculum vitae, minimum GPA of 3.5, master's degree in special education or related field, 3 years of teaching experience. Additional exam requirements/recommendations for international students: Required—TOEFL (paper-based 550; computer-based 220) or Michigan English Language Assessment Battery. *Application deadline:* For fall admission, 7/15 for domestic students, 5/1 for international students; for spring admission, 11/15 for domestic students, 10/1 for international students. Application fee: $55. *Expenses:* Tuition, state resident: full-time $2,855. Tuition, nonresident: full-time $13,062. Required fees: $1,692. *Financial support:* In 2007–08, 13 research assistantships (averaging $12,615 per year), 6 teaching assistantships (averaging $8,000 per year) were awarded. Financial award application deadline: 4/1; financial award applicants required to submit FAFSA. *Faculty research:* Transition to adulthood and self-determination, teaching reading and other academic skills to students with disabilities, alternate assessment, early intervention, preschool education. *Unit head:* David Gilmore, Unit Head, 704-687-8186, Fax: 704-687-2916. *Application contact:* Kathy B. Giddings, Director of Graduate Admissions, 704-687-3366, Fax: 704-687-3279, E-mail: agidding@uncc.edu.

The University of Tennessee at Martin, Graduate Programs, College of Agriculture and Applied Sciences, Department of Family and Consumer Sciences, Martin, TN 38238-1000. Offers dietetics (MSFCS); general family and consumer sciences (MSFCS). Part-time programs available. *Faculty:* 6. *Students:* 19 (all women) 21 applicants, 90% accepted, 8 enrolled. In 2007, 6 degrees awarded. *Degree requirements:* For master's, comprehensive exam, thesis optional. *Entrance requirements:* For master's, GRE General Test, minimum GPA of 2.5. Additional exam requirements/recommendations for international students: Required—TOEFL (minimum score 525 paper-based; 197 computer-based). *Application deadline:* For fall admission, 8/1 priority date for domestic students, 8/1 for international students; for spring admission, 1/1 for domestic and international students. Applications are processed on a rolling basis. Application fee: $30 ($50 for international students). Electronic applications accepted. *Expenses:* Tuition, state resident: full-time $2,893; part-time $323 per credit hour. Tuition, nonresident: full-time $7,913; part-time $881 per credit hour. Required fees: $220 per credit hour. *Financial support:* In 2007–08, 3 students received support. Scholarships/grants, tuition waivers (partial), and unspecified assistantships available. Financial award application deadline: 3/1. *Faculty research:* Children with developmental disabilities, regional food product development and marketing, parent education. *Unit head:* Dr. Lisa LeBleu, Coordinator, 731-881-7116, E-mail: llebleu@utm.edu. *Application contact:* Linda S. Arant, Student Services Specialist, 731-881-7012, Fax: 731-881-7499, E-mail: larant@utm.edu.

The University of Texas at Austin, Graduate School, College of Natural Sciences, Department of Human Ecology, Austin, TX 78712-1111. Offers child development and family relations (MA, PhD); nutritional sciences (MA, PhD), including nutrition (MA), nutritional sciences (PhD). *Degree requirements:* For master's, thesis; for doctorate, thesis/dissertation. *Entrance requirements:* For master's and doctorate, GRE General Test. Electronic applications accepted.

University of Wyoming, Graduate School, College of Agriculture, Department of Family and Consumer Sciences, Laramie, WY 82070. Offers early childhood development (MS); family and consumer sciences (MS); food science and human nutrition (MS). Part-time programs available. *Faculty:* 11 full-time (7 women). *Students:* 2 full-time (both women), 4 part-time (all women); includes 1 minority (American Indian/Alaska Native), 1 international. Average age 33. 8 applicants, 38% accepted, 2 enrolled. In 2007, 2 degrees awarded. *Degree requirements:* For master's, thesis, Project/Plan B. *Entrance requirements:* For master's, GRE General Test or MCAT, minimum GPA of 3.0. Additional exam requirements/recommendations for international students: Required—TOEFL (minimum score 540 paper-based; 207 computer-based; 76 iBT). *Application deadline:* For fall admission, 4/1 priority date for domestic students, 3/1 priority date for international students; for spring admission, 10/1 priority date for domestic students, 9/1 priority date for international students. Applications are processed on a rolling basis. Application fee: $50. Electronic applications accepted. *Financial support:* In 2007–08, 2 research assistantships with full tuition reimbursements (averaging $10,696 per year), 2 teaching assistantships with full tuition reimbursements (averaging $10,696 per year) were awarded; career-related internships or fieldwork, Federal Work-Study, institutionally sponsored loans, scholarships/grants, and health care benefits also available. Support available to part-time students. Financial award application deadline: 5/1; financial award applicants required to submit FAFSA. *Faculty research:* Asthma, obesity and healthy weights, nutrition concerns of children with special health care needs, food product development, food safety, postpartum health, exercise nutrition. *Unit head:* Dr. Karen C. Williams, Professor and Department Head, 307-766-4145, Fax: 307-766-5686, E-mail: fam-consci@uwyo.edu.

Virginia Polytechnic Institute and State University, Graduate School, College of Liberal Arts and Human Sciences, Department of Human Development, Blacksburg, VA 24061. Offers adult development and aging (MS, PhD); adult learning and human resource development (MS, PhD); child development (MS, PhD); family studies (MS, PhD); marriage and family therapy (MS, PhD). *Accreditation:* AAMFT/COAMFTE (one or more programs are accredited). *Entrance requirements:* For master's and doctorate, GRE General Test. Additional exam requirements/recommendations for international students: Required—TOEFL (minimum score 600 paper-based; 250 computer-based). Electronic applications accepted. *Faculty research:* Stress management, children's play, dual-career families, social cognition, relationships of elderly.

Whittier College, Graduate Programs, Department of Education and Child Development, Whittier, CA 90608-0634. Offers educational administration (MA Ed); elementary education (MA Ed); secondary education (MA Ed). Part-time and evening/weekend programs available. *Degree requirements:* For master's, thesis. *Entrance requirements:* For master's, GRE General Test, MAT, minimum GPA of 3.5, academic writing sample.

Clothing and Textiles

Academy of Art University, Graduate Program, School of Fashion, San Francisco, CA 94105-3410. Offers fashion design (MFA); fashion merchandising (MFA); fashion textiles (MFA); knitwear (MFA). Part-time programs available. Postbaccalaureate distance learning degree programs offered (no on-campus study). *Degree requirements:* For master's, thesis, final review. *Entrance requirements:* For master's, minimum GPA of 3.0, portfolio. Electronic applications accepted.

Auburn University, Graduate School, College of Human Sciences, Department of Consumer Affairs, Auburn University, AL 36849. Offers apparel and textiles (MS). Part-time programs available. *Faculty:* 11 full-time (all women), 1 part-time/adjunct (0 women). *Students:* 12 full-time (all women), 5 part-time (all women); includes 1 minority (African American), 3 international. Average age 26. 13 applicants, 85% accepted, 6 enrolled. In 2007, 4 degrees awarded. *Degree requirements:* For master's, thesis (for some programs). *Entrance requirements:* For master's, GRE General Test. *Application deadline:* For fall admission, 7/7 for domestic students; for spring admission, 11/24 for domestic students. Applications are processed on a rolling basis. Application fee: $25 ($50 for international students). Electronic applications accepted. *Financial support:* Fellowships, research assistantships, teaching assistantships, career-related internships or fieldwork and Federal Work-Study available. Support available to part-time students. Financial award application deadline: 3/15. *Faculty research:* Merchandising, consumer behavior, international marketing of textiles and apparel, apparel product development. Total annual research expenditures: $875,000. *Unit head:* Dr. Carol L. Warfield, Head, 334-844-4084, E-mail: cwarfiel@humsci.auburn.edu. *Application contact:* Dr. Joe Pittman, Interim Dean of the Graduate School, 334-844-4700.

Cornell University, Graduate School, Graduate Fields of Human Ecology, Field of Textiles, Ithaca, NY 14853-0001. Offers apparel design (MA, MPS); fiber science (MS, PhD); polymer science (MS, PhD); textile science (MS, PhD). *Faculty:* 18 full-time (7 women). *Students:* 23 full-time (16 women); includes 2 minority (1 African American, 1 Hispanic American), 13 international. Average age 29. 36 applicants, 33% accepted, 8 enrolled. In 2007, 3 master's, 3 doctorates awarded. *Degree requirements:* For master's, thesis (MA, MS), project paper (MPS); for doctorate, comprehensive exam, thesis/dissertation. *Entrance requirements:* For master's, GRE General Test, 2 letters of recommendation, portfolio (functional apparel design); for doctorate, GRE General Test, 2 letters of recommendation. Additional exam requirements/recommendations for international students: Required—TOEFL (minimum score 600 paper-based; 250 computer-based; 77 iBT). *Application deadline:* For fall admission, 3/1 for domestic students; for spring admission, 10/1 for domestic students. Application fee: $70. Electronic applications accepted. *Financial support:* In 2007–08, 21 students received support, including 2 fellowships with full tuition reimbursements available, 12 research assistantships with full tuition reimbursements available, 7 teaching assistantships with full tuition reimbursements available; institutionally sponsored loans, scholarships/grants, health care benefits, tuition waivers (full and partial), and unspecified assistantships also available. Financial award applicants required to submit FAFSA. *Faculty research:* Apparel design, consumption, mass customization, 3-D body scanning. *Unit head:* Director of Graduate Studies, 607-255-3151, Fax: 607-255-1093. *Application contact:* Graduate Field Assistant, 607-255-3151, Fax: 607-255-1093, E-mail: textiles_grad@cornell.edu.

Eastern Michigan University, Graduate School, College of Technology, School of Technology Studies, Program in Apparel, Textile Merchandising, Ypsilanti, MI 48197. Offers MS. Part-time and evening/weekend programs available. Postbaccalaureate distance learning degree programs offered (minimal on-campus study). *Students:* 4 full-time (all women), 9 part-time (8 women); includes 7 minority (5 African Americans, 2 Asian Americans or Pacific Islanders), 3 international. Average age 29. In 2007, 1 degree awarded. *Entrance requirements:* Additional exam requirements/recommendations for international students: Required—TOEFL. *Application deadline:* Applications are processed on a rolling basis. Application fee: $35. *Expenses:* Tuition, state resident: full-time $8,952; part-time $373 per credit hour. Tuition, nonresident: full-time $17,634; part-time $735 per credit hour. Required fees: $896; $34 per credit hour. Tuition and fees vary according to course level, degree level and program. *Financial support:* Fellowships, research assistantships with full tuition reimbursements, teaching assistantships with full tuition reimbursements, career-related internships or fieldwork, Federal Work-Study, institutionally sponsored loans, scholarships/grants, tuition waivers (partial), and unspecified assistantships available. Support available to part-time students. Financial award applicants required to submit FAFSA. *Unit head:* Dr. Subhas Ghosh, Coordinator, 734-487-1161, Fax: 734-487-7690, E-mail: sghosh@emich.edu.

Fashion Institute of Technology, School of Graduate Studies, Programs in Fashion and Textile Studies: History, Theory, and Museum Practice, New York, NY 10001-5992. Offers MA. *Accreditation:* NASAD. *Degree requirements:* For master's, one foreign language, thesis, internship. *Entrance requirements:* For master's, GRE General Test or GRE Subject Test, previous course work in art history and chemistry, 4 semesters of a foreign language. Additional exam requirements/recommendations for international students: Required—TOEFL (minimum score 550 paper-based; 213 computer-based). *Application deadline:* For fall admission, 2/15 priority date for domestic and international students. Applications are processed on a rolling basis. Application fee: $50. Electronic applications accepted. *Expenses:* Tuition, state resident: full-time $7,245; part-time $302 per credit. Tuition, nonresident: full-time $11,466; part-time $478 per credit. Required fees: $440; $35 per term. *Financial support:* Federal Work-Study and scholarships/grants available. Financial award applicants required to submit FAFSA. *Unit head:* Denyse Montegut, Associate Chair, 212-217-4308, Fax: 212-217-5156, E-mail: denyse_montegut@fitnyc.edu. *Application contact:* Carole deSantis, Administrative Secretary, Graduate Admissions, 212-217-4314, Fax: 212-217-5156, E-mail: carole_desantis@fitnyc.edu.

See Close-Up on page 113.

Florida State University, Graduate Studies, College of Human Sciences, Department of Textiles and Consumer Sciences, Tallahassee, FL 32306. Offers apparel product development (MS); apparel/textile product development (PhD); creative design (MS); global product development (MS); professional merchandising (MS); retail merchandising (MS, PhD); textiles (MS). Part-time programs available. *Faculty:* 12 full-time (all women). *Students:* 28 full-time (26 women), 6 part-time (4 women); includes 14 minority (9 African Americans, 2 Asian Americans or Pacific Islanders, 3 Hispanic Americans), 2 international. 44 applicants, 25% accepted, 7 enrolled. In 2007, 13 master's, 5 doctorates awarded. *Degree requirements:* For master's, thesis optional; for doctorate, thesis/dissertation. *Entrance requirements:* For master's and doctorate, GRE General Test, minimum GPA of 3.0. Additional exam requirements/recommendations for international students: Required—TOEFL (minimum score 80 iBT). *Application deadline:* For fall admission, 7/1 priority date for domestic students, 5/1 for international students; for spring admission, 11/1 for domestic students, 12/1 for international students. Applications are processed on a rolling basis. Application fee: $30. Electronic applications accepted. *Expenses:* Tuition, state resident: part-time $248 per credit hour. Tuition, nonresident: part-time $880 per credit hour. Tuition and fees vary according to program. *Financial support:* In 2007–08, 20 students received support, including 1 fellowship with partial tuition reimbursement available (averaging $10,000 per year), research assistantships with partial tuition reimbursements available (averaging $8,000 per year), 15 teaching assistantships with partial tuition reimbursements available (averaging $8,000 per year); career-related internships or fieldwork, Federal Work-Study, institutionally sponsored loans, scholarships/grants, and unspecified assistantships also available. Financial award application deadline: 1/15; financial award applicants required to submit FAFSA. *Faculty research:* Soft goods retailing, small business strategies, textile product performance, consumer behavior, accessible housing. *Unit head:* Dr. Barbara Dyer, Chair, 850-644-2498, Fax: 850-645-4673, E-mail: bdyer@fsu.edu. *Application contact:* Sue Skornia, Academic Support Assistant, 850-644-2498, Fax: 850-645-4673, E-mail: sskornia@fsu.edu.

See Close-Up on page 1073.

Iowa State University of Science and Technology, Graduate College, College of Human Sciences, Department of Apparel, Education Studies, and Hospitality Management, Program in Textiles and Clothing, Ames, IA 50011. Offers MFCS, MS, PhD. *Students:* 26 full-time (22 women), 2 part-time (1 woman); includes 1 minority (American Indian/Alaska Native), 18 international. 33 applicants, 61% accepted, 10 enrolled. In 2007, 6 master's, 4 doctorates awarded. *Degree requirements:* For master's, thesis; for doctorate, thesis/dissertation. *Entrance requirements:* For master's and doctorate, GRE General Test. Additional exam requirements/recommendations for international students: Required—TOEFL (paper-based 550; computer-based 213; iBT 79) or IELTS (6.5). *Application deadline:* For fall admission, 2/1 priority date for domestic and international students. Applications are processed on a rolling basis. Application fee: $30 ($70 for international students). Electronic applications accepted. *Financial support:* In 2007–08, 3 research assistantships with full and partial tuition reimbursements (averaging $20,572 per year), 12 teaching assistantships with full and partial tuition reimbursements (averaging $19,604 per year) were awarded; scholarships/grants also available. *Unit head:* Dr. Ann Marie Fiore, Director of Graduate Education, 515-294-9303, E-mail: amfiore@iastate.edu.

Kansas State University, Graduate School, College of Human Ecology, Department of Apparel, Textiles, and Interior Design, Manhattan, KS 66506. Offers apparel and textiles (MS). *Faculty:* 7 full-time (all women), 2 part-time/adjunct (0 women). *Students:* 17 full-time (15 women), 5 part-time (all women); includes 2 minority (1 African American, 1 Hispanic American), 1 international. Average age 25. 9 applicants, 89% accepted, 2 enrolled. In 2007, 3 degrees awarded. *Degree requirements:* For master's, thesis optional, residency. *Entrance requirements:* For master's, GRE General Test, minimum undergraduate GPA of 3.0. Additional exam requirements/recommendations for international students: Required—TOEFL (minimum score 600 paper-based; 250 computer-based). *Application deadline:* For fall admission, 2/1 priority date for domestic and international students; for spring admission, 9/1 for domestic and international students. Applications are processed on a rolling basis. Application fee: $30 ($55 for international students). Electronic applications accepted. *Financial support:* In 2007–08, 1 teaching assistantship with full tuition reimbursement (averaging $13,000 per year) was awarded; fellowships, research assistantships, career-related internships or fieldwork, Federal Work-Study, institutionally sponsored loans, and scholarships/grants also available. Support available to part-time students. Financial award application deadline: 3/1; financial award applicants required to submit FAFSA. *Faculty research:* Apparel marketing and consumer behavior, protective and functional clothing and textiles, social and environmental responsibility, apparel design, new product development. *Unit head:* Jana Hawley, Head, 785-532-1318, Fax: 785-532-3796, E-mail: hawleyj@ksu.edu. *Application contact:* Deb Brosdahl, Director, 785-532-1314, Fax: 785-532-3796, E-mail: brosdahl@ksu.edu.

Kansas State University, Graduate School, College of Human Ecology, Program in Human Ecology, Manhattan, KS 66506. Offers apparel and textiles (PhD); family life education and consultation (PhD); food service, hospitality management, and administrative dietetics (PhD); institutional management (PhD); lifespan and human development (PhD); marriage and family therapy (PhD). *Students:* 44 full-time (29 women), 23 part-time (12 women); includes 12 minority (9 African Americans, 1 American Indian/Alaska Native, 2 Asian Americans or Pacific Islanders), 14 international. 39 applicants, 54% accepted, 6 enrolled. In 2007, 14 degrees awarded. *Application deadline:* For fall admission, 2/1 priority date for domestic and international students; for spring admission, 8/1 for domestic and international students. Application fee: $30 ($55 for international students). *Unit head:* Elizabeth McCullough, Director, 785-532-2284, Fax: 785-532-3796, E-mail: lizm@ksu.edu.

North Carolina State University, Graduate School, College of Textiles, Program in Textile Technology Management, Raleigh, NC 27695. Offers PhD. *Degree requirements:* For doctorate, one foreign language, thesis/dissertation, cumulative exams. *Entrance requirements:* For doctorate, GRE or GMAT. Electronic applications accepted. *Faculty research:* Niche markets, supply chain, globalization, logistics.

The Ohio State University, Graduate School, College of Education and Human Ecology, Program in Textiles and Clothing, Columbus, OH 43210. Offers MS, PhD. *Faculty:* 8. *Students:* 8 full-time (all women), 4 part-time (all women); includes 1 minority (Asian American or Pacific Islander), 7 international. Average age 34. In 2007, 2 master's, 5 doctorates awarded. *Degree requirements:* For master's, thesis optional; for doctorate, thesis/dissertation. *Entrance requirements:* For master's and doctorate, GRE General Test. Additional exam requirements/recommendations for international students: Required—TOEFL (minimum score 577 paper-based; 233 computer-based). *Application deadline:* For fall admission, 8/15 priority date for domestic students, 7/1 priority date for international students; for winter admission, 12/1 priority date for domestic students, 11/1 priority date for international students; for spring admission, 3/1 priority date for domestic students, 2/1 priority date for international students. Applications are processed on a rolling basis. Application fee: $40 ($50 for international students). Electronic applications accepted. *Financial support:* Fellowships, research assistantships, teaching assistantships, Federal Work-Study, institutionally sponsored loans, and unspecified assistantships available. Support available to part-time students. *Unit head:* Leslie D. Stoel, Graduate Studies Committee Chair, 614-292-8594, Fax: 614-292-2581, E-mail: stoel.1@osu.edu. *Application contact:* 614-292-9444, Fax: 614-292-3895, E-mail: domestic.grad@osu.edu.

Oklahoma State University, College of Human Environmental Sciences, Department of Design, Housing and Merchandising, Stillwater, OK 74078. Offers MS, PhD. *Faculty:* 17 full-time (11 women), 4 part-time/adjunct (3 women). *Students:* 14 full-time (11 women), 22 part-time (20 women); includes 3 minority (1 African American, 1 American Indian/Alaska Native, 1 Asian American or Pacific Islander), 15 international. Average age 31. 15 applicants, 60% accepted, 4 enrolled. In 2007, 4 degrees awarded. *Degree requirements:* For master's, thesis; for doctorate, thesis/dissertation. *Entrance requirements:* For master's and doctorate, GRE or GMAT. Additional exam requirements/recommendations for international students: Required—TOEFL. *Application deadline:* For fall admission, 3/1 priority date for international students; for spring admission, 8/1 priority date for international students. Applications are processed on a rolling basis. Application fee: $40 ($75 for international students). Electronic applications accepted. *Expenses:* Tuition, state resident: full-time $4,993; part-time $148 per credit hour. Tuition, nonresident: full-time $14,755; part-time $555 per credit hour. Tuition and fees vary according to program. *Financial support:* In 2007–08, 21 research assistantships (averaging $9,120 per year), 12 teaching assistantships (averaging $9,057 per year) were awarded; career-related internships or fieldwork, Federal Work-Study, scholarships/grants, health care benefits, tuition waivers (partial), and unspecified assistantships also available. Support available to part-time students. Financial award application deadline: 3/1. *Faculty research:* Environmental sciences design, housing & merchandising, creativity and physical environment; product development, production and evaluation; experimental learning and critical thinking, technology strategies and assessment, customer expectation and satisfaction. *Unit head:* Dr. Paulette Hebert, Head, 405-744-5049.

Oregon State University, Graduate School, College of Health and Human Sciences, Department of Design and Human Environment, Corvallis, OR 97331. Offers MA, MAIS, MS, PhD. *Faculty:* 13 full-time (all women), 1 (woman) part-time/adjunct. *Students:* 29 full-time (27 women), 2 part-time (both women); includes 2 minority (both Asian Americans or Pacific Islanders), 11 international. Average age 30. In 2007, 4 master's, 2 doctorates awarded. Terminal master's awarded for partial completion of doctoral program. *Degree requirements:* For master's, thesis or alternative; for doctorate, thesis/dissertation. *Entrance requirements:* For master's and doctorate, GRE General Test, minimum GPA of 3.0 in last 90 hours. Additional exam requirements/recommendations for international students: Required—TOEFL. *Application deadline:* For fall admission, 2/1 priority date for domestic students. Application fee: $50. *Expenses:* Tuition, state resident: full-time $9,126; part-time $338 per credit. Tuition, nonresident: full-time $14,796; part-time $548 per credit. Required fees: $1,447. *Financial support:* Research assistantships, teaching assistantships, career-related internships or fieldwork, Federal Work-Study, and institutionally sponsored loans available. Support available to part-time students. Financial award application deadline: 2/1. *Unit head:* Dr. Leslie D. Burns, Chair, 541-737-0983, Fax: 541-737-0993, E-mail: leslie.burns@oregonstate.edu. *Application contact:* Dr. Elaine Pedersen, Chair, Graduate Committee, 541-737-0984, Fax: 541-737-0993, E-mail: pedersee@oregonstate.edu.

Philadelphia University, School of Engineering and Textiles, Program in Fashion-Apparel Studies, Philadelphia, PA 19144-5497. Offers MS. Part-time programs available. *Entrance requirements:* For master's, GRE or GMAT, minimum GPA of 2.8. Additional exam requirements/recommendations for international students: Required—TOEFL (minimum score 550 paper-based; 213 computer-based; 79 iBT). Electronic applications accepted.

Purdue University, Graduate School, College of Consumer and Family Sciences, Department of Consumer Sciences and Retailing, West Lafayette, IN 47907. Offers consumer behavior (MS, PhD); family and consumer economics (MS, PhD); retail management (MS, PhD); textile science (MS, PhD). Part-time programs available. *Degree requirements:* For master's, thesis; for doctorate, thesis/dissertation. *Entrance requirements:* For master's and doctorate, GMAT or GRE General Test. Additional exam requirements/recommendations for international students: Required—TOEFL. Electronic applications accepted. *Faculty research:* Family financial resources, retail management and patronage, chemical analysis of textile dyes and finishes.

South Dakota State University, Graduate School, College of Family and Consumer Sciences, Department of Apparel Merchandising and Interior Design, Brookings, SD 57007. Offers MFCS. Part-time and evening/weekend programs available. Postbaccalaureate distance learning degree programs offered. *Entrance requirements:* Additional exam requirements/recommendations for international students: Required—TOEFL (minimum score 550 paper-based; 213 computer-based; 79 iBT). *Faculty research:* Rural internet shopping, professional development in apparel merchandising, gender, aesthetics.

The University of Akron, Graduate School, College of Fine and Applied Arts, School of Family and Consumer Sciences, Program in Clothing, Textiles and Interiors, Akron, OH 44325. Offers MA. *Students:* 4 full-time (3 women), 1 (woman) part-time; includes 1 minority (African American) Average age 31. 1 applicant, 100% accepted, 1 enrolled. In 2007, 4 degrees awarded. *Degree requirements:* For master's, comprehensive exam, thesis optional, thesis or project. *Entrance requirements:* For master's, GRE, minimum GPA of 2.75, letters of recommendation, personal statement of goals, interview. Additional exam requirements/recommendations for international students: Required—TOEFL (minimum score 550 paper-based; 213 computer-based; 79 iBT). *Application deadline:* For fall admission, 3/1 for domestic and international students; for spring admission, 10/1 for domestic and international students. Applications are processed on a rolling basis. Application fee: $30 ($40 for international students). Electronic applications accepted. *Expenses:* Tuition, state resident: full-time $6,164; part-time $342 per credit. Tuition, nonresident: full-time $10,575; part-time $588 per credit. Required fees: $806; $43 per credit. $12 per term. Tuition and fees vary according to course load, degree level and program. *Unit head:* Dr. Sandra Buckland, Associate Professor, 330-972-8090, E-mail: skb@uakron.edu.

The University of Alabama, Graduate School, College of Human Environmental Sciences, Department of Clothing, Textiles, and Interior Design, Tuscaloosa, AL 35487. Offers MSHES. *Faculty:* 3 full-time (all women). *Students:* 1 (woman) full-time. Average age 23. 1 applicant, 0% accepted. In 2007, 4 degrees awarded. *Degree requirements:* For master's, comprehensive exam, thesis optional. *Entrance requirements:* For master's, GRE General Test or MAT, minimum GPA of 3.0. *Application deadline:* For fall admission, 7/6 for domestic students. Applications are processed on a rolling basis. Application fee: $30. *Expenses:* Tuition, state resident: full-time $5,700. Tuition, nonresident: full-time $16,518. *Financial support:* In 2007–08, 1 research assistantship with full tuition reimbursement (averaging $8,100 per year), 2 teaching assistantships with full tuition reimbursements (averaging $8,100 per year) were awarded; fellowships, career-related internships or fieldwork, Federal Work-Study, and scholarships/grants also available. Financial award application deadline: 3/15. *Faculty research:* Archeological textiles, textile science, material culture, social psychology, international trade. *Unit head:* Dr. Carolyn Callis, Chair and Associate Professor, 205-348-6176, Fax: 205-348-0022, E-mail: ccallis@ches.ua.edu.

University of Alberta, Faculty of Graduate Studies and Research, Department of Human Ecology, Edmonton, AB T6G 2E1, Canada. Offers family ecology and practice (M Sc, PhD);

Clothing and Textiles

University of Alberta (continued)
textiles and clothing (M Sc, MA, PhD). Postbaccalaureate distance learning degree programs offered (no on-campus study). *Degree requirements:* For master's, thesis (for some programs); for doctorate, comprehensive exam, thesis/dissertation. *Entrance requirements:* For master's and doctorate, minimum GPA of 7.0 on a 9.0 scale. Additional exam requirements/recommendations for international students: Required—TOEFL (minimum score 580 paper-based; 237 computer-based). *Faculty research:* Families and aging, family and child poverty, paid and unpaid work of families, textiles and clothing, parent-child relationships.

University of California, Davis, Graduate Studies, Graduate Group in Textiles, Davis, CA 95616. Offers MS. *Degree requirements:* For master's, comprehensive exam (for some programs), thesis (for some programs). *Entrance requirements:* For master's, GRE General Test, minimum GPA of 3.0. Additional exam requirements/recommendations for international students: Required—TOEFL (minimum score 550 paper-based; 213 computer-based). Electronic applications accepted. *Faculty research:* Fiber science, social psychology, consumer psychology, chemical and physical properties of fibrous and polymeric materials.

University of Georgia, Graduate School, College of Family and Consumer Sciences, Department of Textiles, Merchandising, and Interiors, Athens, GA 30602. Offers historic costume and textiles (MS); merchandising/international trade (MS); textile analysis (PhD); textile chemical processes (PhD); textile products and standards (PhD); textile science (MS). *Faculty:* 9 full-time (6 women). *Students:* 17 full-time (14 women), 1 part-time; includes 1 minority (African American), 10 international. 20 applicants, 50% accepted, 8 enrolled. In 2007, 5 master's, 4 doctorates awarded. *Degree requirements:* For master's, thesis; for doctorate, thesis/dissertation. *Entrance requirements:* For master's and doctorate, GRE General Test. *Application deadline:* For fall admission, 7/1 priority date for domestic students; for spring admission, 11/15 for domestic students. Application fee: $50. Electronic applications accepted. *Financial support:* Fellowships, research assistantships, teaching assistantships, unspecified assistantships available. *Unit head:* Dr. Patricia Hunt-Hurst, Department Head, 706-542-4891, Fax: 706-542-4862, E-mail: phunt@fcs.uga.edu.

University of Kentucky, Graduate School, College of Design, Program in Interior Design, Merchandising, and Textiles, Lexington, KY 40506-0032. Offers MAIDM, MSIDM. *Faculty:* 8 full-time (7 women). *Students:* 13 full-time (11 women), 3 part-time (all women); includes 2 minority (1 African American, 1 Hispanic American), 2 international. Average age 25. 16 applicants, 38% accepted, 5 enrolled. In 2007, 5 degrees awarded. *Degree requirements:* For master's, comprehensive exam, thesis optional. *Entrance requirements:* For master's, GRE General Test, minimum undergraduate GPA of 2.75. Additional exam requirements/recommendations for international students: Required—TOEFL (minimum score 550 paper-based; 213 computer-based). *Application deadline:* For fall admission, 7/17 priority date for domestic students, 2/1 priority date for international students; for spring admission, 12/13 priority date for domestic students, 6/15 priority date for international students. Application fee: $50 ($65 for international students). Electronic applications accepted. *Expenses:* Tuition, state resident: part-time $437 per credit hour. Tuition, nonresident: part-time $931 per credit hour. *Financial support:* In 2007–08, 11 students received support, including 3 research assistantships with full tuition reimbursements available (averaging $4,803 per year), 8 teaching assistantships with full tuition reimbursements available (averaging $4,803 per year); fellowships with full tuition reimbursements available, Federal Work-Study, scholarships/grants, traineeships, health care benefits, tuition waivers (partial), and unspecified assistantships also available. Support available to part-time students. Financial award application deadline: 3/15; financial award applicants required to submit FAFSA. *Faculty research:* Interior design, apparel merchandising, textile evaluation, creativity in design, social-psychological aspects of dress and interiors. *Unit head:* Dr. Elizabeth Easter, Director of Graduate Studies, 859-257-7777, Fax: 859-257-1275, E-mail: hetliz@uky.edu. *Application contact:* Dr. Brian Jackson, Senior Associate Dean, 859-257-4667, Fax: 859-257-4676, E-mail: brian.jackson@uky.edu.

University of Manitoba, Faculty of Graduate Studies, Faculty of Human Ecology, Department of Clothing and Textiles, Winnipeg, MB R3T 2N2, Canada. Offers M Sc. *Degree requirements:* For master's, thesis.

University of Minnesota, Twin Cities Campus, Graduate School, College of Design, Department of Design, Housing, and Apparel, Minneapolis, MN 55455-0213. Offers apparel (MA, MS, PhD); design communication (MA, MS, PhD); housing studies (MA, MS, PhD, Postbaccalaureate Certificate); interactive design (MFA); interior design (MA, MS, PhD). Part-time programs available. *Faculty:* 24 full-time (18 women), 5 part-time/adjunct (4 women). *Students:* 41 full-time (34 women), 28 part-time (21 women); includes 3 minority (1 African American, 1 Asian American or Pacific Islander, 1 Hispanic American), 20 international. 37 applicants, 54% accepted, 15 enrolled. In 2007, 3 master's, 8 doctorates awarded. *Median time to degree:* Of those who began their doctoral program in fall 1999, 100% received their degree in 8 years or less. *Degree requirements:* For master's and Postbaccalaureate Certificate, comprehensive exam, thesis (for some programs); for doctorate, comprehensive exam, thesis/dissertation. *Entrance requirements:* For master's, GRE General Test, minimum GPA of 3.0 (preferred), portfolio, 3 letters of recommendation; for doctorate, GRE General Test, minimum GPA of 3.0 (preferred), portfolio, 3 letters of recommendation, writing sample; for Postbaccalaureate Certificate, GRE General Test, minimum GPA of 3.0 (preferred). Additional exam requirements/recommendations for international students: Required—TOEFL (minimum score 550 paper-based; 213 computer-based; 79 iBT). *Application deadline:* For fall admission, 1/15 for domestic and international students. Application fee: $55 ($75 for international students). Electronic applications accepted. *Financial support:* In 2007–08, 34 students received support, including 13 research assistantships with partial tuition reimbursements available (averaging $12,652 per year), 24 teaching assistantships with partial tuition reimbursements available (averaging $12,652 per year); Federal Work-Study, institutionally sponsored loans, and unspecified assistantships also available. Financial award application deadline: 2/1; financial award applicants required to submit FAFSA. *Faculty research:* Housing policy and community development; consumer behavior; interactive design; design history; social, cultural, and behavioral issues related to designed environments. Total annual research expenditures: $320,058. *Unit head:* Becky Love Yust, Professor and Department Head, 612-624-7461, Fax: 612-624-2750, E-mail: byust@che.umn.edu. *Application contact:* Charleen Klarquist, Student Support Services Assistant, 612-626-1219, Fax: 612-624-2750, E-mail: dhagrad@umn.edu.

University of Missouri–Columbia, Graduate School, College of Human Environmental Science, Department of Textile and Apparel Management, Columbia, MO 65211. Offers MA, MS. *Entrance requirements:* For master's, GRE General Test, minimum GPA of 3.0. Additional exam requirements/recommendations for international students: Required—TOEFL (minimum score 550 paper-based; 213 computer-based).

University of Nebraska–Lincoln, Graduate College, College of Education and Human Sciences, Department of Textiles, Clothing and Design, Lincoln, NE 68588. Offers MA, MS. Part-time programs available. Postbaccalaureate distance learning degree programs offered (minimal on-campus study). *Degree requirements:* For master's, thesis optional. *Entrance requirements:* For master's, GRE General Test. Additional exam requirements/recommendations for international students: Required—TOEFL (minimum score 550 paper-based; 213 computer-based). Electronic applications accepted. *Faculty research:* Merchandising, textile science, fiber arts, textile history, quilt studies.

University of North Texas, Robert B. Toulouse School of Graduate Studies, School of Merchandising and Hospitality Management, Denton, TX 76203. Offers hospitality management (MS); merchandising (MS). Part-time programs available. Postbaccalaureate distance learning degree programs offered (no on-campus study). *Faculty:* 22 full-time (15 women). *Students:* 28 full-time (25 women), 17 part-time (16 women); includes 13 minority (6 African Americans, 4 Asian Americans or Pacific Islanders, 3 Hispanic Americans), 13 international. Average age 28. 42 applicants, 52% accepted, 10 enrolled. In 2007, 13 degrees awarded. *Degree requirements:* For master's, comprehensive exam, thesis or alternative. *Entrance requirements:* For master's, GRE General Test or GMAT, minimum GPA of 2.8, course work in major area, essay, 3 references, resumè. Additional exam requirements/recommendations for international students: Required—proof of English language proficiency required for non-native English speakers; Recommended—TOEFL (minimum score 550 paper-based; 213 computer-based). *Application deadline:* For fall admission, 7/15 for domestic students; for spring admission, 11/15 for domestic students. Application fee: $50 ($75 for international students). *Financial support:* In 2007–08, 1 fellowship (averaging $10,000 per year), 5 teaching assistantships (averaging $6,300 per year) were awarded; research assistantships, career-related internships or fieldwork, Federal Work-Study, and institutionally sponsored loans also available. Financial award application deadline: 4/1. *Faculty research:* Management, hospitality, merchandising, globalization, consumer behavior and experiences. *Unit head:* Dr. Judith C. Forney, Dean, 940-565-2436, Fax: 940-565-4348, E-mail: jforney@smhm.unt.edu. *Application contact:* Dr. Lisa Kennon, Coordinator, 940-565-4757, Fax: 940-565-4348, E-mail: kennon@smhm.unt.edu.

University of Rhode Island, Graduate School, College of Human Science and Services, Department of Textiles, Fashion Merchandising and Design, Kingston, RI 02881. Offers MS. In 2007, 6 degrees awarded. *Entrance requirements:* For master's, GRE. *Application deadline:* For fall admission, 4/15 priority date for domestic students; for spring admission, 11/15 for domestic students. Applications are processed on a rolling basis. Application fee: $35. *Expenses:* Tuition, state resident: full-time $6,936; part-time $385 per credit. Tuition, nonresident: full-time $19,044; part-time $1,058 per credit. Required fees: $1,508; $48 per credit. $30 per semester. One-time fee: $80 part-time. *Unit head:* Dr. Linda Welters, Chair, 401-874-4525.

The University of Tennessee, Graduate School, College of Education, Health and Human Sciences, Department of Consumer and Industry Services Management, Program in Consumer Services Management, Knoxville, TN 37996. Offers retail and consumer sciences (MS); textile science (MS). Part-time programs available. *Degree requirements:* For master's, thesis or alternative. *Entrance requirements:* For master's, GRE General Test, minimum GPA of 2.7. Additional exam requirements/recommendations for international students: Required—TOEFL. Electronic applications accepted.

The University of Tennessee, Graduate School, College of Education, Health and Human Sciences, Program in Human Ecology, Knoxville, TN 37996. Offers child and family studies (PhD); community health (PhD); nutrition science (PhD); retailing and consumer sciences (PhD); textile science (PhD). *Degree requirements:* For doctorate, thesis/dissertation. *Entrance requirements:* For doctorate, GRE General Test, minimum GPA of 2.7. Additional exam requirements/recommendations for international students: Required—TOEFL. Electronic applications accepted.

Virginia Polytechnic Institute and State University, Graduate School, College of Liberal Arts and Human Sciences, Department of Apparel, Housing, and Resource Management, Blacksburg, VA 24061. Offers apparel business and economics (MS, PhD); apparel product design and analysis (MS, PhD); apparel quality analysis (MS, PhD); consumer studies (MS, PhD); family financial management (MS, PhD); household equipment (MS, PhD); housing (MS, PhD); interior design (MS, PhD); resource management (MS, PhD). *Degree requirements:* For master's, thesis; for doctorate, thesis/dissertation. *Entrance requirements:* For master's and doctorate, GRE General Test. Additional exam requirements/recommendations for international students: Required—TOEFL (minimum score 550 paper-based; 213 computer-based). Electronic applications accepted. *Faculty research:* Housing for elderly, affordable housing, household time use, phosphate laundry study, economic well-living.

Washington State University, Graduate School, College of Agricultural, Human, and Natural Resource Sciences, Department of Apparel, Merchandising, Design, and Textiles, Pullman, WA 99164. Offers apparel, merchandising, design and textiles (MA); interdisciplinary (PhD); interior design (MA). *Faculty:* 8. *Students:* 7 full-time (all women), 2 part-time (both women); includes 1 minority (African American), 2 international. Average age 33. 7 applicants, 43% accepted, 2 enrolled. In 2007, 6 degrees awarded. *Degree requirements:* For master's, comprehensive exam (for some programs), thesis, oral exam; for doctorate, comprehensive exam, thesis/dissertation. *Entrance requirements:* For master's, GRE, minimum GPA of 3.0, 3 writing samples, 3 letters of recommendation, portfolio. Additional exam requirements/recommendations for international students: Required—TOEFL. *Application deadline:* For fall admission, 5/1 priority date for domestic students, 3/1 for international students; for spring admission, 11/1 for domestic students, 7/1 for international students. Applications are processed on a rolling basis. Application fee: $50. Electronic applications accepted. *Financial support:* In 2007–08, 9 students received support, including research assistantships with full and partial tuition reimbursements available (averaging $13,917 per year), 5 teaching assistantships with full and partial tuition reimbursements available (averaging $13,056 per year); career-related internships or fieldwork, Federal Work-Study, institutionally sponsored loans, and scholarships/grants also available. Financial award application deadline: 4/1; financial award applicants required to submit FAFSA. *Faculty research:* Product development, design theory, cultural diversity, computer design accessibility. *Unit head:* Dr. Karen K. Leonas, Department Chair, 509-335-6766, Fax: 509-355-7299, E-mail: amid@wsu.edu. *Application contact:* Graduate School Admissions, 800-GRADWSU, Fax: 509-335-1949, E-mail: gradsch@wsu.edu.

Consumer Economics

California State University, Long Beach, Graduate Studies, College of Health and Human Services, Department of Family and Consumer Sciences, Long Beach, CA 90840. Offers family and consumer sciences (MA); nutritional sciences (MS), including nutritional sciences/dietetics and food administration. Part-time and evening/weekend programs available. *Faculty:* 18 full-time (13 women), 29 part-time/adjunct (25 women). *Students:* 29 full-time (25 women), 44 part-time (37 women); includes 29 minority (1 African American, 17 Asian Americans or Pacific Islanders, 11 Hispanic Americans). Average age 33. *Degree requirements:* For master's, comprehensive exam or thesis. *Entrance requirements:* For master's, GRE (MS), minimum GPA of 3.0. *Application deadline:* For fall admission, 5/1 for domestic students; for spring admission, 11/1 for domestic students. Applications are processed on a rolling basis. Application fee: $55. Electronic applications accepted. *Financial support:* Federal Work-Study, institutionally sponsored loans, and scholarships/grants available. Financial award application deadline: 3/2. *Faculty research:* School uniforms, consumer complaining behavior, nutrition and fitness education and behavior change, curriculum change, teaching experience of interns.

Unit head: Dr. M Sue Stanley, Chair, 562-985-4484, Fax: 562-985-4414, E-mail: stanleym@csulb.edu. *Application contact:* Dr. Mary Jacob, Graduate Coordinator, 562-985-4484, Fax: 562-985-4414, E-mail: marjacob@csulb.edu.

Colorado State University, Graduate School, College of Applied Human Sciences, Department of Design and Merchandising, Fort Collins, CO 80523-0015. Offers MS. Part-time programs available. Postbaccalaureate distance learning degree programs offered (no on-campus study). *Faculty:* 13 full-time (9 women), 1 (woman) part-time/adjunct. *Students:* 9 full-time (6 women), 16 part-time (15 women); includes 4 minority (1 African American, 1 American Indian/Alaska Native, 2 Asian Americans or Pacific Islanders), 4 international. Average age 31. 25 applicants, 48% accepted, 6 enrolled. In 2007, 4 degrees awarded. *Degree requirements:* For master's, thesis. *Entrance requirements:* For master's, GRE General Test, minimum GPA of 3.0, resumé, portfolio (if applicable to area of study). Additional exam requirements/recommendations for international students: Required—TOEFL (minimum score 550 paper-based; 213 computer-based). *Application deadline:* For fall admission, 2/1 priority date for domestic students, 2/15 priority date for international students; for spring admission, 8/1 priority date for domestic students, 7/15 priority date for international students. Applications are processed on a rolling basis. Application fee: $50. Electronic applications accepted. *Expenses:* Tuition, state resident: full-time $4,887; part-time $272 per credit. Tuition, nonresident: full-time $16,425; part-time $913 per credit. Required fees: $1,379; $75 per credit. *Financial support:* In 2007–08, 11 students received support, including 2 research assistantships with partial tuition reimbursements available (averaging $6,362 per year), 9 teaching assistantships with partial tuition reimbursements available (averaging $6,381 per year); fellowships, career-related internships or fieldwork, Federal Work-Study, institutionally sponsored loans, scholarships/grants, traineeships, and unspecified assistantships also available. Support available to part-time students. Financial award application deadline: 1/15; financial award applicants required to submit FAFSA. *Faculty research:* Consumer and textile end use, apparel design, consumer behavior, interior design, historic costume and textiles. Total annual research expenditures: $216,966. *Unit head:* Dr. Mary A. Littrell, Head, 970-491-5811, Fax: 970-491-4855, E-mail: mlittrel@cahs.colostate.edu. *Application contact:* Dr. Jen Ogle, Graduate Coordinator, 970-491-3794, Fax: 970-491-4376, E-mail: ogle@cahs.colostate.edu.

Cornell University, Graduate School, Graduate Fields of Human Ecology, Field of Policy Analysis and Management, Ithaca, NY 14853-0001. Offers consumer policy (PhD); evaluation (PhD); family and social welfare policy (PhD); health administration (MHA); health management and policy (PhD). *Faculty:* 32 full-time (13 women). *Students:* 57 full-time (28 women); includes 16 minority (4 African Americans, 9 Asian Americans or Pacific Islanders, 3 Hispanic Americans), 8 international. Average age 26. 105 applicants, 45% accepted, 26 enrolled. In 2007, 19 master's, 5 doctorates awarded. *Degree requirements:* For master's, thesis; for doctorate, thesis/dissertation. *Entrance requirements:* For master's, GRE General Test or GMAT, 2 letters of recommendation; for doctorate, GRE General Test, 2 letters of recommendation. Additional exam requirements/recommendations for international students: Required—TOEFL (minimum score 550 paper-based; 213 computer-based; 77 iBT). *Application deadline:* For fall admission, 1/15 for domestic students. Application fee: $70. Electronic applications accepted. *Financial support:* In 2007–08, 23 students received support, including 3 fellowships with full and partial tuition reimbursements available, 9 research assistantships with full and partial tuition reimbursements available, 11 teaching assistantships with full and partial tuition reimbursements available; institutionally sponsored loans, scholarships/grants, health care benefits, tuition waivers (full and partial), and unspecified assistantships also available. Financial award applicants required to submit FAFSA. *Faculty research:* Health policy, family policy, social welfare policy, program evaluation, consumer policy. *Unit head:* Director of Graduate Studies, 607-255-7772. *Application contact:* Graduate Field Assistant, 607-255-7772, Fax: 607-255-4071, E-mail: pam_phd@cornell.edu.

Eastern Illinois University, Graduate School, Lumpkin College of Business and Applied Sciences, School of Family and Consumer Sciences, Charleston, IL 61920-3099. Offers dietetics (MS); family and consumer sciences (MS). Part-time programs available. *Faculty:* 12 full-time (10 women). *Students:* 34 full-time (33 women), 29 part-time (all women). In 2007, 40 degrees awarded. *Degree requirements:* For master's, comprehensive exam. *Application deadline:* For fall admission, 7/31 priority date for domestic students. Applications are processed on a rolling basis. Application fee: $30. *Expenses:* Tuition, state resident: part-time $218 per hour. Tuition, nonresident: part-time $654 per hour. *Financial support:* In 2007–08, 2 research assistantships with tuition reimbursements (averaging $7,200 per year), 6 teaching assistantships with tuition reimbursements (averaging $7,200 per year) were awarded; career-related internships or fieldwork also available. *Unit head:* Dr. James Painter, Chairperson, 217-581-6076, Fax: 217-581-6090, E-mail: jepainter@eiu.edu. *Application contact:* Dr. Frances Murphy, Coordinator, 217-581-6997, Fax: 217-581-6090, E-mail: flmurphy@eiu.edu.

Florida State University, Graduate Studies, College of Human Sciences, Department of Textiles and Consumer Sciences, Tallahassee, FL 32306. Offers apparel product development (MS); apparel/textile product development (PhD); creative design (MS); global product development (MS); professional merchandising (MS); retail merchandising (MS, PhD); textiles (MS). Part-time programs available. *Faculty:* 12 full-time (all women). *Students:* 28 full-time (26 women), 6 part-time (4 women); includes 14 minority (9 African Americans, 2 Asian Americans or Pacific Islanders, 3 Hispanic Americans), 2 international. 44 applicants, 25% accepted, 7 enrolled. In 2007, 13 master's, 5 doctorates awarded. *Degree requirements:* For master's, thesis optional; for doctorate, thesis/dissertation. *Entrance requirements:* For master's and doctorate, GRE General Test, minimum GPA of 3.0. Additional exam requirements/recommendations for international students: Required—TOEFL (minimum score 80 iBT). *Application deadline:* For fall admission, 7/1 priority date for domestic students, 5/1 for international students; for spring admission, 11/1 for domestic students, 12/1 for international students. Applications are processed on a rolling basis. Application fee: $30. Electronic applications accepted. *Expenses:* Tuition, state resident: part-time $248 per credit hour. Tuition, nonresident: part-time $880 per credit hour. Tuition and fees vary according to program. *Financial support:* In 2007–08, 20 students received support, including 1 fellowship with partial tuition reimbursement available (averaging $10,000 per year), research assistantships with partial tuition reimbursements available (averaging $8,000 per year), 15 teaching assistantships with partial tuition reimbursements available (averaging $8,000 per year); career-related internships or fieldwork, Federal Work-Study, institutionally sponsored loans, scholarships/grants, and unspecified assistantships also available. Financial award application deadline: 1/15; financial award applicants required to submit FAFSA. *Faculty research:* Soft goods retailing, small business strategies, textile product performance, consumer behavior, accessible housing. *Unit head:* Dr. Barbara Dyer, Chair, 850-644-2498, Fax: 850-645-4673, E-mail: bdyer@fsu.edu. *Application contact:* Sue Skornia, Academic Support Assistant, 850-644-2498, Fax: 850-645-4673, E-mail: sskornia@fsu.edu.

See Close-Up on page 1073.

Indiana State University, School of Graduate Studies, College of Arts and Sciences, Department of Family and Consumer Sciences, Terre Haute, IN 47809-1401. Offers dietetics (MS); family and consumer sciences education (MS); inter-area option (MS). *Accreditation:* ADtA. Part-time programs available. *Faculty:* 5 full-time (4 women). *Students:* 12 full-time (all women), 7 part-time (6 women); includes 4 minority (3 African Americans, 1 Asian American or Pacific Islander), 2 international. Average age 33. 13 applicants, 100% accepted, 5 enrolled. In 2007, 9 degrees awarded. *Degree requirements:* For master's, thesis optional. *Application deadline:* For fall admission, 7/1 priority date for domestic students; for spring admission, 11/1 priority date for domestic students. Applications are processed on a rolling basis. Application fee: $35. Electronic applications accepted. *Expenses:* Tuition, state resident: full-time $7,056; part-time $294 per semester hour. Tuition, nonresident: full-time $14,016; part-time $584 per semester hour. Required fees: $175 per semester. *Financial support:* In 2007–08, 2 research assistantships with partial tuition reimbursements (averaging $7,000 per year) were awarded; teaching assistantships, tuition waivers (partial) also available. Financial award application deadline: 3/1; financial award applicants required to submit FAFSA. *Unit head:* Dr. Frederica Kramer, Chairperson, 812-237-3297.

Iowa State University of Science and Technology, Graduate College, College of Human Sciences, Department of Apparel, Education Studies, and Hospitality Management, Program in Family and Consumer Sciences Education and Studies, Ames, IA 50011. Offers M Ed, MS, PhD. *Students:* 6 full-time (5 women), 36 part-time (33 women); includes 5 minority (all African Americans), 2 international. 17 applicants, 82% accepted, 14 enrolled. In 2007, 5 master's, 4 doctorates awarded. *Degree requirements:* For master's, thesis (for some programs); for doctorate, thesis/dissertation. *Entrance requirements:* For master's and doctorate, GRE General Test. Additional exam requirements/recommendations for international students: Required—TOEFL (paper-based 550; computer-based 213; iBT 80) or IELTS (6.5). *Application deadline:* For fall admission, 1/15 priority date for domestic and international students. Applications are processed on a rolling basis. Application fee: $30 ($70 for international students). Electronic applications accepted. *Financial support:* In 2007–08, 1 research assistantship with full and partial tuition reimbursement (averaging $17,700 per year), 1 teaching assistantship with full and partial tuition reimbursement (averaging $17,700 per year) were awarded; scholarships/grants also available. *Unit head:* Dr. Cheryl O. Hausafus, Director of Graduate Education, 515-294-5307, E-mail: haus@iastate.edu.

North Dakota State University, College of Graduate and Interdisciplinary Studies, College of Human Development and Education, Department of Child Development and Family Science, Fargo, ND 58105. Offers child development and family science (MS); couple and family therapy (MS); family financial planning (MS); gerontology (MS, PhD). *Accreditation:* AAMFT/COAMFTE. Part-time and evening/weekend programs available. Postbaccalaureate distance learning degree programs offered (no on-campus study). *Faculty:* 12 full-time (7 women). *Students:* 39 full-time (35 women), 14 part-time (13 women); includes 5 minority (1 African American, 2 American Indian/Alaska Native, 2 Asian Americans or Pacific Islanders), 1 international. 22 applicants, 64% accepted, 12 enrolled. In 2007, 6 degrees awarded. *Degree requirements:* For master's, thesis or alternative; for doctorate, thesis/dissertation. *Entrance requirements:* Additional exam requirements/recommendations for international students: Required—TOEFL (minimum score 525 paper-based; 197 computer-based; 71 iBT). *Application deadline:* For fall admission, 2/1 for domestic and international students; for spring admission, 10/1 for domestic and international students. Application fee: $45 ($60 for international students). *Expenses:* Tuition, state resident: full-time $5,376; part-time $224 per credit. Tuition, nonresident: full-time $14,354; part-time $598 per credit. Required fees: $962; $40 per credit. Part-time tuition and fees vary according to course load and reciprocity agreements. *Financial support:* In 2007–08, 17 students received support, including research assistantships with full tuition reimbursements available (averaging $3,000 per year), 17 teaching assistantships with full tuition reimbursements available (averaging $3,000 per year); career-related internships or fieldwork, Federal Work-Study, institutionally sponsored loans, and tuition waivers (full) also available. Financial award application deadline: 4/1. *Faculty research:* Family therapy, resilience, parenting, adolescent development, mental health. Total annual research expenditures:$333,582. *Unit head:* Dr. James Deal, Head, 701-231-7568, Fax: 701-231-9645, E-mail: jim_deal@ndsu.edu. *Application contact:* Theresa Anderson, Administrative Assistant, 701-231-8628, Fax: 701-231-9645, E-mail: theresa.anderson@ndsu.edu.

The Ohio State University, Graduate School, College of Education and Human Ecology, Program in Family Resource Management, Columbus, OH 43210. Offers MS, PhD. *Faculty:* 10. *Students:* 7 full-time (5 women), 4 part-time (3 women); includes 1 minority (American Indian/Alaska Native), 9 international. Average age 30. In 2007, 1 master's, 1 doctorate awarded. *Degree requirements:* For master's, thesis optional; for doctorate, thesis/dissertation. *Entrance requirements:* For master's and doctorate, GRE General Test. Additional exam requirements/recommendations for international students: Required—TOEFL (minimum score 577 paper-based; 233 computer-based). *Application deadline:* For fall admission, 8/15 priority date for domestic students, 7/1 priority date for international students; for winter admission, 12/1 priority date for domestic students, 11/1 priority date for international students; for spring admission, 3/1 priority date for domestic students, 2/1 priority date for international students. Applications are processed on a rolling basis. Application fee: $40 ($50 for international students). Electronic applications accepted. *Financial support:* Fellowships, research assistantships, teaching assistantships, Federal Work-Study and institutionally sponsored loans available. Support available to part-time students. *Unit head:* Catherine P. Montalto, Graduate Studies Committee Chair, 614-292-4571, Fax: 614-292-2581, E-mail: montalto.2@osu.edu. *Application contact:* 614-292-9444, Fax: 614-292-3895, E-mail: domestic.grad@osu.edu.

Purdue University, Graduate School, College of Consumer and Family Sciences, Department of Consumer Sciences and Retailing, West Lafayette, IN 47907. Offers consumer behavior (MS, PhD); family and consumer economics (MS, PhD); retail management (MS, PhD); textile science (MS, PhD). Part-time programs available. *Degree requirements:* For master's, thesis; for doctorate, thesis/dissertation. *Entrance requirements:* For master's and doctorate, GMAT or GRE General Test. Additional exam requirements/recommendations for international students: Required—TOEFL. Electronic applications accepted. *Faculty research:* Family financial resources, retail management and patronage, chemical analysis of textile dyes and finishes.

State University of New York at Oswego, Graduate Studies, School of Education, Department of Vocational Teacher Preparation, Oswego, NY 13126. Offers agriculture (MS Ed); business and marketing (MS Ed); family and consumer sciences (MS Ed); health careers (MS Ed); technical education (MS Ed); trade education (MS Ed). *Accreditation:* NCATE. Part-time and evening/weekend programs available. *Faculty:* 5 full-time, 5 part-time/adjunct. *Students:* 23 full-time (10 women), 47 part-time (22 women); includes 6 minority (3 African Americans, 2 Asian Americans or Pacific Islanders, 1 Hispanic American). Average age 40. 33 applicants, 100% accepted. In 2007, 35 degrees awarded. *Degree requirements:* For master's, thesis or alternative. *Entrance requirements:* Additional exam requirements/recommendations for international students: Required—TOEFL (minimum score 560 paper-based; 220 computer-based). *Application deadline:* For fall admission, 4/1 for domestic students; for spring admission, 10/1 for domestic students. Applications are processed on a rolling basis. Application fee: $50. *Expenses:* Tuition, state resident: full-time $6,900; part-time $288 per credit. Tuition, nonresident: full-time $10,920; part-time $455 per credit. Required fees: $607; $32 per credit. $225 per term. Tuition and fees vary according to degree level. *Financial support:* In 2007–08, 4 students received support, including 2 fellowships (averaging $5,100 per year), 2 teaching assistantships (averaging $3,800 per year); career-related internships or fieldwork, Federal Work-Study, institutionally sponsored loans, health care benefits, and unspecified assistantships also available. Support available to part-time students. Financial award application deadline: 4/1; financial award applicants required to submit FAFSA. *Unit head:* Dr. Margaret Martin, Chair, 315-312-2480.

Texas Tech University, Graduate School, College of Human Sciences, Department of Applied and Professional Studies, Lubbock, TX 79409. Offers family and consumer sciences education (MS, PhD); marriage and family therapy (MS, PhD); personal financial planning (MS); JD/MS. Part-time programs available. *Faculty:* 13 full-time (8 women). *Students:* 66 full-time (28 women), 47 part-time (27 women); includes 14 minority (4 African Americans, 2 American Indian/Alaska Native, 2 Asian Americans or Pacific Islanders, 6 Hispanic Americans), 5 international. Average age 30. 120 applicants, 67% accepted, 26 enrolled. In 2007, 18 master's, 11 doctorates awarded. Terminal master's awarded for partial completion of doctoral program. *Degree requirements:* For master's, thesis (for some programs); for doctorate, thesis/dissertation. *Entrance requirements:* For master's and doctorate, GRE General Test. Additional exam requirements/recommendations for international students: Required—TOEFL (minimum score 550 paper-based; 213 computer-based). *Application deadline:* For fall admission, 3/1 priority date for international students; for spring admission, 11/1 priority date for international students. Applications are processed on a rolling basis. Application fee: $50 ($60 for international students). *Expenses:* Tuition, state resident: part-time $373 per credit hour. Tuition, nonresident: part-time $651 per credit hour. Tuition and fees vary according to program. *Financial support:* In 2007–08, 77 students received support, including 20 research assistant-

Consumer Economics

Texas Tech University (continued)
ships with partial tuition reimbursements available (averaging $13,531 per year), 33 teaching assistantships with partial tuition reimbursements available (averaging $13,583 per year); career-related internships or fieldwork, Federal Work-Study, institutionally sponsored loans, and tuition waivers (partial) also available. Support available to part-time students. Financial award application deadline: 4/15; financial award applicants required to submit FAFSA. *Faculty research:* Functional interior design applications for special needs populations; retirement planning and income/expenditure patterns for teachers; surface design, purchase, and consumption of leather products; financial counseling outcome and assessment of college students; multicultural housing environments and behavior correlations. Total annual research expenditures: $939,769. *Unit head:* Dr. Sterling Shumway, Chair, 806-742-5050, Fax: 806-742-5033, E-mail: sterling.shumway@ttu.edu.

Texas Tech University, Graduate School, College of Human Sciences, Department of Design, Program in Personal Financial Planning, Lubbock, TX 79409. Offers PhD. Part-time programs available. *Students:* 18 full-time (6 women), 11 part-time (3 women); includes 6 minority (all African Americans), 5 international. Average age 35. 22 applicants, 86% accepted, 6 enrolled. In 2007, 4 degrees awarded. *Degree requirements:* For doctorate, thesis/dissertation. *Entrance requirements:* For doctorate, GRE General Test, GMAT. Additional exam requirements/recommendations for international students: Required—TOEFL (minimum score 550 paper-based; 213 computer-based). *Application deadline:* For fall admission, 3/1 priority date for international students; for spring admission, 11/1 priority date for international students. Applications are processed on a rolling basis. Application fee: $50 ($60 for international students). *Expenses:* Tuition, state resident: part-time $373 per credit hour. Tuition, nonresident: part-time $651 per credit hour. Tuition and fees vary according to program. *Financial support:* Research assistantships, teaching assistantships, career-related internships or fieldwork, Federal Work-Study, and institutionally sponsored loans available. Support available to part-time students. Financial award application deadline: 4/15; financial award applicants required to submit FAFSA. *Faculty research:* Financial risk tolerance, determinants of success on CFP exam, personal financial wellness, retirement procedures, benchmarks for measuring financial well-being of families. *Unit head:* Dr. Vickie Hampton, Associate Chair of Graduate Programs, 806-742-5050 Ext. 272, Fax: 806-742-5033, E-mail: vickie.hampton@ttu.edu.

Université Laval, Faculty of Agricultural and Food Sciences, Department of Agricultural Economics and Consumer Sciences, Program in Consumer Sciences, Québec, QC G1K 7P4, Canada. Offers Diploma. Part-time programs available. *Entrance requirements:* For degree, knowledge of French and English. Electronic applications accepted.

The University of Alabama, Graduate School, College of Human Environmental Sciences, Department of Consumer Sciences, Tuscaloosa, AL 35487. Offers MS. Part-time and evening/weekend programs available. Postbaccalaureate distance learning degree programs offered (minimal on-campus study). *Faculty:* 4 full-time (2 women). *Students:* 2 full-time (both women), 1 international. Average age 29. 4 applicants, 25% accepted, 1 enrolled. In 2007, 2 degrees awarded. *Degree requirements:* For master's, thesis. *Entrance requirements:* For master's, GRE or MAT. Additional exam requirements/recommendations for international students: Required—TOEFL. *Application deadline:* Applications are processed on a rolling basis. Application fee: $30. *Expenses:* Tuition, state resident: full-time $5,700. Tuition, nonresident: full-time $16,518. *Financial support:* In 2007–08, 2 students received support, including 1 research assistantship (averaging $8,100 per year), 1 teaching assistantship (averaging $8,100 per year); fellowships also available. Financial award application deadline: 3/15. *Faculty research:* Consumer economics, financial planning.

The University of Arizona, Graduate College, College of Agriculture and Life Sciences, School of Family and Consumer Sciences, Division of Family Studies and Human Development, Tucson, AZ 85721. Offers family and consumer sciences education (MS); family studies and human development (PhD). In 2007, 3 master's, 5 doctorates awarded. Terminal master's awarded for partial completion of doctoral program. *Entrance requirements:* For master's, GRE General Test, minimum undergraduate GPA of 3.0, personal resumé, personal statement, 3 letters of recommendation. Additional exam requirements/recommendations for international students: Required—TOEFL. *Application deadline:* For fall admission, 1/15 for domestic and international students. Applications are processed on a rolling basis. Application fee: $50. *Unit head:* Dr. Angela R. Taylor, Division Chair, 520-621-7129, Fax: 520-621-3401, E-mail: artaylor@u.arizona.edu. *Application contact:* Mary Helen Scott, Administrative Assistant, 520-621-5884, Fax: 520-621-3401, E-mail: mhscott@ag.arizona.edu.

The University of Arizona, Graduate College, College of Agriculture and Life Sciences, School of Family and Consumer Sciences, Division of Retailing and Consumer Sciences, Tucson, AZ 85721. Offers MS, PhD. Part-time programs available. In 2007, 2 master's, 1 doctorate awarded. Terminal master's awarded for partial completion of doctoral program. *Median time to degree:* Of those who began their doctoral program in fall 1999, 100% received their degree in 8 years or less. *Degree requirements:* For master's, thesis; for doctorate, thesis/dissertation. *Entrance requirements:* For master's and doctorate, GRE General Test or GMAT, minimum GPA of 3.0. Additional exam requirements/recommendations for international students: Required—TOEFL. *Application deadline:* Applications are processed on a rolling basis. Application fee: $50. Electronic applications accepted. *Financial support:* In 2007–08, 9 students received support; research assistantships with partial tuition reimbursements available, teaching assistantships with partial tuition reimbursements available, career-related internships or fieldwork, institutionally sponsored loans, scholarships/grants, traineeships, health care benefits, and unspecified assistantships available. *Application contact:* Cinda Van Winkle, Administrative Assistant, 520-621-3346, E-mail: cvw@ag.arizona.edu.

University of Georgia, Graduate School, College of Family and Consumer Sciences, Department of Housing and Consumer Economics, Athens, GA 30602. Offers MS, PhD. Part-time programs available. *Faculty:* 13 full-time (6 women). *Students:* 17 full-time (10 women), 5 part-time (3 women); includes 8 minority (6 African Americans, 1 Asian American or Pacific Islander, 1 Hispanic American), 2 international. 16 applicants, 63% accepted, 5 enrolled. In 2007, 2 master's, 2 doctorates awarded. *Degree requirements:* For master's, thesis; for doctorate, thesis/dissertation. *Entrance requirements:* For master's and doctorate, GRE General Test. Additional exam requirements/recommendations for international students: Required—TOEFL (minimum score 575 paper-based; 230 computer-based). *Application deadline:* For fall admission, 7/1 for domestic students, 2/1 for international students; for spring admission, 11/15 for domestic students. Application fee: $50. Electronic applications accepted. *Financial support:* In 2007–08, 10 students received support; fellowships, research assistantships, teaching assistantships, unspecified assistantships available. Financial award application deadline: 2/1. *Faculty research:* Demographics, consumer decision making, home ownership counseling, financial management, economics of divorce and poverty. *Unit head:* Dr. Anne L. Sweaney, Interim Head, 706-542-4856, E-mail: asweaney@fcs.uga.edu. *Application contact:* Dr. Teresa Mauldin, Graduate Coordinator, 706-542-4854, Fax: 706-583-0313, E-mail: tmauldin@fcs.uga.edu.

University of Guelph, Graduate Program Services, College of Management and Economics, Department of Marketing and Consumer Studies, Guelph, ON N1G 2W1, Canada. Offers M Sc. *Faculty:* 16 full-time (6 women). *Students:* 31 full-time (19 women); includes 7 minority (1 African American, 4 Asian Americans or Pacific Islanders, 2 Hispanic Americans), 1 international. Average age 25. In 2007, 5 degrees awarded. *Degree requirements:* For master's, thesis. *Entrance requirements:* For master's, GMAT or GRE General Test, minimum B average during previous 2 years of course work. Additional exam requirements/recommendations for international students: Required—TOEFL (minimum score 575 paper-based; 213 computer-based). *Application deadline:* For fall admission, 4/1 priority date for domestic and international students. Applications are processed on a rolling basis. Application fee: $85. Electronic applications accepted. *Financial support:* In 2007–08, fellowships (averaging $2,000 per year), teaching assistantships (averaging $8,800 per year) were awarded; research assistantships. Financial award application deadline: 4/4. *Faculty research:* Marketing, quality management, consumer economics, housing and real estate management, problem gambling. *Unit head:* Dr. Paulette Padanyi, Chair, 519-824-4120 Ext. 53774, Fax: 519-823-1964, E-mail: ppadanyi@uoguelph.ca. *Application contact:* Dr. May Aung, Graduate Coordinator, 519-824-4120 Ext. 58737, Fax: 519-823-1964, E-mail: maung@uoguelph.ca.

University of Idaho, College of Graduate Studies, College of Agricultural and Life Sciences, Margaret Ritchie School of Family and Consumer Sciences, Moscow, ID 83844-3183. Offers MS. *Students:* 20. In 2007, 5 degrees awarded. *Degree requirements:* For master's, thesis. *Entrance requirements:* For master's, minimum GPA of 2.8. *Application deadline:* For fall admission, 8/1 for domestic students; for spring admission, 12/15 for domestic students. Application fee: $55 ($60 for international students). *Financial support:* Research assistantships, teaching assistantships available. Financial award application deadline: 2/15. *Unit head:* Dr. Sandra Evenson, Interim Chair, 208-885-6546.

University of Illinois at Urbana–Champaign, Graduate College, College of Agricultural, Consumer and Environmental Sciences, Department of Agricultural and Consumer Economics, Champaign, IL 61820. Offers MS, PhD. *Faculty:* 35 full-time (10 women), 1 (woman) part-time/adjunct. *Students:* 49 full-time (22 women), 18 part-time (6 women); includes 6 minority (2 African Americans, 2 Asian Americans or Pacific Islanders, 2 Hispanic Americans), 38 international. 83 applicants, 28% accepted, 12 enrolled. In 2007, 5 master's, 8 doctorates awarded. *Degree requirements:* For master's, thesis; for doctorate, thesis/dissertation. *Entrance requirements:* For master's, minimum GPA of 3.0. *Application deadline:* Applications are processed on a rolling basis. Application fee: $60 ($75 for international students). Electronic applications accepted. *Financial support:* In 2007–08, 10 fellowships, 48 research assistantships, 26 teaching assistantships were awarded; tuition waivers (full and partial) also available. Financial award application deadline: 2/15. *Unit head:* Robert J. Hauser, Head, 217-333-8859, Fax: 217-333-5538, E-mail: r-hauser@uiuc.edu. *Application contact:* Linda Foste, Administrative Assistant, 217-333-1830, Fax: 217-244-7088, E-mail: l-foste@uiuc.edu.

University of Missouri–Columbia, Graduate School, College of Human Environmental Science, Department of Personal Financial Planning, Columbia, MO 65211. Offers MS. *Entrance requirements:* For master's, GRE General Test, minimum GPA of 3.0. Additional exam requirements/recommendations for international students: Required—TOEFL (minimum score 550 paper-based; 213 computer-based).

University of Nebraska–Lincoln, Graduate College, College of Education and Human Sciences, Department of Family and Consumer Sciences, Lincoln, NE 68588. Offers family and consumer sciences (MS); human resources and family sciences (PhD). *Accreditation:* AAMFT/COAMFTE (one or more programs are accredited). Postbaccalaureate distance learning degree programs offered. *Degree requirements:* For master's, thesis optional. *Entrance requirements:* For master's, GRE. Additional exam requirements/recommendations for international students: Required—TOEFL (minimum score 550 paper-based; 213 computer-based). Electronic applications accepted. *Faculty research:* Marriage and family therapy, child development/early childhood education, family financial management.

University of South Carolina, The Graduate School, College of Hospitality, Retail, and Sport Management, Department of Retailing, Columbia, SC 29208. Offers MR. Part-time programs available. *Faculty:* 7 full-time (4 women). *Students:* 12 full-time (10 women); includes 3 minority (all African Americans), 2 international. Average age 25. 6 applicants, 33% accepted, 2 enrolled. In 2007, 9 degrees awarded. *Degree requirements:* For master's, comprehensive exam, Internship or Thesis. *Entrance requirements:* For master's, GMAT or GRE General Test, minimum GPA of 3.0. Additional exam requirements/recommendations for international students: Required—TOEFL (minimum score 80 iBT). *Application deadline:* For fall admission, 7/1 priority date for domestic students, 5/1 priority date for international students; for spring admission, 11/1 priority date for domestic students, 10/1 priority date for international students. Applications are processed on a rolling basis. Application fee: $40. Electronic applications accepted. *Expenses:* Tuition, state resident: part-time $440 per hour. Tuition, nonresident: part-time $936 per hour. Required fees: $17 per hour. Tuition and fees vary according to program. *Financial support:* In 2007–08, 1 student received support, including 1 teaching assistantship with partial tuition reimbursement available (averaging $2,500 per year); research assistantships with partial tuition reimbursements available, career-related internships or fieldwork, health care benefits, and unspecified assistantships also available. Financial award application deadline: 7/1. *Faculty research:* Retail technology, retail strategy, international retailing. *Unit head:* Dr. Richard Clodfelter, Chair, 803-777-4846, Fax: 803-777-4357, E-mail: clodfelt@mailbox.sc.edu. *Application contact:* Dr. Rodney C. Runyan, Graduate Director, 803-777-4295, Fax: 803-777-4357, E-mail: runyanrc@sc.edu.

The University of Tennessee, Graduate School, College of Education, Health and Human Sciences, Department of Consumer and Industry Services Management, Program in Consumer Services Management, Knoxville, TN 37996. Offers retail and consumer sciences (MS); textile science (MS). Part-time programs available. *Degree requirements:* For master's, thesis or alternative. *Entrance requirements:* For master's, GRE General Test, minimum GPA of 2.7. Additional exam requirements/recommendations for international students: Required—TOEFL. Electronic applications accepted.

The University of Tennessee, Graduate School, College of Education, Health and Human Sciences, Program in Human Ecology, Knoxville, TN 37996. Offers child and family studies (PhD); community health (PhD); nutrition science (PhD); retailing and consumer sciences (PhD); textile science (PhD). *Degree requirements:* For doctorate, thesis/dissertation. *Entrance requirements:* For doctorate, GRE General Test, minimum GPA of 2.7. Additional exam requirements/recommendations for international students: Required—TOEFL. Electronic applications accepted.

University of Utah, The Graduate School, College of Social and Behavioral Science, Department of Family and Consumer Studies, Salt Lake City, UT 84112-1107. Offers MS. *Faculty:* 18 full-time (10 women), 1 (woman) part-time/adjunct. *Students:* 9 full-time (7 women), 4 part-time (2 women), 2 international. Average age 31. 15 applicants, 33% accepted, 5 enrolled. In 2007, 5 degrees awarded. *Degree requirements:* For master's, thesis optional. *Entrance requirements:* For master's, GRE General Test, minimum undergraduate GPA of 3.0. Additional exam requirements/recommendations for international students: Required—TOEFL (minimum score 500 paper-based; 173 computer-based). *Application deadline:* For spring admission, 3/1 for domestic students. Application fee: $45 ($65 for international students). *Financial support:* Research assistantships with full tuition reimbursements, teaching assistantships with full tuition reimbursements available. Financial award application deadline: 2/15. *Faculty research:* Social, physical and economic contexts of families and communities. Total annual research expenditures: $14,858. *Unit head:* Dr. Cheryl Wright, Chair, 801-581-4431, E-mail: cheryl.wright@fcs.utah.edu. *Application contact:* Barbara Brown, Graduate Director, 801-581-7111, E-mail: barbara.brown@fcs.utah.edu.

University of Wisconsin–Madison, Graduate School, School of Human Ecology, Program in Consumer Behavior and Family Economics, Madison, WI 53706-1380. Offers MS, PhD. *Degree requirements:* For master's, thesis; for doctorate, comprehensive exam, thesis/dissertation. *Entrance requirements:* For master's and doctorate, GRE General Test, 3 letters of recommendation. Additional exam requirements/recommendations for international students: Required—TOEFL (minimum score 580 paper-based; 237 computer-based). Electronic applications accepted. *Faculty research:* Economic well-being of elderly, finance, financial planning, health care policy, consumer behavior.

University of Wyoming, Graduate School, College of Agriculture, Department of Family and Consumer Sciences, Laramie, WY 82070. Offers early childhood development (MS); family and consumer sciences (MS); food science and human nutrition (MS). Part-time programs available. *Faculty:* 11 full-time (7 women). *Students:* 2 full-time (both women), 4 part-time (all women); includes 1 minority (American Indian/Alaska Native), 1 international. Average age 33. 8 applicants, 38% accepted, 2 enrolled. In 2007, 2 degrees awarded. *Degree requirements:* For master's, thesis, Project/Plan B. *Entrance requirements:* For master's, GRE General Test or MCAT, minimum GPA of 3.0. Additional exam requirements/recommendations for international students: Required—TOEFL (minimum score 540 paper-based; 207 computer-based; 76 iBT). *Application deadline:* For fall admission, 4/1 priority date for domestic students, 3/1 priority date for international students; for spring admission, 10/1 priority date for domestic students, 9/1 priority date for international students. Applications are processed on a rolling basis. Application fee: $50. Electronic applications accepted. *Financial support:* In 2007–08, 2 research assistantships with full tuition reimbursements (averaging $10,696 per year), 2 teaching assistantships with full tuition reimbursements (averaging $10,696 per year) were awarded; career-related internships or fieldwork, Federal Work-Study, institutionally sponsored loans, scholarships/grants, and health care benefits also available. Support available to part-time students. Financial award application deadline: 5/1; financial award applicants required to submit FAFSA. *Faculty research:* Asthma, obesity and healthy weights, nutrition concerns of children with special health care needs, food product development, food safety, postpartum health, exercise nutrition. *Unit head:* Dr. Karen C. Williams, Professor and Department Head, 307-766-4145, Fax: 307-766-5686, E-mail: fam-consci@uwyo.edu.

Utah State University, School of Graduate Studies, College of Agriculture, Department of Agricultural Systems Technology and Education, Logan, UT 84322. Offers agricultural systems technology (MS), including agricultural extension education, agricultural mechanization, international agricultural extension, secondary and postsecondary agricultural education; family and consumer sciences education (MS). Part-time programs available. Postbaccalaureate distance learning degree programs offered (minimal on-campus study). *Degree requirements:* For master's, comprehensive exam (for some programs), thesis (for some programs). *Entrance requirements:* For master's, GRE General Test, MAT, BS in agricultural education, agricultural extension, or related agricultural or science discipline; minimum GPA of 3.0. Additional exam requirements/recommendations for international students: Required—TOEFL. *Faculty research:* Extension and adult education; structures and environment; low-input agriculture; farm safety, systems, and mechanizations.

Virginia Polytechnic Institute and State University, Graduate School, College of Liberal Arts and Human Sciences, Department of Apparel, Housing, and Resource Management, Blacksburg, VA 24061. Offers apparel business and economics (MS, PhD); apparel product design and analysis (MS, PhD); apparel quality analysis (MS, PhD); consumer studies (MS, PhD); family financial management (MS, PhD); household equipment (MS, PhD); housing (MS, PhD); interior design (MS, PhD); resource management (MS, PhD). *Degree requirements:* For master's, thesis; for doctorate, thesis/dissertation. *Entrance requirements:* For master's and doctorate, GRE General Test. Additional exam requirements/recommendations for international students: Required—TOEFL (minimum score 550 paper-based; 213 computer-based). Electronic applications accepted. *Faculty research:* Housing for elderly, affordable housing, household time use, phosphate laundry study, economic well-living.

Gerontology

Abilene Christian University, Graduate School, College of Arts and Sciences, Department of Sociology and Family Studies, Program in Gerontology, Abilene, TX 79699-9100. Offers MS, Certificate. *Faculty:* 3 part-time/adjunct (0 women). *Students:* 2 full-time (both women), 2 part-time (both women); includes 3 minority (1 African American, 1 Asian American or Pacific Islander, 1 Hispanic American). 1 applicant, 100% accepted, 1 enrolled. In 2007, 1 degree awarded. *Degree requirements:* For master's, comprehensive exam. *Entrance requirements:* For master's, GRE General Test or MAT. *Application deadline:* For fall admission, 4/1 priority date for domestic students; for spring admission, 11/1 for domestic students. Applications are processed on a rolling basis. Application fee: $40 ($45 for international students). Electronic applications accepted. *Expenses:* Tuition: Full-time $13,368; part-time $557 per hour. Required fees: $700; $34 per hour. $10 per semester. Tuition and fees vary according to degree level and campus/location. *Financial support:* Career-related internships or fieldwork and Federal Work-Study available. Support available to part-time students. Financial award application deadline: 4/1. *Unit head:* Dr. Charlie D. Pruett, Director of the Center for Aging, 325-674-2350, Fax: 325-674-6804, E-mail: pruettc@acu.edu. *Application contact:* William Horn, Graduate Admissions Counselor, 325-674-2656, Fax: 325-674-6717, E-mail: gradinfo@acu.edu.

Adelphi University, School of Education, Program in Physical Education and Human Performance Science, Garden City, NY 11530-0701. Offers aging (Certificate); physical/educational human performance science (MA). Part-time and evening/weekend programs available. *Students:* 47 full-time (22 women), 97 part-time (47 women); includes 12 minority (5 African Americans, 1 Asian American or Pacific Islander, 6 Hispanic Americans), 2 international. Average age 28. In 2007, 80 degrees awarded. *Degree requirements:* For master's, internship. *Entrance requirements:* For master's, 3 letters of recommendation, resumé. Additional exam requirements/recommendations for international students: Required—TOEFL (minimum score 550 paper-based; 213 computer-based). *Application deadline:* Applications are processed on a rolling basis. Application fee: $50. Electronic applications accepted. *Financial support:* In 2007–08, 4 research assistantships with full and partial tuition reimbursements (averaging $1,500 per year) were awarded; fellowships, teaching assistantships, career-related internships or fieldwork, Federal Work-Study, institutionally sponsored loans, and tuition waivers (full) also available. Support available to part-time students. Financial award application deadline: 2/15; financial award applicants required to submit FAFSA. *Faculty research:* Physical education for the handicapped, sport sociology, sport pedagogy. *Unit head:* Dr. Stephen J. Virgilio, Chair, 516-877-4262, E-mail: virgilio@adelphi.edu. *Application contact:* Christine Murphy, Director of Admissions, 516-877-3050, Fax: 516-877-3039, E-mail: graduateadmissions@adelphi.edu.

Adler School of Professional Psychology, Programs in Psychology, Chicago, IL 60601-7203. Offers art therapy (Certificate); clinical hypnosis (Certificate); clinical psychology (Psy D); counseling psychology (MACP); counseling psychology/art therapy (MACAT); gerontology (MAGP); marriage and family counseling (MAMFC); marriage and family therapy (Certificate); organizational psychology (MAO); substance abuse counseling (MASAC, Certificate); Psy D/Certificate; Psy D/MACAT; Psy D/MACP; Psy D/MAMFC; Psy D/MASAC. *Accreditation:* APA. Part-time and evening/weekend programs available. Terminal master's awarded for partial completion of doctoral program. *Degree requirements:* For master's, thesis or alternative, oral exam, practicum; for doctorate, thesis/dissertation, clinical exam, internship, oral exam, practicum, written qualifying exam. *Entrance requirements:* For master's, 12 semester hours in psychology, minimum GPA of 3.0; for doctorate, 18 semester hours in psychology, minimum GPA of 3.25; for Certificate, appropriate master's or doctoral degree.

See Close-Up on page 1363.

Alliant International University–Los Angeles, California School of Professional Psychology, Program in Marital and Family Therapy, Alhambra, CA 91803-1360. Offers biofeedback (MA); chemical dependency (MA); gerontology (MA); Latin American family therapy (MA). *Accreditation:* AAMFT/COAMFTE.

See Close-Up on page 1373.

Appalachian State University, Cratis D. Williams Graduate School, Department of Sociology and Social Work, Boone, NC 28608. Offers gerontology (MA); social work (MSW). Part-time programs available. *Faculty:* 12 full-time (5 women). *Students:* 22 full-time (19 women), 34 part-time (25 women); includes 2 minority (1 African American, 1 Hispanic American). Average age 23. 49 applicants, 88% accepted, 29 enrolled. In 2007, 9 master's awarded. *Degree requirements:* For master's, comprehensive exam, thesis optional. *Entrance requirements:* For master's, GRE General Test. Additional exam requirements/recommendations for international students: Required—TOEFL (minimum score 570 paper-based; 230 computer-based). *Application deadline:* For fall admission, 7/1 for domestic students, 1/1 for international students; for spring admission, 11/1 for domestic students, 6/1 for international students. Applications are processed on a rolling basis. Application fee: $50. *Expenses:* Tuition, state resident: part-time $127 per semester hour. Tuition, nonresident: part-time $597 per semester hour. Required fees: $18 per semester. *Financial support:* In 2007–08, 8 research assistantships (averaging $3,500 per year), 5 teaching assistantships (averaging $7,000 per year) were awarded; fellowships with partial tuition reimbursements, career-related internships or fieldwork, Federal Work-Study, scholarships/grants, and unspecified assistantships also available. Financial award application deadline: 4/1. *Faculty research:* Aging, criminology, deviance. Total annual research expenditures: $700,841. *Unit head:* Dr. Ed Folts, Chairman, 828-262-2293, E-mail: foltswe@appstate.edu.

Arizona State University at the West campus, College of Human Services, School of Aging and Lifespan Development, Phoenix, AZ 85069-7100. Offers aging and lifespan development (MS); gerontology (Certificate). Part-time and evening/weekend programs available. *Faculty:* 1 (woman) full-time, 2 part-time/adjunct (both women). *Students:* Average age 56. *Degree requirements:* For master's, applied project. *Entrance requirements:* For master's, 3 letters of recommendation, personal statement/essay; for Certificate, 2 letters of recommendation. Additional exam requirements/recommendations for international students: Required—TOEFL (minimum score 550 paper-based; 213 computer-based; 83 iBT). *Application deadline:* For fall admission, 7/15 for domestic and international students; for spring admission, 12/1 for domestic and international students. Applications are processed on a rolling basis. Application fee: $65 ($80 for international students). Electronic applications accepted. *Expenses:* Tuition, state resident: full-time $6,227. Tuition, nonresident: full-time $17,920. Required fees: $146. *Unit head:* Kathleen Waldron, Interim Director, 602-543-6698, Fax: 602-543-6612, E-mail: kathleen.waldron@asu.edu. *Application contact:* Eleanor Avilez, Administrative Assistant, 602-543-6642, Fax: 602-543-6612, E-mail: eavilez@asu.edu.

Arkansas State University, Graduate School, College of Nursing and Health Professions, Program in Health Sciences, Jonesboro, State University, AR 72467. Offers aging studies (Certificate); health sciences (MS); health sciences education (Certificate). Part-time programs available. *Faculty:* 3 full-time (2 women), 1 (woman) part-time/adjunct. *Students:* 3 full-time (2 women), 11 part-time (all women); includes 4 minority (all African Americans), 1 international. Average age 31. 5 applicants, 80% accepted, 4 enrolled. In 2007, 1 degree awarded. *Degree requirements:* For master's, comprehensive exam. *Entrance requirements:* For master's, GRE General Test, Allied Health Professions Admission Test, appropriate bachelor's degree, resumé, writing sample, letters of reference, official transcript. Additional exam requirements/recommendations for international students: Required—TOEFL (minimum score 213 computer-based). *Application deadline:* Applications are processed on a rolling basis. Application fee: $30 ($40 for international students). Electronic applications accepted. *Expenses: Contact institution.* Tuition and fees vary according to course load and program. *Financial support:* Scholarships/grants available. Financial award application deadline: 7/1; financial award applicants required to submit FAFSA. *Faculty research:* Body fluids, clinical laboratory science, immunohematology/immunology/serology, phlebotomy, clinical chemistry. *Unit head:* Dr. Whitney Williams, Director, 870-972-3073, Fax: 870-972-2004, E-mail: wwilliam@astate.edu.

A.T. Still University of Health Sciences, School of Health Management, Kirksville, MO 63501. Offers geriatric healthcare (MGH); health administration (MHA); health education (MH Ed, DH Ed); public health (MPH). Part-time and evening/weekend programs available. Postbaccalaureate distance learning degree programs offered (no on-campus study). *Faculty:* 6 full-time (3 women), 60 part-time/adjunct (20 women). *Students:* 38 full-time (29 women), 373 part-time (231 women); includes 142 minority (72 African Americans, 12 American Indian/Alaska Native, 39 Asian Americans or Pacific Islanders, 19 Hispanic Americans). Average age 32. 89 applicants, 100% accepted, 82 enrolled. In 2007, 78 degrees awarded. *Degree requirements:* For master's, thesis (for some programs), capstone project; for doctorate, thesis/dissertation. *Entrance requirements:* For master's, minimum GPA of 2.5, bachelor's degree or equivalent from U.S. institution; for doctorate, minimum GPA of 2.5, master's or terminal degree, employment. Additional exam requirements/recommendations for international students: Required—TOEFL (minimum score 550 paper-based; 213 computer-based; 80 iBT). *Application deadline:* For fall admission, 7/27 for domestic and international students; for winter admission, 10/26 for domestic and international students; for spring admission, 2/15 for domestic and international students. Applications are processed on a rolling basis. Application fee: $60. Electronic applications accepted. *Expenses: Contact institution.* *Financial support:* In 2007–08, 618 students received support; fellowships, research assistantships, teaching assistantships, scholarships/grants available. Financial award application deadline: 5/1; financial award applicants required to submit FAFSA. *Unit head:* Dr. Jon Persavich, Dean, 660-626-2820, Fax: 660-626-2826, E-mail: jpersavich@atsu.edu. *Application contact:* Donna Sparks, Associate Director for Admissions, 660-626-2237, Fax: 660-626-2969, E-mail: admissions@atsu.edu.

Ball State University, Graduate School, College of Applied Science and Technology, Fisher Institute for Wellness, Program in Applied Gerontology, Muncie, IN 47306-1099. Offers MA. *Faculty:* 1. *Students:* 7 full-time (5 women), 4 part-time (2 women); includes 2 minority (1 African American, 1 Asian American or Pacific Islander), 2 international. Average age 23. 13 applicants, 77% accepted, 5 enrolled. In 2007, 14 degrees awarded. Application fee: $25 ($35 for international students). *Expenses:* Tuition, state resident: full-time $6,864. Tuition, nonresident: full-time $17,932. Required fees: $1,866. *Financial support:* Research assistantships with full tuition reimbursements available. Financial award application deadline: 3/1. *Unit head:* Dr. Kathryn Segrist, Information Contact, 765-285-1296. *Application contact:* Dr. Kathryn Segrist, Information Contact, 765-285-8259, Fax: 765-285-8237, E-mail: ksegrist@gw.bsu.edu.

Bethel University, Graduate School, Department of Anthropology and Sociology, St. Paul, MN 55112-6999. Offers gerontology (MA). Evening/weekend programs available. *Faculty:* 1 full-time (0 women), 2 part-time/adjunct (both women). *Students:* 24 full-time (20 women), 1 (woman) part-time; includes 1 minority (Asian American or Pacific Islander) Average age 45. In 2007, 9 degrees awarded. *Degree requirements:* For master's, thesis. *Entrance requirements:* For master's, interview, 5 years of work experience, minimum GPA of 3.0, letters of reference. Additional exam requirements/recommendations for international students: Required—TOEFL (minimum score 550 paper-based; 213 computer-based). *Application deadline:* For fall admission, 7/1 priority date for domestic students. Applications are processed on a rolling basis. Application fee: $25. Electronic applications accepted. *Expenses:* Tuition: Part-time $415 per credit. Tuition and fees vary according to program. *Financial support:* Institutionally sponsored loans available. Financial award applicants required to submit FAFSA. *Unit head:* Dr. Harley Schreck, Director, 651-638-6104, Fax: 651-635-8004, E-mail: h-schreck@bethel.edu. *Application contact:* Michael Price, Director of Admissions, 651-635-8000 Ext. 8017, Fax: 651-635-8039, E-mail: m-price@bethel.edu.

Gerontology

California State University, Fullerton, Graduate Studies, College of Humanities and Social Sciences, Program in Gerontology, Fullerton, CA 92834-9480. Offers MS. *Students:* 19 full-time (16 women), 25 part-time (20 women); includes 22 minority (3 African Americans, 1 American Indian/Alaska Native, 10 Asian Americans or Pacific Islanders, 8 Hispanic Americans). Average age 43. 25 applicants, 80% accepted, 16 enrolled. In 2007, 15 degrees awarded. *Financial support:* Teaching assistantships available. *Unit head:* Dr. Joseph Weber, Coordinator, 714-278-7057.

California State University, Long Beach, Graduate Studies, College of Health and Human Services, Program in Gerontology, Long Beach, CA 90840. Offers MS. Part-time programs available. *Students:* Average age 32. *Degree requirements:* For master's, thesis optional. *Application deadline:* For fall admission, 7/1 for domestic students; for spring admission, 12/1 for domestic students. Applications are processed on a rolling basis. Application fee: $55. Electronic applications accepted. *Financial support:* Federal Work-Study, institutionally sponsored loans, and scholarships/grants available. Financial award application deadline: 3/2. *Unit head:* Dr. Barbara White, Director, 562-985-1582, Fax: 562-985-4414, E-mail: bwhite@csulb.edu.

California State University, Stanislaus, College of Humanities and Social Sciences, Department of Sociology, Turlock, CA 95382. Offers gerontology (Certificate). *Entrance requirements:* For degree, minimum GPA of 2.5. *Expenses:* Tuition, nonresident: full-time $10,170; part-time $339 per unit. Required fees: $3,972; $2,538 per term. $1,165 per semester. *Financial support:* In 2007–08, 10 students received support. Application deadline: 3/2. *Application contact:* Dr. Paul O'Brien, Chair, 209-667-3408, Fax: 200-664-7034.

Case Western Reserve University, School of Graduate Studies, Department of Communication Sciences, Cleveland, OH 44106. Offers gerontology (Certificate); speech-language pathology (MA, PhD). *Accreditation:* ASHA (one or more programs are accredited). *Faculty:* 5 full-time (all women), 6 part-time/adjunct (4 women). *Students:* 15 full-time (13 women), 6 part-time (all women), 3 international. Average age 24. 31 applicants, 45% accepted, 6 enrolled. In 2007, 8 master's, 1 doctorate awarded. Terminal master's awarded for partial completion of doctoral program. *Degree requirements:* For master's, comprehensive exam, thesis optional; for doctorate, thesis/dissertation. *Entrance requirements:* For master's and doctorate, GRE General Test. Additional exam requirements/recommendations for international students: Required—TOEFL. *Application deadline:* For fall admission, 3/1 for domestic students. Application fee: $50. Electronic applications accepted. *Financial support:* Research assistantships, career-related internships or fieldwork, Federal Work-Study, scholarships/grants, tuition waivers (partial), and unspecified assistantships available. Financial award application deadline: 3/1; financial award applicants required to submit FAFSA. *Faculty research:* Traumatic brain injury, phonological disorders, child language disorders, communication problems in the aged and Alzheimer's patients, cleft palate, voice disorders. *Unit head:* Stephen E. Haynesworth, Interim Chair, 216-368-2470, Fax: 216-368-6078, E-mail: stephen.haynesworth@case.edu. *Application contact:* Julie Clutter, Assistant, 216-368-2470, Fax: 216-368-6078, E-mail: jac34@case.edu.

Chestnut Hill College, School of Graduate Studies, Program in Administration of Human Services, Philadelphia, PA 19118-2693. Offers administration of human services (MS); adult and aging services (CAS); leadership development (CAS). Part-time and evening/weekend programs available. *Faculty:* 4 full-time (3 women), 6 part-time/adjunct (2 women). *Students:* 10 full-time (9 women), 28 part-time (24 women); includes 2 minority (both African Americans) Average age 35. 13 applicants, 100% accepted. In 2007, 32 master's awarded. *Degree requirements:* For master's, special projects or internship. *Entrance requirements:* For master's, GRE General Test or MAT, 100 hours volunteer or 1 year work related human services experience, statement of professional goals writing sample, transcripts, letters of recommendation; for CAS, GRE or MAT, transcripts, letters of recommendation, statement of professional goals writing sample. Additional exam requirements/recommendations for international students: Required—TOEFL (minimum score 500 paper-based; 213 computer-based). *Application deadline:* For fall admission, 7/17 priority date for domestic students, 7/17 for international students; for spring admission, 12/15 priority date for domestic students, 12/15 for international students. Applications are processed on a rolling basis. Application fee: $50. *Financial support:* Institutionally sponsored loans available. *Faculty research:* E-learning/e-training; motivation: a technology perspective; technology, restructured environments, and learning. *Unit head:* Dr. Elaine Green, Dean of the School of Continuing and Professional Studies/Program Coordinator, 215-248-7172, Fax: 215-248-7065, E-mail: green@chc.edu. *Application contact:* Amy Boorse, Administrative Assistant, School of Graduate Studies Office, 215-248-7170, Fax: 215-248-7161, E-mail: gradadmissions@chc.edu.

The College of New Rochelle, Graduate School, Division of Human Services, Program in Gerontology, New Rochelle, NY 10805-2308. Offers MS, Certificate. Part-time and evening/weekend programs available. *Faculty:* 3 full-time (1 woman), 2 part-time/adjunct (both women). *Students:* 3 full-time (all women), 13 part-time (all women); includes 8 minority (all African Americans) Average age 43. In 2007, 6 degrees awarded. *Degree requirements:* For master's, fieldwork, internship. *Entrance requirements:* For master's, interview, minimum GPA of 3.0, writing sample. *Application deadline:* For fall admission, 8/1 priority date for domestic students. Applications are processed on a rolling basis. Application fee: $35. *Expenses:* Tuition: Part-time $650 per credit. Required fees: $90 per term. *Financial support:* In 2007–08, 2 research assistantships were awarded; career-related internships or fieldwork, scholarships/grants, and unspecified assistantships also available. *Unit head:* Dr. Marie Ribarich, Associate Dean, Division of Human Services, 914-654-5561, Fax: 914-654-5593, E-mail: mribarich@cnr.edu.

Concordia University Chicago, College of Arts and Sciences, Program in Gerontology, River Forest, IL 60305-1499. Offers MA. Part-time and evening/weekend programs available. *Degree requirements:* For master's, comprehensive exam, thesis. *Entrance requirements:* For master's, minimum GPA of 2.9. Additional exam requirements/recommendations for international students: Required—TOEFL (minimum score 550 paper-based; 195 computer-based). Electronic applications accepted.

Dominican University of California, Graduate Programs, School of Arts and Sciences, Program in Nursing, San Rafael, CA 94901-2298. Offers geriatric and nurse educator (MS); integrated health practices (clinical nursing specialist) (MS). *Accreditation:* AACN. Part-time and evening/weekend programs available. *Faculty:* 3 full-time (all women), 16 part-time/adjunct (14 women). *Students:* 20 full-time (19 women), 11 part-time (9 women); includes 11 minority (5 African Americans, 1 American Indian/Alaska Native, 4 Asian Americans or Pacific Islanders, 1 Hispanic American). Average age 44. 15 applicants, 47% accepted, 7 enrolled. In 2007, 8 degrees awarded. *Degree requirements:* For master's, thesis. *Entrance requirements:* For master's, minimum GPA of 3.0, clinical experience, course work in nursing research and statistics, CPR certification, professional liability and malpractice insurance, interview. Additional exam requirements/recommendations for international students: Required—TOEFL (minimum score 550 paper-based; 213 computer-based). *Application deadline:* Applications are processed on a rolling basis. Application fee: $40. Electronic applications accepted. *Financial support:* In 2007–08, 20 students received support, including 10 fellowships (averaging $3,200 per year); scholarships/grants also available. Support available to part-time students. Financial award applicants required to submit FAFSA. *Unit head:* Dr. Barbara Ganley, Chair, 415-482-1829, Fax: 415-485-0120, E-mail: bganley@dominican.edu. *Application contact:* Lawrence Schwaltz, Associate Director, 415-458-3748, Fax: 415-485-3214, E-mail: larry.schwaltz@dominican.edu.

Eastern Illinois University, Graduate School, Lumpkin College of Business and Applied Sciences, Program in Gerontology, Charleston, IL 61920-3099. Offers MA. *Faculty:* 7 full-time (3 women). In 2007, 10 degrees awarded. *Application deadline:* For fall admission, 7/31 priority date for domestic students. Applications are processed on a rolling basis. Application fee: $30. *Expenses:* Tuition, state resident: part-time $218 per hour. Tuition, nonresident: part-time $654 per hour. *Financial support:* In 2007–08, research assistantships with tuition reimbursements (averaging $7,200 per year), 4 teaching assistantships with tuition reimbursements (averaging $7,200 per year) were awarded; career-related internships or fieldwork and institutionally sponsored loans also available. *Unit head:* Dr. James Painter, Chairperson, 217-581-6076, Fax: 217-581-6090, E-mail: jepainter@eiu.edu. *Application contact:* Dr. Jeanne Snyder, Coordinator, 217-581-6348, Fax: 217-581-6090, E-mail: jrsnyder@eiu.edu.

Eastern Michigan University, Graduate School, College of Health and Human Services, School of Social Work, Ypsilanti, MI 48197. Offers family and children's services (MSW); gerontology (Graduate Certificate); gerontology-dementia (Graduate Certificate); mental health and chemical dependency (MSW); services to the aging (MSW). *Accreditation:* CSWE.Part-time and evening/weekend programs available. Postbaccalaureate distance learning degree programs offered (minimal on-campus study). *Faculty:* 18 full-time (15 women). *Students:* 26 full-time (21 women), 164 part-time (142 women); includes 78 minority (69 African Americans, 3 American Indian/Alaska Native, 4 Asian Americans or Pacific Islanders, 2 Hispanic Americans), 1 international. Average age 35. In 2007, 117 master's, 17 other advanced degrees awarded. *Entrance requirements:* Additional exam requirements/recommendations for international students: Required—TOEFL. *Application deadline:* Applications are processed on a rolling basis. Application fee: $35. *Expenses:* Tuition, state resident: full-time $8,952; part-time $373 per credit hour. Tuition, nonresident: full-time $17,634; part-time $735 per credit hour. Required fees: $896; $34 per credit hour. Tuition and fees vary according to course level, degree level and program. *Financial support:* Fellowships, research assistantships with full tuition reimbursements, teaching assistantships with full tuition reimbursements, career-related internships or fieldwork, Federal Work-Study, institutionally sponsored loans, scholarships/grants, tuition waivers (partial), and unspecified assistantships available. Support available to part-time students. Financial award applicants required to submit FAFSA. *Unit head:* Prof. Marjorie Ziefert, Director, 734-487-0393, Fax: 734-487-6832, E-mail: marjorie.ziefert@emich.edu. *Application contact:* Julie Harkema, Advisor, 734-487-0393, Fax: 734-487-6832, E-mail: jharkema@emich.edu.

East Tennessee State University, School of Graduate Studies, College of Public and Allied Health, Department of Public Health, Johnson City, TN 37614. Offers community health (MPH); epidemiology (Certificate); gerontology (Certificate); health care management (Certificate); public health (MPH); public health administration (MPH). *Accreditation:* CEPH. Part-time programs available. *Degree requirements:* For master's, comprehensive exam, thesis optional. *Entrance requirements:* For master's, GRE General Test, 2 years of community health experience. Additional exam requirements/recommendations for international students: Required—TOEFL (minimum score 550 paper-based; 213 computer-based). *Faculty research:* Rural health issues, youth and adolescent health, health of the elderly, environmental epidemiology, spatial analysis of data.

Emory University, Nell Hodgson Woodruff School of Nursing, Atlanta, GA 30322-1100. Offers adult and elder health advanced practice nursing (MSN), including acute and critical care, adult nurse practitioner, gerontology, oncology; emergency nurse practitioner (MSN); family nurse practitioner (MSN); family nurse-midwife (MSN); leadership in healthcare (MSN); nurse midwifery (MSN); nursing administration (MSN); pediatric advanced nursing practice (MSN); public health nursing (MSN); women's health nurse practitioner (MSN); MSN/MPH. *Accreditation:* AACN; ACNM/DOA (one or more programs are accredited). Part-time programs available. *Entrance requirements:* For master's, GRE General Test or MAT, minimum GPA of 3.0, BS in nursing, RN license and additional course work, 3 letters of recommendation. Additional exam requirements/recommendations for international students: Required—TOEFL (minimum score 600 paper-based; 250 computer-based). Electronic applications accepted. Expenses: Contact institution. *Faculty research:* Older adult falls and injuries, minority health issues, cardiac symptoms amd quality of life, bio-ethics and decision making, menopausal issues.

Florida Gulf Coast University, College of Health Professions, Geriatric Recreational Therapy Program, Fort Myers, FL 33965-6565. Offers MS. *Faculty:* 41 full-time (32 women), 37 part-time/adjunct (25 women). *Students:* Average age 25. 1 applicant, 0% accepted. *Application deadline:* For fall admission, 2/15 for domestic students. *Expenses:* Tuition, state resident: full-time $4,542. Tuition, nonresident: full-time $19,449. Required fees: $1,297. *Unit head:* Dr. Joan Glacken, Chair, 239-590-7498, Fax: 239-590-7474, E-mail: jglacken@fgcu.edu.

Gannon University, School of Graduate Studies, College of Humanities, Business, and Education, School of Humanities, Program in Gerontology, Erie, PA 16541-0001. Offers Certificate. Part-time and evening/weekend programs available. *Entrance requirements:* For degree, interview. Additional exam requirements/recommendations for international students: Required—TOEFL (minimum score 500 paper-based; 173 computer-based). *Application deadline:* Applications are processed on a rolling basis. Application fee: $25. *Expenses:* Tuition: Full-time $13,050; part-time $725 per credit. Required fees: $502; $16 per credit. Tuition and fees vary according to course load, degree level, campus/location and program. *Financial support:* Career-related internships or fieldwork available. Financial award application deadline: 7/1; financial award applicants required to submit FAFSA. *Unit head:* Charles Murphy, Director, 814-871-7542, E-mail: murphy001@gannon.edu. *Application contact:* Debra Meszaros, Director of Graduate Recruitment, 814-871-5819, Fax: 814-871-5827, E-mail: cfal@gannon.edu.

Georgia State University, College of Arts and Sciences, Gerontology Institute, Atlanta, GA 30303-3083. Offers MA. Part-time programs available. *Faculty:* 25 full-time (19 women). *Students:* 18 full-time (17 women), 9 part-time (7 women); includes 7 minority (6 African Americans, 1 Asian American or Pacific Islander), 4 international. 11 applicants, 73% accepted, 7 enrolled. In 2007, 6 degrees awarded. *Degree requirements:* For master's, thesis, internship. *Entrance requirements:* For master's, GRE, 3 letters of reference. Additional exam requirements/recommendations for international students: Required—TOEFL, TWE. *Application deadline:* For fall admission, 4/15 for domestic and international students; for spring admission, 10/15 for domestic and international students. Applications are processed on a rolling basis. Application fee: $50. Electronic applications accepted. *Expenses:* Tuition, state resident: part-time $221 per credit hour. *Financial support:* In 2007–08, 18 students received support, including 14 research assistantships with full tuition reimbursements available (averaging $9,000 per year); career-related internships or fieldwork, scholarships/grants, and health care benefits also available. Financial award application deadline: 4/15. *Faculty research:* Long-term care, assisted living, ethnicity and aging dementia, memory. Total annual research expenditures: $175,000. *Unit head:* Dr. Frank J. Whittington, Director, 404-413-5213, Fax: 404-413-5219, E-mail: fwhittington@gsu.edu. *Application contact:* Mary MacKinnon, Assistant Director for Student Affairs, 404-413-5211, E-mail: mmackinnon@gsu.edu.

Hofstra University, School of Education and Allied Human Services, Department of Counseling, Research, Special Education and Rehabilitation, Program in Gerontology, Hempstead, NY 11549. Offers MS, Advanced Certificate. Part-time programs available. *Students:* 8 full-time (6 women), 13 part-time (12 women); includes 8 minority (all African Americans) Average age 42. 11 applicants, 100% accepted, 6 enrolled. In 2007, 6 master's, 1 other advanced degree awarded. *Degree requirements:* For master's and Advanced Certificate, thesis optional, Internship. *Entrance requirements:* For master's, interview, letter of recommendation; for Advanced Certificate, letter of recommendation, interview. Additional exam requirements/recommendations for international students: Required—TOEFL (minimum score 550 paper-based; 213 computer-based). *Application deadline:* Applications are processed on a rolling basis. Application fee: $60. Electronic applications accepted. *Expenses:* Tuition: Full-time $14,220; part-time $820 per credit. Required fees: $970; $165 per term. Tuition and fees vary according to program. *Financial support:* In 2007–08, 10 students received support, including 1 fellowship with tuition reimbursement available (averaging $3,000 per year); research assistantships with full and partial tuition reimbursements available, career-related internships or fieldwork, Federal Work-Study, institutionally sponsored loans, scholarships/grants, and tuition waivers (full and partial) also available. Support available to part-time students. Financial award applicants required to submit FAFSA. *Faculty research:* Elder abuse, geropsychology, environmental gerontology, later life education. *Unit head:* Dr. Jeffrey P. Rosenfeld, Director, 516-463-5752, Fax: 516-463-6184, E-mail: cprjzr@hofstra.edu. *Application contact:* Carol Drummer, Dean of Graduate Admissions, 516-463-4876, Fax: 516-463-4664, E-mail: gradstudent@hofstra.edu.

Kent State University, Graduate School of Education, Health, and Human Services, School of Family and Consumer Studies, Program in Family Studies, Kent, OH 44242-0001. Offers gerontology (MA); human development and family studies (MA). *Faculty:* 17 full-time (10 women). *Students:* 3 full-time (all women), 4 part-time (all women). 3 applicants, 0% accepted. In 2007, 1 degree awarded. Application fee: $30. *Financial support:* In 2007–08, research assistantships (averaging $8,313 per year). *Unit head:* Dr. Rhonda Richardson, Coordinator, 330-672-2197, E-mail: rrichard@kent.edu. *Application contact:* Nancy Miller, Academic Program Coordinator, 330-672-2576, Fax: 330-672-9162, E-mail: ogs@kent.edu.

Lakehead University, Graduate Studies, Gerontology Collaborative Program-Northern Educational Center for Aging and Health, Thunder Bay, ON P7B 5E1, Canada. Offers specialization gerontology (M Ed, M Sc, MA, MSW). Part-time programs available. *Degree requirements:* For master's, thesis (for some programs). *Entrance requirements:* Additional exam requirements/recommendations for international students: Required—TOEFL. *Faculty research:* Integrated health information systems.

Lindenwood University, Graduate Programs, Programs in Individualized Education, St. Charles, MO 63301-1695. Offers administration (MSA); business administration (MBA); communication (MS); communications (MA); criminal justice and administration (MS); gerontology (MA); health management (MS); human resource management (MS); information technology (MBA, Certificate); management (MSA); managing information technology (MS); marketing (MSA); writing (MFA). Part-time and evening/weekend programs available. *Faculty:* 13 full-time (7 women), 54 part-time/adjunct (32 women). *Students:* 774 full-time (495 women), 55 part-time (32 women); includes 226 minority (213 African Americans, 9 Asian Americans or Pacific Islanders, 4 Hispanic Americans), 17 international. Average age 35. In 2007, 299 degrees awarded. *Degree requirements:* For master's, thesis (for some programs), minimum GPA of 3.0, 1 colloquium per term. *Entrance requirements:* For master's, interview, minimum GPA of 3.0. Additional exam requirements/recommendations for international students: Required—TOEFL (minimum score 550 paper-based; 213 computer-based; 80 iBT). *Application deadline:* For fall admission, 9/30 priority date for domestic and international students; for winter admission, 12/30 priority date for domestic and international students; for spring admission, 3/30 priority date for domestic and international students. Applications are processed on a rolling basis. Application fee: $30 ($100 for international students). *Expenses:* Tuition: Full-time $12,400; part-time $350 per hour. Full-time tuition and fees vary according to degree level and program. *Financial support:* Career-related internships or fieldwork, institutionally sponsored loans, tuition waivers (partial), and unspecified assistantships available. Financial award application deadline: 6/30; financial award applicants required to submit FAFSA. *Unit head:* Dan Kemper, Dean of Lindenwood College for Individual Education, 636-949-4501, Fax: 636-949-4505, E-mail: dkemper@lindenwood.edu. *Application contact:* Brett Barger, Dean of Evening Admissions and Extension Campuses, 636-949-4934, Fax: 636-949-4109, E-mail: adultadmissions@lindenwood.edu.

Long Island University, C.W. Post Campus, College of Management, Department of Health Care and Public Administration, Brookville, NY 11548-1300. Offers gerontology (Certificate); health care administration (MPA); health care administration/gerontology (MPA); nonprofit management (MPA, Certificate); public administration (MPA). *Accreditation:* NASPAA (one or more programs are accredited). Part-time and evening/weekend programs available. *Faculty:* 8 full-time (4 women), 14 part-time/adjunct (4 women). *Students:* 51 full-time (31 women), 65 part-time (43 women); includes 41 minority (19 African Americans, 15 Asian Americans or Pacific Islanders, 7 Hispanic Americans), 5 international. Average age 32. 232 applicants, 69% accepted, 26 enrolled. In 2007, 44 degrees awarded. *Degree requirements:* For master's, thesis. *Entrance requirements:* For master's, GMAT, minimum GPA of 2.5; for Certificate, minimum GPA of 2.5. *Application deadline:* Applications are processed on a rolling basis. Application fee: $30. Electronic applications accepted. *Expenses:* Tuition: Part-time $825 per credit. Tuition and fees vary according to course load. *Financial support:* In 2007–08, 10 students received support, including 3 research assistantships with partial tuition reimbursements available; Federal Work-Study and unspecified assistantships also available. Support available to part-time students. Financial award application deadline: 5/15; financial award applicants required to submit CSS PROFILE or FAFSA. *Faculty research:* Critical issues in sexuality, social work in religious communities, gerontological social work. *Unit head:* Dr. Linda Vila, Chair, 516-299-2578, E-mail: linda.vila@liu.edu.

Long Island University, Rockland Graduate Campus, Graduate School, Programs in Health and Public Administration, Orangeburg, NY 10962. Offers gerontology (Advanced Certificate); health administration (MPA); public administration (MPA). *Faculty:* 1 full-time (0 women), 3 part-time/adjunct (1 woman). *Students:* 3 full-time (1 woman), 27 part-time (19 women). In 2007, 9 degrees awarded. *Entrance requirements:* For master's, GRE General Test. *Application deadline:* Applications are processed on a rolling basis. Application fee: $30. *Expenses:* Tuition: Part-time $835 per credit. Required fees: $100 per term. *Unit head:* Prof. Patricia Latona, Program Director, 845-359-7200 Ext. 5410, Fax: 845-359-7248, E-mail: patricia.latona@liu.edu. *Application contact:* Peter S. Reiner, Director of Admissions and Marketing, 845-359-7200, Fax: 845-359-7248, E-mail: peter.reiner@liu.edu.

See Close-Up on page 1603.

Marywood University, Academic Affairs, College of Health and Human Services, Department of Nursing and Public Administration, Program in Gerontology, Scranton, PA 18509-1598. Offers MS, Certificate. *Expenses:* Tuition: Full-time $15,290; part-time $695 per credit. Required fees: $990; $370 per term. Tuition and fees vary according to degree level. *Application contact:* Tammy Manka, Assistant Director of Graduate Admissions, 570-340-6002, E-mail: tmanka@marywood.edu.

Miami University, Graduate School, College of Arts and Sciences, Department of Sociology and Gerontology, Program in Gerontology, Oxford, OH 45056. Offers MGS. *Degree requirements:* For master's, final exam. *Entrance requirements:* For master's, GRE General Test, minimum undergraduate GPA of 3.0 during previous 2 years or 2.75 overall. Additional exam requirements/recommendations for international students: Required—TOEFL (minimum score 550 paper-based; 213 computer-based), TWE (minimum score 4). Electronic applications accepted.

Middle Tennessee State University, College of Graduate Studies, Program in Gerontology, Murfreesboro, TN 37132. Offers Graduate Certificate. Part-time and evening/weekend programs available. Postbaccalaureate distance learning degree programs offered. *Entrance requirements:* Additional exam requirements/recommendations for international students: Required—TOEFL (paper-based 525; computer-based 195; IBT 71) or IELTS (6.0). *Financial support:* Application deadline: 5/1. *Unit head:* Dr. Ronald Aday, Head, 615-898-2693.

Minnesota State University Mankato, College of Graduate Studies, College of Social and Behavioral Sciences, Program in Gerontology, Mankato, MN 56001. Offers MS, Certificate. *Students:* 5 full-time (4 women), 4 part-time (all women). Average age 32. In 2007, 3 degrees awarded. *Degree requirements:* For master's, comprehensive exam, thesis. *Entrance requirements:* For master's, GRE, minimum GPA of 3.0 during previous 2 years, letters of recommendation. Additional exam requirements/recommendations for international students: Required—TOEFL. *Application deadline:* For fall admission, 7/1 priority date for domestic students; for spring admission, 11/1 for domestic students. Applications are processed on a rolling basis. Application fee: $40. Electronic applications accepted. *Financial support:* Federal Work-Study and unspecified assistantships available. Support available to part-time students. Financial award application deadline: 3/15. *Unit head:* Jim Tift, Director, 507-389-5188. *Application contact:* 507-389-2321, E-mail: grad@mnsu.edu.

Morehead State University, Graduate Programs, Caudill College of Humanities, Department of Sociology, Social Work and Criminology, Morehead, KY 40351. Offers criminology (MA); general sociology (MA); gerontology (MA). Part-time and evening/weekend programs available. *Faculty:* 8 full-time (3 women), 2 part-time/adjunct (1 woman). *Students:* 14 full-time (8 women), 7 part-time (3 women). Average age 28. In 2007, 3 degrees awarded. *Degree requirements:* For master's, comprehensive exam, thesis optional. *Entrance requirements:* For master's, GRE General Test, minimum GPA of 3.0 in sociology, 2.5 overall; 18 hours of course work in sociology, writing sample. Additional exam requirements/recommendations for international students: Required—TOEFL (minimum score 500 paper-based; 173 computer-based). *Application deadline:* For fall admission, 8/1 priority date for domestic and international students; for spring admission, 12/1 priority date for domestic and international students. Applications are processed on a rolling basis. Application fee: $0 ($55 for international students). Electronic applications accepted. *Financial support:* In 2007–08, 5 teaching assistantships (averaging $6,000 per year) were awarded; career-related internships or fieldwork, Federal Work-Study, and unspecified assistantships also available. Financial award application deadline: 4/1; financial award applicants required to submit FAFSA. *Faculty research:* Death and dying; aging, drinking, and drugs; economic development; adult children of alcoholics. *Unit head:* Dr. Robert Bylund, Chair, 606-783-2656, Fax: 606-783-5027, E-mail: r.bylund@moreheadstate.edu. *Application contact:* Michelle Barber, Graduate Admissions Counselor, 606-783-2039, Fax: 606-783-5061, E-mail: m.barber@moreheadstate.edu.

Mount Saint Vincent University, Graduate Programs, Department of Family Studies and Gerontology, Halifax, NS B3M 2J6, Canada. Offers MA. Part-time programs available. Postbaccalaureate distance learning degree programs offered (minimal on-campus study). *Degree requirements:* For master's, thesis. *Entrance requirements:* For master's, minimum GPA of 3.0; course work in statistics, research methods, family and social theories.

National-Louis University, College of Arts and Sciences, Department of Counseling and Human Services, Chicago, IL 60603. Offers addictions counseling (Certificate); addictions treatment (Certificate); career counseling and development studies (Certificate); community counseling (MS); community wellness and prevention (Certificate); counseling (Certificate); eating disorders counseling (Certificate); employee assistance programs (MS, Certificate); gerontology administration (Certificate); gerontology counseling (MS, Certificate); human services administration (MS, Certificate); long-term care administration (Certificate); school counseling (MS). Part-time programs available. *Students:* 15 full-time (11 women), 229 part-time (187 women); includes 69 minority (56 African Americans, 1 American Indian/Alaska Native, 2 Asian Americans or Pacific Islanders, 10 Hispanic Americans). Average age 38. In 2007, 53 master's, 6 other advanced degrees awarded. *Degree requirements:* For master's and Certificate, internship. *Entrance requirements:* For master's and Certificate, GRE, MAT, or Watson-Glaser Critical Thinking Appraisal, interview, minimum GPA of 3.0. *Application deadline:* Applications are processed on a rolling basis. *Expenses:* Tuition: Full-time $18,900; part-time $630 per credit hour. Required fees: $20 per term. One-time fee: $40 part-time. Tuition and fees vary according to course load, campus/location and program. *Financial support:* Federal Work-Study, institutionally sponsored loans, scholarships/grants, and tuition waivers available. Support available to part-time students. Financial award applicants required to submit FAFSA. *Faculty research:* Religion and aging, drug abuse prevention, hunger, homelessness, multicultural diversity. *Unit head:* Dr. Susan Thorne-Devin, Assistant Professor, 630-874-4560, E-mail: stdevin@nl.edu. *Application contact:* Dr. Larry Poselli, Vice President of Enrollment and Student Services, 800-443-5522 Ext. 5718, Fax: 312-261-3550, E-mail: larry.polselli@nl.edu.

North Dakota State University, College of Graduate and Interdisciplinary Studies, College of Human Development and Education, Department of Child Development and Family Science, Fargo, ND 58105. Offers child development and family science (MS); couple and family therapy (MS); family financial planning (MS); gerontology (MS, PhD). *Accreditation:* AAMFT/COAMFTE. Part-time and evening/weekend programs available. Postbaccalaureate distance learning degree programs offered (no on-campus study). *Faculty:* 12 full-time (7 women). *Students:* 39 full-time (35 women), 14 part-time (13 women); includes 5 minority (1 African American, 2 American Indian/Alaska Native, 2 Asian Americans or Pacific Islanders), 1 international. 22 applicants, 64% accepted, 12 enrolled. In 2007, 6 degrees awarded. *Degree requirements:* For master's, thesis or alternative; for doctorate, thesis/dissertation. *Entrance requirements:* Additional exam requirements/recommendations for international students: Required—TOEFL (minimum score 525 paper-based; 197 computer-based; 71 iBT). *Application deadline:* For fall admission, 2/1 for domestic and international students; for spring admission, 10/1 for domestic and international students. Application fee: $45 ($60 for international students). *Expenses:* Tuition, state resident: full-time $5,376; part-time $224 per credit. Tuition, nonresident: full-time $14,354; part-time $598 per credit. Required fees: $962; $40 per credit. Part-time tuition and fees vary according to course load and reciprocity agreements. *Financial support:* In 2007–08, 17 students received support, including research assistantships with full tuition reimbursements available (averaging $3,000 per year), 17 teaching assistantships with full tuition reimbursements available (averaging $3,000 per year); career-related internships or fieldwork, Federal Work-Study, institutionally sponsored loans, and tuition waivers (full) also available. Financial award application deadline: 4/1. *Faculty research:* Family therapy, resilience, parenting, adolescent development, mental health. Total annual research expenditures:$333,582. *Unit head:* Dr. James Deal, Head, 701-231-7568, Fax: 701-231-9645, E-mail: jim_deal@ndsu.edu. *Application contact:* Theresa Anderson, Administrative Assistant, 701-231-8628, Fax: 701-231-9645, E-mail: theresa.anderson@ndsu.edu.

Northeastern Illinois University, Graduate College, College of Arts and Sciences, Department of Gerontology, Program in Gerontology, Chicago, IL 60625-4699. Offers MA. Part-time and evening/weekend programs available. *Faculty:* 13 full-time (9 women), 6 part-time/adjunct (5 women). *Students:* 3 full-time (all women), 25 part-time (19 women); includes 8 minority (4 African Americans, 3 Asian Americans or Pacific Islanders, 1 Hispanic American), 3 international. Average age 44. 7 applicants, 57% accepted. In 2007, 1 degree awarded. *Degree requirements:* For master's, comprehensive exam, paper and project or thesis, practicum, minimum GPA of 3.0. *Entrance requirements:* For master's, 15 hours in social sciences (3 hours in gerontology), 1 course in research methods or statistics, minimum GPA of 2.75. Additional exam requirements/recommendations for international students: Required—TOEFL (minimum score 550 paper-based; 213 computer-based; 80 iBT). *Application deadline:* For fall admission, 4/1 priority date for domestic students; for spring admission, 8/15 for domestic students. Applications are processed on a rolling basis. Application fee: $25. Electronic applications accepted. *Expenses:* Tuition, state resident: part-time $243 per credit hour. Tuition, nonresident: part-time $443 per credit hour. *Financial support:* In 2007–08, 12 students received support, including 2 research assistantships with full tuition reimbursements available (averaging $6,600 per year); career-related internships or fieldwork, Federal Work-Study, institutionally sponsored loans, scholarships/grants, tuition waivers (full and partial), and unspecified assistantships also available. Support available to part-time students. Financial award applicants required to submit FAFSA. *Faculty research:* Later life development, cultural diversity, humanities and aging, elder abuse, AIDS and aging, computer training.

Notre Dame de Namur University, Division of Academic Affairs, School of Sciences, Department of Clinical Psychology and Gerontology, Program in Clinical Gerontology, Belmont, CA 94002-1908. Offers MA, Certificate. *Application contact:* Helen Valine, Director of Graduate Admissions, 650-508-3534, Fax: 650-508-3426, E-mail: grad.admit@ndnu.edu.

Oklahoma State University, Graduate College, Interdisciplinary Program in Natural and Applied Sciences, Interdisciplinary Program in Gerontology, Stillwater, OK 74078. Offers MS. *Expenses:* Tuition, state resident: full-time $4,993; part-time $148 per credit hour. Tuition, nonresident: full-time $14,755; part-time $555 per credit hour. Tuition and fees vary according to program. *Unit head:* Dr. Tammy Henderson, Program Coordinator, 405-744-8350.

Oregon Health & Science University, School of Nursing, Program in Nursing Education, Portland, OR 97239-3098. Offers MN, MS, Post Master's Certificate. *Application contact:* Office of Recruitment, 503-494-7725, Fax: 503-494-4350, E-mail: proginfo@ohsu.edu.

Oregon State University, Graduate School, College of Health and Human Sciences, Department of Human Development and Family Sciences, Program in Gerontology, Corvallis, OR 97331. Offers MAIS. *Degree requirements:* For master's, thesis optional. *Entrance requirements:* For master's, GRE, minimum GPA of 3.0 in last 90 hours. Additional exam requirements/recommendations for international students: Required—TOEFL. *Application deadline:* For fall admission, 1/15 for domestic students. Application fee: $50. *Expenses:* Tuition, state resident: full-time $9,126; part-time $338 per credit. Tuition, nonresident: full-time $14,796; part-time

Gerontology

Oregon State University (continued)
$548 per credit. Required fees: $1,447. *Financial support:* Research assistantships, teaching assistantships, career-related internships or fieldwork, Federal Work-Study, and institutionally sponsored loans available. Support available to part-time students. Financial award application deadline: 2/1. *Faculty research:* Aging/families, social/psychological aspects of aging, osteoporosis, nutrition, disease and aging. *Unit head:* Dr. Karen Hooker, Director, 541-737-4336, Fax: 541-737-1076, E-mail: hookerk@oregonstate.edu.

Portland State University, Graduate Studies, College of Urban and Public Affairs, School of Community Health, Institute on Aging, Portland, OR 97207-0751. Offers Certificate. Part-time programs available. *Students:* 1 (woman) full-time, 11 part-time (6 women); includes 1 minority (African American) Average age 41. 4 applicants, 100% accepted, 4 enrolled. *Application deadline:* For fall admission, 2/1 for domestic and international students. Application fee: $50. *Expenses:* Tuition, state resident: full-time $7,047. Tuition, nonresident: full-time $11,178. *Financial support:* In 2007–08, 4 research assistantships with full tuition reimbursements (averaging $10,355 per year) were awarded; fellowships, teaching assistantships, career-related internships or fieldwork and Federal Work-Study also available. Support available to part-time students. Financial award application deadline: 3/1; financial award applicants required to submit FAFSA. Total annual research expenditures: $583,289. *Unit head:* Dr. Margaret Neal, Director, 503-725-3952, Fax: 503-725-5199, E-mail: nealm@pdx.edu.

Rochester Institute of Technology, Graduate Enrollment Services, College of Applied Science and Technology, Department of Hospitality and Service Management, Program in Senior Living Management, Rochester, NY 14623-5603. Offers AC. *Entrance requirements:* Additional exam requirements/recommendations for international students: Required—TOEFL (minimum score 550 paper-based; 213 computer-based; 79 iBT). *Expenses:* Tuition: Full-time $28,491; part-time $800 per credit hour. Required fees: $201; $67 per term. *Financial support:* Research assistantships with partial tuition reimbursements, teaching assistantships with partial tuition reimbursements, career-related internships or fieldwork, institutionally sponsored loans, scholarships/grants, and unspecified assistantships available. Support available to part-time students. Financial award applicants required to submit FAFSA. *Unit head:* Linda Underhill, Chair, 585-475-7359, E-mail: lmuism@rit.edu.

Sacred Heart University, Graduate Programs, College of Education and Health Professions, Program in Geriatric Health and Wellness, Fairfield, CT 06825-1000. Offers MS. Part-time and evening/weekend programs available. Postbaccalaureate distance learning degree programs offered. *Faculty:* 6 full-time (4 women). *Students:* Average age 30. *Entrance requirements:* Additional exam requirements/recommendations for international students: Required—TOEFL (minimum score 550 paper-based; 213 computer-based; 75 iBT). *Application deadline:* Applications are processed on a rolling basis. Application fee: $50 ($100 for international students). Electronic applications accepted. *Expenses: Contact institution.* Tuition and fees vary according to program. *Financial support:* Applicants required to submit FAFSA. *Unit head:* Dr. Michelle Lusardi, Director, 203-365-4721. *Application contact:* Kathy Dilks, Assistant Dean of Graduate Admissions, Health Professions, 203-396-8259, Fax: 203-365-4732, E-mail: gradstudies@sacredheart.edu.

Sage Graduate School, Graduate School, Department of Management, Program in Health Services Administration, Troy, NY 12180-4115. Offers gerontology (MS); health education (MS); management (MS). Part-time and evening/weekend programs available. *Faculty:* 2 full-time (1 woman), 7 part-time/adjunct (0 women). *Students:* 2 full-time (both women), 17 part-time (13 women); includes 1 minority (Hispanic American) Average age 37. 8 applicants, 75% accepted, 4 enrolled. In 2007, 5 degrees awarded. *Entrance requirements:* For master's, minimum GPA of 2.75, completed application, current resum&e, essay, official transcripts, 2 letters of recommendation. Additional exam requirements/recommendations for international students: Required—TOEFL (minimum score 550 paper-based; 213 computer-based). Application fee: $40. *Expenses:* Tuition: Full-time $9,720; part-time $540 per credit hour. *Financial support:* Fellowships, research assistantships, Federal Work-Study, scholarships/grants, and unspecified assistantships available. Support available to part-time students. Financial award application deadline: 3/1; financial award applicants required to submit FAFSA. *Application contact:* Shannon K. Easton, Director of Graduate and Adult Admission, 518-244-2443, Fax: 518-244-6880, E-mail: sgsadm@sage.edu.

St. Cloud State University, School of Graduate Studies, College of Social Sciences, Program in Gerontology, St. Cloud, MN 56301-4498. Offers MS. Part-time programs available. *Faculty:* 8 full-time (5 women). *Students:* 8 full-time (7 women), 5 part-time (all women); includes 1 minority (African American), 3 international. 8 applicants, 100% accepted. In 2007, 2 degrees awarded. *Degree requirements:* For master's, thesis or alternative. *Entrance requirements:* For master's, GRE General Test, minimum GPA of 2.75. Additional exam requirements/recommendations for international students: Required—MELAB; Recommended—TOEFL (minimum score 550 paper-based; 213 computer-based), IELTS (minimum score 7). *Application deadline:* For fall admission, 6/1 priority date for domestic students, 6/1 for international students; for spring admission, 10/1 priority date for domestic students, 10/1 for international students. Applications are processed on a rolling basis. Application fee: $35. Electronic applications accepted. *Expenses:* Tuition, state resident: part-time $267 per credit. Tuition, nonresident: part-time $418 per credit. Required fees: $28 per credit. *Financial support:* Federal Work-Study, scholarships/grants, and unspecified assistantships available. Financial award application deadline: 3/1. *Unit head:* Dr. Phyllis Greenberg, Coordinator, 320-308-3947, E-mail: pgreenberg@stcloudstate.edu. *Application contact:* Linda Lou Krueger, School of Graduate Studies, 320-308-2113, Fax: 320-308-5371, E-mail: lekrueger@stcloudstate.edu.

Saint Joseph College, Graduate Division, Institute in Gerontology, West Hartford, CT 06117-2700. Offers human development/gerontology (Certificate). Part-time and evening/weekend programs available. Electronic applications accepted. *Faculty research:* Education, aging, public health.

Saint Joseph's University, College of Arts and Sciences, Program in Gerontological Services, Philadelphia, PA 19131-1395. Offers gerontological counseling (MS); gerontological services (Post-Master's Certificate); human services administration (MS). Evening/weekend programs available. *Students:* 3 full-time (0 women), 9 part-time (4 women); includes 5 minority (all African Americans), 5 international. Average age 34. In 2007, 6 degrees awarded. *Entrance requirements:* For master's, 2 letters of recommendation, application, official transcripts, personal statement. Additional exam requirements/recommendations for international students: Required—TOEFL (minimum score 550 paper-based; 213 computer-based; 79 iBT). *Application deadline:* For fall admission, 7/15 priority date for domestic students, 4/15 for international students; for winter admission, 1/15 for international students; for spring admission, 11/15 priority date for domestic students, 10/15 for international students. Applications are processed on a rolling basis. Application fee: $35. Electronic applications accepted. *Expenses:* Tuition: Part-time $738 per credit. Tuition and fees vary according to degree level and program. *Financial support:* Fellowships available. *Unit head:* Dr. Catherine Murray, Director, 610-660-1805.

San Diego State University, Graduate and Research Affairs, College of Health and Human Services, Department of Gerontology, San Diego, CA 92182. Offers MS. Part-time and evening/weekend programs available. *Students:* 2 full-time (both women), 4 part-time (all women); includes 1 minority (Asian American or Pacific Islander) Average age 31. 5 applicants, 1060% accepted, 2 enrolled. In 2007, 5 degrees awarded. *Degree requirements:* For master's, thesis. *Entrance requirements:* For master's, GRE General Test. Additional exam requirements/recommendations for international students: Required—TOEFL. *Application deadline:* For fall admission, 5/1 for domestic students; for spring admission, 11/1 for domestic students. Applications are processed on a rolling basis. Electronic applications accepted. *Financial support:* In 2007–08, 1 teaching assistantship was awarded; career-related internships or fieldwork and traineeships also available. Total annual research expenditures: $249,000. *Unit head:* Mario Garrett, Chair, 619-594-2818, Fax: 619-594-2811, E-mail: mgarrett@mail.sdsu.edu. *Application contact:* Barbara DuBois, Graduate Adviser, 619-594-6768, Fax: 619-594-2811, E-mail: dubois@mail.sdsu.edu.

San Francisco State University, Division of Graduate Studies, College of Health and Human Services, Gerontology Program, San Francisco, CA 94132-1722. Offers geriatric care management (MA); health, wellness and aging (MA); long-term care administration (MA). Part-time programs available. *Application deadline:* Applications are processed on a rolling basis. *Financial support:* Career-related internships or fieldwork and unspecified assistantships available. *Unit head:* Dr. Anabel Pelham, Director, 415-338-1684, Fax: 415-338-6378, E-mail: apelham@sfsu.edu.

San Jose State University, Graduate Studies and Research, College of Applied Sciences and Arts, Department of Health Science, San Jose, CA 95192-0001. Offers applied social gerontology (Certificate); community health education (MPH). *Accreditation:* CEPH (one or more programs are accredited). Postbaccalaureate distance learning degree programs offered. *Students:* 11 full-time (10 women), 44 part-time (37 women); includes 22 minority (1 African American, 9 Asian Americans or Pacific Islanders, 12 Hispanic Americans), 3 international. Average age 35. 147 applicants, 40% accepted, 21 enrolled. In 2007, 21 degrees awarded. *Entrance requirements:* For master's, GRE General Test. *Application deadline:* For fall admission, 6/29 for domestic students; for spring admission, 11/30 for domestic students. Applications are processed on a rolling basis. Application fee: $59. Electronic applications accepted. *Financial support:* Career-related internships or fieldwork, Federal Work-Study, and institutionally sponsored loans available. Support available to part-time students. Financial award applicants required to submit FAFSA. *Faculty research:* Behavioral science in occupational and health care settings, epidemiology in health care settings. *Unit head:* Dr. Kathleen Roe, Chair, 408-924-2976, Fax: 408-924-2979.

Simon Fraser University, Graduate Studies, Faculty of Arts and Social Sciences, Department of Gerontology, Burnaby, BC V5A 1S6, Canada. Offers MA, PhD. *Degree requirements:* For master's, thesis (for some programs). *Entrance requirements:* For master's, minimum GPA of 3.5. Additional exam requirements/recommendations for international students: Required—TOEFL or IELTS. *Faculty research:* Aging and the built environment, health promotion and aging.

Texas A&M University–Kingsville, College of Graduate Studies, College of Arts and Sciences, Department of Psychology and Sociology, Kingsville, TX 78363. Offers gerontology (MS); psychology (MA, MS); sociology (MA, MS). Part-time and evening/weekend programs available. *Degree requirements:* For master's, comprehensive exam, thesis or alternative. *Entrance requirements:* For master's, GRE General Test, minimum GPA of 2.5. Additional exam requirements/recommendations for international students: Required—TOEFL. *Faculty research:* Hispanic female voting behavior, attitudes toward criminal justice, immigration of aged into south Texas, folk medicine.

Texas Tech University, Graduate School, College of Human Sciences, Department of Human Development and Family Studies, Lubbock, TX 79409. Offers gerontology (MS); human development and family studies (MS, PhD). *Accreditation:* AAMFT/COAMFTE (one or more programs are accredited). Part-time programs available. *Faculty:* 20 full-time (16 women). *Students:* 45 full-time (38 women), 16 part-time (12 women); includes 9 minority (1 African American, 1 American Indian/Alaska Native, 3 Asian Americans or Pacific Islanders, 4 Hispanic Americans), 13 international. Average age 34. 44 applicants, 75% accepted, 16 enrolled. In 2007, 2 master's, 2 doctorates awarded. *Degree requirements:* For master's, thesis; for doctorate, thesis/dissertation. *Entrance requirements:* For master's and doctorate, GRE General Test. Additional exam requirements/recommendations for international students: Required—TOEFL (minimum score 550 paper-based; 213 computer-based). *Application deadline:* For fall admission, 3/1 priority date for international students; for spring admission, 11/1 priority date for international students. Applications are processed on a rolling basis. Application fee: $50 ($60 for international students). Electronic applications accepted. *Expenses:* Tuition, state resident: part-time $373 per credit hour. Tuition, nonresident: part-time $651 per credit hour. Tuition and fees vary according to program. *Financial support:* In 2007–08, 50 students received support, including 11 research assistantships with partial tuition reimbursements available (averaging $12,849 per year), 35 teaching assistantships with partial tuition reimbursements available (averaging $12,986 per year); career-related internships or fieldwork, Federal Work-Study, institutionally sponsored loans, and scholarships/grants also available. Support available to part-time students. Financial award application deadline: 4/15; financial award applicants required to submit FAFSA. *Faculty research:* Parenting, marital and premarital relationships, adolescent drug abuse, life span; child development. Total annual research expenditures: $72,657. *Unit head:* Anisa Zvonkovic, Interim Chair, 806-742-3000 Ext. 279, Fax: 806-742-0285, E-mail: anisa.zvonkovic@ttu.edu. *Application contact:* Judy McMurry, Graduate Secretary, 806-742-3000, Fax: 806-742-0285.

Towson University, College of Graduate Studies and Research, Program in Applied Gerontology, Towson, MD 21252-0001. Offers MS, Certificate. *Students:* 1 (woman) full-time, 12 part-time (all women); includes 1 minority (Asian American or Pacific Islander) Average age 36. 1 applicant, 100% accepted, 1 enrolled. In 2007, 2 degrees awarded. *Entrance requirements:* For master's, minimum of 9 credits of upper-level related coursework, 2 letters of recommendation, admission essay; for Certificate, minimum of 9 credits of upper-level related coursework. *Application deadline:* Applications are processed on a rolling basis. Application fee: $50. Electronic applications accepted. *Expenses:* Tuition, state resident: part-time $286 per credit. Tuition, nonresident: part-time $600 per credit. Required fees: $75 per credit. *Financial support:* Application deadline: 4/1; *Unit head:* Donna L. Wagner, Graduate Program Director, 410-704-4643, E-mail: dwagner@towson.edu. *Application contact:* 410-704-2501, Fax: 410-704-4675, E-mail: grads@towson.edu.

Université de Sherbrooke, Faculty of Letters and Human Sciences, Department of Psychology, Sherbrooke, QC J1K 2R1, Canada. Offers gerontology (MA). *Degree requirements:* For master's, thesis. *Faculty research:* Human relations.

Université Laval, Faculty of Medicine, Post-Professional Programs in Medical Studies, Québec, QC G1K 7P4, Canada. Offers anatomy–pathology (DESS); anesthesiology (DESS); cardiology (DESS); care of older people (Diploma); clinical research (DESS); community health (DESS); dermatology (DESS); diagnostic radiology (DESS); emergency medicine (Diploma); family medicine (DESS); general surgery (DESS); geriatrics (DESS); hematology (DESS); internal medicine (DESS); maternal and fetal medicine (Diploma); medical biochemistry (DESS); medical microbiology and infectious diseases (DESS); medical oncology (DESS); nephrology (DESS); neurology (DESS); neurosurgery (DESS); obstetrics and gynecology (DESS); ophthalmology (DESS); orthopedic surgery (DESS); oto-rhino-laryngology (DESS); palliative medicine (Diploma); pediatrics (DESS); plastic surgery (DESS); psychiatry (DESS); pulmonary medicine (DESS); radiology–oncology (DESS); thoracic surgery (DESS); urology (DESS). *Degree requirements:* For other advanced degree, comprehensive exam. *Entrance requirements:* For degree, knowledge of French. Electronic applications accepted.

University of Arkansas at Little Rock, Graduate School, College of Arts, Humanities, and Social Science, Program in Gerontology, Little Rock, AR 72204-1099. Offers Graduate Certificate. *Students:* Average age 39. *Application deadline:* Applications are processed on a rolling basis. *Financial support:* Research assistantships, career-related internships or fieldwork, Federal Work-Study, institutionally sponsored loans, and unspecified assistantships available. Support available to part-time students. *Application contact:* Shannon M. Clowney, Coordinator, 501-569-8781, E-mail: smclowney@ualr.edu.

University of Central Florida, College of Health and Public Affairs, School of Social Work, Orlando, FL 32816. Offers addictions (Certificate); aging studies (Certificate); children's services (Certificate); school social work (Certificate); social work (MSW); social work administration (Certificate). *Accreditation:* CSWE. Part-time and evening/weekend programs available. *Faculty:*

16 full-time (11 women), 21 part-time/adjunct (16 women). *Degree requirements:* For master's, thesis or alternative, field education. *Entrance requirements:* For master's, resumé. Additional exam requirements/recommendations for international students: Required—TOEFL. *Application deadline:* For fall admission, 3/1 for domestic students. Application fee: $30. Electronic applications accepted. *Expenses:* Tuition, state resident: full-time $6,484. Tuition, nonresident: full-time $23,938. Tuition and fees vary according to program. *Financial support:* Fellowships with partial tuition reimbursements, research assistantships with partial tuition reimbursements, teaching assistantships with partial tuition reimbursements, career-related internships or fieldwork, Federal Work-Study, institutionally sponsored loans, and unspecified assistantships available. Financial award application deadline: 3/1; financial award applicants required to submit FAFSA. *Unit head:* Dr. John Ronnau, Director, 407-823-2208, Fax: 407-823-5697, E-mail: jronnau@mail.ucf.edu.

University of Central Missouri, The Graduate School, College of Health and Human Services, Department of Sociology and Social Work, Warrensburg, MO 64093. Offers social gerontology (MS); sociology (MA). Part-time programs available. *Faculty:* 14 full-time (8 women). *Students:* 10 full-time (9 women), 19 part-time (14 women); includes 5 minority (4 African Americans, 1 Asian American or Pacific Islander), 1 international. Average age 38. 25 applicants, 84% accepted, 9 enrolled. In 2007, 11 degrees awarded. *Degree requirements:* For master's, comprehensive exam. *Entrance requirements:* For master's, minimum GPA of 2.5. Additional exam requirements/recommendations for international students: Required—TOEFL (minimum score 500 paper-based; 173 computer-based). *Application deadline:* For fall admission, 6/1 priority date for domestic students, 5/1 priority date for international students; for spring admission, 10/1 priority date for domestic students, 10/1 for international students. Applications are processed on a rolling basis. Application fee: $30 ($50 for international students). *Expenses:* Tuition, state resident: full-time $6,259; part-time $256 per credit hour. Tuition, nonresident: full-time $11,915; part-time $491 per credit hour. Required fees: $604; $20 per credit hour. *Financial support:* In 2007–08, 5 students received support; teaching assistantships with partial tuition reimbursements available, Federal Work-Study, scholarships/grants, unspecified assistantships, and administrative assistantships available. Support available to part-time students. Financial award application deadline: 3/1; financial award applicants required to submit FAFSA. *Faculty research:* Suicide, end of life decision making, aging/gerontology, race/ethic relations, religion. Total annual research expenditures: $212,400. *Unit head:* Jean Nuernberger, Chair, 660-543-8758, Fax: 660-543-8215, E-mail: nuernberger@ucmo.edu.

University of Central Oklahoma, College of Graduate Studies and Research, College of Education, Department of Occupational and Technical Education, Program in Adult Education, Edmond, OK 73034-5209. Offers community services (M Ed); gerontology (M Ed). *Accreditation:* NCATE. Part-time programs available. *Faculty:* 9 full-time (4 women), 5 part-time/adjunct (3 women). *Students:* 39 full-time (26 women), 77 part-time (64 women); includes 28 minority (18 African Americans, 6 American Indian/Alaska Native, 2 Asian Americans or Pacific Islanders, 2 Hispanic Americans), 10 international. Average age 36. 34 applicants, 100% accepted. In 2007, 35 degrees awarded. *Entrance requirements:* For master's, GRE General Test. Additional exam requirements/recommendations for international students: Required—TOEFL (minimum score 550 paper-based; 213 computer-based). *Application deadline:* For fall admission, 7/1 for international students; for spring admission, 11/1 for international students. Applications are processed on a rolling basis. Application fee: $25. Electronic applications accepted. *Expenses:* Tuition, state resident: full-time $3,516; part-time $147 per hour. Tuition, nonresident: full-time $9,054; part-time $377 per hour. Required fees: $433; $18 per hour. *Financial support:* Unspecified assistantships available. Financial award application deadline: 3/31; financial award applicants required to submit FAFSA. *Unit head:* Shari Villani, Head, 405-974-2855.

University of Georgia, College of Public Health, Institute of Gerontology, Athens, GA 30602. Offers Certificate. *Faculty:* 2 full-time (1 woman). *Students:* 3 applicants, 67% accepted, 2 enrolled. *Unit head:* Dr. Leonard W. Poon, Director, 706-425-3222, E-mail: lpoon@geron.uga.edu. *Application contact:* Dr. Anne H. Glass, Graduate Coordinator, 706-425-3222, E-mail: aglass@geron.uga.edu.

University of Illinois at Springfield, Graduate Programs, College of Education and Human Services, Program in Human Services, Springfield, IL 62703-5407. Offers alcoholism and substance abuse (MA); child and family services (MA); gerontology (MA); social services administration (MA). Part-time and evening/weekend programs available. Postbaccalaureate distance learning degree programs offered. *Faculty:* 4 full-time (3 women), 2 part-time/adjunct (both women). *Students:* 36 full-time (30 women), 64 part-time (53 women); includes 23 minority (21 African Americans, 2 American Indian/Alaska Native), 1 international. Average age 36. 52 applicants, 62% accepted, 27 enrolled. In 2007, 10 degrees awarded. *Degree requirements:* For master's, thesis optional, internship. *Entrance requirements:* For master's, 2 letters of reference, minimum undergraduate GPA of 3.0, prerequisite courses in lifespan development and research methods, personal statement. Additional exam requirements/recommendations for international students: Required—TOEFL (minimum score 550 paper-based; 213 computer-based). *Application deadline:* For fall admission, 2/15 priority date for domestic and international students; for spring admission, 9/15 priority date for domestic and international students. Application fee: $50 ($60 for international students). *Expenses:* Tuition, state resident: full-time $5,424; part-time $226 per credit hour. Tuition, nonresident: part-time $553 per credit hour. Required fees: $618 per term. *Financial support:* In 2007–08, research assistantships with full tuition reimbursements (averaging $7,988 per year), teaching assistantships with full tuition reimbursements (averaging $7,988 per year) were awarded; career-related internships or fieldwork, scholarships/grants, health care benefits, and unspecified assistantships also available. Support available to part-time students. Financial award application deadline: 11/15. *Unit head:* Dr. Carolyn Peck, Program Administrator, 217-206-7577, Fax: 217-206-6775, E-mail: peck.carolyn@uis.edu.

University of Indianapolis, Graduate Programs, Center for Aging and Community, Indianapolis, IN 46227-3697. Offers gerontology (MS, Certificate). Part-time and evening/weekend programs available. Postbaccalaureate distance learning degree programs offered. *Students:* Average age 37. *Degree requirements:* For master's, capstone course. *Entrance requirements:* For master's, 1 page essay, 3 letters of recommendation. Additional exam requirements/recommendations for international students: Required—TOEFL (minimum score 550 paper-based; 213 computer-based). *Application deadline:* Applications are processed on a rolling basis. Application fee: $50. *Financial support:* In 2007–08, 1 research assistantship was awarded; Federal Work-Study and scholarships/grants also available. *Unit head:* Dr. Ellen Miller, Executive Director, 317-791-5930, Fax: 317-791-5945, E-mail: emiller@uindy.edu. *Application contact:* Tamora Wolske, Academic Program Director, 317-791-5930, Fax: 317-791-5945, E-mail: wolsketl@uindy.edu.

University of Indianapolis, Graduate Programs, School of Nursing, Indianapolis, IN 46227-3697. Offers family practice (post-RN) (MSN); gerontological nurse practitioner (MSN); nurse-midwifery (MSN); nursing (MSN); nursing administration (MSN); nursing education (MSN); MBA/MSN. *Accreditation:* AACN; ACNM. *Faculty:* 6 full-time (5 women), 4 part-time/adjunct (all women). *Students:* 26 full-time (23 women), 97 part-time (94 women); includes 18 minority (17 African Americans, 1 Hispanic American). Average age 39. *Entrance requirements:* For master's, minimum GPA of 3.0, interview, letters of recommendation, resumé, IN nursing license, 1 year professional practice. Additional exam requirements/recommendations for international students: Required—TOEFL (minimum score 550 paper-based; 213 computer-based). *Application deadline:* For fall admission, 8/1 for domestic students; for winter admission, 12/15 for domestic students; for spring admission, 4/15 for domestic students. Applications are processed on a rolling basis. Application fee: $50. *Financial support:* Federal Work-Study available. *Unit head:* Dr. Mary McHugh, Dean, 317-788-3206, E-mail: issac@uindy.edu. *Application contact:* T.C. Crum, Information Contact, 317-788-2128, Fax: 317-788-3542, E-mail: tcrum@uindy.edu.

University of Kansas, Research and Graduate Studies, College of Liberal Arts and Sciences, Program in Gerontology, Lawrence, KS 66045. Offers MA, PhD. *Faculty:* 5. *Students:* 1 (woman) full-time, 1 international. Average age 29. 5 applicants, 20% accepted. In 2007, 3 degrees awarded. *Degree requirements:* For master's, thesis; for doctorate, comprehensive exam, thesis/dissertation, written preliminary exam. *Entrance requirements:* For master's and doctorate, GRE, 3 letters of reference. Additional exam requirements/recommendations for international students: Required—TOEFL. *Application deadline:* For fall admission, 2/1 priority date for domestic and international students. Applications are processed on a rolling basis. Application fee: $55 ($60 for international students). Electronic applications accepted. *Expenses:* Tuition, state resident: full-time $5,838. Tuition, nonresident: full-time $13,409. Tuition and fees vary according to program. *Financial support:* Fellowships with full tuition reimbursements, research assistantships with full tuition reimbursements, career-related internships or fieldwork, traineeships, and unspecified assistantships available. Financial award application deadline: 1/15. *Faculty research:* Communication and aging, work and retirement, family studies, cognitive aging, exercise and disability. *Unit head:* David J. Ekerdt, Center Director, 785-864-4130, Fax: 785-864-2666, E-mail: gerontology@ku.edu. *Application contact:* Susan Kemper, Graduate Adviser, 785-864-0748, E-mail: skemper@ku.edu.

University of Kentucky, Graduate School, College of Public Health, Program in Gerontology, Lexington, KY 40506-0032. Offers PhD. *Faculty:* 10 full-time (4 women), 1 part-time/adjunct (0 women). *Students:* 22 full-time (21 women), 7 part-time (6 women); includes 2 minority (both African Americans), 1 international. Average age 35. 22 applicants, 41% accepted, 5 enrolled. In 2007, 4 degrees awarded. *Median time to degree:* Of those who began their doctoral program in fall 1999, 67% received their degree in 8 years or less. *Degree requirements:* For doctorate, comprehensive exam, thesis/dissertation. *Entrance requirements:* For doctorate, GRE General Test, minimum undergraduate GPA of 2.75, graduate work GPA of 3.0. Additional exam requirements/recommendations for international students: Required—TOEFL (minimum score 550 paper-based; 213 computer-based). *Application deadline:* For fall admission, 7/17 for domestic students, 2/1 priority date for international students; for spring admission, 12/13 for domestic students, 6/15 priority date for international students. Application fee: $50 ($65 for international students). Electronic applications accepted. *Expenses:* Tuition, state resident: part-time $437 per credit hour. Tuition, nonresident: part-time $931 per credit hour. *Financial support:* In 2007–08, 17 students received support, including 11 fellowships with full tuition reimbursements available (averaging $16,000 per year), 7 research assistantships with full tuition reimbursements available (averaging $16,000 per year); teaching assistantships, Federal Work-Study, scholarships/grants, traineeships, health care benefits, tuition waivers (partial), and unspecified assistantships also available. Support available to part-time students. Financial award application deadline: 3/15. *Unit head:* Dr. John Watkins, Director of Graduate Studies, 859-323-1450 Ext. 80240, Fax: 859-323-5747, E-mail: geg173@pop.uky.edu. *Application contact:* Dr. Brian Jackson, Senior Associate Dean, 859-257-4667, Fax: 859-257-4676, E-mail: brian.jackson@uky.edu.

University of La Verne, College of Business and Public Management, Program in Gerontology, La Verne, CA 91750-4443. Offers business administration (MS); counseling (MS); gerontology (Certificate); gerontology administration (MS); health services management (MS); public administration (MS). Part-time programs available. *Faculty:* 6 full-time (2 women), 11 part-time/adjunct (5 women). *Students:* 5 full-time (all women), 23 part-time (19 women); includes 16 minority (9 African Americans, 1 American Indian/Alaska Native, 1 Asian American or Pacific Islander, 5 Hispanic Americans). Average age 49. In 2007, 14 degrees awarded. *Entrance requirements:* For master's, minimum GPA of 2.5. Additional exam requirements/recommendations for international students: Required—TOEFL (minimum score 550 paper-based; 213 computer-based). *Application deadline:* Applications are processed on a rolling basis. Application fee: $50. *Expenses: Contact institution.* Tuition and fees vary according to course load and program. *Financial support:* Institutionally sponsored loans available. Financial award application deadline: 3/2; financial award applicants required to submit FAFSA. *Unit head:* Joan Branin, Chairperson, 909-593-3511 Ext. 4247, E-mail: braninj@ulv.edu. *Application contact:* Connie Hamlow, Admissions Information Specialist, 909-593-3511 Ext. 4244, Fax: 909-392-2761, E-mail: gradadmission@ulv.edu.

University of Louisiana at Monroe, Graduate Studies and Research, College of Arts and Sciences, Program in Gerontology, Monroe, LA 71209-0001. Offers MA, CGS. *Faculty:* 2 full-time (0 women). *Students:* 13 full-time (all women), 20 part-time (17 women); includes 12 African Americans, 1 Hispanic American. Average age 32. In 2007, 6 degrees awarded. *Degree requirements:* For master's, thesis optional. *Entrance requirements:* For master's, GRE General Test, minimum GPA of 2.75, 3.0 in last 60 credits. Additional exam requirements/recommendations for international students: Required—TOEFL (minimum score 500 paper-based; 173 computer-based; 61 iBT). *Application deadline:* For fall admission, 8/22 priority date for domestic students, 7/1 for international students; for winter admission, 12/12 priority date for domestic students; for spring admission, 1/17 for domestic students, 11/1 for international students. Applications are processed on a rolling basis. Application fee: $20 ($30 for international students). Electronic applications accepted. *Expenses:* Tuition, state resident: full-time $2,220. Tuition, nonresident: full-time $8,172. *Financial support:* In 2007–08, 3 research assistantships with full tuition reimbursements (averaging $2,500 per year), 1 teaching assistantship with full tuition reimbursement (averaging $2,500 per year) were awarded; career-related internships or fieldwork, Federal Work-Study, and unspecified assistantships also available. Financial award application deadline: 4/1; financial award applicants required to submit FAFSA. *Unit head:* Dr. James Bulot, Unit Head, 318-342-1465, Fax: 318-342-1431, E-mail: bulot@ulm.edu.

University of Maryland, Baltimore, Graduate School, Program in Gerontology, Baltimore, MD 21201. Offers PhD. *Students:* 8 full-time (6 women), 2 part-time (both women); includes 1 minority (African American), 2 international. Average age 35. 6 applicants, 67% accepted, 2 enrolled. In 2007, 2 doctorates awarded. *Degree requirements:* For doctorate, comprehensive exam, thesis/dissertation. *Entrance requirements:* For doctorate, GRE General Test. Additional exam requirements/recommendations for international students: Required—TOEFL (minimum score 550 paper-based; 213 computer-based; 80 iBT), TOEFL or IELTS; Recommended—IELTS (minimum score 7). *Application deadline:* For fall admission, 2/1 for domestic students, 1/15 for international students. Application fee: $50. Electronic applications accepted. *Financial support:* Fellowships, research assistantships available. Financial award applicants required to submit FAFSA. *Unit head:* Dr. Jay Magaziner, Professor and Program Director, 410-706-4926.

University of Maryland, Baltimore County, Graduate School, College of Arts, Humanities and Social Sciences, Department of Sociology and Anthropology, Baltimore, MD 21250. Offers applied sociology (MA, Postbaccalaureate Certificate), including applied sociology (MA), non-profit sector (Postbaccalaureate Certificate). Part-time programs available. *Faculty:* 13 full-time (6 women), 1 (woman) part-time/adjunct. *Students:* 28 full-time (21 women), 32 part-time (24 women); includes 18 minority (11 African Americans, 1 American Indian/Alaska Native, 6 Asian Americans or Pacific Islanders), 2 international. Average age 32. 37 applicants, 100% accepted, 34 enrolled. In 2007, 18 degrees awarded. *Degree requirements:* For master's, thesis or alternative. *Entrance requirements:* For master's, minimum GPA of 3.0, undergrad statistics course. Additional exam requirements/recommendations for international students: Required—TOEFL. *Application deadline:* For fall admission, 7/31 for domestic students; for spring admission, 12/31 for domestic students. Applications are processed on a rolling basis. Application fee: $50. Electronic applications accepted. *Financial support:* In 2007–08, 9 students received support, including 4 research assistantships with partial tuition reimbursements available (averaging $12,500 per year), 5 teaching assistantships with partial tuition reimbursements available (averaging $12,500 per year); scholarships/grants, health care benefits, unspecified assistantships, and tuition remission also available. Financial award application deadline: 2/1. *Faculty research:* Sociology of aging, diversity, medical sociology. *Unit head:* Dr. James E. Trela, Chairperson, 410-455-2076, Fax: 410-455-1154, E-mail: trela@umbc.edu. *Application contact:* Dr. William G. Rothstein, Director, 410-455-2078, Fax: 410-455-1154, E-mail: rothstei@umbc.edu.

University of Maryland, Baltimore County, Graduate School, Program in Gerontology, Baltimore, MD 21250. Offers aging policy for the elderly (PhD); epidemiology of aging (PhD);

Gerontology

University of Maryland, Baltimore County (continued)
social, cultural, and behavioral sciences (PhD). Part-time programs available. *Faculty:* 22 part-time/adjunct (11 women). *Students:* 21 full-time (16 women), 5 part-time (all women); includes 4 minority (all African Americans), 3 international. Average age 33. 19 applicants, 37% accepted, 6 enrolled. In 2007, 2 degrees awarded. *Degree requirements:* For doctorate, comprehensive exam, thesis/dissertation. *Entrance requirements:* For doctorate, GRE General Test. Additional exam requirements/recommendations for international students: Required—TOEFL, TWE. *Application deadline:* For spring admission, 2/1 for domestic and international students. Application fee: $45. Electronic applications accepted. *Financial support:* In 2007–08, 4 fellowships with full tuition reimbursements (averaging $19,000 per year), 8 research assistantships with full tuition reimbursements (averaging $19,000 per year), 1 teaching assistantship with full tuition reimbursement (averaging $19,000 per year) were awarded; career-related internships or fieldwork, scholarships/grants, traineeships, health care benefits, tuition waivers (partial), and unspecified assistantships also available. Support available to part-time students. Financial award application deadline: 2/1. *Faculty research:* Aging and health policy, behavioral aspects of aging, caregiving, LTC, epidemiology of aging. Total annual research expenditures: $32 million. *Unit head:* Dr. Leslie Morgan, Co-Director, 410-455-2074, Fax: 410-455-1154, E-mail: lmorgan@umbc.edu. *Application contact:* Justine Golden, Academic Coordinator, 410-706-4926, E-mail: jgold002@umaryland.edu.

University of Massachusetts Boston, Office of Graduate Studies, John W. McCormack Graduate School of Policy Studies, Program in Gerontology, Boston, MA 02125-3393. Offers gerontology (MS, PhD, Certificate); gerontology research (MA); management in aging services (MA). Part-time programs available. *Degree requirements:* For doctorate, comprehensive exam, thesis/dissertation. *Entrance requirements:* For doctorate, GRE General Test, minimum GPA of 3.0. *Faculty research:* Aging with a chronic disability, pension policy and social security system, elderly minorities, health services research, living arrangements.

University of Missouri–St. Louis, College of Arts and Sciences, Program in Gerontology, St. Louis, MO 63121. Offers gerontology (MS, Certificate); long term care administration (Certificate). Part-time and evening/weekend programs available. *Faculty:* 4 full-time (3 women), 5 part-time/adjunct (4 women). *Students:* 5 full-time (all women), 12 part-time (8 women); includes 4 minority (3 African Americans, 1 Asian American or Pacific Islander), 2 international. Average age 40. In 2007, 5 degrees awarded. *Entrance requirements:* For master's, 3 letters of recommendation. Additional exam requirements/recommendations for international students: Required—TOEFL (minimum score 550 paper-based; 213 computer-based). *Application deadline:* For fall admission, 7/15 priority date for domestic students; for spring admission, 12/15 priority date for domestic students. Applications are processed on a rolling basis. Application fee: $35 ($40 for international students). Electronic applications accepted. *Financial support:* In 2007–08, 1 research assistantship with full tuition reimbursement (averaging $7,200 per year) was awarded; teaching assistantships with full tuition reimbursements, career-related internships or fieldwork and Federal Work-Study also available. *Faculty research:* Health care policy, social support and stress, retirement policy health behavior, ethnic differences in aging. *Unit head:* Thomas Meuser, Director, 314-516-5421. *Application contact:* 314-516-5458, Fax: 314-516-6996, E-mail: gradadm@umsl.edu.

University of Nebraska at Omaha, Graduate Studies and Research, College of Education, Department of Counseling, Omaha, NE 68182. Offers community counseling (MA, MS); counseling gerontology (MA, MS); school counseling (MA, MS); student affairs practice in higher education (MA, MS). *Accreditation:* ACA (one or more programs are accredited); NCATE. Part-time and evening/weekend programs available. *Faculty:* 5 full-time (1 woman). *Students:* 28 full-time (22 women), 123 part-time (104 women); includes 13 minority (9 African Americans, 2 Asian Americans or Pacific Islanders, 2 Hispanic Americans). Average age 34. 40 applicants, 48% accepted, 14 enrolled. In 2007, 50 degrees awarded. *Degree requirements:* For master's, comprehensive exam, thesis (for some programs). *Entrance requirements:* For master's, GRE General Test, MAT, department test, interview, minimum GPA of 3.0. Additional exam requirements/recommendations for international students: Required—TOEFL (minimum score 550 paper-based; 213 computer-based; 80 iBT). *Application deadline:* For fall admission, 3/1 for domestic students; for spring admission, 10/1 for domestic students. Applications are processed on a rolling basis. Application fee: $45. Electronic applications accepted. *Financial support:* In 2007–08, 83 students received support, including 2 research assistantships with tuition reimbursements available; fellowships, Federal Work-Study, institutionally sponsored loans, scholarships/grants, tuition waivers (partial), and unspecified assistantships also available. Support available to part-time students. Financial award application deadline: 3/1; financial award applicants required to submit FAFSA. *Unit head:* Dr. Jeanette Seaberry, Chairperson, 402-554-2727.

University of Nebraska at Omaha, Graduate Studies and Research, College of Public Affairs and Community Service, Department of Gerontology, Omaha, NE 68182. Offers gerontology (Certificate); social gerontology (MA). Part-time and evening/weekend programs available. *Faculty:* 6 full-time (2 women). *Students:* 4 full-time (all women), 7 part-time (6 women); includes 2 minority (both African Americans) Average age 36. 7 applicants, 71% accepted, 5 enrolled. In 2007, 5 degrees awarded. *Degree requirements:* For master's, comprehensive exam, thesis. *Entrance requirements:* For master's, GRE General Test, MAT, minimum GPA of 3.0, writing sample, letters of recommendation. Additional exam requirements/recommendations for international students: Required—TOEFL (minimum score 550 paper-based; 213 computer-based; 80 iBT). *Application deadline:* For fall admission, 7/1 priority date for domestic students; for spring admission, 12/1 priority date for domestic students. Applications are processed on a rolling basis. Application fee: $45. Electronic applications accepted. *Financial support:* In 2007–08, 6 students received support; fellowships, career-related internships or fieldwork, Federal Work-Study, institutionally sponsored loans, scholarships/grants, and tuition waivers (partial) available. Support available to part-time students. Financial award application deadline: 3/1; financial award applicants required to submit FAFSA. *Unit head:* Dr. Karl Kosloski, Chairperson, 402-554-2272.

University of New England, College of Health Professions, School of Social Work, Biddeford, ME 04005-9526. Offers addictions counseling (Certificate); gerontology (Certificate); social work (MSW). *Accreditation:* CSWE. Part-time programs available. *Faculty:* 14 full-time (8 women), 5 part-time/adjunct (4 women). *Students:* 137 full-time (117 women), 7 part-time (all women); includes 2 minority (both American Indian/Alaska Native), 3 international. Average age 32. 110 applicants, 86% accepted, 55 enrolled. In 2007, 55 master's, 1 other advanced degree awarded. *Degree requirements:* For master's, field internships. *Entrance requirements:* Additional exam requirements/recommendations for international students: Required—TOEFL (minimum score 550 paper-based; 213 computer-based). *Application deadline:* For fall admission, 1/15 priority date for domestic students; for spring admission, 3/31 priority date for domestic students, 3/31 for international students. Applications are processed on a rolling basis. Application fee: $40. Electronic applications accepted. *Financial support:* In 2007–08, 40 students received support. Scholarships/grants and tuition waivers (partial) available. Financial award application deadline: 5/1; financial award applicants required to submit FAFSA. *Faculty research:* Domestic violence, solution focused practice, empowerment models, adverse childhood experiences. *Unit head:* Martha Wilson, Director, 207-221-4513, E-mail: mwilson@une.edu. *Application contact:* Peggy Warden, Assistant Director of Graduate Admissions, 207-221-4225, Fax: 207-221-4898, E-mail: gradadmissions@une.edu.

The University of North Carolina at Charlotte, Graduate School, College of Arts and Sciences, Program in Gerontology, Charlotte, NC 28223-0001. Offers MA. *Students:* 3 full-time (all women), 9 part-time (all women); includes 2 African Americans, 1 Hispanic American, 2 international. Average age 25. 4 applicants, 100% accepted, 3 enrolled. In 2007, 7 degrees awarded. *Degree requirements:* For master's, thesis optional. *Entrance requirements:* For master's, GRE or MAT. Additional exam requirements/recommendations for international students: Required—TOEFL (minimum score 557 paper-based; 220 computer-based). *Application deadline:* For fall admission, 7/1 for domestic students, 5/1 for international students; for spring admission, 11/1 for domestic students, 10/1 for international students. Applications are processed on a rolling basis. Application fee: $55. Electronic applications accepted. *Expenses:* Tuition, state resident: full-time $2,855. Tuition, nonresident: full-time $13,062. Required fees: $1,692. *Financial support:* In 2007–08, 3 research assistantships (averaging $10,000 per year) were awarded; fellowships, teaching assistantships, career-related internships or fieldwork, Federal Work-Study, institutionally sponsored loans, scholarships/grants, and unspecified assistantships also available. Support available to part-time students. Financial award application deadline: 4/1; financial award applicants required to submit FAFSA. *Faculty research:* Rural older adults, person-centered dementia care, formal and informal systems of care, health care issues: gay, lesbian, and African American aging. *Unit head:* Dr. Dena Shenk, Director, 704-687-4349, Fax: 704-687-4347, E-mail: dshenk@email.uncc.edu. *Application contact:* Kathy B. Giddings, Director of Graduate Admissions, 704-687-3366, Fax: 704-687-3279, E-mail: agidding@uncc.edu.

The University of North Carolina at Greensboro, Graduate School, Program in Gerontology, Greensboro, NC 27412-5001. Offers MS, Certificate, MS/MBA. *Students:* 11 full-time (10 women), 9 part-time (4 women); includes 2 minority (both Asian Americans or Pacific Islanders) *Application deadline:* For fall admission, 7/1 for domestic students. Application fee: $45. Electronic applications accepted. *Unit head:* Dr. Janice I Wassel, Director/Director of Graduate Studies, 336-256-1020, Fax: 336-256-0174, E-mail: jiwassel@uncg.edu. *Application contact:* Michelle Harkleroad, Director of Graduate Admissions, 336-334-4884, Fax: 336-334-4424, E-mail: mbharkle@uncg.edu.

University of Northern Colorado, Graduate School, College of Natural and Health Sciences, School of Human Sciences, Program in Gerontology, Greeley, CO 80639. Offers MA. Part-time programs available. *Faculty:* 2 full-time (both women). *Students:* 3 full-time (all women), 3 part-time (all women). Average age 37. 3 applicants, 67% accepted, 2 enrolled. In 2007, 3 degrees awarded. *Degree requirements:* For master's, comprehensive exam. *Entrance requirements:* For master's, GRE General Test or MAT, 2 letters of recommendation. *Application deadline:* Applications are processed on a rolling basis. Application fee: $50 ($60 for international students). Electronic applications accepted. *Expenses:* Tuition, state resident: part-time $222 per credit. Tuition, nonresident: part-time $627 per credit. Required fees: $36 per credit. *Financial support:* Fellowships, research assistantships, teaching assistantships, unspecified assistantships available. Financial award application deadline: 3/1; financial award applicants required to submit FAFSA. *Unit head:* Dr. Susan Collins, Program Coordinator, 970-351-2403.

University of North Florida, College of Health, Department of Public Health, Jacksonville, FL 32224-2645. Offers community health (MPH); geriatric management (MSH); health administration (MHA); health behavior research and evaluation (Certificate); nutrition (MSH); rehabilitation counseling (MS). *Accreditation:* CORE. Part-time and evening/weekend programs available. *Faculty:* 23 full-time (18 women). *Students:* 75 full-time (59 women), 55 part-time (47 women); includes 30 minority (20 African Americans, 4 Asian Americans or Pacific Islanders, 6 Hispanic Americans), 8 international. Average age 30. 171 applicants, 52% accepted, 50 enrolled. In 2007, 49 degrees awarded. *Degree requirements:* For master's, thesis optional. *Entrance requirements:* For master's, GRE General Test (MSH, MS, MPH), GMAT or GRE General Test (MHA), minimum GPA of 3.0 in last 60 hours. Additional exam requirements/recommendations for international students: Required—TOEFL (minimum score 500 paper-based; 173 computer-based). *Application deadline:* For fall admission, 7/1 priority date for domestic students, 5/1 for international students; for spring admission, 11/10 priority date for domestic students, 10/1 for international students. Applications are processed on a rolling basis. Application fee: $30. Electronic applications accepted. *Expenses:* Tuition, state resident: part-time $266 per credit hour. Tuition, nonresident: part-time $858 per credit hour. One-time fee: $35 part-time. Tuition and fees vary according to program. *Financial support:* In 2007–08, 66 students received support; research assistantships, teaching assistantships, career-related internships or fieldwork, Federal Work-Study, scholarships/grants, and tuition waivers (partial) available. Support available to part-time students. Financial award application deadline: 4/1; financial award applicants required to submit FAFSA. *Faculty research:* Dietary supplements; alcohol, tobacco, and other drug use prevention; turnover among health professionals; aging; psychosocial aspects of disabilities. Total annual research expenditures:$412,026. *Unit head:* Dr. Judith Perkin, Chair, 904-620-2840, Fax: 904-620-2848, E-mail: jperkin@unf.edu. *Application contact:* Rachel Broderick, Director of Advising, 904-620-2817, Fax: 904-620-1770, E-mail: rbroderi@unf.edu.

University of North Texas, Robert B. Toulouse School of Graduate Studies, College of Public Affairs and Community Service, Department of Applied Gerontology, Denton, TX 76203. Offers aging (Certificate); applied gerontology (PhD); general studies in aging (MA, MS); long term care, senior housing, and aging services (MA, MS). Part-time and evening/weekend programs available. Postbaccalaureate distance learning degree programs offered (minimal on-campus study). *Faculty:* 5 full-time (1 woman). *Students:* 27 full-time (17 women), 41 part-time (35 women); includes 26 minority (21 African Americans, 3 Asian Americans or Pacific Islanders, 2 Hispanic Americans), 7 international. Average age 38. 39 applicants, 51% accepted, 12 enrolled. In 2007, 2 master's, 1 doctorate awarded. *Degree requirements:* For master's, comprehensive exam (for some programs), thesis, internship; for doctorate, thesis/dissertation. *Entrance requirements:* For master's and doctorate, GRE General Test. Additional exam requirements/recommendations for international students: Required—proof of English language proficiency required for non-native English speakers; Recommended—TOEFL (minimum score 550 paper-based; 213 computer-based). *Application deadline:* For fall admission, 7/15 for domestic students; for spring admission, 11/15 for domestic students. Applications are processed on a rolling basis. Application fee: $50 ($75 for international students). *Financial support:* Research assistantships, career-related internships or fieldwork, Federal Work-Study, institutionally sponsored loans, and scholarships/grants available. Financial award application deadline: 6/1; financial award applicants required to submit FAFSA. *Faculty research:* Minority aging, housing for the elderly, aging and developmental disability, caregiving, public policy and aging. *Unit head:* Dr. Richard A. Lusky, Chair, 940-565-2765, Fax: 940-565-4370, E-mail: lusky@scs.unt.edu. *Application contact:* Graduate Advisor, 940-565-2765, Fax: 940-565-4370, E-mail: gerontology@pacs.unt.edu.

University of Pittsburgh, Graduate School of Public Health, Department of Behavioral and Community Health Science, Pittsburgh, PA 15260. Offers behavioral and community health sciences (MPH, Dr PH); lesbian, gay, bisexual and transgender health and wellness (Certificate); minority health and health disparities (Certificate); program evaluation (Certificate); public health and aging (Certificate); public health preparedness (Certificate); MID/MPH; MPH/MPA; MPH/MSW; MPH/PhD. *Accreditation:* CAHME (one or more programs are accredited). Part-time programs available. *Faculty:* 18 full-time (8 women), 16 part-time/adjunct (7 women). *Students:* 61 full-time (50 women), 37 part-time (28 women); includes 17 minority (11 African Americans, 4 Asian Americans or Pacific Islanders, 2 Hispanic Americans), 7 international. Average age 29. 221 applicants, 67% accepted, 45 enrolled. In 2007, 30 master's, 5 doctorates awarded. *Median time to degree:* Of those who began their doctoral program in fall 1999, 100% received their degree in 8 years or less. *Degree requirements:* For master's, thesis; for doctorate, comprehensive exam, thesis/dissertation, preliminary exams. *Entrance requirements:* For master's and Certificate, GRE; for doctorate, GRE, master's degree in public health or related field. Additional exam requirements/recommendations for international students: Required—TOEFL (minimum score 550 paper-based; 213 computer-based; 80 iBT). *Application deadline:* For fall admission, 5/1 priority date for domestic students, 4/1 for international students; for winter admission, 9/1 for international students; for spring admission, 10/1 priority date for domestic students, 2/1 for international students. Applications are processed on a rolling basis. Application fee: $50 ($60 for international students). Electronic applications accepted. *Financial support:* In 2007–08, 17 students received support, including 16 research assistantships with full tuition reimbursements available (averaging $17,745 per year), 1 teaching assistantship with full tuition reimbursement available (averaging $7,535 per year). *Faculty research:* Maternal and child health, program evaluation, community-based participatory research, minority health and health disparities, aging. Total annual research expenditures: $1.3 million. *Unit head:* Dr. Ronald D Stall, Director and Assistant Dean, 412-383-7933, Fax: 412-624-3013, E-mail:

rstall@pitt.edu. *Application contact:* Natalie C Arnold, Recruitment and Academic Affairs Administrator, 412-624-3107, Fax: 412-624-5510, E-mail: narnold@pitt.edu.

University of Pittsburgh, School of Social Work, Program in Social Work, Pittsburgh, PA 15260. Offers gerontology (Certificate); social work (MSW, PhD); M Div/MSW; MPA/MSW; MPH/PhD; MPIA/MSW; MSW/MAJCS. *Accreditation:* CSWE (one or more programs are accredited). Part-time programs available. Postbaccalaureate distance learning degree programs offered (no on-campus study). *Degree requirements:* For master's, practicum; for doctorate, comprehensive exam, thesis/dissertation. *Entrance requirements:* For master's, minimum QPA of 3.0, course work in descriptive statistics and human biology; for doctorate, GRE, MSW or related degree, course work in statistics. Additional exam requirements/recommendations for international students: Required—TOEFL (minimum score 600 paper-based; 250 computer-based). Electronic applications accepted. *Faculty research:* Child abuse and neglect, poverty race relations and community empowerment, family preservation, welfare reform, mental health services research.

University of Puerto Rico, Medical Sciences Campus, Graduate School of Public Health, Department of Human Development, Program in Gerontology, San Juan, PR 00936-5067. Offers MPH, Certificate. Part-time and evening/weekend programs available. *Entrance requirements:* For master's, GRE, previous course work in social sciences, biology, psychology, and algebra.

University of Regina, Faculty of Graduate Studies and Research, Faculty of Arts, Program in Gerontology, Regina, SK S4S 0A2, Canada. Offers M Sc, MA. *Faculty:* 10 full-time (3 women). *Students:* 2 full-time (1 woman), 2 part-time (both women). 4 applicants, 100% accepted, 3 enrolled. *Degree requirements:* For master's, thesis. *Entrance requirements:* Additional exam requirements/recommendations for international students: Required—TOEFL (minimum score 580 paper-based; 237 computer-based; 88 iBT). *Application deadline:* For fall admission, 3/31 for domestic students. Application fee: $85 ($100 for international students). Electronic applications accepted. *Financial support:* In 2007–08, fellowships (averaging $15,750 per year), research assistantships (averaging $13,875 per year), teaching assistantships (averaging $13,060 per year) were awarded. *Unit head:* Dr. John Barden, Program Coordinator, 306-585-4629.

University of Rhode Island, Graduate School, College of Nursing, Kingston, RI 02881. Offers administration (MS); clinical nurse leader (MS); clinical specialist in gerontology (MS); clinical specialist in psychiatric/mental health (MS); family nurse practitioner (MS); gerontological nurse practitioner (MS); nursing (PhD); nursing education (MS). *Accreditation:* AACN; ACNM/DOA (one or more programs are accredited). In 2007, 34 master's, 5 doctorates awarded. *Application deadline:* For fall admission, 4/15 for domestic students. Application fee: $35. *Expenses:* Tuition, state resident: full-time $6,936; part-time $385 per credit. Tuition, nonresident: full-time $19,044; part-time $1,058 per credit. Required fees: $1,508; $48 per credit. $30 per semester. One-time fee: $80 part-time. *Unit head:* Dayle Joseph, Dean, 401-874-2766.

University of South Alabama, Graduate School, College of Arts and Sciences, Program in Gerontology, Mobile, AL 36688-0002. Offers Certificate. Part-time programs available. *Students:* 2 applicants, 50% accepted, 1 enrolled. In 2007, 1 degree awarded. *Entrance requirements:* For degree, GRE General Test. *Application deadline:* For fall admission, 9/1 priority date for domestic students. Applications are processed on a rolling basis. Application fee: $25. *Expenses:* Tuition, state resident: full-time $4,224; part-time $176 per credit hour. Tuition, nonresident: full-time $8,448; part-time $352 per credit hour. Required fees: $802. Full-time tuition and fees vary according to program and student level. *Financial support:* Application deadline: 4/1. *Unit head:* Dr. Roma Hanks, Chair, 251-460-6347.

University of South Carolina, The Graduate School, Program in Gerontology, Columbia, SC 29208. Offers Certificate. Part-time programs available. *Students:* 1 full-time (0 women), 4 part-time (all women); includes 3 minority (all African Americans) Average age 39. 11 applicants, 100% accepted. In 2007, 4 degrees awarded. *Degree requirements:* For Certificate, practicum. Application fee: $35. Electronic applications accepted. *Expenses:* Tuition, state resident: part-time $440 per hour. Tuition, nonresident: part-time $936 per hour. Required fees: $17 per hour. Tuition and fees vary according to program. *Unit head:* Geri Adler, Associate Professor, 803-777-0139, Fax: 803-777-3498. *Application contact:* Geraldine B. Washington, Administrative Assistant, 803-777-4221, Fax: 803-576-5501, E-mail: geraldinew@gwm.sc.edu.

University of Southern California, Graduate School, School of Gerontology, Los Angeles, CA 90089. Offers MA, MS, PhD, Certificate, DDS/MS, JD/MS, M Pl/MS, MAJCS/MS, MBA/MS, MHA/MS, MPA/MS, MSW/MS. Part-time programs available. Postbaccalaureate distance learning degree programs offered (no on-campus study). *Faculty:* 13 full-time (4 women), 4 part-time/adjunct (1 woman). *Students:* 52 full-time (42 women), 16 part-time (10 women); includes 25 minority (4 African Americans, 17 Asian Americans or Pacific Islanders, 4 Hispanic Americans), 6 international. 71 applicants, 68% accepted. In 2007, 20 master's, 2 doctorates awarded. *Degree requirements:* For doctorate, thesis/dissertation. *Entrance requirements:* For master's and doctorate, GRE General Test. *Application deadline:* For fall admission, 12/1 priority date for domestic students; for spring admission, 2/1 priority date for domestic students. Applications are processed on a rolling basis. Application fee: $85. *Financial support:* In 2007–08, 56 students received support; fellowships with full tuition reimbursements available, research assistantships with full tuition reimbursements available, teaching assistantships with full tuition reimbursements available, career-related internships or fieldwork, Federal Work-Study, scholarships/grants, and tuition waivers (partial) available. Financial award application deadline: 2/15; financial award applicants required to submit FAFSA. *Faculty research:* Cognition in aging, biodemographic of aging, health outcomes research, families and intergenerational relatives, care-giving of elderly. *Unit head:* Dr. Eileen Crimmins, Head, 213-740-2311. *Application contact:* Maria Henke, Information Contact, 213-740-2311.

University of South Florida, Graduate School, College of Arts and Sciences, School of Aging Studies, Tampa, FL 33620-9951. Offers aging studies (PhD); gerontology (MA). Part-time and evening/weekend programs available. *Faculty:* 10 full-time (6 women), 3 part-time/adjunct (2 women). *Students:* 32 full-time (29 women), 12 part-time (11 women); includes 10 minority (7 African Americans, 3 Hispanic Americans), 5 international. 35 applicants, 40% accepted, 7 enrolled. In 2007, 10 master's, 3 doctorates awarded. *Degree requirements:* For doctorate, thesis/dissertation. *Entrance requirements:* For master's, GRE General Test, minimum GPA of 3.0 in last 60 hours; for doctorate, GRE General Test, minimum GPA of 3.25, letter of recommendation. Additional exam requirements/recommendations for international students: Required—TOEFL (minimum score 550 paper-based; 213 computer-based). *Application deadline:* For fall admission, 6/1 for domestic students, 1/2 for international students; for spring admission, 10/15 for domestic students. Application fee: $30. Electronic applications accepted. *Financial support:* Health care benefits available. Financial award application deadline: 2/3. *Faculty research:* Minorities, caregiving, guardianship, Alzheimer's disease, cognitive aging. *Unit head:* Dr. William E. Haley, Director, 813-974-9739, Fax: 813-974-9754, E-mail: whaley@luna.cas.usf.edu. *Application contact:* Dr. Cathy L. McEvoy, Director of Graduate Programs, 813-974-1940, Fax: 813-974-9754, E-mail: cmcevoy@cas.usf.edu.

The University of Tennessee, Graduate School, College of Education, Health and Human Sciences, Program in Public Health, Knoxville, TN 37996. Offers community health education (MPH); gerontology (MPH); health planning/administration (MPH); MS/MPH. *Accreditation:* CEPH. *Degree requirements:* For master's, thesis optional. *Entrance requirements:* For master's, minimum GPA of 2.7. Additional exam requirements/recommendations for international students: Required—TOEFL. Electronic applications accepted.

The University of Toledo, College of Graduate Studies, College of Medicine, Biomedical Science Programs, Program in Gerontology, Toledo, OH 43606-3390. Offers contemporary gerontological practice (Certificate). *Students:* 6 full-time (all women), 4 part-time (2 women), 1 international. 6 applicants, 83% accepted, 5 enrolled. In 2007, 16 degrees awarded. Application fee: $45. *Unit head:* Dr. Barbara Kopp-Miller, Chair, 419-530-4630. *Application contact:* Joan Mulligan, Admissions Analyst, 419-530-4186.

University of Utah, The Graduate School, College of Nursing, Gerontology Interdisciplinary Program, Salt Lake City, UT 84112-1107. Offers MS, Certificate. *Accreditation:* AACN.Part-time programs available. *Faculty:* 48 full-time (42 women), 9 part-time/adjunct (8 women). *Students:* 4 full-time (3 women), 5 part-time (all women). Average age 42. 12 applicants, 75% accepted, 8 enrolled. In 2007, 3 degrees awarded. *Degree requirements:* For master's, thesis optional. *Entrance requirements:* For master's, GRE General Test, minimum undergraduate GPA of 3.0. Additional exam requirements/recommendations for international students: Required—TOEFL (minimum score 500 paper-based; 173 computer-based). *Application deadline:* For fall admission, 4/1 priority date for domestic students. Applications are processed on a rolling basis. Application fee: $20. *Expenses: Contact institution. Financial support:* In 2007–08, 1 student received support, including 20 fellowships with partial tuition reimbursements available, 2 research assistantships; teaching assistantships, scholarships/grants also available. Financial award application deadline: 4/1. *Faculty research:* Spousal bereavement, family caregiving, healthy promotion and self-care, environmental issues, geriatric care management. *Unit head:* Dr. Scott O. Wright, Director, 801-585-9542, Fax: 801-581-4642, E-mail: scott.wright@nurs.utah.edu. *Application contact:* Mirela Rankovic, Administrative Assistant, 801-581-8273, Fax: 801-581-4642, E-mail: mirela.milas@nurs.utah.edu.

Valparaiso University, Graduate Division, Program in Liberal Studies, Concentration in Gerontology, Valparaiso, IN 46383. Offers MALS, Post-Master's Certificate, JD/MALS. Part-time and evening/weekend programs available. *Students:* 1 (woman) full-time, 2 part-time (1 woman). Average age 26. *Entrance requirements:* For master's, minimum GPA of 3.0. Additional exam requirements/recommendations for international students: Required—TOEFL (minimum score 550 paper-based; 213 computer-based). *Application deadline:* Applications are processed on a rolling basis. Application fee: $30 ($50 for international students). Electronic applications accepted. *Financial support:* Available to part-time students. Applicants required to submit FAFSA. *Application contact:* Jamie Haney, Coordinator of Recruitment Activities, 219-464-5313, Fax: 219-464-5381, E-mail: jamie.haney@valpo.edu.

Virginia Commonwealth University, Graduate School, School of Allied Health Professions, Department of Gerontology, Richmond, VA 23284-9005. Offers aging studies (CAS); gerontology (MS). *Faculty:* 3 full-time (1 woman). *Students:* 4 full-time (all women), 7 part-time (all women); includes 1 African American. 10 applicants, 80% accepted, 4 enrolled. In 2007, 3 master's, 14 other advanced degrees awarded. *Entrance requirements:* For master's, GRE General Test or MAT. Application fee: $50. *Expenses:* Tuition, state resident: full-time $7,224; part-time $401 per credit. Tuition, nonresident: full-time $16,072; part-time $891 per credit. Required fees: $1,679; $63 per credit. Tuition and fees vary according to campus/location. *Financial support:* Career-related internships or fieldwork available. *Faculty research:* Alzheimer's disease, age-related alcoholism and suicide, pain perception, curriculum development and evaluation in gerontology/geriatrics. *Unit head:* Dr. Iris A. Parham, Chair, 804-828-9060, Fax: 804-828-5259, E-mail: iaparham@vcu.edu.

Virginia Commonwealth University, Graduate School, School of Allied Health Professions, Department of Health Administration, Doctoral Program in Health Related Sciences, Richmond, VA 23284-9005. Offers clinical laboratory sciences (PhD); gerontology (PhD); health administration (PhD); nurse anesthesia (PhD); occupational therapy (PhD); physical therapy (PhD); radiation sciences (PhD); rehabilitation leadership (PhD). *Faculty:* 2 full-time (1 woman). *Students:* 75 full-time (34 women), 40 part-time (22 women); includes 17 minority (8 African Americans, 8 Asian Americans or Pacific Islanders, 1 Hispanic American), 1 international. 36 applicants, 36% accepted, 11 enrolled. In 2007, 2 degrees awarded. *Expenses:* Tuition, state resident: full-time $7,224; part-time $401 per credit. Tuition, nonresident: full-time $16,072; part-time $891 per credit. Required fees: $1,679; $63 per credit. Tuition and fees vary according to campus/location. *Unit head:* Monica L. White, Director of Student Services, 804-828-3273, Fax: 804-828-8656, E-mail: mlwhite1@vcu.edu.

Virginia Polytechnic Institute and State University, Graduate School, College of Liberal Arts and Human Sciences, Department of Human Development, Blacksburg, VA 24061. Offers adult development and aging (MS, PhD); adult learning and human resource development (MS, PhD); child development (MS, PhD); family studies (MS, PhD); marriage and family therapy (MS, PhD). *Accreditation:* AAMFT/COAMFTE (one or more programs are accredited). *Entrance requirements:* For master's and doctorate, GRE General Test. Additional exam requirements/recommendations for international students: Required—TOEFL (minimum score 600 paper-based; 250 computer-based). Electronic applications accepted. *Faculty research:* Stress management, children's play, dual-career families, social cognition, relationships of elderly.

Wayne State University, Graduate School, Interdisciplinary Program in Gerontology, Detroit, MI 48202. Offers Certificate. *Students:* Average age 41. 2 applicants, 0% accepted. In 2007, 2 degrees awarded. *Entrance requirements:* For degree, personal statement; letters of reference; interview. Additional exam requirements/recommendations for international students: Required—TOEFL (minimum score 550 paper-based; 213 computer-based); Recommended—TWE (minimum score 6). *Application deadline:* For fall admission, 7/1 for domestic students, 6/1 for international students; for winter admission, 10/1 for international students; for spring admission, 2/1 for international students. Applications are processed on a rolling basis. Application fee: $30 ($50 for international students). Electronic applications accepted. *Expenses:* Tuition, state resident: part-time $403 per credit hour. Tuition, nonresident: part-time $890 per credit hour. *Financial support:* In 2007–08, 7 research assistantships (averaging $19,998 per year) were awarded; fellowships also available. *Faculty research:* Aging and health, cognitive and neuroscience, aging and disability, minority aging, human factors and aging. *Unit head:* Dr. Jennifer C. Mendez, Director of Education, 313-577-2297, Fax: 313-875-0947, E-mail: j.mendez@wayne.edu.

Webster University, College of Arts and Sciences, Department of Behavioral and Social Sciences, Program in Gerontology, St. Louis, MO 63119-3194. Offers MA. *Students:* 15 full-time (12 women), 33 part-time (28 women); includes 17 minority (8 African Americans, 2 American Indian/Alaska Native, 7 Hispanic Americans). Average age 46. In 2007, 7 degrees awarded. *Application deadline:* Applications are processed on a rolling basis. Application fee: $35 ($50 for international students). *Expenses:* Tuition: Full-time $9,360; part-time $520 per credit. *Financial support:* Federal Work-Study available. Support available to part-time students. Financial award application deadline: 4/1; financial award applicants required to submit FAFSA. *Unit head:* Margaret Cook, Coordinator, 314-246-7709. *Application contact:* Director of Graduate and Evening Student Admissions, Fax: 314-968-7116, E-mail: gadmit@webster.edu.

West Chester University of Pennsylvania, Office of Graduate Studies and Extended Education, College of Arts and Sciences, Department of Anthropology and Sociology, West Chester, PA 19383. Offers gerontology (Certificate); long term health care (MSA). Part-time and evening/weekend programs available. In 2007, 1 degree awarded. *Degree requirements:* For master's, comprehensive exam. *Entrance requirements:* For master's, MAT, GRE, or GMAT, interview. Additional exam requirements/recommendations for international students: Required—TOEFL (minimum score 550 paper-based; 213 computer-based; 80 iBT). *Application deadline:* For fall admission, 4/15 priority date for domestic students; for spring admission, 10/15 for domestic students. Applications are processed on a rolling basis. Application fee: $35. *Expenses:* Tuition, state resident: part-time $345 per credit. Tuition, nonresident: part-time $552 per credit. Tuition and fees vary according to course load. *Financial support:* In 2007–08, research assistantships with full tuition reimbursements (averaging $5,000 per year); unspecified assistantships also available. Support available to part-time students. Financial award application deadline: 2/15; financial award applicants required to submit FAFSA. *Faculty research:* West African communities in the U.S., life long learning-distance education, comparative religions. *Unit head:* Dr. Susan Johnston, Chair, 610-436-2556, E-mail: sjohnston@wcupa.edu. *Application contact:* Dr. Douglas McConatha, Graduate Coordinator, 610-436-3125, E-mail: dmcconatha@wcupa.edu.

Gerontology

West Chester University of Pennsylvania, Office of Graduate Studies and Extended Education, College of Health Sciences, Department of Health, West Chester, PA 19383. Offers emergency preparedness (Certificate); gerontology (MS); health care administration (Certificate); integrative health (Certificate); public health (MPH, MS); school health (M Ed). *Accreditation:* CEPH. Part-time and evening/weekend programs available. *Students:* 47 full-time (23 women), 65 part-time (48 women); includes 20 minority (18 African Americans, 2 Asian Americans or Pacific Islanders), 26 international. Average age 30. 120 applicants, 95% accepted, 38 enrolled. In 2007, 58 degrees awarded. *Degree requirements:* For master's, comprehensive exam, thesis (for some programs). *Entrance requirements:* For master's, GRE. Additional exam requirements/recommendations for international students: Required—TOEFL (minimum score 550 paper-based; 213 computer-based; 80 iBT). *Application deadline:* For fall admission, 4/15 priority date for domestic students; for spring admission, 10/15 for domestic students. Applications are processed on a rolling basis. Application fee: $35. *Expenses:* Tuition, state resident: part-time $345 per credit. Tuition, nonresident: part-time $552 per credit. Tuition and fees vary according to course load. *Financial support:* In 2007–08, 10 research assistantships with full and partial tuition reimbursements (averaging $5,000 per year) were awarded; unspecified assistantships also available. Support available to part-time students. Financial award application deadline: 2/15; financial award applicants required to submit FAFSA. *Faculty research:* HIV/AIDS education, teacher preparation, water quality. *Unit head:* Dr. Roger Mustalish, Chair, 610-436-2931, E-mail: rmustalish@wcupa.edu. *Application contact:* Dr. Bethann Cinelli, Graduate Coordinator, 610-436-2267, E-mail: bcinelli@wcupa.edu.

Wichita State University, Graduate School, Fairmount College of Liberal Arts and Sciences, School of Community Affairs, Wichita, KS 67260. Offers criminal justice (MA); gerontology (MA). Part-time programs available. Electronic applications accepted.

Wilmington University, Division of Nursing and Allied Health, New Castle, DE 19720-6491. Offers adult nurse practitioner (MSN); family nurse practitioner (MSN); gerontology (MSN); leadership (MSN); nursing (MSN); women's nurse practitioner (MSN). *Accreditation:* AACN. Part-time programs available. *Faculty:* 3 full-time (all women). *Students:* 29 full-time (all women), 187 part-time (160 women); includes 9 minority (6 African Americans, 1 American Indian/Alaska Native, 2 Hispanic Americans). Average age 38. 114 applicants, 100% accepted, 69 enrolled. In 2007, 59 degrees awarded. *Degree requirements:* For master's, thesis. *Entrance requirements:* For master's, BSN, RN license, interview, 3 letters of recommendation. Additional exam requirements/recommendations for international students: Required—TOEFL (minimum score 500 paper-based; 173 computer-based). *Application deadline:* For fall admission, 3/31 priority date for domestic students. Applications are processed on a rolling basis. Application fee: $25. Electronic applications accepted. *Expenses:* Tuition: Full-time $6,246; part-time $1,041 per course. Tuition and fees vary according to degree level and campus/location. *Financial support:* In 2007–08, 28 fellowships with tuition reimbursements (averaging $2,200 per year) were awarded; traineeships also available. Financial award applicants required to submit FAFSA. *Faculty research:* Outcomes assessment, student writing ability. *Unit head:* Dr. Mary Letitia Gallagher, Chair, 302-328-9401 Ext. 161, Fax: 302-328-7081, E-mail: tgall@wilmcoll.edu. *Application contact:* Chris Ferguson, Director of Admissions, 302-356-4636 Ext. 256, Fax: 302-328-5164, E-mail: inquire@wilmcoll.edu.

FLORIDA STATE UNIVERSITY

College of Human Sciences

Programs of Study

The College of Human Sciences offers graduate programs with specializations in the following areas.

Family and child sciences (M.S. in family and child sciences; Ph.D. in human sciences, with a concentration in either child development or family relations; Ph.D. in marriage and family therapy): The M.S. degree may be thesis or nonthesis. The Ph.D. is a research degree that focuses on human development, family relationships, research methods and theories, and marriage and family therapy. (http://www.chs.fsu.edu/fcs)

Nutrition, food, and exercise sciences (M.S. in nutrition and food science; M.S. in exercise physiology; Ph.D. in human sciences, with a concentration in either nutrition and food science or exercise physiology): The M.S. degree may be thesis or nonthesis. The Ph.D. is a research degree that focuses on health behaviors, health promotion, physical activity and chronic disease prevention, food quality and safety, and nutritional neuroscience. (http://www.chs.fsu.edu/nfes)

Textiles and consumer sciences (M.S. in apparel design and technology; M.S. in merchandising; M.S. in textiles; Ph.D. in human sciences, with a concentration in apparel design, retail merchandising, or textile product development): The M.S. degree may be thesis or nonthesis. The Ph.D. is a research degree that focuses on further research development, with emphasis in merchandising, textiles, or apparel product development. (http://www.chs.fsu.edu/tcs)

Research Facilities

Facilities are those essential for each area of specialization. Laboratories are equipped for chemical, physical, microbiological, trace-mineral, and small-animal research. The exercise science laboratories are equipped for metabolic studies, exercise and environmental testing, body composition and bone mineral density, and assessment of neuromuscular control. Textile laboratories include a conditioning room and sensory evaluation and colorfastness labs. Also available are CAD and apparel assembly labs, a merchandising technology lab, a historic costume collection of more than 2,700 garments and accessories dating from 1770, and the Carter Collection of pre-Columbian Peruvian textiles. The Department of Family and Child Sciences operates the FSU Family Institute. The University library houses 1.8 million volumes, and the science library has more than 300 databases available through its online searching.

Financial Aid

College and departmental graduate fellowships, scholarships, and assistantships are available on a competitive basis based on academic merit. There are a variety of fellowships, including minority ones, offered through the University. Out-of-state graduate students who have assistantships may apply for out-of-state tuition waivers. (http://www.fsu.edu/gradstudies/finances)

Cost of Study

In 2007–08, tuition for Florida residents was $248.18 per credit hour for graduate courses and thesis and dissertation hours; out-of-state students paid $879.58 per credit hour for graduate courses and thesis and dissertation hours. Residents of states participating in the Academic Common Market (Alabama, Arkansas, Delaware, Georgia, Kentucky, Louisiana, Maryland, Mississippi, North Carolina, Oklahoma, South Carolina, Tennessee, Texas, Virginia, and West Virginia) can also qualify for in-state rates for some programs. Tuition costs are subject to change by the legislature. Books and supplies average $725 per year.

Living and Housing Costs

The University provides housing for married students near the campus on the University shuttle bus routes at rents that ranged from $355 to $606 per month in 2007–08. In addition, there is a graduate hall on campus that rented for $380 to $575 per month in 2007–08. Ragans Hall, the new apartment facility, houses 555 men and women. Of these spaces, a limited number are reserved for single graduate students. Four students share a four-bedroom apartment with two bathrooms, and each apartment has a common study area, living area, and kitchen. Ragans Hall is centrally located on the FSU campus. The 2007–08 was $2600 per person for each semester. There are numerous apartments, duplexes, and houses for rent in the area around the University.

Student Group

The College currently has 195 graduate students and 2,984 undergraduate students. There are 41,065 students enrolled at the University. Students have diverse academic backgrounds and come from all parts of the United States and from other countries. Thirty-one percent of the College's graduate students are members of minority groups, and 13 percent are from other countries.

Location

Florida State University is a major influence in Tallahassee, the capital of Florida, which combines the charm and physical beauty of a southern city with the dynamic spirit of an important political center. The nearby Gulf of Mexico tempers the climate and provides excellent recreational opportunities. A national forest, a federal wildlife preserve, and botanical gardens are nearby. The airport is served by one major and several regional airlines.

The University and The College

Florida State University, founded in 1851, is one of the oldest universities in the state. In addition to its main campus in Tallahassee, the University has branch campuses in Panama City, Florida, and the Panama Canal and operates centers in Florence, Italy, and London, England. The Ringling Center for the Cultural Arts brings together resources to create a comprehensive arts and cultural complex for the state of Florida. The Ringling Center for the Cultural Arts incorporates the world-renowned John and Mable Ringling Museum of Arts located on a 66-acre estate on Sarasota Bay.

The College of Human Sciences, which is one of sixteen colleges at the University, is in the top ten human sciences programs nationally for the number of doctoral degrees granted. The College has an Eminent Scholar Chair, which is currently held in the Department of Family and Child Sciences by Frank Fincham, Ph.D., an internationally known psychologist whose research focuses on relationships, including marriage and personal relationships. Faculty members in the College are active nationally and internationally through research projects, professional organizations, and other activities. The College's policies and procedures are printed in a set of guidelines to lead students through the appropriate sequence of course work, exams, and other steps that culminate in the master's and doctoral degrees.

Applying

Applications may be submitted for any term but should be received by July 1 for fall admission, November 1 for spring admission, or March 1 for summer admission. International students should apply six months to one year prior to the term desired. Applicants are required to furnish transcripts of all academic work taken at or beyond the college level and satisfactory scores on the verbal and quantitative portions of the General Test of the Graduate Record Examinations. Individual programs may require additional application materials. Applicants requesting financial aid should apply between January 1 and February 15 for the following academic year. The application fee is $30.

Correspondence and Information

Requests for information on one or more specific programs should be directed to the chair of the appropriate department. For application forms and information about admissions, students should contact the school.

Office of Graduate Admissions
Florida State University
282 Champions Way
P.O. Box 3062400
Tallahassee, Florida 32306-2400

Phone: 850-644-3420
Web site: http://www.fsu.edu/prospective/admissions (online application)

Florida State University

THE FACULTY AND THEIR RESEARCH

Billie J. Collier, Professor and Dean; Ph.D., Tennessee, Knoxville. Textile processing and properties.

Family and Child Sciences

Kay Pasley, Professor and Chair; Ed.D., Indiana. Mental process in remarriage and stepfamilies, divorce education, relationship development.
Kathryn Bojczyk, Assistant Professor; Ph.D., Purdue. Association between mother's beliefs and practices and children's emergent literary skills, parent-child relationships.
Thomas A. Cornille, Associate Professor; Ph.D., Florida State. Addictions, social support, family services/therapy, program evaluation.
Ming Cui, Assistant Professor; Ph.D., Iowa State. The influence of family characteristics on child and adolescent development.
Carol A. Darling, Margaret Rector Sandels Professor of Human Sciences; Ph.D., Michigan State. Human sexuality, parent-child interaction, family services.
Frank Fincham, Eminent Scholar and Director of the FSU Family Institute; D.Phil., Oxford. Personal relationships, forgiveness in families, substance abuse in families.
Murray Krantz, Professor; Ph.D., Penn State. Child care, social competence of young children, sharing behavior of children.
Robert E. Lee, Norejane Hendrickson Professor and MFT Program Director; Ph.D., Princeton. Marriage and family therapy education and training, best practices in foster care, marital/family resiliency.
Lenore McWey, Assistant Professor; Ph.D., Florida State. Therapeutic interventions with families in the foster-care system, in-home therapy, marriage and family therapy.
Steve Mills, Community Instruction Coordinator; Ph.D., Purdue. Marriage and family therapy, service learning.
Ann K. Mullis, Associate Professor; Ph.D., Iowa State. Public policy, early childhood development, program evaluation.
Ronald L. Mullis, Professor; Ph.D., Iowa State. Parent-child relationships, middle childhood, adolescent development, program evaluation.
Penny A. Ralston, Professor; Ph.D., Illinois. Community-based programs for older adults, program development in higher education.
Christine A. Readdick, Associate Professor; Ph.D., Florida State. Early childhood, middle childhood, child care.
Marsha Rehm, Associate Professor; Ph.D., Minnesota. Vocational development, creativity and aesthetic perspectives in relation to family and consumer sciences education, critical thinking.

Nutrition, Food, and Exercise Sciences

Bahram Arjmandi, Margaret A. Sitton Professor and Chair; Ph.D., Kansas State. Bone and calcium metabolism, osteoporosis and osteoarthritis, sterol biosynthesis, functional food and health.
Doris Abood, Associate Professor; Ph.D., Tennessee. Health behavior, stress, wellness, drug education.
Jodee Dorsey, Associate Professor and Associate Dean; Ph.D., Tennessee. Metabolic aspects of obesity, nutrient-drug interaction.
Arturo Figueroa, Assistant Professor; Ph.D., Arizona; M.D., Guadalajara. Acute and chronic effects of exercise on cardiac autonomic control in obesity, diabetes, and cardiovascular disease.
Emily Haymes, C. Etta Walters Professor of Exercise Science; Ph.D., Penn State. Nutrition and performance, environmental effects of exercise.
Y.-H. Peggy Hsieh, Professor; Ph.D., Florida State. Muscle food chemistry, rapid detection for food safety, functional food product development.
Jasminka Ilich-Ernst, Professor; Ph.D., Zagreb (Croatia) and Ohio State. Bone health and body composition, bioavailability of calcium, magnesium, and zinc.
Jeong-Su Kim, Assistant Professor; Ph.D., Ohio State. Study of sarcopenia (i.e., age-related atrophy of skeletal muscle) and other neuromuscular changes related to aging, exercise, and physical function.
Cathy Levenson, Hazel K. Stiebeling Associate Professor; Ph.D., Chicago. Nutrient regulation of gene expression, molecular regulation of trace mineral metabolism.
Robert J. Moffatt, Georgia Alice Stamford Professor of Exercise Physiology; Ph.D., Michigan. Exercise and lipoprotein metabolism, effects of cigarette smoking and cessation from smoking on energy balance and lipoprotein metabolism.
Lynn Panton, Assistant Professor; Ph.D., Florida. Function in aging, strength training and the effects on the physiological measurements of strength, blood pressure, cholesterol, body composition, and functional outcomes of healthy elderly adults and chronically diseased populations.
Jenice Rankins, Associate Professor; Ed.D., Columbia. Nutrition education interventions in the community, interactions of gender and nutrition in international development, global education.
Shridhar K. Sathe, D. K. Salunkhe Professor of Food Science and Distinguished Teaching Professor; Ph.D., Utah State. Physiochemical and nutritional aspects of food chemistry, with emphasis in protein biochemistry.
Maria Spicer, Assistant Professor; Ph.D., Oklahoma State. Clinical nutrition and dietetics, pathophysiology of obesity and diabetes, cultural foods and international nutrition, community nutrition and development.
Delores Truesdell, Associate in Food Service; M.S., Florida State; RD. Food service management.

Textiles and Consumer Sciences

Barbara Dyer, Associate Professor and Chair; Ph.D., Tennessee, Knoxville. Consumer values: their exploration, application, and connection to retailing and marketing, including research on the personal value of materialism, consumer perceived value relative to retail shopping, home furnishings, salon hair colorants, and apparel.
Catherine Black, Associate Professor; Ph.D., Minnesota. Apparel design, functional and aesthetic apparel design, computer applications in apparel design.
Rinn M. Cloud, Professor; Ph.D., North Carolina at Greensboro. Physical/mechanical properties of textiles, barrier effectiveness of protective clothing fabrics, comfort and health effects of textile products.
Susan S. Fiorito, Associate Professor; Ph.D., Oklahoma State. Apparel retail technologies, financial and marketing analysis of small retail businesses, merchandising.
Elizabeth B. Goldsmith, Professor; Ph.D., Michigan State. Work and family, consumer economics, family finance, resource management.
Kay Grise, Associate Professor; Ph.D., Tennessee. Physical properties and performance of textiles.
Jeanne Heitmeyer, Associate Professor; Ph.D., Florida State. Merchandising, consumer purchase behavior and store patronage.
Eundeok Kim, Assistant Professor; Ph.D., Iowa State. Creative and technological aspects of apparel design, aesthetics, historical and cultural aspects of dress.
Young-A. Lee, Assistant Professor. Apparel product development, with emphasis on design issues and fit satisfaction of the elderly.
Mary Ann Moore, Carol Avery Professor and Associate Dean, Research and Graduate Studies; Ph.D., Florida State. Chemical and physical properties of textiles, textile product development, issues in the textile industry.
Pauline M. Sullivan, Associate Professor; Ph.D., NYU. Out-of-town shopping, hospitality-related retail and sustainable development, small and medium-sized businesses.

UNIVERSITY OF MARYLAND, COLLEGE PARK

School of Public Health
Department of Family Science

Programs of Study

The Department offers a Ph.D. in family science, a Ph.D. in maternal and child health (MCH), and a master's degree in couple and family therapy (CFT).

The Ph.D. program in family science provides an interdisciplinary, research-oriented approach to the discovery and application of knowledge about families. Course work focuses on family theory, research methodology, family policy, family law, family programs, ethnic families, family health, and major issues confronting today's families. Students also learn to design, implement, and evaluate culturally sensitive interventions addressing family needs. Students may enter the program with a bachelor's or master's degree. Those with a bachelor's degree must earn a master's degree in family science (30 credits) or marriage and family therapy (51 credits) with a thesis before advancing to doctoral course work. The Ph.D. program requires 51 graduate credits beyond the master's degree, a comprehensive examination, and a dissertation. Completion requires approximately three years post–master's degree. Ph.D. graduates are prepared for many careers, including university faculty positions and high-level research and administrative positions involving human services and family policy analysis. Students entering with a master's degree who have not completed a thesis using empirical data must complete an empirical research project during their first year of the doctoral program.

The Ph.D. program in maternal and child health provides interdisciplinary training in research, practice, and policy relevant to health problems and services for women, infants, children, adolescents, and their families. The MCH program prepares students to advance research, policy, and practice to improve the health, safety, and well-being of these groups, with a particular emphasis on low-income and ethnic-minority populations. The program equips students to address MCH issues at both the family and population levels. It is unique in its focus on the whole family system and family health policy. The Ph.D. program requires 48 graduate credits beyond the master's degree, including a maternal and child health core (24 credits), a research methods core (12 credits), and the dissertation (12 credits).

Applicants to the MCH Ph.D. program must have completed all of the requirements for a Master of Public Health (M.P.H.) degree or a social/behavioral science master's degree that focuses on family, maternal, and/or child health issues (including mental health) prior to their acceptance into the program. Prior to entry, students must also have completed at least one semester of a university-supervised, graduate-level professional experience in a public health or mental health setting. Students without the five M.P.H. core courses (biostatistics, epidemiology, environmental health sciences, health services administration, and health behavior) must complete missing courses within one academic year of their entry into the program.

The Master of Science program in couple and family therapy provides students with course work and supervised clinical training required in states with marriage and family therapy licensure. The program is accredited by AAMFT/COAMFTE. Course material is continually applied in the 500 hours of therapy that students provide to couples and families. The CFT program may be completed in 2 to 2½ years and requires either 48 (nonthesis) or 51 (thesis) credits.

Research Facilities

The Department of Family Science operates the Family Research Center (FRC) and the Center for Healthy Families. The Family Research Center seeks to enhance family research opportunities by securing external funding and encouraging cooperative ventures within the University and with other institutions. Grants focus on fathering, child care, childhood obesity, welfare reform, family therapy, family and community violence, child and family mental health, adoption and foster care, family financial education, and resiliency of African-American children. The FRC maintains a library of national data sets on families and family issues.

The Center for Healthy Families is the marriage and family therapy clinic that is housed in the Department of Family Science. The center annually provides therapy to 500 families from surrounding communities, training for the Department's clinical graduate students, and a site for clinical research.

The Department also has access to excellent computer facilities, including a computer laboratory located within the same building. The University has an outstanding library system containing approximately 4 million volumes.

Financial Aid

Financial assistance to M.S. and Ph.D. students is available through University fellowships, scholarships, graduate assistantships, and teaching and research assistantships. These awards are competitive, based on student merit and Department need. Some students obtain graduate assistantships in other University departments and units. Students may indicate their interest in fellowships or assistantships on the Graduate School application form. In 2006, financial aid (fellowships, scholarships, assistantships) was provided to 90 percent of the full-time master's students and to 100 percent of the full-time Ph.D. students. Information on other sources of financial assistance can be obtained through the Financial Aid Office on campus. The Web site is http://www.testudo.umd.edu/Financials.html.

Cost of Study

Effective in spring 2007, the cost for graduate student tuition per credit was $411 for Maryland residents and $886 for out-of-state students, plus fees. Students average from 9 to 12 credits per semester.

Living and Housing Costs

Graduate student housing is located adjacent to the College Park campus and in the surrounding communities of Prince George's and Montgomery Counties in Maryland and Washington, D.C. Housing ranges from $700 per month for an efficiency apartment to $900 or more for a two-bedroom apartment. Information on graduate student and off-campus housing may be obtained by calling the Off-Campus Housing Service at 301-314-3645 or online at http://www.och.umd.edu/.

Student Group

The Department of Family Science currently has 22 doctoral and 20 master's students. Of these students, 12 percent are men and 30 percent are members of ethnic minority groups. The Department sponsors a "Preparing Future Faculty" program for Ph.D. students, which is modeled after the national program developed by the Council of Graduate Schools. Doctoral students receive comprehensive preparation for academic jobs and positions in the government, nonprofit, and private sectors. There is an active student-run affiliate of the National Council on Family Relations, the University of Maryland Council on Family Relations.

Location

Located 8 miles from Washington, D.C.; 35 miles from Baltimore; and 30 miles from the state capital in Annapolis, the campus offers unparalleled opportunities for studying family policy and culturally diverse families. Students conduct research in urban, suburban, and rural communities. Nearby resources include the Library of Congress, the National Institutes of Health, and the National Library of Medicine.

The University

The University of Maryland, College Park, is the flagship campus of the University System of Maryland. Family research and training opportunities exist in the revitalized multiethnic city of Baltimore; the international city of Washington, D.C.; the historic Maryland capital of Annapolis; and the suburban and rural communities of Maryland. The Department cooperates with many other academic units on campus, providing students with flexibility in their course of study, as well as access to additional faculty resources.

Applying

Admission requirements for the Ph.D. program include an undergraduate GPA of at least 3.0, a graduate GPA of at least 3.3 (if applicable), a minimum GRE score of 1000 (verbal and quantitative), three letters of recommendation, and a statement of professional goals. Admission requirements for the master's program in couple and family therapy include an undergraduate GPA of at least 3.0, a minimum GRE score of 1000 (verbal and quantitative), three letters of recommendation, and a statement of professional goals. Students may complete a graduate application online at http://www.gradschool.umd.edu/gss/admission.htm. The application deadline is January 15 for both the master's and Ph.D. programs. Applications from members of racial and ethnic minority groups are encouraged.

Correspondence and Information

Graduate Director, Family Science
1204 Marie Mount Hall
University of Maryland, College Park
College Park, Maryland 20742

Phone: 301-405-3672
Fax: 301-314-9161
E-mail: fmsc@umd.edu
Web site: http://www.hhp.umd.edu/FMST

University of Maryland, College Park

THE FACULTY AND THEIR RESEARCH

Department of Family Science Faculty

Sally Koblinsky, Professor and Chair; Ph.D., Oregon State, 1977. Parenting in at-risk families, community violence, homelessness, child development, scholarship of teaching and learning.

Elaine Anderson, Professor; Ph.D., Penn State, 1979. Family policy, at-risk families, work and family issues.

Bonnie Braun, Associate Professor; Ph.D., Missouri, 1979. Family policy, resiliency, low-income families, rural families, educational program evaluation.

Norman Epstein, Professor; Ph.D., UCLA, 1974. Assessment and treatment of couples, depression, anxiety, cross-cultural research, domestic violence, family psychoeducation for schizophrenia.

Ned L. Gaylin, Professor Emeritus; Ph.D., Chicago, 1965. Parent-child relationships, marriage and family therapy and theory.

Sandra Hofferth, Professor; Ph.D., North Carolina at Chapel Hill, 1976. American children's use of time, work and family, fathers and fathering, adolescent pregnancy and childbearing, childhood obesity, family policy.

Jinhee Kim, Assistant Professor; Ph.D., Virginia Tech, 2000. Financial stress, health, and work outcome behavior of employees; credit counseling and debt management; food resource management of low-income families.

Jaslean LaTaillade, Assistant Professor; Ph.D., Washington (Seattle), 1999. African-American interracial couples and families, intimate-partner violence, couple therapy, ethnic-minority families.

Leigh Leslie, Associate Professor; Ph.D., Penn State, 1982. Gender issues, ethnic families, social support.

Manouchehr Mokhtari, Associate Professor; Ph.D., Houston, 1986. Economic transition, fiscal management strategies in transition, tax policy, microeconometric analysis of household behavior.

Noel Myricks, Associate Professor Emeritus; J.D., Howard, 1970; Ed.D., American, 1974. Family law, children's legal rights, family mediation.

Suzanne Randolph, Associate Professor; Ph.D., Michigan, 1981. African-American families, HIV/AIDS, community violence, evaluation of maternal/child health programs.

Kevin Roy, Assistant Professor; Ph.D., Northwestern, 1999. Men in low-income families, fathering, social policy, qualitative methods, poverty across the life course.

Edmond Shenassa, Associate Professor; Sc.D., Harvard. Prenatal and perinatal exposure to toxins, the role of built environment in health disparities.

Jacqueline Wallen, Associate Professor; Ph.D., Chicago, 1976. Women and substance-abuse treatment, treatment of PTSD, adoption and foster care, Latino families, work and family programs.

Carol Werlinich, Instructor; Ph.D., Maryland, 1983. Family therapy, domestic violence, couples communication.

Section 21
Geography

This section contains a directory of institutions offering graduate work in geography, followed by an in-depth entry submitted by an institution that chose to prepare a detailed program description. Additional information about programs listed in the directory but not augmented by an in-depth entry may be obtained by writing directly to the dean of a graduate school or chair of a department at the address given in the directory.

For programs offering related work, see also in this book *Area and Cultural Studies* and *Humanities*. In another guide in this series:

Graduate Programs in the Physical Sciences, Mathematics, Agricultural Sciences, the Environment & Natural Resources

See *Geosciences*

CONTENTS

Program Directories

Close-Ups

See also:

Geographic Information Systems

Boston University, Graduate School of Arts and Sciences, Department of Geography and Environment, Boston, MA 02215. Offers energy and environmental analysis (MA); environmental remote sensing and GIs (MA); geography (MA); geography and environment (PhD); international relations and environmental policy (MA). *Students:* 49 full-time (22 women), 8 part-time (4 women); includes 1 minority (Hispanic American), 28 international. Average age 29. 55 applicants, 27% accepted, 6 enrolled. In 2007, 2 master's, 3 doctorates awarded. Terminal master's awarded for partial completion of doctoral program. *Degree requirements:* For master's, one foreign language, comprehensive exam, thesis; for doctorate, one foreign language, comprehensive exam, thesis/dissertation. *Entrance requirements:* For master's and doctorate, GRE General Test, GRE Subject Test, 3 letters of recommendation. Additional exam requirements/recommendations for international students: Required—TOEFL (minimum score 600 paper-based; 250 computer-based). *Application deadline:* For fall admission, 7/1 for domestic and international students; for spring admission, 11/15 for domestic and international students. Application fee: $70. *Expenses:* Tuition: Full-time $34,930; part-time $1,092 per credit. Tuition and fees vary according to class time, course level and program. *Financial support:* In 2007–08, 33 students received support, including 2 fellowships with full tuition reimbursements available (averaging $18,000 per year), 20 research assistantships with full tuition reimbursements available (averaging $17,500 per year), 9 teaching assistantships with full tuition reimbursements available (averaging $17,500 per year); Federal Work-Study and unspecified assistantships also available. Support available to part-time students. Financial award application deadline: 1/15; financial award applicants required to submit FAFSA. Total annual research expenditures: $1.2 million. *Unit head:* Mark Friedl, Chairman, 617-353-5745, Fax: 617-353-8399, E-mail: friedl@bu.edu. *Application contact:* Erin Wnorowski, Graduate Program Coordinator, 617-353-7554, Fax: 617-353-8399, E-mail: wnorowsk@bu.edu.

Clark University, Graduate School, Department of Geography, Program in Geographic Information Science, Worcester, MA 01610-1477. Offers MA. *Students:* 3 full-time (1 woman), 1 part-time; includes 1 minority (Hispanic American) Average age 23. 4 applicants, 100% accepted, 4 enrolled. In 2007, 2 degrees awarded. *Application deadline:* For fall admission, 2/15 for domestic students. Application fee: $50. *Expenses:* Tuition: Full-time $32,600; part-time $1,019 per credit. Required fees: $30. Tuition and fees vary according to program. *Application contact:* Christine Silva, Admission Coordinator, 508-793-7337, Fax: 508-793-8881, E-mail: geography@clarku.edu.

Clark University, Graduate School, Department of International Development, Community, and Environment, Program in Geographic Information Science for Development and Environment, Worcester, MA 01610-1477. Offers MA. *Students:* 14 full-time (6 women), 1 (woman) part-time; includes 1 minority (African American), 7 international. Average age 33. 72 applicants, 61% accepted, 7 enrolled. In 2007, 13 degrees awarded. *Degree requirements:* For master's, thesis. *Entrance requirements:* Additional exam requirements/recommendations for international students: Required—TOEFL. *Application deadline:* For fall admission, 1/15 for domestic students. Application fee: $55. *Expenses:* Tuition: Full-time $32,600; part-time $1,019 per credit. Required fees: $30. Tuition and fees vary according to program. *Financial support:* In 2007–08, fellowships (averaging $5,000 per year), research assistantships with full and partial tuition reimbursements (averaging $5,000 per year), teaching assistantships with full and partial tuition reimbursements (averaging $5,000 per year) were awarded; tuition waivers (full and partial) also available. *Faculty research:* Dynamic modeling, image processing, land use and land cover change modeling, image classification, spatial econometrics. *Unit head:* Dr. William F. Fisher, Director, 508-421-3765, Fax: 508-793-8820, E-mail: wfisher@clarku.edu. *Application contact:* Paula Hall, IDCE Graduate Admissions, 508-793-7201, Fax: 508-793-8820, E-mail: idce@clarku.edu.

Cleveland State University, College of Graduate Studies, Maxine Goodman Levin College of Urban Affairs, Department of Urban Studies, Cleveland, OH 44115. Offers geographic information systems (Certificate); local and urban management (Certificate); nonprofit management (Certificate); research administration (Certificate); urban economic development (Certificate); urban real estate development and finance (Certificate); urban studies (MS); urban studies and public affairs (PhD). Part-time and evening/weekend programs available. *Faculty:* 26 full-time (10 women), 20 part-time/adjunct (11 women). *Students:* 92 full-time (45 women), 180 part-time (98 women); includes 28 minority (24 African Americans, 1 Asian American or Pacific Islander, 3 Hispanic Americans). Average age 39. 185 applicants, 76% accepted, 86 enrolled. In 2007, 92 master's, 5 doctorates awarded. *Median time to degree:* Of those who began their doctoral program in fall 1999, 40% received their degree in 8 years or less. *Degree requirements:* For master's, thesis or alternative, exit project, capstone course; for doctorate, comprehensive exam, thesis/dissertation. *Entrance requirements:* For master's, GRE General Test, minimum GPA of 3.0; for doctorate, GRE General Test, minimum GPA of 3.5. Additional exam requirements/recommendations for international students: Required—TOEFL (minimum score 525 paper-based; 197 computer-based). *Application deadline:* For fall admission, 7/15 priority date for domestic students, 5/15 for international students; for spring admission, 11/1 for international students. Applications are processed on a rolling basis. Application fee: $30. Electronic applications accepted. *Financial support:* In 2007–08, 60 students received support, including 40 research assistantships with full and partial tuition reimbursements available (averaging $7,632 per year), 1 teaching assistantship with full and partial tuition reimbursement available (averaging $7,800 per year); career-related internships or fieldwork, Federal Work-Study, institutionally sponsored loans, scholarships/grants, tuition waivers (full and partial), and unspecified assistantships also available. Support available to part-time students. Financial award application deadline: 3/1. *Faculty research:* Environmental issues, economic development, urban and public policy, public management. *Unit head:* Dr. Wendy Kellogg, Director, 216-687-5265, Fax: 216-687-9342, E-mail: w.kellogg@csuohio.edu. *Application contact:* Graduate Advisor, 216-523-7522, Fax: 216-687-5398, E-mail: urbanprograms@csuohio.edu.

Cleveland State University, College of Graduate Studies, Maxine Goodman Levin College of Urban Affairs, Program in Environmental Studies, Cleveland, OH 44115. Offers geographic information systems (Certificate); urban real estate development and finance (Certificate); JD/MAES. Part-time and evening/weekend programs available. *Faculty:* 26 full-time (10 women), 3 part-time/adjunct (0 women). *Students:* 75 full-time (31 women), 199 part-time (120 women); includes 71 minority (60 African Americans, 4 Asian Americans or Pacific Islanders, 7 Hispanic Americans), 24 international. 8 applicants, 75% accepted, 5 enrolled. *Degree requirements:* For master's, thesis or alternative, exit project. *Entrance requirements:* For master's, GRE General Test, 40th percentile Q/V, 4.0 aw, minimum GPA of 3.0. Additional exam requirements/recommendations for international students: Required—TOEFL (minimum score 525 paper-based; 197 computer-based). *Application deadline:* For fall admission, 7/15 priority date for domestic students, 5/15 for international students; for spring admission, 11/1 for international students. Applications are processed on a rolling basis. Application fee: $30. Electronic applications accepted. *Financial support:* In 2007–08, 1 student received support, including 1 research assistantship with full and partial tuition reimbursement available (averaging $6,960 per year); career-related internships or fieldwork, Federal Work-Study, scholarships/grants, tuition waivers (full and partial), and unspecified assistantships also available. Support available to part-time students. Financial award application deadline: 3/1. *Faculty research:* Environmental policy and administration, environmental planning, geographic information systems (GIS), nonprofit management. *Unit head:* Dr. Sanda Kaufman, Director, 216-687-2367, Fax: 216-687-9342, E-mail: s.kaufman@csuohio.edu. *Application contact:* Graduate Programs Coordinator, 216-523-7522, Fax: 216-687-5398, E-mail: urbanprogram@csuohio.edu.

Cleveland State University, College of Graduate Studies, Maxine Goodman Levin College of Urban Affairs, Program in Nonprofit Administration and Leadership, Cleveland, OH 44115. Offers geographic information systems (Certificate); local and urban management (Certificate); nonprofit management (Certificate). *Faculty:* 26 full-time (10 women), 6 part-time/adjunct (4 women). *Students:* 8 applicants, 88% accepted, 7 enrolled. *Degree requirements:* For master's, thesis or alternative, capstone course. *Entrance requirements:* For master's, GRE (minimum score: 40th percentile quantitative/verbal, 4.0 analytical writing), minimum GPA of 3.0. Additional exam requirements/recommendations for international students: Required—TOEFL (minimum score 525 paper-based; 197 computer-based). *Application deadline:* For fall admission, 7/15 priority date for domestic students, 5/15 for international students; for spring admission, 11/1 for international students. Applications are processed on a rolling basis. Application fee: $30. Electronic applications accepted. *Financial support:* In 2007–08, research assistantships with full and partial tuition reimbursements (averaging $6,960 per year); career-related internships or fieldwork, Federal Work-Study, scholarships/grants, tuition waivers (full and partial), and unspecified assistantships also available. Support available to part-time students. *Faculty research:* Human resource management, volunteerism, performance measurement in nonprofits, government-nonprofit partnerships. *Unit head:* Dr. Jennifer Alexander, Director, 216-687-5011, Fax: 216-687-2013, E-mail: j.kalexander@csuohio.edu. *Application contact:* Graduate Advisor, 216-523-7522, Fax: 216-687-5398, E-mail: urbanprograms@csuohio.edu.

Cleveland State University, College of Graduate Studies, Maxine Goodman Levin College of Urban Affairs, Program in Public Administration, Cleveland, OH 44115. Offers geographic information systems (Certificate); local and urban management (Certificate); non-profit management (Certificate); public administration (MPA); research administration (Certificate); JD/MPA. *Accreditation:* NASPAA. Part-time and evening/weekend programs available. *Faculty:* 26 full-time (10 women), 14 part-time/adjunct (8 women). *Students:* 36 full-time (17 women), 108 part-time (76 women); includes 46 minority (43 African Americans, 1 Asian American or Pacific Islander, 2 Hispanic Americans), 1 international. Average age 35. 45 applicants, 78% accepted, 23 enrolled. In 2007, 1 degree awarded. *Degree requirements:* For master's, thesis or alternative, capstone course. *Entrance requirements:* For master's, GRE General Test (minimum score: verbal and quantitative 40th percentile, analytical writing 4.0), minimum GPA of 3.0. Additional exam requirements/recommendations for international students: Required—TOEFL (minimum score 525 paper-based; 197 computer-based). *Application deadline:* For fall admission, 7/15 priority date for domestic students, 5/15 for international students; for spring admission, 11/1 for international students. Applications are processed on a rolling basis. Application fee: $30. Electronic applications accepted. *Financial support:* In 2007–08, 17 students received support, including 10 research assistantships with full and partial tuition reimbursements available (averaging $6,960 per year); career-related internships or fieldwork, institutionally sponsored loans, tuition waivers (full and partial), and unspecified assistantships also available. Financial award application deadline: 3/1. *Faculty research:* Health care, public management, economic development, city management. *Unit head:* Dr. Vera Vogelsang–Coombs, Director, 216-687-9223, Fax: 216-687-5398, E-mail: v.vogelsang-coombs@csuohio.edu. *Application contact:* Graduate Advisor, 216-523-7522, Fax: 216-687-5398, E-mail: urbanprograms@csuohio.edu.

Cleveland State University, College of Graduate Studies, Maxine Goodman Levin College of Urban Affairs, Program in Urban Planning, Design, and Development, Cleveland, OH 44115. Offers geographic information systems (Certificate); local and urban management (Certificate); urban economic development (Certificate); urban planning, design, and development (MUPDD); urban real estate development and finance (Certificate); JD/MUPDD. *Accreditation:* ACSP. Part-time and evening/weekend programs available. *Faculty:* 26 full-time (10 women), 12 part-time/adjunct (5 women). *Students:* 25 full-time (10 women), 46 part-time (23 women); includes 13 minority (12 African Americans, 1 Asian American or Pacific Islander), 7 international. Average age 30. 55 applicants, 82% accepted, 23 enrolled. In 2007, 7 degrees awarded. *Degree requirements:* For master's, project or thesis. *Entrance requirements:* For master's, GRE General Test (minimum score: verbal and quantitative 50th percentile, analytical writing 4.0), minimum GPA of 3.0. Additional exam requirements/recommendations for international students: Required—TOEFL (minimum score 525 paper-based; 197 computer-based). *Application deadline:* For fall admission, 7/15 priority date for domestic students, 5/15 for international students; for spring admission, 11/1 for international students. Applications are processed on a rolling basis. Application fee: $30. Electronic applications accepted. *Financial support:* In 2007–08, 21 students received support, including 13 research assistantships with full and partial tuition reimbursements available (averaging $6,960 per year); teaching assistantships with full and partial tuition reimbursements available, career-related internships or fieldwork, Federal Work-Study, tuition waivers (full and partial), and unspecified assistantships also available. Support available to part-time students. Financial award application deadline: 3/1. *Faculty research:* Housing and neighborhood development, urban housing policy, environmental sustainability, economic development. *Unit head:* Dr. W. Dennis Keating, Director, 216-687-2298, Fax: 216-687-2013, E-mail: w.keating@csuohio.edu. *Application contact:* Graduate Advisor, 216-523-7522, Fax: 216-687-5398, E-mail: urbanprograms@csuohio.edu.

Eastern Michigan University, Graduate School, College of Arts and Sciences, Department of Geography and Geology, Program in Geographic Information Systems, Ypsilanti, MI 48197. Offers geographic information systems (MS); GIS educator (Graduate Certificate); GIS professional (Graduate Certificate); GIS-planning (MS). *Students:* 8 full-time (2 women), 25 part-time (8 women); includes 1 minority (American Indian/Alaska Native), 7 international. In 2007, 15 degrees awarded. Application fee: $35. *Expenses:* Tuition, state resident: full-time $8,952; part-time $373 per credit hour. Tuition, nonresident: full-time $17,634; part-time $735 per credit hour. Required fees: $896; $34 per credit hour. Tuition and fees vary according to course level, degree level and program. *Application contact:* Dr. Michael Bradley, Program Advisor, 734-487-0218, Fax: 734-487-6979, E-mail: michael.bradley@emich.edu.

Florida State University, Graduate Studies, College of Social Sciences, Department of Geography, Tallahassee, FL 32306. Offers geographic information systems (MS); geography (MA, MS, PhD). Part-time programs available. *Faculty:* 10 full-time (2 women), 2 part-time/adjunct (0 women). *Students:* 72 full-time (35 women), 13 part-time (3 women); includes 8 minority (2 African Americans, 1 Asian American or Pacific Islander, 5 Hispanic Americans), 5 international. Average age 30. 50 applicants, 60% accepted, 20 enrolled. In 2007, 21 master's, 3 doctorates awarded. Terminal master's awarded for partial completion of doctoral program. *Degree requirements:* For master's, thesis (for some programs); for doctorate, thesis/dissertation. *Entrance requirements:* For master's and doctorate, GRE General Test, minimum GPA of 3.0. Additional exam requirements/recommendations for international students: Required—TOEFL. *Application deadline:* For fall admission, 1/15 priority date for domestic students, 12/15 priority date for international students; for spring admission, 11/1 for domestic students, 9/15 for international students. Applications are processed on a rolling basis. Application fee: $30. Electronic applications accepted. *Expenses:* Tuition, state resident: part-time $248 per credit hour. Tuition, nonresident: part-time $880 per credit hour. Tuition and fees vary according to program. *Financial support:* In 2007–08, 19 students received support, including 6 research assistantships with full tuition reimbursements available (averaging $12,900 per year), 13 teaching assistantships with full tuition reimbursements available (averaging $12,900 per year); fellowships with full tuition reimbursements available, career-related internships or fieldwork, Federal Work-Study, institutionally sponsored loans, scholarships/grants, health care benefits, and unspecified assistantships also available. Financial award application deadline: 1/15; financial award applicants required to submit FAFSA. *Faculty research:* Society-nature interaction, geographic information science. Total annual research expenditures:$210,000. *Unit head:* Dr. Victor Mesev, Chair, 850-645-2498, Fax: 850-644-5913. *Application contact:* Dr. Tony Stallins, Graduate Director, 850-644-8385, Fax: 850-644-5193, E-mail: jastallins@fsu.edu.

George Mason University, College of Science, Department of Earth Systems and Geoinformation Sciences, Fairfax, VA 22030. Offers MS, PhD, Certificate.

George Mason University, College of Science, Department of Geography, Fairfax, VA 22030. Offers geographic and cartographic sciences (MS). *Degree requirements:* For master's, thesis optional. *Entrance requirements:* For master's, GRE General Test, minimum GPA of 3.0 in last 60 hours; BS or BA in geography, cartography, or related field. Electronic applications accepted.

Georgia Institute of Technology, Graduate Studies and Research, College of Architecture, City and Regional Planning Program, Atlanta, GA 30332-0001. Offers architecture (PhD); economic development (MCRP); environmental planning and management (MCRP); geographic information systems (MCRP); land development (MCRP); land use planning (MCRP); transportation (MCRP); urban design (MCRP); MCP/MSCE. *Accreditation:* ACSP. *Degree requirements:* For master's, thesis, internship. *Entrance requirements:* For master's, GRE General Test, minimum GPA of 2.7. Additional exam requirements/recommendations for international students: Required—TOEFL. Electronic applications accepted.

Georgia State University, College of Arts and Sciences, Department of Geosciences, Program in Geographic Information Systems, Atlanta, GA 30303-3083. Offers Certificate. Part-time programs available. *Faculty:* 2 full-time (0 women), 2 part-time/adjunct (1 woman). *Students:* 7 (1 woman). In 2007, 3 degrees awarded. *Entrance requirements:* Additional exam requirements/recommendations for international students: Required—TOEFL. *Application deadline:* For fall admission, 4/15 for domestic and international students; for spring admission, 10/15 for domestic and international students. Applications are processed on a rolling basis. Electronic applications accepted. *Expenses:* Tuition, state resident: part-time $221 per credit hour. *Financial support:* In 2007–08, research assistantships with full tuition reimbursements (averaging $6,000 per year), teaching assistantships with full tuition reimbursements (averaging $6,000 per year) were awarded. *Faculty research:* Cartography, remote sensing. *Unit head:* Jeremy Crampton, Director of Graduate Studies, 404-413-5771, Fax: 404-413-5768, E-mail: jcrampton@gsu.edu.

Hunter College of the City University of New York, Graduate School, School of Arts and Sciences, Department of Geography, New York, NY 10021-5085. Offers analytical geography (MA); earth system science (MA); environmental and social issues (MA); geographic information science (Certificate); geographic information systems (MA); teaching earth science (MA). Part-time and evening/weekend programs available. *Faculty:* 3 full-time (4 women), 10 part-time/adjunct (1 woman). *Students:* 5 full-time (2 women), 25 part-time (12 women). Average age 35. 20 applicants, 85% accepted, 10 enrolled. In 2007, 13 degrees awarded. *Degree requirements:* For master's, comprehensive exam or thesis. *Entrance requirements:* For master's, GRE General Test, minimum B average in major, minimum B- average overall, 18 credits of course work in geography, 2 letters of recommendation; for Certificate, minimum of B average in major, B- overall. Additional exam requirements/recommendations for international students: Required—TOEFL. *Application deadline:* For fall admission, 4/1 for domestic students; for spring admission, 11/1 for domestic students. Applications are processed on a rolling basis. Application fee: $125. *Expenses:* Tuition, state resident: full-time $6,400; part-time $270 per credit. Tuition, nonresident: part-time $500 per credit. One-time fee: $125 full-time. Tuition and fees vary according to program. *Financial support:* In 2007–08, 1 fellowship (averaging $3,000 per year), 2 research assistantships (averaging $10,000 per year), 10 teaching assistantships (averaging $6,000 per year) were awarded; career-related internships or fieldwork, Federal Work-Study, institutionally sponsored loans, and unspecified assistantships also available. Financial award application deadline: 3/1. *Faculty research:* Urban geography, economic geography, geographic information science, demographic methods, climate change. *Unit head:* Prof. William Solecki, Chair, 212-772-4536, Fax: 212-772-5268, E-mail: wsolecki@hunter.cuny.edu. *Application contact:* Prof. Marianna Pavlovskaya, Graduate Adviser, 212-772-5320, Fax: 212-772-5268, E-mail: mpavlov@geo.hunter.cuny.edu.

Idaho State University, Office of Graduate Studies, College of Arts and Sciences, Department of Geosciences, Pocatello, ID 83209. Offers geographic information science (MS); geology (MNS, MS); geophysics/hydrology (MS); geotechnology (Postbaccalaureate Certificate). Part-time programs available. *Faculty:* 8 full-time (1 woman). *Students:* 22 full-time (7 women), 23 part-time (6 women), 6 international. Average age 34. In 2007, 8 master's, 2 other advanced degrees awarded. *Degree requirements:* For master's, comprehensive exam, thesis; for Postbaccalaureate Certificate, thesis optional. *Entrance requirements:* For master's and Postbaccalaureate Certificate, GRE General Test, 3 letters of recommendation. Additional exam requirements/recommendations for international students: Required—TOEFL (minimum score 550 paper-based; 213 computer-based; 80 iBT). *Application deadline:* For fall admission, 7/1 for domestic students, 6/1 for international students; for spring admission, 12/1 for domestic students, 11/1 for international students. Applications are processed on a rolling basis. Application fee: $55. *Expenses:* Tuition, state resident: full-time $2,882; part-time $259 per credit hour. Tuition, nonresident: full-time $11,566; part-time $379 per credit hour. Required fees: $2,278. Full-time tuition and fees vary according to program. Part-time tuition and fees vary according to course load. *Financial support:* In 2007–08, 13 research assistantships with full and partial tuition reimbursements (averaging $9,128 per year), 7 teaching assistantships with full and partial tuition reimbursements (averaging $9,128 per year) were awarded; career-related internships or fieldwork, Federal Work-Study, institutionally sponsored loans, scholarships/grants, health care benefits, tuition waivers (full and partial), and unspecified assistantships also available. Support available to part-time students. Financial award application deadline: 1/1; financial award applicants required to submit FAFSA. *Faculty research:* Structural geography, stratigraphy, geochemistry, remote sensing, geomorphology. *Unit head:* Dr. Scott Hughes, Chairman, 208-282-3365, Fax: 208-282-4414, E-mail: hughscot@isu.edu. *Application contact:* Ellen Combs, Graduate School Technical Records Specialist, 208-282-2150, Fax: 208-282-4847.

Indiana University–Purdue University Indianapolis, School of Liberal Arts, Department of Geography, Indianapolis, IN 46202-2896. Offers geographic information systems (MS, Certificate). *Students:* 5 full-time (1 woman), 16 part-time (7 women); includes 2 Asian Americans or Pacific Islanders. *Entrance requirements:* For master's, GRE, GPA of 3.0. Application fee: $50 ($60 for international students). *Expenses:* Tuition, state resident: full-time $5,818; part-time $242 per credit hour. Tuition, nonresident: full-time $17,106; part-time $713 per credit hour. Required fees: $629. Tuition and fees vary according to course load, campus/location and program. *Financial support:* In 2007–08, 2 fellowships (averaging $9,000 per year), 1 teaching assistantship (averaging $7,067 per year) were awarded. *Application contact:* Joyce Haibe, Department Secretary, 317-274-8877, E-mail: geogdept@iupui.edu.

Montclair State University, The Office of Graduate Admissions and Support Services, College of Science and Mathematics, Department of Earth and Environmental Studies, Montclair, NJ 07043-1624. Offers earth science (Certificate); environmental management (MA, D Env M); environmental studies (MS), including environmental education, environmental health, environmental management, environmental science; geographic information science (Certificate); geoscience (MS, Certificate), including geoscience (MS), water resource management (Certificate). Part-time and evening/weekend programs available. *Faculty:* 15 full-time (2 women), 11 part-time/adjunct (5 women). *Students:* 26 full-time (11 women), 47 part-time (20 women); includes 10 minority (7 African Americans, 1 Asian American or Pacific Islander, 2 Hispanic Americans), 10 international. 63 applicants, 48% accepted, 30 enrolled. In 2007, 18 master's, 2 other advanced degrees awarded. *Degree requirements:* For master's, comprehensive exam, thesis or alternative; for doctorate, thesis/dissertation. *Entrance requirements:* For master's, GRE General Test, 2 letters of recommendation. Additional exam requirements/recommendations for international students: Required—TOEFL (minimum score 83 computer-based). *Application deadline:* For fall admission, 6/1 for international students; for spring admission, 10/1 for international students. Applications are processed on a rolling basis. Application fee: $60. Electronic applications accepted. *Financial support:* In 2007–08, 3 research assistantships with full tuition reimbursements were awarded; Federal Work-Study, scholarships/grants, and unspecified assistantships also available. Support available to part-time students. Financial award application deadline: 3/1; financial award applicants required to submit FAFSA. *Faculty research:* Antarctica, carbon pools, contaminated sediments, wetlands. *Unit head:* Dr. Duke Ophori, Chairperson, 973-655-7558.

North Carolina State University, Graduate School, College of Natural Resources, Department of Parks, Recreation and Tourism Management, Raleigh, NC 27695. Offers geographic information systems (MS); maintenance management (MRRA, MS); parks, recreation and tourism management (PhD); recreation planning (MRRA, MS); recreation resources administration/public administration (MRRA); recreation/park management (MRRA, MS); sports management (MRRA, MS); travel and tourism management (MS). *Degree requirements:* For master's, thesis (for some programs); for doctorate, thesis/dissertation. *Entrance requirements:* For master's and doctorate, GRE General Test. Additional exam requirements/recommendations for international students: Required—TOEFL. Electronic applications accepted. *Faculty research:* Tourism policy and development, spatial information systems, natural resource management, recreational sports management, park and recreation management.

Northern Arizona University, Graduate College, College of Social and Behavioral Sciences, Department of Geography, Planning, and Recreation, Flagstaff, AZ 86011. Offers applied geographic information science (MS); geographic information systems (Certificate); rural geography (MA). *Degree requirements:* For master's, thesis. *Entrance requirements:* For master's, GRE General Test.

Northwest Missouri State University, Graduate School, College of Arts and Sciences, Department of Geology/Geography, Program in Geographic Information Sciences, Maryville, MO 64468-6001. Offers MS, Certificate. Part-time programs available. *Faculty:* 9 full-time (4 women). *Students:* 1 (woman) full-time, 88 part-time (26 women); includes 8 minority (2 American Indian/Alaska Native, 4 Asian Americans or Pacific Islanders, 2 Hispanic Americans), 1 international. 25 applicants, 100% accepted, 23 enrolled. In 2007, 4 degrees awarded. *Degree requirements:* For master's, comprehensive exam, thesis. *Entrance requirements:* For master's, GRE General Test, 2 letters of recommendation, writing sample, minimum undergraduate GPA of 2.5. Additional exam requirements/recommendations for international students: Required—TOEFL (minimum score 550 paper-based; 213 computer-based). *Application deadline:* For fall admission, 4/15 for domestic and international students. Application fee: $0 ($50 for international students). *Financial support:* In 2007–08, teaching assistantships (averaging $6,000 per year). Financial award application deadline: 3/1; financial award applicants required to submit FAFSA. *Unit head:* Dr. Patricia Drews, Head, 660-562-1273, E-mail: drews@nwmissouri.edu. *Application contact:* Dr. Frances Shipley, Dean of Graduate School, 660-562-1145, Fax: 660-562-1096, E-mail: gradsch@nwmissouri.edu.

Saint Louis University, Graduate School, College of Education and Public Service and Graduate School, Department of Public Policy Studies, St. Louis, MO 63103-2097. Offers geographic information systems (Certificate); organizational development (Certificate); public administration (MAPA); public policy analysis (PhD); urban affairs (MAUA); urban planning and real estate development (MUPRED). *Accreditation:* NASPAA. Part-time programs available. *Faculty:* 8 full-time (2 women), 1 part-time/adjunct (0 women). *Students:* 55 full-time (18 women), 57 part-time (27 women); includes 20 minority (15 African Americans, 1 Asian American or Pacific Islander, 4 Hispanic Americans), 7 international. Average age 34. 79 applicants, 76% accepted, 34 enrolled. In 2007, 11 master's, 1 doctorate awarded. *Degree requirements:* For master's, comprehensive exam (for some programs), thesis (for some programs); for doctorate, comprehensive exam, thesis/dissertation, preliminary exams. *Entrance requirements:* For master's and doctorate, GMAT, GRE General Test, or LSAT, letters of recommendation, resumé, interview, transcripts, goal statement. Additional exam requirements/recommendations for international students: Required—TOEFL (minimum score 525 paper-based; 194 computer-based). *Application deadline:* For fall admission, 7/1 for domestic and international students; for spring admission, 11/1 for domestic and international students. Applications are processed on a rolling basis. Application fee: $40. Electronic applications accepted. *Expenses:* Tuition: Part-time $845 per credit hour. Required fees: $105 per semester. *Financial support:* In 2007–08, 36 students received support, including 8 teaching assistantships with full tuition reimbursements available (averaging $12,000 per year); Federal Work-Study, scholarships/grants, traineeships, health care benefits, tuition waivers (partial), and unspecified assistantships also available. Support available to part-time students. Financial award application deadline: 2/1; financial award applicants required to submit FAFSA. *Faculty research:* Urban politics, brown fields, e-government, and administration, evaluation research, community development, electronic government and governance. Total annual research expenditures: $100,000. *Unit head:* Dr. Robert A. Cropf, Chairperson, 314-977-3936, Fax: 314-977-3943, E-mail: cropfra@slu.edu. *Application contact:* Gary U. Behrman, Associate Dean of Graduate School Admissions, 314-977-3827, Fax: 314-977-3943, E-mail: behrmang@slu.edu.

Saint Mary's University of Minnesota, Schools of Graduate and Professional Programs, Graduate School of Business and Technology, Geographic Information Science Program, Winona, MN 55987-1399. Offers MS, Certificate. *Unit head:* Dr. David McConville, Director, 507-457-1542, Fax: 507-457-1633, E-mail: dmcconvi@smumn.edu.

Salisbury University, Graduate Division, Program in Geography Information Systems and Public Administration, Salisbury, MD 21801-6837. Offers MS. *Faculty:* 2 full-time (0 women). *Students:* 6 full-time (1 woman), 4 part-time (2 women). Average age 33. 12 applicants, 83% accepted, 10 enrolled. In 2007, 2 degrees awarded. *Expenses:* Tuition, state resident: part-time $260 per credit hour. Tuition, nonresident: part-time $556 per credit hour. *Unit head:* Dr. Xingzhi Mara Chen, Coordinator, 410-546-6302, E-mail: xmchen@salisbury.edu.

San Jose State University, Graduate Studies and Research, College of Social Sciences, Department of Geography, San Jose, CA 95192-0001. Offers geographic information science (Certificate); geography (MA). *Students:* 10 full-time (8 women), 13 part-time (7 women); includes 6 minority (1 American Indian/Alaska Native, 4 Asian Americans or Pacific Islanders, 1 Hispanic American), 1 international. Average age 36. 18 applicants, 61% accepted, 7 enrolled. In 2007, 4 degrees awarded. *Entrance requirements:* For master's, minimum GPA of 3.0. *Application deadline:* For fall admission, 6/29 for domestic students; for spring admission, 11/30 for domestic students. Applications are processed on a rolling basis. Application fee: $59. Electronic applications accepted. *Financial support:* Applicants required to submit FAFSA. *Unit head:* Dr. Richard Taketa, Chair, 408-924-5425, E-mail: richard.taketa@sjsu.edu.

Texas State University–San Marcos, Graduate School, College of Liberal Arts, Department of Geography, Program in Environmental Geography, Geography Education, and Geography Information Science, San Marcos, TX 78666. Offers environmental geography (PhD); geography education (PhD); information science (PhD). Part-time programs available. *Students:* 38 full-time (19 women), 27 part-time (14 women); includes 12 minority (3 African Americans, 3 Asian Americans or Pacific Islanders, 6 Hispanic Americans), 9 international. Average age 38. 19 applicants, 84% accepted, 14 enrolled. In 2007, 7 degrees awarded. *Degree requirements:* For doctorate, thesis/dissertation. *Entrance requirements:* For doctorate, GRE General Test, minimum GPA of 3.5, master's degree in geography, demonstrated scholarly research. Additional exam requirements/recommendations for international students: Required—TOEFL (minimum score 550 paper-based; 213 computer-based). *Application deadline:* For fall admission, 6/15 priority date for domestic students, 6/1 for international students; for spring admission, 10/15 priority date for domestic students, 10/1 for international students. Applications are processed on a rolling basis. Application fee: $40 ($90 for international students). Electronic applications accepted. *Expenses:* Tuition, state resident: full-time $3,780; part-time $210 per credit hour. Tuition, nonresident: full-time $8,784; part-time $488 per credit hour. Required fees: $493 per semester. Full-time tuition and fees vary according to course load. *Financial support:* In 2007–08, 56 students received support, including 19 research assistantships (averaging $7,119 per year), 23 teaching assistantships (averaging $6,804 per year); career-related internships or fieldwork, Federal Work-Study, and institutionally sponsored loans also available. Support available to part-time students. Financial award application deadline: 4/1; financial award applicants required to submit FAFSA. *Unit head:* Dr. David Butler, Graduate Adviser, 512-245-2170, Fax: 512-245-8353, E-mail: db25@txstate.edu.

Texas State University–San Marcos, Graduate School, College of Liberal Arts, Department of Geography, Program in Geographic Information Science, San Marcos, TX 78666. Offers MAG. Part-time and evening/weekend programs available. *Students:* 6 full-time (2 women), 13 part-time (4 women); includes 3 minority (1 African American, 1 Asian American or Pacific Islander, 1 Hispanic American). Average age 32. 4 applicants, 100% accepted, 4 enrolled. In 2007, 3 master's awarded. *Degree requirements:* For master's, comprehensive exam,

Geographic Information Systems

Texas State University–San Marcos (continued)

internship or thesis. *Entrance requirements:* For master's, GRE General Test, minimum GPA of 3.0 in last 60 hours of course work. Additional exam requirements/recommendations for international students: Required—TOEFL (minimum score 550 paper-based; 213 computer-based). *Application deadline:* For fall admission, 6/15 priority date for domestic students, 6/1 for international students; for spring admission, 10/15 priority date for domestic students, 10/1 for international students. Applications are processed on a rolling basis. Application fee: $40 ($90 for international students). Electronic applications accepted. *Expenses:* Tuition, state resident: full-time $3,780; part-time $210 per credit hour. Tuition, nonresident: full-time $8,784; part-time $488 per credit hour. Required fees: $493 per semester. Full-time tuition and fees vary according to course load. *Financial support:* In 2007–08, 9 students received support, including 1 research assistantship (averaging $3,154 per year), 2 teaching assistantships (averaging $5,386 per year); career-related internships or fieldwork, Federal Work-Study, institutionally sponsored loans, and scholarships/grants also available. Support available to part-time students. Financial award application deadline: 4/1; financial award applicants required to submit FAFSA. *Unit head:* Dr. David Butler, Graduate Adviser, 512-245-2170, Fax: 512-245-8353, E-mail: db25@txstate.edu.

Université du Québec à Montréal, Graduate Programs, Program in Geographical Information Systems, Montréal, QC H3C 3P8, Canada. Offers Diploma. Part-time programs available. *Entrance requirements:* For degree, appropriate bachelor's degree or equivalent, proficiency in French.

University at Albany, State University of New York, College of Arts and Sciences, Department of Geography and Planning, Program in Geography, Albany, NY 12222-0001. Offers geographic information systems and spatial analysis (Certificate); geography (MA). *Degree requirements:* For master's, thesis or alternative. *Entrance requirements:* Additional exam requirements/recommendations for international students: Required—TOEFL (minimum score 550 paper-based; 213 computer-based). *Application deadline:* For fall admission, 3/1 for domestic students, 5/1 for international students; for spring admission, 11/1 for international students. Applications are processed on a rolling basis. Application fee: $75. Electronic applications accepted. *Expenses:* Tuition, state resident: part-time $576 per credit. Tuition, nonresident: part-time $910 per credit. Tuition and fees vary according to program. *Financial support:* Fellowships, teaching assistantships, Federal Work-Study and institutionally sponsored loans available. Financial award application deadline: 6/1. *Faculty research:* Remote sensing, cultural/social geography, urban geography.

University at Buffalo, the State University of New York, Graduate School, College of Arts and Sciences, Department of Geography, Buffalo, NY 14260. Offers geographic information science (Certificate); geography (MA, MS, PhD); transportation and business geographics (Certificate); MA/MBA. *Degree requirements:* For master's, thesis (for some programs), project; for doctorate, thesis/dissertation; for Certificate, portfolio. *Entrance requirements:* For master's, GRE General Test, minimum GPA of 2.9; for doctorate, GRE General Test, minimum GPA of 3.0. Additional exam requirements/recommendations for international students: Required—TOEFL (minimum score 550 paper-based; 213 computer-based; 79 iBT). Electronic applications accepted. *Faculty research:* International business and world trade, geographic information systems and cartography, transportation, urban and regional analysis, physical and environmental geography.

The University of Akron, Graduate School, Buchtel College of Arts and Sciences, Department of Geography and Planning, Program in Geographic Information Science, Akron, OH 44325. Offers MS. *Students:* 13 full-time (3 women), 3 part-time (1 woman); includes 1 minority (African American), 3 international. Average age 28. 15 applicants, 87% accepted, 6 enrolled. In 2007, 6 degrees awarded. *Entrance requirements:* Additional exam requirements/recommendations for international students: Required—TOEFL (minimum score 550 paper-based; 213 computer-based; 79 iBT). *Application deadline:* Applications are processed on a rolling basis. Electronic applications accepted. *Expenses:* Tuition, state resident: full-time $6,164; part-time $342 per credit. Tuition, nonresident: full-time $10,575; part-time $588 per credit. Required fees: $806; $43 per credit. $12 per term. Tuition and fees vary according to course load, degree level and program. *Unit head:* Kevin Butler, Manager, GIS Research, 330-972-7120, E-mail: butler@uakron.edu.

University of Central Arkansas, Graduate School, College of Liberal Arts, Department of Geography, Conway, AR 72035-0001. Offers geographic information systems (MGIS, Certificate). Part-time programs available. Postbaccalaureate distance learning degree programs offered (minimal on-campus study). *Faculty:* 3 full-time (0 women). *Students:* 1 full-time (0 women), 17 part-time (6 women); includes 1 minority (American Indian/Alaska Native), 1 international. 11 applicants, 100% accepted, 11 enrolled. *Entrance requirements:* Additional exam requirements/recommendations for international students: Required—TOEFL (minimum score 550 paper-based; 213 computer-based). *Application deadline:* For fall admission, 3/1 priority date for domestic and international students; for spring admission, 10/1 priority date for domestic and international students. Applications are processed on a rolling basis. Application fee: $25 ($50 for international students). *Expenses:* Tuition, state resident: full-time $4,513; part-time $240 per credit. Tuition, nonresident: full-time $8,805; part-time $440 per credit. International tuition: $9,700 full-time. Required fees: $100 per term. *Financial support:* Applicants required to submit FAFSA. *Unit head:* Dr. Brooks Green, Chairperson, 501-450-5636, Fax: 501-450-5185, E-mail: brooksg@uca.edu. *Application contact:* Brenda Herring, Admissions Assistant, 501-450-5065, Fax: 501-450-5678, E-mail: bherring@uca.edu.

University of Colorado Denver, College of Engineering and Applied Science, Department of Civil Engineering, Denver, CO 80217-3364. Offers civil engineering (MS, PhD); geographic information systems (M Eng). Part-time and evening/weekend programs available. *Faculty:* 10 full-time (1 woman). *Students:* 13 full-time (3 women), 77 part-time (19 women); includes 14 minority (3 African Americans, 4 Asian Americans or Pacific Islanders, 7 Hispanic Americans), 18 international. Average age 34. 45 applicants, 58% accepted, 11 enrolled. In 2007, 24 master's, 2 doctorates awarded. *Degree requirements:* For master's, comprehensive exam, thesis or alternative; for doctorate, comprehensive exam, thesis/dissertation. *Entrance requirements:* For master's and doctorate, GRE. Additional exam requirements/recommendations for international students: Required—TOEFL (minimum score 525 paper-based; 197 computer-based). *Application deadline:* For fall admission, 4/1 for domestic students; for spring admission, 10/1 for domestic students. Applications are processed on a rolling basis. Application fee: $50 ($75 for international students). Electronic applications accepted. *Financial support:* Research assistantships, teaching assistantships, career-related internships or fieldwork and Federal Work-Study available. Financial award application deadline: 4/1; financial award applicants required to submit FAFSA. *Unit head:* Dr. Bruce Janson, Chair, 303-556-2831, Fax: 303-556-2368, E-mail: bjanson@carbon.cudenver.edu. *Application contact:* Dawn Arge, Program Assistant, 303-556-2871, Fax: 303-556-2368, E-mail: darge@carbon.cudenver.edu.

University of Colorado Denver, College of Liberal Arts and Sciences, Department of Geography and Environmental Sciences, Denver, CO 80217-3364. Offers environmental sciences (MS); geographic information science (Certificate). Part-time and evening/weekend programs available. *Students:* 20 full-time (10 women), 23 part-time (15 women); includes 7 minority (2 African Americans, 1 Asian American or Pacific Islander, 4 Hispanic Americans), 6 international. Average age 32. 35 applicants, 69% accepted, 18 enrolled. In 2007, 6 degrees awarded. *Degree requirements:* For master's, thesis or alternative. *Entrance requirements:* For master's, GRE General Test. Additional exam requirements/recommendations for international students: Required—TOEFL (minimum score 525 paper-based; 197 computer-based). *Application deadline:* For fall admission, 4/1 for domestic students; for spring admission, 10/1 for domestic students. Applications are processed on a rolling basis. Application fee: $50 ($75 for international students). Electronic applications accepted. *Financial support:* Research assistantships, teaching assistantships, Federal Work-Study available. Financial award application deadline: 4/1; financial award applicants required to submit FAFSA. *Unit head:* Dr. Brian Page, Chair, 303-556-8332, Fax: 303-556-6197, E-mail: brian.page@cudenver.edu.

University of Connecticut, Graduate School, College of Liberal Arts and Sciences, Department of Geography, Field of Geography, Storrs, CT 06269. Offers geographic information systems (Certificate); geography (MS, PhD). Part-time programs available. *Faculty:* 11 full-time (3 women). *Students:* 18 full-time (6 women), 5 part-time (1 woman); includes 1 minority (Asian American or Pacific Islander), 2 international. Average age 32. 23 applicants, 22% accepted, 4 enrolled. In 2007, 4 master's, 1 doctorate, 8 other advanced degrees awarded. Terminal master's awarded for partial completion of doctoral program. *Degree requirements:* For master's, comprehensive exam; for doctorate, thesis/dissertation. *Entrance requirements:* For master's and doctorate, GRE General Test. Additional exam requirements/recommendations for international students: Required—TOEFL (minimum score 550 paper-based; 213 computer-based). *Application deadline:* For fall admission, 2/1 priority date for domestic and international students; for spring admission, 11/1 for domestic students, 10/1 for international students. Applications are processed on a rolling basis. Application fee: $55. Electronic applications accepted. *Expenses:* Tuition, state resident: part-time $469 per credit hour. Tuition, nonresident: part-time $1,218 per credit hour. *Financial support:* In 2007–08, 2 research assistantships with full tuition reimbursements, 16 teaching assistantships with full tuition reimbursements were awarded; fellowships, Federal Work-Study, scholarships/grants, health care benefits, and unspecified assistantships also available. Financial award application deadline: 2/1; financial award applicants required to submit FAFSA. *Application contact:* Rose Karosi, Administrative Assistant, 860-986-3656, Fax: 860-486-1348, E-mail: rose.karosi@uconn.edu.

University of Denver, University College, Denver, CO 80208. Offers applied communication (MAS, MPS, Certificate); computer information systems (MAS, Certificate); environmental policy and management (MAS, Certificate); geographic information systems (MAS, Certificate); human resource administration (MPS, Certificate); knowledge and information technologies (MAS); liberal studies (MLS, Certificate); modern languages (MLS, Certificate); organizational leadership (MPS, Certificate); security management (Certificate); technology management (MAS, Certificate), including 21st century strategic management (MAS), international markets (MAS), project management (MAS), research and development management (MAS); telecommunications (MAS, Certificate), including broadband (MAS), telecommunications management and policy (MAS), telecommunications technology (MAS), wireless networks (MAS). Part-time and evening/weekend programs available. Postbaccalaureate distance learning degree programs offered (no on-campus study). *Students:* 29 full-time (15 women), 524 part-time (304 women); includes 92 minority (37 African Americans, 3 American Indian/Alaska Native, 17 Asian Americans or Pacific Islanders, 35 Hispanic Americans), 53 international. Average age 36. 625 applicants, 97% accepted, 359 enrolled. In 2007, 151 master's, 2 Certificates awarded. *Entrance requirements:* Additional exam requirements/recommendations for international students: Required—TOEFL (minimum score 550 paper-based; 213 computer-based). *Application deadline:* Applications are processed on a rolling basis. Application fee: $75. Electronic applications accepted. *Expenses: Contact institution. Financial support:* Applicants required to submit FAFSA. *Unit head:* Dr. James Davis, Dean, 303-871-2291, Fax: 303-871-4047, E-mail: jdavis@du.edu. *Application contact:* Information Contact, 303-871-3069.

University of Lethbridge, School of Graduate Studies, Lethbridge, AB T1K 3M4, Canada. Offers accounting (MScM); addictions counseling (M Sc); agricultural biotechnology (M Sc); agricultural studies (M Sc, MA); anthropology (MA); archaeology (MA); art (MA); biochemistry (M Sc); biological sciences (M Sc); biomolecular science (PhD); biosystems and biodiversity (PhD); Canadian studies (MA); chemistry (M Sc); computer science (M Sc); computer science and geographical information science (M Sc); counseling psychology (M Ed); dramatic arts (MA); earth, space, and physical science (PhD); economics (MA); educational leadership (M Ed); English (MA); environmental science (M Sc); evolution and behavior (PhD); exercise science (M Sc); finance (MScM); French (MA); French/German (MA); French/Spanish (MA); general education (M Ed); general management (MScM); geography (M Sc, MA); German (MA); health sciences (M Sc, MA); history (MA); human resource management and labour relations (MScM); individualized multidisciplinary (M Sc, MA); information systems (MScM); international management (MScM); kinesiology (M Sc, MA); management (M Sc, MA); marketing (MScM); mathematics (M Sc); music (MA); Native American studies (MA); neuroscience (M Sc, PhD); new media (MA); nursing (M Sc); philosophy (MA); physics (M Sc); policy and strategy (MScM); political science (MA); psychology (M Sc, MA); religious studies (MA); sociology (MA); theoretical and computational science (PhD); urban and regional studies (MA). Part-time and evening/weekend programs available. *Students:* 215 full-time, 98 part-time. In 2007, 87 master's, 1 doctorate awarded. *Degree requirements:* For doctorate, comprehensive exam, thesis/dissertation. *Entrance requirements:* For master's, GMAT (M Sc in management), bachelor's degree in related field, minimum GPA of 3.0 during previous 20 graded semester courses, 2 years teaching or related experience (M Ed); for doctorate, master's degree, minimum graduate GPA of 3.5. Additional exam requirements/recommendations for international students: Required—TOEFL. Application fee: $60 Canadian dollars. *Financial support:* Fellowships, research assistantships, teaching assistantships, scholarships/grants, health care benefits, and unspecified assistantships available. *Faculty research:* Movement and brain plasticity, gibberellin physiology, photosynthesis, carbon cycling, molecular properties of main-group ring components. *Unit head:* Dr. Jo-Anne Fiske, Interim Dean, 403-329-2121, Fax: 403-329-2097. *Application contact:* Jennifer Geddes, Graduate Liaison Officer, 403-329-2762, Fax: 403-329-5159, E-mail: jennifer.geddes@uleth.ca.

University of Minnesota, Twin Cities Campus, Graduate School, College of Liberal Arts, Department of Geography, Program in Geographic Information Science, Minneapolis, MN 55455-0213. Offers MGIS. Part-time programs available. *Faculty:* 12 full-time (1 woman), 3 part-time/adjunct (0 women). *Students:* 33 full-time (15 women), 30 part-time (7 women); includes 1 minority (Asian American or Pacific Islander), 6 international. 26 applicants, 62% accepted, 10 enrolled. In 2007, 16 degrees awarded. *Degree requirements:* For master's, 3 plan B projects/papers. *Entrance requirements:* For master's, minimum GPA of 3.0; course work in college-level math, statistics, and computer programming. Additional exam requirements/recommendations for international students: Required—TOEFL (minimum score 600 paper-based; 250 computer-based; 100 iBT). *Application deadline:* For fall admission, 1/30 for domestic students; for spring admission, 9/1 for domestic students. Applications are processed on a rolling basis. Application fee: $55 ($75 for international students). *Expenses: Contact institution. Financial support:* In 2007–08, 13 students received support, including 11 research assistantships with full and partial tuition reimbursements available, 2 teaching assistantships with full and partial tuition reimbursements available; career-related internships or fieldwork and unspecified assistantships also available. *Faculty research:* Accuracy assessment, geographic information science and society, spatial analysis and modeling, spatial databases, remote sensing. *Unit head:* Dr. Richard H. Skaggs, Co-Director, 612-625-6080, Fax: 612-624-1044, E-mail: skaggs@umn.edu. *Application contact:* Dr. Susanna A. McMaster, Associate Program Director, 612-624-1498, Fax: 612-624-1044, E-mail: mcmas002@umn.edu.

The University of Montana, Graduate School, College of Arts and Sciences, Department of Geography, Missoula, MT 59812-0002. Offers geography (MA), including cartography and GIS, community and environmental planning. *Entrance requirements:* For master's, GRE General Test. Additional exam requirements/recommendations for international students: Required—TOEFL.

The University of North Carolina at Greensboro, Graduate School, College of Arts and Sciences, Department of Geography, Greensboro, NC 27412-5001. Offers applied geography (MA); geographic information science (Certificate); geography (PhD); urban and economic development (Certificate). *Faculty:* 14 full-time (3 women). *Students:* 55 full-time (17 women), 6 part-time (2 women); includes 17 minority (11 African Americans, 6 Asian Americans or Pacific Islanders). 31 applicants, 52% accepted. *Degree requirements:* For master's, comprehensive exam, thesis or alternative. *Entrance requirements:* For master's, GRE General Test. Additional exam requirements/recommendations for international students: Required—TOEFL. *Application deadline:* For fall admission, 6/15 for domestic students; for spring admission, 3/15 for domestic students. Electronic applications accepted. *Financial support:* Research assistantships with full tuition reimbursements, teaching assistantships with full tuition reimbursements, career-related internships or fieldwork, Federal Work-Study, scholarships/grants, and traineeships available. Support available to part-time students. *Unit head:* Dr. Jeffrey C Patton, Head, 336-334-5388, Fax: 336-334-5864, E-mail: jcpatton@uncg.edu. *Application contact:* Michelle Harkleroad, Director of Graduate Admissions, 336-334-4884, Fax: 336-334-4424, E-mail: mbharkle@uncg.edu.

University of Pittsburgh, School of Arts and Sciences, Department of Geology and Planetary Science, Pittsburgh, PA 15260. Offers geographical information systems (PM Sc); geology and planetary science (MS, PhD). Part-time programs available. *Faculty:* 9 full-time (1 woman), 4 part-time/adjunct (1 woman). *Students:* 17 full-time (5 women), 16 part-time (3 women); includes 3 minority (2 Asian Americans or Pacific Islanders, 1 Hispanic American), 2 international. Average age 30. 31 applicants, 19% accepted, 7 enrolled. In 2007, 5 master's, 2 doctorates awarded. *Median time to degree:* Of those who began their doctoral program in fall 1999, 100% received their degree in 8 years or less. *Degree requirements:* For master's, thesis, oral thesis defense; for doctorate, thesis/dissertation, oral dissertation defense. *Entrance requirements:* For master's and doctorate, GRE General Test. Additional exam requirements/recommendations for international students: Required—TOEFL (minimum score 550 paper-based; 213 computer-based; 80 iBT). *Application deadline:* For fall admission, 8/1 priority date for domestic students, 4/30 for international students; for winter admission, 12/1 priority date for domestic students, 8/30 for international students; for spring admission, 4/1 priority date for domestic students, 1/31 for international students. Applications are processed on a rolling basis. Application fee: $50. Electronic applications accepted. *Financial support:* In 2007–08, 25 students received support, including fellowships with tuition reimbursements available (averaging $13,690 per year), 13 research assistantships with tuition reimbursements available (averaging $13,600 per year), 12 teaching assistantships with tuition reimbursements available (averaging $14,485 per year); career-related internships or fieldwork, Federal Work-Study, institutionally sponsored loans, scholarships/grants, and tuition waivers (full and partial) also available. Support available to part-time students. Financial award application deadline: 2/1; financial award applicants required to submit FAFSA. *Faculty research:* Geographical information systems, hydrology, low temperature geochemistry, volcanology, paleoclimatology. Total annual research expenditures: $1.2 million. *Unit head:* Dr. Brian W Stewart, Chair, 412-624-8783, Fax: 412-624-3914, E-mail: bstewart@pitt.edu. *Application contact:* Dr. Thomas Anderson, Graduate Adviser, 412-624-8870, Fax: 412-624-3914, E-mail: taco@pitt.edu.

University of Redlands, College of Arts and Sciences, Program in Geographic Information Systems, Redlands, CA 92373-0999. Offers MS. *Faculty:* 2 full-time (1 woman), 10 part-time/adjunct (2 women). *Students:* 20 full-time (7 women), 3 part-time (1 woman); includes 2 minority (1 African American, 1 Hispanic American), 3 international. Average age 31. In 2007, 8 degrees awarded. *Entrance requirements:* For master's, 2 years of professional experience using GIS or 2 university-level GIS courses plus internship, minimum undergraduate GPA of 3.0, 2 letters of recommendation. Additional exam requirements/recommendations for international students: Required—TOEFL (minimum score 550 paper-based; 210 computer-based); Recommended—IELTS (minimum score 6). *Application deadline:* For fall admission, 3/31 for domestic students; for spring admission, 7/30 for domestic students. Applications are processed on a rolling basis. Application fee: $40. Electronic applications accepted. *Expenses: Contact institution.* Tuition and fees vary according to course level, course load, degree level and program. *Financial support:* In 2007–08, 5 students received support. Institutionally sponsored loans and scholarships/grants available. Financial award application deadline: 3/2; financial award applicants required to submit FAFSA. *Unit head:* Mark Kumler, Interim Director, 909-748-8649, Fax: 909-748-6334, E-mail: mark_kumler@redlands.edu. *Application contact:* Theresa Ellis, Coordinator, 909-793-2121 Ext. 5128, E-mail: theresa_ellis@redlands.edu.

University of Southern California, Graduate School, College of Letters, Arts and Sciences, Department of Geography, Los Angeles, CA 90089. Offers geographic information science and technology (Graduate Certificate); geography (MA, MS, PhD). Part-time and evening/weekend programs available. Postbaccalaureate distance learning degree programs offered (no on-campus study). *Faculty:* 8 full-time (3 women), 4 part-time/adjunct (1 woman). *Students:* 25 full-time (16 women), 5 part-time (1 woman); includes 6 minority (1 African American, 1 American Indian/Alaska Native, 2 Asian Americans or Pacific Islanders, 2 Hispanic Americans), 8 international. 31 applicants, 42% accepted. In 2007, 4 doctorates, 5 other advanced degrees awarded. Terminal master's awarded for partial completion of doctoral program. *Degree requirements:* For master's, thesis; for doctorate, thesis/dissertation. *Entrance requirements:* For master's and doctorate, GRE General Test. *Application deadline:* For fall admission, 12/1 priority date for domestic students. Applications are processed on a rolling basis. Application fee: $85. *Financial support:* In 2007–08, 2 students received support, including fellowships with full tuition reimbursements available (averaging $18,570 per year), research assistantships with full tuition reimbursements available (averaging $18,570 per year), teaching assistantships with full tuition reimbursements available (averaging $18,570 per year); scholarships/grants, traineeships, and tuition waivers (full) also available. Financial award application deadline: 2/15; financial award applicants required to submit FAFSA. *Faculty research:* Landscape dynamics, geomorphology, geographic information science, urban geography and nature-society relations, GIS. *Unit head:* Dr. John Wilson, Chair, 213-740-2311, E-mail: uscgeog@usc.edu. *Application contact:* Kate Kelsey, Information Contact, 213-740-2311.

The University of Texas at Dallas, School of Economic, Political and Policy Sciences, Program in Geospatial Sciences, Richardson, TX 75083-0688. Offers MS, PhD. Part-time and evening/weekend programs available. *Faculty:* 7 full-time (1 woman), 1 part-time/adjunct (0 women). *Students:* 29 full-time (11 women), 27 part-time (9 women); includes 5 minority (3 African Americans, 1 Asian American or Pacific Islander, 1 Hispanic American), 27 international. Average age 33. 43 applicants, 72% accepted, 16 enrolled. In 2007, 16 degrees awarded. *Degree requirements:* For master's, internship. *Entrance requirements:* For master's, GRE General Test, minimum GPA of 3.0 in upper-level coursework in field. Additional exam requirements/recommendations for international students: Required—TOEFL (minimum score 550 paper-based; 213 computer-based). *Application deadline:* For fall admission, 7/15 for domestic students; for spring admission, 11/15 for domestic students. Applications are processed on a rolling basis. Application fee: $50 ($100 for international students). Electronic applications accepted. *Expenses:* Tuition, state resident: full-time $7,052. Tuition, nonresident: full-time $12,632. Tuition and fees vary according to course load. *Financial support:* In 2007–08, 5 research assistantships with tuition reimbursements (averaging $11,171 per year), 6 teaching assistantships with tuition reimbursements (averaging $10,512 per year) were awarded; fellowships, career-related internships or fieldwork, Federal Work-Study, institutionally sponsored loans, scholarships/grants, and unspecified assistantships also available. Support available to part-time students. Financial award application deadline: 4/30; financial award applicants required to submit FAFSA. *Faculty research:* Neighborhood evaluation using geographical information systems. *Unit head:* Dr. Ronald Briggs, Coordinator, 972-883-6406, Fax: 972-883-2735, E-mail: briggs@utdallas.edu. *Application contact:* Judy C. Robertson, Program Assistant, 972-883-6406, E-mail: judy.robertson@utdallas.edu.

See Close-Up on page 1043.

The University of Toledo, College of Graduate Studies, College of Arts and Sciences, Department of Geography and Planning, Toledo, OH 43606-3390. Offers geographic information systems and applied geographics (Certificate); geography (MA); planning (MA). Part-time programs available. *Faculty:* 10. *Students:* 20 full-time (6 women), 12 part-time (4 women); includes 2 minority (both African Americans), 5 international. Average age 31. 27 applicants, 67% accepted, 9 enrolled. In 2007, 8 master's, 3 other advanced degrees awarded. *Degree requirements:* For master's, thesis. *Entrance requirements:* For master's, GRE General Test. *Application deadline:* For fall admission, 3/15 priority date for domestic students. Applications are processed on a rolling basis. Application fee: $45. Electronic applications accepted. *Financial support:* In 2007–08, 4 research assistantships with full tuition reimbursements (averaging $10,500 per year), 9 teaching assistantships with full tuition reimbursements (averaging $10,500 per year) were awarded; career-related internships or fieldwork, institutionally sponsored loans, scholarships/grants, tuition waivers (full), and unspecified assistantships also available. Support available to part-time students. Financial award application deadline: 4/1. *Unit head:* Dr. Peter Lindquist, Chair, 419-530-4287, Fax: 419-530-7919, E-mail: peter.lindquist@utoledo.edu.

See Close-Up on page 1093.

University of West Georgia, Graduate School, College of Arts and Sciences, Department of Political Science and Planning, Program in Geographic Information Systems, Carrollton, GA 30118. Offers Certificate. *Students:* 1 full-time (0 women), 2 part-time (1 woman). Average age 30.Application fee: $30. *Expenses:* Tuition, state resident: full-time $2,448; part-time $136 per semester hour. Tuition, nonresident: full-time $9,774; part-time $543 per semester hour. Required fees: $26 per semester hour. $173 per semester. *Application contact:* Dr. Charles W. Clark, Interim Dean, 678-839-6508, E-mail: cclark@westga.edu.

University of Wisconsin–Madison, Graduate School, College of Letters and Science, Department of Geography, Madison, WI 53706-1380. Offers cartography and geographic information systems (MS); geographic information systems (Certificate); geography (MS, PhD). Part-time programs available. *Degree requirements:* For master's, thesis; for doctorate, thesis/dissertation; for Certificate, internship. *Entrance requirements:* For master's and doctorate, GRE General Test, minimum GPA of 3.25. Electronic applications accepted. *Faculty research:* Physical geography, urban/historical geography, people-environment, history of cartography, GIS.

Virginia Commonwealth University, Graduate School, College of Humanities and Sciences, Wilder School of Government and Public Affairs, Department of Urban Studies and Planning, Program in Geographic Information Systems, Richmond, VA 23284-9005. Offers Certificate. *Application deadline:* For fall admission, 4/15 for domestic students; for spring admission, 11/15 for domestic students. Applications are processed on a rolling basis. Application fee: $50. *Expenses:* Tuition, state resident: full-time $7,224; part-time $401 per credit. Tuition, nonresident: full-time $16,072; part-time $891 per credit. Required fees: $1,679; $63 per credit. Tuition and fees vary according to campus/location.

See Close-Up on page 457.

West Chester University of Pennsylvania, Office of Graduate Studies and Extended Education, College of Business and Public Affairs, Department of Geography and Planning, West Chester, PA 19383. Offers geographic technology (Certificate); geography (MA); regional planning (MSA). Part-time and evening/weekend programs available. *Students:* 15 full-time (5 women), 12 part-time (2 women); includes 5 minority (4 African Americans, 1 Hispanic American). Average age 28. 19 applicants, 84% accepted, 11 enrolled. In 2007, 6 degrees awarded. *Degree requirements:* For master's, comprehensive exam, thesis optional. *Entrance requirements:* For master's, GRE General Test, interview, minimum GPA of 3.0, resumé. Additional exam requirements/recommendations for international students: Required—TOEFL (minimum score 550 paper-based; 213 computer-based; 80 iBT). *Application deadline:* For fall admission, 4/15 priority date for domestic students; for spring admission, 10/15 for domestic students. Applications are processed on a rolling basis. Application fee: $35. *Expenses:* Tuition, state resident: part-time $345 per credit. Tuition, nonresident: part-time $552 per credit. Tuition and fees vary according to course load. *Financial support:* In 2007–08, 3 research assistantships with full and partial tuition reimbursements (averaging $5,000 per year) were awarded; unspecified assistantships also available. Support available to part-time students. Financial award application deadline: 2/15; financial award applicants required to submit FAFSA. *Faculty research:* Environmental education, land use/suburban planning, landscapes of Catalunya. *Unit head:* Dr. Joan Welch, Chair and Graduate Coordinator, 610-436-2343, E-mail: jwelch@wcupa.edu.

West Virginia University, Eberly College of Arts and Sciences, Department of Geology and Geography, Program in Geography, Morgantown, WV 26506. Offers energy and environmental resources (MA); geographic information systems (PhD); geography-regional development (PhD); GIS/cartographic analysis (MA); regional development (MA). Part-time programs available. *Students:* 20 full-time (10 women), 7 part-time (4 women); includes 1 minority (American Indian/Alaska Native), 4 international. Average age 32. 18 applicants, 56% accepted, 7 enrolled. In 2007, 9 master's, 7 doctorates awarded. *Degree requirements:* For master's, thesis, oral and written exams; for doctorate, comprehensive exam, thesis/dissertation, oral and written exams. *Entrance requirements:* For master's and doctorate, GRE General Test, minimum GPA of 3.0. Additional exam requirements/recommendations for international students: Required—TOEFL. *Application deadline:* For fall admission, 1/1 priority date for domestic students, 11/14 priority date for international students; for spring admission, 5/1 priority date for domestic students, 7/1 priority date for international students. Applications are processed on a rolling basis. Application fee: $45. Electronic applications accepted. *Expenses:* Tuition, state resident: full-time $5,196; part-time $292 per credit hour. Tuition, nonresident: full-time $15,064; part-time $840 per credit hour. Tuition and fees vary according to program. *Financial support:* In 2007–08, 26 students received support, including 1 research assistantship with full tuition reimbursement available (averaging $15,000 per year), 6 teaching assistantships with full tuition reimbursements available (averaging $11,000 per year); career-related internships or fieldwork, Federal Work-Study, institutionally sponsored loans, health care benefits, and tuition waivers (partial) also available. Financial award application deadline: 2/1; financial award applicants required to submit FAFSA. *Faculty research:* Space, place and development, geographic information science, environmental geography. *Application contact:* Dr. Amy Hessl, Associate Professor, 304-293-8210, Fax: 304-293-6522, E-mail: geography-grad-info@mail.wvu.edu.

Geography

Appalachian State University, Cratis D. Williams Graduate School, Department of Geography and Planning, Boone, NC 28608. Offers geography (MA). *Faculty:* 14 full-time (3 women), 1 part-time/adjunct (0 women). *Students:* 16 full-time (4 women), 8 part-time (2 women). 25 applicants, 84% accepted, 15 enrolled. In 2007, 6 master's awarded. *Degree requirements:* For master's, comprehensive exam, thesis or alternative. *Entrance requirements:* For master's, GRE General Test, 3 letters of recommendation. Additional exam requirements/recommendations for international students: Required—TOEFL (minimum score 570 paper-based; 230 computer-based; 79 iBT), IELTS (minimum score 7), TOEFL or IELTS. *Application deadline:* For fall admission, 7/1 for domestic students, 1/1 for international students; for spring admission, 11/1 for domestic students, 6/1 for international students. Applications are processed on a rolling basis. Application fee: $50. Electronic applications accepted. *Expenses:* Tuition, state resident: part-time $127 per semester hour. Tuition, nonresident: part-time $597 per semester hour. Required fees: $18 per semester. *Financial support:* In 2007–08, 10 research assistantships (averaging $7,500 per year) were awarded; fellowships, teaching assistantships, career-

Geography

Appalachian State University (continued)
related internships or fieldwork, Federal Work-Study, scholarships/grants, and unspecified assistantships also available. Financial award application deadline: 4/1. *Faculty research:* Global change, climatology, production cartography, geographic information systems, North Carolina geography, Latin America. Total annual research expenditures: $46,464. *Unit head:* Dr. James Young, Chairperson, 828-262-3000, Fax: 828-262-3067. *Application contact:* Dr. Kathleen Schroeder, Graduate Program Director, 828-262-3000.

Arizona State University, Graduate College, College of Liberal Arts and Sciences, Division of Social Sciences, Department of Geography, Tempe, AZ 85287. Offers MA, MAS, PhD. *Degree requirements:* For master's, thesis; for doctorate, thesis/dissertation. *Entrance requirements:* For master's and doctorate, GRE.

Boston University, Graduate School of Arts and Sciences, Department of Geography and Environment, Boston, MA 02215. Offers energy and environmental analysis (MA); environmental remote sensing and GIs (MA); geography (MA); geography and environment (PhD); international relations and environmental policy (MA). *Students:* 49 full-time (22 women), 8 part-time (4 women); includes 1 minority (Hispanic American), 28 international. Average age 29. 55 applicants, 27% accepted, 6 enrolled. In 2007, 2 master's, 3 doctorates awarded. Terminal master's awarded for partial completion of doctoral program. *Degree requirements:* For master's, one foreign language, comprehensive exam, thesis; for doctorate, one foreign language, comprehensive exam, thesis/dissertation. *Entrance requirements:* For master's and doctorate, GRE General Test, GRE Subject Test, 3 letters of recommendation. Additional exam requirements/recommendations for international students: Required—TOEFL (minimum score 600 paper-based; 250 computer-based). *Application deadline:* For fall admission, 7/1 for domestic and international students; for spring admission, 11/15 for domestic and international students. Application fee: $70. *Expenses:* Tuition: Full-time $34,930; part-time $1,092 per credit. Tuition and fees vary according to class time, course level and program. *Financial support:* In 2007–08, 33 students received support, including 2 fellowships with full tuition reimbursements available (averaging $18,000 per year), 20 research assistantships with full tuition reimbursements available (averaging $17,500 per year), 9 teaching assistantships with full tuition reimbursements available (averaging $17,500 per year); Federal Work-Study and unspecified assistantships also available. Support available to part-time students. Financial award application deadline: 1/15; financial award applicants required to submit FAFSA. Total annual research expenditures: $1.2 million. *Unit head:* Mark Friedl, Chairman, 617-353-5745, Fax: 617-353-8399, E-mail: friedl@bu.edu. *Application contact:* Erin Wnorowski, Graduate Program Coordinator, 617-353-7554, Fax: 617-353-8399, E-mail: wnorowsk@bu.edu.

Brigham Young University, Graduate Studies, College of Family, Home, and Social Sciences, Department of Geography, Provo, UT 84602-1001. Offers MS. *Faculty:* 9 full-time (0 women), 1 part-time/adjunct (0 women). *Students:* 8 full-time (3 women). Average age 32. *Financial support:* In 2007–08, 3 students received support. *Faculty research:* Global studies, physical environment, urban planning, travel and tourism, geospatial intelligence, geographic information systems. *Unit head:* Dr. J. Matthew Shumway, Chair, 801-422-2707, Fax: 801-422-0266, E-mail: jms7@byu.edu.

Brock University, Faculty of Graduate Studies, Faculty of Social Sciences, Program in Geography, St. Catharines, ON L2S 3A1, Canada. Offers MA. Part-time programs available. *Degree requirements:* For master's, thesis optional. *Entrance requirements:* For master's, honors degree. Additional exam requirements/recommendations for international students: Required—TOEFL (minimum score 550 paper-based; 213 computer-based; 80 iBT), IELTS (minimum score 7), TWE (minimum score 4).

California State University, Chico, Graduate School, College of Behavioral and Social Sciences, Department of Geography and Planning, Program in Geography, Chico, CA 95929-0425. Offers MA. Part-time programs available. *Students:* 8 full-time (6 women), 5 part-time (2 women); includes 2 minority (both Hispanic Americans) Average age 33. 5 applicants, 80% accepted, 3 enrolled. In 2007, 4 degrees awarded. *Entrance requirements:* For master's, GRE General Test, 2 letters of recommendation, statement of purpose, writing sample. Additional exam requirements/recommendations for international students: Required—TOEFL (minimum score 550 paper-based; 213 computer-based; 80 iBT), IELTS (minimum score 7). *Application deadline:* For fall admission, 3/1 priority date for domestic students, 3/1 for international students; for spring admission, 9/15 priority date for domestic students, 9/15 for international students. Applications are processed on a rolling basis. Application fee: $55. Electronic applications accepted. *Unit head:* Dr. Dean Fairbanks, Graduate Coordinator, 530-898-5780.

California State University, East Bay, Academic Programs and Graduate Studies, College of Letters, Arts, and Social Sciences, Department of Geography and Environmental Studies, Hayward, CA 94542-3000. Offers geography (MA). Part-time programs available. *Faculty:* 2 full-time (0 women). *Students:* 3 full-time (1 woman), 3 part-time (2 women); includes 3 minority (1 African American, 2 Asian Americans or Pacific Islanders), 1 international. Average age 37. 10 applicants, 80% accepted, 2 enrolled. In 2007, 1 degree awarded. *Degree requirements:* For master's, variable foreign language requirement, project or thesis. *Entrance requirements:* For master's, GRE, minimum GPA of 3.0 in field. Additional exam requirements/recommendations for international students: Required—TOEFL (minimum score 550 paper-based; 213 computer-based). *Application deadline:* For fall admission, 5/31 for domestic students, 4/30 for international students; for winter admission, 9/30 for domestic and international students; for spring admission, 12/31 for domestic students, 11/30 for international students. Applications are processed on a rolling basis. Application fee: $55. Electronic applications accepted. *Expenses:* Required fees: $3,987; $851 per quarter. *Financial support:* Fellowships, teaching assistantships, career-related internships or fieldwork, Federal Work-Study, institutionally sponsored loans, and scholarships/grants available. Support available to part-time students. Financial award application deadline: 3/2. *Unit head:* Dr. David Larson, Chair, 510-885-3193 Ext. 3193, Fax: 510-885-2353, E-mail: david.larson@csueastbay.edu. *Application contact:* My Huynh, Graduate Prospect Specialist, 510-885-2989, Fax: 510-885-4059, E-mail: my.huynh@csueastbay.edu.

California State University, Fullerton, Graduate Studies, College of Humanities and Social Sciences, Department of Geography, Fullerton, CA 92834-9480. Offers MA. *Students:* 5 full-time (3 women), 16 part-time (7 women); includes 8 minority (4 Asian Americans or Pacific Islanders, 4 Hispanic Americans), 1 international. Average age 30. 9 applicants, 67% accepted, 3 enrolled. In 2007, 2 degrees awarded. *Degree requirements:* For master's, comprehensive exam or thesis. *Entrance requirements:* For master's, minimum GPA of 3.0, 18 undergraduate credits in field. Application fee: $55. *Financial support:* Teaching assistantships, career-related internships or fieldwork, Federal Work-Study, institutionally sponsored loans, and scholarships/grants available. Support available to part-time students. Financial award application deadline: 3/1. *Faculty research:* Human geography, physical geography. *Unit head:* Dr. John Carroll, Chair, 714-278-3161.

California State University, Long Beach, Graduate Studies, College of Liberal Arts, Department of Geography, Long Beach, CA 90840. Offers MA. Part-time programs available. *Faculty:* 11 full-time (6 women), 12 part-time/adjunct (4 women). *Students:* 8 full-time (1 woman), 23 part-time (12 women); includes 7 minority (1 African American, 3 Asian Americans or Pacific Islanders, 3 Hispanic Americans). Average age 33. *Degree requirements:* For master's, thesis. *Application deadline:* For fall admission, 7/1 for domestic students; for spring admission, 12/1 for domestic students. Applications are processed on a rolling basis. Application fee: $55. Electronic applications accepted. *Financial support:* Career-related internships or fieldwork, Federal Work-Study, institutionally sponsored loans, and scholarships/grants available. Financial award application deadline: 3/2. *Faculty research:* Demography, geographic information systems, world landforms and societies. *Unit head:* Dr. Christine Rodrigue, Chair, 562-985-4977, Fax: 562-985-8993, E-mail: rodrigue@csulb.edu. *Application contact:* Dr. Christopher T Lee, Graduate Advisor, 562-985-2358, Fax: 562-985-8993, E-mail: clee@csulb.edu.

California State University, Los Angeles, Graduate Studies, College of Natural and Social Sciences, Department of Geography and Urban Analysis, Los Angeles, CA 90032-8530. Offers geography (MA). Part-time and evening/weekend programs available. *Faculty:* 4 full-time (1 woman), 1 part-time/adjunct (0 women). *Students:* 7 full-time (4 women), 16 part-time (10 women); includes 6 minority (2 Asian Americans or Pacific Islanders, 4 Hispanic Americans), 6 international. Average age 36. In 2007, 5 degrees awarded. *Degree requirements:* For master's, one foreign language, comprehensive exam or thesis. *Entrance requirements:* Additional exam requirements/recommendations for international students: Required—TOEFL. *Application deadline:* For fall admission, 6/30 for domestic students; for spring admission, 2/1 for domestic students. Applications are processed on a rolling basis. Application fee: $55. *Financial support:* Career-related internships or fieldwork and Federal Work-Study available. Support available to part-time students. Financial award application deadline: 3/1. *Faculty research:* Technique focus–air photography, cartography, locational analysis. *Unit head:* Dr. Killian Ying, Chair, 323-343-2220, Fax: 323-343-6494, E-mail: kying@calstatela.edu.

California State University, Northridge, Graduate Studies, College of Social and Behavioral Sciences, Department of Geography, Northridge, CA 91330. Offers MA. Part-time programs available. *Faculty:* 15 full-time (4 women), 19 part-time/adjunct (10 women). *Students:* 10 full-time (7 women), 25 part-time (9 women); includes 7 minority (3 Asian Americans or Pacific Islanders, 4 Hispanic Americans), 3 international. Average age 34. 18 applicants, 78% accepted, 9 enrolled. In 2007, 13 degrees awarded. *Degree requirements:* For master's, one foreign language, thesis. *Entrance requirements:* For master's, GRE General Test or minimum GPA of 3.0. Additional exam requirements/recommendations for international students: Required—TOEFL. *Application deadline:* For fall admission, 11/30 for domestic students. Application fee: $55. *Financial support:* Teaching assistantships available. Financial award application deadline: 3/1. *Unit head:* Darrick Danta, Chair, 818-677-3532. *Application contact:* Dr. Edward Jackiewicz, Graduate Advisor, 818-677-4565.

Carleton University, Faculty of Graduate Studies, Faculty of Arts and Social Sciences, Department of Geography and Environmental Studies, Ottawa, ON K1S 5B6, Canada. Offers geography (M Sc, MA, PhD). *Degree requirements:* For master's, thesis, seminar; for doctorate, one foreign language, thesis/dissertation, 2 comprehensive exams. *Entrance requirements:* For master's, honors degree; for doctorate, master's degree in geography. Additional exam requirements/recommendations for international students: Required—TOEFL. Application fee: $77. *Financial support:* Fellowships, research assistantships, teaching assistantships available. *Faculty research:* Human dimensions of global environmental change, winter environments, population studies, historical geography, globalization. *Unit head:* Michael Brklcick, Chair, 613-520-0600 Ext. 2561, Fax: 613-520-4301, E-mail: chair_geography@carleton.ca. *Application contact:* Natalie Pressburger, Graduate Secretary, 613-520-2600 Ext. 2561, Fax: 613-520-4301.

Central Connecticut State University, School of Graduate Studies, School of Arts and Sciences, Department of Geography, New Britain, CT 06050-4010. Offers MS. Part-time and evening/weekend programs available. *Faculty:* 10 full-time (2 women), 8 part-time/adjunct (2 women). *Students:* 6 full-time (0 women), 21 part-time (9 women); includes 2 minority (both African Americans) Average age 35. 20 applicants, 50% accepted, 3 enrolled. In 2007, 5 degrees awarded. *Degree requirements:* For master's, thesis or alternative, comprehensive exam or special project. *Entrance requirements:* For master's, minimum GPA of 2.7. Additional exam requirements/recommendations for international students: Required—TOEFL. *Application deadline:* For fall admission, 7/1 for domestic students; for spring admission, 12/1 for domestic students. Applications are processed on a rolling basis. Application fee: $50. Electronic applications accepted. *Expenses:* Tuition, area resident: Full-time $4,169. Tuition, state resident: full-time $6,253. Tuition, nonresident: full-time $11,614; part-time $400 per credit. Required fees: $3,322. One-time fee: $62 part-time. Tuition and fees vary according to degree level and program. *Financial support:* In 2007–08, 5 students received support, including 1 research assistantship; career-related internships or fieldwork, Federal Work-Study, scholarships/grants, and unspecified assistantships also available. Support available to part-time students. Financial award application deadline: 3/1; financial award applicants required to submit FAFSA. *Faculty research:* Regional planning, environmental protection, tourism, computer mapping and geographic information systems. *Unit head:* Dr. Xieoping Shen, Chair, 860-832-2785.

Chicago State University, School of Graduate and Professional Studies, College of Arts and Sciences, Department of Geography, Sociology, Economics, and Anthropology, Chicago, IL 60628. Offers geography and economic development (MA). *Entrance requirements:* For master's, minimum GPA of 2.75.

Clark University, Graduate School, Department of Geography, Worcester, MA 01610-1477. Offers geographic information science (MA); geography (PhD). *Faculty:* 16 full-time (5 women), 1 part-time/adjunct (0 women). *Students:* 59 full-time (27 women), 1 part-time; includes 2 minority (1 Asian American or Pacific Islander, 1 Hispanic American), 30 international. Average age 31. 87 applicants, 23% accepted, 12 enrolled. In 2007, 5 master's, 6 doctorates awarded. *Degree requirements:* For doctorate, thesis/dissertation. *Entrance requirements:* For doctorate, GRE General Test. Additional exam requirements/recommendations for international students: Required—TOEFL. *Application deadline:* For fall admission, 1/15 priority date for domestic students. Applications are processed on a rolling basis. Application fee: $55. *Expenses:* Tuition: Full-time $32,600; part-time $1,019 per credit. Required fees: $30. Tuition and fees vary according to program. *Financial support:* In 2007–08, 5 fellowships with full tuition reimbursements (averaging $15,700 per year), 14 research assistantships with full tuition reimbursements (averaging $15,700 per year), 15 teaching assistantships with full tuition reimbursements (averaging $15,700 per year) were awarded; career-related internships or fieldwork and tuition waivers (full) also available. *Faculty research:* Global environmental change, geographic information systems, natural and technological hazards, water resources, urbanization. Total annual research expenditures: $1.5 million. *Unit head:* Dr. Billie Lee Turner, Director, 508-793-7336. *Application contact:* Christine Silva, Admission Coordinator, 508-793-7337, Fax: 508-793-8881, E-mail: geography@clarku.edu.

Concordia University, School of Graduate Studies, Faculty of Arts and Science, Department of Geography, Planning and Environment, Montréal, QC H3G 1M8, Canada. Offers environmental impact assessment (Diploma); geography, urban and environmental studies (M Sc).

Concordia University, School of Graduate Studies, Faculty of Arts and Science, Department of Political Science, Montréal, QC H3G 1M8, Canada. Offers political science (PhD); public policy and public administration (MA), including geography. *Degree requirements:* For master's, one foreign language, comprehensive exam, thesis optional, internship. *Entrance requirements:* For master's, honors degree or equivalent. Additional exam requirements/recommendations for international students: Required—TOEFL. *Faculty research:* International public policy and administration, Quebec public administration, public policy and social/political theory, geography and public policy, public administration and decision making.

East Carolina University, Graduate School, Thomas Harriot College of Arts and Sciences, Department of Geography, Greenville, NC 27858-4353. Offers MA. Part-time and evening/weekend programs available. *Faculty:* 14 full-time (3 women). *Students:* 15 full-time (10 women), 10 part-time (5 women); includes 2 minority (both African Americans), 1 international. Average age 28. 10 applicants, 20% accepted, 2 enrolled. In 2007, 6 degrees awarded. *Degree requirements:* For master's, one foreign language, comprehensive exam, thesis optional. *Entrance requirements:* For master's, GRE General Test. Additional exam requirements/recommendations for international students: Required—TOEFL. *Application deadline:* For fall admission, 6/1 priority date for domestic students; for spring admission, 10/15 for domestic students. Applications are processed on a rolling basis. Application fee: $50. *Financial support:* Research assistantships with partial tuition reimbursements, teaching assistantships with partial tuition reimbursements, Federal Work-Study available. Support available to part-time students. Financial award application deadline: 6/1. *Unit head:* Dr. Ron Mitchelson, Chair, 252-328-6230, Fax: 252-328-6054, E-mail: mitchelsonr@ecu.edu.

Eastern Michigan University, Graduate School, College of Arts and Sciences, Department of Geography and Geology, Program in Geography and Geology, Ypsilanti, MI 48197. Offers geography (MA, MS); water resources (Graduate Certificate). Part-time and evening/weekend programs available. Postbaccalaureate distance learning degree programs offered (minimal on-campus study). *Students:* Average age 30. In 2007, 1 master's, 1 other advanced degree awarded. *Degree requirements:* For master's, thesis optional. *Entrance requirements:* Additional exam requirements/recommendations for international students: Required—TOEFL. *Application deadline:* Applications are processed on a rolling basis. Application fee: $35. *Expenses:* Tuition, state resident: full-time $8,952; part-time $373 per credit hour. Tuition, nonresident: full-time $17,634; part-time $735 per credit hour. Required fees: $896; $34 per credit hour. Tuition and fees vary according to course level, degree level and program. *Financial support:* Fellowships, research assistantships with full tuition reimbursements, teaching assistantships with full tuition reimbursements, career-related internships or fieldwork, Federal Work-Study, institutionally sponsored loans, traineeships, tuition waivers (partial), and unspecified assistantships available. Support available to part-time students. Financial award applicants required to submit FAFSA. *Application contact:* Dr. Andrew Nazzaro, Program Advisor, 734-487-0218, Fax: 734-487-6979, E-mail: andrew.nazzaro@emich.edu.

Florida Atlantic University, Charles E. Schmidt College of Science, Department of Geosciences, Program in Geography, Boca Raton, FL 33431-0991. Offers MA, MAT. Part-time programs available. *Degree requirements:* For master's, thesis (for some programs). *Entrance requirements:* For master's, GRE General Test, minimum GPA of 3.0. Electronic applications accepted. *Faculty research:* Remote sensoring/digital images, location-allocation modeling, analysis of less-developed countries, historical settlement patterns, urban form.

Florida State University, Graduate Studies, College of Social Sciences, Department of Geography, Tallahassee, FL 32306. Offers geographic information systems (MS); geography (MA, MS, PhD). Part-time programs available. *Faculty:* 10 full-time (2 women), 2 part-time/adjunct (0 women). *Students:* 72 full-time (35 women), 13 part-time (3 women); includes 8 minority (2 African Americans, 1 Asian American or Pacific Islander, 5 Hispanic Americans), 5 international. Average age 30. 50 applicants, 60% accepted, 20 enrolled. In 2007, 21 master's, 3 doctorates awarded. Terminal master's awarded for partial completion of doctoral program. *Degree requirements:* For master's, thesis (for some programs); for doctorate, thesis/dissertation. *Entrance requirements:* For master's and doctorate, GRE General Test, minimum GPA of 3.0. Additional exam requirements/recommendations for international students: Required—TOEFL. *Application deadline:* For fall admission, 1/15 priority date for domestic students, 12/15 priority date for international students; for spring admission, 11/1 for domestic students, 9/15 for international students. Applications are processed on a rolling basis. Application fee: $30. Electronic applications accepted. *Expenses:* Tuition, state resident: part-time $248 per credit hour. Tuition, nonresident: part-time $880 per credit hour. Tuition and fees vary according to program. *Financial support:* In 2007–08, 19 students received support, including 6 research assistantships with full tuition reimbursements available (averaging $12,900 per year), 13 teaching assistantships with full tuition reimbursements available (averaging $12,900 per year); fellowships with full tuition reimbursements available, career-related internships or fieldwork, Federal Work-Study, institutionally sponsored loans, scholarships/grants, health care benefits, and unspecified assistantships also available. Financial award application deadline: 1/15; financial award applicants required to submit FAFSA. *Faculty research:* Society-nature interaction, geographic information science. Total annual research expenditures:$210,000. *Unit head:* Dr. Victor Mesev, Chair, 850-645-2498, Fax: 850-644-5913. *Application contact:* Dr. Tony Stallins, Graduate Director, 850-644-8385, Fax: 850-644-5193, E-mail: jastallins@fsu.edu.

Fort Hays State University, Graduate School, College of Arts and Sciences, Department of Geosciences, Program in Geosciences, Hays, KS 67601-4099. Offers geography (MS); geology (MS). *Faculty:* 8 full-time (0 women). *Students:* 9 full-time (2 women), 8 part-time (1 woman); includes 3 minority (1 African American, 1 Asian American or Pacific Islander, 1 Hispanic American). Average age 27. 6 applicants, 67% accepted. In 2007, 4 degrees awarded. *Degree requirements:* For master's, comprehensive exam, thesis. *Entrance requirements:* For master's, GRE General Test. Additional exam requirements/recommendations for international students: Required—TOEFL (minimum score 550 paper-based; 213 computer-based). *Application deadline:* For fall admission, 7/1 priority date for domestic students. Applications are processed on a rolling basis. Application fee: $35. Electronic applications accepted. *Expenses:* Tuition, state resident: part-time $155 per credit hour. Tuition, nonresident: part-time $409 per credit hour. Tuition and fees vary according to class time, course level, course load, degree level, campus/location and program. *Financial support:* In 2007–08, 5 teaching assistantships with tuition reimbursements (averaging $7,000 per year) were awarded; research assistantships, career-related internships or fieldwork and institutionally sponsored loans also available. Support available to part-time students. *Faculty research:* Cretaceous and late Cenozoic stratigraphy, sedimentation, paleontology. *Unit head:* Dr. John Heinrichs, Chair, Department of Geosciences, 785-628-5389, E-mail: jheinric@fhsu.edu.

George Mason University, College of Science, Department of Geography, Fairfax, VA 22030. Offers geographic and cartographic sciences (MS). *Degree requirements:* For master's, thesis optional. *Entrance requirements:* For master's, GRE General Test, minimum GPA of 3.0 in last 60 hours; BS or BA in geography, cartography, or related field. Electronic applications accepted.

The George Washington University, Columbian College of Arts and Sciences, Department of Geography, Washington, DC 20052. Offers MA. *Degree requirements:* For master's, comprehensive exam, thesis or alternative. *Entrance requirements:* For master's, GRE General Test, BA in geography or related field, minimum GPA of 3.0. Additional exam requirements/recommendations for international students: Required—TOEFL (minimum score 550 paper-based; 213 computer-based). Electronic applications accepted.

Georgia State University, College of Arts and Sciences, Department of Geosciences, Program in Geography, Atlanta, GA 30303-3083. Offers MA. Part-time programs available. *Faculty:* 7 full-time (1 woman), 2 part-time/adjunct (0 women). *Students:* 17 full-time (7 women), 4 part-time (2 women); includes 2 African Americans. In 2007, 1 degree awarded. *Degree requirements:* For master's, one foreign language, thesis or alternative, written and oral exams. *Entrance requirements:* For master's, GRE General Test. Additional exam requirements/recommendations for international students: Required—TOEFL. *Application deadline:* For fall admission, 4/15 for domestic and international students; for spring admission, 10/15 for domestic and international students. Applications are processed on a rolling basis. Application fee: $50. Electronic applications accepted. *Expenses:* Tuition, state resident: part-time $221 per credit hour. *Financial support:* In 2007–08, research assistantships with full tuition reimbursements (averaging $6,000 per year), teaching assistantships with full tuition reimbursements (averaging $6,000 per year) were awarded. *Faculty research:* Urban economics, biogeography, cartography, GIS, environmental. *Unit head:* Jeremy Crampton, Director of Graduate Studies, 404-413-5771, Fax: 404-413-5768, E-mail: jcrampton@gsu.edu. *Application contact:* Jeremy Crampton, Director of Graduate Studies, 404-413-5771, Fax: 404-413-5768, E-mail: jcrampton@gsu.edu.

Hunter College of the City University of New York, Graduate School, School of Arts and Sciences, Department of Geography, New York, NY 10021-5085. Offers analytical geography (MA); earth system science (MA); environmental and social issues (MA); geographic information science (Certificate); geographic information systems (MA); teaching earth science (MA). Part-time and evening/weekend programs available. *Faculty:* 3 full-time (4 women), 10 part-time/adjunct (1 woman). *Students:* 5 full-time (2 women), 25 part-time (12 women). Average age 35. 20 applicants, 85% accepted, 10 enrolled. In 2007, 13 degrees awarded. *Degree requirements:* For master's, comprehensive exam or thesis. *Entrance requirements:* For master's, GRE General Test, minimum B average in major, minimum B- average overall, 18 credits of course work in geography, 2 letters of recommendation; for Certificate, minimum of B average in major, B- overall. Additional exam requirements/recommendations for international students: Required—TOEFL. *Application deadline:* For fall admission, 4/1 for domestic students; for spring admission, 11/1 for domestic students. Applications are processed on a rolling basis. Application fee: $125. *Expenses:* Tuition, state resident: full-time $6,400; part-time $270 per credit. Tuition, nonresident: part-time $500 per credit. One-time fee: $125 full-time. Tuition and fees vary according to program. *Financial support:* In 2007–08, 1 fellowship (averaging $3,000 per year), 2 research assistantships (averaging $10,000 per year), 10 teaching assistantships (averaging $6,000 per year) were awarded; career-related internships or fieldwork, Federal Work-Study, institutionally sponsored loans, and unspecified assistantships also available. Financial award application deadline: 3/1. *Faculty research:* Urban geography, economic geography, geographic information science, demographic methods, climate change. *Unit head:* Prof. William Solecki, Chair, 212-772-4536, Fax: 212-772-5268, E-mail: wsolecki@hunter.cuny.edu. *Application contact:* Prof. Marianna Pavlovskaya, Graduate Adviser, 212-772-5320, Fax: 212-772-5268, E-mail: mpavlov@geo.hunter.cuny.edu.

Indiana State University, School of Graduate Studies, College of Arts and Sciences, Department of Geography, Geology and Anthropology, Terre Haute, IN 47809-1401. Offers geography (MA); geology (MS); physical geography (PhD). *Faculty:* 15 full-time (4 women), 5 part-time/adjunct (2 women). *Students:* 25 full-time (10 women), 14 part-time (3 women); includes 2 minority (both Asian Americans or Pacific Islanders), 10 international. Average age 33. 21 applicants, 43% accepted, 6 enrolled. In 2007, 7 master's, 2 doctorates awarded. *Degree requirements:* For master's, thesis or alternative; for doctorate, comprehensive exam, thesis/dissertation, departmental qualifying exam. *Entrance requirements:* For doctorate, GRE General Test. Additional exam requirements/recommendations for international students: Required—TOEFL (minimum score 550 paper-based). *Application deadline:* For fall admission, 7/1 priority date for domestic students; for spring admission, 11/1 priority date for domestic students. Applications are processed on a rolling basis. Application fee: $45. Electronic applications accepted. *Expenses:* Tuition, state resident: full-time $7,056; part-time $294 per semester hour. Tuition, nonresident: full-time $14,016; part-time $584 per semester hour. Required fees: $175 per semester. *Financial support:* In 2007–08, 6 research assistantships with partial tuition reimbursements (averaging $10,000 per year), 15 teaching assistantships with partial tuition reimbursements (averaging $9,600 per year) were awarded; tuition waivers (partial) also available. Financial award application deadline: 3/1; financial award applicants required to submit FAFSA. *Unit head:* Dr. Susan Berta, Chairperson, 812-237-2261.

Indiana University Bloomington, University Graduate School, College of Arts and Sciences, Department of Geography, Bloomington, IN 47405-7000. Offers MA, MAT, MS, PhD, MSES/MA, MSES/MS. *Faculty:* 8 full-time (2 women), 5 part-time/adjunct (1 woman). *Students:* 22 full-time (10 women), 7 part-time (2 women); includes 1 minority (Hispanic American), 9 international. Average age 31. 29 applicants, 34% accepted, 5 enrolled. In 2007, 2 master's, 1 doctorate awarded. *Median time to degree:* Of those who began their doctoral program in fall 1999, 50% received their degree in 8 years or less. *Degree requirements:* For master's, comprehensive exam, thesis; for doctorate, comprehensive exam, thesis/dissertation. *Entrance requirements:* For master's and doctorate, GRE General Test, minimum GPA of 3.0. Additional exam requirements/recommendations for international students: Required—TOEFL (minimum score 620 paper-based; 260 computer-based; 104 iBT). *Application deadline:* For fall admission, 2/15 priority date for domestic students, 12/15 priority date for international students; for spring admission, 11/15 priority date for domestic students, 11/1 priority date for international students. Application fee: $50 ($60 for international students). Electronic applications accepted. *Financial support:* Fellowships with full tuition reimbursements, research assistantships with full tuition reimbursements, teaching assistantships with full tuition reimbursements, health care benefits available. Financial award application deadline: 2/15; financial award applicants required to submit FAFSA. *Faculty research:* Synoptic climatology, urban and regional modeling, regional development, hydrology and statistical climatology, migration, atmospheric science, GIS human environment interaction, human geography. Total annual research expenditures: $2 million. *Unit head:* Dr. Scott Robeson, Chair and Professor, 812-855-6303, Fax: 812-855-1661, E-mail: srobeson@indiana.edu. *Application contact:* Susan White, Graduate Secretary, 812-855-6303, Fax: 812-855-1661, E-mail: suswhite@indiana.edu.

Indiana University of Pennsylvania, School of Graduate Studies and Research, College of Humanities and Social Sciences, Department of Geography and Regional Planning, Program in Geography, Indiana, PA 15705-1087. Offers MA, MS. Part-time programs available. *Faculty:* 8 full-time (0 women). *Students:* 17 full-time (6 women), 4 part-time (2 women), 1 international. Average age 28. 17 applicants, 53% accepted, 6 enrolled. In 2007, 7 degrees awarded. *Degree requirements:* For master's, thesis optional. *Entrance requirements:* For master's, GRE, 2 letters of recommendation. Additional exam requirements/recommendations for international students: Required—TOEFL. *Application deadline:* For fall admission, 7/1 priority date for domestic students; for spring admission, 11/1 for domestic students. Applications are processed on a rolling basis. Application fee: $30. *Expenses:* Tuition, state resident: full-time $6,214; part-time $345 per credit. Tuition, nonresident: full-time $9,944; part-time $552 per credit. Required fees: $43 per credit. One-time fee: $140 part-time. Tuition and fees vary according to course load. *Financial support:* In 2007–08, 10 research assistantships with full and partial tuition reimbursements (averaging $2,745 per year) were awarded; Federal Work-Study also available. Support available to part-time students. Financial award application deadline: 3/15; financial award applicants required to submit FAFSA.

The Johns Hopkins University, G. W. C. Whiting School of Engineering, Department of Geography and Environmental Engineering, Baltimore, MD 21218-2699. Offers MA, MS, MSE, PhD. *Faculty:* 14 full-time (5 women), 6 part-time/adjunct (0 women). *Students:* 53 full-time (23 women), 2 part-time (1 woman); includes 3 minority (1 African American, 2 Hispanic Americans), 22 international. Average age 29. 165 applicants, 68% accepted, 74 enrolled. In 2007, 27 master's, 6 doctorates awarded. Terminal master's awarded for partial completion of doctoral program. *Median time to degree:* Of those who began their doctoral program in fall 1999, 100% received their degree in 8 years or less. *Degree requirements:* For master's, thesis (for some programs), 1 year full-time residency; for doctorate, comprehensive exam, thesis/dissertation, oral exam, 2 year full-time residency. *Entrance requirements:* For master's and doctorate, GRE General Test. Additional exam requirements/recommendations for international students: Required—TOEFL (minimum score 670 paper-based; 300 computer-based; 120 iBT); Recommended—IELTS. *Application deadline:* For fall admission, 1/15 priority date for domestic and international students. Applications are processed on a rolling basis. Application fee: $75. Electronic applications accepted. *Financial support:* In 2007–08, 2 fellowships with full tuition reimbursements (averaging $27,000 per year), 26 research assistantships with full tuition reimbursements (averaging $23,496 per year) were awarded; teaching assistantships with full tuition reimbursements, Federal Work-Study, institutionally sponsored loans, scholarships/grants, health care benefits, tuition waivers (full), and unspecified assistantships also available. Financial award application deadline: 2/1. *Faculty research:* Environmental engineering; environmental chemistry; water resources engineering; systems analysis and economics for public decision making; geomorphology, hydrology and ecology. Total annual research expenditures: $1.4 million. *Unit head:* Dr. Edward J. Bouwer, Chair, 410-516-7102, Fax: 410-516-8996, E-mail: bouwer@jhu.edu.

Kansas State University, Graduate School, College of Arts and Sciences, Department of Geography, Manhattan, KS 66506. Offers MA, PhD. *Faculty:* 11 full-time (3 women). *Students:* 39 full-time (7 women), 7 part-time (3 women); includes 2 minority (1 African American, 1 Asian American or Pacific Islander), 6 international. 29 applicants, 66% accepted, 5 enrolled. In 2007, 9 degrees awarded. *Degree requirements:* For master's, thesis optional, oral exam; for doctorate, one foreign language, thesis/dissertation. *Entrance requirements:* For master's and doctorate, GRE General Test, minimum GPA of 3.0. *Application deadline:* For fall admission, 2/15 priority date for domestic students, 2/1 priority date for international students; for spring admission, 11/15 priority date for domestic students, 8/1 priority date for international students. Applications are processed on a rolling basis. Application fee: $30 ($55 for international students). Electronic applications accepted. *Financial support:* In 2007–08, 5 research assistantships (averaging $12,208 per year), 19 teaching assistantships with full tuition reimbursements (averaging $9,379 per year) were awarded; Federal Work-Study, institutionally sponsored

Geography

Kansas State University (continued)
loans, and scholarships/grants also available. Support available to part-time students. Financial award application deadline: 3/1; financial award applicants required to submit FAFSA. *Faculty research:* Human environment interaction, health and population, culture and landscape, physical geography, geospatial analysis and applications. Total annual research expenditures: $274,649. *Unit head:* Richard Marston, Head, 785-532-5412, Fax: 785-532-7310, E-mail: rmarston@ksu.edu. *Application contact:* Kevin Blake, Director, 785-532-3406, Fax: 785-532-7310, E-mail: kblake@ksu.edu.

Kent State University, College of Arts and Sciences, Department of Geography, Kent, OH 44242-0001. Offers MA, PhD. Part-time programs available. *Faculty:* 10 full-time (2 women), 2 part-time/adjunct (0 women). *Students:* 21 full-time (5 women), 10 part-time (6 women); includes 5 minority (4 Asian Americans or Pacific Islanders, 1 Hispanic American), 4 international. In 2007, 8 master's, 2 doctorates awarded. *Median time to degree:* Of those who began their doctoral program in fall 1999, 85% received their degree in 8 years or less. *Degree requirements:* For master's, thesis optional; for doctorate, comprehensive exam, thesis/dissertation. *Entrance requirements:* For master's and doctorate, GRE, minimum GPA of 3.0. Additional exam requirements/recommendations for international students: Required—TOEFL. *Application deadline:* For fall admission, 7/12 for domestic students; for spring admission, 11/29 for domestic students. Applications are processed on a rolling basis. Application fee: $30. Electronic applications accepted. *Financial support:* In 2007–08, 21 teaching assistantships with tuition reimbursements were awarded; fellowships with tuition reimbursements, research assistantships with tuition reimbursements, career-related internships or fieldwork, Federal Work-Study, institutionally sponsored loans, health care benefits, tuition waivers (full), and unspecified assistantships also available. Financial award application deadline: 2/1. Total annual research expenditures: $400,000. *Unit head:* Dr. Jay Lee, Chairman, 330-672-3222, Fax: 330-672-4304, E-mail: jlee@kent.edu. *Application contact:* Dr. Scott Sheridan, Graduate Coordinator, 330-672-3224, E-mail: ssherid1@kent.edu.

Louisiana State University and Agricultural and Mechanical College, Graduate School, College of Arts and Sciences, Department of Geography and Anthropology, Baton Rouge, LA 70803. Offers anthropology (MA); geography (MA, MS, PhD). Part-time programs available. *Faculty:* 27 full-time (7 women). *Students:* 64 full-time (26 women), 21 part-time (12 women); includes 2 African Americans, 1 American Indian/Alaska Native, 1 Hispanic American, 21 international. Average age 31. 51 applicants, 55% accepted, 11 enrolled. In 2007, 18 master's, 10 doctorates awarded. Terminal master's awarded for partial completion of doctoral program. *Degree requirements:* For master's, 2 foreign languages, thesis (for some programs); for doctorate, 2 foreign languages, thesis/dissertation. *Entrance requirements:* For master's and doctorate, GRE General Test, minimum GPA of 3.0. Additional exam requirements/recommendations for international students: Required—TOEFL (minimum score 550 paper-based; 213 computer-based; 79 iBT). *Application deadline:* For fall admission, 1/25 priority date for domestic students, 5/15 for international students; for spring admission, 10/15 for international students. Applications are processed on a rolling basis. Application fee: $25. Electronic applications accepted. *Financial support:* In 2007–08, 65 students received support, including 1 fellowship with full tuition reimbursement available (averaging $7,019 per year), 29 research assistantships with full and partial tuition reimbursements available (averaging $16,246 per year), 16 teaching assistantships with full and partial tuition reimbursements available (averaging $11,794 per year); career-related internships or fieldwork, health care benefits, and unspecified assistantships also available. Financial award application deadline: 3/1; financial award applicants required to submit FAFSA. *Faculty research:* Cultural, coastal, climate, GIS-geography, cultural, linguistics, archaeology-anthropology. Total annual research expenditures: $568,400. *Unit head:* Dr. Patrick A. Hesp, Chair, 225-578-5942, Fax: 225-578-4420, E-mail: gachair@lsu.edu. *Application contact:* Dr. Steve Namikas, Graduate Adviser, 225-578-6142, Fax: 225-578-4420, E-mail: snamik1@lsu.edu.

Marshall University, Academic Affairs Division, College of Liberal Arts, Department of Geography, Huntington, WV 25755. Offers MA, MS. *Faculty:* 6 full-time (2 women), 9 part-time/adjunct (2 women). *Students:* 11 full-time (4 women), 5 part-time (2 women), 2 international. Average age 33. In 2007, 2 degrees awarded. *Degree requirements:* For master's, thesis optional. Application fee: $40. *Unit head:* Larry Jarrett, Chairperson, 304-696-2886, E-mail: jarrettl@marshall.edu. *Application contact:* Information Contact, 304-746-1900, Fax: 304-746-1902, E-mail: services@marshall.edu.

McGill University, Faculty of Graduate and Postdoctoral Studies, Faculty of Science, Department of Geography, Montréal, QC H3A 2T5, Canada. Offers geography (M Sc, MA, PhD); neo-tropical environment (MA, PhD); social statistics (MA). *Faculty:* 21 full-time (5 women), 14 part-time/adjunct (7 women). *Students:* 54 full-time (34 women). 53 applicants, 36% accepted, 14 enrolled. In 2007, 11 master's, 5 doctorates awarded.

McMaster University, School of Graduate Studies, Faculty of Science, School of Geography and Earth Sciences, Hamilton, ON L8S 4M2, Canada. Offers geochemistry (PhD); geology (M Sc, PhD); human geography (MA, PhD); physical geography (M Sc, PhD). Part-time programs available. *Faculty:* 27 full-time, 13 part-time/adjunct. *Students:* 69 full-time, 12 part-time. 51 applicants, 31% accepted.Terminal master's awarded for partial completion of doctoral program. *Degree requirements:* For master's, thesis; for doctorate, comprehensive exam, thesis/dissertation. *Entrance requirements:* For master's, minimum B+ average. Additional exam requirements/recommendations for international students: Required—TOEFL (minimum score 550 paper-based; 213 computer-based). *Application deadline:* For fall admission, 3/15 priority date for domestic students. Applications are processed on a rolling basis. Application fee: $90. *Financial support:* In 2007–08, teaching assistantships (averaging $8,440 per year); scholarships/grants also available. *Unit head:* Dr. Pavlos Kanaroglou, Director, 905-525-9140 Ext. 23525, Fax: 905-546-0463, E-mail: pavlos@mcmaster.ca. *Application contact:* Ann Wallace, Administrative Assistant Graduate Program, 905-525-9140 Ext. 23535, Fax: 905-546-0463, E-mail: wallann@mcmaster.ca.

Memorial University of Newfoundland, School of Graduate Studies, Department of Geography, St. John's, NL A1C 5S7, Canada. Offers M Sc, MA, PhD. *Degree requirements:* For master's, thesis; for doctorate, comprehensive exam, thesis/dissertation, seminar, oral defense of thesis. *Entrance requirements:* For master's, 2nd class degree; for doctorate, master's degree. Electronic applications accepted. *Faculty research:* Cultural/historical geography, physical geography, economic geography, cartography, geographical information systems.

Miami University, Graduate School, College of Arts and Sciences, Department of Geography, Oxford, OH 45056. Offers MA. Part-time programs available. *Degree requirements:* For master's, thesis (for some programs), final exam. *Entrance requirements:* For master's, minimum undergraduate GPA of 3.0 during previous 2 years or 2.75 overall. Additional exam requirements/recommendations for international students: Required—TOEFL (minimum score 550 paper-based; 213 computer-based), TWE (minimum score 4). Electronic applications accepted.

Michigan State University, The Graduate School, College of Social Science, Department of Geography, East Lansing, MI 48824. Offers geographic information science (MS); geography (MA, PhD). *Degree requirements:* For master's, comprehensive exam, thesis (for some programs), presentation of poster/paper or oral defense of thesis; for doctorate, comprehensive exam, thesis/dissertation, presentation of poster/paper, presentation and defense of dissertation proposal, oral exam in defense of dissertation . *Entrance requirements:* Additional exam requirements/recommendations for international students: Required—TOEFL (minimum score 600 paper-based; 250 computer-based). Electronic applications accepted. *Expenses:* Tuition, state resident: part-time $379 per credit hour. Tuition, nonresident: part-time $800 per credit hour. Tuition and fees vary according to program.

Minnesota State University Mankato, College of Graduate Studies, College of Social and Behavioral Sciences, Department of Geography, Mankato, MN 56001. Offers geography (MS); geography education (MT). Part-time programs available. *Students:* 6 full-time (1 woman), 26 part-time (11 women). Average age 30. In 2007, 7 degrees awarded. *Degree requirements:* For master's, one foreign language, comprehensive exam. *Entrance requirements:* For master's, GRE General Test (if GPA is below 2.8 for the last 2 years), minimum GPA of 3.0 during previous 2 years. *Application deadline:* For fall admission, 7/1 priority date for domestic students; for spring admission, 11/1 for domestic students. Applications are processed on a rolling basis. Application fee: $40. Electronic applications accepted. *Financial support:* Research assistantships, teaching assistantships with full tuition reimbursements, career-related internships or fieldwork, Federal Work-Study, institutionally sponsored loans, and unspecified assistantships available. Support available to part-time students. Financial award application deadline: 3/15; financial award applicants required to submit FAFSA. *Unit head:* Dr. Donald Friend, Chairperson, 507-389-2617. *Application contact:* 507-389-2321, E-mail: grad@mnsu.edu.

Missouri State University, Graduate College, College of Natural and Applied Sciences, Department of Geography, Geology, and Planning, Springfield, MO 65804-0094. Offers geography, geology and planning (MNAS); geospatial sciences (MS); secondary education (MS Ed), including earth science, geography. Part-time and evening/weekend programs available. *Faculty:* 19 full-time (3 women). *Students:* 14 full-time (4 women), 14 part-time (5 women), 6 international. Average age 31. 15 applicants, 100% accepted, 12 enrolled. In 2007, 8 degrees awarded. *Degree requirements:* For master's, comprehensive exam, thesis (for some programs). *Entrance requirements:* For master's, GRE General Test (MS, MNAS), minimum undergraduate GPA of 3.0 (MS, MNAS), 9-12 teacher certification (MS Ed). Additional exam requirements/recommendations for international students: Required—TOEFL (minimum score 550 paper-based; 213 computer-based; 79 iBT). *Application deadline:* For fall admission, 7/20 priority date for domestic students; for spring admission, 12/20 priority date for domestic students. Applications are processed on a rolling basis. Application fee: $35. Electronic applications accepted. *Expenses:* Tuition, state resident: full-time $3,708; part-time $206 per credit hour. Tuition, nonresident: full-time $7,236; part-time $206 per credit hour. Required fees: $622. Full-time tuition and fees vary according to course level, course load, program and reciprocity agreements. *Financial support:* In 2007–08, 9 research assistantships with full tuition reimbursements (averaging $8,845 per year), 9 teaching assistantships with full tuition reimbursements (averaging $7,305 per year) were awarded; career-related internships or fieldwork, Federal Work-Study, scholarships/grants, and unspecified assistantships also available. Financial award application deadline: 3/31; financial award applicants required to submit FAFSA. *Faculty research:* Water resources, small town planning, recreation and open space planning. *Unit head:* Dr. Tom Plymate, Head, 417-836-5800, Fax: 417-836-6934, E-mail: tomplymate@missouristate.edu. *Application contact:* Dr. Robert T. Pavlowsky, Graduate Adviser, 417-836-8473, Fax: 417-836-6006, E-mail: bobpavlowsky@missouristate.edu.

New Mexico State University, Graduate School, College of Arts and Sciences, Department of Geography, Las Cruces, NM 88003-8001. Offers MAG. Part-time programs available. *Faculty:* 5 full-time (1 woman). *Students:* 12 full-time (4 women), 9 part-time (4 women); includes 1 American Indian/Alaska Native, 3 Hispanic Americans, 1 international. Average age 33. 8 applicants, 75% accepted, 5 enrolled. In 2007, 6 degrees awarded. *Degree requirements:* For master's, thesis or alternative. *Entrance requirements:* For master's, GRE General Test, previous course work in geography, map use, and physical geography. Additional exam requirements/recommendations for international students: Required—TOEFL. *Application deadline:* For fall admission, 7/1 priority date for domestic students; for spring admission, 11/1 for domestic students. Applications are processed on a rolling basis. Application fee: $30 ($50 for international students). Electronic applications accepted. *Expenses:* Tuition, state resident: full-time $3,602; part-time $199 per credit. Tuition, nonresident: full-time $13,380; part-time $607 per credit. Required fees: $1,178. *Financial support:* In 2007–08, 2 research assistantships, 7 teaching assistantships were awarded; career-related internships or fieldwork and health care benefits also available. Financial award application deadline: 3/1. *Faculty research:* Landscape ecology, land use, geomorphology, Latin America and the U.S.-Mexico border, geographic information systems. *Unit head:* Dr. John Wright, Head, 575-646-3509, Fax: 575-646-7430, E-mail: jowright@nmsu.edu. *Application contact:* Dr. Daniel Dugas, Assistant Professor, 575-646-3509, Fax: 575-646-7430, E-mail: ddugas@nmsu.edu.

Northeastern Illinois University, Graduate College, College of Arts and Sciences, Department of Geography, Environmental Studies and Economics, Program in Geography and Environmental Studies, Chicago, IL 60625-4699. Offers MA. Part-time and evening/weekend programs available. *Faculty:* 6 full-time (0 women), 3 part-time/adjunct (2 women). *Students:* 6 full-time (4 women), 18 part-time (9 women); includes 3 minority (2 African Americans, 1 Hispanic American). Average age 34. 13 applicants, 92% accepted, 8 enrolled. In 2007, 8 degrees awarded. *Degree requirements:* For master's, comprehensive exam, thesis optional, minimum GPA of 3.0. *Entrance requirements:* For master's, undergraduate minor in geography or environmental studies, minimum GPA of 2.75. Additional exam requirements/recommendations for international students: Required—TOEFL (minimum score 550 paper-based; 213 computer-based; 80 iBT). *Application deadline:* For fall admission, 4/1 priority date for domestic students; for spring admission, 8/15 for domestic students. Applications are processed on a rolling basis. Application fee: $25. Electronic applications accepted. *Expenses:* Tuition, state resident: part-time $243 per credit hour. Tuition, nonresident: part-time $443 per credit hour. *Financial support:* In 2007–08, 3 research assistantships with full tuition reimbursements (averaging $6,600 per year) were awarded; career-related internships or fieldwork, Federal Work-Study, institutionally sponsored loans, scholarships/grants, tuition waivers (full and partial), and unspecified assistantships also available. Support available to part-time students. Financial award applicants required to submit FAFSA. *Faculty research:* Segregation and urbanization of minority groups in the Chicago area, scale dependence and parameterization in nonpoint source pollution modeling, ecological land classification and mapping, ecosystem restoration, soil-vegetation relationships.

Northern Arizona University, Graduate College, College of Social and Behavioral Sciences, Department of Geography, Planning, and Recreation, Flagstaff, AZ 86011. Offers applied geographic information science (MS); geographic information systems (Certificate); rural geography (MA). *Degree requirements:* For master's, thesis. *Entrance requirements:* For master's, GRE General Test.

Northern Illinois University, Graduate School, College of Liberal Arts and Sciences, Department of Geography, De Kalb, IL 60115-2854. Offers MS. Part-time programs available. *Faculty:* 8 full-time (2 women). *Students:* 20 full-time (8 women), 13 part-time (8 women); includes 3 minority (1 African American, 1 Asian American or Pacific Islander, 1 Hispanic American), 2 international. Average age 29. 28 applicants, 75% accepted, 12 enrolled. In 2007, 6 degrees awarded. *Degree requirements:* For master's, comprehensive exam, thesis optional, research seminar. *Entrance requirements:* For master's, GRE General Test, minimum GPA of 2.75. Additional exam requirements/recommendations for international students: Required—TOEFL (minimum score 550 paper-based; 213 computer-based). *Application deadline:* For fall admission, 2/1 priority date for domestic students, 5/1 for international students; for spring admission, 10/1 priority date for domestic students, 10/1 for international students. Applications are processed on a rolling basis. Application fee: $30. Electronic applications accepted. *Expenses:* Tuition, area resident: Part-time $226 per credit hour. Tuition, state resident: full-time $5,424; part-time $225 per credit hour. Tuition, nonresident: full-time $10,848. Required fees: $2,416; $64 per credit hour. *Financial support:* In 2007–08, 5 research assistantships with full tuition reimbursements, 13 teaching assistantships with full tuition reimbursements were awarded; fellowships with full tuition reimbursements, career-related internships or fieldwork, Federal Work-Study, scholarships/grants, tuition waivers (full), and unspecified assistantships also available. Support available to part-time students. Financial award applicants required to submit FAFSA. *Faculty research:* Synoptic meteorology, human impacts on soil properties, plant soil relationships, hydrological cycle, climate variability. *Unit head:* Dr. Andrew Krmenec, Chair, 815-753-6826, Fax: 815-753-6872, E-mail: akrmenec@niu.edu. *Application contact:* Dr. Fahui Wang, Coordinator of Graduate Studies, 815-753-6842, E-mail: fwang@niu.edu.

Northwest Missouri State University, Graduate School, College of Arts and Sciences, Department of Geology/Geography, Maryville, MO 64468-6001. Offers geographic information sciences (MS, Certificate). Part-time programs available. *Faculty:* 9 full-time (4 women). *Students:* 1 (woman) full-time, 88 part-time (26 women); includes 8 minority (2 American Indian/Alaska Native, 4 Asian Americans or Pacific Islanders, 2 Hispanic Americans), 1 international. 25 applicants, 100% accepted, 23 enrolled. In 2007, 4 degrees awarded. *Degree requirements:* For master's, comprehensive exam, thesis. *Entrance requirements:* For master's, GRE General Test, 2 letters of recommendation, writing sample, minimum undergraduate GPA of 2.5. *Application deadline:* For fall admission, 4/15 for domestic and international students. Application fee: $0 ($50 for international students). *Financial support:* In 2007–08, teaching assistantships with full and partial tuition reimbursements (averaging $6,000 per year). Financial award application deadline: 3/1; financial award applicants required to submit FAFSA. *Unit head:* Greg Haddock, Chairperson, 660-562-1719. *Application contact:* Dr. Frances Shipley, Dean of Graduate School, 660-562-1145, Fax: 660-562-1096, E-mail: gradsch@nwmissouri.edu.

The Ohio State University, Graduate School, College of Social and Behavioral Sciences, School of Social and Behavioral Science, Department of Geography, Columbus, OH 43210. Offers atmospheric sciences (MS, PhD); geography (MA, PhD). *Faculty:* 24. *Students:* 48 full-time (16 women), 8 part-time (2 women); includes 1 minority (Hispanic American), 16 international. Average age 30. In 2007, 1 master's, 6 doctorates awarded. *Degree requirements:* For doctorate, variable foreign language requirement, thesis/dissertation. *Entrance requirements:* Additional exam requirements/recommendations for international students: Recommended—TOEFL (minimum score 600 paper-based; 250 computer-based). *Application deadline:* For fall admission, 8/15 priority date for domestic students, 7/1 priority date for international students; for winter admission, 12/1 priority date for domestic students, 11/1 priority date for international students; for spring admission, 3/1 priority date for domestic students, 2/1 priority date for international students. Applications are processed on a rolling basis. Application fee: $40 ($50 for international students). Electronic applications accepted. *Financial support:* Fellowships, research assistantships, teaching assistantships, Federal Work-Study and institutionally sponsored loans available. Support available to part-time students. *Unit head:* Mei-Po Kwan, Graduate Studies Committee Chair, 614-292-2514, Fax: 614-292-6213, E-mail: kwan.8@osu.edu. *Application contact:* 614-292-9444, Fax: 614-292-3895, E-mail: domestic.grad@osu.edu.

Ohio University, Graduate College, College of Arts and Sciences, Department of Geography, Athens, OH 45701-2979. Offers MA. Part-time programs available. *Faculty:* 13 full-time (6 women), 6 part-time/adjunct (0 women). *Students:* 14 full-time (8 women), 1 international. Average age 24. 17 applicants, 59% accepted, 6 enrolled. In 2007, 9 degrees awarded. *Degree requirements:* For master's, thesis. *Entrance requirements:* For master's, GRE General Test, minimum GPA of 3.0. Additional exam requirements/recommendations for international students: Required—TOEFL (minimum score 600 paper-based; 250 computer-based). *Application deadline:* For fall admission, 2/1 priority date for domestic students, 2/1 for international students; for winter admission, 11/1 priority date for domestic students; for spring admission, 3/1 priority date for domestic students. Application fee: $50 ($55 for international students). Electronic applications accepted. *Financial support:* In 2007–08, 4 research assistantships with full tuition reimbursements (averaging $12,000 per year), 14 teaching assistantships with full tuition reimbursements (averaging $10,926 per year) were awarded; Federal Work-Study, institutionally sponsored loans, and tuition waivers (full) also available. Financial award application deadline: 3/1. *Faculty research:* Environmental geography, cartography and geographic information systems, cultural ecology, area studies, historical geography. Total annual research expenditures: $81,622. *Unit head:* Dr. Timothy G. Anderson, Graduate Chair, 740-593-1138, Fax: 740-593-1139, E-mail: anderstl@ohio.edu. *Application contact:* Dr. Brad Jokisch, Graduate Chair, 740-593-1143, Fax: 740-593-1139, E-mail: jokisch@ohio.edu.

Oklahoma State University, College of Arts and Sciences, Department of Geography, Stillwater, OK 74078. Offers MS, PhD. *Faculty:* 14 full-time (3 women), 1 part-time/adjunct (0 women). *Students:* 15 full-time (2 women), 22 part-time (7 women); includes 1 minority (Asian American or Pacific Islander), 13 international. Average age 32. 24 applicants, 46% accepted, 6 enrolled. In 2007, 5 degrees awarded. *Degree requirements:* For master's, thesis or alternative; for doctorate, thesis/dissertation. *Entrance requirements:* For master's and doctorate, GRE or GMAT. Additional exam requirements/recommendations for international students: Required—TOEFL. *Application deadline:* For fall admission, 3/1 priority date for international students; for spring admission, 8/1 priority date for international students. Applications are processed on a rolling basis. Application fee: $40 ($75 for international students). Electronic applications accepted. *Expenses:* Tuition, state resident: full-time $4,993; part-time $148 per credit hour. Tuition, nonresident: full-time $14,755; part-time $555 per credit hour. Tuition and fees vary according to program. *Financial support:* In 2007–08, 6 research assistantships (averaging $12,670 per year), 17 teaching assistantships (averaging $16,469 per year) were awarded; career-related internships or fieldwork, Federal Work-Study, scholarships/grants, health care benefits, tuition waivers (partial), and unspecified assistantships also available. Support available to part-time students. Financial award application deadline: 3/1. *Faculty research:* Cultural ecology, resource management, historical/cultural geography, central Asia, geographic information systems. *Unit head:* Dr. Dale R. Lightfoot, Head, 405-744-6250.

Oregon State University, Graduate School, College of Science, Department of Geosciences, Program in Geography, Corvallis, OR 97331. Offers MA, MAIS, MS, PhD. Part-time programs available. *Students:* 28 full-time (10 women), 12 part-time (4 women); includes 2 minority (both Hispanic Americans), 3 international. Average age 35. In 2007, 8 master's, 4 doctorates awarded. Terminal master's awarded for partial completion of doctoral program. *Degree requirements:* For master's, variable foreign language requirement, thesis optional; for doctorate, one foreign language, thesis/dissertation. *Entrance requirements:* For master's and doctorate, GRE General Test, GRE Subject Test, minimum GPA of 3.0 in last 90 hours. Additional exam requirements/recommendations for international students: Required—TOEFL. *Application deadline:* For fall admission, 2/1 for domestic students. Applications are processed on a rolling basis. Application fee: $50. *Expenses:* Tuition, state resident: full-time $9,126; part-time $338 per credit. Tuition, nonresident: full-time $14,796; part-time $548 per credit. Required fees: $1,447. *Financial support:* Fellowships, research assistantships, teaching assistantships, Federal Work-Study and institutionally sponsored loans available. Support available to part-time students. Financial award application deadline: 2/1. *Faculty research:* Resources, physical geography, cartography, remote sensing. *Unit head:* Dr. Lawrence C. Becker, Director, 541-737-9504, E-mail: beckerla@geo.oregonstate.edu. *Application contact:* Dr. Julia A. Jones, Professor, 541-737-1224, Fax: 541-737-1200, E-mail: jonesj@geo.oregonstate.edu.

Penn State University Park, Graduate School, College of Earth and Mineral Sciences, Department of Geography, State College, University Park, PA 16802-1503. Offers geography (MS, PhD). *Expenses:* Tuition, state resident: full-time $14,738; part-time $614 per credit. Tuition, nonresident: full-time $26,050; part-time $1,085 per credit. Tuition and fees vary according to course load, program and student level. *Unit head:* Dr. Karl S. Zimmerer, Head, 814-865-1915, Fax: 814-863-7943. *Application contact:* Noelle Capparrelle, Graduate Admissions, E-mail: geoggradsec@psu.edu.

Portland State University, Graduate Studies, College of Liberal Arts and Sciences, Department of Geography, Portland, OR 97207-0751. Offers MA, MAT, MS, MST, PhD. Part-time programs available. *Faculty:* 11 full-time (2 women). *Students:* 26 full-time (15 women), 36 part-time (10 women); includes 2 minority (1 American Indian/Alaska Native, 1 Asian American or Pacific Islander). Average age 33. 17 applicants, 71% accepted, 8 enrolled. In 2007, 7 degrees awarded. *Degree requirements:* For master's, thesis (for some programs). *Entrance requirements:* For master's, GRE General Test, minimum GPA of 3.0 in upper-division course work or 2.75 overall, 3 letters of recommendation. Additional exam requirements/recommendations for international students: Required—TOEFL (minimum score 550 paper-based; 213 computer-based). *Application deadline:* For fall admission, 4/1 for domestic students, 3/1 for international students. Applications are processed on a rolling basis. Application fee: $50. *Expenses:* Tuition, state resident: full-time $7,047. Tuition, nonresident: full-time $11,178. *Financial support:* In 2007–08, 2 research assistantships with full tuition reimbursements (averaging $5,508 per year), 7 teaching assistantships with full tuition reimbursements (averaging $5,508 per year) were awarded; career-related internships or fieldwork, Federal Work-Study, scholarships/grants, and unspecified assistantships also available. Support available to part-time students. Financial award application deadline: 3/1; financial award applicants required to submit FAFSA. *Faculty research:* Geographic information systems, natural lands, Latin American subsistence farming, climatic change, urban perspectives. Total annual research expenditures: $217,444. *Unit head:* Dr. Martha Works, Head, 503-725-3916, Fax: 503-725-3166. *Application contact:* Angelica Nelson, Coordinator, 503-725-3916, Fax: 503-725-3166, E-mail: anelson@pdx.edu.

Queen's University at Kingston, School of Graduate Studies and Research, Faculty of Arts and Sciences, Department of Geography, Kingston, ON K7L 3N6, Canada. Offers M Sc, MA, PhD. *Degree requirements:* For master's, thesis; for doctorate, comprehensive exam, thesis/dissertation. *Entrance requirements:* Additional exam requirements/recommendations for international students: Required—TOEFL. *Faculty research:* Urban and economic geography, historical-cultural geography, earth system science.

Rutgers, The State University of New Jersey, New Brunswick, Graduate School, Program in Geography, New Brunswick, NJ 08901-1281. Offers MA, MS, PhD. Terminal master's awarded for partial completion of doctoral program. *Degree requirements:* For master's, thesis or alternative; for doctorate, comprehensive exam, thesis/dissertation. *Entrance requirements:* For master's and doctorate, GRE General Test. *Faculty research:* Urban social theory, climate, political biology, hazards, economic development.

St. Cloud State University, School of Graduate Studies, College of Social Sciences, Department of Geography, St. Cloud, MN 56301-4498. Offers MS. *Faculty:* 9 full-time (0 women). *Students:* 5 full-time (2 women), 16 part-time (5 women); includes 1 minority (Asian American or Pacific Islander), 7 international. 5 applicants, 80% accepted. In 2007, 4 degrees awarded. *Degree requirements:* For master's, comprehensive exam (for some programs), thesis or alternative. *Entrance requirements:* For master's, GRE General Test, minimum GPA of 2.75. Additional exam requirements/recommendations for international students: Required—MELAB; Recommended—TOEFL (minimum score 550 paper-based; 213 computer-based), IELTS (minimum score 7). *Application deadline:* For fall admission, 6/1 priority date for domestic students, 4/1 for international students; for spring admission, 10/1 priority date for domestic students, 8/1 for international students. Applications are processed on a rolling basis. Application fee: $35. Electronic applications accepted. *Expenses:* Tuition, state resident: part-time $267 per credit. Tuition, nonresident: part-time $418 per credit. Required fees: $28 per credit. *Financial support:* Federal Work-Study, scholarships/grants, and unspecified assistantships available. Financial award application deadline: 3/1. *Unit head:* Dr. Lewis Wixon, Chairperson, 320-308-3160, Fax: 320-308-5198. *Application contact:* Linda Lou Krueger, School of Graduate Studies, 320-308-2113, Fax: 320-308-5371, E-mail: lekrueger@stcloudstate.edu.

Salem State College, Graduate School, Program in Geo-Information Science, Salem, MA 01970-5353. Offers geo-information science (MS). Part-time and evening/weekend programs available. *Students:* 2 full-time (0 women), 6 part-time (1 woman); includes 1 minority (African American) Average age 33. In 2007, 5 degrees awarded. *Degree requirements:* For master's, thesis optional. *Entrance requirements:* For master's, GRE General Test or MAT. *Application deadline:* Applications are processed on a rolling basis. Application fee: $35. *Unit head:* Keith Ratner, Coordinator, 978-542-6321, E-mail: kratner@salemstate.edu.

San Diego State University, Graduate and Research Affairs, College of Arts and Letters, Department of Geography, San Diego, CA 92182. Offers MA, PhD. *Students:* 14 full-time (5 women), 58 part-time (20 women); includes 7 minority (2 Asian Americans or Pacific Islanders, 5 Hispanic Americans), 14 international. Average age 30. 64 applicants, 44% accepted, 21 enrolled. In 2007, 21 degrees awarded. *Degree requirements:* For master's, thesis; for doctorate, thesis/dissertation. *Entrance requirements:* For master's, GRE General Test, bachelor's degree in related field, 3 letters of recommendation. Additional exam requirements/recommendations for international students: Required—TOEFL. *Application deadline:* For fall admission, 5/1 for domestic and international students; for spring admission, 9/15 for domestic and international students. Applications are processed on a rolling basis. Application fee: $55. Electronic applications accepted. *Financial support:* In 2007–08, 42 teaching assistantships were awarded; fellowships, research assistantships, career-related internships or fieldwork also available. Financial award applicants required to submit FAFSA. *Faculty research:* Physical geography, human geography, biogeography, environmental resources, geographic analysis. Total annual research expenditures: $798,889. *Unit head:* John O'Leary, Chair, 619-594-5437, E-mail: oleary@mail.sdsu.edu. *Application contact:* Ed Aguado, Graduate Advisor, 619-594-5462, Fax: 619-594-4938.

San Francisco State University, Division of Graduate Studies, College of Behavioral and Social Sciences, Department of Geography and Human Environmental Studies, San Francisco, CA 94132-1722. Offers geography (MA), including resource management and environmental planning. *Unit head:* Dr. Nancy Wilkinson, Chair, Graduate Coordinator, 415-338-2049, E-mail: nancyw@sfsu.edu.

San Jose State University, Graduate Studies and Research, College of Social Sciences, Department of Geography, San Jose, CA 95192-0001. Offers geographic information science (Certificate); geography (MA). *Students:* 10 full-time (8 women), 13 part-time (7 women); includes 6 minority (1 American Indian/Alaska Native, 4 Asian Americans or Pacific Islanders, 1 Hispanic American), 1 international. Average age 36. 18 applicants, 61% accepted, 7 enrolled. In 2007, 4 degrees awarded. *Entrance requirements:* For master's, minimum GPA of 3.0. *Application deadline:* For fall admission, 6/29 for domestic students; for spring admission, 11/30 for domestic students. Applications are processed on a rolling basis. Application fee: $59. Electronic applications accepted. *Financial support:* Applicants required to submit FAFSA. *Unit head:* Dr. Richard Taketa, Chair, 408-924-5425, E-mail: richard.taketa@sjsu.edu.

Simon Fraser University, Graduate Studies, Faculty of Arts and Social Sciences, Department of Geography, Burnaby, BC V5A 1S6, Canada. Offers M Sc, MA, PhD. *Degree requirements:* For master's, one foreign language, thesis or alternative; for doctorate, one foreign language, thesis/dissertation, qualifying exams. *Entrance requirements:* For master's, minimum GPA of 3.0; for doctorate, minimum GPA of 3.5. Additional exam requirements/recommendations for international students: Required—TOEFL or IELTS. Electronic applications accepted. *Faculty research:* Theoretical and systematic aspects of geography, ginseng research, geographic information sciences, tourism and community planning, geomorphology.

South Dakota State University, Graduate School, College of Arts and Science, Department of Geography, Brookings, SD 57007. Offers MS. Part-time programs available. *Degree requirements:* For master's, thesis, oral exam. *Entrance requirements:* Additional exam requirements/recommendations for international students: Required—TOEFL (minimum score 550 paper-based). *Faculty research:* Contemporary agriculture and rural land use, geography of Indian casino gambling, geography of illegal drug trade, geography of crop circles.

Southern Illinois University Carbondale, Graduate School, College of Liberal Arts, Department of Geography, Carbondale, IL 62901-4701. Offers MS, PhD. *Faculty:* 7 full-time (1 woman), 1 part-time/adjunct (0 women). *Students:* 13 full-time (6 women), 17 part-time (6 women); includes 4 minority (3 African Americans, 1 Hispanic American), 3 international. Average age 27. 21 applicants, 62% accepted, 5 enrolled. In 2007, 6 master's awarded. *Degree requirements:* For master's, thesis; for doctorate, thesis/dissertation. *Entrance requirements:* For master's, minimum GPA of 2.7; for doctorate, minimum GPA of 3.25. Additional exam requirements/recommendations for international students: Required—TOEFL. *Application deadline:* Applications are processed on a rolling basis. Application fee: $20. *Financial support:* In 2007–08, 21 students received support, including 6 research assistantships with full tuition reimbursements available, 11 teaching assistantships with full tuition reimbursements available; fellowships with full tuition reimbursements available, career-related internships or fieldwork, Federal Work-Study, institutionally sponsored loans, and tuition waivers (full) also available. Support

Geography

Southern Illinois University Carbondale (continued)

available to part-time students. Financial award application deadline: 4/1. *Faculty research:* Natural resources management emphasizing water resources and environmental quality of air, water, and land systems. *Unit head:* Dr. Leslie Duram, Chair, 618-536-3375, Fax: 618-453-2671, E-mail: duram@siu.edu. *Application contact:* Jennie Absher, Administrative Clerk, 618-536-3375, E-mail: jabsher@siu.edu.

Southern Illinois University Edwardsville, Graduate Studies and Research, College of Arts and Sciences, Department of Geography, Edwardsville, IL 62026-0001. Offers MS. Part-time and evening/weekend programs available. *Faculty:* 11 full-time. *Students:* 4 full-time (3 women), 29 part-time (12 women); includes 2 minority (1 American Indian/Alaska Native, 1 Asian American or Pacific Islander), 3 international. Average age 33. 23 applicants, 52% accepted. In 2007, 4 degrees awarded. *Degree requirements:* For master's, thesis or alternative, final exam. *Entrance requirements:* For master's, GRE. Additional exam requirements/recommendations for international students: Required—TOEFL. *Application deadline:* For fall admission, 7/20 for domestic students, 6/1 for international students; for spring admission, 12/14 for domestic students, 10/1 for international students. Application fee: $30. Electronic applications accepted. *Financial support:* Fellowships with full tuition reimbursements, research assistantships with full tuition reimbursements, teaching assistantships with full tuition reimbursements, career-related internships or fieldwork, Federal Work-Study, institutionally sponsored loans, and unspecified assistantships available. Support available to part-time students. Financial award application deadline: 3/1. *Unit head:* Dr. Randall Pearson, Chair, 618-650-2090, E-mail: rapears@siue.edu. *Application contact:* Dr. Michael Starr, Director, 618-650-2492, E-mail: mstarr@siue.edu.

State University of New York at Binghamton, Graduate School, School of Arts and Sciences, Department of Geography, Binghamton, NY 13902-6000. Offers MA. *Faculty:* 7 full-time (2 women), 1 part-time/adjunct (0 women). *Students:* 24 full-time (8 women), 1 part-time; includes 5 minority (1 African American, 1 Asian American or Pacific Islander, 3 Hispanic Americans), 3 international. Average age 26. 23 applicants, 91% accepted, 10 enrolled. In 2007, 8 degrees awarded. *Degree requirements:* For master's, one foreign language, thesis (for some programs), oral and written exams. *Entrance requirements:* For master's, GRE General Test, GRE Subject Test. Additional exam requirements/recommendations for international students: Required—TOEFL. *Application deadline:* For fall admission, 4/15 priority date for domestic students, 1/15 priority date for international students; for spring admission, 11/1 for domestic students, 10/1 priority date for international students. Applications are processed on a rolling basis. Application fee: $60. Electronic applications accepted. *Financial support:* In 2007–08, 13 fellowships with full tuition reimbursements (averaging $800 per year), 9 teaching assistantships with full tuition reimbursements (averaging $9,000 per year) were awarded; research assistantships with full tuition reimbursements, career-related internships or fieldwork, Federal Work-Study, institutionally sponsored loans, tuition waivers (full and partial), and unspecified assistantships also available. Support available to part-time students. Financial award application deadline: 2/15. *Unit head:* Dr. Florence Margai, Chairperson, 607-777-6731, E-mail: margai@binghamton.edu.

Syracuse University, Graduate School, Maxwell School of Citizenship and Public Affairs, Department of Geography, Syracuse, NY 13244. Offers MA, PhD. Part-time and evening/weekend programs available. *Students:* 31 full-time (17 women), 7 part-time (4 women); includes 7 minority (1 African American, 2 Asian Americans or Pacific Islanders, 4 Hispanic Americans), 10 international. 62 applicants, 34% accepted, 4 enrolled. In 2007, 3 master's, 3 doctorates awarded. *Degree requirements:* For master's, thesis or alternative; for doctorate, thesis/dissertation. *Entrance requirements:* For master's and doctorate, GRE General Test. Additional exam requirements/recommendations for international students: Required—TOEFL. *Application deadline:* For fall admission, 2/1 priority date for domestic students. Applications are processed on a rolling basis. Application fee: $75. Electronic applications accepted. *Expenses:* Tuition: Full-time $18,216; part-time $1,012 per credit. Required fees: $980. Tuition and fees vary according to program. *Financial support:* Fellowships with full tuition reimbursements, research assistantships with full tuition reimbursements, teaching assistantships with full and partial tuition reimbursements, tuition waivers (partial) available. *Unit head:* Dr. Donald Mitchell, Chair, 315-443-2607, Fax: 315-443-4227. *Application contact:* Chris Chapman, Recruiting Contact, 315-443-2605, E-mail: cmchapma@maxwell.syr.edu.

Temple University, Graduate School, College of Liberal Arts, Department of Geography and Urban Studies, Philadelphia, PA 19122-6096. Offers geography (MA); urban studies (MA). *Degree requirements:* For master's, comprehensive exam, thesis or alternative. *Entrance requirements:* For master's, GRE General Test, minimum GPA of 3.0. Additional exam requirements/recommendations for international students: Required—TOEFL (minimum score 550 paper-based; 213 computer-based; 79 iBT). Electronic applications accepted. *Faculty research:* Environmental issues, urban political economy, poverty and unemployment, neighborhood development, African and Asian urbanization, housing, computer cartography.

Texas A&M University, College of Geosciences, Department of Geography, College Station, TX 77843. Offers MS, PhD. Part-time programs available. *Faculty:* 17. *Students:* 46 full-time (19 women), 10 part-time (4 women); includes 6 minority (2 African Americans, 1 American Indian/Alaska Native, 3 Hispanic Americans), 27 international. Average age 34. 40 applicants, 43% accepted, 9 enrolled. In 2007, 10 master's, 3 doctorates awarded. *Degree requirements:* For master's, thesis optional; for doctorate, thesis/dissertation. *Entrance requirements:* For master's and doctorate, GRE General Test. Additional exam requirements/recommendations for international students: Required—TOEFL. *Application deadline:* For fall admission, 3/1 priority date for domestic students; for spring admission, 10/1 for domestic students. Applications are processed on a rolling basis. Application fee: $50 ($75 for international students). Electronic applications accepted. *Expenses:* Tuition, state resident: full-time $6,129. Tuition, nonresident: full-time $11,689. Tuition and fees vary according to course load. *Financial support:* Fellowships, research assistantships, teaching assistantships, career-related internships or fieldwork, Federal Work-Study, and institutionally sponsored loans available. Financial award application deadline: 3/1; financial award applicants required to submit FAFSA. *Faculty research:* Geomorphology, historical geography, urban-economic geography, geographic education and technology, human-environment interaction. *Unit head:* Dr. Douglas Sherman, Head, 979-845-7141, Fax: 979-862-4487. *Application contact:* Daniel J. Sui, Graduate Advisor, 979-845-7154, Fax: 979-862-4487, E-mail: d-sui@tamu.edu.

Texas State University–San Marcos, Graduate School, College of Liberal Arts, Department of Geography, Program in Environmental Geography, Geography Education, and Geography Information Science, San Marcos, TX 78666. Offers environmental geography (PhD); geography education (PhD); information science (PhD). Part-time programs available. *Students:* 38 full-time (19 women), 27 part-time (14 women); includes 12 minority (3 African Americans, 3 Asian Americans or Pacific Islanders, 6 Hispanic Americans), 9 international. Average age 38. 19 applicants, 84% accepted, 14 enrolled. In 2007, 7 degrees awarded. *Degree requirements:* For doctorate, thesis/dissertation. *Entrance requirements:* For doctorate, GRE General Test, minimum GPA of 3.5, master's degree in geography, demonstrated scholarly research. Additional exam requirements/recommendations for international students: Required—TOEFL (minimum score 550 paper-based; 213 computer-based). *Application deadline:* For fall admission, 6/15 priority date for domestic students, 6/1 for international students; for spring admission, 10/15 priority date for domestic students, 10/1 for international students. Applications are processed on a rolling basis. Application fee: $40 ($90 for international students). Electronic applications accepted. *Expenses:* Tuition, state resident: full-time $3,780; part-time $210 per credit hour. Tuition, nonresident: full-time $8,784; part-time $488 per credit hour. Required fees: $493 per semester. Full-time tuition and fees vary according to course load. *Financial support:* In 2007–08, 56 students received support, including 19 research assistantships (averaging $7,119 per year), 23 teaching assistantships (averaging $6,804 per year); career-related internships or fieldwork, Federal Work-Study, and institutionally sponsored loans also available. Support available to part-time students. Financial award application deadline: 4/1; financial award applicants required to submit FAFSA. *Unit head:* Dr. David Butler, Graduate Adviser, 512-245-2170, Fax: 512-245-8353, E-mail: db25@txstate.edu.

Texas State University–San Marcos, Graduate School, College of Liberal Arts, Department of Geography, Program in Geography, San Marcos, TX 78666. Offers applied geography (MAG); geography (MS). Part-time and evening/weekend programs available. *Students:* 31 full-time (10 women), 34 part-time (18 women); includes 3 minority (1 African American, 1 Asian American or Pacific Islander, 1 Hispanic American), 2 international. Average age 29. 18 applicants, 100% accepted, 14 enrolled. In 2007, 13 degrees awarded. *Degree requirements:* For master's, comprehensive exam, internship or thesis. *Entrance requirements:* For master's, GRE General Test, minimum GPA of 3.0 in last 60 hours of course work. Additional exam requirements/recommendations for international students: Required—TOEFL (minimum score 550 paper-based; 213 computer-based). *Application deadline:* For fall admission, 6/15 priority date for domestic students, 6/1 for international students; for spring admission, 10/15 priority date for domestic students, 10/1 for international students. Applications are processed on a rolling basis. Application fee: $40 ($90 for international students). Electronic applications accepted. *Expenses:* Tuition, state resident: full-time $3,780; part-time $210 per credit hour. Tuition, nonresident: full-time $8,784; part-time $488 per credit hour. Required fees: $493 per semester. Full-time tuition and fees vary according to course load. *Financial support:* In 2007–08, 36 students received support, including 4 research assistantships (averaging $5,202 per year), 13 teaching assistantships (averaging $5,386 per year); career-related internships or fieldwork, Federal Work-Study, and institutionally sponsored loans also available. Support available to part-time students. Financial award application deadline: 4/1; financial award applicants required to submit FAFSA. *Faculty research:* Applied cartography and geographic information systems, physical and environmental studies, land/area development and management. *Unit head:* Dr. David Butler, Graduate Adviser, 512-245-2170, Fax: 512-245-8353, E-mail: db25@txstate.edu.

Texas State University–San Marcos, Graduate School, College of Liberal Arts, Department of Geography, Program in Land/Area Studies, San Marcos, TX 78666. Offers MAG. Part-time and evening/weekend programs available. *Students:* 7 full-time (0 women), 8 part-time (5 women); includes 2 minority (1 African American, 1 Asian American or Pacific Islander). Average age 27. 7 applicants, 100% accepted, 7 enrolled. In 2007, 1 degree awarded. *Degree requirements:* For master's, comprehensive exam, internship or thesis. *Entrance requirements:* For master's, GRE General Test, minimum GPA of 3.0 in last 60 hours of course work. Additional exam requirements/recommendations for international students: Required—TOEFL (minimum score 550 paper-based; 213 computer-based). *Application deadline:* For fall admission, 6/15 priority date for domestic students, 6/1 for international students; for spring admission, 10/15 priority date for domestic students, 10/1 for international students. Applications are processed on a rolling basis. Application fee: $40 ($90 for international students). Electronic applications accepted. *Expenses:* Tuition, state resident: full-time $3,780; part-time $210 per credit hour. Tuition, nonresident: full-time $8,784; part-time $488 per credit hour. Required fees: $493 per semester. Full-time tuition and fees vary according to course load. *Financial support:* In 2007–08, 1 research assistantship (averaging $5,386 per year) was awarded; teaching assistantships, career-related internships or fieldwork, Federal Work-Study, institutionally sponsored loans, and scholarships/grants also available. Support available to part-time students. Financial award application deadline: 4/1; financial award applicants required to submit FAFSA. *Unit head:* Dr. David Butler, Graduate Adviser, 512-245-2170, Fax: 512-245-8353, E-mail: db25@txstate.edu.

Towson University, College of Graduate Studies and Research, Program in Geography and Environmental Planning, Towson, MD 21252-0001. Offers MA. Part-time and evening/weekend programs available. *Faculty:* 9 full-time (1 woman), 2 part-time/adjunct (0 women). *Students:* 9 full-time (4 women), 24 part-time (13 women); includes 3 minority (all African Americans) Average age 30. 8 applicants, 100% accepted, 6 enrolled. In 2007, 6 degrees awarded. *Degree requirements:* For master's, thesis optional. *Entrance requirements:* For master's, 9 credits of course work in geography, minimum GPA of 3.0 in geography, admission essay, (2) narrative letters of recomendation, official transcripts. Additional exam requirements/recommendations for international students: Required—TOEFL. *Application deadline:* Applications are processed on a rolling basis. Application fee: $50. Electronic applications accepted. *Expenses:* Tuition, state resident: part-time $286 per credit. Tuition, nonresident: part-time $600 per credit. Required fees: $75 per credit. *Financial support:* In 2007–08, 1 teaching assistantship with full tuition reimbursement (averaging $4,000 per year) was awarded; Federal Work-Study and unspecified assistantships also available. Financial award application deadline: 4/1; financial award applicants required to submit FAFSA. *Faculty research:* Geographic information systems, regional planning, hazards, development issues, urban fluvial systems. *Unit head:* Dr. Virginia Thompson, Graduate Program Director, 410-704-4371, Fax: 410-704-3880, E-mail: vthompson@towson.edu. *Application contact:* 410-704-2501, Fax: 410-704-4675, E-mail: grads@towson.edu.

Trent University, Graduate Studies, Program in Applications of Modeling in the Natural and Social Sciences, Peterborough, ON K9J 7B8, Canada. Offers applications of modeling in the natural and social sciences (MA); biology (M Sc, PhD); chemistry (M Sc); computer studies (M Sc); geography (M Sc, PhD); physics (M Sc). Part-time programs available. *Degree requirements:* For master's, thesis. *Entrance requirements:* For master's, honours degree. *Faculty research:* Computation of heat transfer, atmospheric physics, statistical mechanics, stress and coping, evolutionary ecology.

Trent University, Graduate Studies, Program in Watershed Ecosystems and Program in Applications of Modeling in the Natural and Social Sciences, Department of Geography, Peterborough, ON K9J 7B8, Canada. Offers M Sc, PhD. Part-time programs available. *Degree requirements:* For master's, thesis; for doctorate, thesis/dissertation. *Entrance requirements:* For master's, honors degree; for doctorate, master's degree. *Faculty research:* Hydrometeorology, snow and ice, urban hydrology, fluvial geomorphology.

Université de Montréal, Faculty of Arts and Sciences, Department of Geography, Montréal, QC H3C 3J7, Canada. Offers geography (M Sc, PhD, DESS); geomatical and spatial analysis (Certificate). *Faculty:* 27 full-time (5 women). *Students:* 72 full-time (32 women), 2 part-time (1 woman). 39 applicants, 36% accepted, 12 enrolled. In 2007, 15 master's, 3 doctorates, 2 other advanced degrees awarded. *Degree requirements:* For master's, 2 foreign languages, thesis (for some programs); for doctorate, 3 foreign languages, thesis/dissertation, general exam. *Entrance requirements:* For master's, bachelor's degree in related field; for doctorate, MA in geography or related field. *Application deadline:* For fall admission, 2/1 priority date for domestic students; for winter admission, 11/1 priority date for domestic students; for spring admission, 2/1 priority date for domestic students. Applications are processed on a rolling basis. Application fee: $100. Electronic applications accepted. *Financial support:* Fellowships, research assistantships, teaching assistantships, career-related internships or fieldwork and scholarships/grants available. Support available to part-time students. *Faculty research:* Cartography, palynology, geomorphology, economic geography, regional and urban development. *Unit head:* François Courchesne, Chairman, 514-343-8012, Fax: 514-343-8008, E-mail: francois.courchesne@umontreal.ca. *Application contact:* Pierrette Kieffer, Student Files Management Technician, 514-343-8049, Fax: 514-343-8008, E-mail: pierrette.kieffer@umontreal.ca.

Université de Sherbrooke, Faculty of Letters and Human Sciences, Department of Geography and Remote Sensing, Sherbrooke, QC J1K 2R1, Canada. Offers M Sc, PhD. *Degree requirements:* For master's, one foreign language, thesis; for doctorate, thesis/dissertation. *Faculty research:* Cartography.

Université du Québec à Montréal, Graduate Programs, Program in Geography, Montréal, QC H3C 3P8, Canada. Offers M Sc. Part-time programs available. *Degree requirements:* For master's, thesis optional. *Entrance requirements:* For master's, appropriate bachelor's degree or equivalent and proficiency in French.

Université Laval, Faculty of Forestry and Geomatics, Department of Geography, Program in Geographical Sciences, Québec, QC G1K 7P4, Canada. Offers M Sc Geogr, PhD. Terminal master's awarded for partial completion of doctoral program. *Degree requirements:* For master's, thesis; for doctorate, comprehensive exam, thesis/dissertation. *Entrance requirements:* For master's, knowledge of French; for doctorate, knowledge of French, knowledge of a second language. Electronic applications accepted.

University at Albany, State University of New York, College of Arts and Sciences, Department of Geography and Planning, Program in Geography, Albany, NY 12222-0001. Offers geographic information systems and spatial analysis (Certificate); geography (MA). *Degree requirements:* For master's, thesis or alternative. *Entrance requirements:* Additional exam requirements/recommendations for international students: Required—TOEFL (minimum score 550 paper-based; 213 computer-based). *Application deadline:* For fall admission, 3/1 for domestic students, 5/1 for international students; for spring admission, 11/1 for international students. Applications are processed on a rolling basis. Application fee: $75. Electronic applications accepted. *Expenses:* Tuition, state resident: part-time $576 per credit. Tuition, nonresident: part-time $910 per credit. Tuition and fees vary according to program. *Financial support:* Fellowships, teaching assistantships, Federal Work-Study and institutionally sponsored loans available. Financial award application deadline: 6/1. *Faculty research:* Remote sensing, cultural/social geography, urban geography.

University at Buffalo, the State University of New York, Graduate School, College of Arts and Sciences, Department of Geography, Buffalo, NY 14260. Offers geographic information science (Certificate); geography (MA, MS, PhD); transportation and business geographics (Certificate); MA/MBA. *Degree requirements:* For master's, thesis (for some programs), project; for doctorate, thesis/dissertation; for Certificate, portfolio. *Entrance requirements:* For master's, GRE General Test, minimum GPA of 2.9; for doctorate, GRE General Test, minimum GPA of 3.0. Additional exam requirements/recommendations for international students: Required—TOEFL (minimum score 550 paper-based; 213 computer-based; 79 iBT). Electronic applications accepted. *Faculty research:* International business and world trade, geographic information systems and cartography, transportation, urban and regional analysis, physical and environmental geography.

The University of Akron, Graduate School, Buchtel College of Arts and Sciences, Department of Geography and Planning, Akron, OH 44325. Offers geographic information science (MS); urban planning (MA). Part-time and evening/weekend programs available. *Faculty:* 5 full-time (1 woman), 11 part-time/adjunct (1 woman). *Students:* 31 full-time (13 women), 3 part-time (1 woman); includes 2 minority (1 African American, 1 Hispanic American), 9 international. Average age 28. 25 applicants, 80% accepted, 9 enrolled. In 2007, 15 degrees awarded. *Degree requirements:* For master's, thesis optional. *Entrance requirements:* For master's, minimum GPA of 2.75. Additional exam requirements/recommendations for international students: Required—TOEFL (minimum score 550 paper-based; 213 computer-based; 79 iBT). *Application deadline:* Applications are processed on a rolling basis. Application fee: $30 ($40 for international students). Electronic applications accepted. *Expenses:* Tuition, state resident: full-time $6,164; part-time $342 per credit. Tuition, nonresident: full-time $10,575; part-time $588 per credit. Required fees: $806; $43 per credit. $12 per term. Tuition and fees vary according to course load, degree level and program. *Financial support:* In 2007–08, 27 teaching assistantships with full tuition reimbursements were awarded; fellowships with full tuition reimbursements, research assistantships with full tuition reimbursements, career-related internships or fieldwork, Federal Work-Study, institutionally sponsored loans, scholarships/grants, tuition waivers (full), and unspecified assistantships also available. *Faculty research:* Geographic information sciences, urban and regional planning, human geography especially cultural, political, and urban, regional geography, especially Native America, Asia, and Middle East. Total annual research expenditures: $122,323. *Unit head:* Dr. Robert Kent, Chair, 330-972-8032, E-mail: rkent@uakron.edu.

The University of Alabama, Graduate School, College of Arts and Sciences, Department of Geography, Tuscaloosa, AL 35487. Offers MS. Part-time and evening/weekend programs available. *Faculty:* 9 full-time (1 woman). *Students:* 20 full-time (6 women), 5 part-time; includes 3 minority (all African Americans) Average age 25. 14 applicants, 71% accepted, 8 enrolled. In 2007, 12 degrees awarded. *Degree requirements:* For master's, comprehensive exam, thesis or alternative. *Entrance requirements:* For master's, GRE, minimum GPA of 3.0. Additional exam requirements/recommendations for international students: Required—TOEFL. *Application deadline:* For fall admission, 2/1 priority date for domestic and international students; for spring admission, 10/1 priority date for domestic and international students. Applications are processed on a rolling basis. Application fee: $30. Electronic applications accepted. *Expenses:* Tuition, state resident: full-time $5,700. Tuition, nonresident: full-time $16,518. *Financial support:* In 2007–08, 16 students received support, including fellowships (averaging $12,500 per year), 3 research assistantships with full tuition reimbursements available (averaging $10,908 per year), 12 teaching assistantships with full tuition reimbursements available (averaging $10,908 per year); career-related internships or fieldwork, health care benefits, and unspecified assistantships also available. *Faculty research:* Land use, regional and urban planning, geographic information systems, forest ecology, environmental management, geomorphology, climatology, planning urban-economic geography. Total annual research expenditures: $69,876. *Unit head:* Prof. Luoheng Han, Chair, 205-348-5047, Fax: 205-348-2278, E-mail: lhan@bama.ua.edu. *Application contact:* Information Contact, 205-348-5047, Fax: 205-348-2278.

The University of Arizona, Graduate College, College of Social and Behavioral Sciences, Department of Geography and Regional Development, Tucson, AZ 85721. Offers geography (MA, PhD). Part-time programs available. *Faculty:* 21. *Students:* 51 full-time (20 women), 16 part-time (8 women); includes 4 minority (1 American Indian/Alaska Native, 3 Hispanic Americans), 9 international. Average age 32. 65 applicants, 43% accepted, 10 enrolled. In 2007, 5 master's, 3 doctorates awarded. Terminal master's awarded for partial completion of doctoral program. *Degree requirements:* For master's, thesis or additional course work; for doctorate, variable foreign language requirement, thesis/dissertation. *Entrance requirements:* For master's, GRE General Test, minimum GPA of 3.0, master's degree, statement of purpose, 2 letters of recommendation; for doctorate, GRE General Test, minimum GPA of 3.0, statement of purpose, 2 letters of recommendation, master's degree. Additional exam requirements/recommendations for international students: Required—TOEFL (minimum score 550 paper-based). *Application deadline:* For fall admission, 1/15 for domestic students, 12/1 for international students. Application fee: $50. *Financial support:* Fellowships, research assistantships, teaching assistantships, career-related internships or fieldwork and scholarships/grants available. Financial award application deadline: 2/1. *Faculty research:* Population, Latin America, Anglo America, the former Soviet Union, Middle East. Total annual research expenditures: $269,921. *Unit head:* Dr. John Paul Jones, Head, 520-621-1652. *Application contact:* Linda Koski, Information Contact, 520-621-1652, Fax: 520-621-2889, E-mail: lkoski@email.arizona.edu.

University of Arkansas, Graduate School, J. William Fulbright College of Arts and Sciences, Department of Geosciences, Program in Geography, Fayetteville, AR 72701-1201. Offers MA. Part-time programs available. *Students:* 13 full-time (6 women), 10 part-time (3 women); includes 4 minority (1 African American, 2 American Indian/Alaska Native, 1 Asian American or Pacific Islander), 2 international. In 2007, 10 degrees awarded. *Degree requirements:* For master's, thesis. Application fee: $40 ($50 for international students). *Financial support:* In 2007–08, 1 fellowship, 1 research assistantship, 4 teaching assistantships were awarded; career-related internships or fieldwork and Federal Work-Study also available. Support available to part-time students. Financial award application deadline: 4/1; financial award applicants required to submit FAFSA. *Unit head:* David Stahle, Graduate Coordinator, 479-575-3355, Fax: 479-575-3469, E-mail: dstahle@uark.edu.

The University of British Columbia, Faculty of Arts and Faculty of Graduate Studies, Department of Geography, Vancouver, BC V6T 1Z1, Canada. Offers M Sc, MA, PhD. Part-time programs available. *Faculty:* 25 full-time (6 women), 7 part-time/adjunct (0 women). *Students:* 114 full-time (48 women); includes 20 minority (15 Asian Americans or Pacific Islanders, 5 Hispanic Americans). Average age 31. 107 applicants, 22% accepted. In 2007, 17 master's, 2 doctorates awarded. Terminal master's awarded for partial completion of doctoral program. *Median time to degree:* Of those who began their doctoral program in fall 1999, 63% received their degree in 8 years or less. *Degree requirements:* For master's, thesis; for doctorate, comprehensive exam, thesis/dissertation. *Entrance requirements:* For master's and doctorate, minimum B average, 2nd class honors, upper division (class II, division I). Additional exam requirements/recommendations for international students: Required—TOEFL (minimum score 600 paper-based; 250 computer-based; 100 iBT). *Application deadline:* For fall admission, 1/15 for domestic and international students. Applications are processed on a rolling basis. Application fee: $90 Canadian dollars ($150 Canadian dollars for international students). Electronic applications accepted. *Financial support:* Fellowships, research assistantships, teaching assistantships, career-related internships or fieldwork available. Financial award application deadline: 2/1. *Faculty research:* Earth system science, environmental geography, historical geography, social geography, urban geography. *Unit head:* Dr. Graeme Wynn, Head, 604-822-6226, Fax: 604-822-6150, E-mail: head@geog.ubc.ca. *Application contact:* Junnie Cheung, Graduate Secretary, 604-822-2663, Fax: 604-822-6150, E-mail: gradprogram@geog.ubc.ca.

University of Calgary, Faculty of Graduate Studies, Faculty of Social Sciences, Department of Geography, Calgary, AB T2N 1N4, Canada. Offers M Sc, MA, MGIS, PhD. Part-time programs available. *Degree requirements:* For master's, thesis, departmental conference; for doctorate, thesis/dissertation, candidacy exam, departmental conference. *Entrance requirements:* For master's, minimum undergraduate GPA of 3.0 during last 2 years; for doctorate, minimum GPA of 3.0 during previous 2 years, master's degree. Additional exam requirements/recommendations for international students: Required—TOEFL (minimum score 550 paper-based; 213 computer-based). Electronic applications accepted. *Faculty research:* Geographic information systems, remote sensing, geomorphology, earth system processes, urban and required environmental health research.

University of California, Berkeley, Graduate Division, College of Letters and Science, Department of Geography, Berkeley, CA 94720-1500. Offers PhD. *Degree requirements:* For doctorate, thesis/dissertation, qualifying exam. *Entrance requirements:* For doctorate, GRE General Test, minimum GPA of 3.0, 3 letters of recommendation. *Application deadline:* For fall admission, 12/12 for domestic students. Application fee: $70 ($90 for international students). Electronic applications accepted. *Financial support:* Fellowships, research assistantships, teaching assistantships, unspecified assistantships available. *Unit head:* Dr. Michael Johns, Chair, 510-642-0276, E-mail: johns@berkeley.edu. *Application contact:* Carol Page, Graduate Assistant for Admission, 510-642-3904, Fax: 510-642-3370, E-mail: carolpage@socrates.berkeley.edu.

University of California, Davis, Graduate Studies, Graduate Group in Geography, Davis, CA 95616. Offers MA, PhD. Terminal master's awarded for partial completion of doctoral program. *Degree requirements:* For master's, comprehensive exam (for some programs), thesis (for some programs); for doctorate, thesis/dissertation. *Entrance requirements:* For master's, GRE General Test, minimum GPA of 3.0; for doctorate, GRE General Test, master's degree, minimum GPA of 3.0. Additional exam requirements/recommendations for international students: Required—TOEFL (minimum score 550 paper-based; 213 computer-based). Electronic applications accepted. *Faculty research:* Cultural agrosystems, mountain society habitat and South Asia.

University of California, Los Angeles, Graduate Division, College of Letters and Science, Department of Geography, Los Angeles, CA 90095. Offers MA, PhD. *Students:* 50 full-time (22 women); includes 9 minority (1 African American, 5 Asian Americans or Pacific Islanders, 3 Hispanic Americans), 11 international. Average age 31. 54 applicants, 43% accepted, 15 enrolled. In 2007, 5 master's, 2 doctorates awarded. Terminal master's awarded for partial completion of doctoral program. *Median time to degree:* Of those who began their doctoral program in fall 1999, 40% received their degree in 8 years or less. *Degree requirements:* For master's, thesis; for doctorate, thesis/dissertation, oral and written qualifying exams. *Entrance requirements:* For master's, GRE General Test, minimum GPA of 3.3; for doctorate, GRE General Test, minimum undergraduate GPA of 3.3, sample of research writing or thesis. *Application deadline:* For fall admission, 12/15 for domestic students. Application fee: $60. Electronic applications accepted. *Expenses:* Tuition, nonresident: full-time $5,728. Required fees: $8,966. Full-time tuition and fees vary according to program and student level. *Financial support:* In 2007–08, 33 fellowships with full and partial tuition reimbursements, 13 research assistantships with full and partial tuition reimbursements, 28 teaching assistantships with full and partial tuition reimbursements were awarded; Federal Work-Study, institutionally sponsored loans, scholarships/grants, and tuition waivers (full and partial) also available. Financial award application deadline: 3/1; financial award applicants required to submit FAFSA. *Unit head:* Dr. David Rigby, Chair, 310-825-1071. *Application contact:* Departmental Office, 310-825-1071, E-mail: gradapps@geog.ucla.edu.

University of California, Santa Barbara, Graduate Division, College of Letters and Sciences, Division of Mathematics, Life, and Physical Sciences, Department of Geography, Santa Barbara, CA 93106. Offers cognitive science (PhD); quantitative methods in social sciences (PhD); MA/PhD. *Faculty:* 22 full-time (3 women), 11 part-time/adjunct (3 women). *Students:* 66 full-time (28 women); includes 6 minority (2 African Americans, 1 American Indian/Alaska Native, 2 Asian Americans or Pacific Islanders, 1 Hispanic American), 11 international. Average age 30. 98 applicants, 33% accepted, 18 enrolled. In 2007, 9 master's, 8 doctorates awarded. *Median time to degree:* Of those who began their doctoral program in fall 1999, 53% received their degree in 8 years or less. *Degree requirements:* For master's, comprehensive exam (for some programs), thesis; for doctorate, comprehensive exam, thesis/dissertation, candidacy, diagnostic interview, written and oral exam, approved dissertation proposal. *Entrance requirements:* For master's and doctorate, GRE General Test, minimum GPA of 3.25 in junior and senior year. Additional exam requirements/recommendations for international students: Required—TOEFL (minimum score 550 paper-based; 213 computer-based; 80 iBT). *Application deadline:* For fall admission, 12/15 for domestic students, 1/15 for international students. Application fee: $60. Electronic applications accepted. *Expenses:* Tuition, nonresident: full-time $14,888. Required fees: $10,108. *Financial support:* In 2007–08, 66 students received support, including 28 fellowships with full and partial tuition reimbursements available (averaging $12,100 per year), 13 research assistantships with full and partial tuition reimbursements available (averaging $13,000 per year), 24 teaching assistantships with full and partial tuition reimbursements available (averaging $15,000 per year); Federal Work-Study, institutionally sponsored loans, scholarships/grants, health care benefits, and unspecified assistantships also available. Financial award application deadline: 12/15; financial award applicants required to submit FAFSA. *Faculty research:* Earth system science, human environment relations, modeling, measurement and computation, quantitative methods in social sciences. *Unit head:* Dr. Oliver Chadwick, Chair, 805-893-4223, E-mail: oac@geog.ucsb.edu. *Application contact:* Karen Barteld, Graduate Program Assistant, 805-893-8789, Fax: 805-893-3146, E-mail: barteld@geog.ucsb.edu.

University of Central Arkansas, Graduate School, College of Liberal Arts, Department of Geography, Conway, AR 72035-0001. Offers geographic information systems (MGIS, Certificate). Part-time programs available. Postbaccalaureate distance learning degree programs offered (minimal on-campus study). *Faculty:* 3 full-time (0 women). *Students:* 1 full-time (0 women), 17 part-time (6 women); includes 1 minority (American Indian/Alaska Native), 1 international. 11 applicants, 100% accepted, 11 enrolled. *Entrance requirements:* Additional exam requirements/recommendations for international students: Required—TOEFL (minimum score 550 paper-based; 213 computer-based). *Application deadline:* For fall admission, 3/1 priority date for domestic and international students; for spring admission, 10/1 priority date for domestic and international students. Applications are processed on a rolling basis. Application fee: $25 ($50 for international students). *Expenses:* Tuition, state resident: full-time $4,513; part-time $240 per credit. Tuition, nonresident: full-time $8,805; part-time $440 per credit. International tuition: $9,700 full-time. Required fees: $100 per term. *Financial support:* Applicants required to

Geography

University of Central Arkansas (continued)
submit FAFSA. *Unit head:* Dr. Brooks Green, Chairperson, 501-450-5636, Fax: 501-450-5185, E-mail: brooksg@uca.edu. *Application contact:* Brenda Herring, Admissions Assistant, 501-450-5065, Fax: 501-450-5678, E-mail: bherring@uca.edu.

University of Cincinnati, Graduate School, McMicken College of Arts and Sciences, Department of Geography, Cincinnati, OH 45221. Offers MA, PhD. *Faculty:* 9 full-time (3 women). *Students:* 29 full-time (12 women), 9 part-time (3 women); includes 2 minority (1 Asian American or Pacific Islander, 1 Hispanic American), 14 international. Average age 30. 25 applicants, 80% accepted, 12 enrolled. In 2007, 8 master's, 4 doctorates awarded. Terminal master's awarded for partial completion of doctoral program. *Degree requirements:* For master's, thesis optional; for doctorate, one foreign language, comprehensive exam, thesis/dissertation. *Entrance requirements:* For master's and doctorate, GRE General Test. Additional exam requirements/recommendations for international students: Required—TOEFL. *Application deadline:* For fall admission, 7/1 priority date for domestic students, 7/1 for international students. Application fee: $40. Electronic applications accepted. *Financial support:* In 2007–08, 21 students received support, including 6 research assistantships with full tuition reimbursements available (averaging $9,383 per year), 15 teaching assistantships with full tuition reimbursements available (averaging $11,488 per year); tuition waivers (partial) and unspecified assistantships also available. Financial award application deadline: 5/1. *Faculty research:* Urban-economics, GIS, physical-environmental. Total annual research expenditures: $73,855. *Unit head:* Dr. Lin Liu, Head, 513-556-3429, Fax: 513-556-3370, E-mail: lin.liu@uc.edu. *Application contact:* Dr. Nicholas Dunning, Graduate Program Director, 513-556-3436, Fax: 513-556-3370, E-mail: nicholas.dunning@uc.edu.

University of Colorado at Boulder, Graduate School, College of Arts and Sciences, Department of Geography, Boulder, CO 80309. Offers MA, PhD. Part-time programs available. *Faculty:* 17. *Students:* 53 full-time (22 women), 13 part-time (3 women); includes 3 minority (1 American Indian/Alaska Native, 2 Asian Americans or Pacific Islanders), 14 international. Average age 31. 19 applicants, 100% accepted. In 2007, 11 master's, 11 doctorates awarded. Terminal master's awarded for partial completion of doctoral program. *Degree requirements:* For master's, thesis; for doctorate, one foreign language, comprehensive exam, thesis/dissertation. *Entrance requirements:* For master's, GRE General Test, minimum undergraduate GPA of 3.0; for doctorate, GRE General Test. *Application deadline:* For fall admission, 1/15 priority date for domestic students, 12/1 for international students. Application fee: $50 ($60 for international students). *Financial support:* In 2007–08, 21 fellowships (averaging $7,410 per year), 13 research assistantships with tuition reimbursements (averaging $14,468 per year) were awarded. Financial award application deadline: 1/15. *Faculty research:* Physical geography, human geography, environmental society relations, technical geography, GIS and cartography. Total annual research expenditures: $26.1 million. *Unit head:* Susan Beatty, Chair, 303-492-8310, Fax: 303-492-7501, E-mail: susan.beatty@colorado.edu. *Application contact:* Karen Weingarten, Graduate Secretary, 303-492-8311, Fax: 303-492-7501, E-mail: geoggrad@colorado.edu.

University of Colorado at Colorado Springs, Graduate School, College of Letters, Arts and Sciences, Department of Geography and Environmental Studies, Colorado Springs, CO 80933-7150. Offers MA. *Faculty:* 8 full-time (2 women), 1 part-time/adjunct (0 women). *Students:* 24 full-time (10 women), 16 part-time (6 women); includes 6 minority (4 Asian Americans or Pacific Islanders, 2 Hispanic Americans). Average age 36. 6 applicants, 100% accepted, 3 enrolled. In 2007, 4 degrees awarded. *Degree requirements:* For master's, thesis optional. *Entrance requirements:* For master's, GRE. *Application deadline:* For fall admission, 4/1 for domestic students. *Faculty research:* Natural hazard mitigation and policy issues, applied geography, geographic information systems, population geography. Total annual research expenditures: $107,300. *Unit head:* Dr. Robert Larkin, Associate Professor, 719-262-4053, E-mail: rlarkin@uccs.edu.

University of Connecticut, Graduate School, College of Liberal Arts and Sciences, Department of Geography, Field of Geography, Storrs, CT 06269. Offers geographic information systems (Certificate); geography (MS, PhD). Part-time programs available. *Faculty:* 11 full-time (3 women). *Students:* 18 full-time (6 women), 5 part-time (1 woman); includes 1 minority (Asian American or Pacific Islander), 2 international. Average age 32. 23 applicants, 22% accepted, 4 enrolled. In 2007, 4 master's, 1 doctorate, 8 other advanced degrees awarded. Terminal master's awarded for partial completion of doctoral program. *Degree requirements:* For master's, comprehensive exam; for doctorate, thesis/dissertation. *Entrance requirements:* For master's and doctorate, GRE General Test. Additional exam requirements/recommendations for international students: Required—TOEFL (minimum score 550 paper-based; 213 computer-based). *Application deadline:* For fall admission, 2/1 priority date for domestic and international students; for spring admission, 11/1 for domestic students, 10/1 for international students. Applications are processed on a rolling basis. Application fee: $55. Electronic applications accepted. *Expenses:* Tuition, state resident: part-time $469 per credit hour. Tuition, nonresident: part-time $1,218 per credit hour. *Financial support:* In 2007–08, 2 research assistantships with full tuition reimbursements, 16 teaching assistantships with full tuition reimbursements were awarded; fellowships, Federal Work-Study, scholarships/grants, health care benefits, and unspecified assistantships also available. Financial award application deadline: 2/1; financial award applicants required to submit FAFSA. *Application contact:* Rose Karosi, Administrative Assistant, 860-986-3656, Fax: 860-486-1348, E-mail: rose.karosi@uconn.edu.

University of Delaware, College of Arts and Sciences, Department of Geography, Newark, DE 19716. Offers climatology (PhD); geography (MA, MS). *Faculty:* 13 full-time (4 women). *Students:* 37 full-time (20 women), 2 part-time; includes 1 minority (Asian American or Pacific Islander), 4 international. Average age 25. 24 applicants, 67% accepted, 9 enrolled. In 2007, 9 degrees awarded. *Degree requirements:* For master's, thesis; for doctorate, thesis/dissertation. *Entrance requirements:* For master's and doctorate, GRE General Test. Additional exam requirements/recommendations for international students: Required—TOEFL. *Application deadline:* For fall admission, 2/1 for domestic and international students. Application fee: $60. Electronic applications accepted. *Financial support:* In 2007–08, 18 students received support, including 2 fellowships with full tuition reimbursements available (averaging $17,500 per year), 2 research assistantships with full tuition reimbursements available (averaging $17,500 per year), 15 teaching assistantships with full tuition reimbursements available (averaging $17,500 per year); health care benefits and tuition waivers (full) also available. Financial award application deadline: 2/1. *Faculty research:* Permafrost, Glaciers, Climatology, Physical Geography, Human Geography. Total annual research expenditures: $700,000. *Unit head:* Dr. Brian Hanson, Chair, 302-831-8764, Fax: 302-831-6654. *Application contact:* Ingrid Callahan, Assistant to the Chair, 302-831-8998, Fax: 302-831-6654, E-mail: iac@udel.edu.

University of Denver, Faculty of Natural Sciences and Mathematics, Department of Geography, Denver, CO 80208. Offers MA, MS, PhD. Part-time programs available. *Faculty:* 11 full-time (3 women). *Students:* 13 full-time (4 women), 18 part-time (9 women); includes 2 minority (both Asian Americans or Pacific Islanders), 4 international. Average age 32. In 2007, 5 master's awarded. Terminal master's awarded for partial completion of doctoral program. *Degree requirements:* For master's, thesis or alternative; for doctorate, one foreign language, thesis/dissertation. *Entrance requirements:* For master's, GRE General Test; for doctorate, GRE General Test, MA. Additional exam requirements/recommendations for international students: Required—TOEFL. *Application deadline:* Applications are processed on a rolling basis. Application fee: $50. Electronic applications accepted. *Financial support:* In 2007–08, 14 teaching assistantships with full and partial tuition reimbursements (averaging $15,000 per year) were awarded; research assistantships with full and partial tuition reimbursements, career-related internships or fieldwork, Federal Work-Study, institutionally sponsored loans, and scholarships/grants also available. Support available to part-time students. Financial award application deadline: 3/1; financial award applicants required to submit FAFSA. *Faculty research:* Transportation and land use, fluvial geography and water resources, climatology, geographic information systems, biogeography. Total annual research expenditures: $258,000. *Unit head:* Dr. Michael Keables, Graduate Director, 303-871-2513. *Application contact:* Information Contact, 303-871-2513, E-mail: kescobar@du.edu.

University of Florida, Graduate School, College of Liberal Arts and Sciences, Department of Geography, Gainesville, FL 32611. Offers MA, MS, PhD. *Faculty:* 13 full-time (4 women), 1 part-time/adjunct (0 women). *Students:* 51 (24 women); includes 7 minority (3 African Americans, 2 Asian Americans or Pacific Islanders, 2 Hispanic Americans) 15 international. In 2007, 3 degrees awarded. *Degree requirements:* For master's, variable foreign language requirement, thesis (for some programs); for doctorate, thesis/dissertation. *Entrance requirements:* For master's and doctorate, GRE General Test, minimum GPA of 3.0. Additional exam requirements/recommendations for international students: Required—TOEFL (minimum score 550 paper-based; 213 computer-based). *Application deadline:* For fall admission, 6/1 priority date for domestic students. Applications are processed on a rolling basis. Application fee: $30. Electronic applications accepted. *Expenses:* Tuition, state resident: full-time $7,478. Tuition, nonresident: full-time $22,603. *Financial support:* In 2007–08, 18 students received support, including 2 research assistantships (averaging $12,132 per year), 15 teaching assistantships (averaging $13,009 per year); fellowships, career-related internships or fieldwork and unspecified assistantships also available. *Faculty research:* Economic development, physical geography, hydrology, climatology, tropical agriculture. *Unit head:* Peter Waylen, Chair, 352-392-0494 Ext. 203. *Application contact:* Dr. Abe Goldman, Coordinator, 352-392-0494 Ext. 206, Fax: 352-392-8855, E-mail: agoldmn@geog.ufl.edu.

University of Georgia, Graduate School, College of Arts and Sciences, Department of Geography, Athens, GA 30602. Offers MA, MS, PhD. *Faculty:* 19 full-time (6 women), 1 part-time/adjunct (0 women). *Students:* 50 full-time (23 women), 13 part-time (5 women); includes 7 minority (4 African Americans, 2 Asian Americans or Pacific Islanders, 1 Hispanic American), 15 international. 60 applicants, 53% accepted, 17 enrolled. In 2007, 7 master's, 6 doctorates awarded. *Degree requirements:* For master's, one foreign language, thesis; for doctorate, one foreign language, thesis/dissertation. *Entrance requirements:* For master's and doctorate, GRE General Test. *Application deadline:* For fall admission, 7/1 priority date for domestic students; for spring admission, 11/15 for domestic students. Application fee: $50. Electronic applications accepted. *Financial support:* Fellowships, research assistantships, teaching assistantships, unspecified assistantships available. *Unit head:* Dr. George A. Brook, Head, 706-542-2856, E-mail: gabrook@uga.edu. *Application contact:* Dr. David S. Leigh, Graduate Coordinator, 706-542-2856, E-mail: dleigh@uga.edu.

University of Guelph, Graduate Program Services, College of Social and Applied Human Sciences, Department of Geography, Guelph, ON N1G 2W1, Canada. Offers M Sc, MA, PhD. Part-time programs available. *Faculty:* 18 full-time (2 women), 24 part-time/adjunct (5 women). *Students:* 48 full-time (30 women), 1 (woman) part-time. Average age 26. 64 applicants, 33% accepted, 21 enrolled. In 2007, 14 master's, 4 doctorates awarded. *Median time to degree:* Of those who began their doctoral program in fall 1999, 100% received their degree in 8 years or less. *Degree requirements:* For master's, thesis (for some programs); for doctorate, comprehensive exam, thesis/dissertation. *Entrance requirements:* For master's, minimum B average during previous 2 years of course work; for doctorate, minimum A- average. Additional exam requirements/recommendations for international students: Required—TOEFL (minimum score 550 paper-based; 213 computer-based). *Application deadline:* For fall admission, 1/15 priority date for domestic and international students. Applications are processed on a rolling basis. Application fee: $85. Electronic applications accepted. *Financial support:* In 2007–08, 33 fellowships (averaging $2,000 per year), 48 research assistantships (averaging $5,300 per year), 66 teaching assistantships (averaging $5,107 per year) were awarded. *Faculty research:* Rural resource evaluation, environmental analysis, biophysical process, rural settlement and land use, resource assessment. Total annual research expenditures: $1.1 million. *Unit head:* Dr. William G. Nickling, Department Chair, 519-824-4120 Ext. 56722, Fax: 519-837-2940, E-mail: nickling@uoguelph.ca. *Application contact:* Dr. Robert de Loë, Graduate Coordinator, 519-824-4120 Ext. 53525, Fax: 519-837-2940, E-mail: rdeloe@uoguelph.ca.

University of Hawaii at Manoa, Graduate Division, Colleges of Arts and Sciences, College of Social Sciences, Department of Geography, Honolulu, HI 96822. Offers geography (MA, PhD); ocean policy (Graduate Certificate). Part-time programs available. *Faculty:* 20 full-time (7 women), 3 part-time/adjunct (0 women). *Students:* 47 full-time (19 women), 18 part-time (6 women); includes 19 minority (1 American Indian/Alaska Native, 15 Asian Americans or Pacific Islanders, 3 Hispanic Americans), 14 international. Average age 35. 40 applicants, 53% accepted, 15 enrolled. *Median time to degree:* Of those who began their doctoral program in fall 1999, 83% received their degree in 8 years or less. *Degree requirements:* For master's, one foreign language, comprehensive exam, thesis; for doctorate, one foreign language, comprehensive exam, thesis/dissertation. *Entrance requirements:* For master's, GRE General Test; for doctorate, GRE General Test, sample of written work. Additional exam requirements/recommendations for international students: Required—TOEFL (minimum score 500 paper-based; 173 computer-based; 61 iBT), IELTS (minimum score 5). *Application deadline:* For fall admission, 1/15 for domestic and international students. Applications are processed on a rolling basis. Application fee: $50. *Financial support:* In 2007–08, 7 research assistantships (averaging $22,090 per year), 14 teaching assistantships (averaging $16,888 per year) were awarded; career-related internships or fieldwork, Federal Work-Study, institutionally sponsored loans, and tuition waivers (full) also available. Financial award application deadline: 3/1. *Faculty research:* Physical geography, human geography, methodology. Total annual research expenditures: $188,662. *Application contact:* Tom Giambelluca, Information Contact, 808-956-8465, Fax: 808-956-3512, E-mail: thomas@hawaii.edu.

University of Idaho, College of Graduate Studies, College of Science, Department of Geography, Moscow, ID 83844-2282. Offers MAT, MS, PhD. *Students:* 17 (6 women). Average age 34. In 2007, 1 doctorate awarded. *Degree requirements:* For doctorate, one foreign language, thesis/dissertation. *Entrance requirements:* For master's, minimum GPA of 2.8; for doctorate, minimum undergraduate GPA of 2.8, graduate GPA of 3.0. *Application deadline:* For fall admission, 8/1 for domestic students; for spring admission, 12/15 for domestic students. Application fee: $55 ($60 for international students). *Financial support:* Research assistantships, teaching assistantships available. Financial award application deadline: 2/15. *Unit head:* Dr. Harley E. Johansen, Head, 208-885-6216.

University of Illinois at Chicago, Graduate College, College of Liberal Arts and Sciences, Department of Anthropology, Program in Environmental and Urban Geography, Chicago, IL 60607-7128. Offers environmental studies (MA); urban geography (MA). Part-time programs available. *Degree requirements:* For master's, thesis. *Entrance requirements:* For master's, GRE General Test, minimum GPA of 2.75. Additional exam requirements/recommendations for international students: Required—TOEFL. Electronic applications accepted.

University of Illinois at Urbana–Champaign, Graduate College, College of Liberal Arts and Sciences, School of Earth, Society and Environment, Department of Geography, Champaign, IL 61820. Offers MA, MS, PhD. *Faculty:* 14 full-time (2 women). *Students:* 34 full-time (17 women), 5 part-time (1 woman); includes 3 minority (2 African Americans, 1 Asian American or Pacific Islander), 12 international. Average age 27. 45 applicants, 22% accepted, 9 enrolled. In 2007, 6 master's, 2 doctorates awarded. *Degree requirements:* For master's, thesis; for doctorate, thesis/dissertation. *Entrance requirements:* For master's, minimum GPA of 3.0. *Application deadline:* Applications are processed on a rolling basis. Application fee: $60 ($75 for international students). *Financial support:* In 2007–08, 14 fellowships, 10 research assistantships, 13 teaching assistantships were awarded; career-related internships or fieldwork, institutionally sponsored loans, and tuition waivers (full and partial) also available. Financial award application deadline: 2/15. Total annual research expenditures: $250,000. *Unit head:* Bruce Rhoads, Interim Head, 217-333-3342, Fax: 217-244-1785. *Application contact:* Chris Wilcock, Admissions and Records Officer, I, 217-244-3486, Fax: 217-244-1785, E-mail: cwilcock@uiuc.edu.

The University of Iowa, Graduate College, College of Liberal Arts and Sciences, Department of Geography, Iowa City, IA 52242-1316. Offers MA, PhD. *Faculty:* 9 full-time, 6 part-time/

adjunct. *Students:* 7 full-time (2 women), 23 part-time (9 women); includes 2 minority (1 African American, 1 Hispanic American), 15 international. 35 applicants, 3% accepted, 1 enrolled. In 2007, 3 master's, 5 doctorates awarded. *Degree requirements:* For master's, thesis optional, exam; for doctorate, comprehensive exam, thesis/dissertation. *Entrance requirements:* For master's and doctorate, GRE General Test, minimum GPA of 3.0. Additional exam requirements/recommendations for international students: Required—TOEFL (minimum score 550 paper-based; 213 computer-based; 81 iBT). *Application deadline:* For fall admission, 2/1 for domestic and international students. Application fee: $60 ($85 for international students). Electronic applications accepted. *Expenses:* Tuition, state resident: part-time $349 per hour. Tuition, nonresident: part-time $349 per hour. Tuition and fees vary according to course load and program. *Financial support:* In 2007–08, 2 fellowships, 6 research assistantships with partial tuition reimbursements, 9 teaching assistantships with partial tuition reimbursements were awarded. Financial award application deadline: 1/15; financial award applicants required to submit FAFSA. *Unit head:* Marc Armstrong, Chair, 319-335-0153, Fax: 319-335-2725.

University of Kansas, Research and Graduate Studies, College of Liberal Arts and Sciences, Department of Geography, Lawrence, KS 66045. Offers MA, PhD. Part-time programs available. *Faculty:* 20. *Students:* 58 full-time (18 women), 19 part-time (8 women), 14 international. Average age 32. 46 applicants, 61% accepted, 15 enrolled. In 2007, 9 master's, 4 doctorates awarded. *Degree requirements:* For master's, comprehensive exam, thesis; for doctorate, one foreign language, comprehensive exam, thesis/dissertation. *Entrance requirements:* For master's and doctorate, GRE General Test, 3 letters of reference, transcripts, statement of interests. Additional exam requirements/recommendations for international students: Required—TOEFL. *Application deadline:* For fall admission, 2/1 for domestic students, 2/1 priority date for international students; for spring admission, 11/1 for domestic and international students. Applications are processed on a rolling basis. Application fee: $55 ($60 for international students). Electronic applications accepted. *Expenses:* Tuition, state resident: full-time $5,838. Tuition, nonresident: full-time $13,409. Tuition and fees vary according to program. *Financial support:* Fellowships with full tuition reimbursements, research assistantships with full tuition reimbursements, teaching assistantships with full and partial tuition reimbursements, unspecified assistantships available. Financial award application deadline: 2/1. *Faculty research:* Physical geography, techniques (cartography-GIS-remote sensing), cultural/regional geography. *Unit head:* Terry Slocum, Chair, 785-864-5146, Fax: 785-864-5378, E-mail: t-slocum@ku.edu. *Application contact:* Stephen Egbert, Graduate Director, 785-864-4252, Fax: 785-864-5378, E-mail: s-egbert@ku.edu.

University of Kentucky, Graduate School, College of Arts and Sciences, Program in Geography, Lexington, KY 40506-0032. Offers MA, PhD. *Faculty:* 19 full-time (6 women), 2 part-time/adjunct (0 women). *Students:* 36 full-time (21 women), 6 part-time (3 women); includes 3 minority (1 African American, 2 Hispanic Americans), 70 international. Average age 33. 41 applicants, 56% accepted, 5 enrolled. In 2007, 4 master's, 1 doctorate awarded. *Median time to degree:* Of those who began their doctoral program in fall 1999, 89% received their degree in 8 years or less. *Degree requirements:* For master's, comprehensive exam, thesis optional; for doctorate, one foreign language, comprehensive exam, thesis/dissertation. *Entrance requirements:* For master's, GRE General Test, minimum undergraduate GPA of 2.75; for doctorate, GRE General Test, minimum graduate GPA of 3.0. Additional exam requirements/recommendations for international students: Required—TOEFL (minimum score 550 paper-based; 213 computer-based). *Application deadline:* For fall admission, 7/17 priority date for domestic students, 2/1 priority date for international students; for spring admission, 12/13 priority date for domestic students, 6/15 priority date for international students. Application fee: $50 ($65 for international students). Electronic applications accepted. *Expenses:* Tuition, state resident: part-time $437 per credit hour. Tuition, nonresident: part-time $931 per credit hour. *Financial support:* In 2007–08, 28 students received support, including 1 fellowship with full tuition reimbursement available (averaging $4,687 per year), 2 research assistantships with full tuition reimbursements available (averaging $11,056 per year), 19 teaching assistantships with full tuition reimbursements available (averaging $12,500 per year); Federal Work-Study, institutionally sponsored loans, scholarships/grants, traineeships, health care benefits, tuition waivers (partial), and unspecified assistantships also available. Support available to part-time students. Financial award application deadline: 3/15. *Faculty research:* Cultural, industrial, medical, political, social, population, and transportation geography; geographic analysis; Third World (especially Southeast Asia theory); Eastern Europe. *Unit head:* Dr. Richard Schein, Director of Graduate Studies, 859-257-2119, Fax: 859-323-1969. *Application contact:* Dr. Brian Jackson, Senior Associate Dean, 859-257-4667, Fax: 859-257-4676, E-mail: brian.jackson@uky.edu.

University of Lethbridge, School of Graduate Studies, Lethbridge, AB T1K 3M4, Canada. Offers accounting (MScM); addictions counseling (M Sc); agricultural biotechnology (M Sc); agricultural studies (M Sc, MA); anthropology (MA); archaeology (MA); art (MA); biochemistry (M Sc); biological sciences (M Sc); biomolecular science (PhD); biosystems and biodiversity (PhD); Canadian studies (MA); chemistry (M Sc); computer science (M Sc); computer science and geographical information science (M Sc); counseling psychology (M Ed); dramatic arts (MA); earth, space, and physical science (PhD); economics (MA); educational leadership (M Ed); English (MA); environmental science (M Sc); evolution and behavior (PhD); exercise science (M Sc); finance (MScM); French (MA); French/German (MA); French/Spanish (MA); general education (M Ed); general management (MScM); geography (M Sc, MA); German (MA); health sciences (M Sc, MA); history (MA); human resource management and labour relations (MScM); individualized multidisciplinary (M Sc, MA); information systems (MScM); international management (MScM); kinesiology (M Sc, MA); management (M Sc, MA); marketing (MScM); mathematics (M Sc); music (MA); Native American studies (MA); neuroscience (M Sc, PhD); new media (MA); nursing (M Sc); philosophy (MA); physics (M Sc); policy and strategy (MScM); political science (MA); psychology (M Sc, MA); religious studies (MA); sociology (MA); theoretical and computational science (PhD); urban and regional studies (MA). Part-time and evening/weekend programs available. *Students:* 215 full-time, 98 part-time. In 2007, 87 master's, 1 doctorate awarded. *Degree requirements:* For doctorate, comprehensive exam, thesis/dissertation. *Entrance requirements:* For master's, GMAT (M Sc in management), bachelor's degree in related field, minimum GPA of 3.0 during previous 20 graded semester courses, 2 years teaching or related experience (M Ed); for doctorate, master's degree, minimum graduate GPA of 3.5. Additional exam requirements/recommendations for international students: Required—TOEFL. Application fee: $60 Canadian dollars. *Financial support:* Fellowships, research assistantships, teaching assistantships, scholarships/grants, health care benefits, and unspecified assistantships available. *Faculty research:* Movement and brain plasticity, gibberellin physiology, photosynthesis, carbon cycling, molecular properties of main-group ring components. *Unit head:* Dr. Jo-Anne Fiske, Interim Dean, 403-329-2121, Fax: 403-329-2097. *Application contact:* Jennifer Geddes, Graduate Liaison Officer, 403-329-2762, Fax: 403-329-5159, E-mail: jennifer.geddes@uleth.ca.

University of Manitoba, Faculty of Graduate Studies, Faculty of Environment, Earth and Resources, Department of Geography, Winnipeg, MB R3T 2N2, Canada. Offers MA, PhD. *Degree requirements:* For master's, thesis; for doctorate, one foreign language, thesis/dissertation.

University of Maryland, College Park, Graduate Studies, College of Behavioral and Social Sciences, Department of Geography, College Park, MD 20742. Offers MA, PhD, MA/MLS. Part-time and evening/weekend programs available. *Faculty:* 41 full-time (16 women), 12 part-time/adjunct (8 women). *Students:* 58 full-time (20 women), 16 part-time (7 women); includes 16 minority (8 African Americans, 3 Asian Americans or Pacific Islanders, 5 Hispanic Americans), 15 international. 74 applicants, 43% accepted, 21 enrolled. In 2007, 7 master's, 7 doctorates awarded. Terminal master's awarded for partial completion of doctoral program. *Median time to degree:* Of those who began their doctoral program in fall 1999, 100% received their degree in 8 years or less. *Degree requirements:* For master's, thesis, oral exam; for doctorate, comprehensive exam, thesis/dissertation. *Entrance requirements:* For master's, GRE General Test, minimum GPA of 3.0, 3 letters of recommendation; for doctorate, GRE General Test. Additional exam requirements/recommendations for international students: Required—TOEFL, TWE. *Application deadline:* For fall admission, 1/15 for domestic students, 2/1 for international students. Applications are processed on a rolling basis. Application fee: $60. Electronic applications accepted. *Financial support:* In 2007–08, 17 fellowships with full tuition reimbursements (averaging $11,015 per year), 7 research assistantships with tuition reimbursements (averaging $16,571 per year), 37 teaching assistantships with tuition reimbursements (averaging $15,036 per year) were awarded; Federal Work-Study and scholarships/grants also available. Support available to part-time students. Financial award applicants required to submit FAFSA. *Faculty research:* Cartography and automated mapping, environmental systems analysis, metropolitan analysis and planning, historical and human geography, coastal geomorphology. Total annual research expenditures: $6.9 million. *Unit head:* Dr. John Townshend, Chairman, 301-405-4051, Fax: 301-314-9299, E-mail: jtownshe@umd.edu. *Application contact:* Dean of Graduate School, 301-405-0358, Fax: 301-314-9305.

University of Maryland, College Park, Graduate Studies, Interdepartmental Programs, Program in Geography, Library, and Information Services, College Park, MD 20742. Offers MA/MLS. *Application deadline:* For fall admission, 1/15 for domestic and international students. Applications are processed on a rolling basis. Application fee: $60. Electronic applications accepted. *Financial support:* Fellowships, research assistantships, teaching assistantships available. Financial award application deadline: 2/1; financial award applicants required to submit FAFSA. *Unit head:* Dr. Diane Barlow, Associate Dean, 301-405-2042, Fax: 301-314-9145, E-mail: dbarlow@umd.edu. *Application contact:* Dean of Graduate School, 301-405-0358, Fax: 301-314-9305.

University of Massachusetts Amherst, Graduate School, College of Natural Sciences and Mathematics, Department of Geosciences, Program in Geography, Amherst, MA 01003. Offers MS. Part-time programs available. *Students:* 6 full-time (2 women), 4 part-time (3 women); includes 1 minority (American Indian/Alaska Native), 1 international. Average age 31. 19 applicants, 53% accepted, 2 enrolled. In 2007, 3 degrees awarded. *Degree requirements:* For master's, thesis optional. *Entrance requirements:* For master's, GRE General Test. Additional exam requirements/recommendations for international students: Required—TOEFL (minimum score 530 paper-based; 197 computer-based). *Application deadline:* For fall admission, 2/1 priority date for domestic and international students; for spring admission, 10/1 for domestic and international students. Applications are processed on a rolling basis. Application fee: $50 ($65 for international students). Electronic applications accepted. *Expenses:* Tuition, state resident: full-time $2,640; part-time $110 per credit. Tuition, nonresident: full-time $9,936; part-time $414 per credit. Required fees: $7,455. One-time fee: $332. Tuition and fees vary according to course load, campus/location, program and reciprocity agreements. *Financial support:* Fellowships with full tuition reimbursements, research assistantships with full tuition reimbursements, teaching assistantships with full tuition reimbursements, career-related internships or fieldwork, Federal Work-Study, scholarships/grants, traineeships, and unspecified assistantships available. Support available to part-time students. Financial award application deadline: 2/1. *Unit head:* Dr. Richard Wilkie, Director, 413-545-2286, Fax: 413-545-1200, E-mail: rwilkie@geo.umass.edu.

University of Miami, Graduate School, College of Arts and Sciences, Department of Geography and Regional Studies, Coral Gables, FL 33124. Offers geography (MA). Part-time programs available. *Faculty:* 10 full-time (3 women). *Students:* 8 full-time (4 women), 2 part-time (1 woman); includes 3 minority (1 Asian American or Pacific Islander, 2 Hispanic Americans), 2 international. Average age 27. 13 applicants, 38% accepted, 3 enrolled. In 2007, 3 degrees awarded. *Degree requirements:* For master's, thesis. *Entrance requirements:* For master's, GRE, 3 letters of recommendation, official transcripts. Additional exam requirements/recommendations for international students: Required—TOEFL. *Application deadline:* For fall admission, 3/1 priority date for domestic and international students; for spring admission, 11/1 priority date for domestic and international students. Application fee: $50. Electronic applications accepted. *Financial support:* In 2007–08, 8 students received support, including research assistantships with full tuition reimbursements available (averaging $15,000 per year), 2 teaching assistantships with full tuition reimbursements available (averaging $15,500 per year). Financial award application deadline: 3/30. *Faculty research:* Urbanization, globalization, environmental change. Total annual research expenditures: $100,000. *Unit head:* Prof. Douglas O. Fuller, Chair, 305-284-6695, Fax: 305-284-5430, E-mail: dofuller@miami.edu. *Application contact:* Prof. Peter O. Muller, Professor, 305-284-6678, Fax: 305-284-5430, E-mail: pmuller@miami.edu.

University of Minnesota, Twin Cities Campus, Graduate School, College of Liberal Arts, Department of Geography, Program in Geography, Minneapolis, MN 55455-0213. Offers MA, PhD. *Faculty:* 19 full-time (6 women), 13 part-time/adjunct (4 women). *Students:* 53 full-time (24 women), 23 part-time (10 women); includes 3 minority (1 American Indian/Alaska Native, 1 Asian American or Pacific Islander, 1 Hispanic American), 18 international. 71 applicants, 42% accepted, 13 enrolled. In 2007, 5 master's, 17 doctorates awarded. *Degree requirements:* For master's, comprehensive exam, thesis or 3 papers; for doctorate, comprehensive exam, thesis/dissertation. *Entrance requirements:* For master's and doctorate, GRE General Test, minimum GPA of 3.5. Additional exam requirements/recommendations for international students: Required—TOEFL (minimum score 600 paper-based; 250 computer-based; 100 iBT). *Application deadline:* For fall admission, 12/15 for domestic and international students. Application fee: $55 ($75 for international students). Electronic applications accepted. *Financial support:* In 2007–08, 50 students received support, including 16 fellowships with full and partial tuition reimbursements available (averaging $20,500 per year), 6 research assistantships with full and partial tuition reimbursements available (averaging $12,500 per year), 28 teaching assistantships with full and partial tuition reimbursements available (averaging $12,500 per year); career-related internships or fieldwork, Federal Work-Study, institutionally sponsored loans, scholarships/grants, traineeships, health care benefits, tuition waivers (full and partial), and unspecified assistantships also available. Support available to part-time students. Financial award application deadline: 12/15. *Faculty research:* Space, place, and the environment, biogeography/forest dynamics, international labor migration, political economy of development/globalization, historical urban geography. Total annual research expenditures: $425,506. *Application contact:* Bonnie L. Williams, DGS Assistant, 612-625-6080, Fax: 612-624-1044, E-mail: willi046@umn.edu.

University of Missouri–Columbia, Graduate School, College of Arts and Sciences, Department of Geography, Columbia, MO 65211. Offers MA. *Entrance requirements:* For master's, GRE General Test, minimum GPA of 3.0.

The University of Montana, Graduate School, College of Arts and Sciences, Department of Geography, Missoula, MT 59812-0002. Offers geography (MA), including cartography and GIS, community and environmental planning. *Entrance requirements:* For master's, GRE General Test. Additional exam requirements/recommendations for international students: Required—TOEFL.

University of Nebraska at Omaha, Graduate Studies and Research, College of Arts and Sciences, Department of Geography and Geology, Omaha, NE 68182. Offers geographic information science (Certificate); geography (MA). Part-time programs available. *Faculty:* 11 full-time (2 women). *Students:* 10 full-time (4 women), 10 part-time (3 women), 2 international. Average age 29. 11 applicants, 27% accepted, 3 enrolled. In 2007, 5 master's, 2 other advanced degrees awarded. *Degree requirements:* For master's, comprehensive exam, thesis (for some programs). *Entrance requirements:* For master's, GRE, minimum GPA of 3.0, 15 undergraduate geography hours, resumé. Additional exam requirements/recommendations for international students: Required—TOEFL (minimum score 550 paper-based; 213 computer-based; 80 iBT). *Application deadline:* For fall admission, 3/1 priority date for domestic students; for spring admission, 12/1 priority date for domestic students. Applications are processed on a rolling basis. Application fee: $45. Electronic applications accepted. *Financial support:* In 2007–08, 15 students received support; fellowships, research assistantships with tuition reimbursements available, teaching assistantships with tuition reimbursements available, Federal Work-Study, institutionally sponsored loans, scholarships/grants, tuition waivers (partial), and

Geography

University of Nebraska at Omaha (continued)
unspecified assistantships available. Support available to part-time students. Financial award application deadline: 3/1; financial award applicants required to submit FAFSA. *Unit head:* Dr. Jeffrey Peake, Chairperson, 402-554-2662.

University of Nebraska–Lincoln, Graduate College, College of Arts and Sciences, Department of Anthropology and Geography, Program in Geography, Lincoln, NE 68588. Offers MA, PhD. *Degree requirements:* For master's, thesis optional; for doctorate, comprehensive exam, thesis/dissertation. *Entrance requirements:* For master's and doctorate, GRE General Test. Additional exam requirements/recommendations for international students: Required—TOEFL (minimum score 550 paper-based; 213 computer-based). Electronic applications accepted. *Faculty research:* Climatology, historical-cultural geography, geographic information systems/ cartography/remote sensing, human geography, Great Plains studies.

University of Nevada, Reno, Graduate School, College of Science, Mackay School of Earth Sciences and Engineering, Department of Geography, Reno, NV 89557. Offers geography (PhD); land use planning (MS). *Faculty:* 13. *Students:* 12 full-time (4 women), 15 part-time (6 women); includes 2 minority (1 Asian American or Pacific Islander, 1 Hispanic American). Average age 33. 25 applicants, 60% accepted, 8 enrolled. In 2007, 16 degrees awarded. *Degree requirements:* For master's, thesis. *Entrance requirements:* For master's, GRE General Test, minimum GPA of 3.0; for doctorate, GRE. Additional exam requirements/recommendations for international students: Required—TOEFL. *Application deadline:* For fall admission, 2/1 priority date for domestic students. Applications are processed on a rolling basis. Application fee: $60 ($95 for international students). *Expenses:* Tuition, state resident: full-time $2,774; part-time $154 per credit. Tuition, nonresident: full-time $13,578; part-time $330 per credit. Required fees: $49 per semester. *Financial support:* In 2007–08, 6 teaching assistantships were awarded; research assistantships. Financial award application deadline: 3/1. *Faculty research:* Natural resources, education, climatology, biogeography, ethnic/cultural geography. *Unit head:* Dr. Gary Hausladen, Graduate Program Director, 775-784-6995.

University of New Mexico, Graduate School, College of Arts and Sciences, Department of Geography, Albuquerque, NM 87131-2039. Offers MS. Part-time programs available. *Faculty:* 5 full-time (1 woman), 4 part-time/adjunct (0 women). *Students:* 9 full-time (4 women), 9 part-time (1 woman); includes 3 minority (1 American Indian/Alaska Native, 2 Hispanic Americans). Average age 34. 11 applicants, 36% accepted, 4 enrolled. In 2007, 9 degrees awarded. *Degree requirements:* For master's, comprehensive exam (for some programs), thesis (for some programs). *Entrance requirements:* For master's, GRE. Additional exam requirements/ recommendations for international students: Required—TOEFL. *Application deadline:* For fall admission, 4/15 priority date for domestic students; for spring admission, 11/30 for domestic students. Application fee: $50. Electronic applications accepted. *Financial support:* In 2007–08, 3 students received support, including research assistantships with full tuition reimbursements available (averaging $13,500 per year), teaching assistantships with full tuition reimbursements available (averaging $13,500 per year); health care benefits and tuition waivers (full) also available. Financial award applicants required to submit FAFSA. *Faculty research:* Geographic information science, water resources, economic development, environmental management. Total annual research expenditures: $94,525. *Unit head:* Dr. Olen P. Matthews, Chair, 505-277-5007 Ext. 228, Fax: 505-277-3614, E-mail: opmatt@unm.edu. *Application contact:* Dr. Jazmin Knight, Department Administrator, 505-277-5041, Fax: 505-277-3614.

University of New Orleans, Graduate School, College of Liberal Arts, Department of Geography, New Orleans, LA 70148. Offers MA. *Students:* 8 (4 women). Average age 35. In 2007, 5 degrees awarded. *Entrance requirements:* For master's, GRE General Test. Additional exam requirements/recommendations for international students: Required—TOEFL (minimum score 550 paper-based; 213 computer-based; 79 iBT). *Application deadline:* For fall admission, 7/1 priority date for domestic students, 6/1 for international students; for spring admission, 11/15 priority date for domestic students, 10/1 for international students. Applications are processed on a rolling basis. Application fee: $40. Electronic applications accepted. *Financial support:* Application deadline: 3/15; *Unit head:* Dr. Peter Yaukey, Chairperson, 504-280-7133, Fax: 504-280-1123, E-mail: pyaukey@uno.edu. *Application contact:* Dr. James Lowry, Graduate Coordinator, 504-280-6329, Fax: 504-280-1123, E-mail: jlowry@uno.edu.

The University of North Carolina at Chapel Hill, Graduate School, College of Arts and Sciences, Department of Geography, Chapel Hill, NC 27599. Offers MA, PhD. *Degree requirements:* For master's, one foreign language, comprehensive exam, thesis; for doctorate, 2 foreign languages, comprehensive exam, thesis/dissertation. *Entrance requirements:* For master's and doctorate, GRE General Test, minimum GPA of 3.0. *Faculty research:* Geographic information systems, climatology, hydrology, population research, Latino immigration.

The University of North Carolina at Charlotte, Graduate School, College of Arts and Sciences, Department of Geography and Earth Sciences, Charlotte, NC 28223-0001. Offers earth sciences (MS), including climatology and hydrology, environmental systems analysis, solid earth sciences; geography (MA), including community planning, location analysis, transportation studies, urban regional analysis; geography and urban and regional analysis (PhD). Part-time and evening/weekend programs available. *Faculty:* 22 full-time (7 women), 1 part-time/adjunct (0 women). *Students:* 41 full-time (16 women), 47 part-time (19 women); includes 6 minority (4 African Americans, 1 Asian American or Pacific Islander, 1 Hispanic American), 8 international. Average age 30. 50 applicants, 80% accepted, 25 enrolled. In 2007, 18 degrees awarded. *Degree requirements:* For master's, comprehensive exam, project. *Entrance requirements:* For master's, GRE General Test or MAT, Doppelt Mathematical Reasoning Test, minimum GPA of 3.0 in undergraduate major, 2.75 overall. Additional exam requirements/ recommendations for international students: Required—TOEFL (minimum score 557 paper-based; 220 computer-based). *Application deadline:* For fall admission, 7/1 for domestic students, 5/1 for international students; for spring admission, 11/1 for domestic students, 10/1 for international students. Applications are processed on a rolling basis. Application fee: $55. Electronic applications accepted. *Expenses:* Tuition, state resident: full-time $2,855. Tuition, nonresident: full-time $13,062. Required fees: $1,692. *Financial support:* In 2007–08, 13 research assistantships (averaging $12,323 per year), 14 teaching assistantships (averaging $6,552 per year) were awarded; fellowships, career-related internships or fieldwork, Federal Work-Study, institutionally sponsored loans, scholarships/grants, and unspecified assistantships also available. Support available to part-time students. Financial award application deadline: 4/1; financial award applicants required to submit FAFSA. *Faculty research:* Location analysis, applications of GIS technology, community planning and development, regional economic modeling, retail geography. *Unit head:* Dr. Gerald L. Ingalls, Chair, 704-687-2293, Fax: 704-687-3182, E-mail: gingalls@email.uncc.edu. *Application contact:* Kathy B. Giddings, Director of Graduate Admissions, 704-687-3366, Fax: 704-687-3279, E-mail: agidding@ uncc.edu.

The University of North Carolina at Greensboro, Graduate School, College of Arts and Sciences, Department of Geography, Greensboro, NC 27412-5001. Offers applied geography (MA); geographic information science (Certificate); geography (PhD); urban and economic development (Certificate). *Faculty:* 14 full-time (3 women). *Students:* 55 full-time (17 women), 6 part-time (2 women); includes 17 minority (11 African Americans, 6 Asian Americans or Pacific Islanders). 31 applicants, 52% accepted. *Degree requirements:* For master's, comprehensive exam, thesis or alternative. *Entrance requirements:* For master's, GRE General Test. Additional exam requirements/recommendations for international students: Required—TOEFL. *Application deadline:* For fall admission, 6/15 for domestic students; for spring admission, 3/15 for domestic students. Electronic applications accepted. *Financial support:* Research assistantships with full tuition reimbursements, teaching assistantships with full tuition reimbursements, career-related internships or fieldwork, Federal Work-Study, scholarships/grants, and traineeships available. Support available to part-time students. *Unit head:* Dr. Jeffrey C Patton, Head, 336-334-5388, Fax: 336-334-5864, E-mail: jcpatton@uncg.edu. *Application contact:* Michelle Harkleroad, Director of Graduate Admissions, 336-334-4884, Fax: 336-334-4424, E-mail: mbharkle@uncg.edu.

University of North Dakota, Graduate School, College of Arts and Sciences, Department of Geography, Grand Forks, ND 58202. Offers MA, MS. Part-time programs available. *Faculty:* 7 full-time (2 women). *Students:* 8 full-time (4 women), 7 part-time (1 woman). 16 applicants, 56% accepted, 5 enrolled. In 2007, 6 degrees awarded. *Degree requirements:* For master's, comprehensive exam, thesis or alternative. *Entrance requirements:* For master's, minimum GPA of 3.0. Additional exam requirements/recommendations for international students: Required—TOEFL (minimum score 550 paper-based; 213 computer-based; 79 iBT), IELTS (minimum score 7). *Application deadline:* For fall admission, 2/15 priority date for domestic and international students; for spring admission, 10/15 priority date for domestic and international students. Applications are processed on a rolling basis. Application fee: $35. Electronic applications accepted. *Expenses:* Tuition, state resident: full-time $4,050; part-time $225 per credit. Tuition, nonresident: full-time $10,818; part-time $601 per credit. Required fees: $110 per semester. Tuition and fees vary according to class time, campus/location, program and reciprocity agreements. *Financial support:* In 2007–08, 3 research assistantships with full tuition reimbursements (averaging $10,728 per year), 4 teaching assistantships with full tuition reimbursements (averaging $10,413 per year) were awarded; fellowships with full and partial tuition reimbursements, Federal Work-Study, institutionally sponsored loans, scholarships/ grants, health care benefits, tuition waivers (full and partial), and unspecified assistantships also available. Support available to part-time students. Financial award application deadline: 3/15; financial award applicants required to submit FAFSA. *Faculty research:* Regional and urban development, environmental geography, geographic education, geographic techniques. *Unit head:* Dr. Douglas Munski, Graduate Director, 701-777-6195, Fax: 701-777-6195, E-mail: douglas_munski@und.nodak.edu. *Application contact:* Brenda Halle, Admissions Specialist, 701-777-2947, Fax: 701-777-3619, E-mail: brendahalle@mail.und.edu.

University of Northern Iowa, Graduate College, College of Social and Behavioral Sciences, Department of Geography, Cedar Falls, IA 50614. Offers MA. Part-time programs available. *Students:* 9 full-time (2 women), 4 part-time (3 women); includes 1 minority (African American), 3 international. 10 applicants, 70% accepted, 4 enrolled. In 2007, 2 degrees awarded. *Degree requirements:* For master's, thesis or alternative. *Entrance requirements:* For master's, minimum GPA of 3.0; 2 letters of recommendation; a brief statement about professional interests and career objectives. Additional exam requirements/recommendations for international students: Required—TOEFL (minimum score 500 paper-based; 180 computer-based; 61 iBT). *Application deadline:* For fall admission, 8/1 priority date for domestic students. Applications are processed on a rolling basis. Application fee: $30 ($50 for international students). Electronic applications accepted. *Expenses:* Tuition, state resident: full-time $6,246; part-time $694 per credit hour. Tuition, nonresident: full-time $14,554; part-time $694 per credit hour. Required fees: $838; $119 per semester. *Financial support:* Career-related internships or fieldwork, Federal Work-Study, scholarships/grants, and tuition waivers (full and partial) available. Support available to part-time students. Financial award application deadline: 2/1. *Unit head:* Dr. Patrick P. Pease, Interim Head, 319-273-2772, Fax: 319-273-7103, E-mail: patrick.pease@uni.edu.

University of North Texas, Robert B. Toulouse School of Graduate Studies, College of Arts and Sciences, Department of Geography, Denton, TX 76203. Offers MS. *Faculty:* 10 full-time (1 woman). *Students:* 19 full-time (6 women), 22 part-time (12 women); includes 7 minority (1 African American, 1 American Indian/Alaska Native, 1 Asian American or Pacific Islander, 4 Hispanic Americans), 8 international. Average age 32. 30 applicants, 70% accepted, 15 enrolled. In 2007, 10 degrees awarded. *Degree requirements:* For master's, comprehensive exam (for some programs), thesis (for some programs), 36 hours or more total. *Entrance requirements:* For master's, GRE General Test, GPA; BA/BS. Additional exam requirements/ recommendations for international students: Required—proof of English language proficiency required for non-native English speakers; Recommended—TOEFL (minimum score 550 paper-based; 213 computer-based). *Application deadline:* For fall admission, 7/15 for domestic students; for spring admission, 11/15 for domestic students. Application fee: $50 ($75 for international students). *Financial support:* In 2007–08, 1 student received support, including 1 fellowship (averaging $10,000 per year), 14 teaching assistantships (averaging $11,610 per year). *Faculty research:* Environmental monitoring and modeling; health and economic geography; environmental archaeology. Total annual research expenditures: $800,000. *Unit head:* Dr. Paul Hudak, Chair, 940-565-2091, Fax: 940-369-7550, E-mail: hudak@unt.edu. *Application contact:* Dr. Donald Lyons, Graduate Adviser/Coordinator, 940-565-2721, Fax: 940-369-7550, E-mail: dlyons@unt.edu.

University of Oklahoma, Graduate College, College of Atmospheric and Geographic Sciences, Department of Geography, Norman, OK 73019-0390. Offers MA, PhD. Part-time programs available. *Faculty:* 13 full-time (2 women), 2 part-time/adjunct (1 woman). *Students:* 31 full-time (12 women), 24 part-time (11 women); includes 5 minority (2 African Americans, 3 American Indian/Alaska Native), 16 international. 21 applicants, 81% accepted, 9 enrolled. In 2007, 7 master's, 3 doctorates awarded. *Degree requirements:* For master's, thesis, oral and written exams; for doctorate, one foreign language, thesis/dissertation, general exams. *Entrance requirements:* For master's, minimum GPA of 3.0, writing sample, 3 letters of recommendation. Additional exam requirements/recommendations for international students: Required—TOEFL (minimum score 550 paper-based; 213 computer-based). *Application deadline:* For fall admission, 2/1 for domestic students, 4/1 for international students; for spring admission, 12/1 for domestic students, 9/1 for international students. Applications are processed on a rolling basis. Application fee: $40 ($90 for international students). Electronic applications accepted. *Expenses:* Tuition, state resident: full-time $3,451; part-time $144 per credit hour. Tuition, nonresident: full-time $12,432; part-time $518 per credit hour. Required fees: $1,925; $70 per credit hour. $122 per semester. *Financial support:* In 2007–08, 17 students received support, including 6 fellowships with full tuition reimbursements available (averaging $5,000 per year), 1 research assistantship with partial tuition reimbursement available (averaging $32,000 per year), 19 teaching assistantships with partial tuition reimbursements available (averaging $12,926 per year); scholarships/grants and unspecified assistantships also available. Financial award application deadline: 2/1; financial award applicants required to submit FAFSA. *Faculty research:* Geographic information science, applied physical geography, cultural, political and economic geography. Total annual research expenditures: $574,446. *Unit head:* Fred Shelley, Chair, 405-325-5325, Fax: 405-325-6090, E-mail: fshelley@ou.edu. *Application contact:* Dr. Andrew Wood, Graduate Liaison, 405-325-2438, Fax: 405-325-6090, E-mail: gwood@ou.edu.

University of Oregon, Graduate School, College of Arts and Sciences, Department of Geography, Eugene, OR 97403. Offers MA, MS, PhD. *Faculty:* 12 full-time (5 women). *Students:* 27 full-time (18 women), 7 part-time (3 women); includes 3 minority (1 African American, 1 Asian American or Pacific Islander, 1 Hispanic American), 1 international. 72 applicants, 26% accepted. In 2007, 5 master's, 1 doctorate awarded. *Degree requirements:* For master's, one foreign language, thesis; for doctorate, one foreign language, thesis/ dissertation. *Entrance requirements:* For master's and doctorate, GRE General Test, minimum GPA of 3.0. Additional exam requirements/recommendations for international students: Required—TOEFL. *Application deadline:* For fall admission, 1/15 for domestic students. Application fee: $50. *Financial support:* In 2007–08, 30 teaching assistantships were awarded; career-related internships or fieldwork and Federal Work-Study also available. Financial award application deadline: 1/15. *Faculty research:* Place-name research, past climates, quaternary environments, plant diffusions, population redistributions. *Unit head:* Pat McDowell, Head, 541-346-4555. *Application contact:* Mary Milo, Admissions Contact, 541-346-4555, E-mail: uogeog@darkwing.uoregon.edu.

University of Ottawa, Faculty of Graduate and Postdoctoral Studies, Faculty of Arts, Department of Geography, Ottawa, ON K1N 6N5, Canada. Offers M Geog, M Sc, MA, PhD. *Degree requirements:* For master's, one foreign language, thesis; for doctorate, one foreign language, comprehensive exam, thesis/dissertation. *Entrance requirements:* For master's, honors degree or equivalent, minimum B average; for doctorate, master's degree, minimum B+ average.

Electronic applications accepted. *Faculty research:* The physical geography of cold environment; space, place and society, environmental change.

University of Prince Edward Island, Faculty of Arts, Charlottetown, PE C1A 4P3, Canada. Offers island studies (MA). Part-time programs available. *Degree requirements:* For master's, thesis. *Entrance requirements:* Additional exam requirements/recommendations for international students: Required—TOEFL (minimum score 550 paper-based; 213 computer-based; 80 iBT), Canadian Academic English Language Assessment, Michigan English Language Assessment Battery, Canadian Test of English for Scholars and Trainees. *Faculty research:* International island studies.

University of Regina, Faculty of Graduate Studies and Research, Faculty of Arts, Department of Geography, Regina, SK S4S 0A2, Canada. Offers M Sc, MA, PhD. *Faculty:* 12 full-time (3 women), 2 part-time/adjunct (both women). *Students:* 6 full-time (4 women), 4 part-time (2 women). 10 applicants, 50% accepted, 4 enrolled. In 2007, 1 degree awarded. *Degree requirements:* For master's, thesis. *Entrance requirements:* Additional exam requirements/recommendations for international students: Required—TOEFL (minimum score 580 paper-based; 237 computer-based; 88 iBT). *Application deadline:* Applications are processed on a rolling basis. Application fee: $85 ($100 for international students). Electronic applications accepted. *Financial support:* In 2007–08, 1 fellowship (averaging $15,750 per year), 1 research assistantship (averaging $13,875 per year), 1 teaching assistantship (averaging $13,060 per year) were awarded; scholarships/grants also available. Financial award application deadline: 6/15. *Faculty research:* Cultural, historical, economic, rural, and urban geography; cartography; resource management; hydrology. *Unit head:* Dr. Ben Cecil, Graduate Program Coordinator, 306-585-4034, E-mail: ben.cecil@uregina.ca. *Application contact:* Dr. Joe Piwowar, Graduate Program Coordinator, 306-585-5273, E-mail: joe.piwowar@uregina.ca.

University of Saskatchewan, College of Graduate Studies and Research, College of Arts and Sciences, Department of Geography, Saskatoon, SK S7N 5A2, Canada. Offers M Sc, MA, PhD. *Degree requirements:* For master's, thesis; for doctorate, thesis/dissertation. *Entrance requirements:* Additional exam requirements/recommendations for international students: Required—TOEFL.

University of South Africa, College of Agriculture and Environmental Sciences, Pretoria, South Africa. Offers agriculture (MS); consumer science (MCS); environmental management (MA, MS, PhD); environmental science (MA, MS, PhD); geography (MA, MS, PhD); horticulture (M Tech); human ecology (MHE); life sciences (MS); nature conservation (M Tech).

University of South Carolina, The Graduate School, College of Arts and Sciences, Department of Geography, Columbia, SC 29208. Offers geography (MA, MS, PhD); geography education (IMA). IMA and MAT offered in cooperation with the College of Education. Part-time programs available. *Faculty:* 20 full-time (4 women), 2 part-time/adjunct (0 women). *Students:* 36 full-time (17 women), 22 part-time (13 women); includes 2 minority (1 African American, 1 Hispanic American), 10 international. Average age 31. 84 applicants, 52% accepted, 21 enrolled. In 2007, 6 master's, 3 doctorates awarded. *Degree requirements:* For master's, comprehensive exam, thesis (for some programs); for doctorate, comprehensive exam, thesis/dissertation. *Entrance requirements:* For master's, GRE General Test; for doctorate, GRE General Test, master's degree. *Application deadline:* For fall admission, 2/15 priority date for domestic students; for spring admission, 11/1 priority date for domestic students. Applications are processed on a rolling basis. Application fee: $35. Electronic applications accepted. *Expenses:* Tuition, state resident: part-time $440 per hour. Tuition, nonresident: part-time $936 per hour. Required fees: $17 per hour. Tuition and fees vary according to program. *Financial support:* In 2007–08, 42 students received support, including 3 fellowships (averaging $9,000 per year), 25 research assistantships (averaging $9,500 per year), 13 teaching assistantships (averaging $9,500 per year); career-related internships or fieldwork, Federal Work-Study, scholarships/grants, traineeships, tuition waivers (full), and unspecified assistantships also available. Financial award application deadline: 2/15. *Faculty research:* Geographic information processing; economic, cultural, physical, and environmental geography. Total annual research expenditures: $917,949. *Unit head:* Dr. David J. Cowen, Chair, 803-777-5234, Fax: 803-777-4972, E-mail: cowend@gwm.sc.edu. *Application contact:* Dr. John F. Jakubs, Director of Graduate Studies, 803-777-6604, Fax: 803-777-4972, E-mail: jjakubs@sc.edu.

University of Southern California, Graduate School, College of Letters, Arts and Sciences, Department of Geography, Los Angeles, CA 90089. Offers geographic information science and technology (Graduate Certificate); geography (MA, MS, PhD). Part-time and evening/weekend programs available. Postbaccalaureate distance learning degree programs offered (no on-campus study). *Faculty:* 8 full-time (3 women), 4 part-time/adjunct (1 woman). *Students:* 25 full-time (16 women), 5 part-time (1 woman); includes 6 minority (1 African American, 1 American Indian/Alaska Native, 2 Asian Americans or Pacific Islanders, 2 Hispanic Americans), 8 international. 31 applicants, 42% accepted. In 2007, 4 doctorates, 5 other advanced degrees awarded. Terminal master's awarded for partial completion of doctoral program. *Degree requirements:* For master's, thesis; for doctorate, thesis/dissertation. *Entrance requirements:* For master's and doctorate, GRE General Test. *Application deadline:* For fall admission, 12/1 priority date for domestic students. Applications are processed on a rolling basis. Application fee: $85. *Financial support:* In 2007–08, 2 students received support, including fellowships with full tuition reimbursements available (averaging $18,570 per year), research assistantships with full tuition reimbursements available (averaging $18,570 per year), teaching assistantships with full tuition reimbursements available (averaging $18,570 per year); scholarships/grants, traineeships, and tuition waivers (full) also available. Financial award application deadline: 2/15; financial award applicants required to submit FAFSA. *Faculty research:* Landscape dynamics, geomorphology, geographic information science, urban geography and nature-society relations, GIS. *Unit head:* Dr. John Wilson, Chair, 213-740-2311, E-mail: uscgeog@usc.edu. *Application contact:* Kate Kelsey, Information Contact, 213-740-2311.

University of Southern Mississippi, Graduate School, College of Science and Technology, Department of Geography and Geology, Hattiesburg, MS 39406-0001. Offers geography (MS, PhD); geology (MS). Part-time programs available. *Faculty:* 10 full-time (1 woman). *Students:* 12 full-time (2 women), 15 part-time (5 women); includes 2 minority (both African Americans) Average age 29. 12 applicants, 67% accepted, 6 enrolled. In 2007, 2 master's awarded. *Degree requirements:* For master's, comprehensive exam, thesis (for some programs), internships; for doctorate, comprehensive exam, thesis/dissertation. *Entrance requirements:* For master's, GMAT, GRE General Test, minimum GPA of 3.0. Additional exam requirements/recommendations for international students: Required—TOEFL. *Application deadline:* For fall admission, 3/15 for domestic and international students; for spring admission, 1/3 for domestic students. Applications are processed on a rolling basis. Application fee: $30. Electronic applications accepted. *Financial support:* In 2007–08, 1 research assistantship (averaging $7,767 per year), 9 teaching assistantships with full tuition reimbursements (averaging $7,767 per year) were awarded; fellowships with full tuition reimbursements, career-related internships or fieldwork, Federal Work-Study, and institutionally sponsored loans also available. Financial award application deadline: 3/15. *Faculty research:* City and regional planning, geographic techniques, physical geography, human geography. *Unit head:* Dr. Clifton Dixon, Chair, 601-266-4729, Fax: 601-266-6219, E-mail: c.dixon@usm.edu. *Application contact:* Dr. Gail Russell, Graduate Coordinator, 601-266-6519, Fax: 601-266-6219.

University of South Florida, Graduate School, College of Arts and Sciences, Department of Geography, Tampa, FL 33620-9951. Offers MA. Part-time and evening/weekend programs available. *Faculty:* 14 full-time (5 women), 1 part-time/adjunct (0 women). *Students:* 14 full-time (8 women), 16 part-time (7 women); includes 4 minority (all Hispanic Americans), 2 international. 18 applicants, 61% accepted, 4 enrolled. In 2007, 7 degrees awarded. *Degree requirements:* For master's, thesis. *Entrance requirements:* For master's, GRE General Test, minimum GPA of 3.0 in last 60 hours of course work. Additional exam requirements/recommendations for international students: Required—TOEFL (minimum score 550 paper-based; 213 computer-based). *Application deadline:* For fall admission, 3/1 for domestic and international students; for spring admission, 10/1 for domestic and international students. Application fee: $30. *Financial support:* Unspecified assistantships available. Financial award application deadline: 3/1. *Faculty research:* Natural hazards, geographic information systems models, soil contamination, urban geography and social theory. Total annual research expenditures:$56,218. *Unit head:* Dr. Kevin W. Archer, Associate Professor/Chair, 813-974-4843, Fax: 813-974-4808, E-mail: karcher@cas.usf.edu. *Application contact:* Dr. Philip Reeder, Graduate Program Director, 813-974-3292, Fax: 813-974-4808, E-mail: preeder@cas.usf.edu.

The University of Tennessee, Graduate School, College of Arts and Sciences, Department of Geography, Knoxville, TN 37996. Offers MS, PhD. *Degree requirements:* For master's, thesis or alternative; for doctorate, thesis/dissertation. *Entrance requirements:* For master's and doctorate, GRE General Test, minimum GPA of 2.7. Additional exam requirements/recommendations for international students: Required—TOEFL. Electronic applications accepted.

The University of Texas at Austin, Graduate School, College of Liberal Arts, Department of Geography, Austin, TX 78712-1111. Offers MA, PhD, MSCRP/PhD. *Degree requirements:* For master's, thesis or alternative; for doctorate, thesis/dissertation. *Entrance requirements:* For master's and doctorate, GRE General Test. Additional exam requirements/recommendations for international students: Required—TOEFL. Electronic applications accepted. *Faculty research:* Cultural and historical geography, environmental and physical geography, human-environment interactions, electronic technology and hypermedia, international area studies.

The University of Toledo, College of Graduate Studies, College of Arts and Sciences, Department of Geography and Planning, Toledo, OH 43606-3390. Offers geographic information systems and applied geographics (Certificate); geography (MA); planning (MA). Part-time programs available. *Faculty:* 10. *Students:* 20 full-time (6 women), 12 part-time (4 women); includes 2 minority (both African Americans), 5 international. Average age 31. 27 applicants, 67% accepted, 9 enrolled. In 2007, 8 master's, 3 other advanced degrees awarded. *Degree requirements:* For master's, thesis. *Entrance requirements:* For master's, GRE General Test. *Application deadline:* For fall admission, 3/15 priority date for domestic students. Applications are processed on a rolling basis. Application fee: $45. Electronic applications accepted. *Financial support:* In 2007–08, 4 research assistantships with full tuition reimbursements (averaging $10,500 per year), 9 teaching assistantships with full tuition reimbursements (averaging $10,500 per year) were awarded; career-related internships or fieldwork, institutionally sponsored loans, scholarships/grants, tuition waivers (full), and unspecified assistantships also available. Support available to part-time students. Financial award application deadline: 4/1. *Unit head:* Dr. Peter Lindquist, Chair, 419-530-4287, Fax: 419-530-7919, E-mail: peter.lindquist@utoledo.edu.

See Close-Up on page 1093.

University of Toronto, School of Graduate Studies, Social Sciences Division, Department of Geography, Toronto, ON M5S 1A1, Canada. Offers geography (M Sc, MA, PhD); planning (M Sc Pl); urban design studies (MUD). Part-time programs available. *Faculty:* 45 full-time, 19 part-time/adjunct. *Students:* 180 full-time (102 women), 13 part-time, 28 international. 201 applicants, 45% accepted. In 2007, 15 master's, 1 doctorate awarded. *Degree requirements:* For master's, thesis optional; for doctorate, thesis/dissertation. *Entrance requirements:* For master's, bachelor's degree or equivalent in geography or a closely related field, minimum B+ average in each of 2 final years of degree, 3 letters of reference; for doctorate, master of geography degree, minimum A–average. *Application deadline:* For fall admission, 2/2 priority date for domestic students. Application fee: $100 Canadian dollars. *Unit head:* Prof. Amrita Daniere, Graduate Chair, 416-978-3377, Fax: 416-946-3886, E-mail: daniere@geog.utoronto.ca. *Application contact:* Marianne Ishibashi, Graduate Counselor, 416-978-3377, Fax: 416-978-3886, E-mail: ishi@geog.utoronto.ca.

University of Utah, The Graduate School, College of Social and Behavioral Science, Department of Geography, Salt Lake City, UT 84112-1107. Offers MA, MS, PhD. Part-time programs available. *Faculty:* 12 full-time (4 women), 1 (woman) part-time/adjunct. *Students:* 25 full-time (14 women), 26 part-time (8 women); includes 4 minority (1 American Indian/Alaska Native, 1 Asian American or Pacific Islander, 2 Hispanic Americans), 11 international. Average age 34. 45 applicants, 53% accepted, 13 enrolled. In 2007, 1 master's, 5 doctorates awarded. *Median time to degree:* Of those who began their doctoral program in fall 1999, 17% received their degree in 8 years or less. *Degree requirements:* For master's, variable foreign language requirement, thesis or alternative, 6 research hours; for doctorate, comprehensive exam, thesis/dissertation, 14 research hours. *Entrance requirements:* For master's and doctorate, GRE General Test, minimum undergraduate GPA of 3.0. Additional exam requirements/recommendations for international students: Required—TOEFL (minimum score 500 paper-based; 173 computer-based; 61 iBT). *Application deadline:* For fall admission, 4/1 for domestic students, 1/20 for international students. Application fee: $45 ($65 for international students). Electronic applications accepted. *Financial support:* In 2007–08, 1 fellowship with full tuition reimbursement (averaging $24,000 per year), 4 research assistantships with full tuition reimbursements (averaging $10,000 per year), 10 teaching assistantships with full tuition reimbursements (averaging $10,000 per year) were awarded; career-related internships or fieldwork, Federal Work-Study, and health care benefits also available. Financial award application deadline: 2/15; financial award applicants required to submit FAFSA. *Faculty research:* Urban geography, earth system science, geographic information systems, remote sensing, hazards. Total annual research expenditures: $118,119. *Unit head:* Dr. Harvey J. Miller, Chair, 801-581-8218, Fax: 801-581-8219, E-mail: harvey.miller@geog.utah.edu. *Application contact:* Thomas M Kontuly, Director of Graduate Studies, 801-581-8218, Fax: 801-581-8219, E-mail: kontuly@geog.utah.edu.

University of Victoria, Faculty of Graduate Studies, Faculty of Social Sciences, Department of Geography, Victoria, BC V8W 2Y2, Canada. Offers M Sc, MA, PhD. Part-time programs available. *Faculty:* 19 full-time (3 women), 23 part-time/adjunct (8 women). *Students:* Average age 27. 53 applicants, 34% accepted, 16 enrolled. In 2007, 8 master's, 2 doctorates awarded. *Degree requirements:* For master's, thesis; for doctorate, comprehensive exam, thesis/dissertation, candidacy exam. *Entrance requirements:* For master's, minimum B+ average in undergraduate course work; for doctorate, master's degree. Additional exam requirements/recommendations for international students: Required—TOEFL (minimum score 575 paper-based; 233 computer-based), IELTS (minimum score 7). *Application deadline:* For fall admission, 2/15 for domestic students, 12/15 for international students. Applications are processed on a rolling basis. Application fee: $75 ($125 for international students). Electronic applications accepted. *Expenses:* Tuition, state resident: full-time $3,110. International tuition: $3,700 full-time. Tuition and fees vary according to program. *Financial support:* In 2007–08, 2 fellowships, 31 teaching assistantships were awarded; research assistantships, career-related internships or fieldwork and institutionally sponsored loans also available. Financial award application deadline: 1/31. *Faculty research:* Resources and protected areas, remote sensing and forestry, geographic information systems and cartography, urban regional planning, physical climatology. *Unit head:* Dr. Dan J. Smith, Chair, 250-721-7328, Fax: 250-721-6216, E-mail: chair@mail.geog.uvic.ca. *Application contact:* Dr. Dave Duffus, Graduate Adviser, 250-721-7344, Fax: 250-721-6216, E-mail: geograd@office.geog.uvic.ca.

University of Washington, Graduate School, College of Arts and Sciences, Department of Geography, Seattle, WA 98195. Offers MA, PhD. *Degree requirements:* For master's, thesis; for doctorate, thesis/dissertation. *Entrance requirements:* For master's and doctorate, GRE General Test. Additional exam requirements/recommendations for international students: Required—TOEFL. Electronic applications accepted. *Faculty research:* Globalization and social theory, nature and society, regional economic development, urban patterns and processes, geographic information systems.

University of Waterloo, Graduate Studies, Faculty of Environmental Studies, Department of Geography, Waterloo, ON N2L 3G1, Canada. Offers MA, PhD. *Degree requirements:* For master's, thesis optional; for doctorate, one foreign language, comprehensive exam, thesis/dissertation. *Entrance requirements:* For master's, honors degree, minimum B average; for

Geography

University of Waterloo (continued)
doctorate, master's degree, minimum A- average. Additional exam requirements/recommendations for international students: Required—TOEFL, TWE. Electronic applications accepted. *Faculty research:* Urban economic geography; physical geography; resource management; cultural, regional, historical geography; spatial data.

The University of Western Ontario, Faculty of Graduate Studies, Social Sciences Division, Department of Geography, London, ON N6A 5B8, Canada. Offers M Sc, MA, PhD. *Degree requirements:* For master's, thesis; for doctorate, thesis/dissertation. *Entrance requirements:* For master's, honors degree, minimum B average, GRE exam; for doctorate, honors degree, minimum B average. Additional exam requirements/recommendations for international students: Required—TOEFL. *Application deadline:* For fall admission, 7/4 for domestic and international students. Application fee: $50. *Financial support:* Fellowships, career-related internships or fieldwork available. Financial award application deadline: 4/1. *Unit head:* Dr. Dan Shrubsole, Chair, 519-661-5031 Ext. 83126, E-mail: deshrubs@uwo.ca. *Application contact:* Susan Underhill, Graduate Assistant, 519-661-2111 Ext. 85033, E-mail: geogradadmin@uwo.ca.

University of Wisconsin–Madison, Graduate School, College of Letters and Science, Department of Geography, Madison, WI 53706-1380. Offers cartography and geographic information systems (MS); geographic information systems (Certificate); geography (MS, PhD). Part-time programs available. *Degree requirements:* For master's, thesis; for doctorate, thesis/dissertation; for Certificate, internship. *Entrance requirements:* For master's and doctorate, GRE General Test, minimum GPA of 3.25. Electronic applications accepted. *Faculty research:* Physical geography, urban/historical geography, people-environment, history of cartography, GIS.

University of Wisconsin–Milwaukee, Graduate School, College of Letters and Sciences, Department of Geography, Milwaukee, WI 53201-0413. Offers MA, MS, PhD, MLIS/MA. *Faculty:* 11 full-time (4 women). *Students:* 21 full-time (10 women), 12 part-time (4 women); includes 3 minority (2 Asian Americans or Pacific Islanders, 1 Hispanic American), 12 international. 39 applicants, 56% accepted, 10 enrolled. In 2007, 9 master's, 2 doctorates awarded. *Degree requirements:* For master's, thesis. *Application deadline:* For fall admission, 1/1 priority date for domestic students; for spring admission, 9/1 for domestic students. Applications are processed on a rolling basis. Application fee: $45 ($75 for international students). *Expenses:* Tuition, state resident: part-time $530 per credit. Tuition, nonresident: part-time $1,428 per credit. Required fees: $19 per credit. $229 per term. Tuition and fees vary according to course load and program. *Financial support:* In 2007–08, 1 research assistantship, 23 teaching assistantships were awarded; fellowships, career-related internships or fieldwork and unspecified assistantships also available. Support available to part-time students. Financial award application deadline: 4/15. *Unit head:* Rina Ghose, Representative, 414-229-4797, Fax: 414-229-3981, E-mail: rghose@uwm.edu.

University of Wyoming, Graduate School, College of Arts and Sciences, Department of Geography, Laramie, WY 82070. Offers geography (MA, MP, MST); geography/water resources (MA); rural planning and natural resources (MP), including community and regional planning and natural resources. Postbaccalaureate distance learning degree programs offered (minimal on-campus study). *Faculty:* 9 full-time (2 women). *Students:* 10 full-time (5 women), 12 part-time (3 women); includes 1 minority (American Indian/Alaska Native), 1 international. Average age 36. 14 applicants, 86% accepted, 8 enrolled. In 2007, 7 master's awarded. *Degree requirements:* For master's, thesis or alternative. *Entrance requirements:* For master's, GRE General Test, minimum GPA of 3.0. Additional exam requirements/recommendations for international students: Required—TOEFL. *Application deadline:* For fall admission, 2/15 for domestic students. Applications are processed on a rolling basis. Application fee: $50. Electronic applications accepted. *Financial support:* In 2007–08, 3 research assistantships with full and partial tuition reimbursements (averaging $10,696 per year), 6 teaching assistantships with full and partial tuition reimbursements (averaging $10,696 per year) were awarded; career-related internships or fieldwork, Federal Work-Study, scholarships/grants, health care benefits, and unspecified assistantships also available. Financial award application deadline: 3/1; financial award applicants required to submit FAFSA. *Faculty research:* Landscape ecology, landscape change, public land management, rural and small town planning, GIS. Total annual research expenditures: $112,940. *Unit head:* Dr. Gerald R. Webster, Chair, 307-766-3311, Fax: 307-766-3294, E-mail: geography-info@uwyo.edu. *Application contact:* Barbara Powell, Office Associate Senior, 307-766-3311, Fax: 307-766-3294, E-mail: geography-info@uwyo.edu.

Utah State University, School of Graduate Studies, College of Natural Resources, Department of Environment and Society, Logan, UT 84322. Offers bioregional planning (MS); geography (MA, MS); human dimensions of ecosystem science and management (MS, PhD); recreation resource management (MS, PhD). *Degree requirements:* For master's, comprehensive exam, thesis (for some programs). *Entrance requirements:* For master's and doctorate, GRE General Test, minimum GPA of 3.0. Additional exam requirements/recommendations for international students: Required—TOEFL. Electronic applications accepted. *Faculty research:* Geographic information systems/geographic and environmental education, bioregional planning, natural resource and environmental policy, outdoor recreation and tourism, natural resource and environmental management.

Virginia Polytechnic Institute and State University, Graduate School, College of Natural Resources, Department of Geography, Blacksburg, VA 24061. Offers MS, PhD. *Entrance requirements:* For master's, GRE. Additional exam requirements/recommendations for international students: Required—TOEFL (minimum score 550 paper-based; 213 computer-based). Electronic applications accepted. *Faculty research:* Third World development, geographical information systems, remote sensing, critical geopolitics, medical geography.

Wayne State University, College of Liberal Arts and Sciences, Department of Geography and Urban Planning, Detroit, MI 48202. Offers geography (MA); urban planning (MUP). Evening/weekend programs available. *Faculty:* 8 full-time (0 women). *Students:* 16 full-time (11 women), 55 part-time (28 women); includes 27 minority (25 African Americans, 1 Asian American or Pacific Islander, 1 Hispanic American), 5 international. Average age 30. 44 applicants, 59% accepted, 21 enrolled. In 2007, 8 degrees awarded. *Entrance requirements:* For master's, minimum 3.0 GPA; statement of interest; two letters of recommendations. Additional exam requirements/recommendations for international students: Required—TOEFL (minimum score 550 paper-based; 213 computer-based); Recommended—TWE (minimum score 6). *Application deadline:* For fall admission, 7/1 for domestic students, 6/1 for international students; for winter admission, 10/1 for international students; for spring admission, 2/1 for international students. Applications are processed on a rolling basis. Application fee: $30 ($50 for international students). Electronic applications accepted. *Expenses:* Tuition, state resident: part-time $403 per credit hour. Tuition, nonresident: part-time $890 per credit hour. *Financial support:* Teaching assistantships available. *Faculty research:* Housing and community development, urban and regional economic development, urban development and land use, transportation policy and planning, environmental policy and planning. Total annual research expenditures: $7,362. *Unit head:* Robin Boyle, Chair, 313-577-0543, Fax: 313-577-0022, E-mail: aa2815@wayne.edu.

Wayne State University, College of Liberal Arts and Sciences, Program in Geography, Detroit, MI 48202. Offers MA. *Entrance requirements:* For master's, GRE General Test. Additional exam requirements/recommendations for international students: Required—TOEFL (minimum score 550 paper-based; 213 computer-based); Recommended—TWE (minimum score 6). *Application deadline:* For fall admission, 7/1 for domestic students, 6/1 for international students; for winter admission, 10/1 for international students; for spring admission, 2/1 for international students. Applications are processed on a rolling basis. Application fee: $30 ($50 for international students). Electronic applications accepted. *Expenses:* Tuition, state resident: part-time $403 per credit hour. Tuition, nonresident: part-time $890 per credit hour. *Application contact:* Janet Hankin, Professor, 313-577-0841, E-mail: janet.hankin@wayne.edu.

West Chester University of Pennsylvania, Office of Graduate Studies and Extended Education, College of Business and Public Affairs, Department of Geography and Planning, West Chester, PA 19383. Offers geographic technology (Certificate); geography (MA); regional planning (MSA). Part-time and evening/weekend programs available. *Students:* 15 full-time (5 women), 12 part-time (2 women); includes 5 minority (4 African Americans, 1 Hispanic American). Average age 28. 19 applicants, 84% accepted, 11 enrolled. In 2007, 6 degrees awarded. *Degree requirements:* For master's, comprehensive exam, thesis optional. *Entrance requirements:* For master's, GRE General Test, interview, minimum GPA of 3.0, resumé. Additional exam requirements/recommendations for international students: Required—TOEFL (minimum score 550 paper-based; 213 computer-based; 80 iBT). *Application deadline:* For fall admission, 4/15 priority date for domestic students; for spring admission, 10/15 for domestic students. Applications are processed on a rolling basis. Application fee: $35. *Expenses:* Tuition, state resident: part-time $345 per credit. Tuition, nonresident: part-time $552 per credit. Tuition and fees vary according to course load. *Financial support:* In 2007–08, 3 research assistantships with full and partial tuition reimbursements (averaging $5,000 per year) were awarded; unspecified assistantships also available. Support available to part-time students. Financial award application deadline: 2/15; financial award applicants required to submit FAFSA. *Faculty research:* Environmental education, land use/suburban planning, landscapes of Catalunya. *Unit head:* Dr. Joan Welch, Chair and Graduate Coordinator, 610-436-2343, E-mail: jwelch@wcupa.edu.

Western Illinois University, School of Graduate Studies, College of Arts and Sciences, Department of Geography, Macomb, IL 61455-1390. Offers community development (Certificate); geography (MA). Part-time programs available. *Students:* 15 full-time (2 women), 4 part-time (1 woman); includes 3 minority (all Asian Americans or Pacific Islanders), 5 international. Average age 30. 14 applicants, 79% accepted. In 2007, 4 master's awarded. *Degree requirements:* For master's, thesis or alternative. *Entrance requirements:* Additional exam requirements/recommendations for international students: Required—TOEFL (minimum score 550 paper-based; 213 computer-based; 80 iBT). *Application deadline:* Applications are processed on a rolling basis. Application fee: $30. Electronic applications accepted. *Expenses:* Tuition, state resident: part-time $217 per credit hour. Tuition, nonresident: part-time $433 per credit hour. Required fees: $54 per credit hour. *Financial support:* In 2007–08, 14 students received support, including 14 research assistantships with full tuition reimbursements available (averaging $6,800 per year). Financial award applicants required to submit FAFSA. *Unit head:* Dr. Sam Thompson, Interim Chairperson, 309-298-1648. *Application contact:* Dr. Barbara Baily, Director of Graduate Studies/Associate Provost, 309-298-1806, Fax: 309-298-2345, E-mail: grad-office@wiu.edu.

Western Kentucky University, Graduate Studies, Ogden College of Science and Engineering, Department of Geography and Geology, Bowling Green, KY 42101. Offers MAE, MS. *Degree requirements:* For master's, comprehensive exam, thesis or alternative. *Entrance requirements:* For master's, GRE General Test, minimum GPA of 2.75. Additional exam requirements/recommendations for international students: Required—TOEFL (minimum score 555 paper-based; 213 computer-based; 79 iBT). *Faculty research:* Hydroclimatology, electronic data sets, groundwater, sinkhole liquification potential, meteorological analysis.

Western Michigan University, Graduate College, College of Arts and Sciences, Department of Geography, Kalamazoo, MI 49008-5202. Offers MA. *Degree requirements:* For master's, thesis, internship.

Western Washington University, Graduate School, Huxley College of the Environment, Department of Environmental Studies, Program in Geography, Bellingham, WA 98225-5996. Offers MS. *Faculty:* 16. *Students:* 13 full-time (6 women), 1 part-time, 1 international. 28 applicants, 61% accepted, 9 enrolled. In 2007, 4 degrees awarded. *Entrance requirements:* Additional exam requirements/recommendations for international students: Required—TOEFL (minimum score 567 paper-based; 227 computer-based). Application fee: $50. Electronic applications accepted. *Expenses:* Tuition, state resident: part-time $208 per credit. Tuition, nonresident: part-time $541 per credit. Required fees: $241 per quarter. One-time fee: $250 part-time. *Financial support:* In 2007–08, 3 teaching assistantships with partial tuition reimbursements (averaging $9,339 per year) were awarded; Federal Work-Study, institutionally sponsored loans, scholarships/grants, tuition waivers (partial), and unspecified assistantships also available. Support available to part-time students. *Unit head:* Dr. Michael Medler, Graduate Program Adviser, 360-650-3284.

West Virginia University, Eberly College of Arts and Sciences, Department of Geology and Geography, Program in Geography, Morgantown, WV 26506. Offers energy and environmental resources (MA); geographic information systems (PhD); geography-regional development (PhD); GIS/cartographic analysis (MA); regional development (MA). Part-time programs available. *Students:* 20 full-time (10 women), 7 part-time (4 women); includes 1 minority (American Indian/Alaska Native), 4 international. Average age 32. 18 applicants, 56% accepted, 7 enrolled. In 2007, 9 master's, 7 doctorates awarded. *Degree requirements:* For master's, thesis, oral and written exams; for doctorate, comprehensive exam, thesis/dissertation, oral and written exams. *Entrance requirements:* For master's and doctorate, GRE General Test, minimum GPA of 3.0. Additional exam requirements/recommendations for international students: Required—TOEFL. *Application deadline:* For fall admission, 1/1 priority date for domestic students, 11/14 priority date for international students; for spring admission, 5/1 priority date for domestic students, 7/1 priority date for international students. Applications are processed on a rolling basis. Application fee: $45. Electronic applications accepted. *Expenses:* Tuition, state resident: full-time $5,196; part-time $292 per credit hour. Tuition, nonresident: full-time $15,064; part-time $840 per credit hour. Tuition and fees vary according to program. *Financial support:* In 2007–08, 26 students received support, including 1 research assistantship with full tuition reimbursement available (averaging $15,000 per year), 6 teaching assistantships with full tuition reimbursements available (averaging $11,000 per year); career-related internships or fieldwork, Federal Work-Study, institutionally sponsored loans, health care benefits, and tuition waivers (partial) also available. Financial award application deadline: 2/1; financial award applicants required to submit FAFSA. *Faculty research:* Space, place and development, geographic information science, environmental geography. *Application contact:* Dr. Amy Hessl, Associate Professor, 304-293-8210, Fax: 304-293-6522, E-mail: geography-grad-info@mail.wvu.edu.

Wilfrid Laurier University, Faculty of Graduate Studies, Faculty of Arts, Department of Geography and Environmental Studies, Waterloo, ON N2L 3C5, Canada. Offers M Sc, MA, MES, PhD. *Faculty:* 20 full-time, 2 part-time/adjunct. *Students:* 45 full-time, 8 part-time. 119 applicants, 24% accepted, 17 enrolled. In 2007, 10 degrees awarded. *Degree requirements:* For master's, thesis optional; for doctorate, thesis/dissertation. *Entrance requirements:* For master's, honors BA in geography, minimum B average in undergraduate course work; honors BSc with minimum B+ or honors BES or BA in physical geography, environmental or earth sciences or the equivalent; for doctorate, MA in geography, minimum A-average. Additional exam requirements/recommendations for international students: Required—TOEFL (minimum score 230 computer-based; 89 iBT). *Application deadline:* For fall admission, 2/1 priority date for domestic students. Application fee: $75. Electronic applications accepted. *Financial support:* Fellowships, research assistantships, teaching assistantships available. *Faculty research:* Resources management, urban/economic/physical/cultural/earth surfaces/geomatics/historical/regional, spatial data handling. *Unit head:* Dr. Mary-Louise Byrne, Chairperson, 519-884-0710 Ext. 2993, E-mail: wlgpig@wlu.ca.

York University, Faculty of Graduate Studies, Faculty of Arts and Faculty of Science and Engineering, Program in Geography, Toronto, ON M3J 1P3, Canada. Offers M Sc, MA, PhD. Part-time programs available. *Degree requirements:* For master's, thesis or alternative; for doctorate, comprehensive exam, thesis/dissertation. Electronic applications accepted.

UNIVERSITY OF TOLEDO

Department of Geography and Planning

Program of Study

The mission of the Department is to provide a high-quality multifunctional program that supplies service at the general education and baccalaureate levels to the University community, provides high-quality programs, fosters theoretical and applied research in geography and planning, promotes multicultural understanding, complements interdisciplinary work, and engages in community outreach programs.

The master's degree requires completion of 30 credits, including 15 in faculty seminars and the rest in urban and regional planning, geographic techniques and applications, and urban-economic, environmental, or cultural-behavioral tracks. At least one course, but no more than three, may be taken outside the Department. At least 2 hours of thesis credit are required, but many as 6 can be counted within the 30-hour requirement.

The comprehensive examination is scheduled at the end of the first year of study. To qualify, a student must have a 3.0 grade point average (GPA) or better for all graduate course work and at least 15 hours of completed course work, not including teaching practicum or internship credit. The comprehensive examination contains a written examination followed by an oral examination containing general questions related to core material, as well as questions related to the student's area of specialization.

Upon successful completion of the examination, the student chooses a thesis committee of 3 voting members and a thesis adviser whose area of specialization is consistent with the thesis topic. The student then prepares a formal thesis proposal for either a traditional academic thesis or a professional or applied thesis option. A formal defense of the thesis research to faculty members, graduate students, and guests generally completes the program.

Research Facilities

The William S. Carlson Library houses more than 1.6 million volumes and 3,000 periodicals, including more than 5,000 electronic journals. The University Libraries have a fully electronic catalog and circulation service that is available through any terminal on or off campus. The Center for Geographic Information Sciences and Applied Geographics serves as a focal point for GIS contract research on and off campus and as a clearinghouse for GIS research opportunities. The center seeks to solve complex problems related to regional and community issues, environmental protection, land-use planning, economic development, site characterization, resource mapping, and GIS/GPS support. The Lake Erie Research Center's goal is to assemble within a single facility programs in agricultural management, environmental chemistry, geography and land-use planning, aquatic and terrestrial ecology, and other disciplines to explore the linkages between land use and water quality in the western catchment of Lake Erie.

Financial Aid

The out-of-state tuition surcharge normally charged to out-of-state and international students is waived for students whose permanent address is within one of the following Michigan counties: Hillsdale, Lenawee, Macomb, Oakland, Washtenaw, and Wayne. In addition, the University of Toledo offers an out-of-state tuition surcharge waiver to cities and regions that are a part of the Sister Cities Agreement. These regions include Toledo, Spain; Londrina, Brazil; Qinhuangdao, China; Csongrad County, Hungary; Delmenhorst, Germany; Toyohashi, Japan; Tanga, Tanzania; Bekaa Valley, Lebanon; and Poznan, Poland. The University of Toledo Graduate College offers a variety of memorial scholarship awards, including the Ronald E. McNair Postbaccalaureate Achievement Scholarship, the Graduate Opportunity Assistantship Award, and two full University fellowships.

Cost of Study

The graduate tuition rate for the 2008–09 academic year is $434.05 per semester credit hour for in-state students. For nonresidents, the out-of-state surcharge is $389 per semester credit hour. Additional fees are required and include the general fee, technology fee, and mandatory insurance.

Living and Housing Costs

The University of Toledo has a diverse offering of student housing options, including suite-style and traditional residential halls. Housing is offered to graduate students through Residence Life or contracted individually by the student. Affordable, high-quality off-campus apartment-style housing within walking distance of campus is abundant.

Student Group

There are approximately 20,000 students at the University of Toledo. About 4,000 are graduate and professional students. The University has a rich diversity of student organizations. Students join groups that are organized around common cultural, religious, athletic, and educational interests.

Student Outcomes

Graduates of the program occupy positions in academia, government, and industry as planners, GIS analysts, strategic planners, and commercial development and economic development specialists. Many graduates pursue their doctoral degrees at colleges and universities.

Location

The University of Toledo has several campus sites in the city of Toledo. Most graduate students take classes on the Main campus, which is located in suburban western Toledo. With a population of more than 330,000, Toledo is the fiftieth-largest city in the United States. It is located on the western shores of Lake Erie, within a 2-hour drive of Cleveland and Detroit.

The University

The University of Toledo was founded by Jessup W. Scott in 1872 as a municipal institution and became part of the state of Ohio's system of higher education in 1967. On July 1, 2006, the University of Toledo merged with the Medical University of Ohio becoming one of only seventeen American universities to offer professional and graduate academic programs in medicine, law, pharmacy, nursing, health sciences, engineering, and business.

Applying

Admission to the program requires a baccalaureate degree from an accredited institution with a minimum GPA of 2.7, a completed application form, three copies of transcripts from each university previously attended, three letters of recommendation, a statement of purpose, copies of GMAT or GRE test scores of at least 500 in each section, and a nonrefundable $45 application fee.

Correspondence and Information

Department of Geography and Planning
Mail Stop 932
University of Toledo
Toledo, Ohio 43606
Phone: 419-530-2545
Fax: 419-530-7919
E-mail: grdsch@utnet.utoledo.edu
Web site: http://www.geography.utoledo.edu

University of Toledo

THE FACULTY AND THEIR RESEARCH

Kevin Czajkowski, Associate Professor; Ph.D., Michigan. Remote sensing meteorology.

Daniel Hammel, Associate Professor; Ph.D., Minnesota. Urban geography, urban and regional planning, housing.

David Howard, Adjunct Lecturer. Geography education.

Patrick Lawrence, Assistant Professor; Ph.D., Waterloo. Water resources and watershed management, impacts of land cover/land-use change, Great Lakes coastal/shoreline management and geomorphology, land-use policy and planning evaluation, ecosystem planning, parks and protected areas.

Peter Lindquist, Associate Professor and Department Chair; Ph.D., Wisconsin–Milwaukee. GIS, digital cartography, location analysis, transportation.

David Weiguo Liu, Assistant Professor; Ph.D., Boston University. Remote sensing, quantitative methods, artificial intelligence applications.

David "Jim" Nemeth, Professor; Ph.D., UCLA. Critical relativism and extreme geography, enlightened underdevelopment as an alternative to sustainable economic growth.

Neil Reid, Associate Professor; Ph.D., Arizona State. Spatial dynamics of foreign direct investment in the United States, spatial dynamics of growth of the United States service sector.

M. Beth Schlemper, Adjunct Professor; Ph.D., Wisconsin–Madison. Cultural/historical geography; research associate with Association of American Geographers in EDGE Project.

Sujata Shetty, Assistant Professor; Ph.D., Michigan. Urban and regional planning.

Benjamin Tallerico, Visiting Instructor; M.A., Wayne State. Approaches to the study of urban politics, urban administration, urban public policy, urban poverty.

Paul Tecpanecatl, Part-Time Faculty. Urban planning, housing and community development, neighborhood revitalization.

Section 22
Military and Defense Studies

This section contains a directory of institutions offering graduate work in military and defense studies, followed by in-depth entries submitted by institutions that chose to prepare detailed program descriptions. Additional information about programs listed in the directory but not augmented by an in-depth entry may be obtained by writing directly to the dean of a graduate school or chair of a department at the address given in the directory.

For programs offering related work, see also in this book *History* and *Political Science and International Affairs.*

CONTENTS

Program Directories

Close-Ups

See also:

Military and Defense Studies

American Public University System, AMU/APU Graduate Programs, Charles Town, WV 25414. Offers air warfare (MA Military Studies); American Revolution (MA Military Studies); business administration (MBA); Civil War (MA Military Studies); criminal justice (MA); defense management (MA Military Studies); emergency and disaster management (MA); environmental policy and management (MS); fire science management (MA); global engagement (MA); history (MA); homeland security (MA); humanities (MA); intelligence (MA Military Studies, MA Strategic Intelligence); international peace and conflict resolution (MA); international relations and conflict resolution (MA); joint warfare (MA Military Studies); land warfare international perspective (MA Military Studies); management (MA); military history (MA); military leadership (MA Military Studies); national security studies (MA); naval warfare international (MA Military Studies); naval warfare US (MA Military Studies); political science (MA); public administration (MA); public health (MA); security management (MA); space studies (MS); special ops/LIC (MA Military Studies); sports management (MA); transportation and logistics management (MA); transportation management (MA); unconventional warfare (MA Military Studies); World War II (MA Military Studies). Programs offered via distance learning only. Part-time and evening/weekend programs available. Postbaccalaureate distance learning degree programs offered (no on-campus study). *Faculty:* 10 full-time (3 women), 188 part-time/adjunct (57 women). *Students:* 340 full-time (98 women), 3,567 part-time (790 women); includes 615 minority (317 African Americans, 28 American Indian/Alaska Native, 85 Asian Americans or Pacific Islanders, 185 Hispanic Americans), 20 international. Average age 36. 2,123 applicants, 100% accepted, 893 enrolled. In 2007, 829 degrees awarded. *Degree requirements:* For master's, comprehensive exam. *Entrance requirements:* For master's, bachelor's degree or equivalent, minimum GPA of 2.7 in last 60 hours of course work. *Application deadline:* Applications are processed on a rolling basis. Application fee: $0. Electronic applications accepted. *Expenses:* Tuition: Part-time $275 per semester hour. *Financial support:* Applicants required to submit FAFSA. *Faculty research:* Military history, criminal justice, management performance, national security. *Unit head:* Dr. Frank McCluskey, Provost, 877-468-6268, Fax: 304-724-3780. *Application contact:* Terry Grant, Director of Enrollment Management, 877-468-6268, Fax: 304-724-3780, E-mail: info@apus.edu.

Austin Peay State University, College of Graduate Studies, College of Arts and Letters, Department of History and Philosophy, Clarksville, TN 37044. Offers military history (MA). Part-time programs available. Postbaccalaureate distance learning degree programs offered (minimal on-campus study). *Faculty:* 6 full-time (0 women). *Students:* 12 full-time (5 women), 19 part-time (4 women); includes 4 minority (2 African Americans, 2 Asian Americans or Pacific Islanders). Average age 35. *Degree requirements:* For master's, comprehensive exam, thesis optional. *Entrance requirements:* For master's, GRE General Test, minimum GPA of 2.5, 3 letters of recommendation. Additional exam requirements/recommendations for international students: Required—TOEFL (minimum score 500 paper-based; 173 computer-based). *Application deadline:* For fall admission, 7/31 priority date for domestic students; for spring admission, 12/17 priority date for domestic students. Applications are processed on a rolling basis. Application fee: $25. Electronic applications accepted. *Expenses:* Tuition, state resident: full-time $5,446; part-time $288 per credit hour. Tuition, nonresident: full-time $15,722; part-time $734 per credit hour. Required fees: $1,180. Part-time tuition and fees vary according to course load. *Financial support:* In 2007–08, research assistantships (averaging $10,368 per year); career-related internships or fieldwork, Federal Work-Study, institutionally sponsored loans, scholarships/grants, and unspecified assistantships also available. Support available to part-time students. Financial award application deadline: 3/1; financial award applicants required to submit FAFSA. *Unit head:* Dr. Dewey Browder, Chair, 931-221-7919, Fax: 931-221-9917, E-mail: browderd@apsu.edu.

The George Washington University, Elliott School of International Affairs, Program in Security Policy Studies, Washington, DC 20052. Offers MA, JD/MA. Part-time and evening/weekend programs available. *Degree requirements:* For master's, one foreign language, capstone project. *Entrance requirements:* For master's, GRE General Test, 2 semesters of introductory economics, 2 years of a modern foreign language or one semester of statistics. Additional exam requirements/recommendations for international students: Required—TOEFL. Electronic applications accepted. *Faculty research:* U.S. arms transfer policies, military balance in the Third World, U.S. foreign policy, technology and security policy.

Hawai'i Pacific University, College of Liberal Arts, Honolulu, HI 96813. Offers diplomacy and military studies (MA); social work (MA). Part-time and evening/weekend programs available. *Faculty:* 3 full-time (0 women), 5 part-time/adjunct (1 woman). *Students:* 73 full-time (41 women), 88 part-time (51 women); includes 57 minority (7 African Americans, 3 American Indian/Alaska Native, 39 Asian Americans or Pacific Islanders, 8 Hispanic Americans), 15 international. Average age 35. 100 applicants, 98% accepted, 47 enrolled. In 2007, 22 degrees awarded. *Degree requirements:* For master's, thesis. *Entrance requirements:* Additional exam requirements/recommendations for international students: Recommended—TOEFL (minimum score 550 paper-based; 213 computer-based), TWE (minimum score 5). *Application deadline:* For fall admission, 2/15 priority date for domestic students; for spring admission, 10/15 priority date for domestic students. Applications are processed on a rolling basis. Application fee: $50. Electronic applications accepted. *Expenses:* Tuition: Full-time $14,400. Required fees: $1,885. Tuition and fees vary according to course load and program. *Financial support:* In 2007–08, 60 students received support. Career-related internships or fieldwork, Federal Work-Study, scholarships/grants, and unspecified assistantships available. Support available to part-time students. Financial award application deadline: 3/1; financial award applicants required to submit FAFSA. *Unit head:* Dr. Leslie Correa, Associate Vice President and Dean, 808-544-0228, Fax: 808-544-1424, E-mail: lcorrea@hpu.edu. *Application contact:* Danny Lam, Assistant Director of Graduate Admissions, 808-544-1135, Fax: 808-544-0280, E-mail: graduate@hpu.edu.

See Close-Up on page 1099.

The Institute of World Politics, Graduate Programs in National Security, Intelligence, and International Affairs, Washington, DC 20036. Offers American foreign policy (Certificate); comparative political culture (Certificate); counterintelligence (Certificate); democracy building (Certificate); intelligence (Certificate); international politics (Certificate); national security affairs (Certificate); public diplomacy and political warfare (Certificate); statecraft and national security affairs (MA); statecraft and world politics (MA); strategic intelligence studies (MA). Part-time and evening/weekend programs available. *Degree requirements:* For master's, comprehensive exam, thesis optional. *Entrance requirements:* For master's, GRE General Test. Additional exam requirements/recommendations for international students: Required—TOEFL. Electronic applications accepted. *Faculty research:* Intelligence, national security, statecraft.

See Close-Up on page 1151.

The Johns Hopkins University, School of Education, Division of Public Safety Leadership, Baltimore, MD 21218-2699. Offers homeland security (MS); intelligence analysis (MS); management (MS). Part-time and evening/weekend programs available. *Students:* 133 full-time (36 women), 12 part-time (5 women); includes 55 minority (48 African Americans, 5 Asian Americans or Pacific Islanders, 2 Hispanic Americans). Average age 37. 70 applicants, 90% accepted, 60 enrolled. In 2007, 96 degrees awarded. *Entrance requirements:* For master's, minimum GPA of 3.0, interview, resumé, letters of recommendation. Additional exam requirements/recommendations for international students: Required—TOEFL (minimum score 600 paper-based; 250 computer-based; 100 iBT). *Application deadline:* For fall admission, 5/1 for international students; for spring admission, 10/15 for international students. Applications are processed on a rolling basis. Application fee: $60. *Financial support:* Scholarships/grants available. Support available to part-time students. Financial award application deadline: 6/1; financial award applicants required to submit FAFSA. *Faculty research:* Ethics and integrity, counter terrorism, school safety, Homeland Security, identity theft. *Unit head:* Dr. Sheldon Greenberg, Associate Dean, 410-312-4401, Fax: 410-290-1061, E-mail: greenberg@jhu.edu. *Application contact:* Kelly Williams, Academic Administrator, 410-312-4409, Fax: 410-290-1061, E-mail: kelly.williams@jhu.edu.

Joint Military Intelligence College, School of Intelligence Studies, Washington, DC 20340-5100. Offers MSSI, Certificate. Open only to federal government employees. Part-time and evening/weekend programs available. *Degree requirements:* For master's, thesis. *Entrance requirements:* For master's, MAT, authorized nomination. *Faculty research:* Law and intelligence, intelligence and higher education, low-intensity conflict, intelligence information systems.

The Judge Advocate General's School, U.S. Army, Graduate Programs, Charlottesville, VA 22903-1781. Offers military law (LL M). Only active duty military lawyers attend this school. *Accreditation:* ABA. *Degree requirements:* For master's, thesis optional. *Entrance requirements:* For master's, active duty military lawyer, international military officer, or DOD civilian attorney, JD or LL B. *Faculty research:* Criminal law, administrative and civil law, contract law, international law, legal research and writing.

Missouri State University, Graduate College, College of Humanities and Public Affairs, Department of Defense and Strategic Studies, Fairfax, VA 22031. Offers MS. Part-time programs available. *Faculty:* 2 full-time (0 women), 22 part-time/adjunct (3 women). *Students:* 35 full-time (11 women), 10 part-time (1 woman); includes 3 minority (1 African American, 1 Asian American or Pacific Islander, 1 Hispanic American), 2 international. Average age 27. 47 applicants, 100% accepted, 19 enrolled. In 2007, 14 degrees awarded. *Degree requirements:* For master's, comprehensive exam, thesis or alternative. *Entrance requirements:* For master's, GRE, minimum GPA of 2.75, 3 letters of recommendation. Additional exam requirements/recommendations for international students: Required—TOEFL (minimum score 550 paper-based; 213 computer-based; 79 iBT). *Application deadline:* For fall admission, 7/20 priority date for domestic students; for spring admission, 12/20 priority date for domestic students. Applications are processed on a rolling basis. Application fee: $35. Electronic applications accepted. *Expenses:* Tuition, state resident: full-time $3,708; part-time $206 per credit hour. Tuition, nonresident: full-time $7,236; part-time $206 per credit hour. Required fees: $622. Full-time tuition and fees vary according to course level, course load, program and reciprocity agreements. *Financial support:* Career-related internships or fieldwork, Federal Work-Study, institutionally sponsored loans, scholarships/grants, and tuition waivers (partial) available. Financial award application deadline: 3/31; financial award applicants required to submit FAFSA. *Faculty research:* Middle East, terrorism, arms control, U.S.-Soviet military balance, Strategic Defense Initiative. *Unit head:* Dr. Keith Payne, Head, 703-218-3565, Fax: 703-218-3568, E-mail: kbpayne@missouristate.edu.

National Defense University, Industrial College of the Armed Forces, Washington, DC 20319-5066. Offers national resource strategy (MS). Open only to Department of Defense employees and specific federal agencies. *Entrance requirements:* Additional exam requirements/recommendations for international students: Required—TOEFL. *Faculty research:* National security and resources.

National Defense University, Joint Advanced Warfighting School, Washington, DC 20319-5066. Offers joint campaign planning and strategy (MS). Open only to Department of Defense employees and specific federal agencies. *Faculty research:* Military operations.

National Defense University, National War College, Washington, DC 20319-5066. Offers national security strategy (MS). Open only to Department of Defense employees and specific federal agencies. *Faculty research:* International studies.

Naval Postgraduate School, Graduate Programs, Department of Computer Science, Program in Modeling of Virtual Environments and Simulations, Monterey, CA 93943. Offers MS, PhD. Program only open to commissioned officers of the United States and friendly nations and selected United States federal civilian employees. Part-time programs available. *Degree requirements:* For master's, thesis; for doctorate, one foreign language, thesis/dissertation.

Naval Postgraduate School, Graduate Programs, Department of Defense Analysis, Monterey, CA 93943. Offers defense analysis (MS); joint information operations (MS); special operations (MS). Program only open to commissioned officers of the United States and friendly nations and selected United States federal civilian employees. Part-time programs available. *Degree requirements:* For master's, thesis.

Naval Postgraduate School, Graduate Programs, Program in Undersea Warfare, Monterey, CA 93943. Offers applied science (MS); electrical engineering (MS); engineering acoustics (MS); operations research (MS); physical oceanography (MS). Program only open to commissioned officers of the United States and friendly nations and selected United States federal civilian employees. Part-time programs available. *Degree requirements:* For master's, thesis.

Naval Postgraduate School, Graduate Programs, School of Business and Public Policy, Monterey, CA 93943. Offers contract management (MS); defense-focused business administration (MBA); executive business administration (MBA); leadership and human resource development (MS); management (MS); program management (MS); systems engineering management (MS). Program only open to commissioned officers of the United States and friendly nations and selected United States federal civilian employees. *Accreditation:* AACSB; NASPAA. Part-time programs available. Postbaccalaureate distance learning degree programs offered (minimal on-campus study). *Degree requirements:* For master's, thesis.

Norwich University, School of Graduate Studies, Program in Military History, Northfield, VT 05663. Offers MA. Evening/weekend programs available. *Faculty:* 24 part-time/adjunct (2 women). *Students:* 284 full-time (31 women), 1 part-time; includes 18 minority (6 African Americans, 4 Asian Americans or Pacific Islanders, 8 Hispanic Americans). Average age 41. 91 applicants, 98% accepted, 70 enrolled. In 2007, 53 degrees awarded. *Entrance requirements:* For master's, minimum undergraduate GPA of 2.75. Additional exam requirements/recommendations for international students: Required—TOEFL (minimum score 550 paper-based). *Application deadline:* For fall admission, 8/10 for domestic and international students; for winter admission, 11/7 for domestic and international students; for spring admission, 2/6 for domestic and international students. Application fee: $50. Electronic applications accepted. *Expenses:* Tuition: Full-time $15,768; part-time $657 per credit. Tuition and fees vary according to program. *Financial support:* Scholarships/grants available. Financial award applicants required to submit FAFSA. *Unit head:* Dr. James Erhman, Program Director, 802-485-2730, Fax: 802-485-2533. *Application contact:* Lars Nielsen, Administrative Director, 802-485-2853, Fax: 802-485-2533, E-mail: lnielsen@norwich.edu.

Royal Military College of Canada, Division of Graduate Studies and Research, Continuing Studies, Department of History, Kingston, ON K7K 7B4, Canada. Offers defense management and policy (MA); war studies (MA). *Students:* 48 full-time, 100 part-time. In 2007, 41 degrees awarded. *Degree requirements:* For master's, thesis. *Entrance requirements:* For master's, Honours degree with second-class standing; for doctorate, Master's degree. *Application deadline:* For fall admission, 5/1 priority date for domestic students; for winter admission, 9/1 priority date for domestic students. Applications are processed on a rolling basis. Electronic applications accepted. *Application contact:* Peggy Murphy, Administrative Assistant, Graduate Studies, 613-541-6000 Ext. 6361, Fax: 613-542-8612, E-mail: murphy-p@rmc.ca.

School of Advanced Air and Space Studies, Program in Airpower Art and Science, Maxwell AFB, AL 36112-6424. Offers MA. Available to active duty military officers only. *Faculty:* 14 full-time (0 women). *Students:* 42 full-time (2 women); includes 2 African Americans, 3 Asian Americans or Pacific Islanders, 3 Hispanic Americans, 2 international. Average age 37. 174 applicants, 23% accepted, 40 enrolled. In 2007, 42 master's awarded. *Median time to degree:* Of those who began their doctoral program in fall 1999, 100% received their degree in 8 years or less. *Degree requirements:* For master's, comprehensive exam, thesis, minimum

GPA of 3.0. *Entrance requirements:* For master's, less than 16 years total of active commissioned service; master's degree or undergraduate degree with a minimum GPA of 2.75. Additional exam requirements/recommendations for international students: Required—TOEFL. *Application deadline:* For fall admission, 12/31 for domestic students, 12/31 priority date for international students. Application fee: $0. *Faculty research:* Military history, political science, international relations, social history, technology. *Unit head:* Dr. Stephen D. Chiabotti, Assistant Dean, 334-953-5155, Fax: 334-953-3015, E-mail: stephen.chiabotti@us.af.mil.

United States Army Command and General Staff College, Graduate Program, Fort Leavenworth, KS 66027-2301. Offers military art and science (MMAS). Only career military officers are selected to attend United States Army Command and General Staff College; Graduate Program is voluntary for first-year students, but mandatory for second-year students. *Faculty:* 374 full-time (15 women). *Students:* 163 (6 women). Average age 36. In 2007, 124 degrees awarded. *Unit head:* Dr. Bob F. Baumann, Director, Graduate Degree Programs, 913-684-2741, Fax: 913-684-4648.

University of Calgary, Faculty of Graduate Studies, Centre for Military and Strategic Studies, Calgary, AB T2N 1N4, Canada. Offers MSS, PhD. PhD offered in special cases only. Part-time programs available. *Degree requirements:* For master's, thesis; for doctorate, comprehensive exam, thesis/dissertation. *Entrance requirements:* For master's, minimum GPA of 3.4. Additional exam requirements/recommendations for international students: Recommended—TOEFL (minimum score 550 paper-based). *Faculty research:* Military history, Israeli studies, strategic studies, int'l relations, Arctic security.

University of Pittsburgh, Graduate School of Public and International Affairs, International Affairs Division, Program in Security and Intelligence Studies, Pittsburgh, PA 15260. Offers MPIA, JD/MPIA, MBA/MPIA, MID/MPIA, MPA/MPIA, MSIS/MPIA. Part-time and evening/weekend programs available. *Faculty:* 34 full-time (10 women), 18 part-time/adjunct (6 women). *Students:* 79 full-time (26 women), 10 part-time (3 women); includes 6 minority (4 African Americans, 1 Asian American or Pacific Islander, 1 Hispanic American), 1 international. Average age 25. 120 applicants, 86% accepted, 42 enrolled. In 2007, 63 degrees awarded. *Degree requirements:* For master's, thesis optional, internship, capstone seminar. *Entrance requirements:* For master's, GRE General Test, 3 letters of recommendation, resumé, minimum GPA of 3.2. Additional exam requirements/recommendations for international students: Required—TOEFL (minimum score 550 paper-based; 213 computer-based; 80 iBT), TWE (minimum score 4.5); Recommended—IELTS (minimum score 7). *Application deadline:* For fall admission, 3/1 for domestic students, 1/15 for international students; for spring admission, 11/1 for domestic students, 8/1 for international students. Application fee: $50. Electronic applications accepted. *Financial support:* In 2007–08, 41 students received support, including 41 fellowships (averaging $8,280 per year); career-related internships or fieldwork, institutionally sponsored loans, scholarships/grants, and unspecified assistantships also available. Financial award application deadline: 2/1. *Faculty research:* Political economy, international security/defense/intelligence, transnational crime, international trade, international finance, terrorism. Total annual research expenditures: $845,025. *Application contact:* Jessica L. Hatherill, Associate Director of Student Services, 412-648-7640, Fax: 412-648-7641, E-mail: hatherill@gspia.pitt.edu.

National Security

American Public University System, AMU/APU Graduate Programs, Charles Town, WV 25414. Offers air warfare (MA Military Studies); American Revolution (MA Military Studies); business administration (MBA); Civil War (MA Military Studies); criminal justice (MA); defense management (MA Military Studies); emergency and disaster management (MA); environmental policy and management (MS); fire science management (MA); global engagement (MA); history (MA); homeland security (MA); humanities (MA); intelligence (MA Military Studies, MA Strategic Intelligence); international peace and conflict resolution (MA); international relations and conflict resolution (MA); joint warfare (MA Military Studies); land warfare international perspective (MA Military Studies); management (MA); military history (MA); military leadership (MA Military Studies); national security studies (MA); naval warfare international (MA Military Studies); naval warfare US (MA Military Studies); political science (MA); public administration (MA); public health (MA); security management (MA); space studies (MS); special ops/LIC (MA Military Studies); sports management (MA); transportation and logistics management (MA); transportation management (MA); unconventional warfare (MA Military Studies); World War II (MA Military Studies). Programs offered via distance learning only. Part-time and evening/weekend programs available. Postbaccalaureate distance learning degree programs offered (no on-campus study). *Faculty:* 10 full-time (3 women), 188 part-time/adjunct (57 women). *Students:* 340 full-time (98 women), 3,567 part-time (790 women); includes 615 minority (317 African Americans, 28 American Indian/Alaska Native, 85 Asian Americans or Pacific Islanders, 185 Hispanic Americans), 20 international. Average age 36. 2,123 applicants, 100% accepted, 893 enrolled. In 2007, 829 degrees awarded. *Degree requirements:* For master's, comprehensive exam. *Entrance requirements:* For master's, bachelor's degree or equivalent, minimum GPA of 2.7 in last 60 hours of course work. *Application deadline:* Applications are processed on a rolling basis. Application fee: $0. Electronic applications accepted. *Expenses:* Tuition: Part-time $275 per semester hour. *Financial support:* Applicants required to submit FAFSA. *Faculty research:* Military history, criminal justice, management performance, national security. *Unit head:* Dr. Frank McCluskey, Provost, 877-468-6268, Fax: 304-724-3780. *Application contact:* Terry Grant, Director of Enrollment Management, 877-468-6268, Fax: 304-724-3780, E-mail: info@apus.edu.

California State University, San Bernardino, Graduate Studies, College of Social and Behavioral Sciences, National Security Studies Program, San Bernardino, CA 92407-2397. Offers MA. Part-time and evening/weekend programs available. *Faculty:* 6 full-time, 5 part-time/adjunct. *Students:* 50 full-time (15 women), 29 part-time (11 women); includes 2 African Americans, 6 Asian Americans or Pacific Islanders, 13 Hispanic Americans. Average age 27. 39 applicants, 77% accepted, 20 enrolled. In 2007, 10 degrees awarded. *Degree requirements:* For master's, comprehensive exam. *Entrance requirements:* For master's, minimum GPA of 2.5. *Application deadline:* Applications are processed on a rolling basis. Application fee: $55. *Financial support:* Career-related internships or fieldwork, Federal Work-Study, institutionally sponsored loans, and unspecified assistantships available. Support available to part-time students. *Faculty research:* Strategy, arms control, defense policy, terrorism, U.S. foreign policy, operations analysis. *Unit head:* Dr. Mark Clark, Director, 909-537-5534, Fax: 909-537-7018, E-mail: mtclark@csusb.edu.

Georgetown University, Graduate School of Arts and Sciences, Department of National Security Studies, Washington, DC 20057. Offers MA, MA/PhD. *Entrance requirements:* For master's, GRE. Additional exam requirements/recommendations for international students: Required—TOEFL.

Huron University USA in London, Graduate Programs, Program in International Relations, London, United Kingdom. Offers conflict resolution (MA); diplomacy (MA); international public law (MA); international relations (MA); Middle East international security (MA); politics (MA); security studies (MA); terrorism (MA); U.S. foreign policy (MA). Part-time programs available. *Entrance requirements:* Additional exam requirements/recommendations for international students: Required—TOEFL (minimum score 580 paper-based; 237 computer-based), TWE (minimum score 5). Electronic applications accepted. *Faculty research:* American foreign politics, Middle East, security studies.

The Institute of World Politics, Graduate Programs in National Security, Intelligence, and International Affairs, Washington, DC 20036. Offers American foreign policy (Certificate); comparative political culture (Certificate); counterintelligence (Certificate); democracy building (Certificate); intelligence (Certificate); international politics (Certificate); national security affairs (Certificate); public diplomacy and political warfare (Certificate); statecraft and national security affairs (MA); statecraft and world politics (MA); strategic intelligence studies (MA). Part-time and evening/weekend programs available. *Degree requirements:* For master's, comprehensive exam, thesis optional. *Entrance requirements:* For master's, GRE General Test. Additional exam requirements/recommendations for international students: Required—TOEFL. Electronic applications accepted. *Faculty research:* Intelligence, national security, statecraft.

See Close-Up on page 1151.

National Defense University, National War College, Washington, DC 20319-5066. Offers national security strategy (MS). Open only to Department of Defense employees and specific federal agencies. *Faculty research:* International studies.

Naval Postgraduate School, Graduate Programs, Department of National Security Affairs, Monterey, CA 93943. Offers intelligence (MA); international relations (MA); political science (MA); regional security education (MA); security building (MA); security studies (MA). Program only open to commissioned officers of the United States and friendly nations and selected United States federal civilian employees. Part-time programs available. *Degree requirements:* For master's, thesis.

Naval War College, Program in National Security and Strategic Studies, Newport, RI 02841-1207. Offers MA. Program open only to full-time military personnel.

Texas A&M University, George Bush School of Government and Public Service, College Station, TX 77843. Offers advanced international affairs (Certificate); homeland security (Certificate); international affairs (MPIA), including international economics and development, national security affairs; nonprofit management (Certificate); public service and administration (MPSA), including public management, public policy analysis. *Accreditation:* NASPAA. *Faculty:* 39. *Students:* 155 full-time (67 women), 97 part-time (27 women); includes 37 minority (8 African Americans, 2 American Indian/Alaska Native, 4 Asian Americans or Pacific Islanders, 23 Hispanic Americans), 18 international. Average age 24. 249 applicants, 57% accepted, 88 enrolled. In 2007, 69 degrees awarded. *Degree requirements:* For master's, summer internship. *Entrance requirements:* For master's, GRE (preferred) or GMAT. *Application deadline:* For fall admission, 1/24 for domestic and international students. Application fee: $50 ($75 for international students). Electronic applications accepted. *Expenses:* Tuition, state resident: full-time $6,129. Tuition, nonresident: full-time $11,689. Tuition and fees vary according to course load. *Financial support:* In 2007–08, fellowships (averaging $11,000 per year), research assistantships (averaging $11,250 per year) were awarded; career-related internships or fieldwork, Federal Work-Study, and institutionally sponsored loans also available. Financial award application deadline: 2/1; financial award applicants required to submit FAFSA. *Faculty research:* Public policy, Presidential studies, public leadership, economic policy, social policy. *Unit head:* Richard A. Chilcoat, Dean, 979-862-8007, Fax: 979-862-7953, E-mail: bushschool@tamu.edu. *Application contact:* Kathryn Meyer, Recruitment/Placement Officer, 979-458-4767, Fax: 979-845-4155, E-mail: admissions@bushschool.tamu.edu.

See Close-Up on page 1623.

University of New Haven, Graduate School, Henry C. Lee College of Criminal Justice and Forensic Sciences, National Security and Public Safety Program, West Haven, CT 06516-1916. Offers MS. *Expenses:* Tuition: Part-time $630 per credit. Required fees: $40 per term. *Unit head:* Dr. Richard Ward, Dean, Henry C. Lee College of Criminal Justice and Forensic Sciences, 203-932-7260.

University of Pittsburgh, Graduate School of Public and International Affairs, Executive Programs in Public Policy and Management, Pittsburgh, PA 15260. Offers development planning (MPPM); international development (MPPM); international political economy (MPPM); international security studies (MPPM); management of non profit organizations (MPPM); metropolitan management and regional development (MPPM); policy analysis and evaluation (MPPM). Part-time programs available. *Faculty:* 34 full-time (10 women), 18 part-time/adjunct (6 women). *Students:* 11 full-time (3 women), 46 part-time (20 women); includes 4 minority (3 African Americans, 1 Hispanic American), 8 international. Average age 38. 48 applicants, 88% accepted, 29 enrolled. In 2007, 27 degrees awarded. *Degree requirements:* For master's, thesis optional, capstone seminar. *Entrance requirements:* For master's, 2 letters of recommendation, resumé, 5 years of supervisory or budgetary experience. Additional exam requirements/recommendations for international students: Required—TOEFL (minimum score 600 paper-based; 250 computer-based; 100 iBT), TWE (minimum score 4); Recommended—IELTS (minimum score 7). *Application deadline:* For fall admission, 6/1 priority date for domestic students, 2/15 for international students; for spring admission, 1/1 priority date for domestic students, 8/1 for international students. Applications are processed on a rolling basis. Application fee: $50. Electronic applications accepted. *Financial support:* In 2007–08, 4 students received support, including 4 fellowships (averaging $5,075 per year); institutionally sponsored loans and scholarships/grants also available. Support available to part-time students. Financial award application deadline: 2/1. *Faculty research:* Executive training and technical assistance for U.S. and international clients. Total annual research expenditures: $845,025. *Unit head:* Michele Garrity, Director, Executive Education, 412-648-7610, Fax: 412-648-2605, E-mail: garrity@birch.gspia.pitt.edu. *Application contact:* Maureen O'Malley, Admissions Counselor, 412-648-7640, Fax: 412-648-7641, E-mail: pronobis@birch.gspia.pitt.edu.

See Close-Up on page 1645.

HAWAI'I PACIFIC UNIVERSITY

Diplomacy and Military Studies Program

Program of Study

Hawai'i Pacific University's (HPU's) Master of Arts in diplomacy and military studies (M.A./DMS) is designed to provide students with an interdisciplinary view of the role of diplomacy and the military in world affairs from both historical and contemporary perspectives. The program combines courses in history, art history, literature, philosophy, anthropology, international relations, strategic studies, and political science to acquaint students with different approaches and methods in the study of diplomacy and the military.

The M.A./DMS program is an excellent opportunity for those wishing to explore the complex relationships of politics, society, and the military. It is a useful degree for those who are either professional military officers or those who work in a variety of government positions. It is also outstanding preparation for more advanced graduate studies in history, political science, or international relations.

Courses for the diplomacy and military studies degree fall into four major categories: core classes, electives in diplomatic and military history, supporting field electives, and capstone courses. Moreover, unlike other similar programs which have a focus on the United States and Europe, the M.A./DMS integrates a variety of courses in Asia and the Pacific as well as courses of a comparative nature.

The core classes are drawn from the disciplines of history, interdisciplinary humanities, philosophy, and political science and provide students with the historical, ethical, and practical background necessary to fully understand the multifaceted character of the military. They are also intended to give students a sound introduction to the fundamental literature dealing with the history of foreign relations and the military.

Research Facilities

University libraries, with a collection exceeding 153,000 volumes, add an average of 2,500 volumes annually to support the program. Periodical titles number more than 1,700, and 205,000 pieces of microfiche and 5,300 rolls of microfilm are maintained. Libraries are electronically linked to the catalogs and databases of Hawaii's major publicly supported library systems, other specialized libraries on Oahu, and remote-site libraries. HPU students are provided with e-mail as well as Internet and online access to state-of-the-art research databases.

Financial Aid

The University participates in all federal financial aid programs designated for graduate students. These programs provide aid in the form of subsidized (need-based) and unsubsidized (non-need-based) Federal Stafford Student Loans. Through these loans, funds may be available to cover the student's entire cost of education. To apply for aid, students must submit the Free Application for Federal Student Aid (FAFSA) after January 1. Mailing of student award letters usually begins by the end of March. The University also offers several institutional scholarships and assistantships.

Cost of Study

For the 2007–08 academic year, graduate tuition was $560 per credit hour, and books cost approximately $1500 for the entire program.

Living and Housing Costs

The University has both residence halls and an apartment referral service. Including tuition, books, housing, food, health insurance, and miscellaneous expenses, the cost of living for a typical single student for two semesters (nine months) is approximately $26,280.

Student Group

University enrollment currently stands at nearly 9,000, including more than 1,200 graduate students. All fifty states and more than 100 countries are represented.

Location

The University has three campuses linked by shuttle. Hawai'i Pacific combines the excitement of an urban, downtown campus with the serenity of the windward side of the island. The main campus is located in downtown Honolulu, the business and financial center of the Pacific. The Hawai'i Loa Campus is 8 miles away, situated in Kaneohe at the base of the Ko'olau Range; it is the site of the School of Nursing, the marine science program, and a variety of other course offerings. The third campus, the Oceanic Institute, is an applied aquaculture research facility located on a 56-acre site at Makapu'u Point on the windward coast.

The University

Hawai'i Pacific University is the largest private postsecondary institution in the state of Hawaii. The University is coeducational, with a faculty of more than 300 members, a student-faculty ratio of 18:1, and an average class size of 20. A wide range of counseling and student support services are available. There are more than ninety student organizations, including the Graduate Student Organization.

Applying

Hawai'i Pacific University seeks students with academic promise, outstanding career potential, and high motivation. Applicants should complete and forward a graduate admissions application form, have official transcripts sent from all colleges or universities, submit two original, current letters of recommendation, and submit two essays. Admissions decisions are made on a rolling basis, and applicants are notified between one and two weeks after all documents have been submitted. Applicants to Hawai'i Pacific University's graduate program are encouraged to submit applications online at http://www.hpu.edu/grad.

Correspondence and Information

Graduate Admissions
Hawai'i Pacific University
1164 Bishop Street, #911
Honolulu, Hawaii 96813

Phone: 808-544-1135
866-GRAD-HPU (toll-free)
Fax: 808-544-0280
E-mail: graduate@hpu.edu
Web site: http://www.hpu.edu/grad

Hawai'i Pacific University

THE FACULTY

Wayne Andrews, Ph.D. (philosophy), California, Santa Cruz.
Daniel Binkley, Ph.D. (history), Colorado.
Robert Borofsky, Ph.D. (anthropology), Hawai'i at Manoa.
Stanley Carpenter, Ph.D. (history), Florida State.
Grace Cheng, Ph.D. (political science), Hawai'i at Manoa.
Russell Hart, Ph.D. (history), Ohio State.
Carlos Juarez, Ph.D. (international relations), UCLA.
S. Mike Pavelec, Ph.D., (history), Ohio State.
James Primm, Ph.D. (political science), Hawai'i at Manoa.
Capt. Carl Schuster, USN (Ret.), M.A. (international relations), USC.
James Stroble, Ph.D. (philosophy), Hawai'i at Manoa.
William Zanella, Ph.D. (history), Hawai'i at Manoa.

Section 23
Political Science and International Affairs

This section contains a directory of institutions offering graduate work in political science and international affairs, followed by in-depth entries submitted by institutions that chose to prepare detailed program descriptions. Additional information about programs listed in the directory but not augmented by an in-depth entry may be obtained by writing directly to the dean of a graduate school or chair of a department at the address given in the directory.

For programs offering related work, see also in this book *Area and Cultural Studies, History, Language and Literature,* and *Public, Regional, and Industrial Affairs.* In another guide in this series:

Graduate Programs in Business, Education, Health, Information Studies, Law & Social Work

See *International Business*

CONTENTS

Program Directories

Announcements

Close-Ups

See also:

International Affairs

Alliant International University–México City, International Studies Division, Mexico City, Mexico. Offers international relations (MA).

Alliant International University–México City, Marshall Goldsmith School of Management, Mexico City, Mexico. Offers international business administration (MIBA); international relations (MA). Part-time and evening/weekend programs available. *Entrance requirements:* For master's, GMAT, minimum GPA of 3.0. Additional exam requirements/recommendations for international students: Required—TOEFL (minimum score 550 paper-based; 213 computer-based), TWE (minimum score 5). Electronic applications accepted. *Faculty research:* Environmental impact and business in Mexico.

Alliant International University–México City, Programs in Arts and Science, Mexico City, Mexico. Offers counseling psychology (MA); international relations (MA). Part-time programs available. *Degree requirements:* For master's, thesis optional. *Entrance requirements:* For master's, GRE General Test, letters of recommendation. Additional exam requirements/recommendations for international students: Required—TOEFL. Electronic applications accepted.

Alliant International University–San Diego, Marshall Goldsmith School of Management, International Studies Division, San Diego, CA 92131-1799. Offers international relations (MA). Part-time programs available. *Degree requirements:* For master's, thesis. *Entrance requirements:* For master's, GRE, minimum GPA of 2.5, letters of recommendation. Additional exam requirements/recommendations for international students: Required—TOEFL (minimum score 550 paper-based).

American Graduate School of International Relations and Diplomacy, Program in International Relations and Diplomacy, Paris, France. Offers MA, PhD.

See Close-Up on page 1137.

American Public University System, AMU/APU Graduate Programs, Charles Town, WV 25414. Offers air warfare (MA Military Studies); American Revolution (MA Military Studies); business administration (MBA); Civil War (MA Military Studies); criminal justice (MA); defense management (MA Military Studies); emergency and disaster management (MA); environmental policy and management (MS); fire science management (MA); global engagement (MA); history (MA); homeland security (MA); humanities (MA); intelligence (MA Military Studies, MA Strategic Intelligence); international peace and conflict resolution (MA); international relations and conflict resolution (MA); joint warfare (MA Military Studies); land warfare international perspective (MA Military Studies); management (MA); military history (MA); military leadership (MA Military Studies); national security studies (MA); naval warfare international (MA Military Studies); naval warfare US (MA Military Studies); political science (MA); public administration (MA); public health (MA); security management (MA); space studies (MS); special ops/LIC (MA Military Studies); sports management (MA); transportation and logistics management (MA); transportation management (MA); unconventional warfare (MA Military Studies); World War II (MA Military Studies). Programs offered via distance learning only. Part-time and evening/weekend programs available. Postbaccalaureate distance learning degree programs offered (no on-campus study). *Faculty:* 10 full-time (3 women), 188 part-time/adjunct (57 women). *Students:* 340 full-time (98 women), 3,567 part-time (790 women); includes 615 minority (317 African Americans, 28 American Indian/Alaska Native, 85 Asian Americans or Pacific Islanders, 185 Hispanic Americans), 20 international. Average age 36. 2,123 applicants, 100% accepted, 893 enrolled. In 2007, 829 degrees awarded. *Degree requirements:* For master's, comprehensive exam. *Entrance requirements:* For master's, bachelor's degree or equivalent, minimum GPA of 2.7 in last 60 hours of course work. *Application deadline:* Applications are processed on a rolling basis. Application fee: $0. Electronic applications accepted. *Expenses:* Tuition: Part-time $275 per semester hour. *Financial support:* Applicants required to submit FAFSA. *Faculty research:* Military history, criminal justice, management performance, national security. *Unit head:* Dr. Frank McCluskey, Provost, 877-468-6268, Fax: 304-724-3780. *Application contact:* Terry Grant, Director of Enrollment Management, 877-468-6268, Fax: 304-724-3780, E-mail: info@apus.edu.

American University, College of Arts and Sciences, Department of Economics, Washington, DC 20016-8001. Offers applied microeconomics (Certificate); economics (MA, PhD); international economic relations (Certificate). Part-time and evening/weekend programs available. *Faculty:* 25 full-time (11 women), 1 part-time/adjunct (0 women). *Students:* 59 full-time (22 women), 71 part-time (32 women); includes 14 minority (7 African Americans, 3 Asian Americans or Pacific Islanders, 4 Hispanic Americans), 55 international. Average age 29. 181 applicants, 71% accepted, 38 enrolled. In 2007, 29 master's, 5 doctorates, 1 other advanced degree awarded. Terminal master's awarded for partial completion of doctoral program. *Degree requirements:* For master's, comprehensive exam, thesis or alternative; for doctorate, comprehensive exam, thesis/dissertation, 2 research seminars, field requirement. *Entrance requirements:* For master's, GRE; for doctorate, GRE General Test; for Certificate, Bachelor's Degree. Additional exam requirements/recommendations for international students: Required—TOEFL (minimum score 550 paper-based; 213 computer-based). *Application deadline:* For spring admission, 10/1 for domestic students. Applications are processed on a rolling basis. Application fee: $50. *Expenses:* Tuition: Full-time $19,998; part-time $1,111 per credit hour. Required fees: $380. Tuition and fees vary according to program. *Financial support:* Fellowships with full tuition reimbursements, research assistantships, teaching assistantships with full tuition reimbursements, career-related internships or fieldwork, Federal Work-Study, institutionally sponsored loans, and tuition waivers (full and partial) available. Financial award application deadline: 2/1. *Faculty research:* Political economy, development, labor, gender. *Unit head:* Dr. John Willoughby, Chair, 202-885-3759, Fax: 202-885-3790.

American University, School of International Service, Washington, DC 20016-8001. Offers comparative and regional studies (MA); cross-cultural communication (Certificate); development management (MS); environmental policy (MA); ethics, peace, and global affairs (MA); global environmental policy (MA); international communication (MA); international development (MA); international development management (Certificate); international economic policy (MA); international economic relations (Certificate); international peace and conflict resolution (MA); international politics (MA); international relations (PhD); international service (MIS); the Americas (Certificate); U.S. foreign policy (MA); JD/MA; MBA/MA. Part-time and evening/weekend programs available. *Faculty:* 73 full-time (27 women), 34 part-time/adjunct (15 women). *Students:* 528 full-time (339 women), 355 part-time (218 women); includes 137 minority (39 African Americans, 2 American Indian/Alaska Native, 45 Asian Americans or Pacific Islanders, 51 Hispanic Americans), 119 international. Average age 27. 1,840 applicants, 66% accepted, 321 enrolled. In 2007, 347 master's, 5 doctorates, 12 other advanced degrees awarded. Terminal master's awarded for partial completion of doctoral program. *Degree requirements:* For master's, one foreign language, comprehensive exam, thesis or alternative; for doctorate, one foreign language, comprehensive exam, thesis/dissertation, research practicum; for Certificate, minimum 15 credit hours related course work. *Entrance requirements:* For master's, GRE General Test, 24 credits of course work in related social sciences, minimum GPA of 3.5, 2 letters of recommendation, bachelor's Degree, resumé, statement of purpose; for doctorate, GRE General Test, 2 letters of recommendation, 24 credits in related social sciences. Additional exam requirements/recommendations for international students: Required—TOEFL (minimum score 550 paper-based; 213 computer-based). *Application deadline:* For fall admission, 1/15 priority date for domestic students; for spring admission, 10/1 priority date for domestic students. Applications are processed on a rolling basis. Application fee: $50. *Expenses:* Tuition: Full-time $19,998; part-time $1,111 per credit hour. Required fees: $380. Tuition and fees vary according to program. *Financial support:* Career-related internships or fieldwork, Federal Work-Study, and institutionally sponsored loans available. Financial award application deadline: 1/15. *Faculty research:* International intellectual property, international environmental issues, international law and legal order, international telecommunications/technology, international sustainable development. *Unit head:* Dr. Louis W. Goodman, Dean, 202-885-1600, Fax: 202-885-2494. *Application contact:* Amanda Taylor, Director of Graduate Admissions and Financial Aid, 202-885-1599, Fax: 202-885-2494.

See Close-Up on page 1139.

The American University of Paris, Graduate Programs, Paris, France. Offers finance (MSF); global communications (MAGC); international affairs, conflict resolution and civil society development (MA); Middle Eastern and Islamic studies (MA); public administration (MPA). *Degree requirements:* For master's, thesis. *Entrance requirements:* For master's, minimum undergraduate GPA of 3.0.

Arcadia University, Graduate Studies, Program in International Relations and Diplomacy, Glenside, PA 19038-3295. Offers MA.

Baylor University, Graduate School, College of Arts and Sciences, Department of Political Science, Waco, TX 76798. Offers international studies (MA); political science (MA, PhD); public policy and administration (MPPA); JD/MPPA. *Students:* 24 full-time (8 women), 3 part-time (2 women); includes 1 minority (Hispanic American), 3 international. In 2007, 11 degrees awarded. *Entrance requirements:* For master's, GRE General Test. *Application deadline:* Applications are processed on a rolling basis. Application fee: $25. *Financial support:* Research assistantships, career-related internships or fieldwork, Federal Work-Study, and institutionally sponsored loans available. Financial award application deadline: 3/1. *Unit head:* Dr. Dwight Allman, Graduate Program Director, 254-710-3161, Fax: 254-710-3122, E-mail: dwight_allman@baylor.edu. *Application contact:* Suzanne Keener, Administrative Assistant, 254-710-3588, Fax: 254-710-3870.

Baylor University, Graduate School, Hankamer School of Business, Department of Economics, Waco, TX 76798. Offers economics (MS Eco); international economics (MA, MS). *Students:* 15 full-time (7 women), 1 part-time; includes 1 minority (Asian American or Pacific Islander), 10 international. In 2007, 7 degrees awarded. *Entrance requirements:* For master's, GMAT or GRE General Test. *Application deadline:* For fall admission, 8/1 for domestic students; for spring admission, 12/1 for domestic students. Applications are processed on a rolling basis. Application fee: $25. *Financial support:* Research assistantships, Federal Work-Study and institutionally sponsored loans available. Financial award application deadline: 4/1. *Faculty research:* Econometrics, international economics, private enterprise, comparative economic systems. *Unit head:* Dr. Steve Green, Chair, 254-710-2263, Fax: 254-710-3265, E-mail: steve_green@baylor.edu. *Application contact:* Vicky Todd, Administrative Assistant, 254-710-3718, Fax: 254-710-1066, E-mail: mba@hsb.baylor.edu.

Boston University, Graduate School of Arts and Sciences, Department of Geography and Environment, Boston, MA 02215. Offers energy and environmental analysis (MA); environmental remote sensing and GIs (MA); geography (MA); geography and environment (PhD); international relations and environmental policy (MA). *Students:* 49 full-time (22 women), 8 part-time (4 women); includes 1 minority (Hispanic American), 28 international. Average age 29. 55 applicants, 27% accepted, 6 enrolled. In 2007, 2 master's, 3 doctorates awarded. Terminal master's awarded for partial completion of doctoral program. *Degree requirements:* For master's, one foreign language, comprehensive exam, thesis; for doctorate, one foreign language, comprehensive exam, thesis/dissertation. *Entrance requirements:* For master's and doctorate, GRE General Test, GRE Subject Test, 3 letters of recommendation. Additional exam requirements/recommendations for international students: Required—TOEFL (minimum score 600 paper-based; 250 computer-based). *Application deadline:* For fall admission, 7/1 for domestic and international students; for spring admission, 11/15 for domestic and international students. Application fee: $70. *Expenses:* Tuition: Full-time $34,930; part-time $1,092 per credit. Tuition and fees vary according to class time, course level and program. *Financial support:* In 2007–08, 33 students received support, including 2 fellowships with full tuition reimbursements available (averaging $18,000 per year), 20 research assistantships with full tuition reimbursements available (averaging $17,500 per year), 9 teaching assistantships with full tuition reimbursements available (averaging $17,500 per year); Federal Work-Study and unspecified assistantships also available. Support available to part-time students. Financial award application deadline: 1/15; financial award applicants required to submit FAFSA. Total annual research expenditures: $1.2 million. *Unit head:* Mark Friedl, Chairman, 617-353-5745, Fax: 617-353-8399, E-mail: friedl@bu.edu. *Application contact:* Erin Wnorowski, Graduate Program Coordinator, 617-353-7554, Fax: 617-353-8399, E-mail: wnorowsk@bu.edu.

Boston University, Graduate School of Arts and Sciences, Department of International Relations, Boston, MA 02215. Offers African studies (Certificate); international relations (MA); international relations and environmental policy management (MA); international relations and international communication (MA); JD/MA; MBA/MA. *Students:* 60 full-time (33 women), 28 part-time (19 women); includes 12 minority (4 African Americans, 6 Asian Americans or Pacific Islanders, 2 Hispanic Americans), 13 international. Average age 29. 337 applicants, 64% accepted, 48 enrolled. In 2007, 36 degrees awarded. *Degree requirements:* For master's, one foreign language, comprehensive exam, thesis. *Entrance requirements:* For master's, GRE General Test, 3 letters of recommendation; for Certificate, GRE General Test. Additional exam requirements/recommendations for international students: Required—TOEFL (minimum score 600 paper-based; 250 computer-based). *Application deadline:* For fall admission, 4/15 for domestic and international students; for spring admission, 10/15 for domestic and international students. Application fee: $70. *Expenses:* Tuition: Full-time $34,930; part-time $1,092 per credit. Tuition and fees vary according to class time, course level and program. *Financial support:* In 2007–08, 17 students received support. Federal Work-Study, scholarships/grants, and unspecified assistantships available. Support available to part-time students. Financial award application deadline: 1/15; financial award applicants required to submit FAFSA. *Unit head:* Dr. Erik Goldstein, Chairman, 617-353-9280, Fax: 617-353-9290, E-mail: goldstee@bu.edu. *Application contact:* Michael Williams, Graduate Program Administrator, 617-353-9349, Fax: 617-353-9290, E-mail: mawillia@bu.edu.

Brandeis University, International Business School, Waltham, MA 02454-9110. Offers finance (MSF); international business (MBAi); international economics and finance (MA, PhD); international finance/international economics (MBAi). Part-time and evening/weekend programs available. Terminal master's awarded for partial completion of doctoral program. *Degree requirements:* For master's, one foreign language, semester abroad; for doctorate, thesis/dissertation. *Entrance requirements:* For master's, GMAT or GRE General Test (MA), GMAT (MBAi and MSF); for doctorate, GRE General Test. Additional exam requirements/recommendations for international students: Required—TOEFL (minimum score 600 paper-based; 250 computer-based), IELTS (minimum score 7). Electronic applications accepted. *Faculty research:* International finance and business, trade policy, macroeconomics, Asian economic issues, developmental economics.

See Close-Up on page 1025.

British American College London, Webster Graduate School, London, United Kingdom. Offers business (MBA); finance (MS); human resources (MA); information technology management (MA); international business (MA); international non-governmental organizations (MA); international relations (MA); management and leadership (MA); marketing (MA). Part-time programs available.

Brock University, Faculty of Graduate Studies, Faculty of Social Sciences, Program in Political Science, St. Catharines, ON L2S 3A1, Canada. Offers Canadian politics (MA); international and comparative politics (MA); political philosophy (MA); public administration (MA). Part-time programs available. *Degree requirements:* For master's, thesis optional. *Entrance requirements:* For master's, honors degree. Additional exam requirements/recommendations for international students: Required—TOEFL (minimum score 550 paper-based; 213 computer-based; 80 iBT), IELTS (minimum score 7), TWE (minimum score 4). Electronic applications accepted. *Faculty research:* Public administration reform, economic and social justice, politics of societies, Canadian politics, international relations.

Brooklyn College of the City University of New York, Division of Graduate Studies, Department of Political Science, Brooklyn, NY 11210-2889. Offers international affairs (MA); political science (MA, PhD); political science, urban policy and administration (MA). The department offers courses at Brooklyn College that are creditable toward the CUNY doctoral degree (with permission of the executive officer of the doctoral program). Part-time and evening/weekend programs available. *Students:* 6 full-time (3 women), 106 part-time (64 women); includes 65 minority (50 African Americans, 5 Asian Americans or Pacific Islanders, 10 Hispanic Americans), 13 international. 56 applicants, 89% accepted, 30 enrolled. In 2007, 43 degrees awarded. *Degree requirements:* For master's, comprehensive exam (for some programs), thesis or alternative, foreign language exam for international affairs program. *Entrance requirements:* For master's, 2 letters of recommendation, personal statement. *Application deadline:* For fall admission, 3/1 priority date for domestic students, 2/1 priority date for international students; for spring admission, 11/1 priority date for domestic students, 10/1 priority date for international students. Applications are processed on a rolling basis. Application fee: $125. Electronic applications accepted. *Financial support:* Career-related internships or fieldwork and Federal Work-Study available. Support available to part-time students. Financial award application deadline: 5/1; financial award applicants required to submit FAFSA. *Faculty research:* Ethics and politics, politics of criminal justice, Western Europe, international law and politics, labor politics. *Unit head:* Dr. Sally Bermanzohn, Chairperson, 718-951-5306, E-mail: sallyb@brooklyn.cuny.edu. *Application contact:* Hernan Sierra, Graduate Admissions Coordinator, 718-951-4536, Fax: 718-951-4506, E-mail: grads@brooklyn.cuny.edu.

California State University, Fresno, Division of Graduate Studies, College of Social Sciences, Department of Political Science, Program in International Relations, Fresno, CA 93740-8027. Offers MA. Part-time and evening/weekend programs available. *Faculty:* 8 full-time (0 women). *Students:* 61; includes 20 minority (3 African Americans, 1 American Indian/Alaska Native, 5 Asian Americans or Pacific Islanders, 11 Hispanic Americans), 5 international. Average age 28. 7 applicants. In 2007, 22 degrees awarded. *Degree requirements:* For master's, one foreign language, thesis or alternative. *Entrance requirements:* For master's, GRE General Test, minimum GPA of 3.0. Additional exam requirements/recommendations for international students: Required—TOEFL. *Application deadline:* For fall admission, 5/1 for domestic and international students; for spring admission, 10/1 for domestic and international students. Applications are processed on a rolling basis. Application fee: $55. Electronic applications accepted. *Financial support:* Career-related internships or fieldwork, Federal Work-Study, scholarships/grants, and unspecified assistantships available. Support available to part-time students. Financial award application deadline: 3/1; financial award applicants required to submit FAFSA.

California State University, Sacramento, Graduate Studies, College of Social Sciences and Interdisciplinary Studies, International Affairs Graduate Program, Sacramento, CA 95819-6048. Offers MA. Part-time programs available. *Students:* 12 full-time (4 women), 10 part-time (9 women); includes 6 minority (2 African Americans, 1 American Indian/Alaska Native, 1 Asian American or Pacific Islander, 2 Hispanic Americans). Average age 29. 23 applicants, 39% accepted, 4 enrolled. *Degree requirements:* For master's, one foreign language, thesis or alternative, writing proficiency exam. *Entrance requirements:* For master's, GRE General Test, appropriate bachelor's degree, minimum GPA of 3.0 in last 2 years of course work. Additional exam requirements/recommendations for international students: Required—TOEFL. *Application deadline:* Applications are processed on a rolling basis. Application fee: $55. Electronic applications accepted. *Expenses:* Tuition, state resident: full-time $3,414. Tuition, nonresident: full-time $13,584; part-time $339 per unit. Required fees: $786; $393 per semester. *Financial support:* Teaching assistantships, career-related internships or fieldwork and Federal Work-Study available. Support available to part-time students. Financial award application deadline: 3/1. *Unit head:* Bahman Fozouni, Chair, 916-278-6202, Fax: 916-278-6488.

California State University, Stanislaus, College of Humanities and Social Sciences, Department of History, Turlock, CA 95382. Offers history (MA); international relations (MA); secondary school teachers (MA). Part-time programs available. *Faculty:* 9. *Students:* 4 full-time (2 women), 19 part-time (7 women); includes 5 minority (1 African American, 1 Asian American or Pacific Islander, 3 Hispanic Americans). Average age 36. 18 applicants, 100% accepted, 9 enrolled. *Degree requirements:* For master's, one foreign language, comprehensive exam, thesis or alternative. *Entrance requirements:* For master's, GRE General Test, minimum undergraduate GPA of 3.0, personal statement. Additional exam requirements/recommendations for international students: Required—TOEFL (minimum score 550 paper-based; 213 computer-based). Application fee: $55. Electronic applications accepted. *Expenses:* Tuition, nonresident: full-time $10,170; part-time $339 per unit. Required fees: $3,972; $2,538 per term. $1,165 per semester. *Financial support:* Fellowships, Federal Work-Study available. Financial award application deadline: 3/2; financial award applicants required to submit FAFSA. *Faculty research:* History of Ancient Greece, history and ecology of the central valley, acculturation and gender. *Application contact:* Dr. Samuel Relgalado, Chair, 209-667-3238, Fax: 209-667-3132.

Carleton University, Faculty of Graduate Studies, Faculty of Public Affairs and Management, Norman Paterson School of International Affairs, Ottawa, ON K1S 5B6, Canada. Offers MA, PhD. Part-time programs available. *Degree requirements:* For master's, one foreign language, comprehensive exam, thesis optional. *Entrance requirements:* For master's, honors degree. Additional exam requirements/recommendations for international students: Required—TOEFL. *Application deadline:* Applications are processed on a rolling basis. Application fee: $77 Canadian dollars. *Financial support:* Fellowships, research assistantships, teaching assistantships, institutionally sponsored loans, scholarships/grants, and unspecified assistantships available. *Faculty research:* International conflict, development, political economy, conflict analysis. *Unit head:* Fen O. Hampson, Director, 613-520-2600 Ext. 6655, Fax: 613-520-2889, E-mail: international_affairs@carleton.ca. *Application contact:* Dane Rowlands, Graduate Supervisor, 613-520-2600 Ext. 6655, Fax: 613-520-2889, E-mail: international_affairs@carleton.ca.

The Catholic University of America, School of Arts and Sciences, Department of Business and Economics, Washington, DC 20064. Offers international political economics (MA). Part-time and evening/weekend programs available. *Faculty:* 8 full-time (3 women), 9 part-time/adjunct (6 women). *Students:* 3 full-time (all women), 29 part-time (20 women); includes 16 minority (11 African Americans, 2 Asian Americans or Pacific Islanders, 3 Hispanic Americans). Average age 34. 28 applicants, 14% accepted, 0 enrolled. In 2007, 1 degree awarded. *Degree requirements:* For master's, comprehensive exam. *Entrance requirements:* For master's, GRE General Test, 3 letters of recommendation. Additional exam requirements/recommendations for international students: Required—TOEFL (minimum score 580 paper-based; 237 computer-based). *Application deadline:* For fall admission, 2/1 priority date for domestic students; for spring admission, 11/15 priority date for domestic students. Applications are processed on a rolling basis. Application fee: $55. Electronic applications accepted. *Financial support:* Teaching assistantships, career-related internships or fieldwork, Federal Work-Study, scholarships/grants, tuition waivers (full and partial), and unspecified assistantships available. Support available to part-time students. Financial award application deadline: 2/1; financial award applicants required to submit FAFSA. *Unit head:* Dr. Kevin F. Forbes, Chair, 202-319-5236, Fax: 202-319-4426, E-mail: forbes@cua.edu.

The Catholic University of America, School of Arts and Sciences, Department of Politics, Washington, DC 20064. Offers American government (MA, PhD); congressional studies (MA); international affairs (MA); international political economics (MA); political theory (MA, PhD); world politics (MA, PhD); JD/MA. Part-time programs available. *Faculty:* 13 full-time (2 women), 9 part-time/adjunct (1 woman). *Students:* 27 full-time (10 women), 85 part-time (30 women); includes 16 minority (3 African Americans, 7 Asian Americans or Pacific Islanders, 6 Hispanic Americans), 13 international. Average age 31. 110 applicants, 70% accepted, 25 enrolled. In 2007, 27 master's, 6 doctorates awarded. *Degree requirements:* For master's, one foreign language, comprehensive exam, thesis or alternative; for doctorate, 2 foreign languages, comprehensive exam, thesis/dissertation. *Entrance requirements:* For master's and doctorate, GRE General Test, 3 letters of recommendation, minimum GPA of 3.0. Additional exam requirements/recommendations for international students: Required—TOEFL (minimum score 580 paper-based; 237 computer-based). *Application deadline:* For fall admission, 2/1 priority date for domestic students; for spring admission, 11/15 priority date for domestic students. Applications are processed on a rolling basis. Application fee: $55. Electronic applications accepted. *Financial support:* Teaching assistantships, career-related internships or fieldwork, Federal Work-Study, scholarships/grants, tuition waivers (full and partial), and unspecified assistantships available. Support available to part-time students. Financial award application deadline: 2/1; financial award applicants required to submit FAFSA. *Faculty research:* Political philosophy, American political institutions and processes, political economy, national security. *Unit head:* Dr. Stephen Schneck, Chair, 202-319-5128, Fax: 202-319-6289, E-mail: schneck@cua.edu.

Central Connecticut State University, School of Graduate Studies, School of Arts and Sciences, Program in International Area Studies, New Britain, CT 06050-4010. Offers international studies (MS). Part-time and evening/weekend programs available. *Students:* 11 full-time (4 women), 21 part-time (15 women); includes 6 minority (3 African Americans, 1 Asian American or Pacific Islander, 2 Hispanic Americans), 2 international. Average age 32. 9 applicants, 0% accepted. In 2007, 5 degrees awarded. *Degree requirements:* For master's, thesis or alternative, comprehensive exam or special project. *Entrance requirements:* For master's, minimum GPA of 2.7. Additional exam requirements/recommendations for international students: Required—TOEFL. *Application deadline:* For fall admission, 7/1 for domestic students; for spring admission, 12/1 for domestic students. Applications are processed on a rolling basis. Application fee: $50. Electronic applications accepted. *Expenses:* Tuition, area resident: Full-time $4,169. Tuition, state resident: full-time $6,253. Tuition, nonresident: full-time $11,614; part-time $400 per credit. Required fees: $3,322. One-time fee: $62 part-time. Tuition and fees vary according to degree level and program. *Financial support:* In 2007–08, 2 students received support; research assistantships, career-related internships or fieldwork, Federal Work-Study, scholarships/grants, and unspecified assistantships available. Support available to part-time students. Financial award application deadline: 3/1; financial award applicants required to submit FAFSA. *Unit head:* Dr. Evelyn Newman Phillips, Coordinator, 860-832-2617.

Central European University, Graduate Studies, School of Social Sciences and Humanities, Budapest, Hungary. Offers economics (MA, PhD); gender studies (MA, PhD); international relations and European studies (MA, PhD); mathematics and its applications (MS, PhD); medieval studies (MA, PhD); nationalism studies (MA, PhD); philosophy (MA, PhD); political science (MA, PhD); public policy (MA, PhD); sociology and social anthropology (MA, PhD). *Faculty:* 75 full-time (25 women), 46 part-time/adjunct (10 women). *Students:* 625 full-time (355 women). Average age 26. 2,500 applicants, 31% accepted, 540 enrolled. In 2007, 325 master's, 20 doctorates awarded. Terminal master's awarded for partial completion of doctoral program. *Degree requirements:* For master's, one foreign language, thesis; for doctorate, one foreign language, comprehensive exam, thesis/dissertation. *Entrance requirements:* For master's, CEU subject tests, interview; for doctorate, GRE, CEU subject test, interview. Additional exam requirements/recommendations for international students: Required—TOEFL (minimum score 570 paper-based; 230 computer-based). *Application deadline:* For fall admission, 1/15 priority date for domestic and international students. Application fee: $0. Electronic applications accepted. Tuition charges are reported in euros. *Expenses:* Tuition: Full-time 10,000 euros; part-time 315 euros per credit. *Financial support:* In 2007–08, 402 students received support, including 350 fellowships with full and partial tuition reimbursements available (averaging $5,000 per year); career-related internships or fieldwork, institutionally sponsored loans, and scholarships/grants also available. Financial award application deadline: 1/5. *Faculty research:* Civil society, fiscal decentralization, party politics, political philosophy (especially Liberalism, theory of Democracy). Total annual research expenditures: $35,000. *Unit head:* Dr. Howard Michael Robinson, Provost, 361-327-3003, Fax: 361-327-3211, E-mail: robinson@ceu.hu. *Application contact:* Zsuzsanna Jaszberenyi, Admissions Officer, 361-327-3009, Fax: 361-327-3211, E-mail: admissions@ceu.hu.

See Close-Up on page 447.

Central Michigan University, Central Michigan University Off-Campus Programs, Program in Administration, Mount Pleasant, MI 48859. Offers acquisitions administration (MSA, Certificate); general administration (MSA, Certificate); health services administration (MSA, Certificate); human resources administration (MSA, Certificate); information resource management (MSA, Certificate); international administration (MSA, Certificate); leadership (MSA, Certificate); public administration (MSA, Certificate); software engineering administration (MSA); vehicle design and manufacturing administration (MSA, Certificate). Part-time and evening/weekend programs available. Postbaccalaureate distance learning degree programs offered (no on-campus study). *Students:* Average age 38. *Entrance requirements:* For master's, minimum GPA of 2.7 in major. *Application deadline:* Applications are processed on a rolling basis. Application fee: $50. Electronic applications accepted. *Financial support:* Scholarships/grants available. Support available to part-time students. Financial award applicants required to submit FAFSA. *Unit head:* Dr. Scott J. Smith, Head, 989-774-2859, E-mail: smith5sj@cmich.edu. *Application contact:* 877-268-4636, E-mail: cmuoffcampus@cmich.edu.

City College of the City University of New York, Graduate School, College of Liberal Arts and Science, Division of Social Science, Program in International Relations, New York, NY 10031-9198. Offers MA. Part-time programs available. *Students:* 2 full-time (1 woman), 80 part-time (41 women); includes 46 minority (16 African Americans, 9 Asian Americans or Pacific Islanders, 21 Hispanic Americans), 26 international. 55 applicants, 69% accepted, 13 enrolled. In 2007, 32 degrees awarded. *Degree requirements:* For master's, one foreign language, thesis. *Entrance requirements:* For master's, GRE, 3 letters of recommendation. Additional exam requirements/recommendations for international students: Required—TOEFL (minimum score 600 paper-based; 250 computer-based). *Application deadline:* For fall admission, 4/1 for domestic students; for spring admission, 11/1 for domestic students. Application fee: $125. *Financial support:* Fellowships, research assistantships, teaching assistantships, career-related internships or fieldwork available. *Faculty research:* International finance, international economics, European diplomatic history, area studies, international politics and diplomacy. *Unit head:* Bruce Cronin, Director, 212-650-6844, Fax: 212-650-5464, E-mail: bcronin@ccny.cuny.edu.

Claremont Graduate University, Graduate Programs, School of Politics and Economics, Department of Politics and Policy, Claremont, CA 91711-6160. Offers American politics (MA, PhD); comparative politics (PhD); international political economy (MA); international studies (MA); political philosophy (PhD); political science (PhD); politics, economics and business (MA); public policy (MA, PhD); world politics (PhD); MBA/PhD. Part-time programs available. *Faculty:* 7 full-time (3 women), 9 part-time/adjunct (1 woman). *Students:* 181 full-time (69 women), 19 part-time (8 women); includes 35 minority (8 African Americans, 10 Asian Americans or Pacific Islanders, 17 Hispanic Americans), 45 international. Average age 34. In 2007, 27 master's, 19 doctorates awarded. Terminal master's awarded for partial completion of doctoral program. *Degree requirements:* For master's, thesis; for doctorate, one foreign language, thesis/dissertation. *Entrance requirements:* For master's and doctorate, GRE General Test. *Application deadline:* For fall admission, 2/15 priority date for domestic students. Applications are processed on a rolling basis. Electronic applications accepted. *Expenses:* Tuition: Full-time $31,640; part-time $1,376 per unit. Required fees: $145 per semester. Tuition and fees vary according to course load, degree level and program. *Financial support:* Fellowships, research assistantships, teaching assistantships, career-related internships or fieldwork, Federal Work-Study, and institutionally sponsored loans available. Support available to part-time students. Financial award application deadline: 2/15; financial award applicants required to submit FAFSA. *Faculty research:* Environmental policy, international debt, global democratization, Third World

International Affairs

Claremont Graduate University (continued)
development, public sector discrimination. *Unit head:* Jean Schroedel, Chair, 909-621-8696, Fax: 909-621-8545, E-mail: jean.schroedel@cgu.edu.

Colorado School of Mines, Graduate School, Division of Liberal Arts and International Studies, Golden, CO 80401-1887. Offers international political economy (Graduate Certificate); liberal arts and international studies (MIPER); science and technology policy (Graduate Certificate). Part-time programs available. *Faculty:* 54 full-time (26 women), 3 part-time/adjunct (1 woman). *Students:* 10 full-time (2 women), 3 part-time; includes 2 minority (both Hispanic Americans) 11 applicants, 91% accepted, 5 enrolled. In 2007, 7 degrees awarded. *Degree requirements:* For master's, thesis or alternative. *Entrance requirements:* For master's, GRE. Additional exam requirements/recommendations for international students: Required—TOEFL (minimum score 550 paper-based; 213 computer-based; 80 iBT). *Application deadline:* For fall admission, 1/15 priority date for domestic and international students; for spring admission, 9/1 priority date for domestic and international students. Application fee: $50 ($70 for international students). Electronic applications accepted. *Expenses:* Tuition, state resident: full-time $8,964; part-time $448 per credit. Tuition, nonresident: full-time $21,744; part-time $1,130 per credit. Required fees: $1,287; $643 per semester. *Financial support:* In 2007–08, 13 students received support, including fellowships with full tuition reimbursements available (averaging $19,968 per year), research assistantships with full tuition reimbursements available (averaging $19,968 per year), 9 teaching assistantships with full tuition reimbursements available (averaging $19,968 per year); scholarships/grants, health care benefits, and unspecified assistantships also available. Total annual research expenditures: $27,852. *Unit head:* Dr. Eul Soo Pang, Director, 303-273-3596, Fax: 303-273-3751, E-mail: epang@mines.edu. *Application contact:* Connie Warren, Program Assistant, 303-273-3590, Fax: 303-273-3751, E-mail: cwarren@mines.edu.

Columbia University, School of International and Public Affairs, Program in International Affairs, New York, NY 10027. Offers MIA, JD/MIA, MBA/MIA, MIA/MS, MPH/MIA, MSJ/MIA. *Faculty:* 70 full-time (18 women), 203 part-time/adjunct (80 women). *Students:* 720 full-time (410 women). Average age 27. 1,908 applicants, 39% accepted, 342 enrolled. In 2007, 332 degrees awarded. *Degree requirements:* For master's, one foreign language. *Entrance requirements:* For master's, GRE General Test. Additional exam requirements/recommendations for international students: Required—TOEFL (minimum score 600 paper-based; 250 computer-based; 100 iBT). *Application deadline:* For fall admission, 1/5 for domestic and international students; for spring admission, 10/1 for domestic and international students. Application fee: $85. Electronic applications accepted. *Expenses:* Tuition: Part-time $1,452 per credit. Required fees: $152 per term. One-time fee: $75 part-time. Full-time tuition and fees vary according to course level, course load, degree level and program. *Financial support:* In 2007–08, 207 students received support, including 184 fellowships with full and partial tuition reimbursements available (averaging $14,692 per year), 23 teaching assistantships with full and partial tuition reimbursements available (averaging $25,701 per year); research assistantships, career-related internships or fieldwork, Federal Work-Study, and institutionally sponsored loans also available. Financial award application deadline: 1/5; financial award applicants required to submit FAFSA. *Unit head:* Director, 212-854-8690, Fax: 212-854-3010, E-mail: sipa_admission@columbia.edu. *Application contact:* Matt Clemons, Director of Admissions and Financial Aid, 212-854-6216, Fax: 212-854-3010, E-mail: mc2793@columbia.edu.

See Close-Up on page 1143.

Concordia University, School of Business and Professional Studies, Irvine, CA 92612-3299. Offers entrepreneurial business administration (MBA); international studies (MA). Part-time programs available. *Faculty:* 1 full-time (0 women), 11 part-time/adjunct (0 women). *Students:* 111 full-time (51 women), 27 part-time (15 women); includes 33 minority (6 African Americans, 16 Asian Americans or Pacific Islanders, 11 Hispanic Americans), 17 international. Average age 30. In 2007, 31 degrees awarded. *Entrance requirements:* Additional exam requirements/recommendations for international students: Required—TOEFL (minimum score 550 paper-based; 213 computer-based). *Application deadline:* For fall admission, 7/1 for domestic students; for spring admission, 12/1 for domestic students. Applications are processed on a rolling basis. *Financial support:* Applicants required to submit FAFSA. Total annual research expenditures: $10,000. *Unit head:* Dr. Timothy Peters, Dean, 949-854-8002 Ext. 1333, Fax: 949-854-6864, E-mail: tim.peters@cui.edu. *Application contact:* Roberto Marquez, Coordinator of Graduate Enrollment, 949-854-8002 Ext. 1133, Fax: 949-854-6894, E-mail: roberto.marquez@cui.edu.

Cornell University, Graduate School, Graduate Fields of Arts and Sciences, Field of Government, Ithaca, NY 14853-0001. Offers American politics (PhD); comparative politics (PhD); international relations (PhD); political methodology (PhD); political thought (PhD); public policy (PhD). *Faculty:* 39 full-time (13 women). *Students:* 71 full-time (37 women); includes 12 minority (2 African Americans, 1 American Indian/Alaska Native, 6 Asian Americans or Pacific Islanders, 3 Hispanic Americans), 33 international. Average age 30. 305 applicants, 8% accepted, 11 enrolled. In 2007, 9 doctorates awarded. *Degree requirements:* For doctorate, comprehensive exam, thesis/dissertation. *Entrance requirements:* For doctorate, GRE General Test, sample of written work, 3 letters of recommendation. Additional exam requirements/recommendations for international students: Required—TOEFL (minimum score 550 paper-based; 213 computer-based; 77 iBT). *Application deadline:* For fall admission, 1/15 for domestic students. Application fee: $70. Electronic applications accepted. *Financial support:* In 2007–08, 56 students received support, including 29 fellowships with full tuition reimbursements available, 1 research assistantship with full tuition reimbursement available, 26 teaching assistantships with full tuition reimbursements available; institutionally sponsored loans, scholarships/grants, health care benefits, tuition waivers (full and partial), and unspecified assistantships also available. Financial award applicants required to submit FAFSA. *Faculty research:* Political theory, American politics, comparative politics, international relations, methodology. *Unit head:* Director of Graduate Studies, 607-255-3567, Fax: 607-255-4530. *Application contact:* Graduate Field Assistant, 607-255-3567, Fax: 607-255-4530, E-mail: cu_govt@cornell.edu.

Creighton University, Graduate School, College of Arts and Sciences, Program in International Relations, Omaha, NE 68178-0001. Offers MA. Part-time and evening/weekend programs available. *Faculty:* 13 full-time. *Students:* 6 full-time (3 women), 16 part-time (1 woman); includes 4 minority (1 African American, 2 Asian Americans or Pacific Islanders, 1 Hispanic American), 2 international. 10 applicants, 60% accepted, 4 enrolled. In 2007, 4 degrees awarded. *Degree requirements:* For master's, one foreign language, thesis. *Entrance requirements:* For master's, GRE General Test, 3 letters of recommendation. Additional exam requirements/recommendations for international students: Required—TOEFL (minimum score 550 paper-based; 213 computer-based; 80 iBT). *Application deadline:* For fall admission, 3/1 priority date for domestic and international students; for winter admission, 12/1 priority date for domestic and international students; for spring admission, 4/1 priority date for domestic and international students. Applications are processed on a rolling basis. Application fee: $50. Electronic applications accepted. *Financial support:* In 2007–08, fellowships with tuition reimbursements (averaging $10,075 per year), research assistantships with tuition reimbursements (averaging $10,075 per year) were awarded; health care benefits also available. Support available to part-time students. Financial award applicants required to submit FAFSA. *Unit head:* Dr. Terry Clark, Chair, 402-280-4712, E-mail: tclark@creighton.edu. *Application contact:* LuAnn M. Schwery, Assistant Dean, 402-280-2870, Fax: 402-280-5762, E-mail: schwery@creighton.edu.

East Carolina University, Graduate School, Thomas Harriot College of Arts and Sciences, Program in International Studies, Greenville, NC 27858-4353. Offers MA. Part-time programs available. *Students:* 14 full-time (10 women), 9 part-time (8 women); includes 1 minority (Asian American or Pacific Islander), 2 international. Average age 29. 8 applicants, 50% accepted, 3 enrolled. In 2007, 10 degrees awarded. *Degree requirements:* For master's, comprehensive exam. *Entrance requirements:* For master's, GRE General Test. Additional exam requirements/recommendations for international students: Required—TOEFL. *Application deadline:* Applications are processed on a rolling basis. Application fee: $50. *Financial support:* Research assistantships with partial tuition reimbursements available. Financial award application deadline: 6/1. *Unit head:* Dr. Sylvie Henning, Director, 252-328-5520. *Application contact:* Dean of Graduate School, 252-328-6012, Fax: 252-328-6071, E-mail: gradschool@ecu.edu.

Fairleigh Dickinson University, Metropolitan Campus, University College: Arts, Sciences, and Professional Studies, School of History, Political and International Studies, Program in International Studies, Teaneck, NJ 07666-1914. Offers MA. *Students:* 6 full-time (4 women), 6 part-time (3 women), 4 international. Average age 27. 26 applicants, 62% accepted, 8 enrolled. *Application deadline:* Applications are processed on a rolling basis. Application fee: $40. *Expenses:* Tuition: Part-time $869 per credit. Tuition and fees vary according to degree level, campus/location and program. *Unit head:* Dr. Faramarz S. Fatemi, Director, School of History, Political and International Studies, 201-692-2272, Fax: 201-692-9096, E-mail: fatemi@fdu.edu.

Florida Agricultural and Mechanical University, Division of Graduate Studies, Research, and Continuing Education, College of Engineering Science, Technology, and Agriculture, Division of Agricultural Sciences, Tallahassee, FL 32307-3200. Offers agribusiness (MS); animal science (MS); engineering technology (MS); entomology (MS); food science (MS); international programs (MS); plant science (MS). *Degree requirements:* For master's, thesis. *Entrance requirements:* For master's, GRE General Test, minimum GPA of 3.0. Additional exam requirements/recommendations for international students: Required—TOEFL (minimum score 500 paper-based).

Florida International University, College of Arts and Sciences, Department of International Relations, Miami, FL 33199. Offers international relations (PhD); international studies (MA). Fall admission only for PhD. Part-time programs available. *Faculty:* 20 full-time (5 women), 2 part-time/adjunct (1 woman). *Students:* 36 full-time (14 women), 26 part-time (16 women); includes 25 minority (3 African Americans, 1 American Indian/Alaska Native, 6 Asian Americans or Pacific Islanders, 15 Hispanic Americans), 15 international. Average age 33. 66 applicants, 58% accepted, 26 enrolled. In 2007, 10 master's, 3 doctorates awarded. *Degree requirements:* For master's, one foreign language, thesis optional; for doctorate, one foreign language, thesis/dissertation. *Entrance requirements:* For master's and doctorate, GRE General Test, minimum GPA of 3.0, letters of recommendatikon. Additional exam requirements/recommendations for international students: Required—TOEFL (minimum score 550 paper-based; 213 computer-based). *Application deadline:* For fall admission, 1/15 for domestic students, 1/15 priority date for international students; for spring admission, 8/15 for domestic and international students. Applications are processed on a rolling basis. Application fee: $30. *Expenses:* Tuition, state resident: full-time $6,106. Tuition, nonresident: full-time $15,528. Required fees: $284. *Financial support:* Teaching assistantships, Federal Work-Study, institutionally sponsored loans, and tuition waivers (full) available. Financial award application deadline: 1/15. *Faculty research:* International relations theory (particularly constructivist and feminist IR theory), comparative regional studies (including Latin America and the Caribbean, Europe, East and Central Asia, Africa, and the Middle East), foreign policy and security, international law and human rights, identity and geopolitics. *Unit head:* Dr. John Clark, Chairperson, 305-348-3289, Fax: 305-348-6189, E-mail: john.clark@fiu.edu.

Florida State University, Graduate Studies, College of Social Sciences, Program in International Affairs, Tallahassee, FL 32306. Offers MA, MS, JD/MA, JD/MS. Part-time programs available. *Students:* 31 full-time (12 women), 47 part-time (22 women); includes 19 minority (9 African Americans, 1 American Indian/Alaska Native, 1 Asian American or Pacific Islander, 8 Hispanic Americans), 5 international. Average age 25. 90 applicants, 97% accepted, 36 enrolled. In 2007, 46 degrees awarded. *Degree requirements:* For master's, one foreign language, comprehensive exam, thesis optional. *Entrance requirements:* For master's, GRE General Test, minimum GPA of 3.0. *Application deadline:* For fall admission, 7/1 for domestic students; for spring admission, 7/1 for domestic students. Applications are processed on a rolling basis. Application fee: $30. *Expenses:* Tuition, state resident: part-time $248 per credit hour. Tuition, nonresident: part-time $880 per credit hour. Tuition and fees vary according to program. *Financial support:* In 2007–08, 12 students received support, including fellowships with full tuition reimbursements available (averaging $15,000 per year), 5 research assistantships with full tuition reimbursements available (averaging $5,000 per year); career-related internships or fieldwork, Federal Work-Study, and institutionally sponsored loans also available. Financial award application deadline: 3/15; financial award applicants required to submit FAFSA. *Unit head:* Dr. Lee K. Metcalf, Director, 850-644-7327, Fax: 850-645-4981, E-mail: lmetcalf@fsu.edu. *Application contact:* Patty Lollis, Program Assistant, 850-644-4418, Fax: 850-645-4981, E-mail: plollis@mailer.fsu.edu.

Fordham University, Graduate School of Arts and Sciences, Program in International Political Economy and Development, New York, NY 10458. Offers MA, Certificate. Part-time and evening/weekend programs available. *Faculty:* 23. *Students:* 36 full-time (12 women), 20 part-time (9 women); includes 7 minority (1 American Indian/Alaska Native, 4 Asian Americans or Pacific Islanders, 2 Hispanic Americans), 12 international. Average age 28. 202 applicants, 39% accepted, 26 enrolled. In 2007, 37 degrees awarded. *Degree requirements:* For master's, comprehensive exam. *Entrance requirements:* For master's, GRE General Test. Additional exam requirements/recommendations for international students: Required—TOEFL (minimum score 600 paper-based; 250 computer-based). *Application deadline:* For fall admission, 1/4 priority date for domestic students; for spring admission, 11/1 for domestic students. Application fee: $70. Electronic applications accepted. *Expenses:* Tuition: Full-time $23,880; part-time $995 per credit. *Financial support:* In 2007–08, 14 students received support, including 1 fellowship with tuition reimbursement available (averaging $21,100 per year), 13 research assistantships with tuition reimbursements available (averaging $13,769 per year); career-related internships or fieldwork, institutionally sponsored loans, tuition waivers (full and partial), and unspecified assistantships also available. Financial award application deadline: 1/4; financial award applicants required to submit FAFSA. *Faculty research:* International economics, comparative international politics, international banking and finance, international development, emerging markets and country risk analysis. *Unit head:* Dr. Henry Schwalbenberg, Chair, 718-817-3866, Fax: 718-817-3518. *Application contact:* Charlene Dundie, Director of Graduate Admissions, 718-817-4420, Fax: 718-817-3566, E-mail: dundie@fordham.edu.

See Close-Up on page 1147.

George Mason University, School of Public Policy, Program in International Commerce and Policy, Fairfax, VA 22030. Offers MA. Part-time programs available. *Faculty:* 48 full-time (8 women), 41 part-time/adjunct (6 women). *Students:* 74 full-time (37 women), 178 part-time (89 women); includes 51 minority (7 African Americans, 21 Asian Americans or Pacific Islanders, 23 Hispanic Americans), 36 international. 155 applicants, 77% accepted, 69 enrolled. In 2007, 118 degrees awarded. *Degree requirements:* For master's, thesis or alternative. *Entrance requirements:* For master's, minimum undergraduate GPA of 3.0, 2 letters of recommendation, resumé, goals statement. Additional exam requirements/recommendations for international students: Required—TOEFL. *Application deadline:* For fall admission, 6/1 priority date for domestic students, 5/1 priority date for international students; for spring admission, 12/1 priority date for domestic students, 11/1 priority date for international students. Applications are processed on a rolling basis. Application fee: $60. Electronic applications accepted. *Expenses:* Contact institution. *Financial support:* Career-related internships or fieldwork, Federal Work-Study, scholarships/grants, and tuition waivers (partial) available. Support available to part-time students. Financial award application deadline: 3/1; financial award applicants required to submit FAFSA. *Unit head:* Dr. Kenneth Reinert, Director, 703-993-8099, E-mail: spp@gmu.edu. *Application contact:* Leslie Metzger Levin, Director of Graduate Admissions, 703-993-8099, Fax: 703-993-4876, E-mail: lmetzger@gmu.edu.

Georgetown University, Graduate School of Arts and Sciences, BMW Center for German and European Studies, Washington, DC 20057. Offers MA, MA/JD, MA/PhD. *Degree requirements:* For master's, 2 foreign languages, comprehensive exam. *Entrance requirements:* For master's, GRE General Test. Additional exam requirements/recommendations for international students: Required—TOEFL. *Faculty research:* Trans-Atlantic relations, European Union, German and European Studies.

Georgetown University, Graduate School of Arts and Sciences, Department of Government, Washington, DC 20057. Offers American government (MA, PhD); comparative government (PhD); conflict resolution (MA); democracy and governance (MA); international law and government (MA); international relations (PhD); political theory (PhD); MA/PhD. *Faculty:* 41 full-time (8 women), 13 part-time/adjunct (2 women). In 2007, 9 master's, 6 doctorates awarded. Terminal master's awarded for partial completion of doctoral program. *Degree requirements:* For master's, one foreign language, comprehensive exam; for doctorate, one foreign language, comprehensive exam, thesis/dissertation. *Entrance requirements:* For master's, GRE General Test, minimum B average; for doctorate, GRE General Test, MA. Additional exam requirements/recommendations for international students: Required—TOEFL. *Application deadline:* For fall admission, 1/2 priority date for domestic students. Application fee: $50 ($55 for international students). *Financial support:* Research assistantships, teaching assistantships, tuition waivers (full and partial) available. Financial award application deadline: 1/2; financial award applicants required to submit FAFSA. *Faculty research:* Western Europe, Latin America, the Middle East, political theory, international relations and law, methodology, American politics and institutions. *Unit head:* Dr. George Shambaugh, Chair, 202-687-6130. *Application contact:* Graduate School Admissions Office, 202-687-5974.

Georgetown University, Graduate School of Arts and Sciences, Edmund A. Walsh School of Foreign Service, Washington, DC 20057. Offers MS, JD/MS, MBA/MS, MS/MA. *Degree requirements:* For master's, one foreign language, comprehensive exam. *Entrance requirements:* For master's, GRE General Test, 3 semesters of undergraduate course work in economics. Additional exam requirements/recommendations for international students: Required—TOEFL. *Faculty research:* International business diplomacy, political risk analysis, foreign policy decision making, intercultural perspectives on contemporary issues.

The George Washington University, Elliott School of International Affairs, Program in International Affairs, Washington, DC 20052. Offers MA, JD/MA, MBA/MA, MPH/MA. Part-time and evening/weekend programs available. *Degree requirements:* For master's, one foreign language, capstone project. *Entrance requirements:* For master's, GRE General Test, 2 years of a modern foreign language, 2 semesters of introductory economics. Additional exam requirements/recommendations for international students: Required—TOEFL. Electronic applications accepted. *Faculty research:* Area studies, international economics, national security policy studies, international economic development, Sino-Soviet studies.

The George Washington University, Elliott School of International Affairs, Program in International Policy and Practice, Washington, DC 20052. Offers MIPP, MIS. Part-time and evening/weekend programs available. *Degree requirements:* For master's, one foreign language, capstone project. *Entrance requirements:* For master's, GRE (recommended), advanced degree or 8 years experience plus BA. Additional exam requirements/recommendations for international students: Required—TOEFL. Electronic applications accepted.

Georgia Institute of Technology, Graduate Studies and Research, Ivan Allen College of Policy and International Affairs, Sam Nunn School of International Affairs, Atlanta, GA 30332-0001. Offers MS Int A. *Degree requirements:* For master's, one foreign language. *Entrance requirements:* Additional exam requirements/recommendations for international students: Required—TOEFL. Electronic applications accepted. *Faculty research:* International political economy, international security, Asian and European studies.

See Close-Up on page 1149.

Harvard University, Graduate School of Arts and Sciences, Department of Government, Cambridge, MA 02138. Offers political science (PhD), including American politics, comparative politics, international relations, political thought, quantitative methods. *Degree requirements:* For doctorate, one foreign language, thesis/dissertation, general exams. *Entrance requirements:* For doctorate, GRE General Test. Additional exam requirements/recommendations for international students: Required—TOEFL. *Expenses:* Tuition: Full-time $31,456. Full-time tuition and fees vary according to program and student level.

Huron University USA in London, Graduate Programs, Program in International Relations, London, United Kingdom. Offers conflict resolution (MA); diplomacy (MA); international public law (MA); international relations (MA); Middle East international security (MA); politics (MA); security studies (MA); terrorism (MA); U.S. foreign policy (MA). Part-time programs available. *Entrance requirements:* Additional exam requirements/recommendations for international students: Required—TOEFL (minimum score 580 paper-based; 237 computer-based), TWE (minimum score 5). Electronic applications accepted. *Faculty research:* American foreign politics, Middle East, security studies.

Instituto Tecnológico y de Estudios Superiores de Monterrey, Campus Ciudad Obregón, Program in International Relations, Ciudad Obregón, Mexico. Offers MIR.

The Johns Hopkins University, Paul H. Nitze School of Advanced International Studies, Washington, DC 20036. Offers international development (Certificate); international public policy (MIPP); international relations (MA, PhD), including African studies (MA), American foreign policy (MA), Asian studies (MA), Canadian studies (MA), conflict management (MA), European studies (MA), global theory and history (MA), international development (MA), international law, and organizations (MA), international policy (MA), international relations (general) (MA), Latin American studies (MA), Middle East studies (MA), Russian and Eurasian studies (MA), strategic studies (MA); international studies (Certificate); JD/MA; MBA/MA; MHS/MA. *Faculty:* 66 full-time (22 women), 158 part-time/adjunct (54 women). *Students:* 578 full-time (256 women), 46 part-time (16 women); includes 85 minority (18 African Americans, 1 American Indian/Alaska Native, 51 Asian Americans or Pacific Islanders, 15 Hispanic Americans), 193 international. Average age 27. In 2007, 359 master's, 13 doctorates awarded. Terminal master's awarded for partial completion of doctoral program. *Degree requirements:* For master's, one foreign language, 16 non-language courses (8 for MIPP), 2 core examinations, comprehensive oral exam, paper (for some programs); for doctorate, 2 foreign languages, thesis/dissertation, 3 comprehensive exams, defense. *Entrance requirements:* For master's, GMAT or GRE General Test, previous course work in economics, foreign language, undergraduate degree; for doctorate, GRE General Test, master's degree. Additional exam requirements/recommendations for international students: Required—TOEFL (minimum paper-based score of 600, computer-based 250, iBT 100) or IELTS (minimum 7.0). *Application deadline:* For fall admission, 1/7 for domestic students. Application fee: $80. Electronic applications accepted. *Expenses: Contact institution. Financial support:* In 2007–08, 350 students received support, including fellowships (averaging $7,500 per year); career-related internships or fieldwork, Federal Work-Study, and scholarships/grants also available. Financial award application deadline: 2/15; financial award applicants required to submit FAFSA. *Faculty research:* Regional studies and functional fields of international relations, international economics, conflict management, global theory and history, international law and organizations, international policy, strategic studies. *Unit head:* Tara Campbell, Associate Director of Admissions, 202-663-5700, Fax: 202-663-7788. *Application contact:* Dr. Belinda A. Yeomans, Director of Admissions, 202-663-5700, Fax: 202-663-7788, E-mail: admissions.sais@jhu.edu.

Kansas State University, Graduate School, College of Arts and Sciences, Department of Political Science, Program in Political Science, Manhattan, KS 66506. Offers international service (MA); political science (MA). Part-time programs available. *Students:* 39 full-time (16 women), 3 part-time; includes 2 minority (both African Americans), 8 international. Average age 33. In 2007, 9 degrees awarded. *Degree requirements:* For master's, thesis or alternative. *Entrance requirements:* For master's, GRE (recommended), minimum GPA of 3.0. Additional exam requirements/recommendations for international students: Required—TOEFL (minimum score 550 paper-based; 213 computer-based). *Application deadline:* For fall admission, 2/1 priority date for domestic and international students; for spring admission, 10/1 for domestic students, 8/1 priority date for international students. Applications are processed on a rolling basis. Application fee: $30 ($55 for international students). *Financial support:* Fellowships, research assistantships, teaching assistantships, institutionally sponsored loans and scholarships/grants available. Support available to part-time students. Financial award application deadline: 3/1; financial award applicants required to submit FAFSA. *Application contact:* Jeffrey Pickering, Director, 785-532-0454, Fax: 785-532-2339, E-mail: jjp@ksu.edu.

Lebanese American University, School of Arts and Sciences, Beirut, Lebanon. Offers computer science (MS); international affairs (MA).

Lesley University, Graduate School of Arts and Social Sciences, Program in Intercultural Relations, Cambridge, MA 02138-2790. Offers MA, CAGS. Part-time and evening/weekend programs available. *Faculty:* 4 full-time (3 women), 3 part-time/adjunct (2 women). *Students:* 28 full-time (24 women), 44 part-time (41 women); includes 6 minority (4 African Americans, 2 Asian Americans or Pacific Islanders), 13 international. Average age 29. 55 applicants, 91% accepted, 29 enrolled. In 2007, 33 degrees awarded. *Degree requirements:* For master's, one foreign language, internship, practicum; for CAGS, one foreign language, thesis. *Entrance requirements:* For master's, interview; for CAGS, interview, master's degree. Additional exam requirements/recommendations for international students: Required—TOEFL (minimum score 550 paper-based; 213 computer-based; 80 iBT). Application fee: $50. *Financial support:* In 2007–08, 8 students received support, including research assistantships (averaging $3,400 per year), teaching assistantships (averaging $3,400 per year); career-related internships or fieldwork, Federal Work-Study, scholarships/grants, and unspecified assistantships also available. Support available to part-time students. Financial award application deadline: 4/15; financial award applicants required to submit FAFSA. *Faculty research:* Sociolinguistics, cross-cultural feminist theory, immigration and diaspora, intercultural business training. *Unit head:* Sylvia R. Cowan, Coordinator, 617-349-8978, E-mail: scowan@lesley.edu. *Application contact:* Jana Vanderveer, Assistant Director, Advising and Student Services, 617-349-8369, E-mail: jvanderv@lesley.edu.

Long Island University, Brooklyn Campus, Richard L. Conolly College of Liberal Arts and Sciences, Program in Social Science, Brooklyn, NY 11201-8423. Offers history (MS); United Nations studies (Certificate). Part-time and evening/weekend programs available. *Entrance requirements:* For master's, 2 letters of recommendation. Additional exam requirements/recommendations for international students: Required—TOEFL (minimum score 500 paper-based; 173 computer-based). Electronic applications accepted.

Long Island University, C.W. Post Campus, College of Liberal Arts and Sciences, Department of Political Science/International Studies, Brookville, NY 11548-1300. Offers MA. Part-time and evening/weekend programs available. *Faculty:* 4 full-time (0 women), 6 part-time/adjunct (2 women). *Students:* 9 full-time (6 women), 11 part-time (5 women); includes 7 minority (3 African Americans, 4 Asian Americans or Pacific Islanders), 1 international. Average age 26. 17 applicants, 76% accepted, 4 enrolled. In 2007, 7 degrees awarded. *Degree requirements:* For master's, comprehensive exam, thesis or alternative. *Entrance requirements:* For master's, GRE. *Application deadline:* For fall admission, 9/1 priority date for domestic students; for winter admission, 12/15 priority date for domestic students; for spring admission, 1/20 priority date for domestic students. Applications are processed on a rolling basis. Application fee: $30. Electronic applications accepted. *Expenses:* Tuition: Part-time $825 per credit. Tuition and fees vary according to course load. *Financial support:* In 2007–08, 2 research assistantships were awarded; career-related internships or fieldwork and Federal Work-Study also available. Support available to part-time students. Financial award application deadline: 5/15; financial award applicants required to submit CSS PROFILE or FAFSA. *Faculty research:* International relations, Middle Eastern politics, political philosophy. *Unit head:* Dr. Roger Goldstein, Chair, 516-299-2407, Fax: 516-299-4140. *Application contact:* Dr. Michael Soupios, Graduate Advisor, 516-299-3026.

Loyola University Chicago, Graduate School, Department of Political Science, Chicago, IL 60611-2196. Offers American politics and policy (MA, PhD); international studies (MA, PhD); political theory and philosophy (MA, PhD); JD/MA. Part-time and evening/weekend programs available. *Faculty:* 18 full-time (2 women), 1 (woman) part-time/adjunct. *Students:* 27 full-time (13 women), 3 part-time (1 woman), 2 international. Average age 31. 78 applicants, 51% accepted, 12 enrolled. In 2007, 18 master's, 3 doctorates awarded. *Degree requirements:* For master's, thesis or alternative; for doctorate, variable foreign language requirement, comprehensive exam, thesis/dissertation. *Entrance requirements:* For master's and doctorate, GRE General Test. *Application deadline:* For fall admission, 6/1 for domestic students; for spring admission, 10/1 for domestic students. Applications are processed on a rolling basis. Application fee: $50. Electronic applications accepted. *Expenses:* Tuition: Full-time $12,780; part-time $710 per credit hour. Required fees: $55 per semester. Full-time tuition and fees vary according to program. *Financial support:* In 2007–08, 5 fellowships with full tuition reimbursements (averaging $14,000 per year), 5 research assistantships with full tuition reimbursements (averaging $14,000 per year) were awarded; Federal Work-Study, institutionally sponsored loans, scholarships/grants, tuition waivers (partial), and unspecified assistantships also available. Financial award application deadline: 2/15; financial award applicants required to submit FAFSA. *Faculty research:* American parties and elections, state and local politics, American political institutions, international political economy, modern and contemporary political thought. *Unit head:* Prof. Peter M. Sanchez, Chair, 773-508-8658, Fax: 773-508-3131, E-mail: psanche@luc.edu.

Marquette University, Graduate School, College of Arts and Sciences, Department of Political Science/International Affairs, Milwaukee, WI 53201-1881. Offers international affairs (MA), including comparative politics, international political economy, international politics; political science (MA), including American politics, comparative politics, international politics, political philosophy; JD/MA. Part-time programs available. *Faculty:* 16 full-time (3 women), 2 part-time/adjunct (1 woman). *Students:* 17 full-time (3 women), 9 part-time (4 women); includes 1 minority (Hispanic American), 3 international. Average age 28. 75 applicants, 56% accepted, 9 enrolled. In 2007, 8 degrees awarded. *Degree requirements:* For master's, comprehensive exam, thesis optional. *Entrance requirements:* For master's, GRE General Test. Additional exam requirements/recommendations for international students: Required—TOEFL. Application fee: $40. *Financial support:* In 2007–08, 5 research assistantships were awarded; Federal Work-Study, institutionally sponsored loans, scholarships/grants, and tuition waivers (full and partial) also available. Support available to part-time students. Financial award application deadline: 2/15. *Faculty research:* Public opinion and electoral behavior, public policy analysis, Congress and the Presidency, judicial behavior, political system transitions. *Unit head:* Dr. Duane Swank, Chair, 414-288-3418, Fax: 414-288-3360. *Application contact:* Dr. Lowell Barrington, Director of Graduate Studies, 414-288-6842, Fax: 414-288-3360.

McMaster University, School of Graduate Studies, Faculty of Humanities and Faculty of Social Sciences, Institute on Globalization and the Human Condition, Hamilton, ON L8S 4M2, Canada. Offers globalization studies (MA). *Faculty:* 23 full-time. *Students:* 21 full-time. Application fee: $90. *Unit head:* Dr. William Coleman, Director, 905-525-9140 Ext. 23886, Fax: 905-777-8316, E-mail: colemanw@mcmaster.ca. *Application contact:* Kara Vincent, Graduate Secretary, 905-525-9140 Ext. 27877, Fax: 905-527-3071, E-mail: kvincen@mcmaster.ca.

McMaster University, School of Graduate Studies, Faculty of Social Sciences, Department of Political Science, Hamilton, ON L8S 4M2, Canada. Offers international relations (PhD); political science (MA); public and the global economy (MA); public policy (PhD); public policy and administration (MA). Part-time programs available. *Faculty:* 21 full-time. *Students:* 63 full-time, 6 part-time. 140 applicants, 20% accepted. *Degree requirements:* For master's, thesis or alternative. *Entrance requirements:* For master's, minimum B+ average. Additional exam requirements/recommendations for international students: Required—TOEFL (minimum score 580 paper-based; 237 computer-based). *Application deadline:* For fall admission, 2/15 priority date for domestic students. Applications are processed on a rolling basis. Application fee: $90. *Financial support:* In 2007–08, 27 teaching assistantships (averaging $8,440 per year) were awarded; scholarships/grants also available. *Faculty research:* Organizational theory, internationalization of public policy, water resource policies, political interest intermediation,

International Affairs

McMaster University (continued)

comparative politics. *Unit head:* Dr. Robert O'Brien, Chair, 905-525-9140 Ext. 23705, Fax: 905-527-3071, E-mail: obrienr@mcmaster.ca. *Application contact:* Manuela Dozzi, Administrative Secretary, 905-525-9140 Ext. 24742, Fax: 905-527-3071, E-mail: dozzim@mcmaster.ca.

Michigan State University, The Graduate School, College of Social Science, Interdisciplinary Studies in Social Science—Global Applications, East Lansing, MI 48824. Offers MA. *Degree requirements:* For master's, internship/practicum or field experience, policy paper or analytical report. *Entrance requirements:* Additional exam requirements/recommendations for international students: Required—TOEFL, Michigan State University ELT (85), Michigan English Language Assessment Battery (83). Electronic applications accepted. *Expenses:* Tuition, state resident: part-time $379 per credit hour. Tuition, nonresident: part-time $800 per credit hour. Tuition and fees vary according to program.

Missouri State University, Graduate College, College of Humanities and Public Affairs, Department of Political Science, Program in International Affairs and Administration, Springfield, MO 65804-0094. Offers MIAA. *Students:* 20 full-time (6 women), 10 part-time (2 women); includes 4 minority (2 African Americans, 1 Asian American or Pacific Islander, 1 Hispanic American), 4 international. Average age 28. 17 applicants, 100% accepted, 5 enrolled. In 2007, 12 degrees awarded. *Degree requirements:* For master's, 2 foreign languages, comprehensive exam, thesis or alternative. *Entrance requirements:* For master's, GRE, minimum GPA of 3.0. Additional exam requirements/recommendations for international students: Required—TOEFL (minimum score 550 paper-based; 213 computer-based; 79 iBT). *Application deadline:* For fall admission, 7/20 priority date for domestic students; for spring admission, 12/20 priority date for domestic students. Applications are processed on a rolling basis. Application fee: $35. Electronic applications accepted. *Expenses:* Tuition, state resident: full-time $3,708; part-time $206 per credit hour. Tuition, nonresident: full-time $7,236; part-time $206 per credit hour. Required fees: $622. Full-time tuition and fees vary according to course level, course load, program and reciprocity agreements. *Financial support:* In 2007–08, 1 teaching assistantship (averaging $7,050 per year) was awarded; research assistantships, Federal Work-Study, scholarships/grants, and unspecified assistantships also available. Support available to part-time students. Financial award application deadline: 3/31; financial award applicants required to submit FAFSA. *Unit head:* Dr. Gabriel Ondetti, Graduate Director, 417-836-5733, Fax: 417-836-6655, E-mail: gabrielondetti@missouristate.edu.

See Close-Up on page 1155.

Monterey Institute of International Studies, Graduate School of International Policy Studies, Program in International Policy Studies, Monterey, CA 93940-2691. Offers MA. *Students:* 221 full-time (121 women), 10 part-time (6 women); includes 24 minority (3 African Americans, 11 Asian Americans or Pacific Islanders, 10 Hispanic Americans), 49 international. Average age 27. 286 applicants, 95% accepted, 112 enrolled. In 2007, 102 degrees awarded. *Degree requirements:* For master's, one foreign language. *Entrance requirements:* For master's, minimum GPA of 3.0, proficiency in a foreign language. Additional exam requirements/recommendations for international students: Required—TOEFL (minimum score 550 paper-based; 213 computer-based; 80 iBT). *Application deadline:* For fall admission, 3/15 priority date for domestic students; for spring admission, 10/1 priority date for domestic students. Applications are processed on a rolling basis. Application fee: $50. Electronic applications accepted. *Expenses:* Tuition: Full-time $27,750; part-time $1,250 per credit. Required fees: $200. *Financial support:* Application deadline: 3/15. *Application contact:* 831-647-4123, Fax: 831-647-6405, E-mail: admit@miis.edu.

See Close-Up on page 1157.

Monterey Institute of International Studies, Graduate School of International Policy Studies, Program in International Public Administration, Monterey, CA 93940-2691. Offers international management (MPA). *Students:* 61 full-time (41 women), 1 (woman) part-time; includes 4 minority (1 Asian American or Pacific Islander, 3 Hispanic Americans), 23 international. Average age 28. 53 applicants, 94% accepted, 24 enrolled. In 2007, 33 degrees awarded. *Degree requirements:* For master's, one foreign language. *Entrance requirements:* For master's, minimum GPA of 3.0, proficiency in a foreign language. Additional exam requirements/recommendations for international students: Required—TOEFL (minimum score 550 paper-based; 213 computer-based; 80 iBT). *Application deadline:* For fall admission, 3/15 priority date for domestic students; for spring admission, 10/1 priority date for domestic students. Applications are processed on a rolling basis. Application fee: $50. Electronic applications accepted. *Expenses:* Tuition: Full-time $27,750; part-time $1,250 per credit. Required fees: $200. *Financial support:* Career-related internships or fieldwork, Federal Work-Study, and institutionally sponsored loans available. Support available to part-time students. Financial award application deadline: 3/15; financial award applicants required to submit FAFSA. *Application contact:* 831-647-4123, Fax: 831-647-6405, E-mail: admit@miis.edu.

See Close-Up on page 1157.

Morgan State University, School of Graduate Studies, College of Liberal Arts, Department of World Languages and International Studies, Baltimore, MD 21251. Offers international studies (MA). Part-time and evening/weekend programs available. *Faculty:* 7. *Students:* 16 (9 women); includes 10 minority (all African Americans) 3 international. In 2007, 1 degree awarded. *Degree requirements:* For master's, one foreign language, comprehensive exam, thesis. *Entrance requirements:* For master's, GRE. Additional exam requirements/recommendations for international students: Required—TOEFL (minimum score 550 paper-based; 213 computer-based). *Application deadline:* For fall admission, 2/1 priority date for domestic students; for spring admission, 10/1 priority date for domestic students. Applications are processed on a rolling basis. Application fee: $0. *Financial support:* Fellowships, research assistantships, teaching assistantships available. Financial award application deadline: 2/1. *Unit head:* Dr. M'Bare N'Gom, Chair, 443-885-3095, E-mail: mbare.ngom@morgan.edu. *Application contact:* Dr. Mark Garrison, Associate Dean, 443-885-3185, Fax: 443-885-8226, E-mail: mark.garrison@morgan.edu.

Naval Postgraduate School, Graduate Programs, Department of National Security Affairs, Monterey, CA 93943. Offers intelligence (MA); international relations (MA); political science (MA); regional security education (MA); security building (MA); security studies (MA). Program only open to commissioned officers of the United States and friendly nations and selected United States federal civilian employees. Part-time programs available. *Degree requirements:* For master's, thesis.

The New School: A University, The New School for General Studies, Program in International Affairs, New York, NY 10011. Offers global management, trade, and finance (MA, MS); international development (MA, MS); international media and communication (MA, MS); international politics and diplomacy (MA, MS); service, civic, and non-profit management (MS). Part-time programs available. *Faculty:* 10 full-time (6 women), 26 part-time/adjunct (11 women). *Students:* 192 full-time (129 women), 122 part-time (80 women); includes 67 minority (20 African Americans, 17 Asian Americans or Pacific Islanders, 30 Hispanic Americans), 54 international. Average age 30. In 2007, 78 degrees awarded. *Entrance requirements:* Additional exam requirements/recommendations for international students: Required—TOEFL (minimum score 600 paper-based; 250 computer-based; 100 iBT). *Application deadline:* For fall admission, 4/15 for domestic students; for spring admission, 10/15 for domestic students. Application fee: $50. *Financial support:* Fellowships with partial tuition reimbursements, research assistantships, teaching assistantships with partial tuition reimbursements, career-related internships or fieldwork, Federal Work-Study, scholarships/grants, tuition waivers (partial), and unspecified assistantships available. Support available to part-time students. Financial award application deadline: 3/1; financial award applicants required to submit FAFSA. *Unit head:* Dr. Michael Cohen, Director, 212-206-3524, Fax: 212-645-0661, E-mail: cohenm2@newschool.edu. *Application contact:* David Norris, Director of Admissions, 212-229-5630, Fax: 212-989-3887, E-mail: nsadmissions@newschool.edu.

See Close-Up on page 1159.

New York University, Graduate School of Arts and Science, Department of Politics, New York, NY 10012-1019. Offers political campaign management (MA); politics (MA, PhD); JD/MA; MBA/MA. Part-time programs available. *Faculty:* 30 full-time (4 women), 24 part-time/adjunct. *Students:* 147 full-time (75 women), 49 part-time (25 women); includes 23 minority (5 African Americans, 12 Asian Americans or Pacific Islanders, 6 Hispanic Americans), 88 international. Average age 22. 551 applicants, 44% accepted, 72 enrolled. In 2007, 63 master's, 7 doctorates awarded. Terminal master's awarded for partial completion of doctoral program. *Degree requirements:* For master's, one foreign language, thesis or alternative; for doctorate, 2 foreign languages, comprehensive exam, thesis/dissertation. *Entrance requirements:* For master's, GRE General Test; for doctorate, GRE General Test, master's degree in political science, minimum GPA of 2.5. Additional exam requirements/recommendations for international students: Required—TOEFL. *Application deadline:* For fall admission, 12/18 priority date for domestic students. Application fee: $85. *Financial support:* Fellowships with tuition reimbursements, teaching assistantships with tuition reimbursements, career-related internships or fieldwork, Federal Work-Study, and institutionally sponsored loans available. Financial award application deadline: 12/18; financial award applicants required to submit FAFSA. *Faculty research:* Comparative politics, democratic theory and practice, rational choice, political economy; international relations. *Unit head:* Nathaniel Beck, Chair, 212-998-8500, Fax: 212-995-4184, E-mail: politics.program@nyu.edu. *Application contact:* Jonathan Nagler, Director of Graduate Studies, 212-998-8500, Fax: 212-995-4184, E-mail: politics.program@nyu.edu.

New York University, Robert F. Wagner Graduate School of Public Service, Program in Public Administration, New York, NY 10012-1019. Offers public administration (PhD); public and nonprofit management and policy (MPA, Advanced Certificate), including developmental administration (Advanced Certificate), financial management and public finance, human resources management (Advanced Certificate), international administration (Advanced Certificate), management (MPA), management for public and nonprofit organizations (Advanced Certificate), public policy analysis, quantitative analysis and computer applications (Advanced Certificate), urban public policy (Advanced Certificate); JD/MPA; MBA/MPA; MPA/MA. *Accreditation:* NASPAA (one or more programs are accredited). Part-time and evening/weekend programs available. *Faculty:* 16 full-time (10 women), 52 part-time/adjunct (28 women). *Students:* 318 full-time (229 women), 245 part-time (183 women); includes 105 minority (34 African Americans, 43 Asian Americans or Pacific Islanders, 28 Hispanic Americans), 66 international. Average age 28. 803 applicants, 61% accepted, 175 enrolled. In 2007, 206 master's, 3 doctorates awarded. *Degree requirements:* For master's, thesis or alternative, capstone/end event; for doctorate, one foreign language, thesis/dissertation. *Entrance requirements:* For master's, minimum undergraduate GPA of 3.0; for doctorate, GMAT or GRE General Test, minimum GPA of 3.5. Additional exam requirements/recommendations for international students: Required—TOEFL (minimum score 600 paper-based; 250 computer-based; 100 iBT), TWE (minimum score 4). *Application deadline:* For fall admission, 6/1 for domestic students, 1/15 for international students; for spring admission, 11/15 for domestic students, 10/1 for international students. Applications are processed on a rolling basis. Application fee: $70. Electronic applications accepted. *Expenses:* Contact institution. *Financial support:* In 2007–08, 160 fellowships (averaging $9,051 per year), 4 research assistantships with full tuition reimbursements (averaging $16,000 per year) were awarded; career-related internships or fieldwork, Federal Work-Study, institutionally sponsored loans, scholarships/grants, health care benefits, and unspecified assistantships also available. Support available to part-time students. Financial award application deadline: 12/1; financial award applicants required to submit FAFSA. *Unit head:* Prof. Katherine O'Regan, Director, 212-998-7400, Fax: 212-995-4161. *Application contact:* Bethany Godsoe, Assistant Dean, Enrollment and Student Services, 212-998-7414, Fax: 212-995-4164, E-mail: wagner.admissions@nyu.edu.

See Close-Up on page 1611.

New York University, School of Continuing and Professional Studies, Center for Global Affairs, New York, NY 10012-1019. Offers global studies (MS), including energy policy/environment/oil, human rights and humanitarian assistance, international law, dispute settlement, and institutions, international relations, private sector: international business, economics, and development. Part-time and evening/weekend programs available. *Faculty:* 4 full-time (1 woman), 21 part-time/adjunct (11 women). *Students:* 94 full-time (71 women), 120 part-time (86 women); includes 36 minority (11 African Americans, 11 Asian Americans or Pacific Islanders, 14 Hispanic Americans), 24 international. Average age 30. 262 applicants, 52% accepted, 54 enrolled. In 2007, 10 degrees awarded. *Entrance requirements:* For master's, GRE General Test or GMAT (for recent graduates), 2 letters of recommendation, resumé, essay. Additional exam requirements/recommendations for international students: Required—TOEFL (minimum score 600 paper-based; 250 computer-based; 100 iBT), TWE. *Application deadline:* For fall admission, 3/15 priority date for domestic and international students; for spring admission, 10/15 priority date for domestic students, 8/15 priority date for international students. Applications are processed on a rolling basis. Application fee: $75. Electronic applications accepted. *Financial support:* In 2007–08, 132 students received support, including 132 fellowships (averaging $2,215 per year); institutionally sponsored loans, scholarships/grants, and tuition waivers (partial) also available. Support available to part-time students. Financial award application deadline: 3/1; financial award applicants required to submit FAFSA. *Unit head:* Dr. Vera Jelinek, Assistant Dean and Director, 212-992-8380, Fax: 212-995-4597, E-mail: vj1@nyu.edu. *Application contact:* Mykellan Ledden, Interim Associate Director, 212-992-8380, Fax: 212-995-4597, E-mail: mykellan.ledden@nyu.edu.

See Close-Up on page 1161.

North Carolina State University, Graduate School, College of Humanities and Social Sciences, Department of Political Science and Public Administration, Program in International Studies, Raleigh, NC 27695. Offers MAIS. *Degree requirements:* For master's, thesis optional. *Entrance requirements:* For master's, GRE General Test, minimum GPA of 3.0 during previous 2 years. Electronic applications accepted. *Faculty research:* Global environmental policy and climate change, drug policy and the Caribbean, U.S. national security politics, local responses to globalization, the political economy of the European Union.

Northeastern University, College of Arts and Sciences, Department of Political Science, Boston, MA 02115-5096. Offers political science (MA); public administration (MPA, Certificate), including development administration (MPA), health administration and policy (MPA), state and local government (MPA), urban studies (Certificate); public and international affairs (PhD). Part-time and evening/weekend programs available. *Faculty:* 22 full-time (4 women), 3 part-time/adjunct (all women). *Students:* 59 full-time (32 women), 14 part-time (5 women). Average age 30. 165 applicants, 53% accepted. In 2007, 23 master's, 2 doctorates awarded. *Degree requirements:* For master's, thesis optional; for doctorate, thesis/dissertation. *Entrance requirements:* For master's, GRE General Test. Additional exam requirements/recommendations for international students: Required—TOEFL. *Application deadline:* Applications are processed on a rolling basis. Application fee: $50. *Financial support:* In 2007–08, 12 teaching assistantships with tuition reimbursements (averaging $14,035 per year) were awarded; research assistantships with tuition reimbursements, career-related internships or fieldwork, Federal Work-Study, tuition waivers (full and partial), and unspecified assistantships also available. Support available to part-time students. Financial award application deadline: 2/1; financial award applicants required to submit FAFSA. *Faculty research:* Presidency, public opinion, Congress, democratization, national identity. *Unit head:* Dr. John Portz, Chair, 617-373-2796, Fax: 617-373-5311, E-mail: gradpolisci@neu.edu. *Application contact:* Brynn Thompson, Graduate Programs Assistant, 617-373-4404, Fax: 617-373-5311, E-mail: gradpolisci@neu.edu.

Northwestern University, The Graduate School, Center for International and Comparative Studies, Evanston, IL 60208. Offers Certificate.

Northwestern University, Law School, Chicago, IL 60611-3069. Offers executive law (LL M); international human rights (LL M); international law (JD); law (JD, LL M); JD/LL M; JD/MBA; JD/PhD; LL M/Certificate; MSJ/MSL. *Accreditation:* ABA. *Faculty:* 100 full-time (49 women),

71 part-time/adjunct (21 women). *Students:* 771 full-time (357 women); includes 278 minority (63 African Americans, 7 American Indian/Alaska Native, 141 Asian Americans or Pacific Islanders, 67 Hispanic Americans), 31 international. Average age 26. 4,821 applicants, 18% accepted, 238 enrolled. In 2007, 254 degrees awarded. *Entrance requirements:* For JD, LSAT, 1 letter of recommendation, resumé; for master's, law degree or equivalent, letter of recommendation, resumé. Additional exam requirements/recommendations for international students: Required—TOEFL. *Application deadline:* For fall admission, 2/15 for domestic students, 2/1 for international students. Applications are processed on a rolling basis. Application fee: $80 ($85 for international students). Electronic applications accepted. *Expenses:* Contact institution. *Financial support:* In 2007–08, 243 fellowships (averaging $20,000 per year) were awarded; career-related internships or fieldwork, Federal Work-Study, institutionally sponsored loans, and scholarships/grants also available. Financial award application deadline: 2/15; financial award applicants required to submit FAFSA. *Faculty research:* Constitutional law, corporate law, international law, law and social policy, ethical studies. *Unit head:* David Van Zandt, Dean, 312-503-3100, Fax: 847-467-1035. *Application contact:* Johann H. Lee, Assistant Dean of Admissions and Financial Aid, 312-503-8465, Fax: 312-503-0178, E-mail: johann@law.northwestern.edu.

Norwich University, School of Graduate Studies, Program in Diplomacy, Northfield, VT 05663. Offers international commerce (MA); international conflict management (MA); international terrorism (MA). Evening/weekend programs available. *Faculty:* 1 full-time (0 women), 28 part-time/adjunct (3 women). *Students:* 366 full-time (122 women), 9 part-time (1 woman); includes 61 minority (19 African Americans, 1 American Indian/Alaska Native, 18 Asian Americans or Pacific Islanders, 23 Hispanic Americans), 1 international. Average age 33. 151 applicants, 97% accepted, 107 enrolled. In 2007, 145 degrees awarded. *Degree requirements:* For master's, comprehensive exam, thesis optional. *Entrance requirements:* For master's, minimum undergraduate GPA of 2.75. Additional exam requirements/recommendations for international students: Required—TOEFL. *Application deadline:* For fall admission, 8/10 for domestic and international students; for winter admission, 11/7 for domestic and international students; for spring admission, 2/6 for domestic and international students. Application fee: $50. Electronic applications accepted. *Expenses:* Tuition: Full-time $15,768; part-time $657 per credit. Tuition and fees vary according to program. *Financial support:* Scholarships/grants available. Financial award applicants required to submit FAFSA. *Unit head:* Dr. Hal Kearsley, Program Director, 802-485-2730, E-mail: hkearsley@norwich.edu. *Application contact:* Fianna Verret, Administrative Director, 802-485-2783, Fax: 802-485-2533, E-mail: fverret@norwich.edu.

Ohio University, Graduate College, Center for International Studies, Program in Communications and Development Studies, Athens, OH 45701-2979. Offers MA. Part-time programs available. *Faculty:* 13 full-time (5 women), 4 part-time/adjunct (2 women). *Students:* 29 full-time (24 women); includes 1 minority (African American), 21 international. Average age 24. 57 applicants, 79% accepted, 21 enrolled. In 2007, 15 degrees awarded. *Degree requirements:* For master's, one foreign language, thesis optional, internship. *Entrance requirements:* For master's, minimum GPA of 3.0. Additional exam requirements/recommendations for international students: Required—TOEFL (minimum score 550 paper-based; 213 computer-based). *Application deadline:* For fall admission, 3/1 priority date for domestic and international students. Application fee: $50 ($55 for international students). *Financial support:* In 2007–08, 19 students received support, including 6 research assistantships with full tuition reimbursements available (averaging $10,000 per year); Federal Work-Study, institutionally sponsored loans, and tuition waivers (full) also available. Financial award application deadline: 1/1. *Faculty research:* National development processes, public relations and participatory research, audio and video production, health communication, urban development. *Unit head:* Dr. David H. Mould, Associate Dean, 740-593-4885, Fax: 740-593-0459, E-mail: mould@ohio.edu. *Application contact:* Joan Kraynanski, Administrative Assistant, 740-593-1840, Fax: 740-593-1837, E-mail: kraynans@ohio.edu.

Oklahoma State University, Graduate College, Interdisciplinary Program in International Studies, Stillwater, OK 74078. Offers MS. *Application deadline:* Applications are processed on a rolling basis. Electronic applications accepted. *Expenses:* Tuition, state resident: full-time $4,993; part-time $148 per credit hour. Tuition, nonresident: full-time $14,755; part-time $555 per credit hour. Tuition and fees vary according to program. *Financial support:* Research assistantships available. *Unit head:* Dr. Stephen Miller, Associate Director, 405-744-7693.

Old Dominion University, College of Arts and Letters, Programs in International Studies, Norfolk, VA 23529. Offers MA, PhD. Part-time programs available. *Faculty:* 14 full-time (3 women). *Students:* 36 full-time (11 women), 27 part-time (19 women); includes 5 minority (1 African American, 4 Hispanic Americans), 18 international. Average age 31. 99 applicants, 54% accepted, 30 enrolled. In 2007, 18 master's, 3 doctorates awarded. Terminal master's awarded for partial completion of doctoral program. *Degree requirements:* For master's, one foreign language, comprehensive exam, thesis optional; for doctorate, one foreign language, comprehensive exam, thesis/dissertation. *Entrance requirements:* For master's, GRE General Test, sample of written work, 2 letters of recommendation; for doctorate, GRE General Test, sample of written work, 3 letters of recommendation. Additional exam requirements/recommendations for international students: Required—TOEFL (minimum score 570 paper-based; 230 computer-based). *Application deadline:* For fall admission, 3/15 for domestic students, 2/15 for international students; for spring admission, 10/15 for domestic and international students. Application fee: $40. Electronic applications accepted. *Expenses:* Tuition, state resident: part-time $304 per credit hour. Tuition, nonresident: part-time $761 per credit hour. *Financial support:* In 2007–08, 20 students received support, including 2 fellowships (averaging $13,000 per year), 9 research assistantships with tuition reimbursements available (averaging $11,000 per year), 9 teaching assistantships with tuition reimbursements available (averaging $11,000 per year); career-related internships or fieldwork, institutionally sponsored loans, scholarships/grants, and unspecified assistantships also available. Support available to part-time students. Financial award application deadline: 2/15; financial award applicants required to submit FAFSA. *Faculty research:* U.S. foreign policy, international security, transatlantic and transpacific relations, transnational issues, IPE and development. Total annual research expenditures: $330,391. *Unit head:* Dr. Regina Karp, Acting Director, 757-683-5700, Fax: 757-683-5701, E-mail: rkarp@odu.edu.

Pepperdine University, School of Public Policy, Malibu, CA 90263. Offers American politics (MPP); economics (MPP); international relations (MPP); public policy (MPP); state and local policy (MPP). *Entrance requirements:* For master's, GRE, 2 letters of recommendation, resumé. Additional exam requirements/recommendations for international students: Required—TOEFL. Electronic applications accepted.

See Close-Up on page 1619.

Pontificia Universidad Catolica Madre y Maestra, Graduate School, Santiago, Dominican Republic. Offers administration (M Adm, M Ed); architecture of interiors (M Arch); architecture of tourist lodgings (M Arch); construction administration (ME); convergent networks (ME); corporate business law (LL M); criminal procedure law (LL M); earthquake-resistant engineering (ME); environmental engineering (MEE); finance (M Mgmt); human resources (EMBA); international business (M Mgmt); international relations (LL M); labor law and Social Security (M Mgmt); logistics management (ME); marketing (M Mgmt); urban planning (M Urb). *Entrance requirements:* For master's, curriculum vitae, interview.

Princeton University, Graduate School, Woodrow Wilson School of Public and International Affairs, Princeton, NJ 08544-1019. Offers MPA, MPA-URP, MPP, PhD, JD/MPA. Terminal master's awarded for partial completion of doctoral program. *Degree requirements:* For master's, internship; for doctorate, one foreign language, thesis/dissertation. *Entrance requirements:* For master's, GRE General Test, original policy memo; for doctorate, GRE General Test. Additional exam requirements/recommendations for international students: Required—TOEFL (minimum score 600 paper-based; 250 computer-based). Electronic applications accepted.

Rutgers, The State University of New Jersey, Camden, Graduate School of Arts and Sciences, Department of Public Policy and Administration, Camden, NJ 08102-1401. Offers education policy and leadership (MPA); international public service and development (MPA); public management (MPA); JD/MPA. *Accreditation:* NASPAA. Part-time and evening/weekend programs available. *Degree requirements:* For master's, directed study, research workshop. *Entrance requirements:* For master's, GRE General Test, GMAT or LSAT. Additional exam requirements/recommendations for international students: Required—TOEFL (minimum score 550 paper-based; 213 computer-based). Electronic applications accepted. *Faculty research:* Nonprofit management, county and municipal administration, health and human services, government communication, administrative law, educational finance.

Rutgers, The State University of New Jersey, Newark, Graduate School, Division of Global Affairs, Newark, NJ 07102. Offers MS, PhD. Part-time and evening/weekend programs available. *Degree requirements:* For master's, one foreign language, thesis optional. *Entrance requirements:* For master's and doctorate, GRE General Test, minimum B average. Electronic applications accepted. *Faculty research:* International organizations, diplomacy, world history, international political economy, global environment.

Announcement: The Graduate Division of Global Affairs offers two interdisciplinary degrees: PhD and MS in global affairs. Candidates for the MS can apply and be admitted at any time in the academic year. Candidates for the PhD must apply by February 1.

Rutgers, The State University of New Jersey, Newark, Graduate School, Program in Political Science, Newark, NJ 07102. Offers American political system (MA); international relations (MA); JD/MA. Part-time and evening/weekend programs available. *Degree requirements:* For master's, comprehensive exam, thesis optional. *Entrance requirements:* For master's, GRE, minimum undergraduate B average. Electronic applications accepted. *Faculty research:* Policymaking and policy evaluation in the United States; government and politics in Europe, Middle East, Asia, Africa, and Latin America.

Rutgers, The State University of New Jersey, New Brunswick, Graduate School, Department of Political Science, New Brunswick, NJ 08901-1281. Offers American politics (PhD); comparative politics (PhD); international relations (PhD); political theory (PhD); public law (PhD); women and politics (PhD). *Degree requirements:* For doctorate, one foreign language, comprehensive exam, thesis/dissertation. *Entrance requirements:* For doctorate, GRE General Test. Additional exam requirements/recommendations for international students: Required—TOEFL.

St. John Fisher College, Office of the Provost, School of Arts and Sciences, International Studies Program, Rochester, NY 14618-3597. Offers MS. Part-time and evening/weekend programs available. *Faculty:* 4 full-time (0 women), 3 part-time/adjunct (0 women). *Students:* 7 full-time (2 women), 26 part-time (13 women); includes 2 African Americans, 1 American Indian/Alaska Native. Average age 28. 15 applicants, 100% accepted, 10 enrolled. In 2007, 3 degrees awarded. *Degree requirements:* For master's, project. *Entrance requirements:* For master's, minimum GPA of 3.0. Additional exam requirements/recommendations for international students: Required—TOEFL (minimum score 575 paper-based; 233 computer-based; 80 iBT). *Application deadline:* For fall admission, 7/1 for domestic students; for spring admission, 10/30 for domestic students. Applications are processed on a rolling basis. Application fee: $30. *Financial support:* Federal Work-Study and scholarships/grants available. Financial award application deadline: 2/15; financial award applicants required to submit FAFSA. *Faculty research:* International relations, international affairs, international economics, Chinese politics. *Unit head:* Dr. John Roche, Interim Director, 585-385-8119, E-mail: jroche@sjfc.edu. *Application contact:* Holly Smith, Interim Director of Graduate Admissions, 585-385-8161, Fax: 585-385-8344, E-mail: hsmith@sjfc.edu.

St. Mary's University, Graduate School, Department of Political Science, Interdisciplinary Program in International Relations, San Antonio, TX 78228-8507. Offers MA, JD/MA. Part-time programs available. Postbaccalaureate distance learning degree programs offered (no on-campus study). *Students:* 34 full-time (21 women), 111 part-time (44 women); includes 50 minority (1 African American, 7 Asian Americans or Pacific Islanders, 42 Hispanic Americans), 6 international. Average age 30. In 2007, 38 degrees awarded. *Degree requirements:* For master's, one foreign language, comprehensive exam, thesis optional. *Entrance requirements:* For master's, GRE General Test. Additional exam requirements/recommendations for international students: Required—TOEFL (minimum score 550 paper-based; 213 computer-based). *Application deadline:* Applications are processed on a rolling basis. Application fee: $0. Electronic applications accepted. *Financial support:* Fellowships, career-related internships or fieldwork, Federal Work-Study, institutionally sponsored loans, scholarships/grants, health care benefits, tuition waivers (full), and unspecified assistantships available. Financial award application deadline: 3/31; financial award applicants required to submit FAFSA. *Faculty research:* Eastern Europe, Soviet Union, Balkans, modern Asia, Latin America. *Unit head:* Dr. Leona Pallansch, Director, 210-436-3204, Fax: 210-431-4336, E-mail: lpallansch@stmarytx.edu.

Salve Regina University, Graduate Studies, Program in International Relations, Newport, RI 02840-4192. Offers homeland security (Certificate); international relations (MA, Certificate). Part-time and evening/weekend programs available. Postbaccalaureate distance learning degree programs offered (minimal on-campus study). *Entrance requirements:* For master's, GMAT, GRE General Test, MAT or LSAT. Additional exam requirements/recommendations for international students: Required—TOEFL or IELTS. Electronic applications accepted.

San Francisco State University, Division of Graduate Studies, College of Behavioral and Social Sciences, Department of International Relations, San Francisco, CA 94132-1722. Offers MA. *Unit head:* Dr. JoAnn Aviel, Chair, 415-338-2055. *Application contact:* Dr. Jean-Marc Blanchard, Graduate Coordinator, 415-338-2654, E-mail: irgrad@sfsu.edu.

Schiller International University, Graduate Programs, London, Program in International Relations and Diplomacy, London, United Kingdom. Offers MA. Part-time programs available. *Degree requirements:* For master's, thesis optional, GMAT before graduation. *Entrance requirements:* For master's, 1 year of undergraduate economics, 1 foreign language. Additional exam requirements/recommendations for international students: Required—TOEFL (minimum score 550 paper-based; 213 computer-based).

Schiller International University, Program in International Relations and Diplomacy, Paris, France. Offers MA. Part-time and evening/weekend programs available. *Students:* 11 full-time, 8 part-time. Average age 25. *Degree requirements:* For master's, one foreign language, thesis or alternative, final comprehensive exam or thesis. *Entrance requirements:* For master's, undergraduate mathematics (strongly advised). Additional exam requirements/recommendations for international students: Required—TOEFL (minimum score 550 paper-based; 213 computer-based). *Application deadline:* For fall admission, 8/1 priority date for domestic and international students; for spring admission, 12/1 priority date for domestic and international students. Applications are processed on a rolling basis. Application fee: $65. Tuition and fees charges are reported in euros. *Expenses:* Tuition: Full-time 15,960 euros; part-time 1,330 euros per course. Required fees: 170 euros; 90 euros per semester. One-time fee: 170 euros full-time. *Financial support:* Teaching assistantships, scholarships/grants and unspecified assistantships available. Support available to part-time students. Financial award application deadline: 3/30; financial award applicants required to submit FAFSA. *Unit head:* Souha Akiki-Svahn, Adviser, 1-4538-5601, Fax: 1-4538-5430, E-mail: sakiki@schillerparis.com. *Application contact:* Sally Bennett, Associate Director of Admissions—Europe, 20-79-28-1372, Fax: 20-76-20-1226, E-mail: admissions@schillerlondon.ac.uk.

Seton Hall University, Whitehead School of Diplomacy and International Relations, South Orange, NJ 07079-2697. Offers MA, JD/MA, MBA/MA, MPA/MA. Part-time and evening/weekend programs available. *Faculty:* 14 full-time (3 women), 17 part-time/adjunct (6 women). *Students:* Average age 26. 360 applicants, 58% accepted. In 2007, 106 degrees awarded. *Degree requirements:* For master's, thesis (for some programs), research project, internship. *Entrance requirements:* For master's, GMAT, GRE, or LSAT, minimum GPA of 3.2. Additional

International Affairs

Seton Hall University (continued)

exam requirements/recommendations for international students: Required—TOEFL (minimum score 600 paper-based; 250 computer-based; 100 iBT). *Application deadline:* For fall admission, 5/1 priority date for domestic students; for winter admission, 10/1 priority date for domestic students. Applications are processed on a rolling basis. Application fee: $50. Electronic applications accepted. *Financial support:* Career-related internships or fieldwork, scholarships/grants, tuition waivers (full and partial), and unspecified assistantships available. *Faculty research:* International economics and development, global health, United Nations conflict negotiation and conflict management. *Unit head:* Ursula Sanjamino, Assistant Dean of Graduate Studies, 973-313-6210, Fax: 973-275-2519, E-mail: sanjamur@shu.edu. *Application contact:* Catherine Ruby, Director of Graduate Admissions, 973-275-2142, Fax: 973-275-2519, E-mail: rubycath@shu.edu.

See Close-Up on page 1163.

SIT Graduate Institute, Graduate Programs, Master's Programs in Intercultural Service, Leadership, and Management, Brattleboro, VT 05302-0676. Offers conflict transformation (MA); intercultural service, leadership, and management (MA); international education (MA); management (MS); social justice in intercultural relations (MA); sustainable development (MA). Postbaccalaureate distance learning degree programs offered (minimal on-campus study). *Students:* 178 full-time (127 women), 315 part-time (217 women); includes 60 minority (27 African Americans, 1 American Indian/Alaska Native, 12 Asian Americans or Pacific Islanders, 20 Hispanic Americans), 108 international. Average age 30. 540 applicants, 73% accepted, 178 enrolled. In 2007, 179 degrees awarded. *Degree requirements:* For master's, one foreign language, thesis. *Entrance requirements:* For master's, 3 letters of reference. Additional exam requirements/recommendations for international students: Required—TOEFL. *Application deadline:* Applications are processed on a rolling basis. Application fee: $50. *Financial support:* Career-related internships or fieldwork, Federal Work-Study, institutionally sponsored loans, and scholarships/grants available. Financial award application deadline: 3/1; financial award applicants required to submit FAFSA. *Faculty research:* Intercultural communication, conflict resolution, advising and training, world issues, international business. *Unit head:* Marla Solomon, Graduate Dean, 802-258-3325, Fax: 802-258-3241, E-mail: marla.solomon@sit.edu. *Application contact:* Information Contact, 800-336-1616, Fax: 802-258-3500, E-mail: admissions@sit.edu.

Stanford University, School of Humanities and Sciences, Program in International Policy Studies, Stanford, CA 94305-9991. Offers MA. *Degree requirements:* For master's, thesis optional. *Entrance requirements:* For master's, GRE General Test. Additional exam requirements/recommendations for international students: Required—TOEFL. Electronic applications accepted.

Syracuse University, Graduate School, Maxwell School of Citizenship and Public Affairs, Programs in International Relations and S. I. Newhouse School of Public Communications, Program in Public Diplomacy, Syracuse, NY 13244. Offers MS/MA. *Entrance requirements:* Additional exam requirements/recommendations for international students: Required—TOEFL. *Application deadline:* For fall admission, 2/1 for domestic students. Application fee: $75. *Expenses:* Tuition: Full-time $18,216; part-time $1,012 per credit. Required fees: $980. Tuition and fees vary according to program. *Unit head:* Dr. Dennis Kinsey, Director, 315-443-1944, E-mail: publicdiplomacy@syr.edu. *Application contact:* Martha Coria, Office Supervisor, 315-443-5749, Fax: 315-443-1834, E-mail: pcgrad@syr.edu.

Syracuse University, Graduate School, S. I. Newhouse School of Public Communications, Department of Public Relations and Maxwell School of Citizenship and Public Affairs, Program in Public Diplomacy, Syracuse, NY 13244. Offers MS/MA. *Students:* 14. *Entrance requirements:* Additional exam requirements/recommendations for international students: Required—TOEFL. *Application deadline:* For fall admission, 2/1 for domestic students. Application fee: $75. *Expenses:* Tuition: Full-time $18,216; part-time $1,012 per credit. Required fees: $980. Tuition and fees vary according to program. *Unit head:* Dr. Dennis Kinsey, Director, 315-443-1944, E-mail: publicdiplomacy@syr.edu. *Application contact:* Graduate Records Office, 315-443-4039, Fax: 315-443-1834, E-mail: pcgrad@syr.edu.

Texas A&M University, George Bush School of Government and Public Service, College Station, TX 77843. Offers advanced international affairs (Certificate); homeland security (Certificate); international affairs (MPIA), including international economics and development, national security affairs; nonprofit management (Certificate); public service and administration (MPSA), including public management, public policy analysis. *Accreditation:* NASPAA. *Faculty:* 39. *Students:* 155 full-time (67 women), 97 part-time (27 women); includes 37 minority (8 African Americans, 2 American Indian/Alaska Native, 4 Asian Americans or Pacific Islanders, 23 Hispanic Americans), 18 international. Average age 24. 249 applicants, 57% accepted, 88 enrolled. In 2007, 69 degrees awarded. *Degree requirements:* For master's, summer internship. *Entrance requirements:* For master's, GRE (preferred) or GMAT. *Application deadline:* For fall admission, 1/24 for domestic and international students. Application fee: $50 ($75 for international students). Electronic applications accepted. *Expenses:* Tuition, state resident: full-time $6,129. Tuition, nonresident: full-time $11,689. Tuition and fees vary according to course load. *Financial support:* In 2007–08, fellowships (averaging $11,000 per year), research assistantships (averaging $11,250 per year) were awarded; career-related internships or fieldwork, Federal Work-Study, and institutionally sponsored loans also available. Financial award application deadline: 2/1; financial award applicants required to submit FAFSA. *Faculty research:* Public policy, Presidential studies, public leadership, economic policy, social policy. *Unit head:* Richard A. Chilcoat, Dean, 979-862-8007, Fax: 979-862-7953, E-mail: bushschool@tamu.edu. *Application contact:* Kathryn Meyer, Recruitment/Placement Officer, 979-458-4767, Fax: 979-845-4155, E-mail: admissions@bushschool.tamu.edu.

See Close-Up on page 1623.

Texas State University–San Marcos, Graduate School, Program in International Studies, San Marcos, TX 78666. Offers MA. *Faculty:* 2 full-time (both women), 2 part-time/adjunct (1 woman). *Students:* 12 full-time (5 women), 12 part-time (9 women); includes 8 minority (1 Asian American or Pacific Islander, 7 Hispanic Americans), 2 international. Average age 28. 7 applicants, 100% accepted, 7 enrolled. In 2007, 2 degrees awarded. *Degree requirements:* For master's, comprehensive exam. *Entrance requirements:* For master's, minimum 3.0 GPA on last 60 hours of undergraduate work, 2 to 5 page essay, 2 letters of reference. Additional exam requirements/recommendations for international students: Required—TOEFL (minimum score 550 paper-based; 213 computer-based). *Application deadline:* For fall admission, 6/15 priority date for domestic students; for spring admission, 10/15 priority date for domestic students. Applications are processed on a rolling basis. Application fee: $40 ($90 for international students). *Expenses:* Tuition, state resident: full-time $3,780; part-time $210 per credit hour. Tuition, nonresident: full-time $8,784; part-time $488 per credit hour. Required fees: $493 per semester. Full-time tuition and fees vary according to course load. *Financial support:* In 2007–08, 16 students received support, including 3 research assistantships (averaging $4,928 per year), 3 teaching assistantships (averaging $5,301 per year). Financial award application deadline: 4/1; financial award applicants required to submit FAFSA. *Unit head:* Dr. Dennis Dunn, Head, 512-245-2339, E-mail: dd05@txstate.edu.

Troy University, Graduate School, College of Arts and Sciences, Program in International Relations, Troy, AL 36082. Offers MS. Part-time and evening/weekend programs available. Postbaccalaureate distance learning degree programs offered (no on-campus study). *Students:* 126 full-time (46 women), 557 part-time (149 women); includes 169 minority (58 African Americans, 6 American Indian/Alaska Native, 39 Asian Americans or Pacific Islanders, 66 Hispanic Americans). Average age 32. In 2007, 141 degrees awarded. *Degree requirements:* For master's, comprehensive exam (for some programs), thesis optional. *Entrance requirements:* For master's, GRE General Test, MAT, or GMAT, minimum GPA of 2.5. Additional exam requirements/recommendations for international students: Required—TOEFL (minimum score 523 paper-based; 200 computer-based). *Application deadline:* For fall admission, 6/1 for international students; for spring admission, 10/15 for international students. Applications are processed on a rolling basis. Application fee: $50. Electronic applications accepted. *Financial support:* Available to part-time students. Applicants required to submit FAFSA. *Faculty research:* Elections, religion and world politics, terrorism. *Unit head:* Dr. James F. Rinehart, Chairman, 334-670-5646, Fax: 334-670-5647, E-mail: rinehart@troy.edu. *Application contact:* Brenda K. Campbell, Director of Graduate Admissions, 334-670-3178, Fax: 334-670-3733, E-mail: bcamp@troy.edu.

Tufts University, Fletcher School of Law and Diplomacy, Medford, MA 02155. Offers LL M, MA, MAHA, MALD, MIB, PhD, DVM/MA, JD/MALD, MALD/MA, MALD/MBA, MALD/MS, MD/MA. Postbaccalaureate distance learning degree programs offered (minimal on-campus study). *Faculty:* 34 full-time (7 women), 31 part-time/adjunct (8 women). *Students:* 443 full-time (224 women), 7 part-time (4 women); includes 51 minority (6 African Americans, 1 American Indian/Alaska Native, 26 Asian Americans or Pacific Islanders, 18 Hispanic Americans), 165 international. Average age 31. 1,636 applicants, 34% accepted, 183 enrolled. In 2007, 364 master's, 12 doctorates awarded. *Median time to degree:* Of those who began their doctoral program in fall 1999, 75% received their degree in 8 years or less. *Degree requirements:* For master's, one foreign language, thesis; for doctorate, one foreign language, comprehensive exam, thesis/dissertation, dissertation defense. *Entrance requirements:* For master's and doctorate, GMAT or GRE General Test. Additional exam requirements/recommendations for international students: Required—TOEFL (minimum score 600 paper-based; 250 computer-based; 100 iBT), IELTS (minimum score 7). *Application deadline:* For fall admission, 1/15 for domestic and international students; for spring admission, 10/15 for domestic and international students. Application fee: $70. Electronic applications accepted. *Expenses:* Contact institution. *Financial support:* Federal Work-Study, institutionally sponsored loans, scholarships/grants, and tuition waivers (partial) available. Financial award application deadline: 1/15; financial award applicants required to submit FAFSA. *Faculty research:* Negotiation and conflict resolution, international organizations, international business and economic law, security studies, development economics. *Unit head:* Stephen W. Bosworth, Dean, 617-627-3050, Fax: 617-627-3712. *Application contact:* Laurie A. Hurley, Director of Admissions and Financial Aid, 617-627-2410, Fax: 617-627-3712, E-mail: fletcheradmissions@tufts.edu.

See Close-Up on page 1169.

United States International University, School of Arts and Sciences, Nairobi, Kenya. Offers counseling psychology (MA); international relations (MA). Part-time and evening/weekend programs available. *Degree requirements:* For master's, thesis, practicum. *Entrance requirements:* For master's, GRE General Test, 2 letters of recommendation, resumé. Additional exam requirements/recommendations for international students: Required—TOEFL (minimum score 550 paper-based; 213 computer-based). *Faculty research:* Trauma in children, African intellectualism, psychological assessment tools.

Universidad de las Americas, A.C., Program in International Organizations and Institutions, Mexico City, Mexico. Offers MA.

Universidad Nacional Pedro Henriquez Urena, Graduate School, Santo Domingo, Dominican Republic. Offers accounting and auditing (M Acct); animal production (M Agr); business administration (MBA, PhD); Caribbean tropical architecture (M Arch); conservation of monuments and cultural goods (M Arch); economics (M Econ); education (PhD); environmental engineering (MEE); horticulture (M Agr); hospital administration (PhD); humanities (PhD); international relations (MPS); management of natural resources (MNRM); project management (M Man, MPM); public administration (MPS); sanitary engineering (ME); social science (PhD); veterinary medicine (DVM).

Université Laval, Québec Institute for Advanced International Studies, Program in International Relations, Québec, QC G1K 7P4, Canada. Offers MA. *Degree requirements:* For master's, thesis (for some programs). *Entrance requirements:* For master's, English exam, French exam. Electronic applications accepted.

University of Bridgeport, International College, Bridgeport, CT 06604. Offers global development and peace (MA). *Expenses:* Tuition: Part-time $635 per credit. Tuition and fees vary according to course load, degree level and program. *Unit head:* Dr. Thomas Ward, Dean, 203-576-4966, E-mail: ward@bridgeport.edu.

The University of British Columbia, Faculty of Graduate Studies, Institute of Asian Research, Vancouver, BC V6T 1Z1, Canada. Offers MAPPS. Part-time programs available. *Faculty:* 9 full-time (1 woman), 2 part-time/adjunct (0 women). *Students:* 28 full-time (16 women). Average age 30. 60 applicants, 42% accepted, 14 enrolled. In 2007, 15 degrees awarded. *Degree requirements:* For master's, thesis optional. *Entrance requirements:* Additional exam requirements/recommendations for international students: Required—TOEFL (minimum score 600 paper-based; 250 computer-based; 100 iBT), GRE (recommended). *Application deadline:* For fall admission, 3/30 for domestic students, 3/1 for international students. Application fee: $90 ($150 for international students). Electronic applications accepted. *Financial support:* In 2007–08, 7 fellowships with tuition reimbursements (averaging $70,000 Canadian dollars per year), 16 research assistantships (averaging $3,500 Canadian dollars per year) were awarded; career-related internships or fieldwork, institutionally sponsored loans, scholarships/grants, and tuition waivers (partial) also available. *Faculty research:* Social cohesion, globalization, social safety nets, research and development alliances, knowledge-based workshops. *Unit head:* Pitman B. Potter, Director and Professor of Law, 604-822-4686, Fax: 604-822-5207, E-mail: potter@interchg.ubc.ca. *Application contact:* Marietta T. Lao, Administrator, 604-822-2746, Fax: 604-822-5207, E-mail: mlao@interchg.ubc.ca.

University of California, Berkeley, Graduate Division, Group in International and Area Studies, Berkeley, CA 94720-1500. Offers MA, JD/MA, MBA/MA, MJ/MA. Application fee: $70 ($90 for international students). *Unit head:* John Lie, Chair, 510-642-0656, E-mail: iasone@berkeley.edu.

University of California, Berkeley, Graduate Division, Haas School of Business and Group in International and Area Studies, Concurrent MBA/MIAS Program in International and Area Studies, Berkeley, CA 94720-1500. Offers MBA/MIAS. *Accreditation:* AACSB. *Entrance requirements:* Additional exam requirements/recommendations for international students: Required—TOEFL. *Application deadline:* For fall admission, 3/10 for domestic and international students. Application fee: $175. *Financial support:* Fellowships with full tuition reimbursements, research assistantships, teaching assistantships with partial tuition reimbursements, career-related internships or fieldwork, scholarships/grants, and unspecified assistantships available. Support available to part-time students. Financial award application deadline: 3/2; financial award applicants required to submit FAFSA. *Unit head:* Julia Hwang, Director, MBA Program, 510-642-1405, Fax: 510-643-6659, E-mail: julia_hwang@haas.berkeley.edu. *Application contact:* 510-642-1405, Fax: 510-643-6659.

University of California, San Diego, Office of Graduate Studies, Department of Economics, La Jolla, CA 92093. Offers economics (PhD); economics and international affairs (PhD). *Degree requirements:* For doctorate, thesis/dissertation. *Entrance requirements:* For doctorate, GRE General Test. Electronic applications accepted. *Faculty research:* Microfoundations of macroeconomics, econometric model specification and testing, industrial organization.

University of California, San Diego, Office of Graduate Studies, Department of Political Science, La Jolla, CA 92093. Offers Latin American studies (MA); political science (PhD); political science and international affairs (PhD). *Entrance requirements:* For master's and doctorate, GRE General Test. Electronic applications accepted.

University of California, San Diego, Office of Graduate Studies, Graduate School of International Relations and Pacific Studies, La Jolla, CA 92093-0520. Offers economics and international affairs (PhD); Pacific international affairs (MPIA); political science and international affairs (PhD). *Degree requirements:* For master's, one foreign language; for doctorate, thesis/dissertation. *Entrance requirements:* For master's, GMAT or GRE General Test; for doctorate, GRE General Test. Additional exam requirements/recommendations for international students: Required—TOEFL (minimum score 550 paper-based; 213 computer-

International Affairs

University of Indianapolis (continued)
to submit FAFSA. *Unit head:* Dr. Lawrence Sondhaus, Chairperson, 317-788-2196, Fax: 317-788-3480, E-mail: sondhaus@uindy.edu.

University of Kansas, Research and Graduate Studies, College of Liberal Arts and Sciences, Program in International Studies, Lawrence, KS 66045. Offers MA. Part-time and evening/weekend programs available. *Faculty:* 9. *Students:* 16 full-time (10 women), 34 part-time (15 women); includes 11 minority (3 African Americans, 4 Asian Americans or Pacific Islanders, 4 Hispanic Americans), 6 international. Average age 33. 24 applicants, 46% accepted, 8 enrolled. In 2007, 6 degrees awarded. *Degree requirements:* For master's, one foreign language, thesis optional, exam (in lieu of thesis). *Entrance requirements:* For master's, GRE, minimum GPA of 3.0, 3 letters of reference, curriculum vitae. Additional exam requirements/recommendations for international students: Required—TOEFL. *Application deadline:* For fall admission, 6/1 priority date for domestic students; for spring admission, 11/1 priority date for domestic students. Applications are processed on a rolling basis. Application fee: $55 ($60 for international students). Electronic applications accepted. *Expenses:* Tuition, state resident: full-time $5,838. Tuition, nonresident: full-time $13,409. Tuition and fees vary according to program. *Financial support:* Scholarships/grants available. *Unit head:* Dr. Gary Reich, Program Director, 913-897-8510, Fax: 913-897-8491, E-mail: greich@ku.edu. *Application contact:* Noel Rasor, Program Advisor, 913-897-8510, Fax: 913-897-8491, E-mail: noel@ku.edu.

University of Kentucky, Graduate School, Patterson School of Diplomacy and International Commerce, Lexington, KY 40506-0027. Offers MA. *Faculty:* 5 full-time (1 woman), 1 part-time/adjunct (0 women). *Students:* 62 full-time (31 women), 10 part-time (6 women); includes 1 minority (African American), 10 international. Average age 27. 101 applicants, 51% accepted, 37 enrolled. In 2007, 32 degrees awarded. *Degree requirements:* For master's, one foreign language, comprehensive exam, 30 credit hours, statistics. *Entrance requirements:* For master's, GRE General Test, minimum undergraduate GPA of 3.0. Additional exam requirements/recommendations for international students: Required—TOEFL (minimum score 550 paper-based; 213 computer-based; 79 iBT). *Application deadline:* For fall admission, 2/1 for domestic students. Application fee: $40 ($55 for international students). Electronic applications accepted. *Expenses:* Tuition, state resident: part-time $437 per credit hour. Tuition, nonresident: part-time $931 per credit hour. *Financial support:* Over half of the incoming students received institutionally-sponsored financial assistance ranging from one-half of tuition up to $20,000 available. Financial award application deadline: 3/15; financial award applicants required to submit FAFSA. *Faculty research:* International relations, foreign and defense policy, cross-cultural negotiation, international science and technology, diplomacy, international economics and development, geopolitical modeling. Total annual research expenditures: $100,000. *Unit head:* Dr. Evan Hillebrand, Director of Graduate Studies, 859-257-6928, Fax: 859-257-4676, E-mail: evan.hillebrand@uky.edu. *Application contact:* Dr. Brian Jackson, Senior Associate Dean, 859-257-4667, Fax: 859-257-4676, E-mail: brian.jackson@uky.edu.

University of Miami, Graduate School, College of Arts and Sciences, Department of International Studies, Coral Gables, FL 33124. Offers MA, PhD. *Faculty:* 8 full-time (1 woman), 7 part-time/adjunct (4 women). *Students:* 27 full-time (15 women), 6 part-time (2 women); includes 15 minority (4 African Americans, 2 Asian Americans or Pacific Islanders, 9 Hispanic Americans), 5 international. Average age 33. In 2007, 7 master's, 5 doctorates awarded. *Degree requirements:* For master's, one foreign language, comprehensive exam; for doctorate, one foreign language, comprehensive exam, thesis/dissertation. *Entrance requirements:* For master's, GRE General Test, minimum GPA of 3.0; for doctorate, GRE General Test. Additional exam requirements/recommendations for international students: Required—TOEFL. *Application deadline:* For fall admission, 1/15 for domestic and international students. Application fee: $50. Electronic applications accepted. *Financial support:* In 2007–08, 17 students received support, including 4 fellowships with tuition reimbursements available (averaging $18,000 per year), 4 research assistantships with tuition reimbursements available (averaging $16,000 per year), 5 teaching assistantships with tuition reimbursements available (averaging $16,000 per year); Federal Work-Study, institutionally sponsored loans, and unspecified assistantships also available. Financial award application deadline: 1/15; financial award applicants required to submit FAFSA. *Faculty research:* Latin American studies, international economics, international security and conflict, comparative development, international health policy. *Unit head:* Dr. Bruce Bagley, Director of Graduate Studies, 305-284-4406. *Application contact:* Steven Ralph, Director of Student Services, 305-284-3117, Fax: 305-284-4406.

University of Miami, Graduate School, Program in International Administration, Coral Gables, FL 33124. Offers MAIA. Part-time and evening/weekend programs available. *Faculty:* 3 full-time (1 woman), 2 part-time/adjunct (0 women). *Students:* 16 full-time (10 women), 32 part-time (19 women); includes 26 minority (4 African Americans, 22 Hispanic Americans), 5 international. Average age 25. 41 applicants, 51% accepted, 18 enrolled. In 2007, 16 degrees awarded. *Degree requirements:* For master's, practicum. *Entrance requirements:* For master's, GRE General Test. Additional exam requirements/recommendations for international students: Required—TOEFL (minimum score 550 paper-based; 213 computer-based), IELTS (minimum score 7). *Application deadline:* For fall admission, 3/1 priority date for domestic and international students; for spring admission, 10/1 priority date for domestic and international students. Applications are processed on a rolling basis. Application fee: $50. Electronic applications accepted. *Financial support:* In 2007–08, 14 students received support. Career-related internships or fieldwork, institutionally sponsored loans, and scholarships/grants available. Financial award applicants required to submit FAFSA. *Unit head:* Prof. Vendulka Kubalkova, Director, 305-284-8783, Fax: 305-284-2023, E-mail: vkubalkova@miami.edu. *Application contact:* Manuel Niño, Director of Student Services, 305-284-8782, Fax: 305-284-2023, E-mail: mnino@miami.edu.

University of Northern British Columbia, Office of Graduate Studies, Prince George, BC V2N 4Z9, Canada. Offers business administration (Diploma); community health science (M Sc); disability management (MA); education (M Ed); first nations studies (MA); gender studies (MA); history (MA); interdisciplinary studies (MA); international studies (MA); mathematical, computer and physical sciences (M Sc); natural resources and environmental studies (M Sc, MA, MNRES, PhD); political science (MA); psychology (M Sc, PhD); social work (MSW). Part-time and evening/weekend programs available. Postbaccalaureate distance learning degree programs offered (no on-campus study). *Degree requirements:* For master's, thesis; for doctorate, thesis/dissertation. *Entrance requirements:* For master's, GRE, minimum B average in undergraduate course work; for doctorate, candidacy exam, minimum A average in graduate course work.

University of Oklahoma, Graduate College, College of Arts and Sciences, School of International and Area Studies, Norman, OK 73019-0390. Offers international studies (MA), including global affairs, global management. *Faculty:* 9 full-time (1 woman), 1 part-time/adjunct (0 women). *Students:* 5 full-time (3 women), 4 part-time (1 woman); includes 1 minority (Hispanic American), 1 international. 9 applicants, 78% accepted, 3 enrolled. *Degree requirements:* For master's, one foreign language, thesis optional. *Entrance requirements:* For master's, GMAT or GRE. Additional exam requirements/recommendations for international students: Required—TOEFL (minimum score 550 paper-based; 213 computer-based). *Application deadline:* For fall admission, 2/15 for domestic students, 4/1 for international students; for spring admission, 10/15 for domestic students, 9/1 for international students. Applications are processed on a rolling basis. Application fee: $40 ($90 for international students). Electronic applications accepted. *Expenses:* Tuition, state resident: full-time $3,451; part-time $144 per credit hour. Tuition, nonresident: full-time $12,432; part-time $518 per credit hour. Required fees: $1,925; $70 per credit hour. $122 per semester. *Financial support:* In 2007–08, 2 students received support, including 2 research assistantships (averaging $11,449 per year), 3 teaching assistantships with partial tuition reimbursements available (averaging $12,750 per year); tuition waivers (full) and unspecified assistantships also available. Financial award applicants required to submit FAFSA. *Faculty research:* Political economy; foreign policy; linguistics; environmental affairs; international law. Total annual research expenditures: $183,057. *Unit head:* Dr. Robert Cox, Director, 405-325-1584, Fax: 405-325-7402, E-mail: rhcox@ou.edu. *Application contact:* Mitchell Smith, Associate Professor, 405-325-8893, Fax: 405-325-0718, E-mail: mps@ou.edu.

University of Oregon, Graduate School, College of Arts and Sciences, Program in International Studies, Eugene, OR 97403. Offers MA. Part-time programs available. *Faculty:* 2 full-time (1 woman). *Students:* 18 full-time (11 women), 4 part-time (all women); includes 3 minority (1 African American, 1 Asian American or Pacific Islander, 1 Hispanic American), 6 international. 75 applicants, 17% accepted. In 2007, 19 degrees awarded. *Degree requirements:* For master's, one foreign language, thesis, internship. *Entrance requirements:* For master's, minimum GPA of 3.0. Additional exam requirements/recommendations for international students: Required—TOEFL. *Application deadline:* For fall admission, 2/1 for domestic students. Application fee: $50. *Financial support:* In 2007–08, 9 teaching assistantships were awarded; career-related internships or fieldwork and Federal Work-Study also available. Financial award application deadline: 2/1. *Faculty research:* International development studies; environmental studies; cross-cultural communications; planning, public policy, and management; several world regions. *Unit head:* Dennis Galvan, Director, 541-346-5051. *Application contact:* Daniel Gorman, Coordinator, 541-346-2850, Fax: 541-346-0802, E-mail: dqgorman@uoregon.edu.

University of Pennsylvania, School of Arts and Sciences, Graduate Group in International Studies, Philadelphia, PA 19104. Offers AM.

University of Pittsburgh, Graduate School of Public and International Affairs, Doctoral Program in Public and International Affairs, Pittsburgh, PA 15260. Offers development policy (PhD); foreign and security policy (PhD); international political economy (PhD); public administration (PhD); public policy (PhD). *Accreditation:* NASPAA. Part-time programs available. *Faculty:* 34 full-time (10 women), 18 part-time/adjunct (6 women). *Students:* 39 full-time (15 women), 8 part-time (6 women); includes 6 minority (2 African Americans, 3 Asian Americans or Pacific Islanders, 1 Hispanic American), 10 international. Average age 30. 61 applicants, 30% accepted, 11 enrolled. In 2007, 8 degrees awarded. *Degree requirements:* For doctorate, comprehensive exam, thesis/dissertation. *Entrance requirements:* For doctorate, GRE, 3 letters of recommendation, resumé, minimum GPA of 3.0, writing sample. Additional exam requirements/recommendations for international students: Required—TOEFL (minimum score 600 paper-based; 250 computer-based; 100 iBT), TWE (minimum score 4); Recommended—IELTS (minimum score 7). *Application deadline:* For fall admission, 2/1 for domestic students, 1/15 for international students. Application fee: $50. Electronic applications accepted. *Financial support:* In 2007–08, 13 students received support, including 13 fellowships (averaging $28,580 per year); scholarships/grants and unspecified assistantships also available. Financial award application deadline: 2/1. *Faculty research:* International political economy, international development, public administration, public policy, foreign policy, international security policy. Total annual research expenditures: $845,025. *Unit head:* Dr. Phyllis Coontz, Doctoral Program Coordinator, 412-648-2654, Fax: 412-648-2605, E-mail: pcoontz@gspia.pitt.edu. *Application contact:* Jessica L. Hatherill, Associate Director of Student Services, 412-648-7640, Fax: 412-648-7641, E-mail: hatherill@gspia.pitt.edu.

See Close-Up on page 1645.

University of Pittsburgh, Graduate School of Public and International Affairs, International Affairs Division, Pittsburgh, PA 15260. Offers global political economy (MPIA); human security (MPIA); security and intelligence studies (MPIA); JD/MPIA; MBA/MPIA; MID/MPIA; MPA/MPIA; MSIS/MPIA. Part-time and evening/weekend programs available. *Faculty:* 34 full-time (10 women), 18 part-time/adjunct (6 women). *Students:* 121 full-time (52 women), 21 part-time (11 women); includes 13 minority (8 African Americans, 4 Asian Americans or Pacific Islanders, 1 Hispanic American), 7 international. Average age 25. 223 applicants, 87% accepted, 75 enrolled. In 2007, 63 degrees awarded. *Degree requirements:* For master's, thesis optional, internship, capstone seminar. *Entrance requirements:* For master's, GRE General Test, 3 letters of recommendation, resumé, minimum GPA of 3.2. Additional exam requirements/recommendations for international students: Required—TOEFL (minimum score 550 paper-based; 213 computer-based), TWE (minimum score 4); Recommended—IELTS (minimum score 7). *Application deadline:* For fall admission, 3/1 for domestic students, 1/15 for international students; for spring admission, 11/1 for domestic students, 8/1 for international students. Application fee: $50. Electronic applications accepted. *Financial support:* In 2007–08, 41 students received support, including 41 fellowships (averaging $8,280 per year); career-related internships or fieldwork, scholarships/grants, and unspecified assistantships also available. Financial award application deadline: 2/1. *Faculty research:* Political economy, international security, transnational crime, international trade, international finance, terrorism. Total annual research expenditures: $845,025. *Unit head:* Dr. Martin Staniland, Director, International Affairs and International Development Divisions, 412-648-7656, Fax: 412-648-2605, E-mail: mstan@pitt.edu. *Application contact:* Jessica L. Hatherill, Associate Director of Student Services, 412-648-7640, Fax: 412-648-7641, E-mail: hatherill@gspia.pitt.edu.

See Close-Up on page 1645.

University of Pittsburgh, University Center for International Studies, Pittsburgh, PA 15260. Offers African studies (Certificate); Asian studies (Certificate); European Union studies (Certificate); global studies (Certificate); Latin American studies (Certificate); Russian and East European studies (Certificate); West European studies (Certificate). *Unit head:* Lawrence F. Feick, Director, University Center for International Studies, 412-648-7374, Fax: 412-624-4672, E-mail: feick@pitt.edu.

University of Rhode Island, Graduate School, College of Arts and Sciences, Department of Political Science, Kingston, RI 02881. Offers political science (MA), including American politics, comparative government, international relations, public policy; public policy and administration (MA, MPA, Certificate). In 2007, 6 degrees awarded. *Application deadline:* For fall admission, 4/15 priority date for domestic students. Applications are processed on a rolling basis. Application fee: $35. *Expenses:* Tuition, state resident: full-time $6,936; part-time $385 per credit. Tuition, nonresident: full-time $19,044; part-time $1,058 per credit. Required fees: $1,508; $48 per credit. $30 per semester. One-time fee: $80 part-time. *Unit head:* Dr. Gerry Tyler, Chairperson, 401-874-4053.

University of San Diego, College of Arts and Sciences, Department of Political Science and International Relations, San Diego, CA 92110-2492. Offers international relations (MA); JD/MA. Part-time and evening/weekend programs available. *Faculty:* 2 full-time (0 women), 2 part-time/adjunct (1 woman). *Students:* 14 full-time (10 women), 13 part-time (7 women); includes 9 minority (2 Asian Americans or Pacific Islanders, 7 Hispanic Americans). Average age 28. 46 applicants, 57% accepted, 15 enrolled. In 2007, 17 degrees awarded. *Degree requirements:* For master's, one foreign language, comprehensive exam. *Entrance requirements:* For master's, GRE General Test, minimum GPA of 3.0. Additional exam requirements/recommendations for international students: Required—TOEFL (minimum score 580 paper-based; 237 computer-based), TWE. *Application deadline:* For fall admission, 5/1 priority date for domestic students; for spring admission, 11/15 for domestic students. Applications are processed on a rolling basis. Application fee: $45. Electronic applications accepted. *Expenses:* Tuition: Part-time $1,095 per unit. Tuition and fees vary according to degree level and program. *Financial support:* Federal Work-Study, institutionally sponsored loans, tuition waivers (partial), and unspecified assistantships available. Support available to part-time students. Financial award application deadline: 5/1; financial award applicants required to submit FAFSA. *Faculty research:* Soviet politics, Latin American politics, China, Canada, international organizations. *Unit head:* Dr. Emily Edmonds-Poli, Graduate Program Director, 619-260-7802, Fax: 619-260-6840, E-mail: edmonds@sandiego.edu. *Application contact:* Stephen Pultz, Director of Admissions, 619-260-4524, Fax: 619-260-4158, E-mail: grads@sandiego.edu.

University of San Francisco, College of Arts and Sciences, Department of Economics, Program in International and Development Economics, San Francisco, CA 94117-1080. Offers MA. *Expenses:* Tuition: Part-time $1,005 per unit. Tuition and fees vary according to degree level, campus/location and program. *Unit head:* Dr. Elizabeth Katz, Co-Director, 415-422-2711, Fax: 415-422-6983.

based). Electronic applications accepted. *Faculty research:* Pacific Rim as system and placement in global relations; studies in international economics, management and finance; analysis of patterns of policymaking in countries of the Pacific.

Announcement: The School of International Relations and Pacific Studies (IR/PS) at UC, San Diego, is among the leading institutions of international relations in the world. Learn about the world from where economics, business, politics, and culture intersect. More than 33 percent of students focus their studies on Latin America; at IR/PS, learn how to join them.

See Close-Up on page 1171.

University of California, Santa Barbara, Graduate Division, College of Letters and Sciences, Division of Social Sciences, Department of Global and International Studies, Santa Barbara, CA 93106. Offers MA. *Faculty:* 5 full-time (1 woman), 8 part-time/adjunct (4 women). *Students:* 19 full-time (11 women); includes 7 minority (1 African American, 6 Asian Americans or Pacific Islanders), 3 international. Average age 25. 74 applicants, 62% accepted, 16 enrolled. *Degree requirements:* For master's, comprehensive exam (for some programs), thesis or alternative, internship/study abroad. *Entrance requirements:* For master's, GRE. Additional exam requirements/recommendations for international students: Required—TOEFL (minimum score 550 paper-based; 213 computer-based; 80 iBT). *Application deadline:* For fall admission, 12/15 for domestic and international students. Application fee: $60. Electronic applications accepted. *Expenses:* Tuition, nonresident: full-time $14,888. Required fees: $10,108. *Financial support:* In 2007–08, 30 students received support, including 22 fellowships with full and partial tuition reimbursements available (averaging $3,579 per year), 2 research assistantships with full and partial tuition reimbursements available (averaging $5,000 per year), 41 teaching assistantships with partial tuition reimbursements available (averaging $25,863 per year); career-related internships or fieldwork, Federal Work-Study, institutionally sponsored loans, scholarships/grants, health care benefits, tuition waivers (partial), and travel stipends also available. Financial award application deadline: 12/15; financial award applicants required to submit FAFSA. *Faculty research:* Globalization, NGO/non-profit organizations, world system theory, international/global conflict resolution, international/global ethics. Total annual research expenditures: $30,000. *Unit head:* Dr. Giles Gunn, Chair, 805-893-4299, E-mail: ggunn@global.ucsb.edu. *Application contact:* Jessea Gay Marie, Graduate Program Advisor, Internship Assistance Officer, 805-893-4668, Fax: 805-893-8003, E-mail: jmarie@global.ucsb.edu.

University of California, Santa Cruz, Division of Graduate Studies, Division of Social Sciences, Program in International Economics, Santa Cruz, CA 95064. Offers PhD. *Faculty:* 22 full-time (3 women). *Students:* 40 full-time (18 women), 1 (woman) part-time; includes 2 minority (both Hispanic Americans), 28 international. 121 applicants, 26% accepted, 11 enrolled. In 2007, 6 doctorates awarded. *Degree requirements:* For doctorate, thesis/dissertation, 4 field exams, econometrics project. *Entrance requirements:* For doctorate, GRE General Test. *Application deadline:* For fall admission, 1/15 for domestic students. Application fee: $60. *Expenses:* Tuition, nonresident: full-time $14,694. Required fees: $11,360. *Financial support:* Research assistantships, teaching assistantships, career-related internships or fieldwork, Federal Work-Study, institutionally sponsored loans, and tuition waivers (partial) available. Financial award application deadline: 2/1. *Faculty research:* Current and emerging issues in taxation, industrial policy, environmental regulation, market structure. *Unit head:* Phillip McCalman, Director, 831-59-4381, E-mail: mccalman@ucsc.edu. *Application contact:* Cristina M. Intintoli, Graduate Assistant, 831-459-2219, E-mail: cmintint@cats.ucsc.edu.

University of Central Florida, College of Sciences, Department of Political Science, Orlando, FL 32816. Offers environmental politics (MA); international studies (MA); political analysis and policy (MA). Part-time and evening/weekend programs available. *Faculty:* 24 full-time (7 women), 8 part-time/adjunct (2 women). *Students:* Average age 30. *Degree requirements:* For master's, comprehensive exam, thesis. *Entrance requirements:* For master's, GRE General Test, minimum GPA of 3.0 in last 60 hours. Additional exam requirements/recommendations for international students: Required—TOEFL. *Application deadline:* For fall admission, 7/15 for domestic students; for spring admission, 12/1 for domestic students. Application fee: $30. Electronic applications accepted. *Expenses:* Tuition, state resident: full-time $6,484. Tuition, nonresident: full-time $23,938. Tuition and fees vary according to program. *Financial support:* Fellowships with partial tuition reimbursements, research assistantships with partial tuition reimbursements, teaching assistantships with partial tuition reimbursements, career-related internships or fieldwork, Federal Work-Study, institutionally sponsored loans, tuition waivers (partial), and unspecified assistantships available. Financial award application deadline: 3/1; financial award applicants required to submit FAFSA. *Faculty research:* Environment, presidential campaigning, term limits for elected officials. *Unit head:* Dr. Roger Handberg, Chair, 407-823-2608, Fax: 407-823-0051.

University of Central Oklahoma, College of Graduate Studies and Research, College of Liberal Arts, Department of Political Science, Program in International Affairs, Edmond, OK 73034-5209. Offers MA. Part-time programs available. *Faculty:* 6 full-time (1 woman), 1 part-time/adjunct (0 women). *Students:* 2 full-time (0 women), 1 part-time. Average age 24. 7 applicants, 100% accepted. In 2007, 2 degrees awarded. *Entrance requirements:* Additional exam requirements/recommendations for international students: Required—TOEFL (minimum score 550 paper-based; 213 computer-based). *Application deadline:* For fall admission, 7/1 for international students; for spring admission, 11/1 for international students. Applications are processed on a rolling basis. Application fee: $25. Electronic applications accepted. *Expenses:* Tuition, state resident: full-time $3,516; part-time $147 per hour. Tuition, nonresident: full-time $9,054; part-time $377 per hour. Required fees: $433; $18 per hour. *Financial support:* Unspecified assistantships available. Financial award application deadline: 3/31; financial award applicants required to submit FAFSA. *Faculty research:* Korean and Japanese politics. *Unit head:* Dr. Jan Hardt, Adviser, 405-974-5840, E-mail: jhardt@aix1.ucok.edu.

University of Chicago, Division of Social Sciences, Committee on International Relations, Chicago, IL 60637-1513. Offers AM, MBA/AM. Part-time programs available. *Students:* 46. In 2007, 40 degrees awarded. *Degree requirements:* For master's, thesis. *Entrance requirements:* For master's, GRE General Test. Additional exam requirements/recommendations for international students: Required—TOEFL. *Application deadline:* For fall admission, 12/28 for domestic students. Application fee: $55. Electronic applications accepted. *Financial support:* Federal Work-Study, institutionally sponsored loans, and scholarships/grants available. Financial award application deadline: 12/28. *Unit head:* Prof. Duncan Snidal, Chair, 773-702-8078. *Application contact:* Office of the Dean of Students, 773-702-8415.

University of Colorado at Boulder, Graduate School, College of Arts and Sciences, Department of Political Science, Boulder, CO 80309. Offers international affairs (MA); political science (MA, PhD); public policy (MA). *Faculty:* 27. *Students:* 49 full-time (22 women), 20 part-time (8 women); includes 5 minority (3 Asian Americans or Pacific Islanders, 2 Hispanic Americans), 9 international. Average age 29. 64 applicants, 50% accepted. In 2007, 16 master's, 7 doctorates awarded. Terminal master's awarded for partial completion of doctoral program. *Degree requirements:* For master's, comprehensive exam, thesis; for doctorate, one foreign language, thesis/dissertation. *Entrance requirements:* For master's, GRE General Test, minimum undergraduate GPA of 3.0; for doctorate, GRE General Test, minimum GPA of 3.5 (undergraduate), 3.0 (graduate). *Application deadline:* For fall admission, 12/31 priority date for domestic students, 12/31 for international students. Application fee: $50 ($60 for international students). *Financial support:* In 2007–08, 5 fellowships (averaging $3,024 per year), 1 research assistantship (averaging $16,252 per year) were awarded; Federal Work-Study also available. Financial award application deadline: 12/31. *Faculty research:* American government and politics, comparative politics, international relations, law and politics, public policy, political philosophy, empirical theory and methodology. Total annual research expenditures: $427,386. *Unit head:* Steven Chan, Chair, 303-492-8601, Fax: 303-492-0978, E-mail: steve.chan@colorado.edu. *Application contact:* Mary Gregory, Graduate Program Assistant, 303-492-7872, Fax: 303-492-0978, E-mail: pscigrad@colorado.edu.

University of Connecticut, Graduate School, College of Liberal Arts and Sciences, Field of International Studies, Program in International Studies, Storrs, CT 06269. Offers MA. *Faculty:* 46 full-time (23 women). *Students:* 6 full-time (3 women), 2 part-time (1 woman); includes 1 minority (African American), 4 international. Average age 27. 12 applicants, 17% accepted, 2 enrolled. In 2007, 2 degrees awarded. *Degree requirements:* For master's, comprehensive exam. *Entrance requirements:* For master's, GRE General Test. Additional exam requirements/recommendations for international students: Required—TOEFL (minimum score 550 paper-based; 213 computer-based). *Application deadline:* For fall admission, 2/1 priority date for domestic and international students; for spring admission, 11/1 for domestic students, 10/1 for international students. Applications are processed on a rolling basis. Electronic applications accepted. *Expenses:* Tuition, state resident: part-time $469 per credit hour. Tuition, nonresident: part-time $1,218 per credit hour. *Financial support:* In 2007–08, 3 research assistantships with full tuition reimbursements, 1 teaching assistantship with full tuition reimbursement were awarded; Federal Work-Study, scholarships/grants, health care benefits, and unspecified assistantships also available. Financial award application deadline: 2/1. *Unit head:* M. Elizabeth Mahan, Director, Field of International Studies, 860-486-2908, Fax: 860-486-2963, E-mail: elizabeth.mahan@uconn.edu.

University of Delaware, College of Arts and Sciences, Department of Political Science and International Relations, Newark, DE 19716. Offers MA, PhD. *Faculty:* 19 full-time (6 women). *Students:* 44 full-time (17 women), 2 part-time (both women); includes 4 minority (2 African Americans, 2 Hispanic Americans), 20 international. Average age 28. 82 applicants, 35% accepted, 10 enrolled. In 2007, 10 master's, 1 doctorate awarded. Terminal master's awarded for partial completion of doctoral program. *Degree requirements:* For master's, research paper; for doctorate, one foreign language, comprehensive exam, thesis/dissertation. *Entrance requirements:* For master's and doctorate, GRE General Test, minimum GPA of 3.2 in major, 3.0 overall. Additional exam requirements/recommendations for international students: Required—TOEFL (minimum score 600 paper-based). *Application deadline:* For fall admission, 5/15 priority date for domestic students. Application fee: $60. Electronic applications accepted. *Financial support:* In 2007–08, 31 students received support, including 2 fellowships with full tuition reimbursements available (averaging $14,600 per year), 23 teaching assistantships with full tuition reimbursements available (averaging $14,600 per year); research assistantships with full tuition reimbursements available, career-related internships or fieldwork, Federal Work-Study, institutionally sponsored loans, scholarships/grants, and tuition waivers (full and partial) also available. Financial award application deadline: 2/1. *Faculty research:* Social constructivism. international migration, international security, democratization, human rights. Total annual research expenditures: $246,882. *Unit head:* Dr. Gretchen M. Bauer, Chair, 302-831-2355, Fax: 302-831-4452. *Application contact:* Prof. Daniel Green, Graduate Director, 302-831-1933, Fax: 302-831-4452, E-mail: dgreen@udel.edu.

University of Denver, Faculty of Arts and Humanities/Social Sciences, School of Communication, Program in International and Intercultural Communication, Denver, CO 80208. Offers MA. *Students:* 23 full-time (18 women), 7 part-time (6 women); includes 3 minority (1 African American, 1 Asian American or Pacific Islander, 1 Hispanic American), 4 international. Average age 28. In 2007, 11 degrees awarded. *Degree requirements:* For master's, one foreign language. *Entrance requirements:* For master's, GRE. Additional exam requirements/recommendations for international students: Required—TOEFL, TWE. *Application deadline:* Applications are processed on a rolling basis. Application fee: $50. Electronic applications accepted. *Financial support:* Career-related internships or fieldwork, Federal Work-Study, institutionally sponsored loans, and scholarships/grants available. Support available to part-time students. Financial award application deadline: 3/1; financial award applicants required to submit FAFSA. *Unit head:* Dr. Margaret Thompson, Chairperson, 303-871-2088. *Application contact:* Information Contact, 303-871-2088, Fax: 303-871-4949, E-mail: icc@du.edu.

University of Denver, Graduate School of International Studies, Denver, CO 80208. Offers global studies (MGS); international studies (MA, PhD). Part-time and evening/weekend programs available. *Faculty:* 23 full-time (6 women). *Students:* 392 full-time (227 women), 48 part-time (24 women); includes 39 minority (15 African Americans, 8 Asian Americans or Pacific Islanders, 16 Hispanic Americans), 42 international. Average age 27. 842 applicants, 76% accepted, 209 enrolled. In 2007, 188 master's, 10 doctorates awarded. *Degree requirements:* For master's, one foreign language, thesis; for doctorate, one foreign language, thesis/dissertation. *Entrance requirements:* For master's and doctorate, GRE General Test. Additional exam requirements/recommendations for international students: Required—TOEFL. *Application deadline:* For fall admission, 1/15 priority date for domestic students. Applications are processed on a rolling basis. Application fee: $65. Electronic applications accepted. *Financial support:* Career-related internships or fieldwork, Federal Work-Study, institutionally sponsored loans, and scholarships/grants available. Support available to part-time students. Financial award application deadline: 2/15; financial award applicants required to submit FAFSA. *Faculty research:* International politics and economics, international technology analysis and management, human rights and international security, economic-social and political development, homeland security. Total annual research expenditures: $305,000. *Unit head:* Dr. Tom Farer, Dean, 303-871-2544. *Application contact:* Information Contact, 303-871-3585, E-mail: gsisadm@du.edu.

University of Florida, Graduate School, College of Liberal Arts and Sciences, Department of Political Science, Program in International Relations, Gainesville, FL 32611. Offers MA, MAT. Part-time programs available. *Faculty:* 6. Terminal master's awarded for partial completion of doctoral program. *Degree requirements:* For master's, variable foreign language requirement, thesis or alternative. *Entrance requirements:* For master's, GRE General Test, minimum GPA of 3.0. Additional exam requirements/recommendations for international students: Required—TOEFL (minimum score 550 paper-based; 213 computer-based). *Application deadline:* For fall admission, 3/16 priority date for domestic students. Applications are processed on a rolling basis. Application fee: $30. Electronic applications accepted. *Expenses:* Tuition, state resident: full-time $7,478. Tuition, nonresident: full-time $22,603. *Faculty research:* American and comparative foreign policy, North-South relations, international political economy. *Unit head:* Ido Oren, Head, E-mail: oren@polisci.ufl.edu. *Application contact:* Dr. J. Samuel Barkin, Coordinator, 352-392-0262 Ext. 222, Fax: 352-392-8127, E-mail: barkin@polisci.ufl.edu.

University of Hawaii at Manoa, Graduate Division, East-West Center, Honolulu, HI 96822. Offers international cultural studies (Graduate Certificate). Part-time programs available. *Students:* 22 full-time (14 women), 5 part-time (4 women); includes 7 minority (6 Asian Americans or Pacific Islanders, 1 Hispanic American), 11 international. 8 applicants, 13% accepted, 1 enrolled. *Entrance requirements:* For degree, GRE General Test. Additional exam requirements/recommendations for international students: Required—TOEFL (minimum score 540 paper-based; 207 computer-based; 76 iBT), IELTS (minimum score 5). *Application deadline:* For fall admission, 3/1 for domestic and international students; for spring admission, 9/1 for domestic and international students. Application fee: $50. *Financial support:* In 2007–08, 2 research assistantships (averaging $17,847 per year), 6 teaching assistantships (averaging $14,574 per year) were awarded. *Application contact:* Mari Yoshihara, Graduate Chairperson, 808-956-8542, Fax: 808-956-4733, E-mail: myoshiha@hawaii.edu.

University of Indianapolis, Graduate Programs, College of Arts and Sciences, Department of History and Political Science, Indianapolis, IN 46227-3697. Offers history (MA); international relations (MA). Part-time and evening/weekend programs available. *Faculty:* 5 full-time (2 women). *Students:* 3 full-time (2 women), 28 part-time (15 women); includes 4 minority (3 African Americans, 1 Hispanic American), 2 international. Average age 30. *Degree requirements:* For master's, thesis optional. *Entrance requirements:* For master's, GRE Subject Test, minimum GPA of 3.0, 3 letters of recommendation, statement of purpose. Additional exam requirements/recommendations for international students: Required—TOEFL (minimum score 550 paper-based; 213 computer-based). *Application deadline:* Applications are processed on a rolling basis. Application fee: $30. Electronic applications accepted. *Financial support:* Federal Work-Study available. Financial award application deadline: 5/1; financial award applicants required

University of South Carolina, The Graduate School, College of Arts and Sciences, Department of Political Science, Program in International Studies, Columbia, SC 29208. Offers MA, PhD. Part-time programs available. *Faculty:* 32 full-time (8 women). *Students:* 17 full-time (8 women), 8 part-time (4 women); includes 1 minority (African American), 6 international. Average age 25. 27 applicants, 70% accepted, 8 enrolled. In 2007, 4 master's, 3 doctorates awarded. Terminal master's awarded for partial completion of doctoral program. *Degree requirements:* For master's, one foreign language, thesis or alternative; for doctorate, one foreign language, comprehensive exam, thesis/dissertation. *Entrance requirements:* For master's, GRE General Test, minimum GPA of 3.3; for doctorate, GRE General Test, minimum GPA of 3.5. Additional exam requirements/recommendations for international students: Required—TOEFL. *Application deadline:* For fall admission, 6/1 for domestic and international students; for spring admission, 11/15 for domestic and international students. Applications are processed on a rolling basis. Application fee: $40. Electronic applications accepted. *Expenses:* Tuition, state resident: part-time $440 per hour. Tuition, nonresident: part-time $936 per hour. Required fees: $17 per hour. Tuition and fees vary according to program. *Financial support:* In 2007–08, 6 students received support, including 3 fellowships (averaging $3,000 per year); research assistantships with partial tuition reimbursements available, teaching assistantships with partial tuition reimbursements available, career-related internships or fieldwork, Federal Work-Study, institutionally sponsored loans, and tuition waivers (partial) also available. Financial award application deadline: 2/15. *Faculty research:* International relations, international organization, foreign policy, comparative politics. *Unit head:* Dr. Donald J. Puchala, Graduate Director, 803-777-6801, Fax: 803-777-8255. *Application contact:* Tamara Lorraine Gordon, Student Services Coordinator, 803-777-3869, Fax: 803-777-8255, E-mail: gordontl@gwm.sc.edu.

University of Southern California, Graduate School, Annenberg School for Communication, School of Communication, Program in Public Diplomacy, Los Angeles, CA 90089. Offers MPD. *Students:* 34 full-time (27 women), 1 (woman) part-time; includes 2 minority (1 African American, 1 Hispanic American), 6 international. 71 applicants, 76% accepted, 20 enrolled. In 2007, 2 degrees awarded. *Degree requirements:* For master's, thesis. *Entrance requirements:* For master's, GRE, resumé, writing samples, recommendation letters. Additional exam requirements/recommendations for international students: Required—TOEFL (minimum score 280 computer-based; 114 iBT). *Application deadline:* For fall admission, 12/14 priority date for domestic and international students. Application fee: $85. Electronic applications accepted. *Financial support:* Career-related internships or fieldwork, Federal Work-Study, scholarships/grants, and tuition waivers available. Support available to part-time students. Financial award application deadline: 1/15; financial award applicants required to submit FAFSA. *Unit head:* Dr. Nicholas Cull, Director, 213-821-4080, E-mail: cull@usc.edu. *Application contact:* Allyson Hill, Director of Admissions, 213-821-0770, Fax: 213-821-5574, E-mail: ascadm@usc.edu.

See Close-Up on page 945.

University of Southern California, Graduate School, College of Letters, Arts and Sciences, Department of Political Science, Los Angeles, CA 90089. Offers politics and international relations (MA, PhD). *Faculty:* 32 full-time (11 women), 1 part-time/adjunct (0 women). *Students:* 34 full-time (17 women); includes 12 minority (2 African Americans, 1 American Indian/Alaska Native, 4 Asian Americans or Pacific Islanders, 5 Hispanic Americans), 10 international. In 2007, 8 degrees awarded. *Degree requirements:* For doctorate, one foreign language, thesis/dissertation. *Entrance requirements:* For doctorate, GRE General Test. *Application deadline:* For fall admission, 12/1 for domestic students. Application fee: $85. *Financial support:* In 2007–08, 38 students received support, including 14 fellowships with tuition reimbursements available (averaging $19,000 per year), 7 research assistantships with tuition reimbursements available (averaging $18,500 per year), 17 teaching assistantships with tuition reimbursements available (averaging $18,500 per year); scholarships/grants and tuition waivers (partial) also available. Financial award application deadline: 2/15; financial award applicants required to submit FAFSA. *Faculty research:* Public law, urban politics, political communication, Pacific Rim studies, environmental politics. *Unit head:* Dr. Daniel Lynch, Chair, 213-740-2311. *Application contact:* Alex Venegas, Information Contact, 213-740-2311.

University of Southern California, Graduate School, College of Letters, Arts and Sciences, School of International Relations, Los Angeles, CA 90089. Offers politics and international relations (PhD); public diplomacy (MPD); JD/MA; MPA/MA. Part-time programs available. *Students:* 25 full-time (10 women), 2 part-time (both women); includes 4 minority (3 Asian Americans or Pacific Islanders, 1 Hispanic American), 9 international. 25 applicants, 28% accepted. In 2007, 4 master's, 3 doctorates awarded. Terminal master's awarded for partial completion of doctoral program. *Degree requirements:* For master's, one foreign language, thesis optional, substantive paper; for doctorate, one foreign language, thesis/dissertation, substantive paper, written/oral exams. *Entrance requirements:* For master's and doctorate, GRE General Test. *Application deadline:* For fall admission, 12/1 priority date for domestic students. Applications are processed on a rolling basis. Application fee: $85. *Financial support:* In 2007–08, research assistantships with full tuition reimbursements (averaging $18,500 per year), teaching assistantships with full tuition reimbursements (averaging $18,500 per year) were awarded; fellowships with full tuition reimbursements, career-related internships or fieldwork, Federal Work-Study, institutionally sponsored loans, and scholarships/grants also available. Financial award application deadline: 2/15; financial award applicants required to submit FAFSA. *Faculty research:* International environmental agreements and regimes, Middle East regional and domestic political economies, negotiation and conflict among states on economic issues. *Unit head:* Dr. Laurie Brand, Chair, 213-740-2136, E-mail: brand@usc.edu. *Application contact:* Luda Spilewsky, Information Contact, 213-740-8629, E-mail: ludas@usc.edu.

University of Southern Mississippi, Graduate School, College of Arts and Letters, Department of Political Science, International Development, and International Affairs, Hattiesburg, MS 39406-0001. Offers international development (PhD); political science (MA, MS). Part-time programs available. *Faculty:* 17 full-time (3 women). *Students:* 23 full-time (8 women), 45 part-time (12 women); includes 14 minority (10 African Americans, 1 American Indian/Alaska Native, 1 Asian American or Pacific Islander, 2 Hispanic Americans), 3 international. Average age 40. 29 applicants, 66% accepted, 16 enrolled. In 2007, 8 master's, 3 doctorates awarded. *Degree requirements:* For master's, comprehensive exam, thesis (for some programs). *Entrance requirements:* For master's, GRE General Test, minimum GPA of 2.75 in last 2 years, 3.0 in field of study. *Application deadline:* For fall admission, 3/1 priority date for domestic students, 3/1 for international students. Applications are processed on a rolling basis. Application fee: $30. *Financial support:* In 2007–08, 3 research assistantships with full and partial tuition reimbursements (averaging $7,942 per year), 8 teaching assistantships (averaging $7,942 per year) were awarded; career-related internships or fieldwork, Federal Work-Study, scholarships/grants, and unspecified assistantships also available. Financial award application deadline: 3/15. *Faculty research:* American politics, international politics, political theory, comparative politics, public law. *Unit head:* Dr. Thomas Lansford, Interim Chair, 601-266-4310. *Application contact:* Dr. Robert Pauley, Graduate Coordinator, 601-266-4310, Fax: 601-266-4172.

University of South Florida, Graduate School, College of Arts and Sciences, Department of Government and International Affairs, Tampa, FL 33620-9951. Offers political science (MA); public administration (MPA). Part-time and evening/weekend programs available. *Faculty:* 14 full-time (3 women), 5 part-time/adjunct (3 women). *Students:* 38 full-time (24 women), 85 part-time (41 women); includes 34 minority (17 African Americans, 5 Asian Americans or Pacific Islanders, 12 Hispanic Americans), 7 international. 95 applicants, 59% accepted, 31 enrolled. In 2007, 33 degrees awarded. *Degree requirements:* For master's, comprehensive exam, thesis. *Entrance requirements:* For master's, GRE (minimum score: 470 verbal, 470 quantitative), minimum GPA of 3.0 in last 60 hours of course work. *Application deadline:* For fall admission, 6/1 for domestic students; for spring admission, 10/15 for domestic students. Applications are processed on a rolling basis. Application fee: $30. Electronic applications accepted. *Financial support:* Scholarships/grants and unspecified assistantships available. Financial award application deadline: 4/1. *Unit head:* Dr. Mohsen Milani, Chairperson, 813-974-2384, Fax: 813-974-0832, E-mail: milani@chuma1.cas.usf.edu. *Application contact:* Dr. Stephen Tauber, Graduate Coordinator, 813-974-0781, Fax: 813-974-0832, E-mail: stauber@chuma1.cas.usf.edu.

University of the Pacific, McGeorge School of Law, Sacramento, CA 95817. Offers government and public policy (LL M); international law (LL M); international waters resources law (LL M); law (JD); transnational business practice (LL M); JD/MBA; JD/MPPA. *Accreditation:* ABA. Part-time and evening/weekend programs available. *Faculty:* 65 full-time (26 women), 64 part-time/adjunct (16 women). *Students:* 660 full-time (295 women), 361 part-time (178 women); includes 272 minority (33 African Americans, 10 American Indian/Alaska Native, 142 Asian Americans or Pacific Islanders, 87 Hispanic Americans). Average age 24. 2,881 applicants, 40% accepted. In 2007, 292 JDs, 25 master's awarded. *Degree requirements:* For master's, thesis (for some programs); for doctorate, thesis/dissertation. *Entrance requirements:* For JD, LSAT; for master's, JD; for doctorate, LL M. Additional exam requirements/recommendations for international students: Required—TOEFL (minimum score 600 paper-based; 250 computer-based; 100 iBT). *Application deadline:* For fall admission, 3/15 priority date for domestic students. Applications are processed on a rolling basis. Application fee: $50. Electronic applications accepted. *Expenses:* Contact institution. *Financial support:* In 2007–08, 902 students received support, including 9 fellowships, 20 research assistantships (averaging $6,485 per year); career-related internships or fieldwork, Federal Work-Study, institutionally sponsored loans, and scholarships/grants also available. Support available to part-time students. Financial award applicants required to submit FAFSA. *Faculty research:* Taxation and business, family and juvenile law, governmental affairs, environmental law, intellectual property law. *Unit head:* Elizabeth Rindskopf Parker, Dean, 916-739-7151, E-mail: elizabeth@uop.edu. *Application contact:* 916-739-7105, Fax: 916-739-7134, E-mail: admissionsmcgeorge@uop.edu.

University of the Pacific, School of International Studies, Program in Intercultural Relations, Stockton, CA 95211-0197. Offers MA. In 2007, 2 degrees awarded. *Entrance requirements:* Additional exam requirements/recommendations for international students: Required—TOEFL (minimum score 475 paper-based; 150 computer-based). Application fee: $75. *Financial support:* Application deadline: 3/1; *Unit head:* Dr. Margee Ensign, Dean, School of International Studies, 209-946-2650, E-mail: mensign@pacific.edu.

University of Utah, The Graduate School, College of Social and Behavioral Science, Department of Political Science, Program in Public Policy, Salt Lake City, UT 84112-1107. Offers international affairs and global enterprises (MS); public policy (MPP). *Application contact:* Mary Ann Underwood, Graduate Coordinator, 801-581-8608, Fax: 801-585-6492, E-mail: maryann.underwood@poli-sci.utah.edu.

University of Virginia, College and Graduate School of Arts and Sciences, Department of Politics, Program in Foreign Affairs, Charlottesville, VA 22903. Offers MA, PhD. *Students:* 46 full-time (17 women); includes 2 minority (both Asian Americans or Pacific Islanders), 14 international. Average age 29. 138 applicants, 20% accepted, 8 enrolled. In 2007, 11 master's, 4 doctorates awarded. *Degree requirements:* For master's, one foreign language, thesis; for doctorate, one foreign language, thesis/dissertation. *Entrance requirements:* For master's and doctorate, GRE General Test, GRE Subject Test. *Application deadline:* Applications are processed on a rolling basis. Application fee: $60. Electronic applications accepted. *Financial support:* Applicants required to submit FAFSA.

University of Washington, Graduate School, College of Arts and Sciences, Henry M. Jackson School of International Studies, Seattle, WA 98195. Offers China studies (MAIS); comparative religion (MAIS); international studies (MAIS); Japan studies (MAIS); Korea studies (MAIS); Middle Eastern studies (MAIS); Russian, East European and Central Asian studies (MAIS), including Central Asian studies, East European studies, Russian studies; South Asian studies (MAIS); JD/MAIS; MBA/MAIS; MFR/MAIS; MMA/MAIS; MPA/MAIS; MPH/MAIS. *Students:* 153 full-time (83 women); includes 23 minority (5 African Americans, 14 Asian Americans or Pacific Islanders, 4 Hispanic Americans), 16 international. Average age 28. 305 applicants, 53% accepted, 67 enrolled. In 2007, 57 degrees awarded. *Entrance requirements:* For master's, GRE General Test, minimum GPA of 3.0. Additional exam requirements/recommendations for international students: Required—TOEFL (minimum score 500 paper-based; 213 computer-based). Application fee: $50. Electronic applications accepted. *Financial support:* Fellowships with tuition reimbursements, research assistantships with full tuition reimbursements, teaching assistantships with full tuition reimbursements, career-related internships or fieldwork, Federal Work-Study, institutionally sponsored loans, and summer language study awards available. Financial award application deadline: 1/15; financial award applicants required to submit FAFSA. *Unit head:* Prof. Anand A. Yang, Director, 206-543-4373. *Application contact:* 206-543-6001, Fax: 206-616-3170, E-mail: jsisinfo@u.washington.edu.

University of Waterloo, Graduate Studies, Faculty of Arts, Department of Political Science, Global Governance Program, Waterloo, ON N2L 3G1, Canada. Offers MA, PhD. *Students:* 15. *Entrance requirements:* For master's, BA, B+ average; for doctorate, MA. Additional exam requirements/recommendations for international students: Required—TOEFL. Application fee: $75. Electronic applications accepted. *Financial support:* Fellowships, research assistantships, teaching assistantships, career-related internships or fieldwork available. *Faculty research:* Global political economy, global environment, peace and security, global justice and human rights, multilateral institutions and diplomacy. *Unit head:* Dr. Eric Helleiner, Graduate Officer, 519-888-4567 Ext. 33955, E-mail: ehelleine@uwaterloo.ca.

University of Wyoming, Graduate School, College of Arts and Sciences, Program in International Studies, Laramie, WY 82070. Offers international peace corps (MA); international studies (MA). Part-time programs available. *Faculty:* 24 part-time/adjunct (7 women). *Students:* 11 full-time (7 women), 12 part-time (7 women); includes 1 minority (African American), 3 international. Average age 30. 2 applicants, 500% accepted, 4 enrolled. In 2007, 6 degrees awarded. *Degree requirements:* For master's, thesis or alternative. *Entrance requirements:* For master's, GRE General Test, minimum GPA of 3.0. Additional exam requirements/recommendations for international students: Required—TOEFL (minimum score 525 paper-based; 195 computer-based). *Application deadline:* For fall admission, 2/1 for domestic and international students. Applications are processed on a rolling basis. Application fee: $50. Electronic applications accepted. *Financial support:* In 2007–08, 5 teaching assistantships with full and partial tuition reimbursements (averaging $10,062 per year) were awarded. Financial award application deadline: 2/1. *Faculty research:* International political economy, comparative social institutions, foreign policy, economic development. *Unit head:* Dr. Garth M. Massey, Director, 307-766-3423, Fax: 307-766-3812, E-mail: dirinst@uwyo.edu.

Virginia Polytechnic Institute and State University, Graduate School, College of Architecture and Urban Studies, School of Public and International Affairs, Blacksburg, VA 24061. Offers environmental planning and policy (MURP); government and international affairs (MPIA); housing, community and economic development (MURP); international development planning (MURP); land use and physical planning (MURP); planning, governance and globalization (PhD), including environmental planning and landscape analysis, physical planning and urban design, public and international affairs, urban and environmental design and planning; urban and regional planning (MURP). *Accreditation:* ACSP. *Entrance requirements:* Additional exam requirements/recommendations for international students: Required—TOEFL (minimum score 550 paper-based; 213 computer-based). Electronic applications accepted. *Faculty research:* Design theory, environmental planning, town planning, transportation planning.

Walden University, Graduate Programs, School of Public Policy and Administration, Minneapolis, MN 55401. Offers criminal justice (MPA, PhD); health services (MPA, PhD); homeland security policy and coordination (MPA, PhD); international nongovernmental organizations (MPA, PhD); knowledge management (MPA, PhD); nonprofit management and leadership (MPA, PhD); public management and leadership (MPA, PhD); public policy (MPA, PhD); public safety management (MPA, PhD). Part-time and evening/weekend programs available. Postbaccalaureate distance learning degree programs offered (minimal on-campus study). *Students:* 433 full-time (228 women), 148 part-time (79 women); includes 265 minority (234 African Americans, 6 American Indian/Alaska Native, 11 Asian Americans or Pacific Islanders, 14

International Affairs

Walden University (continued)
Hispanic Americans), 4 international. Average age 42. 475 applicants, 76% accepted, 220 enrolled. In 2007, 71 master's, 7 doctorates awarded. *Degree requirements:* For doctorate, thesis/dissertation. *Entrance requirements:* For master's, minimum GPA of 3.0; for doctorate, 3 years of professional experience, master's degree. Additional exam requirements/recommendations for international students: Required—TOEFL (minimum score 550 paper-based; 213 computer-based), IELTS (minimum score 7). *Application deadline:* For fall admission, 8/15 priority date for domestic and international students; for winter admission, 11/15 priority date for domestic and international students; for spring admission, 12/15 priority date for domestic and international students. Applications are processed on a rolling basis. Application fee: $50. Electronic applications accepted. *Financial support:* Fellowships with partial tuition reimbursements, Federal Work-Study, institutionally sponsored loans, scholarships/grants, and unspecified assistantships available. Financial award application deadline: 6/1; financial award applicants required to submit FAFSA. *Unit head:* Gary Kelsey, Associate Dean, 800-925-3368, Fax: 612-338-5092. *Application contact:* 866-4-WALDEN, Fax: 410-843-8780, E-mail: request@waldenu.edu.

Washington State University, Graduate School, College of Liberal Arts, Edward R. Murrow College of Communication, Pullman, WA 99164. Offers health communications (MA, PhD); intercultural and international communications (MA, PhD); media and society (MA, PhD); media process and effects (MA, PhD); organizational communications (MA, PhD). *Faculty:* 30. *Students:* 43 full-time (26 women), 6 part-time (4 women); includes 2 minority (1 Asian American or Pacific Islander, 1 Hispanic American), 19 international. Average age 30. 120 applicants, 22% accepted, 19 enrolled. In 2007, 22 master's, 1 doctorate awarded. *Degree requirements:* For master's, comprehensive exam (for some programs), thesis optional, oral exam; for doctorate, comprehensive exam, thesis/dissertation. *Entrance requirements:* For master's, GRE General Test, minimum GPA of 3.25, 3 letters of recommendation; for doctorate, GRE General Test, minimum undergraduate GPA of 3.25, graduate 3.5; MA in communication; 3 letters of recommendation. Additional exam requirements/recommendations for international students: Required—TOEFL (minimum score 580 paper-based; 237 computer-based). *Application deadline:* For fall admission, 1/15 priority date for domestic students, 3/1 for international students. Applications are processed on a rolling basis. Application fee: $50. Electronic applications accepted. *Financial support:* In 2007–08, 46 students received support, including 2 fellowships (averaging $4,477 per year), 7 research assistantships with full and partial tuition reimbursements available (averaging $13,917 per year), 34 teaching assistantships with full and partial tuition reimbursements available (averaging $13,056 per year); career-related internships or fieldwork, Federal Work-Study, institutionally sponsored loans, tuition waivers (partial), and teaching associateships also available. Financial award application deadline: 4/1; financial award applicants required to submit FAFSA. *Faculty research:* Advocacy communication, mediated communication in decision making, communication technology policy and effects, multicultural and international psychology and physiology of communication. Total annual research expenditures: $550,455. *Unit head:* Dr. Erica Austin, Interim Director, 509-335-1556, E-mail: eaustin@wsu.edu. *Application contact:* Graduate School Admissions, 800-GRADWSU, Fax: 509-335-1949, E-mail: gradsch@wsu.edu.

Webster University, College of Arts and Sciences, Department of History, Politics and International Relations, Program in International Relations, St. Louis, MO 63119-3194. Offers MA. Part-time and evening/weekend programs available. *Students:* 147 full-time (74 women), 206 part-time (88 women); includes 76 minority (41 African Americans, 5 American Indian/Alaska Native, 7 Asian Americans or Pacific Islanders, 23 Hispanic Americans), 48 international. Average age 31. In 2007, 81 degrees awarded. *Degree requirements:* For master's, thesis optional. *Application deadline:* Applications are processed on a rolling basis. Application fee: $35 ($50 for international students). *Expenses:* Tuition: Full-time $9,360; part-time $520 per credit. *Financial support:* Career-related internships or fieldwork and Federal Work-Study available. Support available to part-time students. Financial award application deadline: 4/1; financial award applicants required to submit FAFSA. *Faculty research:* International organizations, international political economy, politics of development, environmental law, Latin American law. *Unit head:* Dan Hellinger, Director, 314-968-7064. *Application contact:* Director of Graduate and Evening Student Admissions, Fax: 314-968-7116, E-mail: gadmit@webster.edu.

West Virginia University, Eberly College of Arts and Sciences, Department of Political Science, Morgantown, WV 26506. Offers American public policy and politics (MA); international and comparative public policy and politics (MA); political science (PhD); public policy analysis (PhD). *Faculty:* 15 full-time (3 women), 6 part-time/adjunct (2 women). *Students:* 56 full-time (22 women), 20 part-time (9 women); includes 7 minority (5 African Americans, 1 Asian American or Pacific Islander, 1 Hispanic American), 17 international. Average age 31. 55 applicants, 85% accepted, 24 enrolled. In 2007, 10 master's, 8 doctorates awarded. Terminal master's awarded for partial completion of doctoral program. *Degree requirements:* For master's, thesis optional; for doctorate, comprehensive exam, thesis/dissertation. *Entrance requirements:* For master's, GRE General Test, minimum GPA of 2.75; for doctorate, GRE General Test, minimum GPA of 3.0. Additional exam requirements/recommendations for international students: Required—TOEFL. *Application deadline:* For fall admission, 4/1 priority date for domestic students. Applications are processed on a rolling basis. Application fee: $45. *Expenses:* Tuition, state resident: full-time $5,196; part-time $292 per credit hour. Tuition, nonresident: full-time $15,064; part-time $840 per credit hour. Tuition and fees vary according to program. *Financial support:* In 2007–08, 65 students received support, including 1 research assistantship (averaging $15,000 per year), 15 teaching assistantships (averaging $9,000 per year); career-related internships or fieldwork, Federal Work-Study, institutionally sponsored loans, tuition waivers (full and partial), and unspecified assistantships also available. Financial award application deadline: 2/1; financial award applicants required to submit FAFSA. *Faculty research:* Public policy, research methods, foreign policy analysis, judicial politics, environmental and energy policy. Total annual research expenditures: $8,421. *Unit head:* Dr. Joe D. Hagan, Chair, 304-293-3811 Ext. 5283, Fax: 304-293-8644, E-mail: jhagan@wvu.edu. *Application contact:* Dr. Jeff Worsham, Director, Graduate Studies, 304-293-3811 Ext. 5277, Fax: 304-293-8644, E-mail: jeff.worsham@mail.wvu.edu.

Wilfrid Laurier University, Faculty of Graduate Studies, Faculty of Arts and School of Business and Economics, Global Governance Program, Waterloo, ON N2L 3C5, Canada. Offers PhD. *Faculty:* 29 full-time. *Students:* 4 full-time. 26 applicants, 23% accepted, 4 enrolled. *Degree requirements:* For doctorate, thesis/dissertation. *Entrance requirements:* For doctorate, MA in political science, history, economics, international development studies, international peace studies, globalization studies, environmental studies or related field with minimum A-. Additional exam requirements/recommendations for international students: Required—TOEFL (minimum score 230 computer-based; 89 iBT). *Application deadline:* For fall admission, 2/1 priority date for domestic students. Application fee: $75. Electronic applications accepted. *Financial support:* Fellowships, research assistantships, teaching assistantships available. *Faculty research:* Global political economy, global environment, conflict and security, global justice and human rights, multilateral institutions and diplomacy. *Unit head:* Dr. Jorge Heine, Head, 519-884-1970. *Application contact:* Jennifer Poppe, Student Contact, 519-884-0710 Ext. 3536, Fax: 519-884-1020, E-mail: gradstudies@wlu.ca.

Wilfrid Laurier University, Faculty of Graduate Studies, Faculty of Arts and School of Business and Economics, International Public Policy Program, Waterloo, ON N2L 3C5, Canada. Offers MIPP. *Faculty:* 21 full-time. *Students:* 13 full-time. 74 applicants, 27% accepted, 15 enrolled. *Entrance requirements:* For master's, honours BA with minimum B average. Additional exam requirements/recommendations for international students: Required—TOEFL (minimum score 230 computer-based; 89 iBT). *Application deadline:* For fall admission, 2/1 priority date for domestic students. Application fee: $75. Electronic applications accepted. *Financial support:* Fellowships, research assistantships, teaching assistantships available. *Faculty research:* International environmental policy, international economic relations, human security, global governance. *Unit head:* Tracy Snodden, Director, 519-884-0710 Ext. 3215, E-mail: tsnodden@wlu.ca. *Application contact:* Jennifer Poppe, Student Contact, 519-884-0710 Ext. 3536, Fax: 519-884-1020, E-mail: gradstudies@wlu.ca.

Yale University, Graduate School of Arts and Sciences, Department of Economics, Program in International and Development Economics, New Haven, CT 06520. Offers MA. *Entrance requirements:* For master's, GRE General Test.

Yale University, Graduate School of Arts and Sciences, Graduate Program in International Relations, New Haven, CT 06520. Offers MA, JD/MA, MBA/MA, MEM/MA, MES/MA, MF/MA, MFS/MA, MPH/MA. *Faculty:* 206. *Students:* 42 full-time (21 women), 1 part-time; includes 6 minority (2 African Americans, 4 Asian Americans or Pacific Islanders), 14 international. Average age 26. 261 applicants, 21% accepted, 20 enrolled. In 2007, 20 degrees awarded. *Degree requirements:* For master's, one foreign language, research paper, summer project, specified grade average. *Entrance requirements:* For master's, GRE General Test, previous course work in microeconomics and macroeconomics, professional experience (preferred). Additional exam requirements/recommendations for international students: Required—TOEFL (minimum score 610 paper-based; 253 computer-based; 102 iBT). *Application deadline:* For fall admission, 1/2 for domestic and international students. Application fee: $85. Electronic applications accepted. *Financial support:* In 2007–08, 29 students received support, including 29 fellowships with full and partial tuition reimbursements available (averaging $10,250 per year), 33 teaching assistantships (averaging $7,000 per year); research assistantships, career-related internships or fieldwork, institutionally sponsored loans, scholarships/grants, tuition waivers (full and partial), and unspecified assistantships also available. Financial award application deadline: 1/2. *Faculty research:* International security studies, international human rights, international economic development, political economy, policy studies, religion and politics. *Unit head:* Prof. Cheryl Doss, Director of Graduate Studies, 203-432-3418, Fax: 203-432-9886, E-mail: international.relations@yale.edu. *Application contact:* Alice J. Kustenbauder, Registrar, 203-432-3418, Fax: 203-432-9886, E-mail: international.relations@yale.edu.

York University, Faculty of Graduate Studies, Glendon College, Program in Public and International Affairs, Toronto, ON M3J 1P3, Canada. Offers MA.

International Development

American University, School of International Service, Washington, DC 20016-8001. Offers comparative and regional studies (MA); cross-cultural communication (Certificate); development management (MS); environmental policy (MA); ethics, peace, and global affairs (MA); global environmental policy (MA); international communication (MA); international development (MA); international development management (Certificate); international economic policy (MA); international economic relations (Certificate); international peace and conflict resolution (MA); international politics (MA); international relations (PhD); international service (MIS); the Americas (Certificate); U.S. foreign policy (MA); JD/MA; MBA/MA. Part-time and evening/weekend programs available. *Faculty:* 73 full-time (27 women), 34 part-time/adjunct (15 women). *Students:* 528 full-time (339 women), 355 part-time (218 women); includes 137 minority (39 African Americans, 2 American Indian/Alaska Native, 45 Asian Americans or Pacific Islanders, 51 Hispanic Americans), 119 international. Average age 27. 1,840 applicants, 66% accepted, 321 enrolled. In 2007, 347 master's, 5 doctorates, 12 other advanced degrees awarded. Terminal master's awarded for partial completion of doctoral program. *Degree requirements:* For master's, one foreign language, comprehensive exam, thesis or alternative; for doctorate, one foreign language, comprehensive exam, thesis/dissertation, research practicum; for Certificate, minimum 15 credit hours related course work. *Entrance requirements:* For master's, GRE General Test, 24 credits of course work in related social sciences, minimum GPA of 3.5, 2 letters of recommendation, bachelor's Degree, resumé, statement of purpose; for doctorate, GRE General Test, 2 letters of recommendation, 24 credits in related social sciences. Additional exam requirements/recommendations for international students: Required—TOEFL (minimum score 550 paper-based; 213 computer-based). *Application deadline:* For fall admission, 1/15 priority date for domestic students; for spring admission, 10/1 priority date for domestic students. Applications are processed on a rolling basis. Application fee: $50. *Expenses:* Tuition: Full-time $19,998; part-time $1,111 per credit hour. Required fees: $380. Tuition and fees vary according to program. *Financial support:* Career-related internships or fieldwork, Federal Work-Study, and institutionally sponsored loans available. Financial award application deadline: 1/15. *Faculty research:* International intellectual property, international environmental issues, international law and legal order, international telecommunications/technology, international sustainable development. *Unit head:* Dr. Louis W. Goodman, Dean, 202-885-1600, Fax: 202-885-2494. *Application contact:* Amanda Taylor, Director of Graduate Admissions and Financial Aid, 202-885-1599, Fax: 202-885-2494.

See Close-Up on page 1139.

Andrews University, School of Graduate Studies, College of Arts and Sciences, Department of Behavioral Science, Program in International Development, Berrien Springs, MI 49104. Offers MSA. Postbaccalaureate distance learning degree programs offered. *Entrance requirements:* For master's, GRE General Test.

Athabasca University, Centre for Integrated Studies, Athabasca, AB T9S 3A3, Canada. Offers adult education (MA); community studies (MA); cultural studies (MA); educational studies (MA); global change (MA); work, organization, and leadership (MA). Part-time and evening/weekend programs available. Postbaccalaureate distance learning degree programs offered (no on-campus study). *Faculty:* 8 full-time (3 women), 16 part-time/adjunct (13 women). *Students:* Average age 36. 150 applicants, 87% accepted, 112 enrolled. In 2007, 39 degrees awarded. *Degree requirements:* For master's, project. *Entrance requirements:* For master's, 3- or 4-year BA. Additional exam requirements/recommendations for international students: Required—TOEFL (minimum score 560 paper-based; 220 computer-based). *Application deadline:* For fall admission, 3/1 for domestic and international students; for winter admission, 10/1 for domestic and international students. Application fee: $65. Electronic applications accepted. Tuition and fees charges are reported in Canadian dollars. *Expenses:* Tuition, state resident: part-time $1,795 Canadian dollars per credit. Required fees: $70 Canadian dollars per year. One-time fee: $360 Canadian dollars part-time. Part-time tuition and fees vary according to program. *Faculty research:* Women's history, literature and culture studies, sustainable development, labor and education. *Unit head:* Dr. Michael Gismondi, Program Director, 780-675-6218, Fax: 780-675-6921, E-mail: mikeg@athabascau.ca. *Application contact:* Derek Stovin, Program Administrator, 780-675-6236, Fax: 780-675-6921, E-mail: dereks@athabascau.ca.

Brandeis University, The Heller School for Social Policy and Management, Program in Sustainable International Development, Waltham, MA 02454-9110. Offers international development (MA); sustainable development (MA). *Degree requirements:* For master's, 2nd-year fieldwork or internship. *Entrance requirements:* For master's, 3 letters of recommendation; curriculum vitae or resumé. Additional exam requirements/recommendations for international students: Required—TOEFL, IELTS. Electronic applications accepted. Expenses: Contact institution. *Faculty research:* Water resource management, human rights, biosphere management, rural development, public policy and governance.

See Close-Up on page 1141.

Clark University, Graduate School, Department of International Development, Community, and Environment, Program in International Development and Social Change, Worcester, MA 01610-1477. Offers MA. *Students:* 36 full-time (23 women), 21 part-time (15 women); includes 3 minority (1 American Indian/Alaska Native, 2 Asian Americans or Pacific Islanders), 23 international. Average age 30. 147 applicants, 82% accepted, 33 enrolled. In 2007, 33 degrees awarded. *Degree requirements:* For master's, thesis. *Application deadline:* For fall admission, 1/15 for domestic students. Application fee: $55. *Expenses:* Tuition: Full-time $32,600; part-time $1,019 per credit. Required fees: $30. Tuition and fees vary according to program. *Financial support:* In 2007–08, fellowships (averaging $5,000 per year), research assistantships with full and partial tuition reimbursements (averaging $5,000 per year), teaching assistantships with full and partial tuition reimbursements (averaging $5,000 per year) were awarded; tuition waivers (full and partial) also available. *Faculty research:* Participatory rural appraisal, gender issues, sustainable resource management, community building, geographic information sciences, AIDS research. *Unit head:* Dr. William F. Fisher, Director, 508-421-3765, Fax: 508-793-8820, E-mail: wfisher@clarku.edu. *Application contact:* Paula Hall, IDCE Graduate Admissions, 508-793-7201, Fax: 508-793-8820, E-mail: idce@clarku.edu.

Cornell University, Graduate School, Graduate Fields of Arts and Sciences, Field of International Development, Ithaca, NY 14853-0001. Offers development policy (MPS); international nutrition (MPS); international planning (MPS); international population (MPS); science and technology policy (MPS). *Faculty:* 53 full-time (17 women). *Students:* 28 full-time (15 women); includes 2 minority (both African Americans), 24 international. Average age 32. 30 applicants, 60% accepted, 11 enrolled. In 2007, 5 degrees awarded. *Degree requirements:* For master's, project paper. *Entrance requirements:* For master's, GRE General Test (recommended), 2 academic recommendations, 2 years of development experience. Additional exam requirements/recommendations for international students: Required—TOEFL (minimum score 77 iBT). *Application deadline:* Applications are processed on a rolling basis. Application fee: $70. Electronic applications accepted. *Financial support:* In 2007–08, 21 students received support, including 18 fellowships with full tuition reimbursements available, 3 teaching assistantships with full tuition reimbursements available; research assistantships with full tuition reimbursements available, institutionally sponsored loans, scholarships/grants, health care benefits, tuition waivers (full and partial), and unspecified assistantships also available. Financial award applicants required to submit FAFSA. *Faculty research:* Development policy, international nutrition, international planning, science and technology policy, international population. *Unit head:* Director of Graduate Studies, 607-255-3037, Fax: 607-255-1005. *Application contact:* Graduate Field Assistant, 607-255-0831, Fax: 607-255-1005, E-mail: mpsid@cornell.edu.

Dalhousie University, Faculty of Arts and Social Science, Department of International Development Studies, Halifax, NS B3H 4R2, Canada. Offers MA. Part-time programs available. *Faculty:* 36 full-time (11 women), 4 part-time/adjunct (2 women). *Students:* 13 full-time (10 women), 1 part-time; includes 3 Asian Americans or Pacific Islanders, 2 international. 40 applicants, 15% accepted. In 2007, 2 degrees awarded. *Degree requirements:* For master's, thesis. *Entrance requirements:* For master's, honors degree in international development studies or equivalent. Additional exam requirements/recommendations for international students: Required—TOEFL. *Application deadline:* For fall admission, 2/1 priority date for domestic students. Applications are processed on a rolling basis. Application fee: $60. Electronic applications accepted. *Financial support:* In 2007–08, 2 fellowships (averaging $15,000 Canadian dollars per year), 6 teaching assistantships were awarded; career-related internships or fieldwork also available. *Faculty research:* Development theory, development methods, development practice, environment and development, gender and development. *Unit head:* Dr. David Black, Coordinator, 902-494-3814, Fax: 902-494-2105. *Application contact:* Dr. Owen Willis, Graduate Coordinator, 902-494-3814, Fax: 902-494-2105, E-mail: idsgrad@dal.ca.

Duke University, Graduate School, Terry Sanford Institute of Public Policy, Program in International Development Policy, Durham, NC 27708-0237. Offers AM, Certificate. *Faculty:* 18 full-time (5 women). *Students:* 64 full-time (25 women); includes 3 minority (all Hispanic Americans), 57 international. Average age 33. 149 applicants, 56% accepted, 39 enrolled. In 2007, 34 master's awarded. *Degree requirements:* For master's, internship, project. *Entrance requirements:* For master's, minimum 3 years of professional experience in a development-related field. Additional exam requirements/recommendations for international students: Required—TOEFL (minimum score 550 paper-based; 213 computer-based; 83 iBT), IELTS (minimum score 7). *Application deadline:* For fall admission, 12/15 priority date for domestic and international students. Applications are processed on a rolling basis. Application fee: $75. Electronic applications accepted. *Expenses: Contact institution. Financial support:* In 2007–08, teaching assistantships (averaging $16,000 per year); fellowships, research assistantships, scholarships/grants, tuition waivers (partial), and unspecified assistantships also available. Financial award application deadline: 12/15; financial award applicants required to submit FAFSA. *Unit head:* Dr. Corinne Krupp, Director of Graduate Studies, 919-613-9221, Fax: 919-684-2861, E-mail: pidinfo@duke.edu. *Application contact:* Elizabeth Dixon, Program Coordinator, 919-613-9223, Fax: 919-684-2861, E-mail: pidinfo@duke.edu.

See Close-Up on page 1145.

Fordham University, Graduate School of Arts and Sciences, Program in International Political Economy and Development, New York, NY 10458. Offers MA, Certificate. Part-time and evening/weekend programs available. *Faculty:* 23. *Students:* 36 full-time (12 women), 20 part-time (9 women); includes 7 minority (1 American Indian/Alaska Native, 4 Asian Americans or Pacific Islanders, 2 Hispanic Americans), 12 international. Average age 28. 202 applicants, 39% accepted, 26 enrolled. In 2007, 37 degrees awarded. *Degree requirements:* For master's, comprehensive exam. *Entrance requirements:* For master's, GRE General Test. Additional exam requirements/recommendations for international students: Required—TOEFL (minimum score 600 paper-based; 250 computer-based). *Application deadline:* For fall admission, 1/4 priority date for domestic students; for spring admission, 11/1 for domestic students. Application fee: $70. Electronic applications accepted. *Expenses:* Tuition: Full-time $23,880; part-time $995 per credit. *Financial support:* In 2007–08, 14 students received support, including 1 fellowship with tuition reimbursement available (averaging $21,100 per year), 13 research assistantships with tuition reimbursements available (averaging $13,769 per year); career-related internships or fieldwork, institutionally sponsored loans, tuition waivers (full and partial), and unspecified assistantships also available. Financial award application deadline: 1/4; financial award applicants required to submit FAFSA. *Faculty research:* International economics, comparative international politics, international banking and finance, international development, emerging markets and country risk analysis. *Unit head:* Dr. Henry Schwalbenberg, Chair, 718-817-3866, Fax: 718-817-3518. *Application contact:* Charlene Dundie, Director of Graduate Admissions, 718-817-4420, Fax: 718-817-3566, E-mail: dundie@fordham.edu.

See Close-Up on page 1147.

The George Washington University, Columbian College of Arts and Sciences, School of Public Policy and Public Administration, Programs in Public Policy and Public Administration, Washington, DC 20052. Offers budget and public finance (MPA); federal policy, politics, and management (MPA); international development management (MPA); managing public organizations (MPA); managing state and local governments and urban policy (MPA); nonprofit management (MPA); policy analysis and evaluation (MPA); public administration (MPA). *Accreditation:* NASPAA. Part-time programs available. *Entrance requirements:* For master's, GRE General Test. Additional exam requirements/recommendations for international students: Required—TOEFL. *Faculty research:* Regulatory reform, policy and program evaluation, ethics and public management, managing not-for-profits, policy making in the White House and Congress.

The George Washington University, Elliott School of International Affairs, Program in International Development Studies, Washington, DC 20052. Offers MA, JD/MA, MPH/MA. *Degree requirements:* For master's, one foreign language, capstone project. *Entrance requirements:* For master's, GRE General Test, 2 years (or the equivalent) of a modern foreign language, introductory course in microeconomics and 1 semester of statistics. Additional exam requirements/recommendations for international students: Required—TOEFL. Electronic applications accepted. *Faculty research:* Development, anthropology, health and development, political science, education.

Harvard University, John F. Kennedy School of Government, Master in Public Administration/International Development Program, Cambridge, MA 02138. Offers MPAID. *Students:* 60 full-time (30 women); includes 4 minority (1 African American, 2 Asian Americans or Pacific Islanders, 1 Hispanic American), 40 international. Average age 26. 351 applicants, 27% accepted, 60 enrolled. *Entrance requirements:* For master's, GMAT or GRE General Test (for joint Business School applicants only), one course each in microeconomics and macroeconomics; two college-level calculus courses (one must contain multivariable calculus); bachelor's degree; 2-3 years of professional experience in development (strongly encouraged). Additional exam requirements/recommendations for international students: Required—TOEFL (minimum score 600 paper-based; 250 computer-based; 100 iBT). *Application deadline:* For fall admission, 1/9 for domestic students. Application fee: $80. Electronic applications accepted. *Expenses:* Tuition: Full-time $31,456. Full-time tuition and fees vary according to program and student level. *Financial support:* Fellowships, research assistantships, teaching assistantships, career-related internships or fieldwork, Federal Work-Study, institutionally sponsored loans, scholarships/grants, health care benefits, and unspecified assistantships available. Financial award application deadline: 2/2; financial award applicants required to submit CSS PROFILE or FAFSA. *Unit head:* Carol Finney, Director, 617-495-7799, E-mail: carol_finney@harvard.edu. *Application contact:* 617-495-2133.

Hope International University, School of Graduate Studies, Program in Business Administration, Fullerton, CA 92831-3138. Offers business administration (MBA); educational administration (MSM); international development (MBA, MSM); management (MBA); nonprofit management (MBA). Part-time programs available. Postbaccalaureate distance learning degree programs offered (no on-campus study). *Faculty:* 4. *Students:* 15 full-time (7 women), 32 part-time (9 women); includes 16 minority (5 African Americans, 4 Asian Americans or Pacific Islanders, 7 Hispanic Americans), 11 international. Average age 34. 47 applicants, 83% accepted, 34 enrolled. In 2007, 49 degrees awarded. *Degree requirements:* For master's, comprehensive exam (for some programs), thesis (for some programs), project. *Entrance requirements:* For master's, minimum GPA of 3.0; Bachelor's degree/official transcripts; 2 references; statement of purpose. Additional exam requirements/recommendations for international students: Required—TOEFL (minimum score 550 paper-based; 213 computer-based; 86 iBT); Recommended—IELTS (minimum score 7). *Application deadline:* For fall admission, 8/3 priority date for domestic and international students; for winter admission, 12/14 priority date for domestic and international students; for spring admission, 1/4 priority date for domestic and international students. Applications are processed on a rolling basis. Application fee: $75. Electronic applications accepted. *Expenses: Contact institution. Financial support:* In 2007–08, 33 students received support. Scholarships/grants and health care benefits available. Support available to part-time students. Financial award applicants required to submit FAFSA. *Unit head:* Dr. Lind W. Coop, Chair, 714-879-3901 Ext. 2264, Fax: 714-681-7450, E-mail: lwcoop@hiu.edu. *Application contact:* Annette Mativo, Assistant Director of Admissions, 714-879-3901 Ext. 2244, Fax: 714-681-7450, E-mail: anmativo@hiu.edu.

The Johns Hopkins University, Paul H. Nitze School of Advanced International Studies, Washington, DC 20036. Offers international development (Certificate); international public policy (MIPP); international relations (MA, PhD), including African studies (MA), American foreign policy (MA), Asian studies (MA), Canadian studies (MA), conflict management (MA), European studies (MA), global theory and history (MA), international development (MA), international law, and organizations (MA), international policy (MA), international relations (general) (MA), Latin American studies (MA), Middle East studies (MA), Russian and Eurasian studies (MA), strategic studies (MA); international studies (Certificate); JD/MA; MBA/MA; MHS/MA. *Faculty:* 66 full-time (22 women), 158 part-time/adjunct (54 women). *Students:* 578 full-time (256 women), 46 part-time (16 women); includes 85 minority (18 African Americans, 1 American Indian/Alaska Native, 51 Asian Americans or Pacific Islanders, 15 Hispanic Americans), 193 international. Average age 27. In 2007, 359 master's, 13 doctorates awarded. Terminal master's awarded for partial completion of doctoral program. *Degree requirements:* For master's, one foreign language, 16 non-language courses (8 for MIPP), 2 core examinations, comprehensive oral exam, paper (for some programs); for doctorate, 2 foreign languages, thesis/dissertation, 3 comprehensive exams, defense. *Entrance requirements:* For master's, GMAT or GRE General Test, previous course work in economics, foreign language, undergraduate degree; for doctorate, GRE General Test, master's degree. Additional exam requirements/recommendations for international students: Required—TOEFL (minimum paper-based score of 600, computer-based 250, iBT 100) or IELTS (minimum 7.0). *Application deadline:* For fall admission, 1/7 for domestic students. Application fee: $80. Electronic applications accepted. *Expenses: Contact institution. Financial support:* In 2007–08, 350 students received support, including fellowships (averaging $7,500 per year); career-related internships or fieldwork, Federal Work-Study, and scholarships/grants also available. Financial award application deadline: 2/15; financial award applicants required to submit FAFSA. *Faculty research:* Regional studies and functional fields of international relations, international economics, conflict management, global theory and history, international law and organizations, international policy, strategic studies. *Unit head:* Tara Campbell, Associate Director of Admissions, 202-663-5700, Fax: 202-663-7788. *Application contact:* Dr. Belinda A. Yeomans, Director of Admissions, 202-663-5700, Fax: 202-663-7788, E-mail: admissions.sais@jhu.edu.

McGill University, Faculty of Graduate and Postdoctoral Studies, Desautels Faculty of Management, Montréal, QC H3A 2T5, Canada. Offers administration (PhD); entrepreneurial studies (MBA); finance (MBA); general management (Post Master's Certificate); information systems (MBA); international business (exchange program) (MBA); international Master's program in practicing management (MM); management (MBA); management for development (MBA); manufacturing management (MMM); marketing (MBA); operations management (MBA); public accountancy (Diploma); strategic management (MBA); MBA/LL B; MD/MBA. *Faculty:* 78 full-time (21 women), 46 part-time/adjunct (17 women). *Students:* 277 full-time (103 women), 336 part-time (100 women). 637 applicants, 33% accepted, 143 enrolled. In 2007, 223 master's, 9 doctorates, 38 other advanced degrees awarded.

The New School: A University, The New School for General Studies, Program in International Affairs, New York, NY 10011. Offers global management, trade, and finance (MA, MS); international development (MA, MS); international media and communication (MA, MS); international politics and diplomacy (MA, MS); service, civic, and non-profit management (MS). Part-time programs available. *Faculty:* 10 full-time (6 women), 26 part-time/adjunct (11 women). *Students:* 192 full-time (129 women), 122 part-time (80 women); includes 67 minority (20 African Americans, 17 Asian Americans or Pacific Islanders, 30 Hispanic Americans), 54 international. Average age 30. In 2007, 78 degrees awarded. *Entrance requirements:* Additional exam requirements/recommendations for international students: Required—TOEFL (minimum score 600 paper-based; 250 computer-based; 100 iBT). *Application deadline:* For fall admission, 4/15 for domestic students; for spring admission, 10/15 for domestic students. Application fee: $50. *Financial support:* Fellowships with partial tuition reimbursements, research assistantships, teaching assistantships with partial tuition reimbursements, career-related internships or fieldwork, Federal Work-Study, scholarships/grants, tuition waivers (partial), and unspecified assistantships available. Support available to part-time students. Financial award application deadline: 3/1; financial award applicants required to submit FAFSA. *Unit head:* Dr. Michael

International Development

The New School: A University (continued)
Cohen, Director, 212-206-3524, Fax: 212-645-0661, E-mail: cohenm2@newschool.edu. *Application contact:* David Norris, Director of Admissions, 212-229-5630, Fax: 212-989-3887, E-mail: nsadmissions@newschool.edu.

See Close-Up on page 1159.

Ohio University, Graduate College, Center for International Studies, Program in Development Studies, Athens, OH 45701-2979. Offers MA. Part-time programs available. *Students:* 37 full-time (21 women), 2 part-time; includes 2 minority (both Asian Americans or Pacific Islanders), 25 international. 116 applicants, 49% accepted, 26 enrolled. In 2007, 22 degrees awarded. *Degree requirements:* For master's, one foreign language, thesis optional. *Entrance requirements:* For master's, minimum GPA of 3.0. Additional exam requirements/recommendations for international students: Required—TOEFL (minimum score 550 paper-based; 213 computer-based). *Application deadline:* For fall admission, 1/1 for domestic and international students. Application fee: $50 ($55 for international students). *Financial support:* In 2007–08, 21 students received support, including 6 research assistantships with full tuition reimbursements available (averaging $10,000 per year); career-related internships or fieldwork, Federal Work-Study, institutionally sponsored loans, tuition waivers (full), and unspecified assistantships also available. Financial award application deadline: 1/1. *Faculty research:* Problems and issues in social, economic, political, health and environmental development. *Unit head:* Dr. Ann R. Tickamyer, Director, 740-593-1832, Fax: 740-593-1837. *Application contact:* Joan Kraynanski, Administrative Assistant, 740-593-1840, Fax: 740-593-1837, E-mail: kraynans@ohio.edu.

Rutgers, The State University of New Jersey, Camden, Graduate School of Arts and Sciences, Department of Public Policy and Administration, Camden, NJ 08102-1401. Offers education policy and leadership (MPA); international public service and development (MPA); public management (MPA); JD/MPA. *Accreditation:* NASPAA. Part-time and evening/weekend programs available. *Degree requirements:* For master's, directed study, research workshop. *Entrance requirements:* For master's, GRE General Test, GMAT or LSAT. Additional exam requirements/recommendations for international students: Required—TOEFL (minimum score 550 paper-based; 213 computer-based). Electronic applications accepted. *Faculty research:* Nonprofit management, county and municipal administration, health and human services, government communication, administrative law, educational finance.

Saint Mary's University, Faculty of Arts, International Development Studies Program, Halifax, NS B3H 3C3, Canada. Offers MA. Part-time programs available. *Degree requirements:* For master's, thesis. *Entrance requirements:* For master's, honors degree. *Faculty research:* Dynamics of global development, gender and development, policy analysis, models and strategies for development, Latin American and Caribbean development.

Texas A&M University, George Bush School of Government and Public Service, College Station, TX 77843. Offers advanced international affairs (Certificate); homeland security (Certificate); international affairs (MPIA), including international economics and development, national security affairs; nonprofit management (Certificate); public service and administration (MPSA), including public management, public policy analysis. *Accreditation:* NASPAA. *Faculty:* 39. *Students:* 155 full-time (67 women), 97 part-time (27 women); includes 37 minority (8 African Americans, 2 American Indian/Alaska Native, 4 Asian Americans or Pacific Islanders, 23 Hispanic Americans), 18 international. Average age 24. 249 applicants, 57% accepted, 88 enrolled. In 2007, 69 degrees awarded. *Degree requirements:* For master's, summer internship. *Entrance requirements:* For master's, GRE (preferred) or GMAT. *Application deadline:* For fall admission, 1/24 for domestic and international students. Application fee: $50 ($75 for international students). Electronic applications accepted. *Expenses:* Tuition, state resident: full-time $6,129. Tuition, nonresident: full-time $11,689. Tuition and fees vary according to course load. *Financial support:* In 2007–08, fellowships (averaging $11,000 per year), research assistantships (averaging $11,250 per year) were awarded; career-related internships or fieldwork, Federal Work-Study, and institutionally sponsored loans also available. Financial award application deadline: 2/1; financial award applicants required to submit FAFSA. *Faculty research:* Public policy, Presidential studies, public leadership, economic policy, social policy. *Unit head:* Richard A. Chilcoat, Dean, 979-862-8007, Fax: 979-862-7953, E-mail: bushschool@tamu.edu. *Application contact:* Kathryn Meyer, Recruitment/Placement Officer, 979-458-4767, Fax: 979-845-4155, E-mail: admissions@bushschool.tamu.edu.

See Close-Up on page 1623.

Tufts University, Fletcher School of Law and Diplomacy, Medford, MA 02155. Offers LL M, MA, MAHA, MALD, MIB, PhD, DVM/MA, JD/MALD, MALD/MA, MALD/MBA, MALD/MS, MD/MA. Postbaccalaureate distance learning degree programs offered (minimal on-campus study). *Faculty:* 34 full-time (7 women), 31 part-time/adjunct (8 women). *Students:* 443 full-time (224 women), 7 part-time (4 women); includes 51 minority (6 African Americans, 1 American Indian/Alaska Native, 26 Asian Americans or Pacific Islanders, 18 Hispanic Americans), 165 international. Average age 31. 1,636 applicants, 34% accepted, 183 enrolled. In 2007, 364 master's, 12 doctorates awarded. *Median time to degree:* Of those who began their doctoral program in fall 1999, 75% received their degree in 8 years or less. *Degree requirements:* For master's, one foreign language, thesis; for doctorate, one foreign language, comprehensive exam, thesis/dissertation, dissertation defense. *Entrance requirements:* For master's and doctorate, GMAT or GRE General Test. Additional exam requirements/recommendations for international students: Required—TOEFL (minimum score 600 paper-based; 250 computer-based; 100 iBT), IELTS (minimum score 7). *Application deadline:* For fall admission, 1/15 for domestic and international students; for spring admission, 10/15 for domestic and international students. Application fee: $70. Electronic applications accepted. *Expenses: Contact institution.* *Financial support:* Federal Work-Study, institutionally sponsored loans, scholarships/grants, and tuition waivers (partial) available. Financial award application deadline: 1/15; financial award applicants required to submit FAFSA. *Faculty research:* Negotiation and conflict resolution, international organizations, international business and economic law, security studies, development economics. *Unit head:* Stephen W. Bosworth, Dean, 617-627-3050, Fax: 617-627-3712. *Application contact:* Laurie A. Hurley, Director of Admissions and Financial Aid, 617-627-2410, Fax: 617-627-3712, E-mail: fletcheradmissions@tufts.edu.

See Close-Up on page 1169.

Tufts University, Graduate School of Arts and Sciences, Department of Urban and Environmental Policy and Planning, Medford, MA 02155. Offers community development (MA); environmental policy (MA); health and human welfare (MA); housing policy (MA); international environment/development policy (MA); public policy (MPP); public policy and citizen participation (MA); MA/MS; MALD/MA. *Accreditation:* ACSP (one or more programs are accredited). Part-time programs available. *Faculty:* 8 full-time, 9 part-time/adjunct. *Students:* 135 (93 women); includes 23 minority (9 African Americans, 5 Asian Americans or Pacific Islanders, 9 Hispanic Americans) 9 international. 174 applicants, 82% accepted, 55 enrolled. In 2007, 32 degrees awarded. *Degree requirements:* For master's, thesis, internship. *Entrance requirements:* For master's, GRE General Test. Additional exam requirements/recommendations for international students: Required—TOEFL (minimum score 550 paper-based; 213 computer-based; 80 iBT). *Application deadline:* For fall admission, 1/15 for domestic students, 12/30 for international students. Applications are processed on a rolling basis. Application fee: $70. Electronic applications accepted. *Expenses: Contact institution.* *Financial support:* Teaching assistantships with full and partial tuition reimbursements, career-related internships or fieldwork, Federal Work-Study, scholarships/grants, and tuition waivers (partial) available. Support available to part-time students. Financial award application deadline: 1/15; financial award applicants required to submit FAFSA. *Unit head:* Julian Agyeman, Chair, 617-627-3394, Fax: 617-627-3377.

See Close-Up on page 1625.

Tulane University, School of Liberal Arts, The Payson Center for International Development and Technology Transfer, New Orleans, LA 70118-5669. Offers international development (MS, PhD). Part-time programs available. *Degree requirements:* For master's, comprehensive exam (for some programs), thesis optional; for doctorate, comprehensive exam, thesis/dissertation. *Entrance requirements:* For master's, GRE General Test, minimum B average in undergraduate course work. Additional exam requirements/recommendations for international students: Required—TOEFL. Electronic applications accepted. *Faculty research:* Third World development.

University of Florida, Graduate School, College of Liberal Arts and Sciences, Department of Political Science, Gainesville, FL 32611. Offers international development policy and administration (MA, Certificate); international relations (MA, MAT); political campaigning (MA, Certificate); political science (MA, MAT, PhD); public affairs (MA, Certificate); JD/MA. Part-time programs available. *Faculty:* 32 full-time (6 women). *Students:* 123 (44 women); includes 7 minority (1 African American, 1 Asian American or Pacific Islander, 5 Hispanic Americans) 12 international. In 2007, 25 master's, 7 doctorates awarded. Terminal master's awarded for partial completion of doctoral program. *Degree requirements:* For master's, variable foreign language requirement, thesis or alternative; for doctorate, variable foreign language requirement, thesis/dissertation. *Entrance requirements:* For master's and doctorate, GRE General Test, minimum GPA of 3.0. Additional exam requirements/recommendations for international students: Required—TOEFL (minimum score 550 paper-based; 213 computer-based). *Application deadline:* For fall admission, 3/16 priority date for domestic students. Applications are processed on a rolling basis. Application fee: $30. Electronic applications accepted. *Expenses:* Tuition, state resident: full-time $7,478. Tuition, nonresident: full-time $22,603. *Financial support:* In 2007–08, 1 research assistantship (averaging $16,666 per year), 39 teaching assistantships (averaging $17,071 per year) were awarded; fellowships, career-related internships or fieldwork, Federal Work-Study, institutionally sponsored loans, and unspecified assistantships also available. Financial award application deadline: 1/15. *Faculty research:* U.S. political development, religion and politics, environmental politics and policy, developing societies, international relations. *Unit head:* Philip J. Williams, Chair, 352-392-0262 Ext. 247, Fax: 352-392-8127, E-mail: pjw@polisci.ufl.edu. *Application contact:* Dr. J. Samuel Barkin, Coordinator, 352-392-0262 Ext. 222, Fax: 352-392-8127, E-mail: barkin@polisci.ufl.edu.

University of Guelph, Graduate Program Services, Collaborative International Development Studies, Guelph, ON N1G 2W1, Canada. Offers M Eng, M Sc, MA, MBA, PhD. Part-time programs available. *Faculty:* 62 full-time (14 women). *Students:* 41 full-time (28 women); includes 12 minority (2 African Americans, 7 Asian Americans or Pacific Islanders, 3 Hispanic Americans), 11 international. In 2007, 10 master's awarded. *Degree requirements:* For master's, thesis (for some programs), seminar, economics course, sociology/anthropology course, geography course, political science course; for doctorate, comprehensive exam (for some programs), thesis/dissertation. *Entrance requirements:* For master's, honour's degree with courses in economics, social science, and empirical methods. *Application deadline:* Applications are processed on a rolling basis. Application fee: $75. *Financial support:* In 2007–08, 3 fellowships (averaging $2,000 per year), 2 teaching assistantships (averaging $4,246 per year) were awarded; research assistantships. *Faculty research:* Transformation of developing societies, regional differences, national and international processes of development, long-term change. *Application contact:* Dr. Kerry Preibisch, Graduate Coordinator, E-mail: kpreibis@uoguelph.ca.

University of Ottawa, Faculty of Graduate and Postdoctoral Studies, Program in Globalization and International Development, Ottawa, ON K1N 6N5, Canada. Offers MA. *Degree requirements:* For master's, thesis or alternative. *Entrance requirements:* For master's, honours bachelor's degree or equivalent, minimum B average.

University of Pittsburgh, Graduate School of Public and International Affairs, Division of International Development, Program in Human Security, Pittsburgh, PA 15260. Offers MID, MPA/MID, MID/JD, MID/MBA, MID/MPH, MID/MPIA, MID/MSIS, MID/MSW. *Faculty:* 34 full-time (10 women), 18 part-time/adjunct (6 women). *Students:* 12 full-time (11 women). Average age 25. 21 applicants, 90% accepted, 8 enrolled. In 2007, 29 degrees awarded. *Degree requirements:* For master's, thesis optional, internship, capstone seminar. *Entrance requirements:* For master's, GRE General Test, 3 letters of recommendation, minimum GPA of 3.2, resumé. Additional exam requirements/recommendations for international students: Required—TOEFL (minimum score 550 paper-based; 213 computer-based; 80 iBT), TWE (minimum score 4); Recommended—IELTS (minimum score 7). *Application deadline:* For fall admission, 2/1 for domestic students, 1/15 for international students; for spring admission, 11/1 for domestic students, 8/1 for international students. Application fee: $50. Electronic applications accepted. *Financial support:* In 2007–08, 25 students received support, including 25 fellowships (averaging $8,840 per year); scholarships/grants and unspecified assistantships also available. Financial award application deadline: 2/1. *Faculty research:* Human rights, threats to civilian populations, human trafficking, child soldiers, post-conflict reconstruction. Total annual research expenditures: $845,025. *Application contact:* Elizabeth Hruby, Graduate Enrollment Counselor, 412-648-7640, Fax: 412-648-7641, E-mail: eah44@pitt.edu.

University of Pittsburgh, Graduate School of Public and International Affairs, Division of International Development, Program in Nongovernmental Organizations and Civil Society, Pittsburgh, PA 15260. Offers MID, MPA/MID, MID/JD, MID/MBA, MID/MPH, MID/MPIA, MID/MSIS, MID/MSW. Part-time programs available. *Faculty:* 34 full-time (10 women), 18 part-time/adjunct (6 women). *Students:* 29 full-time (22 women), 3 part-time (2 women); includes 7 minority (3 African Americans, 2 Asian Americans or Pacific Islanders, 2 Hispanic Americans), 8 international. Average age 25. 37 applicants, 92% accepted, 12 enrolled. In 2007, 29 degrees awarded. *Degree requirements:* For master's, thesis optional, internship, capstone seminar. *Entrance requirements:* For master's, GRE General Test, 3 letters of recommendation, resumé, minimum GPA of 3.2. Additional exam requirements/recommendations for international students: Required—TOEFL (minimum score 550 paper-based; 213 computer-based; 80 iBT), TWE (minimum score 4); Recommended—IELTS (minimum score 7). *Application deadline:* For fall admission, 2/1 for domestic students, 1/5 for international students; for spring admission, 11/1 for domestic students, 8/1 for international students. Application fee: $50. Electronic applications accepted. *Financial support:* In 2007–08, 25 students received support, including 25 fellowships (averaging $8,840 per year); scholarships/grants and unspecified assistantships also available. Financial award application deadline: 2/1. *Faculty research:* Project/program evaluation, population and environment, international development, development economics, civil society. Total annual research expenditures: $845,025. *Application contact:* Elizabeth Hruby, Graduate Enrollment Counselor, 412-648-7640, Fax: 412-648-7641, E-mail: eah44@pitt.edu.

University of Pittsburgh, Graduate School of Public and International Affairs, Executive Programs in Public Policy and Management, Pittsburgh, PA 15260. Offers development planning (MPPM); international development (MPPM); international political economy (MPPM); international security studies (MPPM); management of non profit organizations (MPPM); metropolitan management and regional development (MPPM); policy analysis and evaluation (MPPM). Part-time programs available. *Faculty:* 34 full-time (10 women), 18 part-time/adjunct (6 women). *Students:* 11 full-time (3 women), 46 part-time (20 women); includes 4 minority (3 African Americans, 1 Hispanic American), 8 international. Average age 38. 48 applicants, 88% accepted, 29 enrolled. In 2007, 27 degrees awarded. *Degree requirements:* For master's, thesis optional, capstone seminar. *Entrance requirements:* For master's, 2 letters of recommendation, resumé, 5 years of supervisory or budgetary experience. Additional exam requirements/recommendations for international students: Required—TOEFL (minimum score 600 paper-based; 250 computer-based; 100 iBT), TWE (minimum score 4); Recommended—IELTS (minimum score 7). *Application deadline:* For fall admission, 6/1 priority date for domestic students, 2/15 for international students; for spring admission, 1/1 priority date for domestic students, 8/1 for international students. Applications are processed on a rolling basis. Application fee: $50. Electronic applications accepted. *Financial support:* In 2007–08, 4 students received support, including 4 fellowships (averaging $5,075 per year); institutionally sponsored loans and scholarships/grants also available. Support available to part-time students. Financial award application deadline: 2/1. *Faculty research:* Executive training and technical assistance for U.S. and international clients. Total annual research expenditures: $845,025. *Unit head:*

Michele Garrity, Director, Executive Education, 412-648-7610, Fax: 412-648-2605, E-mail: garrity@birch.gspia.pitt.edu. *Application contact:* Maureen O'Malley, Admissions Counselor, 412-648-7640, Fax: 412-648-7641, E-mail: pronobis@birch.gspia.pitt.edu.

See Close-Up on page 1645.

University of San Francisco, College of Arts and Sciences, Department of Economics, San Francisco, CA 94117-1080. Offers economics (MA); financial analysis (MS); international and development economics (MA). Part-time and evening/weekend programs available. *Faculty:* 8 full-time (1 woman), 6 part-time/adjunct (0 women). *Students:* 171 full-time (87 women), 13 part-time (3 women); includes 36 minority (2 African Americans, 27 Asian Americans or Pacific Islanders, 7 Hispanic Americans), 77 international. Average age 28. 499 applicants, 74% accepted, 108 enrolled. In 2007, 73 degrees awarded. *Degree requirements:* For master's, comprehensive exam, thesis or alternative. *Entrance requirements:* For master's, GRE General Test (recommended), BA in economics (preferred). Additional exam requirements/recommendations for international students: Required—TOEFL. *Application deadline:* For fall admission, 7/15 priority date for domestic students; for spring admission, 12/15 for domestic students. Applications are processed on a rolling basis. Application fee: $55 ($65 for international students). *Expenses:* Tuition: Part-time $1,005 per unit. Tuition and fees vary according to degree level, campus/location and program. *Financial support:* In 2007–08, 138 students received support; fellowships, teaching assistantships, career-related internships or fieldwork available. Financial award application deadline: 3/2; financial award applicants required to submit FAFSA. *Faculty research:* Economic development, forecasting and planning, labor markets, Pacific Rim, financial markets. *Unit head:* John Veitch, Chair, 415-422-6784, Fax: 415-422-5784.

University of Southern Mississippi, Graduate School, College of Arts and Letters, Department of Political Science, International Development, and International Affairs, Hattiesburg, MS 39406-0001. Offers international development (PhD); political science (MA, MS). Part-time programs available. *Faculty:* 17 full-time (3 women). *Students:* 23 full-time (8 women), 45 part-time (12 women); includes 14 minority (10 African Americans, 1 American Indian/Alaska Native, 1 Asian American or Pacific Islander, 2 Hispanic Americans), 3 international. Average age 40. 29 applicants, 66% accepted, 16 enrolled. In 2007, 8 master's, 3 doctorates awarded. *Degree requirements:* For master's, comprehensive exam, thesis (for some programs). *Entrance requirements:* For master's, GRE General Test, minimum GPA of 2.75 in last 2 years, 3.0 in field of study. *Application deadline:* For fall admission, 3/1 priority date for domestic students, 3/1 for international students. Applications are processed on a rolling basis. Application fee: $30. *Financial support:* In 2007–08, 3 research assistantships with full and partial tuition reimbursements (averaging $7,942 per year), 8 teaching assistantships (averaging $7,942 per year) were awarded; career-related internships or fieldwork, Federal Work-Study, scholarships/grants, and unspecified assistantships also available. Financial award application deadline: 3/15. *Faculty research:* American politics, international politics, political theory, comparative politics, public law. *Unit head:* Dr. Thomas Lansford, Interim Chair, 601-266-4310. *Application contact:* Dr. Robert Pauley, Graduate Coordinator, 601-266-4310, Fax: 601-266-4172.

Virginia Polytechnic Institute and State University, Graduate School, College of Architecture and Urban Studies, School of Public and International Affairs, Blacksburg, VA 24061. Offers environmental planning and policy (MURP); government and international affairs (MPIA); housing, community and economic development (MURP); international development planning (MURP); land use and physical planning (MURP); planning, governance and globalization (PhD), including environmental planning and landscape analysis, physical planning and urban design, public and international affairs, urban and environmental design and planning; urban and regional planning (MURP). *Accreditation:* ACSP. *Entrance requirements:* Additional exam requirements/recommendations for international students: Required—TOEFL (minimum score 550 paper-based; 213 computer-based). Electronic applications accepted. *Faculty research:* Design theory, environmental planning, town planning, transportation planning.

International Trade Policy

The George Washington University, Elliott School of International Affairs, Program in International Trade and Investment Policy, Washington, DC 20052. Offers MA, JD/MA, MBA/MA. Part-time and evening/weekend programs available. *Degree requirements:* For master's, one foreign language, capstone project. *Entrance requirements:* For master's, GRE General Test, 2 years of a modern foreign language and 2 semesters of introductory economics. Additional exam requirements/recommendations for international students: Required—TOEFL. Electronic applications accepted.

Monterey Institute of International Studies, Graduate School of International Policy Studies, Program in International Trade Policy, Monterey, CA 93940-2691. Offers MA. *Students:* 35 full-time (21 women), 2 part-time (1 woman); includes 7 minority (1 African American, 6 Asian Americans or Pacific Islanders), 7 international. Average age 27. 33 applicants, 97% accepted, 14 enrolled. In 2007, 14 degrees awarded. *Degree requirements:* For master's, one foreign language. *Entrance requirements:* For master's, minimum GPA of 3.0, proficiency in a foreign language. Additional exam requirements/recommendations for international students: Required—TOEFL (minimum score 550 paper-based; 213 computer-based; 80 iBT). *Application deadline:* For fall admission, 3/15 priority date for domestic students; for spring admission, 10/1 priority date for domestic students. Applications are processed on a rolling basis. Application fee: $50. Electronic applications accepted. *Expenses:* Tuition: Full-time $27,750; part-time $1,250 per credit. Required fees: $200. *Financial support:* Application deadline: 3/15. *Application contact:* 831-647-4123, Fax: 831-647-6405, E-mail: admit@miis.edu.

See Close-Up on page 1157.

Political Science

Acadia University, Faculty of Arts, Department of Political Science, Wolfville, NS B4P 2R6, Canada. Offers MA. *Faculty:* 7 full-time (2 women), 1 part-time/adjunct (0 women). *Students:* 1 (woman) full-time, 4 part-time (1 woman). Average age 26. 3 applicants, 33% accepted, 1 enrolled. *Degree requirements:* For master's, thesis. *Entrance requirements:* For master's, honors degree or equivalent. Additional exam requirements/recommendations for international students: Required—TOEFL (minimum score 580 paper-based; 237 computer-based), IELTS (minimum score 7). *Application deadline:* For fall admission, 2/1 priority date for domestic and international students. Application fee: $50. *Financial support:* In 2007–08, 1 student received support, including 1 teaching assistantship (averaging $9,000 per year). Financial award application deadline: 2/1. *Faculty research:* Atlantic Canada, international relations and organization, human rights, Canadian politics, political thought, technology. *Unit head:* Dr. Greg Pyrez, Head, 902-585-1293, Fax: 902-585-1070, E-mail: greg.pyrez@acadiau.ca. *Application contact:* Danielle Fraser, Administrative Secretary, 902-585-1506, Fax: 902-585-1070, E-mail: polisci@acadiau.ca.

American Public University System, AMU/APU Graduate Programs, Charles Town, WV 25414. Offers air warfare (MA Military Studies); American Revolution (MA Military Studies); business administration (MBA); Civil War (MA Military Studies); criminal justice (MA); defense management (MA Military Studies); emergency and disaster management (MA); environmental policy and management (MS); fire science management (MA); global engagement (MA); history (MA); homeland security (MA); humanities (MA); intelligence (MA Military Studies, MA Strategic Intelligence); international peace and conflict resolution (MA); international relations and conflict resolution (MA); joint warfare (MA Military Studies); land warfare international perspective (MA Military Studies); management (MA); military history (MA); military leadership (MA Military Studies); national security studies (MA); naval warfare international (MA Military Studies); naval warfare US (MA Military Studies); political science (MA); public administration (MA); public health (MA); security management (MA); space studies (MS); special ops/LIC (MA Military Studies); sports management (MA); transportation and logistics management (MA); transportation management (MA); unconventional warfare (MA Military Studies); World War II (MA Military Studies). Programs offered via distance learning only. Part-time and evening/weekend programs available. Postbaccalaureate distance learning degree programs offered (no on-campus study). *Faculty:* 10 full-time (3 women), 188 part-time/adjunct (57 women). *Students:* 340 full-time (98 women), 3,567 part-time (790 women); includes 615 minority (317 African Americans, 28 American Indian/Alaska Native, 85 Asian Americans or Pacific Islanders, 185 Hispanic Americans), 20 international. Average age 36. 2,123 applicants, 100% accepted, 893 enrolled. In 2007, 829 degrees awarded. *Degree requirements:* For master's, comprehensive exam. *Entrance requirements:* For master's, bachelor's degree or equivalent, minimum GPA of 2.7 in last 60 hours of course work. *Application deadline:* Applications are processed on a rolling basis. Application fee: $0. Electronic applications accepted. *Expenses:* Tuition: Part-time $275 per semester hour. *Financial support:* Applicants required to submit FAFSA. *Faculty research:* Military history, criminal justice, management performance, national security. *Unit head:* Dr. Frank McCluskey, Provost, 877-468-6268, Fax: 304-724-3780. *Application contact:* Terry Grant, Director of Enrollment Management, 877-468-6268, Fax: 304-724-3780, E-mail: info@apus.edu.

American University, School of Public Affairs, Department of Government, Washington, DC 20016-8001. Offers advanced leadership studies (Certificate); political science (MA, PhD), including American politics (MA), comparative politics (MA). Part-time and evening/weekend programs available. *Faculty:* 29 full-time (13 women), 25 part-time/adjunct (10 women). *Students:* 43 full-time (24 women), 43 part-time (18 women); includes 7 minority (2 African Americans, 1 American Indian/Alaska Native, 2 Asian Americans or Pacific Islanders, 2 Hispanic Americans), 6 international. Average age 27. 131 applicants, 50% accepted, 21 enrolled. In 2007, 28 master's, 3 doctorates, 4 other advanced degrees awarded. Terminal master's awarded for partial completion of doctoral program. *Degree requirements:* For master's, comprehensive exam; for doctorate, comprehensive exam, thesis/dissertation. *Entrance requirements:* For master's, GRE General Test, statement of purpose; 2 recommendations; for doctorate, GRE General Test, statement of purpose; 3 recommendations; for Certificate, Bachelor's Degree. *Application deadline:* For fall admission, 2/1 for domestic students; for spring admission, 11/1 for domestic students. Application fee: $50. *Expenses:* Tuition: Full-time $19,998; part-time $1,111 per credit hour. Required fees: $380. Tuition and fees vary according to program. *Financial support:* Fellowships, research assistantships, teaching assistantships, career-related internships or fieldwork and institutionally sponsored loans available. Financial award application deadline: 2/1. *Faculty research:* Political leadership, interest groups, politics of regulation, public law, political behavior. *Unit head:* Dr. Candance Nelson, Chair, 202-885-2338.

The American University in Cairo, Graduate Studies and Research, School of Humanities and Social Sciences, Department of Political Science, Cairo, Egypt. Offers MA. *Degree requirements:* For master's, thesis. *Entrance requirements:* Additional exam requirements/recommendations for international students: Required—English entrance exam and/or TOEFL. Electronic applications accepted. *Faculty research:* African and Middle East politics, international relations, development of human rights, international law.

The American University of Athens, The School of Graduate Studies, Athens, Greece. Offers biomedical sciences (MS); business (MBA); business communication (MA); computer sciences (MS); engineering and applied sciences (MS); politics and policy making (MA); systems engineering (MS); telecommunications (MS). *Faculty:* 15 full-time (2 women), 13 part-time/adjunct (4 women). *Students:* 20 full-time (2 women), 8 part-time, 10 international. *Entrance requirements:* For master's, University Degree/Resum&e, 2 recommendation letters/TOEFL score 550. Additional exam requirements/recommendations for international students: Required—TOEFL (minimum score 550 paper-based; 213 computer-based). Application fee: 100 euros. *Expenses:* Tuition: Part-time $400 per credit. Required fees: $400 per credit. Tuition and fees vary according to program. *Faculty research:* Nanotechnology, environmental sciences, rock mechanics, human skin studies, Monte Carlo algorithms and software. *Unit head:* Dr. Rita Roussos, Director of the School of Graduate Studies, 302-725-9301-3, Fax: 302-10-7259304, E-mail: rroussos@aua.edu.

American University of Beirut, Graduate Programs, Faculty of Arts and Sciences, Beirut, Lebanon. Offers anthropology (MA); Arabic language and literature (MA); archaeology (MA); biology (MS); chemistry (MS); computer science (MS); economics (MA); education (MA); English language (MA); English literature (MA); environmental policy planning (MSES); financial economics (MAFE); geology (MS); history (MA); mathematics (MA, MS); Middle Eastern studies (MA); philosophy (MA); physics (MS); political studies (MA); psychology (MA); public administration (MA); sociology (MA); statistics (MA, MS). Part-time programs available. *Faculty:* 108 full-time (29 women), 5 part-time/adjunct (3 women). *Students:* 134 full-time (92 women), 228 part-time (167 women). Average age 25. 319 applicants, 67% accepted, 91 enrolled. In 2007, 144 degrees awarded. *Degree requirements:* For master's, one foreign language, comprehensive exam, thesis (for some programs). *Entrance requirements:* For master's, GRE, letter of recommendation. Additional exam requirements/recommendations for international students: Required—TOEFL (minimum score 600 paper-based; 250 computer-based; 100 iBT), IELTS (minimum score 8). *Application deadline:* For fall admission, 4/30 for domestic and international students; for spring admission, 11/1 for domestic and international

Political Science

American University of Beirut (continued)
students. Application fee: $50. *Expenses:* Tuition: Full-time $9,954; part-time $553 per credit. Tuition and fees vary according to course load and program. *Financial support:* In 2007–08, 28 students received support. Career-related internships or fieldwork, institutionally sponsored loans, scholarships/grants, health care benefits, and unspecified assistantships available. Financial award application deadline: 2/4; financial award applicants required to submit FAFSA. *Faculty research:* String theory and supergravity; computer graphics; algebra and number theory; popular Arabic literature; marine and freshwater biology; integrating science, math and technology. Total annual research expenditures: $132,270. *Unit head:* Khalil Bitar, Dean, 961-1374374 Ext. 3800, Fax: 961-1744461, E-mail: kmb@aub.edu.lb. *Application contact:* Dr. Salim Kanaan, Director, Admissions Office, 961-1350000 Ext. 2594, Fax: 961-1750775, E-mail: sk00@aub.edu.lb.

Appalachian State University, Cratis D. Williams Graduate School, Department of Government and Justice Studies, Boone, NC 28608. Offers criminal justice (MS); political science (MA); public administration (MPA). Part-time programs available. *Faculty:* 26 full-time (5 women). *Students:* 51 full-time (20 women), 71 part-time (30 women); includes 11 minority (8 African Americans, 1 American Indian/Alaska Native, 2 Asian Americans or Pacific Islanders), 4 international. 77 applicants, 77% accepted, 47 enrolled. In 2007, 45 degrees awarded. *Degree requirements:* For master's, variable foreign language requirement, comprehensive exam, thesis optional. *Entrance requirements:* For master's, GRE General Test. Additional exam requirements/recommendations for international students: Required—TOEFL (minimum score 570 paper-based; 230 computer-based; 79 iBT), IELTS (minimum score 7), TOEFL or IELTS. *Application deadline:* For fall admission, 7/1 for domestic students, 1/1 for international students; for spring admission, 11/1 for domestic students, 6/1 for international students. Applications are processed on a rolling basis. Application fee: $50. Electronic applications accepted. *Expenses:* Tuition, state resident: part-time $127 per semester hour. Tuition, nonresident: part-time $597 per semester hour. Required fees: $18 per semester. *Financial support:* In 2007–08, 35 research assistantships (averaging $7,000 per year) were awarded; fellowships, teaching assistantships, career-related internships or fieldwork, Federal Work-Study, scholarships/grants, and unspecified assistantships also available. Financial award application deadline: 4/1. *Faculty research:* Campaign finance, emerging democracies, bureaucratic politics, judicial behavior, administration of justice. Total annual research expenditures: $43,054. *Unit head:* Dr. Brian Ellison, Chairperson, 828-262-3085, E-mail: ellisonba@appstate.edu.

Arizona State University, Graduate College, College of Liberal Arts and Sciences, Division of Social Sciences, Department of Political Science, Tempe, AZ 85287. Offers MA, PhD. *Degree requirements:* For master's, thesis or alternative; for doctorate, thesis/dissertation. *Entrance requirements:* For master's and doctorate, GRE.

Arkansas State University, Graduate School, College of Humanities and Social Sciences, Department of Political Science, Jonesboro, State University, AR 72467. Offers political science (MA); political science education (SCCT); public administration (MPA). *Accreditation:* NASPAA (one or more programs are accredited). Part-time programs available. *Faculty:* 8 full-time (3 women), 1 (woman) part-time/adjunct. *Students:* 25 full-time (11 women), 21 part-time (14 women); includes 9 minority (all African Americans), 3 international. Average age 30. 22 applicants, 91% accepted, 17 enrolled. In 2007, 15 degrees awarded. *Degree requirements:* For master's, comprehensive exam, thesis or alternative; for SCCT, comprehensive exam. *Entrance requirements:* For master's, GRE General Test or MAT, GMAT, appropriate bachelor's degree, letters of reference, official transcript; for SCCT, GRE General Test or MAT, GMAT, interview, master's degree, official transcript. Additional exam requirements/recommendations for international students: Required—TOEFL (minimum score 213 computer-based). *Application deadline:* Applications are processed on a rolling basis. Application fee: $30 ($40 for international students). Electronic applications accepted. *Expenses:* Tuition, state resident: full-time $3,528; part-time $196 per hour. Tuition, nonresident: full-time $8,928; part-time $496 per hour. Required fees: $842; $44 per hour. $25 per term. Tuition and fees vary according to course load and program. *Financial support:* Teaching assistantships, career-related internships or fieldwork, scholarships/grants, and unspecified assistantships available. Financial award application deadline: 7/1; financial award applicants required to submit FAFSA. *Faculty research:* Peace Corps, political communication, political psychology, public opinion, elections. *Unit head:* Dr. Richard Wang, Chair, 870-972-3048, Fax: 870-972-2720, E-mail: rwang@astate.edu.

Ashland University, College of Arts and Sciences, Program in American History and Government, Ashland, OH 44805-3702. Offers MAHG. Part-time programs available. *Faculty:* 4 full-time (0 women), 12 part-time/adjunct (0 women). *Students:* 38 full-time (17 women), 38 part-time (16 women); includes 3 minority (2 Asian Americans or Pacific Islanders, 1 Hispanic American). Average age 38. *Degree requirements:* For master's, thesis optional. *Entrance requirements:* For master's, minimum GPA of 3.0. *Application deadline:* Applications are processed on a rolling basis. Application fee: $30. Electronic applications accepted. *Expenses:* Contact institution. *Financial support:* In 2007–08, 25 students received support. Application deadline: 4/15. *Faculty research:* American founding, civil war, progressives. *Unit head:* Dr. Peter W. Schramm, Executive Director, Ashbrook Center, 419-289-5414, Fax: 419-289-5425, E-mail: pschramm@ashland.edu. *Application contact:* Roger L. Beckett, Deputy Director, Ashbrook Center, 419-289-5413, Fax: 419-289-5425, E-mail: rbeckett@ashland.edu.

Auburn University, Graduate School, College of Liberal Arts, Department of Political Science, Auburn University, AL 36849. Offers public administration (MPA, PhD); MPA/MCP. Part-time programs available. *Faculty:* 20 full-time (7 women). *Students:* 24 full-time (9 women), 36 part-time (22 women); includes 18 minority (16 African Americans, 2 Hispanic Americans), 2 international. Average age 35. 69 applicants, 54% accepted, 18 enrolled. In 2007, 19 master's, 5 doctorates awarded. *Degree requirements:* For doctorate, thesis/dissertation. *Entrance requirements:* For master's, GRE General Test, minimum GPA of 3.0 in political science, 2.5 overall; for doctorate, GRE General Test. *Application deadline:* For fall admission, 7/7 for domestic students; for spring admission, 11/24 for domestic students. Applications are processed on a rolling basis. Application fee: $25 ($50 for international students). Electronic applications accepted. *Financial support:* Fellowships, research assistantships, teaching assistantships, career-related internships or fieldwork and Federal Work-Study available. Support available to part-time students. Financial award application deadline: 3/15. *Faculty research:* Policy evaluation, political economy, privatization, participation, election administration. Total annual research expenditures: $200,000. *Unit head:* Dr. Gerard Gryski, Chair, 334-844-5370. *Application contact:* Dr. Joe Pittman, Interim Dean of the Graduate School, 334-844-4700.

Auburn University Montgomery, School of Sciences, Department of Public Administration and Political Science, Montgomery, AL 36124-4023. Offers MPA, MPS, PhD. *Accreditation:* NASPAA (one or more programs are accredited). Part-time and evening/weekend programs available. *Faculty:* 4 full-time (0 women), 4 part-time/adjunct (1 woman). *Students:* 20 full-time (8 women), 90 part-time (54 women); includes 42 minority (37 African Americans, 2 Asian Americans or Pacific Islanders, 3 Hispanic Americans). Average age 34. In 2007, 16 degrees awarded. *Degree requirements:* For master's, comprehensive exam; for doctorate, thesis/dissertation. *Entrance requirements:* For master's, GRE General Test or MAT; for doctorate, GRE General Test. *Application deadline:* Applications are processed on a rolling basis. Application fee: $25. Electronic applications accepted. *Expenses:* Tuition, state resident: full-time $4,536; part-time $189 per credit hour. Tuition, nonresident: full-time $13,608; part-time $567 per credit hour. Required fees: $234. *Financial support:* In 2007–08, 1 research assistantship was awarded; career-related internships or fieldwork and scholarships/grants also available. Support available to part-time students. Financial award application deadline: 3/1; financial award applicants required to submit FAFSA. *Unit head:* Dr. Thomas Vocino, Head, 334-244-3696, Fax: 334-244-3826, E-mail: vocino@mail.aum.edu.

Augusta State University, Graduate Studies, College of Arts and Sciences, Department of Political Science, Augusta, GA 30904-2200. Offers MPA. Part-time and evening/weekend programs available. *Faculty:* 4 full-time (1 woman), 4 part-time/adjunct (2 women). *Students:* 10 full-time (3 women), 22 part-time (18 women); includes 10 African Americans, 3 Hispanic Americans. Average age 31. 10 applicants, 100% accepted, 10 enrolled. In 2007, 10 degrees awarded. *Degree requirements:* For master's, comprehensive exam, thesis. *Entrance requirements:* For master's, GRE General Test. *Application deadline:* For fall admission, 7/16 priority date for domestic students. Applications are processed on a rolling basis. Application fee: $20. Electronic applications accepted. *Expenses:* Tuition, state resident: full-time $3,192; part-time $133 per hour. Tuition, nonresident: full-time $12,792; part-time $533 per hour. Required fees: $536; $268 per semester. *Financial support:* In 2007–08, 1 student received support. Federal Work-Study and institutionally sponsored loans available. Financial award application deadline: 4/15; financial award applicants required to submit FAFSA. *Faculty research:* Political behavior, administrative law, political participation, human resources administration. *Unit head:* Dr. Sudha Ratan, Chair, 706-737-1710, E-mail: sratan@aug.edu. *Application contact:* Dr. Saundra J. Reinke, MPA Director, 706-667-4424, Fax: 706-667-4083, E-mail: sreinke@aug.edu.

Ball State University, Graduate School, College of Sciences and Humanities, Department of Political Science, Program in Political Science, Muncie, IN 47306-1099. Offers MA. *Faculty:* 16. *Students:* 6 full-time (1 woman), 14 part-time (5 women); includes 2 minority (1 African American, 1 Hispanic American), 4 international. Average age 25. 11 applicants, 100% accepted, 9 enrolled. In 2007, 8 degrees awarded. Application fee: $25 ($35 for international students). *Expenses:* Tuition, state resident: full-time $6,864. Tuition, nonresident: full-time $17,932. Required fees: $1,866. *Financial support:* Teaching assistantships with full tuition reimbursements, career-related internships or fieldwork available. Financial award application deadline: 3/1. *Faculty research:* Survey research, public policy. *Unit head:* Dr. Roger Hollands, Director, 765-285-8800, Fax: 765-285-5345.

Baylor University, Graduate School, College of Arts and Sciences, Department of Political Science, Waco, TX 76798. Offers international studies (MA); political science (MA, PhD); public policy and administration (MPPA); JD/MPPA. *Students:* 24 full-time (8 women), 3 part-time (2 women); includes 1 minority (Hispanic American), 3 international. In 2007, 11 degrees awarded. *Entrance requirements:* For master's, GRE General Test. *Application deadline:* Applications are processed on a rolling basis. Application fee: $25. *Financial support:* Research assistantships, career-related internships or fieldwork, Federal Work-Study, and institutionally sponsored loans available. Financial award application deadline: 3/1. *Unit head:* Dr. Dwight Allman, Graduate Program Director, 254-710-3161, Fax: 254-710-3122, E-mail: dwight_allman@baylor.edu. *Application contact:* Suzanne Keener, Administrative Assistant, 254-710-3588, Fax: 254-710-3870.

Baylor University, Graduate School, College of Arts and Sciences, J. M. Dawson Institute of Church-State Studies, Waco, TX 76798. Offers MA, PhD. *Students:* 36 full-time (10 women), 1 (woman) part-time; includes 4 minority (2 Asian Americans or Pacific Islanders, 2 Hispanic Americans), 5 international. In 2007, 3 master's, 2 doctorates awarded. *Degree requirements:* For master's, thesis, oral exam; for doctorate, one foreign language, thesis/dissertation, preliminary exams. *Entrance requirements:* For master's, GRE General Test; for doctorate, GRE General Test, MA or equivalent. *Application deadline:* For fall admission, 3/1 for domestic students. Applications are processed on a rolling basis. Application fee: $25. *Financial support:* Fellowships, research assistantships, teaching assistantships, Federal Work-Study and institutionally sponsored loans available. Financial award application deadline: 3/1. *Faculty research:* Religion and politics, religion and public education, religious freedom and international politics, First Amendment jurisprudence. *Unit head:* Dr. Derek H. Davis, Director, 254-710-1510, Fax: 254-710-1571, E-mail: derek_davis@baylor.edu. *Application contact:* Suzanne Keener, Administrative Assistant, 254-710-3588, Fax: 254-710-3870.

Boston College, Graduate School of Arts and Sciences, Department of Political Science, Chestnut Hill, MA 02467-3800. Offers MA, PhD. *Students:* 53 full-time (16 women), 6 part-time (2 women); includes 2 minority (1 Asian American or Pacific Islander, 1 Hispanic American), 13 international. 193 applicants, 38% accepted, 17 enrolled. In 2007, 13 master's, 2 doctorates awarded. Terminal master's awarded for partial completion of doctoral program. *Degree requirements:* For master's, thesis or alternative; for doctorate, one foreign language, thesis/dissertation. *Entrance requirements:* For master's and doctorate, GRE General Test. Additional exam requirements/recommendations for international students: Required—TOEFL (minimum score 590 paper-based; 250 computer-based; 91 iBT). *Application deadline:* For fall admission, 1/15 for domestic students. Application fee: $70. Electronic applications accepted. *Financial support:* Fellowships with full tuition reimbursements, research assistantships with full tuition reimbursements, teaching assistantships with full tuition reimbursements, Federal Work-Study and scholarships/grants available. Support available to part-time students. Financial award application deadline: 3/1; financial award applicants required to submit FAFSA. *Faculty research:* Political theory, American politics, international politics. *Unit head:* Dr. Susan Shell, Chairperson, 617-552-4161, E-mail: susan.shell@bc.edu. *Application contact:* Dr. Christopher Kelly, Graduate Program Director, 617-552-1565, E-mail: christopher.kelly@bc.edu.

Boston University, Graduate School of Arts and Sciences, Department of Political Science, Boston, MA 02215. Offers MA, PhD. *Students:* 44 full-time (16 women), 8 part-time (5 women); includes 2 minority (1 African American, 1 Asian American or Pacific Islander), 27 international. Average age 32. 164 applicants, 25% accepted, 12 enrolled. In 2007, 3 master's, 6 doctorates awarded. Terminal master's awarded for partial completion of doctoral program. *Degree requirements:* For master's, one foreign language; for doctorate, 2 foreign languages, comprehensive exam, thesis/dissertation. *Entrance requirements:* For master's and doctorate, GRE General Test, 3 letters of recommendation. Additional exam requirements/recommendations for international students: Required—TOEFL (minimum score 600 paper-based; 250 computer-based). *Application deadline:* For fall admission, 3/1 for domestic and international students. Application fee: $70. *Expenses:* Tuition: Full-time $34,930; part-time $1,092 per credit. Tuition and fees vary according to class time, course level and program. *Financial support:* In 2007–08, 17 students received support, including 1 fellowship with full tuition reimbursement available (averaging $18,000 per year), 11 teaching assistantships with full tuition reimbursements available (averaging $16,500 per year); career-related internships or fieldwork, Federal Work-Study, and stipends also available. Support available to part-time students. Financial award application deadline: 1/15; financial award applicants required to submit FAFSA. *Unit head:* Walter Connor, Chairman, 617-353-7003, Fax: 617-353-5508, E-mail: wdconnor@bu.edu. *Application contact:* Linda Simons, Graduate Program Coordinator, 617-353-2541, Fax: 617-353-5508, E-mail: pograd@bu.edu.

Bowling Green State University, Graduate College, College of Arts and Sciences, Department of Political Science, Program in Political Science, Bowling Green, OH 43403. Offers MA/MA. *Students:* 1 (woman) full-time. Average age 25. 3 applicants, 33% accepted, 0 enrolled. *Entrance requirements:* Additional exam requirements/recommendations for international students: Required—TOEFL. *Application deadline:* For fall admission, 3/1 priority date for domestic students. Application fee: $30. Electronic applications accepted. *Financial support:* Research assistantships with full tuition reimbursements, teaching assistantships with full tuition reimbursements, Federal Work-Study and unspecified assistantships available. Financial award applicants required to submit FAFSA.

Brandeis University, Graduate School of Arts and Sciences, Department of Politics, Waltham, MA 02454-9110. Offers MA, PhD. *Faculty:* 18 full-time (4 women). *Students:* 28 full-time (17 women), 8 international. 59 applicants, 10% accepted, 4 enrolled.Terminal master's awarded for partial completion of doctoral program. *Degree requirements:* For master's, thesis; for doctorate, one foreign language, comprehensive exam, thesis/dissertation. *Entrance requirements:* For master's and doctorate, GRE General Test, sample of written work, resumé, 3 letters of recommendation. Additional exam requirements/recommendations for international students: Required—TOEFL (minimum score 600 paper-based; 250 computer-based; 100 iBT), IELTS (minimum score 7). *Application deadline:* For fall admission, 1/15 for domestic and international students. Application fee: $55. Electronic applications accepted. *Financial support:* In 2007–08, 15 students received support, including 11 fellowships with full and partial tuition reimbursements available (averaging $16,500 per year), 4 teaching assistantships (averaging $3,000 per year); scholarships/grants, health care benefits, tuition waivers (full and partial), and unspecified assistantships also available. Financial award application deadline: 2/1; financial award applicants required to submit CSS PROFILE or FAFSA. *Faculty research:* American institutions, international law and foreign policy, political theory, comparative politics, European politics. *Unit head:* Dr. Robert Art, Graduate Director, 781-736-2754, Fax: 781-736-2777, E-mail: art@brandeis.edu. *Application contact:* Claire Cincotta, Information Contact, 781-736-2750, Fax: 781-736-2777, E-mail: cincott@brandeis.edu.

Brigham Young University, Graduate Studies, College of Family, Home, and Social Sciences, Department of Political Science—Public Policy, Provo, UT 84602-1001. Offers MPP, JD/MPP. Part-time programs available. *Faculty:* 6 full-time (0 women), 2 part-time/adjunct (1 woman). *Students:* 10 full-time (6 women); includes 1 minority (Asian American or Pacific Islander), 1 international. Average age 28. 10 applicants, 70% accepted, 4 enrolled. In 2007, 7 degrees awarded. *Degree requirements:* For master's, Internship. *Entrance requirements:* For master's, GRE, Prerequisites: Econ 110 Math, Stat 221. Additional exam requirements/recommendations for international students: Required—TOEFL. *Application deadline:* For fall admission, 3/1 priority date for domestic and international students. Application fee: $50. Electronic applications accepted. *Financial support:* In 2007–08, 10 students received support, including 5 fellowships (averaging $5,000 per year), 5 research assistantships (averaging $5,000 per year). *Unit head:* Sven E. Wilson, Graduate Director, 801-422-9018, Fax: 801-422-0224, E-mail: sven_wilson@byu.edu. *Application contact:* Jessica A. McArthur, Department Secretary, 801-422-7146, Fax: 801-422-0224, E-mail: publicpolicy@byu.edu.

Brock University, Faculty of Graduate Studies, Faculty of Social Sciences, Program in Political Science, St. Catharines, ON L2S 3A1, Canada. Offers Canadian politics (MA); international and comparative politics (MA); political philosophy (MA); public administration (MA). Part-time programs available. *Degree requirements:* For master's, thesis optional. *Entrance requirements:* For master's, honors degree. Additional exam requirements/recommendations for international students: Required—TOEFL (minimum score 550 paper-based; 213 computer-based; 80 iBT), IELTS (minimum score 7), TWE (minimum score 4). Electronic applications accepted. *Faculty research:* Public administration reform, economic and social justice, politics of societies, Canadian politics, international relations.

Brooklyn College of the City University of New York, Division of Graduate Studies, Department of Political Science, Brooklyn, NY 11210-2889. Offers international affairs (MA); political science (MA, PhD); political science, urban policy and administration (MA). The department offers courses at Brooklyn College that are creditable toward the CUNY doctoral degree (with permission of the executive officer of the doctoral program). Part-time and evening/weekend programs available. *Students:* 6 full-time (3 women), 106 part-time (64 women); includes 65 minority (50 African Americans, 5 Asian Americans or Pacific Islanders, 10 Hispanic Americans), 13 international. 56 applicants, 89% accepted, 30 enrolled. In 2007, 43 degrees awarded. *Degree requirements:* For master's, comprehensive exam (for some programs), thesis or alternative, foreign language exam for international affairs program. *Entrance requirements:* For master's, 2 letters of recommendation, personal statement. *Application deadline:* For fall admission, 3/1 priority date for domestic students, 2/1 priority date for international students; for spring admission, 11/1 priority date for domestic students, 10/1 priority date for international students. Applications are processed on a rolling basis. Application fee: $125. Electronic applications accepted. *Financial support:* Career-related internships or fieldwork and Federal Work-Study available. Support available to part-time students. Financial award application deadline: 5/1; financial award applicants required to submit FAFSA. *Faculty research:* Ethics and politics, politics of criminal justice, Western Europe, international law and politics, labor politics. *Unit head:* Dr. Sally Bermanzohn, Chairperson, 718-951-5306, E-mail: sallyb@brooklyn.cuny.edu. *Application contact:* Hernan Sierra, Graduate Admissions Coordinator, 718-951-4536, Fax: 718-951-4506, E-mail: grads@brooklyn.cuny.edu.

Brown University, Graduate School, Department of Political Science, Providence, RI 02912. Offers AM, PhD. *Degree requirements:* For master's, thesis, oral exam; for doctorate, thesis/dissertation. *Entrance requirements:* For master's and doctorate, GRE General Test.

California Institute of Technology, Division of the Humanities and Social Sciences, Social Science Program, Pasadena, CA 91125-0001. Offers economics (PhD); political science (PhD); social science (MS). *Faculty:* 29 full-time (3 women). *Students:* 37 full-time (10 women); includes 9 minority (7 Asian Americans or Pacific Islanders, 2 Hispanic Americans), 14 international. Average age 26. 186 applicants, 10% accepted, 11 enrolled. In 2007, 5 master's, 7 doctorates awarded. Terminal master's awarded for partial completion of doctoral program. *Degree requirements:* For doctorate, thesis/dissertation. *Entrance requirements:* For doctorate, GRE General Test. *Application deadline:* For fall admission, 1/1 for domestic students. Application fee: $80. Electronic applications accepted. *Financial support:* In 2007–08, 34 students received support, including 12 fellowships (averaging $25,000 per year), 16 research assistantships (averaging $25,000 per year), 10 teaching assistantships (averaging $25,000 per year); Federal Work-Study, institutionally sponsored loans, scholarships/grants, and unspecified assistantships also available. *Faculty research:* Individual and group decision making, design of political and economic institutions, experimental social science, public policy, quantitative history. *Application contact:* Laurel Auchampaugh, Graduate Secretary, 626-395-4206, Fax: 626-405-9841, E-mail: gradsec@hss.caltech.edu.

California Polytechnic State University, San Luis Obispo, College of Liberal Arts, Department of Political Science, San Luis Obispo, CA 93407. Offers MPP. Part-time programs available. *Faculty:* 2 full-time (both women), 1 part-time/adjunct (0 women). *Students:* 16 full-time (9 women), 20 part-time (12 women); includes 9 minority (2 African Americans, 1 American Indian/Alaska Native, 2 Asian Americans or Pacific Islanders, 4 Hispanic Americans). 29 applicants, 69% accepted, 17 enrolled. In 2007, 12 degrees awarded. *Degree requirements:* For master's, thesis or alternative. *Entrance requirements:* For master's, minimum GPA of 2.75 in last 90 quarter units of course work, three letters of recommendation. Additional exam requirements/recommendations for international students: Required—TOEFL (minimum score 550 paper-based; 213 computer-based), TWE (minimum score 4.5). *Application deadline:* For fall admission, 5/1 for domestic students, 11/30 for international students; for winter admission, 6/30 for international students. Application fee: $55. *Expenses:* Tuition, nonresident: part-time $226 per unit. Required fees: $1,777 per quarter. *Financial support:* Career-related internships or fieldwork, Federal Work-Study, and scholarships/grants available. Support available to part-time students. Financial award application deadline: 3/2; financial award applicants required to submit FAFSA. *Unit head:* Dr. Elizabeth Lowham, Graduate Coordinator, 805-756-2919, Fax: 805-756-7168, E-mail: elowham@calpoly.edu.

California State University, Chico, Graduate School, College of Behavioral and Social Sciences, Department of Political Science, Program in Political Science, Chico, CA 95929-0455. Offers MA. Part-time programs available. *Students:* 11 full-time (4 women), 9 part-time (2 women); includes 3 minority (1 American Indian/Alaska Native, 1 Asian American or Pacific Islander, 1 Hispanic American), 1 international. Average age 35. 22 applicants, 68% accepted, 9 enrolled. In 2007, 6 degrees awarded. *Entrance requirements:* For master's, 2 letters of recommendation, statement of purpose. Additional exam requirements/recommendations for international students: Required—TOEFL (minimum score 550 paper-based; 213 computer-based; 80 iBT), IELTS (minimum score 7). *Application deadline:* For fall admission, 3/1 priority date for domestic students, 3/1 for international students; for spring admission, 9/15 priority date for domestic students, 9/15 for international students. Applications are processed on a rolling basis. Application fee: $55. Electronic applications accepted. *Financial support:* Career-related internships or fieldwork available. *Unit head:* Dr. Charles Turner, Graduate Coordinator, 530-898-5960.

California State University, Fullerton, Graduate Studies, College of Humanities and Social Sciences, Division of Politics, Administration, and Justice, Fullerton, CA 92834-9480. Offers political science (MA); public administration (MPA). *Accreditation:* NASPAA (one or more programs are accredited). Part-time programs available. *Students:* 61 full-time (35 women), 158 part-time (79 women); includes 112 minority (10 African Americans, 38 Asian Americans or Pacific Islanders, 64 Hispanic Americans), 7 international. Average age 30. 179 applicants, 78% accepted, 91 enrolled. In 2007, 30 degrees awarded. *Degree requirements:* For master's, comprehensive exam, project or thesis. *Entrance requirements:* For master's, minimum GPA of 2.5 in last 60 units of course work, 12 units of course work in social sciences. Application fee: $55. *Financial support:* Teaching assistantships, career-related internships or fieldwork, Federal Work-Study, institutionally sponsored loans, and scholarships/grants available. Support available to part-time students. Financial award application deadline: 3/1. *Faculty research:* Emergency management plans. *Unit head:* Dr. Phil Gianos, Chair, 714-278-3521.

California State University, Long Beach, Graduate Studies, College of Liberal Arts, Department of Political Science, Long Beach, CA 90840. Offers MA. Part-time programs available. *Faculty:* 15 full-time (4 women), 15 part-time/adjunct (5 women). *Students:* 13 full-time (2 women), 26 part-time (12 women); includes 1 African American, 2 Asian Americans or Pacific Islanders, 11 Hispanic Americans. Average age 33. *Degree requirements:* For master's, one foreign language, comprehensive exam or thesis. *Entrance requirements:* For master's, GRE General Test, minimum GPA of 3.0 in field. *Application deadline:* For fall admission, 7/1 for domestic students; for spring admission, 12/1 for domestic students. Applications are processed on a rolling basis. Application fee: $55. Electronic applications accepted. *Financial support:* In 2007–08, 6 students received support; teaching assistantships, Federal Work-Study, institutionally sponsored loans, and scholarships/grants available. Financial award application deadline: 3/2. *Faculty research:* Social welfare policy, international political economy, Marxism, voting behavior. *Unit head:* Dr. Charles Noble, Chair, 562-985-4704, Fax: 562-985-4979, E-mail: cnoble@csulb.edu. *Application contact:* Dr. Ron J Schmidt, Graduate Advisor, 562-985-4717, Fax: 562-985-4979, E-mail: rschmidt@csulb.edu.

California State University, Los Angeles, Graduate Studies, College of Natural and Social Sciences, Department of Political Science, Major in Political Science, Los Angeles, CA 90032-8530. Offers MA. *Students:* 6 full-time (4 women), 27 part-time (12 women); includes 13 minority (2 African Americans, 3 Asian Americans or Pacific Islanders, 8 Hispanic Americans), 9 international. Average age 29. In 2007, 8 degrees awarded. *Degree requirements:* For master's, comprehensive exam or thesis. *Entrance requirements:* For master's, minimum GPA of 3.0 in last 90 units. Additional exam requirements/recommendations for international students: Required—TOEFL. *Application deadline:* For fall admission, 6/30 for domestic students; for spring admission, 2/1 for domestic students. Applications are processed on a rolling basis. Application fee: $55. *Financial support:* Application deadline: 3/1. *Faculty research:* American government and politics, public policy, legal systems, international politics and economic relations. *Unit head:* Dr. Naomi Caiden, Acting Chair, Department of Political Science, 323-343-2230, Fax: 323-343-6452, E-mail: ncaiden@calstatela.edu.

California State University, Northridge, Graduate Studies, College of Social and Behavioral Sciences, Department of Political Science, Northridge, CA 91330. Offers MA. *Faculty:* 17 full-time (8 women), 7 part-time/adjunct (2 women). *Students:* 12 full-time (9 women), 25 part-time (12 women); includes 8 minority (3 Asian Americans or Pacific Islanders, 5 Hispanic Americans), 1 international. Average age 33. 274 applicants, 81% accepted, 17 enrolled. In 2007, 124 degrees awarded. *Degree requirements:* For master's, comprehensive exam. *Entrance requirements:* For master's, GRE if cumulative undergraduate GPA below 3.0, 2 letters of recommendation. Additional exam requirements/recommendations for international students: Required—TOEFL. *Application deadline:* For fall admission, 11/30 for domestic students. Application fee: $55. *Financial support:* Application deadline: 3/1. *Unit head:* Dr. Matthew Cahn, Chair, 818-677-3566.

California State University, Sacramento, Graduate Studies, College of Social Sciences and Interdisciplinary Studies, Department of Government, Sacramento, CA 95819-6048. Offers MA. Part-time programs available. *Students:* 11 full-time (2 women), 21 part-time (7 women); includes 7 minority (3 African Americans, 1 American Indian/Alaska Native, 3 Hispanic Americans), 1 international. Average age 32. 22 applicants, 50% accepted, 9 enrolled. *Degree requirements:* For master's, thesis or alternative, writing proficiency exam. *Entrance requirements:* For master's, GRE General Test, minimum GPA of 3.0 during previous 2 years. Additional exam requirements/recommendations for international students: Required—TOEFL. *Application deadline:* Applications are processed on a rolling basis. Application fee: $55. Electronic applications accepted. *Expenses:* Tuition, state resident: full-time $3,414. Tuition, nonresident: full-time $13,584; part-time $339 per unit. Required fees: $786; $393 per semester. *Financial support:* Career-related internships or fieldwork and Federal Work-Study available. Support available to part-time students. Financial award application deadline: 3/1. *Unit head:* Bahman Fozouni, Chair, 916-278-6202, Fax: 916-278-6488.

Carleton University, Faculty of Graduate Studies, Faculty of Public Affairs and Management, Department of Political Science, Ottawa, ON K1S 5B6, Canada. Offers MA, PhD. *Degree requirements:* For master's, one foreign language, comprehensive exam, thesis optional; for doctorate, one foreign language, comprehensive exam, thesis/dissertation. *Entrance requirements:* For master's, honors degree in political science, minimum B average; for doctorate, master's degree in political science. Additional exam requirements/recommendations for international students: Required—TOEFL. *Application deadline:* Applications are processed on a rolling basis. Application fee: $77. *Financial support:* Fellowships, research assistantships, teaching assistantships, institutionally sponsored loans, scholarships/grants, and unspecified assistantships available. *Faculty research:* Canadian politics, comparative politics, international relations, public administration and policy analysis, political theory. *Unit head:* Laura MacDonald, Chair, 613-520-2600 Ext. 2777, Fax: 613-520-4064, E-mail: political_science@carleton.ca. *Application contact:* Fiona Robinson, Supervisor of Graduate Studies, 613-520-2600 Ext. 6614, Fax: 613-520-4064, E-mail: political_science@carleton.ca.

Carleton University, Faculty of Graduate Studies, Faculty of Public Affairs and Management, Institute of Political Economy, Ottawa, ON K1S 5B6, Canada. Offers MA, PhD. *Degree requirements:* For master's, thesis optional. *Entrance requirements:* For master's, honors degree. Additional exam requirements/recommendations for international students: Required—TOEFL. *Application deadline:* Applications are processed on a rolling basis. Application fee: $77 Canadian dollars. *Financial support:* Fellowships, research assistantships, teaching assistantships, institutionally sponsored loans, scholarships/grants, and unspecified assistantships available. *Faculty research:* Relationships between economy and politics as they affect the political, social and cultural life of societies; historical processes whereby social change is located in the interaction of the economic, political and cultural, and ideological moments of social life. *Unit head:* Rianne Mahon, Director, 613-520-2600 Ext. 7414, Fax: 613-260-2154. *Application contact:* Donna Coghill, Institute Administrator, 613-520-2600 Ext. 7414, Fax: 613-520-2154, E-mail: donna_coghill@carleton.ca.

Case Western Reserve University, School of Graduate Studies, Department of Political Science, Cleveland, OH 44106. Offers MA, PhD. Part-time programs available. *Faculty:* 9 full-time (3 women), 3 part-time/adjunct (1 woman). *Students:* 3 full-time (2 women), 2 part-time (1 woman). 11 applicants, 55% accepted, 3 enrolled. In 2007, 1 master's awarded. Terminal master's awarded for partial completion of doctoral program. *Degree requirements:* For doctorate, thesis/dissertation. *Entrance requirements:* For master's, GRE General Test, 18 hours in political science; for doctorate, GRE General Test, GRE Subject Test (political science), master's degree in political science. Additional exam requirements/recommendations for international students: Required—TOEFL. *Application deadline:* For fall admission, 5/1 for domestic students; for spring admission, 11/1 for domestic students. Applications are processed on a rolling basis. Application fee: $50. Electronic applications accepted. *Financial support:* Federal Work-Study available. *Faculty research:* American cultural politics and policy, Western and Eastern European governments, African politics in international affairs, American legislative and presidential politics, women and politics, Southern politics. *Unit head:* Joseph White, Chairman, 216-368-2426, Fax: 216-368-4681, E-mail: joseph.white@case.edu. *Application*

Political Science

Case Western Reserve University (continued)

contact: Sharon Skowronski, Department Assistant, 216-368-2424, Fax: 216-368-4681, E-mail: sxs22@po.cwru.edu.

The Catholic University of America, School of Arts and Sciences, Department of Politics, Washington, DC 20064. Offers American government (MA, PhD); congressional studies (MA); international affairs (MA); international political economics (MA); political theory (MA, PhD); world politics (MA, PhD); JD/MA. Part-time programs available. *Faculty:* 13 full-time (2 women), 9 part-time/adjunct (1 woman). *Students:* 27 full-time (10 women), 85 part-time (30 women); includes 16 minority (3 African Americans, 7 Asian Americans or Pacific Islanders, 6 Hispanic Americans), 13 international. Average age 31. 110 applicants, 70% accepted, 25 enrolled. In 2007, 27 master's, 6 doctorates awarded. *Degree requirements:* For master's, one foreign language, comprehensive exam, thesis or alternative; for doctorate, 2 foreign languages, comprehensive exam, thesis/dissertation. *Entrance requirements:* For master's and doctorate, GRE General Test, 3 letters of recommendation, minimum GPA of 3.0. Additional exam requirements/recommendations for international students: Required—TOEFL (minimum score 580 paper-based; 237 computer-based). *Application deadline:* For fall admission, 2/1 priority date for domestic students; for spring admission, 11/15 priority date for domestic students. Applications are processed on a rolling basis. Application fee: $55. Electronic applications accepted. *Financial support:* Teaching assistantships, career-related internships or fieldwork, Federal Work-Study, scholarships/grants, tuition waivers (full and partial), and unspecified assistantships available. Support available to part-time students. Financial award application deadline: 2/1; financial award applicants required to submit FAFSA. *Faculty research:* Political philosophy, American political institutions and processes, political economy, national security. *Unit head:* Dr. Stephen Schneck, Chair, 202-319-5128, Fax: 202-319-6289, E-mail: schneck@cua.edu.

Central European University, Graduate Studies, School of Social Sciences and Humanities, Budapest, Hungary. Offers economics (MA, PhD); gender studies (MA, PhD); international relations and European studies (MA, PhD); mathematics and its applications (MS, PhD); medieval studies (MA, PhD); nationalism studies (MA, PhD); philosophy (MA, PhD); political science (MA, PhD); public policy (MA, PhD); sociology and social anthropology (MA, PhD). *Faculty:* 75 full-time (25 women), 46 part-time/adjunct (10 women). *Students:* 625 full-time (355 women). Average age 26. 2,500 applicants, 31% accepted, 540 enrolled. In 2007, 325 master's, 20 doctorates awarded. Terminal master's awarded for partial completion of doctoral program. *Degree requirements:* For master's, one foreign language, thesis; for doctorate, one foreign language, comprehensive exam, thesis/dissertation. *Entrance requirements:* For master's, CEU subject tests, interview; for doctorate, GRE, CEU subject test, interview. Additional exam requirements/recommendations for international students: Required—TOEFL (minimum score 570 paper-based; 230 computer-based). *Application deadline:* For fall admission, 1/15 priority date for domestic and international students. Application fee: $0. Electronic applications accepted. Tuition charges are reported in euros. *Expenses:* Tuition: Full-time 10,000 euros; part-time 315 euros per credit. *Financial support:* In 2007–08, 402 students received support, including 350 fellowships with full and partial tuition reimbursements available (averaging $5,000 per year); career-related internships or fieldwork, institutionally sponsored loans, and scholarships/grants also available. Financial award application deadline: 1/5. *Faculty research:* Civil society, fiscal decentralization, party politics, political philosophy (especially Liberalism, theory of Democracy). Total annual research expenditures: $35,000. *Unit head:* Dr. Howard Michael Robinson, Provost, 361-327-3003, Fax: 361-327-3211, E-mail: robinson@ceu.hu. *Application contact:* Zsuzsanna Jaszberenyi, Admissions Officer, 361-327-3009, Fax: 361-327-3211, E-mail: admissions@ceu.hu.

See Close-Up on page 447.

Central Michigan University, College of Graduate Studies, College of Humanities and Social and Behavioral Sciences, Department of Political Science, Program in Political Science, Mount Pleasant, MI 48859. Offers MA. *Degree requirements:* For master's, thesis or alternative. *Entrance requirements:* For master's, GRE.

Claremont Graduate University, Graduate Programs, School of Politics and Economics, Department of Politics and Policy, Claremont, CA 91711-6160. Offers American politics (MA, PhD); comparative politics (PhD); international political economy (MA); international studies (MA); political philosophy (PhD); political science (PhD); politics, economics and business (MA); public policy (MA, PhD); world politics (PhD); MBA/PhD. Part-time programs available. *Faculty:* 7 full-time (3 women), 9 part-time/adjunct (1 woman). *Students:* 181 full-time (69 women), 19 part-time (8 women); includes 35 minority (8 African Americans, 10 Asian Americans or Pacific Islanders, 17 Hispanic Americans), 45 international. Average age 34. In 2007, 27 master's, 19 doctorates awarded. Terminal master's awarded for partial completion of doctoral program. *Degree requirements:* For master's, thesis; for doctorate, one foreign language, thesis/dissertation. *Entrance requirements:* For master's and doctorate, GRE General Test. *Application deadline:* For fall admission, 2/15 priority date for domestic students. Applications are processed on a rolling basis. Electronic applications accepted. *Expenses:* Tuition: Full-time $31,640; part-time $1,376 per unit. Required fees: $145 per semester. Tuition and fees vary according to course load, degree level and program. *Financial support:* Fellowships, research assistantships, teaching assistantships, career-related internships or fieldwork, Federal Work-Study, and institutionally sponsored loans available. Support available to part-time students. Financial award application deadline: 2/15; financial award applicants required to submit FAFSA. *Faculty research:* Environmental policy, international debt, global democratization, Third World development, public sector discrimination. *Unit head:* Jean Schroedel, Chair, 909-621-8696, Fax: 909-621-8545, E-mail: jean.schroedel@cgu.edu.

Clark Atlanta University, School of Arts and Sciences, Department of Political Science, Atlanta, GA 30314. Offers MA, PhD. Part-time programs available. *Faculty:* 5 full-time (0 women), 2 part-time/adjunct (1 woman). *Students:* 11 full-time (5 women), 46 part-time (21 women); includes 52 minority (all African Americans) Average age 37. 15 applicants, 100% accepted, 4 enrolled. In 2007, 2 master's, 3 doctorates awarded. Terminal master's awarded for partial completion of doctoral program. *Degree requirements:* For master's, one foreign language, thesis; for doctorate, 2 foreign languages, thesis/dissertation. *Entrance requirements:* For master's, GRE General Test, minimum GPA of 2.5; for doctorate, GRE General Test, minimum graduate GPA of 3.0. Additional exam requirements/recommendations for international students: Required—TOEFL (minimum score 500 paper-based; 173 computer-based). *Application deadline:* For fall admission, 4/1 for domestic and international students; for spring admission, 11/1 for domestic and international students. Applications are processed on a rolling basis. Application fee: $40 ($55 for international students). *Expenses:* Tuition: Full-time $11,664; part-time $648 per credit hour. Required fees: $550; $275 per semester. *Financial support:* In 2007–08, 8 fellowships, 5 teaching assistantships were awarded; career-related internships or fieldwork, Federal Work-Study, scholarships/grants, and unspecified assistantships also available. Support available to part-time students. Financial award application deadline: 4/30; financial award applicants required to submit FAFSA. *Faculty research:* Public policy and education, rural politics, women and state economic programs, reconstruction after war in Africa, environmental policies. *Unit head:* Dr. Abi Awomolo, Chairperson, 404-880-8721, Fax: 404-880-8717, E-mail: aawomolo@cau.edu. *Application contact:* Michelle Clark-Davis, Graduate Program Admissions, 404-880-8709, E-mail: mdowis@cau.edu.

The College of Saint Rose, Graduate Studies, School of Arts and Humanities, Program in History/Political Science, Albany, NY 12203-1419. Offers MA. Part-time and evening/weekend programs available. *Faculty:* 13 full-time (7 women), 15 part-time/adjunct (6 women). *Students:* 8 full-time (3 women), 14 part-time (5 women); includes 1 minority (Asian American or Pacific Islander) Average age 34. 12 applicants, 83% accepted, 10 enrolled. *Degree requirements:* For master's, final paper/project, thesis or comprehensive exam. *Entrance requirements:* For master's, minimum undergraduate GPA of 3.0, 12 undergraduate credits in US history and/or political science. Additional exam requirements/recommendations for international students: Required—TOEFL (minimum score 550 paper-based; 213 computer-based). *Application deadline:* For fall admission, 7/15 priority date for domestic and international students; for spring admission, 11/15 priority date for domestic and international students. Applications are processed on a rolling basis. Application fee: $35. Electronic applications accepted. *Financial support:* Career-related internships or fieldwork, scholarships/grants, tuition waivers (partial), and unspecified assistantships available. Support available to part-time students. Financial award application deadline: 3/1; financial award applicants required to submit FAFSA. *Unit head:* Dr. Angela Ledford, Graduate Coordinator, 518-458-5326, Fax: 518-454-2862, E-mail: ledforda@strose.edu. *Application contact:* Susan Patterson, Assistant Vice President for Graduate Admission, 518-454-5136, Fax: 518-458-5479, E-mail: ace@strose.edu.

Colorado State University, Graduate School, College of Liberal Arts, Department of Political Science, Fort Collins, CO 80523-0015. Offers MA, PhD. Part-time programs available. *Faculty:* 17 full-time (6 women). *Students:* 23 full-time (12 women), 25 part-time (10 women); includes 3 minority (1 African American, 2 Hispanic Americans), 1 international. Average age 30. 46 applicants, 65% accepted, 17 enrolled. In 2007, 5 master's, 3 doctorates awarded. *Median time to degree:* Of those who began their doctoral program in fall 1999, 25% received their degree in 8 years or less. *Degree requirements:* For master's, thesis optional; for doctorate, comprehensive exam, thesis/dissertation. *Entrance requirements:* For master's, GRE General Test, minimum GPA of 3.0, BA/BS; for doctorate, GRE General Test, minimum GPA of 3.5, 15-page writing sample, MA/MS or at least 24 credits in a master's program. Additional exam requirements/recommendations for international students: Required—TOEFL (minimum score 600 paper-based; 250 computer-based). *Application deadline:* For fall admission, 2/15 for domestic and international students; for spring admission, 10/15 for domestic and international students. Applications are processed on a rolling basis. Application fee: $50. Electronic applications accepted. *Expenses:* Tuition, state resident: full-time $4,887; part-time $272 per credit. Tuition, nonresident: full-time $16,425; part-time $913 per credit. Required fees: $1,379; $75 per credit. *Financial support:* In 2007–08, 26 teaching assistantships with full tuition reimbursements (averaging $11,740 per year) were awarded; fellowships, research assistantships, career-related internships or fieldwork, Federal Work-Study, institutionally sponsored loans, scholarships/grants, traineeships, and unspecified assistantships also available. Financial award application deadline: 3/1; financial award applicants required to submit FAFSA. *Faculty research:* Environmental politics and policy, international relations, politics of developing nations, state and local politics and administration, political behavior. Total annual research expenditures: $1,857. *Unit head:* Dr. Robert Duffy, Chair, 970-491-5157, Fax: 970-491-2490, E-mail: robert.duffy@colostate.edu. *Application contact:* Dr. Sandra K. Davis, Coordinator, 970-491-5281, Fax: 970-491-2490, E-mail: sandra.davis@colostate.edu.

Columbia University, Graduate School of Arts and Sciences, Division of Social Sciences, Department of Political Science, New York, NY 10027. Offers M Phil, MA, PhD, JD/MA, JD/PhD. *Faculty:* 44 full-time, 10 part-time/adjunct. *Students:* 190 full-time (78 women), 23 part-time (9 women). Average age 32. 555 applicants, 25% accepted. In 2007, 32 master's, 29 doctorates awarded. *Degree requirements:* For master's, one foreign language; for doctorate, 2 foreign languages, thesis/dissertation. *Entrance requirements:* For master's and doctorate, GRE General Test. Additional exam requirements/recommendations for international students: Required—TOEFL. Application fee: $90. *Expenses:* Tuition: Part-time $1,452 per credit. Required fees: $152 per term. One-time fee: $75 part-time. Full-time tuition and fees vary according to course level, course load, degree level and program. *Financial support:* Fellowships, teaching assistantships, Federal Work-Study and institutionally sponsored loans available. Support available to part-time students. Financial award application deadline: 1/5; financial award applicants required to submit FAFSA. *Faculty research:* Comparative politics, American government, international relations. *Unit head:* John Huber, Chair, 212-854-7208, Fax: 212-222-0598, E-mail: jdh39@columbia.edu.

Concordia University, School of Graduate Studies, Faculty of Arts and Science, Department of Political Science, Montréal, QC H3G 1M8, Canada. Offers political science (PhD); public policy and public administration (MA), including geography. *Degree requirements:* For master's, one foreign language, comprehensive exam, thesis optional, internship. *Entrance requirements:* For master's, honors degree or equivalent. Additional exam requirements/recommendations for international students: Required—TOEFL. *Faculty research:* International public policy and administration, Quebec public administration, public policy and social/political theory, geography and public policy, public administration and decision making.

Converse College, School of Education and Graduate Studies, Program in Liberal Arts, Spartanburg, SC 29302-0006. Offers English (MLA); history (MLA); political science (MLA). *Degree requirements:* For master's, capstone paper. *Entrance requirements:* For master's, minimum GPA of 3.0, 2 recommendations.

Cornell University, Graduate School, Graduate Fields of Arts and Sciences, Field of Government, Ithaca, NY 14853-0001. Offers American politics (PhD); comparative politics (PhD); international relations (PhD); political methodology (PhD); political thought (PhD); public policy (PhD). *Faculty:* 39 full-time (13 women). *Students:* 71 full-time (37 women); includes 12 minority (2 African Americans, 1 American Indian/Alaska Native, 6 Asian Americans or Pacific Islanders, 3 Hispanic Americans), 33 international. Average age 30. 305 applicants, 8% accepted, 11 enrolled. In 2007, 9 doctorates awarded. *Degree requirements:* For doctorate, comprehensive exam, thesis/dissertation. *Entrance requirements:* For doctorate, GRE General Test, sample of written work, 3 letters of recommendation. Additional exam requirements/recommendations for international students: Required—TOEFL (minimum score 550 paper-based; 213 computer-based; 77 iBT). *Application deadline:* For fall admission, 1/15 for domestic students. Application fee: $70. Electronic applications accepted. *Financial support:* In 2007–08, 56 students received support, including 29 fellowships with full tuition reimbursements available, 1 research assistantship with full tuition reimbursement available, 26 teaching assistantships with full tuition reimbursements available; institutionally sponsored loans, scholarships/grants, health care benefits, tuition waivers (full and partial), and unspecified assistantships also available. Financial award applicants required to submit FAFSA. *Faculty research:* Political theory, American politics, comparative politics, international relations, methodology. *Unit head:* Director of Graduate Studies, 607-255-3567, Fax: 607-255-4530. *Application contact:* Graduate Field Assistant, 607-255-3567, Fax: 607-255-4530, E-mail: cu_govt@cornell.edu.

Dalhousie University, Faculty of Arts and Social Science, Department of Political Science, Halifax, NS B3H 4R2, Canada. Offers MA, PhD. Part-time programs available. *Faculty:* 13 full-time (3 women), 5 part-time/adjunct (1 woman). *Students:* 29 full-time (17 women), 5 part-time (2 women). In 2007, 16 master's, 6 doctorates awarded. *Degree requirements:* For master's, thesis; for doctorate, one foreign language, comprehensive exam, thesis/dissertation. *Entrance requirements:* For master's, minimum GPA of 3.3; for doctorate, minimum GPA of 3.7. Additional exam requirements/recommendations for international students: Required—TOEFL. *Application deadline:* For fall admission, 6/1 for domestic students. Applications are processed on a rolling basis. Application fee: $60. *Financial support:* In 2007–08, 14 fellowships (averaging $8,000 per year), 4 research assistantships (averaging $2,500 per year), 12 teaching assistantships (averaging $2,565 per year) were awarded; institutionally sponsored loans, scholarships/grants, and unspecified assistantships also available. Financial award application deadline: 3/31. *Faculty research:* Canadian political behavior and institutions, international politics, foreign policy, African politics, liberalism and modern political theory. *Unit head:* Dr. Robert Finbow, Graduate Coordinator, 902-494-3825, Fax: 902-494-3825, E-mail: pscience@dal.ca. *Application contact:* Dr. Louise Carbert, Graduate Coordinator, 902-494-2396, Fax: 902-494-3825, E-mail: pscience@dal.ca.

Duke University, Graduate School, Department of Political Science, Durham, NC 27708. Offers AM, PhD, JD/AM, JD/PhD. *Faculty:* 40 full-time. *Students:* 92 full-time (32 women); includes 14 minority (5 African Americans, 5 Asian Americans or Pacific Islanders, 4 Hispanic Americans), 29 international. 307 applicants, 18% accepted, 25 enrolled. In 2007, 8 master's, 9 doctorates awarded. Terminal master's awarded for partial completion of doctoral program. *Degree requirements:* For doctorate, 2 foreign languages, thesis/dissertation. *Entrance requirements:* For master's and doctorate, GRE General Test. Additional exam requirements/

recommendations for international students: Required—TOEFL (minimum score 550 paper-based; 213 computer-based; 83 iBT), IELTS (minimum score 7). *Application deadline:* For fall admission, 12/15 priority date for domestic and international students. Application fee: $75. Electronic applications accepted. *Financial support:* Fellowships, research assistantships, teaching assistantships, Federal Work-Study available. Financial award application deadline: 12/31. *Unit head:* Emerson Niou, Director of Graduate Studies, 919-660-4327, Fax: 919-660-4330, E-mail: knigh021@duke.edu.

East Carolina University, Graduate School, Thomas Harriot College of Arts and Sciences, Department of Political Science, Greenville, NC 27858-4353. Offers public administration (MPA). *Accreditation:* NASPAA. Part-time and evening/weekend programs available. *Faculty:* 21 full-time (7 women). *Students:* 23 full-time (16 women), 28 part-time (11 women); includes 9 minority (7 African Americans, 2 Asian Americans or Pacific Islanders), 3 international. Average age 28. 49 applicants, 53% accepted. In 2007, 22 degrees awarded. *Degree requirements:* For master's, one foreign language, comprehensive exam. *Entrance requirements:* For master's, GRE General Test. Additional exam requirements/recommendations for international students: Required—TOEFL. *Application deadline:* For fall admission, 6/1 priority date for domestic students; for spring admission, 10/15 for domestic students. Applications are processed on a rolling basis. Application fee: $50. *Financial support:* Research assistantships with partial tuition reimbursements, teaching assistantships with partial tuition reimbursements, Federal Work-Study available. Support available to part-time students. Financial award application deadline: 6/1. *Unit head:* Dr. Robert J. Thompson, Interim Chair, 252-328-5686, Fax: 252-328-4134, E-mail: thompsonr@ecu.edu. *Application contact:* Dean of Graduate School, 252-328-6012, Fax: 252-328-6071, E-mail: gradschool@ecu.edu.

Eastern Illinois University, Graduate School, College of Sciences, Department of Political Science, Charleston, IL 61920-3099. Offers MA. *Faculty:* 11 full-time (2 women). In 2007, 11 degrees awarded. *Application deadline:* For fall admission, 7/31 priority date for domestic students. Applications are processed on a rolling basis. Application fee: $30. *Expenses:* Tuition, state resident: part-time $218 per hour. Tuition, nonresident: part-time $654 per hour. *Financial support:* In 2007–08, research assistantships with tuition reimbursements (averaging $7,200 per year), 4 teaching assistantships with tuition reimbursements (averaging $7,200 per year) were awarded. *Unit head:* Dr. Richard Wandling, Chairperson, 217-581-2523, E-mail: rawandling@eiu.edu. *Application contact:* Dr. Ryan Hendrickson, Coordinator, 217-581-6224, E-mail: rchendrickson@eiu.edu.

Eastern Kentucky University, The Graduate School, College of Arts and Sciences, Department of Government, Program in Political Science, Richmond, KY 40475-3102. Offers MA. *Students:* 2 full-time (1 woman), 4 part-time (2 women). Average age 26. 9 applicants, 56% accepted, 3 enrolled. *Entrance requirements:* For master's, GRE General Test, minimum GPA of 2.5. Application fee: $30. *Unit head:* Dr. Sara Zeigler, Chair, Department of Government, 859-622-5931.

Eastern Michigan University, Graduate School, College of Arts and Sciences, Department of Political Science, Program in Political Science, Ypsilanti, MI 48197. Offers MPA. *Faculty:* 15 full-time (3 women). *Students:* Average age 27. *Expenses:* Tuition, state resident: full-time $8,952; part-time $373 per credit hour. Tuition, nonresident: full-time $17,634; part-time $735 per credit hour. Required fees: $896; $34 per credit hour. Tuition and fees vary according to course level, degree level and program. *Unit head:* Dr. Joseph Ohren, Director, 734-487-2522, Fax: 734-487-3440, E-mail: joseph.ohren@emich.edu. *Application contact:* Dr. Dogan Koyluoglu, Program Coordinator, 734-487-0063, E-mail: sukru.koyuoglu@emich.edu.

East Stroudsburg University of Pennsylvania, Graduate School, College of Arts and Sciences, Department of Political Science, East Stroudsburg, PA 18301-2999. Offers M Ed, MA. Part-time and evening/weekend programs available. *Faculty:* 9 full-time (4 women), 2 part-time/adjunct (1 woman). *Students:* 33 full-time (17 women), 17 part-time (9 women); includes 13 minority (4 African Americans, 9 Hispanic Americans), 4 international. Average age 30. In 2007, 7 degrees awarded. *Degree requirements:* For master's, variable foreign language requirement, comprehensive exam, thesis or alternative. *Entrance requirements:* Additional exam requirements/recommendations for international students: Required—TOEFL (minimum score 560 paper-based; 220 computer-based; 83 iBT). *Application deadline:* For fall admission, 7/31 priority date for domestic students, 5/1 priority date for international students; for spring admission, 11/30 for domestic students, 10/1 for international students. Applications are processed on a rolling basis. Application fee: $50. *Expenses:* Tuition, state resident: full-time $6,214; part-time $345 per credit. Tuition, nonresident: full-time $9,944; part-time $552 per credit. Required fees: $1,441; $120 per credit. *Financial support:* In 2007–08, 16 research assistantships with full and partial tuition reimbursements (averaging $1,947 per year) were awarded; Federal Work-Study and institutionally sponsored loans also available. Financial award application deadline: 3/1; financial award applicants required to submit FAFSA. *Unit head:* Dr. Patricia Crotty, Graduate Coordinator, 570-422-3271, Fax: 570-422-3506, E-mail: pcrotty@po-box.esu.edu. *Application contact:* Dr. Henry Gardner, Associate Provost for Enrollment Management, 570-422-2870, Fax: 570-422-2843, E-mail: hgardner@po-box.esu.edu.

Emory University, Graduate School of Arts and Sciences, Department of Political Science, Atlanta, GA 30322-1100. Offers PhD. *Degree requirements:* For doctorate, comprehensive exam, thesis/dissertation. *Entrance requirements:* For doctorate, GRE General Test, minimum GPA of 3.0. Additional exam requirements/recommendations for international students: Required—TOEFL. Electronic applications accepted. *Faculty research:* Post-Soviet politics, comparative politics, international politics, judicial politics and methodology, American national political institutions.

Fairleigh Dickinson University, Metropolitan Campus, University College: Arts, Sciences, and Professional Studies, School of History, Political and International Studies, Program in Political Science, Teaneck, NJ 07666-1914. Offers MA. *Students:* 1 full-time (0 women), 2 part-time (1 woman). Average age 35. 6 applicants, 33% accepted, 0 enrolled. In 2007, 1 degree awarded. *Application deadline:* Applications are processed on a rolling basis. Application fee: $40. *Expenses:* Tuition: Part-time $869 per credit. Tuition and fees vary according to degree level, campus/location and program.

Fayetteville State University, Graduate School, Department of Geography, History and Political Science, Fayetteville, NC 28301-4298. Offers history (MA); political science (MA). Part-time and evening/weekend programs available. *Faculty:* 6 full-time (1 woman). *Students:* 6 full-time (3 women), 9 part-time (4 women); includes 10 minority (all African Americans) Average age 40. 2 applicants, 100% accepted, 2 enrolled. In 2007, 11 degrees awarded. *Degree requirements:* For master's, comprehensive exam, internship. *Entrance requirements:* For master's, GRE General Test. *Application deadline:* For fall admission, 7/1 for domestic students; for spring admission, 12/1 for domestic students. Applications are processed on a rolling basis. Application fee: $25. Electronic applications accepted. *Expenses:* Tuition, state resident: full-time $2,118; part-time $265 per credit hour. Tuition, nonresident: full-time $11,708; part-time $1,464 per credit hour. Required fees: $1,218; $152 per credit hour. *Unit head:* Dr. Adeguke Ademiluyi, Chairperson, 910-672-1137, E-mail: aademiluyi@uncfsu.edu.

Florida Agricultural and Mechanical University, Division of Graduate Studies, Research, and Continuing Education, College of Arts and Sciences, Division of History and Political Sciences, Program in Applied Social Science, Tallahassee, FL 32307-3200. Offers African American history (MASS); criminal justice (MASS); economics (MASS); history (MASS); political science (MASS); public administration (MASS); public management (MASS); social work (MASS); sociology (MASS). Part-time programs available. *Degree requirements:* For master's, thesis optional. *Entrance requirements:* For master's, GRE General Test, minimum GPA of 3.0. *Faculty research:* Southern history, black history, election trends, presidential history.

Florida Atlantic University, Dorothy F. Schmidt College of Arts and Letters, Department of Political Science, Boca Raton, FL 33431-0991. Offers MA, MAT. Part-time programs available. *Degree requirements:* For master's, one foreign language, thesis or alternative. *Entrance requirements:* For master's, GRE General Test, minimum GPA of 3.0 during last 60 hours of course work. Electronic applications accepted. *Faculty research:* Public policy, comparative policy affecting women, Congress, international system, urban policy.

Florida International University, College of Arts and Sciences, Department of Political Science, Miami, FL 33199. Offers MS, PhD. Part-time and evening/weekend programs available. *Faculty:* 15 full-time (6 women), 1 part-time/adjunct (0 women). *Students:* 22 full-time (9 women), 14 part-time (8 women); includes 19 minority (2 African Americans, 17 Hispanic Americans), 9 international. Average age 33. 24 applicants, 33% accepted, 3 enrolled. In 2007, 3 master's, 2 doctorates awarded. *Degree requirements:* For master's, one foreign language, thesis, research project; for doctorate, one foreign language, thesis/dissertation. *Entrance requirements:* For master's, GRE General Test, minimum GPA of 3.2, 2 letters of recommendation; for doctorate, GRE General Test, minimum GPA of 3.2 (undergraduate), 3.25 (graduate), 2 letters of recommendation. Additional exam requirements/recommendations for international students: Required—TOEFL (minimum score 550 paper-based; 213 computer-based). *Application deadline:* For fall admission, 3/15 for domestic and international students. Application fee: $30. Electronic applications accepted. *Expenses:* Tuition, state resident: full-time $6,106. Tuition, nonresident: full-time $15,528. Required fees: $284. *Financial support:* Teaching assistantships, scholarships/grants available. *Unit head:* Dr. Richard Olson, Chairperson, 305-348-2226, Fax: 305-348-3765, E-mail: richard.olson@fiu.edu.

Florida State University, Graduate Studies, College of Social Sciences, Department of Political Science, Tallahassee, FL 32306. Offers MA, MS, PhD. Part-time programs available. *Faculty:* 27 full-time (6 women). *Students:* 65 full-time (23 women), 28 part-time (7 women); includes 11 minority (4 African Americans, 3 Asian Americans or Pacific Islanders, 4 Hispanic Americans), 9 international. Average age 25. 116 applicants, 57% accepted, 46 enrolled. In 2007, 27 master's, 6 doctorates awarded. Terminal master's awarded for partial completion of doctoral program. *Median time to degree:* Of those who began their doctoral program in fall 1999, 100% received their degree in 8 years or less. *Degree requirements:* For master's, thesis optional; for doctorate, comprehensive exam, thesis/dissertation. *Entrance requirements:* For master's, GRE General Test, minimum undergraduate GPA of 3.0; for doctorate, GRE General Test, minimum graduate GPA of 3.5 and/or minimum undergraduate GPA of 3.0. Additional exam requirements/recommendations for international students: Required—TOEFL (minimum score 600 paper-based). *Application deadline:* For fall admission, 1/15 priority date for domestic and international students. Applications are processed on a rolling basis. Application fee: $30. Electronic applications accepted. *Expenses:* Tuition, state resident: part-time $248 per credit hour. Tuition, nonresident: part-time $880 per credit hour. Tuition and fees vary according to program. *Financial support:* In 2007–08, 35 students received support, including 2 fellowships with full tuition reimbursements available (averaging $18,000 per year), 23 research assistantships with full tuition reimbursements available (averaging $17,000 per year), 10 teaching assistantships with full tuition reimbursements available (averaging $17,000 per year); Federal Work-Study, institutionally sponsored loans, scholarships/grants, and unspecified assistantships also available. Financial award application deadline: 1/15; financial award applicants required to submit FAFSA. *Faculty research:* American government, international relations, comparative government, public policy. *Unit head:* Dr. Charles Barrilleaux, Director of Graduate Studies, 850-644-7643, Fax: 850-644-1367, E-mail: cbarrile@fsu.edu. *Application contact:* Jerry Fisher, Academic Coordinator, 850-644-7305, Fax: 850-644-1367, E-mail: jfisher@admin.fsu.edu.

Fordham University, Graduate School of Arts and Sciences, Department of Political Science, New York, NY 10458. Offers elections and campaign management (MA). Part-time and evening/weekend programs available. *Faculty:* 18 full-time (2 women). *Students:* 6 full-time (4 women), 9 part-time (3 women); includes 1 minority (Hispanic American), 2 international. Average age 30. 80 applicants, 58% accepted, 7 enrolled. In 2007, 8 master's awarded. *Degree requirements:* For master's, comprehensive exam. *Entrance requirements:* For master's, GRE General Test. Additional exam requirements/recommendations for international students: Required—TOEFL (minimum score 600 paper-based; 250 computer-based). *Application deadline:* For fall admission, 1/4 priority date for domestic students; for spring admission, 11/1 for domestic students. Application fee: $70. Electronic applications accepted. *Expenses:* Tuition: Full-time $23,880; part-time $995 per credit. *Financial support:* In 2007–08, 4 students received support, including 3 research assistantships with tuition reimbursements available (averaging $14,916 per year), 1 teaching assistantship with tuition reimbursement available (averaging $4,750 per year); fellowships with tuition reimbursements available, institutionally sponsored loans, tuition waivers (full and partial), and unspecified assistantships also available. Financial award application deadline: 1/4; financial award applicants required to submit FAFSA. *Faculty research:* Protest in emerging democracies, impact of religion on presidential elections, increasing partisan polarization in U.S. politics, comparative urban development, democracy vs. authoritarianism in the Middle East, election and campaign management. *Unit head:* Dr. Bruce Berg, Chair, 718-817-3950, Fax: 718-817-3972, E-mail: berg@fordham.edu. *Application contact:* Charlene Dundie, Director of Graduate Admissions, 718-817-4420, Fax: 718-817-3566, E-mail: dundie@fordham.edu.

Fordham University, Graduate School of Arts and Sciences, Program in International Political Economy and Development, Program in Elections and Campaign Management, New York, NY 10458. Offers MA. *Students:* 8 full-time (2 women), 2 part-time (1 woman); includes 2 minority (1 Asian American or Pacific Islander, 1 Hispanic American), 1 international. 30 applicants, 70% accepted, 14 enrolled. In 2007, 9 degrees awarded. Application fee: $70. *Expenses:* Tuition: Full-time $23,880; part-time $995 per credit. *Unit head:* Dr. Costas Panagopoulos, Director, 718-817-3967.

George Mason University, College of Humanities and Social Sciences, Department of Public and International Affairs, Fairfax, VA 22030. Offers biodefense (MS, PhD); political science (MA, PhD); public administration (MPA). *Accreditation:* NASPAA (one or more programs are accredited). *Faculty:* 40 full-time (14 women), 48 part-time/adjunct (11 women). *Students:* 59 full-time (41 women), 214 part-time (146 women); includes 46 minority (18 African Americans, 1 American Indian/Alaska Native, 15 Asian Americans or Pacific Islanders, 12 Hispanic Americans), 7 international. Average age 30. 492 applicants, 55% accepted, 172 enrolled. In 2007, 99 degrees awarded. *Entrance requirements:* For master's, GRE General Test, minimum GPA of 3.0 in last 60 hours of course work. *Application deadline:* For fall admission, 5/1 for domestic students; for spring admission, 11/1 for domestic students. Application fee: $60 ($75 for international students). Electronic applications accepted. *Financial support:* Fellowships, research assistantships, teaching assistantships available. Support available to part-time students. Financial award application deadline: 3/1; financial award applicants required to submit FAFSA. *Unit head:* Dr. Robert Dudley, Chair, 703-993-1400, Fax: 703-993-1399, E-mail: rdudley@gmu.edu. *Application contact:* Dr. Ming Wan, Information Contact, 703-993-2955, Fax: 703-993-1399, E-mail: mpa@gmu.edu.

Georgetown University, Graduate School of Arts and Sciences, Department of Government, Program in Democracy and Governance, Washington, DC 20057. Offers MA. *Students:* 23 full-time (10 women), 1 part-time; includes 3 minority (all Asian Americans or Pacific Islanders), 2 international. *Application contact:* Jennifer Counts, Program Coordinator, 202-687-0513, Fax: 202-687-0597, E-mail: jac252@georgetown.edu.

The George Washington University, College of Professional Studies, Graduate School of Political Management, Program in Legislative Affairs, Washington, DC 20052. Offers MA. Part-time and evening/weekend programs available. *Degree requirements:* For master's, comprehensive exam. *Entrance requirements:* For master's, GRE General Test, minimum GPA of 3.0. Additional exam requirements/recommendations for international students: Required—TOEFL (minimum score 550 paper-based; 213 computer-based). Electronic applications accepted.

The George Washington University, Columbian College of Arts and Sciences, Department of Political Science, Washington, DC 20052. Offers MA, PhD. Part-time and evening/weekend

Political Science

The George Washington University (continued)

programs available. Terminal master's awarded for partial completion of doctoral program. *Degree requirements:* For master's, one foreign language, comprehensive exam, thesis or alternative; for doctorate, 2 foreign languages, thesis/dissertation, general exam. *Entrance requirements:* For master's and doctorate, GRE General Test, minimum GPA of 3.0. Additional exam requirements/recommendations for international students: Required—TOEFL (minimum score 550 paper-based; 213 computer-based). Electronic applications accepted.

The George Washington University, Elliott School of International Affairs, Program in Security Policy Studies, Washington, DC 20052. Offers MA, JD/MA. Part-time and evening/weekend programs available. *Degree requirements:* For master's, one foreign language, capstone project. *Entrance requirements:* For master's, GRE General Test, 2 semesters of introductory economics, 2 years of a modern foreign language or one semester of statistics. Additional exam requirements/recommendations for international students: Required—TOEFL. Electronic applications accepted. *Faculty research:* U.S. arms transfer policies, military balance in the Third World, U.S. foreign policy, technology and security policy.

Georgia State University, College of Arts and Sciences, Department of Political Science, Atlanta, GA 30303-3083. Offers MA, PhD. Part-time and evening/weekend programs available. *Faculty:* 27 full-time (9 women), 4 part-time/adjunct (1 woman). *Students:* 44 full-time (22 women), 23 part-time (12 women); includes 9 minority (7 African Americans, 1 Asian American or Pacific Islander, 1 Hispanic American), 12 international. 60 applicants, 45% accepted, 17 enrolled. In 2007, 11 master's, 1 doctorate awarded. Terminal master's awarded for partial completion of doctoral program. *Degree requirements:* For master's, thesis or alternative, exam; for doctorate, one foreign language, comprehensive exam, thesis/dissertation, exam. *Entrance requirements:* For master's, GRE General Test, 2 letters of recommendation; for doctorate, GRE General Test, 3 letters of recommendation, writing sample. Additional exam requirements/recommendations for international students: Required—TOEFL. *Application deadline:* For fall admission, 4/15 for domestic and international students; for spring admission, 10/15 for domestic and international students. Applications are processed on a rolling basis. Application fee: $50. Electronic applications accepted. *Expenses:* Tuition, state resident: part-time $221 per credit hour. *Financial support:* In 2007–08, 24 research assistantships with tuition reimbursements (averaging $14,000 per year), 12 teaching assistantships with tuition reimbursements (averaging $14,000 per year) were awarded; career-related internships or fieldwork, Federal Work-Study, institutionally sponsored loans, health care benefits, and unspecified assistantships also available. Support available to part-time students. Financial award application deadline: 2/15; financial award applicants required to submit FAFSA. *Faculty research:* International politics, American politics, comparative politics, public administration, international political economy. *Unit head:* Dr. William M. Downs, Chair, 404-413-6170, E-mail: polwmd@langate.gsu.edu. *Application contact:* Dr. Carrie Manning, Director of Graduate Studies, 404-413-6169, Fax: 404-413-6156, E-mail: polgraddirector@langate.gsu.edu.

Governors State University, College of Arts and Sciences, Program in Political and Justice Studies, University Park, IL 60466-0975. Offers MA. Part-time and evening/weekend programs available. *Students:* 11 full-time, 43 part-time. Average age 35. *Degree requirements:* For master's, thesis or alternative. *Entrance requirements:* For master's, bachelor's degree in related field. *Application deadline:* For fall admission, 7/15 priority date for domestic students; for spring admission, 11/10 for domestic students. Applications are processed on a rolling basis. Application fee: $25. *Financial support:* Research assistantships, Federal Work-Study, institutionally sponsored loans, and scholarships/grants available. Support available to part-time students. Financial award application deadline: 5/1. *Unit head:* Dr. Eric V. Martin, Dean, College of Arts and Sciences, 708-534-4101.

Graduate School and University Center of the City University of New York, Graduate Studies, Program in Political Science, New York, NY 10016-4039. Offers MA, PhD. *Faculty:* 56 full-time (10 women). *Students:* 135 full-time (68 women), 41 part-time (17 women); includes 26 minority (10 African Americans, 1 American Indian/Alaska Native, 3 Asian Americans or Pacific Islanders, 12 Hispanic Americans), 33 international. Average age 35. 188 applicants, 29% accepted, 16 enrolled. In 2007, 19 master's, 9 doctorates awarded. Terminal master's awarded for partial completion of doctoral program. *Degree requirements:* For master's, one foreign language, thesis; for doctorate, one foreign language, thesis/dissertation. *Entrance requirements:* For master's and doctorate, GRE General Test. Additional exam requirements/recommendations for international students: Required—TOEFL. *Application deadline:* For fall admission, 1/15 for domestic students. Application fee: $125. Electronic applications accepted. *Financial support:* In 2007–08, 90 students received support, including 74 fellowships, 6 research assistantships, 7 teaching assistantships; career-related internships or fieldwork, Federal Work-Study, institutionally sponsored loans, and tuition waivers (full and partial) also available. Financial award application deadline: 2/1; financial award applicants required to submit FAFSA. *Unit head:* Dr. Joan Tronto, Executive Officer, 212-817-8671, Fax: 212-817-1532.

Harvard University, Graduate School of Arts and Sciences, Committee on Political Economy and Government, Cambridge, MA 02138. Offers PhD. *Entrance requirements:* For doctorate, GRE General Test or GMAT. Additional exam requirements/recommendations for international students: Required—TOEFL. *Expenses:* Tuition: Full-time $31,456. Full-time tuition and fees vary according to program and student level.

Harvard University, Graduate School of Arts and Sciences, Department of Government, Cambridge, MA 02138. Offers political science (PhD), including American politics, comparative politics, international relations, political thought, quantitative methods. *Degree requirements:* For doctorate, one foreign language, thesis/dissertation, general exams. *Entrance requirements:* For doctorate, GRE General Test. Additional exam requirements/recommendations for international students: Required—TOEFL. *Expenses:* Tuition: Full-time $31,456. Full-time tuition and fees vary according to program and student level.

Harvard University, John F. Kennedy School of Government, Cambridge, MA 02138. Offers MPA, MPAID, MPP, MPPUP, PhD, JD/MPP, MBA/MPP, MD/MPP. *Accreditation:* NASPAA. *Faculty:* 70. *Students:* 522 full-time (229 women); includes 97 minority (24 African Americans, 3 American Indian/Alaska Native, 35 Asian Americans or Pacific Islanders, 35 Hispanic Americans), 218 international. Average age 30. 2,386 applicants, 35% accepted, 522 enrolled. *Degree requirements:* For doctorate, thesis/dissertation. *Entrance requirements:* For master's and doctorate, GMAT or GRE General Test. Additional exam requirements/recommendations for international students: Required—TOEFL (minimum score 600 paper-based; 250 computer-based; 100 iBT), TWE. Application fee: $80. Electronic applications accepted. *Expenses:* Tuition: Full-time $31,456. Full-time tuition and fees vary according to program and student level. *Financial support:* Fellowships, research assistantships, teaching assistantships, career-related internships or fieldwork, Federal Work-Study, institutionally sponsored loans, scholarships/grants, and unspecified assistantships available. Support available to part-time students. Financial award applicants required to submit CSS PROFILE or FAFSA. *Unit head:* Dr. David Ellwood, Dean, 617-495-1122. *Application contact:* 617-495-1155, Fax: 617-496-1165, E-mail: ksg_admissions@harvard.edu.

Howard University, Graduate School, Department of Political Science, Program in Political Science, Washington, DC 20059-0002. Offers MA, PhD. *Degree requirements:* For master's, comprehensive exam. *Entrance requirements:* For master's, GRE General Test, minimum GPA of 3.0; for doctorate, GRE General Test, minimum GPA of 2.8. *Expenses:* Tuition: Full-time $16,175; part-time $899 per credit hour. Required fees: $805.

Huron University USA in London, Graduate Programs, Program in International Relations, London, United Kingdom. Offers conflict resolution (MA); diplomacy (MA); international public law (MA); international relations (MA); Middle East international security (MA); politics (MA); security studies (MA); terrorism (MA); U.S. foreign policy (MA). Part-time programs available. *Entrance requirements:* Additional exam requirements/recommendations for international students: Required—TOEFL (minimum score 580 paper-based; 237 computer-based), TWE (minimum score 5). Electronic applications accepted. *Faculty research:* American foreign politics, Middle East, security studies.

Idaho State University, Office of Graduate Studies, College of Arts and Sciences, Department of Political Science, Pocatello, ID 83209. Offers political science (MA, DA); public administration (MPA). Part-time programs available. *Faculty:* 7 full-time (0 women). *Students:* 30 full-time (12 women), 31 part-time (14 women); includes 5 minority (2 African Americans, 3 Hispanic Americans). Average age 35. In 2007, 17 master's, 1 doctorate awarded. *Degree requirements:* For master's, comprehensive exam, thesis optional, coursework in 2 subfields; for doctorate, comprehensive exam, thesis/dissertation, teaching internship. *Entrance requirements:* For master's, GRE General Test, minimum GPA of 3.0 in last 2 years of undergraduate study, 3 letters of recommendation; for doctorate, GRE General Test, major field of American politics, minimum GPA of 3.0 in last 2 years of undergraduate study, 3 letters of recommendation. Additional exam requirements/recommendations for international students: Required—TOEFL (minimum score 550 paper-based; 213 computer-based; 80 iBT). *Application deadline:* For fall admission, 7/1 for domestic students, 6/1 for international students; for spring admission, 12/1 for domestic students, 11/1 for international students. Applications are processed on a rolling basis. Application fee: $55. Electronic applications accepted. *Expenses:* Tuition, state resident: full-time $2,882; part-time $259 per credit hour. Tuition, nonresident: full-time $11,566; part-time $379 per credit hour. Required fees: $2,278. Full-time tuition and fees vary according to program. Part-time tuition and fees vary according to course load. *Financial support:* In 2007–08, 6 fellowships with full and partial tuition reimbursements (averaging $12,772 per year), 3 teaching assistantships with full and partial tuition reimbursements (averaging $9,128 per year) were awarded; career-related internships or fieldwork, Federal Work-Study, institutionally sponsored loans, scholarships/grants, health care benefits, tuition waivers (full and partial), and unspecified assistantships also available. Support available to part-time students. Financial award application deadline: 1/1; financial award applicants required to submit FAFSA. *Faculty research:* International affairs, environmental policy, decision making, Constitution, executive/legislative relations. *Unit head:* Dr. Wayne Gabardi, Chairman, 208-282-4536, Fax: 208-282-4833, E-mail: gabawayn@isu.edu. *Application contact:* Ellen Combs, Graduate School Technical Records Specialist, 208-282-2150, Fax: 208-282-4847.

Illinois State University, Graduate School, College of Arts and Sciences, Department of Politics and Government, Normal, IL 61790-2200. Offers MA, MS. *Faculty:* 13 full-time (3 women), 1 part-time/adjunct (0 women). *Students:* 25 full-time (15 women), 13 part-time (4 women); includes 4 minority (1 Asian American or Pacific Islander, 3 Hispanic Americans), 2 international. 18 applicants, 56% accepted. In 2007, 16 degrees awarded. *Degree requirements:* For master's, thesis or alternative. *Entrance requirements:* For master's, GRE General Test, minimum GPA of 3.0 in last 60 hours of course work, 15 hours of course work in political science. *Application deadline:* Applications are processed on a rolling basis. Application fee: $40. *Expenses:* Tuition, state resident: full-time $3,492; part-time $194 per credit hour. Tuition, nonresident: full-time $7,272; part-time $404 per credit hour. Required fees: $1,024; $57 per credit hour. *Financial support:* In 2007–08, 11 research assistantships (averaging $7,355 per year), 12 teaching assistantships (averaging $4,836 per year) were awarded; tuition waivers (full) and unspecified assistantships also available. Financial award application deadline: 4/1. *Faculty research:* Political tolerance in a democracy under external threats: a survey of public opinion. Total annual research expenditures: $25,000. *Unit head:* Dr. Ali Riaz, Acting Chairperson, 309-438-8638.

Indiana State University, School of Graduate Studies, College of Arts and Sciences, Department of Political Science, Terre Haute, IN 47809-1401. Offers political science (MA, MS); public administration (MPA). *Faculty:* 6 full-time (1 woman), 6 part-time/adjunct (2 women). *Students:* 14 full-time (7 women), 31 part-time (14 women); includes 9 minority (5 African Americans, 2 Asian Americans or Pacific Islanders, 2 Hispanic Americans), 4 international. Average age 34. 40 applicants, 75% accepted, 18 enrolled. In 2007, 9 degrees awarded. *Degree requirements:* For master's, thesis (for some programs). *Entrance requirements:* For master's, GRE or minimum undergraduate GPA of 2.75, 18 semester hours of course work in political science. Additional exam requirements/recommendations for international students: Required—TOEFL (minimum score 550 paper-based). *Application deadline:* For fall admission, 7/1 priority date for domestic students; for spring admission, 11/1 priority date for domestic students. Applications are processed on a rolling basis. Application fee: $20. Electronic applications accepted. *Expenses:* Tuition, state resident: full-time $7,056; part-time $294 per semester hour. Tuition, nonresident: full-time $14,016; part-time $584 per semester hour. Required fees: $175 per semester. *Financial support:* In 2007–08, 1 research assistantship with partial tuition reimbursement (averaging $7,000 per year), 6 teaching assistantships (averaging $7,000 per year) were awarded; career-related internships or fieldwork, Federal Work-Study, institutionally sponsored loans, and tuition waivers (partial) also available. Support available to part-time students. Financial award application deadline: 3/1; financial award applicants required to submit FAFSA. *Unit head:* Dr. Michael Chambers, Interim Chairperson, 812-237-2429.

Indiana University Bloomington, University Graduate School, College of Arts and Sciences, Department of Political Science, Bloomington, IN 47405-7000. Offers MA, PhD. *Faculty:* 20 full-time (7 women). *Students:* 55 full-time (23 women), 33 part-time (14 women); includes 10 minority (4 African Americans, 4 Asian Americans or Pacific Islanders, 2 Hispanic Americans), 22 international. Average age 30. 126 applicants, 20% accepted, 13 enrolled. In 2007, 1 master's, 4 doctorates awarded. Terminal master's awarded for partial completion of doctoral program. *Median time to degree:* Of those who began their doctoral program in fall 1999, 29% received their degree in 8 years or less. *Degree requirements:* For master's, thesis, 30 credit hours; for doctorate, comprehensive exam, thesis/dissertation, 90 credit hours. *Entrance requirements:* For master's, GRE, personal statement, transcripts, 3 letters of recommendation; for doctorate, GRE, sample of written work, personal statement, 3 letters of recommendation. Additional exam requirements/recommendations for international students: Required—TOEFL (minimum score 640 paper-based; 273 computer-based; 112 iBT). *Application deadline:* For fall admission, 1/15 for domestic students, 12/1 for international students. Application fee: $50 ($60 for international students). Electronic applications accepted. *Financial support:* In 2007–08, 51 students received support; fellowships with full tuition reimbursements available, research assistantships with full tuition reimbursements available, teaching assistantships with full tuition reimbursements available, Federal Work-Study, institutionally sponsored loans, scholarships/grants, health care benefits, and unspecified assistantships available. Financial award application deadline: 2/26. *Faculty research:* Democracy, public opinion, quantitative methodology, parties and voting, conflict. Total annual research expenditures: $291,773. *Unit head:* Jeffrey C. Issac, Chair, 812-855-1209, Fax: 812-855-2027, E-mail: isaac@indiana.edu. *Application contact:* Sharon LaRoche, Graduate Secretary, 812-855-1208, Fax: 812-855-2027, E-mail: laroches@indiana.edu.

Indiana University of Pennsylvania, School of Graduate Studies and Research, College of Humanities and Social Sciences, Department of Political Science, Indiana, PA 15705-1087. Offers public affairs (MA). Part-time programs available. *Faculty:* 5 full-time (3 women). *Students:* 10 full-time (2 women), 6 part-time (2 women); includes 1 minority (African American), 3 international. Average age 30. 9 applicants, 56% accepted, 5 enrolled. In 2007, 8 degrees awarded. *Degree requirements:* For master's, thesis optional. *Entrance requirements:* For master's, GRE, 2 letters of recommendation. Additional exam requirements/recommendations for international students: Required—TOEFL. *Application deadline:* For fall admission, 7/1 priority date for domestic students; for spring admission, 11/1 for domestic students. Applications are processed on a rolling basis. Application fee: $30. *Expenses:* Tuition, state resident: full-time $6,214; part-time $345 per credit. Tuition, nonresident: full-time $9,944; part-time $552 per credit. Required fees: $43 per credit. One-time fee: $140 part-time. Tuition and fees vary according to course load. *Financial support:* In 2007–08, 7 research assistantships with full and partial tuition reimbursements (averaging $2,495 per year) were awarded; Federal Work-Study also available. Support available to part-time students. Financial award application deadline: 3/15; financial award applicants required to submit FAFSA. *Unit* *head:* Dr. Steven Jackson, Chairperson, 724-357-2776, E-mail: sjackson@iup.edu. *Application contact:* Dr. David Chambers, Graduate Coordinator, 724-357-2776, E-mail: chambers@iup.edu.

Indiana University–Purdue University Indianapolis, School of Liberal Arts, Department of Political Science, Indianapolis, IN 46202-2896. Offers MA, Certificate. *Students:* 5 full-time (4 women), 4 part-time (all women); includes 3 minority (2 Asian Americans or Pacific Islanders, 1 Hispanic American). Average age 26. *Expenses:* Tuition, state resident: full-time $5,818; part-time $242 per credit hour. Tuition, nonresident: full-time $17,106; part-time $713 per credit hour. Required fees: $629. Tuition and fees vary according to course load, campus/location and program. *Unit head:* John McCormick, Chair, 317-274-7387.

Institute for Christian Studies, Graduate Programs, Toronto, ON M5T 1R4, Canada. Offers education (M Phil F, PhD); history of philosophy (M Phil F, PhD); philosophical aesthetics (M Phil F, PhD); philosophy of religion (M Phil F, PhD); political theory (M Phil F, PhD); systematic philosophy (M Phil F, PhD); theology (M Phil F, PhD); worldview studies (MWS). Part-time programs available. Postbaccalaureate distance learning degree programs offered (minimal on-campus study). *Degree requirements:* For master's, one foreign language, thesis; for doctorate, 2 foreign languages, thesis/dissertation. *Entrance requirements:* For master's and doctorate, philosophy background. Additional exam requirements/recommendations for international students: Required—TOEFL (minimum score 600 paper-based; 250 computer-based). *Faculty research:* Human rights, anthropology of self, medieval discourse, gender and body, post-modern thought; biblical hermeneutics, creational aesthetics, ecumenism, epistemology, political theory and public policy, relational psychotherapy.

The Institute of World Politics, Graduate Programs in National Security, Intelligence, and International Affairs, Washington, DC 20036. Offers American foreign policy (Certificate); comparative political culture (Certificate); counterintelligence (Certificate); democracy building (Certificate); intelligence (Certificate); international politics (Certificate); national security affairs (Certificate); public diplomacy and political warfare (Certificate); statecraft and national security affairs (MA); statecraft and world politics (MA); strategic intelligence studies (MA). Part-time and evening/weekend programs available. *Degree requirements:* For master's, comprehensive exam, thesis optional. *Entrance requirements:* For master's, GRE General Test. Additional exam requirements/recommendations for international students: Required—TOEFL. Electronic applications accepted. *Faculty research:* Intelligence, national security, statecraft.

See Close-Up on page 1151.

Iowa State University of Science and Technology, Graduate College, College of Liberal Arts and Sciences, Department of Political Science, Ames, IA 50011. Offers political science (MA); public administration (MPA); JD/MA. *Accreditation:* NASPAA. *Faculty:* 12 full-time (4 women), 2 part-time/adjunct (1 woman). *Students:* 26 full-time (12 women), 33 part-time (10 women); includes 3 minority (2 African Americans, 1 Asian American or Pacific Islander), 5 international. 31 applicants, 77% accepted, 15 enrolled. In 2007, 16 degrees awarded. *Degree requirements:* For master's, thesis (for some programs). *Entrance requirements:* For master's, GRE General Test or GMAT or LSAT. Additional exam requirements/recommendations for international students: Required—TOEFL (paper-based 570; computer-based 230; iBT 80) or IELTS (6.0). *Application deadline:* For fall admission, 1/1 priority date for domestic and international students; for spring admission, 10/1 for domestic and international students. Applications are processed on a rolling basis. Application fee: $30 ($70 for international students). Electronic applications accepted. *Financial support:* In 2007–08, 18 research assistantships with full and partial tuition reimbursements (averaging $16,052 per year) were awarded; fellowships, teaching assistantships with full and partial tuition reimbursements, scholarships/grants, health care benefits, and unspecified assistantships also available. *Unit head:* Dr. James M. McCormick, Chair, 515-294-8682, Fax: 515-294-1003, E-mail: polsc@iastate.edu. *Application contact:* Dr. Richard Mansback, Director of Graduate Education, 515-294-3764, E-mail: polsci@iastate.edu.

Jackson State University, Graduate School, School of Liberal Arts, Department of Political Science, Jackson, MS 39217. Offers MA. Part-time and evening/weekend programs available. *Degree requirements:* For master's, comprehensive exam, thesis or alternative. *Entrance requirements:* For master's, GRE General Test. Additional exam requirements/recommendations for international students: Required—TOEFL.

Jacksonville State University, College of Graduate Studies and Continuing Education, College of Arts and Sciences, Department of Political Science, Jacksonville, AL 36265-1602. Offers MPA. *Faculty:* 6 full-time (1 woman), 1 part-time/adjunct (0 women). *Students:* 28 full-time (21 women), 119 part-time (56 women); includes 51 minority (48 African Americans, 1 American Indian/Alaska Native, 1 Asian American or Pacific Islander, 1 Hispanic American), 3 international. In 2007, 30 degrees awarded. *Degree requirements:* For master's, thesis optional. *Entrance requirements:* For master's, GRE General Test or MAT. *Application deadline:* Applications are processed on a rolling basis. Application fee: $20. *Financial support:* In 2007–08, 2 research assistantships were awarded. Support available to part-time students. Financial award application deadline: 4/1. *Unit head:* Dr. Lawson Veasey, Head, 256-782-8130. *Application contact:* 256-782-5329, Fax: 256-782-5321, E-mail: graduate@jsu.edu.

The Johns Hopkins University, Zanvyl Krieger School of Arts and Sciences, Advanced Academic Programs, Program in Government, Washington, DC 20036. Offers government (MA); national securities study (Certificate); MA/MBA. Part-time and evening/weekend programs available. *Faculty:* 8 full-time, 16 part-time/adjunct. *Students:* 132 applicants, 73% accepted, 91 enrolled. *Degree requirements:* For master's, thesis. *Entrance requirements:* For master's, minimum GPA of 3.0. Additional exam requirements/recommendations for international students: Required—TOEFL (minimum score 250 computer-based; 100 iBT). *Application deadline:* For fall admission, 5/31 priority date for domestic students, 4/30 priority date for international students; for spring admission, 10/31 priority date for domestic and international students. Applications are processed on a rolling basis. Application fee: $70. Electronic applications accepted. *Financial support:* Applicants required to submit FAFSA. *Unit head:* Dr. Kathy Hill, Associate Program Chair, 202-452-1953, E-mail: kathyhill@jhu.edu. *Application contact:* Rachel C. Jenkins, Admissions Manager, 202-452-1941, Fax: 202-452-1970, E-mail: aapadmissions@jhu.edu.

See Close-Up on page 1153.

The Johns Hopkins University, Zanvyl Krieger School of Arts and Sciences, Department of Political Science, Baltimore, MD 21218-2699. Offers MA, PhD. *Faculty:* 18 full-time (6 women), 3 part-time/adjunct (0 women). *Students:* 68 full-time (31 women), 1 part-time; includes 6 minority (1 African American, 4 Asian Americans or Pacific Islanders, 1 Hispanic American), 28 international. Average age 27. 229 applicants, 9% accepted, 8 enrolled. In 2007, 1 master's, 5 doctorates awarded. *Median time to degree:* Of those who began their doctoral program in fall 1999, 100% received their degree in 8 years or less. *Degree requirements:* For doctorate, one foreign language, thesis/dissertation. *Entrance requirements:* For doctorate, GRE General Test. Additional exam requirements/recommendations for international students: Required—TOEFL. *Application deadline:* For fall admission, 1/15 for domestic and international students. Application fee: $65. Electronic applications accepted. *Financial support:* In 2007–08, 52 students received support, including 26 fellowships with full tuition reimbursements available (averaging $15,000 per year), 26 teaching assistantships with full tuition reimbursements available (averaging $15,000 per year); research assistantships with full tuition reimbursements available, Federal Work-Study and institutionally sponsored loans also available. Financial award application deadline: 4/15; financial award applicants required to submit FAFSA. *Faculty research:* American politics, comparative politics, international relations, political theory, urban politics. Total annual research expenditures: $21,557. *Unit head:* Dr. Jane Bennet, Chair, 410-516-5230, Fax: 410-516-5515, E-mail: janebennet@jhu.edu. *Application contact:* Barbara Lazarek, Academic Program Coordinator, 410-516-7540, Fax: 410-516-5515, E-mail: blazarek@jhu.edu.

Kansas State University, Graduate School, College of Arts and Sciences, Department of Political Science, Program in Political Science, Manhattan, KS 66506. Offers international service (MA); political science (MA). Part-time programs available. *Students:* 39 full-time (16 women), 3 part-time; includes 2 minority (both African Americans), 8 international. Average age 33. In 2007, 9 degrees awarded. *Degree requirements:* For master's, thesis or alternative. *Entrance requirements:* For master's, GRE (recommended), minimum GPA of 3.0. Additional exam requirements/recommendations for international students: Required—TOEFL (minimum score 550 paper-based; 213 computer-based). *Application deadline:* For fall admission, 2/1 priority date for domestic and international students; for spring admission, 10/1 for domestic students, 8/1 priority date for international students. Applications are processed on a rolling basis. Application fee: $30 ($55 for international students). *Financial support:* Fellowships, research assistantships, teaching assistantships, institutionally sponsored loans and scholarships/grants available. Support available to part-time students. Financial award application deadline: 3/1; financial award applicants required to submit FAFSA. *Application contact:* Jeffrey Pickering, Director, 785-532-0454, Fax: 785-532-2339, E-mail: jjp@ksu.edu.

Kaplan University–Davenport, School of Legal Studies, Davenport, IA 52807-2095. Offers health care delivery (MS); pathway to paralegal (Postbaccalaureate Certificate); state and local government (MS). Part-time and evening/weekend programs available. Postbaccalaureate distance learning degree programs offered (no on-campus study). *Students:* 4 full-time (3 women), 60 part-time (55 women). Average age 34. *Entrance requirements:* For master's, GPA requirement. Additional exam requirements/recommendations for international students: Required—TOEFL (minimum score 550 paper-based; 218 computer-based; 80 iBT). *Expenses:* Tuition: Full-time $12,972; part-time $395 per credit. Required fees: $100 per term. Tuition and fees vary according to course load and program. *Financial support:* Applicants required to submit FAFSA.

Kean University, College of Humanities and Social Sciences, Program in Political Science, Union, NJ 07083. Offers MA. Part-time and evening/weekend programs available. *Faculty:* 7 full-time (0 women). *Students:* 12 full-time (5 women), 6 part-time (3 women); includes 3 African Americans, 1 Hispanic American, 1 international. Average age 27. 12 applicants, 75% accepted, 6 enrolled. In 2007, 3 degrees awarded. *Degree requirements:* For master's, comprehensive exam, thesis. *Entrance requirements:* For master's, GRE General Test, 3 letters of recommendation. *Application deadline:* For fall admission, 5/1 for domestic students; for spring admission, 11/1 for domestic students. Application fee: $60 ($150 for international students). Electronic applications accepted. *Expenses:* Tuition, state resident: full-time $9,384; part-time $391 per credit. Tuition, nonresident: full-time $12,720; part-time $530 per credit. Required fees: $2,382; $99 per credit. Part-time tuition and fees vary according to course load. *Financial support:* In 2007–08, 1 research assistantship with full tuition reimbursement (averaging $3,217 per year) was awarded; unspecified assistantships also available. *Unit head:* Dr. Lawrence S. Chang, Program Coordinator, 908-737-3998, E-mail: lchang@kean.edu. *Application contact:* Joanne Morris, Director of Graduate Admissions, 908-737-3355, Fax: 908-737-3354, E-mail: grad-adm@kean.edu.

Kent State University, College of Arts and Sciences, Department of Political Science, Kent, OH 44242-0001. Offers political science (MA); public administration (MPA); public policy (PhD). Part-time programs available. Postbaccalaureate distance learning degree programs offered. *Faculty:* 17 full-time (7 women), 3 part-time/adjunct (1 woman). *Students:* 46 full-time (15 women), 9 part-time (3 women); includes 3 minority (all African Americans), 18 international. Average age 35. 54 applicants, 44% accepted, 12 enrolled. In 2007, 2 degrees awarded. *Degree requirements:* For master's, thesis optional; for doctorate, 2 foreign languages, thesis/dissertation. *Entrance requirements:* For master's, GRE General Test, minimum GPA of 2.75; for doctorate, GRE General Test, minimum GPA of 3.0. Additional exam requirements/recommendations for international students: Required—TOEFL. *Application deadline:* For fall admission, 7/12 for domestic students; for spring admission, 11/29 for domestic students. Applications are processed on a rolling basis. Application fee: $30. Electronic applications accepted. *Financial support:* In 2007–08, 21 research assistantships with full tuition reimbursements (averaging $19,000 per year) were awarded; fellowships with full tuition reimbursements, teaching assistantships with full tuition reimbursements, career-related internships or fieldwork, Federal Work-Study, institutionally sponsored loans, and tuition waivers (full) also available. Financial award application deadline: 2/1. *Unit head:* Dr. John A Logue, Chairman, 330-672-2060, Fax: 330-672-3362, E-mail: jlogue@kent.edu. *Application contact:* Andrew Barnes, Graduate Coordinator, 330-672-2060, E-mail: abarnes3@kent.edu.

Lamar University, College of Graduate Studies, College of Arts and Sciences, Department of Political Science, Beaumont, TX 77710. Offers public administration (MPA). Part-time programs available. *Faculty:* 6 full-time (1 woman), 1 part-time/adjunct (0 women). *Students:* 3 full-time (0 women), 3 part-time (2 women); includes 2 minority (1 African American, 1 Asian American or Pacific Islander), 1 international. Average age 26. 11 applicants, 36% accepted, 3 enrolled. In 2007, 5 degrees awarded. *Entrance requirements:* For master's, GRE General Test. Additional exam requirements/recommendations for international students: Required—TOEFL. *Application deadline:* For fall admission, 8/1 for domestic students; for spring admission, 12/1 for domestic students. Applications are processed on a rolling basis. Application fee: $25 ($50 for international students). *Expenses:* Tuition, state resident: part-time $348 per semester hour. Tuition, nonresident: part-time $626 per semester hour. Tuition and fees vary according to course load. *Financial support:* Fellowships, research assistantships, teaching assistantships, career-related internships or fieldwork, Federal Work-Study, and institutionally sponsored loans available. Financial award application deadline: 4/1. *Faculty research:* Political activities of administrators, administrative response to Hurricane Rita, budgeting, environmental politics, urban planning. *Unit head:* Dr. Glenn Utter, Chair, 409-880-8526, Fax: 409-880-8710. *Application contact:* Dr. Terri Davis, Director, 409-880-8533, Fax: 409-880-1710, E-mail: davistb@hal.lamar.edu.

Lehigh University, College of Arts and Sciences, Department of Political Science, Bethlehem, PA 18015-3094. Offers politics and policy (MA). Part-time programs available. *Faculty:* 9 full-time (3 women). *Students:* 7 full-time (5 women), 3 part-time; includes 1 minority (Asian American or Pacific Islander), 1 international. Average age 26. 16 applicants, 38% accepted, 4 enrolled. In 2007, 15 degrees awarded. *Degree requirements:* For master's, comprehensive exam, thesis optional. *Entrance requirements:* For master's, GRE General Test. Additional exam requirements/recommendations for international students: Required—TOEFL (minimum score 560 paper-based; 223 computer-based). *Application deadline:* For fall admission, 7/15 for domestic and international students; for spring admission, 12/1 for domestic and international students. Applications are processed on a rolling basis. Application fee: $65. Electronic applications accepted. *Financial support:* Fellowships, research assistantships, teaching assistantships with partial tuition reimbursements, career-related internships or fieldwork and tuition waivers (partial) available. Financial award application deadline: 1/15. *Faculty research:* American politics and institutions. *Unit head:* Dr. Richard K. Matthews, Chairman, 610-758-3340, Fax: 610-758-3348, E-mail: rm02@lehigh.edu. *Application contact:* Dr. Frank L. Davis, Director, Graduate Studies, 610-758-5987, Fax: 610-758-3348, E-mail: fld1@lehigh.edu.

Lincoln University, School of Graduate Studies and Continuing Education, College of Liberal Arts, Education and Journalism, Department of Social and Behavioral Sciences, Jefferson City, MO 65102. Offers history (MA); social science (MA), including history, political science, sociology; sociology (MA); sociology/criminal justice (MA). Part-time and evening/weekend programs available. *Faculty:* 12 part-time/adjunct (4 women). *Students:* 13 full-time (9 women), 17 part-time (7 women); includes 16 minority (13 African Americans, 1 American Indian/Alaska Native, 2 Hispanic Americans), 3 international. Average age 33. 9 applicants, 89% accepted, 5 enrolled. In 2007, 6 degrees awarded. *Degree requirements:* For master's, comprehensive exam, thesis optional. *Entrance requirements:* For master's, GRE General Test or MAT, 15 undergraduate hours of course work in social science including 6 hours upper-division, with 9 hours in the area of concentration; see parent units for general requirements. Additional exam requirements/recommendations for international students: Required—TOEFL (minimum score 500 paper-based; 173 computer-based; 61 iBT). *Application deadline:* For fall admission, 7/1

Political Science

Lincoln University (continued)
priority date for domestic and international students; for spring admission, 12/1 priority date for domestic and international students. Applications are processed on a rolling basis. Application fee: $20. *Expenses:* Tuition, state resident: full-time $5,400; part-time $225 per credit hour. Tuition, nonresident: full-time $10,020; part-time $417 per credit hour. Required fees: $360; $15 per credit hour. $20 per semester. *Financial support:* Federal Work-Study and scholarships/grants available. Financial award application deadline: 4/1; financial award applicants required to submit FAFSA. *Faculty research:* Suicide prevention. *Unit head:* Dr. Antonio Holland, Department Head, 573-681-5145, Fax: 573-681-5150, E-mail: hollanda@lincolnu.edu.

Long Island University, Brooklyn Campus, Richard L. Conolly College of Liberal Arts and Sciences, Department of Political Science, Brooklyn, NY 11201-8423. Offers MA. Part-time and evening/weekend programs available. *Degree requirements:* For master's, thesis or alternative. *Entrance requirements:* For master's, 2 letters of recommendation. Additional exam requirements/recommendations for international students: Required—TOEFL (minimum score 550 paper-based; 173 computer-based). Electronic applications accepted.

Long Island University, C.W. Post Campus, College of Liberal Arts and Sciences, Department of Political Science/International Studies, Brookville, NY 11548-1300. Offers MA. Part-time and evening/weekend programs available. *Faculty:* 4 full-time (0 women), 6 part-time/adjunct (2 women). *Students:* 9 full-time (6 women), 11 part-time (5 women); includes 7 minority (3 African Americans, 4 Asian Americans or Pacific Islanders), 1 international. Average age 26. 17 applicants, 76% accepted, 4 enrolled. In 2007, 7 degrees awarded. *Degree requirements:* For master's, comprehensive exam, thesis or alternative. *Entrance requirements:* For master's, GRE. *Application deadline:* For fall admission, 9/1 priority date for domestic students; for winter admission, 12/15 priority date for domestic students; for spring admission, 1/20 priority date for domestic students. Applications are processed on a rolling basis. Application fee: $30. Electronic applications accepted. *Expenses:* Tuition: Part-time $825 per credit. Tuition and fees vary according to course load. *Financial support:* In 2007–08, 2 research assistantships were awarded; career-related internships or fieldwork and Federal Work-Study also available. Support available to part-time students. Financial award application deadline: 5/15; financial award applicants required to submit CSS PROFILE or FAFSA. *Faculty research:* International relations, Middle Eastern politics, political philosophy. *Unit head:* Dr. Roger Goldstein, Chair, 516-299-2407, Fax: 516-299-4140. *Application contact:* Dr. Michael Soupios, Graduate Advisor, 516-299-3026.

Louisiana State University and Agricultural and Mechanical College, Graduate School, College of Arts and Sciences, Department of Political Science, Baton Rouge, LA 70803. Offers MA, PhD. *Faculty:* 23 full-time (4 women). *Students:* 40 full-time (22 women), 10 part-time (4 women); includes 5 minority (1 African American, 2 Asian Americans or Pacific Islanders, 2 Hispanic Americans), 7 international. Average age 29. 44 applicants, 52% accepted, 10 enrolled. In 2007, 6 master's, 3 doctorates awarded. Terminal master's awarded for partial completion of doctoral program. *Degree requirements:* For master's, thesis or alternative; for doctorate, one foreign language, thesis/dissertation. *Entrance requirements:* For master's and doctorate, GRE General Test, minimum GPA of 3.0. Additional exam requirements/recommendations for international students: Required—TOEFL (minimum score 550 paper-based; 213 computer-based; 79 iBT). *Application deadline:* For fall admission, 2/15 priority date for domestic students, 5/15 for international students; for spring admission, 10/15 for domestic and international students. Application fee: $25. Electronic applications accepted. *Financial support:* In 2007–08, 43 students received support, including 3 fellowships with full and partial tuition reimbursements available (averaging $24,314 per year), 6 research assistantships with full and partial tuition reimbursements available (averaging $17,567 per year), 24 teaching assistantships with full and partial tuition reimbursements available (averaging $13,379 per year); Federal Work-Study, institutionally sponsored loans, health care benefits, tuition waivers (full), and unspecified assistantships also available. Financial award application deadline: 3/1; financial award applicants required to submit FAFSA. *Faculty research:* American government and policy, political theory, international relations and comparative politics. Total annual research expenditures: $81,934. *Unit head:* Dr. Greg Stoner, Chair, 225-578-2141, Fax: 225-578-2540. *Application contact:* Dr. James Garand, Director of Graduate Studies, 225-578-2548, Fax: 225-578-2540, E-mail: pogara@lsu.edu.

Loyola University Chicago, Graduate School, Department of Political Science, Chicago, IL 60611-2196. Offers American politics and policy (MA, PhD); international studies (MA, PhD); political theory and philosophy (MA, PhD); JD/MA. Part-time and evening/weekend programs available. *Faculty:* 18 full-time (2 women), 1 (woman) part-time/adjunct. *Students:* 27 full-time (13 women), 3 part-time (1 woman), 2 international. Average age 31. 78 applicants, 51% accepted, 12 enrolled. In 2007, 18 master's, 3 doctorates awarded. *Degree requirements:* For master's, thesis or alternative; for doctorate, variable foreign language requirement, comprehensive exam, thesis/dissertation. *Entrance requirements:* For master's and doctorate, GRE General Test. *Application deadline:* For fall admission, 6/1 for domestic students; for spring admission, 10/1 for domestic students. Applications are processed on a rolling basis. Application fee: $50. Electronic applications accepted. *Expenses:* Tuition: Full-time $12,780; part-time $710 per credit hour. Required fees: $55 per semester. Full-time tuition and fees vary according to program. *Financial support:* In 2007–08, 5 fellowships with full tuition reimbursements (averaging $14,000 per year), 5 research assistantships with full tuition reimbursements (averaging $14,000 per year) were awarded; Federal Work-Study, institutionally sponsored loans, scholarships/grants, tuition waivers (partial), and unspecified assistantships also available. Financial award application deadline: 2/15; financial award applicants required to submit FAFSA. *Faculty research:* American parties and elections, state and local politics, American political institutions, international political economy, modern and contemporary political thought. *Unit head:* Prof. Peter M. Sanchez, Chair, 773-508-8658, Fax: 773-508-3131, E-mail: psanche@luc.edu.

Marquette University, Graduate School, College of Arts and Sciences, Department of Political Science/International Affairs, Milwaukee, WI 53201-1881. Offers international affairs (MA), including comparative politics, international political economy, international politics; political science (MA), including American politics, comparative politics, international politics, political philosophy; JD/MA. Part-time programs available. *Faculty:* 16 full-time (3 women), 2 part-time/adjunct (1 woman). *Students:* 17 full-time (3 women), 9 part-time (4 women); includes 1 minority (Hispanic American), 3 international. Average age 28. 75 applicants, 56% accepted, 9 enrolled. In 2007, 8 degrees awarded. *Degree requirements:* For master's, comprehensive exam, thesis optional. *Entrance requirements:* For master's, GRE General Test. Additional exam requirements/recommendations for international students: Required—TOEFL. Application fee: $40. *Financial support:* In 2007–08, 5 research assistantships were awarded; Federal Work-Study, institutionally sponsored loans, scholarships/grants, and tuition waivers (full and partial) also available. Support available to part-time students. Financial award application deadline: 2/15. *Faculty research:* Public opinion and electoral behavior, public policy analysis, Congress and the Presidency, judicial behavior, political system transitions. *Unit head:* Dr. Duane Swank, Chair, 414-288-3418, Fax: 414-288-3360. *Application contact:* Dr. Lowell Barrington, Director of Graduate Studies, 414-288-6842, Fax: 414-288-3360.

Marshall University, Academic Affairs Division, College of Liberal Arts, Department of Political Science, Huntington, WV 25755. Offers MA. *Faculty:* 7 full-time (3 women), 5 part-time/adjunct (2 women). *Students:* 9 full-time (4 women), 3 part-time (1 woman); includes 2 minority (1 African American, 1 American Indian/Alaska Native), 2 international. Average age 26. In 2007, 7 degrees awarded. *Degree requirements:* For master's, thesis optional. *Entrance requirements:* For master's, GRE General Test. Application fee: $40. *Unit head:* Dr. Robert W. Behrman, Chairperson, 304-696-2762, Fax: 304-696-3245, E-mail: behrmanr@marshall.edu. *Application contact:* Information Contact, 304-746-1900, Fax: 304-746-1902, E-mail: services@marshall.edu.

Massachusetts Institute of Technology, School of Humanities, Arts, and Social Sciences, Department of Political Science, Cambridge, MA 02139-4307. Offers SM, PhD. *Faculty:* 20 full-time (6 women). *Students:* 62 full-time (22 women); includes 12 minority (1 African American, 5 Asian Americans or Pacific Islanders, 6 Hispanic Americans), 11 international. Average age 30. 351 applicants, 9% accepted, 12 enrolled. In 2007, 4 master's, 6 doctorates awarded. Terminal master's awarded for partial completion of doctoral program. *Degree requirements:* For master's, thesis; for doctorate, one foreign language, comprehensive exam, thesis/dissertation. *Entrance requirements:* For master's and doctorate, GRE General Test. Additional exam requirements/recommendations for international students: Required—TOEFL (minimum score 600 paper-based; 250 computer-based). *Application deadline:* For fall admission, 12/31 for domestic and international students. Application fee: $70. *Expenses:* Tuition: Full-time $34,760; part-time $545 per unit. Required fees: $236. *Financial support:* In 2007–08, 53 students received support, including 16 fellowships with tuition reimbursements available (averaging $25,888 per year), 17 research assistantships with tuition reimbursements available (averaging $26,352 per year), 15 teaching assistantships with tuition reimbursements available (averaging $27,000 per year); Federal Work-Study, institutionally sponsored loans, scholarships/grants, health care benefits, and unspecified assistantships also available. Financial award applicants required to submit FAFSA. *Faculty research:* International security; American politics; political economy; ethnic conflict and politics; democratization. Total annual research expenditures: $970,000. *Unit head:* Prof. Charles Stewart, Head, 617-253-5262, Fax: 617-258-6164. *Application contact:* Graduate Administrator, 617-253-8336, Fax: 617-258-6164, E-mail: twarog@mit.edu.

McGill University, Faculty of Graduate and Postdoctoral Studies, Faculty of Arts, Department of Political Science, Montréal, QC H3A 2T5, Canada. Offers MA, PhD. *Faculty:* 32 full-time (8 women), 8 part-time/adjunct (2 women). *Students:* 88 full-time (52 women), 5 part-time (1 woman). 460 applicants, 17% accepted, 35 enrolled. In 2007, 19 master's, 10 doctorates awarded.

McMaster University, School of Graduate Studies, Faculty of Social Sciences, Department of Political Science, Hamilton, ON L8S 4M2, Canada. Offers international relations (PhD); political science (MA); public and the global economy (MA); public policy (PhD); public policy and administration (MA). Part-time programs available. *Faculty:* 21 full-time. *Students:* 63 full-time, 6 part-time. 140 applicants, 20% accepted. *Degree requirements:* For master's, thesis or alternative. *Entrance requirements:* For master's, minimum B+ average. Additional exam requirements/recommendations for international students: Required—TOEFL (minimum score 580 paper-based; 237 computer-based). *Application deadline:* For fall admission, 2/15 priority date for domestic students. Applications are processed on a rolling basis. Application fee: $90. *Financial support:* In 2007–08, 27 teaching assistantships (averaging $8,440 per year) were awarded; scholarships/grants also available. *Faculty research:* Organizational theory, internationalization of public policy, water resource policies, political interest intermediation, comparative politics. *Unit head:* Dr. Robert O'Brien, Chair, 905-525-9140 Ext. 23705, Fax: 905-527-3071, E-mail: obrienr@mcmaster.ca. *Application contact:* Manuela Dozzi, Administrative Secretary, 905-525-9140 Ext. 24742, Fax: 905-527-3071, E-mail: dozzim@mcmaster.ca.

Memorial University of Newfoundland, School of Graduate Studies, Department of Political Science, St. John's, NL A1C 5S7, Canada. Offers MA. Part-time and evening/weekend programs available. *Degree requirements:* For master's, thesis optional. *Entrance requirements:* For master's, minimum 2nd class bachelor's degree. Electronic applications accepted. *Faculty research:* Comparative politics, Canadian government and politics, Newfoundland politics, and the politics of multi-level systems.

Miami University, Graduate School, College of Arts and Sciences, Department of Political Science, Oxford, OH 45056. Offers MA, MAT, PhD. *Degree requirements:* For master's, thesis (for some programs), final exam; for doctorate, comprehensive exam, thesis/dissertation, final exams. *Entrance requirements:* For master's, GRE, minimum undergraduate GPA of 3.0 during previous 2 years or 2.75 overall; for doctorate, GRE, minimum undergraduate GPA of 2.75, 3.0 graduate. Additional exam requirements/recommendations for international students: Required—TOEFL (minimum score 550 paper-based; 213 computer-based), TWE (minimum score 4). Electronic applications accepted.

Michigan State University, The Graduate School, College of Social Science, Department of Political Science, East Lansing, MI 48824. Offers political science (MA, PhD); public policy (MPP). *Degree requirements:* For master's, practicum; for doctorate, comprehensive exam, presentation of dissertation. *Entrance requirements:* Additional exam requirements/recommendations for international students: Required—TOEFL. Electronic applications accepted. *Expenses:* Tuition, state resident: part-time $379 per credit hour. Tuition, nonresident: part-time $800 per credit hour. Tuition and fees vary according to program.

Midwestern State University, Graduate Studies, College of Humanities and Social Sciences, Department of Political Science, Wichita Falls, TX 76308. Offers MA. *Degree requirements:* For master's, one foreign language, comprehensive exam. *Entrance requirements:* For master's, GRE General Test. Additional exam requirements/recommendations for international students: Required—TOEFL (minimum score 550 paper-based; 213 computer-based). Electronic applications accepted.

Minnesota State University Mankato, College of Graduate Studies, College of Social and Behavioral Sciences, Department of Political Science and Law Enforcement, Program in Political Science, Mankato, MN 56001. Offers MA, MS, MT. *Students:* 8 full-time (2 women), 7 part-time (3 women). Average age 33. In 2007, 14 degrees awarded. *Degree requirements:* For master's, one foreign language, comprehensive exam, thesis or alternative. *Entrance requirements:* For master's, minimum GPA of 3.0 during previous 2 years, 2 letters of recommendation. *Application deadline:* For fall admission, 7/1 priority date for domestic students; for spring admission, 11/1 for domestic students. Applications are processed on a rolling basis. Application fee: $40. Electronic applications accepted. *Financial support:* Research assistantships with full tuition reimbursements, teaching assistantships with full tuition reimbursements, unspecified assistantships available. Financial award application deadline: 3/15; financial award applicants required to submit FAFSA. *Unit head:* Dr. Scott Granberg-Rademacker, Graduate Coordinator, 507-389-6939. *Application contact:* 507-389-2321, E-mail: grad@mnsu.edu.

Mississippi College, Graduate School, College of Arts and Sciences, School of Humanities and Social Sciences, Department of History and Political Science, Clinton, MS 39058. Offers administration of justice (MSS); history (M Ed, MA, MSS); paralegal studies (Certificate); political science (MSS); social sciences (M Ed, MSS). Part-time programs available. *Faculty:* 5 full-time (1 woman), 2 part-time/adjunct (0 women). *Students:* 12 full-time (7 women), 17 part-time (14 women); includes 7 minority (6 African Americans, 1 American Indian/Alaska Native), 1 international. Average age 27. In 2007, 5 master's, 2 other advanced degrees awarded. *Degree requirements:* For master's, one foreign language, comprehensive exam, thesis (for some programs). *Entrance requirements:* For master's, GRE or NTE, minimum GPA of 2.5. Additional exam requirements/recommendations for international students: Recommended—IELTS. *Application deadline:* For fall admission, 8/15 priority date for domestic students. Applications are processed on a rolling basis. Application fee: $25. Electronic applications accepted. *Expenses:* Tuition: Full-time $7,470; part-time $415 per hour. Required fees: $1,160 per term. Part-time tuition and fees vary according to course load and degree level. *Financial support:* Teaching assistantships, Federal Work-Study, scholarships/grants, and unspecified assistantships available. Support available to part-time students. Financial award application deadline: 4/1; financial award applicants required to submit FAFSA. *Unit head:* Dr. Kirk Ford, Chair, 601-925-3326, E-mail: ford@mc.edu.

Mississippi State University, College of Arts and Sciences, Department of Political Science and Public Administration, Mississippi State, MS 39762. Offers political science (MA); public policy and administration (MPPA, PhD). *Accreditation:* NASPAA (one or more programs are accredited). Evening/weekend programs available. *Faculty:* 13 full-time (3 women), 2 part-time/adjunct (both women). *Students:* 47 full-time (24 women), 34 part-time (19 women); includes 25 minority (22 African Americans, 3 Hispanic Americans), 2 international. Average age 32. 33 applicants, 76% accepted, 20 enrolled. In 2007, 23 master's, 3 doctorates awarded. *Degree* *requirements:* For master's, comprehensive oral or written exam; for doctorate, thesis/dissertation, comprehensive oral and written exam. *Entrance requirements:* For master's, minimum GPA of 3.0; for doctorate, GRE General Test, minimum graduate GPA of 3.35. Additional exam requirements/recommendations for international students: Required—TOEFL. *Application deadline:* For fall admission, 8/1 priority date for domestic students; for spring admission, 12/1 priority date for domestic students. Applications are processed on a rolling basis. Application fee: $30. *Expenses:* Tuition, state resident: full-time $4,978; part-time $274 per hour. Tuition, nonresident: full-time $11,469; part-time $635 per hour. *Financial support:* In 2007–08, 8 teaching assistantships with full tuition reimbursements (averaging $9,044 per year) were awarded; Federal Work-Study, institutionally sponsored loans, and unspecified assistantships also available. Financial award application deadline: 4/15. *Faculty research:* American politics, international relations, state and local government, comparative government, public administration. Total annual research expenditures: $890,000. *Unit head:* Dr. David A. Breaux, Head, 662-325-2711, Fax: 662-325-2716, E-mail: dab1@ps.msstate.edu. *Application contact:* Dr. William A. Person, Interim Associate Vice President for Academic Affairs/Interim Dean of Graduate Studies, 662-325-7400, Fax: 662-325-1967, E-mail: grad@grad.msstate.edu.

Missouri State University, Graduate College, College of Humanities and Public Affairs, Department of Political Science, Springfield, MO 65804-0094. Offers international affairs and administration (MIAA); public administration (MPA). Part-time and evening/weekend programs available. *Faculty:* 14 full-time (2 women). *Students:* 34 full-time (13 women), 18 part-time (6 women); includes 6 minority (3 African Americans, 2 Asian Americans or Pacific Islanders, 1 Hispanic American), 7 international. Average age 29. 26 applicants, 100% accepted, 10 enrolled. In 2007, 18 degrees awarded. *Degree requirements:* For master's, variable foreign language requirement, comprehensive exam, thesis or alternative. *Entrance requirements:* For master's, GRE, minimum GPA of 3.0. Additional exam requirements/recommendations for international students: Required—TOEFL (minimum score 550 paper-based; 213 computer-based; 79 iBT). *Application deadline:* For fall admission, 7/20 priority date for domestic students; for spring admission, 12/20 priority date for domestic students. Applications are processed on a rolling basis. Application fee: $35. Electronic applications accepted. *Expenses:* Tuition, state resident: full-time $3,708; part-time $206 per credit hour. Tuition, nonresident: full-time $7,236; part-time $206 per credit hour. Required fees: $622. Full-time tuition and fees vary according to course level, course load, program and reciprocity agreements. *Financial support:* In 2007–08, 1 teaching assistantship with full tuition reimbursement (averaging $7,050 per year) was awarded; research assistantships with full tuition reimbursements, career-related internships or fieldwork, Federal Work-Study, scholarships/grants, and unspecified assistantships also available. Support available to part-time students. Financial award application deadline: 3/31; financial award applicants required to submit FAFSA. *Faculty research:* Health care, global environmental problems, legislatures. *Unit head:* Dr. George Connor, Acting Head, 417-836-5630, Fax: 417-836-6655, E-mail: beatkernen@missouristate.edu.

Naval Postgraduate School, Graduate Programs, Department of National Security Affairs, Monterey, CA 93943. Offers intelligence (MA); international relations (MA); political science (MA); regional security education (MA); security building (MA); security studies (MA). Program only open to commissioned officers of the United States and friendly nations and selected United States federal civilian employees. Part-time programs available. *Degree requirements:* For master's, thesis.

New Mexico State University, Graduate School, College of Arts and Sciences, Department of Government, Las Cruces, NM 88003-8001. Offers MA, MPA. *Accreditation:* NASPAA (one or more programs are accredited). Part-time and evening/weekend programs available. *Faculty:* 7 full-time (2 women). *Students:* 24 full-time (12 women), 10 part-time (3 women); includes 1 American Indian/Alaska Native, 1 Asian American or Pacific Islander, 8 Hispanic Americans, 3 international. Average age 31. 10 applicants, 60% accepted, 5 enrolled. In 2007, 22 degrees awarded. *Degree requirements:* For master's, comprehensive exam (for some programs), thesis optional. *Entrance requirements:* For master's, GRE (if GPA is below 3.0), writing sample, 3 letters of recommendation, resumé. Additional exam requirements/recommendations for international students: Required—TOEFL (minimum score 530 paper-based; 197 computer-based). *Application deadline:* Applications are processed on a rolling basis. Application fee: $30 ($50 for international students). Electronic applications accepted. *Expenses:* Tuition, state resident: full-time $3,602; part-time $199 per credit. Tuition, nonresident: full-time $13,380; part-time $607 per credit. Required fees: $1,178. *Financial support:* In 2007–08, 11 teaching assistantships with tuition reimbursements were awarded; research assistantships, career-related internships or fieldwork, Federal Work-Study, scholarships/grants, health care benefits, and unspecified assistantships also available. Support available to part-time students. Financial award application deadline: 3/1. *Faculty research:* U.S./Mexico border studies, public administration and policy, international relations, Latin America, American politics and theory. *Unit head:* Dr. Nancy Baker, Head, 575-646-4935, Fax: 575-646-2052, E-mail: nbaker@nmsu.edu. *Application contact:* Rona M. Lujan, Department Secretary, 575-646-4734, Fax: 575-646-2052, E-mail: rona@nmsu.edu.

The New School: A University, The New School for Social Research, Department of Political Science, New York, NY 10011. Offers MA, DS Sc, PhD. Part-time and evening/weekend programs available. *Faculty:* 13 full-time (5 women), 2 part-time/adjunct (1 woman). *Students:* 129 full-time (59 women), 36 part-time (17 women); includes 17 minority (7 African Americans, 2 Asian Americans or Pacific Islanders, 8 Hispanic Americans), 72 international. Average age 32. In 2007, 13 master's, 9 doctorates awarded. Terminal master's awarded for partial completion of doctoral program. *Degree requirements:* For master's, exam or major paper; for doctorate, one foreign language, thesis/dissertation, qualifying exam. *Entrance requirements:* For master's, GRE General Test; for doctorate, GRE General Test, MA. Additional exam requirements/recommendations for international students: Required—TOEFL (minimum score 600 paper-based; 250 computer-based; 100 iBT). *Application deadline:* For fall admission, 1/15 priority date for domestic students. Applications are processed on a rolling basis. Application fee: $50. *Financial support:* Fellowships, research assistantships, teaching assistantships, career-related internships or fieldwork, Federal Work-Study, scholarships/grants, and tuition waivers (full and partial) available. Financial award application deadline: 3/1; financial award applicants required to submit FAFSA. *Faculty research:* Democratic transitions and institution; race, class and gender; immigration and incorporation. *Unit head:* Dr. Victoria Hattam, Chair, 212-229-5747 Ext. 3082, Fax: 212-229-5315, E-mail: hattamv@newschool.edu. *Application contact:* Robert MacDonald, Director of Admissions, 800-523-5710 Ext. 3007, Fax: 212-989-7102, E-mail: macdonar@newschool.edu.

See Close-Up on page 1653.

New York University, Graduate School of Arts and Science, Department of Politics, New York, NY 10012-1019. Offers political campaign management (MA); politics (MA, PhD); JD/MA; MBA/MA. Part-time programs available. *Faculty:* 30 full-time (4 women), 24 part-time/adjunct. *Students:* 147 full-time (75 women), 49 part-time (25 women); includes 23 minority (5 African Americans, 12 Asian Americans or Pacific Islanders, 6 Hispanic Americans), 88 international. Average age 22. 551 applicants, 44% accepted, 72 enrolled. In 2007, 63 master's, 7 doctorates awarded. Terminal master's awarded for partial completion of doctoral program. *Degree requirements:* For master's, one foreign language, thesis or alternative; for doctorate, 2 foreign languages, comprehensive exam, thesis/dissertation. *Entrance requirements:* For master's, GRE General Test; for doctorate, GRE General Test, master's degree in political science, minimum GPA of 2.5. Additional exam requirements/recommendations for international students: Required—TOEFL. *Application deadline:* For fall admission, 12/18 priority date for domestic students. Application fee: $85. *Financial support:* Fellowships with tuition reimbursements, teaching assistantships with tuition reimbursements, career-related internships or fieldwork, Federal Work-Study, and institutionally sponsored loans available. Financial award application deadline: 12/18; financial award applicants required to submit FAFSA. *Faculty research:* Comparative politics, democratic theory and practice, rational choice, political economy; international relations. *Unit head:* Nathaniel Beck, Chair, 212-998-8500, Fax: 212-995-4184, E-mail: politics.program@nyu.edu. *Application contact:* Jonathan Nagler, Director of Graduate Studies, 212-998-8500, Fax: 212-995-4184, E-mail: politics.program@nyu.edu.

Northeastern Illinois University, Graduate College, College of Arts and Sciences, Department of Political Science, Program in Political Science, Chicago, IL 60625-4699. Offers MA. Part-time and evening/weekend programs available. *Faculty:* 9 full-time (2 women), 4 part-time/adjunct (3 women). *Students:* 10 full-time (4 women), 17 part-time (8 women); includes 10 minority (4 African Americans, 2 Asian Americans or Pacific Islanders, 4 Hispanic Americans), 2 international. Average age 36. 27 applicants, 85% accepted. In 2007, 14 degrees awarded. *Degree requirements:* For master's, comprehensive exam, thesis optional, minimum GPA of 3.0. *Entrance requirements:* For master's, minimum GPA of 2.75. Additional exam requirements/recommendations for international students: Required—TOEFL (minimum score 550 paper-based; 213 computer-based; 80 iBT). *Application deadline:* For fall admission, 4/1 priority date for domestic students; for spring admission, 8/15 for domestic students. Applications are processed on a rolling basis. Application fee: $25. Electronic applications accepted. *Expenses:* Tuition, state resident: part-time $243 per credit hour. Tuition, nonresident: part-time $443 per credit hour. *Financial support:* In 2007–08, 13 students received support, including 3 research assistantships with full tuition reimbursements available (averaging $6,600 per year); career-related internships or fieldwork, Federal Work-Study, institutionally sponsored loans, scholarships/grants, tuition waivers (full and partial), and unspecified assistantships also available. Support available to part-time students. Financial award applicants required to submit FAFSA. *Faculty research:* Chinese politics, Latin American democratization, Jewish feminism, administration and delegation.

Northeastern University, College of Arts and Sciences, Department of Political Science, Boston, MA 02115-5096. Offers political science (MA); public administration (MPA, Certificate), including development administration (MPA), health administration and policy (MPA), state and local government (MPA), urban studies (Certificate); public and international affairs (PhD). Part-time and evening/weekend programs available. *Faculty:* 22 full-time (4 women), 3 part-time/adjunct (all women). *Students:* 59 full-time (32 women), 14 part-time (5 women). Average age 30. 165 applicants, 53% accepted. In 2007, 23 master's, 2 doctorates awarded. *Degree requirements:* For master's, thesis optional; for doctorate, thesis/dissertation. *Entrance requirements:* For master's, GRE General Test. Additional exam requirements/recommendations for international students: Required—TOEFL. *Application deadline:* Applications are processed on a rolling basis. Application fee: $50. *Financial support:* In 2007–08, 12 teaching assistantships with tuition reimbursements (averaging $14,035 per year) were awarded; research assistantships with tuition reimbursements, career-related internships or fieldwork, Federal Work-Study, tuition waivers (full and partial), and unspecified assistantships also available. Support available to part-time students. Financial award application deadline: 2/1; financial award applicants required to submit FAFSA. *Faculty research:* Presidency, public opinion, Congress, democratization, national identity. *Unit head:* Dr. John Portz, Chair, 617-373-2796, Fax: 617-373-5311, E-mail: gradpolisci@neu.edu. *Application contact:* Brynn Thompson, Graduate Programs Assistant, 617-373-4404, Fax: 617-373-5311, E-mail: gradpolisci@neu.edu.

Northern Arizona University, Graduate College, College of Social and Behavioral Sciences, Department of Political Science, Program in Political Science, Flagstaff, AZ 86011. Offers political science (MA); public management (Certificate); public policy (PhD). *Degree requirements:* For master's, thesis optional; for doctorate, one foreign language, thesis/dissertation. *Entrance requirements:* For doctorate, GRE General Test.

Northern Illinois University, Graduate School, College of Liberal Arts and Sciences, Department of Political Science, De Kalb, IL 60115-2854. Offers political science (MA, PhD); public administration (MPA). Part-time and evening/weekend programs available. *Faculty:* 24 full-time (5 women), 8 part-time/adjunct (2 women). *Students:* 100 full-time (34 women), 92 part-time (34 women); includes 22 minority (11 African Americans, 5 Asian Americans or Pacific Islanders, 6 Hispanic Americans), 23 international. Average age 32. 91 applicants, 56% accepted, 30 enrolled. In 2007, 14 master's, 5 doctorates awarded. Terminal master's awarded for partial completion of doctoral program. *Degree requirements:* For master's, comprehensive exam, thesis optional; for doctorate, variable foreign language requirement, thesis/dissertation, candidacy exam, dissertation defense. *Entrance requirements:* For master's, GRE General Test, minimum GPA of 2.75, 9 hours of course work in political science; for doctorate, GRE General Test, minimum GPA of 2.75 (undergraduate), 3.2 (graduate); undergraduate major in related field. Additional exam requirements/recommendations for international students: Required—TOEFL (minimum score 550 paper-based; 213 computer-based). *Application deadline:* For fall admission, 3/1 priority date for domestic students, 5/1 for international students; for spring admission, 11/1 for domestic students, 10/1 for international students. Applications are processed on a rolling basis. Application fee: $30. Electronic applications accepted. *Expenses:* Tuition, area resident: Part-time $226 per credit hour. Tuition, state resident: full-time $5,424; part-time $225 per credit hour. Tuition, nonresident: full-time $10,848. Required fees: $2,416; $64 per credit hour. *Financial support:* In 2007–08, 4 research assistantships with full tuition reimbursements, 22 teaching assistantships with full tuition reimbursements were awarded; fellowships with full tuition reimbursements, career-related internships or fieldwork, Federal Work-Study, scholarships/grants, tuition waivers (full), and unspecified assistantships also available. Support available to part-time students. Financial award applicants required to submit FAFSA. *Faculty research:* Terrorism and dynamics of trade, U.S. foreign policy, political economy of development, biopolitical theory, women and politics. *Unit head:* Dr. Christopher Jones, Chair, 815-753-7040, Fax: 815-753-6302. *Application contact:* Dr. Dwight King, Director, Graduate Studies, 815-753-7054, E-mail: dking@niu.edu.

Northwestern University, The Graduate School, Judd A. and Marjorie Weinberg College of Arts and Sciences, Department of Political Science, Evanston, IL 60208. Offers MA, PhD, JD/PhD. Admissions and degrees offered through The Graduate School. Terminal master's awarded for partial completion of doctoral program. *Degree requirements:* For master's, thesis or alternative; for doctorate, thesis/dissertation, qualifying exams. *Entrance requirements:* For master's and doctorate, GRE General Test, sample of written work. Additional exam requirements/recommendations for international students: Required—TOEFL. *Faculty research:* Formal theory/formal political economy, political economy of development/state-business relations, labor market institutions and welfare policy, public opinion and political behavior, feminist political theory.

The Ohio State University, Graduate School, College of Social and Behavioral Sciences, School of Social and Behavioral Science, Department of Political Science, Columbus, OH 43210. Offers MA, PhD. *Faculty:* 40. *Students:* 104 full-time (40 women), 1 part-time; includes 13 minority (7 African Americans, 4 Asian Americans or Pacific Islanders, 2 Hispanic Americans), 32 international. Average age 27. In 2007, 24 master's, 9 doctorates awarded. *Degree requirements:* For master's, thesis optional; for doctorate, thesis/dissertation. *Entrance requirements:* For master's and doctorate, GRE General Test. Additional exam requirements/recommendations for international students: Recommended—TOEFL (minimum score 620 paper-based; 260 computer-based). *Application deadline:* For fall admission, 8/15 priority date for domestic students, 7/1 priority date for international students; for winter admission, 12/1 priority date for domestic students, 11/1 priority date for international students; for spring admission, 3/1 priority date for domestic students, 2/1 priority date for international students. Applications are processed on a rolling basis. Application fee: $40 ($50 for international students). Electronic applications accepted. *Financial support:* Fellowships, research assistantships, teaching assistantships, Federal Work-Study and institutionally sponsored loans available. Support available to part-time students. *Faculty research:* American, comparative, and international politics; political theory. *Unit head:* Dr. Kathleen M. McGraw, Graduate Studies Committee Chair, 614-292-2880, Fax: 614-292-1146, E-mail: mcgraw.36@osu.edu. *Application contact:* 614-292-9444, Fax: 614-292-3895, E-mail: domestic.grad@osu.edu.

Ohio University, Graduate College, College of Arts and Sciences, Department of Political Science, Athens, OH 45701-2979. Offers political science (MA); public administration (MPA).

Political Science

Ohio University (continued)

Part-time programs available. *Faculty:* 24 full-time (8 women). *Students:* 39 full-time (12 women), 29 part-time (11 women); includes 4 minority (3 African Americans, 1 American Indian/Alaska Native), 15 international. 54 applicants, 76% accepted, 31 enrolled. In 2007, 31 degrees awarded. *Degree requirements:* For master's, comprehensive exam, thesis or alternative. *Entrance requirements:* For master's, GRE General Test, minimum GPA of 3.0. Additional exam requirements/recommendations for international students: Required—TOEFL. *Application deadline:* For fall admission, 3/1 priority date for domestic students. Applications are processed on a rolling basis. Application fee: $50 ($55 for international students). Electronic applications accepted. *Financial support:* In 2007–08, 30 students received support, including 10 research assistantships with full tuition reimbursements available (averaging $8,000 per year), 6 teaching assistantships with full tuition reimbursements available (averaging $8,000 per year); career-related internships or fieldwork, Federal Work-Study, institutionally sponsored loans, and tuition waivers (full and partial) also available. Financial award application deadline: 2/15. *Faculty research:* International relations, Latin American politics, public policy, economic development, political theory. *Unit head:* Dr. John Gilliom, Chair, 740-593-4368, Fax: 740-593-0394. *Application contact:* Dr. Judith Millesen, Graduate Director, 740-593-4381, Fax: 740-593-0394.

Oklahoma State University, College of Arts and Sciences, Department of Political Science, Stillwater, OK 74078. Offers fire and emergency management administration (MS); political science (MA). *Faculty:* 20 full-time (4 women), 3 part-time/adjunct (1 woman). *Students:* 16 full-time (5 women), 37 part-time (6 women); includes 13 minority (2 African Americans, 5 American Indian/Alaska Native, 2 Asian Americans or Pacific Islanders, 4 Hispanic Americans), 3 international. Average age 33. 24 applicants, 50% accepted, 7 enrolled. In 2007, 17 degrees awarded. *Degree requirements:* For master's, comprehensive exam, thesis or creative component. *Entrance requirements:* For master's, GRE or GMAT. Additional exam requirements/recommendations for international students: Required—TOEFL. *Application deadline:* For fall admission, 3/1 priority date for international students; for spring admission, 8/1 priority date for international students. Applications are processed on a rolling basis. Application fee: $40 ($75 for international students). Electronic applications accepted. *Expenses:* Tuition, state resident: full-time $4,993; part-time $148 per credit hour. Tuition, nonresident: full-time $14,755; part-time $555 per credit hour. Tuition and fees vary according to program. *Financial support:* In 2007–08, 2 research assistantships (averaging $8,650 per year), 11 teaching assistantships (averaging $10,090 per year) were awarded; Federal Work-Study, scholarships/grants, health care benefits, tuition waivers (partial), and unspecified assistantships also available. Support available to part-time students. Financial award application deadline: 3/1. *Faculty research:* Fire and emergency management, environmental dispute resolution, voting and elections, women and politics, urban politics. *Unit head:* Dr. James Scott, Head, 405-744-5569, Fax: 405-744-6534.

Penn State University Park, Graduate School, College of the Liberal Arts, Department of Political Science, State College, University Park, PA 16802-1503. Offers MA, PhD. *Expenses:* Tuition, state resident: full-time $14,738; part-time $614 per credit. Tuition, nonresident: full-time $26,050; part-time $1,085 per credit. Tuition and fees vary according to course load, program and student level. *Unit head:* Dr. Donna Bahry, Head, 814-863-1449, E-mail: dlb46@psu.edu.

Pepperdine University, School of Public Policy, Malibu, CA 90263. Offers American politics (MPP); economics (MPP); international relations (MPP); public policy (MPP); state and local policy (MPP). *Entrance requirements:* For master's, GRE, 2 letters of recommendation, resumé. Additional exam requirements/recommendations for international students: Required—TOEFL. Electronic applications accepted.

See Close-Up on page 1619.

Portland State University, Graduate Studies, College of Urban and Public Affairs, Hatfield School of Government, Division of Political Science, Portland, OR 97207-0751. Offers MA, MAT, MS, MST, PhD. Part-time programs available. *Faculty:* 11 full-time (4 women), 7 part-time/adjunct (1 woman). *Students:* 9 full-time (3 women), 8 part-time (4 women), 3 international. Average age 28. 14 applicants, 50% accepted, 4 enrolled. In 2007, 1 degree awarded. *Degree requirements:* For master's, one foreign language, comprehensive exam, thesis; for doctorate, comprehensive exam, thesis/dissertation, residency. *Entrance requirements:* For master's, GRE General Test or MAT, minimum GPA of 3.1, 2 letters of recommendation; for doctorate, GRE General Test. Additional exam requirements/recommendations for international students: Required—TOEFL (minimum score 550 paper-based; 213 computer-based). *Application deadline:* For fall admission, 4/1 priority date for domestic students, 3/1 priority date for international students. Applications are processed on a rolling basis. Application fee: $50. *Expenses:* Tuition, state resident: full-time $7,047. Tuition, nonresident: full-time $11,178. *Financial support:* In 2007–08, 2 research assistantships with full tuition reimbursements (averaging $10,730 per year) were awarded; teaching assistantships, career-related internships or fieldwork, Federal Work-Study, and unspecified assistantships also available. Support available to part-time students. Financial award application deadline: 3/1; financial award applicants required to submit FAFSA. *Faculty research:* Congress, presidency, political reform, international environment, hate speech. *Unit head:* Melody Rose, Chair, 503-725-3921, Fax: 503-725-8444, E-mail: rosem@pdx.edu.

Princeton University, Graduate School, Department of Politics, Princeton, NJ 08544-1019. Offers political philosophy (PhD); politics (PhD). *Degree requirements:* For doctorate, comprehensive exam, thesis/dissertation, teaching experience. *Entrance requirements:* For doctorate, GRE General Test, sample of written work, letters of recommendation. Additional exam requirements/recommendations for international students: Required—TOEFL (minimum score 600 paper-based; 250 computer-based). Electronic applications accepted. *Faculty research:* American politics, comparative politics, formal and quantitative methods, international relations, public law, political theory.

Purdue University, Graduate School, College of Liberal Arts, Department of Political Science, West Lafayette, IN 47907. Offers MA, PhD. Part-time and evening/weekend programs available. Terminal master's awarded for partial completion of doctoral program. *Degree requirements:* For doctorate, 2 foreign languages, thesis/dissertation. *Entrance requirements:* For master's and doctorate, GRE General Test, minimum GPA of 3.0. Additional exam requirements/recommendations for international students: Required—TOEFL. Electronic applications accepted. *Faculty research:* American politics, comparative politics, political theory, public policy/public administration, international relations.

Purdue University Calumet, Graduate School, School of Liberal Arts and Sciences, Department of History and Political Science, Hammond, IN 46323-2094. Offers MA. Part-time and evening/weekend programs available. *Entrance requirements:* Additional exam requirements/recommendations for international students: Required—TOEFL. *Faculty research:* Mid-east, German history, US regional history, US social history, holocaust.

Queen's University at Kingston, School of Graduate Studies and Research, Faculty of Arts and Sciences, Department of Political Studies, Kingston, ON K7L 3N6, Canada. Offers MA, PhD. *Degree requirements:* For master's, thesis or alternative; for doctorate, one foreign language, thesis/dissertation, qualifying exams. *Entrance requirements:* Additional exam requirements/recommendations for international students: Required—TOEFL (minimum score 600 paper-based; 250 computer-based). *Faculty research:* Canadian politics, comparative politics, political thought, international politics, women and politics.

Regent University, Graduate School, Robertson School of Government, Virginia Beach, VA 23464-9800. Offers health care policy and administration (MA); international politics (MA); law and public policy (MA); political leadership and management (MA); political management (MA); public administration (MA); public policy (MA); terrorism and homeland defense (MA); world economies and political development (MA); JD/MA; M Div/MA; M Ed/MA; MBA/MA. Part-time programs available. *Faculty:* 6 full-time (2 women), 11 part-time/adjunct (1 woman). *Students:* 50 full-time (31 women), 67 part-time (32 women); includes 31 minority (20 African Americans, 1 American Indian/Alaska Native, 2 Asian Americans or Pacific Islanders, 8 Hispanic Americans), 2 international. Average age 31. 147 applicants, 50% accepted, 28 enrolled. In 2007, 47 degrees awarded. *Degree requirements:* For master's, thesis optional, internship. *Entrance requirements:* For master's, GRE General Test or LSAT, minimum undergraduate GPA of 3.0, writing sample, resumé, interview, references, transcripts. Additional exam requirements/recommendations for international students: Required—TOEFL (minimum score 577 paper-based; 233 computer-based). *Application deadline:* For fall admission, 5/1 priority date for domestic students; for spring admission, 11/1 priority date for domestic students. Applications are processed on a rolling basis. Application fee: $50. Electronic applications accepted. *Expenses: Contact institution. Financial support:* In 2007–08, 123 students received support. Career-related internships or fieldwork, scholarships/grants, tuition waivers (full and partial), and unspecified assistantships available. Support available to part-time students. Financial award application deadline: 9/1; financial award applicants required to submit FAFSA. *Faculty research:* Education reform, political character issues, social capital concerns, administrative ethics, biblical law and public policy. *Unit head:* Dr. Charles W. Dunn, Dean, 757-226-4322, Fax: 757-226-4643, E-mail: cwdunn@regent.edu. *Application contact:* Althea Bishard, Registrar and Executive Director of Enrollment and Academic Services, 800-373-5504, Fax: 757-226-4381, E-mail: admissions@regent.edu.

Rice University, Graduate Programs, School of Social Sciences, Department of Political Science, Houston, TX 77251-1892. Offers MA, PhD. Terminal master's awarded for partial completion of doctoral program. *Degree requirements:* For master's, thesis optional; for doctorate, comprehensive exam, thesis/dissertation. *Entrance requirements:* For doctorate, GRE General Test. Additional exam requirements/recommendations for international students: Required—TOEFL (minimum score 600 paper-based; 250 computer-based; 90 iBT). Electronic applications accepted. *Faculty research:* Comparative government in Western Europe and the former Soviet Union, international relations, Congress and public policy in American government, minority politics.

Roosevelt University, Graduate Division, College of Arts and Sciences, Department of Political Science and Public Administration, Program in Political Science, Chicago, IL 60605-1394. Offers MA. Part-time and evening/weekend programs available. *Students:* 1 (woman) full-time, 5 part-time (2 women); includes 5 minority (3 African Americans, 2 Hispanic Americans), 1 international. Average age 41. 10 applicants, 30% accepted, 2 enrolled. In 2007, 6 degrees awarded. *Degree requirements:* For master's, thesis or alternative. *Entrance requirements:* For master's, minimum GPA of 2.7. *Application deadline:* For fall admission, 6/1 priority date for domestic students. Applications are processed on a rolling basis. Application fee: $25 ($35 for international students). *Financial support:* Application deadline: 2/15. *Faculty research:* Metropolitan social movements, American politics, comparative politics, political theory. *Unit head:* Jeffrey Edwards, Head, 312-341-3670. *Application contact:* Joanne Canyon-Heller, Coordinator of Graduate Admission, 877-APPLY RU, Fax: 312-281-3356, E-mail: applyru@roosevelt.edu.

Rutgers, The State University of New Jersey, Newark, Graduate School, Program in Political Science, Newark, NJ 07102. Offers American political system (MA); international relations (MA); JD/MA. Part-time and evening/weekend programs available. *Degree requirements:* For master's, comprehensive exam, thesis optional. *Entrance requirements:* For master's, GRE, minimum undergraduate B average. Electronic applications accepted. *Faculty research:* Policymaking and policy evaluation in the United States; government and politics in Europe, Middle East, Asia, Africa, and Latin America.

Rutgers, The State University of New Jersey, New Brunswick, Graduate School, Department of Political Science, New Brunswick, NJ 08901-1281. Offers American politics (PhD); comparative politics (PhD); international relations (PhD); political theory (PhD); public law (PhD); women and politics (PhD). *Degree requirements:* For doctorate, one foreign language, comprehensive exam, thesis/dissertation. *Entrance requirements:* For doctorate, GRE General Test. Additional exam requirements/recommendations for international students: Required—TOEFL.

St. John's University, St. John's College of Liberal Arts and Sciences, Department of Government and Politics, Program in Government and Politics, Queens, NY 11439. Offers MA, Adv C, JD/MA. Part-time and evening/weekend programs available. *Faculty:* 11 full-time (4 women), 11 part-time/adjunct (7 women). *Students:* 23 full-time (12 women), 75 part-time (37 women); includes 24 minority (6 African Americans, 1 American Indian/Alaska Native, 4 Asian Americans or Pacific Islanders, 13 Hispanic Americans), 14 international. Average age 28. 112 applicants, 61% accepted, 45 enrolled. In 2007, 50 master's, 4 other advanced degrees awarded. *Degree requirements:* For master's, comprehensive exam, thesis optional. *Entrance requirements:* For master's, minimum GPA of 3.0. Additional exam requirements/recommendations for international students: Required—TOEFL (minimum score 500 paper-based; 173 computer-based; 61 iBT), IELTS (minimum score 6). *Application deadline:* For fall admission, 5/1 priority date for domestic and international students; for spring admission, 11/1 priority date for domestic and international students. Applications are processed on a rolling basis. Application fee: $40. Electronic applications accepted. *Financial support:* Research assistantships, scholarships/grants available. Support available to part-time students. Financial award application deadline: 3/1; financial award applicants required to submit FAFSA. *Application contact:* Br. Shamus McGrenra, Senior Associate Director, Office of Admission, 718-990-1601, Fax: 718-990-2346, E-mail: gradhelp@stjohns.edu.

St. John's University, St. John's College of Liberal Arts and Sciences, Department of Government and Politics and Division of Library and Information Science, Program in Government Information Specialist, Queens, NY 11439. Offers MA/MLS. Part-time and evening/weekend programs available. *Students:* 2 applicants, 50% accepted, 0 enrolled. *Entrance requirements:* Additional exam requirements/recommendations for international students: Required—TOEFL (minimum score 500 paper-based; 173 computer-based; 61 iBT), IELTS (minimum score 6). *Application deadline:* For fall admission, 5/1 priority date for domestic and international students; for spring admission, 11/1 priority date for domestic and international students. Applications are processed on a rolling basis. Application fee: $40. *Financial support:* Research assistantships, career-related internships or fieldwork and scholarships/grants available. Support available to part-time students. Financial award application deadline: 3/1; financial award applicants required to submit FAFSA. *Application contact:* Br. Shamus McGrenra, Senior Associate Director, Office of Admission, 718-990-1601, Fax: 718-990-2346, E-mail: gradhelp@stjohns.edu.

Saint Louis University, Graduate School, College of Arts and Sciences and Graduate School, Department of Political Science, St. Louis, MO 63103-2097. Offers MA. Part-time programs available. *Faculty:* 5 full-time (1 woman). *Students:* 4 full-time (3 women), 1 part-time; includes 1 minority (Asian American or Pacific Islander) Average age 22. 10 applicants, 90% accepted, 4 enrolled. *Entrance requirements:* For master's, GRE or LSAT, letters of recommendation, resumé, writing sample, goal statement, transcripts. Additional exam requirements/recommendations for international students: Required—TOEFL (minimum score 525 paper-based; 194 computer-based). *Application deadline:* For fall admission, 1/30 priority date for domestic and international students. Applications are processed on a rolling basis. Application fee: $40. Electronic applications accepted. *Expenses:* Tuition: Part-time $845 per credit hour. Required fees: $105 per semester. *Financial support:* Application deadline: 2/1; *Faculty research:* Part of Asia, Africa, Latin America, and Russia; international political economy; diplomacy and international organization; theories of democracy and justice; American political institutions. *Unit head:* Dr. Wynne W. Moskop, Chairman, 314-977-2897, Fax: 314-977-1462, E-mail: moskopww@slu.edu. *Application contact:* Gary U. Behrman, Associate Dean of Graduate School Admissions, 314-977-3827, Fax: 314-977-3943, E-mail: behrmang@slu.edu.

St. Mary's University, Graduate School, Department of Political Science, San Antonio, TX 78228-8507. Offers international relations (MA); political communications and applied science (MA); political science (MA); public administration (MPA), including inter-American administration, public management; JD/MA; JD/MPA. Part-time programs available. *Students:*

43 full-time (28 women), 126 part-time (55 women); includes 67 minority (3 African Americans, 7 Asian Americans or Pacific Islanders, 57 Hispanic Americans), 7 international. Average age 29. In 2007, 55 degrees awarded. *Degree requirements:* For master's, thesis optional. *Entrance requirements:* For master's, GRE General Test. Additional exam requirements/recommendations for international students: Required—TOEFL (minimum score 550 paper-based; 213 computer-based). *Application deadline:* Applications are processed on a rolling basis. Application fee: $0. Electronic applications accepted. *Financial support:* Fellowships, research assistantships, career-related internships or fieldwork, Federal Work-Study, institutionally sponsored loans, scholarships/grants, health care benefits, and unspecified assistantships available. Financial award application deadline: 3/31; financial award applicants required to submit FAFSA. *Faculty research:* Voting rights, natural resources and urban policy, comparative politics and international relations. *Unit head:* Dr. Sonia Garcia, Chair, 210-436-2013, Fax: 210-431-4336, E-mail: sgarcia@stmarytx.edu.

Sam Houston State University, College of Humanities and Social Sciences, Department of Political Science, Huntsville, TX 77341. Offers political science (MA); public administration (MPA). Evening/weekend programs available. *Faculty:* 15 full-time (7 women). *Students:* 6 full-time (3 women), 16 part-time (9 women); includes 8 minority (3 African Americans, 1 Asian American or Pacific Islander, 4 Hispanic Americans). Average age 30. In 2007, 10 degrees awarded. *Degree requirements:* For master's, thesis or alternative. *Entrance requirements:* For master's, GRE General Test. Additional exam requirements/recommendations for international students: Required—TOEFL (minimum score 550 paper-based; 213 computer-based). *Application deadline:* For fall admission, 8/1 for domestic students; for spring admission, 12/1 for domestic students. Applications are processed on a rolling basis. Application fee: $20. *Expenses:* Tuition, state resident: full-time $5,026; part-time $184 per semester hour. Tuition, nonresident: full-time $10,586; part-time $462 per semester hour. Required fees: $494 per semester. *Financial support:* Research assistantships, teaching assistantships, career-related internships or fieldwork and institutionally sponsored loans available. Support available to part-time students. Financial award application deadline: 5/31; financial award applicants required to submit FAFSA. *Unit head:* Dr. John Holcombe, Chair, 936-294-1467, E-mail: pol_jwh@shsu.edu. *Application contact:* Dr. Corliss Lentz, Advisor, 936-294-1459.

San Diego State University, Graduate and Research Affairs, College of Arts and Letters, Department of Political Science, San Diego, CA 92182. Offers MA. Part-time programs available. *Students:* 19 full-time (8 women), 24 part-time (9 women); includes 8 minority (1 African American, 4 Asian Americans or Pacific Islanders, 3 Hispanic Americans), 3 international. Average age 29. 52 applicants, 52% accepted, 18 enrolled. In 2007, 11 degrees awarded. *Degree requirements:* For master's, thesis. *Entrance requirements:* For master's, GRE General Test, minimum GPA of 3.0, 2 letters of reference. Additional exam requirements/recommendations for international students: Required—TOEFL. *Application deadline:* For fall admission, 5/1 for domestic and international students; for spring admission, 11/1 for domestic students, 10/1 for international students. Applications are processed on a rolling basis. Application fee: $55. Electronic applications accepted. *Financial support:* In 2007–08, 16 teaching assistantships were awarded; fellowships, career-related internships or fieldwork, Federal Work-Study, and institutionally sponsored loans also available. Financial award applicants required to submit FAFSA. Total annual research expenditures: $264,400. *Unit head:* Dr. Ronald F. King, Chair, 619-594-6245, Fax: 619-594-7302, E-mail: rking@mail.sdsu.edu. *Application contact:* Kristen Hill Maher, Graduate Advisor, 619-594-4873, Fax: 619-594-7302, E-mail: kmaher@mail.sdsu.edu.

San Francisco State University, Division of Graduate Studies, College of Behavioral and Social Sciences, Department of Political Science, San Francisco, CA 94132-1722. Offers MA. *Financial support:* Research assistantships, teaching assistantships available. *Unit head:* Dr. James Martel, Chair, 415-338-1178, Fax: 415-338-2391. *Application contact:* Dr. Sujian Guo, Graduate Coordinator, 415-338-1178, E-mail: sguo@sfsu.edu.

Simon Fraser University, Graduate Studies, Faculty of Arts and Social Sciences, Department of Political Science, Burnaby, BC V5A 1S6, Canada. Offers MA, PhD. *Degree requirements:* For master's, thesis (for some programs); for doctorate, one foreign language, comprehensive exam, thesis/dissertation. *Entrance requirements:* For master's, minimum GPA of 3.0; for doctorate, minimum GPA of 3.67, master's in political science. Additional exam requirements/recommendations for international students: Required—TOEFL or IELTS. *Faculty research:* Theory, comparative government, public policy and administration, federalism, international relations, Canadian politics.

Sonoma State University, School of Social Sciences, Department of Political Science, Rohnert Park, CA 94928-3609. Offers public administration (MPA). Part-time and evening/weekend programs available. *Faculty:* 5 full-time (1 woman), 8 part-time/adjunct (4 women). *Students:* 21 full-time (14 women), 26 part-time (20 women); includes 7 minority (1 African American, 2 Asian Americans or Pacific Islanders, 4 Hispanic Americans). Average age 35. 13 applicants, 85% accepted, 10 enrolled. In 2007, 10 degrees awarded. *Degree requirements:* For master's, thesis or alternative. *Entrance requirements:* For master's, GRE General Test, minimum GPA of 3.0. *Application deadline:* For fall admission, 11/30 for domestic students; for spring admission, 8/31 for domestic students. Application fee: $55. *Financial support:* Career-related internships or fieldwork available. Financial award application deadline: 3/2. *Faculty research:* Cross-disciplinary viewpoint in public administration, public policy implementation and evaluation with emphasis on state & local politics and non-profit organizations. *Unit head:* Dr. Diane Parness, Chair, 707-664-2179. *Application contact:* Dr. David McCuan, Graduate Program Coordinator, 707-664-3309, Fax: 707-664-3920, E-mail: david.mccuan@sonoma.edu.

Southern Connecticut State University, School of Graduate Studies, School of Arts and Sciences, Department of Political Science, New Haven, CT 06515-1355. Offers MS. Part-time and evening/weekend programs available. *Faculty:* 6 full-time. *Students:* 8 full-time (3 women), 21 part-time (9 women); includes 4 minority (all African Americans) 17 applicants, 29% accepted, 4 enrolled. In 2007, 6 degrees awarded. *Degree requirements:* For master's, thesis or alternative. *Entrance requirements:* For master's, interview. *Application deadline:* For fall admission, 7/15 priority date for domestic students. Applications are processed on a rolling basis. Application fee: $50. Electronic applications accepted. *Financial support:* Application deadline: 4/15; *Unit head:* Dr. John Critzer, Interim Chair, 203-392-5658, Fax: 203-392-5670, E-mail: critzerj1@southernct.edu. *Application contact:* Dr. Paul Best, Graduate Coordinator, 203-392-5660, Fax: 203-392-5670, E-mail: bestp1@southernct.edu.

Southern Illinois University Carbondale, Graduate School, College of Liberal Arts, Department of Political Science, Program in Political Science, Carbondale, IL 62901-4701. Offers MA, PhD, JD/PhD. Part-time programs available. *Faculty:* 17 full-time (1 woman), 2 part-time/adjunct (0 women). *Students:* 17 full-time (8 women), 21 part-time (8 women); includes 3 minority (2 African Americans, 1 Hispanic American), 13 international. 43 applicants, 28% accepted, 6 enrolled. In 2007, 4 master's awarded. *Degree requirements:* For doctorate, thesis/dissertation. *Entrance requirements:* For master's, GRE General Test, minimum GPA of 2.7; for doctorate, GRE General Test, minimum GPA of 3.5. Additional exam requirements/recommendations for international students: Required—TOEFL. *Application deadline:* Applications are processed on a rolling basis. Application fee: $20. *Financial support:* In 2007–08, 3 fellowships with full tuition reimbursements, 5 research assistantships with full tuition reimbursements, 10 teaching assistantships with full tuition reimbursements were awarded; career-related internships or fieldwork, Federal Work-Study, institutionally sponsored loans, and tuition waivers (full) also available. Support available to part-time students. Financial award application deadline: 2/1. *Faculty research:* Public law, international relations, comparative government, American government. *Unit head:* Dr. Steven Shulman, Head, E-mail: shulman@siu.edu. *Application contact:* Andrea Steen, Administrative Clerk, 618-453-3165, E-mail: asteen@siu.edu.

Announcement: The University and department were honored to have a most-respected American political voice on campus. For more than 40 years, U.S. Senator Paul Simon nurtured a celebrated career in public service that was built on a foundation of integrity, trust, and compassion. Following his 1997 retirement, SIU welcomed Senator Simon to be the first holder of the Paul Simon Endowed Chair in Public Policy. He taught courses in political science, journalism, and history and also headed the Public Policy Institute at Southern Illinois University.

See Close-Up on page 1165.

Southern University and Agricultural and Mechanical College, Graduate School, Nelson Mandela School of Public Policy and Urban Affairs, Department of Political Science and Geography, Baton Rouge, LA 70813. Offers social sciences (MA). *Students:* Average age 25. *Degree requirements:* For master's, thesis. *Entrance requirements:* For master's; GMAT or GRE General Test, minimum GPA of 3.0. Additional exam requirements/recommendations for international students: Required—TOEFL. *Application deadline:* For fall admission, 6/1 priority date for domestic students; for spring admission, 11/1 for domestic students. Applications are processed on a rolling basis. Application fee: $25. *Financial support:* In 2007–08, research assistantships (averaging $7,000 per year), teaching assistantships (averaging $7,000 per year) were awarded. Financial award application deadline: 4/15; financial award applicants required to submit FAFSA. *Faculty research:* Redistricting, comparative studies, environmental politics, political geography, mayoral elections. *Unit head:* Dr. Kingsley Esedo, Chairman, 225-771-3210, Fax: 225-771-3105.

Stanford University, School of Humanities and Sciences, Department of Political Science, Stanford, CA 94305-9991. Offers MA, PhD. Terminal master's awarded for partial completion of doctoral program. *Degree requirements:* For doctorate, one foreign language, thesis/dissertation, oral exam. *Entrance requirements:* For master's and doctorate, GRE General Test. Additional exam requirements/recommendations for international students: Required—TOEFL. Electronic applications accepted.

State University of New York at Binghamton, Graduate School, School of Arts and Sciences, Department of Political Science, Binghamton, NY 13902-6000. Offers political science (MA, PhD); public policy (MA, PhD). *Faculty:* 11 full-time (2 women), 1 part-time/adjunct (0 women). *Students:* 37 full-time (12 women), 12 part-time (7 women); includes 5 minority (4 African Americans, 1 Asian American or Pacific Islander), 22 international. Average age 27. 73 applicants, 41% accepted, 11 enrolled. In 2007, 10 master's, 2 doctorates awarded. Terminal master's awarded for partial completion of doctoral program. *Degree requirements:* For master's, thesis or alternative, written exam; for doctorate, 2 foreign languages, thesis/dissertation, written exam. *Entrance requirements:* For master's and doctorate, GRE General Test, GRE Subject Test. Additional exam requirements/recommendations for international students: Required—TOEFL. *Application deadline:* For fall admission, 4/15 priority date for domestic students, 1/15 priority date for international students; for spring admission, 11/1 for domestic students, 10/1 priority date for international students. Applications are processed on a rolling basis. Application fee: $60. Electronic applications accepted. *Financial support:* In 2007–08, 24 students received support, including 5 fellowships with full tuition reimbursements available (averaging $5,000 per year), 2 research assistantships with full tuition reimbursements available (averaging $10,500 per year), 14 teaching assistantships with full tuition reimbursements available (averaging $14,700 per year); career-related internships or fieldwork, Federal Work-Study, institutionally sponsored loans, tuition waivers (full and partial), and unspecified assistantships also available. Support available to part-time students. Financial award application deadline: 2/15. *Unit head:* Dr. David Clark, Chairperson, 607-777-6786, E-mail: dclark@binghamton.edu.

Stony Brook University, State University of New York, Graduate School, College of Arts and Sciences, Department of Political Science, Stony Brook, NY 11794. Offers political science (MA, PhD); public policy (MAPP). Evening/weekend programs available. *Faculty:* 17 full-time (3 women), 2 part-time/adjunct (0 women). *Students:* 68 full-time (22 women), 23 part-time (13 women); includes 15 minority (4 African Americans, 6 Asian Americans or Pacific Islanders, 5 Hispanic Americans), 21 international. Average age 27. 90 applicants, 70% accepted. In 2007, 29 master's, 3 doctorates awarded. *Degree requirements:* For doctorate, thesis/dissertation. *Entrance requirements:* For master's and doctorate, GRE General Test. *Application deadline:* For fall admission, 1/15 for domestic students. Application fee: $60. *Financial support:* In 2007–08, 25 teaching assistantships were awarded; fellowships, research assistantships also available. Total annual research expenditures: $349,872. *Unit head:* Dr. Jeffrey Segal, Chair, 631-632-7640. *Application contact:* Dr. Stanley Feldman, Director, 631-632-7667, Fax: 631-632-4116, E-mail: stanley.feldman@stonybrook.edu.

Announcement: The PhD in political science prepares students for academic research and teaching positions with a focus on American politics, political psychology, and political economy. The Master of Arts in Public Policy (MAPP) prepares students for analytic and management positions in state, local, and federal agencies; in nonprofit organizations that interact with government; and in corporations that deal with public policy. Many graduates have had successful careers in each of these venues, while others have used the MA program as a launching pad to advanced graduate study in the social sciences and law.

See Close-Up on page 1167.

Suffolk University, College of Arts and Sciences, Department of Government, Boston, MA 02108-2770. Offers political science (MS); MS/MPA. Part-time and evening/weekend programs available. *Faculty:* 9 full-time (4 women), 5 part-time/adjunct (1 woman). *Students:* 16 full-time (8 women), 18 part-time (7 women); includes 1 African American, 1 Asian American or Pacific Islander, 3 Hispanic Americans, 6 international. Average age 27. 60 applicants, 83% accepted, 25 enrolled. In 2007, 12 degrees awarded. *Degree requirements:* For master's, thesis optional. *Entrance requirements:* For master's, GRE General Test or MAT. Additional exam requirements/recommendations for international students: Required—TOEFL (minimum score 550 paper-based; 213 computer-based; 80 iBT). *Application deadline:* For fall admission, 6/15 priority date for domestic students, 6/15 for international students; for spring admission, 11/1 priority date for domestic students, 11/1 for international students. Applications are processed on a rolling basis. Application fee: $50. Electronic applications accepted. *Expenses:* Contact institution. *Financial support:* In 2007–08, 30 students received support, including 26 fellowships with full and partial tuition reimbursements available (averaging $4,346 per year); career-related internships or fieldwork, Federal Work-Study, and institutionally sponsored loans also available. Support available to part-time students. Financial award application deadline: 4/1; financial award applicants required to submit FAFSA. *Faculty research:* Political parties, women in politics, Canadian politics, public policy, legislative policies. *Unit head:* John Berg, Chairperson, 617-573-8123, Fax: 617-367-5762, E-mail: jberg@suffolk.edu. *Application contact:* Judith Reynolds, Director of Graduate Admissions, 617-573-8302, Fax: 617-523-0116, E-mail: grad.admission@suffolk.edu.

Sul Ross State University, School of Arts and Sciences, Department of Behavioral and Social Sciences, Program in Political Science, Alpine, TX 79832. Offers MA. Part-time and evening/weekend programs available. *Degree requirements:* For master's, thesis optional. *Entrance requirements:* For master's, GRE General Test, minimum undergraduate GPA of 2.5 in last 60 hours. *Faculty research:* Local government, state government, borderland studies, British studies.

Syracuse University, Graduate School, Maxwell School of Citizenship and Public Affairs, Department of Political Science, Syracuse, NY 13244. Offers MA, PhD. *Students:* 60 full-time (30 women), 4 part-time (3 women); includes 1 minority (Hispanic American), 31 international. 144 applicants, 19% accepted, 14 enrolled. In 2007, 10 master's, 4 doctorates awarded. *Degree requirements:* For doctorate, thesis/dissertation. *Entrance requirements:* For master's and doctorate, GRE General Test. Additional exam requirements/recommendations for international students: Required—TOEFL. *Application deadline:* For fall admission, 2/1 priority date for domestic students. Applications are processed on a rolling basis. Application fee: $75. Electronic applications accepted. *Expenses:* Tuition: Full-time $18,216; part-time $1,012 per credit. Required fees: $980. Tuition and fees vary according to program. *Financial support:* Fellowships with full and partial tuition reimbursements, research assistantships with full tuition

Political Science

Syracuse University (continued)
reimbursements, teaching assistantships with full and partial tuition reimbursements, tuition waivers (partial) available. *Unit head:* Dr. Mark Rupert, Chair, 315-443-2416, Fax: 315-443-9082, E-mail: polisci@maxwell.syr.edu. *Application contact:* Candy Brooks, Recruiting Contact, 315-443-2416, E-mail: cbrooks01@syr.edu.

Tarleton State University, College of Graduate Studies, College of Liberal and Fine Arts, Department of Social Sciences, Stephenville, TX 76402. Offers history (MA); political science (MA). Part-time and evening/weekend programs available. Postbaccalaureate distance learning degree programs offered (minimal on-campus study). *Faculty:* 8 full-time (1 woman), 3 part-time/adjunct (0 women). *Students:* 7 full-time (2 women), 28 part-time (10 women); includes 6 minority (2 African Americans, 1 American Indian/Alaska Native, 3 Hispanic Americans), 1 international. Average age 37. 15 applicants, 93% accepted, 10 enrolled. In 2007, 3 degrees awarded. *Degree requirements:* For master's, variable foreign language requirement, comprehensive exam, thesis optional. *Entrance requirements:* For master's, GRE General Test, minimum GPA of 3.0. Additional exam requirements/recommendations for international students: Required—TOEFL (minimum score 550 paper-based; 213 computer-based). *Application deadline:* For fall admission, 8/5 priority date for domestic students; for spring admission, 12/1 for domestic students. Applications are processed on a rolling basis. Application fee: $25 ($125 for international students). Electronic applications accepted. *Expenses:* Tuition, state resident: full-time $2,520; part-time $140 per credit hour. Tuition, nonresident: full-time $7,344; part-time $408 per credit hour. Required fees: $948; $39 per credit hour. *Financial support:* Research assistantships, teaching assistantships, career-related internships or fieldwork and Federal Work-Study available. Support available to part-time students. Financial award application deadline: 5/1; financial award applicants required to submit FAFSA. *Unit head:* Dr. Dean A. Minix, Interim Department Head, 254-968-9141, Fax: 254-968-9798, E-mail: minix@tarleton.edu.

Teachers College, Columbia University, Graduate Faculty of Education, Department of Organization and Leadership, Program in Politics and Education, New York, NY 10027-6696. Offers Ed M, MA, Ed D, PhD. *Faculty:* 2 part-time/adjunct. *Students:* 12 full-time (5 women), 22 part-time (12 women); includes 11 minority (4 African Americans, 4 Asian Americans or Pacific Islanders, 3 Hispanic Americans). Average age 30. 49 applicants, 61% accepted, 9 enrolled. In 2007, 10 master's, 1 doctorate awarded. *Degree requirements:* For doctorate, thesis/dissertation. *Application deadline:* For fall admission, 5/15 for domestic students. Application fee: $70. *Financial support:* Career-related internships or fieldwork, Federal Work-Study, institutionally sponsored loans, and tuition waivers (full and partial) available. Support available to part-time students. Financial award application deadline: 2/1. *Faculty research:* Urban and social programs in education. *Application contact:* Debbie Lesperance, Assistant Director of Admission, 212-678-3710, Fax: 212-678-4171.

Temple University, Graduate School, College of Liberal Arts, Department of Political Science, Philadelphia, PA 19122-6096. Offers MA, PhD. Part-time programs available. Terminal master's awarded for partial completion of doctoral program. *Degree requirements:* For master's, comprehensive exam; for doctorate, thesis/dissertation, preliminary and oral exams. *Entrance requirements:* For master's and doctorate, GRE General Test, minimum GPA of 3.0. Additional exam requirements/recommendations for international students: Required—TOEFL (minimum score 550 paper-based; 213 computer-based; 79 iBT). Electronic applications accepted. *Faculty research:* American politics, international politics, comparative politics, political theory, urban politics, public policy.

Texas A&M International University, Office of Graduate Studies and Research, College of Arts and Sciences, Department of Social Sciences, Laredo, TX 78041-1900. Offers history (MA); political science (MA); public administration (MPA). *Faculty:* 8 full-time (3 women), 2 part-time/adjunct (1 woman). *Students:* 14 full-time (8 women), 65 part-time (34 women); includes 68 minority (1 Asian American or Pacific Islander, 67 Hispanic Americans), 4 international. Average age 34. 35 applicants, 97% accepted, 23 enrolled. In 2007, 10 degrees awarded. *Degree requirements:* For master's, thesis (for some programs). *Entrance requirements:* For master's, GRE General Test. Additional exam requirements/recommendations for international students: Required—TOEFL (minimum score 550 paper-based; 213 computer-based). *Application deadline:* For fall admission, 7/15 priority date for domestic students; for spring admission, 11/12 for domestic students. Applications are processed on a rolling basis. Application fee: $25. *Financial support:* In 2007–08, 29 students received support. Application deadline: 11/1. *Unit head:* Dr. William W. Riggs, Chair, 956-328-2540, E-mail: wriggs@tamiu.edu. *Application contact:* Rosie Espinoza-Dickinson, Director of Admissions, 956-326-2200, Fax: 956-326-2199, E-mail: enroll@tamiu.edu.

Texas A&M University, College of Liberal Arts, Department of Political Science, College Station, TX 77843. Offers MA, PhD. *Faculty:* 21. *Students:* 52 full-time (22 women), 11 part-time (5 women); includes 12 minority (5 African Americans, 1 Asian American or Pacific Islander, 6 Hispanic Americans), 15 international. Average age 30. 79 applicants, 30% accepted, 17 enrolled. In 2007, 2 master's, 11 doctorates awarded. *Degree requirements:* For master's, thesis optional; for doctorate, comprehensive exam, thesis/dissertation. *Entrance requirements:* For master's and doctorate, GRE General Test, minimum GPA of 3.4. Additional exam requirements/recommendations for international students: Required—TOEFL. *Application deadline:* For fall admission, 12/20 for domestic and international students. Application fee: $50 ($75 for international students). Electronic applications accepted. *Expenses:* Tuition, state resident: full-time $6,129. Tuition, nonresident: full-time $11,689. Tuition and fees vary according to course load. *Financial support:* In 2007–08, fellowships (averaging $3,000 per year), research assistantships (averaging $15,600 per year) were awarded; institutionally sponsored loans and assistant lecturer positions also available. Financial award application deadline: 12/20; financial award applicants required to submit FAFSA. *Faculty research:* American politics, international relations, comparative politics, political theory, public policy. *Unit head:* Dr. Patricia A. Hurley, Head, 979-845-2511, Fax: 979-847-8924, E-mail: pat_hurley@polisci.tamu.edu. *Application contact:* Dr. Cary J. Nederman, Graduate Advisor, 979-845-4845, Fax: 979-845-4845, E-mail: nederman@polisci.tamu.edu.

Texas A&M University–Kingsville, College of Graduate Studies, College of Arts and Sciences, Program in History and Political Science, Kingsville, TX 78363. Offers MA, MS. Part-time and evening/weekend programs available. *Degree requirements:* For master's, comprehensive exam, thesis or alternative. *Entrance requirements:* For master's, GRE General Test. Additional exam requirements/recommendations for international students: Required—TOEFL.

Texas State University–San Marcos, Graduate School, College of Liberal Arts, Department of Political Science, Program in Political Science, San Marcos, TX 78666. Offers MA. Part-time and evening/weekend programs available. *Students:* 35 full-time (18 women), 33 part-time (10 women); includes 18 minority (3 African Americans, 2 Asian Americans or Pacific Islanders, 13 Hispanic Americans), 1 international. Average age 30. 38 applicants, 97% accepted, 23 enrolled. In 2007, 12 degrees awarded. *Degree requirements:* For master's, comprehensive exam, thesis (for some programs). *Entrance requirements:* For master's, minimum GPA of 2.9 in last 60 hours of course work. Additional exam requirements/recommendations for international students: Required—TOEFL (minimum score 550 paper-based; 213 computer-based). *Application deadline:* For fall admission, 6/15 priority date for domestic students, 6/1 priority date for international students; for spring admission, 10/15 priority date for domestic students, 10/1 priority date for international students. Applications are processed on a rolling basis. Application fee: $40 ($90 for international students). Electronic applications accepted. *Expenses:* Tuition, state resident: full-time $3,780; part-time $210 per credit hour. Tuition, nonresident: full-time $8,784; part-time $488 per credit hour. Required fees: $493 per semester. Full-time tuition and fees vary according to course load. *Financial support:* In 2007–08, 49 students received support, including 1 research assistantship (averaging $4,928 per year), 10 teaching assistantships (averaging $5,173 per year); career-related internships or fieldwork, Federal Work-Study, and institutionally sponsored loans also available. Support available to part-time students. Financial award application deadline: 4/1; financial award applicants required to submit FAFSA. *Faculty research:* Religion in American public life, international humanitarian and refugee policy, judicial biography and history, citizenship and ethics, business and government policy making. *Unit head:* Dr. Cecilia Castillio, Graduate Adviser, 512-245-2143, Fax: 512-345-7815, E-mail: cr09@txstate.edu.

Texas State University–San Marcos, Graduate School, Interdisciplinary Studies in Political Science, San Marcos, TX 78666. Offers MAIS. *Degree requirements:* For master's, comprehensive exam. *Application deadline:* For fall admission, 6/15 priority date for domestic students; for spring admission, 10/15 priority date for domestic students. Applications are processed on a rolling basis. Application fee: $40 ($90 for international students). *Expenses:* Tuition, state resident: full-time $3,780; part-time $210 per credit hour. Tuition, nonresident: full-time $8,784; part-time $488 per credit hour. Required fees: $493 per semester. Full-time tuition and fees vary according to course load. *Financial support:* Application deadline: 4/1; *Unit head:* Dr. Cecilia Castillio, Graduate Advisor, 512-245-3255, Fax: 512-345-7815, E-mail: cr09@txstate.edu.

Texas Tech University, Graduate School, College of Arts and Sciences, Department of Political Science, Lubbock, TX 79409. Offers political science (MA, PhD); public administration (MPA); JD/MPA. *Accreditation:* NASPAA (one or more programs are accredited). Part-time programs available. *Faculty:* 10 full-time (1 woman). *Students:* 59 full-time (23 women), 19 part-time (7 women); includes 19 minority (2 African Americans, 2 American Indian/Alaska Native, 3 Asian Americans or Pacific Islanders, 12 Hispanic Americans), 9 international. Average age 28. 64 applicants, 78% accepted, 22 enrolled. In 2007, 32 master's, 2 doctorates awarded. *Degree requirements:* For master's, thesis or alternative; for doctorate, thesis/dissertation. *Entrance requirements:* For master's and doctorate, GRE General Test. Additional exam requirements/recommendations for international students: Required—TOEFL (minimum score 550 paper-based; 213 computer-based). *Application deadline:* For fall admission, 3/1 priority date for international students; for spring admission, 11/1 priority date for international students. Applications are processed on a rolling basis. Application fee: $50 ($60 for international students). Electronic applications accepted. *Expenses:* Tuition, state resident: part-time $373 per credit hour. Tuition, nonresident: part-time $651 per credit hour. Tuition and fees vary according to program. *Financial support:* In 2007–08, 64 students received support, including 1 research assistantship with partial tuition reimbursement available (averaging $9,000 per year), 26 teaching assistantships with partial tuition reimbursements available (averaging $12,024 per year); Federal Work-Study and institutionally sponsored loans also available. Support available to part-time students. Financial award application deadline: 4/15; financial award applicants required to submit FAFSA. *Faculty research:* State politics, American institutions and behavior, Asian politics, international and comparative political relations and economics, public administration and organizations. Total annual research expenditures:$45,033. *Unit head:* Dr. Philip H. Marshall, Chair, 806-742-3121, Fax: 806-742-0850, E-mail: philip.marshall@ttu.edu.

Texas Woman's University, Graduate School, College of Arts and Sciences, Department of History and Government, Denton, TX 76201. Offers government (MA); history (MA). Part-time and evening/weekend programs available. *Students:* 9 full-time (all women), 30 part-time (25 women); includes 9 minority (5 African Americans, 1 Asian American or Pacific Islander, 3 Hispanic Americans). Average age 35. In 2007, 16 master's awarded. *Degree requirements:* For master's, thesis. *Entrance requirements:* For master's, minimum GPA of 3.3, writing sample/portfolio. Additional exam requirements/recommendations for international students: Required—TOEFL (minimum score 550 paper-based; 213 computer-based; 79 iBT). *Application deadline:* For fall admission, 4/1 for international students; for spring admission, 8/1 for international students. Applications are processed on a rolling basis. Application fee: $30 ($50 for international students). Electronic applications accepted. *Expenses:* Tuition, state resident: full-time $3,294; part-time $183 per credit. Tuition, nonresident: full-time $8,298; part-time $461 per credit. Required fees: $985; $55 per credit. Tuition and fees vary according to degree level. *Financial support:* In 2007–08, 14 teaching assistantships (averaging $9,684 per year) were awarded; career-related internships or fieldwork, Federal Work-Study, institutionally sponsored loans, scholarships/grants, traineeships, health care benefits, and unspecified assistantships also available. Support available to part-time students. Financial award application deadline: 3/1; financial award applicants required to submit FAFSA. *Faculty research:* Recent American history, civil liberties, military history, legal studies, women and politics. *Unit head:* Dr. Barbara Presnall, Interim Chair, 940-898-2133, Fax: 940-898-2130, E-mail: bpresnall@twu.edu. *Application contact:* Samuel Wheeler, Assistant Director of Admissions, 940-898-3188, Fax: 940-898-3081, E-mail: wheelersr@twu.edu.

Tulane University, School of Liberal Arts, Department of Political Science, New Orleans, LA 70118-5669. Offers MA, PhD, MA/JD. *Degree requirements:* For master's, one foreign language, thesis optional, seminar; for doctorate, 2 foreign languages, thesis/dissertation. *Entrance requirements:* For master's, GRE General Test, minimum B average in undergraduate course work; for doctorate, GRE General Test. Additional exam requirements/recommendations for international students: Required—TOEFL. Electronic applications accepted.

Université de Montréal, Faculty of Arts and Sciences, Department of Political Science, Montréal, QC H3C 3J7, Canada. Offers M Sc, PhD. *Faculty:* 27 full-time (6 women), 5 part-time/adjunct (1 woman). *Students:* 207 applicants, 23% accepted, 40 enrolled. In 2007, 45 master's, 4 doctorates awarded. *Degree requirements:* For master's, thesis; for doctorate, thesis/dissertation, general exam. *Entrance requirements:* For master's, minimum GPA of 2.8; for doctorate, master's degree, minimum GPA of 3.0. *Application deadline:* For fall admission, 2/1 priority date for domestic students; for winter admission, 11/1 priority date for domestic students; for spring admission, 2/1 priority date for domestic students. Application fee: $100. Electronic applications accepted. *Financial support:* Fellowships, research assistantships, teaching assistantships, career-related internships or fieldwork available. *Unit head:* Philippe Faucher, Chairman, 514-343-6588, Fax: 514-343-2360, E-mail: philippe.faucher@umontreal.ca. *Application contact:* Richard Nadeau, Graduate Chairman, 514-343-2163, Fax: 514-343-2360, E-mail: richard.nadeau@umontreal.ca.

Université du Québec à Montréal, Graduate Programs, Program in Political Science, Montréal, QC H3C 3P8, Canada. Offers MA, PhD. Part-time programs available. *Degree requirements:* For master's, thesis; for doctorate, thesis/dissertation. *Entrance requirements:* For master's, appropriate bachelor's degree or equivalent, proficiency in French; for doctorate, appropriate master's degree or equivalent, proficiency in French.

Université Laval, Faculty of Social Sciences, Department of Political Science, Program in Politics Analysis, Québec, QC G1K 7P4, Canada. Offers MA. *Degree requirements:* For master's, thesis (for some programs). *Entrance requirements:* For master's, knowledge of French, comprehension of written English. Electronic applications accepted.

Université Laval, Faculty of Social Sciences, Department of Political Science, Programs in Political Science, Québec, QC G1K 7P4, Canada. Offers MA, PhD. Terminal master's awarded for partial completion of doctoral program. *Degree requirements:* For master's, thesis (for some programs); for doctorate, comprehensive exam, thesis/dissertation. *Entrance requirements:* For master's, knowledge of French; for doctorate, knowledge of French, comprehension of written English. Electronic applications accepted.

University at Albany, State University of New York, Nelson A. Rockefeller College of Public Affairs and Policy, Department of Political Science, Albany, NY 12222-0001. Offers MA, PhD. *Students:* 39 full-time (18 women), 36 part-time (12 women). Average age 33. In 2007, 7 master's, 4 doctorates awarded. *Degree requirements:* For doctorate, one foreign language, thesis/dissertation. *Entrance requirements:* For doctorate, GRE General Test. Additional exam requirements/recommendations for international students: Required—TOEFL (minimum score 550 paper-based; 213 computer-based). *Application deadline:* For fall admission, 2/1 priority date for domestic students, 5/1 for international students; for spring admission, 11/1 for international students. Applications are processed on a rolling basis. Application fee: $75. Electronic applications accepted. *Expenses:* Tuition, state resident: part-time $576 per credit.

Tuition, nonresident: part-time $910 per credit. Tuition and fees vary according to program. *Financial support:* Fellowships available. Financial award application deadline: 2/1. *Unit head:* Dr. Thomas Church, Chair, 518-442-5255.

University at Buffalo, the State University of New York, Graduate School, College of Arts and Sciences, Department of Political Science, Buffalo, NY 14260. Offers MA, PhD. Terminal master's awarded for partial completion of doctoral program. *Degree requirements:* For master's, thesis or alternative, paper, project; for doctorate, comprehensive exam, thesis/dissertation. *Entrance requirements:* For master's, GRE General Test, minimum GPA of 3.0; for doctorate, GRE General Test, minimum GPA of 3.3. Additional exam requirements/recommendations for international students: Required—TOEFL (minimum score 550 paper-based; 213 computer-based; 79 iBT). Electronic applications accepted. *Faculty research:* American politics, public law, comparative politics, international politics.

The University of Akron, Graduate School, Buchtel College of Arts and Sciences, Department of Political Science, Akron, OH 44325. Offers applied politics (MA); political science (MA); JD/MAP. Part-time programs available. *Faculty:* 10 full-time (2 women), 9 part-time/adjunct (3 women). *Students:* 47 full-time (21 women), 28 part-time (8 women); includes 11 minority (9 African Americans, 2 Hispanic Americans). Average age 30. 42 applicants, 76% accepted, 23 enrolled. In 2007, 27 degrees awarded. *Degree requirements:* For master's, comprehensive exam, essay, seminars (political science); portfolio (applied politics). *Entrance requirements:* For master's, minimum GPA of 2.75, letters of recommendation. Additional exam requirements/recommendations for international students: Required—TOEFL (minimum score 550 paper-based; 213 computer-based; 79 iBT). *Application deadline:* Applications are processed on a rolling basis. Application fee: $30 ($40 for international students). Electronic applications accepted. *Expenses:* Tuition, state resident: full-time $6,164; part-time $342 per credit. Tuition, nonresident: full-time $10,575; part-time $588 per credit. Required fees: $806; $43 per credit. $12 per term. Tuition and fees vary according to course load, degree level and program. *Financial support:* In 2007–08, 2 research assistantships with full tuition reimbursements, 16 teaching assistantships with full tuition reimbursements were awarded; tuition waivers (full) also available. *Faculty research:* Public opinion and public policy, applied/electrical politics, international/comparative politics, the politics of criminal justice, conflict management. Total annual research expenditures: $422,767. *Unit head:* Dr. William Lyons, Interim Chair, 330-972-6291, E-mail: wtlyons@uakron.edu. *Application contact:* Dr. Ronald Gelleny, Graduate Director, 330-972-7406, E-mail: gelleny@uakron.edu.

The University of Alabama, Graduate School, College of Arts and Sciences, Department of Political Science, Tuscaloosa, AL 35487. Offers political science (MA, PhD); public administration (MPA). Part-time programs available. *Faculty:* 15 full-time (3 women). *Students:* 42 full-time (15 women), 14 part-time (8 women); includes 4 minority (2 African Americans, 2 Hispanic Americans), 7 international. Average age 30. 44 applicants, 52% accepted, 12 enrolled. In 2007, 21 master's, 4 doctorates awarded. Terminal master's awarded for partial completion of doctoral program. *Median time to degree:* Of those who began their doctoral program in fall 1999, 100% received their degree in 8 years or less. *Degree requirements:* For master's, thesis optional; for doctorate, comprehensive exam, thesis/dissertation. *Entrance requirements:* For master's and doctorate, GRE (minimum score: 1000), minimum GPA of 3.0 UG. Additional exam requirements/recommendations for international students: Required—TOEFL. *Application deadline:* For fall admission, 6/30 for domestic and international students; for spring admission, 10/15 for domestic and international students. Applications are processed on a rolling basis. Application fee: $30. *Expenses:* Tuition, state resident: full-time $5,700. Tuition, nonresident: full-time $16,518. *Financial support:* In 2007–08, 15 students received support, including teaching assistantships with full tuition reimbursements available (averaging $10,908 per year); career-related internships or fieldwork and Federal Work-Study also available. Financial award application deadline: 2/15. *Faculty research:* American politics, comparative politics, international relations, public administration, political theory. *Unit head:* Dr. David U. Lanoue, Chair and Professor, 205-348-5981, Fax: 205-348-5298, E-mail: dlanoue@bama.ua.edu. *Application contact:* Dr. Terry Royed, Graduate Advisor, 205-348-3801, Fax: 205-348-5248, E-mail: troyed@tenhoor.as.ua.edu.

University of Alberta, Faculty of Graduate Studies and Research, Department of Political Science, Edmonton, AB T6G 2E1, Canada. Offers MA, PhD. Part-time programs available. *Degree requirements:* For master's, thesis (for some programs); for doctorate, one foreign language, thesis/dissertation. *Entrance requirements:* Additional exam requirements/recommendations for international students: Required—TOEFL. *Faculty research:* Canadian politics, international relations, globalization, classical and contemporary political theory, gender and politics.

The University of Arizona, Graduate College, College of Social and Behavioral Sciences, Department of Political Science, Tucson, AZ 85721. Offers MA, PhD. *Faculty:* 22. *Students:* 34 full-time (20 women), 3 part-time (2 women); includes 4 minority (1 American Indian/Alaska Native, 1 Asian American or Pacific Islander, 2 Hispanic Americans), 6 international. Average age 28. 84 applicants, 13% accepted, 10 enrolled. In 2007, 11 master's, 2 doctorates awarded. Terminal master's awarded for partial completion of doctoral program. *Degree requirements:* For master's, thesis or alternative; for doctorate, variable foreign language requirement, comprehensive exam, thesis/dissertation. *Entrance requirements:* For master's and doctorate, GRE General Test, GRE Subject Test, minimum GPA of 3.2, 3 letters of recommendation, statement of purpose, writing sample. Additional exam requirements/recommendations for international students: Required—TOEFL (minimum score 550 paper-based). *Application deadline:* For fall admission, 1/1 for domestic and international students. Applications are processed on a rolling basis. Application fee: $50. Electronic applications accepted. *Financial support:* In 2007–08, 28 students received support, including 4 fellowships with tuition reimbursements available (averaging $5,000 per year); research assistantships with tuition reimbursements available, teaching assistantships with tuition reimbursements available, institutionally sponsored loans, scholarships/grants, health care benefits, tuition waivers (full), and unspecified assistantships also available. Financial award application deadline: 3/6. *Faculty research:* Voting behavior, political participation, Soviet domestic and Sino-Soviet relations, presidential leadership and congressional behavior. Total annual research expenditures: $74,250. *Unit head:* Dr. William Dixon, Head, 520-621-5728, Fax: 520-621-5051, E-mail: dixonw@email.arizona.edu. *Application contact:* Victoria Healey, Coordinator, 520-621-7601, Fax: 520-621-5051, E-mail: vhealey@email.arizona.edu.

University of Arkansas, Graduate School, J. William Fulbright College of Arts and Sciences, Department of Political Science, Program in Political Science, Fayetteville, AR 72701-1201. Offers MA. *Students:* 15 full-time (10 women), 7 part-time (2 women); includes 5 minority (2 African Americans, 1 American Indian/Alaska Native, 2 Hispanic Americans). In 2007, 9 degrees awarded. *Degree requirements:* For master's, thesis or alternative. *Entrance requirements:* For master's, GRE General Test. Application fee: $40 ($50 for international students). *Financial support:* In 2007–08, 1 fellowship, 5 teaching assistantships were awarded; research assistantships, career-related internships or fieldwork and Federal Work-Study also available. Support available to part-time students. Financial award application deadline: 4/1; financial award applicants required to submit FAFSA. *Unit head:* Dr. Margaret Reid, Graduate Coordinator, 479-575-3356, E-mail: mreid@uark.edu.

The University of British Columbia, Faculty of Arts and Faculty of Graduate Studies, Department of Political Science, Vancouver, BC V6T 1Z1, Canada. Offers MA, PhD. Part-time programs available. *Faculty:* 30 full-time (8 women), 3 part-time/adjunct (0 women). *Students:* 76 full-time (40 women); includes 9 minority (8 Asian Americans or Pacific Islanders, 1 Hispanic American). Average age 24. 254 applicants, 28% accepted, 23 enrolled. In 2007, 16 master's awarded. *Degree requirements:* For master's, thesis; for doctorate, comprehensive exam, thesis/dissertation. *Entrance requirements:* For master's, BA in political science; for doctorate, GRE, BA and MA in political science. Additional exam requirements/recommendations for international students: Required—TOEFL (minimum score 580 paper-based; 237 computer-based), TWE (minimum score 5). *Application deadline:* For fall admission, 1/15 for domestic and international students. Application fee: $90 Canadian dollars ($150 Canadian dollars for international students). Electronic applications accepted. *Financial support:* In 2007–08, 11 fellowships with full tuition reimbursements (averaging $16,000 Canadian dollars per year), 23 research assistantships with full tuition reimbursements (averaging $15,000 Canadian dollars per year), 48 teaching assistantships with full tuition reimbursements (averaging $10,000 Canadian dollars per year) were awarded; scholarships/grants and unspecified assistantships also available. Financial award application deadline: 10/15. *Faculty research:* Canadian politics, international relations, political theory, comparative politics, public policy. Total annual research expenditures: $969,086 Canadian dollars. *Unit head:* Dr. Allan Tupper, Head, 604-822-3387, Fax: 604-822-5540, E-mail: allan.tupper@interchange.ubc.ca. *Application contact:* Prof. Maxwell A. Cameron, Director of Graduate Studies, 604-822-3129, Fax: 604-822-5540, E-mail: cameron@politics.ubc.ca.

University of Calgary, Faculty of Graduate Studies, Faculty of Social Sciences, Department of Political Science, Calgary, AB T2N 1N4, Canada. Offers MA, PhD. *Degree requirements:* For master's, thesis; for doctorate, one foreign language, comprehensive exam, thesis/dissertation, prospectus, oral and written candidacy exams. *Entrance requirements:* For master's, minimum GPA of 3.4; for doctorate, minimum GPA of 3.7. Additional exam requirements/recommendations for international students: Required—TOEFL (minimum score 620 paper-based; 260 computer-based). Electronic applications accepted. *Faculty research:* Canadian politics, international relations, comparative politics, theory, public policy.

University of California, Berkeley, Graduate Division, College of Letters and Science, Department of Political Science, Berkeley, CA 94720-1500. Offers PhD. *Faculty:* 44 full-time, 1 part-time/adjunct. *Degree requirements:* For doctorate, thesis/dissertation, oral qualifying exams. *Entrance requirements:* For doctorate, GRE General Test, minimum GPA of 3.0, 3 letters of recommendation. *Application deadline:* For fall admission, 12/2 for domestic students. Application fee: $70 ($90 for international students). Electronic applications accepted. *Financial support:* Fellowships, research assistantships, teaching assistantships, unspecified assistantships available. *Unit head:* Pradeep Chhibber, Chair, 510-643-4408, E-mail: chhibber@berkeley.edu. *Application contact:* Janet Eva Newhall, Information Contact, 510-643-4408, E-mail: pscadmit@berkeley.edu.

University of California, Davis, Graduate Studies, Program in Political Science, Davis, CA 95616. Offers MA, PhD. Terminal master's awarded for partial completion of doctoral program. *Degree requirements:* For master's, thesis; for doctorate, thesis/dissertation. *Entrance requirements:* For master's and doctorate, GRE General Test, minimum GPA of 3.0, writing sample. Additional exam requirements/recommendations for international students: Required—TOEFL (minimum score 550 paper-based; 213 computer-based). Electronic applications accepted. *Faculty research:* American government and politics, political theory, comparative politics, international relations, public law.

University of California, Irvine, Office of Graduate Studies, School of Social Sciences, Department of Political Science, Irvine, CA 92697. Offers political psychology (PhD); political sciences (PhD); public choice (PhD). *Students:* 65 full-time (29 women); includes 13 minority (3 African Americans, 7 Asian Americans or Pacific Islanders, 3 Hispanic Americans), 3 international. In 2007, 6 doctorates awarded. *Degree requirements:* For doctorate, thesis/dissertation. *Entrance requirements:* For doctorate, GRE General Test, minimum GPA of 3.0. Additional exam requirements/recommendations for international students: Required—TOEFL (minimum score 550 paper-based; 213 computer-based). *Application deadline:* For fall admission, 1/15 priority date for domestic students; for winter admission, 10/15 priority date for domestic students. Applications are processed on a rolling basis. Application fee: $60. Electronic applications accepted. *Financial support:* Fellowships, research assistantships with full tuition reimbursements, teaching assistantships, institutionally sponsored loans, traineeships, health care benefits, and unspecified assistantships available. Financial award application deadline: 3/1; financial award applicants required to submit FAFSA. *Faculty research:* Political behavior, political economy, international relations. *Unit head:* Katherine Tate, Chair, 949-824-4012, E-mail: ktate@uci.edu. *Application contact:* Diane Enriquez, Graduate Counselor, 949-824-5924, Fax: 949-824-3548, E-mail: dmvargas@uci.edu.

University of California, Los Angeles, Graduate Division, College of Letters and Science, Department of Political Science, Los Angeles, CA 90095. Offers MA, PhD. *Students:* 142 full-time (62 women); includes 34 minority (8 African Americans, 12 Asian Americans or Pacific Islanders, 14 Hispanic Americans), 25 international. Average age 30. 341 applicants, 23% accepted, 27 enrolled. In 2007, 16 master's, 15 doctorates awarded. *Median time to degree:* Of those who began their doctoral program in fall 1999, 30% received their degree in 8 years or less. *Degree requirements:* For master's, comprehensive exam; for doctorate, one foreign language, thesis/dissertation, oral and written qualifying exams. *Entrance requirements:* For master's, GRE General Test, minimum GPA of 3.0, sample of written work, degree objective of Ph.D; for doctorate, GRE General Test, minimum undergraduate GPA of 3.0, sample of written work. *Application deadline:* For fall admission, 12/15 for domestic students. Application fee: $60. Electronic applications accepted. *Expenses:* Tuition, nonresident: full-time $5,728. Required fees: $8,966. Full-time tuition and fees vary according to program and student level. *Financial support:* In 2007–08, 78 fellowships with full tuition reimbursements, 21 research assistantships with full tuition reimbursements, 78 teaching assistantships with full tuition reimbursements were awarded; Federal Work-Study, institutionally sponsored loans, scholarships/grants, and tuition waivers (full and partial) also available. Financial award application deadline: 3/1; financial award applicants required to submit FAFSA. *Unit head:* Dr. Michael F. Lofchie, Chair, 310-825-3372. *Application contact:* Glenda Jones, Graduate Advisor, 310-825-3372, Fax: 310-825-0778, E-mail: joseph@polisci.ucla.edu.

University of California, Riverside, Graduate Division, Department of Political Science, Riverside, CA 92521-0102. Offers MA, PhD. Part-time programs available. *Faculty:* 15 full-time (4 women). *Students:* 41 full-time (13 women); includes 6 minority (2 Asian Americans or Pacific Islanders, 4 Hispanic Americans), 3 international. Average age 33. In 2007, 8 master's, 1 doctorate awarded. Terminal master's awarded for partial completion of doctoral program. *Median time to degree:* Of those who began their doctoral program in fall 1999, 100% received their degree in 8 years or less. *Degree requirements:* For master's, comprehensive exams or thesis; for doctorate, thesis/dissertation, qualifying exams. *Entrance requirements:* For master's and doctorate, GRE General Test, minimum GPA of 3.2. Additional exam requirements/recommendations for international students: Required—TOEFL (minimum score 550 paper-based; 213 computer-based; 80 iBT). *Application deadline:* For fall admission, 4/1 for domestic students, 2/1 for international students. Applications are processed on a rolling basis. Application fee: $60 ($75 for international students). Electronic applications accepted. *Financial support:* In 2007–08, fellowships with full and partial tuition reimbursements (averaging $12,000 per year), teaching assistantships with full and partial tuition reimbursements (averaging $16,500 per year) were awarded; research assistantships, career-related internships or fieldwork also available. Financial award application deadline: 12/1; financial award applicants required to submit FAFSA. *Faculty research:* American politics, mass political behavior, comparative politics, international relations, political theory. *Unit head:* Dr. John Medearis, Graduate Advisor, 951-827-4345, Fax: 951-827-3933, E-mail: politics@ucr.edu. *Application contact:* Renee D'Aguilar, Graduate Program Assistant, 951-827-5597, Fax: 951-827-3933, E-mail: politics@ucr.edu.

University of California, San Diego, Office of Graduate Studies, Department of Political Science, La Jolla, CA 92093. Offers Latin American studies (MA); political science (PhD); political science and international affairs (PhD). *Entrance requirements:* For master's and doctorate, GRE General Test. Electronic applications accepted.

University of California, San Diego, Office of Graduate Studies, Graduate School of International Relations and Pacific Studies, La Jolla, CA 92093-0520. Offers economics and international affairs (PhD); Pacific international affairs (MPIA); political science and international affairs (PhD). *Degree requirements:* For master's, one foreign language; for doctorate, thesis/dissertation. *Entrance requirements:* For master's, GMAT or GRE General Test; for

Political Science

University of California, San Diego (continued)
doctorate, GRE General Test. Additional exam requirements/recommendations for international students: Required—TOEFL (minimum score 550 paper-based; 213 computer-based). Electronic applications accepted. *Faculty research:* Pacific Rim as system and placement in global relations; studies in international economics, management and finance; analysis of patterns of policymaking in countries of the Pacific.

See Close-Up on page 1171.

University of California, Santa Barbara, Graduate Division, College of Letters and Sciences, Division of Social Sciences, Department of Political Science, Santa Barbara, CA 93106. Offers MA, PhD, MA/PhD. Part-time programs available. *Faculty:* 21 full-time (9 women), 7 part-time/adjunct (3 women). *Students:* 57 full-time (27 women); includes 11 minority (3 Asian Americans or Pacific Islanders, 8 Hispanic Americans), 6 international. Average age 30. 90 applicants, 33% accepted, 8 enrolled. In 2007, 3 master's, 8 doctorates awarded. Terminal master's awarded for partial completion of doctoral program. *Median time to degree:* Of those who began their doctoral program in fall 1999, 14% received their degree in 8 years or less. *Degree requirements:* For master's, comprehensive exam, thesis optional; for doctorate, one foreign language, comprehensive exam, thesis/dissertation. *Entrance requirements:* For master's, GRE General Test, bachelor's degree with minimum GPA of 3.0; for doctorate, GRE General Test, master's degree with minimum GPA of 3.0. Additional exam requirements/recommendations for international students: Required—TOEFL (minimum score 600 paper-based; 250 computer-based; 100 iBT). *Application deadline:* For fall admission, 1/1 for domestic and international students. Applications are processed on a rolling basis. Application fee: $60. Electronic applications accepted. *Expenses:* Tuition, nonresident: full-time $14,888. Required fees: $10,108. *Financial support:* In 2007–08, 22 students received support, including 11 fellowships (averaging $10,159 per year), 76 teaching assistantships (averaging $16,389 per year); Federal Work-Study, scholarships/grants, and health care benefits also available. Financial award application deadline: 1/1; financial award applicants required to submit FAFSA. *Faculty research:* Identity and politics communication and politics, politics of public policy. *Unit head:* Dr. John Woolley, Chair, 805-893-3623, E-mail: wooley@polsci.ucsb.edu. *Application contact:* Linda James, Graduate Program Assistant, 805-893-3626, Fax: 805-893-3309, E-mail: james@polsci.ucsb.edu.

University of California, Santa Cruz, Division of Graduate Studies, Division of Social Sciences, Politics Department, Santa Cruz, CA 95064. Offers PhD. *Faculty:* 15 full-time (5 women). *Students:* 35 full-time (23 women). 67 applicants, 15% accepted, 3 enrolled. *Entrance requirements:* Additional exam requirements/recommendations for international students: Required—TOEFL. *Application deadline:* For fall admission, 1/15 for domestic students. Application fee: $60. Electronic applications accepted. *Expenses:* Tuition, nonresident: full-time $14,694. Required fees: $11,360. *Unit head:* Michael K. Brown, Chair, 831-459-2052, E-mail: popcorn@ucsc.edu. *Application contact:* Judy L. Glass, Reporting Analyst for Graduate Admissions, 831-459-5906, Fax: 831-459-4843, E-mail: jlglass@ucsc.edu.

University of Central Florida, College of Sciences, Department of Political Science, Orlando, FL 32816. Offers environmental politics (MA); international studies (MA); political analysis and policy (MA). Part-time and evening/weekend programs available. *Faculty:* 24 full-time (7 women), 8 part-time/adjunct (2 women). *Students:* Average age 30. *Degree requirements:* For master's, comprehensive exam, thesis. *Entrance requirements:* For master's, GRE General Test, minimum GPA of 3.0 in last 60 hours. Additional exam requirements/recommendations for international students: Required—TOEFL. *Application deadline:* For fall admission, 7/15 for domestic students; for spring admission, 12/1 for domestic students. Application fee: $30. Electronic applications accepted. *Expenses:* Tuition, state resident: full-time $6,484. Tuition, nonresident: full-time $23,938. Tuition and fees vary according to program. *Financial support:* Fellowships with partial tuition reimbursements, research assistantships with partial tuition reimbursements, teaching assistantships with partial tuition reimbursements, career-related internships or fieldwork, Federal Work-Study, institutionally sponsored loans, tuition waivers (partial), and unspecified assistantships available. Financial award application deadline: 3/1; financial award applicants required to submit FAFSA. *Faculty research:* Environment, presidential campaigning, term limits for elected officials. *Unit head:* Dr. Roger Handberg, Chair, 407-823-2608, Fax: 407-823-0051.

University of Central Oklahoma, College of Graduate Studies and Research, College of Liberal Arts, Department of Political Science, Program in Political Science, Edmond, OK 73034-5209. Offers MA. Part-time programs available. *Faculty:* 6 full-time (1 woman), 1 part-time/adjunct (0 women). *Students:* Average age 22. 2 applicants, 100% accepted. *Entrance requirements:* Additional exam requirements/recommendations for international students: Required—TOEFL (minimum score 550 paper-based; 213 computer-based). *Application deadline:* For fall admission, 7/1 for international students; for spring admission, 11/1 for international students. Applications are processed on a rolling basis. Application fee: $25. Electronic applications accepted. *Expenses:* Tuition, state resident: full-time $3,516; part-time $147 per hour. Tuition, nonresident: full-time $9,054; part-time $377 per hour. Required fees: $433; $18 per hour. *Financial support:* Unspecified assistantships available. Financial award application deadline: 3/31; financial award applicants required to submit FAFSA. *Faculty research:* U. S. Congress. *Unit head:* Dr. Jan Hardt, Adviser, 405-974-5840, E-mail: jhardt@aix1.ucok.edu.

University of Chicago, Division of Social Sciences, Department of Political Science, Chicago, IL 60637-1513. Offers PhD. *Students:* 148. In 2007, 10 degrees awarded. *Degree requirements:* For doctorate, one foreign language, thesis/dissertation, exam, qualifying paper. *Entrance requirements:* For doctorate, GRE General Test. Additional exam requirements/recommendations for international students: Required—TOEFL, IELTS (minimum score 7). *Application deadline:* For fall admission, 12/15 for domestic and international students. Application fee: $55. Electronic applications accepted. *Financial support:* Fellowships, research assistantships, teaching assistantships, Federal Work-Study, institutionally sponsored loans, scholarships/grants, traineeships, health care benefits, and unspecified assistantships available. Financial award application deadline: 12/15. *Faculty research:* Political philosophy, international political economy, strategic studies, public policy and race relations, comparative politics (China, Middle East, Soviet Union, Africa, India, Japan). *Unit head:* Prof. Lisa Wedeen, Chair, 773-702-8050. *Application contact:* Office of the Dean of Students, 773-702-8415.

University of Cincinnati, Graduate School, McMicken College of Arts and Sciences, Department of Political Science, Cincinnati, OH 45221. Offers MA, PhD. *Faculty:* 12 full-time (2 women). *Students:* 37 full-time (11 women), 7 part-time (4 women); includes 2 minority (1 African American, 1 Asian American or Pacific Islander), 21 international. Average age 29. 25 applicants, 44% accepted, 4 enrolled. In 2007, 4 master's awarded. Terminal master's awarded for partial completion of doctoral program. *Degree requirements:* For master's, thesis (for some programs); for doctorate, thesis/dissertation. *Entrance requirements:* For master's and doctorate, GRE General Test, GRE Subject Test. Additional exam requirements/recommendations for international students: Required—TOEFL. *Application deadline:* For fall admission, 1/15 for domestic and international students. Application fee: $30. Electronic applications accepted. *Financial support:* In 2007–08, 17 students received support, including 10 fellowships with tuition reimbursements available (averaging $10,050 per year); tuition waivers (partial) and unspecified assistantships also available. Financial award application deadline: 1/15; financial award applicants required to submit FAFSA. *Faculty research:* International security, methodology, American politics, comparative politics. *Unit head:* Dr. Joel Wolfe, Head, 513-556-3307, Fax: 513-556-2314, E-mail: joel.wolfe@uc.edu. *Application contact:* Joseph Waddle, Administrative Assistant, 513-556-3300, Fax: 513-556-2314, E-mail: waddlejw@email.uc.edu.

University of Colorado at Boulder, Graduate School, College of Arts and Sciences, Department of Political Science, Boulder, CO 80309. Offers international affairs (MA); political science (MA, PhD); public policy (MA). *Faculty:* 27. *Students:* 49 full-time (22 women), 20 part-time (8 women); includes 5 minority (3 Asian Americans or Pacific Islanders, 2 Hispanic Americans), 9 international. Average age 29. 64 applicants, 50% accepted. In 2007, 16 master's, 7 doctorates awarded. Terminal master's awarded for partial completion of doctoral program. *Degree requirements:* For master's, comprehensive exam, thesis; for doctorate, one foreign language, thesis/dissertation. *Entrance requirements:* For master's, GRE General Test, minimum undergraduate GPA of 3.0; for doctorate, GRE General Test, minimum GPA of 3.5 (undergraduate), 3.0 (graduate). *Application deadline:* For fall admission, 12/31 priority date for domestic students, 12/31 for international students. Application fee: $50 ($60 for international students). *Financial support:* In 2007–08, 5 fellowships (averaging $3,024 per year), 1 research assistantship (averaging $16,252 per year) were awarded; Federal Work-Study also available. Financial award application deadline: 12/31. *Faculty research:* American government and politics, comparative politics, international relations, law and politics, public policy, political philosophy, empirical theory and methodology. Total annual research expenditures: $427,386. *Unit head:* Steven Chan, Chair, 303-492-8601, Fax: 303-492-0978, E-mail: steve.chan@colorado.edu. *Application contact:* Mary Gregory, Graduate Program Assistant, 303-492-7872, Fax: 303-492-0978, E-mail: pscigrad@colorado.edu.

University of Colorado Denver, College of Liberal Arts and Sciences, Department of Political Science, Denver, CO 80217-3364. Offers MA. Part-time and evening/weekend programs available. *Faculty:* 12 full-time (4 women). *Students:* 14 full-time (8 women), 47 part-time (26 women); includes 12 minority (1 African American, 4 American Indian/Alaska Native, 7 Hispanic Americans), 4 international. Average age 35. 28 applicants, 71% accepted, 11 enrolled. In 2007, 24 degrees awarded. *Degree requirements:* For master's, thesis or alternative. *Entrance requirements:* For master's, GRE, 18 hours of course work in political science. Additional exam requirements/recommendations for international students: Required—TOEFL (minimum score 525 paper-based; 197 computer-based). *Application deadline:* For fall admission, 6/1 for domestic students; for spring admission, 11/1 for domestic students. Applications are processed on a rolling basis. Application fee: $50 ($75 for international students). Electronic applications accepted. *Financial support:* Research assistantships, teaching assistantships, Federal Work-Study available. Financial award application deadline: 4/1; financial award applicants required to submit FAFSA. *Faculty research:* Palestinian peace process, post-Soviet governmental corruption, gender/racial/ethnic politics in the U.S.A., U.S. immigration. *Unit head:* Jana Everett, Chair, 303-556-3515, Fax: 303-556-4861, E-mail: jana.everett@cudenver.edu. *Application contact:* Cory Gruebele, Program Assistant, 303-556-3556, Fax: 303-556-6041, E-mail: corwin.lydel.gruebele@cudenver.edu.

University of Connecticut, Graduate School, College of Liberal Arts and Sciences, Department of Political Science, Field of Political Science, Storrs, CT 06269. Offers MA, PhD. *Faculty:* 34 full-time (11 women). *Students:* 64 full-time (21 women), 17 part-time (3 women); includes 8 minority (2 African Americans, 1 Asian American or Pacific Islander, 5 Hispanic Americans), 14 international. Average age 32. 109 applicants, 21% accepted, 19 enrolled. In 2007, 7 master's, 3 doctorates awarded. Terminal master's awarded for partial completion of doctoral program. *Degree requirements:* For master's, comprehensive exam; for doctorate, 2 foreign languages, thesis/dissertation. *Entrance requirements:* For master's and doctorate, GRE General Test. Additional exam requirements/recommendations for international students: Required—TOEFL (minimum score 550 paper-based; 213 computer-based). *Application deadline:* For fall admission, 2/1 priority date for domestic and international students; for spring admission, 11/1 for domestic students, 10/1 for international students. Applications are processed on a rolling basis. Application fee: $55. Electronic applications accepted. *Expenses:* Tuition, state resident: part-time $469 per credit hour. Tuition, nonresident: part-time $1,218 per credit hour. *Financial support:* In 2007–08, 13 research assistantships with full tuition reimbursements, 39 teaching assistantships with full tuition reimbursements were awarded; fellowships, career-related internships or fieldwork, Federal Work-Study, scholarships/grants, health care benefits, and unspecified assistantships also available. Financial award application deadline: 2/1; financial award applicants required to submit FAFSA. *Application contact:* Prof. John Garry Clifford, Director of Graduate Studies, 860-486-2079, Fax: 860-486-3347, E-mail: john.clifford@uconn.edu.

University of Dallas, Braniff Graduate School of Liberal Arts, Institute of Philosophic Studies, Doctoral Program in Politics, Irving, TX 75062-4736. Offers PhD. *Faculty:* 3 part-time/adjunct (0 women). *Students:* 17 full-time (2 women), 3 part-time, 5 international. Average age 30. 9 applicants, 67% accepted, 4 enrolled. In 2007, 1 degree awarded. *Degree requirements:* For doctorate, 2 foreign languages, comprehensive exam, thesis/dissertation. *Entrance requirements:* For doctorate, GRE General Test. Additional exam requirements/recommendations for international students: Required—TOEFL. *Application deadline:* For fall admission, 2/15 priority date for domestic students. Application fee: $50. *Expenses:* Tuition: Part-time $600 per credit. Required fees: $15 per credit. *Financial support:* In 2007–08, 18 students received support. Scholarships/grants available. Financial award application deadline: 2/15. *Faculty research:* Classical, medieval, and modern political philosophy; American political thought and institutions; politics and literature. *Unit head:* Dr. Leo Paul de Alvarez, Chair, 972-721-5344, Fax: 972-721-4007, E-mail: alvarez@udallas.edu. *Application contact:* Graduate Coordinator, 972-721-5106, Fax: 972-721-5280, E-mail: graduate@acad.udallas.edu.

University of Dallas, Braniff Graduate School of Liberal Arts, Master's Program in Politics, Irving, TX 75062-4736. Offers M Pol, MA. Part-time programs available. *Faculty:* 2 part-time/adjunct (0 women). *Students:* 7 full-time (4 women), 2 part-time (1 woman); includes 4 minority (1 African American, 1 Asian American or Pacific Islander, 2 Hispanic Americans). Average age 24. 8 applicants, 100% accepted, 6 enrolled. In 2007, 9 degrees awarded. *Degree requirements:* For master's, one foreign language, comprehensive exam, thesis. *Entrance requirements:* For master's, GRE General Test. Additional exam requirements/recommendations for international students: Required—TOEFL. *Application deadline:* For fall admission, 2/15 priority date for domestic students; for spring admission, 11/15 for domestic students. Applications are processed on a rolling basis. Application fee: $50. *Expenses:* Tuition: Part-time $600 per credit. Required fees: $15 per credit. *Financial support:* In 2007–08, 8 students received support. Scholarships/grants available. Financial award application deadline: 2/15. *Faculty research:* Classical, medieval, and modern political philosophy; American political thought and institutions; politics and literature. *Unit head:* Dr. Leo Paul de Alvarez, Chair, 972-721-5344, Fax: 972-721-4007, E-mail: alvarez@udallas.edu. *Application contact:* Graduate Coordinator, 972-721-5106, Fax: 972-721-5280, E-mail: graduate@acad.udallas.edu.

University of Delaware, College of Arts and Sciences, Department of Political Science and International Relations, Newark, DE 19716. Offers MA, PhD. *Faculty:* 19 full-time (6 women). *Students:* 44 full-time (17 women), 2 part-time (both women); includes 4 minority (2 African Americans, 2 Hispanic Americans), 20 international. Average age 28. 82 applicants, 35% accepted, 10 enrolled. In 2007, 10 master's, 1 doctorate awarded. Terminal master's awarded for partial completion of doctoral program. *Degree requirements:* For master's, research paper; for doctorate, one foreign language, comprehensive exam, thesis/dissertation. *Entrance requirements:* For master's and doctorate, GRE General Test, minimum GPA of 3.2 in major, 3.0 overall. Additional exam requirements/recommendations for international students: Required—TOEFL (minimum score 600 paper-based). *Application deadline:* For fall admission, 5/15 priority date for domestic students. Application fee: $60. Electronic applications accepted. *Financial support:* In 2007–08, 31 students received support, including 2 fellowships with full tuition reimbursements available (averaging $14,600 per year), 23 teaching assistantships with full tuition reimbursements available (averaging $14,600 per year); research assistantships with full tuition reimbursements available, career-related internships or fieldwork, Federal Work-Study, institutionally sponsored loans, scholarships/grants, and tuition waivers (full and partial) also available. Financial award application deadline: 2/1. *Faculty research:* Social constructivism, international migration, international security, democratization, human rights. Total annual research expenditures: $246,882. *Unit head:* Dr. Gretchen M. Bauer, Chair, 302-831-2355, Fax: 302-831-4452. *Application contact:* Prof. Daniel Green, Graduate Director, 302-831-1933, Fax: 302-831-4452, E-mail: dgreen@udel.edu.

University of Florida, Graduate School, College of Liberal Arts and Sciences, Department of Political Science, Gainesville, FL 32611. Offers international development policy and administration (MA, Certificate); international relations (MA, MAT); political campaigning (MA,

Certificate); political science (MA, MAT, PhD); public affairs (MA, Certificate); JD/MA. Part-time programs available. *Faculty:* 32 full-time (6 women). *Students:* 123 (44 women); includes 7 minority (1 African American, 1 Asian American or Pacific Islander, 5 Hispanic Americans) 12 international. In 2007, 25 master's, 7 doctorates awarded. Terminal master's awarded for partial completion of doctoral program. *Degree requirements:* For master's, variable foreign language requirement, thesis or alternative; for doctorate, variable foreign language requirement, thesis/dissertation. *Entrance requirements:* For master's and doctorate, GRE General Test, minimum GPA of 3.0. Additional exam requirements/recommendations for international students: Required—TOEFL (minimum score 550 paper-based; 213 computer-based). *Application deadline:* For fall admission, 3/16 priority date for domestic students. Applications are processed on a rolling basis. Application fee: $30. Electronic applications accepted. *Expenses:* Tuition, state resident: full-time $7,478. Tuition, nonresident: full-time $22,603. *Financial support:* In 2007–08, 1 research assistantship (averaging $16,666 per year), 39 teaching assistantships (averaging $17,071 per year) were awarded; fellowships, career-related internships or fieldwork, Federal Work-Study, institutionally sponsored loans, and unspecified assistantships also available. Financial award application deadline: 1/15. *Faculty research:* U.S. political development, religion and politics, environmental politics and policy, developing societies, international relations. *Unit head:* Philip J. Williams, Chair, 352-392-0262 Ext. 247, Fax: 352-392-8127, E-mail: pjw@polisci.ufl.edu. *Application contact:* Dr. J. Samuel Barkin, Coordinator, 352-392-0262 Ext. 222, Fax: 352-392-8127, E-mail: barkin@polisci.ufl.edu.

University of Georgia, School of Public and International Affairs, Program in Political Science, Athens, GA 30602. Offers MA, PhD. *Faculty:* 15 full-time (3 women). *Students:* 65 full-time (21 women), 10 part-time (3 women); includes 2 minority (1 African American, 1 Asian American or Pacific Islander), 22 international. 148 applicants, 20% accepted, 17 enrolled. In 2007, 17 master's, 4 doctorates awarded. *Degree requirements:* For master's, one foreign language, thesis; for doctorate, one foreign language, thesis/dissertation. *Entrance requirements:* For master's and doctorate, GRE General Test. *Application deadline:* For fall admission, 7/1 priority date for domestic students; for spring admission, 11/15 for domestic students. Application fee: $50. Electronic applications accepted. *Financial support:* Fellowships, research assistantships, teaching assistantships, unspecified assistantships available. *Unit head:* Dr. Robert Grafstein, Head, 706-542-2057, E-mail: bobgraf@uga.edu. *Application contact:* Dr. Audrey A. Haynes, Graduate Coordinator, 706-542-2933, Fax: 706-542-4421, E-mail: polaah@uga.edu.

University of Guelph, Graduate Program Services, College of Social and Applied Human Sciences, Department of Political Science, Guelph, ON N1G 2W1, Canada. Offers comparative politics (MA); international development (MA); political science (MA); public policy and public administration (MA); the Americas (Canada emphasis) (MA). MA in public policy and public administration offered in collaboration with Department of Political Science of McMaster University. *Faculty:* 20 full-time (8 women), 2 part-time/adjunct (0 women). *Students:* 41 full-time (25 women). Average age 26. 130 applicants, 23% accepted, 25 enrolled. In 2007, 19 degrees awarded. *Degree requirements:* For master's, thesis or paper. *Entrance requirements:* For master's, minimum B average during previous 2 years of course work, 4 year Honours Degree in Political Science. Additional exam requirements/recommendations for international students: Required—TOEFL. *Application deadline:* For fall admission, 2/1 for domestic and international students. Application fee: $85. Electronic applications accepted. *Financial support:* In 2007–08, 9 research assistantships (averaging $2,000 per year), 58 teaching assistantships (averaging $5,106 per year) were awarded; scholarships/grants also available. *Faculty research:* Political ethics, constitutional power. *Unit head:* Dr. B. Sheldrick, Chair, 519-824-4120 Ext. 56503, Fax: 519-822-7703, E-mail: sheldric@uoguelph.ca. *Application contact:* Dr. C. Johnson, Coordinator, 519-824-4120, Fax: 519-822-7703, E-mail: cajohnso@uoguelph.ca.

University of Hawaii at Manoa, Graduate Division, Colleges of Arts and Sciences, College of Social Sciences, Department of Political Science, Honolulu, HI 96822. Offers MA, PhD. Part-time programs available. *Faculty:* 32 full-time (14 women), 7 part-time/adjunct (1 woman). *Students:* 91 full-time (43 women), 47 part-time (24 women); includes 46 minority (2 African Americans, 2 American Indian/Alaska Native, 39 Asian Americans or Pacific Islanders, 3 Hispanic Americans), 36 international. Average age 33. 169 applicants, 33% accepted, 31 enrolled.Terminal master's awarded for partial completion of doctoral program. *Median time to degree:* Of those who began their doctoral program in fall 1999, 36% received their degree in 8 years or less. *Degree requirements:* For master's, thesis optional; for doctorate, comprehensive exam, thesis/dissertation. *Entrance requirements:* Additional exam requirements/recommendations for international students: Required—TOEFL (minimum score 540 paper-based; 207 computer-based; 76 iBT), IELTS (minimum score 5). *Application deadline:* For fall admission, 2/1 for domestic students, 1/15 for international students. Application fee: $50. *Financial support:* In 2007–08, 10 research assistantships (averaging $16,937 per year), 16 teaching assistantships (averaging $14,638 per year) were awarded; career-related internships or fieldwork, Federal Work-Study, and institutionally sponsored loans also available. Support available to part-time students. Financial award application deadline: 3/1. *Faculty research:* Asia/Pacific, political economy, human rights, futures, postmodernism. *Application contact:* Manfred Henningsen, Graduate Chair, 808-956-7513, E-mail: hennings@hawaii.edu.

University of Houston, College of Liberal Arts and Social Sciences, Department of Political Science, Houston, TX 77204. Offers MA, PhD. Part-time and evening/weekend programs available. *Faculty:* 12 full-time (2 women), 3 part-time/adjunct (1 woman). *Students:* 32 full-time (17 women), 45 part-time (16 women); includes 14 minority (5 African Americans, 1 American Indian/Alaska Native, 4 Asian Americans or Pacific Islanders, 4 Hispanic Americans), 10 international. Average age 35. 29 applicants, 69% accepted, 13 enrolled. In 2007, 13 master's, 3 doctorates awarded. *Degree requirements:* For doctorate, thesis/dissertation. *Entrance requirements:* For master's and doctorate, GRE General Test, minimum GPA of 3.0. *Application deadline:* For fall admission, 4/1 for domestic students; for spring admission, 10/1 for domestic students. Applications are processed on a rolling basis. Application fee: $0. *Expenses:* Tuition, state resident: full-time $6,297; part-time $262 per credit. Tuition, nonresident: full-time $12,969; part-time $540 per credit. Required fees: $2,696. *Financial support:* In 2007–08, 26 teaching assistantships with full tuition reimbursements (averaging $12,850 per year) were awarded; fellowships with full tuition reimbursements, research assistantships with full tuition reimbursements, career-related internships or fieldwork, Federal Work-Study, institutionally sponsored loans, scholarships/grants, health care benefits, and unspecified assistantships also available. Support available to part-time students. Financial award application deadline: 2/1. *Faculty research:* American politics, political theory, judicial process, public policy, comparative politics. *Unit head:* Dr. Harrell Rodgers, Chairperson, 713-743-3890, Fax: 713-743-3927, E-mail: hrodgers@uh.edu. *Application contact:* Director of Graduate Studies, 713-743-3890, E-mail: polsgrad@bayou.uh.edu.

University of Idaho, College of Graduate Studies, College of Letters, Arts and Social Sciences, Department of Political Science and Public Affairs Research, Program in Political Science, Moscow, ID 83844-2282. Offers MA, PhD. *Students:* 13 (5 women). Average age 37. In 2007, 2 master's, 1 doctorate awarded. *Degree requirements:* For doctorate, thesis/dissertation. *Entrance requirements:* For master's, minimum GPA of 2.8; for doctorate, minimum undergraduate GPA of 2.8, 3.0 graduate. *Application deadline:* For fall admission, 8/1 for domestic students; for spring admission, 12/15 for domestic students. Application fee: $55 ($60 for international students). *Financial support:* Application deadline: 2/15. *Unit head:* Dr. Donald W. Crowley, Chair, Department of Political Science and Public Affairs Research, 208-885-6328.

University of Illinois at Chicago, Graduate College, College of Liberal Arts and Sciences, Department of Political Science, Chicago, IL 60607-7128. Offers MA, PhD. Part-time programs available. Terminal master's awarded for partial completion of doctoral program. *Degree requirements:* For master's, thesis or comprehensive exam. *Entrance requirements:* For master's, GRE General Test, minimum GPA of 3.0. Additional exam requirements/recommendations for international students: Required—TOEFL. Electronic applications accepted. *Faculty research:* Policy analysis/national urban politics and policy, electoral behavior.

University of Illinois at Springfield, Graduate Programs, College of Public Affairs and Administration, Program in Political Studies, Springfield, IL 62703-5407. Offers MA. Part-time and evening/weekend programs available. *Faculty:* 12 full-time (2 women), 1 part-time/adjunct (0 women). *Students:* 22 full-time (8 women), 52 part-time (20 women); includes 14 minority (10 African Americans, 2 Asian Americans or Pacific Islanders, 2 Hispanic Americans), 1 international. Average age 29. 36 applicants, 86% accepted, 23 enrolled. In 2007, 17 degrees awarded. *Degree requirements:* For master's, group research project, comprehensive exam, project, or thesis. *Entrance requirements:* For master's, minimum undergraduate GPA of 3.0. Additional exam requirements/recommendations for international students: Required—TOEFL (minimum score 550 paper-based; 213 computer-based). *Application deadline:* Applications are processed on a rolling basis. Application fee: $50 ($60 for international students). Electronic applications accepted. *Expenses:* Tuition, state resident: full-time $5,424; part-time $226 per credit hour. Tuition, nonresident: part-time $553 per credit hour. Required fees: $618 per term. *Financial support:* In 2007–08, research assistantships with full tuition reimbursements (averaging $7,988 per year), teaching assistantships with full tuition reimbursements (averaging $7,988 per year) were awarded; career-related internships or fieldwork, Federal Work-Study, scholarships/grants, health care benefits, and unspecified assistantships also available. Support available to part-time students. Financial award application deadline: 11/15; financial award applicants required to submit FAFSA. *Unit head:* Dr. Calvin Mouw, Program Administrator, 217-206-7884, Fax: 217-206-7807, E-mail: mouw.calvin@uis.edu.

University of Illinois at Urbana–Champaign, Graduate College, College of Liberal Arts and Sciences, Department of Political Science, Champaign, IL 61820. Offers MA, PhD. *Faculty:* 31 full-time (10 women), 3 part-time/adjunct (0 women). *Students:* 66 full-time (31 women), 1 (woman) part-time; includes 7 minority (4 African Americans, 3 Asian Americans or Pacific Islanders), 15 international. 151 applicants, 9% accepted, 15 enrolled. In 2007, 4 master's, 4 doctorates awarded. *Degree requirements:* For doctorate, thesis/dissertation. *Entrance requirements:* For master's, GRE General Test, minimum GPA of 3.0; for doctorate, GRE. *Application deadline:* For fall admission, 1/2 for domestic students; for spring admission, 1/2 for domestic students. Applications are processed on a rolling basis. Application fee: $60 ($75 for international students). Electronic applications accepted. *Financial support:* In 2007–08, 46 fellowships, 27 research assistantships, 37 teaching assistantships were awarded. Financial award application deadline: 2/15. *Unit head:* William Bernhard, Head, 217-333-3880, Fax: 217-244-5712, E-mail: bernhard@uiuc.edu. *Application contact:* Brenda R. Stamm, Secretary, 217-333-2602, Fax: 217-244-5712, E-mail: stamm@uiuc.edu.

The University of Iowa, Graduate College, College of Liberal Arts and Sciences, Department of Political Science, Iowa City, IA 52242-1316. Offers MA, PhD. *Faculty:* 26 full-time, 2 part-time/adjunct. *Students:* 32 full-time (5 women), 18 part-time (8 women); includes 3 minority (1 African American, 1 Asian American or Pacific Islander, 1 Hispanic American), 13 international. 85 applicants, 47% accepted, 15 enrolled. In 2007, 10 master's, 5 doctorates awarded. *Degree requirements:* For master's, thesis optional, exam; for doctorate, comprehensive exam, thesis/dissertation. *Entrance requirements:* For master's and doctorate, GRE General Test, minimum GPA of 3.0. Additional exam requirements/recommendations for international students: Required—TOEFL (minimum score 600 paper-based; 250 computer-based; 100 iBT). *Application deadline:* For fall admission, 2/1 priority date for domestic and international students. Applications are processed on a rolling basis. Application fee: $60 ($85 for international students). Electronic applications accepted. *Expenses:* Tuition, state resident: part-time $349 per hour. Tuition, nonresident: part-time $349 per hour. Tuition and fees vary according to course load and program. *Financial support:* In 2007–08, 2 fellowships, 4 research assistantships with partial tuition reimbursements, 24 teaching assistantships with partial tuition reimbursements were awarded. Financial award application deadline: 2/1; financial award applicants required to submit FAFSA. *Unit head:* Tom Rice, Chair, 319-335-2358, Fax: 319-335-3400.

University of Kansas, Research and Graduate Studies, College of Liberal Arts and Sciences, Department of Political Science, Lawrence, KS 66045. Offers MA, PhD. Part-time programs available. *Faculty:* 25 full-time. *Students:* 41 full-time (16 women), 4 part-time (1 woman); includes 1 minority (Asian American or Pacific Islander), 11 international. Average age 30. 67 applicants, 61% accepted, 12 enrolled. In 2007, 4 master's, 3 doctorates awarded. Terminal master's awarded for partial completion of doctoral program. *Degree requirements:* For master's, comprehensive exam, thesis or alternative; for doctorate, comprehensive exam, thesis/dissertation, Research skills. *Entrance requirements:* For master's and doctorate, GRE General Test, 3 letters of recommendation, transcripts, personal statement, CV. Additional exam requirements/recommendations for international students: Required—TOEFL. *Application deadline:* For fall admission, 1/10 for domestic and international students. Application fee: $55 ($60 for international students). Electronic applications accepted. *Expenses:* Tuition, state resident: full-time $5,838. Tuition, nonresident: full-time $13,409. Tuition and fees vary according to program. *Financial support:* Fellowships with full tuition reimbursements, research assistantships, teaching assistantships with full tuition reimbursements, scholarships/grants, health care benefits, and unspecified assistantships available. Financial award application deadline: 1/10. *Faculty research:* Public policy, political economy and development, political institutions and organized interests, international conflict and cooperation. *Unit head:* Elaine Sharp, Chair, 785-864-3523, Fax: 785-864-5700, E-mail: esharp@ku.edu. *Application contact:* Juliet Kaarbo, Graduate Director, 785-864-3523, Fax: 785-864-5700, E-mail: jkaarbo@ku.edu.

University of Kentucky, Graduate School, College of Arts and Sciences, Program in Political Science, Lexington, KY 40506-0032. Offers MA, PhD. *Faculty:* 18 full-time (3 women). *Students:* 34 full-time (4 women), 7 part-time (1 woman), 11 international. Average age 32. 69 applicants, 52% accepted, 10 enrolled. In 2007, 4 master's, 2 doctorates awarded. *Median time to degree:* Of those who began their doctoral program in fall 1999, 83% received their degree in 8 years or less. *Degree requirements:* For master's, comprehensive exam, thesis optional; for doctorate, comprehensive exam, thesis/dissertation. *Entrance requirements:* For master's, GRE General Test, minimum undergraduate GPA of 2.75; for doctorate, GRE General Test, minimum graduate GPA of 3.0. Additional exam requirements/recommendations for international students: Required—TOEFL (minimum score 550 paper-based; 213 computer-based). *Application deadline:* For fall admission, 7/17 priority date for domestic students, 2/1 priority date for international students; for spring admission, 12/13 priority date for domestic students, 6/15 priority date for international students. Application fee: $50 ($65 for international students). Electronic applications accepted. *Expenses:* Tuition, state resident: part-time $437 per credit hour. Tuition, nonresident: part-time $931 per credit hour. *Financial support:* In 2007–08, 17 students received support, including 4 research assistantships (averaging $12,050 per year), 15 teaching assistantships (averaging $12,100 per year); fellowships, Federal Work-Study, institutionally sponsored loans, scholarships/grants, traineeships, tuition waivers (partial), and unspecified assistantships also available. Support available to part-time students. Financial award application deadline: 3/15. *Faculty research:* International political economy, critical policy studies, regional conflict and integration, race and American politics, media studies. Total annual research expenditures: $25,000. *Unit head:* Dr. Horace A. Bartilow, Director of Graduate Studies, 859-257-7031, Fax: 859-257-7034. *Application contact:* Dr. Brian Jackson, Senior Associate Dean, 859-257-4667, Fax: 859-257-4676, E-mail: brian.jackson@uky.edu.

University of Lethbridge, School of Graduate Studies, Lethbridge, AB T1K 3M4, Canada. Offers accounting (MScM); addictions counseling (M Sc); agricultural biotechnology (M Sc); agricultural studies (M Sc, MA); anthropology (MA); archaeology (MA); art (MA); biochemistry (M Sc); biological sciences (M Sc); biomolecular science (PhD); biosystems and biodiversity (PhD); Canadian studies (MA); chemistry (M Sc); computer science (M Sc); computer science and geographical information science (M Sc); counseling psychology (M Ed); dramatic arts (MA); earth, space, and physical science (PhD); economics (MA); educational leadership (M Ed); English (MA); environmental science (M Sc); evolution and behavior (PhD); exercise science (M Sc); finance (MScM); French (MA); French/German (MA); French/Spanish (MA); general education (M Ed); general management (MScM); geography (M Sc, MA); German (MA); health sciences (M Sc, MA); history (MA); human resource management and labour relations (MScM); individualized multidisciplinary (M Sc, MA); information systems (MScM); international management (MScM); kinesiology (M Sc, MA); management (M Sc, MA); marketing

Political Science

University of Lethbridge (continued)

(MScM); mathematics (M Sc); music (MA); Native American studies (MA); neuroscience (M Sc, PhD); new media (MA); nursing (M Sc); philosophy (MA); physics (M Sc); policy and strategy (MScM); political science (MA); psychology (M Sc, MA); religious studies (MA); sociology (MA); theoretical and computational science (PhD); urban and regional studies (MA). Part-time and evening/weekend programs available. *Students:* 215 full-time, 98 part-time. In 2007, 87 master's, 1 doctorate awarded. *Degree requirements:* For doctorate, comprehensive exam, thesis/dissertation. *Entrance requirements:* For master's, GMAT (M Sc in management), bachelor's degree in related field, minimum GPA of 3.0 during previous 20 graded semester courses, 2 years teaching or related experience (M Ed); for doctorate, master's degree, minimum graduate GPA of 3.5. Additional exam requirements/recommendations for international students: Required—TOEFL. Application fee: $60 Canadian dollars. *Financial support:* Fellowships, research assistantships, teaching assistantships, scholarships/grants, health care benefits, and unspecified assistantships available. *Faculty research:* Movement and brain plasticity, gibberellin physiology, photosynthesis, carbon cycling, molecular properties of main-group ring components. *Unit head:* Dr. Jo-Anne Fiske, Interim Dean, 403-329-2121, Fax: 403-329-2097. *Application contact:* Jennifer Geddes, Graduate Liaison Officer, 403-329-2762, Fax: 403-329-5159, E-mail: jennifer.geddes@uleth.ca.

University of Louisville, Graduate School, College of Arts and Sciences, Department of Political Science, Louisville, KY 40292-0001. Offers MA. *Students:* 12 full-time (3 women), 13 part-time (10 women); includes 4 minority (2 African Americans, 1 Asian American or Pacific Islander, 1 Hispanic American), 1 international. Average age 29. In 2007, 21 degrees awarded. *Degree requirements:* For master's, thesis (for some programs), thesis or directed research paper. *Entrance requirements:* For master's, GRE General Test, letters of recommendation. *Application deadline:* For fall admission, 8/1 for domestic students; for spring admission, 12/1 for domestic students. Applications are processed on a rolling basis. Application fee: $50. *Financial support:* In 2007–08, 2 research assistantships with full tuition reimbursements (averaging $12,000 per year) were awarded. *Unit head:* Dr. Charles E. Ziegler, Chair, 502-852-3248, Fax: 502-852-7923, E-mail: cezieg01@louisville.edu.

University of Manitoba, Faculty of Graduate Studies, Faculty of Arts, Department of Political Studies, Winnipeg, MB R3T 2N2, Canada. Offers MA. *Degree requirements:* For master's, one foreign language, thesis or alternative.

University of Maryland, College Park, Graduate Studies, College of Behavioral and Social Sciences, Department of Government and Politics, College Park, MD 20742. Offers American politics (PhD); comparative politics (PhD); international relations (PhD); political economy (PhD); political theory (PhD). Part-time and evening/weekend programs available. *Faculty:* 47 full-time (11 women), 11 part-time/adjunct (3 women). *Students:* 132 full-time (59 women), 22 part-time (9 women); includes 29 minority (8 African Americans, 15 Asian Americans or Pacific Islanders, 6 Hispanic Americans), 24 international. 277 applicants, 18% accepted, 16 enrolled. In 2007, 9 doctorates awarded. *Median time to degree:* Of those who began their doctoral program in fall 1999, 41% received their degree in 8 years or less. *Degree requirements:* For doctorate, comprehensive exam, thesis/dissertation, written exams in 2 fields. *Entrance requirements:* For doctorate, GRE General Test, minimum GPA of 3.5, writing sample. Additional exam requirements/recommendations for international students: Required—TOEFL. *Application deadline:* For fall admission, 2/1 for domestic and international students. Applications are processed on a rolling basis. Application fee: $60. Electronic applications accepted. *Financial support:* In 2007–08, 10 fellowships with full tuition reimbursements (averaging $17,695 per year), 3 research assistantships with tuition reimbursements (averaging $15,383 per year), 66 teaching assistantships with tuition reimbursements (averaging $14,997 per year) were awarded; career-related internships or fieldwork, Federal Work-Study, scholarships/grants, and unspecified assistantships also available. Support available to part-time students. Financial award applicants required to submit FAFSA. *Faculty research:* International development/conflict, international security, post-communist society, public service, dynamics of conflict and conflict resolution. Total annual research expenditures: $2.3 million. *Unit head:* Dr. Mark Lichbach, Chairman, 301-405-4160, Fax: 301-314-9690, E-mail: mlichbac@umd.edu. *Application contact:* Dean of Graduate School, 301-405-0358, Fax: 301-314-9305.

University of Massachusetts Amherst, Graduate School, College of Social and Behavioral Sciences, Department of Political Science, Amherst, MA 01003. Offers MA, PhD. Part-time programs available. *Faculty:* 26 full-time (9 women). *Students:* 41 full-time (20 women), 22 part-time (8 women); includes 6 minority (1 African American, 2 Asian Americans or Pacific Islanders, 3 Hispanic Americans), 17 international. Average age 30. 119 applicants, 36% accepted, 11 enrolled. In 2007, 3 master's, 4 doctorates awarded. Terminal master's awarded for partial completion of doctoral program. *Degree requirements:* For master's, thesis or alternative; for doctorate, one foreign language, thesis/dissertation. *Entrance requirements:* For master's and doctorate, GRE General Test, writing sample, 3 letters of recommendation. Additional exam requirements/recommendations for international students: Required—TOEFL (minimum score 530 paper-based; 197 computer-based). *Application deadline:* For fall admission, 2/1 for domestic and international students. Applications are processed on a rolling basis. Application fee: $50 ($65 for international students). Electronic applications accepted. *Expenses:* Tuition, state resident: full-time $2,640; part-time $110 per credit. Tuition, nonresident: full-time $9,936; part-time $414 per credit. Required fees: $7,455. One-time fee: $332. Tuition and fees vary according to course load, campus/location, program and reciprocity agreements. *Financial support:* In 2007–08, 9 fellowships with full tuition reimbursements (averaging $2,799 per year), 20 research assistantships with full tuition reimbursements (averaging $6,278 per year), 34 teaching assistantships with full tuition reimbursements (averaging $12,036 per year) were awarded; career-related internships or fieldwork, Federal Work-Study, scholarships/grants, traineeships, and unspecified assistantships also available. Support available to part-time students. Financial award application deadline: 2/1. *Unit head:* Dr. John Hird, Chair, 413-545-2438, Fax: 413-545-3349, E-mail: jhird@pubpol.umass.edu.

University of Massachusetts Boston, Office of Graduate Studies, Division of Continuing Education and John W. McCormack Graduate School of Policy Studies, Program in Women in Politics and Government, Boston, MA 02125-3393. Offers Certificate. Part-time and evening/weekend programs available. *Degree requirements:* For Certificate, practicum, final project. *Entrance requirements:* For degree, interview, minimum GPA of 2.75.

University of Massachusetts Boston, Office of Graduate Studies, John W. McCormack Graduate School of Policy Studies, Boston, MA 02125-3393. Offers gerontology (MA, MS, PhD, Certificate), including gerontology (MS, PhD, Certificate), gerontology research (MA), management in aging services (MA); public affairs (MS); public policy (PhD); women in politics and government (Certificate). Certificate program in women in politics and government offered jointly with Division of Continuing Education. Part-time and evening/weekend programs available. *Degree requirements:* For doctorate, thesis/dissertation; for Certificate, practicum, final project. *Entrance requirements:* For doctorate, GRE General Test; for Certificate, interview, minimum GPA of 2.5.

University of Memphis, Graduate School, College of Arts and Sciences, Department of Political Science, Memphis, TN 38152. Offers MA. *Faculty:* 3 full-time (0 women), 2 part-time/adjunct (0 women). *Students:* 12 full-time (7 women), 6 part-time (2 women). Average age 29. 22 applicants, 73% accepted, 9 enrolled. In 2007, 4 degrees awarded. *Degree requirements:* For master's, comprehensive exam, thesis or alternative, internship. *Entrance requirements:* For master's, GRE General Test or GMAT, minimum GPA of 3.0. *Application deadline:* For fall admission, 8/1 for domestic students; for spring admission, 12/1 for domestic students. Applications are processed on a rolling basis. Application fee: $35 ($60 for international students). *Expenses:* Tuition, state resident: full-time $6,990; part-time $377 per hour. Tuition, nonresident: full-time $17,818; part-time $830 per hour. Tuition and fees vary according to course load and program. *Financial support:* In 2007–08, 10 research assistantships with full tuition reimbursements (averaging $7,150 per year) were awarded. *Faculty research:* Political philosophy, comparative judicial studies, conflict studies, legislative studies, foreign policy. *Unit head:* Dr. Shannon L. Blanton, Chair, 901-678-2395, Fax: 901-678-2983, E-mail: sblanton@memphis.edu. *Application contact:* Dr. Doug Imig, Graduate Program Coordinator, 901-678-2395, Fax: 901-678-2983, E-mail: dimig@memphis.edu.

University of Miami, Graduate School, College of Arts and Sciences, Department of Political Science, Coral Gables, FL 33124. Offers MPA, MPA/MPH. Part-time and evening/weekend programs available. *Faculty:* 11 full-time (4 women), 6 part-time/adjunct (2 women). *Students:* 13 full-time (6 women), 17 part-time (10 women); includes 5 African Americans, 9 Hispanic Americans, 1 international. Average age 30. 16 applicants, 44% accepted, 3 enrolled. In 2007, 6 degrees awarded. *Degree requirements:* For master's, thesis optional. *Entrance requirements:* For master's, GRE General Test. Additional exam requirements/recommendations for international students: Required—TOEFL. *Application deadline:* For fall admission, 7/15 priority date for domestic students, 5/31 for international students; for spring admission, 1/31 for domestic students, 10/31 for international students. Applications are processed on a rolling basis. Application fee: $50. *Financial support:* In 2007–08, 8 students received support; research assistantships, career-related internships or fieldwork and Federal Work-Study available. Financial award application deadline: 3/1. *Unit head:* Dr. Fred Frohock, Chairperson, 305-284-2401, Fax: 305-284-3636. *Application contact:* Dr. Jonathan P. West, Director of Graduate Program in Public Administration, 305-284-2401, Fax: 305-284-3636, E-mail: jwest@miami.edu.

University of Michigan, Horace H. Rackham School of Graduate Studies, College of Literature, Science, and the Arts, Department of Political Science, Ann Arbor, MI 48109. Offers political science (AM, PhD); social work and political science (PhD); JD/AM. *Faculty:* 30 full-time (8 women), 11 part-time/adjunct (3 women). *Students:* 111 full-time (60 women); includes 31 minority (15 African Americans, 2 American Indian/Alaska Native, 8 Asian Americans or Pacific Islanders, 6 Hispanic Americans), 24 international. Average age 25. 383 applicants, 10% accepted, 21 enrolled. In 2007, 5 master's, 12 doctorates awarded. Terminal master's awarded for partial completion of doctoral program. *Median time to degree:* Of those who began their doctoral program in fall 1999, 40% received their degree in 8 years or less. *Degree requirements:* For master's, thesis; for doctorate, comprehensive exam, thesis/dissertation, oral defense of dissertation, preliminary exam. *Entrance requirements:* For master's and doctorate, GRE General Test. Additional exam requirements/recommendations for international students: Required—TOEFL. *Application deadline:* For fall admission, 12/15 for domestic and international students. Application fee: $65 ($75 for international students). Electronic applications accepted. *Financial support:* In 2007–08, 27 fellowships with full tuition reimbursements (averaging $16,000 per year), 10 research assistantships with full tuition reimbursements (averaging $16,000 per year), 41 teaching assistantships with full tuition reimbursements (averaging $16,000 per year) were awarded; career-related internships or fieldwork also available. Financial award application deadline: 12/15. *Faculty research:* Political theory, American politics, world politics, comparative politics. *Unit head:* Donald R. Kinder, Chair, 734-764-6313, Fax: 734-764-3522. *Application contact:* Michelle L. Spornhauer, Student Services Associate, 734-763-2226, Fax: 734-764-3522, E-mail: migalita@umich.edu.

University of Minnesota, Twin Cities Campus, Graduate School, College of Liberal Arts, Department of Political Science, Minneapolis, MN 55455-0213. Offers PhD. Part-time programs available. *Faculty:* 28 full-time (12 women), 6 part-time/adjunct (1 woman). *Students:* 78 full-time (39 women), 16 part-time (7 women); includes 10 minority (1 African American, 1 American Indian/Alaska Native, 7 Asian Americans or Pacific Islanders, 1 Hispanic American), 27 international. Average age 28. 274 applicants, 10% accepted, 12 enrolled. In 2007, 9 doctorates awarded. *Median time to degree:* Of those who began their doctoral program in fall 1999, 50% received their degree in 8 years or less. *Degree requirements:* For doctorate, thesis/dissertation, 1 foreign language or statistics. *Entrance requirements:* For doctorate, GRE. Additional exam requirements/recommendations for international students: Required—TOEFL; Recommended—IELTS. *Application deadline:* For fall admission, 1/1 for domestic and international students. Application fee: $55 ($75 for international students). Electronic applications accepted. *Financial support:* In 2007–08, 14 fellowships with full tuition reimbursements (averaging $15,000 per year), 9 research assistantships with full tuition reimbursements (averaging $15,000 per year), 92 teaching assistantships with full tuition reimbursements (averaging $15,000 per year) were awarded; career-related internships or fieldwork also available. Financial award application deadline: 1/1. *Faculty research:* Political psychology, political economy, social policy, legislative studies, history of political thought. Total annual research expenditures: $38,811. *Unit head:* Raymond Duvall, Chair, 612-624-4144, Fax: 612-626-7599. *Application contact:* Judith Mitchell, Assistant to Director of Graduate Studies, 612-624-4144, Fax: 612-626-7599, E-mail: office@polisci.umn.edu.

University of Mississippi, Graduate School, College of Liberal Arts, Department of Political Science, Oxford, University, MS 38677. Offers MA, PhD. *Faculty:* 14 full-time (2 women), 3 part-time/adjunct (1 woman). *Students:* 16 full-time (6 women), 2 part-time (both women), 1 international. In 2007, 2 master's, 3 doctorates awarded. *Degree requirements:* For doctorate, thesis/dissertation. *Entrance requirements:* For master's, GRE General Test, minimum GPA of 3.0; for doctorate, GRE General Test. Additional exam requirements/recommendations for international students: Required—TOEFL. *Application deadline:* For fall admission, 2/15 for domestic students; for spring admission, 10/1 for domestic students. Applications are processed on a rolling basis. Application fee: $25. Electronic applications accepted. *Expenses:* Tuition, state resident: full-time $4,932. Tuition, nonresident: full-time $11,436. *Financial support:* Scholarships/grants available. Financial award application deadline: 3/1; financial award applicants required to submit FAFSA. *Unit head:* Dr. Richard G. Forgette, Chairman, 662-915-7401, Fax: 662-915-7808.

University of Missouri–Columbia, Graduate School, College of Arts and Sciences, Department of Political Science, Columbia, MO 65211. Offers MA, PhD. Terminal master's awarded for partial completion of doctoral program. *Degree requirements:* For doctorate, one foreign language, thesis/dissertation. *Entrance requirements:* For master's and doctorate, GRE General Test, minimum GPA of 3.0.

University of Missouri–Kansas City, College of Arts and Sciences, Department of Political Science, Kansas City, MO 64110-2499. Offers MA, PhD. PhD offered through the School of Graduate Studies. Part-time and evening/weekend programs available. *Faculty:* 7 full-time (1 woman), 4 part-time/adjunct (1 woman). *Students:* 1 full-time (0 women), 9 part-time (4 women). Average age 34. 6 applicants, 50% accepted, 3 enrolled. In 2007, 1 degree awarded. Terminal master's awarded for partial completion of doctoral program. *Degree requirements:* For master's, thesis optional; for doctorate, thesis/dissertation. *Entrance requirements:* For master's, GRE, minimum GPA of 3.0, course work in political science, a letter of application, 2 letters of recommendation; for doctorate, GRE, minimum GPA of 3.0, MA in political science or related area, writing sample. Additional exam requirements/recommendations for international students: Required—TOEFL. *Application deadline:* For fall admission, 4/1 priority date for domestic and international students; for spring admission, 11/1 priority date for domestic and international students. Applications are processed on a rolling basis. Application fee: $35 ($50 for international students). Electronic applications accepted. *Expenses:* Tuition, state resident: part-time $287 per hour. Tuition, nonresident: part-time $741 per hour. Required fees: $31 per hour. Tuition and fees vary according to program. *Financial support:* In 2007–08, 2 research assistantships (averaging $11,400 per year) were awarded; teaching assistantships with partial tuition reimbursements, career-related internships or fieldwork and institutionally sponsored loans also available. Financial award application deadline: 3/1; financial award applicants required to submit FAFSA. *Faculty research:* Sex and gender, Chinese politics, voting behavior, politics of presidency and social security, public law. *Unit head:* Dr. Harris Mirkin, Chair, 816-235-2792, Fax: 816-235-5594, E-mail: mirkinh@umkc.edu.

University of Missouri–St. Louis, College of Arts and Sciences, Department of Political Science, St. Louis, MO 63121. Offers American politics (MA); comparative politics (MA); international politics (MA); political process and behavior (MA); political science (PhD); public administration and public policy (MA); urban and regional politics (MA). Part-time and evening/

weekend programs available. *Faculty:* 20 full-time (8 women), 2 part-time/adjunct (both women). *Students:* 28 full-time (13 women), 20 part-time (15 women); includes 9 minority (6 African Americans, 2 American Indian/Alaska Native, 1 Asian American or Pacific Islander), 6 international. Average age 36. In 2007, 10 master's, 3 doctorates awarded. Terminal master's awarded for partial completion of doctoral program. *Degree requirements:* For master's, thesis optional; for doctorate, thesis/dissertation. *Entrance requirements:* For master's, GRE General Test, 2 letters of recommendation; for doctorate, GRE General Test, 3 letters of recommendation. Additional exam requirements/recommendations for international students: Required—TOEFL (minimum score 550 paper-based; 213 computer-based). *Application deadline:* For fall admission, 2/15 for domestic students; for spring admission, 10/15 for domestic students. Applications are processed on a rolling basis. Application fee: $35 ($40 for international students). Electronic applications accepted. *Financial support:* In 2007–08, 9 research assistantships with full and partial tuition reimbursements (averaging $12,000 per year), 6 teaching assistantships with full and partial tuition reimbursements (averaging $12,000 per year) were awarded; fellowships, career-related internships or fieldwork also available. Support available to part-time students. Financial award application deadline: 3/15. *Faculty research:* Public policy, urban politics and administration, American government. *Unit head:* Dr. Eduardo Silva, Director of Graduate Studies, 314-516-5522, Fax: 314-516-5268, E-mail: umslpolisci@umsl.edu. *Application contact:* 314-516-5458, Fax: 314-516-6996, E-mail: gradadm@umsl.edu.

The University of Montana, Graduate School, College of Arts and Sciences, Department of Political Science, Program in Political Science, Missoula, MT 59812-0002. Offers MA. *Degree requirements:* For master's, thesis. *Entrance requirements:* For master's, GRE General Test.

University of Nebraska at Omaha, Graduate Studies and Research, College of Arts and Sciences, Department of Political Science, Omaha, NE 68182. Offers MS. Part-time and evening/weekend programs available. *Faculty:* 12 full-time (4 women). *Students:* 15 full-time (6 women), 29 part-time (17 women); includes 3 minority (1 African American, 1 American Indian/Alaska Native, 1 Hispanic American), 3 international. Average age 32. 21 applicants, 81% accepted, 14 enrolled. In 2007, 3 degrees awarded. *Degree requirements:* For master's, comprehensive exam, thesis (for some programs). *Entrance requirements:* For master's, 15 undergraduate political science hours, minimum undergraduate GPA of 3.0, 2 letters of recommendation. Additional exam requirements/recommendations for international students: Required—TOEFL (minimum score 500 paper-based; 173 computer-based; 61 iBT). *Application deadline:* For fall admission, 3/15 priority date for domestic students; for spring admission, 11/1 priority date for domestic students. Applications are processed on a rolling basis. Application fee: $45. Electronic applications accepted. *Financial support:* In 2007–08, 28 students received support; fellowships, research assistantships, teaching assistantships, Federal Work-Study, scholarships/grants, tuition waivers (partial), and unspecified assistantships available. Financial award application deadline: 3/1; financial award applicants required to submit FAFSA. *Unit head:* Dr. Loree Bykerk, Chairperson, 402-554-2624. *Application contact:* Dr. Randall Adkins, Student Contact, 402-554-2624.

University of Nebraska–Lincoln, Graduate College, College of Arts and Sciences, Department of Political Science, Lincoln, NE 68588. Offers MA, PhD, JD/MA. *Degree requirements:* For master's, thesis optional; for doctorate, variable foreign language requirement, comprehensive exam, thesis/dissertation. *Entrance requirements:* For master's and doctorate, GRE General Test, writing sample. Additional exam requirements/recommendations for international students: Required—TOEFL (minimum score 600 paper-based; 250 computer-based). Electronic applications accepted. *Faculty research:* Public policy; comparative politics; international relations; political theory, behavior, and methodology; American politics.

University of Nevada, Las Vegas, Graduate College, College of Liberal Arts, Department of Political Science, Las Vegas, NV 89154-9900. Offers ethics and policy studies (MA); political science (MA). Part-time programs available. *Faculty:* 20 full-time (3 women). *Students:* 10 full-time (4 women), 12 part-time (4 women); includes 4 minority (2 Asian Americans or Pacific Islanders, 2 Hispanic Americans). 21 applicants, 57% accepted, 10 enrolled. In 2007, 1 degree awarded. *Degree requirements:* For master's, comprehensive exam (for some programs), thesis (for some programs). *Entrance requirements:* For master's, GRE General Test, minimum GPA of 3.0. Additional exam requirements/recommendations for international students: Required—TOEFL (minimum score 550 paper-based; 213 computer-based; 80 iBT). *Application deadline:* For fall admission, 3/1 for domestic and international students; for spring admission, 11/1 for domestic students, 10/1 for international students. Application fee: $60 ($75 for international students). Electronic applications accepted. *Expenses:* Tuition, state resident: part-time $198 per credit. Tuition, nonresident: part-time $416 per credit. Required fees: $256 per semester. Tuition and fees vary according to course load and reciprocity agreements. *Financial support:* In 2007–08, 5 research assistantships with partial tuition reimbursements (averaging $10,000 per year), 3 teaching assistantships with partial tuition reimbursements (averaging $10,000 per year) were awarded; career-related internships or fieldwork, Federal Work-Study, institutionally sponsored loans, scholarships/grants, health care benefits, and unspecified assistantships also available. Support available to part-time students. Financial award application deadline: 3/1. *Unit head:* Dr. Mehran Tamadonfar, Chair, 702-895-5258, E-mail: mehran.tamadorfar@unlv.edu. *Application contact:* Graduate College Admissions Evaluator, 702-895-3320, Fax: 702-895-4180, E-mail: gradcollege@unlv.edu.

University of Nevada, Reno, Graduate School, College of Liberal Arts, Department of Political Science, Program in Political Science, Reno, NV 89557. Offers MA, PhD. Part-time and evening/weekend programs available. *Faculty:* 15. *Students:* 10 full-time (2 women), 28 part-time (13 women); includes 5 minority (1 African American, 1 American Indian/Alaska Native, 3 Hispanic Americans), 2 international. Average age 40. In 2007, 2 degrees awarded. Terminal master's awarded for partial completion of doctoral program. *Degree requirements:* For master's, comprehensive exam, oral exam/thesis or professional paper; for doctorate, thesis/dissertation, 2 field exams, oral exam. *Entrance requirements:* For master's, GRE General Test, GMAT, LSAT, minimum GPA of 2.75; for doctorate, GRE General Test, GMAT, LSAT, minimum GPA of 3.0. Additional exam requirements/recommendations for international students: Required—TOEFL. *Application deadline:* For fall admission, 2/1 priority date for domestic students. Applications are processed on a rolling basis. Application fee: $60 ($95 for international students). *Expenses:* Tuition, state resident: full-time $2,774; part-time $154 per credit. Tuition, nonresident: full-time $13,578; part-time $330 per credit. Required fees: $49 per semester. *Financial support:* Research assistantships, teaching assistantships, Federal Work-Study, institutionally sponsored loans, tuition waivers (full), and unspecified assistantships available. Financial award application deadline: 3/1. *Unit head:* Leah Wilds, Chair, 775-682-7773, Fax: 775-784-1473.

University of New Brunswick Fredericton, School of Graduate Studies, Faculty of Arts, Department of Political Science, Fredericton, NB E3B 5A3, Canada. Offers MA. Part-time programs available. *Faculty:* 10 full-time (3 women). *Students:* 10 full-time (2 women), 3 part-time (1 woman). In 2007, 5 degrees awarded. *Degree requirements:* For master's, thesis. *Entrance requirements:* For master's, minimum GPA of 3.0. Additional exam requirements/recommendations for international students: Required—TOEFL, TWE. *Application deadline:* For fall admission, 3/1 priority date for domestic students. Applications are processed on a rolling basis. Application fee: $50 Canadian dollars. *Financial support:* In 2007–08, 2 research assistantships, 4 teaching assistantships were awarded; fellowships also available. *Faculty research:* Canadian politics, political theory, public policy, gender and politics, international studies. *Unit head:* Dr. Joanne Wright, Director of Graduate Studies, 506-458-7422, Fax: 506-453-4755, E-mail: jwright@unb.ca. *Application contact:* Deborah Sloan, Graduate Secretary, 506-453-4826, Fax: 506-453-4755, E-mail: dsloan@unb.ca.

University of New Hampshire, Graduate School, College of Liberal Arts, Department of Political Science, Program in Political Science, Durham, NH 03824. Offers MA. Part-time programs available. *Faculty:* 15 full-time. *Students:* 11 full-time (8 women), 10 part-time (3 women); includes 6 minority (3 African Americans, 1 American Indian/Alaska Native, 1 Asian American or Pacific Islander, 1 Hispanic American), 1 international. Average age 28. 12 applicants, 92% accepted, 5 enrolled. In 2007, 4 degrees awarded. *Degree requirements:* For master's, thesis. *Entrance requirements:* For master's, GRE General Test. Additional exam requirements/recommendations for international students: Required—TOEFL (minimum score 550 paper-based; 213 computer-based; 80 iBT). *Application deadline:* For fall admission, 4/1 priority date for domestic students, 4/1 for international students; for winter admission, 12/1 for domestic students. Applications are processed on a rolling basis. Application fee: $60. Electronic applications accepted. *Financial support:* In 2007–08, 3 teaching assistantships were awarded; fellowships, research assistantships, career-related internships or fieldwork, Federal Work-Study, scholarships/grants, and tuition waivers (full and partial) also available. Support available to part-time students. Financial award application deadline: 2/15. *Application contact:* Tama Andrews, Administrative Assistant, 603-862-1750, E-mail: mpa.ma.political.science.grad@unh.edu.

University of New Mexico, Graduate School, College of Arts and Sciences, Department of Political Science, Albuquerque, NM 87131-2039. Offers MA, PhD. Part-time programs available. *Faculty:* 15 full-time (7 women), 6 part-time/adjunct (1 woman). *Students:* 28 full-time (10 women), 5 part-time (4 women); includes 8 minority (1 African American, 2 American Indian/Alaska Native, 1 Asian American or Pacific Islander, 4 Hispanic Americans), 7 international. Average age 32. 44 applicants, 27% accepted, 6 enrolled. In 2007, 7 master's, 2 doctorates awarded. Terminal master's awarded for partial completion of doctoral program. *Degree requirements:* For master's, comprehensive exam, thesis optional, minimum cumulative GPA of 3.2; for doctorate, comprehensive exam, thesis/dissertation, field research paper, minimum cumulative GPA of 3.5. *Entrance requirements:* For master's and doctorate, GRE, 3 letters of recommendation, writing sample, letter of intent. Additional exam requirements/recommendations for international students: Required—TOEFL. *Application deadline:* For fall admission, 2/1 priority date for domestic students. Application fee: $50. Electronic applications accepted. *Financial support:* In 2007–08, 10 students received support, including research assistantships with tuition reimbursements available (averaging $14,634 per year), teaching assistantships with tuition reimbursements available (averaging $14,634 per year); scholarships/grants, health care benefits, and unspecified assistantships also available. Financial award application deadline: 2/1; financial award applicants required to submit FAFSA. *Faculty research:* Latin American politics, American politics, comparative politics, public policy, international relations, methodology. Total annual research expenditures: $589,246. *Unit head:* Dr. Mark Peceny, Chair, 505-277-5104, Fax: 505-277-2821, E-mail: markpec@unm.edu. *Application contact:* Beth Leahy, Graduate Program Assistant, 505-277-5104, Fax: 505-288-2821, E-mail: bleahy@unm.edu.

University of New Orleans, Graduate School, College of Liberal Arts, Department of Political Science, New Orleans, LA 70148. Offers political science (MA, PhD); public administration (MPA). Evening/weekend programs available. *Students:* 41 (21 women). Average age 34. In 2007, 5 master's, 1 doctorate awarded. *Degree requirements:* For master's, one foreign language, thesis or alternative; for doctorate, one foreign language, thesis/dissertation. *Entrance requirements:* For master's, GRE General Test; for doctorate, GRE General Test, GRE Subject Test. Additional exam requirements/recommendations for international students: Required—TOEFL (minimum score 550 paper-based; 213 computer-based; 79 iBT). *Application deadline:* For fall admission, 7/1 priority date for domestic students, 6/1 for international students; for spring admission, 11/15 priority date for domestic students, 10/1 for international students. Applications are processed on a rolling basis. Application fee: $40. Electronic applications accepted. *Financial support:* Fellowships, research assistantships, teaching assistantships, institutionally sponsored loans available. Financial award application deadline: 3/15; financial award applicants required to submit FAFSA. *Faculty research:* Judicial politics, public policy, voting rights, Southern politics, presidential-congressional relations. *Unit head:* Dr. Christine Day, Chairperson, 504-280-6997, Fax: 504-280-6468. *Application contact:* Dr. Michael Huelshoff, Graduate Coordinator, 504-280-6460, Fax: 504-280-6468.

The University of North Carolina at Chapel Hill, Graduate School, College of Arts and Sciences, Department of Political Science, Program in Political Science, Chapel Hill, NC 27599. Offers MA, PhD. *Degree requirements:* For master's, comprehensive exam, thesis; for doctorate, one foreign language, comprehensive exam, thesis/dissertation. *Entrance requirements:* For master's and doctorate, GRE General Test, GRE Subject Test, minimum GPA of 3.0.

The University of North Carolina at Greensboro, Graduate School, College of Arts and Sciences, Department of Political Science, Greensboro, NC 27412-5001. Offers nonprofit management (Certificate); public affairs (MPA); urban and economic development (Certificate). *Accreditation:* NASPAA. *Faculty:* 14 full-time (4 women). *Students:* 35 full-time (21 women), 28 part-time (20 women); includes 62 minority (13 African Americans, 1 American Indian/Alaska Native, 48 Hispanic Americans). 55 applicants, 27% accepted. *Degree requirements:* For master's, comprehensive exam. *Entrance requirements:* For master's, GRE General Test. Additional exam requirements/recommendations for international students: Required—TOEFL. *Application deadline:* For fall admission, 3/15 priority date for domestic students; for spring admission, 11/1 for domestic students. Applications are processed on a rolling basis. Electronic applications accepted. *Financial support:* In 2007–08, 19 students received support, including 4 research assistantships with full tuition reimbursements available; teaching assistantships with full tuition reimbursements available, career-related internships or fieldwork, Federal Work-Study, scholarships/grants, and traineeships also available. Support available to part-time students. *Faculty research:* U.S. Constitution, Canadian parliament, public management, ethical challenge of public service. *Unit head:* Dr. Ruth H. DeHoog, Head, 336-256-0511, Fax: 336-334-4315, E-mail: rhdehoog@uncg.edu. *Application contact:* Michelle Harkleroad, Director of Graduate Admissions, 336-334-4884, Fax: 336-334-4424, E-mail: mbharkle@uncg.edu.

University of Northern British Columbia, Office of Graduate Studies, Prince George, BC V2N 4Z9, Canada. Offers business administration (Diploma); community health science (M Sc); disability management (MA); education (M Ed); first nations studies (MA); gender studies (MA); history (MA); interdisciplinary studies (MA); international studies (MA); mathematical, computer and physical sciences (M Sc); natural resources and environmental studies (M Sc, MA, MNRES, PhD); political science (MA); psychology (M Sc, PhD); social work (MSW). Part-time and evening/weekend programs available. Postbaccalaureate distance learning degree programs offered (no on-campus study). *Degree requirements:* For master's, thesis; for doctorate, thesis/dissertation. *Entrance requirements:* For master's, GRE, minimum B average in undergraduate course work; for doctorate, candidacy exam, minimum A average in graduate course work.

University of North Texas, Robert B. Toulouse School of Graduate Studies, College of Arts and Sciences, Department of Political Science, Denton, TX 76203. Offers MA, MS, PhD. Evening/weekend programs available. *Faculty:* 25 full-time (5 women). *Students:* 37 full-time (12 women), 22 part-time (8 women); includes 10 minority (4 African Americans, 1 American Indian/Alaska Native, 2 Asian Americans or Pacific Islanders, 3 Hispanic Americans), 12 international. Average age 29. 62 applicants, 48% accepted, 14 enrolled. In 2007, 7 master's, 2 doctorates awarded. *Degree requirements:* For master's, comprehensive exam, thesis (for some programs); for doctorate, 2 foreign languages, comprehensive exam, thesis/dissertation. *Entrance requirements:* For master's, GRE General Test, minimum GPA of 3.0, 3 letters of recommendation, statement of interest; for doctorate, GRE General Test, 3 letters of recommendation, statement of interest. Additional exam requirements/recommendations for international students: Required—proof of English language proficiency; Recommended—TOEFL (minimum score 550 paper-based; 213 computer-based). *Application deadline:* For fall admission, 7/15 for domestic students; for spring admission, 11/15 for domestic students. Application fee: $50 ($75 for international students). *Financial support:* In 2007–08, 2 fellowships with tuition reimbursements (averaging $20,000 per year), 7 research assistantships with tuition reimbursements (averaging $12,000 per year), 22 teaching assistantships with tuition reimbursements (averaging $12,000 per year) were awarded; career-related internships or fieldwork, Federal Work-Study, and institutionally sponsored loans also available. *Faculty research:* Political parties, international conflict, judicial politics, comparative politics. Total annual research expenditures: $45,000. *Unit head:* Dr. James Meernik, Chair, 940-545-2276, Fax: 940-565-

Political Science

University of North Texas (continued)

4818, E-mail: meernik@unt.edu. *Application contact:* Dr. Andrew Enterline, Graduate Advisor, 940-565-2276, Fax: 940-565-4818, E-mail: ajentier@unt.edu.

University of Notre Dame, Graduate School, College of Arts and Letters, Division of Social Science, Department of Political Science, Notre Dame, IN 46556. Offers PhD. *Faculty:* 42 full-time (8 women), 5 part-time/adjunct (1 woman). *Students:* 83 full-time (32 women); includes 14 minority (2 African Americans, 1 American Indian/Alaska Native, 1 Asian American or Pacific Islander, 10 Hispanic Americans), 26 international. 263 applicants, 8% accepted, 12 enrolled. In 2007, 5 doctorates awarded. *Median time to degree:* Of those who began their doctoral program in fall 1999, 67% received their degree in 8 years or less. *Degree requirements:* For doctorate, one foreign language, comprehensive exam, thesis/dissertation, candidacy exam. *Entrance requirements:* For doctorate, GRE General Test. Additional exam requirements/recommendations for international students: Required—TOEFL (minimum score 600 paper-based; 250 computer-based; 80 iBT). *Application deadline:* For fall admission, 2/1 priority date for domestic students, 2/1 for international students. Application fee: $50. Electronic applications accepted. *Financial support:* In 2007–08, 9 fellowships with full tuition reimbursements (averaging $22,000 per year), 4 research assistantships with full tuition reimbursements (averaging $30,000 per year), 49 teaching assistantships with full tuition reimbursements (averaging $16,000 per year) were awarded; career-related internships or fieldwork and tuition waivers (full) also available. Financial award application deadline: 2/1. *Faculty research:* American government, comparative politics, international relations, political theory. *Unit head:* Dr. Ben Radcliff, Director of Graduate Studies, 574-631-9017, Fax: 574-631-4405, E-mail: govtgrad@nd.edu. *Application contact:* Dr. Jarren Gonzales, Director of Graduate Admissions, 574-631-7706, Fax: 574-631-4183.

University of Oklahoma, Graduate College, College of Arts and Sciences, Department of Political Science, Program in Political Science, Norman, OK 73019-0390. Offers MA, PhD. *Students:* 41 full-time (13 women), 28 part-time (12 women); includes 8 minority (2 African Americans, 3 American Indian/Alaska Native, 1 Asian American or Pacific Islander, 2 Hispanic Americans), 14 international. 42 applicants, 71% accepted, 17 enrolled. In 2007, 8 master's, 2 doctorates awarded. Terminal master's awarded for partial completion of doctoral program. *Degree requirements:* For master's, thesis or alternative; for doctorate, thesis/dissertation, language or quantitative techniques. *Entrance requirements:* For master's and doctorate, GRE General Test, 3 letters of recommendation. Additional exam requirements/recommendations for international students: Required—TOEFL (minimum score 600 paper-based; 250 computer-based). *Application deadline:* For fall admission, 2/1 for domestic and international students; for spring admission, 10/15 for domestic students, 9/1 for international students. Applications are processed on a rolling basis. Application fee: $40 ($90 for international students). Electronic applications accepted. *Expenses:* Tuition, state resident: full-time $3,451; part-time $144 per credit hour. Tuition, nonresident: full-time $12,432; part-time $518 per credit hour. Required fees: $1,925; $70 per credit hour. $122 per semester. *Financial support:* In 2007–08, 25 students received support; fellowships with full tuition reimbursements available, research assistantships with partial tuition reimbursements available, teaching assistantships with partial tuition reimbursements available, tuition waivers (partial) and unspecified assistantships available. *Faculty research:* American politics; institutions, processes and political behavior; Democratization; international security; terrorism; knowledge utilization in the policy process; comparative administration systems. *Application contact:* Mitchell P. Smith, Graduate Programs Director, 405-325-8893, Fax: 405-325-0718, E-mail: mps@ou.edu.

University of Oregon, Graduate School, College of Arts and Sciences, Department of Political Science, Eugene, OR 97403. Offers MA, MS, PhD. *Faculty:* 15 full-time (6 women), 2 part-time/adjunct (0 women). *Students:* 39 full-time (9 women), 3 part-time (2 women); includes 1 minority (African American), 9 international. 99 applicants, 24% accepted. In 2007, 4 master's, 2 doctorates awarded. Terminal master's awarded for partial completion of doctoral program. *Degree requirements:* For master's, thesis or alternative; for doctorate, thesis/dissertation. *Entrance requirements:* For master's and doctorate, GRE General Test, minimum GPA of 3.0. Additional exam requirements/recommendations for international students: Required—TOEFL. *Application deadline:* For fall admission, 2/15 for domestic students. Application fee: $50. *Financial support:* In 2007–08, 25 teaching assistantships were awarded; career-related internships or fieldwork also available. Financial award application deadline: 3/1. *Faculty research:* Public policy, public choice, comparative politics, political economy, international relations. *Unit head:* Lars Skalnes, Head, 541-346-4866, Fax: 541-346-4860. *Application contact:* Tara Thompson, Admissions Contact, 541-346-1326, Fax: 541-346-4860, E-mail: tarat@uoregon.edu.

University of Ottawa, Faculty of Graduate and Postdoctoral Studies, Faculty of Social Sciences, Department of Political Studies, Ottawa, ON K1N 6N5, Canada. Offers MA, PhD. *Degree requirements:* For master's, thesis or alternative, fluency in English and French; for doctorate, comprehensive exam, thesis/dissertation. *Entrance requirements:* For master's, honors bachelor's degree or equivalent, minimum B average; for doctorate, master's degree, minimum B+ average. Electronic applications accepted. *Faculty research:* Political thought and analysis of ideologies, Canadian and Québécois policies, international and comparative policies.

University of Pennsylvania, School of Arts and Sciences, Graduate Group in Political Science, Philadelphia, PA 19104. Offers AM, PhD, MGA/AM. Terminal master's awarded for partial completion of doctoral program. *Degree requirements:* For doctorate, one foreign language, thesis/dissertation. *Entrance requirements:* For master's and doctorate, GRE General Test. Additional exam requirements/recommendations for international students: Required—TOEFL. Electronic applications accepted.

University of Pittsburgh, Graduate School of Public and International Affairs, Executive Programs in Public Policy and Management, Pittsburgh, PA 15260. Offers development planning (MPPM); international development (MPPM); international political economy (MPPM); international security studies (MPPM); management of non profit organizations (MPPM); metropolitan management and regional development (MPPM); policy analysis and evaluation (MPPM). Part-time programs available. *Faculty:* 34 full-time (10 women), 18 part-time/adjunct (6 women). *Students:* 11 full-time (3 women), 46 part-time (20 women); includes 4 minority (3 African Americans, 1 Hispanic American), 8 international. Average age 38. 48 applicants, 88% accepted, 29 enrolled. In 2007, 27 degrees awarded. *Degree requirements:* For master's, thesis optional, capstone seminar. *Entrance requirements:* For master's, 2 letters of recommendation, resumé, 5 years of supervisory or budgetary experience. Additional exam requirements/recommendations for international students: Required—TOEFL (minimum score 600 paper-based; 250 computer-based; 100 iBT), TWE (minimum score 4); Recommended—IELTS (minimum score 7). *Application deadline:* For fall admission, 6/1 priority date for domestic students, 2/15 for international students; for spring admission, 1/1 priority date for domestic students, 8/1 for international students. Applications are processed on a rolling basis. Application fee: $50. Electronic applications accepted. *Financial support:* In 2007–08, 4 students received support, including 4 fellowships (averaging $5,075 per year); institutionally sponsored loans and scholarships/grants also available. Support available to part-time students. Financial award application deadline: 2/1. *Faculty research:* Executive training and technical assistance for U.S. and international clients. Total annual research expenditures: $845,025. *Unit head:* Michele Garrity, Director, Executive Education, 412-648-7610, Fax: 412-648-2605, E-mail: garrity@birch.gspia.pitt.edu. *Application contact:* Maureen O'Malley, Admissions Counselor, 412-648-7640, Fax: 412-648-7641, E-mail: pronobis@birch.gspia.pitt.edu.

See Close-Up on page 1645.

University of Pittsburgh, Graduate School of Public and International Affairs, International Affairs Division, Program in Global Political Economy, Pittsburgh, PA 15260. Offers MPIA, JD/MPIA, MBA/MPIA, MID/MPIA, MPA/MPIA, MSIS/MPIA. Part-time and evening/weekend programs available. *Faculty:* 34 full-time (10 women), 18 part-time/adjunct (6 women). *Students:* 21 full-time (12 women), 9 part-time (5 women); includes 3 minority (1 African American, 2 Asian Americans or Pacific Islanders), 5 international. Average age 25. 55 applicants, 87% accepted, 15 enrolled. In 2007, 63 degrees awarded. *Degree requirements:* For master's, thesis optional, internship, capstone seminar. *Entrance requirements:* For master's, GRE General Test, 3 letters of recommendation, resumé, minimum GPA of 3.2 . Additional exam requirements/recommendations for international students: Required—TOEFL (minimum score 550 paper-based; 213 computer-based; 80 iBT), TWE (minimum score 4); Recommended—IELTS (minimum score 7). *Application deadline:* For fall admission, 2/1 for domestic students, 1/15 for international students; for spring admission, 11/1 for domestic students, 8/1 for international students. Application fee: $50. Electronic applications accepted. *Financial support:* In 2007–08, 41 students received support, including 41 fellowships (averaging $8,280 per year); career-related internships or fieldwork, scholarships/grants, and unspecified assistantships also available. Financial award application deadline: 2/1. *Faculty research:* Political economy, international security/defense/intelligence, transnational crime, international trade, international finance, terrorism. Total annual research expenditures: $845,025. *Application contact:* Michael Rizzi, Graduate Enrollment Counselor, 412-648-7643, Fax: 412-648-7641, E-mail: rizzim@pitt.edu.

University of Pittsburgh, School of Arts and Sciences, Department of Political Science, Pittsburgh, PA 15260. Offers MA, PhD. Part-time programs available. *Faculty:* 26 full-time (6 women), 2 part-time/adjunct (0 women). *Students:* 55 full-time (30 women), 1 part-time; includes 23 minority (1 African American, 9 Asian Americans or Pacific Islanders, 13 Hispanic Americans), 6 international. Average age 25. 156 applicants, 12% accepted, 10 enrolled. In 2007, 3 master's, 6 doctorates awarded. Terminal master's awarded for partial completion of doctoral program. *Median time to degree:* Of those who began their doctoral program in fall 1999, 25% received their degree in 8 years or less. *Degree requirements:* For master's, comprehensive exam; for doctorate, comprehensive exam, thesis/dissertation. *Entrance requirements:* For master's and doctorate, GRE General Test, minimum QPA of 3.0. Additional exam requirements/recommendations for international students: Required—TOEFL. *Application deadline:* For fall admission, 1/15 for domestic and international students. Applications are processed on a rolling basis. Application fee: $50. Electronic applications accepted. *Financial support:* In 2007–08, 34 students received support, including 18 fellowships with tuition reimbursements available (averaging $17,162 per year), 16 teaching assistantships with tuition reimbursements available (averaging $15,010 per year); research assistantships with tuition reimbursements available, tuition waivers (partial) also available. Financial award application deadline: 1/15. *Unit head:* Dr. Barry Ames, Chairman, 412-648-7290, Fax: 412-648-7277, E-mail: barrya@pitt.edu. *Application contact:* David Barker, Director of Graduate Students, 412-648-7275, Fax: 412-648-7277, E-mail: dbarker@pitt.edu.

University of Regina, Faculty of Graduate Studies and Research, Faculty of Arts, Department of Philosophy, Regina, SK S4S 0A2, Canada. Offers philosophy (MA); social and political thought (MA). *Faculty:* 9 full-time (3 women). *Students:* 1 (woman) full-time. *Degree requirements:* For master's, thesis. *Entrance requirements:* Additional exam requirements/recommendations for international students: Required—TOEFL (minimum score 580 paper-based; 237 computer-based; 88 iBT). *Application deadline:* Applications are processed on a rolling basis. Application fee: $85 ($100 for international students). Electronic applications accepted. *Financial support:* In 2007–08, fellowships (averaging $15,750 per year), research assistantships (averaging $13,875 per year), teaching assistantships (averaging $13,060 per year) were awarded; scholarships/grants also available. Financial award application deadline: 6/15. *Faculty research:* History of philosophy, ethics, aesthetics, metaphysics, epistemology. *Unit head:* Dr. Eldon Soifer, Head, 306-585-4301, Fax: 306-585-4827, E-mail: eldon.soifer@uregina.ca.

University of Regina, Faculty of Graduate Studies and Research, Faculty of Arts, Department of Political Science, Regina, SK S4S 0A2, Canada. Offers MA. Part-time programs available. *Faculty:* 10 full-time (3 women), 1 (woman) part-time/adjunct. *Students:* 10 full-time (5 women), 6 part-time (4 women). 11 applicants, 64% accepted, 6 enrolled. In 2007, 3 degrees awarded. *Degree requirements:* For master's, thesis. *Entrance requirements:* Additional exam requirements/recommendations for international students: Required—TOEFL (minimum score 580 paper-based; 237 computer-based; 88 iBT). *Application deadline:* For fall admission, 3/15 for domestic students. Applications are processed on a rolling basis. Application fee: $85 ($100 for international students). Electronic applications accepted. *Financial support:* In 2007–08, 4 fellowships (averaging $15,750 per year), 2 research assistantships (averaging $13,875 per year), 2 teaching assistantships (averaging $13,060 per year) were awarded; scholarships/grants also available. Financial award application deadline: 6/15. *Faculty research:* Canadian politics, comparative politics, international politics. *Unit head:* Dr. Jeremy Rayner, Head, 306-585-5679, Fax: 306-585-4815, E-mail: jeremy.rayner@uregina.ca. *Application contact:* Dr. Yuchao Zhu, Graduate Coordinator, 306-585-4060, E-mail: yuchao.zhu@uregina.ca.

University of Regina, Faculty of Graduate Studies and Research, Faculty of Arts, Program in Social and Political Thought, Regina, SK S4S 0A2, Canada. Offers MA. *Faculty:* 9 full-time (3 women). *Students:* 5 full-time (1 woman), 1 part-time. 7 applicants, 71% accepted, 4 enrolled. *Degree requirements:* For master's, thesis. *Entrance requirements:* Additional exam requirements/recommendations for international students: Required—TOEFL (minimum score 580 paper-based; 237 computer-based; 88 iBT). *Application deadline:* For fall admission, 3/15 for domestic students. Application fee: $85 ($100 for international students). Electronic applications accepted. *Financial support:* In 2007–08, 1 fellowship (averaging $15,750 per year), 1 research assistantship (averaging $13,875 per year), teaching assistantships (averaging $13,060 per year) were awarded. *Unit head:* Dr. Shadia Drury, Program Coordinator, 306-585-4073, E-mail: shadia.drury@uregina.ca.

University of Rhode Island, Graduate School, College of Arts and Sciences, Department of Political Science, Kingston, RI 02881. Offers political science (MA), including American politics, comparative government, international relations, public policy; public policy and administration (MA, MPA, Certificate). In 2007, 6 degrees awarded. *Application deadline:* For fall admission, 4/15 priority date for domestic students. Applications are processed on a rolling basis. Application fee: $35. *Expenses:* Tuition, state resident: full-time $6,936; part-time $385 per credit. Tuition, nonresident: full-time $19,044; part-time $1,058 per credit. Required fees: $1,508; $48 per credit. $30 per semester. One-time fee: $80 part-time. *Unit head:* Dr. Gerry Tyler, Chairperson, 401-874-4053.

University of Rochester, The College, Arts and Sciences, Department of Political Science, Rochester, NY 14627-0250. Offers MA, PhD, MPH/MS, MS/PhD. Terminal master's awarded for partial completion of doctoral program. *Degree requirements:* For doctorate, thesis/dissertation, qualifying exam. *Entrance requirements:* For master's and doctorate, GRE General Test. Additional exam requirements/recommendations for international students: Required—TOEFL.

University of Saskatchewan, College of Graduate Studies and Research, College of Arts and Sciences, Department of Political Studies, Saskatoon, SK S7N 5A2, Canada. Offers MA. *Degree requirements:* For master's, thesis. *Entrance requirements:* Additional exam requirements/recommendations for international students: Required—TOEFL.

University of South Africa, College of Human Sciences, Pretoria, South Africa. Offers adult education (M Ed); African languages (MA, PhD); African politics (MA, PhD); Afrikaans (MA, PhD); ancient history (MA, PhD); ancient Near Eastern studies (MA, PhD); anthropology (MA, PhD); applied linguistics (MA); Arabic (MA, PhD); archaeology (MA); art history (MA); Biblical archaeology (MA); Biblical studies (M Th, D Th, PhD); Christian spirituality (M Th, D Th); church history (M Th, D Th); classical studies (MA, PhD); clinical psychology (MA); communication (MA, PhD); comparative education (M Ed, Ed D); consulting psychology (D Admin, D Com, PhD); curriculum studies (M Ed, Ed D); development studies (M Admin, MA, D Admin, PhD); didactics (M Ed, Ed D); education (M Tech); education management (M Ed, Ed D); educational psychology (M Ed); English (MA); environmental education (M Ed); French (MA, PhD); German (MA, PhD); Greek (MA); guidance and counseling (M Ed); health studies (MA, PhD), including health sciences education (MA), health services management (MA), medical and surgical nursing science (critical care general) (MA), midwifery and neonatal nursing science (MA), trauma and emergency care (MA); history (MA, PhD); history of education

(Ed D); inclusive education (M Ed, Ed D); information and communications technology policy and regulation (MA); information science (MA, MIS, PhD); international politics (MA, PhD); Islamic studies (MA, PhD); Italian (MA, PhD); Judaica (MA, PhD); linguistics (MA, PhD); mathematical education (M Ed); mathematics education (MA); missiology (M Th, D Th); modern Hebrew (MA, PhD); musicology (MA, MMus, D Mus, PhD); natural science education (M Ed); New Testament (M Th, D Th); Old Testament (D Th); pastoral therapy (M Th, D Th); philosophy (MA); philosophy of education (M Ed, Ed D); politics (MA, PhD); Portuguese (MA, PhD); practical theology (M Th, D Th); psychology (MA, MS, PhD); psychology of education (M Ed, Ed D); public health (MA); religious studies (MA, D Th, PhD); Romance languages (MA); Russian (MA, PhD); Semitic languages (MA, PhD); social behavior studies in HIV/AIDS (MA); social science (mental health) (MA); social science in development studies (MA); social science in psychology (MA); social science in social work (MA); social science in sociology (MA); social work (MSW, DSW, PhD); socio-education (M Ed, Ed D); sociolinguistics (MA); sociology (MA, PhD); Spanish (MA, PhD); systematic theology (M Th, D Th); TESOL (teaching English to speakers of other languages) (MA); theological ethics (M Th, D Th); theory of literature (MA, PhD); urban ministries (D Th); urban ministry (M Th).

University of South Carolina, The Graduate School, College of Arts and Sciences, Department of Political Science, Program in Political Science, Columbia, SC 29208. Offers MA, PhD. Part-time programs available. *Faculty:* 32 full-time (8 women). *Students:* 38 full-time (19 women), 17 part-time (9 women); includes 7 minority (6 African Americans, 1 Asian American or Pacific Islander), 20 international. Average age 28. 53 applicants, 66% accepted, 15 enrolled. In 2007, 1 master's awarded. Terminal master's awarded for partial completion of doctoral program. *Median time to degree:* Of those who began their doctoral program in fall 1999, 25% received their degree in 8 years or less. *Degree requirements:* For master's, one foreign language, thesis; for doctorate, one foreign language, comprehensive exam, thesis/dissertation. *Entrance requirements:* For master's and doctorate, GRE General Test, minimum GPA of 3.5. Additional exam requirements/recommendations for international students: Required—TOEFL. *Application deadline:* For fall admission, 6/1 for domestic and international students. Applications are processed on a rolling basis. Application fee: $40. Electronic applications accepted. *Expenses:* Tuition, state resident: part-time $440 per hour. Tuition, nonresident: part-time $936 per hour. Required fees: $17 per hour. Tuition and fees vary according to program. *Financial support:* In 2007–08, 2 fellowships with partial tuition reimbursements (averaging $3,000 per year), 5 research assistantships with full tuition reimbursements (averaging $12,250 per year), 15 teaching assistantships with full tuition reimbursements (averaging $12,250 per year) were awarded; Federal Work-Study and institutionally sponsored loans also available. Financial award application deadline: 2/15. *Faculty research:* American government and politics, comparative politics, political theory, international politics, public administration and policy. *Unit head:* Dr. Donald J. Puchala, Graduate Director, 803-777-6801, Fax: 803-777-8255. *Application contact:* Tamara Lorraine Gordon, Student Services Coordinator, 803-777-3869, Fax: 803-777-8255, E-mail: gordontl@gwm.sc.edu.

The University of South Dakota, Graduate School, College of Arts and Sciences, Department of Political Science, Vermillion, SD 57069-2390. Offers American political institutions (PhD); political science (MA); public administration (MPA, PhD); public policy (PhD); JD/MA; JD/MPA. *Accreditation:* NASPAA (one or more programs are accredited). Part-time programs available. Postbaccalaureate distance learning degree programs offered. *Faculty:* 16 full-time (3 women), 1 part-time/adjunct (0 women). *Students:* 55 (29 women). In 2007, 65 degrees awarded. *Degree requirements:* For master's, comprehensive exam, thesis (for some programs). *Entrance requirements:* For master's, GRE or LSAT (MPA), GRE General Test (MA), minimum GPA of 2.7. Additional exam requirements/recommendations for international students: Required—TOEFL (minimum score 550 paper-based; 213 computer-based; 79 iBT). *Application deadline:* Applications are processed on a rolling basis. Application fee: $35. Electronic applications accepted. *Financial support:* In 2007–08, 4 research assistantships with partial tuition reimbursements (averaging $4,626 per year), 3 teaching assistantships with partial tuition reimbursements (averaging $4,626 per year) were awarded; Federal Work-Study also available. Support available to part-time students. Financial award applicants required to submit FAFSA. *Unit head:* Dr. William Richardson, Chair, 605-677-5242, Fax: 605-677-6302, E-mail: wrichard@usd.edu. *Application contact:* Dr. Richard Braunstein, Graduate Student Advisor, MPA Program, 605-677-5242, Fax: 605-677-6302, E-mail: rich.braunstein@usd.edu.

University of Southern California, Graduate School, Annenberg School for Communication, School of Communication, Program in Public Diplomacy, Los Angeles, CA 90089. Offers MPD. *Students:* 34 full-time (27 women), 1 (woman) part-time; includes 2 minority (1 African American, 1 Hispanic American), 6 international. 71 applicants, 76% accepted, 20 enrolled. In 2007, 2 degrees awarded. *Degree requirements:* For master's, thesis. *Entrance requirements:* For master's, GRE, resumé, writing samples, recommendation letters. Additional exam requirements/recommendations for international students: Required—TOEFL (minimum score 280 computer-based; 114 iBT). *Application deadline:* For fall admission, 12/14 priority date for domestic and international students. Application fee: $85. Electronic applications accepted. *Financial support:* Career-related internships or fieldwork, Federal Work-Study, scholarships/grants, and tuition waivers available. Support available to part-time students. Financial award application deadline: 1/15; financial award applicants required to submit FAFSA. *Unit head:* Dr. Nicholas Cull, Director, 213-821-4080, E-mail: cull@usc.edu. *Application contact:* Allyson Hill, Director of Admissions, 213-821-0770, Fax: 213-821-5574, E-mail: ascadm@usc.edu.

See Close-Up on page 945.

University of Southern California, Graduate School, College of Letters, Arts and Sciences, Department of Political Science, Los Angeles, CA 90089. Offers politics and international relations (MA, PhD). *Faculty:* 32 full-time (11 women), 1 part-time/adjunct (0 women). *Students:* 34 full-time (17 women); includes 12 minority (2 African Americans, 1 American Indian/Alaska Native, 4 Asian Americans or Pacific Islanders, 5 Hispanic Americans), 10 international. In 2007, 8 degrees awarded. *Degree requirements:* For doctorate, one foreign language, thesis/dissertation. *Entrance requirements:* For doctorate, GRE General Test. *Application deadline:* For fall admission, 12/1 for domestic students. Application fee: $85. *Financial support:* In 2007–08, 38 students received support, including 14 fellowships with tuition reimbursements available (averaging $19,000 per year), 7 research assistantships with tuition reimbursements available (averaging $18,500 per year), 17 teaching assistantships with tuition reimbursements available (averaging $18,500 per year); scholarships/grants and tuition waivers (partial) also available. Financial award application deadline: 2/15; financial award applicants required to submit FAFSA. *Faculty research:* Public law, urban politics, political communication, Pacific Rim studies, environmental politics. *Unit head:* Dr. Daniel Lynch, Chair, 213-740-2311. *Application contact:* Alex Venegas, Information Contact, 213-740-2311.

University of Southern Mississippi, Graduate School, College of Arts and Letters, Department of Political Science, International Development, and International Affairs, Hattiesburg, MS 39406-0001. Offers international development (PhD); political science (MA, MS). Part-time programs available. *Faculty:* 17 full-time (3 women). *Students:* 23 full-time (8 women), 45 part-time (12 women); includes 14 minority (10 African Americans, 1 American Indian/Alaska Native, 1 Asian American or Pacific Islander, 2 Hispanic Americans), 3 international. Average age 40. 29 applicants, 66% accepted, 16 enrolled. In 2007, 8 master's, 3 doctorates awarded. *Degree requirements:* For master's, comprehensive exam, thesis (for some programs). *Entrance requirements:* For master's, GRE General Test, minimum GPA of 2.75 in last 2 years, 3.0 in field of study. *Application deadline:* For fall admission, 3/1 priority date for domestic students, 3/1 for international students. Applications are processed on a rolling basis. Application fee: $30. *Financial support:* In 2007–08, 3 research assistantships with full and partial tuition reimbursements (averaging $7,942 per year), 8 teaching assistantships (averaging $7,942 per year) were awarded; career-related internships or fieldwork, Federal Work-Study, scholarships/grants, and unspecified assistantships also available. Financial award application deadline: 3/15. *Faculty research:* American politics, international politics, political theory, comparative politics, public law. *Unit head:* Dr. Thomas Lansford, Interim Chair, 601-266-4310. *Application contact:* Dr. Robert Pauley, Graduate Coordinator, 601-266-4310, Fax: 601-266-4172.

University of South Florida, Graduate School, College of Arts and Sciences, Department of Government and International Affairs, Tampa, FL 33620-9951. Offers political science (MA); public administration (MPA). Part-time and evening/weekend programs available. *Faculty:* 14 full-time (3 women), 5 part-time/adjunct (3 women). *Students:* 38 full-time (24 women), 85 part-time (41 women); includes 34 minority (17 African Americans, 5 Asian Americans or Pacific Islanders, 12 Hispanic Americans), 7 international. 95 applicants, 59% accepted, 31 enrolled. In 2007, 33 degrees awarded. *Degree requirements:* For master's, comprehensive exam, thesis. *Entrance requirements:* For master's, GRE (minimum score: 470 verbal, 470 quantitative), minimum GPA of 3.0 in last 60 hours of course work. *Application deadline:* For fall admission, 6/1 for domestic students; for spring admission, 10/15 for domestic students. Applications are processed on a rolling basis. Application fee: $30. Electronic applications accepted. *Financial support:* Scholarships/grants and unspecified assistantships available. Financial award application deadline: 4/1. *Unit head:* Dr. Mohsen Milani, Chairperson, 813-974-2384, Fax: 813-974-0832, E-mail: milani@chuma1.cas.usf.edu. *Application contact:* Dr. Stephen Tauber, Graduate Coordinator, 813-974-0781, Fax: 813-974-0832, E-mail: stauber@chuma1.cas.usf.edu.

The University of Tennessee, Graduate School, College of Arts and Sciences, Department of Political Science, Program in Political Science, Knoxville, TN 37996. Offers MA, PhD. Part-time programs available. *Degree requirements:* For master's, thesis or alternative; for doctorate, one foreign language, thesis/dissertation. *Entrance requirements:* For master's and doctorate, GRE General Test, minimum GPA of 2.7. Additional exam requirements/recommendations for international students: Required—TOEFL. Electronic applications accepted.

The University of Tennessee, Graduate School, College of Arts and Sciences, Department of Sociology, Knoxville, TN 37996. Offers criminology (MA, PhD); energy, environment, and resource policy (MA, PhD); political economy (MA, PhD). Part-time programs available. *Degree requirements:* For master's, thesis or alternative; for doctorate, thesis/dissertation. *Entrance requirements:* For master's, GRE General Test, minimum GPA of 3.0; for doctorate, GRE General Test, minimum GPA of 3.5. Additional exam requirements/recommendations for international students: Required—TOEFL. Electronic applications accepted.

The University of Texas at Arlington, Graduate School, College of Liberal Arts, Department of Political Science, Arlington, TX 76019. Offers MA. Part-time and evening/weekend programs available. *Faculty:* 4 full-time (1 woman). *Students:* 10 full-time (8 women), 29 part-time (12 women); includes 9 minority (5 African Americans, 1 Asian American or Pacific Islander, 3 Hispanic Americans), 4 international. 18 applicants, 50% accepted, 9 enrolled. In 2007, 5 degrees awarded. *Degree requirements:* For master's, comprehensive exam, thesis optional. *Entrance requirements:* For master's, minimum GPA of 3.0 in last 60 hours of course work. Additional exam requirements/recommendations for international students: Required—TOEFL (minimum score 550 paper-based; 213 computer-based). *Application deadline:* For fall admission, 6/16 for domestic students. Applications are processed on a rolling basis. Application fee: $35 ($50 for international students). *Expenses:* Tuition, state resident: full-time $5,934. Tuition, nonresident: full-time $10,938. *Financial support:* In 2007–08, 1 student received support; fellowships, teaching assistantships, career-related internships or fieldwork, institutionally sponsored loans, and scholarships/grants available. Support available to part-time students. Financial award application deadline: 6/1; financial award applicants required to submit FAFSA. *Unit head:* Dr. Rebecca Deen, Chair, 817-272-2991, Fax: 817-272-2525, E-mail: deen@uta.edu.

The University of Texas at Austin, Graduate School, College of Liberal Arts, Department of Government, Austin, TX 78712-1111. Offers MA, PhD. *Degree requirements:* For master's, thesis; for doctorate, comprehensive exam, thesis/dissertation. *Entrance requirements:* For master's and doctorate, GRE General Test. Electronic applications accepted.

The University of Texas at Brownsville, Graduate Studies, College of Liberal Arts, Department of Government, Brownsville, TX 78520-4991. Offers MAIS. Part-time and evening/weekend programs available. *Degree requirements:* For master's, comprehensive exam, thesis optional. *Entrance requirements:* For master's, GRE General Test. Additional exam requirements/recommendations for international students: Required—TOEFL.

The University of Texas at Dallas, School of Economic, Political and Policy Sciences, Program in Political Science, Richardson, TX 75083-0688. Offers PhD. Part-time and evening/weekend programs available. *Faculty:* 12 full-time (4 women), 2 part-time/adjunct (0 women). *Students:* 36 full-time (12 women), 8 part-time; includes 11 minority (4 African Americans, 1 American Indian/Alaska Native, 3 Asian Americans or Pacific Islanders, 3 Hispanic Americans), 7 international. Average age 39. 22 applicants, 64% accepted, 6 enrolled. In 2007, 1 degree awarded. *Degree requirements:* For doctorate, thesis/dissertation. *Entrance requirements:* For doctorate, GRE General Test, minimum GPA of 3.0 in upper-level course work in field. Additional exam requirements/recommendations for international students: Required—TOEFL (minimum score 550 paper-based; 213 computer-based). *Application deadline:* For fall admission, 7/15 for domestic students; for spring admission, 11/15 for domestic students. Application fee: $50 ($100 for international students). *Expenses:* Tuition, state resident: full-time $7,052. Tuition, nonresident: full-time $12,632. Tuition and fees vary according to course load. *Financial support:* In 2007–08, 20 teaching assistantships with tuition reimbursements (averaging $10,980 per year) were awarded; fellowships, research assistantships with tuition reimbursements, career-related internships or fieldwork, Federal Work-Study, institutionally sponsored loans, and scholarships/grants also available. Support available to part-time students. Financial award application deadline: 4/30; financial award applicants required to submit FAFSA. *Unit head:* Dr. Robert Lowry, Program Head, 972-883-2932, Fax: 972-883-2735, E-mail: robert.lowry@utdallas.edu. *Application contact:* Lynne Boyer, Program Assistant, 972-883-2932, E-mail: lynne.boyer@utdallas.edu.

The University of Texas at El Paso, Graduate School, College of Liberal Arts, Department of Political Science, El Paso, TX 79968-0001. Offers MA, MPA. Part-time and evening/weekend programs available. *Degree requirements:* For master's, thesis (for some programs). *Entrance requirements:* For master's, GMAT, GRE General Test, minimum GPA of 3.0. Electronic applications accepted.

The University of Texas at San Antonio, College of Liberal and Fine Arts, Department of Political Science and Geography, San Antonio, TX 78249-0617. Offers political science (MA). Part-time and evening/weekend programs available. *Faculty:* 13 full-time (5 women). *Students:* 16 full-time (8 women), 29 part-time (16 women); includes 28 minority (6 African Americans, 1 Asian American or Pacific Islander, 21 Hispanic Americans). Average age 30. 21 applicants, 90% accepted, 19 enrolled. In 2007, 3 degrees awarded. *Degree requirements:* For master's, thesis optional. *Entrance requirements:* For master's, GRE General Test. Additional exam requirements/recommendations for international students: Required—TOEFL (minimum score 500 paper-based; 173 computer-based). *Application deadline:* For fall admission, 7/1 for domestic students, 4/1 for international students; for spring admission, 11/1 for domestic students, 9/1 for international students. Applications are processed on a rolling basis. Application fee: $45 ($80 for international students). Electronic applications accepted. *Financial support:* In 2007–08, 10 students received support, including 8 research assistantships (averaging $7,488 per year), 1 teaching assistantship (averaging $8,892 per year); career-related internships or fieldwork, Federal Work-Study, scholarships/grants, and unspecified assistantships also available. *Unit head:* Dr. Mansour El-Kikhia, Chair, 210-458-5600, Fax: 210-458-5615, E-mail: mansour.elkikhia@utsa.edu. *Application contact:* Martha Luna, Administrative Associate, 210-458-5883, Fax: 210-458-5430.

The University of Texas at Tyler, College of Arts and Sciences, Department of Political Science, Tyler, TX 75799-0001. Offers MA. Part-time and evening/weekend programs available. *Faculty:* 3 full-time (1 woman), 2 part-time/adjunct (0 women). *Students:* 6 full-time (3 women), 3 part-time (1 woman); includes 1 African American, 1 American Indian/Alaska Native. 2 applicants, 100% accepted, 2 enrolled. In 2007, 6 degrees awarded. *Degree requirements:* For master's, comprehensive exam, thesis optional, 36 hours of course work, minimum GPA of

Political Science

The University of Texas at Tyler (continued)
3.0. *Expenses:* Tuition, state resident: part-time $627 per semester hour. Tuition, nonresident: part-time $908 per semester hour. Required fees: $107 per semester hour. Tuition and fees vary according to course load. *Financial support:* In 2007–08, fellowships (averaging $500 per year), 1 teaching assistantship (averaging $6,750 per year) were awarded; scholarships/grants also available. *Faculty research:* American Politics Comparative Politics, international relations, political theory and philosophy. *Unit head:* Dr. Marcus Stadelmann, Head, 903-566-7412, Fax: 903-565-5537, E-mail: mstadelmann@uttyler.edu. *Application contact:* Dr. Randy LeBlanc, Information Contact, 903-566-7415, E-mail: rlblanc@uttyler.edu.

The University of Toledo, College of Graduate Studies, College of Arts and Sciences, Department of Political Science and Public Administration, Program in Political Science, Toledo, OH 43606-3390. Offers MA. *Students:* 8 full-time (7 women), 4 part-time (1 woman); includes 3 minority (all African Americans), 1 international. Average age 27. 7 applicants, 71% accepted, 4 enrolled. In 2007, 4 degrees awarded. *Degree requirements:* For master's, thesis. *Entrance requirements:* For master's, GRE General Test, GRE Subject Test, minimum GPA of 2.7. *Application deadline:* For fall admission, 1/15 priority date for domestic students; for spring admission, 4/1 for domestic students. Applications are processed on a rolling basis. Application fee: $45. Electronic applications accepted. *Financial support:* Research assistantships, teaching assistantships, scholarships/grants, tuition waivers (full), and unspecified assistantships available. Financial award application deadline: 4/1. *Faculty research:* Economic policy, development, Third World, Eastern Europe, Africa. *Application contact:* Renee Heberle, Director, 419-530-2265, E-mail: renee.herberle@utoledo.edu.

University of Toronto, School of Graduate Studies, Social Sciences Division, Department of Political Science, Toronto, ON M5S 1A1, Canada. Offers MA, PhD. Part-time programs available. *Faculty:* 58 full-time, 19 part-time/adjunct. *Students:* 204 full-time (107 women), 5 part-time, 40 international. 717 applicants, 29% accepted. In 2007, 24 master's, 8 doctorates awarded. *Degree requirements:* For master's, thesis optional; for doctorate, one foreign language, thesis/dissertation, reading competency in a language other than English. *Entrance requirements:* For master's, 3 letters of recommendation, writing sample; for doctorate, 4 letters of recommendation, writing sample. *Application deadline:* For fall admission, 2/1 priority date for domestic students. Application fee: $100 Canadian dollars. *Unit head:* Prof. David Cameron, Graduate Director, 416-978-6385, Fax: 416-978-2027. *Application contact:* Joan Kalis, Secretary, 416-978-7170, Fax: 416-978-5566, E-mail: poliscm@artsci.utoronto.ca.

University of Utah, The Graduate School, College of Humanities, Program in Middle East Studies, Salt Lake City, UT 84112-1107. Offers anthropology (MA); Arabic (MA, PhD); Arabic and linguistics (MA, PhD); Hebrew (MA); history (MA, PhD); Persian (MA, PhD); political science (MA, PhD); Turkish (MA). *Faculty:* 12 full-time (3 women). *Students:* 26 full-time (12 women), 10 part-time (2 women); includes 1 minority (Asian American or Pacific Islander), 10 international. Average age 36. 36 applicants, 78% accepted, 10 enrolled. In 2007, 6 master's awarded. Terminal master's awarded for partial completion of doctoral program. *Median time to degree:* Of those who began their doctoral program in fall 1999, 100% received their degree in 8 years or less. *Degree requirements:* For master's, 2 foreign languages, comprehensive exam, thesis optional; for doctorate, 3 foreign languages, comprehensive exam, thesis/dissertation. *Entrance requirements:* For master's, GRE General Test, minimum GPA of 3.2; for doctorate, GRE General Test, MA in Middle East studies or equivalent, minimum GPA of 3.2. Additional exam requirements/recommendations for international students: Required—TOEFL (minimum score 580 paper-based; 237 computer-based; 92 iBT). *Application deadline:* For fall admission, 1/15 for domestic and international students; for spring admission, 9/15 for domestic and international students. Application fee: $45 ($65 for international students). *Financial support:* In 2007–08, 17 students received support, including 14 fellowships with full tuition reimbursements available (averaging $14,000 per year), 2 teaching assistantships with full tuition reimbursements available (averaging $12,000 per year); unspecified assistantships also available. Financial award application deadline: 1/15. *Faculty research:* Arabic literature and linguistics, Islamic studies, Middle East history, political science, Judaic studies. *Unit head:* Dr. Ibrahim A. Karawan, Director, 801-581-6181, Fax: 801-581-6183, E-mail: ibrahim.karawan@poli-sci.utah.edu. *Application contact:* Peter von Sivers, Director of Graduate Studies, 801-581-8073, Fax: 801-581-6183, E-mail: peter.vonsivers@utah.edu.

University of Utah, The Graduate School, College of Social and Behavioral Science, Department of Political Science, Program in Political Science, Salt Lake City, UT 84112-1107. Offers MA, MS, PhD. Part-time programs available. *Students:* 24 full-time (7 women), 34 part-time (12 women); includes 4 minority (3 Asian Americans or Pacific Islanders, 1 Hispanic American), 13 international. Average age 34. 55 applicants, 40% accepted, 11 enrolled. In 2007, 5 master's, 5 doctorates awarded. *Median time to degree:* Of those who began their doctoral program in fall 1999, 50% received their degree in 8 years or less. *Degree requirements:* For master's, one foreign language, thesis or research paper; for doctorate, variable foreign language requirement, thesis/dissertation. *Entrance requirements:* For master's, GRE General Test, minimum GPA of 3.2; for doctorate, GRE General Test. Additional exam requirements/recommendations for international students: Required—TOEFL (minimum score 500 paper-based; 173 computer-based). *Application deadline:* For fall admission, 7/1 priority date for domestic and international students; for winter admission, 8/1 priority date for domestic and international students. Application fee: $45 ($65 for international students). *Financial support:* In 2007–08, 15 students received support, including 3 fellowships with full tuition reimbursements available (averaging $9,000 per year), 10 teaching assistantships (averaging $9,000 per year); research assistantships with full tuition reimbursements available, career-related internships or fieldwork also available. Financial award application deadline: 1/15; financial award applicants required to submit FAFSA. *Faculty research:* Middle East politics, environmental politics, democratic theory, political participation, Latin-American politics. *Application contact:* Jessica Peterson, Graduate Coordinator, 801-585-7031, Fax: 801-585-6492, E-mail: jessica.peterson@poli-sci.utah.edu.

University of Victoria, Faculty of Graduate Studies, Faculty of Social Sciences, Department of Political Science, Victoria, BC V8W 2Y2, Canada. Offers MA, PhD. Part-time programs available. *Faculty:* 11 full-time (4 women), 9 part-time/adjunct (0 women). *Students:* 7. Average age 24. 95 applicants, 32% accepted, 5 enrolled. In 2007, 3 degrees awarded. *Degree requirements:* For master's, thesis; for doctorate, thesis/dissertation, candidacy exam. *Entrance requirements:* For master's, minimum B+ average in last 2 years of undergraduate course work. Additional exam requirements/recommendations for international students: Required—TOEFL (minimum score 600 paper-based; 250 computer-based). *Application deadline:* For fall admission, 1/15 priority date for domestic students, 12/15 priority date for international students. Applications are processed on a rolling basis. Application fee: $75 ($125 for international students). Electronic applications accepted. *Expenses:* Tuition, state resident: full-time $3,110. International tuition: $3,700 full-time. Tuition and fees vary according to program. *Financial support:* In 2007–08, 2 fellowships (averaging $12,400 per year), 1 research assistantship (averaging $6,000 per year), 5 teaching assistantships (averaging $6,000 per year) were awarded; institutionally sponsored loans also available. Financial award application deadline: 2/15. *Faculty research:* Political theory, political parties, international political economy, comparative public policy, British Columbian politics. *Unit head:* Dr. Colin Bennett, Chair, 250-721-7495, Fax: 250-721-7485, E-mail: chairpol@uvic.ca. *Application contact:* Amy Verdun, Graduate Adviser, 250-472-5466, Fax: 250-721-7485, E-mail: gradpol@uvic.ca.

University of Virginia, College and Graduate School of Arts and Sciences, Department of Politics, Program in Government, Charlottesville, VA 22903. Offers MA, PhD, JD/MA, MBA/MA. *Students:* 39 full-time (12 women), 3 part-time (1 woman); includes 1 minority (African American), 12 international. Average age 29. 66 applicants, 33% accepted, 6 enrolled. In 2007, 10 master's, 5 doctorates awarded. *Degree requirements:* For master's, thesis; for doctorate, variable foreign language requirement, thesis/dissertation. *Entrance requirements:* For master's and doctorate, GRE General Test, GRE Subject Test. *Application deadline:* Applications are processed on a rolling basis. Application fee: $60. Electronic applications accepted. *Financial support:* Applicants required to submit FAFSA.

University of Washington, Graduate School, College of Arts and Sciences, Department of Political Science, Seattle, WA 98195. Offers MA, PhD. *Degree requirements:* For doctorate, thesis/dissertation. *Entrance requirements:* For master's and doctorate, GRE General Test, minimum GPA of 3.0. Additional exam requirements/recommendations for international students: Required—TOEFL. Electronic applications accepted. *Faculty research:* American politics, comparative politics, international relations, political theory, political economy.

University of Waterloo, Graduate Studies, Faculty of Arts, Department of Political Science, Global Governance Program, Waterloo, ON N2L 3G1, Canada. Offers MA, PhD. *Students:* 15. *Entrance requirements:* For master's, BA, B+ average; for doctorate, MA. Additional exam requirements/recommendations for international students: Required—TOEFL. Application fee: $75. Electronic applications accepted. *Financial support:* Fellowships, research assistantships, teaching assistantships, career-related internships or fieldwork available. *Faculty research:* Global political economy, global environment, peace and security, global justice and human rights, multilateral institutions and diplomacy. *Unit head:* Dr. Eric Helleiner, Graduate Officer, 519-888-4567 Ext. 33955, E-mail: ehelleine@uwaterloo.ca.

The University of Western Ontario, Faculty of Graduate Studies, Social Sciences Division, Department of Political Science, London, ON N6A 5B8, Canada. Offers MA, MPA, PhD. Part-time programs available. *Degree requirements:* For master's, thesis; for doctorate, comprehensive exam, thesis/dissertation. *Entrance requirements:* For master's, minimum B average, honors BA in political science or equivalent, sample of written work; for doctorate, MA in political science or equivalent. *Application deadline:* For fall admission, 2/1 for domestic students. Applications are processed on a rolling basis. Application fee: $50. *Financial support:* Fellowships, research assistantships, teaching assistantships available. Financial award application deadline: 4/1. *Faculty research:* Political theory, Canadian politics, local government, comparative politics, international relations. *Unit head:* Dr. Donald E. Abelson, Graduate Chair, 519-661-4185 Ext. 84185, Fax: 519-661-3904, E-mail: dabelson@uwo.ca. *Application contact:* Teresa McLauchlan, Graduate Assistant, 519-661-2111 Ext. 83657, Fax: 519-661-4093, E-mail: polscigrading@uwo.ca.

University of West Florida, College of Arts and Sciences: Arts, Department of Government, Pensacola, FL 32514-5750. Offers political science (MA), including public administration, security and diplomacy. Part-time and evening/weekend programs available. *Faculty:* 3 full-time (0 women), 1 part-time/adjunct (0 women). *Students:* 9 full-time (4 women), 9 part-time (1 woman); includes 2 minority (both Hispanic Americans) Average age 32. 25 applicants, 68% accepted, 11 enrolled. In 2007, 8 degrees awarded. *Degree requirements:* For master's, thesis or alternative. *Entrance requirements:* For master's, GRE General Test, minimum GPA of 3.0. Additional exam requirements/recommendations for international students: Required—TOEFL (minimum score 550 paper-based; 213 computer-based). *Application deadline:* For fall admission, 6/1 for domestic students, 5/15 for international students; for spring admission, 11/1 for domestic students, 10/1 for international students. Applications are processed on a rolling basis. Application fee: $30. *Expenses:* Tuition, state resident: full-time $6,054; part-time $252 per credit. Tuition, nonresident: full-time $21,886; part-time $912 per credit. *Financial support:* Fellowships, research assistantships with partial tuition reimbursements, career-related internships or fieldwork, Federal Work-Study, institutionally sponsored loans, and tuition waivers (full and partial) available. Support available to part-time students. Financial award application deadline: 4/15; financial award applicants required to submit FAFSA. *Faculty research:* Political campaigns, elections, law enforcement, growth management. *Unit head:* Dr. A. Cuzan, Chairperson, 850-474-2337.

University of Windsor, Faculty of Graduate Studies, Faculty of Arts and Social Sciences, Department of Political Science, Windsor, ON N9B 3P4, Canada. Offers MA. Part-time programs available. *Faculty:* 13 full-time (4 women). *Students:* 37 full-time (14 women), 3 part-time. 76 applicants, 68% accepted. In 2007, 17 degrees awarded. *Entrance requirements:* For master's, minimum B+ average. Additional exam requirements/recommendations for international students: Required—TOEFL (minimum score 600 paper-based; 250 computer-based). *Application deadline:* For fall admission, 7/1 for domestic students; for winter admission, 11/1 for domestic students; for spring admission, 3/1 for domestic students. Applications are processed on a rolling basis. Application fee: $55. Electronic applications accepted. *Financial support:* In 2007–08, 21 teaching assistantships (averaging $8,901 per year) were awarded; Federal Work-Study, tuition waivers (full and partial), unspecified assistantships, and bursary also available. *Faculty research:* Canadian politics and government, local government, comparative political Canadian public administration, public policy. *Unit head:* Dr. John Sutcliffe, Head, 519-253-3000 Ext. 2347, Fax: 519-973-7094, E-mail: sutclif@uwindsor.ca. *Application contact:* 519-253-3000 Ext. 6459, Fax: 519-971-3653, E-mail: gradadmit@uwindsor.ca.

University of Wisconsin–Madison, Graduate School, College of Letters and Science, Department of Political Science, Madison, WI 53706-1380. Offers MA, PhD. *Degree requirements:* For doctorate, thesis/dissertation. *Entrance requirements:* For master's and doctorate, GRE General Test. Electronic applications accepted. *Faculty research:* Comparative politics, American politics, international relations, political theory, political methodology.

University of Wisconsin–Milwaukee, Graduate School, College of Letters and Sciences, Department of Political Science, Milwaukee, WI 53201-0413. Offers MA, PhD. *Faculty:* 18 full-time (4 women). *Students:* 34 full-time (14 women), 18 part-time (11 women); includes 6 minority (2 African Americans, 2 Asian Americans or Pacific Islanders, 2 Hispanic Americans), 6 international. 73 applicants, 47% accepted, 18 enrolled. In 2007, 9 master's, 4 doctorates awarded. *Degree requirements:* For master's, thesis or alternative; for doctorate, one foreign language, thesis/dissertation. *Entrance requirements:* For master's, GRE General Test, minimum GPA of 3.0. *Application deadline:* For fall admission, 1/1 priority date for domestic students; for spring admission, 9/1 for domestic students. Applications are processed on a rolling basis. Application fee: $45 ($75 for international students). *Expenses:* Tuition, state resident: part-time $530 per credit. Tuition, nonresident: part-time $1,428 per credit. Required fees: $19 per credit. $229 per term. Tuition and fees vary according to course load and program. *Financial support:* In 2007–08, 20 teaching assistantships were awarded; fellowships, research assistantships, career-related internships or fieldwork and unspecified assistantships also available. Support available to part-time students. Financial award application deadline: 4/15. *Unit head:* John Bohte, Representative, 414-229-4328, Fax: 414-229-5021, E-mail: jbohte@uwm.edu.

University of Wyoming, Graduate School, College of Arts and Sciences, Department of Political Science, Program in Political Science, Laramie, WY 82070. Offers MA. Part-time programs available. *Faculty:* 5 full-time (0 women), 3 part-time/adjunct (2 women). *Students:* 16 full-time (6 women), 28 part-time (17 women); includes 4 minority (1 African American, 1 American Indian/Alaska Native, 2 Hispanic Americans), 2 international. Average age 32. 22 applicants, 64% accepted. In 2007, 2 degrees awarded. *Degree requirements:* For master's, thesis or alternative. *Entrance requirements:* For master's, GRE General Test, bachelor's degree in political science, minimum GPA of 3.0. Additional exam requirements/recommendations for international students: Required—TOEFL (minimum score 525 paper-based; 195 computer-based). *Application deadline:* For fall admission, 6/1 priority date for domestic students. Applications are processed on a rolling basis. Application fee: $50. Electronic applications accepted. *Financial support:* In 2007–08, 6 students received support, including 5 research assistantships with full tuition reimbursements available (averaging $10,062 per year), 1 teaching assistantship with full tuition reimbursement available (averaging $10,062 per year); career-related internships or fieldwork and unspecified assistantships also available. Financial award application deadline: 3/15. *Faculty research:* American government, public law, judicial politics, political theory, international relations. *Application contact:* Jamie L. LeJambre, Graduate Coordinator, 307-766-6484, Fax: 307-766-6771, E-mail: lejambre@uwyo.edu.

Utah State University, School of Graduate Studies, College of Humanities, Arts and Social Sciences, Department of Political Science, Logan, UT 84322. Offers MA, MS. Part-time programs available. *Degree requirements:* For master's, one foreign language, thesis. *Entrance requirements:* For master's, GRE General Test, minimum GPA of 3.0. Additional exam requirements/recommendations for international students: Required—TOEFL. *Faculty research:* Political parties; social choice; international political economics; foreign policy; politics, markets, and public policy.

Vanderbilt University, Graduate School, Department of Political Science, Nashville, TN 37240-1001. Offers MA, MAT, PhD. *Faculty:* 21 full-time (6 women), 3 part-time/adjunct (0 women). *Students:* 32 full-time (16 women); includes 5 minority (2 African Americans, 3 Hispanic Americans), 11 international. Average age 29. 130 applicants, 15% accepted, 8 enrolled. In 2007, 2 master's, 1 doctorate awarded. *Degree requirements:* For master's, thesis; for doctorate, thesis/dissertation, final and qualifying exams. *Entrance requirements:* For master's and doctorate, GRE General Test. *Application deadline:* For fall admission, 1/15 for domestic and international students. Application fee: $0. Electronic applications accepted. *Financial support:* Fellowships with full tuition reimbursements, research assistantships with full tuition reimbursements, teaching assistantships with full tuition reimbursements, Federal Work-Study, institutionally sponsored loans, and health care benefits available. Financial award application deadline: 1/15; financial award applicants required to submit CSS PROFILE or FAFSA. *Faculty research:* American politics, comparative politics, international politics, political theory, political culture and life. *Unit head:* Neal Tate, Chair, 615-322-6222, Fax: 615-343-6003, E-mail: n.tate@vanderbilt.edu. *Application contact:* Marc Hetherington, Director of Graduate Studies, 615-322-6222, Fax: 615-343-6003, E-mail: marc.j.hetherington@vanderbilt.edu.

Villanova University, Graduate School of Liberal Arts and Sciences, Department of Political Science, Program in Political Science, Villanova, PA 19085-1699. Offers MA. *Students:* 19 full-time (7 women), 27 part-time (11 women); includes 2 minority (both Asian Americans or Pacific Islanders), 2 international. Average age 27. 36 applicants, 81% accepted. In 2007, 22 degrees awarded. *Degree requirements:* For master's, thesis or alternative. *Entrance requirements:* For master's, GRE, minimum GPA of 3.0. *Application deadline:* For fall admission, 8/1 for domestic and international students; for spring admission, 12/1 for domestic and international students. Applications are processed on a rolling basis. Application fee: $50. Electronic applications accepted. *Financial support:* Scholarships/grants and unspecified assistantships available. Financial award application deadline: 3/15; financial award applicants required to submit FAFSA. *Application contact:* Matthew Kerbel, Information Contact, 610-519-4553, Fax: 610-519-7487, E-mail: matthew.kerbel@villanova.edu.

See Close-Up on page 1173.

Virginia Commonwealth University, Graduate School, College of Humanities and Sciences, Wilder School of Government and Public Affairs, Richmond, VA 23284-9005. Offers MA, MPA, MS, MURP, PhD, CASR, CCJA, CPM, CURP, Certificate, Graduate Certificate, JD/MURP, MSW/Certificate. *Expenses:* Tuition, state resident: full-time $7,224; part-time $401 per credit. Tuition, nonresident: full-time $16,072; part-time $891 per credit. Required fees: $1,679; $63 per credit. Tuition and fees vary according to campus/location. *Application contact:* Dr. Sherry T. Sandkam, Associate Dean, 804-828-6916, Fax: 804-827-4546, E-mail: ssandkam@vcu.edu.

Virginia Polytechnic Institute and State University, Graduate School, College of Liberal Arts and Human Sciences, Department of Political Science, Blacksburg, VA 24061. Offers MA. *Entrance requirements:* For master's, GRE General Test. Additional exam requirements/recommendations for international students: Required—TOEFL (minimum score 600 paper-based; 250 computer-based). Electronic applications accepted. *Faculty research:* Comparative politics, international relations, American government and politics, research methods.

Washington State University, Graduate School, College of Liberal Arts, Department of Political Science, Program in Political Science, Pullman, WA 99164. Offers MA, PhD. *Faculty:* 22. *Students:* 30 full-time (7 women), 13 part-time (3 women); includes 7 minority (1 African American, 1 American Indian/Alaska Native, 5 Hispanic Americans), 4 international. Average age 32. 45 applicants, 27% accepted, 4 enrolled. In 2007, 9 master's, 3 doctorates awarded. Terminal master's awarded for partial completion of doctoral program. *Degree requirements:* For master's, comprehensive exam (for some programs), thesis, oral exam; for doctorate, comprehensive exam, thesis/dissertation, oral exam, written exam. *Entrance requirements:* For master's, GRE General Test, minimum GPA of 3.0; for doctorate, GRE General Test, minimum GPA of 3.5. Additional exam requirements/recommendations for international students: Required—TOEFL. *Application deadline:* For fall admission, 2/1 for domestic and international students; for spring admission, 11/1 for domestic students, 7/1 for international students. Application fee: $50. Electronic applications accepted. *Financial support:* In 2007–08, 34 students received support, including 4 fellowships (averaging $2,656 per year), 6 research assistantships with full and partial tuition reimbursements available (averaging $13,917 per year), 12 teaching assistantships with full and partial tuition reimbursements available (averaging $13,056 per year). Financial award application deadline: 2/1; financial award applicants required to submit FAFSA. *Faculty research:* Political psychology and image theory, grass roots environmental policy, federal juvenile policy. *Unit head:* Dr. Andrew Mark Appleton, Director, 509-335-4025, Fax: 509-335-7990, E-mail: appleton@wsu.edu. *Application contact:* Graduate School Admissions, 800-GRADWSU, Fax: 509-335-1949, E-mail: gradsch@wsu.edu.

Washington University in St. Louis, Graduate School of Arts and Sciences, Department of Political Science, St. Louis, MO 63130-4899. Offers political economy and public policy (MA); political science (MA, PhD); JD/MA. Terminal master's awarded for partial completion of doctoral program. *Degree requirements:* For master's, thesis or alternative; for doctorate, thesis/dissertation. *Entrance requirements:* For master's and doctorate, GRE General Test. Electronic applications accepted.

Wayne State University, College of Liberal Arts and Sciences, Department of Political Science, Program in Political Science, Detroit, MI 48202. Offers MA, PhD, JD/MA. *Students:* 27 full-time (15 women), 28 part-time (11 women); includes 7 minority (all African Americans), 6 international. Average age 36. 32 applicants, 41% accepted, 5 enrolled. In 2007, 6 master's, 4 doctorates awarded. *Degree requirements:* For doctorate, thesis/dissertation. *Entrance requirements:* For master's, GRE General Test, minimum GPA of 3.0; for doctorate, GRE General Test, minimum GPA of 3.0, 3 letters of recommendation. Additional exam requirements/recommendations for international students: Required—TOEFL (minimum score 550 paper-based; 213 computer-based); Recommended—TWE (minimum score 6). *Application deadline:* For fall admission, 6/1 for domestic students, 5/1 for international students. Applications are processed on a rolling basis. Application fee: $81. Electronic applications accepted. *Expenses:* Tuition, state resident: part-time $403 per credit hour. Tuition, nonresident: part-time $890 per credit hour. *Financial support:* Fellowships, research assistantships, teaching assistantships, career-related internships or fieldwork, Federal Work-Study, and institutionally sponsored loans available. *Faculty research:* Political theory and thought, international relations, American politics, comparative politics, public policy, public administration, urban politics. *Application contact:* Application Contact, 313-577-2630, Fax: 313-993-3435.

Western Illinois University, School of Graduate Studies, College of Arts and Sciences, Department of Political Science, Macomb, IL 61455-1390. Offers political science (MA); public and non-profit management (Certificate). Part-time programs available. *Students:* 13 full-time (5 women), 9 part-time (2 women); includes 4 minority (3 African Americans, 1 Hispanic American), 5 international. Average age 26. 20 applicants, 55% accepted. In 2007, 8 master's, 1 other advanced degree awarded. *Degree requirements:* For master's, comprehensive exam, thesis or alternative. *Entrance requirements:* For master's, minimum GPA of 2.75. Additional exam requirements/recommendations for international students: Required—TOEFL (minimum score 550 paper-based; 213 computer-based; 80 iBT). *Application deadline:* Applications are processed on a rolling basis. Electronic applications accepted. *Expenses:* Tuition, state resident: part-time $217 per credit hour. Tuition, nonresident: part-time $433 per credit hour. Required fees: $54 per credit hour. *Financial support:* In 2007–08, 8 students received support, including 8 research assistantships with full tuition reimbursements available (averaging $6,800 per year). Financial award applicants required to submit FAFSA. *Unit head:* Dr. Richard Hardy, Chairperson, 309-298-1055. *Application contact:* Dr. Barbara Baily, Director of Graduate Studies/Associate Provost, 309-298-1806, Fax: 309-298-2345, E-mail: grad-office@wiu.edu.

Western Kentucky University, Graduate Studies, Potter College of Arts and Letters, Department of Political Science, Bowling Green, KY 42101. Offers MPA. Part-time and evening/weekend programs available. *Degree requirements:* For master's, comprehensive exam, final exam. *Entrance requirements:* For master's, GRE General Test, minimum GPA of 2.75. Additional exam requirements/recommendations for international students: Required—TOEFL (minimum score 555 paper-based; 213 computer-based; 79 iBT). *Faculty research:* Role of non-profits, comparative policy analysis, social welfare policy, rural administration, ethics and bureaucracy.

Western Michigan University, Graduate College, College of Arts and Sciences, Department of Political Science, Program in Political Science, Kalamazoo, MI 49008-5202. Offers MA, PhD. *Degree requirements:* For master's, thesis optional, oral exams; for doctorate, thesis/dissertation, oral exam. *Entrance requirements:* For doctorate, GRE General Test.

Western Washington University, Graduate School, College of Humanities and Social Sciences, Department of Political Science, Bellingham, WA 98225-5996. Offers MA. Part-time programs available. *Faculty:* 12. *Students:* 11 full-time (4 women), 7 part-time (3 women); includes 2 minority (1 Asian American or Pacific Islander, 1 Hispanic American), 1 international. 16 applicants, 13% accepted, 9 enrolled. In 2007, 2 degrees awarded. *Degree requirements:* For master's, comprehensive exam, thesis (for some programs). *Entrance requirements:* For master's, GRE General Test, minimum GPA of 3.0 in last 60 semester hours or last 90 quarter hours. Additional exam requirements/recommendations for international students: Required—TOEFL (minimum score 567 paper-based; 227 computer-based). *Application deadline:* For fall admission, 2/1 priority date for domestic students; for winter admission, 10/1 for domestic students; for spring admission, 2/1 for domestic students. Applications are processed on a rolling basis. Application fee: $50. Electronic applications accepted. *Expenses:* Tuition, state resident: part-time $208 per credit. Tuition, nonresident: part-time $541 per credit. Required fees: $241 per quarter. One-time fee: $250 part-time. *Financial support:* In 2007–08, 4 teaching assistantships with partial tuition reimbursements (averaging $9,339 per year) were awarded; career-related internships or fieldwork, Federal Work-Study, institutionally sponsored loans, scholarships/grants, tuition waivers (partial), and unspecified assistantships also available. Support available to part-time students. Financial award application deadline: 2/15; financial award applicants required to submit FAFSA. *Faculty research:* Elections, environment, identity, international relations. *Unit head:* Dr. Sara Weir, Chair, 360-650-2912. *Application contact:* Dr. Vernon D. Johnson, Graduate Adviser, 360-650-4874.

West Texas A&M University, College of Education and Social Sciences, Department of History and Political Science, Program in Political Science, Canyon, TX 79016-0001. Offers MA. Part-time and evening/weekend programs available. *Degree requirements:* For master's, comprehensive exam, thesis optional. *Entrance requirements:* For master's, GRE General Test. Additional exam requirements/recommendations for international students: Required—TOEFL (minimum score 550 paper-based). Electronic applications accepted. *Faculty research:* American government, public administration, state and local government, international politics.

West Virginia University, Eberly College of Arts and Sciences, Department of Political Science, Morgantown, WV 26506. Offers American public policy and politics (MA); international and comparative public policy and politics (MA); political science (PhD); public policy analysis (PhD). *Faculty:* 15 full-time (3 women), 6 part-time/adjunct (2 women). *Students:* 56 full-time (22 women), 20 part-time (9 women); includes 7 minority (5 African Americans, 1 Asian American or Pacific Islander, 1 Hispanic American), 17 international. Average age 31. 55 applicants, 85% accepted, 24 enrolled. In 2007, 10 master's, 8 doctorates awarded. Terminal master's awarded for partial completion of doctoral program. *Degree requirements:* For master's, thesis optional; for doctorate, comprehensive exam, thesis/dissertation. *Entrance requirements:* For master's, GRE General Test, minimum GPA of 2.75; for doctorate, GRE General Test, minimum GPA of 3.0. Additional exam requirements/recommendations for international students: Required—TOEFL. *Application deadline:* For fall admission, 4/1 priority date for domestic students. Applications are processed on a rolling basis. Application fee: $45. *Expenses:* Tuition, state resident: full-time $5,196; part-time $292 per credit hour. Tuition, nonresident: full-time $15,064; part-time $840 per credit hour. Tuition and fees vary according to program. *Financial support:* In 2007–08, 65 students received support, including 1 research assistantship (averaging $15,000 per year), 15 teaching assistantships (averaging $9,000 per year); career-related internships or fieldwork, Federal Work-Study, institutionally sponsored loans, tuition waivers (full and partial), and unspecified assistantships also available. Financial award application deadline: 2/1; financial award applicants required to submit FAFSA. *Faculty research:* Public policy, research methods, foreign policy analysis, judicial politics, environmental and energy policy. Total annual research expenditures: $8,421. *Unit head:* Dr. Joe D. Hagan, Chair, 304-293-3811 Ext. 5283, Fax: 304-293-8644, E-mail: jhagan@wvu.edu. *Application contact:* Dr. Jeff Worsham, Director, Graduate Studies, 304-293-3811 Ext. 5277, Fax: 304-293-8644, E-mail: jeff.worsham@mail.wvu.edu.

Wichita State University, Graduate School, Fairmount College of Liberal Arts and Sciences, Department of Political Science, Wichita, KS 67260. Offers MA. Part-time and evening/weekend programs available. *Degree requirements:* For master's, comprehensive exam, thesis optional, internship. *Entrance requirements:* For master's, GRE, minimum GPA of 3.0. Additional exam requirements/recommendations for international students: Required—TOEFL. Electronic applications accepted. *Faculty research:* Foreign intelligence, political participation of U.S. parties, Southern civil rights policy.

Wilfrid Laurier University, Faculty of Graduate Studies, Faculty of Arts, Department of Political Science, Waterloo, ON N2L 3C5, Canada. Offers MA. *Faculty:* 15 full-time. *Students:* 20 full-time, 1 part-time. 60 applicants, 42% accepted, 16 enrolled. In 2007, 11 degrees awarded. *Degree requirements:* For master's, thesis optional. *Entrance requirements:* For master's, honors bachelor's degree or the equivalent in political science, minimum B average in undergraduate course work. Additional exam requirements/recommendations for international students: Required—TOEFL (minimum score 230 computer-based; 89 iBT). *Application deadline:* For fall admission, 2/1 priority date for domestic students. Application fee: $75. Electronic applications accepted. *Financial support:* Fellowships, research assistantships, teaching assistantships available. *Faculty research:* Political behavior/political psychology, Canadian political studies, comparative, politics/relations, public opinion and electoral studies, international. *Unit head:* Dr. Brian Tanguay, Chairperson, 519-884-0710 Ext. 3663. *Application contact:* Jennifer Poppe, Student Contact, 519-884-0710 Ext. 3536, Fax: 519-884-1020, E-mail: gradstudies@wlu.ca.

Yale University, Graduate School of Arts and Sciences, Department of Political Science, New Haven, CT 06520. Offers PhD. *Degree requirements:* For doctorate, one foreign language, thesis/dissertation. *Entrance requirements:* For doctorate, GRE General Test. *Faculty research:* U.N. and international security.

York University, Faculty of Graduate Studies, Faculty of Arts, Program in Political Science, Toronto, ON M3J 1P3, Canada. Offers MA, PhD. Part-time programs available. *Degree requirements:* For master's, thesis or alternative; for doctorate, one foreign language, comprehensive exam, thesis/dissertation. Electronic applications accepted.

York University, Faculty of Graduate Studies, Faculty of Arts, Program in Social and Political Thought, Toronto, ON M3J 1P3, Canada. Offers MA, PhD. Part-time programs available. *Degree requirements:* For master's, one foreign language, thesis or alternative, oral exams; for doctorate, one foreign language, comprehensive exam, thesis/dissertation. Electronic applications accepted.

AMERICAN GRADUATE SCHOOL OF INTERNATIONAL RELATIONS AND DIPLOMACY

International Relations and Diplomacy Programs

Programs of Study

The American Graduate School of International Relations and Diplomacy (AGSIRD) is an American institution of higher education located in Paris and specializing in international relations as well as related complementary disciplines such as international law and peace studies. It is located in Paris and accredited in the United States as an affiliated campus of Arcadia University in Pennsylvania. All AGSIRD courses are taught in English and based on the American model of higher education. They also take advantage of the cultural, institutional, and academic resources of Paris. Along with the master's programs, students have the opportunity to take courses in the French language at the School's world-renowned partner institution, Alliance Française.

Students at AGSIRD are prepared to begin or advance careers in international organizations, nongovernmental organizations (NGOs), government, and diplomacy as well as international business, journalism, academics, and other fields that require interaction with disparate countries and cultures.

AGSIRD offers full-time and part-time programs. The programs available are the Master of Arts (M.A.) in international relations and diplomacy (a two-year, full-time M.A. program; an accelerated eighteen-month program; and extended part-time programs), including optional specialization certificates; a Ph.D. program in international relations and diplomacy; a dual-degree program—American M.A. and French master's program in diplomacy and strategic negotiations, in partnership with University of Paris–Sud 11; a dual-degree program—American M.A. and European LL.M. in French and European union law, in partnership with the University of Cergy-Pontoise, France; a one-month intensive summer program in French language and French and European history, politics, and diplomacy, in partnership with Alliance Française (open to graduates and undergraduates); and two-course certificate programs in various subjects, such as conflict resolution, conflict and geopolitics, foreign policy, economics, and international law (for a complete list, students should visit the Web site). Single courses can also be chosen "à la carte".

Research Facilities

In addition to the School's specialized collection of international relations materials available for loan, students have access to the libraries at the two French partner universities and a wide variety of libraries in Paris, including the Bibliothèque Nationale de France and the specialized libraries of UNESCO, the Organisation for Economic Co-operation and Development (OECD), and other institutions. Students also have access to Arcadia University's online resources.

Financial Aid

AGSIRD offers financial aid, such as loans and scholarships, to open its program to all motivated and deserving students, whatever their financial possibilities. American students studying at AGSIRD are eligible for Federal Stafford Student Loans (up to $20,500) and can apply for private loans from Sallie Mae up to the full cost of attendance. For non-U.S. students, AGSIRD also offers school loans up to 50 percent of the tuition.

Need-based grants can be awarded by the financial aid office, and students of high academic merit can apply for the John A. Lee Memorial Scholarship. Students can work in France up to 19½ hours per week during the school year and full-time during breaks.

Cost of Study

Tuition for each 3-credit course is €2000. From the time of the student's enrollment, this price remains unchanged for up to three years. Unless credits are transferred from another university, the full tuition for the M.A. program is €30,000, including the French language option (€28,000 otherwise). The typical breakdown by semester is given on the School's Web site. A registration fee of €70 per semester is added; no other fee is levied.

Living and Housing Costs

Housing and living costs for students in the two-year M.A. program range from €13,400 to €19,200 in the first year and from €12,100 to €16,800 in the second year. This includes rent, books, medical coverage, local transportation, two overseas travels, food, and utilities as well as recreation and other personal expenses. The breakdown and additional details are on the School's Web site.

Student Group

AGSIRD welcomes students from various backgrounds. Although Americans represent the largest single national group, students at AGSIRD come from more than twenty different countries. They range from recent graduates to professionals seeking knowledge or career advancement. The student body is around 50, allowing for close interaction with professors, which AGSIRD believes is very important, especially at the graduate level.

Student Outcomes

AGSIRD graduates often pursue careers in diplomacy and other areas of government service; intergovernmental organizations, such as the UN and UNESCO; NGOs; think tanks; journalism and other media; international banks and businesses; consultancies; and academics.

Location

AGSIRD is located in Paris in a lively area between the traditional student district of the Latin Quarter and the historical artists' district of Montparnasse. In addition to the rich culture of France, the programs take advantage of the presence in Paris of many NGOs, international organizations (OECD, UNESCO), diplomatic missions, and headquarters of multinational corporations. Students also enjoy visiting France and Europe during the breaks.

The School

The American Graduate School of International Relations and Diplomacy was established in 1994 and was originally designed for diplomats posted in Paris. It is now open to both students who have recently completed their undergraduate degree and professionals seeking knowledge and career advancement. It is an affiliated campus of Arcadia University, which is located on the outskirts of Philadelphia, Pennsylvania, and is accredited in the United States by the Commission on Higher Education of the Middle States Association of Colleges and Schools.

Applying

Applicants come from a wide variety of national backgrounds and educational histories. AGSIRD admissions are selective, but the School emphasizes individual consideration of each of its candidates. Students are encouraged to have as much preparation as possible in history, economics, or social sciences. The School also values personal experience in other cultures as well as practical, professional work experience. No knowledge of French is required to apply, but language ability is appreciated. To be considered for admission, master's applicants must have completed the equivalent of a bachelor's degree, and Ph.D. applicants must hold a master's degree in international relations or a related discipline.

Applicants should submit an application form (available at http://www.agsird.edu/images/pdf/agsird_ma_application_form.pdf), official transcripts of all previous university work, a one- to three-page personal statement, two letters of recommendation, and a nonrefundable €50 application fee. A GRE score of at least 1100 (combined verbal and quantitative) and an analytical writing score of at least 5 are normally required (school code: 0632). Nonnative speakers of English who did not graduate from an American university must submit their official TOEFL scores. A minimum score of 600 on the paper-based test or 90 on the Internet-based test is required (school code: 0230). All documents in a language other than English or French must be accompanied by certified translations. In some cases, AGSIRD may request additional material, and applicants may be asked to take an interview.

Applications are considered up to six weeks before the beginning of the semester applied for. Admission decisions are made on a rolling basis, and notifications of admission status are mailed within four weeks of receipt of completed application materials. Admitted candidates confirm their enrollment with a €350 nonrefundable deposit that is credited toward their first semester's tuition.

Correspondence and Information

American Graduate School of International Relations and Diplomacy
101 Boulevard Raspail
75006 Paris
France

Phone: 33(0) 1 47 20 00 94
Fax: 33(0) 1 47 20 81 89
E-mail: info@agsird.edu
Web site: http://www.agsird.edu/

American Graduate School of International Relations and Diplomacy

THE FACULTY

The faculty is composed of both accomplished scholars and professional diplomats. It draws from a dozen countries.

Ruchi Anand (India), Ph.D., Purdue.
Bixio Barenco (Switzerland), Ph.D., Berkeley.
Mariam Habibi (Iran), Ph.D., Paris Institute of Political Studies.
Nikita Harwich (Venezuela), Ph.D., London School of Economics.
Oleg Kobtzeff (United States, France), Ph.D., Paris I (Pantheon-Sorbonne).
Anton Koslov (Russia, France), D.E.A., School for Advanced Studies in the Social Sciences (Paris).
Virginia Lindsay (United States, Ireland), J.D., California, San Francisco; LL.M., Georgetown.
Matthias Maass (Germany), Ph.D., Tufts (Fletcher).
Sir Christopher MacRae, KCMG (United Kingdom), B.A. (Hons), Oxford; Henry Fellow, Harvard.
Steven McGiffen (United Kingdom), Ph.D., Manchester (England).
David Pike (United States, France), Ph.D., Stanford; Ph.D., Toulouse (France).
Kaveh Rahnema (Iran, France), D.E.A., Paris X (Nanterre).
Eileen Servidio-Delabre (United States, France), D.E.A., Paris II (Pantheon-Assas).
Joav Toker (Israel, France), M.I.A., Columbia.
Paul Vallet (United States, France), Ph.D., Cambridge.
John West (Australia), Head of Public Affairs Division at OECD and Director of OECD Forum; M.Com., South Wales (Australia).
Fawn Wilderson-Legros (United States), J.D., Georgetown.
Douglas Yates (United States), Ph.D., Boston University.

AMERICAN UNIVERSITY

School of International Service

Programs of Study

A founding member of the Association of Professional Schools of International Affairs, American University's (AU) School of International Service (SIS) is the largest and most-applied-to school of international affairs in the United States. SIS offers two-year standard master's programs in the following fields: comparative and regional studies, global environmental politics, international communication, international development, international economic relations, international politics, international peace and conflict resolution, and U.S. foreign policy.

SIS also offers a one-year executive master's program (Master of International Service) for midcareer professionals with five to seven years of work experience, preferably in international affairs, and a Ph.D. program in international relations. In addition, the School has dual-degree programs with Ritsumeikan University in Japan, Korea University and Sookmyung Women's University in Korea, and the University of Peace in Costa Rica. Joint-degree programs in international media, ethics, peace, and global affairs and dual J.D./M.A., M.A./M.B.A., M.A./M.A.T., and M.A./M.T.S. programs are also available on the American University campus.

Within the graduate curriculum, students can tailor their programs to reflect their special interest and career paths and are also encouraged to integrate professional experience, including internships. General M.A. degree requirements include 39–42 credit hours of approved graduate course work, a comprehensive examination, demonstration of research and writing skills through completion of a master's thesis, substantial research paper requirement or research practicum, and proficiency in a modern foreign language. General Ph.D. degree requirements include 72 credit hours of approved graduate course work consisting of 60 hours of course credits and 12 credit hours of independent dissertation supervision.

Teaching styles at SIS are highly collegial. The curriculum is distinguished by linking theory and practice and addressing emerging issues both conceptually and empirically. SIS students have the opportunity to participate in cutting-edge faculty-led research projects and are constantly challenged to care about the moral, philosophical, and practical implications of an increasingly interdependent world.

The University's nationally recognized Career Center and SIS partner with domestic and international employers to offer substantive internship experiences for which students may earn academic credit. SIS students have interned and worked at such organizations as the International Monetary Fund, Amnesty International, Global Fund for Women, U.N. Higher Commissioner for Refugees, the U.S. Department of State, the World Bank, Search for Common Ground, foreign embassies, and many others.

Research Facilities

The School of International Service offers research opportunities through a number of research programs and centers, such as the Center for Asian Studies, the Center for Global Peace, Intercultural Management Institute, Center for Human Rights, Peacebuilding and Development Institute, and Public International Law and Policy Program.

During the summer, SIS also offers specialized study tours to sites including South Africa, Japan, Malaysia, Egypt, Italy, India, China, and the United Arab Emirates, where students are encouraged to pursue self-designed research in conjunction with a faculty adviser.

The American University's Bender Library and Learning Resources Center house more than 780,000 titles, as well as journals, film/video/multimedia recordings, and microforms. The library also contains special collections in music, mathematics, Japanese materials, and broadcast journalism. The library provides online access to 2,000 other member libraries. The University is also ranked by Intel as one of the top ten "most unwired college campuses" and was selected as T-Mobile's first HotSpot WiFi Internet campus.

Financial Aid

SIS offers merit-based awards to a limited number of eligible domestic and international graduate students upon notification of admission. Only full-time students are eligible to receive merit-based assistance. These awards are normally awarded for two years, provided that the recipient follows American University academic regulations and remains in good academic standing. The award amounts and types vary but can include partial- to full-tuition remission and/or a monthly stipend and/or a research assistantship with a faculty member. All admitted Ph.D. students are fully funded for their course work during their study at SIS. Students should note that all required application materials need to be received by the posted deadline in order to be considered for merit-based aid.

Cost of Study

Tuition for the 2007–08 academic year cost $19,998, based on two semesters of full-time enrollment, 9 credits/semester, at the rate of $1111 per credit. Fees cost $1880, which includes an SIS fee of $750 per semester for full-time students (registering for 9 credits or above) or $500 per semester for part-time students (registering for 6 to 8 credits), plus $300 for other estimated University fees. Students should anticipate an increase of 5 to 8 percent for each succeeding academic year.

Living and Housing Costs

Washington, D.C., is a diverse and eclectic city with many options for graduate students looking for housing. The best place to start searching is the American University Housing and Dining Web site (http://www.american.edu/ocl/housing/index1.html), where information about housing in Washington, D.C., and current postings for a variety of accommodations are listed. Some students choose to live on their own, renting a studio or one-bedroom apartment in the AU neighborhood or in one of the many centers around the city; others opt for group housing, sharing costs with several people in a house or apartment. Washington, D.C., has plenty of options from which to choose. There are many resources for finding housing in the city, including American University Housing and Dining Programs (http://www.american.edu/ocl/housing/index1.html), Apartment Search (http://www.apartmentsearch.com), Craig's List–Washington D.C. (http://www.washingtondc.craigslist.org), Off Campus Network (http://www.offcampusnetwork.com/index.asp), Washington City Paper Classifieds (http://www.washingtoncitypaper.com/class/classifieds.html), Washington Post Classifieds (http://www.washingtonpost.com), Washington D.C. for Rent (http://www.washingtondc.forrent.com), Washington D.C. Convention and Visitors Bureau (http://www.washington.org), and Washington Metropolitan Transit Authority (http://www.wmata.com).

Student Group

With a graduate student body of more than 700, SIS is the largest and most-applied-to school of international affairs in the U.S. A very diverse student body is composed of about 20 percent international students from more than 130 countries, and an additional 25 percent are members of domestic minority groups. The number of M.A. applications for the 2007 entering class was more than 2,000, and the size of the entering class was 330. More than 150 students applied for the Ph.D. program, which has an incoming cohort of 8 students.

Location

American University is located in northwest Washington, D.C., home to some 192 foreign embassies, chanceries, and the headquarters of many international organizations. In addition, the Smithsonian Institution, National Institutes of Health, John F. Kennedy Center for the Performing Arts, National Archives, Brookings Institute, World Bank, and Library of Congress are all just a short distance from the campus. There are also a host of research and internship sites related to each field, including the Office of European Union Commission, Organization of American States, TransAfrica Forum, and Asia Society.

The University and The School

American University was chartered by an Act of the United States Congress in 1893. The first graduate students were admitted in 1914, and President Woodrow Wilson officially dedicated the University on May 27, 1914. Today, as a premiere global university, American University has more than 11,000 students enrolled and attracts students from all fifty states, the District of Columbia, Puerto Rico and the territories, and nearly 150 other countries.

During the Cold War, U.S. President Dwight Eisenhower was aware that the world needed to prepare for a time when the U.S.-Soviet rivalry no longer dominated foreign policy. He encouraged thirteen university presidents, including AU's Hurst Anderson, to incorporate human-focused international affairs into higher education. Anderson and the Methodist Bishop of Washington shared a similar vision: a school predicated on service to the global community. Eisenhower embraced the idea and spoke at the School's groundbreaking ceremony in 1957. The School of International Service opened in 1958 to an inaugural class of 80 students from thirty-six countries.

Applying

To be considered for admission to the master's programs, all applicants must possess a bachelor's degree or its equivalent from an accredited institution and submit the application form; a resume; a statement of purpose; two letters of recommendation (three for the Ph.D. program); official transcripts; official test scores, such as GRE scores and/or TOEFL/IELTS scores (if applicable, for international students); and a $50 application fee. GRE scores are required for all Ph.D. applicants. The minimum TOEFL requirement for international students is 100 on the iBT, 250 on the CBT, or 600 on the PBT. The minimum IELTS requirement is 7.0. International students who do not hold a higher education degree from an English-speaking university are not required to take the GRE but do need to take the TOEFL/IELTS. The M.A. application deadline for spring semester is October 1 for domestic students and September 15 for international students; the M.A. application deadline for fall semester is January 15 for all applicants. The Ph.D. application deadline is January 1. All application materials must reach the Graduate Admissions Office by the deadline if students wish to be considered for merit-based financial aid.

Correspondence and Information

Office of Graduate Admissions
School of International Service
American University
4400 Massachusetts Avenue, NW
Washington, D.C. 20016-8071

Phone: 202-885-1646
Fax: 202-885-1109
E-mail: sisgrad@american.edu
Web site: http://www.american.edu/sis

American University

THE FACULTY AND THEIR RESEARCH

The diversity of SIS faculty members exemplifies the multidisciplinary and cross-cultural aspects of international relations. Bringing cutting-edge research into their classrooms, the faculty members use a variety of interactive approaches, such as simulations and case studies, in their teaching. The School regularly appoints adjunct and visiting professors and benefits from their expertise in the field of international relations.

Comparative and Regional Studies: Quansheng Zhao, Director
Global Environmental Politics: Paul Wapner, Director
International Communication: Shalini Venturelli, Director
International Development: David Hirschmann, Director
International Economic Relations: Tamar Gutner, Interim Director
International Peace and Conflict Resolution: Ronald Fisher, Director
International Politics: Tamar Gutner, Director
U.S. Foreign Policy: Philip Brenner, Director

BRANDEIS UNIVERSITY

Heller School for Social Policy and Management
Sustainable International Development Graduate Program

Program of Study

The Master of Arts (M.A.) program in sustainable international development (SID) at Brandeis University considers the state of world development, probes issues that affect future generations, and broadens skills necessary to plan, negotiate, implement, monitor, and evaluate development programs. SID examines models of development for their achievements in reducing poverty and inequality, raising quality of life, and conserving the environment. SID seeks fresh thinking about complex relationships, bridging areas of concern reserved traditionally for scientists or social scientists, policymakers, human rights advocates, or development practitioners.

SID aims to impart knowledge and skills that are necessary to design and manage local, regional, and national or international development. The program is designed for early-career to midcareer planning professionals from government or nongovernment entities who are responsible for enterprise creation, poverty alleviation, biodiversity and natural resource management, refugee settlement and disaster mitigation, food security, and civil society institutions.

SID has an innovative professional curriculum that includes a year in residence studying with senior researchers and field-level development practitioners and a second-year field project, internship, or advanced study applying and evaluating methods and models of development. Field projects and internships have included water and sanitation (India), agrarian reform planning (Eritrea, Ukraine), microcredit projects (Uganda, a Tibetan community in India, Indonesia, Serbia), natural resource management (Jamaica, Kazakhstan, Armenia, Western Samoa), rain forest conservation (Sri Lanka), ecotourism (Sri Lanka, Guatemala), gender equality (Eritrea, Ethiopia, Benin), refugees (Burundi), and the Central Bank (Uganda, Botswana, Zimbabwe, England), among others.

SID participates in applied research and development programs overseas in integrated conservation and development within rain forest buffer zones, ecotourism, biodiversity, conservation, food security, technology transfer, health-care financing, small industrial development, youth entrepreneurship, and NGO capacity building.

Research Facilities

The SID program is affiliated with the Center for International Development (CID) at the Heller School for Social Policy and Management. CID faculty members, researchers, and students are engaged in research that furthers knowledge about sustainable development and helps build local capacity to solve problems and plan sound development strategies. SID students also participate in seminars and discussions with visiting scholars and practitioners from such institutions as the United Nations Development Programme, the World Bank, the U.S. Agency for International Development, Oxfam, and the Woods Hole Oceanographic Institute.

The SID program houses its own specialized library collection, including books, CDs, videos, training manuals, and working papers in the field of sustainable development. As part of the Brandeis community, SID students have access to all on-campus libraries as well as other local community and college libraries through the Boston Library Consortium.

Financial Aid

The program awards a number of generous partial tuition remission scholarships to U.S. and international students based on both merit and need. SID also advises candidates on applying for international scholarships, foundation support, and other sources of funds. Students are supported by such donors as the Fulbright and Muskie programs of the United States, the World Bank Scholars Program, the Ford Foundation, the United Nations Development Programme, the United States Agency for International Development, the Soros Foundation, the Asian Development Bank, and the Africa Capacity Building Foundation, among others.

Cost of Study

Tuition for the 2007–08 year in residence was $34,566. The mandatory health insurance fee (unless covered by another acceptable policy) was $1475. During the postresidence year, there is no tuition and students pay continuation and program fees that amount to approximately $3000.

Living and Housing Costs

The minimum yearly cost of living is estimated at $12,000. Limited graduate housing is available on campus; rent for a one-bedroom apartment nearby ranges from $500 to $800 per month.

Student Group

SID limits its enrollment to emphasize close student-faculty interaction in teaching and research. Currently, there are 85 full-time students in residence, part of a total enrollment of 163. The student body is diverse, with students coming from more than fifty-four countries; 66 percent are international and 58 percent are women. SID students are involved in extracurricular activities, cultural events, conferences, and travel within the U.S.

Student Outcomes

Virtually all SID graduates are employed in positions utilizing their planning skills with their local or national governments, research institutions, NGOs, and private companies. Among the organizations employing SID alumni are the Canadian International Development Agency (Ethiopia); Care International (Senegal); the National Council on Economic Education; J. P. Morgan Investment Bank (England); the Ministry of Development and Planning, Burundi; the U.S. Peace Corps, Washington, D.C.; the Latin American Studies Program, Costa Rica; the World Wildlife Fund, South Pacific; and Population Services International, Eritrea.

Location

Located in Waltham, Massachusetts, 16 miles west of Boston, Brandeis University is part of a metropolitan area that includes educational institutions, museums and galleries, theaters, cultural events, and other attractions of the city. Students are able to travel easily into Cambridge or Boston via either the commuter train or public bus, both of which stop within steps of the campus.

The University and The School

Brandeis University is ranked in the top tier of the nation's universities. It is the youngest private research university in the country. The Heller School is committed to developing new knowledge and insights in the fields of social policy, sustainable development, and health and human services management. As a research institution, Heller has pioneered in a variety of policy areas, including mental health, substance abuse, international and community development, developmental disabilities, and poverty and hunger.

Applying

Admission decisions are based on intellectual ability, academic preparation, work experience, and demonstrated commitment to development. Applications are accepted from individuals, while nominations from development agencies are particularly welcome. Completed applications are reviewed as they are received throughout the year. Applying early is encouraged to allow lead time for outside scholarship deadlines that require a university admission. All applications must include university-level transcripts, three letters of recommendation, a statement of purpose, a curriculum vitae or resume, and a completed application, which can be downloaded from the School's Web site or submitted online. All international applicants must submit TOEFL or IELTS scores or otherwise satisfy English proficiency requirements. The application fee is waived for citizens of developing nations, returned Peace Corps volunteers, and AmeriCorps and City Year members. Inquiries and applications should include fax and e-mail contact information if possible.

Correspondence and Information

Office of Admissions and Recruitment
The Heller School for Social Policy and Management
P.O. Box 549110
Brandeis University/MS 035
Waltham, Massachusetts 02454-9110

Phone: 781-736-3820
Fax: 781-736-2774
E-mail: helleradmissions@brandeis.edu
Web site: http://heller.brandeis.edu/sid

Brandeis University

THE FACULTY AND THEIR TEACHING/RESEARCH AREAS

Jeffrey Ashe, M.A., Boston University, is a specialist in microcredit lending and enterprise development.
Sarita Bhalotra, M.B.B.S., Delhi (India), is an experienced health researcher and policy analyst.
David Boyer, B.S., Colorado, is a community-based research management specialist working with Oxfam America and its indigenous partners in the Amazon and the Andes Mountains in Peru, Bolivia, and Ecuador. He has also provided technical assistance and strategic planning in the Environmental Impact Assessment to community groups in Cambodia and Vietnam.
Susan Curnan, M.F.S., Yale, is the Director of the Center for Youth and Communities. She has developed and directed many innovative national evaluations and community building projects aimed at improving the quality of life for youth, their families, and their neighborhoods.
Barry Friedman, Ph.D., MIT, is an economist working on research related to the design and management of social protection programs internationally. He has studied the social security system of China and frequently consults on management issues in the Chinese social security system. Recently, he completed a study on enterprise benefits in Hungary.
Ricardo Godoy, Ph.D., Columbia, specializes in insurance mechanisms in rain forest societies in Latin America, private time preference, tenure rights, and the use of natural resources among Amerindians in Bolivia and Panama.
Maria Green, J.D., Harvard, is a specialist on human rights and development. Her work focuses on the intersection of human rights standards with economic and social policy at both the national and international levels.
Andrew Hahn, Ph.D., Brandeis, focuses his work on employment and training policies, evaluations of training strategies, and evaluation methodologies for assessing community needs and the impacts of community interventions. He also studies the effects of media coverage of social problems and the relationship of these effects to the work of nonprofit groups.
Anita Hill, J.D., Yale, teaches law and society: race, class, and gender equality. She is the author of numerous articles on international commercial law, bankruptcy, and civil rights.
Susan Holcombe, Ph.D., NYU, is a specialist in the field of demographics and development. She was most recently the director of the Global Program department for Oxfam America and has worked as a senior program adviser for UNFPA China, was director of UNIFEM's Asia and Pacific program, and has been an independent consultant to the World Bank.
Marion Howard, M.A., Brandeis, teaches planning and implementation and conservation-related courses. Her work focuses on participatory planning, coastal and marine management, protected areas, and small-island development.
Milton Obote Joshua, M.A., Nairobi, is an Engaged Scholar specializing in masculinity and gender relations in development.
Sajed Kamal, Ph.D., Boston University, is a specialist in energy alternatives and appropriate technology.
Attila O. Klein, Ph.D., Indiana, is a plant biochemist who has worked on plant-environmental relations and is currently studying the ecology of river watersheds.
Ravi Lakshmikanthan, M.A., Brandeis, teaches geographic information systems in the SID program. He is an SID graduate with fieldwork experience both at the United Nations and with a World Bank water project in India.
Jeffrey Prottas, Ph.D., MIT, is a specialist in human services delivery and implementation and has developed qualitative and survey methods to study organizational behavior.
Jehan Raheem, M.B.A., CUNY, Baruch, is a specialist in development program planning and evaluation, the United Nations system, and technical assistance.
Carol A. (Kelley) Ready, Ph.D., CUNY Graduate Center, is an anthropologist who has worked on issues of gender, sexuality, and Latin America. Her work with women and social movements has centered on Central America. In addition to teaching courses on women and development, she serves as the Assistant Director of External Relations for the SID program.
Ann W. Seidman, Ph.D., Wisconsin–Madison, is a recognized expert in the area of law and sustainable development. Her research includes numerous economic development, planning policy, and strategy studies in southern and eastern Africa.
Robert B. Seidman, LL.M., Columbia, has been a distinguished member of the Boston University School of Law faculty since 1972. His work includes several books on law and development, as well as articles on comparative law of the Third World and transitional worlds.
Donald S. Shepard, Ph.D., Harvard, is a health economist who specializes in cost-effectiveness analysis and health financing in developing countries. He has been an adviser to the World Health Organization, the World Bank, the Sabin Foundation, and the Institute of Medicine of the National Academy of Sciences.
Joe Short, Ph.D., Columbia, specializes in civil society, international NGOs, and leadership and management of NGOs.
Laurence R. Simon, Ph.D., Clark, is Director of the SID Graduate Program and an economic geographer specializing in regional planning, including integrated conservation and development and agrarian reform. He has been an adviser to the United Nations Development Programme and the World Bank on poverty alleviation and nongovernmental organizations. He is Chair of Grain Protection International, the postharvest research and training foundation.

Associated Faculty, Advisers, and Research Partners
Clark Abt, Ph.D., MIT, is Chairman of Abt Associates, Inc. Dr. Abt is also the author of *Solar-Powered Economic Growth,* an exploration of renewable energy development economics and technologies.
Seyom Brown, Ph.D., Chicago, is a political scientist and specialist in human rights conventions and practices.
Steven Burg, Ph.D., Chicago, is a political scientist specializing in ethnic politics and is one of the leaders of the SID Yugoslavia Project.
Neela de Zoysa, M.A., Oxford, is a tropical ecologist specializing in south Asia.
Gordon Fellman, Ph.D., Harvard, is a sociologist specializing in peace and conflict studies.
David Gil, D.S.W., Pennsylvania, is Director of the Center for Social Change and teaches social policy.
Shulamit Reinharz, Ph.D., Brandeis, is a sociologist who heads the Women's Studies Program and is a specialist in qualitative research methods and feminine research.

COLUMBIA UNIVERSITY

School of International and Public Affairs
Master of International Affairs and Master of Public Administration

Programs of Study

The School of International and Public Affairs (SIPA) offers two full-time graduate policy degree programs: the Master of International Affairs (M.I.A.) and the Master of Public Administration (M.P.A.). These programs and their student bodies share a great deal in common. Employers demand the reliable skill set of a common core curriculum and an area of solid specialization of both sets of graduates. The School offers the same concentration choices to students in both programs, reflecting the fact that most policy questions can no longer be neatly categorized as domestic or international issues. As a result, the content and the structure of SIPA's M.I.A. and M.P.A. programs have slowly converged. Prospective students still notice differences in the programs that reflect their histories and student bodies: There is more flexibility and more international content in the M.I.A. core; the M.P.A. core has more national and local policy content and a tighter set of requirements. Students in both programs choose SIPA for its balance of theory and practice, and find their classmates' perspectives are as varied as their diverse backgrounds. Nonetheless, most students would say that an M.I.A. student tends toward a more global and theoretical approach to policy questions, while an M.P.A. student is more likely to focus on questions of policy processes and implementation at a local level.

The School of International and Public Affairs also participates in combined programs with the Graduate School of Business; the School of Law; the School of Public Health; the Graduate School of Journalism; the Graduate School of Architecture, Planning, and Preservation; the Graduate School of Arts and Sciences; Institut d'Études Politiques (Paris); the London School of Economics; and the National University of Singapore.

Research Facilities

The International Affairs Building contains Lehman Library, which holds 265,000 volumes, including virtually all significant American and international publications in foreign relations, foreign policy, and the areas covered by the Regional Institutes. The Lehman Library is part of the University library system, with holdings in excess of 6 million volumes.

Associated with the School are the University's eight regional institutes, the Institute of War and Peace Studies, the Center for the Study of Human Rights, the United Nations Study Program, and the Columbia Earth Institute. Scholars from all parts of the world are invited to study and participate in the institutes' activities and, while in residence, to teach courses.

Financial Aid

The School offers a number of fellowships. In 2006–07 approximately 10 percent of first-year students received fellowship funding, while over 68 percent of second-year students received funding. The average first-year fellowship award was $10,135, and the average second-year fellowship amount was $18,000. Students are also encouraged to apply for outside fellowships. Long-term loans at low interest rates are available to help pay for tuition, fees, and living expenses. For additional information about financial aid, interested students should visit http://www.sipa.columbia.edu/FINAID/index.html.

Cost of Study

Tuition and fees for the 2006–07 academic year were $36,573. Additional expenses for the academic year, including housing in New York City, food, and books, are estimated to be approximately $19,560.

Living and Housing Costs

The University provides housing for a limited number of single and married graduate students at varying costs. Inquiries about accommodations should be directed to the Office of University Apartment Housing. International House, a privately owned student residence near the campus, also has accommodations for graduate students. Inquiries should be addressed to the Committee on Admissions, International House, 500 Riverside Drive, New York, New York 10027. The Off-Campus Housing Registry in the Office of University Apartment Housing maintains a listing of privately owned apartments and rooms for rent.

Student Group

The School's student body, with approximately 1,200 students across six degree programs, consists of men and women from the United States and many other countries. In 2006–07 students at SIPA came from more than ninety different countries. Approximately 40 percent of the students are international scholars, and about 60 percent are women.

Location

New York City is truly an exciting city in which to live and study. Its educational and cultural opportunities are unparalleled in their scope and diversity, as are its professional options.

The University and The School

Established as King's College in 1754, Columbia was given a state charter and a new name after the Revolutionary War. Today, the University community of over 26,000 students and faculty members has at its disposal extensive library collections and a computer center for academic research projects. The University is one of the world's leading centers for studies in international affairs.

The School of International and Public Affairs is a graduate professional school established in 1946 for the purpose of training students for careers in such fields as international business and banking, government service, international organizations, and journalism. The School has an active placement program that is constantly seeking the best opportunities for its graduates. Apart from its own resources, the School draws upon the faculties of the Graduate School of Arts and Sciences, the School of Law, the Graduate School of Business, Teachers College, the Graduate School of Journalism, and the School of Public Health.

Applying

A bachelor's degree or the equivalent, with undergraduate work in at least one foreign language, is required. It is also recommended that students submit GRE General Test scores. Six credits in the principles of macroeconomics and microeconomics are strongly recommended. The application deadline for fall admission is the first Friday in January. Students are encouraged to apply early. The School prefers to accept students for September (fall) matriculation; however, applications for admission to the spring semester (starting in January) are also accepted. The January application deadline is October 1. Fellowships are not awarded to January entrants. All qualified applicants receive consideration for admission without regard to race, creed, color, sex, or national origin.

Correspondence and Information

Office of Admissions and Financial Aid
420 West 118th Street, Room 408
Mail Code 3325
School of International and Public Affairs
Columbia University
New York, New York 10027
Phone: 212-854-6216
Fax: 212-854-3010
E-mail: sipa_admission@columbia.edu
Web site: http://sipa.columbia.edu/admissions

Columbia University

FACULTY HEADS AND SPECIALIZATIONS

ADMINISTRATION

John H. Coatsworth, Ph.D., Dean.
Patrick Bohan, M.A., Associate Dean.
Robert Garris, Ph.D., Associate Dean.
Sara Mason, M.A., Associate Dean.
Meg Heenehan, M.Ed., Director, Office of Career Services.
Matt Clemons, M.B.A., Director, Office of Admissions and Financial Aid.

CONCENTRATIONS

Students ordinarily follow a program of study that involves either functional or regional concentration. However, they may wish to employ the option of dual concentrations by taking either two functional concentrations or a combination of a functional and a regional concentration.

Functional

Advanced Policy Analysis (APA), Economic and Political Development (EPD), Environmental Policy Studies (EPS), Human Rights (HR), International Energy Management and Policy (IEMP), International Economic Policy (IEP), International Finance and Policy (IFP), International Media and Communications (IMC), International Security Policy (ISP), and Management and Institutional Analysis.

Regional

Africa, East Asia, East Central Europe, Latin America and Iberia, Middle East, Southern Asia, former Soviet Union (Harriman Institute), and Western Europe.

Students should note that the regional concentration option has a substantial language proficiency requirement and is usually only available to M.I.A. degree candidates.

DUKE UNIVERSITY

Duke Center for International Development
Terry Sanford Institute of Public Policy

M.A. in International Development Policy

Program of Study

The Program in International Development Policy (PIDP) at the Duke Center for International Development (DCID) is an interdisciplinary program designed for midcareer professionals with three or more years of work experience, who plan to dedicate their careers to policy making and public service in developing and transitional countries.

The PIDP provides sound training in policy analysis on issues related to long-term social and economic development. To achieve this, participants in the program—known as PIDP Fellows—self-design their course of study with the help of academic advisers. Fellows may select from PIDP seminars and elective courses from across Duke University and other nearby universities through Duke's inter-institutional agreement.

To help in their curriculum design, students self-select into one of PIDP's five areas of specialization: applied economics, development management, environmental management and policy, peace and conflict resolution, and social policy. They are then assigned accordingly to the appropriate academic adviser who assists them with their course selection each semester. To ensure that all students have an adequate understanding of basic policy issues, all participants are required to enroll in three core courses during their first year of study: Policy Analysis of Development, Economic Foundations of Development, and Economic Analysis of Development.

In contrast to most other development-related programs, PIDP Fellows find that Duke's faculty members take a practitioner-oriented approach in the classroom, asking participants to work together in teams to analyze development issues ranging from NGO development in Africa to tax restructuring in Southeast Asia. To ensure that Fellows experience a true simulation of the diverse nature of the development field, PIDP strives to bring together midcareer professionals from many regions of the world and fields of development. Through this diverse makeup, Fellows not only have the opportunity to learn from each other in the classroom, but they also develop invaluable intercultural communication and teamwork skills that are so important to the International Development career force.

Fellows also gain hands-on development experience in both their summer internship and the final master's project. PIDP alumni, who work in more than sixty-five countries as senior government officials, policy analysts, and consultants for international agencies, researchers, and NGO directors, are instrumental in working with PIDP faculty and staff members to assist current Fellows in securing meaningful internships and clients for their master's projects. Through successful completion of the PIDP, Fellows join this network of alumni, effectively impacting policy change and innovation throughout the developing world.

Research Facilities

The Duke libraries, with more than 5 million volumes, rank among the top 10 private research libraries in the United States. The William R. Perkins Library system comprises a main library, seven branch libraries, and a state-of-the-art shelving facility. There are also four professional school libraries. Duke's main library houses government documents, maps, newspapers, and microforms. Its special collections library contains 11 million manuscripts and other printed and pictorial matter. A $55-million expansion of the main Perkins Library includes the 110,00-square-foot, five-story Bostock Library building and the von der Heyden Pavilion.

An international focus is evident throughout the library collections, reflecting the global strengths of area programs at the University. A large collection of U.S., European, and Latin American public documents and newspapers are held here. Included are extensive research collections from and about South Asia, Latin America, Africa, Europe, Russia, and Poland as well as the country's largest collection of Canadiana. The East Asian collection offers resources in Japanese, Chinese, and Korean on a variety of topics—predominantly history, politics, literature, and language. The newspaper collection includes many eighteenth-century titles, nineteenth-century New England papers, and antebellum and Civil War papers.

In addition, the Terry Sanford Institute of Public Policy provides a state-of-the-art campus hub for interdisciplinary research centers exploring vital policy questions in the field and in the classroom. Support for students' computer work is provided by hundreds of public terminals throughout the campus, all available for student use.

Financial Aid

Limited financial aid is available from the PIDP in the form of partial tuition waivers and teaching and graduate assistantships. Assistantships are generally reserved for second-year Fellows. The PIDP also has a number of strategic partnerships with funding organizations of international students.

Cost of Study

For the nine-month 2008–09 academic year, tuition is $24,888 (24 credits at $1037 per credit). Additional fees include the Graduate School registration fee of $5090, a health fee of $570, a medical insurance fee estimate of $2000, a transcript fee of $40 (first year only), Student Government dues of $20, and a recreation fee of $70, for a total annual cost of $32,678

Living and Housing Costs

The monthly standard of living in the Raleigh-Durham area is about $1830 per month. For on-campus housing information, students should contact the Housing Management Office. For information regarding off-campus housing, students should contact Duke Community Housing (919-684-6711; communityhousing@duke.edu).

Student Group

PIDP Fellows represent diverse nationalities, academic interests, and professional backgrounds. Most are citizens of developing and transitional countries and have worked for their government or for nongovernmental organizations, the private sector, and research institutions. Other participants are citizens of developed nations who are committed to helping developing countries through their service in foreign assistance agencies, international organizations, nongovernmental organizations, or other development institutions.

The PIDP program usually has about 45 to 65 Fellows enrolled each year, chosen from the best applicants from throughout the world. Fellows average about eight years of professional work experience prior to entering the program. The program is highly international, with a student population of about 35 percent Asian, 25 percent Latin American, 10 percent North American and European, 5 percent African, and 25 percent former Soviet Republics.

Student Outcomes

Economists, urban planners, environmental activists, engineers, lawyers, agronomists, educators, legislators, diplomats, researchers, and other professionals from the public and private sector have all taken part in the PIDP. After completing the program, Fellows have served both in their home countries and in international agencies at senior levels as public officials, policy analysts, independent researchers, and leaders of nongovernmental organizations.

Location

Duke University is located in Durham, North Carolina. Set in the midst of the 7,700-acre Duke Forest, the University blends impressive Gothic- and Georgian-style architecture with a lush botanical setting unique to the region. Along with nearby Raleigh and Chapel Hill, Durham is one of three small cities that make up the Research Triangle, an area with a total population of approximately 1 million. Duke is minutes away from Research Triangle Park, a center of sophisticated research facilities and high-technology industry that attracts professionals from around the world. Graduate programs at Duke are also enhanced by collaboration with nearby North Carolina State University and the University of North Carolina at Chapel Hill, where Duke students may also take classes.

Adding to the quality of life are the city's many parks, which make Durham a remarkably green, livable place. Spring comes early, fall lasts into November, and snow falls perhaps once each winter. Temperatures are moderate throughout the year, allowing outdoor recreation all year long. Some of the country's most beautiful beaches are 3 hours to the east by car, and the Blue Ridge and Appalachian Mountains are a 4-hour drive to the west.

The University and The Program

Duke has been consistently ranked among the nation's top 10 colleges and universities. Created in 1924, Duke traces its roots to 1838 in nearby Randolph County, when local religious communities joined forces to support a permanent school, which became Duke University in Durham.

Duke University's Public Policy Studies program began in the early 1970s under the leadership of then-University president Terry Sanford, a former North Carolina governor and U.S. senator and a well-known local, regional, and national public policy leader. The Terry Sanford Institute houses the Department of Public Policy Studies, the Duke Center for International Development (DCID), and a variety of multidisciplinary research centers and programs. Dozens of leaders from around the world come to the Institute each year. The Institute also sponsors colloquiums and conferences that engage students, faculty members, and alumni in ongoing international development and public policy discussions.

Applying

Interested applicants should have at least three years (preferably five) of professional work experience as well as the required official transcripts from all colleges and universities previously attended, a curriculum vitae or resume, a personal statement, a policy essay, and three letters of recommendation. TOEFL or IELTS scores are required for nonnative English speakers. The GRE is not required. Application forms can be found online at http://www.gradschool.duke.edu/admissions.

Correspondence and Information

Program in International Development Policy (PIDP)
Duke University Center for International Development (DCID)
Duke University
Durham, North Carolina 27708

Phone: 919-613-9223
Fax: 919-684-2861
E-mail: pidpinfo@duke.edu
Web site: http://www.pubpol.duke.edu/dcid

Duke University

THE FACULTY AND THEIR RESEARCH

Catherine Admay, Lecturing Fellow, School of Law; J.D., Yale. Public international law, human rights law, comparative property law, water law, law and development.
Marc F. Bellemare, Assistant Professor of Public Policy and Economics; Ph.D., Cornell. Development microeconomics, applied econometrics, applied contract theory, economics, international development.
Robert Conrad, Associate Professor of Public Policy Studies and of Economics; Ph.D., Wisconsin. Public finance, tax policy, natural resource economics.
Thomas Cook, Visiting Lecturer; Ph.D., Florida State. Poverty, local economic development, public organization capacity building, monitoring and evaluation.
Fernando Fernholz, Associate Professor of the Practice, Public Policy Studies; Ph.D., Boston University. International trade, macroeconomics, debt and public finance, investment appraisal, economic development.
Rosemary Morales Fernholz, Senior Research Scholar; Ph.D., Harvard. Environmental policy analysis, indigenous peoples, educational and social development, community management of natural resources, policy analysis.
Gary Gereffi, Professor of Sociology and Director, Center for Globalization, Governance, and Competitiveness; Ph.D., Yale. Sociology of development, multinational corporations, economic sociology, research methods in macrosociology, global commodity chains.
Graham Glenday, Professor of the Practice, Public Policy Studies; Ph.D., Harvard. International tax policy and administration, public finance and public administration, economic development.
F. Henry Healey, Visiting Lecturer; Ph.D., Cornell. Social sector reform, role of democratic structures as mechanisms of social sector reform, political economy of reform, development, and ethics.
Robert Healy, Professor, Nicholas School of the Environment and of Public Policy Studies; Ph.D., UCLA. Environmental policy, land use, parks and tourism.
Bruce Jentleson, Professor of Public Policy Studies and of Political Science; Ph.D., Cornell. Post–Cold War international affairs, U.S. foreign policy, preventive diplomacy and peacekeeping, Middle East peace process.
Roy Kelly, Professor of the Practice, Public Policy Studies; Ph.D., Harvard. Public finance, international tax, fiscal decentralization, financial management in government.
Randall Kramer, Professor, Nicholas School of the Environment and of Economics; Ph.D., California, Davis. Resource and environmental economics, development economics.
Anirudh Krishna, Assistant Professor of Public Policy Studies; Ph.D., Cornell. Social capital, rural development, economic development and democratic governance.
Corinne Krupp, Associate Professor of the Practice of Public Policy Studies and Director of Graduate Studies, PIDP; Ph.D., Pennsylvania. International trade economics, competition policy.
Bruce Kuniholm, Professor of Public Policy Studies and of History; Chairman, Department of Public Policy Studies; and Director, Terry Sanford Institute of Public Policy; Ph.D., Duke. National security, U.S. policy in the Near East.
Francis Lethem, Professor of the Practice, Public Policy Studies; Ph.D., Neuchatel (Switzerland). Institutional development, design and management of development projects.
Frederick Mayer, Associate Professor of Public Policy Studies; Ph.D., Harvard. International trade, American foreign policy, negotiation processes.
Margaret McKean, Professor of Political Science; Ph.D., Berkeley. Environmental policy, property rights and environment, common property regimes for resource management.
Ellen Mickiewicz, Professor of Public Policy Studies and of Political Science and Director, DeWitt Wallace Center for Communication and Journalism; Ph.D., Yale. Media policy, political issues of transitional systems.
Natalia Mirovitskaya, Senior Research Scholar; Ph.D., Academy of Science (Russia). International environmental politics and policy, sustainable development, diversity issues in development and resource management, environmental security.
Gangadhar Prasad (G. P.) Shukla, Professor of the Practice, Public Policy Studies; Ph.D., Harvard. Tax analysis and revenue forecasting, public finance, investment appraisal, mineral taxation, economic development.
Joel Rosch, Senior Research Scholar/Research Associate; Ph.D., Washington (Seattle). Crime policy, implementation, structure of service-delivery systems, collaboration/networked government, the framing of public dialogue about the effectiveness of public programs, service delivery systems.
Joseph Tham, Visiting Assistant Professor; Ed.D., Harvard. Project appraisal, cash flow valuation, economic analysis of expenditures in the health and education sectors, economic development.
Edward Tower, Professor of Economics; Ph.D., Harvard. International trade, financial policy.
Jerry VanSant, Visiting Lecturer, Public Policy Studies; M.B.A., Pace. International management and organizational development, management training, project design, performance monitoring and evaluation, NGO roles in development.
Stephen Wallenstein, Senior Lecturing Fellow, School of Law; J.D., Yale. International financial institutions, international capital markets.
Leila Webster, Visiting Lecturer; M.B.A., Georgetown. Small and medium enterprise development, microfinance.

FORDHAM UNIVERSITY

Graduate Program in International Political Economy and Development

Programs of Study

The Graduate Program in International Political Economy and Development (IPED) is internationally known for its academic excellence. This excellence is achieved through a unique and innovative interdisciplinary approach to analyzing contemporary global economic relations as well as international development issues. The program is a twelve-course curriculum designed primarily for future and present professionals involved with international economic issues as financial analysts, economists, policy analysts, and program administrators. The IPED curriculum begins by providing a rigorous graduate-level foundation in economic, political, and quantitative analysis. Building on this solid foundation, the curriculum then offers an advanced interdisciplinary study of global economic relations and international development issues. Students can complete their professional training in the IPED Master of Arts (M.A.) curriculum with specializations in international banking and finance, international development studies, international economics, or international policy analysis. As a capstone experience, students must pass a comprehensive examination. A full-time student can complete the program in three semesters. Part-time students can complete the program in two years, including two summers.

The M.A. program also provides important practical training. Students must complete an approved internship with an international organization in the business, government, or nonprofit sector if they do not already possess relevant professional experience. The IPED program sponsors a number of internships, both in the United States and abroad, as well as an emerging markets travel program. On a competitive basis, the Graduate Program also offers several international travel scholarships, overseas language immersion study awards, and internship fellowships.

As part of their twelve M.A. courses, IPED students may also fulfill the requirements for two Advanced Certificates: one in Emerging Markets and Country Risk Analysis and the other in Financial Econometrics and Data Analysis. These certificates are also open to qualified visiting students from other universities as well as currently employed professionals. IPED students who wish to strengthen their financial analysis skills may take an additional five courses in the Business School and earn an Advanced Certificate in International Business and Finance.

Two dual-degree programs are offered: IPED students may pursue a second M.A. in economics or a J.D. from Fordham's Law School.

Research Facilities

Fordham University supports academic and scientific research with exceptional resources that include sophisticated computer facilities and state-of-the-art laboratories. The combined libraries of the University contain more than 1.8 million bound volumes and more than 15,500 periodicals and serials. The 240,000-square-foot William D. Walsh Family Library, one of the most technologically advanced academic libraries in the world, is an open-stack library that seats 1,600 readers. The Law School library and the Gerald Quinn Library Lincoln Center may also be used by Fordham students. In addition to the University libraries, graduate students may use the New York Public Library system, and they also have access to the libraries of the City University of New York, Columbia University, the New School, and New York University.

Financial Aid

Each year, the Graduate Program in International Political Economy and Development offers a number of fellowships. In addition to regular fellowships, there are specialized fellowships that enable the recruitment of an extremely talented and diverse student body. For example, Ricci Fellowships ensure that individuals who are actively involved in international affairs, usually from the UN diplomatic community, are enrolled; Global Markets Assistantships attract highly qualified individuals interested in the analysis of international commercial and financial markets; Public Service Assistantships are available for U.S. citizens with international experience who wish to pursue a career with the U.S. federal government; and Arrupe Fellowships attract very promising students who want to pursue a career with a nonprofit international relief and development organization. The program also participates in the U.S. Peace Corps Fellows/U.S.A. Program. Once enrolled in the IPED program, students become eligible for additional scholarships that help them prepare for the job market by gaining overseas experience (International Peace and Development Scholarships, Emerging Markets Travel Program), enhancing their language proficiency (Language Immersion Study Awards), or interning with a specially selected organization (Intern Fellowships). Educational Loans are also available for most students.

Cost of Study

Tuition for the 2008–09 academic year is $1120 per credit. Annual general fees are $268.

Living and Housing Costs

Rental costs for single students living in University apartments range from $7700 to $8775 per year. Shared rental units range from $700 to $950 per month in the immediate off-campus neighborhood. An up-to-date rental database is maintained by the Office of the Associate Dean.

Student Group

The IPED program has an entering class of approximately 25 students each year from diverse backgrounds who share a common enthusiasm for international and development issues. About 40 percent of the students come from Africa, Asia, Eastern Europe, and Latin America.

Student Outcomes

Approximately half of the program's alumni are employed in the business sector, usually as analysts in the financial services industry with firms such as Merrill Lynch and Morgan Stanley. About a quarter work in the public sector as economists, analysts, or managers at agencies ranging from the U.S. International Trade Administration to the United Nations Development Programme. About 15 percent work in the nonprofit sector, usually as project managers with organizations such as Catholic Relief Services and Freedom House. On average over the last five years, more than 20 percent of the program's graduates have won distinguished awards, ranging from Fulbrights and Soros Foundation Scholarships to U.S. Presidential Management Fellowships.

Location

The program's New York City location is ideal for anyone who wishes to be at the center of the world economy. New York City exposes students to the best the world has to offer in art, culture, and business and has the highly diversified atmosphere of a truly international city. Professors draw upon the resources of the city to enrich their courses.

The University

Fordham is a university in the Jesuit tradition. Founded in 1841, it is governed as an institution under a charter granted by the State of New York. The IPED program is offered through the Graduate School of Arts and Sciences. Founded in 1916, it carries on Fordham's oldest academic tradition, the education of talented men and women in the liberal arts and sciences, at the postgraduate level.

Applying

Admission to the program is very selective. Students are chosen from among the top 50 percent of applicants to U.S. graduate programs. Fellowship recipients are selected from among the top 15 percent of applicants to U.S. graduate schools. All applicants must have the equivalent of a U.S. bachelor's degree with a B or better average and must submit a statement of purpose, the general aptitude scores of the GRE, transcripts of all previous undergraduate and graduate course work, and three letters of recommendation. International applicants must also submit TOEFL scores. Applicants who do not wish to be considered for University financial aid may substitute LSAT scores or GMAT scores in place of the GRE. These individuals are still eligible for financial aid in the form of loans. There are additional admission materials required for some of the fellowship programs. Admission is for fall entrance only. To guarantee full consideration, the Graduate Admissions Office must receive students' complete applications by January 2 if aid is also applied for and by April 1 for applications without aid as well as those for Ricci Fellowships.

Correspondence and Information

International Political Economy and Development Program
Fordham University
Bronx, New York 10458

Phone: 718-817-4064
E-mail: iped@fordham.edu
Web site: http://www.fordham.edu/iped

Fordham University

THE FACULTY AND THEIR RESEARCH

All of the faculty members in the program are full-time, and all have doctorates from prominent universities. The faculty members are not only distinguished by their research and consultancy work, but also by their personal interest in mentoring and teaching the students. To complement the faculty, up to 2 visiting lecturers who are practitioners in their fields also teach each year. Currently, there is a visiting lecturer from the U.S. State Department and another from the United Nations.

Economists

Robert Brent, Professor; Ph.D., Manchester (UK). Project evaluation, taxation and development, tax reform, health evaluations and developing countries.
Mary Burke, Associate Clinical Professor; Ph.D., Fordham. Banking, management consulting.
Mary Beth Combs, Associate Professor; Ph.D., Iowa. Economic rights of women, economic history.
Edward T. Dowling, S.J., Professor; M.Div., Woodstock; Ph.D., Cornell. Development economics, global oil market, Philippines.
Ralf Hepp, Assistant Professor; Ph.D., California, Santa Cruz. International finance, open macroeconomics.
Baybars Karacaovali, Assistant Professor; Ph.D., Maryland, College Park. International trade, international political economy.
Subha Mani, Assistant Professor, Ph.D., USC. Microeconomics of development, microfinance, health, education, demography, applied econometrics.
Darryl L. McLeod, Associate Professor; Ph.D., Berkeley. Consultant to the World Bank, Inter-American Development Bank, the Organization of American States, and Lehman Brothers Emerging Markets Group. Development economics, stabilization and developing countries, poverty and income distribution in Latin America and Asia.
Sophie Mitra, Assistant Professor; Ph.D., Paris. Sustainable development, agricultural economics, and labor.
Dominick Salvatore, Distinguished Professor; Ph.D., CUNY Graduate Center. Consultant to UN. Fulbright Awardee (Europe). Commercial policies and trade protectionism, international trade and economic development, international and European monetary systems.
Henry M. Schwalbenberg, Associate Professor and Director of the Graduate Program in International Political Economy and Development; Ph.D., Columbia. Political economy of trade and development, Southeast Asia and the Pacific economies, North-South capital flows.
Troy Tassier, Assistant Professor; Ph.D., Iowa. Microeconomics, public policy, economics of networks, complex systems, epidemics and development.
Booi Themeli, Assistant Clinical Professor of Economics and Director of the Africa Rising Project; M.Comm., Rhodes (South Africa); Ph.D., Fordham. Rockefeller Fellow, Fulbright Fellow, Mandela Fellow. Privatization and development, the economies of Sub-Saharan Africa.

Political Scientists

Bruce E. Andrews, Associate Professor; Ph.D., Harvard. Political economy of the world system, interpretation of foreign policy, theories of international politics.
Susan A. Berger, Associate Professor; Ph.D., Columbia. Political economy of development, comparative politics, political economy of Latin America and the Caribbean.
Jonathan Crystal, Associate Professor; Ph.D., Harvard. Political economy of direct foreign investment.
John P. Entelis, Professor; Ph.D., NYU. Comparative politics, political risk analysis, political economy of the Middle East and North Africa.

Sociologists and Anthropologists

O. Hugo Benavides, Assistant Professor of Anthropology; Ph.D., CUNY Graduate Center. Ethnographic research in Ecuador.
Evelyn L. Bush, Assistant Professor; Ph.D., Cornell. Social movements and transnational politics, sociology of religion, human rights.
Rosemary S. Cooney, Professor; Ph.D., Texas at Austin. Social demography, ethnic and gender labor force inequalities, immigrant adaptation.
Greta Gilbertson, Associate Professor; Ph.D., Texas at Austin. Gender, ethnicity, and migration.
Donald F. Heisel, Research Director, Center for Migration Studies; Ph.D., Wisconsin. International migration, population, and social-economic development.
E. Doyle McCarthy, Professor; Ph.D., Fordham. Sociology of knowledge and culture, social psychology, social theory.

Historians

Michael Latham, Associate Professor of History; Ph.D., UCLA. Diplomatic history, the Kennedy administration and the Alliance for Progress.
Hector Lindo-Fuentes, Professor of History; Ph.D., Chicago. Economic history, nineteenth- and twentieth-century Latin America.

Visiting Lecturers

Andrew S. Hillman, Visiting Lecturer of Diplomacy; M.I.A., Columbia. U.S. Foreign Service Officer and Political Advisor to the U.S. Ambassador to the United Nations.
William Seltzer, Senior Research Scholar and Chair of the American Statistical Association's Committee on Professional Ethics; B.A., Chicago. Consultant, UN International Criminal Tribunal for Rwanda (1996); Director of the UN Statistics Division (1986–94); Chief of Demographic and Social Statistics, UN Statistics Division (1974–86). Demographic measurement, statistical organization and policy, the interface between human rights and population data systems, the promotion of ethical standards in demographic and statistical work.

GEORGIA INSTITUTE OF TECHNOLOGY

Ivan Allen College
Sam Nunn School of International Affairs

Program of Study

The M.S. degree in international affairs at Georgia Tech is an eighteen-month program designed to provide students with the quantitative and qualitative analytic skills and advanced theoretical knowledge necessary to engage in international analysis and planning. The program includes core courses in comparative politics, empirical research methods, international political economy, international relations theory, international security, and modeling, forecasting, and decision making.

The Ph.D. program provides an unparalleled opportunity for students with backgrounds in either politics or science and technology to deepen their understanding of international affairs through the advanced study of subfields such as international relations theory, international security, international political economy, comparative politics, and methods for social scientific research.

Students also have the opportunity to tailor the program to their individual interests through elective offerings in the Sam Nunn School of International Affairs and through interdisciplinary work in the Schools of Economics and Public Policy and the Colleges of Computing, Engineering, Management, and others. M.S. graduates are prepared for professional careers in corporate planning and strategy, policy analysis, government service, or admissions to top Ph.D. programs.

Research Facilities

In addition to housing more than 2.7 million volumes and more than 11,000 current periodicals, the Library and Information Center contains more than 5 million patents and is a depository for U.S. government documents. Its collections are a major resource for graduate students in all fields. The catalog record of the library is online as part of the Georgia Tech Electronic Library (GTEL) and is available to faculty members and staff members and students throughout the campus computer network. GTEL also contains databases that index the contents of periodicals, conference proceedings, and research reports. In addition, Georgia Tech is an active participant in ARCHE, an institutional agreement that allows for shared library privileges and course enrollment across twenty-one Atlanta-area colleges and universities.

The Office of Information Technology provides computing services in support of education, research, and administration. Accounts issued to all students provide universal access to powerful computing, communication, and information services. Access to computing via the campuswide fiber-optic network is available at the computer lab in Habersham Building, which houses the Sam Nunn School of International Affairs. Wireless access and other clusters are also located throughout the campus.

Financial Aid

Various forms of financial assistance are available, including loans and grants at the federal and state level. The School offers a selected number of research and teaching assistantships in which participating graduate students receive stipends and a tuition waiver. The School also awards scholarships on a meritocratic basis. Applicants may also compete for Institute fellowships that provide stipends and a tuition waiver. Awards are based on academic promise. Additional grants and fellowship opportunities are available through the Georgia Tech Graduate Office; they include National Science Foundation and Georgia Regents Opportunity scholarships.

Cost of Study

Tuition figures for 2008-09 are approximately $3000 per semester for state residents and $12,000 per semester for students from out of state. The estimated cost of attendance for the 2007–08 academic year is $20,000 for in-state graduate students and $36,500 for out-of-state graduate students. These figures include estimated costs of tuition and fees, room and board, books and supplies, and personal expenses.

Living and Housing Costs

A wide variety of reasonably priced off-campus apartments are available around the Institute and in surrounding communities. On-campus apartments for graduate students are also available for approximately $3000 per semester.

Student Group

The School admits a diverse and high-quality group of 40 to 50 graduate students in August each year. The graduate student population at Georgia Tech numbers approximately 5,500 students.

Student Outcomes

Students from the School's graduating classes have assumed positions in policy, business, international organizations, and education. Graduates are working at the U.S. Departments of State and Defense, the Central Intelligence Agency, the Centers for Disease Control, Booz Allen Hamilton, SAIC Corporation, Home Depot, the Carter Center, and in Ph.D. programs at MIT and the Universities of Michigan and Southern California. The School has a full-time placement coordinator to assist students in locating positions and internships in government, the private sector, nonprofit organizations, and education.

Location

Georgia Tech is located in midtown Atlanta, the cultural, social, business, and economic capital of the Southeast. Its convenient location enables the School to enhance its international offerings through numerous conferences and seminars that feature prominent U.S. and international government officials, diplomats, corporate leaders, and journalists. The city is also home to internationally known centers such as the Carter Center; the Martin Luther King, Jr. Center for Nonviolent Social Change; and the Southern Center for International Studies. Numerous cultural activities and special events, a moderate cost of living, and one of the best public transportation systems in North America contribute to Atlanta's appeal. Atlanta consistently ranks among the best American cities in which to live and work.

The Institute and The School

Since 1888, Georgia Tech has been a leader in technological education and a catalyst for economic development in the Southeast. In the twenty-first century, Georgia Tech plans to build on its traditional strengths and transcend disciplinary boundaries to provide greater understanding of the scientific, social, environmental, political, and international factors that shape technological development and economic growth. The Sam Nunn School of International Affairs provides interdisciplinary education that enables its graduates to assume responsible positions in government, business, organizations, and academia in an international environment characterized by the globalization of politics, economics, and communications and increasing interdependence.

Applying

The School encourages applications from individuals with backgrounds in the natural sciences and engineering as well as those from the social sciences or humanities. GRE test scores, three letters of recommendation, undergraduate transcripts, a resume, and a career objective statement are required of applicants. Applications should be received by April 1 for fall admission. The priority deadline for financial aid consideration is January 15 for fall admission.

Correspondence and Information

Graduate Coordinator
Sam Nunn School of International Affairs
Georgia Institute of Technology
Atlanta, Georgia 30332-0610

Phone: 404-894-1905
Fax: 404-894-1900
E-mail: vince.pedicino@inta.gatech.edu
Web site: http://www.inta.gatech.edu

Georgia Institute of Technology

THE FACULTY AND THEIR RESEARCH

Michael Best, Ph.D., MIT. Information and communication technologies for social, economic, and political development.
Vicki Birchfield, Ph.D., Georgia. European politics, comparative politics, international political economy.
Kirk Bowman, Ph.D., North Carolina. Comparative politics and Latin American politics.
Peter Brecke, Ph.D., MIT. Global modeling, computer simulation, international political processes.
Dan Breznitz, Ph.D., MIT. Science and technology policies and the role of the state, globalization, state-society interactions.
Molly Cochran, Ph.D., London School of Economics. Ethics and international affairs, international relations theory.
Michelle Dion, Ph.D., North Carolina at Chapel Hill. International political economy, comparative politics, Latin American politics.
John E. Endicott, Emeritus; Ph.D., Tufts. East Asian security affairs, Japanese studies, American defense policy, nuclear nonproliferation.
Miklus Fabry, Ph.D., British Columbia. International relations, theory, human rights, international law.
John W. Garver, Ph.D., Colorado. Asian international relations, Chinese foreign policy, theories of international relations.
Seymour Goodman, Ph.D., Caltech. Information technology and policy.
Justin O. Hastings, Ph.D., Berkeley. International relations, terrorism, Southeast and East Asian politics.
Edward Keene, Ph.D., London School of Economics. International law and political theory, comparative politics.
Robert Kennedy, Ph.D., Georgetown. American foreign and defense policy, European security issues, decision making and crisis management.
Austin Long, Ph.D., MIT. International relations, international security, organization theory.
William J. Long, Ph.D., Columbia. International relations, international political economy, trade and technology transfer.
Michael D. Salomone, Ph.D., Pittsburgh. International arms and technology transfer, organization theory, capabilities of military organizations.
Adam Stulberg, Ph.D., UCLA. International relations, comparative politics, Soviet-Russian studies.
Mark Zachary Taylor, Ph.D., MIT. International relations, political economy, comparative politics with a focus on technological innovation.
Fei-Ling Wang, Ph.D., Pennsylvania. International politics, international political economy, development and modernization, East Asia.
Katja Weber, Ph.D., UCLA. International political economy, European politics.
Brian Woodall, Ph.D., Berkeley. International political economy, comparative politics, Japanese and East Asian politics.

THE INSTITUTE OF WORLD POLITICS

A Graduate School of National Security and International Affairs Master of Arts in Statecraft and World Politics, Master of Arts in Statecraft and National Security Affairs, and Master of Arts in Strategic Intelligence Studies

Program of Study

The Institute of World Politics (IWP) is an accredited graduate school of national security, intelligence, and international affairs dedicated to developing leaders with a sound understanding of international realities and the ethical conduct of statecraft, based on knowledge and appreciation of the principles of the American political economy and the Western moral tradition. The Institute's curriculum includes the study of all the elements of statecraft, including the arts of war, peacemaking, and diplomacy; public diplomacy and cultural diplomacy; psychological strategy and political action; economic strategy; intelligence and counterintelligence; the exercise of intangible instruments of power such as moral leadership, will-power, courage, rhetoric, etc.; and the integration of these elements into overall national strategy.

The Institute emphasizes the development of a capacity to think strategically so as to detect and understand strategic threats and opportunities; prevent, manage, resolve, and prevail in international conflicts; match the ends and means of policy; and do all of these in ways that minimize the necessity to use force.

Because true statesmanship requires that power not be misused, IWP's educational philosophy posits that the responsible conduct of statecraft must be guided by ethics and personal and civic virtue. Hence it incorporates character development and the study of applied ethics—another aspect that contributes to its uniqueness.

IWP currently offers three Master of Arts degree programs: Statecraft and National Security Affairs, Statecraft and World Politics, and Strategic Intelligence Studies. Statecraft and World Politics includes a foreign language requirement. All degrees contain the same foundational core curriculum in history, international politics, comparative ideologies, the Western moral tradition and the application of ethics to the use of power, American founding principles, and an overview of all the elements of statecraft. The Statecraft and National Security Affairs program offers specializations in intelligence, national security affairs, and public diplomacy and political warfare. The Statecraft and World Politics program offers specializations in comparative political culture, international politics, American foreign policy, and democracy building. The Strategic Intelligence Studies program is designed for recent graduates who seek careers in the intelligence field as well as professionals whose agencies or clientele are charged with the acquisition and interpretation of intelligence. Each degree consists of eight core courses (4 credits each) and four elective courses in one of the specializations. All students also take or test out of two shorter courses (2-credits) on strategic geography and economics. Students may study full-time or part-time. Most classes are offered in the evenings for the convenience of those students who are midcareer professionals.

For their foreign language requirement, students in the Statecraft and World Politics program must demonstrate a professional reading knowledge of a widely used foreign language. IWP provides a list of these languages.

IWP also offers eight graduate-level certificate programs: American foreign policy, comparative political culture, democracy building, intelligence, counterintelligence, international politics, national security affairs, and public diplomacy and political warfare. The certificate programs are designed for students who wish to pursue graduate studies but do not need or seek a degree and/or those students who already have an advanced degree yet require additional graduate credentials. These programs are also intended to encourage students' continued professional growth and to serve as valuable indicators of achievement and knowledge for current or prospective employers and professional colleagues and peers.

Research Facilities

The IWP library contains more than 30,000 volumes, including the private library of William J. Casey, a former Director of Central Intelligence. In addition, the library maintains an extensive collection of foreign affairs periodicals and reference works, many of which are unique and available only through IWP. The IWP library also has specialized collections in U.S. foreign policy, Soviet/Russian affairs, Middle Eastern history, and intelligence/counterintelligence. High-speed Internet access is available to students through the library, as are extensive electronic databases.

Financial Aid

IWP offers merit-based scholarships to attract and retain high-achieving, academically talented graduate students. A more modest, need-based grant program is also available. IWP is currently in the application process to participate in Title IV student aid programs and VA educational benefits programs. IWP has partnered with several lenders. Prospective students should visit the IWP Web site for complete details.

Cost of Study

Tuition for the 2007–08 academic year was $975 per credit hour; each 4-credit course was $3900 ($1950 for each 2-credit course). An application fee of $50 (nonrefundable and nontransferable) and a $300 deposit (applied toward tuition) are required to seek and hold an accepted student's place in the entering class. In addition, there is a mandatory Student Services fee of $115 per semester ($50 in the summer session). Classes are held throughout the year, with sessions beginning in spring, summer, and fall. Classes are small, conducted in seminar settings, and most are held during evening and weekend hours for the convenience of the students and their employers.

Living and Housing Costs

The Institute does not provide student housing. However, housing is available at several locations near the Institute. Students are responsible for making their own housing arrangements. Neighborhoods in northwest Washington, D.C., and many areas of Maryland and Virginia are proximate and accessible via public transportation. Students should consider personal safety and transportation availability as well as price when searching for housing. For a list of off-campus housing search engines and apartment locator services, students should visit the Institute's Web site.

Student Group

IWP's average class size per course is 10. In addition to recent college graduates, midcareer professionals from a wide range of U.S. and foreign government agencies and private organizations enroll at the Institute to advance their careers. The result is an ever-expanding network of IWP students and alumni from—and graduates earning key positions throughout—the organizations that develop and implement policy for the United States and countries around the world.

Student Outcomes

Successful recipients of IWP's master's degrees are prepared for a wide range of careers, including defense, intelligence, foreign policy making and implementation, policy research, journalism, and a variety of private-sector professions. These advanced degrees complement many undergraduate pursuits, thereby enhancing a bachelor's degree in political science, history, international relations, economics, or business.

Location

The Institute of World Politics is located in the historical Marlatt Mansion and Bently Hall on 16th Street, NW, in downtown Washington, D.C. The school's location, just eight blocks from the White House, offers students access to the seat of federal government and to the heart of U.S. foreign policy and governmental decision-making processes. Experts at the Institute, whether they are faculty members, guest lecturers, or speakers at extracurricular functions are drawn from the highest ranks of the U.S. government, foreign embassies, and domestic and international organizations specializing in national security affairs.

Applying

Admission to the master's degree programs is competitive. The Institute of World Politics seeks a culturally diverse student body to enhance the international classroom experience. Half the student body consists of recent college graduates who have an interest in international affairs, foreign policy, intelligence, or national security. Other students include personnel from the U.S. government, international diplomats, and working professionals with interests in international affairs and national security.

An earned bachelor's degree from a regionally accredited or similarly recognized college or university is required. Applicants without significant undergraduate course work or job experience in IWP's subject fields may be required to complete related prerequisite course work. Application requirements include a current resume, official (sealed) transcripts from all institutions attended, Graduate Record Examinations (GRE) General Test scores (or the LSAT), three letters of recommendation, a short description of educational and professional goals, and an essay. Prospective students may apply online or request further information through the Institute's address, phone number, or Web site.

Correspondence and Information

Jason Johnsrud
Director of Student Affairs and Admissions Coordinator
The Institute of World Politics
1521 16th Street, NW
Washington, D.C. 20036-1464
Phone: 202-462-2101
888-KNOW-IWP (toll-free)
E-mail: info@iwp.edu
Web site: http://www.iwp.edu

The Institute of World Politics

THE FACULTY

Norman A. Bailey, Adjunct Professor; Ph.D., Columbia, 1962. Mission Manager for Cuba and Venezuela, Office of the Director of National Intelligence; former Senior Director of International Economic Affairs, National Security Council.
Raymond J. Batvinis, Adjunct Professor; Ph.D., Catholic University, 2002. Consultant/investigator for RJB Associates; former supervisory special agent, FBI.
David Burgess, Adjunct Professor; J.D., Georgetown, 1978. Senior official, U.S. Peace Corps and former State Department official.
Marek Jan Chodakiewicz, Professor of History and Academic Dean; Ph.D., Columbia, 2002.
Kenneth deGraffenreid, Professor of Intelligence Studies; M.A., Catholic University, 1977. Former Deputy National Counterintelligence Executive and former Senior Director of Intelligence Programs, National Security Council.
John J. Dziak, Adjunct Professor; Ph.D., Georgetown, 1971. Consultant; retired from the Defense Intelligence Agency.
Lee Edwards, Adjunct Professor; Ph.D., Catholic University, 1986. Distinguished Scholar, The Heritage Foundation.
Roger W. Fontaine, Adjunct Professor; Ph.D., Johns Hopkins (SAIS), 1970. Former Director of Latin American Affairs, National Security Council.
Paul A. Goble, Adjunct Professor; M.A., Chicago, 1973. Formerly with the International Broadcasting Bureau, CIA, and Department of State.
Christopher C. Harmon, Adjunct Professor; Ph.D., Claremont, 1984. Author, *Terrorism Today;* Professor, Marine Corps University.
Walter Jajko, Defense Advanced Research Projects Agency Professor of Defense Studies; M.A., Columbia, 1964. Former Assistant to the Secretary of Defense for Intelligence Oversight; Brigadier General, USAF (retired).
Brian Kelley, Adjunct Professor; M.A., Florida State, 1974. Retired senior CIA official.
David M. L. Klocek, Professor of Political Science, Faculty Chairman, and Director of Admissions; Ph.D., Georgetown, 2000. Former analyst, CIA.
Sven F. Kraemer, Adjunct Professor; M.A., Berkeley, 1964. Department of Defense consultant, former policy adviser to the Under Secretary of Defense for Policy; former Director of Arms Control, National Security Council.
Mark P. Lagon, Adjunct Professor; Ph.D., Georgetown, 1991. Deputy Assistant Secretary of State; formerly with the Senate Foreign Relations Committee.
John Lenczowski, Professor, Founder, and President of The Institute of World Politics; Ph.D., Johns Hopkins (SAIS), 1980. Former Director of European and Soviet Affairs, National Security Council; formerly with the Department of State.
Thomas P. Melady, Senior Diplomat in Residence; Ph.D., Catholic University, 1954. Former U.S. Ambassador to the Vatican, Uganda, and Burundi.
Ross H. Munro, Adjunct Professor; B.A., British Columbia, 1965. Director of Asian Studies, Center for Security Studies.
Joshua Muravchik, Adjunct Professor; Ph.D., Georgetown, 1984. Resident Scholar, American Enterprise Institute.
Alberto M. Piedra, Donald E. Bently Professor of Political Economy; Ph.D., Madrid, 1957; Ph.D., Georgetown, 1962. Former U.S. Ambassador to Guatemala.
Juliana Geran Pilon, Adjunct Research Professor and Earhart Fellow; Ph.D., Chicago, 1974.
S. Eugene Poteat, Adjunct Professor; M.A., Institute of World Politics, 2001. President, Association for Intelligence Officers; former CIA official.
Herbert Romerstein, Adjunct Professor. Author, researcher, and former Director, Office to Counter Soviet Disinformation and Active Measures, U.S. Information Agency.
Charles R. Smith, Adjunct Professor; Ph.D., Catholic University, 1982.
Henry D. Sokolski, Adjunct Professor; M.A., Chicago, 1980. Former Deputy for Nonproliferation, Department of Defense.
Robert W. Stephan, Adjunct Professor; Ph.D., George Washington, 1997. Senior CIA official.
Douglas E. Streusand, Adjunct Professor; Ph.D., Chicago, 1987. Associate Professor, Marine Corps Command and Staff College.
David Thomas, Adjunct Professor; D.Phil., Oxford, 1980. Department of Defense.
John J. Tierney Jr., Walter Kohler Professor of International Relations; Ph.D., Pennsylvania, 1969.
J. Michael Waller, Walter and Leonore Annenberg Professor of International Communication; Ph.D., Boston University, 1993.
John J. Yurechko, Adjunct Professor; Ph.D., Berkeley, 1980. Director of Analysis and Collection, Office of the National Counterintelligence Executive; formerly with Defense Intelligence Agency.

THE JOHNS HOPKINS UNIVERSITY

Zanvyl Krieger School of Arts and Sciences
Advanced Academic Programs
Master of Arts in Government

Program of Study

Students in the Master of Arts in Government program are given the tools to examine the governmental and social institutions in society, to assess prospects for reform, and to effect change. At the Johns Hopkins University Washington Center for the Study of American Government, students use their graduate studies to better inform their work, and they find that their practical work experience augments their graduate studies.

The Government Program brings the theory and practice of government, politics, and policymaking together for those working in the Washington, D.C., area while completing their master's degrees. It is designed as a part-time graduate program, but students have the option of accelerating their course of study by attending full-time.

Students have the option of specializing in one of three concentrations offered in the Government Program: political communication, security studies, and legal studies. The concentration in political communication provides students with the opportunity to study with practitioners in the field: reporters, political operatives, journalists, and campaign and news and media professionals. Security studies covers the fundamentals of administering and preserving American security, with a range of course offerings on defense policy, military strategy, nuclear weapons, theories of terrorism, and comparative politics, to name a few. Courses in the legal studies concentration provide students with an opportunity to better understand the interaction between political and governmental institutions in the legal and criminal justice system and related legal and ethical issues.

Johns Hopkins University's Certificate in National Security Studies program provides a unique approach to the subject of national security by bringing together experts from three critical areas: government and policy, international relations, and bioscience. The certificate meets the needs of working professionals seeking further training in this demanding and developing field. Courses for the certificate program intersect the political, theoretical, and scientific analysis of security issues and lead to direct application.

Research Facilities

The Sheridan Libraries encompass the Milton S. Eisenhower Library and its collections at the Albert D. Hutzler Reading Room, the John Work Garrett Library at Evergreen House, and the George Peabody Library at Mt. Vernon Place. Together, these collections provide the major research library resources for the University. The Milton S. Eisenhower Library, the University's principal research library, includes specialized facilities and collections in medicine, public health, engineering, international affairs, and music. The Sheridan Libraries collections contain more than 2.6 million books, over 30,000 print and electronic journal subscriptions, more than 600,000 e-books, over 7,000 videos and DVDs, 215,000 maps, and 4.1 million microforms. University students have access to the libraries at five academic centers in the Baltimore-Washington metropolitan area. In addition, the interlibrary loan department makes the research collection of the nation available to faculty members and students.

Students in Washington may utilize the Library Resource Center at 1717 Massachusetts Avenue, NW, to conduct research. The center's staff facilitates interlibrary loans, reserve services, and a collection of program-specific reference materials, books, and videos. The Library Resource Center has eleven workstations in the electronic research room that connect to the Eisenhower Library's online catalog search tool and a vast array of electronic databases, journals, and periodicals.

Financial Aid

Federal financial aid in the form of student loans is available on a limited basis to degree candidates who are enrolled in two or more courses per semester or term. More information is available from the Office of Student Financial Services.

Cost of Study

Tuition is $2560 per course in 2008–09. Eleven courses are required to complete the degree.

Living and Housing Costs

Students make their own arrangements for housing.

Student Group

Students in the Government Program come from all walks of life. There are lawyers, staffers on Capitol Hill, economists, lobbyists and interest group staffers, consultants, policy analysts, and managers working in government, business, or social organizations—all seeking to benefit from a more comprehensive knowledge of the various governmental components, how they interact, and how they comply with their mandated accountability in administering the affairs of the state.

Location

The Government Program is housed at the Johns Hopkins Washington Center near Dupont Circle in Washington, D.C. The faculty includes tenured Hopkins faculty members, leading consultants, public relations executives, social scientists, government officials, and experts in political communication.

The University and The School

Privately endowed, the Johns Hopkins University was founded in 1876 as the first true American university based on the European model—a graduate institution with an associated preparatory college, a place where knowledge would be created and assembled as well as taught. The Zanvyl Krieger School of Arts and Sciences is at the heart of a small but unusually diverse coeducational university. The core institution of the Johns Hopkins complex of schools, centers, and institutes, the School recognizes the intellectual strength and education requirements of working adults. Through the Advanced Academic Programs, the School offers a Hopkins education to those wishing to attend graduate school.

Applying

Students must submit the completed application form, the nonrefundable application fee, official transcripts of all previous college work, a resume, and one letter of recommendation.

Students may apply throughout the year and begin study during any of the three terms. When an application is received, every effort is made to render a decision and notify an applicant in time for the upcoming term. For more information, students should visit http://advanced.jhu.edu/admissions.

Correspondence and Information

Advanced Academic Programs
Zanvyl Krieger School of Arts and Sciences
The Johns Hopkins University
1717 Massachusetts Avenue, NW, Suite 101
Washington, D.C. 20036-1717
Phone: 800-847-3330 (toll-free)
E-mail: advanced@jhu.edu
Web site: http://government.jhu.edu

The Johns Hopkins University

THE FACULTY

Charles Bingman, M.B.A., Lecturer.
Peter Black, Supervisory Special Agent, Office of the Inspector General, Department of Defense.
Mark Blyth, Ph.D., Associate Professor of Political Science, Johns Hopkins University.
J. Richard Broughton, LL.M., Trial Attorney, Capital Case Unit, United States Department of Justice.
Brett M. Decker, Senior Vice President, Export-Import Bank of the United States.
Milad Doueihi, Ph.D., Honorary Professorial Fellow, University of Glasgow.
Jill Egeth, Ph.D., Social, Behavioral, and Linguistic Sciences, MITRE Corporation.
Brian Feldman, Legislator, Maryland House of Delegates.
Benjamin Ginsberg, Ph.D., David Bernstein Professor of Political Science; Program Chair, Master of Arts in Government, Advanced Academic Programs; and Director, Center for the Study of American Government, Johns Hopkins University.
Dan Guttman, Attorney, Public Interest Law Program, Peking University School of Law.
Robert J. Guttman, Director, Center on Politics & Foreign Relations, Paul H. Nitze School of Advanced International Studies, Johns Hopkins University.
Robert P. Haffa Jr., Ph.D., Corporate Director, Northrop Grumman Analysis Center, Northrop Grumman Corporation.
Douglas B. Harris, Ph.D., Associate Professor of Political Science, Loyola College.
Kathy Wagner Hill, Ph.D., Associate Program Chair.
Lisa Jaeger, J.D., Partner, Bracewell & Giuliani LLP.
Jack L. Kangas, Ph.D., Professor, Center for the Defense Leadership and Management Program, National Defense University.
John J. Kornacki, Ph.D., Adjunct Associate Professor, Graduate School of Political Management, George Washington University.
James Lacey, Analyst, Institute for Defense Analyses.
Joseph Libonati, Ph.D., Lecturer.
Mark Lowenthal, Ph.D., President and CEO, Intelligence & Security Academy, LLC.
Mark Luckner, Policy Analyst, Office of the Hon. Martin O'Malley, Governor, Maryland.
Glenn Marcus, Documentary Writer/Producer, New Voyage Communication.
Susan W. Morris, Ph.D., Fellow, Department of History of Science & Technology, Johns Hopkins University.
Williamson Murray, Ph.D., Senior Fellow, Institute for Defense Analyses.
Douglas T. Nelson, J.D., Ph.D., Executive Vice President, General Counsel, and Secretary, CropLife America.
James L. Pavlik, M.A., Assistant Inspector General, Office of the Inspector General, Department of Defense.
W. Edward Perlman, M.A., Poetry Advisor and Lecturer, Writing Program, Advanced Academic Programs, Johns Hopkins University.
Alexander Rosenthal, Ph.D., Program Coordinator.
Ariel Ilan Roth, Ph.D., Assistant Professor of International Relations, Goucher College.
John Samples, Director, Center for Representative Government, Cato Institute.
David Satter, Visiting Scholar, School of Advanced International Studies, Johns Hopkins University.
Andrew D. Selee, Ph.D., Director, Mexico Institute, Woodrow Wilson Center.
Adam Sheingate, Ph.D., Assistant Professor of Political Science, Johns Hopkins University.
Robert Shogan, Author.
Michael Eric Siegel, Ph.D., Senior Training Specialist, the Federal Judicial Center in Washington, D.C.
Thomas H. Stanton, Esq., Attorney-at-Law.
Paul Weinstein Jr., Chief Operating Officer/Visiting Fellow, Progressive Policy Institute/Johns Hopkins University.
Kenneth D. Wilde, Ph.D., Chief, Division of Environmental Microbiology (Retired), Maryland Public Health Laboratories.
Jim Wilkinson, Chief of Staff, United States Department of the Treasury.
Mary Ellen Coster Williams, J.D., Judge, U.S. Court of Federal Claims.
Dorothea I. Wolfson, Ph.D., Program Coordinator and Thesis Advisor.

MISSOURI STATE UNIVERSITY

Department of Political Science
Master of International Affairs and Administration

Program of Study

The Department of Political Science offers a Master of International Affairs and Administration (M.I.A.A.) degree to meet the growing societal and occupational needs in a highly competitive and yet increasingly interdependent world. The main mission of the M.I.A.A. program is to produce well-rounded and educated persons who understand and appreciate the diversity and complexity of international affairs and the role of global citizenship and who can bring imaginative and creative problem-solving skills to problems faced by the global community.

The M.I.A.A. is designed to equip students with skills in areas such as quantitative analysis, policy analysis, administration/management, foreign languages, communication, and problem solving that allow them to pursue careers in both public and private-sector agencies in an international environment. The M.I.A.A. also prepares students to continue their education at the doctoral level in international relations, political science, or other related fields.

Students enrolled in the M.I.A.A. program must complete a series of core courses that have been crafted to provide them with a firm foundation in international affairs and administration. These courses include seminars in international relations theory, international organizations and administration, international political economy, comparative politics, foreign policy decision making, and comparative public administration. In addition to the core curriculum, each student selects a cognate field and specializes in it. These fields include international relations and comparative political systems, international economics and business, defense and strategic studies, and public administration and management. The student completes a total of 15 to 18 hours in his or her cognate field. Students also must either complete an independent research project supervised by a faculty member or opt for the 6-hour thesis option, whereby the student writes a full-fledged thesis. Finally, students must complete the equivalent of two years of training in a modern foreign language. Those students who earn a grade point average of less than 3.75 in the program must pass a comprehensive exam composed of both written and oral assessments. This exam is designed to measure the extent to which these students have absorbed the core body of knowledge included in the curriculum.

Students are encouraged to enroll in an internship. In the past, students have secured positions in internships in locations ranging from the local area to Japan. Students may receive 3 hours of credit for the internship, and it may be counted in the cognate field portion of the program requirements. Graduate students enrolled in the M.I.A.A. program also participate in numerous international conferences and a wide variety of other academic-related events. Such activities play a critical role in helping students learn about the global community (and help make them more competitive job candidates after graduation).

The M.I.A.A. program also encourages students to participate in study-abroad trips. Past study tours have included China and various European countries, including Russia. In addition, the M.I.A.A. program has established an exchange program with the Graduate Institute of Political Science at National Sun Yat-sen University (NSYSU) in Kaohsiung, Taiwan. NSYSU has been named by the Ministry of Education as one of Taiwan's seven major research-intensive universities. With a population of over 2 million, Kaohsiung is the second-largest city in Taiwan. NSYSU's Political Science Program only has exchange programs with a small number of other universities—including the two best universities in China (Peking University and Fudan University). M.I.A.A. students may spend a semester studying international relations and/or Chinese at NSYSU (all graduate classes are taught in English) and receive credit for those classes. In addition to the exchange program with NSYSU, there are other exchange program opportunities.

Research Facilities

Missouri State University libraries have comprehensive electronic resources, including an online catalog, electronic indexes and full-text resources, and Internet accessibility. The University is a member of the Center for Research Libraries and is both a U.S. and United Nations document depository.

Financial Aid

Graduate assistantships are awarded on a competitive basis in the Department and elsewhere on campus. The Department typically awards up to five graduate assistantships per year to students in the M.I.A.A. program. All students applying for a graduate assistantship must have their GRE scores (verbal and quantitative) on file at the time of application. Each award is granted for an academic year. A stipend and a waiver of tuition accompany the assistantship. Student research grants of up to $2000 are available to students who wish to conduct research in East Asia.

Cost of Study

Missouri residents pay $3708 for 9 hours plus approximately $1400 in fees; nonresidents pay $7326 for 9 hours plus approximately $1400 in fees.

Living and Housing Costs

Graduate student housing with meal plans costs between $5358 and $5606 per person; without a meal plan, it costs $3420 per person. The married student option without a meal plan costs between $461 and $613 per month for a furnished apartment. Two-bedroom apartments in the community rent for approximately $570 a month.

Student Group

The total enrollment at Missouri State University is approximately 20,000 students, of whom 16 percent are graduate students. Students come from across the United States and from more than sixty countries. There are 40 students enrolled in the M.I.A.A. program. Students in the program come from the surrounding area, the state of Missouri, across the U.S., and from many other nations.

Student Outcomes

The M.I.A.A. program enjoys a record of nearly 100 percent in placing its graduates in Ph.D. programs in America and abroad. Graduates have been admitted to the American University, Cambridge University, University of New Mexico, Catholic University, University of Southern California, University of Missouri, University of Northern Illinois, University of North Texas, University of South Carolina and University of Essex. It is noteworthy that many of these students have received prestigious and highly competitive scholarships and/or graduate assistantships.

A vast majority of graduates who have opted for a career have managed to secure employment in prestigious organizations. These include the National Defense University, Television Tokyo, the Landmine Survivors Network, and the United Nations in New York City or the UN branch offices in various countries overseas. Some international students who have earned the M.I.A.A. degree have found employment with their respective home governments or with international businesses.

Location

Missouri State University is located in Springfield, the third-largest city in Missouri, with a metropolitan service region of 398,000. Located in the heart of the Ozarks recreational area, the University is within easy driving distance of numerous lakes, streams, and parks. The community of Springfield is supported by an industrial/manufacturing base and an expanding service industry in tourism, with people drawn by the natural beauty and recreation of the Ozarks and the musical attractions in nearby Branson. Springfield has an extensive health and medical economy serving southwest Missouri, northwest Arkansas, southeast Kansas, and northeast Oklahoma.

The University

Missouri State University, founded in 1905, is a multicampus metropolitan university system with a statewide mission in public affairs. The University offers more than 150 undergraduate majors and forty-three graduate programs, many of which are the strongest of their kind in the state. The students experience college life at its best, with NCAA Division I athletics and more than 250 student organizations.

Applying

Individuals interested in applying to the M.I.A.A. program may obtain an application from the Graduate College, Carrington Hall, Room 306, Missouri State University, 901 South National, Springfield, Missouri 65897 (417-836-5335). Downloadable forms and an online application are provided at the Graduate College Web site at http://graduate.missouristate.edu/admissions.htm/. International students must also follow all directions as outlined on the Graduate College Web site at http://graduate.missouristate.edu/international.htm/.

Correspondence and Information

Dr. Beat Kernen
M.I.A.A. Program Director
Missouri State University
Springfield, Missouri 65897
Phone: 417-836-5733
E-mail: beatkernen@missouristate.edu
Web site: http://polsci.missouristate.edu/miaa/

Missouri State University

THE FACULTY AND THEIR RESEARCH

M.I.A.A. faculty members are student oriented. They are also among the most productive and visible faculty at MSU. M.I.A.A. faculty members have published a string of policy-relevant publications (books and articles) focusing on international affairs. As a consequence, M.I.A.A. faculty have been asked to provide testimony before the U.S. Congress and served as consultants to various agencies and departments within the executive branch of the national government. Moreover, they are regularly invited to appear on local television and radio programs and have made appearances on national or international television broadcasts including *Dateline, CNN World News, Nightline, The Oprah Winfrey Show,* and the Voice of America's *Issues & Opinions* (a television program broadcast into China) and China Central Television (CCTV). With respect to the print media, faculty members have contributed opinion pieces to many of the world's major newspapers, including the *China Daily, Wall Street Journal, Los Angeles Times, Chicago Tribune, Denver Post, Taipei Times, Rocky Mountain News,* and *Kansas City Star.* Not surprisingly, the M.I.A.A. program has hosted a number of important international conferences. Students are strongly encouraged to participate in these events.

Dennis Hickey, Professor; Ph.D., Texas. Dr. Hickey's research and teaching interests include international relations, Asian politics, national security, and American foreign policy. During the spring semester of 2008, Dr. Hickey was a Fulbright Exchange Scholar at the China Foreign Affairs University in Beijing, China. His most recent book, *Foreign Policy Making in Taiwan: From Principle to Pragmatism,* was published by Routledge in 2007. (dennishickey@missouristate.edu)

Beat R. Kernen, Professor and Director of the M.I.A.A. Program; Ph.D., Kansas. Dr. Kernen's teaching and research interests include international relations, post-Soviet politics, and the politics of the European Union. His most recent research focuses on Russia's geo-strategic interests in other former Soviet republics, especially in the Caucasus. He has published articles in *The Soviet and Post-Soviet Review, Crossroads, Political Chronicle, Yearbook of East European Economies,* and *East European Quarterly.* (beatkernen@missouristate.edu)

Gabriel Ondetti, Assistant Professor; Ph.D., North Carolina at Chapel Hill. Dr. Ondetti's teaching and research interests include Latin American politics and international political economy. His current research focuses on the impact of democracy on redistributive policies in Latin America. In spring 2008 he published *Land, Protest, and Politics: The Landless Movement and the Struggle for Agrarian Reform in Brazil* (Penn State Press). (gabrielondetti@missouristate.edu)

Kenneth R. Rutherford, Associate Professor; M.B.A., Colorado; M.A.L.S., Ph.D., Georgetown. Dr. Rutherford's research and teaching interests include international law, international organization, and international security. He is cofounder of Survivor Corps, formerly the Landmine Survivors Network. His most recent book is *Humanitarianism Under Fire: The United States and United Nations Intervention in Somalia* (Kumarian Press) published in July 2008. (kenrutherford@missouristate.edu)

MONTEREY INSTITUTE OF INTERNATIONAL STUDIES

Graduate School of International Policy Studies

Programs of Study

The Graduate School of International Policy Studies (GSIPS) offers four 2-year professional master's degree programs: the Master of Arts in international policy studies (MAIPS), the Master of Public Administration (M.P.A.) in international management, the Master of Arts in international environmental policy (MAIEP), and the Master of Arts in international trade policy (MAITP).

The MAIPS program combines language and policy studies to train students for careers in the public, nonprofit, or private sectors in cross-cultural settings. The curriculum combines courses in policy analysis, economics, quantitative analysis, international relations, comparative politics, area studies, and language, with an in-depth focus on specific policy problems or sectors.

Complementing the MAIPS program, GSIPS offers one certificate program in nonproliferation studies and various specializations in international development, international negotiation/conflict resolution, international norms/humans rights/justice, Asian studies, terrorism studies, international organizations/nonprofit management. To accommodate the unique interests and career goals of individual students, customized specializations are also available.

The M.P.A. program focuses on the knowledge, professional skills, and leadership abilities needed to effectively help local, national, and global organizations build or improve community developments. The curriculum includes courses in public and nonprofit management, organizational theory, data analysis, budgeting, accounting, and program evaluation.

The MAIEP program responds to the growing need for policymakers to address environmental problems with international dimensions, such as biodiversity protection, climate-change policy, sustainable development, renewable energy, water and air quality, coastal watersheds, and marine policy. Courses include the scientific foundations of environmental policy, international environmental law and policy, environmental economics, and conflict management

The MAITP program represents a cutting-edge curriculum and degree program that focuses on the trade-policy process and the development of related professional skills, including analysis, institutional dynamics, law, negotiations, and business-government relations. The program trains graduates to be effective managers of trade policy representing government, business, or nongovernmental organizations.

In addition to the degree programs, GSIPS offers stand-alone certificate programs structured around defined clusters of courses that examine specific policy areas: Nonproliferation Studies, Conflict Resolution, International Environmental Policy, and International Trade Policy.

Research Facilities

Innovative and challenging curricula at the Institute require appropriate facilities and cutting-edge technology. Classrooms vary in size from large halls where plenary sessions with simultaneous interpretation can be held to smaller classrooms and labs befitting seminar-style classes for 5 to 15 students.

Internships and research opportunities are available through the Institute's Center for Nonproliferation Studies; Center for East Asian Studies; the Monterey Center for Humanitarian Assistance, Development, and Security; and the Monterey Terrorism Research and Education Program.

The Max Kade Language and Technology Center is a fully equipped language-learning center. It provides multimedia classrooms and conference rooms with state-of-the-art technology, including a multimedia resource center and the campus Teaching and Learning Collaborative.

In addition to numerous computer labs, the campus is fully wireless. Every student is encouraged to have a personal laptop computer adapted for wireless connectivity.

The William Tell Coleman Library includes 95,000 volumes, more than 500 print periodicals, over 50 online databases, more than 400 academic journals, about thirty-five newspapers, and approximately 15,000 electronic books. One third of the collection is in languages other than English.

Financial Aid

Candidates with a minimum grade point average of 3.3 on a 4.0 scale (or equivalent) are considered for merit scholarships ranging from $4000 to $14,000 per year. Scholarships are renewable for a second year depending on the recipient's program and academic performance.

Under the Federal Stafford Loan program, students may borrow up to $8500 in subsidized loans or $18,500 in unsubsidized loans. Graduate PLUS Loans cover the cost of college minus other financial aid resources. The Federal Work-Study Program allows students to work up to 20 hours per week for up to $4000 per year.

Many faculty members employ research assistants, and numerous part-time jobs are available on campus. Some of these opportunities are awarded along with scholarships, and others are available when students enroll.

Cost of Study

Tuition and fees for 2008–09 are $29,300.

Living and Housing Costs

The estimated variable expense for books, supplies, housing, food, local transportation, personal expenses, and health insurance is $16,160.

Student Group

Institute enrollment is approximately 800. About one third of the students are from outside the United States, representing more than sixty countries. More than 90 percent of students from the U.S. have worked or studied abroad. More than fifty languages are spoken by students on campus. Language classes are regularly offered in English, Spanish, Arabic, French, Russian, Japanese, Chinese (Mandarin), and German. Other languages are offered by request.

Student Outcomes

GSIPS graduates are prepared for careers in policy research, project coordination and management in international development (UNDP, World Bank), environmental protection (UNEP, World Wildlife Fund), intergovernmental organizations (World Trade Organization, United Nations), national governments (Japan, China, Kazakhstan, Russia, India), U.S. government (Departments of State, Energy, and Commerce; USAID; DIA; CIA), and international NGOs (Save the Children, Mercy Corps).

Location

The Monterey Institute is situated in one of the most spectacular natural environments in the world. The Monterey Peninsula is 130 miles south of San Francisco on California's central coast, surrounded by ocean and mountains. Silicon Valley is only a short drive away. With a population of 100,000, the area combines a variety of rich cultural resources and agricultural activities.

The Institute

Established in 1955 with summer classes in language and culture, the Monterey Institute of Foreign Studies was the first institute dedicated to the then-revolutionary concept that a living language should be taught as such: French in French, German in German, etc. Year-round degree programs began in 1961. By 1979, the Institute had grown to international distinction and was renamed the Monterey Institute of International Studies.

The Monterey Institute is an affiliate of Middlebury College. Founded in 1800, Middlebury is one of the country's top liberal arts colleges. It offers students a broad curriculum embracing the arts, humanities, literature, foreign languages, social sciences, and natural sciences. The affiliation further enriches the curriculum, creates a bicoastal presence, and offers valuable connections to build greater global connection.

Applying

The Monterey Institute of International Studies has a rolling application process and allows students to begin in either the fall or spring semesters. Priority deadlines for the fall semester for applicants who wish to be considered for merit-based scholarship consideration are December 1, February 1, or March 15.

Prospective students are required to have a U.S. bachelor's degree or the equivalent from an accredited college/university and a minimum GPA of 3.0 on a 4.0. scale. Applicants with a GPA below 3.0 should submit a GRE score; otherwise, a GRE score is optional. Prospective students must also submit the following: a completed application form, a personal statement (600 words), a resume/CV, official transcripts from all colleges attended, two letters of recommendation, and a nonrefundable $50 application fee.

Nonnative English speakers must also provide a TOEFL or IELTS score. The minimum TOEFL/IELTS requirements are as follows: Paper-based test, 550; Test of Written English, 4.0; Computer-based test: 213, Test of Written English: 4.0; Internet-based test: 80, Test of Written English: 23, no other subscores below 19; IELTS minimums: 6.5 overall score with no subscore below 6.0 on the Academic module. International students should apply three months before enrollment to allow enough time for the visa process.

Correspondence and Information

Admissions Office
Monterey Institute of International Studies
460 Pierce Street
Monterey, California 93940

Phone: 831-647-4123
800-824-7235 (toll-free within the United States)
Fax: 831-647-6405
E-mail: admit@miis.edu
Web site: http://www.miis.edu

Monterey Institute of International Studies

THE FULL-TIME FACULTY AND THEIR RESEARCH

Tsuneo Akaha, Professor and Director, Center for East Asian Studies; Ph.D. (political science), USC. Dr. Akaha teaches courses on security in Northeast Asia and public policy in Japan, especially foreign and environmental.

William Arrocha, Assistant Professor; Ph.D. (international relations), Queen's at Kingston. Dr. Arrocha teaches courses on international political economy, trade policy with special reference to NAFTA, and politics of Mexico.

Mahabat Baimyrzaeva; Ph.D. (public administration), USC. Professor Baimyrzaeva teaches courses in public administration, management, policy, and international development.

Jeffrey M. Bale, Assistant Professor and Director, Monterey Terrorism Research and Education Program (MonTREP); Ph.D. (European history), Berkeley. Dr. Bale teaches courses in terrorism and security issues.

Jan Knippers Black, Professor; Ph.D. (international studies), American. Dr. Black teaches courses on Latin American politics and development (media, foreign policy, women, and human rights).

Fernando DePaolis, Assistant Professor, Ph.D. (regional analysis), UCLA. Dr. DePaolis teaches courses on regional analysis, data analysis, and the labor and income effects of trade policies.

Stephen Garrett, Professor; Ph.D. (international affairs), Virginia. Dr. Garrett spent academic year 1978–79 in Bangkok, Thailand, as a senior lecturer on a Fulbright Fellowship and was appointed to the Gordon Paul Smith Chair of International Policy Studies in 1988–89. Dr. Garrett teaches courses on ethics and force in international relations, comparative approaches to transitional justice, and humanitarian intervention.

Nuket Kardam, Associate Professor; Ph.D. (political science), Michigan State. Dr. Kardam teaches courses on international organizations, organization behavior, and women and civil society in Islamic countries, especially Turkey.

Jeffrey Langholz, Professor; Ph.D. (natural resource policy and management), Cornell. Dr. Langholz teaches courses on natural resource policy and management, international environmental policy, and sustainable development.

Edward J. Laurance, Dean; Ph.D. (international relations), Pennsylvania. Dr. Laurance has served as a consultant to the UN Department of Disarmament Affairs since 1992. He also cofounded the International Action Network on Small Arms, the largest transnational small arms NGO. In addition to his position as Dean, Dr. Laurance teaches courses on international organizations, multilateral problem solving, and small arms control.

Beryl Levinger, Distinguished Professor of Nonprofit Management; Ph.D. (educational planning), Alabama. Dr. Levinger teaches courses on nonprofit organization and management, and human capacity building.

Wei Liang, Assistant Professor; Ph.D. (international relations), USC. Dr. Liang teaches courses in international trade negotiation, international relations, international political economy, and Asian studies.

Robert McCleery, Professor; Ph.D. (economics), Stanford. Dr. McCleery teaches courses on international economics, quantitative analysis for trade policy, and economic development, especially East Asia and Mexico.

William Monning, Professor of Negotiation and Conflict Resolution; J.D., San Francisco. Professor Monning teaches classes on negotiations, mediation, and conflict resolution. He is also a practicing attorney.

William Potter, Professor and Director, Center for Russian and Eurasian Studies and the James Martin Center for Nonproliferation Studies; Ph.D. (political science), Michigan. Dr. Potter teaches courses on disarmament and nonproliferation of weapons of mass destruction.

Moyara de Moraes Ruehsen, Associate Professor; Ph.D. (international economics and Middle Eastern studies), Johns Hopkins. Dr. Ruehsen teaches courses on international economics, illegal markets, and data analysis.

Jason Scorse, Assistant Professor; Ph.D. (environmental economics and policy), Berkeley. Dr. Scorse teaches courses on environmental and resource economics, sustainable development, international trade, and international economics.

Sheikh Shahnawaz, Assistant Professor; Ph.D. (economics), USC. Dr. Shahnawaz teaches courses on trade services, international economics, and the political economy of the Middle East.

Fred Wehling, Assistant Professor; Ph.D. (political science), UCLA. Dr. Wehling teaches courses on international security, fissile material control, terrorism with nuclear/chemical/biological/radiological weapons, and nuclear nonproliferation

Jing-dong Yuan, Associate Professor; Ph.D. (political science), Queen's at Kingston. Dr. Yuan teaches courses on Chinese security and foreign policy, Chinese politics, arms control, East Asia security, Sino-Indian relations, and Sino-U.S. relations.

Lyuba Zarsky, Associate Professor; Ph.D. (economics), Massachusetts Amherst. Dr. Zarsky teaches courses in trade, sustainable development, globalization, environmental governance, development economics, and macroeconomics of sustainable development.

THE NEW SCHOOL
A UNIVERSITY

THE NEW SCHOOL: A UNIVERSITY

International Affairs

Programs of Study

The graduate program in international affairs offers two degree options: a 42-credit Master of Arts in international affairs designed for students who wish to enter the field, and a 30-credit Master of Science in international affairs for those with prior professional experience in the field. Both programs of study combine a set of core courses with a wide range of electives and opportunities for hands-on experience. Students may pursue the M.A. or M.S. degree on a full-time or part-time basis; courses are offered both days and evenings.

The New School's International Affairs programs emphasize practice and real-world problem solving. They combine analysis of the changing global economy and culture with an examination of the economic and social problems facing developing countries. Upon graduation, students are in a position to begin or advance careers in public service, nongovernmental organizations, academia, media, the private sector, and more.

The curriculum is supplemented by internships, fieldwork, conferences, weekly seminars on international affairs, conferences, and other special workshops and talks. The program also offers opportunities for fieldwork overseas during the summer, in such locations as Barcelona, Bombay, Buenos Aires, Cameroon, Geneva, Ghana, Hong Kong, Johannesburg, and Kenya. Students also have access to The New School's extensive academic resources, including the graduate program in media studies, Milano The New School for Management and Urban Policy, and the World Policy and India China institutes.

The program's full-time and part-time M.A. and M.S. students come from a wide range of backgrounds; they include former UN staff members, Peace Corps volunteers, NGO workers, journalists, filmmakers, lawyers, and stockbrokers. Some seek new careers, whereas others are looking for ways to address the limitations of their current ones. Above all, students enroll in the program because they want to expand and build upon their unique experiences in the service of a better world.

Research Facilities

The New School is a member of the Research Library Association of South Manhattan, one of the largest interuniversity library consortia in the country. Members of the consortium include The New School's Raymond Fogelman Library, which houses 173,000 volumes in the social sciences and philosophy; New York University's Elmer Holmes Bobst Library; and the Cooper Union Library. Total holdings of these libraries exceed 4.1 million volumes and 25,000 journals. Beyond the consortium are the rich resources of New York City, including 250 METRO-member libraries and the public library systems of the five New York boroughs. Extensive computer facilities are available.

Financial Aid

Scholarships and awards are available to all matriculated students, whether full-time or part-time. The University considers both merit and need in granting available funds. The University Scholars fund provides additional financial support for students from underrepresented groups. An extended payment plan allows students to pay tuition in installments throughout the academic year.

Cost of Study

Tuition for the 2008–09 academic year is $1124 per credit. A $100 University services fee and a $15 student services fee are charged each term. Prospective students should visit http://www.newschool.edu/tuition for more information.

Living and Housing Costs

The University Housing Office maintains a comprehensive resource center with apartment listings. University-operated apartments and residence halls are also an option for graduate students. The cost of housing, food, transportation, and living expenses averages $17,000 per year. For more information, students should visit: http://www.newschool.edu/studentservices.

Student Group

More than 300 students from 62 countries work directly with international practitioners and scholars and focus on today's top global issues, including global economics, poverty and development, cities and urbanization, international institutions, NGOs, human rights, conflict and security, and media and culture.

Location

New York City offers numerous opportunities for students of international affairs. The U.N. General Assembly is located there, as are many major NGOs and multinational corporations. New York is an international center for media business and production and is the financial center of the world.

The University and The School

Located in the heart of New York's Greenwich Village, The New School is a center of academic excellence where intellectual and artistic freedoms thrive. The 9,000 matriculated students and more than 6,000 continuing education students who attend the university's eight schools enjoy a disciplined education supported by small class sizes, superior resources, and renowned working faculty members who practice what they teach. When The New School was founded in 1919, its mission was to create a place where global peace and justice were more than theoretical goals. Today, The New School continues to pursue that mission and strives to foster worthy and just citizens of the world. For more information about the University, students should visit http://www.newschool.edu.

The eight schools that make up The New School are The New School for General Studies, The New School for Social Research, Milano The New School for Management and Urban Policy, Parsons The New School for Design, Eugene Lang College The New School for Liberal Arts, Mannes College The New School for Music, The New School for Drama, and The New School for Jazz and Contemporary Music.

Applying

Applications are welcome from students in all academic disciplines. Students must submit official transcripts, letters of recommendation, a statement of purpose, an academic writing sample, a one-page resume, and a $40 application fee. A personal interview is conducted after the application has been reviewed. Standardized test scores are not required. Application deadlines are February 15 for fall and October 15 for spring admission. Early application is strongly encouraged.

Correspondence and Information

International Affairs Program
Office of Admissions
The New School
66 West 12th Street, Room 401
New York, New York 10011

Phone: 212-229-5630
E-mail: nsadmissions@newschool.edu
Web site: http://www.ia.newschool.edu

The New School: A University

THE FACULTY

Michael A. Cohen, Program Director; Ph.D., Chicago.
Jonathan Bach, Associate Director; Ph.D., Syracuse.

Core Faculty
Stephen J. Collier, Ph.D., Berkeley.
David Gold, Ph.D., City University of New York.
Ashok Gurung, M.I.A., Columbia.
Nina Khrushcheva, Ph.D., Princeton.
Lily Ling, Ph.D., MIT.

For a complete listing of courses and faculty members, including visiting and part-time faculty members, students should visit the Web site at http://www.ia.newschool.edu.

NEW YORK UNIVERSITY

School of Continuing and Professional Studies
Master of Science in Global Affairs

Program of Study

The Master of Science in Global Affairs program at the School of Continuing and Professional Studies' (SCPS) Center for Global Affairs is designed to familiarize students with critical issues in international politics, economics, dispute settlement, law, human rights, humanitarian assistance, energy, the environment, and related areas. With its emphasis on current issues in world affairs, the program meets the needs of those seeking careers with the United Nations and its affiliated agencies, diplomatic missions, foreign offices, government agencies, international and nongovernmental organizations (NGOs), international business, press and media, law firms, foundations, and a host of allied institutions.

Concentrations are available in international relations; private sector: international business, economics, and development; international law, dispute settlement, and institutions; human rights and humanitarian assistance; and environment/energy policy.

The program's 42-credit curriculum consists of 21 credits of core courses, 18 credits of concentration courses, and a 3-credit advanced independent research study or capstone project. Through full-time study, students can complete this program in two years and part-time in up to five years. The curriculum for the M.S. in Global Affairs is continually reevaluated and updated in response to industry needs to provide the most up-to-date and relevant course of study.

Research Facilities

The Elmer Holmes Bobst Library and Study Center, one of the largest open-stack research libraries in the world, houses more than 3 million of New York University's (NYU) nearly 4.4 million volumes. In addition to books, journals, and other print materials, the library provides access to many nonprint resources. These include microforms, databases, and other electronic resources that students can connect to from their home or residence hall; extensive video and audio collections; and a variety of computer equipment and software programs.

NYU's central source for computing, information, network, and telecommunications services is Information Technology Services (ITS). ITS maintains four large, modern computer labs with high-end Macintosh and Windows computers, laser printers, multimedia equipment, and a wide variety of up-to-date software. The Client Services division of ITS provides comprehensive help on the materials and equipment available to students via telephone and e-mail, online, and in person.

Financial Aid

There are many financial aid options to consider, including fellowships and low-interest educational loans. NYU's centralized Office of Financial Aid assists students with loan packages, scholarships, and the NYU monthly payment plan, which enables students to spread out their tuition payments. For more information, students should visit http://www.nyu.edu/financial.aid.

Cost of Study

Tuition for part-time students for the 2008–09 academic year is $1326 per credit plus fees. For full-time students (10–12 credits per semester), the cost of tuition and related fees is $13,260 per semester. Fees vary somewhat by program. The Board of Trustees of New York University reserves the right to alter these costs without notice.

Living and Housing Costs

Graduate student housing is available on the University campus and is administered through the Office of Housing and Residence Life. However, students may choose to live off campus. NYU's Off-Campus Housing Office (OCHO) offers assistance to members of the NYU community in their search for non-University housing options. OCHO provides, exclusively to NYU students, listings of available locations for rent through private landlords, property managers, brokers, and real estate agents. Updated daily, these listings are accessible through OCHO's computer terminals or online for members of the NYU community.

Student Group

In 2007–08, there were 240 students enrolled in the Master of Science in Global Affairs. The median age was 28, and 74 percent of the students were women. Part-time students accounted for 56 percent of those enrolled.

Location

The Center for Global Affairs at NYU's School of Continuing and Professional Studies is located in SCPS' state-of-the-art facility in the Woolworth Building in Lower Manhattan—one of downtown New York's architectural treasures. The Center's location in Manhattan is itself an asset to this program. The United Nations headquarters, major international organizations, NGOs, diplomatic missions, and Wall Street, the center of international financial activity, are located in this major hub of global activity.

The University, The School, and The Center

NYU is a private university, composed of fourteen schools and colleges. The University was founded in 1831 and the School of Continuing and Professional Studies in 1934. The Center for Global Affairs, which offers seminars, professional development courses, certificate programs, summer intensives, and the Master of Science degree, was founded in 1991.

Applying

Students may apply for fall or spring admission. Matriculated students may take summer courses. Factors that are considered in evaluating an applicant include official transcripts of academic achievement in previous undergraduate and graduate course work, scores from the GRE or GMAT, TOEFL scores (for international students whose native language is not English), professional recommendations, and a statement of purpose.

Correspondence and Information

Office of Admissions
Master of Science in Global Affairs
New York University
145 Fourth Avenue, Room 219
New York, New York 10003
Phone: 212-998-7200 Ext. 535
Fax: 212-995-4674
E-mail: scps.gradadmissions@nyu.edu
Web site: http://www.scps.nyu.edu/535

New York University

THE ADMINISTRATION AND THE FACULTY

The Administration

Robert S. Lapiner, Ph.D., Dean, School of Continuing and Professional Studies.
Vera Jelinek, Ph.D., Divisional Dean and Clinical Associate Professor, Center for Global Affairs.
MyKellann Ledden, M.S., Associate Director, Graduate Program in Global Affairs, Center for Global Affairs.

The Faculty

Carolyn Kissane, Ph.D., Clinical Assistant Professor, Graduate Program in Global Affairs, Center for Global Affairs.
Louis Klaveras, Ph.D., Clinical Assistant Professor, Graduate Program in Global Affairs, Center for Global Affairs.
Michael Oppenheimer, M.A., Clinical Assistant Professor, Graduate Program in Global Affairs, Center for Global Affairs.
Howard S. Schiffman, LL.M., Clinical Associate Professor, Graduate Program in Global Affairs, Center for Global Affairs.

SETON HALL UNIVERSITY

The Whitehead School of Diplomacy and International Relations

Programs of Study

The John C. Whitehead School of Diplomacy and International Relations educates students from around the world to bring diplomatic skills and a solid understanding of international affairs to careers in public service, business, law, and the nonprofit sector. The only school of its kind in the United States to share a unique link with the United Nations Association of the USA, the Whitehead School of Diplomacy exposes students to the policymakers and practitioners addressing today's worldwide concerns. Innovative graduate and undergraduate degree programs, taught by a distinguished faculty of scholars and professionals, prepare students to be effective and ethical leaders in their professional careers. The Whitehead School of Diplomacy is an affiliate member of the Association of Professional Schools of International Affairs (APSIA).

The graduate curriculum combines interdisciplinary global studies with research methodology and policy analysis, culminating in a professional internship and significant research project. To attain the M.A. degree, students complete a total of 45 credit hours, satisfying core curriculum requirements, and two specializations. Students select from an array of functional and regional specializations structuring their academic studies according to their particular interests, career goals, and backgrounds. Functional specializations include foreign policy analysis, global health and human security, global negotiation and conflict management, human rights, international security, international economics and development, international law, and international organizations. Regional specializations in Africa, Asia, Europe, Latin America and the Caribbean, and the Middle East are also available.

Joint graduate degree programs combine an M.A. in diplomacy and international relations with a J.D., an M.B.A., an M.P.A. (with a focus on government or nonprofit management), an M.A. in corporate communications, or an M.A. in Asian studies.

At the Whitehead School, graduate students of diverse cultural, educational, and professional backgrounds form an international academic community. The graduate program fosters leadership and civic responsibility and sharpens analytical and practical skills. Small classes create a supportive environment that encourages mentoring relationships. An active graduate student association takes on a variety of projects and activities. Graduate assistantships, scholarships, and positions on the student-edited *Whitehead Journal of Diplomacy and International Relations* are awarded on a competitive basis.

Research Facilities

Walsh Library is a state-of-the-art facility built in 1994. In addition to housing print materials, library services include expert research support, bibliographic searching with online text retrieval (also available remotely), extensive CD-ROM databases, and interlibrary borrowing. As a U.N. depository, optical disk technology makes available up-to-date documentation from the U.N. The library's computer labs and study carrels are all Internet-linked.

Financial Aid

In addition to federal loan and work-study programs, the Whitehead School of Diplomacy may award graduate assistantships and scholarships to full-time students who exhibit high academic and professional potential. The School's Office of Internships and Career Development guides students' career development activities.

Cost of Study

In 2008–09, tuition is $875 per credit. Full-time students pay $305 per semester in University and technology fees; part-time students pay $185.

Living and Housing Costs

On-campus housing is not available for graduate students. Housing and living costs in South Orange and surrounding towns are comparable to most suburban cities, with studio and one-bedroom apartments renting for $750 to $1000 per month.

Student Group

Approximately 250 full-time graduate students are enrolled in the program. Students come from throughout the United States and nearly fifty countries. Their diverse backgrounds are a tremendous asset, offering students a truly international experience. The student body includes recent college graduates as well as midcareer professionals from various disciplines. The School's graduate student association organizes academic, professional, and social events and serves as a support network for mentoring new students.

Location

Nestled on 58 acres in the suburban town of South Orange, New Jersey, Seton Hall is just 30 minutes by train from New York City.

The University and The School

For 150 years, Seton Hall University has been a catalyst for leadership, developing the whole student—mind, heart, and spirit. Seton Hall combines the resources of a large university with the personal attention of a small liberal arts college. Composed of 5,200 undergraduate students and 4,800 graduate students, Seton Hall is a Catholic university that embraces students of all races and religions, challenging each to better the world through integrity, compassion, and a commitment to serving others.

Through a unique alliance with the United Nations Association of the USA, the Whitehead School of Diplomacy and International Relations provides students with a link to the United Nations system, the diplomatic community, nongovernmental organizations, and global business. A continuous exchange of people and ideas between the School and the U.N. brings students in direct contact with policymakers and practitioners and exposes them to ongoing opportunities to foster professional growth and development. The curriculum is enhanced by the perspectives and insights of practitioners from all sectors of the international community who participate in panel discussions, video conferences, and as adjunct professors and guest lecturers.

Beyond the classroom, the Whitehead School actively promotes dialogue on critical global issues. A prestigious World Leaders Forum has brought to the campus thought-provoking lectures and discussions with former Polish President Lech Walesa, former Soviet President Mikhail Gorbachev, United Nations Secretary-General Kofi Annan, Iranian President Mohammad Khatami, former Prime Minister of Israel Shimon Peres, and many others.

Applying

The Whitehead School of Diplomacy and International Relations selects students from around the world who have completed undergraduate degrees in a variety of disciplines, and whose academic record, international experience, or professional achievements and personal goals show promise of leadership. English proficiency is a requirement, and students whose education was not in English are required to submit scores of the TOEFL. Applications are evaluated on a rolling basis, and students may begin the program in September, January, or May. Students applying to the dual-degree programs should submit separate applications to each school.

Correspondence and Information

Catherine Ruby, Ph.D., Director
Office of Graduate Admissions
The Whitehead School of Diplomacy and International Relations
Seton Hall University
400 South Orange Avenue
South Orange, New Jersey 07079

Phone: 973-275-2515
Fax: 973-275-2519
E-mail: diplomat@shu.edu
Web site: http://diplomacy.shu.edu

Seton Hall University

THE FACULTY

Administrative Organization
Ambassador John K. Menzies, Ph.D., Dean.
Rosa Alves-Ferreira, J.D., Associate Dean of Administration.
Courtney Smith, Ph.D., Associate Dean of Academic Affairs.
Ursula Sanjamino, M.A., Assistant Dean of Graduate Studies.
Catherine Ruby, Ph.D., Director of Graduate Admissions.
Elisa Varon, M.Ed., Director of Internships and Career Development.

Faculty
Margarita Balmaceda, Associate Professor; Ph.D., Princeton. Central and Eastern Europe, security and energy policy.
Assefaw Bariagaber, Professor; Ph.D., Southern Illinois. Ethno-political analysis, refugee policy, Africa.
Martin Edwards, Assistant Professor; Ph.D., Rutgers. International organizations and international political economy.
Omer Gokcekus, Associate Professor; Ph.D., Duke. Interest groups and trade policy, organizational architecture and corruption.
Benjamin Goldfrank, Assistant Professor; Ph.D., Berkeley. Comparative analysis of Latin American politics, sub-national governments, participatory budgeting, political parties.
Yinan He, Assistant Professor; Ph.D., M.I.T. Security studies.
Yanzhong Huang, Associate Professor; Ph.D., Chicago. Global health studies, U.S.-China relations, Chinese politics.
Philip Moremen, Associate Professor; J.D., UCLA; Ph.D., Tufts (Fletcher). International law, environmental policy.
Ann Marie Murphy, Assistant Professor; Ph.D., Columbia. Comparative foreign policy.
Jesse Russell, Assistant Professor; Ph.D., California, Santa Barbara. International relations theory, research methods.
Courtney Smith, Associate Professor; Ph.D., Ohio State. United Nations studies.
Yui Suzuki, Assistant Professor; Ph.D., Michigan. International macro/finance, economic development and transition, macroeconomics and international trade.
Zheng Wang, Assistant Professor; Ph.D., George Mason. Negotiation and conflict management.

Distinguished Adjunct Faculty Members
Ambassador S. Azmat Hassan, M.A., M.Sc., former Ambassador of Pakistan to Morocco, Syria, and Malaysia.
Ambassador Ahmad Kamal, M.A., former Permanent Representative of Pakistan to the United Nations.
Ambassador Laszlo Molnar, Ph.D., former Permanent Representative of Hungary to the United Nations.
Ambassador Slavi Pachovski, J.D., Ph.D., former Permanent Representative of Bulgaria to the United Nations.
Giandomenico Picco, M.A., a former Under-Secretary-General of the United Nations and former U.N. Chief Hostage Negotiator.

SOUTHERN ILLINOIS UNIVERSITY CARBONDALE

Department of Political Science
Ph.D. Program

Program of Study

The Doctor of Philosophy (Ph.D.) in political science at Southern Illinois University Carbondale (SIUC) provides advanced specialized training for careers in teaching and research in colleges, universities, and the public sector. The minimum requirements to graduate are 33 semester credit hours in three different fields, 9 credit hours in research methodology, and a dissertation, for a total of 66 credit hours. Credits earned at the master's level may apply toward this total. The fields of study are American politics and government, comparative politics, international relations, political theory, public administration and policy, public law, and methodology. The normal time commitment for completion of the Ph.D. is three to four years beyond the M.A.

The program strives to accommodate divergent career goals. Students preparing to teach in traditional liberal arts colleges where teaching loads are spread across several fields may generalize by studying in four fields. Students anticipating careers in larger institutions where a more specialized research focus is demanded may study in three. Students may also choose between a quantitative or qualitative emphasis in methodology, depending on their research objectives.

The Department of Political Science is dedicated to providing a stimulating and challenging environment for its students and to advancing knowledge in the political and social sciences. A highly favorable faculty-student ratio guarantees small class size, individualized instruction, and opportunities for research collaboration. The Department also cooperates with the Law School in offering a concurrent Ph.D./J.D. program to serve the needs of both the political science and legal education communities.

Research Facilities

SIUC's Morris Library is a member of the Association of Research Libraries, the Center of Research Libraries in Chicago, the Online Computer Library Center (OCLC), and ILLINET Online (IO), the statewide automated catalog and interlibrary loan system, with records of more than 600 libraries. The library's own collection holds 2.8 million volumes, 4.5 million microforms, and more than 12,200 current serial subscriptions. It is a regional depository for U.S. government publications. SIUC offers abundant and accessible computing facilities, and it is among the 180 universities working in partnership with industry and government to develop Internet2. Students also have access to important data archives, including full membership with the Interuniversity Consortium for Political and Social Research and the Roper Public Opinion Archive.

Financial Aid

Graduate students with a graduate assistant appointment of at least 25 percent receive a tuition waiver and stipend sufficient to cover all expenses of the student's education; any admitted student is eligible to apply. Students with outstanding qualifications may be nominated for fellowships awarded by the Graduate School. SIUC provides a large number of on-campus work opportunities, while federally subsidized loans are available through the Office of Financial Aid.

Cost of Study

In-state graduate tuition is $313.90 per credit hour in 2008–09. Out-of-state tuition is 2.5 times the in-state tuition rate ($784.75 per credit hour). Graduate students with at least a 25 percent appointment as a graduate assistant receive a tuition scholarship. Fees vary from $511.26 (1 credit hour) to $1416.05 (12 credit hours). Students with a graduate assistantship receive a 25 percent reduction in the Primary Care Medical Fee.

Living and Housing Costs

For married couples, students with families, and single graduate students, the University has 690 efficiency and one-, two-, three-, and four-bedroom apartments that rent for $484 to $686 per month in 2008–09. Residence halls for single graduate students are also available, as are accessible residence hall rooms and apartments for students with disabilities.

Student Group

The Ph.D. program enrolls about two dozen students annually. Including students in M.A. and M.P.A. programs, total graduate student enrollment in the Department is about 100. In 2006, forty percent of Ph.D. students are women and twenty-five percent are international. About half of all Ph.D. students work as graduate assistants in the Department, while the remainder are supported by fellowships or hold jobs on campus.

Student Outcomes

The large majority of Ph.D. graduates look forward to careers in teaching and research in colleges and universities, although a few find employment as researchers in the private and public sectors. Recent graduates hold positions at the University of Illinois, National Defense University, Clarion University, Austin Peay University, Seton Hall University, Loras College (Dubuque), Georgia Southern University, University of Missouri–Rolla, and Hankuk University (Korea). Graduates are also employed in various governmental agencies at the national, state, and local levels and in the private sector.

Location

Carbondale is approximately 100 miles southeast of St. Louis, Missouri, and on the edge of the 263,000-acre Shawnee National Forest. Two state parks and four recreational lakes are located within 10 miles of campus, which is noted for its landscaping and wooded areas. Surrounded by forest, farmland, and Illinois's nascent wine industry, the city of Carbondale has been cited as one of the fifty most desirable places to live in the United States.

The University and The Department

Founded in 1869, Southern Illinois University Carbondale enrolls 21,000 students, of whom 4,000 are graduate and professional students. SIUC has fifty-eight master's and twenty-seven doctoral degree programs, placing it in the Carnegie Foundation's premier category, Doctoral/Research University–Extensive.

The Political Science Graduate Student Association and the Public Administration Student Organization (PASO) host visiting speakers, brown-bag seminars, and social events throughout the year. The Mileur Endowment enables the Department to bring noted scholars and public figures to campus for varying periods of time. The Public Policy Institute, founded by the late Senator Paul Simon, provides additional opportunities for students to participate in discussions of major issues facing government leaders and society at large.

Applying

Applications may be obtained by writing to the Director of Graduate Studies or downloading forms from the Department's Web site. Applications must include the standard forms, transcripts from all colleges and universities previously attended, three letters of reference, a statement of purpose, and GRE scores. An appropriate M.A. degree is normally a prerequisite, but suitably qualified students lacking the M.A. may apply for direct entry to the doctoral program. Deadlines for applications that include a request for financial assistance are January 15 for doctoral fellowships and February 15 for graduate assistantships. Applications for admission without assistance should be received no later than three months (domestic students) or six months (international students) before the start of the semester. Admission to spring semester (starting in January) is possible.

Correspondence and Information

Director of Graduate Studies
Department of Political Science
Southern Illinois University Carbondale
Carbondale, Illinois 62901-4501

Phone: 618-536-2371
E-mail: polsdept@siu.edu
Web site: http://www.siu.edu/~polysci

Southern Illinois University Carbondale

THE FACULTY AND THEIR RESEARCH

Stephen Bloom, Assistant Professor; Ph.D., UCLA, 2004. Comparative politics, international relations, nationalism, ethnic politics, political economy, Ukraine and Latvia.

Randolph Burnside, Assistant Professor; Ph.D., New Orleans, 2005. American political institutions, public opinion, urban and minority politics.

Robert Clinton, Professor; Ph.D., Texas, 1984. Public law and political theory, challenge of long-held assumptions about the power of the Supreme Court.

Scott A. Comparato, Assistant Professor; Ph.D., Washington (St. Louis), 2000. Public law, judicial politics and interest-group strategies in argumentation before the courts.

Uday Desai, Professor, Chair, and Editor, *Policy Studies Journal;* Ph.D., Pittsburgh, 1973. Public management, organizational theory and behavior, environmental policy and administration.

John L. Foster, Associate Professor; Ph.D., Minnesota, 1971. Simulation of policy processes, American politics, bureaucratic structure and personality, bureaucratic attitudes toward innovation, management of local government.

J. Tobin Grant, Associate Professor; Ph.D., Ohio State, 2001. American politics, campaign finance reform, sessional lawmaking, religion in politics.

Phillip Habel, Assistant Professor; Ph.D., Illinois at Urbana-Champaign, 2006. American politics, media and politics, political methodology.

Laura Hatcher, Assistant Professor; Ph.D., Massachusetts, 2002. Public law, law and society, the legal profession, conservative legal movements, regulation and administrative law, qualitative research methods.

John A. Hamman, Associate Professor; Ph.D., Illinois, 1988. The American presidency, executive leadership, public management.

Roudy W. Hildreth, Assistant Professor; Ph.D., Minnesota, 2005. Democratic theory, American political thought, political theory of John Dewey, youth civic engagement.

Celeste Montoya Kirk, Assistant Professor; Ph.D., Washington (St. Louis), 2005. Comparative politics, social movements and civil society, gender politics, European politics.

Scott D. McClurg, Assistant Professor; Ph.D., Washington (St. Louis), 2000. American politics, political participation, public opinion, electoral behavior, political geography, spatial statistics, campaign dynamics.

Debra H. Moore, Assistant Professor; Ph.D., Missouri–St. Louis, 2004; postdoctoral study at Harvard. Public administration and policy, state and local politics, women in politics.

Ken Mulligan, Assistant Professor; Ph.D., Ohio State, 2004. American politics, mass political behavior, political psychology, voting behavior, religion and politics.

Stephen Shulman, Associate Professor; Ph.D., Michigan, 1996; postdoctoral study at Yale. National identity and the role of culture in international politics, with special reference to Ukraine and Russia.

Keith Snavely, Professor and Director of the M.P.A. Program; Ph.D., California, Davis, 1984. Domestic and international nonprofit organizations, local economic development.

Frederick Solt, Assistant Professor; Ph.D., North Carolina, 2003. Comparative politics, democratization, institutions, Latin America.

William S. Turley, Professor and Director of Graduate Studies; Ph.D., Washington (Seattle). 1972. International political economy and Southeast Asia politics, Vietnamese politics, politics of economic policy reform, political change.

STONY BROOK UNIVERSITY, STATE UNIVERSITY OF NEW YORK

Department of Political Science

Programs of Study

The Department offers research and teaching resources in three specialized fields—American politics, policy and political economy, and political psychology. Students take foundation courses in these fields during their first year. In subsequent years, they do advanced course work in two of these three fields as well as select a specialized field for dissertation research.

The American politics concentration provides a broad perspective on national political institutions and processes. Courses are taught in political parties and elections, the legislative process, the American judiciary, political ideology, electoral behavior, and social choice theory. Members of the faculty are currently doing research on Supreme Court decision making, voting in congressional and presidential elections, congressional strategy, separation of powers, federalism, and public opinion.

Political economy and public policy emphasize the interaction between politics and the institutions (both public and private) that shape economic policies. Students choosing this concentration analyze important policy issues by focusing on decision making and organizational behavior as shaped by individual incentives and institutional structures. In addition to the foundation course in public policy required of all students, elective courses in this field include policy evaluation, organizational decision making, bureaucracy, regulation, and comparative institutional analysis as well as courses on urban politics and economic development.

The doctoral concentration in political psychology/behavior applies contemporary psychological theories, concepts, and research methods to the study of political behavior. Students are trained in topics and methods associated with psychology as well as political science. Methodological concerns focus on experimentation and survey research. In addition to formal training in experimental methods, students are apprenticed throughout their course of training to ongoing laboratory research projects. Students become familiar with the Department's extensive and well-equipped laboratories and the regular subject pool. The substantive concerns of the political psychology concentration include those facets of psychology that can be applied to the study of political behavior, such as communication and interaction, group influence, attribution, attitude change, political cognition, public opinion, cognitive processes, and decision making.

Since the Department believes that a strong background in research methods is essential for political scientists in the twenty-first century, it provides a rigorous training in the application of statistical methods and formal models to political analysis. Course work in analytic methods includes introductory training in mathematical methods and statistics as well as more advanced modeling, econometric, measurement, and time series analysis. The Department believes, however, that it is the application of research methods, first as part of faculty and class research projects and then in the student's own dissertation research, that makes the student a competent researcher with the skills required for success in research and academic careers.

The Master of Arts in Public Policy (M.A.P.P.) degree prepares students for analytic and management positions in state, local, and federal agencies; in nonprofit organizations that interact with government; and in corporations that deal with public policy. Graduates have had successful careers in each of these venues, while others have used the M.A. program as a launching pad to advanced graduate study in the social sciences and law. The degree provides additional credentials and field experience to students launching their careers and enhances the skills and credentials of those already employed. Classes are held in the evenings so the degree can be completed in one calendar year of full- or part-time study, as the student's schedule permits.

Research Facilities

The Department has extensive research facilities equal to any in the country. Students in the program have access to the Social and Behavioral Sciences Data Laboratory, which provides access to state-of-the-art personal computers tied to a local computer network that provides connections to all computers on campus. Students also have access to two experimental research laboratories and a modern survey research center.

Financial Aid

Many Ph.D. students receive tuition scholarships and graduate assistantships, and several fellowship opportunities exist on a competitive basis. The Department of Political Science generally does not have graduate assistantships available for M.A.P.P. students. Given the reasonable tuition, short nature of the program, and good job opportunities available after graduation, most students can finance this degree. However, students in need can seek financial support elsewhere on the campus. The Office of Financial Aid and Student Employment assists graduate students in taking full advantage of their financial aid opportunities, providing information about available grants, work opportunities, and student loan programs. Financial assistance is available as a resource to help students and their families meet educational costs.

Cost of Study

In 2008–09, full-time tuition at 12 credits for entering in-state residents is $3450 per semester, while out-of-state residents and international students pay $5460. Additional fees for each semester, including (but not limited to) the infirmary, activity, technology, and transportation fees, total about $875. International students also pay a service fee of approximately $35 per semester and an orientation fee of $50. Fees for the mandatory Student Health Insurance Plan vary depending on citizenship and employment status.

Living and Housing Costs

For 2008–09, Stony Brook calculates the cost of education excluding tuition, fees, and insurance at $14,228 per year. On-campus apartments range in cost from approximately $336 per month to approximately $1456 per month, depending on the size of the unit and the number of students sharing the space. Off-campus housing options include rooms, houses, and apartments that can be rented from approximately $350 to $2500 per month. Costs including books, food, and transportation may vary depending on academic program and/or personal circumstances.

Student Group

There are approximately 30 students currently enrolled in the Ph.D. program and about 70 students in the M.A.P.P. program, with a nearly even ratio of men and women. Faculty members look for qualities such as interest and/or experience in the areas of concentration in our Ph.D. program and demonstrated interest in public policy-related activities and issues for M.A.P.P. applicants, as well as solid grades and recommendation letters when making admissions decisions.

Student Outcomes

Recent Ph.D. students have been placed at a wide range of excellent universities, including Oxford, Michigan State, Princeton, Washington (St. Louis), and the University of Arizona. Some examples of employment for recent M.A. graduates are policy analyst, New York City Office of Emergency Management; policy analyst, New York City Comptroller's Office; director, Department of Parks, Suffolk County; executive director, Long Island American Lung Association; budget analyst, Suffolk County Executive's Office; urban fellow, New York City Government; and legislative assistant, Suffolk County legislator. Several other graduates have gone on to law school, including Hofstra, Albany, Brooklyn, and St. John's.

Location

The University is located in one of the East Coast's most desirable spots—the North Shore of Long Island about 60 miles east of New York City, midway between Montauk and Manhattan. The tranquil waters of Long Island Sound are just minutes away to the north, and the white sandy beaches of the Atlantic Ocean beckon southward.

The University

Stony Brook is a 1,100-acre university where world-renowned faculty members have created a stimulating, highly interactive environment for graduate studies. Campus refurbishment efforts have enhanced the University environment. Bicycle paths, an apple orchard, park benches, a duck pond, and spacious plazas complement the more than 120 modern laboratories and classroom buildings. Diversity is a byword at Stony Brook, where 31 percent of graduate students hail from other countries. Stony Brook's Political Science Department is one of the leading departments in the country, ranked among the top twenty nationwide in the study of American politics and in the top five in research grants and publications.

Applying

Applications must be submitted online (http://www.grad.sunysb.edu). In addition to completing the online application form, applicants need to provide two official transcripts of all undergraduate and graduate course work, official Graduate Record Examinations (GRE) scores (Stony Brook's code for score reporting is 2548), a minimum score of 550 on the TOEFL for international students, three letters of recommendation, and a nonrefundable $50 fee. Ph.D. applications are accepted for fall admission only. M.A. applications are accepted on a rolling basis for both fall and spring admission.

Correspondence and Information

For program information:

Matthew Lebo, Graduate Director, Ph.D. Program
Peter Salins, Director, M.A.P.P. Program
Alethia Stanley, Graduate Coordinator
Department of Political Science
Stony Brook University, State University of New York
Stony Brook, New York 11794-4392

Phone: 631-632-7667
E-mail: matthew.lebo@sunysb.edu
peter.salins@sunysb.edu
alethia.stanley@sunysb.edu

For an application:
Web site: http://www.grad.sunysb.edu

Stony Brook University, State University of New York

THE FACULTY

Ph.D. Program Faculty Members
Brandon Bartels, Assistant Professor.
Albert D. Cover, Associate Professor.
Stanley Feldman, Professor.
Leonie Huddy, Associate Professor.
Lee E. Koppelman, Professor.
Gallya Lahav, Assistant Professor.
Howard Lavine, Associate Professor.
Matthew Lebo, Assistant Professor.
Lindsey Clark Levitan, Assistant Professor.
Milton Lodge, Distinguished University Professor.
Frank Myers, Professor.
Helmut Norpoth, Professor.
Mark Schneider, Professor.
Jeffrey A. Segal, Professor and Chair.
Joel W. Simmons, Assistant Professor.
Oleg Smirnov, Assistant Professor.
Charles S. Taber, Associate Professor and Director of Graduate Studies.

M.A. Program Faculty Members
Leonie Huddy, Professor.
Lee Koppelman, Professor and Director, Center for Regional Policy Studies.
Matthew Lebo, Assistant Professor.
Peter Salins, Professor and Director, M.A.P.P.
Mark Schneider, Professor.
Oleg Smirnov, Assistant Professor.

Adjunct Faculty Members
Seth Forman holds an M.P.A. from SUNY at Albany and a Ph.D. in history from SUNY at Stony Brook. He is Deputy Director of the Suffolk County Planning Department. He has published books and other research on racial and ethnic politics as well as Long Island issues.
Kenneth LaValle holds a J.D. from Touro Law Center. He has been a New York State senator since 1976 and devotes considerable energy to issues of higher education and environmental preservation. He is also a practicing attorney on Long Island.
Harold Withers holds a Ph.D. in political science from Fordham University. He is Deputy Director of the Suffolk County Planning Department and previously served as Suffolk County Commissioner of Consumer Affairs and Commissioner of Elections. He has also been an elected councilman in the town of Babylon.

TUFTS UNIVERSITY

The Fletcher School

Programs of Study The Fletcher School provides students with the theoretical knowledge and practical skills needed to be leaders in the global community. A Fletcher education is designed to be as flexible as it is rigorous. A variety of degree programs allows students to tailor their Fletcher education to meet a specific international interest or career goal. All students are required to pass written and oral comprehension exams in a language other than their native tongue. The master's degrees require the completion of a substantial thesis. Ph.D. candidates must write and defend a dissertation. In addition, each degree program has specific graduation requirements.

The School offers several degree programs. The Master of Arts in Law and Diplomacy (M.A.L.D.) is a two-year, highly flexible, interdisciplinary, professional degree in international affairs.

The Master of International Business (M.I.B.) is a two-year hybrid international business/international affairs professional degree.

The Master of Arts (M.A.) is a one-year degree program designed for midcareer or senior-level professionals with eight or more years of professional experience.

The Master of Laws (L.L.M.) is a one-year program in international law for professionals practicing law or for those eligible to practice law.

The Global Master of Arts Program (GMAP) is a twelve-month program for midcareer or senior-level professionals with eight or more years of professional experience. Courses are conducted through a combination of Internet-mediated instruction and three 2-week residencies.

The Doctor of Philosophy (Ph.D.) is an advanced interdisciplinary study of international affairs.

Upon graduation, students pursue careers in government, business, journalism, international agencies, teaching, and research in international affairs.

The School takes a multidisciplinary approach to the study of international issues, offering courses in three divisions: international law and organizations; diplomacy, history, and politics; and economics and international business. Students choose from an array of fields of study in which they concentrate their studies. The program is conducted on a semester basis.

Through cooperative arrangements, Fletcher students may take approved courses in the graduate departments and professional schools of Tufts University and Harvard University. Formal exchange programs exist with prominent institutions throughout the world. In addition, the Fletcher School offers several formal joint programs with other institutions: a four-year joint program leading to the M.A.L.D. from Fletcher and the J.D. from the law schools at Harvard or Berkeley (Boalt Hall); a three-year joint program leading to the M.A.L.D. from Fletcher and the M.B.A. from the Amos Tuck School of Business Administration at Dartmouth, from Instituto de Empressa, Madrid, or from HEC M.B.A. Program, HEC School of Management; and joint programs of international affairs studies leading to the M.A.L.D. from Fletcher and the M.A.I.S. from the Diplomatische Akademie, Vienna, or the MIA from University of St. Gallen, Switzerland. Fletcher also offers joint degrees with several programs at Tufts University, including the Department of Urban and Environmental Policy, the Cummings School of Veterinary Medicine, the Gerald J. and Dorothy R. Friedman School of Nutrition Science and Policy, the Faculty of Arts and Sciences, the College of Engineering, and the School of Medicine. Students who wish to enroll in a joint-degree program must be admitted independently to both the Fletcher School and the other institution. Ad hoc joint-degree programs also may be arranged with other law, business, or professional schools.

Research Facilities The research facilities available to Fletcher students are unparalleled. The Edwin Ginn Library of the Fletcher School is one of the largest specialized international affairs teaching libraries in the world. In addition, Fletcher students have full access to the libraries of Tufts and Harvard Universities and the major public and private libraries participating in the Boston Library Consortium. Extensive microcomputer facilities are also available at the School.

Financial Aid Fellowship grants are available up to the cost of tuition. Loan programs and work-study funds are also available, as are teaching assistantships at Tufts University and research assistantships at Fletcher.

Cost of Study Tuition varies by the program, depending on special program features. In 2007–08, tuition for the M.A.L.D., M.A., and Ph.D. programs at the Fletcher School was $32,394. Reduced fees are charged to doctoral candidates once they have completed course work.

Living and Housing Costs Single first-year students are encouraged to live in the Fletcher residence hall. For 2007–08, room rates were $4650; full board was $4750. Off-campus room and board expenses ranged from $12,000 to $14,500 on average.

Student Group Students are drawn to the Fletcher School from all parts of the United States and throughout the world. Diversity is a hallmark of the school. In most years, 46 percent of Fletcher's students come from abroad, while 25 percent of the U.S. citizens attending are members of minority groups. The very first class in 1933 included women and international and minority students; the School remains firmly committed to enrolling a multinational and multiethnic student body. In addition to recent college graduates, the student body includes midcareer executives and government officials from the United States and abroad. Total enrollment is approximately 400 students; 190 master's degree candidates are admitted annually.

Location The Fletcher School is located on the Tufts campus in Medford, Massachusetts. The metropolitan area of Cambridge and Boston, with its famous academic institutions, is 10 minutes away, providing students with easy access to many intellectual, cultural, and social opportunities. At the same time, the small-campus environment of the School fosters the contemplative pursuit of academic interests and contributes to a supportive and cohesive student community.

The School Established by Tufts with the assistance of Harvard University in 1933, the Fletcher School was the first graduate and professional school in the United States devoted to the study of international relations. The curriculum is designed to combine practice and theory. Fletcher students live, study, and attend classes within the School's own complex of four contiguous buildings and share social, cultural, and intellectual interests to a degree unusual in graduate school. Since its founding, Fletcher has graduated more than 7,000 students, and its alumni are engaged in careers in public service; in business, banking, and other private pursuits; and in education and research in international affairs. Fletcher alumni, students, administrators, and faculty and staff members share a sense of pride in the School, motivation for high endeavor, and desire to be of service. All members of the faculty are in residence at the School; most have had practical experience in international public, not-for-profit, or private organizations. They regularly contribute to the policy and scholarly debates of the day in print and broadcast media, in refereed journals, and in books on topics in international affairs.

Applying The School selects students whose academic background, interest in international affairs, related experience and achievements, and personal qualities support expectation of distinguished graduate study and professional careers. The School welcomes applications from college graduates in all areas of concentration—the social sciences, the humanities, the physical sciences, engineering, and business. Applicants who are graduates of colleges and universities where the language of instruction is English are required to take the GRE General Test or the GMAT. International applicants whose native language is not English are required to take the TOEFL or the IELTS and are encouraged to take the GRE General Test or the GMAT. Application materials, including requests for financial assistance, should be filed no later than January 15 for admission for the following September. Notification of admission for fall is mailed by April 1. In addition, Fletcher offers limited admission to the spring semester class; the deadline for applying is October 15.

Correspondence and Information

Director of Admissions and Financial Aid
The Fletcher School
Tufts University
Medford, Massachusetts 02155

Phone: 617-627-3040
Fax: 617-627-3712
E-mail: fletcheradmissions@tufts.edu
Web site: http://fletcher.tufts.edu

Tufts University

THE RESIDENT FACULTY

The faculty members listed here teach the majority of courses offered each year at the Fletcher School. They also serve as students' primary advisers and directors of thesis and dissertation writing. Additional courses may be offered to enhance the curriculum by professors from other units of Tufts University, experts in the field, and international affairs practitioners.

Stephen W. Bosworth, Dean; LL.D. (hon.), B.A., Dartmouth.
Eileen Babbitt, Professor of International Conflict Management Practice; Ph.D., MIT.
Steven A. Block, Associate Professor of International Economics; Ph.D., Harvard.
Jonathan Brookfield, Associate Professor of Strategic Management and International Business; Ph.D., Pennsylvania.
Katrina Burgess, Associate Professor of International Political Economy; Ph.D., Princeton.
Daniel Drezner, Associate Director of International Politics; Ph.D., Stanford.
Leila Fawaz, Issam M. Fares Professor of Lebanese and Eastern Mediterranean Studies; Ph.D., Harvard.
Carolyn Gideon, Assistant Professor of International Communications and Technology Policy; Ph.D., Harvard.
Michael J. Glennon, Professor of International Law; J.D., Minnesota.
John Hammock, Associate Professor of Public Policy; Ph.D., Tufts.
Hurst Hannum, Professor of International Law; J.D., Berkeley.
Alan K. Henrikson, Associate Professor of Diplomatic History; Ph.D., Harvard.
Andrew C. Hess, Professor of Diplomacy; Ph.D., Harvard.
Shirley A. Hunter, Assistant Professor of International Accounting; Ph.D., Texas A&M.
Laurent L. Jacque, Walter B. Wriston Professor of International Business; Ph.D., Pennsylvania.
Ayesha Jalal, Professor of History; Ph.D., Cambridge.
Ian Johnstone, Associate Professor of International Law; LL.M., Columbia.
Michael W. Klein, Professor of International Economics; Ph.D., Columbia.
Carsten Kowalczyk, Associate Professor of International Economics; Ph.D., Rochester.
Lisa M. Lynch, William L. Clayton Professor of International Economic Affairs; Ph.D., London School of Economics.
William C. Martel, Associate Professor of International Security Studies; Ph.D., Massachusetts Amherst.
William R. Moomaw, Professor of International Environmental Policy; Ph.D., MIT.
Vali Nasr, Professor of International Politics; Ph.D., MIT.
John C. Perry, Henry Willard Denison Professor of Japanese Diplomacy; Ph.D., Harvard.
Robert L. Pfaltzgraff Jr., Shelby Cullom Davis Professor of International Security Studies; Ph.D., Pennsylvania.
Jeswald W. Salacuse, Henry J. Braker Professor of Commercial Law; J.D., Harvard.
Richard H. Shultz, Professor of International Politics; Ph.D., Miami (Ohio).
Bernard Simonin, Associate Professor of Marketing and International Business; Ph.D., Michigan.
Joel P. Trachtman, Professor of International Law; J.D., Harvard.
Peter Uvin, Henry J. Leir Associate Professor of International Humanitarian Studies; Ph.D., Geneva.
Alan Wachman, Assistant Professor of International Politics; Ph.D., Harvard.

The Fletcher School.

Stephen W. Bosworth, Dean of the Fletcher School.

University of California, San Diego
School of International Relations
and Pacific Studies

UNIVERSITY OF CALIFORNIA, SAN DIEGO

School of International Relations and Pacific Studies (IR/PS)

Programs of Study

The School of International Relations and Pacific Studies (IR/PS) offers a professional Master of Pacific International Affairs (M.P.I.A.) degree and a joint Ph.D. program in political science and international affairs. The M.P.I.A. program provides professional training for graduates pursuing careers in international business, policymaking, government, consulting, finance and banking, journalism, and development assistance. The program is designed to integrate the diverse subject areas of international management, international relations, comparative public policy, international development and nonprofit management, and international environmental policy as well as regional studies and foreign language. Elective course work allows for flexibility in order to suit students' professional and personal needs. Students choose a career concentration and are required to declare a regional concentration in China, Japan, Korea, Southeast Asia, or Latin America.

The Ph.D. program offers interdisciplinary academic education to a very small number of elite students pursuing international careers requiring advanced research capabilities in economics and political science within the international arena. Within the general requirements, programs of study are structured to fit individual interests. The School also sponsors a certificate program, the Global Leadership Institute (GLI), which is designed for working professionals seeking to expand their international knowledge and experience within their field, as well as enhance their professional development in public and private finance, international economics, public policy and program evaluation, management, marketing, accounting, nonprofit management, quantitative methods, econometrics, long-range strategic planning, and international affairs.

Research Facilities

IR/PS houses the first academic library in the United States to focus exclusively on contemporary political, economic, and business affairs in the countries of the Pacific Basin. The library's current collection consists of more than 60,000 bound volumes and some 2,000 periodical subscriptions in Japanese, Chinese, Spanish, Portuguese, Korean, English, and other languages as well as company annual reports, computerized data files, maps, and other special materials. The language laboratory currently has facilities for instruction in Mandarin Chinese, Japanese, Korean, Portuguese, Vietnamese, Bahasa Indonesian, and Spanish. Computers equipped with Chinese and Japanese software and several Japanese word processors are also available. Supporting resources include the Center for Iberian and Latin American Studies, the Center for U.S.-Mexican Studies, the Institute of the Americas, the Program in Chinese Studies, the Program in Japanese Studies, the Melanesian Studies Resource Center, the Institute for Global Conflict and Cooperation, and the numerous University departments of science and engineering. The University of California, San Diego (UCSD), library contains more than 2 million volumes. An additional 7.6 million titles are available through the MELVYL online catalog, which provides easy access to the other University of California campus libraries.

Financial Aid

Financial assistance is available in the form of merit-based awards, campus employment, and need-based financial aid. Many students receive partial- or full-tuition scholarships or fellowship awards each year. More than $1.3 million is awarded to the incoming class. International and U.S. applicants are eligible.

Cost of Study

The 2008–09 fees are approximately $13,600. Out-of-state tuition and fees are approximately $26,200.

Living and Housing Costs

The University provides housing for both single and married graduate students. It is somewhat limited, but ample housing is available in the region surrounding the campus, particularly in an area called University Town Center. About 25 percent of master's students live in University apartments or affiliated housing.

Student Group

Approximately 250 graduate students from the United States and overseas are enrolled in the School. About 56 percent are women, 37 percent are international, and 19 percent are members of minority groups. The students represent a variety of universities and backgrounds.

Student Outcomes

IR/PS has firmly established itself as a leader in training people to compete in the global arena. M.P.I.A. program graduates have gone on to rewarding positions in the private and public sectors in Japan, Korea, Hong Kong, Taiwan, and other parts of Asia as well as in the United States, Mexico, South America, and Europe. They have skills in finance, marketing, management, foreign languages and culture, and trade and public policy. Program graduates are employed in media/telecommunications, nonprofit organizations, international trade, manufacturing/high technology, financial services, consulting, and government. Major private-sector employers include Andersen Consulting, AT&T, Fujitsu, Hewlett-Packard, PricewaterhouseCoopers, Salomon Brothers, Sony, and Wells Fargo Bank. Major public-sector organizations that have hired IR/PS graduates include the Asia Foundation, the Centers for Disease Control and Prevention, Conservation International, the Ford Foundation, Inter-American Development Bank, NASA, Project Concern International, the State of California Trade and Commerce Agency, the U.S. Department of Commerce, the Environmental Protection Agency, the State Department, and WorldShare.

Location

UCSD is located minutes from downtown San Diego, which offers a rich variety of social and cultural opportunities, coupled with widespread recreational activities. With a strong concentration of academic institutions, San Diego has become an important center for advanced research. The city hosts a large number of rapidly growing international trade and service firms and has more Ph.D.'s, more personal computers, and more miles of fiber-optic cable per capita than any other American city.

San Diego borders Tijuana, one of Mexico's most dynamic cities. The San Diego/Tijuana area is one of the most important economic centers on the Pacific Rim. San Diego is in a prime location for international businesses involved in the Maquiladora industry, and more than 2,000 companies have U.S.-Mexico production-sharing operations. In recognition of the increasing influence of international business on the economy, the San Diego World Trade Center serves the business community to promote increased trade in the Pacific Rim.

The University and The School

UCSD, part of the ten-campus University of California System, is recognized as one of the top teaching and research institutions in the United States. The University has a total enrollment of approximately 30,000 students. Its graduate and professional students are drawn from the upper ranks of the nation's finest colleges and universities and from institutions of comparable standing throughout the world. IR/PS is the University of California's only professional school of international affairs and the only one in the United States focused exclusively on the Pacific Rim.

Applying

The Admissions Committee looks for students who have strong academic records, previous professional employment, a history of meaningful international experience, and demonstrated leadership ability. Students interested in pursuing a degree program at IR/PS must have earned a B.A. or its equivalent at an institution of comparable standing to that of the University of California System. An applicant must submit a completed application, three letters of recommendation, transcripts, and scores on the GRE General Test. (Waivers of the GRE requirement are offered on a case-by-case basis. In addition, scores from the GMAT may be substituted for the GRE for M.P.I.A. applicants.) A minimum score of 575 on the paper-based version of the TOEFL or 7.0 on the IELTS is required of international applicants whose native language is not English and whose undergraduate education was conducted in a language other than English. The Priority deadline for M.P.I.A. applications for admission is December 1, and the Round 2 deadline is January 12; late applications are considered on a rolling admissions basis. The deadline for Ph.D. applications is January 12. Students are admitted without regard to race, creed, color, sex, or national origin. The application process is online.

Correspondence and Information

Admissions Office
School of International Relations and Pacific Studies
University of California, San Diego
9500 Gilman Drive, 0520
La Jolla, California 92093-0520

Phone: 858-534-5914
Fax: 858-534-1135
E-mail: irps-apply@ucsd.edu
Web site: http://irps.ucsd.edu

University of California, San Diego

THE FACULTY

Peter F. Cowhey, Dean; Ph.D., Berkeley.
Roger E. Bohn, Ph.D., MIT.
Richard E. Feinberg, Ph.D., Stanford
Peter A. Gourevitch, Ph.D., Harvard.
Stephan M. Haggard, Ph.D., Berkeley.
Gordon H. Hanson, Ph.D., MIT.
Takeo Hoshi, Ph.D., MIT.
Miles E. Kahler, Ph.D., Harvard.
Alex Kane, Ph.D., NYU.
Ellis S. Krauss, Ph.D., Stanford.
Bruce N. Lehmann, Ph.D., Chicago.
Edmund J. Malesky, Ph.D., Duke.
Craig T. McIntosh, Ph.D., Berkeley.
Barry J. Naughton, Ph.D., Yale.
Krislert Samphantharak, Ph.D. candidate, Chicago.
Ulrike Scheade, Ph.D., Marburg (Germany).
Susan L. Shirk, Ph.D., MIT.
Matthew F. Shugart, Ph.D., California, Irvine.
Y.-H. Tohsaku, Ph.D., California, San Diego.
Barbara F. Walter, Ph.D., Chicago.
Christopher M. Woodruff, Ph.D., Texas at Austin.

Language Instructors
Nohemi Lugo, M.A., Western Michigan.
Sandra Pedregal, M.A., California, San Diego.
Vanda Poirier, M.A., San Diego State.
Yvonee Swun, M.B.A., National.
Eiko Uchida, Ph.D., Carnegie Mellon.

Adjunct Faculty
Julian R. Betts, Ph.D., Queen's at Kingston.
Ann T. Brownlee, Ph.D., Boston University.
Marsha A. Chandler, Ph.D., North Carolina at Chapel Hill.
William M. Chandler, Ph.D., North Carolina at Chapel Hill.
Wayne A. Cornelius, Ph.D., Stanford.
Jeffrey Davidow, M.A., Minnesota.
Paul W. Drake, Ph.D., Stanford.
Theodore Groves, Ph.D., Berkeley.
Germaine A. Hoston, Ph.D., Harvard.
David A. Lake, Ph.D., Cornell.
David R. Mares, Ph.D., Harvard.
Michael M. May, Ph.D., Berkeley.
James E. Rauch, Ph.D., Yale.
Lisa R. Shaffer, Ph.D., George Washington.
Peter H. Smith, Ph.D., Columbia.
Dale E. Squires, Ph.D., Cornell.
Christena L. Turner, Ph.D., Stanford.

Emeritus Faculty
Lawrence Krause, Ph.D., Harvard.

The Robinson Building Complex, home to the School of International Relations and Pacific Studies.

Students at the School of International Relations and Pacific Studies.

VILLANOVA UNIVERSITY

Graduate Studies
Liberal Arts and Sciences
Department of Political Science

Program of Study

The Department of Political Science at Villanova University offers two graduate programs: the Master of Arts (M.A.) in political science and the Master of Public Administration (M.P.A.).

The M.A. program features courses on American government, comparative government, international relations, and political theory. A degree requires ten courses and a capstone oral exam that involves the defense of the student's portfolio or eight courses and a 6-credit thesis. All students pursuing the M.A. must complete PSC 7000 and one course from each of the three concentrations: American government, international relations, and political philosophy.

The M.P.A. is a 36- to 39-credit program, designed to prepare students for management careers in the public and nonprofit sectors. Required courses provide students with knowledge of public administration theory and history, statistical analysis and research methods, organization theory and design, and how to manage financial and human resources in order to be successful in their careers. Elective courses include 3-credit and 1-credit courses.

Both graduate programs also offer graduate certificates (five courses or 15 credits are required) for students not seeking a master's degree or for those looking for a specialization within their degree. Both graduate degree programs admit part-time students. Class size ranges from 4 to 20 students, with the average around 12. Courses meet for 2 hours once per week in the evening.

Research Facilities

The Falvey Memorial Library provides resources and facilities for study and research by students and faculty members, with a book capacity of more than half a million volumes. The Office of University Information Technologies (UNIT) provides data and voice communication, computing services, and access to remote computing and information services over the Internet. Student computer laboratories throughout campus are open 24 hours a day.

Financial Aid

Financial support (tuition remission and/or stipends) is available through the political science department in the form of graduate assistantships and tuition scholarships. Loan programs and need-based financial aid are available through the Office of Financial Assistance, Kennedy Hall, Villanova University, Villanova, Pennsylvania 19085; telephone: 610-519-4010.

Cost of Study

Graduate tuition was approximately $585 per credit hour in 2007–08. In addition, there is a University fee of $60 each semester.

Living and Housing Costs

Various affordable housing possibilities are available near the Villanova University campus or are easily accessible by public transportation. Housing costs vary in accordance with the option chosen. Room and board for a single graduate student may average about $8000 for a twelve-month period. Villanova University does not provide on-campus housing for graduate students.

Student Group

Students in the M.A. and M.P.A. programs combine a variety of academic backgrounds, professional interests, and personal aims. The M.A. program enrolls 40 to 50 students per year, and the M.P.A. program enrolls 45 to 55 students per year. The ratio of men to women is 1:1. About 20 percent of the students in both programs are international. The majority of students in both programs are part-time.

Student Outcomes

Recent graduates of both programs have been admitted to doctoral programs at schools such as Cornell, Penn, Emory, Johns Hopkins, Duke, Maryland, Michigan, NYU, and Penn State. Others attend law schools, such as Georgetown, George Washington, Seton Hall, and Villanova. Graduates also pursue public service careers in the national, state, and local governments and with nonprofit organizations.

Location

Villanova University provides a tranquil setting for study and reflection. Situated on the historic Main Line, a western suburb of Philadelphia, Villanova is located on Lancaster Avenue (Route 30), 2 minutes from the Blue Route (Route 476) and 5 minutes from the Pennsylvania Turnpike, Schuylkill Expressway, and Route 202. Philadelphia's revitalized Center City is 25 minutes away by train, and historic Valley Forge and the Brandywine Valley are easily accessible by car. Villanova is within easy driving distance of several other premier institutions of higher learning, including Bryn Mawr, Haverford, and Swarthmore Colleges; Temple University; and the University of Pennsylvania. With ample parking and mass transit stops right on University grounds, the campus allows for easy travel by car, bus, or train.

The University

Villanova University is an institute rich in history and tradition. For more than 150 years, Villanova has been directed by one of the oldest teaching orders of the Catholic Church, the Order of St. Augustine. From modest beginnings on a country estate of a Revolutionary War officer, the University has seen significant growth in its student population as well as its position as a leading coeducational institute of higher learning.

Applying

Applications for admission and financial aid are available from the Office of Graduate Studies. Applications should be sent to the Office of Graduate Studies, College of Liberal Arts and Sciences, Villanova University, 800 Lancaster Avenue, Villanova, Pennsylvania 19085. Completed applications include an application for admission, nonrefundable application fee of $50, official postsecondary academic transcripts, and GRE scores (General Test only). In addition, applicants should send three letters of recommendation and a two-page narrative explaining anticipated career objectives and reasons for seeking admission to the Director of Graduate Studies at the address listed below. No interviews are necessary. Applicants from non-English-speaking countries must submit TOEFL scores. Applications are considered on a rolling basis. Financial aid decisions are made by April 15. Only applicants seeking full-time admission are considered for financial aid.

Correspondence and Information

Director of Graduate Studies (specify M.A. or M.P.A. or both)
Department of Political Science
Villanova University
Villanova, Pennsylvania 19085
Phone: 610-519-4710
Fax: 610-519-7487
Web site: http://www.villanova.edu/artsci/psc/graduate

Villanova University

THE FACULTY AND THEIR RESEARCH

David Barrett, Ph.D., Notre Dame. National security policy, intelligence policy, foreign policy formation.
Lara Brown, Ph.D., UCLA. Presidents, elections, political parties, congress.
Kail C. Ellis, O.S.A., Dean, College of Arts and Sciences; Ph.D., Catholic University. Comparative politics of Arab states.
Lowell S. Gustafson, Chair; Ph.D., Virginia. Latin American politics, international political economy, theories of international relations.
Jeffrey W. Hahn, Ph.D., Duke. Russian politics and government, Russian foreign policy.
John R. Johannes, Vice President for Academic Affairs; Ph.D., Harvard. American government, congress.
Christine Kelleher, Ph.D., North Carolina at Chapel Hill. American politics, state and local government, urban politics, methodology.
Matthew R. Kerbel, Ph.D., Michigan. Political communications, the presidency.
Marcus L. Kreuzer, Ph.D., Columbia. Parties, comparative political economy, democratization, European politics.
Robert W. Langran, Ph.D., Bryn Mawr. Constitutional development, constitutional law, civil rights and civil liberties, congress, government and business, women and politics.
Hafeez Malik, Ph.D., Syracuse. International relations, politics of the communist world, South Asia, problems of nationalism.
Robert A. Maranto, Ph.D., Minnesota. Public policy, public administration, American government.
Colleen A. Sheehan, Ph.D., Claremont. American political theory.
Thomas W. Smith, Ph.D., Notre Dame. Ancient political theory, religion and politics.
Joseph E. Thompson, Ph.D., Catholic University. International relations, American foreign policy, comparative politics, Ireland.
A. Maria Toyoda, Ph.D., Georgetown. East Asia, comparative politics.
Catherine E. Warrick, Ph.D., Georgetown. Comparative politics, Middle East, South Asia, gender and Islamic politics.
Craig Wheeland, Associate Vice President for Academic Affairs; Ph.D., Penn State. Public administration, urban politics, intergovernmental management.
Catherine Wilson, Ph.D., Penn. Public administration, nonprofit management, immigration, religion and politics.

Section 24
Psychology and Counseling

This section contains a directory of institutions offering graduate work in psychology and counseling, followed by in-depth entries submitted by institutions that chose to prepare detailed program descriptions. Additional information about programs listed in the directory but not augmented by an in-depth entry may be obtained by writing directly to the dean of a graduate school or chair of a department at the address given in the directory.

For programs offering related work, see also in this book *Criminology and Forensics, Family and Consumer Sciences,* and *Sociology, Anthropology, and Archaeology.* In the other guides in this series:

Graduate Programs in the Biological Sciences

See *Biological and Biomedical Sciences; Genetics, Developmental Biology, and Reproductive Biology; Neuroscience and Neurobiology;* and *Pharmacology and Toxicology*

Graduate Programs in Business, Education, Health, Information Studies, Law & Social Work

See *Education, Nursing (Psychiatric Nursing), Pharmacy and Pharmaceutical Sciences, Public Health,* and *Social Work*

CONTENTS

Program Directories

Announcements

Cross-Discipline Announcement

Close-Ups

Psychology—General

Abilene Christian University, Graduate School, College of Arts and Sciences, Department of Psychology, Program in General Psychology, Abilene, TX 79699-9100. Offers MS. *Students:* 7 full-time (4 women), 3 part-time (all women); includes 1 minority (African American), 1 international. 10 applicants, 90% accepted, 6 enrolled. In 2007, 3 degrees awarded. *Degree requirements:* For master's, comprehensive exam, thesis optional. *Entrance requirements:* For master's, GRE General Test. *Application deadline:* For fall admission, 4/1 priority date for domestic students; for spring admission, 11/1 for domestic students. Applications are processed on a rolling basis. Application fee: $40 ($45 for international students). Electronic applications accepted. *Expenses:* Tuition: Full-time $13,368; part-time $557 per hour. Required fees: $700; $34 per hour. $10 per semester. Tuition and fees vary according to degree level and campus/location. *Financial support:* Federal Work-Study available. Support available to part-time students. Financial award application deadline: 4/1. *Unit head:* Dr. Jeffrey Wherry, Graduate Advisor, 325-674-2471, Fax: 325-674-6968, E-mail: jnw04c@acu.edu. *Application contact:* William Horn, Graduate Admissions Counselor, 325-674-2656, Fax: 325-674-6717, E-mail: gradinfo@acu.edu.

Acadia University, Faculty of Pure and Applied Science, Department of Psychology, Wolfville, NS B4P 2R6, Canada. Offers clinical psychology (M Sc). *Faculty:* 12 full-time (6 women), 11 part-time/adjunct (5 women). *Students:* 10 full-time (8 women). Average age 26. 39 applicants, 18% accepted, 5 enrolled. In 2007, 7 degrees awarded. *Degree requirements:* For master's, thesis. *Entrance requirements:* For master's, GRE General Test, GRE Subject Test, honors degree or equivalent. Additional exam requirements/recommendations for international students: Required—TOEFL (minimum score 580 paper-based; 237 computer-based), IELTS (minimum score 7). *Application deadline:* For fall admission, 2/1 priority date for domestic students. Applications are processed on a rolling basis. Application fee: $50. Electronic applications accepted. *Financial support:* In 2007–08, 5 students received support; teaching assistantships, career-related internships or fieldwork and scholarships/grants available. Financial award application deadline: 2/1. *Faculty research:* Social psychology, job stress, psychotherapy, cognition perception, development. *Unit head:* Dr. Douglas K. Symons, Head, 902-585-1301, Fax: 902-585-1078, E-mail: doug.symons@acadiau.ca. *Application contact:* Dr. Peter Horvath, Information Contact, 902-585-1200, Fax: 902-585-1078, E-mail: peter.horvath@acadiau.ca.

Adelphi University, Derner Institute of Advanced Psychological Studies, Garden City, NY 11530-0701. Offers clinical psychology (PhD, Post-Doctoral Certificate); general psychology (MA); mental health counseling (MA); school psychology (MA). *Accreditation:* APA (one or more programs are accredited). *Faculty:* 23 full-time (10 women). *Students:* 174 full-time (144 women), 201 part-time (161 women); includes 37 minority (20 African Americans, 9 Asian Americans or Pacific Islanders, 8 Hispanic Americans), 21 international. Average age 31. 541 applicants, 42% accepted, 118 enrolled. In 2007, 92 master's, 26 doctorates, 26 other advanced degrees awarded. *Degree requirements:* For master's, comprehensive exam; for doctorate, thesis/dissertation, research (second year), 1 year internship; for Post-Doctoral Certificate, 2 years of full-time study and supervised clinical practice, 1 year full-time internship. *Entrance requirements:* For master's, 3 letters of recommendation, minimum GPA of 3.0; for doctorate, GRE General Test, GRE Subject Test, interview; resumé; undergraduate course work in psychology, experimental psychology, statistics, developmental psychology, and abnormal psychology; for Post-Doctoral Certificate, doctoral degree in psychology, 2 interviews. Additional exam requirements/recommendations for international students: Required—TOEFL (minimum score 550 paper-based; 213 computer-based). *Application deadline:* For fall admission, 1/15 priority date for domestic students, 5/1 priority date for international students; for spring admission, 12/1 priority date for international students. Application fee: $50. Electronic applications accepted. *Expenses:* Contact institution. *Financial support:* In 2007–08, 74 research assistantships with full and partial tuition reimbursements (averaging $6,343 per year) were awarded; teaching assistantships, career-related internships or fieldwork, Federal Work-Study, institutionally sponsored loans, and unspecified assistantships also available. Financial award application deadline: 2/15; financial award applicants required to submit FAFSA. *Faculty research:* Psychoanalytic processes, victimization, women's issues, program evaluation, psychotherapy process. *Unit head:* Dr. Jeau Lau Chir, Dean, 516-877-4800, E-mail: Chir@adelphi.edu. *Application contact:* Christine Murphy, Director of Admissions, 516-877-3050, Fax: 516-877-3039, E-mail: graduateadmissions@adelphi.edu.

See Close-Up on page 1361.

Adler School of Professional Psychology, Programs in Psychology, Chicago, IL 60601-7203. Offers art therapy (Certificate); clinical hypnosis (Certificate); clinical psychology (Psy D); counseling psychology (MACP); counseling psychology/art therapy (MACAT); gerontology (MAGP); marriage and family counseling (MAMFC); marriage and family therapy (Certificate); organizational psychology (MAO); substance abuse counseling (MASAC, Certificate); Psy D/Certificate; Psy D/MACAT; Psy D/MACP; Psy D/MAMFC; Psy D/MASAC. *Accreditation:* APA. Part-time and evening/weekend programs available. Terminal master's awarded for partial completion of doctoral program. *Degree requirements:* For master's, thesis or alternative, oral exam, practicum; for doctorate, thesis/dissertation, clinical exam, internship, oral exam, practicum, written qualifying exam. *Entrance requirements:* For master's, 12 semester hours in psychology, minimum GPA of 3.0; for doctorate, 18 semester hours in psychology, minimum GPA of 3.25; for Certificate, appropriate master's or doctoral degree.

See Close-Up on page 1363.

Alabama Agricultural and Mechanical University, School of Graduate Studies, School of Education, Department of Counseling and Special Education, Huntsville, AL 35811. Offers communicative disorders (M Ed, MS); psychology and counseling (MS, Ed S), including clinical psychology (MS), counseling and guidance, counseling psychology (MS), personnel management (MS), psychometry (MS), school psychology (MS); special education (M Ed, MS). *Accreditation:* CORE; NCATE. Part-time and evening/weekend programs available. *Faculty:* 4 full-time (3 women), 3 part-time/adjunct (1 woman). *Students:* 24 full-time (16 women), 58 part-time (48 women); includes 59 minority (56 African Americans, 1 American Indian/Alaska Native, 2 Hispanic Americans), 2 international. In 2007, 55 master's, 2 other advanced degrees awarded. *Degree requirements:* For master's, comprehensive exam. *Entrance requirements:* For master's, GRE General Test. *Application deadline:* For fall admission, 5/1 for domestic students. Application fee: $15 ($20 for international students). *Financial support:* Career-related internships or fieldwork available. Support available to part-time students. Financial award application deadline: 4/1. *Faculty research:* Increasing numbers of minorities in special education and speech-language pathology. Total annual research expenditures: $300,000. *Unit head:* Dr. Shirley King, Chair, 256-372-5520, Fax: 256-372-5526.

Alliant International University–Fresno, California School of Professional Psychology, Fresno, CA 93727. Offers PhD, Psy D. *Accreditation:* APA. *Degree requirements:* For doctorate, thesis/dissertation. *Entrance requirements:* For doctorate, interview, 3.0 GPA, letters of recommendation, essay. *Faculty research:* Child and family, body image, psychoanalysis, neuropsychology, teaching of psychology.

See Close-Up on page 1367.

Alliant International University–Los Angeles, California School of Professional Psychology, Alhambra, CA 91803-1360. Offers MA, PhD, Psy D. *Accreditation:* APA. *Degree requirements:* For doctorate, comprehensive exam, thesis/dissertation. *Entrance requirements:* For doctorate, interview, minimum GPA of 3.0 in psychology and overall, letters of recommendation, essay. Additional exam requirements/recommendations for international students: Required—TOEFL (minimum score 600 paper-based; 250 computer-based), TWE (minimum score 5). Electronic applications accepted. *Faculty research:* Family therapy, pregnancy-related issues, multicultural psychology, post-traumatic stress.

See Close-Up on page 1367.

Alliant International University–Sacramento, California School of Professional Psychology, Sacramento, CA 95825. Offers MA, Psy D. Electronic applications accepted.

See Close-Ups on pages 1369 and 1373.

Alliant International University–San Diego, California School of Professional Psychology, San Diego, CA 92131-1799. Offers MA, PhD, Psy D. *Accreditation:* APA. Part-time programs available. *Degree requirements:* For doctorate, thesis/dissertation. *Entrance requirements:* For doctorate, interview, minimum GPA of 3.0 in both psychology and overall. *Faculty research:* Native American studies, cross-cultural family therapy, families.

Alliant International University–San Francisco, California School of Professional Psychology, San Francisco, CA 94133-1221. Offers Post-Doctoral MS, PhD, Psy D, Certificate. *Accreditation:* APA (one or more programs are accredited). *Degree requirements:* For doctorate, comprehensive exam, thesis/dissertation. *Entrance requirements:* For master's and doctorate, interview, minimum GPA of 3.0. Additional exam requirements/recommendations for international students: Required—TOEFL (minimum score 600 paper-based; 250 computer-based), TWE (minimum score 5). Electronic applications accepted. *Faculty research:* Multicultural issues, lesbian/gay/bisexual/transgender issues, health psychology, family systems, substance abuse.

See Close-Ups on pages 1367 and 1369.

American International College, School of Arts, Education and Science, Department of Psychology, Springfield, MA 01109-3189. Offers child development (MA, Ed D), including educational psychology; clinical psychology (MA); forensic psychology (MS). Part-time and evening/weekend programs available. *Faculty:* 4 full-time (1 woman), 5 part-time/adjunct (2 women). *Students:* 76 full-time (65 women), 52 part-time (43 women); includes 28 minority (15 African Americans, 1 American Indian/Alaska Native, 4 Asian Americans or Pacific Islanders, 8 Hispanic Americans), 1 international. Average age 35. In 2007, 24 master's, 2 doctorates awarded. *Median time to degree:* Of those who began their doctoral program in fall 1999, 100% received their degree in 8 years or less. *Degree requirements:* For master's, comprehensive exam (for some programs), thesis (for some programs), practicum. *Entrance requirements:* For master's, minimum GPA of 3.0, BS or BA; for doctorate, GRE General Test, interview. Additional exam requirements/recommendations for international students: Required—TOEFL. *Application deadline:* For fall admission, 4/1 for domestic students, 4/15 for international students. Applications are processed on a rolling basis. Application fee: $50. Electronic applications accepted. *Expenses:* Tuition: Part-time $615 per credit hour. Full-time tuition and fees vary according to degree level, campus/location and program. *Financial support:* In 2007–08, 6 fellowships were awarded; career-related internships or fieldwork and institutionally sponsored loans also available. Financial award applicants required to submit FAFSA. *Unit head:* Dr. John DeFrancesco, Director, 413-205-3343, Fax: 413-205-3943, E-mail: john.defrancesco@aic.edu. *Application contact:* Barbara Z. Benoit, Director of Graduate Admissions, 413-205-3700, Fax: 413-205-3051, E-mail: barbara.benoit@aic.edu.

American University, College of Arts and Sciences, Department of Psychology, Washington, DC 20016-8001. Offers behavior, cognition, and neuroscience (PhD); clinical psychology (PhD); psychology (MA), including experimental/biological psychology, general psychology, personality/social psychology. *Accreditation:* APA. Part-time programs available. *Faculty:* 18 full-time (6 women), 8 part-time/adjunct (4 women). *Students:* 75 full-time (57 women), 45 part-time (38 women); includes 21 minority (10 African Americans, 6 Asian Americans or Pacific Islanders, 5 Hispanic Americans), 3 international. Average age 27. 426 applicants, 20% accepted, 35 enrolled. In 2007, 28 master's, 9 doctorates awarded. *Degree requirements:* For master's, comprehensive exam, thesis or alternative; for doctorate, comprehensive exam, thesis/dissertation, Tools of research. *Entrance requirements:* For master's, GRE General Test, GRE Subject Test, recommendations; for doctorate, GRE General Test, GRE Subject Test. Additional exam requirements/recommendations for international students: Required—TOEFL (minimum score 550 paper-based; 213 computer-based). Application fee: $50. *Expenses:* Tuition: Full-time $19,998; part-time $1,111 per credit hour. Required fees: $380. Tuition and fees vary according to program. *Financial support:* Fellowships, research assistantships, teaching assistantships, career-related internships or fieldwork, Federal Work-Study, institutionally sponsored loans, tuition waivers (full and partial), and unspecified assistantships available. Support available to part-time students. Financial award application deadline: 2/1. *Faculty research:* Anxiety disorders, cognitive assessment, neuropsychology, conditioning and learning, psychopharmacology. *Unit head:* Dr. Anthony Riley, Chair, 202-885-1720. *Application contact:* Sara Holland, Senior Administrative Assistant, 202-885-1717, Fax: 202-885-1023.

American University of Beirut, Graduate Programs, Faculty of Arts and Sciences, Beirut, Lebanon. Offers anthropology (MA); Arabic language and literature (MA); archaeology (MA); biology (MS); chemistry (MS); computer science (MS); economics (MA); education (MA); English language (MA); English literature (MA); environmental policy planning (MSES); financial economics (MAFE); geology (MS); history (MA); mathematics (MA, MS); Middle Eastern studies (MA); philosophy (MA); physics (MS); political studies (MA); psychology (MA); public administration (MA); sociology (MA); statistics (MA, MS). Part-time programs available. *Faculty:* 108 full-time (29 women), 5 part-time/adjunct (3 women). *Students:* 134 full-time (92 women), 228 part-time (167 women). Average age 25. 319 applicants, 67% accepted, 91 enrolled. In 2007, 144 degrees awarded. *Degree requirements:* For master's, one foreign language, comprehensive exam, thesis (for some programs). *Entrance requirements:* For master's, GRE, letter of recommendation. Additional exam requirements/recommendations for international students: Required—TOEFL (minimum score 600 paper-based; 250 computer-based; 100 iBT), IELTS (minimum score 8). *Application deadline:* For fall admission, 4/30 for domestic and international students; for spring admission, 11/1 for domestic and international students. Application fee: $50. *Expenses:* Tuition: Full-time $9,954; part-time $553 per credit. Tuition and fees vary according to course load and program. *Financial support:* In 2007–08, 28 students received support. Career-related internships or fieldwork, institutionally sponsored loans, scholarships/grants, health care benefits, and unspecified assistantships available. Financial award application deadline: 2/4; financial award applicants required to submit FAFSA. *Faculty research:* String theory and supergravity; computer graphics; algebra and number theory; popular Arabic literature; marine and freshwater biology; integrating science, math and technology. Total annual research expenditures: $132,270. *Unit head:* Khalil Bitar, Dean, 961-1374374 Ext. 3800, Fax: 961-1744461, E-mail: kmb@aub.edu.lb. *Application contact:* Dr. Salim Kanaan, Director, Admissions Office, 961-1350000 Ext. 2594, Fax: 961-1750775, E-mail: sk00@aub.edu.lb.

Andrews University, School of Graduate Studies, School of Education, Department of Educational and Counseling Psychology, Berrien Springs, MI 49104. Offers community counseling (MA); counseling psychology (PhD); educational and developmental psychology (MA, Ed D, PhD), including educational and developmental psychology (MA), educational psychology (Ed D, PhD); school counseling (MA); school psychology (Ed S). *Accreditation:* ACA (one or more programs are accredited). Part-time programs available. Terminal master's awarded for partial completion of doctoral program. *Degree requirements:* For master's, thesis optional; for doctorate, thesis/dissertation. *Entrance requirements:* For master's, GRE Subject Test, minimum GPA of 2.6; for doctorate, GRE General Test, MA, minimum GPA of 3.5, sample of research. *Faculty research:* Testing methods, temperament, African-American studies, counseling process, multicultural issues.

Angelo State University, College of Graduate Studies, College of Liberal and Fine Arts, Department of Psychology and Sociology, San Angelo, TX 76909. Offers psychology (MS), including counseling psychology, general psychology, industrial and organizational psychology. Part-time and evening/weekend programs available. *Faculty:* 8 full-time (2 women). *Students:* 11 full-time (8 women), 39 part-time (21 women); includes 8 minority (2 African Americans, 1 American Indian/Alaska Native, 5 Hispanic Americans), 1 international. Average age 26. 35

Psychology—General

Angelo State University (continued)

applicants, 66% accepted, 17 enrolled. In 2007, 27 degrees awarded. *Degree requirements:* For master's, comprehensive exam, thesis optional. *Entrance requirements:* For master's, GRE General Test. Additional exam requirements/recommendations for international students: Required—TOEFL or IELTS. *Application deadline:* For fall admission, 7/15 priority date for domestic students, 6/10 for international students; for spring admission, 12/8 for domestic students, 11/1 for international students. Applications are processed on a rolling basis. Application fee: $40 ($50 for international students). Electronic applications accepted. *Financial support:* In 2007–08, 44 students received support, including 3 teaching assistantships (averaging $10,251 per year); career-related internships or fieldwork, Federal Work-Study, scholarships/grants, and unspecified assistantships also available. Support available to part-time students. Financial award application deadline: 3/1; financial award applicants required to submit FAFSA. *Faculty research:* Toddlers use of actors' intentions to learn verbs. Total annual research expenditures: $116,915. *Unit head:* Dr. William B. Davidson, Department Head, 325-942-2068 Ext. 248, E-mail: bill.davidson@angelo.edu.

Antioch University Los Angeles, Graduate Programs, Program in Psychology, Culver City, CA 90230. Offers clinical psychology (MA); psychology (MA). Part-time programs available. *Degree requirements:* For master's, thesis (for some programs), internship. *Entrance requirements:* For master's, interview. Additional exam requirements/recommendations for international students: Required—TOEFL. *Faculty research:* Creativity and humor, ethnic humor, adult development, Jungian theory, psychoanalytic theory.

Antioch University McGregor, Graduate Programs, Individualized Liberal and Professional Studies Program, Yellow Springs, OH 45387-1609. Offers liberal and professional studies (MA), including counseling, creative writing, education, film studies, liberal studies, management, modern literature, psychology, theatre, visual arts. Part-time and evening/weekend programs available. Postbaccalaureate distance learning degree programs offered (minimal on-campus study). *Faculty:* 2 full-time (1 woman), 3 part-time/adjunct (2 women). *Students:* Average age 40. 35 applicants, 63% accepted, 17 enrolled. In 2007, 31 degrees awarded. *Degree requirements:* For master's, thesis or alternative. *Entrance requirements:* For master's, resumé, 2 letters of reference. *Application deadline:* For fall admission, 8/25 for domestic students; for winter admission, 12/5 for domestic students; for spring admission, 3/8 for domestic students. Applications are processed on a rolling basis. Application fee: $50. Electronic applications accepted. *Expenses:* Contact institution. *Financial support:* Federal Work-Study available. Financial award applicants required to submit FAFSA. *Unit head:* Suzanne Fest, Chair, 937-769-1876, Fax: 937-769-1807, E-mail: sfest@mcgregor.edu. *Application contact:* Seth Gordon, Assistant Director of Admissions, 937-769-1800 Ext. 1825, Fax: 937-769-1804, E-mail: sgordon@mcgregor.edu.

See Close-Up on page 443.

Antioch University New England, Graduate School, Department of Applied Psychology, Keene, NH 03431-3552. Offers autism spectrum disorders (Certificate); clinical mental health counseling (MA); dance/movement therapy and counseling (M Ed, MA); marriage and family therapy (MA, PhD). *Faculty:* 9 full-time (7 women), 14 part-time/adjunct (9 women). *Students:* 176 full-time (152 women), 29 part-time (19 women); includes 9 minority (4 African Americans, 1 American Indian/Alaska Native, 4 Hispanic Americans), 5 international. Average age 36. 179 applicants, 82% accepted, 94 enrolled. In 2007, 104 degrees awarded. *Degree requirements:* For master's, internship, practicum. *Entrance requirements:* For master's, previous course work and work experience in psychology. Additional exam requirements/recommendations for international students: Required—TOEFL (minimum score 600 paper-based; 250 computer-based). *Application deadline:* For fall admission, 7/15 for domestic and international students; for spring admission, 12/1 for domestic and international students. Applications are processed on a rolling basis. Application fee: $50. Electronic applications accepted. *Expenses:* Contact institution. Tuition and fees vary according to degree level, program and student level. *Financial support:* In 2007–08, 181 students received support, including 31 fellowships (averaging $1,576 per year), 3 research assistantships (averaging $5,700 per year); career-related internships or fieldwork, Federal Work-Study, and scholarships/grants also available. Financial award applicants required to submit FAFSA. *Faculty research:* Diversity, descendents of survivors of the Holocaust and American slavery. *Unit head:* Dr. Katherine Clarke, Chair, 603-283-2150, Fax: 306-357-0718, E-mail: kclarke@antiochne.edu. *Application contact:* Leatrice A. Oram, Co-Director of Admissions, 800-490-3310, Fax: 603-357-0718, E-mail: admissions@antiochne.edu.

See Close-Up on page 1375.

Antioch University Santa Barbara, Program in Psychology, Santa Barbara, CA 93101-1581. Offers MA. Part-time and evening/weekend programs available. *Faculty:* 13 full-time (9 women), 34 part-time/adjunct (19 women). *Students:* 100 full-time (89 women), 23 part-time (22 women); includes 36 minority (5 African Americans, 3 Asian Americans or Pacific Islanders, 28 Hispanic Americans), 5 international. In 2007, 59 degrees awarded. *Degree requirements:* For master's, internship. *Entrance requirements:* Additional exam requirements/recommendations for international students: Required—TOEFL (minimum score 550 paper-based; 213 computer-based). *Application deadline:* For fall admission, 7/16 priority date for domestic students; for winter admission, 11/5 priority date for domestic students. Applications are processed on a rolling basis. Application fee: $60 ($100 for international students). Electronic applications accepted. *Financial support:* Federal Work-Study and traineeships available. Support available to part-time students. Financial award application deadline: 8/8; financial award applicants required to submit FAFSA. *Unit head:* Dr. Catherine Radecki-Bush, Chair, 805-962-8179 Ext. 229, Fax: 805-962-4786, E-mail: cradecki-bush@antiochsb.edu. *Application contact:* Director of Admissions, 805-962-8179, Fax: 805-962-4786, E-mail: admissions@antiochsb.edu.

Antioch University Seattle, Graduate Programs, Program in Psychology, Seattle, WA 98121-1814. Offers MA, Psy D. Part-time and evening/weekend programs available. *Degree requirements:* For master's, internship. Electronic applications accepted. *Faculty research:* Trauma and post-traumatic stress disorders, workplace harassment and violence, multicultural issues and diversity.

Appalachian State University, Cratis D. Williams Graduate School, Department of Psychology, Boone, NC 28608. Offers clinical health psychology (MA); general experimental psychology (MA); industrial and organizational psychology (MA). Part-time programs available. *Faculty:* 31 full-time (11 women). *Students:* 43 full-time (31 women), 37 part-time (30 women); includes 4 minority (3 African Americans, 1 Asian American or Pacific Islander), 4 international. 197 applicants, 30% accepted, 30 enrolled. In 2007, 23 master's, 6 other advanced degrees awarded. *Degree requirements:* For master's and MS/SSP, comprehensive exam, thesis optional, GRE Subject Test exit exam. *Entrance requirements:* For master's, GRE General Test, 3 letters of recommendation. Additional exam requirements/recommendations for international students: Required—TOEFL (minimum score 550 paper-based; 230 computer-based; 79 iBT), IELTS (minimum score 7). *Application deadline:* For fall admission, 3/1 for domestic students, 1/1 for international students. Applications are processed on a rolling basis. Application fee: $50. *Expenses:* Tuition, state resident: part-time $127 per semester hour. Tuition, nonresident: part-time $597 per semester hour. Required fees: $18 per semester. *Financial support:* In 2007–08, 34 research assistantships (averaging $3,500 per year), 25 teaching assistantships (averaging $3,500 per year) were awarded; fellowships, career-related internships or fieldwork, Federal Work-Study, scholarships/grants, and unspecified assistantships also available. Financial award application deadline: 4/1. *Faculty research:* Eating disorders, school-based consultations, organizational behavior management, brain mechanisms of sound localization, parenting styles. Total annual research expenditures: $158,688. *Unit head:* Dr. Paul Fox, Chair, 828-262-2272, Fax: 828-262-2974, E-mail: foxpa@appstate.edu. *Application contact:* Dr. Denise Martz, Graduate Coordinator, 828-262-2715, E-mail: martzdm@appstate.edu.

Arcadia University, Graduate Studies, Department of Education, Glenside, PA 19038-3295. Offers art education (M Ed, MA Ed); biology education (MA Ed); chemistry education (MA Ed); child development (CAS); computer education (M Ed, CAS); computer education 7–12 (MA Ed); early childhood education (M Ed, CAS), including individualized (M Ed), master teacher (M Ed), research in child development (M Ed); educational leadership (M Ed, CAS); educational psychology (CAS); elementary education (M Ed, CAS); English education (MA Ed); environmental education (MA Ed, CAS); history education (MA Ed); language arts (M Ed, CAS); mathematics education (M Ed, MA Ed, CAS); music education (MA Ed); psychology (MA Ed); pupil personnel services (CAS); reading (M Ed, CAS); school library science (M Ed); science education (M Ed, CAS); secondary education (M Ed, CAS); special education (M Ed, Ed D, CAS); theater arts (MA Ed); written communication (MA Ed). *Accreditation:* NASAD. Part-time and evening/weekend programs available. Postbaccalaureate distance learning degree programs offered (minimal on-campus study). Electronic applications accepted.

Arcadia University, Graduate Studies, Department of Psychology, Glenside, PA 19038-3295. Offers community counseling (MACP); school counseling (MACP). Part-time programs available. *Degree requirements:* For master's, practicum. *Entrance requirements:* For master's, GRE General Test or MAT.

Argosy University, Atlanta, College of Psychology and Behavioral Sciences, Atlanta, GA 30328. Offers clinical psychology (MA, Psy D, Postdoctoral Respecialization Certificate), including child and family psychology (Psy D), general adult clinical (Psy D), health psychology (Psy D), neuropsychology/geropsychology (Psy D); community counseling (MA), including marriage and family therapy; counselor education and supervision (Ed D); marriage and family therapy (Certificate). *Accreditation:* APA.

See Close-Up on page 1377.

Argosy University, Chicago, College of Psychology and Behavioral Sciences, Chicago, IL 60654. Offers clinical psychology (MA, Psy D), including child and adolescent psychology (Psy D), client-centered and experiential psychotherapies (Psy D), diversity and multicultural psychology (Psy D), family psychology (Psy D), forensic psychology (Psy D), health psychology (Psy D), psychoanalytic psychology (Psy D), psychology and spirituality (Psy D); community counseling (MA); counseling psychology (Ed D), including counselor education and supervision; counselor education and supervision (Ed D); organizational leadership (Ed D). *Accreditation:* APA (one or more programs are accredited). Postbaccalaureate distance learning degree programs offered (minimal on-campus study).

See Close-Up on page 1379.

Argosy University, Dallas, College of Psychology and Behavioral Sciences, Dallas, TX 75231. Offers MA, Psy D.

See Close-Up on page 1381.

Argosy University, Denver, College of Psychology and Behavioral Sciences, Denver, CO 80203. Offers clinical psychology (MA, Psy D); community counseling (MA); counseling psychology (Ed D), including counselor education and supervision; counselor education and supervision (Ed D); forensic psychology (MA); marriage and family therapy (MA); organizational leadership (Ed D).

See Close-Up on page 1383.

Argosy University, Hawai'i, College of Psychology and Behavioral Sciences, Honolulu, HI 96813. Offers MA, MS, Ed D, Psy D, Certificate, Postdoctoral Respecialization Certificate. *Accreditation:* APA.

See Close-Up on page 1385.

Argosy University, Inland Empire, College of Psychology and Behavioral Sciences, San Bernardino, CA 92408. Offers clinical psychology/marriage and family therapy (MA); counseling psychology (MA, Ed D); counseling psychology/marriage and family therapy (MA); forensic psychology (MA).

See Close-Up on page 1387.

Argosy University, Los Angeles, College of Psychology and Behavioral Sciences, Santa Monica, CA 90405. Offers clinical psychology/marriage and family therapy (MA); counseling psychology (Ed D); counseling psychology/marriage and family therapy (MA); organizational leadership (Ed D).

See Close-Up on page 1389.

Argosy University, Nashville, College of Psychology and Behavioral Sciences, Nashville, TN 37214. Offers counselor education and supervision (Ed D); mental health counseling (MA).

See Close-Up on page 1391.

Argosy University, Orange County, College of Psychology and Behavioral Sciences, Santa Ana, CA 92704. Offers MA, Ed D, Psy D, Postdoctoral Respecialization Certificate. *Accreditation:* APA. Part-time and evening/weekend programs available. *Faculty:* 8 full-time (5 women), 19 part-time/adjunct (6 women). *Students:* 160 full-time (118 women), 41 part-time (30 women). Average age 30. 217 applicants, 69 enrolled. In 2007, 6 master's, 2 doctorates awarded. *Degree requirements:* For master's, comprehensive exam; for doctorate, comprehensive exam, thesis/dissertation. *Entrance requirements:* For master's and doctorate, 3 letters of recommendation, interview, resumé. Additional exam requirements/recommendations for international students: Required—TOEFL. *Application deadline:* Applications are processed on a rolling basis. Application fee: $50. Electronic applications accepted. *Financial support:* In 2007–08, 15 students received support. Career-related internships or fieldwork, Federal Work-Study, institutionally sponsored loans, and scholarships/grants available. Support available to part-time students. Financial award applicants required to submit FAFSA. *Faculty research:* The psychological aspects of infertility medicine, depression, psychoanalytic therapy, experiential approaches to teaching. *Unit head:* Dr. Gary Bruss, Dean, 800-716-9598, Fax: 714-437-1284, E-mail: gbruss@argosy.edu. *Application contact:* Mark Betz, Director of Admissions, 800-716-9598, Fax: 714-437-1697, E-mail: mbetz@argosy.edu.

See Close-Up on page 1393.

Argosy University, Phoenix, College of Psychology and Behavioral Sciences, Phoenix, AZ 85021. Offers MA, Psy D.

See Close-Up on page 1395.

Argosy University, Salt Lake City, College of Psychology and Behavioral Sciences, Draper, UT 84020. Offers counseling psychology (Ed D); marriage and family therapy (MA).

See Close-Up on page 1397.

Argosy University, San Diego, College of Psychology and Behavioral Sciences, San Diego, CA 92108. Offers clinical psychology/marriage and family therapy (MA); counseling psychology (MA, Ed D); counseling psychology/marriage and family therapy (MA).

See Close-Up on page 1399.

Argosy University, San Francisco Bay Area, College of Psychology and Behavioral Sciences, Alameda, CA 94501. Offers clinical psychology (MA, Psy D); counseling psychology (MA, Ed D); forensic psychology (MA); organizational leadership (Ed D). *Accreditation:* APA (one or more programs are accredited).

See Close-Up on page 1401.

Argosy University, Sarasota, College of Psychology and Behavioral Sciences, Sarasota, FL 34235. Offers community counseling (MA); counseling psychology (Ed D); counselor education and supervision (Ed D); forensic psychology (MA); marriage and family therapy (MA); mental health counseling (MA); organizational leadership (Ed D); pastoral community counseling (Ed D); school counseling (MA, Ed S); school psychology (MA).

See Close-Up on page 1403.

Argosy University, Schaumburg, College of Psychology and Behavioral Sciences, Schaumburg, IL 60173-5403. Offers clinical health psychology (Post-Graduate Certificate); clinical psychology (MA, Psy D), including child and family psychology (Psy D), clinical health psychology (Psy D), diversity and multicultural psychology (Psy D), forensic psychology (Psy D); community counseling (MA); counseling psychology (Ed D), including counselor education and supervision; counselor education and supervision (Ed D); forensic psychology (Post-Graduate Certificate); organizational leadership (Ed D). *Accreditation:* ACA; APA.

See Close-Up on page 1405.

Argosy University, Seattle, College of Psychology and Behavioral Sciences, Seattle, WA 98121. Offers MA, Ed D, Psy D, Postdoctoral Respecialization Certificate.

See Close-Up on page 1407.

Argosy University, Tampa, College of Psychology and Behavioral Sciences, Tampa, FL 33614. Offers clinical psychology (MA, Psy D), including clinical psychology; counselor education and supervision (Ed D); marriage and family therapy (MA); mental health counseling (MA); organizational leadership (Ed D); school counseling (MA).

See Close-Up on page 1409.

Argosy University, Twin Cities, College of Psychology and Behavioral Sciences, Eagan, MN 55121. Offers clinical psychology (MA, Psy D), including child and family psychology (Psy D), forensic psychology (Psy D), health psychology (Psy D), marriage/couples and family therapy (Psy D), neuropsychology (Psy D); forensic counseling (Post-Graduate Certificate); forensic psychology (MA); marriage and family therapy (MA, DMFT), including forensic counseling (MA); organizational leadership (Ed D). *Accreditation:* APA.

See Close-Up on page 1411.

Argosy University, Washington DC, College of Psychology and Behavioral Sciences, Arlington, VA 22209. Offers clinical psychology (MA, Psy D), including child and family psychology (Psy D), diversity and multicultural psychology (Psy D), forensic psychology (Psy D), health and neuropsychology (Psy D); community counseling (MA); counseling psychology (Ed D), including counselor education and supervision; counselor education and supervision (Ed D); forensic psychology (MA); organizational leadership (Ed D). *Accreditation:* APA.

See Close-Up on page 1413.

Arizona State University, Graduate College, College of Liberal Arts and Sciences, Division of Natural Sciences and Mathematics, Department of Psychology, Tempe, AZ 85287. Offers behavioral neuroscience (PhD); clinical psychology (PhD); cognitive/behavioral systems (PhD); developmental psychology (PhD); environmental psychology (PhD); quantitative research methods (PhD); social psychology (PhD). *Accreditation:* APA. *Degree requirements:* For doctorate, thesis/dissertation. *Entrance requirements:* For doctorate, GRE General Test, GRE Subject Test.

Arizona State University at the Polytechnic Campus, School of Applied Arts and Sciences, Applied Psychology Program, Mesa, AZ 85212. Offers MS. *Faculty:* 6 full-time (1 woman). *Students:* 9 full-time (7 women), 4 part-time; includes 2 minority (1 Asian American or Pacific Islander, 1 Hispanic American), 1 international. Average age 29. In 2007, 5 degrees awarded. *Degree requirements:* For master's, thesis or applied project with oral defense. *Entrance requirements:* For master's, GRE, 3 letters of recommendation, minimum GPA of 3.0. Additional exam requirements/recommendations for international students: Required—TOEFL (minimum score 550 paper-based; 213 computer-based; 83 iBT); Recommended—TWE. *Application deadline:* For fall admission, 1/31 priority date for domestic and international students; for spring admission, 9/15 priority date for domestic and international students. Application fee: $50. Electronic applications accepted. *Expenses:* Tuition, state resident: full-time $4,620. Tuition, nonresident: full-time $16,853. Tuition and fees vary according to course level, course load and program. *Financial support:* Fellowships, research assistantships with full tuition reimbursements, teaching assistantships with full tuition reimbursements, career-related internships or fieldwork, scholarships/grants, traineeships, health care benefits, and unspecified assistantships available. Support available to part-time students. Total annual research expenditures: $816,852. *Unit head:* Dr. David Vaughn Becker, Assistant Professor/Graduate Program Director, 480-727-1151, Fax: 480-727-1538, E-mail: vaughn.becker@asu.edu.

Athabasca University, Graduate Centre for Applied Psychology, Athabasca, AB T9S 3A3, Canada. Offers art therapy (MC); career counseling (MC); counseling (Advanced Certificate); counseling psychology (MC); school counseling (MC). *Faculty:* 3 full-time (2 women), 2 part-time/adjunct (0 women). Tuition and fees charges are reported in Canadian dollars. *Expenses:* Tuition, state resident: part-time $1,795 Canadian dollars per credit. Required fees: $70 Canadian dollars per year. One-time fee: $360 Canadian dollars part-time. Part-time tuition and fees vary according to program. *Unit head:* Dr. Sandra Collins, Program Director, 888-611-7121, E-mail: sandrac@athabascau.ca.

Auburn University, Graduate School, College of Liberal Arts, Department of Psychology, Auburn University, AL 36849. Offers applied behavior analysis in developmental disabilities (MS); clinical psychology (PhD); experimental psychology (PhD); industrial/organizational psychology (PhD). *Accreditation:* APA (one or more programs are accredited). Part-time programs available. *Faculty:* 22 full-time (5 women). *Students:* 30 full-time (18 women), 65 part-time (44 women); includes 10 minority (5 African Americans, 1 American Indian/Alaska Native, 2 Asian Americans or Pacific Islanders, 2 Hispanic Americans), 2 international. Average age 28. 298 applicants, 15% accepted, 27 enrolled. In 2007, 15 master's, 3 doctorates awarded. *Degree requirements:* For doctorate, thesis/dissertation. *Entrance requirements:* For master's, GRE General Test, GRE Subject Test, minimum GPA of 3.25 in psychology, 3.0 overall; for doctorate, GRE General Test, GRE Subject Test. *Application deadline:* For fall admission, 7/7 for domestic students; for spring admission, 11/24 for domestic students. Applications are processed on a rolling basis. Application fee: $25 ($50 for international students). Electronic applications accepted. *Financial support:* Research assistantships, teaching assistantships, Federal Work-Study available. Support available to part-time students. Financial award application deadline: 3/15. *Faculty research:* Clinical psychology, learning, industrial psychology, organizational psychology. Total annual research expenditures: $200,000. *Unit head:* Dr. Barry Burkhart, Chair, 334-844-4412. *Application contact:* Dr. Joe Pittman, Interim Dean of the Graduate School, 334-844-4700.

Auburn University Montgomery, School of Sciences, Department of Psychology, Montgomery, AL 36124-4023. Offers MSPG. Part-time and evening/weekend programs available. *Faculty:* 7 full-time (3 women). *Students:* 12 full-time (10 women), 10 part-time (all women); includes 10 minority (9 African Americans, 1 Asian American or Pacific Islander). Average age 27. In 2007, 8 degrees awarded. *Degree requirements:* For master's, comprehensive exam, thesis optional. *Entrance requirements:* For master's, GRE General Test or MAT. *Application deadline:* Applications are processed on a rolling basis. Application fee: $25. Electronic applications accepted. *Expenses:* Tuition, state resident: full-time $4,536; part-time $189 per credit hour. Tuition, nonresident: full-time $13,608; part-time $567 per credit hour. Required fees: $234. *Financial support:* In 2007–08, 7 teaching assistantships were awarded; career-related internships or fieldwork and scholarships/grants also available. Support available to part-time students. Financial award application deadline: 3/1; financial award applicants required to submit FAFSA. *Faculty research:* Community service, diagnosis, behavior modification. *Unit head:* Dr. Peter Zachar, Chair, 334-244-3311, Fax: 334-244-3826, E-mail: pzachar@mail.aum.edu. *Application contact:* Dr. Steve LoBello, Graduate Coordinator, 334-244-3309, Fax: 334-244-3826, E-mail: slobello@mail.aum.edu.

Augusta State University, Graduate Studies, College of Arts and Sciences, Department of Psychology, Augusta, GA 30904-2200. Offers MS. Part-time programs available. *Faculty:* 8 full-time (5 women). *Students:* 25 full-time (19 women), 7 part-time (6 women); includes 12 minority (10 African Americans, 1 Asian American or Pacific Islander, 1 Hispanic American). Average age 27. 25 applicants, 72% accepted, 14 enrolled. In 2007, 15 degrees awarded. *Degree requirements:* For master's, thesis optional, written/oral exam. *Entrance requirements:* For master's, GRE General Test, minimum GPA of 2.5, bachelor's degree in psychology or equivalent course work. *Application deadline:* For fall admission, 8/1 priority date for domestic students. Applications are processed on a rolling basis. Application fee: $20. *Expenses:* Tuition, state resident: full-time $3,192; part-time $133 per hour. Tuition, nonresident: full-time $12,792; part-time $533 per hour. Required fees: $536; $268 per semester. *Financial support:* Research assistantships with partial tuition reimbursements, career-related internships or fieldwork, Federal Work-Study, and institutionally sponsored loans available. Financial award application deadline: 4/15; financial award applicants required to submit FAFSA. *Faculty research:* Developmental, cognitive, gender and aging issues; consumer behavior; conditioned taste aversions; circadian rhythms; use of slang and offensive language. *Unit head:* Dr. Deborah S. Richardson, Chair, 706-737-1694. *Application contact:* Connie Bradley, Degree Program Specialist, 706-737-1694, Fax: 706-737-1773, E-mail: cbradley@aug.edu.

Austin Peay State University, College of Graduate Studies, College of Professional Programs and Social Sciences, Department of Psychology, Clarksville, TN 37044. Offers counseling (MS); psychology (MA). Part-time programs available. Postbaccalaureate distance learning degree programs offered (no on-campus study). *Faculty:* 14 full-time (6 women), 2 part-time/adjunct (1 woman). *Students:* 47 full-time (37 women), 28 part-time (27 women); includes 4 minority (3 African Americans, 1 Asian American or Pacific Islander). Average age 32. In 2007, 12 degrees awarded. *Degree requirements:* For master's, comprehensive exam, thesis (for some programs). *Entrance requirements:* For master's, GRE General Test, minimum GPA of 2.5, 3 letters of recommendation. Additional exam requirements/recommendations for international students: Required—TOEFL (minimum score 500 paper-based; 173 computer-based). *Application deadline:* For fall admission, 3/31 priority date for domestic students; for spring admission, 11/1 priority date for domestic students. Applications are processed on a rolling basis. Application fee: $25. Electronic applications accepted. *Expenses:* Tuition, state resident: full-time $5,446; part-time $288 per credit hour. Tuition, nonresident: full-time $15,722; part-time $734 per credit hour. Required fees: $1,180. Part-time tuition and fees vary according to course load. *Financial support:* In 2007–08, research assistantships (averaging $10,368 per year); career-related internships or fieldwork, Federal Work-Study, institutionally sponsored loans, scholarships/grants, and unspecified assistantships also available. Support available to part-time students. Financial award application deadline: 3/1; financial award applicants required to submit FAFSA. *Unit head:* Dr. Samuel Fung, Chair, 931-221-7233, Fax: 931-221-6267, E-mail: fungs@apsu.edu.

Avila University, Department of Psychology, Kansas City, MO 64145-1698. Offers counseling and art therapy (MS); counseling psychology (MS); general psychology (MS). Part-time and evening/weekend programs available. *Faculty:* 7 full-time (5 women), 12 part-time/adjunct (9 women). *Students:* 109 full-time (94 women), 19 part-time (15 women); includes 24 minority (19 African Americans, 1 Asian American or Pacific Islander, 4 Hispanic Americans), 4 international. Average age 35. In 2007, 30 degrees awarded. *Entrance requirements:* For master's, minimum GPA of 3.0 in last 60 hours, 2 letters of recommendation, transcripts, application with letter of intent. Additional exam requirements/recommendations for international students: Required—TOEFL. *Application deadline:* Applications are processed on a rolling basis. Application fee: $0. *Expenses:* Tuition: Part-time $435 per credit hour. Required fees: $19 per credit hour. Tuition and fees vary according to program. *Financial support:* Career-related internships or fieldwork and scholarships/grants available. Support available to part-time students. Financial award applicants required to submit FAFSA. *Faculty research:* Preparation for working in mental health services. *Unit head:* Dr. Regina Staves, Director of Graduate Psychology, 816-501-3665, Fax: 816-501-2455, E-mail: gradpsych@avila.edu.

Azusa Pacific University, School of Behavioral and Applied Sciences, Department of Graduate Psychology, Azusa, CA 91702-7000. Offers clinical psychology (MA, Psy D), including family therapy (MA). *Accreditation:* APA (one or more programs are accredited). Part-time and evening/weekend programs available. *Degree requirements:* For master's, comprehensive exam, 250 hours of clinical experience, individual and group therapy. *Entrance requirements:* For master's, interview, minimum GPA of 3.0, Minnesota Multiphasic Personality Inventory. Additional exam requirements/recommendations for international students: Required—TOEFL (minimum score 600 paper-based).

Ball State University, Graduate School, College of Sciences and Humanities, Department of Psychological Science, Muncie, IN 47306-1099. Offers clinical psychology (MA); cognitive and social processes (MA). *Faculty:* 20. *Students:* 37 full-time (24 women), 2 part-time (1 woman); includes 6 minority (1 African American, 1 American Indian/Alaska Native, 3 Asian Americans or Pacific Islanders, 1 Hispanic American), 6 international. Average age 24. 61 applicants, 52% accepted, 19 enrolled. In 2007, 13 degrees awarded. Application fee: $25 ($35 for international students). *Expenses:* Tuition, state resident: full-time $6,864. Tuition, nonresident: full-time $17,932. Required fees: $1,866. *Financial support:* In 2007–08, 19 teaching assistantships (averaging $7,959 per year) were awarded; research assistantships with full tuition reimbursements. Financial award application deadline: 3/1. *Unit head:* Dr. Bernard Whitley, Chairman, 765-285-1690, Fax: 765-285-8980. *Application contact:* Dr. Kerri Pickel, Graduate Program Director, 765-285-1690, Fax: 765-285-8980, E-mail: kpickel@bsu.edu.

Barry University, School of Arts and Sciences, Department of Psychology, Miami Shores, FL 33161-6695. Offers clinical psychology (MS); school psychology (MS, SSP). Part-time and evening/weekend programs available. *Students:* 6 full-time (0 women), 56 part-time (52 women); includes 34 minority (14 African Americans, 2 Asian Americans or Pacific Islanders, 18 Hispanic Americans), 8 international. *Degree requirements:* For master's, thesis, practicum. *Entrance requirements:* For master's, GRE General Test, minimum GPA of 3.0, course work in psychology. *Application deadline:* Applications are processed on a rolling basis. Application fee: $30. Electronic applications accepted. *Financial support:* In 2007–08, 5 research assistantships with partial tuition reimbursements (averaging $3,000 per year) were awarded; career-related internships or fieldwork and tuition waivers (partial) also available. Support available to part-time students. Financial award application deadline: 5/1; financial award applicants required to submit FAFSA. *Faculty research:* Closed head injury, memory and aging, infant/mother interaction, evolutionary aspects of behavior, gender roles. *Unit head:* Dr. Lenore Szuchman, Chair, 305-899-3278, Fax: 305-899-3279, E-mail: lszuchman@mail.barry.edu. *Application contact:* Dave Fletcher, Director of Graduate Admissions, 305-899-3113, Fax: 305-899-2971, E-mail: dfletcher@mail.barry.edu.

See Close-Up on page 1415.

Bayamón Central University, Graduate Programs, Program in Psychology, Bayamón, PR 00960-1725. Offers MA. Part-time and evening/weekend programs available. *Degree requirements:* For master's, comprehensive exam. *Entrance requirements:* For master's, EXADEP, bachelor's degree in psychology or related field.

Baylor University, Graduate School, College of Arts and Sciences, Department of Psychology and Neuroscience, Waco, TX 76798. Offers clinical psychology (MSCP, Psy D); neuroscience (MA, PhD). *Accreditation:* APA (one or more programs are accredited). *Students:* 34 full-time (25 women), 1 (woman) part-time; includes 7 minority (4 Asian Americans or Pacific Islanders, 3 Hispanic Americans). In 2007, 9 master's, 8 doctorates awarded. *Degree requirements:* For doctorate, comprehensive exam. *Entrance requirements:* For master's, GRE General Test; for doctorate, GRE General Test, GRE Subject Test (Psy D). *Application*

Psychology—General

Baylor University (continued)
deadline: Applications are processed on a rolling basis. Application fee: $25. *Financial support:* Research assistantships, teaching assistantships, career-related internships or fieldwork, Federal Work-Study, institutionally sponsored loans, tuition waivers (partial), and practicum stipends available. Financial award applicants required to submit FAFSA. *Application contact:* Suzanne Keener, Administrative Assistant, 254-710-3588, Fax: 254-710-3870.

Biola University, Rosemead School of Psychology, La Mirada, CA 90639-0001. Offers MA, PhD, Psy D. *Accreditation:* APA. Terminal master's awarded for partial completion of doctoral program. *Degree requirements:* For master's, thesis, internship; for doctorate, comprehensive exam, thesis/dissertation, internship. *Entrance requirements:* For master's and doctorate, GRE General Test, GRE Subject Test, Minnesota Multiphasic Personality Inventory, interview, 30 undergraduate credits in psychology. Additional exam requirements/recommendations for international students: Required—TOEFL (minimum score 250 computer-based). Expenses: Contact institution. *Faculty research:* Integration of psychology and theology, practice of psychotherapy, therapy process and outcomes.

Boston College, Graduate School of Arts and Sciences, Department of Psychology, Chestnut Hill, MA 02467-3800. Offers MA, PhD. *Students:* 26 full-time (21 women), 2 part-time (both women); includes 3 minority (2 Asian Americans or Pacific Islanders, 1 Hispanic American), 1 international. 193 applicants, 8% accepted, 9 enrolled. In 2007, 4 master's, 1 doctorate awarded. *Degree requirements:* For doctorate, thesis/dissertation, fieldwork. *Entrance requirements:* For master's, GRE General Test; for doctorate, GRE General Test, GRE Subject Test. Additional exam requirements/recommendations for international students: Required—TOEFL (minimum score 590 paper-based; 250 computer-based; 91 iBT). *Application deadline:* For fall admission, 1/2 for domestic students. Application fee: $70. Electronic applications accepted. *Financial support:* Fellowships with full tuition reimbursements, research assistantships with full tuition reimbursements, teaching assistantships with full tuition reimbursements, career-related internships or fieldwork available. Support available to part-time students. Financial award application deadline: 3/1; financial award applicants required to submit FAFSA. *Faculty research:* Social, cognitive, and biological processes. *Unit head:* Dr. James Russell, Chairperson, 617-552-4100, E-mail: james.russell@bc.edu. *Application contact:* Dr. Jon Horvitz, Graduate Program Director, 617-552-2999, E-mail: jon.horvitz@bc.edu.

Boston Graduate School of Psychoanalysis, Master's Program—New York, New York, NY 10011. Offers MA. Part-time programs available. *Faculty:* 12 full-time (10 women), 11 part-time/adjunct (7 women). *Students:* 8 full-time (7 women), 13 part-time (6 women), 1 international. In 2007, 5 degrees awarded. *Entrance requirements:* For master's, interview, writing sample. *Application deadline:* Applications are processed on a rolling basis. Application fee: $100. *Expenses:* Tuition: Full-time $5,400; part-time $1,350 per course. Required fees: $460 per semester. Tuition and fees vary according to course load, campus/location and program. *Financial support:* Career-related internships or fieldwork available. Financial award applicants required to submit FAFSA. *Unit head:* Dr. Mimi Crowell, Dean, 212-260-7050, Fax: 212-228-6410, E-mail: bgsp-ny.registrar@bgsp.edu. *Application contact:* Stephen Guttman, Registrar, 212-260-7050, Fax: 212-228-6410, E-mail: bgsp-ny.registrar@bgsp.edu.

See Close-Up on page 1417.

Boston University, Graduate School of Arts and Sciences, Department of Psychology, Boston, MA 02215. Offers MA, PhD. *Accreditation:* APA (one or more programs are accredited). *Students:* 138 full-time (104 women), 13 part-time (9 women); includes 17 minority (5 African Americans, 9 Asian Americans or Pacific Islanders, 3 Hispanic Americans), 18 international. Average age 29. 984 applicants, 19% accepted, 60 enrolled. In 2007, 84 master's, 16 doctorates awarded. Terminal master's awarded for partial completion of doctoral program. *Degree requirements:* For master's, one foreign language, comprehensive exam; for doctorate, one foreign language, comprehensive exam, thesis/dissertation. *Entrance requirements:* For master's and doctorate, GRE General Test. Additional exam requirements/recommendations for international students: Required—TOEFL. *Application deadline:* For fall admission, 1/15 for domestic and international students. Application fee: $70. *Expenses:* Tuition: Full-time $34,930; part-time $1,092 per credit. Tuition and fees vary according to class time, course level and program. *Financial support:* In 2007–08, 85 students received support, including 4 fellowships (averaging $18,000 per year), 54 research assistantships with full tuition reimbursements available (averaging $17,500 per year), 23 teaching assistantships with full and partial tuition reimbursements available (averaging $17,500 per year); career-related internships or fieldwork, Federal Work-Study, and unspecified assistantships also available. Support available to part-time students. Financial award application deadline: 1/15; financial award applicants required to submit FAFSA. *Unit head:* Howard Eichenbaum, Chairman, 617-353-1426, Fax: 617-353-6933, E-mail: hbe@bu.edu. *Application contact:* Howard Eichenbaum, Chairman, 617-353-1426, Fax: 617-353-6933, E-mail: hbe@bu.edu.

Boston University, School of Medicine, Division of Graduate Medical Sciences, Program in Mental Health Counseling and Behavioral Medicine, Boston, MA 02215. Offers mental health and behavioral medicine (MA). *Entrance requirements:* For master's, GRE General Test. Additional exam requirements/recommendations for international students: Required—TOEFL. *Expenses:* Tuition: Full-time $34,930; part-time $1,092 per credit. Tuition and fees vary according to class time, course level and program. *Faculty research:* HIV/AIDS, trauma, behavioral medicine (obesity, breast cancer), neurosciences, autism, serious mental illness, sports psychology.

See Close-Up on page 1419.

Bowling Green State University, Graduate College, College of Arts and Sciences, Department of Psychology, Bowling Green, OH 43403. Offers clinical psychology (MA, PhD); developmental psychology (MA, PhD); experimental psychology (MA, PhD); industrial/organizational psychology (MA, PhD); quantitative psychology (MA, PhD). *Accreditation:* APA (one or more programs are accredited). *Faculty:* 29 full-time (9 women), 14 part-time/adjunct (5 women). *Students:* 88 full-time (61 women), 27 part-time (19 women); includes 10 minority (5 Asian Americans or Pacific Islanders, 5 Hispanic Americans), 12 international. Average age 27. 225 applicants, 15% accepted, 19 enrolled. In 2007, 22 master's, 14 doctorates awarded. *Degree requirements:* For doctorate, thesis/dissertation. *Entrance requirements:* For doctorate, GRE General Test, GRE Subject Test. Additional exam requirements/recommendations for international students: Required—TOEFL. *Application deadline:* For fall admission, 1/1 for domestic students. Application fee: $30. Electronic applications accepted. *Financial support:* In 2007–08, 5 fellowships with full tuition reimbursements (averaging $16,187 per year), 50 research assistantships with full tuition reimbursements (averaging $11,844 per year), 29 teaching assistantships with full tuition reimbursements (averaging $11,805 per year) were awarded; career-related internships or fieldwork, Federal Work-Study, institutionally sponsored loans, tuition waivers (full), and unspecified assistantships also available. Financial award applicants required to submit FAFSA. *Faculty research:* Personnel psychology, developmental-mathematical models, behavioral medication, brain process, child/adolescent social cognition. *Unit head:* Dr. Dale Klopfer, Chair, 419-372-2733.

Brandeis University, Graduate School of Arts and Sciences, Department of Psychology, Program in General Psychology, Waltham, MA 02454-9110. Offers MA. Part-time programs available. *Faculty:* 16 full-time (3 women), 3 part-time/adjunct (all women). *Students:* 8 full-time (7 women), 2 part-time (1 woman), 4 international. Average age 27. 43 applicants, 23% accepted, 8 enrolled. In 2007, 4 degrees awarded. *Degree requirements:* For master's, thesis. *Entrance requirements:* For master's, GRE General Test, 3 letters of recommendation. Additional exam requirements/recommendations for international students: Required—TOEFL (minimum score 600 paper-based; 250 computer-based). *Application deadline:* For fall admission, 5/1 for domestic and international students. Application fee: $55. Electronic applications accepted. *Financial support:* In 2007–08, 8 students received support, including research assistantships (averaging $2,000 per year); institutionally sponsored loans and scholarships/grants also available. Financial award applicants required to submit CSS PROFILE. *Faculty research:* Developmental, cognition, social aging, perception. Total annual research expenditures: $5.1 million. *Unit head:* Department Administrator, 781-736-3300. *Application contact:* Donna J. Coletti, Graduate Admissions Coordinator, 781-736-3303, Fax: 781-736-3291, E-mail: coletti@brandeis.edu.

Brenau University, Graduate Programs, School of Health and Science, Gainesville, GA 30501. Offers family nurse practitioner (MSN); nurse educator (MSN); occupational therapy (MS); psychology (MS). *Accreditation:* AOTA; NLN. Part-time and evening/weekend programs available. *Faculty:* 15 full-time (14 women), 10 part-time/adjunct (7 women). *Students:* 61 full-time (57 women), 47 part-time (44 women); includes 31 minority (22 African Americans, 2 American Indian/Alaska Native, 4 Asian Americans or Pacific Islanders, 3 Hispanic Americans). Average age 31. 97 applicants, 60% accepted, 30 enrolled. In 2007, 28 degrees awarded. *Degree requirements:* For master's, clinical practicum hours. *Entrance requirements:* For master's, GRE General Test or MAT. Additional exam requirements/recommendations for international students: Required—TOEFL (minimum score 550 paper-based). *Application deadline:* Applications are processed on a rolling basis. Application fee: $30. *Expenses:* Contact institution. *Financial support:* In 2007–08, 20 students received support. Scholarships/grants and traineeships available. Support available to part-time students. Financial award application deadline: 7/15; financial award applicants required to submit FAFSA. *Unit head:* Dr. Gale Starich, Dean, 777-718-5305, Fax: 770-297-5929, E-mail: gstarich@brenau.edu. *Application contact:* Nathan Goss, Admissions Coordinator, 770-534-6162, Fax: 770-538-4701, E-mail: ngoss@brenau.edu.

Bridgewater State College, School of Graduate Studies, School of Arts and Sciences, Department of Psychology, Bridgewater, MA 02325-0001. Offers MA. Part-time and evening/weekend programs available. *Entrance requirements:* For master's, GRE General Test. *Application deadline:* For fall admission, 4/1 priority date for domestic students; for spring admission, 10/1 priority date for domestic students. Application fee: $50. *Financial support:* Career-related internships or fieldwork, health care benefits, and unspecified assistantships available. Support available to part-time students.

Brigham Young University, Graduate Studies, College of Family, Home, and Social Sciences, Department of Psychology, Provo, UT 84602-1001. Offers clinical psychology (PhD); general psychology (MS); psychology (PhD), including applied social psychology, behavioral neurobiology, theoretical/philosophical psychology. *Accreditation:* APA (one or more programs are accredited). *Faculty:* 30 full-time (7 women), 10 part-time/adjunct (4 women). *Students:* 99 full-time (30 women); includes 11 minority (3 African Americans, 6 Asian Americans or Pacific Islanders, 2 Hispanic Americans), 7 international. Average age 24. 107 applicants, 23% accepted, 25 enrolled. In 2007, 9 master's, 14 doctorates awarded. *Degree requirements:* For master's, thesis; for doctorate, thesis/dissertation, publishable paper. *Entrance requirements:* For master's and doctorate, GRE General Test, minimum GPA of 3.0 in last 60 hours of course work. Additional exam requirements/recommendations for international students: Required—TOEFL. *Application deadline:* For fall admission, 1/1 for domestic students. Application fee: $50. Electronic applications accepted. *Financial support:* In 2007–08, 85 students received support, including 13 research assistantships with partial tuition reimbursements available (averaging $3,000 per year), 26 teaching assistantships with partial tuition reimbursements available (averaging $3,000 per year); fellowships, career-related internships or fieldwork, scholarships/grants, tuition waivers (partial), and unspecified assistantships also available. Financial award application deadline: 5/31. *Faculty research:* Psychotherapy process, Alzheimer's disease/dementia, psychology and law, health, psychology. Total annual research expenditures: $533,878. *Unit head:* Dr. Ramona Hopkins, Chair, 801-422-1170, Fax: 801-422-0602, E-mail: ramona_hopkins@byu.edu. *Application contact:* Karen A. Christensen, Coordinator of Student Programs, 801-422-4560, Fax: 801-422-0602, E-mail: karen_christensen@byu.edu.

Brock University, Faculty of Graduate Studies, Faculty of Social Sciences, Program in Psychology, St. Catharines, ON L2S 3A1, Canada. Offers behavioral neuroscience (MA, PhD); life span development (MA, PhD); social personality (MA, PhD). Part-time programs available. *Degree requirements:* For master's, thesis; for doctorate, thesis/dissertation. *Entrance requirements:* For master's, GRE, honors degree; for doctorate, GRE, master's degree. Additional exam requirements/recommendations for international students: Required—TOEFL (minimum score 550 paper-based; 213 computer-based; 80 iBT), IELTS (minimum score 7), TWE (minimum score 4). Electronic applications accepted. *Faculty research:* Social personality, behavioral neuroscience, life-span development.

Brooklyn College of the City University of New York, Division of Graduate Studies, Department of Psychology, Brooklyn, NY 11210-2889. Offers experimental psychology (MA); industrial and organizational psychology (MA), including industrial and organizational psychology-human relations, psychology-organizational psychology and behavior; mental health counseling (MA); psychology (PhD). The City University doctoral program in experimental psychology is based at Brooklyn College; candidates who complete the MA may apply for admission to the doctoral program. MA programs in industrial and organizational psychology and mental health counseling are fall admissions only. Part-time programs available. *Students:* 57 full-time (49 women), 91 part-time (73 women); includes 67 minority (39 African Americans, 1 American Indian/Alaska Native, 13 Asian Americans or Pacific Islanders, 14 Hispanic Americans), 9 international. 207 applicants, 60% accepted, 77 enrolled. In 2007, 37 degrees awarded. *Degree requirements:* For master's, comprehensive exam, thesis (for some programs). *Entrance requirements:* For master's, minimum GPA of 3.0, 2 letters of recommendation, essay; for doctorate, GRE. Additional exam requirements/recommendations for international students: Required—TOEFL. *Application deadline:* For fall admission, 3/1 for domestic students, 2/1 for international students; for spring admission, 11/1 for domestic students, 10/1 for international students. Applications are processed on a rolling basis. Application fee: $125. Electronic applications accepted. *Financial support:* Career-related internships or fieldwork, Federal Work-Study, institutionally sponsored loans, scholarships/grants, and tuition waivers (partial) available. Support available to part-time students. Financial award application deadline: 5/1; financial award applicants required to submit FAFSA. *Unit head:* Dr. Glen Hass, Chairperson, 718-951-5601, Fax: 718-951-4814, E-mail: ghass@brooklyn.cuny.edu. *Application contact:* Hernan Sierra, Graduate Admissions Coordinator, 718-951-4536, Fax: 718-951-4506, E-mail: grads@brooklyn.cuny.edu.

Brown University, Graduate School, Department of Psychology, Providence, RI 02912. Offers AM, Sc M, PhD. *Degree requirements:* For master's, thesis; for doctorate, thesis/dissertation. *Entrance requirements:* For master's and doctorate, GRE General Test, GRE Subject Test.

Bryn Mawr College, Graduate School of Arts and Sciences, Department of Psychology, Bryn Mawr, PA 19010-2899. Offers clinical developmental psychology (PhD). Part-time programs available. *Faculty:* 11. *Students:* 24 full-time (23 women), 10 part-time (all women); includes 2 minority (1 Asian American or Pacific Islander, 1 Hispanic American), 2 international. 56 applicants, 20% accepted, 4 enrolled. In 2007, 3 doctorates awarded. *Degree requirements:* For doctorate, one foreign language, comprehensive exam, thesis/dissertation. *Entrance requirements:* For doctorate, GRE General Test. Additional exam requirements/recommendations for international students: Required—TOEFL (minimum score 600 paper-based; 250 computer-based). *Application deadline:* For fall admission, 1/3 for domestic and international students. Application fee: $30. *Financial support:* Teaching assistantships with partial tuition reimbursements, career-related internships or fieldwork and scholarships/grants available. Support available to part-time students. Financial award application deadline: 1/3. *Unit head:* Dr. Marc Schulz, Chair, 610-526-5039, E-mail: mschulz@brynmawr.edu. *Application contact:* Lea R. Miller, Secretary, 610-526-5072, Fax: 610-526-5076, E-mail: lrmiller@brynmawr.edu.

Bucknell University, Graduate Studies, College of Arts and Sciences, Department of Psychology, Lewisburg, PA 17837. Offers MA, MS. Part-time programs available. *Faculty:* 12 full-time (3 women). *Students:* 5 full-time (4 women). *Degree requirements:* For master's, thesis. *Entrance requirements:* For master's, GRE General Test, GRE Subject Test, minimum GPA of 2.8. Additional exam requirements/recommendations for international students: Required—TOEFL. *Application deadline:* For fall admission, 6/1 priority date for domestic students; for spring admission, 12/1 priority date for domestic students. Applications are processed on a rolling basis. Application fee: $25. *Expenses:* Tuition: Full-time $16,660; part-time $1,041 per credit hour. *Financial support:* Unspecified assistantships available. Financial award application deadline: 3/1. *Unit head:* Dr. T. Joel Wade, Chair, 570-577-1200.

Caldwell College, Graduate Studies, Program in Applied Behavior Analysis, Caldwell, NJ 07006-6195. Offers MA. *Entrance requirements:* For master's, GRE, minimum GPA of 3.0, writing sample. Additional exam requirements/recommendations for international students: Required—TOEFL (minimum score 580 paper-based; 237 computer-based).

California Coast University, Program in Psychology, Santa Ana, CA 92701. Offers MS. Part-time programs available. Postbaccalaureate distance learning degree programs offered (no on-campus study). Application fee: $75. *Expenses:* Tuition: Full-time $3,780; part-time $420 per unit.

California Institute of Integral Studies, Graduate Programs, School of Consciousness and Transformation, San Francisco, CA 94103. Offers cultural anthropology and social transformation (MA); East-West psychology (MA, PhD); integrative health studies (MA); philosophy and religion (MA, PhD), including Asian and comparative studies, philosophy, cosmology, and consciousness, social and cultural anthropology (PhD), transformative leadership (MA), transformative studies (PhD), women's spirituality, women's spirituality flex format; social and cultural anthropology (PhD); transformative leadership (MA); transformative studies (PhD). Part-time and evening/weekend programs available. Postbaccalaureate distance learning degree programs offered (minimal on-campus study). *Faculty:* 30 full-time, 28 part-time/adjunct. *Students:* 456; includes 92 minority (32 African Americans, 3 American Indian/Alaska Native, 40 Asian Americans or Pacific Islanders, 17 Hispanic Americans), 1 international. Average age 37. 206 applicants, 93% accepted, 114 enrolled. In 2007, 26 degrees awarded. Terminal master's awarded for partial completion of doctoral program. *Degree requirements:* For master's, comprehensive exam (for some programs), thesis optional; for doctorate, comprehensive exam, thesis/dissertation. *Entrance requirements:* For master's, minimum GPA of 3.0, letters of recommendation, writing sample; for doctorate, master's degree, minimum GPA of 3.0, letters of recommendation, writing sample. Additional exam requirements/recommendations for international students: Required—TOEFL. *Application deadline:* For fall admission, 2/15 priority date for domestic and international students; for spring admission, 10/15 priority date for domestic and international students. Applications are processed on a rolling basis. Application fee: $65. Electronic applications accepted. *Expenses:* Tuition: Full-time $16,930; part-time $780 per unit. Tuition and fees vary according to course load and program. *Financial support:* In 2007–08, 292 students received support; research assistantships, teaching assistantships, career-related internships or fieldwork, Federal Work-Study, institutionally sponsored loans, scholarships/grants, and tuition waivers (partial) available. Support available to part-time students. Financial award application deadline: 3/15; financial award applicants required to submit FAFSA. *Faculty research:* Altered states of consciousness, dreams, cosmology, postcolonial studies, integrative health studies. *Application contact:* Allyson Werner, Senior Admissions Counselor, 415-575-6155, Fax: 415-575-1268.

See Close-Up on page 445.

California Institute of Integral Studies, Graduate Programs, School of Professional Psychology, San Francisco, CA 94103. Offers clinical psychology (Psy D); community mental health (MA); drama therapy (MA); expressive arts therapy (MA); integral counseling psychology (MA); integral counseling, psychology-weekend (MA); psychology (Psy D), including clinical psychology; somatic psychology (MA). *Accreditation:* APA. Part-time programs available. *Faculty:* 28 full-time, 54 part-time/adjunct. *Students:* 591; includes 113 minority (19 African Americans, 3 American Indian/Alaska Native, 48 Asian Americans or Pacific Islanders, 43 Hispanic Americans). Average age 37. 383 applicants, 75% accepted, 155 enrolled. In 2007, 109 master's, 20 doctorates awarded. *Degree requirements:* For master's, comprehensive exam; for doctorate, comprehensive exam, thesis/dissertation. *Entrance requirements:* For master's, minimum GPA of 3.0, letters of recommendation, writing sample; for doctorate, GRE, MA in psychology or social work with appropriate practical experience for advanced standing, or BA with a minimum GPA of 3.1; letters of recommendation; writing sample. Additional exam requirements/recommendations for international students: Required—TOEFL. *Application deadline:* For fall admission, 2/1 priority date for domestic and international students; for spring admission, 10/15 priority date for domestic and international students. Applications are processed on a rolling basis. Application fee: $65. Electronic applications accepted. *Expenses:* Tuition: Full-time $16,930; part-time $780 per unit. Tuition and fees vary according to course load and program. *Financial support:* In 2007–08, 393 students received support; research assistantships with tuition reimbursements available, teaching assistantships with tuition reimbursements available, career-related internships or fieldwork, Federal Work-Study, institutionally sponsored loans, scholarships/grants, and tuition waivers (partial) available. Support available to part-time students. Financial award application deadline: 3/15; financial award applicants required to submit FAFSA. *Faculty research:* Somatic psychology, comparative psychology, art therapy, transpersonal psychology, eco-psychology. *Application contact:* David Townes, Senior Admissions Counselor, 415-575-6152, Fax: 415-575-1268, E-mail: dtownes@ciis.edu.

See Close-Up on page 1421.

California Lutheran University, Graduate Studies, Department of Psychology, Thousand Oaks, CA 91360-2787. Offers clinical psychology (MS); marital and family therapy (MS). Part-time programs available. *Degree requirements:* For master's, thesis or comprehensive exams. *Entrance requirements:* For master's, GRE General Test, interview, minimum GPA of 3.0.

California Polytechnic State University, San Luis Obispo, College of Liberal Arts, Department of Psychology and Child Development, San Luis Obispo, CA 93407. Offers psychology (MS). Part-time programs available. *Faculty:* 4 full-time (2 women). *Students:* 23 full-time (19 women), 9 part-time (all women); includes 6 minority (1 African American, 2 Asian Americans or Pacific Islanders, 3 Hispanic Americans). 69 applicants, 23% accepted, 12 enrolled. In 2007, 8 degrees awarded. *Degree requirements:* For master's, comprehensive exam, thesis (for some programs). *Entrance requirements:* For master's, GRE General Test, minimum GPA of 3.0 in last 90 quarter units of course work, 4 letters of recommendation, interview. Additional exam requirements/recommendations for international students: Required—TOEFL, TWE. *Application deadline:* For fall admission, 1/15 for domestic students, 11/30 for international students. Application fee: $55. Electronic applications accepted. *Expenses:* Tuition, nonresident: part-time $226 per unit. Required fees: $1,777 per quarter. *Financial support:* Career-related internships or fieldwork, Federal Work-Study, and institutionally sponsored loans available. Support available to part-time students. Financial award application deadline: 3/2; financial award applicants required to submit FAFSA. *Faculty research:* Eating disorders, mood disorders, neuropsychology, forensic psychology, group therapy. *Unit head:* Dr. Kelly Moreno, Graduate Coordinate, 805-756-2805, Fax: 805-756-1134, E-mail: kmoreno@calpoly.edu. *Application contact:* Margaret Booker, Administrative Analyst, 805-756-2456, Fax: 805-756-1134, E-mail: mbooker@calpoly.edu.

California State Polytechnic University, Pomona, Academic Affairs, College of Letters, Arts, and Social Sciences, Program in Psychology, Pomona, CA 91768-2557. Offers MS. *Students:* 23 full-time (21 women), 6 part-time (5 women); includes 13 minority (2 African Americans, 3 Asian Americans or Pacific Islanders, 8 Hispanic Americans). Average age 27. 54 applicants, 26% accepted, 13 enrolled. In 2007, 11 degrees awarded. *Degree requirements:* For master's, thesis or alternative. *Application deadline:* For fall admission, 4/15 for domestic students. Applications are processed on a rolling basis. Application fee: $55. Electronic applications accepted. *Expenses:* Tuition, nonresident: full-time $7,232; part-time $226 per unit. Required fees: $3,920. One-time fee: $2,486 part-time. *Financial support:* Application deadline: 3/2. *Unit head:* Dr. Laurie A. Roades, Chair, 909-869-3910.

California State University, Bakersfield, Division of Graduate Studies, School of Humanities and Social Sciences, Program in Psychology, Bakersfield, CA 93311-1022. Offers MA. Part-time programs available. *Degree requirements:* For master's, comprehensive exam, thesis. *Entrance requirements:* For master's, GRE General Test, 3 letters of recommendation.

California State University, Chico, Graduate School, College of Behavioral and Social Sciences, Department of Psychology, Program in Psychological Science, Chico, CA 95929-0722. Offers MA. *Students:* 15 full-time (5 women), 5 part-time (3 women); includes 4 minority (1 African American, 2 Asian Americans or Pacific Islanders, 1 Hispanic American). Average age 24. 21 applicants, 86% accepted, 8 enrolled. In 2007, 4 degrees awarded. *Degree requirements:* For master's, thesis or alternative. *Entrance requirements:* For master's, GRE General Test or MAT, 3 letters of recommendation on departmental form, statement of purpose. Additional exam requirements/recommendations for international students: Required—TOEFL (minimum score 550 paper-based; 213 computer-based; 80 iBT), IELTS (minimum score 7). *Application deadline:* For fall admission, 3/1 for domestic and international students. Application fee: $55. *Unit head:* Dr. Linda Kline, Graduate Coordinator, 530-898-6263.

California State University, Dominguez Hills, College of Natural and Behavioral Science, Program in Psychology, Carson, CA 90747-0001. Offers clinical psychology (MA); general psychology (MA). Part-time and evening/weekend programs available. *Faculty:* 6 full-time (5 women), 3 part-time/adjunct (0 women). *Students:* 18 full-time (14 women), 14 part-time (10 women); includes 19 minority (7 African Americans, 12 Hispanic Americans), 2 international. Average age 31. 22 applicants, 45% accepted, 6 enrolled. In 2007, 14 degrees awarded. Terminal master's awarded for partial completion of doctoral program. *Degree requirements:* For master's, comprehensive exam, thesis optional. *Entrance requirements:* For master's, GRE General Test or MAT, interview, minimum GPA of 3.0, prerequisite psychology courses. Additional exam requirements/recommendations for international students: Required—TOEFL (minimum score 550 paper-based). *Application deadline:* For fall admission, 3/1 for domestic and international students. Application fee: $55. Electronic applications accepted. *Faculty research:* Culture and health, neuropsychology and HIV, psychohistory of the Holocaust, community and adolescents, malingering. Total annual research expenditures: $10,000. *Unit head:* Dr. L. Mark Carrier, Chair, 310-243-3499, E-mail: lcarrier@csudh.edu. *Application contact:* Dr. Karen I. Mason, Coordinator, 310-243-3642, Fax: 310-516-3642, E-mail: kmason@csudh.edu.

California State University, Fresno, Division of Graduate Studies, College of Science and Mathematics, Department of Psychology, Fresno, CA 93740-8027. Offers MA, MS. *Faculty:* 14 full-time (7 women). *Students:* 55; includes 16 minority (1 African American, 4 Asian Americans or Pacific Islanders, 11 Hispanic Americans), 1 international. Average age 28. 5 applicants. In 2007, 12 degrees awarded. *Degree requirements:* For master's, thesis. *Entrance requirements:* For master's, GRE General Test, GRE Subject Test, minimum GPA of 3.0. Additional exam requirements/recommendations for international students: Required—TOEFL. *Application deadline:* For fall admission, 5/1 for domestic and international students; for spring admission, 10/1 for domestic and international students. Applications are processed on a rolling basis. Application fee: $55. Electronic applications accepted. *Financial support:* Teaching assistantships, career-related internships or fieldwork, Federal Work-Study, scholarships/grants, and unspecified assistantships available. Support available to part-time students. Financial award application deadline: 3/1; financial award applicants required to submit FAFSA. *Faculty research:* Oncology prediction, parenting stress, wellness, aging and memory, retrieval inhibition, anger, minority mental health. *Unit head:* Dr. Lynnette Zelenzy, Chair, 559-278-2691, Fax: 559-278-7910, E-mail: lynnette@csufresno.edu. *Application contact:* Dr. Marilyn Wilson, MS Program Coordinator, 559-278-5129, Fax: 559-278-7910, E-mail: marilyn_wilson@csufresno.edu.

California State University, Fullerton, Graduate Studies, College of Humanities and Social Sciences, Department of Psychology, Fullerton, CA 92834-9480. Offers clinical/community psychology (MS); psychology (MA). Part-time programs available. *Students:* 56 full-time (43 women), 11 part-time (5 women); includes 22 minority (2 African Americans, 6 Asian Americans or Pacific Islanders, 14 Hispanic Americans), 6 international. Average age 28. 138 applicants, 28% accepted, 34 enrolled. In 2007, 22 degrees awarded. *Degree requirements:* For master's, thesis. *Entrance requirements:* For master's, GRE General Test, GRE Subject Test, undergraduate major in psychology or related field. *Application deadline:* For fall admission, 3/15 for domestic students. Application fee: $55. *Financial support:* Teaching assistantships, career-related internships or fieldwork, Federal Work-Study, institutionally sponsored loans, and scholarships/grants available. Support available to part-time students. Financial award application deadline: 3/1. *Unit head:* Dr. Daniel Kee, Chair, 714-278-3514.

California State University, Long Beach, Graduate Studies, College of Liberal Arts, Department of Psychology, Long Beach, CA 90840. Offers MA, MS. Part-time and evening/weekend programs available. *Faculty:* 32 full-time (15 women), 29 part-time/adjunct (17 women). *Students:* 57 full-time (39 women), 22 part-time (13 women); includes 28 minority (1 African American, 3 American Indian/Alaska Native, 12 Asian Americans or Pacific Islanders, 12 Hispanic Americans). Average age 30. *Degree requirements:* For master's, comprehensive exam, thesis. *Entrance requirements:* For master's, GRE General Test, GRE Subject Test. *Application deadline:* For fall admission, 3/1 for domestic students. Applications are processed on a rolling basis. Application fee: $55. Electronic applications accepted. *Financial support:* Federal Work-Study, institutionally sponsored loans, and scholarships/grants available. Financial award application deadline: 3/2. *Faculty research:* Physiological psychology, social and personality psychology, community-clinical psychology, industrial-organizational psychology, developmental psychology. *Unit head:* Dr. Kenneth F Green, Chair, 562-985-5001, Fax: 562-985-8004, E-mail: kgreen@csulb.edu. *Application contact:* Diane Roe, Graduate Adviser, 562-985-5000, Fax: 562-985-8004, E-mail: droe@csulb.edu.

California State University, Los Angeles, Graduate Studies, College of Natural and Social Sciences, Department of Psychology, Los Angeles, CA 90032-8530. Offers MA, MS. Part-time and evening/weekend programs available. *Faculty:* 4 full-time (2 women), 2 part-time/adjunct (1 woman). *Students:* 65 full-time (49 women), 61 part-time (48 women); includes 61 minority (4 African Americans, 15 Asian Americans or Pacific Islanders, 42 Hispanic Americans), 23 international. Average age 31. In 2007, 27 degrees awarded. *Degree requirements:* For master's, comprehensive exam or thesis. *Entrance requirements:* Additional exam requirements/recommendations for international students: Required—TOEFL. *Application deadline:* For fall admission, 6/30 for domestic students; for spring admission, 2/1 for domestic students. Applications are processed on a rolling basis. Application fee: $55. *Financial support:* Career-related internships or fieldwork and Federal Work-Study available. Support available to part-time students. Financial award application deadline: 3/1. *Faculty research:* Binaural resolution of the size of an acoustic array, response and generalization of matching to sample in children. *Unit head:* Dr. Fary Cachelin, Chair, 323-343-2250, Fax: 323-343-2281, E-mail: fcachel@calstatela.edu.

California State University, Northridge, Graduate Studies, College of Social and Behavioral Sciences, Department of Psychology, Northridge, CA 91330. Offers clinical psychology (MA); general-experimental psychology (MA); human factors and applied experimental psychology (MA). *Faculty:* 26 full-time (17 women), 32 part-time/adjunct (15 women). *Students:* 51 full-time (29 women), 18 part-time (13 women); includes 21 minority (1 African American, 4 Asian Americans or Pacific Islanders, 16 Hispanic Americans), 9 international. Average age 28. 102 applicants, 48% accepted, 38 enrolled. In 2007, 13 degrees awarded. *Degree requirements:* For master's, thesis. *Entrance requirements:* For master's, GRE General Test, GRE Subject Test, minimum GPA of 3.0, letters of recommendation. Additional exam requirements/recommendations for international students: Required—TOEFL. *Application deadline:* For fall admission, 11/30 for domestic students. Application fee: $55. *Financial support:* Application deadline: 3/1. *Unit head:* Dr. Paul Skolnick, Chair, 818-677-2827.

California State University, Sacramento, Graduate Studies, College of Social Sciences and Interdisciplinary Studies, Department of Psychology, Sacramento, CA 95819-6048. Offers counseling psychology (MA). Part-time programs available. *Students:* 36 full-time (27 women), 75 part-time (55 women); includes 26 minority (4 African Americans, 14 Asian Americans or Pacific Islanders, 8 Hispanic Americans), 2 international. Average age 28. 68 applicants, 66%

Psychology—General

California State University, Sacramento (continued)
accepted, 29 enrolled. *Degree requirements:* For master's, thesis, writing proficiency exam. *Entrance requirements:* For master's, GRE Subject Test, minimum GPA of 3.0 during previous 2 years. Additional exam requirements/recommendations for international students: Required—TOEFL. *Application deadline:* Applications are processed on a rolling basis. Application fee: $55. Electronic applications accepted. *Expenses:* Tuition, state resident: full-time $3,414. Tuition, nonresident: full-time $13,584; part-time $339 per unit. Required fees: $786; $393 per semester. *Financial support:* Career-related internships or fieldwork and Federal Work-Study available. Support available to part-time students. Financial award application deadline: 3/1. *Unit head:* Bruce Behrman, Chair, 916-2748-6254, Fax: 916-278-6820.

California State University, San Bernardino, Graduate Studies, College of Social and Behavioral Sciences, Department of Psychology, San Bernardino, CA 92407-2397. Offers child development (MA); clinical/counseling psychology (MS); general/experimental psychology (MA); industrial/organizational psychology (MS). *Faculty:* 29 full-time, 30 part-time/adjunct. *Students:* 97 full-time (74 women), 35 part-time (24 women); includes 40 minority (6 African Americans, 5 Asian Americans or Pacific Islanders, 29 Hispanic Americans), 4 international. Average age 26. 166 applicants, 37% accepted, 43 enrolled. *Entrance requirements:* For master's, minimum GPA of 3.0 in major. *Application deadline:* For fall admission, 8/31 priority date for domestic students. Application fee: $55. *Financial support:* Fellowships, research assistantships, teaching assistantships, career-related internships or fieldwork, Federal Work-Study, institutionally sponsored loans, and unspecified assistantships available. *Faculty research:* Perceptual development, human memory, psychopharmacology, psychology of women, language acquisition. *Unit head:* Dr. Joanna S. Worthley, Chair, 909-537-5570, Fax: 909-537-7003, E-mail: jworthley@csusb.edu. *Application contact:* Stacy Brooks, Graduate Secretary, 909-537-5570, Fax: 909-537-7003, E-mail: sbrooks@csusb.edu.

California State University, San Marcos, College of Arts and Sciences, Program in Psychology, San Marcos, CA 92096-0001. Offers MA. *Faculty:* 15 full-time (8 women), 17 part-time/adjunct (11 women). *Students:* 11 full-time (10 women), 11 part-time (9 women); includes 8 minority (2 African Americans, 6 Hispanic Americans). Average age 29. In 2007, 2 degrees awarded. *Degree requirements:* For master's, thesis. *Entrance requirements:* For master's, GRE General Test, GRE Subject Test (recommended), 3 letters of recommendation. Additional exam requirements/recommendations for international students: Required—TOEFL (minimum score 550 paper-based). *Application deadline:* For fall admission, 3/15 priority date for domestic students. Application fee: $55. *Financial support:* Research assistantships, teaching assistantships available. *Faculty research:* Psychopharmacology, recovery from major surgery, computer literacy in children, neuropsychology of hemispheric differences, conservation psychology. *Unit head:* Dr. Sharon Hamill, Department Chair, 760-750-4102, Fax: 760-750-3418, E-mail: mthomas@csusm.edu. *Application contact:* Margie Stagner-Kidd, Administrative Coordinator, 760-750-4102, E-mail: mkidd@csusm.edu.

California State University, Stanislaus, College of Human and Health Sciences, Department of Psychology, Turlock, CA 95382. Offers behavior analysis (MS); child development (Graduate Certificate); counseling (MS); psychology (MA, MS). Part-time programs available. *Faculty:* 18. *Students:* 22 full-time (18 women), 25 part-time (20 women); includes 11 minority (1 African American, 1 Asian American or Pacific Islander, 9 Hispanic Americans). Average age 31. 15 applicants, 100% accepted, 9 enrolled. In 2007, 16 degrees awarded. *Degree requirements:* For master's, thesis. *Entrance requirements:* For master's, GRE General Test, minimum GPA of 3.0, 3 letters of reference, personal statement. Additional exam requirements/recommendations for international students: Required—TOEFL (minimum score 550 paper-based; 213 computer-based). *Application deadline:* For fall admission, 2/1 for domestic and international students. Application fee: $55. Electronic applications accepted. *Expenses:* Tuition, nonresident: full-time $10,170; part-time $339 per unit. Required fees: $3,972; $2,538 per term. $1,165 per semester. *Financial support:* Fellowships, career-related internships or fieldwork and Federal Work-Study available. Financial award application deadline: 3/2; financial award applicants required to submit FAFSA. *Faculty research:* Hedonic tone judgement, syntax and autism, early literacy assessment and native and non-native languages. *Application contact:* Dr. Gina M. Pallotta, Chair, 209-667-3386.

Cameron University, Office of Graduate Studies, Program in Behavioral Sciences, Lawton, OK 73505-6377. Offers MS. Part-time and evening/weekend programs available. *Degree requirements:* For master's, comprehensive exam, thesis optional. *Entrance requirements:* Additional exam requirements/recommendations for international students: Required—TOEFL (minimum score 550 paper-based; 213 computer-based). Electronic applications accepted. *Faculty research:* Student burnout, attention deficit hyperactivity disorder, group decision making, counseling outcomes, smoking cessation.

Capella University, Harold Abel School of Psychology, Minneapolis, MN 55402. Offers clinical psychology (MS); counseling psychology (MS); educational psychology (MS, PhD); general psychology (MS, PhD); industrial/organizational psychology (MS, PhD); school psychology (MS, Certificate); sport psychology (MS). Part-time and evening/weekend programs available. Postbaccalaureate distance learning degree programs offered (minimal on-campus study). Terminal master's awarded for partial completion of doctoral program. *Degree requirements:* For master's, thesis optional, project; for doctorate, thesis/dissertation. *Entrance requirements:* For degree, master's degree in school psychology. Additional exam requirements/recommendations for international students: Required—TOEFL (minimum score 550 paper-based; 213 computer-based), TWE (minimum score 4). Electronic applications accepted. *Faculty research:* Correctional mental health delivery, community mental health, attachment and caregiving in adult and family relationships, influence of encouragement on motivation, and moral dilemmas in business.

Cardinal Stritch University, College of Arts and Sciences, Department of Psychology, Milwaukee, WI 53217-3985. Offers clinical psychology (MA). Part-time and evening/weekend programs available. *Degree requirements:* For master's, thesis, portfolio, clinical practicum. *Entrance requirements:* For master's, GRE General Test, GRE Subject Test (psychology), interview, minimum GPA of 3.0, 3 letters of recommendation.

Carleton University, Faculty of Graduate Studies, Faculty of Arts and Social Sciences, Department of Psychology, Ottawa, ON K1S 5B6, Canada. Offers neuroscience (M Sc); psychology (MA, PhD). Part-time programs available. *Degree requirements:* For master's, thesis; for doctorate, comprehensive exam, thesis/dissertation. *Entrance requirements:* For master's, honors degree; for doctorate, GRE, master's degree. Additional exam requirements/recommendations for international students: Required—TOEFL. Application fee: $77. *Financial support:* Fellowships, research assistantships, teaching assistantships, institutionally sponsored loans, scholarships/grants, and unspecified assistantships available. *Faculty research:* Behavioral neuroscience, social and personality psychology, cognitive/perception, developmental psychology, computer user research and evaluation, forensic psychology, health psychology. *Unit head:* Janet Mantler, Chair, 613-520-2600 Ext. 2644, Fax: 613-520-3667. *Application contact:* Etelle Bourassa, Graduate Studies Assistant, 613-520-2600 Ext. 2644, Fax: 613-520-3667.

Carlos Albizu University, Graduate Programs in Psychology, San Juan, PR 00901. Offers clinical psychology (MS, PhD, Psy D); general psychology (PhD); industrial/organizational psychology (MS, PhD); speech and language pathology (MS). *Accreditation:* APA (one or more programs are accredited). Part-time and evening/weekend programs available. *Degree requirements:* For master's, one foreign language, comprehensive exam, thesis; for doctorate, one foreign language, comprehensive exam, thesis/dissertation, written qualifying exams. *Entrance requirements:* For master's, GRE General Test or EXADEP, interview, minimum GPA of 3.0; for doctorate, GRE General Test or EXADEP, interview, minimum GPA of 3.0 (industrial/organizational psychology), minimum GPA of 3.25 (clinical psychology). *Faculty research:* Psychotherapeutic techniques for Hispanics, psychology of the aged, school dropouts, stress, violence.

Carlos Albizu University, Miami Campus, Graduate Programs, Miami, FL 33172-2209. Offers clinical psychology (Psy D); entrepreneurship (MBA); exceptional student education (MS); industrial/organizational psychology (MS); marriage and family therapy (MS); mental health counseling (MS); nonprofit management (MBA); organizational management (MBA); psychology (MS); school counseling (MS); teaching English as a second language (MS). *Accreditation:* APA. Part-time and evening/weekend programs available. *Faculty:* 20 full-time (13 women), 65 part-time/adjunct (39 women). *Students:* 514 full-time (409 women), 143 part-time (119 women); includes 465 minority (54 African Americans, 1 American Indian/Alaska Native, 4 Asian Americans or Pacific Islanders, 406 Hispanic Americans). Average age 35. 194 applicants, 73% accepted, 130 enrolled. In 2007, 208 master's, 37 doctorates awarded. Terminal master's awarded for partial completion of doctoral program. *Median time to degree:* Of those who began their doctoral program in fall 1999, 65% received their degree in 8 years or less. *Degree requirements:* For master's, one foreign language, comprehensive exam, integrative project (MBA), research project (MSESE and MSTESOL); for doctorate, one foreign language, comprehensive exam, internship, doctoral project. *Entrance requirements:* For master's, 3 letters of recommendation, interview, minimum GPA of 3.0, resumé, statement of purpose, official transcripts; for doctorate, 3 letters of recommendation, minimum GPA of 3.0, resumé, interview. *Application deadline:* For fall admission, 8/1 priority date for domestic students; for spring admission, 11/30 priority date for domestic students. Applications are processed on a rolling basis. Application fee: $50. *Expenses:* Tuition: Full-time $9,090; part-time $505 per credit. Required fees: $298 per term. Tuition and fees vary according to course load and degree level. *Financial support:* In 2007–08, 37 students received support. Federal Work-Study and scholarships/grants available. Financial award application deadline: 6/1; financial award applicants required to submit FAFSA. *Faculty research:* Psychotherapy, forensic psychology, neuropsychology, marketing strategy, entrepreneurship, special education. *Unit head:* Dr. Carmen S. Roca, Interim Chancellor, 305-593-1223 Ext. 120, Fax: 305-629-8052, E-mail: croca@albizu.edu. *Application contact:* Barbara De la Cruz, Admission Officer, 305-593-1223 Ext. 218, Fax: 305-593-1854, E-mail: bdelacruz@albizu.edu.

Carnegie Mellon University, College of Humanities and Social Sciences, Department of Psychology, Pittsburgh, PA 15213-3891. Offers cognitive neuroscience (PhD); cognitive psychology (PhD); developmental psychology (PhD); social/personality/health psychology (PhD). *Degree requirements:* For doctorate, comprehensive exam, thesis/dissertation. *Entrance requirements:* For doctorate, GRE General Test. Additional exam requirements/recommendations for international students: Required—TOEFL. *Faculty research:* Artificial intelligence, stress and the immune system, children's learning strategies, neural basis of cognition.

Case Western Reserve University, School of Graduate Studies, Department of Psychology, Cleveland, OH 44106. Offers clinical psychology (PhD); experimental psychology (PhD). *Accreditation:* APA. *Faculty:* 16 full-time (8 women), 11 part-time/adjunct (4 women). *Students:* 36 full-time (32 women); includes 7 minority (2 African Americans, 1 Asian American or Pacific Islander, 4 Hispanic Americans). Average age 26. 126 applicants, 6% accepted, 6 enrolled. In 2007, 4 doctorates awarded. *Degree requirements:* For doctorate, thesis/dissertation, internship. *Entrance requirements:* For doctorate, GRE General Test, GRE Subject Test. Additional exam requirements/recommendations for international students: Required—TOEFL. *Application deadline:* For fall admission, 1/15 for domestic students. Application fee: $50. Electronic applications accepted. *Financial support:* Fellowships, research assistantships, teaching assistantships, tuition waivers (full and partial) available. Financial award application deadline: 2/1. *Faculty research:* Adolescent suicide, cognitive processing, repressive responses, visual perception, impact of HIV infection, neuropsychology. *Unit head:* Dr. Robert Greene, Chair, 216-368-6473, Fax: 216-368-4891, E-mail: robert.greene@case.edu. *Application contact:* Dr. James C. Overholser, Director of Clinical Training, 216-368-2686, Fax: 216-368-4891, E-mail: overholser@case.edu.

Castleton State College, Division of Graduate Studies, Department of Psychology, Castleton, VT 05735. Offers forensic psychology (MA). *Degree requirements:* For master's, thesis. *Entrance requirements:* For master's, GRE General Test, minimum undergraduate GPA of 3.5, previous course work in research methodology and statistics. Additional exam requirements/recommendations for international students: Required—TOEFL. *Faculty research:* Psychology and law, juvenile delinquency, criminal psychology, correctional psychology, police psychology.

The Catholic University of America, School of Arts and Sciences, Department of Psychology, Washington, DC 20064. Offers applied experimental psychology (MA, PhD); clinical psychology (PhD); general psychology (MA, PhD); human development (PhD); human factors (MA); JD/MA. *Accreditation:* APA (one or more programs are accredited). Part-time programs available. *Faculty:* 12 full-time (6 women), 2 part-time/adjunct (0 women). *Students:* 46 full-time (37 women), 30 part-time (21 women); includes 14 minority (6 African Americans, 4 Asian Americans or Pacific Islanders, 4 Hispanic Americans), 2 international. Average age 28. 270 applicants, 27% accepted, 25 enrolled. In 2007, 22 master's, 9 doctorates awarded. Terminal master's awarded for partial completion of doctoral program. *Degree requirements:* For master's, comprehensive exam; for doctorate, comprehensive exam, thesis/dissertation. *Entrance requirements:* For master's, GRE General Test, 3 letters of recommendation; for doctorate, GRE General Test, GRE Subject Test, 3 letters of recommendation. Additional exam requirements/recommendations for international students: Required—TOEFL (minimum score 580 paper-based; 237 computer-based). *Application deadline:* For fall admission, 2/1 priority date for domestic students; for spring admission, 11/15 priority date for domestic students. Applications are processed on a rolling basis. Application fee: $55. Electronic applications accepted. *Financial support:* Fellowships, research assistantships, teaching assistantships, career-related internships or fieldwork, Federal Work-Study, scholarships/grants, tuition waivers (full and partial), and unspecified assistantships available. Support available to part-time students. Financial award application deadline: 2/1; financial award applicants required to submit FAFSA. *Faculty research:* Social development, family interaction, human perception and cognition, applied cognitive science, individual and group psychotherapy. *Unit head:* Dr. Marc M. Sebrechts, Chair, 202-319-5750, Fax: 202-319-6263, E-mail: sebrechts@cua.edu.

Central Connecticut State University, School of Graduate Studies, School of Arts and Sciences, Department of Psychology, New Britain, CT 06050-4010. Offers community psychology (MA); general psychology (MA); health psychology (MA). Part-time and evening/weekend programs available. *Faculty:* 21 full-time (11 women), 22 part-time/adjunct (10 women). *Students:* 21 full-time (13 women), 20 part-time (15 women); includes 5 minority (1 African American, 4 Hispanic Americans), 3 international. Average age 29. 42 applicants, 40% accepted, 11 enrolled. In 2007, 11 degrees awarded. *Degree requirements:* For master's, thesis, comprehensive exam or special project. *Entrance requirements:* For master's, minimum GPA of 2.7. Additional exam requirements/recommendations for international students: Required—TOEFL. *Application deadline:* For fall admission, 4/25 for domestic students; for spring admission, 12/1 for domestic students. Applications are processed on a rolling basis. Application fee: $50. Electronic applications accepted. *Expenses:* Tuition, area resident: Full-time $4,169. Tuition, state resident: full-time $6,253. Tuition, nonresident: full-time $11,614; part-time $400 per credit. Required fees: $3,322. One-time fee: $62 part-time. Tuition and fees vary according to degree level and program. *Financial support:* In 2007–08, 3 students received support, including 6 research assistantships; career-related internships or fieldwork, Federal Work-Study, scholarships/grants, and unspecified assistantships also available. Support available to part-time students. Financial award application deadline: 3/1; financial award applicants required to submit FAFSA. *Faculty research:* Clinical psychology, general psychology, child development, cognitive development, drugs/behavior. *Unit head:* Dr. Bradley M. Waite, Chair, 860-832-3100.

Central Michigan University, College of Graduate Studies, College of Humanities and Social and Behavioral Sciences, Department of Psychology, Mount Pleasant, MI 48859. Offers clinical psychology (PhD); general, applied, and experimental psychology (MS, PhD), including applied experimental psychology (PhD), general/experimental psychology (MS); industrial/organizational psychology (MA, PhD); neuroscience (MS, PhD); school psychology (PhD, S Psy S). *Accreditation:* APA (one or more programs are accredited). Terminal master's awarded for partial completion of doctoral program. *Degree requirements:* For master's, thesis or alternative;

for S Psy S, thesis. *Entrance requirements:* For doctorate, GRE. *Faculty research:* Occupational stress, hyperamnesia, humor, problem solving, behavioral neuroscience.

Central Washington University, Graduate Studies, Research and Continuing Education, College of the Sciences, Department of Psychology, Ellensburg, WA 98926. Offers experimental psychology (MS); mental health counseling (MS); school counseling (M Ed); school psychology (M Ed). Evening/weekend programs available. *Faculty:* 27 full-time (13 women). *Students:* 45 full-time (34 women), 19 part-time (16 women); includes 10 minority (1 African American, 1 American Indian/Alaska Native, 1 Asian American or Pacific Islander, 7 Hispanic Americans), 1 international. 65 applicants, 74% accepted, 48 enrolled. In 2007, 19 degrees awarded. *Degree requirements:* For master's, thesis. *Entrance requirements:* For master's, GRE General Test, minimum GPA of 3.0. Additional exam requirements/recommendations for international students: Required—TOEFL (minimum score 550 paper-based; 213 computer-based; 79 iBT). *Application deadline:* For fall admission, 4/1 for domestic students. Application fee: $50. *Expenses:* Tuition, state resident: full-time $2,209; part-time $221 per credit. Tuition, nonresident: full-time $4,939; part-time $442 per credit. Required fees: $207 per quarter. Tuition and fees vary according to degree level. *Financial support:* In 2007–08, 13 research assistantships with partial tuition reimbursements (averaging $8,100 per year), 3 teaching assistantships (averaging $8,100 per year) were awarded; career-related internships or fieldwork, Federal Work-Study, health care benefits, and unspecified assistantships also available. Financial award application deadline: 3/1; financial award applicants required to submit FAFSA. *Unit head:* Dr. Stephanie Stein, Chair, 509-963-2381. *Application contact:* Justine Eason, Admissions Program Coordinator, 509-963-3103, Fax: 509-963-1799, E-mail: masters@cwu.edu.

Chestnut Hill College, School of Graduate Studies, Division of Psychology, Philadelphia, PA 19118-2693. Offers clinical and counseling psychology (MA, MS, CAS); clinical psychology (Psy D); MS/Psy D. Part-time and evening/weekend programs available. *Faculty:* 11 full-time (4 women), 29 part-time/adjunct (13 women). *Students:* 122 full-time (102 women), 225 part-time (187 women); includes 59 minority (48 African Americans, 5 Asian Americans or Pacific Islanders, 6 Hispanic Americans), 2 international. Average age 33. 80 applicants, 93% accepted. In 2007, 66 master's, 8 doctorates awarded. *Degree requirements:* For master's, thesis optional, practica; for doctorate, comprehensive exam, thesis/dissertation, internship, practica, clinical competency exam. *Entrance requirements:* For master's, GRE General Test, statement of professional goals writing sample, official transcripts, letters of recommendation; for doctorate, GRE General Test, master's degree in clinical counseling or closely related field, transcripts, letters of recommendation, statement of professional goals writing sample; for CAS, GRE General Test, official transcripts, letters of recommendation, statement of professional goals writing sample. Additional exam requirements/recommendations for international students: Required—TOEFL (minimum score 500 paper-based; 213 computer-based). *Application deadline:* For fall admission, 7/17 priority date for domestic students, 7/17 for international students; for spring admission, 12/15 priority date for domestic students, 12/15 for international students. Applications are processed on a rolling basis. *Faculty research:* Child and adolescent therapy and clinical issues; phychoanalytic psychotherapy, object relations, and cognitive-behavioral therapy; marriage and family issues; clinical issues and interventions with diverse populations. *Unit head:* Dr. Joseph Micucci, Division Chair, 215-248-7162, Fax: 215-248-7155. *Application contact:* Amy Boorse, Administrative Assistant, School of Graduate Studies Office, 215-248-7170, Fax: 215-248-7161, E-mail: gradadmissions@chc.edu.

The Chicago School of Professional Psychology, Graduate School, Program in Clinical Psychology, Chicago, IL 60610. Offers applied behavior analysis (MA, Psy D, Certificate); clinical psychology (Psy D); counseling (MA); Latino mental health (Certificate); psychology (Certificate). *Students:* 756. Average age 26. 628 applicants, 64% accepted, 177 enrolled. *Degree requirements:* For master's, thesis (for some programs); for doctorate, comprehensive exam, thesis/dissertation. *Entrance requirements:* For master's, minimum undergraduate GPA of 3.0; 1 course in psychology and 1 course in either statistics or research methods; for doctorate, GRE, 18 hours of psychology credit (including courses in statistics, normal psychology and human development); minimum GPA of 3.2. Additional exam requirements/recommendations for international students: Required—TOEFL (minimum score 550 paper-based; 213 computer-based; 79 iBT). Application fee: $50. Electronic applications accepted. *Financial support:* Fellowships, Federal Work-Study and scholarships/grants available. Financial award applicants required to submit FAFSA. *Application contact:* Yarelli Meza, Director of Admission, 312-329-6666, Fax: 312-644-3333, E-mail: admissions@thechicagoschool.edu.

See Close-Up on page 1425.

The Citadel, The Military College of South Carolina, Citadel Graduate College, Department of Psychology, Charleston, SC 29409. Offers MA. Part-time and evening/weekend programs available. *Students:* 29 full-time (25 women), 35 part-time (33 women); includes 4 minority (2 African Americans, 2 American Indian/Alaska Native), 1 international. Average age 27. In 2007, 20 degrees awarded. *Entrance requirements:* For master's, GRE General Test or MAT. Additional exam requirements/recommendations for international students: Required—TOEFL (minimum score 550 paper-based; 213 computer-based). *Application deadline:* For fall admission, 3/15 for domestic students. Application fee: $30. *Expenses:* Tuition, state resident: part-time $280 per credit hour. Tuition, nonresident: part-time $503 per credit hour. *Financial support:* Research assistantships, teaching assistantships, career-related internships or fieldwork and unspecified assistantships available. Financial award application deadline: 7/1; financial award applicants required to submit FAFSA. *Faculty research:* Childhood depression, victimization, early intervention, mental retardation. *Unit head:* Dr. Steve Nida, Head, 843-953-5320, Fax: 843-953-7084, E-mail: steve.nida@citadel.edu. *Application contact:* Dr. Julie Lipovsky, Coordinator, 843-953-5323, Fax: 843-953-7084, E-mail: lipovskyj@citadel.edu.

City College of the City University of New York, Graduate School, College of Liberal Arts and Science, Division of Social Science, Department of Psychology, New York, NY 10031-9198. Offers clinical psychology (PhD); experimental cognition (PhD); general psychology (MA); mental health counseling (MA). *Accreditation:* APA (one or more programs are accredited). Part-time programs available. *Students:* 17 full-time (12 women), 98 part-time (72 women); includes 79 minority (28 African Americans, 13 Asian Americans or Pacific Islanders, 38 Hispanic Americans), 23 international. 40 applicants, 55% accepted, 30 enrolled. In 2007, 43 degrees awarded. *Degree requirements:* For master's, one foreign language, comprehensive exam, thesis. *Entrance requirements:* For master's, GRE. Additional exam requirements/recommendations for international students: Required—TOEFL (minimum score 550 paper-based; 213 computer-based). *Application deadline:* For fall admission, 4/15 for domestic students; for spring admission, 11/15 for domestic students. Application fee: $125. *Financial support:* Fellowships, teaching assistantships, career-related internships or fieldwork, Federal Work-Study, and tuition waivers (full and partial) available. Support available to part-time students. Financial award application deadline: 5/1. *Faculty research:* Social/personality psychology, physiological psychology, cognition and development. *Unit head:* Vivien Tartter, Graduate Adviser, 212-650-5709, Fax: 212-650-5865, E-mail: vtartter@ccny.cuny.edu.

Claremont Graduate University, Graduate Programs, School of Behavioral and Organizational Sciences, Department of Psychology, Claremont, CA 91711-6160. Offers advanced study in evaluation (Certificate); cognitive psychology (MA, PhD); developmental psychology (MA, PhD); evaluation and applied research methods (MA, PhD); health behavior research and evaluation (MA, PhD); human resource development and evaluation (MA); industrial/organizational psychology (MA, PhD); organizational behavior (MA, PhD); organizational psychology (MA, PhD); social psychology (MA, PhD); MBA/PhD. Part-time programs available. *Faculty:* 15 full-time (7 women), 4 part-time/adjunct (2 women). *Students:* 184 full-time (137 women), 24 part-time (20 women); includes 51 minority (13 African Americans, 1 American Indian/Alaska Native, 26 Asian Americans or Pacific Islanders, 11 Hispanic Americans), 12 international. Average age 29. In 2007, 42 master's, 10 doctorates, 2 other advanced degrees awarded. Terminal master's awarded for partial completion of doctoral program. *Degree requirements:* For master's, thesis (for some programs); for doctorate, comprehensive exam, thesis/dissertation. *Entrance requirements:* For master's and doctorate, GRE General Test. *Application deadline:* For fall admission, 2/15 priority date for domestic students. Applications are processed on a rolling basis. Electronic applications accepted. *Expenses:* Tuition: Full-time $31,640; part-time $1,376 per unit. Required fees: $145 per semester. Tuition and fees vary according to course load, degree level and program. *Financial support:* Fellowships, research assistantships, teaching assistantships, career-related internships or fieldwork, Federal Work-Study, institutionally sponsored loans, and tuition waivers (full and partial) available. Support available to part-time students. Financial award application deadline: 2/15; financial award applicants required to submit FAFSA. *Faculty research:* Social intervention, diversity in organizations, eyewitness memory, aging and cognition, drug policy. *Unit head:* Natalie Brown, Program Coordinator, 909-621-8084, Fax: 909-621-8905, E-mail: natalie.brown@cgu.edu.

Clark University, Graduate School, Department of Psychology, Worcester, MA 01610-1477. Offers clinical psychology (PhD); developmental psychology (PhD); social-personality psychology (PhD). *Accreditation:* APA. *Faculty:* 16 full-time (8 women), 6 part-time/adjunct (4 women). *Students:* 42 full-time (33 women), 1 (woman) part-time; includes 5 minority (1 African American, 4 Hispanic Americans), 12 international. Average age 30. 181 applicants, 8% accepted, 8 enrolled. In 2007, 11 doctorates awarded. *Degree requirements:* For doctorate, thesis/dissertation. *Entrance requirements:* For doctorate, GRE General Test. Additional exam requirements/recommendations for international students: Required—TOEFL. *Application deadline:* For fall admission, 1/1 priority date for domestic students. Applications are processed on a rolling basis. Application fee: $55. *Expenses:* Tuition: Full-time $32,600; part-time $1,019 per credit. Required fees: $30. Tuition and fees vary according to program. *Financial support:* In 2007–08, 2 fellowships with full tuition reimbursements (averaging $15,700 per year), 11 research assistantships with full tuition reimbursements (averaging $15,700 per year), 15 teaching assistantships with full tuition reimbursements (averaging $15,700 per year) were awarded; career-related internships or fieldwork and tuition waivers (full and partial) also available. *Faculty research:* Development of psychological processes in sociocultural context, conceptualizing and reasoning, symbolization, psychotherapy, metaphor, emotions and personalities. Total annual research expenditures: $842,000. *Unit head:* Dr. Wendy Grolnick, Chair, 508-793-7273. *Application contact:* Peggy Moskowitz, Graduate School Secretary, 508-793-7274, Fax: 508-793-7265, E-mail: psychology@clarku.edu.

Clemson University, Graduate School, College of Business and Behavioral Science, Department of Psychology, Program in Applied Psychology, Clemson, SC 29634. Offers MS. *Students:* 9 full-time (4 women), 1 (woman) part-time. 40 applicants, 3% accepted, 0 enrolled. In 2007, 4 degrees awarded. *Degree requirements:* For master's, thesis, internship. *Entrance requirements:* For master's, GRE General Test, 18 hours of course work in psychology. Additional exam requirements/recommendations for international students: Required—TOEFL. *Application deadline:* For fall admission, 3/15 for domestic students, 4/15 for international students; for spring admission, 9/15 for international students. Application fee: $55. *Financial support:* In 2007–08, 3 research assistantships were awarded; teaching assistantships, career-related internships or fieldwork and unspecified assistantships also available. Financial award application deadline: 3/15; financial award applicants required to submit FAFSA. *Faculty research:* Personnel selection and validation; performance evaluation; training, motivation and decision making; human factors; TOEFL. *Unit head:* Chris Pagano, Coordinator, 864-656-4984, Fax: 864-656-0358, E-mail: cpagano@clemson.edu.

Clemson University, Graduate School, College of Business and Behavioral Science, Department of Psychology, Program in Human Factors Psychology, Clemson, SC 29634. Offers PhD. *Students:* 9 full-time (6 women). 17 applicants, 24% accepted, 3 enrolled. Application fee: $55. *Unit head:* Chris Pagano, Coordinator, 864-656-4984, Fax: 864-656-0358, E-mail: cpagano@clemson.edu.

Cleveland State University, College of Graduate Studies, College of Science, Department of Psychology, Cleveland, OH 44115. Offers clinical psychology (MA); consumer/industrial research (MA); diversity management (MA); experimental research psychology (MA); school psychology (Psy S). Part-time programs available. *Faculty:* 17 full-time (5 women), 16 part-time/adjunct (10 women). *Students:* 76 full-time (52 women), 44 part-time (37 women); includes 19 minority (15 African Americans, 1 American Indian/Alaska Native, 2 Asian Americans or Pacific Islanders, 1 Hispanic American), 3 international. Average age 29. 153 applicants, 27% accepted, 37 enrolled. In 2007, 26 master's, 9 other advanced degrees awarded. *Degree requirements:* For master's, thesis (for some programs). *Entrance requirements:* For master's, GRE General Test. Additional exam requirements/recommendations for international students: Required—TOEFL (minimum score 525 paper-based; 197 computer-based). *Application deadline:* For fall admission, 2/1 priority date for domestic and international students. Applications are processed on a rolling basis. Application fee: $30. Electronic applications accepted. *Financial support:* In 2007–08, 45 students received support. Career-related internships or fieldwork, Federal Work-Study, tuition waivers (partial), and unspecified assistantships available. Financial award applicants required to submit FAFSA. Total annual research expenditures: $112,607. *Unit head:* Dr. David M. Grilly, Chairperson, 216-687-2545, Fax: 216-687-9294, E-mail: d.grilly@csuohio.edu. *Application contact:* Karen Colston, Administrative Coordinator, 216-687-2552, E-mail: k.colston@csuohio.edu.

The College at Brockport, State University of New York, School of Letters and Sciences, Department of Psychology, Brockport, NY 14420-2997. Offers MA. *Students:* 9 full-time (6 women), 7 part-time (1 woman); includes 3 minority (all Asian Americans or Pacific Islanders) 14 applicants, 50% accepted, 5 enrolled. In 2007, 11 degrees awarded. *Degree requirements:* For master's, thesis optional. *Entrance requirements:* For master's, GRE General Test, letters of recommendation, interview, minimum GPA of 3.0. Additional exam requirements/recommendations for international students: Required—TOEFL (minimum score 550 paper-based; 213 computer-based; 79 iBT). *Application deadline:* For fall admission, 5/15 for domestic and international students. Application fee: $50. *Expenses:* Tuition, state resident: full-time $6,900; part-time $288 per credit. Tuition, nonresident: full-time $10,920; part-time $455 per credit. Required fees: $738; $31 per credit. *Financial support:* In 2007–08, 2 teaching assistantships with tuition reimbursements (averaging $6,000 per year) were awarded; Federal Work-Study, scholarships/grants, and unspecified assistantships also available. Support available to part-time students. Financial award application deadline: 3/15; financial award applicants required to submit FAFSA. *Faculty research:* Positive psychology, decision-making and applied behavior analysis, family processes and close relationships, cognition and neuropsychology, social/personality and industrial/organizational psychology. *Unit head:* Dr. Melissa Brown, Chairperson, 585-395-2488, Fax: 585-395-2116, E-mail: mbrown@brockport.edu. *Application contact:* Dr. Janet Gillespie, Graduate Director, 585-395-2433, E-mail: jgillesp@brockport.edu.

College of Saint Elizabeth, Department of Psychology, Morristown, NJ 07960-6989. Offers counseling psychology (MA); forensic psychology (MA); student affairs in higher education (Certificate). Part-time and evening/weekend programs available. *Faculty:* 5 full-time (2 women), 6 part-time/adjunct (4 women). *Students:* 7 full-time (all women), 61 part-time (58 women); includes 21 minority (7 African Americans, 2 Asian Americans or Pacific Islanders, 12 Hispanic Americans), 2 international. Average age 30. In 2007, 8 degrees awarded. *Degree requirements:* For master's, thesis or alternative, portfolio. *Entrance requirements:* For master's, minimum GPA of 3.0, BA in psychology (preferred), 12 credits of course work in psychology. *Application deadline:* For fall admission, 4/14 priority date for domestic students; for spring admission, 11/15 for domestic students. Applications are processed on a rolling basis. Application fee: $35. Electronic applications accepted. *Expenses:* Tuition: Full-time $17,016; part-time $709 per credit. Required fees: $1,300; $370 per term. Full-time tuition and fees vary according to program and student's religious affiliation. Part-time tuition and fees vary according to campus/location and student's religious affiliation. *Financial support:* Career-related internships or fieldwork, tuition waivers (partial), and unspecified assistantships available. Support available to part-time students. Financial award application deadline: 3/15; financial award applicants required to submit FAFSA. *Faculty research:* Family systems, dissociative identity disorder, multicultural counseling, outcomes assessment. *Unit head:* Dr. Valerie Scott, Director of the Graduate Program in Counseling Psychology, 973-290-4102, Fax: 973-290-4676, E-mail:

Psychology—General

College of Saint Elizabeth (continued)
vscott@cse.edu. *Application contact:* Michael Szarek, Director of Enrollment Management, 973-290-4112, Fax: 973-290-4167, E-mail: mszarek@cse.edu.

College of St. Joseph, Graduate Programs, Division of Psychology and Human Services, Rutland, VT 05701-3899. Offers alcohol and substance abuse counseling (MS); clinical mental health counseling (MS); clinical psychology (MS); community counseling (MS); school guidance counseling (MS). Part-time and evening/weekend programs available. *Faculty:* 4 full-time (1 woman), 8 part-time/adjunct (4 women). *Students:* 20 full-time (16 women), 44 part-time (31 women), 1 international. Average age 35. 20 applicants, 90% accepted, 15 enrolled. In 2007, 16 degrees awarded. *Degree requirements:* For master's, comprehensive exam, thesis. *Entrance requirements:* For master's, 2 letters of reference, interview. *Application deadline:* Applications are processed on a rolling basis. Application fee: $35. Electronic applications accepted. *Expenses:* Tuition: Full-time $12,000; part-time $325 per credit. Required fees: $45 per semester. *Financial support:* In 2007–08, 3 students received support, including teaching assistantships with tuition reimbursements available (averaging $3,000 per year); career-related internships or fieldwork, Federal Work-Study, and unspecified assistantships also available. Support available to part-time students. Financial award application deadline: 3/1. *Unit head:* Dr. Craig Knapp, Chair, 802-773-5900 Ext. 3219, Fax: 802-776-5258, E-mail: cknapp@csj.edu. *Application contact:* Tracy Gallipo, Director of Admissions, 802-773-5900 Ext. 3262, Fax: 802-773-5900, E-mail: tracygallipo@csj.edu.

The College of William and Mary, Faculty of Arts and Sciences, Department of Psychology, Williamsburg, VA 23187-8795. Offers clinical psychology (Psy D); general experimental psychology (MA). Psy D is offered through the Virginia Consortium for Professional Psychology. *Faculty:* 9 full-time (3 women), 1 part-time/adjunct (0 women). *Students:* 14 full-time (13 women); includes 2 minority (1 African American, 1 Asian American or Pacific Islander). Average age 24. 93 applicants, 11% accepted, 7 enrolled. In 2007, 6 degrees awarded. *Degree requirements:* For master's, comprehensive exam, thesis, oral exams. *Entrance requirements:* For master's, GRE, passed course work in statistics and experimental psychology. Additional exam requirements/recommendations for international students: Required—TOEFL. *Application deadline:* For fall admission, 2/15 for domestic and international students. Application fee: $45. Electronic applications accepted. *Expenses:* Tuition, state resident: full-time $6,250; part-time $275 per credit hour. Tuition, nonresident: part-time $760 per credit hour. Required fees: $3,550. Tuition and fees vary according to program. *Financial support:* In 2007–08, 14 students received support, including 1 research assistantship with full tuition reimbursement available (averaging $9,000 per year), 13 teaching assistantships with full tuition reimbursements available (averaging $9,000 per year); institutionally sponsored loans, scholarships/grants, and tuition waivers also available. Financial award application deadline: 2/15. *Faculty research:* Personality, developmental, cognition, applied decision theory, social psychology. *Unit head:* Dr. Constance J. Pilkington, Chair, 757-221-3875, Fax: 757-221-3896. *Application contact:* Barbara B. Pumilia, Graduate Administrator, Psychology, 757-221-3872, Fax: 757-221-3896, E-mail: bbpumi@wm.edu.

Colorado State University, Graduate School, College of Natural Sciences, Department of Psychology, Fort Collins, CO 80523-0015. Offers MS, PhD. *Accreditation:* APA. *Faculty:* 28 full-time (15 women), 1 part-time/adjunct (0 women). *Students:* 74 full-time (52 women), 34 part-time (25 women); includes 21 minority (1 African American, 6 American Indian/Alaska Native, 4 Asian Americans or Pacific Islanders, 10 Hispanic Americans), 4 international. Average age 28. 386 applicants, 6% accepted. In 2007, 17 master's, 11 doctorates awarded. *Median time to degree:* Of those who began their doctoral program in fall 1999, 100% received their degree in 8 years or less. *Degree requirements:* For master's, thesis; for doctorate, comprehensive exam, thesis/dissertation. *Entrance requirements:* For master's and doctorate, GRE General Test, GRE Subject Test, minimum GPA of 3.5; transcripts; 3 letters of recommendation; resumé or vita. Additional exam requirements/recommendations for international students: Required—TOEFL. *Application deadline:* For fall admission, 12/15 for domestic students, 2/15 for international students. Application fee: $50. Electronic applications accepted. *Expenses:* Tuition, state resident: full-time $4,887; part-time $272 per credit. Tuition, nonresident: full-time $16,425; part-time $913 per credit. Required fees: $1,379; $75 per credit. *Financial support:* In 2007–08, 14 research assistantships with full tuition reimbursements (averaging $8,290 per year), 52 teaching assistantships with full tuition reimbursements (averaging $10,187 per year) were awarded; career-related internships or fieldwork, Federal Work-Study, institutionally sponsored loans, scholarships/grants, and unspecified assistantships also available. Financial award application deadline: 1/15; financial award applicants required to submit FAFSA. *Faculty research:* Environmental psychology, cognitive learning, health psychology, counseling and clinical issues. Total annual research expenditures: $2.4 million. *Unit head:* Ernest L. Chavez, Chair and Professor, 970-491-6364, Fax: 970-491-1032, E-mail: ernest.chavez@colostate.edu. *Application contact:* Joanne Moran, Program Assistant I, 970-491-7298, Fax: 970-491-1032, E-mail: joanne.moran@colostate.edu.

Columbia University, Graduate School of Arts and Sciences, Division of Natural Sciences, Department of Psychology, New York, NY 10027. Offers experimental psychology (M Phil, MA, PhD); psychobiology (M Phil, MA, PhD); social psychology (M Phil, MA, PhD); JD/MA; JD/PhD; MD/PhD. *Faculty:* 23 full-time. *Students:* 35 full-time (19 women), 2 part-time. Average age 28. 156 applicants, 7% accepted. In 2007, 7 master's, 6 doctorates awarded. *Degree requirements:* For master's, thesis; for doctorate, thesis/dissertation. *Entrance requirements:* For master's and doctorate, GRE General Test. Additional exam requirements/recommendations for international students: Required—TOEFL. Application fee: $90. *Expenses:* Tuition: Part-time $1,452 per credit. Required fees: $152 per term. One-time fee: $75 part-time. Full-time tuition and fees vary according to course level, course load, degree level and program. *Financial support:* Fellowships, teaching assistantships, Federal Work-Study and institutionally sponsored loans available. Support available to part-time students. Financial award application deadline: 1/5; financial award applicants required to submit FAFSA. *Unit head:* Norma Graham, Chair, 212-854-5591, Fax: 212-854-3609, E-mail: nb2229@columbia.edu.

Concordia University, School of Graduate Studies, Faculty of Arts and Science, Department of Psychology, Program in Psychology (General), Montréal, QC H3G 1M8, Canada. Offers MA, PhD. *Degree requirements:* For master's, comprehensive exam, thesis; for doctorate, comprehensive exam, thesis/dissertation. *Entrance requirements:* For master's, GRE General Test, GRE Subject Test, honors degree in psychology or equivalent; for doctorate, master's degree in psychology. *Faculty research:* Appetitive motivation and drug dependence, human information processing, psychology of physical activity.

Concordia University Chicago, College of Arts and Sciences, Program in Psychology, River Forest, IL 60305-1499. Offers MA. Part-time and evening/weekend programs available. *Degree requirements:* For master's, comprehensive exam, thesis optional. *Entrance requirements:* For master's, minimum GPA of 2.9. Additional exam requirements/recommendations for international students: Required—TOEFL (minimum score 550 paper-based; 195 computer-based). Electronic applications accepted. *Faculty research:* Lutheran high school counseling research.

Concordia University Wisconsin, Graduate Programs, Department of Psychology, Mequon, WI 53097-2402. Offers professional counseling (MPC).

Connecticut College, Graduate School, Department of Psychology, New London, CT 06320-4196. Offers MA. Part-time programs available. *Students:* 8 full-time (all women), 3 part-time (all women), 1 international. Average age 25. 13 applicants, 62% accepted, 4 enrolled. In 2007, 1 degree awarded. *Degree requirements:* For master's, comprehensive exam, thesis or alternative. *Entrance requirements:* For master's, GRE General Test, GRE Subject Test. Additional exam requirements/recommendations for international students: Required—TOEFL (minimum score 600 paper-based). *Application deadline:* For fall admission, 2/1 for domestic and international students. Application fee: $60. *Expenses:* Tuition: Full-time $9,300; part-time $388 per credit. *Financial support:* 2 course remissions for each of 5 students available. Financial award application deadline: 2/1; financial award applicants required to submit CSS PROFILE or FAFSA. *Faculty research:* Behavioral medicine, personality-social psychology, clinical, neuroscience/psychobiology. *Unit head:* Dr. Ann Sloan Devlin, Chair, 860-439-2333. *Application contact:* Nancy M. MacLeod, Academic Department Assistant, 860-439-2330, Fax: 860-439-5300, E-mail: nancy.macleod@conncoll.edu.

Cornell University, Graduate School, Graduate Fields of Arts and Sciences, Field of Psychology, Ithaca, NY 14853-0001. Offers biopsychology (PhD); human experimental psychology (PhD); personality and social psychology (PhD). *Faculty:* 42 full-time (15 women). *Students:* 33 full-time (18 women); includes 5 minority (2 African Americans, 2 Asian Americans or Pacific Islanders, 1 Hispanic American), 10 international. Average age 29. 175 applicants, 8% accepted, 8 enrolled. In 2007, 4 doctorates awarded. *Degree requirements:* For doctorate, comprehensive exam, thesis/dissertation, 2 semesters of teaching experience. *Entrance requirements:* For doctorate, GRE General Test, 3 letters of recommendation. Additional exam requirements/recommendations for international students: Required—TOEFL (minimum score 550 paper-based; 213 computer-based; 77 iBT). *Application deadline:* For fall admission, 12/15 for domestic students. Application fee: $70. Electronic applications accepted. *Financial support:* In 2007–08, 33 students received support, including 11 fellowships with full tuition reimbursements available, 22 teaching assistantships with full tuition reimbursements available; research assistantships with full tuition reimbursements available, institutionally sponsored loans, scholarships/grants, health care benefits, tuition waivers (full and partial), and unspecified assistantships also available. Financial award applicants required to submit FAFSA. *Faculty research:* Sensory and perceptual systems, social cognition, cognitive development, quantitative and computational modeling, behavioral neuroscience. *Unit head:* Director of Graduate Studies, 607-255-6364, Fax: 607-255-8433. *Application contact:* Graduate Field Assistant, 607-255-3834, Fax: 607-255-8433, E-mail: psychapp@cornell.edu.

Dalhousie University, Faculty of Science, Department of Psychology, Halifax, NS B3H 4R2, Canada. Offers clinical psychology (PhD); psychology (M Sc, PhD); psychology/neuroscience (M Sc, PhD). *Accreditation:* APA (one or more programs are accredited). *Faculty:* 30 full-time (8 women), 34 part-time/adjunct (14 women). *Students:* 56 full-time (35 women); includes 2 minority (both Asian Americans or Pacific Islanders) 200 applicants, 8% accepted. In 2007, 8 master's, 7 doctorates awarded. *Degree requirements:* For master's, thesis; for doctorate, thesis/dissertation. *Entrance requirements:* For doctorate, GRE General Test. Additional exam requirements/recommendations for international students: Required—TOEFL. *Application deadline:* For fall admission, 2/1 priority date for domestic students. Applications are processed on a rolling basis. Application fee: $60. *Financial support:* In 2007–08, 19 fellowships, 26 teaching assistantships (averaging $1,853 per year) were awarded; career-related internships or fieldwork also available. Financial award application deadline: 2/1. *Faculty research:* Physiological psychology, psychology of learning, learning and behavior, forensic clinical health psychology, development perception and cognition. Total annual research expenditures: $1.9 million. *Unit head:* Dr. Richard Brown, Chair, 902-494-3417, Fax: 902-494-6585, E-mail: richard.brown@dal.ca. *Application contact:* Dr. Raymond Klein, Graduate Coordinator, 902-494-6551, Fax: 902-494-6585, E-mail: ray.klein@dal.ca.

Dartmouth College, Arts and Sciences Graduate Programs, Department of Psychological and Brain Sciences, Hanover, NH 03755. Offers cognitive neuroscience (PhD); psychology (PhD). *Faculty:* 16 full-time (3 women), 4 part-time/adjunct (2 women). *Students:* 33 full-time (19 women); includes 2 minority (both Asian Americans or Pacific Islanders), 6 international. Average age 28. 78 applicants, 14% accepted, 4 enrolled. In 2007, 2 degrees awarded. *Degree requirements:* For doctorate, thesis/dissertation. *Entrance requirements:* For doctorate, GRE General Test, GRE Subject Test. Additional exam requirements/recommendations for international students: Required—TOEFL. *Application deadline:* For fall admission, 1/15 priority date for domestic students. Application fee: $40. *Financial support:* In 2007–08, 26 students received support, including fellowships with full tuition reimbursements available (averaging $22,464 per year), research assistantships with full tuition reimbursements available (averaging $22,464 per year); Federal Work-Study, institutionally sponsored loans, and tuition waivers (full) also available. *Faculty research:* Behavioral neuroscience, cognitive neuroscience, cognitive science, social/personality psychology. Total annual research expenditures: $3.5 million. *Unit head:* Dr. Howard C. Hughes, Chair, 603-646-3181, Fax: 603-646-1419, E-mail: howard.hughes@dartmouth.edu. *Application contact:* Nancy Tenney, Departmental Administrative, 603-646-3181, E-mail: nancy.4.tenney@dartmouth.edu.

DePaul University, College of Liberal Arts and Sciences, Department of Psychology, Chicago, IL 60604-2287. Offers clinical psychology (MA, PhD), including child clinical psychology, community clinical psychology; experimental psychology (MA, PhD); general psychology (MS); industrial/organizational psychology (MA, PhD); MA/PhD. *Accreditation:* APA (one or more programs are accredited). *Faculty:* 31 full-time (19 women), 6 part-time/adjunct (4 women). *Students:* 57 full-time (36 women), 53 part-time (36 women); includes 24 minority (14 African Americans, 1 American Indian/Alaska Native, 3 Asian Americans or Pacific Islanders, 6 Hispanic Americans), 1 international. Average age 28. 332 applicants, 14% accepted, 23 enrolled. In 2007, 14 master's, 17 doctorates awarded. *Median time to degree:* Of those who began their doctoral program in fall 1999, 60% received their degree in 8 years or less. *Degree requirements:* For master's, thesis, oral exam; for doctorate, comprehensive exam, thesis/dissertation, oral and written exams. *Entrance requirements:* For master's and doctorate, GRE General Test, GRE Subject Test, 32 quarter hours of course work in psychology, 3 letters of recommendation. Additional exam requirements/recommendations for international students: Required—TOEFL. Application fee: $40. Electronic applications accepted. *Financial support:* In 2007–08, 48 students received support, including 35 research assistantships with full tuition reimbursements available (averaging $11,800 per year), 13 teaching assistantships with full tuition reimbursements available (averaging $11,800 per year); career-related internships or fieldwork, scholarships/grants, traineeships, tuition waivers (full and partial), and unspecified assistantships also available. Financial award application deadline: 1/10. *Faculty research:* Adolescent stress and depression, minority adolescents sexuality, public policy, community influences in child adjustment. *Unit head:* Dr. Christopher B Keys, Chairman, 773-325-7887, Fax: 773-325-7888. *Application contact:* Alison Pereida Knapp, Graduate Admissions Assistant, 773-325-7887, Fax: 773-325-7888.

Drexel University, College of Arts and Sciences, Department of Psychology, Philadelphia, PA 19104-2875. Offers clinical psychology (MA, MS, PhD), including clinical psychology (MA, MS), forensic psychology (PhD), health psychology (PhD), neuropsychology (PhD); law-psychology (PhD); JD/PhD. *Accreditation:* APA (one or more programs are accredited). *Degree requirements:* For doctorate, thesis/dissertation, internship. *Entrance requirements:* For doctorate, GRE General Test. Additional exam requirements/recommendations for international students: Required—TOEFL. Electronic applications accepted. Expenses: Contact institution. *Faculty research:* Neurosciences, rehabilitation psychology, cognitive science, neurological assessment.

Duke University, Graduate School, Department of Psychology, Durham, NC 27708-0586. Offers biological psychology (PhD); clinical psychology (PhD); cognitive psychology (PhD); developmental psychology (PhD); experimental psychology (PhD); health psychology (PhD); human social development (PhD); JD/MA. *Accreditation:* APA (one or more programs are accredited). *Faculty:* 40 full-time. *Students:* 91 full-time (71 women); includes 15 minority (9 African Americans, 1 Asian American or Pacific Islander, 5 Hispanic Americans), 13 international. 468 applicants, 7% accepted, 19 enrolled. In 2007, 14 doctorates awarded. *Degree requirements:* For doctorate, thesis/dissertation. *Entrance requirements:* For doctorate, GRE General Test. Additional exam requirements/recommendations for international students: Required—TOEFL (minimum score 550 paper-based; 213 computer-based; 83 iBT), IELTS (minimum score 7). *Application deadline:* For fall admission, 12/15 priority date for domestic and international students. Application fee: $75. Electronic applications accepted. *Financial support:* Fellowships, research assistantships, teaching assistantships, career-related internships or fieldwork and Federal Work-Study available. Financial award application deadline: 12/31. *Unit head:* Amy Needham, Co-Director of Graduate Studies, 919-660-5715, Fax: 919-660-5726, E-mail: morrell@duke.edu.

Duquesne University, Graduate School of Liberal Arts, Department of Psychology, Pittsburgh, PA 15282-0001. Offers clinical psychology (PhD). *Accreditation:* APA. *Faculty:* 14 full-time (5 women). *Students:* 54 full-time (27 women), 3 part-time (1 woman). Average age 25. In 2007, 11 doctorates awarded. *Degree requirements:* For doctorate, comprehensive exam, thesis/dissertation. *Entrance requirements:* For doctorate, GRE General Test, MA in psychology. Additional exam requirements/recommendations for international students: Required—TOEFL. *Application deadline:* For fall admission, 12/15 for domestic and international students. Application fee: $50. *Expenses:* Tuition: Part-time $774 per credit. Required fees: $74 per credit. Tuition and fees vary according to program. *Financial support:* In 2007–08, 1 research assistantship with full tuition reimbursement (averaging $11,200 per year), 14 teaching assistantships with full tuition reimbursements (averaging $11,200 per year) were awarded; fellowships with full tuition reimbursements, career-related internships or fieldwork, scholarships/grants, tuition waivers (partial), and unspecified assistantships also available. Financial award application deadline: 5/1. *Faculty research:* Emotion, language motivation, imagination, development. *Unit head:* Dr. Daniel Burston, Chair, 412-396-5067.

East Carolina University, Graduate School, Thomas Harriot College of Arts and Sciences, Department of Psychology, Program in General Psychology, Greenville, NC 27858-4353. Offers MA. *Students:* 26 full-time (21 women), 15 part-time (14 women); includes 4 minority (1 African American, 3 Asian Americans or Pacific Islanders). Average age 27. 34 applicants, 88% accepted, 0 enrolled. In 2007, 9 degrees awarded. *Degree requirements:* For master's, one foreign language, comprehensive exam, thesis. *Entrance requirements:* For master's, GRE General Test, GRE Subject Test. Additional exam requirements/recommendations for international students: Required—TOEFL. *Application deadline:* Applications are processed on a rolling basis. Application fee: $50. *Financial support:* Application deadline: 6/1. *Unit head:* Dr. John Cope, Director of Graduate Studies, 252-328-6497, Fax: 252-328-6283, E-mail: copej@ecu.edu. *Application contact:* Dean of Graduate School, 252-328-6012, Fax: 252-328-6071, E-mail: gradschool@ecu.edu.

East Central University, School of Graduate Studies, Department of Psychology, Ada, OK 74820-6899. Offers MSPS. Part-time and evening/weekend programs available. *Faculty:* 7 part-time/adjunct (3 women). *Students:* 14 full-time (10 women), 8 part-time (6 women); includes 3 minority (all American Indian/Alaska Native). Average age 32. 12 applicants, 83% accepted. In 2007, 6 degrees awarded. *Entrance requirements:* For master's, GRE General Test, MAT. *Application deadline:* Applications are processed on a rolling basis. Application fee: $0 ($50 for international students). Electronic applications accepted. *Expenses:* Tuition, state resident: full-time $2,784. Required fees: $53. *Financial support:* Teaching assistantships, career-related internships or fieldwork, Federal Work-Study, institutionally sponsored loans, and tuition waivers (partial) available. *Unit head:* Dr. Joanna Harris, Chair, 580-332-8000 Ext. 319. *Application contact:* Juanita L. Pratt, Secretary, 580-310-5708, Fax: 580-282-8691, E-mail: jpratt@ecok.edu.

Eastern Illinois University, Graduate School, College of Sciences, Department of Psychology, Charleston, IL 61920-3099. Offers clinical psychology (MA); school psychology (SSP). *Faculty:* 18 full-time (4 women). In 2007, 10 master's, 11 other advanced degrees awarded. *Degree requirements:* For master's, comprehensive exam; for SSP, thesis. *Entrance requirements:* For master's and SSP, GRE General Test. *Application deadline:* For fall admission, 7/31 priority date for domestic students. Applications are processed on a rolling basis. Application fee: $30. *Expenses:* Tuition, state resident: part-time $218 per hour. Tuition, nonresident: part-time $654 per hour. *Financial support:* In 2007–08, research assistantships with tuition reimbursements (averaging $7,200 per year), 9 teaching assistantships with tuition reimbursements (averaging $7,200 per year) were awarded; career-related internships or fieldwork also available. *Unit head:* Dr. John H. Mace, Chairperson, 217-581-2127, Fax: 217-581-6764, E-mail: jhmace@eiu.edu.

Eastern Kentucky University, The Graduate School, College of Arts and Sciences, Department of Psychology, Richmond, KY 40475-3102. Offers clinical psychology (MS); industrial/organizational psychology (MS); school psychology (Psy S). Part-time programs available. *Faculty:* 11 full-time (5 women). *Students:* 64 full-time (47 women), 10 part-time (8 women); includes 5 minority (4 African Americans, 1 Asian American or Pacific Islander). Average age 25. 166 applicants, 31% accepted, 18 enrolled. In 2007, 32 master's, 11 other advanced degrees awarded. *Entrance requirements:* For master's and Psy S, GRE General Test, minimum GPA of 2.5. *Application deadline:* For fall admission, 3/15 priority date for domestic students. Applications are processed on a rolling basis. Application fee: $35. *Financial support:* In 2007–08, 30 students received support, including research assistantships (averaging $10,000 per year), teaching assistantships (averaging $10,000 per year); career-related internships or fieldwork and Federal Work-Study also available. Support available to part-time students. *Faculty research:* Autism, social psychology, parenting, assessment of depression/anxiety, reading. Total annual research expenditures: $40,000. *Unit head:* Dr. Robert Brubaker, Chair, 859-622-1105, Fax: 859-622-5871, E-mail: robert.brubaker@eku.edu.

Eastern Michigan University, Graduate School, College of Arts and Sciences, Department of Psychology, Ypsilanti, MI 48197. Offers clinical behavioral psychology (MS); clinical psychology (MS, PhD); psychology (MS). *Accreditation:* APA. *Faculty:* 22 full-time (11 women). *Students:* 40 full-time (27 women), 49 part-time (33 women); includes 3 African Americans, 2 Asian Americans or Pacific Islanders, 2 Hispanic Americans, 5 international. Average age 28. In 2007, 38 master's, 5 doctorates awarded. Application fee: $35. *Expenses:* Tuition, state resident: full-time $8,952; part-time $373 per credit hour. Tuition, nonresident: full-time $17,634; part-time $735 per credit hour. Required fees: $896; $34 per credit hour. Tuition and fees vary according to course level, degree level and program. *Unit head:* Dr. Carol Freedman-Doan, Interim Head, 734-487-1155, Fax: 734-487-6553, E-mail: cfreedman@emich.edu.

Eastern Washington University, Graduate Studies, College of Education and Human Development, Department of Counseling, Educational, and Developmental Psychology, Cheney, WA 99004-2431. Offers school counseling (MS), including counseling psychology, school counseling; school psychology (MS); special education (M Ed). *Accreditation:* ACA (one or more programs are accredited); NCATE (one or more programs are accredited). *Degree requirements:* For master's, comprehensive exam, thesis or alternative. *Entrance requirements:* For master's, GRE General Test, minimum GPA of 3.0. *Faculty research:* 21.

Eastern Washington University, Graduate Studies, College of Social and Behavioral Sciences, Department of Psychology, Cheney, WA 99004-2431. Offers psychology (MS); school psychology (MS). *Degree requirements:* For master's, comprehensive exam, thesis or alternative. *Entrance requirements:* For master's, GRE General Test, minimum GPA of 3.0.

East Tennessee State University, School of Graduate Studies, College of Arts and Sciences, Department of Psychology, Johnson City, TN 37614. Offers clinical psychology (MA); general psychology (MA). *Degree requirements:* For master's, thesis, oral exams. *Entrance requirements:* For master's, GRE General Test, GRE Subject Test, minimum GPA of 3.0. Additional exam requirements/recommendations for international students: Required—TOEFL (minimum score 550 paper-based; 213 computer-based). *Faculty research:* Language acquisition, recovery of brain function after injury or damage, violence in domestic relationships and road rage, reasons for living, unhealthy tanning behaviors.

Edinboro University of Pennsylvania, Graduate Studies and Research, School of Liberal Arts, Department of Psychology, Edinboro, PA 16444. Offers clinical psychology (MA). Part-time and evening/weekend programs available. *Faculty:* 3 full-time (1 woman). *Students:* 27 full-time (20 women), 5 part-time (3 women); includes 1 minority (Asian American or Pacific Islander), 1 international. Average age 29. In 2007, 17 degrees awarded. *Degree requirements:* For master's, comprehensive exam, thesis or alternative, project. *Entrance requirements:* For master's, GRE or MAT, minimum QPA of 2.5. *Application deadline:* For fall admission, 3/15 priority date for domestic students. Applications are processed on a rolling basis. Application fee: $30. Electronic applications accepted. *Expenses:* Tuition, state resident: full-time $6,214; part-time $345 per credit. Tuition, nonresident: full-time $9,944; part-time $552 per credit. Required fees: $46 per credit. *Financial support:* In 2007–08, 10 research assistantships with full and partial tuition reimbursements (averaging $3,850 per year) were awarded; career-related internships or fieldwork, Federal Work-Study, scholarships/grants, and unspecified assistantships also available. Support available to part-time students. Financial award application deadline: 2/15; financial award applicants required to submit FAFSA. *Unit head:* Dr. Cynthia Legin-Bucell, Chairperson, 814-732-2774, E-mail: leginbucell@edinboro.edu. *Application contact:* Dr. R. Scott Baldwin, Dean, 814-732-2752, Fax: 814-732-2268, E-mail: sbaldwin@edinboro.edu.

Emory University, Graduate School of Arts and Sciences, Department of Psychology, Atlanta, GA 30322-1100. Offers clinical psychology (PhD); cognition and development (PhD); neuroscience and animal behavior (PhD). *Accreditation:* APA. *Degree requirements:* For doctorate, comprehensive exam, thesis/dissertation. *Entrance requirements:* For doctorate, GRE General Test, minimum GPA of 3.25. Additional exam requirements/recommendations for international students: Required—TOEFL. Electronic applications accepted. *Faculty research:* Neuroscience and animal behavior; adult and child psychopathology, cognition development assessment.

Emporia State University, School of Graduate Studies, The Teachers College, Department of Psychology and Special Education, Program in Psychology, Emporia, KS 66801-5087. Offers general psychology (MS); industrial/organizational psychology (MS). Part-time programs available. *Students:* 11 full-time (5 women), 20 part-time (15 women); includes 1 minority (Hispanic American), 3 international. 16 applicants, 69% accepted, 11 enrolled. In 2007, 10 degrees awarded. *Degree requirements:* For master's, comprehensive exam or thesis, internship. *Entrance requirements:* For master's, GRE General Test or MAT, graduate essay exam, appropriate bachelor's degree, letters of recommendation. Additional exam requirements/recommendations for international students: Required—TOEFL. *Application deadline:* For fall admission, 6/1 priority date for domestic students; for spring admission, 10/1 for domestic students. Applications are processed on a rolling basis. Application fee: $30 ($75 for international students). Electronic applications accepted. *Expenses:* Tuition, state resident: part-time $157 per credit hour. Tuition, nonresident: part-time $475 per credit hour. Required fees: $47 per credit hour. Tuition and fees vary according to campus/location. *Financial support:* Career-related internships or fieldwork, Federal Work-Study, institutionally sponsored loans, health care benefits, and unspecified assistantships available. Financial award application deadline: 3/15; financial award applicants required to submit FAFSA. *Faculty research:* Driving under the influence (DUI) personality, lifestyles and imposter phenomenon. *Unit head:* Dr. Kenneth A. Weaver, Chair, Department of Psychology and Special Education, 620-341-5317, E-mail: kweaver@emporia.edu.

Evangel University, Department of Psychology, Springfield, MO 65802-2191. Offers clinical psychology (MS); counseling psychology (MS). Part-time and evening/weekend programs available. *Faculty:* 4 full-time (2 women), 1 part-time/adjunct (0 women). *Students:* 19 full-time (16 women), 6 part-time (5 women). Average age 30. 17 applicants, 100% accepted, 15 enrolled. In 2007, 9 degrees awarded. *Degree requirements:* For master's, comprehensive exam, thesis (for some programs). *Entrance requirements:* For master's, GRE General Test or MAT, minimum undergraduate GPA of 3.0, undergraduate major or minor in psychology, teaching certificate (school counseling). Additional exam requirements/recommendations for international students: Required—TOEFL (minimum score 550 paper-based; 213 computer-based). *Application deadline:* For fall admission, 2/1 priority date for domestic students; for spring admission, 10/15 priority date for domestic students. Applications are processed on a rolling basis. Application fee: $25. *Financial support:* In 2007–08, 6 students received support; research assistantships with partial tuition reimbursements available, teaching assistantships with partial tuition reimbursements available, career-related internships or fieldwork, institutionally sponsored loans, scholarships/grants, and unspecified assistantships available. Support available to part-time students. Financial award application deadline: 3/1; financial award applicants required to submit FAFSA. *Unit head:* Dr. Grant Jones, Chair, 417-865-2815 Ext. 8619, E-mail: jonesg@evangel.edu. *Application contact:* Charity H. Fahlstrom, Admissions Representative, Graduate and Professional Studies Admissions, 417-865-2811 Ext. 7227, Fax: 417-575-5484.

Fairfield University, Graduate School of Education and Allied Professions, Department of Psychology and Special Education, Fairfield, CT 06824-5195. Offers applied psychology (MA); school psychology (MA, CAS); special education (MA, CAS). Part-time and evening/weekend programs available. *Faculty:* 7 full-time (4 women), 7 part-time/adjunct (4 women). *Students:* 44 full-time (39 women), 114 part-time (87 women). 74 applicants, 46% accepted, 26 enrolled. In 2007, 40 master's, 17 other advanced degrees awarded. *Degree requirements:* For master's, comprehensive exam, thesis optional, educational technology course. *Entrance requirements:* For master's, PRAXIS I (PPST), minimum QPA of 2.67, 2 recommendations, resumé, essay. Additional exam requirements/recommendations for international students: Required—TOEFL (minimum score 550 paper-based; 213 computer-based; 79 iBT). *Application deadline:* For fall admission, 2/15 for domestic students; for spring admission, 10/15 for domestic students. Applications are processed on a rolling basis. Application fee: $60. Electronic applications accepted. *Financial support:* Scholarships/grants, tuition waivers (partial), and unspecified assistantships available. Financial award applicants required to submit FAFSA. *Faculty research:* School university collaboration, special education consultation, child neuropsychology, disabilities, effect of pretreatment orientation on treatment. *Unit head:* Dr. Daniel Geller, Chair, 203-254-4000 Ext. 2324, Fax: 203-254-4047, E-mail: dgeller@mail.fairfield.edu. *Application contact:* Marianne Gumpper, Director of Graduate and Continuing Studies Admissions, 203-254-4184, Fax: 203-254-4073, E-mail: gradadmis@mail.fairfield.edu.

Fairleigh Dickinson University, College at Florham, Maxwell Becton College of Arts and Sciences, Department of Psychology, Madison, NJ 07940-1099. Offers counseling (MA); industrial/organizational psychology (MA); organizational behavior (MA, Certificate), including organizational behavior (MA), organizational leadership (Certificate); MA/MBA. *Students:* 76 full-time (49 women), 77 part-time (51 women), 5 international. Average age 29. 116 applicants, 80% accepted, 38 enrolled. In 2007, 58 degrees awarded. *Application deadline:* Applications are processed on a rolling basis. Application fee: $40. *Expenses:* Tuition: Part-time $869 per credit. *Unit head:* Dr. Diane Wentworth, Chairperson, 973-443-8548.

See Close-Up on page 1431.

Fairleigh Dickinson University, Metropolitan Campus, University College: Arts, Sciences, and Professional Studies, School of Psychology, Teaneck, NJ 07666-1914. Offers clinical psychology (MA, PhD); clinical psychopharmacology (MA); forensic psychology (MA); general-theoretical psychology (MA, Certificate); school psychology (MA, Psy D). *Accreditation:* APA (one or more programs are accredited). *Students:* 163 full-time (118 women), 52 part-time (29 women), 6 international. Average age 33. 139 applicants, 70% accepted, 60 enrolled. In 2007, 52 master's, 28 doctorates awarded. *Application deadline:* Applications are processed on a rolling basis. Application fee: $40. *Expenses:* Tuition: Part-time $869 per credit. Tuition and fees vary according to degree level, campus/location and program. *Unit head:* Dr. Christopher Capuano, Director, 201-692-2000.

Fayetteville State University, Graduate School, Program in Psychology, Fayetteville, NC 28301-4298. Offers MA. Part-time and evening/weekend programs available. *Faculty:* 13 full-time (5 women). *Students:* 32 full-time (27 women), 7 part-time (all women); includes 22 minority (19 African Americans, 1 American Indian/Alaska Native, 2 Hispanic Americans). Average age 31. 14 applicants, 100% accepted, 14 enrolled. In 2007, 13 degrees awarded. *Degree requirements:* For master's, comprehensive exam, internship. *Application deadline:* For fall admission, 7/1 for domestic students; for spring admission, 12/1 for domestic students. Applications are processed on a rolling basis. Application fee: $25. Electronic applications accepted. *Expenses:* Tuition, state resident: full-time $2,118; part-time $265 per credit hour. Tuition, nonresident: full-time $11,708; part-time $1,464 per credit hour. Required fees: $1,218; $152 per credit hour. *Faculty research:* Coping strategies, reasons for living, hypnosis, cultural differences in expression of emotions, ethics, morals, stress, adult development. *Unit head:* Dr. Susan Franzblau, Head, 910-672-1574, E-mail: sfranzblau@uncfsu.edu.

Psychology—General

Fielding Graduate University, Graduate Programs, School of Psychology, Santa Barbara, CA 93105-3538. Offers clinical psychology (PhD); clinical psychology respecialization (Post-Doctoral Certificate); media psychology (PhD); media psychology and social change (MA); neuropsychology (Certificate). *Accreditation:* APA. Evening/weekend programs available. *Faculty:* 36 full-time (17 women), 22 part-time/adjunct (9 women). *Students:* 537 full-time (384 women), 66 part-time (44 women); includes 120 minority (41 African Americans, 5 American Indian/Alaska Native, 21 Asian Americans or Pacific Islanders, 53 Hispanic Americans), 9 international. Average age 46. 333 applicants, 41% accepted, 98 enrolled. In 2007, 50 doctorates, 32 other advanced degrees awarded. *Degree requirements:* For doctorate, comprehensive exam, thesis/dissertation. *Entrance requirements:* For doctorate, writing sample, minimum GPA of 3.0, 3 letters of recommendation, resum[00e9]. *Application deadline:* For fall admission, 2/23 for domestic students; for spring admission, 8/25 for domestic students. Application fee: $75. Electronic applications accepted. *Expenses:* Contact institution. *Financial support:* In 2007–08, 419 students received support, including 2 research assistantships (averaging $1,000 per year); career-related internships or fieldwork and scholarships/grants also available. Financial award application deadline: 3/1; financial award applicants required to submit FAFSA. *Unit head:* Dr. Raymond Trybus, Dean, 805-898-2909, E-mail: rtrybus@fielding.edu. *Application contact:* Addie Merrill, Admission Counselor, 800-340-1099, Fax: 805-687-9793, E-mail: amerrill@fielding.edu.

See Close-Up on page 1433.

Fisk University, Graduate Programs, Department of Psychology, Nashville, TN 37208-3051. Offers clinical psychology (MA); psychology (MA). *Degree requirements:* For master's, thesis. *Entrance requirements:* For master's, GRE General Test, GRE Subject Test, minimum GPA of 3.0. *Faculty research:* Ethnic and gender identity, development, female adolescent development, juvenile delinquency prevention.

Florida Agricultural and Mechanical University, Division of Graduate Studies, Research, and Continuing Education, College of Arts and Sciences, Department of Psychology, Tallahassee, FL 32307-3200. Offers community psychology (MS); school psychology (MS). *Degree requirements:* For master's, thesis. *Entrance requirements:* For master's, GRE General Test, minimum GPA of 3.0. Additional exam requirements/recommendations for international students: Required—TOEFL.

Florida Atlantic University, Charles E. Schmidt College of Science, Department of Psychology, Boca Raton, FL 33431-0991. Offers MA, PhD. Terminal master's awarded for partial completion of doctoral program. *Degree requirements:* For master's, one foreign language, thesis or alternative; for doctorate, one foreign language, comprehensive exam, thesis/dissertation. *Entrance requirements:* For master's and doctorate, GRE General Test, minimum GPA of 3.0 during previous 2 years. Electronic applications accepted. *Faculty research:* Cognition, psychobiology, developmental psychology, social psychology, neuroscience.

Florida Institute of Technology, Graduate Programs, College of Psychology and Liberal Arts, School of Psychology, Melbourne, FL 32901-6975. Offers applied behavior analysis (MS); clinical psychology (Psy D); industrial/organizational psychology (MS, PhD). *Accreditation:* APA (one or more programs are accredited). Part-time programs available. *Faculty:* 17 full-time (7 women), 8 part-time/adjunct (2 women). *Students:* 188 full-time (145 women), 14 part-time (9 women); includes 24 minority (8 African Americans, 4 Asian Americans or Pacific Islanders, 12 Hispanic Americans), 14 international. Average age 27. 304 applicants, 50% accepted, 72 enrolled. In 2007, 62 master's, 21 doctorates awarded. *Degree requirements:* For master's, comprehensive exam (for some programs), thesis (for some programs); for doctorate, comprehensive exam, thesis/dissertation (for some programs), internship. *Entrance requirements:* For master's, GRE General Test, 3 letters of recommendation, minimum GPA of 3.0, resumé; for doctorate, GRE General Test, GRE Subject Test, 3 letters of recommendation, minimum GPA of 3.2, resumé. Additional exam requirements/recommendations for international students: Required—TOEFL (minimum score 550 paper-based; 213 computer-based). *Application deadline:* For fall admission, 3/15 for domestic students. Applications are processed on a rolling basis. Application fee: $50. Electronic applications accepted. *Expenses:* Tuition: Part-time $945 per credit. *Financial support:* In 2007–08, 12 students received support, including 5 research assistantships with full and partial tuition reimbursements available (averaging $7,575 per year), 7 teaching assistantships with full and partial tuition reimbursements available (averaging $5,926 per year); career-related internships or fieldwork, institutionally sponsored loans, tuition waivers (partial), unspecified assistantships, and tuition remissions also available. Financial award application deadline: 3/1; financial award applicants required to submit FAFSA. *Faculty research:* Addictions, neuropsychology, child abuse, assessment, psychological trauma. Total annual research expenditures: $69,032. *Application contact:* Thomas M. Shea, Director of Graduate Admissions, 321-674-7577, Fax: 321-723-9468, E-mail: tshea@fit.edu.

See Close-Up on page 1435.

Florida International University, College of Arts and Sciences, Department of Psychology, Miami, FL 33199. Offers developmental psychology (PhD); general psychology (MS); psychology (MS). Part-time programs available. *Faculty:* 24 full-time (12 women). *Students:* 108 full-time (75 women), 34 part-time (22 women); includes 75 minority (12 African Americans, 2 Asian Americans or Pacific Islanders, 61 Hispanic Americans), 18 international. Average age 29. 194 applicants, 25% accepted, 26 enrolled. In 2007, 49 master's, 10 doctorates awarded. Terminal master's awarded for partial completion of doctoral program. *Degree requirements:* For master's, thesis; for doctorate, comprehensive exam, thesis/dissertation. *Entrance requirements:* For master's, GRE General Test, minimum GPA of 3.0, resumé, writing samples; for doctorate, GRE General Test, 3 letters of recommendation, resumé, writing samples, minimum GPA of 3.0. Additional exam requirements/recommendations for international students: Required—TOEFL (minimum score 550 paper-based; 213 computer-based). *Application deadline:* For fall admission, 12/5 for domestic students, 12/15 for international students. Application fee: $30. Electronic applications accepted. *Expenses:* Tuition, state resident: full-time $6,106. Tuition, nonresident: full-time $15,528. Required fees: $284. *Financial support:* Fellowships, research assistantships, teaching assistantships, Federal Work-Study, institutionally sponsored loans, and scholarships/grants available. Support available to part-time students. *Faculty research:* Community psychology. *Unit head:* Dr. Suzanna Rose, Chairperson, 305-348-2408, Fax: 305-348-3143, E-mail: suzanna.rose@fiu.edu.

Florida State University, Graduate Studies, College of Arts and Sciences, Department of Psychology, Tallahassee, FL 32306. Offers applied behavior analysis (MS); clinical psychology (PhD); cognitive psychology (PhD); developmental psychology (PhD); neuroscience (PhD); social psychology (PhD). *Accreditation:* APA (one or more programs are accredited). *Faculty:* 44 full-time (15 women), 1 part-time/adjunct (0 women). *Students:* 158 full-time (109 women); includes 23 minority (8 African Americans, 1 American Indian/Alaska Native, 1 Asian American or Pacific Islander, 13 Hispanic Americans), 5 international. Average age 26. 395 applicants, 10% accepted, 38 enrolled. In 2007, 38 master's, 17 doctorates awarded. Terminal master's awarded for partial completion of doctoral program. *Median time to degree:* Of those who began their doctoral program in fall 1999, 74% received their degree in 8 years or less. *Degree requirements:* For master's, comprehensive exam; for doctorate, thesis/dissertation, preliminary exam. *Entrance requirements:* For master's and doctorate, GRE General Test, minimum GPA of 3.0. Additional exam requirements/recommendations for international students: Required—TOEFL (minimum score 550 paper-based; 213 computer-based; 80 iBT). Application fee: $30. Electronic applications accepted. *Expenses:* Tuition, state resident: part-time $248 per credit hour. Tuition, nonresident: part-time $880 per credit hour. Tuition and fees vary according to program. *Financial support:* In 2007–08, 27 fellowships with full tuition reimbursements (averaging $18,000 per year), 75 research assistantships with full tuition reimbursements (averaging $18,000 per year), 39 teaching assistantships with full tuition reimbursements (averaging $15,000 per year) were awarded; career-related internships or fieldwork, Federal Work-Study, institutionally sponsored loans, scholarships/grants, traineeships, health care benefits, and unspecified assistantships also available. Financial award applicants required to submit FAFSA. Total annual research expenditures: $5.1 million. *Unit head:* Dr. Janet Kistner, Chairman, 850-644-2040, Fax: 850-644-7739, E-mail: kistner@psy.fsu.edu. *Application contact:* Cherie P. Miller, Graduate Program Assistant, 850-644-2499, Fax: 850-644-7739, E-mail: grad-info@psy.fsu.edu.

Fordham University, Graduate School of Arts and Sciences, Department of Psychology, New York, NY 10458. Offers applied developmental psychology (PhD); clinical psychology (PhD); psychometrics (PhD). *Faculty:* 25 full-time (8 women), 3 part-time/adjunct (2 women). *Students:* 91 full-time (62 women), 25 part-time (17 women); includes 33 minority (9 African Americans, 9 Asian Americans or Pacific Islanders, 15 Hispanic Americans), 12 international. Average age 29. 369 applicants, 13% accepted, 17 enrolled. In 2007, 18 doctorates awarded. Terminal master's awarded for partial completion of doctoral program. *Median time to degree:* Of those who began their doctoral program in fall 1999, 58% received their degree in 8 years or less. *Degree requirements:* For doctorate, comprehensive exam, thesis/dissertation. *Entrance requirements:* For doctorate, GRE General Test, GRE Subject Test. Additional exam requirements/recommendations for international students: Required—TOEFL (minimum score 600 paper-based; 250 computer-based). *Application deadline:* For fall admission, 12/14 for domestic students. Application fee: $65. Electronic applications accepted. *Expenses:* Tuition: Full-time $23,880; part-time $995 per credit. *Financial support:* In 2007–08, 73 students received support, including 4 fellowships with tuition reimbursements available (averaging $18,500 per year), 40 research assistantships with tuition reimbursements available (averaging $15,125 per year), 16 teaching assistantships with tuition reimbursements available (averaging $10,209 per year); career-related internships or fieldwork, institutionally sponsored loans, tuition waivers (full and partial), and unspecified assistantships also available. Financial award application deadline: 12/14; financial award applicants required to submit FAFSA. Total annual research expenditures: $848,459. *Unit head:* Dr. Frederick Wertz, Chair, 718-817-3777, Fax: 718-817-3785, E-mail: wertz@fordham.edu. *Application contact:* Charlene Dundie, Director of Graduate Admissions, 718-817-4420, Fax: 718-817-3566, E-mail: dundie@fordham.edu.

Fort Hays State University, Graduate School, College of Arts and Sciences, Department of Psychology, Hays, KS 67601-4099. Offers psychology (MS); school psychology (Ed S). *Faculty:* 7 full-time (1 woman). *Students:* 18 full-time (15 women), 17 part-time (13 women); includes 1 minority (Hispanic American) Average age 31. 34 applicants, 82% accepted. In 2007, 10 master's, 5 other advanced degrees awarded. *Degree requirements:* For master's and Ed S, comprehensive exam, thesis. *Entrance requirements:* For master's, GRE General Test. Additional exam requirements/recommendations for international students: Required—TOEFL (minimum score 550 paper-based; 213 computer-based). *Application deadline:* For fall admission, 3/1 priority date for domestic students. Applications are processed on a rolling basis. Application fee: $35. Electronic applications accepted. *Expenses:* Tuition, state resident: part-time $155 per credit hour. Tuition, nonresident: part-time $409 per credit hour. Tuition and fees vary according to class time, course level, course load, degree level, campus/location and program. *Financial support:* In 2007–08, 12 teaching assistantships (averaging $7,000 per year) were awarded; research assistantships, career-related internships or fieldwork, institutionally sponsored loans, and tuition waivers (full) also available. Support available to part-time students. *Faculty research:* Memory, learning, motivation, clinical and experimental psychology, history and systems of psychological stressors in rural environments. *Unit head:* Dr. Heath Marrs, Chair, 785-628-4405, E-mail: hmarrs@fhsu.edu.

Framingham State College, Division of Graduate and Continuing Education, Program in Counseling Psychology, Framingham, MA 01701-9101. Offers MA. Part-time and evening/weekend programs available. *Faculty:* 4 full-time, 3 part-time/adjunct. *Students:* 102. In 2007, 36 degrees awarded. *Unit head:* Prof. Deborah McMakin, Coordinator, 508-626-4550, Fax: 508-626-4030, E-mail: dmcmakin@frc.mass.edu. *Application contact:* Graduate Office, 508-626-4550, Fax: 508-626-4030, E-mail: dgce@frc.mass.edu.

Francis Marion University, Graduate Programs, Department of Psychology, Florence, SC 29501-0547. Offers applied clinical psychology (MS); applied community psychology (MS); school psychology (MS). Part-time and evening/weekend programs available. *Faculty:* 10 full-time (3 women), 6 part-time/adjunct (3 women). *Students:* 12 full-time (all women), 34 part-time (31 women); includes 5 minority (all African Americans), 1 international. Average age 28. 34 applicants, 100% accepted, 9 enrolled. In 2007, 9 degrees awarded. *Degree requirements:* For master's, internship. *Entrance requirements:* For master's, GRE General Test. *Application deadline:* For fall admission, 4/15 for domestic students; for spring admission, 10/15 for domestic students. Applications are processed on a rolling basis. Application fee: $30. *Expenses:* Tuition, state resident: full-time $7,547; part-time $377 per credit hour. Tuition, nonresident: full-time $15,094; part-time $755 per credit hour. Required fees: $285; $10 per credit hour. $45 per term. *Financial support:* In 2007–08, 2 research assistantships (averaging $7,000 per year), 3 teaching assistantships (averaging $8,000 per year) were awarded; career-related internships or fieldwork and unspecified assistantships also available. Support available to part-time students. Financial award application deadline: 3/1; financial award applicants required to submit FAFSA. *Faculty research:* Critical thinking, spatial localization, cognition and aging, family psychology. *Unit head:* Dr. John R. Hester, Chair, 843-661-1635, Fax: 843-661-1628. *Application contact:* Jennifer Taylor, Administrative Assistant, 843-661-1378, Fax: 843-661-1628.

Frostburg State University, Graduate School, College of Liberal Arts and Sciences, Department of Psychology, Frostburg, MD 21532-1099. Offers counseling psychology (MS). Part-time and evening/weekend programs available. *Faculty:* 7 full-time (3 women), 3 part-time/adjunct (2 women). *Students:* 38 full-time (31 women), 7 part-time (6 women); includes 6 minority (4 African Americans, 1 Asian American or Pacific Islander, 1 Hispanic American), 4 international. Average age 28. 38 applicants, 47% accepted, 15 enrolled. In 2007, 6 degrees awarded. *Degree requirements:* For master's, internship. *Entrance requirements:* For master's, GRE General Test or MAT, interview, minimum GPA of 3.0, resumé. *Application deadline:* For fall admission, 2/1 for domestic students. Applications are processed on a rolling basis. Application fee: $30. Electronic applications accepted. *Expenses:* Tuition, state resident: full-time $5,706; part-time $317 per credit hour. Tuition, nonresident: full-time $6,552; part-time $364 per credit hour. Required fees: $77 per credit hour. $11 per term. *Financial support:* In 2007–08, 7 research assistantships with full tuition reimbursements (averaging $5,000 per year) were awarded; career-related internships or fieldwork and Federal Work-Study also available. Financial award application deadline: 4/1; financial award applicants required to submit FAFSA. *Unit head:* Dr. Kevin Peterson, Chair, 301-687-4193. *Application contact:* Vickie Mazer, Director, Graduate Services, 301-687-7053, Fax: 301-687-4597, E-mail: vmmazer@frostburg.edu.

Fuller Theological Seminary, Graduate School of Psychology, Pasadena, CA 91182. Offers MA, MS, PhD, Psy D, MACL/PhD, MACL/Psy D. *Accreditation:* APA (one or more programs are accredited). Terminal master's awarded for partial completion of doctoral program. *Degree requirements:* For master's, practicum; for doctorate, thesis/dissertation, internships. *Entrance requirements:* For master's, GRE General Test; for doctorate, GRE General Test, GRE Subject Test, interview. Additional exam requirements/recommendations for international students: Required—TOEFL. *Faculty research:* Psychology of religion, depression, shame, psychoneuroimmunology, marital intimacy, sex roles, psychoanalytic theory, men's issues, family relations.

Gallaudet University, The Graduate School, College of Arts and Sciences, Department of Psychology, Washington, DC 20002-3625. Offers clinical psychology (PhD); school psychology (MA, Psy S), including developmental psychology (MA), school psychology (Psy S). *Accreditation:* APA (one or more programs are accredited). *Degree requirements:* For master's, thesis optional; for doctorate, thesis/dissertation. *Entrance requirements:* For master's, GRE General Test or MAT; for doctorate, GRE General Test or MAT, interview. *Application deadline:* For fall admission, 2/15 for domestic students. Application fee: $50. Electronic applications accepted. *Expenses:* Tuition: Full-time $5,790. Required fees: $1,886. *Financial support:* Application deadline: 8/1. *Unit head:* Dr. Virginia Gutman, Chair, 202-651-5540. *Application* *contact:* Wednesday Luria, Coordinator of Prospective Graduate Student Services, 202-651-5647, Fax: 202-651-5295, E-mail: wednesday.luria@gallaudet.edu.

Gardner-Webb University, Graduate School, School of Psychology, Boiling Springs, NC 28017. Offers mental health counseling (MA); school counseling (MA). Part-time and evening/weekend programs available. *Faculty:* 7 full-time (4 women), 1 part-time/adjunct (0 women). *Students:* 4 full-time (all women), 87 part-time (72 women); includes 19 minority (13 African Americans, 1 Asian American or Pacific Islander, 5 Hispanic Americans). Average age 32. In 2007, 19 degrees awarded. *Degree requirements:* For master's, comprehensive exam. *Entrance requirements:* For master's, GRE General Test, MAT, minimum GPA of 2.7. *Application deadline:* For fall admission, 7/1 priority date for domestic students. Applications are processed on a rolling basis. Application fee: $25. Electronic applications accepted. *Expenses:* Tuition: Part-time $275 per hour. *Financial support:* Unspecified assistantships available. *Unit head:* Dr. David Carscaddon, Chair, 704-406-4437, Fax: 704-406-4329, E-mail: dcarscaddon@gardner-webb.edu.

Geneva College, Program in Counseling, Beaver Falls, PA 15010-3599. Offers marriage and family (MA); mental health (MA); school counseling (MA). *Accreditation:* ACA. Part-time and evening/weekend programs available. *Degree requirements:* For master's, internship. *Entrance requirements:* For master's, GRE General Test or MAT, minimum GPA of 3.0, letters of recommendation, faith statement, 12 credits in undergraduate psychology. Additional exam requirements/recommendations for international students: Required—TOEFL. Electronic applications accepted.

George Fox University, Graduate Department of Clinical Psychology, Newberg, OR 97132-2697. Offers clinical psychology (Psy D); psychology (MA). *Accreditation:* APA. *Faculty:* 8 full-time (3 women), 11 part-time/adjunct (5 women). *Students:* 97 full-time (58 women), 11 part-time (6 women); includes 7 minority (1 African American, 1 American Indian/Alaska Native, 3 Asian Americans or Pacific Islanders, 2 Hispanic Americans), 1 international. Average age 29. 71 applicants, 51% accepted, 22 enrolled. In 2007, 23 master's, 14 doctorates awarded. *Degree requirements:* For doctorate, thesis/dissertation, internship. *Entrance requirements:* For master's, GRE General Test, GRE Subject Test, minimum undergraduate GPA of 3.0 during previous 2 years. Additional exam requirements/recommendations for international students: Required—TOEFL (minimum score 550 paper-based; 213 computer-based). *Application deadline:* For fall admission, 1/15 priority date for domestic students, 1/1 for international students. Application fee: $40. Electronic applications accepted. *Expenses: Contact institution. Financial support:* Career-related internships or fieldwork and scholarships/grants available. Financial award applicants required to submit FAFSA. *Faculty research:* Spiritual well-being, psychosocial development, value and ethics development. *Unit head:* Dr. Wayne Adams, Director, 800-765-4369 Ext. 2760, E-mail: wadams@georgefox.edu. *Application contact:* Adina McConaughey, Admission Counselor, 800-631-0921, Fax: 503-554-2263, E-mail: amcconaughey@georgefox.edu.

See Close-Up on page 1437.

George Mason University, College of Humanities and Social Sciences, Department of Psychology, Fairfax, VA 22030. Offers applied developmental psychology (MA, PhD); biopsychology (MA, PhD); clinical psychology (MA, PhD); human factors engineering psychology (MA, PhD); industrial/organizational psychology (MA, PhD); psychology (MA, PhD); school psychology (MA). *Accreditation:* APA. *Faculty:* 44 full-time (17 women), 16 part-time/adjunct (10 women). *Students:* 101 full-time (80 women), 135 part-time (88 women); includes 30 minority (6 African Americans, 13 Asian Americans or Pacific Islanders, 11 Hispanic Americans), 14 international. Average age 27. 734 applicants, 22% accepted, 86 enrolled. In 2007, 49 master's, 17 doctorates awarded. Terminal master's awarded for partial completion of doctoral program. *Median time to degree:* Of those who began their doctoral program in fall 1999, 97% received their degree in 8 years or less. *Degree requirements:* For master's, thesis (for applied developmental psychology and biopsychology); for doctorate, comprehensive exam, thesis/dissertation or alternative. *Entrance requirements:* For master's, GRE General Test, minimum GPA of 3.0 in last 60 hours of course work, undergraduate course work in psychology; for doctorate, GRE General Test, minimum undergraduate GPA of 3.0, 3.3 in major. Additional exam requirements/recommendations for international students: Required—TOEFL (minimum score 575 paper-based; 230 computer-based; 88 iBT), IELTS (minimum score 6). Application fee: $60 ($75 for international students). Electronic applications accepted. *Financial support:* In 2007–08, 15 fellowships with partial tuition reimbursements (averaging $2,300 per year), 33 research assistantships with partial tuition reimbursements (averaging $12,200 per year), 21 teaching assistantships with partial tuition reimbursements (averaging $12,200 per year) were awarded; career-related internships or fieldwork, scholarships/grants, traineeships, tuition waivers (partial), and unspecified assistantships also available. Financial award application deadline: 3/1; financial award applicants required to submit FAFSA. *Unit head:* Dr. Deborah Boehm-Davis, Chairperson, 703-993-1398, Fax: 703-993-1359, E-mail: bsmith@gmu.edu. *Application contact:* Dr. James Maddux, Information Contact, 703-993-3590, Fax: 703-993-1355, E-mail: psycgrad@gmu.edu.

Georgetown University, Graduate School of Arts and Sciences, Department of Psychology, Washington, DC 20057. Offers PhD. *Degree requirements:* For doctorate, thesis/dissertation. *Entrance requirements:* For doctorate, GRE General Test, GRE Subject Test. Additional exam requirements/recommendations for international students: Required—TOEFL.

The George Washington University, Columbian College of Arts and Sciences, Department of Psychology, Washington, DC 20052. Offers applied social psychology (PhD); clinical psychology (PhD); cognitive neuropsychology (PhD); industrial-organizational psychology (PhD). *Accreditation:* APA. Part-time and evening/weekend programs available. *Degree requirements:* For doctorate, thesis/dissertation or alternative, general exam. *Entrance requirements:* For doctorate, GRE General Test, minimum GPA of 3.0. Additional exam requirements/recommendations for international students: Required—TOEFL (minimum score 550 paper-based; 213 computer-based).

The George Washington University, Columbian College of Arts and Sciences, Program in Professional Psychology, Washington, DC 20052. Offers Psy D. *Accreditation:* APA. *Entrance requirements:* For doctorate, GRE General Test, interview, minimum GPA of 3.0. Additional exam requirements/recommendations for international students: Required—TOEFL (minimum score 550 paper-based; 213 computer-based). Electronic applications accepted.

Georgia Institute of Technology, Graduate Studies and Research, College of Sciences, School of Psychology, Atlanta, GA 30332-0001. Offers human computer interaction (MSHCI); psychology (MS, MS Psy, PhD). Terminal master's awarded for partial completion of doctoral program. *Degree requirements:* For master's, thesis; for doctorate, thesis/dissertation. *Entrance requirements:* For master's and doctorate, GRE General Test, GRE Subject Test, minimum GPA of 3.0. Additional exam requirements/recommendations for international students: Required—TOEFL. Electronic applications accepted. *Faculty research:* Experimental, industrial-organizational, and engineering psychology; cognitive aging and processes; leadership; human factors.

Georgia Southern University, Jack N. Averitt College of Graduate Studies, College of Liberal Arts and Social Sciences, Department of Psychology, Statesboro, GA 30460. Offers MS, Psy D. *Students:* 24 full-time (18 women); includes 6 minority (4 African Americans, 1 Asian American or Pacific Islander, 1 Hispanic American). Average age 25. 27 applicants, 56% accepted, 8 enrolled. In 2007, 13 degrees awarded. *Degree requirements:* For master's, thesis (for some programs), terminal exam; for doctorate, practical internship. *Entrance requirements:* For master's, GRE General Test, minimum GPA of 3.0, introductory courses in psychology and statistics, letter of recommendation; for doctorate, minimum 3.25 undergraduate GPA; 3 letters of reference; statement of purpose. Additional exam requirements/recommendations for international students: Required—TOEFL (minimum score 550 paper-based; 213 computer-based; 80 iBT). *Application deadline:* For fall admission, 3/1 priority date for domestic students, 3/1 for international students. Applications are processed on a rolling basis. Application fee: $50. Electronic applications accepted. *Expenses:* Tuition, state resident: full-time $3,516; part-time $147 per semester hour. Tuition, nonresident: full-time $14,060; part-time $586 per semester hour. Required fees: $562 per term. *Financial support:* In 2007–08, 22 students received support, including research assistantships with partial tuition reimbursements available (averaging $6,850 per year), teaching assistantships with partial tuition reimbursements available (averaging $6,850 per year); career-related internships or fieldwork, Federal Work-Study, scholarships/grants, tuition waivers (partial), and unspecified assistantships also available. Support available to part-time students. Financial award application deadline: 4/15; financial award applicants required to submit FAFSA. *Faculty research:* Scholarship related to the teaching of psychology, psychology of religion, animal models of stress, reading and discourse processing, health and psychological response to illness. Total annual research expenditures: $50,396. *Unit head:* Dr. John Murray, Chair, 912-478-5539, Fax: 912-478-0751, E-mail: jmurray@kmccurdy@georgiasouthern.edu. *Application contact:* 912-478-5384, Fax: 912-478-0740, E-mail: gradadmissions@georgiasouthern.edu.

Georgia State University, College of Arts and Sciences, Department of Psychology, Atlanta, GA 30303-3083. Offers MA, PhD. *Accreditation:* APA (one or more programs are accredited). *Faculty:* 33 full-time (17 women). *Students:* 91 full-time (69 women), 10 part-time (9 women); includes 21 minority (12 African Americans, 9 Asian Americans or Pacific Islanders), 6 international. Average age 30. 445 applicants, 7% accepted, 15 enrolled. In 2007, 13 degrees awarded. *Degree requirements:* For master's, thesis; for doctorate, comprehensive exam, thesis/dissertation. *Entrance requirements:* For doctorate, GRE General Test, departmental supplemental form. Additional exam requirements/recommendations for international students: Required—TOEFL. *Application deadline:* For fall admission, 12/5 for domestic and international students. Application fee: $50. Electronic applications accepted. *Expenses:* Tuition, state resident: part-time $221 per credit hour. *Financial support:* In 2007–08, 98 students received support, including fellowships with full tuition reimbursements available (averaging $21,000 per year), research assistantships with full tuition reimbursements available (averaging $16,031 per year), teaching assistantships with full tuition reimbursements available (averaging $16,031 per year); career-related internships or fieldwork, Federal Work-Study, institutionally sponsored loans, health care benefits, and unspecified assistantships also available. Financial award applicants required to submit FAFSA. *Faculty research:* Social psychology, developmental and comparative psychology, neuropsychology, clinical psychology, neuropsychology. Total annual research expenditures: $1.1 million. *Unit head:* Dr. David A. Washburn, Chair, 404-413-6203, E-mail: dwashburn@gsu.edu. *Application contact:* Dr. Marise B. Parent, Director of Graduate Studies, 404-413-6286, E-mail: mbparent@gsu.edu.

Golden Gate University, Ageno School of Business, San Francisco, CA 94105-2968. Offers accounting (MBA); business administration (EMBA, MBA, DBA); finance (MBA, MS, Certificate); financial planning (MS, Certificate); human resource management (MBA, MS); human resources management (Certificate); information technology (MBA); information technology management (MS, Certificate); integrated marketing and communications (MS, Certificate); international business (MBA); management (MBA); marketing (MBA, MS, Certificate); operations management (Certificate); psychology (MA, Certificate); public relations (MS, Certificate); JD/MBA. Part-time and evening/weekend programs available. *Students:* 320 full-time (175 women), 749 part-time (388 women); includes 339 minority (75 African Americans, 1 American Indian/Alaska Native, 202 Asian Americans or Pacific Islanders, 61 Hispanic Americans), 177 international. Average age 34. 664 applicants, 68% accepted, 229 enrolled. In 2007, 545 master's, 21 doctorates awarded. *Degree requirements:* For doctorate, thesis/dissertation. *Entrance requirements:* For master's, GMAT (MBA), minimum GPA of 2.5 (MS). Additional exam requirements/recommendations for international students: Required—TOEFL. *Application deadline:* Applications are processed on a rolling basis. Application fee: $55 ($90 for international students). *Financial support:* Career-related internships or fieldwork, Federal Work-Study, and institutionally sponsored loans available. Support available to part-time students. Financial award applicants required to submit FAFSA. *Unit head:* Terry Connelly, Dean, 415-442-6519, Fax: 415-442-5369. *Application contact:* Enrollment Services, 415-442-7800, Fax: 415-442-7807, E-mail: info@ggu.edu.

Governors State University, College of Education, Program in Psychology, University Park, IL 60466-0975. Offers MA. Part-time and evening/weekend programs available. *Students:* 4 full-time, 33 part-time. Average age 34. *Degree requirements:* For master's, thesis or alternative, practicum. *Entrance requirements:* For master's, GRE or MAT. *Application deadline:* For fall admission, 7/15 priority date for domestic students; for spring admission, 11/10 for domestic students. Applications are processed on a rolling basis. Application fee: $25. *Financial support:* Career-related internships or fieldwork, Federal Work-Study, institutionally sponsored loans, and tuition waivers (full and partial) available. Support available to part-time students. Financial award application deadline: 5/1. *Application contact:* John Powers, Adviser, 708-534-6363.

Graduate School and University Center of the City University of New York, Graduate Studies, Program in Psychology, New York, NY 10016-4039. Offers basic applied neurocognition (PhD); biopsychology (PhD); clinical psychology (PhD); developmental psychology (PhD); environmental psychology (PhD); experimental psychology (PhD); industrial psychology (PhD); learning processes (PhD); neuropsychology (PhD); psychology (PhD); social personality (PhD). *Faculty:* 119 full-time (40 women). *Students:* 510 full-time (379 women), 1 (woman) part-time; includes 98 minority (39 African Americans, 1 American Indian/Alaska Native, 21 Asian Americans or Pacific Islanders, 37 Hispanic Americans), 63 international. Average age 33. 747 applicants, 17% accepted, 78 enrolled. In 2007, 59 degrees awarded. *Degree requirements:* For doctorate, one foreign language, thesis/dissertation. *Entrance requirements:* For doctorate, GRE General Test. Additional exam requirements/recommendations for international students: Required—TOEFL. *Application deadline:* For fall admission, 12/15 for domestic students. Application fee: $125. Electronic applications accepted. *Financial support:* In 2007–08, 371 students received support, including 308 fellowships, 34 research assistantships, 33 teaching assistantships; career-related internships or fieldwork, Federal Work-Study, institutionally sponsored loans, and tuition waivers (full and partial) also available. Financial award application deadline: 2/1; financial award applicants required to submit FAFSA. *Unit head:* Dr. Joseph Glick, Executive Officer, 212-817-8706, Fax: 212-817-1533, E-mail: jglick@gc.cuny.edu.

Hardin-Simmons University, Graduate School, Cynthia Ann Parker College of Liberal Arts, Department of Psychology, Abilene, TX 79698-0001. Offers family psychology (MA). Part-time programs available. *Faculty:* 5 full-time (1 woman), 1 (woman) part-time/adjunct. *Students:* 18 full-time (12 women), 10 part-time (5 women); includes 3 minority (1 African American, 2 Hispanic Americans). Average age 27. 18 applicants, 67% accepted, 11 enrolled. In 2007, 8 degrees awarded. *Degree requirements:* For master's, comprehensive exam, clinical experience, project. *Entrance requirements:* For master's, 21 semester hours of course work in psychology (18 in upper division classes), minimum undergraduate GPA of 3.0 in major, minimum GPA of 2.7 overall, writing sample, letters of recommendation. Additional exam requirements/recommendations for international students: Required—TOEFL (minimum score 550 paper-based; 213 computer-based). *Application deadline:* For fall admission, 8/15 priority date for domestic students; for spring admission, 1/5 priority date for domestic students. Applications are processed on a rolling basis. Application fee: $50 ($100 for international students). *Expenses:* Tuition: Full-time $9,810; part-time $545 per hour. Required fees: $590; $75 per semester. One-time fee: $50 part-time. *Financial support:* In 2007–08, 21 students received support, including 20 fellowships (averaging $690 per year); career-related internships or fieldwork and scholarships/grants also available. Support available to part-time students. Financial award application deadline: 6/30; financial award applicants required to submit FAFSA. *Faculty research:* Spirituality in marriage, intimacy and sexuality in marriage, sex education in the church, role of faith in marital satisfaction, family stress management. *Unit head:* Dr. Doug Thomas, Head, 325-670-1534, Fax: 325-670-1458, E-mail: dthomas@hsutx.edu. *Application contact:* Dr. Gary Stanlake, Dean of Graduate Studies, 325-670-1298, Fax: 325-670-1564, E-mail: gradoff@hsutx.edu.

Harvard University, Graduate School of Arts and Sciences, Department of Psychology, Cambridge, MA 02138. Offers psychology (PhD), including behavior and decision analysis,

Psychology—General

Harvard University (continued)
cognition, developmental psychology, experimental psychology, personality, psychobiology, psychopathology; social psychology (PhD). *Degree requirements:* For doctorate, thesis/dissertation, general exams. *Entrance requirements:* For doctorate, GRE General Test. Additional exam requirements/recommendations for international students: Required—TOEFL. *Expenses:* Tuition: Full-time $31,456. Full-time tuition and fees vary according to program and student level.

Hodges University, Graduate Programs, Naples, FL 34119. Offers business administration (MBA); computer information technology (MS); criminal justice (MCJ); education (MPS); information systems management (MIS); interdisciplinary (MPS); law (MPS); management (MSM); professional studies (MPS); psychology (MPS); public administration (MPA). Part-time and evening/weekend programs available. Postbaccalaureate distance learning degree programs offered (no on-campus study). *Faculty:* 16 full-time (4 women), 2 part-time/adjunct (1 woman). *Students:* 37 full-time (25 women), 175 part-time (104 women); includes 64 minority (29 African Americans, 2 Asian Americans or Pacific Islanders, 33 Hispanic Americans). Average age 36. In 2007, 75 degrees awarded. *Degree requirements:* For master's, comprehensive exam (for some programs). *Entrance requirements:* For master's, in-house entrance exam. *Application deadline:* Applications are processed on a rolling basis. Application fee: $50. Electronic applications accepted. *Expenses:* Tuition: Full-time $10,260; part-time $570 per credit hour. Required fees: $190 per trimester. *Financial support:* In 2007–08, 181 students received support. Federal Work-Study and scholarships/grants available. Financial award application deadline: 7/8; financial award applicants required to submit FAFSA. *Unit head:* Terry McMahan, President, 239-513-1122, Fax: 239-598-6253, E-mail: tmcmahan@hodges.edu. *Application contact:* Rita Lampus, Vice President of Student Enrollment Management, 239-513-1122, Fax: 239-598-6253, E-mail: rlampus@internationalcollege.edu.

Hofstra University, College of Liberal Arts and Sciences, Department of Psychology, Hempstead, NY 11549. Offers applied organizational psychology (PhD); clinical and school psychology (PhD); clinical psychology (Psy D); industrial/organizational psychology (MA); school and community psychology (Psy D); school-community psychology (MS, CAS). Part-time and evening/weekend programs available. *Faculty:* 26 full-time (7 women), 10 part-time/adjunct (2 women). *Students:* 184 full-time (123 women), 52 part-time (29 women); includes 29 minority (11 African Americans, 11 Asian Americans or Pacific Islanders, 7 Hispanic Americans), 3 international. Average age 27. 423 applicants, 28% accepted, 56 enrolled. In 2007, 42 master's, 27 doctorates, 8 other advanced degrees awarded. Terminal master's awarded for partial completion of doctoral program. *Degree requirements:* For master's, comprehensive exam, thesis optional, internship; for doctorate, comprehensive exam, thesis/dissertation, oral defense. *Entrance requirements:* For master's, GRE, interview, essay, minimum GPA; for doctorate, GRE General Test, GRE Subject Test (psychology), letters of recommendation, interview, essay. Additional exam requirements/recommendations for international students: Required—TOEFL (minimum score 550 paper-based; 213 computer-based). *Application deadline:* For fall admission, 1/15 priority date for domestic and international students. Application fee: $60. Electronic applications accepted. *Expenses:* Tuition: Full-time $14,220; part-time $820 per credit. Required fees: $970; $165 per term. Tuition and fees vary according to program. *Financial support:* In 2007–08, 147 students received support, including 96 fellowships with tuition reimbursements available (averaging $5,621 per year), 10 research assistantships with full and partial tuition reimbursements available (averaging $9,567 per year); career-related internships or fieldwork, Federal Work-Study, scholarships/grants, tuition waivers (full and partial), and unspecified assistantships also available. Support available to part-time students. Financial award applicants required to submit FAFSA. *Faculty research:* Treatment of anger; performance management; childhood and adult trauma; organizational health; virtual reality treatment of phobias. Total annual research expenditures: $130,000. *Unit head:* Dr. Charles Levinthal, Chairperson, 516-463-5627, Fax: 516-463-6052, E-mail: psycfl@hofstra.edu. *Application contact:* Carol Drummer, Dean of Graduate Admissions, 516-463-4876, Fax: 516-463-4664, E-mail: gradstudent@hofstra.edu.

Hood College, Graduate School, Programs in Human Sciences, Frederick, MD 21701-8575. Offers human sciences (MA); thanatology (MA, Certificate). Part-time and evening/weekend programs available. *Degree requirements:* For master's, comprehensive exam, thesis or alternative. *Entrance requirements:* For master's, minimum GPA of 2.5. *Faculty research:* Mind-body medicine and multicultural healing, the New Orleans jazz funeral, death practices in African-American culture, bereavement theories and gender differences, Piaget's theory of cognitive development as a formal mathematical model.

Houston Baptist University, College of Education and Behavioral Sciences, Program in Psychology, Houston, TX 77074-3298. Offers MAP. Part-time and evening/weekend programs available. *Faculty:* 5 full-time (3 women), 8 part-time/adjunct (7 women). *Students:* 50 full-time (45 women), 24 part-time (20 women); includes 30 minority (13 African Americans, 2 American Indian/Alaska Native, 4 Asian Americans or Pacific Islanders, 11 Hispanic Americans), 3 international. Average age 31. 42 applicants, 74% accepted, 14 enrolled. In 2007, 25 degrees awarded. *Degree requirements:* For master's, comprehensive exam. *Entrance requirements:* For master's, GRE General Test, minimum GPA of 3.0. Additional exam requirements/recommendations for international students: Required—TOEFL (minimum score 550 paper-based; 213 computer-based). *Application deadline:* For fall admission, 7/1 priority date for domestic and international students; for winter admission, 10/1 priority date for domestic and international students; for spring admission, 1/1 priority date for domestic and international students. Applications are processed on a rolling basis. Application fee: $25 ($100 for international students). *Expenses:* Tuition: Part-time $1,416 per course. Required fees: $190 per quarter. *Financial support:* Federal Work-Study available. Support available to part-time students. Financial award application deadline: 3/1; financial award applicants required to submit FAFSA. *Unit head:* Dr. Renata Nero, Director, 281-649-3000 Ext. 2436, Fax: 281-649-3361, E-mail: rnero@hbu.edu. *Application contact:* Becky Greer, Secretary, 281-649-3000 Ext. 3095, Fax: 281-649-3361, E-mail: bgreer@hbu.edu.

Howard University, Graduate School, Department of Psychology, Washington, DC 20059-0002. Offers clinical psychology (PhD); developmental psychology (PhD); experimental psychology (PhD); neuropsychology (PhD); personality psychology (PhD); psychology (MS); social psychology (PhD). *Accreditation:* APA (one or more programs are accredited). Part-time programs available. *Degree requirements:* For master's, thesis; for doctorate, comprehensive exam, thesis/dissertation, qualifying exam. *Entrance requirements:* For master's, GRE General Test, minimum GPA of 2.5, bachelor's degree in psychology or related field; for doctorate, GRE General Test, minimum GPA of 3.0. *Expenses:* Tuition: Full-time $16,175; part-time $899 per credit hour. Required fees: $805. *Faculty research:* Personality and psychophysiology, educational and social development of African-American children, child and adult psychopathology.

Humboldt State University, Graduate Studies, College of Natural Resources and Sciences, Department of Psychology, Arcata, CA 95521-8299. Offers MA. *Students:* 59 full-time (49 women), 11 part-time (8 women); includes 14 minority (1 African American, 3 American Indian/Alaska Native, 3 Asian Americans or Pacific Islanders, 7 Hispanic Americans). Average age 30. 71 applicants, 45% accepted, 26 enrolled. In 2007, 14 degrees awarded. *Degree requirements:* For master's, thesis. *Entrance requirements:* For master's, appropriate bachelor's degree, minimum GPA of 2.5. Additional exam requirements/recommendations for international students: Required—TOEFL (minimum score 500 paper-based; 173 computer-based). *Application deadline:* For fall admission, 2/15 for domestic and international students. Applications are processed on a rolling basis. Application fee: $55. *Financial support:* Career-related internships or fieldwork available. Financial award application deadline: 3/1; financial award applicants required to submit FAFSA. *Faculty research:* School psychology, counseling, eating disorders, mood induction, depression. *Unit head:* Dr. Sengi Hu, Chair, 707-826-3755, Fax: 707-826-4993, E-mail: sh4@humboldt.edu.

Hunter College of the City University of New York, Graduate School, School of Arts and Sciences, Department of Psychology, New York, NY 10021-5085. Offers applied and evaluative psychology (MA); biopsychology and comparative psychology (MA); social, cognitive, and developmental psychology (MA). Part-time and evening/weekend programs available. *Faculty:* 8 full-time (2 women), 4 part-time/adjunct (2 women). *Students:* 7 full-time (5 women), 68 part-time (57 women); includes 10 minority (2 African Americans, 1 Asian American or Pacific Islander, 7 Hispanic Americans). Average age 29. 100 applicants, 47% accepted, 21 enrolled. In 2007, 30 degrees awarded. *Degree requirements:* For master's, comprehensive exam, thesis. *Entrance requirements:* For master's, GRE General Test, minimum 12 credits of course work in psychology, including statistics and experimental psychology; 2 letters of recommendation. Additional exam requirements/recommendations for international students: Required—TOEFL. *Application deadline:* For fall admission, 4/1 for domestic students, 2/1 for international students; for spring admission, 11/1 for domestic students, 9/1 for international students. Applications are processed on a rolling basis. Application fee: $125. *Expenses:* Tuition, state resident: full-time $6,400; part-time $270 per credit. Tuition, nonresident: part-time $500 per credit. One-time fee: $125 full-time. Tuition and fees vary according to program. *Financial support:* Federal Work-Study, scholarships/grants, and tuition waivers (partial) available. Support available to part-time students. *Faculty research:* Personality, cognitive and linguistic development, hormonal and neural control of behavior, gender and culture, social cognition of health and attitudes. *Unit head:* Dr. Gordon A. Barr, Acting Chair, 212-772-5550. *Application contact:* William Zlata, Director for Graduate Admissions, 212-772-4482, Fax: 212-650-3336, E-mail: admissions@hunter.cuny.edu.

Idaho State University, Office of Graduate Studies, College of Arts and Sciences, Department of Psychology, Pocatello, ID 83209. Offers clinical psychology (PhD); psychology (MS). *Accreditation:* APA (one or more programs are accredited). Part-time programs available. *Faculty:* 9 full-time (4 women). *Students:* 31 full-time (23 women), 10 part-time (8 women); includes 1 minority (Hispanic American), 2 international. Average age 28. In 2007, 9 master's, 4 doctorates awarded. *Degree requirements:* For master's, comprehensive exam, thesis, active participation in the research process; for doctorate, comprehensive exam, thesis/dissertation, 1 year full-time clinical internship. *Entrance requirements:* For master's, GRE General Test, GRE Subject Test, BS in psychology, minimum GPA of 3.0 in last 2 years of undergraduate courses; for doctorate, GRE General Test, GRE Subject Test, MS in psychology, recommendation from Clinical Admissions Committee. Additional exam requirements/recommendations for international students: Required—TOEFL (minimum score 550 paper-based; 213 computer-based; 80 iBT). *Application deadline:* For fall admission, 7/1 for domestic students, 6/1 for international students; for spring admission, 12/1 for domestic students, 11/1 for international students. Applications are processed on a rolling basis. Application fee: $55. Electronic applications accepted. *Expenses:* Tuition, state resident: full-time $2,882; part-time $259 per credit hour. Tuition, nonresident: full-time $11,566; part-time $379 per credit hour. Required fees: $2,278. Full-time tuition and fees vary according to program. Part-time tuition and fees vary according to course load. *Financial support:* In 2007–08, 9 research assistantships with full and partial tuition reimbursements (averaging $9,128 per year), 17 teaching assistantships with full and partial tuition reimbursements (averaging $9,128 per year) were awarded; career-related internships or fieldwork, Federal Work-Study, institutionally sponsored loans, scholarships/grants, traineeships, health care benefits, tuition waivers (full and partial), and unspecified assistantships also available. Support available to part-time students. Financial award application deadline: 1/1; financial award applicants required to submit FAFSA. *Faculty research:* Decision making, social psychology, personality and affective disorders, marital satisfaction, child pathology. *Unit head:* Dr. Kandi Turley-Ames, Chairman, 208-282-2462, Fax: 208-282-4832, E-mail: turlkand@isu.edu. *Application contact:* Ellen Combs, Graduate School Technical Records Specialist, 208-282-2150, Fax: 208-282-4847.

Illinois Institute of Technology, Graduate College, Institute of Psychology, Chicago, IL 60616-3793. Offers clinical psychology (PhD); industrial/organizational psychology (PhD); personnel/human resource development (MS); psychology (MS); rehabilitation counseling (MS); rehabilitation counselor education (PhD). *Accreditation:* APA (one or more programs are accredited); CORE. Evening/weekend programs available. *Faculty:* 18 full-time (8 women), 4 part-time/adjunct (2 women). *Students:* 122 full-time (95 women), 66 part-time (45 women); includes 44 minority (15 African Americans, 1 American Indian/Alaska Native, 17 Asian Americans or Pacific Islanders, 11 Hispanic Americans), 22 international. Average age 29. 261 applicants, 34% accepted, 32 enrolled. In 2007, 31 master's, 12 doctorates awarded. Terminal master's awarded for partial completion of doctoral program. *Degree requirements:* For master's, comprehensive exam, thesis (for some programs); for doctorate, comprehensive exam, thesis/dissertation, qualifying exams. *Entrance requirements:* For master's, GRE General Test, minimum GPA of 3.0; for doctorate, GRE General Test, minimum GPA of 3.2. Additional exam requirements/recommendations for international students: Required—TOEFL (minimum score 550 paper-based; 213 computer-based; 80 iBT). *Application deadline:* For fall admission, 1/15 for domestic and international students. Application fee: $40. Electronic applications accepted. *Expenses:* Tuition: Full-time $14,004; part-time $778 per credit. Required fees: $7 per credit. $235 per term. Tuition and fees vary according to class time, course level, course load, program and student level. *Financial support:* In 2007–08, 39 fellowships with partial tuition reimbursements (averaging $2,798 per year), 1 research assistantship with partial tuition reimbursement, 24 teaching assistantships with partial tuition reimbursements (averaging $4,405 per year) were awarded; career-related internships or fieldwork, Federal Work-Study, institutionally sponsored loans, scholarships/grants, traineeships, health care benefits, tuition waivers (partial), and unspecified assistantships also available. Support available to part-time students. Financial award applicants required to submit FAFSA. *Faculty research:* Stigma and mental illness, depression, couples communication, leadership, psychometric theory. Total annual research expenditures: $636,382. *Unit head:* Dr. M. Ellen Mitchell, Dean, 312-567-3362, Fax: 312-567-3493, E-mail: mitchelle@iit.edu. *Application contact:* Application Contact, 312-567-3500, Fax: 312-567-3493, E-mail: psychology@iit.edu.

Illinois State University, Graduate School, College of Arts and Sciences, Department of Psychology, Normal, IL 61790-2200. Offers psychology (MA, MS), including clinical psychology, counseling psychology, developmental psychology, educational psychology, experimental psychology, measurement-evaluation, organizational-industrial psychology; school psychology (PhD, SSP). *Accreditation:* APA. *Faculty:* 36 full-time (14 women). *Students:* 49 full-time (37 women), 19 part-time (14 women); includes 3 minority (all Asian Americans or Pacific Islanders), 7 international. 91 applicants, 43% accepted. In 2007, 24 degrees awarded. *Degree requirements:* For master's, thesis or alternative; for doctorate, variable foreign language requirement, thesis/dissertation, 2 terms of residency, internship, practicum. *Entrance requirements:* For master's, GRE General Test, GRE Subject Test, minimum GPA of 3.0 in last 60 hours of course work; for doctorate, GRE General Test. *Application deadline:* Applications are processed on a rolling basis. Application fee: $40. *Expenses:* Tuition, state resident: full-time $3,492; part-time $194 per credit hour. Tuition, nonresident: full-time $7,272; part-time $404 per credit hour. Required fees: $1,024; $57 per credit hour. *Financial support:* In 2007–08, 33 research assistantships (averaging $6,252 per year), 49 teaching assistantships (averaging $4,217 per year) were awarded; tuition waivers (full) and unspecified assistantships also available. Financial award application deadline: 4/1. *Faculty research:* Comprehensive evaluation system for the central region professional development grant, Illinois school psychology internship consortium, for children's sake. Total annual research expenditures: $292,085. *Unit head:* Dr. Neil Skaggs, Acting Chairperson, 309-438-8651.

Immaculata University, College of Graduate Studies, Department of Psychology, Immaculata, PA 19345. Offers clinical psychology (Psy D); counseling psychology (MA, Certificate), including school guidance counselor (Certificate), school psychologist (Certificate). *Accreditation:* APA. Part-time and evening/weekend programs available. *Students:* 106 full-time (71 women), 207 part-time (194 women); includes 30 minority (20 African Americans, 6 Asian Americans or Pacific Islanders, 4 Hispanic Americans). Average age 34. 182 applicants, 62% accepted, 56 enrolled. In 2007, 38 master's, 10 doctorates awarded. *Degree requirements:* For master's, comprehensive exam, thesis optional; for doctorate, comprehensive exam, thesis/dissertation. *Entrance requirements:* For master's, GRE General Test or MAT, minimum GPA of 3.0; for doctorate, GRE General Test, minimum GPA of 3.5. Additional exam requirements/recommendations for international students: Required—TOEFL, IELTS. *Application deadline:*

Applications are processed on a rolling basis. Application fee: $35. *Financial support:* Application deadline: 5/1. *Faculty research:* Supervision ethics, psychology of teaching, gender. *Unit head:* Dr. Jed A. Yalof, Chair, 610-647-4400 Ext. 3503, Fax: 610-993-8550, E-mail: jyalof@immaculata.edu. *Application contact:* Office of Graduate Admission, 610-647-4400 Ext. 3211, Fax: 610-993-8550, E-mail: graduate@immaculata.edu.

Indiana State University, School of Graduate Studies, College of Arts and Sciences, Department of Psychology, Terre Haute, IN 47809-1401. Offers clinical psychology (Psy D); general psychology (MA, MS). *Accreditation:* APA (one or more programs are accredited). *Faculty:* 9 full-time (6 women), 4 part-time/adjunct (1 woman). *Students:* 39 full-time (23 women), 17 part-time (12 women); includes 6 minority (1 African American, 3 Asian Americans or Pacific Islanders, 2 Hispanic Americans), 1 international. Average age 28. 185 applicants, 9% accepted, 15 enrolled. In 2007, 12 master's, 6 doctorates awarded. Terminal master's awarded for partial completion of doctoral program. *Degree requirements:* For master's, thesis (for some programs); for doctorate, comprehensive exam, thesis/dissertation, internship, professional research project. *Entrance requirements:* For master's, GRE General Test, 12 semester hours of course work in psychology, minimum GPA of 2.75; for doctorate, GRE General Test, minimum GPA of 3.0. Additional exam requirements/recommendations for international students: Required—TOEFL (minimum score 550 paper-based). *Application deadline:* For fall admission, 2/1 for domestic students; for spring admission, 11/1 priority date for domestic students. Applications are processed on a rolling basis. Application fee: $35. Electronic applications accepted. *Expenses:* Tuition, state resident: full-time $7,056; part-time $294 per semester hour. Tuition, nonresident: full-time $14,016; part-time $584 per semester hour. Required fees: $175 per semester. *Financial support:* In 2007–08, 4 research assistantships with partial tuition reimbursements (averaging $7,000 per year), 22 teaching assistantships with partial tuition reimbursements (averaging $7,000 per year) were awarded; fellowships with partial tuition reimbursements, career-related internships or fieldwork, Federal Work-Study, institutionally sponsored loans, and tuition waivers (full) also available. Financial award application deadline: 3/1; financial award applicants required to submit FAFSA. *Unit head:* Dr. Virgil L. Sheets, Chairperson, 812-237-2456. *Application contact:* Application Contact, 812-237-2456.

Indiana University Bloomington, University Graduate School, College of Arts and Sciences, Department of Psychological and Brain Sciences, Bloomington, IN 47405-7000. Offers biology and behavior (PhD); clinical science (PhD); cognitive psychology (PhD); developmental psychology (PhD); psychological and brain sciences (MA); social psychology (PhD). *Accreditation:* APA (one or more programs are accredited). *Faculty:* 53 full-time (16 women). *Students:* 79 full-time (42 women), 14 part-time (7 women); includes 10 minority (3 African Americans, 3 Asian Americans or Pacific Islanders, 4 Hispanic Americans), 16 international. Average age 28. 240 applicants, 10% accepted, 20 enrolled. In 2007, 5 master's, 15 doctorates awarded. *Median time to degree:* Of those who began their doctoral program in fall 1999, 86% received their degree in 8 years or less. *Degree requirements:* For doctorate, comprehensive exam, thesis/dissertation, 1st and 2nd year projects, 1 year as associate instructor, qualifying exam, teaching. *Entrance requirements:* For doctorate, GRE. Additional exam requirements/recommendations for international students: Required—TOEFL (minimum score 550 paper-based; 213 computer-based). *Application deadline:* For fall admission, 12/15 for domestic students, 12/1 for international students. Application fee: $50 ($60 for international students). Electronic applications accepted. *Financial support:* Fellowships with full tuition reimbursements, research assistantships with full tuition reimbursements, teaching assistantships with full tuition reimbursements, scholarships/grants, health care benefits, and unspecified assistantships available. *Unit head:* Dr. Linda B. Smith, Chair, 812-855-3991, Fax: 812-855-4691, E-mail: smith4@indiana.edu. *Application contact:* Patricia G. Crouch, Academic Services Coordinator, 812-855-4528, Fax: 812-855-4691, E-mail: pcrouch@indiana.edu.

Indiana University of Pennsylvania, School of Graduate Studies and Research, College of Natural Sciences and Mathematics, Department of Psychology, Indiana, PA 15705-1087. Offers clinical psychology (Psy D); psychology (MA). *Accreditation:* APA (one or more programs are accredited). Part-time programs available. *Faculty:* 15 full-time (10 women). *Students:* 44 full-time (39 women), 25 part-time (19 women); includes 4 minority (1 African American, 1 Asian American or Pacific Islander, 2 Hispanic Americans). Average age 28. 97 applicants, 14% accepted, 13 enrolled. In 2007, 8 master's, 8 doctorates awarded. Terminal master's awarded for partial completion of doctoral program. *Degree requirements:* For doctorate, comprehensive exam, thesis/dissertation, internship, practicum. *Entrance requirements:* For master's, GRE General Test; for doctorate, GRE General Test, minimum GPA of 3.0, interview, letters of recommendation. Additional exam requirements/recommendations for international students: Required—TOEFL. *Application deadline:* For fall admission, 1/10 for domestic students. Applications are processed on a rolling basis. Application fee: $30. *Expenses:* Tuition, state resident: full-time $6,214; part-time $345 per credit. Tuition, nonresident: full-time $9,944; part-time $552 per credit. Required fees: $43 per credit. One-time fee: $140 part-time. Tuition and fees vary according to course load. *Financial support:* In 2007–08, 7 fellowships (averaging $1,000 per year), 39 research assistantships with full and partial tuition reimbursements (averaging $3,040 per year), 2 teaching assistantships (averaging $17,001 per year) were awarded; Federal Work-Study and scholarships/grants also available. Financial award application deadline: 3/15; financial award applicants required to submit FAFSA. *Unit head:* Dr. Mary Lou Zanich, Chairperson, 724-357-2426, E-mail: mtzanich@iup.edu. *Application contact:* Dr. Donald Robertson, Graduate Coordinator, 724-357-4522, E-mail: durobert@iup.edu.

Indiana University–Purdue University Indianapolis, School of Science, Department of Psychology, Indianapolis, IN 46202-3275. Offers clinical rehabilitation psychology (MS); industrial/organizational psychology (MS); psychobiology of addictions (MS, PhD). *Accreditation:* APA (one or more programs are accredited). *Faculty:* 10 full-time (2 women). *Students:* 21 full-time (19 women), 5 part-time (all women); includes 4 minority (2 African Americans, 2 Asian Americans or Pacific Islanders). Average age 26. In 2007, 7 degrees awarded. Terminal master's awarded for partial completion of doctoral program. *Degree requirements:* For master's, thesis; for doctorate, thesis/dissertation. *Entrance requirements:* For master's, GRE General Test, minimum undergraduate GPA of 3.0; for doctorate, GRE General Test, GRE Subject Test (clinical rehabilitation psychology), minimum undergraduate GPA of 3.2. *Application deadline:* For fall admission, 1/1 priority date for domestic students. Application fee: $50 ($60 for international students). *Expenses:* Tuition, state resident: full-time $5,818; part-time $242 per credit hour. Tuition, nonresident: full-time $17,106; part-time $713 per credit hour. Required fees: $629. Tuition and fees vary according to course load, campus/location and program. *Financial support:* In 2007–08, 5 fellowships with partial tuition reimbursements (averaging $12,218 per year), 23 teaching assistantships with partial tuition reimbursements (averaging $7,553 per year) were awarded; research assistantships with partial tuition reimbursements, career-related internships or fieldwork, Federal Work-Study, and institutionally sponsored loans also available. Financial award application deadline: 3/1; financial award applicants required to submit FAFSA. *Faculty research:* Psychiatric rehabilitation, chronic stress, neurological research, language and cognitive development in infants, alcoholism and psychopathology. *Unit head:* Dr. J. Gregor Fetterman, Chairman, 317-274-6945, Fax: 317-274-6756, E-mail: gfetter@iupui.edu.

Indiana University South Bend, College of Liberal Arts and Sciences, South Bend, IN 46634-7111. Offers applied mathematics and computer science (MS); applied psychology (MA); English (MA); liberal studies (MLS). Part-time and evening/weekend programs available. *Faculty:* 79 full-time (33 women). *Students:* 11 full-time (6 women), 71 part-time (44 women); includes 14 minority (8 African Americans, 1 American Indian/Alaska Native, 3 Asian Americans or Pacific Islanders, 2 Hispanic Americans), 8 international. Average age 37. In 2007, 24 degrees awarded. *Degree requirements:* For master's, thesis (for some programs). *Entrance requirements:* For master's, minimum GPA of 3.0. Additional exam requirements/recommendations for international students: Required—TOEFL. *Application deadline:* For fall admission, 7/31 priority date for domestic students, 7/1 priority date for international students; for spring admission, 3/31 priority date for domestic students, 11/1 priority date for international students. Applications are processed on a rolling basis. Application fee: $46 ($58 for international students). *Expenses:* Tuition, state resident: full-time $4,762; part-time $198 per credit hour. Tuition, nonresident: full-time $11,720; part-time $488 per credit hour. Required fees: $422; $422 per year. Full-time tuition and fees vary according to course load, campus/location and program. *Financial support:* In 2007–08, 5 students received support, including 5 teaching assistantships; Federal Work-Study also available. Support available to part-time students. *Faculty research:* Artificial intelligence, bioinformatics, English language and literature, creative writing, computer networks. Total annual research expenditures: $127,000. *Unit head:* Dr. Lynn R. Williams, Dean, 574-520-4322, Fax: 574-520-4528, E-mail: lwilliam@iusb.edu.

Institute of Transpersonal Psychology, Global Programs, Palo Alto, CA 94303. Offers psychology (PhD); transpersonal psychology (MTP); transpersonal studies (Certificate). Post-baccalaureate distance learning degree programs offered (minimal on-campus study). *Faculty:* 8 full-time (4 women), 26 part-time/adjunct (19 women). *Students:* 154 full-time (123 women), 32 part-time (25 women); includes 29 minority (9 African Americans, 2 American Indian/Alaska Native, 5 Asian Americans or Pacific Islanders, 13 Hispanic Americans), 20 international. Average age 44. 112 applicants, 88% accepted, 80 enrolled. In 2007, 19 master's, 8 doctorates awarded. Terminal master's awarded for partial completion of doctoral program. *Degree requirements:* For master's, thesis (for some programs); for doctorate, thesis/dissertation. *Entrance requirements:* For master's and doctorate, bachelor's degree. Additional exam requirements/recommendations for international students: Required—TOEFL. *Application deadline:* Applications are processed on a rolling basis. Application fee: $55. *Expenses:* *Contact institution.* Tuition and fees vary according to degree level and student level. *Financial support:* In 2007–08, 68 students received support. Federal Work-Study and scholarships/grants available. Support available to part-time students. Financial award application deadline: 6/30; financial award applicants required to submit FAFSA. *Unit head:* Dr. Paul Roy, Academic Vice President, 650-493-4430 Ext. 243, Fax: 650-493-6835, E-mail: proy@itp.edu. *Application contact:* Hana Schneider, Admissions Assistant, 650-493-4430 Ext. 240, Fax: 650-493-6835, E-mail: itpinfo@itp.edu.

Institute of Transpersonal Psychology, Residential Programs, Palo Alto, CA 94303. Offers clinical psychology (PhD); counseling psychology (MA); transpersonal psychology (MA, PhD); women's spirituality (PhD). Part-time and evening/weekend programs available. *Faculty:* 17 full-time (9 women), 31 part-time/adjunct (18 women). *Students:* 239 full-time (164 women), 48 part-time (33 women); includes 46 minority (8 African Americans, 4 American Indian/Alaska Native, 18 Asian Americans or Pacific Islanders, 16 Hispanic Americans), 16 international. Average age 38. 132 applicants, 80% accepted, 79 enrolled. In 2007, 47 master's, 16 doctorates awarded. Terminal master's awarded for partial completion of doctoral program. *Degree requirements:* For doctorate, thesis/dissertation. *Entrance requirements:* For master's and doctorate, bachelor's degree. *Application deadline:* For fall admission, 2/15 priority date for domestic students. Applications are processed on a rolling basis. Application fee: $55. *Expenses:* Tuition: Full-time $11,877; part-time $3,959 per quarter. Tuition and fees vary according to degree level and student level. *Financial support:* In 2007–08, 178 students received support; teaching assistantships, career-related internships or fieldwork, Federal Work-Study, and scholarships/grants available. Support available to part-time students. Financial award application deadline: 7/1; financial award applicants required to submit FAFSA. *Unit head:* Dr. Paul Roy, Academic Vice President, 650-493-4430 Ext. 243, Fax: 650-493-6835, E-mail: proy@itp.edu. *Application contact:* 650-493-4430 Ext. 16, Fax: 650-493-6835, E-mail: itpinfo@itp.edu.

See Close-Up on page 1439.

Instituto Tecnologico de Santo Domingo, Graduate School, Santo Domingo, Dominican Republic. Offers applied linguistics (MA); corporate finance (M Mgmt); education (M Ed); engineering (M Eng), including data telecommunications, industrial engineering, sanitary and environmental engineering, structural engineering; environmental science (M En S), including environmental education, environmental management, marine and coastal ecosystems, natural resources management; human resources administration (M Mgmt); management (M Mgmt); psychology (MA); social science (M Ed). *Entrance requirements:* For master's, birth certificate, minimum GPA of 2.0.

Inter American University of Puerto Rico, Metropolitan Campus, School of Psychology, San Juan, PR 00919-1293. Offers MA. *Degree requirements:* For master's, comprehensive exam. *Entrance requirements:* For master's, GRE or EXADEP, interview. Electronic applications accepted.

Inter American University of Puerto Rico, San Germán Campus, Graduate Studies Center, Program in Psychology, San Germán, PR 00683-5008. Offers counseling psychology (MA, PhD); school psychology (MA, PhD). Part-time and evening/weekend programs available. *Faculty:* 8 full-time, 24 part-time/adjunct. *Students:* 223. In 2007, 51 master's, 2 doctorates awarded. *Degree requirements:* For master's, comprehensive exam, thesis; for doctorate, comprehensive exam, thesis/dissertation. *Entrance requirements:* For master's, GRE General Test or EXADEP, minimum GPA of 3.0; for doctorate, GRE, EXADEP or MAT, minimum GPA of 3.0. *Application deadline:* For fall admission, 4/30 priority date for domestic students; for spring admission, 11/15 for domestic students. Applications are processed on a rolling basis. Application fee: $31. *Expenses:* Tuition: Full-time $3,258; part-time $181 per credit. Required fees: $258 per semester. Tuition and fees vary according to degree level. *Financial support:* Teaching assistantships, unspecified assistantships available. *Application contact:* Dr. Ines Canabel, Program Coordinator, 787-264-1912 Ext. 7646, Fax: 787-892-7510, E-mail: icanabal@sg.intev.edu.

Iona College, School of Arts and Science, Department of Psychology, New Rochelle, NY 10801-1890. Offers experimental psychology (MA); industrial-organizational psychology (MA); mental health counseling (MA); psychology (MA); school psychology (MA). Part-time and evening/weekend programs available. *Faculty:* 12 full-time (6 women), 5 part-time/adjunct (2 women). *Students:* 77 full-time (62 women), 21 part-time (19 women); includes 19 minority (5 African Americans, 2 Asian Americans or Pacific Islanders, 12 Hispanic Americans). Average age 25. 105 applicants, 66% accepted, 33 enrolled. In 2007, 29 degrees awarded. *Degree requirements:* For master's, thesis. *Entrance requirements:* For master's, GRE or minimum GPA of 3.0. Additional exam requirements/recommendations for international students: Required—TOEFL (minimum score 550 paper-based; 213 computer-based). *Application deadline:* Applications are processed on a rolling basis. Application fee: $50. Electronic applications accepted. *Expenses:* Tuition: Part-time $712 per credit. Required fees: $150 per term. *Financial support:* Career-related internships or fieldwork, tuition waivers (partial), and unspecified assistantships available. Support available to part-time students. *Unit head:* Dr. Pauline Jirik-Babb, Chair, 914-633-2191, E-mail: pjirikbabb@iona.edu. *Application contact:* Veronica Jarek-Prinz, Director of Graduate Admissions, 914-633-2420, Fax: 914-633-2277, E-mail: vjarekprinz@iona.edu.

Iowa State University of Science and Technology, Graduate College, College of Liberal Arts and Sciences, Department of Psychology, Ames, IA 50011. Offers cognitive psychology (PhD); counseling psychology (PhD); social psychology (PhD). *Accreditation:* APA. *Faculty:* 25 full-time (8 women), 8 part-time/adjunct (4 women). *Students:* 63 full-time (43 women); includes 10 minority (3 African Americans, 7 Asian Americans or Pacific Islanders), 4 international. Average age 26. 117 applicants, 14% accepted, 11 enrolled. In 2007, 8 doctorates awarded. Terminal master's awarded for partial completion of doctoral program. *Median time to degree:* Of those who began their doctoral program in fall 1999, 100% received their degree in 8 years or less. *Degree requirements:* For doctorate, thesis/dissertation. *Entrance requirements:* For doctorate, GRE General Test, GRE Subject Test (psychology). Additional exam requirements/recommendations for international students: Required—TOEFL (minimum score 560 paper-based; 220 computer-based). *Application deadline:* For fall admission, 1/5 priority date for domestic and international students. Application fee: $30 ($70 for international students). Electronic applications accepted. *Financial support:* In 2007–08, 45 students received support, including 2 fellowships with full tuition reimbursements available (averaging $14,055 per year), 13 research assistantships with full tuition reimbursements available (averaging $12,200 per

Psychology—General

Iowa State University of Science and Technology (continued)
year), 30 teaching assistantships with full tuition reimbursements available (averaging $12,200 per year); scholarships/grants, health care benefits, and unspecified assistantships also available. *Faculty research:* Counseling psychology, cognitive psychology, social psychology, health psychology, psychology and public policy. Total annual research expenditures: $2 million. *Unit head:* Dr. David L Vogel, Director of Graduate Education, 515-294-1742, Fax: 515-294-6424, E-mail: dvogel@iastate.edu. *Application contact:* Ann K Schmidt, Graduate Admissions Secretary, 515-294-1743, Fax: 515-294-6424, E-mail: psychadm@iastate.edu.

Jackson State University, Graduate School, School of Liberal Arts, Department of Psychology, Jackson, MS 39217. Offers clinical psychology (PhD). *Accreditation:* APA. *Degree requirements:* For doctorate, comprehensive exam, thesis/dissertation. *Entrance requirements:* For doctorate, MAT, GRE.

Jacksonville State University, College of Graduate Studies and Continuing Education, College of Arts and Sciences, Department of Psychology, Jacksonville, AL 36265-1602. Offers MS. *Faculty:* 10 full-time (6 women), 3 part-time/adjunct (1 woman). *Students:* 18 full-time (14 women), 20 part-time (14 women); includes 7 minority (6 African Americans, 1 Hispanic American), 3 international. In 2007, 6 degrees awarded. *Degree requirements:* For master's, thesis optional. *Entrance requirements:* For master's, GRE General Test or MAT. *Application deadline:* Applications are processed on a rolling basis. Application fee: $20. *Financial support:* Available to part-time students. Application deadline: 4/1. *Unit head:* Dr. Steven Dworkin, Interim Department Head, 256-782-5804. *Application contact:* 256-782-5329, Fax: 256-782-5321, E-mail: graduate@jsu.edu.

James Madison University, The Graduate School, College of Integrated Science and Technology, Department of Graduate Psychology, Harrisonburg, VA 22807. Offers assessment and measurement (PhD); college student personnel administration (M Ed); combined-integrated clinical and school psychology (Psy D); community counseling psychology (MA, Ed S); psychological sciences (MA); school counseling (Ed S); school psychology (M Ed, MA, Ed S), including school counseling (M Ed, Ed S), school psychology (MA, Ed S). *Accreditation:* ACA (one or more programs are accredited); APA (one or more programs are accredited). Part-time and evening/weekend programs available. *Faculty:* 29 full-time (15 women), 13 part-time/adjunct (8 women). *Students:* 119 full-time (88 women), 56 part-time (40 women); includes 19 minority (12 African Americans, 5 Asian Americans or Pacific Islanders, 2 Hispanic Americans), 6 international. Average age 27. In 2007, 43 master's, 5 doctorates, 21 other advanced degrees awarded. *Degree requirements:* For doctorate, thesis/dissertation; for Ed S, thesis. *Entrance requirements:* For master's, GRE General Test, GRE Subject Test; for doctorate, GRE General Test. Additional exam requirements/recommendations for international students: Required—TOEFL. *Application deadline:* For fall admission, 2/1 priority date for domestic students; for spring admission, 9/1 for domestic students. Applications are processed on a rolling basis. Application fee: $55. Electronic applications accepted. *Expenses:* Tuition, state resident: full-time $6,720; part-time $280 per credit hour. Tuition, nonresident: full-time $19,104; part-time $796 per credit hour. *Financial support:* In 2007–08, 91 students received support, including 3 teaching assistantships with full tuition reimbursements available (averaging $8,494 per year); research assistantships, career-related internships or fieldwork, Federal Work-Study, unspecified assistantships, and 88 assistantships also available. Financial award application deadline: 3/1; financial award applicants required to submit FAFSA. *Unit head:* Sheena J. Rogers, Academic Unit Head, 540-568-6439, Fax: 540-568-3322, E-mail: rogerssj@cisat.jmu.edu.

John F. Kennedy University, Graduate School of Holistic Studies, Department of Integral Studies, Program in Integral Psychology, Pleasant Hill, CA 94523-4817. Offers dream studies (Certificate); integral psychology (MA); life coaching (Certificate). Part-time and evening/weekend programs available.

John F. Kennedy University, Graduate School of Professional Psychology, Pleasant Hill, CA 94523-4817. Offers MA, Psy D, Certificate. *Accreditation:* APA. Part-time and evening/weekend programs available. *Degree requirements:* For master's, thesis or alternative. *Entrance requirements:* For master's, interview. Additional exam requirements/recommendations for international students: Required—TOEFL.

The Johns Hopkins University, Zanvyl Krieger School of Arts and Sciences, Department of Psychological and Brain Sciences, Baltimore, MD 21218-2699. Offers PhD. *Faculty:* 12 full-time (4 women), 12 part-time/adjunct (3 women). *Students:* 24 full-time (10 women); includes 5 minority (1 African American, 3 Asian Americans or Pacific Islanders, 1 Hispanic American), 2 international. Average age 24. 94 applicants, 12% accepted, 4 enrolled. In 2007, 5 doctorates awarded. *Median time to degree:* Of those who began their doctoral program in fall 1999, 100% received their degree in 8 years or less. *Degree requirements:* For doctorate, thesis/dissertation, research project, teaching experience. *Entrance requirements:* For doctorate, GRE General Test, GRE Subject Test. Additional exam requirements/recommendations for international students: Required—TOEFL. *Application deadline:* For fall admission, 12/15 priority date for domestic students. Application fee: $75. Electronic applications accepted. *Financial support:* In 2007–08, 8 fellowships with tuition reimbursements (averaging $28,000 per year), 2 research assistantships (averaging $18,500 per year), 13 teaching assistantships with tuition reimbursements (averaging $16,000 per year) were awarded; Federal Work-Study, tuition waivers (full), and unspecified assistantships also available. Financial award application deadline: 4/15; financial award applicants required to submit FAFSA. *Faculty research:* Bio-psychology, cognitive psychology, cognitive neuroscience, developmental psychology, neurobiology. Total annual research expenditures: $4.7 million. *Unit head:* Dr. Peter Holland, Chair, 410-516-6396, Fax: 410-516-4478, E-mail: psychair@jhu.edu. *Application contact:* Hope Stein, Admissions Coordinator, 410-516-6175, Fax: 410-516-4478, E-mail: hope.stein@jhu.edu.

Kansas State University, Graduate School, College of Arts and Sciences, Department of Psychology, Manhattan, KS 66506. Offers MS, PhD. Part-time programs available. *Faculty:* 12 full-time (3 women), 2 part-time/adjunct (0 women). *Students:* 61 full-time (36 women), 42 part-time (28 women); includes 12 minority (5 African Americans, 2 Asian Americans or Pacific Islanders, 5 Hispanic Americans), 6 international. Average age 24. 100 applicants, 19% accepted, 8 enrolled. In 2007, 16 master's, 3 doctorates awarded. *Degree requirements:* For master's, thesis or alternative; for doctorate, thesis/dissertation, preliminary exam. *Entrance requirements:* For master's, GRE General Test, minimum undergraduate GPA of 3.0; for doctorate, GRE General Test, minimum GPA of 3.0. Additional exam requirements/recommendations for international students: Required—TOEFL (minimum score 600 paper-based; 250 computer-based). *Application deadline:* For fall admission, 2/1 priority date for domestic and international students; for spring admission, 10/1 for domestic students, 8/1 priority date for international students. Applications are processed on a rolling basis. Application fee: $30 ($55 for international students). Electronic applications accepted. *Financial support:* In 2007–08, 7 research assistantships (averaging $11,694 per year), 20 teaching assistantships with full tuition reimbursements (averaging $10,015 per year) were awarded; fellowships, career-related internships or fieldwork, institutionally sponsored loans, and scholarships/grants also available. Support available to part-time students. Financial award application deadline: 3/1; financial award applicants required to submit FAFSA. *Faculty research:* Behavioral neuroscience, human factors, industrial/organizational psychology, social/personality psychology, health psychology. Total annual research expenditures: $362,463. *Unit head:* Jerry Frieman, Head, 785-532-0607, Fax: 785-532-5401, E-mail: frieman@ksu.edu. *Application contact:* Clive Fullagar, Director, 785-532-0608, Fax: 785-532-5401, E-mail: fullagar@ksu.edu.

Kent State University, College of Arts and Sciences, Department of Psychology, Kent, OH 44242-0001. Offers clinical psychology (MA, PhD); experimental psychology (MA, PhD). *Accreditation:* APA (one or more programs are accredited). *Faculty:* 28 full-time (12 women). *Students:* 119 full-time (87 women). 324 applicants, 7% accepted. In 2007, 16 master's, 16 doctorates awarded. *Degree requirements:* For master's, thesis; for doctorate, thesis/dissertation. *Entrance requirements:* For master's, GRE, minimum GPA of 3.0, minimum 18 semester hours in psychology with one course in statistics and one experimental course with a lab component; for doctorate, GRE, minimum GPA of 3.0. Additional exam requirements/recommendations for international students: Required—TOEFL (minimum score 525 paper-based), Michigan English Language Assessment Battery (minimum score: 77). *Application deadline:* For fall admission, 1/1 for domestic and international students. Application fee: $30. *Financial support:* Fellowships, research assistantships, teaching assistantships, career-related internships or fieldwork, Federal Work-Study, institutionally sponsored loans, health care benefits, and tuition waivers (full) available. Financial award application deadline: 1/1. *Unit head:* Dr. Mary Ann Parris Stephens, Chair, 330-672-2027, Fax: 330-672-3786, E-mail: mstephen@kent.edu. *Application contact:* Jack Graham, Coordinator of Graduate Studies, E-mail: jgraham@kent.edu.

Lakehead University, Graduate Studies, Department of Psychology, Thunder Bay, ON P7B 5E1, Canada. Offers clinical psychology (MA, PhD); experimental psychology (MA). Part-time and evening/weekend programs available. *Degree requirements:* For master's, thesis optional; for doctorate, thesis/dissertation, 2 comprehensive exams, internship. *Entrance requirements:* For master's, GRE, honors degree in psychology, advanced course work in statistics, minimum B average; for doctorate, GRE, minimum B average. Additional exam requirements/recommendations for international students: Required—TOEFL. *Faculty research:* Chaos theory, health psychology, counseling psychology, gerontology, women's studies.

Lamar University, College of Graduate Studies, College of Arts and Sciences, Department of Psychology, Beaumont, TX 77710. Offers community/clinical psychology (MS); industrial/organizational psychology (MS). Part-time programs available. *Faculty:* 6 full-time (3 women). *Students:* 19 full-time (11 women), 10 part-time (8 women); includes 6 minority (2 African Americans, 1 Asian American or Pacific Islander, 3 Hispanic Americans), 1 international. Average age 25. 37 applicants, 43% accepted, 10 enrolled. In 2007, 6 degrees awarded. *Degree requirements:* For master's, thesis, practicum. *Entrance requirements:* For master's, GRE General Test, minimum GPA of 2.75 in last 60 hours of undergraduate course work. Additional exam requirements/recommendations for international students: Required—TOEFL. *Application deadline:* For fall admission, 8/1 for domestic students; for spring admission, 12/1 for domestic students. Application fee: $25 ($50 for international students). *Expenses:* Tuition, state resident: part-time $348 per semester hour. Tuition, nonresident: part-time $626 per semester hour. Tuition and fees vary according to course load. *Financial support:* In 2007–08, 12 students received support, including 3 teaching assistantships (averaging $4,500 per year); fellowships, research assistantships, career-related internships or fieldwork, Federal Work-Study, scholarships/grants, and tuition waivers (partial) also available. Support available to part-time students. Financial award application deadline: 4/1. *Faculty research:* Groupthink, health psychology, school psychology, behavioral neuroscience. *Unit head:* Dr. Oney D. Fitzpatrick, Chair, 409-880-8285, Fax: 409-880-1779, E-mail: fitzpatrod@hal.lamar.edu.

La Salle University, School of Arts and Sciences, Program in Psychology, Philadelphia, PA 19141-1199. Offers clinical psychology (Psy D); family psychology (Psy D); rehabilitation psychology (Psy D). Part-time and evening/weekend programs available. *Faculty:* 8 full-time (4 women), 5 part-time/adjunct (2 women). *Students:* 91 full-time (80 women), 18 part-time (11 women); includes 13 minority (6 African Americans, 4 Asian Americans or Pacific Islanders, 3 Hispanic Americans), 1 international. Average age 27. 111 applicants, 48% accepted, 23 enrolled. In 2007, 21 doctorates awarded. *Entrance requirements:* For doctorate, GRE, minimum GPA of 3.0. *Application deadline:* For fall admission, 3/1 for domestic students. Application fee: $35. *Expenses:* Contact institution. Tuition and fees vary according to program. *Financial support:* In 2007–08, 94 students received support. Scholarships/grants available. Financial award applicants required to submit FAFSA. *Faculty research:* Cognitive therapy, attribution theory, treatment of addiction. *Unit head:* Dr. Frank Gardner, Director, 215-951-5016, Fax: 215-951-1351.

Leadership Institute of Seattle, School of Applied Behavioral Science, Kenmore, WA 98028-4966. Offers consulting and coaching in organizations (MA); systems counseling (MA). *Degree requirements:* For master's, thesis (for some programs), oral exams. *Entrance requirements:* For master's, bachelor's degree from an accredited university or college.

Lehigh University, College of Arts and Sciences, Department of Psychology, Bethlehem, PA 18015-3094. Offers human cognition and development (MS, PhD). *Faculty:* 10 full-time (7 women). *Students:* 17 full-time (12 women), 17 part-time (12 women), 4 international. Average age 25. 57 applicants, 21% accepted, 4 enrolled. In 2007, 4 master's, 1 doctorate awarded. *Degree requirements:* For doctorate, comprehensive exam, thesis/dissertation. *Entrance requirements:* For doctorate, GRE General Test. Additional exam requirements/recommendations for international students: Required—TOEFL. *Application deadline:* For fall admission, 1/15 for domestic and international students. Application fee: $65. Electronic applications accepted. *Expenses:* Contact institution. *Financial support:* In 2007–08, 1 fellowship with full tuition reimbursement (averaging $20,000 per year), 4 research assistantships with full tuition reimbursements (averaging $15,100 per year), 11 teaching assistantships with full tuition reimbursements (averaging $15,100 per year) were awarded; scholarships/grants, tuition waivers (full and partial), and unspecified assistantships also available. Financial award application deadline: 1/15. *Faculty research:* Social-cognitive developmental psychology, cognition and language, social cognition. Total annual research expenditures: $258,519. *Unit head:* Diane Hyland, Chairperson, 610-758-3631, Fax: 610-758-6277, E-mail: dthl@lehigh.edu. *Application contact:* Dr. Ageliki Nicolopoulu, Program Director, 610-758-3630, Fax: 610-758-6277, E-mail: inpsy@lehigh.edu.

Lesley University, Graduate School of Arts and Social Sciences, Cambridge, MA 02138-2790. Offers clinical mental health counseling (MA), including expressive therapies counseling, holistic counseling, school and community counseling; counseling psychology (MA, CAGS), including professional counseling (MA), school counseling (MA); creative arts in learning (CAGS); creative writing (MFA); ecological teaching and learning (MS); environmental education (MS); expressive therapies (MA, PhD, CAGS), including art (MA), dance (MA), expressive therapies, music (MA); independent studies (CAGS); independent study (MA); intercultural relations (MA, CAGS); interdisciplinary studies (MA), including individualized studies, integrative holistic health, women's studies; visual arts (MFA). Part-time and evening/weekend programs available. Postbaccalaureate distance learning degree programs offered (minimal on-campus study). *Faculty:* 49 full-time (41 women), 185 part-time/adjunct (137 women). *Students:* 653 full-time (580 women), 1,972 part-time (1,795 women); includes 191 minority (103 African Americans, 11 American Indian/Alaska Native, 19 Asian Americans or Pacific Islanders, 58 Hispanic Americans), 61 international. Average age 37. 1,011 applicants, 87% accepted, 645 enrolled. In 2007, 1,107 master's, 1 doctorate, 3 other advanced degrees awarded. *Degree requirements:* For master's, internship, practicum, thesis (expressive therapies); for doctorate, thesis/dissertation, arts apprenticeship, field placement; for CAGS, thesis, internship (counseling psychology, expressive therapies). *Entrance requirements:* For master's, MAT (counseling psychology), interview, writing samples, art portfolio; for doctorate, GRE or MAT; for CAGS, interview, master's degree. Additional exam requirements/recommendations for international students: Required—TOEFL (minimum score 550 paper-based; 213 computer-based; 80 iBT). *Application deadline:* Applications are processed on a rolling basis. Application fee: $50. Electronic applications accepted. *Financial support:* In 2007–08, 64 students received support, including research assistantships (averaging $3,400 per year), 1 teaching assistantship (averaging $7,298 per year); career-related internships or fieldwork, Federal Work-Study, scholarships/grants, and unspecified assistantships also available. Support available to part-time students. Financial award application deadline: 4/15; financial award applicants required to submit FAFSA. *Faculty research:* Psychotherapy and culture; psychotherapy and psychological trauma; women's issues in art, teaching and psychotherapy; community based art, psycho-spiritual inquiry. *Unit head:* Dr. Julia Halevy, Dean, 617-349-8317, Fax: 617-349-8366, E-mail: jhalevy@lesley.edu. *Application contact:* Christina Murray, Senior Assistant Director, On-Campus Admissions, 617-349-8827, Fax: 617-349-8313, E-mail: cmurray3@lesley.edu.

Lipscomb University, Program in Counseling, Nashville, TN 37204-3951. Offers counseling psychology (Certificate); professional counseling (MS); psychology (MS). Part-time and evening/

weekend programs available. Postbaccalaureate distance learning degree programs offered (minimal on-campus study). *Faculty:* 3 full-time (1 woman), 1 part-time/adjunct (0 women). *Students:* 21 full-time (16 women), 8 part-time (5 women); includes 1 African American, 1 international. Average age 30. *Entrance requirements:* For master's, GRE, resumé, 3 reference letters, minimum GPA of 3.0. *Application deadline:* For fall admission, 3/1 for domestic students. Application fee: $25. Electronic applications accepted. *Expenses:* Tuition: Part-time $599 per semester hour. *Faculty research:* Cognitive psychology, neuroscience, health psychology, grief issues. *Unit head:* Dr. Roy Hamley, Co-Director, 615-966-5753, E-mail: roy.hamley@lipscomb.edu. *Application contact:* Elena Zemmel, Administrative Assistant, 615-966-5906, E-mail: elena.zemmel@lipscomb.edu.

Loma Linda University, School of Science and Technology, Department of Psychology, Loma Linda, CA 92350. Offers PhD, Psy D. *Accreditation:* APA. *Faculty:* 12 full-time (5 women), 30 part-time/adjunct (9 women). *Students:* 108 full-time (72 women), 26 part-time (17 women); includes 52 minority (9 African Americans, 22 Asian Americans or Pacific Islanders, 21 Hispanic Americans), 2 international. *Degree requirements:* For doctorate, comprehensive exam, thesis/dissertation. *Entrance requirements:* For doctorate, GRE General Test. Additional exam requirements/recommendations for international students: Required—TOEFL (minimum score 550 paper-based; 213 computer-based), MTELP. Application fee: $60. Electronic applications accepted. *Financial support:* Tuition waivers (full and partial) available. *Unit head:* Dr. Louis E. Jenkins, Chair, 909-824-8577.

Long Island University, Brooklyn Campus, Richard L. Conolly College of Liberal Arts and Sciences, Department of Psychology, Brooklyn, NY 11201-8423. Offers clinical psychology (PhD); psychology (MA). *Accreditation:* APA (one or more programs are accredited). Part-time and evening/weekend programs available. Terminal master's awarded for partial completion of doctoral program. *Degree requirements:* For master's, thesis or alternative; for doctorate, thesis/dissertation. *Entrance requirements:* For master's, GRE Subject Test, GRE General Test, 2 letters of recommendation; for doctorate, GRE Subject Test, GRE General Test. Additional exam requirements/recommendations for international students: Required—TOEFL (minimum score 500 paper-based; 173 computer-based). Electronic applications accepted.

Long Island University, C.W. Post Campus, College of Liberal Arts and Sciences, Department of Psychology, Brookville, NY 11548-1300. Offers clinical psychology (Psy D); psychology (MA). *Accreditation:* APA. Part-time programs available. *Faculty:* 13 full-time (6 women), 12 part-time/adjunct (6 women). *Students:* 50 full-time (40 women), 41 part-time (34 women); includes 17 minority (3 African Americans, 2 American Indian/Alaska Native, 4 Asian Americans or Pacific Islanders, 8 Hispanic Americans), 2 international. Average age 29. 322 applicants, 29% accepted, 44 enrolled. In 2007, 8 master's, 9 doctorates awarded. *Degree requirements:* For master's, thesis; for doctorate, thesis/dissertation, internship. *Entrance requirements:* For master's, GRE General Test, GRE Subject Test, minimum GPA of 3.0 in psychology, 2.8 overall; for doctorate, GRE General Test, GRE Subject Test, bachelor's degree in psychology, minimum GPA of 3.25. Application fee: $30. Electronic applications accepted. *Expenses:* Tuition: Part-time $825 per credit. Tuition and fees vary according to course load. *Financial support:* In 2007–08, 10 fellowships with full tuition reimbursements, 12 research assistantships, 7 teaching assistantships were awarded; career-related internships or fieldwork, Federal Work-Study, institutionally sponsored loans, tuition waivers (full and partial), and unspecified assistantships also available. Support available to part-time students. Financial award application deadline: 5/15; financial award applicants required to submit CSS PROFILE or FAFSA. *Faculty research:* Visual perception, animal learning, attachment, neuropsychology, developmental disabilities, severe mental illness. *Unit head:* Dr. Gerald Lachter, Chair, 516-299-2184, E-mail: glachter@liu.edu. *Application contact:* Dr. Ethel Matin, Graduate Advisor, 516-299-2063, E-mail: ethel.matin@liu.edu.

Loras College, Graduate Division, Program in Applied Psychology, Dubuque, IA 52004-0178. Offers MA. Part-time and evening/weekend programs available. *Faculty:* 1 (woman) full-time, 4 part-time/adjunct (3 women). *Students:* 7 full-time (5 women), 13 part-time (12 women), 1 international. Average age 29. 9 applicants, 78% accepted, 3 enrolled. In 2007, 4 degrees awarded. *Degree requirements:* For master's, comprehensive exam, thesis (for some programs). *Entrance requirements:* For master's, Ohio State University Psychological Test or GRE General Test, minimum undergraduate GPA of 2.75. *Application deadline:* Applications are processed on a rolling basis. Application fee: $25. *Expenses:* Tuition: Full-time $7,920; part-time $440 per credit. *Financial support:* Applicants required to submit FAFSA. *Unit head:* Dr. Mary Johnson, Graduate Coordinator, 563-588-7938. *Application contact:* Michelle Rice, Graduate Admissions Counselor, 563-588-7166, E-mail: michelle.rice@loras.edu.

Louisiana State University and Agricultural and Mechanical College, Graduate School, College of Arts and Sciences, Department of Psychology, Baton Rouge, LA 70803. Offers biological psychology (MA, PhD); clinical psychology (MA, PhD); cognitive psychology (MA, PhD); developmental psychology (MA, PhD); industrial/organizational psychology (MA, PhD); school psychology (MA, PhD). *Accreditation:* APA (one or more programs are accredited). *Faculty:* 25 full-time (9 women). *Students:* 81 full-time (60 women), 23 part-time (15 women); includes 15 minority (6 African Americans, 4 American Indian/Alaska Native, 2 Asian Americans or Pacific Islanders, 3 Hispanic Americans), 3 international. Average age 28. 199 applicants, 15% accepted, 23 enrolled. In 2007, 11 master's, 13 doctorates awarded. Terminal master's awarded for partial completion of doctoral program. *Degree requirements:* For master's, thesis; for doctorate, thesis/dissertation, 1 year internship. *Entrance requirements:* For master's and doctorate, GRE General Test, minimum GPA of 3.0. Additional exam requirements/recommendations for international students: Required—TOEFL (minimum score 550 paper-based; 213 computer-based; 79 iBT). *Application deadline:* For fall admission, 1/15 for domestic and international students. Applications are processed on a rolling basis. Application fee: $25. Electronic applications accepted. *Financial support:* In 2007–08, 101 students received support, including 5 fellowships (averaging $26,557 per year), 55 teaching assistantships with partial tuition reimbursements available (averaging $13,218 per year); research assistantships with partial tuition reimbursements available, career-related internships or fieldwork, Federal Work-Study, institutionally sponsored loans, scholarships/grants, health care benefits, and tuition waivers (full and partial) also available. Financial award applicants required to submit FAFSA. *Faculty research:* Clinical psychology, autism, anxiety, addition, neuro-psychology, school psychology, cognitive psychology, experimental psychology. Total annual research expenditures: $582,678. *Unit head:* Dr. Alan Baumeister, Chair, 225-578-4099, Fax: 225-578-4125, E-mail: abaumei@lsu.edu. *Application contact:* Dr. Janet McDonald, Coordinator of Graduate Studies, 225-578-4116, Fax: 225-578-4125, E-mail: psmcdo@lsu.edu.

Louisiana Tech University, Graduate School, College of Education, Department of Behavioral Sciences and Psychology, Ruston, LA 71272. Offers counseling (MA); counseling psychology (PhD); industrial/organizational psychology (MA); special education (MA). *Accreditation:* APA (one or more programs are accredited). Part-time programs available. *Degree requirements:* For master's, thesis or alternative; for doctorate, thesis/dissertation. *Entrance requirements:* For master's and doctorate, GRE General Test. *Application deadline:* For fall admission, 7/29 for domestic students; for spring admission, 2/3 for domestic students. Application fee: $20 ($30 for international students). *Financial support:* Fellowships, research assistantships, teaching assistantships, career-related internships or fieldwork available. Financial award application deadline: 2/1. *Unit head:* Dr. Tilman Sheets, Head, 318-257-4315, Fax: 318-257-2379. *Application contact:* Dr. Cathy Stockton, Director of Graduate Studies, 318-257-3229, Fax: 318-257-2379, E-mail: cstock@latech.edu.

Loyola College in Maryland, Graduate Programs, College of Arts and Sciences, Department of Psychology, Baltimore, MD 21210-2699. Offers clinical psychology (MS, Psy D, CAS); counseling psychology (MS, CAS), including counseling psychology (MS), employee assistance and substance abuse (CAS). *Accreditation:* APA. Part-time and evening/weekend programs available. *Entrance requirements:* For master's, doctorate, and CAS, GRE General Test, GRE Subject Test (recommended). Additional exam requirements/recommendations for international students: Required—TOEFL (minimum score 550 paper-based; 213 computer-based).

See Close-Up on page 1445.

Loyola University Chicago, Graduate School, Department of Psychology, Chicago, IL 60611-2196. Offers applied human perception and performance (MS); applied social psychology (MA, PhD); clinical psychology (PhD); developmental psychology (PhD). *Accreditation:* APA (one or more programs are accredited). *Faculty:* 27 full-time (12 women), 1 part-time/adjunct (0 women). *Students:* 90 full-time (76 women), 4 part-time (3 women); includes 16 minority (7 African Americans, 1 American Indian/Alaska Native, 4 Asian Americans or Pacific Islanders, 4 Hispanic Americans), 4 international. Average age 28. 363 applicants, 9% accepted, 18 enrolled. In 2007, 11 master's, 13 doctorates awarded. Terminal master's awarded for partial completion of doctoral program. *Median time to degree:* Of those who began their doctoral program in fall 1999, 70% received their degree in 8 years or less. *Degree requirements:* For master's, comprehensive exam, thesis; for doctorate, comprehensive exam, thesis/dissertation. *Entrance requirements:* For master's and doctorate, GRE General Test, GRE Subject Test. Application fee: $50. Electronic applications accepted. *Expenses:* Tuition: Full-time $12,780; part-time $710 per credit hour. Required fees: $55 per semester. Full-time tuition and fees vary according to program. *Financial support:* In 2007–08, 7 fellowships with full tuition reimbursements (averaging $12,000 per year), 24 research assistantships with full tuition reimbursements (averaging $12,000 per year), 10 teaching assistantships with full tuition reimbursements (averaging $12,000 per year) were awarded; career-related internships or fieldwork, Federal Work-Study, scholarships/grants, and traineeships also available. Financial award applicants required to submit FAFSA. *Faculty research:* Cognitive development, hearing and vision, attitude and prejudice, child and family, AIDS and health promotion. Total annual research expenditures: $2.5 million. *Unit head:* Dr. R. Scott Tindale, Chair, 773-508-3014, E-mail: rtindal@luc.edu.

Lynn University, College of Arts and Sciences, Boca Raton, FL 33431-5598. Offers applied psychology (MS); criminal justice administration (MS); emergency planning and administration (MS, Certificate). Part-time and evening/weekend programs available. Postbaccalaureate distance learning degree programs offered. *Entrance requirements:* For master's, GRE, resumé, 2 letters of recommendation, minimum undergraduate GPA of 3.0. Additional exam requirements/recommendations for international students: Required—TOEFL (minimum score 550 paper-based; 213 computer-based). *Faculty research:* Terrorism, criminological theory, corrections, emergency planning.

Madonna University, Department of Psychology, Livonia, MI 48150-1173. Offers clinical psychology (MSCP). Part-time and evening/weekend programs available. *Degree requirements:* For master's, thesis or alternative. *Entrance requirements:* Additional exam requirements/recommendations for international students: Required—TOEFL. Electronic applications accepted.

Marietta College, Program in Psychology, Marietta, OH 45750-4000. Offers MAP. *Faculty:* 3 full-time (1 woman). *Students:* 12 full-time (9 women), 8 part-time (all women). *Unit head:* Dr. Mark E. Sibicky, Chair, 740-376-4762, E-mail: sibickym@marietta.edu.

Marist College, Graduate Programs, School of Social and Behavioral Sciences, Poughkeepsie, NY 12601-1387. Offers counseling psychology (MA); education (M Ed); education psychology (MA); school psychology (MA, Adv C). Part-time and evening/weekend programs available. *Faculty:* 20 full-time (10 women), 18 part-time/adjunct (7 women). *Students:* 98 full-time (82 women), 121 part-time (97 women); includes 23 minority (7 African Americans, 3 Asian Americans or Pacific Islanders, 13 Hispanic Americans), 4 international. Average age 29. 100 applicants, 56% accepted, 45 enrolled. In 2007, 87 master's, 3 other advanced degrees awarded. *Degree requirements:* For master's, thesis optional. *Entrance requirements:* For master's, GRE General Test, letters of recommendation, minimum undergraduate GPA of 3.0, interview, essay, official transcript. Additional exam requirements/recommendations for international students: Required—TOEFL (minimum score 550 paper-based; 213 computer-based; 80 iBT); Recommended—IELTS (minimum score 7). *Application deadline:* For fall admission, 8/1 for domestic students, 6/1 for international students; for spring admission, 12/1 for domestic students, 10/31 for international students. Applications are processed on a rolling basis. Application fee: $50. Electronic applications accepted. *Expenses:* Tuition: Part-time $665 per credit. *Financial support:* In 2007–08, 130 students received support. Career-related internships or fieldwork, scholarships/grants, and unspecified assistantships available. Support available to part-time students. Financial award application deadline: 8/15; financial award applicants required to submit FAFSA. *Faculty research:* AIDS prevention, educational intervention, humanistic counseling research, aging and development, neuroimaging. *Unit head:* Margaret Calista, Dean, 845-575-3000 Ext. 2960, E-mail: margaret.calista@marist.edu. *Application contact:* Kelly Holmes, Director of Admissions, 845-575-3800, Fax: 845-575-3166, E-mail: graduate@marist.edu.

Marquette University, Graduate School, College of Arts and Sciences, Department of Psychology, Milwaukee, WI 53201-1881. Offers clinical psychology (MS); psychology (PhD). *Accreditation:* APA. Part-time programs available. *Faculty:* 17 full-time (8 women), 2 part-time/adjunct (1 woman). *Students:* 42 full-time (29 women), 7 part-time (6 women); includes 5 minority (3 African Americans, 1 American Indian/Alaska Native, 1 Hispanic American), 1 international. Average age 28. 111 applicants, 16% accepted, 13 enrolled. In 2007, 7 master's, 9 doctorates awarded. *Degree requirements:* For master's, comprehensive exam, thesis or alternative; for doctorate, thesis/dissertation, internship, qualifying exam. *Entrance requirements:* For master's, GRE General Test, GRE Subject Test, MAT; for doctorate, GRE General Test, GRE Subject Test, sample of scholarly writing. Additional exam requirements/recommendations for international students: Required—TOEFL. *Application deadline:* For fall admission, 2/15 for domestic students. Application fee: $40. *Financial support:* In 2007–08, 3 research assistantships, 16 teaching assistantships were awarded; career-related internships or fieldwork, Federal Work-Study, institutionally sponsored loans, scholarships/grants, and tuition waivers (full and partial) also available. Support available to part-time students. Financial award application deadline: 2/15. *Faculty research:* Mental imagery, moral development, organizational behavior, depression, psychotherapy outcomes. Total annual research expenditures: $122,416. *Unit head:* Dr. Mike Wierzbicki, Chair, 414-288-7218, Fax: 414-288-5333. *Application contact:* Dr. Steve Saunders, Information Contact, 414-288-7459.

Marshall University, Academic Affairs Division, College of Liberal Arts, Department of Psychology, Huntington, WV 25755. Offers clinical psychology (MA); general psychology (MA); industrial and organizational psychology (MA); psychology (Psy D). *Accreditation:* APA. *Faculty:* 20 full-time (8 women), 1 part-time/adjunct (0 women). *Students:* 94 full-time (60 women), 31 part-time (23 women); includes 3 minority (1 Asian American or Pacific Islander, 2 Hispanic Americans), 4 international. Average age 29. In 2007, 26 master's, 3 doctorates awarded. *Degree requirements:* For master's, thesis optional. *Entrance requirements:* For master's, GRE General Test or MAT. *Application deadline:* For fall admission, 3/1 for domestic students; for spring admission, 11/1 for domestic students. Application fee: $40. *Financial support:* Teaching assistantships with tuition reimbursements available. *Unit head:* Dr. Martin Amerikaner, Chairperson, 304-696-2783, E-mail: amerikan@marshall.edu. *Application contact:* Information Contact, 304-746-1900, Fax: 304-746-1902, E-mail: services@marshall.edu.

Martin University, Division of Psychology, Indianapolis, IN 46218-3867. Offers community psychology (MS). Part-time and evening/weekend programs available. *Degree requirements:* For master's, thesis. *Entrance requirements:* For master's, GRE General Test, GRE Subject Test.

Marywood University, Academic Affairs, College of Education and Human Development, Department of Psychology and Counseling, Program in Psychology, Scranton, PA 18509-1598. Offers child/clinical school psychology (MA); clinical services (MA); general theoretical psychology (MA). Part-time and evening/weekend programs available. *Students:* 41 full-time (34 women), 15 part-time (11 women); includes 5 minority (2 African Americans, 3 Asian Americans or Pacific Islanders). Average age 28. 62 applicants, 66% accepted. In 2007, 24 degrees awarded. *Degree requirements:* For master's, comprehensive exam, thesis or alternative, internship/practicum. *Entrance requirements:* For master's, GRE or MAT. Additional exam requirements/recommendations for international students: Required—TOEFL (minimum score 550 paper-based; 213 computer-based). *Application deadline:* For fall admission, 4/15 priority date for domestic and international students; for spring admission, 11/15 priority date

Psychology—General

Marywood University (continued)
for domestic and international students. Applications are processed on a rolling basis. Application fee: $30. Electronic applications accepted. *Expenses:* Tuition: Full-time $15,290; part-time $695 per credit. Required fees: $990; $370 per term. Tuition and fees vary according to degree level. *Financial support:* Research assistantships with tuition reimbursements, career-related internships or fieldwork, scholarships/grants, tuition waivers (partial), and unspecified assistantships available. Support available to part-time students. Financial award application deadline: 2/15; financial award applicants required to submit FAFSA. *Faculty research:* Personality disorders, counselor training, preschool development, self-esteem measurement, family dynamics. *Unit head:* Dr. Edward J. O'Brien, Chairperson, 570-348-6211 Ext. 2459, E-mail: obrien@es.marywood.edu. *Application contact:* Tammy Manka, Assistant Director of Graduate Admissions, 570-340-6002, E-mail: tmanka@marywood.edu.

Massachusetts School of Professional Psychology, Graduate Programs, Boston, MA 02132. Offers clinical psychology (Psy D); clinical psychopharmacology (Post-Doctoral MS); counseling psychology (MA); executive coaching (Graduate Certificate); forensic psychology (MA); organizational psychology (MA); respecialization in clinical psychology (Certificate); MA/CAGS. *Accreditation:* APA. *Faculty:* 24 full-time (11 women), 13 part-time/adjunct (9 women). *Students:* 223 full-time (177 women), 81 part-time (68 women); includes 22 minority (3 African Americans, 8 Asian Americans or Pacific Islanders, 11 Hispanic Americans), 9 international. Average age 28. 415 applicants, 42% accepted, 77 enrolled. In 2007, 14 master's, 37 doctorates awarded. *Degree requirements:* For master's, comprehensive exam; for doctorate, thesis/dissertation. *Entrance requirements:* For doctorate, GRE General Test. Additional exam requirements/recommendations for international students: Required—TOEFL (minimum score 550 paper-based; 213 computer-based). *Application deadline:* For fall admission, 1/3 for domestic and international students. Application fee: $50. Electronic applications accepted. *Expenses:* Tuition: Full-time $25,952; part-time $811 per credit. Required fees: $200. *Financial support:* In 2007–08, 20 teaching assistantships (averaging $3,300 per year) were awarded; career-related internships or fieldwork also available. Financial award applicants required to submit FAFSA. *Unit head:* Dr. Nicholas A. Covino, President, 617-327-6777, Fax: 617-327-4447. *Application contact:* 617-327-6777 Ext. 210, Fax: 617-327-4447, E-mail: admissions@mspp.edu.

See Close-Up on page 1447.

McGill University, Faculty of Graduate and Postdoctoral Studies, Faculty of Medicine, Department of Psychiatry, Montréal, QC H3A 2T5, Canada. Offers M Sc. *Faculty:* 61 full-time (22 women), 231 part-time/adjunct (88 women). *Students:* 30 full-time (20 women). 21 applicants, 48% accepted, 7 enrolled. In 2007, 6 degrees awarded. Application fee: $60 Canadian dollars.

McGill University, Faculty of Graduate and Postdoctoral Studies, Faculty of Science, Department of Psychology, Montréal, QC H3A 2T5, Canada. Offers clinical psychology (PhD); experimental psychology (M Sc, MA, PhD). *Accreditation:* APA (one or more programs are accredited). *Faculty:* 45 full-time (17 women), 67 part-time/adjunct (38 women). *Students:* 100 full-time (72 women), 2 part-time (both women). 256 applicants, 11% accepted, 26 enrolled. In 2007, 3 master's, 12 doctorates awarded.

McMaster University, School of Graduate Studies, Faculty of Science, Department of Psychology, Hamilton, ON L8S 4M2, Canada. Offers M Sc, PhD. *Faculty:* 24 full-time. *Students:* 72 full-time, 1 part-time. Average age 27. 82 applicants, 12% accepted. *Degree requirements:* For doctorate, comprehensive exam, thesis/dissertation. *Entrance requirements:* For doctorate, GRE General Test, honors degree, minimum B+ average. Additional exam requirements/recommendations for international students: Required—TOEFL (minimum score 550 paper-based; 213 computer-based). *Application deadline:* For fall admission, 1/15 priority date for domestic students. Applications are processed on a rolling basis. Application fee: $90. *Financial support:* In 2007–08, 24 fellowships, 41 teaching assistantships (averaging $8,440 per year) were awarded; career-related internships or fieldwork, institutionally sponsored loans, and scholarships/grants also available. *Unit head:* Dr. Betty Ann Levy, Chair, 905-525-9140 Ext. 23019, Fax: 905-529-6225. *Application contact:* Nancy Riddell, Graduate Secretary, 905-525-9140 Ext. 23298, Fax: 905-529-6225, E-mail: riddeln@mcmaster.ca.

McNeese State University, Graduate School, College of Education, Department of Psychology, Lake Charles, LA 70609. Offers counseling psychology (MA); general psychology (MA). Evening/weekend programs available. *Faculty:* 7 full-time (3 women), 1 (woman) part-time/adjunct. *Students:* 31 full-time (24 women), 36 part-time (28 women); includes 14 minority (9 African Americans, 1 American Indian/Alaska Native, 2 Asian Americans or Pacific Islanders, 2 Hispanic Americans), 3 international. In 2007, 2 degrees awarded. *Entrance requirements:* For master's, GRE. *Application deadline:* For fall admission, 5/15 priority date for domestic students. Applications are processed on a rolling basis. Application fee: $20 ($30 for international students). *Expenses:* Tuition, state resident: full-time $2,226; part-time $193 per hour. Required fees: $935; $110 per hour. Tuition and fees vary according to course load. *Financial support:* Application deadline: 5/1. *Unit head:* Dr. Dena L. Matzenbacher, Head, 337-475-5457, Fax: 337-562-4115, E-mail: dena@mcneese.edu.

Medaille College, Programs in Psychology, Buffalo, NY 14214-2695. Offers mental health counseling (MA); psychology (MA). Part-time and evening/weekend programs available. *Faculty:* 6 full-time (3 women), 10 part-time/adjunct (8 women). *Students:* 139 full-time (111 women); includes 28 minority (27 African Americans, 1 Hispanic American). Average age 34. 86 applicants, 93% accepted, 75 enrolled. In 2007, 25 degrees awarded. *Degree requirements:* For master's, comprehensive exam (for some programs), thesis (for some programs). *Entrance requirements:* For master's, GRE General Test (psychology), minimum GPA of 2.75 (psychology). Additional exam requirements/recommendations for international students: Required—TOEFL (minimum score 550 paper-based; 213 computer-based). *Application deadline:* Applications are processed on a rolling basis. Application fee: $35. Electronic applications accepted. *Expenses:* Tuition: Full-time $14,760; part-time $615 per credit hour. *Financial support:* In 2007–08, 88 students received support. Federal Work-Study available. Financial award applicants required to submit FAFSA. *Faculty research:* Schizophrenia, Parkinson's Disease, eyewitness testimony, methodology. *Unit head:* Dr. Judith Horowitz, Interim Dean of Adult and Graduate Studies, 716-880-2229 Ext. 229, Fax: 716-884-0291, E-mail: jhorowitz@medaille.edu. *Application contact:* Jacqueline Matheny, Executive Director of Marketing and Enrollment, 716-932-2541, Fax: 716-632-1811, E-mail: jmatheny@medaille.edu.

Memorial University of Newfoundland, School of Graduate Studies, Department of Psychology, St. John's, NL A1C 5S7, Canada. Offers applied social psychology (MASP); experimental psychology (M Sc, PhD). Part-time programs available. *Degree requirements:* For master's, workterms (MASP), thesis (M Sc); for doctorate, comprehensive exam, thesis/dissertation, oral thesis defense. *Entrance requirements:* For master's, GRE, honors bachelor's degree of high second class standing or equivalent; for doctorate, GRE, master's or honors degree. Electronic applications accepted. *Faculty research:* Behavioral neuroscience, cognition, theory and research on abnormal behavior.

Mercy College, Division of Social and Behavioral Sciences, Program in Psychology, Dobbs Ferry, NY 10522-1189. Offers psychology (MS); school psychology (MS). *Students:* 28 full-time (22 women), 40 part-time (30 women); includes 35 minority (12 African Americans, 2 American Indian/Alaska Native, 1 Asian American or Pacific Islander, 20 Hispanic Americans), 1 international. Average age 32. In 2007, 17 degrees awarded. *Entrance requirements:* For master's, BA in psychology, sociology, behavioral science or education; interview; letters of recommendation. *Expenses:* Tuition: Part-time $575 per credit. Required fees: $220 per semester. Tuition and fees vary according to program. *Unit head:* Dr. Barbara Melamed, Program Director, 914-674-7345, E-mail: bmelamed@mercy.edu.

Metropolitan State University, College of Professional Studies, St. Paul, MN 55106-5000. Offers psychology (MA). Part-time and evening/weekend programs available. *Faculty:* 7 full-time (4 women), 8 part-time/adjunct (3 women). *Students:* 8 full-time (6 women), 15 part-time (13 women); includes 7 African Americans, 1 international. Average age 35. In 2007, 6 degrees awarded. *Degree requirements:* For master's, thesis. *Entrance requirements:* For master's, transcripts, resum&e, letters of reference, BA, 3.0 GPA. Additional exam requirements/recommendations for international students: Required—TOEFL (minimum score 550 paper-based; 213 computer-based). *Application deadline:* For fall admission, 8/1 priority date for domestic students; for spring admission, 12/1 priority date for domestic students. *Expenses:* Tuition, state resident: full-time $5,080; part-time $254 per credit. Tuition, nonresident: full-time $10,160; part-time $508 per credit. Required fees: $189; $34 per credit. *Financial support:* Applicants required to submit FAFSA. *Unit head:* Dr. Carmen Coballes-Vega, Dean, 651-793-1333, Fax: 651-793-1355, E-mail: carmen.coballesvega@metrostate.edu.

Miami University, Graduate School, College of Arts and Sciences, Department of Psychology, Oxford, OH 45056. Offers clinical psychology (PhD); experimental psychology (PhD); social psychology (PhD). *Accreditation:* APA. *Degree requirements:* For doctorate, comprehensive exam, thesis/dissertation, final exams. *Entrance requirements:* For doctorate, GRE General Test, GRE Subject Test, minimum GPA of 2.75 (undergraduate), 3.0 (graduate). Additional exam requirements/recommendations for international students: Required—TOEFL (minimum score 550 paper-based; 213 computer-based), TWE (minimum score 4). Electronic applications accepted.

Michigan School of Professional Psychology, Programs in Humanistic and Clinical Psychology, Farmington Hills, MI 48334. Offers humanistic and clinical psychology (MA, Psy D). *Faculty:* 3 full-time (1 woman), 20 part-time/adjunct (11 women). *Students:* 109 full-time (86 women); includes 20 minority (13 African Americans, 7 Asian Americans or Pacific Islanders). Average age 38. 200 applicants, 40% accepted, 69 enrolled. In 2007, 39 master's, 11 doctorates awarded. *Median time to degree:* Of those who began their doctoral program in fall 1999, 100% received their degree in 8 years or less. *Degree requirements:* For master's, thesis, practicum; for doctorate, thesis/dissertation, internship, practicum. *Entrance requirements:* For master's, 1 year of work experience, interview, minimum GPA of 3.0, curriculum vitae, personal essay, Bachelor's completion; for doctorate, 3 years of work experience, 2 interviews, minimum graduate GPA of 3.0, scholarly writing sample, curriculum vitae, personal essay, MA degree completion. Additional exam requirements/recommendations for international students: Required—TOEFL. *Application deadline:* For fall admission, 1/15 priority date for domestic students. Applications are processed on a rolling basis. Application fee: $75. Electronic applications accepted. *Expenses:* Tuition: Full-time $21,255. One-time fee: $200 full-time. *Financial support:* In 2007–08, 39 students received support. Application deadline: 6/30; *Faculty research:* Qualitative research, existential-phenomenological psychology, applications to clinical practice. *Unit head:* Dr. Kerry Moustakas, President, 248-476-1122, Fax: 248-476-1125, E-mail: kmoustakas@mispp.edu. *Application contact:* Linda Potter-Gallant, Admissions Advisor, 248-476-1122 Ext. 117, Fax: 248-476-1125, E-mail: lpgallant@mispp.edu.

Michigan State University, The Graduate School, College of Social Science, Department of Psychology, East Lansing, MI 48824. Offers MA, PhD. *Accreditation:* APA (one or more programs are accredited). *Entrance requirements:* Additional exam requirements/recommendations for international students: Required—TOEFL (minimum score 550 paper-based; 213 computer-based), Michigan State University ELT (85), Michigan ELAB (83). Electronic applications accepted. *Expenses:* Tuition, state resident: part-time $379 per credit hour. Tuition, nonresident: part-time $800 per credit hour. Tuition and fees vary according to program.

Middle Tennessee State University, College of Graduate Studies, College of Education and Behavioral Science, Department of Psychology, Program in Psychology, Murfreesboro, TN 37132. Offers MA. Part-time and evening/weekend programs available. Postbaccalaureate distance learning degree programs offered. *Students:* 17 full-time (13 women), 86 part-time (57 women); includes 15 minority (7 African Americans, 7 Asian Americans or Pacific Islanders, 1 Hispanic American). 185 applicants, 57% accepted. In 2007, 31 degrees awarded. *Degree requirements:* For master's, one foreign language, comprehensive exam, thesis. *Entrance requirements:* For master's, GRE. Additional exam requirements/recommendations for international students: Required—TOEFL (paper-based 525; computer-based 195; IBT 71) or IELTS (6.0). *Application deadline:* For fall admission, 8/1 priority date for domestic students. Applications are processed on a rolling basis. Application fee: $25. Electronic applications accepted. *Financial support:* In 2007–08, 8 students received support. Career-related internships or fieldwork and institutionally sponsored loans available. Support available to part-time students. Financial award application deadline: 5/1. *Unit head:* Dr. Dennis Papini, Interim Chair, Department of Psychology, 615-898-2706, Fax: 615-898-5027.

Midwestern State University, Graduate Studies, College of Humanities and Social Sciences, Department of Psychology, Wichita Falls, TX 76308. Offers MA. Part-time and evening/weekend programs available. *Degree requirements:* For master's, one foreign language, comprehensive exam, thesis optional. *Entrance requirements:* For master's, GRE General Test, 3 recommendation forms. Additional exam requirements/recommendations for international students: Required—TOEFL (minimum score 550 paper-based; 213 computer-based). Electronic applications accepted. *Faculty research:* Personality disorders, child sexual abuse and sexual coercion, educational psychology.

Millersville University of Pennsylvania, Graduate School, School of Education, Department of Psychology, Millersville, PA 17551-0302. Offers psychology (MS), including clinical psychology, school psychology; school counseling (M Ed). Part-time and evening/weekend programs available. *Faculty:* 20 full-time (14 women), 13 part-time/adjunct (9 women). *Students:* 55 full-time (45 women), 84 part-time (69 women); includes 7 minority (6 African Americans, 1 Hispanic American), 1 international. Average age 28. 70 applicants, 66% accepted, 33 enrolled. In 2007, 48 degrees awarded. *Degree requirements:* For master's, thesis optional, departmental exam. *Entrance requirements:* For master's, GRE General Test, minimum undergraduate GPA of 2.75, 6 or 18 undergraduate hours of course work in psychology, interview, letters of recommendation, writing sample. Additional exam requirements/recommendations for international students: Required—TOEFL (minimum score 500 paper-based; 183 computer-based). *Application deadline:* For fall admission, 2/29 for domestic students; for winter admission, 10/1 for domestic students; for spring admission, 10/1 for domestic students. Application fee: $40. Electronic applications accepted. *Expenses:* Tuition, state resident: full-time $6,214; part-time $345 per credit. Tuition, nonresident: full-time $9,944; part-time $552 per credit. Required fees: $1,442. Tuition and fees vary according to course load. *Financial support:* In 2007–08, 47 students received support, including 47 research assistantships with full and partial tuition reimbursements available (averaging $5,200 per year); institutionally sponsored loans and unspecified assistantships also available. Support available to part-time students. Financial award application deadline: 3/15; financial award applicants required to submit FAFSA. *Unit head:* Dr. Helena Tuleya-Payne, Chair, 717-872-3925, Fax: 717-871-2480, E-mail: helena.tuleya-payne@millersville.edu. *Application contact:* Dr. Victor S. DeSantis, Dean of Graduate Studies, 717-872-3099, Fax: 717-871-2022, E-mail: victor.desantis@millersville.edu.

Minnesota State University Mankato, College of Graduate Studies, College of Social and Behavioral Sciences, Department of Psychology, Mankato, MN 56001. Offers clinical psychology (MA); industrial/organizational psychology (MA); psychology (MT). Part-time programs available. *Students:* 43 full-time (26 women), 5 part-time (3 women). Average age 26. In 2007, 11 degrees awarded. *Degree requirements:* For master's, one foreign language, comprehensive exam, thesis (for some programs). *Entrance requirements:* For master's, GRE General Test, GRE Subject Test (clinical psychology), minimum GPA of 3.0 during previous 2 years, 3 letters of reference. Additional exam requirements/recommendations for international students: Required—TOEFL. *Application deadline:* For fall admission, 3/1 for domestic students; for spring admission, 11/27 for domestic students. Applications are processed on a rolling basis. Application fee: $40. Electronic applications accepted. *Financial support:* Research assistantships, teaching assistantships with full tuition reimbursements, career-related internships or fieldwork, Federal Work-Study, institutionally sponsored loans, and unspecified assistantships available. Support available to part-time students. Financial award application deadline: 3/15; financial award applicants required to submit FAFSA. *Faculty research:* Professional competency in hospitals, mood disturbance, 360-degree feedback, employee selection, planning fallacy. *Unit head:* Dr. Rosemary Krawczyk, Chairperson, 507-389-2724. *Application contact:* 507-389-2321, E-mail: grad@mnsu.edu.

Mississippi State University, College of Arts and Sciences, Department of Psychology, Mississippi State, MS 39762. Offers clinical psychology (MS); cognitive science (PhD); experimental psychology (MS). *Faculty:* 16 full-time (7 women), 2 part-time/adjunct (1 woman). *Students:* 31 full-time (21 women), 14 part-time (7 women); includes 2 minority (1 African American, 1 American Indian/Alaska Native), 2 international. Average age 26. 32 applicants, 47% accepted, 8 enrolled. In 2007, 8 master's awarded. Terminal master's awarded for partial completion of doctoral program. *Degree requirements:* For master's, comprehensive exam, thesis; for doctorate, thesis/dissertation, qualifying exam, comprehensive written and oral exam. *Entrance requirements:* For master's, GRE General Test, minimum GPA of 2.75; for doctorate, GRE General Test, proficiency in at least 1 computer language. Additional exam requirements/recommendations for international students: Required—TOEFL. *Application deadline:* For fall admission, 7/1 priority date for domestic students; for spring admission, 11/1 for domestic students. Applications are processed on a rolling basis. Application fee: $30. *Expenses:* Tuition, state resident: full-time $4,978; part-time $274 per hour. Tuition, nonresident: full-time $11,469; part-time $635 per hour. *Financial support:* In 2007–08, 13 teaching assistantships with full tuition reimbursements (averaging $8,877 per year) were awarded; research assistantships with full tuition reimbursements, career-related internships or fieldwork, Federal Work-Study, institutionally sponsored loans, scholarships/grants, and unspecified assistantships also available. Financial award applicants required to submit FAFSA. *Faculty research:* Personality type, alcoholism, blindness and low vision, mental retardation, language comprehension. Total annual research expenditures: $4.5 million. *Unit head:* Dr. Stephen B. Klein, Head, 662-325-3202, Fax: 662-325-7212, E-mail: sbkl@ra.msstate.edu. *Application contact:* Dr. William A. Person, Interim Associate Vice President for Academic Affairs/Interim Dean of Graduate Studies, 662-325-7400, Fax: 662-325-1967, E-mail: grad@grad.msstate.edu.

Missouri State University, Graduate College, College of Health and Human Services, Department of Psychology, Springfield, MO 65804-0094. Offers MS. *Faculty:* 27 full-time (10 women), 1 part-time/adjunct (0 women). *Students:* 42 full-time (31 women), 2 part-time (both women); includes 3 minority (1 African American, 2 Hispanic Americans), 2 international. Average age 26. 70 applicants, 41% accepted, 19 enrolled. In 2007, 16 degrees awarded. *Degree requirements:* For master's, comprehensive exam, thesis. *Entrance requirements:* For master's, GRE General Test, GRE Subject Test, minimum GPA of 3.25 in major, 3.0 overall; 20 hours of course work in psychology (experimental and statistics). Additional exam requirements/recommendations for international students: Required—TOEFL (minimum score 550 paper-based; 213 computer-based; 79 iBT). *Application deadline:* For fall admission, 3/1 priority date for domestic students. Applications are processed on a rolling basis. Application fee: $35. Electronic applications accepted. *Expenses:* Tuition, state resident: full-time $3,708; part-time $206 per credit hour. Tuition, nonresident: full-time $7,236; part-time $206 per credit hour. Required fees: $622. Full-time tuition and fees vary according to course level, course load, program and reciprocity agreements. *Financial support:* In 2007–08, 11 research assistantships with full tuition reimbursements (averaging $7,050 per year), 3 teaching assistantships with full tuition reimbursements (averaging $9,360 per year) were awarded; career-related internships or fieldwork, Federal Work-Study, scholarships/grants, and unspecified assistantships also available. Financial award application deadline: 3/31; financial award applicants required to submit FAFSA. *Faculty research:* Sports psychology, information processing, motivational processes, interpersonal dynamics, infant visual processing. *Unit head:* Dr. Robert G. Jones, Head, 417-836-5797, Fax: 417-836-830, E-mail: psychology@missouristate.edu.

Monmouth University, Graduate School, Department of Psychology, West Long Branch, NJ 07764-1898. Offers professional counseling (PMC); psychological counseling (MA). Part-time and evening/weekend programs available. *Faculty:* 7 full-time (3 women), 4 part-time/adjunct (all women). *Students:* 68 full-time (54 women), 112 part-time (96 women); includes 23 minority (12 African Americans, 1 American Indian/Alaska Native, 3 Asian Americans or Pacific Islanders, 7 Hispanic Americans), 3 international. Average age 31. 72 applicants, 88% accepted, 33 enrolled. In 2007, 47 degrees awarded. *Degree requirements:* For master's, thesis optional, fieldwork. *Entrance requirements:* For master's, GRE General Test, minimum GPA of 3.0 in major, 24 credits in psychology. Additional exam requirements/recommendations for international students: Required—TOEFL (minimum score 550 paper-based; 213 computer-based; 79 iBT), IELTS (minimum score 5), MELAB 77, Cambridge A, B, C. *Application deadline:* For fall admission, 7/15 priority date for domestic students, 6/1 for international students; for spring admission, 11/15 priority date for domestic students, 11/1 for international students. Applications are processed on a rolling basis. Application fee: $50. Electronic applications accepted. *Financial support:* In 2007–08, 90 students received support, including 90 fellowships (averaging $1,884 per year), 4 research assistantships (averaging $9,804 per year); career-related internships or fieldwork, scholarships/grants, tuition waivers (partial), and unspecified assistantships also available. Support available to part-time students. Financial award application deadline: 3/1; financial award applicants required to submit FAFSA. *Faculty research:* Violent crime, single parenting, the African-American male, counseling older women, successful behavior for under-achieving youth. *Unit head:* Dr. Frances K. Trotman, Director, 732-571-7593, Fax: 732-263-5159, E-mail: ftrotman@monmouth.edu. *Application contact:* Kevin Roane, Director, Office of Graduate Admission, 732-571-3452, Fax: 732-263-5123, E-mail: gradadm@monmouth.edu.

Montana State University, College of Graduate Studies, College of Letters and Science, Department of Psychology, Bozeman, MT 59717. Offers MS. Part-time programs available. *Faculty:* 8 full-time (2 women), 3 part-time/adjunct (2 women). *Students:* 8 full-time (4 women), 3 part-time (2 women). Average age 27. 14 applicants, 57% accepted, 7 enrolled. In 2007, 6 degrees awarded. *Degree requirements:* For master's, comprehensive exam, thesis (for some programs). *Entrance requirements:* For master's, GRE General Test. Additional exam requirements/recommendations for international students: Required—TOEFL (minimum score 550 paper-based; 213 computer-based). *Application deadline:* For fall admission, 7/15 priority date for domestic students, 5/15 priority date for international students; for spring admission, 12/1 priority date for domestic students, 10/1 priority date for international students. Applications are processed on a rolling basis. Application fee: $30. Electronic applications accepted. *Expenses:* Tuition, state resident: full-time $5,176. Tuition, nonresident: full-time $13,070. *Financial support:* In 2007–08, 11 teaching assistantships with full tuition reimbursements (averaging $10,010 per year) were awarded; unspecified assistantships also available. Financial award application deadline: 3/1; financial award applicants required to submit FAFSA. *Faculty research:* Cognitive psychology, social psychology, biopsychology, health psychology. Total annual research expenditures: $47,914. *Unit head:* Dr. Richard Block, Interim Department Head, 406-994-5173, Fax: 406-994-3804, E-mail: block@montana.edu.

Montana State University–Billings, College of Arts and Sciences, Department of Psychology, Billings, MT 59101-0298. Offers MS. Part-time programs available. *Students:* 18. 9 applicants, 100% accepted, 9 enrolled. In 2007, 4 degrees awarded. *Degree requirements:* For master's, thesis optional. *Entrance requirements:* For master's, GRE General Test, 3 letters of recommendation, resumé. *Application deadline:* For fall admission, 3/15 for domestic students, 7/15 for international students; for spring admission, 12/1 for international students. Applications are processed on a rolling basis. Application fee: $40. *Expenses:* Tuition, state resident: full-time $4,665. Tuition, nonresident: full-time $11,096. *Financial support:* Teaching assistantships with partial tuition reimbursements, career-related internships or fieldwork, Federal Work-Study, institutionally sponsored loans, scholarships/grants, tuition waivers (partial), and unspecified assistantships available. Support available to part-time students. Financial award application deadline: 5/1; financial award applicants required to submit FAFSA. *Unit head:* Dr. Mike Havens, Chair, 406-657-2242, E-mail: mhavens@msubillings.edu. *Application contact:* David M. Sullivan, Graduate Studies Counselor, 406-657-2053, Fax: 406-657-2299, E-mail: dsullivan@msubillings.edu.

Montclair State University, The Office of Graduate Admissions and Support Services, College of Humanities and Social Sciences, Department of Psychology, Montclair, NJ 07043-1624. Offers educational psychology (MA), including child/adolescent clinical psychology, clinical psychology for Spanish/English bilinguals; psychology (MA, Certificate), including industrial and organizational psychology (MA); school psychologist (Certificate). Part-time and evening/weekend programs available. *Faculty:* 27 full-time (11 women), 27 part-time/adjunct (20 women). *Students:* 27 full-time (21 women), 39 part-time (32 women); includes 26 minority (7 African Americans, 4 Asian Americans or Pacific Islanders, 15 Hispanic Americans), 3 international. 86 applicants, 21% accepted, 13 enrolled. In 2007, 22 master's, 11 other advanced degrees awarded. *Degree requirements:* For master's, comprehensive exam, thesis or alternative. *Entrance requirements:* For master's, GRE General Test, GRE Subject Test, previous course work in psychology, interview, 2 letters of recommendation. Additional exam requirements/recommendations for international students: Required—TOEFL (minimum score 83 computer-based). *Application deadline:* For fall admission, 2/1 for domestic and international students; for spring admission, 10/1 for domestic and international students. Applications are processed on a rolling basis. Application fee: $60. Electronic applications accepted. *Financial support:* In 2007–08, 10 research assistantships with full tuition reimbursements (averaging $7,000 per year) were awarded; Federal Work-Study, scholarships/grants, and unspecified assistantships also available. Support available to part-time students. Financial award application deadline: 3/1; financial award applicants required to submit FAFSA. *Faculty research:* Engaged learning, academic and civic development. Total annual research expenditures: $10,000. *Unit head:* Dr. Peter Vietze, Chairperson, 973-655-5201.

Morehead State University, Graduate Programs, College of Science and Technology, Department of Psychology, Morehead, KY 40351. Offers clinical psychology (MA); counseling psychology (MA); experimental/general psychology (MA). Part-time programs available. *Faculty:* 7 full-time (3 women), 3 part-time/adjunct (1 woman). *Students:* 21 full-time (18 women), 4 part-time (1 woman); includes 1 minority (African American) Average age 26. In 2007, 12 degrees awarded. *Degree requirements:* For master's, comprehensive exam, thesis optional. *Entrance requirements:* For master's, GRE General Test, 18 undergraduate hours in psychology, minimum GPA of 3.0. Additional exam requirements/recommendations for international students: Required—TOEFL (minimum score 500 paper-based; 173 computer-based). *Application deadline:* For fall admission, 8/1 priority date for domestic and international students; for spring admission, 12/1 for domestic students, 12/1 priority date for international students. Applications are processed on a rolling basis. Application fee: $0 ($55 for international students). Electronic applications accepted. *Financial support:* In 2007–08, 19 research assistantships (averaging $6,000 per year) were awarded; career-related internships or fieldwork, Federal Work-Study, and institutionally sponsored loans also available. Financial award application deadline: 4/1; financial award applicants required to submit FAFSA. *Faculty research:* Mood induction effects, serotonin receptor activity, stress, perceptual processes. *Application contact:* Michelle Barber, Graduate Admissions Counselor, 606-783-2039, Fax: 606-783-5061, E-mail: m.barber@moreheadstate.edu.

Morgan State University, School of Graduate Studies, College of Liberal Arts, Department of Psychology, Baltimore, MD 21251. Offers psychometrics (MS, PhD). *Faculty:* 6. *Students:* 2. *Entrance requirements:* For master's and doctorate, GRE. Application fee: $0. *Financial support:* Fellowships, research assistantships, teaching assistantships available. Financial award application deadline: 2/1. *Unit head:* Dr. Pamela Scott-Johnson, Chairperson, 443-885-3290. *Application contact:* Dr. Mark Garrison, Associate Dean, 443-885-3185, Fax: 443-885-8226, E-mail: mark.garrison@morgan.edu.

Mount Aloysius College, Program in Psychology, Cresson, PA 16630-1999. Offers MS. *Entrance requirements:* For master's, GRE General Test.

Mount Holyoke College, Department of Psychology and Education, South Hadley, MA 01075. Offers MA.

Murray State University, College of Humanities and Fine Arts, Program in Psychology, Murray, KY 42071. Offers clinical psychology (MA, MS); psychology (MA, MS). Part-time programs available. *Degree requirements:* For master's, one foreign language, comprehensive exam (for some programs), thesis. *Entrance requirements:* For master's, GRE General Test. Additional exam requirements/recommendations for international students: Required—TOEFL.

National-Louis University, College of Arts and Sciences, Program in Psychology, Chicago, IL 60603. Offers cultural psychology (MA); health psychology (MA); human development (MA); organizational psychology (MA); psychology (Certificate). Part-time and evening/weekend programs available. *Students:* 37 full-time (33 women), 147 part-time (127 women); includes 99 minority (79 African Americans, 1 American Indian/Alaska Native, 6 Asian Americans or Pacific Islanders, 13 Hispanic Americans). Average age 38. *Degree requirements:* For master's, thesis, internship (health psychology). *Entrance requirements:* For master's, GRE, MAT, or Watson-Glaser Critical Thinking Appraisal, interview, minimum GPA of 3.0; for Certificate, GRE, MAT, or Watson-Glaser Critical Thinking Appraisal, interview, minimum GPA of 3.0, undergraduate course work in psychology. *Application deadline:* Applications are processed on a rolling basis. *Expenses:* Tuition: Full-time $18,900; part-time $630 per credit hour. Required fees: $20 per term. One-time fee: $40 part-time. Tuition and fees vary according to course load, campus/location and program. *Financial support:* Federal Work-Study, institutionally sponsored loans, scholarships/grants, and tuition waivers available. Support available to part-time students. Financial award applicants required to submit FAFSA. *Faculty research:* Human development, personality theory, abnormal psychology. *Unit head:* Dr. Edward Risinger, Professor, 224-233-2533, Fax: 224-233-2533, E-mail: erisinger@nl.edu. *Application contact:* David McCulloch, Vice President for University Services, 800-443-5522 Ext. 5151, Fax: 847-465-0593, E-mail: dmcc@wheeling1.nl.edu.

National University, Academic Affairs, College of Letters and Sciences, Department of Psychology, La Jolla, CA 92037-1011. Offers counseling psychology (MA); human behavior (MA). Part-time and evening/weekend programs available. Postbaccalaureate distance learning degree programs offered (no on-campus study). *Faculty:* 18 full-time (9 women), 201 part-time/adjunct (120 women). *Students:* 349 full-time (260 women), 388 part-time (297 women); includes 228 minority (90 African Americans, 6 American Indian/Alaska Native, 37 Asian Americans or Pacific Islanders, 95 Hispanic Americans), 8 international. Average age 36. 486 applicants, 368 enrolled. In 2007, 246 degrees awarded. *Degree requirements:* For master's, thesis (for some programs). *Entrance requirements:* For master's, interview, minimum GPA of 2.5. Additional exam requirements/recommendations for international students: Required—TOEFL (minimum score 550 paper-based; 213 computer-based; 80 iBT), IELTS (minimum score 6). *Application deadline:* Applications are processed on a rolling basis. Application fee: $60 ($65 for international students). Electronic applications accepted. *Expenses:* Tuition: Full-time $8,262; part-time $306 per unit. One-time fee: $60. *Financial support:* Career-related internships or fieldwork, institutionally sponsored loans, scholarships/grants, and tuition waivers (partial) available. Support available to part-time students. Financial award application deadline: 6/30; financial award applicants required to submit FAFSA. *Unit head:* Dr. Maureen O'Hara, Chair and Professor, 858-642-8464, Fax: 858-642-8715, E-mail: mohara@nu.edu. *Application contact:* Dominick Giovanniello, Associate Regional Dean—San Diego, 800-NAT-UNIV, Fax: 858-642-8709, E-mail: dgiovann@nu.edu.

New Jersey City University, Graduate Studies and Continuing Education, College of Arts and Sciences, Department of Psychology, Jersey City, NJ 07305-1597. Offers counseling (MA); educational psychology (MA, PD), including educational psychology (MA), school psychology (PD). *Faculty:* 9. *Students:* 12 full-time (9 women), 93 part-time (71 women); includes 27 minority (10 African Americans, 3 Asian Americans or Pacific Islanders, 14 Hispanic Americans), 3 international. Average age 30. In 2007, 75 degrees awarded. *Degree requirements:* For PD, summer internship or externship. *Entrance requirements:* For master's, GRE General Test or MAT; for PD, GRE General Test. Additional exam requirements/recommendations for international students: Required—TOEFL. *Application deadline:* For fall admission, 8/1 priority date for domestic students; for spring admission, 12/1 for domestic students. Applications are processed on a rolling basis. Application fee: $0. *Expenses:* Tuition, state resident: full-time $7,462. Tuition, nonresident: full-time $13,762. Required fees: $1,296.

Psychology—General

New Jersey City University (continued)

Financial support: Career-related internships or fieldwork and unspecified assistantships available. *Unit head:* Dr. David Hallerman, Chairperson, 201-200-3062, E-mail: dhallerman@njcu.edu.

New Mexico Highlands University, Graduate Studies, College of Arts and Sciences, Department of Behavioral Sciences, Las Vegas, NM 87701. Offers psychology (MS), including clinical psychology, general psychology;). Part-time programs available. *Faculty:* 4 full-time (2 women). *Students:* 17 full-time (11 women), 6 part-time (1 woman); includes 10 minority (1 African American, 9 Hispanic Americans), 1 international. Average age 28. 20 applicants, 75% accepted, 11 enrolled. In 2007, 4 degrees awarded. *Degree requirements:* For master's, comprehensive exam, thesis or alternative. *Entrance requirements:* For master's, minimum undergraduate GPA of 3.0. Additional exam requirements/recommendations for international students: Required—TOEFL (minimum score 540 paper-based; 190 computer-based). *Application deadline:* For fall admission, 8/1 priority date for domestic students. Applications are processed on a rolling basis. Application fee: $15. *Expenses:* Tuition, state resident: full-time $2,642; part-time $110 per credit hour. Tuition, nonresident: full-time $3,964; part-time $165 per credit hour. International tuition: $5,285 full-time. One-time fee: $20 full-time. *Financial support:* In 2007–08, 15 students received support, including 12 teaching assistantships with full and partial tuition reimbursements available (averaging $6,500 per year); career-related internships or fieldwork, Federal Work-Study, institutionally sponsored loans, scholarships/grants, tuition waivers (full and partial), and unspecified assistantships also available. Support available to part-time students. Financial award application deadline: 3/1; financial award applicants required to submit FAFSA. *Faculty research:* Sense of community, memory deficits, shame and guilt, neurochemistry of personality, at risk youth. *Unit head:* Dr. Tom Ward, Chair, 505-454-3343, Fax: 505-454-3331, E-mail: tsward@nmhu.edu. *Application contact:* Diane Trujillo, Administrative Assistant Graduate Studies, 505-454-3266, Fax: 505-454-3558, E-mail: dtrujillo@nmhu.edu.

New Mexico State University, Graduate School, College of Arts and Sciences, Department of Psychology, Las Cruces, NM 88003-8001. Offers MA, PhD. Part-time programs available. *Faculty:* 8 full-time (3 women). *Students:* 40 full-time (20 women), 6 part-time (2 women); includes 5 Hispanic Americans, 4 international. Average age 31. 42 applicants, 38% accepted, 7 enrolled. In 2007, 6 master's, 4 doctorates awarded. *Degree requirements:* For master's, thesis; for doctorate, comprehensive exam, thesis/dissertation. *Entrance requirements:* For master's, GRE General Test, letters of recommendation, curriculum vitae; for doctorate, GRE General Test, letters of recommendation, master's thesis or proposal, curriculum vitae. *Application deadline:* For fall admission, 2/1 priority date for domestic students, 2/1 for international students. Applications are processed on a rolling basis. Application fee: $30 ($50 for international students). Electronic applications accepted. *Expenses:* Tuition, state resident: full-time $3,602; part-time $199 per credit. Tuition, nonresident: full-time $13,380; part-time $607 per credit. Required fees: $1,178. *Financial support:* In 2007–08, 10 research assistantships with partial tuition reimbursements, 26 teaching assistantships with partial tuition reimbursements were awarded; fellowships, career-related internships or fieldwork, Federal Work-Study, and health care benefits also available. Support available to part-time students. Financial award application deadline: 2/15. *Faculty research:* Engineering, cognitive, and social psychology; human/computer interaction; cognitive science. *Unit head:* Dr. James E. McDonald, Head, 575-646-5130, Fax: 575-646-6212, E-mail: jemcdon@nmsu.edu. *Application contact:* Dr. Laura J Madson, Associate Professor/Chair of Graduate Committee, 575-646-6207, Fax: 575-646-6212, E-mail: lmadson@nmsu.edu.

The New School: A University, The New School for Social Research, Department of Psychology, New York, NY 10011. Offers clinical psychology (PhD); general psychology (MA, PhD). *Accreditation:* APA (one or more programs are accredited). Part-time and evening/weekend programs available. *Faculty:* 17 full-time (8 women), 6 part-time/adjunct (1 woman). *Students:* 147 full-time (108 women), 74 part-time (64 women); includes 48 minority (14 African Americans, 3 American Indian/Alaska Native, 12 Asian Americans or Pacific Islanders, 19 Hispanic Americans), 20 international. Average age 29. In 2007, 55 master's, 2 doctorates awarded. Terminal master's awarded for partial completion of doctoral program. *Degree requirements:* For doctorate, one foreign language, thesis/dissertation, qualifying exam. *Entrance requirements:* For master's, GRE General Test; for doctorate, GRE General Test, MA. Additional exam requirements/recommendations for international students: Required—TOEFL (minimum score 600 paper-based; 250 computer-based; 100 iBT). *Application deadline:* For fall admission, 1/15 priority date for domestic students. Applications are processed on a rolling basis. Application fee: $50. *Financial support:* Fellowships, research assistantships, teaching assistantships, career-related internships or fieldwork, Federal Work-Study, scholarships/grants, and tuition waivers (full and partial) available. Financial award application deadline: 3/1; financial award applicants required to submit FAFSA. *Faculty research:* Consciousness, memory, language, perceptions, psychopathology. *Unit head:* Dr. Joan Miller, Chair, 212-229-5727 Ext. 3106. *Application contact:* Robert MacDonald, Director of Admissions, 800-523-5710 Ext. 3007, Fax: 212-989-7102, E-mail: macdonar@newschool.edu.

See Close-Up on page 1653.

New York University, Graduate School of Arts and Science, Department of Psychology, New York, NY 10012-1019. Offers cognition and perception (PhD); community psychology (PhD); general psychology (MA); industrial/organizational psychology (MA); psychotherapy and psychoanalysis (Advanced Certificate); social/personality psychology (PhD). Part-time programs available. *Faculty:* 38 full-time (13 women), 78 part-time/adjunct. *Students:* 155 full-time (115 women), 305 part-time (218 women); includes 77 minority (24 African Americans, 29 Asian Americans or Pacific Islanders, 24 Hispanic Americans), 53 international. Average age 32. 767 applicants, 46% accepted, 112 enrolled. In 2007, 80 master's, 15 doctorates awarded. Terminal master's awarded for partial completion of doctoral program. *Degree requirements:* For master's, comprehensive exam, thesis or alternative; for doctorate, thesis/dissertation. *Entrance requirements:* For master's, GRE General Test, minimum GPA of 3.0; for doctorate, GRE General Test, GRE Subject Test; for Advanced Certificate, doctoral degree, minimum GPA of 3.0. Additional exam requirements/recommendations for international students: Required—TOEFL. *Application deadline:* For fall admission, 12/18 for domestic students. Application fee: $85. *Financial support:* Fellowships with tuition reimbursements, research assistantships with tuition reimbursements, teaching assistantships with tuition reimbursements, career-related internships or fieldwork, Federal Work-Study, institutionally sponsored loans, scholarships/grants, traineeships, health care benefits, and unspecified assistantships available. Financial award application deadline: 12/18; financial award applicants required to submit FAFSA. *Faculty research:* Vision, memory, social cognition, social and cognitive development, relationships. *Unit head:* Marisa Carrasco, Chair, 212-998-7900, Fax: 212-995-4018, E-mail: psychq@psych.nyu.edu. *Application contact:* Laurence Maloney, Director of Graduate Studies, 212-998-7900, Fax: 212-995-4018, E-mail: psychq@psych.nyu.edu.

New York University, Steinhardt School of Culture, Education and Human Development, Department of Applied Psychology, New York, NY 10012-1019. Offers counselor education (MA, PhD, Advanced Certificate), including counseling and guidance (MA, Advanced Certificate), counseling for mental health and wellness (MA), counseling psychology (PhD); educational and developmental psychology (MA, PhD), including educational psychology (MA), psychological development (PhD), school psychology (PhD). *Accreditation:* APA (one or more programs are accredited). Part-time and evening/weekend programs available. *Faculty:* 35 full-time (23 women), 43 part-time/adjunct (29 women). *Students:* 207 full-time (172 women), 137 part-time (121 women); includes 99 minority (38 African Americans, 22 Asian Americans or Pacific Islanders, 39 Hispanic Americans), 34 international. 770 applicants, 35% accepted, 116 enrolled. In 2007, 93 master's, 18 doctorates, 1 other advanced degree awarded. Terminal master's awarded for partial completion of doctoral program. *Degree requirements:* For master's, thesis (for some programs); for doctorate, thesis/dissertation. *Entrance requirements:* For doctorate, GRE General Test, interview. Additional exam requirements/recommendations for international students: Required—TOEFL. *Application deadline:* For fall admission, 12/15 priority date for domestic students, 12/1 priority date for international students; for spring admission, 11/1 for domestic students, 12/1 for international students. Applications are processed on a rolling basis. Application fee: $50. *Financial support:* Fellowships with full and partial tuition reimbursements, research assistantships with full and partial tuition reimbursements, teaching assistantships with full and partial tuition reimbursements, career-related internships or fieldwork, Federal Work-Study, institutionally sponsored loans, scholarships/grants, tuition waivers (partial), and unspecified assistantships available. Support available to part-time students. Financial award application deadline: 2/1; financial award applicants required to submit FAFSA. *Faculty research:* Urban children; adolescents and families; culture, race and ethnicity; risk-taking behaviors and health; early childhood. *Unit head:* Dr. Carola Suarez-Orozco, Chairperson, 212-998-5282, Fax: 212-995-4358, E-mail: cs02@nyu.edu. *Application contact:* 212-998-5030, Fax: 212-995-4328, E-mail: steinhardt.gradadmissions@nyu.edu.

Norfolk State University, School of Graduate Studies, School of Liberal Arts, Department of Psychology, Norfolk, VA 23504. Offers community/clinical psychology (MA); psychology (Psy D). Psy D offered through the Virginia Consortium for Professional Psychology; for information call 757-431-4950. Part-time programs available. *Degree requirements:* For master's, comprehensive exam, thesis or alternative; for doctorate, comprehensive exam, thesis/dissertation. *Entrance requirements:* For master's, minimum GPA of 2.7.

North Carolina Central University, Division of Academic Affairs, College of Arts and Sciences, Department of Psychology, Durham, NC 27707-3129. Offers MA. Part-time and evening/weekend programs available. *Degree requirements:* For master's, one foreign language, comprehensive exam, thesis. *Entrance requirements:* For master's, GRE, minimum GPA of 3.0 in major, 2.5 overall. Additional exam requirements/recommendations for international students: Required—TOEFL. *Faculty research:* Aggression, hypertension, faces, anger, teaching.

North Carolina State University, Graduate School, College of Humanities and Social Sciences, Department of Psychology, Raleigh, NC 27695. Offers developmental psychology (PhD); ergonomics and experimental psychology (PhD); industrial/organizational psychology (PhD); psychology in the public interest (PhD); school psychology (PhD). *Accreditation:* APA. *Degree requirements:* For doctorate, comprehensive exam, thesis/dissertation. *Entrance requirements:* For doctorate, GRE General Test, GRE Subject Test (industrial/organizational psychology), MAT (recommended), minimum GPA of 3.0 in major. Electronic applications accepted. *Faculty research:* Cognitive and social development (human factors, families, the workplace, community issues and health, aging).

Northcentral University, Graduate Studies, Prescott Valley, AZ 86314. Offers business (MBA, DBA, PhD, CAGS); education (M Ed, Ed D, PhD, CAGS); psychology (MA, PhD, CAGS).

North Dakota State University, College of Graduate and Interdisciplinary Studies, College of Science and Mathematics, Department of Psychology, Fargo, ND 58105. Offers clinical psychology (MS); cognitive and visual neuroscience (PhD); health and social psychology (PhD); psychology (MS). *Faculty:* 18 full-time (4 women), 2 part-time/adjunct (1 woman). *Students:* 36 full-time (27 women); includes 4 minority (1 African American, 2 Asian Americans or Pacific Islanders, 1 Hispanic American), 1 international. Average age 24. 48 applicants, 33% accepted, 10 enrolled. In 2007, 3 master's, 1 doctorate awarded. *Degree requirements:* For master's, thesis; for doctorate, thesis/dissertation. *Entrance requirements:* For master's and doctorate, GRE General Test, GRE Subject Test. Additional exam requirements/recommendations for international students: Required—TOEFL (minimum score 525 paper-based; 197 computer-based; 71 iBT). *Application deadline:* For fall admission, 3/1 for domestic and international students. Application fee: $45 ($60 for international students). Electronic applications accepted. *Expenses:* Tuition, state resident: full-time $5,376; part-time $224 per credit. Tuition, nonresident: full-time $14,354; part-time $598 per credit. Required fees: $962; $40 per credit. Part-time tuition and fees vary according to course load and reciprocity agreements. *Financial support:* In 2007–08, 36 students received support, including 2 fellowships with full tuition reimbursements available (averaging $16,000 per year), 23 research assistantships with full tuition reimbursements available (averaging $16,000 per year), 11 teaching assistantships with full tuition reimbursements available (averaging $6,000 per year); career-related internships or fieldwork, Federal Work-Study, institutionally sponsored loans, tuition waivers (full and partial), and unspecified assistantships also available. Support available to part-time students. Financial award application deadline: 3/1. *Faculty research:* Cognition science, neuropsychology, group behavior, applied behavior analysis, behavior therapy. Total annual research expenditures: $2 million. *Unit head:* Dr. Paul D. Rokke, Chair, 701-231-8622, Fax: 701-231-8426, E-mail: paul.rokke@ndsu.edu.

Northeastern State University, Graduate College, College of Education, Department of Psychology and Counseling, Tahlequah, OK 74464-2399. Offers counseling psychology (MS); school counseling (M Ed). Part-time and evening/weekend programs available. *Students:* 87 full-time (67 women), 58 part-time (46 women); includes 40 minority (9 African Americans, 29 American Indian/Alaska Native, 1 Asian American or Pacific Islander, 1 Hispanic American), 1 international. In 2007, 40 degrees awarded. *Degree requirements:* For master's, thesis (for some programs); written and oral examinations. *Entrance requirements:* For master's, GRE, minimum GPA of 2.5. *Application deadline:* Applications are processed on a rolling basis. Application fee: $0. *Financial support:* Teaching assistantships, career-related internships or fieldwork and Federal Work-Study available. Financial award application deadline: 3/1. *Unit head:* Dr. Kathryn Sanders, Chair, 918-456-5511 Ext. 3016, Fax: 918-458-2397, E-mail: sanderka@nsuok.edu.

Northeastern University, Bouvé College of Health Sciences Graduate School, Department of Counseling and Applied Educational Psychology, Boston, MA 02115-5096. Offers applied behavior analysis (MS); applied educational psychology (MS), including school counseling, school psychology; college student development and counseling (MS); counseling psychology (MS, PhD, CAGS); school psychology (PhD, CAGS); special needs and intensive special needs (MS Ed). *Accreditation:* APA (one or more programs are accredited). Part-time and evening/weekend programs available. *Degree requirements:* For doctorate, comprehensive exam, thesis/dissertation, qualifying exams; for CAGS, comprehensive exam. *Entrance requirements:* For master's and CAGS, GRE General Test or MAT; for doctorate, GRE General Test. Additional exam requirements/recommendations for international students: Required—TOEFL. *Faculty research:* Early intervention, career development and choice, crisis intervention, family systems, bilingual education in special education.

Northern Arizona University, Graduate College, College of Social and Behavioral Sciences, Department of Psychology, Flagstaff, AZ 86011. Offers applied health psychology (MA); general (MA). Part-time programs available. *Degree requirements:* For master's, thesis, oral defense. *Entrance requirements:* For master's, GRE General Test.

Northern Illinois University, Graduate School, College of Liberal Arts and Sciences, Department of Psychology, De Kalb, IL 60115-2854. Offers MA, PhD. *Accreditation:* APA (one or more programs are accredited). *Faculty:* 26 full-time (11 women), 5 part-time/adjunct (1 woman). *Students:* 126 full-time (86 women), 20 part-time (15 women); includes 20 minority (6 African Americans, 4 American Indian/Alaska Native, 5 Asian Americans or Pacific Islanders, 5 Hispanic Americans), 7 international. Average age 27. 376 applicants, 14% accepted, 36 enrolled. In 2007, 33 master's, 13 doctorates awarded. *Degree requirements:* For master's, comprehensive exam, thesis optional; for doctorate, thesis/dissertation, candidacy exam, dissertation defense. *Entrance requirements:* For master's, GRE General Test, minimum GPA of 3.0 for last 2 years of undergraduate work; for doctorate, GRE General Test, minimum undergraduate GPA of 2.75, graduate GPA of 3.2; master's degree with research thesis. Additional exam requirements/recommendations for international students: Required—TOEFL (minimum score 550 paper-based; 213 computer-based). *Application deadline:* For fall admission, 3/1 for domestic students, 5/1 for international students; for spring admission, 11/1 for domestic students, 10/1 for international students. Applications are processed on a rolling basis. Application fee: $30. Electronic applications accepted. *Expenses:* Tuition, area resident: Part-time $226 per credit hour. Tuition, state resident: full-time $5,424; part-time $225 per credit hour.

Tuition, nonresident: full-time $10,848. Required fees: $2,416; $64 per credit hour. *Financial support:* In 2007–08, 41 research assistantships with full tuition reimbursements, 52 teaching assistantships with full tuition reimbursements were awarded; fellowships with full tuition reimbursements, career-related internships or fieldwork, Federal Work-Study, scholarships/grants, tuition waivers (full), and unspecified assistantships also available. Support available to part-time students. Financial award applicants required to submit FAFSA. *Faculty research:* Neglect syndrome, ADHD, workplace discrimination, adolescent suicide, social dilemmas. *Unit head:* Dr. Charles Miller, Chair, 815-753-7070, E-mail: cmiller@niu.edu. *Application contact:* Dr. Greg Waas, Director, Graduate Studies, 815-753-7070, E-mail: gwaas@niu.edu.

Northern Michigan University, College of Graduate Studies, College of Professional Studies, Department of Psychology, Marquette, MI 49855-5301. Offers MS. Part-time and evening/weekend programs available. *Degree requirements:* For master's, thesis (for some programs). *Entrance requirements:* For master's, GRE, minimum GPA of 3.0.

Northwestern State University of Louisiana, Graduate Studies and Research, Department of Psychology, Natchitoches, LA 71497. Offers clinical psychology (MS). *Faculty:* 5 full-time (4 women), 1 (woman) part-time/adjunct. *Students:* 14 full-time (10 women), 8 part-time (6 women); includes 10 minority (6 African Americans, 1 American Indian/Alaska Native, 3 Hispanic Americans). Average age 26. In 2007, 7 degrees awarded. *Degree requirements:* For master's, comprehensive exam, thesis or alternative. *Entrance requirements:* For master's, GRE General Test, GRE Subject Test, minimum undergraduate GPA of 2.5. *Application deadline:* For fall admission, 8/1 priority date for domestic students; for spring admission, 1/10 for domestic students. Applications are processed on a rolling basis. Application fee: $20 ($30 for international students). *Financial support:* Application deadline: 7/15. *Unit head:* Dr. Cynthia Lindsey, Head, 318-357-6594, Fax: 318-357-6802, E-mail: lindseyc@nsula.edu. *Application contact:* Dr. Steven G. Horton, Associate Provost/Dean, Graduate Studies, Research, and Information Systems, 318-357-5851, Fax: 318-357-5019, E-mail: grad_school@nsula.edu.

Northwestern University, The Graduate School, Judd A. and Marjorie Weinberg College of Arts and Sciences, Department of Psychology, Evanston, IL 60208. Offers brain, behavior and cognition (PhD); clinical psychology (PhD); cognitive psychology (PhD); personality (PhD); social psychology (PhD); JD/PhD. Admissions and degrees offered through The Graduate School. *Accreditation:* APA (one or more programs are accredited). Part-time programs available. *Degree requirements:* For doctorate, thesis/dissertation. *Entrance requirements:* For doctorate, GRE General Test, GRE Subject Test. Additional exam requirements/recommendations for international students: Required—TOEFL. Electronic applications accepted. *Faculty research:* Memory and higher order cognition, anxiety and depression, effectiveness of psychotherapy, social cognition, molecular basis of memory.

Announcement: The Department of Psychology offers PhD programs in brain, behavior, and cognition (BBC); cognitive psychology; social psychology; personality; and clinical psychology. There is a special emphasis on genuine interdisciplinary cooperation. Study and research programs are tailored to the individual. Write to Graduate Admissions Coordinator.

Northwest Missouri State University, Graduate School, College of Education and Human Services, Department of Psychology and Sociology, Maryville, MO 64468-6001. Offers guidance and counseling (MS Ed). Part-time programs available. *Faculty:* 8 full-time (5 women). *Students:* 9 full-time (8 women), 26 part-time (21 women); includes 2 minority (both African Americans) 15 applicants, 93% accepted, 13 enrolled. In 2007, 6 degrees awarded. *Degree requirements:* For master's, comprehensive exam, thesis. *Entrance requirements:* For master's, GRE General Test, minimum undergraduate GPA of 2.5, 3.0 in major; writing sample. Additional exam requirements/recommendations for international students: Required—TOEFL (minimum score 550 paper-based; 213 computer-based). *Application deadline:* For fall admission, 3/1 for domestic and international students. Applications are processed on a rolling basis. Application fee: $0 ($50 for international students). Electronic applications accepted. *Financial support:* In 2007–08, 3 research assistantships with full tuition reimbursements (averaging $6,000 per year) were awarded; teaching assistantships, unspecified assistantships also available. Financial award application deadline: 3/1; financial award applicants required to submit FAFSA. *Unit head:* Dr. Jackie Kibler, Chairperson, 660-562-1852. *Application contact:* Dr. Frances Shipley, Dean of Graduate School, 660-562-1145, Fax: 660-562-1096, E-mail: gradsch@nwmissouri.edu.

Northwest University, School of Graduate Psychology, Kirkland, WA 98033. Offers counseling psychology (MA). Evening/weekend programs available. *Entrance requirements:* For master's, essay, 3 character references. Additional exam requirements/recommendations for international students: Required—TOEFL (minimum score 580 paper-based; 237 computer-based). Expenses: Contact institution.

Notre Dame de Namur University, Division of Academic Affairs, School of Sciences, Department of Clinical Psychology and Gerontology, Belmont, CA 94002-1908. Offers chemical dependency (MACP); clinical gerontology (MA, Certificate); counseling psychology (MACP); marital and family therapy (MACP, MAMFT). Part-time and evening/weekend programs available. *Faculty:* 2 full-time (both women), 6 part-time/adjunct (5 women). *Students:* 29 full-time (25 women), 65 part-time (56 women); includes 31 minority (5 African Americans, 11 Asian Americans or Pacific Islanders, 15 Hispanic Americans), 1 international. Average age 35. 26 applicants, 81% accepted, 16 enrolled. In 2007, 23 degrees awarded. *Entrance requirements:* For master's, interview, minimum GPA of 2.5. Additional exam requirements/recommendations for international students: Required—TOEFL. *Application deadline:* For fall admission, 8/1 priority date for domestic students; for spring admission, 12/1 priority date for domestic students. Applications are processed on a rolling basis. Application fee: $50. Electronic applications accepted. *Financial support:* Career-related internships or fieldwork available. Support available to part-time students. Financial award applicants required to submit FAFSA. *Unit head:* Dr. Nusha Askari, Chair, 650-508-3728, E-mail: naskari@ndnu.edu. *Application contact:* Helen Valine, Director of Graduate Admissions, 650-508-3534, Fax: 650-508-3426, E-mail: grad.admit@ndnu.edu.

Nova Southeastern University, Center for Psychological Studies, Fort Lauderdale, FL 33314-7796. Offers MS, PhD, Psy D, Psy S, SPS. *Accreditation:* APA (one or more programs are accredited). Postbaccalaureate distance learning degree programs offered. *Faculty:* 34 full-time (11 women), 68 part-time/adjunct (32 women). *Students:* 810 full-time (687 women), 625 part-time (556 women); includes 574 minority (271 African Americans, 5 American Indian/Alaska Native, 30 Asian Americans or Pacific Islanders, 268 Hispanic Americans), 25 international. 1,433 applicants, 49% accepted, 520 enrolled. In 2007, 315 master's, 91 doctorates, 34 other advanced degrees awarded. Terminal master's awarded for partial completion of doctoral program. *Degree requirements:* For master's, comprehensive exam, 3 practica; for doctorate, thesis/dissertation, clinical internship, competency exam; for other advanced degree, comprehensive exam, internship. *Entrance requirements:* For doctorate, GRE General Test, GRE Subject Test (recommended), minimum undergraduate GPA of 3.0; for other advanced degree, GRE General Test. Additional exam requirements/recommendations for international students: Required—TOEFL (minimum score 550 paper-based; 213 computer-based). *Application deadline:* Applications are processed on a rolling basis. Application fee: $50. Electronic applications accepted. *Expenses: Contact institution. Financial support:* In 2007–08, 5 research assistantships, 34 teaching assistantships (averaging $1,000 per year) were awarded; career-related internships or fieldwork, Federal Work-Study, institutionally sponsored loans, scholarships/grants, and unspecified assistantships also available. Support available to part-time students. Financial award application deadline: 4/1. *Faculty research:* Clinical and child clinical psychology, geriatrics, interpersonal violence. *Unit head:* Karen Grosby, Dean, 954-262-5701, Fax: 954-262-3859, E-mail: grosby@nova.edu. *Application contact:* Carlos Perez, Enrollment Management, 954-262-5790, Fax: 954-262-3893, E-mail: cpsinfo@cps.nova.edu.

The Ohio State University, Graduate School, College of Social and Behavioral Sciences, School of Social and Behavioral Science, Department of Psychology, Columbus, OH 43210. Offers behavioral neuroscience (PhD); clinical psychology (PhD); cognitive psychology (PhD); developmental psychology (PhD); mental retardation and developmental disabilities (PhD); psychology (MA); quantitative psychology (PhD); social psychology (PhD). *Accreditation:* APA (one or more programs are accredited). *Faculty:* 60. *Students:* 111 full-time (78 women), 6 part-time (4 women); includes 19 minority (6 African Americans, 1 American Indian/Alaska Native, 3 Asian Americans or Pacific Islanders, 9 Hispanic Americans), 16 international. Average age 27. In 2007, 17 master's, 41 doctorates awarded. *Degree requirements:* For doctorate, thesis/dissertation. *Entrance requirements:* For master's and doctorate, GRE General Test. Additional exam requirements/recommendations for international students: Required—TOEFL (minimum score 600 paper-based; 250 computer-based). *Application deadline:* For fall admission, 12/31 for domestic students, 11/30 for international students. Applications are processed on a rolling basis. Application fee: $40 ($50 for international students). Electronic applications accepted. *Financial support:* Fellowships, research assistantships, teaching assistantships available. *Unit head:* Marilynn B. Brewer, Graduate Studies Committee Chair, 614-292-3038, Fax: 614-292-4537. *Application contact:* 614-292-9444, Fax: 614-292-3895, E-mail: domestic.grad@osu.edu.

Ohio University, Graduate College, College of Arts and Sciences, Department of Psychology, Athens, OH 45701-2979. Offers clinical psychology (PhD); experimental psychology (PhD); organizational psychology (PhD). *Accreditation:* APA. *Faculty:* 23 full-time (10 women), 6 part-time/adjunct (3 women). *Students:* 65 full-time (44 women), 15 part-time (5 women); includes 6 minority (1 American Indian/Alaska Native, 2 Asian Americans or Pacific Islanders, 3 Hispanic Americans), 13 international. Average age 28. 226 applicants, 15% accepted, 20 enrolled. In 2007, 14 doctorates awarded. *Degree requirements:* For doctorate, one foreign language, comprehensive exam, thesis/dissertation. *Entrance requirements:* For doctorate, GRE General Test, GRE Subject Test. Additional exam requirements/recommendations for international students: Required—TOEFL. *Application deadline:* For fall admission, 1/1 for domestic students. Application fee: $50 ($55 for international students). *Financial support:* In 2007–08, 67 students received support, including 12 fellowships with full tuition reimbursements available (averaging $16,400 per year), 10 research assistantships with full tuition reimbursements available (averaging $13,200 per year), 14 teaching assistantships with full tuition reimbursements available (averaging $13,200 per year); career-related internships or fieldwork, Federal Work-Study, institutionally sponsored loans, traineeships, tuition waivers (full), and unspecified assistantships also available. Financial award application deadline: 1/15. *Faculty research:* Health, cognitive, child clinical, and social psychology. Total annual research expenditures: $11.2 million. *Unit head:* Dr. Bruce Carlson, Head, 740-593-1077, Fax: 740-593-0053, E-mail: carlsonb@ohio.edu. *Application contact:* Karyl Jones, Administrative Secretary, 740-593-1090, Fax: 740-593-0579, E-mail: psychology@ohio.edu.

Oklahoma State University, College of Arts and Sciences, Department of Psychology, Stillwater, OK 74078. Offers clinical psychology (PhD); experimental psychology (PhD); general psychology (MS). *Accreditation:* APA (one or more programs are accredited). *Faculty:* 24 full-time (13 women), 1 part-time/adjunct (0 women). *Students:* 36 full-time (20 women), 13 part-time (10 women); includes 13 minority (2 African Americans, 5 American Indian/Alaska Native, 2 Asian Americans or Pacific Islanders, 4 Hispanic Americans), 2 international. Average age 28. 154 applicants, 7% accepted, 10 enrolled. In 2007, 12 master's, 7 doctorates awarded. *Degree requirements:* For doctorate, thesis/dissertation. *Entrance requirements:* For master's and doctorate, GRE General Test or GMAT. Additional exam requirements/recommendations for international students: Required—TOEFL. *Application deadline:* For fall admission, 3/1 priority date for international students; for spring admission, 8/1 priority date for international students. Applications are processed on a rolling basis. Application fee: $40 ($75 for international students). Electronic applications accepted. *Expenses:* Tuition, state resident: full-time $4,993; part-time $148 per credit hour. Tuition, nonresident: full-time $14,755; part-time $555 per credit hour. Tuition and fees vary according to program. *Financial support:* In 2007–08, 12 research assistantships (averaging $13,222 per year), 34 teaching assistantships (averaging $14,372 per year) were awarded; career-related internships or fieldwork, Federal Work-Study, scholarships/grants, health care benefits, tuition waivers (partial), and unspecified assistantships also available. Support available to part-time students. Financial award application deadline: 3/1. *Unit head:* Dr. Maureen A. Sullivan, Head, 405-744-6028.

Old Dominion University, College of Sciences, Doctoral Program in Psychology, Norfolk, VA 23529. Offers applied experimental psychology (PhD); human factors psychology (PhD); industrial/organizational psychology (PhD). *Faculty:* 17 full-time (7 women), 1 part-time/adjunct (0 women). *Students:* 15 full-time (12 women), 16 part-time (10 women); includes 3 minority (1 African American, 1 Asian American or Pacific Islander, 1 Hispanic American). Average age 29. 42 applicants, 29% accepted, 6 enrolled. In 2007, 5 degrees awarded. *Degree requirements:* For doctorate, thesis/dissertation, qualifying exam. *Entrance requirements:* For doctorate, GRE, GRE Subject Test, 3 recommendation letters. Additional exam requirements/recommendations for international students: Required—TOEFL (minimum score 550 paper-based). *Application deadline:* For winter admission, 1/15 for domestic and international students. Application fee: $40. *Expenses:* Tuition, state resident: part-time $304 per credit hour. Tuition, nonresident: part-time $761 per credit hour. *Financial support:* In 2007–08, 6 students received support, including 2 fellowships with full tuition reimbursements available (averaging $18,000 per year), research assistantships with full tuition reimbursements available (averaging $12,000 per year), 3 teaching assistantships with full tuition reimbursements available (averaging $12,000 per year). Financial award application deadline: 1/15. *Faculty research:* Human-computer interaction, simulation, neuroergonomics, attention and workload. Total annual research expenditures: $399,161. *Unit head:* Dr. James Bliss, Graduate Program Director, 757-683-4051, Fax: 757-683-5087, E-mail: psychppd@odu.edu.

Old Dominion University, College of Sciences, Program in Psychology, Norfolk, VA 23529. Offers MS. Part-time programs available. *Faculty:* 17 full-time (7 women), 1 part-time/adjunct (0 women). *Students:* 11 full-time (6 women), 11 part-time (8 women); includes 6 minority (all African Americans) Average age 26. 53 applicants, 25% accepted, 7 enrolled. In 2007, 9 degrees awarded. *Degree requirements:* For master's, comprehensive exam, thesis optional. *Entrance requirements:* For master's, GRE General Test, minimum GPA of 3.0 in major, previous course work in psychology. Additional exam requirements/recommendations for international students: Required—TOEFL. *Application deadline:* For fall admission, 5/15 for domestic and international students. Applications are processed on a rolling basis. Application fee: $40. Electronic applications accepted. *Expenses:* Tuition, state resident: part-time $304 per credit hour. Tuition, nonresident: part-time $761 per credit hour. *Financial support:* In 2007–08, 10 students received support, including research assistantships with partial tuition reimbursements available (averaging $9,000 per year), 4 teaching assistantships with partial tuition reimbursements available (averaging $9,000 per year); career-related internships or fieldwork, scholarships/grants, and tuition waivers (partial) also available. Financial award application deadline: 2/15; financial award applicants required to submit FAFSA. *Faculty research:* Social psychology, developmental psychology, physiopsychology, community psychology, industrial/organizational psychology. *Unit head:* Dr. Louis H. Janda, Graduate Program Director, 757-683-4211, Fax: 757-683-5087, E-mail: ljanda@odu.edu.

Our Lady of the Lake University of San Antonio, School of Education and Clinical Studies, Program in Counseling Psychology, San Antonio, TX 78207-4689. Offers counseling psychology (MS, Psy D); marriage and family therapy (MS); school psychology (MS). *Accreditation:* APA (one or more programs are accredited). Part-time and evening/weekend programs available. *Degree requirements:* For master's, comprehensive exam, thesis optional, practicum; for doctorate, thesis/dissertation, internship, qualifying exam. *Entrance requirements:* For master's and doctorate, GRE General Test or MAT, interview. Additional exam requirements/recommendations for international students: Required—TOEFL. Electronic applications accepted. *Faculty research:* Marriage and family therapy, supervision, cross-cultural counseling, violence.

Pace University, Dyson College of Arts and Sciences, Department of Psychology, New York, NY 10038. Offers bilingual school psychology (MS Ed); counseling-substance abuse (MS); psychology (MA); school psychology (MS Ed); school-clinical child psychology (Psy D).

Psychology—General

Pace University (continued)
Accreditation: APA (one or more programs are accredited). Part-time and evening/weekend programs available. *Students:* 18 full-time (14 women), 11 part-time (9 women); includes 9 minority (2 African Americans, 1 American Indian/Alaska Native, 2 Asian Americans or Pacific Islanders, 4 Hispanic Americans), 4 international. Average age 28. 68 applicants, 66% accepted, 6 enrolled. In 2007, 40 master's, 12 doctorates awarded. Terminal master's awarded for partial completion of doctoral program. *Degree requirements:* For master's, comprehensive exam, qualifying exams, internship; for doctorate, comprehensive exam, qualifying exams, externship, internship, project. *Entrance requirements:* For master's, interview; for doctorate, GRE General Test, GRE Subject Test, interview. *Application deadline:* Applications are processed on a rolling basis. Application fee: $65. Electronic applications accepted. *Expenses:* Tuition: Part-time $856 per credit. Tuition and fees vary according to degree level and program. *Financial support:* Research assistantships, teaching assistantships, career-related internships or fieldwork, Federal Work-Study, tuition waivers (partial), and unspecified assistantships available. Support available to part-time students. Financial award applicants required to submit FAFSA. *Unit head:* Dr. Florence Denmark, Chairperson, 212-346-1506. *Application contact:* Joanna Broda, Director of Admissions, 212-346-1652, Fax: 212-346-1585, E-mail: gradnyc@pace.edu.

See Close-Up on page 1461.

Pacifica Graduate Institute, Graduate Programs, Carpinteria, CA 93013. Offers clinical psychology (PhD); counseling psychology (MA); depth psychology (MA, PhD); mythological studies (MA, PhD). Terminal master's awarded for partial completion of doctoral program. *Degree requirements:* For master's, thesis (for some programs), practicum; for doctorate, comprehensive exam, thesis/dissertation, internship. *Entrance requirements:* For master's, resumé, 3 letters of recommendation, writing sample, interview; for doctorate, resumé, 4 letters of recommendation, writing sample, interview. Additional exam requirements/recommendations for international students: Required—TOEFL. *Faculty research:* Imaginal and archetypal theory; post-Colonial psychoanalytic and Jungian theory; myth literature as it applies to the theory and practice of psychology.

Pacific Graduate School of Psychology, Distance Learning Program in Psychology, Palo Alto, CA 94303-4232. Offers MS. Postbaccalaureate distance learning degree programs offered (no on-campus study). *Entrance requirements:* For master's, GRE General Test. Additional exam requirements/recommendations for international students: Required—TOEFL (minimum score 550 paper-based; 220 computer-based). Electronic applications accepted.

Pacific Graduate School of Psychology, Program in Clinical Psychology, Palo Alto, CA 94303-4232. Offers PhD, JD/PhD, MBA/PhD. *Accreditation:* APA. *Degree requirements:* For doctorate, comprehensive exam, thesis/dissertation, 2000 hour clinical internship, oral clinical competency exam. *Entrance requirements:* For doctorate, GRE General Test, BA or MA in psychology or related area, minimum undergraduate GPA of 3.0, 3.3 graduate. Additional exam requirements/recommendations for international students: Required—TOEFL. Electronic applications accepted. *Faculty research:* Child/family studies, health psychology, neuropsychology, personality development, assessment.

See Close-Up on page 1463.

Pacific University, School of Professional Psychology, Forest Grove, OR 97116-1797. Offers clinical psychology (MS, Psy D); counseling psychology (MA). *Accreditation:* APA (one or more programs are accredited). Part-time programs available. *Faculty:* 22 full-time (14 women), 20 part-time/adjunct (10 women). *Students:* 260 full-time (180 women), 71 part-time (55 women); includes 33 minority (3 African Americans, 4 American Indian/Alaska Native, 21 Asian Americans or Pacific Islanders, 5 Hispanic Americans). Average age 30. 336 applicants, 49% accepted, 55 enrolled. In 2007, 66 master's, 25 doctorates awarded. *Median time to degree:* Of those who began their doctoral program in fall 1999, 73% received their degree in 8 years or less. *Degree requirements:* For master's, comprehensive exam (for some programs), thesis (for some programs); for doctorate, comprehensive exam, thesis/dissertation. *Entrance requirements:* For master's, course work in introductory psychology, statistics, and abnormal psychology; minimum GPA of 3.0; for doctorate, GRE General Test, minimum GPA of 3.0, undergraduate course work in psychology, minimum GPA of 3.1 in last 2 years. Additional exam requirements/recommendations for international students: Required—TOEFL (minimum score 600 paper-based; 105 computer-based). *Application deadline:* For fall admission, 1/10 priority date for domestic students; for winter admission, 3/5 priority date for domestic students. Application fee: $40. Electronic applications accepted. *Expenses: Contact institution. Financial support:* In 2007–08, 86 students received support; fellowships, research assistantships, teaching assistantships, career-related internships or fieldwork, Federal Work-Study, scholarships/grants, and unspecified assistantships available. Support available to part-time students. Financial award applicants required to submit FAFSA. *Faculty research:* Neuropsychological assessment, assessment and treatment of anxiety, forensic psychology, cross-cultural psychology, child and adolescent psychopathology. *Unit head:* Dr. Michel Hersen, Dean, 503-352-7330, Fax: 503-352-7320, E-mail: spp@pacificu.edu. *Application contact:* Janelle Holmboe, Assistant Director of Graduate and Professional Admissions, 503-352-2218, Fax: 503-352-2975, E-mail: admissions@pacificu.edu.

Penn State Harrisburg, Graduate School, School of Behavioral Sciences and Education, Middletown, PA 17057-4898. Offers adult education (D Ed); applied behavior analysis (MA); applied clinical psychology (MA); applied psychological research (MA); community psychology and social change (MA); health education (M Ed); teaching and curriculum (M Ed); training and development (M Ed). Part-time and evening/weekend programs available. *Financial support:* Career-related internships or fieldwork available. *Unit head:* Dr. William D. Milheim, Director, 717-948-6205, Fax: 717-948-6209, E-mail: wdm2@psu.edu.

Penn State University Park, Graduate School, College of the Liberal Arts, Department of Psychology, State College, University Park, PA 16802-1503. Offers clinical psychology (MS, PhD); cognitive psychology (MS, PhD); developmental psychology (MS, PhD); industrial/organizational psychology (MS, PhD); psychobiology (MS, PhD); social psychology (MS, PhD). *Accreditation:* APA (one or more programs are accredited). *Expenses:* Tuition, state resident: full-time $14,738; part-time $614 per credit. Tuition, nonresident: full-time $26,050; part-time $1,085 per credit. Tuition and fees vary according to course load, program and student level. *Unit head:* Dr. Melvin M. Mark, Interim Head, 814-865-9515, Fax: 814-863-7002, E-mail: m5m@psu.edu.

Pepperdine University, Graduate School of Education and Psychology, Division of Psychology, Malibu, CA 90263. Offers clinical psychology (MA). *Entrance requirements:* For master's, GRE General Test or MAT, 2 professional recommendations. Additional exam requirements/recommendations for international students: Required—TOEFL (minimum score 550 paper-based; 220 computer-based).

Pepperdine University, Graduate School of Education and Psychology, Division of Psychology, Los Angeles, CA 90045. Offers clinical psychology (MA); psychology (MA, Psy D). Part-time and evening/weekend programs available. *Faculty:* 32 full-time (11 women), 76 part-time/adjunct (42 women). *Students:* 156 full-time (135 women), 185 part-time (149 women); includes 105 minority (30 African Americans, 3 American Indian/Alaska Native, 29 Asian Americans or Pacific Islanders, 43 Hispanic Americans), 6 international. 630 applicants, 70% accepted, 238 enrolled. In 2007, 313 master's, 27 doctorates awarded. *Entrance requirements:* For master's and doctorate, GRE General Test. Additional exam requirements/recommendations for international students: Required—TOEFL. *Application deadline:* For fall admission, 2/1 for domestic students. Applications are processed on a rolling basis. Application fee: $55. *Expenses: Contact institution. Financial support:* Research assistantships, teaching assistantships, career-related internships or fieldwork and scholarships/grants available. Support available to part-time students. Financial award application deadline: 7/1; financial award applicants required to submit FAFSA. *Unit head:* Dr. Robert deMayo, Associate Dean, 310-568-5747, E-mail: robert.demayo@pepperdine.edu. *Application contact:* Brenden Wysocki, Admissions Manager, 310-568-5786.

See Close-Up on page 1467.

Philadelphia College of Osteopathic Medicine, Graduate and Professional Programs, Department of Psychology, Philadelphia, PA 19131-1694. Offers clinical psychology (Psy D); counseling and clinical health psychology (MS); organizational leadership and development (MS); psychology (Certificate); school psychology (MS, Psy D, Ed S). *Accreditation:* APA. *Degree requirements:* For master's, thesis; for doctorate, comprehensive exam, thesis/dissertation, final project, fieldwork. *Entrance requirements:* For master's, GRE or MAT, minimum GPA of 3.0; course work in biology, chemistry, English, physics; for other advanced degree, PRAXIS. *Faculty research:* Depression in primary care, integrated primary care, geriatric mental health.

See Close-Up on page 1469.

Pittsburg State University, Graduate School, College of Education, Department of Psychology and Counseling, Program in Psychology, Pittsburg, KS 66762. Offers MS. *Degree requirements:* For master's, thesis or alternative. *Entrance requirements:* For master's, GRE General Test, minimum GPA of 2.8.

Polytechnic Institute of NYU, Department of Humanities and Social Sciences, Major in Environment-Behavior Studies, Brooklyn, NY 11201-2990. Offers MS. Part-time and evening/weekend programs available. *Students:* 2 applicants, 0% accepted. *Degree requirements:* For master's, comprehensive exam (for some programs), thesis (for some programs). *Entrance requirements:* Additional exam requirements/recommendations for international students: Required—TOEFL (minimum score 550 paper-based; 213 computer-based); Recommended—IELTS (minimum score 7). *Application deadline:* For fall admission, 7/15 priority date for domestic students, 4/1 priority date for international students; for spring admission, 12/15 priority date for domestic students, 10/1 priority date for international students. Applications are processed on a rolling basis. Application fee: $55. Electronic applications accepted. *Expenses:* Tuition: Full-time $18,486; part-time $1,027 per credit. Required fees: $352 per semester.

Pontifical Catholic University of Puerto Rico, Institute of Graduate Studies in Behavioral Science and Community Affairs, Ponce, PR 00717-0777. Offers clinical psychology (MA, MS, PhD); clinical social work (MSW); criminology (MA); industrial psychology (MS, PhD); psychology (PhD); public administration (MA); vocational rehabilitation counseling (MSS). Part-time and evening/weekend programs available. *Degree requirements:* For master's, thesis; for doctorate, comprehensive exam, thesis/dissertation. *Entrance requirements:* For master's, EXADEP, GRE, 3 letters of recommendation, interview, minimum GPA of 2.75.

Portland State University, Graduate Studies, College of Liberal Arts and Sciences, Department of Psychology, Portland, OR 97207-0751. Offers MA, MS, PhD. *Faculty:* 19 full-time (10 women), 12 part-time/adjunct (5 women). *Students:* 44 full-time (33 women), 5 part-time (4 women); includes 7 minority (1 African American, 1 American Indian/Alaska Native, 5 Hispanic Americans), 4 international. Average age 32. 70 applicants, 26% accepted, 15 enrolled. In 2007, 6 master's, 3 doctorates awarded. *Degree requirements:* For master's, variable foreign language requirement, thesis; for doctorate, variable foreign language requirement, comprehensive exam, thesis/dissertation. *Entrance requirements:* For master's, GRE General Test, minimum GPA of 3.0 in upper-division course work or 2.75 overall, 3 letters of recommendation. Additional exam requirements/recommendations for international students: Required—TOEFL (minimum score 550 paper-based; 213 computer-based). *Application deadline:* For fall admission, 1/15 for domestic and international students. Application fee: $50. *Expenses:* Tuition, state resident: full-time $7,047. Tuition, nonresident: full-time $11,178. *Financial support:* In 2007–08, 10 research assistantships with full tuition reimbursements (averaging $9,065 per year), 40 teaching assistantships with full tuition reimbursements (averaging $8,988 per year) were awarded; career-related internships or fieldwork, Federal Work-Study, scholarships/grants, tuition waivers (partial), and unspecified assistantships also available. Support available to part-time students. Financial award application deadline: 3/1; financial award applicants required to submit FAFSA. *Faculty research:* Organizational psychology, work and the family, quantitative psychology, decision making, psychosocial factors affecting health. Total annual research expenditures: $760,591. *Unit head:* Sherwin Davidson, Chair, 503-725-3923, Fax: 503-725-3904, E-mail: davidsons@pdx.edu.

Portland State University, Graduate Studies, Systems Science Program, Portland, OR 97207-0751. Offers computational intelligence (Certificate); computer modeling and simulation (Certificate); systems science (MS); systems science/anthropology (PhD); systems science/business administration (PhD); systems science/civil engineering (PhD); systems science/economics (PhD); systems science/engineering management (PhD); systems science/general (PhD); systems science/mathematical sciences (PhD); systems science/mechanical engineering (PhD); systems science/psychology (PhD); systems science/sociology (PhD). *Faculty:* 3 full-time (0 women). *Students:* 9 full-time (2 women), 11 part-time (2 women); includes 6 minority (3 Asian Americans or Pacific Islanders, 3 Hispanic Americans), 13 international. Average age 38. 8 applicants, 100% accepted, 6 enrolled. In 2007, 4 master's, 6 doctorates awarded. *Degree requirements:* For doctorate, variable foreign language requirement, thesis/dissertation. *Entrance requirements:* For master's, 2 letters of recommendation; for doctorate, GMAT, GRE General Test, minimum undergraduate GPA of 3.0. Additional exam requirements/recommendations for international students: Required—TOEFL. *Application deadline:* For fall admission, 2/1 for domestic students; for spring admission, 11/1 for domestic students. Application fee: $50. *Expenses:* Tuition, state resident: full-time $7,047. Tuition, nonresident: full-time $11,178. *Financial support:* In 2007–08, 1 research assistantship with full tuition reimbursement (averaging $5,980 per year) was awarded; teaching assistantships with full tuition reimbursements, career-related internships or fieldwork, Federal Work-Study, scholarships/grants, and unspecified assistantships also available. Support available to part-time students. Financial award application deadline: 3/1; financial award applicants required to submit FAFSA. *Faculty research:* Systems theory and methodology, artificial intelligence neural networks, information theory, nonlinear dynamics/chaos, modeling and simulation. Total annual research expenditures: $5,370. *Unit head:* George Lendaris, Acting Director, 503-725-4960. *Application contact:* Dawn Sharafi, Administrative Assistant, 503-725-4960, E-mail: dawn@sysc.pdx.edu.

Princeton University, Graduate School, Department of Psychology, Princeton, NJ 08544-1019. Offers neuroscience (PhD); psychology (PhD). *Degree requirements:* For doctorate, thesis/dissertation. *Entrance requirements:* For doctorate, GRE General Test, GRE Subject Test. Additional exam requirements/recommendations for international students: Required—TOEFL (minimum score 550 paper-based). Electronic applications accepted.

Purdue University, Graduate School, College of Liberal Arts, Department of Psychological Sciences, West Lafayette, IN 47907. Offers PhD. *Accreditation:* APA. *Entrance requirements:* For doctorate, GRE General Test. Additional exam requirements/recommendations for international students: Required—TOEFL. Electronic applications accepted. *Faculty research:* Career development of women in science, development of friendships during childhood and adolescence, social competence, human information processing.

Queens College of the City University of New York, Division of Graduate Studies, Mathematics and Natural Sciences Division, Department of Psychology, Flushing, NY 11367-1597. Offers clinical behavioral applications in mental health settings (MA); psychology (MA). Part-time programs available. *Faculty:* 27 full-time (13 women). *Students:* 21 full-time (16 women), 61 part-time (46 women). 111 applicants, 73% accepted, 49 enrolled. In 2007, 21 degrees awarded. *Degree requirements:* For master's, comprehensive exam, thesis or alternative. *Entrance requirements:* For master's, GRE, minimum GPA of 3.0. Additional exam requirements/recommendations for international students: Required—TOEFL. *Application deadline:* For fall admission, 4/1 for domestic students; for spring admission, 11/1 for domestic students. Applications are processed on a rolling basis. Application fee: $125. *Financial* *support:* Career-related internships or fieldwork, Federal Work-Study, institutionally sponsored loans, and tuition waivers (partial) available. Support available to part-time students. Financial award application deadline: 4/1; financial award applicants required to submit FAFSA. *Unit head:* Dr. Richard Bodnar, Chairperson, 718-997-3200. *Application contact:* Dr. Philip Ramsey, Graduate Adviser, 718-997-3200, E-mail: philip_ramsey@qc.edu.

Queen's University at Kingston, School of Graduate Studies and Research, Faculty of Arts and Sciences, Department of Psychology, Kingston, ON K7L 3N6, Canada. Offers brain behavior and cognitive science (MA, PhD); clinical psychology (MA, PhD); developmental psychology (MA, PhD); social personality psychology (MA, PhD). *Accreditation:* APA (one or more programs are accredited). *Degree requirements:* For master's, thesis; for doctorate, comprehensive exam, thesis/dissertation. *Entrance requirements:* For master's and doctorate, GRE General Test. Additional exam requirements/recommendations for international students: Required—TOEFL. *Faculty research:* Human development, social, personality, behavioral neuroscience, forensic.

Radford University, Graduate College, College of Humanities and Behavioral Sciences, Department of Psychology, Radford, VA 24142. Offers clinical psychology (MA, MS); counseling psychology (Psy D); experimental psychology (MA); industrial-organizational psychology (MA, MS); school psychology (Ed S). Part-time programs available. *Faculty:* 24 full-time (10 women). *Students:* 38 full-time (31 women), 52 part-time (39 women); includes 5 minority (4 African Americans, 1 Asian American or Pacific Islander), 2 international. Average age 25. 128 applicants, 64% accepted, 38 enrolled. In 2007, 45 degrees awarded. *Degree requirements:* For master's, comprehensive exam, thesis (for some programs); for doctorate, comprehensive exam, thesis/dissertation; for Ed S, comprehensive exam. *Entrance requirements:* For master's, GRE, minimum GPA 3.0; for doctorate, GRE; for Ed S, GMAT, GRE General Test, MAT, NTE. Additional exam requirements/recommendations for international students: Required—TOEFL. *Application deadline:* For fall admission, 3/1 priority date for domestic students, 12/1 for international students; for spring admission, 10/1 for domestic students, 7/1 for international students. Applications are processed on a rolling basis. Application fee: $40. Electronic applications accepted. *Financial support:* In 2007–08, 42 research assistantships with partial tuition reimbursements (averaging $8,000 per year), 12 teaching assistantships with partial tuition reimbursements (averaging $8,700 per year) were awarded; career-related internships or fieldwork, Federal Work-Study, institutionally sponsored loans, scholarships/grants, and unspecified assistantships also available. Financial award application deadline: 3/1; financial award applicants required to submit FAFSA. *Unit head:* Dr. Hilary M. Lips, Chair, 540-831-5387, Fax: 540-831-6113, E-mail: hlips@radford.edu.

Regis University, College for Professional Studies, MA Program, Denver, CO 80221-1099. Offers criminology (MA); fine arts administration (Certificate); language and communication (MA); mediation (Certificate); psychology (MA); self-designed major (MA); social justice, peace, and reconciliation (Certificate); social science (MA); technical communication (Certificate). Program also offered in Henderson and Las Vegas (Summerlin), NV. Part-time and evening/weekend programs available. Postbaccalaureate distance learning degree programs offered (minimal on-campus study). *Faculty:* 84. *Students:* 218 (167 women). Average age 41. In 2007, 52 degrees awarded. *Degree requirements:* For master's, thesis, research project. *Entrance requirements:* For master's, resumé, recommendations, essays. Additional exam requirements/recommendations for international students: Required—TOEFL (minimum score 213 computer-based), TWE (minimum score 5). *Application deadline:* For fall admission, 8/13 priority date for domestic students, 7/13 priority date for international students; for winter admission, 10/8 priority date for domestic students, 9/8 priority date for international students; for spring admission, 12/17 priority date for domestic students, 11/17 for international students. Applications are processed on a rolling basis. Application fee: $75. Electronic applications accepted. *Expenses: Contact institution. Financial support:* Federal Work-Study available. Support available to part-time students. Financial award application deadline: 3/15; financial award applicants required to submit FAFSA. *Faculty research:* Independent/nonresidential graduate study: new methods and models, adult learning and the capstone experience, Goal Setting, behavior of Adult students, Innovative Studies for Community Colleges. *Unit head:* Dr. Robert Collins, Chair, 303-458-4302, Fax: 303-964-5538. *Application contact:* Graduate Admissions, 800-677-9270 Ext. 4080, Fax: 303-964-5538, E-mail: masters@regis.edu.

Rhode Island College, School of Graduate Studies, Faculty of Arts and Sciences, Department of Psychology, Providence, RI 02908-1991. Offers MA. Part-time and evening/weekend programs available. *Faculty:* 12 full-time (5 women), 1 (woman) part-time/adjunct. *Students:* 3 full-time (1 woman), 8 part-time (7 women); includes 3 minority (1 African American, 2 Hispanic Americans). Average age 29. In 2007, 5 degrees awarded. *Degree requirements:* For master's, comprehensive exam. *Entrance requirements:* For master's, GRE or MAT, 3 letters of recommendation. *Application deadline:* For fall admission, 4/1 for domestic students; for spring admission, 11/1 for domestic students. Applications are processed on a rolling basis. Application fee: $50. *Expenses:* Tuition, state resident: full-time $6,240; part-time $260 per credit hour. Tuition, nonresident: full-time $13,104; part-time $546 per credit hour. Required fees: $332; $14 per credit hour. One-time fee: $66 part-time. *Financial support:* In 2007–08, 1 teaching assistantship with full tuition reimbursement (averaging $4,000 per year) was awarded; Federal Work-Study, scholarships/grants, health care benefits, and unspecified assistantships also available. Support available to part-time students. Financial award application deadline: 5/15; financial award applicants required to submit FAFSA. *Unit head:* Dr. David Sugarman, Chair, 401-456-8107, E-mail: dsugarman@ric.edu.

Rice University, Graduate Programs, School of Social Sciences, Department of Psychology, Houston, TX 77251-1892. Offers cognitive sciences (MA, PhD); industrial-organizational/social psychology (MA, PhD); psychology (MA, PhD). Terminal master's awarded for partial completion of doctoral program. *Degree requirements:* For master's, thesis; for doctorate, thesis/dissertation. *Entrance requirements:* For doctorate, GRE General Test, minimum GPA of 3.0. Additional exam requirements/recommendations for international students: Required—TOEFL. Electronic applications accepted. *Faculty research:* Learning and memory, information processing, decision theory.

Rochester Institute of Technology, Graduate Enrollment Services, College of Liberal Arts, Department of Psychology, Rochester, NY 14623-5603. Offers MS. *Students:* 10 full-time (6 women), 3 part-time (1 woman); includes 1 minority (African American) 8 applicants, 100% accepted, 6 enrolled. *Entrance requirements:* Additional exam requirements/recommendations for international students: Required—TOEFL. *Application deadline:* For fall admission, 2/15 for domestic students. *Expenses:* Tuition: Full-time $28,491; part-time $800 per credit hour. Required fees: $201; $67 per term. *Financial support:* Research assistantships with partial tuition reimbursements, teaching assistantships with partial tuition reimbursements, career-related internships or fieldwork, institutionally sponsored loans, scholarships/grants, and unspecified assistantships available. Support available to part-time students. Financial award applicants required to submit FAFSA. *Unit head:* Dr. Kathleen Chen, Chair, 585-475-2405, E-mail: kccgss@rit.edu.

Roosevelt University, Graduate Division, College of Arts and Sciences, Department of Psychology, Program in Psychology, Chicago, IL 60605-1394. Offers Psy D. *Students:* 57 full-time (43 women), 22 part-time (14 women); includes 15 minority (10 African Americans, 2 Asian Americans or Pacific Islanders, 3 Hispanic Americans), 1 international. Average age 30. 144 applicants, 12% accepted, 17 enrolled. In 2007, 5 degrees awarded. Application fee: $25 ($35 for international students). *Unit head:* Steven Kvaal, Director, 312-341-6374.

Rosalind Franklin University of Medicine and Science, College of Health Professions, Department of Psychology, North Chicago, IL 60064-3095. Offers clinical counseling (MS); psychology (MS, PhD). *Faculty:* 9 full-time (2 women), 6 part-time/adjunct (3 women). *Students:* 56 full-time (40 women); includes 8 minority (2 African Americans, 6 Asian Americans or Pacific Islanders), 1 international. 63 applicants, 33% accepted, 12 enrolled. In 2007, 7 master's, 14 doctorates awarded. Terminal master's awarded for partial completion of doctoral program. *Degree requirements:* For master's, capstone experience. *Entrance requirements:* For master's, GRE (optional), minimum 3.0 GPA, bachelor's degree (preferably in related subject); for doctorate, GRE, minimum 3.0 GPA, bachelors or master's degree. Additional exam requirements/recommendations for international students: Required—TOEFL. Application fee: $25. *Financial support:* In 2007–08, 13 fellowships with partial tuition reimbursements (averaging $10,000 per year), 5 research assistantships with partial tuition reimbursements (averaging $10,000 per year), 6 teaching assistantships (averaging $10,000 per year) were awarded; career-related internships or fieldwork and Federal Work-Study also available. *Faculty research:* Anxiety, pain, psychopathy, epilepsy, neuropsychology. *Unit head:* Dr. John E. Calamari, Acting Chair, 847-578-8747, Fax: 847-578-8765, E-mail: john.calamari@rosalindfranklin.edu. *Application contact:* Patricia Rigwood, Administrative Assistant, 847-578-3305, Fax: 847-578-8765, E-mail: patricia.rigwood@rosalindfranklin.edu.

Rowan University, Graduate School, College of Liberal Arts and Sciences, Program in Mental Health Counseling and Applied Psychology, Glassboro, NJ 08028-1701. Offers MA, CAGS. Part-time and evening/weekend programs available. *Faculty:* 18 full-time (13 women), 4 part-time/adjunct (1 woman). *Students:* 22 full-time (17 women), 9 part-time (all women); includes 5 minority (1 African American, 2 Asian Americans or Pacific Islanders, 2 Hispanic Americans). Average age 27. 26 applicants, 27% accepted, 6 enrolled. In 2007, 7 degrees awarded. *Entrance requirements:* Additional exam requirements/recommendations for international students: Required—TOEFL. *Application deadline:* Applications are processed on a rolling basis. Application fee: $50. Electronic applications accepted. *Expenses:* Tuition, nonresident: full-time $9,882; part-time $549 per credit. Required fees: $104,385 per credit. *Financial support:* Career-related internships or fieldwork, Federal Work-Study, and unspecified assistantships available. Support available to part-time students. *Unit head:* Dr. David Angelone, Adviser, 856-256-4500 Ext. 3780.

Rutgers, The State University of New Jersey, Camden, Graduate School of Arts and Sciences, Program in Psychology, Camden, NJ 08102-1401. Offers MA. *Faculty research:* Cognitive psychology, sexuality, health psychology, personality psychology, clinical psychology.

Rutgers, The State University of New Jersey, Newark, Graduate School, Program in Psychology, Newark, NJ 07102. Offers cognitive neuroscience (PhD); cognitive science (PhD); perception (PhD); psychobiology (PhD); social cognition (PhD). *Degree requirements:* For doctorate, comprehensive exam, thesis/dissertation. *Entrance requirements:* For doctorate, GRE General Test, GRE Subject Test, minimum undergraduate B average. Electronic applications accepted. *Faculty research:* Visual perception (luminance, motion), neuroendocrine mechanisms in behavior (reproduction, pain), attachment theory, connectionist modeling of cognition.

See Close-Up on page 1475.

Rutgers, The State University of New Jersey, New Brunswick, Graduate School of Applied and Professional Psychology, New Brunswick, NJ 08901-1281. Offers Psy M, Psy D. *Accreditation:* APA (one or more programs are accredited). *Degree requirements:* For doctorate, comprehensive exam, thesis/dissertation, 1 year internship. *Entrance requirements:* For doctorate, GRE General Test, GRE Subject Test, bachelor's degree in psychology or equivalent. Additional exam requirements/recommendations for international students: Required—TOEFL. Electronic applications accepted. Expenses: Contact institution. *Faculty research:* Organizational psychology, behavior modification, long- and short-term dynamic therapy, school psychology, addictive behaviors.

Rutgers, The State University of New Jersey, New Brunswick, Graduate School, Program in Psychology, New Brunswick, NJ 08901-1281. Offers behavioral neuroscience (PhD); clinical psychology (PhD); cognitive psychology (PhD); interdisciplinary health psychology (PhD); social psychology (PhD). *Accreditation:* APA. *Degree requirements:* For doctorate, thesis/dissertation. *Entrance requirements:* For doctorate, GRE General Test, 3 letters of recommendation. Additional exam requirements/recommendations for international students: Required—TOEFL (minimum score 577 paper-based; 233 computer-based). Electronic applications accepted. *Faculty research:* Learning and memory, behavioral ecology, hormones and behavior, psychopharmacology, anxiety disorders.

Sage Graduate School, Graduate School, Department of Psychology, Troy, NY 12180-4115. Offers community psychology (MA), including child care and children's services, community counseling, community health education, general psychology; forensic psychology (Certificate). Part-time and evening/weekend programs available. *Faculty:* 4 full-time (all women), 4 part-time/adjunct (1 woman). *Students:* 38 full-time (36 women), 66 part-time (61 women); includes 13 minority (8 African Americans, 2 American Indian/Alaska Native, 1 Asian American or Pacific Islander, 2 Hispanic Americans). Average age 30. 67 applicants, 51% accepted, 19 enrolled. In 2007, 35 master's, 2 other advanced degrees awarded. *Degree requirements:* For master's, thesis or alternative. *Entrance requirements:* For master's, GRE General Test. Additional exam requirements/recommendations for international students: Required—TOEFL (minimum score 550 paper-based; 213 computer-based). *Application deadline:* Applications are processed on a rolling basis. Application fee: $40. *Expenses:* Tuition: Full-time $9,720; part-time $540 per credit hour. *Financial support:* Fellowships, research assistantships, Federal Work-Study, scholarships/grants, and unspecified assistantships available. Support available to part-time students. Financial award application deadline: 3/1; financial award applicants required to submit FAFSA. *Faculty research:* Effectiveness of arts integration program in elementary/secondary schools, literacy based substance abuse program, outcome evaluation of program to increase college entry among urban youth. Total annual research expenditures: $10,000. *Unit head:* Dr. Jean Poppei, Chair, 518-244-2076, Fax: 518-244-4545, E-mail: poppei@sage.edu. *Application contact:* Shannon K. Easton, Director of Graduate and Adult Admission, 518-244-2443, Fax: 518-244-6880, E-mail: sgsadm@sage.edu.

St. Cloud State University, School of Graduate Studies, College of Education, Department of Counselor Education and Educational Psychology, St. Cloud, MN 56301-4498. Offers college counseling and student development (MS); rehabilitation counseling (MS); school counseling (MS). *Faculty:* 12 full-time (5 women). *Students:* 97 full-time (79 women), 57 part-time (55 women); includes 4 minority (2 Asian Americans or Pacific Islanders, 2 Hispanic Americans), 10 international. 99 applicants, 47% accepted. In 2007, 40 degrees awarded. *Degree requirements:* For master's, thesis or alternative. *Entrance requirements:* For master's, GRE General Test, minimum GPA of 2.75. Additional exam requirements/recommendations for international students: Required—MELAB; Recommended—TOEFL (minimum score 550 paper-based; 213 computer-based), IELTS (minimum score 7). *Application deadline:* Applications are processed on a rolling basis. Application fee: $35. Electronic applications accepted. *Expenses:* Tuition, state resident: part-time $267 per credit. Tuition, nonresident: part-time $418 per credit. Required fees: $28 per credit. *Financial support:* Career-related internships or fieldwork, Federal Work-Study, scholarships/grants, and unspecified assistantships available. Financial award application deadline: 3/1. *Unit head:* Dr. Steve Hoorer, Chairperson, 320-308-4089, Fax: 320-308-4082, E-mail: smhoover@stcloudstate.edu. *Application contact:* Linda Lou Krueger, School of Graduate Studies, 320-308-2113, Fax: 320-308-5371, E-mail: lekrueger@stcloudstate.edu.

St. Cloud State University, School of Graduate Studies, College of Education, Department of Educational Leadership and Community Psychology, Program in Applied Behavior Analysis, St. Cloud, MN 56301-4498. Offers MS. Part-time programs available. Postbaccalaureate distance learning degree programs offered (no on-campus study). *Faculty:* 2 full-time (1 woman). *Students:* 9 full-time (all women), 59 part-time (51 women); includes 5 minority (1 African American, 1 American Indian/Alaska Native, 3 Hispanic Americans), 14 international. Average age 27. 92 applicants, 53% accepted. In 2007, 16 degrees awarded. *Degree requirements:* For master's, comprehensive exam (for some programs), thesis or alternative. *Entrance requirements:* For master's, GRE General Test, minimum GPA of 2.75. Additional exam requirements/recommendations for international students: Required—MELAB; Recommended—TOEFL (minimum score 550 paper-based; 213 computer-based), IELTS (minimum score 7). *Application deadline:* For fall admission, 4/1 for domestic and international students. Applications are processed on a rolling basis. Application fee: $35. *Expenses:*

Psychology—General

St. Cloud State University (continued)

Tuition, state resident: part-time $267 per credit. Tuition, nonresident: part-time $418 per credit. Required fees: $28 per credit. *Financial support:* Career-related internships or fieldwork, Federal Work-Study, scholarships/grants, and unspecified assistantships available. Financial award application deadline: 3/1; financial award applicants required to submit FAFSA. *Unit head:* Dr. Kimberly Schulze, Coordinator, 320-308-4155. *Application contact:* Linda Lou Krueger, School of Graduate Studies, 320-308-2113, Fax: 320-308-5371, E-mail: lekrueger@stcloudstate.edu.

St. John's University, St. John's College of Liberal Arts and Sciences, Department of Psychology, Queens, NY 11439. Offers clinical psychology (PhD), including clinical psychology-child, clinical psychology-general; general experimental psychology (MA); school psychology (MS, Psy D). *Accreditation:* APA (one or more programs are accredited). Part-time and evening/weekend programs available. *Faculty:* 29 full-time (13 women), 30 part-time/adjunct (15 women). *Students:* 159 full-time (139 women), 95 part-time (80 women); includes 39 minority (12 African Americans, 15 Asian Americans or Pacific Islanders, 12 Hispanic Americans), 5 international. Average age 28. 459 applicants, 24% accepted, 58 enrolled. In 2007, 55 master's, 39 doctorates awarded. *Median time to degree:* Of those who began their doctoral program in fall 1999, 74% received their degree in 8 years or less. *Degree requirements:* For master's, comprehensive exam, thesis optional; for doctorate, comprehensive exam, thesis/dissertation, internship. *Entrance requirements:* For master's, GRE, minimum GPA of 3.0, 2 writing samples; for doctorate, GRE General Test, GRE Subject Test, interview. Additional exam requirements/recommendations for international students: Required—TOEFL (minimum score 500 paper-based; 173 computer-based; 61 iBT), IELTS (minimum score 6). *Application deadline:* For fall admission, 2/1 for domestic students, 5/1 priority date for international students; for spring admission, 11/1 priority date for international students. Applications are processed on a rolling basis. Application fee: $40. Electronic applications accepted. *Expenses:* Contact institution. *Financial support:* Fellowships, research assistantships, career-related internships or fieldwork, scholarships/grants, and unspecified assistantships available. Support available to part-time students. Financial award application deadline: 3/1; financial award applicants required to submit FAFSA. *Faculty research:* Clinical psychology, school psychology, developmental psychology, health psychology and psychotherapies. *Unit head:* Dr. Raymond DiGiuseppe, Chair, 718-990-1955, E-mail: digiuser@stjohns.edu. *Application contact:* Br. Shamus McGrenra, Senior Associate Director, Office of Admission, 718-990-1601, Fax: 718-990-2346, E-mail: gradhelp@stjohns.edu.

Saint Joseph's University, College of Arts and Sciences, Department of Criminal Justice, Philadelphia, PA 19131-1395. Offers administration/police executive (MS); behavior analysis (MS, Post-Master's Certificate); criminal justice (MS, Post-Master's Certificate); criminology (MS); federal law (MS); intelligence and crime (MS); probation, parole, and corrections (MS). Evening/weekend programs available. *Students:* 2 full-time (1 woman), 178 part-time (107 women); includes 56 minority (49 African Americans, 1 Asian American or Pacific Islander, 6 Hispanic Americans), 2 international. Average age 33. In 2007, 118 degrees awarded. *Degree requirements:* For master's, thesis. *Entrance requirements:* For master's, GRE General Test or minimum GPA of 3.0, 2 letters of recommendation, personal statement, application, official transcripts. Additional exam requirements/recommendations for international students: Required—TOEFL (minimum score 550 paper-based; 213 computer-based; 79 iBT). *Application deadline:* For fall admission, 7/15 priority date for domestic students, 4/15 for international students; for winter admission, 1/15 for international students; for spring admission, 11/15 priority date for domestic students, 10/15 for international students. Applications are processed on a rolling basis. Application fee: $35. Electronic applications accepted. *Expenses:* Tuition: Part-time $738 per credit. Tuition and fees vary according to degree level and program. *Financial support:* Career-related internships or fieldwork and unspecified assistantships available. *Unit head:* Patricia Griffin, Director, 610-660-1294.

Saint Joseph's University, College of Arts and Sciences, Department of Psychology, Philadelphia, PA 19131-1395. Offers MS. *Students:* 17 full-time (13 women); includes 2 minority (1 African American, 1 Hispanic American), 1 international. Average age 24. In 2007, 8 degrees awarded. *Entrance requirements:* For master's, GRE General Test, minimum GPA of 3.25, 2 letters of recommendation, application, official transcripts, personal statement. Additional exam requirements/recommendations for international students: Required—TOEFL (minimum score 550 paper-based; 213 computer-based; 79 iBT). *Application deadline:* For fall admission, 7/15 priority date for domestic students, 4/15 priority date for international students; for winter admission, 1/15 for international students; for spring admission, 11/15 priority date for domestic students, 10/15 priority date for international students. Applications are processed on a rolling basis. Application fee: $35. Electronic applications accepted. *Expenses:* Tuition: Part-time $738 per credit. Tuition and fees vary according to degree level and program. *Financial support:* In 2007–08, 7,200 teaching assistantships with full tuition reimbursements were awarded; unspecified assistantships also available. *Unit head:* Dr. Jodi Mindell, Director, 610-660-1801.

Saint Louis University, Graduate School, College of Arts and Sciences and Graduate School, Department of Psychology, St. Louis, MO 63103-2097. Offers clinical psychology (MS-R, PhD); experimental psychology (MS-R, PhD); industrial-organizational psychology (PhD); psychology (PhD). *Accreditation:* APA (one or more programs are accredited). Part-time programs available. *Faculty:* 18 full-time (7 women). *Students:* 77 full-time (53 women), 8 part-time (5 women); includes 14 minority (12 African Americans, 1 American Indian/Alaska Native, 1 Asian American or Pacific Islander). Average age 27. 234 applicants, 11% accepted, 20 enrolled. In 2007, 11 master's, 10 doctorates awarded. *Median time to degree:* Of those who began their doctoral program in fall 1999, 90% received their degree in 8 years or less. *Degree requirements:* For master's, comprehensive exam, thesis; for doctorate, thesis/dissertation, clinical internship (for clinical psychology PhD). *Entrance requirements:* For master's and doctorate, GRE General Test, interview, letters of recommendation, resumé, transcripts, goal statement. Additional exam requirements/recommendations for international students: Required—TOEFL (minimum score 550 paper-based; 213 computer-based). *Application deadline:* For fall admission, 1/1 for domestic and international students. Application fee: $40. Electronic applications accepted. *Expenses:* Tuition: Part-time $845 per credit hour. Required fees: $105 per semester. *Financial support:* In 2007–08, 71 students received support, including 16 research assistantships with full tuition reimbursements available (averaging $14,000 per year), 14 teaching assistantships with full tuition reimbursements available (averaging $12,000 per year); career-related internships or fieldwork, Federal Work-Study, scholarships/grants, traineeships, health care benefits, tuition waivers, and unspecified assistantships also available. Support available to part-time students. Financial award application deadline: 2/1; financial award applicants required to submit FAFSA. *Faculty research:* Violence and trauma; neural basis of learning and memory function; eating disorders; body image and health behavior; prejudice, stereotyping, and victimization; memory, cognitive aging and language processing. Total annual research expenditures: $514,559. *Unit head:* Dr. Donna J. LaVoie, Chairperson, 314-977-3676, Fax: 314-977-3679, E-mail: lavoiedj@slu.edu. *Application contact:* Gary U. Behrman, Associate Dean of Graduate School Admissions, 314-977-3827, Fax: 314-977-3943, E-mail: behrmang@slu.edu.

Saint Mary's University, Faculty of Science, Department of Psychology, Halifax, NS B3H 3C3, Canada. Offers applied psychology (M Sc), including clinical psychology, industrial/organizational psychology. M Sc (clinical psychology) offered jointly with Dalhousie University. Part-time programs available. *Degree requirements:* For master's, thesis, internship. *Entrance requirements:* For master's, GRE General Test, honors degree, minimum QPA of 3.25. *Faculty research:* Assessment, health psychology, social psychology, cognition.

St. Mary's University, Graduate School, Department of Psychology, San Antonio, TX 78228-8507. Offers clinical psychology (MA, MS); industrial/organizational psychology (MA, MS); school psychology (MA). Part-time programs available. *Students:* 30 full-time (20 women), 15 part-time (12 women); includes 13 minority (2 African Americans, 11 Hispanic Americans). Average age 28. In 2007, 25 degrees awarded. *Degree requirements:* For master's, comprehensive exam, thesis optional. *Entrance requirements:* For master's, GRE General Test, letters of recommendation, work experience. Additional exam requirements/recommendations for international students: Required—TOEFL (minimum score 550 paper-based; 213 computer-based). *Application deadline:* Applications are processed on a rolling basis. Application fee: $0. Electronic applications accepted. *Financial support:* Research assistantships, career-related internships or fieldwork, Federal Work-Study, institutionally sponsored loans, scholarships/grants, and health care benefits available. Financial award application deadline: 3/31; financial award applicants required to submit FAFSA. *Unit head:* Dr. Patricia Owen, Director, 210-436-3314, Fax: 210-431-4301, E-mail: psycpat@stmarytx.edu.

Saint Xavier University, Graduate Studies, School of Arts and Sciences, Department of Psychology, Chicago, IL 60655-3105. Offers adult counseling (Certificate); child/adolescent counseling (Certificate); core counseling (Certificate); counseling psychology (MA). Part-time and evening/weekend programs available. In 2007, 11 degrees awarded. *Entrance requirements:* For master's, GRE General Test, minimum GPA of 3.0, interview. *Application deadline:* For fall admission, 8/15 priority date for domestic students. Applications are processed on a rolling basis. Application fee: $35. *Financial support:* Career-related internships or fieldwork available. Support available to part-time students. Financial award applicants required to submit FAFSA. *Unit head:* Dr. Anthony Rotatori, Director, 773-298-3477, Fax: 773-779-9061. *Application contact:* Beth Gierach, Managing Director of Admission, 773-298-3053, Fax: 773-298-3076, E-mail: gierach@sxu.edu.

Salem State College, Graduate School, Program in Counseling and Psychological Services, Salem, MA 01970-5353. Offers MS. Part-time and evening/weekend programs available. *Faculty:* 8 part-time/adjunct (3 women). *Students:* 24 full-time (21 women), 33 part-time (29 women); includes 4 minority (1 African American, 1 Asian American or Pacific Islander, 2 Hispanic Americans), 2 international. Average age 33. In 2007, 15 degrees awarded. *Entrance requirements:* For master's, GRE General Test or MAT. *Application deadline:* Applications are processed on a rolling basis. Application fee: $35. *Unit head:* Dr. Patrice Miller, Coordinator, 978-542-6457, Fax: 978-542-6596, E-mail: pmiller@salemstate.edu.

Sam Houston State University, College of Humanities and Social Sciences, Department of Psychology and Philosophy, Huntsville, TX 77341. Offers clinical psychology (MA, PhD); psychology (MA); school psychology (MA). *Accreditation:* APA. Part-time programs available. *Faculty:* 22 full-time (6 women). *Students:* 59 full-time (47 women), 36 part-time (35 women); includes 15 minority (4 African Americans, 2 American Indian/Alaska Native, 3 Asian Americans or Pacific Islanders, 6 Hispanic Americans), 2 international. Average age 27. In 2007, 25 master's, 6 doctorates awarded. *Degree requirements:* For master's, thesis. *Entrance requirements:* For master's, GRE General Test or MAT, minimum GPA of 3.0. *Application deadline:* For fall admission, 8/1 for domestic students; for spring admission, 12/1 for domestic students. Applications are processed on a rolling basis. Application fee: $20. *Expenses:* Tuition, state resident: full-time $5,026; part-time $184 per semester hour. Tuition, nonresident: full-time $10,586; part-time $462 per semester hour. Required fees: $494 per semester. *Financial support:* Research assistantships, teaching assistantships, career-related internships or fieldwork and institutionally sponsored loans available. Support available to part-time students. Financial award application deadline: 5/31; financial award applicants required to submit FAFSA. *Unit head:* Dr. Donna M. Desforges, Chair, 936-294-1178, Fax: 936-294-3798. *Application contact:* Dr. Rowland Miller, Graduate Coordinator, 936-294-1176, Fax: 936-294-3798, E-mail: psy_rsm@shsu.edu.

San Diego State University, Graduate and Research Affairs, College of Sciences, Department of Psychology, San Diego, CA 92182. Offers clinical psychology (MS, PhD); industrial and organizational psychology (MS); program evaluation (MS); psychology (MA). *Accreditation:* APA (one or more programs are accredited). *Students:* 141 full-time (108 women), 32 part-time (24 women); includes 41 minority (4 African Americans, 1 American Indian/Alaska Native, 14 Asian Americans or Pacific Islanders, 22 Hispanic Americans), 8 international. Average age 25. 445 applicants, 20% accepted, 63 enrolled. In 2007, 52 master's, 14 doctorates awarded. Terminal master's awarded for partial completion of doctoral program. *Degree requirements:* For master's, thesis, oral exam; for doctorate, thesis/dissertation. *Entrance requirements:* For master's, GRE General Test, GRE Subject Test, 3 letters of recommendation; for doctorate, GRE General Test, GRE Subject Test, minimum GPA of 3.0, 3 letters of recommendation. Additional exam requirements/recommendations for international students: Required—TOEFL. *Application deadline:* For fall admission, 2/1 for domestic students, 2/1 priority date for international students. Application fee: $55. Electronic applications accepted. *Financial support:* Fellowships, research assistantships, teaching assistantships, career-related internships or fieldwork, scholarships/grants, and unspecified assistantships available. Financial award applicants required to submit FAFSA. Total annual research expenditures: $8 million. *Unit head:* Dr. Claire Murphy, Chair, 619-594-4559, Fax: 619-594-1332, E-mail: cmurphy@sunstroke.sdsu.edu. *Application contact:* Judy Price, Graduate Advisor, 619-594-5401, Fax: 619-594-1332, E-mail: judyprice@sunstroke.sdsu.edu.

San Francisco State University, Division of Graduate Studies, College of Behavioral and Social Sciences, Department of Psychology, San Francisco, CA 94132-1722. Offers MA, MS. *Financial support:* Teaching assistantships available. Financial award application deadline:3/1. *Unit head:* Dr. Kathleen Mosier, Chair, 415-338-1390. *Application contact:* Dr. Linda Juang, Graduate Coordinator, 415-338-1390, E-mail: ljuang@sfsu.edu.

San Jose State University, Graduate Studies and Research, College of Social Sciences, Department of Psychology, San Jose, CA 95192-0001. Offers clinical psychology (MS); experimental psychology (MA); industrial/organizational psychology (MS); psychology (MA). *Students:* 53 full-time (41 women), 16 part-time (11 women); includes 18 minority (11 Asian Americans or Pacific Islanders, 7 Hispanic Americans), 7 international. Average age 27. 124 applicants, 34% accepted, 38 enrolled. In 2007, 27 degrees awarded. *Degree requirements:* For master's, comprehensive exam, thesis (for some programs). *Entrance requirements:* For master's, GRE General Test, minimum GPA of 3.0. *Application deadline:* For fall admission, 6/29 for domestic students; for spring admission, 11/30 for domestic students. Applications are processed on a rolling basis. Application fee: $59. Electronic applications accepted. *Financial support:* In 2007–08, 15 teaching assistantships were awarded; career-related internships or fieldwork and institutionally sponsored loans also available. Financial award application deadline: 3/1; financial award applicants required to submit FAFSA. *Faculty research:* Drug and alcohol abuse, neurohormonal mechanisms in motion sickness, behavior modification, sleep research, genetics. *Unit head:* Dr. Sheila Bienenfeld, Chair, 408-924-5600, Fax: 408-924-5605, E-mail: sheila.bienenfeld@sjsu.edu.

Saybrook Graduate School and Research Center, Programs in Psychology, Human Science and Organizational Systems, San Francisco, CA 94111-1920. Offers clinical psychology (PhD); creativity studies (MA); human science (MA, PhD), including consciousness and spirituality, individualized (PhD), integrative health studies, organizational systems, social transformation; marriage and family therapy (MA); organizational systems (MA, PhD), including individualized (PhD), organizational systems; psychology (MA, PhD), including consciousness and spirituality, humanistic and transpersonal psychology, individualized (PhD), integrative health studies, licensure track (MA), organizational systems, social transformation. Postbaccalaureate distance learning degree programs offered (minimal on-campus study). Terminal master's awarded for partial completion of doctoral program. *Degree requirements:* For master's, thesis or alternative; for doctorate, thesis/dissertation. Electronic applications accepted. *Faculty research:* Humanistic theory, health studies, organizational systems, consciousness and spirituality, social transformation.

The School of Professional Psychology at Forest Institute, Graduate Programs, Springfield, MO 65807. Offers clinical psychology (Psy D); marriage and family therapy (PGC); psychology (MA). *Accreditation:* AAMFT/COAMFTE; APA (one or more programs are accredited). *Faculty:* 20 full-time (13 women), 22 part-time/adjunct (9 women). *Students:* 198 full-time (145 women), 20 part-time (10 women). Average age 32. 122 applicants, 72% accepted, 70 enrolled. In 2007, 40 master's, 40 doctorates awarded. Terminal master's awarded for partial completion of doctoral program. *Median time to degree:* Of those who began their doctoral program in fall 1999, 100% received their degree in 8 years or less. *Degree requirements:* For master's, thesis, practice; for doctorate, comprehensive exam, thesis/dissertation, internship, practice. *Entrance requirements:* For master's, GRE General Test, interview, minimum GPA of 3.0, 12 hours in psychology; for doctorate, GRE General Test, interview, minimum GPA of 3.0, 18 hours in psychology. Additional exam requirements/recommendations for international students: Required—TOEFL (minimum score 550 paper-based; 213 computer-based). *Application deadline:* For fall admission, 8/1 priority date for domestic students, 5/1 for international students; for winter admission, 11/1 priority date for domestic students, 8/1 for international students. Applications are processed on a rolling basis. Application fee: $50. Electronic applications accepted. *Expenses:* Tuition: Part-time $565 per credit hour. Required fees: $385 per term. One-time fee: $275 part-time. Tuition and fees vary according to program. *Financial support:* In 2007–08, 91 students received support. Career-related internships or fieldwork, Federal Work-Study, and scholarships/grants available. Support available to part-time students. Financial award applicants required to submit FAFSA. *Faculty research:* Pain management, clinical supervision, addictions, women's issues, forensics. *Unit head:* Dr. Mark E. Skrade, President, 417-823-3477, Fax: 417-823-3442, E-mail: mskrade@forest.edu. *Application contact:* Phillip Raleigh, Director of Admissions, 417-823-3477, Fax: 417-823-3442, E-mail: praleigh@forest.edu.

Seattle University, College of Arts and Sciences, Department of Psychology, Seattle, WA 98122-1090. Offers existential and phenomenological therapeutic psychology (MA Psych). *Degree requirements:* For master's, thesis. *Entrance requirements:* For master's, interview, minimum GPA of 3.0, previous undergraduate course work in psychology. *Faculty research:* Healing, transformations in relationships, therapy, dialogical research.

Seton Hall University, College of Arts and Sciences, Department of Psychology, South Orange, NJ 07079-2697. Offers experimental psychology (MS), including behavioral neuroscience. *Entrance requirements:* Additional exam requirements/recommendations for international students: Required—TOEFL. Electronic applications accepted. *Faculty research:* Behavioral neuroscience, cognitive psychology, social psychology, perception/motor skills, memory.

See Close-Up on page 1477.

Seton Hall University, College of Education and Human Services, Department of Professional Psychology and Family Therapy, South Orange, NJ 07079-2697. Offers counseling psychology (MA, PhD); marriage and family therapy (MS, PhD, Ed S); psychological studies (MA); school psychology (Ed S). *Accreditation:* APA. Part-time and evening/weekend programs available. Postbaccalaureate distance learning degree programs offered (minimal on-campus study). *Faculty:* 17 full-time (8 women). *Students:* 149 full-time (124 women), 290 part-time (238 women); includes 60 minority (41 African Americans, 2 American Indian/Alaska Native, 3 Asian Americans or Pacific Islanders, 14 Hispanic Americans), 7 international. Average age 31. 324 applicants, 88% accepted, 102 enrolled. In 2007, 52 master's, 10 doctorates, 37 other advanced degrees awarded. Terminal master's awarded for partial completion of doctoral program. *Degree requirements:* For master's, comprehensive exam, case study; for doctorate, comprehensive exam, thesis/dissertation, internship; for Ed S, comprehensive exam, internship. *Entrance requirements:* For master's, GRE or MAT; for doctorate, GRE, interview; for Ed S, GRE or MAT, interview. *Application deadline:* For fall admission, 2/15 for domestic students. Applications are processed on a rolling basis. Application fee: $50. *Financial support:* In 2007–08, 4 research assistantships with full tuition reimbursements (averaging $4,500 per year) were awarded; career-related internships or fieldwork also available. Financial award application deadline: 2/1. *Faculty research:* Counseling process, ethics, family systems, child pathology. *Unit head:* Dr. Laura Palmer, Chair, 973-761-9450, E-mail: palmerla@shu.edu. *Application contact:* Information Contact, 973-761-9451.

Shippensburg University of Pennsylvania, School of Graduate Studies, College of Arts and Sciences, Department of Psychology, Shippensburg, PA 17257-2299. Offers MS. Part-time and evening/weekend programs available. *Faculty:* 8 full-time (3 women). *Students:* 16 full-time (7 women), 14 part-time (10 women), 1 international. Average age 28. 26 applicants, 73% accepted, 8 enrolled. In 2007, 11 degrees awarded. *Degree requirements:* For master's, thesis optional. *Entrance requirements:* For master's, minimum GPA of 2.75, 1 course in statistics, 6 undergraduate credit hours of course work in psychology, essay/goals statement. Additional exam requirements/recommendations for international students: Required—TOEFL (minimum score 560 paper-based; 220 computer-based). *Application deadline:* For fall admission, 4/1 priority date for domestic students, 3/1 for international students; for spring admission, 11/1 priority date for domestic students, 7/1 for international students. Applications are processed on a rolling basis. Application fee: $30. Electronic applications accepted. *Expenses:* Tuition, state resident: part-time $345 per credit. Tuition, nonresident: part-time $552 per credit. Required fees: $28 per credit. Tuition and fees vary according to course load. *Financial support:* In 2007–08, 9 research assistantships with full tuition reimbursements (averaging $3,575 per year) were awarded; career-related internships or fieldwork, scholarships/grants, and unspecified assistantships also available. Support available to part-time students. Financial award application deadline: 3/1; financial award applicants required to submit FAFSA. *Unit head:* Dr. Suzanne Morin, Chairperson, 717-477-1657, Fax: 717-477-4057, E-mail: smmori@ship.edu. *Application contact:* Renee Payne, Associate Dean of Graduate Admissions, 717-477-1231, Fax: 717-477-4016, E-mail: rmpayn@ship.edu.

Simon Fraser University, Graduate Studies, Faculty of Arts and Social Sciences, Department of Psychology, Burnaby, BC V5A 1S6, Canada. Offers MA, PhD. *Accreditation:* APA (one or more programs are accredited). *Degree requirements:* For master's, thesis; for doctorate, thesis/dissertation. *Entrance requirements:* For master's and doctorate, GRE, minimum GPA of 3.5. Additional exam requirements/recommendations for international students: Required—TOEFL or IELTS. Expenses: Contact institution. *Faculty research:* Social cognition/biological neuropsychology, theory and methods.

Southeastern Baptist Theological Seminary, Graduate and Professional Programs, Wake Forest, NC 27588-1889. Offers advanced biblical studies (M Div); Christian education (M Div, MACE); Christian ethics (PhD); Christian ministry (M Div); Christian planting (M Div); church music (MACM); counseling (MACO); evangelism (PhD); language (M Div); ministry (D Min); New Testament (PhD); Old Testament (PhD); philosophy (PhD); theology (Th M, PhD); women's studies (M Div). *Accreditation:* ACIPE; ATS (one or more programs are accredited). *Degree requirements:* For master's, thesis (for some programs), oral exam; for doctorate, thesis/dissertation, fieldwork; for M Div, supervised ministry. *Entrance requirements:* For master's, Cooperative English Test, minimum GPA of 2.0, M Div or equivalent (Th M); for doctorate, GRE General Test or MAT, Cooperative English Test, M Div or equivalent, 3 years of professional experience.

Southeastern Louisiana University, College of Arts, Humanities and Social Sciences, Department of Psychology, Hammond, LA 70402. Offers MA. Part-time programs available. *Faculty:* 7 full-time (2 women), 1 (woman) part-time/adjunct. *Students:* 19 full-time (13 women), 4 part-time (2 women), 1 international. Average age 25. 23 applicants, 91% accepted, 14 enrolled. In 2007, 2 degrees awarded. *Degree requirements:* For master's, comprehensive exam, thesis. *Entrance requirements:* For master's, GRE General Test, minimum GPA of 3.0, 18 undergraduate hours in psychology/educational psychology, 3 letters of reference. Additional exam requirements/recommendations for international students: Required—TOEFL (minimum score 500 paper-based; 173 computer-based). *Application deadline:* For fall admission, 7/15 priority date for domestic students, 6/1 priority date for international students; for spring admission, 12/1 priority date for domestic students, 10/1 priority date for international students. Applications are processed on a rolling basis. Application fee: $20 ($30 for international students). Electronic applications accepted. *Expenses:* Tuition, state resident: full-time $2,216; part-time $123 per credit. Tuition, nonresident: full-time $6,716; part-time $373 per credit. Required fees: $1,105; $61 per credit. *Financial support:* In 2007–08, 10 research assistantships with full tuition reimbursements (averaging $6,750 per year) were awarded; career-related internships or fieldwork, Federal Work-Study, institutionally sponsored loans, unspecified assistantships, and administrative assistantship also available. Support available to part-time students. Financial award application deadline: 5/1; financial award applicants required to submit FAFSA. *Faculty research:* Social cognition, police lineup identification, memory for unusual events, body image, cross-cultural parenting strategy. *Unit head:* Dr. Matt Rossano, Department Head, 985-549-2154, Fax: 985-549-6892, E-mail: mrossano@selu.edu. *Application contact:* Sandra Meyers, Graduate Admissions Analyst, 985-549-2066, Fax: 985-549-5632, E-mail: admissions@selu.edu.

Southern Adventist University, School of Education and Psychology, Collegedale, TN 37315-0370. Offers curriculum and instruction (MS Ed); educational administration and supervision (MS Ed); inclusive education (MS Ed); literacy education (MS Ed); outdoor teacher education (MS Ed); professional counseling (MS); school counseling (MS). *Accreditation:* NCATE. Part-time and evening/weekend programs available. *Faculty:* 6 full-time (2 women), 2 part-time/adjunct (1 woman). *Students:* 27 full-time (21 women), 9 part-time (4 women); includes 14 minority (10 African Americans, 1 Asian American or Pacific Islander, 3 Hispanic Americans). Average age 30. 20 applicants, 85% accepted, 15 enrolled. In 2007, 23 degrees awarded. *Degree requirements:* For master's, comprehensive exam (for some programs), thesis optional, position paper (MS), portfolio (MS Ed in outdoor teacher education). *Entrance requirements:* For master's, GRE General Test, interview (MS); 9 semester hours of upper division course work in psychology or related field, including 1 course in psychology research or statistics; 9 semester hours of education (MS Ed). Additional exam requirements/recommendations for international students: Required—TOEFL (minimum score 600 paper-based; 250 computer-based; 100 iBT). *Application deadline:* For fall admission, 5/15 priority date for domestic and international students; for winter admission, 10/15 priority date for domestic and international students; for spring admission, 3/31 priority date for domestic and international students. Applications are processed on a rolling basis. Application fee: $25. Electronic applications accepted. *Financial support:* In 2007–08, 7 students received support, including 1 research assistantship with full tuition reimbursement available (averaging $10,000 per year), 5 teaching assistantships with full tuition reimbursements available (averaging $10,000 per year); career-related internships or fieldwork, scholarships/grants, tuition waivers (partial), and unspecified assistantships also available. Support available to part-time students. Financial award application deadline: 4/1; financial award applicants required to submit FAFSA. *Unit head:* Dr. Denise Dunzweiler, Dean, 423-236-2776, Fax: 423-236-1765, E-mail: denise@southern.edu. *Application contact:* Mikhaile Spence, Information Contact, 423-236-2496, Fax: 423-236-1765, E-mail: maspence@southern.edu.

Southern California Seminary, Graduate and Professional Programs, El Cajon, CA 92019. Offers biblical studies (MA); counseling psychology (MACP); psychology (Psy D); religious studies (MRS); theology (M Div). Part-time and evening/weekend programs available. Postbaccalaureate distance learning degree programs offered (minimal on-campus study). *Faculty:* 7 full-time (0 women), 17 part-time/adjunct (2 women). *Students:* 56 full-time (21 women), 68 part-time (30 women); includes 44 minority (24 African Americans, 2 Asian Americans or Pacific Islanders, 18 Hispanic Americans), 4 international. Average age 38. In 2007, 42 degrees awarded. *Degree requirements:* For master's, thesis (for some programs); for doctorate, thesis/dissertation; for M Div, 2 foreign languages. *Entrance requirements:* For doctorate, master's degree in psychology. Additional exam requirements/recommendations for international students: Required—TOEFL (minimum score 550 paper-based). *Application deadline:* For fall admission, 8/13 for domestic and international students; for spring admission, 12/11 for domestic students, 12/15 for international students. Applications are processed on a rolling basis. Application fee: $27 ($109 for international students). Electronic applications accepted. *Expenses:* Tuition: Part-time $290 per unit. Tuition and fees vary according to campus/location and program. *Financial support:* In 2007–08, 14 students received support. Federal Work-Study, scholarships/grants, and tuition waivers (partial) available. Financial award application deadline: 3/1; financial award applicants required to submit FAFSA. *Unit head:* Dr. Al Letting, Vice-President of Academics, 619-590-2131, E-mail: aletting@socalsem.edu. *Application contact:* Steve Perdue, Director of Admissions, 888-389-7244, E-mail: sperdue@socalsem.edu.

Southern Connecticut State University, School of Graduate Studies, School of Arts and Sciences, Department of Psychology, New Haven, CT 06515-1355. Offers MA. Part-time and evening/weekend programs available. *Faculty:* 6 full-time, 1 part-time/adjunct. *Students:* 16 full-time (14 women), 25 part-time (21 women); includes 6 minority (4 African Americans, 2 Hispanic Americans). 64 applicants, 45% accepted, 17 enrolled. In 2007, 21 degrees awarded. *Degree requirements:* For master's, thesis or alternative. *Entrance requirements:* For master's, interview, previous course work in psychology. *Application deadline:* For fall admission, 5/15 priority date for domestic students. Applications are processed on a rolling basis. Application fee: $50. Electronic applications accepted. *Financial support:* Teaching assistantships available. Financial award application deadline: 4/15; financial award applicants required to submit FAFSA. *Unit head:* Dr. Claire Novosad, Chairperson, 203-392-6863, Fax: 203-392-6805, E-mail: novosadc1@southernct.edu. *Application contact:* Dr. William Hauselt, Coordinator, 203-392-6874, Fax: 203-392-6805, E-mail: hauseltw1@southernct.edu.

Southern Illinois University Carbondale, Graduate School, College of Education, Department of Behavior Analysis and Therapy, Carbondale, IL 62901-4701. Offers MS. *Students:* 40 full-time (35 women), 35 part-time (33 women); includes 3 minority (2 African Americans, 1 Hispanic American), 11 international. 63 applicants, 33% accepted, 14 enrolled. In 2007, 19 degrees awarded. *Unit head:* Dr. Mark Dixon, Coordinator, 618-536-7704, E-mail: mdixon@siu.edu. *Application contact:* Char Burrell, Administrative Clerk, 618-453-6411, E-mail: cburrell@siu.edu.

Southern Illinois University Carbondale, Graduate School, College of Liberal Arts, Department of Psychology, Carbondale, IL 62901-4701. Offers clinical psychology (MA, MS, PhD); counseling psychology (MA, MS, PhD); experimental psychology (MA, MS, PhD). *Accreditation:* APA (one or more programs are accredited). *Faculty:* 27 full-time (14 women), 1 part-time/adjunct (0 women). *Students:* 81 full-time (54 women), 43 part-time (32 women); includes 25 minority (13 African Americans, 1 American Indian/Alaska Native, 6 Asian Americans or Pacific Islanders, 5 Hispanic Americans), 13 international. 291 applicants, 9% accepted, 13 enrolled. In 2007, 17 master's, 15 doctorates awarded. *Degree requirements:* For master's, thesis; for doctorate, thesis/dissertation. *Entrance requirements:* For master's, GRE General Test, GRE Subject Test, minimum GPA of 2.7; for doctorate, GRE General Test, GRE Subject Test, minimum GPA of 3.25. Additional exam requirements/recommendations for international students: Required—TOEFL. *Application deadline:* For fall admission, 3/1 priority date for domestic students. Applications are processed on a rolling basis. Application fee: $20. *Financial support:* In 2007–08, 82 students received support, including 14 fellowships with full tuition reimbursements available, 23 research assistantships with full tuition reimbursements available, 22 teaching assistantships with full tuition reimbursements available; Federal Work-Study, institutionally sponsored loans, and tuition waivers (full) also available. *Faculty research:* Developmental neuropsychology; smoking, affect, and cognition; personality measurement; vocational psychology; program evaluation. *Unit head:* Dr. Jane Swanson, Chair, 618-453-3529, E-mail: swanson@siu.edu. *Application contact:* Connie Childers, Office Specialist, 618-453-3564, E-mail: childers@siu.edu.

Announcement: The revitalization of the faculty is one of the most exciting recent developments in the department. Ten new faculty members have been hired since 1996—bringing exciting new research programs in relationship violence, agent-based models of sensorimotor cognition, computational modeling of learning, health psychology, and prevention of delinquency.

See Close-Up on page 1479.

Southern Illinois University Edwardsville, Graduate Studies and Research, School of Education, Department of Psychology, Edwardsville, IL 62026-0001. Offers clinical child and school psychology (MS); clinical-adult psychology (MA); industrial-organizational psychology (MA); psychology (MA, MS); school psychology (SD). Part-time programs available. *Faculty:* 19 full-time (8 women). *Students:* 41 full-time (35 women), 40 part-time (32 women); includes

Psychology—General

Southern Illinois University Edwardsville (continued)
5 minority (4 African Americans, 1 Hispanic American), 1 international. Average age 33. 167 applicants, 19% accepted. In 2007, 26 master's, 8 other advanced degrees awarded. *Degree requirements:* For master's, thesis (for some programs), research paper; for SD, thesis. *Entrance requirements:* For master's, GRE. Additional exam requirements/recommendations for international students: Required—TOEFL. *Application deadline:* For fall admission, 3/1 for domestic and international students. Application fee: $30. Electronic applications accepted. *Financial support:* In 2007–08, 1 fellowship with full tuition reimbursement, 1 research assistantship, 1 teaching assistantship with full tuition reimbursement were awarded; career-related internships or fieldwork, Federal Work-Study, institutionally sponsored loans, traineeships, and unspecified assistantships also available. Support available to part-time students. Financial award application deadline: 3/1; financial award applicants required to submit FAFSA. *Unit head:* Dr. Bryce Sullivan, Chair, 618-650-2202, E-mail: bsulliv@siue.edu. *Application contact:* Dr. Lynn Bartels, Director, 618-650-2202, E-mail: lbartel@siue.edu.

Southern Methodist University, Dedman College, Department of Psychology, Dallas, TX 75275. Offers clinical psychology (PhD). Part-time programs available. *Faculty:* 11 full-time (5 women), 3 part-time/adjunct (2 women). *Students:* 16 full-time (14 women), 1 (woman) part-time; includes 6 minority (1 African American, 1 American Indian/Alaska Native, 2 Asian Americans or Pacific Islanders, 2 Hispanic Americans), 1 international. Average age 31. 164 applicants, 10% accepted, 8 enrolled. In 2007, 1 doctorate awarded. *Degree requirements:* For doctorate, comprehensive exam, thesis/dissertation, oral exam, practicum, research presentation and publication. *Entrance requirements:* For doctorate, GRE General Test, minimum GPA of 3.0. Additional exam requirements/recommendations for international students: Required—TOEFL (minimum score 550 paper-based). *Application deadline:* For fall admission, 2/1 priority date for domestic and international students. Application fee: $60. Electronic applications accepted. *Financial support:* In 2007–08, 9 students received support, including 8 research assistantships with tuition reimbursements available (averaging $14,000 per year); teaching assistantships, career-related internships or fieldwork, Federal Work-Study, and institutionally sponsored loans also available. Support available to part-time students. Financial award application deadline: 1/1; financial award applicants required to submit FAFSA. *Faculty research:* Experimental, social, developmental, and cognitive psychology; anger/violence; mood disorders; depression and anxiety; family assessment and development; chronic pain and mental health. *Unit head:* Dr. Ernest Jouriles, Chair, 214-768-2360, Fax: 214-768-3910, E-mail: ejourile@mail.smu.edu. *Application contact:* Dr. Robert B. Hampson, Director, 214-768-2734, Fax: 214-768-3910, E-mail: rhampson@smu.edu.

Southern Nazarene University, Graduate College, School of Psychology, Bethany, OK 73008. Offers counseling psychology (MSCP); marriage and family therapy (MA). *Degree requirements:* For master's, thesis optional. *Entrance requirements:* For master's, English proficiency exam, minimum GPA of 3.0 in last 60 hours/major, 2.7 overall.

Southern New Hampshire University, School of Liberal Arts, Manchester, NH 03106-1045. Offers clinical services for adults psychiatric disabilities (Certificate); clinical services for children and adolescents with psychiatric disabilities (Certificate); clinical services for persons with co-occurring substance abuse and psychiatric disabilities (Certificate); community mental health (MS); fiction writing (MFA); non-fiction writing (MFA); teaching English as a foreign language (MS). Part-time and evening/weekend programs available. *Faculty:* 18 full-time. *Students:* 187 full-time, 12 part-time. Average age 35. In 2007, 35 degrees awarded. *Degree requirements:* For master's, one foreign language, thesis. *Entrance requirements:* For master's, minimum GPA of 2.75: MS-TEFL, 3.0: MFA. Additional exam requirements/recommendations for international students: Required—TOEFL (minimum score 550 paper-based; 213 computer-based; 79 iBT), IELTS (minimum score 7), TWE (minimum score 5). *Application deadline:* For fall admission, 7/1 priority date for domestic students; for winter admission, 11/1 priority date for domestic students; for spring admission, 6/1 priority date for domestic students. Applications are processed on a rolling basis. Application fee: $40. Electronic applications accepted. *Expenses:* Contact institution. *Financial support:* In 2007–08, 4 research assistantships were awarded; career-related internships or fieldwork and scholarships/grants also available. Financial award applicants required to submit FAFSA. *Faculty research:* Action research, state of the art practice in behavioral health services, wraparound approaches to working with youth, learning styles. *Unit head:* Dr. Karen Erickson, Dean, 603-668-2211, E-mail: k.erickson@snhu.edu. *Application contact:* Scott Durand, Director of Graduate Enrollment Services, 603-644-3102 Ext. 3338, Fax: 603-644-3144, E-mail: s.durand@snhu.edu.

Southern Oregon University, Graduate Studies, School of Social Sciences, Department of Psychology, Ashland, OR 97520. Offers applied psychology (MAP); human service-organizational training and development (MA, MS); social science (MA, MS), including professional counseling, psychology. Part-time programs available. *Degree requirements:* For master's, thesis, portfolio and oral defense. *Entrance requirements:* For master's, GRE General Test, minimum GPA of 3.0. Electronic applications accepted.

Southern University and Agricultural and Mechanical College, Graduate School, College of Sciences, Department of Psychology, Baton Rouge, LA 70813. Offers rehabilitation counseling (MS). *Faculty:* 7 full-time (5 women). *Students:* 16 full-time (13 women), 29 part-time (21 women); includes 32 minority (28 African Americans, 1 American Indian/Alaska Native, 3 Asian Americans or Pacific Islanders), 1 international. Average age 32. 6 applicants, 67% accepted, 4 enrolled. In 2007, 5 degrees awarded. *Degree requirements:* For master's, comprehensive exam, thesis optional. *Entrance requirements:* For master's, GMAT or GRE General Test. Additional exam requirements/recommendations for international students: Required—TOEFL (minimum score 525 paper-based; 193 computer-based). *Application deadline:* For fall admission, 4/15 priority date for domestic and international students; for spring admission, 11/1 priority date for domestic and international students. Applications are processed on a rolling basis. Application fee: $25. *Financial support:* In 2007–08, 20 research assistantships (averaging $11,500 per year) were awarded; scholarships/grants also available. Financial award application deadline: 4/15. *Faculty research:* Cultural diversity, professional preparation and participation of minorities, needs and satisfaction of students with disabilities, prediction model for rehabilitation outcome, diabetes. *Unit head:* Murelle G. Harrison, Interim Chair, 225-771-2990, Fax: 225-771-2993.

Southwestern College, Program in Psychodrama and Action Methods, Santa Fe, NM 87502-4788. Offers Certificate. *Faculty:* 2 part-time/adjunct (both women). *Students:* Average age 41. 9 applicants, 100% accepted, 9 enrolled. *Entrance requirements:* For degree, 3 letters of reference, interview application. *Application deadline:* Applications are processed on a rolling basis. Application fee: $28. *Expenses:* Tuition: Full-time $16,416. *Unit head:* Kate Cook, Director, Fax: 877-471-4071. *Application contact:* Dru Phoenix, Director of Admissions, 505-471-5756 Ext. 26, Fax: 505-471-4071, E-mail: admissions@swc.edu.

Spalding University, Graduate Studies, College of Social Sciences and Humanities, School of Professional Psychology, Louisville, KY 40203-2188. Offers clinical psychology (MA, Psy D). *Accreditation:* APA (one or more programs are accredited). Part-time programs available. Terminal master's awarded for partial completion of doctoral program. *Degree requirements:* For master's, comprehensive exam; for doctorate, thesis/dissertation. *Entrance requirements:* For master's, GRE General Test, 18 hours of undergraduate course work in psychology, interview; for doctorate, GRE General Test, interview, 18 hours of coursework in psychology. Additional exam requirements/recommendations for international students: Required—TOEFL. *Faculty research:* Substance abuse, prayer research, end-of-life issues, complementary and alternative medicine, research methodology and statistical inference.

Stanford University, School of Humanities and Sciences, Department of Psychology, Stanford, CA 94305-9991. Offers PhD. *Degree requirements:* For doctorate, thesis/dissertation, oral exam. *Entrance requirements:* For doctorate, GRE General Test, GRE Subject Test. Additional exam requirements/recommendations for international students: Required—TOEFL. Electronic applications accepted.

State University of New York at Binghamton, Graduate School, School of Arts and Sciences, Department of Psychology, Binghamton, NY 13902-6000. Offers behavioral neuroscience (MA, PhD); clinical psychology (MA, PhD); cognitive and behavioral science (MA, PhD). *Accreditation:* APA (one or more programs are accredited). *Faculty:* 27 full-time (11 women), 7 part-time/adjunct (2 women). *Students:* 73 full-time (49 women), 16 part-time (11 women); includes 14 minority (4 African Americans, 1 American Indian/Alaska Native, 2 Asian Americans or Pacific Islanders, 7 Hispanic Americans), 4 international. Average age 27. 269 applicants, 13% accepted, 19 enrolled. In 2007, 14 master's, 11 doctorates awarded. Terminal master's awarded for partial completion of doctoral program. *Degree requirements:* For master's, thesis; for doctorate, thesis/dissertation, departmental qualifying exam. *Entrance requirements:* For master's and doctorate, GRE General Test, GRE Subject Test. Additional exam requirements/recommendations for international students: Required—TOEFL. *Application deadline:* For fall admission, 4/15 priority date for domestic students, 1/15 priority date for international students; for spring admission, 11/1 for domestic students, 10/1 priority date for international students. Applications are processed on a rolling basis. Application fee: $60. Electronic applications accepted. *Financial support:* In 2007–08, 15 fellowships with full tuition reimbursements (averaging $13,000 per year), 24 research assistantships with full tuition reimbursements (averaging $12,500 per year), 38 teaching assistantships with full tuition reimbursements (averaging $16,500 per year) were awarded; career-related internships or fieldwork, Federal Work-Study, institutionally sponsored loans, and unspecified assistantships also available. Support available to part-time students. Financial award application deadline: 2/15. *Unit head:* Dr. Peter Gerhardstein, Chair, 607-777-4387, E-mail: gerhard@binghamton.edu.

State University of New York at New Paltz, Graduate School, Faculty of Liberal Arts and Sciences, Department of Psychology, New Paltz, NY 12561. Offers mental health counseling (MS); psychology (MA). Part-time and evening/weekend programs available. *Faculty:* 15 full-time (8 women), 7 part-time/adjunct (all women). *Students:* 26 full-time (21 women), 14 part-time (11 women); includes 2 minority (1 Asian American or Pacific Islander, 1 Hispanic American). Average age 27. In 2007, 11 degrees awarded. *Degree requirements:* For master's, comprehensive exam, thesis. *Entrance requirements:* For master's, GRE General Test, minimum GPA of 3.0. Additional exam requirements/recommendations for international students: Required—TOEFL (minimum score 550 paper-based; 213 computer-based; 80 iBT). *Application deadline:* For fall admission, 3/15 priority date for domestic students, 3/15 for international students; for spring admission, 11/15 for domestic and international students. Application fee: $50. Electronic applications accepted. *Expenses:* Tuition, state resident: full-time $6,900; part-time $288 per credit hour. Tuition, nonresident: full-time $10,920; part-time $455 per credit hour. Required fees: $1,040; $30 per credit hour. $153 per credit hour. Tuition and fees vary according to program. *Financial support:* In 2007–08, 5 students received support, including 5 teaching assistantships with partial tuition reimbursements available (averaging $5,000 per year); career-related internships or fieldwork, Federal Work-Study, and institutionally sponsored loans also available. *Faculty research:* Industrial/Organizational Psychology, Disaster Mental Health, Human Cognition, Gender Socialization, Defense Mechanisms. *Unit head:* Dr. Douglas Maynard, Chair, 845-257-3426, E-mail: maynardd@newpaltz.edu. *Application contact:* Dr. Jonathan Raskin, Coordinator, 845-257-3471, E-mail: raskinj@newpaltz.edu.

State University of New York at Plattsburgh, Faculty of Arts and Science, Department of Psychology, Plattsburgh, NY 12901-2681. Offers school psychology (MA, CAS). Part-time programs available. *Faculty:* 2 full-time (1 woman), 3 part-time/adjunct (2 women). *Students:* 18 full-time (13 women), 14 part-time (10 women); includes 4 minority (1 African American, 3 Hispanic Americans). Average age 26. 22 applicants, 86% accepted, 11 enrolled. In 2007, 4 master's, 4 other advanced degrees awarded. *Degree requirements:* For master's, thesis, internship. *Entrance requirements:* For master's, GRE General Test, minimum GPA of 3.0. Additional exam requirements/recommendations for international students: Required—TOEFL (minimum score 550 paper-based). *Application deadline:* For fall admission, 3/1 priority date for domestic students. Applications are processed on a rolling basis. Application fee: $50. *Expenses:* Tuition, state resident: full-time $6,900; part-time $288 per credit hour. Tuition, nonresident: full-time $10,920; part-time $455 per credit hour. Required fees: $1,036. *Financial support:* Federal Work-Study available. Support available to part-time students. Financial award application deadline: 4/15; financial award applicants required to submit FAFSA. *Faculty research:* Alzheimer's disease, adolescent behavior, intellectual assessment, learning disabilities, reading skill acquisition. *Unit head:* Dr. Jeanne Ryan, Chair, 518-564-3380. *Application contact:* Dr. Ronald Dumont, Chair, Graduate Admissions Committee, 518-564-2000.

Stephen F. Austin State University, Graduate School, College of Liberal Arts, Department of Psychology, Nacogdoches, TX 75962. Offers MA. *Degree requirements:* For master's, comprehensive exam, thesis. *Entrance requirements:* For master's, GRE General Test. Additional exam requirements/recommendations for international students: Required—TOEFL.

Stony Brook University, State University of New York, Graduate School, College of Arts and Sciences, Department of Psychology, Stony Brook, NY 11794. Offers biopsychology (PhD); clinical psychology (PhD); cognitive/experimental psychology (PhD); social and health psychology (PhD). *Accreditation:* APA. *Faculty:* 31 full-time (14 women), 1 (woman) part-time/adjunct. *Students:* 106 full-time (84 women), 2 part-time (1 woman); includes 14 minority (3 African Americans, 4 Asian Americans or Pacific Islanders, 7 Hispanic Americans), 12 international. Average age 27. 506 applicants, 8% accepted. In 2007, 16 doctorates awarded. *Degree requirements:* For doctorate, thesis/dissertation. *Entrance requirements:* For doctorate, GRE General Test, GRE Subject Test. Additional exam requirements/recommendations for international students: Required—TOEFL. *Application deadline:* For fall admission, 1/15 for domestic students. Application fee: $60. *Financial support:* In 2007–08, 9 fellowships, 29 research assistantships, 44 teaching assistantships were awarded; career-related internships or fieldwork also available. *Faculty research:* Behavior therapy, memory and cognition, child and family studies, quantitative methods, health psychology. Total annual research expenditures: $4.4 million. *Unit head:* Dr. Nancy Squires, Chair, 631-632-7805, E-mail: nancy.squires@stonybrook.edu. *Application contact:* Dr. Arthur Samuel, Graduate Director, 631-632-7792, Fax: 631-632-7876.

See Close-Ups on pages 1495, 1497, and 1499.

Suffolk University, College of Arts and Sciences, Department of Psychology, Boston, MA 02108-2770. Offers clinical-developmental psychology (PhD). *Accreditation:* APA. *Faculty:* 16 full-time (11 women). *Students:* 36 full-time (31 women), 15 part-time (11 women); includes 5 minority (2 African Americans, 2 Asian Americans or Pacific Islanders, 1 Hispanic American), 2 international. Average age 28. 315 applicants, 10% accepted, 13 enrolled. In 2007, 16 degrees awarded. *Degree requirements:* For doctorate, thesis/dissertation, practicum. *Entrance requirements:* For doctorate, GRE General Test or MAT. Additional exam requirements/recommendations for international students: Required—TOEFL (minimum score 550 paper-based; 213 computer-based; 80 iBT). *Application deadline:* For fall admission, 12/15 for domestic and international students. Applications are processed on a rolling basis. Application fee: $50. Electronic applications accepted. *Expenses:* Contact institution. *Financial support:* In 2007–08, 46 students received support, including 36 fellowships with full and partial tuition reimbursements available (averaging $16,747 per year); career-related internships or fieldwork, Federal Work-Study, and institutionally sponsored loans also available. Support available to part-time students. Financial award application deadline: 4/1; financial award applicants required to submit FAFSA. *Faculty research:* Olfaction decision-making in substance-dependent individuals, ego development, experiential avoidance in generalized anxiety disorder. *Unit head:* Dr. Robert Webb, Chair, 617-573-8293, Fax: 617-367-2924, E-mail: rwebb@suffolk.edu. *Application contact:* Judith Reynolds, Director of Graduate Admissions, 617-573-8302, Fax: 617-523-0116, E-mail: grad.admission@suffolk.edu.

Sul Ross State University, School of Arts and Sciences, Department of Behavioral and Social Sciences, Program in Psychology, Alpine, TX 79832. Offers MA. *Entrance requirements:* For master's, GRE General Test, minimum GPA of 2.5 in last 60 hours of undergraduate work.

Syracuse University, Graduate School, College of Arts and Sciences, Department of Psychology, Syracuse, NY 13244. Offers clinical psychology (PhD); experimental psychology (PhD); school psychology (PhD); social psychology (PhD). *Accreditation:* APA. Part-time programs available. *Students:* 56 full-time (44 women), 5 part-time (all women); includes 6 minority (2 African Americans, 1 Asian American or Pacific Islander, 3 Hispanic Americans), 6 international. 202 applicants, 11% accepted, 11 enrolled. In 2007, 7 doctorates awarded. *Degree requirements:* For doctorate, thesis/dissertation. *Entrance requirements:* For doctorate, GRE General Test. Additional exam requirements/recommendations for international students: Required—TOEFL. *Application deadline:* For fall admission, 1/10 for domestic students. Applications are processed on a rolling basis. Application fee: $75. *Expenses:* Tuition: Full-time $18,216; part-time $1,012 per credit. Required fees: $980. Tuition and fees vary according to program. *Financial support:* Fellowships with full tuition reimbursements, research assistantships with full tuition reimbursements, teaching assistantships with full tuition reimbursements, tuition waivers (partial) available. *Unit head:* Dr. Barbara Fiese, Chair, 315-443-2354, E-mail: bhfiese@syr.edu. *Application contact:* Sue Bova, Information Contact, 315-443-1050, E-mail: skbova@syr.edu.

Temple University, Graduate School, College of Liberal Arts, Department of Psychology, Philadelphia, PA 19122-6096. Offers clinical psychology (PhD); cognitive psychology (PhD); developmental psychology (PhD); social psychology (PhD). *Accreditation:* APA. *Degree requirements:* For doctorate, thesis/dissertation. *Entrance requirements:* For doctorate, GRE General Test, minimum GPA of 3.0. Additional exam requirements/recommendations for international students: Required—TOEFL (minimum score 550 paper-based; 213 computer-based; 79 iBT). Electronic applications accepted.

Tennessee State University, The School of Graduate Studies and Research, College of Education, Department of Psychology, Nashville, TN 37209-1561. Offers counseling and guidance (MS), including counseling, elementary school counseling, organizational counseling, secondary school counseling; counseling psychology (PhD); psychology (MS, PhD); school psychology (MS, PhD). *Accreditation:* APA. *Faculty:* 15 full-time (9 women), 1 (woman) part-time/adjunct. *Students:* 91 full-time (74 women), 114 part-time (91 women); includes 141 minority (136 African Americans, 1 American Indian/Alaska Native, 3 Asian Americans or Pacific Islanders, 1 Hispanic American), 2 international. Average age 33. 205 applicants, 45% accepted, 44 enrolled. In 2007, 17 master's, 10 doctorates awarded. *Degree requirements:* For doctorate, thesis/dissertation (for some programs). *Entrance requirements:* For master's, GRE General Test or MAT; for doctorate, GRE General Test or MAT, minimum GPA of 3.25, work experience. Application fee: $25. *Expenses:* Tuition, state resident: full-time $6,271; part-time $490 per hour. Tuition, nonresident: full-time $16,550; part-time $936 per hour. *Unit head:* Dr. Linda Guthrie, Head, 615-963-2920, Fax: 615-963-5140, E-mail: lguthrie@tnstate.edu.

Texas A&M International University, Office of Graduate Studies and Research, College of Arts and Sciences, Department of Behavioral, Applied Sciences, and Criminal Justice, Laredo, TX 78041-1900. Offers counseling psychology (MACP); criminal justice (MS); psychology (MS); sociology (MA). *Faculty:* 10 full-time (5 women), 1 (woman) part-time/adjunct. *Students:* 14 full-time (11 women), 68 part-time (40 women); includes 76 minority (1 Asian American or Pacific Islander, 75 Hispanic Americans), 2 international. Average age 30. 40 applicants, 88% accepted, 21 enrolled. In 2007, 24 degrees awarded. *Degree requirements:* For master's, thesis (for some programs). *Entrance requirements:* For master's, GRE General Test. Additional exam requirements/recommendations for international students: Required—TOEFL (minimum score 550 paper-based; 213 computer-based). *Application deadline:* For fall admission, 7/15 priority date for domestic students; for spring admission, 11/12 for domestic students. Applications are processed on a rolling basis. Application fee: $25. *Financial support:* In 2007–08, 44 students received support. Application deadline: 11/1. *Unit head:* Dr. John Kilburn, Chair, 956-326-2667, Fax: 956-326-2459, E-mail: jkilburn@tamiu.edu. *Application contact:* Rosie Espinoza-Dickinson, Director of Admissions, 956-326-2200, Fax: 956-326-2199, E-mail: enroll@tamiu.edu.

Texas A&M University, College of Liberal Arts, Department of Psychology, College Station, TX 77843. Offers behavioral and cellular neuroscience (MS, PhD); clinical psychology (MS, PhD); cognitive psychology (MS, PhD); developmental psychology (MS, PhD); industrial/organizational psychology (MS, PhD); social psychology (MS, PhD). *Accreditation:* APA (one or more programs are accredited). *Faculty:* 33. *Students:* 69 full-time (46 women), 14 part-time (10 women); includes 27 minority (7 African Americans, 1 American Indian/Alaska Native, 5 Asian Americans or Pacific Islanders, 14 Hispanic Americans), 8 international. 274 applicants, 11% accepted, 15 enrolled. In 2007, 11 master's, 7 doctorates awarded. *Degree requirements:* For master's, thesis; for doctorate, comprehensive exam (for some programs), thesis/dissertation. *Entrance requirements:* For master's and doctorate, GRE General Test. Additional exam requirements/recommendations for international students: Required—TOEFL. *Application deadline:* For fall admission, 1/5 for domestic and international students. Application fee: $50 ($75 for international students). Electronic applications accepted. *Expenses:* Tuition, state resident: full-time $6,129. Tuition, nonresident: full-time $11,689. Tuition and fees vary according to course load. *Financial support:* Fellowships with partial tuition reimbursements, research assistantships with partial tuition reimbursements, teaching assistantships with partial tuition reimbursements, career-related internships or fieldwork, institutionally sponsored loans, health care benefits, and unspecified assistantships available. Financial award application deadline: 1/5; financial award applicants required to submit FAFSA. *Unit head:* Dr. Steve Rholes, Head, 979-845-2581, Fax: 979-845-4727, E-mail: wsr@psyc.tamu.edu. *Application contact:* Sharon Starr, Graduate Admissions Supervisor, 979-458-1710, Fax: 979-845-4727, E-mail: gradadv@psyc.tamu.edu.

Texas A&M University–Commerce, Graduate School, College of Education and Human Services, Department of Psychology and Special Education, Commerce, TX 75429-3011. Offers cognition and instruction (PhD); psychology (MA, MS); special education (M Ed, MA, MS). Part-time programs available. *Faculty:* 19 full-time (8 women), 6 part-time/adjunct (5 women). *Students:* 29 full-time (25 women), 94 part-time (79 women); includes 25 minority (16 African Americans, 2 American Indian/Alaska Native, 1 Asian American or Pacific Islander, 6 Hispanic Americans), 3 international. In 2007, 28 master's, 3 doctorates awarded. Terminal master's awarded for partial completion of doctoral program. *Degree requirements:* For master's, comprehensive exam, thesis (for some programs); for doctorate, thesis/dissertation, departmental qualifying exam. *Entrance requirements:* For master's, GRE General Test; for doctorate, GRE General Test, 3 letters of recommendation. *Application deadline:* For fall admission, 6/1 priority date for domestic students; for spring admission, 11/1 priority date for domestic students. Applications are processed on a rolling basis. Application fee: $0 ($25 for international students). Electronic applications accepted. *Financial support:* In 2007–08, research assistantships (averaging $7,875 per year), teaching assistantships (averaging $7,875 per year) were awarded; career-related internships or fieldwork, Federal Work-Study, institutionally sponsored loans, and scholarships/grants also available. Financial award application deadline: 5/1; financial award applicants required to submit FAFSA. *Faculty research:* Human learning, study skills, multicultural bilingual, diversity and special education, educationally handicapped. Total annual research expenditures: $65,078. *Unit head:* Tracy Henley, Head, 903-886-5594. *Application contact:* Tammi Thompson, Graduate Admissions Adviser, 843-886-5167, Fax: 843-886-5165, E-mail: tammi_thompson@tamu-commerce.edu.

Texas A&M University–Corpus Christi, Graduate Studies and Research, College of Liberal Arts, Program in Psychology, Corpus Christi, TX 78412-5503. Offers MA. Part-time and evening/weekend programs available. *Students:* 17 full-time (11 women); 17 part-time (11 women); includes 12 minority (2 African Americans, 10 Hispanic Americans), 1 international. 35 applicants, 57% accepted, 12 enrolled. In 2007, 16 degrees awarded. *Degree requirements:* For master's, comprehensive exam, thesis (for some programs). *Entrance requirements:* For master's, GRE General Test. Additional exam requirements/recommendations for international students: Required—TOEFL. *Application deadline:* For fall admission, 7/15 priority date for domestic students, 5/1 priority date for international students; for spring admission, 11/15 priority date for domestic students, 9/1 priority date for international students. Applications are processed on a rolling basis. Application fee: $30 ($50 for international students). Electronic applications accepted. *Expenses:* Tuition, state resident: part-time $63 per credit hour. Tuition, nonresident: part-time $341 per credit hour. Tuition and fees vary according to course load. *Financial support:* Research assistantships, teaching assistantships, career-related internships or fieldwork, Federal Work-Study, institutionally sponsored loans, scholarships/grants, health care benefits, and unspecified assistantships available. Support available to part-time students. Financial award application deadline: 3/15; financial award applicants required to submit FAFSA. *Unit head:* Dr. Pamela Brouillard, Chair, 361-825-2619, E-mail: pamela.brouillard@tamucc.edu. *Application contact:* Maria Martinez, Graduate Admissions Coordinator, 361-825-2177, Fax: 361-825-2755, E-mail: gradweb@tamucc.edu.

Texas A&M University–Kingsville, College of Graduate Studies, College of Arts and Sciences, Department of Psychology and Sociology, Kingsville, TX 78363. Offers gerontology (MS); psychology (MA, MS); sociology (MA, MS). Part-time and evening/weekend programs available. *Degree requirements:* For master's, comprehensive exam, thesis or alternative. *Entrance requirements:* For master's, GRE General Test, minimum GPA of 2.5. Additional exam requirements/recommendations for international students: Required—TOEFL. *Faculty research:* Hispanic female voting behavior, attitudes toward criminal justice, immigration of aged into south Texas, folk medicine.

Texas A&M University–Texarkana, Graduate Studies and Research, College of Health and Behavioral Sciences, Texarkana, TX 75505-5518. Offers counseling psychology (MS). Part-time and evening/weekend programs available. *Degree requirements:* For master's, comprehensive exam (for some programs), thesis or alternative. *Entrance requirements:* For master's, minimum GPA of 3.0 in last 60 hours of bachelor's degree. Additional exam requirements/recommendations for international students: Required—TOEFL. Electronic applications accepted.

Texas Christian University, College of Science and Engineering, Department of Psychology, Fort Worth, TX 76129-0002. Offers MA, MS, PhD. Part-time and evening/weekend programs available. *Degree requirements:* For master's, thesis, foreign language (MA); for doctorate, thesis/dissertation. *Entrance requirements:* For master's and doctorate, GRE General Test. Additional exam requirements/recommendations for international students: Required—TOEFL. *Application deadline:* For fall admission, 3/1 for domestic students; for spring admission, 12/1 for domestic students. Applications are processed on a rolling basis. Application fee: $0. *Expenses:* Tuition: Part-time $865 per credit hour. Required fees: $48 per year. *Financial support:* Fellowships, teaching assistantships, unspecified assistantships available. Financial award application deadline: 3/1. *Unit head:* Dr. Timothy Barth, Chairperson, 817-257-7410, E-mail: t.barth@tcu.edu. *Application contact:* Dr. Bonnie Melhart, Associate Dean, College of Science and Engineering, E-mail: b.melhart@tcu.edu.

Texas Southern University, Graduate School, College of Liberal Arts and Behavioral Sciences, Department of Psychology, Houston, TX 77004-4584. Offers MA. *Faculty:* 6 full-time (3 women). *Students:* 41 full-time (36 women), 33 part-time (28 women); includes 71 minority (65 African Americans, 6 Hispanic Americans), 1 international. Average age 32. 25 applicants, 96% accepted, 16 enrolled. In 2007, 7 degrees awarded. Application fee: $50. *Unit head:* Dr. Leon H Belcher, Chair, 713-313-7062, E-mail: belcher_lh@tsu.edu.

Texas State University–San Marcos, Graduate School, College of Liberal Arts, Department of Psychology, San Marcos, TX 78666. Offers health psychology (MA). *Faculty:* 6 full-time (2 women), 1 part-time/adjunct (0 women). *Students:* 29 full-time (22 women), 5 part-time (2 women); includes 8 minority (2 African Americans, 6 Hispanic Americans), 3 international. Average age 28. 35 applicants, 91% accepted, 21 enrolled. In 2007, 10 degrees awarded. *Degree requirements:* For master's, thesis, 450 hours of practicum courses. *Entrance requirements:* For master's, GRE General Test, minimum GPA of 3.0 in last 60 hours and in psychology, 3 letters of rec, 3.0 GPA in psy core courses, statement of purpose. Additional exam requirements/recommendations for international students: Required—TOEFL (minimum score 550 paper-based; 213 computer-based). *Application deadline:* For fall admission, 3/15 for domestic and international students. Applications are processed on a rolling basis. Application fee: $40 ($90 for international students). Electronic applications accepted. *Expenses:* Tuition, state resident: full-time $3,780; part-time $210 per credit hour. Tuition, nonresident: full-time $8,784; part-time $488 per credit hour. Required fees: $493 per semester. Full-time tuition and fees vary according to course load. *Financial support:* In 2007–08, 29 students received support, including 1 research assistantship (averaging $4,928 per year), 7 teaching assistantships (averaging $3,444 per year). Financial award application deadline: 4/1. *Unit head:* Dr. Francisco Barrios, Chair, 512-245-2526, Fax: 512-245-3153, E-mail: fb12@txstate.edu.

Texas State University–San Marcos, Graduate School, Interdisciplinary Studies Program in Educational Administration and Psychological Services, San Marcos, TX 78666. Offers MAIS. *Students:* 1 full-time (0 women), 1 (woman) part-time. Average age 27. *Degree requirements:* For master's, comprehensive exam. *Application deadline:* For fall admission, 6/15 priority date for domestic students; for spring admission, 10/15 priority date for domestic students. Applications are processed on a rolling basis. Application fee: $40 ($90 for international students). *Expenses:* Tuition, state resident: full-time $3,780; part-time $210 per credit hour. Tuition, nonresident: full-time $8,784; part-time $488 per credit hour. Required fees: $493 per semester. Full-time tuition and fees vary according to course load. *Financial support:* Application deadline: 4/1; *Unit head:* Dr. Stan Carpenter, Dean, 512-245-2575, Fax: 512-245-8345, E-mail: sc33@txstate.edu.

Texas State University–San Marcos, Graduate School, Interdisciplinary Studies Program in Psychology, San Marcos, TX 78666. Offers MAIS. *Students:* Average age 49. *Degree requirements:* For master's, comprehensive exam. *Application deadline:* For fall admission, 6/15 priority date for domestic students; for spring admission, 10/15 priority date for domestic students. Applications are processed on a rolling basis. Application fee: $40 ($90 for international students). *Expenses:* Tuition, state resident: full-time $3,780; part-time $210 per credit hour. Tuition, nonresident: full-time $8,784; part-time $488 per credit hour. Required fees: $493 per semester. Full-time tuition and fees vary according to course load. *Financial support:* In 2007–08, 1 student received support. Application deadline: 4/1; *Unit head:* Dr. Francisco Barrios, Advisor, 512-245-3159, Fax: 512-245-3153, E-mail: fb12@txstate.edu.

Texas Tech University, Graduate School, College of Arts and Sciences, Department of Psychology, Lubbock, TX 79409. Offers clinical psychology (PhD); counseling psychology (MA, PhD); experimental psychology (MA, PhD); psychology (MA, PhD). *Accreditation:* APA (one or more programs are accredited). Part-time programs available. *Faculty:* 25 full-time (11 women). *Students:* 91 full-time (59 women), 11 part-time (8 women); includes 16 minority (6 African Americans, 2 Asian Americans or Pacific Islanders, 8 Hispanic Americans), 4 international. Average age 28. 264 applicants, 10% accepted, 17 enrolled. In 2007, 15 master's, 16 doctorates awarded. *Degree requirements:* For doctorate, thesis/dissertation. *Entrance requirements:* For master's and doctorate, GRE General Test, GRE Subject Test. Additional exam requirements/recommendations for international students: Required—TOEFL (minimum score 550 paper-based; 213 computer-based). *Application deadline:* For fall admission, 3/1 priority date for international students; for spring admission, 11/1 priority date for international students. Applications are processed on a rolling basis. Application fee: $50 ($60 for international students). Electronic applications accepted. *Expenses:* Tuition, state resident: part-time $373 per credit hour. Tuition, nonresident: part-time $651 per credit hour. Tuition and fees vary according to program. *Financial support:* In 2007–08, 99 students received support, including 8 research assistantships with partial tuition reimbursements available (averaging $11,462 per year), 64 teaching assistantships with partial tuition reimbursements available (averaging $11,759 per year); career-related internships or fieldwork, Federal Work-Study, and institutionally sponsored loans also available. Support available to part-time students. Financial award application deadline: 4/15; financial award applicants required to submit FAFSA. *Faculty research:* Failure/success in relationships, peer rejection in school, stress and coping, group processes, clinical and health psychology. Total annual research expenditures: $459,933. *Unit head:* Dr. M. David Rudd, Chair, 806-742-3711 Ext. 224, Fax: 806-742-0818, E-mail: david.

Psychology—General

Texas Tech University (continued)
rudd@ttu.edu. *Application contact:* Dr. Steve Richards, Graduate Advisor, 806-742-3711 Ext. 254, Fax: 806-742-0818, E-mail: steven.richards@ttu.edu.

Texas Wesleyan University, Graduate Programs, Programs in Education, Fort Worth, TX 76105-1536. Offers education (M Ed); professional counseling (MA); psychology (MSP); school counseling (MS). Part-time and evening/weekend programs available. Postbaccalaureate distance learning degree programs offered (no on-campus study). *Faculty:* 37 full-time (11 women), 40 part-time/adjunct (13 women). *Students:* 58 full-time (46 women), 171 part-time (146 women); includes 69 minority (38 African Americans, 1 American Indian/Alaska Native, 2 Asian Americans or Pacific Islanders, 28 Hispanic Americans). Average age 34. In 2007, 52 degrees awarded. *Entrance requirements:* For master's, GRE General Test, minimum GPA of 3.0 in final 60 hours of undergraduate course work, interview, essay. *Application deadline:* For fall admission, 6/15 priority date for domestic students; for spring admission, 10/15 priority date for domestic students. Applications are processed on a rolling basis. Application fee: $40 ($50 for international students). *Expenses:* Tuition: Full-time $4,500; part-time $500 per credit hour. Required fees: $56 per credit hour. Tuition and fees vary according to degree level and program. *Financial support:* Career-related internships or fieldwork, Federal Work-Study, scholarships/grants, and tuition waivers (full and partial) available. Support available to part-time students. Financial award application deadline: 3/15; financial award applicants required to submit FAFSA. *Faculty research:* Teacher effectiveness, bilingual education, analytic teaching. *Unit head:* Dr. Carlos Martinez, Dean, School of Education, 817-531-4940, Fax: 817-531-4943. *Application contact:* DeTrae Warren, Graduate Admission Recruiter, 817-531-4931, Fax: 817-531-4935, E-mail: dwarren@txwes.edu.

Texas Woman's University, Graduate School, College of Arts and Sciences, Department of Psychology and Philosophy, Denton, TX 76201. Offers counseling psychology (MA, PhD); school psychology (PhD, SSP). *Accreditation:* APA (one or more programs are accredited). *Students:* 74 full-time (66 women), 50 part-time (46 women); includes 22 minority (7 African Americans, 7 Asian Americans or Pacific Islanders, 8 Hispanic Americans), 3 international. Average age 29. In 2007, 18 master's, 5 doctorates awarded. Terminal master's awarded for partial completion of doctoral program. *Median time to degree:* Of those who began their doctoral program in fall 1999, 25% received their degree in 8 years or less. *Degree requirements:* For master's, thesis; for doctorate, comprehensive exam, thesis/dissertation, internship, residency. *Entrance requirements:* For master's, 2 letters of reference, resumé, interview; for doctorate, 3 letters of reference; resumé; interview; minimum overall GPA of 3.0, 3.5 for all undergraduate psychology courses; autobiographical statement; BS/BA in psychology or 18 hours of required psychology classes. Additional exam requirements/recommendations for international students: Required—TOEFL (minimum score 550 paper-based; 213 computer-based; 79 iBT). *Application deadline:* For fall admission, 12/15 for domestic and international students. Applications are processed on a rolling basis. Application fee: $30 ($50 for international students). Electronic applications accepted. *Expenses:* Tuition, state resident: full-time $3,294; part-time $183 per credit. Tuition, nonresident: full-time $8,298; part-time $461 per credit. Required fees: $985; $55 per credit. Tuition and fees vary according to degree level. *Financial support:* In 2007–08, 1 teaching assistantship (averaging $10,746 per year) was awarded; career-related internships or fieldwork, Federal Work-Study, institutionally sponsored loans, scholarships/grants, traineeships, health care benefits, and unspecified assistantships also available. Support available to part-time students. Financial award application deadline: 3/1; financial award applicants required to submit FAFSA. *Faculty research:* Women's anger, pre-school assessments, body image dysfunction, traumatic stress, classical ethics. *Unit head:* Dr. Dan Miller, Chair, 940-898-2303, Fax: 940-898-2301, E-mail: dmiller@twu.edu. *Application contact:* Samuel Wheeler, Assistant Director of Admissions, 940-898-3188, Fax: 940-898-3081, E-mail: wheelersr@twu.edu.

Trevecca Nazarene University, Graduate Division, Graduate Psychology Programs, Nashville, TN 37210-2877. Offers clinical counseling (Ed D); counseling (MA); counseling psychology (MA); marriage and family therapy (MMFT). Part-time and evening/weekend programs available. *Faculty:* 4 full-time (1 woman), 14 part-time/adjunct (9 women). *Students:* 178 full-time (135 women), 39 part-time (27 women); includes 27 minority (23 African Americans, 2 American Indian/Alaska Native, 2 Hispanic Americans). Average age 34. In 2007, 62 degrees awarded. *Degree requirements:* For master's, comprehensive exam; for doctorate, comprehensive exam, thesis/dissertation. *Entrance requirements:* For master's, GRE General Test or MAT, minimum GPA of 2.7, 2 reference assessment forms; for doctorate, GRE, minimum GPA of 3.25, 3 recommendation forms, 400-word letter of intent, interview. Additional exam requirements/recommendations for international students: Required—TOEFL. *Application deadline:* Applications are processed on a rolling basis. *Expenses:* Contact institution. Tuition and fees vary according to degree level and program. *Financial support:* Applicants required to submit FAFSA. *Unit head:* Dr. Peter Wilson, Director, 615-248-1384, Fax: 615-248-1662, E-mail: pwilson@trevecca.edu. *Application contact:* Heather Ambrefe, Department Secretary, 615-248-1384, Fax: 615-248-1662, E-mail: admissions_psy@trevecca.edu.

Tufts University, Graduate School of Arts and Sciences, Department of Psychology, Medford, MA 02155. Offers MS, PhD. *Faculty:* 15 full-time, 10 part-time/adjunct. *Students:* 36 (24 women); includes 5 minority (2 African Americans, 3 Asian Americans or Pacific Islanders) 4 international. 134 applicants, 11% accepted, 6 enrolled. In 2007, 9 master's, 1 doctorate awarded. Terminal master's awarded for partial completion of doctoral program. *Degree requirements:* For master's, thesis; for doctorate, one foreign language, thesis/dissertation. *Entrance requirements:* For master's and doctorate, GRE General Test, GRE Subject Test. Additional exam requirements/recommendations for international students: Required—TOEFL (minimum score 550 paper-based; 213 computer-based; 80 iBT). *Application deadline:* For fall admission, 1/15 for domestic students, 12/30 for international students. Applications are processed on a rolling basis. Application fee: $70. Electronic applications accepted. *Expenses:* Tuition: Full-time $35,052. *Financial support:* Fellowships, research assistantships with full and partial tuition reimbursements, teaching assistantships with full and partial tuition reimbursements, Federal Work-Study, scholarships/grants, and tuition waivers (partial) available. Support available to part-time students. Financial award application deadline: 1/15; financial award applicants required to submit FAFSA. *Unit head:* Robert Cook, Chair, 617-627-2546. *Application contact:* Holly Taylor, Head, 617-627-3523, Fax: 617-627-3181.

Tulane University, School of Science and Engineering, Department of Psychology, New Orleans, LA 70118-5669. Offers MS, PhD. *Accreditation:* APA (one or more programs are accredited). Terminal master's awarded for partial completion of doctoral program. *Degree requirements:* For master's, variable foreign language requirement, thesis; for doctorate, thesis/dissertation. *Entrance requirements:* For master's, GRE General Test, minimum B average in undergraduate course work; for doctorate, GRE General Test. Additional exam requirements/recommendations for international students: Required—TOEFL. Electronic applications accepted. *Faculty research:* Hormones and behavior, aggression, personnel selection, cognitive development, stereotyping, diabetes.

Uniformed Services University of the Health Sciences, School of Medicine, Programs in Biomedical Sciences, Department of Medical and Clinical Psychology, Bethesda, MD 20814-4799. Offers clinical psychology (PhD); medical psychology (PhD). Clinical psychology available to active duty military only. *Accreditation:* APA. *Faculty:* 8 full-time (3 women), 42 part-time/adjunct (13 women). *Students:* 32 full-time (23 women); includes 5 minority (3 African Americans, 1 American Indian/Alaska Native, 1 Hispanic American). Average age 27. 69 applicants, 16% accepted, 8 enrolled. In 2007, 3 doctorates awarded. Terminal master's awarded for partial completion of doctoral program. *Median time to degree:* Of those who began their doctoral program in fall 1999, 100% received their degree in 8 years or less. *Degree requirements:* For doctorate, comprehensive exam, thesis/dissertation, qualifying exam. *Entrance requirements:* For doctorate, GRE General Test, minimum GPA of 3.0, U.S. citizenship. Additional exam requirements/recommendations for international students: Required—TOEFL. *Application deadline:* For fall admission, 1/15 priority date for domestic and international students. Applications are processed on a rolling basis. Application fee: $0. Electronic applications accepted. *Financial support:* In 2007–08, fellowships with full tuition reimbursements (averaging $25,000 per year); tuition waivers (full) also available. *Faculty research:* Addictive and appetitive behavior, psychopharmacology, stress and eating, obesity, health. *Unit head:* Dr. David S. Krantz, Chair, 301-295-3270, Fax: 301-295-3034, E-mail: dskrantz@usuhs.mil. *Application contact:* Janet M. Anastasi, Graduate Program Coordinator, 301-295-9474, Fax: 301-295-6772, E-mail: janastasi@usuhs.mil.

Union Institute & University, Online MA Programs, Cincinnati, OH 45206-1925. Offers health and wellness (MA); history and culture (MA); leadership (MA); literature and writing (MA); psychology (MA). Part-time programs available. Postbaccalaureate distance learning degree programs offered (no on-campus study). *Faculty:* 3 full-time (1 woman), 15 part-time/adjunct (11 women). *Students:* 204 full-time (143 women); includes 19 minority (14 African Americans, 2 American Indian/Alaska Native, 3 Hispanic Americans). Average age 39. In 2007, 46 degrees awarded. *Degree requirements:* For master's, thesis. *Application deadline:* Applications are processed on a rolling basis. Application fee: $50. *Expenses:* Contact institution. *Financial support:* Career-related internships or fieldwork and tuition waivers available. Financial award applicants required to submit FAFSA. *Unit head:* Dr. Brian Webb, Assistant Vice President, Academic Affairs, 802-828-8777, E-mail: brian.webb@tui.edu.

Union Institute & University, Program in Psychology and Counseling, Cincinnati, OH 45206-1925. Offers MA. *Expenses:* Tuition: Full-time $20,176; part-time $760 per credit hour. Tuition and fees vary according to course load, degree level and program. *Unit head:* Dr. Nicholas Young, Director, 802-257-8911.

Universidad de las Americas, A.C., Program in Psychology, Mexico City, Mexico. Offers family therapy (MA).

Universidad de las Américas–Puebla, Division of Graduate Studies, School of Social Sciences, Program in Psychology, Puebla, Mexico. Offers MA. Part-time and evening/weekend programs available. *Degree requirements:* For master's, one foreign language, thesis. *Entrance requirements:* For master's, minimum B+ average. *Faculty research:* Testing, social hemispheric specialization, clinical psychology.

Université de Montréal, Faculty of Arts and Sciences, Department of Psychology, Montréal, QC H3C 3J7, Canada. Offers M Sc, PhD. *Faculty:* 75 full-time (29 women), 7 part-time/adjunct (3 women). *Students:* 280 full-time (198 women), 1 part-time. 295 applicants, 18% accepted, 53 enrolled. In 2007, 36 master's, 26 doctorates awarded. Terminal master's awarded for partial completion of doctoral program. *Degree requirements:* For master's, one foreign language, thesis; for doctorate, one foreign language, thesis/dissertation, general exam. *Application deadline:* For fall admission, 2/1 for domestic students. Application fee: $100. Electronic applications accepted. *Faculty research:* Vision, marital counseling, memory. *Unit head:* Michel Sabourin, Director, 514-343-6503, Fax: 514-343-2285, E-mail: michel.sabourin@umontreal.ca. *Application contact:* Marcelle Cossette-Ricard, Graduate Studies Chairman, 514-343-5827, Fax: 514-343-2285, E-mail: marcelle.cossette-ricard@umontreal.ca.

Université de Sherbrooke, Faculty of Letters and Human Sciences, Department of Psychology, Sherbrooke, QC J1K 2R1, Canada. Offers gerontology (MA). *Degree requirements:* For master's, thesis. *Faculty research:* Human relations.

Université du Québec à Montréal, Graduate Programs, Program in Psychology, Montréal, QC H3C 3P8, Canada. Offers D Ps, PhD. Part-time programs available. *Degree requirements:* For doctorate, thesis/dissertation. *Entrance requirements:* For doctorate, appropriate master's degree or equivalent, proficiency in French.

Université du Québec à Trois-Rivières, Graduate Programs, Program in Psychology, Trois-Rivières, QC G9A 5H7, Canada. Offers MA, PhD. Part-time programs available. *Degree requirements:* For master's, thesis; for doctorate, thesis/dissertation. *Entrance requirements:* For master's, appropriate bachelor's degree, proficiency in French; for doctorate, appropriate master's degree, proficiency in French. *Faculty research:* Child and family development, gerontology, mental health.

Université Laval, Faculty of Social Sciences, School of Psychology, Programs in Psychology, Québec, QC G1K 7P4, Canada. Offers clinical psychology (PhD); community psychology (PhD); psychology (PhD, Psy D). *Degree requirements:* For doctorate, comprehensive exam, thesis/dissertation. *Entrance requirements:* For doctorate, comprehension of written English, knowledge of French, interview. Electronic applications accepted.

University at Albany, State University of New York, College of Arts and Sciences, Department of Psychology, Albany, NY 12222-0001. Offers autism (Certificate); biopsychology (PhD); clinical psychology (PhD); general/experimental psychology (PhD); industrial/organizational psychology (PhD); psychology (MA); social/personality psychology (PhD). *Accreditation:* APA (one or more programs are accredited). *Students:* 51 full-time (32 women), 47 part-time (40 women). Average age 30. In 2007, 8 master's, 15 doctorates, 7 other advanced degrees awarded. *Degree requirements:* For doctorate, thesis/dissertation. *Entrance requirements:* For doctorate, GRE General Test, GRE Subject Test. Additional exam requirements/recommendations for international students: Required—TOEFL (minimum score 550 paper-based; 213 computer-based). *Application deadline:* For fall admission, 1/15 for domestic and international students. Application fee: $75. Electronic applications accepted. *Expenses:* Tuition, state resident: part-time $576 per credit. Tuition, nonresident: part-time $910 per credit. Tuition and fees vary according to program. *Financial support:* Fellowships, research assistantships, teaching assistantships, career-related internships or fieldwork available. Financial award application deadline: 2/1. *Unit head:* Kevin J. Williams, Chair, 518-442-4820.

University at Buffalo, the State University of New York, Graduate School, College of Arts and Sciences, Department of Psychology, Buffalo, NY 14260. Offers behavioral neuroscience (PhD); clinical psychology (PhD); cognitive psychology (PhD); general psychology (MA); social-personality psychology (PhD). *Accreditation:* APA (one or more programs are accredited). Terminal master's awarded for partial completion of doctoral program. *Degree requirements:* For master's, project; for doctorate, thesis/dissertation. *Entrance requirements:* For master's and doctorate, GRE General Test. Additional exam requirements/recommendations for international students: Required—TOEFL (minimum score 550 paper-based; 213 computer-based; 79 iBT). Electronic applications accepted. *Faculty research:* Neural, endocrine, and molecular bases of behavior; adult mood and anxiety disorders; relationship dysfunction; attention deficit/hyperactivity disorder; psycho-linguistics.

The University of Akron, Graduate School, Buchtel College of Arts and Sciences, Department of Psychology, Akron, OH 44325. Offers applied cognitive aging (MA, PhD); counseling psychology (MA, PhD); industrial/gerontological psychology (PhD); industrial/organizational psychology (MA, PhD); psychology (MA). *Accreditation:* APA (one or more programs are accredited). *Faculty:* 18 full-time (6 women), 7 part-time/adjunct (3 women). *Students:* 56 full-time (41 women), 30 part-time (22 women); includes 10 minority (5 African Americans, 3 Asian Americans or Pacific Islanders, 2 Hispanic Americans), 8 international. Average age 33. 133 applicants, 13% accepted, 4 enrolled. In 2007, 13 master's, 10 doctorates awarded. Terminal master's awarded for partial completion of doctoral program. *Degree requirements:* For master's, thesis optional, thesis or specialty exam; for doctorate, one foreign language, comprehensive exam, thesis/dissertation. *Entrance requirements:* For master's, GRE General Test, GRE Subject Test, minimum GPA of 2.75, letters of recommendation, minimum GPA of 3.0 in psychology courses; for doctorate, GRE General Test, GRE Subject Test, minimum graduate GPA of 3.25, letters of recommendation, personal statement. Additional exam requirements/recommendations for international students: Required—TOEFL (minimum score 550 paper-based; 213 computer-based; 79 iBT). *Application deadline:* For fall admission, 1/15 for domestic and international students. Applications are processed on a rolling basis. Application fee: $30 ($40 for international students). Electronic applications accepted. *Expenses:* Tuition, state resident: full-time $6,164; part-time $342 per credit. Tuition, nonresident: full-time $10,575;

part-time $588 per credit. Required fees: $806; $43 per credit. $12 per term. Tuition and fees vary according to course load, degree level and program. *Financial support:* In 2007–08, 43 teaching assistantships with full tuition reimbursements were awarded; fellowships with full tuition reimbursements, research assistantships with full tuition reimbursements, career-related internships or fieldwork, Federal Work-Study, institutionally sponsored loans, and tuition waivers (full) also available. *Faculty research:* Social cognitive determinants of behaviour, the application of psychological principles to the workplace and career planning/development, the psychological processes of aging. Total annual research expenditures: $129,304. *Unit head:* Dr. Paul Levy, Chair, 330-972-8367, E-mail: plevy@uakron.edu.

The University of Alabama, Graduate School, College of Arts and Sciences, Department of Psychology, Tuscaloosa, AL 35487. Offers clinical psychology (PhD); experimental psychology (PhD). *Accreditation:* APA. *Faculty:* 23 full-time (10 women), 1 part-time/adjunct (0 women). *Students:* 74 full-time (57 women), 12 part-time (11 women); includes 14 minority (8 African Americans, 3 Asian Americans or Pacific Islanders, 3 Hispanic Americans), 4 international. Average age 27. 231 applicants, 11% accepted, 15 enrolled. In 2007, 14 doctorates awarded. *Median time to degree:* Of those who began their doctoral program in fall 1999, 64% received their degree in 8 years or less. *Degree requirements:* For doctorate, thesis/dissertation. *Entrance requirements:* For doctorate, GRE. Additional exam requirements/recommendations for international students: Required—TOEFL (minimum score 550 paper-based). *Application deadline:* For fall admission, 12/1 for domestic and international students. Application fee: $30. Electronic applications accepted. *Expenses:* Tuition, state resident: full-time $5,700. Tuition, nonresident: full-time $16,518. *Financial support:* In 2007–08, 73 students received support, including 12 fellowships with full tuition reimbursements available (averaging $15,000 per year), 34 research assistantships with full and partial tuition reimbursements available (averaging $11,142 per year), 26 teaching assistantships with tuition reimbursements available (averaging $11,142 per year); career-related internships or fieldwork, institutionally sponsored loans, scholarships/grants, health care benefits, and unspecified assistantships also available. Financial award application deadline: 12/1. *Faculty research:* Cognitive development/disability, child clinical, psychology and law, health/aging, social psychology. Total annual research expenditures: $2.5 million. *Unit head:* Dr. Kenneth Lichstein, Chair, 205-348-4962, Fax: 205-348-8648, E-mail: lichstein@ua.edu. *Application contact:* Mary Beth Hubbard, Information Contact, 205-348-1919, Fax: 205-348-8648, E-mail: mbhubbard@as.ua.edu.

The University of Alabama at Birmingham, School of Social and Behavioral Sciences, Department of Psychology, Birmingham, AL 35294. Offers MA, PhD. *Accreditation:* APA (one or more programs are accredited). *Students:* 55 full-time (47 women), 5 part-time (2 women); includes 10 minority (8 African Americans, 2 Hispanic Americans), 3 international. Average age 28. In 2007, 9 master's, 13 doctorates awarded. *Application deadline:* Applications are processed on a rolling basis. Application fee: $35 ($60 for international students). Electronic applications accepted. *Financial support:* Career-related internships or fieldwork available. *Faculty research:* Biological basis of behavior structure, function of the nervous system. *Unit head:* Dr. Carl E. McFarland, Chair, 205-934-3850, E-mail: cmcfarla@uab.edu.

The University of Alabama in Huntsville, School of Graduate Studies, College of Liberal Arts, Department of Psychology, Huntsville, AL 35899. Offers MA. Part-time and evening/weekend programs available. *Faculty:* 5 full-time (2 women). *Students:* 6 full-time (5 women), 4 part-time (2 women); includes 1 minority (Hispanic American) Average age 27. 12 applicants, 42% accepted, 5 enrolled. In 2007, 4 degrees awarded. *Degree requirements:* For master's, one foreign language, comprehensive exam, thesis or alternative, oral and written exams. *Entrance requirements:* For master's, GRE General Test, 15 hours of course work in psychology, minimum GPA of 3.25, sample of written work. Additional exam requirements/recommendations for international students: Required—TOEFL (minimum score 500 paper-based; 173 computer-based; 62 iBT). *Application deadline:* For fall admission, 7/18 for domestic students, 4/1 for international students; for spring admission, 11/30 for domestic students, 9/1 for international students. Applications are processed on a rolling basis. Application fee: $40 ($50 for international students). Electronic applications accepted. *Expenses:* Tuition, state resident: full-time $6,548; part-time $276 per credit hour. Tuition, nonresident: full-time $13,466; part-time $565 per credit hour. *Financial support:* In 2007–08, 5 students received support, including 2 teaching assistantships with full and partial tuition reimbursements available (averaging $8,460 per year); fellowships with full and partial tuition reimbursements available, research assistantships with full and partial tuition reimbursements available, career-related internships or fieldwork, Federal Work-Study, institutionally sponsored loans, scholarships/grants, health care benefits, and unspecified assistantships also available. Support available to part-time students. Financial award application deadline: 4/1; financial award applicants required to submit FAFSA. *Faculty research:* Personal and social cognition, development and aging, human factors, perception, biological psychology: hormones and behavior. Total annual research expenditures: $23,580. *Unit head:* Dr. Sandra L. Carpenter, Chair, 256-824-6191, Fax: 256-824-2387, E-mail: carpens@email.uah.edu.

University of Alaska Anchorage, College of Arts and Sciences, Department of Psychology, Anchorage, AK 99508-8060. Offers clinical psychology (MS); clinical-community psychology with rural-indigenous emphasis (PhD). Part-time programs available. *Degree requirements:* For master's, thesis. *Entrance requirements:* For master's, GRE General Test, GRE Subject Test, interview, references; for doctorate, interview, bachelor's or master's degree in psychology. Additional exam requirements/recommendations for international students: Required—TOEFL (minimum score 550 paper-based; 213 computer-based). *Faculty research:* Substance abuse, childhood autism, biofeedback, psychological assessment, mental health in Native Alaskans.

University of Alaska Fairbanks, College of Liberal Arts, Department of Psychology, Fairbanks, AK 99775-7520. Offers clinical-community psychology (PhD), including rural cross-cultural emphasis. *Degree requirements:* For doctorate, comprehensive exam, thesis/dissertation. *Entrance requirements:* For doctorate, GRE General Test, minimum GPA of 3.0, letters of reference. Additional exam requirements/recommendations for international students: Required—TOEFL (minimum score 550 paper-based; 213 computer-based). *Faculty research:* Clinical and community psychology, rural, indigenous, and cultural psychology.

University of Alberta, Faculty of Graduate Studies and Research, Department of Psychology, Edmonton, AB T6G 2E1, Canada. Offers M Sc, MA, PhD. Terminal master's awarded for partial completion of doctoral program. *Degree requirements:* For master's, thesis (for some programs); for doctorate, thesis/dissertation. *Entrance requirements:* For master's and doctorate, GRE. Additional exam requirements/recommendations for international students: Required—TOEFL (minimum score 550 paper-based; 213 computer-based). Electronic applications accepted. *Faculty research:* Animal behavior processes; cognitive, social and perceptual processes; development and aging; neuroscience.

The University of Arizona, Graduate College, College of Social and Behavioral Sciences, Department of Psychology, Tucson, AZ 85721. Offers PhD, JD/PhD. *Accreditation:* APA (one or more programs are accredited). *Faculty:* 52. *Students:* 77 full-time (49 women), 17 part-time (12 women); includes 18 minority (2 African Americans, 1 American Indian/Alaska Native, 6 Asian Americans or Pacific Islanders, 9 Hispanic Americans), 13 international. Average age 30. 366 applicants, 5% accepted, 18 enrolled. In 2007, 9 doctorates awarded. *Median time to degree:* Of those who began their doctoral program in fall 1999, 44% received their degree in 8 years or less. *Degree requirements:* For doctorate, comprehensive exam, thesis/dissertation. *Entrance requirements:* For doctorate, GRE General Test, GRE Subject Test, 3 letters of recommendation, statement of purpose. Additional exam requirements/recommendations for international students: Required—TOEFL (minimum score 550 paper-based; 80 iBT). *Application deadline:* For fall admission, 12/15 for domestic and international students. Applications are processed on a rolling basis. Application fee: $50. Electronic applications accepted. *Financial support:* In 2007–08, 3 fellowships with partial tuition reimbursements (averaging $10,000 per year), 25 research assistantships with partial tuition reimbursements (averaging $12,710 per year), 38 teaching assistantships with partial tuition reimbursements (averaging $12,710 per year) were awarded; scholarships/grants, health care benefits, and unspecified assistantships also available. Financial award application deadline: 1/1; financial award applicants required to submit FAFSA. *Faculty research:* Cognitive neuroscience, aging, law and psychology, psycholinguistics, family psychology. Total annual research expenditures: $7 million. *Unit head:* Dr. Alfred W. Kaszniak, Head, 520-621-5149, Fax: 520-621-9306, E-mail: kaszniak@u.arizona.edu. *Application contact:* Beth Owens, Information Contact, 520-621-7456, Fax: 520-621-9306, E-mail: psycgrad@u.arizona.edu.

University of Arkansas, Graduate School, J. William Fulbright College of Arts and Sciences, Department of Psychology, Fayetteville, AR 72701-1201. Offers MA, PhD. *Accreditation:* APA (one or more programs are accredited). *Students:* 33 full-time (20 women), 15 part-time (11 women); includes 3 minority (1 African American, 1 American Indian/Alaska Native, 1 Hispanic American). In 2007, 3 master's, 6 doctorates awarded. *Degree requirements:* For master's, thesis; for doctorate, variable foreign language requirement, thesis/dissertation. *Entrance requirements:* For doctorate, GRE General Test, GRE Subject Test. Application fee: $40 ($50 for international students). *Financial support:* In 2007–08, 25 fellowships with tuition reimbursements, 12 research assistantships, 8 teaching assistantships were awarded; career-related internships or fieldwork, Federal Work-Study, and traineeships also available. Support available to part-time students. Financial award application deadline: 4/1; financial award applicants required to submit FAFSA. *Unit head:* Dr. Doug Behrend, Departmental Chairperson, 479-575-4253, Fax: 479-575-3219, E-mail: psycapp@uark.edu.

University of Arkansas at Little Rock, Graduate School, College of Arts, Humanities, and Social Science, Department of Psychology, Little Rock, AR 72204-1099. Offers applied psychology (MAP). Part-time and evening/weekend programs available. *Students:* Average age 33. *Entrance requirements:* For master's, GRE General Test, minimum GPA of 2.7. *Application deadline:* Applications are processed on a rolling basis. *Financial support:* Fellowships with tuition reimbursements, research assistantships with tuition reimbursements, teaching assistantships with tuition reimbursements, career-related internships or fieldwork, Federal Work-Study, institutionally sponsored loans, and unspecified assistantships available. Support available to part-time students. *Faculty research:* Psychological methods and theories in business industry, government, and organizations; personnel program evaluation; training; affirmative action; organizational analysis and development. *Unit head:* Dr. Belinda L. Blevens-Knabe, Chairperson, 501-569-3171, Fax: 501-569-3039, E-mail: blblevens@ualr.edu. *Application contact:* Dr. Robert J. Hines, Coordinator, 501-569-3527, E-mail: rjhines@ualr.edu.

University of Baltimore, Graduate School, The Yale Gordon College of Liberal Arts, Division of Applied Sciences, Baltimore, MD 21201-5779. Offers applied psychology (MS), including counseling, industrial and organizational psychology, psychological applications; human services (MS). Part-time and evening/weekend programs available. *Faculty:* 7 full-time (5 women), 7 part-time/adjunct (2 women). *Students:* 61 full-time (49 women), 43 part-time (34 women); includes 30 minority (23 African Americans, 5 Asian Americans or Pacific Islanders, 2 Hispanic Americans), 6 international. Average age 28. 112 applicants, 64% accepted, 27 enrolled. In 2007, 31 degrees awarded. *Degree requirements:* For master's, thesis optional. *Entrance requirements:* For master's, GRE, minimum GPA of 3.0. Additional exam requirements/recommendations for international students: Required—TOEFL (minimum score 550 paper-based; 213 computer-based). *Application deadline:* For fall admission, 8/1 for domestic students, 6/1 for international students; for spring admission, 12/1 for domestic students, 11/1 for international students. Applications are processed on a rolling basis. Application fee: $45. Electronic applications accepted. *Expenses: Contact institution.* Tuition and fees vary according to program. *Financial support:* In 2007–08, 5 research assistantships with full and partial tuition reimbursements were awarded; fellowships, career-related internships or fieldwork and Federal Work-Study also available. Support available to part-time students. Financial award application deadline: 4/1; financial award applicants required to submit FAFSA. *Faculty research:* Participatory decision making, counter productive workplace behavior, organizational consulting, substance abuse treatment, cognitive functioning in head injured. Total annual research expenditures: $93,146. *Unit head:* Dr. Thomas Mitchell, Director of Program in Applied Psychology, 410-837-5348, Fax: 410-837-4793, E-mail: tmitchell@ubalt.edu. *Application contact:* Wendy Bolyard.

See Close-Up on page 1505.

The University of British Columbia, Faculty of Arts and Faculty of Graduate Studies, Department of Psychology, Vancouver, BC V6T 1Z1, Canada. Offers behavioral neuroscience (MA, PhD); clinical psychology (MA, PhD); cognitive science (MA, PhD); developmental psychology (MA, PhD); forensic psychology (PhD); health psychology (MA, PhD); quantitative methods (MA, PhD); social/personality psychology (MA, PhD). *Accreditation:* APA (one or more programs are accredited). *Faculty:* 46 full-time (20 women), 26 part-time/adjunct (13 women). *Students:* 102 full-time (69 women). Average age 29. 247 applicants, 14% accepted, 18 enrolled. In 2007, 14 master's, 11 doctorates awarded. Terminal master's awarded for partial completion of doctoral program. *Median time to degree:* Of those who began their doctoral program in fall 1999, 91% received their degree in 8 years or less. *Degree requirements:* For master's, thesis; for doctorate, comprehensive exam, thesis/dissertation. *Entrance requirements:* For master's and doctorate, GRE General Test, GRE Subject Test. Additional exam requirements/recommendations for international students: Required—TOEFL (minimum score 550 paper-based; 230 computer-based; 80 iBT). *Application deadline:* For fall admission, 1/15 for domestic and international students. Applications are processed on a rolling basis. Application fee: $90 Canadian dollars ($150 Canadian dollars for international students). Electronic applications accepted. *Financial support:* In 2007–08, 95 students received support, including 27 fellowships with full and partial tuition reimbursements available (averaging $16,500 per year), 50 research assistantships with full and partial tuition reimbursements available (averaging $6,775 per year), 80 teaching assistantships with full and partial tuition reimbursements available (averaging $8,065 per year); career-related internships or fieldwork, Federal Work-Study, institutionally sponsored loans, scholarships/grants, health care benefits, tuition waivers (full and partial), and unspecified assistantships also available. Financial award application deadline: 1/15. *Faculty research:* Clinical, developmental, social/personality, cognition, behavioral neuroscience. Total annual research expenditures: $5.5 million Canadian dollars. *Unit head:* Dr. Eric Eich, Head, 604-822-3078, Fax: 604-822-6923, E-mail: ee@psych.ubc.ca. *Application contact:* Rose Tam, Graduate Secretary, 604-822-3144, Fax: 604-822-6923, E-mail: gradsec@psych.ubc.ca.

University of Calgary, Faculty of Graduate Studies, Faculty of Social Sciences, Department of Psychology, Calgary, AB T2N 1N4, Canada. Offers clinical psychology (M Sc, PhD); psychology (M Sc, PhD). *Degree requirements:* For master's, thesis; for doctorate, thesis/dissertation. *Entrance requirements:* For master's, GRE General Test, bachelor's degree in psychology, minimum GPA of 3.4. Additional exam requirements/recommendations for international students: Required—TOEFL (minimum score 550 paper-based; 213 computer-based). Electronic applications accepted. *Faculty research:* Cognition and cognitive development, social psychology, theoretical psychology, perception, aging.

University of California, Berkeley, Graduate Division, College of Letters and Science, Department of Psychology, Berkeley, CA 94720-1500. Offers PhD. *Accreditation:* APA. *Degree requirements:* For doctorate, thesis/dissertation, qualifying exam. *Entrance requirements:* For doctorate, GRE General Test, GRE Subject Test, minimum GPA of 3.0, 3 letters of recommendation. *Application deadline:* For fall admission, 12/3 for domestic students. Application fee: $70 ($90 for international students). Electronic applications accepted. *Financial support:* Unspecified assistantships available. *Unit head:* Stephen Hinshaw, Chair, 510-643-8586, E-mail: hinshaw@socrates.berkeley.edu. *Application contact:* Michael Ortt, Graduate Admissions Officer, 510-643-1382, Fax: 510-642-5293, E-mail: psychapp@berkeley.edu.

University of California, Davis, Graduate Studies, Program in Psychology, Davis, CA 95616. Offers PhD. *Degree requirements:* For doctorate, thesis/dissertation. *Entrance requirements:* For doctorate, GRE General Test, GRE Subject Test, minimum GPA of 3.0. Additional exam requirements/recommendations for international students: Required—TOEFL (minimum score

Psychology—General

University of California, Davis (continued)
550 paper-based; 213 computer-based). Electronic applications accepted. *Faculty research:* Social personality, perception, cognition, psychobiology.

University of California, Irvine, Office of Graduate Studies, School of Social Ecology, Department of Psychology and Social Behavior, Irvine, CA 92697. Offers PhD. *Students:* 66 full-time (49 women); includes 12 minority (1 African American, 10 Asian Americans or Pacific Islanders, 1 Hispanic American), 1 international. In 2007, 3 degrees awarded. *Degree requirements:* For doctorate, thesis/dissertation, research project. *Entrance requirements:* For doctorate, GRE General Test, minimum GPA of 3.0. Additional exam requirements/recommendations for international students: Required—TOEFL (minimum score 550 paper-based; 213 computer-based). *Application deadline:* For fall admission, 1/15 priority date for domestic students; for winter admission, 10/15 priority date for domestic students. Applications are processed on a rolling basis. Application fee: $60. Electronic applications accepted. *Financial support:* Fellowships, research assistantships with full tuition reimbursements, teaching assistantships, institutionally sponsored loans, traineeships, health care benefits, and unspecified assistantships available. Financial award application deadline: 3/1; financial award applicants required to submit FAFSA. *Faculty research:* Psychosocial development in children, adolescents, and adults; gerontology, childhood behavior disorders, and developmental psychopathology; sex differences; attitude change; social psychology. *Unit head:* Chuansheng Chen, Chair, 949-824-4184, E-mail: ksrook@uci.edu. *Application contact:* Jill Vidas, Academic Counselor, 949-824-5918, Fax: 949-824-2056, E-mail: jjvidas@uci.edu.

University of California, Irvine, Office of Graduate Studies, School of Social Sciences, Department of Cognitive Science, Irvine, CA 92697. Offers psychology (PhD). *Students:* 60 full-time (29 women); includes 16 minority (9 Asian Americans or Pacific Islanders, 7 Hispanic Americans), 11 international. In 2007, 1 doctorate awarded. *Degree requirements:* For doctorate, thesis/dissertation. *Entrance requirements:* For doctorate, GRE General Test, minimum GPA of 3.0. Additional exam requirements/recommendations for international students: Required—TOEFL (minimum score 550 paper-based; 213 computer-based). *Application deadline:* For fall admission, 1/15 priority date for domestic students; for winter admission, 10/15 priority date for domestic students. Applications are processed on a rolling basis. Application fee: $60. Electronic applications accepted. *Financial support:* Fellowships, research assistantships with full tuition reimbursements, teaching assistantships, institutionally sponsored loans, traineeships, health care benefits, and unspecified assistantships available. Financial award application deadline: 3/1; financial award applicants required to submit FAFSA. *Faculty research:* Mathematical psychology, visual and auditory perception, cognitive development, problem solving, experimental psychology. *Unit head:* Charles (Ted) Wright, Chair, 949-824-7589, Fax: 949-824-2307, E-mail: cewright@uci.edu. *Application contact:* Diane Enriquez, Graduate Counselor, 949-824-5924, Fax: 949-824-3548, E-mail: dmvargas@uci.edu.

University of California, Los Angeles, Graduate Division, College of Letters and Science, Department of Psychology, Los Angeles, CA 90095. Offers MA, PhD. *Accreditation:* APA (one or more programs are accredited). *Students:* 170 full-time (106 women); includes 39 minority (7 African Americans, 15 Asian Americans or Pacific Islanders, 17 Hispanic Americans), 10 international. Average age 27. 562 applicants, 12% accepted, 39 enrolled. In 2007, 31 master's, 22 doctorates awarded. Terminal master's awarded for partial completion of doctoral program. *Median time to degree:* Of those who began their doctoral program in fall 1999, 73% received their degree in 8 years or less. *Degree requirements:* For master's, comprehensive exam; for doctorate, thesis/dissertation, oral and written qualifying exams, teaching experience. *Entrance requirements:* For master's, GRE General Test, GRE Subject Test, minimum GPA of 3.0, degree objective of Ph.D; for doctorate, GRE General Test, GRE Subject Test, MAT, minimum undergraduate GPA of 3.0. Additional exam requirements/recommendations for international students: Required—TOEFL. Application fee: $60. Electronic applications accepted. *Expenses:* Tuition, nonresident: full-time $5,728. Required fees: $8,966. Full-time tuition and fees vary according to program and student level. *Financial support:* In 2007–08, 104 fellowships with full and partial tuition reimbursements, 36 research assistantships with full and partial tuition reimbursements, 98 teaching assistantships with full and partial tuition reimbursements were awarded; Federal Work-Study, institutionally sponsored loans, scholarships/grants, and tuition waivers (full and partial) also available. Financial award application deadline: 3/1; financial award applicants required to submit FAFSA. *Unit head:* Robert Bjork, Chair, 310-825-7028. *Application contact:* Departmental Office, 310-825-2617, E-mail: gradadm@psych.ucla.edu.

University of California, Riverside, Graduate Division, Department of Psychology, Riverside, CA 92521-0102. Offers MA, PhD. *Accreditation:* APA. *Faculty:* 26 full-time (12 women). *Students:* 67 full-time (42 women); includes 14 minority (8 Asian Americans or Pacific Islanders, 6 Hispanic Americans), 3 international. Average age 29. In 2007, 8 master's, 12 doctorates awarded. *Degree requirements:* For doctorate, comprehensive exam, thesis/dissertation, 3 quarters of teaching experience, qualifying exams. *Entrance requirements:* For doctorate, GRE General Test, minimum GPA of 3.2. Additional exam requirements/recommendations for international students: Required—TOEFL (minimum score 550 paper-based; 213 computer-based; 80 iBT). *Application deadline:* For fall admission, 1/3 priority date for domestic and international students. Applications are processed on a rolling basis. Application fee: $60 ($75 for international students). Electronic applications accepted. *Financial support:* In 2007–08, fellowships with tuition reimbursements (averaging $12,500 per year), research assistantships with partial tuition reimbursements (averaging $18,000 per year), teaching assistantships with partial tuition reimbursements (averaging $16,500 per year) were awarded; institutionally sponsored loans, health care benefits, and tuition waivers (full and partial) also available. Financial award application deadline: 1/3; financial award applicants required to submit FAFSA. *Faculty research:* Neuroscience, personality and social psychology, developmental psychology, cognition, health psychology, quantitative psychology. Total annual research expenditures: $6,000. *Unit head:* Dr. Christine Chiarello, Graduate Advisor, 951-827-5096, Fax: 951-827-3985, E-mail: chris@faculty.ucr.edu. *Application contact:* Faye Harmer, Graduate Program Assistant, 951-827-6306, Fax: 951-827-3985, E-mail: psychadvisor@ucr.edu.

University of California, San Diego, Office of Graduate Studies, Department of Psychology, La Jolla, CA 92093. Offers PhD. *Degree requirements:* For doctorate, thesis/dissertation. *Entrance requirements:* For doctorate, GRE General Test. Electronic applications accepted.

University of California, San Diego, Office of Graduate Studies, Interdisciplinary Program in Cognitive Science, La Jolla, CA 92093. Offers cognitive science/anthropology (PhD); cognitive science/communication (PhD); cognitive science/computer science and engineering (PhD); cognitive science/linguistics (PhD); cognitive science/neuroscience (PhD); cognitive science/philosophy (PhD); cognitive science/psychology (PhD); cognitive science/sociology (PhD). Admissions offered through affiliated departments. *Faculty:* 65 full-time (14 women). *Students:* 7 full-time (3 women). Average age 26. 2 applicants, 100% accepted, 2 enrolled. In 2007, 1 degree awarded. *Degree requirements:* For doctorate, thesis/dissertation. *Entrance requirements:* For doctorate, GRE General Test, acceptance into one of the 8 participating departments. *Application deadline:* Applications are processed on a rolling basis. Application fee: $0. *Faculty research:* Language and cognition, philosophy of mind, visual perception, biological anthropology, sociolinguistics. *Unit head:* Gary Cottrell, Director, 858-534-7141, Fax: 858-534-1128, E-mail: gcottrell@ucsd.edu. *Application contact:* Beverley Walton, Coordinator, 858-534-4387, E-mail: bwalton@ucsd.edu.

University of California, Santa Barbara, Graduate Division, College of Letters and Sciences, Division of Mathematics, Life, and Physical Sciences, Department of Psychology, Santa Barbara, CA 93106. Offers PhD. *Faculty:* 30 full-time (10 women). *Students:* 78 full-time (44 women); includes 10 minority (3 African Americans, 7 Asian Americans or Pacific Islanders), 1 international. Average age 27. 247 applicants, 19% accepted, 20 enrolled. In 2007, 10 doctorates awarded. *Median time to degree:* Of those who began their doctoral program in fall 1999, 75% received their degree in 8 years or less. *Degree requirements:* For doctorate, comprehensive exam, thesis/dissertation, TA training, progress report, papers, mini-convention presentation, 1 quarter teaching or TA class with section lab. *Entrance requirements:* For doctorate, GRE General Test. Additional exam requirements/recommendations for international students: Required—TOEFL (minimum score 550 paper-based; 213 computer-based; 80 iBT). *Application deadline:* For fall admission, 12/1 for domestic and international students. Application fee: $60. Electronic applications accepted. *Expenses:* Tuition, nonresident: full-time $14,888. Required fees: $10,108. *Financial support:* In 2007–08, 21 fellowships with full and partial tuition reimbursements (averaging $13,100 per year), 18 research assistantships with full and partial tuition reimbursements (averaging $18,600 per year), 46 teaching assistantships with full and partial tuition reimbursements (averaging $18,200 per year) were awarded; Federal Work-Study, institutionally sponsored loans, scholarships/grants, health care benefits, and unspecified assistantships also available. Financial award application deadline: 12/15; financial award applicants required to submit FAFSA. *Faculty research:* Social psychology; developmental and evolutionary psychology; neuroscience and behavior; cognition, perception and cognitive neuroscience. Total annual research expenditures: $4.8 million. *Unit head:* Dr. Daphne J. Bugental, Chair, 805-893-2858, E-mail: bugental@psych.ucsb.edu. *Application contact:* Sondra Gordon, Staff Graduate Advisor, 805-893-2793, Fax: 805-893-4303, E-mail: gordon@psych.ucsb.edu.

University of California, Santa Cruz, Division of Graduate Studies, Division of Social Sciences, Program in Psychology, Santa Cruz, CA 95064. Offers PhD. *Faculty:* 29 full-time (16 women). *Students:* 69 (51 women). 121 applicants, 18% accepted, 13 enrolled. In 2007, 12 doctorates awarded. *Degree requirements:* For doctorate, thesis/dissertation, qualifying exam. *Entrance requirements:* For doctorate, GRE General Test. *Application deadline:* For fall admission, 12/15 for domestic students. Application fee: $60. *Expenses:* Tuition, nonresident: full-time $14,694. Required fees: $11,360. *Financial support:* Fellowships, research assistantships, teaching assistantships, career-related internships or fieldwork, Federal Work-Study, and institutionally sponsored loans available. Financial award application deadline: 1/1. *Faculty research:* Cognitive psychology, human information processing, sensation perceptions, psychobiology. *Unit head:* Maureen A. Callanan, Director, 831-459-3147, E-mail: callanan@ucsc.edu. *Application contact:* Judy L. Glass, Reporting Analyst for Graduate Admissions, 831-459-5906, Fax: 831-459-4843, E-mail: jlglass@ucsc.edu.

University of Central Arkansas, Graduate School, College of Health and Behavioral Sciences, Department of Counseling and Psychology, Conway, AR 72035-0001. Offers community service counseling (MS); counseling psychology (MS); school psychology (MS, PhD). *Accreditation:* APA. *Faculty:* 17 full-time (4 women). *Students:* 86 full-time (71 women), 31 part-time (25 women); includes 12 minority (9 African Americans, 3 American Indian/Alaska Native), 3 international. 50 applicants, 88% accepted, 44 enrolled. In 2007, 20 degrees awarded. Terminal master's awarded for partial completion of doctoral program. *Degree requirements:* For master's, comprehensive exam, thesis optional, internship; for doctorate, comprehensive exam, thesis/dissertation, internship. *Entrance requirements:* For master's, GRE General Test, minimum GPA of 2.75; for doctorate, GRE General Test, minimum GPA of 3.25. Additional exam requirements/recommendations for international students: Required—TOEFL (minimum score 550 paper-based; 213 computer-based). *Application deadline:* For fall admission, 3/1 priority date for domestic students; for spring admission, 10/1 priority date for domestic students. Applications are processed on a rolling basis. Application fee: $25 ($50 for international students). *Expenses:* Tuition, state resident: full-time $4,513; part-time $240 per credit. Tuition, nonresident: full-time $8,805; part-time $440 per credit. International tuition: $9,700 full-time. Required fees: $100 per term. *Financial support:* In 2007–08, 17 research assistantships with partial tuition reimbursements (averaging $6,000 per year) were awarded; career-related internships or fieldwork, Federal Work-Study, scholarships/grants, tuition waivers (partial), and unspecified assistantships also available. Support available to part-time students. Financial award application deadline: 6/30; financial award applicants required to submit FAFSA. *Unit head:* Dr. David Skotko, Chair, 501-450-3175, Fax: 501-450-5424, E-mail: davids@uca.edu. *Application contact:* Patti Hornor, Administrative Assistant, 501-450-5063, Fax: 501-450-5678, E-mail: pattih@uca.edu.

University of Central Florida, College of Sciences, Department of Psychology, Orlando, FL 32816. Offers applied experimental and human factors psychology (MA, PhD); clinical psychology (MA, MS, PhD); industrial/organizational psychology (MS, PhD). *Accreditation:* APA. Part-time and evening/weekend programs available. *Faculty:* 40 full-time (16 women), 13 part-time/adjunct (7 women). *Degree requirements:* For doctorate, thesis/dissertation, candidacy exam. *Entrance requirements:* For master's, GRE General Test, minimum GPA of 3.0 in last 60 hours. Additional exam requirements/recommendations for international students: Required—TOEFL. *Application deadline:* For fall admission, 2/15 for domestic students. Application fee: $30. Electronic applications accepted. *Expenses:* Tuition, state resident: full-time $6,484. Tuition, nonresident: full-time $23,938. Tuition and fees vary according to program. *Financial support:* Fellowships with partial tuition reimbursements, research assistantships with partial tuition reimbursements, teaching assistantships with partial tuition reimbursements, career-related internships or fieldwork, Federal Work-Study, institutionally sponsored loans, tuition waivers (partial), and unspecified assistantships available. Financial award application deadline: 3/1; financial award applicants required to submit FAFSA. *Faculty research:* Professional ethical decision making, electronic selection systems, psychometrics. *Unit head:* Dr. Robert Dipboye, Chair, 407-823-2216, E-mail: rdipboye@mail.ucf.edu.

University of Central Missouri, The Graduate School, College of Health and Human Services, Department of Psychology, Warrensburg, MO 64093. Offers MS. Part-time programs available. *Faculty:* 12 full-time (3 women). *Students:* 13 full-time (9 women), 13 part-time (11 women), 1 international. Average age 28. 15 applicants, 67% accepted, 8 enrolled. In 2007, 1 degree awarded. *Degree requirements:* For master's, comprehensive exam, thesis optional. *Entrance requirements:* For master's, GRE General Test, GRE Subject Test, minimum GPA of 2.75, Missouri teaching certificate, course work in psychology, 3 letters of recommendation. Additional exam requirements/recommendations for international students: Required—TOEFL (minimum score 500 paper-based; 173 computer-based). *Application deadline:* For fall admission, 6/1 priority date for domestic students, 5/1 priority date for international students; for spring admission, 10/1 priority date for domestic students, 10/1 for international students. Applications are processed on a rolling basis. Application fee: $30 ($50 for international students). *Expenses:* Tuition, state resident: full-time $6,259; part-time $256 per credit hour. Tuition, nonresident: full-time $11,915; part-time $491 per credit hour. Required fees: $604; $20 per credit hour. *Financial support:* In 2007–08, 7 students received support. Federal Work-Study, scholarships/grants, unspecified assistantships, and 3 administrative and 2 laboratory assistantships available. Support available to part-time students. Financial award application deadline: 3/1; financial award applicants required to submit FAFSA. *Unit head:* Dr. Joe Ryan, Chair, 660-543-4185, Fax: 660-543-8505, E-mail: ryan@ucmo.edu.

University of Central Oklahoma, College of Graduate Studies and Research, College of Education, Department of Psychology, Program in General Psychology, Edmond, OK 73034-5209. Offers MA. *Faculty:* 11 full-time (6 women), 2 part-time/adjunct (1 woman). *Students:* 16 full-time (12 women), 10 part-time (8 women); includes 6 minority (1 African American, 3 American Indian/Alaska Native, 1 Asian American or Pacific Islander, 1 Hispanic American), 1 international. Average age 30. 7 applicants, 100% accepted. In 2007, 15 degrees awarded. *Degree requirements:* For master's, thesis. *Entrance requirements:* For master's, GRE General Test. Additional exam requirements/recommendations for international students: Required—TOEFL (minimum score 550 paper-based; 213 computer-based). *Application deadline:* For fall admission, 7/1 for international students; for spring admission, 11/1 for international students. Applications are processed on a rolling basis. Application fee: $25. Electronic applications accepted. *Expenses:* Tuition, state resident: full-time $3,516; part-time $147 per hour. Tuition, nonresident: full-time $9,054; part-time $377 per hour. Required fees: $433; $18 per hour. *Financial support:* Career-related internships or fieldwork and unspecified assistantships available. Financial award application deadline: 3/31; financial award applicants required to submit FAFSA. *Unit head:* Dr. Mike Knight, Chairman, Department of Psychology, 405-974-5707.

University of Chicago, Division of Social Sciences, Department of Psychology, Chicago, IL 60637-1513. Offers PhD. *Students:* 58. In 2007, 11 degrees awarded. *Degree requirements:*

For doctorate, one foreign language, thesis/dissertation, exams. *Entrance requirements:* For doctorate, GRE General Test, GRE Subject Test. Additional exam requirements/recommendations for international students: Required—TOEFL, IELTS (minimum score 7). *Application deadline:* For fall admission, 12/10 for domestic and international students. Application fee: $55. Electronic applications accepted. *Financial support:* Fellowships, research assistantships, teaching assistantships, Federal Work-Study, institutionally sponsored loans, scholarships/grants, traineeships, health care benefits, and unspecified assistantships available. Financial award application deadline: 12/10. *Unit head:* Prof. Howard Nusbaum, Chair, 773-702-8861. *Application contact:* Office of the Dean of Students, 773-702-8415.

University of Cincinnati, Graduate School, McMicken College of Arts and Sciences, Department of Psychology, Cincinnati, OH 45221. Offers clinical psychology (PhD); experimental psychology (PhD). *Accreditation:* APA. *Faculty:* 26 full-time (8 women), 5 part-time/adjunct (2 women). *Students:* 66 full-time (45 women), 6 part-time (3 women); includes 15 minority (8 African Americans, 4 Asian Americans or Pacific Islanders, 3 Hispanic Americans), 6 international. Average age 28. 274 applicants, 5% accepted, 9 enrolled. In 2007, 16 doctorates awarded. *Median time to degree:* Of those who began their doctoral program in fall 1999, 100% received their degree in 8 years or less. *Degree requirements:* For doctorate, comprehensive exam, thesis/dissertation. *Entrance requirements:* For doctorate, GRE General Test. Additional exam requirements/recommendations for international students: Required—TOEFL. *Application deadline:* For fall admission, 1/3 for domestic and international students. Application fee: $35. *Financial support:* Fellowships with full tuition reimbursements, research assistantships with full tuition reimbursements, teaching assistantships with full tuition reimbursements, scholarships/grants, traineeships, tuition waivers (partial), and unspecified assistantships available. Financial award application deadline: 5/1. *Faculty research:* Neuropsychology, human factors, health. Total annual research expenditures: $509,418. *Unit head:* Dr. Steven J. Howe, Head, 513-556-5572, Fax: 513-556-1904, E-mail: steven.howe@uc.edu. *Application contact:* Dr. Paula K. Shear, Graduate Program Director, 513-556-5577, Fax: 513-556-1904, E-mail: paula.shear@uc.edu.

University of Colorado at Boulder, Graduate School, College of Arts and Sciences, Department of Psychology, Boulder, CO 80309. Offers MA, PhD. *Accreditation:* APA (one or more programs are accredited). *Faculty:* 42. *Students:* 89 full-time (48 women), 15 part-time (11 women); includes 6 minority (2 African Americans, 1 American Indian/Alaska Native, 3 Hispanic Americans), 6 international. Average age 30. 18 applicants, 100% accepted. In 2007, 12 master's, 8 doctorates awarded. *Degree requirements:* For master's, comprehensive exam; for doctorate, thesis/dissertation. *Entrance requirements:* For master's, GRE General Test, minimum undergraduate GPA of 2.75; for doctorate, GRE General Test. *Application deadline:* For fall admission, 1/1 for domestic students, 12/1 for international students. Application fee: $50 ($60 for international students). *Financial support:* In 2007–08, 55 fellowships (averaging $8,047 per year), 25 research assistantships (averaging $13,340 per year) were awarded; tuition waivers (full) also available. Financial award application deadline: 1/1. *Faculty research:* Clinical psychology, behavioral genetics, behavioral neuroscience, cognitive psychology, social psychology. Total annual research expenditures: $16.2 million. *Unit head:* Edward Craighead, Chair, 303-492-4498, Fax: 303-492-2967, E-mail: wade.craighead@colorado.edu. *Application contact:* Graduate Secretary, 303-492-8662, Fax: 303-492-2967, E-mail: grad-admissions@psych.colorado.edu.

University of Colorado at Colorado Springs, Graduate School, College of Letters, Arts and Sciences, Department of Psychology, Colorado Springs, CO 80933-7150. Offers geropsychology (PhD); psychology (MA). *Accreditation:* APA. Part-time programs available. *Faculty:* 14 full-time (5 women), 3 part-time/adjunct (1 woman). *Students:* 63 full-time (45 women), 22 part-time (16 women); includes 12 minority (2 African Americans, 6 Asian Americans or Pacific Islanders, 4 Hispanic Americans), 2 international. Average age 29. 22 applicants, 68% accepted, 11 enrolled. In 2007, 11 degrees awarded. *Degree requirements:* For master's, thesis; for doctorate, comprehensive exam, thesis/dissertation. *Entrance requirements:* For master's, GRE, BA in psychology or equivalent background; minimum GPA of 3.0. *Application deadline:* For fall admission, 1/1 for domestic students. Applications are processed on a rolling basis. *Financial support:* Research assistantships, teaching assistantships, career-related internships or fieldwork and Federal Work-Study available. Support available to part-time students. Financial award applicants required to submit FAFSA. *Faculty research:* Aging, social psychology, learning and memory, personality disorders, psychology and law. Total annual research expenditures: $429,985. *Unit head:* , Dr. Kelli Klebe, Chair, 719-262-4181, E-mail: kklebe@uccs.edu. *Application contact:* Dr. Hasker Davis, Graduate Student Adviser, 719-262-4148, Fax: 719-262-4166, E-mail: hdavis@uccs.edu.

University of Colorado Denver, College of Liberal Arts and Sciences, Department of Psychology, Denver, CO 80217-3364. Offers MA. Part-time and evening/weekend programs available. *Faculty:* 17 full-time (9 women). *Students:* 15 full-time (10 women), 12 part-time (7 women); includes 4 minority (all Hispanic Americans), 1 international. Average age 28. 103 applicants, 12% accepted, 10 enrolled. In 2007, 5 degrees awarded. *Degree requirements:* For master's, comprehensive exam, thesis or alternative. *Entrance requirements:* For master's, GRE General Test, GRE Subject Test, minimum GPA of 2.75. Additional exam requirements/recommendations for international students: Required—TOEFL (minimum score 525 paper-based; 197 computer-based). *Application deadline:* For fall admission, 3/1 for domestic students. Applications are processed on a rolling basis. Application fee: $50 ($75 for international students). Electronic applications accepted. *Financial support:* Research assistantships, teaching assistantships, career-related internships or fieldwork, Federal Work-Study, and scholarships/grants available. Financial award application deadline: 4/1; financial award applicants required to submit FAFSA. *Faculty research:* Organizational behavior, body image perception, professional ethics, infant perception and cognition, charismatic leadership. *Unit head:* Dr. Peter Kaplan, Chair, 303-556-26001, Fax: 303-556-3520, E-mail: peter.kaplan@cudenver.edu. *Application contact:* Gay Freebern, Program Assistant, 303-556-8565, Fax: 303-556-3520, E-mail: gay.freeborn@cudenver.edu.

University of Connecticut, Graduate School, College of Liberal Arts and Sciences, Department of Psychology, Field of Psychology, Storrs, CT 06269. Offers behavioral neuroscience (PhD); biopsychology (PhD); clinical psychology (MA, PhD); cognition and instruction (PhD); developmental psychology (MA, PhD); ecological psychology (PhD); experimental psychology (PhD); general psychology (MA, PhD); health psychology (Graduate Certificate); industrial/organizational psychology (PhD); language and cognition (PhD); neuroscience (PhD); occupational health psychology (Graduate Certificate); social psychology (MA, PhD). *Accreditation:* APA (one or more programs are accredited). *Faculty:* 52 full-time (23 women). *Students:* 130 full-time (94 women), 25 part-time (11 women); includes 24 minority (8 African Americans, 6 Asian Americans or Pacific Islanders, 10 Hispanic Americans), 18 international. Average age 28. 531 applicants, 7% accepted, 35 enrolled. In 2007, 19 master's, 20 doctorates, 2 other advanced degrees awarded. Terminal master's awarded for partial completion of doctoral program. *Degree requirements:* For master's, comprehensive exam; for doctorate, thesis/dissertation. *Entrance requirements:* For master's and doctorate, GRE General Test, GRE Subject Test. Additional exam requirements/recommendations for international students: Required—TOEFL (minimum score 550 paper-based; 213 computer-based). *Application deadline:* For fall admission, 2/1 priority date for domestic and international students; for spring admission, 11/1 for domestic students, 10/1 for international students. Applications are processed on a rolling basis. Application fee: $55. Electronic applications accepted. *Expenses:* Tuition, state resident: part-time $469 per credit hour. Tuition, nonresident: part-time $1,218 per credit hour. *Financial support:* In 2007–08, 54 research assistantships with full tuition reimbursements, 69 teaching assistantships with full tuition reimbursements were awarded; fellowships, career-related internships or fieldwork, Federal Work-Study, scholarships/grants, health care benefits, and unspecified assistantships also available. Financial award application deadline: 2/1; financial award applicants required to submit FAFSA. *Application contact:* Deborah Doucette, Administrative Assistant, 860-486-2057, Fax: 860-486-2760, E-mail: futuregr@psych.psy.uconn.edu.

University of Dallas, Braniff Graduate School of Liberal Arts, Program in Psychology, Irving, TX 75062-4736. Offers M Psych, MA. Part-time programs available. *Faculty:* 2 full-time (1 woman), 2 part-time/adjunct (1 woman). *Students:* 5 full-time (all women), 4 part-time (3 women); includes 2 minority (1 Asian American or Pacific Islander, 1 Hispanic American), 1 international. Average age 30. 7 applicants, 71% accepted, 4 enrolled. In 2007, 2 degrees awarded. *Degree requirements:* For master's, one foreign language, comprehensive exam (for some programs), thesis (for some programs). *Entrance requirements:* Additional exam requirements/recommendations for international students: Required—TOEFL. *Application deadline:* For fall admission, 2/15 priority date for domestic students; for spring admission, 11/15 for domestic students. Application fee: $50. *Expenses:* Tuition: Part-time $600 per credit. Required fees: $15 per credit. *Financial support:* Scholarships/grants available. *Unit head:* Dr. Scott Churchill, Chairman, 972-721-5106, Fax: 972-721-4034. *Application contact:* Graduate Coordinator, 972-721-5106, Fax: 972-721-5280, E-mail: graduate@acad.udallas.edu.

University of Dayton, Graduate School, College of Arts and Sciences, Department of Psychology, Dayton, OH 45469-1300. Offers clinical psychology (MA); general psychology (MA). Part-time programs available. *Faculty:* 17 full-time (5 women), 2 part-time/adjunct (1 woman). *Students:* 31 full-time (21 women), 6 part-time (4 women); includes 5 minority (1 African American, 1 Asian American or Pacific Islander, 3 Hispanic Americans), 1 international. Average age 25. 128 applicants, 28% accepted, 19 enrolled. In 2007, 12 degrees awarded. *Degree requirements:* For master's, thesis. *Entrance requirements:* For master's, GRE General Test, GRE Subject Test (recommended). Additional exam requirements/recommendations for international students: Required—TOEFL (minimum score 550 paper-based; 213 computer-based; 80 iBT). *Application deadline:* For fall admission, 3/1 priority date for domestic and international students. Application fee: $0 ($50 for international students). Electronic applications accepted. *Financial support:* In 2007–08, 24 students received support, including 13 research assistantships with full tuition reimbursements available (averaging $9,660 per year); institutionally sponsored loans, traineeships, and tuition waivers (partial) also available. Financial award application deadline: 3/1; financial award applicants required to submit FAFSA. *Faculty research:* Cognitive processes, television and children, interpersonal process, modes and mechanisms of therapy. *Unit head:* Dr. David W. Biers, Chair, 937-229-2713, Fax: 937-229-3900, E-mail: biers@udayton.edu. *Application contact:* Angela Jones-Glukhov, Associate Director of Graduate Admissions, 937-229-4305, Fax: 937-229-4729.

University of Delaware, College of Arts and Sciences, Department of Psychology, Newark, DE 19716. Offers behavioral neuroscience (PhD); clinical psychology (PhD); cognitive psychology (PhD); social psychology (PhD). *Accreditation:* APA. *Faculty:* 28 full-time (10 women), 3 part-time/adjunct (1 woman). *Students:* 46 full-time (32 women), 3 part-time (2 women); includes 5 minority (4 African Americans, 1 Asian American or Pacific Islander), 3 international. Average age 27. 252 applicants, 8% accepted, 7 enrolled. In 2007, 6 doctorates awarded. *Degree requirements:* For doctorate, thesis/dissertation. *Entrance requirements:* For doctorate, GRE General Test. Additional exam requirements/recommendations for international students: Required—TOEFL (minimum score 600 paper-based; 250 computer-based). *Application deadline:* For fall admission, 1/7 priority date for domestic students. Application fee: $60. Electronic applications accepted. *Financial support:* In 2007–08, 47 students received support, including 7 fellowships with full tuition reimbursements available (averaging $16,000 per year), 14 research assistantships with full tuition reimbursements available (averaging $15,500 per year), 20 teaching assistantships with full tuition reimbursements available (averaging $16,000 per year); career-related internships or fieldwork, Federal Work-Study, institutionally sponsored loans, scholarships/grants, and tuition waivers (full and partial) also available. Financial award application deadline: 1/7. *Faculty research:* Emotion development, neural and cognitive aspects of memory, neural control of feeding, intergroup relations, social cognition and communication. Total annual research expenditures: $2.5 million. *Unit head:* Dr. Thomas M. DiLorenzo, Chair, 302-831-2271, Fax: 302-831-3645. *Application contact:* Linda Scarpitti, Information Contact, 302-831-2271, Fax: 302-831-3645, E-mail: linnie@udel.edu.

University of Denver, Faculty of Arts and Humanities/Social Sciences, Department of Psychology, Denver, CO 80208. Offers MA, PhD. *Accreditation:* APA (one or more programs are accredited). *Faculty:* 18 full-time (9 women). *Students:* 28 full-time (23 women), 2 part-time (both women); includes 5 minority (4 Asian Americans or Pacific Islanders, 1 Hispanic American). Average age 26. In 2007, 9 master's, 8 doctorates awarded. *Degree requirements:* For doctorate, thesis/dissertation. *Entrance requirements:* For master's and doctorate, GRE General Test. Additional exam requirements/recommendations for international students: Required—TOEFL. *Application deadline:* Applications are processed on a rolling basis. Application fee: $50. Electronic applications accepted. *Financial support:* In 2007–08, 12 research assistantships with full and partial tuition reimbursements (averaging $12,500 per year), 23 teaching assistantships with full and partial tuition reimbursements (averaging $13,700 per year) were awarded; career-related internships or fieldwork, Federal Work-Study, institutionally sponsored loans, and scholarships/grants also available. Support available to part-time students. Financial award application deadline: 1/1; financial award applicants required to submit FAFSA. *Faculty research:* Developmental neuropsychology, self-esteem and peer relationships, child abuse and neglect, marital and family interactions, adolescent peer and romantic relationships. Total annual research expenditures: $2.4 million. *Unit head:* Dr. Ralph J. Roberts, Chairperson, 303-871-3803. *Application contact:* Paula Houghtaling, Information Contact, 303-871-3803.

University of Denver, Graduate School of Professional Psychology, Denver, CO 80208. Offers clinical psychology (Psy D); psychology (MA). *Accreditation:* APA. *Faculty:* 10 full-time (6 women). *Students:* 194 full-time (165 women), 23 part-time (14 women); includes 24 minority (3 African Americans, 2 American Indian/Alaska Native, 9 Asian Americans or Pacific Islanders, 10 Hispanic Americans), 10 international. Average age 26. 541 applicants, 33% accepted, 96 enrolled. In 2007, 60 master's, 24 doctorates awarded. *Degree requirements:* For doctorate, paper, internship. *Entrance requirements:* For master's and doctorate, GRE General Test. Additional exam requirements/recommendations for international students: Required—TOEFL. *Application deadline:* For fall admission, 1/5 for domestic students. Application fee: $50. Electronic applications accepted. *Financial support:* In 2007–08, 25 teaching assistantships with full and partial tuition reimbursements (averaging $3,500 per year) were awarded; career-related internships or fieldwork, Federal Work-Study, institutionally sponsored loans, scholarships/grants, and clinical assistantships also available. Support available to part-time students. Financial award application deadline: 3/1; financial award applicants required to submit FAFSA. *Unit head:* Dr. Peter Buirski, Dean, 303-871-3873. *Application contact:* Admissions, 303-871-3873, Fax: 303-871-4220, E-mail: gsppiwfo@du.edu.

University of Detroit Mercy, College of Liberal Arts and Education, Department of Psychology, Detroit, MI 48221. Offers clinical psychology (MA, PhD); industrial/organizational psychology (MA); school psychology (Spec). *Accreditation:* APA. Evening/weekend programs available. *Degree requirements:* For doctorate, departmental qualifying exam. *Faculty research:* Gerontology.

University of Florida, Graduate School, College of Liberal Arts and Sciences, Department of Psychology, Gainesville, FL 32611. Offers behavior analysis (PhD); behavioral neuroscience (MS, PhD); cognitive and sensory processes (PhD); counseling psychology (PhD); developmental psychology (PhD); social psychology (MS, PhD); JD/PhD. *Faculty:* 42 full-time (12 women), 3 part-time/adjunct (1 woman). *Students:* 136 (90 women); includes 22 minority (7 African Americans, 1 American Indian/Alaska Native, 5 Asian Americans or Pacific Islanders, 9 Hispanic Americans) 22 international. In 2007, 25 master's, 14 doctorates awarded. *Degree requirements:* For master's, thesis or alternative; for doctorate, thesis/dissertation. *Entrance requirements:* For master's and doctorate, GRE General Test, minimum GPA of 3.0. Additional exam requirements/recommendations for international students: Required—TOEFL (minimum score 550 paper-based; 213 computer-based). *Application deadline:* For fall admission, 1/15 priority date for domestic students. Applications are processed on a rolling basis. Application fee: $30.

Psychology—General

University of Florida (continued)
Electronic applications accepted. *Expenses:* Tuition, state resident: full-time $7,478. Tuition, nonresident: full-time $22,603. *Financial support:* In 2007–08, 33 research assistantships (averaging $16,597 per year), 64 teaching assistantships (averaging $16,703 per year) were awarded; fellowships, career-related internships or fieldwork and unspecified assistantships also available. Financial award application deadline: 1/15. *Faculty research:* Experimental analysis of behavior, psychobiology, cognition and sensory processes, counseling psychology, social psychology, developmental psychology. *Unit head:* Dr. Martin Heesacker, Chair, 352-392-0601 Ext. 200, Fax: 352-392-7985, E-mail: heesack@ufl.edu. *Application contact:* Dr. Gregory Neimeyer, Coordinator, 352-392-0601 Ext. 259, Fax: 352-392-7985, E-mail: neimeyer@ufl.edu.

University of Georgia, Graduate School, College of Arts and Sciences, Department of Psychology, Athens, GA 30602. Offers MS, PhD. *Accreditation:* APA (one or more programs are accredited). *Faculty:* 35 full-time (13 women). *Students:* 96 full-time (65 women), 12 part-time (10 women); includes 13 minority (6 African Americans, 3 Asian Americans or Pacific Islanders, 4 Hispanic Americans), 10 international. 288 applicants, 16% accepted, 23 enrolled. In 2007, 20 master's, 22 doctorates awarded. *Degree requirements:* For master's, thesis; for doctorate, one foreign language, thesis/dissertation. *Entrance requirements:* For master's and doctorate, GRE General Test. Additional exam requirements/recommendations for international students: Required—TOEFL. *Application deadline:* For fall admission, 12/1 for domestic students; for spring admission, 11/15 for domestic students. Application fee: $50. Electronic applications accepted. *Financial support:* Fellowships, research assistantships, teaching assistantships, unspecified assistantships available. *Unit head:* Dr. Patricia H. Miller, Head, 706-542-2174, E-mail: phmiller@uga.edu. *Application contact:* Dr. B. Randy Hammond, Graduate Coordinator, 706-542-4812, Fax: 706-542-3275, E-mail: bhammond@uga.edu.

University of Guelph, Graduate Program Services, College of Social and Applied Human Sciences, Department of Psychology, Guelph, ON N1G 2W1, Canada. Offers applied social psychology (MA, PhD); clinical psychology applied development emphasis (PhD); clinical psychology applied developmental emphasis (MA); industrial/organizational psychology (MA, PhD); neuroscience and applied cognitive science (MA, PhD). *Faculty:* 34 full-time (14 women). *Students:* 95 full-time (72 women), 6 part-time (all women); includes 6 minority (2 African Americans, 4 Asian Americans or Pacific Islanders). 230 applicants, 28% accepted, 35 enrolled. In 2007, 8 master's, 2 doctorates awarded. *Median time to degree:* Of those who began their doctoral program in fall 1999, 100% received their degree in 8 years or less. *Degree requirements:* For master's, thesis; for doctorate, comprehensive exam, thesis/dissertation. *Entrance requirements:* For master's, GRE General Test, GRE Subject Test, minimum B+ average during previous 2 years of course work; for doctorate, GRE General Test, GRE Subject Test, minimum A- average. Additional exam requirements/recommendations for international students: Required—TOEFL (minimum score 89 iBT). *Application deadline:* For fall admission, 12/15 priority date for domestic students, 1/15 priority date for international students; for spring admission, 12/15 priority date for domestic students. Application fee: $85. Electronic applications accepted. *Financial support:* In 2007–08, 108 teaching assistantships with partial tuition reimbursements (averaging $10,213 per year) were awarded. *Faculty research:* Organizational psychology, reading comprehension and mathematical ability, drug addiction and relapse, gender issues and culture, memory, clinical psychology. *Unit head:* Dr. Harvey Marmurek, Chair, 519-824-4120 Ext. 53673, Fax: 519-837-8629, E-mail: marmurek@psy.uoguelph.ca. *Application contact:* Dr. Ian Newby-Clark, Graduate Coordinator, 519-824-4120 Ext. 53307, Fax: 519-837-8629, E-mail: newby-clark@psy.uogeulph.ca.

University of Hartford, College of Arts and Sciences, Department of Psychology, West Hartford, CT 06117-1599. Offers clinical practices (MA, Psy D), including clinical practices (Psy D), psychology (MA); general experimental psychology (MA); organizational behavior (MS); school psychology (MS). *Accreditation:* APA. Part-time programs available. *Faculty:* 14 full-time (7 women), 11 part-time/adjunct (4 women). *Students:* 126 full-time (103 women), 99 part-time (79 women); includes 26 minority (7 African Americans, 2 American Indian/Alaska Native, 4 Asian Americans or Pacific Islanders, 13 Hispanic Americans), 5 international. Average age 29. 272 applicants, 51% accepted, 76 enrolled. In 2007, 53 master's, 38 doctorates awarded. *Degree requirements:* For master's, comprehensive exam, thesis (for some programs). *Entrance requirements:* For master's, GRE General Test, GRE Subject Test, minimum GPA of 3.0; for doctorate, GRE General Test, GRE Subject Test. Additional exam requirements/recommendations for international students: Required—TOEFL (minimum score 550 paper-based; 213 computer-based). *Application deadline:* For fall admission, 2/15 priority date for domestic students. Applications are processed on a rolling basis. Application fee: $45. Electronic applications accepted. *Expenses:* Contact institution. *Financial support:* In 2007–08, 8 research assistantships (averaging $2,200 per year), 15 teaching assistantships (averaging $2,700 per year) were awarded; career-related internships or fieldwork and Federal Work-Study also available. Support available to part-time students. Financial award application deadline: 6/1; financial award applicants required to submit FAFSA. *Unit head:* Dr. Caryn Christensen, Chair, 860-768-4720, E-mail: christens@hartford.edu. *Application contact:* Reneé Murphy, Assistant Director of Graduate Admissions, 860-768-4371, Fax: 860-768-5160, E-mail: rmurphy@hartford.edu.

University of Hawaii at Manoa, Graduate Division, Colleges of Arts and Sciences, College of Social Sciences, Department of Psychology, Honolulu, HI 96822. Offers clinical psychology (PhD); community and cultural psychology (PhD); community and culture (MA); psychology (MA, PhD, Graduate Certificate). *Accreditation:* APA (one or more programs are accredited). Part-time programs available. *Faculty:* 35 full-time (13 women), 8 part-time/adjunct (1 woman). *Students:* 86 full-time (61 women), 7 part-time (5 women); includes 30 minority (1 African American, 1 American Indian/Alaska Native, 26 Asian Americans or Pacific Islanders, 2 Hispanic Americans), 11 international. 199 applicants, 14% accepted, 16 enrolled.Terminal master's awarded for partial completion of doctoral program. *Median time to degree:* Of those who began their doctoral program in fall 1999, 83% received their degree in 8 years or less. *Degree requirements:* For master's, comprehensive exam, thesis; for doctorate, comprehensive exam, thesis/dissertation. *Entrance requirements:* For master's and doctorate, GRE General Test, GRE Subject Test. Additional exam requirements/recommendations for international students: Required—TOEFL (minimum score 600 paper-based; 250 computer-based; 100 iBT), IELTS (minimum score 7). *Application deadline:* For fall admission, 1/1 for domestic and international students. Application fee: $50. *Financial support:* In 2007–08, 44 research assistantships (averaging $16,926 per year), 18 teaching assistantships (averaging $14,042 per year) were awarded; career-related internships or fieldwork, institutionally sponsored loans, and tuition waivers (full and partial) also available. Financial award application deadline: 1/1. *Faculty research:* Cross-cultural psychology, health psychology, marine mammals, child/adult psychopathology. Total annual research expenditures: $1.1 million. *Application contact:* Catherine Sophian, Graduate Chair, 808-956-8414, Fax: 808-956-4700, E-mail: csophian@hawaii.edu.

University of Houston, College of Liberal Arts and Social Sciences, Department of Psychology, Houston, TX 77204. Offers clinical psychology (PhD); industrial/organizational psychology (PhD); psychology (MA); social psychology (PhD). *Accreditation:* APA (one or more programs are accredited). *Faculty:* 24 full-time (9 women), 3 part-time/adjunct (1 woman). *Students:* 102 full-time (77 women), 16 part-time (12 women); includes 22 minority (4 African Americans, 8 Asian Americans or Pacific Islanders, 10 Hispanic Americans), 8 international. Average age 27. 187 applicants, 13% accepted, 22 enrolled. In 2007, 10 master's, 12 doctorates awarded. *Degree requirements:* For doctorate, thesis/dissertation. *Entrance requirements:* For doctorate, GRE General Test, minimum GPA of 3.0. *Application deadline:* For fall admission, 1/1 for domestic students. Application fee: $40 ($75 for international students). *Expenses:* Tuition, state resident: full-time $6,297; part-time $262 per credit. Tuition, nonresident: full-time $12,969; part-time $540 per credit. Required fees: $2,696. *Financial support:* In 2007–08, 12 fellowships with full tuition reimbursements (averaging $11,200 per year), 13 research assistantships with full tuition reimbursements (averaging $10,050 per year), 74 teaching assistantships with full tuition reimbursements (averaging $10,250 per year) were awarded; career-related internships or fieldwork, Federal Work-Study, institutionally sponsored loans, scholarships/grants, health care benefits, and unspecified assistantships also available. Support available to part-time students. Financial award application deadline: 2/1; financial award applicants required to submit FAFSA. *Faculty research:* Health psychology, depression, child/family process, organizational effectiveness, close relationships. *Unit head:* Dr. David Francis, Chairperson, 713-743-7036, Fax: 713-743-8588, E-mail: dfrancis@uh.edu. *Application contact:* Sherry A. Berun, Coordinator—Academic Affairs, 713-743-8508, Fax: 713-743-8588, E-mail: sherryr@uh.edu.

University of Houston–Clear Lake, School of Human Sciences and Humanities, Programs in Human Sciences, Houston, TX 77058-1098. Offers behavioral sciences (MA), including behavioral sciences-general, behavioral sciences-psychology, behavioral sciences-sociology; clinical psychology (MA); criminology (MA); cross-cultural studies (MA); family therapy (MA); fitness and human performance (MA); school psychology (MA). *Accreditation:* AAMFT/COAMFTE. Part-time and evening/weekend programs available. Postbaccalaureate distance learning degree programs offered (minimal on-campus study). *Degree requirements:* For master's, thesis or alternative. *Entrance requirements:* For master's, GRE General Test. Additional exam requirements/recommendations for international students: Required—TOEFL (minimum score 550 paper-based; 213 computer-based). Electronic applications accepted. *Faculty research:* Smoking cessation, adolescent sexuality, white collar crime, serial murder, human factors/human computer interaction.

University of Houston–Victoria, School of Arts and Sciences, Program in Psychology, Victoria, TX 77901-4450. Offers counseling psychology (MA); school psychology (MA). Part-time and evening/weekend programs available. Postbaccalaureate distance learning degree programs offered. *Faculty:* 4 full-time (2 women). *Students:* 18 full-time (15 women), 47 part-time (36 women); includes 18 minority (3 African Americans, 2 Asian Americans or Pacific Islanders, 13 Hispanic Americans). In 2007, 8 degrees awarded. *Degree requirements:* For master's, project or thesis. *Entrance requirements:* For master's, GRE General Test. Additional exam requirements/recommendations for international students: Required—TOEFL (minimum score 550 paper-based; 213 computer-based). *Application deadline:* Applications are processed on a rolling basis. Application fee: $0. Electronic applications accepted. *Expenses:* Tuition, state resident: full-time $3,492; part-time $194 per semester hour. Tuition, nonresident: full-time $7,596; part-time $422 per semester hour. Required fees: $774; $43 per semester hour. Tuition and fees vary according to course load. *Financial support:* In 2007–08, research assistantships with partial tuition reimbursements (averaging $2,000 per year), teaching assistantships with partial tuition reimbursements (averaging $2,000 per year) were awarded; career-related internships or fieldwork, Federal Work-Study, scholarships/grants, and unspecified assistantships also available. Support available to part-time students. Financial award application deadline: 4/15. *Unit head:* Dr. Rick Harrington, Head, 361-570-4205, Fax: 361-570-4229, E-mail: harringtonr@unh.edu. *Application contact:* Admissions and Records, E-mail: admissions@uhv.edu.

University of Idaho, College of Graduate Studies, College of Letters, Arts and Social Sciences, Department of Psychology and Communication Studies, Moscow, ID 83844-2282. Offers psychology (MS). *Students:* 29 (13 women). Average age 29. In 2007, 15 degrees awarded. *Entrance requirements:* For master's, GRE, minimum GPA of 2.8. *Application deadline:* For fall admission, 8/1 for domestic students; for spring admission, 12/15 for domestic students. Application fee: $55 ($60 for international students). *Financial support:* Fellowships, research assistantships, teaching assistantships available. Financial award application deadline: 2/15. *Faculty research:* Clinical, experimental, and cognitive psychology. *Unit head:* Dr. Richard D. Locke, Chair, 208-885-6324.

University of Illinois at Chicago, Graduate College, College of Liberal Arts and Sciences, Department of Psychology, Chicago, IL 60607-7128. Offers PhD. *Accreditation:* APA. *Degree requirements:* For doctorate, thesis/dissertation, departmental qualifying exam. *Entrance requirements:* For doctorate, GRE General Test, minimum GPA of 2.75. Additional exam requirements/recommendations for international students: Required—TOEFL. Electronic applications accepted.

University of Illinois at Urbana–Champaign, Graduate College, College of Liberal Arts and Sciences, Department of Psychology, Champaign, IL 61820. Offers MA, MS, PhD. *Accreditation:* APA (one or more programs are accredited). *Faculty:* 59 full-time (21 women), 2 part-time/adjunct (both women). *Students:* 179 full-time (117 women), 6 part-time (3 women); includes 28 minority (9 African Americans, 12 Asian Americans or Pacific Islanders, 7 Hispanic Americans), 55 international. 520 applicants, 13% accepted, 34 enrolled. In 2007, 31 master's, 20 doctorates awarded. *Degree requirements:* For doctorate, thesis/dissertation. *Entrance requirements:* For master's, GRE General Test, GRE Subject Test (recommended), minimum GPA of 3.0; for doctorate, GRE General Test, GRE Subject Test (recommended). Additional exam requirements/recommendations for international students: Required—TOEFL. *Application deadline:* For fall admission, 1/4 for domestic students. Application fee: $60 ($75 for international students). Electronic applications accepted. *Financial support:* In 2007–08, 37 fellowships with full tuition reimbursements, 103 research assistantships with full tuition reimbursements, 95 teaching assistantships with full tuition reimbursements were awarded; career-related internships or fieldwork, traineeships, and tuition waivers (full) also available. Financial award application deadline: 12/1. Total annual research expenditures: $5.7 million. *Unit head:* Dr. David Irwin, Head, 217-333-0632, Fax: 217-244-5876, E-mail: irwin@uiuc.edu. *Application contact:* Cheryl Berger, Assistant Head for Graduate Affairs, 217-333-0631, Fax: 217-244-5876, E-mail: gradstdy@cyrus.psych.uiuc.edu.

University of Indianapolis, Graduate Programs, School of Psychological Sciences, Indianapolis, IN 46227-3697. Offers clinical psychology (Psy D); clinical psychology/mental health counseling (MA). *Accreditation:* APA. *Faculty:* 7 full-time (2 women). *Students:* 107 full-time (90 women), 44 part-time (31 women); includes 4 minority (3 African Americans, 1 Hispanic American), 6 international. Average age 27. *Degree requirements:* For master's, practicum; for doctorate, comprehensive exam, thesis/dissertation, 1200 hours of clinical practicum, 2000 hour internship. *Entrance requirements:* For master's, GRE, 3 letters of recommendation; for doctorate, GRE, minimum GPA of 3.0, 18 hours of course work in psychology, 3 letters of recommendation. Additional exam requirements/recommendations for international students: Required—TOEFL (minimum score 550 paper-based; 213 computer-based). *Application deadline:* For fall admission, 2/25 for domestic students. Application fee: $50. *Financial support:* Federal Work-Study available. *Unit head:* Dr. E. John McIlvried, Dean, 317-788-3247, Fax: 317-788-3480, E-mail: jmcilvried@uindy.edu.

The University of Iowa, Graduate College, College of Education, Department of Psychological and Quantitative Foundations, Iowa City, IA 52242-1316. Offers counseling psychology (PhD); educational measurement and statistics (MA, PhD); educational psychology (MA, PhD); school psychology (PhD, Ed S); JD/PhD. *Accreditation:* APA. *Faculty:* 23 full-time, 21 part-time/adjunct. *Students:* 85 full-time (59 women), 81 part-time (61 women); includes 23 minority (8 African Americans, 8 Asian Americans or Pacific Islanders, 7 Hispanic Americans), 39 international. 147 applicants, 31% accepted, 23 enrolled. In 2007, 7 master's, 16 doctorates, 3 other advanced degrees awarded. *Degree requirements:* For master's, thesis optional, exam; for doctorate, comprehensive exam, thesis/dissertation; for Ed S, exam. *Entrance requirements:* For master's, doctorate, and Ed S, GRE General Test, minimum GPA of 3.0. Additional exam requirements/recommendations for international students: Required—TOEFL (minimum score 550 paper-based; 213 computer-based; 81 iBT). Application fee: $60 ($85 for international students). Electronic applications accepted. *Expenses:* Tuition, state resident: part-time $349 per hour. Tuition, nonresident: part-time $349 per hour. Tuition and fees vary according to course load and program. *Financial support:* In 2007–08, 9 fellowships, 61 research assistantships with partial tuition reimbursements, 15 teaching assistantships with partial tuition reimbursements were awarded. Financial award applicants required to submit FAFSA. *Unit head:* Timothy Ansley, Chair, 319-335-5579, Fax: 319-335-6145.

The University of Iowa, Graduate College, College of Liberal Arts and Sciences, Department of Psychology, Iowa City, IA 52242-1316. Offers neural and behavioral sciences (PhD);

psychology (MA, PhD). *Faculty:* 32 full-time, 24 part-time/adjunct. *Students:* 39 full-time (26 women), 53 part-time (32 women); includes 15 minority (3 African Americans, 3 Asian Americans or Pacific Islanders, 9 Hispanic Americans), 8 international. 262 applicants, 10% accepted, 12 enrolled. In 2007, 9 master's, 10 doctorates awarded. *Degree requirements:* For master's, thesis optional, exam; for doctorate, comprehensive exam, thesis/dissertation. *Entrance requirements:* For master's and doctorate, GRE General Test, minimum GPA of 3.0. Additional exam requirements/recommendations for international students: Required—TOEFL (minimum score 550 paper-based; 213 computer-based; 81 iBT). *Application deadline:* For fall admission, 1/1 for domestic and international students. Application fee: $60 ($85 for international students). Electronic applications accepted. *Expenses:* Tuition, state resident: part-time $349 per hour. Tuition, nonresident: part-time $349 per hour. Tuition and fees vary according to course load and program. *Financial support:* In 2007–08, 7 fellowships, 37 research assistantships with partial tuition reimbursements, 31 teaching assistantships with partial tuition reimbursements were awarded. Financial award applicants required to submit FAFSA. *Unit head:* Alan Christensen, Chair, 319-335-2405, Fax: 319-335-0191.

University of Kansas, Research and Graduate Studies, College of Liberal Arts and Sciences, Department of Applied Behavioral Science, Lawrence, KS 66045. Offers applied behavioral science (MA); behavioral psychology (PhD); clinical child psychology (PhD); developmental and child psychology (PhD); human development (MA). *Faculty:* 18. *Students:* 38 full-time (27 women), 9 part-time (8 women); includes 7 minority (2 African Americans, 2 Asian Americans or Pacific Islanders, 3 Hispanic Americans), 2 international. Average age 33. 41 applicants, 17% accepted, 3 enrolled. In 2007, 7 master's, 9 doctorates awarded. Terminal master's awarded for partial completion of doctoral program. *Degree requirements:* For master's, thesis; for doctorate, thesis/dissertation, comprehensive oral and written exams, journal reviews. *Entrance requirements:* Additional exam requirements/recommendations for international students: Required—TOEFL, TWE. *Application deadline:* For fall admission, 1/15 priority date for domestic and international students. Application fee: $55 ($60 for international students). Electronic applications accepted. *Expenses:* Tuition, state resident: full-time $5,838. Tuition, nonresident: full-time $13,409. Tuition and fees vary according to program. *Financial support:* Fellowships, research assistantships with full and partial tuition reimbursements, teaching assistantships with full and partial tuition reimbursements, career-related internships or fieldwork, traineeships, tuition waivers (full), and unspecified assistantships available. Financial award application deadline: 2/1. *Faculty research:* Early childhood, developmental disabilities, community health and development, adults with disabilities, applied behavior analysis. *Unit head:* Edward K. Morris, Chair, 785-864-4840, Fax: 785-864-5202, E-mail: ekm@ku.edu. *Application contact:* Gregory J. Madden, Graduate Director, 785-864-4840, Fax: 785-864-5202, E-mail: gmadden@ku.edu.

University of Kansas, Research and Graduate Studies, College of Liberal Arts and Sciences, Department of Psychology, Lawrence, KS 66045. Offers clinical child psychology (MA, PhD); psychology (MA, PhD). *Accreditation:* APA (one or more programs are accredited). *Faculty:* 36. *Students:* 113 full-time (81 women), 15 part-time (11 women); includes 22 minority (5 African Americans, 3 American Indian/Alaska Native, 10 Asian Americans or Pacific Islanders, 4 Hispanic Americans), 8 international. Average age 27. 311 applicants, 9% accepted, 10 enrolled. In 2007, 16 master's, 17 doctorates awarded. *Degree requirements:* For master's, thesis; for doctorate, comprehensive exam, thesis/dissertation. *Entrance requirements:* For doctorate, GRE General Test, minimum GPA of 3.0. Additional exam requirements/recommendations for international students: Required—TOEFL. *Application deadline:* For fall admission, 1/15 for domestic and international students. Application fee: $55 ($60 for international students). Electronic applications accepted. *Expenses:* Tuition, state resident: full-time $5,838. Tuition, nonresident: full-time $13,409. Tuition and fees vary according to program. *Financial support:* Fellowships with full tuition reimbursements, research assistantships with partial tuition reimbursements, teaching assistantships with full and partial tuition reimbursements, career-related internships or fieldwork and unspecified assistantships available. Financial award application deadline: 1/4; financial award applicants required to submit FAFSA. *Faculty research:* Cognitive psychology, methodology and statistics, developmental clinical/health psychology. *Unit head:* Greg Simpson, Chair, 785-864-9821, Fax: 785-864-5696, E-mail: gsimpson@ku.edu. *Application contact:* Cathy L. O'Keefe, Graduate Admissions Officer, 785-864-4195, Fax: 785-864-5696, E-mail: psycgrad@ku.edu.

University of Kentucky, Graduate School, College of Arts and Sciences, Program in Psychology, Lexington, KY 40506-0032. Offers clinical psychology (MA); experimental psychology (MA). *Accreditation:* APA (one or more programs are accredited). *Faculty:* 39 full-time (12 women), 1 part-time/adjunct (0 women). *Students:* 73 full-time (58 women), 6 part-time (4 women); includes 9 minority (4 African Americans, 1 American Indian/Alaska Native, 4 Hispanic Americans), 2 international. Average age 29. 286 applicants, 5% accepted, 14 enrolled. In 2007, 10 master's, 9 doctorates awarded. *Median time to degree:* Of those who began their doctoral program in fall 1999, 87% received their degree in 8 years or less. *Degree requirements:* For master's, comprehensive exam, thesis; for doctorate, comprehensive exam, thesis/dissertation. *Entrance requirements:* For master's, GRE General Test, minimum undergraduate GPA of 2.75; for doctorate, GRE General Test, minimum graduate GPA of 3.0. Additional exam requirements/recommendations for international students: Required—TOEFL (minimum score 550 paper-based; 213 computer-based). *Application deadline:* For fall admission, 7/17 for domestic students, 2/1 priority date for international students; for spring admission, 12/13 for domestic students, 6/15 priority date for international students. Application fee: $50 ($65 for international students). Electronic applications accepted. *Expenses:* Tuition, state resident: part-time $437 per credit hour. Tuition, nonresident: part-time $931 per credit hour. *Financial support:* In 2007–08, 64 students received support, including 20 fellowships with full tuition reimbursements available (averaging $3,461 per year), 30 research assistantships with full tuition reimbursements available (averaging $14,000 per year), 24 teaching assistantships with full tuition reimbursements available (averaging $14,000 per year); career-related internships or fieldwork, Federal Work-Study, institutionally sponsored loans, scholarships/grants, traineeships, health care benefits, tuition waivers (partial), and unspecified assistantships also available. Support available to part-time students. Financial award application deadline: 3/15; financial award applicants required to submit FAFSA. *Faculty research:* Psychopharmacology and teratology, behavioral neuroscience, social psychology, cognitive psychology, development and developmental psychobiology. *Unit head:* Dr. David Berry, Director of Graduate Studies, 859-257-5451, Fax: 859-323-1979, E-mail: dtrb@pop.uky.edu. *Application contact:* Dr. Brian Jackson, Senior Associate Dean, 859-257-4667, Fax: 859-257-4676, E-mail: brian.jackson@uky.edu.

University of La Verne, College of Arts and Sciences, Department of Psychology, La Verne, CA 91750-4443. Offers clinical-community psychology (Psy D); counseling (MS), including general counseling, higher education counseling, marriage and family therapy. *Accreditation:* APA (one or more programs are accredited). Part-time programs available. *Faculty:* 10 full-time (2 women), 14 part-time/adjunct (9 women). *Students:* 79 full-time (68 women), 86 part-time (75 women); includes 93 minority (19 African Americans, 8 Asian Americans or Pacific Islanders, 66 Hispanic Americans). Average age 30. In 2007, 24 master's, 20 doctorates awarded. *Degree requirements:* For master's, thesis, competency exam, personal psychotherapy; for doctorate, thesis/dissertation, clinical internship, competency exams, practicum, personal psychotherapy. *Entrance requirements:* For master's, minimum undergraduate GPA of 3.0, 3 letters of recommendation, interview; for doctorate, minimum GPA of 3.25 undergraduate, 3.65 graduate; 3 recommendations; interview; curriculum vitae. Additional exam requirements/recommendations for international students: Required—TOEFL (minimum score 600 paper-based; 250 computer-based). *Application deadline:* Applications are processed on a rolling basis. *Expenses:* *Contact institution.* Tuition and fees vary according to course load and program. *Financial support:* Career-related internships or fieldwork, institutionally sponsored loans, and scholarships/grants available. Financial award application deadline: 3/2; financial award applicants required to submit FAFSA. *Faculty research:* Developmental therapy and counseling. *Unit head:* Dr. Glenn Gamst, Department Chair, 909-593-3511, E-mail: gamstg@ulv.edu. *Application contact:* Connie Hamlow, Admissions Information Specialist, 909-593-3511 Ext. 4244, Fax: 909-392-2761, E-mail: gradadmission@ulv.edu.

University of Lethbridge, School of Graduate Studies, Lethbridge, AB T1K 3M4, Canada. Offers accounting (MScM); addictions counseling (M Sc); agricultural biotechnology (M Sc); agricultural studies (M Sc, MA); anthropology (MA); archaeology (MA); art (MA); biochemistry (M Sc); biological sciences (M Sc); biomolecular science (PhD); biosystems and biodiversity (PhD); Canadian studies (MA); chemistry (M Sc); computer science (M Sc); computer science and geographical information science (M Sc); counseling psychology (M Ed); dramatic arts (MA); earth, space, and physical science (PhD); economics (MA); educational leadership (M Ed); English (MA); environmental science (M Sc); evolution and behavior (PhD); exercise science (M Sc); finance (MScM); French (MA); French/German (MA); French/Spanish (MA); general education (M Ed); general management (MScM); geography (M Sc, MA); German (MA); health sciences (M Sc, MA); history (MA); human resource management and labour relations (MScM); individualized multidisciplinary (M Sc, MA); information systems (MScM); international management (MScM); kinesiology (M Sc, MA); management (M Sc, MA); marketing (MScM); mathematics (M Sc); music (MA); Native American studies (MA); neuroscience (M Sc, PhD); new media (MA); nursing (M Sc); philosophy (MA); physics (M Sc); policy and strategy (MScM); political science (MA); psychology (M Sc, MA); religious studies (MA); sociology (MA); theoretical and computational science (PhD); urban and regional studies (MA). Part-time and evening/weekend programs available. *Students:* 215 full-time, 98 part-time. In 2007, 87 master's, 1 doctorate awarded. *Degree requirements:* For doctorate, comprehensive exam, thesis/dissertation. *Entrance requirements:* For master's, GMAT (M Sc in management), bachelor's degree in related field, minimum GPA of 3.0 during previous 20 graded semester courses, 2 years teaching or related experience (M Ed); for doctorate, master's degree, minimum graduate GPA of 3.5. Additional exam requirements/recommendations for international students: Required—TOEFL. Application fee: $60 Canadian dollars. *Financial support:* Fellowships, research assistantships, teaching assistantships, scholarships/grants, health care benefits, and unspecified assistantships available. *Faculty research:* Movement and brain plasticity, gibberellin physiology, photosynthesis, carbon cycling, molecular properties of main-group ring components. *Unit head:* Dr. Jo-Anne Fiske, Interim Dean, 403-329-2121, Fax: 403-329-2097. *Application contact:* Jennifer Geddes, Graduate Liaison Officer, 403-329-2762, Fax: 403-329-5159, E-mail: jennifer.geddes@uleth.ca.

University of Louisiana at Lafayette, Graduate School, College of Liberal Arts, Department of Psychology, Program in Psychology, Lafayette, LA 70504. Offers MS. *Degree requirements:* For master's, comprehensive exam, thesis (for some programs). *Entrance requirements:* For master's, GRE General Test. Additional exam requirements/recommendations for international students: Required—TOEFL (minimum score 550 paper-based; 213 computer-based).

University of Louisiana at Monroe, Graduate Studies and Research, College of Education and Human Development, Department of Psychology, Monroe, LA 71209-0001. Offers psychology (MS); school psychology (SSP). Part-time and evening/weekend programs available. *Faculty:* 6 full-time (2 women), 2 part-time/adjunct (1 woman). *Students:* 16 full-time (9 women), 18 part-time (17 women); includes 8 African Americans, 2 Asian Americans or Pacific Islanders. Average age 29. In 2007, 12 master's, 2 other advanced degrees awarded. *Degree requirements:* For master's and SSP, thesis. *Entrance requirements:* For master's, GRE, minimum GPA of 2.5 or GRE General Test; for SSP, GRE General Test, minimum GPA of 2.5. Additional exam requirements/recommendations for international students: Required—TOEFL (minimum score 500 paper-based; 173 computer-based; 61 iBT). *Application deadline:* For fall admission, 8/22 priority date for domestic students, 7/1 for international students; for winter admission, 12/12 priority date for domestic students; for spring admission, 1/17 for domestic students, 11/1 for international students. Applications are processed on a rolling basis. Application fee: $20 ($30 for international students). Electronic applications accepted. *Expenses:* Tuition, state resident: full-time $2,220. Tuition, nonresident: full-time $8,172. *Financial support:* In 2007–08, 8 research assistantships with tuition reimbursements (averaging $2,500 per year) were awarded; teaching assistantships with full tuition reimbursements, career-related internships or fieldwork, Federal Work-Study, and unspecified assistantships also available. Financial award application deadline: 4/1; financial award applicants required to submit FAFSA. *Faculty research:* Identity development comparison, alcohol and drug problems. *Unit head:* Dr. James D. Williamson, Head, 318-342-1330, Fax: 318-342-1352, E-mail: williamson@ulm.edu.

University of Louisville, Graduate School, College of Arts and Sciences, Department of Psychological and Brain Sciences, Louisville, KY 40292-0001. Offers clinical psychology (MA, PhD); experimental psychology (PhD); psychology (MA). *Accreditation:* APA (one or more programs are accredited). *Students:* 88 full-time (63 women), 4 part-time (2 women); includes 6 minority (2 African Americans, 3 Asian Americans or Pacific Islanders, 1 Hispanic American), 7 international. Average age 28. In 2007, 27 master's, 8 doctorates awarded. *Degree requirements:* For doctorate, thesis/dissertation, internship. *Entrance requirements:* For master's and doctorate, GRE General Test. *Application deadline:* Applications are processed on a rolling basis. Application fee: $50. *Financial support:* In 2007–08, 29 teaching assistantships with tuition reimbursements (averaging $20,500 per year) were awarded; career-related internships or fieldwork also available. *Unit head:* Dr. Barbara Burns, Chair, 502-852-5947, Fax: 502-852-8904, E-mail: bburns@louisville.edu.

University of Maine, Graduate School, College of Liberal Arts and Sciences, Department of Psychology, Orono, ME 04469. Offers clinical psychology (PhD); developmental psychology (MA); experimental psychology (MA, PhD); social psychology (MA). *Accreditation:* APA (one or more programs are accredited). *Faculty:* 24. *Students:* 28 full-time (17 women), 10 part-time (6 women); includes 2 minority (1 American Indian/Alaska Native, 1 Hispanic American), 1 international. Average age 29. 129 applicants, 9% accepted, 8 enrolled. In 2007, 5 master's, 2 doctorates awarded. *Degree requirements:* For master's, thesis; for doctorate, thesis/dissertation. *Entrance requirements:* For master's and doctorate, GRE General Test, GRE Subject Test. Additional exam requirements/recommendations for international students: Required—TOEFL. *Application deadline:* For fall admission, 2/1 priority date for domestic students. Applications are processed on a rolling basis. Application fee: $60. Electronic applications accepted. *Financial support:* In 2007–08, 3 research assistantships with tuition reimbursements (averaging $13,400 per year), 21 teaching assistantships with tuition reimbursements (averaging $9,010 per year) were awarded; fellowships with tuition reimbursements, Federal Work-Study, institutionally sponsored loans, and tuition waivers (full and partial) also available. Financial award application deadline: 3/1. *Faculty research:* Social development, hypertension and aging, attitude change, self-confidence in achievement situations, health psychology. *Unit head:* Dr. Jeffrey Hecker, Chair, 207-581-2032, Fax: 207-581-6128. *Application contact:* Scott G. Delcourt, Associate Dean of the Graduate School, 207-581-3219, Fax: 207-581-3232, E-mail: graduate@maine.edu.

University of Manitoba, Faculty of Graduate Studies, Faculty of Arts, Department of Psychology, Winnipeg, MB R3T 2N2, Canada. Offers clinical psychology (PhD); psychology (MA, PhD). *Accreditation:* APA (one or more programs are accredited). *Degree requirements:* For master's, thesis; for doctorate, one foreign language, thesis/dissertation. *Entrance requirements:* For master's and doctorate, GRE General Test.

University of Mary Hardin-Baylor, College of Sciences and Humanities, Department of Psychology, Belton, TX 76513. Offers community counseling (MA); marriage and family Christian counseling (MA); psychology and counseling (MA); school counseling and psychology (MA). Part-time and evening/weekend programs available. *Degree requirements:* For master's, comprehensive exam. *Entrance requirements:* For master's, GRE General Test, minimum GPA of 3.0 in last 60 hours or 2.75 overall. Electronic applications accepted.

University of Maryland, Baltimore County, Graduate School, College of Arts, Humanities and Social Sciences, Department of Psychology, Baltimore, MD 21250. Offers applied developmental psychology (PhD); human services psychology (MA, PhD), including applied behavioral analysis (MA), human services psychology/clinical (PhD); industrial and organizational psychology (MPS); psychology (MPS). *Accreditation:* APA (one or more programs are accredited). *Faculty:* 28 full-time (12 women), 11 part-time/adjunct (2 women). *Students:* 100

Psychology—General

University of Maryland, Baltimore County (continued)
full-time (85 women), 23 part-time (21 women); includes 29 minority (13 African Americans, 1 American Indian/Alaska Native, 7 Asian Americans or Pacific Islanders, 8 Hispanic Americans). Average age 30. 207 applicants, 27% accepted, 32 enrolled. In 2007, 23 master's, 13 doctorates awarded. Terminal master's awarded for partial completion of doctoral program. *Degree requirements:* For master's, thesis or alternative; for doctorate, comprehensive exam, thesis/dissertation. *Entrance requirements:* For master's, GRE General Test; for doctorate, GRE General Test, GRE Subject Test. Additional exam requirements/recommendations for international students: Required—TOEFL. *Application deadline:* For fall admission, 12/1 for domestic and international students. Application fee: $50. Electronic applications accepted. *Financial support:* In 2007–08, 2 fellowships (averaging $22,000 per year), 32 research assistantships with full and partial tuition reimbursements (averaging $14,566 per year), 28 teaching assistantships with full and partial tuition reimbursements (averaging $14,566 per year) were awarded; career-related internships or fieldwork, Federal Work-Study, health care benefits, and tuition waivers (full and partial) also available. Financial award application deadline: 3/1; financial award applicants required to submit FAFSA. *Faculty research:* Prevention and treatment of behavior problems, early intervention, cultural contexts, applications to education, behavioral medicine. Total annual research expenditures: $2.5 million. *Unit head:* Dr. Linda Baker, Chair, 410-455-2415, Fax: 410-455-1055, E-mail: baker@umbc.edu. *Application contact:* Cara Lane, Program Management Specialist, 410-455-2567, Fax: 410-455-1055, E-mail: psycdept@umbc.edu.

University of Maryland, College Park, Graduate Studies, College of Behavioral and Social Sciences, Department of Psychology, College Park, MD 20742. Offers clinical psychology (PhD); developmental psychology (PhD); experimental psychology (PhD); industrial psychology (MA, MS, PhD); social psychology (PhD). *Accreditation:* APA (one or more programs are accredited). *Faculty:* 53 full-time (23 women), 12 part-time/adjunct (6 women). *Students:* 92 full-time (70 women), 4 part-time (3 women); includes 15 minority (2 African Americans, 1 American Indian/Alaska Native, 6 Asian Americans or Pacific Islanders, 6 Hispanic Americans), 12 international. 609 applicants, 4% accepted, 13 enrolled. In 2007, 13 master's, 18 doctorates awarded. *Median time to degree:* Of those who began their doctoral program in fall 1999, 71% received their degree in 8 years or less. *Degree requirements:* For master's, thesis; for doctorate, variable foreign language requirement, comprehensive exam, thesis/dissertation. *Entrance requirements:* For master's and doctorate, GRE General Test, GRE Subject Test, minimum GPA of 3.5, research and/or work experience, 3 letters of recommendation. *Application deadline:* For fall admission, 12/15 for domestic students, 2/1 for international students. Applications are processed on a rolling basis. Application fee: $60. Electronic applications accepted. *Financial support:* In 2007–08, 11 fellowships with full tuition reimbursements (averaging $15,736 per year), 9 research assistantships (averaging $15,312 per year), 56 teaching assistantships with tuition reimbursements (averaging $15,292 per year) were awarded; career-related internships or fieldwork, Federal Work-Study, and scholarships/grants also available. Support available to part-time students. Financial award applicants required to submit FAFSA. *Faculty research:* Social stereotyping and prejudice, anxiety disorders, auditory neuroethology, counseling and social psychology. Total annual research expenditures: $4.4 million. *Unit head:* Thomas S. Wallsten, Chair, 301-405-5862, Fax: 301-314-9566, E-mail: twallsten@psyc.umd.edu. *Application contact:* Dean of Graduate School, 301-405-0358, Fax: 301-314-9305.

University of Massachusetts Amherst, Graduate School, College of Social and Behavioral Sciences, Department of Psychology, Amherst, MA 01003. Offers clinical psychology (MS, PhD). *Accreditation:* APA (one or more programs are accredited). *Faculty:* 51 full-time (24 women). *Students:* 57 full-time (39 women), 15 part-time (9 women); includes 12 minority (5 African Americans, 3 Asian Americans or Pacific Islanders, 4 Hispanic Americans), 14 international. Average age 28. 303 applicants, 6% accepted, 9 enrolled. In 2007, 7 master's, 16 doctorates awarded. Terminal master's awarded for partial completion of doctoral program. *Degree requirements:* For master's, thesis; for doctorate, thesis/dissertation. *Entrance requirements:* For master's and doctorate, GRE General Test, 3 letters of recommendation. Additional exam requirements/recommendations for international students: Required—TOEFL (minimum score 530 paper-based; 197 computer-based). *Application deadline:* For fall admission, 12/1 priority date for domestic and international students. Applications are processed on a rolling basis. Application fee: $50 ($65 for international students). Electronic applications accepted. *Expenses:* Tuition, state resident: full-time $2,640; part-time $110 per credit. Tuition, nonresident: full-time $9,936; part-time $414 per credit. Required fees: $7,455. One-time fee: $332. Tuition and fees vary according to course load, campus/location, program and reciprocity agreements. *Financial support:* In 2007–08, 7 fellowships with full tuition reimbursements (averaging $16,610 per year), 86 research assistantships with full tuition reimbursements (averaging $8,002 per year), 52 teaching assistantships with full tuition reimbursements (averaging $9,449 per year) were awarded; career-related internships or fieldwork, Federal Work-Study, scholarships/grants, traineeships, and unspecified assistantships also available. Support available to part-time students. Financial award application deadline: 12/15. *Unit head:* Dr. Melinda Novak, Chair, 413-545-2387, Fax: 413-545-0996, E-mail: mnovak@psych.umass.edu. *Application contact:* Graduate Secretary, 413-545-2503.

University of Massachusetts Dartmouth, Graduate School, College of Arts and Sciences, Department of Psychology, North Dartmouth, MA 02747-2300. Offers clinical psychology (MA); general psychology (MA). Part-time programs available. *Faculty:* 16 full-time (6 women), 8 part-time/adjunct (5 women). *Students:* 17 full-time (13 women), 29 part-time (22 women); includes 5 minority (2 African Americans, 2 Asian Americans or Pacific Islanders, 1 Hispanic American). Average age 27. 68 applicants, 41% accepted, 18 enrolled. In 2007, 15 degrees awarded. *Degree requirements:* For master's, thesis (for some programs). *Entrance requirements:* For master's, GRE General Test, minimum GPA of 2.75, 3 letters of recommendation. Additional exam requirements/recommendations for international students: Required—TOEFL (minimum score 500 paper-based). *Application deadline:* For fall admission, 3/31 for domestic students, 1/31 for international students. Application fee: $40 ($60 for international students). Electronic applications accepted. *Expenses:* Tuition, state resident: full-time $2,071; part-time $86 per credit. Tuition, nonresident: full-time $8,099; part-time $337 per credit. Part-time tuition and fees vary according to course load and program. *Financial support:* In 2007–08, 10 teaching assistantships with full tuition reimbursements (averaging $3,500 per year) were awarded; research assistantships with full tuition reimbursements, career-related internships or fieldwork, Federal Work-Study, and unspecified assistantships also available. Support available to part-time students. Financial award application deadline: 3/1; financial award applicants required to submit FAFSA. *Faculty research:* Psychosocial stress, intimate relationships, sports psychology, behavior modification. Total annual research expenditures: $52,000. *Unit head:* Dr. Paul Donnelly, Director, Clinical Psychology, 508-999-8334, E-mail: pdonnelly@umassd.edu. *Application contact:* Carol Novo, Graduate Admissions Officer, 508-999-8604, Fax: 508-999-8183, E-mail: graduate@umassd.edu.

University of Massachusetts Lowell, College of Arts and Sciences, Department of Psychology, Lowell, MA 01854-2881. Offers community social psychology (MA). Part-time programs available. *Faculty:* 22. *Degree requirements:* For master's, thesis optional. *Entrance requirements:* For master's, GRE General Test or MAT. *Application deadline:* For fall admission, 4/1 priority date for domestic students; for spring admission, 10/1 for domestic students. Applications are processed on a rolling basis. Application fee: $20 ($35 for international students). Electronic applications accepted. *Financial support:* Research assistantships with full tuition reimbursements, teaching assistantships with full tuition reimbursements, career-related internships or fieldwork, Federal Work-Study, scholarships/grants, and traineeships available. Financial award application deadline: 4/1. *Faculty research:* Domestic violence, youth sports, teen pregnancy, substance abuse, family and work roles. *Unit head:* Dr. Nina Coppens, Chair, 978-934-3954, E-mail: nina_coppens@uml.edu. *Application contact:* Dr. Khanh T. Dinh, Graduate Coordinator, 978-934-3916, E-mail: khanh_dinh@uml.edu.

University of Memphis, Graduate School, College of Arts and Sciences, Department of Psychology, Memphis, TN 38152. Offers clinical psychology (PhD); experimental psychology (PhD); general psychology (MS); school psychology (MA, PhD). Part-time programs available. *Faculty:* 29 full-time (8 women), 4 part-time/adjunct (1 woman). *Students:* 92 full-time (56 women), 29 part-time (19 women); includes 18 minority (11 African Americans, 3 Asian Americans or Pacific Islanders, 4 Hispanic Americans), 10 international. Average age 28. 269 applicants, 16% accepted, 37 enrolled. In 2007, 14 master's, 8 doctorates awarded. Terminal master's awarded for partial completion of doctoral program. *Degree requirements:* For master's, comprehensive exam, thesis (for some programs), oral exam (MS); for doctorate, thesis/dissertation, internship. *Entrance requirements:* For master's, GRE General Test, 18 undergraduate hours in psychology, minimum GPA of 2.5; for doctorate, GRE General Test, GRE Subject Test. *Application deadline:* For fall admission, 2/1 for domestic students. Applications are processed on a rolling basis. Application fee: $35 ($60 for international students). *Expenses:* Tuition, state resident: full-time $6,990; part-time $377 per hour. Tuition, nonresident: full-time $17,818; part-time $830 per hour. Tuition and fees vary according to course load and program. *Financial support:* In 2007–08, 75 research assistantships with full tuition reimbursements (averaging $4,500 per year), 13 teaching assistantships with full tuition reimbursements (averaging $4,600 per year) were awarded; fellowships with full tuition reimbursements, tuition waivers (partial) and unspecified assistantships also available. *Faculty research:* Psychotherapy and psychopathology, behavioral medicine and community psychology, child and family studies, cognitive and social processes, neuropsychology and behavioral neuroscience. *Unit head:* Dr. Arthur C. Graesser, Chair, 901-678-2146, Fax: 901-678-2579, E-mail: a-graesser@memphis.edu. *Application contact:* Dr. Robert Cohen, Graduate Studies Coordinator, 901-678-2146.

University of Miami, Graduate School, College of Arts and Sciences, Department of Psychology, Coral Gables, FL 33124. Offers adult clinical (PhD); behavioral neuroscience (PhD); child clinical (PhD); developmental psychology (PhD); health clinical (PhD); psychology (MS). *Accreditation:* APA (one or more programs are accredited). *Faculty:* 27 full-time (13 women). *Students:* 88 full-time (69 women); includes 28 minority (5 African Americans, 7 Asian Americans or Pacific Islanders, 16 Hispanic Americans), 5 international. Average age 27. 340 applicants, 6% accepted, 14 enrolled. In 2007, 13 master's, 15 doctorates awarded. *Median time to degree:* Of those who began their doctoral program in fall 1999, 88% received their degree in 8 years or less. *Degree requirements:* For doctorate, comprehensive exam, thesis/dissertation. *Entrance requirements:* For doctorate, GRE General Test, minimum GPA of 3.5. Additional exam requirements/recommendations for international students: Required—TOEFL. *Application deadline:* For fall admission, 12/1 for domestic and international students. Application fee: $50. Electronic applications accepted. *Financial support:* In 2007–08, 88 students received support, including 9 fellowships with full tuition reimbursements available (averaging $22,000 per year), 24 research assistantships with full tuition reimbursements available (averaging $22,000 per year), 18 teaching assistantships with full tuition reimbursements available (averaging $16,500 per year); career-related internships or fieldwork, institutionally sponsored loans, scholarships/grants, and traineeships also available. Financial award applicants required to submit FAFSA. *Faculty research:* Behavioral factors in cardiovascular disease and cancer adult psychopathology, developmental disabilities, social and emotional development, mechanisms of coping. Total annual research expenditures: $12.4 million. *Unit head:* Dr. A. Rodney Wellens, Chairman, 305-284-2814, Fax: 305-284-3402. *Application contact:* Prof. Phil McCabe, Director of Graduate Studies, 305-284-2814, Fax: 305-284-3402, E-mail: inquire@psy.miami.edu.

University of Michigan, Horace H. Rackham School of Graduate Studies, College of Literature, Science, and the Arts, Department of Psychology, Ann Arbor, MI 48109. Offers biopsychology (PhD); clinical psychology (PhD); cognition and perception (PhD); developmental psychology (PhD); personality and social contexts (PhD); social psychology (PhD). *Accreditation:* APA. *Faculty:* 86 full-time, 69 part-time/adjunct. *Students:* 157 full-time (112 women); includes 51 minority (21 African Americans, 1 American Indian/Alaska Native, 17 Asian Americans or Pacific Islanders, 12 Hispanic Americans), 32 international. Average age 25. 698 applicants, 9% accepted, 29 enrolled. In 2007, 25 degrees awarded. *Degree requirements:* For doctorate, comprehensive exam, thesis/dissertation, oral defense of dissertation, preliminary exam. *Entrance requirements:* For doctorate, GRE General Test (optional), GRE Subject Test (optional). Additional exam requirements/recommendations for international students: Required—TOEFL. *Application deadline:* For fall admission, 12/15 for domestic students. Application fee: $60 ($75 for international students). Electronic applications accepted. *Financial support:* Fellowships with full tuition reimbursements, research assistantships with full tuition reimbursements, teaching assistantships with full tuition reimbursements, career-related internships or fieldwork available. Financial award application deadline: 4/15. *Unit head:* Theresa Lee, Chair, 734-764-7429. *Application contact:* Laurie Brannan, Psychology Student Academic Affairs, 731-764-2580, Fax: 734-615-7584, E-mail: psych.saa@umich.edu.

University of Michigan, Horace H. Rackham School of Graduate Studies, College of Literature, Science, and the Arts, Department of Women's Studies, Ann Arbor, MI 48109. Offers English and women's studies (PhD); history and women's studies (PhD); lesbian, gay, bisexual, transgender, queer (LGBTQ) studies (Certificate); psychology and women's studies (PhD); sociology and women's studies (PhD); women's studies (Certificate). *Faculty:* 71 full-time (68 women). *Students:* 70 full-time (69 women); includes 12 minority (4 African Americans, 5 Asian Americans or Pacific Islanders, 3 Hispanic Americans), 9 international. Average age 30. 140 applicants, 9% accepted. In 2007, 6 doctorates, 5 other advanced degrees awarded. *Degree requirements:* For doctorate, variable foreign language requirement, thesis/dissertation. *Entrance requirements:* For doctorate, GRE General Test, previous undergraduate course work in women's studies. *Application deadline:* For fall admission, 12/15 for domestic students. Application fee: $60 ($75 for international students). Electronic applications accepted. *Financial support:* In 2007–08, 23 fellowships with full tuition reimbursements (averaging $16,000 per year), 19 teaching assistantships with full and partial tuition reimbursements (averaging $15,199 per year) were awarded; career-related internships or fieldwork, institutionally sponsored loans, scholarships/grants, traineeships, health care benefits, and unspecified assistantships also available. *Faculty research:* Gender issues; LGBTQ studies; sexuality; women and science; global feminism. *Unit head:* Valerie Traub, Chair, 734-763-2047, Fax: 734-647-4943, E-mail: traubv@umich.edu. *Application contact:* Jen Sarafin, Graduate Student Services Coordinator, 734-763-2047, Fax: 734-647-4943, E-mail: jsarafin@umich.edu.

University of Michigan, Horace H. Rackham School of Graduate Studies, Combined Program in Education and Psychology, Ann Arbor, MI 48109. Offers PhD. *Faculty:* 19 part-time/adjunct (9 women). *Students:* 23 full-time; includes 9 minority (6 African Americans, 1 Asian American or Pacific Islander, 2 Hispanic Americans), 2 international. Average age 28. 77 applicants, 12% accepted, 4 enrolled. In 2007, 7 degrees awarded. *Median time to degree:* Of those who began their doctoral program in fall 1999, 71% received their degree in 8 years or less. *Degree requirements:* For doctorate, thesis/dissertation, oral defense of dissertation, preliminary exam, independent research project. *Entrance requirements:* For doctorate, GRE General Test. Additional exam requirements/recommendations for international students: Required—TOEFL (minimum score 600 paper-based; 250 computer-based; 100 iBT). *Application deadline:* For fall admission, 12/15 for domestic and international students. Application fee: $60 ($75 for international students). Electronic applications accepted. *Financial support:* In 2007–08, 23 students received support, including 14 fellowships with full tuition reimbursements available (averaging $25,912 per year), 8 research assistantships with full tuition reimbursements available (averaging $26,312 per year), 7 teaching assistantships with full tuition reimbursements available (averaging $26,350 per year); institutionally sponsored loans, scholarships/grants, traineeships, and unspecified assistantships also available. Financial award application deadline: 1/1. *Faculty research:* Classroom research, instructional psychology. *Unit head:* Kevin F Miller, Director, 734-647-0626, Fax: 734-615-2164, E-mail: kevinmil@umich.edu. *Application contact:* Janie Knieper, Administrative Specialist, 734-647-0626, Fax: 734-615-2164, E-mail: cpep@umich.edu.

University of Minnesota, Twin Cities Campus, Graduate School, College of Liberal Arts, Department of Psychology, Minneapolis, MN 55455-0213. Offers biological psychopathology (PhD); clinical psychology (PhD); cognitive and biological psychology (PhD); counseling psychology (PhD); industrial/organizational psychology (PhD); personality, individual differences, and behavior genetics (PhD); quantitative/psychometric methods (PhD); school psychology (PhD); social psychology (PhD). *Accreditation:* APA. *Faculty:* 44 full-time (10 women), 40 part-time/adjunct (11 women). *Students:* 134 full-time (71 women), 16 part-time (11 women); includes 30 minority (2 African Americans, 25 Asian Americans or Pacific Islanders, 3 Hispanic Americans), 18 international. 509 applicants, 5% accepted, 16 enrolled. In 2007, 19 doctorates awarded. *Median time to degree:* Of those who began their doctoral program in fall 1999, 54% received their degree in 8 years or less. *Degree requirements:* For doctorate, comprehensive exam, thesis/dissertation. *Entrance requirements:* For doctorate, GRE General Test, GRE Subject Test (recommended), 12 credits of upper-level psychology courses, including a course in statistics or psychological measurement. Additional exam requirements/recommendations for international students: Required—TOEFL (minimum score 550 paper-based; 213 computer-based; 79 iBT). *Application deadline:* For fall admission, 12/1 for domestic and international students. Application fee: $55 ($75 for international students). *Financial support:* In 2007–08, fellowships with full tuition reimbursements (averaging $21,000 per year), research assistantships with full tuition reimbursements (averaging $12,254 per year), teaching assistantships with full tuition reimbursements (averaging $12,254 per year) were awarded; career-related internships or fieldwork, traineeships, and tuition waivers (partial) also available. Financial award application deadline: 12/1. Total annual research expenditures: $6.5 million. *Unit head:* Gordon Legge, Chair, 612-625-0846, Fax: 612-626-2079. *Application contact:* Coordinator, 612-624-4181, Fax: 612-626-2079, E-mail: psyapply@tc.umn.edu.

University of Mississippi, Graduate School, College of Liberal Arts, Department of Psychology, Oxford, University, MS 38677. Offers clinical psychology (PhD); experimental psychology (PhD); psychology (MA). *Accreditation:* APA (one or more programs are accredited). *Faculty:* 16 full-time (7 women), 5 part-time/adjunct (3 women). *Students:* 45 full-time (34 women), 8 part-time (6 women); includes 11 minority (8 African Americans, 1 American Indian/Alaska Native, 2 Hispanic Americans). In 2007, 6 master's, 13 doctorates awarded. *Degree requirements:* For master's, thesis; for doctorate, thesis/dissertation. *Entrance requirements:* For master's, GRE General Test, minimum GPA of 3.0; for doctorate, GRE General Test. Additional exam requirements/recommendations for international students: Required—TOEFL. *Application deadline:* For fall admission, 1/15 for domestic students; for spring admission, 10/1 for domestic students. Applications are processed on a rolling basis. Application fee: $25. Electronic applications accepted. *Expenses:* Tuition, state resident: full-time $4,932. Tuition, nonresident: full-time $11,436. *Financial support:* Scholarships/grants available. Financial award application deadline: 3/1; financial award applicants required to submit FAFSA. *Unit head:* Dr. Michael T. Allen, Chairman, 662-915-5190, Fax: 662-915-5398, E-mail: mta1@olemiss.edu.

University of Missouri–Columbia, Graduate School, College of Arts and Sciences, Department of Psychological Sciences, Columbia, MO 65211. Offers MA, MS, PhD. *Accreditation:* APA (one or more programs are accredited). Terminal master's awarded for partial completion of doctoral program. *Degree requirements:* For doctorate, thesis/dissertation. *Entrance requirements:* For master's and doctorate, GRE General Test, minimum GPA of 3.0.

University of Missouri–Kansas City, College of Arts and Sciences, Department of Psychology, Kansas City, MO 64110-2499. Offers psychology (MA, PhD), including clinical psychology (PhD), community psychology (PhD). *Accreditation:* APA. *Faculty:* 16 full-time (12 women). *Students:* 14 full-time (10 women), 10 part-time (8 women); includes 2 minority (1 African American, 1 Hispanic American). Average age 31. 72 applicants, 6% accepted, 3 enrolled. In 2007, 4 master's, 4 doctorates awarded. Terminal master's awarded for partial completion of doctoral program. *Degree requirements:* For master's, thesis; for doctorate, comprehensive exam, thesis/dissertation, residency. *Entrance requirements:* For master's, GRE, minimum GPA of 3.5, letter of recommendation; for doctorate, GRE, minimum GPA of 3.25. Additional exam requirements/recommendations for international students: Required—TOEFL. *Application deadline:* For fall admission, 1/15 for domestic and international students. Applications are processed on a rolling basis. Application fee: $35 ($50 for international students). Electronic applications accepted. *Expenses:* Tuition, state resident: part-time $287 per hour. Tuition, nonresident: part-time $741 per hour. Required fees: $31 per hour. Tuition and fees vary according to program. *Financial support:* In 2007–08, 10 research assistantships (averaging $13,294 per year), 9 teaching assistantships (averaging $12,083 per year) were awarded; career-related internships or fieldwork, Federal Work-Study, and institutionally sponsored loans also available. Support available to part-time students. Financial award application deadline: 3/1; financial award applicants required to submit FAFSA. *Faculty research:* HIV/AIDS research group, psycho-oncology, sensory and cognitive neuroscience, cognitive psychophysiology, obesity and related metabolic disorders. Total annual research expenditures: $666,164. *Unit head:* Dr. Diane Filion, Chairperson, 816-235-1061. *Application contact:* 816-235-1111.

University of Missouri–St. Louis, College of Arts and Sciences, Department of Psychology, St. Louis, MO 63121. Offers behavioral neuroscience (PhD); clinical psychology respecialization (Certificate); community psychology (PhD); general psychology (MA); industrial/organizational psychology (PhD). *Accreditation:* APA (one or more programs are accredited). Evening/weekend programs available. *Faculty:* 20 full-time (9 women), 2 part-time/adjunct (both women). *Students:* 51 full-time (40 women), 22 part-time (16 women); includes 5 minority (1 African American, 3 Asian Americans or Pacific Islanders, 1 Hispanic American), 2 international. Average age 29. In 2007, 11 master's, 8 doctorates awarded. Terminal master's awarded for partial completion of doctoral program. *Degree requirements:* For doctorate, thesis/dissertation. *Entrance requirements:* For master's and doctorate, GRE General Test, GRE Subject Test, 3 letters of recommendation. Additional exam requirements/recommendations for international students: Required—TOEFL (minimum score 550 paper-based; 213 computer-based). *Application deadline:* For fall admission, 2/1 priority date for domestic students. Applications are processed on a rolling basis. Application fee: $35 ($40 for international students). Electronic applications accepted. *Financial support:* In 2007–08, 11 research assistantships with full and partial tuition reimbursements (averaging $11,333 per year), 18 teaching assistantships with full and partial tuition reimbursements (averaging $10,525 per year) were awarded; fellowships with full tuition reimbursements also available. *Faculty research:* Bereavement and loss, neuroscience, post-traumatic stress disorder, conflict and negotiation, social psychology. *Unit head:* Dr. Robert Calsyn, Chair, 314-516-5391, Fax: 314-516-5392, E-mail: umslpsychology@msx.umsl.edu. *Application contact:* 314-516-5458, Fax: 314-516-6996, E-mail: gradadm@umsl.edu.

The University of Montana, Graduate School, College of Arts and Sciences, Department of Psychology, Missoula, MT 59812-0002. Offers clinical psychology (PhD); experimental psychology (PhD), including animal behavior psychology, developmental psychology; school psychology (MA, PhD, Ed S). *Accreditation:* APA (one or more programs are accredited). Terminal master's awarded for partial completion of doctoral program. *Degree requirements:* For master's, thesis; for doctorate, thesis/dissertation. *Entrance requirements:* For master's, doctorate, and Ed S, GRE General Test. Additional exam requirements/recommendations for international students: Required—TOEFL.

University of Nebraska at Omaha, Graduate Studies and Research, College of Arts and Sciences, Department of Psychology, Omaha, NE 68182. Offers developmental psychology (PhD); industrial/organizational psychology (MS, PhD); psychobiology (PhD); psychology (MA); school psychology (MS, Ed S). Part-time programs available. *Faculty:* 17 full-time (8 women). *Students:* 33 full-time (24 women), 32 part-time (26 women); includes 4 minority (2 African Americans, 1 Asian American or Pacific Islander, 1 Hispanic American), 3 international. Average age 28. 89 applicants, 56% accepted, 25 enrolled. In 2007, 16 master's, 5 other advanced degrees awarded. *Degree requirements:* For master's, comprehensive exam, thesis (for some programs). *Entrance requirements:* For master's, GRE General Test, GRE Subject Test, previous course work in psychology, including statistics and a laboratory course; minimum GPA of 3.0, 3 letters of recommendation; for doctorate, GRE General Test. Additional exam requirements/recommendations for international students: Required—TOEFL (minimum score 500 paper-based; 173 computer-based; 61 iBT). *Application deadline:* For fall admission, 1/5 for domestic students. Application fee: $45. Electronic applications accepted. *Financial support:* In 2007–08, 55 students received support; fellowships, research assistantships with tuition reimbursements available, teaching assistantships with tuition reimbursements available, career-related internships or fieldwork, Federal Work-Study, institutionally sponsored loans, scholarships/grants, tuition waivers (partial), and unspecified assistantships available. Support available to part-time students. Financial award application deadline: 3/1; financial award applicants required to submit FAFSA. *Unit head:* Dr. Kenneth Deffenbacher, Chairperson, 402-554-2592. *Application contact:* Dr. Joseph Brown, Student Contact, 402-554-2592.

University of Nebraska–Lincoln, Graduate College, College of Arts and Sciences, Department of Psychology, Lincoln, NE 68588. Offers MA, PhD, JD/MA, JD/PhD. *Accreditation:* APA (one or more programs are accredited). *Degree requirements:* For master's, thesis optional; for doctorate, comprehensive exam, thesis/dissertation. *Entrance requirements:* For master's and doctorate, GRE General Test. Additional exam requirements/recommendations for international students: Required—TOEFL (minimum score 550 paper-based; 213 computer-based). Electronic applications accepted. *Faculty research:* Law and psychology, rural mental health, chronic mental illness, neuropsychology, child clinical psychology.

University of Nebraska–Lincoln, Graduate College, College of Education and Human Services, Interdepartmental Area of Psychological and Cultural Studies, Lincoln, NE 68588. Offers Ed D, PhD. *Degree requirements:* For doctorate, comprehensive exam, thesis/dissertation. *Entrance requirements:* For doctorate, GRE. Additional exam requirements/recommendations for international students: Required—TOEFL. Electronic applications accepted.

University of Nevada, Las Vegas, Graduate College, College of Liberal Arts, Department of Psychology, Las Vegas, NV 89154-9900. Offers clinical psychology (PhD); experimental psychology (PhD); general psychology (MA). *Accreditation:* APA. Part-time programs available. *Faculty:* 24 full-time (7 women), 2 part-time/adjunct (both women). *Students:* 63 full-time (48 women), 16 part-time (10 women); includes 11 minority (4 African Americans, 1 Asian American or Pacific Islander, 6 Hispanic Americans), 3 international. 89 applicants, 13% accepted, 11 enrolled. In 2007, 11 master's, 9 doctorates awarded. *Degree requirements:* For master's, comprehensive exam, thesis, oral exam; for doctorate, comprehensive exam, thesis/dissertation, oral exam. *Entrance requirements:* For master's, GRE General Test, GRE Subject Test, minimum GPA of 3.2; for doctorate, GRE General Test, GRE Subject Test, minimum undergraduate GPA of 3.2, graduate 3.5. Additional exam requirements/recommendations for international students: Required—TOEFL (minimum score 550 paper-based; 213 computer-based; 80 iBT). *Application deadline:* For fall admission, 1/15 for domestic and international students. Application fee: $60 ($75 for international students). Electronic applications accepted. *Expenses:* Tuition, state resident: part-time $198 per credit. Tuition, nonresident: part-time $416 per credit. Required fees: $256 per semester. Tuition and fees vary according to course load and reciprocity agreements. *Financial support:* In 2007–08, 24 research assistantships with full and partial tuition reimbursements (averaging $12,000 per year), 25 teaching assistantships with partial tuition reimbursements (averaging $12,000 per year) were awarded; career-related internships or fieldwork, Federal Work-Study, institutionally sponsored loans, scholarships/grants, health care benefits, and unspecified assistantships also available. Support available to part-time students. Financial award application deadline: 3/1. *Unit head:* Dr. Mark Ashcraft, Chair, 702-895-0195. *Application contact:* Graduate College Admissions Evaluator, 702-895-3320, Fax: 702-895-4180, E-mail: gradcollege@unlv.edu.

University of Nevada, Reno, Graduate School, College of Liberal Arts, Department of Psychology, Reno, NV 89557. Offers behavior analysis (MA, PhD); clinical psychology (PhD); cognitive brain science (MA, PhD). *Accreditation:* APA (one or more programs are accredited). Postbaccalaureate distance learning degree programs offered. *Faculty:* 34. *Students:* 80 full-time (59 women), 88 part-time (60 women); includes 27 minority (2 African Americans, 1 American Indian/Alaska Native, 16 Asian Americans or Pacific Islanders, 8 Hispanic Americans), 15 international. Average age 30. 211 applicants, 23% accepted, 41 enrolled. In 2007, 15 master's, 12 doctorates awarded. Terminal master's awarded for partial completion of doctoral program. *Degree requirements:* For master's, thesis optional; for doctorate, thesis/dissertation. *Entrance requirements:* For master's and doctorate, GRE General Test, GRE Subject Test, minimum GPA of 3.0. Additional exam requirements/recommendations for international students: Required—TOEFL. *Application deadline:* For fall admission, 1/1 for domestic students. Applications are processed on a rolling basis. Application fee: $60 ($95 for international students). *Expenses:* Tuition, state resident: full-time $2,774; part-time $154 per credit. Tuition, nonresident: full-time $13,578; part-time $330 per credit. Required fees: $49 per semester. *Financial support:* In 2007–08, 43 research assistantships, 20 teaching assistantships were awarded; Federal Work-Study, institutionally sponsored loans, and unspecified assistantships also available. Financial award application deadline: 3/1. *Faculty research:* Cognitive psychology, social psychological theory, animal and human intelligence, psychotherapy outcome, perception. *Unit head:* Dr. Victoria Follette, Chair, 775-784-6828.

University of New Brunswick Fredericton, School of Graduate Studies, Faculty of Arts, Department of Psychology, Fredericton, NB E3B 5A3, Canada. Offers clinical psychology (PhD); experimental and applied psychology (MA). *Accreditation:* APA. Part-time programs available. *Faculty:* 14 full-time (9 women). *Students:* 43 full-time (38 women), 1 (woman) part-time. In 2007, 4 doctorates awarded. *Degree requirements:* For doctorate, thesis/dissertation. *Entrance requirements:* For master's, GRE, minimum GPA of 3.5; for doctorate, GRE, minimum GPA of 3.7. Additional exam requirements/recommendations for international students: Required—TOEFL, TWE. *Application deadline:* For fall admission, 1/15 priority date for domestic and international students. Applications are processed on a rolling basis. Application fee: $50 Canadian dollars. *Financial support:* In 2007–08, 4 fellowships (averaging $3,750 per year), 11 research assistantships, 11 teaching assistantships were awarded. Financial award application deadline: 1/15. *Faculty research:* Depression, adolescence, human sexuality, family violence, autism. *Unit head:* Dr. Janet Stoppard, Acting Director of Graduate Studies, 506-458-7994, Fax: 506-447-3063, E-mail: stoppard@unb.ca. *Application contact:* Theresa Mills, Graduate Secretary, 506-453-4707, Fax: 506-447-3063, E-mail: tmills@unb.ca.

University of New Brunswick Saint John, Faculty of Arts, Saint John, NB E2L 4L5, Canada. Offers applied and experimental psychology (PhD); clinical psychology (PhD); experimental psychology (MA). *Faculty:* 9 full-time (4 women), 1 part-time/adjunct (0 women). *Students:* 5 full-time (4 women). Average age 23. 4 applicants, 75% accepted, 2 enrolled. In 2007, 2 master's, 1 doctorate awarded. *Degree requirements:* For master's, thesis. *Entrance requirements:* For master's, GRE General Test. Additional exam requirements/recommendations for international students: Required—TOEFL (minimum score 550 paper-based). *Application deadline:* For fall admission, 2/1 for domestic students. Application fee: $50. Electronic applications accepted. *Financial support:* In 2007–08, 7 research assistantships (averaging $2,550 per year), 5 teaching assistantships (averaging $3,600 per year) were awarded; fellowships, unspecified assistantships also available. Support available to part-time students. Financial award application deadline: 2/1. *Faculty research:* Psychopharmacology and addictions; forensic psychology and criminal justice; interpersonal relations; perception and graphical perception; lie detection. *Unit head:* Dr. Enrico DiTommaso, Director of Graduate Studies, 506-648-5636, Fax: 506-648-5780, E-mail: rico@unb.ca. *Application contact:* Frances Stevens, Secretary, 506-648-5640, Fax: 506-648-5780, E-mail: fstevens@unb.ca.

University of New Hampshire, Graduate School, College of Liberal Arts, Department of Psychology, Durham, NH 03824. Offers PhD. *Faculty:* 21 full-time. *Students:* 29 full-time (17 women), 2 international. Average age 27. 67 applicants, 10% accepted, 6 enrolled. In 2007, 5 doctorates awarded. *Degree requirements:* For doctorate, thesis/dissertation. *Entrance requirements:* For doctorate, GRE General Test, GRE Subject Test. Additional exam requirements/recommendations for international students: Required—TOEFL (minimum score 550 paper-based; 213 computer-based; 80 iBT). *Application deadline:* For fall admission, 2/15 priority date for domestic students, 2/15 for international students. Applications are processed on a rolling basis. Application fee: $60. Electronic applications accepted. *Financial support:* In 2007–08, 1 research assistantship, 27 teaching assistantships were awarded; fellowships, career-related internships or fieldwork, Federal Work-Study, scholarships/grants, and tuition waivers (full and partial) also available. Support available to part-time students. Financial

Psychology—General

University of New Hampshire (continued)
award application deadline: 2/15. *Faculty research:* History of psychology; cognition and perception; learning, developmental, physiological, and social psychology. *Unit head:* Dr. Robert Mair, Chairperson, 603-862-3198. *Application contact:* Janice Chadwich, Administrative Assistant, 603-862-3105, E-mail: psychology.ph.d@unh.edu.

University of New Mexico, Graduate School, College of Arts and Sciences, Department of Psychology, Albuquerque, NM 87131-2039. Offers clinical psychology (MS, PhD); psychology (PhD). *Accreditation:* APA (one or more programs are accredited). *Faculty:* 26 full-time (9 women), 12 part-time/adjunct (7 women). *Students:* 72 full-time (50 women), 9 part-time (7 women); includes 12 minority (1 African American, 11 Hispanic Americans), 6 international. Average age 33. 180 applicants, 8% accepted, 12 enrolled. In 2007, 9 master's, 8 doctorates awarded. *Degree requirements:* For master's, thesis; for doctorate, comprehensive exam, thesis/dissertation, pre-doctoral internship. *Entrance requirements:* For doctorate, GRE General Test, GRE Subject Test (psychology), minimum GPA of 3.0. Additional exam requirements/recommendations for international students: Required—TOEFL. *Application deadline:* For fall admission, 1/15 priority date for domestic students. Applications are processed on a rolling basis. Application fee: $50. Electronic applications accepted. *Financial support:* In 2007–08, 39 students received support; fellowships, research assistantships with full and partial tuition reimbursements available, teaching assistantships with full and partial tuition reimbursements available, career-related internships or fieldwork, Federal Work-Study, institutionally sponsored loans, scholarships/grants, health care benefits, and unspecified assistantships available. Financial award application deadline: 3/1; financial award applicants required to submit FAFSA. *Faculty research:* Addictions, learning cognition and memory, neuropsychology, quantitative behavioral neuroscience, evolutionary development psychology, physiological psychology, cognitive neuroscience. Total annual research expenditures: $953,743. *Unit head:* Dr. Ron Yeo, Chair, 505-277-4121, Fax: 505-277-1394, E-mail: ryeo@unm.edu. *Application contact:* Patricia Aragon-Mascurenas, Program Advisement Coordinator, 505-277-5009, Fax: 505-277-1394, E-mail: trishara@unm.edu.

University of New Orleans, Graduate School, College of Sciences, Department of Psychology, New Orleans, LA 70148. Offers MS, PhD. *Students:* 17 (12 women). Average age 32. In 2007, 6 master's, 7 doctorates awarded. *Degree requirements:* For doctorate, thesis/dissertation. *Entrance requirements:* For doctorate, GRE General Test, minimum GPA of 3.0, 21 hours of course work in psychology. Additional exam requirements/recommendations for international students: Required—TOEFL (minimum score 550 paper-based; 213 computer-based; 79 iBT). *Application deadline:* For fall admission, 7/1 priority date for domestic students, 6/1 for international students; for spring admission, 11/15 priority date for domestic students, 10/1 for international students. Applications are processed on a rolling basis. Application fee: $40. Electronic applications accepted. *Financial support:* Fellowships, research assistantships, teaching assistantships, career-related internships or fieldwork and unspecified assistantships available. Financial award application deadline: 5/15; financial award applicants required to submit FAFSA. *Faculty research:* Biofeedback, visual and auditory perception, psychopharmacology, neuropeptides. *Unit head:* Dr. Paul Frick, Graduate Coordinator, 504-280-6012, Fax: 504-280-6049, E-mail: pfrick@uno.edu. *Application contact:* Dr. Laura Scaramella, Graduate Coordinator, 504-280-6012, Fax: 504-280-6049, E-mail: lscarame@uno.edu.

The University of North Carolina at Chapel Hill, Graduate School, College of Arts and Sciences, Department of Psychology, Chapel Hill, NC 27599. Offers biological psychology (PhD); clinical psychology (PhD); cognitive psychology (PhD); developmental psychology (PhD); quantitative psychology (PhD); social psychology (PhD). *Accreditation:* APA. *Degree requirements:* For doctorate, comprehensive exam, thesis/dissertation. *Entrance requirements:* For doctorate, GRE General Test, minimum GPA of 3.0. Electronic applications accepted. *Faculty research:* Expressed emotion, cognitive development, social cognitive neuroscience, human memory personality.

The University of North Carolina at Charlotte, Graduate School, College of Arts and Sciences, Department of Psychology, Charlotte, NC 28223-0001. Offers community/clinical psychology (MA); health psychology (PhD); industrial/organizational psychology (MA); organizational science (PhD). Part-time programs available. *Faculty:* 31 full-time (13 women), 2 part-time/adjunct (0 women). *Students:* 53 full-time (41 women), 28 part-time (25 women); includes 13 minority (6 African Americans, 1 Asian American or Pacific Islander, 6 Hispanic Americans), 3 international. Average age 26. 215 applicants, 10% accepted, 18 enrolled. In 2007, 21 degrees awarded. *Degree requirements:* For master's, thesis. *Entrance requirements:* For master's, GRE General Test, GRE Subject Test, minimum GPA of 3.0 in undergraduate major, 2.8 overall. Additional exam requirements/recommendations for international students: Required—TOEFL (minimum score 557 paper-based; 220 computer-based). *Application deadline:* Applications are processed on a rolling basis. Application fee: $55. Electronic applications accepted. *Expenses:* Tuition, state resident: full-time $2,855. Tuition, nonresident: full-time $13,062. Required fees: $1,692. *Financial support:* In 2007–08, 2 fellowships (averaging $20,000 per year), 30 research assistantships (averaging $10,362 per year), 9 teaching assistantships (averaging $9,167 per year) were awarded; career-related internships or fieldwork, Federal Work-Study, institutionally sponsored loans, scholarships/grants, and unspecified assistantships also available. Support available to part-time students. Financial award application deadline: 4/1; financial award applicants required to submit FAFSA. *Faculty research:* Health psychology, industrial-organizational psychology, cognitive science. *Unit head:* Dr. Brian L. Cutler, Chair, 704-687-4731, Fax: 704-687-3096, E-mail: blcutler@email.uncc.edu. *Application contact:* Kathy B. Giddings, Director of Graduate Admissions, 704-687-3366, Fax: 704-687-3279, E-mail: agidding@uncc.edu.

The University of North Carolina at Greensboro, Graduate School, College of Arts and Sciences, Department of Psychology, Greensboro, NC 27412-5001. Offers clinical psychology (MA, PhD); cognitive psychology (MA, PhD); developmental psychology (MA, PhD); social psychology (MA, PhD). *Accreditation:* APA (one or more programs are accredited). *Faculty:* 23 full-time (8 women). *Students:* 46 full-time (31 women), 13 part-time (10 women); includes 7 minority (3 African Americans, 1 American Indian/Alaska Native, 1 Asian American or Pacific Islander, 2 Hispanic Americans). 218 applicants, 7% accepted.Terminal master's awarded for partial completion of doctoral program. *Degree requirements:* For master's, comprehensive exam, thesis; for doctorate, one foreign language, thesis/dissertation, preliminary exam. *Entrance requirements:* For master's and doctorate, GRE General Test. Additional exam requirements/recommendations for international students: Required—TOEFL. *Application deadline:* For fall admission, 2/1 for domestic students. Application fee: $45. Electronic applications accepted. *Financial support:* Fellowships with full tuition reimbursements, research assistantships with full tuition reimbursements, teaching assistantships with full tuition reimbursements, unspecified assistantships available. *Faculty research:* Sensory and perceptual determinants; evoked potential: disorders, deafness, and development. *Unit head:* Dr. George Michel, Head, 336-336-5013, E-mail: gfmichel@uncg.edu. *Application contact:* Michelle Harkleroad, Director of Graduate Admissions, 336-334-4884, Fax: 336-334-4424, E-mail: mbharkle@uncg.edu.

The University of North Carolina Wilmington, College of Arts and Sciences, Department of Psychology, Wilmington, NC 28403-3297. Offers MA. Part-time programs available. *Students:* 34 full-time (26 women), 32 part-time (20 women); includes 4 minority (2 African Americans, 1 Asian American or Pacific Islander, 1 Hispanic American), 4 international. Average age 27. 100 applicants, 26% accepted, 20 enrolled. In 2007, 18 degrees awarded. *Degree requirements:* For master's, comprehensive exam, thesis. *Entrance requirements:* For master's, GRE General Test, GRE Subject Test, minimum B average in undergraduate major. *Application deadline:* For fall admission, 1/15 for domestic students. Applications are processed on a rolling basis. Application fee: $45. *Expenses:* Tuition, state resident: full-time $2,714. Tuition, nonresident: full-time $12,579. Required fees: $1,985. *Financial support:* In 2007–08, 16 teaching assistantships were awarded; career-related internships or fieldwork and Federal Work-Study also available. Financial award application deadline: 3/15. *Unit head:* Dr. Mark Galizio, Chairman, 910-962-3813, Fax: 910-962-7010, E-mail: galizio@uncw.edu. *Application contact:* Dr. Robert D. Roer, Dean, Graduate School, 910-962-4117, Fax: 910-962-3787, E-mail: roer@uncw.edu.

University of North Dakota, Graduate School, College of Arts and Sciences, Department of Psychology, Grand Forks, ND 58202. Offers clinical psychology (PhD); counseling psychology (PhD); experimental psychology (PhD); forensic psychology (MA, MS); psychology (MA). *Accreditation:* APA (one or more programs are accredited). *Faculty:* 15 full-time (3 women). *Students:* 79 full-time (60 women), 15 part-time (11 women); includes 19 minority (2 African Americans, 15 American Indian/Alaska Native, 2 Asian Americans or Pacific Islanders), 9 international. 168 applicants, 24% accepted, 32 enrolled. In 2007, 4 master's, 16 doctorates awarded. *Degree requirements:* For master's, thesis, final exam; for doctorate, comprehensive exam, thesis/dissertation, internship, final exam. *Entrance requirements:* For master's, GRE General Test, GRE Subject Test, minimum GPA of 3.0; for doctorate, GRE General Test, GRE Subject Test, minimum GPA of 3.5. Additional exam requirements/recommendations for international students: Required—TOEFL (minimum score 550 paper-based; 213 computer-based; 79 iBT), IELTS (minimum score 7). *Application deadline:* For fall admission, 1/15 for domestic and international students. Application fee: $35. Electronic applications accepted. *Expenses:* Tuition, state resident: full-time $4,050; part-time $225 per credit. Tuition, nonresident: full-time $10,818; part-time $601 per credit. Required fees: $110 per semester. Tuition and fees vary according to class time, campus/location, program and reciprocity agreements. *Financial support:* In 2007–08, 34 students received support, including 8 research assistantships with full tuition reimbursements available (averaging $11,476 per year), 23 teaching assistantships with full tuition reimbursements available (averaging $8,993 per year); fellowships with full and partial tuition reimbursements available, career-related internships or fieldwork, Federal Work-Study, institutionally sponsored loans, scholarships/grants, health care benefits, tuition waivers (full and partial), and unspecified assistantships also available. Support available to part-time students. Financial award application deadline: 3/15; financial award applicants required to submit FAFSA. *Faculty research:* Developmental psychology, clinical social psychology, educational psychology, personality disorders. *Unit head:* Dr. Jeffrey N. Weatherly, Chairperson, 701-777-3470, E-mail: jeffrey.weatherly@und.nodak.edu. *Application contact:* Brenda Halle, Admissions Specialist, 701-777-2947, Fax: 701-777-3619, E-mail: brendahalle@mail.und.edu.

University of Northern British Columbia, Office of Graduate Studies, Prince George, BC V2N 4Z9, Canada. Offers business administration (Diploma); community health science (M Sc); disability management (MA); education (M Ed); first nations studies (MA); gender studies (MA); history (MA); interdisciplinary studies (MA); international studies (MA); mathematical, computer and physical sciences (M Sc); natural resources and environmental studies (M Sc, MA, MNRES, PhD); political science (MA); psychology (M Sc, PhD); social work (MSW). Part-time and evening/weekend programs available. Postbaccalaureate distance learning degree programs offered (no on-campus study). *Degree requirements:* For master's, thesis; for doctorate, thesis/dissertation. *Entrance requirements:* For master's, GRE, minimum B average in undergraduate course work; for doctorate, candidacy exam, minimum A average in graduate course work.

University of Northern Colorado, Graduate School, College of Education and Behavioral Sciences, School of Psychological Sciences, Greeley, CO 80639. Offers MA, PhD. Part-time programs available. *Faculty:* 15 full-time (6 women). *Students:* 27 full-time (19 women), 14 part-time (9 women); includes 5 minority (2 Asian Americans or Pacific Islanders, 3 Hispanic Americans), 7 international. Average age 35. 20 applicants, 90% accepted, 9 enrolled. In 2007, 3 master's, 1 doctorate awarded. *Degree requirements:* For master's, comprehensive exam, thesis or alternative; for doctorate, comprehensive exam, thesis/dissertation. *Entrance requirements:* For master's and doctorate, GRE General Test, letters of recommendation. *Application deadline:* Applications are processed on a rolling basis. Application fee: $50 ($60 for international students). Electronic applications accepted. *Expenses:* Tuition, state resident: part-time $222 per credit. Tuition, nonresident: part-time $627 per credit. Required fees: $36 per credit. *Financial support:* In 2007–08, 9 research assistantships (averaging $7,214 per year), 3 teaching assistantships (averaging $2,905 per year) were awarded; fellowships, unspecified assistantships also available. Financial award application deadline: 3/1; financial award applicants required to submit FAFSA. *Unit head:* Dr. Mark Alcorn, Director, 970-351-2957, Fax: 970-351-1103.

University of Northern Iowa, Graduate College, College of Social and Behavioral Sciences, Department of Psychology, Cedar Falls, IA 50614. Offers MA. Part-time programs available. *Students:* 34 full-time (23 women), 1 (woman) part-time; includes 7 minority (3 African Americans, 1 American Indian/Alaska Native, 3 Asian Americans or Pacific Islanders), 2 international. 102 applicants, 29% accepted, 22 enrolled. In 2007, 17 degrees awarded. *Degree requirements:* For master's, comprehensive exam, thesis. *Entrance requirements:* For master's, GRE, minimum GPA of 3.0; 3 letters of recommendation; dept. app. Additional exam requirements/recommendations for international students: Required—TOEFL (minimum score 500 paper-based; 180 computer-based; 61 iBT). *Application deadline:* For fall admission, 4/30 for domestic students. Applications are processed on a rolling basis. Application fee: $30 ($50 for international students). Electronic applications accepted. *Expenses:* Tuition, state resident: full-time $6,246; part-time $694 per credit hour. Tuition, nonresident: full-time $14,554; part-time $694 per credit hour. Required fees: $838; $119 per semester. *Financial support:* Career-related internships or fieldwork, Federal Work-Study, and tuition waivers (full and partial) available. Support available to part-time students. Financial award application deadline: 2/1. *Unit head:* Dr. Kimberly MacLin, Acting Head, 319-273-2302, Fax: 319-273-6188, E-mail: kim.maclin@uni.edu.

University of North Florida, College of Arts and Sciences, Department of Psychology, Jacksonville, FL 32224-2645. Offers counseling psychology (MAC); general psychology (MA). Part-time and evening/weekend programs available. *Faculty:* 18 full-time (8 women). *Students:* 44 full-time (38 women), 8 part-time (5 women); includes 9 minority (4 African Americans, 1 Asian American or Pacific Islander, 4 Hispanic Americans), 1 international. Average age 27. 115 applicants, 34% accepted, 26 enrolled. In 2007, 24 degrees awarded. *Degree requirements:* For master's, comprehensive exam, thesis optional, practicum. *Entrance requirements:* For master's, GRE General Test, 2 letters of recommendation, minimum GPA of 3.0 in last 60 hours of course work. Additional exam requirements/recommendations for international students: Required—TOEFL (minimum score 500 paper-based; 173 computer-based). *Application deadline:* For fall admission, 3/1 priority date for domestic students, 3/1 for international students. Applications are processed on a rolling basis. Application fee: $30. Electronic applications accepted. *Expenses:* Tuition, state resident: part-time $266 per credit hour. Tuition, nonresident: part-time $858 per credit hour. One-time fee: $35 part-time. Tuition and fees vary according to program. *Financial support:* In 2007–08, 32 students received support, including 3 teaching assistantships (averaging $3,435 per year); Federal Work-Study and tuition waivers (partial) also available. Support available to part-time students. Financial award application deadline: 4/1; financial award applicants required to submit FAFSA. *Faculty research:* Sensory perception, social cognition, sexual behavior, evolutionary psychology, psychology and law. Total annual research expenditures: $131,349. *Unit head:* Dr. Linda Foley, Chair, 904-620-2807, E-mail: lfoley@unf.edu. *Application contact:* Dr. Randy Russac, Graduate Coordinator for General Psychology, 904-620-2807, E-mail: rrussac@unf.edu.

University of North Texas, Robert B. Toulouse School of Graduate Studies, College of Arts and Sciences, Department of Psychology, Denton, TX 76203. Offers clinical psychology (PhD); counseling psychology (MA, MS, PhD); experimental psychology (MA, MS, PhD); health psychology and behavioral medicine (PhD). *Accreditation:* APA (one or more programs are accredited). *Faculty:* 26 full-time (8 women). *Students:* 101 full-time (74 women), 105 part-time (77 women); includes 27 minority (8 African Americans, 1 American Indian/Alaska Native, 5 Asian Americans or Pacific Islanders, 13 Hispanic Americans), 7 international. Average age 29. 472 applicants, 9% accepted, 36 enrolled. In 2007, 28 master's, 23 doctorates awarded. Terminal master's awarded for partial completion of doctoral program. *Degree requirements:* For master's, comprehensive exam, thesis or alternative; for doctorate, one foreign language, comprehensive exam, thesis/dissertation. *Entrance requirements:* For master's and doctorate, GRE General Test, interview. Additional exam requirements/recommendations for international students: Required—proof of English language proficiency required for non-native English speakers; Recommended—TOEFL (minimum score 550 paper-based; 213 computer-based). *Application deadline:* For fall admission, 7/15 for domestic students; for spring admission, 11/15 for domestic students. Application fee: $50 ($75 for international students). *Financial support:* In 2007–08, 2 fellowships (averaging $20,000 per year), 18 research assistantships (averaging $9,000 per year), 38 teaching assistantships (averaging $9,000 per year) were awarded; career-related internships or fieldwork, Federal Work-Study, and institutionally sponsored loans also available. Financial award application deadline: 8/1. *Faculty research:* Very broad range of topics and approaches. *Unit head:* Dr. Linda Marshall, Chair, 940-565-2339, Fax: 940-546-4682, E-mail: psychair@unt.edu. *Application contact:* Amy Mayfield, Graduate Coordinator, 940-565-2671, Fax: 940-565-4682, E-mail: amym@unt.edu.

University of North Texas, Robert B. Toulouse School of Graduate Studies, College of Public Affairs and Community Service, Department of Behavior Analysis, Denton, TX 76203. Offers MS. *Accreditation:* APA. *Faculty:* 7 full-time (3 women). *Students:* 32 full-time (26 women), 79 part-time (69 women); includes 15 minority (3 African Americans, 2 Asian Americans or Pacific Islanders, 10 Hispanic Americans), 2 international. Average age 30. 148 applicants, 66% accepted, 28 enrolled. In 2007, 18 degrees awarded. *Degree requirements:* For master's, thesis. *Entrance requirements:* For master's, GRE General Test. Additional exam requirements/recommendations for international students: Required—proof of English language proficiency required for non-native English speakers; Recommended—TOEFL (minimum score 550 paper-based; 213 computer-based). *Application deadline:* For fall admission, 7/15 priority date for domestic students; for spring admission, 11/15 for domestic students. Applications are processed on a rolling basis. Application fee: $50 ($75 for international students). *Financial support:* In 2007–08, 10 fellowships (averaging $7,500 per year), teaching assistantships (averaging $4,000 per year) were awarded; research assistantships, career-related internships or fieldwork, Federal Work-Study, scholarships/grants, and tuition waivers (partial) also available. Support available to part-time students. Financial award applicants required to submit FAFSA. *Faculty research:* Human operant research, applied behavior analysis, animal training autism. Total annual research expenditures: $500,000. *Unit head:* Dr. Richard Smith, Chair, 940-565-2274, Fax: 940-565-2467. *Application contact:* Dr. Cloyd Hyten, Graduate Advisor for MS Program, 940-565-4071, Fax: 940-565-2467, E-mail: hyten@unt.edu.

University of Notre Dame, Graduate School, College of Arts and Letters, Division of Social Science, Department of Psychology, Notre Dame, IN 46556. Offers cognitive psychology (PhD); counseling psychology (PhD); developmental psychology (PhD); quantitative psychology (PhD). *Accreditation:* APA. *Faculty:* 28 full-time (11 women), 5 part-time/adjunct (4 women). *Students:* 62 full-time (43 women); includes 9 minority (3 African Americans, 2 Asian Americans or Pacific Islanders, 4 Hispanic Americans), 9 international. 166 applicants, 15% accepted, 8 enrolled. In 2007, 13 doctorates awarded. *Degree requirements:* For doctorate, comprehensive exam, thesis/dissertation, candidacy exam. *Entrance requirements:* For doctorate, GRE General Test, GRE Subject Test (strongly recommended). Additional exam requirements/recommendations for international students: Required—TOEFL (minimum score 600 paper-based; 250 computer-based; 80 iBT). *Application deadline:* For fall admission, 1/2 for domestic and international students. Application fee: $50. Electronic applications accepted. *Financial support:* In 2007–08, 4 fellowships with full tuition reimbursements (averaging $22,000 per year), 14 research assistantships with full tuition reimbursements (averaging $16,000 per year), 41 teaching assistantships with full tuition reimbursements (averaging $16,000 per year) were awarded; career-related internships or fieldwork and tuition waivers (full) also available. Financial award application deadline: 1/2. *Faculty research:* Cognitive and socio-emotional development, statistical methods and quantitative models applicable to psychology, interpersonal relations, life span development and developmental delay, childhood depression, structural equation and dynamical systems. *Unit head:* Dr. Dawn Gondoli, Director of Graduate Studies, 574-631-6650, Fax: 574-631-8883. *Application contact:* Dr. Jarren Gonzales, Director of Graduate Admissions, 574-631-7706, Fax: 574-631-4183.

University of Oklahoma, Graduate College, College of Arts and Sciences, Department of Psychology, Norman, OK 73019-0390. Offers organizational dynamics (MS); psychology (MS, PhD). *Faculty:* 20 full-time (9 women). *Students:* 63 full-time (35 women), 42 part-time (26 women); includes 14 minority (3 African Americans, 3 American Indian/Alaska Native, 1 Asian American or Pacific Islander, 7 Hispanic Americans), 4 international. 75 applicants, 36% accepted, 24 enrolled. In 2007, 26 master's, 5 doctorates awarded. Terminal master's awarded for partial completion of doctoral program. *Degree requirements:* For master's, thesis or alternative; for doctorate, thesis/dissertation, general exam. *Entrance requirements:* For master's, GRE General Test, GRE Subject Test, minimum GPA of 3.0, 3 letters of recommendation; for doctorate, GRE General Test, GRE Subject Test, 3 letters of recommendation. Additional exam requirements/recommendations for international students: Required—TOEFL (minimum score 550 paper-based; 213 computer-based). *Application deadline:* For fall admission, 4/1 priority date for domestic students, 4/1 for international students; for spring admission, 11/1 for domestic students, 9/1 for international students. Applications are processed on a rolling basis. Application fee: $40 ($90 for international students). Electronic applications accepted. *Expenses:* Tuition, state resident: full-time $3,451; part-time $144 per credit hour. Tuition, nonresident: full-time $12,432; part-time $518 per credit hour. Required fees: $1,925; $70 per credit hour. $122 per semester. *Financial support:* In 2007–08, 38 students received support, including 12 fellowships with full tuition reimbursements available (averaging $5,416 per year), 8 research assistantships with partial tuition reimbursements available (averaging $12,291 per year), 31 teaching assistantships with partial tuition reimbursements available (averaging $13,071 per year); scholarships/grants, tuition waivers (partial), and unspecified assistantships also available. Support available to part-time students. Financial award application deadline: 3/1; financial award applicants required to submit FAFSA. *Faculty research:* Attention human judgement and decision-making; human performance; creativity of leadership; comparative psychology. Total annual research expenditures: $1.5 million. *Unit head:* Dr. Jorge Mendoza, Chair, 405-325-4511, Fax: 405-325-4737, E-mail: jmendoza@ou.edu. *Application contact:* Kathryn Paine, Graduate Admissions Coordinator, 405-325-4512, Fax: 405-325-4737, E-mail: kpaine@ou.edu.

University of Oregon, Graduate School, College of Arts and Sciences, Department of Psychology, Eugene, OR 97403. Offers clinical psychology (PhD); cognitive psychology (MA, MS, PhD); developmental psychology (MA, MS, PhD); physiological psychology (MA, MS, PhD); psychology (MA, MS, PhD); social/personality psychology (MA, MS, PhD). *Accreditation:* APA (one or more programs are accredited). *Faculty:* 27 full-time (11 women), 11 part-time/adjunct (8 women). *Students:* 76 full-time (48 women), 10 part-time (7 women); includes 11 minority (1 African American, 7 Asian Americans or Pacific Islanders, 3 Hispanic Americans), 15 international. 320 applicants, 8% accepted. In 2007, 21 master's, 11 doctorates awarded. Terminal master's awarded for partial completion of doctoral program. *Degree requirements:* For doctorate, thesis/dissertation. *Entrance requirements:* For master's, GRE General Test, minimum GPA of 3.0; for doctorate, GRE General Test. Additional exam requirements/recommendations for international students: Required—TOEFL. *Application deadline:* For fall admission, 12/1 for domestic students. Application fee: $50. *Financial support:* In 2007–08, 48 teaching assistantships were awarded; research assistantships, career-related internships or fieldwork also available. *Unit head:* Louis Moses, Head, 541-346-4918, Fax: 541-346-4911. *Application contact:* Lori Olsen, Admissions Contact, 541-346-5060, Fax: 541-346-4911, E-mail: gradsec@psych.uoregon.edu.

University of Ottawa, Faculty of Graduate and Postdoctoral Studies, Faculty of Social Sciences, School of Psychology, Ottawa, ON K1N 6N5, Canada. Offers PhD. *Accreditation:* APA. *Degree requirements:* For doctorate, thesis/dissertation. *Entrance requirements:* For doctorate, minimum B+ average. Electronic applications accepted. *Faculty research:* Behavioral neuroscience, social psychology, developmental psychology, cognition.

University of Pennsylvania, School of Arts and Sciences, Graduate Group in Psychology, Philadelphia, PA 19104. Offers PhD. *Accreditation:* APA. *Degree requirements:* For doctorate, thesis/dissertation. *Entrance requirements:* For doctorate, GRE General Test, GRE Subject Test. Additional exam requirements/recommendations for international students: Required—TOEFL. Electronic applications accepted. *Faculty research:* Cognitive psychology, sensation and perception, biological psychology, clinical psychology, social psychology.

University of Phoenix, The Artemis School, College of Health and Human Services, Phoenix, AZ 85034-7209. Offers administration of justice and security (MS); health care administration (MHA); health care management (MBA, MSN); nurse practitioner (MSN); nursing (MSN); nursing education (MSN); psychology (MS); MSN/MBA-HCM; MSN/MHA. *Accreditation:* AACN. Evening/weekend programs available. *Degree requirements:* For master's, thesis (for some programs). *Entrance requirements:* For master's, 3 years of work experience, minimum undergraduate GPA of 2.5, RN license. Additional exam requirements/recommendations for international students: Required—TOEFL (minimum score 550 paper-based; 213 computer-based; 79 iBT). Electronic applications accepted.

University of Phoenix–Austin Campus, College of Social and Behavioral Science, Austin, TX 78759. Offers administration of justice and security (MS); psychology (MS).

University of Phoenix–Cheyenne Campus, College of Social and Behavioral Science, Cheyenne, WY 82009. Offers administration of justice and security (MS); psychology (MS).

University of Phoenix–Cleveland Campus, The Artemis School, College of Health and Human Services, Independence, OH 44131-2194. Offers administration of justice and security (MS); health care management (MBA); nursing (MSN); psychology (MS). Evening/weekend programs available. *Degree requirements:* For master's, thesis (for some programs). *Entrance requirements:* For master's, minimum undergraduate GPA of 2.5, 3 years of work experience. Additional exam requirements/recommendations for international students: Required—TOEFL (minimum score 550 paper-based; 213 computer-based; 79 iBT). Electronic applications accepted.

University of Phoenix–Harrisburg Campus, College of Social and Behavioral Science, Harrisburg, PA 17112. Offers administration of justice and security (MS); psychology (MS).

University of Phoenix–Hawaii Campus, The Artemis School, College of Health and Human Services, Honolulu, HI 96813-4317. Offers administration of justice and security (MS); community counseling (MSC); family nurse practitioner (MSN); health administration (MHA); health care management (MBA); marriage, family and child therapy (MSC); nursing (MSN); psychology (MS). Evening/weekend programs available. *Degree requirements:* For master's, thesis (for some programs). *Entrance requirements:* For master's, minimum undergraduate GPA of 2.5, 3 years of work experience, RN license. Additional exam requirements/recommendations for international students: Required—TOEFL (minimum score 550 paper-based; 213 computer-based; 79 iBT). Electronic applications accepted.

University of Phoenix–Idaho Campus, The Artemis School, College of Health and Human Services, Meridian, ID 83642-3014. Offers health administration (MHA); health care management (MBA); psychology (MS). Evening/weekend programs available. *Degree requirements:* For master's, thesis (for some programs). *Entrance requirements:* For master's, minimum undergraduate GPA of 2.5, 3 years of work experience. Additional exam requirements/recommendations for international students: Required—TOEFL (minimum score 550 paper-based; 213 computer-based). Electronic applications accepted.

University of Phoenix–Indianapolis Campus, The Artemis School, College of Health and Human Services, Indianapolis, IN 46250-932. Offers administration of justice and security (MS); health administration (MHA); health care management (MBA); nursing (MSN); psychology (MS). Evening/weekend programs available. *Degree requirements:* For master's, thesis. *Entrance requirements:* For master's, 3 years work experience, minimum undergraduate GPA of 2.5. Additional exam requirements/recommendations for international students: Required—TOEFL (minimum score 500 paper-based; 213 computer-based). Electronic applications accepted.

University of Phoenix–Jersey City Campus, College of Social and Behavioral Science, Jersey City, NJ 07310. Offers administration of justice and security (MS); psychology (MS).

University of Phoenix–Louisiana Campus, The Artemis School, College of Health and Human Services, Metairie, LA 70001-2082. Offers administration of justice and security (MS); health care management (MBA); nursing (MSN); psychology (MS); MSN/MBA. Evening/weekend programs available. *Degree requirements:* For master's, thesis (for some programs). *Entrance requirements:* For master's, minimum undergraduate GPA of 2.5, 3 years work experience, RN license. Additional exam requirements/recommendations for international students: Required—TOEFL (minimum score 550 paper-based; 213 computer-based; 79 iBT). Electronic applications accepted.

University of Phoenix–Maryland Campus, The Artemis School, College of Health and Human Services, Columbia, MD 21045-5424. Offers administration of justice and security (MS); nursing (MSN); nursing education (MSN); psychology (MS); MSN/MBA; MSN/MHA. Evening/weekend programs available. *Degree requirements:* For master's, thesis (for some programs). *Entrance requirements:* For master's, minimum undergraduate GPA of 2.5, 3 years work experience. Additional exam requirements/recommendations for international students: Required—TOEFL (minimum score 550 paper-based; 213 computer-based; 79 iBT). Electronic applications accepted.

University of Phoenix–Northern Nevada Campus, College of Social and Behavioral Science, Reno, NV 89511. Offers administration of justice and security (MS); marriage, family and child therapy (MSC); psychology (MS); school counseling (MSC).

University of Phoenix–Oregon Campus, The Artemis School, College of Health and Human Services, Tigard, OR 97223. Offers administration of justice and security (MS); health administration (MHA); health care management (MBA); nursing (MSN); psychology (MS); MSN/MBA. Evening/weekend programs available. *Degree requirements:* For master's, thesis (for some programs). *Entrance requirements:* For master's, minimum undergraduate GPA of 2.5, 3 years of work experience, current RN license (nursing). Additional exam requirements/recommendations for international students: Required—TOEFL (minimum score 550 paper-based; 213 computer-based; 79 iBT). Electronic applications accepted.

University of Phoenix–Pittsburgh Campus, The Artemis School, College of Health and Human Services, Pittsburgh, PA 15276. Offers administration of justice and security (MS); health administration (MHA); health care management (MBA); nursing (MSN); nursing education (MSN); psychology (MS); MSN/MBA; MSN/MHA. Evening/weekend programs available. *Degree requirements:* For master's, thesis (for some programs). *Entrance requirements:* For master's, minimum undergraduate GPA of 2.5, 3 years work experience, current RN license (nursing). Additional exam requirements/recommendations for international students: Required—TOEFL (minimum score 550 paper-based; 213 computer-based; 79 iBT). Electronic applications accepted.

University of Phoenix–Richmond Campus, The Artemis School, College of Health and Human Services, Richmond, VA 23230. Offers administration of justice and security (MS); health administration (MHA); health care management (MBA); nursing (MSN); psychology (MS). Evening/weekend programs available. *Degree requirements:* For master's, thesis (for some programs). *Entrance requirements:* For master's, minimum undergraduate GPA of 2.5, 3 years work experience, current RN license for nursing programs. Additional exam requirements/recommendations for international students: Required—TOEFL (minimum score 500 paper-based; 213 computer-based; 79 iBT). Electronic applications accepted.

Psychology—General

University of Phoenix–San Antonio Campus, College of Social and Behavioral Science, San Antonio, TX 78230. Offers administration of justice and security (MS); psychology (MS).

University of Pittsburgh, School of Arts and Sciences, Department of Psychology, Pittsburgh, PA 15260. Offers MS, PhD. *Accreditation:* APA (one or more programs are accredited). *Faculty:* 40 full-time (17 women), 52 part-time/adjunct (19 women). *Students:* 91 full-time (73 women); includes 8 minority (5 African Americans, 3 Hispanic Americans), 11 international. 425 applicants, 6% accepted, 10 enrolled. In 2007, 13 master's, 12 doctorates awarded. Terminal master's awarded for partial completion of doctoral program. *Median time to degree:* Of those who began their doctoral program in fall 1999, 100% received their degree in 8 years or less. *Degree requirements:* For master's, comprehensive exam, thesis; for doctorate, comprehensive exam, thesis/dissertation. *Entrance requirements:* For doctorate, GRE General Test, minimum GPA of 3.0. Additional exam requirements/recommendations for international students: Required—TOEFL (minimum score 550 paper-based; 213 computer-based), TOEFL (paper-based 550, computer-based 213) or IELTS (score 7). *Application deadline:* For fall admission, 12/1 for domestic and international students. Application fee: $50. Electronic applications accepted. *Financial support:* In 2007–08, 13 fellowships with full tuition reimbursements (averaging $17,500 per year), 29 research assistantships with full tuition reimbursements (averaging $13,500 per year), 35 teaching assistantships with full tuition reimbursements (averaging $14,800 per year) were awarded; career-related internships or fieldwork, scholarships/grants, traineeships, health care benefits, and unspecified assistantships also available. Financial award application deadline: 12/1. *Faculty research:* Behavioral medicine and psychoneuroimmunology; learning, reasoning and memory; psychopathology and behavioral problems; social cognition; social influence and group processes; social and cognitive development. Total annual research expenditures: $16.5 million. *Unit head:* Dr. Anthony R. Caggiula, Chairman, 412-624-4501, Fax: 412-624-4428, E-mail: tonypsy@pitt.edu. *Application contact:* Maria Milleville, Graduate Program Administrator, 412-624-4502, Fax: 412-624-4428, E-mail: psygrad@pitt.edu.

University of Puerto Rico, Río Piedras, College of Social Sciences, Department of Psychology, San Juan, PR 00931-3300. Offers clinical psychology (MA); industrial organizational psychology (MA); investigative academic psychology (MA); psychology (PhD). Part-time programs available. *Students:* 177 full-time (136 women), 55 part-time (42 women). Average age 30. In 2007, 18 master's, 21 doctorates awarded. *Degree requirements:* For master's, comprehensive exam, thesis; for doctorate, comprehensive exam, thesis/dissertation, internship. *Entrance requirements:* For master's, GRE or PAEG, interview, minimum GPA of 3.0; for doctorate, GRE or PAEG, interview, master's degree, minimum GPA of 3.0. *Application deadline:* For fall admission, 2/1 for domestic and international students. Application fee: $17. *Expenses:* Tuition, state resident: full-time $1,808; part-time $113 per credit. Tuition, nonresident: full-time $5,248; part-time $328 per credit. Required fees: $72 per term. *Financial support:* Fellowships, research assistantships, teaching assistantships, career-related internships or fieldwork, Federal Work-Study, institutionally sponsored loans, and tuition waivers (partial) available. Financial award application deadline: 5/31. *Faculty research:* Intervention on Depressed Latino Youth, biosychosocial training. *Unit head:* Dr. Dolores Miranda, Director, 787-764-0000 Ext. 2094. *Application contact:* Information Contact, 787-764-0000, Fax: 787-763-4599.

University of Regina, Faculty of Graduate Studies and Research, Faculty of Arts, Department of Psychology, Regina, SK S4S 0A2, Canada. Offers clinical psychology (MA, PhD); experimental and applied psychology (MA, PhD). *Faculty:* 18 full-time (10 women). *Students:* 45 full-time (37 women), 6 part-time (all women). 66 applicants, 32% accepted. In 2007, 6 master's, 2 doctorates awarded. *Degree requirements:* For master's, thesis; for doctorate, comprehensive exam, thesis/dissertation. *Entrance requirements:* For master's, GRE General Test, GRE Subject Test; for doctorate, GRE General Test, GRE Subject Test (optional for students who hold a master's degree from a Canadian university). Additional exam requirements/recommendations for international students: Required—TOEFL (minimum score 580 paper-based; 237 computer-based; 88 iBT). *Application deadline:* For fall admission, 2/15 for domestic students. Application fee: $85 ($100 for international students). Electronic applications accepted. *Financial support:* In 2007–08, 19 fellowships (averaging $15,750 per year), 4 research assistantships (averaging $13,875 per year), 10 teaching assistantships (averaging $13,060 per year) were awarded; career-related internships or fieldwork and scholarships/grants also available. Financial award application deadline: 6/15. *Faculty research:* Clinical and experimental and applied psychology. *Unit head:* Dr. William E. Smythe, Head, 306-585-4157, Fax: 306-585-5429, E-mail: william.smythe@uregina.ca.

University of Rhode Island, Graduate School, College of Arts and Sciences, Department of Psychology, Program in Behavioral Science, Kingston, RI 02881. Offers PhD. In 2007, 2 doctorates awarded. *Application deadline:* For fall admission, 4/15 priority date for domestic students. Applications are processed on a rolling basis. Application fee: $35. *Expenses:* Tuition, state resident: full-time $6,936; part-time $385 per credit. Tuition, nonresident: full-time $19,044; part-time $1,058 per credit. Required fees: $1,508; $48 per credit. $30 per semester. One-time fee: $80 part-time. *Unit head:* Kathryn Quina, Director, 401-277-5164.

University of Rochester, The College, Arts and Sciences, Department of Clinical and Social Sciences in Psychology, Rochester, NY 14627-0250. Offers clinical psychology (PhD); developmental psychology (PhD); psychology (MA); social-personality psychology (PhD). *Accreditation:* APA (one or more programs are accredited). Terminal master's awarded for partial completion of doctoral program. *Degree requirements:* For doctorate, thesis/dissertation, qualifying exam. *Entrance requirements:* For doctorate, GRE General Test. Additional exam requirements/recommendations for international students: Required—TOEFL.

University of Saint Francis, Graduate School, Department of Psychology and Counseling, Fort Wayne, IN 46808-3994. Offers general psychology (MS); mental health counseling (MS); pastoral counseling (MS); school counseling (MS Ed). Part-time and evening/weekend programs available. *Faculty:* 4 full-time (1 woman), 3 part-time/adjunct (0 women). *Students:* 28 full-time (24 women), 41 part-time (35 women); includes 7 minority (3 African Americans, 4 Hispanic Americans). Average age 35. 16 applicants, 88% accepted. In 2007, 8 degrees awarded. *Entrance requirements:* For master's, interview, minimum undergraduate GPA of 3.0. *Application deadline:* For fall admission, 7/1 for domestic students; for spring admission, 11/1 for domestic students. Applications are processed on a rolling basis. Application fee: $20. *Financial support:* In 2007–08, 4 students received support. Federal Work-Study, scholarships/grants, and unspecified assistantships available. *Unit head:* Dr. Rolf Daniel, Dean, 260-399-7700 Ext. 8403, Fax: 260-399-8170, E-mail: rdaniel@sf.edu. *Application contact:* Michelle Kuhlhorst, Admissions Counselor, 260-434-7748, Fax: 260-434-7590, E-mail: mkuhlhorst@st.edu.

University of Saint Mary, Graduate Programs, Program in Psychology, Leavenworth, KS 66048-5082. Offers MA. Part-time and evening/weekend programs available. *Degree requirements:* For master's, thesis. *Entrance requirements:* For master's, minimum undergraduate GPA of 2.75.

University of St. Thomas, Graduate Studies, Graduate School of Professional Psychology, St. Paul, MN 55105-1096. Offers counseling psychology (MA, Psy D); family psychology (Certificate). *Accreditation:* APA. Part-time and evening/weekend programs available. *Degree requirements:* For master's, comprehensive exam, practicum; for doctorate, comprehensive exam, thesis/dissertation, qualifying exam, practicum, internship. *Entrance requirements:* For master's, MAT or GRE, minimum GPA of 2.75, letters of recommendation; for doctorate, GRE, minimum GPA of 3.2, letters of recommendation. Additional exam requirements/recommendations for international students: Required—TOEFL. Expenses: Contact institution. *Faculty research:* Elderly, eating disorders, anxiety.

University of Saskatchewan, College of Graduate Studies and Research, College of Arts and Sciences, Department of Psychology, Saskatoon, SK S7N 5A2, Canada. Offers MA, PhD. *Accreditation:* APA (one or more programs are accredited). *Degree requirements:* For master's, thesis; for doctorate, thesis/dissertation. *Entrance requirements:* Additional exam requirements/recommendations for international students: Required—TOEFL.

University of South Africa, College of Human Sciences, Pretoria, South Africa. Offers adult education (M Ed); African languages (MA, PhD); African politics (MA, PhD); Afrikaans (MA, PhD); ancient history (MA, PhD); ancient Near Eastern studies (MA, PhD); anthropology (MA, PhD); applied linguistics (MA); Arabic (MA, PhD); archaeology (MA); art history (MA); Biblical archaeology (MA); Biblical studies (M Th, D Th, PhD); Christian spirituality (M Th, D Th); church history (M Th, D Th); classical studies (MA, PhD); clinical psychology (MA); communication (MA, PhD); comparative education (M Ed, Ed D); consulting psychology (D Admin, D Com, PhD); curriculum studies (M Ed, Ed D); development studies (M Admin, MA, D Admin, PhD); didactics (M Ed, Ed D); education (M Tech); education management (M Ed, Ed D); educational psychology (M Ed); English (MA); environmental education (M Ed); French (MA, PhD); German (MA, PhD); Greek (MA); guidance and counseling (M Ed); health studies (MA, PhD), including health sciences education (MA), health services management (MA), medical and surgical nursing science (critical care general) (MA), midwifery and neonatal nursing science (MA), trauma and emergency care (MA); history (MA, PhD); history of education (Ed D); inclusive education (M Ed, Ed D); information and communications technology policy and regulation (MA); information science (MA, MIS, PhD); international politics (MA, PhD); Islamic studies (MA, PhD); Italian (MA, PhD); Judaica (MA, PhD); linguistics (MA, PhD); mathematical education (M Ed); mathematics education (MA); missiology (M Th, D Th); modern Hebrew (MA, PhD); musicology (MA, MMus, D Mus, PhD); natural science education (M Ed); New Testament (M Th, D Th); Old Testament (D Th); pastoral therapy (M Th, D Th); philosophy (MA); philosophy of education (M Ed, Ed D); politics (MA, PhD); Portuguese (MA, PhD); practical theology (M Th, D Th); psychology (MA, MS, PhD); psychology of education (M Ed, Ed D); public health (MA); religious studies (MA, D Th, PhD); Romance languages (MA); Russian (MA, PhD); Semitic languages (MA, PhD); social behavior studies in HIV/AIDS (MA); social science (mental health) (MA); social science in development studies (MA); social science in psychology (MA); social science in social work (MA); social science in sociology (MA); social work (MSW, DSW, PhD); socio-education (M Ed, Ed D); sociolinguistics (MA); sociology (MA, PhD); Spanish (MA, PhD); systematic theology (M Th, D Th); TESOL (teaching English to speakers of other languages) (MA); theological ethics (M Th, D Th); theory of literature (MA, PhD); urban ministries (D Th); urban ministry (M Th).

University of South Alabama, Graduate School, College of Arts and Sciences, Department of Psychology, Mobile, AL 36688-0002. Offers MS. Part-time and evening/weekend programs available. *Faculty:* 10 full-time (5 women), 4 part-time/adjunct (1 woman). *Students:* 22 full-time (17 women), 6 part-time (5 women); includes 3 minority (1 African American, 2 Asian Americans or Pacific Islanders). 24 applicants, 54% accepted, 8 enrolled. In 2007, 6 degrees awarded. *Degree requirements:* For master's, comprehensive exam, thesis optional. *Entrance requirements:* For master's, GRE General Test, GRE Subject Test (recommended), minimum GPA of 3.0, major in psychology or equivalent. *Application deadline:* For fall admission, 9/1 priority date for domestic students. Applications are processed on a rolling basis. Application fee: $25. *Expenses:* Tuition, state resident: full-time $4,224; part-time $176 per credit hour. Tuition, nonresident: full-time $8,448; part-time $352 per credit hour. Required fees: $802. Full-time tuition and fees vary according to program and student level. *Financial support:* Fellowships, research assistantships available. Support available to part-time students. Financial award application deadline: 4/1. *Faculty research:* Language acquisition and development. *Unit head:* Dr. Larry Christensen, Chair, 251-460-6321.

University of South Carolina, The Graduate School, College of Arts and Sciences, Department of Psychology, Columbia, SC 29208. Offers clinical/community psychology (MA, PhD), including clinical/community psychology (PhD), general psychology (MA); experimental psychology (MA, PhD); school psychology (PhD). *Accreditation:* APA (one or more programs are accredited). *Faculty:* 29 full-time (8 women), 4 part-time/adjunct (2 women). *Students:* 75 full-time (56 women), 31 part-time (23 women); includes 20 minority (11 African Americans, 6 Asian Americans or Pacific Islanders, 3 Hispanic Americans), 6 international. Average age 29. 260 applicants, 12% accepted. In 2007, 7 master's awarded. Terminal master's awarded for partial completion of doctoral program. *Degree requirements:* For master's, thesis; for doctorate, comprehensive exam, thesis/dissertation. *Entrance requirements:* For master's and doctorate, GRE General Test. Additional exam requirements/recommendations for international students: Required—TOEFL. *Application deadline:* For fall admission, 1/1 for domestic and international students. Application fee: $35. Electronic applications accepted. *Expenses:* Tuition, state resident: part-time $440 per hour. Tuition, nonresident: part-time $936 per hour. Required fees: $17 per hour. Tuition and fees vary according to program. *Financial support:* In 2007–08, 9 fellowships with full tuition reimbursements, 16 research assistantships with full tuition reimbursements (averaging $12,000 per year), 14 teaching assistantships with full tuition reimbursements (averaging $12,000 per year) were awarded; career-related internships or fieldwork, Federal Work-Study, and institutionally sponsored loans also available. Support available to part-time students. *Faculty research:* Developmental cognitive neuroscience, alcohol and drug addictions, reading and language processing, child and family, prevention. Total annual research expenditures: $3.2 million. *Unit head:* Dr. John E. Richards, Chair, 803-777-4263, Fax: 803-777-9558, E-mail: richards_john@sc.edu. *Application contact:* Doris Davis, Graduate Secretary, 803-777-2312, Fax: 803-777-9558, E-mail: doris@gwm.sc.edu.

The University of South Dakota, Graduate School, College of Arts and Sciences, Department of Psychology, Vermillion, SD 57069-2390. Offers clinical psychology (MA, PhD); human factors (MA, PhD). *Accreditation:* APA (one or more programs are accredited). *Faculty:* 24. *Students:* 68 (42 women). In 2007, 10 master's, 6 doctorates awarded. *Degree requirements:* For master's, comprehensive exam, thesis; for doctorate, comprehensive exam, thesis/dissertation. *Entrance requirements:* For master's, GRE, minimum GPA of 2.7; for doctorate, GRE General Test, GRE Subject Test, minimum GPA of 2.7. Additional exam requirements/recommendations for international students: Required—TOEFL (minimum score 550 paper-based; 213 computer-based; 79 iBT). *Application deadline:* For fall admission, 2/1 for domestic students. Application fee: $35. Electronic applications accepted. *Financial support:* In 2007–08, 1 fellowship (averaging $6,000 per year), 12 research assistantships with partial tuition reimbursements (averaging $6,000 per year), 31 teaching assistantships with partial tuition reimbursements (averaging $6,000 per year) were awarded; unspecified assistantships also available. Financial award applicants required to submit FAFSA. *Faculty research:* Human-computer interactions, perceptual-cognitive processing, medical psychology, depression, moral psychology. *Unit head:* Dr. Randal Quevillon, Chair, 605-677-5153, E-mail: askpsyc@usd.edu. *Application contact:* Dr. Barbara Yutrzenka, Graduate Student Adviser—Clinical, 605-677-5153, E-mail: byutrzen@usd.edu.

University of Southern California, Graduate School, College of Letters, Arts and Sciences, Department of Psychology, Los Angeles, CA 90089. *Accreditation:* APA. *Faculty:* 33 full-time (9 women). *Students:* 87 full-time (56 women), 4 part-time (3 women); includes 19 minority (4 African Americans, 6 Asian Americans or Pacific Islanders, 9 Hispanic Americans), 15 international. 447 applicants, 7% accepted. *Application deadline:* For fall admission, 12/1 for domestic students. Application fee: $85. *Financial support:* In 2007–08, 84 students received support, including fellowships with full tuition reimbursements available (averaging $23,500 per year), research assistantships with full tuition reimbursements available (averaging $18,570 per year), teaching assistantships with full tuition reimbursements available (averaging $18,570 per year); traineeships also available. Financial award application deadline: 2/15; financial award applicants required to submit FAFSA. *Faculty research:* Affective neuroscience, vision, aggression and violence, language and reading development, substance abuse. *Unit head:* Dr. Margaret Gatz, Chair, 213-740-2311. *Application contact:* Irene Takaragawa, Graduate Advisor, 213-740-2205.

University of Southern Mississippi, Graduate School, College of Education and Psychology, Department of Psychology, Hattiesburg, MS 39406-0001. Offers clinical psychology (MA, PhD); counseling psychology (PhD); experimental psychology (MA, PhD); psychology (MS); school psychology (MA, PhD). *Accreditation:* ACA; APA (one or more programs are accredited). *Faculty:* 33 full-time (12 women), 1 (woman) part-time/adjunct. *Students:* 111 full-time (87 women), 32 part-time (22 women); includes 11 minority (6 African Americans, 3 Asian Americans or Pacific Islanders, 2 Hispanic Americans), 8 international. Average age 28. 201 applicants,

21% accepted, 33 enrolled. In 2007, 32 master's, 15 doctorates awarded. Terminal master's awarded for partial completion of doctoral program. *Degree requirements:* For master's, comprehensive exam, thesis; for doctorate, comprehensive exam, thesis/dissertation. *Entrance requirements:* For master's, GRE General Test, minimum GPA of 3.0; for doctorate, GRE General Test, interview, minimum GPA of 3.0. Additional exam requirements/recommendations for international students: Required—TOEFL. *Application deadline:* For fall admission, 3/1 priority date for domestic students, 3/1 for international students. Applications are processed on a rolling basis. Application fee: $30. *Financial support:* In 2007–08, 46 research assistantships with full tuition reimbursements (averaging $7,731 per year), 49 teaching assistantships with full tuition reimbursements (averaging $7,731 per year) were awarded; career-related internships or fieldwork, Federal Work-Study, and institutionally sponsored loans also available. Financial award application deadline: 3/15. *Faculty research:* Dolphin cognition, sleep, neuropsychology, health-related behaviors, psychopathology. Total annual research expenditures: $101,200. *Unit head:* Dr. Stan Kuczaj, Chair, 601-266-4177, Fax: 601-266-5580. *Application contact:* Dr. Heather Sterling-Tairner, Graduate Coordinator, 601-266-4177, Fax: 601-266-5580.

University of South Florida, Graduate School, College of Arts and Sciences, Department of Psychology, Tampa, FL 33620-9951. Offers clinical psychology (MA, PhD); cognitive and neural sciences (MA, PhD); industrial-organizational psychology (MA, PhD). *Accreditation:* APA (one or more programs are accredited). *Faculty:* 32 full-time (8 women), 1 (woman) part-time/adjunct. *Students:* 106 full-time (65 women), 21 part-time (16 women); includes 17 minority (4 African Americans, 4 Asian Americans or Pacific Islanders, 9 Hispanic Americans), 17 international. 398 applicants, 6% accepted, 22 enrolled. In 2007, 16 master's, 21 doctorates awarded. *Degree requirements:* For master's, thesis; for doctorate, comprehensive exam, thesis/dissertation. *Entrance requirements:* For master's and doctorate, GRE General Test, minimum GPA of 3.0 in last 60 hours of course work. Application fee: $30. Electronic applications accepted. *Expenses: Contact institution. Financial support:* In 2007–08, 13 fellowships with full and partial tuition reimbursements (averaging $17,500 per year), 50 research assistantships with partial tuition reimbursements (averaging $13,000 per year), 50 teaching assistantships with partial tuition reimbursements (averaging $13,000 per year) were awarded; career-related internships or fieldwork, scholarships/grants, tuition waivers (partial), and unspecified assistantships also available. Financial award applicants required to submit FAFSA. *Faculty research:* Human memory; job analysis; stress, drug and alcohol abuse; neuroscience. *Unit head:* Michael T. Brannick, Director of Graduate Program, 813-974-0478, Fax: 813-974-4617, E-mail: mbrannick@cas.usf.edu. *Application contact:* Laura Pierce, Program Assistant, 813-974-0497, Fax: 813-974-4617, E-mail: lpierce@cas.usf.edu.

The University of Tennessee, Graduate School, College of Arts and Sciences, Department of Psychology, Knoxville, TN 37996. Offers clinical psychology (PhD); experimental psychology (MA, PhD); psychology (MA). *Accreditation:* APA (one or more programs are accredited). Terminal master's awarded for partial completion of doctoral program. *Degree requirements:* For master's, thesis; for doctorate, thesis/dissertation. *Entrance requirements:* For master's and doctorate, GRE General Test, GRE Subject Test, minimum GPA of 2.7. Additional exam requirements/recommendations for international students: Required—TOEFL. Electronic applications accepted.

The University of Tennessee at Chattanooga, Graduate School, College of Arts and Sciences, Department of Psychology, Chattanooga, TN 37403-2598. Offers industrial/organizational psychology (MS); research psychology (MS). Part-time and evening/weekend programs available. *Faculty:* 8 full-time (1 woman), 1 (woman) part-time/adjunct. *Students:* 40 full-time (28 women), 8 part-time (7 women); includes 9 minority (4 African Americans, 3 Asian Americans or Pacific Islanders, 2 Hispanic Americans), 2 international. Average age 26. 88 applicants, 85% accepted, 28 enrolled. In 2007, 27 degrees awarded. *Degree requirements:* For master's, comprehensive exam (for some programs), thesis optional, practicum (industrial/organizational psychology). *Entrance requirements:* For master's, GRE General Test, minimum GPA of 2.5 on all undergraduate coursework or 3.0 in senior year. Additional exam requirements/recommendations for international students: Required—TOEFL (minimum score 550 paper-based; 213 computer-based; 79 iBT); Recommended—IELTS (minimum score 6). *Application deadline:* For fall admission, 8/1 priority date for domestic students, 6/1 for international students; for spring admission, 12/1 priority date for domestic students, 10/1 for international students. Applications are processed on a rolling basis. Application fee: $30 ($35 for international students). *Expenses:* Tuition, state resident: full-time $5,854; part-time $393 per hour. Tuition, nonresident: full-time $15,816; part-time $946 per hour. Required fees: $1,090; $256 per hour. *Financial support:* In 2007–08, 12 fellowships with full and partial tuition reimbursements (averaging $3,438 per year) were awarded; career-related internships or fieldwork, Federal Work-Study, institutionally sponsored loans, scholarships/grants, tuition waivers (partial), and unspecified assistantships also available. Support available to part-time students. Financial award application deadline: 4/1; financial award applicants required to submit FAFSA. *Faculty research:* Decision processes; philosophical psychology; memory; social cognition; employee selection. *Unit head:* Dr. Paul J. Watson, Head, 423-425-4262, Fax: 423-425-4284. *Application contact:* Dr. Deborah E. Arfken, Dean of Graduate Studies, 423-425-4666, Fax: 423-425-5223, E-mail: deborah-arfken@utc.edu.

The University of Texas at Arlington, Graduate School, College of Science, Department of Psychology, Arlington, TX 76019. Offers experimental psychology (PhD); health psychology (PhD); psychology (MS). Part-time programs available. *Faculty:* 8 full-time (2 women), 1 (woman) part-time/adjunct. *Students:* 60 full-time (45 women), 6 part-time (4 women); includes 8 minority (2 African Americans, 1 Asian American or Pacific Islander, 5 Hispanic Americans), 18 international. 51 applicants, 29% accepted, 17 enrolled. In 2007, 13 master's, 3 doctorates awarded. Terminal master's awarded for partial completion of doctoral program. *Median time to degree:* Of those who began their doctoral program in fall 1999, 100% received their degree in 8 years or less. *Degree requirements:* For master's, comprehensive exam or thesis; for doctorate, thesis/dissertation (for some programs). *Entrance requirements:* For master's and doctorate, GRE General Test, minimum GPA of 3.0 in last 60 hours of course work. Additional exam requirements/recommendations for international students: Required—TOEFL (minimum score 550 paper-based; 213 computer-based). *Application deadline:* For fall admission, 6/16 for domestic students. Applications are processed on a rolling basis. Application fee: $35 ($50 for international students). *Expenses:* Tuition, state resident: full-time $5,934. Tuition, nonresident: full-time $10,938. *Financial support:* In 2007–08, 4 fellowships (averaging $1,000 per year), 2 research assistantships with tuition reimbursements (averaging $15,000 per year), 28 teaching assistantships with tuition reimbursements (averaging $15,000 per year) were awarded; career-related internships or fieldwork, Federal Work-Study, institutionally sponsored loans, scholarships/grants, traineeships, tuition waivers (partial), and unspecified assistantships also available. Financial award application deadline: 6/1; financial award applicants required to submit FAFSA. *Unit head:* Dr. Robert Gatchel, Chair, 817-272-2281, Fax: 817-272-2364, E-mail: gatchel@uta.edu. *Application contact:* Dr. Jared Kenworthy, Graduate Advisor, 817-272-2281, Fax: 817-272-2364, E-mail: kenworthy@uta.edu.

The University of Texas at Austin, Graduate School, College of Liberal Arts, Department of Psychology, Austin, TX 78712-1111. Offers PhD. *Accreditation:* APA. *Degree requirements:* For doctorate, thesis/dissertation. *Entrance requirements:* For doctorate, GRE General Test. Electronic applications accepted. *Faculty research:* Behavioral neuroscience, sensory neuroscience, evolutionary psychology, cognitive processes in psychopathology, cognitive processes and their development.

The University of Texas at Brownsville, Graduate Studies, College of Liberal Arts, Department of Behavioral Sciences, Brownsville, TX 78520-4991. Offers MAIS. Part-time and evening/weekend programs available. *Degree requirements:* For master's, thesis or comprehensive exam. *Entrance requirements:* For master's, GRE General Test. Additional exam requirements/recommendations for international students: Required—TOEFL. *Faculty research:* Memory, socio-political structure of South America, cartography of Mexico and Central America, family economic structure of Spain.

The University of Texas at Dallas, School of Behavioral and Brain Sciences, Program in Psychological Sciences, Richardson, TX 75083-0688. Offers early childhood disorders (MS); psychological sciences (MS, PhD). Part-time and evening/weekend programs available. *Faculty:* 30 full-time (15 women), 1 (woman) part-time/adjunct. *Students:* 30 full-time (27 women), 15 part-time (all women); includes 9 minority (3 African Americans, 4 Asian Americans or Pacific Islanders, 2 Hispanic Americans), 10 international. Average age 30. 51 applicants, 63% accepted, 16 enrolled. In 2007, 16 master's, 2 doctorates awarded. *Degree requirements:* For master's, directed project or internship. *Entrance requirements:* For master's, GRE General Test, minimum GPA of 3.0 in upper-level course work. Additional exam requirements/recommendations for international students: Required—TOEFL (minimum score 550 paper-based; 213 computer-based). *Application deadline:* For fall admission, 7/15 for domestic students; for spring admission, 11/15 for domestic students. Applications are processed on a rolling basis. Application fee: $50 ($100 for international students). Electronic applications accepted. *Expenses:* Tuition, state resident: full-time $7,052. Tuition, nonresident: full-time $12,632. Tuition and fees vary according to course load. *Financial support:* In 2007–08, 13 teaching assistantships with tuition reimbursements (averaging $10,131 per year) were awarded; fellowships, research assistantships with tuition reimbursements, career-related internships or fieldwork, Federal Work-Study, scholarships/grants, and unspecified assistantships also available. Support available to part-time students. Financial award application deadline: 4/30; financial award applicants required to submit FAFSA. *Faculty research:* Social competence in normal and hyperactive youth, preschool number development, social-emotional development, family and peer relationships. *Unit head:* Dr. Melanie J. Spence, Head, PhD Programs, 972-883-2206, Fax: 972-883-2491, E-mail: mspence@utdallas.edu. *Application contact:* Dr. Robert D. Stillman, Head, 972-883-3106, Fax: 972-883-3022, E-mail: stillman@utdallas.edu.

The University of Texas at El Paso, Graduate School, College of Liberal Arts, Department of Psychology, El Paso, TX 79968-0001. Offers clinical psychology (MA); experimental psychology (MA); psychology (PhD). Part-time and evening/weekend programs available. *Degree requirements:* For master's, thesis; for doctorate, thesis/dissertation. *Entrance requirements:* For master's and doctorate, GRE General Test. Additional exam requirements/recommendations for international students: Required—TOEFL. Electronic applications accepted.

The University of Texas at San Antonio, College of Liberal and Fine Arts, Department of Psychology, San Antonio, TX 78249-0617. Offers MS. Part-time and evening/weekend programs available. *Faculty:* 12 full-time (6 women). *Students:* 20 full-time (13 women), 11 part-time (5 women); includes 8 minority (all Hispanic Americans) Average age 27. 33 applicants, 67% accepted, 22 enrolled. In 2007, 8 degrees awarded. *Degree requirements:* For master's, comprehensive exam, thesis. *Entrance requirements:* For master's, GRE General Test, minimum GPA of 3.0 in last 60 hours and in all psychology courses. Additional exam requirements/recommendations for international students: Required—TOEFL (minimum score 500 paper-based; 173 computer-based). *Application deadline:* For fall admission, 7/1 for domestic students, 4/1 for international students; for spring admission, 11/1 for domestic students, 9/1 for international students. Applications are processed on a rolling basis. Application fee: $45 ($80 for international students). Electronic applications accepted. *Financial support:* In 2007–08, 6 research assistantships (averaging $7,880 per year), 2 teaching assistantships (averaging $9,094 per year) were awarded; career-related internships or fieldwork, Federal Work-Study, scholarships/grants, and unspecified assistantships also available. Total annual research expenditures: $109,487. *Unit head:* Dr. Robert W. Fuhrman, Chair, 210-458-4372, Fax: 210-458-7352, E-mail: rfuhrman@utsa.edu. *Application contact:* Dr. Stella Garcia-Lopez, Graduate Advisor, 210-458-5731.

The University of Texas at Tyler, College of Education and Psychology, Department of Psychology, Tyler, TX 75799-0001. Offers clinical psychology (MS), including neuropsychology, school psychology; counseling psychology (MA), including general, marriage and family; interdisciplinary studies (MSIS); school counseling (MA). Part-time and evening/weekend programs available. *Faculty:* 10 full-time (2 women), 8 part-time/adjunct (5 women). *Students:* 67 full-time (50 women), 60 part-time (50 women); includes 12 minority (4 African Americans, 1 American Indian/Alaska Native, 2 Asian Americans or Pacific Islanders, 5 Hispanic Americans). 37 applicants, 97% accepted, 32 enrolled. In 2007, 16 degrees awarded. *Degree requirements:* For master's, comprehensive exam, thesis optional. *Entrance requirements:* For master's, GRE General Test, minimum GPA of 3.0. *Application deadline:* For fall admission, 2/1 for domestic students; for spring admission, 10/1 for domestic students. Application fee: $0 ($50 for international students). Electronic applications accepted. *Expenses:* Tuition, state resident: part-time $627 per semester hour. Tuition, nonresident: part-time $908 per semester hour. Required fees: $107 per semester hour. Tuition and fees vary according to course load. *Financial support:* In 2007–08, fellowships with partial tuition reimbursements (averaging $3,000 per year), research assistantships (averaging $5,000 per year), teaching assistantships (averaging $1,500 per year) were awarded; career-related internships or fieldwork, Federal Work-Study, and institutionally sponsored loans also available. Support available to part-time students. Financial award application deadline: 7/1. *Faculty research:* Neuropsychology, child abuse, psychometric properties of psychological instruments, maternal behavior, clinical practice issues, victimization of women, post-traumatic stress disorder. *Unit head:* Dr. Charles B. Barke, Interim Chair, 903-565-5875, Fax: 903-565-5560, E-mail: cbarke@uttyler.edu. *Application contact:* Pam Morrow, Assistant to Dean for Enrollment Management, 903-566-7205, Fax: 903-566-7068, E-mail: pmorrow@uttyler.edu.

The University of Texas of the Permian Basin, Office of Graduate Studies, College of Arts and Sciences, Department of Behavioral Science, Program in Psychology, Odessa, TX 79762-0001. Offers applied behavioral analysis (MA); clinical psychology (MA). Part-time and evening/weekend programs available. *Degree requirements:* For master's, comprehensive exam, thesis, practicum. *Entrance requirements:* For master's, GRE General Test, 3 letters of recommendation. Additional exam requirements/recommendations for international students: Required—TOEFL (minimum score 550 paper-based; 213 computer-based).

The University of Texas–Pan American, College of Social and Behavioral Sciences, Department of Psychology and Anthropology, Edinburg, TX 78541-2999. Offers psychology (MA), including clinical psychology, experimental psychology. Part-time and evening/weekend programs available. *Faculty:* 10 full-time (2 women). *Students:* 24 full-time (17 women), 12 part-time (7 women); includes 29 minority (all Hispanic Americans) Average age 29. 15 applicants, 60% accepted, 9 enrolled. In 2007, 3 degrees awarded. *Degree requirements:* For master's, comprehensive exam, thesis optional, internship. *Entrance requirements:* For master's, GRE, letters of recommendation. Additional exam requirements/recommendations for international students: Required—TOEFL. *Application deadline:* For fall admission, 7/1 priority date for domestic and international students; for spring admission, 11/1 priority date for domestic and international students. Application fee: $0. Electronic applications accepted. *Financial support:* In 2007–08, 1 research assistantship (averaging $10,000 per year), 3 teaching assistantships (averaging $6,000 per year) were awarded; career-related internships or fieldwork, Federal Work-Study, and institutionally sponsored loans also available. *Faculty research:* Biofeedback, acculturation, health, stress/trauma, neuropsychological assessment, false memories, children's theory of mind. Total annual research expenditures: $60,000. *Unit head:* Dr. Philip G. Gasquoine, Director, 956-381-2155, Fax: 956-381-3333, E-mail: pgasquoine@panam.edu.

University of the Pacific, College of the Pacific, Department of Psychology, Stockton, CA 95211-0197. Offers MA. *Faculty:* 7 full-time (4 women). *Students:* Average age 26. 16 applicants, 69% accepted, 6 enrolled. In 2007, 4 degrees awarded. *Degree requirements:* For master's, thesis. *Entrance requirements:* For master's, GRE General Test. Additional exam requirements/recommendations for international students: Required—TOEFL (minimum score 475 paper-based; 150 computer-based). *Application deadline:* For fall admission, 3/1 priority date for domestic students. Applications are processed on a rolling basis. Application fee: $75. *Financial support:* In 2007–08, 7 teaching assistantships were awarded; institutionally sponsored loans also available. Support available to part-time students. Financial award application

Psychology—General

University of the Pacific (continued)
deadline: 3/1; financial award applicants required to submit FAFSA. *Unit head:* Dr. Roseann Hannon, Chairperson, 209-946-2133, E-mail: rhannon@pacific.edu.

The University of Toledo, College of Graduate Studies, College of Arts and Sciences, Department of Psychology, Toledo, OH 43606-3390. Offers behavioral (PhD), including cognitive, psychobiology and learning, social; clinical psychology (PhD); experimental psychology (MA). *Accreditation:* APA. *Faculty:* 22. *Students:* 34 full-time (24 women), 4 part-time (2 women); includes 2 minority (1 Asian American or Pacific Islander, 1 Hispanic American), 4 international. Average age 26. 150 applicants, 13% accepted, 9 enrolled. In 2007, 9 master's, 7 doctorates awarded. *Degree requirements:* For master's, thesis; for doctorate, one foreign language, thesis/dissertation. *Entrance requirements:* For master's and doctorate, GRE General Test, GRE Subject Test. *Application deadline:* For fall admission, 1/15 priority date for domestic students. Application fee: $45. *Financial support:* In 2007–08, 13 research assistantships (averaging $8,400 per year), 18 teaching assistantships (averaging $11,000 per year) were awarded; career-related internships or fieldwork, Federal Work-Study, institutionally sponsored loans, scholarships/grants, and unspecified assistantships also available. Support available to part-time students. Financial award application deadline: 1/15; financial award applicants required to submit FAFSA. *Faculty research:* Neural taste response. *Unit head:* Dr. Joseph Hovey, Chair, 419-530-2693, Fax: 419-530-8479.

See Close-Up on page 1509.

University of Toronto, School of Graduate Studies, Life Sciences Division, Department of Psychology, Toronto, ON M5S 1A1, Canada. Offers MA, PhD. *Accreditation:* APA (one or more programs are accredited). *Faculty:* 95 full-time, 1 part-time/adjunct. *Students:* 139 full-time (94 women), 25 international. 290 applicants, 26% accepted. In 2007, 15 master's, 5 doctorates awarded. *Degree requirements:* For master's, thesis; for doctorate, thesis/dissertation, oral exam. *Entrance requirements:* For master's, minimum A– average in last two years, 6 full courses in psychology, laboratory experience; for doctorate, minimum A– average, research experience. Application fee: $100 Canadian dollars. *Unit head:* Prof. Peter Herman, Interim Chair, 416-978-3404, Fax: 416-978-4811, E-mail: grad@psych.utoronto.ca. *Application contact:* Ann Lang, Graduate Administrator, 416-978-3404, Fax: 416-978-4811, E-mail: lang@psych.utoronto.ca.

University of Tulsa, Graduate School, College of Arts and Sciences, Department of Psychology, Tulsa, OK 74104-3189. Offers clinical psychology (MA, PhD); industrial/organizational psychology (MA, PhD); JD/MA. *Accreditation:* APA (one or more programs are accredited). Part-time programs available. *Faculty:* 13 full-time (5 women). *Students:* 43 full-time (35 women), 25 part-time (16 women); includes 7 minority (3 African Americans, 3 American Indian/Alaska Native, 1 Hispanic American), 3 international. Average age 28. 115 applicants, 35% accepted, 11 enrolled. In 2007, 8 master's, 7 doctorates awarded. Terminal master's awarded for partial completion of doctoral program. *Degree requirements:* For doctorate, comprehensive exam, thesis/dissertation. *Entrance requirements:* For master's and doctorate, GRE General Test. Additional exam requirements/recommendations for international students: Required—TOEFL (minimum score 575 paper-based; 231 computer-based; 91 iBT), IELTS (minimum score 7). *Application deadline:* For fall admission, 2/1 priority date for domestic students. Applications are processed on a rolling basis. Application fee: $40. Electronic applications accepted. *Expenses:* Tuition: Full-time $14,004; part-time $778 per credit hour. Required fees: $60; $30 per term. Tuition and fees vary according to course load. *Financial support:* In 2007–08, 46 students received support, including 9 fellowships with full and partial tuition reimbursements available (averaging $10,500 per year), 15 research assistantships with full and partial tuition reimbursements available (averaging $7,625 per year), 25 teaching assistantships with full and partial tuition reimbursements available (averaging $11,000 per year); career-related internships or fieldwork, Federal Work-Study, scholarships/grants, tuition waivers (full and partial), and unspecified assistantships also available. Support available to part-time students. Financial award application deadline: 2/1; financial award applicants required to submit FAFSA. *Faculty research:* Personality and social psychology, cognitive psychology, neuropsychology, training assessment, trauma studies. Total annual research expenditures: $2.1 million. *Unit head:* Dr. Judy Berry, Chairperson, 918-631-2834, Fax: 918-631-2833, E-mail: judy-berry@utulsa.edu. *Application contact:* Graduate School, 918-631-2336, Fax: 918-631-2156, E-mail: grad@utulsa.edu.

University of Utah, The Graduate School, College of Social and Behavioral Science, Department of Psychology, Salt Lake City, UT 84112-1107. Offers clinical psychology (PhD); psychology (PhD). *Accreditation:* APA. *Faculty:* 32 full-time (14 women), 4 part-time/adjunct (1 woman). *Students:* 44 full-time (28 women), 15 part-time (11 women); includes 7 minority (3 Asian Americans or Pacific Islanders, 4 Hispanic Americans), 3 international. Average age 31. 194 applicants, 10% accepted, 10 enrolled. In 2007, 5 doctorates awarded. *Median time to degree:* Of those who began their doctoral program in fall 1999, 78% received their degree in 8 years or less. *Degree requirements:* For doctorate, thesis/dissertation. *Entrance requirements:* For doctorate, GRE General Test. Additional exam requirements/recommendations for international students: Required—TOEFL (minimum score 500 paper-based; 173 computer-based). *Application deadline:* For fall admission, 12/15 for domestic and international students. Applications are processed on a rolling basis. Application fee: $45 ($65 for international students). *Financial support:* In 2007–08, 54 students received support, including 3 fellowships with full tuition reimbursements available (averaging $11,000 per year), 14 research assistantships with full tuition reimbursements available (averaging $11,000 per year), 37 teaching assistantships with full tuition reimbursements available (averaging $10,500 per year); career-related internships or fieldwork also available. Financial award applicants required to submit FAFSA. *Faculty research:* Cognitive neuroscience, health, social cognition, psychopathology, cognitive and social development. Total annual research expenditures: $1.9 million. *Unit head:* Frances J Friedrich, Chair, 801-581-6124, Fax: 801-581-5841, E-mail: friedrich@psych.utah.edu. *Application contact:* Nancy Seegmiller, Administrative Assistant, 801-581-6124, Fax: 801-581-5841, E-mail: nancy.seegmiller@psych.utah.edu.

University of Vermont, Graduate College, College of Arts and Sciences, Department of Psychology, Burlington, VT 05405. Offers clinical psychology (PhD); psychology (PhD). *Accreditation:* APA. *Students:* 50 (42 women); includes 6 minority (1 African American, 1 Asian American or Pacific Islander, 4 Hispanic Americans) 3 international. 220 applicants, 6% accepted, 8 enrolled. In 2007, 4 doctorates awarded. *Degree requirements:* For doctorate, thesis/dissertation. *Entrance requirements:* For doctorate, GRE General Test, GRE Subject Test. Additional exam requirements/recommendations for international students: Required—TOEFL (minimum score 550 paper-based; 213 computer-based; 80 iBT). *Application deadline:* For fall admission, 12/1 for domestic students. Application fee: $40. Electronic applications accepted. *Financial support:* Fellowships, research assistantships, teaching assistantships available. Financial award application deadline: 2/1. *Unit head:* Dr. William Falls, Chairperson, 802-656-2670. *Application contact:* Holly Olmstead, Information Contact, 802-656-2670.

University of Victoria, Faculty of Graduate Studies, Faculty of Social Sciences, Department of Psychology, Victoria, BC V8W 2Y2, Canada. Offers clinical psychology (PhD); clinical psychology (neuropsychology) (M Sc); cognition and brain science (M Sc, PhD); experimental neuropsychology (M Sc, PhD); individualized study (M Sc, PhD); life span development psychology (PhD); life span developmental psychology (M Sc); social psychology (M Sc, PhD). *Accreditation:* APA (one or more programs are accredited). *Faculty:* 24 full-time (12 women), 14 part-time/adjunct (7 women). *Students:* 26, 4 international. Average age 25. 146 applicants, 21% accepted, 14 enrolled. In 2007, 36 master's, 2 doctorates awarded. *Degree requirements:* For master's, thesis; for doctorate, thesis/dissertation, candidacy exam. *Entrance requirements:* For master's and doctorate, GRE General Test. Additional exam requirements/recommendations for international students: Required—TOEFL (minimum score 600 paper-based; 250 computer-based). *Application deadline:* For fall admission, 1/1 for domestic students, 12/15 priority date for international students. Applications are processed on a rolling basis. Application fee: $65 ($100 for international students). Electronic applications accepted. *Expenses:* Tuition, state resident: full-time $3,110. International tuition: $3,700 full-time. Tuition and fees vary according to program. *Financial support:* In 2007–08, 4 fellowships (averaging $13,000 per year), 23 research assistantships, 22 teaching assistantships (averaging $2,750 per year) were awarded; career-related internships or fieldwork and institutionally sponsored loans also available. Financial award application deadline: 1/15. *Faculty research:* Life span development psychology and aging, behavioral neuroscience, cognitive psychology, behavioral psychology, environmental psychology. *Unit head:* Dr. Elizabeth Brimacombe, Chair, 250-721-7547, Fax: 250-721-8929, E-mail: psychair@uvic.ca. *Application contact:* Paul Taylor, Graduate Secretary, 250-721-6109, Fax: 250-721-8929, E-mail: ptaylor@uvic.ca.

University of Virginia, College and Graduate School of Arts and Sciences, Department of Psychology, Program in Psychology, Charlottesville, VA 22903. Offers MA, PhD. *Accreditation:* APA. *Students:* 79 full-time (53 women), 1 (woman) part-time; includes 6 minority (3 African Americans, 3 Asian Americans or Pacific Islanders), 10 international. Average age 27. 491 applicants, 5% accepted, 11 enrolled. In 2007, 21 master's, 15 doctorates awarded. *Degree requirements:* For master's, thesis; for doctorate, comprehensive exam, thesis/dissertation. *Entrance requirements:* For master's and doctorate, GRE General Test, GRE Subject Test. *Application deadline:* Applications are processed on a rolling basis. Application fee: $60. Electronic applications accepted. *Financial support:* Applicants required to submit FAFSA.

University of Washington, Graduate School, College of Arts and Sciences, Department of Psychology, Seattle, WA 98195. Offers PhD. *Accreditation:* APA. *Degree requirements:* For doctorate, thesis/dissertation. *Entrance requirements:* For doctorate, GRE General Test, minimum GPA of 3.0. Electronic applications accepted. *Faculty research:* Addictive behaviors, artificial intelligence, child psychopathology, mechanisms and development of vision, physiology of ingestive behaviors.

University of Waterloo, Graduate Studies, Faculty of Arts, Department of Psychology, Waterloo, ON N2L 3G1, Canada. Offers MA, MA Sc, PhD. *Accreditation:* APA (one or more programs are accredited). *Faculty:* 34 full-time (11 women), 27 part-time/adjunct (12 women). *Students:* 207. 183 applicants, 24% accepted, 17 enrolled. In 2007, 13 master's, 16 doctorates awarded. Terminal master's awarded for partial completion of doctoral program. *Degree requirements:* For master's, thesis (for some programs); for doctorate, thesis/dissertation. *Entrance requirements:* For master's, GRE, honors degree in psychology, minimum B average; for doctorate, GRE, master's degree in psychology, minimum B average. Additional exam requirements/recommendations for international students: Required—TOEFL, TWE. *Application deadline:* For fall admission, 12/15 priority date for domestic students. Application fee: $75 Canadian dollars. Electronic applications accepted. *Financial support:* Research assistantships, teaching assistantships, career-related internships or fieldwork available. *Faculty research:* Memory and attention, attitudes and behavior in the workplace, object recognition, judgment and decision making, communication and knowledge in toddlers. *Unit head:* Dr. J. A. Cheyne, Chair, 519-888-4567 Ext. 32629, Fax: 519-746-8631, E-mail: acheyne@watarts.uwaterloo.ca. *Application contact:* Rita A. Cherkewski, Graduate Program Assistant, 519-888-4567 Ext. 32043, Fax: 519-746-8631, E-mail: gradpsyc@watarts.uwaterloo.ca.

The University of Western Ontario, Faculty of Graduate Studies, Biosciences Division, Department of Psychology, London, ON N6A 5B8, Canada. Offers MA, PhD. *Faculty:* 53 full-time (10 women). *Students:* 84 full-time (62 women), 7 part-time (5 women). Average age 29. 214 applicants. In 2007, 12 master's, 5 doctorates awarded. *Degree requirements:* For master's, thesis; for doctorate, thesis/dissertation. *Entrance requirements:* For master's, minimum B average during last 2 years; for doctorate, MA in psychology. Additional exam requirements/recommendations for international students: Required—TOEFL. *Application deadline:* For fall admission, 1/15 for domestic students. Application fee: $50. *Financial support:* In 2007–08, 41 fellowships with full and partial tuition reimbursements (averaging $15,000 per year), 4 research assistantships with partial tuition reimbursements, 76 teaching assistantships with partial tuition reimbursements (averaging $9,048 per year) were awarded; career-related internships or fieldwork also available. Financial award application deadline: 4/1. *Faculty research:* Clinical, applied and social/personality psychology; psychobiology; cognitive processes. *Unit head:* Dr. Albert Katz, Chair, 519-661-2111 Ext. 82066, Fax: 519-661-3961. *Application contact:* Dr. Ken McRae, Graduate Chair, 519-661-2064, Fax: 519-661-3961, E-mail: psych-grad@uwo.ca.

University of West Florida, College of Arts and Sciences: Arts, Department of Psychology, Pensacola, FL 32514-5750. Offers counseling (MA); counseling-licensed mental health counselor (MA); general (MA); industrial-organizational (MA). Part-time programs available. *Faculty:* 14 full-time (5 women), 1 (woman) part-time/adjunct. *Students:* 52 full-time (41 women), 29 part-time (23 women); includes 18 minority (10 African Americans, 2 American Indian/Alaska Native, 2 Asian Americans or Pacific Islanders, 4 Hispanic Americans), 3 international. Average age 29. 120 applicants, 53% accepted, 26 enrolled. In 2007, 18 degrees awarded. *Degree requirements:* For master's, thesis (for some programs). *Entrance requirements:* For master's, GRE General Test, GRE Subject Test, minimum GPA of 3.0. Additional exam requirements/recommendations for international students: Required—TOEFL (minimum score 550 paper-based; 213 computer-based). *Application deadline:* For fall admission, 6/1 for domestic students, 5/15 for international students; for spring admission, 11/1 for domestic students, 10/1 for international students. Applications are processed on a rolling basis. Application fee: $30. *Expenses:* Tuition, state resident: full-time $6,054; part-time $252 per credit. Tuition, nonresident: full-time $21,886; part-time $912 per credit. *Financial support:* In 2007–08, 3 research assistantships with partial tuition reimbursements (averaging $17,440 per year), 2 teaching assistantships with partial tuition reimbursements (averaging $4,948 per year) were awarded; fellowships with partial tuition reimbursements, career-related internships or fieldwork and Federal Work-Study also available. Financial award application deadline: 4/15; financial award applicants required to submit FAFSA. *Faculty research:* Prose recall, brain imaging, peak performance, biofeedback and pain control, comparable worth. Total annual research expenditures: $15,000. *Unit head:* Dr. Laura Koppes, Chairperson, 850-474-3493.

University of West Georgia, Graduate School, College of Arts and Sciences, Department of Psychology, Carrollton, GA 30118. Offers individual, organizational, and community transformation: consciousness and society (Psy D); psychology (MA). Part-time programs available. *Faculty:* 12 full-time (2 women). *Students:* 36 full-time (20 women), 16 part-time (11 women); includes 5 minority (3 African Americans, 2 Hispanic Americans), 2 international. Average age 32. In 2007, 16 degrees awarded. *Degree requirements:* For master's, one foreign language, comprehensive exam, thesis optional; for doctorate, comprehensive exam, thesis/dissertation. *Entrance requirements:* For master's, GRE General Test, interview, minimum GPA of 2.5, written statement; for doctorate, GRE or MAT, interview, written statement. *Application deadline:* For fall admission, 7/18 priority date for domestic students; for spring admission, 11/27 for domestic students. Application fee: $30. Electronic applications accepted. *Expenses:* Tuition, state resident: full-time $2,448; part-time $136 per semester hour. Tuition, nonresident: full-time $9,774; part-time $543 per semester hour. Required fees: $26 per semester hour. $173 per semester. *Financial support:* In 2007–08, 12 research assistantships with full tuition reimbursements (averaging $3,000 per year) were awarded; career-related internships or fieldwork, tuition waivers (full), and unspecified assistantships also available. Support available to part-time students. Financial award applicants required to submit FAFSA. *Faculty research:* Creativity, inspiration and consciousness; symbolism and metaphor in psychotherapy; spirituality of children; feminism and culture; mind/body connection. Total annual research expenditures: $30,000. *Unit head:* Dr. Tobbin R. Hart, Interim Chair, 678-839-6510, Fax: 678-839-0611, E-mail: thart@westga.edu. *Application contact:* Dr. Charles W. Clark, Interim Dean, 678-839-6508, E-mail: cclark@westga.edu.

University of Windsor, Faculty of Graduate Studies, Faculty of Arts and Social Sciences, Department of Psychology, Windsor, ON N9B 3P4, Canada. Offers adult clinical (MA, PhD); applied social psychology (MA, PhD); child clinical (MA, PhD); clinical neuropsychology (MA, PhD). *Accreditation:* APA (one or more programs are accredited). *Faculty:* 30 full-time (12 women). *Students:* 106 full-time (89 women). 183 applicants, 19% accepted. In 2007, 19 master's, 10 doctorates awarded. *Degree requirements:* For master's, thesis; for doctorate, comprehensive exam, thesis/dissertation. *Entrance requirements:* For master's, GRE General Test, GRE Subject Test in psychology, minimum B average; for doctorate, GRE General Test, GRE Subject Test in psychology, master's degree. Additional exam requirements/recommendations for international students: Required—TOEFL (minimum score 600 paper-based; 250 computer-based). *Application deadline:* For fall admission, 1/15 for domestic students. Application fee: $55. Electronic applications accepted. *Financial support:* In 2007–08, 67 teaching assistantships (averaging $9,409 per year) were awarded; Federal Work-Study, scholarships/grants, tuition waivers (full and partial), unspecified assistantships, and bursaries also available. Financial award application deadline: 2/15. *Faculty research:* Gambling, suicidology, emotional competence, psychotherapy and trauma. *Unit head:* Dr. Shelagh Towson, Head, 519-253-3000 Ext. 2215, Fax: 519-973-7021, E-mail: towson@uwindsor.ca. *Application contact:* Applicant Services, 519-253-3000 Ext. 6459, Fax: 519-971-3653, E-mail: gradadmit@uwindsor.ca.

University of Wisconsin–Eau Claire, College of Arts and Sciences, Department of Psychology, Eau Claire, WI 54702-4004. Offers school psychology (MSE, Ed S). *Faculty:* 13 full-time (7 women). *Students:* 14 full-time (12 women), 9 part-time (7 women), 1 international. Average age 25. 42 applicants, 36% accepted, 14 enrolled. In 2007, 17 degrees awarded. *Degree requirements:* For master's, comprehensive exam, thesis. *Entrance requirements:* For master's, GRE, minimum undergraduate GPA of 3.07. *Application deadline:* For fall admission, 3/1 for domestic students. Applications are processed on a rolling basis. Application fee: $45. Electronic applications accepted. *Expenses:* Tuition, state resident: full-time $6,870; part-time $381 per credit. Tuition, nonresident: full-time $17,480; part-time $971 per credit. Tuition and fees vary according to reciprocity agreements. *Financial support:* In 2007–08, 15 students received support, including 6 teaching assistantships (averaging $3,600 per year); Federal Work-Study also available. Financial award application deadline: 4/15; financial award applicants required to submit FAFSA. *Unit head:* Dr. Barbara Lozar, Program Director, 715-836-5733, Fax: 715-836-2214, E-mail: lozarb@uwec.edu.

University of Wisconsin–La Crosse, Office of University Graduate Studies, College of Liberal Studies, Department of Psychology, La Crosse, WI 54601-3742. Offers college student development and administration (MS Ed); school psychology (MS Ed, Ed S). *Faculty:* 9 full-time (6 women), 15 part-time/adjunct (9 women). *Students:* 43 full-time (30 women), 51 part-time (43 women); includes 6 minority (1 African American, 3 Asian Americans or Pacific Islanders, 2 Hispanic Americans). Average age 25. 86 applicants, 72% accepted, 20 enrolled. In 2007, 39 degrees awarded. *Degree requirements:* For master's, thesis, seminar, or comprehensive exams. *Entrance requirements:* For master's, GRE General Test, minimum GPA of 2.85, interview, writing sample, resumé. Additional exam requirements/recommendations for international students: Required—TOEFL (minimum score 550 paper-based; 213 computer-based). *Application deadline:* For fall admission, 2/15 for domestic students. Application fee: $45. *Financial support:* Research assistantships with partial tuition reimbursements, career-related internships or fieldwork, Federal Work-Study, institutionally sponsored loans, scholarships/grants, health care benefits, and unspecified assistantships available. Support available to part-time students. *Unit head:* Dr. Emily Johnson, Chair, 608-785-6888, Fax: 608-785-8443, E-mail: johnson.emil@uwlax.edu. *Application contact:* Kathryn Kiefer, Associate Director of Admissions, 608-785-8939, E-mail: admissions@uwlax.edu.

University of Wisconsin–Madison, Graduate School, College of Letters and Science, Department of Psychology, Madison, WI 53706-1380. Offers biology of brain and behavior (PhD); clinical psychology (PhD); cognitive neurosciences (PhD); developmental psychology (PhD); perception (PhD); psychology (PhD); social and personality psychology (PhD). *Accreditation:* APA. *Degree requirements:* For doctorate, comprehensive exam, thesis/dissertation. *Entrance requirements:* For doctorate, GRE General Test, minimum undergraduate GPA of 3.0. Additional exam requirements/recommendations for international students: Required—TOEFL. Electronic applications accepted.

University of Wisconsin–Milwaukee, Graduate School, College of Letters and Sciences, Department of Psychology, Milwaukee, WI 53201-0413. Offers clinical psychology (MS, PhD); psychology (MS, PhD). *Accreditation:* APA (one or more programs are accredited). *Faculty:* 19 full-time (4 women). *Students:* 60 full-time (38 women), 11 part-time (5 women); includes 13 minority (2 African Americans, 4 Asian Americans or Pacific Islanders, 7 Hispanic Americans), 4 international. 165 applicants, 14% accepted, 14 enrolled. In 2007, 8 master's, 11 doctorates awarded. *Degree requirements:* For master's, thesis; for doctorate, variable foreign language requirement, thesis/dissertation. *Entrance requirements:* For master's and doctorate, GRE General Test, GRE Subject Test. *Application deadline:* For fall admission, 1/1 priority date for domestic students; for spring admission, 9/1 for domestic students. Applications are processed on a rolling basis. Application fee: $45 ($75 for international students). *Expenses:* Tuition, state resident: part-time $530 per credit. Tuition, nonresident: part-time $1,428 per credit. Required fees: $19 per credit. $229 per term. Tuition and fees vary according to course load and program. *Financial support:* In 2007–08, 2 research assistantships, 42 teaching assistantships were awarded; fellowships, career-related internships or fieldwork and unspecified assistantships also available. Support available to part-time students. Financial award application deadline: 4/15. *Unit head:* Hobart Davies, Representative, 414-229-6594, Fax: 414-229-5219, E-mail: hobart@uwm.edu.

University of Wisconsin–Oshkosh, The Office of Graduate Studies, College of Letters and Science, Department of Psychology, Oshkosh, WI 54901. Offers experimental psychology (MS); industrial/organizational psychology (MS). *Faculty:* 10 full-time (3 women). *Students:* 27. Average age 26. 22 applicants, 100% accepted. In 2007, 9 degrees awarded. *Degree requirements:* For master's, thesis. *Entrance requirements:* For master's, GRE, 10 semester hours of undergraduate course work in psychology. Additional exam requirements/recommendations for international students: Required—TOEFL (minimum score 550 paper-based; 213 computer-based; 79 iBT). *Application deadline:* For fall admission, 4/1 priority date for domestic students. Applications are processed on a rolling basis. Application fee: $45. Electronic applications accepted. *Financial support:* Fellowships, research assistantships with partial tuition reimbursements, career-related internships or fieldwork, institutionally sponsored loans, scholarships/grants, tuition waivers (partial), and unspecified assistantships available. Financial award application deadline: 3/15; financial award applicants required to submit FAFSA. *Faculty research:* Performance evaluation, training, biological bases of behavior, tactile perception, aging. *Unit head:* Dr. Jim Koch, Chair, 920-424-2303, E-mail: kochj@uwosh.edu. *Application contact:* Dr. Gary Adams, Graduate Program Coordinator, 920-424-2300, E-mail: psychology@uwosh.edu.

University of Wisconsin–Stout, Graduate School, College of Human Development, Program in Applied Psychology, Menomonie, WI 54751. Offers MS. Part-time programs available. *Faculty:* 7 full-time (2 women). *Students:* 18 full-time (12 women), 1 (woman) part-time; includes 2 minority (both Hispanic Americans), 1 international. Average age 26. 21 applicants, 86% accepted, 10 enrolled. In 2007, 16 degrees awarded. *Degree requirements:* For master's, thesis. *Entrance requirements:* For master's, GRE General Test, GRE Subject Test, minimum GPA of 3.0, 15 semester credits of undergraduate course work in psychology, 8 semester credits in research methods and statistics. Additional exam requirements/recommendations for international students: Required—TOEFL (minimum score 500 paper-based; 173 computer-based; 61 iBT). *Application deadline:* For fall admission, 2/1 priority date for domestic and international students; for spring admission, 10/1 priority date for domestic and international students. Application fee: $45. Electronic applications accepted. *Expenses:* Tuition, state resident: part-time $332 per credit. Tuition, nonresident: part-time $553 per credit. *Financial support:* In 2007–08, 15 research assistantships with partial tuition reimbursements (averaging $4,592 per year), 1 teaching assistantship with tuition reimbursement (averaging $3,485 per year) were awarded; Federal Work-Study, scholarships/grants, tuition waivers (partial), and unspecified assistantships also available. Support available to part-time students. Financial award application deadline: 4/1; financial award applicants required to submit FAFSA. *Faculty research:* Health complementary therapies, motivation, group dynamics, social reasoning, stress. *Unit head:* Dr. Kristina Gorbatenko-Roth, Director, 715-232-2451, E-mail: gorbatenkok@uwstout.edu. *Application contact:* Anne E. Johnson, Graduate Student Evaluator, 715-232-1322, Fax: 715-232-2413, E-mail: johnsona@uwstout.edu.

University of Wisconsin–Whitewater, School of Graduate Studies, College of Letters and Sciences, Department of Psychology, Whitewater, WI 53190-1790. Offers school psychology (MS Ed, Ed S). Part-time and evening/weekend programs available. Postbaccalaureate distance learning degree programs offered (no on-campus study). *Students:* 21 full-time (17 women), 13 part-time (10 women); includes 3 minority (1 African American, 2 Asian Americans or Pacific Islanders). Average age 26. 21 applicants, 90% accepted, 18 enrolled. In 2007, 12 degrees awarded. *Degree requirements:* For master's, comprehensive exam or thesis. *Entrance requirements:* For master's, MAT or GRE, interview, minimum GPA of 3.0, 3 letters of recommendation. Additional exam requirements/recommendations for international students: Required—TOEFL (minimum score 550 paper-based; 213 computer-based). *Application deadline:* For fall and spring admission, 3/1 for domestic and international students. Applications are processed on a rolling basis. Application fee: $45. Electronic applications accepted. *Expenses:* Tuition, state resident: full-time $3,451; part-time $244 per credit. Tuition, nonresident: full-time $8,756; part-time $560 per credit. *Financial support:* In 2007–08, 2 research assistantships (averaging $7,000 per year) were awarded; Federal Work-Study, unspecified assistantships, and out of state fee waiver also available. Support available to part-time students. Financial award application deadline: 3/15; financial award applicants required to submit FAFSA. *Faculty research:* School violence/youth violence; anger/aggression interventions; women's mental health; pedagogy of empathy, social psychology, and personality. *Unit head:* Dr. James Larson, Coordinator, 262-472-5412, Fax: 262-472-1863, E-mail: larsonj@uww.edu. *Application contact:* Sally A. Lange, School of Graduate Studies, 262-472-1006, Fax: 262-472-5027, E-mail: gradschl@uww.edu.

University of Wyoming, Graduate School, College of Arts and Sciences, Department of Psychology, Laramie, WY 82070. Offers MA, MS, PhD. *Accreditation:* APA (one or more programs are accredited). *Faculty:* 13 full-time (4 women), 1 (woman) part-time/adjunct. *Students:* 30 full-time (20 women), 12 part-time (6 women); includes 3 minority (1 American Indian/Alaska Native, 2 Asian Americans or Pacific Islanders), 1 international. Average age 28. 18 applicants, 44% accepted, 0 enrolled. In 2007, 10 master's, 8 doctorates awarded. Terminal master's awarded for partial completion of doctoral program. *Median time to degree:* Of those who began their doctoral program in fall 1999, 13% received their degree in 8 years or less. *Degree requirements:* For master's, thesis; for doctorate, comprehensive exam, thesis/dissertation. *Entrance requirements:* For master's and doctorate, GRE General Test, GRE Subject Test, minimum GPA of 3.0. Additional exam requirements/recommendations for international students: Required—TOEFL. *Application deadline:* For fall admission, 1/15 for domestic and international students. Application fee: $50. *Financial support:* In 2007–08, 17 research assistantships with full tuition reimbursements (averaging $10,100 per year), 12 teaching assistantships with full tuition reimbursements (averaging $10,100 per year) were awarded; career-related internships or fieldwork, Federal Work-Study, and institutionally sponsored loans also available. Financial award application deadline: 3/1. *Faculty research:* Child development, health psychology, psychology and law, social psychology, mood/anxiety disorders. Total annual research expenditures: $1.1 million. *Unit head:* Dr. Narina Nunez, Chair, 307-766-6303, Fax: 307-766-2926, E-mail: narina@uwyo.edu. *Application contact:* Cheryl Hamilton, Graduate Admission Coordinator, 307-766-6303, Fax: 307-766-2926, E-mail: psyc-uw@uwyo.edu.

Utah State University, School of Graduate Studies, College of Education and Human Services, Department of Psychology, Logan, UT 84322. Offers clinical/counseling/school psychology (PhD); research and evaluation methodology (PhD); school counseling (MS); school psychology (MS). *Accreditation:* APA (one or more programs are accredited). Part-time and evening/weekend programs available. Postbaccalaureate distance learning degree programs offered (no on-campus study). Terminal master's awarded for partial completion of doctoral program. *Degree requirements:* For master's, thesis (for some programs); for doctorate, thesis/dissertation. *Entrance requirements:* For master's, GRE General Test (school psychology), MAT (school counseling), minimum GPA of 3.5; for doctorate, GRE General Test, minimum GPA of 3.5. Additional exam requirements/recommendations for international students: Required—TOEFL. *Faculty research:* Hearing loss detection in infancy, ADHD, eating disorders, domestic violence, neuropsychology, bilingual/Spanish speaking students/parents.

Valdosta State University, Graduate School, College of Education, Department of Psychology and Counseling, Valdosta, GA 31698. Offers clinical/counseling psychology (MS); industrial/organizational psychology (MS); school counseling (M Ed, Ed S); school psychology (Ed S). Part-time and evening/weekend programs available. *Faculty:* 16 full-time (2 women). *Students:* 61 full-time (48 women), 38 part-time (31 women); includes 22 minority (19 African Americans, 1 American Indian/Alaska Native, 1 Asian American or Pacific Islander, 1 Hispanic American). Average age 27. 103 applicants, 31% accepted, 22 enrolled. In 2007, 25 degrees awarded. *Degree requirements:* For master's, thesis or alternative, comprehensive written and/or oral exams; for Ed S, thesis. *Entrance requirements:* For master's and Ed S, GRE General Test or MAT. Additional exam requirements/recommendations for international students: Required—TOEFL (minimum score 523 paper-based; 193 computer-based). *Application deadline:* For fall admission, 7/1 for domestic and international students; for spring admission, 11/15 for domestic and international students. Applications are processed on a rolling basis. Application fee: $40. Electronic applications accepted. *Expenses:* Tuition, state resident: part-time $147 per hour. Tuition, nonresident: part-time $586 per hour. Required fees: $520 per semester. Tuition and fees vary according to course level, course load, campus/location and program. *Financial support:* In 2007–08, 2 students received support, including 2 research assistantships with full tuition reimbursements available (averaging $2,452 per year); institutionally sponsored loans and unspecified assistantships also available. Support available to part-time students. Financial award application deadline: 7/1; financial award applicants required to submit FAFSA. *Faculty research:* Using Bender-Gestalt to predict graphomotor dimensions of the draw-a-person test, neurobehavioral hemispheric dominance. *Unit head:* Dr. Robert Bauer, Chair, 229-333-5930, Fax: 229-259-5576, E-mail: bbauer@valdosta.edu.

Valparaiso University, Graduate Division, Department of Psychology, Valparaiso, IN 46383. Offers business management (for counseling students) (Certificate); clinical mental health counseling (MA); community counseling (MA); JD/MA. Part-time and evening/weekend programs available. *Faculty:* 7 part-time/adjunct (1 woman). *Students:* 35 full-time (25 women), 11 part-time (9 women); includes 2 minority (1 African American, 1 Hispanic American), 5 international. Average age 30. In 2007, 13 degrees awarded. *Degree requirements:* For master's, thesis or alternative, internship. *Entrance requirements:* For master's, minimum GPA of 3.0. Additional exam requirements/recommendations for international students: Required—TOEFL (minimum score 550 paper-based; 213 computer-based). *Application deadline:* For fall admission, 3/1 priority date for domestic students. Applications are processed on a rolling basis. Application fee: $30 ($50 for international students). Electronic applications accepted. *Financial support:* Career-related internships or fieldwork, traineeships, and unspecified assistantships available. Support available to part-time students. Financial award applicants required to submit FAFSA. *Faculty research:* Environmental psychology, human sexuality, racial identity development models, social psychology. *Unit head:* Dr. James Nelson, Graduate Program Director, 219-464-5443, Fax: 219-464-6878, E-mail: jim.nelson@valpo.edu. *Application contact:* Jamie Haney, Coordinator of Recruitment Activities, 219-464-5313, Fax: 219-464-5381, E-mail: jamie.haney@valpo.edu.

Vanderbilt University, Graduate School, Program in Psychological Sciences, Nashville, TN 37240-1001. Offers MA, PhD. *Accreditation:* APA (one or more programs are accredited). *Faculty:* 90 full-time (35 women). *Students:* 93 full-time (68 women); includes 14 minority (7 African Americans, 3 Asian Americans or Pacific Islanders, 4 Hispanic Americans), 17 international. Average age 27. 390 applicants, 6% accepted, 13 enrolled. In 2007, 13 master's, 7 doctorates awarded. *Degree requirements:* For doctorate, thesis/dissertation, final and qualifying exams. *Entrance requirements:* For master's, GRE General Test; for doctorate, GRE

Psychology—General

Vanderbilt University (continued)
General Test, GRE Subject Test. *Application deadline:* For fall admission, 1/15 for domestic and international students. Application fee: $0. Electronic applications accepted. *Financial support:* Fellowships with full and partial tuition reimbursements, research assistantships, teaching assistantships with full and partial tuition reimbursements, career-related internships or fieldwork, Federal Work-Study, institutionally sponsored loans, traineeships, and health care benefits available. Financial award application deadline: 1/15; financial award applicants required to submit CSS PROFILE or FAFSA. *Faculty research:* Clinical, cognitive, developmental, and social psychology; neuroscience; vision; behavior. *Unit head:* Andrew J. Tomarken, Chair, 615-322-2874, Fax: 615-343-8449, E-mail: andrew.j.tomarken@vanderbilt.edu. *Application contact:* Thomas J. Palmeri, Director of Graduate Studies, 615-322-2874, Fax: 615-343-8449, E-mail: tom.palmeri@vanderbilt.edu.

Vanderbilt University, Peabody College, Department of Psychology and Human Development, Nashville, TN 37240-1001. Offers child studies (M Ed). *Accreditation:* APA. Part-time programs available. *Faculty:* 25 full-time (13 women), 2 part-time/adjunct (0 women). *Students:* 15 full-time (12 women), 3 part-time (all women); includes 3 minority (1 African American, 1 Asian American or Pacific Islander, 1 Hispanic American). Average age 25. 18 applicants, 89% accepted, 9 enrolled. In 2007, 13 degrees awarded. *Degree requirements:* For master's, comprehensive exam, thesis optional. *Entrance requirements:* For master's, GRE General Test. Additional exam requirements/recommendations for international students: Required—TOEFL (minimum score 550 paper-based; 213 computer-based). *Application deadline:* For fall admission, 12/31 for domestic and international students; for spring admission, 11/1 for domestic and international students. Applications are processed on a rolling basis. Application fee: $0. Electronic applications accepted. *Financial support:* In 2007–08, 12 students received support, including 4 fellowships with full and partial tuition reimbursements available, 8 research assistantships with full and partial tuition reimbursements available; teaching assistantships with full and partial tuition reimbursements available, Federal Work-Study, institutionally sponsored loans, scholarships/grants, and unspecified assistantships also available. Financial award application deadline: 2/1; financial award applicants required to submit FAFSA. *Faculty research:* Cognitive, language and social development; stress, coping and emotion; quantitative methods and evaluation; clinical intervention and prevention; individual differences, disabilities and developmental psychopathology. *Unit head:* John Rieser, Acting Chair, 615-322-8141, Fax: 615-343-9494, E-mail: j.rieser@vanderbilt.edu. *Application contact:* Sharone Hall, Educational Coordinator, 615-343-4963, Fax: 615-343-9494, E-mail: sharone.k.hall@vanderbilt.edu.

Villanova University, Graduate School of Liberal Arts and Sciences, Department of Psychology, Villanova, PA 19085-1699. Offers MS. Part-time and evening/weekend programs available. *Faculty:* 8 full-time (3 women), 2 part-time/adjunct (both women). *Students:* 39 full-time (26 women); includes 2 minority (both African Americans), 1 international. Average age 25. 122 applicants, 39% accepted. In 2007, 11 degrees awarded. *Degree requirements:* For master's, thesis. *Entrance requirements:* For master's, GRE General Test, minimum GPA of 3.0. *Application deadline:* For fall admission, 8/1 for domestic and international students; for spring admission, 12/1 for domestic and international students. Applications are processed on a rolling basis. Application fee: $50. Electronic applications accepted. *Financial support:* Research assistantships, Federal Work-Study and scholarships/grants available. Financial award applicants required to submit FAFSA. *Unit head:* Dr. Thomas Toppino, Chair, 610-519-4720.

See Close-Up on page 1511.

Virginia Commonwealth University, Graduate School, College of Humanities and Sciences, Department of Psychology, Program in General Psychology, Richmond, VA 23284-9005. Offers PhD. *Students:* 27 full-time (22 women), 6 part-time (3 women); includes 6 minority (4 African Americans, 1 American Indian/Alaska Native, 1 Asian American or Pacific Islander), 2 international. 79 applicants, 14% accepted, 9 enrolled. In 2007, 5 doctorates awarded. *Degree requirements:* For doctorate, thesis/dissertation. *Entrance requirements:* For doctorate, GRE General Test. *Application deadline:* For fall admission, 2/15 for domestic students. Application fee: $50. *Expenses:* Tuition, state resident: full-time $7,224; part-time $401 per credit. Tuition, nonresident: full-time $16,072; part-time $891 per credit. Required fees: $1,679; $63 per credit. Tuition and fees vary according to campus/location. *Financial support:* Fellowships, research assistantships, teaching assistantships, Federal Work-Study, institutionally sponsored loans, and scholarships/grants available. Support available to part-time students. *Unit head:* Dr. Wendy L. Kliewer, Head, 804-828-1793. *Application contact:* Dr. J. Donelson Forsyth, Director, Graduate Programs in Psychology, 804-828-6754, Fax: 804-828-2237, E-mail: jforsyth@vcu.edu.

See Close-Up on page 457.

Virginia Polytechnic Institute and State University, Graduate School, College of Science, Department of Psychology, Blacksburg, VA 24061. Offers bio-behavioral sciences (PhD); clinical psychology (PhD); developmental psychology (PhD); industrial/organizational psychology (PhD); psychology (MS). *Accreditation:* APA (one or more programs are accredited). *Entrance requirements:* For master's and doctorate, GRE General Test. Additional exam requirements/recommendations for international students: Required—TOEFL (minimum score 550 paper-based; 213 computer-based). Electronic applications accepted. *Faculty research:* Infant development from electrophysical point of view, work motivation and personnel selection, EEG, ERP and hypnosis with reference to chronic pain, intimate violence.

Virginia State University, School of Graduate Studies, Research, and Outreach, School of Engineering, Science and Technology, Department of Psychology, Petersburg, VA 23806-0001. Offers MS. *Degree requirements:* For master's, one foreign language, thesis. *Entrance requirements:* For master's, GRE General Test.

Wake Forest University, Graduate School of Arts and Sciences, Department of Psychology, Winston-Salem, NC 27109. Offers MA. *Faculty:* 16 full-time (7 women), 4 part-time/adjunct (0 women). *Students:* 21 full-time (14 women); includes 1 minority (Asian American or Pacific Islander), 1 international. Average age 25. 123 applicants, 14% accepted, 9 enrolled. In 2007, 10 master's awarded. *Degree requirements:* For master's, one foreign language, comprehensive exam, thesis. *Entrance requirements:* For master's, GRE General Test. Additional exam requirements/recommendations for international students: Required—TOEFL (minimum score 213 computer-based; 79 iBT). *Application deadline:* For fall admission, 1/15 for domestic and international students. Application fee: $45 ($55 for international students). Electronic applications accepted. *Financial support:* In 2007–08, 19 students received support, including 4 research assistantships with full tuition reimbursements available (averaging $8,500 per year), 13 teaching assistantships with full tuition reimbursements available (averaging $8,500 per year); fellowships, scholarships/grants, tuition waivers (full), and unspecified assistantships also available. Financial award application deadline: 1/15; financial award applicants required to submit FAFSA. *Faculty research:* Developmental, social, personality, experimental, and physiological psychology. *Unit head:* Dr. Catherine Seta, Director, 336-758-4722, Fax: 336-758-4773, E-mail: seta@wfu.edu.

Walden University, Graduate Programs, School of Psychology, Minneapolis, MN 55401. Offers clinical assessment (Post-Doctoral Certificate); clinical child psychology (Post-Doctoral Certificate); clinical psychology (PhD, Post-Doctoral Certificate); counseling psychology (PhD, Post-Doctoral Certificate); general psychology (MS, PhD, Post-Doctoral Certificate); health psychology (PhD, Post-Doctoral Certificate); organizational psychology (PhD, Post-Doctoral Certificate); organizational psychology and development (MS); school psychology (PhD, Post-Doctoral Certificate); teaching online (Post-Doctoral Certificate). Part-time and evening/weekend programs available. Postbaccalaureate distance learning degree programs offered (minimal on-campus study). *Students:* 1,428 full-time (1,130 women), 1,933 part-time (1,483 women); includes 959 minority (737 African Americans, 35 American Indian/Alaska Native, 53 Asian Americans or Pacific Islanders, 134 Hispanic Americans), 39 international. Average age 40. 1,254 applicants, 75% accepted, 548 enrolled. In 2007, 182 master's, 43 doctorates awarded. *Degree requirements:* For master's, thesis; for doctorate, thesis/dissertation, brief dispersed residency sessions. *Entrance requirements:* For master's, minimum GPA of 3.0; for doctorate, 3 years of professional experience, master's degree; for Post-Doctoral Certificate, PhD in related field, 3 years of professional experience. Additional exam requirements/recommendations for international students: Required—TOEFL (minimum score 550 paper-based; 213 computer-based), IELTS (minimum score 7). *Application deadline:* For fall admission, 8/15 priority date for domestic and international students; for winter admission, 11/15 priority date for domestic and international students; for spring admission, 12/15 priority date for domestic and international students. Applications are processed on a rolling basis. Application fee: $50. Electronic applications accepted. *Financial support:* Fellowships with partial tuition reimbursements, career-related internships or fieldwork, Federal Work-Study, institutionally sponsored loans, scholarships/grants, tuition waivers (partial), and unspecified assistantships available. Support available to part-time students. Financial award applicants required to submit FAFSA. *Faculty research:* Clinical psychology, organizational psychology, forensic psychology, group processes, educational psychology. *Unit head:* Dr. Nina Nabors, Associate Dean, 800-925-3368. *Application contact:* 866-4-WALDEN, Fax: 410-843-8780, E-mail: request@waldenu.edu.

Washburn University, College of Arts and Sciences, Department of Psychology, Topeka, KS 66621. Offers clinical psychology (MA). Part-time programs available. *Faculty:* 8 full-time (5 women), 6 part-time/adjunct (4 women). *Students:* 27 full-time (18 women), 4 part-time (2 women). Average age 25. In 2007, 4 degrees awarded. *Degree requirements:* For master's, thesis. *Entrance requirements:* For master's, GRE General Test, 15 hours of course work in psychology. *Application deadline:* For fall admission, 3/15 for domestic students; for spring admission, 12/1 for domestic students. Application fee: $0. Electronic applications accepted. *Expenses:* Tuition, state resident: full-time $4,590; part-time $255 per credit hour. Tuition, nonresident: full-time $9,360; part-time $520 per credit hour. Required fees: $86; $43 per semester. Tuition and fees vary according to program. *Financial support:* Application deadline: 2/15; *Faculty research:* Animal behavior, correctional psychology, children's social development, metacognition and metamemory, psychology of exercise, Gibsonian Ecological Psychology, treatment of anxiety disorders. *Unit head:* Dr. David Provorse, Chair, 785-670-1565, Fax: 785-670-1004, E-mail: dave.provorse@washburn.edu.

Washington College, Graduate Programs, Department of Psychology, Chestertown, MD 21620-1197. Offers MA. Part-time and evening/weekend programs available. *Entrance requirements:* For master's, GRE General Test.

Washington State University, Graduate School, College of Liberal Arts, Department of Psychology, Pullman, WA 99164. Offers clinical psychology (PhD); experimental psychology (PhD); psychology (MS). *Accreditation:* APA (one or more programs are accredited). *Faculty:* 28. *Students:* 58 full-time (37 women), 2 part-time (1 woman); includes 9 minority (1 African American, 1 Asian American or Pacific Islander, 7 Hispanic Americans), 7 international. Average age 29. 238 applicants, 6% accepted, 12 enrolled. In 2007, 4 master's, 8 doctorates awarded. *Degree requirements:* For master's, comprehensive exam (for some programs), thesis (for some programs), oral exam; for doctorate, comprehensive exam, thesis/dissertation, oral exam, written exam. *Entrance requirements:* For master's, GRE General Test, minimum GPA of 3.0, research or clinical experience, 3 letters of recommendation; for doctorate, GRE General Test, minimum GPA of 3.0, 1 course in statistics and research methodology, research or clinical experience, 3 letters of recommendation. *Application deadline:* For fall admission, 1/1 for domestic students. Applications are processed on a rolling basis. Application fee: $50. *Financial support:* In 2007–08, 47 students received support, including 5 research assistantships with full and partial tuition reimbursements available (averaging $13,917 per year), 39 teaching assistantships with full and partial tuition reimbursements available (averaging $13,056 per year); fellowships, career-related internships or fieldwork, Federal Work-Study, institutionally sponsored loans, and unspecified assistantships also available. Financial award application deadline: 4/1; financial award applicants required to submit FAFSA. *Faculty research:* Childhood conduct disorders, etiology of depression, treatment of reading disorders, applied behavior analysis, selective attention. Total annual research expenditures: $240,986. *Unit head:* Dr. John Hinson, Chair, 509-335-2631, E-mail: hinson@mail.wsu.edu. *Application contact:* Graduate School Admissions, 800-GRADWSU, Fax: 509-335-16949, E-mail: gradsch@wsu.edu.

Washington University in St. Louis, Graduate School of Arts and Sciences, Department of Philosophy, Program in Philosophy/Neuroscience/Psychology, St. Louis, MO 63130-4899. Offers PhD. *Degree requirements:* For doctorate, thesis/dissertation. *Entrance requirements:* For doctorate, GRE General Test, sample of written work. Electronic applications accepted.

Washington University in St. Louis, Graduate School of Arts and Sciences, Department of Psychology, St. Louis, MO 63130-4899. Offers clinical psychology (PhD); general experimental psychology (MA, PhD); social psychology (MA, PhD). *Accreditation:* APA (one or more programs are accredited). Terminal master's awarded for partial completion of doctoral program. *Degree requirements:* For master's, thesis or alternative; for doctorate, thesis/dissertation. *Entrance requirements:* For master's and doctorate, GRE General Test. Electronic applications accepted.

Wayne State University, College of Liberal Arts and Sciences, Department of Psychology, Detroit, MI 48202. Offers human development (MA); psychology (MA, MS, PhD), including behavioral and cognitive neuroscience (PhD), clinical psychology (PhD), cognitive and social psychology (PhD), industrial/organizational psychology (PhD), psychology (MA, MS). *Accreditation:* APA (one or more programs are accredited). *Faculty:* 22 full-time (8 women). *Students:* 106 full-time (81 women), 48 part-time (38 women); includes 17 minority (9 African Americans, 4 Asian Americans or Pacific Islanders, 4 Hispanic Americans), 15 international. Average age 27. 234 applicants, 18% accepted, 32 enrolled. In 2007, 16 master's, 12 doctorates awarded. *Degree requirements:* For doctorate, thesis/dissertation. *Entrance requirements:* For doctorate, GRE General Test, GRE Subject Test, personal statement; letters of recommendation. Additional exam requirements/recommendations for international students: Required—TOEFL (minimum score 550 paper-based; 213 computer-based); Recommended—TWE (minimum score 6). *Application deadline:* For fall admission, 6/1 for international students; for winter admission, 10/1 for international students; for spring admission, 2/1 for international students. Applications are processed on a rolling basis. Application fee: $30 ($50 for international students). Electronic applications accepted. *Expenses:* Tuition, state resident: part-time $403 per credit hour. Tuition, nonresident: part-time $890 per credit hour. *Financial support:* In 2007–08, 5 fellowships with tuition reimbursements (averaging $15,001 per year), 14 research assistantships with tuition reimbursements (averaging $15,053 per year), 47 teaching assistantships with tuition reimbursements (averaging $13,715 per year) were awarded; career-related internships or fieldwork also available. Financial award application deadline: 2/1. *Faculty research:* Clinical neuropsychology; high risk factors in development; human aging and neuroscience; industrial/organizational psychology; health psychology. Total annual research expenditures: $172,430. *Unit head:* Douglas Whitman, Chair, 313-577-2803, Fax: 313-577-7636, E-mail: dwhitman@wayne.edu. *Application contact:* Dr. Melissa Kaplan-Estrin, Graduate Director, 313-577-2824, Fax: 313-577-7636, E-mail: mkestrin@sun.science.wayne.edu.

Wesleyan University, Graduate Programs, Department of Psychology, Middletown, CT 06459-0260. Offers MA. *Faculty:* 12 full-time (4 women), 3 part-time/adjunct (1 woman). *Students:* 3 full-time (all women); includes 1 minority (African American), 1 international. In 2007, 4 degrees awarded. *Degree requirements:* For master's, thesis. *Entrance requirements:* For master's, GRE General Test, GRE Subject Test, MAT. Additional exam requirements/recommendations for international students: Required—TOEFL. *Application deadline:* For fall admission, 3/1 for domestic and international students. Applications are processed on a rolling basis. Application fee: $0. Electronic applications accepted. *Financial support:* In 2007–08, 1 research assistantship with tuition reimbursement, 3 teaching assistantships with tuition reimbursements were awarded. Financial award application deadline: 4/15. *Faculty research:* Human perception and cognition; cognitive, social, and moral development; history of psychology; biopsychology; psycholinguistics. *Unit head:* Dr. Ruth Striegel-Moore, Chair, 876-685-2868,

E-mail: jseamon@wesleyan.edu. *Application contact:* Tina Velasquez-Lange, Administrative Assistant, 860-685-2342, Fax: 860-685-2761, E-mail: tvelasquez@wesleyan.edu.

West Chester University of Pennsylvania, Office of Graduate Studies and Extended Education, College of Arts and Sciences, Department of Psychology, West Chester, PA 19383. Offers clinical mental health (Certificate); clinical psychology (MA); general psychology (MA); industrial organizational psychology (MA). Part-time and evening/weekend programs available. *Students:* 61 full-time (44 women), 29 part-time (18 women); includes 6 minority (4 African Americans, 1 Asian American or Pacific Islander, 1 Hispanic American), 2 international. Average age 27. 177 applicants, 68% accepted, 37 enrolled. In 2007, 22 degrees awarded. *Degree requirements:* For master's, comprehensive exam, thesis (for some programs). *Entrance requirements:* For master's, GRE General Test or MAT, interview. Additional exam requirements/recommendations for international students: Required—TOEFL (minimum score 550 paper-based; 213 computer-based; 80 iBT). *Application deadline:* For fall admission, 4/15 priority date for domestic students; for spring admission, 10/15 for domestic students. Applications are processed on a rolling basis. Application fee: $35. *Expenses:* Tuition, state resident: part-time $345 per credit. Tuition, nonresident: part-time $552 per credit. Tuition and fees vary according to course load. *Financial support:* In 2007–08, 13 research assistantships with full and partial tuition reimbursements (averaging $5,000 per year) were awarded; unspecified assistantships also available. Support available to part-time students. Financial award application deadline: 2/15; financial award applicants required to submit FAFSA. *Faculty research:* Animal learning and cognition. *Unit head:* Dr. Sandra Kerr, Chair, 610-436-2945, E-mail: skerr@wcupa.edu. *Application contact:* Dr. Loretta Rieser-Danner, Graduate Coordinator, 610-436-3106, E-mail: lriserdanner@wcupa.edu.

Western Carolina University, Graduate School, College of Education and Allied Professions, Department of Psychology, Cullowhee, NC 28723. Offers general psychology (MA); school psychology (MA). Part-time programs available. *Faculty:* 20 full-time (6 women). *Students:* 41 full-time (28 women), 1 part-time; includes 3 minority (2 African Americans, 1 Asian American or Pacific Islander). Average age 25. 60 applicants, 45% accepted, 13 enrolled. In 2007, 10 degrees awarded. *Degree requirements:* For master's, comprehensive exam, thesis. *Entrance requirements:* For master's, GRE General Test, appropriate undergraduate, interview, 3 letters of recommendation, personal statement. Additional exam requirements/recommendations for international students: Required—TOEFL (minimum score 550 paper-based; 270 computer-based; 79 iBT). *Application deadline:* For fall admission, 2/1 for domestic students. Application fee: $40. *Expenses:* Tuition, state resident: full-time $2,314. Tuition, nonresident: full-time $11,899. Required fees: $2,033. Tuition and fees vary according to course load. *Financial support:* In 2007–08, 32 students received support, including 32 teaching assistantships with full and partial tuition reimbursements available (averaging $7,000 per year); fellowships, research assistantships with full and partial tuition reimbursements available, career-related internships or fieldwork, institutionally sponsored loans, scholarships/grants, and unspecified assistantships also available. Financial award application deadline: 3/31; financial award applicants required to submit FAFSA. *Faculty research:* Five-factor model of personality, evolutionary psychology, stress and worry, body image and physical attractiveness, moral decision-making, memory, learning styles. *Unit head:* Dr. David McCord, Head, 828-227-7361, Fax: 828-227-7005, E-mail: mccord@email.wcu.edu. *Application contact:* Admissions Specialist for Psychology, 828-227-7398, Fax: 828-227-7480, E-mail: gradsch@email.wcu.edu.

Western Illinois University, School of Graduate Studies, College of Arts and Sciences, Department of Psychology, Macomb, IL 61455-1390. Offers clinical/community mental health (MS); general psychology (MS); psychology (MS, SSP); school psychology (SSP). Part-time programs available. *Students:* 40 full-time (24 women), 18 part-time (10 women); includes 1 minority (Asian American or Pacific Islander), 1 international. Average age 25. 78 applicants, 35% accepted. In 2007, 15 master's, 8 other advanced degrees awarded. *Degree requirements:* For master's, comprehensive exam (for some programs), thesis or alternative. *Entrance requirements:* For master's and SSP, GRE General Test. Additional exam requirements/recommendations for international students: Required—TOEFL (minimum score 550 paper-based; 213 computer-based; 80 iBT). *Application deadline:* Applications are processed on a rolling basis. Application fee: $30. Electronic applications accepted. *Expenses:* Tuition, state resident: part-time $217 per credit hour. Tuition, nonresident: part-time $433 per credit hour. Required fees: $54 per credit hour. *Financial support:* In 2007–08, 38 students received support, including 38 research assistantships with full tuition reimbursements available (averaging $6,800 per year). Financial award applicants required to submit FAFSA. *Unit head:* Dr. Virginia Diehl, Chairperson, 309-298-1593. *Application contact:* Dr. Barbara Baily, Director of Graduate Studies/Associate Provost, 309-298-1806, Fax: 309-298-2345, E-mail: grad-office@wiu.edu.

Western Kentucky University, Graduate Studies, College of Education and Behavioral Sciences, Department of Psychology, Bowling Green, KY 42101. Offers psychology (MA); school psychology (Ed S). *Degree requirements:* For master's, comprehensive exam, thesis (for some programs); for Ed S, thesis, oral exam. *Entrance requirements:* For master's, GRE General Test; for Ed S, GRE General Test, minimum GPA of 3.5. Additional exam requirements/recommendations for international students: Required—TOEFL (minimum score 555 paper-based; 213 computer-based; 79 iBT). *Faculty research:* Neural regeneration, enhancing mobility in the elderly, improvement in visual processing in older adults, lifespan development.

Western Michigan University, Graduate College, College of Arts and Sciences, Department of Psychology, Kalamazoo, MI 49008-5202. Offers applied behavior analysis (MA, PhD); clinical psychology (MA, PhD); experimental analysis of behavior (PhD); experimental psychology (MA); industrial/organizational psychology (MA); school psychology (PhD, Ed S). *Accreditation:* APA (one or more programs are accredited). *Degree requirements:* For master's, variable foreign language requirement, thesis, oral exams; for doctorate, 2 foreign languages, comprehensive exam, thesis/dissertation, oral exams; for Ed S, thesis, oral exams. *Entrance requirements:* For master's, doctorate, and Ed S, GRE General Test.

Western Washington University, Graduate School, College of Humanities and Social Sciences, Department of Psychology, Bellingham, WA 98225-5996. Offers experimental psychology (MS); mental health counseling (MS); school counseling (M Ed). *Accreditation:* ACA (one or more programs are accredited). *Faculty:* 31. *Degree requirements:* For master's, comprehensive exam, thesis (for some programs). *Entrance requirements:* For master's, GRE General Test, minimum GPA of 3.0 in last 60 semester hours or last 90 quarter hours. Additional exam requirements/recommendations for international students: Required—TOEFL (minimum score 567 paper-based; 227 computer-based). *Application deadline:* For fall admission, 2/1 priority date for domestic students; for winter admission, 10/1 for domestic students; for spring admission, 2/1 for domestic students. Application fee: $50. *Expenses:* Tuition, state resident: part-time $208 per credit. Tuition, nonresident: part-time $541 per credit. Required fees: $241 per quarter. One-time fee: $250 part-time. *Financial support:* In 2007–08, teaching assistantships with partial tuition reimbursements (averaging $9,339 per year); career-related internships or fieldwork, Federal Work-Study, institutionally sponsored loans, scholarships/grants, tuition waivers (partial), and unspecified assistantships also available. Support available to part-time students. Financial award application deadline: 2/15; financial award applicants required to submit FAFSA. *Faculty research:* Social, cognitive, behavioral neuroscience, counseling/clinical, developmental. *Unit head:* Dr. Dale Dinnel, Chair, 360-650-352, E-mail: dale.dinnel@wwu.edu. *Application contact:* Lynn Graham, Graduate Coordinator, 360-650-3184, E-mail: lynn.graham@wwu.edu.

Westfield State College, Division of Graduate and Continuing Education, Department of Psychology, Westfield, MA 01086. Offers mental health counseling (MA); school guidance (MA). Part-time and evening/weekend programs available. *Degree requirements:* For master's, comprehensive exam. *Entrance requirements:* For master's, GRE General Test, MAT, minimum undergraduate GPA of 2.7.

West Texas A&M University, College of Education and Social Sciences, Department of Behavioral Sciences, Canyon, TX 79016-0001. Offers psychology (MA). Part-time and evening/weekend programs available. *Degree requirements:* For master's, comprehensive exam, thesis optional. *Entrance requirements:* For master's, GRE General Test, 3 letters of recommendation; interview; minimum GPA of 3.25 in psychology, 3.0 overall. Additional exam requirements/recommendations for international students: Required—TOEFL (minimum score 550 paper-based). Electronic applications accepted. *Faculty research:* Application of sociological principles to historical and contemporary analyses of social systems.

West Virginia University, Eberly College of Arts and Sciences, Department of Psychology, Morgantown, WV 26506. Offers behavior analysis (PhD); clinical psychology (MA, PhD); development psychology (PhD); psychology (MS). *Accreditation:* APA (one or more programs are accredited). Part-time programs available. *Faculty:* 21 full-time (10 women), 2 part-time/adjunct (both women). *Students:* 67 full-time (41 women), 6 part-time (all women); includes 4 minority (2 African Americans, 1 Asian American or Pacific Islander, 1 Hispanic American), 8 international. Average age 27. 195 applicants, 10% accepted, 20 enrolled. In 2007, 7 master's, 12 doctorates awarded. Terminal master's awarded for partial completion of doctoral program. *Degree requirements:* For master's, thesis optional; for doctorate, comprehensive exam, thesis/dissertation. *Entrance requirements:* For master's and doctorate, GRE General Test, minimum GPA of 3.0. Additional exam requirements/recommendations for international students: Required—TOEFL. *Application deadline:* For fall admission, 1/15 for domestic students. Application fee: $45. *Expenses:* Tuition, state resident: full-time $5,196; part-time $292 per credit hour. Tuition, nonresident: full-time $15,064; part-time $840 per credit hour. Tuition and fees vary according to program. *Financial support:* In 2007–08, 73 students received support, including 28 research assistantships (averaging $13,000 per year), 34 teaching assistantships (averaging $10,000 per year); fellowships, career-related internships or fieldwork, Federal Work-Study, institutionally sponsored loans, and tuition waivers (full and partial) also available. Financial award application deadline: 1/15; financial award applicants required to submit FAFSA. *Faculty research:* Adult and child clinical psychology, behavioral assessment and therapy, child and adolescent behavior, life span development, experimental and applied behavior analysis. Total annual research expenditures: $415,123. *Unit head:* Dr. Michael T. Perone, Chair, 304-293-2001 Ext. 31604, Fax: 304-293-6606, E-mail: michael.perone@mail.wvu.edu. *Application contact:* Dr. Barry Edelstein, Director, Graduate Training, 304-293-2001 Ext. 31661, Fax: 304-293-6606, E-mail: barry.edelstein@mail.wvu.edu.

Wheaton College, Graduate School, Department of Psychology, Wheaton, IL 60187-5593. Offers clinical psychology (MA, Psy D); counseling ministries (MA). *Accreditation:* APA (one or more programs are accredited). *Faculty:* 18 full-time (9 women), 10 part-time/adjunct (3 women). *Students:* 141. 159 applicants, 52% accepted, 54 enrolled. In 2007, 44 master's, 13 doctorates awarded. Terminal master's awarded for partial completion of doctoral program. *Degree requirements:* For master's, thesis or alternative; for doctorate, thesis/dissertation, internship. *Entrance requirements:* For master's, GRE General Test, 18 hours of course work in psychology; for doctorate, GRE General Test. *Financial support:* In 2007–08, 3 research assistantships (averaging $4,800 per year) were awarded; career-related internships or fieldwork, Federal Work-Study, scholarships/grants, and unspecified assistantships also available. Financial award application deadline: 6/1; financial award applicants required to submit FAFSA. *Unit head:* Dr. Robert Gregory, Chair, 630-752-7053. *Application contact:* Julie A. Huebner, Director of Graduate Admissions, 630-752-5195, Fax: 630-752-5935, E-mail: gradadm@wheaton.edu.

Wichita State University, Graduate School, Fairmount College of Liberal Arts and Sciences, Department of Psychology, Wichita, KS 67260. Offers community/clinical psychology (PhD); human factors (PhD); psychology (MA). *Accreditation:* APA. Part-time programs available. *Degree requirements:* For doctorate, thesis/dissertation. *Entrance requirements:* For doctorate, GRE. Additional exam requirements/recommendations for international students: Required—TOEFL. Electronic applications accepted. *Faculty research:* Behavioral evolution, women and alcohol, behavioral medicine, delinquency prevention.

Widener University, School of Human Service Professions, Institute for Graduate Clinical Psychology, Law-Psychology Program, Chester, PA 19013-5792. Offers JD/Psy D. *Faculty:* 15 full-time (6 women), 18 part-time/adjunct (10 women). *Students:* 17 full-time (11 women); includes 2 minority (1 American Indian/Alaska Native, 1 Asian American or Pacific Islander), 1 international. Average age 23. 21 applicants, 19% accepted. *Application deadline:* For fall admission, 2/1 for domestic students. Applications are processed on a rolling basis. Application fee: $60. Electronic applications accepted. *Expenses:* Tuition: Part-time $570 per credit. Tuition and fees vary according to course load and program. *Financial support:* In 2007–08, 12 students received support; research assistantships, career-related internships or fieldwork, Federal Work-Study, institutionally sponsored loans, and scholarships/grants available. Financial award application deadline: 5/31. *Unit head:* Dr. Amiram Elwork, Director, 610-499-1206, Fax: 610-499-4625, E-mail: amiram.elwork@widener.edu. *Application contact:* Maureen A. Brennan, Admissions Coordinator, 610-499-1206, Fax: 610-499-4625, E-mail: maureen.a.brennan@widener.edu.

See Close-Up on page 1513.

Wilfrid Laurier University, Faculty of Graduate Studies, Faculty of Science, Department of Psychology, Waterloo, ON N2L 3C5, Canada. Offers brain and cognition (M Sc, PhD); community psychology (MA, PhD); social and developmental psychology (MA, PhD). *Faculty:* 32 full-time, 3 part-time/adjunct. *Students:* 61 full-time, 4 part-time. 129 applicants, 27% accepted, 27 enrolled. In 2007, 3 degrees awarded. *Degree requirements:* For master's, thesis; for doctorate, thesis/dissertation. *Entrance requirements:* For master's, honors BA or the equivalent in psychology, minimum B average in undergraduate course work, GRE (General Test); for doctorate, master's degree, minimum A- average, GRE (General Test). Additional exam requirements/recommendations for international students: Required—TOEFL (minimum score 230 computer-based; 89 iBT). *Application deadline:* For fall admission, 2/1 priority date for domestic students. Application fee: $75. Electronic applications accepted. *Financial support:* Fellowships, research assistantships, teaching assistantships available. *Faculty research:* Brain and cognition, community psychology, social and developmental psychology. *Unit head:* Dr. Mark Pancer, Chairperson, 519-884-1970 Ext. 3149. *Application contact:* Jennifer Poppe, Student Contact, 519-884-0710 Ext. 3536, Fax: 519-884-1020, E-mail: gradstudies@wlu.ca.

William Carey University, School of Psychology and Counseling, Hattiesburg, MS 39401-5499. Offers counseling psychology (MS). Part-time programs available. *Entrance requirements:* For master's, GRE, PRAXIS, MAT, minimum GPA of 2.5. Additional exam requirements/recommendations for international students: Required—TOEFL (minimum score 550 paper-based; 213 computer-based). Expenses: Contact institution. *Faculty research:* Addiction prevention, psychometric measurement, crisis counseling, gerontology.

Winthrop University, College of Arts and Sciences, Department of Psychology, Rock Hill, SC 29733. Offers MS, SSP. *Faculty:* 6 full-time (2 women), 6 part-time/adjunct (5 women). *Students:* 28 full-time (27 women), 3 part-time (all women); includes 5 minority (3 African Americans, 2 Hispanic Americans). Average age 21. In 2007, 8 master's, 10 other advanced degrees awarded. *Degree requirements:* For master's and SSP, comprehensive exam. *Entrance requirements:* For master's, GRE General Test, interview, minimum GPA of 3.0, 3 letters of recommendation, 15 hours of psychology courses in specified subject areas. *Application deadline:* For fall admission, 2/15 priority date for domestic students. Application fee: $50. Electronic applications accepted. *Expenses:* Tuition, state resident: full-time $9,834; part-time $412 per credit hour. Tuition, nonresident: full-time $18,280; part-time $763 per credit hour. *Financial support:* In 2007–08, 23 research assistantships with full tuition reimbursements (averaging $3,600 per year) were awarded; career-related internships or fieldwork, Federal Work-Study, scholarships/grants, and unspecified assistantships also available. Support available to part-time students. Financial award application deadline: 2/1; financial award applicants required to submit FAFSA. *Unit head:* Dr. Joe Prus, Chair, 803-323-2117, E-mail: prusj@winthrop.edu. *Application contact:* 800-411-7041, Fax: 803-323-2292, E-mail: graduatestu@winthrop.edu.

Wisconsin School of Professional Psychology, Program in Clinical Psychology, Milwaukee, WI 53225-4960. Offers MA, Psy D. *Accreditation:* APA. Part-time and evening/weekend

Psychology—General

Wisconsin School of Professional Psychology (continued)

programs available. *Faculty:* 3 full-time (all women), 32 part-time/adjunct (13 women). *Students:* 23 full-time (20 women), 39 part-time (31 women); includes 7 minority (6 African Americans, 1 Asian American or Pacific Islander). Average age 38. 48 applicants, 21% accepted. In 2007, 11 master's, 3 doctorates awarded. Terminal master's awarded for partial completion of doctoral program. *Median time to degree:* Of those who began their doctoral program in fall 1999, 90% received their degree in 8 years or less. *Degree requirements:* For master's, candidacy exam, 500 hours of supervised clinical practica; for doctorate, thesis/dissertation, 1 year clinical intern and practicum experience (2000 hrs), candidacy and clinical exams. *Entrance requirements:* For master's, GRE General Test, GRE Subject Test, bachelor's degree in psychology, writing sample; for doctorate, GRE General Test, GRE Subject Test, master's degree in clinical psychology or equivalent, writing sample. *Application deadline:* For fall admission, 4/15 priority date for domestic students; for spring admission, 10/15 priority date for domestic students. Applications are processed on a rolling basis. Application fee: $75. *Financial support:* In 2007–08, 6 students received support. Scholarships/grants and clinical service assistantships, library aid assistantships available. Support available to part-time students. *Faculty research:* Violence prevention, psychology of women, forensic psychology, custody evaluation, aging, harm reduction in AODA. *Application contact:* Sheri Lindgren, Assistant to the President, 414-464-9777, Fax: 414-358-5590, E-mail: admissions@wspp.edu.

Wright Institute, Program in Clinical Psychology, Berkeley, CA 94704-1796. Offers Psy D. *Accreditation:* APA. *Degree requirements:* For doctorate, thesis/dissertation. *Entrance requirements:* Additional exam requirements/recommendations for international students: Required—TOEFL (minimum score 600 paper-based). Electronic applications accepted.

Wright State University, School of Graduate Studies, College of Liberal Arts, Program in Applied Behavioral Science, Dayton, OH 45435. Offers criminal justice and social problems (MA); international and comparative politics (MA). *Degree requirements:* For master's, thesis optional. *Entrance requirements:* Additional exam requirements/recommendations for international students: Required—TOEFL. *Faculty research:* Training and development, criminal justice and social problems, community systems, human factors, industrial/organizational psychology.

Wright State University, School of Graduate Studies, College of Science and Mathematics, Department of Psychology, Dayton, OH 45435. Offers human factors and industrial/organizational psychology (MS, PhD). *Degree requirements:* For master's, thesis; for doctorate, thesis/dissertation. *Entrance requirements:* For master's, GRE General Test. Additional exam requirements/recommendations for international students: Required—TOEFL.

Wright State University, School of Professional Psychology, Dayton, OH 45435. Offers clinical psychology (Psy D). *Accreditation:* APA. *Degree requirements:* For doctorate, thesis/dissertation. *Entrance requirements:* For doctorate, GRE General Test, GRE Subject Test. Additional exam requirements/recommendations for international students: Required—TOEFL. Expenses: Contact institution.

Xavier University, College of Social Sciences, Health and Education, Department of Psychology, Cincinnati, OH 45207. Offers clinical psychology (Psy D); psychology (MA), including general experimental, industrial-organizational. *Accreditation:* APA (one or more programs are accredited). *Faculty:* 16 full-time (8 women), 10 part-time/adjunct (5 women). *Students:* 83 full-time (62 women), 27 part-time (20 women); includes 9 minority (4 African Americans, 4 Asian Americans or Pacific Islanders, 1 Hispanic American), 2 international. Average age 29. 275 applicants, 28% accepted, 27 enrolled. In 2007, 27 master's, 12 doctorates awarded. Terminal master's awarded for partial completion of doctoral program. *Median time to degree:* Of those who began their doctoral program in fall 1999, 100% received their degree in 8 years or less. *Degree requirements:* For master's, one foreign language, comprehensive exam, thesis, internship; for doctorate, one foreign language, comprehensive exam, thesis/dissertation, internship, practicum. *Entrance requirements:* For master's, GRE, minimum GPA of 3.0, 18 hours of course work in psychology; for doctorate, GRE, 18 hours of course work in psychology or a master's degree in clinical psychology, minimum GPA of 3.0. Additional exam requirements/recommendations for international students: Required—TOEFL (minimum score 550 paper-based; 213 computer-based). *Application deadline:* For fall admission, 1/15 priority date for domestic students. Application fee: $35. Electronic applications accepted. *Expenses:* Contact institution. *Financial support:* In 2007–08, 50 students received support, including 16 research assistantships with partial tuition reimbursements available, 4 teaching assistantships with partial tuition reimbursements available; career-related internships or fieldwork, traineeships, health care benefits, and unspecified assistantships also available. Financial award application deadline: 3/1; financial award applicants required to submit FAFSA. *Faculty research:* Cognitive development in children, weight management, psychodiagnostics, psychotherapy, gerontology I-O psychology. *Unit head:* Dr. Christine M. Dacey, Chair, 513-745-3533, Fax: 513-745-3327, E-mail: dacey@xavier.edu. *Application contact:* Margaret Maybury, Assistant Director-Enrollment and Student Services, 513-745-1053, Fax: 513-745-3327, E-mail: maybury@xavier.edu.

Yale University, Graduate School of Arts and Sciences, Department of Psychology, New Haven, CT 06520. Offers PhD. *Accreditation:* APA. *Degree requirements:* For doctorate, thesis/dissertation. *Entrance requirements:* For doctorate, GRE General Test.

Yeshiva University, Ferkauf Graduate School of Psychology, New York, NY 10033-3201. Offers MA, PhD, Psy D. *Accreditation:* APA (one or more programs are accredited). Part-time programs available. *Degree requirements:* For doctorate, comprehensive exam, thesis/dissertation. *Entrance requirements:* For master's and doctorate, GRE General Test.

York University, Faculty of Graduate Studies, Faculty of Health, Program in Psychology, Toronto, ON M3J 1P3, Canada. Offers MA, PhD. *Accreditation:* APA (one or more programs are accredited). Part-time programs available. *Degree requirements:* For master's, thesis, practicum; for doctorate, thesis/dissertation, practicum. *Entrance requirements:* For master's, GRE. Electronic applications accepted.

Addictions/Substance Abuse Counseling

Adler School of Professional Psychology, Programs in Psychology, Chicago, IL 60601-7203. Offers art therapy (Certificate); clinical hypnosis (Certificate); clinical psychology (Psy D); counseling psychology (MACP); counseling psychology/art therapy (MACAT); gerontology (MAGP); marriage and family counseling (MAMFC); marriage and family therapy (Certificate); organizational psychology (MAO); substance abuse counseling (MASAC, Certificate); Psy D/Certificate; Psy D/MACAT; Psy D/MACP; Psy D/MAMFC; Psy D/MASAC. *Accreditation:* APA. Part-time and evening/weekend programs available. Terminal master's awarded for partial completion of doctoral program. *Degree requirements:* For master's, thesis or alternative, oral exam, practicum; for doctorate, thesis/dissertation, clinical exam, internship, oral exam, practicum, written qualifying exam. *Entrance requirements:* For master's, 12 semester hours in psychology, minimum GPA of 3.0; for doctorate, 18 semester hours in psychology, minimum GPA of 3.25; for Certificate, appropriate master's or doctoral degree.

See Close-Up on page 1363.

Alliant International University–Los Angeles, California School of Professional Psychology, Program in Marital and Family Therapy, Alhambra, CA 91803-1360. Offers biofeedback (MA); chemical dependency (MA); gerontology (MA); Latin American family therapy (MA). *Accreditation:* AAMFT/COAMFTE.

See Close-Up on page 1373.

Argosy University, Hawai'i, College of Psychology and Behavioral Sciences, Program in Substance Abuse Counseling, Honolulu, HI 96813. Offers Certificate.

See Close-Up on page 1385.

Capella University, School of Human Services, Minneapolis, MN 55402. Offers addictions counseling (Certificate); counseling studies (MS, PhD); criminal justice (MS, PhD, Certificate); diversity studies (Certificate); general human services (MS, PhD); health care administration (MS, PhD, Certificate); management of nonprofit agencies (MS, PhD, Certificate); marital, couple and family counseling/therapy (MS); marriage and family services (Certificate); mental health counseling (MS); professional counseling (Certificate); social and community services (MS, PhD, Certificate). Part-time and evening/weekend programs available. Postbaccalaureate distance learning degree programs offered (minimal on-campus study). Terminal master's awarded for partial completion of doctoral program. *Degree requirements:* For master's, thesis optional, integrative project; for doctorate, comprehensive exam, thesis/dissertation. *Entrance requirements:* Additional exam requirements/recommendations for international students: Required—TOEFL (minimum score 550 paper-based; 213 computer-based), TWE (minimum score 4). Electronic applications accepted. *Faculty research:* Compulsive and addictive behaviors, substance abuse, assessment of psychopathology and neuropsychology.

The College of New Jersey, Graduate Division, School of Education, Department of Counselor Education, Program in Community Counseling: Substance Abuse and Addiction Specialization, Ewing, NJ 08628. Offers MA, Certificate. *Students:* 1 (woman) full-time, 6 part-time (all women). 6 applicants, 50% accepted. In 2007, 4 degrees awarded. *Degree requirements:* For master's, comprehensive exam. *Entrance requirements:* For master's, GRE, minimum GPA of 3.0 in field or 2.75 overall; for Certificate, M Ed. Additional exam requirements/recommendations for international students: Required—TOEFL. *Application deadline:* For fall admission, 4/15 for domestic students; for spring admission, 10/15 for domestic students. Application fee: $60. Electronic applications accepted. *Financial support:* Application deadline: 5/1. *Application contact:* Susan L. Hydro, Office of Graduate Studies, Assistant Dean, 609-771-2300, Fax: 609-637-5105, E-mail: graduate@tcnj.edu.

College of St. Joseph, Graduate Programs, Division of Psychology and Human Services, Program in Alcohol and Substance Abuse Counseling, Rutland, VT 05701-3899. Offers MS. Part-time programs available. *Faculty:* 4 full-time (1 woman), 8 part-time/adjunct (4 women). *Students:* 1 full-time (0 women), 1 part-time. 2 applicants, 100% accepted, 1 enrolled. *Entrance requirements:* For master's, 2 letters of reference, interview. *Application deadline:* Applications are processed on a rolling basis. Application fee: $35. Electronic applications accepted. *Expenses:* Tuition: Full-time $12,000; part-time $325 per credit. Required fees: $45 per semester. *Financial support:* Application deadline: 3/1. *Application contact:* Tracy Gallipo, Director of Admissions, 802-773-5900 Ext. 3262, Fax: 802-773-5900, E-mail: tracygallipo@csj.edu.

The College of William and Mary, School of Education, Program in Counselor Education, Williamsburg, VA 23187-8795. Offers community and addictions counseling (M Ed); community counseling (M Ed); educational counseling (PhD); family counseling (M Ed); school counseling (M Ed). *Accreditation:* ACA; NCATE. Part-time and evening/weekend programs available. *Faculty:* 5 full-time (2 women), 5 part-time/adjunct (3 women). *Students:* 62 full-time (49 women), 13 part-time (12 women); includes 7 minority (4 African Americans, 1 American Indian/Alaska Native, 2 Hispanic Americans), 1 international. Average age 32. 112 applicants, 50% accepted, 35 enrolled. In 2007, 37 master's, 2 doctorates awarded. *Degree requirements:* For doctorate, comprehensive exam, thesis/dissertation. *Entrance requirements:* For master's, GRE, minimum GPA of 2.5; for doctorate, GRE, minimum GPA of 3.5. Additional exam requirements/recommendations for international students: Required—TOEFL. *Application deadline:* For fall admission, 1/15 for domestic and international students. Application fee: $45. Electronic applications accepted. *Expenses:* Tuition, state resident: full-time $6,250; part-time $275 per credit hour. Tuition, nonresident: part-time $760 per credit hour. Required fees:$3,550. Tuition and fees vary according to program. *Financial support:* In 2007–08, 1 fellowship with full tuition reimbursement (averaging $20,000 per year), 43 research assistantships with full tuition reimbursements (averaging $9,000 per year) were awarded; career-related internships or fieldwork, Federal Work-Study, institutionally sponsored loans, scholarships/grants, and unspecified assistantships also available. Financial award application deadline: 1/15; financial award applicants required to submit FAFSA. *Faculty research:* Sexuality, multicultural education, substance abuse, transpersonal psychology. *Unit head:* Dr. Charles McAdams, Area Coordinator, 757-221-2338, E-mail: crmcad@wm.edu. *Application contact:* Dorothy Smith Osborne, Director of Admissions, 757-221-2317, Fax: 757-221-2293, E-mail: dsosbo@wm.edu.

Coppin State University, Division of Graduate Studies, Division of Arts and Sciences, Department of Applied Psychology and Rehabilitation Counseling, Program in Alcohol and Substance Abuse Counseling, Baltimore, MD 21216-3698. Offers MS. Part-time programs available. *Students:* 11 full-time (9 women), 17 part-time (10 women); all minorities (all African Americans) Average age 45. 17 applicants, 71% accepted, 6 enrolled. In 2007, 7 degrees awarded. *Degree requirements:* For master's, comprehensive exam (for some programs), thesis optional, internship, clinical requirement. *Entrance requirements:* For master's, GRE General Test, interview, minimum GPA of 3.0. *Application deadline:* For fall admission, 8/15 for domestic students; for spring admission, 12/15 for domestic students. Applications are processed on a rolling basis. Application fee: $45. *Expenses:* Tuition, state resident: part-time $217 per credit. Tuition, nonresident: part-time $400 per credit. *Financial support:* Federal Work-Study available. Financial award application deadline: 6/30; financial award applicants required to submit FAFSA. *Unit head:* Dr. Janet D. Spry, Coordinator, 410-951-3514, E-mail: jspry@coppin.edu.

East Carolina University, Graduate School, School of Allied Health Sciences, Program in Rehabilitation Studies, Greenville, NC 27858-4353. Offers rehabilitation counseling (MS); substance abuse and clinical counseling (MS); vocational evaluation (MS). *Accreditation:* CORE. Part-time and evening/weekend programs available. *Students:* 61 full-time (45 women), 10 part-time (8 women); includes 9 minority (8 African Americans, 1 American Indian/Alaska Native), 2 international. Average age 31. 22 applicants, 14% accepted, 3 enrolled. In 2007, 21 degrees awarded. *Degree requirements:* For master's, comprehensive exam, thesis or alternative, internship. *Entrance requirements:* For master's, GRE General Test or MAT. Additional exam requirements/recommendations for international students: Required—TOEFL. *Application deadline:* For fall admission, 3/1 priority date for domestic students; for spring admission, 10/1 priority date for domestic students. Applications are processed on a rolling basis. Application fee: $50. *Financial support:* Research assistantships with partial tuition reimbursements, teaching assistantships with partial tuition reimbursements, Federal Work-Study and scholarships/grants available. Support available to part-time students. Financial award application deadline: 3/1. *Unit head:* Dr. Paul Alston, Chair, 252-744-6290, Fax: 252-328-0725, E-mail: alstonp@ecu.edu. *Application contact:* Dean of Graduate School, 252-328-6012, Fax: 252-328-6071, E-mail: gradschool@ecu.edu.

Eastern Michigan University, Graduate School, College of Health and Human Services, School of Social Work, Ypsilanti, MI 48197. Offers family and children's services (MSW); gerontology (Graduate Certificate); gerontology-dementia (Graduate Certificate); mental health and chemical dependency (MSW); services to the aging (MSW). *Accreditation:* CSWE. Part-time and evening/weekend programs available. Postbaccalaureate distance learning degree programs offered (minimal on-campus study). *Faculty:* 18 full-time (15 women). *Students:* 26 full-time (21 women), 164 part-time (142 women); includes 78 minority (69 African Americans, 3 American Indian/Alaska Native, 4 Asian Americans or Pacific Islanders, 2 Hispanic Americans), 1 international. Average age 35. In 2007, 117 master's, 17 other advanced degrees awarded. *Entrance requirements:* Additional exam requirements/recommendations for international students: Required—TOEFL. *Application deadline:* Applications are processed on a rolling basis. Application fee: $35. *Expenses:* Tuition, state resident: full-time $8,952; part-time $373 per credit hour. Tuition, nonresident: full-time $17,634; part-time $735 per credit hour. Required fees: $896; $34 per credit hour. Tuition and fees vary according to course level, degree level and program. *Financial support:* Fellowships, research assistantships with full tuition reimbursements, teaching assistantships with full tuition reimbursements, career-related internships or fieldwork, Federal Work-Study, institutionally sponsored loans, scholarships/grants, tuition waivers (partial), and unspecified assistantships available. Support available to part-time students. Financial award applicants required to submit FAFSA. *Unit head:* Prof. Marjorie Ziefert, Director, 734-487-0393, Fax: 734-487-6832, E-mail: marjorie.ziefert@emich.edu. *Application contact:* Julie Harkema, Advisor, 734-487-0393, Fax: 734-487-6832, E-mail: jharkema@emich.edu.

Governors State University, College of Health Professions, Program in Addictions Studies, University Park, IL 60466-0975. Offers MHS. Part-time and evening/weekend programs available. *Students:* 14 full-time, 66 part-time. Average age 39. *Degree requirements:* For master's, comprehensive exam, thesis or alternative, internship. *Entrance requirements:* For master's, minimum undergraduate GPA of 2.5; 9 hours of course work in behavioral sciences; 6 hours of course work in biological sciences or chemistry, statistics or research methods. *Application deadline:* For fall admission, 7/15 priority date for domestic students; for spring admission, 11/10 for domestic students. Applications are processed on a rolling basis. Application fee: $25. *Financial support:* Research assistantships, career-related internships or fieldwork, Federal Work-Study, institutionally sponsored loans, scholarships/grants, and tuition waivers (full and partial) available. Support available to part-time students. Financial award application deadline: 5/1. *Unit head:* Dr. Judith Lewis, Head, 708-534-4918.

Grand Canyon University, College of Nursing and Health Sciences, Phoenix, AZ 85017-1097. Offers addiction counseling (MS); nursing (MS); professional counseling (MS). Part-time and evening/weekend programs available. Postbaccalaureate distance learning degree programs offered (no on-campus study). *Faculty:* 4 full-time (3 women), 23 part-time/adjunct (22 women). *Students:* 35 full-time (31 women), 288 part-time (266 women); includes 26 minority (9 African Americans, 2 American Indian/Alaska Native, 4 Asian Americans or Pacific Islanders, 11 Hispanic Americans). Average age 44. In 2007, 35 master's awarded. *Entrance requirements:* For master's, Contact for details. Additional exam requirements/recommendations for international students: Required—TOEFL (minimum score 575 paper-based; 233 computer-based; 90 iBT), IELTS (minimum score 7). Application fee: $100. *Expenses:* Tuition: Part-time $645 per credit. *Financial support:* Federal Work-Study available. Support available to part-time students. Financial award applicants required to submit FAFSA. *Unit head:* Fran Roberts, Vice President, 602-639-6163, E-mail: froberts@gcu.edu. *Application contact:* Andrea Wolochuk, Information Contact, 602-639-6429, E-mail: awolochuk@gcu.edu.

Hazelden Graduate School of Addiction Studies, Graduate Programs, Center City, MN 55012. Offers addiction counseling (MA, Certificate). Part-time programs available. *Faculty:* 4 full-time (1 woman), 11 part-time/adjunct (7 women). *Students:* 30 full-time (19 women), 28 part-time (19 women); includes 1 American Indian/Alaska Native. In 2007, 36 degrees awarded. *Entrance requirements:* Additional exam requirements/recommendations for international students: Required—TOEFL. Application fee: $30. *Application contact:* Nancy Kaminski, Graduate School Admission Specialist, 651-213-4175, E-mail: nkaminski@hazelden.org.

Hofstra University, School of Education and Allied Human Services, Department of Health Professions and Family Studies, Program in Marriage and Family Therapy, Hempstead, NY 11549. Offers addiction studies (Advanced Certificate); marriage and family therapy (MA, PD). Part-time programs available. *Students:* 35 full-time (32 women), 15 part-time (all women); includes 10 minority (6 African Americans, 1 Asian American or Pacific Islander, 3 Hispanic Americans), 1 international. Average age 27. 50 applicants, 94% accepted, 19 enrolled. In 2007, 17 master's, 9 other advanced degrees awarded. *Degree requirements:* For master's, comprehensive exam, internship, clinic hours. *Entrance requirements:* For master's, GRE General Test, interview, letters of recommendation; for other advanced degree, 3 letters of recommendation, interview, resumé, essay, masters degree. Additional exam requirements/recommendations for international students: Required—TOEFL (minimum score 550 paper-based; 213 computer-based). *Application deadline:* Applications are processed on a rolling basis. Application fee: $60. Electronic applications accepted. *Expenses:* Tuition: Full-time $14,220; part-time $820 per credit. Required fees: $970; $165 per term. Tuition and fees vary according to program. *Financial support:* In 2007–08, 19 students received support, including 1 fellowship with tuition reimbursement available (averaging $3,000 per year), 2 research assistantships with full and partial tuition reimbursements available (averaging $11,100 per year); career-related internships or fieldwork, Federal Work-Study, institutionally sponsored loans, scholarships/grants, tuition waivers (full and partial), and unspecified assistantships also available. Support available to part-time students. Financial award applicants required to submit FAFSA. *Faculty research:* Marriage and family therapy, addiction studies, divorce mediation, human sexuality. *Unit head:* Prof. Lauren B. Mangino, Program Director, 516-463-5224. *Application contact:* Carol Drummer, Dean of Graduate Admissions, 516-463-4876, Fax: 516-463-4664, E-mail: gradstudent@hofstra.edu.

Indiana University–Purdue University Indianapolis, School of Science, Department of Psychology, Psychobiology of Addictions Program, Indianapolis, IN 46202-2896. Offers MS, PhD. *Faculty:* 7 full-time (3 women). *Students:* 9 full-time (5 women); includes 1 minority (African American) Average age 26. *Entrance requirements:* For master's, GRE General Test, minimum undergraduate GPA of 3.2. *Application deadline:* For fall admission, 1/1 for domestic students. Application fee: $50 ($60 for international students). *Expenses:* Tuition, state resident: full-time $5,818; part-time $242 per credit hour. Tuition, nonresident: full-time $17,106; part-time $713 per credit hour. Required fees: $629. Tuition and fees vary according to course load, campus/location and program. *Financial support:* Fellowships with partial tuition reimbursements, research assistantships with partial tuition reimbursements, teaching assistantships with partial tuition reimbursements, career-related internships or fieldwork and Federal Work-Study available. Financial award application deadline: 3/1; financial award applicants required to submit FAFSA. *Faculty research:* Behavioral genetics, behavior pharmacology, animal models, developmental psychology, neurobehavioral toxicology, neuropsychology of learning and memory, animal models of fetal alcohol syndrome.

The Johns Hopkins University, Bloomberg School of Public Health, Department of Mental Health, Baltimore, MD 21218-2699. Offers children's mental health services (PhD); drug dependence epidemiology (PhD); mental health (MHS); psychiatric epidemiology (PhD). *Faculty:* 26 full-time (15 women), 35 part-time/adjunct (13 women). *Students:* 42 full-time (32 women), 3 part-time (1 woman); includes 10 minority (4 African Americans, 5 Asian Americans or Pacific Islanders, 1 Hispanic American), 8 international. Average age 29. 69 applicants, 71% accepted, 27 enrolled. In 2007, 10 master's, 5 doctorates awarded. *Median time to degree:* Of those who began their doctoral program in fall 1999, 90% received their degree in 8 years or less. *Degree requirements:* For master's, thesis (for some programs); for doctorate, thesis/dissertation, 1 year full-time residency, oral and written exams. *Entrance requirements:* For master's, GRE General Test, MCAT, 3 letters of recommendation, curriculum vitae; for doctorate, GRE General Test, MCAT or GMAT, 3 letters of recommendation, curriculum vitae. Additional exam requirements/recommendations for international students: Required—TOEFL (minimum score 550 paper-based; 250 computer-based). *Application deadline:* For fall admission, 12/1 priority date for domestic students. Applications are processed on a rolling basis. Application fee: $45. Electronic applications accepted. *Financial support:* In 2007–08, 61 students received support, including 1 fellowship (averaging $32,000 per year); Federal Work-Study, institutionally sponsored loans, scholarships/grants, traineeships, and stipends also available. Support available to part-time students. Financial award application deadline: 3/15; financial award applicants required to submit FAFSA. *Faculty research:* Etiology, development and prevention of aggressive and antisocial behavior; epidemiology of mental disorders; genetic epidemiology of mental disorders. Total annual research expenditures: $14.5 million. *Unit head:* Dr. William W. Eaton, Chair, 410-955-3910, Fax: 410-614-7469, E-mail: weaton@jhsph.edu. *Application contact:* Patricia E. Scott, Senior Academic Program Coordinator, 410-955-1906, Fax: 410-955-9088, E-mail: mhdept@jhsph.edu.

The Johns Hopkins University, School of Education, Department of Counseling and Human Services, Baltimore, MD 21218-2699. Offers addictions counseling (Certificate); clinical community counseling (Certificate); clinical supervision (Certificate); contemporary trauma (Certificate); counseling (MS, CAGS); counseling at-risk youth (Certificate); organizational counseling (Certificate); play therapy (Certificate); spiritual and existential counseling and therapy (Certificate). Part-time and evening/weekend programs available. *Students:* 51 full-time (45 women), 389 part-time (330 women); includes 103 minority (77 African Americans, 2 American Indian/Alaska Native, 13 Asian Americans or Pacific Islanders, 11 Hispanic Americans), 10 international. Average age 33. 142 applicants, 80% accepted, 77 enrolled. In 2007, 110 master's, 31 other advanced degrees awarded. *Entrance requirements:* For master's, minimum GPA of 3.0, interview, resumé, letters of recommendation; for other advanced degree, master's or doctoral degree, interview, resumé, minimum GPA of 3.0, letters of recommendation. Additional exam requirements/recommendations for international students: Required—TOEFL (minimum score 600 paper-based; 250 computer-based; 100 iBT). *Application deadline:* For fall admission, 5/1 for international students; for spring admission, 10/15 for international students. Applications are processed on a rolling basis. Application fee: $60. *Financial support:* Scholarships/grants available. Support available to part-time students. Financial award application deadline: 6/1; financial award applicants required to submit FAFSA. *Unit head:* Dr. Mary Guindon, Chair, 301-294-7040. *Application contact:* Carol Herrman, Admissions Coordinator, 410-872-1234, Fax: 410-872-1251, E-mail: onestop.admissions@jhu.edu.

Kean University, College of Education, Program in Counselor Education, Union, NJ 07083. Offers alcohol and drug abuse counseling (MA); business and industry counseling (MA); community/agency counseling (MA); school counseling (MA). *Accreditation:* ACA; NCATE. Part-time programs available. *Faculty:* 5 full-time (2 women). *Students:* 49 full-time (43 women), 189 part-time (159 women); includes 40 African Americans, 3 Asian Americans or Pacific Islanders, 21 Hispanic Americans. Average age 32. 109 applicants, 74% accepted, 49 enrolled. In 2007, 45 degrees awarded. *Degree requirements:* For master's, comprehensive exam, thesis, practicum, internship. *Entrance requirements:* For master's, GRE General Test or MAT, 2 letters of recommendation, interview, minimum 3.0 GPA, initial teaching certificate (school counseling). *Application deadline:* For fall admission, 5/1 for domestic students; for spring admission, 11/1 for domestic students. Application fee: $60 ($150 for international students). Electronic applications accepted. *Expenses:* Tuition, state resident: full-time $9,384; part-time $391 per credit. Tuition, nonresident: full-time $12,720; part-time $530 per credit. Required fees: $2,382; $99 per credit. Part-time tuition and fees vary according to course load. *Financial support:* In 2007–08, 8 research assistantships with full tuition reimbursements (averaging $3,217 per year) were awarded; unspecified assistantships also available. *Unit head:* Dr. Juneau Gary, Coordinator, 908-737-3842, E-mail: jgary@kean.edu. *Application contact:* Joanne Morris, Director of Graduate Admissions, 908-737-3355, Fax: 908-737-3354, E-mail: grad-adm@kean.edu.

Lewis & Clark College, Graduate School of Education and Counseling, Department of Counseling Psychology, Program in Addictions Treatment, Portland, OR 97219-7899. Offers MA. Part-time and evening/weekend programs available. *Faculty:* 6 full-time (2 women), 18 part-time/adjunct (8 women). *Students:* 16 full-time (13 women), 25 part-time (19 women); includes 5 minority (1 African American, 1 Asian American or Pacific Islander, 3 Hispanic Americans). Average age 32. 17 applicants, 100% accepted, 10 enrolled. In 2007, 14 degrees awarded. *Entrance requirements:* For master's, GRE General Test, minimum undergraduate GPA of 2.75. Additional exam requirements/recommendations for international students: Required—TOEFL (minimum score 575 paper-based; 233 computer-based). *Application deadline:* For fall admission, 2/1 priority date for domestic and international students; for spring admission, 10/1 priority date for domestic and international students. Application fee: $50. Electronic applications accepted. *Expenses:* Tuition: Part-time $645 per credit. Tuition and fees vary according to campus/location. *Financial support:* In 2007–08, 36 students received support. Career-related internships or fieldwork, Federal Work-Study, institutionally sponsored loans, scholarships/grants, health care benefits, and tuition waivers (partial) available. Support available to part-time students. Financial award applicants required to submit FAFSA. *Unit head:* Dr. Boyd Pidcock, Program Coordinator, 503-768-6060, Fax: 503-768-6065, E-mail: cpsy@lclark.edu. *Application contact:* Becky Haas, Director of Admissions, 503-768-6200, Fax: 503-768-6205, E-mail: gseadmit@lclark.edu.

Loyola College in Maryland, Graduate Programs, College of Arts and Sciences, Department of Psychology, Program in Counseling Psychology, Baltimore, MD 21210-2699. Offers counseling psychology (MS); employee assistance and substance abuse (CAS). Part-time and evening/weekend programs available. *Entrance requirements:* For master's and CAS, GRE General Test, GRE Subject Test (recommended). Additional exam requirements/recommendations for international students: Required—TOEFL (minimum score 550 paper-based; 213 computer-based).

Maryville University of Saint Louis, School of Health Professions, Program in Rehabilitation Counseling, St. Louis, MO 63141-7299. Offers marriage and family therapy (MARC); music therapy (MARC); substance abuse (MARC). *Accreditation:* CORE. Part-time and evening/weekend programs available. *Degree requirements:* For master's, internship, seminar. *Entrance requirements:* For master's, minimum cumulative GPA of 3.0, 2 letters of recommendation, interview. *Application deadline:* For fall admission, 1/15 for domestic students; for spring admission, 10/1 for domestic students. Application fee: $35. Electronic applications accepted. *Expenses:* Tuition: Full-time $18,600; part-time $580 per credit. Required fees: $75 per semester. *Financial support:* Career-related internships or fieldwork, Federal Work-Study, and campus employment available. Financial award application deadline: 7/31. *Unit head:* Barbara Parker, Director, 314-529-9437.

Marywood University, Academic Affairs, College of Education and Human Development, Department of Psychology and Counseling, Program in Mental Health Counseling, Scranton, PA 18509-1598. Offers addiction (MA); general (MA); pastoral (MA). *Accreditation:* ACA. *Students:* 9 full-time (6 women), 9 part-time (6 women); includes 1 minority (African American), 1 international. Average age 33. In 2007, 5 degrees awarded. Application fee: $30. *Expenses:* Tuition: Full-time $15,290; part-time $695 per credit. Required fees: $990; $370 per term. Tuition and fees vary according to degree level. *Unit head:* Dr. John Lemoncelli, Director, 570-348-6211 Ext. 2317, E-mail: lemoncelli@marywood.edu.

Mercy College, Division of Social and Behavioral Sciences, Program in Counseling, Dobbs Ferry, NY 10522-1189. Offers alcohol and substance abuse counseling (AC); counseling (MS); family counseling (AC); retirement counseling (AC). *Students:* 85 full-time (79 women), 213 part-time (174 women); includes 202 minority (94 African Americans, 1 Asian American or Pacific Islander, 107 Hispanic Americans). Average age 34. In 2007, 74 master's, 14 other advanced degrees awarded. *Entrance requirements:* For master's, interview, letters of recommendation, minimum undergraduate GPA of 3.0. *Expenses:* Tuition: Part-time $575 per credit. Required fees: $220 per semester. Tuition and fees vary according to program. *Unit head:* Dr. Fernando Cabrera, Program Director, 914-674-7334, E-mail: fcabrera@mercy.edu.

Addictions/Substance Abuse Counseling

Minnesota State University Mankato, College of Graduate Studies, College of Allied Health and Nursing, Department of Health Science, Mankato, MN 56001. Offers chemical dependency studies (MS); community health (MS); health science (MS, MT); school health (MS). Part-time programs available. *Students:* 10 full-time (6 women), 40 part-time (29 women). Average age 32. In 2007, 10 degrees awarded. *Degree requirements:* For master's, comprehensive exam, thesis or alternative. *Entrance requirements:* For master's, minimum GPA of 3.0 during previous 2 years. *Application deadline:* For fall admission, 7/1 for domestic students, 5/1 for international students; for spring admission, 11/1 for domestic students, 10/1 for international students. Applications are processed on a rolling basis. Application fee: $40. Electronic applications accepted. *Financial support:* Research assistantships with full tuition reimbursements, teaching assistantships with full tuition reimbursements, career-related internships or fieldwork and Federal Work-Study available. Support available to part-time students. Financial award application deadline: 3/15; financial award applicants required to submit FAFSA. *Faculty research:* Teaching methods, stress prophylaxis and management, effects of alcohol. *Unit head:* Dr. Dawn Larsen, Graduate Coordinator, 507-389-2113. *Application contact:* 507-389-2321, E-mail: grad@mnsu.edu.

Monmouth University, Graduate School, The Marjorie K. Unterberg School of Nursing and Health Studies, West Long Branch, NJ 07764-1898. Offers advanced practice nursing (Post-Master's Certificate); nursing (MSN); school nursing (Certificate); substance awareness coordinator (Certificate). *Accreditation:* AACN. Part-time and evening/weekend programs available. *Faculty:* 10 full-time (all women), 2 part-time/adjunct (1 woman). *Students:* 6 full-time (5 women), 199 part-time (192 women); includes 29 minority (6 African Americans, 19 Asian Americans or Pacific Islanders, 4 Hispanic Americans). Average age 43. 66 applicants, 98% accepted, 48 enrolled. In 2007, 36 degrees awarded. *Degree requirements:* For master's, 7 different tracks—39-45 credits each, some require practicum. *Entrance requirements:* For master's, GRE General Test, RN license, 1 year of work experience, minimum undergraduate GPA of 2.75. Additional exam requirements/recommendations for international students: Required—TOEFL (minimum score 550 paper-based; 213 computer-based; 79 iBT), IELTS (minimum score 5), MELAB 77, Cambridge A, B, C. *Application deadline:* For fall admission, 7/15 priority date for domestic students, 6/1 for international students; for spring admission, 11/15 priority date for domestic students, 11/1 for international students. Applications are processed on a rolling basis. Application fee: $50. Electronic applications accepted. *Financial support:* In 2007–08, 141 students received support, including 140 fellowships (averaging $1,473 per year), 4 research assistantships (averaging $3,676 per year); career-related internships or fieldwork, scholarships/grants, tuition waivers (partial), and unspecified assistantships also available. Support available to part-time students. Financial award application deadline: 3/1; financial award applicants required to submit FAFSA. *Faculty research:* Relationship of undergraduate GPA and GRE to succeed in a graduate nursing program. *Unit head:* Dr. Janet Mahoney, Director, 732-571-3443, Fax: 732-263-5131, E-mail: jmahoney@monmouth.edu. *Application contact:* Kevin Roane, Director, Office of Graduate Admission, 732-571-3452, Fax: 732-263-5123, E-mail: gradadm@monmouth.edu.

Montclair State University, The Office of Graduate Admissions and Support Services, College of Education and Human Services, Department of Counseling, Human Development, and Educational Leadership, Montclair, NJ 07043-1624. Offers administration and supervision (MA), including administration and supervision, educator/trainer; advanced counseling (Certificate); counseling and guidance (MA), including addictions counseling, community counseling, student affairs; principal (Certificate); school administrator (Certificate); school business administrator (Certificate); school counselor (Certificate); substance awareness coordinator (Certificate). *Accreditation:* NCATE. Part-time and evening/weekend programs available. *Faculty:* 19 full-time (14 women), 18 part-time/adjunct (8 women). *Students:* 119 full-time (98 women), 582 part-time (427 women); includes 131 minority (68 African Americans, 14 Asian Americans or Pacific Islanders, 49 Hispanic Americans), 3 international. Average age 33. 581 applicants, 54% accepted, 270 enrolled. In 2007, 187 master's, 25 other advanced degrees awarded. *Degree requirements:* For master's, comprehensive exam, thesis or alternative. *Entrance requirements:* For master's, GRE General Test, interview, 2 letters of recommendation. Additional exam requirements/recommendations for international students: Required—TOEFL (minimum score 83 computer-based). *Application deadline:* For fall admission, 6/1 for international students; for spring admission, 10/1 for international students. Applications are processed on a rolling basis. Application fee: $60. Electronic applications accepted. *Financial support:* In 2007–08, 15 research assistantships with full tuition reimbursements (averaging $7,000 per year) were awarded; Federal Work-Study, scholarships/grants, and unspecified assistantships also available. Support available to part-time students. Financial award application deadline: 3/1; financial award applicants required to submit FAFSA. *Faculty research:* K-12 education, data collection. *Unit head:* Dr. Catherine Roland, Chairperson, 973-655-7216, E-mail: rolandc@mail.montclair.edu.

National-Louis University, College of Arts and Sciences, Department of Counseling and Human Services, Chicago, IL 60603. Offers addictions counseling (Certificate); addictions treatment (Certificate); career counseling and development studies (Certificate); community counseling (MS); community wellness and prevention (Certificate); counseling (Certificate); eating disorders counseling (Certificate); employee assistance programs (MS, Certificate); gerontology administration (Certificate); gerontology counseling (MS, Certificate); human services administration (MS, Certificate); long-term care administration (Certificate); school counseling (MS). Part-time programs available. *Students:* 15 full-time (11 women), 229 part-time (187 women); includes 69 minority (56 African Americans, 1 American Indian/Alaska Native, 2 Asian Americans or Pacific Islanders, 10 Hispanic Americans). Average age 38. In 2007, 53 master's, 6 other advanced degrees awarded. *Degree requirements:* For master's and Certificate, internship. *Entrance requirements:* For master's and Certificate, GRE, MAT, or Watson-Glaser Critical Thinking Appraisal, interview, minimum GPA of 3.0. *Application deadline:* Applications are processed on a rolling basis. *Expenses:* Tuition: Full-time $18,900; part-time $630 per credit hour. Required fees: $20 per term. One-time fee: $40 part-time. Tuition and fees vary according to course load, campus/location and program. *Financial support:* Federal Work-Study, institutionally sponsored loans, scholarships/grants, and tuition waivers available. Support available to part-time students. Financial award applicants required to submit FAFSA. *Faculty research:* Religion and aging, drug abuse prevention, hunger, homelessness, multicultural diversity. *Unit head:* Dr. Susan Thorne-Devin, Assistant Professor, 630-874-4560, E-mail: stdevin@nl.edu. *Application contact:* Dr. Larry Poselli, Vice President of Enrollment and Student Services, 800-443-5522 Ext. 5718, Fax: 312-261-3550, E-mail: larry.polselli@nl.edu.

Notre Dame de Namur University, Division of Academic Affairs, School of Sciences, Department of Clinical Psychology and Gerontology, Belmont, CA 94002-1908. Offers chemical dependency (MACP); clinical gerontology (MA, Certificate); counseling psychology (MACP); marital and family therapy (MACP, MAMFT). Part-time and evening/weekend programs available. *Faculty:* 2 full-time (both women), 6 part-time/adjunct (5 women). *Students:* 29 full-time (25 women), 65 part-time (56 women); includes 31 minority (5 African Americans, 11 Asian Americans or Pacific Islanders, 15 Hispanic Americans), 1 international. Average age 35. 26 applicants, 81% accepted, 16 enrolled. In 2007, 23 degrees awarded. *Entrance requirements:* For master's, interview, minimum GPA of 2.5. Additional exam requirements/recommendations for international students: Required—TOEFL. *Application deadline:* For fall admission, 8/1 priority date for domestic students; for spring admission, 12/1 priority date for domestic students. Applications are processed on a rolling basis. Application fee: $50. Electronic applications accepted. *Financial support:* Career-related internships or fieldwork available. Support available to part-time students. Financial award applicants required to submit FAFSA. *Unit head:* Dr. Nusha Askari, Chair, 650-508-3728, E-mail: naskari@ndnu.edu. *Application contact:* Helen Valine, Director of Graduate Admissions, 650-508-3534, Fax: 650-508-3426, E-mail: grad.admit@ndnu.edu.

Pace University, Dyson College of Arts and Sciences, Department of Psychology, Program in Counseling-Substance Abuse, New York, NY 10038. Offers MS. Offered at Pleasantville, NY location only. Part-time and evening/weekend programs available. *Students:* 47 full-time (39 women), 58 part-time (47 women); includes 12 African Americans, 5 Asian Americans or Pacific Islanders, 6 Hispanic Americans, 4 international. Average age 34. 84 applicants, 90% accepted, 35 enrolled. In 2007, 47 degrees awarded. *Degree requirements:* For master's, comprehensive exam, qualifying exams, internship. *Entrance requirements:* For master's, GRE, interview. *Application deadline:* For fall admission, 8/1 priority date for domestic students; for spring admission, 12/1 priority date for domestic students. Applications are processed on a rolling basis. Application fee: $65. Electronic applications accepted. *Expenses:* Tuition: Part-time $856 per credit. Tuition and fees vary according to degree level and program. *Financial support:* Research assistantships, teaching assistantships, career-related internships or fieldwork, Federal Work-Study, and tuition waivers (partial) available. Financial award applicants required to submit FAFSA. *Unit head:* Dr. Ross Robak, Head, 914-773-3673. *Application contact:* Joanna Broda, Director of Admissions, 914-422-4283, Fax: 914-422-4287, E-mail: gradwp@pace.edu.

See Close-Up on page 1459.

Palm Beach Atlantic University, School of Education and Behavioral Studies, West Palm Beach, FL 33416-4708. Offers counseling psychology (MSCP), including addictions/mental health, marriage and family therapy, mental health counseling, school guidance counseling; elementary education (M Ed). Part-time and evening/weekend programs available. *Faculty:* 11 full-time (5 women), 10 part-time/adjunct (5 women). *Students:* 223 full-time (178 women), 65 part-time (48 women); includes 114 minority (62 African Americans, 5 Asian Americans or Pacific Islanders, 47 Hispanic Americans), 9 international. Average age 36. 145 applicants, 60% accepted, 73 enrolled. In 2007, 56 degrees awarded. *Entrance requirements:* For master's, GRE General Test, minimum GPA of 3.0 in last 60 hours of course work. Additional exam requirements/recommendations for international students: Required—TOEFL (minimum score 550 paper-based; 213 computer-based). *Application deadline:* For fall admission, 7/15 priority date for domestic students; for spring admission, 11/15 priority date for domestic students. Applications are processed on a rolling basis. Application fee: $45. Electronic applications accepted. *Expenses:* Tuition: Full-time $7,560; part-time $420 per credit. Required fees: $260; $95 per semester. Tuition and fees vary according to degree level, campus/location and program. *Financial support:* Career-related internships or fieldwork and unspecified assistantships available. Support available to part-time students. Financial award applicants required to submit FAFSA. *Unit head:* Dr. Melise Bunker, Dean, 561-803-2350, Fax: 561-803-2186, E-mail: melise_bunker@pba.edu. *Application contact:* Myra Santiago, Assistant Director of Graduate and Evening Admissions, 888-468-6722, Fax: 561-803-2115, E-mail: grad@pba.edu.

St. Mary's University, Graduate School, Department of Counseling and Human Services, San Antonio, TX 78228-8507. Offers community counseling (MA); counseling (Sp C); counseling education and supervision (PhD); marriage and family relations (Certificate); marriage and family therapy (MA, PhD); mental health (MA); mental health and substance abuse counseling (Certificate); substance abuse (MA). *Accreditation:* AAMFT/COAMFTE (one or more programs are accredited); ACA (one or more programs are accredited). Postbaccalaureate distance learning degree programs offered (minimal on-campus study). *Students:* 87 full-time (64 women), 84 part-time (66 women); includes 58 minority (8 African Americans, 3 Asian Americans or Pacific Islanders, 47 Hispanic Americans), 9 international. Average age 34. In 2007, 25 master's, 5 doctorates awarded. *Degree requirements:* For master's, comprehensive exam (for some programs), thesis optional, internship; for doctorate, comprehensive exam, thesis/dissertation, internship. *Entrance requirements:* For master's, GRE General Test, MAT; for doctorate, GRE General Test, recommendation from employers, admissions committee and department faculty. Additional exam requirements/recommendations for international students: Required—TOEFL (minimum score 550 paper-based; 213 computer-based). *Application deadline:* Applications are processed on a rolling basis. Application fee: $0. Electronic applications accepted. *Expenses:* Contact institution. *Financial support:* Research assistantships, career-related internships or fieldwork, Federal Work-Study, institutionally sponsored loans, scholarships/grants, and health care benefits available. Financial award application deadline: 3/31; financial award applicants required to submit FAFSA. *Unit head:* Dr. Dana Comstock, Chair, 210-436-3226, Fax: 210-431-6886, E-mail: dcomstock@stmarytx.edu.

Southern New Hampshire University, School of Liberal Arts, Manchester, NH 03106-1045. Offers clinical services for adults psychiatric disabilities (Certificate); clinical services for children and adolescents with psychiatric disabilities (Certificate); clinical services for persons with co-occurring substance abuse and psychiatric disabilities (Certificate); community mental health (MS); fiction writing (MFA); non-fiction writing (MFA); teaching English as a foreign language (MS). Part-time and evening/weekend programs available. *Faculty:* 18 full-time. *Students:* 187 full-time, 12 part-time. Average age 35. In 2007, 35 degrees awarded. *Degree requirements:* For master's, one foreign language, thesis. *Entrance requirements:* For master's, minimum GPA of 2.75; MS-TEFL, 3.0: MFA. Additional exam requirements/recommendations for international students: Required—TOEFL (minimum score 550 paper-based; 213 computer-based; 79 iBT), IELTS (minimum score 7), TWE (minimum score 5). *Application deadline:* For fall admission, 7/1 priority date for domestic students; for winter admission, 11/1 priority date for domestic students; for spring admission, 6/1 priority date for domestic students. Applications are processed on a rolling basis. Application fee: $40. Electronic applications accepted. *Expenses:* Contact institution. *Financial support:* In 2007–08, 4 research assistantships were awarded; career-related internships or fieldwork and scholarships/grants also available. Financial award applicants required to submit FAFSA. *Faculty research:* Action research, state of the art practice in behavioral health services, wraparound approaches to working with youth, learning styles. *Unit head:* Dr. Karen Erickson, Dean, 603-668-2211, E-mail: k.erickson@snhu.edu. *Application contact:* Scott Durand, Director of Graduate Enrollment Services, 603-644-3102 Ext. 3338, Fax: 603-644-3144, E-mail: s.durand@snhu.edu.

Springfield College, Graduate Programs, Programs in Rehabilitation Counseling and Services, Springfield, MA 01109-3797. Offers alcohol rehabilitation/substance abuse counseling (M Ed, MS, CAS); deaf counseling (M Ed, MS, CAS); developmental disabilities (M Ed, MS, CAS); general counseling and casework (M Ed, MS, CAS); psychiatric rehabilitation/mental health counseling (M Ed, MS, CAS); special services (M Ed, MS, CAS). *Accreditation:* CORE (one or more programs are accredited). Part-time and evening/weekend programs available. *Faculty:* 8 full-time (2 women), 4 part-time/adjunct (3 women). *Students:* 31 full-time, 9 part-time. Average age 31. 27 applicants, 89% accepted, 16 enrolled. In 2007, 13 degrees awarded. *Degree requirements:* For master's, comprehensive exam, thesis (for some programs). *Entrance requirements:* For master's and CAS, interview. Additional exam requirements/recommendations for international students: Required—TOEFL (minimum score 550 paper-based; 213 computer-based). *Application deadline:* For fall admission, 1/15 for domestic students; for winter admission, 11/1 for domestic students; for spring admission, 12/1 for domestic students. Applications are processed on a rolling basis. Application fee: $50. Electronic applications accepted. *Expenses:* Tuition: Full-time $12,942; part-time $719 per semester hour. Required fees: $25. Tuition and fees vary according to program. *Financial support:* In 2007–08, 4 teaching assistantships with partial tuition reimbursements were awarded; fellowships with partial tuition reimbursements, career-related internships or fieldwork, Federal Work-Study, institutionally sponsored loans, traineeships, and tuition waivers (full and partial) also available. Financial award application deadline: 3/1. *Faculty research:* Mental health, multicultural counseling, alcohol and substance abuse, developmental disabilities, families and disabilities, rehabilitation treatment outcomes. *Unit head:* Thomas J. Ruscio, Director, 413-748-3318, E-mail: thomas_ruscio@spfldcol.edu. *Application contact:* Donald James Shaw, Director of Graduate Admissions, 413-748-3060, Fax: 413-748-3069, E-mail: donald_shaw_jr@spfldcol.edu.

Stony Brook University, State University of New York, Stony Brook University Medical Center, School of Medicine, Program in Public Health, Stony Brook, NY 11794. Offers community health (MPH); evaluation sciences (MPH); family violence (MPH); health economics (MPH); population health (MPH); substance abuse (MPH). *Faculty:* 7 full-time (3 women), 1 part-time/adjunct (0 women). *Students:* 10 full-time (9 women), 28 part-time (23 women); includes 6 minority (4 African Americans, 2 Asian Americans or Pacific Islanders), 3 international. Average age 39. 83 applicants, 57% accepted. In 2007, 3 degrees awarded. *Entrance requirements:* For master's, GRE, 3 references. Additional exam requirements/recommendations for international students: Required—TOEFL. *Application deadline:* For fall admission, 1/15 for domestic and international students. Application fee: $60. Electronic applications accepted. *Faculty research:* Population health, health service research, health economics. *Unit head:* Dr. Raymond L. Goldsteen, Director, 631-444-2074, Fax: 631-444-3480, E-mail: raymond.goldsteen@stonybrook.edu.

Universidad Central del Caribe, Program in Substance Abuse Counseling, Bayamón, PR 00960-6032. Offers MHS.

Université de Montréal, Faculty of Arts and Sciences, School of Social Service, Montréal, QC H3C 3J7, Canada. Offers social administration (Certificate, DESS); social work (M Sc, PhD); the phenomenon of narcotics (Certificate, DESS). Part-time programs available. *Faculty:* 26 full-time (14 women), 7 part-time/adjunct (6 women). *Students:* 117 full-time (99 women), 75 part-time (59 women). 144 applicants, 24% accepted, 31 enrolled. In 2007, 37 master's, 2 doctorates awarded. *Degree requirements:* For master's, one foreign language, thesis (for some programs). *Application deadline:* For fall admission, 2/1 priority date for domestic students; for winter admission, 11/1 priority date for domestic students; for spring admission, 2/1 priority date for domestic students. Application fee: $100. Electronic applications accepted. *Financial support:* Research assistantships, teaching assistantships, career-related internships or fieldwork and institutionally sponsored loans available. Financial award application deadline: 9/1. *Faculty research:* Family violence, social policies analysis, community development, gerontology, prevention. *Unit head:* Dominique Damant, Director, 514-343-6596, Fax: 514-343-2493, E-mail: dominique.damant@umontreal.ca. *Application contact:* Gilbert Renaud, Responsible, 514-343-2063, Fax: 514-343-2493, E-mail: gilbert.renaud@umontreal.ca.

University of Central Florida, College of Health and Public Affairs, School of Social Work, Orlando, FL 32816. Offers addictions (Certificate); aging studies (Certificate); children's services (Certificate); school social work (Certificate); social work (MSW); social work administration (Certificate). *Accreditation:* CSWE. Part-time and evening/weekend programs available. *Faculty:* 16 full-time (11 women), 21 part-time/adjunct (16 women). *Degree requirements:* For master's, thesis or alternative, field education. *Entrance requirements:* For master's, resumé. Additional exam requirements/recommendations for international students: Required—TOEFL. *Application deadline:* For fall admission, 3/1 for domestic students. Application fee: $30. Electronic applications accepted. *Expenses:* Tuition, state resident: full-time $6,484. Tuition, nonresident: full-time $23,938. Tuition and fees vary according to program. *Financial support:* Fellowships with partial tuition reimbursements, research assistantships with partial tuition reimbursements, teaching assistantships with partial tuition reimbursements, career-related internships or fieldwork, Federal Work-Study, institutionally sponsored loans, and unspecified assistantships available. Financial award application deadline: 3/1; financial award applicants required to submit FAFSA. *Unit head:* Dr. John Ronnau, Director, 407-823-2208, Fax: 407-823-5697, E-mail: jronnau@mail.ucf.edu.

University of Central Oklahoma, College of Graduate Studies and Research, College of Liberal Arts, Department of Sociology, Criminal Justice and Substance Abuse Studies, Edmond, OK 73034-5209. Offers criminal justice management and administration (MA). Part-time programs available. *Faculty:* 10 full-time (5 women), 6 part-time/adjunct (4 women). *Students:* 9 full-time (4 women), 18 part-time (11 women); includes 7 minority (5 African Americans, 1 American Indian/Alaska Native, 1 Hispanic American). Average age 32. 26 applicants, 100% accepted. In 2007, 4 degrees awarded. *Entrance requirements:* Additional exam requirements/recommendations for international students: Required—TOEFL (minimum score 550 paper-based; 213 computer-based). *Application deadline:* For fall admission, 7/1 for international students; for spring admission, 11/1 for international students. Applications are processed on a rolling basis. Application fee: $25. Electronic applications accepted. *Expenses:* Tuition, state resident: full-time $3,516; part-time $147 per hour. Tuition, nonresident: full-time $9,054; part-time $377 per hour. Required fees: $433; $18 per hour. *Financial support:* Unspecified assistantships available. Financial award application deadline: 3/31; financial award applicants required to submit FAFSA. *Faculty research:* Gender issues, violent offenders. *Unit head:* Dr. David Ford, Chairperson, 405-974-5622. *Application contact:* Dr. Sid Brown, Director, Program in Criminal Justice Management, 405-974-5271, Fax: 405-974-3823, E-mail: sbrown@ucok.edu.

University of Detroit Mercy, College of Liberal Arts and Education, Department of Counseling and Addiction Studies, Program in Addiction Studies, Detroit, MI 48221. Offers Certificate. Part-time programs available.

University of Detroit Mercy, College of Liberal Arts and Education, Department of Counseling and Addiction Studies, Program in Counseling, Detroit, MI 48221. Offers addiction counseling (MA); community counseling (MA); school counseling (MA). *Accreditation:* ACA. Part-time and evening/weekend programs available. *Degree requirements:* For master's, thesis or alternative. *Entrance requirements:* For master's, minimum GPA of 2.75.

University of Great Falls, Graduate Studies, Program in Addictions Counseling, Great Falls, MT 59405. Offers Certificate. Part-time and evening/weekend programs available. *Faculty:* 2 full-time (both women), 4 part-time/adjunct (2 women). *Students:* 1 full-time (0 women), 4 part-time (all women); includes 1 minority (American Indian/Alaska Native). Average age 39. 4 applicants, 75% accepted, 3 enrolled. In 2007, 10 degrees awarded. *Degree requirements:* For Certificate, thesis optional. *Entrance requirements:* For degree, GRE General Test or MAT, 3 letters of recommendation. Additional exam requirements/recommendations for international students: Required—TOEFL (minimum score 500 paper-based; 205 computer-based). *Application deadline:* For fall admission, 8/15 priority date for domestic students, 6/15 priority date for international students; for spring admission, 12/15 priority date for domestic students, 10/15 priority date for international students. Application fee: $50. Electronic applications accepted. *Expenses:* Tuition: Part-time $520 per credit. Required fees: $60 per semester. Tuition and fees vary according to course load. *Financial support:* In 2007–08, 5 students received support. Career-related internships or fieldwork, Federal Work-Study, and institutionally sponsored loans available. Support available to part-time students. Financial award application deadline: 6/1; financial award applicants required to submit FAFSA. *Unit head:* Mary Ann Dubay, Head, 406-791-5365, Fax: 406-791-5990, E-mail: mdubay@ugf.edu.

University of Illinois at Springfield, Graduate Programs, College of Education and Human Services, Program in Human Services, Springfield, IL 62703-5407. Offers alcoholism and substance abuse (MA); child and family services (MA); gerontology (MA); social services administration (MA). Part-time and evening/weekend programs available. Postbaccalaureate distance learning degree programs offered. *Faculty:* 4 full-time (3 women), 2 part-time/adjunct (both women). *Students:* 36 full-time (30 women), 64 part-time (53 women); includes 23 minority (21 African Americans, 2 American Indian/Alaska Native), 1 international. Average age 36. 52 applicants, 62% accepted, 27 enrolled. In 2007, 10 degrees awarded. *Degree requirements:* For master's, thesis optional, internship. *Entrance requirements:* For master's, 2 letters of reference, minimum undergraduate GPA of 3.0, prerequisite courses in lifespan development and research methods, personal statement. Additional exam requirements/recommendations for international students: Required—TOEFL (minimum score 550 paper-based; 213 computer-based). *Application deadline:* For fall admission, 2/15 priority date for domestic and international students; for spring admission, 9/15 priority date for domestic and international students. Application fee: $50 ($60 for international students). *Expenses:* Tuition, state resident: full-time $5,424; part-time $226 per credit hour. Tuition, nonresident: part-time $553 per credit hour. Required fees: $618 per term. *Financial support:* In 2007–08, research assistantships with full tuition reimbursements (averaging $7,988 per year), teaching assistantships with full tuition reimbursements (averaging $7,988 per year) were awarded; career-related internships or fieldwork, scholarships/grants, health care benefits, and unspecified assistantships also available. Support available to part-time students. Financial award application deadline: 11/15. *Unit head:* Dr. Carolyn Peck, Program Administrator, 217-206-7577, Fax: 217-206-6775, E-mail: peck.carolyn@uis.edu.

University of Lethbridge, School of Graduate Studies, Lethbridge, AB T1K 3M4, Canada. Offers accounting (MScM); addictions counseling (M Sc); agricultural biotechnology (M Sc); agricultural studies (M Sc, MA); anthropology (MA); archaeology (MA); art (MA); biochemistry (M Sc); biological sciences (M Sc); biomolecular science (PhD); biosystems and biodiversity (PhD); Canadian studies (MA); chemistry (M Sc); computer science (M Sc); computer science and geographical information science (M Sc); counseling psychology (M Ed); dramatic arts (MA); earth, space, and physical science (PhD); economics (MA); educational leadership (M Ed); English (MA); environmental science (M Sc); evolution and behavior (PhD); exercise science (M Sc); finance (MScM); French (MA); French/German (MA); French/Spanish (MA); general education (M Ed); general management (MScM); geography (M Sc, MA); German (MA); health sciences (M Sc, MA); history (MA); human resource management and labour relations (MScM); individualized multidisciplinary (M Sc, MA); information systems (MScM); international management (MScM); kinesiology (M Sc, MA); management (M Sc, MA); marketing (MScM); mathematics (M Sc); music (MA); Native American studies (MA); neuroscience (M Sc, PhD); new media (MA); nursing (M Sc); philosophy (MA); physics (M Sc); policy and strategy (MScM); political science (MA); psychology (M Sc, MA); religious studies (MA); sociology (MA); theoretical and computational science (PhD); urban and regional studies (MA). Part-time and evening/weekend programs available. *Students:* 215 full-time, 98 part-time. In 2007, 87 master's, 1 doctorate awarded. *Degree requirements:* For doctorate, comprehensive exam, thesis/dissertation. *Entrance requirements:* For master's, GMAT (M Sc in management), bachelor's degree in related field, minimum GPA of 3.0 during previous 20 graded semester courses, 2 years teaching or related experience (M Ed); for doctorate, master's degree, minimum graduate GPA of 3.5. Additional exam requirements/recommendations for international students: Required—TOEFL. Application fee: $60 Canadian dollars. *Financial support:* Fellowships, research assistantships, teaching assistantships, scholarships/grants, health care benefits, and unspecified assistantships available. *Faculty research:* Movement and brain plasticity, gibberellin physiology, photosynthesis, carbon cycling, molecular properties of main-group ring components. *Unit head:* Dr. Jo-Anne Fiske, Interim Dean, 403-329-2121, Fax: 403-329-2097. *Application contact:* Jennifer Geddes, Graduate Liaison Officer, 403-329-2762, Fax: 403-329-5159, E-mail: jennifer.geddes@uleth.ca.

University of Louisiana at Monroe, Graduate Studies and Research, College of Education and Human Development, Department of Educational Leadership and Counseling, Program in Substance Abuse Counseling, Monroe, LA 71209-0001. Offers MA. Part-time and evening/weekend programs available. *Students:* 8 full-time (5 women), 4 part-time (all women); includes 4 minority (3 African Americans, 1 Asian American or Pacific Islander). Average age 33. *Degree requirements:* For master's, comprehensive exam, internship. *Entrance requirements:* For master's, GRE General Test, minimum GPA of 2.8 in last 60 hours, interview. Additional exam requirements/recommendations for international students: Required—TOEFL (minimum score 500 paper-based; 173 computer-based; 61 iBT). *Application deadline:* For fall admission, 8/22 priority date for domestic students, 7/1 for international students; for winter admission, 12/12 for domestic students; for spring admission, 1/17 for domestic students, 11/1 for international students. Applications are processed on a rolling basis. Application fee: $20 ($30 for international students). Electronic applications accepted. *Expenses:* Tuition, state resident: full-time $2,220. Tuition, nonresident: full-time $8,172. *Financial support:* Research assistantships with full tuition reimbursements, teaching assistantships with full tuition reimbursements, career-related internships or fieldwork, Federal Work-Study, and unspecified assistantships available. Financial award application deadline: 4/1; financial award applicants required to submit FAFSA. *Faculty research:* Addictionology. *Unit head:* Dr. Mitchell Young, Coordinator, 318-342-1255, Fax: 318-342-3131, E-mail: myoung@ulm.edu.

University of Nevada, Las Vegas, Graduate College, College of Education, Department of Counselor Education, Las Vegas, NV 89154-9900. Offers addiction studies (Certificate); community mental health (MS); rehabilitation counseling (Certificate); school counseling (M Ed). *Faculty:* 7 full-time (4 women). *Students:* 27 full-time (24 women), 20 part-time (all women); includes 12 minority (2 African Americans, 3 Asian Americans or Pacific Islanders, 7 Hispanic Americans). 26 applicants, 38% accepted, 9 enrolled. In 2007, 21 master's, 2 other advanced degrees awarded. *Entrance requirements:* Additional exam requirements/recommendations for international students: Required—TOEFL (minimum score 550 paper-based; 213 computer-based; 80 iBT). *Application deadline:* For fall and winter admission, 2/1 for domestic and international students. Electronic applications accepted. *Expenses:* Tuition, state resident: part-time $198 per credit. Tuition, nonresident: part-time $416 per credit. Required fees: $256 per semester. Tuition and fees vary according to course load and reciprocity agreements. *Financial support:* In 2007–08, 4 research assistantships with partial tuition reimbursements (averaging $10,000 per year), 5 teaching assistantships with partial tuition reimbursements (averaging $10,000 per year) were awarded. *Unit head:* Dr. Pat Markos, Chair, 702-895-5994. *Application contact:* Graduate College Admissions Evaluator, 702-895-3320, E-mail: gradcollege@unlv.edu.

University of New England, College of Health Professions, School of Social Work, Biddeford, ME 04005-9526. Offers addictions counseling (Certificate); gerontology (Certificate); social work (MSW). *Accreditation:* CSWE. Part-time programs available. *Faculty:* 14 full-time (8 women), 5 part-time/adjunct (4 women). *Students:* 137 full-time (117 women), 7 part-time (all women); includes 2 minority (both American Indian/Alaska Native), 3 international. Average age 32. 110 applicants, 86% accepted, 55 enrolled. In 2007, 55 master's, 1 other advanced degree awarded. *Degree requirements:* For master's, field internships. *Entrance requirements:* Additional exam requirements/recommendations for international students: Required—TOEFL (minimum score 550 paper-based; 213 computer-based). *Application deadline:* For fall admission, 1/15 priority date for domestic students; for spring admission, 3/31 priority date for domestic students, 3/31 for international students. Applications are processed on a rolling basis. Application fee: $40. Electronic applications accepted. *Financial support:* In 2007–08, 40 students received support. Scholarships/grants and tuition waivers (partial) available. Financial award application deadline: 5/1; financial award applicants required to submit FAFSA. *Faculty research:* Domestic violence, solution focused practice, empowerment models, adverse childhood experiences. *Unit head:* Martha Wilson, Director, 207-221-4513, E-mail: mwilson@une.edu. *Application contact:* Peggy Warden, Assistant Director of Graduate Admissions, 207-221-4225, Fax: 207-221-4898, E-mail: gradadmissions@une.edu.

Wayne State University, Graduate School, Interdisciplinary Program in Alcohol and Drug Abuse Studies, Detroit, MI 48202. Offers Certificate. *Students:* Average age 34. 2 applicants, 100% accepted, 2 enrolled. In 2007, 1 degree awarded. *Entrance requirements:* For degree, graduate degree or enrolled in graduate program; letter of reference. Additional exam requirements/recommendations for international students: Required—TOEFL (minimum score 550 paper-based; 213 computer-based); Recommended—TWE (minimum score 6). *Application deadline:* For fall admission, 7/1 for domestic students, 6/1 for international students; for winter admission, 10/1 for international students; for spring admission, 2/1 for international students. Applications are processed on a rolling basis. Application fee: $30 ($50 for international students). Electronic applications accepted. *Expenses:* Tuition, state resident: part-time $403 per credit hour. Tuition, nonresident: part-time $890 per credit hour. *Faculty research:* Epidemiology and etiology of substance use, substance abuse prevention and treatment; treatment for substance abuse and co-occurring disorders; faculty and professional development in substance abuse. *Unit head:* Dr. Eugene Schoener, Director, 313-577-1388, E-mail: eschoen@med.wayne.edu. *Application contact:* Cheryl Madeja, Research Assistant, 313-993-9747, Fax: 313-577-6685, E-mail: cmadeja@med.wayne.edu.

Clinical Psychology

Abilene Christian University, Graduate School, College of Arts and Sciences, Department of Psychology, Program in Clinical Psychology, Abilene, TX 79699-9100. Offers MS. Part-time programs available. *Students:* 17 full-time (13 women), 1 (woman) part-time; includes 1 minority (Hispanic American), 1 international. 15 applicants, 73% accepted, 8 enrolled. In 2007, 3 degrees awarded. *Degree requirements:* For master's, comprehensive exam, thesis. *Entrance requirements:* For master's, GRE General Test. *Application deadline:* For fall admission, 4/1 priority date for domestic students; for spring admission, 11/1 for domestic students. Applications are processed on a rolling basis. Application fee: $40 ($45 for international students). Electronic applications accepted. *Expenses:* Tuition: Full-time $13,368; part-time $557 per hour. Required fees: $700; $34 per hour. $10 per semester. Tuition and fees vary according to degree level and campus/location. *Financial support:* Career-related internships or fieldwork and Federal Work-Study available. Support available to part-time students. Financial award application deadline: 4/1. *Unit head:* Dr. Jeffrey Wherry, Graduate Advisor, 325-674-2471, Fax: 325-674-6968, E-mail: jnw04c@acu.edu. *Application contact:* William Horn, Graduate Admissions Counselor, 325-674-2656, Fax: 325-674-6717, E-mail: gradinfo@acu.edu.

Acadia University, Faculty of Pure and Applied Science, Department of Psychology, Wolfville, NS B4P 2R6, Canada. Offers clinical psychology (M Sc). *Faculty:* 12 full-time (6 women), 11 part-time/adjunct (5 women). *Students:* 10 full-time (8 women). Average age 26. 39 applicants, 18% accepted, 5 enrolled. In 2007, 7 degrees awarded. *Degree requirements:* For master's, thesis. *Entrance requirements:* For master's, GRE General Test, GRE Subject Test, honors degree or equivalent. Additional exam requirements/recommendations for international students: Required—TOEFL (minimum score 580 paper-based; 237 computer-based), IELTS (minimum score 7). *Application deadline:* For fall admission, 2/1 priority date for domestic students. Applications are processed on a rolling basis. Application fee: $50. Electronic applications accepted. *Financial support:* In 2007–08, 5 students received support; teaching assistantships, career-related internships or fieldwork and scholarships/grants available. Financial award application deadline: 2/1. *Faculty research:* Social psychology, job stress, psychotherapy, cognition perception, development. *Unit head:* Dr. Douglas K. Symons, Head, 902-585-1301, Fax: 902-585-1078, E-mail: doug.symons@acadiau.ca. *Application contact:* Dr. Peter Horvath, Information Contact, 902-585-1200, Fax: 902-585-1078, E-mail: peter.horvath@acadiau.ca.

Adelphi University, Derner Institute of Advanced Psychological Studies, Program in Clinical Psychology, Garden City, NY 11530-0701. Offers PhD. *Students:* 69 full-time (56 women), 55 part-time (38 women); includes 9 minority (3 African Americans, 5 Asian Americans or Pacific Islanders, 1 Hispanic American), 16 international. Average age 33. In 2007, 26 doctorates awarded. *Degree requirements:* For doctorate, thesis/dissertation, research (second year), 1 year internship. *Entrance requirements:* For doctorate, GRE General Test, GRE Subject Test, interview; resumé, undergraduate courses in psychology, experimental psychology, statistics, developmental psychology, and abnormal psychology. Additional exam requirements/recommendations for international students: Required—TOEFL (minimum score 550 paper-based; 213 computer-based). *Application deadline:* For fall admission, 1/15 priority date for domestic and international students. Application fee: $50. Electronic applications accepted. *Financial support:* Research assistantships with full and partial tuition reimbursements, teaching assistantships, career-related internships or fieldwork, Federal Work-Study, institutionally sponsored loans, and unspecified assistantships available. Financial award application deadline: 2/15; financial award applicants required to submit FAFSA. *Unit head:* Unit Head, 516-877-4800. *Application contact:* Christine Murphy, Director of Admissions, 516-877-3050, Fax: 516-877-3039, E-mail: graduateadmissions@adelphi.edu.

Adelphi University, Derner Institute of Advanced Psychological Studies, Respecialization Program in Clinical Psychology, Garden City, NY 11530-0701. Offers Post-Doctoral Certificate. *Students:* Average age 44. In 2007, 26 degrees awarded. *Degree requirements:* For Post-Doctoral Certificate, 2 years of full-time study and supervised clinical practice, 1 year full-time internship. *Entrance requirements:* For degree, doctoral degree in psychology, 2 interviews, 2 years clinical courses and clerkships, 1 year internship. Additional exam requirements/recommendations for international students: Required—TOEFL (minimum score 550 paper-based; 213 computer-based). *Application deadline:* Applications are processed on a rolling basis. Application fee: $50. *Financial support:* Research assistantships with partial tuition reimbursements, teaching assistantships, career-related internships or fieldwork and institutionally sponsored loans available. Financial award application deadline: 2/15; financial award applicants required to submit FAFSA. *Unit head:* Dr. Marybeth Cresci, Professor, 516-877-4826, E-mail: cresci@adelphi.edu. *Application contact:* Christine Murphy, Director of Admissions, 516-877-3050, Fax: 516-877-3039, E-mail: graduateadmissions@adelphi.edu.

Adler School of Professional Psychology, Programs in Psychology, Chicago, IL 60601-7203. Offers art therapy (Certificate); clinical hypnosis (Certificate); clinical psychology (Psy D); counseling psychology (MACP); counseling psychology/art therapy (MACAT); gerontology (MAGP); marriage and family counseling (MAMFC); marriage and family therapy (Certificate); organizational psychology (MAO); substance abuse counseling (MASAC, Certificate); Psy D/Certificate; Psy D/MACAT; Psy D/MACP; Psy D/MAMFC; Psy D/MASAC. *Accreditation:* APA. Part-time and evening/weekend programs available. Terminal master's awarded for partial completion of doctoral program. *Degree requirements:* For master's, thesis or alternative, oral exam, practicum; for doctorate, thesis/dissertation, clinical exam, internship, oral exam, practicum, written qualifying exam. *Entrance requirements:* For master's, 12 semester hours in psychology, minimum GPA of 3.0; for doctorate, 18 semester hours in psychology, minimum GPA of 3.25; for Certificate, appropriate master's or doctoral degree.

See Close-Up on page 1363.

Alabama Agricultural and Mechanical University, School of Graduate Studies, School of Education, Department of Counseling and Special Education, Huntsville, AL 35811. Offers communicative disorders (M Ed, MS); psychology and counseling (MS, Ed S), including clinical psychology (MS), counseling and guidance, counseling psychology (MS), personnel management (MS), psychometry (MS), school psychology (MS); special education (M Ed, MS). *Accreditation:* CORE; NCATE. Part-time and evening/weekend programs available. *Faculty:* 4 full-time (3 women), 3 part-time/adjunct (1 woman). *Students:* 24 full-time (16 women), 58 part-time (48 women); includes 59 minority (56 African Americans, 1 American Indian/Alaska Native, 2 Hispanic Americans), 2 international. In 2007, 55 master's, 2 other advanced degrees awarded. *Degree requirements:* For master's, comprehensive exam. *Entrance requirements:* For master's, GRE General Test. *Application deadline:* For fall admission, 5/1 for domestic students. Application fee: $15 ($20 for international students). *Financial support:* Career-related internships or fieldwork available. Support available to part-time students. Financial award application deadline: 4/1. *Faculty research:* Increasing numbers of minorities in special education and speech-language pathology. Total annual research expenditures: $300,000. *Unit head:* Dr. Shirley King, Chair, 256-372-5520, Fax: 256-372-5526.

Alliant International University–Fresno, California School of Professional Psychology, PhD Program in Clinical Psychology, Fresno, CA 93727. Offers PhD. *Degree requirements:* For doctorate, thesis/dissertation. *Entrance requirements:* For doctorate, interview, minimum GPA of 3.0 in both psychology and overall, letters of recommendation, essay. Additional exam requirements/recommendations for international students: Required—TOEFL (minimum score 600 paper-based; 250 computer-based), TWE (minimum score 5). *Faculty research:* Teaching, ecosystemic child psychology, health psychology, clinical forensic psychology.

See Close-Up on page 1367.

Alliant International University–Fresno, California School of Professional Psychology, Psy D Program in Clinical Psychology, Fresno, CA 93727. Offers Psy D. *Accreditation:* APA. *Degree requirements:* For doctorate, comprehensive exam, thesis/dissertation. *Entrance requirements:* For doctorate, interview, minimum GPA of 3.0 in both psychology and overall, letters of recommendation, essay. Additional exam requirements/recommendations for international students: Required—TOEFL (minimum score 600 paper-based; 250 computer-based), TWE (minimum score 5). Electronic applications accepted. *Faculty research:* Ecosystemic child clinical health psychology, eating disorders.

See Close-Up on page 1369.

Alliant International University–Los Angeles, California School of Professional Psychology, PhD Program in Clinical Psychology, Alhambra, CA 91803-1360. Offers PhD. *Accreditation:* APA. *Degree requirements:* For doctorate, comprehensive exam, thesis/dissertation. *Entrance requirements:* For doctorate, interview, minimum GPA of 3.0 in both psychology and overall. Additional exam requirements/recommendations for international students: Required—TOEFL (minimum score 600 paper-based; 250 computer-based), TWE (minimum score 5). Electronic applications accepted. *Faculty research:* Multicultural and community clinical psychology, health psychology, individual and family psychology.

See Close-Up on page 1367.

Alliant International University–Los Angeles, California School of Professional Psychology, Psy D Program in Clinical Psychology, Alhambra, CA 91803-1360. Offers Psy D. *Accreditation:* APA. *Degree requirements:* For doctorate, thesis/dissertation. *Entrance requirements:* For doctorate, interview, minimum GPA of 3.0 in both psychology and overall. Additional exam requirements/recommendations for international students: Required—TOEFL (minimum score 600 paper-based; 250 computer-based), TWE. Electronic applications accepted. *Faculty research:* Child and family psychology, multicultural and community psychology, acculturation, lesbian and gay issues, women's health.

See Close-Up on page 1369.

Alliant International University–Sacramento, California School of Professional Psychology, Program in Clinical Psychology, Sacramento, CA 95825. Offers Psy D. *Entrance requirements:* For doctorate, minimum GPA of 3.0, letters of recommendation, interview. Electronic applications accepted. *Faculty research:* Health psychology, infant-preschool mental health, community mental, health trauma, aging.

See Close-Up on page 1369.

Alliant International University–San Diego, California School of Professional Psychology, PhD Program in Clinical Psychology, San Diego, CA 92131-1799. Offers PhD. *Accreditation:* APA. *Degree requirements:* For doctorate, thesis/dissertation. *Entrance requirements:* For doctorate, interview, minimum GPA of 3.0 in both psychology and overall. Additional exam requirements/recommendations for international students: Required—TOEFL (minimum score 600 paper-based; 250 computer-based), TWE (minimum score 5). Electronic applications accepted. *Faculty research:* Family conflict in adolescence, anxiety disorders, PTSD, childhood psychopathology, regressed memory.

See Close-Up on page 1367.

Alliant International University–San Diego, California School of Professional Psychology, Psy D Program in Clinical Psychology, San Diego, CA 92131-1799. Offers Psy D. *Accreditation:* APA. *Degree requirements:* For doctorate, thesis/dissertation. *Entrance requirements:* For doctorate, interview, minimum GPA of 3.0 in both psychology and overall. Additional exam requirements/recommendations for international students: Required—TOEFL (minimum score 600 paper-based; 250 computer-based), TWE (minimum score 5). Electronic applications accepted. *Faculty research:* Forensic psychology, health psychology, integrative psychology, family and child psychology.

See Close-Up on page 1369.

Alliant International University–San Diego, Marshall Goldsmith School of Management, Organizational Psychology Division, San Diego, CA 92131-1799. Offers clinical/industrial organizational psychology (PhD); consulting psychology (PhD); industrial/organizational psychology (MA, MS, PhD); organizational behavior (MA). Part-time and evening/weekend programs available. Terminal master's awarded for partial completion of doctoral program. *Degree requirements:* For doctorate, thesis/dissertation. *Entrance requirements:* For master's and doctorate, interview, minimum GPA of 3.0 in both psychology and overall. Additional exam requirements/recommendations for international students: Required—TOEFL (minimum score 600 paper-based; 250 computer-based), TWE (minimum score 5). Electronic applications accepted. *Faculty research:* Cultural diversity in the workplace, work motivation, personnel, performance management.

Alliant International University–San Francisco, California School of Professional Psychology, PhD Program in Clinical Psychology, San Francisco, CA 94133-1221. Offers PhD. *Degree requirements:* For doctorate, thesis/dissertation. *Entrance requirements:* For doctorate, interview, minimum GPA of 3.0 in both psychology and overall. Additional exam requirements/recommendations for international students: Required—TOEFL (minimum score 600 paper-based; 250 computer-based), TWE (minimum score 5). Electronic applications accepted. *Faculty research:* Social model of disability, feminist models of clinical training, post-traumatic stress disorder, HIV, psychology of women.

See Close-Up on page 1367.

Alliant International University–San Francisco, California School of Professional Psychology, Psy D Program in Clinical Psychology, San Francisco, CA 94133-1221. Offers Psy D, Certificate. *Accreditation:* APA (one or more programs are accredited). *Degree requirements:* For doctorate, thesis/dissertation. *Entrance requirements:* For doctorate, interview, minimum GPA of 3.0 in both psychology and overall. Additional exam requirements/recommendations for international students: Required—TOEFL (minimum score 600 paper-based; 250 computer-based), TWE (minimum score 5). Electronic applications accepted. *Faculty research:* Health psychology, family and child psychology, psychodynamic psychology, multicultural and community psychology, gender issues.

See Close-Up on page 1369.

American International College, School of Arts, Education and Science, Department of Psychology, Program in Clinical Psychology, Springfield, MA 01109-3189. Offers MA. *Faculty:* 2 full-time (1 woman), 4 part-time/adjunct (2 women). *Students:* 25 full-time (20 women), 14 part-time (10 women); includes 13 minority (8 African Americans, 2 Asian Americans or Pacific Islanders, 3 Hispanic Americans). Average age 29. In 2007, 4 degrees awarded. *Degree requirements:* For master's, practicum. *Entrance requirements:* For master's, minimum B average in undergraduate course work, BS or BA. Additional exam requirements/recommendations for international students: Required—TOEFL. *Application deadline:* For fall admission, 4/15 for domestic and international students. Applications are processed on a rolling basis. Application fee: $50. Electronic applications accepted. *Expenses:* Tuition: Part-time $615 per credit hour. Full-time tuition and fees vary according to degree level, campus/location and program. *Financial support:* Fellowships, career-related internships or fieldwork available. Financial award applicants required to submit FAFSA. *Application contact:* Barbara Z. Benoit, Director of Graduate Admissions, 413-205-3700, Fax: 413-205-3051, E-mail: barbara.benoit@aic.edu.

American University, College of Arts and Sciences, Department of Psychology, Program in Clinical Psychology, Washington, DC 20016-8001. Offers PhD. *Accreditation:* APA. *Students:* 22 full-time (18 women), 18 part-time (17 women); includes 6 minority (3 African Americans, 1 Asian American or Pacific Islander, 2 Hispanic Americans). Average age 29. In 2007, 6 degrees awarded. *Degree requirements:* For doctorate, comprehensive exam, thesis/dissertation, internship. *Entrance requirements:* For doctorate, GRE General Test, GRE Subject Test, recommendations. *Application deadline:* For fall admission, 1/1 for domestic students. Application fee: $50. *Expenses:* Tuition: Full-time $19,998; part-time $1,111 per credit hour. Required fees: $380. Tuition and fees vary according to program. *Financial support:* Fellowships, research assistantships, teaching assistantships, career-related internships or fieldwork, Federal Work-Study, institutionally sponsored loans, tuition waivers (full and partial), and unspecified assistantships available. Support available to part-time students. Financial award application deadline: 2/1. *Faculty research:* Depression, eating disorders, anxiety disorders, addictions, behavior therapy. *Application contact:* Sara Holland, Senior Administrative Assistant, 202-885-1717, Fax: 202-885-1023.

Antioch University Los Angeles, Graduate Programs, Program in Psychology, Culver City, CA 90230. Offers clinical psychology (MA); psychology (MA). Part-time programs available. *Degree requirements:* For master's, thesis (for some programs), internship. *Entrance requirements:* For master's, interview. Additional exam requirements/recommendations for international students: Required—TOEFL. *Faculty research:* Creativity and humor, ethnic humor, adult development, Jungian theory, psychoanalytic theory.

Antioch University New England, Graduate School, Department of Applied Psychology, Program in Clinical Mental Health Counseling, Keene, NH 03431-3552. Offers MA. *Faculty:* 9 full-time (7 women), 14 part-time/adjunct (9 women). *Students:* 75 full-time (62 women), 44 part-time (37 women); includes 4 minority (2 African Americans, 1 American Indian/Alaska Native, 1 Hispanic American), 5 international. Average age 35. 65 applicants, 75% accepted, 34 enrolled. In 2007, 38 degrees awarded. *Degree requirements:* For master's, internship, practicum. *Entrance requirements:* For master's, previous course work and work experience in psychology. Additional exam requirements/recommendations for international students: Required—TOEFL (minimum score 600 paper-based; 250 computer-based). *Application deadline:* For fall admission, 7/15 for domestic and international students; for spring admission, 12/1 for domestic and international students. Applications are processed on a rolling basis. Application fee: $50. Electronic applications accepted. *Expenses: Contact institution.* Tuition and fees vary according to degree level, program and student level. *Financial support:* In 2007–08, 23 fellowships (averaging $1,767 per year) were awarded; career-related internships or fieldwork and Federal Work-Study also available. Financial award applicants required to submit FAFSA. *Faculty research:* Multicultural issues in field supervision. *Unit head:* Dr. Carlotta Willis, Director, Clinical Mental Health Counseling Program, 603-283-2147, Fax: 603-357-0718, E-mail: cwillis@antiochne.edu. *Application contact:* Leatrice A. Oram, Co-Director of Admissions, 800-490-3310, Fax: 603-357-0718, E-mail: admissions@antiochne.edu.

Antioch University New England, Graduate School, Department of Clinical Psychology, Keene, NH 03431-3552. Offers Psy D. *Accreditation:* APA. *Faculty:* 8 full-time (4 women), 6 part-time/adjunct (3 women). *Students:* 165 full-time (130 women); includes 7 minority (2 African Americans, 5 Hispanic Americans), 4 international. Average age 39. 102 applicants, 61% accepted, 36 enrolled. In 2007, 25 degrees awarded. *Degree requirements:* For doctorate, thesis/dissertation, internship, practicum. *Entrance requirements:* For doctorate, GRE General Test, GRE Subject Test, previous course work in psychology. Additional exam requirements/recommendations for international students: Required—TOEFL (minimum score 600 paper-based; 250 computer-based). *Application deadline:* For fall admission, 1/13 for domestic and international students. Application fee: $75. *Expenses: Contact institution.* Tuition and fees vary according to degree level, program and student level. *Financial support:* In 2007–08, 123 students received support, including 17 fellowships (averaging $1,647 per year), 1 research assistantship (averaging $5,284 per year), 5 teaching assistantships (averaging $3,048 per year); career-related internships or fieldwork, Federal Work-Study, and scholarships/grants also available. Financial award applicants required to submit FAFSA. *Faculty research:* Psychotherapy outcome and process in private practice, neuropsychiatric evaluations, effects of trauma on adults, supervision, clinical training evaluation. *Unit head:* Dr. Roger L. Peterson, Chairperson, 603-283-2178, Fax: 603-357-1679, E-mail: rpeterson@antiochne.edu. *Application contact:* Leatrice A. Oram, Co-Director of Admissions, 800-490-3310, Fax: 603-357-0718, E-mail: admissions@antiochne.edu.

Antioch University Santa Barbara, Program in Clinical Psychology, Santa Barbara, CA 93101-1581. Offers Psy D. *Faculty:* 13 full-time (9 women), 34 part-time/adjunct (19 women). *Students:* 43 full-time (28 women); includes 9 minority (1 African American, 2 Asian Americans or Pacific Islanders, 6 Hispanic Americans), 1 international. *Application deadline:* For fall admission, 1/31 priority date for domestic students. Applications are processed on a rolling basis. Application fee: $60 ($100 for international students). Electronic applications accepted. *Unit head:* Dr. Michele Harway, Director, 805-962-8179 Ext. 320, Fax: 805-962-4786, E-mail: mharway@antiochsb.edu. *Application contact:* Director of Admissions, 805-962-8179, Fax: 805-962-4786, E-mail: admissions@antiochsb.edu.

Appalachian State University, Cratis D. Williams Graduate School, Department of Psychology, Boone, NC 28608. Offers clinical health psychology (MA); general experimental psychology (MA); industrial and organizational psychology (MA). Part-time programs available. *Faculty:* 31 full-time (11 women). *Students:* 43 full-time (31 women), 37 part-time (30 women); includes 4 minority (3 African Americans, 1 Asian American or Pacific Islander), 4 international. 197 applicants, 30% accepted, 30 enrolled. In 2007, 23 master's, 6 other advanced degrees awarded. *Degree requirements:* For master's and MS/SSP, comprehensive exam, thesis optional, GRE Subject Test exit exam. *Entrance requirements:* For master's, GRE General Test, 3 letters of recommendation. Additional exam requirements/recommendations for international students: Required—TOEFL (minimum score 550 paper-based; 230 computer-based; 79 iBT), IELTS (minimum score 7). *Application deadline:* For fall admission, 3/1 for domestic students, 1/1 for international students. Applications are processed on a rolling basis. Application fee: $50. *Expenses:* Tuition, state resident: part-time $127 per semester hour. Tuition, nonresident: part-time $597 per semester hour. Required fees: $18 per semester. *Financial support:* In 2007–08, 34 research assistantships (averaging $3,500 per year), 25 teaching assistantships (averaging $3,500 per year) were awarded; fellowships, career-related internships or fieldwork, Federal Work-Study, scholarships/grants, and unspecified assistantships also available. Financial award application deadline: 4/1. *Faculty research:* Eating disorders, school-based consultations, organizational behavior management, brain mechanisms of sound localization, parenting styles. Total annual research expenditures: $158,688. *Unit head:* Dr. Paul Fox, Chair, 828-262-2272, Fax: 828-262-2974, E-mail: foxpa@appstate.edu. *Application contact:* Dr. Denise Martz, Graduate Coordinator, 828-262-2715, E-mail: martzdm@appstate.edu.

Argosy University, Atlanta, College of Psychology and Behavioral Sciences, Atlanta, GA 30328. Offers clinical psychology (MA, Psy D, Postdoctoral Respecialization Certificate), including child and family psychology (Psy D), general adult clinical (Psy D), health psychology (Psy D), neuropsychology/geropsychology (Psy D); community counseling (MA), including marriage and family therapy; counselor education and supervision (Ed D); marriage and family therapy (Certificate). *Accreditation:* APA.

See Close-Up on page 1377.

Argosy University, Chicago, College of Psychology and Behavioral Sciences, Master's Program in Clinical Psychology, Chicago, IL 60654. Offers MA.

See Close-Up on page 1379.

Argosy University, Dallas, College of Psychology and Behavioral Sciences, Program in Clinical Psychology, Dallas, TX 75231. Offers MA, Psy D.

See Close-Up on page 1381.

Argosy University, Denver, College of Psychology and Behavioral Sciences, Denver, CO 80203. Offers clinical psychology (MA, Psy D); community counseling (MA); counseling psychology (Ed D), including counselor education and supervision; counselor education and supervision (Ed D); forensic psychology (MA); marriage and family therapy (MA); organizational leadership (Ed D).

See Close-Up on page 1383.

Argosy University, Hawai'i, College of Psychology and Behavioral Sciences, Program in Clinical Psychology, Honolulu, HI 96813. Offers clinical psychology (MA, Psy D, Postdoctoral Respecialization Certificate), including child and family clinical practice (Psy D), diversity in clinical practice (Psy D). *Accreditation:* APA.

See Close-Up on page 1385.

Argosy University, Inland Empire, College of Psychology and Behavioral Sciences, San Bernardino, CA 92408. Offers clinical psychology/marriage and family therapy (MA); counseling psychology (MA, Ed D); counseling psychology/marriage and family therapy (MA); forensic psychology (MA).

See Close-Up on page 1387.

Argosy University, Los Angeles, College of Psychology and Behavioral Sciences, Santa Monica, CA 90405. Offers clinical psychology/marriage and family therapy (MA); counseling psychology (Ed D); counseling psychology/marriage and family therapy (MA); organizational leadership (Ed D).

See Close-Up on page 1389.

Argosy University, Orange County, College of Psychology and Behavioral Sciences, Program in Clinical Psychology, Santa Ana, CA 92704. Offers child and adolescent psychology (Psy D); forensic psychology (Psy D); marriage and family therapy (MA).

See Close-Up on page 1393.

Argosy University, Phoenix, College of Psychology and Behavioral Sciences, Program in Clinical Psychology, Phoenix, AZ 85021. Offers clinical psychology (MA); sports-exercise psychology (Psy D). *Accreditation:* APA (one or more programs are accredited).

See Close-Up on page 1395.

Argosy University, San Diego, College of Psychology and Behavioral Sciences, San Diego, CA 92108. Offers clinical psychology/marriage and family therapy (MA); counseling psychology (MA, Ed D); counseling psychology/marriage and family therapy (MA).

See Close-Up on page 1399.

Argosy University, San Francisco Bay Area, College of Psychology and Behavioral Sciences, Alameda, CA 94501. Offers clinical psychology (MA, Psy D); counseling psychology (MA, Ed D); forensic psychology (MA); organizational leadership (Ed D). *Accreditation:* APA (one or more programs are accredited).

See Close-Up on page 1401.

Argosy University, Schaumburg, College of Psychology and Behavioral Sciences, Schaumburg, IL 60173-5403. Offers clinical health psychology (Post-Graduate Certificate); clinical psychology (MA, Psy D), including child and family psychology (Psy D), clinical health psychology (Psy D), diversity and multicultural psychology (Psy D), forensic psychology (Psy D); community counseling (MA); counseling psychology (Ed D), including counselor education and supervision; counselor education and supervision (Ed D); forensic psychology (Post-Graduate Certificate); organizational leadership (Ed D). *Accreditation:* ACA; APA.

See Close-Up on page 1405.

Argosy University, Seattle, College of Psychology and Behavioral Sciences, Program in Clinical Psychology, Seattle, WA 98121. Offers MA, Psy D, Postdoctoral Respecialization Certificate.

See Close-Up on page 1407.

Argosy University, Tampa, College of Psychology and Behavioral Sciences, Program in Clinical Psychology, Tampa, FL 33614. Offers clinical psychology (MA, Psy D), including child and adolescent psychology (Psy D), geropsychology (Psy D), marriage/couples and family therapy (Psy D), neuropsychology (Psy D). *Accreditation:* APA.

See Close-Up on page 1409.

Argosy University, Twin Cities, College of Psychology and Behavioral Sciences, Eagan, MN 55121. Offers clinical psychology (MA, Psy D), including child and family psychology (Psy D), forensic psychology (Psy D), health psychology (Psy D), marriage/couples and family therapy (Psy D), neuropsychology (Psy D); forensic counseling (Post-Graduate Certificate); forensic psychology (MA); marriage and family therapy (MA, DMFT), including forensic counseling (MA); organizational leadership (Ed D). *Accreditation:* APA.

See Close-Up on page 1411.

Argosy University, Washington DC, College of Psychology and Behavioral Sciences, Arlington, VA 22209. Offers clinical psychology (MA, Psy D), including child and family psychology (Psy D), diversity and multicultural psychology (Psy D), forensic psychology (Psy D), health and neuropsychology (Psy D); community counseling (MA); counseling psychology (Ed D), including counselor education and supervision; counselor education and supervision (Ed D); forensic psychology (MA); organizational leadership (Ed D). *Accreditation:* APA.

See Close-Up on page 1413.

Arizona State University, Graduate College, College of Liberal Arts and Sciences, Division of Natural Sciences and Mathematics, Department of Psychology, Tempe, AZ 85287. Offers behavioral neuroscience (PhD); clinical psychology (PhD); cognitive/behavioral systems (PhD); developmental psychology (PhD); environmental psychology (PhD); quantitative research methods (PhD); social psychology (PhD). *Accreditation:* APA. *Degree requirements:* For doctorate, thesis/dissertation. *Entrance requirements:* For doctorate, GRE General Test, GRE Subject Test.

Azusa Pacific University, School of Behavioral and Applied Sciences, Department of Graduate Psychology, Azusa, CA 91702-7000. Offers clinical psychology (MA, Psy D), including family therapy (MA). *Accreditation:* APA (one or more programs are accredited). Part-time and evening/weekend programs available. *Degree requirements:* For master's, comprehensive exam, 250 hours of clinical experience, individual and group therapy. *Entrance requirements:* For master's, interview, minimum GPA of 3.0, Minnesota Multiphasic Personality Inventory. Additional exam requirements/recommendations for international students: Required—TOEFL (minimum score 600 paper-based).

Ball State University, Graduate School, College of Sciences and Humanities, Department of Psychological Science, Program in Clinical Psychology, Muncie, IN 47306-1099. Offers MA. *Faculty:* 20. *Students:* 23 full-time (15 women), 1 (woman) part-time; includes 5 minority (1 African American, 3 Asian Americans or Pacific Islanders, 1 Hispanic American), 2 international. Average age 23. 47 applicants, 49% accepted, 12 enrolled. In 2007, 10 degrees awarded. *Entrance requirements:* For master's, GRE General Test, interview. Application fee: $25 ($35 for international students). *Expenses:* Tuition, state resident: full-time $6,864. Tuition, nonresident: full-time $17,932. Required fees: $1,866. *Financial support:* Research assistantships with full tuition reimbursements, teaching assistantships available. Financial award application deadline: 3/1. *Unit head:* Dr. Kerri Pickel, Graduate Program Director, 765-285-1690, Fax: 765-285-8980, E-mail: kpickel@bsu.edu.

Barry University, School of Arts and Sciences, Department of Psychology, Miami Shores, FL 33161-6695. Offers clinical psychology (MS); school psychology (MS, SSP). Part-time and

Clinical Psychology

Barry University (continued)

evening/weekend programs available. *Students:* 6 full-time (0 women), 56 part-time (52 women); includes 34 minority (14 African Americans, 2 Asian Americans or Pacific Islanders, 18 Hispanic Americans), 8 international. *Degree requirements:* For master's, thesis, practicum. *Entrance requirements:* For master's, GRE General Test, minimum GPA of 3.0, course work in psychology. *Application deadline:* Applications are processed on a rolling basis. Application fee: $30. Electronic applications accepted. *Financial support:* In 2007–08, 5 research assistantships with partial tuition reimbursements (averaging $3,000 per year) were awarded; career-related internships or fieldwork and tuition waivers (partial) also available. Support available to part-time students. Financial award application deadline: 5/1; financial award applicants required to submit FAFSA. *Faculty research:* Closed head injury, memory and aging, infant/mother interaction, evolutionary aspects of behavior, gender roles. *Unit head:* Dr. Lenore Szuchman, Chair, 305-899-3278, Fax: 305-899-3279, E-mail: lszuchman@mail.barry.edu. *Application contact:* Dave Fletcher, Director of Graduate Admissions, 305-899-3113, Fax: 305-899-2971, E-mail: dfletcher@mail.barry.edu.

See Close-Up on page 1415.

Baylor University, Graduate School, College of Arts and Sciences, Department of Psychology and Neuroscience, Program in Clinical Psychology, Waco, TX 76798. Offers MSCP, Psy D. *Accreditation:* APA. *Students:* 23 full-time (18 women), 1 (woman) part-time; includes 6 minority (4 Asian Americans or Pacific Islanders, 2 Hispanic Americans). In 2007, 5 master's, 8 doctorates awarded. *Degree requirements:* For doctorate, comprehensive exam. *Entrance requirements:* For master's, GRE General Test; for doctorate, GRE General Test, interview. *Application deadline:* For fall admission, 2/1 for domestic students. Applications are processed on a rolling basis. Application fee: $25. *Financial support:* Research assistantships, teaching assistantships, career-related internships or fieldwork, institutionally sponsored loans, tuition waivers (partial), and practicum stipends available. Financial award applicants required to submit FAFSA. *Faculty research:* Professional training in clinical psychology, human systems and dynamics, social skills validation, child therapy and assessment. *Unit head:* Dr. David Rudd, Graduate Program Director, 254-710-2961, Fax: 254-710-3033, E-mail: david_rudd@baylor.edu. *Application contact:* Judy Mills, Graduate Coordinator, 254-710-2811, Fax: 254-710-3033.

Benedictine University, Graduate Programs, Program in Clinical Psychology, Lisle, IL 60532-0900. Offers MS. Part-time programs available. *Faculty:* 1 full-time (0 women), 7 part-time/adjunct (4 women). *Students:* 13 full-time (10 women), 5 part-time (1 woman); includes 1 minority (Hispanic American) Average age 33. 46 applicants, 54% accepted. In 2007, 27 degrees awarded. *Degree requirements:* For master's, comprehensive exam, internship. *Entrance requirements:* For master's, MAT. Additional exam requirements/recommendations for international students: Required—TOEFL (minimum score 550 paper-based; 213 computer-based). *Application deadline:* For fall admission, 9/1 for domestic students; for winter admission, 12/1 for domestic students; for spring admission, 2/15 for domestic students. Applications are processed on a rolling basis. Application fee: $40. Electronic applications accepted. *Expenses:* Tuition: Full-time $12,825; part-time $475 per credit hour. *Financial support:* Career-related internships or fieldwork and health care benefits available. Support available to part-time students. *Unit head:* Dr. James Crissmon, Director, 630-829-6490, E-mail: jcrissmon@ben.edu. *Application contact:* Kari Gibbons, Director, Admissions, 630-829-6200, Fax: 630-829-6584, E-mail: kgibbons@ben.edu.

Bethany University, Program in Clinical Psychology, Scotts Valley, CA 95066-2820. Offers MS. Part-time and evening/weekend programs available. *Faculty:* 3 full-time (2 women), 4 part-time/adjunct (3 women). *Students:* 11 full-time (9 women), 17 part-time (13 women); includes 7 minority (1 American Indian/Alaska Native, 1 Asian American or Pacific Islander, 5 Hispanic Americans), 1 international. 34 applicants, 59% accepted, 11 enrolled. In 2007, 13 degrees awarded. *Application deadline:* For fall admission, 3/31 priority date for domestic students. Applications are processed on a rolling basis. Application fee: $30. *Expenses:* Tuition: Full-time $9,520; part-time $595 per unit. Required fees: $25; $225 per term. One-time fee: $170. Tuition and fees vary according to course load and program. *Financial support:* In 2007–08, 13 students received support, including 4 teaching assistantships (averaging $1,000 per year); scholarships/grants and tuition waivers (partial) also available. Financial award application deadline: 3/31; financial award applicants required to submit FAFSA. *Unit head:* Dr. William Snow, Director, 831-438-3800 Ext. 3981, E-mail: wsnow@fc.bethany.edu. *Application contact:* Kim Tortora, Program Assistant, 831-438-3800 Ext. 3900, E-mail: ktortora@fc.bethany.edu.

Bowling Green State University, Graduate College, College of Arts and Sciences, Department of Psychology, Bowling Green, OH 43403. Offers clinical psychology (MA, PhD); developmental psychology (MA, PhD); experimental psychology (MA, PhD); industrial/organizational psychology (MA, PhD); quantitative psychology (MA, PhD). *Accreditation:* APA (one or more programs are accredited). *Faculty:* 29 full-time (9 women), 14 part-time/adjunct (5 women). *Students:* 88 full-time (61 women), 27 part-time (19 women); includes 10 minority (5 Asian Americans or Pacific Islanders, 5 Hispanic Americans), 12 international. Average age 27. 225 applicants, 15% accepted, 19 enrolled. In 2007, 22 master's, 14 doctorates awarded. *Degree requirements:* For doctorate, thesis/dissertation. *Entrance requirements:* For doctorate, GRE General Test, GRE Subject Test. Additional exam requirements/recommendations for international students: Required—TOEFL. *Application deadline:* For fall admission, 1/1 for domestic students. Application fee: $30. Electronic applications accepted. *Financial support:* In 2007–08, 5 fellowships with full tuition reimbursements (averaging $16,187 per year), 50 research assistantships with full tuition reimbursements (averaging $11,844 per year), 29 teaching assistantships with full tuition reimbursements (averaging $11,805 per year) were awarded; career-related internships or fieldwork, Federal Work-Study, institutionally sponsored loans, tuition waivers (full), and unspecified assistantships also available. Financial award applicants required to submit FAFSA. *Faculty research:* Personnel psychology, developmental-mathematical models, behavioral medication, brain process, child/adolescent social cognition. *Unit head:* Dr. Dale Klopfer, Chair, 419-372-2733.

Brigham Young University, Graduate Studies, College of Family, Home, and Social Sciences, Department of Psychology, Provo, UT 84602-1001. Offers clinical psychology (PhD); general psychology (MS); psychology (PhD), including applied social psychology, behavioral neurobiology, theoretical/philosophical psychology. *Accreditation:* APA (one or more programs are accredited). *Faculty:* 30 full-time (7 women), 10 part-time/adjunct (4 women). *Students:* 99 full-time (30 women); includes 11 minority (3 African Americans, 6 Asian Americans or Pacific Islanders, 2 Hispanic Americans), 7 international. Average age 24. 107 applicants, 23% accepted, 25 enrolled. In 2007, 9 master's, 14 doctorates awarded. *Degree requirements:* For master's, thesis; for doctorate, thesis/dissertation, publishable paper. *Entrance requirements:* For master's and doctorate, GRE General Test, minimum GPA of 3.0 in last 60 hours of course work. Additional exam requirements/recommendations for international students: Required—TOEFL. *Application deadline:* For fall admission, 1/1 for domestic students. Application fee: $50. Electronic applications accepted. *Financial support:* In 2007–08, 85 students received support, including 13 research assistantships with partial tuition reimbursements available (averaging $3,000 per year), 26 teaching assistantships with partial tuition reimbursements available (averaging $3,000 per year); fellowships, career-related internships or fieldwork, scholarships/grants, tuition waivers (partial), and unspecified assistantships also available. Financial award application deadline: 5/31. *Faculty research:* Psychotherapy process, Alzheimer's disease/dementia, psychology and law, health, psychology. Total annual research expenditures: $533,878. *Unit head:* Dr. Ramona Hopkins, Chair, 801-422-1170, Fax: 801-422-0602, E-mail: ramona_hopkins@byu.edu. *Application contact:* Karen A. Christensen, Coordinator of Student Programs, 801-422-4560, Fax: 801-422-0602, E-mail: karen_christensen@byu.edu.

Bryn Mawr College, Graduate School of Arts and Sciences, Department of Psychology, Bryn Mawr, PA 19010-2899. Offers clinical developmental psychology (PhD). Part-time programs available. *Faculty:* 11. *Students:* 24 full-time (23 women), 10 part-time (all women); includes 2 minority (1 Asian American or Pacific Islander, 1 Hispanic American), 2 international. 56 applicants, 20% accepted, 4 enrolled. In 2007, 3 doctorates awarded. *Degree requirements:* For doctorate, one foreign language, comprehensive exam, thesis/dissertation. *Entrance requirements:* For doctorate, GRE General Test. Additional exam requirements/recommendations for international students: Required—TOEFL (minimum score 600 paper-based; 250 computer-based). *Application deadline:* For fall admission, 1/3 for domestic and international students. Application fee: $30. *Financial support:* Teaching assistantships with partial tuition reimbursements, career-related internships or fieldwork and scholarships/grants available. Support available to part-time students. Financial award application deadline: 1/3. *Unit head:* Dr. Marc Schulz, Chair, 610-526-5039, E-mail: mschulz@brynmawr.edu. *Application contact:* Lea R. Miller, Secretary, 610-526-5072, Fax: 610-526-5076, E-mail: lrmiller@brynmawr.edu.

California Institute of Integral Studies, Graduate Programs, School of Professional Psychology, San Francisco, CA 94103. Offers clinical psychology (Psy D); community mental health (MA); drama therapy (MA); expressive arts therapy (MA); integral counseling psychology (MA); integral counseling, psychology-weekend (MA); psychology (Psy D), including clinical psychology; somatic psychology (MA). *Accreditation:* APA. Part-time programs available. *Faculty:* 28 full-time, 54 part-time/adjunct. *Students:* 591; includes 113 minority (19 African Americans, 3 American Indian/Alaska Native, 48 Asian Americans or Pacific Islanders, 43 Hispanic Americans). Average age 37. 383 applicants, 75% accepted, 155 enrolled. In 2007, 109 master's, 20 doctorates awarded. *Degree requirements:* For master's, comprehensive exam; for doctorate, comprehensive exam, thesis/dissertation. *Entrance requirements:* For master's, minimum GPA of 3.0, letters of recommendation, writing sample; for doctorate, GRE, MA in psychology or social work with appropriate practical experience for advanced standing, or BA with a minimum GPA of 3.1; letters of recommendation; writing sample. Additional exam requirements/recommendations for international students: Required—TOEFL. *Application deadline:* For fall admission, 2/1 priority date for domestic and international students; for spring admission, 10/15 priority date for domestic and international students. Applications are processed on a rolling basis. Application fee: $65. Electronic applications accepted. *Expenses:* Tuition: Full-time $16,930; part-time $780 per unit. Tuition and fees vary according to course load and program. *Financial support:* In 2007–08, 393 students received support; research assistantships with tuition reimbursements available, teaching assistantships with tuition reimbursements available, career-related internships or fieldwork, Federal Work-Study, institutionally sponsored loans, scholarships/grants, and tuition waivers (partial) available. Support available to part-time students. Financial award application deadline: 3/15; financial award applicants required to submit FAFSA. *Faculty research:* Somatic psychology, comparative psychology, art therapy, transpersonal psychology, eco-psychology. *Application contact:* David Townes, Senior Admissions Counselor, 415-575-6152, Fax: 415-575-1268, E-mail: dtownes@ciis.edu.

See Close-Up on page 1421.

California Lutheran University, Graduate Studies, Department of Psychology, Thousand Oaks, CA 91360-2787. Offers clinical psychology (MS); marital and family therapy (MS). Part-time programs available. *Degree requirements:* For master's, thesis or comprehensive exams. *Entrance requirements:* For master's, GRE General Test, interview, minimum GPA of 3.0.

California State University, Dominguez Hills, College of Natural and Behavioral Science, Program in Psychology, Carson, CA 90747-0001. Offers clinical psychology (MA); general psychology (MA). Part-time and evening/weekend programs available. *Faculty:* 6 full-time (5 women), 3 part-time/adjunct (0 women). *Students:* 18 full-time (14 women), 14 part-time (10 women); includes 19 minority (7 African Americans, 12 Hispanic Americans), 2 international. Average age 31. 22 applicants, 45% accepted, 6 enrolled. In 2007, 14 degrees awarded. Terminal master's awarded for partial completion of doctoral program. *Degree requirements:* For master's, comprehensive exam, thesis optional. *Entrance requirements:* For master's, GRE General Test or MAT, interview, minimum GPA of 3.0, prerequisite psychology courses. Additional exam requirements/recommendations for international students: Required—TOEFL (minimum score 550 paper-based). *Application deadline:* For fall admission, 3/1 for domestic and international students. Application fee: $55. Electronic applications accepted. *Faculty research:* Culture and health, neuropsychology and HIV, psychohistory of the Holocaust, community and adolescents, malingering. Total annual research expenditures: $10,000. *Unit head:* Dr. L. Mark Carrier, Chair, 310-243-3499, E-mail: lcarrier@csudh.edu. *Application contact:* Dr. Karen I. Mason, Coordinator, 310-243-3642, Fax: 310-516-3642, E-mail: kmason@csudh.edu.

California State University, Fullerton, Graduate Studies, College of Humanities and Social Sciences, Department of Psychology, Fullerton, CA 92834-9480. Offers clinical/community psychology (MS); psychology (MA). Part-time programs available. *Students:* 56 full-time (43 women), 11 part-time (5 women); includes 22 minority (2 African Americans, 6 Asian Americans or Pacific Islanders, 14 Hispanic Americans), 6 international. Average age 28. 138 applicants, 28% accepted, 34 enrolled. In 2007, 22 degrees awarded. *Degree requirements:* For master's, thesis. *Entrance requirements:* For master's, GRE General Test, GRE Subject Test, undergraduate major in psychology or related field. *Application deadline:* For fall admission, 3/15 for domestic students. Application fee: $55. *Financial support:* Teaching assistantships, career-related internships or fieldwork, Federal Work-Study, institutionally sponsored loans, and scholarships/grants available. Support available to part-time students. Financial award application deadline: 3/1. *Unit head:* Dr. Daniel Kee, Chair, 714-278-3514.

California State University, Northridge, Graduate Studies, College of Social and Behavioral Sciences, Department of Psychology, Northridge, CA 91330. Offers clinical psychology (MA); general-experimental psychology (MA); human factors and applied experimental psychology (MA). *Faculty:* 26 full-time (17 women), 32 part-time/adjunct (15 women). *Students:* 51 full-time (29 women), 18 part-time (13 women); includes 21 minority (1 African American, 4 Asian Americans or Pacific Islanders, 16 Hispanic Americans), 9 international. Average age 28. 102 applicants, 48% accepted, 38 enrolled. In 2007, 13 degrees awarded. *Degree requirements:* For master's, thesis. *Entrance requirements:* For master's, GRE General Test, GRE Subject Test, minimum GPA of 3.0, letters of recommendation. Additional exam requirements/recommendations for international students: Required—TOEFL. *Application deadline:* For fall admission, 11/30 for domestic students. Application fee: $55. *Financial support:* Application deadline: 3/1. *Unit head:* Dr. Paul Skolnick, Chair, 818-677-2827.

California State University, San Bernardino, Graduate Studies, College of Social and Behavioral Sciences, Department of Psychology, Program in Clinical/Counseling Psychology, San Bernardino, CA 92407-2397. Offers MS. *Faculty:* 10 full-time. *Students:* 25 full-time (22 women); includes 8 minority (3 African Americans, 5 Hispanic Americans), 1 international. Average age 24. 66 applicants, 29% accepted, 13 enrolled. In 2007, 13 degrees awarded. *Degree requirements:* For master's, comprehensive exam or thesis. *Entrance requirements:* For master's, minimum GPA of 3.0 in major. *Application deadline:* For fall admission, 8/31 priority date for domestic students. Application fee: $55. *Financial support:* Fellowships, research assistantships, teaching assistantships, career-related internships or fieldwork, Federal Work-Study, and unspecified assistantships available. Financial award application deadline: 3/1. *Faculty research:* Psychology of women, fathering, depression, families, cross-cultural counseling. *Unit head:* Dr. David Chavez, Head, 909-537-5572, Fax: 909-537-7003, E-mail: dchavez@csusb.edu. *Application contact:* Stacy Brooks, Graduate Secretary, 909-880-5570, Fax: 909-880-7003, E-mail: sbrooks@csusb.edu.

Capella University, Harold Abel School of Psychology, Minneapolis, MN 55402. Offers clinical psychology (MS); counseling psychology (MS); educational psychology (MS, PhD); general psychology (MS, PhD); industrial/organizational psychology (MS, PhD); school psychology (MS, Certificate); sport psychology (MS). Part-time and evening/weekend programs available. Postbaccalaureate distance learning degree programs offered (minimal on-campus study). Terminal master's awarded for partial completion of doctoral program. *Degree requirements:* For master's, thesis optional, project; for doctorate, thesis/dissertation. *Entrance requirements:* For degree, master's degree in school psychology. Additional exam requirements/recommendations for international students: Required—TOEFL (minimum score 550 paper-based; 213 computer-based), TWE (minimum score 4). Electronic applications accepted. *Faculty research:* Correctional mental health delivery, community mental health, attachment and caregiving in adult and family relationships, influence of encouragement on motivation, and moral dilemmas in business.

Cardinal Stritch University, College of Arts and Sciences, Department of Psychology, Milwaukee, WI 53217-3985. Offers clinical psychology (MA). Part-time and evening/weekend programs available. *Degree requirements:* For master's, thesis, portfolio, clinical practicum. *Entrance requirements:* For master's, GRE General Test, GRE Subject Test (psychology), interview, minimum GPA of 3.0, 3 letters of recommendation.

Carlos Albizu University, Graduate Programs in Psychology, San Juan, PR 00901. Offers clinical psychology (MS, PhD, Psy D); general psychology (PhD); industrial/organizational psychology (MS, PhD); speech and language pathology (MS). *Accreditation:* APA (one or more programs are accredited). Part-time and evening/weekend programs available. *Degree requirements:* For master's, one foreign language, comprehensive exam, thesis; for doctorate, one foreign language, comprehensive exam, thesis/dissertation, written qualifying exams. *Entrance requirements:* For master's, GRE General Test or EXADEP, interview, minimum GPA of 3.0; for doctorate, GRE General Test or EXADEP, interview, minimum GPA of 3.0 (industrial/organizational psychology), minimum GPA of 3.25 (clinical psychology). *Faculty research:* Psychotherapeutic techniques for Hispanics, psychology of the aged, school dropouts, stress, violence.

Carlos Albizu University, Miami Campus, Graduate Programs, Miami, FL 33172-2209. Offers clinical psychology (Psy D); entrepreneurship (MBA); exceptional student education (MS); industrial/organizational psychology (MS); marriage and family therapy (MS); mental health counseling (MS); nonprofit management (MBA); organizational management (MBA); psychology (MS); school counseling (MS); teaching English as a second language (MS). *Accreditation:* APA. Part-time and evening/weekend programs available. *Faculty:* 20 full-time (13 women), 65 part-time/adjunct (39 women). *Students:* 514 full-time (409 women), 143 part-time (119 women); includes 465 minority (54 African Americans, 1 American Indian/Alaska Native, 4 Asian Americans or Pacific Islanders, 406 Hispanic Americans). Average age 35. 194 applicants, 73% accepted, 130 enrolled. In 2007, 208 master's, 37 doctorates awarded. Terminal master's awarded for partial completion of doctoral program. *Median time to degree:* Of those who began their doctoral program in fall 1999, 65% received their degree in 8 years or less. *Degree requirements:* For master's, one foreign language, comprehensive exam, integrative project (MBA), research project (MSESE and MSTESOL); for doctorate, one foreign language, comprehensive exam, internship, doctoral project. *Entrance requirements:* For master's, 3 letters of recommendation, interview, minimum GPA of 3.0, resumé, statement of purpose, official transcripts; for doctorate, 3 letters of recommendation, minimum GPA of 3.0, resumé, interview. *Application deadline:* For fall admission, 8/1 priority date for domestic students; for spring admission, 11/30 priority date for domestic students. Applications are processed on a rolling basis. Application fee: $50. *Expenses:* Tuition: Full-time $9,090; part-time $505 per credit. Required fees: $298 per term. Tuition and fees vary according to course load and degree level. *Financial support:* In 2007–08, 37 students received support. Federal Work-Study and scholarships/grants available. Financial award application deadline: 6/1; financial award applicants required to submit FAFSA. *Faculty research:* Psychotherapy, forensic psychology, neuropsychology, marketing strategy, entrepreneurship, special education. *Unit head:* Dr. Carmen S. Roca, Interim Chancellor, 305-593-1223 Ext. 120, Fax: 305-629-8052, E-mail: croca@albizu.edu. *Application contact:* Barbara De la Cruz, Admission Officer, 305-593-1223 Ext. 218, Fax: 305-593-1854, E-mail: bdelacruz@albizu.edu.

Case Western Reserve University, School of Graduate Studies, Department of Psychology, Program in Clinical Psychology, Cleveland, OH 44106. Offers PhD. *Accreditation:* APA. *Faculty:* 7 full-time (4 women), 2 part-time/adjunct (both women). *Students:* 28 full-time (27 women); includes 6 minority (2 African Americans, 4 Hispanic Americans). *Degree requirements:* For doctorate, thesis/dissertation, internship. *Entrance requirements:* For doctorate, GRE General Test, GRE Subject Test. Additional exam requirements/recommendations for international students: Required—TOEFL. *Application deadline:* For fall admission, 1/15 for domestic students. Application fee: $50. Electronic applications accepted. *Financial support:* Fellowships, research assistantships available. *Faculty research:* Pediatric psychology, family functioning, depression, geriatric psychopathology, creativity and play. *Unit head:* Dr. James C. Overholser, Director of Clinical Training, 216-368-2686, Fax: 216-368-4891, E-mail: overholser@case.edu.

The Catholic University of America, School of Arts and Sciences, Department of Psychology, Program in Clinical Psychology, Washington, DC 20064. Offers PhD. *Accreditation:* APA. *Students:* 18 full-time (15 women), 8 part-time (6 women); includes 5 minority (1 African American, 2 Asian Americans or Pacific Islanders, 2 Hispanic Americans). Average age 29. 156 applicants, 8% accepted, 6 enrolled. In 2007, 7 degrees awarded. *Degree requirements:* For doctorate, comprehensive exam, thesis/dissertation. *Entrance requirements:* For doctorate, GRE General Test, GRE Subject Test, 3 letters of recommendation. Additional exam requirements/recommendations for international students: Required—TOEFL (minimum score 580 paper-based; 237 computer-based). *Application deadline:* For fall admission, 2/1 priority date for domestic students; for spring admission, 11/15 priority date for domestic students. Applications are processed on a rolling basis. Application fee: $55. Electronic applications accepted. *Financial support:* Fellowships, research assistantships, teaching assistantships, career-related internships or fieldwork, Federal Work-Study, scholarships/grants, tuition waivers (full and partial), and unspecified assistantships available. Support available to part-time students. Financial award application deadline: 2/1; financial award applicants required to submit FAFSA. *Faculty research:* Individual and group psychotherapy, marital and family interaction, suicide and depression, anxiety, paraphilias. *Unit head:* Dr. David A. Jobes, Director, 202-319-5750, Fax: 202-319-6263, E-mail: jobes@cua.edu.

Central Michigan University, College of Graduate Studies, College of Humanities and Social and Behavioral Sciences, Department of Psychology, Program in Clinical Psychology, Mount Pleasant, MI 48859. Offers PhD. *Accreditation:* APA. *Degree requirements:* For doctorate, thesis/dissertation. *Entrance requirements:* For doctorate, GRE. *Faculty research:* Intervention strategies, personal problem solving.

Chestnut Hill College, School of Graduate Studies, Division of Psychology, Program in Clinical and Counseling Psychology, Philadelphia, PA 19118-2693. Offers MA, MS, CAS. Part-time and evening/weekend programs available. *Faculty:* 11 full-time (4 women), 29 part-time/adjunct (13 women). *Students:* 80 full-time (70 women), 157 part-time (128 women); includes 50 minority (42 African Americans, 3 Asian Americans or Pacific Islanders, 5 Hispanic Americans), 1 international. Average age 33. 80 applicants, 30% accepted. In 2007, 66 degrees awarded. *Degree requirements:* For master's, thesis optional, practica. *Entrance requirements:* For master's, GRE, statement of professional goals writing sample, transcripts, letters of recommendation; for CAS, GRE, Master's degree in counseling or a related discipline, transcripts, letters of recommendation, statement of professional goals writing sample. Additional exam requirements/recommendations for international students: Required—TOEFL (minimum score 550 paper-based; 213 computer-based). *Application deadline:* For fall admission, 7/17 priority date for domestic students, 7/17 for international students; for spring admission, 12/15 priority date for domestic students, 12/15 for international students. Applications are processed on a rolling basis. Application fee: $50. *Faculty research:* Child and adolescent therapy and clinical issues; psychoanalytic psychotherapy; object relations and cognitive-behavior therapy; marriage and family issues; clinical issues and interventions with diverse populations. *Application contact:* Amy Boorse, Administrative Assistant, School of Graduate Studies Office, 215-248-7170, Fax: 215-248-7161, E-mail: gradadmissions@chc.edu.

Chestnut Hill College, School of Graduate Studies, Division of Psychology, Program in Clinical Psychology, Philadelphia, PA 19118-2693. Offers Psy D, MS/Psy D. *Accreditation:* APA. Part-time and evening/weekend programs available. *Faculty:* 11 full-time (4 women), 29 part-time/adjunct (13 women). *Students:* 42 full-time (32 women), 68 part-time (59 women); includes 9 minority (6 African Americans, 2 Asian Americans or Pacific Islanders, 1 Hispanic American), 1 international. Average age 33. In 2007, 8 degrees awarded. *Degree requirements:* For doctorate, comprehensive exam, thesis/dissertation, internships, practica. *Entrance requirements:* For doctorate, GRE, transcripts, letters of recommendation, statement of professional goals writing sample, master's degree in clinical/counseling psychology or closely related field. Additional exam requirements/recommendations for international students: Required—TOEFL (minimum score 500 paper-based; 213 computer-based). *Application deadline:* For fall admission, 7/17 priority date for domestic students, 7/17 for international students; for spring admission, 12/15 priority date for domestic students, 12/15 for international students. Applications are processed on a rolling basis. Application fee: $75. *Faculty research:* Psychoanalytic psychotherapy; marriage and family issues; stepfamilies, couples and family therapy with adolescents; clinical issues and interventions with diverse populations; child and adolescent therapy and clinical issues; object relations and cognitive-behavior therapy. *Application contact:* Mary Steinmetz, Director of Psy D Admissions, 215-248-7077, Fax: 215-753-3619, E-mail: profpsyc@chc.edu.

The Chicago School of Professional Psychology, Graduate School, Program in Clinical Psychology, Chicago, IL 60610. Offers applied behavior analysis (MA, Psy D, Certificate); clinical psychology (Psy D); counseling (MA); Latino mental health (Certificate); psychology (Certificate). *Students:* 756. Average age 26. 628 applicants, 64% accepted, 177 enrolled. *Degree requirements:* For master's, thesis (for some programs); for doctorate, comprehensive exam, thesis/dissertation. *Entrance requirements:* For master's, minimum undergraduate GPA of 3.0; 1 course in psychology and 1 course in either statistics or research methods; for doctorate, GRE, 18 hours of psychology credit (including courses in statistics, normal psychology and human development); minimum GPA of 3.2. Additional exam requirements/recommendations for international students: Required—TOEFL (minimum score 550 paper-based; 213 computer-based; 79 iBT). Application fee: $50. Electronic applications accepted. *Financial support:* Fellowships, Federal Work-Study and scholarships/grants available. Financial award applicants required to submit FAFSA. *Application contact:* Yarelli Meza, Director of Admission, 312-329-6666, Fax: 312-644-3333, E-mail: admissions@thechicagoschool.edu.

See Close-Up on page 1425.

City College of the City University of New York, Graduate School, College of Liberal Arts and Science, Division of Social Science, Department of Psychology, New York, NY 10031-9198. Offers clinical psychology (PhD); experimental cognition (PhD); general psychology (MA); mental health counseling (MA). *Accreditation:* APA (one or more programs are accredited). Part-time programs available. *Students:* 17 full-time (12 women), 98 part-time (72 women); includes 79 minority (28 African Americans, 13 Asian Americans or Pacific Islanders, 38 Hispanic Americans), 23 international. 40 applicants, 55% accepted, 30 enrolled. In 2007, 43 degrees awarded. *Degree requirements:* For master's, one foreign language, comprehensive exam, thesis. *Entrance requirements:* For master's, GRE. Additional exam requirements/recommendations for international students: Required—TOEFL (minimum score 550 paper-based; 213 computer-based). *Application deadline:* For fall admission, 4/15 for domestic students; for spring admission, 11/15 for domestic students. Application fee: $125. *Financial support:* Fellowships, teaching assistantships, career-related internships or fieldwork, Federal Work-Study, and tuition waivers (full and partial) available. Support available to part-time students. Financial award application deadline: 5/1. *Faculty research:* Social/personality psychology, physiological psychology, cognition and development. *Unit head:* Vivien Tartter, Graduate Adviser, 212-650-5709, Fax: 212-650-5865, E-mail: vtartter@ccny.cuny.edu.

Clark University, Graduate School, Department of Psychology, Program in Clinical Psychology, Worcester, MA 01610-1477. Offers PhD. *Accreditation:* APA. *Degree requirements:* For doctorate, thesis/dissertation. *Entrance requirements:* For doctorate, GRE General Test. Additional exam requirements/recommendations for international students: Required—TOEFL. *Application deadline:* For fall admission, 1/1 priority date for domestic students. Applications are processed on a rolling basis. Application fee: $55. *Expenses:* Tuition: Full-time $32,600; part-time $1,019 per credit. Required fees: $30. Tuition and fees vary according to program. *Financial support:* In 2007–08, fellowships with full tuition reimbursements (averaging $15,700 per year), research assistantships with full tuition reimbursements (averaging $15,700 per year), teaching assistantships with full tuition reimbursements (averaging $15,700 per year) were awarded; tuition waivers (full) also available. *Unit head:* Dr. James Cordova, Chair, 508-793-7268. *Application contact:* Peggy Moskowitz, Graduate School Secretary, 508-793-7274, Fax: 508-793-7265, E-mail: psychology@clarku.edu.

Cleveland State University, College of Graduate Studies, College of Science, Department of Psychology, Cleveland, OH 44115. Offers clinical psychology (MA); consumer/industrial research (MA); diversity management (MA); experimental research psychology (MA); school psychology (Psy S). Part-time programs available. *Faculty:* 17 full-time (5 women), 16 part-time/adjunct (10 women). *Students:* 76 full-time (52 women), 44 part-time (37 women); includes 19 minority (15 African Americans, 1 American Indian/Alaska Native, 2 Asian Americans or Pacific Islanders, 1 Hispanic American), 3 international. Average age 29. 153 applicants, 27% accepted, 37 enrolled. In 2007, 26 master's, 9 other advanced degrees awarded. *Degree requirements:* For master's, thesis (for some programs). *Entrance requirements:* For master's, GRE General Test. Additional exam requirements/recommendations for international students: Required—TOEFL (minimum score 525 paper-based; 197 computer-based). *Application deadline:* For fall admission, 2/1 priority date for domestic and international students. Applications are processed on a rolling basis. Application fee: $30. Electronic applications accepted. *Financial support:* In 2007–08, 45 students received support. Career-related internships or fieldwork, Federal Work-Study, tuition waivers (partial), and unspecified assistantships available. Financial award applicants required to submit FAFSA. Total annual research expenditures: $112,607. *Unit head:* Dr. David M. Grilly, Chairperson, 216-687-2545, Fax: 216-687-9294, E-mail: d.grilly@csuohio.edu. *Application contact:* Karen Colston, Administrative Coordinator, 216-687-2552, E-mail: k.colston@csuohio.edu.

College of St. Joseph, Graduate Programs, Division of Psychology and Human Services, Program in Clinical Mental Health Counseling, Rutland, VT 05701-3899. Offers MS. Part-time programs available. *Faculty:* 4 full-time (1 woman), 8 part-time/adjunct (4 women). *Students:* 2 full-time (both women), 14 part-time (11 women). Average age 30. 4 applicants, 75% accepted, 2 enrolled. In 2007, 7 degrees awarded. *Degree requirements:* For master's, comprehensive exam. *Entrance requirements:* For master's, 2 letters of reference, interview. *Application deadline:* Applications are processed on a rolling basis. Application fee: $35. Electronic applications accepted. *Expenses:* Tuition: Full-time $12,000; part-time $325 per credit. Required fees: $45 per semester. *Financial support:* In 2007–08, 1 student received support. Career-related internships or fieldwork, Federal Work-Study, and unspecified assistantships available. Support available to part-time students. Financial award application deadline: 3/1. *Application contact:* Tracy Gallipo, Director of Admissions, 802-773-5900 Ext. 3262, Fax: 802-773-5900, E-mail: tracygallipo@csj.edu.

College of St. Joseph, Graduate Programs, Division of Psychology and Human Services, Program in Clinical Psychology, Rutland, VT 05701-3899. Offers MS. Part-time and evening/weekend programs available. *Faculty:* 4 full-time (1 woman), 8 part-time/adjunct (4 women). *Students:* 8 full-time (6 women), 18 part-time (12 women), 1 international. Average age 36. 5 applicants, 80% accepted, 4 enrolled. In 2007, 6 degrees awarded. *Degree requirements:* For master's, comprehensive exam, thesis optional. *Entrance requirements:* For master's, 2 letters of reference, interview. *Application deadline:* Applications are processed on a rolling basis. Application fee: $35. Electronic applications accepted. *Expenses:* Tuition: Full-time $12,000; part-time $325 per credit. Required fees: $45 per semester. *Financial support:* In 2007–08, 2 students received support, including teaching assistantships with tuition reimbursements available (averaging $3,000 per year); unspecified assistantships also available. Financial award application deadline: 3/1. *Application contact:* Tracy Gallipo, Director of Admissions, 802-773-5900 Ext. 3262, Fax: 802-773-5900, E-mail: tracygallipo@csj.edu.

Clinical Psychology

The College of William and Mary, Faculty of Arts and Sciences, Department of Psychology, Virginia Consortium Program in Clinical Psychology, Williamsburg, VA 23187-8795. Offers Psy D. Offered through the Virginia Consortium for Professional Psychology; for information call 757-518-2550. *Accreditation:* APA. *Degree requirements:* For doctorate, comprehensive exam, thesis/dissertation, internship. *Entrance requirements:* For doctorate, GRE General Test. Additional exam requirements/recommendations for international students: Required—TOEFL. Expenses: Contact institution. Tuition and fees vary according to program.

Concordia University, School of Graduate Studies, Faculty of Arts and Science, Department of Psychology, Program in Psychology (Clinical), Montréal, QC H3G 1M8, Canada. Offers MA, PhD, Certificate. *Accreditation:* APA (one or more programs are accredited). *Degree requirements:* For master's, comprehensive exam, thesis; for doctorate, comprehensive exam, thesis/dissertation. *Entrance requirements:* For master's, GRE General Test, GRE Subject Test, honors degree in psychology or equivalent; for doctorate, master's degree in psychology. *Faculty research:* Developmental-clinical psychology, sensory deficits, sexual dysfunction.

Dalhousie University, Faculty of Science, Department of Psychology, Halifax, NS B3H 4R2, Canada. Offers clinical psychology (PhD); psychology (M Sc, PhD); psychology/neuroscience (M Sc, PhD). *Accreditation:* APA (one or more programs are accredited). *Faculty:* 30 full-time (8 women), 34 part-time/adjunct (14 women). *Students:* 56 full-time (35 women); includes 2 minority (both Asian Americans or Pacific Islanders) 200 applicants, 8% accepted. In 2007, 8 master's, 7 doctorates awarded. *Degree requirements:* For master's, thesis; for doctorate, thesis/dissertation. *Entrance requirements:* For doctorate, GRE General Test. Additional exam requirements/recommendations for international students: Required—TOEFL. *Application deadline:* For fall admission, 2/1 priority date for domestic students. Applications are processed on a rolling basis. Application fee: $60. *Financial support:* In 2007–08, 19 fellowships, 26 teaching assistantships (averaging $1,853 per year) were awarded; career-related internships or fieldwork also available. Financial award application deadline: 2/1. *Faculty research:* Physiological psychology, psychology of learning, learning and behavior, forensic clinical health psychology, development perception and cognition. Total annual research expenditures: $1.9 million. *Unit head:* Dr. Richard Brown, Chair, 902-494-3417, Fax: 902-494-6585, E-mail: richard.brown@dal.ca. *Application contact:* Dr. Raymond Klein, Graduate Coordinator, 902-494-6551, Fax: 902-494-6585, E-mail: ray.klein@dal.ca.

DePaul University, College of Liberal Arts and Sciences, Department of Psychology, Chicago, IL 60604-2287. Offers clinical psychology (MA, PhD), including child clinical psychology, community clinical psychology; experimental psychology (MA, PhD); general psychology (MS); industrial/organizational psychology (MA, PhD); MA/PhD. *Accreditation:* APA (one or more programs are accredited). *Faculty:* 31 full-time (19 women), 6 part-time/adjunct (4 women). *Students:* 57 full-time (36 women), 53 part-time (36 women); includes 24 minority (14 African Americans, 1 American Indian/Alaska Native, 3 Asian Americans or Pacific Islanders, 6 Hispanic Americans), 1 international. Average age 28. 332 applicants, 14% accepted, 23 enrolled. In 2007, 14 master's, 17 doctorates awarded. *Median time to degree:* Of those who began their doctoral program in fall 1999, 60% received their degree in 8 years or less. *Degree requirements:* For master's, thesis, oral exam; for doctorate, comprehensive exam, thesis/dissertation, oral and written exams. *Entrance requirements:* For master's and doctorate, GRE General Test, GRE Subject Test, 32 quarter hours of course work in psychology, 3 letters of recommendation. Additional exam requirements/recommendations for international students: Required—TOEFL. Application fee: $40. Electronic applications accepted. *Financial support:* In 2007–08, 48 students received support, including 35 research assistantships with full tuition reimbursements available (averaging $11,800 per year), 13 teaching assistantships with full tuition reimbursements available (averaging $11,800 per year); career-related internships or fieldwork, scholarships/grants, traineeships, tuition waivers (full and partial), and unspecified assistantships also available. Financial award application deadline: 1/10. *Faculty research:* Adolescent stress and depression, minority adolescents sexuality, public policy, community influences in child adjustment. *Unit head:* Dr. Christopher B Keys, Chairman, 773-325-7887, Fax: 773-325-7888. *Application contact:* Alison Pereida Knapp, Graduate Admissions Assistant, 773-325-7887, Fax: 773-325-7888.

Drexel University, College of Arts and Sciences, Department of Psychology, Clinical Psychology Program, Philadelphia, PA 19104-2875. Offers clinical psychology (MA, MS); forensic psychology (PhD); health psychology (PhD); neuropsychology (PhD). *Accreditation:* APA. Terminal master's awarded for partial completion of doctoral program. *Degree requirements:* For master's, comprehensive exam, thesis; for doctorate, thesis/dissertation, qualifying exam. *Entrance requirements:* For master's, GRE General Test, minimum GPA of 3.0; for doctorate, GRE General Test, GRE Subject Test, minimum GPA of 3.0. Electronic applications accepted. Expenses: Contact institution. *Faculty research:* Cognitive behavioral therapy, stress and coping, eating disorders, substance abuse, developmental disabilities.

Drexel University, College of Arts and Sciences, Department of Psychology, Program in Law-Psychology, Philadelphia, PA 19104-2875. Offers PhD, JD/PhD. *Degree requirements:* For doctorate, thesis/dissertation, qualifying exam. *Entrance requirements:* For doctorate, GRE General Test, GRE Subject Test, minimum GPA of 3.0. Electronic applications accepted. Expenses: Contact institution. *Faculty research:* Mental health law issues, professional ethics, social science applications to law.

Duke University, Graduate School, Department of Psychology, Durham, NC 27708-0586. Offers biological psychology (PhD); clinical psychology (PhD); cognitive psychology (PhD); developmental psychology (PhD); experimental psychology (PhD); health psychology (PhD); human social development (PhD); JD/MA. *Accreditation:* APA (one or more programs are accredited). *Faculty:* 40 full-time. *Students:* 91 full-time (71 women); includes 15 minority (9 African Americans, 1 Asian American or Pacific Islander, 5 Hispanic Americans), 13 international. 468 applicants, 7% accepted, 19 enrolled. In 2007, 14 doctorates awarded. *Degree requirements:* For doctorate, thesis/dissertation. *Entrance requirements:* For doctorate, GRE General Test. Additional exam requirements/recommendations for international students: Required—TOEFL (minimum score 550 paper-based; 213 computer-based; 83 iBT), IELTS (minimum score 7). *Application deadline:* For fall admission, 12/15 priority date for domestic and international students. Application fee: $75. Electronic applications accepted. *Financial support:* Fellowships, research assistantships, teaching assistantships, career-related internships or fieldwork and Federal Work-Study available. Financial award application deadline: 12/31. *Unit head:* Amy Needham, Co-Director of Graduate Studies, 919-660-5715, Fax: 919-660-5726, E-mail: morrell@duke.edu.

Duquesne University, Graduate School of Liberal Arts, Department of Psychology, Pittsburgh, PA 15282-0001. Offers clinical psychology (PhD). *Accreditation:* APA. *Faculty:* 14 full-time (5 women). *Students:* 54 full-time (27 women), 3 part-time (1 woman). Average age 25. In 2007, 11 doctorates awarded. *Degree requirements:* For doctorate, comprehensive exam, thesis/dissertation. *Entrance requirements:* For doctorate, GRE General Test, MA in psychology. Additional exam requirements/recommendations for international students: Required—TOEFL. *Application deadline:* For fall admission, 12/15 for domestic and international students. Application fee: $50. *Expenses:* Tuition: Part-time $774 per credit. Required fees: $74 per credit. Tuition and fees vary according to program. *Financial support:* In 2007–08, 1 research assistantship with full tuition reimbursement (averaging $11,200 per year), 14 teaching assistantships with full tuition reimbursements (averaging $11,200 per year) were awarded; fellowships with full tuition reimbursements, career-related internships or fieldwork, scholarships/grants, tuition waivers (partial), and unspecified assistantships also available. Financial award application deadline: 5/1. *Faculty research:* Emotion, language motivation, imagination, development. *Unit head:* Dr. Daniel Burston, Chair, 412-396-5067.

East Carolina University, Graduate School, Thomas Harriot College of Arts and Sciences, Department of Psychology, Program in Clinical Psychology, Greenville, NC 27858-4353. Offers MA. *Students:* 11 full-time (9 women), 3 part-time (2 women); includes 1 minority (African American) Average age 23. 7 applicants, 71% accepted, 0 enrolled. In 2007, 6 degrees awarded. *Degree requirements:* For master's, one foreign language, comprehensive exam, thesis. *Entrance requirements:* For master's, GRE General Test, GRE Subject Test. Additional exam requirements/recommendations for international students: Required—TOEFL. *Application deadline:* For fall admission, 3/15 priority date for domestic students. Applications are processed on a rolling basis. Application fee: $50. *Financial support:* Research assistantships with partial tuition reimbursements, teaching assistantships with partial tuition reimbursements, traineeships available. Support available to part-time students. Financial award application deadline: 6/1. *Unit head:* Dr. Thomas Durham, Director of Graduate Studies, 252-328-6118, Fax: 252-328-6283, E-mail: durhamt@ecu.edu. *Application contact:* Dean of Graduate School, 252-328-6012, Fax: 252-328-6071, E-mail: gradschool@ecu.edu.

Eastern Illinois University, Graduate School, College of Sciences, Charleston, IL 61920-3099. Offers biological sciences (MS); chemistry (MS); communication disorders and sciences (MS); economics (MA); mathematics and computer science (MA), including mathematics, mathematics education; natural sciences (MS); political science (MA); psychology (MA, SSP), including clinical psychology (MA), school psychology (SSP). Part-time programs available. *Faculty:* 193 full-time (40 women). In 2007, 83 master's, 11 other advanced degrees awarded. *Degree requirements:* For SSP, thesis. *Entrance requirements:* For degree, GRE General Test. *Application deadline:* For fall admission, 7/31 priority date for domestic students. Applications are processed on a rolling basis. Application fee: $30. *Expenses:* Tuition, state resident: part-time $218 per hour. Tuition, nonresident: part-time $654 per hour. *Financial support:* In 2007–08, research assistantships with tuition reimbursements (averaging $7,200 per year), teaching assistantships with tuition reimbursements (averaging $7,200 per year) were awarded; career-related internships or fieldwork and Federal Work-Study also available. Support available to part-time students. *Unit head:* Dr. Mary Ann Hanner, Dean, 217-581-3328, Fax: 217-581-7110, E-mail: mahanner@eiu.edu.

Eastern Illinois University, Graduate School, College of Sciences, Department of Psychology, Program in Clinical Psychology, Charleston, IL 61920-3099. Offers MA. In 2007, 10 degrees awarded. *Degree requirements:* For master's, comprehensive exam. *Entrance requirements:* For master's, GRE General Test. *Application deadline:* For fall admission, 7/31 priority date for domestic students. Applications are processed on a rolling basis. Application fee: $30. *Expenses:* Tuition, state resident: part-time $218 per hour. Tuition, nonresident: part-time $654 per hour. *Financial support:* In 2007–08, research assistantships with tuition reimbursements (averaging $7,200 per year), 5 teaching assistantships with tuition reimbursements (averaging $7,200 per year) were awarded. *Unit head:* Dr. Anu Sharma, Coordinator, 217-581-2127, Fax: 217-581-6764, E-mail: asharma@eiu.edu.

Eastern Kentucky University, The Graduate School, College of Arts and Sciences, Department of Psychology, Richmond, KY 40475-3102. Offers clinical psychology (MS); industrial/organizational psychology (MS); school psychology (Psy S). Part-time programs available. *Faculty:* 11 full-time (5 women). *Students:* 64 full-time (47 women), 10 part-time (8 women); includes 5 minority (4 African Americans, 1 Asian American or Pacific Islander). Average age 25. 166 applicants, 31% accepted, 18 enrolled. In 2007, 32 master's, 11 other advanced degrees awarded. *Entrance requirements:* For master's and Psy S, GRE General Test, minimum GPA of 2.5. *Application deadline:* For fall admission, 3/15 priority date for domestic students. Applications are processed on a rolling basis. Application fee: $35. *Financial support:* In 2007–08, 30 students received support, including research assistantships (averaging $10,000 per year), teaching assistantships (averaging $10,000 per year); career-related internships or fieldwork and Federal Work-Study also available. Support available to part-time students. *Faculty research:* Autism, social psychology, parenting, assessment of depression/anxiety, reading. Total annual research expenditures: $40,000. *Unit head:* Dr. Robert Brubaker, Chair, 859-622-1105, Fax: 859-622-5871, E-mail: robert.brubaker@eku.edu.

Eastern Michigan University, Graduate School, College of Arts and Sciences, Department of Psychology, Ypsilanti, MI 48197. Offers clinical behavioral psychology (MS); clinical psychology (MS, PhD); psychology (MS). *Accreditation:* APA. *Faculty:* 22 full-time (11 women). *Students:* 40 full-time (27 women), 49 part-time (33 women); includes 3 African Americans, 2 Asian Americans or Pacific Islanders, 2 Hispanic Americans, 5 international. Average age 28. In 2007, 38 master's, 5 doctorates awarded. Application fee: $35. *Expenses:* Tuition, state resident: full-time $8,952; part-time $373 per credit hour. Tuition, nonresident: full-time $17,634; part-time $735 per credit hour. Required fees: $896; $34 per credit hour. Tuition and fees vary according to course level, degree level and program. *Unit head:* Dr. Carol Freedman-Doan, Interim Head, 734-487-1155, Fax: 734-487-6553, E-mail: cfreedman@emich.edu.

Eastern Virginia Medical School, The Virginia Consortium Program in Clinical Psychology, Norfolk, VA 23501-1980. Offers Psy D. *Accreditation:* APA. *Faculty:* 33. *Students:* 48 full-time (37 women); includes 14 minority (9 African Americans, 3 Asian Americans or Pacific Islanders, 2 Hispanic Americans). 228 applicants, 7% accepted, 10 enrolled. In 2007, 10 degrees awarded. *Entrance requirements:* For doctorate, GRE, BS in behavioral sciences or equivalent. Additional exam requirements/recommendations for international students: Required—TOEFL. *Application deadline:* For fall admission, 1/15 for domestic students. Application fee: $40. *Expenses:* Contact institution. *Unit head:* Dr. Michael L. Stutts, Director, 757-446-8400, Fax: 757-446-8401, E-mail: stuttsml@evms.edu. *Application contact:* Eileen O'Neill, Administrative Coordinator, 757-368-1820, Fax: 757-446-8401, E-mail: exoneill@odu.edu.

East Tennessee State University, School of Graduate Studies, College of Arts and Sciences, Department of Psychology, Johnson City, TN 37614. Offers clinical psychology (MA); general psychology (MA). *Degree requirements:* For master's, thesis, oral exams. *Entrance requirements:* For master's, GRE General Test, GRE Subject Test, minimum GPA of 3.0. Additional exam requirements/recommendations for international students: Required—TOEFL (minimum score 550 paper-based; 213 computer-based). *Faculty research:* Language acquisition, recovery of brain function after injury or damage, violence in domestic relationships and road rage, reasons for living, unhealthy tanning behaviors.

Edinboro University of Pennsylvania, Graduate Studies and Research, School of Liberal Arts, Department of Psychology, Edinboro, PA 16444. Offers clinical psychology (MA). Part-time and evening/weekend programs available. *Faculty:* 3 full-time (1 woman). *Students:* 27 full-time (20 women), 5 part-time (3 women); includes 1 minority (Asian American or Pacific Islander), 1 international. Average age 29. In 2007, 17 degrees awarded. *Degree requirements:* For master's, comprehensive exam, thesis or alternative, project. *Entrance requirements:* For master's, GRE or MAT, minimum QPA of 2.5. *Application deadline:* For fall admission, 3/15 priority date for domestic students. Applications are processed on a rolling basis. Application fee: $30. Electronic applications accepted. *Expenses:* Tuition, state resident: full-time $6,214; part-time $345 per credit. Tuition, nonresident: full-time $9,944; part-time $552 per credit. Required fees: $46 per credit. *Financial support:* In 2007–08, 10 research assistantships with full and partial tuition reimbursements (averaging $3,850 per year) were awarded; career-related internships or fieldwork, Federal Work-Study, scholarships/grants, and unspecified assistantships also available. Support available to part-time students. Financial award application deadline: 2/15; financial award applicants required to submit FAFSA. *Unit head:* Dr. Cynthia Legin-Bucell, Chairperson, 814-732-2774, E-mail: leginbucell@edinboro.edu. *Application contact:* Dr. R. Scott Baldwin, Dean, 814-732-2752, Fax: 814-732-2268, E-mail: sbaldwin@edinboro.edu.

Emory University, Graduate School of Arts and Sciences, Department of Psychology, Atlanta, GA 30322-1100. Offers clinical psychology (PhD); cognition and development (PhD); neuroscience and animal behavior (PhD). *Accreditation:* APA. *Degree requirements:* For doctorate, comprehensive exam, thesis/dissertation. *Entrance requirements:* For doctorate, GRE General Test, minimum GPA of 3.25. Additional exam requirements/recommendations for international students: Required—TOEFL. Electronic applications accepted. *Faculty research:* Neuroscience and animal behavior; adult and child psychopathology, cognition development assessment.

Emporia State University, School of Graduate Studies, The Teachers College, Department of Psychology and Special Education, Program in Clinical Psychology, Emporia, KS 66801-5087. Offers MS. Part-time programs available. *Students:* 2 full-time (0 women), 19 part-time (14 women); includes 1 minority (African American), 1 international. 12 applicants, 42% accepted,

5 enrolled. In 2007, 9 degrees awarded. *Degree requirements:* For master's, comprehensive exam, clinical internship. *Entrance requirements:* For master's, GRE or MAT, 24 hours of course work in undergraduate psychology, 3 letters of recommendation. Additional exam requirements/recommendations for international students: Required—TOEFL (minimum score 450 paper-based; 133 computer-based). *Application deadline:* For fall admission, 8/15 for domestic students. Applications are processed on a rolling basis. Application fee: $30 ($75 for international students). Electronic applications accepted. *Expenses:* Tuition, state resident: part-time $157 per credit hour. Tuition, nonresident: part-time $475 per credit hour. Required fees: $47 per credit hour. Tuition and fees vary according to campus/location. *Financial support:* Career-related internships or fieldwork, Federal Work-Study, institutionally sponsored loans, health care benefits, and unspecified assistantships available. Support available to part-time students. Financial award application deadline: 3/15; financial award applicants required to submit FAFSA. *Unit head:* Dr. Kenneth A. Weaver, Chair, Department of Psychology and Special Education, 620-341-5317, E-mail: kweaver@emporia.edu.

Evangel University, Department of Psychology, Springfield, MO 65802-2191. Offers clinical psychology (MS); counseling psychology (MS). Part-time and evening/weekend programs available. *Faculty:* 4 full-time (2 women), 1 part-time/adjunct (0 women). *Students:* 19 full-time (16 women), 6 part-time (5 women). Average age 30. 17 applicants, 100% accepted, 15 enrolled. In 2007, 9 degrees awarded. *Degree requirements:* For master's, comprehensive exam, thesis (for some programs). *Entrance requirements:* For master's, GRE General Test or MAT, minimum undergraduate GPA of 3.0, undergraduate major or minor in psychology, teaching certificate (school counseling). Additional exam requirements/recommendations for international students: Required—TOEFL (minimum score 550 paper-based; 213 computer-based). *Application deadline:* For fall admission, 2/1 priority date for domestic students; for spring admission, 10/15 priority date for domestic students. Applications are processed on a rolling basis. Application fee: $25. *Financial support:* In 2007–08, 6 students received support; research assistantships with partial tuition reimbursements available, teaching assistantships with partial tuition reimbursements available, career-related internships or fieldwork, institutionally sponsored loans, scholarships/grants, and unspecified assistantships available. Support available to part-time students. Financial award application deadline: 3/1; financial award applicants required to submit FAFSA. *Unit head:* Dr. Grant Jones, Chair, 417-865-2815 Ext. 8619, E-mail: jonesg@evangel.edu. *Application contact:* Charity H. Fahlstrom, Admissions Representative, Graduate and Professional Studies Admissions, 417-865-2811 Ext. 7227, Fax: 417-575-5484.

Fairleigh Dickinson University, Metropolitan Campus, University College: Arts, Sciences, and Professional Studies, School of Psychology, Program in Clinical Psychology, Teaneck, NJ 07666-1914. Offers MA, PhD. *Accreditation:* APA. *Students:* 83 full-time (60 women), 1 (woman) part-time, 3 international. Average age 33. 17 applicants, 76% accepted, 10 enrolled. In 2007, 14 degrees awarded. *Application deadline:* Applications are processed on a rolling basis. Application fee: $40. *Expenses:* Tuition: Part-time $869 per credit. Tuition and fees vary according to degree level, campus/location and program.

See Close-Up on page 1431.

Fairleigh Dickinson University, Metropolitan Campus, University College: Arts, Sciences, and Professional Studies, School of Psychology, Program in Clinical Psychopharmacology, Teaneck, NJ 07666-1914. Offers MA. *Students:* Average age 45. 27 applicants, 100% accepted, 18 enrolled. In 2007, 8 degrees awarded. *Expenses:* Tuition: Part-time $869 per credit. Tuition and fees vary according to degree level, campus/location and program. *Unit head:* Dr. Christopher Capuano, Director, School of Psychology, 201-692-2000.

Fielding Graduate University, Graduate Programs, School of Psychology, Santa Barbara, CA 93105-3538. Offers clinical psychology (PhD); clinical psychology respecialization (Post-Doctoral Certificate); media psychology (PhD); media psychology and social change (MA); neuropsychology (Certificate). *Accreditation:* APA. Evening/weekend programs available. *Faculty:* 36 full-time (17 women), 22 part-time/adjunct (9 women). *Students:* 537 full-time (384 women), 66 part-time (44 women); includes 120 minority (41 African Americans, 5 American Indian/Alaska Native, 21 Asian Americans or Pacific Islanders, 53 Hispanic Americans), 9 international. Average age 46. 333 applicants, 41% accepted, 98 enrolled. In 2007, 50 doctorates, 32 other advanced degrees awarded. *Degree requirements:* For doctorate, comprehensive exam, thesis/dissertation. *Entrance requirements:* For doctorate, writing sample, minimum GPA of 3.0, 3 letters of recommendation, resum[00e9]. *Application deadline:* For fall admission, 2/23 for domestic students; for spring admission, 8/25 for domestic students. Application fee: $75. Electronic applications accepted. *Expenses: Contact institution. Financial support:* In 2007–08, 419 students received support, including 2 research assistantships (averaging $1,000 per year); career-related internships or fieldwork and scholarships/grants also available. Financial award application deadline: 3/1; financial award applicants required to submit FAFSA. *Unit head:* Dr. Raymond Trybus, Dean, 805-898-2909, E-mail: rtrybus@fielding.edu. *Application contact:* Addie Merrill, Admission Counselor, 800-340-1099, Fax: 805-687-9793, E-mail: amerrill@fielding.edu.

See Close-Up on page 1433.

Fisk University, Graduate Programs, Department of Psychology, Nashville, TN 37208-3051. Offers clinical psychology (MA); psychology (MA). *Degree requirements:* For master's, thesis. *Entrance requirements:* For master's, GRE General Test, GRE Subject Test, minimum GPA of 3.0. *Faculty research:* Ethnic and gender identity, development, female adolescent development, juvenile delinquency prevention.

Florida Institute of Technology, Graduate Programs, College of Psychology and Liberal Arts, School of Psychology, Melbourne, FL 32901-6975. Offers applied behavior analysis (MS); clinical psychology (Psy D); industrial/organizational psychology (MS, PhD). *Accreditation:* APA (one or more programs are accredited). Part-time programs available. *Faculty:* 17 full-time (7 women), 8 part-time/adjunct (2 women). *Students:* 188 full-time (145 women), 14 part-time (9 women); includes 24 minority (8 African Americans, 4 Asian Americans or Pacific Islanders, 12 Hispanic Americans), 14 international. Average age 27. 304 applicants, 50% accepted, 72 enrolled. In 2007, 62 master's, 21 doctorates awarded. *Degree requirements:* For master's, comprehensive exam (for some programs), thesis (for some programs); for doctorate, comprehensive exam, thesis/dissertation (for some programs), internship. *Entrance requirements:* For master's, GRE General Test, 3 letters of recommendation, minimum GPA of 3.0, resumé; for doctorate, GRE General Test, GRE Subject Test, 3 letters of recommendation, minimum GPA of 3.2, resumé. Additional exam requirements/recommendations for international students: Required—TOEFL (minimum score 550 paper-based; 213 computer-based). *Application deadline:* For fall admission, 3/15 for domestic students. Applications are processed on a rolling basis. Application fee: $50. Electronic applications accepted. *Expenses:* Tuition: Part-time $945 per credit. *Financial support:* In 2007–08, 12 students received support, including 5 research assistantships with full and partial tuition reimbursements available (averaging $7,575 per year), 7 teaching assistantships with full and partial tuition reimbursements available (averaging $5,926 per year); career-related internships or fieldwork, institutionally sponsored loans, tuition waivers (partial), unspecified assistantships, and tuition remissions also available. Financial award application deadline: 3/1; financial award applicants required to submit FAFSA. *Faculty research:* Addictions, neuropsychology, child abuse, assessment, psychological trauma. Total annual research expenditures: $69,032. *Application contact:* Thomas M. Shea, Director of Graduate Admissions, 321-674-7577, Fax: 321-723-9468, E-mail: tshea@fit.edu.

See Close-Up on page 1435.

Florida State University, Graduate Studies, College of Arts and Sciences, Department of Psychology, Program in Clinical Psychology, Tallahassee, FL 32306. Offers PhD. *Accreditation:* APA. *Faculty:* 12 full-time (6 women), 1 part-time/adjunct (0 women). *Students:* 60 full-time (43 women); includes 12 minority (5 African Americans, 1 American Indian/Alaska Native, 6 Hispanic Americans). Average age 25. 189 applicants, 5% accepted, 10 enrolled. In 2007, 5 doctorates awarded. *Median time to degree:* Of those who began their doctoral program in fall 1999, 64% received their degree in 8 years or less. *Degree requirements:* For doctorate, thesis/dissertation, preliminary exam, independent project. *Entrance requirements:* For doctorate, GRE General Test, minimum GPA of 3.2, research experience, letters of recommendation. Additional exam requirements/recommendations for international students: Required—TOEFL (minimum score 550 paper-based; 213 computer-based; 80 iBT). *Application deadline:* For fall admission, 12/1 for domestic and international students. Application fee: $30. Electronic applications accepted. *Expenses:* Tuition, state resident: part-time $248 per credit hour. Tuition, nonresident: part-time $880 per credit hour. Tuition and fees vary according to program. *Financial support:* In 2007–08, 11 fellowships with full tuition reimbursements (averaging $18,000 per year), 21 research assistantships with full tuition reimbursements (averaging $16,000 per year), 15 teaching assistantships with full tuition reimbursements (averaging $15,000 per year) were awarded; career-related internships or fieldwork, Federal Work-Study, institutionally sponsored loans, scholarships/grants, traineeships, health care benefits, and unspecified assistantships also available. Financial award applicants required to submit FAFSA. *Faculty research:* Antisocial behavior, depression, addictive behavior, developmental psychopathology, anxiety. Total annual research expenditures: $2.4 million. *Unit head:* Dr. Norman Bradley Schmidt, Director, 850-644-1707, Fax: 850-644-7739, E-mail: schmidt@psy.fsu.edu. *Application contact:* Cherie P. Miller, Graduate Program Assistant, 850-644-2499, Fax: 850-644-7739, E-mail: grad-info@psy.fsu.edu.

Fordham University, Graduate School of Arts and Sciences, Department of Psychology, Program in Clinical Psychology, New York, NY 10458. Offers PhD. *Students:* 57 full-time (39 women), 18 part-time (13 women); includes 25 minority (9 African Americans, 1 American Indian/Alaska Native, 8 Asian Americans or Pacific Islanders, 7 Hispanic Americans), 2 international. Average age 28. 398 applicants, 5% accepted, 11 enrolled. In 2007, 8 degrees awarded. Terminal master's awarded for partial completion of doctoral program. *Median time to degree:* Of those who began their doctoral program in fall 1999, 50% received their degree in 8 years or less. *Degree requirements:* For doctorate, comprehensive exam, thesis/dissertation, clinical internship. *Entrance requirements:* For doctorate, GRE General Test, GRE Subject Test. Additional exam requirements/recommendations for international students: Required—TOEFL (minimum score 600 paper-based; 250 computer-based). *Application deadline:* For fall admission, 12/14 for domestic students. Application fee: $70. Electronic applications accepted. *Expenses:* Tuition: Full-time $23,880; part-time $995 per credit. *Financial support:* In 2007–08, 33 students received support, including 3 fellowships with tuition reimbursements available (averaging $21,183 per year), 22 research assistantships with tuition reimbursements available (averaging $17,725 per year), 8 teaching assistantships with tuition reimbursements available (averaging $17,012 per year); career-related internships or fieldwork, institutionally sponsored loans, tuition waivers (full and partial), and unspecified assistantships also available. Financial award application deadline: 12/14. Total annual research expenditures: $2 million. *Unit head:* Dr. Barry Rosenfeld, Director, 718-817-3782, Fax: 718-817-3785. *Application contact:* Charlene Dundie, Director of Graduate Admissions, 718-817-4420, Fax: 718-817-3566, E-mail: dundie@fordham.edu.

Francis Marion University, Graduate Programs, Department of Psychology, Florence, SC 29501-0547. Offers applied clinical psychology (MS); applied community psychology (MS); school psychology (MS). Part-time and evening/weekend programs available. *Faculty:* 10 full-time (3 women), 6 part-time/adjunct (3 women). *Students:* 12 full-time (all women), 34 part-time (31 women); includes 5 minority (all African Americans), 1 international. Average age 28. 34 applicants, 100% accepted, 9 enrolled. In 2007, 9 degrees awarded. *Degree requirements:* For master's, internship. *Entrance requirements:* For master's, GRE General Test. *Application deadline:* For fall admission, 4/15 for domestic students; for spring admission, 10/15 for domestic students. Applications are processed on a rolling basis. Application fee: $30. *Expenses:* Tuition, state resident: full-time $7,547; part-time $377 per credit hour. Tuition, nonresident: full-time $15,094; part-time $755 per credit hour. Required fees: $285; $10 per credit hour. $45 per term. *Financial support:* In 2007–08, 2 research assistantships (averaging $7,000 per year), 3 teaching assistantships (averaging $8,000 per year) were awarded; career-related internships or fieldwork and unspecified assistantships also available. Support available to part-time students. Financial award application deadline: 3/1; financial award applicants required to submit FAFSA. *Faculty research:* Critical thinking, spatial localization, cognition and aging, family psychology. *Unit head:* Dr. John R. Hester, Chair, 843-661-1635, Fax: 843-661-1628. *Application contact:* Jennifer Taylor, Administrative Assistant, 843-661-1378, Fax: 843-661-1628.

Fuller Theological Seminary, Graduate School of Psychology, Department of Psychology, Pasadena, CA 91182. Offers clinical psychology (PhD, Psy D); psychology (MA, MS); MACL/PhD; MACL/Psy D. *Accreditation:* APA (one or more programs are accredited). *Degree requirements:* For doctorate, thesis/dissertation, internships. *Entrance requirements:* For doctorate, GRE General Test, GRE Subject Test, interview. Additional exam requirements/recommendations for international students: Required—TOEFL. Expenses: Contact institution. *Faculty research:* Psychoneuroimmunology, psychology of religion, coping, shame, depression.

Gallaudet University, The Graduate School, College of Arts and Sciences, Department of Psychology, Program in Clinical Psychology, Washington, DC 20002-3625. Offers PhD. MA in psychology given as part of PhD program. *Accreditation:* APA. *Degree requirements:* For doctorate, thesis/dissertation. *Entrance requirements:* For doctorate, GRE General Test or MAT, interview. *Application deadline:* For fall admission, 2/15 for domestic students. Application fee: $50. Electronic applications accepted. *Expenses:* Tuition: Full-time $5,790. Required fees: $1,886. *Financial support:* Application deadline: 8/1. *Application contact:* Wednesday Luria, Coordinator of Prospective Graduate Student Services, 202-651-5647, Fax: 202-651-5295, E-mail: wednesday.luria@gallaudet.edu.

George Fox University, Graduate Department of Clinical Psychology, Newberg, OR 97132-2697. Offers clinical psychology (Psy D); psychology (MA). *Accreditation:* APA. *Faculty:* 8 full-time (3 women), 11 part-time/adjunct (5 women). *Students:* 97 full-time (58 women), 11 part-time (6 women); includes 7 minority (1 African American, 1 American Indian/Alaska Native, 3 Asian Americans or Pacific Islanders, 2 Hispanic Americans), 1 international. Average age 29. 71 applicants, 51% accepted, 22 enrolled. In 2007, 23 master's, 14 doctorates awarded. *Degree requirements:* For doctorate, thesis/dissertation, internship. *Entrance requirements:* For master's, GRE General Test, GRE Subject Test, minimum undergraduate GPA of 3.0 during previous 2 years. Additional exam requirements/recommendations for international students: Required—TOEFL (minimum score 550 paper-based; 213 computer-based). *Application deadline:* For fall admission, 1/15 priority date for domestic students, 1/1 for international students. Application fee: $40. Electronic applications accepted. *Expenses: Contact institution. Financial support:* Career-related internships or fieldwork and scholarships/grants available. Financial award applicants required to submit FAFSA. *Faculty research:* Spiritual well-being, psychosocial development, value and ethics development. *Unit head:* Dr. Wayne Adams, Director, 800-765-4369 Ext. 2760, E-mail: wadams@georgefox.edu. *Application contact:* Adina McConaughey, Admission Counselor, 800-631-0921, Fax: 503-554-2263, E-mail: amcconaughey@georgefox.edu.

See Close-Up on page 1437.

George Mason University, College of Humanities and Social Sciences, Department of Psychology, Fairfax, VA 22030. Offers applied developmental psychology (MA, PhD); biopsychology (MA, PhD); clinical psychology (MA, PhD); human factors engineering psychology (MA, PhD); industrial/organizational psychology (MA, PhD); psychology (MA, PhD); school psychology (MA). *Accreditation:* APA. *Faculty:* 44 full-time (17 women), 16 part-time/adjunct (10 women). *Students:* 101 full-time (80 women), 135 part-time (88 women); includes 30 minority (6 African Americans, 13 Asian Americans or Pacific Islanders, 11 Hispanic Americans), 14 international. Average age 27. 734 applicants, 22% accepted, 86 enrolled. In 2007, 49 master's, 17 doctorates awarded. Terminal master's awarded for partial completion of doctoral program. *Median time to degree:* Of those who began their doctoral program in fall 1999, 97% received their degree in 8 years or less. *Degree requirements:* For master's, thesis (for applied developmental psychology and biopsychology); for doctorate, comprehensive

Clinical Psychology

George Mason University (continued)
exam, thesis/dissertation or alternative. *Entrance requirements:* For master's, GRE General Test, minimum GPA of 3.0 in last 60 hours of course work, undergraduate course work in psychology; for doctorate, GRE General Test, minimum undergraduate GPA of 3.0, 3.3 in major. Additional exam requirements/recommendations for international students: Required—TOEFL (minimum score 575 paper-based; 230 computer-based; 88 iBT), IELTS (minimum score 6). Application fee: $60 ($75 for international students). Electronic applications accepted. *Financial support:* In 2007–08, 15 fellowships with partial tuition reimbursements (averaging $2,300 per year), 33 research assistantships with partial tuition reimbursements (averaging $12,200 per year), 21 teaching assistantships with partial tuition reimbursements (averaging $12,200 per year) were awarded; career-related internships or fieldwork, scholarships/grants, traineeships, tuition waivers (partial), and unspecified assistantships also available. Financial award application deadline: 3/1; financial award applicants required to submit FAFSA. *Unit head:* Dr. Deborah Boehm-Davis, Chairperson, 703-993-1398, Fax: 703-993-1359, E-mail: bsmith@gmu.edu. *Application contact:* Dr. James Maddux, Information Contact, 703-993-3590, Fax: 703-993-1355, E-mail: psycgrad@gmu.edu.

The George Washington University, Columbian College of Arts and Sciences, Department of Psychology, Washington, DC 20052. Offers applied social psychology (PhD); clinical psychology (PhD); cognitive neuropsychology (PhD); industrial-organizational psychology (PhD). *Accreditation:* APA. Part-time and evening/weekend programs available. *Degree requirements:* For doctorate, thesis/dissertation or alternative, general exam. *Entrance requirements:* For doctorate, GRE General Test, minimum GPA of 3.0. Additional exam requirements/recommendations for international students: Required—TOEFL (minimum score 550 paper-based; 213 computer-based).

Graduate School and University Center of the City University of New York, Graduate Studies, Program in Psychology, New York, NY 10016-4039. Offers basic applied neurocognition (PhD); biopsychology (PhD); clinical psychology (PhD); developmental psychology (PhD); environmental psychology (PhD); experimental psychology (PhD); industrial psychology (PhD); learning processes (PhD); neuropsychology (PhD); psychology (PhD); social personality (PhD). *Faculty:* 119 full-time (40 women). *Students:* 510 full-time (379 women), 1 (woman) part-time; includes 98 minority (39 African Americans, 1 American Indian/Alaska Native, 21 Asian Americans or Pacific Islanders, 37 Hispanic Americans), 63 international. Average age 33. 747 applicants, 17% accepted, 78 enrolled. In 2007, 59 degrees awarded. *Degree requirements:* For doctorate, one foreign language, thesis/dissertation. *Entrance requirements:* For doctorate, GRE General Test. Additional exam requirements/recommendations for international students: Required—TOEFL. *Application deadline:* For fall admission, 12/15 for domestic students. Application fee: $125. Electronic applications accepted. *Financial support:* In 2007–08, 371 students received support, including 308 fellowships, 34 research assistantships, 33 teaching assistantships; career-related internships or fieldwork, Federal Work-Study, institutionally sponsored loans, and tuition waivers (full and partial) also available. Financial award application deadline: 2/1; financial award applicants required to submit FAFSA. *Unit head:* Dr. Joseph Glick, Executive Officer, 212-817-8706, Fax: 212-817-1533, E-mail: jglick@gc.cuny.edu.

Hofstra University, College of Liberal Arts and Sciences, Department of Psychology, Program in Clinical and School Psychology, Hempstead, NY 11549. Offers MS, PhD. *Accreditation:* APA (one or more programs are accredited); NCATE (one or more programs are accredited). *Students:* 79 full-time (54 women), 11 part-time (8 women); includes 10 minority (2 African Americans, 4 Asian Americans or Pacific Islanders, 4 Hispanic Americans), 3 international. Average age 28. 194 applicants, 15% accepted, 14 enrolled. In 2007, 13 master's, 12 doctorates awarded. *Median time to degree:* Of those who began their doctoral program in fall 1999, 95% received their degree in 8 years or less. *Degree requirements:* For doctorate, comprehensive exam, thesis/dissertation, oral defense. *Entrance requirements:* For doctorate, GRE General Test, GRE Subject Test (psychology), 3 letters of recommendation, interview, essay, curriculum vitae. Additional exam requirements/recommendations for international students: Required—TOEFL (minimum score 550 paper-based; 213 computer-based). *Application deadline:* For fall admission, 1/15 for domestic and international students. Application fee: $60. Electronic applications accepted. *Expenses:* Tuition: Full-time $14,220; part-time $820 per credit. Required fees: $970; $165 per term. Tuition and fees vary according to program. *Financial support:* In 2007–08, 61 students received support, including 39 fellowships with tuition reimbursements available (averaging $6,337 per year), 4 research assistantships with full and partial tuition reimbursements available (averaging $4,500 per year); career-related internships or fieldwork, Federal Work-Study, institutionally sponsored loans, scholarships/grants, tuition waivers (full and partial), and unspecified assistantships also available. Support available to part-time students. Financial award applicants required to submit FAFSA. *Faculty research:* Self-help approach to cigarette cessation, treatment of anger, cognitions of cocaine-addicted schizophrenics, use of mindfulness in treatment of chronic medical conditions, virtual reality treatment in phobia. *Unit head:* Dr. Mitchell L. Schare, Program Director, 516-463-5009, Fax: 516-463-6052, E-mail: psymls@hofstra.edu. *Application contact:* Carol Drummer, Dean of Graduate Admissions, 516-463-4876, Fax: 516-463-4664, E-mail: gradstudent@hofstra.edu.

Howard University, Graduate School, Department of Psychology, Washington, DC 20059-0002. Offers clinical psychology (PhD); developmental psychology (PhD); experimental psychology (PhD); neuropsychology (PhD); personality psychology (PhD); psychology (MS); social psychology (PhD). *Accreditation:* APA (one or more programs are accredited). Part-time programs available. *Degree requirements:* For master's, thesis; for doctorate, comprehensive exam, thesis/dissertation, qualifying exam. *Entrance requirements:* For master's, GRE General Test, minimum GPA of 2.5, bachelor's degree in psychology or related field; for doctorate, GRE General Test, minimum GPA of 3.0. *Expenses:* Tuition: Full-time $16,175; part-time $899 per credit hour. Required fees: $805. *Faculty research:* Personality and psychophysiology, educational and social development of African-American children, child and adult psychopathology.

Idaho State University, Office of Graduate Studies, College of Arts and Sciences, Department of Psychology, Department of Clinical Psychology, Pocatello, ID 83209. Offers PhD. *Students:* 27 full-time (20 women), 7 part-time (6 women); includes 1 minority (Hispanic American), 1 international. Average age 29. In 2007, 4 degrees awarded. *Degree requirements:* For doctorate, comprehensive exam, thesis/dissertation, 1 year full-time clinical internship. *Entrance requirements:* For doctorate, GRE General Test, GRE Subject Test, MS in psychology. Additional exam requirements/recommendations for international students: Required—TOEFL (minimum score 550 paper-based; 213 computer-based; 80 iBT). *Application deadline:* For fall admission, 7/1 for domestic students, 6/1 for international students; for spring admission, 12/1 for domestic students, 11/1 for international students. Applications are processed on a rolling basis. Application fee: $55. Electronic applications accepted. *Expenses:* Tuition, state resident: full-time $2,882; part-time $259 per credit hour. Tuition, nonresident: full-time $11,566; part-time $379 per credit hour. Required fees: $2,278. Full-time tuition and fees vary according to program. Part-time tuition and fees vary according to course load. *Financial support:* Career-related internships or fieldwork, Federal Work-Study, institutionally sponsored loans, scholarships/grants, traineeships, health care benefits, tuition waivers (full and partial), and unspecified assistantships available. Support available to part-time students. Financial award application deadline: 1/1; financial award applicants required to submit FAFSA. *Faculty research:* Pre-adolescent behavior, substance abuse training, trauma related problems. *Application contact:* Ellen Combs, Graduate School Technical Records Specialist, 208-282-2150, Fax: 208-282-4847.

Illinois Institute of Technology, Graduate College, Institute of Psychology, Chicago, IL 60616-3793. Offers clinical psychology (PhD); industrial/organizational psychology (PhD); personnel/human resource development (MS); psychology (MS); rehabilitation counseling (MS); rehabilitation counselor education (PhD). *Accreditation:* APA (one or more programs are accredited); CORE. Evening/weekend programs available. *Faculty:* 18 full-time (8 women), 4 part-time/adjunct (2 women). *Students:* 122 full-time (95 women), 66 part-time (45 women); includes 44 minority (15 African Americans, 1 American Indian/Alaska Native, 17 Asian Americans or Pacific Islanders, 11 Hispanic Americans), 22 international. Average age 29. 261 applicants, 34% accepted, 32 enrolled. In 2007, 31 master's, 12 doctorates awarded. Terminal master's awarded for partial completion of doctoral program. *Degree requirements:* For master's, comprehensive exam, thesis (for some programs); for doctorate, comprehensive exam, thesis/dissertation, qualifying exams. *Entrance requirements:* For master's, GRE General Test, minimum GPA of 3.0; for doctorate, GRE General Test, minimum GPA of 3.2. Additional exam requirements/recommendations for international students: Required—TOEFL (minimum score 550 paper-based; 213 computer-based; 80 iBT). *Application deadline:* For fall admission, 1/15 for domestic and international students. Application fee: $40. Electronic applications accepted. *Expenses:* Tuition: Full-time $14,004; part-time $778 per credit. Required fees: $7 per credit. $235 per term. Tuition and fees vary according to class time, course level, course load, program and student level. *Financial support:* In 2007–08, 39 fellowships with partial tuition reimbursements (averaging $2,798 per year), 1 research assistantship with partial tuition reimbursement, 24 teaching assistantships with partial tuition reimbursements (averaging $4,405 per year) were awarded; career-related internships or fieldwork, Federal Work-Study, institutionally sponsored loans, scholarships/grants, traineeships, health care benefits, tuition waivers (partial), and unspecified assistantships also available. Support available to part-time students. Financial award applicants required to submit FAFSA. *Faculty research:* Stigma and mental illness, depression, couples communication, leadership, psychometric theory. Total annual research expenditures: $636,382. *Unit head:* Dr. M. Ellen Mitchell, Dean, 312-567-3362, Fax: 312-567-3493, E-mail: mitchelle@itt.edu. *Application contact:* Application Contact, 312-567-3500, Fax: 312-567-3493, E-mail: psychology@iit.edu.

Illinois State University, Graduate School, College of Arts and Sciences, Department of Psychology, Normal, IL 61790-2200. Offers psychology (MA, MS), including clinical psychology, counseling psychology, developmental psychology, educational psychology, experimental psychology, measurement-evaluation, organizational-industrial psychology; school psychology (PhD, SSP). *Accreditation:* APA. *Faculty:* 36 full-time (14 women). *Students:* 49 full-time (37 women), 19 part-time (14 women); includes 3 minority (all Asian Americans or Pacific Islanders), 7 international. 91 applicants, 43% accepted. In 2007, 24 degrees awarded. *Degree requirements:* For master's, thesis or alternative; for doctorate, variable foreign language requirement, thesis/dissertation, 2 terms of residency, internship, practicum. *Entrance requirements:* For master's, GRE General Test, GRE Subject Test, minimum GPA of 3.0 in last 60 hours of course work; for doctorate, GRE General Test. *Application deadline:* Applications are processed on a rolling basis. Application fee: $40. *Expenses:* Tuition, state resident: full-time $3,492; part-time $194 per credit hour. Tuition, nonresident: full-time $7,272; part-time $404 per credit hour. Required fees: $1,024; $57 per credit hour. *Financial support:* In 2007–08, 33 research assistantships (averaging $6,252 per year), 49 teaching assistantships (averaging $4,217 per year) were awarded; tuition waivers (full) and unspecified assistantships also available. Financial award application deadline: 4/1. *Faculty research:* Comprehensive evaluation system for the central region professional development grant, Illinois school psychology internship consortium, for children's sake. Total annual research expenditures: $292,085. *Unit head:* Dr. Neil Skaggs, Acting Chairperson, 309-438-8651.

Immaculata University, College of Graduate Studies, Department of Psychology, Immaculata, PA 19345. Offers clinical psychology (Psy D); counseling psychology (MA, Certificate), including school guidance counselor (Certificate), school psychologist (Certificate). *Accreditation:* APA. Part-time and evening/weekend programs available. *Students:* 106 full-time (71 women), 207 part-time (194 women); includes 30 minority (20 African Americans, 6 Asian Americans or Pacific Islanders, 4 Hispanic Americans). Average age 34. 182 applicants, 62% accepted, 56 enrolled. In 2007, 38 master's, 10 doctorates awarded. *Degree requirements:* For master's, comprehensive exam, thesis optional; for doctorate, comprehensive exam, thesis/dissertation. *Entrance requirements:* For master's, GRE General Test or MAT, minimum GPA of 3.0; for doctorate, GRE General Test, minimum GPA of 3.5. Additional exam requirements/recommendations for international students: Required—TOEFL, IELTS. *Application deadline:* Applications are processed on a rolling basis. Application fee: $35. *Financial support:* Application deadline: 5/1. *Faculty research:* Supervision ethics, psychology of teaching, gender. *Unit head:* Dr. Jed A. Yalof, Chair, 610-647-4400 Ext. 3503, Fax: 610-993-8550, E-mail: jyalof@immaculata.edu. *Application contact:* Office of Graduate Admission, 610-647-4400 Ext. 3211, Fax: 610-993-8550, E-mail: graduate@immaculata.edu.

Indiana State University, School of Graduate Studies, College of Arts and Sciences, Department of Psychology, Terre Haute, IN 47809-1401. Offers clinical psychology (Psy D); general psychology (MA, MS). *Accreditation:* APA (one or more programs are accredited). *Faculty:* 9 full-time (6 women), 4 part-time/adjunct (1 woman). *Students:* 39 full-time (23 women), 17 part-time (12 women); includes 6 minority (1 African American, 3 Asian Americans or Pacific Islanders, 2 Hispanic Americans), 1 international. Average age 28. 185 applicants, 9% accepted, 15 enrolled. In 2007, 12 master's, 6 doctorates awarded. Terminal master's awarded for partial completion of doctoral program. *Degree requirements:* For master's, thesis (for some programs); for doctorate, comprehensive exam, thesis/dissertation, internship, professional research project. *Entrance requirements:* For master's, GRE General Test, 12 semester hours of course work in psychology, minimum GPA of 2.75; for doctorate, GRE General Test, minimum GPA of 3.0. Additional exam requirements/recommendations for international students: Required—TOEFL (minimum score 550 paper-based). *Application deadline:* For fall admission, 2/1 for domestic students; for spring admission, 11/1 priority date for domestic students. Applications are processed on a rolling basis. Application fee: $35. Electronic applications accepted. *Expenses:* Tuition, state resident: full-time $7,056; part-time $294 per semester hour. Tuition, nonresident: full-time $14,016; part-time $584 per semester hour. Required fees: $175 per semester. *Financial support:* In 2007–08, 4 research assistantships with partial tuition reimbursements (averaging $7,000 per year), 22 teaching assistantships with partial tuition reimbursements (averaging $7,000 per year) were awarded; fellowships with partial tuition reimbursements, career-related internships or fieldwork, Federal Work-Study, institutionally sponsored loans, and tuition waivers (full) also available. Financial award application deadline: 3/1; financial award applicants required to submit FAFSA. *Unit head:* Dr. Virgil L. Sheets, Chairperson, 812-237-2456. *Application contact:* Application Contact, 812-237-2456.

Indiana University of Pennsylvania, School of Graduate Studies and Research, College of Natural Sciences and Mathematics, Department of Psychology, Program in Clinical Psychology, Indiana, PA 15705-1087. Offers Psy D. *Accreditation:* APA. Part-time programs available. *Faculty:* 15 full-time (10 women). *Students:* 44 full-time (39 women), 25 part-time (19 women); includes 4 minority (1 African American, 1 Asian American or Pacific Islander, 2 Hispanic Americans). Average age 28. 83 applicants, 17% accepted, 13 enrolled. In 2007, 8 doctorates awarded. *Degree requirements:* For doctorate, comprehensive exam, thesis/dissertation, internship, practicum. *Entrance requirements:* For doctorate, GRE General Test, minimum GPA of 3.0, 3 letters of recommendation, interview. Additional exam requirements/recommendations for international students: Required—TOEFL. *Application deadline:* For fall admission, 1/10 for domestic students. Application fee: $30. *Expenses:* Tuition, state resident: full-time $6,214; part-time $345 per credit. Tuition, nonresident: full-time $9,944; part-time $552 per credit. Required fees: $43 per credit. One-time fee: $140 part-time. Tuition and fees vary according to course load. *Financial support:* In 2007–08, 7 fellowships (averaging $1,000 per year), 39 research assistantships with full and partial tuition reimbursements (averaging $3,040 per year), 2 teaching assistantships (averaging $17,001 per year) were awarded; Federal Work-Study and scholarships/grants also available. Financial award application deadline: 3/15; financial award applicants required to submit FAFSA. *Unit head:* Dr. Donald Robertson, Graduate Coordinator, 724-357-4522, E-mail: durobert@iup.edu.

Indiana University–Purdue University Indianapolis, School of Science, Department of Psychology, Indianapolis, IN 46202-3275. Offers clinical rehabilitation psychology (MS); industrial/organizational psychology (MS); psychobiology of addictions (MS, PhD). *Accreditation:* APA (one or more programs are accredited). *Faculty:* 10 full-time (2 women). *Students:* 21 full-time (19 women), 5 part-time (all women); includes 4 minority (2 African Americans, 2 Asian

Americans or Pacific Islanders). Average age 26. In 2007, 7 degrees awarded. Terminal master's awarded for partial completion of doctoral program. *Degree requirements:* For master's, thesis; for doctorate, thesis/dissertation. *Entrance requirements:* For master's, GRE General Test, minimum undergraduate GPA of 3.0; for doctorate, GRE General Test, GRE Subject Test (clinical rehabilitation psychology), minimum undergraduate GPA of 3.2. *Application deadline:* For fall admission, 1/1 priority date for domestic students. Application fee: $50 ($60 for international students). *Expenses:* Tuition, state resident: full-time $5,818; part-time $242 per credit hour. Tuition, nonresident: full-time $17,106; part-time $713 per credit hour. Required fees: $629. Tuition and fees vary according to course load, campus/location and program. *Financial support:* In 2007–08, 5 fellowships with partial tuition reimbursements (averaging $12,218 per year), 23 teaching assistantships with partial tuition reimbursements (averaging $7,553 per year) were awarded; research assistantships with partial tuition reimbursements, career-related internships or fieldwork, Federal Work-Study, and institutionally sponsored loans also available. Financial award application deadline: 3/1; financial award applicants required to submit FAFSA. *Faculty research:* Psychiatric rehabilitation, chronic stress, neurological research, language and cognitive development in infants. alcoholism and psychopathology. *Unit head:* Dr. J. Gregor Fetterman, Chairman, 317-274-6945, Fax: 317-274-6756, E-mail: gfetter@iupui.edu.

Institute of Transpersonal Psychology, Residential Programs, Palo Alto, CA 94303. Offers clinical psychology (PhD); counseling psychology (MA); transpersonal psychology (MA, PhD); women's spirituality (PhD). Part-time and evening/weekend programs available. *Faculty:* 17 full-time (9 women), 31 part-time/adjunct (18 women). *Students:* 239 full-time (164 women), 48 part-time (33 women); includes 46 minority (8 African Americans, 4 American Indian/Alaska Native, 18 Asian Americans or Pacific Islanders, 16 Hispanic Americans), 16 international. Average age 38. 132 applicants, 80% accepted, 79 enrolled. In 2007, 47 master's, 16 doctorates awarded. Terminal master's awarded for partial completion of doctoral program. *Degree requirements:* For doctorate, thesis/dissertation. *Entrance requirements:* For master's and doctorate, bachelor's degree. *Application deadline:* For fall admission, 2/15 priority date for domestic students. Applications are processed on a rolling basis. Application fee: $55. *Expenses:* Tuition: Full-time $11,877; part-time $3,959 per quarter. Tuition and fees vary according to degree level and student level. *Financial support:* In 2007–08, 178 students received support; teaching assistantships, career-related internships or fieldwork, Federal Work-Study, and scholarships/grants available. Support available to part-time students. Financial award application deadline: 7/1; financial award applicants required to submit FAFSA. *Unit head:* Dr. Paul Roy, Academic Vice President, 650-493-4430 Ext. 243, Fax: 650-493-6835, E-mail: proy@itp.edu. *Application contact:* 650-493-4430 Ext. 16, Fax: 650-493-6835, E-mail: itpinfo@itp.edu.

See Close-Up on page 1439.

Jackson State University, Graduate School, School of Liberal Arts, Department of Psychology, Jackson, MS 39217. Offers clinical psychology (PhD). *Accreditation:* APA. *Degree requirements:* For doctorate, comprehensive exam, thesis/dissertation. *Entrance requirements:* For doctorate, MAT, GRE.

James Madison University, The Graduate School, College of Integrated Science and Technology, Department of Graduate Psychology, Program in Combined-Integrated Clinical and School Psychology, Harrisonburg, VA 22807. Offers Psy D. Part-time and evening/weekend programs available. *Students:* 19 full-time (16 women), 3 part-time (2 women); includes 2 minority (1 African American, 1 Asian American or Pacific Islander), 4 international. Average age 27. In 2007, 2 degrees awarded. *Degree requirements:* For doctorate, thesis/dissertation, 12-month internship. *Entrance requirements:* For doctorate, GRE General Test, GRE Subject Test (advanced psychology), 3 letters of recommendation. Additional exam requirements/recommendations for international students: Required—TOEFL. *Application deadline:* For fall admission, 2/1 for domestic students. Applications are processed on a rolling basis. Application fee: $55. Electronic applications accepted. *Expenses:* Tuition, state resident: full-time $6,720; part-time $280 per credit hour. Tuition, nonresident: full-time $19,104; part-time $796 per credit hour. *Financial support:* In 2007–08, 12 students received support. 12 doctoral assistantships ($14,216) available. Financial award application deadline: 3/1; financial award applicants required to submit FAFSA. *Unit head:* Dr. Gregg R. Henriques, Program Director, 540-568-7857.

The Johns Hopkins University, Bloomberg School of Public Health, Department of Mental Health, Baltimore, MD 21218-2699. Offers children's mental health services (PhD); drug dependence epidemiology (PhD); mental health (MHS); psychiatric epidemiology (PhD). *Faculty:* 26 full-time (15 women), 35 part-time/adjunct (13 women). *Students:* 42 full-time (32 women), 3 part-time (1 woman); includes 10 minority (4 African Americans, 5 Asian Americans or Pacific Islanders, 1 Hispanic American), 8 international. Average age 29. 69 applicants, 71% accepted, 27 enrolled. In 2007, 10 master's, 5 doctorates awarded. *Median time to degree:* Of those who began their doctoral program in fall 1999, 90% received their degree in 8 years or less. *Degree requirements:* For master's, thesis (for some programs); for doctorate, thesis/dissertation, 1 year full-time residency, oral and written exams. *Entrance requirements:* For master's, GRE General Test, MCAT, 3 letters of recommendation, curriculum vitae; for doctorate, GRE General Test, MCAT or GMAT, 3 letters of recommendation, curriculum vitae. Additional exam requirements/recommendations for international students: Required—TOEFL (minimum score 550 paper-based; 250 computer-based). *Application deadline:* For fall admission, 12/1 priority date for domestic students. Applications are processed on a rolling basis. Application fee: $45. Electronic applications accepted. *Financial support:* In 2007–08, 61 students received support, including 1 fellowship (averaging $32,000 per year); Federal Work-Study, institutionally sponsored loans, scholarships/grants, traineeships, and stipends also available. Support available to part-time students. Financial award application deadline: 3/15; financial award applicants required to submit FAFSA. *Faculty research:* Etiology, development and prevention of aggressive and antisocial behavior; epidemiology of mental disorders; genetic epidemiology of mental disorders. Total annual research expenditures: $14.5 million. *Unit head:* Dr. William W. Eaton, Chair, 410-955-3910, Fax: 410-614-7469, E-mail: weaton@jhsph.edu. *Application contact:* Patricia E. Scott, Senior Academic Program Coordinator, 410-955-1906, Fax: 410-955-9088, E-mail: mhdept@jhsph.edu.

Kent State University, College of Arts and Sciences, Department of Psychology, Kent, OH 44242-0001. Offers clinical psychology (MA, PhD); experimental psychology (MA, PhD). *Accreditation:* APA (one or more programs are accredited). *Faculty:* 28 full-time (12 women). *Students:* 119 full-time (87 women). 324 applicants, 7% accepted. In 2007, 16 master's, 16 doctorates awarded. *Degree requirements:* For master's, thesis; for doctorate, thesis/dissertation. *Entrance requirements:* For master's, GRE, minimum GPA of 3.0, minimum 18 semester hours in psychology with one course in statistics and one experimental course with a lab component; for doctorate, GRE, minimum GPA of 3.0. Additional exam requirements/recommendations for international students: Required—TOEFL (minimum score 525 paper-based), Michigan English Language Assessment Battery (minimum score: 77). *Application deadline:* For fall admission, 1/1 for domestic and international students. Application fee: $30. *Financial support:* Fellowships, research assistantships, teaching assistantships, career-related internships or fieldwork, Federal Work-Study, institutionally sponsored loans, health care benefits, and tuition waivers (full) available. Financial award application deadline: 1/1. *Unit head:* Dr. Mary Ann Parris Stephens, Chair, 330-672-2027, Fax: 330-672-3786, E-mail: mstephen@kent.edu. *Application contact:* Jack Graham, Coordinator of Graduate Studies, E-mail: jgraham@kent.edu.

Lakehead University, Graduate Studies, Department of Psychology, Thunder Bay, ON P7B 5E1, Canada. Offers clinical psychology (MA, PhD); experimental psychology (MA). Part-time and evening/weekend programs available. *Degree requirements:* For master's, thesis optional; for doctorate, thesis/dissertation, 2 comprehensive exams, internship. *Entrance requirements:* For master's, GRE, honors degree in psychology, advanced course work in statistics, minimum B average; for doctorate, GRE, minimum B average. Additional exam requirements/recommendations for international students: Required—TOEFL. *Faculty research:* Chaos theory, health psychology, counseling psychology, gerontology, women's studies.

Lamar University, College of Graduate Studies, College of Arts and Sciences, Department of Psychology, Beaumont, TX 77710. Offers community/clinical psychology (MS); industrial/organizational psychology (MS). Part-time programs available. *Faculty:* 6 full-time (3 women). *Students:* 19 full-time (11 women), 10 part-time (8 women); includes 6 minority (2 African Americans, 1 Asian American or Pacific Islander, 3 Hispanic Americans), 1 international. Average age 25. 37 applicants, 43% accepted, 10 enrolled. In 2007, 6 degrees awarded. *Degree requirements:* For master's, thesis, practicum. *Entrance requirements:* For master's, GRE General Test, minimum GPA of 2.75 in last 60 hours of undergraduate course work. Additional exam requirements/recommendations for international students: Required—TOEFL. *Application deadline:* For fall admission, 8/1 for domestic students; for spring admission, 12/1 for domestic students. Application fee: $25 ($50 for international students). *Expenses:* Tuition, state resident: part-time $348 per semester hour. Tuition, nonresident: part-time $626 per semester hour. Tuition and fees vary according to course load. *Financial support:* In 2007–08, 12 students received support, including 3 teaching assistantships (averaging $4,500 per year); fellowships, research assistantships, career-related internships or fieldwork, Federal Work-Study, scholarships/grants, and tuition waivers (partial) also available. Support available to part-time students. Financial award application deadline: 4/1. *Faculty research:* Groupthink, health psychology, school psychology, behavioral neuroscience. *Unit head:* Dr. Oney D. Fitzpatrick, Chair, 409-880-8285, Fax: 409-880-1779, E-mail: fitzpatrod@hal.lamar.edu.

La Salle University, School of Arts and Sciences, Program in Clinical-Counseling Psychology, Philadelphia, PA 19141-1199. Offers MA. *Accreditation:* APA. Part-time and evening/weekend programs available. *Faculty:* 10 full-time (6 women), 17 part-time/adjunct (4 women). *Students:* 90 full-time (72 women), 217 part-time (166 women); includes 64 minority (44 African Americans, 9 Asian Americans or Pacific Islanders, 11 Hispanic Americans), 2 international. Average age 31. 197 applicants, 73% accepted, 80 enrolled. In 2007, 61 degrees awarded. *Degree requirements:* For master's, comprehensive exam. *Entrance requirements:* For master's, GRE or MAT, 15 undergraduate credits in psychology. *Application deadline:* Applications are processed on a rolling basis. Application fee: $35. *Expenses: Contact institution.* Tuition and fees vary according to program. *Financial support:* In 2007–08, 211 students received support; teaching assistantships, career-related internships or fieldwork, institutionally sponsored loans, scholarships/grants, and tuition waivers (partial) available. Support available to part-time students. Financial award application deadline: 8/15; financial award applicants required to submit FAFSA. *Faculty research:* Cognitive therapy, attribution theory, work habits, single parent families, treatment of addictions. *Unit head:* Dr. John Rooney, Director, 215-951-1767, Fax: 215-951-1843, E-mail: rooney@lasalle.edu.

La Salle University, School of Arts and Sciences, Program in Psychology, Philadelphia, PA 19141-1199. Offers clinical psychology (Psy D); family psychology (Psy D); rehabilitation psychology (Psy D). Part-time and evening/weekend programs available. *Faculty:* 8 full-time (4 women), 5 part-time/adjunct (2 women). *Students:* 91 full-time (80 women), 18 part-time (11 women); includes 13 minority (6 African Americans, 4 Asian Americans or Pacific Islanders, 3 Hispanic Americans), 1 international. Average age 27. 111 applicants, 48% accepted, 23 enrolled. In 2007, 21 doctorates awarded. *Entrance requirements:* For doctorate, GRE, minimum GPA of 3.0. *Application deadline:* For fall admission, 3/1 for domestic students. Application fee: $35. *Expenses: Contact institution.* Tuition and fees vary according to program. *Financial support:* In 2007–08, 94 students received support. Scholarships/grants available. Financial award applicants required to submit FAFSA. *Faculty research:* Cognitive therapy, attribution theory, treatment of addiction. *Unit head:* Dr. Frank Gardner, Director, 215-951-5016, Fax: 215-951-1351.

Lesley University, Graduate School of Arts and Social Sciences, Cambridge, MA 02138-2790. Offers clinical mental health counseling (MA), including expressive therapies counseling, holistic counseling, school and community counseling; counseling psychology (MA, CAGS), including professional counseling (MA), school counseling (MA); creative arts in learning (CAGS); creative writing (MFA); ecological teaching and learning (MS); environmental education (MS); expressive therapies (MA, PhD, CAGS), including art (MA), dance (MA), expressive therapies, music (MA); independent studies (CAGS); independent study (MA); intercultural relations (MA, CAGS); interdisciplinary studies (MA), including individualized studies, integrative holistic health, women's studies; visual arts (MFA). Part-time and evening/weekend programs available. Postbaccalaureate distance learning degree programs offered (minimal on-campus study). *Faculty:* 49 full-time (41 women), 185 part-time/adjunct (137 women). *Students:* 653 full-time (580 women), 1,972 part-time (1,795 women); includes 191 minority (103 African Americans, 11 American Indian/Alaska Native, 19 Asian Americans or Pacific Islanders, 58 Hispanic Americans), 61 international. Average age 37. 1,011 applicants, 87% accepted, 645 enrolled. In 2007, 1,107 master's, 1 doctorate, 3 other advanced degrees awarded. *Degree requirements:* For master's, internship, practicum, thesis (expressive therapies); for doctorate, thesis/dissertation, arts apprenticeship, field placement; for CAGS, thesis, internship (counseling psychology, expressive therapies). *Entrance requirements:* For master's, MAT (counseling psychology), interview, writing samples, art portfolio; for doctorate, GRE or MAT; for CAGS, interview, master's degree. Additional exam requirements/recommendations for international students: Required—TOEFL (minimum score 550 paper-based; 213 computer-based; 80 iBT). *Application deadline:* Applications are processed on a rolling basis. Application fee: $50. Electronic applications accepted. *Financial support:* In 2007–08, 64 students received support, including research assistantships (averaging $3,400 per year), 1 teaching assistantship (averaging $7,298 per year); career-related internships or fieldwork, Federal Work-Study, scholarships/grants, and unspecified assistantships also available. Support available to part-time students. Financial award application deadline: 4/15; financial award applicants required to submit FAFSA. *Faculty research:* Psychotherapy and culture; psychotherapy and psychological trauma; women's issues in art, teaching and psychotherapy; community based art, psycho-spiritual inquiry. *Unit head:* Dr. Julia Halevy, Dean, 617-349-8317, Fax: 617-349-8366, E-mail: jhalevy@lesley.edu. *Application contact:* Christina Murray, Senior Assistant Director, On-Campus Admissions, 617-349-8827, Fax: 617-349-8313, E-mail: cmurray3@lesley.edu.

Long Island University, Brooklyn Campus, Richard L. Conolly College of Liberal Arts and Sciences, Department of Psychology, Program in Clinical Psychology, Brooklyn, NY 11201-8423. Offers PhD. *Accreditation:* APA. *Degree requirements:* For doctorate, thesis/dissertation. *Entrance requirements:* For doctorate, GRE Subject Test, GRE General Test. Additional exam requirements/recommendations for international students: Required—TOEFL (minimum score 500 paper-based; 173 computer-based). Electronic applications accepted. *Faculty research:* Ethnicity and human development.

Long Island University, C.W. Post Campus, College of Liberal Arts and Sciences, Department of Psychology, Program in Clinical Psychology, Brookville, NY 11548-1300. Offers Psy D. *Accreditation:* APA. *Degree requirements:* For doctorate, thesis/dissertation, internship. *Entrance requirements:* For doctorate, GRE General Test, GRE Subject Test, GRE analytical writing, bachelor's degree in psychology, minimum GPA of 3.25, 18 credit hours of undergraduate psychology, 3 letters of recommendation. Expenses: Contact institution. Tuition and fees vary according to course load. *Faculty research:* Family violence, schizophrenia, developmental disabilities, psychotherapy, terror and trauma.

Louisiana State University and Agricultural and Mechanical College, Graduate School, College of Arts and Sciences, Department of Psychology, Baton Rouge, LA 70803. Offers biological psychology (MA, PhD); clinical psychology (MA, PhD); cognitive psychology (MA, PhD); developmental psychology (MA, PhD); industrial/organizational psychology (MA, PhD); school psychology (MA, PhD). *Accreditation:* APA (one or more programs are accredited). *Faculty:* 25 full-time (9 women). *Students:* 81 full-time (60 women), 23 part-time (15 women); includes 15 minority (6 African Americans, 4 American Indian/Alaska Native, 2 Asian Americans or Pacific Islanders, 3 Hispanic Americans), 3 international. Average age 28. 199 applicants,

Clinical Psychology

Louisiana State University and Agricultural and Mechanical College (continued)

15% accepted, 23 enrolled. In 2007, 11 master's, 13 doctorates awarded. Terminal master's awarded for partial completion of doctoral program. *Degree requirements:* For master's, thesis; for doctorate, thesis/dissertation, 1 year internship. *Entrance requirements:* For master's and doctorate, GRE General Test, minimum GPA of 3.0. Additional exam requirements/recommendations for international students: Required—TOEFL (minimum score 550 paper-based; 213 computer-based; 79 iBT). *Application deadline:* For fall admission, 1/15 for domestic and international students. Applications are processed on a rolling basis. Application fee: $25. Electronic applications accepted. *Financial support:* In 2007–08, 101 students received support, including 5 fellowships (averaging $26,557 per year), 55 teaching assistantships with partial tuition reimbursements available (averaging $13,218 per year); research assistantships with partial tuition reimbursements available, career-related internships or fieldwork, Federal Work-Study, institutionally sponsored loans, scholarships/grants, health care benefits, and tuition waivers (full and partial) also available. Financial award applicants required to submit FAFSA. *Faculty research:* Clinical psychology, autism, anxiety, addition, neuro-psychology, school psychology, cognitive psychology, experimental psychology. Total annual research expenditures: $582,678. *Unit head:* Dr. Alan Baumeister, Chair, 225-578-4099, Fax: 225-578-4125, E-mail: abaumei@lsu.edu. *Application contact:* Dr. Janet McDonald, Coordinator of Graduate Studies, 225-578-4116, Fax: 225-578-4125, E-mail: psmcdo@lsu.edu.

Loyola College in Maryland, Graduate Programs, College of Arts and Sciences, Department of Psychology, Program in Clinical Psychology, Baltimore, MD 21210-2699. Offers MS, Psy D, CAS. *Accreditation:* APA. Part-time and evening/weekend programs available. *Entrance requirements:* For master's, doctorate, and CAS, GRE General Test, GRE Subject Test (recommended). Additional exam requirements/recommendations for international students: Required—TOEFL (minimum score 550 paper-based; 213 computer-based).

Loyola University Chicago, Graduate School, Department of Psychology, Program in Clinical Psychology, Chicago, IL 60611-2196. Offers PhD. *Accreditation:* APA. *Faculty:* 10 full-time (5 women). *Students:* 37 full-time (33 women); includes 6 minority (4 African Americans, 2 Hispanic Americans). Average age 27. 260 applicants, 3% accepted, 6 enrolled. In 2007, 7 degrees awarded. Terminal master's awarded for partial completion of doctoral program. *Degree requirements:* For doctorate, comprehensive exam, thesis/dissertation. *Entrance requirements:* For doctorate, GRE General Test, GRE Subject Test, letters of recommendation. *Application deadline:* For fall admission, 12/1 for domestic students. Application fee: $50. Electronic applications accepted. *Expenses:* Tuition: Full-time $12,780; part-time $710 per credit hour. Required fees: $55 per semester. Full-time tuition and fees vary according to program. *Financial support:* In 2007–08, 2 fellowships with full tuition reimbursements (averaging $15,000 per year), 17 research assistantships with full tuition reimbursements (averaging $15,000 per year), 7 teaching assistantships with full tuition reimbursements (averaging $15,000 per year) were awarded; career-related internships or fieldwork, Federal Work-Study, scholarships/grants, traineeships, and unspecified assistantships also available. Financial award application deadline: 12/1; financial award applicants required to submit FAFSA. *Faculty research:* Child and family, AIDS, ethics and professional practice, psychotherapy, stress and coping, positive youth development, pediatric psychology, adolescence, inner city youth. *Unit head:* Dr. Grayson Holmbeck, Director, 773-508-2967, Fax: 773-508-8713, E-mail: gholmbe@luc.edu. *Application contact:* Jacquie Hamilton, Senior Secretary, 773-508-2974, Fax: 773-508-8713, E-mail: jhamilt@luc.edu.

Madonna University, Department of Psychology, Livonia, MI 48150-1173. Offers clinical psychology (MSCP). Part-time and evening/weekend programs available. *Degree requirements:* For master's, thesis or alternative. *Entrance requirements:* Additional exam requirements/recommendations for international students: Required—TOEFL. Electronic applications accepted.

Marquette University, Graduate School, College of Arts and Sciences, Department of Psychology, Milwaukee, WI 53201-1881. Offers clinical psychology (MS); psychology (PhD). *Accreditation:* APA. Part-time programs available. *Faculty:* 17 full-time (8 women), 2 part-time/adjunct (1 woman). *Students:* 42 full-time (29 women), 7 part-time (6 women); includes 5 minority (3 African Americans, 1 American Indian/Alaska Native, 1 Hispanic American), 1 international. Average age 28. 111 applicants, 16% accepted, 13 enrolled. In 2007, 7 master's, 9 doctorates awarded. *Degree requirements:* For master's, comprehensive exam, thesis or alternative; for doctorate, thesis/dissertation, internship, qualifying exam. *Entrance requirements:* For master's, GRE General Test, GRE Subject Test, MAT; for doctorate, GRE General Test, GRE Subject Test, sample of scholarly writing. Additional exam requirements/recommendations for international students: Required—TOEFL. *Application deadline:* For fall admission, 2/15 for domestic students. Application fee: $40. *Financial support:* In 2007–08, 3 research assistantships, 16 teaching assistantships were awarded; career-related internships or fieldwork, Federal Work-Study, institutionally sponsored loans, scholarships/grants, and tuition waivers (full and partial) also available. Support available to part-time students. Financial award application deadline: 2/15. *Faculty research:* Mental imagery, moral development, organizational behavior, depression, psychotherapy outcomes. Total annual research expenditures: $122,416. *Unit head:* Dr. Mike Wierzbicki, Chair, 414-288-7218, Fax: 414-288-5333. *Application contact:* Dr. Steve Saunders, Information Contact, 414-288-7459.

Marshall University, Academic Affairs Division, College of Liberal Arts, Department of Psychology, Huntington, WV 25755. Offers clinical psychology (MA); general psychology (MA); industrial and organizational psychology (MA); psychology (Psy D). *Accreditation:* APA. *Faculty:* 20 full-time (8 women), 1 part-time/adjunct (0 women). *Students:* 94 full-time (60 women), 31 part-time (23 women); includes 3 minority (1 Asian American or Pacific Islander, 2 Hispanic Americans), 4 international. Average age 29. In 2007, 26 master's, 3 doctorates awarded. *Degree requirements:* For master's, thesis optional. *Entrance requirements:* For master's, GRE General Test or MAT. *Application deadline:* For fall admission, 3/1 for domestic students; for spring admission, 11/1 for domestic students. Application fee: $40. *Financial support:* Teaching assistantships with tuition reimbursements available. *Unit head:* Dr. Martin Amerikaner, Chairperson, 304-696-2783, E-mail: amerikan@marshall.edu. *Application contact:* Information Contact, 304-746-1900, Fax: 304-746-1902, E-mail: services@marshall.edu.

Marywood University, Academic Affairs, College of Education and Human Development, Department of Psychology and Counseling, Program in Clinical Psychology, Scranton, PA 18509-1598. Offers Psy D. *Accreditation:* APA. *Faculty:* 13. *Students:* 26 full-time (19 women), 10 part-time (all women). Average age 28. *Entrance requirements:* For doctorate, GRE, official transcripts, 3 letters of recomendation, personal statement, minimum overall GPA of 3.3. *Application deadline:* For fall admission, 1/9 for domestic students. Application fee: $30. *Expenses:* Tuition: Full-time $15,290; part-time $695 per credit. Required fees: $990; $370 per term. Tuition and fees vary according to degree level. *Unit head:* Dr. Brooke Cannon, Director, 570-348-6211 Ext. 2324.

Marywood University, Academic Affairs, College of Education and Human Development, Department of Psychology and Counseling, Program in Psychology, Scranton, PA 18509-1598. Offers child/clinical school psychology (MA); clinical services (MA); general theoretical psychology (MA). Part-time and evening/weekend programs available. *Students:* 41 full-time (34 women), 15 part-time (11 women); includes 5 minority (2 African Americans, 3 Asian Americans or Pacific Islanders). Average age 28. 62 applicants, 66% accepted. In 2007, 24 degrees awarded. *Degree requirements:* For master's, comprehensive exam, thesis or alternative, internship/practicum. *Entrance requirements:* For master's, GRE or MAT. Additional exam requirements/recommendations for international students: Required—TOEFL (minimum score 550 paper-based; 213 computer-based). *Application deadline:* For fall admission, 4/15 priority date for domestic and international students; for spring admission, 11/15 priority date for domestic and international students. Applications are processed on a rolling basis. Application fee: $30. Electronic applications accepted. *Expenses:* Tuition: Full-time $15,290; part-time $695 per credit. Required fees: $990; $370 per term. Tuition and fees vary according to degree level. *Financial support:* Research assistantships with tuition reimbursements, career-related internships or fieldwork, scholarships/grants, tuition waivers (partial), and unspecified assistantships available. Support available to part-time students. Financial award application deadline: 2/15; financial award applicants required to submit FAFSA. *Faculty research:* Personality disorders, counselor training, preschool development, self-esteem measurement, family dynamics. *Unit head:* Dr. Edward J. O'Brien, Chairperson, 570-348-6211 Ext. 2459, E-mail: obrien@es.marywood.edu. *Application contact:* Tammy Manka, Assistant Director of Graduate Admissions, 570-340-6002, E-mail: tmanka@marywood.edu.

Massachusetts School of Professional Psychology, Graduate Programs, Boston, MA 02132. Offers clinical psychology (Psy D); clinical psychopharmacology (Post-Doctoral MS); counseling psychology (MA); executive coaching (Graduate Certificate); forensic psychology (MA); organizational psychology (MA); respecialization in clinical psychology (Certificate); MA/CAGS. *Accreditation:* APA. *Faculty:* 24 full-time (11 women), 13 part-time/adjunct (9 women). *Students:* 223 full-time (177 women), 81 part-time (68 women); includes 22 minority (3 African Americans, 8 Asian Americans or Pacific Islanders, 11 Hispanic Americans), 9 international. Average age 28. 415 applicants, 42% accepted, 77 enrolled. In 2007, 14 master's, 37 doctorates awarded. *Degree requirements:* For master's, comprehensive exam; for doctorate, thesis/dissertation. *Entrance requirements:* For doctorate, GRE General Test. Additional exam requirements/recommendations for international students: Required—TOEFL (minimum score 550 paper-based; 213 computer-based). *Application deadline:* For fall admission, 1/3 for domestic and international students. Application fee: $50. Electronic applications accepted. *Expenses:* Tuition: Full-time $25,952; part-time $811 per credit. Required fees: $200. *Financial support:* In 2007–08, 20 teaching assistantships (averaging $3,300 per year) were awarded; career-related internships or fieldwork also available. Financial award applicants required to submit FAFSA. *Unit head:* Dr. Nicholas A. Covino, President, 617-327-6777, Fax: 617-327-4447. *Application contact:* 617-327-6777 Ext. 210, Fax: 617-327-4447, E-mail: admissions@mspp.edu.

See Close-Up on page 1447.

McGill University, Faculty of Graduate and Postdoctoral Studies, Faculty of Science, Department of Psychology, Montréal, QC H3A 2T5, Canada. Offers clinical psychology (PhD); experimental psychology (M Sc, MA, PhD). *Accreditation:* APA (one or more programs are accredited). *Faculty:* 45 full-time (17 women), 67 part-time/adjunct (38 women). *Students:* 100 full-time (72 women), 2 part-time (both women). 256 applicants, 11% accepted, 26 enrolled. In 2007, 3 master's, 12 doctorates awarded.

Miami University, Graduate School, College of Arts and Sciences, Department of Psychology, Oxford, OH 45056. Offers clinical psychology (PhD); experimental psychology (PhD); social psychology (PhD). *Accreditation:* APA. *Degree requirements:* For doctorate, comprehensive exam, thesis/dissertation, final exams. *Entrance requirements:* For doctorate, GRE General Test, GRE Subject Test, minimum GPA of 2.75 (undergraduate), 3.0 (graduate). Additional exam requirements/recommendations for international students: Required—TOEFL (minimum score 550 paper-based; 213 computer-based), TWE (minimum score 4). Electronic applications accepted.

Michigan School of Professional Psychology, Programs in Humanistic and Clinical Psychology, Farmington Hills, MI 48334. Offers humanistic and clinical psychology (MA, Psy D). *Faculty:* 3 full-time (1 woman), 20 part-time/adjunct (11 women). *Students:* 109 full-time (86 women); includes 20 minority (13 African Americans, 7 Asian Americans or Pacific Islanders). Average age 38. 200 applicants, 40% accepted, 69 enrolled. In 2007, 39 master's, 11 doctorates awarded. *Median time to degree:* Of those who began their doctoral program in fall 1999, 100% received their degree in 8 years or less. *Degree requirements:* For master's, thesis, practicum; for doctorate, thesis/dissertation, internship, practicum. *Entrance requirements:* For master's, 1 year of work experience, interview, minimum GPA of 3.0, curriculum vitae, personal essay, Bachelor's completion; for doctorate, 3 years of work experience, 2 interviews, minimum graduate GPA of 3.0, scholarly writing sample, curriculum vitae, personal essay, MA degree completion. Additional exam requirements/recommendations for international students: Required—TOEFL. *Application deadline:* For fall admission, 1/15 priority date for domestic students. Applications are processed on a rolling basis. Application fee: $75. Electronic applications accepted. *Expenses:* Tuition: Full-time $21,255. One-time fee: $200 full-time. *Financial support:* In 2007–08, 39 students received support. Application deadline: 6/30; *Faculty research:* Qualitative research, existential-phenomenological psychology, applications to clinical practice. *Unit head:* Dr. Kerry Moustakas, President, 248-476-1122, Fax: 248-476-1125, E-mail: kmoustakas@mispp.edu. *Application contact:* Linda Potter-Gallant, Admissions Advisor, 248-476-1122 Ext. 117, Fax: 248-476-1125, E-mail: lpgallant@mispp.edu.

Midwestern University, Downers Grove Campus, College of Health Sciences, Illinois Campus, Program in Clinical Psychology, Downers Grove, IL 60515-1235. Offers MA, Psy D. *Faculty:* 1 part-time/adjunct (0 women). *Students:* 79 full-time (68 women), 1 (woman) part-time; includes 13 minority (8 African Americans, 3 Asian Americans or Pacific Islanders, 2 Hispanic Americans), 2 international. Average age 27. 78 applicants, 62% accepted, 24 enrolled. In 2007, 16 degrees awarded. *Degree requirements:* For doctorate, thesis/dissertation, qualifying examination. *Entrance requirements:* For master's and doctorate, GRE, minimum overall GPA of 2.75, 3 letters of recommendation. Additional exam requirements/recommendations for international students: Required—TOEFL. *Application deadline:* Applications are processed on a rolling basis. Application fee: $50. *Unit head:* Dr. Frank J. Prerost, Director, 630-515-7405, Fax: 630-971-6402, E-mail: fprero@midwestern.edu. *Application contact:* Michael Laken, Director of Admissions, 630-515-6171, Fax: 630-971-6086, E-mail: admissil@midwestern.edu.

Announcement: Midwestern University is committed to educating the health-care team of the new century. The University administers the Chicago College of Osteopathic Medicine, the Chicago College of Pharmacy, the College of Health Sciences, the Arizona College of Osteopathic Medicine, and the College of Pharmacy-Glendale. The University operates campuses in Downers Grove, Illinois, and in Glendale, Arizona. The Clinical Psychology Program offers an MA/Doctor of Psychology (PsyD) degree on the Downers Grove campus. The four-year curriculum incorporates didactic courses, practical experiences, internships, and a clinical dissertation. The Master of Arts degree is awarded after the successful completion of the first two years of the program, and the Doctor of Psychology degree is awarded after two additional years of study. Contact the Office of Admissions, Midwestern University (Downers Grove campus); 800-458-6253; e-mail: admissil@midwestern.edu; Web site: http://www.midwestern.edu.

Midwestern University, Glendale Campus, College of Health Sciences, Arizona Campus, Program in Clinical Psychology, Glendale, AZ 85308. Offers Psy D. *Students:* 5 full-time (3 women); includes 1 minority (African American) Average age 25. 15 applicants, 47% accepted, 5 enrolled. *Unit head:* Dr. Philinda Hutchings, Program Director and Professor, 623-572-3861, Fax: 623-572-3449.

Millersville University of Pennsylvania, Graduate School, School of Education, Department of Psychology, Program in Psychology, Millersville, PA 17551-0302. Offers clinical psychology (MS); school psychology (MS). Part-time and evening/weekend programs available. *Faculty:* 20 full-time (14 women), 13 part-time/adjunct (9 women). *Students:* 47 full-time (37 women), 44 part-time (34 women); includes 6 minority (5 African Americans, 1 Hispanic American), 1 international. Average age 28. 53 applicants, 75% accepted, 30 enrolled. In 2007, 33 degrees awarded. *Degree requirements:* For master's, thesis optional, departmental exam. *Entrance requirements:* For master's, GRE General Test, minimum undergraduate GPA of 2.75, 18 undergraduate hours of course work in psychology, group interview, letters of recommendation, writing sample. Additional exam requirements/recommendations for international students: Required—TOEFL (minimum score 500 paper-based; 183 computer-based). *Application deadline:* For fall admission, 2/29 for domestic students; for winter admission, 10/1 for domestic students; for spring admission, 10/1 for domestic students. Application fee: $40. Electronic applications accepted. *Expenses:* Tuition, state resident: full-time $6,214; part-time $345 per credit. Tuition, nonresident: full-time $9,944; part-time $552 per credit. Required fees: $1,442. Tuition and fees vary according to course load. *Financial support:* In 2007–08, 33 students received support, including 33 research assistantships with full and partial tuition reimbursements available (averaging $5,200 per year); institutionally sponsored loans and unspecified assistantships also available. Support available to part-time students. Financial award application deadline: 3/15; financial award applicants required to submit FAFSA. *Faculty research:* Childhood disorders, family stress, anxiety and worry treatments, solution focused counseling, creativity and personality correlates. *Application contact:* Dr. Victor S. DeSantis, Dean of Graduate Studies, 717-872-3099, Fax: 717-871-2022, E-mail: victor.desantis@millersville.edu.

Minnesota State University Mankato, College of Graduate Studies, College of Social and Behavioral Sciences, Department of Psychology, Mankato, MN 56001. Offers clinical psychology (MA); industrial/organizational psychology (MA); psychology (MT). Part-time programs available. *Students:* 43 full-time (26 women), 5 part-time (3 women). Average age 26. In 2007, 11 degrees awarded. *Degree requirements:* For master's, one foreign language, comprehensive exam, thesis (for some programs). *Entrance requirements:* For master's, GRE General Test, GRE Subject Test (clinical psychology), minimum GPA of 3.0 during previous 2 years, 3 letters of reference. Additional exam requirements/recommendations for international students: Required—TOEFL. *Application deadline:* For fall admission, 3/1 for domestic students; for spring admission, 11/27 for domestic students. Applications are processed on a rolling basis. Application fee: $40. Electronic applications accepted. *Financial support:* Research assistantships, teaching assistantships with full tuition reimbursements, career-related internships or fieldwork, Federal Work-Study, institutionally sponsored loans, and unspecified assistantships available. Support available to part-time students. Financial award application deadline: 3/15; financial award applicants required to submit FAFSA. *Faculty research:* Professional competency in hospitals, mood disturbance, 360-degree feedback, employee selection, planning fallacy. *Unit head:* Dr. Rosemary Krawczyk, Chairperson, 507-389-2724. *Application contact:* 507-389-2321, E-mail: grad@mnsu.edu.

Mississippi State University, College of Arts and Sciences, Department of Psychology, Mississippi State, MS 39762. Offers clinical psychology (MS); cognitive science (PhD); experimental psychology (MS). *Faculty:* 16 full-time (7 women), 2 part-time/adjunct (1 woman). *Students:* 31 full-time (21 women), 14 part-time (7 women); includes 2 minority (1 African American, 1 American Indian/Alaska Native), 2 international. Average age 26. 32 applicants, 47% accepted, 8 enrolled. In 2007, 8 master's awarded. Terminal master's awarded for partial completion of doctoral program. *Degree requirements:* For master's, comprehensive exam, thesis; for doctorate, thesis/dissertation, qualifying exam, comprehensive written and oral exam. *Entrance requirements:* For master's, GRE General Test, minimum GPA of 2.75; for doctorate, GRE General Test, proficiency in at least 1 computer language. Additional exam requirements/recommendations for international students: Required—TOEFL. *Application deadline:* For fall admission, 7/1 priority date for domestic students; for spring admission, 11/1 for domestic students. Applications are processed on a rolling basis. Application fee: $30. *Expenses:* Tuition, state resident: full-time $4,978; part-time $274 per hour. Tuition, nonresident: full-time $11,469; part-time $635 per hour. *Financial support:* In 2007–08, 13 teaching assistantships with full tuition reimbursements (averaging $8,877 per year) were awarded; research assistantships with full tuition reimbursements, career-related internships or fieldwork, Federal Work-Study, institutionally sponsored loans, scholarships/grants, and unspecified assistantships also available. Financial award applicants required to submit FAFSA. *Faculty research:* Personality type, alcoholism, blindness and low vision, mental retardation, language comprehension. Total annual research expenditures: $4.5 million. *Unit head:* Dr. Stephen B. Klein, Head, 662-325-3202, Fax: 662-325-7212, E-mail: sbkl@ra.msstate.edu. *Application contact:* Dr. William A. Person, Interim Associate Vice President for Academic Affairs/Interim Dean of Graduate Studies, 662-325-7400, Fax: 662-325-1967, E-mail: grad@grad.msstate.edu.

Montclair State University, The Office of Graduate Admissions and Support Services, College of Humanities and Social Sciences, Department of Psychology, Montclair, NJ 07043-1624. Offers educational psychology (MA), including child/adolescent clinical psychology, clinical psychology for Spanish/English bilinguals; psychology (MA, Certificate), including industrial and organizational psychology (MA); school psychologist (Certificate). Part-time and evening/weekend programs available. *Faculty:* 27 full-time (11 women), 27 part-time/adjunct (20 women). *Students:* 27 full-time (21 women), 39 part-time (32 women); includes 26 minority (7 African Americans, 4 Asian Americans or Pacific Islanders, 15 Hispanic Americans), 3 international. 86 applicants, 21% accepted, 13 enrolled. In 2007, 22 master's, 11 other advanced degrees awarded. *Degree requirements:* For master's, comprehensive exam, thesis or alternative. *Entrance requirements:* For master's, GRE General Test, GRE Subject Test, previous course work in psychology, interview, 2 letters of recommendation. Additional exam requirements/recommendations for international students: Required—TOEFL (minimum score 83 computer-based). *Application deadline:* For fall admission, 2/1 for domestic and international students; for spring admission, 10/1 for domestic and international students. Applications are processed on a rolling basis. Application fee: $60. Electronic applications accepted. *Financial support:* In 2007–08, 10 research assistantships with full tuition reimbursements (averaging $7,000 per year) were awarded; Federal Work-Study, scholarships/grants, and unspecified assistantships also available. Support available to part-time students. Financial award application deadline: 3/1; financial award applicants required to submit FAFSA. *Faculty research:* Engaged learning, academic and civic development. Total annual research expenditures: $10,000. *Unit head:* Dr. Peter Vietze, Chairperson, 973-655-5201.

Morehead State University, Graduate Programs, College of Science and Technology, Department of Psychology, Morehead, KY 40351. Offers clinical psychology (MA); counseling psychology (MA); experimental/general psychology (MA). Part-time programs available. *Faculty:* 7 full-time (3 women), 3 part-time/adjunct (1 woman). *Students:* 21 full-time (18 women), 4 part-time (1 woman); includes 1 minority (African American) Average age 26. In 2007, 12 degrees awarded. *Degree requirements:* For master's, comprehensive exam, thesis optional. *Entrance requirements:* For master's, GRE General Test, 18 undergraduate hours in psychology, minimum GPA of 3.0. Additional exam requirements/recommendations for international students: Required—TOEFL (minimum score 500 paper-based; 173 computer-based). *Application deadline:* For fall admission, 8/1 priority date for domestic and international students; for spring admission, 12/1 for domestic students, 12/1 priority date for international students. Applications are processed on a rolling basis. Application fee: $0 ($55 for international students). Electronic applications accepted. *Financial support:* In 2007–08, 19 research assistantships (averaging $6,000 per year) were awarded; career-related internships or fieldwork, Federal Work-Study, and institutionally sponsored loans also available. Financial award application deadline: 4/1; financial award applicants required to submit FAFSA. *Faculty research:* Mood induction effects, serotonin receptor activity, stress, perceptual processes. *Application contact:* Michelle Barber, Graduate Admissions Counselor, 606-783-2039, Fax: 606-783-5061, E-mail: m.barber@moreheadstate.edu.

Murray State University, College of Humanities and Fine Arts, Program in Psychology, Murray, KY 42071. Offers clinical psychology (MA, MS); psychology (MA, MS). Part-time programs available. *Degree requirements:* For master's, one foreign language, comprehensive exam (for some programs), thesis. *Entrance requirements:* For master's, GRE General Test. Additional exam requirements/recommendations for international students: Required—TOEFL.

Naropa University, Graduate Programs, Program in Transpersonal Psychology, Boulder, CO 80302-6697. Offers ecopsychology (MA); transpersonal psychology (MA). *Faculty:* 2 full-time (0 women). *Students:* Average age 40. 45 applicants, 71% accepted, 23 enrolled. In 2007, 23 degrees awarded. *Degree requirements:* For master's, thesis. *Entrance requirements:* For master's, interview (by phone or in-person), technology form. Additional exam requirements/recommendations for international students: Required—TOEFL (minimum score 600 paper-based). *Application deadline:* For fall admission, 1/15 for domestic and international students; for spring admission, 10/15 for domestic students. Applications are processed on a rolling basis. Application fee: $60. Electronic applications accepted. *Expenses:* Tuition: Full-time $15,070; part-time $685 per credit. Required fees: $250 per semester. Tuition and fees vary according to course load. *Financial support:* In 2007–08, 2 students received support. Career-related internships or fieldwork, Federal Work-Study, scholarships/grants, health care benefits, and tuition waivers (partial) available. Support available to part-time students. Financial award application deadline: 3/1; financial award applicants required to submit FAFSA. *Unit head:* Dr. John Davis, Director, 303-245-4654, Fax: 303-546-4044, E-mail: jdavis@naropa.edu. *Application contact:* Kate Levene, Assistant Director of Admissions, 303-245-4657, Fax: 303-546-3583, E-mail: klevene@naropa.edu.

See Close-Up on page 1449.

New Mexico Highlands University, Graduate Studies, College of Arts and Sciences, Department of Behavioral Sciences, Las Vegas, NM 87701. Offers psychology (MS), including clinical psychology, general psychology;). Part-time programs available. *Faculty:* 4 full-time (2 women). *Students:* 17 full-time (11 women), 6 part-time (1 woman); includes 10 minority (1 African American, 9 Hispanic Americans), 1 international. Average age 28. 20 applicants, 75% accepted, 11 enrolled. In 2007, 4 degrees awarded. *Degree requirements:* For master's, comprehensive exam, thesis or alternative. *Entrance requirements:* For master's, minimum undergraduate GPA of 3.0. Additional exam requirements/recommendations for international students: Required—TOEFL (minimum score 540 paper-based; 190 computer-based). *Application deadline:* For fall admission, 8/1 priority date for domestic students. Applications are processed on a rolling basis. Application fee: $15. *Expenses:* Tuition, state resident: full-time $2,642; part-time $110 per credit hour. Tuition, nonresident: full-time $3,964; part-time $165 per credit hour. International tuition: $5,285 full-time. One-time fee: $20 full-time. *Financial support:* In 2007–08, 15 students received support, including 12 teaching assistantships with full and partial tuition reimbursements available (averaging $6,500 per year); career-related internships or fieldwork, Federal Work-Study, institutionally sponsored loans, scholarships/grants, tuition waivers (full and partial), and unspecified assistantships also available. Support available to part-time students. Financial award application deadline: 3/1; financial award applicants required to submit FAFSA. *Faculty research:* Sense of community, memory deficits, shame and guilt, neurochemistry of personality, at risk youth. *Unit head:* Dr. Tom Ward, Chair, 505-454-3343, Fax: 505-454-3331, E-mail: tsward@nmhu.edu. *Application contact:* Diane Trujillo, Administrative Assistant Graduate Studies, 505-454-3266, Fax: 505-454-3558, E-mail: dtrujillo@nmhu.edu.

The New School: A University, The New School for Social Research, Department of Psychology, New York, NY 10011. Offers clinical psychology (PhD); general psychology (MA, PhD). *Accreditation:* APA (one or more programs are accredited). Part-time and evening/weekend programs available. *Faculty:* 17 full-time (8 women), 6 part-time/adjunct (1 woman). *Students:* 147 full-time (108 women), 74 part-time (64 women); includes 48 minority (14 African Americans, 3 American Indian/Alaska Native, 12 Asian Americans or Pacific Islanders, 19 Hispanic Americans), 20 international. Average age 29. In 2007, 55 master's, 2 doctorates awarded. Terminal master's awarded for partial completion of doctoral program. *Degree requirements:* For doctorate, one foreign language, thesis/dissertation, qualifying exam. *Entrance requirements:* For master's, GRE General Test; for doctorate, GRE General Test, MA. Additional exam requirements/recommendations for international students: Required—TOEFL (minimum score 600 paper-based; 250 computer-based; 100 iBT). *Application deadline:* For fall admission, 1/15 priority date for domestic students. Applications are processed on a rolling basis. Application fee: $50. *Financial support:* Fellowships, research assistantships, teaching assistantships, career-related internships or fieldwork, Federal Work-Study, scholarships/grants, and tuition waivers (full and partial) available. Financial award application deadline: 3/1; financial award applicants required to submit FAFSA. *Faculty research:* Consciousness, memory, language, perceptions, psychopathology. *Unit head:* Dr. Joan Miller, Chair, 212-229-5727 Ext. 3106. *Application contact:* Robert MacDonald, Director of Admissions, 800-523-5710 Ext. 3007, Fax: 212-989-7102, E-mail: macdonar@newschool.edu.

See Close-Up on page 1653.

Norfolk State University, School of Graduate Studies, School of Liberal Arts, Department of Psychology, Program in Community/Clinical Psychology, Norfolk, VA 23504. Offers MA. *Degree requirements:* For master's, comprehensive exam, thesis or alternative. *Entrance requirements:* For master's, minimum GPA of 2.7.

North Dakota State University, College of Graduate and Interdisciplinary Studies, College of Science and Mathematics, Department of Psychology, Fargo, ND 58105. Offers clinical psychology (MS); cognitive and visual neuroscience (PhD); health and social psychology (PhD); psychology (MS). *Faculty:* 18 full-time (4 women), 2 part-time/adjunct (1 woman). *Students:* 36 full-time (27 women); includes 4 minority (1 African American, 2 Asian Americans or Pacific Islanders, 1 Hispanic American), 1 international. Average age 24. 48 applicants, 33% accepted, 10 enrolled. In 2007, 3 master's, 1 doctorate awarded. *Degree requirements:* For master's, thesis; for doctorate, thesis/dissertation. *Entrance requirements:* For master's and doctorate, GRE General Test, GRE Subject Test. Additional exam requirements/recommendations for international students: Required—TOEFL (minimum score 525 paper-based; 197 computer-based; 71 iBT). *Application deadline:* For fall admission, 3/1 for domestic and international students. Application fee: $45 ($60 for international students). Electronic applications accepted. *Expenses:* Tuition, state resident: full-time $5,376; part-time $224 per credit. Tuition, nonresident: full-time $14,354; part-time $598 per credit. Required fees: $962; $40 per credit. Part-time tuition and fees vary according to course load and reciprocity agreements. *Financial support:* In 2007–08, 36 students received support, including 2 fellowships with full tuition reimbursements available (averaging $16,000 per year), 23 research assistantships with full tuition reimbursements available (averaging $16,000 per year), 11 teaching assistantships with full tuition reimbursements available (averaging $6,000 per year); career-related internships or fieldwork, Federal Work-Study, institutionally sponsored loans, tuition waivers (full and partial), and unspecified assistantships also available. Support available to part-time students. Financial award application deadline: 3/1. *Faculty research:* Cognition science, neuropsychology, group behavior, applied behavior analysis, behavior therapy. Total annual research expenditures: $2 million. *Unit head:* Dr. Paul D. Rokke, Chair, 701-231-8622, Fax: 701-231-8426, E-mail: paul.rokke@ndsu.edu.

Northwestern State University of Louisiana, Graduate Studies and Research, Department of Psychology, Natchitoches, LA 71497. Offers clinical psychology (MS). *Faculty:* 5 full-time (4 women), 1 (woman) part-time/adjunct. *Students:* 14 full-time (10 women), 8 part-time (6 women); includes 10 minority (6 African Americans, 1 American Indian/Alaska Native, 3 Hispanic Americans). Average age 26. In 2007, 7 degrees awarded. *Degree requirements:* For master's, comprehensive exam, thesis or alternative. *Entrance requirements:* For master's, GRE General Test, GRE Subject Test, minimum undergraduate GPA of 2.5. *Application deadline:* For fall admission, 8/1 priority date for domestic students; for spring admission, 1/10 for domestic students. Applications are processed on a rolling basis. Application fee: $20 ($30 for international students). *Financial support:* Application deadline: 7/15. *Unit head:* Dr. Cynthia Lindsey, Head, 318-357-6594, Fax: 318-357-6802, E-mail: lindseyc@nsula.edu. *Application contact:* Dr. Steven G. Horton, Associate Provost/Dean, Graduate Studies, Research, and Information Systems, 318-357-5851, Fax: 318-357-5019, E-mail: grad_school@nsula.edu.

Northwestern University, The Graduate School, Judd A. and Marjorie Weinberg College of Arts and Sciences, Department of Psychology, Evanston, IL 60208. Offers brain, behavior and cognition (PhD); clinical psychology (PhD); cognitive psychology (PhD); personality (PhD); social psychology (PhD); JD/PhD. Admissions and degrees offered through The Graduate School. *Accreditation:* APA (one or more programs are accredited). Part-time programs available. *Degree requirements:* For doctorate, thesis/dissertation. *Entrance requirements:* For doctorate, GRE General Test, GRE Subject Test. Additional exam requirements/recommendations for international students: Required—TOEFL. Electronic applications accepted. *Faculty research:* Memory and higher order cognition, anxiety and depression, effectiveness of psychotherapy, social cognition, molecular basis of memory.

Northwestern University, The Graduate School and Northwestern University Feinberg School of Medicine, Program in Clinical Psychology, Evanston, IL 60208. Offers clinical psychology

Clinical Psychology

Northwestern University (continued)
(PhD), including clinical neuropsychology, general clinical. PhD admissions and degree offered through The Graduate School. *Accreditation:* APA. *Degree requirements:* For doctorate, thesis/dissertation, clinical internship. *Entrance requirements:* For doctorate, GRE General Test, GRE Subject Test, minimum GPA of 3.2, course work in psychology. Additional exam requirements/recommendations for international students: Required—TOEFL. *Faculty research:* Cancer and cardiovascular risk reduction, evaluation of mental health services and policy, neuropsychological assessment, outcome of psychotherapy, cognitive therapy, pediatric and clinical child psychology.

Nova Southeastern University, Center for Psychological Studies, Program in Clinical Psychology, Fort Lauderdale, FL 33314-7796. Offers PhD, Psy D, SPS. *Accreditation:* APA. *Faculty:* 31 full-time (9 women), 12 part-time/adjunct (6 women). *Students:* 503 full-time (414 women); includes 128 minority (32 African Americans, 1 American Indian/Alaska Native, 13 Asian Americans or Pacific Islanders, 82 Hispanic Americans), 8 international. 474 applicants, 30% accepted, 95 enrolled. In 2007, 91 degrees awarded. *Median time to degree:* Of those who began their doctoral program in fall 1999, 95% received their degree in 8 years or less. *Degree requirements:* For doctorate, thesis/dissertation, clinical internship, competency exam; for SPS, comprehensive exam, internship. *Entrance requirements:* For doctorate, GRE General Test, GRE Subject Test (recommended), 18 credits of course work in psychology including 1 hour of experimental psychology and 3 hours of statistics, minimum undergraduate GPA of 3.0; for SPS, GRE General Test. Additional exam requirements/recommendations for international students: Required—TOEFL (minimum score 550 paper-based; 213 computer-based). *Application deadline:* For fall admission, 1/8 for domestic students. Application fee: $50. Electronic applications accepted. *Expenses:* Contact institution. *Financial support:* In 2007–08, 5 research assistantships, 33 teaching assistantships (averaging $1,000 per year) were awarded; career-related internships or fieldwork, Federal Work-Study, scholarships/grants, and unspecified assistantships also available. Financial award application deadline: 4/1. *Faculty research:* Eating disorders, neuropsychology, family violence, sports psychology, child-pediatric psychology. *Unit head:* Karen Grosby, Dean, 954-262-5701, Fax: 954-262-3859, E-mail: grosby@nova.edu. *Application contact:* Carlos Perez, Enrollment Management, 954-262-5790, Fax: 954-262-3893, E-mail: cpsinfo@cps.nova.edu.

See Close-Up on page 1453.

The Ohio State University, Graduate School, College of Social and Behavioral Sciences, School of Social and Behavioral Science, Department of Psychology, Columbus, OH 43210. Offers behavioral neuroscience (PhD); clinical psychology (PhD); cognitive psychology (PhD); developmental psychology (PhD); mental retardation and developmental disabilities (PhD); psychology (MA); quantitative psychology (PhD); social psychology (PhD). *Accreditation:* APA (one or more programs are accredited). *Faculty:* 60. *Students:* 111 full-time (78 women), 6 part-time (4 women); includes 19 minority (6 African Americans, 1 American Indian/Alaska Native, 3 Asian Americans or Pacific Islanders, 9 Hispanic Americans), 16 international. Average age 27. In 2007, 17 master's, 41 doctorates awarded. *Degree requirements:* For doctorate, thesis/dissertation. *Entrance requirements:* For master's and doctorate, GRE General Test. Additional exam requirements/recommendations for international students: Required—TOEFL (minimum score 600 paper-based; 250 computer-based). *Application deadline:* For fall admission, 12/31 for domestic students, 11/30 for international students. Applications are processed on a rolling basis. Application fee: $40 ($50 for international students). Electronic applications accepted. *Financial support:* Fellowships, research assistantships, teaching assistantships available. *Unit head:* Marilynn B. Brewer, Graduate Studies Committee Chair, 614-292-3038, Fax: 614-292-4537. *Application contact:* 614-292-9444, Fax: 614-292-3895, E-mail: domestic.grad@osu.edu.

Ohio University, Graduate College, College of Arts and Sciences, Department of Psychology, Program in Clinical Psychology, Athens, OH 45701-2979. Offers PhD. *Accreditation:* APA. *Faculty:* 11 full-time (6 women). *Students:* 43 full-time (32 women), 9 part-time (5 women); includes 5 minority (1 American Indian/Alaska Native, 1 Asian American or Pacific Islander, 3 Hispanic Americans), 7 international. Average age 28. 176 applicants, 10% accepted, 11 enrolled. In 2007, 11 degrees awarded. *Degree requirements:* For doctorate, one foreign language, comprehensive exam, thesis/dissertation. *Entrance requirements:* For doctorate, GRE General Test, GRE Subject Test, minimum graduate GPA of 3.4. Additional exam requirements/recommendations for international students: Required—TOEFL. *Application deadline:* For fall admission, 1/1 for domestic students. Application fee: $50 ($55 for international students). *Financial support:* In 2007–08, 41 students received support, including 6 fellowships with full tuition reimbursements available (averaging $16,400 per year), 1 research assistantship with full tuition reimbursement available (averaging $13,200 per year), 9 teaching assistantships with full tuition reimbursements available (averaging $13,200 per year); career-related internships or fieldwork, Federal Work-Study, institutionally sponsored loans, traineeships, tuition waivers (full), and unspecified assistantships also available. Financial award application deadline: 1/15. *Faculty research:* Health psychology, child clinical psychology, psychotherapy outcome. Total annual research expenditures: $7.3 million. *Unit head:* Christine Gidycz, Director of Clinical Studies, 740-593-1092, Fax: 740-593-0579, E-mail: gidycz@ohio.edu. *Application contact:* Karyl Jones, Administrative Secretary, 740-593-1090, Fax: 740-593-0579, E-mail: psychology@ohio.edu.

Oklahoma State University, College of Arts and Sciences, Department of Psychology, Stillwater, OK 74078. Offers clinical psychology (PhD); experimental psychology (PhD); general psychology (MS). *Accreditation:* APA (one or more programs are accredited). *Faculty:* 24 full-time (13 women), 1 part-time/adjunct (0 women). *Students:* 36 full-time (20 women), 13 part-time (10 women); includes 13 minority (2 African Americans, 5 American Indian/Alaska Native, 2 Asian Americans or Pacific Islanders, 4 Hispanic Americans), 2 international. Average age 28. 154 applicants, 7% accepted, 10 enrolled. In 2007, 12 master's, 7 doctorates awarded. *Degree requirements:* For doctorate, thesis/dissertation. *Entrance requirements:* For master's and doctorate, GRE General Test or GMAT. Additional exam requirements/recommendations for international students: Required—TOEFL. *Application deadline:* For fall admission, 3/1 priority date for international students; for spring admission, 8/1 priority date for international students. Applications are processed on a rolling basis. Application fee: $40 ($75 for international students). Electronic applications accepted. *Expenses:* Tuition, state resident: full-time $4,993; part-time $148 per credit hour. Tuition, nonresident: full-time $14,755; part-time $555 per credit hour. Tuition and fees vary according to program. *Financial support:* In 2007–08, 12 research assistantships (averaging $13,222 per year), 34 teaching assistantships (averaging $14,372 per year) were awarded; career-related internships or fieldwork, Federal Work-Study, scholarships/grants, health care benefits, tuition waivers (partial), and unspecified assistantships also available. Support available to part-time students. Financial award application deadline: 3/1. *Unit head:* Dr. Maureen A. Sullivan, Head, 405-744-6028.

Old Dominion University, College of Sciences, Virginia Consortium Program in Clinical Psychology, Norfolk, VA 23529. Offers Psy D. *Accreditation:* APA. *Faculty:* 10 full-time (5 women). *Students:* 20 full-time (13 women), 29 part-time (26 women); includes 14 minority (7 African Americans, 5 Asian Americans or Pacific Islanders, 2 Hispanic Americans). Average age 28. 207 applicants, 8% accepted, 10 enrolled. In 2007, 3 degrees awarded. *Median time to degree:* Of those who began their doctoral program in fall 1999, 90% received their degree in 8 years or less. *Degree requirements:* For doctorate, comprehensive exam, thesis/dissertation, internship. *Entrance requirements:* For doctorate, GRE General Test. Additional exam requirements/recommendations for international students: Required—TOEFL. *Application deadline:* For fall admission, 1/2 for domestic and international students. Application fee: $40. *Expenses:* Contact institution. *Financial support:* In 2007–08, 29 students received support, including 26 research assistantships with partial tuition reimbursements available (averaging $7,550 per year), 3 teaching assistantships with partial tuition reimbursements available (averaging $8,000 per year); career-related internships or fieldwork, scholarships/grants, and unspecified assistantships also available. Financial award application deadline: 1/2; financial award applicants required to submit FAFSA. *Faculty research:* Body image, depression, coping with stress, minority and women's issues, family therapy, neuropsychology. *Unit head:* Dr. Robin J. Lewis, Graduate Program Director, 757-683-4210, Fax: 757-368-1823, E-mail: psydgpd@odu.edu. *Application contact:* Eileen O'Neill, Coordinator, 757-368-1820, Fax: 757-368-1823, E-mail: exoneill@odu.edu.

Pace University, Dyson College of Arts and Sciences, Department of Psychology, Program in School-Clinical Child Psychology, New York, NY 10038. Offers Psy D. *Accreditation:* APA. *Students:* 74 full-time (63 women), 29 part-time (26 women); includes 16 minority (4 African Americans, 8 Asian Americans or Pacific Islanders, 4 Hispanic Americans), 5 international. Average age 27. 253 applicants, 27% accepted, 25 enrolled. In 2007, 14 doctorates awarded. Terminal master's awarded for partial completion of doctoral program. *Degree requirements:* For doctorate, comprehensive exam, qualifying exams, externship, internship, project. *Entrance requirements:* For doctorate, GRE General Test, GRE Subject Test, interview. *Application deadline:* For fall admission, 2/1 priority date for domestic students. Applications are processed on a rolling basis. Application fee: $65. Electronic applications accepted. *Expenses:* Tuition: Part-time $856 per credit. Tuition and fees vary according to degree level and program. *Financial support:* Research assistantships, teaching assistantships, career-related internships or fieldwork, Federal Work-Study, and tuition waivers (partial) available. Support available to part-time students. Financial award applicants required to submit FAFSA. *Unit head:* Dr. Barbara Mowder, Director, 212-346-1506. *Application contact:* Joanna Broda, Director of Admissions, 212-346-1652, Fax: 212-346-1585, E-mail: gradnyc@pace.edu.

See Close-Up on page 1461.

Pacifica Graduate Institute, Graduate Programs, Carpinteria, CA 93013. Offers clinical psychology (PhD); counseling psychology (MA); depth psychology (MA, PhD); mythological studies (MA, PhD). Terminal master's awarded for partial completion of doctoral program. *Degree requirements:* For master's, thesis (for some programs), practicum; for doctorate, comprehensive exam, thesis/dissertation, internship. *Entrance requirements:* For master's, resumé, 3 letters of recommendation, writing sample, interview; for doctorate, resumé, 4 letters of recommendation, writing sample, interview. Additional exam requirements/recommendations for international students: Required—TOEFL. *Faculty research:* Imaginal and archetypal theory; post-Colonial psychoanalytic and Jungian theory; myth literature as it applies to the theory and practice of psychology.

Pacific Graduate School of Psychology, PGSP-Stanford Psy D Consortium Program, Palo Alto, CA 94303-4232. Offers Psy D. *Degree requirements:* For doctorate, thesis/dissertation. *Entrance requirements:* For doctorate, GRE, BA or MA in psychology or related area, minimum undergraduate GPA of 3.0, minimum graduate GPA of 3.3. Additional exam requirements/recommendations for international students: Required—TOEFL. Electronic applications accepted. *Faculty research:* Biopsychosocial research, neurobiology, psychopharmacology.

See Close-Up on page 1465.

Pacific Graduate School of Psychology, Program in Clinical Psychology, Palo Alto, CA 94303-4232. Offers PhD, JD/PhD, MBA/PhD. *Accreditation:* APA. *Degree requirements:* For doctorate, comprehensive exam, thesis/dissertation, 2000 hour clinical internship, oral clinical competency exam. *Entrance requirements:* For doctorate, GRE General Test, BA or MA in psychology or related area, minimum undergraduate GPA of 3.0, 3.3 graduate. Additional exam requirements/recommendations for international students: Required—TOEFL. Electronic applications accepted. *Faculty research:* Child/family studies, health psychology, neuropsychology, personality development, assessment.

See Close-Up on page 1463.

Penn State Harrisburg, Graduate School, School of Behavioral Sciences and Education, Middletown, PA 17057-4898. Offers adult education (D Ed); applied behavior analysis (MA); applied clinical psychology (MA); applied psychological research (MA); community psychology and social change (MA); health education (M Ed); teaching and curriculum (M Ed); training and development (M Ed). Part-time and evening/weekend programs available. *Financial support:* Career-related internships or fieldwork available. *Unit head:* Dr. William D. Milheim, Director, 717-948-6205, Fax: 717-948-6209, E-mail: wdm2@psu.edu.

Penn State University Park, Graduate School, College of the Liberal Arts, Department of Psychology, State College, University Park, PA 16802-1503. Offers clinical psychology (MS, PhD); cognitive psychology (MS, PhD); developmental psychology (MS, PhD); industrial/organizational psychology (MS, PhD); psychobiology (MS, PhD); social psychology (MS, PhD). *Accreditation:* APA (one or more programs are accredited). *Expenses:* Tuition, state resident: full-time $14,738; part-time $614 per credit. Tuition, nonresident: full-time $26,050; part-time $1,085 per credit. Tuition and fees vary according to course load, program and student level. *Unit head:* Dr. Melvin M. Mark, Interim Head, 814-865-9515, Fax: 814-863-7002, E-mail: m5m@psu.edu.

Pepperdine University, Graduate School of Education and Psychology, Division of Psychology, Malibu, CA 90263. Offers clinical psychology (MA). *Entrance requirements:* For master's, GRE General Test or MAT, 2 professional recommendations. Additional exam requirements/recommendations for international students: Required—TOEFL (minimum score 550 paper-based; 220 computer-based).

Pepperdine University, Graduate School of Education and Psychology, Division of Psychology, Program in Clinical Psychology, Los Angeles, CA 90045. Offers MA. *Accreditation:* APA. Part-time and evening/weekend programs available. *Students:* 77 full-time (68 women), 67 part-time (55 women); includes 41 minority (12 African Americans, 3 American Indian/Alaska Native, 13 Asian Americans or Pacific Islanders, 13 Hispanic Americans), 1 international. 297 applicants, 88% accepted, 161 enrolled. In 2007, 195 degrees awarded. *Entrance requirements:* For master's, GRE General Test, bachelor's degree in psychology or related field. Additional exam requirements/recommendations for international students: Required—TOEFL. *Application deadline:* For fall admission, 2/1 for domestic students. Applications are processed on a rolling basis. Application fee: $55. *Financial support:* Research assistantships, teaching assistantships available. Financial award application deadline: 7/1; financial award applicants required to submit FAFSA. *Unit head:* Dr. Cary Mitchell, Director, 310-568-8553, E-mail: cary.mitchell@pepperdine.edu. *Application contact:* Lindsy Blanco, Recruitment and Admissions Manager, 310-506-5605.

See Close-Up on page 1467.

Philadelphia College of Osteopathic Medicine, Graduate and Professional Programs, Department of Psychology, Philadelphia, PA 19131-1694. Offers clinical psychology (Psy D); counseling and clinical health psychology (MS); organizational leadership and development (MS); psychology (Certificate); school psychology (MS, Psy D, Ed S). *Accreditation:* APA. *Degree requirements:* For master's, thesis; for doctorate, comprehensive exam, thesis/dissertation, final project, fieldwork. *Entrance requirements:* For master's, GRE or MAT, minimum GPA of 3.0; course work in biology, chemistry, English, physics; for other advanced degree, PRAXIS. *Faculty research:* Depression in primary care, integrated primary care, geriatric mental health.

See Close-Up on page 1469.

Phillips Graduate Institute, Program in Clinical Family Psychology and Organizational Consulting, Encino, CA 91316-1509. Offers clinical psychology (Psy D); organizational consulting (Psy D). Evening/weekend programs available. *Faculty:* 13 full-time, 30 part-time/adjunct. *Students:* 39 full-time (32 women), 30 part-time (22 women); includes 19 minority (4 African Americans, 1 American Indian/Alaska Native, 2 Asian Americans or Pacific Islanders, 12 Hispanic Americans). *Degree requirements:* For doctorate, thesis/dissertation. *Entrance requirements:* For doctorate, minimum GPA of 3.0, interview. *Application deadline:* For fall admission, 6/1 priority date for domestic students; for spring admission, 12/1 priority date for domestic students. Applications are processed on a rolling basis. Application fee: $75. *Expenses:*

Tuition: Part-time $820 per unit. Required fees: $300 per semester. Tuition and fees vary according to course load, degree level and program. *Financial support:* Tuition waivers (full and partial) available. *Application contact:* Kim Bell, Assistant Director of Admission, 818-386-5639, Fax: 818-386-5699, E-mail: admit@pgi.edu.

Ponce School of Medicine, Program in Clinical Psychology, Ponce, PR 00732-7004. Offers Psy D. *Accreditation:* APA. *Faculty:* 17 full-time (13 women), 5 part-time/adjunct (2 women). *Students:* 178 full-time (143 women); all minorities (all Hispanic Americans), 1 international. Average age 28. 92 applicants, 33% accepted, 30 enrolled. In 2007, 21 degrees awarded. *Degree requirements:* For doctorate, one foreign language, comprehensive exam, thesis/dissertation, internship. *Entrance requirements:* For doctorate, GRE General Test or EXADEP, proficiency in Spanish and English, 2 letters of recommendation, minimum undergraduate GPA of 2.7. *Application deadline:* For fall admission, 4/15 for domestic and international students. Application fee: $100. *Financial support:* In 2007–08, 155 students received support; fellowships, scholarships/grants available. Financial award application deadline: 4/30; financial award applicants required to submit FAFSA. *Unit head:* Dr. José Pons, Head, 787-840-2575, E-mail: jpons@psm.edu. *Application contact:* Dr. Maria Colón, Admissions Officer, 787-840-2575 Ext. 2143, E-mail: mcolon@psm.edu.

Pontifical Catholic University of Puerto Rico, Institute of Graduate Studies in Behavioral Science and Community Affairs, Program in Clinical Psychology (Doctorate), Ponce, PR 00717-0777. Offers PhD. Part-time and evening/weekend programs available. *Degree requirements:* For doctorate, comprehensive exam, thesis/dissertation. *Entrance requirements:* For doctorate, EXADEP, minimum GPA of 2.75.

Pontifical Catholic University of Puerto Rico, Institute of Graduate Studies in Behavioral Science and Community Affairs, Program in Clinical Psychology (Master's), Ponce, PR 00717-0777. Offers MA, MS. Part-time and evening/weekend programs available. *Degree requirements:* For master's, thesis. *Entrance requirements:* For master's, EXADEP, 3 letters of recommendation, interview, minimum GPA of 2.75.

Prairie View A&M University, College of Juvenile Justice and Psychology, Prairie View, TX 77446-0519. Offers clinical adolescent psychology (PhD); juvenile forensic psychology (MSJFP); juvenile justice (MSJJ, PhD). Part-time and evening/weekend programs available. *Faculty:* 11 full-time (5 women), 2 part-time/adjunct (1 woman). *Students:* 45 full-time (37 women), 54 part-time (42 women); includes 76 minority (70 African Americans, 2 Asian Americans or Pacific Islanders, 4 Hispanic Americans), 4 international. Average age 30. 55 applicants, 60% accepted, 33 enrolled. In 2007, 5 master's, 5 doctorates awarded. *Degree requirements:* For master's, comprehensive exam (for some programs), thesis (for some programs); for doctorate, comprehensive exam, thesis/dissertation. *Entrance requirements:* For master's, GRE, minimum GPA of 2.75; for doctorate, GRE, previous course work in clinical adolescent psychology, minimum GPA of 3.5. Additional exam requirements/recommendations for international students: Required—TOEFL. *Application deadline:* For fall admission, 3/1 for domestic and international students; for spring admission, 10/1 for domestic and international students. Applications are processed on a rolling basis. Application fee: $50. *Financial support:* In 2007–08, 18 students received support; research assistantships, teaching assistantships, career-related internships or fieldwork, Federal Work-Study, institutionally sponsored loans, tuition waivers (full and partial), and unspecified assistantships available. Support available to part-time students. Financial award application deadline: 3/1; financial award applicants required to submit FAFSA. *Faculty research:* Juvenile justice, juvenile forensic psychology, teen court, graduate education, capital punishment. Total annual research expenditures: $2,888. *Unit head:* Dr. Elaine Rodney, Dean, 936-261-520, Fax: 936-261-5252, E-mail: ehrodney@pvamu.edu. *Application contact:* Sandy Siegmund, Executive Secretary, Graduate Program, 936-857-5234, Fax: 936-857-5249, E-mail: sisiegmund@pvamu.edu.

Queens College of the City University of New York, Division of Graduate Studies, Mathematics and Natural Sciences Division, Department of Psychology, Flushing, NY 11367-1597. Offers clinical behavioral applications in mental health settings (MA); psychology (MA). Part-time programs available. *Faculty:* 27 full-time (13 women). *Students:* 21 full-time (16 women), 61 part-time (46 women). 111 applicants, 73% accepted, 49 enrolled. In 2007, 21 degrees awarded. *Degree requirements:* For master's, comprehensive exam, thesis or alternative. *Entrance requirements:* For master's, GRE, minimum GPA of 3.0. Additional exam requirements/recommendations for international students: Required—TOEFL. *Application deadline:* For fall admission, 4/1 for domestic students; for spring admission, 11/1 for domestic students. Applications are processed on a rolling basis. Application fee: $125. *Financial support:* Career-related internships or fieldwork, Federal Work-Study, institutionally sponsored loans, and tuition waivers (partial) available. Support available to part-time students. Financial award application deadline: 4/1; financial award applicants required to submit FAFSA. *Unit head:* Dr. Richard Bodnar, Chairperson, 718-997-3200. *Application contact:* Dr. Philip Ramsey, Graduate Adviser, 718-997-3200, E-mail: philip_ramsey@qc.edu.

Queen's University at Kingston, School of Graduate Studies and Research, Faculty of Arts and Sciences, Department of Psychology, Kingston, ON K7L 3N6, Canada. Offers brain behavior and cognitive science (MA, PhD); clinical psychology (MA, PhD); developmental psychology (MA, PhD); social personality psychology (MA, PhD). *Accreditation:* APA (one or more programs are accredited). *Degree requirements:* For master's, thesis; for doctorate, comprehensive exam, thesis/dissertation. *Entrance requirements:* For master's and doctorate, GRE General Test. Additional exam requirements/recommendations for international students: Required—TOEFL. *Faculty research:* Human development, social, personality, behavioral neuroscience, forensic.

Radford University, Graduate College, College of Humanities and Behavioral Sciences, Department of Psychology, Radford, VA 24142. Offers clinical psychology (MA, MS); counseling psychology (Psy D); experimental psychology (MA); industrial-organizational psychology (MA, MS); school psychology (Ed S). Part-time programs available. *Faculty:* 24 full-time (10 women). *Students:* 38 full-time (31 women), 52 part-time (39 women); includes 5 minority (4 African Americans, 1 Asian American or Pacific Islander), 2 international. Average age 25. 128 applicants, 64% accepted, 38 enrolled. In 2007, 45 degrees awarded. *Degree requirements:* For master's, comprehensive exam, thesis (for some programs); for doctorate, comprehensive exam, thesis/dissertation; for Ed S, comprehensive exam. *Entrance requirements:* For master's, GRE, minimum GPA 3.0; for doctorate, GRE; for Ed S, GMAT, GRE General Test, MAT, NTE. Additional exam requirements/recommendations for international students: Required—TOEFL. *Application deadline:* For fall admission, 3/1 priority date for domestic students, 12/1 for international students; for spring admission, 10/1 for domestic students, 7/1 for international students. Applications are processed on a rolling basis. Application fee: $40. Electronic applications accepted. *Financial support:* In 2007–08, 42 research assistantships with partial tuition reimbursements (averaging $8,000 per year), 12 teaching assistantships with partial tuition reimbursements (averaging $8,700 per year) were awarded; career-related internships or fieldwork, Federal Work-Study, institutionally sponsored loans, scholarships/grants, and unspecified assistantships also available. Financial award application deadline: 3/1; financial award applicants required to submit FAFSA. *Unit head:* Dr. Hilary M. Lips, Chair, 540-831-5387, Fax: 540-831-6113, E-mail: hlips@radford.edu.

Regent University, Graduate School, School of Psychology and Counseling, Virginia Beach, VA 23464-9800. Offers clinical psychology (Psy D); counseling (MA), including clinical psychology, community counseling, human services counseling, school guidance; counseling studies (CAGS); counselor education and supervision (PhD); M Div/MA; M Ed/MA; MBA/MA. PhD program offered online only. *Accreditation:* ACA; APA (one or more programs are accredited). Part-time programs available. Postbaccalaureate distance learning degree programs offered. *Faculty:* 25 full-time (14 women), 17 part-time/adjunct (7 women). *Students:* 223 full-time (176 women), 187 part-time (141 women); includes 110 minority (89 African Americans, 2 American Indian/Alaska Native, 9 Asian Americans or Pacific Islanders, 10 Hispanic Americans), 11 international. Average age 31. 293 applicants, 58% accepted, 99 enrolled. In 2007, 79 master's, 23 doctorates awarded. *Degree requirements:* For master's, thesis or alternative, internship, practicum, written competency exam; for doctorate, thesis/dissertation or alternative. *Entrance requirements:* For master's, GRE General Test including writing exam, minimum undergraduate GPA of 2.75, 3 recommendations, resumé, transcripts, writing sample; for doctorate, GRE General Test including writing exam, GRE Subject Test, minimum undergraduate GPA of 3.0, 3.5 (PhD), 10-15 minute VHS tape demonstrating counseling skills, writing sample, 3 recommendations, resumé, transcripts. Additional exam requirements/recommendations for international students: Required—TOEFL (minimum score 577 paper-based; 233 computer-based). *Application deadline:* For fall admission, 4/1 priority date for domestic students; for spring admission, 11/1 priority date for domestic students. Applications are processed on a rolling basis. Application fee: $50. Electronic applications accepted. *Expenses: Contact institution. Financial support:* In 2007–08, 362 students received support, including 15 research assistantships with full and partial tuition reimbursements available (averaging $4,439 per year), 6 teaching assistantships with full and partial tuition reimbursements available (averaging $12,699 per year); career-related internships or fieldwork, scholarships/grants, and tuition waivers (full and partial) also available. Support available to part-time students. Financial award application deadline: 9/1. *Faculty research:* Marriage enrichment, AIDS counseling, troubled youth. Total annual research expenditures: $12,000. *Unit head:* Dr. Rosemarie Hughes, Dean, 757-226-4269, Fax: 757-226-4282, E-mail: rosehug@regent.edu. *Application contact:* Althea Bishard, Registrar and Executive Director of Enrollment and Academic Services, 800-373-5504, Fax: 757-226-4381, E-mail: admissions@regent.edu.

Roosevelt University, Graduate Division, College of Arts and Sciences, Department of Psychology, Program in Clinical Professional Psychology, Chicago, IL 60605-1394. Offers MA, Psy D. *Accreditation:* APA. *Students:* 85 full-time (75 women), 102 part-time (92 women); includes 27 minority (4 African Americans, 11 Asian Americans or Pacific Islanders, 12 Hispanic Americans), 2 international. Average age 30. 117 applicants, 46% accepted, 35 enrolled. In 2007, 43 master's, 4 doctorates awarded. *Unit head:* Judith Dygdon, Director, 312-341-6362. *Application contact:* Joanne Canyon-Heller, Coordinator of Graduate Admission, 877-APPLY RU, Fax: 312-281-3356, E-mail: applyru@roosevelt.edu.

Rosalind Franklin University of Medicine and Science, School of Graduate and Postdoctoral Studies, Department of Clinical Psychology, North Chicago, IL 60064-3095. Offers MS, PhD. *Accreditation:* APA. Terminal master's awarded for partial completion of doctoral program. *Degree requirements:* For master's, thesis; for doctorate, comprehensive exam, thesis/dissertation, 1 year full-time clinical internship. *Entrance requirements:* For master's, GRE General Test; for doctorate, GRE General Test, GRE Subject Test. Additional exam requirements/recommendations for international students: Required—TOEFL, TWE. Expenses: Contact institution. *Faculty research:* Hormonal influences on human sexually dimorphic behavior, nutrition and mood, aging, anxiety disorders.

Rutgers, The State University of New Jersey, New Brunswick, Graduate School of Applied and Professional Psychology, Department of Clinical Psychology, New Brunswick, NJ 08901-1281. Offers Psy M, Psy D. *Accreditation:* APA (one or more programs are accredited). *Degree requirements:* For doctorate, comprehensive exam, thesis/dissertation, 1 year internship. *Entrance requirements:* For doctorate, GRE General Test, GRE Subject Test, bachelor's degree in psychology or equivalent. Additional exam requirements/recommendations for international students: Required—TOEFL. Electronic applications accepted. Expenses: Contact institution. *Faculty research:* Long- and short-term dynamic therapy, community psychology, cognitive-behavioral therapy: anxiety and depressive disorders, addictive behaviors: eating disorders and alcoholism.

Rutgers, The State University of New Jersey, New Brunswick, Graduate School, Program in Psychology, New Brunswick, NJ 08901-1281. Offers behavioral neuroscience (PhD); clinical psychology (PhD); cognitive psychology (PhD); interdisciplinary health psychology (PhD); social psychology (PhD). *Accreditation:* APA. *Degree requirements:* For doctorate, thesis/dissertation. *Entrance requirements:* For doctorate, GRE General Test, 3 letters of recommendation. Additional exam requirements/recommendations for international students: Required—TOEFL (minimum score 577 paper-based; 233 computer-based). Electronic applications accepted. *Faculty research:* Learning and memory, behavioral ecology, hormones and behavior, psychopharmacology, anxiety disorders.

St. John's University, St. John's College of Liberal Arts and Sciences, Department of Psychology, Program in Clinical Psychology, Queens, NY 11439. Offers clinical psychology-child (PhD); clinical psychology-general (PhD). *Accreditation:* APA. *Students:* 39 full-time (31 women), 25 part-time (19 women); includes 18 minority (5 African Americans, 8 Asian Americans or Pacific Islanders, 5 Hispanic Americans), 3 international. Average age 28. 27 applicants, 100% accepted, 10 enrolled. In 2007, 15 degrees awarded. *Median time to degree:* Of those who began their doctoral program in fall 1999, 93% received their degree in 8 years or less. *Degree requirements:* For doctorate, comprehensive exam, thesis/dissertation, internship, externship. *Entrance requirements:* For doctorate, GRE General Test, GRE Subject Test, 24 credits of undergraduate course work in psychology, 2 writing samples. Additional exam requirements/recommendations for international students: Required—TOEFL (minimum score 500 paper-based; 173 computer-based; 61 iBT), IELTS (minimum score 6). *Application deadline:* For fall admission, 2/1 for domestic students, 5/1 priority date for international students; for spring admission, 11/1 priority date for international students. Applications are processed on a rolling basis. Application fee: $40. Electronic applications accepted. *Expenses: Contact institution. Financial support:* Fellowships, research assistantships, career-related internships or fieldwork and scholarships/grants available. Support available to part-time students. Financial award application deadline: 3/1; financial award applicants required to submit FAFSA. *Faculty research:* Cognitive-behavioral therapy, sucking cessation pedagogical research and implicit attitudes. *Unit head:* Dr. Jeffrey S. Nevid, Director, 718-990-1548, E-mail: nevidj@stjohns.edu. *Application contact:* Beth Evans, Associate Vice President and Executive Director, Enrollment Management, 718-990-6999, Fax: 718-990-5686, E-mail: gradhelp@stjohns.edu.

Saint Louis University, Graduate School, College of Arts and Sciences and Graduate School, Department of Psychology, St. Louis, MO 63103-2097. Offers clinical psychology (MS-R, PhD); experimental psychology (MS-R, PhD); industrial-organizational psychology (PhD); psychology (PhD). *Accreditation:* APA (one or more programs are accredited). Part-time programs available. *Faculty:* 18 full-time (7 women). *Students:* 77 full-time (53 women), 8 part-time (5 women); includes 14 minority (12 African Americans, 1 American Indian/Alaska Native, 1 Asian American or Pacific Islander). Average age 27. 234 applicants, 11% accepted, 20 enrolled. In 2007, 11 master's, 10 doctorates awarded. *Median time to degree:* Of those who began their doctoral program in fall 1999, 90% received their degree in 8 years or less. *Degree requirements:* For master's, comprehensive exam, thesis; for doctorate, thesis/dissertation, clinical internship (for clinical psychology PhD). *Entrance requirements:* For master's and doctorate, GRE General Test, interview, letters of recommendation, resumé, transcripts, goal statement. Additional exam requirements/recommendations for international students: Required—TOEFL (minimum score 550 paper-based; 213 computer-based). *Application deadline:* For fall admission, 1/1 for domestic and international students. Application fee: $40. Electronic applications accepted. *Expenses:* Tuition: Part-time $845 per credit hour. Required fees: $105 per semester. *Financial support:* In 2007–08, 71 students received support, including 16 research assistantships with full tuition reimbursements available (averaging $14,000 per year), 14 teaching assistantships with full tuition reimbursements available (averaging $12,000 per year); career-related internships or fieldwork, Federal Work-Study, scholarships/grants, traineeships, health care benefits, tuition waivers, and unspecified assistantships also available. Support available to part-time students. Financial award application deadline: 2/1; financial award applicants required to submit FAFSA. *Faculty research:* Violence and trauma; neural basis of learning and memory function; eating disorders; body image and health behavior; prejudice, stereotyping, and victimization; memory, cognitive aging and language processing. Total annual research expenditures: $514,559. *Unit head:* Dr. Donna J. LaVoie, Chairperson, 314-977-3676, Fax: 314-977-3679, E-mail: lavoiedj@slu.edu. *Application contact:* Gary U.

Clinical Psychology

Saint Louis University (continued)

Behrman, Associate Dean of Graduate School Admissions, 314-977-3827, Fax: 314-977-3943, E-mail: behrmang@slu.edu.

Saint Mary's University, Faculty of Science, Department of Psychology, Halifax, NS B3H 3C3, Canada. Offers applied psychology (M Sc), including clinical psychology, industrial/organizational psychology. M Sc (clinical psychology) offered jointly with Dalhousie University. Part-time programs available. *Degree requirements:* For master's, thesis, internship. *Entrance requirements:* For master's, GRE General Test, honors degree, minimum QPA of 3.25. *Faculty research:* Assessment, health psychology, social psychology, cognition.

St. Mary's University, Graduate School, Department of Psychology, Program in Clinical Psychology, San Antonio, TX 78228-8507. Offers MA, MS. *Students:* 16 full-time (12 women), 8 part-time (6 women); includes 9 minority (1 African American, 8 Hispanic Americans). Average age 27. In 2007, 8 degrees awarded. *Degree requirements:* For master's, comprehensive exam, thesis optional, practica. *Entrance requirements:* For master's, GRE General Test. Additional exam requirements/recommendations for international students: Required—TOEFL (minimum score 550 paper-based; 213 computer-based). Application fee: $0. *Financial support:* Career-related internships or fieldwork, Federal Work-Study, institutionally sponsored loans, scholarships/grants, health care benefits, and unspecified assistantships available. Financial award application deadline: 3/31; financial award applicants required to submit FAFSA. *Unit head:* Dr. Patricia Owen, Interim Director, 210-436-3314, Fax: 210-431-4301, E-mail: powen@stmarytx.edu.

Saint Michael's College, Graduate Programs, Program in Clinical Psychology, Colchester, VT 05439. Offers MA. Part-time and evening/weekend programs available. *Faculty:* 5 full-time (1 woman), 12 part-time/adjunct (6 women). *Students:* 24 full-time (16 women), 23 part-time (15 women); includes 1 minority (American Indian/Alaska Native), 1 international. Average age 32. 31 applicants, 74% accepted, 16 enrolled. In 2007, 8 degrees awarded. *Degree requirements:* For master's, thesis or alternative, internship, practicum, research seminar. *Entrance requirements:* For master's, GRE General Test, GRE Subject Test, undergraduate major in psychology or related area, minimum 12 credits in psychology, minimum GPA of 3.0. *Application deadline:* For fall admission, 6/1 priority date for domestic students. Applications are processed on a rolling basis. Application fee: $35. Electronic applications accepted. *Expenses:* Tuition: Full-time $13,650. *Financial support:* Teaching assistantships with partial tuition reimbursements, career-related internships or fieldwork, Federal Work-Study, scholarships/grants, tuition waivers (partial), and unspecified assistantships available. Financial award application deadline: 5/1; financial award applicants required to submit FAFSA. *Faculty research:* Psychodynamic psychotherapy, family therapy, philosophical foundations of clinical psychology. *Unit head:* Dr. Ronald B. Miller, Director, 802-654-2206, Fax: 802-654-2664, E-mail: rmiller@smcvt.edu.

Sam Houston State University, College of Humanities and Social Sciences, Department of Psychology and Philosophy, Huntsville, TX 77341. Offers clinical psychology (MA, PhD); psychology (MA); school psychology (MA). *Accreditation:* APA. Part-time programs available. *Faculty:* 22 full-time (6 women). *Students:* 59 full-time (47 women), 36 part-time (35 women); includes 15 minority (4 African Americans, 2 American Indian/Alaska Native, 3 Asian Americans or Pacific Islanders, 6 Hispanic Americans), 2 international. Average age 27. In 2007, 25 master's, 6 doctorates awarded. *Degree requirements:* For master's, thesis. *Entrance requirements:* For master's, GRE General Test or MAT, minimum GPA of 3.0. *Application deadline:* For fall admission, 8/1 for domestic students; for spring admission, 12/1 for domestic students. Applications are processed on a rolling basis. Application fee: $20. *Expenses:* Tuition, state resident: full-time $5,026; part-time $184 per semester hour. Tuition, nonresident: full-time $10,586; part-time $462 per semester hour. Required fees: $494 per semester. *Financial support:* Research assistantships, teaching assistantships, career-related internships or fieldwork and institutionally sponsored loans available. Support available to part-time students. Financial award application deadline: 5/31; financial award applicants required to submit FAFSA. *Unit head:* Dr. Donna M. Desforges, Chair, 936-294-1178, Fax: 936-294-3798. *Application contact:* Dr. Rowland Miller, Graduate Coordinator, 936-294-1176, Fax: 936-294-3798, E-mail: psy_rsm@shsu.edu.

San Diego State University, Graduate and Research Affairs, College of Sciences, Department of Psychology, San Diego, CA 92182. Offers clinical psychology (MS, PhD); industrial and organizational psychology (MS); program evaluation (MS); psychology (MA). *Accreditation:* APA (one or more programs are accredited). *Students:* 141 full-time (108 women), 32 part-time (24 women); includes 41 minority (4 African Americans, 1 American Indian/Alaska Native, 14 Asian Americans or Pacific Islanders, 22 Hispanic Americans), 8 international. Average age 25. 445 applicants, 20% accepted, 63 enrolled. In 2007, 52 master's, 14 doctorates awarded. Terminal master's awarded for partial completion of doctoral program. *Degree requirements:* For master's, thesis, oral exam; for doctorate, thesis/dissertation. *Entrance requirements:* For master's, GRE General Test, GRE Subject Test, 3 letters of recommendation; for doctorate, GRE General Test, GRE Subject Test, minimum GPA of 3.0, 3 letters of recommendation. Additional exam requirements/recommendations for international students: Required—TOEFL. *Application deadline:* For fall admission, 2/1 for domestic students, 2/1 priority date for international students. Application fee: $55. Electronic applications accepted. *Financial support:* Fellowships, research assistantships, teaching assistantships, career-related internships or fieldwork, scholarships/grants, and unspecified assistantships available. Financial award applicants required to submit FAFSA. Total annual research expenditures: $8 million. *Unit head:* Dr. Claire Murphy, Chair, 619-594-4559, Fax: 619-594-1332, E-mail: cmurphy@sunstroke.sdsu.edu. *Application contact:* Judy Price, Graduate Advisor, 619-594-5401, Fax: 619-594-1332, E-mail: judyprice@sunstroke.sdsu.edu.

San Jose State University, Graduate Studies and Research, College of Social Sciences, Department of Psychology, San Jose, CA 95192-0001. Offers clinical psychology (MS); experimental psychology (MA); industrial/organizational psychology (MS); psychology (MA). *Students:* 53 full-time (41 women), 16 part-time (11 women); includes 18 minority (11 Asian Americans or Pacific Islanders, 7 Hispanic Americans), 7 international. Average age 27. 124 applicants, 34% accepted, 38 enrolled. In 2007, 27 degrees awarded. *Degree requirements:* For master's, comprehensive exam, thesis (for some programs). *Entrance requirements:* For master's, GRE General Test, minimum GPA of 3.0. *Application deadline:* For fall admission, 6/29 for domestic students; for spring admission, 11/30 for domestic students. Applications are processed on a rolling basis. Application fee: $59. Electronic applications accepted. *Financial support:* In 2007–08, 15 teaching assistantships were awarded; career-related internships or fieldwork and institutionally sponsored loans also available. Financial award application deadline: 3/1; financial award applicants required to submit FAFSA. *Faculty research:* Drug and alcohol abuse, neurohormonal mechanisms in motion sickness, behavior modification, sleep research, genetics. *Unit head:* Dr. Sheila Bienenfeld, Chair, 408-924-5600, Fax: 408-924-5605, E-mail: sheila.bienenfeld@sjsu.edu.

Saybrook Graduate School and Research Center, Programs in Psychology, Human Science and Organizational Systems, San Francisco, CA 94111-1920. Offers clinical psychology (PhD); creativity studies (MA); human science (MA, PhD), including consciousness and spirituality, individualized (PhD), integrative health studies, organizational systems, social transformation; marriage and family therapy (MA); organizational systems (MA, PhD), including individualized (PhD), organizational systems; psychology (MA, PhD), including consciousness and spirituality, humanistic and transpersonal psychology, individualized (PhD), integrative health studies, licensure track (MA), organizational systems, social transformation. Postbaccalaureate distance learning degree programs offered (minimal on-campus study). Terminal master's awarded for partial completion of doctoral program. *Degree requirements:* For master's, thesis or alternative; for doctorate, thesis/dissertation. Electronic applications accepted. *Faculty research:* Humanistic theory, health studies, organizational systems, consciousness and spirituality, social transformation.

The School of Professional Psychology at Forest Institute, Graduate Programs, Springfield, MO 65807. Offers clinical psychology (Psy D); marriage and family therapy (PGC); psychology (MA). *Accreditation:* AAMFT/COAMFTE; APA (one or more programs are accredited). *Faculty:* 20 full-time (13 women), 22 part-time/adjunct (9 women). *Students:* 198 full-time (145 women), 20 part-time (10 women). Average age 32. 122 applicants, 72% accepted, 70 enrolled. In 2007, 40 master's, 40 doctorates awarded. Terminal master's awarded for partial completion of doctoral program. *Median time to degree:* Of those who began their doctoral program in fall 1999, 100% received their degree in 8 years or less. *Degree requirements:* For master's, thesis, practice; for doctorate, comprehensive exam, thesis/dissertation, internship, practice. *Entrance requirements:* For master's, GRE General Test, interview, minimum GPA of 3.0, 12 hours in psychology; for doctorate, GRE General Test, interview, minimum GPA of 3.0, 18 hours in psychology. Additional exam requirements/recommendations for international students: Required—TOEFL (minimum score 550 paper-based; 213 computer-based). *Application deadline:* For fall admission, 8/1 priority date for domestic students, 5/1 for international students; for winter admission, 11/1 priority date for domestic students, 8/1 for international students. Applications are processed on a rolling basis. Application fee: $50. Electronic applications accepted. *Expenses:* Tuition: Part-time $565 per credit hour. Required fees: $385 per term. One-time fee: $275 part-time. Tuition and fees vary according to program. *Financial support:* In 2007–08, 91 students received support. Career-related internships or fieldwork, Federal Work-Study, and scholarships/grants available. Support available to part-time students. Financial award applicants required to submit FAFSA. *Faculty research:* Pain management, clinical supervision, addictions, women's issues, forensics. *Unit head:* Dr. Mark E. Skrade, President, 417-823-3477, Fax: 417-823-3442, E-mail: mskrade@forest.edu. *Application contact:* Phillip Raleigh, Director of Admissions, 417-823-3477, Fax: 417-823-3442, E-mail: praleigh@forest.edu.

Seattle Pacific University, Graduate School, School of Psychology, Family and Community, Program in Clinical Psychology, Seattle, WA 98119-1997. Offers PhD. *Accreditation:* APA. *Students:* 47 full-time (38 women), 36 part-time (30 women); includes 11 minority (2 African Americans, 1 American Indian/Alaska Native, 7 Asian Americans or Pacific Islanders, 1 Hispanic American). Average age 30. 60 applicants, 23% accepted, 14 enrolled. In 2007, 33 degrees awarded. *Degree requirements:* For doctorate, thesis/dissertation, clinical internship, practicum. *Entrance requirements:* For doctorate, GRE General Test or MAT. *Application deadline:* For fall admission, 2/1 for domestic students. *Expenses:* Contact institution. Tuition and fees vary according to program. *Financial support:* In 2007–08, 2 research assistantships (averaging $6,000 per year) were awarded; career-related internships or fieldwork and unspecified assistantships also available. Financial award applicants required to submit FAFSA. *Faculty research:* Social network support, attachment, integration of faith and family psychology, developmental psychology. Total annual research expenditures: $10,000. *Unit head:* Dr. Jay Skidmore, Chair, 706-281-2916. *Application contact:* Marie Baldwin, Program Coordinator, 206-281-2839, Fax: 206-281-2695, E-mail: mbaldwin@spu.edu.

Southern Illinois University Carbondale, Graduate School, College of Liberal Arts, Department of Psychology, Carbondale, IL 62901-4701. Offers clinical psychology (MA, MS, PhD); counseling psychology (MA, MS, PhD); experimental psychology (MA, MS, PhD). *Accreditation:* APA (one or more programs are accredited). *Faculty:* 27 full-time (14 women), 1 part-time/adjunct (0 women). *Students:* 81 full-time (54 women), 43 part-time (32 women); includes 25 minority (13 African Americans, 1 American Indian/Alaska Native, 6 Asian Americans or Pacific Islanders, 5 Hispanic Americans), 13 international. 291 applicants, 9% accepted, 13 enrolled. In 2007, 17 master's, 15 doctorates awarded. *Degree requirements:* For master's, thesis; for doctorate, thesis/dissertation. *Entrance requirements:* For master's, GRE General Test, GRE Subject Test, minimum GPA of 2.7; for doctorate, GRE General Test, GRE Subject Test, minimum GPA of 3.25. Additional exam requirements/recommendations for international students: Required—TOEFL. *Application deadline:* For fall admission, 3/1 priority date for domestic students. Applications are processed on a rolling basis. Application fee: $20. *Financial support:* In 2007–08, 82 students received support, including 14 fellowships with full tuition reimbursements available, 23 research assistantships with full tuition reimbursements available, 22 teaching assistantships with full tuition reimbursements available; Federal Work-Study, institutionally sponsored loans, and tuition waivers (full) also available. *Faculty research:* Developmental neuropsychology; smoking, affect, and cognition; personality measurement; vocational psychology; program evaluation. *Unit head:* Dr. Jane Swanson, Chair, 618-453-3529, E-mail: swanson@siu.edu. *Application contact:* Connie Childers, Office Specialist, 618-453-3564, E-mail: childers@siu.edu.

See Close-Up on page 1479.

Southern Illinois University Edwardsville, Graduate Studies and Research, School of Education, Department of Psychology, Program in Clinical-Adult Psychology, Edwardsville, IL 62026-0001. Offers MA. *Students:* 12 full-time (10 women), 14 part-time (11 women); includes 2 minority (1 African American, 1 Hispanic American), 1 international. In 2007, 9 degrees awarded. *Degree requirements:* For master's, thesis. *Application deadline:* For fall admission, 3/1 for domestic and international students. Applications are processed on a rolling basis. Application fee: $30. Electronic applications accepted. *Unit head:* Dr. Lynn Bartels, Director, 618-650-2202, E-mail: lbartel@siue.edu.

Southern Illinois University Edwardsville, Graduate Studies and Research, School of Education, Department of Psychology, Program in Clinical Child and School Psychology, Edwardsville, IL 62026-0001. Offers MS. *Students:* 12 full-time (11 women), 7 part-time (all women). In 2007, 8 degrees awarded. *Degree requirements:* For master's, thesis. *Application deadline:* For fall admission, 3/1 for domestic and international students. Applications are processed on a rolling basis. Application fee: $30. Electronic applications accepted. *Unit head:* Dr. Lynn Bartels, Director, 618-650-2202, E-mail: lbartel@siue.edu.

Southern Methodist University, Dedman College, Department of Psychology, Program in Clinical Psychology, Dallas, TX 75275. Offers PhD. *Faculty:* 11 full-time (5 women), 3 part-time/adjunct (2 women). *Students:* 16 full-time (14 women); includes 4 minority (1 American Indian/Alaska Native, 1 Asian American or Pacific Islander, 2 Hispanic Americans). Average age 32. 84 applicants, 8% accepted, 4 enrolled. In 2007, 1 degree awarded. *Degree requirements:* For doctorate, comprehensive exam, thesis/dissertation, research presentation and publication. *Entrance requirements:* For doctorate, GRE General Test, minimum GPA of 3.0, 3 letters of recommendation. Additional exam requirements/recommendations for international students: Required—TOEFL (minimum score 550 paper-based). *Application deadline:* For fall admission, 1/1 priority date for domestic and international students. Application fee: $60. Electronic applications accepted. *Financial support:* In 2007–08, 9 students received support, including 8 research assistantships with full tuition reimbursements available (averaging $14,000 per year); career-related internships or fieldwork also available. Financial award application deadline: 1/1; financial award applicants required to submit FAFSA. *Faculty research:* Family violence, family assessment, anxiety disorders, personality disorders. Total annual research expenditures: $500,000. *Unit head:* Dr. Robert B. Hampson, Director, 214-768-2734, Fax: 214-768-3910, E-mail: rhampson@smu.edu. *Application contact:* Ann Conner, Assistant to Director of Graduate Studies, 214-768-4924, Fax: 214-768-3910, E-mail: aconner@smu.edu.

Southern New Hampshire University, School of Liberal Arts, Manchester, NH 03106-1045. Offers clinical services for adults psychiatric disabilities (Certificate); clinical services for children and adolescents with psychiatric disabilities (Certificate); clinical services for persons with co-occurring substance abuse and psychiatric disabilities (Certificate); community mental health (MS); fiction writing (MFA); non-fiction writing (MFA); teaching English as a foreign language (MS). Part-time and evening/weekend programs available. *Faculty:* 18 full-time. *Students:* 187 full-time, 12 part-time. Average age 35. In 2007, 35 degrees awarded. *Degree requirements:* For master's, one foreign language, thesis. *Entrance requirements:* For master's, minimum GPA of 2.75: MS-TEFL, 3.0: MFA. Additional exam requirements/recommendations for international students: Required—TOEFL (minimum score 550 paper-based; 213 computer-based; 79 iBT), IELTS (minimum score 7), TWE (minimum score 5). *Application deadline:* For fall admission, 7/1 priority date for domestic students; for winter admission, 11/1 priority date for domestic students; for spring admission, 6/1 priority date for domestic students. Applications are processed on a rolling basis. Application fee: $40. Electronic applications accepted. *Expenses:* Contact institution. *Financial support:* In 2007–08, 4 research assistantships were awarded; career-related internships or fieldwork and scholarships/grants also available. Financial award applicants required to submit FAFSA. *Faculty research:* Action research, state of the art practice in behavioral health services, wraparound approaches to working with youth, learning styles. *Unit head:* Dr. Karen Erickson, Dean, 603-668-2211, E-mail: k.erickson@snhu.edu. *Application contact:* Scott Durand, Director of Graduate Enrollment Services, 603-644-3102 Ext. 3338, Fax: 603-644-3144, E-mail: s.durand@snhu.edu.

Spalding University, Graduate Studies, College of Social Sciences and Humanities, School of Professional Psychology, Louisville, KY 40203-2188. Offers clinical psychology (MA, Psy D). *Accreditation:* APA (one or more programs are accredited). Part-time programs available. Terminal master's awarded for partial completion of doctoral program. *Degree requirements:* For master's, comprehensive exam; for doctorate, thesis/dissertation. *Entrance requirements:* For master's, GRE General Test, 18 hours of undergraduate course work in psychology, interview; for doctorate, GRE General Test, interview, 18 hours of coursework in psychology. Additional exam requirements/recommendations for international students: Required—TOEFL. *Faculty research:* Substance abuse, prayer research, end-of-life issues, complementary and alternative medicine, research methodology and statistical inference.

State University of New York at Binghamton, Graduate School, School of Arts and Sciences, Department of Psychology, Specialization in Clinical Psychology, Binghamton, NY 13902-6000. Offers MA, PhD. *Accreditation:* APA (one or more programs are accredited). *Students:* 32 full-time (24 women), 11 part-time (8 women); includes 7 minority (3 African Americans, 4 Hispanic Americans), 2 international. Average age 28. 213 applicants, 7% accepted, 8 enrolled. In 2007, 10 master's, 7 doctorates awarded. *Degree requirements:* For master's, thesis; for doctorate, thesis/dissertation, departmental qualifying exam. *Entrance requirements:* For master's and doctorate, GRE General Test, GRE Subject Test. Additional exam requirements/recommendations for international students: Required—TOEFL. *Application deadline:* For fall admission, 4/15 priority date for domestic students, 1/15 priority date for international students; for spring admission, 11/1 for domestic students, 10/1 priority date for international students. Applications are processed on a rolling basis. Application fee: $60. Electronic applications accepted. *Financial support:* In 2007–08, 40 students received support, including 6 fellowships with full tuition reimbursements available (averaging $12,000 per year), 10 research assistantships with full tuition reimbursements available (averaging $10,000 per year), 13 teaching assistantships with full tuition reimbursements available (averaging $16,500 per year); career-related internships or fieldwork, Federal Work-Study, institutionally sponsored loans, and unspecified assistantships also available. Support available to part-time students. Financial award application deadline: 2/15. *Unit head:* Dr. Steven Lisman, Graduate Coordinator, 607-777-4929, E-mail: slisman@binghamton.edu.

Stony Brook University, State University of New York, Graduate School, College of Arts and Sciences, Department of Psychology, Program in Clinical Psychology, Stony Brook, NY 11794. Offers PhD. *Accreditation:* APA. *Students:* 42 full-time (35 women); includes 2 minority (1 Asian American or Pacific Islander, 1 Hispanic American). Average age 27. 305 applicants, 4% accepted. In 2007, 7 degrees awarded. *Degree requirements:* For doctorate, thesis/dissertation. *Entrance requirements:* For doctorate, GRE General Test, GRE Subject Test. Additional exam requirements/recommendations for international students: Required—TOEFL. *Application deadline:* For fall admission, 1/15 for domestic students. Application fee: $60. *Unit head:* Dr. Daniel O'Leary, Head, 631-632-7850, E-mail: k.d.oleary@stonybrook.edu.

Announcement: The Clinical Psychology Program was identified in 2001 by *U.S. News & World Report* as one of the top 10 clinical psychology doctoral programs in the US. In 1999, Stony Brook was the first program in the country designated "Outstanding Clinical Training Program" by the Association for the Advancement of Behavior Therapy.

See Close-Up on page 1495.

Suffolk University, College of Arts and Sciences, Department of Psychology, Boston, MA 02108-2770. Offers clinical-developmental psychology (PhD). *Accreditation:* APA. *Faculty:* 16 full-time (11 women). *Students:* 36 full-time (31 women), 15 part-time (11 women); includes 5 minority (2 African Americans, 2 Asian Americans or Pacific Islanders, 1 Hispanic American), 2 international. Average age 28. 315 applicants, 10% accepted, 13 enrolled. In 2007, 16 degrees awarded. *Degree requirements:* For doctorate, thesis/dissertation, practicum. *Entrance requirements:* For doctorate, GRE General Test or MAT. Additional exam requirements/recommendations for international students: Required—TOEFL (minimum score 550 paper-based; 213 computer-based; 80 iBT). *Application deadline:* For fall admission, 12/15 for domestic and international students. Applications are processed on a rolling basis. Application fee: $50. Electronic applications accepted. *Expenses:* Contact institution. *Financial support:* In 2007–08, 46 students received support, including 36 fellowships with full and partial tuition reimbursements available (averaging $16,747 per year); career-related internships or fieldwork, Federal Work-Study, and institutionally sponsored loans also available. Support available to part-time students. Financial award application deadline: 4/1; financial award applicants required to submit FAFSA. *Faculty research:* Olfaction decision-making in substance-dependent individuals, ego development, experiential avoidance in generalized anxiety disorder. *Unit head:* Dr. Robert Webb, Chair, 617-573-8293, Fax: 617-367-2924, E-mail: rwebb@suffolk.edu. *Application contact:* Judith Reynolds, Director of Graduate Admissions, 617-573-8302, Fax: 617-523-0116, E-mail: grad.admission@suffolk.edu.

Syracuse University, Graduate School, College of Arts and Sciences, Department of Psychology, Program in Clinical Psychology, Syracuse, NY 13244. Offers PhD. *Accreditation:* APA. *Students:* 29 full-time (22 women), 2 part-time (both women); includes 3 minority (2 African Americans, 1 American Indian/Alaska Native), 3 international. 111 applicants, 9% accepted, 6 enrolled. In 2007, 2 doctorates awarded. *Degree requirements:* For doctorate, thesis/dissertation. *Entrance requirements:* For doctorate, GRE General Test, GRE Subject Test. Additional exam requirements/recommendations for international students: Required—TOEFL. *Application deadline:* For fall admission, 1/1 for domestic students. Applications are processed on a rolling basis. Application fee: $65. Electronic applications accepted. *Expenses:* Tuition: Full-time $18,216; part-time $1,012 per credit. Required fees: $980. Tuition and fees vary according to program. *Financial support:* Fellowships with full tuition reimbursements, research assistantships with full tuition reimbursements, teaching assistantships with full tuition reimbursements available. *Unit head:* Dr. Kevin S. Masters, Graduate Director, 315-443-3666, Fax: 315-443-4085, E-mail: kemaster@syr.edu. *Application contact:* Sue Bova, Information Contact, 315-443-1050, E-mail: skbova@syr.edu.

Teachers College, Columbia University, Graduate Faculty of Education, Department of Counseling and Clinical Psychology, Program in Clinical Psychology, New York, NY 10027-6696. Offers PhD. *Accreditation:* APA. *Faculty:* 4 full-time (2 women), 8 part-time/adjunct. *Students:* 34 full-time (25 women), 19 part-time (15 women); includes 16 minority (2 African Americans, 10 Asian Americans or Pacific Islanders, 4 Hispanic Americans), 2 international. Average age 31. 75 applicants, 5% accepted, 4 enrolled. In 2007, 7 doctorates awarded. *Application deadline:* For fall admission, 12/15 for domestic students. Application fee: $70. *Financial support:* Career-related internships or fieldwork, Federal Work-Study, institutionally sponsored loans, and tuition waivers (partial) available. Support available to part-time students. Financial award application deadline: 2/1. *Faculty research:* Psychotherapy education, trauma, stress, psychopathology, life span and aging issues. *Application contact:* Melba Remice, Assistant Director of Admission, 212-678-4035, Fax: 212-678-4171, E-mail: ms2545@columbia.edu.

Teachers College, Columbia University, Graduate Faculty of Education, Department of Counseling and Clinical Psychology, Program in Clinical Psychology—Master's, New York, NY 10027-6696. Offers MA. *Students:* 76 full-time (62 women), 75 part-time (64 women); includes 50 minority (15 African Americans, 13 Asian Americans or Pacific Islanders, 22 Hispanic Americans), 11 international. Average age 26. 313 applicants, 97% accepted, 86 enrolled. In 2007, 73 degrees awarded. *Application deadline:* For fall admission, 5/15 for domestic students. Application fee: $70. *Financial support:* Application deadline: 2/1. *Application contact:* Melba Remice, Assistant Director of Admission, 212-678-4035, Fax: 212-678-4171, E-mail: ms2545@columbia.edu.

Temple University, Graduate School, College of Liberal Arts, Department of Psychology, Program in Clinical Psychology, Philadelphia, PA 19122-6096. Offers PhD. *Accreditation:* APA. *Degree requirements:* For doctorate, thesis/dissertation. *Entrance requirements:* For doctorate, GRE General Test, minimum GPA of 3.0. Additional exam requirements/recommendations for international students: Required—TOEFL (minimum score 550 paper-based; 213 computer-based; 79 iBT). Electronic applications accepted. *Faculty research:* Depression, addictive disorders, parenting and families, social phobia, child and adolescent treatment research.

Texas A&M University, College of Liberal Arts, Department of Psychology, College Station, TX 77843. Offers behavioral and cellular neuroscience (MS, PhD); clinical psychology (MS, PhD); cognitive psychology (MS, PhD); developmental psychology (MS, PhD); industrial/organizational psychology (MS, PhD); social psychology (MS, PhD). *Accreditation:* APA (one or more programs are accredited). *Faculty:* 33. *Students:* 69 full-time (46 women), 14 part-time (10 women); includes 27 minority (7 African Americans, 1 American Indian/Alaska Native, 5 Asian Americans or Pacific Islanders, 14 Hispanic Americans), 8 international. 274 applicants, 11% accepted, 15 enrolled. In 2007, 11 master's, 7 doctorates awarded. *Degree requirements:* For master's, thesis; for doctorate, comprehensive exam (for some programs), thesis/dissertation. *Entrance requirements:* For master's and doctorate, GRE General Test. Additional exam requirements/recommendations for international students: Required—TOEFL. *Application deadline:* For fall admission, 1/5 for domestic and international students. Application fee: $50 ($75 for international students). Electronic applications accepted. *Expenses:* Tuition, state resident: full-time $6,129. Tuition, nonresident: full-time $11,689. Tuition and fees vary according to course load. *Financial support:* Fellowships with partial tuition reimbursements, research assistantships with partial tuition reimbursements, teaching assistantships with partial tuition reimbursements, career-related internships or fieldwork, institutionally sponsored loans, health care benefits, and unspecified assistantships available. Financial award application deadline: 1/5; financial award applicants required to submit FAFSA. *Unit head:* Dr. Steve Rholes, Head, 979-845-2581, Fax: 979-845-4727, E-mail: wsr@psyc.tamu.edu. *Application contact:* Sharon Starr, Graduate Admissions Supervisor, 979-458-1710, Fax: 979-845-4727, E-mail: gradadv@psyc.tamu.edu.

Texas Tech University, Graduate School, College of Arts and Sciences, Department of Psychology, Lubbock, TX 79409. Offers clinical psychology (PhD); counseling psychology (MA, PhD); experimental psychology (MA, PhD); psychology (MA, PhD). *Accreditation:* APA (one or more programs are accredited). Part-time programs available. *Faculty:* 25 full-time (11 women). *Students:* 91 full-time (59 women), 11 part-time (8 women); includes 16 minority (6 African Americans, 2 Asian Americans or Pacific Islanders, 8 Hispanic Americans), 4 international. Average age 28. 264 applicants, 10% accepted, 17 enrolled. In 2007, 15 master's, 16 doctorates awarded. *Degree requirements:* For doctorate, thesis/dissertation. *Entrance requirements:* For master's and doctorate, GRE General Test, GRE Subject Test. Additional exam requirements/recommendations for international students: Required—TOEFL (minimum score 550 paper-based; 213 computer-based). *Application deadline:* For fall admission, 3/1 priority date for international students; for spring admission, 11/1 priority date for international students. Applications are processed on a rolling basis. Application fee: $50 ($60 for international students). Electronic applications accepted. *Expenses:* Tuition, state resident: part-time $373 per credit hour. Tuition, nonresident: part-time $651 per credit hour. Tuition and fees vary according to program. *Financial support:* In 2007–08, 99 students received support, including 8 research assistantships with partial tuition reimbursements available (averaging $11,462 per year), 64 teaching assistantships with partial tuition reimbursements available (averaging $11,759 per year); career-related internships or fieldwork, Federal Work-Study, and institutionally sponsored loans also available. Support available to part-time students. Financial award application deadline: 4/15; financial award applicants required to submit FAFSA. *Faculty research:* Failure/success in relationships, peer rejection in school, stress and coping, group processes, clinical and health psychology. Total annual research expenditures: $459,933. *Unit head:* Dr. M. David Rudd, Chair, 806-742-3711 Ext. 224, Fax: 806-742-0818, E-mail: david.rudd@ttu.edu. *Application contact:* Dr. Steve Richards, Graduate Advisor, 806-742-3711 Ext. 254, Fax: 806-742-0818, E-mail: steven.richards@ttu.edu.

Towson University, College of Graduate Studies and Research, Program in Clinical Psychology, Towson, MD 21252-0001. Offers MA. Part-time and evening/weekend programs available. *Faculty:* 11 full-time (3 women), 2 part-time/adjunct (both women). *Students:* 101 full-time (87 women), 43 part-time (33 women); includes 23 minority (11 African Americans, 8 Asian Americans or Pacific Islanders, 4 Hispanic Americans), 1 international. Average age 26. 58 applicants, 88% accepted, 44 enrolled. In 2007, 58 degrees awarded. *Degree requirements:* For master's, thesis (for some programs), exams. *Entrance requirements:* For master's, GRE, minimum GPA of 3.0, 15 credits in related course work. Additional exam requirements/recommendations for international students: Required—TOEFL. *Application deadline:* For fall admission, 2/1 for domestic and international students. Application fee: $50. Electronic applications accepted. *Expenses:* Tuition, state resident: part-time $286 per credit. Tuition, nonresident: part-time $600 per credit. Required fees: $75 per credit. *Financial support:* Federal Work-Study and unspecified assistantships available. Financial award application deadline: 4/1; financial award applicants required to submit FAFSA. *Faculty research:* Cognitive behavior, issues affecting the aging, relaxation hypnosis and imagery, medicalization of male sexuality. *Unit head:* Dr. Elizabeth Katz, Graduate Program Director, 410-704-3201, Fax: 410-704-3800, E-mail: ekatz@towson.edu. *Application contact:* The Graduate School, 410-704-2501, Fax: 410-704-4675, E-mail: grads@towson.edu.

Troy University, Graduate School, College of Education, Program in Counseling and Psychology, Troy, AL 36082. Offers clinical mental health (MS); community counseling (MS); school psychology (MS); student affairs counseling (MS). *Accreditation:* ACA; CORE; NCATE. Part-time and evening/weekend programs available. *Students:* 355 full-time (303 women), 555 part-time (461 women); includes 598 minority (550 African Americans, 20 American Indian/Alaska Native, 6 Asian Americans or Pacific Islanders, 22 Hispanic Americans). Average age 32. In 2007, 328 degrees awarded. *Degree requirements:* For master's, comprehensive exam, thesis. *Entrance requirements:* For master's, MAT, minimum GPA of 2.5. Additional exam requirements/recommendations for international students: Required—TOEFL (minimum score 523 paper-based; 200 computer-based). *Application deadline:* Applications are processed on a rolling basis. Application fee: $50. Electronic applications accepted. *Unit head:* Dr. Andrew Creamer, Chair, 334-670-3350, Fax: 334-670-32961, E-mail: drcreamer@troy.edu. *Application contact:* Brenda K. Campbell, Director of Graduate Admissions, 334-670-3178, Fax: 334-670-3733, E-mail: bcamp@troy.edu.

Uniformed Services University of the Health Sciences, School of Medicine, Programs in Biomedical Sciences, Department of Medical and Clinical Psychology, Bethesda, MD 20814-4799. Offers clinical psychology (PhD); medical psychology (PhD). Clinical psychology available to active duty military only. *Accreditation:* APA. *Faculty:* 8 full-time (3 women), 42 part-time/adjunct (13 women). *Students:* 32 full-time (23 women); includes 5 minority (3 African Americans, 1 American Indian/Alaska Native, 1 Hispanic American). Average age 27. 69 applicants, 16% accepted, 8 enrolled. In 2007, 3 doctorates awarded. Terminal master's awarded for partial completion of doctoral program. *Median time to degree:* Of those who began their doctoral program in fall 1999, 100% received their degree in 8 years or less. *Degree requirements:* For doctorate, comprehensive exam, thesis/dissertation, qualifying exam. *Entrance requirements:* For doctorate, GRE General Test, minimum GPA of 3.0, U.S. citizenship. Additional exam requirements/recommendations for international students: Required—TOEFL. *Application deadline:* For fall admission, 1/15 priority date for domestic and international students. Applications are processed on a rolling basis. Application fee: $0. Electronic applications accepted.

Clinical Psychology

Uniformed Services University of the Health Sciences (continued)
Financial support: In 2007–08, fellowships with full tuition reimbursements (averaging $25,000 per year); tuition waivers (full) also available. *Faculty research:* Addictive and appetitive behavior, psychopharmacology, stress and eating, obesity, health. *Unit head:* Dr. David S. Krantz, Chair, 301-295-3270, Fax: 301-295-3034, E-mail: dskrantz@usuhs.mil. *Application contact:* Janet M. Anastasi, Graduate Program Coordinator, 301-295-9474, Fax: 301-295-6772, E-mail: janastasi@usuhs.mil.

Union Institute & University, Program in Clinical Psychology, Cincinnati, OH 45206-1925. Offers Psy D. *Faculty:* 5 full-time (1 woman), 6 part-time/adjunct (2 women). *Students:* 17 full-time (14 women); includes 3 minority (1 African American, 2 Hispanic Americans). Average age 51. *Degree requirements:* For doctorate, thesis/dissertation, internship, residency, practicum. *Entrance requirements:* For doctorate, master's degree, letters of recommendation, interview. *Application deadline:* Applications are processed on a rolling basis. Application fee: $50. *Expenses:* Tuition: Full-time $20,176; part-time $760 per credit hour. Tuition and fees vary according to course load, degree level and program. *Financial support:* Federal Work-Study, scholarships/grants, and tuition waivers (partial) available. Financial award application deadline: 5/1; financial award applicants required to submit FAFSA. *Unit head:* Dr. William Lax, Dean, 802-254-0152.

Universidad de Iberoamerica, Graduate School, San Jose, Costa Rica. Offers clinical psychology (M Psych); educational psychology (M Psych); forensic psychology (M Psych); hospital and health services management (MHA); intensive care nursing (MN); medicine (MD). *Entrance requirements:* For master's, 2 letters of recommendation, interview.

Université Laval, Faculty of Social Sciences, School of Psychology, Programs in Psychology, Québec, QC G1K 7P4, Canada. Offers clinical psychology (PhD); community psychology (PhD); psychology (PhD, Psy D). *Degree requirements:* For doctorate, comprehensive exam, thesis/dissertation. *Entrance requirements:* For doctorate, comprehension of written English, knowledge of French, interview. Electronic applications accepted.

University at Albany, State University of New York, College of Arts and Sciences, Department of Psychology, Albany, NY 12222-0001. Offers autism (Certificate); biopsychology (PhD); clinical psychology (PhD); general/experimental psychology (PhD); industrial/organizational psychology (PhD); psychology (MA); social/personality psychology (PhD). *Accreditation:* APA (one or more programs are accredited). *Students:* 51 full-time (32 women), 47 part-time (40 women). Average age 30. In 2007, 8 master's, 15 doctorates, 7 other advanced degrees awarded. *Degree requirements:* For doctorate, thesis/dissertation. *Entrance requirements:* For doctorate, GRE General Test, GRE Subject Test. Additional exam requirements/recommendations for international students: Required—TOEFL (minimum score 550 paper-based; 213 computer-based). *Application deadline:* For fall admission, 1/15 for domestic and international students. Application fee: $75. Electronic applications accepted. *Expenses:* Tuition, state resident: part-time $576 per credit. Tuition, nonresident: part-time $910 per credit. Tuition and fees vary according to program. *Financial support:* Fellowships, research assistantships, teaching assistantships, career-related internships or fieldwork available. Financial award application deadline: 2/1. *Unit head:* Kevin J. Williams, Chair, 518-442-4820.

University at Buffalo, the State University of New York, Graduate School, College of Arts and Sciences, Department of Psychology, Buffalo, NY 14260. Offers behavioral neuroscience (PhD); clinical psychology (PhD); cognitive psychology (PhD); general psychology (MA); social-personality psychology (PhD). *Accreditation:* APA (one or more programs are accredited). Terminal master's awarded for partial completion of doctoral program. *Degree requirements:* For master's, project; for doctorate, thesis/dissertation. *Entrance requirements:* For master's and doctorate, GRE General Test. Additional exam requirements/recommendations for international students: Required—TOEFL (minimum score 550 paper-based; 213 computer-based; 79 iBT). Electronic applications accepted. *Faculty research:* Neural, endocrine, and molecular bases of behavior; adult mood and anxiety disorders; relationship dysfunction; attention deficit/hyperactivity disorder; psycho-linguistics.

The University of Alabama, Graduate School, College of Arts and Sciences, Department of Psychology, Tuscaloosa, AL 35487. Offers clinical psychology (PhD); experimental psychology (PhD). *Accreditation:* APA. *Faculty:* 23 full-time (10 women), 1 part-time/adjunct (0 women). *Students:* 74 full-time (57 women), 12 part-time (11 women); includes 14 minority (8 African Americans, 3 Asian Americans or Pacific Islanders, 3 Hispanic Americans), 4 international. Average age 27. 231 applicants, 11% accepted, 15 enrolled. In 2007, 14 doctorates awarded. *Median time to degree:* Of those who began their doctoral program in fall 1999, 64% received their degree in 8 years or less. *Degree requirements:* For doctorate, thesis/dissertation. *Entrance requirements:* For doctorate, GRE. Additional exam requirements/recommendations for international students: Required—TOEFL (minimum score 550 paper-based). *Application deadline:* For fall admission, 12/1 for domestic and international students. Application fee: $30. Electronic applications accepted. *Expenses:* Tuition, state resident: full-time $5,700. Tuition, nonresident: full-time $16,518. *Financial support:* In 2007–08, 73 students received support, including 12 fellowships with full tuition reimbursements available (averaging $15,000 per year), 34 research assistantships with full and partial tuition reimbursements available (averaging $11,142 per year), 26 teaching assistantships with tuition reimbursements available (averaging $11,142 per year); career-related internships or fieldwork, institutionally sponsored loans, scholarships/grants, health care benefits, and unspecified assistantships also available. Financial award application deadline: 12/1. *Faculty research:* Cognitive development/disability, child clinical, psychology and law, health/aging, social psychology. Total annual research expenditures: $2.5 million. *Unit head:* Dr. Kenneth Lichstein, Chair, 205-348-4962, Fax: 205-348-8648, E-mail: lichstein@ua.edu. *Application contact:* Mary Beth Hubbard, Information Contact, 205-348-1919, Fax: 205-348-8648, E-mail: mbhubbard@as.ua.edu.

University of Alaska Anchorage, College of Arts and Sciences, Department of Psychology, Anchorage, AK 99508-8060. Offers clinical psychology (MS); clinical-community psychology with rural-indigenous emphasis (PhD). Part-time programs available. *Degree requirements:* For master's, thesis. *Entrance requirements:* For master's, GRE General Test, GRE Subject Test, interview, references; for doctorate, interview, bachelor's or master's degree in psychology. Additional exam requirements/recommendations for international students: Required—TOEFL (minimum score 550 paper-based; 213 computer-based). *Faculty research:* Substance abuse, childhood autism, biofeedback, psychological assessment, mental health in Native Alaskans.

University of Alaska Fairbanks, College of Liberal Arts, Department of Psychology, Fairbanks, AK 99775-7520. Offers clinical-community psychology (PhD), including rural cross-cultural emphasis. *Degree requirements:* For doctorate, comprehensive exam, thesis/dissertation. *Entrance requirements:* For doctorate, GRE General Test, minimum GPA of 3.0, letters of reference. Additional exam requirements/recommendations for international students: Required—TOEFL (minimum score 550 paper-based; 213 computer-based). *Faculty research:* Clinical and community psychology, rural, indigenous, and cultural psychology.

The University of British Columbia, Faculty of Arts and Faculty of Graduate Studies, Department of Psychology, Vancouver, BC V6T 1Z1, Canada. Offers behavioral neuroscience (MA, PhD); clinical psychology (MA, PhD); cognitive science (MA, PhD); developmental psychology (MA, PhD); forensic psychology (PhD); health psychology (MA, PhD); quantitative methods (MA, PhD); social/personality psychology (MA, PhD). *Accreditation:* APA (one or more programs are accredited). *Faculty:* 46 full-time (20 women), 26 part-time/adjunct (13 women). *Students:* 102 full-time (69 women). Average age 29. 247 applicants, 14% accepted, 18 enrolled. In 2007, 14 master's, 11 doctorates awarded. Terminal master's awarded for partial completion of doctoral program. *Median time to degree:* Of those who began their doctoral program in fall 1999, 91% received their degree in 8 years or less. *Degree requirements:* For master's, thesis; for doctorate, comprehensive exam, thesis/dissertation. *Entrance requirements:* For master's and doctorate, GRE General Test, GRE Subject Test. Additional exam requirements/recommendations for international students: Required—TOEFL (minimum score 550 paper-based; 230 computer-based; 80 iBT). *Application deadline:* For fall admission, 1/15 for domestic and international students. Applications are processed on a rolling basis. Application fee: $90 Canadian dollars ($150 Canadian dollars for international students). Electronic applications accepted. *Financial support:* In 2007–08, 95 students received support, including 27 fellowships with full and partial tuition reimbursements available (averaging $16,500 per year), 50 research assistantships with full and partial tuition reimbursements available (averaging $6,775 per year), 80 teaching assistantships with full and partial tuition reimbursements available (averaging $8,065 per year); career-related internships or fieldwork, Federal Work-Study, institutionally sponsored loans, scholarships/grants, health care benefits, tuition waivers (full and partial), and unspecified assistantships also available. Financial award application deadline: 1/15. *Faculty research:* Clinical, developmental, social/personality, cognition, behavioral neuroscience. Total annual research expenditures: $5.5 million Canadian dollars. *Unit head:* Dr. Eric Eich, Head, 604-822-3078, Fax: 604-822-6923, E-mail: ee@psych.ubc.ca. *Application contact:* Rose Tam, Graduate Secretary, 604-822-3144, Fax: 604-822-6923, E-mail: gradsec@psych.ubc.ca.

University of Calgary, Faculty of Graduate Studies, Faculty of Social Sciences, Department of Psychology, Program in Clinical Psychology, Calgary, AB T2N 1N4, Canada. Offers M Sc, PhD. *Degree requirements:* For master's, thesis, practical training; for doctorate, thesis/dissertation, practical training. *Entrance requirements:* For master's, GRE General Test, bachelor's degree in psychology or equivalent, minimum GPA of 3.6; for doctorate, GRE General Test, bachelor's degree in psychology, master's degree. Additional exam requirements/recommendations for international students: Required—TOEFL (minimum score 600 paper-based; 250 computer-based). Electronic applications accepted. *Faculty research:* Depression, schizophrenia, aging, neuropsychology, cognitive and linguistic development in infancy.

University of California, San Diego, Office of Graduate Studies, Group in Clinical Psychology, La Jolla, CA 92093. Offers PhD. Electronic applications accepted.

University of California, Santa Barbara, Graduate Division, Gevirtz Graduate School of Education, Santa Barbara, CA 93106. Offers counseling, clinical and school psychology (PhD), including clinical psychology, counseling psychology; education (MA, PhD), including child and adolescent development, cultural perspectives and comparative education, educational leadership and organizations, research methodology, special education disabilities and risk studies (MA), special education, disabilities and risk studies (PhD), teaching and learning; educational leadership (Ed D); school psychology (M Ed); MA/PhD. *Accreditation:* APA (one or more programs are accredited). Postbaccalaureate distance learning degree programs offered (minimal on-campus study). *Faculty:* 36 full-time (18 women), 7 part-time/adjunct (3 women). *Students:* 400 full-time (308 women); includes 119 minority (11 African Americans, 6 American Indian/Alaska Native, 46 Asian Americans or Pacific Islanders, 56 Hispanic Americans), 18 international. Average age 31. 721 applicants, 41% accepted, 189 enrolled. In 2007, 157 master's, 35 doctorates awarded. Terminal master's awarded for partial completion of doctoral program. *Median time to degree:* Of those who began their doctoral program in fall 1999, 60% received their degree in 8 years or less. *Degree requirements:* For master's, comprehensive exam (for some programs), thesis (for some programs); for doctorate, comprehensive exam (for some programs), thesis/dissertation, qualifying exam. *Entrance requirements:* For master's, GRE, MAT (M Ed); for doctorate, GRE. Additional exam requirements/recommendations for international students: Required—TOEFL (minimum score 550 paper-based; 213 computer-based; 80 iBT). *Application deadline:* For fall admission, 12/15 priority date for domestic and international students. Application fee: $60. Electronic applications accepted. *Expenses:* Tuition, nonresident: full-time $14,888. Required fees: $10,108. *Financial support:* In 2007–08, 292 students received support, including 170 fellowships with full and partial tuition reimbursements available (averaging $5,200 per year), 80 research assistantships with full and partial tuition reimbursements available, 124 teaching assistantships with full and partial tuition reimbursements available; career-related internships or fieldwork, Federal Work-Study, institutionally sponsored loans, scholarships/grants, traineeships, health care benefits, and unspecified assistantships also available. Financial award applicants required to submit FAFSA. *Faculty research:* Professional development, early childhood development, school violence, literacy, science/math initiative. Total annual research expenditures: $4.2 million. *Unit head:* Carol Dixon, Associate Dean of Students, 805-893-2137, Fax: 805-893-7264, E-mail: sao@education.ucsb.edu. *Application contact:* Katie Tucciarone, Student Affairs Officer, 805-893-2137, Fax: 805-893-2588, E-mail: katiet@education.ucsb.edu.

University of Central Florida, College of Sciences, Department of Psychology, Program in Clinical Psychology, Orlando, FL 32816. Offers MA, MS, PhD. *Accreditation:* APA. Part-time and evening/weekend programs available. *Degree requirements:* For master's, thesis or alternative, clinical internship; for doctorate, thesis/dissertation, candidacy exam, internship. *Entrance requirements:* For master's and doctorate, GRE General Test, minimum GPA of 3.0 in last 60 hours, resumé. Additional exam requirements/recommendations for international students: Required—TOEFL. *Application deadline:* For fall admission, 2/15 for domestic students. Application fee: $30. Electronic applications accepted. *Expenses:* Tuition, state resident: full-time $6,484. Tuition, nonresident: full-time $23,938. Tuition and fees vary according to program. *Financial support:* Fellowships with partial tuition reimbursements, research assistantships with partial tuition reimbursements, teaching assistantships with partial tuition reimbursements, career-related internships or fieldwork, Federal Work-Study, institutionally sponsored loans, tuition waivers (partial), and unspecified assistantships available. Financial award application deadline: 3/1; financial award applicants required to submit FAFSA. *Faculty research:* Professional ethical decision making, computer experience and anxiety, effects of expert testimony on decision making in a rape trial, religiosity, relationship beliefs and marital adjustment. *Unit head:* Dr. Deborah Beidel, Director, 407-254-3908, E-mail: dbeidel@mail.ucf.edu.

University of Cincinnati, Graduate School, McMicken College of Arts and Sciences, Department of Psychology, Cincinnati, OH 45221. Offers clinical psychology (PhD); experimental psychology (PhD). *Accreditation:* APA. *Faculty:* 26 full-time (8 women), 5 part-time/adjunct (2 women). *Students:* 66 full-time (45 women), 6 part-time (3 women); includes 15 minority (8 African Americans, 4 Asian Americans or Pacific Islanders, 3 Hispanic Americans), 6 international. Average age 28. 274 applicants, 5% accepted, 9 enrolled. In 2007, 16 doctorates awarded. *Median time to degree:* Of those who began their doctoral program in fall 1999, 100% received their degree in 8 years or less. *Degree requirements:* For doctorate, comprehensive exam, thesis/dissertation. *Entrance requirements:* For doctorate, GRE General Test. Additional exam requirements/recommendations for international students: Required—TOEFL. *Application deadline:* For fall admission, 1/3 for domestic and international students. Application fee: $35. *Financial support:* Fellowships with full tuition reimbursements, research assistantships with full tuition reimbursements, teaching assistantships with full tuition reimbursements, scholarships/grants, traineeships, tuition waivers (partial), and unspecified assistantships available. Financial award application deadline: 5/1. *Faculty research:* Neuropsychology, human factors, health. Total annual research expenditures: $509,418. *Unit head:* Dr. Steven J. Howe, Head, 513-556-5572, Fax: 513-556-1904, E-mail: steven.howe@uc.edu. *Application contact:* Dr. Paula K. Shear, Graduate Program Director, 513-556-5577, Fax: 513-556-1904, E-mail: paula.shear@uc.edu.

University of Connecticut, Graduate School, College of Liberal Arts and Sciences, Department of Psychology, Field of Psychology, Storrs, CT 06269. Offers behavioral neuroscience (PhD); biopsychology (PhD); clinical psychology (MA, PhD); cognition and instruction (PhD); developmental psychology (MA, PhD); ecological psychology (PhD); experimental psychology (PhD); general psychology (MA, PhD); health psychology (Graduate Certificate); industrial/organizational psychology (PhD); language and cognition (PhD); neuroscience (PhD); occupational health psychology (Graduate Certificate); social psychology (MA, PhD). *Accreditation:* APA (one or more programs are accredited). *Faculty:* 52 full-time (23 women). *Students:* 130 full-time (94 women), 25 part-time (11 women); includes 24 minority (8 African Americans, 6 Asian Americans or Pacific Islanders, 10 Hispanic Americans), 18 international. Average age 28. 531 applicants, 7% accepted, 35 enrolled. In 2007, 19 master's, 20 doctorates,

2 other advanced degrees awarded. Terminal master's awarded for partial completion of doctoral program. *Degree requirements:* For master's, comprehensive exam; for doctorate, thesis/dissertation. *Entrance requirements:* For master's and doctorate, GRE General Test, GRE Subject Test. Additional exam requirements/recommendations for international students: Required—TOEFL (minimum score 550 paper-based; 213 computer-based). *Application deadline:* For fall admission, 2/1 priority date for domestic and international students; for spring admission, 11/1 for domestic students, 10/1 for international students. Applications are processed on a rolling basis. Application fee: $55. Electronic applications accepted. *Expenses:* Tuition, state resident: part-time $469 per credit hour. Tuition, nonresident: part-time $1,218 per credit hour. *Financial support:* In 2007–08, 54 research assistantships with full tuition reimbursements, 69 teaching assistantships with full tuition reimbursements were awarded; fellowships, career-related internships or fieldwork, Federal Work-Study, scholarships/grants, health care benefits, and unspecified assistantships also available. Financial award application deadline: 2/1; financial award applicants required to submit FAFSA. *Application contact:* Deborah Doucette, Administrative Assistant, 860-486-2057, Fax: 860-486-2760, E-mail: futuregr@psych.psy.uconn.edu.

University of Dayton, Graduate School, College of Arts and Sciences, Department of Psychology, Program in Clinical Psychology, Dayton, OH 45469-1300. Offers MA. Part-time programs available. *Faculty:* 8 full-time (3 women), 2 part-time/adjunct (1 woman). *Students:* 21 full-time (17 women), 3 part-time (2 women); includes 3 minority (1 African American, 1 Asian American or Pacific Islander, 1 Hispanic American). Average age 26. 96 applicants, 24% accepted, 12 enrolled. In 2007, 10 degrees awarded. *Degree requirements:* For master's, thesis. *Entrance requirements:* For master's, GRE General Test, GRE Subject Test (recommended), minimum undergraduate GPA of 3.0 or 3.3 during final 2 years of course work. Additional exam requirements/recommendations for international students: Required—TOEFL (minimum score 550 paper-based; 213 computer-based; 80 iBT). *Application deadline:* For fall admission, 3/1 priority date for domestic and international students; for winter admission, 7/1 priority date for international students; for spring admission, 1/1 priority date for international students. Application fee: $0 ($50 for international students). Electronic applications accepted. *Financial support:* In 2007–08, 18 students received support, including 6 research assistantships with full tuition reimbursements available (averaging $9,660 per year); institutionally sponsored loans, traineeships, and tuition waivers (partial) also available. Financial award application deadline: 3/1. *Faculty research:* Family issues, modes and mechanisms of therapy, gender issues, personality disorders, stress and coping. *Unit head:* Dr. Roger N. Reeb, Director, 937-229-2395, Fax: 937-229-3900, E-mail: roger.reeb@notes.udayton.edu. *Application contact:* Angela Jones-Glukhov, Associate Director of Graduate Admissions, 937-229-4305, Fax: 937-229-4729.

University of Delaware, College of Arts and Sciences, Department of Psychology, Newark, DE 19716. Offers behavioral neuroscience (PhD); clinical psychology (PhD); cognitive psychology (PhD); social psychology (PhD). *Accreditation:* APA. *Faculty:* 28 full-time (10 women), 3 part-time/adjunct (1 woman). *Students:* 46 full-time (32 women), 3 part-time (2 women); includes 5 minority (4 African Americans, 1 Asian American or Pacific Islander), 3 international. Average age 27. 252 applicants, 8% accepted, 7 enrolled. In 2007, 6 doctorates awarded. *Degree requirements:* For doctorate, thesis/dissertation. *Entrance requirements:* For doctorate, GRE General Test. Additional exam requirements/recommendations for international students: Required—TOEFL (minimum score 600 paper-based; 250 computer-based). *Application deadline:* For fall admission, 1/7 priority date for domestic students. Application fee: $60. Electronic applications accepted. *Financial support:* In 2007–08, 47 students received support, including 7 fellowships with full tuition reimbursements available (averaging $16,000 per year), 14 research assistantships with full tuition reimbursements available (averaging $15,500 per year), 20 teaching assistantships with full tuition reimbursements available (averaging $16,000 per year); career-related internships or fieldwork, Federal Work-Study, institutionally sponsored loans, scholarships/grants, and tuition waivers (full and partial) also available. Financial award application deadline: 1/7. *Faculty research:* Emotion development, neural and cognitive aspects of memory, neural control of feeding, intergroup relations, social cognition and communication. Total annual research expenditures: $2.5 million. *Unit head:* Dr. Thomas M. DiLorenzo, Chair, 302-831-2271, Fax: 302-831-3645. *Application contact:* Linda Scarpitti, Information Contact, 302-831-2271, Fax: 302-831-3645, E-mail: linnie@udel.edu.

University of Denver, Graduate School of Professional Psychology, Denver, CO 80208. Offers clinical psychology (Psy D); psychology (MA). *Accreditation:* APA. *Faculty:* 10 full-time (6 women). *Students:* 194 full-time (165 women), 23 part-time (14 women); includes 24 minority (3 African Americans, 2 American Indian/Alaska Native, 9 Asian Americans or Pacific Islanders, 10 Hispanic Americans), 10 international. Average age 26. 541 applicants, 33% accepted, 96 enrolled. In 2007, 60 master's, 24 doctorates awarded. *Degree requirements:* For doctorate, paper, internship. *Entrance requirements:* For master's and doctorate, GRE General Test. Additional exam requirements/recommendations for international students: Required—TOEFL. *Application deadline:* For fall admission, 1/5 for domestic students. Application fee: $50. Electronic applications accepted. *Financial support:* In 2007–08, 25 teaching assistantships with full and partial tuition reimbursements (averaging $3,500 per year) were awarded; career-related internships or fieldwork, Federal Work-Study, institutionally sponsored loans, scholarships/grants, and clinical assistantships also available. Support available to part-time students. Financial award application deadline: 3/1; financial award applicants required to submit FAFSA. *Unit head:* Dr. Peter Buirski, Dean, 303-871-3873. *Application contact:* Admissions, 303-871-3873, Fax: 303-871-4220, E-mail: gsppiwfo@du.edu.

University of Detroit Mercy, College of Liberal Arts and Education, Department of Psychology, Program in Clinical Psychology, Detroit, MI 48221. Offers MA, PhD. *Accreditation:* APA. *Degree requirements:* For doctorate, departmental qualifying exam.

University of Florida, Graduate School, College of Public Health and Health Professions, Department of Clinical and Health Psychology, Gainesville, FL 32611. Offers PhD. *Accreditation:* APA. *Faculty:* 19 full-time (10 women), 1 part-time/adjunct (0 women). *Students:* 87 (69 women); includes 14 minority (5 African Americans, 6 Asian Americans or Pacific Islanders, 3 Hispanic Americans) 4 international. In 2007, 9 doctorates awarded. *Degree requirements:* For doctorate, thesis/dissertation. *Entrance requirements:* For doctorate, GRE General Test, minimum GPA of 3.0. Additional exam requirements/recommendations for international students: Required—TOEFL (minimum score 550 paper-based; 213 computer-based). *Application deadline:* For fall admission, 12/1 for domestic students. Application fee: $30. Electronic applications accepted. *Expenses:* Tuition, state resident: full-time $7,478. Tuition, nonresident: full-time $22,603. *Financial support:* In 2007–08, 53 research assistantships with partial tuition reimbursements (averaging $10,164 per year) were awarded; fellowships with partial tuition reimbursements, teaching assistantships with partial tuition reimbursements, career-related internships or fieldwork, Federal Work-Study, institutionally sponsored loans, scholarships/grants, and unspecified assistantships also available. Financial award application deadline: 12/1. *Faculty research:* Child psychology, pediatric psychology, health/medical psychology, neuropsychology. *Unit head:* Dr. Ronald H. Rozensky, Chair, 352-273-6033, Fax: 352-273-6156, E-mail: rrozensky@phhp.ufl.edu. *Application contact:* Dr. Russell M. Bauer, Coordinator, 352-273-6455, Fax: 352-273-6156, E-mail: rbauer@phhp.ufl.edu.

University of Guelph, Graduate Program Services, College of Social and Applied Human Sciences, Department of Psychology, Guelph, ON N1G 2W1, Canada. Offers applied social psychology (MA, PhD); clinical psychology applied development emphasis (PhD); clinical psychology applied developmental emphasis (MA); industrial/organizational psychology (MA, PhD); neuroscience and applied cognitive science (MA, PhD). *Faculty:* 34 full-time (14 women). *Students:* 95 full-time (72 women), 6 part-time (all women); includes 6 minority (2 African Americans, 4 Asian Americans or Pacific Islanders). 230 applicants, 28% accepted, 35 enrolled. In 2007, 8 master's, 2 doctorates awarded. *Median time to degree:* Of those who began their doctoral program in fall 1999, 100% received their degree in 8 years or less. *Degree requirements:* For master's, thesis; for doctorate, comprehensive exam, thesis/dissertation. *Entrance requirements:* For master's, GRE General Test, GRE Subject Test, minimum B+ average during previous 2 years of course work; for doctorate, GRE General Test, GRE Subject Test, minimum A- average. Additional exam requirements/recommendations for international students: Required—TOEFL (minimum score 89 iBT). *Application deadline:* For fall admission, 12/15 priority date for domestic students, 1/15 priority date for international students; for spring admission, 12/15 priority date for domestic students. Application fee: $85. Electronic applications accepted. *Financial support:* In 2007–08, 108 teaching assistantships with partial tuition reimbursements (averaging $10,213 per year) were awarded. *Faculty research:* Organizational psychology, reading comprehension and mathematical ability, drug addiction and relapse, gender issues and culture, memory, clinical psychology. *Unit head:* Dr. Harvey Marmurek, Chair, 519-824-4120 Ext. 53673, Fax: 519-837-8629, E-mail: marmurek@psy.uoguelph.ca. *Application contact:* Dr. Ian Newby-Clark, Graduate Coordinator, 519-824-4120 Ext. 53307, Fax: 519-837-8629, E-mail: newby-clark@psy.uogeulph.ca.

University of Hartford, College of Arts and Sciences, Department of Psychology, Program in Clinical Practices, West Hartford, CT 06117-1599. Offers clinical practices (Psy D); psychology (MA). *Accreditation:* APA. *Faculty:* 5 full-time (4 women), 6 part-time/adjunct (4 women). *Students:* 94 full-time (79 women), 60 part-time (51 women); includes 19 minority (5 African Americans, 1 American Indian/Alaska Native, 4 Asian Americans or Pacific Islanders, 9 Hispanic Americans), 3 international. Average age 29. 195 applicants, 41% accepted, 37 enrolled. In 2007, 34 master's, 38 doctorates awarded. *Degree requirements:* For master's, comprehensive exam, thesis optional. *Entrance requirements:* For master's, GRE General Test, GRE Subject Test, minimum GPA of 3.0, 3 letters of recommendation. Additional exam requirements/recommendations for international students: Required—TOEFL (minimum score 550 paper-based; 213 computer-based). *Application deadline:* For fall admission, 2/15 priority date for domestic students. Applications are processed on a rolling basis. Application fee: $45. Electronic applications accepted. *Expenses:* Tuition: Part-time $595 per credit. Required fees: $200 per term. *Financial support:* In 2007–08, 5 research assistantships (averaging $2,000 per year), 4 teaching assistantships (averaging $2,600 per year) were awarded. Financial award application deadline: 6/1; financial award applicants required to submit FAFSA. *Faculty research:* Attachment issues, child abuse prevention, master's psychologist issues, neuropsychology. *Unit head:* Dr. Tony Crespi, Director, 860-768-5081, Fax: 860-768-5292, E-mail: crespi@hartford.edu. *Application contact:* Reneé Murphy, Assistant Director of Graduate Admissions, 860-768-4371, Fax: 860-768-5160, E-mail: rmurphy@hartford.edu.

University of Hawaii at Manoa, Graduate Division, Colleges of Arts and Sciences, College of Social Sciences, Department of Psychology, Honolulu, HI 96822. Offers clinical psychology (PhD); community and cultural psychology (PhD); community and culture (MA); psychology (MA, PhD, Graduate Certificate). *Accreditation:* APA (one or more programs are accredited). Part-time programs available. *Faculty:* 35 full-time (13 women), 8 part-time/adjunct (1 woman). *Students:* 86 full-time (61 women), 7 part-time (5 women); includes 30 minority (1 African American, 1 American Indian/Alaska Native, 26 Asian Americans or Pacific Islanders, 2 Hispanic Americans), 11 international. 199 applicants, 14% accepted, 16 enrolled.Terminal master's awarded for partial completion of doctoral program. *Median time to degree:* Of those who began their doctoral program in fall 1999, 83% received their degree in 8 years or less. *Degree requirements:* For master's, comprehensive exam, thesis; for doctorate, comprehensive exam, thesis/dissertation. *Entrance requirements:* For master's and doctorate, GRE General Test, GRE Subject Test. Additional exam requirements/recommendations for international students: Required—TOEFL (minimum score 600 paper-based; 250 computer-based; 100 iBT), IELTS (minimum score 7). *Application deadline:* For fall admission, 1/1 for domestic and international students. Application fee: $50. *Financial support:* In 2007–08, 44 research assistantships (averaging $16,926 per year), 18 teaching assistantships (averaging $14,042 per year) were awarded; career-related internships or fieldwork, institutionally sponsored loans, and tuition waivers (full and partial) also available. Financial award application deadline: 1/1. *Faculty research:* Cross-cultural psychology, health psychology, marine mammals, child/adult psychopathology. Total annual research expenditures: $1.1 million. *Application contact:* Catherine Sophian, Graduate Chair, 808-956-8414, Fax: 808-956-4700, E-mail: csophian@hawaii.edu.

University of Houston, College of Liberal Arts and Social Sciences, Department of Psychology, Houston, TX 77204. Offers clinical psychology (PhD); industrial/organizational psychology (PhD); psychology (MA); social psychology (PhD). *Accreditation:* APA (one or more programs are accredited). *Faculty:* 24 full-time (9 women), 3 part-time/adjunct (1 woman). *Students:* 102 full-time (77 women), 16 part-time (12 women); includes 22 minority (4 African Americans, 8 Asian Americans or Pacific Islanders, 10 Hispanic Americans), 8 international. Average age 27. 187 applicants, 13% accepted, 22 enrolled. In 2007, 10 master's, 12 doctorates awarded. *Degree requirements:* For doctorate, thesis/dissertation. *Entrance requirements:* For doctorate, GRE General Test, minimum GPA of 3.0. *Application deadline:* For fall admission, 1/1 for domestic students. Application fee: $40 ($75 for international students). *Expenses:* Tuition, state resident: full-time $6,297; part-time $262 per credit. Tuition, nonresident: full-time $12,969; part-time $540 per credit. Required fees: $2,696. *Financial support:* In 2007–08, 12 fellowships with full tuition reimbursements (averaging $11,200 per year), 13 research assistantships with full tuition reimbursements (averaging $10,050 per year), 74 teaching assistantships with full tuition reimbursements (averaging $10,250 per year) were awarded; career-related internships or fieldwork, Federal Work-Study, institutionally sponsored loans, scholarships/grants, health care benefits, and unspecified assistantships also available. Support available to part-time students. Financial award application deadline: 2/1; financial award applicants required to submit FAFSA. *Faculty research:* Health psychology, depression, child/family process, organizational effectiveness, close relationships. *Unit head:* Dr. David Francis, Chairperson, 713-743-7036, Fax: 713-743-8588, E-mail: dfrancis@uh.edu. *Application contact:* Sherry A. Berun, Coordinator—Academic Affairs, 713-743-8508, Fax: 713-743-8588, E-mail: sherryr@uh.edu.

University of Houston–Clear Lake, School of Human Sciences and Humanities, Programs in Human Sciences, Houston, TX 77058-1098. Offers behavioral sciences (MA), including behavioral sciences-general, behavioral sciences-psychology, behavioral sciences-sociology; clinical psychology (MA); criminology (MA); cross-cultural studies (MA); family therapy (MA); fitness and human performance (MA); school psychology (MA). *Accreditation:* AAMFT/COAMFTE. Part-time and evening/weekend programs available. Postbaccalaureate distance learning degree programs offered (minimal on-campus study). *Degree requirements:* For master's, thesis or alternative. *Entrance requirements:* For master's, GRE General Test. Additional exam requirements/recommendations for international students: Required—TOEFL (minimum score 550 paper-based; 213 computer-based). Electronic applications accepted. *Faculty research:* Smoking cessation, adolescent sexuality, white collar crime, serial murder, human factors/human computer interaction.

University of Indianapolis, Graduate Programs, School of Psychological Sciences, Indianapolis, IN 46227-3697. Offers clinical psychology (Psy D); clinical psychology/mental health counseling (MA). *Accreditation:* APA. *Faculty:* 7 full-time (2 women). *Students:* 107 full-time (90 women), 44 part-time (31 women); includes 4 minority (3 African Americans, 1 Hispanic American), 6 international. Average age 27. *Degree requirements:* For master's, practicum; for doctorate, comprehensive exam, thesis/dissertation, 1200 hours of clinical practicum, 2000 hour internship. *Entrance requirements:* For master's, GRE, 3 letters of recommendation; for doctorate, GRE, minimum GPA of 3.0, 18 hours of course work in psychology, 3 letters of recommendation. Additional exam requirements/recommendations for international students: Required—TOEFL (minimum score 550 paper-based; 213 computer-based). *Application deadline:* For fall admission, 2/25 for domestic students. Application fee: $50. *Financial support:* Federal Work-Study available. *Unit head:* Dr. E. John McIlvried, Dean, 317-788-3247, Fax: 317-788-3480, E-mail: jmcilvried@uindy.edu.

University of Kansas, Research and Graduate Studies, College of Liberal Arts and Sciences, Department of Applied Behavioral Science and Department of Psychology, Program in Clinical Child Psychology, Lawrence, KS 66045. Offers PhD. *Accreditation:* APA. *Faculty:* 16. *Students:* 22 full-time (13 women), 5 part-time (4 women); includes 7 minority (1 African American, 1 American Indian/Alaska Native, 4 Asian Americans or Pacific Islanders, 1 Hispanic American). Average age 28. 95 applicants, 4% accepted, 4 enrolled. In 2007, 2 doctorates awarded. *Degree requirements:* For doctorate, comprehensive exam, thesis/dissertation, clinical internship.

Clinical Psychology

University of Kansas (continued)
Entrance requirements: For doctorate, GRE General Test, GRE Subject Test, minimum GPA of 3.5. Additional exam requirements/recommendations for international students: Required—TOEFL. *Application deadline:* For fall admission, 12/1 for domestic and international students. Application fee: $55 ($60 for international students). Electronic applications accepted. *Expenses:* Tuition, state resident: full-time $5,838. Tuition, nonresident: full-time $13,409. Tuition and fees vary according to program. *Financial support:* Fellowships with tuition reimbursements, research assistantships with tuition reimbursements, teaching assistantships with tuition reimbursements, career-related internships or fieldwork, scholarships/grants, traineeships, health care benefits, and unspecified assistantships available. Financial award application deadline: 12/1. *Faculty research:* Pediatric psychology, serious emotional disorders, responses to disasters and terrorism, anxiety, stress, and coping, psychotherapy with children. *Unit head:* Michael Roberts, Director, 785-864-4226, Fax: 785-864-5024, E-mail: mroberts@ku.edu. *Application contact:* Graduate Admissions, 785-864-4226, Fax: 785-864-5024, E-mail: ccpp@ku.edu.

University of Kansas, Research and Graduate Studies, College of Liberal Arts and Sciences, Department of Psychology, Lawrence, KS 66045. Offers clinical child psychology (MA, PhD); psychology (MA, PhD). *Accreditation:* APA (one or more programs are accredited). *Faculty:* 36. *Students:* 113 full-time (81 women), 15 part-time (11 women); includes 22 minority (5 African Americans, 3 American Indian/Alaska Native, 10 Asian Americans or Pacific Islanders, 4 Hispanic Americans), 8 international. Average age 27. 311 applicants, 9% accepted, 10 enrolled. In 2007, 16 master's, 17 doctorates awarded. *Degree requirements:* For master's, thesis; for doctorate, comprehensive exam, thesis/dissertation. *Entrance requirements:* For doctorate, GRE General Test, minimum GPA of 3.0. Additional exam requirements/recommendations for international students: Required—TOEFL. *Application deadline:* For fall admission, 1/15 for domestic and international students. Application fee: $55 ($60 for international students). Electronic applications accepted. *Expenses:* Tuition, state resident: full-time $5,838. Tuition, nonresident: full-time $13,409. Tuition and fees vary according to program. *Financial support:* Fellowships with full tuition reimbursements, research assistantships with partial tuition reimbursements, teaching assistantships with full and partial tuition reimbursements, career-related internships or fieldwork and unspecified assistantships available. Financial award application deadline: 1/4; financial award applicants required to submit FAFSA. *Faculty research:* Cognitive psychology, methodology and statistics, developmental clinical/health psychology. *Unit head:* Greg Simpson, Chair, 785-864-9821, Fax: 785-864-5696, E-mail: gsimpson@ku.edu. *Application contact:* Cathy L. O'Keefe, Graduate Admissions Officer, 785-864-4195, Fax: 785-864-5696, E-mail: psycgrad@ku.edu.

University of Kentucky, Graduate School, College of Arts and Sciences, Program in Psychology, Lexington, KY 40506-0032. Offers clinical psychology (MA); experimental psychology (MA). *Accreditation:* APA (one or more programs are accredited). *Faculty:* 39 full-time (12 women), 1 part-time/adjunct (0 women). *Students:* 73 full-time (58 women), 6 part-time (4 women); includes 9 minority (4 African Americans, 1 American Indian/Alaska Native, 4 Hispanic Americans), 2 international. Average age 29. 286 applicants, 5% accepted, 14 enrolled. In 2007, 10 master's, 9 doctorates awarded. *Median time to degree:* Of those who began their doctoral program in fall 1999, 87% received their degree in 8 years or less. *Degree requirements:* For master's, comprehensive exam, thesis; for doctorate, comprehensive exam, thesis/dissertation. *Entrance requirements:* For master's, GRE General Test, minimum undergraduate GPA of 2.75; for doctorate, GRE General Test, minimum graduate GPA of 3.0. Additional exam requirements/recommendations for international students: Required—TOEFL (minimum score 550 paper-based; 213 computer-based). *Application deadline:* For fall admission, 7/17 for domestic students, 2/1 priority date for international students; for spring admission, 12/13 for domestic students, 6/15 priority date for international students. Application fee: $50 ($65 for international students). Electronic applications accepted. *Expenses:* Tuition, state resident: part-time $437 per credit hour. Tuition, nonresident: part-time $931 per credit hour. *Financial support:* In 2007–08, 64 students received support, including 20 fellowships with full tuition reimbursements available (averaging $3,461 per year), 30 research assistantships with full tuition reimbursements available (averaging $14,000 per year), 24 teaching assistantships with full tuition reimbursements available (averaging $14,000 per year); career-related internships or fieldwork, Federal Work-Study, institutionally sponsored loans, scholarships/grants, traineeships, health care benefits, tuition waivers (partial), and unspecified assistantships also available. Support available to part-time students. Financial award application deadline: 3/15; financial award applicants required to submit FAFSA. *Faculty research:* Psychopharmacology and teratology, behavioral neuroscience, social psychology, cognitive psychology, development and developmental psychobiology. *Unit head:* Dr. David Berry, Director of Graduate Studies, 859-257-5451, Fax: 859-323-1979, E-mail: dtrb@pop.uky.edu. *Application contact:* Dr. Brian Jackson, Senior Associate Dean, 859-257-4667, Fax: 859-257-4676, E-mail: brian.jackson@uky.edu.

University of La Verne, College of Arts and Sciences, Department of Psychology, Program in Clinical-Community Psychology, La Verne, CA 91750-4443. Offers Psy D. Part-time programs available. *Faculty:* 8 full-time (1 woman), 5 part-time/adjunct (1 woman). *Students:* 47 full-time (38 women), 22 part-time (19 women); includes 40 minority (7 African Americans, 11 American Indian/Alaska Native, 4 Asian Americans or Pacific Islanders, 18 Hispanic Americans). Average age 29. In 2007, 20 degrees awarded. *Degree requirements:* For doctorate, thesis/dissertation, clinical internship, competency exams, practicum, personal psychotherapy. *Entrance requirements:* For doctorate, minimum GPA of 3.25 undergraduate, 3.65 graduate; 3 recommendations; interview; curriculum vitae. Additional exam requirements/recommendations for international students: Required—TOEFL (minimum score 600 paper-based; 250 computer-based). *Application deadline:* For fall admission, 1/15 for domestic and international students. Application fee: $75. *Expenses: Contact institution.* Tuition and fees vary according to course load and program. *Financial support:* Career-related internships or fieldwork, institutionally sponsored loans, scholarships/grants, and unspecified assistantships available. Financial award application deadline: 3/2; financial award applicants required to submit FAFSA. *Unit head:* Dr. Raymond Scott, Chairperson, 909-593-3511 Ext. 4181, E-mail: rscott@ulv.edu. *Application contact:* Connie Hamlow, Admissions Information Specialist, 909-593-3511 Ext. 4244, Fax: 909-392-2761, E-mail: gradadmission@ulv.edu.

University of Louisville, Graduate School, College of Arts and Sciences, Department of Psychological and Brain Sciences, Program in Clinical Psychology, Louisville, KY 40292-0001. Offers MA, PhD. *Accreditation:* APA. *Students:* 42 full-time (31 women), 1 (woman) part-time; includes 2 minority (1 African American, 1 Asian American or Pacific Islander), 1 international. Average age 29. In 2007, 1 master's, 6 doctorates awarded. *Degree requirements:* For doctorate, thesis/dissertation. *Entrance requirements:* For doctorate, GRE General Test. *Application deadline:* Applications are processed on a rolling basis. Application fee: $50. *Financial support:* Career-related internships or fieldwork available. *Unit head:* Dr. Richard Lewine, Director of Clinical Training, 502-852-3243, Fax: 502-852-8904, E-mail: rrlewi02@louisville.edu.

University of Maine, Graduate School, College of Liberal Arts and Sciences, Department of Psychology, Orono, ME 04469. Offers clinical psychology (PhD); developmental psychology (MA); experimental psychology (MA, PhD); social psychology (MA). *Accreditation:* APA (one or more programs are accredited). *Faculty:* 24. *Students:* 28 full-time (17 women), 10 part-time (6 women); includes 2 minority (1 American Indian/Alaska Native, 1 Hispanic American), 1 international. Average age 29. 129 applicants, 9% accepted, 8 enrolled. In 2007, 5 master's, 2 doctorates awarded. *Degree requirements:* For master's, thesis; for doctorate, thesis/dissertation. *Entrance requirements:* For master's and doctorate, GRE General Test, GRE Subject Test. Additional exam requirements/recommendations for international students: Required—TOEFL. *Application deadline:* For fall admission, 2/1 priority date for domestic students. Applications are processed on a rolling basis. Application fee: $60. Electronic applications accepted. *Financial support:* In 2007–08, 3 research assistantships with tuition reimbursements (averaging $13,400 per year), 21 teaching assistantships with tuition reimbursements (averaging $9,010 per year) were awarded; fellowships with tuition reimbursements, Federal Work-Study, institutionally sponsored loans, and tuition waivers (full and partial) also available. Financial award application deadline: 3/1. *Faculty research:* Social development, hypertension and aging, attitude change, self-confidence in achievement situations, health psychology. *Unit head:* Dr. Jeffrey Hecker, Chair, 207-581-2032, Fax: 207-581-6128. *Application contact:* Scott G. Delcourt, Associate Dean of the Graduate School, 207-581-3219, Fax: 207-581-3232, E-mail: graduate@maine.edu.

University of Manitoba, Faculty of Graduate Studies, Faculty of Arts, Department of Psychology, Winnipeg, MB R3T 2N2, Canada. Offers clinical psychology (PhD); psychology (MA, PhD). *Accreditation:* APA (one or more programs are accredited). *Degree requirements:* For master's, thesis; for doctorate, one foreign language, thesis/dissertation. *Entrance requirements:* For master's and doctorate, GRE General Test.

University of Maryland, College Park, Graduate Studies, College of Behavioral and Social Sciences, Department of Psychology, College Park, MD 20742. Offers clinical psychology (PhD); developmental psychology (PhD); experimental psychology (PhD); industrial psychology (MA, MS, PhD); social psychology (PhD). *Accreditation:* APA (one or more programs are accredited). *Faculty:* 53 full-time (23 women), 12 part-time/adjunct (6 women). *Students:* 92 full-time (70 women), 4 part-time (3 women); includes 15 minority (2 African Americans, 1 American Indian/Alaska Native, 6 Asian Americans or Pacific Islanders, 6 Hispanic Americans), 12 international. 609 applicants, 4% accepted, 13 enrolled. In 2007, 13 master's, 18 doctorates awarded. *Median time to degree:* Of those who began their doctoral program in fall 1999, 71% received their degree in 8 years or less. *Degree requirements:* For master's, thesis; for doctorate, variable foreign language requirement, comprehensive exam, thesis/dissertation. *Entrance requirements:* For master's and doctorate, GRE General Test, GRE Subject Test, minimum GPA of 3.5, research and/or work experience, 3 letters of recommendation. *Application deadline:* For fall admission, 12/15 for domestic students, 2/1 for international students. Applications are processed on a rolling basis. Application fee: $60. Electronic applications accepted. *Financial support:* In 2007–08, 11 fellowships with full tuition reimbursements (averaging $15,736 per year), 9 research assistantships (averaging $15,312 per year), 56 teaching assistantships with tuition reimbursements (averaging $15,292 per year) were awarded; career-related internships or fieldwork, Federal Work-Study, and scholarships/grants also available. Support available to part-time students. Financial award applicants required to submit FAFSA. *Faculty research:* Social stereotyping and prejudice, anxiety disorders, auditory neuroethology, counseling and social psychology. Total annual research expenditures: $4.4 million. *Unit head:* Thomas S. Wallsten, Chair, 301-405-5862, Fax: 301-314-9566, E-mail: twallsten@psyc.umd.edu. *Application contact:* Dean of Graduate School, 301-405-0358, Fax: 301-314-9305.

University of Massachusetts Amherst, Graduate School, College of Social and Behavioral Sciences, Department of Psychology, Amherst, MA 01003. Offers clinical psychology (MS, PhD). *Accreditation:* APA (one or more programs are accredited). *Faculty:* 51 full-time (24 women). *Students:* 57 full-time (39 women), 15 part-time (9 women); includes 12 minority (5 African Americans, 3 Asian Americans or Pacific Islanders, 4 Hispanic Americans), 14 international. Average age 28. 303 applicants, 6% accepted, 9 enrolled. In 2007, 7 master's, 16 doctorates awarded. Terminal master's awarded for partial completion of doctoral program. *Degree requirements:* For master's, thesis; for doctorate, thesis/dissertation. *Entrance requirements:* For master's and doctorate, GRE General Test, 3 letters of recommendation. Additional exam requirements/recommendations for international students: Required—TOEFL (minimum score 530 paper-based; 197 computer-based). *Application deadline:* For fall admission, 12/1 priority date for domestic and international students. Applications are processed on a rolling basis. Application fee: $50 ($65 for international students). Electronic applications accepted. *Expenses:* Tuition, state resident: full-time $2,640; part-time $110 per credit. Tuition, nonresident: full-time $9,936; part-time $414 per credit. Required fees: $7,455. One-time fee: $332. Tuition and fees vary according to course load, campus/location, program and reciprocity agreements. *Financial support:* In 2007–08, 7 fellowships with full tuition reimbursements (averaging $16,610 per year), 86 research assistantships with full tuition reimbursements (averaging $8,002 per year), 52 teaching assistantships with full tuition reimbursements (averaging $9,449 per year) were awarded; career-related internships or fieldwork, Federal Work-Study, scholarships/grants, traineeships, and unspecified assistantships also available. Support available to part-time students. Financial award application deadline: 12/15. *Unit head:* Dr. Melinda Novak, Chair, 413-545-2387, Fax: 413-545-0996, E-mail: mnovak@psych.umass.edu. *Application contact:* Graduate Secretary, 413-545-2503.

University of Massachusetts Boston, Office of Graduate Studies, College of Liberal Arts, Program in Clinical Psychology, Boston, MA 02125-3393. Offers PhD. *Accreditation:* APA. Part-time and evening/weekend programs available. *Degree requirements:* For doctorate, comprehensive exam, thesis/dissertation, oral exams, practicum. *Entrance requirements:* For doctorate, GRE General Test, GRE Subject Test, minimum GPA of 2.75. *Faculty research:* Community psychology, psychology, racism and mental health, gender and culture, posttraumatic stress disorder.

University of Massachusetts Dartmouth, Graduate School, College of Arts and Sciences, Department of Psychology, North Dartmouth, MA 02747-2300. Offers clinical psychology (MA); general psychology (MA). Part-time programs available. *Faculty:* 16 full-time (6 women), 8 part-time/adjunct (5 women). *Students:* 17 full-time (13 women), 29 part-time (22 women); includes 5 minority (2 African Americans, 2 Asian Americans or Pacific Islanders, 1 Hispanic American). Average age 27. 68 applicants, 41% accepted, 18 enrolled. In 2007, 15 degrees awarded. *Degree requirements:* For master's, thesis (for some programs). *Entrance requirements:* For master's, GRE General Test, minimum GPA of 2.75, 3 letters of recommendation. Additional exam requirements/recommendations for international students: Required—TOEFL (minimum score 500 paper-based). *Application deadline:* For fall admission, 3/31 for domestic students, 1/31 for international students. Application fee: $40 ($60 for international students). Electronic applications accepted. *Expenses:* Tuition, state resident: full-time $2,071; part-time $86 per credit. Tuition, nonresident: full-time $8,099; part-time $337 per credit. Part-time tuition and fees vary according to course load and program. *Financial support:* In 2007–08, 10 teaching assistantships with full tuition reimbursements (averaging $3,500 per year) were awarded; research assistantships with full tuition reimbursements, career-related internships or fieldwork, Federal Work-Study, and unspecified assistantships also available. Support available to part-time students. Financial award application deadline: 3/1; financial award applicants required to submit FAFSA. *Faculty research:* Psychosocial stress, intimate relationships, sports psychology, behavior modification. Total annual research expenditures: $52,000. *Unit head:* Dr. Paul Donnelly, Director, Clinical Psychology, 508-999-8334, E-mail: pdonnelly@umassd.edu. *Application contact:* Carol Novo, Graduate Admissions Officer, 508-999-8604, Fax: 508-999-8183, E-mail: graduate@umassd.edu.

University of Memphis, Graduate School, College of Arts and Sciences, Department of Psychology, Memphis, TN 38152. Offers clinical psychology (PhD); experimental psychology (PhD); general psychology (MS); school psychology (MA, PhD). Part-time programs available. *Faculty:* 29 full-time (8 women), 4 part-time/adjunct (1 woman). *Students:* 92 full-time (56 women), 29 part-time (19 women); includes 18 minority (11 African Americans, 3 Asian Americans or Pacific Islanders, 4 Hispanic Americans), 10 international. Average age 28. 269 applicants, 16% accepted, 37 enrolled. In 2007, 14 master's, 8 doctorates awarded. Terminal master's awarded for partial completion of doctoral program. *Degree requirements:* For master's, comprehensive exam, thesis (for some programs), oral exam (MS); for doctorate, thesis/dissertation, internship. *Entrance requirements:* For master's, GRE General Test, 18 undergraduate hours in psychology, minimum GPA of 2.5; for doctorate, GRE General Test, GRE Subject Test. *Application deadline:* For fall admission, 2/1 for domestic students. Applications are processed on a rolling basis. Application fee: $35 ($60 for international students). *Expenses:* Tuition, state resident: full-time $6,990; part-time $377 per hour. Tuition, nonresident: full-time $17,818; part-time $830 per hour. Tuition and fees vary according to course load and program. *Financial support:* In 2007–08, 75 research assistantships with full tuition reimbursements (averaging $4,500 per year), 13 teaching assistantships with full tuition reimbursements (averaging $4,600 per year) were awarded; fellowships with full tuition reimbursements, tuition waivers (partial) and unspecified assistantships also available. *Faculty research:* Psychotherapy and psychopathology, behavioral medicine and community psychology, child and family studies, cognitive and social processes, neuropsychology and behavioral neuroscience. *Unit head:* Dr. Arthur C. Graesser, Chair, 901-678-2146, Fax: 901-678-2579, E-mail: a-graesser@memphis.edu. *Application contact:* Dr. Robert Cohen, Graduate Studies Coordinator, 901-678-2146.

University of Miami, Graduate School, College of Arts and Sciences, Department of Psychology, Coral Gables, FL 33124. Offers adult clinical (PhD); behavioral neuroscience (PhD); child clinical (PhD); developmental psychology (PhD); health clinical (PhD); psychology (MS). *Accreditation:* APA (one or more programs are accredited). *Faculty:* 27 full-time (13 women). *Students:* 88 full-time (69 women); includes 28 minority (5 African Americans, 7 Asian Americans or Pacific Islanders, 16 Hispanic Americans), 5 international. Average age 27. 340 applicants, 6% accepted, 14 enrolled. In 2007, 13 master's, 15 doctorates awarded. *Median time to degree:* Of those who began their doctoral program in fall 1999, 88% received their degree in 8 years or less. *Degree requirements:* For doctorate, comprehensive exam, thesis/dissertation. *Entrance requirements:* For doctorate, GRE General Test, minimum GPA of 3.5. Additional exam requirements/recommendations for international students: Required—TOEFL. *Application deadline:* For fall admission, 12/1 for domestic and international students. Application fee: $50. Electronic applications accepted. *Financial support:* In 2007–08, 88 students received support, including 9 fellowships with full tuition reimbursements available (averaging $22,000 per year), 24 research assistantships with full tuition reimbursements available (averaging $22,000 per year), 18 teaching assistantships with full tuition reimbursements available (averaging $16,500 per year); career-related internships or fieldwork, institutionally sponsored loans, scholarships/grants, and traineeships also available. Financial award applicants required to submit FAFSA. *Faculty research:* Behavioral factors in cardiovascular disease and cancer adult psychopathology, developmental disabilities, social and emotional development, mechanisms of coping. Total annual research expenditures: $12.4 million. *Unit head:* Dr. A. Rodney Wellens, Chairman, 305-284-2814, Fax: 305-284-3402. *Application contact:* Prof. Phil McCabe, Director of Graduate Studies, 305-284-2814, Fax: 305-284-3402, E-mail: inquire@psy.miami.edu.

University of Michigan, Horace H. Rackham School of Graduate Studies, College of Literature, Science, and the Arts, Department of Psychology, Ann Arbor, MI 48109. Offers biopsychology (PhD); clinical psychology (PhD); cognition and perception (PhD); developmental psychology (PhD); personality and social contexts (PhD); social psychology (PhD). *Accreditation:* APA. *Faculty:* 86 full-time, 69 part-time/adjunct. *Students:* 157 full-time (112 women); includes 51 minority (21 African Americans, 1 American Indian/Alaska Native, 17 Asian Americans or Pacific Islanders, 12 Hispanic Americans), 32 international. Average age 25. 698 applicants, 9% accepted, 29 enrolled. In 2007, 25 degrees awarded. *Degree requirements:* For doctorate, comprehensive exam, thesis/dissertation, oral defense of dissertation, preliminary exam. *Entrance requirements:* For doctorate, GRE General Test (optional), GRE Subject Test (optional). Additional exam requirements/recommendations for international students: Required—TOEFL. *Application deadline:* For fall admission, 12/15 for domestic students. Application fee: $60 ($75 for international students). Electronic applications accepted. *Financial support:* Fellowships with full tuition reimbursements, research assistantships with full tuition reimbursements, teaching assistantships with full tuition reimbursements, career-related internships or fieldwork available. Financial award application deadline: 4/15. *Unit head:* Theresa Lee, Chair, 734-764-7429. *Application contact:* Laurie Brannan, Psychology Student Academic Affairs, 731-764-2580, Fax: 734-615-7584, E-mail: psych.saa@umich.edu.

University of Michigan–Dearborn, College of Arts, Sciences, and Letters, Department of Behavioral Sciences, Dearborn, MI 48128-1491. Offers clinical health psychology (MS); health psychology (MS). Part-time programs available. *Faculty:* 8 full-time (4 women), 1 part-time/adjunct (0 women). *Students:* 15 full-time (11 women), 13 part-time (10 women); includes 9 minority (2 African Americans, 1 American Indian/Alaska Native, 4 Asian Americans or Pacific Islanders, 2 Hispanic Americans). Average age 34. 57 applicants, 35% accepted, 16 enrolled. In 2007, 9 degrees awarded. *Degree requirements:* For master's, thesis or alternative, oral defense of thesis. *Entrance requirements:* For master's, GRE, 3 letters of recommendation, statement of purpose. Additional exam requirements/recommendations for international students: Required—TOEFL (minimum score 560 paper-based; 220 computer-based). *Application deadline:* For fall admission, 3/15 for domestic and international students. Application fee: $60 ($75 for international students). *Expenses:* Tuition, state resident: part-time $318 per credit hour. Tuition, nonresident: part-time $722 per credit hour. Tuition and fees vary according to course load and program. *Financial support:* In 2007–08, 4 students received support. Scholarships/grants available. *Faculty research:* Cardiovascular reactivity, coping, addiction, psychoneuroimmunology. *Unit head:* Dr. Pam McAuslan, Program Director, 313-593-5376, E-mail: pmcausla@umd.umich.edu. *Application contact:* Carol Ligienza, Administrative Coordinator, CASL Graduate Programs, 313-593-1183, Fax: 313-583-6498, E-mail: caslgrad@umd.umich.edu.

University of Minnesota, Twin Cities Campus, Graduate School, College of Liberal Arts, Department of Psychology, Program in Clinical Psychology, Minneapolis, MN 55455-0213. Offers PhD. *Accreditation:* APA. *Faculty:* 7 full-time (1 woman). *Students:* 29 full-time (19 women); includes 2 minority (both Hispanic Americans), 3 international. 167 applicants, 6% accepted, 5 enrolled. In 2007, 4 doctorates awarded. *Median time to degree:* Of those who began their doctoral program in fall 1999, 75% received their degree in 8 years or less. *Degree requirements:* For doctorate, comprehensive exam, thesis/dissertation, internship. *Entrance requirements:* For doctorate, GRE General Test, minimum GPA of 3.5; 12 credits of upper-level psychology courses, including statistics or psychological measurement; previous course work in abnormal psychology. Additional exam requirements/recommendations for international students: Required—TOEFL (minimum score 550 paper-based; 213 computer-based; 79 iBT). *Application deadline:* For fall admission, 12/1 for domestic and international students. Application fee: $55 ($75 for international students). *Financial support:* In 2007–08, fellowships with full tuition reimbursements (averaging $21,000 per year), research assistantships with full tuition reimbursements (averaging $12,254 per year), teaching assistantships with full tuition reimbursements (averaging $12,254 per year) were awarded; career-related internships or fieldwork, traineeships, and tuition waivers (partial) also available. Financial award application deadline: 12/1. *Unit head:* Christopher Patrick, Area Director, 612-626-9918. *Application contact:* Coordinator, 612-624-4181, Fax: 612-626-2079, E-mail: psyapply@tc.umn.edu.

University of Mississippi, Graduate School, College of Liberal Arts, Department of Psychology, Oxford, University, MS 38677. Offers clinical psychology (PhD); experimental psychology (PhD); psychology (MA). *Accreditation:* APA (one or more programs are accredited). *Faculty:* 16 full-time (7 women), 5 part-time/adjunct (3 women). *Students:* 45 full-time (34 women), 8 part-time (6 women); includes 11 minority (8 African Americans, 1 American Indian/Alaska Native, 2 Hispanic Americans). In 2007, 6 master's, 13 doctorates awarded. *Degree requirements:* For master's, thesis; for doctorate, thesis/dissertation. *Entrance requirements:* For master's, GRE General Test, minimum GPA of 3.0; for doctorate, GRE General Test. Additional exam requirements/recommendations for international students: Required—TOEFL. *Application deadline:* For fall admission, 1/15 for domestic students; for spring admission, 10/1 for domestic students. Applications are processed on a rolling basis. Application fee: $25. Electronic applications accepted. *Expenses:* Tuition, state resident: full-time $4,932. Tuition, nonresident: full-time $11,436. *Financial support:* Scholarships/grants available. Financial award application deadline: 3/1; financial award applicants required to submit FAFSA. *Unit head:* Dr. Michael T. Allen, Chairman, 662-915-5190, Fax: 662-915-5398, E-mail: mta1@olemiss.edu.

University of Missouri–Kansas City, College of Arts and Sciences, Department of Psychology, Kansas City, MO 64110-2499. Offers psychology (MA, PhD), including clinical psychology (PhD), community psychology (PhD). *Accreditation:* APA. *Faculty:* 16 full-time (12 women). *Students:* 14 full-time (10 women), 10 part-time (8 women); includes 2 minority (1 African American, 1 Hispanic American). Average age 31. 72 applicants, 6% accepted, 3 enrolled. In 2007, 4 master's, 4 doctorates awarded. Terminal master's awarded for partial completion of doctoral program. *Degree requirements:* For master's, thesis; for doctorate, comprehensive exam, thesis/dissertation, residency. *Entrance requirements:* For master's, GRE, minimum GPA of 3.5, letter of recommendation; for doctorate, GRE, minimum GPA of 3.25. Additional exam requirements/recommendations for international students: Required—TOEFL. *Application deadline:* For fall admission, 1/15 for domestic and international students. Applications are processed on a rolling basis. Application fee: $35 ($50 for international students). Electronic applications accepted. *Expenses:* Tuition, state resident: part-time $287 per hour. Tuition, nonresident: part-time $741 per hour. Required fees: $31 per hour. Tuition and fees vary according to program. *Financial support:* In 2007–08, 10 research assistantships (averaging $13,294 per year), 9 teaching assistantships (averaging $12,083 per year) were awarded; career-related internships or fieldwork, Federal Work-Study, and institutionally sponsored loans also available. Support available to part-time students. Financial award application deadline: 3/1; financial award applicants required to submit FAFSA. *Faculty research:* HIV/AIDS research group, psycho-oncology, sensory and cognitive neuroscience, cognitive psychophysiology, obesity and related metabolic disorders. Total annual research expenditures: $666,164. *Unit head:* Dr. Diane Filion, Chairperson, 816-235-1061. *Application contact:* 816-235-1111.

University of Missouri–St. Louis, College of Arts and Sciences, Department of Psychology, St. Louis, MO 63121. Offers behavioral neuroscience (PhD); clinical psychology respecialization (Certificate); community psychology (PhD); general psychology (MA); industrial/organizational psychology (PhD). *Accreditation:* APA (one or more programs are accredited). Evening/weekend programs available. *Faculty:* 20 full-time (9 women), 2 part-time/adjunct (both women). *Students:* 51 full-time (40 women), 22 part-time (16 women); includes 5 minority (1 African American, 3 Asian Americans or Pacific Islanders, 1 Hispanic American), 2 international. Average age 29. In 2007, 11 master's, 8 doctorates awarded. Terminal master's awarded for partial completion of doctoral program. *Degree requirements:* For doctorate, thesis/dissertation. *Entrance requirements:* For master's and doctorate, GRE General Test, GRE Subject Test, 3 letters of recommendation. Additional exam requirements/recommendations for international students: Required—TOEFL (minimum score 550 paper-based; 213 computer-based). *Application deadline:* For fall admission, 2/1 priority date for domestic students. Applications are processed on a rolling basis. Application fee: $35 ($40 for international students). Electronic applications accepted. *Financial support:* In 2007–08, 11 research assistantships with full and partial tuition reimbursements (averaging $11,333 per year), 18 teaching assistantships with full and partial tuition reimbursements (averaging $10,525 per year) were awarded; fellowships with full tuition reimbursements also available. *Faculty research:* Bereavement and loss, neuroscience, post-traumatic stress disorder, conflict and negotiation, social psychology. *Unit head:* Dr. Robert Calsyn, Chair, 314-516-5391, Fax: 314-516-5392, E-mail: umslpsychology@msx.umsl.edu. *Application contact:* 314-516-5458, Fax: 314-516-6996, E-mail: gradadm@umsl.edu.

The University of Montana, Graduate School, College of Arts and Sciences, Department of Psychology, Missoula, MT 59812-0002. Offers clinical psychology (PhD); experimental psychology (PhD), including animal behavior psychology, developmental psychology; school psychology (MA, PhD, Ed S). *Accreditation:* APA (one or more programs are accredited). Terminal master's awarded for partial completion of doctoral program. *Degree requirements:* For master's, thesis; for doctorate, thesis/dissertation. *Entrance requirements:* For master's, doctorate, and Ed S, GRE General Test. Additional exam requirements/recommendations for international students: Required—TOEFL.

University of Nevada, Las Vegas, Graduate College, College of Liberal Arts, Department of Psychology, Las Vegas, NV 89154-9900. Offers clinical psychology (PhD); experimental psychology (PhD); general psychology (MA). *Accreditation:* APA. Part-time programs available. *Faculty:* 24 full-time (7 women), 2 part-time/adjunct (both women). *Students:* 63 full-time (48 women), 16 part-time (10 women); includes 11 minority (4 African Americans, 1 Asian American or Pacific Islander, 6 Hispanic Americans), 3 international. 89 applicants, 13% accepted, 11 enrolled. In 2007, 11 master's, 9 doctorates awarded. *Degree requirements:* For master's, comprehensive exam, thesis, oral exam; for doctorate, comprehensive exam, thesis/dissertation, oral exam. *Entrance requirements:* For master's, GRE General Test, GRE Subject Test, minimum GPA of 3.2; for doctorate, GRE General Test, GRE Subject Test, minimum undergraduate GPA of 3.2, graduate 3.5. Additional exam requirements/recommendations for international students: Required—TOEFL (minimum score 550 paper-based; 213 computer-based; 80 iBT). *Application deadline:* For fall admission, 1/15 for domestic and international students. Application fee: $60 ($75 for international students). Electronic applications accepted. *Expenses:* Tuition, state resident: part-time $198 per credit. Tuition, nonresident: part-time $416 per credit. Required fees: $256 per semester. Tuition and fees vary according to course load and reciprocity agreements. *Financial support:* In 2007–08, 24 research assistantships with full and partial tuition reimbursements (averaging $12,000 per year), 25 teaching assistantships with partial tuition reimbursements (averaging $12,000 per year) were awarded; career-related internships or fieldwork, Federal Work-Study, institutionally sponsored loans, scholarships/grants, health care benefits, and unspecified assistantships also available. Support available to part-time students. Financial award application deadline: 3/1. *Unit head:* Dr. Mark Ashcraft, Chair, 702-895-0195. *Application contact:* Graduate College Admissions Evaluator, 702-895-3320, Fax: 702-895-4180, E-mail: gradcollege@unlv.edu.

University of Nevada, Reno, Graduate School, College of Liberal Arts, Department of Psychology, Program in Clinical Psychology, Reno, NV 89557. Offers PhD. *Students:* 34 full-time (26 women), 13 part-time (8 women); includes 1 African American, 2 Asian Americans or Pacific Islanders, 2 Hispanic Americans, 6 international. *Expenses:* Tuition, state resident: full-time $2,774; part-time $154 per credit. Tuition, nonresident: full-time $13,578; part-time $330 per credit. Required fees: $49 per semester. *Unit head:* Dr. William Follette, Program Director, 775-784-6828.

University of New Brunswick Fredericton, School of Graduate Studies, Faculty of Arts, Department of Psychology, Fredericton, NB E3B 5A3, Canada. Offers clinical psychology (PhD); experimental and applied psychology (MA). *Accreditation:* APA. Part-time programs available. *Faculty:* 14 full-time (9 women). *Students:* 43 full-time (38 women), 1 (woman) part-time. In 2007, 4 doctorates awarded. *Degree requirements:* For doctorate, thesis/dissertation. *Entrance requirements:* For master's, GRE, minimum GPA of 3.5; for doctorate, GRE, minimum GPA of 3.7. Additional exam requirements/recommendations for international students: Required—TOEFL, TWE. *Application deadline:* For fall admission, 1/15 priority date for domestic and international students. Applications are processed on a rolling basis. Application fee: $50 Canadian dollars. *Financial support:* In 2007–08, 4 fellowships (averaging $3,750 per year), 11 research assistantships, 11 teaching assistantships were awarded. Financial award application deadline: 1/15. *Faculty research:* Depression, adolescence, human sexuality, family violence, autism. *Unit head:* Dr. Janet Stoppard, Acting Director of Graduate Studies, 506-458-7994, Fax: 506-447-3063, E-mail: stoppard@unb.ca. *Application contact:* Theresa Mills, Graduate Secretary, 506-453-4707, Fax: 506-447-3063, E-mail: tmills@unb.ca.

University of New Brunswick Saint John, Faculty of Arts, Saint John, NB E2L 4L5, Canada. Offers applied and experimental psychology (PhD); clinical psychology (PhD); experimental psychology (MA). *Faculty:* 9 full-time (4 women), 1 part-time/adjunct (0 women). *Students:* 5 full-time (4 women). Average age 23. 4 applicants, 75% accepted, 2 enrolled. In 2007, 2 master's, 1 doctorate awarded. *Degree requirements:* For master's, thesis. *Entrance requirements:* For master's, GRE General Test. Additional exam requirements/recommendations for international students: Required—TOEFL (minimum score 550 paper-based). *Application deadline:* For fall admission, 2/1 for domestic students. Application fee: $50. Electronic applications accepted. *Financial support:* In 2007–08, 7 research assistantships (averaging $2,550 per year), 5 teaching assistantships (averaging $3,600 per year) were awarded; fellowships, unspecified assistantships also available. Support available to part-time students. Financial award application deadline: 2/1. *Faculty research:* Psychopharmacology and addictions; forensic psychology and criminal justice; interpersonal relations; perception and graphical perception; lie detection. *Unit head:* Dr. Enrico DiTommaso, Director of Graduate Studies, 506-648-5636,

Clinical Psychology

University of New Brunswick Saint John (continued)
Fax: 506-648-5780, E-mail: rico@unb.ca. *Application contact:* Frances Stevens, Secretary, 506-648-5640, Fax: 506-648-5780, E-mail: fstevens@unb.ca.

University of New Mexico, Graduate School, College of Arts and Sciences, Department of Psychology, Program in Clinical Psychology, Albuquerque, NM 87131-2039. Offers MS, PhD. *Accreditation:* APA (one or more programs are accredited). *Students:* 39 full-time (30 women), 7 part-time (all women); includes 9 minority (1 African American, 8 Hispanic Americans), 1 international. Average age 33. 7 applicants, 71% accepted, 5 enrolled. In 2007, 1 doctorate awarded. *Degree requirements:* For master's, thesis; for doctorate, comprehensive exam, thesis/dissertation, pre-doctoral internship. *Entrance requirements:* For doctorate, GRE General Test, GRE Subject Test (psychology), minimum GPA of 3.0. Additional exam requirements/recommendations for international students: Required—TOEFL. *Application deadline:* For fall admission, 1/15 priority date for domestic students. Applications are processed on a rolling basis. Application fee: $50. Electronic applications accepted. *Financial support:* In 2007–08, fellowships (averaging $27,492 per year), research assistantships with tuition reimbursements (averaging $14,000 per year), teaching assistantships with tuition reimbursements (averaging $12,283 per year) were awarded; career-related internships or fieldwork, Federal Work-Study, scholarships/grants, health care benefits, and unspecified assistantships also available. Financial award application deadline: 3/1; financial award applicants required to submit FAFSA. *Unit head:* Dr. Jane Elle Smith, Director of Clinical Training, 505-277-4121, Fax: 505-277-1394, E-mail: janellen@unm.edu. *Application contact:* Patricia Aragon-Mascurenas, Program Advisement Coordinator, 505-277-5009, Fax: 505-277-1394, E-mail: trishara@unm.edu.

The University of North Carolina at Chapel Hill, Graduate School, College of Arts and Sciences, Department of Psychology, Chapel Hill, NC 27599. Offers biological psychology (PhD); clinical psychology (PhD); cognitive psychology (PhD); developmental psychology (PhD); quantitative psychology (PhD); social psychology (PhD). *Accreditation:* APA. *Degree requirements:* For doctorate, comprehensive exam, thesis/dissertation. *Entrance requirements:* For doctorate, GRE General Test, minimum GPA of 3.0. Electronic applications accepted. *Faculty research:* Expressed emotion, cognitive development, social cognitive neuroscience, human memory personality.

The University of North Carolina at Charlotte, Graduate School, College of Arts and Sciences, Department of Psychology, Program in Community/Clinical Psychology, Charlotte, NC 28223-0001. Offers MA. *Students:* 10 full-time (9 women), 18 part-time (16 women); includes 8 minority (4 African Americans, 1 Asian American or Pacific Islander, 3 Hispanic Americans), 2 international. Average age 26. 94 applicants, 5% accepted, 5 enrolled. In 2007, 12 degrees awarded. *Degree requirements:* For master's, comprehensive exam, thesis. *Entrance requirements:* For master's, GRE General Test, GRE Subject Test, minimum GPA of 3.0 in undergraduate major, 2.8 overall. Additional exam requirements/recommendations for international students: Required—TOEFL (minimum score 557 paper-based; 220 computer-based). *Application deadline:* For fall admission, 3/1 for domestic and international students. Application fee: $55. Electronic applications accepted. *Expenses:* Tuition, state resident: full-time $2,855. Tuition, nonresident: full-time $13,062. Required fees: $1,692. *Financial support:* In 2007–08, 1 research assistantship (averaging $9,000 per year), 2 teaching assistantships (averaging $9,000 per year) were awarded; fellowships, career-related internships or fieldwork, Federal Work-Study, institutionally sponsored loans, scholarships/grants, and unspecified assistantships also available. Support available to part-time students. Financial award application deadline: 4/1; financial award applicants required to submit FAFSA. *Unit head:* Dr. Richard G. Tedeschi, Coordinator, 704-687-4754, Fax: 704-687-3096, E-mail: rtedesch@email.uncc.edu. *Application contact:* Kathy B. Giddings, Director of Graduate Admissions, 704-687-3366, Fax: 704-687-3279, E-mail: agidding@uncc.edu.

The University of North Carolina at Greensboro, Graduate School, College of Arts and Sciences, Department of Psychology, Greensboro, NC 27412-5001. Offers clinical psychology (MA, PhD); cognitive psychology (MA, PhD); developmental psychology (MA, PhD); social psychology (MA, PhD). *Accreditation:* APA (one or more programs are accredited). *Faculty:* 23 full-time (8 women). *Students:* 46 full-time (31 women), 13 part-time (10 women); includes 7 minority (3 African Americans, 1 American Indian/Alaska Native, 1 Asian American or Pacific Islander, 2 Hispanic Americans). 218 applicants, 7% accepted.Terminal master's awarded for partial completion of doctoral program. *Degree requirements:* For master's, comprehensive exam, thesis; for doctorate, one foreign language, thesis/dissertation, preliminary exam. *Entrance requirements:* For master's and doctorate, GRE General Test. Additional exam requirements/recommendations for international students: Required—TOEFL. *Application deadline:* For fall admission, 2/1 for domestic students. Application fee: $45. Electronic applications accepted. *Financial support:* Fellowships with full tuition reimbursements, research assistantships with full tuition reimbursements, teaching assistantships with full tuition reimbursements, unspecified assistantships available. *Faculty research:* Sensory and perceptual determinants; evoked potential: disorders, deafness, and development. *Unit head:* Dr. George Michel, Head, 336-336-5013, E-mail: gfmichel@uncg.edu. *Application contact:* Michelle Harkleroad, Director of Graduate Admissions, 336-334-4884, Fax: 336-334-4424, E-mail: mbharkle@uncg.edu.

University of North Dakota, Graduate School, College of Arts and Sciences, Department of Psychology, Grand Forks, ND 58202. Offers clinical psychology (PhD); counseling psychology (PhD); experimental psychology (PhD); forensic psychology (MA, MS); psychology (MA). *Accreditation:* APA (one or more programs are accredited). *Faculty:* 15 full-time (3 women). *Students:* 79 full-time (60 women), 15 part-time (11 women); includes 19 minority (2 African Americans, 15 American Indian/Alaska Native, 2 Asian Americans or Pacific Islanders), 9 international. 168 applicants, 24% accepted, 32 enrolled. In 2007, 4 master's, 16 doctorates awarded. *Degree requirements:* For master's, thesis, final exam; for doctorate, comprehensive exam, thesis/dissertation, internship, final exam. *Entrance requirements:* For master's, GRE General Test, GRE Subject Test, minimum GPA of 3.0; for doctorate, GRE General Test, GRE Subject Test, minimum GPA of 3.5. Additional exam requirements/recommendations for international students: Required—TOEFL (minimum score 550 paper-based; 213 computer-based; 79 iBT), IELTS (minimum score 7). *Application deadline:* For fall admission, 1/15 for domestic and international students. Application fee: $35. Electronic applications accepted. *Expenses:* Tuition, state resident: full-time $4,050; part-time $225 per credit. Tuition, nonresident: full-time $10,818; part-time $601 per credit. Required fees: $110 per semester. Tuition and fees vary according to class time, campus/location, program and reciprocity agreements. *Financial support:* In 2007–08, 34 students received support, including 8 research assistantships with full tuition reimbursements available (averaging $11,476 per year), 23 teaching assistantships with full tuition reimbursements available (averaging $8,993 per year); fellowships with full and partial tuition reimbursements available, career-related internships or fieldwork, Federal Work-Study, institutionally sponsored loans, scholarships/grants, health care benefits, tuition waivers (full and partial), and unspecified assistantships also available. Support available to part-time students. Financial award application deadline: 3/15; financial award applicants required to submit FAFSA. *Faculty research:* Developmental psychology, clinical social psychology, educational psychology, personality disorders. *Unit head:* Dr. Jeffrey N. Weatherly, Chairperson, 701-777-3470, E-mail: jeffrey.weatherly@und.nodak.edu. *Application contact:* Brenda Halle, Admissions Specialist, 701-777-2947, Fax: 701-777-3619, E-mail: brendahalle@mail.und.edu.

University of North Texas, Robert B. Toulouse School of Graduate Studies, College of Arts and Sciences, Department of Psychology, Denton, TX 76203. Offers clinical psychology (PhD); counseling psychology (MA, MS, PhD); experimental psychology (MA, MS, PhD); health psychology and behavioral medicine (PhD). *Accreditation:* APA (one or more programs are accredited). *Faculty:* 26 full-time (8 women). *Students:* 101 full-time (74 women), 105 part-time (77 women); includes 27 minority (8 African Americans, 1 American Indian/Alaska Native, 5 Asian Americans or Pacific Islanders, 13 Hispanic Americans), 7 international. Average age 29. 472 applicants, 9% accepted, 36 enrolled. In 2007, 28 master's, 23 doctorates awarded. Terminal master's awarded for partial completion of doctoral program. *Degree requirements:* For master's, comprehensive exam, thesis or alternative; for doctorate, one foreign language, comprehensive exam, thesis/dissertation. *Entrance requirements:* For master's and doctorate, GRE General Test, interview. Additional exam requirements/recommendations for international students: Required—proof of English language proficiency required for non-native English speakers; Recommended—TOEFL (minimum score 550 paper-based; 213 computer-based). *Application deadline:* For fall admission, 7/15 for domestic students; for spring admission, 11/15 for domestic students. Application fee: $50 ($75 for international students). *Financial support:* In 2007–08, 2 fellowships (averaging $20,000 per year), 18 research assistantships (averaging $9,000 per year), 38 teaching assistantships (averaging $9,000 per year) were awarded; career-related internships or fieldwork, Federal Work-Study, and institutionally sponsored loans also available. Financial award application deadline: 8/1. *Faculty research:* Very broad range of topics and approaches. *Unit head:* Dr. Linda Marshall, Chair, 940-565-2339, Fax: 940-546-4682, E-mail: psychair@unt.edu. *Application contact:* Amy Mayfield, Graduate Coordinator, 940-565-2671, Fax: 940-565-4682, E-mail: amym@unt.edu.

University of Oregon, Graduate School, College of Arts and Sciences, Department of Psychology, Program in Clinical Psychology, Eugene, OR 97403. Offers PhD. *Accreditation:* APA. *Students:* 169 applicants, 2% accepted. In 2007, 6 degrees awarded. *Degree requirements:* For doctorate, thesis/dissertation. *Entrance requirements:* For doctorate, GRE General Test. Additional exam requirements/recommendations for international students: Required—TOEFL. *Application deadline:* For fall admission, 12/1 for domestic students. Application fee: $50. *Financial support:* Research assistantships, teaching assistantships, career-related internships or fieldwork available. *Unit head:* Ann Simons, Head, 541-346-5561. *Application contact:* Lori Olsen, Admissions Contact, 541-346-5060, Fax: 541-346-4911, E-mail: gradsec@psych.uoregon.edu.

University of Pennsylvania, Graduate School of Education, Division of Applied Psychology and Human Development, Program in School, Community, and Clinical Child Psychology, Philadelphia, PA 19104. Offers PhD. *Degree requirements:* For doctorate, thesis/dissertation, exams. *Entrance requirements:* For doctorate, GRE General Test, GRE Subject Test. Electronic applications accepted. Expenses: Contact institution. *Faculty research:* Therapeutic interventions at a preschool level, childhood stress, college psychology, school and community psychology.

University of Puerto Rico, Río Piedras, College of Social Sciences, Department of Psychology, San Juan, PR 00931-3300. Offers clinical psychology (MA); industrial organizational psychology (MA); investigative academic psychology (MA); psychology (PhD). Part-time programs available. *Students:* 177 full-time (136 women), 55 part-time (42 women). Average age 30. In 2007, 18 master's, 21 doctorates awarded. *Degree requirements:* For master's, comprehensive exam, thesis; for doctorate, comprehensive exam, thesis/dissertation, internship. *Entrance requirements:* For master's, GRE or PAEG, interview, minimum GPA of 3.0; for doctorate, GRE or PAEG, interview, master's degree, minimum GPA of 3.0. *Application deadline:* For fall admission, 2/1 for domestic and international students. Application fee: $17. *Expenses:* Tuition, state resident: full-time $1,808; part-time $113 per credit. Tuition, nonresident: full-time $5,248; part-time $328 per credit. Required fees: $72 per term. *Financial support:* Fellowships, research assistantships, teaching assistantships, career-related internships or fieldwork, Federal Work-Study, institutionally sponsored loans, and tuition waivers (partial) available. Financial award application deadline: 5/31. *Faculty research:* Intervention on Depressed Latino Youth, biosychosocial training. *Unit head:* Dr. Dolores Miranda, Director, 787-764-0000 Ext. 2094. *Application contact:* Information Contact, 787-764-0000, Fax: 787-763-4599.

University of Regina, Faculty of Graduate Studies and Research, Faculty of Arts, Department of Psychology, Regina, SK S4S 0A2, Canada. Offers clinical psychology (MA, PhD); experimental and applied psychology (MA, PhD). *Faculty:* 18 full-time (10 women). *Students:* 45 full-time (37 women), 6 part-time (all women). 66 applicants, 32% accepted. In 2007, 6 master's, 2 doctorates awarded. *Degree requirements:* For master's, thesis; for doctorate, comprehensive exam, thesis/dissertation. *Entrance requirements:* For master's, GRE General Test, GRE Subject Test; for doctorate, GRE General Test, GRE Subject Test (optional for students who hold a master's degree from a Canadian university). Additional exam requirements/recommendations for international students: Required—TOEFL (minimum score 580 paper-based; 237 computer-based; 88 iBT). *Application deadline:* For fall admission, 2/15 for domestic students. Application fee: $85 ($100 for international students). Electronic applications accepted. *Financial support:* In 2007–08, 19 fellowships (averaging $15,750 per year), 4 research assistantships (averaging $13,875 per year), 10 teaching assistantships (averaging $13,060 per year) were awarded; career-related internships or fieldwork and scholarships/grants also available. Financial award application deadline: 6/15. *Faculty research:* Clinical and experimental and applied psychology. *Unit head:* Dr. William E. Smythe, Head, 306-585-4157, Fax: 306-585-5429, E-mail: william.smythe@uregina.ca.

University of Rhode Island, Graduate School, College of Arts and Sciences, Department of Psychology, Program in Clinical Psychology, Kingston, RI 02881. Offers PhD. *Accreditation:* APA. In 2007, 5 doctorates awarded. *Application deadline:* For fall admission, 1/1 for domestic students. Application fee: $35. *Expenses:* Tuition, state resident: full-time $6,936; part-time $385 per credit. Tuition, nonresident: full-time $19,044; part-time $1,058 per credit. Required fees: $1,508; $48 per credit. $30 per semester. One-time fee: $80 part-time. *Unit head:* Dr. Allan Berman, Director, 401-874-4257.

University of Rochester, The College, Arts and Sciences, Department of Clinical and Social Sciences in Psychology, Rochester, NY 14627-0250. Offers clinical psychology (PhD); developmental psychology (PhD); psychology (MA); social-personality psychology (PhD). *Accreditation:* APA (one or more programs are accredited). Terminal master's awarded for partial completion of doctoral program. *Degree requirements:* For doctorate, thesis/dissertation, qualifying exam. *Entrance requirements:* For doctorate, GRE General Test. Additional exam requirements/recommendations for international students: Required—TOEFL.

University of South Africa, College of Human Sciences, Pretoria, South Africa. Offers adult education (M Ed); African languages (MA, PhD); African politics (MA, PhD); Afrikaans (MA, PhD); ancient history (MA, PhD); ancient Near Eastern studies (MA, PhD); anthropology (MA, PhD); applied linguistics (MA); Arabic (MA, PhD); archaeology (MA); art history (MA); Biblical archaeology (MA); Biblical studies (M Th, D Th, PhD); Christian spirituality (M Th, D Th); church history (M Th, D Th); classical studies (MA, PhD); clinical psychology (MA); communication (MA, PhD); comparative education (M Ed, Ed D); consulting psychology (D Admin, D Com, PhD); curriculum studies (M Ed, Ed D); development studies (M Admin, MA, D Admin, PhD); didactics (M Ed, Ed D); education (M Tech); education management (M Ed, Ed D); educational psychology (M Ed); English (MA); environmental education (M Ed); French (MA, PhD); German (MA, PhD); Greek (MA); guidance and counseling (M Ed); health studies (MA, PhD), including health sciences education (MA), health services management (MA), medical and surgical nursing science (critical care general) (MA), midwifery and neonatal nursing science (MA), trauma and emergency care (MA); history (MA, PhD); history of education (Ed D); inclusive education (M Ed, Ed D); information and communications technology policy and regulation (MA); information science (MA, MIS, PhD); international politics (MA, PhD); Islamic studies (MA, PhD); Italian (MA, PhD); Judaica (MA, PhD); linguistics (MA, PhD); mathematical education (M Ed); mathematics education (MA); missiology (M Th, D Th); modern Hebrew (MA, PhD); musicology (MA, MMus, D Mus, PhD); natural science education (M Ed); New Testament (M Th, D Th); Old Testament (D Th); pastoral therapy (M Th, D Th); philosophy (MA); philosophy of education (M Ed, Ed D); politics (MA, PhD); Portuguese (MA, PhD); practical theology (M Th, D Th); psychology (MA, MS, PhD); psychology of education (M Ed, Ed D); public health (MA); religious studies (MA, D Th, PhD); Romance languages (MA); Russian (MA, PhD); Semitic languages (MA, PhD); social behavior studies in HIV/AIDS (MA); social science (mental health) (MA); social science in development studies (MA); social science in psychology (MA); social science in social work (MA); social science in sociology

(MA); social work (MSW, DSW, PhD); socio-education (M Ed, Ed D); sociolinguistics (MA); sociology (MA, PhD); Spanish (MA, PhD); systematic theology (M Th, D Th); TESOL (teaching English to speakers of other languages) (MA); theological ethics (M Th, D Th); theory of literature (MA, PhD); urban ministries (D Th); urban ministry (M Th).

University of South Carolina, The Graduate School, College of Arts and Sciences, Department of Psychology, Program in Clinical/Community Psychology, Columbia, SC 29208. Offers clinical/ community psychology (PhD); general psychology (MA). *Accreditation:* APA. *Faculty:* 14 full-time (6 women), 2 part-time/adjunct (both women). *Students:* 31 full-time (23 women), 18 part-time (13 women); includes 14 minority (10 African Americans, 2 Asian Americans or Pacific Islanders, 2 Hispanic Americans), 2 international. Average age 31. 110 applicants, 8% accepted, 5 enrolled. In 2007, 9 master's, 8 doctorates awarded. *Median time to degree:* Of those who began their doctoral program in fall 1999, 77% received their degree in 8 years or less. *Degree requirements:* For master's, comprehensive exam, thesis; for doctorate, comprehensive exam, thesis/dissertation. *Entrance requirements:* For doctorate, GRE General Test, minimum GPA of 3.2. Additional exam requirements/recommendations for international students: Required—TOEFL. *Application deadline:* For fall admission, 1/4 priority date for domestic students. Applications are processed on a rolling basis. Application fee: $35. Electronic applications accepted. *Expenses:* Tuition, state resident: part-time $440 per hour. Tuition, nonresident: part-time $936 per hour. Required fees: $17 per hour. Tuition and fees vary according to program. *Financial support:* In 2007–08, 43 students received support, including 3 fellowships with full tuition reimbursements available (averaging $16,000 per year), 6 research assistantships with full tuition reimbursements available (averaging $12,000 per year), 6 teaching assistantships with full tuition reimbursements available (averaging $12,000 per year); career-related internships or fieldwork, Federal Work-Study, and institutionally sponsored loans also available. Support available to part-time students. *Faculty research:* Developmental psychopathology, health disparities, community-level interventions for psychological well being. *Unit head:* Jeffrey C. Schatz, Director, 803-777-8439, Fax: 803-777-9558, E-mail: schatz@sc.edu. *Application contact:* Marti Brown, Student Services Program Coordinator, 803-777-9482, Fax: 803-777-0670, E-mail: marthab@gwm.sc.edu.

University of South Carolina Aiken, Program in Applied Clinical Psychology, Aiken, SC 29801-6309. Offers MS. Part-time and evening/weekend programs available. *Faculty:* 7 full-time (5 women). *Students:* 17 full-time (15 women), 11 part-time (9 women). In 2007, 12 degrees awarded. *Degree requirements:* For master's, thesis. *Entrance requirements:* For master's, GRE General Test, GRE Subject Test (psychology). *Application deadline:* Applications are processed on a rolling basis. Application fee: $45. Electronic applications accepted. *Expenses:* Tuition, state resident: full-time $8,888; part-time $440 per semester hour. Tuition, nonresident: full-time $19,180; part-time $936 per semester hour. Required fees: $230; $115 per semester. *Unit head:* Dr. Edward Callen, Chair, 803-641-3446, Fax: 803-641-3726, E-mail: edc@usca.edu. *Application contact:* Karen Morris, Graduate Studies Coordinator, 803-641-3489, E-mail: karenm@usca.edu.

The University of South Dakota, Graduate School, College of Arts and Sciences, Department of Psychology, Vermillion, SD 57069-2390. Offers clinical psychology (MA, PhD); human factors (MA, PhD). *Accreditation:* APA (one or more programs are accredited). *Faculty:* 24. *Students:* 68 (42 women). In 2007, 10 master's, 6 doctorates awarded. *Degree requirements:* For master's, comprehensive exam, thesis; for doctorate, comprehensive exam, thesis/ dissertation. *Entrance requirements:* For master's, GRE, minimum GPA of 2.7; for doctorate, GRE General Test, GRE Subject Test, minimum GPA of 2.7. Additional exam requirements/ recommendations for international students: Required—TOEFL (minimum score 550 paper-based; 213 computer-based; 79 iBT). *Application deadline:* For fall admission, 2/1 for domestic students. Application fee: $35. Electronic applications accepted. *Financial support:* In 2007–08, 1 fellowship (averaging $6,000 per year), 12 research assistantships with partial tuition reimbursements (averaging $6,000 per year), 31 teaching assistantships with partial tuition reimbursements (averaging $6,000 per year) were awarded; unspecified assistantships also available. Financial award applicants required to submit FAFSA. *Faculty research:* Human-computer interactions, perceptual-cognitive processing, medical psychology, depression, moral psychology. *Unit head:* Dr. Randal Quevillon, Chair, 605-677-5153, E-mail: askpsyc@usd.edu. *Application contact:* Dr. Barbara Yutrzenka, Graduate Student Adviser—Clinical, 605-677-5153, E-mail: byutrzen@usd.edu.

University of Southern Mississippi, Graduate School, College of Education and Psychology, Department of Psychology, Hattiesburg, MS 39406-0001. Offers clinical psychology (MA, PhD); counseling psychology (PhD); experimental psychology (MA, PhD); psychology (MS); school psychology (MA, PhD). *Accreditation:* ACA; APA (one or more programs are accredited). *Faculty:* 33 full-time (12 women), 1 (woman) part-time/adjunct. *Students:* 111 full-time (87 women), 32 part-time (22 women); includes 11 minority (6 African Americans, 3 Asian Americans or Pacific Islanders, 2 Hispanic Americans), 8 international. Average age 28. 201 applicants, 21% accepted, 33 enrolled. In 2007, 32 master's, 15 doctorates awarded. Terminal master's awarded for partial completion of doctoral program. *Degree requirements:* For master's, comprehensive exam, thesis; for doctorate, comprehensive exam, thesis/dissertation. *Entrance requirements:* For master's, GRE General Test, minimum GPA of 3.0; for doctorate, GRE General Test, interview, minimum GPA of 3.0. Additional exam requirements/recommendations for international students: Required—TOEFL. *Application deadline:* For fall admission, 3/1 priority date for domestic students, 3/1 for international students. Applications are processed on a rolling basis. Application fee: $30. *Financial support:* In 2007–08, 46 research assistantships with full tuition reimbursements (averaging $7,731 per year), 49 teaching assistantships with full tuition reimbursements (averaging $7,731 per year) were awarded; career-related internships or fieldwork, Federal Work-Study, and institutionally sponsored loans also available. Financial award application deadline: 3/15. *Faculty research:* Dolphin cognition, sleep, neuropsychology, health-related behaviors, psychopathology. Total annual research expenditures: $101,200. *Unit head:* Dr. Stan Kuczaj, Chair, 601-266-4177, Fax: 601-266-5580. *Application contact:* Dr. Heather Sterling-Tairner, Graduate Coordinator, 601-266-4177, Fax: 601-266-5580.

University of South Florida, Graduate School, College of Arts and Sciences, Department of Psychology, Tampa, FL 33620-9951. Offers clinical psychology (MA, PhD); cognitive and neural sciences (MA, PhD); industrial-organizational psychology (MA, PhD). *Accreditation:* APA (one or more programs are accredited). *Faculty:* 32 full-time (8 women), 1 (woman) part-time/adjunct. *Students:* 106 full-time (65 women), 21 part-time (16 women); includes 17 minority (4 African Americans, 4 Asian Americans or Pacific Islanders, 9 Hispanic Americans), 17 international. 398 applicants, 6% accepted, 22 enrolled. In 2007, 16 master's, 21 doctorates awarded. *Degree requirements:* For master's, thesis; for doctorate, comprehensive exam, thesis/dissertation. *Entrance requirements:* For master's and doctorate, GRE General Test, minimum GPA of 3.0 in last 60 hours of course work. Application fee: $30. Electronic applications accepted. *Expenses:* Contact institution. *Financial support:* In 2007–08, 13 fellowships with full and partial tuition reimbursements (averaging $17,500 per year), 50 research assistantships with partial tuition reimbursements (averaging $13,000 per year), 50 teaching assistantships with partial tuition reimbursements (averaging $13,000 per year) were awarded; career-related internships or fieldwork, scholarships/grants, tuition waivers (partial), and unspecified assistantships also available. Financial award applicants required to submit FAFSA. *Faculty research:* Human memory; job analysis; stress, drug and alcohol abuse; neuroscience. *Unit head:* Michael T. Brannick, Director of Graduate Program, 813-974-0478, Fax: 813-974-4617, E-mail: mbrannick@cas.usf.edu. *Application contact:* Laura Pierce, Program Assistant, 813-974-0497, Fax: 813-974-4617, E-mail: lpierce@cas.usf.edu.

The University of Tennessee, Graduate School, College of Arts and Sciences, Department of Psychology, Knoxville, TN 37996. Offers clinical psychology (PhD); experimental psychology (MA, PhD); psychology (MA). *Accreditation:* APA (one or more programs are accredited). Terminal master's awarded for partial completion of doctoral program. *Degree requirements:* For master's, thesis; for doctorate, thesis/dissertation. *Entrance requirements:* For master's and doctorate, GRE General Test, GRE Subject Test, minimum GPA of 2.7. Additional exam requirements/recommendations for international students: Required—TOEFL. Electronic applications accepted.

The University of Texas at El Paso, Graduate School, College of Liberal Arts, Department of Psychology, El Paso, TX 79968-0001. Offers clinical psychology (MA); experimental psychology (MA); psychology (PhD). Part-time and evening/weekend programs available. *Degree requirements:* For master's, thesis; for doctorate, thesis/dissertation. *Entrance requirements:* For master's and doctorate, GRE General Test. Additional exam requirements/recommendations for international students: Required—TOEFL. Electronic applications accepted.

The University of Texas at Tyler, College of Education and Psychology, Department of Psychology, Tyler, TX 75799-0001. Offers clinical psychology (MS), including neuropsychology, school psychology; counseling psychology (MA), including general, marriage and family; interdisciplinary studies (MSIS); school counseling (MA). Part-time and evening/weekend programs available. *Faculty:* 10 full-time (2 women), 8 part-time/adjunct (5 women). *Students:* 67 full-time (50 women), 60 part-time (50 women); includes 12 minority (4 African Americans, 1 American Indian/Alaska Native, 2 Asian Americans or Pacific Islanders, 5 Hispanic Americans). 37 applicants, 97% accepted, 32 enrolled. In 2007, 16 degrees awarded. *Degree requirements:* For master's, comprehensive exam, thesis optional. *Entrance requirements:* For master's, GRE General Test, minimum GPA of 3.0. *Application deadline:* For fall admission, 2/1 for domestic students; for spring admission, 10/1 for domestic students. Application fee: $0 ($50 for international students). Electronic applications accepted. *Expenses:* Tuition, state resident: part-time $627 per semester hour. Tuition, nonresident: part-time $908 per semester hour. Required fees: $107 per semester hour. Tuition and fees vary according to course load. *Financial support:* In 2007–08, fellowships with partial tuition reimbursements (averaging $3,000 per year), research assistantships (averaging $5,000 per year), teaching assistantships (averaging $1,500 per year) were awarded; career-related internships or fieldwork, Federal Work-Study, and institutionally sponsored loans also available. Support available to part-time students. Financial award application deadline: 7/1. *Faculty research:* Neuropsychology, child abuse, psychometric properties of psychological instruments, maternal behavior, clinical practice issues, victimization of women, post-traumatic stress disorder. *Unit head:* Dr. Charles B. Barke, Interim Chair, 903-565-5875, Fax: 903-565-5560, E-mail: cbarke@uttyler.edu. *Application contact:* Pam Morrow, Assistant to Dean for Enrollment Management, 903-566-7205, Fax: 903-566-7068, E-mail: pmorrow@uttyler.edu.

The University of Texas of the Permian Basin, Office of Graduate Studies, College of Arts and Sciences, Department of Behavioral Science, Program in Psychology, Odessa, TX 79762-0001. Offers applied behavioral analysis (MA); clinical psychology (MA). Part-time and evening/ weekend programs available. *Degree requirements:* For master's, comprehensive exam, thesis, practicum. *Entrance requirements:* For master's, GRE General Test, 3 letters of recommendation. Additional exam requirements/recommendations for international students: Required—TOEFL (minimum score 550 paper-based; 213 computer-based).

The University of Texas–Pan American, College of Social and Behavioral Sciences, Department of Psychology and Anthropology, Edinburg, TX 78541-2999. Offers psychology (MA), including clinical psychology, experimental psychology. Part-time and evening/weekend programs available. *Faculty:* 10 full-time (2 women). *Students:* 24 full-time (17 women), 12 part-time (7 women); includes 29 minority (all Hispanic Americans) Average age 29. 15 applicants, 60% accepted, 9 enrolled. In 2007, 3 degrees awarded. *Degree requirements:* For master's, comprehensive exam, thesis optional, internship. *Entrance requirements:* For master's, GRE, letters of recommendation. Additional exam requirements/recommendations for international students: Required—TOEFL. *Application deadline:* For fall admission, 7/1 priority date for domestic and international students; for spring admission, 11/1 priority date for domestic and international students. Application fee: $0. Electronic applications accepted. *Financial support:* In 2007–08, 1 research assistantship (averaging $10,000 per year), 3 teaching assistantships (averaging $6,000 per year) were awarded; career-related internships or fieldwork, Federal Work-Study, and institutionally sponsored loans also available. *Faculty research:* Biofeedback, acculturation, health, stress/trauma, neuropsychological assessment, false memories, children's theory of mind. Total annual research expenditures: $60,000. *Unit head:* Dr. Philip G. Gasquoine, Director, 956-381-2155, Fax: 956-381-3333, E-mail: pgasquoine@panam.edu.

The University of Texas Southwestern Medical Center at Dallas, Southwestern Graduate School of Biomedical Sciences, Division of Clinical Science, Clinical Psychology Program, Dallas, TX 75390. Offers PhD. *Accreditation:* APA. *Faculty:* 41 full-time (20 women), 30 part-time/adjunct (11 women). *Students:* 52 full-time (37 women); includes 12 minority (2 African Americans, 3 Asian Americans or Pacific Islanders, 7 Hispanic Americans). Average age 30. 155 applicants, 6% accepted, 10 enrolled. In 2007, 10 degrees awarded. *Degree requirements:* For doctorate, thesis/dissertation, clinical and qualifying exams. *Entrance requirements:* For doctorate, GRE General Test, minimum undergraduate GPA of 3.0. *Application deadline:* For fall admission, 1/1 for domestic students. Application fee: $0. Electronic applications accepted. *Financial support:* Research assistantships, career-related internships or fieldwork and institutionally sponsored loans available. Financial award application deadline: 3/1; financial award applicants required to submit FAFSA. *Faculty research:* Health psychology, depression, cross-cultural research, neuropsychology, sequelae children's illness. *Unit head:* Dr. C. Munro Cullum, Chair, 214-648-4640, Fax: 214-648-5250, E-mail: munro.cullum@utsouthwestern.edu. *Application contact:* Kelsey Stutzman, Education Coordinator, 214-648-5267, Fax: 214-648-5297, E-mail: kelsey.stutzman@utsouthwestern.edu.

University of the District of Columbia, College of Arts and Sciences, Department of Psychology and Counseling, Program in Clinical Psychology, Washington, DC 20008-1175. Offers MS. *Students:* 6 full-time (4 women), 7 part-time (6 women); includes 11 minority (9 African Americans, 1 Asian American or Pacific Islander, 1 Hispanic American). *Application contact:* LaVerne Hill Flannigan, Director of Admission, 202-274-6069.

The University of Toledo, College of Graduate Studies, College of Arts and Sciences, Department of Psychology, Toledo, OH 43606-3390. Offers behavioral (PhD), including cognitive, psychobiology and learning, social; clinical psychology (PhD); experimental psychology (MA). *Accreditation:* APA. *Faculty:* 22. *Students:* 34 full-time (24 women), 4 part-time (2 women); includes 2 minority (1 Asian American or Pacific Islander, 1 Hispanic American), 4 international. Average age 26. 150 applicants, 13% accepted, 9 enrolled. In 2007, 9 master's, 7 doctorates awarded. *Degree requirements:* For master's, thesis; for doctorate, one foreign language, thesis/dissertation. *Entrance requirements:* For master's and doctorate, GRE General Test, GRE Subject Test. *Application deadline:* For fall admission, 1/15 priority date for domestic students. Application fee: $45. *Financial support:* In 2007–08, 13 research assistantships (averaging $8,400 per year), 18 teaching assistantships (averaging $11,000 per year) were awarded; career-related internships or fieldwork, Federal Work-Study, institutionally sponsored loans, scholarships/grants, and unspecified assistantships also available. Support available to part-time students. Financial award application deadline: 1/15; financial award applicants required to submit FAFSA. *Faculty research:* Neural taste response. *Unit head:* Dr. Joseph Hovey, Chair, 419-530-2693, Fax: 419-530-8479.

See Close-Up on page 1509.

University of Tulsa, Graduate School, College of Arts and Sciences, Department of Psychology, Program in Clinical Psychology, Tulsa, OK 74104-3189. Offers MA, PhD, JD/MA. *Accreditation:* APA (one or more programs are accredited). Part-time programs available. *Faculty:* 10 full-time (3 women). *Students:* 30 full-time (27 women), 18 part-time (13 women); includes 5 minority (1 African American, 3 American Indian/Alaska Native, 1 Hispanic American), 1 international. Average age 29. 68 applicants, 25% accepted, 4 enrolled. In 2007, 2 master's, 6 doctorates awarded. Terminal master's awarded for partial completion of doctoral program. *Degree requirements:* For master's, thesis (for some programs), 6 credit hours of practicum training; for doctorate, comprehensive exam, thesis/dissertation, 1 year pre-doctoral internship.

Clinical Psychology

University of Tulsa (continued)

Entrance requirements: For master's and doctorate, GRE General Test, interview. Additional exam requirements/recommendations for international students: Required—TOEFL (minimum score 575 paper-based; 231 computer-based; 91 iBT), IELTS (minimum score 7). *Application deadline:* For fall admission, 12/1 for domestic and international students. Application fee: $40. Electronic applications accepted. *Expenses:* Tuition: Full-time $14,004; part-time $778 per credit hour. Required fees: $60; $30 per term. Tuition and fees vary according to course load. *Financial support:* In 2007–08, 35 students received support, including 9 fellowships with full and partial tuition reimbursements available (averaging $10,500 per year), 13 research assistantships with full and partial tuition reimbursements available (averaging $7,200 per year), 15 teaching assistantships with full and partial tuition reimbursements available (averaging $11,200 per year); career-related internships or fieldwork, Federal Work-Study, tuition waivers (full and partial), and unspecified assistantships also available. Support available to part-time students. Financial award application deadline: 2/1; financial award applicants required to submit FAFSA. Total annual research expenditures: $2 million. *Unit head:* Dr. Elana Newman, Director, 918-631-3151, Fax: 918-631-2836, E-mail: elana-newman@utulsa.edu. *Application contact:* Information Contact, E-mail: grad@utulsa.edu.

University of Utah, The Graduate School, College of Social and Behavioral Science, Department of Psychology, Salt Lake City, UT 84112-1107. Offers clinical psychology (PhD); psychology (PhD). *Accreditation:* APA. *Faculty:* 32 full-time (14 women), 4 part-time/adjunct (1 woman). *Students:* 44 full-time (28 women), 15 part-time (11 women); includes 7 minority (3 Asian Americans or Pacific Islanders, 4 Hispanic Americans), 3 international. Average age 31. 194 applicants, 10% accepted, 10 enrolled. In 2007, 5 doctorates awarded. *Median time to degree:* Of those who began their doctoral program in fall 1999, 78% received their degree in 8 years or less. *Degree requirements:* For doctorate, thesis/dissertation. *Entrance requirements:* For doctorate, GRE General Test. Additional exam requirements/recommendations for international students: Required—TOEFL (minimum score 500 paper-based; 173 computer-based). *Application deadline:* For fall admission, 12/15 for domestic and international students. Applications are processed on a rolling basis. Application fee: $45 ($65 for international students). *Financial support:* In 2007–08, 54 students received support, including 3 fellowships with full tuition reimbursements available (averaging $11,000 per year), 14 research assistantships with full tuition reimbursements available (averaging $11,000 per year), 37 teaching assistantships with full tuition reimbursements available (averaging $10,500 per year); career-related internships or fieldwork also available. Financial award applicants required to submit FAFSA. *Faculty research:* Cognitive neuroscience, health, social cognition, psychopathology, cognitive and social development. Total annual research expenditures: $1.9 million. *Unit head:* Frances J Friedrich, Chair, 801-581-6124, Fax: 801-581-5841, E-mail: friedrich@psych.utah.edu. *Application contact:* Nancy Seegmiller, Administrative Assistant, 801-581-6124, Fax: 801-581-5841, E-mail: nancy.seegmiller@psych.utah.edu.

University of Vermont, Graduate College, College of Arts and Sciences, Department of Psychology, Burlington, VT 05405. Offers clinical psychology (PhD); psychology (PhD). *Accreditation:* APA. *Students:* 50 (42 women); includes 6 minority (1 African American, 1 Asian American or Pacific Islander, 4 Hispanic Americans) 3 international. 220 applicants, 6% accepted, 8 enrolled. In 2007, 4 doctorates awarded. *Degree requirements:* For doctorate, thesis/dissertation. *Entrance requirements:* For doctorate, GRE General Test, GRE Subject Test. Additional exam requirements/recommendations for international students: Required—TOEFL (minimum score 550 paper-based; 213 computer-based; 80 iBT). *Application deadline:* For fall admission, 12/1 for domestic students. Application fee: $40. Electronic applications accepted. *Financial support:* Fellowships, research assistantships, teaching assistantships available. Financial award application deadline: 2/1. *Unit head:* Dr. William Falls, Chairperson, 802-656-2670. *Application contact:* Holly Olmstead, Information Contact, 802-656-2670.

University of Victoria, Faculty of Graduate Studies, Faculty of Social Sciences, Department of Psychology, Victoria, BC V8W 2Y2, Canada. Offers clinical psychology (PhD); clinical psychology (neuropsychology) (M Sc); cognition and brain science (M Sc, PhD); experimental neuropsychology (M Sc, PhD); individualized study (M Sc, PhD); life span development psychology (PhD); life span developmental psychology (M Sc); social psychology (M Sc, PhD). *Accreditation:* APA (one or more programs are accredited). *Faculty:* 24 full-time (12 women), 14 part-time/adjunct (7 women). *Students:* 26, 4 international. Average age 25. 146 applicants, 21% accepted, 14 enrolled. In 2007, 36 master's, 2 doctorates awarded. *Degree requirements:* For master's, thesis; for doctorate, thesis/dissertation, candidacy exam. *Entrance requirements:* For master's and doctorate, GRE General Test. Additional exam requirements/recommendations for international students: Required—TOEFL (minimum score 600 paper-based; 250 computer-based). *Application deadline:* For fall admission, 1/1 for domestic students, 12/15 priority date for international students. Applications are processed on a rolling basis. Application fee: $65 ($100 for international students). Electronic applications accepted. *Expenses:* Tuition, state resident: full-time $3,110. International tuition: $3,700 full-time. Tuition and fees vary according to program. *Financial support:* In 2007–08, 4 fellowships (averaging $13,000 per year), 23 research assistantships, 22 teaching assistantships (averaging $2,750 per year) were awarded; career-related internships or fieldwork and institutionally sponsored loans also available. Financial award application deadline: 1/15. *Faculty research:* Life span development psychology and aging, behavioral neuroscience, cognitive psychology, behavioral psychology, environmental psychology. *Unit head:* Dr. Elizabeth Brimacombe, Chair, 250-721-7547, Fax: 250-721-8929, E-mail: psychair@uvic.ca. *Application contact:* Paul Taylor, Graduate Secretary, 250-721-6109, Fax: 250-721-8929, E-mail: ptaylor@uvic.ca.

University of Virginia, Curry School of Education, Department of Human Services, Charlottesville, VA 22903. Offers clinical and school psychology (Ed D, PhD); communication disorders (M Ed); counselor education (M Ed, Ed D, Ed S); health and physical education (M Ed, Ed D), including kinesiology. *Accreditation:* APA (one or more programs are accredited). *Faculty:* 28 full-time (15 women), 1 (woman) part-time/adjunct. *Students:* 130 full-time (109 women), 9 part-time (7 women); includes 12 minority (5 African Americans, 7 Asian Americans or Pacific Islanders), 3 international. Average age 25. 238 applicants, 48% accepted, 48 enrolled. In 2007, 83 master's, 1 doctorate awarded. *Entrance requirements:* For master's, doctorate, and Ed S, GRE General Test. Additional exam requirements/recommendations for international students: Required—TOEFL (minimum score 600 paper-based; 250 computer-based). *Application deadline:* Applications are processed on a rolling basis. Application fee: $60. *Financial support:* Fellowships with tuition reimbursements, research assistantships with tuition reimbursements, teaching assistantships with tuition reimbursements available. Financial award applicants required to submit FAFSA. *Unit head:* Ronald E. Reeve, Chair, 434-924-6254. *Application contact:* Lynn Renfroe, Information Contact, 434-924-6254, E-mail: ldr9t@virginia.edu.

University of Washington, Graduate School, College of Arts and Sciences, Department of Psychology, Seattle, WA 98195. Offers PhD. *Accreditation:* APA. *Degree requirements:* For doctorate, thesis/dissertation. *Entrance requirements:* For doctorate, GRE General Test, minimum GPA of 3.0. Electronic applications accepted. *Faculty research:* Addictive behaviors, artificial intelligence, child psychopathology, mechanisms and development of vision, physiology of ingestive behaviors.

University of Windsor, Faculty of Graduate Studies, Faculty of Arts and Social Sciences, Department of Psychology, Windsor, ON N9B 3P4, Canada. Offers adult clinical (MA, PhD); applied social psychology (MA, PhD); child clinical (MA, PhD); clinical neuropsychology (MA, PhD). *Accreditation:* APA (one or more programs are accredited). *Faculty:* 30 full-time (12 women). *Students:* 106 full-time (89 women). 183 applicants, 19% accepted. In 2007, 19 master's, 10 doctorates awarded. *Degree requirements:* For master's, thesis; for doctorate, comprehensive exam, thesis/dissertation. *Entrance requirements:* For master's, GRE General Test, GRE Subject Test in psychology, minimum B average; for doctorate, GRE General Test, GRE Subject Test in psychology, master's degree. Additional exam requirements/recommendations for international students: Required—TOEFL (minimum score 600 paper-based; 250 computer-based). *Application deadline:* For fall admission, 1/15 for domestic students. Application fee: $55. Electronic applications accepted. *Financial support:* In 2007–08, 67 teaching assistantships (averaging $9,409 per year) were awarded; Federal Work-Study, scholarships/grants, tuition waivers (full and partial), unspecified assistantships, and bursaries also available. Financial award application deadline: 2/15. *Faculty research:* Gambling, suicidology, emotional competence, psychotherapy and trauma. *Unit head:* Dr. Shelagh Towson, Head, 519-253-3000 Ext. 2215, Fax: 519-973-7021, E-mail: towson@uwindsor.ca. *Application contact:* Applicant Services, 519-253-3000 Ext. 6459, Fax: 519-971-3653, E-mail: gradadmit@uwindsor.ca.

University of Wisconsin–Madison, Graduate School, College of Letters and Science, Department of Psychology, Program in Clinical Psychology, Madison, WI 53706-1380. Offers PhD. *Accreditation:* APA. *Degree requirements:* For doctorate, comprehensive exam, thesis/dissertation. *Entrance requirements:* For doctorate, GRE General Test, minimum undergraduate GPA of 3.0. Additional exam requirements/recommendations for international students: Required—TOEFL. Electronic applications accepted.

University of Wisconsin–Milwaukee, Graduate School, College of Letters and Sciences, Department of Psychology, Milwaukee, WI 53201-0413. Offers clinical psychology (MS, PhD); psychology (MS, PhD). *Accreditation:* APA (one or more programs are accredited). *Faculty:* 19 full-time (4 women). *Students:* 60 full-time (38 women), 11 part-time (5 women); includes 13 minority (2 African Americans, 4 Asian Americans or Pacific Islanders, 7 Hispanic Americans), 4 international. 165 applicants, 14% accepted, 14 enrolled. In 2007, 8 master's, 11 doctorates awarded. *Degree requirements:* For master's, thesis; for doctorate, variable foreign language requirement, thesis/dissertation. *Entrance requirements:* For master's and doctorate, GRE General Test, GRE Subject Test. *Application deadline:* For fall admission, 1/1 priority date for domestic students; for spring admission, 9/1 for domestic students. Applications are processed on a rolling basis. Application fee: $45 ($75 for international students). *Expenses:* Tuition, state resident: part-time $530 per credit. Tuition, nonresident: part-time $1,428 per credit. Required fees: $19 per credit. $229 per term. Tuition and fees vary according to course load and program. *Financial support:* In 2007–08, 2 research assistantships, 42 teaching assistantships were awarded; fellowships, career-related internships or fieldwork and unspecified assistantships also available. Support available to part-time students. Financial award application deadline: 4/15. *Unit head:* Hobart Davies, Representative, 414-229-6594, Fax: 414-229-5219, E-mail: hobart@uwm.edu.

Utah State University, School of Graduate Studies, College of Education and Human Services, Department of Psychology, Logan, UT 84322. Offers clinical/counseling/school psychology (PhD); research and evaluation methodology (PhD); school counseling (MS); school psychology (MS). *Accreditation:* APA (one or more programs are accredited). Part-time and evening/weekend programs available. Postbaccalaureate distance learning degree programs offered (no on-campus study). Terminal master's awarded for partial completion of doctoral program. *Degree requirements:* For master's, thesis (for some programs); for doctorate, thesis/dissertation. *Entrance requirements:* For master's, GRE General Test (school psychology), MAT (school counseling), minimum GPA of 3.5; for doctorate, GRE General Test, minimum GPA of 3.5. Additional exam requirements/recommendations for international students: Required—TOEFL. *Faculty research:* Hearing loss detection in infancy, ADHD, eating disorders, domestic violence, neuropsychology, bilingual/Spanish speaking students/parents.

Valdosta State University, Graduate School, College of Education, Department of Psychology and Counseling, Valdosta, GA 31698. Offers clinical/counseling psychology (MS); industrial/organizational psychology (MS); school counseling (M Ed, Ed S); school psychology (Ed S). Part-time and evening/weekend programs available. *Faculty:* 16 full-time (2 women). *Students:* 61 full-time (48 women), 38 part-time (31 women); includes 22 minority (19 African Americans, 1 American Indian/Alaska Native, 1 Asian American or Pacific Islander, 1 Hispanic American). Average age 27. 103 applicants, 31% accepted, 22 enrolled. In 2007, 25 degrees awarded. *Degree requirements:* For master's, thesis or alternative, comprehensive written and/or oral exams; for Ed S, thesis. *Entrance requirements:* For master's and Ed S, GRE General Test or MAT. Additional exam requirements/recommendations for international students: Required—TOEFL (minimum score 523 paper-based; 193 computer-based). *Application deadline:* For fall admission, 7/1 for domestic and international students; for spring admission, 11/15 for domestic and international students. Applications are processed on a rolling basis. Application fee: $40. Electronic applications accepted. *Expenses:* Tuition, state resident: part-time $147 per hour. Tuition, nonresident: part-time $586 per hour. Required fees: $520 per semester. Tuition and fees vary according to course level, course load, campus/location and program. *Financial support:* In 2007–08, 2 students received support, including 2 research assistantships with full tuition reimbursements available (averaging $2,452 per year); institutionally sponsored loans and unspecified assistantships also available. Support available to part-time students. Financial award application deadline: 7/1; financial award applicants required to submit FAFSA. *Faculty research:* Using Bender-Gestalt to predict graphomotor dimensions of the draw-a-person test, neurobehavioral hemispheric dominance. *Unit head:* Dr. Robert Bauer, Chair, 229-333-5930, Fax: 229-259-5576, E-mail: bbauer@valdosta.edu.

Valparaiso University, Graduate Division, Department of Psychology, Valparaiso, IN 46383. Offers business management (for counseling students) (Certificate); clinical mental health counseling (MA); community counseling (MA); JD/MA. Part-time and evening/weekend programs available. *Faculty:* 7 part-time/adjunct (1 woman). *Students:* 35 full-time (25 women), 11 part-time (9 women); includes 2 minority (1 African American, 1 Hispanic American), 5 international. Average age 30. In 2007, 13 degrees awarded. *Degree requirements:* For master's, thesis or alternative, internship. *Entrance requirements:* For master's, minimum GPA of 3.0. Additional exam requirements/recommendations for international students: Required—TOEFL (minimum score 550 paper-based; 213 computer-based). *Application deadline:* For fall admission, 3/1 priority date for domestic students. Applications are processed on a rolling basis. Application fee: $30 ($50 for international students). Electronic applications accepted. *Financial support:* Career-related internships or fieldwork, traineeships, and unspecified assistantships available. Support available to part-time students. Financial award applicants required to submit FAFSA. *Faculty research:* Environmental psychology, human sexuality, racial identity development models, social psychology. *Unit head:* Dr. James Nelson, Graduate Program Director, 219-464-5443, Fax: 219-464-6878, E-mail: jim.nelson@valpo.edu. *Application contact:* Jamie Haney, Coordinator of Recruitment Activities, 219-464-5313, Fax: 219-464-5381, E-mail: jamie.haney@valpo.edu.

Vanguard University of Southern California, School of Psychology, Costa Mesa, CA 92626-9601. Offers clinical psychology (MS). Part-time and evening/weekend programs available. *Faculty:* 3 full-time (all women), 7 part-time/adjunct (4 women). *Students:* 41 full-time (33 women), 25 part-time (20 women); includes 16 minority (2 African Americans, 1 American Indian/Alaska Native, 2 Asian Americans or Pacific Islanders, 11 Hispanic Americans). Average age 30. 92 applicants, 47% accepted, 26 enrolled. In 2007, 24 degrees awarded. *Degree requirements:* For master's, thesis or alternative. *Entrance requirements:* For master's, minimum GPA of 3.0. Additional exam requirements/recommendations for international students: Required—TOEFL (minimum score 550 paper-based; 213 computer-based; 79 iBT). *Application deadline:* For fall admission, 4/1 priority date for domestic and international students; for winter admission, 10/1 for domestic and international students. Applications are processed on a rolling basis. Application fee: $45. Electronic applications accepted. *Expenses:* Contact institution. *Financial support:* In 2007–08, 62 students received support, including 16 teaching assistantships (averaging $2,469 per year); scholarships/grants and unspecified assistantships also available. Financial award application deadline: 3/2; financial award applicants required to submit FAFSA. *Faculty research:* Children, play therapy, death and dying, trauma, marital and family counseling. *Unit head:* Dr. Jerre White, Dean, 714-556-3610 Ext. 3550, Fax: 714-662-5226, E-mail: jwhite@vanguard.edu. *Application contact:* Asha Harrington, Graduate Psychology Coordinator, 714-556-3610 Ext. 3550, Fax: 714-662-5226, E-mail: gradpsych@vanguard.edu.

Virginia Commonwealth University, Graduate School, College of Humanities and Sciences, Department of Psychology, Program in Clinical Psychology, Richmond, VA 23284-9005. Offers PhD. *Accreditation:* APA. *Students:* 40 full-time (34 women), 6 part-time (5 women); includes 8 minority (1 African American, 2 Asian Americans or Pacific Islanders, 5 Hispanic Americans). 204 applicants, 7% accepted, 11 enrolled. In 2007, 7 doctorates awarded. *Degree requirements:* For doctorate, thesis/dissertation. *Entrance requirements:* For doctorate, GRE General Test. *Application deadline:* For fall admission, 1/15 for domestic students. Application fee: $50. *Expenses:* Tuition, state resident: full-time $7,224; part-time $401 per credit. Tuition, nonresident: full-time $16,072; part-time $891 per credit. Required fees: $1,679; $63 per credit. Tuition and fees vary according to campus/location. *Financial support:* Fellowships, research assistantships, teaching assistantships, Federal Work-Study, institutionally sponsored loans, and scholarships/grants available. Support available to part-time students. *Unit head:* Dr. Wendy L. Kliewer, Head, 804-828-1793. *Application contact:* Dr. J. Donelson Forsyth, Director, Graduate Programs in Psychology, 804-828-6754, Fax: 804-828-2237, E-mail: jforsyth@vcu.edu.

See Close-Up on page 457.

Virginia Polytechnic Institute and State University, Graduate School, College of Science, Department of Psychology, Blacksburg, VA 24061. Offers bio-behavioral sciences (PhD); clinical psychology (PhD); developmental psychology (PhD); industrial/organizational psychology (PhD); psychology (MS). *Accreditation:* APA (one or more programs are accredited). *Entrance requirements:* For master's and doctorate, GRE General Test. Additional exam requirements/recommendations for international students: Required—TOEFL (minimum score 550 paper-based; 213 computer-based). Electronic applications accepted. *Faculty research:* Infant development from electrophysical point of view, work motivation and personnel selection, EEG, ERP and hypnosis with reference to chronic pain, intimate violence.

Walden University, Graduate Programs, School of Psychology, Minneapolis, MN 55401. Offers clinical assessment (Post-Doctoral Certificate); clinical child psychology (Post-Doctoral Certificate); clinical psychology (PhD, Post-Doctoral Certificate); counseling psychology (PhD, Post-Doctoral Certificate); general psychology (MS, PhD, Post-Doctoral Certificate); health psychology (PhD, Post-Doctoral Certificate); organizational psychology (PhD, Post-Doctoral Certificate); organizational psychology and development (MS); school psychology (PhD, Post-Doctoral Certificate); teaching online (Post-Doctoral Certificate). Part-time and evening/weekend programs available. Postbaccalaureate distance learning degree programs offered (minimal on-campus study). *Students:* 1,428 full-time (1,130 women), 1,933 part-time (1,483 women); includes 959 minority (737 African Americans, 35 American Indian/Alaska Native, 53 Asian Americans or Pacific Islanders, 134 Hispanic Americans), 39 international. Average age 40. 1,254 applicants, 75% accepted, 548 enrolled. In 2007, 182 master's, 43 doctorates awarded. *Degree requirements:* For master's, thesis; for doctorate, thesis/dissertation, brief dispersed residency sessions. *Entrance requirements:* For master's, minimum GPA of 3.0; for doctorate, 3 years of professional experience, master's degree; for Post-Doctoral Certificate, PhD in related field, 3 years of professional experience. Additional exam requirements/recommendations for international students: Required—TOEFL (minimum score 550 paper-based; 213 computer-based), IELTS (minimum score 7). *Application deadline:* For fall admission, 8/15 priority date for domestic and international students; for winter admission, 11/15 priority date for domestic and international students; for spring admission, 12/15 priority date for domestic and international students. Applications are processed on a rolling basis. Application fee: $50. Electronic applications accepted. *Financial support:* Fellowships with partial tuition reimbursements, career-related internships or fieldwork, Federal Work-Study, institutionally sponsored loans, scholarships/grants, tuition waivers (partial), and unspecified assistantships available. Support available to part-time students. Financial award applicants required to submit FAFSA. *Faculty research:* Clinical psychology, organizational psychology, forensic psychology, group processes, educational psychology. *Unit head:* Dr. Nina Nabors, Associate Dean, 800-925-3368. *Application contact:* 866-4-WALDEN, Fax: 410-843-8780, E-mail: request@waldenu.edu.

Washburn University, College of Arts and Sciences, Department of Psychology, Topeka, KS 66621. Offers clinical psychology (MA). Part-time programs available. *Faculty:* 8 full-time (5 women), 6 part-time/adjunct (4 women). *Students:* 27 full-time (18 women), 4 part-time (2 women). Average age 25. In 2007, 4 degrees awarded. *Degree requirements:* For master's, thesis. *Entrance requirements:* For master's, GRE General Test, 15 hours of course work in psychology. *Application deadline:* For fall admission, 3/15 for domestic students; for spring admission, 12/1 for domestic students. Application fee: $0. Electronic applications accepted. *Expenses:* Tuition, state resident: full-time $4,590; part-time $255 per credit hour. Tuition, nonresident: full-time $9,360; part-time $520 per credit hour. Required fees: $86; $43 per semester. Tuition and fees vary according to program. *Financial support:* Application deadline: 2/15; *Faculty research:* Animal behavior, correctional psychology, children's social development, metacognition and metamemory, psychology of exercise, Gibsonian Ecological Psychology, treatment of anxiety disorders. *Unit head:* Dr. David Provorse, Chair, 785-670-1565, Fax: 785-670-1004, E-mail: dave.provorse@washburn.edu.

Washington State University, Graduate School, College of Liberal Arts, Department of Psychology, Pullman, WA 99164. Offers clinical psychology (PhD); experimental psychology (PhD); psychology (MS). *Accreditation:* APA (one or more programs are accredited). *Faculty:* 28. *Students:* 58 full-time (37 women), 2 part-time (1 woman); includes 9 minority (1 African American, 1 Asian American or Pacific Islander, 7 Hispanic Americans), 7 international. Average age 29. 238 applicants, 6% accepted, 12 enrolled. In 2007, 4 master's, 8 doctorates awarded. *Degree requirements:* For master's, comprehensive exam (for some programs), thesis (for some programs), oral exam; for doctorate, comprehensive exam, thesis/dissertation, oral exam, written exam. *Entrance requirements:* For master's, GRE General Test, minimum GPA of 3.0, research or clinical experience, 3 letters of recommendation; for doctorate, GRE General Test, minimum GPA of 3.0, 1 course in statistics and research methodology, research or clinical experience, 3 letters of recommendation. *Application deadline:* For fall admission, 1/1 for domestic students. Applications are processed on a rolling basis. Application fee: $50. *Financial support:* In 2007–08, 47 students received support, including 5 research assistantships with full and partial tuition reimbursements available (averaging $13,917 per year), 39 teaching assistantships with full and partial tuition reimbursements available (averaging $13,056 per year); fellowships, career-related internships or fieldwork, Federal Work-Study, institutionally sponsored loans, and unspecified assistantships also available. Financial award application deadline: 4/1; financial award applicants required to submit FAFSA. *Faculty research:* Childhood conduct disorders, etiology of depression, treatment of reading disorders, applied behavior analysis, selective attention. Total annual research expenditures: $240,986. *Unit head:* Dr. John Hinson, Chair, 509-335-2631, E-mail: hinson@mail.wsu.edu. *Application contact:* Graduate School Admissions, 800-GRADWSU, Fax: 509-335-16949, E-mail: gradsch@wsu.edu.

Washington University in St. Louis, Graduate School of Arts and Sciences, Department of Psychology, St. Louis, MO 63130-4899. Offers clinical psychology (PhD); general experimental psychology (MA, PhD); social psychology (MA, PhD). *Accreditation:* APA (one or more programs are accredited). Terminal master's awarded for partial completion of doctoral program. *Degree requirements:* For master's, thesis or alternative; for doctorate, thesis/dissertation. *Entrance requirements:* For master's and doctorate, GRE General Test. Electronic applications accepted.

Wayne State University, College of Education, Division of Theoretical and Behavioral Foundations, Detroit, MI 48202. Offers counseling (M Ed, MA, Ed D, PhD, Ed S); education evaluation and research (M Ed, Ed D, PhD); educational psychology (M Ed, Ed D, PhD, Ed S); educational sociology (M Ed, Ed D, PhD, Ed S); history and philosophy of education (M Ed, Ed D, PhD); rehabilitation counseling and community inclusion (MA, Ed S); school and community psychology (MA, Ed S); school clinical psychology (Ed S). *Accreditation:* ACA (one or more programs are accredited); CORE (one or more programs are accredited). Evening/weekend programs available. *Students:* 166 full-time (135 women), 215 part-time (173 women); includes 141 minority (127 African Americans, 3 American Indian/Alaska Native, 6 Asian Americans or Pacific Islanders, 5 Hispanic Americans), 17 international. Average age 35. 149 applicants, 50% accepted, 58 enrolled. In 2007, 90 master's, 16 doctorates, 2 other advanced degrees awarded. *Degree requirements:* For doctorate, thesis/dissertation. *Entrance requirements:* For master's, GRE; for doctorate, GRE, interview, minimum GPA of 3.0, curriculum vitae, references. Additional exam requirements/recommendations for international students: Required—TOEFL (minimum score 550 paper-based; 213 computer-based), TWE (minimum score 6). *Application deadline:* For fall admission, 7/1 for domestic students, 6/1 for international students; for winter admission, 10/1 for international students; for spring admission, 2/1 for international students. Application fee: $20 ($30 for international students). Electronic applications accepted. *Expenses:* Tuition, state resident: part-time $403 per credit hour. Tuition, nonresident: part-time $890 per credit hour. *Financial support:* In 2007–08, 1 fellowship with tuition reimbursement (averaging $14,201 per year), 2 research assistantships with tuition reimbursements (averaging $13,627 per year) were awarded; career-related internships or fieldwork, Federal Work-Study, and institutionally sponsored loans also available. *Faculty research:* Adolescents at risk, supervision of counseling. *Unit head:* Dr. JoAnne Holbert, Assistant Dean, 313-577-1721, E-mail: jholbert@wayne.edu.

Wayne State University, College of Liberal Arts and Sciences, Department of Psychology, Program in Psychology, Detroit, MI 48202. Offers behavioral and cognitive neuroscience (PhD); clinical psychology (PhD); cognitive and social psychology (PhD); industrial/organizational psychology (PhD); psychology (MA, MS). *Accreditation:* APA (one or more programs are accredited). *Students:* 99 full-time (74 women), 20 part-time (16 women); includes 14 minority (7 African Americans, 4 Asian Americans or Pacific Islanders, 3 Hispanic Americans), 13 international. Average age 27. 219 applicants, 17% accepted, 23 enrolled. In 2007, 13 master's, 12 doctorates awarded. *Degree requirements:* For doctorate, thesis/dissertation. *Entrance requirements:* For doctorate, GRE General Test, GRE Subject Test. Additional exam requirements/recommendations for international students: Required—TOEFL (minimum score 550 paper-based; 213 computer-based); Recommended—TWE (minimum score 6). *Application deadline:* For fall admission, 2/1 for domestic students, 6/1 for international students; for winter admission, 10/1 for international students; for spring admission, 2/1 for international students. Applications are processed on a rolling basis. Application fee: $30 ($50 for international students). Electronic applications accepted. *Expenses:* Tuition, state resident: part-time $403 per credit hour. Tuition, nonresident: part-time $890 per credit hour. *Financial support:* Application deadline: 2/1. *Application contact:* Dr. Melissa Kaplan-Estrin, Graduate Director, 313-577-2824, Fax: 313-577-7636, E-mail: mkestrin@sun.science.wayne.edu.

West Chester University of Pennsylvania, Office of Graduate Studies and Extended Education, College of Arts and Sciences, Department of Psychology, West Chester, PA 19383. Offers clinical mental health (Certificate); clinical psychology (MA); general psychology (MA); industrial organizational psychology (MA). Part-time and evening/weekend programs available. *Students:* 61 full-time (44 women), 29 part-time (18 women); includes 6 minority (4 African Americans, 1 Asian American or Pacific Islander, 1 Hispanic American), 2 international. Average age 27. 177 applicants, 68% accepted, 37 enrolled. In 2007, 22 degrees awarded. *Degree requirements:* For master's, comprehensive exam, thesis (for some programs). *Entrance requirements:* For master's, GRE General Test or MAT, interview. Additional exam requirements/recommendations for international students: Required—TOEFL (minimum score 550 paper-based; 213 computer-based; 80 iBT). *Application deadline:* For fall admission, 4/15 priority date for domestic students; for spring admission, 10/15 for domestic students. Applications are processed on a rolling basis. Application fee: $35. *Expenses:* Tuition, state resident: part-time $345 per credit. Tuition, nonresident: part-time $552 per credit. Tuition and fees vary according to course load. *Financial support:* In 2007–08, 13 research assistantships with full and partial tuition reimbursements (averaging $5,000 per year) were awarded; unspecified assistantships also available. Support available to part-time students. Financial award application deadline: 2/15; financial award applicants required to submit FAFSA. *Faculty research:* Animal learning and cognition. *Unit head:* Dr. Sandra Kerr, Chair, 610-436-2945, E-mail: skerr@wcupa.edu. *Application contact:* Dr. Loretta Rieser-Danner, Graduate Coordinator, 610-436-3106, E-mail: lriserdanner@wcupa.edu.

Western Illinois University, School of Graduate Studies, College of Arts and Sciences, Department of Psychology, Macomb, IL 61455-1390. Offers clinical/community mental health (MS); general psychology (MS); psychology (MS, SSP); school psychology (SSP). Part-time programs available. *Students:* 40 full-time (24 women), 18 part-time (10 women); includes 1 minority (Asian American or Pacific Islander), 1 international. Average age 25. 78 applicants, 35% accepted. In 2007, 15 master's, 8 other advanced degrees awarded. *Degree requirements:* For master's, comprehensive exam (for some programs), thesis or alternative. *Entrance requirements:* For master's and SSP, GRE General Test. Additional exam requirements/recommendations for international students: Required—TOEFL (minimum score 550 paper-based; 213 computer-based; 80 iBT). *Application deadline:* Applications are processed on a rolling basis. Application fee: $30. Electronic applications accepted. *Expenses:* Tuition, state resident: part-time $217 per credit hour. Tuition, nonresident: part-time $433 per credit hour. Required fees: $54 per credit hour. *Financial support:* In 2007–08, 38 students received support, including 38 research assistantships with full tuition reimbursements available (averaging $6,800 per year). Financial award applicants required to submit FAFSA. *Unit head:* Dr. Virginia Diehl, Chairperson, 309-298-1593. *Application contact:* Dr. Barbara Baily, Director of Graduate Studies/Associate Provost, 309-298-1806, Fax: 309-298-2345, E-mail: grad-office@wiu.edu.

Western Michigan University, Graduate College, College of Arts and Sciences, Department of Psychology, Kalamazoo, MI 49008-5202. Offers applied behavior analysis (MA, PhD); clinical psychology (MA, PhD); experimental analysis of behavior (PhD); experimental psychology (MA); industrial/organizational psychology (MA); school psychology (PhD, Ed S). *Accreditation:* APA (one or more programs are accredited). *Degree requirements:* For master's, variable foreign language requirement, thesis, oral exams; for doctorate, 2 foreign languages, comprehensive exam, thesis/dissertation, oral exams; for Ed S, thesis, oral exams. *Entrance requirements:* For master's, doctorate, and Ed S, GRE General Test.

West Virginia University, Eberly College of Arts and Sciences, Department of Psychology, Morgantown, WV 26506. Offers behavior analysis (PhD); clinical psychology (MA, PhD); development psychology (PhD); psychology (MS). *Accreditation:* APA (one or more programs are accredited). Part-time programs available. *Faculty:* 21 full-time (10 women), 2 part-time/adjunct (both women). *Students:* 67 full-time (41 women), 6 part-time (all women); includes 4 minority (2 African Americans, 1 Asian American or Pacific Islander, 1 Hispanic American), 8 international. Average age 27. 195 applicants, 10% accepted, 20 enrolled. In 2007, 7 master's, 12 doctorates awarded. Terminal master's awarded for partial completion of doctoral program. *Degree requirements:* For master's, thesis optional; for doctorate, comprehensive exam, thesis/dissertation. *Entrance requirements:* For master's and doctorate, GRE General Test, minimum GPA of 3.0. Additional exam requirements/recommendations for international students: Required—TOEFL. *Application deadline:* For fall admission, 1/15 for domestic students. Application fee: $45. *Expenses:* Tuition, state resident: full-time $5,196; part-time $292 per credit hour. Tuition, nonresident: full-time $15,064; part-time $840 per credit hour. Tuition and fees vary according to program. *Financial support:* In 2007–08, 73 students received support, including 28 research assistantships (averaging $13,000 per year), 34 teaching assistantships (averaging $10,000 per year); fellowships, career-related internships or fieldwork, Federal Work-Study, institutionally sponsored loans, and tuition waivers (full and partial) also available. Financial award application deadline: 1/15; financial award applicants required to submit FAFSA. *Faculty research:* Adult and child clinical psychology, behavioral assessment and therapy, child and adolescent behavior, life span development, experimental and applied behavior analysis. Total annual research expenditures: $415,123. *Unit head:* Dr. Michael T. Perone, Chair, 304-293-2001 Ext. 31604, Fax: 304-293-6606, E-mail: michael.perone@mail.wvu.edu. *Application contact:* Dr. Barry Edelstein, Director, Graduate Training, 304-293-2001 Ext. 31661, Fax: 304-293-6606, E-mail: barry.edelstein@mail.wvu.edu.

Wheaton College, Graduate School, Department of Psychology, Wheaton, IL 60187-5593. Offers clinical psychology (MA, Psy D); counseling ministries (MA). *Accreditation:* APA (one or more programs are accredited). *Faculty:* 18 full-time (9 women), 10 part-time/adjunct (3 women). *Students:* 141. 159 applicants, 52% accepted, 54 enrolled. In 2007, 44 master's, 13

Clinical Psychology

Wheaton College (continued)

doctorates awarded. Terminal master's awarded for partial completion of doctoral program. *Degree requirements:* For master's, thesis or alternative; for doctorate, thesis/dissertation, internship. *Entrance requirements:* For master's, GRE General Test, 18 hours of course work in psychology; for doctorate, GRE General Test. *Financial support:* In 2007–08, 3 research assistantships (averaging $4,800 per year) were awarded; career-related internships or fieldwork, Federal Work-Study, scholarships/grants, and unspecified assistantships also available. Financial award application deadline: 6/1; financial award applicants required to submit FAFSA. *Unit head:* Dr. Robert Gregory, Chair, 630-752-7053. *Application contact:* Julie A. Huebner, Director of Graduate Admissions, 630-752-5195, Fax: 630-752-5935, E-mail: gradadm@wheaton.edu.

Wichita State University, Graduate School, Fairmount College of Liberal Arts and Sciences, Department of Psychology, Wichita, KS 67260. Offers community/clinical psychology (PhD); human factors (PhD); psychology (MA). *Accreditation:* APA. Part-time programs available. *Degree requirements:* For doctorate, thesis/dissertation. *Entrance requirements:* For doctorate, GRE. Additional exam requirements/recommendations for international students: Required—TOEFL. Electronic applications accepted. *Faculty research:* Behavioral evolution, women and alcohol, behavioral medicine, delinquency prevention.

Widener University, School of Human Service Professions, Institute for Graduate Clinical Psychology, Program in Clinical Psychology, Chester, PA 19013-5792. Offers Psy D, Psy D/M Ed, Psy D/MA, Psy D/MBA, Psy D/MHA, Psy D/MPA, Psy D/MSHR. *Accreditation:* APA. *Students:* Average age 24. In 2007, 34 degrees awarded. *Degree requirements:* For doctorate, thesis/dissertation, final oral and written qualifying exams. *Entrance requirements:* For doctorate, GRE General Test or MAT. *Application deadline:* For fall admission, 12/31 for domestic students. Application fee: $75. Electronic applications accepted. *Expenses: Contact institution.* Tuition and fees vary according to course load and program. *Financial support:* Career-related internships or fieldwork, Federal Work-Study, institutionally sponsored loans, scholarships/grants, and stipends available. Financial award application deadline: 4/15. *Faculty research:* Cognitive and personality diagnostic testing, depression, child and adolescent competencies, learning disabilities, family therapy. *Unit head:* Dr. Virginia Brabender, Associate Dean/Director, 610-499-1208, Fax: 610-499-4625, E-mail: graduate.psychology@widener.edu. *Application contact:* Ellen Madison, Admissions Coordinator, 611-499-1206, Fax: 610-499-4625, E-mail: ellen.t.madison@widener.edu.

See Close-Up on page 1513.

Widener University, School of Human Service Professions, Institute for Graduate Clinical Psychology, Program in Clinical Psychology and Health and Medical Services Administration, Chester, PA 19013-5792. Offers Psy D/MBA, Psy D/MHA. *Accreditation:* APA (one or more programs are accredited); CAHME. *Faculty:* 15 full-time (6 women), 18 part-time/adjunct (10 women). *Students:* 21 full-time (13 women); includes 4 minority (3 African Americans, 1 Asian American or Pacific Islander). Average age 28. *Application deadline:* For fall admission, 12/31 for domestic students. Application fee: $75. Electronic applications accepted. *Expenses:* Tuition: Part-time $570 per credit. Tuition and fees vary according to course load and program. *Financial support:* Career-related internships or fieldwork, Federal Work-Study, and institutionally sponsored loans available. Financial award application deadline: 5/31. *Faculty research:* Psychosocial competence, family systems, medical care systems and financing. *Unit head:* Dr. Geoffrey Marczyk, Director, 610-499-4598, Fax: 610-499-4625. *Application contact:* Ellen Madison, Admissions Coordinator, 611-499-1206, Fax: 610-499-4625, E-mail: ellen.t.madison@widener.edu.

See Close-Up on page 1513.

William Paterson University of New Jersey, College of the Humanities and Social Sciences, Program in Clinical and Counseling Psychology, Wayne, NJ 07470-8420. Offers MA. *Students:* 29 full-time (22 women), 23 part-time (17 women); includes 14 minority (7 African Americans, 1 Asian American or Pacific Islander, 6 Hispanic Americans), 1 international. In 2007, 13 degrees awarded. *Entrance requirements:* For master's, GRE General Test. *Application deadline:* For fall admission, 3/1 for domestic students. Applications are processed on a rolling basis. Application fee: $50. Electronic applications accepted. *Financial support:* Research assistantships with full tuition reimbursements available. Financial award application deadline: 4/1; financial award applicants required to submit FAFSA. *Unit head:* Dr. Bruce Diamond, Program Director, 973-720-3629, E-mail: psychgrad@wpunj.edu. *Application contact:* Danielle Liautaud, Director, 973-720-3579, Fax: 973-720-2035, E-mail: liautaudd@wpunj.edu.

Wisconsin School of Professional Psychology, Program in Clinical Psychology, Milwaukee, WI 53225-4960. Offers MA, Psy D. *Accreditation:* APA. Part-time and evening/weekend programs available. *Faculty:* 3 full-time (all women), 32 part-time/adjunct (13 women). *Students:* 23 full-time (20 women), 39 part-time (31 women); includes 7 minority (6 African Americans, 1 Asian American or Pacific Islander). Average age 38. 48 applicants, 21% accepted. In 2007, 11 master's, 3 doctorates awarded. Terminal master's awarded for partial completion of doctoral program. *Median time to degree:* Of those who began their doctoral program in fall 1999, 90% received their degree in 8 years or less. *Degree requirements:* For master's, candidacy exam, 500 hours of supervised clinical practica; for doctorate, thesis/dissertation, 1 year clinical intern and practicum experience (2000 hrs), candidacy and clinical exams. *Entrance requirements:* For master's, GRE General Test, GRE Subject Test, bachelor's degree in psychology, writing sample; for doctorate, GRE General Test, GRE Subject Test, master's degree in clinical psychology or equivalent, writing sample. *Application deadline:* For fall admission, 4/15 priority date for domestic students; for spring admission, 10/15 priority date for domestic students. Applications are processed on a rolling basis. Application fee: $75. *Financial support:* In 2007–08, 6 students received support. Scholarships/grants and clinical service assistantships, library aid assistantships available. Support available to part-time students. *Faculty research:* Violence prevention, psychology of women, forensic psychology, custody evaluation, aging, harm reduction in AODA. *Application contact:* Sheri Lindgren, Assistant to the President, 414-464-9777, Fax: 414-358-5590, E-mail: admissions@wspp.edu.

Wright Institute, Program in Clinical Psychology, Berkeley, CA 94704-1796. Offers Psy D. *Accreditation:* APA. *Degree requirements:* For doctorate, thesis/dissertation. *Entrance requirements:* Additional exam requirements/recommendations for international students: Required—TOEFL (minimum score 600 paper-based). Electronic applications accepted.

Wright State University, School of Professional Psychology, Dayton, OH 45435. Offers clinical psychology (Psy D). *Accreditation:* APA. *Degree requirements:* For doctorate, thesis/dissertation. *Entrance requirements:* For doctorate, GRE General Test, GRE Subject Test. Additional exam requirements/recommendations for international students: Required—TOEFL. Expenses: Contact institution.

Xavier University, College of Social Sciences, Health and Education, Department of Psychology, Cincinnati, OH 45207. Offers clinical psychology (Psy D); psychology (MA), including general experimental, industrial-organizational. *Accreditation:* APA (one or more programs are accredited). *Faculty:* 16 full-time (8 women), 10 part-time/adjunct (5 women). *Students:* 83 full-time (62 women), 27 part-time (20 women); includes 9 minority (4 African Americans, 4 Asian Americans or Pacific Islanders, 1 Hispanic American), 2 international. Average age 29. 275 applicants, 28% accepted, 27 enrolled. In 2007, 27 master's, 12 doctorates awarded. Terminal master's awarded for partial completion of doctoral program. *Median time to degree:* Of those who began their doctoral program in fall 1999, 100% received their degree in 8 years or less. *Degree requirements:* For master's, one foreign language, comprehensive exam, thesis, internship; for doctorate, one foreign language, comprehensive exam, thesis/dissertation, internship, practicum. *Entrance requirements:* For master's, GRE, minimum GPA of 3.0, 18 hours of course work in psychology; for doctorate, GRE, 18 hours of course work in psychology or a master's degree in clinical psychology, minimum GPA of 3.0. Additional exam requirements/recommendations for international students: Required—TOEFL (minimum score 550 paper-based; 213 computer-based). *Application deadline:* For fall admission, 1/15 priority date for domestic students. Application fee: $35. Electronic applications accepted. *Expenses: Contact institution. Financial support:* In 2007–08, 50 students received support, including 16 research assistantships with partial tuition reimbursements available, 4 teaching assistantships with partial tuition reimbursements available; career-related internships or fieldwork, traineeships, health care benefits, and unspecified assistantships also available. Financial award application deadline: 3/1; financial award applicants required to submit FAFSA. *Faculty research:* Cognitive development in children, weight management, psychodiagnostics, psychotherapy, gerontology I-O psychology. *Unit head:* Dr. Christine M. Dacey, Chair, 513-745-3533, Fax: 513-745-3327, E-mail: dacey@xavier.edu. *Application contact:* Margaret Maybury, Assistant Director-Enrollment and Student Services, 513-745-1053, Fax: 513-745-3327, E-mail: maybury@xavier.edu.

Yeshiva University, Ferkauf Graduate School of Psychology, Program in Clinical Psychology, New York, NY 10033-3201. Offers Psy D. *Accreditation:* APA. Part-time programs available. *Degree requirements:* For doctorate, comprehensive exam, thesis/dissertation. *Entrance requirements:* For doctorate, GRE General Test. *Faculty research:* Psychotherapy, family therapy, psychoanalysis, cognitive behavior therapy.

Yeshiva University, Ferkauf Graduate School of Psychology, Program in School/Clinical-Child Psychology, New York, NY 10033-3201. Offers Psy D. *Accreditation:* APA. Part-time programs available. *Degree requirements:* For doctorate, comprehensive exam, thesis/dissertation. *Entrance requirements:* For doctorate, GRE General Test. *Faculty research:* Testing, early childhood intervention, child and adolescent psychotherapy, clinical child psychology.

Cognitive Sciences

Arizona State University, Graduate College, College of Liberal Arts and Sciences, Division of Natural Sciences and Mathematics, Department of Psychology, Tempe, AZ 85287. Offers behavioral neuroscience (PhD); clinical psychology (PhD); cognitive/behavioral systems (PhD); developmental psychology (PhD); environmental psychology (PhD); quantitative research methods (PhD); social psychology (PhD). *Accreditation:* APA. *Degree requirements:* For doctorate, thesis/dissertation. *Entrance requirements:* For doctorate, GRE General Test, GRE Subject Test.

Ball State University, Graduate School, College of Sciences and Humanities, Department of Psychological Science, Program in Cognitive and Social Processes, Muncie, IN 47306-1099. Offers MA. *Faculty:* 20. *Students:* 14 full-time (9 women), 1 part-time; includes 1 minority (American Indian/Alaska Native), 4 international. Average age 27. 14 applicants, 64% accepted, 7 enrolled. In 2007, 3 degrees awarded. *Expenses:* Tuition, state resident: full-time $6,864. Tuition, nonresident: full-time $17,932. Required fees: $1,866. *Financial support:* Research assistantships with full tuition reimbursements, teaching assistantships available. *Unit head:* Dr. Kerri Pickel, Graduate Program Director, 765-285-1690, Fax: 765-285-8980, E-mail: kpickel@bsu.edu.

Boston University, Graduate School of Arts and Sciences, Department of Cognitive and Neural Systems, Boston, MA 02215. Offers MA, PhD. *Students:* 56 full-time (8 women), 7 part-time (1 woman); includes 5 minority (1 African American, 3 Asian Americans or Pacific Islanders, 1 Hispanic American), 26 international. Average age 30. 70 applicants, 59% accepted, 15 enrolled. Terminal master's awarded for partial completion of doctoral program. *Degree requirements:* For master's, one foreign language, comprehensive exam; for doctorate, one foreign language, comprehensive exam, thesis/dissertation. *Entrance requirements:* For master's and doctorate, GRE General Test, GRE Subject Test (recommended), 3 letters of recommendation. Additional exam requirements/recommendations for international students: Required—TOEFL (minimum score 550 paper-based; 213 computer-based). *Application deadline:* For fall admission, 5/1 for domestic and international students; for spring admission, 11/15 for domestic and international students. Application fee: $70. *Expenses:* Tuition: Full-time $34,930; part-time $1,092 per credit. Tuition and fees vary according to class time, course level and program. *Financial support:* In 2007–08, 3 fellowships with full tuition reimbursements (averaging $18,000 per year), 48 research assistantships with full tuition reimbursements (averaging $17,500 per year), 2 teaching assistantships with full tuition reimbursements were awarded; Federal Work-Study and unspecified assistantships also available. Support available to part-time students. Financial award application deadline: 1/15; financial award applicants required to submit FAFSA. *Unit head:* Stephen Grossberg, Chairman, 617-353-7858, Fax: 617-353-7755, E-mail: steve@bu.edu. *Application contact:* Carol Y. Jefferson, Administrative Assistant, 617-353-7676, Fax: 617-353-7755, E-mail: caroly@bu.edu.

Brandeis University, Graduate School of Arts and Sciences, Department of Psychology, Waltham, MA 02454-9110. Offers cognitive neuroscience (PhD); general psychology (MA); social/developmental psychology (PhD). MA program offered to students enrolled in PhD program only. *Faculty:* 16 full-time (3 women), 3 part-time/adjunct (all women). *Students:* 26 full-time (19 women), 8 international. Average age 26. 44 applicants, 20% accepted, 5 enrolled. In 2007, 5 master's, 3 doctorates awarded. *Median time to degree:* Of those who began their doctoral program in fall 1999, 100% received their degree in 8 years or less. *Degree requirements:* For doctorate, comprehensive exam, thesis/dissertation. *Entrance requirements:* For doctorate, GRE General Test, GRE Subject Test (recommended), 3 letters of recommendation. Additional exam requirements/recommendations for international students: Required—TOEFL (minimum score 600 paper-based; 250 computer-based). *Application deadline:* For fall admission, 1/15 for domestic and international students. Application fee: $55. Electronic applications accepted. *Financial support:* In 2007–08, 21 fellowships with full tuition reimbursements (averaging $18,000 per year), teaching assistantships with full tuition reimbursements (averaging $3,000 per year) were awarded; institutionally sponsored loans, scholarships/grants, traineeships, health care benefits, tuition waivers (full), and unspecified assistantships also available. *Faculty research:* Development, cognition, social aging, perception. Total annual research expenditures: $5.1 million. *Unit head:* Paul DiZio, Director of Graduate Studies, 781-736-3300, Fax: 781-736-3291, E-mail: dizio@brandeis.edu. *Application contact:* Donna J. Coletti, Graduate Admissions Coordinator, 781-736-3303, Fax: 781-736-3291, E-mail: coletti@brandeis.edu.

Brown University, Graduate School, Department of Cognitive and Linguistic Sciences, Providence, RI 02912. Offers cognitive science (Sc M, PhD); linguistics (AM, PhD). *Degree requirements:* For master's, one foreign language, thesis or alternative; for doctorate, 2 foreign languages, thesis/dissertation.

Carleton University, Faculty of Graduate Studies, Faculty of Arts and Social Sciences, Program in Cognitive Science, Ottawa, ON K1S 5B6, Canada. Offers PhD. *Degree requirements:*

For doctorate, thesis/dissertation. *Entrance requirements:* For doctorate, master's degree. Application fee: $77. *Financial support:* Fellowships, research assistantships, teaching assistantships, institutionally sponsored loans, scholarships/grants, and unspecified assistantships available. *Faculty research:* Language, attention, artificial intelligence, symbol recognition, consciousness. *Unit head:* Andrew Brook, Director, 613-520-2600 Ext. 2368, Fax: 613-520-3985. *Application contact:* Colleen Fulton, Administrator, 613-520-2600 Ext. 2368, E-mail: iis@carleton.ca.

Carnegie Mellon University, College of Humanities and Social Sciences, Department of Psychology, Area of Cognitive Neuroscience, Pittsburgh, PA 15213-3891. Offers PhD. *Degree requirements:* For doctorate, comprehensive exam, thesis/dissertation. *Entrance requirements:* For doctorate, GRE General Test. Additional exam requirements/recommendations for international students: Required—TOEFL.

Carnegie Mellon University, College of Humanities and Social Sciences, Department of Psychology, Area of Cognitive Psychology, Pittsburgh, PA 15213-3891. Offers PhD. *Degree requirements:* For doctorate, comprehensive exam, thesis/dissertation. *Entrance requirements:* For doctorate, GRE General Test. Additional exam requirements/recommendations for international students: Required—TOEFL.

Case Western Reserve University, School of Graduate Studies, Department of Cognitive Science, Cleveland, OH 44106. Offers cognitive linguistics (MA). Part-time programs available. *Faculty:* 5 full-time (2 women), 2 part-time/adjunct (1 woman). *Degree requirements:* For master's, thesis. *Entrance requirements:* For master's, GRE, writing sample, recommendations. Additional exam requirements/recommendations for international students: Required—TOEFL. *Application deadline:* For fall admission, 3/1 priority date for domestic students. Application fee: $50. Electronic applications accepted. *Faculty research:* Application of metaphor and conceptual integration theories to a wide range of non-linguistic phenomena. *Unit head:* Dr. Mark Turner, Chair, 216-368-4753, E-mail: cogsci@case.edu. *Application contact:* Dr. Todd Oakley, Co-Director of Admission, 216-368-4753, E-mail: coglingadmission@case.edu.

Claremont Graduate University, Graduate Programs, School of Behavioral and Organizational Sciences, Department of Psychology, Claremont, CA 91711-6160. Offers advanced study in evaluation (Certificate); cognitive psychology (MA, PhD); developmental psychology (MA, PhD); evaluation and applied research methods (MA, PhD); health behavior research and evaluation (MA, PhD); human resource development and evaluation (MA); industrial/organizational psychology (MA, PhD); organizational behavior (MA, PhD); organizational psychology (MA, PhD); social psychology (MA, PhD); MBA/PhD. Part-time programs available. *Faculty:* 15 full-time (7 women), 4 part-time/adjunct (2 women). *Students:* 184 full-time (137 women), 24 part-time (20 women); includes 51 minority (13 African Americans, 1 American Indian/Alaska Native, 26 Asian Americans or Pacific Islanders, 11 Hispanic Americans), 12 international. Average age 29. In 2007, 42 master's, 10 doctorates, 2 other advanced degrees awarded. Terminal master's awarded for partial completion of doctoral program. *Degree requirements:* For master's, thesis (for some programs); for doctorate, comprehensive exam, thesis/dissertation. *Entrance requirements:* For master's and doctorate, GRE General Test. *Application deadline:* For fall admission, 2/15 priority date for domestic students. Applications are processed on a rolling basis. Electronic applications accepted. *Expenses:* Tuition: Full-time $31,640; part-time $1,376 per unit. Required fees: $145 per semester. Tuition and fees vary according to course load, degree level and program. *Financial support:* Fellowships, research assistantships, teaching assistantships, career-related internships or fieldwork, Federal Work-Study, institutionally sponsored loans, and tuition waivers (full and partial) available. Support available to part-time students. Financial award application deadline: 2/15; financial award applicants required to submit FAFSA. *Faculty research:* Social intervention, diversity in organizations, eyewitness memory, aging and cognition, drug policy. *Unit head:* Natalie Brown, Program Coordinator, 909-621-8084, Fax: 909-621-8905, E-mail: natalie.brown@cgu.edu.

Cornell University, Graduate School, Graduate Fields of Arts and Sciences, Field of Information Science, Ithaca, NY 14853-0001. Offers cognition (PhD); human computer interaction (PhD); information systems (PhD); social aspects of information (PhD). *Faculty:* 29 full-time (8 women). *Students:* 10 full-time (4 women), 6 international. Average age 30. 66 applicants, 9% accepted, 3 enrolled. *Degree requirements:* For doctorate, comprehensive exam, thesis/dissertation. *Entrance requirements:* For doctorate, GRE General Test, 3 letters of recommendation. Additional exam requirements/recommendations for international students: Required—TOEFL (minimum score 550 paper-based; 213 computer-based; 77 iBT). *Application deadline:* For fall admission, 1/1 for domestic students. Application fee: $70. Electronic applications accepted. *Financial support:* In 2007–08, 10 students received support, including 1 fellowship with full tuition reimbursement available, 4 research assistantships with full tuition reimbursements available, 5 teaching assistantships with full tuition reimbursements available; institutionally sponsored loans, scholarships/grants, tuition waivers (full and partial), and unspecified assistantships also available. Financial award applicants required to submit FAFSA. *Faculty research:* Digital libraries, game theory, data mining, human-computer interaction, computational linguistics. *Unit head:* Director of Graduate Studies, 607-255-5925. *Application contact:* Graduate Field Assistant, 607-255-5925, E-mail: info@infosci.cornell.edu.

Dartmouth College, Arts and Sciences Graduate Programs, Department of Psychological and Brain Sciences, Hanover, NH 03755. Offers cognitive neuroscience (PhD); psychology (PhD). *Faculty:* 16 full-time (3 women), 4 part-time/adjunct (2 women). *Students:* 33 full-time (19 women); includes 2 minority (both Asian Americans or Pacific Islanders), 6 international. Average age 28. 78 applicants, 14% accepted, 4 enrolled. In 2007, 2 degrees awarded. *Degree requirements:* For doctorate, thesis/dissertation. *Entrance requirements:* For doctorate, GRE General Test, GRE Subject Test. Additional exam requirements/recommendations for international students: Required—TOEFL. *Application deadline:* For fall admission, 1/15 priority date for domestic students. Application fee: $40. *Financial support:* In 2007–08, 26 students received support, including fellowships with full tuition reimbursements available (averaging $22,464 per year), research assistantships with full tuition reimbursements available (averaging $22,464 per year); Federal Work-Study, institutionally sponsored loans, and tuition waivers (full) also available. *Faculty research:* Behavioral neuroscience, cognitive neuroscience, cognitive science, social/personality psychology. Total annual research expenditures: $3.5 million. *Unit head:* Dr. Howard C. Hughes, Chair, 603-646-3181, Fax: 603-646-1419, E-mail: howard.hughes@dartmouth.edu. *Application contact:* Nancy Tenney, Departmental Administrative, 603-646-3181, E-mail: nancy.4.tenney@dartmouth.edu.

Duke University, Graduate School, Department of Psychology, Durham, NC 27708-0586. Offers biological psychology (PhD); clinical psychology (PhD); cognitive psychology (PhD); developmental psychology (PhD); experimental psychology (PhD); health psychology (PhD); human social development (PhD); JD/MA. *Accreditation:* APA (one or more programs are accredited). *Faculty:* 40 full-time. *Students:* 91 full-time (71 women); includes 15 minority (9 African Americans, 1 Asian American or Pacific Islander, 5 Hispanic Americans), 13 international. 468 applicants, 7% accepted, 19 enrolled. In 2007, 14 doctorates awarded. *Degree requirements:* For doctorate, thesis/dissertation. *Entrance requirements:* For doctorate, GRE General Test. Additional exam requirements/recommendations for international students: Required—TOEFL (minimum score 550 paper-based; 213 computer-based; 83 iBT), IELTS (minimum score 7). *Application deadline:* For fall admission, 12/15 priority date for domestic and international students. Application fee: $75. Electronic applications accepted. *Financial support:* Fellowships, research assistantships, teaching assistantships, career-related internships or fieldwork and Federal Work-Study available. Financial award application deadline: 12/31. *Unit head:* Amy Needham, Co-Director of Graduate Studies, 919-660-5715, Fax: 919-660-5726, E-mail: morrell@duke.edu.

Emory University, Graduate School of Arts and Sciences, Department of Psychology, Atlanta, GA 30322-1100. Offers clinical psychology (PhD); cognition and development (PhD); neuroscience and animal behavior (PhD). *Accreditation:* APA. *Degree requirements:* For doctorate, comprehensive exam, thesis/dissertation. *Entrance requirements:* For doctorate, GRE General Test, minimum GPA of 3.25. Additional exam requirements/recommendations for international students: Required—TOEFL. Electronic applications accepted. *Faculty research:* Neuroscience and animal behavior; adult and child psychopathology, cognition development assessment.

Florida State University, Graduate Studies, College of Arts and Sciences, Department of Psychology, Program in Cognitive Psychology, Tallahassee, FL 32306. Offers PhD. *Faculty:* 9 full-time (1 woman). *Students:* 20 full-time (9 women), 3 international. Average age 28. 27 applicants, 19% accepted, 5 enrolled. In 2007, 4 doctorates awarded. *Median time to degree:* Of those who began their doctoral program in fall 1999, 100% received their degree in 8 years or less. *Degree requirements:* For doctorate, thesis/dissertation, preliminary exam. *Entrance requirements:* For doctorate, GRE General Test, minimum GPA of 3.0, research experience, letters of recommendation. Additional exam requirements/recommendations for international students: Required—TOEFL (minimum score 550 paper-based; 213 computer-based; 80 iBT). *Application deadline:* For fall admission, 1/15 for domestic and international students. Application fee: $30. Electronic applications accepted. *Expenses:* Tuition, state resident: part-time $248 per credit hour. Tuition, nonresident: part-time $880 per credit hour. Tuition and fees vary according to program. *Financial support:* In 2007–08, 4 fellowships with full tuition reimbursements (averaging $18,000 per year), 8 research assistantships with full tuition reimbursements (averaging $15,000 per year), 7 teaching assistantships with full tuition reimbursements (averaging $15,000 per year) were awarded; Federal Work-Study, institutionally sponsored loans, scholarships/grants, traineeships, health care benefits, and unspecified assistantships also available. *Faculty research:* Memory, learning and reading disabilities, expert performance, aging. Total annual research expenditures: $675,711. *Unit head:* Dr. Colleen Kelley, Director, 850-644-3816, Fax: 850-644-7739, E-mail: kelley@psy.fsu.edu. *Application contact:* Cherie P. Miller, Graduate Program Assistant, 850-644-2499, Fax: 850-644-7739, E-mail: grad-info@psy.fsu.edu.

The George Washington University, Columbian College of Arts and Sciences, Department of Psychology, Washington, DC 20052. Offers applied social psychology (PhD); clinical psychology (PhD); cognitive neuropsychology (PhD); industrial-organizational psychology (PhD). *Accreditation:* APA. Part-time and evening/weekend programs available. *Degree requirements:* For doctorate, thesis/dissertation or alternative, general exam. *Entrance requirements:* For doctorate, GRE General Test, minimum GPA of 3.0. Additional exam requirements/recommendations for international students: Required—TOEFL (minimum score 550 paper-based; 213 computer-based).

Graduate School and University Center of the City University of New York, Graduate Studies, Program in Psychology, New York, NY 10016-4039. Offers basic applied neurocognition (PhD); biopsychology (PhD); clinical psychology (PhD); developmental psychology (PhD); environmental psychology (PhD); experimental psychology (PhD); industrial psychology (PhD); learning processes (PhD); neuropsychology (PhD); psychology (PhD); social personality (PhD). *Faculty:* 119 full-time (40 women). *Students:* 510 full-time (379 women), 1 (woman) part-time; includes 98 minority (39 African Americans, 1 American Indian/Alaska Native, 21 Asian Americans or Pacific Islanders, 37 Hispanic Americans), 63 international. Average age 33. 747 applicants, 17% accepted, 78 enrolled. In 2007, 59 degrees awarded. *Degree requirements:* For doctorate, one foreign language, thesis/dissertation. *Entrance requirements:* For doctorate, GRE General Test. Additional exam requirements/recommendations for international students: Required—TOEFL. *Application deadline:* For fall admission, 12/15 for domestic students. Application fee: $125. Electronic applications accepted. *Financial support:* In 2007–08, 371 students received support, including 308 fellowships, 34 research assistantships, 33 teaching assistantships; career-related internships or fieldwork, Federal Work-Study, institutionally sponsored loans, and tuition waivers (full and partial) also available. Financial award application deadline: 2/1; financial award applicants required to submit FAFSA. *Unit head:* Dr. Joseph Glick, Executive Officer, 212-817-8706, Fax: 212-817-1533, E-mail: jglick@gc.cuny.edu.

Harvard University, Graduate School of Arts and Sciences, Department of Psychology, Cambridge, MA 02138. Offers psychology (PhD), including behavior and decision analysis, cognition, developmental psychology, experimental psychology, personality, psychobiology, psychopathology; social psychology (PhD). *Degree requirements:* For doctorate, thesis/dissertation, general exams. *Entrance requirements:* For doctorate, GRE General Test. Additional exam requirements/recommendations for international students: Required—TOEFL. *Expenses:* Tuition: Full-time $31,456. Full-time tuition and fees vary according to program and student level.

Harvard University, Graduate School of Education, Master's Programs in Education, Cambridge, MA 02138. Offers arts in education (Ed M); education policy and management (Ed M); higher education (Ed M); human development and psychology (Ed M); international education policy (Ed M); language and literacy (Ed M); learning and teaching (Ed M); mid-career mathematics and science (teaching certificate) (Ed M); mind brain and education (Ed M); risk and prevention (Ed M); school leadership (Ed M); special studies (Ed M); teaching and curriculum (teaching certificate) (Ed M); technology innovation and education (Ed M). Part-time programs available. *Faculty:* 67 full-time (34 women), 31 part-time/adjunct (15 women). *Students:* 515 full-time (395 women), 71 part-time (55 women); includes 135 minority (46 African Americans, 1 American Indian/Alaska Native, 55 Asian Americans or Pacific Islanders, 33 Hispanic Americans), 72 international. Average age 28. 1,219 applicants, 61% accepted, 537 enrolled. In 2007, 610 degrees awarded. *Entrance requirements:* For master's, GRE General Test, 3 letters of recommendation, official transcripts, statement of purpose. Additional exam requirements/recommendations for international students: Required—TOEFL (minimum score 600 paper-based; 250 computer-based; 100 iBT), TWE (minimum score 5). *Application deadline:* For fall admission, 1/4 for domestic and international students. Application fee: $85. Electronic applications accepted. *Expenses:* Contact institution. *Financial support:* In 2007–08, 375 students received support, including 31 fellowships with full and partial tuition reimbursements available (averaging $17,189 per year); career-related internships or fieldwork, Federal Work-Study, institutionally sponsored loans, scholarships/grants, health care benefits, tuition waivers (full and partial), and unspecified assistantships also available. Support available to part-time students. Financial award application deadline: 2/1; financial award applicants required to submit FAFSA. *Faculty research:* Learning and development; educational leadership and organizations; educational policy analysis. Total annual research expenditures: $16.7 million. *Unit head:* Jennifer L. Petrallia, Assistant Dean for Master's Studies, 617-495-8445. *Application contact:* Information Contact, 617-495-3414, Fax: 617-496-3577, E-mail: gseadmissions@harvard.edu.

Hunter College of the City University of New York, Graduate School, School of Arts and Sciences, Department of Psychology, New York, NY 10021-5085. Offers applied and evaluative psychology (MA); biopsychology and comparative psychology (MA); social, cognitive, and developmental psychology (MA). Part-time and evening/weekend programs available. *Faculty:* 8 full-time (2 women), 4 part-time/adjunct (2 women). *Students:* 7 full-time (5 women), 68 part-time (57 women); includes 10 minority (2 African Americans, 1 Asian American or Pacific Islander, 7 Hispanic Americans). Average age 29. 100 applicants, 47% accepted, 21 enrolled. In 2007, 30 degrees awarded. *Degree requirements:* For master's, comprehensive exam, thesis. *Entrance requirements:* For master's, GRE General Test, minimum 12 credits of course work in psychology, including statistics and experimental psychology; 2 letters of recommendation. Additional exam requirements/recommendations for international students: Required—TOEFL. *Application deadline:* For fall admission, 4/1 for domestic students, 2/1 for international students; for spring admission, 11/1 for domestic students, 9/1 for international students. Applications are processed on a rolling basis. Application fee: $125. *Expenses:* Tuition, state resident: full-time $6,400; part-time $270 per credit. Tuition, nonresident: part-time $500 per credit. One-time fee: $125 full-time. Tuition and fees vary according to program. *Financial support:* Federal Work-Study, scholarships/grants, and tuition waivers (partial) available. Support available to part-time students. *Faculty research:* Personality, cognitive and linguistic development, hormonal and neural control of behavior, gender and culture, social cognition of health and attitudes. *Unit head:* Dr. Gordon A. Barr, Acting Chair, 212-772-5550. *Application contact:* William Zlata, Director for Graduate Admissions, 212-772-4482, Fax: 212-650-3336, E-mail: admissions@hunter.cuny.edu.

Cognitive Sciences

Indiana University Bloomington, University Graduate School, College of Arts and Sciences, Cognitive Science Program, Bloomington, IN 47405-7000. Offers PhD. *Students:* 10 full-time (1 woman), 2 part-time (both women); includes 2 minority (both Hispanic Americans), 5 international. Average age 32. 49 applicants, 10% accepted, 5 enrolled. In 2007, 10 degrees awarded. *Median time to degree:* Of those who began their doctoral program in fall 1999, 67% received their degree in 8 years or less. Application fee: $50 ($60 for international students). *Financial support:* Fellowships, research assistantships available. *Unit head:* Robert Goldstone, Director, 812-856-3889, E-mail: rgoldsto@indiana.edu. *Application contact:* Susan Towle, Information Contact, 812-855-0031, E-mail: stowle@indiana.edu.

Indiana University Bloomington, University Graduate School, College of Arts and Sciences, Department of Psychological and Brain Sciences, Bloomington, IN 47405-7000. Offers biology and behavior (PhD); clinical science (PhD); cognitive psychology (PhD); developmental psychology (PhD); psychological and brain sciences (MA); social psychology (PhD). *Accreditation:* APA (one or more programs are accredited). *Faculty:* 53 full-time (16 women). *Students:* 79 full-time (42 women), 14 part-time (7 women); includes 10 minority (3 African Americans, 3 Asian Americans or Pacific Islanders, 4 Hispanic Americans), 16 international. Average age 28. 240 applicants, 10% accepted, 20 enrolled. In 2007, 5 master's, 15 doctorates awarded. *Median time to degree:* Of those who began their doctoral program in fall 1999, 86% received their degree in 8 years or less. *Degree requirements:* For doctorate, comprehensive exam, thesis/dissertation, 1st and 2nd year projects, 1 year as associate instructor, qualifying exam, teaching. *Entrance requirements:* For doctorate, GRE. Additional exam requirements/recommendations for international students: Required—TOEFL (minimum score 550 paper-based; 213 computer-based). *Application deadline:* For fall admission, 12/15 for domestic students, 12/1 for international students. Application fee: $50 ($60 for international students). Electronic applications accepted. *Financial support:* Fellowships with full tuition reimbursements, research assistantships with full tuition reimbursements, teaching assistantships with full tuition reimbursements, scholarships/grants, health care benefits, and unspecified assistantships available. *Unit head:* Dr. Linda B. Smith, Chair, 812-855-3991, Fax: 812-855-4691, E-mail: smith4@indiana.edu. *Application contact:* Patricia G. Crouch, Academic Services Coordinator, 812-855-4528, Fax: 812-855-4691, E-mail: pcrouch@indiana.edu.

Iowa State University of Science and Technology, Graduate College, College of Liberal Arts and Sciences, Department of Psychology, Ames, IA 50011. Offers cognitive psychology (PhD); counseling psychology (PhD); social psychology (PhD). *Accreditation:* APA. *Faculty:* 25 full-time (8 women), 8 part-time/adjunct (4 women). *Students:* 63 full-time (43 women); includes 10 minority (3 African Americans, 7 Asian Americans or Pacific Islanders), 4 international. Average age 26. 117 applicants, 14% accepted, 11 enrolled. In 2007, 8 doctorates awarded. Terminal master's awarded for partial completion of doctoral program. *Median time to degree:* Of those who began their doctoral program in fall 1999, 100% received their degree in 8 years or less. *Degree requirements:* For doctorate, thesis/dissertation. *Entrance requirements:* For doctorate, GRE General Test, GRE Subject Test (psychology). Additional exam requirements/recommendations for international students: Required—TOEFL (minimum score 560 paper-based; 220 computer-based). *Application deadline:* For fall admission, 1/5 priority date for domestic and international students. Application fee: $30 ($70 for international students). Electronic applications accepted. *Financial support:* In 2007–08, 45 students received support, including 2 fellowships with full tuition reimbursements available (averaging $14,055 per year), 13 research assistantships with full tuition reimbursements available (averaging $12,200 per year), 30 teaching assistantships with full tuition reimbursements available (averaging $12,200 per year); scholarships/grants, health care benefits, and unspecified assistantships also available. *Faculty research:* Counseling psychology, cognitive psychology, social psychology, health psychology, psychology and public policy. Total annual research expenditures: $2 million. *Unit head:* Dr. David L Vogel, Director of Graduate Education, 515-294-1742, Fax: 515-294-6424, E-mail: dvogel@iastate.edu. *Application contact:* Ann K Schmidt, Graduate Admissions Secretary, 515-294-1743, Fax: 515-294-6424, E-mail: psychadm@iastate.edu.

The Johns Hopkins University, Zanvyl Krieger School of Arts and Sciences, Department of Cognitive Science, Baltimore, MD 21218-2699. Offers PhD. *Faculty:* 8 full-time (3 women), 2 part-time/adjunct (1 woman). *Students:* 26 full-time (14 women); includes 5 minority (1 African American, 4 Hispanic Americans), 2 international. Average age 25. 27 applicants, 30% accepted, 6 enrolled. In 2007, 1 doctorate awarded. *Median time to degree:* Of those who began their doctoral program in fall 1999, 100% received their degree in 8 years or less. *Degree requirements:* For doctorate, one foreign language, thesis/dissertation, 2 research papers. *Entrance requirements:* For doctorate, GRE General Test, letters of recommendation, sample of work. Additional exam requirements/recommendations for international students: Required—TOEFL (minimum score 600 paper-based; 250 computer-based). *Application deadline:* For fall admission, 1/15 for domestic and international students. Application fee: $65. Electronic applications accepted. *Financial support:* In 2007–08, 22 students received support, including 5 fellowships with full tuition reimbursements available (averaging $30,000 per year), 3 research assistantships with full tuition reimbursements available (averaging $20,000 per year), 14 teaching assistantships with full tuition reimbursements available (averaging $25,000 per year); Federal Work-Study, institutionally sponsored loans, scholarships/grants, health care benefits, tuition waivers (full and partial), and unspecified assistantships also available. Financial award application deadline: 1/15; financial award applicants required to submit FAFSA. *Faculty research:* Acquisition and development, cognitive neuropsychology and neuroscience, computational studies, psycholinguistics and cognitive psychology, theoretical linguistics. Total annual research expenditures: $10.2 million. *Unit head:* Dr. Barbara Landau, Chair, 410-516-5255, Fax: 410-516-8020, E-mail: landau@cogsci.jhu.edu. *Application contact:* Pat Creswell, Secretary, 410-516-5250, Fax: 410-516-8020, E-mail: creswell@cogsci.jhu.edu.

Louisiana State University and Agricultural and Mechanical College, Graduate School, College of Arts and Sciences, Department of Psychology, Baton Rouge, LA 70803. Offers biological psychology (MA, PhD); clinical psychology (MA, PhD); cognitive psychology (MA, PhD); developmental psychology (MA, PhD); industrial/organizational psychology (MA, PhD); school psychology (MA, PhD). *Accreditation:* APA (one or more programs are accredited). *Faculty:* 25 full-time (9 women). *Students:* 81 full-time (60 women), 23 part-time (15 women); includes 15 minority (6 African Americans, 4 American Indian/Alaska Native, 2 Asian Americans or Pacific Islanders, 3 Hispanic Americans), 3 international. Average age 28. 199 applicants, 15% accepted, 23 enrolled. In 2007, 11 master's, 13 doctorates awarded. Terminal master's awarded for partial completion of doctoral program. *Degree requirements:* For master's, thesis; for doctorate, thesis/dissertation, 1 year internship. *Entrance requirements:* For master's and doctorate, GRE General Test, minimum GPA of 3.0. Additional exam requirements/recommendations for international students: Required—TOEFL (minimum score 550 paper-based; 213 computer-based; 79 iBT). *Application deadline:* For fall admission, 1/15 for domestic and international students. Applications are processed on a rolling basis. Application fee: $25. Electronic applications accepted. *Financial support:* In 2007–08, 101 students received support, including 5 fellowships (averaging $26,557 per year), 55 teaching assistantships with partial tuition reimbursements available (averaging $13,218 per year); research assistantships with partial tuition reimbursements available, career-related internships or fieldwork, Federal Work-Study, institutionally sponsored loans, scholarships/grants, health care benefits, and tuition waivers (full and partial) also available. Financial award applicants required to submit FAFSA. *Faculty research:* Clinical psychology, autism, anxiety, addition, neuro-psychology, school psychology, cognitive psychology, experimental psychology. Total annual research expenditures: $582,678. *Unit head:* Dr. Alan Baumeister, Chair, 225-578-4099, Fax: 225-578-4125, E-mail: abaumei@lsu.edu. *Application contact:* Dr. Janet McDonald, Coordinator of Graduate Studies, 225-578-4116, Fax: 225-578-4125, E-mail: psmcdo@lsu.edu.

Loyola University Chicago, Graduate School, Department of Psychology, Program in Applied Human Perception and Performance, Chicago, IL 60611-2196. Offers MS. *Entrance requirements:* For master's, two letters of recommendation, 3.5 GPA. Application fee: $50. *Expenses:* Tuition: Full-time $12,780; part-time $710 per credit hour. Required fees: $55 per semester. Full-time tuition and fees vary according to program. *Faculty research:* Auditory information processing, visual information processing, attention, sensory memory, decision theory. *Unit head:* Dr. Raymond Dye, Program Director, 773-508-3018, Fax: 773-508-8713, E-mail: rdye@luc.edu.

Massachusetts Institute of Technology, School of Science, Department of Brain and Cognitive Sciences, Cambridge, MA 02139-4307. Offers cognitive science (PhD); neuroscience (PhD). *Faculty:* 37 full-time (12 women). *Students:* 90 full-time (38 women); includes 20 minority (4 African Americans, 1 American Indian/Alaska Native, 11 Asian Americans or Pacific Islanders, 4 Hispanic Americans), 16 international. Average age 27. 328 applicants, 11% accepted, 19 enrolled. In 2007, 6 degrees awarded. *Degree requirements:* For doctorate, comprehensive exam, thesis/dissertation. *Entrance requirements:* For doctorate, GRE General Test. Additional exam requirements/recommendations for international students: Required—TOEFL (minimum score 577 paper-based; 233 computer-based). *Application deadline:* For fall admission, 12/15 for domestic and international students. Application fee: $70. Electronic applications accepted. *Expenses:* Tuition: Full-time $34,760; part-time $545 per unit. Required fees: $236. *Financial support:* In 2007–08, 88 students received support, including 66 fellowships with tuition reimbursements available (averaging $22,618 per year), 21 research assistantships with tuition reimbursements available (averaging $22,950 per year), 2 teaching assistantships with tuition reimbursements available (averaging $19,800 per year); Federal Work-Study, institutionally sponsored loans, scholarships/grants, traineeships, health care benefits, and unspecified assistantships also available. *Faculty research:* Vision, learning and memory, motor control, plasticity. Total annual research expenditures: $20.3 million. *Unit head:* Prof. Mriganka Sur, Head, 617-253-5748, Fax: 617-258-9216, E-mail: bcs-info@mit.edu. *Application contact:* Academic Office, 617-253-7403, Fax: 617-253-9767, E-mail: bcs-admissions@mit.edu.

Mississippi State University, College of Arts and Sciences, Department of Psychology, Mississippi State, MS 39762. Offers clinical psychology (MS); cognitive science (PhD); experimental psychology (MS). *Faculty:* 16 full-time (7 women), 2 part-time/adjunct (1 woman). *Students:* 31 full-time (21 women), 14 part-time (7 women); includes 2 minority (1 African American, 1 American Indian/Alaska Native), 2 international. Average age 26. 32 applicants, 47% accepted, 8 enrolled. In 2007, 8 master's awarded. Terminal master's awarded for partial completion of doctoral program. *Degree requirements:* For master's, comprehensive exam, thesis; for doctorate, thesis/dissertation, qualifying exam, comprehensive written and oral exam. *Entrance requirements:* For master's, GRE General Test, minimum GPA of 2.75; for doctorate, GRE General Test, proficiency in at least 1 computer language. Additional exam requirements/recommendations for international students: Required—TOEFL. *Application deadline:* For fall admission, 7/1 priority date for domestic students; for spring admission, 11/1 for domestic students. Applications are processed on a rolling basis. Application fee: $30. *Expenses:* Tuition, state resident: full-time $4,978; part-time $274 per hour. Tuition, nonresident: full-time $11,469; part-time $635 per hour. *Financial support:* In 2007–08, 13 teaching assistantships with full tuition reimbursements (averaging $8,877 per year) were awarded; research assistantships with full tuition reimbursements, career-related internships or fieldwork, Federal Work-Study, institutionally sponsored loans, scholarships/grants, and unspecified assistantships also available. Financial award applicants required to submit FAFSA. *Faculty research:* Personality type, alcoholism, blindness and low vision, mental retardation, language comprehension. Total annual research expenditures: $4.5 million. *Unit head:* Dr. Stephen B. Klein, Head, 662-325-3202, Fax: 662-325-7212, E-mail: sbkl@ra.msstate.edu. *Application contact:* Dr. William A. Person, Interim Associate Vice President for Academic Affairs/Interim Dean of Graduate Studies, 662-325-7400, Fax: 662-325-1967, E-mail: grad@grad.msstate.edu.

New York University, Graduate School of Arts and Science, Department of Psychology, New York, NY 10012-1019. Offers cognition and perception (PhD); community psychology (PhD); general psychology (MA); industrial/organizational psychology (MA); psychotherapy and psychoanalysis (Advanced Certificate); social/personality psychology (PhD). Part-time programs available. *Faculty:* 38 full-time (13 women), 78 part-time/adjunct. *Students:* 155 full-time (115 women), 305 part-time (218 women); includes 77 minority (24 African Americans, 29 Asian Americans or Pacific Islanders, 24 Hispanic Americans), 53 international. Average age 32. 767 applicants, 46% accepted, 112 enrolled. In 2007, 80 master's, 15 doctorates awarded. Terminal master's awarded for partial completion of doctoral program. *Degree requirements:* For master's, comprehensive exam, thesis or alternative; for doctorate, thesis/dissertation. *Entrance requirements:* For master's, GRE General Test, minimum GPA of 3.0; for doctorate, GRE General Test, GRE Subject Test; for Advanced Certificate, doctoral degree, minimum GPA of 3.0. Additional exam requirements/recommendations for international students: Required—TOEFL. *Application deadline:* For fall admission, 12/18 for domestic students. Application fee: $85. *Financial support:* Fellowships with tuition reimbursements, research assistantships with tuition reimbursements, teaching assistantships with tuition reimbursements, career-related internships or fieldwork, Federal Work-Study, institutionally sponsored loans, scholarships/grants, traineeships, health care benefits, and unspecified assistantships available. Financial award application deadline: 12/18; financial award applicants required to submit FAFSA. *Faculty research:* Vision, memory, social cognition, social and cognitive development, relationships. *Unit head:* Marisa Carrasco, Chair, 212-998-7900, Fax: 212-995-4018, E-mail: psychq@psych.nyu.edu. *Application contact:* Laurence Maloney, Director of Graduate Studies, 212-998-7900, Fax: 212-995-4018, E-mail: psychq@psych.nyu.edu.

North Dakota State University, College of Graduate and Interdisciplinary Studies, College of Science and Mathematics, Department of Psychology, Fargo, ND 58105. Offers clinical psychology (MS); cognitive and visual neuroscience (PhD); health and social psychology (PhD); psychology (MS). *Faculty:* 18 full-time (4 women), 2 part-time/adjunct (1 woman). *Students:* 36 full-time (27 women); includes 4 minority (1 African American, 2 Asian Americans or Pacific Islanders, 1 Hispanic American), 1 international. Average age 24. 48 applicants, 33% accepted, 10 enrolled. In 2007, 3 master's, 1 doctorate awarded. *Degree requirements:* For master's, thesis; for doctorate, thesis/dissertation. *Entrance requirements:* For master's and doctorate, GRE General Test, GRE Subject Test. Additional exam requirements/recommendations for international students: Required—TOEFL (minimum score 525 paper-based; 197 computer-based; 71 iBT). *Application deadline:* For fall admission, 3/1 for domestic and international students. Application fee: $45 ($60 for international students). Electronic applications accepted. *Expenses:* Tuition, state resident: full-time $5,376; part-time $224 per credit. Tuition, nonresident: full-time $14,354; part-time $598 per credit. Required fees: $962; $40 per credit. Part-time tuition and fees vary according to course load and reciprocity agreements. *Financial support:* In 2007–08, 36 students received support, including 2 fellowships with full tuition reimbursements available (averaging $16,000 per year), 23 research assistantships with full tuition reimbursements available (averaging $16,000 per year), 11 teaching assistantships with full tuition reimbursements available (averaging $6,000 per year); career-related internships or fieldwork, Federal Work-Study, institutionally sponsored loans, tuition waivers (full and partial), and unspecified assistantships also available. Support available to part-time students. Financial award application deadline: 3/1. *Faculty research:* Cognition science, neuropsychology, group behavior, applied behavior analysis, behavior therapy. Total annual research expenditures: $2 million. *Unit head:* Dr. Paul D. Rokke, Chair, 701-231-8622, Fax: 701-231-8426, E-mail: paul.rokke@ndsu.edu.

Northwestern University, The Graduate School, Judd A. and Marjorie Weinberg College of Arts and Sciences, Department of Psychology, Evanston, IL 60208. Offers brain, behavior and cognition (PhD); clinical psychology (PhD); cognitive psychology (PhD); personality (PhD); social psychology (PhD); JD/PhD. Admissions and degrees offered through The Graduate School. *Accreditation:* APA (one or more programs are accredited). Part-time programs available. *Degree requirements:* For doctorate, thesis/dissertation. *Entrance requirements:* For doctorate, GRE General Test, GRE Subject Test. Additional exam requirements/recommendations for international students: Required—TOEFL. Electronic applications accepted. *Faculty research:* Memory and higher order cognition, anxiety and depression, effectiveness of psychotherapy, social cognition, molecular basis of memory.

The Ohio State University, Graduate School, College of Social and Behavioral Sciences, School of Social and Behavioral Science, Department of Psychology, Columbus, OH 43210.

Offers behavioral neuroscience (PhD); clinical psychology (PhD); cognitive psychology (PhD); developmental psychology (PhD); mental retardation and developmental disabilities (PhD); psychology (MA); quantitative psychology (PhD); social psychology (PhD). *Accreditation:* APA (one or more programs are accredited). *Faculty:* 60. *Students:* 111 full-time (78 women), 6 part-time (4 women); includes 19 minority (6 African Americans, 1 American Indian/Alaska Native, 3 Asian Americans or Pacific Islanders, 9 Hispanic Americans), 16 international. Average age 27. In 2007, 17 master's, 41 doctorates awarded. *Degree requirements:* For doctorate, thesis/dissertation. *Entrance requirements:* For master's and doctorate, GRE General Test. Additional exam requirements/recommendations for international students: Required—TOEFL (minimum score 600 paper-based; 250 computer-based). *Application deadline:* For fall admission, 12/31 for domestic students, 11/30 for international students. Applications are processed on a rolling basis. Application fee: $40 ($50 for international students). Electronic applications accepted. *Financial support:* Fellowships, research assistantships, teaching assistantships available. *Unit head:* Marilynn B. Brewer, Graduate Studies Committee Chair, 614-292-3038, Fax: 614-292-4537. *Application contact:* 614-292-9444, Fax: 614-292-3895, E-mail: domestic.grad@osu.edu.

Penn State University Park, Graduate School, College of the Liberal Arts, Department of Psychology, State College, University Park, PA 16802-1503. Offers clinical psychology (MS, PhD); cognitive psychology (MS, PhD); developmental psychology (MS, PhD); industrial/organizational psychology (MS, PhD); psychobiology (MS, PhD); social psychology (MS, PhD). *Accreditation:* APA (one or more programs are accredited). *Expenses:* Tuition, state resident: full-time $14,738; part-time $614 per credit. Tuition, nonresident: full-time $26,050; part-time $1,085 per credit. Tuition and fees vary according to course load, program and student level. *Unit head:* Dr. Melvin M. Mark, Interim Head, 814-865-9515, Fax: 814-863-7002, E-mail: m5m@psu.edu.

Queen's University at Kingston, School of Graduate Studies and Research, Faculty of Arts and Sciences, Department of Psychology, Kingston, ON K7L 3N6, Canada. Offers brain behavior and cognitive science (MA, PhD); clinical psychology (MA, PhD); developmental psychology (MA, PhD); social personality psychology (MA, PhD). *Accreditation:* APA (one or more programs are accredited). *Degree requirements:* For master's, thesis; for doctorate, comprehensive exam, thesis/dissertation. *Entrance requirements:* For master's and doctorate, GRE General Test. Additional exam requirements/recommendations for international students: Required—TOEFL. *Faculty research:* Human development, social, personality, behavioral neuroscience, forensic.

Rensselaer Polytechnic Institute, Graduate School, School of Humanities and Social Sciences, Department of Cognitive Science, Troy, NY 12180-3590. Offers PhD. *Faculty:* 20 full-time (2 women), 4 part-time/adjunct (1 woman). *Students:* Average age 23. 26 applicants, 15% accepted, 1 enrolled. *Degree requirements:* For doctorate, thesis/dissertation. *Entrance requirements:* For doctorate, GRE General Test. Additional exam requirements/recommendations for international students: Required—TOEFL (minimum score 600 paper-based; 250 computer-based), IELTS (minimum score 8). *Application deadline:* For fall admission, 1/15 priority date for domestic students. Applications are processed on a rolling basis. Application fee: $75. Electronic applications accepted. *Expenses:* Tuition: Full-time $34,900; part-time $1,454 per credit. Required fees: $1,802. *Financial support:* In 2007–08, 1 fellowship with full tuition reimbursement (averaging $21,000 per year), 7 research assistantships with full tuition reimbursements (averaging $16,000 per year), 3 teaching assistantships with full tuition reimbursements (averaging $14,500 per year) were awarded; career-related internships or fieldwork, institutionally sponsored loans, and unspecified assistantships also available. Financial award application deadline: 2/1. *Faculty research:* Perception and action, logic, artificial intelligence, cognitive engineering, computational cognitive modeling. Total annual research expenditures: $1.3 million. *Unit head:* Dr. Selmer Bringsjord, Professor and Chair, 518-276-8105, Fax: 518-276-8268, E-mail: brings@rpi.edu. *Application contact:* Betty Osganian, Program Coordinator, 518-276-6473, Fax: 518-276-8268, E-mail: osgane@rpi.edu.

See Close-Up on page 1471.

Rice University, Graduate Programs, School of Social Sciences, Department of Psychology, Houston, TX 77251-1892. Offers cognitive sciences (MA, PhD); industrial-organizational/social psychology (MA, PhD); psychology (MA, PhD). Terminal master's awarded for partial completion of doctoral program. *Degree requirements:* For master's, thesis; for doctorate, thesis/dissertation. *Entrance requirements:* For doctorate, GRE General Test, minimum GPA of 3.0. Additional exam requirements/recommendations for international students: Required—TOEFL. Electronic applications accepted. *Faculty research:* Learning and memory, information processing, decision theory.

Rutgers, The State University of New Jersey, Newark, Graduate School, Program in Psychology, Newark, NJ 07102. Offers cognitive neuroscience (PhD); cognitive science (PhD); perception (PhD); psychobiology (PhD); social cognition (PhD). *Degree requirements:* For doctorate, comprehensive exam, thesis/dissertation. *Entrance requirements:* For doctorate, GRE General Test, GRE Subject Test, minimum undergraduate B average. Electronic applications accepted. *Faculty research:* Visual perception (luminance, motion), neuroendocrine mechanisms in behavior (reproduction, pain), attachment theory, connectionist modeling of cognition.

See Close-Up on page 1475.

Rutgers, The State University of New Jersey, New Brunswick, Graduate School, Program in Psychology, New Brunswick, NJ 08901-1281. Offers behavioral neuroscience (PhD); clinical psychology (PhD); cognitive psychology (PhD); interdisciplinary health psychology (PhD); social psychology (PhD). *Accreditation:* APA. *Degree requirements:* For doctorate, thesis/dissertation. *Entrance requirements:* For doctorate, GRE General Test, 3 letters of recommendation. Additional exam requirements/recommendations for international students: Required—TOEFL (minimum score 577 paper-based; 233 computer-based). Electronic applications accepted. *Faculty research:* Learning and memory, behavioral ecology, hormones and behavior, psychopharmacology, anxiety disorders.

State University of New York at Binghamton, Graduate School, School of Arts and Sciences, Department of Psychology, Specialization in Cognitive and Behavioral Science, Binghamton, NY 13902-6000. Offers MA, PhD. *Students:* 15 full-time (8 women), 4 part-time (2 women); includes 2 minority (both Asian Americans or Pacific Islanders), 2 international. Average age 27. 18 applicants, 44% accepted, 4 enrolled. In 2007, 3 master's, 2 doctorates awarded. *Degree requirements:* For master's, thesis; for doctorate, thesis/dissertation, departmental qualifying exam. *Entrance requirements:* For master's and doctorate, GRE General Test, GRE Subject Test. Additional exam requirements/recommendations for international students: Required—TOEFL. *Application deadline:* For fall admission, 4/15 priority date for domestic students, 1/15 priority date for international students; for spring admission, 11/1 for domestic students, 10/1 priority date for international students. Applications are processed on a rolling basis. Application fee: $60. Electronic applications accepted. *Financial support:* In 2007–08, 3 fellowships with full tuition reimbursements (averaging $2,333 per year), 10 research assistantships (averaging $10,000 per year), 13 teaching assistantships with full tuition reimbursements (averaging $16,500 per year) were awarded; career-related internships or fieldwork, Federal Work-Study, institutionally sponsored loans, and unspecified assistantships also available. Support available to part-time students. Financial award application deadline: 2/15. *Unit head:* Dr. Cynthia Connine, Graduate Coordinator, 607-777-2286, E-mail: connine@binghamton.edu.

Stevens Institute of Technology, Graduate School, Arthur E. Imperatore School of Sciences and Arts, Department of Humanities and Social Sciences, Program in Cognitive Science, Hoboken, NJ 07030. Offers Certificate.

Temple University, Graduate School, College of Liberal Arts, Department of Psychology, Program in Cognitive Psychology, Philadelphia, PA 19122-6096. Offers PhD. *Degree requirements:* For doctorate, thesis/dissertation. *Entrance requirements:* For doctorate, GRE General Test, minimum GPA of 3.0. Additional exam requirements/recommendations for international students: Required—TOEFL (minimum score 550 paper-based; 213 computer-based; 79 iBT). Electronic applications accepted. *Faculty research:* Language development, creativity, childhood memory, visual perception, aging.

Texas A&M University, College of Liberal Arts, Department of Psychology, College Station, TX 77843. Offers behavioral and cellular neuroscience (MS, PhD); clinical psychology (MS, PhD); cognitive psychology (MS, PhD); developmental psychology (MS, PhD); industrial/organizational psychology (MS, PhD); social psychology (MS, PhD). *Accreditation:* APA (one or more programs are accredited). *Faculty:* 33. *Students:* 69 full-time (46 women), 14 part-time (10 women); includes 27 minority (7 African Americans, 1 American Indian/Alaska Native, 5 Asian Americans or Pacific Islanders, 14 Hispanic Americans), 8 international. 274 applicants, 11% accepted, 15 enrolled. In 2007, 11 master's, 7 doctorates awarded. *Degree requirements:* For master's, thesis; for doctorate, comprehensive exam (for some programs), thesis/dissertation. *Entrance requirements:* For master's and doctorate, GRE General Test. Additional exam requirements/recommendations for international students: Required—TOEFL. *Application deadline:* For fall admission, 1/5 for domestic and international students. Application fee: $50 ($75 for international students). Electronic applications accepted. *Expenses:* Tuition, state resident: full-time $6,129. Tuition, nonresident: full-time $11,689. Tuition and fees vary according to course load. *Financial support:* Fellowships with partial tuition reimbursements, research assistantships with partial tuition reimbursements, teaching assistantships with partial tuition reimbursements, career-related internships or fieldwork, institutionally sponsored loans, health care benefits, and unspecified assistantships available. Financial award application deadline: 1/5; financial award applicants required to submit FAFSA. *Unit head:* Dr. Steve Rholes, Head, 979-845-2581, Fax: 979-845-4727, E-mail: wsr@psyc.tamu.edu. *Application contact:* Sharon Starr, Graduate Admissions Supervisor, 979-458-1710, Fax: 979-845-4727, E-mail: gradadv@psyc.tamu.edu.

Texas A&M University–Commerce, Graduate School, College of Education and Human Services, Department of Psychology and Special Education, Commerce, TX 75429-3011. Offers cognition and instruction (PhD); psychology (MA, MS); special education (M Ed, MA, MS). Part-time programs available. *Faculty:* 19 full-time (8 women), 6 part-time/adjunct (5 women). *Students:* 29 full-time (25 women), 94 part-time (79 women); includes 25 minority (16 African Americans, 2 American Indian/Alaska Native, 1 Asian American or Pacific Islander, 6 Hispanic Americans), 3 international. In 2007, 28 master's, 3 doctorates awarded. Terminal master's awarded for partial completion of doctoral program. *Degree requirements:* For master's, comprehensive exam, thesis (for some programs); for doctorate, thesis/dissertation, departmental qualifying exam. *Entrance requirements:* For master's, GRE General Test; for doctorate, GRE General Test, 3 letters of recommendation. *Application deadline:* For fall admission, 6/1 priority date for domestic students; for spring admission, 11/1 priority date for domestic students. Applications are processed on a rolling basis. Application fee: $0 ($25 for international students). Electronic applications accepted. *Financial support:* In 2007–08, research assistantships (averaging $7,875 per year), teaching assistantships (averaging $7,875 per year) were awarded; career-related internships or fieldwork, Federal Work-Study, institutionally sponsored loans, and scholarships/grants also available. Financial award application deadline: 5/1; financial award applicants required to submit FAFSA. *Faculty research:* Human learning, study skills, multicultural bilingual, diversity and special education, educationally handicapped. Total annual research expenditures: $65,078. *Unit head:* Tracy Henley, Head, 903-886-5594. *Application contact:* Tammi Thompson, Graduate Admissions Adviser, 843-886-5167, Fax: 843-886-5165, E-mail: tammi_thompson@tamu-commerce.edu.

University at Buffalo, the State University of New York, Graduate School, College of Arts and Sciences, Department of Psychology, Buffalo, NY 14260. Offers behavioral neuroscience (PhD); clinical psychology (PhD); cognitive psychology (PhD); general psychology (MA); social-personality psychology (PhD). *Accreditation:* APA (one or more programs are accredited). Terminal master's awarded for partial completion of doctoral program. *Degree requirements:* For master's, project; for doctorate, thesis/dissertation. *Entrance requirements:* For master's and doctorate, GRE General Test. Additional exam requirements/recommendations for international students: Required—TOEFL (minimum score 550 paper-based; 213 computer-based; 79 iBT). Electronic applications accepted. *Faculty research:* Neural, endocrine, and molecular bases of behavior; adult mood and anxiety disorders; relationship dysfunction; attention deficit/hyperactivity disorder; psycho-linguistics.

The University of Akron, Graduate School, Buchtel College of Arts and Sciences, Department of Psychology, Program in Applied Cognitive Aging, Akron, OH 44325. Offers MA, PhD. *Students:* Average age 29. 4 applicants. In 2007, 1 degree awarded. *Degree requirements:* For master's, thesis optional, thesis or specialty exam; for doctorate, one foreign language, comprehensive exam, thesis/dissertation. *Entrance requirements:* For master's, GRE General Test, GRE Subject Test, minimum GPA of 2.75, letters of recommendation; for doctorate, GRE General Test, GRE Subject Test, minimum graduate GPA of 3.25, letters of recommendation, personal statement. Additional exam requirements/recommendations for international students: Required—TOEFL (minimum score 550 paper-based; 213 computer-based; 79 iBT). *Application deadline:* For fall admission, 1/15 for domestic and international students. Applications are processed on a rolling basis. Application fee: $30 ($40 for international students). Electronic applications accepted. *Expenses:* Tuition, state resident: full-time $6,164; part-time $342 per credit. Tuition, nonresident: full-time $10,575; part-time $588 per credit. Required fees: $806; $43 per credit. $12 per term. Tuition and fees vary according to course load, degree level and program. *Financial support:* Fellowships with full tuition reimbursements, research assistantships with full tuition reimbursements, teaching assistantships with full tuition reimbursements available. *Faculty research:* Changes in memory and cognition with age, automaticity and effects of training, models of visual word recognition, and experimental neuropsychology. *Unit head:* Dr. Phil Allen, Coordinator, 330-972-6177, E-mail: paallen@uakron.edu.

The University of British Columbia, Faculty of Arts and Faculty of Graduate Studies, Department of Psychology, Vancouver, BC V6T 1Z1, Canada. Offers behavioral neuroscience (MA, PhD); clinical psychology (MA, PhD); cognitive science (MA, PhD); developmental psychology (MA, PhD); forensic psychology (PhD); health psychology (MA, PhD); quantitative methods (MA, PhD); social/personality psychology (MA, PhD). *Accreditation:* APA (one or more programs are accredited). *Faculty:* 46 full-time (20 women), 26 part-time/adjunct (13 women). *Students:* 102 full-time (69 women). Average age 29. 247 applicants, 14% accepted, 18 enrolled. In 2007, 14 master's, 11 doctorates awarded. Terminal master's awarded for partial completion of doctoral program. *Median time to degree:* Of those who began their doctoral program in fall 1999, 91% received their degree in 8 years or less. *Degree requirements:* For master's, thesis; for doctorate, comprehensive exam, thesis/dissertation. *Entrance requirements:* For master's and doctorate, GRE General Test, GRE Subject Test. Additional exam requirements/recommendations for international students: Required—TOEFL (minimum score 550 paper-based; 230 computer-based; 80 iBT). *Application deadline:* For fall admission, 1/15 for domestic and international students. Applications are processed on a rolling basis. Application fee: $90 Canadian dollars ($150 Canadian dollars for international students). Electronic applications accepted. *Financial support:* In 2007–08, 95 students received support, including 27 fellowships with full and partial tuition reimbursements available (averaging $16,500 per year), 50 research assistantships with full and partial tuition reimbursements available (averaging $6,775 per year), 80 teaching assistantships with full and partial tuition reimbursements available (averaging $8,065 per year); career-related internships or fieldwork, Federal Work-Study, institutionally sponsored loans, scholarships/grants, health care benefits, tuition waivers (full and partial), and unspecified assistantships also available. Financial award application deadline: 1/15. *Faculty research:* Clinical, developmental, social/personality, cognition, behavioral neuroscience. Total annual research expenditures: $5.5 million Canadian dollars. *Unit head:* Dr. Eric Eich, Head, 604-822-3078, Fax: 604-822-6923, E-mail: ee@psych.ubc.ca. *Application contact:* Rose Tam, Graduate Secretary, 604-822-3144, Fax: 604-822-6923, E-mail: gradsec@psych.ubc.ca.

Cognitive Sciences

University of California, San Diego, Office of Graduate Studies, Department of Cognitive Science, La Jolla, CA 92093. Offers PhD. *Faculty:* 16 full-time (6 women), 4 part-time/adjunct (2 women). *Students:* 40 full-time (15 women); includes 4 minority (2 African Americans, 2 Hispanic Americans), 6 international. 118 applicants, 20% accepted, 12 enrolled. In 2007, 3 doctorates awarded. *Median time to degree:* Of those who began their doctoral program in fall 1999, 84% received their degree in 8 years or less. *Degree requirements:* For doctorate, one foreign language, thesis/dissertation. *Entrance requirements:* For doctorate, GRE General Test. Additional exam requirements/recommendations for international students: Required—TOEFL (minimum score 550 paper-based; 213 computer-based). *Application deadline:* For fall admission, 12/1 for domestic and international students. Application fee: $60 ($80 for international students). Electronic applications accepted. *Financial support:* In 2007–08, 40 students received support, including fellowships with full and partial tuition reimbursements available (averaging $22,620 per year), research assistantships with full tuition reimbursements available (averaging $18,882 per year), teaching assistantships with full and partial tuition reimbursements available (averaging $14,571 per year). Financial award applicants required to submit FAFSA. *Faculty research:* Neural networks, neurobiology of cognition, cognitive modeling, distributed cognition, psycholinguistics. *Unit head:* Marta Kutas, Chair, 858-534-7141, Fax: 858-534-1128, E-mail: gradinfo@cogsci.ucad.edu. *Application contact:* Beverley Walton, Coordinator, 858-534-4387, E-mail: bwalton@ucsd.edu.

University of California, San Diego, Office of Graduate Studies, Interdisciplinary Program in Cognitive Science, La Jolla, CA 92093. Offers cognitive science/anthropology (PhD); cognitive science/communication (PhD); cognitive science/computer science and engineering (PhD); cognitive science/linguistics (PhD); cognitive science/neuroscience (PhD); cognitive science/philosophy (PhD); cognitive science/psychology (PhD); cognitive science/sociology (PhD). Admissions offered through affiliated departments. *Faculty:* 65 full-time (14 women). *Students:* 7 full-time (3 women). Average age 26. 2 applicants, 100% accepted, 2 enrolled. In 2007, 1 degree awarded. *Degree requirements:* For doctorate, thesis/dissertation. *Entrance requirements:* For doctorate, GRE General Test, acceptance into one of the 8 participating departments. *Application deadline:* Applications are processed on a rolling basis. Application fee: $0. *Faculty research:* Language and cognition, philosophy of mind, visual perception, biological anthropology, sociolinguistics. *Unit head:* Gary Cottrell, Director, 858-534-7141, Fax: 858-534-1128, E-mail: gcottrell@ucsd.edu. *Application contact:* Beverley Walton, Coordinator, 858-534-4387, E-mail: bwalton@ucsd.edu.

University of California, Santa Barbara, Graduate Division, College of Letters and Sciences, Division of Humanities and Fine Arts, Department of Linguistics, Santa Barbara, CA 93106. Offers linguistics (PhD), including applied linguistics, cognitive science, human development, language interaction, social organizations; MA/PhD. *Faculty:* 27 full-time (20 women). *Students:* 27 full-time (20 women); includes 3 minority (2 Asian Americans or Pacific Islanders, 1 Hispanic American), 3 international. Average age 32. 46 applicants, 22% accepted, 4 enrolled. In 2007, 3 doctorates awarded. *Median time to degree:* Of those who began their doctoral program in fall 1999, 40% received their degree in 8 years or less. *Degree requirements:* For doctorate, one foreign language, thesis/dissertation, 48 units of coursework, minimum GPA of 3.7. *Entrance requirements:* For doctorate, GRE. Additional exam requirements/recommendations for international students: Required—TOEFL (minimum score 550 paper-based; 213 computer-based; 80 iBT). *Application deadline:* For fall admission, 12/1 for domestic and international students. Application fee: $60. Electronic applications accepted. *Expenses:* Tuition, nonresident: full-time $14,888. Required fees: $10,108. *Financial support:* In 2007–08, 27 students received support, including 18 fellowships with full tuition reimbursements available (averaging $10,500 per year), 4 research assistantships with full tuition reimbursements available (averaging $15,000 per year), 22 teaching assistantships (averaging $10,310 per year); Federal Work-Study, institutionally sponsored loans, scholarships/grants, health care benefits, and unspecified assistantships also available. Financial award application deadline: 12/1; financial award applicants required to submit FAFSA. *Faculty research:* Syntax, sociolinguistics, discourse and grammar, phonetics and phonology, corpus linguistics. *Unit head:* Prof. Patricia M. Clancy, Chair, 805-893-8658, E-mail: pclancy@linguistics.ucsb.edu. *Application contact:* Prof. Matthew K. Gordon, Information Contact, 805-893-5954, Fax: 805-893-7769, E-mail: mgordon@linguistics.ucsb.edu.

University of California, Santa Barbara, Graduate Division, College of Letters and Sciences, Division of Mathematics, Life, and Physical Sciences, Department of Geography, Santa Barbara, CA 93106. Offers cognitive science (PhD); quantitative methods in social sciences (PhD); MA/PhD. *Faculty:* 22 full-time (3 women), 11 part-time/adjunct (3 women). *Students:* 66 full-time (28 women); includes 6 minority (2 African Americans, 1 American Indian/Alaska Native, 2 Asian Americans or Pacific Islanders, 1 Hispanic American), 11 international. Average age 30. 98 applicants, 33% accepted, 18 enrolled. In 2007, 9 master's, 8 doctorates awarded. *Median time to degree:* Of those who began their doctoral program in fall 1999, 53% received their degree in 8 years or less. *Degree requirements:* For master's, comprehensive exam (for some programs), thesis; for doctorate, comprehensive exam, thesis/dissertation, candidacy, diagnostic interview, written and oral exam, approved dissertation proposal. *Entrance requirements:* For master's and doctorate, GRE General Test, minimum GPA of 3.25 in junior and senior year. Additional exam requirements/recommendations for international students: Required—TOEFL (minimum score 550 paper-based; 213 computer-based; 80 iBT). *Application deadline:* For fall admission, 12/15 for domestic students, 1/15 for international students. Application fee: $60. Electronic applications accepted. *Expenses:* Tuition, nonresident: full-time $14,888. Required fees: $10,108. *Financial support:* In 2007–08, 66 students received support, including 28 fellowships with full and partial tuition reimbursements available (averaging $12,100 per year), 13 research assistantships with full and partial tuition reimbursements available (averaging $13,000 per year), 24 teaching assistantships with full and partial tuition reimbursements available (averaging $15,000 per year); Federal Work-Study, institutionally sponsored loans, scholarships/grants, health care benefits, and unspecified assistantships also available. Financial award application deadline: 12/15; financial award applicants required to submit FAFSA. *Faculty research:* Earth system science, human environment relations, modeling, measurement and computation, quantitative methods in social sciences. *Unit head:* Dr. Oliver Chadwick, Chair, 805-893-4223, E-mail: oac@geog.ucsb.edu. *Application contact:* Karen Barteld, Graduate Program Assistant, 805-893-8789, Fax: 805-893-3146, E-mail: barteld@geog.ucsb.edu.

University of Colorado at Colorado Springs, Graduate School, College of Letters, Arts and Sciences, Department of Psychology, Colorado Springs, CO 80933-7150. Offers geropsychology (PhD); psychology (MA). *Accreditation:* APA. Part-time programs available. *Faculty:* 14 full-time (5 women), 3 part-time/adjunct (1 woman). *Students:* 63 full-time (45 women), 22 part-time (16 women); includes 12 minority (2 African Americans, 6 Asian Americans or Pacific Islanders, 4 Hispanic Americans), 2 international. Average age 29. 22 applicants, 68% accepted, 11 enrolled. In 2007, 11 degrees awarded. *Degree requirements:* For master's, thesis; for doctorate, comprehensive exam, thesis/dissertation. *Entrance requirements:* For master's, GRE, BA in psychology or equivalent background; minimum GPA of 3.0. *Application deadline:* For fall admission, 1/1 for domestic students. Applications are processed on a rolling basis. *Financial support:* Research assistantships, teaching assistantships, career-related internships or fieldwork and Federal Work-Study available. Support available to part-time students. Financial award applicants required to submit FAFSA. *Faculty research:* Aging, social psychology, learning and memory, personality disorders, psychology and law. Total annual research expenditures: $429,985. *Unit head:* Dr. Kelli Klebe, Chair, 719-262-4181, E-mail: kklebe@uccs.edu. *Application contact:* Dr. Hasker Davis, Graduate Student Adviser, 719-262-4148, Fax: 719-262-4166, E-mail: hdavis@uccs.edu.

University of Connecticut, Graduate School, College of Liberal Arts and Sciences, Department of Psychology, Field of Psychology, Storrs, CT 06269. Offers behavioral neuroscience (PhD); biopsychology (PhD); clinical psychology (MA, PhD); cognition and instruction (PhD); developmental psychology (MA, PhD); ecological psychology (PhD); experimental psychology (PhD); general psychology (MA, PhD); health psychology (Graduate Certificate); industrial/organizational psychology (PhD); language and cognition (PhD); neuroscience (PhD); occupational health psychology (Graduate Certificate); social psychology (MA, PhD). *Accreditation:* APA (one or more programs are accredited). *Faculty:* 52 full-time (23 women). *Students:* 130 full-time (94 women), 25 part-time (11 women); includes 24 minority (8 African Americans, 6 Asian Americans or Pacific Islanders, 10 Hispanic Americans), 18 international. Average age 28. 531 applicants, 7% accepted, 35 enrolled. In 2007, 19 master's, 20 doctorates, 2 other advanced degrees awarded. Terminal master's awarded for partial completion of doctoral program. *Degree requirements:* For master's, comprehensive exam; for doctorate, thesis/dissertation. *Entrance requirements:* For master's and doctorate, GRE General Test, GRE Subject Test. Additional exam requirements/recommendations for international students: Required—TOEFL (minimum score 550 paper-based; 213 computer-based). *Application deadline:* For fall admission, 2/1 priority date for domestic and international students; for spring admission, 11/1 for domestic students, 10/1 for international students. Applications are processed on a rolling basis. Application fee: $55. Electronic applications accepted. *Expenses:* Tuition, state resident: part-time $469 per credit hour. Tuition, nonresident: part-time $1,218 per credit hour. *Financial support:* In 2007–08, 54 research assistantships with full tuition reimbursements, 69 teaching assistantships with full tuition reimbursements were awarded; fellowships, career-related internships or fieldwork, Federal Work-Study, scholarships/grants, health care benefits, and unspecified assistantships also available. Financial award application deadline: 2/1; financial award applicants required to submit FAFSA. *Application contact:* Deborah Doucette, Administrative Assistant, 860-486-2057, Fax: 860-486-2760, E-mail: futuregr@psych.psy.uconn.edu.

University of Connecticut, Graduate School, Neag School of Education, Department of Educational Psychology, Storrs, CT 06269. Offers educational psychology (MA, PhD, Post-Master's Certificate), including cognition and instruction, counseling psychology, gifted and talented education, learning technology, measurement, evaluation, and assessment, school psychology, special education. *Faculty:* 39 full-time (17 women). *Students:* 163 full-time (119 women), 141 part-time (104 women); includes 40 minority (18 African Americans, 1 American Indian/Alaska Native, 8 Asian Americans or Pacific Islanders, 13 Hispanic Americans), 18 international. Average age 34. 348 applicants, 38% accepted, 126 enrolled. In 2007, 65 master's, 24 doctorates, 19 other advanced degrees awarded. *Degree requirements:* For master's, comprehensive exam; for doctorate, thesis/dissertation. *Entrance requirements:* For doctorate, GRE General Test. Additional exam requirements/recommendations for international students: Required—TOEFL (minimum score 550 paper-based; 213 computer-based). *Application deadline:* For fall admission, 2/1 priority date for domestic and international students; for spring admission, 11/1 for domestic students, 10/1 for international students. Applications are processed on a rolling basis. Application fee: $55. Electronic applications accepted. *Expenses:* Tuition, state resident: part-time $469 per credit hour. Tuition, nonresident: part-time $1,218 per credit hour. *Financial support:* In 2007–08, 80 research assistantships with full tuition reimbursements, 3 teaching assistantships with full tuition reimbursements were awarded; fellowships, Federal Work-Study, scholarships/grants, health care benefits, and unspecified assistantships also available. Financial award application deadline: 2/1; financial award applicants required to submit FAFSA. *Unit head:* Hariharan Swaminathan, Head, 860-486-4031, Fax: 860-486-0210, E-mail: hariharan.swaminathan@uconn.edu. *Application contact:* Lisa Rasicot, Graduate Coordinator, 860-486-3065, Fax: 860-486-0210, E-mail: l.rasicot@uconn.edu.

University of Connecticut, Graduate School, Neag School of Education, Department of Educational Psychology, Field of Educational Psychology, Program in Cognition and Instruction, Storrs, CT 06269. Offers MA, PhD, Post-Master's Certificate. *Faculty:* 18 full-time (6 women). *Students:* 11 full-time (6 women), 6 part-time (2 women); includes 2 minority (both Hispanic Americans), 4 international. Average age 35. 19 applicants, 37% accepted, 7 enrolled. In 2007, 1 master's, 5 doctorates awarded. *Degree requirements:* For master's, comprehensive exam; for doctorate, thesis/dissertation. *Entrance requirements:* For doctorate, GRE General Test. Additional exam requirements/recommendations for international students: Required—TOEFL (minimum score 550 paper-based; 213 computer-based). *Application deadline:* For fall admission, 2/1 priority date for domestic and international students; for spring admission, 11/1 for domestic students, 10/1 for international students. Applications are processed on a rolling basis. Application fee: $55. Electronic applications accepted. *Expenses:* Tuition, state resident: part-time $469 per credit hour. Tuition, nonresident: part-time $1,218 per credit hour. *Financial support:* In 2007–08, 9 research assistantships with full tuition reimbursements were awarded; fellowships, teaching assistantships with full tuition reimbursements, Federal Work-Study, scholarships/grants, health care benefits, and unspecified assistantships also available. Financial award application deadline: 2/1; financial award applicants required to submit FAFSA. *Application contact:* Lisa Rasicot, Graduate Coordinator, 860-486-3065, Fax: 860-486-0210, E-mail: l.rasicot@uconn.edu.

University of Delaware, College of Arts and Sciences, Department of Psychology, Newark, DE 19716. Offers behavioral neuroscience (PhD); clinical psychology (PhD); cognitive psychology (PhD); social psychology (PhD). *Accreditation:* APA. *Faculty:* 28 full-time (10 women), 3 part-time/adjunct (1 woman). *Students:* 46 full-time (32 women), 3 part-time (2 women); includes 5 minority (4 African Americans, 1 Asian American or Pacific Islander), 3 international. Average age 27. 252 applicants, 8% accepted, 7 enrolled. In 2007, 6 doctorates awarded. *Degree requirements:* For doctorate, thesis/dissertation. *Entrance requirements:* For doctorate, GRE General Test. Additional exam requirements/recommendations for international students: Required—TOEFL (minimum score 600 paper-based; 250 computer-based). *Application deadline:* For fall admission, 1/7 priority date for domestic students. Application fee: $60. Electronic applications accepted. *Financial support:* In 2007–08, 47 students received support, including 7 fellowships with full tuition reimbursements available (averaging $16,000 per year), 14 research assistantships with full tuition reimbursements available (averaging $15,500 per year), 20 teaching assistantships with full tuition reimbursements available (averaging $16,000 per year); career-related internships or fieldwork, Federal Work-Study, institutionally sponsored loans, scholarships/grants, and tuition waivers (full and partial) also available. Financial award application deadline: 1/7. *Faculty research:* Emotion development, neural and cognitive aspects of memory, neural control of feeding, intergroup relations, social cognition and communication. Total annual research expenditures: $2.5 million. *Unit head:* Dr. Thomas M. DiLorenzo, Chair, 302-831-2271, Fax: 302-831-3645. *Application contact:* Linda Scarpitti, Information Contact, 302-831-2271, Fax: 302-831-3645, E-mail: linnie@udel.edu.

University of Florida, Graduate School, College of Liberal Arts and Sciences, Department of Psychology, Gainesville, FL 32611. Offers behavior analysis (PhD); behavioral neuroscience (MS, PhD); cognitive and sensory processes (PhD); counseling psychology (PhD); developmental psychology (PhD); social psychology (MS, PhD); JD/PhD. *Faculty:* 42 full-time (12 women), 3 part-time/adjunct (1 woman). *Students:* 136 (90 women); includes 22 minority (7 African Americans, 1 American Indian/Alaska Native, 5 Asian Americans or Pacific Islanders, 9 Hispanic Americans) 22 international. In 2007, 25 master's, 14 doctorates awarded. *Degree requirements:* For master's, thesis or alternative; for doctorate, thesis/dissertation. *Entrance requirements:* For master's and doctorate, GRE General Test, minimum GPA of 3.0. Additional exam requirements/recommendations for international students: Required—TOEFL (minimum score 550 paper-based; 213 computer-based). *Application deadline:* For fall admission, 1/15 priority date for domestic students. Applications are processed on a rolling basis. Application fee: $30. Electronic applications accepted. *Expenses:* Tuition, state resident: full-time $7,478. Tuition, nonresident: full-time $22,603. *Financial support:* In 2007–08, 33 research assistantships (averaging $16,597 per year), 64 teaching assistantships (averaging $16,703 per year) were awarded; fellowships, career-related internships or fieldwork and unspecified assistantships also available. Financial award application deadline: 1/15. *Faculty research:* Experimental analysis of behavior, psychobiology, cognition and sensory processes, counseling psychology, social psychology, developmental psychology. *Unit head:* Dr. Martin Heesacker, Chair, 352-392-0601 Ext. 200, Fax: 352-392-7985, E-mail: heesack@ufl.edu. *Application contact:* Dr. Gregory Neimeyer, Coordinator, 352-392-0601 Ext. 259, Fax: 352-392-7985, E-mail: neimeyer@ufl.edu.

University of Guelph, Graduate Program Services, College of Social and Applied Human Sciences, Department of Psychology, Guelph, ON N1G 2W1, Canada. Offers applied social psychology (MA, PhD); clinical psychology applied development emphasis (PhD); clinical psychology applied developmental emphasis (MA); industrial/organizational psychology (MA, PhD); neuroscience and applied cognitive science (MA, PhD). *Faculty:* 34 full-time (14 women). *Students:* 95 full-time (72 women), 6 part-time (all women); includes 6 minority (2 African Americans, 4 Asian Americans or Pacific Islanders). 230 applicants, 28% accepted, 35 enrolled. In 2007, 8 master's, 2 doctorates awarded. *Median time to degree:* Of those who began their doctoral program in fall 1999, 100% received their degree in 8 years or less. *Degree requirements:* For master's, thesis; for doctorate, comprehensive exam, thesis/dissertation. *Entrance requirements:* For master's, GRE General Test, GRE Subject Test, minimum B+ average during previous 2 years of course work; for doctorate, GRE General Test, GRE Subject Test, minimum A- average. Additional exam requirements/recommendations for international students: Required—TOEFL (minimum score 89 iBT). *Application deadline:* For fall admission, 12/15 priority date for domestic students, 1/15 priority date for international students; for spring admission, 12/15 priority date for domestic students. Application fee: $85. Electronic applications accepted. *Financial support:* In 2007–08, 108 teaching assistantships with partial tuition reimbursements (averaging $10,213 per year) were awarded. *Faculty research:* Organizational psychology, reading comprehension and mathematical ability, drug addiction and relapse, gender issues and culture, memory, clinical psychology. *Unit head:* Dr. Harvey Marmurek, Chair, 519-824-4120 Ext. 53673, Fax: 519-837-8629, E-mail: marmurek@psy.uoguelph.ca. *Application contact:* Dr. Ian Newby-Clark, Graduate Coordinator, 519-824-4120 Ext. 53307, Fax: 519-837-8629, E-mail: newby-clark@psy.uoguelph.ca.

University of Louisiana at Lafayette, Graduate School, College of Sciences, Institute of Cognitive Science, Lafayette, LA 70504. Offers PhD. *Degree requirements:* For doctorate, comprehensive exam, thesis/dissertation. *Entrance requirements:* For doctorate, GRE General Test, minimum GPA of 3.25. Additional exam requirements/recommendations for international students: Required—TOEFL (minimum score 550 paper-based; 213 computer-based). Electronic applications accepted. *Faculty research:* Computational models of cognition, comparative cognition, cognitive development, computational cognitive neuroscience, memory.

University of Maryland, Baltimore County, Graduate School, College of Natural and Mathematical Sciences, Department of Biological Sciences and Department of Psychology, Program in Neurosciences and Cognitive Sciences, Baltimore, MD 21250. Offers PhD. *Faculty:* 18 full-time (8 women). *Students:* 5 full-time (4 women); includes 3 minority (1 African American, 1 Asian American or Pacific Islander, 1 Hispanic American). 12 applicants, 25% accepted, 0 enrolled. In 2007, 1 degree awarded. *Degree requirements:* For doctorate, comprehensive exam (for some programs), thesis/dissertation. *Entrance requirements:* For doctorate, GRE General Test, minimum GPA of 3.0. Additional exam requirements/recommendations for international students: Required—TOEFL. *Application deadline:* For fall admission, 1/15 for domestic students, 12/15 for international students. Applications are processed on a rolling basis. Application fee: $50. Electronic applications accepted. *Financial support:* In 2007–08, 5 students received support, including 1 fellowship with tuition reimbursement available (averaging $22,500 per year), research assistantships with tuition reimbursements available (averaging $21,500 per year), teaching assistantships with tuition reimbursements available (averaging $20,500 per year). *Unit head:* Dr. Phyllis Robinson, Director, 410-455-3669, Fax: 410-455-3875, E-mail: biograd@umbc.edu.

University of Maryland, College Park, Graduate Studies, Interdepartmental Programs, Program in Neurosciences and Cognitive Sciences, College Park, MD 20742. Offers PhD. *Students:* 45 full-time (27 women), 1 part-time; includes 8 minority (3 African Americans, 1 American Indian/Alaska Native, 3 Asian Americans or Pacific Islanders, 1 Hispanic American), 19 international. 74 applicants, 26% accepted, 13 enrolled. In 2007, 4 degrees awarded. *Degree requirements:* For doctorate, comprehensive exam, thesis/dissertation. *Entrance requirements:* For doctorate, GRE General Test, 3 letters of recommendation. Additional exam requirements/recommendations for international students: Required—TOEFL. *Application deadline:* For fall admission, 12/1 for domestic students, 2/1 for international students. Applications are processed on a rolling basis. Application fee: $60. Electronic applications accepted. *Financial support:* In 2007–08, 9 fellowships (averaging $14,553 per year) were awarded; teaching assistantships, Federal Work-Study and scholarships/grants also available. Support available to part-time students. Financial award applicants required to submit FAFSA. *Faculty research:* Molecular neurobiology, cognition, neural and behavioral systems language, memory, human development. *Unit head:* Dr. Cynthia F. Moss, Director, 301-405-0353, Fax: 301-405-7104, E-mail: moss@umd.edu.

University of Minnesota, Twin Cities Campus, Graduate School, College of Liberal Arts, Department of Psychology, Program in Cognitive and Biological Psychology, Minneapolis, MN 55455-0213. Offers PhD. *Faculty:* 18 full-time (3 women). *Students:* 26 full-time (13 women); includes 4 minority (1 African American, 3 Asian Americans or Pacific Islanders), 4 international. 56 applicants, 20% accepted, 2 enrolled. In 2007, 5 doctorates awarded. *Median time to degree:* Of those who began their doctoral program in fall 1999, 50% received their degree in 8 years or less. *Degree requirements:* For doctorate, comprehensive exam, thesis/dissertation. *Entrance requirements:* For doctorate, GRE General Test, GRE Subject Test (recommended), 12 credits of upper-level psychology courses, including a course in statistics or psychological measurement. Additional exam requirements/recommendations for international students: Required—TOEFL (minimum score 550 paper-based; 213 computer-based; 79 iBT). *Application deadline:* For fall admission, 12/1 for domestic and international students. Application fee: $55 ($75 for international students). *Financial support:* In 2007–08, fellowships with full tuition reimbursements (averaging $21,000 per year), research assistantships with full tuition reimbursements (averaging $12,254 per year), teaching assistantships with full tuition reimbursements (averaging $12,254 per year) were awarded; career-related internships or fieldwork, traineeships, and tuition waivers (partial) also available. Financial award application deadline: 12/1. *Unit head:* Sheng He, Area Director, 612-626-0752. *Application contact:* Coordinator, 612-624-4181, Fax: 612-626-2079, E-mail: psyapply@tc.umn.edu.

University of Nevada, Reno, Graduate School, College of Liberal Arts, Department of Psychology, Program in Cognitive Brain Science, Reno, NV 89557. Offers MA, PhD. *Expenses:* Tuition, state resident: full-time $2,774; part-time $154 per credit. Tuition, nonresident: full-time $13,578; part-time $330 per credit. Required fees: $49 per semester. *Unit head:* Dr. Michael Crognale, Program Director, 775-784-6828.

The University of North Carolina at Chapel Hill, Graduate School, College of Arts and Sciences, Department of Psychology, Chapel Hill, NC 27599. Offers biological psychology (PhD); clinical psychology (PhD); cognitive psychology (PhD); developmental psychology (PhD); quantitative psychology (PhD); social psychology (PhD). *Accreditation:* APA. *Degree requirements:* For doctorate, comprehensive exam, thesis/dissertation. *Entrance requirements:* For doctorate, GRE General Test, minimum GPA of 3.0. Electronic applications accepted. *Faculty research:* Expressed emotion, cognitive development, social cognitive neuroscience, human memory personality.

The University of North Carolina at Greensboro, Graduate School, College of Arts and Sciences, Department of Psychology, Greensboro, NC 27412-5001. Offers clinical psychology (MA, PhD); cognitive psychology (MA, PhD); developmental psychology (MA, PhD); social psychology (MA, PhD). *Accreditation:* APA (one or more programs are accredited). *Faculty:* 23 full-time (8 women). *Students:* 46 full-time (31 women), 13 part-time (10 women); includes 7 minority (3 African Americans, 1 American Indian/Alaska Native, 1 Asian American or Pacific Islander, 2 Hispanic Americans). 218 applicants, 7% accepted.Terminal master's awarded for partial completion of doctoral program. *Degree requirements:* For master's, comprehensive exam, thesis; for doctorate, one foreign language, thesis/dissertation, preliminary exam. *Entrance requirements:* For master's and doctorate, GRE General Test. Additional exam requirements/recommendations for international students: Required—TOEFL. *Application deadline:* For fall admission, 2/1 for domestic students. Application fee: $45. Electronic applications accepted. *Financial support:* Fellowships with full tuition reimbursements, research assistantships with full tuition reimbursements, teaching assistantships with full tuition reimbursements, unspecified assistantships available. *Faculty research:* Sensory and perceptual determinants; evoked potential: disorders, deafness, and development. *Unit head:* Dr. George Michel, Head, 336-336-5013, E-mail: gfmichel@uncg.edu. *Application contact:* Michelle Harkleroad, Director of Graduate Admissions, 336-334-4884, Fax: 336-334-4424, E-mail: mbharkle@uncg.edu.

University of Notre Dame, Graduate School, College of Arts and Letters, Division of Social Science, Department of Psychology, Notre Dame, IN 46556. Offers cognitive psychology (PhD); counseling psychology (PhD); developmental psychology (PhD); quantitative psychology (PhD). *Accreditation:* APA. *Faculty:* 28 full-time (11 women), 5 part-time/adjunct (4 women). *Students:* 62 full-time (43 women); includes 9 minority (3 African Americans, 2 Asian Americans or Pacific Islanders, 4 Hispanic Americans), 9 international. 166 applicants, 15% accepted, 8 enrolled. In 2007, 13 doctorates awarded. *Degree requirements:* For doctorate, comprehensive exam, thesis/dissertation, candidacy exam. *Entrance requirements:* For doctorate, GRE General Test, GRE Subject Test (strongly recommended). Additional exam requirements/recommendations for international students: Required—TOEFL (minimum score 600 paper-based; 250 computer-based; 80 iBT). *Application deadline:* For fall admission, 1/2 for domestic and international students. Application fee: $50. Electronic applications accepted. *Financial support:* In 2007–08, 4 fellowships with full tuition reimbursements (averaging $22,000 per year), 14 research assistantships with full tuition reimbursements (averaging $16,000 per year), 41 teaching assistantships with full tuition reimbursements (averaging $16,000 per year) were awarded; career-related internships or fieldwork and tuition waivers (full) also available. Financial award application deadline: 1/2. *Faculty research:* Cognitive and socio-emotional development, statistical methods and quantitative models applicable to psychology, interpersonal relations, life span development and developmental delay, childhood depression, structural equation and dynamical systems. *Unit head:* Dr. Dawn Gondoli, Director of Graduate Studies, 574-631-6650, Fax: 574-631-8883. *Application contact:* Dr. Jarren Gonzales, Director of Graduate Admissions, 574-631-7706, Fax: 574-631-4183.

University of Oregon, Graduate School, College of Arts and Sciences, Department of Psychology, Eugene, OR 97403. Offers clinical psychology (PhD); cognitive psychology (MA, MS, PhD); developmental psychology (MA, MS, PhD); physiological psychology (MA, MS, PhD); psychology (MA, MS, PhD); social/personality psychology (MA, MS, PhD). *Accreditation:* APA (one or more programs are accredited). *Faculty:* 27 full-time (11 women), 11 part-time/adjunct (8 women). *Students:* 76 full-time (48 women), 10 part-time (7 women); includes 11 minority (1 African American, 7 Asian Americans or Pacific Islanders, 3 Hispanic Americans), 15 international. 320 applicants, 8% accepted. In 2007, 21 master's, 11 doctorates awarded. Terminal master's awarded for partial completion of doctoral program. *Degree requirements:* For doctorate, thesis/dissertation. *Entrance requirements:* For master's, GRE General Test, minimum GPA of 3.0; for doctorate, GRE General Test. Additional exam requirements/recommendations for international students: Required—TOEFL. *Application deadline:* For fall admission, 12/1 for domestic students. Application fee: $50. *Financial support:* In 2007–08, 48 teaching assistantships were awarded; research assistantships, career-related internships or fieldwork also available. *Unit head:* Louis Moses, Head, 541-346-4918, Fax: 541-346-4911. *Application contact:* Lori Olsen, Admissions Contact, 541-346-5060, Fax: 541-346-4911, E-mail: gradsec@psych.uoregon.edu.

University of Pittsburgh, School of Education, Department of Instruction and Learning, Program in Cognitive Studies, Pittsburgh, PA 15260. Offers PhD. *Students:* 7 full-time (5 women), 2 international. 5 applicants, 40% accepted, 0 enrolled. In 2007, 1 doctorate awarded. *Degree requirements:* For doctorate, thesis/dissertation. *Entrance requirements:* For doctorate, GRE General Test. Additional exam requirements/recommendations for international students: Required—TOEFL. *Application deadline:* For fall admission, 2/1 for domestic and international students. Application fee: $50. Electronic applications accepted. *Financial support:* Research assistantships available. Financial award application deadline: 3/15; financial award applicants required to submit FAFSA. *Application contact:* Information Contact, 412-648-2230, Fax: 412-648-1899, E-mail: soeinfo@pitt.edu.

University of Rochester, The College, Arts and Sciences, Department of Brain and Cognitive Sciences, Rochester, NY 14627-0250. Offers MS, PhD. Terminal master's awarded for partial completion of doctoral program. *Degree requirements:* For doctorate, thesis/dissertation, qualifying exam. *Entrance requirements:* For master's and doctorate, GRE General Test. Additional exam requirements/recommendations for international students: Required—TOEFL. Electronic applications accepted.

University of South Florida, Graduate School, College of Arts and Sciences, Department of Psychology, Tampa, FL 33620-9951. Offers clinical psychology (MA, PhD); cognitive and neural sciences (MA, PhD); industrial-organizational psychology (MA, PhD). *Accreditation:* APA (one or more programs are accredited). *Faculty:* 32 full-time (8 women), 1 (woman) part-time/adjunct. *Students:* 106 full-time (65 women), 21 part-time (16 women); includes 17 minority (4 African Americans, 4 Asian Americans or Pacific Islanders, 9 Hispanic Americans), 17 international. 398 applicants, 6% accepted, 22 enrolled. In 2007, 16 master's, 21 doctorates awarded. *Degree requirements:* For master's, thesis; for doctorate, comprehensive exam, thesis/dissertation. *Entrance requirements:* For master's and doctorate, GRE General Test, minimum GPA of 3.0 in last 60 hours of course work. Application fee: $30. Electronic applications accepted. *Expenses: Contact institution. Financial support:* In 2007–08, 13 fellowships with full and partial tuition reimbursements (averaging $17,500 per year), 50 research assistantships with partial tuition reimbursements (averaging $13,000 per year), 50 teaching assistantships with partial tuition reimbursements (averaging $13,000 per year) were awarded; career-related internships or fieldwork, scholarships/grants, tuition waivers (partial), and unspecified assistantships also available. Financial award applicants required to submit FAFSA. *Faculty research:* Human memory; job analysis; stress, drug and alcohol abuse; neuroscience. *Unit head:* Michael T. Brannick, Director of Graduate Program, 813-974-0478, Fax: 813-974-4617, E-mail: mbrannick@cas.usf.edu. *Application contact:* Laura Pierce, Program Assistant, 813-974-0497, Fax: 813-974-4617, E-mail: lpierce@cas.usf.edu.

The University of Texas at Austin, Graduate School, College of Education, Department of Educational Psychology, Austin, TX 78712-1111. Offers academic educational psychology (M Ed, MA); counseling education (M Ed); counseling psychology (PhD); human development and education (PhD); learning cognition and instruction (PhD); quantitative methods (PhD); school psychology (PhD). *Accreditation:* APA (one or more programs are accredited). *Degree requirements:* For master's, thesis optional; for doctorate, thesis/dissertation. *Entrance requirements:* For master's and doctorate, GRE General Test, 3 letters of recommendation. Additional exam requirements/recommendations for international students: Required—TOEFL.

The University of Texas at Dallas, School of Behavioral and Brain Sciences, Program in Cognition and Neuroscience, Richardson, TX 75083-0688. Offers MS, PhD. Part-time and evening/weekend programs available. *Faculty:* 19 full-time (5 women), 1 part-time/adjunct (0 women). *Students:* 62 full-time (28 women), 29 part-time (17 women); includes 24 minority (3 African Americans, 14 Asian Americans or Pacific Islanders, 7 Hispanic Americans), 20 international. Average age 32. 45 applicants, 80% accepted, 24 enrolled. In 2007, 26 master's, 8 doctorates awarded. *Degree requirements:* For master's, internship. *Entrance requirements:* For master's, GRE General Test, minimum GPA of 3.0 in upper-level coursework in field. Additional exam requirements/recommendations for international students: Required—TOEFL (minimum score 550 paper-based; 213 computer-based). *Application deadline:* For fall admission, 7/15 for domestic students; for spring admission, 11/15 for domestic students. Applications are processed on a rolling basis. Application fee: $50 ($100 for international students). Electronic applications accepted. *Expenses:* Tuition, state resident: full-time $7,052. Tuition, nonresident: full-time $12,632. Tuition and fees vary according to course load. *Financial support:* In 2007–08, 9 research assistantships with tuition reimbursements (averaging $11,920 per year), 28 teaching assistantships with tuition reimbursements (averaging $10,118 per year) were awarded; fellowships, career-related internships or fieldwork, Federal Work-Study, institutionally sponsored loans, scholarships/grants, and unspecified assistantships also available. Support available to part-time students. Financial award application deadline: 4/30; financial award applicants

Cognitive Sciences

The University of Texas at Dallas (continued)
required to submit FAFSA. *Faculty research:* Combination of biological, behavioral, and computational approaches for evaluating biological and artificial information processing systems. *Unit head:* Dr. Jim Bartlett, Head, PhD Program, 972-883-2079, Fax: 972-883-2491, E-mail: jbartlet@utdallas.edu. *Application contact:* Dr. Robert D. Stillman, Head, 972-883-3106, Fax: 972-883-3022, E-mail: stillman@utdallas.edu.

The University of Toledo, College of Graduate Studies, College of Arts and Sciences, Department of Psychology, Toledo, OH 43606-3390. Offers behavioral (PhD), including cognitive, psychobiology and learning, social; clinical psychology (PhD); experimental psychology (MA). *Accreditation:* APA. *Faculty:* 22. *Students:* 34 full-time (24 women), 4 part-time (2 women); includes 2 minority (1 Asian American or Pacific Islander, 1 Hispanic American), 4 international. Average age 26. 150 applicants, 13% accepted, 9 enrolled. In 2007, 9 master's, 7 doctorates awarded. *Degree requirements:* For master's, thesis; for doctorate, one foreign language, thesis/dissertation. *Entrance requirements:* For master's and doctorate, GRE General Test, GRE Subject Test. *Application deadline:* For fall admission, 1/15 priority date for domestic students. Application fee: $45. *Financial support:* In 2007–08, 13 research assistantships (averaging $8,400 per year), 18 teaching assistantships (averaging $11,000 per year) were awarded; career-related internships or fieldwork, Federal Work-Study, institutionally sponsored loans, scholarships/grants, and unspecified assistantships also available. Support available to part-time students. Financial award application deadline: 1/15; financial award applicants required to submit FAFSA. *Faculty research:* Neural taste response. *Unit head:* Dr. Joseph Hovey, Chair, 419-530-2693, Fax: 419-530-8479.

See Close-Up on page 1509.

University of Wisconsin–Madison, Graduate School, College of Letters and Science, Department of Psychology, Program in Cognitive Neurosciences, Madison, WI 53706-1380. Offers PhD. *Degree requirements:* For doctorate, comprehensive exam, thesis/dissertation. *Entrance requirements:* For doctorate, GRE General Test, minimum undergraduate GPA of 3.0. Additional exam requirements/recommendations for international students: Required—TOEFL. Electronic applications accepted.

University of Wisconsin–Madison, Graduate School, College of Letters and Science, Department of Psychology, Program in Perception, Madison, WI 53706-1380. Offers PhD. *Degree requirements:* For doctorate, comprehensive exam, thesis/dissertation. *Entrance requirements:* For doctorate, GRE General Test, minimum GPA of 3.0. Electronic applications accepted.

Wayne State University, College of Liberal Arts and Sciences, Department of Psychology, Program in Psychology, Detroit, MI 48202. Offers behavioral and cognitive neuroscience (PhD); clinical psychology (PhD); cognitive and social psychology (PhD); industrial/organizational psychology (PhD); psychology (MA, MS). *Accreditation:* APA (one or more programs are accredited). *Students:* 99 full-time (74 women), 20 part-time (16 women); includes 14 minority (7 African Americans, 4 Asian Americans or Pacific Islanders, 3 Hispanic Americans), 13 international. Average age 27. 219 applicants, 17% accepted, 23 enrolled. In 2007, 13 master's, 12 doctorates awarded. *Degree requirements:* For doctorate, thesis/dissertation. *Entrance requirements:* For doctorate, GRE General Test, GRE Subject Test. Additional exam requirements/recommendations for international students: Required—TOEFL (minimum score 550 paper-based; 213 computer-based); Recommended—TWE (minimum score 6). *Application deadline:* For fall admission, 2/1 for domestic students, 6/1 for international students; for winter admission, 10/1 for international students; for spring admission, 2/1 for international students. Applications are processed on a rolling basis. Application fee: $30 ($50 for international students). Electronic applications accepted. *Expenses:* Tuition, state resident: part-time $403 per credit hour. Tuition, nonresident: part-time $890 per credit hour. *Financial support:* Application deadline:2/1. *Application contact:* Dr. Melissa Kaplan-Estrin, Graduate Director, 313-577-2824, Fax: 313-577-7636, E-mail: mkestrin@sun.science.wayne.edu.

Wilfrid Laurier University, Faculty of Graduate Studies, Faculty of Science, Department of Psychology, Waterloo, ON N2L 3C5, Canada. Offers brain and cognition (M Sc, PhD); community psychology (MA, PhD); social and developmental psychology (MA, PhD). *Faculty:* 32 full-time, 3 part-time/adjunct. *Students:* 61 full-time, 4 part-time. 129 applicants, 27% accepted, 27 enrolled. In 2007, 3 degrees awarded. *Degree requirements:* For master's, thesis; for doctorate, thesis/dissertation. *Entrance requirements:* For master's, honors BA or the equivalent in psychology, minimum B average in undergraduate course work, GRE (General Test); for doctorate, master's degree, minimum A- average, GRE (General Test). Additional exam requirements/recommendations for international students: Required—TOEFL (minimum score 230 computer-based; 89 iBT). *Application deadline:* For fall admission, 2/1 priority date for domestic students. Application fee: $75. Electronic applications accepted. *Financial support:* Fellowships, research assistantships, teaching assistantships available. *Faculty research:* Brain and cognition, community psychology, social and developmental psychology. *Unit head:* Dr. Mark Pancer, Chairperson, 519-884-1970 Ext. 3149. *Application contact:* Jennifer Poppe, Student Contact, 519-884-0710 Ext. 3536, Fax: 519-884-1020, E-mail: gradstudies@wlu.ca.

Counseling Psychology

Abilene Christian University, Graduate School, College of Arts and Sciences, Department of Psychology, Program in Counseling Psychology, Abilene, TX 79699-9100. Offers MS. *Students:* 8 full-time (4 women); includes 1 minority (African American), 1 international. 19 applicants, 53% accepted, 5 enrolled. In 2007, 5 degrees awarded. *Degree requirements:* For master's, comprehensive exam, thesis optional. *Entrance requirements:* For master's, GRE General Test. *Application deadline:* For fall admission, 4/1 priority date for domestic students; for spring admission, 11/1 for domestic students. Applications are processed on a rolling basis. Application fee: $40 ($45 for international students). Electronic applications accepted. *Expenses:* Tuition: Full-time $13,368; part-time $557 per hour. Required fees: $700; $34 per hour. $10 per semester. Tuition and fees vary according to degree level and campus/location. *Unit head:* Dr. Jeffrey Wherry, Graduate Advisor, 325-674-2471, Fax: 325-674-6968, E-mail: jnw04c@acu.edu. *Application contact:* William Horn, Graduate Admissions Counselor, 325-674-2656, Fax: 325-674-6717, E-mail: gradinfo@acu.edu.

Adelphi University, Derner Institute of Advanced Psychological Studies, Program in Mental Health Counseling, Garden City, NY 11530-0701. Offers MA. *Students:* 23 full-time (20 women), 11 part-time (8 women); includes 2 minority (both Hispanic Americans), 10 international. Average age 29. In 2007, 12 degrees awarded. *Degree requirements:* For master's, comprehensive exam. *Entrance requirements:* For master's, GRE General Test, GRE Subject Test, minimum cumulative GPA of 3.1; interview; course work in developmental psychology, research methods, and psycho-pathology; 2 letters of recommendation. Additional exam requirements/recommendations for international students: Required—TOEFL (minimum score 550 paper-based; 213 computer-based). *Application deadline:* For fall admission, 6/1 priority date for domestic students, 5/1 priority date for international students. Application fee: $50. Electronic applications accepted. *Financial support:* Research assistantships with full and partial tuition reimbursements, career-related internships or fieldwork, Federal Work-Study, institutionally sponsored loans, and unspecified assistantships available. *Unit head:* Dr. Lenore Heller, Assistant Dean and Director, 516-877-4829, E-mail: heller@adelphi.edu. *Application contact:* Christine Murphy, Director of Admissions, 516-877-3050, Fax: 516-877-3039, E-mail: graduateadmissions@adelphi.edu.

Adler Graduate School, Program in Adlerian Studies, Richfield, MN 55423. Offers art therapy specialization (MA); clinical counseling track (MA); coaching and consulting in organizations (Certificate); management consulting and organizational leadership (MA); marriage and family track (MA); non-clinical Adlerian studies track (MA); personal and professional life coaching (Certificate); school counseling (MA). Part-time and evening/weekend programs available. *Faculty:* 4 full-time (1 woman), 44 part-time/adjunct (27 women). *Students:* Average age 37. 46 applicants, 96% accepted, 44 enrolled. In 2007, 37 degrees awarded. *Degree requirements:* For master's, thesis or alternative, 500-700 hour internship, depending on license choice. *Entrance requirements:* For master's, minimum undergraduate GPA of 3.0, 12 credits of course work in psychology or related field. *Application deadline:* For fall admission, 10/1 priority date for domestic students; for winter admission, 1/1 priority date for domestic students; for spring admission, 4/1 priority date for domestic students. Applications are processed on a rolling basis. Application fee: $50. *Expenses:* Tuition: Part-time $430 per credit. Required fees: $85 per term. *Financial support:* In 2007–08, 121 students received support. Career-related internships or fieldwork and tuition waivers available. Support available to part-time students. Financial award applicants required to submit FAFSA. *Unit head:* Dr. Dennis Rislove, President, 612-861-7554 Ext. 106, Fax: 612-861-7559, E-mail: rislove@alfredadler.edu. *Application contact:* Evelyn B. Haas, Director of Student Services and Admissions, 612-861-7554 Ext. 103, Fax: 612-861-7559, E-mail: ev@alfredadler.edu.

Adler School of Professional Psychology, Programs in Psychology, Chicago, IL 60601-7203. Offers art therapy (Certificate); clinical hypnosis (Certificate); clinical psychology (Psy D); counseling psychology (MACP); counseling psychology/art therapy (MACAT); gerontology (MAGP); marriage and family counseling (MAMFC); marriage and family therapy (Certificate); organizational psychology (MAO); substance abuse counseling (MASAC, Certificate); Psy D/Certificate; Psy D/MACAT; Psy D/MACP; Psy D/MAMFC; Psy D/MASAC. *Accreditation:* APA. Part-time and evening/weekend programs available. Terminal master's awarded for partial completion of doctoral program. *Degree requirements:* For master's, thesis or alternative, oral exam, practicum; for doctorate, thesis/dissertation, clinical exam, internship, oral exam, practicum, written qualifying exam. *Entrance requirements:* For master's, 12 semester hours in psychology, minimum GPA of 3.0; for doctorate, 18 semester hours in psychology, minimum GPA of 3.25; for Certificate, appropriate master's or doctoral degree.

See Close-Up on page 1363.

Alabama Agricultural and Mechanical University, School of Graduate Studies, School of Education, Department of Counseling and Special Education, Huntsville, AL 35811. Offers communicative disorders (M Ed, MS); psychology and counseling (MS, Ed S), including clinical psychology (MS), counseling and guidance, counseling psychology (MS), personnel management (MS), psychometry (MS), school psychology (MS); special education (M Ed, MS). *Accreditation:* CORE; NCATE. Part-time and evening/weekend programs available. *Faculty:* 4 full-time (3 women), 3 part-time/adjunct (1 woman). *Students:* 24 full-time (16 women), 58 part-time (48 women); includes 59 minority (56 African Americans, 1 American Indian/Alaska Native, 2 Hispanic Americans), 2 international. In 2007, 55 master's, 2 other advanced degrees awarded. *Degree requirements:* For master's, comprehensive exam. *Entrance requirements:* For master's, GRE General Test. *Application deadline:* For fall admission, 5/1 for domestic students. Application fee: $15 ($20 for international students). *Financial support:* Career-related internships or fieldwork available. Support available to part-time students. Financial award application deadline: 4/1. *Faculty research:* Increasing numbers of minorities in special education and speech-language pathology. Total annual research expenditures: $300,000. *Unit head:* Dr. Shirley King, Chair, 256-372-5520, Fax: 256-372-5526.

Alaska Pacific University, Graduate Programs, Department of Counseling, Psychological Studies, and Human Services, Program in Counseling Psychology, Anchorage, AK 99508-4672. Offers MSCP. *Faculty:* 5 full-time (3 women), 1 (woman) part-time/adjunct. *Students:* 45 full-time (36 women), 1 (woman) part-time; includes 9 minority (1 African American, 3 American Indian/Alaska Native, 3 Asian Americans or Pacific Islanders, 2 Hispanic Americans). Average age 35. In 2007, 22 degrees awarded. *Expenses:* Tuition: Full-time $12,510. One-time fee: $110 full-time. *Financial support:* In 2007–08, 3 teaching assistantships (averaging $9,583 per year) were awarded. *Unit head:* Dr. Ellen Cole, Director, 907-564-8216.

Alliant International University–México City, Programs in Arts and Science, Mexico City, Mexico. Offers counseling psychology (MA); international relations (MA). Part-time programs available. *Degree requirements:* For master's, thesis optional. *Entrance requirements:* For master's, GRE General Test, letters of recommendation. Additional exam requirements/recommendations for international students: Required—TOEFL. Electronic applications accepted.

Amberton University, Graduate School, Program in Counseling, Garland, TX 75041-5595. Offers MA. *Faculty:* 5 full-time (2 women), 8 part-time/adjunct (4 women). *Students:* 100 full-time (50 women), 250 part-time (200 women); includes 70 minority (50 African Americans, 5 American Indian/Alaska Native, 5 Asian Americans or Pacific Islanders, 10 Hispanic Americans). Average age 35. *Entrance requirements:* For master's, minimum GPA of 3.0. *Application deadline:* Applications are processed on a rolling basis. *Expenses:* Tuition: Full-time $5,400; part-time $225 per hour. *Application contact:* Adviser, 972-279-6511 Ext. 180, Fax: 972-279-9773, E-mail: advisor@amberton.edu.

Amridge University, Graduate and Professional Programs, Montgomery, AL 36117. Offers behavioral leadership and management (MA); biblical studies (MA, D Min, PhD); Christian ministry (M Div); family therapy (D Min, PhD), including marriage and family therapy (PhD), professional counseling (PhD); leadership and management (MS); marriage and family therapy (M Div, MA); ministerial leadership (M Div, MS); pastoral counseling (M Div, MS); practical theology (MA); professional counseling (M Div, MA). *Accreditation:* ATS. Part-time and evening/weekend programs available. Postbaccalaureate distance learning degree programs offered (no on-campus study). *Faculty:* 50 full-time (12 women), 36 part-time/adjunct (10 women). *Students:* 165 full-time (85 women), 212 part-time (111 women); includes 174 minority (164 African Americans, 1 American Indian/Alaska Native, 1 Asian American or Pacific Islander, 8 Hispanic Americans). Average age 35. In 2007, 8 first professional degrees, 35 master's, 5 doctorates awarded. *Degree requirements:* For master's, one foreign language, comprehensive exam (for some programs), thesis (for some programs); for doctorate, comprehensive exam (for some programs), thesis/dissertation; for M Div, comprehensive exam (for some programs). *Entrance requirements:* For M Div, master's, and doctorate, GRE General Test or MAT. Additional exam requirements/recommendations for international students: Required—TOEFL. *Application deadline:* For fall admission, 9/1 priority date for domestic students; for spring admission, 1/1 priority date for domestic students. Applications are processed on a rolling basis. Application fee: $50. Electronic applications accepted. *Expenses:* Tuition: Full-time $9,180; part-time $510 per semester hour. Required fees: $400 per term. Tuition and fees vary according to course load and degree level. *Financial support:* Federal Work-Study and scholarships/grants available. Support available to part-time students. Financial award applicants required to submit FAFSA. *Faculty research:* Homiletics, hermeneutics, ancient Near Eastern history. *Unit head:* Rick Johnson, Director of Enrollment Management, 800-351-4040 Ext. 7513, Fax: 334-387-3878,

E-mail: rickjohnson@amridgeuniversity.edu. *Application contact:* Ora Davis, Admissions Officer, 334-387-3877 Ext. 7524, Fax: 334-387-3878, E-mail: oradavis@amridgeuniversity.edu.

Andrews University, School of Graduate Studies, School of Education, Department of Educational and Counseling Psychology, Program in Counseling Psychology, Berrien Springs, MI 49104. Offers PhD. *Degree requirements:* For doctorate, thesis/dissertation.

Angelo State University, College of Graduate Studies, College of Liberal and Fine Arts, Department of Psychology and Sociology, San Angelo, TX 76909. Offers psychology (MS), including counseling psychology, general psychology, industrial and organizational psychology. Part-time and evening/weekend programs available. *Faculty:* 8 full-time (2 women). *Students:* 11 full-time (8 women), 39 part-time (21 women); includes 8 minority (2 African Americans, 1 American Indian/Alaska Native, 5 Hispanic Americans), 1 international. Average age 26. 35 applicants, 66% accepted, 17 enrolled. In 2007, 27 degrees awarded. *Degree requirements:* For master's, comprehensive exam, thesis optional. *Entrance requirements:* For master's, GRE General Test. Additional exam requirements/recommendations for international students: Required—TOEFL or IELTS. *Application deadline:* For fall admission, 7/15 priority date for domestic students, 6/10 for international students; for spring admission, 12/8 for domestic students, 11/1 for international students. Applications are processed on a rolling basis. Application fee: $40 ($50 for international students). Electronic applications accepted. *Financial support:* In 2007–08, 44 students received support, including 3 teaching assistantships (averaging $10,251 per year); career-related internships or fieldwork, Federal Work-Study, scholarships/grants, and unspecified assistantships also available. Support available to part-time students. Financial award application deadline: 3/1; financial award applicants required to submit FAFSA. *Faculty research:* Toddlers use of actors' intentions to learn verbs. Total annual research expenditures: $116,915. *Unit head:* Dr. William B. Davidson, Department Head, 325-942-2068 Ext. 248, E-mail: bill.davidson@angelo.edu.

Anna Maria College, Graduate Division, Program in Counseling Psychology, Paxton, MA 01612. Offers counseling psychology (MA). Part-time and evening/weekend programs available. *Faculty:* 1 full-time (0 women), 7 part-time/adjunct (5 women). *Students:* 12 full-time (9 women), 26 part-time (22 women); includes 3 minority (2 African Americans, 1 Asian American or Pacific Islander). Average age 34. In 2007, 16 degrees awarded. *Degree requirements:* For master's, comprehensive exam, practicum. *Entrance requirements:* Additional exam requirements/recommendations for international students: Required—TOEFL (minimum score 500 paper-based). *Application deadline:* For fall admission, 3/1 priority date for domestic and international students; for spring admission, 11/1 priority date for domestic and international students. Applications are processed on a rolling basis. Application fee: $40. Electronic applications accepted. *Expenses:* Tuition: Part-time $1,272 per course. *Financial support:* Applicants required to submit FAFSA. *Unit head:* Richard L. Connors, Director, 508-849-3413, Fax: 508-849-3339, E-mail: rconnors@annamaria.edu. *Application contact:* Dennis Braun, Director, Graduate and Continuing Education Recruitment, 508-849-3293, Fax: 508-819-3362, E-mail: dbraun@annamaria.edu.

Antioch University McGregor, Graduate Programs, Individualized Liberal and Professional Studies Program, Yellow Springs, OH 45387-1609. Offers liberal and professional studies (MA), including counseling, creative writing, education, film studies, liberal studies, management, modern literature, psychology, theatre, visual arts. Part-time and evening/weekend programs available. Postbaccalaureate distance learning degree programs offered (minimal on-campus study). *Faculty:* 2 full-time (1 woman), 3 part-time/adjunct (2 women). *Students:* Average age 40. 35 applicants, 63% accepted, 17 enrolled. In 2007, 31 degrees awarded. *Degree requirements:* For master's, thesis or alternative. *Entrance requirements:* For master's, resumé, 2 letters of reference. *Application deadline:* For fall admission, 8/25 for domestic students; for winter admission, 12/5 for domestic students; for spring admission, 3/8 for domestic students. Applications are processed on a rolling basis. Application fee: $50. Electronic applications accepted. *Expenses: Contact institution. Financial support:* Federal Work-Study available. Financial award applicants required to submit FAFSA. *Unit head:* Suzanne Fest, Chair, 937-769-1876, Fax: 937-769-1807, E-mail: sfest@mcgregor.edu. *Application contact:* Seth Gordon, Assistant Director of Admissions, 937-769-1800 Ext. 1825, Fax: 937-769-1804, E-mail: sgordon@mcgregor.edu.

See Close-Up on page 443.

Antioch University New England, Graduate School, Department of Applied Psychology, Program in Clinical Mental Health Counseling, Keene, NH 03431-3552. Offers MA. *Faculty:* 9 full-time (7 women), 14 part-time/adjunct (9 women). *Students:* 75 full-time (62 women), 44 part-time (37 women); includes 4 minority (2 African Americans, 1 American Indian/Alaska Native, 1 Hispanic American), 5 international. Average age 35. 65 applicants, 75% accepted, 34 enrolled. In 2007, 38 degrees awarded. *Degree requirements:* For master's, internship, practicum. *Entrance requirements:* For master's, previous course work and work experience in psychology. Additional exam requirements/recommendations for international students: Required—TOEFL (minimum score 600 paper-based; 250 computer-based). *Application deadline:* For fall admission, 7/15 for domestic and international students; for spring admission, 12/1 for domestic and international students. Applications are processed on a rolling basis. Application fee: $50. Electronic applications accepted. *Expenses: Contact institution.* Tuition and fees vary according to degree level, program and student level. *Financial support:* In 2007–08, 23 fellowships (averaging $1,767 per year) were awarded; career-related internships or fieldwork and Federal Work-Study also available. Financial award applicants required to submit FAFSA. *Faculty research:* Multicultural issues in field supervision. *Unit head:* Dr. Carlotta Willis, Director, Clinical Mental Health Counseling Program, 603-283-2147, Fax: 603-357-0718, E-mail: cwillis@antiochne.edu. *Application contact:* Leatrice A. Oram, Co-Director of Admissions, 800-490-3310, Fax: 603-357-0718, E-mail: admissions@antiochne.edu.

Argosy University, Chicago, College of Psychology and Behavioral Sciences, Doctoral Program in Clinical Psychology, Chicago, IL 60654. Offers child and adolescent psychology (Psy D); client-centered and experiential psychotherapies (Psy D); diversity and multicultural psychology (Psy D); family psychology (Psy D); forensic psychology (Psy D); health psychology (Psy D); psychoanalytic psychology (Psy D); psychology and spirituality (Psy D). *Accreditation:* APA.

See Close-Up on page 1379.

Argosy University, Chicago, College of Psychology and Behavioral Sciences, Program in Counseling Psychology, Chicago, IL 60654. Offers counselor education and supervision (Ed D). Postbaccalaureate distance learning degree programs offered (minimal on-campus study).

See Close-Up on page 1379.

Argosy University, Denver, College of Psychology and Behavioral Sciences, Denver, CO 80203. Offers clinical psychology (MA, Psy D); community counseling (MA); counseling psychology (Ed D), including counselor education and supervision; counselor education and supervision (Ed D); forensic psychology (MA); marriage and family therapy (MA); organizational leadership (Ed D).

See Close-Up on page 1383.

Argosy University, Hawai'i, College of Psychology and Behavioral Sciences, Program in Counseling Psychology, Honolulu, HI 96813. Offers Ed D.

See Close-Up on page 1385.

Argosy University, Inland Empire, College of Psychology and Behavioral Sciences, San Bernardino, CA 92408. Offers clinical psychology/marriage and family therapy (MA); counseling psychology (MA, Ed D); counseling psychology/marriage and family therapy (MA); forensic psychology (MA).

See Close-Up on page 1387.

Argosy University, Los Angeles, College of Psychology and Behavioral Sciences, Santa Monica, CA 90405. Offers clinical psychology/marriage and family therapy (MA); counseling psychology (Ed D); counseling psychology/marriage and family therapy (MA); organizational leadership (Ed D).

See Close-Up on page 1389.

Argosy University, Nashville, College of Psychology and Behavioral Sciences, Nashville, TN 37214. Offers counselor education and supervision (Ed D); mental health counseling (MA).

See Close-Up on page 1391.

Argosy University, Orange County, College of Psychology and Behavioral Sciences, Program in Counseling Psychology, Santa Ana, CA 92704. Offers counseling psychology (Ed D); marriage and family therapy (MA).

See Close-Up on page 1393.

Argosy University, Phoenix, College of Psychology and Behavioral Sciences, Program in Mental Health Counseling, Phoenix, AZ 85021. Offers MA.

See Close-Up on page 1395.

Argosy University, Salt Lake City, College of Psychology and Behavioral Sciences, Draper, UT 84020. Offers counseling psychology (Ed D); marriage and family therapy (MA).

See Close-Up on page 1397.

Argosy University, San Diego, College of Psychology and Behavioral Sciences, San Diego, CA 92108. Offers clinical psychology/marriage and family therapy (MA); counseling psychology (MA, Ed D); counseling psychology/marriage and family therapy (MA).

See Close-Up on page 1399.

Argosy University, San Francisco Bay Area, College of Psychology and Behavioral Sciences, Program in Counseling Psychology, Alameda, CA 94501. Offers MA, Ed D.

See Close-Up on page 1401.

Argosy University, Sarasota, College of Psychology and Behavioral Sciences, Sarasota, FL 34235. Offers community counseling (MA); counseling psychology (Ed D); counselor education and supervision (Ed D); forensic psychology (MA); marriage and family therapy (MA); mental health counseling (MA); organizational leadership (Ed D); pastoral community counseling (Ed D); school counseling (MA, Ed S); school psychology (MA).

See Close-Up on page 1403.

Argosy University, Schaumburg, College of Psychology and Behavioral Sciences, Schaumburg, IL 60173-5403. Offers clinical health psychology (Post-Graduate Certificate); clinical psychology (MA, Psy D), including child and family psychology (Psy D), clinical health psychology (Psy D), diversity and multicultural psychology (Psy D), forensic psychology (Psy D); community counseling (MA); counseling psychology (Ed D), including counselor education and supervision; counselor education and supervision (Ed D); forensic psychology (Post-Graduate Certificate); organizational leadership (Ed D). *Accreditation:* ACA; APA.

See Close-Up on page 1405.

Argosy University, Seattle, College of Psychology and Behavioral Sciences, Program in Counseling Psychology, Seattle, WA 98121. Offers MA, Ed D.

See Close-Up on page 1407.

Argosy University, Tampa, College of Psychology and Behavioral Sciences, Tampa, FL 33614. Offers clinical psychology (MA, Psy D), including clinical psychology; counselor education and supervision (Ed D); marriage and family therapy (MA); mental health counseling (MA); organizational leadership (Ed D); school counseling (MA).

See Close-Up on page 1409.

Argosy University, Washington DC, College of Psychology and Behavioral Sciences, Arlington, VA 22209. Offers clinical psychology (MA, Psy D), including child and family psychology (Psy D), diversity and multicultural psychology (Psy D), forensic psychology (Psy D), health and neuropsychology (Psy D); community counseling (MA); counseling psychology (Ed D), including counselor education and supervision; counselor education and supervision (Ed D); forensic psychology (MA); organizational leadership (Ed D). *Accreditation:* APA.

See Close-Up on page 1413.

Arizona State University, Graduate College, College of Education, Division of Psychology in Education, Academic Program in Counseling Psychology, Tempe, AZ 85287. Offers PhD. *Accreditation:* APA. *Degree requirements:* For doctorate, thesis/dissertation. *Entrance requirements:* For doctorate, GRE General Test or MAT.

Assumption College, Graduate School, Counseling Psychology Program, Worcester, MA 01609-1296. Offers MA, CAGS. Part-time and evening/weekend programs available. *Faculty:* 3 full-time (0 women), 7 part-time/adjunct (3 women). *Students:* 55 full-time (48 women), 25 part-time (20 women); includes 4 minority (1 African American, 3 Hispanic Americans), 4 international. Average age 25. 75 applicants, 79% accepted. In 2007, 38 master's awarded. *Degree requirements:* For master's, comprehensive exam, internship, practicum. *Entrance requirements:* For master's, 3 letters of recommendation, resumé, essay; for CAGS, 3 letters of recommendation, resumé, interview, essay. Additional exam requirements/recommendations for international students: Required—TOEFL, IELTS. *Application deadline:* For fall admission, 6/1 priority date for domestic students, 5/1 priority date for international students; for spring admission, 11/1 priority date for domestic students, 10/1 priority date for international students. Applications are processed on a rolling basis. Application fee: $30. Electronic applications accepted. *Expenses:* Tuition: Part-time $450 per credit. Required fees: $20 per semester. *Financial support:* In 2007–08, 84 students received support, including 19 fellowships with partial tuition reimbursements available (averaging $6,808 per year), 2 teaching assistantships with full tuition reimbursements available (averaging $9,940 per year). Financial award application deadline: 3/1; financial award applicants required to submit FAFSA. *Faculty research:* Mood disorders, adjustment to life-threatening illness, perception of movement, socioemotional development of young children, discovery versus disclosure. *Unit head:* Dr. Leonard A. Doerfler, Director, 508-767-7549, Fax: 508-767-7263, E-mail: doerfler@assumption.edu. *Application contact:* Adrian O. Dumas, Director of Graduate Enrollment Management and Services, 508-767-7365, Fax: 508-767-7030, E-mail: adumas@assumption.edu.

Athabasca University, Graduate Centre for Applied Psychology, Athabasca, AB T9S 3A3, Canada. Offers art therapy (MC); career counseling (MC); counseling (Advanced Certificate); counseling psychology (MC); school counseling (MC). *Faculty:* 3 full-time (2 women), 2 part-time/adjunct (0 women). Tuition and fees charges are reported in Canadian dollars. *Expenses:* Tuition, state resident: part-time $1,795 Canadian dollars per credit. Required fees: $70 Canadian dollars per year. One-time fee: $360 Canadian dollars part-time. Part-time tuition and fees vary according to program. *Unit head:* Dr. Sandra Collins, Program Director, 888-611-7121, E-mail: sandrac@athabascau.ca.

Auburn University, Graduate School, College of Education, Department of Counseling and Counseling Psychology, Auburn University, AL 36849. Offers community agency counseling (M Ed, MS, Ed D, PhD, Ed S); counseling psychology (PhD); counselor education (Ed D, PhD); school counseling (M Ed, MS, Ed D, PhD, Ed S); school psychometry (M Ed, MS, Ed D, PhD, Ed S). *Accreditation:* ACA (one or more programs are accredited); APA (one or more programs are accredited); NCATE. Part-time programs available. *Faculty:* 10 full-time (6 women). *Students:* 51 full-time (35 women), 41 part-time (33 women); includes 27 minority (26

Counseling Psychology

Auburn University (continued)

African Americans, 1 Hispanic American), 5 international. Average age 31. 140 applicants, 42% accepted, 30 enrolled. In 2007, 20 master's, 9 doctorates, 4 other advanced degrees awarded. *Degree requirements:* For master's, thesis (for some programs); for doctorate, thesis/dissertation; for Ed S, thesis or alternative. *Entrance requirements:* For master's and Ed S, GRE General Test; for doctorate, GRE General Test, GRE Subject Test. *Application deadline:* For fall admission, 5/15 for domestic students. Application fee: $25 ($50 for international students). Electronic applications accepted. *Financial support:* Research assistantships, Federal Work-Study and traineeships available. Support available to part-time students. Financial award application deadline: 3/15. *Faculty research:* At-risk students, substance abuse, gender roles, AIDS, professional ethics. *Unit head:* Dr. Holly Stadler, Head, 334-844-5160. *Application contact:* Dr. Joe Pittman, Interim Dean of the Graduate School, 334-844-4700.

Avila University, Department of Psychology, Kansas City, MO 64145-1698. Offers counseling and art therapy (MS); counseling psychology (MS); general psychology (MS). Part-time and evening/weekend programs available. *Faculty:* 7 full-time (5 women), 12 part-time/adjunct (9 women). *Students:* 109 full-time (94 women), 19 part-time (15 women); includes 24 minority (19 African Americans, 1 Asian American or Pacific Islander, 4 Hispanic Americans), 4 international. Average age 35. In 2007, 30 degrees awarded. *Entrance requirements:* For master's, minimum GPA of 3.0 in last 60 hours, 2 letters of recommendation, transcripts, application with letter of intent. Additional exam requirements/recommendations for international students: Required—TOEFL. *Application deadline:* Applications are processed on a rolling basis. Application fee: $0. *Expenses:* Tuition: Part-time $435 per credit hour. Required fees: $19 per credit hour. Tuition and fees vary according to program. *Financial support:* Career-related internships or fieldwork and scholarships/grants available. Support available to part-time students. Financial award applicants required to submit FAFSA. *Faculty research:* Preparation for working in mental health services. *Unit head:* Dr. Regina Staves, Director of Graduate Psychology, 816-501-3665, Fax: 816-501-2455, E-mail: gradpsych@avila.edu.

Ball State University, Graduate School, Teachers College, Department of Counseling Psychology and Guidance Services, Program in Counseling Psychology, Muncie, IN 47306-1099. Offers MA, PhD. *Accreditation:* ACA. *Faculty:* 12. *Students:* 94 full-time (71 women), 52 part-time (43 women); includes 8 minority (3 African Americans, 1 American Indian/Alaska Native, 1 Asian American or Pacific Islander, 3 Hispanic Americans), 12 international. Average age 24. 171 applicants, 42% accepted, 48 enrolled. In 2007, 37 master's, 5 doctorates awarded. *Degree requirements:* For doctorate, thesis/dissertation. *Entrance requirements:* For doctorate, GRE General Test, interview, minimum graduate GPA of 3.2, resumé. Application fee: $25 ($35 for international students). *Expenses:* Tuition, state resident: full-time $6,864. Tuition, nonresident: full-time $17,932. Required fees: $1,866. *Financial support:* Research assistantships with full tuition reimbursements, teaching assistantships available. Financial award application deadline: 3/1. *Unit head:* Dr. Charlene Alexander, Head, 765-285-8040.

Bemidji State University, School of Graduate Studies, College of Social and Natural Sciences, Field of Counseling Psychology, Bemidji, MN 56601-2699. Offers psychology (MS). Part-time programs available. *Faculty:* 9 full-time (4 women), 2 part-time/adjunct (both women). *Students:* 8 full-time (5 women), 14 part-time (12 women); includes 2 minority (both Asian Americans or Pacific Islanders) Average age 28. 16 applicants, 88% accepted. *Entrance requirements:* For master's, GRE General Test, letters of recommendation, letter of intent, curriculum vitae/resumé. Additional exam requirements/recommendations for international students: Required—TOEFL. *Application deadline:* For fall admission, 5/1 for domestic and international students. Application fee: $20. Electronic applications accepted. *Expenses:* Tuition, state resident: full-time $5,310; part-time $295 per credit. Required fees: $833; $81 per credit. $1 per term. One-time fee: $20. Tuition and fees vary according to course load, campus/location and reciprocity agreements. *Financial support:* In 2007–08, 1 research assistantship with tuition reimbursement (averaging $8,250 per year), teaching assistantships with tuition reimbursements (averaging $8,250 per year) were awarded; career-related internships or fieldwork, Federal Work-Study, scholarships/grants, health care benefits, and unspecified assistantships also available. Support available to part-time students. *Faculty research:* Exercise and working memory; age and stability of self-esteem in rural women; traumatic stress; Post-Traumatic Stress Disorder treatment for vets; learning outcomes assessment. *Unit head:* Dr. Louise Jackson, Graduate Coordinator, 218-755-2803, E-mail: ljackson@bemidjistate.edu.

Bethel University, Graduate School, Department of Psychology, St. Paul, MN 55112-6999. Offers child and adolescent mental health (Certificate); counseling psychology (MA). Evening/weekend programs available. *Faculty:* 12 full-time (3 women), 6 part-time/adjunct (1 woman). *Students:* 94 full-time (82 women), 2 part-time (both women); includes 8 minority (4 African Americans, 4 Asian Americans or Pacific Islanders). Average age 32. In 2007, 31 master's awarded. *Degree requirements:* For master's, comprehensive exam, thesis, practicum. *Entrance requirements:* For master's, MAT, interview, minimum GPA of 3.0, course work in psychology and statistics, letters of reference. Additional exam requirements/recommendations for international students: Required—TOEFL (minimum score 550 paper-based; 213 computer-based). *Application deadline:* For fall admission, 3/1 priority date for domestic students. Application fee: $25. Electronic applications accepted. *Expenses:* Tuition: Part-time $415 per credit. Tuition and fees vary according to program. *Financial support:* Institutionally sponsored loans and scholarships/grants available. Financial award applicants required to submit FAFSA. *Unit head:* Dr. James E. Koch, Director, 651-638-6415, Fax: 651-635-8004, E-mail: je-koch@bethel.edu. *Application contact:* Michael Price, Director of Admissions, 651-635-8000 Ext. 8017, Fax: 651-635-8039, E-mail: m-price@bethel.edu.

Boston College, Lynch Graduate School of Education, Department of Counseling Psychology, Developmental, and Educational Psychology, Program in Counseling Psychology, Chestnut Hill, MA 02467-3800. Offers MA, PhD, MA/MA. *Accreditation:* APA (one or more programs are accredited). *Students:* 195 full-time (159 women), 10 part-time (all women); includes 41 minority (14 African Americans, 1 American Indian/Alaska Native, 14 Asian Americans or Pacific Islanders, 12 Hispanic Americans), 22 international. 536 applicants, 50% accepted, 86 enrolled. In 2007, 65 master's, 7 doctorates awarded. Terminal master's awarded for partial completion of doctoral program. *Degree requirements:* For master's, comprehensive exam; for doctorate, comprehensive exam, thesis/dissertation. *Entrance requirements:* For master's and doctorate, GRE General Test. Additional exam requirements/recommendations for international students: Required—TOEFL. Application fee: $60. Electronic applications accepted. *Financial support:* Fellowships with full and partial tuition reimbursements, research assistantships with full and partial tuition reimbursements, teaching assistantships with full and partial tuition reimbursements, career-related internships or fieldwork, Federal Work-Study, scholarships/grants, traineeships, health care benefits, tuition waivers (full and partial), and unspecified assistantships available. Support available to part-time students. Financial award applicants required to submit FAFSA. *Faculty research:* Reducing non-academic barriers to learning; race, gender, culture and social class issues in mental health; domestic violence; career development; community intervention and prevention. *Application contact:* Adam Poluzzi, Director, Graduate Admission and Financial Aid, 617-552-4214, Fax: 617-552-0398, E-mail: poluzzi@bc.edu.

Boston Graduate School of Psychoanalysis, Program in Psychoanalytic Counseling, Brookline, MA 02446-4602. Offers MA. *Faculty:* 11 full-time (7 women), 16 part-time/adjunct (8 women). *Students:* 18 full-time (12 women), 1 (woman) part-time; includes 5 minority (2 African Americans, 2 Asian Americans or Pacific Islanders, 1 Hispanic American), 4 international. 21 applicants, 90% accepted, 19 enrolled. *Degree requirements:* For master's, 100-hour practicum, 600-hour internship. *Entrance requirements:* For master's, interview, writing sample. *Application deadline:* For fall admission, 5/15 priority date for domestic and international students; for spring admission, 11/15 priority date for domestic and international students. Applications are processed on a rolling basis. Application fee: $100. Electronic applications accepted. *Expenses:* Tuition: Full-time $5,400; part-time $1,350 per course. Required fees: $460 per semester. Tuition and fees vary according to course load, campus/location and program. *Financial support:* Career-related internships or fieldwork and unspecified assistantships available. Financial award applicants required to submit FAFSA. *Faculty research:* Emotional learning in the classroom, addictions, the effect of extra-analytic contact with analysis, the geriatric setting, siblings. *Unit head:* Dr. Jane Snyder, Provost, 617-277-3915, Fax: 617-277-0312, E-mail: bgsp@bgsp.edu. *Application contact:* Caroline Egnaczyk, Admissions Coordinator, 617-277-3915, Fax: 617-277-0312, E-mail: bgsp@bgsp.edu.

See Close-Up on page 1417.

Boston University, School of Education, Department of Literacy and Language, Counseling and Development, Program in Counseling Psychology, Boston, MA 02215. Offers Ed D. *Students:* 2 full-time (1 woman), 5 part-time (3 women); includes 1 minority (Hispanic American), 1 international. Average age 32. 6 applicants, 33% accepted. In 2007, 4 degrees awarded. *Degree requirements:* For doctorate, comprehensive exam, thesis/dissertation. *Entrance requirements:* For doctorate, GRE General Test or MAT. Additional exam requirements/recommendations for international students: Required—TOEFL. *Application deadline:* For fall admission, 2/15 priority date for domestic students; for winter admission, 11/1 priority date for domestic students. Applications are processed on a rolling basis. Application fee: $70. Electronic applications accepted. *Expenses:* Tuition: Full-time $34,930; part-time $1,092 per credit. Tuition and fees vary according to class time, course level and program. *Financial support:* Application deadline: 2/15. *Faculty research:* Cross-cultural counseling, parenting, women's development, mental health. *Unit head:* Dr. Steven Broder, Coordinator, 617-358-4766, E-mail: snbroder@bu.edu. *Application contact:* 617-353-4237, Fax: 617-353-8937, E-mail: sedgrad@bu.edu.

Boston University, School of Medicine, Division of Graduate Medical Sciences, Program in Mental Health Counseling and Behavioral Medicine, Boston, MA 02215. Offers mental health and behavioral medicine (MA). *Entrance requirements:* For master's, GRE General Test. Additional exam requirements/recommendations for international students: Required—TOEFL. *Expenses:* Tuition: Full-time $34,930; part-time $1,092 per credit. Tuition and fees vary according to class time, course level and program. *Faculty research:* HIV/AIDS, trauma, behavioral medicine (obesity, breast cancer), neurosciences, autism, serious mental illness, sports psychology.

See Close-Up on page 1419.

Bowie State University, Graduate Programs, Program in Counseling Psychology, Bowie, MD 20715-9465. Offers MA. Part-time and evening/weekend programs available. *Degree requirements:* For master's, comprehensive exam, thesis optional, research paper, practicum. *Entrance requirements:* For master's, self statement, 2.5 minimum GPA, 3 recommendations. Electronic applications accepted.

Bowie State University, Graduate Programs, Program in Mental Health Counseling, Bowie, MD 20715-9465. Offers MA. Part-time and evening/weekend programs available. *Degree requirements:* For master's, comprehensive exam. *Entrance requirements:* For master's, 3 letters of recommendation, 3.0 GPA, personal statement, 12 undergraduate credit hours in couseling or psycology. Electronic applications accepted.

Bowling Green State University, Graduate College, College of Education and Human Development, School of Education and Intervention Services, Intervention Services Division, Program in Counseling, Bowling Green, OH 43403. Offers mental health counseling (MA); school counseling (M Ed). *Accreditation:* NCATE. Part-time programs available. *Students:* 37 full-time (30 women), 24 part-time (18 women); includes 7 African Americans, 4 Hispanic Americans, 1 international. Average age 30. 44 applicants, 64% accepted, 14 enrolled. In 2007, 34 degrees awarded. *Degree requirements:* For master's, thesis or alternative. *Entrance requirements:* For master's, GRE General Test. Additional exam requirements/recommendations for international students: Required—TOEFL. *Application deadline:* For fall admission, 3/1 priority date for domestic students. Applications are processed on a rolling basis. Application fee: $30. Electronic applications accepted. *Financial support:* In 2007–08, 15 research assistantships with full tuition reimbursements (averaging $5,323 per year) were awarded; teaching assistantships with full tuition reimbursements, career-related internships or fieldwork and unspecified assistantships also available. Financial award applicants required to submit FAFSA. *Faculty research:* Perfectionism, multicultural counseling, suicide, ethics and legal issues related to counseling, play therapy. *Application contact:* Dr. Greg Garske, Graduate Coordinator, 415-372-7319.

Brigham Young University, Graduate Studies, David O. McKay School of Education, Department of Counseling Psychology and Special Education, Provo, UT 84602-1001. Offers counseling psychology (PhD); school psychology (Ed S); special education (MS). *Accreditation:* NCATE. Part-time programs available. *Faculty:* 13 full-time (8 women), 10 part-time/adjunct (2 women). *Students:* 72 full-time (47 women), 15 part-time (14 women); includes 19 minority (1 African American, 3 American Indian/Alaska Native, 8 Asian Americans or Pacific Islanders, 7 Hispanic Americans), 5 international. Average age 31. 82 applicants, 45% accepted, 26 enrolled. In 2007, 3 master's, 4 doctorates, 11 other advanced degrees awarded. *Degree requirements:* For master's, comprehensive exam, thesis; for doctorate, comprehensive exam, thesis/dissertation. *Entrance requirements:* For master's and doctorate, GRE General Test, minimum GPA of 3.0 in last 60 hours of undergrad coursework. Additional exam requirements/recommendations for international students: Required—TOEFL (minimum score 580 paper-based; 237 computer-based), IELTS (minimum score 7). *Application deadline:* For fall admission, 1/15 for domestic and international students. Application fee: $50. Electronic applications accepted. *Financial support:* In 2007–08, 51 students received support, including 30 research assistantships with partial tuition reimbursements available (averaging $4,500 per year), 3 teaching assistantships with partial tuition reimbursements available (averaging $5,140 per year); career-related internships or fieldwork, institutionally sponsored loans, and tuition waivers (partial) also available. Financial award application deadline: 4/30. *Faculty research:* Gender issues in education, psychotherapy progress and outcome, and behavior disorders and ABA. Total annual research expenditures: $195,507. *Unit head:* Dr. Mary Anne Prater, Chair, 801-422-3857, Fax: 801-422-0198, E-mail: prater@byu.edu. *Application contact:* Diane E. Hancock, Department Secretary, 801-422-3859, Fax: 801-422-0198, E-mail: diane_hancock@byu.edu.

Brooklyn College of the City University of New York, Division of Graduate Studies, Department of Health and Nutrition Science, Brooklyn, NY 11210-2889. Offers community health (MA, MPH, MS), including community health education (MA), computer science and health science (MS), health care management (MPH), health care policy and administration (MPH), thanatology (MA); grief counseling (CAS); nutrition (MS); public health (MPH). Part-time and evening/weekend programs available. *Students:* 10 full-time (9 women), 150 part-time (126 women); includes 67 minority (49 African Americans, 10 Asian Americans or Pacific Islanders, 8 Hispanic Americans), 19 international. 109 applicants, 84% accepted, 37 enrolled. In 2007, 40 degrees awarded. *Degree requirements:* For master's, thesis or alternative. *Entrance requirements:* For master's, GRE, 18 credits, essay, 2 letters of recommendation. Additional exam requirements/recommendations for international students: Required—TOEFL. *Application deadline:* For fall admission, 3/1 priority date for domestic students, 2/1 priority date for international students; for spring admission, 11/1 priority date for domestic students, 10/1 priority date for international students. Applications are processed on a rolling basis. Application fee: $125. Electronic applications accepted. *Financial support:* Career-related internships or fieldwork, Federal Work-Study, institutionally sponsored loans, and scholarships/grants available. Support available to part-time students. Financial award application deadline: 5/1; financial award applicants required to submit FAFSA. *Faculty research:* Medical ethics, relocation stress, risk reduction, disease prevention, history of public health, computer applications. *Unit head:* Dr. Janet Kolmer Grommet, Chairperson, 718-951-5026, Fax: 718-951-4670, E-mail: jgrommet@brooklyn.cuny.edu. *Application contact:* Hernan Sierra, Graduate Admissions Coordinator, 718-951-4536, Fax: 718-951-4506, E-mail: grads@brooklyn.cuny.edu.

Brooklyn College of the City University of New York, Division of Graduate Studies, Department of Psychology, Brooklyn, NY 11210-2889. Offers experimental psychology (MA); industrial and organizational psychology (MA), including industrial and organizational psychology-human relations, psychology-organizational psychology and behavior; mental health counseling (MA); psychology (PhD). The City University doctoral program in experimental psychology is based at Brooklyn College; candidates who complete the MA may apply for admission to the doctoral program. MA programs in industrial and organizational psychology and mental health counseling are fall admissions only. Part-time programs available. *Students:* 57 full-time (49 women), 91 part-time (73 women); includes 67 minority (39 African Americans, 1 American Indian/Alaska Native, 13 Asian Americans or Pacific Islanders, 14 Hispanic Americans), 9 international. 207 applicants, 60% accepted, 77 enrolled. In 2007, 37 degrees awarded. *Degree requirements:* For master's, comprehensive exam, thesis (for some programs). *Entrance requirements:* For master's, minimum GPA of 3.0, 2 letters of recommendation, essay; for doctorate, GRE. Additional exam requirements/recommendations for international students: Required—TOEFL. *Application deadline:* For fall admission, 3/1 for domestic students, 2/1 for international students; for spring admission, 11/1 for domestic students, 10/1 for international students. Applications are processed on a rolling basis. Application fee: $125. Electronic applications accepted. *Financial support:* Career-related internships or fieldwork, Federal Work-Study, institutionally sponsored loans, scholarships/grants, and tuition waivers (partial) available. Support available to part-time students. Financial award application deadline: 5/1; financial award applicants required to submit FAFSA. *Unit head:* Dr. Glen Hass, Chairperson, 718-951-5601, Fax: 718-951-4814, E-mail: ghass@brooklyn.cuny.edu. *Application contact:* Hernan Sierra, Graduate Admissions Coordinator, 718-951-4536, Fax: 718-951-4506, E-mail: grads@brooklyn.cuny.edu.

Caldwell College, Graduate Studies, Program in Counseling Psychology, Caldwell, NJ 07006-6195. Offers art therapy (MA); counseling psychology (MA); school counseling (MA). Part-time and evening/weekend programs available. *Degree requirements:* For master's, comprehensive exam, practicum. *Entrance requirements:* For master's, GRE General Test, minimum GPA of 3.0. Additional exam requirements/recommendations for international students: Required—TOEFL (minimum score 580 paper-based; 237 computer-based). Electronic applications accepted.

California Baptist University, Program in Marriage and Family Therapy, Riverside, CA 92504-3206. Offers counseling psychology (MS). Part-time programs available. *Faculty:* 8 full-time (3 women), 7 part-time/adjunct (2 women). *Students:* 82 full-time (68 women), 53 part-time (43 women); includes 61 minority (21 African Americans, 6 American Indian/Alaska Native, 4 Asian Americans or Pacific Islanders, 30 Hispanic Americans), 2 international. 96 applicants, 43% accepted, 34 enrolled. In 2007, 66 degrees awarded. *Degree requirements:* For master's, comprehensive exam, 24 hours (individual) or 50 hours (group) psychotherapy. *Entrance requirements:* For master's, Minnesota Multiphasic Personality Inventory and Myers-Briggs Type Inventory, course work in developmental psychology, theories of personality, and statistics; minimum undergraduate GPA of 2.75. Additional exam requirements/recommendations for international students: Required—TOEFL (minimum score 575 paper-based; 230 computer-based), IELTS (minimum score 7). *Application deadline:* For fall admission, 9/1 for domestic students, 7/1 priority date for international students; for spring admission, 1/3 for domestic students, 10/15 priority date for international students. Applications are processed on a rolling basis. Application fee: $45. Electronic applications accepted. *Expenses: Contact institution. Financial support:* Career-related internships or fieldwork and Federal Work-Study available. Support available to part-time students. Financial award applicants required to submit FAFSA. *Unit head:* Dr. Gary Collins, Director and Associate Dean, School of Business, 951-343-4304, Fax: 951-343-4569, E-mail: gcollins@calbaptist.edu. *Application contact:* Gail Ronveaux, Dean of Graduate Enrollment, 951-343-5045, Fax: 951-343-5095, E-mail: graduateadmissions@calbaptist.edu.

California Institute of Integral Studies, Graduate Programs, School of Professional Psychology, San Francisco, CA 94103. Offers clinical psychology (Psy D); community mental health (MA); drama therapy (MA); expressive arts therapy (MA); integral counseling psychology (MA); integral counseling, psychology-weekend (MA); psychology (Psy D), including clinical psychology; somatic psychology (MA). *Accreditation:* APA. Part-time programs available. *Faculty:* 28 full-time, 54 part-time/adjunct. *Students:* 591; includes 113 minority (19 African Americans, 3 American Indian/Alaska Native, 48 Asian Americans or Pacific Islanders, 43 Hispanic Americans). Average age 37. 383 applicants, 75% accepted, 155 enrolled. In 2007, 109 master's, 20 doctorates awarded. *Degree requirements:* For master's, comprehensive exam; for doctorate, comprehensive exam, thesis/dissertation. *Entrance requirements:* For master's, minimum GPA of 3.0, letters of recommendation, writing sample; for doctorate, GRE, MA in psychology or social work with appropriate practical experience for advanced standing, or BA with a minimum GPA of 3.1; letters of recommendation; writing sample. Additional exam requirements/recommendations for international students: Required—TOEFL. *Application deadline:* For fall admission, 2/1 priority date for domestic and international students; for spring admission, 10/15 priority date for domestic and international students. Applications are processed on a rolling basis. Application fee: $65. Electronic applications accepted. *Expenses:* Tuition: Full-time $16,930; part-time $780 per unit. Tuition and fees vary according to course load and program. *Financial support:* In 2007–08, 393 students received support; research assistantships with tuition reimbursements available, teaching assistantships with tuition reimbursements available, career-related internships or fieldwork, Federal Work-Study, institutionally sponsored loans, scholarships/grants, and tuition waivers (partial) available. Support available to part-time students. Financial award application deadline: 3/15; financial award applicants required to submit FAFSA. *Faculty research:* Somatic psychology, comparative psychology, art therapy, transpersonal psychology, eco-psychology. *Application contact:* David Townes, Senior Admissions Counselor, 415-575-6152, Fax: 415-575-1268, E-mail: dtownes@ciis.edu.

See Close-Up on page 1421.

California State University, Bakersfield, Division of Graduate Studies, School of Humanities and Social Sciences, Program in Counseling Psychology, Bakersfield, CA 93311-1022. Offers MS.

California State University, Sacramento, Graduate Studies, College of Social Sciences and Interdisciplinary Studies, Department of Psychology, Sacramento, CA 95819-6048. Offers counseling psychology (MA). Part-time programs available. *Students:* 36 full-time (27 women), 75 part-time (55 women); includes 26 minority (4 African Americans, 14 Asian Americans or Pacific Islanders, 8 Hispanic Americans), 2 international. Average age 28. 68 applicants, 66% accepted, 29 enrolled. *Degree requirements:* For master's, thesis, writing proficiency exam. *Entrance requirements:* For master's, GRE Subject Test, minimum GPA of 3.0 during previous 2 years. Additional exam requirements/recommendations for international students: Required—TOEFL. *Application deadline:* Applications are processed on a rolling basis. Application fee: $55. Electronic applications accepted. *Expenses:* Tuition, state resident: full-time $3,414. Tuition, nonresident: full-time $13,584; part-time $339 per unit. Required fees: $786; $393 per semester. *Financial support:* Career-related internships or fieldwork and Federal Work-Study available. Support available to part-time students. Financial award application deadline: 3/1. *Unit head:* Bruce Behrman, Chair, 916-2748-6254, Fax: 916-278-6820.

California State University, San Bernardino, Graduate Studies, College of Social and Behavioral Sciences, Department of Psychology, Program in Clinical/Counseling Psychology, San Bernardino, CA 92407-2397. Offers MS. *Faculty:* 10 full-time. *Students:* 25 full-time (22 women); includes 8 minority (3 African Americans, 5 Hispanic Americans), 1 international. Average age 24. 66 applicants, 29% accepted, 13 enrolled. In 2007, 13 degrees awarded. *Degree requirements:* For master's, comprehensive exam or thesis. *Entrance requirements:* For master's, minimum GPA of 3.0 in major. *Application deadline:* For fall admission, 8/31 priority date for domestic students. Application fee: $55. *Financial support:* Fellowships, research assistantships, teaching assistantships, career-related internships or fieldwork, Federal Work-Study, and unspecified assistantships available. Financial award application deadline: 3/1. *Faculty research:* Psychology of women, fathering, depression, families, cross-cultural counseling. *Unit head:* Dr. David Chavez, Head, 909-537-5572, Fax: 909-537-7003, E-mail: dchavez@csusb.edu. *Application contact:* Stacy Brooks, Graduate Secretary, 909-880-5570, Fax: 909-880-7003, E-mail: sbrooks@csusb.edu.

Cambridge College, Program in Counseling Psychology, Cambridge, MA 02138-5304. Offers M Ed, CAGS. Part-time and evening/weekend programs available. *Faculty:* 6 full-time (2 women), 68 part-time/adjunct (40 women). *Students:* 437 full-time (345 women), 323 part-time (255 women); includes 355 minority (267 African Americans, 8 Asian Americans or Pacific Islanders, 80 Hispanic Americans), 19 international. Average age 37. 232 applicants, 98% accepted, 206 enrolled. In 2007, 233 master's, 6 CAGSs awarded. *Degree requirements:* For master's, thesis, internship/practicum. *Entrance requirements:* Additional exam requirements/recommendations for international students: Required—TOEFL. *Application deadline:* Applications are processed on a rolling basis. Application fee: $30. *Financial support:* Career-related internships or fieldwork and Federal Work-Study available. Financial award applicants required to submit FAFSA. *Unit head:* Dr. Niti Seth, Director, 617-873-0208, Fax: 617-349-3545. *Application contact:* Dahiana Alcon, Admission Counselor, 800-877-4723 Ext. 1622, E-mail: dahiana.alcon@cambridgecollege.edu.

Capella University, Harold Abel School of Psychology, Minneapolis, MN 55402. Offers clinical psychology (MS); counseling psychology (MS); educational psychology (MS, PhD); general psychology (MS, PhD); industrial/organizational psychology (MS, PhD); school psychology (MS, Certificate); sport psychology (MS). Part-time and evening/weekend programs available. Postbaccalaureate distance learning degree programs offered (minimal on-campus study). Terminal master's awarded for partial completion of doctoral program. *Degree requirements:* For master's, thesis optional, project; for doctorate, thesis/dissertation. *Entrance requirements:* For degree, master's degree in school psychology. Additional exam requirements/recommendations for international students: Required—TOEFL (minimum score 550 paper-based; 213 computer-based), TWE (minimum score 4). Electronic applications accepted. *Faculty research:* Correctional mental health delivery, community mental health, attachment and caregiving in adult and family relationships, influence of encouragement on motivation, and moral dilemmas in business.

Capella University, School of Human Services, Minneapolis, MN 55402. Offers addictions counseling (Certificate); counseling studies (MS, PhD); criminal justice (MS, PhD, Certificate); diversity studies (Certificate); general human services (MS, PhD); health care administration (MS, PhD, Certificate); management of nonprofit agencies (MS, PhD, Certificate); marital, couple and family counseling/therapy (MS); marriage and family services (Certificate); mental health counseling (MS); professional counseling (Certificate); social and community services (MS, PhD, Certificate). Part-time and evening/weekend programs available. Postbaccalaureate distance learning degree programs offered (minimal on-campus study). Terminal master's awarded for partial completion of doctoral program. *Degree requirements:* For master's, thesis optional, integrative project; for doctorate, comprehensive exam, thesis/dissertation. *Entrance requirements:* Additional exam requirements/recommendations for international students: Required—TOEFL (minimum score 550 paper-based; 213 computer-based), TWE (minimum score 4). Electronic applications accepted. *Faculty research:* Compulsive and addictive behaviors, substance abuse, assessment of psychopathology and neuropsychology.

Carlos Albizu University, Miami Campus, Graduate Programs, Miami, FL 33172-2209. Offers clinical psychology (Psy D); entrepreneurship (MBA); exceptional student education (MS); industrial/organizational psychology (MS); marriage and family therapy (MS); mental health counseling (MS); nonprofit management (MBA); organizational management (MBA); psychology (MS); school counseling (MS); teaching English as a second language (MS). *Accreditation:* APA. Part-time and evening/weekend programs available. *Faculty:* 20 full-time (13 women), 65 part-time/adjunct (39 women). *Students:* 514 full-time (409 women), 143 part-time (119 women); includes 465 minority (54 African Americans, 1 American Indian/Alaska Native, 4 Asian Americans or Pacific Islanders, 406 Hispanic Americans). Average age 35. 194 applicants, 73% accepted, 130 enrolled. In 2007, 208 master's, 37 doctorates awarded. Terminal master's awarded for partial completion of doctoral program. *Median time to degree:* Of those who began their doctoral program in fall 1999, 65% received their degree in 8 years or less. *Degree requirements:* For master's, one foreign language, comprehensive exam, integrative project (MBA), research project (MSESE and MSTESOL); for doctorate, one foreign language, comprehensive exam, internship, doctoral project. *Entrance requirements:* For master's, 3 letters of recommendation, interview, minimum GPA of 3.0, resumé, statement of purpose, official transcripts; for doctorate, 3 letters of recommendation, minimum GPA of 3.0, resumé, interview. *Application deadline:* For fall admission, 8/1 priority date for domestic students; for spring admission, 11/30 priority date for domestic students. Applications are processed on a rolling basis. Application fee: $50. *Expenses:* Tuition: Full-time $9,090; part-time $505 per credit. Required fees: $298 per term. Tuition and fees vary according to course load and degree level. *Financial support:* In 2007–08, 37 students received support. Federal Work-Study and scholarships/grants available. Financial award application deadline: 6/1; financial award applicants required to submit FAFSA. *Faculty research:* Psychotherapy, forensic psychology, neuropsychology, marketing strategy, entrepreneurship, special education. *Unit head:* Dr. Carmen S. Roca, Interim Chancellor, 305-593-1223 Ext. 120, Fax: 305-629-8052, E-mail: croca@albizu.edu. *Application contact:* Barbara De la Cruz, Admission Officer, 305-593-1223 Ext. 218, Fax: 305-593-1854, E-mail: bdelacruz@albizu.edu.

Carlow University, School for Social Change, Pittsburgh, PA 15213-3165. Offers management of non-profit organization (MS); organizational influence (MS); professional counseling (MSPC); training and development (MS). Part-time and evening/weekend programs available. *Entrance requirements:* For master's, interview, minimum GPA of 3.0, resumé, 3 letters of recommendation, 1 year professional experience. Additional exam requirements/recommendations for international students: Required—TOEFL (minimum score 550 paper-based; 213 computer-based). Electronic applications accepted. *Faculty research:* Gender and leadership, cross cultural communications and leadership, organizational culture.

Centenary College, Program in Counseling Psychology, Hackettstown, NJ 07840-2100. Offers counseling (MA); counseling psychology (MA). Part-time and evening/weekend programs available. Postbaccalaureate distance learning degree programs offered (minimal on-campus study). *Degree requirements:* For master's, thesis, fieldwork.

Central Washington University, Graduate Studies, Research and Continuing Education, College of the Sciences, Department of Psychology, Program in Mental Health Counseling, Ellensburg, WA 98926. Offers MS. *Accreditation:* ACA. *Faculty:* 27 full-time (13 women). *Students:* 14 full-time (11 women), 2 part-time (both women); includes 2 minority (both Hispanic Americans) 30 applicants, 30% accepted, 9 enrolled. *Degree requirements:* For master's, thesis, internship. *Entrance requirements:* For master's, GRE General Test, minimum GPA of 3.0. Additional exam requirements/recommendations for international students: Required—TOEFL (minimum score 550 paper-based; 213 computer-based; 79 iBT). *Application deadline:* For fall admission, 4/1 for domestic students. Application fee: $50. *Expenses:* Tuition, state resident: full-time $2,209; part-time $221 per credit. Tuition, nonresident: full-time $4,939; part-time $442 per credit. Required fees: $207 per quarter. Tuition and fees vary according to degree level. *Financial support:* Research assistantships with partial tuition reimbursements, teaching assistantships, career-related internships or fieldwork, Federal Work-Study, health care benefits, and unspecified assistantships available. Financial award application deadline: 3/1; financial award applicants required to submit FAFSA. *Unit head:* Dr. Jeff Penick, Program Coordinator, 509-963-3660, E-mail: penickj@cwu.edu. *Application contact:* Justine Eason, Admissions Program Coordinator, 509-963-3103, Fax: 509-963-1799, E-mail: masters@cwu.edu.

Chaminade University of Honolulu, Graduate Services, Program in Counseling Psychology, Honolulu, HI 96816-1578. Offers MSCP. Part-time and evening/weekend programs available. *Faculty:* 6 full-time (3 women), 17 part-time/adjunct (10 women). *Students:* 175 full-time (134 women), 60 part-time (41 women); includes 179 minority (11 African Americans, 4 American

Counseling Psychology

Chaminade University of Honolulu (continued)
Indian/Alaska Native, 151 Asian Americans or Pacific Islanders, 13 Hispanic Americans), 1 international. Average age 31. 86 applicants, 83% accepted, 70 enrolled. In 2007, 80 degrees awarded. *Degree requirements:* For master's, comprehensive exam. *Entrance requirements:* For master's, minimum undergraduate GPA of 3.0, 3 letters of recommendation. Additional exam requirements/recommendations for international students: Required—TOEFL (minimum score 550 paper-based). *Application deadline:* For fall admission, 9/1 priority date for domestic students; for winter admission, 11/15 for domestic students; for spring admission, 3/1 for domestic students. Applications are processed on a rolling basis. Application fee: $50. *Expenses:* Tuition: Part-time $490 per credit hour. *Financial support:* In 2007–08, 163 students received support. Career-related internships or fieldwork, Federal Work-Study, and institutionally sponsored loans available. Support available to part-time students. Financial award application deadline: 3/1; financial award applicants required to submit FAFSA. *Faculty research:* Taoist/Buddhist psychology, psychology of T'ai Chi Ch'uan, sleep disorders, drug/alcohol prevention with adolescent girls, anger/aggression with kids. *Unit head:* Dr. Robert G. Santee, Dean, 808-735-4720, Fax: 808-739-4670, E-mail: rsantee@chaminade.edu. *Application contact:* Janet C. Martin, Assistant to the Director, 808-735-4751, Fax: 808-739-4670, E-mail: mscp@chaminade.edu.

Chatham University, Program in Counseling Psychology, Pittsburgh, PA 15232-2826. Offers MSCP. Part-time and evening/weekend programs available. *Students:* 127 full-time (107 women), 83 part-time (69 women). Average age 29. 105 applicants, 85% accepted, 66 enrolled. In 2007, 63 degrees awarded. *Degree requirements:* For master's, thesis optional, supervised internship, optional advanced research project. *Entrance requirements:* For master's, minimum GPA of 3.0; 2 letters of recommendation; resumé; prerequisite coursework in statistics, biology, and psychology. Additional exam requirements/recommendations for international students: Recommended—TOEFL (minimum score 600 paper-based; 250 computer-based; 100 iBT), IELTS (minimum score 7). *Application deadline:* Applications are processed on a rolling basis. Application fee: $45. Electronic applications accepted. *Financial support:* Career-related internships or fieldwork available. Financial award applicants required to submit FAFSA. *Faculty research:* Trauma and recovery, hypnosis, psychospiritual dimensions of healing, psychotherapy of schizophrenia. *Unit head:* Dr. Mary Beth Mannarino, Director, 412-365-1196, Fax: 412-365-1505, E-mail: mmannarino@chatham.edu. *Application contact:* 412-365-1825, Fax: 412-365-1609, E-mail: admissions@chatham.edu.

Chestnut Hill College, School of Graduate Studies, Division of Psychology, Program in Clinical and Counseling Psychology, Philadelphia, PA 19118-2693. Offers MA, MS, CAS. Part-time and evening/weekend programs available. *Faculty:* 11 full-time (4 women), 29 part-time/adjunct (13 women). *Students:* 80 full-time (70 women), 157 part-time (128 women); includes 50 minority (42 African Americans, 3 Asian Americans or Pacific Islanders, 5 Hispanic Americans), 1 international. Average age 33. 80 applicants, 30% accepted. In 2007, 66 degrees awarded. *Degree requirements:* For master's, thesis optional, practica. *Entrance requirements:* For master's, GRE, statement of professional goals writing sample, transcripts, letters of recommendation; for CAS, GRE, Master's degree in counseling or a related discipline, transcripts, letters of recommendation, statement of professional goals writing sample. Additional exam requirements/recommendations for international students: Required—TOEFL (minimum score 550 paper-based; 213 computer-based). *Application deadline:* For fall admission, 7/17 priority date for domestic students, 7/17 for international students; for spring admission, 12/15 priority date for domestic students, 12/15 for international students. Applications are processed on a rolling basis. Application fee: $50. *Faculty research:* Child and adolescent therapy and clinical issues; psychoanalytic psychotherapy; object relations and cognitive-behavior therapy; marriage and family issues; clinical issues and interventions with diverse populations. *Application contact:* Amy Boorse, Administrative Assistant, School of Graduate Studies Office, 215-248-7170, Fax: 215-248-7161, E-mail: gradadmissions@chc.edu.

The Chicago School of Professional Psychology, Graduate School, Program in Clinical Psychology, Chicago, IL 60610. Offers applied behavior analysis (MA, Psy D, Certificate); clinical psychology (Psy D); counseling (MA); Latino mental health (Certificate); psychology (Certificate). *Students:* 756. Average age 26. 628 applicants, 64% accepted, 177 enrolled. *Degree requirements:* For master's, thesis (for some programs); for doctorate, comprehensive exam, thesis/dissertation. *Entrance requirements:* For master's, minimum undergraduate GPA of 3.0; 1 course in psychology and 1 course in either statistics or research methods; for doctorate, GRE, 18 hours of psychology credit (including courses in statistics, normal psychology and human development); minimum GPA of 3.2. Additional exam requirements/recommendations for international students: Required—TOEFL (minimum score 550 paper-based; 213 computer-based; 79 iBT). Application fee: $50. Electronic applications accepted. *Financial support:* Fellowships, Federal Work-Study and scholarships/grants available. Financial award applicants required to submit FAFSA. *Application contact:* Yarelli Meza, Director of Admission, 312-329-6666, Fax: 312-644-3333, E-mail: admissions@thechicagoschool.edu.

See Close-Up on page 1425.

City College of the City University of New York, Graduate School, College of Liberal Arts and Science, Program in Mental Health Counseling, New York, NY 10031-9198. Offers MA. *Students:* 209. 22 applicants, 95% accepted, 16 enrolled. *Unit head:* Robert Malera, Head, 212-650-1380. *Application contact:* Cynthia Grace, Advisor, 212-650-5713, E-mail: cgrace@ccny.cony.edu.

City University of Seattle, Graduate Division, Division of Arts and Sciences, Bellevue, WA 98005. Offers counseling psychology (MA). Part-time and evening/weekend programs available. Postbaccalaureate distance learning degree programs offered (no on-campus study). *Faculty:* 5 full-time (4 women), 58 part-time/adjunct (37 women). *Students:* 308. Average age 36. 124 applicants, 100% accepted, 1 enrolled. In 2007, 99 degrees awarded. *Application deadline:* Applications are processed on a rolling basis. Application fee: $50. Electronic applications accepted. *Expenses: Contact institution. Financial support:* In 2007–08, 29 students received support. Federal Work-Study available. Support available to part-time students. Financial award applicants required to submit FAFSA. *Unit head:* Judy Hinrichs, Interim Dean, 425-637-101 Ext. 5465, Fax: 425-709-5363, E-mail: jhinrichs@cityu.edu. *Application contact:* 800-426-5596, Fax: 425-709-5361, E-mail: info@citryu.edu.

Cleveland State University, College of Graduate Studies, College of Education and Human Services, Program in Urban Education, Cleveland, OH 44115. Offers counseling (PhD); counseling psychology (PhD); leadership and lifelong learning (PhD); learning and development (PhD); policy studies (PhD); school administration (PhD). Part-time programs available. *Faculty:* 14 full-time (9 women), 4 part-time/adjunct (2 women). *Students:* 16 full-time (11 women), 78 part-time (47 women); includes 22 minority (20 African Americans, 2 Asian Americans or Pacific Islanders), 5 international. Average age 43. 45 applicants, 62% accepted, 23 enrolled. In 2007, 9 degrees awarded. *Degree requirements:* For doctorate, one foreign language, comprehensive exam, thesis/dissertation. *Entrance requirements:* For doctorate, GRE General Test, minimum graduate GPA of 3.25. Additional exam requirements/recommendations for international students: Required—TOEFL (minimum score 525 paper-based; 197 computer-based), IELTS (minimum score 6). *Application deadline:* For fall admission, 2/5 for domestic students. Application fee: $30. *Financial support:* In 2007–08, 7 students received support, including 4 research assistantships with full and partial tuition reimbursements available (averaging $7,800 per year), 3 teaching assistantships with full and partial tuition reimbursements available (averaging $7,800 per year); tuition waivers (full) and unspecified assistantships also available. Financial award applicants required to submit FAFSA. *Faculty research:* Equity issues (race, ethnicity, and gender), education development consequences for special needs of urban populations, urban education programming, counseling the violent or aggressive adolescent. Total annual research expenditures: $5,662. *Unit head:* Dr. Joshua Bagakas, Director, 216-687-4591, Fax: 216-875-9697, E-mail: j.bagakas@csuohio.edu. *Application contact:* Wanda Butler, Administrative Assistant, 216-687-4697, Fax: 216-875-9697, E-mail: w.pruett-butler@csuohio.edu.

The College at Brockport, State University of New York, School of Professions, Department of Counselor Education, Brockport, NY 14420-2997. Offers college counseling (MS Ed); mental health counseling (MS); school counseling (MS Ed, CAS). *Accreditation:* ACA (one or more programs are accredited). Part-time programs available. *Students:* 27 full-time (19 women), 54 part-time (41 women); includes 21 minority (18 African Americans, 3 Hispanic Americans), 1 international. 47 applicants, 36% accepted, 15 enrolled. In 2007, 24 master's, 2 other advanced degrees awarded. *Degree requirements:* For master's, internship, project. *Entrance requirements:* For master's, interview, letters of recommendation; for CAS, master's degree, New York state school counselor certificate. Additional exam requirements/recommendations for international students: Required—TOEFL (minimum score 550 paper-based; 213 computer-based; 79 iBT). *Application deadline:* For fall admission, 2/1 for domestic and international students; for spring admission, 9/1 for domestic and international students. Application fee: $80. *Expenses:* Tuition, state resident: full-time $6,900; part-time $288 per credit. Tuition, nonresident: full-time $10,920; part-time $455 per credit. Required fees: $738; $31 per credit. *Financial support:* In 2007–08, 2 teaching assistantships with tuition reimbursements (averaging $6,000 per year) were awarded; Federal Work-Study, scholarships/grants, and unspecified assistantships also available. Support available to part-time students. Financial award application deadline: 3/15; financial award applicants required to submit FAFSA. *Faculty research:* Gender and diversity issues, counseling outcomes, qualitative research, school counseling, mental health counseling and obesity. *Unit head:* Dr. Susan R. Seem, Chairperson, 585-395-2258, E-mail: sseem@brockport.edu.

The College of New Rochelle, Graduate School, Division of Human Services, Program in Guidance and Counseling, New Rochelle, NY 10805-2308. Offers MS. Part-time programs available. *Faculty:* 6 full-time (3 women), 6 part-time/adjunct (3 women). *Students:* 40 full-time (34 women), 94 part-time (84 women); includes 57 minority (44 African Americans, 1 American Indian/Alaska Native, 12 Hispanic Americans), 2 international. Average age 36. In 2007, 75 degrees awarded. *Degree requirements:* For master's, internship. *Entrance requirements:* For master's, interview, minimum GPA of 3.0. *Application deadline:* For fall admission, 8/1 priority date for domestic students. Applications are processed on a rolling basis. Application fee: $35. *Expenses:* Tuition: Part-time $650 per credit. Required fees: $90 per term. *Financial support:* Career-related internships or fieldwork and scholarships/grants available. *Unit head:* Dr. Marie Ribarich, Associate Dean, Division of Human Services, 914-654-5561, Fax: 914-654-5593, E-mail: mribarich@cnr.edu.

The College of New Rochelle, Graduate School, Division of Human Services, Program in Mental Health Counseling, New Rochelle, NY 10805-2308. Offers Certificate. *Students:* 13 full-time (12 women), 38 part-time (36 women); includes 21 minority (16 African Americans, 5 Hispanic Americans). Average age 42. *Degree requirements:* For Certificate, internship. *Application deadline:* For fall admission, 8/1 for domestic students. Applications are processed on a rolling basis. Application fee: $35. *Expenses:* Tuition: Part-time $650 per credit. Required fees: $90 per term. *Unit head:* Dr. Marie Ribarich, Associate Dean, Division of Human Services, 914-654-5561, Fax: 914-654-5593, E-mail: mribarich@cnr.edu.

College of Saint Elizabeth, Department of Psychology, Morristown, NJ 07960-6989. Offers counseling psychology (MA); forensic psychology (MA); student affairs in higher education (Certificate). Part-time and evening/weekend programs available. *Faculty:* 5 full-time (2 women), 6 part-time/adjunct (4 women). *Students:* 7 full-time (all women), 61 part-time (58 women); includes 21 minority (7 African Americans, 2 Asian Americans or Pacific Islanders, 12 Hispanic Americans), 2 international. Average age 30. In 2007, 8 degrees awarded. *Degree requirements:* For master's, thesis or alternative, portfolio. *Entrance requirements:* For master's, minimum GPA of 3.0, BA in psychology (preferred), 12 credits of course work in psychology. *Application deadline:* For fall admission, 4/14 priority date for domestic students; for spring admission, 11/15 for domestic students. Applications are processed on a rolling basis. Application fee: $35. Electronic applications accepted. *Expenses:* Tuition: Full-time $17,016; part-time $709 per credit. Required fees: $1,300; $370 per term. Full-time tuition and fees vary according to program and student's religious affiliation. Part-time tuition and fees vary according to campus/location and student's religious affiliation. *Financial support:* Career-related internships or fieldwork, tuition waivers (partial), and unspecified assistantships available. Support available to part-time students. Financial award application deadline: 3/15; financial award applicants required to submit FAFSA. *Faculty research:* Family systems, dissociative identity disorder, multicultural counseling, outcomes assessment. *Unit head:* Dr. Valerie Scott, Director of the Graduate Program in Counseling Psychology, 973-290-4102, Fax: 973-290-4676, E-mail: vscott@cse.edu. *Application contact:* Michael Szarek, Director of Enrollment Management, 973-290-4112, Fax: 973-290-4167, E-mail: mszarek@cse.edu.

College of St. Joseph, Graduate Programs, Division of Psychology and Human Services, Program in Clinical Mental Health Counseling, Rutland, VT 05701-3899. Offers MS. Part-time programs available. *Faculty:* 4 full-time (1 woman), 8 part-time/adjunct (4 women). *Students:* 2 full-time (both women), 14 part-time (11 women). Average age 30. 4 applicants, 75% accepted, 2 enrolled. In 2007, 7 degrees awarded. *Degree requirements:* For master's, comprehensive exam. *Entrance requirements:* For master's, 2 letters of reference, interview. *Application deadline:* Applications are processed on a rolling basis. Application fee: $35. Electronic applications accepted. *Expenses:* Tuition: Full-time $12,000; part-time $325 per credit. Required fees: $45 per semester. *Financial support:* In 2007–08, 1 student received support. Career-related internships or fieldwork, Federal Work-Study, and unspecified assistantships available. Support available to part-time students. Financial award application deadline: 3/1. *Application contact:* Tracy Gallipo, Director of Admissions, 802-773-5900 Ext. 3262, Fax: 802-773-5900, E-mail: tracygallipo@csj.edu.

Colorado Christian University, Program in Counseling, Lakewood, CO 80226. Offers MA. Part-time and evening/weekend programs available. *Degree requirements:* For master's, thesis optional. *Entrance requirements:* For master's, GRE General Test, 3 letters of recommendation. Additional exam requirements/recommendations for international students: Required—TOEFL. Electronic applications accepted. Expenses: Contact institution.

Columbus State University, Graduate Studies, College of Education, Department of Counseling, Educational Leadership and Professional Studies, Columbus, GA 31907-5645. Offers community counseling (MS); educational leadership (M Ed, Ed S); school counseling (M Ed). *Accreditation:* ACA; NCATE. Part-time and evening/weekend programs available. Postbaccalaureate distance learning degree programs offered (minimal on-campus study). *Faculty:* 11 full-time (4 women), 12 part-time/adjunct (7 women). *Students:* 131 full-time (89 women), 81 part-time (69 women); includes 69 minority (66 African Americans, 1 Asian American or Pacific Islander, 2 Hispanic Americans), 1 international. Average age 36. 102 applicants, 77% accepted, 56 enrolled. In 2007, 40 master's, 33 other advanced degrees awarded. *Degree requirements:* For master's, thesis, exit exam; for Ed S, thesis or alternative. *Entrance requirements:* For master's, GRE General Test, minimum GPA of 2.75; for Ed S, GRE General Test. Additional exam requirements/recommendations for international students: Required—TOEFL (minimum score 550 paper-based; 213 computer-based). *Application deadline:* For fall admission, 5/1 priority date for domestic students, 5/1 for international students; for spring admission, 11/1 for domestic and international students. Applications are processed on a rolling basis. Application fee: $25. Electronic applications accepted. *Expenses:* Tuition, state resident: part-time $143 per semester hour. Tuition, nonresident: part-time $569 per semester hour. Required fees: $273 per term. Tuition and fees vary according to course load. *Financial support:* In 2007–08, 93 students received support, including 5 research assistantships with partial tuition reimbursements available (averaging $3,000 per year); career-related internships or fieldwork, Federal Work-Study, institutionally sponsored loans, scholarships/grants, tuition waivers (partial), and unspecified assistantships also available. Support available to part-time students. Financial award application deadline: 5/1; financial award applicants required to submit FAFSA. *Unit head:* Dr. Paul Tom Hackett, Chair, 706-568-5061, Fax: 706-569-3134, E-mail: hackett_paul@colstate.edu. *Application contact:* Katie Thornton, Graduate Admissions Specialist, 706-568-2035, Fax: 706-568-2462, E-mail: thornton_katie@colstate.edu.

Concordia University Chicago, College of Arts and Sciences, Program in Community Counseling, River Forest, IL 60305-1499. Offers MA. *Accreditation:* ACA. *Degree requirements:* For master's, final project. *Entrance requirements:* For master's, minimum GPA of 2.9. Additional exam requirements/recommendations for international students: Required—TOEFL (minimum score 550 paper-based; 195 computer-based). Electronic applications accepted.

Concordia University Wisconsin, Graduate Programs, Department of Psychology, Program in Professional Counseling, Mequon, WI 53097-2402. Offers MPC. Postbaccalaureate distance learning degree programs offered (minimal on-campus study). *Degree requirements:* For master's, comprehensive exam, thesis or alternative. *Entrance requirements:* For master's, minimum GPA of 3.0. Additional exam requirements/recommendations for international students: Required—TOEFL.

Dallas Baptist University, College of Humanities and Social Sciences, Counseling Program (Main Campus), Dallas, TX 75211-9299. Offers MA. Part-time and evening/weekend programs available. *Faculty:* 55 full-time (22 women), 114 part-time/adjunct (44 women). *Students:* 6 full-time, 165 part-time. 70 applicants, 56% accepted, 33 enrolled. In 2007, 29 degrees awarded. *Entrance requirements:* For master's, GRE General Test, minimum GPA of 3.0. Additional exam requirements/recommendations for international students: Required—TOEFL. *Application deadline:* Applications are processed on a rolling basis. Application fee: $25. Electronic applications accepted. *Expenses:* Tuition: Full-time $9,144; part-time $508 per credit hour. *Financial support:* Federal Work-Study, institutionally sponsored loans, scholarships/grants, and tuition waivers (full and partial) available. Support available to part-time students. Financial award applicants required to submit FAFSA. *Faculty research:* Therapy effectiveness. *Unit head:* Dr. Mary Becerril, Director, 214-333-5273, Fax: 214-333-5323, E-mail: graduate@dbu.edu. *Application contact:* Kit P. Montgomery, Director of Graduate Programs, 214-333-5242, Fax: 214-333-5579, E-mail: graduate@dbu.edu.

Dallas Baptist University, College of Humanities and Social Sciences, Counseling Program (North Campus), Dallas, TX 75211-9299. Offers). Part-time and evening/weekend programs available. *Faculty:* 55 full-time (22 women), 114 part-time/adjunct (44 women). *Students:* 39 applicants, 49% accepted, 18 enrolled.Application fee: $25. *Expenses:* Tuition: Full-time $9,144; part-time $508 per credit hour. *Financial support:* Applicants required to submit FAFSA. *Unit head:* Dr. Joe Cook, Director, 214-333-5787, Fax: 214-333-5579.

Dominican University of California, Graduate Programs, School of Arts and Sciences, Program in Counseling Psychology, San Rafael, CA 94901-2298. Offers MS. Part-time programs available. *Faculty:* 3 full-time (2 women), 8 part-time/adjunct (7 women). *Students:* 61 full-time (56 women), 37 part-time (32 women); includes 11 minority (2 African Americans, 3 Asian Americans or Pacific Islanders, 6 Hispanic Americans), 2 international. Average age 40. 31 applicants, 61% accepted, 19 enrolled. In 2007, 22 degrees awarded. *Degree requirements:* For master's, comprehensive exam, fieldwork. *Entrance requirements:* For master's, interview, minimum GPA of 3.0. Additional exam requirements/recommendations for international students: Required—TOEFL (minimum score 550 paper-based; 213 computer-based). *Application deadline:* For fall admission, 3/2 priority date for domestic students. Applications are processed on a rolling basis. Application fee: $40. Electronic applications accepted. *Financial support:* In 2007–08, 53 students received support, including 22 fellowships (averaging $2,144 per year); Federal Work-Study, scholarships/grants, and tuition discounts also available. Support available to part-time students. Financial award applicants required to submit FAFSA. *Unit head:* Dr. Charles R. Billings, Chair, 415-485-3263, Fax: 415-458-3700, E-mail: billings@dominican.edu. *Application contact:* Lawrence Schwaltz, Associate Director, 415-458-3748, Fax: 415-485-3214, E-mail: larry.schwaltz@dominican.edu.

Eastern Nazarene College, Adult and Graduate Studies, Program in Family Counseling, Quincy, MA 02170-2999. Offers marriage and family therapy (MS). Part-time and evening/weekend programs available. *Entrance requirements:* For master's, 3 letters of recommendation, resumé. Additional exam requirements/recommendations for international students: Required—TOEFL (minimum score 550 paper-based).

Eastern University, Programs in Counseling, St. Davids, PA 19087-3696. Offers community/clinical counseling (MA); educational counseling (MA, MS), including school counseling (MA), school psychology (MS); marriage and family (MA); student development (MA). *Degree requirements:* For master's, internship. *Entrance requirements:* For master's, minimum GPA of 2.5. Additional exam requirements/recommendations for international students: Required—TOEFL.

Eastern Washington University, Graduate Studies, College of Education and Human Development, Department of Counseling, Educational, and Developmental Psychology, Program in School Counseling, Cheney, WA 99004-2431. Offers counseling psychology (MS); school counseling (MS). *Accreditation:* ACA; NCATE. *Degree requirements:* For master's, comprehensive exam, thesis or alternative. *Entrance requirements:* For master's, GRE General Test, minimum GPA of 3.0.

Emporia State University, School of Graduate Studies, The Teachers College, Department of Psychology and Special Education, Program in Mental Health Counseling, Emporia, KS 66801-5087. Offers MS. *Accreditation:* ACA. Part-time programs available. *Students:* 2 full-time (both women), 25 part-time (19 women); includes 2 minority (1 African American, 1 Hispanic American), 4 international. 8 applicants, 88% accepted, 7 enrolled. In 2007, 9 degrees awarded. *Degree requirements:* For master's, comprehensive exam, internship. *Entrance requirements:* For master's, GRE or MAT. Additional exam requirements/recommendations for international students: Required—TOEFL (minimum score 450 paper-based; 133 computer-based). *Application deadline:* For fall admission, 8/15 for domestic students. Applications are processed on a rolling basis. Application fee: $30 ($75 for international students). Electronic applications accepted. *Expenses:* Tuition, state resident: part-time $157 per credit hour. Tuition, nonresident: part-time $475 per credit hour. Required fees: $47 per credit hour. Tuition and fees vary according to campus/location. *Financial support:* Federal Work-Study, institutionally sponsored loans, health care benefits, and unspecified assistantships available. Financial award application deadline: 3/15; financial award applicants required to submit FAFSA. *Unit head:* Dr. Kenneth A. Weaver, Chair, Department of Psychology and Special Education, 620-341-5317, E-mail: kweaver@emporia.edu.

Evangel University, Department of Psychology, Springfield, MO 65802-2191. Offers clinical psychology (MS); counseling psychology (MS). Part-time and evening/weekend programs available. *Faculty:* 4 full-time (2 women), 1 part-time/adjunct (0 women). *Students:* 19 full-time (16 women), 6 part-time (5 women). Average age 30. 17 applicants, 100% accepted, 15 enrolled. In 2007, 9 degrees awarded. *Degree requirements:* For master's, comprehensive exam, thesis (for some programs). *Entrance requirements:* For master's, GRE General Test or MAT, minimum undergraduate GPA of 3.0, undergraduate major or minor in psychology, teaching certificate (school counseling). Additional exam requirements/recommendations for international students: Required—TOEFL (minimum score 550 paper-based; 213 computer-based). *Application deadline:* For fall admission, 2/1 priority date for domestic students; for spring admission, 10/15 priority date for domestic students. Applications are processed on a rolling basis. Application fee: $25. *Financial support:* In 2007–08, 6 students received support; research assistantships with partial tuition reimbursements available, teaching assistantships with partial tuition reimbursements available, career-related internships or fieldwork, institutionally sponsored loans, scholarships/grants, and unspecified assistantships available. Support available to part-time students. Financial award application deadline: 3/1; financial award applicants required to submit FAFSA. *Unit head:* Dr. Grant Jones, Chair, 417-865-2815 Ext. 8619, E-mail: jonesg@evangel.edu. *Application contact:* Charity H. Fahlstrom, Admissions Representative, Graduate and Professional Studies Admissions, 417-865-2811 Ext. 7227, Fax: 417-575-5484.

Fairleigh Dickinson University, College at Florham, Maxwell Becton College of Arts and Sciences, Department of Psychology, Program in Counseling, Madison, NJ 07940-1099. Offers MA. *Students:* 41 full-time (25 women), 24 part-time (15 women), 2 international. Average age 31. 46 applicants, 87% accepted, 19 enrolled. In 2007, 40 degrees awarded. *Expenses:* Tuition: Part-time $869 per credit. *Unit head:* Dr. Diane Wentworth, Chairperson, Department of Psychology, 973-443-8548.

Fitchburg State College, Division of Graduate and Continuing Education, Programs in Counseling, Fitchburg, MA 01420-2697. Offers elementary school guidance counseling (MS); marriage and family therapy (Certificate); mental health counseling (MS); secondary school guidance counseling (MS). *Accreditation:* NCATE. Part-time and evening/weekend programs available. *Students:* 16 full-time (13 women), 65 part-time (55 women); includes 6 minority (1 African American, 1 American Indian/Alaska Native, 4 Hispanic Americans), 2 international. Average age 31. 20 applicants, 85% accepted, 15 enrolled. In 2007, 17 degrees awarded. *Entrance requirements:* For master's, GRE General Test or MAT, letters of recommendation, resumé; for Certificate, master's degree. Additional exam requirements/recommendations for international students: Required—TOEFL (minimum score 550 paper-based; 213 computer-based; 79 iBT). *Application deadline:* Applications are processed on a rolling basis. Application fee: $25 ($50 for international students). *Expenses:* Tuition, nonresident: part-time $150 per credit. Required fees: $109 per credit. *Financial support:* In 2007–08, research assistantships with partial tuition reimbursements (averaging $5,500 per year); Federal Work-Study, scholarships/grants, and unspecified assistantships also available. Support available to part-time students. Financial award application deadline: 3/1; financial award applicants required to submit FAFSA. *Unit head:* Dr. John Hancock, Chair, 978-665-3604, Fax: 978-665-3658, E-mail: gce@fsc.edu. *Application contact:* Director of Admissions, 978-665-3144, Fax: 978-665-4540, E-mail: admissions@fsc.edu.

Florida Atlantic University, College of Education, Department of Counselor Education, Boca Raton, FL 33431-0991. Offers counselor education (M Ed); family counseling (Ed S); mental health counseling (M Ed, Ed S); rehabilitation counseling (M Ed); school counseling (Ed S). *Accreditation:* ACA; NCATE. Part-time and evening/weekend programs available. *Degree requirements:* For Ed S, departmental qualifying exam. *Entrance requirements:* For master's, GRE General Test, minimum GPA of 3.0 during previous 2 years; for Ed S, GRE General Test, minimum graduate GPA of 3.25. Additional exam requirements/recommendations for international students: Required—TOEFL. *Faculty research:* Brief therapy, psychological type, marriage and family counseling, international programs, integrated services.

Florida International University, College of Education, Department of Educational and Psychological Studies, Program in Counselor Education, Miami, FL 33199. Offers mental health counseling (MS); rehabilitation counseling (MS); school counseling (MS). *Accreditation:* ACA; NCATE. Part-time and evening/weekend programs available. *Entrance requirements:* For master's, General Knowledge test, College Level Academic Skills Test, GRE or PRAXIS (school counseling track), minimum GPA of 3.0, interview. Additional exam requirements/recommendations for international students: Required—TOEFL (minimum score 550 paper-based; 213 computer-based; 80 iBT), IELTS (minimum score 6). Electronic applications accepted. *Expenses:* Tuition, state resident: full-time $6,106. Tuition, nonresident: full-time $15,528. Required fees: $284.

Florida State University, Graduate Studies, College of Education, Department of Educational Psychology and Learning Systems, Program in Psychological Services, Tallahassee, FL 32306. Offers MS, PhD, Ed S. *Accreditation:* ACA (one or more programs are accredited). *Faculty:* 7 full-time (3 women), 1 part-time/adjunct (0 women). *Students:* 51 full-time (45 women), 39 part-time (27 women); includes 22 minority (13 African Americans, 7 Asian Americans or Pacific Islanders, 2 Hispanic Americans). Average age 20. 83 applicants, 27% accepted, 17 enrolled. In 2007, 18 master's, 6 doctorates, 19 other advanced degrees awarded. *Degree requirements:* For master's and Ed S, comprehensive exam, thesis optional. *Entrance requirements:* For master's and Ed S, GRE General Test, minimum GPA of 3.0. *Application deadline:* For fall admission, 7/1 priority date for domestic students; for spring admission, 11/1 for domestic students. Applications are processed on a rolling basis. Application fee: $30. *Expenses:* Tuition, state resident: part-time $248 per credit hour. Tuition, nonresident: part-time $880 per credit hour. Tuition and fees vary according to program. *Financial support:* In 2007–08, fellowships with partial tuition reimbursements (averaging $5,000 per year), research assistantships with partial tuition reimbursements (averaging $18,000 per year), teaching assistantships with partial tuition reimbursements (averaging $18,000 per year) were awarded; career-related internships or fieldwork also available. Financial award applicants required to submit FAFSA. *Unit head:* Dr. Frances Prevatt, Program Leader, 850-644-9445, Fax: 850-644-8776, E-mail: fprevatt@coe.fsu.edu. *Application contact:* Sally Gadson, Program Assistant, 850-644-8046, Fax: 850-644-5067, E-mail: gadson@coe.fsu.edu.

Fordham University, Graduate School of Education, Division of Psychological and Educational Services, New York, NY 10023. Offers counseling and personnel services (MSE, Adv C); counseling psychology (PhD); educational psychology (MSE, PhD); school psychology (PhD); urban and urban bilingual school psychology (Adv C). *Accreditation:* APA (one or more programs are accredited); NCATE. *Degree requirements:* For doctorate, thesis/dissertation. *Entrance requirements:* For doctorate, GRE General Test. *Expenses:* Tuition: Full-time $23,880; part-time $995 per credit.

Fort Valley State University, College of Graduate Studies and Extended Education, Department of Counseling Psychology, Program in Mental Health Counseling, Fort Valley, GA 31030-4313. Offers MS. Part-time programs available. *Faculty:* 2 full-time (0 women), 1 part-time/adjunct (0 women). *Students:* 1 (woman) full-time, 258 part-time (253 women); all African Americans Average age 51. In 2007, 7 degrees awarded. *Degree requirements:* For master's, comprehensive exam (for some programs), thesis optional. *Entrance requirements:* For master's, GRE General Test or MAT. *Application deadline:* For fall admission, 8/23 for domestic students. Application fee: $20. *Expenses:* Tuition, state resident: full-time $3,390; part-time $142 per credit hour. Tuition, nonresident: full-time $13,550; part-time $565 per credit hour. Required fees: $920; $50 per credit hour. *Financial support:* Federal Work-Study available. Support available to part-time students. Financial award application deadline: 5/1; financial award applicants required to submit FAFSA. *Unit head:* Dr. Teri Kulkosky, Department Head, 478-825-6232, Fax: 478-825-6161, E-mail: kulkoskyt@fvsu.edu. *Application contact:* Donovan Coley, Director of Admissions, 478-825-6672, E-mail: coleyd@fvsu.edu.

Franciscan University of Steubenville, Graduate Programs, Department of Counseling, Steubenville, OH 43952-1763. Offers MA. Part-time programs available. *Degree requirements:* For master's, case presentation, integrative paper. *Entrance requirements:* For master's, GRE General Test or MAT, minimum undergraduate GPA of 3.0.

Frostburg State University, Graduate School, College of Liberal Arts and Sciences, Department of Psychology, Program in Counseling Psychology, Frostburg, MD 21532-1099. Offers MS. Part-time and evening/weekend programs available. *Faculty:* 7 full-time (3 women), 3 part-time/adjunct (2 women). *Students:* 38 full-time (31 women), 7 part-time (6 women); includes 6 minority (4 African Americans, 1 Asian American or Pacific Islander, 1 Hispanic American), 4 international. Average age 28. 38 applicants, 47% accepted, 15 enrolled. In 2007, 6 degrees awarded. *Degree requirements:* For master's, internship. *Entrance requirements:* For master's, GRE General Test or MAT, interview, minimum GPA of 3.0, resumé. *Application deadline:* For fall admission, 2/1 for domestic students. Applications are processed on a rolling basis. Application fee: $30. Electronic applications accepted. *Expenses:* Tuition, state resident: full-time $5,706; part-time $317 per credit hour. Tuition, nonresident: full-time $6,552; part-time $364 per credit hour. Required fees: $77 per credit hour. $11 per term. *Financial support:* In 2007–08, 7 research assistantships with full tuition reimbursements (averaging $5,000 per year) were awarded; career-related internships or fieldwork and Federal Work-Study also available. Financial award application deadline: 4/1; financial award applicants required to submit FAFSA. *Unit head:* Dr. Mike Murtagh, Coordinator, 301-687-4193. *Application contact:* Vickie Mazer, Director, Graduate Services, 301-687-7053, Fax: 301-687-4597, E-mail: vmmazer@frostburg.edu.

Counseling Psychology

Gallaudet University, The Graduate School, Department of Counseling, Washington, DC 20002-3625. Offers mental health counseling (MA); school counseling (MA). *Accreditation:* ACA; NCATE. *Degree requirements:* For master's, thesis optional. *Entrance requirements:* For master's, GRE General Test or MAT. *Application deadline:* For fall admission, 2/15 priority date for domestic students. Applications are processed on a rolling basis. Application fee: $50. Electronic applications accepted. *Expenses:* Tuition: Full-time $5,790. Required fees: $1,886. *Financial support:* Career-related internships or fieldwork and Federal Work-Study available. Financial award application deadline: 8/1. *Unit head:* Dr. Roger Beach, Chair, 202-651-5515. *Application contact:* Wednesday Luria, Coordinator of Prospective Graduate Student Services, 202-651-5647, Fax: 202-651-5295, E-mail: wednesday.luria@gallaudet.edu.

Gannon University, School of Graduate Studies, College of Humanities, Business, and Education, School of Humanities, Program in Counseling Psychology, Erie, PA 16541-0001. Offers PhD. Part-time and evening/weekend programs available. *Students:* 8 full-time (5 women), 26 part-time (22 women); includes 1 minority (Asian American or Pacific Islander), 2 international. Average age 38. 8 applicants, 63% accepted, 3 enrolled. In 2007, 2 degrees awarded. *Degree requirements:* For doctorate, thesis/dissertation, internship. *Entrance requirements:* For doctorate, GRE General Test, minimum GPA of 3.25, master's degree. Additional exam requirements/recommendations for international students: Required—TOEFL (minimum score 500 paper-based; 173 computer-based). *Application deadline:* Applications are processed on a rolling basis. Application fee: $50. *Expenses:* Tuition: Full-time $13,050; part-time $725 per credit. Required fees: $502; $16 per credit. Tuition and fees vary according to course load, degree level, campus/location and program. *Financial support:* Career-related internships or fieldwork, Federal Work-Study, and unspecified assistantships available. Support available to part-time students. Financial award application deadline: 7/1; financial award applicants required to submit FAFSA. *Unit head:* Dr. Linda Fleming, Director, 814-871-7262, Fax: 814-871-5511, E-mail: fleming006@gannon.edu. *Application contact:* Debra Meszaros, Director of Graduate Recruitment, 814-871-5819, Fax: 814-871-5827, E-mail: cfal@gannon.edu.

Gardner-Webb University, Graduate School, School of Psychology, Program in Mental Health Counseling, Boiling Springs, NC 28017. Offers MA. *Accreditation:* ACA. Part-time and evening/weekend programs available. *Faculty:* 7 full-time (4 women), 1 part-time/adjunct (0 women). *Students:* 2 full-time (both women), 46 part-time (40 women); includes 9 minority (4 African Americans, 5 Hispanic Americans). Average age 31. In 2007, 13 degrees awarded. *Degree requirements:* For master's, comprehensive exam. *Entrance requirements:* For master's, GRE General Test, MAT, minimum GPA of 2.7. *Application deadline:* For fall admission, 7/1 priority date for domestic students. Applications are processed on a rolling basis. Application fee: $25. Electronic applications accepted. *Expenses:* Tuition: Part-time $275 per hour. *Financial support:* Unspecified assistantships available. *Unit head:* Dr. Frieda Brown, Coordinator, 704-406-4436, Fax: 704-406-4329, E-mail: fbrown@gardner-webb.edu.

Geneva College, Program in Counseling, Beaver Falls, PA 15010-3599. Offers marriage and family (MA); mental health (MA); school counseling (MA). *Accreditation:* ACA. Part-time and evening/weekend programs available. *Degree requirements:* For master's, internship. *Entrance requirements:* For master's, GRE General Test or MAT, minimum GPA of 3.0, letters of recommendation, faith statement, 12 credits in undergraduate psychology. Additional exam requirements/recommendations for international students: Required—TOEFL. Electronic applications accepted.

George Fox University, School of Education, Graduate Department of Counseling, Newberg, OR 97132-2697. Offers counseling (MA); marriage and family therapy (MA, Certificate); mental health trauma (Certificate); school counseling (MA); school psychology (MS, Certificate). Part-time programs available. *Faculty:* 10 full-time (7 women), 12 part-time/adjunct (8 women). *Students:* 101 full-time (82 women), 134 part-time (111 women); includes 19 minority (3 African Americans, 2 American Indian/Alaska Native, 8 Asian Americans or Pacific Islanders, 6 Hispanic Americans), 1 international. Average age 36. 86 applicants, 65% accepted, 56 enrolled. In 2007, 60 master's, 4 other advanced degrees awarded. *Degree requirements:* For master's, thesis optional. *Application deadline:* For fall admission, 5/30 for domestic students. Applications are processed on a rolling basis. Application fee: $40. Electronic applications accepted. *Expenses:* Contact institution. *Financial support:* Career-related internships or fieldwork available. *Unit head:* Dr. Richard Shaw, Director, 503-554-6142, E-mail: rshaw@georgefox.edu. *Application contact:* Carol Namburi, Admissions Counselor, 800-631-0921, Fax: 503-554-6111, E-mail: counseling@georgefox.edu.

Georgian Court University, School of Sciences and Mathematics, Lakewood, NJ 08701-2697. Offers biology (MS); counseling psychology (MA); holistic health (Certificate); holistic health studies (MA); mathematics (MA); professional counselor (Certificate); school psychology (Certificate). Part-time and evening/weekend programs available. *Faculty:* 17 full-time (10 women), 8 part-time/adjunct (5 women). *Students:* 46 full-time (40 women), 113 part-time (97 women); includes 17 minority (8 African Americans, 4 Asian Americans or Pacific Islanders, 5 Hispanic Americans), 1 international. Average age 34. 118 applicants, 73% accepted, 69 enrolled. In 2007, 39 master's, 5 other advanced degrees awarded. *Degree requirements:* For master's, comprehensive exam (for some programs), thesis (for some programs). *Entrance requirements:* For master's, GRE General Test, GRE Subject Test in biology (MS), 3 letters of recommendation. Additional exam requirements/recommendations for international students: Required—TOEFL (minimum score 550 paper-based; 213 computer-based). *Application deadline:* For fall admission, 8/1 priority date for domestic students, 4/1 for international students; for spring admission, 1/1 priority date for domestic students, 7/1 for international students. Applications are processed on a rolling basis. Application fee: $40. Electronic applications accepted. *Expenses:* Tuition: Full-time $15,456; part-time $644 per credit. Required fees: $760; $200 per term. Tuition and fees vary according to campus/location. *Financial support:* Scholarships/grants, health care benefits, and unspecified assistantships available. Financial award application deadline: 4/15; financial award applicants required to submit FAFSA. *Unit head:* Dr. Linda James, Dean, 732-987-2617, Fax: 732-987-2007. *Application contact:* Eugene Soltys, Director of Graduate Admissions, 732-987-2770, Fax: 732-987-2084, E-mail: graduateadmissions@georgian.edu.

Georgia State University, College of Education, Department of Counseling and Psychological Services, Program in Professional Counseling, Atlanta, GA 30303-3083. Offers counseling psychology (PhD); counselor education and practice (PhD); professional counseling (MS, Ed S). *Accreditation:* ACA (one or more programs are accredited); APA (one or more programs are accredited). *Students:* Average age 32. 242 applicants, 43% accepted. In 2007, 60 master's, 7 doctorates, 11 other advanced degrees awarded. *Degree requirements:* For master's, comprehensive exam; for doctorate, comprehensive exam, thesis/dissertation. *Entrance requirements:* For master's, GRE General Test, minimum GPA of 2.5; for doctorate, GRE General Test, minimum GPA of 3.3; for Ed S, GRE General Test, minimum graduate GPA of 3.25. Application fee: $50. *Expenses:* Tuition, state resident: part-time $221 per credit hour. *Financial support:* Scholarships/grants available. Financial award application deadline: 4/1. *Faculty research:* Dropout prevention, school reform, school violence, lifestyle correlates, stress management. *Unit head:* Dr. Joanna White, Chairperson, Department of Counseling and Psychological Services, 404-413-8010, E-mail: cpsjfw@langate.gsu.edu.

Goddard College, Graduate Program, Program in Psychology and Counseling, Plainfield, VT 05667-9432. Offers organizational development (MA); psychology and counseling (MA). Postbaccalaureate distance learning degree programs offered (minimal on-campus study). *Faculty:* 7 part-time/adjunct (4 women). *Students:* 54 full-time. Average age 42. 18 applicants, 94% accepted, 17 enrolled. *Degree requirements:* For master's, thesis. *Entrance requirements:* For master's, previous coursework in psychology. *Application deadline:* Applications are processed on a rolling basis. Application fee: $40. Electronic applications accepted. *Expenses:* Tuition: Full-time $14,038. *Financial support:* In 2007–08, 44 students received support. Applicants required to submit FAFSA. *Unit head:* Dr. Steve James, Director, 802-454-8311 Ext. 247, Fax: 802-454-8017, E-mail: jamess@goddard.edu. *Application contact:* David DeLucca, Admissions Counselor, 800-906-8312 Ext. 248, Fax: 802-454-1029, E-mail: david.delucca@goddard.edu.

Gonzaga University, School of Education, Program in Counseling Psychology, Spokane, WA 99258. Offers MAC, MAP. *Accreditation:* ACA. *Faculty:* 4 full-time (1 woman), 7 part-time/adjunct (5 women). *Students:* 19 full-time (13 women), 67 part-time (56 women); includes 6 minority (4 African Americans, 1 American Indian/Alaska Native, 1 Hispanic American), 1 international. Average age 33. In 2007, 49 degrees awarded. *Degree requirements:* For master's, comprehensive exam. *Entrance requirements:* For master's, GRE General Test or MAT, minimum B average in undergraduate course work. Additional exam requirements/recommendations for international students: Required—TOEFL. *Application deadline:* For fall admission, 3/1 for domestic students. Application fee: $40. *Financial support:* Teaching assistantships available. Support available to part-time students. Financial award application deadline: 3/1. *Unit head:* Dr. Lisa Bennett, Director, 509-328-4220 Ext. 3512.

Governors State University, College of Education, Program in Counseling, University Park, IL 60466-0975. Offers MA. *Accreditation:* ACA. Part-time and evening/weekend programs available. *Students:* 90 full-time, 123 part-time. Average age 34. *Degree requirements:* For master's, practicum. *Entrance requirements:* For master's, minimum GPA of 2.5 in last 60 hours of course work or minimum GPA of 2.25 and GRE General Test. *Application deadline:* For fall admission, 7/15 priority date for domestic students; for spring admission, 11/10 for domestic students. Applications are processed on a rolling basis. Application fee: $25. *Financial support:* Career-related internships or fieldwork, Federal Work-Study, institutionally sponsored loans, and tuition waivers (full and partial) available. Support available to part-time students. Financial award application deadline: 5/1. *Application contact:* John Powers, Adviser, 708-534-6363.

Grace College, Graduate School in Counseling and Interpersonal Relations, Program in Counseling, Winona Lake, IN 46590-1294. Offers counseling (MA); interpersonal relations (MA). *Accreditation:* ACA. Part-time and evening/weekend programs available. *Faculty:* 3 full-time (2 women), 8 part-time/adjunct (3 women). *Students:* 18 full-time (10 women), 36 part-time (27 women); includes 2 minority (1 African American, 1 Asian American or Pacific Islander), 2 international. Average age 30. 35 applicants, 86% accepted, 24 enrolled. In 2007, 13 degrees awarded. *Degree requirements:* For master's, comprehensive exam, portfolio. *Entrance requirements:* For master's, GRE (counseling). Additional exam requirements/recommendations for international students: Required—TOEFL. *Application deadline:* For fall admission, 8/1 priority date for domestic students. Applications are processed on a rolling basis. Application fee: $25. Electronic applications accepted. *Expenses:* Tuition: Part-time $417 per credit hour. Tuition and fees vary according to course load. *Financial support:* In 2007–08, 2 teaching assistantships (averaging $2,000 per year) were awarded; career-related internships or fieldwork, scholarships/grants, and unspecified assistantships also available. Financial award application deadline: 3/10; financial award applicants required to submit FAFSA. *Application contact:* Jessie Schroeder, Graduate Admissions Office, 800-54 GRACE, Fax: 574-372-6413.

Grace University, College of Graduate Studies, Counseling Program, Omaha, NE 68108. Offers MA. *Entrance requirements:* For master's, minimum undergraduate GPA of 3.0.

Harding University, College of Bible and Religion, Program in Marriage and Family Therapy, Searcy, AR 72149-0001. Offers marriage and family therapy (MS); mental health counseling (MS). Part-time programs available. *Faculty:* 4 full-time (0 women), 4 part-time/adjunct (2 women). *Students:* 25 full-time (12 women), 2 part-time; includes 1 minority (African American), 2 international. Average age 27. 19 applicants, 79% accepted, 14 enrolled. In 2007, 8 degrees awarded. *Degree requirements:* For master's, comprehensive exam, 15-month practicum. *Entrance requirements:* For master's, GRE General Test, minimum undergraduate GPA of 2.75, graduate 3.0. *Application deadline:* For fall admission, 4/1 priority date for domestic students. Applications are processed on a rolling basis. Application fee: $25. *Expenses:* Tuition: Part-time $485 per credit hour. Required fees: $21 per credit hour. *Financial support:* Career-related internships or fieldwork, Federal Work-Study, institutionally sponsored loans, and scholarships/grants available. Financial award application deadline: 4/1. *Faculty research:* Forgiveness, substance abuse, PTSD. *Unit head:* Dr. Lewis L. Moore, Chairman, 501-279-4347, Fax: 501-279-4417, E-mail: lmoore@harding.edu. *Application contact:* Ruth Ann Dawson, Office Manager, 501-279-4347, Fax: 501-279-4417, E-mail: radawson@harding.edu.

Heidelberg College, Program in Counseling, Tiffin, OH 44883-2462. Offers MA. Part-time and evening/weekend programs available. *Faculty:* 3 full-time (2 women), 6 part-time/adjunct (3 women). *Students:* 5 full-time (all women), 76 part-time (68 women); includes 9 minority (6 African Americans, 1 American Indian/Alaska Native, 2 Hispanic Americans). 26 applicants, 88% accepted, 23 enrolled. In 2007, 15 degrees awarded. *Degree requirements:* For master's, thesis or alternative, counseling practicum, internship. *Entrance requirements:* For master's, GRE General Test, 12 hours course work in behavioral sciences, minimum GPA of 2.9, 3 letters of reference. Additional exam requirements/recommendations for international students: Required—TOEFL. *Application deadline:* Applications are processed on a rolling basis. Application fee: $25. *Financial support:* In 2007–08, 51 students received support, including 1 teaching assistantship; Federal Work-Study also available. Support available to part-time students. Financial award applicants required to submit FAFSA. *Unit head:* Dr. Jo-Ann Lipford Sanders, Director of Graduate Studies in Counseling, 419-448-2312, Fax: 419-448-2072, E-mail: jsanders@heidelberg.edu. *Application contact:* Dr. G. Michael Pratt, Graduate Studies Office, 419-448-2288, Fax: 419-448-2072, E-mail: mpratt@heidelberg.edu.

Hofstra University, School of Education and Allied Human Services, Department of Counseling, Research, Special Education and Rehabilitation, Program in Rehabilitation Counseling, Hempstead, NY 11549. Offers rehabilitation administration (PD); rehabilitation counseling (MS Ed); rehabilitation counseling in mental health (MS Ed). *Accreditation:* CORE. Part-time and evening/weekend programs available. *Students:* 25 full-time (20 women), 3 part-time (all women); includes 12 minority (10 African Americans, 2 Hispanic Americans), 2 international. Average age 33. 9 applicants, 78% accepted, 7 enrolled. In 2007, 10 degrees awarded. *Degree requirements:* For master's, comprehensive exam, 600 hour internship and 100 hour practicum; for PD, internship in rehabilitation administration. *Entrance requirements:* For master's, 4 letters of recommendation, interview, essay, professional experience; for PD, 3 letters of recommendation, masters degree in related field, CRC/CRC elig. professional experience. Additional exam requirements/recommendations for international students: Required—TOEFL (minimum score 550 paper-based; 213 computer-based). *Application deadline:* Applications are processed on a rolling basis. Application fee: $60. Electronic applications accepted. *Expenses:* Tuition: Full-time $14,220; part-time $820 per credit. Required fees: $970; $165 per term. Tuition and fees vary according to program. *Financial support:* In 2007–08, 44 students received support, including 3 fellowships with tuition reimbursements available (averaging $3,083 per year), 2 research assistantships with full and partial tuition reimbursements available (averaging $12,210 per year); career-related internships or fieldwork, Federal Work-Study, institutionally sponsored loans, scholarships/grants, traineeships, tuition waivers (full and partial), and unspecified assistantships also available. Support available to part-time students. Financial award applicants required to submit FAFSA. *Faculty research:* Workplace socialization and individuals with disabilities; collaboration among rehabilitation agencies and consumer outcomes; job retention among rehabilitation counseling professionals; transition services for youth with disabilities. Total annual research expenditures: $90,000. *Unit head:* Dr. Jamie Mitus, Director, 516-463-7453, Fax: 516-463-6184, E-mail: cprjsm@hofstra.edu. *Application contact:* Carol Drummer, Dean of Graduate Admissions, 516-463-4876, Fax: 516-463-4664, E-mail: gradstudent@hofstra.edu.

Holy Family University, Graduate School, School of Arts and Sciences, Philadelphia, PA 19114-2094. Offers counseling psychology (MS). Part-time and evening/weekend programs available. *Degree requirements:* For master's, comprehensive exam, thesis optional. *Entrance requirements:* For master's, MAT, interview, minimum GPA of 3.0.

Holy Names University, Graduate Division, Department of Counseling Psychology, Oakland, CA 94619-1699. Offers counseling psychology (MA); forensic psychology (MA, Certificate); pastoral counseling (MA, Certificate). Part-time and evening/weekend programs available. *Faculty:* 3 full-time (1 woman), 11 part-time/adjunct (6 women). *Students:* 36 full-time (33 women), 16 part-time (15 women); includes 32 minority (23 African Americans, 3 Asian Americans or Pacific Islanders, 6 Hispanic Americans), 2 international. Average age 35. 21 applicants, 81% accepted, 16 enrolled. In 2007, 13 master's awarded. *Degree requirements:* For master's, comprehensive paper, seminars. *Entrance requirements:* For master's, minimum undergraduate GPA of 2.6 overall, 3.0 in major. Additional exam requirements/recommendations for international students: Required—TOEFL. *Application deadline:* For fall admission, 8/1 priority date for domestic students; for spring admission, 12/1 priority date for domestic students. Applications are processed on a rolling basis. Application fee: $65. *Expenses:* Tuition: Part-time $635 per unit. One-time fee: $340 part-time. Tuition and fees vary according to program. *Financial support:* In 2007–08, 34 students received support. Available to part-time students. Application deadline: 3/2; *Faculty research:* Cognitive psychology, anger management, grief and grief counseling, post-modernism and psychotherapy, spirituality and psychology. *Unit head:* Helen Shoemaker, Program Director, 510-436-1543, E-mail: shoemaker@hnu.edu. *Application contact:* 800-430-1351, Fax: 510-436-1325, E-mail: admissions@hnu.edu.

Houston Baptist University, College of Education and Behavioral Sciences, Program in Christian Counseling, Houston, TX 77074-3298. Offers MACC. *Faculty:* 3 full-time (2 women), 1 (woman) part-time/adjunct. *Students:* 5 full-time (4 women), 7 part-time (all women); includes 4 minority (all African Americans) Average age 36. 16 applicants, 50% accepted, 1 enrolled. In 2007, 6 degrees awarded. *Degree requirements:* For master's, comprehensive exam. *Entrance requirements:* For master's, GRE General Test, minimum GPA of 3.0. Additional exam requirements/recommendations for international students: Required—TOEFL (minimum score 550 paper-based; 213 computer-based). *Application deadline:* For fall admission, 7/1 priority date for domestic and international students; for winter admission, 10/1 priority date for domestic and international students; for spring admission, 1/1 priority date for domestic and international students. Applications are processed on a rolling basis. Application fee: $25 ($100 for international students). *Expenses:* Tuition: Part-time $1,416 per course. Required fees: $190 per quarter. *Financial support:* Federal Work-Study available. Support available to part-time students. Financial award application deadline: 3/1; financial award applicants required to submit FAFSA. *Unit head:* Dr. Renata Nero, Director, 281-649-3000 Ext. 2436, Fax: 281-649-3361, E-mail: rnero@hbu.edu. *Application contact:* Becky Greer, Secretary, 281-649-3000 Ext. 3095, Fax: 281-649-3361, E-mail: bgreer@hbu.edu.

Howard University, School of Education, Department of Human Development and Psychoeducational Studies, Program in Counseling Psychology, Washington, DC 20059-0002. Offers M Ed, MA, PhD, CAGS. *Accreditation:* APA. Part-time programs available. *Faculty:* 4 full-time (1 woman), 1 (woman) part-time/adjunct. *Students:* 29 full-time (22 women), 12 part-time (9 women); includes 38 minority (37 African Americans, 1 Asian American or Pacific Islander), 2 international. Average age 29. 55 applicants, 29% accepted, 2 enrolled. In 2007, 12 master's, 3 doctorates awarded. Terminal master's awarded for partial completion of doctoral program. *Median time to degree:* Of those who began their doctoral program in fall 1999, 64% received their degree in 8 years or less. *Degree requirements:* For master's, comprehensive exam, thesis (for some programs), expository writing exam; for doctorate, one foreign language, comprehensive exam, thesis/dissertation, expository writing exam, internship. *Entrance requirements:* For master's, GRE General Test (MA), minimum GPA of 2.7; for doctorate, GRE General Test, minimum GPA of 3.4; for CAGS, GRE General Test, minimum graduate GPA of 3.0. *Application deadline:* For fall admission, 4/1 priority date for domestic students; for spring admission, 11/1 for domestic students. Application fee: $45. *Expenses:* Tuition: Full-time $16,175; part-time $899 per credit hour. Required fees: $805. *Financial support:* Fellowships, research assistantships, teaching assistantships, career-related internships or fieldwork, institutionally sponsored loans, scholarships/grants, and unspecified assistantships available. Financial award application deadline: 3/15. *Faculty research:* Cultural issues in counseling and psychotherapy, counseling theory construction, self–actualization black psychology. *Unit head:* Dr. Angela D. Ferguson, Assistant Professor/Coordinator Doctoral Program, 202-806-6412, Fax: 202-806-5205, E-mail: adferguson@howard.edu. *Application contact:* Dr. Ivory Toldson, Assistant Professor/Coordinator Master's Program, 202-806-6410, Fax: 202-806-5205, E-mail: itoldson@howard.edu.

Idaho State University, Office of Graduate Studies, Kasiska College of Health Professions, Department of Counseling, Pocatello, ID 83209. Offers counseling (M Coun, Ed S, Post-baccalaureate Certificate), including family-centered practice (Postbaccalaureate Certificate), marriage and family counseling (M Coun), mental health counseling (M Coun), school counseling (M Coun), student affairs and college counseling (M Coun); counselor education and counseling (PhD). *Accreditation:* ACA (one or more programs are accredited). *Faculty:* 6 full-time (3 women). *Students:* 62 full-time (40 women), 28 part-time (21 women); includes 6 minority (1 American Indian/Alaska Native, 1 Asian American or Pacific Islander, 4 Hispanic Americans). Average age 34. In 2007, 28 master's, 2 doctorates awarded. *Degree requirements:* For master's, comprehensive exam, thesis; for doctorate, comprehensive exam, thesis/dissertation, internship; for other advanced degree, comprehensive exam, thesis, case studies, oral exam. *Entrance requirements:* For master's, GRE General Test, MAT, minimum GPA of 3.0; for doctorate, GRE General Test, MAT, minimum graduate GPA of 3.0, resumé, interview, counseling license; for other advanced degree, GRE General Test, minimum graduate GPA of 3.0, master's degree in counseling, 3 letters of recommendation, 2 years work experience. Additional exam requirements/recommendations for international students: Required—TOEFL (minimum score 600 paper-based; 213 computer-based; 80 iBT). *Application deadline:* For fall admission, 7/1 for domestic students, 6/1 for international students; for spring admission, 12/1 for domestic students, 11/1 for international students. Applications are processed on a rolling basis. Application fee: $55. *Expenses:* Tuition, state resident: full-time $2,882; part-time $259 per credit hour. Tuition, nonresident: full-time $11,566; part-time $379 per credit hour. Required fees: $2,278. Full-time tuition and fees vary according to program. Part-time tuition and fees vary according to course load. *Financial support:* In 2007–08, 14 teaching assistantships with full and partial tuition reimbursements (averaging $9,128 per year) were awarded; career-related internships or fieldwork, Federal Work-Study, institutionally sponsored loans, scholarships/grants, traineeships, health care benefits, tuition waivers (full), and unspecified assistantships also available. Financial award application deadline: 1/1; financial award applicants required to submit FAFSA. *Faculty research:* Group counseling, multicultural counseling, family counseling, child therapy, supervision. *Unit head:* Dr. Stephen Feit, Chair, 208-282-3663, Fax: 208-282-2583, E-mail: feitstep@isu.edu. *Application contact:* Ellen Combs, Graduate School Technical Records Specialist, 208-282-2150, Fax: 208-282-4847.

Illinois State University, Graduate School, College of Arts and Sciences, Department of Psychology, Normal, IL 61790-2200. Offers psychology (MA, MS), including clinical psychology, counseling psychology, developmental psychology, educational psychology, experimental psychology, measurement-evaluation, organizational-industrial psychology; school psychology (PhD, SSP). *Accreditation:* APA. *Faculty:* 36 full-time (14 women). *Students:* 49 full-time (37 women), 19 part-time (14 women); includes 3 minority (all Asian Americans or Pacific Islanders), 7 international. 91 applicants, 43% accepted. In 2007, 24 degrees awarded. *Degree requirements:* For master's, thesis or alternative; for doctorate, variable foreign language requirement, thesis/dissertation, 2 terms of residency, internship, practicum. *Entrance requirements:* For master's, GRE General Test, GRE Subject Test, minimum GPA of 3.0 in last 60 hours of course work; for doctorate, GRE General Test. *Application deadline:* Applications are processed on a rolling basis. Application fee: $40. *Expenses:* Tuition, state resident: full-time $3,492; part-time $194 per credit hour. Tuition, nonresident: full-time $7,272; part-time $404 per credit hour. Required fees: $1,024; $57 per credit hour. *Financial support:* In 2007–08, 33 research assistantships (averaging $6,252 per year), 49 teaching assistantships (averaging $4,217 per year) were awarded; tuition waivers (full) and unspecified assistantships also available. Financial award application deadline: 4/1. *Faculty research:* Comprehensive evaluation system for the central region professional development grant, Illinois school psychology internship consortium, for children's sake. Total annual research expenditures: $292,085. *Unit head:* Dr. Neil Skaggs, Acting Chairperson, 309-438-8651.

Immaculata University, College of Graduate Studies, Department of Psychology, Immaculata, PA 19345. Offers clinical psychology (Psy D); counseling psychology (MA, Certificate), including school guidance counselor (Certificate), school psychologist (Certificate). *Accreditation:* APA. Part-time and evening/weekend programs available. *Students:* 106 full-time (71 women), 207 part-time (194 women); includes 30 minority (20 African Americans, 6 Asian Americans or Pacific Islanders, 4 Hispanic Americans). Average age 34. 182 applicants, 62% accepted, 56 enrolled. In 2007, 38 master's, 10 doctorates awarded. *Degree requirements:* For master's, comprehensive exam, thesis optional; for doctorate, comprehensive exam, thesis/dissertation. *Entrance requirements:* For master's, GRE General Test or MAT, minimum GPA of 3.0; for doctorate, GRE General Test, minimum GPA of 3.5. Additional exam requirements/recommendations for international students: Required—TOEFL, IELTS. *Application deadline:* Applications are processed on a rolling basis. Application fee: $35. *Financial support:* Application deadline: 5/1. *Faculty research:* Supervision ethics, psychology of teaching, gender. *Unit head:* Dr. Jed A. Yalof, Chair, 610-647-4400 Ext. 3503, Fax: 610-993-8550, E-mail: jyalof@immaculata.edu. *Application contact:* Office of Graduate Admission, 610-647-4400 Ext. 3211, Fax: 610-993-8550, E-mail: graduate@immaculata.edu.

Indiana State University, School of Graduate Studies, College of Education, Department of Communication Disorders, Counseling and School and Educational Psychology, Terre Haute, IN 47809-1401. Offers counseling psychology (MS, PhD); counselor education (PhD); mental health counseling (MS); school counseling (M Ed); school psychology (PhD, Ed S); MA/MS. *Accreditation:* ACA; NCATE. Part-time and evening/weekend programs available. *Faculty:* 10 full-time (5 women), 9 part-time/adjunct (8 women). *Students:* 104 full-time (82 women), 88 part-time (70 women); includes 29 minority (22 African Americans, 1 American Indian/Alaska Native, 2 Asian Americans or Pacific Islanders, 4 Hispanic Americans), 4 international. Average age 30. 154 applicants, 38% accepted, 40 enrolled. In 2007, 75 master's, 12 doctorates, 8 other advanced degrees awarded. *Degree requirements:* For master's, thesis optional; for doctorate, thesis/dissertation, research tools proficiency tests. *Entrance requirements:* For master's, GRE General Test or MAT, minimum undergraduate GPA of 2.75; for doctorate, GRE General Test, master's degree, minimum undergraduate GPA of 3.5. *Application deadline:* For fall admission, 2/15 for domestic students. Applications are processed on a rolling basis. Application fee: $35. Electronic applications accepted. *Expenses:* Tuition, state resident: full-time $7,056; part-time $294 per semester hour. Tuition, nonresident: full-time $14,016; part-time $584 per semester hour. Required fees: $175 per semester. *Financial support:* In 2007–08, 37 research assistantships with partial tuition reimbursements (averaging $6,300 per year) were awarded; teaching assistantships, career-related internships or fieldwork and tuition waivers (partial) also available. Financial award application deadline: 3/1; financial award applicants required to submit FAFSA. *Faculty research:* Vocational development supervision. *Unit head:* Dr. Michele Boyer, Chairperson, 812-237-2832.

Indiana University Bloomington, School of Education, Department of Counseling and Educational Psychology, Bloomington, IN 47405-7000. Offers counseling (MS, PhD, Ed S); counseling psychology (PhD); counselor education (MS, Ed S); educational psychology (MS, PhD); learning and developmental sciences (MS, PhD); school psychology (PhD, Ed S). PhD offered through the University Graduate School. *Accreditation:* ACA (one or more programs are accredited); APA (one or more programs are accredited); NCATE. *Students:* 96 full-time (72 women), 79 part-time (56 women); includes 16 minority (10 African Americans, 4 Asian Americans or Pacific Islanders, 2 Hispanic Americans), 38 international. Average age 29. In 2007, 50 degrees awarded. Terminal master's awarded for partial completion of doctoral program. *Degree requirements:* For master's, thesis optional; for doctorate, thesis/dissertation; for Ed S, comprehensive exam or project. *Entrance requirements:* For master's, doctorate, and Ed S, GRE General Test. *Application deadline:* For fall admission, 6/1 for domestic students, 3/1 for international students; for winter admission, 11/1 for domestic students; for spring admission, 9/1 for international students. Applications are processed on a rolling basis. Application fee: $50 ($60 for international students). Electronic applications accepted. *Financial support:* Fellowships with partial tuition reimbursements, research assistantships with partial tuition reimbursements, teaching assistantships with partial tuition reimbursements, career-related internships or fieldwork, Federal Work-Study, institutionally sponsored loans, tuition waivers (full and partial), and unspecified assistantships available. Support available to part-time students. *Faculty research:* Affective and maturational factors in learning complex cognitive tasks, children's strategies for representing depth, prime time evaluation, rural school psychology. *Unit head:* Dr. Joyce Alexander, Chairperson, 812-856-8300.

Indiana Wesleyan University, College of Graduate Studies, Program in Counseling, Marion, IN 46953-4974. Offers community counseling (MS); marriage and family counseling (MS); school counseling (MS). *Accreditation:* ACA. Part-time programs available. *Faculty:* 3 full-time (1 woman), 3 part-time/adjunct (2 women). *Students:* 41 full-time (31 women), 62 part-time (47 women); includes 5 minority (4 African Americans, 1 Hispanic American). Average age 32. In 2007, 23 degrees awarded. *Degree requirements:* For master's, thesis or alternative. *Entrance requirements:* For master's, GRE General Test. *Application deadline:* For fall admission, 4/1 priority date for domestic students; for spring admission, 10/1 priority date for domestic students. Application fee: $25. Electronic applications accepted. *Expenses:* Contact institution. *Financial support:* In 2007–08, 1 research assistantship with tuition reimbursement, 1 teaching assistantship with partial tuition reimbursement (averaging $1,000 per year) were awarded. Financial award application deadline: 3/1; financial award applicants required to submit FAFSA. *Unit head:* Dr. Mark Gerig, Director of Graduate Counseling Studies, 765-677-2995, Fax: 765-677-2504, E-mail: mark.gerig@indwes.edu. *Application contact:* David McMillan, Assistant Director of Enrollment Management, 765-677-2688, E-mail: david.mcmillan@indwes.edu.

Institute of Transpersonal Psychology, Residential Programs, Palo Alto, CA 94303. Offers clinical psychology (PhD); counseling psychology (MA); transpersonal psychology (MA, PhD); women's spirituality (PhD). Part-time and evening/weekend programs available. *Faculty:* 17 full-time (9 women), 31 part-time/adjunct (18 women). *Students:* 239 full-time (164 women), 48 part-time (33 women); includes 46 minority (8 African Americans, 4 American Indian/Alaska Native, 18 Asian Americans or Pacific Islanders, 16 Hispanic Americans), 16 international. Average age 38. 132 applicants, 80% accepted, 79 enrolled. In 2007, 47 master's, 16 doctorates awarded. Terminal master's awarded for partial completion of doctoral program. *Degree requirements:* For doctorate, thesis/dissertation. *Entrance requirements:* For master's and doctorate, bachelor's degree. *Application deadline:* For fall admission, 2/15 priority date for domestic students. Applications are processed on a rolling basis. Application fee: $55. *Expenses:* Tuition: Full-time $11,877; part-time $3,959 per quarter. Tuition and fees vary according to degree level and student level. *Financial support:* In 2007–08, 178 students received support; teaching assistantships, career-related internships or fieldwork, Federal Work-Study, and scholarships/grants available. Support available to part-time students. Financial award application deadline: 7/1; financial award applicants required to submit FAFSA. *Unit head:* Dr. Paul Roy, Academic Vice President, 650-493-4430 Ext. 243, Fax: 650-493-6835, E-mail: proy@itp.edu. *Application contact:* 650-493-4430 Ext. 16, Fax: 650-493-6835, E-mail: itpinfo@itp.edu.

See Close-Up on page 1439.

Inter American University of Puerto Rico, Aguadilla Campus, Graduate School, Aguadilla, PR 00605. Offers counseling psychology with an emphasis in family (MS); criminal justice (MA); educative management and leadership (MA); elementary education (MA); industrial mangement (MBA); marketing (MBA). Part-time and evening/weekend programs available. *Degree requirements:* For master's, comprehensive exam. *Entrance requirements:* For master's, EXADEP, 2 letters of recommendation, minimum GPA of 2.5. Electronic applications accepted.

Inter American University of Puerto Rico, San Germán Campus, Graduate Studies Center, Program in Psychology, San Germán, PR 00683-5008. Offers counseling psychology (MA, PhD); school psychology (MA, PhD). Part-time and evening/weekend programs available. *Faculty:* 8 full-time, 24 part-time/adjunct. *Students:* 223. In 2007, 51 master's, 2 doctorates awarded. *Degree requirements:* For master's, comprehensive exam, thesis; for doctorate, comprehensive exam, thesis/dissertation. *Entrance requirements:* For master's, GRE General Test or EXADEP, minimum GPA of 3.0; for doctorate, GRE, EXADEP or MAT, minimum GPA of 3.0. *Application*

Counseling Psychology

Inter American University of Puerto Rico, San Germán Campus (continued)
deadline: For fall admission, 4/30 priority date for domestic students; for spring admission, 11/15 for domestic students. Applications are processed on a rolling basis. Application fee: $31. *Expenses:* Tuition: Full-time $3,258; part-time $181 per credit. Required fees: $258 per semester. Tuition and fees vary according to degree level. *Financial support:* Teaching assistantships, unspecified assistantships available. *Application contact:* Dr. Ines Canabel, Program Coordinator, 787-264-1912 Ext. 7646, Fax: 787-892-7510, E-mail: icanabal@sg.intev.edu.

Iona College, School of Arts and Science, Department of Psychology, New Rochelle, NY 10801-1890. Offers experimental psychology (MA); industrial-organizational psychology (MA); mental health counseling (MA); psychology (MA); school psychology (MA). Part-time and evening/weekend programs available. *Faculty:* 12 full-time (6 women), 5 part-time/adjunct (2 women). *Students:* 77 full-time (62 women), 21 part-time (19 women); includes 19 minority (5 African Americans, 2 Asian Americans or Pacific Islanders, 12 Hispanic Americans). Average age 25. 105 applicants, 66% accepted, 33 enrolled. In 2007, 29 degrees awarded. *Degree requirements:* For master's, thesis. *Entrance requirements:* For master's, GRE or minimum GPA of 3.0. Additional exam requirements/recommendations for international students: Required—TOEFL (minimum score 550 paper-based; 213 computer-based). *Application deadline:* Applications are processed on a rolling basis. Application fee: $50. Electronic applications accepted. *Expenses:* Tuition: Part-time $712 per credit. Required fees: $150 per term. *Financial support:* Career-related internships or fieldwork, tuition waivers (partial), and unspecified assistantships available. Support available to part-time students. *Unit head:* Dr. Pauline Jirik-Babb, Chair, 914-633-2191, E-mail: pjirikbabb@iona.edu. *Application contact:* Veronica Jarek-Prinz, Director of Graduate Admissions, 914-633-2420, Fax: 914-633-2277, E-mail: vjarekprinz@iona.edu.

Iowa State University of Science and Technology, Graduate College, College of Liberal Arts and Sciences, Department of Psychology, Ames, IA 50011. Offers cognitive psychology (PhD); counseling psychology (PhD); social psychology (PhD). *Accreditation:* APA. *Faculty:* 25 full-time (8 women), 8 part-time/adjunct (4 women). *Students:* 63 full-time (43 women); includes 10 minority (3 African Americans, 7 Asian Americans or Pacific Islanders), 4 international. Average age 26. 117 applicants, 14% accepted, 11 enrolled. In 2007, 8 doctorates awarded. Terminal master's awarded for partial completion of doctoral program. *Median time to degree:* Of those who began their doctoral program in fall 1999, 100% received their degree in 8 years or less. *Degree requirements:* For doctorate, thesis/dissertation. *Entrance requirements:* For doctorate, GRE General Test, GRE Subject Test (psychology). Additional exam requirements/recommendations for international students: Required—TOEFL (minimum score 560 paper-based; 220 computer-based). *Application deadline:* For fall admission, 1/5 priority date for domestic and international students. Application fee: $30 ($70 for international students). Electronic applications accepted. *Financial support:* In 2007–08, 45 students received support, including 2 fellowships with full tuition reimbursements available (averaging $14,055 per year), 13 research assistantships with full tuition reimbursements available (averaging $12,200 per year), 30 teaching assistantships with full tuition reimbursements available (averaging $12,200 per year); scholarships/grants, health care benefits, and unspecified assistantships also available. *Faculty research:* Counseling psychology, cognitive psychology, social psychology, health psychology, psychology and public policy. Total annual research expenditures: $2 million. *Unit head:* Dr. David L Vogel, Director of Graduate Education, 515-294-1742, Fax: 515-294-6424, E-mail: dvogel@iastate.edu. *Application contact:* Ann K Schmidt, Graduate Admissions Secretary, 515-294-1743, Fax: 515-294-6424, E-mail: psychadm@iastate.edu.

James Madison University, The Graduate School, College of Integrated Science and Technology, Department of Graduate Psychology, Program in Community Counseling Psychology, Harrisonburg, VA 22807. Offers MA, Ed S. *Accreditation:* ACA (one or more programs are accredited); APA (one or more programs are accredited). Part-time and evening/weekend programs available. *Students:* 54 full-time (38 women), 39 part-time (27 women); includes 10 minority (8 African Americans, 1 Asian American or Pacific Islander, 1 Hispanic American), 1 international. Average age 27. In 2007, 28 master's, 16 other advanced degrees awarded. *Degree requirements:* For Ed S, comprehensive exam, thesis, internship. *Entrance requirements:* For master's, GRE General Test, 3 reference forms, interview, criminal history check. Additional exam requirements/recommendations for international students: Required—TOEFL. *Application deadline:* For fall admission, 2/1 priority date for domestic students. Applications are processed on a rolling basis. Application fee: $55. Electronic applications accepted. *Expenses:* Tuition, state resident: full-time $6,720; part-time $280 per credit hour. Tuition, nonresident: full-time $19,104; part-time $796 per credit hour. *Financial support:* In 2007–08, 44 students received support; teaching assistantships with full tuition reimbursements available, career-related internships or fieldwork, Federal Work-Study, unspecified assistantships, and 44 graduate assistantships ($7,237) available. Financial award application deadline: 3/1; financial award applicants required to submit FAFSA. *Unit head:* Dr. Lennis G. Echerling, Program Director, 540-568-6552.

John Carroll University, Graduate School, Program in Community Counseling, University Heights, OH 44118-4581. Offers clinical counseling (Certificate); community counseling (MA). *Accreditation:* ACA. Part-time and evening/weekend programs available. *Faculty:* 7 full-time (4 women), 15 part-time/adjunct (10 women). *Students:* 36 full-time (33 women), 12 part-time (8 women); includes 4 minority (3 African Americans, 1 Hispanic American). Average age 32. 53 applicants, 40% accepted, 21 enrolled. In 2007, 22 degrees awarded. *Degree requirements:* For master's, comprehensive exam, internship, practicum. *Entrance requirements:* For master's, MAT or GRE, minimum GPA of 2.75, statement of volunteer experience, interview, 12-18 hours social science course work, survey. Additional exam requirements/recommendations for international students: Required—TOEFL. *Application deadline:* For fall admission, 8/15 priority date for domestic students; for spring admission, 1/3 for domestic students. Applications are processed on a rolling basis. Application fee: $25 ($35 for international students). Electronic applications accepted. *Financial support:* In 2007–08, 20 students received support, including 1 teaching assistantship with full tuition reimbursement available (averaging $8,000 per year); career-related internships or fieldwork, institutionally sponsored loans, and unspecified assistantships also available. Financial award application deadline: 3/1; financial award applicants required to submit FAFSA. *Faculty research:* Child and adolescent development, HIV, hypnosis, wellness, women's issues. *Unit head:* Dr. Christopher M. Faiver, Coordinator, 216-397-3001, Fax: 216-397-3045, E-mail: faiver@jcu.edu.

John F. Kennedy University, Graduate School of Holistic Studies, Department of Counseling Psychology, Program in Counseling Psychology, Pleasant Hill, CA 94523-4817. Offers holistic studies (MA); somatic psychology (MA); transpersonal psychology (MA). Part-time and evening/weekend programs available. *Degree requirements:* For master's, thesis or alternative. *Entrance requirements:* For master's, interview. Additional exam requirements/recommendations for international students: Required—TOEFL.

John F. Kennedy University, Graduate School of Professional Psychology, Program in Counseling Psychology, Pleasant Hill, CA 94523-4817. Offers MA. *Accreditation:* APA.Part-time and evening/weekend programs available. *Degree requirements:* For master's, thesis or alternative. *Entrance requirements:* For master's, interview. Additional exam requirements/recommendations for international students: Required—TOEFL.

Kean University, College of Humanities and Social Sciences, Program in Behavioral Sciences, Union, NJ 07083. Offers human behavior and organizational psychology (MA); psychological services (MA). Part-time and evening/weekend programs available. *Faculty:* 20 full-time (13 women). *Students:* 22 full-time (19 women), 21 part-time (20 women); includes 8 African Americans, 2 Asian Americans or Pacific Islanders, 4 Hispanic Americans, 4 international. Average age 27. 32 applicants, 78% accepted, 17 enrolled. In 2007, 16 degrees awarded. *Degree requirements:* For master's, comprehensive exam, thesis, research. *Entrance requirements:* For master's, GRE General Test, 2 letters of recommendation, interview, prerequisite courses in behavioral sciences. *Application deadline:* For fall admission, 5/1 for domestic students; for spring admission, 11/1 for domestic students. Application fee: $60 ($150 for international students). Electronic applications accepted. *Expenses:* Tuition, state resident: full-time $9,384; part-time $391 per credit. Tuition, nonresident: full-time $12,720; part-time $530 per credit. Required fees: $2,382; $99 per credit. Part-time tuition and fees vary according to course load. *Financial support:* In 2007–08, 4 research assistantships with full tuition reimbursements (averaging $3,217 per year) were awarded; unspecified assistantships also available. *Unit head:* Dr. Henry L. Kaplowitz, Program Coordinator, 908-737-4018, E-mail: hkaplowi@kean.edu. *Application contact:* Joanne Morris, Director of Graduate Admissions, 908-737-3355, Fax: 908-737-3354, E-mail: grad-adm@kean.edu.

Kent State University, Graduate School of Education, Health, and Human Services, Department of Adult, Counseling, Health and Vocational Education, Program in Community Counseling, Kent, OH 44242-0001. Offers M Ed, MA. *Accreditation:* ACA; NCATE. *Faculty:* 6 full-time (3 women), 7 part-time/adjunct (4 women). *Students:* 58 full-time (52 women), 77 part-time (67 women); includes 16 minority (15 African Americans, 1 American Indian/Alaska Native), 4 international. 55 applicants, 65% accepted. In 2007, 31 degrees awarded. *Degree requirements:* For master's, thesis (for some programs). *Entrance requirements:* Additional exam requirements/recommendations for international students: Required—TOEFL. *Application deadline:* For fall admission, 6/1 for domestic students; for spring admission, 10/1 for domestic students. Application fee: $30. Electronic applications accepted. *Financial support:* In 2007–08, research assistantships with full tuition reimbursements (averaging $7,903 per year); fellowships with full tuition reimbursements, teaching assistantships with full tuition reimbursements, career-related internships or fieldwork, Federal Work-Study, institutionally sponsored loans, scholarships/grants, health care benefits, and unspecified assistantships also available. Support available to part-time students. Financial award application deadline: 4/1; financial award applicants required to submit FAFSA. *Faculty research:* Group work, personality assessment, family/child therapy, substance abuse counseling, clinical supervision. *Unit head:* Dr. Jason McGlothlin, Coordinator, 330-672-2662, E-mail: jmcgloth@kent.edu. *Application contact:* Nancy Miller, Academic Program Coordinator, Office of Graduate Student Services, 330-672-2576, Fax: 330-672-9162, E-mail: ogs@kent.edu.

Kutztown University of Pennsylvania, College of Graduate Studies and Extended Learning, Program in Counseling Psychology, Kutztown, PA 19530-0730. Offers agency counseling (MA); marital and family therapy (MA). Part-time and evening/weekend programs available. *Faculty:* 5 full-time (2 women). *Students:* 28 full-time (22 women), 21 part-time (18 women); includes 2 minority (1 African American, 1 Hispanic American). Average age 29. 45 applicants, 67% accepted, 14 enrolled. In 2007, 16 degrees awarded. *Degree requirements:* For master's, comprehensive exam, thesis optional. *Entrance requirements:* For master's, GRE General Test, interview. Additional exam requirements/recommendations for international students: Required—TOEFL. *Application deadline:* For fall admission, 3/1 for domestic students; for spring admission, 9/1 for domestic students. Application fee: $35. Electronic applications accepted. *Expenses:* Tuition, state resident: full-time $6,214; part-time $345 per credit. Tuition, nonresident: full-time $9,944; part-time $552 per credit. Required fees: $1,536; $78 per credit. $65 per semester. *Financial support:* Career-related internships or fieldwork, Federal Work-Study, scholarships/grants, and unspecified assistantships available. Financial award application deadline: 3/15; financial award applicants required to submit FAFSA. *Faculty research:* Addicted families. *Unit head:* Dr. Margaret Herrick, Chairperson, 610-683-4204, Fax: 610-683-1585, E-mail: herrick@kutztown.edu.

La Salle University, School of Arts and Sciences, Program in Clinical-Counseling Psychology, Philadelphia, PA 19141-1199. Offers MA. *Accreditation:* APA. Part-time and evening/weekend programs available. *Faculty:* 10 full-time (6 women), 17 part-time/adjunct (4 women). *Students:* 90 full-time (72 women), 217 part-time (166 women); includes 64 minority (44 African Americans, 9 Asian Americans or Pacific Islanders, 11 Hispanic Americans), 2 international. Average age 31. 197 applicants, 73% accepted, 80 enrolled. In 2007, 61 degrees awarded. *Degree requirements:* For master's, comprehensive exam. *Entrance requirements:* For master's, GRE or MAT, 15 undergraduate credits in psychology. *Application deadline:* Applications are processed on a rolling basis. Application fee: $35. *Expenses: Contact institution.* Tuition and fees vary according to program. *Financial support:* In 2007–08, 211 students received support; teaching assistantships, career-related internships or fieldwork, institutionally sponsored loans, scholarships/grants, and tuition waivers (partial) available. Support available to part-time students. Financial award application deadline: 8/15; financial award applicants required to submit FAFSA. *Faculty research:* Cognitive therapy, attribution theory, work habits, single parent families, treatment of addictions. *Unit head:* Dr. John Rooney, Director, 215-951-1767, Fax: 215-951-1843, E-mail: rooney@lasalle.edu.

Leadership Institute of Seattle, School of Applied Behavioral Science, Systems Counseling Track, Kenmore, WA 98028-4966. Offers MA. *Degree requirements:* For master's, thesis (for some programs), oral exams. *Entrance requirements:* For master's, bachelor's degree from an accredited university or college. *Faculty research:* Family systems theory, marriage and family therapy, systems consultation, family and culture of origin, personal authority.

Lee University, Program in Behavioral Sciences, Cleveland, TN 37320-3450. Offers mental health counseling (MS); school counseling (MS). Part-time programs available. *Faculty:* 12 full-time (4 women), 5 part-time/adjunct (3 women). *Students:* 49 full-time (41 women), 28 part-time (21 women); includes 2 minority (both Hispanic Americans), 5 international. Average age 27. 24 applicants, 96% accepted, 23 enrolled. In 2007, 27 degrees awarded. *Degree requirements:* For master's, variable foreign language requirement, comprehensive exam, thesis, internship. *Entrance requirements:* For master's, GRE General Test or MAT, minimum undergraduate GPA of 3.0, 3 letters of recommendation, interview. Additional exam requirements/recommendations for international students: Required—TOEFL. *Application deadline:* For fall admission, 4/1 priority date for domestic and international students; for spring admission, 10/1 for domestic and international students. Applications are processed on a rolling basis. Application fee: $25. *Expenses:* Tuition: Full-time $10,392; part-time $433 per credit. Required fees: $65 per term. Tuition and fees vary according to course load. *Financial support:* Teaching assistantships, career-related internships or fieldwork, Federal Work-Study, institutionally sponsored loans, scholarships/grants, and unspecified assistantships available. Financial award application deadline: 3/1; financial award applicants required to submit FAFSA. *Unit head:* Dr. Doyle Goff, Director, 423-614-8126, Fax: 423-614-8129, E-mail: drgoff@leeuniversity.edu. *Application contact:* Vicki Glasscock, Graduate Admissions Director, 423-614-8059, E-mail: vglasscock@leeuniversity.edu.

Lehigh University, College of Education, Program in Counseling Psychology, Bethlehem, PA 18015-3094. Offers counseling and human services (M Ed); counseling psychology (PhD); elementary and secondary school counseling (M Ed); international counseling (M Ed, Certificate). *Accreditation:* APA (one or more programs are accredited). Part-time and evening/weekend programs available. *Faculty:* 5 full-time (3 women), 11 part-time/adjunct (6 women). *Students:* 52 full-time (43 women), 52 part-time (40 women); includes 16 minority (8 African Americans, 1 American Indian/Alaska Native, 3 Asian Americans or Pacific Islanders, 4 Hispanic Americans), 12 international. Average age 30. 172 applicants, 30% accepted, 18 enrolled. In 2007, 32 master's, 5 doctorates awarded. *Degree requirements:* For doctorate, comprehensive exam, thesis/dissertation. *Entrance requirements:* For master's, minimum GPA of 3.0, 2 letters of recommendation, essay, transcript; for doctorate, GRE General Test, 2 letters of recommendation, supplemental application, transcript, essay. Additional exam requirements/recommendations for international students: Required—TOEFL (minimum score 600 paper-based; 250 computer-based; 93 iBT). *Application deadline:* For fall admission, 1/1 for domestic and international students; for winter admission, 3/1 for domestic and international students. Application fee: $65. Electronic applications accepted. *Financial support:* In 2007–08, 2 research assistantships with full and partial tuition reimbursements (averaging $13,000 per year) were awarded; fellowships with full and partial tuition reimbursements, career-related internships or fieldwork, Federal Work-Study, institutionally sponsored loans, scholarships/grants, and tuition waivers (full and partial) also available. Financial award application deadline: 1/31. *Faculty research:* Supervision, violence prevention, multicultural training and counseling, career development and health interventions. *Unit head:* Dr. Tina Richardson, Coordinator, 610-758-3250, Fax: 610-758-3227, E-mail: tqr0@lehigh.edu.

Lesley University, Graduate School of Arts and Social Sciences, Program in Counseling Psychology, Cambridge, MA 02138-2790. Offers professional counseling (MA); school counseling (MA). Part-time and evening/weekend programs available. Postbaccalaureate distance learning degree programs offered (no on-campus study). *Faculty:* 11 full-time (8 women), 40 part-time/adjunct (26 women). *Students:* 143 full-time (132 women), 140 part-time (121 women); includes 15 minority (8 African Americans, 2 Asian Americans or Pacific Islanders, 5 Hispanic Americans), 5 international. Average age 33. 108 applicants, 84% accepted, 63 enrolled. In 2007, 90 master's awarded. Terminal master's awarded for partial completion of doctoral program. *Degree requirements:* For master's, internship, practicum. *Entrance requirements:* For master's, MAT. Additional exam requirements/recommendations for international students: Required—TOEFL (minimum score 550 paper-based; 213 computer-based; 80 iBT). Application fee: $50. *Financial support:* In 2007–08, 5 students received support, including research assistantships (averaging $3,400 per year), teaching assistantships (averaging $3,400 per year); Federal Work-Study, scholarships/grants, and unspecified assistantships also available. Support available to part-time students. Financial award application deadline: 4/15; financial award applicants required to submit FAFSA. *Unit head:* Dr. Susan Gere, Associate Professor and Division Director, 617-349-8342, E-mail: sgere@lesley.edu. *Application contact:* John Gearin, Assistant Director of Advising and Student Services, 617-349-8339, E-mail: jgearin@mail.lesley.edu.

See Close-Up on page 1441.

Lewis & Clark College, Graduate School of Education and Counseling, Department of Counseling Psychology, Portland, OR 97219-7899. Offers addictions treatment (MA); counseling psychology (MA, MS); marriage, couple and family therapy (MA); psychological and cultural studies (MA); school psychology (MS, Ed S). Part-time and evening/weekend programs available. *Faculty:* 6 full-time (2 women), 26 part-time/adjunct (15 women). *Students:* 98 full-time (80 women), 127 part-time (102 women); includes 19 minority (4 African Americans, 5 Asian Americans or Pacific Islanders, 10 Hispanic Americans). Average age 31. 162 applicants, 81% accepted, 70 enrolled. In 2007, 57 master's, 14 other advanced degrees awarded. *Degree requirements:* For master's, thesis proposal (MS). *Entrance requirements:* For master's, GRE General Test, minimum undergraduate GPA of 2.75. Additional exam requirements/recommendations for international students: Required—TOEFL (minimum score 575 paper-based; 233 computer-based). *Application deadline:* For fall admission, 2/1 priority date for domestic and international students; for spring admission, 10/1 priority date for domestic and international students. Application fee: $50. Electronic applications accepted. *Expenses:* Tuition: Part-time $645 per credit. Tuition and fees vary according to campus/location. *Financial support:* In 2007–08, 183 students received support, including fellowships (averaging $22,000 per year); career-related internships or fieldwork, Federal Work-Study, institutionally sponsored loans, scholarships/grants, health care benefits, and tuition waivers (partial) also available. Support available to part-time students. Financial award applicants required to submit FAFSA. *Faculty research:* Treatment of depression, substance abuse, child-family problems, health psychology, marital relations. *Unit head:* Dr. Tod Sloan, Chair, 503-768-6060, Fax: 503-768-6065, E-mail: cpsy@lclark.edu. *Application contact:* Becky Haas, Director of Admissions, 503-768-6200, Fax: 503-768-6205, E-mail: gseadmit@lclark.edu.

Lewis University, College of Arts and Sciences, Program in Counseling Psychology, Romeoville, IL 60446. Offers child and adolescent counseling (MA); mental health counseling (MA). Part-time and evening/weekend programs available. *Faculty:* 6 full-time (2 women). *Students:* 24 full-time (23 women), 55 part-time (48 women); includes 11 minority (all African Americans) Average age 30. 55 applicants, 47% accepted, 26 enrolled. *Degree requirements:* For master's, thesis optional. *Entrance requirements:* For master's, 15 hours of psychology, including statistics or research; 2 letters of recommendation; writing assessment; minimum GPA of 3.0 in last 60 hours, interview. Additional exam requirements/recommendations for international students: Required—TOEFL (minimum score 550 paper-based; 213 computer-based). *Application deadline:* For fall admission, 5/1 priority date for international students; for spring admission, 11/15 priority date for international students. Applications are processed on a rolling basis. Application fee: $40. Electronic applications accepted. *Financial support:* Federal Work-Study, scholarships/grants, tuition waivers, and unspecified assistantships available. Financial award application deadline: 5/1; financial award applicants required to submit FAFSA. *Faculty research:* Cognitive development, attitude formation, juvenile delinquency, gender issues, work-family conflict. *Unit head:* Dr. Katherine Helm, Director, 815-838-0500 Ext. 5604, Fax: 815-836-5032, E-mail: helmka@lewisu.edu. *Application contact:* Nancy Hanley, Information Contact, 815-838-0500 Ext. 5604, E-mail: hanleyna@lewisu.edu.

Liberty University, College of Arts and Sciences, Lynchburg, VA 24502. Offers counseling (MA); nursing (MSN); pastoral care and counseling (PhD); professional counseling (PhD). *Accreditation:* AACN. Part-time programs available. Postbaccalaureate distance learning degree programs offered (minimal on-campus study). *Faculty:* 15 full-time (5 women), 74 part-time/adjunct (31 women). *Students:* 783 full-time (575 women), 2,031 part-time (1,505 women); includes 721 minority (610 African Americans, 12 American Indian/Alaska Native, 26 Asian Americans or Pacific Islanders, 73 Hispanic Americans), 69 international. Average age 36. In 2007, 164 master's, 2 doctorates awarded. *Degree requirements:* For master's, comprehensive exam (for some programs); for doctorate, comprehensive exam, thesis/dissertation. *Entrance requirements:* For master's, GRE General Test (MSN), minimum undergraduate GPA of 3.0; for doctorate, GRE General Test, minimum master's GPA of 3.25. Additional exam requirements/recommendations for international students: Required—TOEFL (minimum score 600 paper-based; 250 computer-based). *Application deadline:* For fall admission, 6/1 priority date for domestic students; for spring admission, 11/1 priority date for domestic students. Applications are processed on a rolling basis. Application fee: $50. Electronic applications accepted. *Expenses:* Tuition: Full-time $7,110; part-time $395 per credit. Required fees: $950. Tuition and fees vary according to program. *Financial support:* In 2007–08, 817 students received support, including 9 teaching assistantships with tuition reimbursements available; Federal Work-Study also available. *Faculty research:* God concept and adult attachment, building marital strength, image of God and gender, breastfeeding behavior among adolescent mothers, osteoporosis. *Unit head:* Dr. Ronald E. Hawkins, Dean, 434-592-4030, Fax: 434-522-0416, E-mail: rehawkin@liberty.edu. *Application contact:* Kyle A Falce, Director of Graduate Admissions, 800-424-9596, Fax: 800-628-7977, E-mail: gradadmissions@liberty.edu.

Lindenwood University, Graduate Programs, Division of Education, St. Charles, MO 63301-1695. Offers education (MA); educational administration (MA, Ed D, Ed S); instructional leadership (Ed D, Ed S); library media (MA); professional and school counseling (MA); professional counseling (MA); school counseling (MA); teaching (MA). Part-time and evening/weekend programs available. *Faculty:* 29 full-time (18 women), 185 part-time/adjunct (110 women). *Students:* 556 full-time (445 women), 1,952 part-time (1,502 women); includes 624 minority (594 African Americans, 5 American Indian/Alaska Native, 13 Asian Americans or Pacific Islanders, 12 Hispanic Americans), 9 international. Average age 37. In 2007, 869 master's, 3 doctorates, 39 other advanced degrees awarded. *Degree requirements:* For master's, thesis (for some programs), minimum GPA of 3.0; for doctorate, thesis/dissertation, minimum GPA of 3.0; for Ed S, specialist project, minimum GPA of 3.0. *Entrance requirements:* For master's, interview, minimum GPA of 3.0, writing sample; for Ed S, master's degree in education, relevant work experience. Additional exam requirements/recommendations for international students: Required—TOEFL (minimum score 550 paper-based; 213 computer-based; 80 iBT). *Application deadline:* For fall admission, 8/30 priority date for domestic and international students; for spring admission, 12/30 priority date for domestic and international students. Applications are processed on a rolling basis. Application fee: $30 ($100 for international students). Electronic applications accepted. *Expenses:* Tuition: Full-time $12,400; part-time $350 per hour. Full-time tuition and fees vary according to degree level and program. *Financial support:* Career-related internships or fieldwork, institutionally sponsored loans, tuition waivers (partial), and unspecified assistantships available. Financial award applicants required to submit FAFSA. *Unit head:* Dr. John Dougherty, Dean of Education, 636-949-4937, Fax: 636-949-4197, E-mail: jdougherty@lindenwood.edu. *Application contact:* Brett Barger, Dean of Evening Admissions and Extension Campuses, 636-949-4934, Fax: 636-949-4109, E-mail: adultadmissions@lindenwood.edu.

Lindsey Wilson College, School of Professional Counseling, Columbia, KY 42728-1298. Offers counseling and human development (M Ed). *Accreditation:* ACA. Part-time and evening/weekend programs available.

Lipscomb University, Program in Counseling, Nashville, TN 37204-3951. Offers counseling psychology (Certificate); professional counseling (MS); psychology (MS). Part-time and evening/weekend programs available. Postbaccalaureate distance learning degree programs offered (minimal on-campus study). *Faculty:* 3 full-time (1 woman), 1 part-time/adjunct (0 women). *Students:* 21 full-time (16 women), 8 part-time (5 women); includes 1 African American, 1 international. Average age 30. *Entrance requirements:* For master's, GRE, resumé, 3 reference letters, minimum GPA of 3.0. *Application deadline:* For fall admission, 3/1 for domestic students. Application fee: $25. Electronic applications accepted. *Expenses:* Tuition: Part-time $599 per semester hour. *Faculty research:* Cognitive psychology, neuroscience, health psychology, grief issues. *Unit head:* Dr. Roy Hamley, Co-Director, 615-966-5753, E-mail: roy.hamley@lipscomb.edu. *Application contact:* Elena Zemmel, Administrative Assistant, 615-966-5906, E-mail: elena.zemmel@lipscomb.edu.

Long Island University, Brentwood Campus, School of Education, Brentwood, NY 11717. Offers childhood education (MS); early childhood education (MS); literacy (MS); mental health counseling (MS); school counseling (MS); special education (MS). Part-time and evening/weekend programs available. *Faculty:* 19 full-time (3 women), 101 part-time/adjunct (33 women). *Students:* 150 full-time (130 women), 450 part-time (400 women); includes 10 African Americans, 2 Asian Americans or Pacific Islanders, 10 Hispanic Americans. Average age 36. 217 applicants, 74% accepted, 130 enrolled. *Application deadline:* Applications are processed on a rolling basis. Application fee: $0. *Expenses:* Tuition: Full-time $15,030; part-time $835 per credit. Required fees: $460; $230 per term. Full-time tuition and fees vary according to program. *Financial support:* Federal Work-Study, scholarships/grants, and unspecified assistantships available. *Unit head:* Dr. Robert Manheimer, Dean, 516-299-2210.

Long Island University, Rockland Graduate Campus, Graduate School, Program in Counseling and Development, Orangeburg, NY 10962. Offers mental health counseling (MS); school counselor (MS). *Faculty:* 2 full-time (both women), 6 part-time/adjunct (2 women). *Students:* 19 full-time (14 women), 53 part-time (46 women). In 2007, 23 degrees awarded. Application fee: $30. *Expenses:* Tuition: Part-time $835 per credit. Required fees: $100 per term. *Unit head:* Dr. Kathleen Keefe-Cooperman, Program Director, 845-359-7200 Ext. 5406, Fax: 845-359-7248, E-mail: kathleen.keefe-cooperman@liu.edu. *Application contact:* Peter S. Reiner, Director of Admissions and Marketing, 845-359-7200, Fax: 845-359-7248, E-mail: peter.reiner@liu.edu.

See Close-Up on page 1443.

Long Island University, Westchester Graduate Campus, Program in Mental Health Counseling, Purchase, NY 10577. Offers MS. *Faculty:* 2 full-time (both women), 10 part-time/adjunct (6 women). *Application deadline:* Applications are processed on a rolling basis. Application fee: $30. *Unit head:* Prof. Beth Weiner, Director, 914-831-2717, Fax: 914-251-5959, E-mail: beth.weiner@liu.edu. *Application contact:* Cindy Doctor, Enrollment Specialist, 914-831-2701, Fax: 914-251-5959, E-mail: cindy.doctor@liu.edu.

Louisiana State University in Shreveport, College of Education and Human Development, Program in Counseling Psychology, Shreveport, LA 71115-2399. Offers MS. *Faculty:* 6 full-time (2 women), 1 part-time/adjunct (0 women). *Students:* 27 full-time (25 women), 23 part-time (16 women); includes 8 minority (7 African Americans, 1 American Indian/Alaska Native). Average age 32. 16 applicants, 56% accepted, 8 enrolled. In 2007, 15 degrees awarded. *Degree requirements:* For master's, comprehensive exam, 30 credit-hour curriculum and internship (600 clock hours). *Entrance requirements:* For master's, GRE, references, undergrad prerequisites. Additional exam requirements/recommendations for international students: Required—TOEFL (minimum score 500 paper-based; 173 computer-based; 61 iBT). *Application deadline:* For fall admission, 6/30 for domestic and international students; for spring admission, 11/30 for domestic and international students. Applications are processed on a rolling basis. Application fee: $10. *Financial support:* In 2007–08, 3 research assistantships with partial tuition reimbursements (averaging $30,000 per year) were awarded. *Unit head:* Dr. Meredith G. Nelson, Program Director, 318-797-5199, E-mail: mnelson@pilot.lsus.edu.

Louisiana Tech University, Graduate School, College of Education, Department of Behavioral Sciences and Psychology, Ruston, LA 71272. Offers counseling (MA); counseling psychology (PhD); industrial/organizational psychology (MA); special education (MA). *Accreditation:* APA (one or more programs are accredited). Part-time programs available. *Degree requirements:* For master's, thesis or alternative; for doctorate, thesis/dissertation. *Entrance requirements:* For master's and doctorate, GRE General Test. *Application deadline:* For fall admission, 7/29 for domestic students; for spring admission, 2/3 for domestic students. Application fee: $20 ($30 for international students). *Financial support:* Fellowships, research assistantships, teaching assistantships, career-related internships or fieldwork available. Financial award application deadline: 2/1. *Unit head:* Dr. Tilman Sheets, Head, 318-257-4315, Fax: 318-257-2379. *Application contact:* Dr. Cathy Stockton, Director of Graduate Studies, 318-257-3229, Fax: 318-257-2379, E-mail: cstock@latech.edu.

Loyola College in Maryland, Graduate Programs, College of Arts and Sciences, Department of Psychology, Program in Counseling Psychology, Baltimore, MD 21210-2699. Offers counseling psychology (MS); employee assistance and substance abuse (CAS). Part-time and evening/weekend programs available. *Entrance requirements:* For master's and CAS, GRE General Test, GRE Subject Test (recommended). Additional exam requirements/recommendations for international students: Required—TOEFL (minimum score 550 paper-based; 213 computer-based).

Loyola University Chicago, School of Education, Program in Counseling Psychology, Chicago, IL 60611-2196. Offers PhD. Offered through the Graduate School. *Accreditation:* APA. *Faculty:* 5 full-time (4 women), 4 part-time/adjunct (2 women). *Students:* 30. Average age 26. 50 applicants, 12% accepted, 4 enrolled. In 2007, 5 degrees awarded. *Degree requirements:* For doctorate, comprehensive exam, thesis/dissertation. *Entrance requirements:* For doctorate, GRE General Test, GRE Subject Test, interview; minimum graduate GPA of 3.5, undergraduate 3.0; letters of recommendation. Additional exam requirements/recommendations for international students: Required—TOEFL (minimum score 550 paper-based; 213 computer-based; 79 iBT). *Application deadline:* For fall admission; 12/1 for domestic and international students. Application fee: $50. Electronic applications accepted. *Expenses:* Tuition: Full-time $12,780; part-time $710 per credit hour. Required fees: $55 per semester. Full-time tuition and fees vary according to program. *Financial support:* In 2007–08, 3 fellowships with full tuition reimbursements (averaging $14,000 per year), 11 research assistantships with full tuition reimbursements (averaging $12,500 per year) were awarded; teaching assistantships with full tuition reimbursements, career-related internships or fieldwork, Federal Work-Study, traineeships, and unspecified assistantships also available. Financial award application deadline: 2/15; financial award applicants required to submit FAFSA. *Faculty research:* Career choice and development, multicultural counseling, psychological measurement, prevention and intervention, family therapy. *Unit head:* Dr. Suzette Speight, Director, 312-915-6937, E-mail: sspeigh@luc.edu. *Application contact:* Marie Rosin-Dittmar, Information Contact, 312-915-6800, E-mail: schleduc@luc.edu.

Marist College, Graduate Programs, School of Social and Behavioral Sciences, Poughkeepsie, NY 12601-1387. Offers counseling psychology (MA); education (M Ed); education psychology (MA); school psychology (MA, Adv C). Part-time and evening/weekend programs available. *Faculty:* 20 full-time (10 women), 18 part-time/adjunct (7 women). *Students:* 98 full-time (82

Counseling Psychology

Marist College (continued)
women), 121 part-time (97 women); includes 23 minority (7 African Americans, 3 Asian Americans or Pacific Islanders, 13 Hispanic Americans), 4 international. Average age 29. 100 applicants, 56% accepted, 45 enrolled. In 2007, 87 master's, 3 other advanced degrees awarded. *Degree requirements:* For master's, thesis optional. *Entrance requirements:* For master's, GRE General Test, letters of recommendation, minimum undergraduate GPA of 3.0, interview, essay, official transcript. Additional exam requirements/recommendations for international students: Required—TOEFL (minimum score 550 paper-based; 213 computer-based; 80 iBT); Recommended—IELTS (minimum score 7). *Application deadline:* For fall admission, 8/1 for domestic students, 6/1 for international students; for spring admission, 12/1 for domestic students, 10/31 for international students. Applications are processed on a rolling basis. Application fee: $50. Electronic applications accepted. *Expenses:* Tuition: Part-time $665 per credit. *Financial support:* In 2007–08, 130 students received support. Career-related internships or fieldwork, scholarships/grants, and unspecified assistantships available. Support available to part-time students. Financial award application deadline: 8/15; financial award applicants required to submit FAFSA. *Faculty research:* AIDS prevention, educational intervention, humanistic counseling research, aging and development, neuroimaging. *Unit head:* Margaret Calista, Dean, 845-575-3000 Ext. 2960, E-mail: margaret.calista@marist.edu. *Application contact:* Kelly Holmes, Director of Admissions, 845-575-3800, Fax: 845-575-3166, E-mail: graduate@marist.edu.

Marylhurst University, Department of Art Therapy Counseling, Marylhurst, OR 97036-0261. Offers art therapy (PGC); art therapy counseling (MA); counseling (PGC). Part-time and evening/weekend programs available. *Faculty:* 2 full-time (both women), 6 part-time/adjunct (all women). *Students:* 50 full-time (47 women), 7 part-time (all women); includes 1 minority (African American) Average age 32. In 2007, 11 degrees awarded. *Degree requirements:* For master's, comprehensive exam. *Entrance requirements:* For master's, MAT, minimum GPA of 3.0, course work in psychology and art, slide portfolio, letters of reference, resumé, autobiography, personal statement. Additional exam requirements/recommendations for international students: Required—TOEFL. *Application deadline:* For fall admission, 2/15 priority date for domestic and international students. Applications are processed on a rolling basis. Application fee: $40 ($50 for international students). *Expenses: Contact institution.* One-time fee: $85 part-time. Tuition and fees vary according to course load and program. *Financial support:* Federal Work-Study and scholarships/grants available. Support available to part-time students. Financial award applicants required to submit FAFSA. *Faculty research:* Scientific approaches to art therapy research, child and adolescent psychotherapy, multicultural counseling. *Unit head:* Christine Turner, Chair, 503-636-8141, Fax: 503-636-9526, E-mail: cturner@marylhurst.edu. *Application contact:* Kathleen Schneff, Admissions Specialist, 800-634-9982 Ext. 3322, Fax: 503-635-6585, E-mail: admissions@marylhurst.edu.

Marymount University, School of Education and Human Services, Program in Community Counseling, Arlington, VA 22207-4299. Offers MA, Certificate. *Accreditation:* ACA (one or more programs are accredited). Part-time and evening/weekend programs available. *Students:* 41 full-time (35 women), 44 part-time (40 women); includes 17 minority (10 African Americans, 1 American Indian/Alaska Native, 2 Asian Americans or Pacific Islanders, 4 Hispanic Americans), 1 international. Average age 31. 61 applicants, 84% accepted, 32 enrolled. In 2007, 21 degrees awarded. *Entrance requirements:* For master's, GRE, interview, 2 letters of recommendation, resumé, personal statement. Additional exam requirements/recommendations for international students: Required—TOEFL (minimum score 600 paper-based; 250 computer-based; 100 iBT). *Application deadline:* For fall admission, 2/15 for domestic students; for spring admission, 9/21 for domestic students. Application fee: $40. *Expenses:* Tuition: Full-time $11,790; part-time $655 per credit. Required fees: $121; $6.7 per credit. *Financial support:* Research assistantships with full tuition reimbursements, career-related internships or fieldwork, scholarships/grants, and unspecified assistantships available. Support available to part-time students. Financial award applicants required to submit FAFSA. *Unit head:* Dr. Lisa Jackson-Cherry, Chair, 703-284-1633, Fax: 703-284-5708, E-mail: lisa.jackson-cherry@marymount.edu.

Marywood University, Academic Affairs, College of Education and Human Development, Department of Psychology and Counseling, Program in Mental Health Counseling, Scranton, PA 18509-1598. Offers addiction (MA); general (MA); pastoral (MA). *Accreditation:* ACA. *Students:* 9 full-time (6 women), 9 part-time (6 women); includes 1 minority (African American), 1 international. Average age 33. In 2007, 5 degrees awarded. Application fee: $30. *Expenses:* Tuition: Full-time $15,290; part-time $695 per credit. Required fees: $990; $370 per term. Tuition and fees vary according to degree level. *Unit head:* Dr. John Lemoncelli, Director, 570-348-6211 Ext. 2317, E-mail: lemoncelli@marywood.edu.

Massachusetts School of Professional Psychology, Graduate Programs, Boston, MA 02132. Offers clinical psychology (Psy D); clinical psychopharmacology (Post-Doctoral MS); counseling psychology (MA); executive coaching (Graduate Certificate); forensic psychology (MA); organizational psychology (MA); respecialization in clinical psychology (Certificate); MA/CAGS. *Accreditation:* APA. *Faculty:* 24 full-time (11 women), 13 part-time/adjunct (9 women). *Students:* 223 full-time (177 women), 81 part-time (68 women); includes 22 minority (3 African Americans, 8 Asian Americans or Pacific Islanders, 11 Hispanic Americans), 9 international. Average age 28. 415 applicants, 42% accepted, 77 enrolled. In 2007, 14 master's, 37 doctorates awarded. *Degree requirements:* For master's, comprehensive exam; for doctorate, thesis/dissertation. *Entrance requirements:* For doctorate, GRE General Test. Additional exam requirements/recommendations for international students: Required—TOEFL (minimum score 550 paper-based; 213 computer-based). *Application deadline:* For fall admission, 1/3 for domestic and international students. Application fee: $50. Electronic applications accepted. *Expenses:* Tuition: Full-time $25,952; part-time $811 per credit. Required fees: $200. *Financial support:* In 2007–08, 20 teaching assistantships (averaging $3,300 per year) were awarded; career-related internships or fieldwork also available. Financial award applicants required to submit FAFSA. *Unit head:* Dr. Nicholas A. Covino, President, 617-327-6777, Fax: 617-327-4447. *Application contact:* 617-327-6777 Ext. 210, Fax: 617-327-4447, E-mail: admissions@mspp.edu.

See Close-Up on page 1447.

McGill University, Faculty of Graduate and Postdoctoral Studies, Faculty of Education, Department of Educational and Counseling Psychology, Montréal, QC H3A 2T5, Canada. Offers counseling psychology (MA, PhD); educational psychology (M Ed, MA, PhD); school/applied child psychology and applied developmental psychology (M Ed, MA, PhD, Diploma), including school psychology. *Accreditation:* APA. *Faculty:* 33 full-time (19 women), 36 part-time/adjunct (23 women). *Students:* 198 full-time (172 women), 70 part-time (61 women). 327 applicants, 37% accepted, 92 enrolled. In 2007, 78 master's, 16 doctorates awarded.

McKendree University, Graduate Programs, Lebanon, IL 62254-1299. Offers business administration (MBA); counseling (MA); education (M Ed); nursing (MSN).

McNeese State University, Graduate School, College of Education, Department of Psychology, Lake Charles, LA 70609. Offers counseling psychology (MA); general psychology (MA). Evening/weekend programs available. *Faculty:* 7 full-time (3 women), 1 (woman) part-time/adjunct. *Students:* 31 full-time (24 women), 36 part-time (28 women); includes 14 minority (9 African Americans, 1 American Indian/Alaska Native, 2 Asian Americans or Pacific Islanders, 2 Hispanic Americans), 3 international. In 2007, 2 degrees awarded. *Entrance requirements:* For master's, GRE. *Application deadline:* For fall admission, 5/15 priority date for domestic students. Applications are processed on a rolling basis. Application fee: $20 ($30 for international students). *Expenses:* Tuition, state resident: full-time $2,226; part-time $193 per hour. Required fees: $935; $110 per hour. Tuition and fees vary according to course load. *Financial support:* Application deadline: 5/1. *Unit head:* Dr. Dena L. Matzenbacher, Head, 337-475-5457, Fax: 337-562-4115, E-mail: dena@mcneese.edu.

Medaille College, Programs in Psychology, Buffalo, NY 14214-2695. Offers mental health counseling (MA); psychology (MA). Part-time and evening/weekend programs available. *Faculty:* 6 full-time (3 women), 10 part-time/adjunct (8 women). *Students:* 139 full-time (111 women); includes 28 minority (27 African Americans, 1 Hispanic American). Average age 34. 86 applicants, 93% accepted, 75 enrolled. In 2007, 25 degrees awarded. *Degree requirements:* For master's, comprehensive exam (for some programs), thesis (for some programs). *Entrance requirements:* For master's, GRE General Test (psychology), minimum GPA of 2.75 (psychology). Additional exam requirements/recommendations for international students: Required—TOEFL (minimum score 550 paper-based; 213 computer-based). *Application deadline:* Applications are processed on a rolling basis. Application fee: $35. Electronic applications accepted. *Expenses:* Tuition: Full-time $14,760; part-time $615 per credit hour. *Financial support:* In 2007–08, 88 students received support. Federal Work-Study available. Financial award applicants required to submit FAFSA. *Faculty research:* Schizophrenia, Parkinson's Disease, eyewitness testimony, methodology. *Unit head:* Dr. Judith Horowitz, Interim Dean of Adult and Graduate Studies, 716-880-2229 Ext. 229, Fax: 716-884-0291, E-mail: jhorowitz@medaille.edu. *Application contact:* Jacqueline Matheny, Executive Director of Marketing and Enrollment, 716-932-2541, Fax: 716-632-1811, E-mail: jmatheny@medaille.edu.

Mercy College, Division of Social and Behavioral Sciences, Program in Counseling, Dobbs Ferry, NY 10522-1189. Offers alcohol and substance abuse counseling (AC); counseling (MS); family counseling (AC); retirement counseling (AC). *Students:* 85 full-time (79 women), 213 part-time (174 women); includes 202 minority (94 African Americans, 1 Asian American or Pacific Islander, 107 Hispanic Americans). Average age 34. In 2007, 74 master's, 14 other advanced degrees awarded. *Entrance requirements:* For master's, interview, letters of recommendation, minimum undergraduate GPA of 3.0. *Expenses:* Tuition: Part-time $575 per credit. Required fees: $220 per semester. Tuition and fees vary according to program. *Unit head:* Dr. Fernando Cabrera, Program Director, 914-674-7334, E-mail: fcabrera@mercy.edu.

Michigan Theological Seminary, Graduate Programs, Plymouth, MI 48170. Offers Christian education (MA); counseling psychology (MA); divinity (M Div); expository communication (D Min); theological studies (MA). *Accreditation:* ATS. Part-time and evening/weekend programs available. *Degree requirements:* For master's, one foreign language, thesis; for doctorate, 2 foreign languages, thesis/dissertation; for M Div, 2 foreign languages. *Faculty research:* Judaism, cults, world religions.

MidAmerica Nazarene University, Graduate Studies in Counseling, Olathe, KS 66062-1899. Offers MAC. Evening/weekend programs available. *Faculty:* 11. *Students:* 62 full-time (44 women); includes 5 minority (2 African Americans, 1 American Indian/Alaska Native, 2 Hispanic Americans). Average age 34. 42 applicants, 64% accepted. In 2007, 25 degrees awarded. *Entrance requirements:* For master's, Minnesota Multiphasic Personality Inventory, minimum GPA of 3.0. *Application deadline:* For fall admission, 6/15 for domestic students. Application fee: $75. *Expenses: Contact institution.* One-time fee: $211 full-time. Tuition and fees vary according to program. *Unit head:* Dr. Todd Frye, Director, 913-971-3449, Fax: 913-971-3402, E-mail: tmfrye@mnu.edu. *Application contact:* Aileen Douglas, Secretary, 913-791-3449, Fax: 913-791-3402, E-mail: adouglas@mnu.edu.

Mississippi College, Graduate School, School of Education, Department of Psychology and Counseling, Clinton, MS 39058. Offers counseling (Ed S); marriage and family counseling (MS); mental health counseling (MS); school counseling (M Ed). Part-time programs available. *Faculty:* 8 full-time (3 women), 4 part-time/adjunct (0 women). *Students:* 27 full-time (24 women), 64 part-time (56 women); includes 35 minority (33 African Americans, 2 American Indian/Alaska Native), 5 international. Average age 31. In 2007, 31 degrees awarded. *Degree requirements:* For master's and Ed S, comprehensive exam, thesis optional. *Entrance requirements:* For master's, GRE or NTE. Additional exam requirements/recommendations for international students: Recommended—IELTS. *Application deadline:* Applications are processed on a rolling basis. Application fee: $25. Electronic applications accepted. *Expenses:* Tuition: Full-time $7,470; part-time $415 per hour. Required fees: $1,160 per term. Part-time tuition and fees vary according to course load and degree level. *Financial support:* Career-related internships or fieldwork, Federal Work-Study, and unspecified assistantships available. Support available to part-time students. Financial award applicants required to submit FAFSA. *Unit head:* Dr. Buddy Wagner, Interim Chair, 601-925-3354, E-mail: bwagner@mc.edu.

Monmouth University, Graduate School, Department of Psychology, West Long Branch, NJ 07764-1898. Offers professional counseling (PMC); psychological counseling (MA). Part-time and evening/weekend programs available. *Faculty:* 7 full-time (3 women), 4 part-time/adjunct (all women). *Students:* 68 full-time (54 women), 112 part-time (96 women); includes 23 minority (12 African Americans, 1 American Indian/Alaska Native, 3 Asian Americans or Pacific Islanders, 7 Hispanic Americans), 3 international. Average age 31. 72 applicants, 88% accepted, 33 enrolled. In 2007, 47 degrees awarded. *Degree requirements:* For master's, thesis optional, fieldwork. *Entrance requirements:* For master's, GRE General Test, minimum GPA of 3.0 in major, 24 credits in psychology. Additional exam requirements/recommendations for international students: Required—TOEFL (minimum score 550 paper-based; 213 computer-based; 79 iBT), IELTS (minimum score 5), MELAB 77, Cambridge A, B, C. *Application deadline:* For fall admission, 7/15 priority date for domestic students, 6/1 for international students; for spring admission, 11/15 priority date for domestic students, 11/1 for international students. Applications are processed on a rolling basis. Application fee: $50. Electronic applications accepted. *Financial support:* In 2007–08, 90 students received support, including 90 fellowships (averaging $1,884 per year), 4 research assistantships (averaging $9,804 per year); career-related internships or fieldwork, scholarships/grants, tuition waivers (partial), and unspecified assistantships also available. Support available to part-time students. Financial award application deadline: 3/1; financial award applicants required to submit FAFSA. *Faculty research:* Violent crime, single parenting, the African-American male, counseling older women, successful behavior for under-achieving youth. *Unit head:* Dr. Frances K. Trotman, Director, 732-571-7593, Fax: 732-263-5159, E-mail: ftrotman@monmouth.edu. *Application contact:* Kevin Roane, Director, Office of Graduate Admission, 732-571-3452, Fax: 732-263-5123, E-mail: gradadm@monmouth.edu.

Montclair State University, The Office of Graduate Admissions and Support Services, College of Education and Human Services, Department of Counseling, Human Development, and Educational Leadership, Montclair, NJ 07043-1624. Offers administration and supervision (MA), including administration and supervision, educator/trainer; advanced counseling (Certificate); counseling and guidance (MA), including addictions counseling, community counseling, student affairs; principal (Certificate); school administrator (Certificate); school business administrator (Certificate); school counselor (Certificate); substance awareness coordinator (Certificate). *Accreditation:* NCATE. Part-time and evening/weekend programs available. *Faculty:* 19 full-time (14 women), 18 part-time/adjunct (8 women). *Students:* 119 full-time (98 women), 582 part-time (427 women); includes 131 minority (68 African Americans, 14 Asian Americans or Pacific Islanders, 49 Hispanic Americans), 3 international. Average age 33. 581 applicants, 54% accepted, 270 enrolled. In 2007, 187 master's, 25 other advanced degrees awarded. *Degree requirements:* For master's, comprehensive exam, thesis or alternative. *Entrance requirements:* For master's, GRE General Test, interview, 2 letters of recommendation. Additional exam requirements/recommendations for international students: Required—TOEFL (minimum score 83 computer-based). *Application deadline:* For fall admission, 6/1 for international students; for spring admission, 10/1 for international students. Applications are processed on a rolling basis. Application fee: $60. Electronic applications accepted. *Financial support:* In 2007–08, 15 research assistantships with full tuition reimbursements (averaging $7,000 per year) were awarded; Federal Work-Study, scholarships/grants, and unspecified assistantships also available. Support available to part-time students. Financial award application deadline: 3/1; financial award applicants required to submit FAFSA. *Faculty research:* K-12 education, data collection. *Unit head:* Dr. Catherine Roland, Chairperson, 973-655-7216, E-mail: rolandc@mail.montclair.edu.

Morehead State University, Graduate Programs, College of Science and Technology, Department of Psychology, Morehead, KY 40351. Offers clinical psychology (MA); counseling psychology (MA); experimental/general psychology (MA). Part-time programs available. *Faculty:*

7 full-time (3 women), 3 part-time/adjunct (1 woman). *Students:* 21 full-time (18 women), 4 part-time (1 woman); includes 1 minority (African American) Average age 26. In 2007, 12 degrees awarded. *Degree requirements:* For master's, comprehensive exam, thesis optional. *Entrance requirements:* For master's, GRE General Test, 18 undergraduate hours in psychology, minimum GPA of 3.0. Additional exam requirements/recommendations for international students: Required—TOEFL (minimum score 500 paper-based; 173 computer-based). *Application deadline:* For fall admission, 8/1 priority date for domestic and international students; for spring admission, 12/1 for domestic students, 12/1 priority date for international students. Applications are processed on a rolling basis. Application fee: $0 ($55 for international students). Electronic applications accepted. *Financial support:* In 2007–08, 19 research assistantships (averaging $6,000 per year) were awarded; career-related internships or fieldwork, Federal Work-Study, and institutionally sponsored loans also available. Financial award application deadline: 4/1; financial award applicants required to submit FAFSA. *Faculty research:* Mood induction effects, serotonin receptor activity, stress, perceptual processes. *Application contact:* Michelle Barber, Graduate Admissions Counselor, 606-783-2039, Fax: 606-783-5061, E-mail: m.barber@moreheadstate.edu.

Mount St. Mary's College, Graduate Division, Program in Counseling Psychology, Los Angeles, CA 90049-1599. Offers MS. Part-time and evening/weekend programs available. *Faculty:* 2 full-time (both women), 5 part-time/adjunct (3 women). *Students:* 13 full-time (10 women), 22 part-time (20 women); includes 22 minority (6 African Americans, 2 Asian Americans or Pacific Islanders, 14 Hispanic Americans). Average age 35. In 2007, 9 degrees awarded. *Degree requirements:* For master's, research project. *Entrance requirements:* For master's, MAT, minimum GPA of 2.75. *Application deadline:* For fall admission, 7/15 for domestic students; for spring admission, 11/15 for domestic students. Application fee: $50 ($75 for international students). *Expenses:* Tuition: Part-time $662 per unit. *Financial support:* Institutionally sponsored loans and tuition waivers (partial) available. Support available to part-time students. Financial award application deadline: 3/15. *Unit head:* Dr. Corinne Mabry, Chair, 213-477-2654. *Application contact:* Jessica M. Bibeau, Director of Graduate Admission, 213-477-2800 Ext. 2798, Fax: 213-477-2797, E-mail: jbibeau@msmc.la.edu.

Naropa University, Graduate Programs, Program in Transpersonal Counseling Psychology, Boulder, CO 80302-6697. Offers art therapy (MA); counseling psychology (MA); wilderness therapy (MA). *Faculty:* 10 full-time (6 women), 40 part-time/adjunct (29 women). *Students:* 130 full-time (97 women), 71 part-time (54 women); includes 14 minority (3 African Americans, 3 Asian Americans or Pacific Islanders, 8 Hispanic Americans), 18 international. Average age 33. 123 applicants, 50% accepted, 38 enrolled. In 2007, 37 degrees awarded. *Degree requirements:* For master's, internship. *Entrance requirements:* For master's, in-person interview, course work in psychology. Additional exam requirements/recommendations for international students: Required—TOEFL (minimum score 600 paper-based; 250 computer-based). *Application deadline:* For fall admission, 1/15 priority date for domestic and international students; for spring admission, 10/15 priority date for domestic students. Applications are processed on a rolling basis. Application fee: $60. Electronic applications accepted. *Expenses:* Tuition: Full-time $15,070; part-time $685 per credit. Required fees: $250 per semester. Tuition and fees vary according to course load. *Financial support:* In 2007–08, 41 students received support, including 3 research assistantships with partial tuition reimbursements available (averaging $3,000 per year), 1 teaching assistantship with partial tuition reimbursement available (averaging $3,000 per year); career-related internships or fieldwork, Federal Work-Study, scholarships/grants, and tuition waivers (partial) also available. Support available to part-time students. Financial award application deadline: 3/1; financial award applicants required to submit FAFSA. *Unit head:* Carla Clements, Chair, 303-546-3577. *Application contact:* Alice Di Tullio, Admissions Counselor, 303-546-3598, Fax: 303-546-3583, E-mail: aliced@naropa.edu.

See Close-Up on page 1449.

National University, Academic Affairs, College of Letters and Sciences, Department of Psychology, La Jolla, CA 92037-1011. Offers counseling psychology (MA); human behavior (MA). Part-time and evening/weekend programs available. Postbaccalaureate distance learning degree programs offered (no on-campus study). *Faculty:* 18 full-time (9 women), 201 part-time/adjunct (120 women). *Students:* 349 full-time (260 women), 388 part-time (297 women); includes 228 minority (90 African Americans, 6 American Indian/Alaska Native, 37 Asian Americans or Pacific Islanders, 95 Hispanic Americans), 8 international. Average age 36. 486 applicants, 368 enrolled. In 2007, 246 degrees awarded. *Degree requirements:* For master's, thesis (for some programs). *Entrance requirements:* For master's, interview, minimum GPA of 2.5. Additional exam requirements/recommendations for international students: Required—TOEFL (minimum score 550 paper-based; 213 computer-based; 80 iBT), IELTS (minimum score 6). *Application deadline:* Applications are processed on a rolling basis. Application fee: $60 ($65 for international students). Electronic applications accepted. *Expenses:* Tuition: Full-time $8,262; part-time $306 per unit. One-time fee: $60. *Financial support:* Career-related internships or fieldwork, institutionally sponsored loans, scholarships/grants, and tuition waivers (partial) available. Support available to part-time students. Financial award application deadline: 6/30; financial award applicants required to submit FAFSA. *Unit head:* Dr. Maureen O'Hara, Chair and Professor, 858-642-8464, Fax: 858-642-8715, E-mail: mohara@nu.edu. *Application contact:* Dominick Giovanniello, Associate Regional Dean—San Diego, 800-NAT-UNIV, Fax: 858-642-8709, E-mail: dgiovann@nu.edu.

New England College, Program in Community Mental Health Counseling, Henniker, NH 03242-3293. Offers human services (MS); mental health counseling (MS). Part-time and evening/weekend programs available. *Degree requirements:* For master's, internship.

New Jersey City University, Graduate Studies and Continuing Education, College of Arts and Sciences, Department of Psychology, Program in Counseling, Jersey City, NJ 07305-1597. Offers MA. *Faculty:* 9. *Students:* 5 full-time (2 women), 62 part-time (49 women); includes 17 minority (6 African Americans, 1 Asian American or Pacific Islander, 10 Hispanic Americans), 2 international. Average age 30. In 2007, 42 degrees awarded. *Expenses:* Tuition, state resident: full-time $7,462. Tuition, nonresident: full-time $13,762. Required fees: $1,296. *Unit head:* Dr. Patrice Dow-Nelson, Coordinator, 201-200-3124, E-mail: pnelson@njcu.edu.

New Mexico State University, Graduate School, College of Education, Department of Counseling and Educational Psychology, Las Cruces, NM 88003-8001. Offers counseling and guidance (MA); counseling psychology (PhD); school psychology (Ed S). *Accreditation:* ACA; APA (one or more programs are accredited); NCATE. Part-time programs available. *Faculty:* 7 full-time (4 women). *Students:* 70 full-time (52 women), 23 part-time (14 women); includes 48 minority (5 African Americans, 1 American Indian/Alaska Native, 1 Asian American or Pacific Islander, 41 Hispanic Americans), 4 international. Average age 33. 35 applicants, 46% accepted, 11 enrolled. In 2007, 15 master's, 6 doctorates, 6 other advanced degrees awarded. *Degree requirements:* For master's, comprehensive exam, thesis optional, internship; for doctorate, comprehensive exam, thesis/dissertation, internship; for Ed S, thesis or alternative, internship. *Entrance requirements:* For master's, doctorate, and Ed S, GRE General Test, 3.0 GPA. *Application deadline:* For fall admission, 12/15 for domestic students; for spring admission, 4/1 priority date for domestic students. Application fee: $30 ($50 for international students). Electronic applications accepted. *Expenses:* Tuition, state resident: full-time $3,602; part-time $199 per credit. Tuition, nonresident: full-time $13,380; part-time $607 per credit. Required fees: $1,178. *Financial support:* In 2007–08, 30 students received support, including 8 fellowships with partial tuition reimbursements available, 10 research assistantships, 25 teaching assistantships with partial tuition reimbursements available; career-related internships or fieldwork, Federal Work-Study, institutionally sponsored loans, scholarships/grants, traineeships, health care benefits, and unspecified assistantships also available. Support available to part-time students. Financial award application deadline: 4/1. *Faculty research:* Multicultural counseling, integrative health psychology group, career development school counseling. *Unit head:* Dr. Eve Adams, Head, 575-646-2121, Fax: 575-646-8035, E-mail: eadams@nmsu.edu.

New York Institute of Technology, Graduate Division, School of Education and Professional Services, Program in Mental Health Counseling and School Counseling, Old Westbury, NY 11568-8000. Offers MS. *Students:* 3 full-time (all women), 15 part-time (11 women); includes 2 African Americans, 1 Hispanic American, 3 international. Average age 34. 71 applicants, 69% accepted. In 2007, 24 degrees awarded. *Degree requirements:* For master's, thesis, internship. *Entrance requirements:* For master's, minimum GPA of 3.0, interview, 3 letters of reference. Additional exam requirements/recommendations for international students: Required—TOEFL. *Application deadline:* For fall admission, 7/1 priority date for domestic students; for spring admission, 12/1 priority date for domestic students. Application fee: $50. *Expenses:* Tuition: Part-time $739 per credit. Required fees: $75 per semester. *Financial support:* Research assistantships with partial tuition reimbursements, career-related internships or fieldwork, institutionally sponsored loans, and unspecified assistantships available. Support available to part-time students. Financial award applicants required to submit FAFSA. *Unit head:* Dr. Carol Dahir, Coordinator, 516-686-7616, Fax: 516-686-7655, E-mail: cdahir@nyit.edu. *Application contact:* Jacquelyn Nealon, Dean of Admissions and Financial Aid, 516-686-7925, Fax: 516-686-7613, E-mail: jnealon@nyit.edu.

New York University, Steinhardt School of Culture, Education and Human Development, Department of Applied Psychology, Program in Counselor Education, New York, NY 10012-1019. Offers counseling and guidance (MA, Advanced Certificate), including bilingual school counseling (MA), school counseling (MA); counseling for mental health and wellness (MA); counseling psychology (PhD). *Accreditation:* APA (one or more programs are accredited). Part-time and evening/weekend programs available. *Faculty:* 7 full-time (5 women). *Students:* 142 full-time (115 women), 77 part-time (63 women); includes 61 minority (21 African Americans, 15 Asian Americans or Pacific Islanders, 25 Hispanic Americans), 18 international. 611 applicants, 29% accepted, 89 enrolled. In 2007, 72 master's, 8 doctorates, 1 other advanced degree awarded. Terminal master's awarded for partial completion of doctoral program. *Degree requirements:* For master's, thesis (for some programs); for doctorate, thesis/dissertation. *Entrance requirements:* For doctorate, GRE General Test, interview. Additional exam requirements/recommendations for international students: Required—TOEFL. *Application deadline:* For fall admission, 1/15 priority date for domestic and international students; for spring admission, 11/1 for domestic and international students. Applications are processed on a rolling basis. Application fee: $50. *Financial support:* Fellowships with full and partial tuition reimbursements, teaching assistantships with partial tuition reimbursements, career-related internships or fieldwork, Federal Work-Study, institutionally sponsored loans, scholarships/grants, tuition waivers (partial), and unspecified assistantships available. Support available to part-time students. Financial award application deadline: 2/1; financial award applicants required to submit FAFSA. *Faculty research:* Cross-cultural counseling; group dynamics; culture, race and ethnicity; religiosity and psychological development; well-being and mental health. *Unit head:* Dr. Mary Sue Richardson, Director, 212-998-5559, Fax: 212-995-4358. *Application contact:* 212-998-5030, Fax: 212-995-4328, E-mail: steinhardt.gradadmissions@nyu.edu.

Nicholls State University, Graduate Studies, College of Education, Department of Psychology and Counselor Education, Thibodaux, LA 70310. Offers psychological counseling (MA); school psychology (SSP). *Accreditation:* NCATE. Part-time and evening/weekend programs available. *Faculty:* 8 full-time (2 women). *Students:* 29 full-time (25 women), 20 part-time (16 women); includes 16 minority (13 African Americans, 2 American Indian/Alaska Native, 1 Hispanic American), 1 international. Average age 27. In 2007, 15 master's, 7 other advanced degrees awarded. *Degree requirements:* For master's, comprehensive exam; for SSP, comprehensive exam, internship. *Entrance requirements:* For master's, GRE General Test. *Application deadline:* For fall admission, 6/17 priority date for domestic students; for spring admission, 11/15 priority date for domestic students. Applications are processed on a rolling basis. Application fee: $20 ($30 for international students). Electronic applications accepted. *Financial support:* In 2007–08, 12 teaching assistantships with tuition reimbursements (averaging $7,000 per year) were awarded; research assistantships with tuition reimbursements. Financial award application deadline: 6/17. *Unit head:* Dr. J. Steven Welsh, Head, 985-448-4371, Fax: 985-448-4435, E-mail: steven.welsh@nicholls.edu.

Northeastern State University, Graduate College, College of Education, Department of Psychology and Counseling, Program in Counseling Psychology, Tahlequah, OK 74464-2399. Offers MS. Part-time and evening/weekend programs available. *Students:* 58 full-time (40 women), 37 part-time (30 women); includes 27 minority (7 African Americans, 19 American Indian/Alaska Native, 1 Hispanic American), 1 international. In 2007, 22 degrees awarded. *Degree requirements:* For master's, thesis, internship, practicum. *Entrance requirements:* For master's, GRE, minimum GPA of 2.5. Additional exam requirements/recommendations for international students: Required—TOEFL (minimum score 213 computer-based). *Application deadline:* For fall admission, 3/1 priority date for domestic students; for spring admission, 10/1 for domestic students. Applications are processed on a rolling basis. Application fee: $0 ($25 for international students). Electronic applications accepted. *Financial support:* Teaching assistantships, career-related internships or fieldwork and Federal Work-Study available. Financial award application deadline: 3/1.

Northeastern University, Bouvé College of Health Sciences Graduate School, Department of Counseling and Applied Educational Psychology, Program in Counseling Psychology, Boston, MA 02115-5096. Offers MS, PhD, CAGS. *Accreditation:* APA (one or more programs are accredited). Part-time programs available. *Degree requirements:* For doctorate, comprehensive exam, thesis/dissertation, qualifying exams; for CAGS, comprehensive exam. *Entrance requirements:* For master's and CAGS, GRE General Test or MAT; for doctorate, GRE General Test. Additional exam requirements/recommendations for international students: Required—TOEFL. *Faculty research:* Crisis intervention, family systems.

Northern Arizona University, Graduate College, College of Education, Program in Educational Psychology, Flagstaff, AZ 86011. Offers counseling psychology (Ed D); learning and instruction (Ed D); school psychology (Ed D). *Degree requirements:* For doctorate, comprehensive exam, thesis/dissertation, internship. *Entrance requirements:* For doctorate, GRE General Test.

Northern Kentucky University, Office of Graduate Programs, College of Education and Human Services, Highland Heights, KY 41099. Offers advance studies in counseling (Certificate); community counseling (MSCC); education (M Ed); instructional leadership (MA); school counseling (MASC); teaching (MAT). *Accreditation:* NCATE. Part-time and evening/weekend programs available. *Faculty:* 41 full-time (22 women), 17 part-time/adjunct (7 women). *Students:* 53 full-time (46 women), 468 part-time (367 women); includes 21 minority (11 African Americans, 1 American Indian/Alaska Native, 3 Asian Americans or Pacific Islanders, 6 Hispanic Americans), 2 international. Average age 32. 263 applicants, 63% accepted, 148 enrolled. In 2007, 212 degrees awarded. *Degree requirements:* For master's, thesis optional, portfolio. *Entrance requirements:* For master's, GRE, teaching certificate, bachelor's degree in appropriate subject area (MAT). Additional exam requirements/recommendations for international students: Required—TOEFL (minimum score 550 paper-based; 213 computer-based; 79 iBT), Michigan English Language Assessment Battery (must be taken at NKU). *Application deadline:* For fall admission, 8/1 priority date for domestic students, 6/1 for international students; for spring admission, 12/1 priority date for domestic students, 10/1 for international students. Applications are processed on a rolling basis. Application fee: $40. Electronic applications accepted. *Financial support:* Unspecified assistantships available. *Faculty research:* Teacher disposition, mathematics teacher strategies, middle school structure. *Unit head:* Dr. Elaine McNally Jarchow, Dean, 859-572-5229, Fax: 859-572-6623, E-mail: jarchowe1@nku.edu. *Application contact:* Dr. Peg Griffin, Director of Graduate Programs, 859-572-1555, Fax: 859-572-6670, E-mail: gradprog@nku.edu.

Northwestern Oklahoma State University, School of Professional Studies, Program in Counseling Psychology, Alva, OK 73717-2799. Offers MCP. Part-time programs available. *Faculty:* 5 full-time (1 woman). *Students:* 39 full-time (31 women), 23 part-time (19 women); includes 4 minority (1 African American, 1 American Indian/Alaska Native, 2 Hispanic Americans). Average age 31. 29 applicants, 76% accepted, 20 enrolled. In 2007, 17 degrees awarded. *Degree requirements:* For master's, comprehensive exam (for some programs). *Entrance requirements:* For master's, GRE General Test or MAT, minimum GPA of 2.75. *Application*

Counseling Psychology

Northwestern Oklahoma State University (continued)
deadline: Applications are processed on a rolling basis. Application fee: $15. *Expenses:* Tuition, area resident: Part-time $152 per hour. Tuition, nonresident: part-time $373 per hour. *Financial support:* Fellowships, Federal Work-Study available. Support available to part-time students. Financial award application deadline: 5/1. *Unit head:* Dr. Nancy Knous, Coordinator, 580-327-8443.

Northwestern University, The Graduate School, Interdepartmental Degree Programs, Program in Counseling Psychology, Evanston, IL 60208. Offers MA. Admissions and degrees offered through The Graduate School. Part-time programs available. *Degree requirements:* For master's, comprehensive exam. *Entrance requirements:* For master's, GRE General Test. Electronic applications accepted. *Faculty research:* Family psychology, adult development and pathology, minority counseling, groups and systems, clinical training, stress and coping, health psychology.

See Close-Up on page 1451.

Northwest University, School of Graduate Psychology, Kirkland, WA 98033. Offers counseling psychology (MA). Evening/weekend programs available. *Entrance requirements:* For master's, essay, 3 character references. Additional exam requirements/recommendations for international students: Required—TOEFL (minimum score 580 paper-based; 237 computer-based). Expenses: Contact institution.

Notre Dame de Namur University, Division of Academic Affairs, School of Sciences, Department of Clinical Psychology and Gerontology, Belmont, CA 94002-1908. Offers chemical dependency (MACP); clinical gerontology (MA, Certificate); counseling psychology (MACP); marital and family therapy (MACP, MAMFT). Part-time and evening/weekend programs available. *Faculty:* 2 full-time (both women), 6 part-time/adjunct (5 women). *Students:* 29 full-time (25 women), 65 part-time (56 women); includes 31 minority (5 African Americans, 11 Asian Americans or Pacific Islanders, 15 Hispanic Americans), 1 international. Average age 35. 26 applicants, 81% accepted, 16 enrolled. In 2007, 23 degrees awarded. *Entrance requirements:* For master's, interview, minimum GPA of 2.5. Additional exam requirements/recommendations for international students: Required—TOEFL. *Application deadline:* For fall admission, 8/1 priority date for domestic students; for spring admission, 12/1 priority date for domestic students. Applications are processed on a rolling basis. Application fee: $50. Electronic applications accepted. *Financial support:* Career-related internships or fieldwork available. Support available to part-time students. Financial award applicants required to submit FAFSA. *Unit head:* Dr. Nusha Askari, Chair, 650-508-3728, E-mail: naskari@ndnu.edu. *Application contact:* Helen Valine, Director of Graduate Admissions, 650-508-3534, Fax: 650-508-3426, E-mail: grad.admit@ndnu.edu.

Nova Southeastern University, Center for Psychological Studies, Master's Programs in Counseling, Mental Health, School Guidance, and Clinical Pharmacology, Fort Lauderdale, FL 33314-7796. Offers clinical pharmacology (MS); mental health counseling (MS); school guidance and counseling (MS). Part-time and evening/weekend programs available. *Faculty:* 7 full-time (2 women), 27 part-time/adjunct (8 women). *Students:* 247 full-time (219 women), 538 part-time (476 women); includes 380 minority (203 African Americans, 4 American Indian/Alaska Native, 11 Asian Americans or Pacific Islanders, 162 Hispanic Americans), 13 international. 562 applicants, 65% accepted, 262 enrolled. In 2007, 315 degrees awarded. *Degree requirements:* For master's, comprehensive exam, 3 practica. *Entrance requirements:* Additional exam requirements/recommendations for international students: Required—TOEFL (minimum score 550 paper-based; 213 computer-based). *Application deadline:* For fall admission, 7/29 for domestic students; for winter admission, 11/29 for domestic students; for spring admission, 3/29 for domestic students. Applications are processed on a rolling basis. Application fee: $50. Electronic applications accepted. *Financial support:* Career-related internships or fieldwork, Federal Work-Study, and institutionally sponsored loans available. Financial award application deadline: 4/1. *Faculty research:* Clinical and child clinical psychology, geriatrics, interpersonal violence. *Unit head:* Karen S. Grosby, Dean, 954-262-5701, Fax: 954-262-3859. *Application contact:* Carlos Perez, Enrollment Management, 954-262-5790, Fax: 954-262-3893, E-mail: cpsinfo@cps.nova.edu.

See Close-Up on page 1455.

Oakland University, Graduate Study and Lifelong Learning, School of Education and Human Services, Department of Counseling, Rochester, MI 48309-4401. Offers MA, PhD, Certificate. *Accreditation:* ACA (one or more programs are accredited). Part-time and evening/weekend programs available. *Faculty:* 11 full-time (3 women), 5 part-time/adjunct (3 women). *Students:* 233 full-time (199 women), 192 part-time (164 women); includes 49 minority (30 African Americans, 6 American Indian/Alaska Native, 3 Asian Americans or Pacific Islanders, 10 Hispanic Americans), 8 international. Average age 33. 149 applicants, 70% accepted, 101 enrolled. In 2007, 142 master's, 1 doctorate awarded. *Degree requirements:* For doctorate, thesis/dissertation. *Entrance requirements:* Additional exam requirements/recommendations for international students: Required—TOEFL (minimum score 550 paper-based; 213 computer-based). *Application deadline:* For fall admission, 4/15 for domestic and international students; for winter admission, 10/1 for domestic students, 9/1 priority date for international students. Application fee: $35. Electronic applications accepted. *Expenses:* Tuition, state resident: full-time $9,936; part-time $414 per credit. Tuition, nonresident: full-time $17,202; part-time $716 per credit. *Financial support:* Career-related internships or fieldwork, Federal Work-Study, institutionally sponsored loans, and tuition waivers (full) available. Financial award application deadline: 3/1; financial award applicants required to submit FAFSA. *Unit head:* Dr. Luellen Ramey, Chair, 248-370-4179, E-mail: ramey@oakland.edu.

Ottawa University, Graduate Studies-Arizona, Program in Professional Counseling, Ottawa, KS 66067-3399. Offers Christian counseling (MA); expressive arts therapy (MA); marriage and family therapy (MA); treatment of trauma, abuse and deprivation (MA). Programs offered in Mesa, Phoenix, Tempe and West Valley, AZ. Part-time and evening/weekend programs available. Postbaccalaureate distance learning degree programs offered. *Degree requirements:* For master's, comprehensive exam, thesis or alternative, field experience, practicum. *Entrance requirements:* For master's, minimum undergraduate GPA of 3.0; course work in theories of personality, abnormal psychology, and human growth and development. Additional exam requirements/recommendations for international students: Required—TOEFL (minimum score 550 paper-based; 213 computer-based).

Our Lady of the Lake University of San Antonio, School of Education and Clinical Studies, Program in Counseling Psychology, San Antonio, TX 78207-4689. Offers counseling psychology (MS, Psy D); marriage and family therapy (MS); school psychology (MS). *Accreditation:* APA (one or more programs are accredited). Part-time and evening/weekend programs available. *Degree requirements:* For master's, comprehensive exam, thesis optional, practicum; for doctorate, thesis/dissertation, internship, qualifying exam. *Entrance requirements:* For master's and doctorate, GRE General Test or MAT, interview. Additional exam requirements/recommendations for international students: Required—TOEFL. Electronic applications accepted. *Faculty research:* Marriage and family therapy, supervision, cross-cultural counseling, violence.

Pacifica Graduate Institute, Graduate Programs, Carpinteria, CA 93013. Offers clinical psychology (PhD); counseling psychology (MA); depth psychology (MA, PhD); mythological studies (MA, PhD). Terminal master's awarded for partial completion of doctoral program. *Degree requirements:* For master's, thesis (for some programs), practicum; for doctorate, comprehensive exam, thesis/dissertation, internship. *Entrance requirements:* For master's, resumé, 3 letters of recommendation, writing sample, interview; for doctorate, resumé, 4 letters of recommendation, writing sample, interview. Additional exam requirements/recommendations for international students: Required—TOEFL. *Faculty research:* Imaginal and archetypal theory; post-Colonial psychoanalytic and Jungian theory; myth literature as it applies to the theory and practice of psychology.

Palm Beach Atlantic University, School of Education and Behavioral Studies, West Palm Beach, FL 33416-4708. Offers counseling psychology (MSCP), including addictions/mental health, marriage and family therapy, mental health counseling, school guidance counseling; elementary education (M Ed). Part-time and evening/weekend programs available. *Faculty:* 11 full-time (5 women), 10 part-time/adjunct (5 women). *Students:* 223 full-time (178 women), 65 part-time (48 women); includes 114 minority (62 African Americans, 5 Asian Americans or Pacific Islanders, 47 Hispanic Americans), 9 international. Average age 36. 145 applicants, 60% accepted, 73 enrolled. In 2007, 56 degrees awarded. *Entrance requirements:* For master's, GRE General Test, minimum GPA of 3.0 in last 60 hours of course work. Additional exam requirements/recommendations for international students: Required—TOEFL (minimum score 550 paper-based; 213 computer-based). *Application deadline:* For fall admission, 7/15 priority date for domestic students; for spring admission, 11/15 priority date for domestic students. Applications are processed on a rolling basis. Application fee: $45. Electronic applications accepted. *Expenses:* Tuition: Full-time $7,560; part-time $420 per credit. Required fees: $260; $95 per semester. Tuition and fees vary according to degree level, campus/location and program. *Financial support:* Career-related internships or fieldwork and unspecified assistantships available. Support available to part-time students. Financial award applicants required to submit FAFSA. *Unit head:* Dr. Melise Bunker, Dean, 561-803-2350, Fax: 561-803-2186, E-mail: melise_bunker@pba.edu. *Application contact:* Myra Santiago, Assistant Director of Graduate and Evening Admissions, 888-468-6722, Fax: 561-803-2115, E-mail: grad@pba.edu.

Penn State University Park, Graduate School, College of Education, Department of Counselor Education, Counseling Psychology and Rehabilitation Services, State College, University Park, PA 16802-1503. Offers counseling psychology (PhD); counselor education (M Ed, MS), including elementary counseling; counselor education, counseling psychology and rehabilitation services (D Ed). *Accreditation:* ACA (one or more programs are accredited); APA (one or more programs are accredited); NCATE. *Expenses:* Tuition, state resident: full-time $14,738; part-time $614 per credit. Tuition, nonresident: full-time $26,050; part-time $1,085 per credit. Tuition and fees vary according to course load, program and student level. *Unit head:* Dr. Spencer A. Niles, Head, 814-863-2412, Fax: 814-863-7750, E-mail: sgn3@psu.edu.

Philadelphia College of Osteopathic Medicine, Graduate and Professional Programs, Department of Psychology, Philadelphia, PA 19131-1694. Offers clinical psychology (Psy D); counseling and clinical health psychology (MS); organizational leadership and development (MS); psychology (Certificate); school psychology (MS, Psy D, Ed S). *Accreditation:* APA. *Degree requirements:* For master's, thesis; for doctorate, comprehensive exam, thesis/dissertation, final project, fieldwork. *Entrance requirements:* For master's, GRE or MAT, minimum GPA of 3.0; course work in biology, chemistry, English, physics; for other advanced degree, PRAXIS. *Faculty research:* Depression in primary care, integrated primary care, geriatric mental health.

See Close-Up on page 1469.

Prescott College, Graduate Programs, Program in Counseling and Psychology, Prescott, AZ 86301. Offers MA. Part-time programs available. Postbaccalaureate distance learning degree programs offered (minimal on-campus study). *Faculty:* 1 full-time (0 women), 42 part-time/adjunct (29 women). *Students:* 71 full-time (58 women), 27 part-time (22 women); includes 14 minority (5 African Americans, 1 American Indian/Alaska Native, 8 Hispanic Americans), 4 international. Average age 38. 62 applicants, 76% accepted, 34 enrolled. In 2007, 29 degrees awarded. *Degree requirements:* For master's, thesis, fieldwork or internship, practicum. *Entrance requirements:* For master's, 2 letters of recommendation, resumé. Additional exam requirements/recommendations for international students: Required—TOEFL (minimum score 550 paper-based; 213 computer-based). *Application deadline:* For fall admission, 5/1 priority date for domestic and international students; for spring admission, 11/1 priority date for domestic and international students. Applications are processed on a rolling basis. Application fee: $40. Electronic applications accepted. *Expenses:* Tuition: Full-time $6,480; part-time $540 per credit. *Financial support:* Career-related internships or fieldwork and Federal Work-Study available. Financial award applicants required to submit FAFSA. *Unit head:* Dr. Les McAllan, Chair, 928-350-3207, Fax: 928-776-5151, E-mail: lmcallan@prescott.edu. *Application contact:* Kerstin Alicki, Admissions Counselor, 877-350-2102, Fax: 928-776-5242, E-mail: admissions@prescott.edu.

Providence College and Theological Seminary, Theological Seminary, Otterburne, MB R0A 1G0, Canada. Offers children's ministry (Certificate); Christian studies (MA, Certificate); counseling (MA); cross-cultural discipleship (Certificate); divinity (M Div); educational studies (MA), including counseling psychology, educational ministries, student development, teaching English to speakers of other languages, training teachers of English to speakers of other languages; global studies (MA); lay counseling (Diploma); ministry (D Min); teaching English to speakers of other languages (Certificate); theological studies (MA); training teacher of English to speakers of other languages (Certificate); youth ministry (Certificate). *Accreditation:* ATS. Part-time programs available. *Degree requirements:* For master's, variable foreign language requirement, thesis (for some programs); for doctorate, thesis/dissertation; for M Div, 2 foreign languages, comprehensive exam, thesis/dissertation (for some programs). *Entrance requirements:* Additional exam requirements/recommendations for international students: Recommended—TOEFL (minimum score 550 paper-based; 213 computer-based). *Faculty research:* Studies in Isaiah, theology of sin.

Radford University, Graduate College, College of Humanities and Behavioral Sciences, Department of Psychology, Radford, VA 24142. Offers clinical psychology (MA, MS); counseling psychology (Psy D); experimental psychology (MA); industrial-organizational psychology (MA, MS); school psychology (Ed S). Part-time programs available. *Faculty:* 24 full-time (10 women). *Students:* 38 full-time (31 women), 52 part-time (39 women); includes 5 minority (4 African Americans, 1 Asian American or Pacific Islander), 2 international. Average age 25. 128 applicants, 64% accepted, 38 enrolled. In 2007, 45 degrees awarded. *Degree requirements:* For master's, comprehensive exam, thesis (for some programs); for doctorate, comprehensive exam, thesis/dissertation; for Ed S, comprehensive exam. *Entrance requirements:* For master's, GRE, minimum GPA 3.0; for doctorate, GRE; for Ed S, GMAT, GRE General Test, MAT, NTE. Additional exam requirements/recommendations for international students: Required—TOEFL. *Application deadline:* For fall admission, 3/1 priority date for domestic students, 12/1 for international students; for spring admission, 10/1 for domestic students, 7/1 for international students. Applications are processed on a rolling basis. Application fee: $40. Electronic applications accepted. *Financial support:* In 2007–08, 42 research assistantships with partial tuition reimbursements (averaging $8,000 per year), 12 teaching assistantships with partial tuition reimbursements (averaging $8,700 per year) were awarded; career-related internships or fieldwork, Federal Work-Study, institutionally sponsored loans, scholarships/grants, and unspecified assistantships also available. Financial award application deadline: 3/1; financial award applicants required to submit FAFSA. *Unit head:* Dr. Hilary M. Lips, Chair, 540-831-5387, Fax: 540-831-6113, E-mail: hlips@radford.edu.

Regent University, Graduate School, School of Psychology and Counseling, Virginia Beach, VA 23464-9800. Offers clinical psychology (Psy D); counseling (MA), including clinical psychology, community counseling, human services counseling, school guidance; counseling studies (CAGS); counselor education and supervision (PhD); M Div/MA; M Ed/MA; MBA/MA. PhD program offered online only. *Accreditation:* ACA; APA (one or more programs are accredited). Part-time programs available. Postbaccalaureate distance learning degree programs offered. *Faculty:* 25 full-time (14 women), 17 part-time/adjunct (7 women). *Students:* 223 full-time (176 women), 187 part-time (141 women); includes 110 minority (89 African Americans, 2 American Indian/Alaska Native, 9 Asian Americans or Pacific Islanders, 10 Hispanic Americans), 11 international. Average age 31. 293 applicants, 58% accepted, 99 enrolled. In 2007, 79 master's, 23 doctorates awarded. *Degree requirements:* For master's, thesis or alternative, internship, practicum, written competency exam; for doctorate, thesis/dissertation or alternative. *Entrance requirements:* For master's, GRE General Test including writing exam, minimum undergraduate GPA of 2.75, 3 recommendations, resumé, transcripts, writing sample; for doctorate, GRE General Test including writing exam, GRE Subject Test, minimum undergraduate GPA of 3.0, 3.5 (PhD), 10-15 minute VHS tape demonstrating counseling skills, writing sample, 3 recommendations, resumé, transcripts. Additional exam requirements/recommendations for international students: Required—TOEFL (minimum score 577 paper-based; 233 computer-based). *Application deadline:* For fall admission, 4/1 priority date for domestic students; for spring admission, 11/1 priority date for domestic students. Applications are processed on a rolling basis. Application fee: $50. Electronic applications accepted. *Expenses: Contact institution. Financial support:* In 2007–08, 362 students received support, including 15 research assistantships with full and partial tuition reimbursements available (averaging $4,439 per year), 6 teaching assistantships with full and partial tuition reimbursements available (averaging $12,699 per year); career-related internships or fieldwork, scholarships/grants, and tuition waivers (full and partial) also available. Support available to part-time students. Financial award application deadline: 9/1. *Faculty research:* Marriage enrichment, AIDS counseling, troubled youth. Total annual research expenditures: $12,000. *Unit head:* Dr. Rosemarie Hughes, Dean, 757-226-4269, Fax: 757-226-4282, E-mail: rosehug@regent.edu. *Application contact:* Althea Bishard, Registrar and Executive Director of Enrollment and Academic Services, 800-373-5504, Fax: 757-226-4381, E-mail: admissions@regent.edu.

Regis University, College for Professional Studies, Graduate Counseling Program, Denver, CO 80221-1099. Offers community counseling (MAC); counseling children and adolescents (Post-Graduate Certificate); marriage and family therapy (Post-Graduate Certificate). Program offered in Henderson and Las Vegas (Summerlin), NV. *Accreditation:* ACA. Part-time and evening/weekend programs available. *Faculty:* 18. *Students:* 231 (189 women). In 2007, 50 degrees awarded. *Degree requirements:* For master's, internships, practicum. *Entrance requirements:* For master's, 2 admissions essays, interview, 2 recommendations, resumé, criminal background check. Additional exam requirements/recommendations for international students: Required—TOEFL (minimum score 213 computer-based), TWE (minimum score 5). *Application deadline:* For fall admission, 8/6 for domestic students, 7/6 for international students; for spring admission, 12/14 for domestic students, 11/14 for international students. Application fee: $75. *Expenses: Contact institution. Faculty research:* Group Development, Counselor Education, Counsel and Therapy, Influence of Technology on Psychology, Dream finding groups, Adult Development, Depression. *Unit head:* Dr. Jolynne Reynolds, Head, 303-458-4100.

Rivier College, School of Graduate Studies, Department of Education, Nashua, NH 03060. Offers curriculum and instruction (M Ed); early childhood education (M Ed); educational administration (M Ed); educational studies (M Ed); elementary education (M Ed); elementary education and general special education (M Ed); emotional and behavioral disorders (M Ed); general social education (M Ed); leadership and learning (CAGS); learning disabilities (M Ed); learning disabilities and reading (M Ed); mental health counseling (MA); reading (M Ed); school counseling (M Ed). Part-time and evening/weekend programs available. *Degree requirements:* For master's, comprehensive exam (for some programs), internships. *Entrance requirements:* For master's, GRE General Test or MAT.

Rosemont College, Graduate School, Program in Counseling Psychology, Rosemont, PA 19010-1699. Offers human services (MA); school counseling (MA). Part-time and evening/weekend programs available. *Faculty:* 3 full-time (2 women), 7 part-time/adjunct (3 women). *Students:* 19 full-time (18 women), 99 part-time (89 women); includes 9 minority (6 African Americans, 2 Asian Americans or Pacific Islanders, 1 Hispanic American), 1 international. Average age 34. 23 applicants, 96% accepted. In 2007, 16 degrees awarded. *Degree requirements:* For master's, thesis or alternative, practicum. *Entrance requirements:* For master's, 3.0 baccalaureate GPA, statement of purpose, 3 letters of recommendation. Additional exam requirements/recommendations for international students: Required—TOEFL. *Application deadline:* Applications are processed on a rolling basis. Application fee: $50. Electronic applications accepted. *Expenses: Contact institution.* Tuition and fees vary according to program. *Financial support:* Institutionally sponsored loans available. *Faculty research:* Addictions counseling. *Unit head:* Dr. Christine M. Erdner, Director, 610-527-0200 Ext. 2342, Fax: 610-526-2964, E-mail: cerdner@rosemont.edu. *Application contact:* Karen Scales, Director, Enrollment and Student Services, 610-527-0200 Ext. 2187, Fax: 610-526-2964, E-mail: gradstudies@rosemont.edu.

Rowan University, Graduate School, College of Liberal Arts and Sciences, Program in Mental Health Counseling and Applied Psychology, Glassboro, NJ 08028-1701. Offers MA, CAGS. Part-time and evening/weekend programs available. *Faculty:* 18 full-time (13 women), 4 part-time/adjunct (1 woman). *Students:* 22 full-time (17 women), 9 part-time (all women); includes 5 minority (1 African American, 2 Asian Americans or Pacific Islanders, 2 Hispanic Americans). Average age 27. 26 applicants, 27% accepted, 6 enrolled. In 2007, 7 degrees awarded. *Entrance requirements:* Additional exam requirements/recommendations for international students: Required—TOEFL. *Application deadline:* Applications are processed on a rolling basis. Application fee: $50. Electronic applications accepted. *Expenses:* Tuition, nonresident: full-time $9,882; part-time $549 per credit. Required fees: $104,385 per credit. *Financial support:* Career-related internships or fieldwork, Federal Work-Study, and unspecified assistantships available. Support available to part-time students. *Unit head:* Dr. David Angelone, Adviser, 856-256-4500 Ext. 3780.

Rutgers, The State University of New Jersey, New Brunswick, Graduate School of Education, Department of Educational Psychology, Program in Counseling Psychology, New Brunswick, NJ 08901-1281. Offers Ed M. Part-time and evening/weekend programs available. *Entrance requirements:* For master's, GRE General Test, 3 letters of recommendation. Additional exam requirements/recommendations for international students: Required—TOEFL (minimum score 550 paper-based; 233 computer-based; 83 iBT). Electronic applications accepted. *Faculty research:* Children and family in a cross-cultural context, attachment theory, multicultural counseling, therapy relationship.

St. Edward's University, New College, Program in Counseling, Austin, TX 78704. Offers MA. Part-time and evening/weekend programs available. *Faculty:* 4 full-time (3 women), 20 part-time/adjunct (12 women). *Students:* 63 full-time (52 women), 156 part-time (113 women); includes 52 minority (13 African Americans, 1 American Indian/Alaska Native, 6 Asian Americans or Pacific Islanders, 32 Hispanic Americans). Average age 34. 90 applicants, 73% accepted, 54 enrolled. In 2007, 63 degrees awarded. *Degree requirements:* For master's, minimum 24 resident hours. *Entrance requirements:* For master's, GRE General Test, minimum GPA of 3.0 in last 60 hours or 2.75 overall. Additional exam requirements/recommendations for international students: Required—TOEFL (minimum score 550 paper-based; 213 computer-based; 79 iBT). *Application deadline:* For fall admission, 8/1 for domestic students, 7/1 for international students; for spring admission, 12/1 for domestic students, 11/1 for international students. Applications are processed on a rolling basis. Application fee: $45 ($50 for international students). Electronic applications accepted. *Expenses:* Tuition: Full-time $12,672; part-time $704 per credit hour. Full-time tuition and fees vary according to program. Part-time tuition and fees vary according to course load. *Financial support:* In 2007–08, 4 students received support. Scholarships/grants available. Financial award applicants required to submit FAFSA. *Unit head:* Dr. Elizabeth Katz, Director, 512-464-8833, Fax: 512-448-8492, E-mail: elizk@stedwards.edu. *Application contact:* Anna Alkin, Graduate Admissions Coordinator, 512-448-8745, Fax: 512-428-1032, E-mail: annaa@stedwards.edu.

St. John Fisher College, Office of the Provost, Wegmans School of Nursing, Mental Health Counseling Program, Rochester, NY 14618-3597. Offers MS. *Accreditation:* ACA. Part-time programs available. *Faculty:* 3 full-time (2 women), 2 part-time/adjunct (1 woman). *Students:* 33 full-time (31 women), 15 part-time (11 women); includes 6 African Americans, 2 Hispanic Americans. Average age 31. 51 applicants, 76% accepted, 24 enrolled. In 2007, 10 degrees awarded. *Degree requirements:* For master's, thesis optional, internships. *Entrance requirements:* For master's, GRE, minimum GPA of 3.0; course work in abnormal psychology. Additional exam requirements/recommendations for international students: Required—TOEFL (minimum score 575 paper-based; 233 computer-based; 80 iBT). *Application deadline:* For fall admission, 7/1 for domestic students; for spring admission, 10/30 for domestic students. Applications are processed on a rolling basis. Application fee: $30. *Financial support:* In 2007–08, 1 student received support. Federal Work-Study and scholarships/grants available. Financial award applicants required to submit FAFSA. *Faculty research:* Social class issues; clinical supervision; counselor education; play therapy. *Unit head:* Dr. Signe M. Kastberg, Director, 585-385-7222, E-mail: skastberg@sjfc.edu. *Application contact:* Holly Smith, Interim Director of Graduate Admissions, 585-385-8161, Fax: 585-385-8344, E-mail: hsmith@sjfc.edu.

Saint Joseph College, Graduate Division, Department of Counselor Education, West Hartford, CT 06117-2700. Offers community counseling (MA), including child welfare, pastoral counseling, school counseling; spirituality (Certificate). Part-time and evening/weekend programs available. *Degree requirements:* For master's, comprehensive exam, thesis optional, Capstone project. *Entrance requirements:* For master's, PRAXIS I (school counseling), 2 letters of recommendation. Electronic applications accepted.

Saint Martin's University, Graduate Programs, Program in Counseling Psychology, Lacey, WA 98503-1297. Offers MAC. Part-time and evening/weekend programs available. *Faculty:* 3 full-time (2 women), 3 part-time/adjunct (all women). *Students:* 40 full-time (29 women), 58 part-time (52 women); includes 14 minority (3 African Americans, 1 American Indian/Alaska Native, 6 Asian Americans or Pacific Islanders, 4 Hispanic Americans), 1 international. Average age 36. 24 applicants, 79% accepted, 18 enrolled. In 2007, 17 degrees awarded. *Degree requirements:* For master's, clinical experience, interview. *Entrance requirements:* For master's, BA in psychology or related field, clinical experience. Additional exam requirements/recommendations for international students: Required—TOEFL. *Application deadline:* For fall admission, 7/1 for domestic students, 2/15 for international students; for spring admission, 11/1 priority date for domestic students, 7/1 for international students. Applications are processed on a rolling basis. Application fee: $35. *Expenses:* Tuition: Part-time $742 per credit. Tuition and fees vary according to course level, campus/location and program. *Financial support:* In 2007–08, 97 students received support. Career-related internships or fieldwork, Federal Work-Study, and institutionally sponsored loans available. Support available to part-time students. Financial award application deadline: 3/1. *Faculty research:* Alcohol studies, clinical effectiveness, social justice, parent adolescent interaction. *Unit head:* Dr. Godfrey J. Ellis, Director, 360-438-4560, E-mail: gellis@stmartin.edu. *Application contact:* Sandy Brandt, Administrative Assistant, 360-438-4560, E-mail: sbrandt@stmartin.edu.

St. Mary's University, Graduate School, Department of Counseling and Human Services, Program in Mental Health, San Antonio, TX 78228-8507. Offers MA. *Students:* 13 full-time (10 women), 2 part-time (both women); includes 3 minority (all Hispanic Americans), 1 international. Average age 33. *Degree requirements:* For master's, thesis optional, internship. *Entrance requirements:* For master's, GRE. Additional exam requirements/recommendations for international students: Required—TOEFL (minimum score 550 paper-based; 213 computer-based). Application fee: $0. *Financial support:* Research assistantships available. Financial award application deadline: 3/31; financial award applicants required to submit FAFSA. *Unit head:* Dr. Ray Wooten, Director, 210-436-3226, Fax: 210-431-6886, E-mail: hrwooten@stmarytx.edu.

Saint Mary's University of Minnesota, Schools of Graduate and Professional Programs, Graduate School of Health and Human Services, Counseling and Psychological Services Program, Winona, MN 55987-1399. Offers MA. *Unit head:* Dr. Christina Huck, Director, 612-728-5113, Fax: 612-728-5121, E-mail: chuck@smumn.edu.

Saint Paul University, Faculty of Human Sciences, Program in Counseling and Spirituality, Ottawa, ON K1S 1C4, Canada. Offers individual or marital/couple counseling (MA); spiritual care (MA). Part-time programs available. *Students:* 57 applicants, 72% accepted, 32 enrolled. In 2007, 18 degrees awarded. *Degree requirements:* For master's, research project or thesis. *Entrance requirements:* For master's, honors BA in human sciences, minimum B average, 12 theology credits. *Application deadline:* For fall admission, 3/31 priority date for domestic and international students; for spring admission, 5/1 priority date for domestic students. Application fee: $60. *Unit head:* Manal Guirguis-Younger, Head, 613-236-1393 Ext. 2390, E-mail: jlowe@ustpaul.ca. *Application contact:* Diane Boudreault, Head, 613-236-1393 Ext. 2292, E-mail: dboudreault@ustpaul.ca.

St. Thomas University, Biscayne College, Department of Social Sciences and Counseling, Program in Mental Health Counseling, Miami Gardens, FL 33054-6459. Offers MS. Part-time and evening/weekend programs available. *Students:* 10 full-time (8 women), 28 part-time (26 women); includes 33 minority (14 African Americans, 19 Hispanic Americans), 1 international. Average age 34. In 2007, 6 degrees awarded. *Degree requirements:* For master's, comprehensive exam. *Entrance requirements:* For master's, interview, minimum GPA of 3.0 or GRE. Additional exam requirements/recommendations for international students: Required—TOEFL (minimum score 550 paper-based; 213 computer-based; 79 iBT). *Application deadline:* For fall admission, 6/15 priority date for domestic students; for spring admission, 11/15 for domestic students. Applications are processed on a rolling basis. Application fee: $40. Electronic applications accepted. *Financial support:* Career-related internships or fieldwork and unspecified assistantships available. Support available to part-time students. Financial award application deadline: 4/15; financial award applicants required to submit FAFSA. *Unit head:* Dr. Lawrence Rubin, Adviser, 305-628-6585, Fax: 305-628-6510, E-mail: lrubin@stu.edu. *Application contact:* Marilyn Carballosa, Assistant Director of Admissions, 305-628-6546, Fax: 305-628-6591, E-mail: graduate@stu.edu.

Saint Xavier University, Graduate Studies, School of Arts and Sciences, Department of Psychology, Chicago, IL 60655-3105. Offers adult counseling (Certificate); child/adolescent counseling (Certificate); core counseling (Certificate); counseling psychology (MA). Part-time and evening/weekend programs available. In 2007, 11 degrees awarded. *Entrance requirements:* For master's, GRE General Test, minimum GPA of 3.0, interview. *Application deadline:* For fall admission, 8/15 priority date for domestic students. Applications are processed on a rolling basis. Application fee: $35. *Financial support:* Career-related internships or fieldwork available. Support available to part-time students. Financial award applicants required to submit FAFSA. *Unit head:* Dr. Anthony Rotatori, Director, 773-298-3477, Fax: 773-779-9061. *Application contact:* Beth Gierach, Managing Director of Admission, 773-298-3053, Fax: 773-298-3076, E-mail: gierach@sxu.edu.

Salem State College, Graduate School, Program in Counseling and Psychological Services, Salem, MA 01970-5353. Offers MS. Part-time and evening/weekend programs available. *Faculty:* 8 part-time/adjunct (3 women). *Students:* 24 full-time (21 women), 33 part-time (29 women); includes 4 minority (1 African American, 1 Asian American or Pacific Islander, 2 Hispanic Americans), 2 international. Average age 33. In 2007, 15 degrees awarded. *Entrance requirements:* For master's, GRE General Test or MAT. *Application deadline:* Applications are processed on a rolling basis. Application fee: $35. *Unit head:* Dr. Patrice Miller, Coordinator, 978-542-6457, Fax: 978-542-6596, E-mail: pmiller@salemstate.edu.

Salve Regina University, Graduate Studies, Program in Holistic Counseling, Newport, RI 02840-4192. Offers expressive and creative arts (CAGS); holistic counseling (MA); mental health (CAGS). Part-time and evening/weekend programs available. *Degree requirements:* For master's, internship, project. *Entrance requirements:* For master's, GMAT, GRE General Test, or MAT. Additional exam requirements/recommendations for international students: Required—TOEFL or IELTS. Electronic applications accepted.

Salve Regina University, Graduate Studies, Program in Rehabilitation Counseling, Newport, RI 02840-4192. Offers mental health counseling (CAGS); rehabilitation counseling (MA). Part-time programs available. Postbaccalaureate distance learning degree programs offered. *Entrance requirements:* For master's, GMAT, GRE General Test or MAT. Additional exam requirements/recommendations for international students: Required—TOEFL or IELTS. Electronic applications accepted.

Counseling Psychology

San Francisco State University, Division of Graduate Studies, College of Health and Human Services, Department of Counseling, San Francisco, CA 94132-1722. Offers counseling (MS); marriage, family, and child counseling (MSC); rehabilitation counseling (MS). *Accreditation:* ACA (one or more programs are accredited). Part-time programs available. *Application deadline:* Applications are processed on a rolling basis. *Unit head:* Dr. Robert Chope, Chair, 415-338-2005. *Application contact:* Couryll Pineda, Academic Office Coordinator, 415-338-2005, E-mail: counsel@sfsu.edu.

Santa Clara University, School of Education, Counseling Psychology, and Pastoral Ministries, Santa Clara, CA 95053. Offers MA, Certificate. Part-time and evening/weekend programs available. *Faculty:* 30 full-time (12 women), 32 part-time/adjunct (19 women). *Students:* 153 full-time (137 women), 449 part-time (349 women); includes 155 minority (6 African Americans, 1 American Indian/Alaska Native, 65 Asian Americans or Pacific Islanders, 83 Hispanic Americans), 21 international. Average age 34. 333 applicants, 78% accepted, 209 enrolled. In 2007, 147 master's, 174 other advanced degrees awarded. *Degree requirements:* For master's and Certificate, comprehensive exam. *Entrance requirements:* Additional exam requirements/recommendations for international students: Required—TOEFL. *Application deadline:* Applications are processed on a rolling basis. Application fee: $50. *Expenses: Contact institution. Financial support:* Fellowships, teaching assistantships, career-related internships or fieldwork, Federal Work-Study, institutionally sponsored loans, and scholarships/grants available. Support available to part-time students. Financial award application deadline: 3/1; financial award applicants required to submit FAFSA. *Unit head:* Dr. Dale Larson, Interim Dean, 408-554-4320.

Santa Clara University, School of Education, Counseling Psychology, and Pastoral Ministries, Department of Counseling Psychology, Program in Counseling Psychology, Santa Clara, CA 95053. Offers MA. Part-time and evening/weekend programs available. *Students:* 89 full-time (82 women), 113 part-time (90 women); includes 55 minority (1 African American, 21 Asian Americans or Pacific Islanders, 33 Hispanic Americans), 6 international. Average age 32. 88 applicants, 72% accepted, 40 enrolled. In 2007, 59 degrees awarded. *Degree requirements:* For master's, comprehensive exam, thesis optional. *Entrance requirements:* For master's, GRE or MAT, minimum GPA of 3.0, 1 year of related experience. Additional exam requirements/recommendations for international students: Required—TOEFL. *Application deadline:* Applications are processed on a rolling basis. *Financial support:* Fellowships, teaching assistantships, career-related internships or fieldwork, Federal Work-Study, institutionally sponsored loans, and scholarships/grants available. Support available to part-time students. Financial award application deadline: 3/1; financial award applicants required to submit FAFSA.

Seton Hall University, College of Education and Human Services, Department of Professional Psychology and Family Therapy, Program in Counseling Psychology, South Orange, NJ 07079-2697. Offers MA, PhD. *Accreditation:* APA. *Faculty:* 5 full-time (1 woman). *Students:* 44 full-time (33 women), 104 part-time (86 women); includes 59 minority (41 African Americans, 2 American Indian/Alaska Native, 2 Asian Americans or Pacific Islanders, 14 Hispanic Americans), 7 international. Average age 31. 222 applicants, 92% accepted, 84 enrolled. In 2007, 61 master's, 7 doctorates awarded. *Degree requirements:* For doctorate, comprehensive exam, thesis/dissertation, internship. *Entrance requirements:* For doctorate, GRE, interview. *Application deadline:* For fall admission, 1/15 for domestic students. Application fee: $50. *Financial support:* In 2007–08, 1 research assistantship with full tuition reimbursement (averaging $4,500 per year) was awarded; career-related internships or fieldwork also available. Financial award application deadline: 2/1. *Faculty research:* Vocational indecision, coping skills, cognitive behavioral interventions, vocational development. *Application contact:* Information Contact, 973-761-9451.

Sonoma State University, School of Social Sciences, Department of Counseling, Rohnert Park, CA 94928-3609. Offers counseling (MA); marriage, family, and child counseling (MA); pupil personnel services (MA). *Accreditation:* ACA. Part-time programs available. *Faculty:* 6 full-time (4 women), 3 part-time/adjunct (2 women). *Students:* 86 full-time (66 women), 6 part-time (all women); includes 14 minority (3 African Americans, 2 American Indian/Alaska Native, 4 Asian Americans or Pacific Islanders, 5 Hispanic Americans). Average age 33. 111 applicants, 40% accepted, 40 enrolled. In 2007, 26 degrees awarded. *Degree requirements:* For master's, internship. *Entrance requirements:* For master's, minimum GPA of 3.0. *Application deadline:* For fall admission, 11/30 for domestic students. Application fee: $55. *Financial support:* Career-related internships or fieldwork available. Financial award application deadline: 3/2. *Faculty research:* Self-esteem, relationship of emotion and health, at-risk youth, feminist issues, supervision strategies. *Unit head:* Maureen Buckley, Chair, 707-664-2544, E-mail: maureen.buckley@sonoma.edu. *Application contact:* Stephanie Wilkinson, Administrative Analyst, 707-664-2544, Fax: 707-664-2038, E-mail: stephanie.wilkinson@sonoma.edu.

Southern Adventist University, School of Education and Psychology, Collegedale, TN 37315-0370. Offers curriculum and instruction (MS Ed); educational administration and supervision (MS Ed); inclusive education (MS Ed); literacy education (MS Ed); outdoor teacher education (MS Ed); professional counseling (MS); school counseling (MS). *Accreditation:* NCATE. Part-time and evening/weekend programs available. *Faculty:* 6 full-time (2 women), 2 part-time/adjunct (1 woman). *Students:* 27 full-time (21 women), 9 part-time (4 women); includes 14 minority (10 African Americans, 1 Asian American or Pacific Islander, 3 Hispanic Americans). Average age 30. 20 applicants, 85% accepted, 15 enrolled. In 2007, 23 degrees awarded. *Degree requirements:* For master's, comprehensive exam (for some programs), thesis optional, position paper (MS), portfolio (MS Ed in outdoor teacher education). *Entrance requirements:* For master's, GRE General Test, interview (MS); 9 semester hours of upper division course work in psychology or related field, including 1 course in psychology research or statistics; 9 semester hours of education (MS Ed). Additional exam requirements/recommendations for international students: Required—TOEFL (minimum score 600 paper-based; 250 computer-based; 100 iBT). *Application deadline:* For fall admission, 5/15 priority date for domestic and international students; for winter admission, 10/15 priority date for domestic and international students; for spring admission, 3/31 priority date for domestic and international students. Applications are processed on a rolling basis. Application fee: $25. Electronic applications accepted. *Financial support:* In 2007–08, 7 students received support, including 1 research assistantship with full tuition reimbursement available (averaging $10,000 per year), 5 teaching assistantships with full tuition reimbursements available (averaging $10,000 per year); career-related internships or fieldwork, scholarships/grants, tuition waivers (partial), and unspecified assistantships also available. Support available to part-time students. Financial award application deadline: 4/1; financial award applicants required to submit FAFSA. *Unit head:* Dr. Denise Dunzweiler, Dean, 423-236-2776, Fax: 423-236-1765, E-mail: denise@southern.edu. *Application contact:* Mikhaile Spence, Information Contact, 423-236-2496, Fax: 423-236-1765, E-mail: maspence@southern.edu.

Southern Arkansas University–Magnolia, Graduate Programs, Magnolia, AR 71753. Offers agriculture (MS); computer and information sciences (MS); counseling (MS); education (M Ed), including counseling and development, educational administration and supervision, elementary education, secondary education; kinesiology (MS); library media and information specialist (M Ed); public administration (EMPA); school counseling (M Ed); teaching (MAT). *Accreditation:* NCATE. Part-time and evening/weekend programs available. *Faculty:* 28 full-time (13 women), 6 part-time/adjunct (5 women). *Students:* 90 full-time (61 women), 254 part-time (195 women); includes 75 minority (74 African Americans, 1 Asian American or Pacific Islander), 14 international. Average age 34. In 2007, 77 degrees awarded. *Degree requirements:* For master's, comprehensive exam, thesis optional. *Entrance requirements:* For master's, GRE or MAT, minimum GPA of 2.75. *Application deadline:* Applications are processed on a rolling basis. Application fee: $0. *Expenses:* Tuition, state resident: full-time $3,348; part-time $186 per hour. Tuition, nonresident: full-time $4,734; part-time $263 per hour. Required fees: $438; $35 per hour. *Financial support:* Career-related internships or fieldwork, Federal Work-Study, scholarships/grants, tuition waivers (full), and unspecified assistantships available. Financial award applicants required to submit FAFSA. *Faculty research:* Alternative certification for teachers, supervision of instruction, instructional leadership, counseling. *Unit head:* Dr. Kim F. Shirey, Interim Dean, Graduate Studies, 870-235-4055, Fax: 870-235-5035, E-mail: kfshirey@saumag.edu.

Southern California Seminary, Graduate and Professional Programs, El Cajon, CA 92019. Offers biblical studies (MA); counseling psychology (MACP); psychology (Psy D); religious studies (MRS); theology (M Div). Part-time and evening/weekend programs available. Postbaccalaureate distance learning degree programs offered (minimal on-campus study). *Faculty:* 7 full-time (0 women), 17 part-time/adjunct (2 women). *Students:* 56 full-time (21 women), 68 part-time (30 women); includes 44 minority (24 African Americans, 2 Asian Americans or Pacific Islanders, 18 Hispanic Americans), 4 international. Average age 38. In 2007, 42 degrees awarded. *Degree requirements:* For master's, thesis (for some programs); for doctorate, thesis/dissertation; for M Div, 2 foreign languages. *Entrance requirements:* For doctorate, master's degree in psychology. Additional exam requirements/recommendations for international students: Required—TOEFL (minimum score 550 paper-based). *Application deadline:* For fall admission, 8/13 for domestic and international students; for spring admission, 12/11 for domestic students, 12/15 for international students. Applications are processed on a rolling basis. Application fee: $27 ($109 for international students). Electronic applications accepted. *Expenses:* Tuition: Part-time $290 per unit. Tuition and fees vary according to campus/location and program. *Financial support:* In 2007–08, 14 students received support. Federal Work-Study, scholarships/grants, and tuition waivers (partial) available. Financial award application deadline: 3/1; financial award applicants required to submit FAFSA. *Unit head:* Dr. Al Letting, Vice-President of Academics, 619-590-2131, E-mail: aletting@socalsem.edu. *Application contact:* Steve Perdue, Director of Admissions, 888-389-7244, E-mail: sperdue@socalsem.edu.

Southern Illinois University Carbondale, Graduate School, College of Liberal Arts, Department of Psychology, Carbondale, IL 62901-4701. Offers clinical psychology (MA, MS, PhD); counseling psychology (MA, MS, PhD); experimental psychology (MA, MS, PhD). *Accreditation:* APA (one or more programs are accredited). *Faculty:* 27 full-time (14 women), 1 part-time/adjunct (0 women). *Students:* 81 full-time (54 women), 43 part-time (32 women); includes 25 minority (13 African Americans, 1 American Indian/Alaska Native, 6 Asian Americans or Pacific Islanders, 5 Hispanic Americans), 13 international. 291 applicants, 9% accepted, 13 enrolled. In 2007, 17 master's, 15 doctorates awarded. *Degree requirements:* For master's, thesis; for doctorate, thesis/dissertation. *Entrance requirements:* For master's, GRE General Test, GRE Subject Test, minimum GPA of 2.7; for doctorate, GRE General Test, GRE Subject Test, minimum GPA of 3.25. Additional exam requirements/recommendations for international students: Required—TOEFL. *Application deadline:* For fall admission, 3/1 priority date for domestic students. Applications are processed on a rolling basis. Application fee: $20. *Financial support:* In 2007–08, 82 students received support, including 14 fellowships with full tuition reimbursements available, 23 research assistantships with full tuition reimbursements available, 22 teaching assistantships with full tuition reimbursements available; Federal Work-Study, institutionally sponsored loans, and tuition waivers (full) also available. *Faculty research:* Developmental neuropsychology; smoking, affect, and cognition; personality measurement; vocational psychology; program evaluation. *Unit head:* Dr. Jane Swanson, Chair, 618-453-3529, E-mail: swanson@siu.edu. *Application contact:* Connie Childers, Office Specialist, 618-453-3564, E-mail: childers@siu.edu.

See Close-Up on page 1479.

Southern Nazarene University, Graduate College, School of Psychology, Bethany, OK 73008. Offers counseling psychology (MSCP); marriage and family therapy (MA). *Degree requirements:* For master's, thesis optional. *Entrance requirements:* For master's, English proficiency exam, minimum GPA of 3.0 in last 60 hours/major, 2.7 overall.

South University, Graduate Programs, College of Arts and Sciences, Program in Professional Counseling, Savannah, GA 31406. Offers MA.

See Close-Up on page 1489.

South University, Program in Professional Counseling, Montgomery, AL 36116-1120. Offers MA.

See Close-Up on page 1487.

South University, Program in Professional Counseling, Columbia, SC 29203-6400. Offers MA.

See Close-Up on page 1485.

South University, Program in Professional Counseling, West Palm Beach, FL 33409. Offers MA.

See Close-Up on page 1491.

Southwestern Assemblies of God University, Thomas F. Harrison School of Graduate Studies, Program in Counseling Psychology, Waxahachie, TX 75165-5735. Offers MS, MS/MA. Part-time programs available. *Degree requirements:* For master's, comprehensive written and oral exams. *Entrance requirements:* For master's, GRE General Test, minimum GPA of 2.5. Electronic applications accepted.

Southwestern College, Program in Art Therapy/Counseling, Santa Fe, NM 87502-4788. Offers MA. Part-time and evening/weekend programs available. *Faculty:* 2 full-time (both women), 8 part-time/adjunct (all women). *Students:* 53 full-time (50 women), 17 part-time (all women); includes 2 African Americans, 1 American Indian/Alaska Native, 4 Hispanic Americans. Average age 31. 48 applicants, 44% accepted, 21 enrolled. In 2007, 16 degrees awarded. *Degree requirements:* For master's, internship. *Entrance requirements:* For master's, resumé, slide portfolio, interview, 3 letters of reference, personal statement of 3 pages. *Application deadline:* For fall admission, 6/1 priority date for domestic students; for winter admission, 10/15 priority date for domestic students; for spring admission, 1/30 priority date for domestic students. Applications are processed on a rolling basis. Application fee: $50. *Expenses:* Tuition: Full-time $16,416. *Financial support:* In 2007–08, 25 students received support. Career-related internships or fieldwork, institutionally sponsored loans, and scholarships/grants available. Support available to part-time students. Financial award application deadline: 6/1; financial award applicants required to submit FAFSA. *Unit head:* Debbie Schroder, Chair, 505-471-5756. *Application contact:* Dru Phoenix, Director of Admissions, 505-471-5756 Ext. 26, Fax: 505-471-4071, E-mail: admissions@swc.edu.

Southwestern College, Program in Counseling, Santa Fe, NM 87502-4788. Offers MA. Part-time and evening/weekend programs available. *Faculty:* 5 full-time (4 women), 20 part-time/adjunct (13 women). *Students:* 45 full-time (32 women), 15 part-time (11 women); includes 11 minority (1 African American, 3 American Indian/Alaska Native, 7 Hispanic Americans). Average age 37. 44 applicants, 39% accepted, 17 enrolled. In 2007, 17 degrees awarded. *Degree requirements:* For master's, internship. *Entrance requirements:* For master's, resumé, 3 letters of reference, interview, personal statement of 3 pages. *Application deadline:* For fall admission, 6/1 priority date for domestic students; for winter admission, 10/15 priority date for domestic students; for spring admission, 1/15 priority date for domestic students. Applications are processed on a rolling basis. Application fee: $50. *Expenses:* Tuition: Full-time $16,416. *Financial support:* In 2007–08, 46 students received support. Career-related internships or fieldwork, institutionally sponsored loans, and scholarships/grants available. Support available to part-time students. Financial award application deadline: 6/1; financial award applicants required to submit FAFSA. *Unit head:* Dr. Carol Parker, Chair, 877-471-5756 Ext. 13. *Application contact:* Dru Phoenix, Director of Admissions, 505-471-5756 Ext. 26, Fax: 505-471-4071, E-mail: admissions@swc.edu.

See Close-Up on page 1493.

Southwestern College, Program in Grief, Loss and Trauma Counseling, Santa Fe, NM 87502-4788. Offers MA, Certificate. Part-time and evening/weekend programs available. Postbaccalaureate distance learning degree programs offered (minimal on-campus study). *Faculty:* 1 (woman) full-time, 7 part-time/adjunct (4 women). *Students:* 12 full-time (9 women), 6 part-time (5 women); includes 1 American Indian/Alaska Native, 1 Asian American or Pacific

Islander, 1 Hispanic American. Average age 37. 12 applicants, 58% accepted, 6 enrolled. In 2007, 11 degrees awarded. *Entrance requirements:* For master's, personal statement of 3 pages, interview, references, resumé; for Certificate, 3 letters of reference, interview. *Application deadline:* For fall admission, 6/1 priority date for domestic students; for winter admission, 10/15 priority date for domestic students; for spring admission, 1/30 priority date for domestic students. Applications are processed on a rolling basis. Application fee: $50. *Expenses:* Tuition: Full-time $16,416. *Unit head:* Dr. Janet Schreiber, Director, Fax: 877-471-4071. *Application contact:* Dru Phoenix, Director of Admissions, 505-471-5756 Ext. 26, Fax: 505-471-4071, E-mail: admissions@swc.edu.

Spring Arbor University, School of Adult Studies, Spring Arbor, MI 49283-9799. Offers counseling (MAC); family studies (MAFS); organizational management (MAOM). Part-time and evening/weekend programs available. Postbaccalaureate distance learning degree programs offered (no on-campus study). *Faculty:* 4 full-time (2 women), 155 part-time/adjunct (72 women). *Students:* 691 full-time (557 women), 182 part-time (140 women); includes 210 minority (187 African Americans, 2 American Indian/Alaska Native, 7 Asian Americans or Pacific Islanders, 14 Hispanic Americans), 3 international. In 2007, 249 degrees awarded. *Entrance requirements:* For master's, minimum GPA of 3.0, interview, writing sample, 2 professional references. Additional exam requirements/recommendations for international students: Required—TOEFL (minimum score 550 paper-based; 220 computer-based). *Application deadline:* Applications are processed on a rolling basis. Application fee: $40. Electronic applications accepted. *Expenses:* Tuition: Full-time $4,560; part-time $380 per credit. Required fees: $75 per term. One-time fee: $40 part-time. Tuition and fees vary according to course load and program. *Financial support:* Scholarships/grants available. Support available to part-time students. Financial award applicants required to submit FAFSA. *Unit head:* Natalie Gianetti, Dean of Adult Studies, 517-750-1200 Ext. 1343, Fax: 517-750-6602, E-mail: gianetti@arbor.edu. *Application contact:* Dr. Carl Pavey, Director of Graduate Studies, 517-750-1200 Ext. 1653, Fax: 517-750-6602, E-mail: cpavey@arbor.edu.

Springfield College, Graduate Programs, Program in Human Services, Springfield, MA 01109-3797. Offers human services (MS), including community counseling psychology, mental health counseling, organizational management and leadership. Part-time and evening/weekend programs available. *Faculty:* 28 full-time (19 women), 74 part-time/adjunct (41 women). *Students:* 464; includes 339 minority (250 African Americans, 5 American Indian/Alaska Native, 5 Asian Americans or Pacific Islanders, 79 Hispanic Americans). Average age 39. 335 applicants, 53% accepted, 160 enrolled. In 2007, 245 degrees awarded. *Degree requirements:* For master's, project. *Entrance requirements:* Additional exam requirements/recommendations for international students: Required—TOEFL (minimum score 550 paper-based; 213 computer-based). *Application deadline:* For fall admission, 8/15 priority date for domestic students; for winter admission, 12/15 for domestic students; for spring admission, 4/15 priority date for domestic students. Applications are processed on a rolling basis. Application fee: $40. Electronic applications accepted. *Expenses: Contact institution.* Tuition and fees vary according to program. *Financial support:* Federal Work-Study and scholarships/grants available. Support available to part-time students. Financial award application deadline: 7/15. *Faculty research:* Social justice, organizational management and leadership, counseling, education and criminal justice. *Unit head:* Dr. Robert J. Willey, Dean, 413-748-3985, Fax: 413-748-3557, E-mail: rwilley@spfldcol.edu. *Application contact:* Joanna Marie Lenfest, Associate Director of Admissions, 413-748-3972, Fax: 413-748-3557, E-mail: jlenfest@spfldcol.edu.

Springfield College, Graduate Programs, Programs in Psychology and Counseling, Springfield, MA 01109-3797. Offers athletic counseling (M Ed, MS, CAGS); industrial/organizational psychology (M Ed, MS, CAGS); marriage and family therapy (M Ed, MS, CAGS); mental health counseling (M Ed, MS, CAGS); school guidance and counseling (M Ed, MS, CAGS); student personnel in higher education (M Ed, MS, CAGS). Part-time and evening/weekend programs available. *Faculty:* 14 full-time (8 women), 17 part-time/adjunct (7 women). *Students:* 157 full-time, 44 part-time. Average age 28. 220 applicants, 72% accepted, 97 enrolled. In 2007, 93 master's, 1 other advanced degree awarded. *Degree requirements:* For master's, comprehensive exam, thesis (for some programs), research project, internship. *Entrance requirements:* For master's and CAGS, interview. Additional exam requirements/recommendations for international students: Required—TOEFL (minimum score 550 paper-based; 213 computer-based). *Application deadline:* For fall admission, 1/15 priority date for domestic students; for winter admission, 11/1 for domestic students; for spring admission, 12/1 for domestic students. Applications are processed on a rolling basis. Application fee: $50. Electronic applications accepted. *Expenses:* Tuition: Full-time $12,942; part-time $719 per semester hour. Required fees: $25. Tuition and fees vary according to program. *Financial support:* In 2007–08, 8 fellowships with partial tuition reimbursements (averaging $2,000 per year), 2 research assistantships (averaging $4,000 per year), 7 teaching assistantships (averaging $1,800 per year) were awarded; career-related internships or fieldwork, Federal Work-Study, institutionally sponsored loans, scholarships/grants, and tuition waivers (full and partial) also available. Financial award application deadline: 3/1. *Faculty research:* Sport psychology, leadership and emotional intelligence, violence and terrorism, performance enhancement, cognitive function. Total annual research expenditures: $715,109. *Unit head:* Dr. Anna L. Moriarty, Director, 413-748-3322, Fax: 413-748-3854, E-mail: anna_l_moriarty@spfldcol.edu. *Application contact:* Donald James Shaw, Director of Graduate Admissions, 413-748-3060, Fax: 413-748-3069, E-mail: donald_shaw_jr@spfldcol.edu.

Stanford University, School of Education, Program in Psychological Studies in Education, Stanford, CA 94305-9991. Offers child and adolescent development (PhD); counseling psychology (PhD); educational psychology (PhD). *Degree requirements:* For doctorate, thesis/dissertation. *Entrance requirements:* For doctorate, GRE General Test. Electronic applications accepted.

State University of New York at New Paltz, Graduate School, Faculty of Liberal Arts and Sciences, Department of Psychology, New Paltz, NY 12561. Offers mental health counseling (MS); psychology (MA). Part-time and evening/weekend programs available. *Faculty:* 15 full-time (8 women), 7 part-time/adjunct (all women). *Students:* 26 full-time (21 women), 14 part-time (11 women); includes 2 minority (1 Asian American or Pacific Islander, 1 Hispanic American). Average age 27. In 2007, 11 degrees awarded. *Degree requirements:* For master's, comprehensive exam, thesis. *Entrance requirements:* For master's, GRE General Test, minimum GPA of 3.0. Additional exam requirements/recommendations for international students: Required—TOEFL (minimum score 550 paper-based; 213 computer-based; 80 iBT). *Application deadline:* For fall admission, 3/15 priority date for domestic students, 3/15 for international students; for spring admission, 11/15 for domestic and international students. Application fee: $50. Electronic applications accepted. *Expenses:* Tuition, state resident: full-time $6,900; part-time $288 per credit hour. Tuition, nonresident: full-time $10,920; part-time $455 per credit hour. Required fees: $1,040; $30 per credit hour. $153 per credit hour. Tuition and fees vary according to program. *Financial support:* In 2007–08, 5 students received support, including 5 teaching assistantships with partial tuition reimbursements available (averaging $5,000 per year); career-related internships or fieldwork, Federal Work-Study, and institutionally sponsored loans also available. *Faculty research:* Industrial/Organizational Psychology, Disaster Mental Health, Human Cognition, Gender Socialization, Defense Mechanisms. *Unit head:* Dr. Douglas Maynard, Chair, 845-257-3426, E-mail: maynardd@newpaltz.edu. *Application contact:* Dr. Jonathan Raskin, Coordinator, 845-257-3471, E-mail: raskinj@newpaltz.edu.

State University of New York at Oswego, Graduate Studies, School of Education, Department of Counseling and Psychological Services, Program in Counseling Services, Oswego, NY 13126. Offers MS, CAS, MS/CAS. *Faculty:* 6 full-time, 8 part-time/adjunct. *Students:* 23 full-time (19 women), 18 part-time (15 women); includes 1 minority (African American) Average age 31. 46 applicants, 63% accepted. In 2007, 18 master's, 3 other advanced degrees awarded. *Degree requirements:* For master's, comprehensive exam, fieldwork; for CAS, thesis, fieldwork. *Entrance requirements:* For master's, GRE General Test, interview, minimum GPA of 3.0; for CAS, GRE General Test, GRE Subject Test, 18 hours of course work in behavioral science or education, interview, minimum GPA of 3.0. Additional exam requirements/recommendations for international students: Required—TOEFL (minimum score 560 paper-based; 220 computer-based). *Application deadline:* For fall admission, 2/1 for domestic students. Application fee: $50. *Expenses:* Tuition, state resident: full-time $6,900; part-time $288 per credit. Tuition, nonresident: full-time $10,920; part-time $455 per credit. Required fees: $607; $32 per credit. $225 per term. Tuition and fees vary according to degree level. *Financial support:* Teaching assistantships with partial tuition reimbursements, career-related internships or fieldwork, Federal Work-Study, institutionally sponsored loans, and scholarships/grants available. Support available to part-time students. Financial award application deadline: 4/1; financial award applicants required to submit FAFSA. *Faculty research:* Psychological applications in education and human services, evaluation of standard tests for admissions criteria. *Unit head:* Michael LeBlanc, Coordinator, 315-312-3494.

State University of New York at Oswego, Graduate Studies, School of Education, Department of Counseling and Psychological Services, Program in Human Services/Counseling, Oswego, NY 13126. Offers MS. Part-time programs available. *Faculty:* 6 full-time, 8 part-time/adjunct. *Students:* 27 full-time (25 women), 11 part-time (4 women); includes 2 minority (both Hispanic Americans), 1 international. Average age 31. 21 applicants, 100% accepted. In 2007, 15 degrees awarded. *Degree requirements:* For master's, comprehensive exam. *Entrance requirements:* For master's, GRE General Test, interview, minimum GPA of 3.0. Additional exam requirements/recommendations for international students: Required—TOEFL (minimum score 560 paper-based; 220 computer-based). *Application deadline:* For fall admission, 2/1 for domestic students. Application fee: $50. *Expenses:* Tuition, state resident: full-time $6,900; part-time $288 per credit. Tuition, nonresident: full-time $10,920; part-time $455 per credit. Required fees: $607; $32 per credit. $225 per term. Tuition and fees vary according to degree level. *Financial support:* Career-related internships or fieldwork, Federal Work-Study, institutionally sponsored loans, and scholarships/grants available. Support available to part-time students. Financial award application deadline: 4/1; financial award applicants required to submit FAFSA. *Unit head:* Jodi Mullen, Coordinator, 315-312-3234.

Tarleton State University, College of Graduate Studies, College of Education, Department of Psychology and Counseling, Stephenville, TX 76402. Offers counseling and psychology (M Ed), including counseling, counseling psychology, educational psychology; educational administration (M Ed); secondary education (Certificate); special education (Certificate). Part-time and evening/weekend programs available. Postbaccalaureate distance learning degree programs offered (minimal on-campus study). *Faculty:* 14 full-time (6 women), 7 part-time/adjunct (3 women). *Students:* 52 full-time (43 women), 223 part-time (199 women); includes 64 minority (49 African Americans, 1 American Indian/Alaska Native, 2 Asian Americans or Pacific Islanders, 12 Hispanic Americans). Average age 37. 127 applicants, 86% accepted, 71 enrolled. In 2007, 53 degrees awarded. *Degree requirements:* For master's, comprehensive exam, thesis optional. *Entrance requirements:* For master's, GRE General Test, minimum GPA of 3.0. Additional exam requirements/recommendations for international students: Required—TOEFL (minimum score 550 paper-based; 213 computer-based). *Application deadline:* For fall admission, 8/5 priority date for domestic students; for spring admission, 12/1 for domestic students. Applications are processed on a rolling basis. Application fee: $25 ($125 for international students). Electronic applications accepted. *Expenses:* Tuition, state resident: full-time $2,520; part-time $140 per credit hour. Tuition, nonresident: full-time $7,344; part-time $408 per credit hour. Required fees: $948; $39 per credit hour. *Financial support:* Research assistantships, teaching assistantships, career-related internships or fieldwork, Federal Work-Study, institutionally sponsored loans, and tuition waivers (partial) available. Support available to part-time students. Financial award application deadline: 5/1; financial award applicants required to submit FAFSA. *Unit head:* Dr. Robert Newby, Head, 254-968-9945, Fax: 254-968-1991, E-mail: newby@tarleton.edu.

Teachers College, Columbia University, Graduate Faculty of Education, Department of Counseling and Clinical Psychology, Program in Counseling Psychology, New York, NY 10027-6696. Offers Ed M, Ed D, PhD. *Accreditation:* APA (one or more programs are accredited). Part-time programs available. *Faculty:* 7 full-time (4 women). *Students:* 163 full-time (140 women), 71 part-time (60 women); includes 80 minority (33 African Americans, 24 Asian Americans or Pacific Islanders, 23 Hispanic Americans), 21 international. Average age 27. 424 applicants, 47% accepted, 87 enrolled. In 2007, 172 master's, 3 doctorates awarded. *Degree requirements:* For doctorate, thesis/dissertation. *Entrance requirements:* For doctorate, GRE General Test. *Application deadline:* For fall admission, 5/15 for domestic students. Application fee: $70. *Financial support:* Fellowships, research assistantships, teaching assistantships, career-related internships or fieldwork, Federal Work-Study, institutionally sponsored loans, and tuition waivers (full and partial) available. Support available to part-time students. Financial award application deadline: 2/1. *Faculty research:* Career development, mentoring racial identity, adult development, gender issues. *Application contact:* Melba Remice, Assistant Director of Admission, 212-678-4035, Fax: 212-678-4171, E-mail: ms2545@columbia.edu.

See Close-Up on page 1501.

Temple University, Graduate School, College of Education, Department of Psychological Studies in Education, Counseling Psychology Program, Philadelphia, PA 19122-6096. Offers Ed M, PhD. *Accreditation:* APA (one or more programs are accredited). Part-time programs available. Terminal master's awarded for partial completion of doctoral program. *Degree requirements:* For master's, thesis or alternative; for doctorate, thesis/dissertation. *Entrance requirements:* For master's, GRE General Test or MAT, minimum GPA of 2.8; for doctorate, GRE General Test, GRE Subject Test in psychology. *Faculty research:* Multi-cultural and diversity training, health psychology/supervision/addictions.

Tennessee State University, The School of Graduate Studies and Research, College of Education, Department of Psychology, Nashville, TN 37209-1561. Offers counseling and guidance (MS), including counseling, elementary school counseling, organizational counseling, secondary school counseling; counseling psychology (PhD); psychology (MS, PhD); school psychology (MS, PhD). *Accreditation:* APA. *Faculty:* 15 full-time (9 women), 1 (woman) part-time/adjunct. *Students:* 91 full-time (74 women), 114 part-time (91 women); includes 141 minority (136 African Americans, 1 American Indian/Alaska Native, 3 Asian Americans or Pacific Islanders, 1 Hispanic American), 2 international. Average age 33. 205 applicants, 45% accepted, 44 enrolled. In 2007, 17 master's, 10 doctorates awarded. *Degree requirements:* For doctorate, thesis/dissertation (for some programs). *Entrance requirements:* For master's, GRE General Test or MAT; for doctorate, GRE General Test or MAT, minimum GPA of 3.25, work experience. Application fee: $25. *Expenses:* Tuition, state resident: full-time $6,271; part-time $490 per hour. Tuition, nonresident: full-time $16,550; part-time $936 per hour. *Unit head:* Dr. Linda Guthrie, Head, 615-963-2920, Fax: 615-963-5140, E-mail: lguthrie@tnstate.edu.

Texas A&M International University, Office of Graduate Studies and Research, College of Arts and Sciences, Department of Behavioral, Applied Sciences, and Criminal Justice, Laredo, TX 78041-1900. Offers counseling psychology (MACP); criminal justice (MS); psychology (MS); sociology (MA). *Faculty:* 10 full-time (5 women), 1 (woman) part-time/adjunct. *Students:* 14 full-time (11 women), 68 part-time (40 women); includes 76 minority (1 Asian American or Pacific Islander, 75 Hispanic Americans), 2 international. Average age 30. 40 applicants, 88% accepted, 21 enrolled. In 2007, 24 degrees awarded. *Degree requirements:* For master's, thesis (for some programs). *Entrance requirements:* For master's, GRE General Test. Additional exam requirements/recommendations for international students: Required—TOEFL (minimum score 550 paper-based; 213 computer-based). *Application deadline:* For fall admission, 7/15 priority date for domestic students; for spring admission, 11/12 for domestic students. Applications are processed on a rolling basis. Application fee: $25. *Financial support:* In 2007–08, 44 students received support. Application deadline: 11/1. *Unit head:* Dr. John Kilburn, Chair, 956-326-2667, Fax: 956-326-2459, E-mail: jkilburn@tamiu.edu. *Application contact:* Rosie Espinoza-Dickinson, Director of Admissions, 956-326-2200, Fax: 956-326-2199, E-mail: enroll@tamiu.edu.

Counseling Psychology

Texas A&M University, College of Education and Human Development, Department of Educational Psychology, College Station, TX 77843. Offers counseling psychology (PhD); educational psychology (PhD); educational technology (M Ed); gifted and talented education (M Ed, MS); Hispanic bilingual education (M Ed, PhD); human learning and development (MS); intelligence, creativity, and giftedness (PhD); learning, development, and instruction (PhD); research, measurement and statistics (MS); research, measurement, and statistics (PhD); school counseling (M Ed); school psychology (PhD); special education (M Ed, PhD). *Accreditation:* APA (one or more programs are accredited); NCATE. Part-time and evening/weekend programs available. Postbaccalaureate distance learning degree programs offered (no on-campus study). *Faculty:* 43. *Students:* 140 full-time (109 women), 153 part-time (129 women); includes 77 minority (27 African Americans, 1 American Indian/Alaska Native, 7 Asian Americans or Pacific Islanders, 42 Hispanic Americans), 41 international. 222 applicants, 61% accepted, 90 enrolled. In 2007, 42 master's, 24 doctorates awarded. *Median time to degree:* Of those who began their doctoral program in fall 1999, 89% received their degree in 8 years or less. *Degree requirements:* For master's, thesis optional; for doctorate, thesis/dissertation. *Entrance requirements:* For master's and doctorate, GRE General Test. Additional exam requirements/recommendations for international students: Required—TOEFL. Application fee: $50 ($75 for international students). Electronic applications accepted. *Expenses:* Tuition, state resident: full-time $6,129. Tuition, nonresident: full-time $11,689. Tuition and fees vary according to course load. *Financial support:* In 2007–08, fellowships (averaging $12,000 per year), research assistantships (averaging $9,000 per year), teaching assistantships (averaging $9,000 per year) were awarded; career-related internships or fieldwork, institutionally sponsored loans, scholarships/grants, and unspecified assistantships also available. Financial award applicants required to submit FAFSA. *Unit head:* Dr. Michael R. Benz, Head, 979-845-1394, Fax: 979-862-1256, E-mail: mbanz@tamu.edu. *Application contact:* Carol A. Wagner, Director of Advising, 979-845-1833, Fax: 979-862-1256, E-mail: c-wagner@tamu.edu.

Texas A&M University–Commerce, Graduate School, College of Education and Human Services, Department of Counseling, Commerce, TX 75429-3011. Offers M Ed, MS, PhD. *Accreditation:* ACA (one or more programs are accredited). Part-time programs available. *Faculty:* 13 full-time (5 women), 4 part-time/adjunct (3 women). *Students:* 43 full-time (35 women), 208 part-time (180 women); includes 61 minority (42 African Americans, 1 American Indian/Alaska Native, 2 Asian Americans or Pacific Islanders, 16 Hispanic Americans), 5 international. Average age 36. In 2007, 27 master's, 4 doctorates awarded. Terminal master's awarded for partial completion of doctoral program. *Degree requirements:* For master's, comprehensive exam, thesis (for some programs); for doctorate, thesis/dissertation, departmental qualifying exam. *Entrance requirements:* For master's and doctorate, GRE General Test. *Application deadline:* For fall admission, 6/1 priority date for domestic students; for spring admission, 11/1 priority date for domestic students. Applications are processed on a rolling basis. Application fee: $0 ($25 for international students). *Financial support:* In 2007–08, research assistantships (averaging $7,875 per year), teaching assistantships (averaging $7,875 per year) were awarded; Federal Work-Study, institutionally sponsored loans, and scholarships/grants also available. Financial award application deadline: 5/1; financial award applicants required to submit FAFSA. *Faculty research:* Emergency responders, efficacy and effect of web-based instruction, family violence, play therapy. *Unit head:* Dr. Stephen J. Freeman, Chair, 903-886-5637. *Application contact:* Tammi Thompson, Graduate Admissions Adviser, 843-886-5167, Fax: 843-886-5165, E-mail: tammi_thompson@tamu-commerce.edu.

Texas A&M University–Texarkana, Graduate Studies and Research, College of Health and Behavioral Sciences, Texarkana, TX 75505-5518. Offers counseling psychology (MS). Part-time and evening/weekend programs available. *Degree requirements:* For master's, comprehensive exam (for some programs), thesis or alternative. *Entrance requirements:* For master's, minimum GPA of 3.0 in last 60 hours of bachelor's degree. Additional exam requirements/recommendations for international students: Required—TOEFL. Electronic applications accepted.

Texas Tech University, Graduate School, College of Arts and Sciences, Department of Psychology, Lubbock, TX 79409. Offers clinical psychology (PhD); counseling psychology (MA, PhD); experimental psychology (MA, PhD); psychology (MA, PhD). *Accreditation:* APA (one or more programs are accredited). Part-time programs available. *Faculty:* 25 full-time (11 women). *Students:* 91 full-time (59 women), 11 part-time (8 women); includes 16 minority (6 African Americans, 2 Asian Americans or Pacific Islanders, 8 Hispanic Americans), 4 international. Average age 28. 264 applicants, 10% accepted, 17 enrolled. In 2007, 15 master's, 16 doctorates awarded. *Degree requirements:* For doctorate, thesis/dissertation. *Entrance requirements:* For master's and doctorate, GRE General Test, GRE Subject Test. Additional exam requirements/recommendations for international students: Required—TOEFL (minimum score 550 paper-based; 213 computer-based). *Application deadline:* For fall admission, 3/1 priority date for international students; for spring admission, 11/1 priority date for international students. Applications are processed on a rolling basis. Application fee: $50 ($60 for international students). Electronic applications accepted. *Expenses:* Tuition, state resident: part-time $373 per credit hour. Tuition, nonresident: part-time $651 per credit hour. Tuition and fees vary according to program. *Financial support:* In 2007–08, 99 students received support, including 8 research assistantships with partial tuition reimbursements available (averaging $11,462 per year), 64 teaching assistantships with partial tuition reimbursements available (averaging $11,759 per year); career-related internships or fieldwork, Federal Work-Study, and institutionally sponsored loans also available. Support available to part-time students. Financial award application deadline: 4/15; financial award applicants required to submit FAFSA. *Faculty research:* Failure/success in relationships, peer rejection in school, stress and coping, group processes, clinical and health psychology. Total annual research expenditures: $459,933. *Unit head:* Dr. M. David Rudd, Chair, 806-742-3711 Ext. 224, Fax: 806-742-0818, E-mail: david.rudd@ttu.edu. *Application contact:* Dr. Steve Richards, Graduate Advisor, 806-742-3711 Ext. 254, Fax: 806-742-0818, E-mail: steven.richards@ttu.edu.

Texas Wesleyan University, Graduate Programs, Programs in Education, Fort Worth, TX 76105-1536. Offers education (M Ed); professional counseling (MA); psychology (MSP); school counseling (MS). Part-time and evening/weekend programs available. Postbaccalaureate distance learning degree programs offered (no on-campus study). *Faculty:* 37 full-time (11 women), 40 part-time/adjunct (13 women). *Students:* 58 full-time (46 women), 171 part-time (146 women); includes 69 minority (38 African Americans, 1 American Indian/Alaska Native, 2 Asian Americans or Pacific Islanders, 28 Hispanic Americans). Average age 34. In 2007, 52 degrees awarded. *Entrance requirements:* For master's, GRE General Test, minimum GPA of 3.0 in final 60 hours of undergraduate course work, interview, essay. *Application deadline:* For fall admission, 6/15 priority date for domestic students; for spring admission, 10/15 priority date for domestic students. Applications are processed on a rolling basis. Application fee: $40 ($50 for international students). *Expenses:* Tuition: Full-time $4,500; part-time $500 per credit hour. Required fees: $56 per credit hour. Tuition and fees vary according to degree level and program. *Financial support:* Career-related internships or fieldwork, Federal Work-Study, scholarships/grants, and tuition waivers (full and partial) available. Support available to part-time students. Financial award application deadline: 3/15; financial award applicants required to submit FAFSA. *Faculty research:* Teacher effectiveness, bilingual education, analytic teaching. *Unit head:* Dr. Carlos Martinez, Dean, School of Education, 817-531-4940, Fax: 817-531-4943. *Application contact:* DeTrae Warren, Graduate Admission Recruiter, 817-531-4931, Fax: 817-531-4935, E-mail: dwarren@txwes.edu.

Texas Woman's University, Graduate School, College of Arts and Sciences, Department of Psychology and Philosophy, Denton, TX 76201. Offers counseling psychology (MA, PhD); school psychology (PhD, SSP). *Accreditation:* APA (one or more programs are accredited). *Students:* 74 full-time (66 women), 50 part-time (46 women); includes 22 minority (7 African Americans, 7 Asian Americans or Pacific Islanders, 8 Hispanic Americans), 3 international. Average age 29. In 2007, 18 master's, 5 doctorates awarded. Terminal master's awarded for partial completion of doctoral program. *Median time to degree:* Of those who began their doctoral program in fall 1999, 25% received their degree in 8 years or less. *Degree requirements:* For master's, thesis; for doctorate, comprehensive exam, thesis/dissertation, internship, residency. *Entrance requirements:* For master's, 2 letters of reference, resumé, interview; for doctorate, 3 letters of reference; resumé; interview; minimum overall GPA of 3.0, 3.5 for all undergraduate psychology courses; autobiographical statement; BS/BA in psychology or 18 hours of required psychology classes. Additional exam requirements/recommendations for international students: Required—TOEFL (minimum score 550 paper-based; 213 computer-based; 79 iBT). *Application deadline:* For fall admission, 12/15 for domestic and international students. Applications are processed on a rolling basis. Application fee: $30 ($50 for international students). Electronic applications accepted. *Expenses:* Tuition, state resident: full-time $3,294; part-time $183 per credit. Tuition, nonresident: full-time $8,298; part-time $461 per credit. Required fees: $985; $55 per credit. Tuition and fees vary according to degree level. *Financial support:* In 2007–08, 1 teaching assistantship (averaging $10,746 per year) was awarded; career-related internships or fieldwork, Federal Work-Study, institutionally sponsored loans, scholarships/grants, traineeships, health care benefits, and unspecified assistantships also available. Support available to part-time students. Financial award application deadline: 3/1; financial award applicants required to submit FAFSA. *Faculty research:* Women's anger, pre-school assessments, body image dysfunction, traumatic stress, classical ethics. *Unit head:* Dr. Dan Miller, Chair, 940-898-2303, Fax: 940-898-2301, E-mail: dmiller@twu.edu. *Application contact:* Samuel Wheeler, Assistant Director of Admissions, 940-898-3188, Fax: 940-898-3081, E-mail: wheelersr@twu.edu.

Towson University, College of Graduate Studies and Research, Program in Counseling Psychology, Towson, MD 21252-0001. Offers CAS. Part-time and evening/weekend programs available. *Students:* 1 (woman) full-time, 14 part-time (11 women); includes 3 minority (all African Americans), 1 international. Average age 43. 289 applicants, 31% accepted. Application fee: $50. *Expenses:* Tuition, state resident: part-time $286 per credit. Tuition, nonresident: part-time $600 per credit. Required fees: $75 per credit. *Financial support:* Application deadline: 4/1. *Unit head:* Julie Quimby, Graduate Program Director, 410-704-3063, E-mail: jquimby@towson.edu. *Application contact:* The Graduate School, 410-704-2501, Fax: 410-704-4675, E-mail: grads@towson.edu.

Trevecca Nazarene University, Graduate Division, Graduate Psychology Programs, Major in Counseling Psychology, Nashville, TN 37210-2877. Offers MA. Part-time and evening/weekend programs available. *Students:* 24 full-time (13 women); includes 5 minority (4 African Americans, 1 Hispanic American). In 2007, 3 degrees awarded. *Degree requirements:* For master's, comprehensive exam, thesis, practicum. *Entrance requirements:* For master's, GRE General Test or MAT, minimum GPA of 2.7, 2 reference assessment forms. Additional exam requirements/recommendations for international students: Required—TOEFL (minimum score 500 paper-based; 173 computer-based). *Application deadline:* Applications are processed on a rolling basis. Application fee: $25. *Expenses: Contact institution.* Tuition and fees vary according to degree level and program. *Financial support:* Applicants required to submit FAFSA. *Application contact:* Heather Ambrefe, Department Secretary, 615-248-1384, Fax: 615-248-1662, E-mail: admissions_psy@trevecca.edu.

Trinity International University, Trinity Evangelical Divinity School, Deerfield, IL 60015-1284. Offers Biblical and Near Eastern archaeology and languages (MA); Christian studies (MA, Certificate); Christian thought (MA); church history (MA, Th M); congregational ministry: pastor-teacher (M Div); congregational ministry: team ministry (M Div); counseling ministries (MA); counseling psychology (MA); cross-cultural ministry (M Div); educational studies (PhD); evangelism (MA); history of Christianity in America (MA); intercultural studies (MA, PhD); leadership and ministry management (D Min); military chaplaincy (D Min); ministry (MA); mission and evangelism (Th M); missions and evangelism (D Min); New Testament (MA, Th M); Old Testament (Th M); Old Testament and Semitic languages (MA); pastoral care (M Div); pastoral care and counseling (D Min); pastoral counseling and psychology (Th M); pastoral theology (Th M); philosophy of religion (MA); preaching (D Min); religion (MA); research ministry (M Div); systematic theology (Th M); theological studies (PhD); urban ministry (MA). *Accreditation:* ATS (one or more programs are accredited). Part-time programs available. Postbaccalaureate distance learning degree programs offered (minimal on-campus study). *Faculty:* 41 full-time (4 women), 77 part-time/adjunct (17 women). *Students:* 578 full-time (141 women), 711 part-time (202 women). In 2007, 92 first professional degrees, 78 master's, 47 doctorates, 23 other advanced degrees awarded. *Degree requirements:* For master's, comprehensive exam, thesis, fieldwork; for doctorate, comprehensive exam (for some programs), thesis/dissertation; for M Div, 2 foreign languages, fieldwork; for Certificate, comprehensive exam, integrative papers. *Entrance requirements:* For M Div, GRE, MAT; for master's, GRE, MAT, minimum cumulative undergraduate GPA of 3.0; for doctorate, GRE, minimum cumulative graduate GPA of 3.2; for Certificate, GRE, MAT, minimum undergraduate GPA of 2.5. Additional exam requirements/recommendations for international students: Required—TOEFL (minimum score 580 paper-based; 237 computer-based), TWE (minimum score 4). *Application deadline:* For fall admission, 7/15 priority date for domestic and international students. Applications are processed on a rolling basis. Application fee: $25. Electronic applications accepted. *Expenses:* Tuition: Full-time $13,200; part-time $630 per credit. Required fees: $170. *Financial support:* In 2007–08, 770 students received support, including 10 fellowships with partial tuition reimbursements available (averaging $6,920 per year); teaching assistantships with partial tuition reimbursements available, career-related internships or fieldwork, Federal Work-Study, scholarships/grants, and tuition waivers (partial) also available. Financial award application deadline: 4/1; financial award applicants required to submit FAFSA. *Unit head:* Dr. Tite Tiénou, Academic Dean, 847-317-8086, Fax: 847-317-8014, E-mail: ttienou@teds.edu. *Application contact:* Ron Campbell, Director of Admissions, 800-345-8337, Fax: 847-317-8097, E-mail: rcampbel@tiu.edu.

Trinity International University, Trinity Graduate School, Deerfield, IL 60015-1284. Offers bioethics (MA); communication and culture (MA); counseling psychology (MA); instructional leadership (M Ed); teaching (MA). Part-time and evening/weekend programs available. Postbaccalaureate distance learning degree programs offered (minimal on-campus study). *Faculty:* 4 full-time (3 women), 34 part-time/adjunct (12 women). *Students:* 92 full-time (71 women), 91 part-time (52 women). In 2007, 55 degrees awarded. *Degree requirements:* For master's, comprehensive exam. *Entrance requirements:* For master's, GRE General Test or MAT, minimum undergraduate GPA of 3.0. Additional exam requirements/recommendations for international students: Required—TOEFL (minimum score 580 paper-based; 237 computer-based), TWE (minimum score 4). *Application deadline:* For fall admission, 7/15 priority date for domestic and international students. Applications are processed on a rolling basis. Application fee: $25. Electronic applications accepted. *Expenses:* Tuition: Full-time $13,200; part-time $630 per credit. Required fees: $170. *Financial support:* Career-related internships or fieldwork, Federal Work-Study, institutionally sponsored loans, and tuition waivers (partial) available. Support available to part-time students. Financial award application deadline: 4/1; financial award applicants required to submit FAFSA. *Unit head:* Dr. James Stamoolis, Academic Dean, 847-317-7001, Fax: 847-317-4786. *Application contact:* Ken Botton, Director of Enrollment Services for University Records and Graduate Admissions, 800-533-0975, Fax: 847-317-8097, E-mail: kbotton@tiu.edu.

Trinity International University, South Florida Campus, Program in Counseling Psychology, Miami, FL 33132-1996. Offers MA.

Trinity Western University, Faculty of Graduate Studies, Program in Counseling Psychology, Langley, BC V2Y 1Y1, Canada. Offers MA. *Accreditation:* ACA. Part-time programs available. *Faculty:* 4 full-time (0 women), 9 part-time/adjunct (5 women). *Students:* 55 full-time (43 women), 14 part-time (all women). Average age 27. 34 applicants, 62% accepted, 17 enrolled. In 2007, 25 degrees awarded. *Degree requirements:* For master's, comprehensive exam, thesis. *Entrance requirements:* For master's, GRE if out of school for 5 years prior to applying, BA in honors psychology; 3.0 GPA for 3rd and 4th year of BA. Additional exam requirements/recommendations for international students: Required—TOEFL (minimum score 600 paper-based; 250 computer-based). *Application deadline:* For fall admission, 2/15 priority date for domestic and international students; for spring admission, 10/15 priority date for domestic and international students. Application fee: $0 Canadian dollars. *Financial support:* Research assistantships, teaching assistantships available. Financial award application deadline: 2/28.

Faculty research: Meaning, group counseling, trauma, counseling supervision. *Unit head:* Dr. Marvin McDonald, Director, 604-888-7511 Ext. 3223, Fax: 604-513-2010, E-mail: mcdonald@twu.edu. *Application contact:* Vic Cornish, Director, Graduate Admissions, 604-888-7511 Ext. 3130, Fax: 604-513-2064, E-mail: vic.cornish@twu.edu.

Union Institute & University, Program in Psychology and Counseling, Cincinnati, OH 45206-1925. Offers MA. *Expenses:* Tuition: Full-time $20,176; part-time $760 per credit hour. Tuition and fees vary according to course load, degree level and program. *Unit head:* Dr. Nicholas Young, Director, 802-257-8911.

United States International University, School of Arts and Sciences, Nairobi, Kenya. Offers counseling psychology (MA); international relations (MA). Part-time and evening/weekend programs available. *Degree requirements:* For master's, thesis, practicum. *Entrance requirements:* For master's, GRE General Test, 2 letters of recommendation, resumé. Additional exam requirements/recommendations for international students: Required—TOEFL (minimum score 550 paper-based; 213 computer-based). *Faculty research:* Trauma in children, African intellectualism, psychological assessment tools.

Universidad del Turabo, Graduate Programs, School of Social Sciences and Humanities, Programs in Psychology, Program in Counseling Psychology, Gurabo, PR 00778-3030. Offers MSS. *Students:* 134 full-time (107 women), 119 part-time (92 women); all Hispanic Americans Average age 32. In 2007, 33 degrees awarded. *Expenses:* Tuition: Full-time $5,560.

University at Albany, State University of New York, School of Education, Department of Educational and Counseling Psychology, Albany, NY 12222-0001. Offers counseling psychology (MS, PhD, CAS); educational psychology (Ed D); educational psychology and statistics (MS); measurements and evaluation (Ed D); rehabilitation counseling (MS), including counseling psychology; school counselor (CAS); school psychology (Psy D, CAS); special education (MS); statistics and research design (Ed D). *Accreditation:* APA (one or more programs are accredited). Evening/weekend programs available. *Students:* 121 full-time (101 women), 79 part-time (61 women). Average age 28. In 2007, 86 master's, 13 doctorates, 13 other advanced degrees awarded. *Degree requirements:* For doctorate, thesis/dissertation. *Entrance requirements:* For doctorate, GRE General Test. Additional exam requirements/recommendations for international students: Required—TOEFL (minimum score 550 paper-based; 213 computer-based). Application fee: $75. Electronic applications accepted. *Expenses:* Tuition, state resident: part-time $576 per credit. Tuition, nonresident: part-time $910 per credit. Tuition and fees vary according to program. *Financial support:* Fellowships, career-related internships or fieldwork available. *Unit head:* Kevin Quinn, Chair, 518-442-5050.

University at Buffalo, the State University of New York, Graduate School, Graduate School of Education, Department of Counseling, School, and Educational Psychology, Buffalo, NY 14260. Offers counseling/school psychology (PhD); counselor education (PhD); educational psychology (MA, PhD); mental health counseling (MS); rehabilitation counseling (MS); school counseling (Ed M, Certificate); school psychology (MA). *Accreditation:* CORE (one or more programs are accredited). *Degree requirements:* For master's, comprehensive exam (for some programs), thesis (for some programs); for doctorate, comprehensive exam, thesis/dissertation. *Entrance requirements:* For master's and doctorate, GRE General Test, interview, letters of reference. Additional exam requirements/recommendations for international students: Required—TOEFL. Electronic applications accepted. *Faculty research:* Multicultural counseling, class size effects, quality of life, eating disorders, outcome assessment.

The University of Akron, Graduate School, Buchtel College of Arts and Sciences, Department of Psychology, Program in Counseling Psychology, Akron, OH 44325. Offers MA, PhD. *Accreditation:* APA (one or more programs are accredited). *Students:* 17 full-time (14 women), 14 part-time (12 women); includes 2 minority (both African Americans), 2 international. Average age 27. 69 applicants, 7% accepted, 2 enrolled. In 2007, 1 master's, 5 doctorates awarded. *Degree requirements:* For master's, thesis optional, thesis or specialty exam; for doctorate, comprehensive exam, thesis/dissertation. *Entrance requirements:* For master's, GRE General Test, GRE Subject Test, minimum GPA of 2.75, letters of recommendation; for doctorate, GRE General Test, GRE Subject Test, minimum GPA of 3.25, letters of recommendation, personal statement. Additional exam requirements/recommendations for international students: Required—TOEFL (minimum score 550 paper-based; 213 computer-based; 79 iBT). *Application deadline:* For fall admission, 1/15 for domestic and international students. Applications are processed on a rolling basis. Application fee: $30 ($40 for international students). Electronic applications accepted. *Expenses:* Tuition, state resident: full-time $6,164; part-time $342 per credit. Tuition, nonresident: full-time $10,575; part-time $588 per credit. Required fees: $806; $43 per credit. $12 per term. Tuition and fees vary according to course load, degree level and program. *Financial support:* Fellowships with full tuition reimbursements, research assistantships with full tuition reimbursements, teaching assistantships with full tuition reimbursements, career-related internships or fieldwork, Federal Work-Study, institutionally sponsored loans, and tuition waivers (full) available. *Faculty research:* Counseling process and outcome, suicide, diversity issues and counseling psychology (e.g., gender, race, ethnicity, sexual orientation) vocational psychology, assessment. *Unit head:* Dr. Linda Subich, Coordinator, 330-972-8379, E-mail: lsubich@uakron.edu.

The University of Akron, Graduate School, College of Education, Department of Counseling, Program in Counseling Psychology, Akron, OH 44325. Offers PhD. *Accreditation:* APA. *Students:* 13 full-time (11 women), 14 part-time (12 women); includes 2 minority (both African Americans) Average age 33. 24 applicants, 17% accepted, 4 enrolled. In 2007, 2 degrees awarded. *Degree requirements:* For doctorate, one foreign language, comprehensive exam, thesis/dissertation, written and oral exams. *Entrance requirements:* For doctorate, GRE, interview, minimum GPA of 3.25, letters of recommendation, supplemental forms, department doctoral application. Additional exam requirements/recommendations for international students: Required—TOEFL (minimum score 550 paper-based; 213 computer-based). *Application deadline:* For fall admission, 1/15 for domestic and international students. Applications are processed on a rolling basis. Application fee: $30 ($40 for international students). Electronic applications accepted. *Expenses:* Tuition, state resident: full-time $6,164; part-time $342 per credit. Tuition, nonresident: full-time $10,575; part-time $588 per credit. Required fees: $806; $43 per credit. $12 per term. Tuition and fees vary according to course load, degree level and program. *Financial support:* In 2007–08, 8 research assistantships, 7 teaching assistantships were awarded. *Unit head:* Dr. James Rogers, Coordinator, 330-972-8635, E-mail: jrrogers@uakron.edu.

University of Alberta, Faculty of Graduate Studies and Research, Department of Educational Psychology, Edmonton, AB T6G 2E1, Canada. Offers counseling psychology (M Ed, PhD); educational psychology (M Ed, PhD); instructional technology (M Ed); school counseling (M Ed); school psychology (M Ed, PhD); special education (M Ed, PhD); special education-deafness studies (M Ed); teaching English as a second language (M Ed). Part-time programs available. *Degree requirements:* For master's, thesis optional; for doctorate, comprehensive exam, thesis/dissertation. *Entrance requirements:* For master's and doctorate, minimum GPA of 3.0. Additional exam requirements/recommendations for international students: Required—TOEFL. *Faculty research:* Human learning, development and assessment.

University of Baltimore, Graduate School, The Yale Gordon College of Liberal Arts, Division of Applied Sciences, Baltimore, MD 21201-5779. Offers applied psychology (MS), including counseling, industrial and organizational psychology, psychological applications; human services (MS). Part-time and evening/weekend programs available. *Faculty:* 7 full-time (5 women), 7 part-time/adjunct (2 women). *Students:* 61 full-time (49 women), 43 part-time (34 women); includes 30 minority (23 African Americans, 5 Asian Americans or Pacific Islanders, 2 Hispanic Americans), 6 international. Average age 28. 112 applicants, 64% accepted, 27 enrolled. In 2007, 31 degrees awarded. *Degree requirements:* For master's, thesis optional. *Entrance requirements:* For master's, GRE, minimum GPA of 3.0. Additional exam requirements/recommendations for international students: Required—TOEFL (minimum score 550 paper-based; 213 computer-based). *Application deadline:* For fall admission, 8/1 for domestic students, 6/1 for international students; for spring admission, 12/1 for domestic students, 11/1 for international students. Applications are processed on a rolling basis. Application fee: $45. Electronic applications accepted. *Expenses: Contact institution.* Tuition and fees vary according to program. *Financial support:* In 2007–08, 5 research assistantships with full and partial tuition reimbursements were awarded; fellowships, career-related internships or fieldwork and Federal Work-Study also available. Support available to part-time students. Financial award application deadline: 4/1; financial award applicants required to submit FAFSA. *Faculty research:* Participatory decision making, counter productive workplace behavior, organizational consulting, substance abuse treatment, cognitive functioning in head injured. Total annual research expenditures: $93,146. *Unit head:* Dr. Thomas Mitchell, Director of Program in Applied Psychology, 410-837-5348, Fax: 410-837-4793, E-mail: tmitchell@ubalt.edu. *Application contact:* Wendy Bolyard.

See Close-Up on page 1505.

The University of British Columbia, Faculty of Graduate Studies, Faculty of Education, Department of Educational and Counseling Psychology, and Special Education, Vancouver, BC V6T 1Z1, Canada. Offers counseling psychology (M Ed, MA, PhD); development, learning and culture (PhD); guidance studies (Diploma); human development, learning and culture (M Ed, MA); measurement and evaluation and research methodology (M Ed); measurement, evaluation and research methodology (MA); measurement, evaluation, and research methodology (PhD); school psychology (M Ed, MA, PhD); special education (M Ed, MA, PhD, Diploma). Part-time programs available. *Faculty:* 37 full-time (25 women). *Students:* 293 full-time (237 women), 102 part-time (86 women). 269 applicants, 41% accepted, 108 enrolled. In 2007, 91 master's, 17 doctorates awarded. *Median time to degree:* Of those who began their doctoral program in fall 1999, 95% received their degree in 8 years or less. *Degree requirements:* For master's, thesis (for some programs); for doctorate, comprehensive exam, thesis/dissertation. *Entrance requirements:* For master's, GRE General Test (counseling psychology MA); for doctorate, GRE General Test. Additional exam requirements/recommendations for international students: Required—TOEFL. *Application deadline:* For fall admission, 12/1 for domestic and international students. Application fee: $90 Canadian dollars ($150 Canadian dollars for international students). Electronic applications accepted. *Financial support:* In 2007–08, 14 fellowships (averaging $35,000 per year), 50 research assistantships (averaging $12,000 per year), 40 teaching assistantships (averaging $5,000 per year) were awarded; career-related internships or fieldwork, Federal Work-Study, institutionally sponsored loans, scholarships/grants, health care benefits, tuition waivers (full and partial), and unspecified assistantships also available. *Faculty research:* Women, family, social problems, career transition, stress and coping problems. *Unit head:* Dr. Shelley Hymel, Head, 604-822-6022, Fax: 604-822-3302, E-mail: shelley.hymel@ubc.ca. *Application contact:* Karen Yan, Graduate Program Assistant, 604-822-6371, Fax: 604-822-3302, E-mail: karen.yan@ubc.ca.

University of Calgary, Faculty of Graduate Studies, Faculty of Education, Division of Applied Psychology, Calgary, AB T2N 1N4, Canada. Offers counseling psychology (M Ed, M Sc, PhD); human development and learning (M Ed, M Sc, PhD); school psychology (M Ed, M Sc, PhD); special education (M Ed, M Sc, PhD). Part-time programs available. *Degree requirements:* For master's, thesis (for some programs), final oral exam; for doctorate, thesis/dissertation, candidacy exam, final oral exam. *Entrance requirements:* For master's, minimum GPA of 3.0, 3 letters of reference; for doctorate, minimum GPA of 3.5, 3 letters of reference. *Faculty research:* Counselor education, family life studies, learning and cognition.

University of California, Santa Barbara, Graduate Division, Gevirtz Graduate School of Education, Santa Barbara, CA 93106. Offers counseling, clinical and school psychology (PhD), including clinical psychology, counseling psychology; education (MA, PhD), including child and adolescent development, cultural perspectives and comparative education, educational leadership and organizations, research methodology, special education disabilities and risk studies (MA), special education, disabilities and risk studies (PhD), teaching and learning; educational leadership (Ed D); school psychology (M Ed); MA/PhD. *Accreditation:* APA (one or more programs are accredited). Postbaccalaureate distance learning degree programs offered (minimal on-campus study). *Faculty:* 36 full-time (18 women), 7 part-time/adjunct (3 women). *Students:* 400 full-time (308 women); includes 119 minority (11 African Americans, 6 American Indian/Alaska Native, 46 Asian Americans or Pacific Islanders, 56 Hispanic Americans), 18 international. Average age 31. 721 applicants, 41% accepted, 189 enrolled. In 2007, 157 master's, 35 doctorates awarded. Terminal master's awarded for partial completion of doctoral program. *Median time to degree:* Of those who began their doctoral program in fall 1999, 60% received their degree in 8 years or less. *Degree requirements:* For master's, comprehensive exam (for some programs), thesis (for some programs); for doctorate, comprehensive exam (for some programs), thesis/dissertation, qualifying exam. *Entrance requirements:* For master's, GRE, MAT (M Ed); for doctorate, GRE. Additional exam requirements/recommendations for international students: Required—TOEFL (minimum score 550 paper-based; 213 computer-based; 80 iBT). *Application deadline:* For fall admission, 12/15 priority date for domestic and international students. Application fee: $60. Electronic applications accepted. *Expenses:* Tuition, nonresident: full-time $14,888. Required fees: $10,108. *Financial support:* In 2007–08, 292 students received support, including 170 fellowships with full and partial tuition reimbursements available (averaging $5,200 per year), 80 research assistantships with full and partial tuition reimbursements available, 124 teaching assistantships with full and partial tuition reimbursements available; career-related internships or fieldwork, Federal Work-Study, institutionally sponsored loans, scholarships/grants, traineeships, health care benefits, and unspecified assistantships also available. Financial award applicants required to submit FAFSA. *Faculty research:* Professional development, early childhood development, school violence, literacy, science/math initiative. Total annual research expenditures: $4.2 million. *Unit head:* Carol Dixon, Associate Dean of Students, 805-893-2137, Fax: 805-893-7264, E-mail: sao@education.ucsb.edu. *Application contact:* Katie Tucciarone, Student Affairs Officer, 805-893-2137, Fax: 805-893-2588, E-mail: katiet@education.ucsb.edu.

University of Central Arkansas, Graduate School, College of Health and Behavioral Sciences, Department of Counseling and Psychology, Program in Counseling Psychology, Conway, AR 72035-0001. Offers MS. *Students:* 34 full-time (27 women), 8 part-time (6 women); includes 4 minority (all African Americans) 22 applicants, 77% accepted, 17 enrolled. In 2007, 9 degrees awarded. *Degree requirements:* For master's, comprehensive exam, thesis optional. *Entrance requirements:* For master's, GRE General Test, minimum GPA of 2.7. Additional exam requirements/recommendations for international students: Required—TOEFL (minimum score 550 paper-based; 213 computer-based). *Application deadline:* For fall admission, 3/1 priority date for domestic and international students; for spring admission, 10/1 priority date for domestic and international students. Applications are processed on a rolling basis. Application fee: $25 ($40 for international students). *Expenses:* Tuition, state resident: full-time $4,513; part-time $240 per credit. Tuition, nonresident: full-time $8,805; part-time $440 per credit. International tuition: $9,700 full-time. Required fees: $100 per term. *Financial support:* Federal Work-Study, scholarships/grants, and unspecified assistantships available. Financial award applicants required to submit FAFSA. *Unit head:* Dr. Elson Bihm, Head, 501-450-3193, Fax: 501-450-5424, E-mail: elsonb@uca.edu. *Application contact:* Patti Hornor, Administrative Assistant, 501-450-5063, Fax: 501-450-5678, E-mail: pattih@uca.edu.

University of Central Oklahoma, College of Graduate Studies and Research, College of Education, Department of Psychology, Program in Counseling Psychology, Edmond, OK 73034-5209. Offers MS. *Faculty:* 11 full-time (6 women), 2 part-time/adjunct (1 woman). *Students:* 48 full-time (34 women), 22 part-time (19 women); includes 12 minority (6 African Americans, 4 American Indian/Alaska Native, 1 Asian American or Pacific Islander, 1 Hispanic American), 2 international. Average age 30. 21 applicants, 95% accepted. In 2007, 8 degrees awarded. *Entrance requirements:* For master's, GRE General Test. Additional exam requirements/recommendations for international students: Required—TOEFL (minimum score 550 paper-based; 213 computer-based). *Application deadline:* For fall admission, 7/1 for international students; for spring admission, 11/1 for international students. Applications are processed on a

Counseling Psychology

University of Central Oklahoma (continued)
rolling basis. Application fee: $25. Electronic applications accepted. *Expenses:* Tuition, state resident: full-time $3,516; part-time $147 per hour. Tuition, nonresident: full-time $9,054; part-time $377 per hour. Required fees: $433; $18 per hour. *Financial support:* Career-related internships or fieldwork and unspecified assistantships available. Financial award application deadline: 3/31; financial award applicants required to submit FAFSA. *Unit head:* Dr. Mike Knight, Chairman, Department of Psychology, 405-974-5707.

University of Colorado Denver, School of Education and Human Development, Program in Counseling Psychology and Counselor Education, Denver, CO 80217-3364. Offers counseling psychology and counselor education (MA); school psychology (Ed S). *Accreditation:* ACA (one or more programs are accredited); NCATE. Part-time and evening/weekend programs available. *Faculty:* 11 full-time (8 women). *Students:* 71 full-time (62 women), 147 part-time (129 women); includes 21 minority (7 African Americans, 2 American Indian/Alaska Native, 2 Asian Americans or Pacific Islanders, 10 Hispanic Americans), 1 international. Average age 33. 154 applicants, 27% accepted, 33 enrolled. In 2007, 59 master's, 21 other advanced degrees awarded. *Degree requirements:* For master's, comprehensive exam, thesis optional. *Entrance requirements:* For master's, GRE or MAT, minimum GPA of 2.75, 4 letters of recommendation, interview, resumé. Additional exam requirements/recommendations for international students: Required—TOEFL (minimum score 525 paper-based; 197 computer-based). *Application deadline:* For fall admission, 2/15 for domestic students; for spring admission, 9/15 for domestic students. Applications are processed on a rolling basis. Application fee: $50 ($75 for international students). Electronic applications accepted. *Financial support:* Research assistantships, teaching assistantships, Federal Work-Study available. Financial award application deadline: 4/1; financial award applicants required to submit FAFSA. *Faculty research:* Spiritual issues in counseling, multicultural and diversity issues in counseling, adolescent suicide, career development. *Unit head:* Dr. Marsha Wiggins-Frame, Division Coordinator, 303-556-6032, Fax: 303-556-4479, E-mail: marsha.frame@cudenver.edu. *Application contact:* Lori Sisneros, Student Services Coordinator, 303-556-8854, Fax: 303-556-4479, E-mail: bri.sisneros@cudenver.edu.

University of Connecticut, Graduate School, Neag School of Education, Department of Educational Psychology, Storrs, CT 06269. Offers educational psychology (MA, PhD, Post-Master's Certificate), including cognition and instruction, counseling psychology, gifted and talented education, learning technology, measurement, evaluation, and assessment, school psychology, special education. *Faculty:* 39 full-time (17 women). *Students:* 163 full-time (119 women), 141 part-time (104 women); includes 40 minority (18 African Americans, 1 American Indian/Alaska Native, 8 Asian Americans or Pacific Islanders, 13 Hispanic Americans), 18 international. Average age 34. 348 applicants, 38% accepted, 126 enrolled. In 2007, 65 master's, 24 doctorates, 19 other advanced degrees awarded. *Degree requirements:* For master's, comprehensive exam; for doctorate, thesis/dissertation. *Entrance requirements:* For doctorate, GRE General Test. Additional exam requirements/recommendations for international students: Required—TOEFL (minimum score 550 paper-based; 213 computer-based). *Application deadline:* For fall admission, 2/1 priority date for domestic and international students; for spring admission, 11/1 for domestic students, 10/1 for international students. Applications are processed on a rolling basis. Application fee: $55. Electronic applications accepted. *Expenses:* Tuition, state resident: part-time $469 per credit hour. Tuition, nonresident: part-time $1,218 per credit hour. *Financial support:* In 2007–08, 80 research assistantships with full tuition reimbursements, 3 teaching assistantships with full tuition reimbursements were awarded; fellowships, Federal Work-Study, scholarships/grants, health care benefits, and unspecified assistantships also available. Financial award application deadline: 2/1; financial award applicants required to submit FAFSA. *Unit head:* Hariharan Swaminathan, Head, 860-486-4031, Fax: 860-486-0210, E-mail: hariharan.swaminathan@uconn.edu. *Application contact:* Lisa Rasicot, Graduate Coordinator, 860-486-3065, Fax: 860-486-0210, E-mail: l.rasicot@uconn.edu.

University of Connecticut, Graduate School, Neag School of Education, Department of Educational Psychology, Field of Educational Psychology, Program in Counseling Psychology, Storrs, CT 06269. Offers counseling psychology (PhD); school counseling (MA, Post-Master's Certificate). *Accreditation:* ACA. *Faculty:* 15 full-time (5 women). *Students:* 35 full-time (26 women), 14 part-time (7 women); includes 9 minority (4 African Americans, 1 Asian American or Pacific Islander, 4 Hispanic Americans), 4 international. Average age 30. 51 applicants, 35% accepted, 16 enrolled. In 2007, 10 master's, 2 doctorates, 3 other advanced degrees awarded. Terminal master's awarded for partial completion of doctoral program. *Degree requirements:* For master's, comprehensive exam, thesis or alternative; for doctorate, thesis/dissertation. *Entrance requirements:* For doctorate, GRE General Test. Additional exam requirements/recommendations for international students: Required—TOEFL (minimum score 550 paper-based; 213 computer-based). *Application deadline:* For fall admission, 2/1 priority date for domestic and international students; for spring admission, 11/1 for domestic students, 10/1 for international students. Applications are processed on a rolling basis. Application fee: $55. Electronic applications accepted. *Expenses:* Tuition, state resident: part-time $469 per credit hour. Tuition, nonresident: part-time $1,218 per credit hour. *Financial support:* In 2007–08, 15 research assistantships with full tuition reimbursements, 3 teaching assistantships with full tuition reimbursements were awarded; fellowships, Federal Work-Study, scholarships/grants, health care benefits, and unspecified assistantships also available. Financial award application deadline: 2/1; financial award applicants required to submit FAFSA. *Application contact:* Lisa Rasicot, Graduate Coordinator, 860-486-3065, Fax: 860-486-0210, E-mail: l.rasicot@uconn.edu.

University of Denver, College of Education, Denver, CO 80208. Offers counseling psychology (MA, PhD); curriculum and instruction (MA, PhD, Certificate), including curriculum leadership (MA, PhD); educational administration and policy studies (Certificate); educational psychology (MA, PhD, Ed S), including child and family studies (MA, PhD), quantitative research methods (MA, PhD), school psychology (PhD, Ed S); higher education and adult studies (MA, PhD); library and information science (MLIS); library and information sciences (Certificate); school administration (PhD). *Accreditation:* ALA; APA (one or more programs are accredited). Part-time and evening/weekend programs available. Postbaccalaureate distance learning degree programs offered (no on-campus study). *Faculty:* 26 full-time (18 women). *Students:* 327 full-time (260 women), 438 part-time (343 women); includes 119 minority (31 African Americans, 7 American Indian/Alaska Native, 14 Asian Americans or Pacific Islanders, 67 Hispanic Americans), 15 international. Average age 34. 778 applicants, 76% accepted, 368 enrolled. In 2007, 183 master's, 29 doctorates, 54 other advanced degrees awarded. Terminal master's awarded for partial completion of doctoral program. *Degree requirements:* For master's, comprehensive exam; for doctorate, 2 foreign languages, comprehensive exam, thesis/dissertation. *Entrance requirements:* For master's and doctorate, GRE General Test or MAT. *Application deadline:* Applications are processed on a rolling basis. Application fee: $50. Electronic applications accepted. *Financial support:* In 2007–08, 58 teaching assistantships with full and partial tuition reimbursements (averaging $6,300 per year) were awarded; career-related internships or fieldwork, Federal Work-Study, institutionally sponsored loans, and scholarships/grants also available. Support available to part-time students. Financial award application deadline: 3/1; financial award applicants required to submit FAFSA. *Faculty research:* Parkinson's disease, personnel training, development and assessments, gifted education, service learning, transportation, public schools. Total annual research expenditures: $340,000. *Unit head:* Dr. Virginia Maloney, Dean, 303-871-2509. *Application contact:* Linda McCarthy, Student Services Coordinator, 303-871-2509, E-mail: edinfo@du.edu.

University of Florida, Graduate School, College of Liberal Arts and Sciences, Department of Psychology, Gainesville, FL 32611. Offers behavior analysis (PhD); behavioral neuroscience (MS, PhD); cognitive and sensory processes (PhD); counseling psychology (PhD); developmental psychology (PhD); social psychology (MS, PhD); JD/PhD. *Faculty:* 42 full-time (12 women), 3 part-time/adjunct (1 woman). *Students:* 136 (90 women); includes 22 minority (7 African Americans, 1 American Indian/Alaska Native, 5 Asian Americans or Pacific Islanders, 9 Hispanic Americans) 22 international. In 2007, 25 master's, 14 doctorates awarded. *Degree requirements:* For master's, thesis or alternative; for doctorate, thesis/dissertation. *Entrance requirements:* For master's and doctorate, GRE General Test, minimum GPA of 3.0. Additional exam requirements/recommendations for international students: Required—TOEFL (minimum score 550 paper-based; 213 computer-based). *Application deadline:* For fall admission, 1/15 priority date for domestic students. Applications are processed on a rolling basis. Application fee: $30. Electronic applications accepted. *Expenses:* Tuition, state resident: full-time $7,478. Tuition, nonresident: full-time $22,603. *Financial support:* In 2007–08, 33 research assistantships (averaging $16,597 per year), 64 teaching assistantships (averaging $16,703 per year) were awarded; fellowships, career-related internships or fieldwork and unspecified assistantships also available. Financial award application deadline: 1/15. *Faculty research:* Experimental analysis of behavior, psychobiology, cognition and sensory processes, counseling psychology, social psychology, developmental psychology. *Unit head:* Dr. Martin Heesacker, Chair, 352-392-0601 Ext. 200, Fax: 352-392-7985, E-mail: heesack@ufl.edu. *Application contact:* Dr. Gregory Neimeyer, Coordinator, 352-392-0601 Ext. 259, Fax: 352-392-7985, E-mail: neimeyer@ufl.edu.

University of Great Falls, Graduate Studies, Program in Counseling, Great Falls, MT 59405. Offers counseling psychology (MSC). Part-time and evening/weekend programs available. *Faculty:* 3 full-time (2 women), 6 part-time/adjunct (4 women). *Students:* 17 full-time (15 women), 15 part-time (13 women). Average age 36. 6 applicants, 83% accepted, 4 enrolled. In 2007, 9 degrees awarded. *Degree requirements:* For master's, thesis optional, internship. *Entrance requirements:* For master's, GRE General Test, 3 letters of recommendation. Additional exam requirements/recommendations for international students: Required—TOEFL (minimum score 500 paper-based; 205 computer-based). *Application deadline:* For fall admission, 8/15 priority date for domestic students, 6/15 priority date for international students; for spring admission, 12/15 priority date for domestic students, 10/15 priority date for international students. Applications are processed on a rolling basis. Application fee: $50. Electronic applications accepted. *Expenses:* Tuition: Part-time $520 per credit. Required fees: $60 per semester. Tuition and fees vary according to course load. *Financial support:* In 2007–08, 24 students received support. Career-related internships or fieldwork, Federal Work-Study, institutionally sponsored loans, and scholarships/grants available. Support available to part-time students. Financial award application deadline: 6/1. *Faculty research:* Self concept and adolescent offenders, juvenile delinquency, community mental health counseling. *Unit head:* Dr. Molly Cox, Head, 406-791-5348, Fax: 406-791-5990.

University of Houston, College of Education, Department of Educational Psychology, Houston, TX 77204. Offers counseling psychology (M Ed, PhD); educational psychology (M Ed); educational psychology and individual differences (PhD); special education (M Ed, Ed D). *Accreditation:* NCATE. Part-time and evening/weekend programs available. *Faculty:* 20 full-time (10 women), 9 part-time/adjunct (5 women). *Students:* 96 full-time (83 women), 107 part-time (97 women); includes 55 minority (20 African Americans, 16 Asian Americans or Pacific Islanders, 19 Hispanic Americans), 6 international. Average age 33. 122 applicants, 49% accepted, 36 enrolled. In 2007, 49 master's, 13 doctorates awarded. *Degree requirements:* For master's, comprehensive exam or thesis; for doctorate, comprehensive exam, thesis/dissertation. *Entrance requirements:* For master's, GRE General Test or MAT, interview (counseling psychology); for doctorate, GRE General Test, interview. *Application deadline:* For fall admission, 2/1 for domestic students. Application fee: $35 ($75 for international students). *Expenses:* Tuition, state resident: full-time $6,297; part-time $262 per credit. Tuition, nonresident: full-time $12,969; part-time $540 per credit. Required fees: $2,696. *Financial support:* In 2007–08, 2 fellowships with full tuition reimbursements (averaging $9,500 per year), 3 research assistantships with full tuition reimbursements (averaging $10,225 per year), 39 teaching assistantships with full tuition reimbursements (averaging $10,225 per year) were awarded; career-related internships or fieldwork, Federal Work-Study, institutionally sponsored loans, scholarships/grants, health care benefits, and unspecified assistantships also available. Support available to part-time students. Financial award application deadline: 2/1. *Faculty research:* Cross-cultural assessment and counseling, cognitive and psychosocial development, learning and emotional disturbances. *Unit head:* Dr. Doris Prater, Interim Chairperson, 713-743-9827, Fax: 713-743-4996, E-mail: dlprater@uh.edu. *Application contact:* Graduate Adviser, 713-743-5019, Fax: 713-743-4996, E-mail: epsy@uh.edu.

University of Houston–Victoria, School of Arts and Sciences, Program in Psychology, Victoria, TX 77901-4450. Offers counseling psychology (MA); school psychology (MA). Part-time and evening/weekend programs available. Postbaccalaureate distance learning degree programs offered. *Faculty:* 4 full-time (2 women). *Students:* 18 full-time (15 women), 47 part-time (36 women); includes 18 minority (3 African Americans, 2 Asian Americans or Pacific Islanders, 13 Hispanic Americans). In 2007, 8 degrees awarded. *Degree requirements:* For master's, project or thesis. *Entrance requirements:* For master's, GRE General Test. Additional exam requirements/recommendations for international students: Required—TOEFL (minimum score 550 paper-based; 213 computer-based). *Application deadline:* Applications are processed on a rolling basis. Application fee: $0. Electronic applications accepted. *Expenses:* Tuition, state resident: full-time $3,492; part-time $194 per semester hour. Tuition, nonresident: full-time $7,596; part-time $422 per semester hour. Required fees: $774; $43 per semester hour. Tuition and fees vary according to course load. *Financial support:* In 2007–08, research assistantships with partial tuition reimbursements (averaging $2,000 per year), teaching assistantships with partial tuition reimbursements (averaging $2,000 per year) were awarded; career-related internships or fieldwork, Federal Work-Study, scholarships/grants, and unspecified assistantships also available. Support available to part-time students. Financial award application deadline: 4/15. *Unit head:* Dr. Rick Harrington, Head, 361-570-4205, Fax: 361-570-4229, E-mail: harringtonr@unh.edu. *Application contact:* Admissions and Records, E-mail: admissions@uhv.edu.

University of Indianapolis, Graduate Programs, School of Psychological Sciences, Indianapolis, IN 46227-3697. Offers clinical psychology (Psy D); clinical psychology/mental health counseling (MA). *Accreditation:* APA. *Faculty:* 7 full-time (2 women). *Students:* 107 full-time (90 women), 44 part-time (31 women); includes 4 minority (3 African Americans, 1 Hispanic American), 6 international. Average age 27. *Degree requirements:* For master's, practicum; for doctorate, comprehensive exam, thesis/dissertation, 1200 hours of clinical practicum, 2000 hour internship. *Entrance requirements:* For master's, GRE, 3 letters of recommendation; for doctorate, GRE, minimum GPA of 3.0, 18 hours of course work in psychology, 3 letters of recommendation. Additional exam requirements/recommendations for international students: Required—TOEFL (minimum score 550 paper-based; 213 computer-based). *Application deadline:* For fall admission, 2/25 for domestic students. Application fee: $50. *Financial support:* Federal Work-Study available. *Unit head:* Dr. E. John McIlvried, Dean, 317-788-3247, Fax: 317-788-3480, E-mail: jmcilvried@uindy.edu.

The University of Iowa, Graduate College, College of Education, Department of Psychological and Quantitative Foundations, Iowa City, IA 52242-1316. Offers counseling psychology (PhD); educational measurement and statistics (MA, PhD); educational psychology (MA, PhD); school psychology (PhD, Ed S); JD/PhD. *Accreditation:* APA. *Faculty:* 23 full-time, 21 part-time/adjunct. *Students:* 85 full-time (59 women), 81 part-time (61 women); includes 23 minority (8 African Americans, 8 Asian Americans or Pacific Islanders, 7 Hispanic Americans), 39 international. 147 applicants, 31% accepted, 23 enrolled. In 2007, 7 master's, 16 doctorates, 3 other advanced degrees awarded. *Degree requirements:* For master's, thesis optional, exam; for doctorate, comprehensive exam, thesis/dissertation; for Ed S, exam. *Entrance requirements:* For master's, doctorate, and Ed S, GRE General Test, minimum GPA of 3.0. Additional exam requirements/recommendations for international students: Required—TOEFL (minimum score 550 paper-based; 213 computer-based; 81 iBT). Application fee: $60 ($85 for international students). Electronic applications accepted. *Expenses:* Tuition, state resident: part-time $349 per hour. Tuition, nonresident: part-time $349 per hour. Tuition and fees vary according to course load and program. *Financial support:* In 2007–08, 9 fellowships, 61 research assistantships with partial tuition reimbursements, 15 teaching assistantships with partial tuition reimbursements were awarded. Financial award applicants required to submit FAFSA. *Unit head:* Timothy Ansley, Chair, 319-335-5579, Fax: 319-335-6145.

University of Kansas, Research and Graduate Studies, School of Education, Department of Psychology and Research in Education, Program in Counseling Psychology, Lawrence, KS 66045. Offers MS, PhD. *Accreditation:* APA (one or more programs are accredited). Part-time programs available. *Faculty:* 6. *Students:* 70 full-time (49 women), 19 part-time (16 women); includes 11 minority (4 African Americans, 1 American Indian/Alaska Native, 3 Asian Americans or Pacific Islanders, 3 Hispanic Americans), 5 international. Average age 30. 103 applicants, 40% accepted, 22 enrolled. In 2007, 14 master's, 6 doctorates awarded. Terminal master's awarded for partial completion of doctoral program. *Degree requirements:* For master's, thesis or alternative; for doctorate, comprehensive exam, thesis/dissertation. *Entrance requirements:* For master's and doctorate, GRE General Test, minimum GPA of 3.0. Additional exam requirements/recommendations for international students: Required—TOEFL. *Application deadline:* For fall admission, 1/15 for domestic and international students. Application fee: $55 ($60 for international students). Electronic applications accepted. *Expenses:* Tuition, state resident: full-time $5,838. Tuition, nonresident: full-time $13,409. Tuition and fees vary according to program. *Financial support:* Fellowships, research assistantships with full and partial tuition reimbursements, teaching assistantships with full and partial tuition reimbursements, career-related internships or fieldwork, scholarships/grants, and unspecified assistantships available. Financial award application deadline: 1/15. *Faculty research:* Career development, assessment and intervention, multi-cultural counseling, counselor training, positive psychology. *Unit head:* Tom Krieshok, Professor and Director of Training, 785-864-3931, Fax: 785-864-3820. *Application contact:* Admissions Coordinator, 785-864-3931, Fax: 785-864-3820, E-mail: preadmit@ku.edu.

University of Kentucky, Graduate School, College of Education, Program in Educational and Counseling Psychology, Lexington, KY 40506-0032. Offers counseling psychology (MS Ed, PhD, Ed S); educational and counseling psychology (MS Ed); educational psychology (Ed D, PhD, Ed S); school psychometrist and school psychology (MA Ed). *Accreditation:* APA (one or more programs are accredited); NCATE. *Faculty:* 14 full-time (8 women), 1 part-time/adjunct (0 women). *Students:* 123 full-time (103 women), 16 part-time (12 women); includes 23 minority (19 African Americans, 4 Hispanic Americans), 7 international. Average age 31. 250 applicants, 20% accepted, 37 enrolled. In 2007, 20 master's, 14 doctorates, 12 other advanced degrees awarded. *Degree requirements:* For master's, comprehensive exam, thesis optional; for doctorate, comprehensive exam, thesis/dissertation; for Ed S, comprehensive exam. *Entrance requirements:* For master's, GRE General Test, minimum undergraduate GPA of 2.75; for doctorate, GRE General Test, minimum graduate GPA of 3.0; for Ed S, GRE General Test. Additional exam requirements/recommendations for international students: Required—TOEFL (minimum score 550 paper-based; 213 computer-based). *Application deadline:* For fall admission, 7/17 priority date for domestic students, 2/1 priority date for international students; for spring admission, 12/13 priority date for domestic students, 6/15 priority date for international students. Application fee: $50 ($65 for international students). Electronic applications accepted. *Expenses:* Tuition, state resident: part-time $437 per credit hour. Tuition, nonresident: part-time $931 per credit hour. *Financial support:* In 2007–08, 73 students received support, including 16 fellowships with full tuition reimbursements available (averaging $2,250 per year), 38 research assistantships with full tuition reimbursements available (averaging $12,874 per year), 31 teaching assistantships with full tuition reimbursements available (averaging $9,700 per year); career-related internships or fieldwork, Federal Work-Study, institutionally sponsored loans, scholarships/grants, traineeships, health care benefits, tuition waivers (partial), and unspecified assistantships also available. Support available to part-time students. Financial award application deadline: 3/15. *Unit head:* Dr. Lynley Anderman, Director of Graduate Studies, 859-257-8647, Fax: 859-257-5662, E-mail: lynley.anderman@uky.edu. *Application contact:* Dr. Brian Jackson, Senior Associate Dean, 859-257-4667, Fax: 859-257-4676, E-mail: brian.jackson@uky.edu.

University of La Verne, College of Arts and Sciences, Department of Psychology, Programs in Counseling, La Verne, CA 91750-4443. Offers general counseling (MS); higher education counseling (MS); marriage and family therapy (MS). Part-time programs available. *Faculty:* 2 full-time (1 woman), 9 part-time/adjunct (8 women). *Students:* 32 full-time (30 women), 64 part-time (56 women); includes 64 minority (12 African Americans, 4 Asian Americans or Pacific Islanders, 48 Hispanic Americans). Average age 30. In 2007, 24 degrees awarded. *Degree requirements:* For master's, thesis, competency exam, personal psychotherapy. *Entrance requirements:* For master's, minimum undergraduate GPA of 3.0, 3 recommendations, interview. Additional exam requirements/recommendations for international students: Required—TOEFL (minimum score 600 paper-based; 250 computer-based). *Application deadline:* Applications are processed on a rolling basis. Application fee: $50. *Expenses: Contact institution.* Tuition and fees vary according to course load and program. *Financial support:* Career-related internships or fieldwork, institutionally sponsored loans, and scholarships/grants available. Financial award application deadline: 3/2; financial award applicants required to submit FAFSA. *Application contact:* Connie Hamlow, Admissions Information Specialist, 909-593-3511 Ext. 4244, Fax: 909-392-2761, E-mail: gradadmission@ulv.edu.

University of Lethbridge, School of Graduate Studies, Lethbridge, AB T1K 3M4, Canada. Offers accounting (MScM); addictions counseling (M Sc); agricultural biotechnology (M Sc); agricultural studies (M Sc, MA); anthropology (MA); archaeology (MA); art (MA); biochemistry (M Sc); biological sciences (M Sc); biomolecular science (PhD); biosystems and biodiversity (PhD); Canadian studies (MA); chemistry (M Sc); computer science (M Sc); computer science and geographical information science (M Sc); counseling psychology (M Ed); dramatic arts (MA); earth, space, and physical science (PhD); economics (MA); educational leadership (M Ed); English (MA); environmental science (M Sc); evolution and behavior (PhD); exercise science (M Sc); finance (MScM); French (MA); French/German (MA); French/Spanish (MA); general education (M Ed); general management (MScM); geography (M Sc, MA); German (MA); health sciences (M Sc, MA); history (MA); human resource management and labour relations (MScM); individualized multidisciplinary (M Sc, MA); information systems (MScM); international management (MScM); kinesiology (M Sc, MA); management (M Sc, MA); marketing (MScM); mathematics (M Sc); music (MA); Native American studies (MA); neuroscience (M Sc, PhD); new media (MA); nursing (M Sc); philosophy (MA); physics (M Sc); policy and strategy (MScM); political science (MA); psychology (M Sc, MA); religious studies (MA); sociology (MA); theoretical and computational science (PhD); urban and regional studies (MA). Part-time and evening/weekend programs available. *Students:* 215 full-time, 98 part-time. In 2007, 87 master's, 1 doctorate awarded. *Degree requirements:* For doctorate, comprehensive exam, thesis/dissertation. *Entrance requirements:* For master's, GMAT (M Sc in management), bachelor's degree in related field, minimum GPA of 3.0 during previous 20 graded semester courses, 2 years teaching or related experience (M Ed); for doctorate, master's degree, minimum graduate GPA of 3.5. Additional exam requirements/recommendations for international students: Required—TOEFL. Application fee: $60 Canadian dollars. *Financial support:* Fellowships, research assistantships, teaching assistantships, scholarships/grants, health care benefits, and unspecified assistantships available. *Faculty research:* Movement and brain plasticity, gibberellin physiology, photosynthesis, carbon cycling, molecular properties of main-group ring components. *Unit head:* Dr. Jo-Anne Fiske, Interim Dean, 403-329-2121, Fax: 403-329-2097. *Application contact:* Jennifer Geddes, Graduate Liaison Officer, 403-329-2762, Fax: 403-329-5159, E-mail: jennifer.geddes@uleth.ca.

University of Louisville, Graduate School, College of Education and Human Development, Department of Educational and Counseling Psychology, Louisville, KY 40292-0001. Offers college student personnel services (M Ed); counseling and personnel services (M Ed, PhD), including expressive therapies (M Ed), school counseling and guidance; counseling psychology (M Ed, PhD); mental health counseling (PhD). *Accreditation:* APA; NCATE. *Students:* 142 full-time (110 women), 96 part-time (80 women); includes 46 minority (42 African Americans, 1 American Indian/Alaska Native, 3 Asian Americans or Pacific Islanders), 7 international. Average age 33. In 2007, 66 master's, 4 doctorates awarded. *Degree requirements:* For doctorate, thesis/dissertation. *Entrance requirements:* For master's and doctorate, GRE General Test. *Application deadline:* Applications are processed on a rolling basis. Application fee: $50. Electronic applications accepted. *Financial support:* Fellowships, research assistantships, teaching assistantships, Federal Work-Study and scholarships/grants available. *Unit head:* Dr. Linda T. Shapiro, Acting Chair, 502-852-6884, Fax: 502-852-0629, E-mail: linda.shapiro@louisville.edu.

University of Mary Hardin-Baylor, College of Sciences and Humanities, Department of Psychology, Belton, TX 76513. Offers community counseling (MA); marriage and family Christian counseling (MA); psychology and counseling (MA); school counseling and psychology (MA). Part-time and evening/weekend programs available. *Degree requirements:* For master's, comprehensive exam. *Entrance requirements:* For master's, GRE General Test, minimum GPA of 3.0 in last 60 hours or 2.75 overall. Electronic applications accepted.

University of Maryland, College Park, Graduate Studies, College of Education, Department of Counseling and Personnel Services, College Park, MD 20742. Offers college student personnel (M Ed, MA); college student personnel administration (PhD); community counseling (CAGS); community/career counseling (M Ed, MA); counseling and personnel services (M Ed, MA, PhD); counseling psychology (PhD); counselor education (PhD); rehabilitation counseling (M Ed, MA, AGSC); school counseling (M Ed, MA); school psychology (M Ed, MA, PhD). *Accreditation:* ACA (one or more programs are accredited); APA (one or more programs are accredited); CORE (one or more programs are accredited); NCATE. Part-time and evening/weekend programs available. Postbaccalaureate distance learning degree programs offered (no on-campus study). *Faculty:* 41 full-time (29 women), 2 part-time/adjunct (both women). *Students:* 157 full-time (114 women), 19 part-time (13 women); includes 63 minority (34 African Americans, 3 American Indian/Alaska Native, 14 Asian Americans or Pacific Islanders, 12 Hispanic Americans), 11 international. 375 applicants, 20% accepted, 48 enrolled. In 2007, 44 master's, 6 doctorates, 4 other advanced degrees awarded. *Degree requirements:* For master's, thesis (for some programs); for doctorate, thesis/dissertation. *Entrance requirements:* For master's, GRE General Test or MAT, minimum GPA of 3.0, 3 letters of recommendation; for doctorate, GRE General Test or MAT, minimum GPA of 3.5, 3 letters of recommendation. Additional exam requirements/recommendations for international students: Required—TOEFL. *Application deadline:* For fall admission, 3/1 for domestic students, 2/1 for international students; for spring admission, 9/1 for domestic students, 6/1 for international students. Applications are processed on a rolling basis. Application fee: $60. Electronic applications accepted. *Financial support:* In 2007–08, 20 fellowships with full tuition reimbursements (averaging $8,362 per year), 5 research assistantships (averaging $14,192 per year), 105 teaching assistantships with tuition reimbursements (averaging $14,702 per year) were awarded; career-related internships or fieldwork, Federal Work-Study, and scholarships/grants also available. Support available to part-time students. Financial award applicants required to submit FAFSA. *Faculty research:* Educational psychology, counseling, health. Total annual research expenditures: $2.1 million. *Unit head:* Dr. Ruth Fassingel, Dean, 301-405-2860, Fax: 301-405-9995, E-mail: rfassing@umd.edu. *Application contact:* Dean of Graduate School, 301-405-0358, Fax: 301-314-9305.

University of Massachusetts Boston, Office of Graduate Studies, Graduate College of Education, Counseling and School Psychology Department, Boston, MA 02125-3393. Offers family therapy (M Ed, CAGS); forensic counseling (M Ed, CAGS); mental health counseling (M Ed, CAGS); rehabilitation counseling (M Ed, CAGS); school guidance counseling (M Ed, CAGS); school psychology (M Ed, CAGS). *Degree requirements:* For master's and CAGS, comprehensive exam. *Entrance requirements:* For master's, GRE General Test or MAT; for CAGS, minimum GPA of 2.75.

University of Medicine and Dentistry of New Jersey, School of Health Related Professions, Department of Psychiatric Rehabilitation and Counseling Professions, Scotch Plains, NJ 07076. Offers professional counseling (Certificate); psychiatric rehabilitation (MS, PhD); rehabilitation counseling (MS), including psychiatric rehabilitation, vocational rehabilitation. *Accreditation:* CORE. *Degree requirements:* For master's, internship, practicum. *Entrance requirements:* For master's, minimum 2 years of psychiatric rehabilitation or related professional experience or GRE General Test, interview; for doctorate, GRE General Test. Additional exam requirements/recommendations for international students: Required—TOEFL. *Application deadline:* Applications are processed on a rolling basis. Application fee: $50. Electronic applications accepted. *Financial support:* Traineeships available. *Unit head:* Dr. Kenneth J. Gill, Chairperson/Director, 908-889-2438, Fax: 908-889-2432, E-mail: kgill@umdnj.edu.

University of Memphis, Graduate School, College of Education, Department of Counseling, Educational Psychology and Research, Memphis, TN 38152. Offers counseling (MS, Ed D), including community counseling (MS), rehabilitation counseling (MS), school counseling (MS); counseling psychology (PhD); educational psychology and research (MS, PhD), including educational psychology, educational research. *Accreditation:* ACA (one or more programs are accredited); APA (one or more programs are accredited); CORE (one or more programs are accredited); NCATE. *Faculty:* 35 full-time (17 women), 9 part-time/adjunct (5 women). *Students:* 9 full-time (6 women), 29 part-time (25 women); includes 10 African Americans, 1 American Indian/Alaska Native, 2 international. Average age 32. 77 applicants, 51% accepted, 35 enrolled. In 2007, 49 master's, 16 doctorates awarded. *Degree requirements:* For master's, comprehensive exam, thesis or alternative; for doctorate, comprehensive exam, thesis/dissertation. *Entrance requirements:* For master's, GRE General Test or MAT, minimum GPA of 2.5; for doctorate, GRE General Test. *Application deadline:* For fall admission, 10/1 for domestic students; for spring admission, 4/1 for domestic students. Application fee: $35 ($60 for international students). *Expenses:* Tuition, state resident: full-time $6,990; part-time $377 per hour. Tuition, nonresident: full-time $17,818; part-time $830 per hour. Tuition and fees vary according to course load and program. *Financial support:* In 2007–08, 15 research assistantships with full tuition reimbursements (averaging $6,650 per year), 4 teaching assistantships with full tuition reimbursements (averaging $6,000 per year) were awarded; fellowships with full tuition reimbursements, career-related internships or fieldwork also available. *Faculty research:* Anger management, aging and disability, supervision, multicultural counseling. *Unit head:* Dr. Douglas C. Strohmer, Chair, 901-678-2841, Fax: 901-678-5114.

University of Miami, Graduate School, School of Education, Department of Educational and Psychological Studies, Program in Counseling Psychology, Coral Gables, FL 33124. Offers PhD. *Accreditation:* APA. *Faculty:* 7 full-time (2 women), 2 part-time/adjunct (1 woman). *Students:* 20 full-time (17 women), 5 part-time (4 women); includes 8 minority (2 African Americans, 6 Hispanic Americans). Average age 32. 105 applicants, 7% accepted, 5 enrolled. In 2007, 5 degrees awarded. *Median time to degree:* Of those who began their doctoral program in fall 1999, 85% received their degree in 8 years or less. *Degree requirements:* For doctorate, comprehensive exam, thesis/dissertation. *Entrance requirements:* For doctorate, GRE General Test. Additional exam requirements/recommendations for international students: Required—TOEFL (minimum score 550 paper-based; 212 computer-based). *Application deadline:* For fall admission, 1/2 for domestic students, 12/1 priority date for international students. Application fee: $50. Electronic applications accepted. *Financial support:* In 2007–08, 2 fellowships with full tuition reimbursements (averaging $20,000 per year), 8 research assistantships with full tuition reimbursements (averaging $18,000 per year), 7 teaching assistantships with full tuition reimbursements (averaging $18,000 per year) were awarded; career-related internships or fieldwork, Federal Work-Study, institutionally sponsored loans, and unspecified assistantships also available. Support available to part-time students. Financial award application deadline: 4/1; financial award applicants required to submit FAFSA. *Faculty research:* Cocaine recidivism, family systems, behavior and health, nontraditional families, stress and coping. *Unit head:* Dr. Brian Lewis, Director of Training, 305-284-2260, Fax: 305-284-3003. *Application contact:* Shelley Lue Foung, Senior Administrative Assistant, 305-284-3001, Fax: 305-284-3003, E-mail: sluefoung@miami.edu.

University of Minnesota, Twin Cities Campus, Graduate School, College of Liberal Arts, Department of Psychology, Program in Counseling Psychology, Minneapolis, MN 55455-0213. Offers PhD. *Accreditation:* APA. *Faculty:* 3 full-time (2 women). *Students:* 25 full-time (19 women); includes 6 minority (all Asian Americans or Pacific Islanders), 4 international. 87 applicants, 7% accepted, 5 enrolled. In 2007, 51 doctorates awarded. *Median time to degree:* Of those who began their doctoral program in fall 1999, 50% received their degree in 8 years or less. *Degree requirements:* For doctorate, comprehensive exam, thesis/dis-

Counseling Psychology

University of Minnesota, Twin Cities Campus (continued)
sertation, internship. *Entrance requirements:* For doctorate, GRE General Test, GRE Subject Test (recommended), 12 credits of upper-level psychology courses, including a course in statistics or psychological measurement. Additional exam requirements/recommendations for international students: Required—TOEFL (minimum score 550 paper-based; 213 computer-based; 79 iBT). *Application deadline:* For fall admission, 12/1 for domestic and international students. Application fee: $55 ($75 for international students). *Financial support:* In 2007–08, fellowships with full tuition reimbursements (averaging $21,000 per year), research assistantships with full tuition reimbursements (averaging $12,254 per year), teaching assistantships with full tuition reimbursements (averaging $12,254 per year) were awarded; career-related internships or fieldwork and tuition waivers (partial) also available. Financial award application deadline: 12/1. *Unit head:* Jo-Ida C Hansen, Area Director, 612-625-3873. *Application contact:* Coordinator, 612-624-4181, Fax: 612-626-2079, E-mail: psyapply@tc.umn.edu.

University of Missouri–Columbia, Graduate School, College of Education, Department of Educational, School, and Counseling Psychology, Columbia, MO 65211. Offers counseling psychology (M Ed, MA, PhD, Ed S); educational psychology (M Ed, MA, PhD, Ed S); learning and instruction (M Ed); school psychology (M Ed, MA, PhD, Ed S). *Accreditation:* APA (one or more programs are accredited); CORE. Part-time programs available. *Degree requirements:* For doctorate, thesis/dissertation. *Entrance requirements:* For master's, doctorate, and Ed S, GRE General Test, minimum GPA of 3.0.

University of Missouri–Kansas City, School of Education, Kansas City, MO 64110-2499. Offers administration (Ed D); counseling and guidance (MA, Ed S); counseling psychology (PhD); curriculum and instruction (MA, Ed S); education (PhD); educational administration (Ed S); reading education (MA, Ed S); special education (MA). *Accreditation:* NCATE.Part-time and evening/weekend programs available. *Faculty:* 59 full-time (44 women), 58 part-time/adjunct (45 women). *Students:* 207 full-time (160 women), 442 part-time (316 women); includes 153 minority (120 African Americans, 6 American Indian/Alaska Native, 8 Asian Americans or Pacific Islanders, 19 Hispanic Americans), 13 international. Average age 34. 299 applicants, 61% accepted, 123 enrolled. In 2007, 156 master's, 5 doctorates, 39 other advanced degrees awarded. *Degree requirements:* For doctorate, thesis/dissertation, internship, practicum. *Entrance requirements:* For master's, GRE, minimum GPA of 2.75, 2 letters of references, a written statement of purpose; for doctorate, GRE, minimum GPA of 3.0; for Ed S, minimum GPA of 3.0. Additional exam requirements/recommendations for international students: Required—TOEFL (minimum score 550 paper-based; 213 computer-based). *Application deadline:* For fall admission, 4/1 priority date for domestic and international students; for spring admission, 11/1 priority date for domestic and international students. Applications are processed on a rolling basis. Application fee: $35 ($50 for international students). *Expenses:* Tuition, state resident: part-time $287 per hour. Tuition, nonresident: part-time $741 per hour. Required fees: $31 per hour. Tuition and fees vary according to program. *Financial support:* In 2007–08, 361 students received support, including 15 research assistantships with partial tuition reimbursements available (averaging $11,024 per year); fellowships with full tuition reimbursements available, teaching assistantships, career-related internships or fieldwork, Federal Work-Study, institutionally sponsored loans, and tuition waivers (full and partial) also available. Support available to part-time students. Financial award application deadline: 3/1; financial award applicants required to submit FAFSA. *Faculty research:* Urban education, inquiry-based field study, theories of counseling and psychotherapy, school literacy, educational technology. Total annual research expenditures: $2.5 million. *Unit head:* Dr. Linda Edwards, Dean, 816-235-2236, Fax: 816-235-5270, E-mail: edwardsli@umkc.edu. *Application contact:* Dr. Lori Reesor, Assistant Dean, 816-235-1473, Fax: 816-235-5270, E-mail: reesorl@umkc.edu.

The University of Montana, Graduate School, School of Education, Department of Educational Leadership and Counseling, Program in Counselor Education, Missoula, MT 59812-0002. Offers counselor education (Ed S); counselor education and supervision (Ed D); mental health counseling (MA); school counseling (MA). *Accreditation:* ACA; NCATE. *Degree requirements:* For doctorate, thesis/dissertation. *Entrance requirements:* For master's, doctorate, and Ed S, GRE General Test. Additional exam requirements/recommendations for international students: Required—TOEFL.

The University of North Carolina at Greensboro, Graduate School, School of Education, Department of Counseling and Educational Development, Greensboro, NC 27412-5001. Offers advanced school counseling (PMC); counseling and counselor education (PhD); counseling and educational development (MS); couple and family counseling (PMC); school counseling (PMC); MS/Ed S. *Accreditation:* ACA (one or more programs are accredited); NCATE. *Faculty:* 10 full-time (5 women), 1 part-time/adjunct (0 women). *Students:* 106 full-time (92 women), 18 part-time (14 women); includes 21 minority (12 African Americans, 1 American Indian/Alaska Native, 4 Asian Americans or Pacific Islanders, 4 Hispanic Americans). 314 applicants, 22% accepted. *Degree requirements:* For master's, comprehensive exam, practicum, internship; for doctorate, comprehensive exam, thesis/dissertation. *Entrance requirements:* For master's, doctorate, and PMC, GRE General Test. Additional exam requirements/recommendations for international students: Required—TOEFL. *Application deadline:* For fall admission, 2/15 for domestic students. Application fee: $45. Electronic applications accepted. *Financial support:* In 2007–08, 57 students received support; fellowships with full tuition reimbursements available, research assistantships with full tuition reimbursements available, teaching assistantships with full tuition reimbursements available, career-related internships or fieldwork, Federal Work-Study, scholarships/grants, traineeships, and unspecified assistantships available. Support available to part-time students. *Faculty research:* Gerontology, invitational theory, career development, marriage and family therapy, drug and alcohol abuse prevention. *Unit head:* Dr. DiAnne Borders, Chair and Director of Graduate Studies, 336-334-3425, Fax: 336-334-4120, E-mail: borders@uncg.edu. *Application contact:* Michelle Harkleroad, Director of Graduate Admissions, 336-334-4884, Fax: 336-334-4424, E-mail: mbharkle@uncg.edu.

University of North Dakota, Graduate School, College of Education and Human Development, Department of Counseling, Grand Forks, ND 58202. Offers MA. *Faculty:* 7 full-time (4 women). *Students:* 55 full-time (43 women), 28 part-time (23 women); includes 9 minority (1 African American, 4 American Indian/Alaska Native, 2 Asian Americans or Pacific Islanders, 2 Hispanic Americans), 3 international. 68 applicants, 35% accepted, 24 enrolled. In 2007, 18 master's awarded. *Degree requirements:* For master's, comprehensive exam, thesis or alternative. *Entrance requirements:* For master's, GRE General Test or MAT, minimum GPA of 3.0. Additional exam requirements/recommendations for international students: Required—TOEFL (minimum score 550 paper-based; 213 computer-based; 79 iBT), IELTS (minimum score 7). *Application deadline:* For fall admission, 2/1 for domestic and international students. Application fee: $35. Electronic applications accepted. *Expenses:* Tuition, state resident: full-time $4,050; part-time $225 per credit. Tuition, nonresident: full-time $10,818; part-time $601 per credit. Required fees: $110 per semester. Tuition and fees vary according to class time, campus/location, program and reciprocity agreements. *Financial support:* In 2007–08, 25 students received support, including 12 research assistantships with full tuition reimbursements available (averaging $7,768 per year), 6 teaching assistantships with full tuition reimbursements available (averaging $6,351 per year); fellowships with full and partial tuition reimbursements available, career-related internships or fieldwork, Federal Work-Study, institutionally sponsored loans, scholarships/grants, tuition waivers (full and partial), and unspecified assistantships also available. Support available to part-time students. Financial award application deadline: 3/15; financial award applicants required to submit FAFSA. *Faculty research:* Group dynamics, addictive behavior, item response theory, geopsychology, women's health. *Unit head:* Dr. David Perry, Director, Doctoral Program, 701-777-3738, Fax: 701-777-3184, E-mail: david_whitcomb@und.nodak.edu. *Application contact:* Staci Wells, Admissions Associate, 701-777-2945, Fax: 701-777-3619, E-mail: gradschool@mail.und.nodak.edu.

University of Northern Colorado, Graduate School, College of Education and Behavioral Sciences, School of Applied Psychology and Counselor Education, Program in Counseling Psychology, Greeley, CO 80639. Offers Psy D. *Accreditation:* ACA; APA; NCATE. Part-time and evening/weekend programs available. *Faculty:* 5 full-time (3 women). *Students:* 17 full-time (15 women), 12 part-time (8 women); includes 1 minority (Hispanic American) Average age 37. 51 applicants, 29% accepted, 4 enrolled. In 2007, 4 degrees awarded. *Degree requirements:* For doctorate, comprehensive exam, thesis/dissertation. *Entrance requirements:* For doctorate, GRE General Test, 3 letters of reference. *Application deadline:* Applications are processed on a rolling basis. Application fee: $50 ($60 for international students). *Expenses:* Tuition, state resident: part-time $222 per credit. Tuition, nonresident: part-time $627 per credit. Required fees: $36 per credit. *Financial support:* Fellowships, research assistantships, teaching assistantships, unspecified assistantships available. Financial award application deadline: 3/1; financial award applicants required to submit FAFSA. *Unit head:* Dr. Brian Johnson, Program Coordinator, 970-351-2731.

University of North Florida, College of Arts and Sciences, Department of Psychology, Jacksonville, FL 32224-2645. Offers counseling psychology (MAC); general psychology (MA). Part-time and evening/weekend programs available. *Faculty:* 18 full-time (8 women). *Students:* 44 full-time (38 women), 8 part-time (5 women); includes 9 minority (4 African Americans, 1 Asian American or Pacific Islander, 4 Hispanic Americans), 1 international. Average age 27. 115 applicants, 34% accepted, 26 enrolled. In 2007, 24 degrees awarded. *Degree requirements:* For master's, comprehensive exam, thesis optional, practicum. *Entrance requirements:* For master's, GRE General Test, 2 letters of recommendation, minimum GPA of 3.0 in last 60 hours of course work. Additional exam requirements/recommendations for international students: Required—TOEFL (minimum score 500 paper-based; 173 computer-based). *Application deadline:* For fall admission, 3/1 priority date for domestic students, 3/1 for international students. Applications are processed on a rolling basis. Application fee: $30. Electronic applications accepted. *Expenses:* Tuition, state resident: part-time $266 per credit hour. Tuition, nonresident: part-time $858 per credit hour. One-time fee: $35 part-time. Tuition and fees vary according to program. *Financial support:* In 2007–08, 32 students received support, including 3 teaching assistantships (averaging $3,435 per year); Federal Work-Study and tuition waivers (partial) also available. Support available to part-time students. Financial award application deadline: 4/1; financial award applicants required to submit FAFSA. *Faculty research:* Sensory perception, social cognition, sexual behavior, evolutionary psychology, psychology and law. Total annual research expenditures: $131,349. *Unit head:* Dr. Linda Foley, Chair, 904-620-2807, E-mail: lfoley@unf.edu. *Application contact:* Dr. Randy Russac, Graduate Coordinator for General Psychology, 904-620-2807, E-mail: rrussac@unf.edu.

University of North Florida, College of Education and Human Services, Department of Counseling and Educational Leadership, Program in Counselor Education, Jacksonville, FL 32224-2645. Offers mental health counseling (M Ed); school counseling (M Ed). *Accreditation:* ACA; NCATE. Part-time and evening/weekend programs available. *Faculty:* 17 full-time (9 women). *Students:* 48 full-time (43 women), 47 part-time (43 women); includes 23 minority (14 African Americans, 3 Asian Americans or Pacific Islanders, 6 Hispanic Americans). Average age 33. 66 applicants, 26% accepted, 16 enrolled. In 2007, 32 degrees awarded. *Entrance requirements:* For master's, GRE General Test, minimum GPA of 3.0 in last 60 hours, 3 letters of recommendation, interview, writing sample. Additional exam requirements/recommendations for international students: Required—TOEFL (minimum score 500 paper-based; 173 computer-based). *Application deadline:* For fall admission, 5/1 for domestic students, 4/23 for international students; for spring admission, 9/26 for domestic students. Application fee: $30. Electronic applications accepted. *Expenses:* Tuition, state resident: part-time $266 per credit hour. Tuition, nonresident: part-time $858 per credit hour. One-time fee: $35 part-time. Tuition and fees vary according to program. *Financial support:* In 2007–08, 59 students received support; teaching assistantships, career-related internships or fieldwork, Federal Work-Study, and tuition waivers (partial) available. Support available to part-time students. Financial award application deadline: 4/1; financial award applicants required to submit FAFSA. *Faculty research:* Legal and ethical issues in working with minors in schools; gay, lesbian, bisexual, and transgender issues; collaboration between school counselors and classroom teachers; therapist distress and self care; school counselors as advocates for academic achievement. *Unit head:* Jennifer Jackson Kane, Chair, E-mail: jkane@unf.edu. *Application contact:* Dr. David Whittinghill, Graduate Coordinator for Mental Health Counseling, 904-620-2838, E-mail: dwhittin@unf.edu.

University of North Texas, Robert B. Toulouse School of Graduate Studies, College of Arts and Sciences, Department of Psychology, Denton, TX 76203. Offers clinical psychology (PhD); counseling psychology (MA, MS, PhD); experimental psychology (MA, MS, PhD); health psychology and behavioral medicine (PhD). *Accreditation:* APA (one or more programs are accredited). *Faculty:* 26 full-time (8 women). *Students:* 101 full-time (74 women), 105 part-time (77 women); includes 27 minority (8 African Americans, 1 American Indian/Alaska Native, 5 Asian Americans or Pacific Islanders, 13 Hispanic Americans), 7 international. Average age 29. 472 applicants, 9% accepted, 36 enrolled. In 2007, 28 master's, 23 doctorates awarded. Terminal master's awarded for partial completion of doctoral program. *Degree requirements:* For master's, comprehensive exam, thesis or alternative; for doctorate, one foreign language, comprehensive exam, thesis/dissertation. *Entrance requirements:* For master's and doctorate, GRE General Test, interview. Additional exam requirements/recommendations for international students: Required—proof of English language proficiency required for non-native English speakers; Recommended—TOEFL (minimum score 550 paper-based; 213 computer-based). *Application deadline:* For fall admission, 7/15 for domestic students; for spring admission, 11/15 for domestic students. Application fee: $50 ($75 for international students). *Financial support:* In 2007–08, 2 fellowships (averaging $20,000 per year), 18 research assistantships (averaging $9,000 per year), 38 teaching assistantships (averaging $9,000 per year) were awarded; career-related internships or fieldwork, Federal Work-Study, and institutionally sponsored loans also available. Financial award application deadline: 8/1. *Faculty research:* Very broad range of topics and approaches. *Unit head:* Dr. Linda Marshall, Chair, 940-565-2339, Fax: 940-546-4682, E-mail: psychair@unt.edu. *Application contact:* Amy Mayfield, Graduate Coordinator, 940-565-2671, Fax: 940-565-4682, E-mail: amym@unt.edu.

University of Notre Dame, Graduate School, College of Arts and Letters, Division of Social Science, Department of Psychology, Notre Dame, IN 46556. Offers cognitive psychology (PhD); counseling psychology (PhD); developmental psychology (PhD); quantitative psychology (PhD). *Accreditation:* APA. *Faculty:* 28 full-time (11 women), 5 part-time/adjunct (4 women). *Students:* 62 full-time (43 women); includes 9 minority (3 African Americans, 2 Asian Americans or Pacific Islanders, 4 Hispanic Americans), 9 international. 166 applicants, 15% accepted, 8 enrolled. In 2007, 13 doctorates awarded. *Degree requirements:* For doctorate, comprehensive exam, thesis/dissertation, candidacy exam. *Entrance requirements:* For doctorate, GRE General Test, GRE Subject Test (strongly recommended). Additional exam requirements/recommendations for international students: Required—TOEFL (minimum score 600 paper-based; 250 computer-based; 80 iBT). *Application deadline:* For fall admission, 1/2 for domestic and international students. Application fee: $50. Electronic applications accepted. *Financial support:* In 2007–08, 4 fellowships with full tuition reimbursements (averaging $22,000 per year), 14 research assistantships with full tuition reimbursements (averaging $16,000 per year), 41 teaching assistantships with full tuition reimbursements (averaging $16,000 per year) were awarded; career-related internships or fieldwork and tuition waivers (full) also available. Financial award application deadline: 1/2. *Faculty research:* Cognitive and socio-emotional development, statistical methods and quantitative models applicable to psychology, interpersonal relations, life span development and developmental delay, childhood depression, structural equation and dynamical systems. *Unit head:* Dr. Dawn Gondoli, Director of Graduate Studies, 574-631-6650, Fax: 574-631-8883. *Application contact:* Dr. Jarren Gonzales, Director of Graduate Admissions, 574-631-7706, Fax: 574-631-4183.

University of Oklahoma, Graduate College, College of Education, Department of Educational Psychology, Program in Counseling Psychology, Norman, OK 73019-0390. Offers PhD. *Accreditation:* APA. *Students:* 25 full-time (15 women), 21 part-time (12 women); includes 12 minority (3 African Americans, 4 American Indian/Alaska Native, 1 Asian American or Pacific Islander, 4 Hispanic Americans), 2 international. 30 applicants, 7% accepted, 2 enrolled. In 2007, 7 degrees awarded. *Degree requirements:* For doctorate, thesis/dissertation, general exam.

Entrance requirements: For doctorate, GRE General Test, master's degree, 3 letters of recommendation, interview, curriculum vitae. Additional exam requirements/recommendations for international students: Required—TOEFL (minimum score 550 paper-based; 213 computer-based). *Application deadline:* For fall admission, 1/10 for domestic and international students; for spring admission, 11/1 for domestic students, 9/1 for international students. Applications are processed on a rolling basis. Application fee: $40 ($90 for international students). Electronic applications accepted. *Expenses:* Tuition, state resident: full-time $3,451; part-time $144 per credit hour. Tuition, nonresident: full-time $12,432; part-time $518 per credit hour. Required fees: $1,925; $70 per credit hour. $122 per semester. *Financial support:* Career-related internships or fieldwork, institutionally sponsored loans, scholarships/grants, health care benefits, tuition waivers (partial), and unspecified assistantships available. Financial award application deadline: 3/1; financial award applicants required to submit FAFSA. *Faculty research:* Counseling assessment; process and outcome; diversity issues; health psychology; marriage and family; education, training and supervision. *Application contact:* Rindi Ledo, Applications Officer, 405-325-4525, Fax: 405-325-6655, E-mail: gpoedpsych@ou.edu.

University of Pennsylvania, Graduate School of Education, Division of Applied Psychology and Human Development, Program in Psychological Services, Philadelphia, PA 19104. Offers counseling psychology (MS Ed). *Degree requirements:* For master's, exam. *Entrance requirements:* For master's, GRE General Test. Electronic applications accepted. Expenses: Contact institution. *Faculty research:* Counseling in school, college, or agency.

University of Phoenix–Las Vegas Campus, The Artemis School, College of Health and Human Services, Las Vegas, NV 89128. Offers marriage, family, and child therapy (MSC); mental health counseling (MSC). *Entrance requirements:* For master's, minimum undergraduate GPA of 2.5, 3 years of work experience. Additional exam requirements/recommendations for international students: Required—TOEFL (minimum score 550 paper-based; 213 computer-based; 79 iBT). Electronic applications accepted.

University of Phoenix–Puerto Rico Campus, The Artemis School, College of Health and Human Services, Guaynabo, PR 00968. Offers marriage, family and child therapy (MSC); mental health counseling (MSC). Evening/weekend programs available. *Degree requirements:* For master's, thesis (for some programs). *Entrance requirements:* For master's, Counselor Preparation Comprehensive Examination, minimum undergraduate GPA of 2.5, 3 years work experience. Additional exam requirements/recommendations for international students: Required—TOEFL (minimum score 550 paper-based; 213 computer-based; 79 iBT). Electronic applications accepted.

University of Phoenix–Utah Campus, The Artemis School, College of Health and Human Services, Salt Lake City, UT 84123-4617. Offers business administration healthcare (MSN); mental health counseling (MSC); nursing (MSN). Evening/weekend programs available. *Degree requirements:* For master's, thesis (for some programs). *Entrance requirements:* For master's, minimum undergraduate GPA of 2.5, 3 years work experience, RN license. Additional exam requirements/recommendations for international students: Required—TOEFL (minimum score 550 paper-based; 213 computer-based; 79 iBT). Electronic applications accepted.

University of Rhode Island, Graduate School, College of Human Science and Services, Department of Human Development and Family Studies, Kingston, RI 02881. Offers college student personnel (MS); human development and family studies (MS); marriage and family therapy (MS). *Accreditation:* AAMFT/COAMFTE. Evening/weekend programs available. *Entrance requirements:* For master's, GRE or MAT. *Application deadline:* For fall admission, 4/15 priority date for domestic students; for spring admission, 11/15 for domestic students. Applications are processed on a rolling basis. Application fee: $35. *Expenses:* Tuition, state resident: full-time $6,936; part-time $385 per credit. Tuition, nonresident: full-time $19,044; part-time $1,058 per credit. Required fees: $1,508; $48 per credit. $30 per semester. One-time fee: $80 part-time. *Financial support:* Career-related internships or fieldwork available. *Unit head:* Dr. Jerome Adams, Chair, 401-874-5962.

University of Saint Francis, Graduate School, Department of Psychology and Counseling, Fort Wayne, IN 46808-3994. Offers general psychology (MS); mental health counseling (MS); pastoral counseling (MS); school counseling (MS Ed). Part-time and evening/weekend programs available. *Faculty:* 4 full-time (1 woman), 3 part-time/adjunct (0 women). *Students:* 28 full-time (24 women), 41 part-time (35 women); includes 7 minority (3 African Americans, 4 Hispanic Americans). Average age 35. 16 applicants, 88% accepted. In 2007, 8 degrees awarded. *Entrance requirements:* For master's, interview, minimum undergraduate GPA of 3.0. *Application deadline:* For fall admission, 7/1 for domestic students; for spring admission, 11/1 for domestic students. Applications are processed on a rolling basis. Application fee: $20. *Financial support:* In 2007–08, 4 students received support. Federal Work-Study, scholarships/grants, and unspecified assistantships available. *Unit head:* Dr. Rolf Daniel, Dean, 260-399-7700 Ext. 8403, Fax: 260-399-8170, E-mail: rdaniel@sf.edu. *Application contact:* Michelle Kuhlhorst, Admissions Counselor, 260-434-7748, Fax: 260-434-7590, E-mail: mkuhlhorst@st.edu.

University of St. Thomas, Graduate Studies, Graduate School of Professional Psychology, St. Paul, MN 55105-1096. Offers counseling psychology (MA, Psy D); family psychology (Certificate). *Accreditation:* APA. Part-time and evening/weekend programs available. *Degree requirements:* For master's, comprehensive exam, practicum; for doctorate, comprehensive exam, thesis/dissertation, qualifying exam, practicum, internship. *Entrance requirements:* For master's, MAT or GRE, minimum GPA of 2.75, letters of recommendation; for doctorate, GRE, minimum GPA of 3.2, letters of recommendation. Additional exam requirements/recommendations for international students: Required—TOEFL. Expenses: Contact institution. *Faculty research:* Elderly, eating disorders, anxiety.

University of San Francisco, School of Education, Department of Counseling Psychology, San Francisco, CA 94117-1080. Offers counseling (MA), including educational counseling, life transitions counseling, marital and family therapy; counseling psychology (Ed D). *Faculty:* 7 full-time (3 women), 34 part-time/adjunct (25 women). *Students:* 240 full-time (206 women), 38 part-time (29 women); includes 92 minority (21 African Americans, 4 American Indian/Alaska Native, 30 Asian Americans or Pacific Islanders, 37 Hispanic Americans), 7 international. Average age 33. 345 applicants, 82% accepted, 131 enrolled. In 2007, 133 master's awarded. *Degree requirements:* For doctorate, thesis/dissertation. *Entrance requirements:* For doctorate, GRE General Test. Application fee: $55 ($65 for international students). *Expenses:* Tuition: Part-time $1,005 per unit. Tuition and fees vary according to degree level, campus/location and program. *Financial support:* In 2007–08, 211 students received support; fellowships, research assistantships, teaching assistantships available. Financial award application deadline: 3/2; financial award applicants required to submit FAFSA. *Unit head:* Dr. Brian Gerrard, Chair, 415-422-6868.

The University of Scranton, Graduate School, Department of Counseling and Human Services, Scranton, PA 18510. Offers community counseling (MS); professional counseling (CAGS); rehabilitation counseling (MS); school counseling (MS). *Accreditation:* ACA (one or more programs are accredited). Part-time and evening/weekend programs available. *Degree requirements:* For master's, comprehensive exam, capstone experience. *Entrance requirements:* For master's, minimum GPA of 2.75. Additional exam requirements/recommendations for international students: Required—TOEFL (minimum score 500 paper-based; 173 computer-based), IELTS (minimum score 6).

University of South Africa, College of Human Sciences, Pretoria, South Africa. Offers adult education (M Ed); African languages (MA, PhD); African politics (MA, PhD); Afrikaans (MA, PhD); ancient history (MA, PhD); ancient Near Eastern studies (MA, PhD); anthropology (MA, PhD); applied linguistics (MA); Arabic (MA, PhD); archaeology (MA); art history (MA); Biblical archaeology (MA); Biblical studies (M Th, D Th, PhD); Christian spirituality (M Th, D Th); church history (M Th, D Th); classical studies (MA, PhD); clinical psychology (MA); communication (MA, PhD); comparative education (M Ed, Ed D); consulting psychology (D Admin, D Com, PhD); curriculum studies (M Ed, Ed D); development studies (M Admin, MA, D Admin, PhD); didactics (M Ed, Ed D); education (M Tech); education management (M Ed, Ed D); educational psychology (M Ed); English (MA); environmental education (M Ed); French (MA, PhD); German (MA, PhD); Greek (MA); guidance and counseling (M Ed); health studies (MA, PhD), including health sciences education (MA), health services management (MA), medical and surgical nursing science (critical care general) (MA), midwifery and neonatal nursing science (MA), trauma and emergency care (MA); history (MA, PhD); history of education (Ed D); inclusive education (M Ed, Ed D); information and communications technology policy and regulation (MA); information science (MA, MIS, PhD); international politics (MA, PhD); Islamic studies (MA, PhD); Italian (MA, PhD); Judaica (MA, PhD); linguistics (MA, PhD); mathematical education (M Ed); mathematics education (MA); missiology (M Th, D Th); modern Hebrew (MA, PhD); musicology (MA, MMus, D Mus, PhD); natural science education (M Ed); New Testament (M Th, D Th); Old Testament (D Th); pastoral therapy (M Th, D Th); philosophy (MA); philosophy of education (M Ed, Ed D); politics (MA, PhD); Portuguese (MA, PhD); practical theology (M Th, D Th); psychology (MA, MS, PhD); psychology of education (M Ed, Ed D); public health (MA); religious studies (MA, D Th, PhD); Romance languages (MA); Russian (MA, PhD); Semitic languages (MA, PhD); social behavior studies in HIV/AIDS (MA); social science (mental health) (MA); social science in development studies (MA); social science in psychology (MA); social science in social work (MA); social science in sociology (MA); social work (MSW, DSW, PhD); socio-education (M Ed, Ed D); sociolinguistics (MA); sociology (MA, PhD); Spanish (MA, PhD); systematic theology (M Th, D Th); TESOL (teaching English to speakers of other languages) (MA); theological ethics (M Th, D Th); theory of literature (MA, PhD); urban ministries (D Th); urban ministry (M Th).

University of Southern California, Graduate School, School of Education, Master's Programs in Education, Los Angeles, CA 90089. Offers counseling psychology (ME); curriculum and teaching (MS); instructional technology (MS); marriage, family and child counseling (MMFT); postsecondary administration and student affairs [PASA] (ME); school counseling (ME); teaching and teaching credential program (MAT); teaching English as a foreign language (ME); teaching English to speakers of other languages (MS). Part-time and evening/weekend programs available. *Faculty:* 24 full-time (17 women), 21 part-time/adjunct (13 women). *Students:* 364 full-time (289 women), 80 part-time (57 women); includes 201 minority (34 African Americans, 1 American Indian/Alaska Native, 90 Asian Americans or Pacific Islanders, 76 Hispanic Americans), 68 international. 427 applicants, 72% accepted. In 2007, 268 degrees awarded. *Entrance requirements:* For master's, GRE. Application fee: $85. *Financial support:* Career-related internships or fieldwork, Federal Work-Study, and scholarships/grants available. Support available to part-time students. *Unit head:* Dr. Kristan Venegas, Head, 213-740-2311.

University of Southern Mississippi, Graduate School, College of Education and Psychology, Department of Psychology, Hattiesburg, MS 39406-0001. Offers clinical psychology (MA, PhD); counseling psychology (PhD); experimental psychology (MA, PhD); psychology (MS); school psychology (MA, PhD). *Accreditation:* ACA; APA (one or more programs are accredited). *Faculty:* 33 full-time (12 women), 1 (woman) part-time/adjunct. *Students:* 111 full-time (87 women), 32 part-time (22 women); includes 11 minority (6 African Americans, 3 Asian Americans or Pacific Islanders, 2 Hispanic Americans), 8 international. Average age 28. 201 applicants, 21% accepted, 33 enrolled. In 2007, 32 master's, 15 doctorates awarded. Terminal master's awarded for partial completion of doctoral program. *Degree requirements:* For master's, comprehensive exam, thesis; for doctorate, comprehensive exam, thesis/dissertation. *Entrance requirements:* For master's, GRE General Test, minimum GPA of 3.0; for doctorate, GRE General Test, interview, minimum GPA of 3.0. Additional exam requirements/recommendations for international students: Required—TOEFL. *Application deadline:* For fall admission, 3/1 priority date for domestic students, 3/1 for international students. Applications are processed on a rolling basis. Application fee: $30. *Financial support:* In 2007–08, 46 research assistantships with full tuition reimbursements (averaging $7,731 per year), 49 teaching assistantships with full tuition reimbursements (averaging $7,731 per year) were awarded; career-related internships or fieldwork, Federal Work-Study, and institutionally sponsored loans also available. Financial award application deadline: 3/15. *Faculty research:* Dolphin cognition, sleep, neuropsychology, health-related behaviors, psychopathology. Total annual research expenditures: $101,200. *Unit head:* Dr. Stan Kuczaj, Chair, 601-266-4177, Fax: 601-266-5580. *Application contact:* Dr. Heather Sterling-Tairner, Graduate Coordinator, 601-266-4177, Fax: 601-266-5580.

The University of Tennessee, Graduate School, College of Education, Health and Human Sciences, Department of Educational Psychology and Counseling, Knoxville, TN 37996. Offers adult education (MS); applied educational psychology (MS); collaborative learning (Ed D); college student personnel (MS); mental health counseling (MS); rehabilitation counseling (MS); school counseling (MS). *Accreditation:* ACA (one or more programs are accredited); CORE (one or more programs are accredited); NCATE. Part-time and evening/weekend programs available. *Degree requirements:* For master's, thesis optional. *Entrance requirements:* For master's, GRE General Test, minimum GPA of 2.7. Additional exam requirements/recommendations for international students: Required—TOEFL. Electronic applications accepted.

The University of Texas at Austin, Graduate School, College of Education, Department of Educational Psychology, Austin, TX 78712-1111. Offers academic educational psychology (M Ed, MA); counseling education (M Ed); counseling psychology (PhD); human development and education (PhD); learning cognition and instruction (PhD); quantitative methods (PhD); school psychology (PhD). *Accreditation:* APA (one or more programs are accredited). *Degree requirements:* For master's, thesis optional; for doctorate, thesis/dissertation. *Entrance requirements:* For master's and doctorate, GRE General Test, 3 letters of recommendation. Additional exam requirements/recommendations for international students: Required—TOEFL.

The University of Texas at Tyler, College of Education and Psychology, Department of Psychology, Tyler, TX 75799-0001. Offers clinical psychology (MS), including neuropsychology, school psychology; counseling psychology (MA), including general, marriage and family; interdisciplinary studies (MSIS); school counseling (MA). Part-time and evening/weekend programs available. *Faculty:* 10 full-time (2 women), 8 part-time/adjunct (5 women). *Students:* 67 full-time (50 women), 60 part-time (50 women); includes 12 minority (4 African Americans, 1 American Indian/Alaska Native, 2 Asian Americans or Pacific Islanders, 5 Hispanic Americans). 37 applicants, 97% accepted, 32 enrolled. In 2007, 16 degrees awarded. *Degree requirements:* For master's, comprehensive exam, thesis optional. *Entrance requirements:* For master's, GRE General Test, minimum GPA of 3.0. *Application deadline:* For fall admission, 2/1 for domestic students; for spring admission, 10/1 for domestic students. Application fee: $0 ($50 for international students). Electronic applications accepted. *Expenses:* Tuition, state resident: part-time $627 per semester hour. Tuition, nonresident: part-time $908 per semester hour. Required fees: $107 per semester hour. Tuition and fees vary according to course load. *Financial support:* In 2007–08, fellowships with partial tuition reimbursements (averaging $3,000 per year), research assistantships (averaging $5,000 per year), teaching assistantships (averaging $1,500 per year) were awarded; career-related internships or fieldwork, Federal Work-Study, and institutionally sponsored loans also available. Support available to part-time students. Financial award application deadline: 7/1. *Faculty research:* Neuropsychology, child abuse, psychometric properties of psychological instruments, maternal behavior, clinical practice issues, victimization of women, post-traumatic stress disorder. *Unit head:* Dr. Charles B. Barke, Interim Chair, 903-565-5875, Fax: 903-565-5560, E-mail: cbarke@uttyler.edu. *Application contact:* Pam Morrow, Assistant to Dean for Enrollment Management, 903-566-7205, Fax: 903-566-7068, E-mail: pmorrow@uttyler.edu.

University of the District of Columbia, College of Arts and Sciences, Department of Psychology and Counseling, Program in Counseling, Washington, DC 20008-1175. Offers MS. *Students:* 9 full-time (4 women), 13 part-time (8 women); includes 19 minority (17 African Americans, 2 Asian Americans or Pacific Islanders). Average age 34.*Application contact:* LaVerne Hill Flannigan, Director of Admission, 202-274-6069.

University of Utah, The Graduate School, College of Education, Department of Educational Psychology, Salt Lake City, UT 84112-1107. Offers counseling psychology (PhD); educational

Counseling Psychology

University of Utah (continued)

psychology (MA); professional counseling (MS); professional psychology (M Ed); school counseling (M Ed, MS); school psychology (MS, PhD); statistics (M Stat). *Accreditation:* APA (one or more programs are accredited). Evening/weekend programs available. *Faculty:* 18 full-time (7 women), 8 part-time/adjunct (3 women). *Students:* 79 full-time (47 women), 85 part-time (57 women); includes 17 minority (1 African American, 3 American Indian/Alaska Native, 5 Asian Americans or Pacific Islanders, 8 Hispanic Americans), 5 international. Average age 32. 193 applicants, 32% accepted, 62 enrolled. In 2007, 41 master's, 15 doctorates awarded. *Degree requirements:* For master's, variable foreign language requirement, comprehensive exam, thesis (for some programs); for doctorate, variable foreign language requirement, thesis/dissertation, oral exam. *Entrance requirements:* For master's and doctorate, GRE General Test, minimum GPA of 3.0. Additional exam requirements/recommendations for international students: Required—TOEFL (minimum score 500 paper-based; 173 computer-based). *Application deadline:* For fall admission, 4/1 for domestic and international students; for spring admission, 11/1 for domestic and international students. Application fee: $45 ($65 for international students). *Financial support:* In 2007–08, 20 fellowships with full tuition reimbursements (averaging $10,000 per year), 5 research assistantships with full tuition reimbursements (averaging $10,000 per year), 32 teaching assistantships with full and partial tuition reimbursements (averaging $10,000 per year) were awarded; career-related internships or fieldwork, Federal Work-Study, institutionally sponsored loans, scholarships/grants, and unspecified assistantships also available. Financial award application deadline: 2/1; financial award applicants required to submit FAFSA. *Faculty research:* Autism, computer technology and instruction, cognitive behavior, aging, group counseling 50728. Total annual research expenditures:$50,728. *Unit head:* Dr. Elaine Clark, Chair, 801-581-7148, Fax: 801-581-5566, E-mail: clark@ed.utah.edu. *Application contact:* Sherrill Christensen, Academic Program Specialist, 801-581-7148, Fax: 801-581-5566, E-mail: sherrill.christensen@ed.utah.edu.

University of Vermont, Graduate College, College of Education and Social Services, Department of Integrated Professional Studies, Counseling Program, Burlington, VT 05405. Offers MS. *Accreditation:* ACA; NCATE. *Faculty:* 3 full-time (2 women), 6 part-time/adjunct (2 women). *Students:* 42 (34 women); includes 3 minority (2 American Indian/Alaska Native, 1 Hispanic American). 47 applicants, 60% accepted, 14 enrolled. In 2007, 18 degrees awarded. *Entrance requirements:* For master's, GRE General Test, resumé. Additional exam requirements/recommendations for international students: Required—TOEFL (minimum score 550 paper-based; 213 computer-based; 80 iBT). *Application deadline:* For fall admission, 2/1 priority date for domestic students. Applications are processed on a rolling basis. Application fee: $40. Electronic applications accepted. *Financial support:* Fellowships, research assistantships, teaching assistantships available. Financial award application deadline: 2/1. *Faculty research:* Women and tenure, counseling children and adolescents. *Unit head:* Dr. Eric C. Nichols, Coordinator, 802-656-3888, Fax: 802-656-3173, E-mail: ecnichol@zoo.uvm.edu.

University of Victoria, Faculty of Graduate Studies, Faculty of Education, Department of Educational Psychology and Leadership Studies, Victoria, BC V8W 2Y2, Canada. Offers aboriginal communities counseling (M Ed); counseling (M Ed, MA); educational psychology (M Ed, MA, PhD), including counseling psychology (M Ed, MA), leadership studies (PhD), learning and development (MA, PhD), measurement and evaluation, special education (M Ed, MA); leadership studies (M Ed, MA). Part-time programs available. *Faculty:* 18 full-time (10 women), 4 part-time/adjunct (2 women). *Students:* 133, 8 international. Average age 30. In 2007, 48 master's, 2 doctorates awarded. *Degree requirements:* For master's, thesis (for some programs), comprehensive exam (M Ed); for doctorate, comprehensive exam, thesis/dissertation, candidacy exam. *Entrance requirements:* For master's, 2 years of work experience in a relevant field, minimum B average; for doctorate, GRE, 2 years of work experience in a relevant field, minimum B average. Additional exam requirements/recommendations for international students: Required—TOEFL (minimum score 575 paper-based; 233 computer-based), IELTS (minimum score 7). *Application deadline:* Applications are processed on a rolling basis. Application fee: $75 ($125 for international students). *Expenses:* Tuition, state resident: full-time $3,110. International tuition: $3,700 full-time. Tuition and fees vary according to program. *Financial support:* In 2007–08, 29 students received support; fellowships, research assistantships, teaching assistantships, institutionally sponsored loans available. Financial award application deadline: 2/15. *Faculty research:* Learning and development (child, adolescent and adult), special education and exceptional children. *Unit head:* Dr. John Walsh, Chair, 250-721-7799, Fax: 250-721-6190. *Application contact:* Gloria F. Bennett, Graduate Program Assistant, 250-472-5005, Fax: 250-721-6190, E-mail: gbennett@uvic.ca.

The University of Western Ontario, Faculty of Graduate Studies, Social Sciences Division, Faculty of Education, Program in Counseling Psychology, London, ON N6A 5B8, Canada. Offers M Ed. Part-time programs available. *Entrance requirements:* For master's, minimum B average, 3 yr experience in helping profession. *Application deadline:* For fall admission, 2/1 for domestic students. Application fee: $80. *Financial support:* Research assistantships, teaching assistantships, career-related internships or fieldwork available. Financial award application deadline: 4/1. *Faculty research:* Women's issues in counseling, causes for sexual harassment in the workplace, counselor memory and confidence in clinical judgements. *Unit head:* Dr. Robert McMillan, Associate Dean, 519-661-2111 Ext. 82099, E-mail: macmil@uwo.ca. *Application contact:* L. Kulak, Graduate Education Manager, 519-661-2099, Fax: 519-661-3833, E-mail: kulak@edu.uwo.ca.

University of West Florida, College of Arts and Sciences: Arts, Department of Psychology, Pensacola, FL 32514-5750. Offers counseling (MA); counseling-licensed mental health counselor (MA); general (MA); industrial-organizational (MA). Part-time programs available. *Faculty:* 14 full-time (5 women), 1 (woman) part-time/adjunct. *Students:* 52 full-time (41 women), 29 part-time (23 women); includes 18 minority (10 African Americans, 2 American Indian/Alaska Native, 2 Asian Americans or Pacific Islanders, 4 Hispanic Americans), 3 international. Average age 29. 120 applicants, 53% accepted, 26 enrolled. In 2007, 18 degrees awarded. *Degree requirements:* For master's, thesis (for some programs). *Entrance requirements:* For master's, GRE General Test, GRE Subject Test, minimum GPA of 3.0. Additional exam requirements/recommendations for international students: Required—TOEFL (minimum score 550 paper-based; 213 computer-based). *Application deadline:* For fall admission, 6/1 for domestic students, 5/15 for international students; for spring admission, 11/1 for domestic students, 10/1 for international students. Applications are processed on a rolling basis. Application fee: $30. *Expenses:* Tuition, state resident: full-time $6,054; part-time $252 per credit. Tuition, nonresident: full-time $21,886; part-time $912 per credit. *Financial support:* In 2007–08, 3 research assistantships with partial tuition reimbursements (averaging $17,440 per year), 2 teaching assistantships with partial tuition reimbursements (averaging $4,948 per year) were awarded; fellowships with partial tuition reimbursements, career-related internships or fieldwork and Federal Work-Study also available. Financial award application deadline: 4/15; financial award applicants required to submit FAFSA. *Faculty research:* Prose recall, brain imaging, peak performance, biofeedback and pain control, comparable worth. Total annual research expenditures: $15,000. *Unit head:* Dr. Laura Koppes, Chairperson, 850-474-3493.

University of Wisconsin–Madison, Graduate School, School of Education, Department of Counseling Psychology, Program in Counseling Psychology, Madison, WI 53706-1380. Offers PhD. *Accreditation:* APA. *Degree requirements:* For doctorate, thesis/dissertation. Application fee: $38. *Unit head:* Dr. Mary Lee Nelson, Chair, Department of Counseling Psychology, 608-262-0461.

University of Wisconsin–Stout, Graduate School, College of Human Development, Program in Mental Health Counseling, Menomonie, WI 54751. Offers MS. Part-time programs available. *Faculty:* 3 full-time (1 woman). *Students:* 32 full-time (27 women), 11 part-time (all women). Average age 31. 64 applicants, 28% accepted, 11 enrolled. In 2007, 24 degrees awarded. *Degree requirements:* For master's, comprehensive exam or thesis. *Entrance requirements:* For master's, minimum GPA of 2.75. Additional exam requirements/recommendations for international students: Required—TOEFL (minimum score 500 paper-based; 173 computer-based). *Application deadline:* For fall admission, 2/1 for domestic and international students; for spring admission, 10/1 for domestic and international students. Application fee: $45. *Expenses:* Tuition, state resident: part-time $332 per credit. Tuition, nonresident: part-time $553 per credit. *Financial support:* In 2007–08, 3 research assistantships with partial tuition reimbursements (averaging $6,671 per year), 1 teaching assistantship with partial tuition reimbursement (averaging $6,671 per year) were awarded; Federal Work-Study, scholarships/grants, health care benefits, tuition waivers (partial), and unspecified assistantships also available. Support available to part-time students. Financial award application deadline: 4/1; financial award applicants required to submit FAFSA. *Faculty research:* Body image, gender issues, eating disorders, cognitive behavioral therapy. *Unit head:* Dr. Julia Champe, Director, 715-232-3094. *Application contact:* Anne E. Johnson, Graduate Student Evaluator, 715-232-1322, Fax: 715-232-2413, E-mail: johnsona@uwstout.edu.

University of Wisconsin–Stout, Graduate School, School of Education, Program in School Counseling, Menomonie, WI 54751. Offers MS. Part-time programs available. *Faculty:* 15 full-time (8 women). *Students:* 50 full-time (41 women), 17 part-time (14 women); includes 4 minority (1 American Indian/Alaska Native, 2 Asian Americans or Pacific Islanders, 1 Hispanic American). Average age 27. 48 applicants, 54% accepted, 18 enrolled. In 2007, 30 degrees awarded. *Degree requirements:* For master's, thesis. *Entrance requirements:* For master's, minimum GPA of 2.75. Additional exam requirements/recommendations for international students: Required—TOEFL (minimum score 500 paper-based; 173 computer-based; 61 iBT). *Application deadline:* For fall admission, 2/1 for domestic and international students; for spring admission, 10/1 for domestic and international students. Application fee: $45. Electronic applications accepted. *Expenses:* Tuition, state resident: part-time $332 per credit. Tuition, nonresident: part-time $553 per credit. *Financial support:* In 2007–08, 5 research assistantships with partial tuition reimbursements (averaging $3,326 per year) were awarded; Federal Work-Study, scholarships/grants, health care benefits, tuition waivers (partial), and unspecified assistantships also available. Support available to part-time students. Financial award application deadline: 4/1; financial award applicants required to submit FAFSA. *Faculty research:* Adventure-based learning, body image, domestic violence, resilience, school climate. *Unit head:* Dr. Barbara Flom, Director, 715-232-1343, E-mail: flomb@uwstout.edu. *Application contact:* Anne E. Johnson, Graduate Student Evaluator, 715-232-1322, Fax: 715-232-2413, E-mail: johnsona@uwstout.edu.

Utah State University, School of Graduate Studies, College of Education and Human Services, Department of Psychology, Logan, UT 84322. Offers clinical/counseling/school psychology (PhD); research and evaluation methodology (PhD); school counseling (MS); school psychology (MS). *Accreditation:* APA (one or more programs are accredited). Part-time and evening/weekend programs available. Postbaccalaureate distance learning degree programs offered (no on-campus study). Terminal master's awarded for partial completion of doctoral program. *Degree requirements:* For master's, thesis (for some programs); for doctorate, thesis/dissertation. *Entrance requirements:* For master's, GRE General Test (school psychology), MAT (school counseling), minimum GPA of 3.5; for doctorate, GRE General Test, minimum GPA of 3.5. Additional exam requirements/recommendations for international students: Required—TOEFL. *Faculty research:* Hearing loss detection in infancy, ADHD, eating disorders, domestic violence, neuropsychology, bilingual/Spanish speaking students/parents.

Valdosta State University, Graduate School, College of Education, Department of Psychology and Counseling, Valdosta, GA 31698. Offers clinical/counseling psychology (MS); industrial/organizational psychology (MS); school counseling (M Ed, Ed S); school psychology (Ed S). Part-time and evening/weekend programs available. *Faculty:* 16 full-time (2 women). *Students:* 61 full-time (48 women), 38 part-time (31 women); includes 22 minority (19 African Americans, 1 American Indian/Alaska Native, 1 Asian American or Pacific Islander, 1 Hispanic American). Average age 27. 103 applicants, 31% accepted, 22 enrolled. In 2007, 25 degrees awarded. *Degree requirements:* For master's, thesis or alternative, comprehensive written and/or oral exams; for Ed S, thesis. *Entrance requirements:* For master's and Ed S, GRE General Test or MAT. Additional exam requirements/recommendations for international students: Required—TOEFL (minimum score 523 paper-based; 193 computer-based). *Application deadline:* For fall admission, 7/1 for domestic and international students; for spring admission, 11/15 for domestic and international students. Applications are processed on a rolling basis. Application fee: $40. Electronic applications accepted. *Expenses:* Tuition, state resident: part-time $147 per hour. Tuition, nonresident: part-time $586 per hour. Required fees: $520 per semester. Tuition and fees vary according to course level, course load, campus/location and program. *Financial support:* In 2007–08, 2 students received support, including 2 research assistantships with full tuition reimbursements available (averaging $2,452 per year); institutionally sponsored loans and unspecified assistantships also available. Support available to part-time students. Financial award application deadline: 7/1; financial award applicants required to submit FAFSA. *Faculty research:* Using Bender-Gestalt to predict graphomotor dimensions of the draw-a-person test, neurobehavioral hemispheric dominance. *Unit head:* Dr. Robert Bauer, Chair, 229-333-5930, Fax: 229-259-5576, E-mail: bbauer@valdosta.edu.

Valparaiso University, Graduate Division, Department of Psychology, Valparaiso, IN 46383. Offers business management (for counseling students) (Certificate); clinical mental health counseling (MA); community counseling (MA); JD/MA. Part-time and evening/weekend programs available. *Faculty:* 7 part-time/adjunct (1 woman). *Students:* 35 full-time (25 women), 11 part-time (9 women); includes 2 minority (1 African American, 1 Hispanic American), 5 international. Average age 30. In 2007, 13 degrees awarded. *Degree requirements:* For master's, thesis or alternative, internship. *Entrance requirements:* For master's, minimum GPA of 3.0. Additional exam requirements/recommendations for international students: Required—TOEFL (minimum score 550 paper-based; 213 computer-based). *Application deadline:* For fall admission, 3/1 priority date for domestic students. Applications are processed on a rolling basis. Application fee: $30 ($50 for international students). Electronic applications accepted. *Financial support:* Career-related internships or fieldwork, traineeships, and unspecified assistantships available. Support available to part-time students. Financial award applicants required to submit FAFSA. *Faculty research:* Environmental psychology, human sexuality, racial identity development models, social psychology. *Unit head:* Dr. James Nelson, Graduate Program Director, 219-464-5443, Fax: 219-464-6878, E-mail: jim.nelson@valpo.edu. *Application contact:* Jamie Haney, Coordinator of Recruitment Activities, 219-464-5313, Fax: 219-464-5381, E-mail: jamie.haney@valpo.edu.

Virginia Commonwealth University, Graduate School, College of Humanities and Sciences, Department of Psychology, Program in Counseling Psychology, Richmond, VA 23284-9005. Offers PhD. *Accreditation:* APA. *Students:* 32 full-time (27 women), 12 part-time (8 women); includes 8 minority (7 African Americans, 1 Asian American or Pacific Islander), 1 international. 128 applicants, 10% accepted, 7 enrolled. In 2007, 9 doctorates awarded. *Degree requirements:* For doctorate, thesis/dissertation. *Entrance requirements:* For doctorate, GRE General Test, GRE Subject Test. *Application deadline:* For fall admission, 1/15 for domestic students. Application fee: $50. *Expenses:* Tuition, state resident: full-time $7,224; part-time $401 per credit. Tuition, nonresident: full-time $16,072; part-time $891 per credit. Required fees: $1,679; $63 per credit. Tuition and fees vary according to campus/location. *Financial support:* Fellowships, research assistantships, teaching assistantships, Federal Work-Study, institutionally sponsored loans, and scholarships/grants available. Support available to part-time students. *Faculty research:* Life span development counseling, couple/family therapy, health psychology, psychotherapy. *Unit head:* Dr. Wendy L. Kliewer, Head, 804-828-1793. *Application contact:* Dr. J. Donelson Forsyth, Director, Graduate Programs in Psychology, 804-828-6754, Fax: 804-828-2237, E-mail: jforsyth@vcu.edu.

See Close-Up on page 457.

Virginia Commonwealth University, Graduate School, School of Allied Health Professions, Program in Patient Counseling, Richmond, VA 23284-9005. Offers MS, CPC. *Faculty:* 7 full-time (4 women). *Students:* 14 full-time (10 women), 5 part-time (4 women); includes 5 African Americans, 2 international. 29 applicants, 48% accepted, 13 enrolled. In 2007, 8 master's, 1 other advanced degree awarded. *Entrance requirements:* For master's, GRE General Test. *Application deadline:* Applications are processed on a rolling basis. Application fee: $50. *Expenses:* Tuition, state resident: full-time $7,224; part-time $401 per credit. Tuition, nonresident: full-time $16,072; part-time $891 per credit. Required fees: $1,679; $63 per credit. Tuition and fees vary according to campus/location. *Financial support:* Application deadline: 3/1. *Unit head:* Dr. Alexander F. Tartaglia, Director, 804-828-0540, E-mail: aftartag@vcu.edu.

Walden University, Graduate Programs, School of Counseling and Social Science, Minneapolis, MN 55401. Offers human services (PhD), including clinical social work, counseling, criminal justice, family studies and intervention strategies, general program in human services, human services administration, self-designed program in human services, social policy analysis and planning; mental health counseling (MS). Part-time and evening/weekend programs available. *Students:* 586 full-time (496 women), 505 part-time (410 women); includes 413 minority (351 African Americans, 14 American Indian/Alaska Native, 11 Asian Americans or Pacific Islanders, 37 Hispanic Americans), 10 international. Average age 39. 538 applicants, 72% accepted, 207 enrolled. In 2007, 4 degrees awarded. *Degree requirements:* For master's, residency requirements; for doctorate, thesis/dissertation, residency requirements. *Entrance requirements:* For master's, BS in related field; for doctorate, 3 years of professional experience (preferred), minimum GPA of 3.0, master's degree. Additional exam requirements/recommendations for international students: Required—TOEFL (minimum score 550 paper-based; 213 computer-based), IELTS (minimum score 7). *Application deadline:* For fall admission, 8/15 priority date for domestic and international students; for winter admission, 11/15 priority date for domestic and international students; for spring admission, 12/15 priority date for domestic and international students. Applications are processed on a rolling basis. Application fee: $50. Electronic applications accepted. *Financial support:* Fellowships, Federal Work-Study, institutionally sponsored loans, scholarships/grants, and unspecified assistantships available. Financial award applicants required to submit FAFSA. *Unit head:* Savitri Dixon-Saxon, Associate Dean, 800-925-3368, Fax: 612-338-5092. *Application contact:* Office of Student Enrollment, 866-4-WALDEN, Fax: 410-843-8780.

Walden University, Graduate Programs, School of Psychology, Minneapolis, MN 55401. Offers clinical assessment (Post-Doctoral Certificate); clinical child psychology (Post-Doctoral Certificate); clinical psychology (PhD, Post-Doctoral Certificate); counseling psychology (PhD, Post-Doctoral Certificate); general psychology (MS, PhD, Post-Doctoral Certificate); health psychology (PhD, Post-Doctoral Certificate); organizational psychology (PhD, Post-Doctoral Certificate); organizational psychology and development (MS); school psychology (PhD, Post-Doctoral Certificate); teaching online (Post-Doctoral Certificate). Part-time and evening/weekend programs available. Postbaccalaureate distance learning degree programs offered (minimal on-campus study). *Students:* 1,428 full-time (1,130 women), 1,933 part-time (1,483 women); includes 959 minority (737 African Americans, 35 American Indian/Alaska Native, 53 Asian Americans or Pacific Islanders, 134 Hispanic Americans), 39 international. Average age 40. 1,254 applicants, 75% accepted, 548 enrolled. In 2007, 182 master's, 43 doctorates awarded. *Degree requirements:* For master's, thesis; for doctorate, thesis/dissertation, brief dispersed residency sessions. *Entrance requirements:* For master's, minimum GPA of 3.0; for doctorate, 3 years of professional experience, master's degree; for Post-Doctoral Certificate, PhD in related field, 3 years of professional experience. Additional exam requirements/recommendations for international students: Required—TOEFL (minimum score 550 paper-based; 213 computer-based), IELTS (minimum score 7). *Application deadline:* For fall admission, 8/15 priority date for domestic and international students; for winter admission, 11/15 priority date for domestic and international students; for spring admission, 12/15 priority date for domestic and international students. Applications are processed on a rolling basis. Application fee: $50. Electronic applications accepted. *Financial support:* Fellowships with partial tuition reimbursements, career-related internships or fieldwork, Federal Work-Study, institutionally sponsored loans, scholarships/grants, tuition waivers (partial), and unspecified assistantships available. Support available to part-time students. Financial award applicants required to submit FAFSA. *Faculty research:* Clinical psychology, organizational psychology, forensic psychology, group processes, educational psychology. *Unit head:* Dr. Nina Nabors, Associate Dean, 800-925-3368. *Application contact:* 866-4-WALDEN, Fax: 410-843-8780, E-mail: request@waldenu.edu.

Walla Walla University, Graduate School, School of Education and Psychology, Specialization in Counseling Psychology, College Place, WA 99324-1198. Offers MA. Part-time programs available. *Faculty:* 8 full-time (3 women), 3 part-time/adjunct (1 woman). *Degree requirements:* For master's, thesis (for some programs). *Entrance requirements:* For master's, GRE General Test, minimum GPA of 2.75, course work in education and psychology. *Application deadline:* For fall admission, 4/1 priority date for domestic students. Applications are processed on a rolling basis. Application fee: $50. Electronic applications accepted. *Expenses:* Tuition: Full-time $21,333; part-time $547 per quarter hour. *Financial support:* Teaching assistantships with partial tuition reimbursements available. Financial award application deadline: 4/1; financial award applicants required to submit FAFSA. *Faculty research:* Instructional psychology, moral development. *Application contact:* Dr. Joe G. Galusha, Dean of Graduate Studies, 509-527-2421, Fax: 509-527-2237, E-mail: joe.galusha@wallawalla.edu.

Walsh University, Graduate Programs, Program in Counseling and Human Development, North Canton, OH 44720-3396. Offers mental health counseling (MA); school counseling (MA). *Accreditation:* ACA. Part-time and evening/weekend programs available. *Faculty:* 4 full-time (all women), 2 part-time/adjunct (both women). *Students:* 33 full-time (30 women), 60 part-time (51 women); includes 4 minority (1 African American, 1 American Indian/Alaska Native, 2 Hispanic Americans), 2 international. Average age 30. 35 applicants, 51% accepted, 18 enrolled. In 2007, 27 degrees awarded. *Degree requirements:* For master's, comprehensive exam, internship, practicum. *Entrance requirements:* For master's, GRE General Test, MAT, interview, minimum GPA of 3.0, writing sample. Additional exam requirements/recommendations for international students: Required—TOEFL (minimum score 500 paper-based; 173 computer-based). *Application deadline:* For fall admission, 7/15 priority date for domestic students. Applications are processed on a rolling basis. Application fee: $25. Electronic applications accepted. *Expenses:* Tuition: Full-time $9,270; part-time $575 per credit. *Financial support:* In 2007–08, 29 students received support, including 7 research assistantships with tuition reimbursements available (averaging $4,128 per year); tuition waivers (partial) and tuition discounts also available. Financial award application deadline: 12/31. *Faculty research:* Student perspectives on beneficial and non-beneficial aspects of counseling graduate school experiences; grief counseling competencies of practicing counselors; improving response of counselor education to current market demands; methods to help supervisors improve multicultural counseling; intro text on mental health counseling strategies for teaching case conceptualization to mental health counselors. *Unit head:* Dr. Linda Barclay, Coordinator, 330-490-7264, Fax: 330-490-7165, E-mail: lbarclay@walsh.edu. *Application contact:* Brett Freshour, Vice President of Enrollment Management, 330-490-7286, Fax: 330-490-7165, E-mail: bfreshour@walsh.edu.

Washington State University, Graduate School, College of Education, Department of Educational Leadership and Counseling Psychology, Program in Counseling Psychology, Pullman, WA 99164. Offers counseling psychology (Ed M, MA, PhD); school psychologist (Certificate). *Accreditation:* APA (one or more programs are accredited). *Faculty:* 15. *Students:* 49 full-time (34 women), 17 part-time (13 women); includes 24 minority (4 African Americans, 2 American Indian/Alaska Native, 8 Asian Americans or Pacific Islanders, 10 Hispanic Americans), 4 international. Average age 27. 113 applicants, 28% accepted, 16 enrolled. In 2007, 20 master's, 8 doctorates awarded. Terminal master's awarded for partial completion of doctoral program. *Degree requirements:* For master's, comprehensive exam (for some programs), thesis (for some programs), oral or written exam; for doctorate, comprehensive exam, thesis/dissertation, oral and written exam. *Entrance requirements:* For master's and doctorate, GRE General Test, minimum GPA of 3.0, 3 letters of recommendation. Additional exam requirements/recommendations for international students: Required—TOEFL (minimum score 550 paper-based; 213 computer-based). *Application deadline:* For fall admission, 2/1 for domestic and international students. Application fee: $50. Electronic applications accepted. *Financial support:* In 2007–08, research assistantships with partial tuition reimbursements (averaging $13,917 per year), teaching assistantships with partial tuition reimbursements (averaging $13,056 per year) were awarded; career-related internships or fieldwork, Federal Work-Study, institutionally sponsored loans, scholarships/grants, tuition waivers (partial), and unspecified assistantships also available. Financial award application deadline: 4/1; financial award applicants required to submit FAFSA. *Faculty research:* Hypnosis supervision, multicultural counseling, American Indian mental health, eating disorders. *Unit head:* Dr. Marianne Barabasz, Director of Training, 509-335-3416, Fax: 509-335-7977, E-mail: mbarabasz@wsu.edu. *Application contact:* Graduate School Admissions, 800-GRADWSU, Fax: 509-335-1949, E-mail: gradsch@wsu.edu.

Wayland Baptist University, Graduate Programs, Program in Counseling, Plainview, TX 79072-6998. Offers counseling (MA); government administration (MPA); justice administration (MPA). Part-time and evening/weekend programs available. Postbaccalaureate distance learning degree programs offered. *Faculty:* 2 full-time (1 woman), 2 part-time/adjunct (1 woman). *Students:* 2 full-time (both women), 78 part-time (64 women); includes 16 minority (1 African American, 15 Hispanic Americans). Average age 33. 42 applicants, 100% accepted. *Degree requirements:* For master's, comprehensive exam. *Entrance requirements:* For master's, GRE, MAT. Application fee: $35. *Expenses:* Tuition: Full-time $6,390; part-time $355 per credit hour. Required fees: $600; $50 per term. Full-time tuition and fees vary according to course load. *Financial support:* Federal Work-Study, institutionally sponsored loans, and scholarships/grants available. Support available to part-time students. Financial award application deadline: 5/1; financial award applicants required to submit FAFSA. *Unit head:* Dr. Estelle Owens, Chairman, 806-291-1171, Fax: 806-291-1972, E-mail: owensest@wbu.edu.

Webster University, College of Arts and Sciences, Department of Behavioral and Social Sciences, Program in Counseling, St. Louis, MO 63119-3194. Offers MA. *Students:* 944 full-time (803 women), 1,066 part-time (932 women); includes 1,299 minority (1,069 African Americans, 17 American Indian/Alaska Native, 13 Asian Americans or Pacific Islanders, 200 Hispanic Americans), 23 international. Average age 35. In 2007, 628 degrees awarded. *Application deadline:* Applications are processed on a rolling basis. Application fee: $35 ($50 for international students). *Expenses:* Tuition: Full-time $9,360; part-time $520 per credit. *Financial support:* Federal Work-Study available. Support available to part-time students. Financial award application deadline: 4/1; financial award applicants required to submit FAFSA. *Unit head:* Brett Newcombe, Head, 314-968-6970. *Application contact:* Director of Graduate and Evening Student Admissions, 314-968-6983, Fax: 314-968-7116, E-mail: gadmit@webster.edu.

Western Michigan University, Graduate College, College of Education, Department of Counselor Education and Counseling Psychology, Kalamazoo, MI 49008-5202. Offers counseling psychology (PhD); counselor education (MA, Ed D, PhD); counselor education and counseling psychology (MA, PhD); counselor psychology (MA); marriage and family therapy (MA). *Accreditation:* ACA (one or more programs are accredited); APA (one or more programs are accredited); CORE; NCATE. *Degree requirements:* For doctorate, thesis/dissertation, oral exams. *Entrance requirements:* For doctorate, GRE General Test.

Western Washington University, Graduate School, College of Humanities and Social Sciences, Department of Psychology, Program in Mental Health Counseling, Bellingham, WA 98225-5996. Offers MS. *Accreditation:* ACA. *Students:* 10 full-time (all women), 2 international. 50 applicants, 18% accepted, 6 enrolled. In 2007, 6 degrees awarded. *Degree requirements:* For master's, thesis optional. *Entrance requirements:* For master's, GRE General Test, minimum GPA of 3.0 in last 60 semester hours or last 90 quarter hours. Additional exam requirements/recommendations for international students: Required—TOEFL (minimum score 567 paper-based; 227 computer-based). *Application deadline:* For fall admission, 2/1 priority date for domestic students. Application fee: $50. Electronic applications accepted. *Expenses:* Tuition, state resident: part-time $208 per credit. Tuition, nonresident: part-time $541 per credit. Required fees: $241 per quarter. One-time fee: $250 part-time. *Financial support:* In 2007–08, 3 teaching assistantships with partial tuition reimbursements (averaging $9,339 per year) were awarded; career-related internships or fieldwork, Federal Work-Study, institutionally sponsored loans, scholarships/grants, tuition waivers (partial), and unspecified assistantships also available. Support available to part-time students. Financial award application deadline: 2/15; financial award applicants required to submit FAFSA. *Unit head:* Dr. Christina Byrne, Adviser, 360-650-7945. *Application contact:* Lynn Graham, Graduate Coordinator, 360-650-3184, E-mail: lynn.graham@wwu.edu.

Westfield State College, Division of Graduate and Continuing Education, Department of Psychology, Westfield, MA 01086. Offers mental health counseling (MA); school guidance (MA). Part-time and evening/weekend programs available. *Degree requirements:* For master's, comprehensive exam. *Entrance requirements:* For master's, GRE General Test, MAT, minimum undergraduate GPA of 2.7.

Westminster College, Program in Counseling Psychology, Salt Lake City, UT 84105-3697. Offers MSPC. Part-time and evening/weekend programs available. Postbaccalaureate distance learning degree programs offered (no on-campus study). *Faculty:* 5 full-time (all women). *Students:* 14 full-time (11 women); includes 3 minority (1 American Indian/Alaska Native, 1 Asian American or Pacific Islander, 1 Hispanic American). Average age 33. 36 applicants, 47% accepted, 14 enrolled. *Degree requirements:* For master's, comprehensive exam, thesis or alternative, internship. *Entrance requirements:* For master's, GRE, 3 professional recommendations, personal statement, official transcripts, background check, baccalaurette information, minimum GPA of 3.0. Additional exam requirements/recommendations for international students: Required—TOEFL (minimum score 600 paper-based). *Application deadline:* For fall admission, 8/1 priority date for domestic students. Applications are processed on a rolling basis. Application fee: $40. Electronic applications accepted. *Expenses:* Contact institution. *Financial support:* In 2007–08, 12 students received support. Career-related internships or fieldwork available. Support available to part-time students. *Unit head:* Janine Wanlass, Director, 801-832-2428, E-mail: jwanlass@westminstercollege.edu. *Application contact:* Joel Bauman, Vice President of Enrollment Services, 801-832-2200, Fax: 801-832-3101, E-mail: admission@westminstercollege.edu.

West Virginia University, College of Human Resources and Education, Department of Counseling, Rehabilitation Counseling, and Counseling Psychology, Program in Counseling Psychology, Morgantown, WV 26506. Offers PhD. *Accreditation:* ACA; APA. *Students:* 19 full-time (13 women), 13 part-time (8 women); includes 3 minority (2 African Americans, 1 Hispanic American), 2 international. Average age 35. 30 applicants, 23% accepted, 6 enrolled. In 2007, 7 degrees awarded. *Median time to degree:* Of those who began their doctoral program in fall 1999, 100% received their degree in 8 years or less. *Degree requirements:* For doctorate, comprehensive exam, thesis/dissertation, APA-approved 1 year internship. *Entrance requirements:* For doctorate, GRE General Test, interview. Additional exam requirements/recommendations for international students: Required—TOEFL (minimum score 550 paper-based; 213 computer-based; 65 iBT). *Application deadline:* For fall admission, 12/1 for domestic and international students. Application fee: $50. Electronic applications accepted. *Expenses:* Tuition, state resident: full-time $5,196; part-time $292 per credit hour. Tuition, nonresident: full-time $15,064; part-time $840 per credit hour. Tuition and fees vary according to program. *Financial support:* In 2007–08, 23 students received support, including 2 fellowships with full tuition reimbursements available (averaging $15,000 per year), 7 research assistantships with full tuition reimbursements available (averaging $8,864 per year), 2 teaching assistantships with full tuition reimbursements available (averaging $8,864 per year); Federal Work-Study and unspecified assistantships also available. Financial award application deadline: 2/1. *Unit head:* Dr. James Bartee, Assistant Professor, 304-293-2227 Ext. 1209, Fax: 304-293-4082, E-mail: james.bartee@mail.wvu.edu.

William Carey University, School of Psychology and Counseling, Hattiesburg, MS 39401-5499. Offers counseling psychology (MS). Part-time programs available. *Entrance requirements:* For master's, GRE, PRAXIS, MAT, minimum GPA of 2.5. Additional exam requirements/

Counseling Psychology

William Carey University (continued)
recommendations for international students: Required—TOEFL (minimum score 550 paper-based; 213 computer-based). Expenses: Contact institution. *Faculty research:* Addiction prevention, psychometric measurement, crisis counseling, gerontology.

William Paterson University of New Jersey, College of the Humanities and Social Sciences, Program in Clinical and Counseling Psychology, Wayne, NJ 07470-8420. Offers MA. *Students:* 29 full-time (22 women), 23 part-time (17 women); includes 14 minority (7 African Americans, 1 Asian American or Pacific Islander, 6 Hispanic Americans), 1 international. In 2007, 13 degrees awarded. *Entrance requirements:* For master's, GRE General Test. *Application deadline:* For fall admission, 3/1 for domestic students. Applications are processed on a rolling basis. Application fee: $50. Electronic applications accepted. *Financial support:* Research assistantships with full tuition reimbursements available. Financial award application deadline: 4/1; financial award applicants required to submit FAFSA. *Unit head:* Dr. Bruce Diamond, Program Director, 973-720-3629, E-mail: psychgrad@wpunj.edu. *Application contact:* Danielle Liautaud, Director, 973-720-3579, Fax: 973-720-2035, E-mail: liautaudd@wpunj.edu.

Yeshiva University, Ferkauf Graduate School of Psychology, Program in Mental Health Counseling Psychology, New York, NY 10033-3201. Offers MA. Part-time programs available. *Entrance requirements:* For master's, GRE General Test. *Faculty research:* Substance abuse treatment, group therapy.

Developmental Psychology

Andrews University, School of Graduate Studies, School of Education, Department of Educational and Counseling Psychology, Program in Educational and Developmental Psychology, Berrien Springs, MI 49104. Offers educational and developmental psychology (MA); educational psychology (Ed D, PhD). *Degree requirements:* For master's, thesis optional.

Arizona State University, Graduate College, College of Liberal Arts and Sciences, Division of Natural Sciences and Mathematics, Department of Psychology, Tempe, AZ 85287. Offers behavioral neuroscience (PhD); clinical psychology (PhD); cognitive/behavioral systems (PhD); developmental psychology (PhD); environmental psychology (PhD); quantitative research methods (PhD); social psychology (PhD). *Accreditation:* APA. *Degree requirements:* For doctorate, thesis/dissertation. *Entrance requirements:* For doctorate, GRE General Test, GRE Subject Test.

Boston College, Lynch Graduate School of Education, Department of Counseling Psychology, Developmental, and Educational Psychology, Program in Developmental and Educational Psychology, Chestnut Hill, MA 02467-3800. Offers MA, PhD. Part-time and evening/weekend programs available. *Students:* 29 full-time (26 women), 5 part-time (4 women); includes 4 minority (2 Asian Americans or Pacific Islanders, 2 Hispanic Americans), 6 international. 113 applicants, 53% accepted, 17 enrolled. In 2007, 12 master's, 5 doctorates awarded. Terminal master's awarded for partial completion of doctoral program. *Degree requirements:* For master's, comprehensive exam; for doctorate, comprehensive exam, thesis/dissertation. *Entrance requirements:* For master's, GRE General Test or MAT; for doctorate, GRE General Test. Additional exam requirements/recommendations for international students: Required—TOEFL. Application fee: $60. Electronic applications accepted. *Financial support:* Fellowships with full and partial tuition reimbursements, research assistantships with full and partial tuition reimbursements, teaching assistantships with full and partial tuition reimbursements, career-related internships or fieldwork, Federal Work-Study, scholarships/grants, traineeships, health care benefits, tuition waivers (full and partial), and unspecified assistantships available. Support available to part-time students. Financial award applicants required to submit FAFSA. *Faculty research:* Cognitive learning and culture, effects of social policy reform on children and families, youth empowerment, impact of poverty and violence on families and communities, psychosocial trauma, human rights and international justice. *Application contact:* Adam Poluzzi, Director, Graduate Admission and Financial Aid, 617-552-4214, Fax: 617-552-0398, E-mail: poluzzi@bc.edu.

Bowling Green State University, Graduate College, College of Arts and Sciences, Department of Psychology, Bowling Green, OH 43403. Offers clinical psychology (MA, PhD); developmental psychology (MA, PhD); experimental psychology (MA, PhD); industrial/organizational psychology (MA, PhD); quantitative psychology (MA, PhD). *Accreditation:* APA (one or more programs are accredited). *Faculty:* 29 full-time (9 women), 14 part-time/adjunct (5 women). *Students:* 88 full-time (61 women), 27 part-time (19 women); includes 10 minority (5 Asian Americans or Pacific Islanders, 5 Hispanic Americans), 12 international. Average age 27. 225 applicants, 15% accepted, 19 enrolled. In 2007, 22 master's, 14 doctorates awarded. *Degree requirements:* For doctorate, thesis/dissertation. *Entrance requirements:* For doctorate, GRE General Test, GRE Subject Test. Additional exam requirements/recommendations for international students: Required—TOEFL. *Application deadline:* For fall admission, 1/1 for domestic students. Application fee: $30. Electronic applications accepted. *Financial support:* In 2007–08, 5 fellowships with full tuition reimbursements (averaging $16,187 per year), 50 research assistantships with full tuition reimbursements (averaging $11,844 per year), 29 teaching assistantships with full tuition reimbursements (averaging $11,805 per year) were awarded; career-related internships or fieldwork, Federal Work-Study, institutionally sponsored loans, tuition waivers (full), and unspecified assistantships also available. Financial award applicants required to submit FAFSA. *Faculty research:* Personnel psychology, developmental-mathematical models, behavioral medication, brain process, child/adolescent social cognition. *Unit head:* Dr. Dale Klopfer, Chair, 419-372-2733.

Brandeis University, Graduate School of Arts and Sciences, Department of Psychology, Waltham, MA 02454-9110. Offers cognitive neuroscience (PhD); general psychology (MA); social/developmental psychology (PhD). MA program offered to students enrolled in PhD program only. *Faculty:* 16 full-time (3 women), 3 part-time/adjunct (all women). *Students:* 26 full-time (19 women), 8 international. Average age 26. 44 applicants, 20% accepted, 5 enrolled. In 2007, 5 master's, 3 doctorates awarded. *Median time to degree:* Of those who began their doctoral program in fall 1999, 100% received their degree in 8 years or less. *Degree requirements:* For doctorate, comprehensive exam, thesis/dissertation. *Entrance requirements:* For doctorate, GRE General Test, GRE Subject Test (recommended), 3 letters of recommendation. Additional exam requirements/recommendations for international students: Required—TOEFL (minimum score 600 paper-based; 250 computer-based). *Application deadline:* For fall admission, 1/15 for domestic and international students. Application fee: $55. Electronic applications accepted. *Financial support:* In 2007–08, 21 fellowships with full tuition reimbursements (averaging $18,000 per year), teaching assistantships with full tuition reimbursements (averaging $3,000 per year) were awarded; institutionally sponsored loans, scholarships/grants, traineeships, health care benefits, tuition waivers (full), and unspecified assistantships also available. *Faculty research:* Development, cognition, social aging, perception. Total annual research expenditures: $5.1 million. *Unit head:* Paul DiZio, Director of Graduate Studies, 781-736-3300, Fax: 781-736-3291, E-mail: dizio@brandeis.edu. *Application contact:* Donna J. Coletti, Graduate Admissions Coordinator, 781-736-3303, Fax: 781-736-3291, E-mail: coletti@brandeis.edu.

Bryn Mawr College, Graduate School of Arts and Sciences, Department of Psychology, Bryn Mawr, PA 19010-2899. Offers clinical developmental psychology (PhD). Part-time programs available. *Faculty:* 11. *Students:* 24 full-time (23 women), 10 part-time (all women); includes 2 minority (1 Asian American or Pacific Islander, 1 Hispanic American), 2 international. 56 applicants, 20% accepted, 4 enrolled. In 2007, 3 doctorates awarded. *Degree requirements:* For doctorate, one foreign language, comprehensive exam, thesis/dissertation. *Entrance requirements:* For doctorate, GRE General Test. Additional exam requirements/recommendations for international students: Required—TOEFL (minimum score 600 paper-based; 250 computer-based). *Application deadline:* For fall admission, 1/3 for domestic and international students. Application fee: $30. *Financial support:* Teaching assistantships with partial tuition reimbursements, career-related internships or fieldwork and scholarships/grants available. Support available to part-time students. Financial award application deadline: 1/3. *Unit head:* Dr. Marc Schulz, Chair, 610-526-5039, E-mail: mschulz@brynmawr.edu. *Application contact:* Lea R. Miller, Secretary, 610-526-5072, Fax: 610-526-5076, E-mail: lrmiller@brynmawr.edu.

Carnegie Mellon University, College of Humanities and Social Sciences, Department of Psychology, Area of Developmental Psychology, Pittsburgh, PA 15213-3891. Offers PhD. *Degree requirements:* For doctorate, comprehensive exam, thesis/dissertation. *Entrance requirements:* For doctorate, GRE General Test. Additional exam requirements/recommendations for international students: Required—TOEFL. *Faculty research:* Cognitive development, language acquisition.

Claremont Graduate University, Graduate Programs, School of Behavioral and Organizational Sciences, Department of Psychology, Claremont, CA 91711-6160. Offers advanced study in evaluation (Certificate); cognitive psychology (MA, PhD); developmental psychology (MA, PhD); evaluation and applied research methods (MA, PhD); health behavior research and evaluation (MA, PhD); human resource development and evaluation (MA); industrial/organizational psychology (MA, PhD); organizational behavior (MA, PhD); organizational psychology (MA, PhD); social psychology (MA, PhD); MBA/PhD. Part-time programs available. *Faculty:* 15 full-time (7 women), 4 part-time/adjunct (2 women). *Students:* 184 full-time (137 women), 24 part-time (20 women); includes 51 minority (13 African Americans, 1 American Indian/Alaska Native, 26 Asian Americans or Pacific Islanders, 11 Hispanic Americans), 12 international. Average age 29. In 2007, 42 master's, 10 doctorates, 2 other advanced degrees awarded. Terminal master's awarded for partial completion of doctoral program. *Degree requirements:* For master's, thesis (for some programs); for doctorate, comprehensive exam, thesis/dissertation. *Entrance requirements:* For master's and doctorate, GRE General Test. *Application deadline:* For fall admission, 2/15 priority date for domestic students. Applications are processed on a rolling basis. Electronic applications accepted. *Expenses:* Tuition: Full-time $31,640; part-time $1,376 per unit. Required fees: $145 per semester. Tuition and fees vary according to course load, degree level and program. *Financial support:* Fellowships, research assistantships, teaching assistantships, career-related internships or fieldwork, Federal Work-Study, institutionally sponsored loans, and tuition waivers (full and partial) available. Support available to part-time students. Financial award application deadline: 2/15; financial award applicants required to submit FAFSA. *Faculty research:* Social intervention, diversity in organizations, eyewitness memory, aging and cognition, drug policy. *Unit head:* Natalie Brown, Program Coordinator, 909-621-8084, Fax: 909-621-8905, E-mail: natalie.brown@cgu.edu.

Clark University, Graduate School, Department of Psychology, Program in Developmental Psychology, Worcester, MA 01610-1477. Offers PhD. *Degree requirements:* For doctorate, thesis/dissertation. *Entrance requirements:* For doctorate, GRE General Test. Additional exam requirements/recommendations for international students: Required—TOEFL. *Application deadline:* For fall admission, 1/1 priority date for domestic students. Applications are processed on a rolling basis. Application fee: $55. *Expenses:* Tuition: Full-time $32,600; part-time $1,019 per credit. Required fees: $30. Tuition and fees vary according to program. *Financial support:* In 2007–08, fellowships with full tuition reimbursements (averaging $15,700 per year), research assistantships with full tuition reimbursements (averaging $15,700 per year), teaching assistantships with full tuition reimbursements (averaging $15,700 per year) were awarded; tuition waivers (full) also available. *Unit head:* Dr. Michael Bambert, Chair, 508-793-7274. *Application contact:* Peggy Moskowitz, Graduate School Secretary, 508-793-7274, Fax: 508-793-7265, E-mail: psychology@clarku.edu.

Cornell University, Graduate School, Graduate Fields of Human Ecology, Field of Human Development, Ithaca, NY 14853-0001. Offers developmental psychology (PhD), including cognitive development, developmental psychopathology, ecology of human development, social and personality development; human development and family studies (PhD), including ecology of human development, family studies and the life course. *Faculty:* 35 full-time (12 women). *Students:* 29 full-time (22 women); includes 4 minority (2 Asian Americans or Pacific Islanders, 2 Hispanic Americans), 10 international. Average age 27. 63 applicants, 19% accepted, 5 enrolled. In 2007, 5 doctorates awarded. *Degree requirements:* For doctorate, comprehensive exam, thesis/dissertation, pre-doctoral research project, teaching experience. *Entrance requirements:* For doctorate, GRE General Test, 2 letters of recommendation. Additional exam requirements/recommendations for international students: Required—TOEFL (minimum score 550 paper-based; 213 computer-based; 77 iBT). *Application deadline:* For fall admission, 1/15 for domestic students. Application fee: $70. Electronic applications accepted. *Financial support:* In 2007–08, 28 students received support, including 6 fellowships with full tuition reimbursements available, 6 research assistantships with full tuition reimbursements available, 16 teaching assistantships with full tuition reimbursements available; institutionally sponsored loans, scholarships/grants, health care benefits, tuition waivers (full and partial), and unspecified assistantships also available. Financial award applicants required to submit FAFSA. *Faculty research:* Cognitive development, developmental psychopathology, ecology of human development, family studies and the life course, social and personality development. *Unit head:* Director of Graduate Studies, 607-255-3181, Fax: 607-255-9856. *Application contact:* Graduate Field Assistant, 607-255-3181, Fax: 607-255-9856, E-mail: hdfs@cornell.edu.

Duke University, Graduate School, Department of Psychology, Durham, NC 27708-0586. Offers biological psychology (PhD); clinical psychology (PhD); cognitive psychology (PhD); developmental psychology (PhD); experimental psychology (PhD); health psychology (PhD); human social development (PhD); JD/MA. *Accreditation:* APA (one or more programs are accredited). *Faculty:* 40 full-time. *Students:* 91 full-time (71 women); includes 15 minority (9 African Americans, 1 Asian American or Pacific Islander, 5 Hispanic Americans), 13 international. 468 applicants, 7% accepted, 19 enrolled. In 2007, 14 doctorates awarded. *Degree requirements:* For doctorate, thesis/dissertation. *Entrance requirements:* For doctorate, GRE General Test. Additional exam requirements/recommendations for international students: Required—TOEFL (minimum score 550 paper-based; 213 computer-based; 83 iBT), IELTS (minimum score 7). *Application deadline:* For fall admission, 12/15 priority date for domestic and international students. Application fee: $75. Electronic applications accepted. *Financial support:* Fellowships, research assistantships, teaching assistantships, career-related internships or fieldwork and Federal Work-Study available. Financial award application deadline: 12/31. *Unit head:* Amy Needham, Co-Director of Graduate Studies, 919-660-5715, Fax: 919-660-5726, E-mail: morrell@duke.edu.

Emory University, Graduate School of Arts and Sciences, Department of Psychology, Atlanta, GA 30322-1100. Offers clinical psychology (PhD); cognition and development (PhD); neuroscience and animal behavior (PhD). *Accreditation:* APA. *Degree requirements:* For doctorate, comprehensive exam, thesis/dissertation. *Entrance requirements:* For doctorate, GRE General Test, minimum GPA of 3.25. Additional exam requirements/recommendations for international students: Required—TOEFL. Electronic applications accepted. *Faculty research:* Neuroscience and animal behavior; adult and child psychopathology, cognition development assessment.

Erikson Institute, Academic Programs, Chicago, IL 60611-5627. Offers administration (Certificate); bilingual/ESL (Certificate); child development (MS); early childhood education (MS); infant mental health (Certificate); infant studies (Certificate); MS/MSW. Part-time and evening/weekend programs available. *Degree requirements:* For master's, comprehensive exam, internship; for Certificate, internship. *Entrance requirements:* For master's and Certificate, minimum GPA of 2.75. Additional exam requirements/recommendations for international students: Required—TOEFL. *Faculty research:* Assessment strategies from early childhood through elementary years; language, literacy, and the arts in children's development; inclusive special education; parent-child relationships; cognitive development.

Florida International University, College of Arts and Sciences, Department of Psychology, Miami, FL 33199. Offers developmental psychology (PhD); general psychology (MS); psychology (MS). Part-time programs available. *Faculty:* 24 full-time (12 women). *Students:* 108 full-time (75 women), 34 part-time (22 women); includes 75 minority (12 African Americans, 2 Asian Americans or Pacific Islanders, 61 Hispanic Americans), 18 international. Average age 29. 194 applicants, 25% accepted, 26 enrolled. In 2007, 49 master's, 10 doctorates awarded. Terminal master's awarded for partial completion of doctoral program. *Degree requirements:* For master's, thesis; for doctorate, comprehensive exam, thesis/dissertation. *Entrance requirements:* For master's, GRE General Test, minimum GPA of 3.0, resumé, writing samples; for doctorate, GRE General Test, 3 letters of recommendation, resumé, writing samples, minimum GPA of 3.0. Additional exam requirements/recommendations for international students: Required—TOEFL (minimum score 550 paper-based; 213 computer-based). *Application deadline:* For fall admission, 12/5 for domestic students, 12/15 for international students. Application fee: $30. Electronic applications accepted. *Expenses:* Tuition, state resident: full-time $6,106. Tuition, nonresident: full-time $15,528. Required fees: $284. *Financial support:* Fellowships, research assistantships, teaching assistantships, Federal Work-Study, institutionally sponsored loans, and scholarships/grants available. Support available to part-time students. *Faculty research:* Community psychology. *Unit head:* Dr. Suzanna Rose, Chairperson, 305-348-2408, Fax: 305-348-3143, E-mail: suzanna.rose@fiu.edu.

Florida State University, Graduate Studies, College of Arts and Sciences, Department of Psychology, Program in Developmental Psychology, Tallahassee, FL 32306. Offers PhD. *Faculty:* 8 full-time (1 woman). *Students:* 10 full-time (9 women); includes 1 minority (Hispanic American) Average age 26. 14 applicants. In 2007, 1 doctorate awarded. *Degree requirements:* For doctorate, thesis/dissertation, preliminary exam. *Entrance requirements:* For doctorate, GRE, minimum GPA of 3.0, research experience, letters of recommendation. Additional exam requirements/recommendations for international students: Required—TOEFL (minimum score 550 paper-based; 213 computer-based; 80 iBT). *Application deadline:* For fall admission, 12/15 for domestic and international students. Application fee: $30. Electronic applications accepted. *Expenses:* Tuition, state resident: part-time $248 per credit hour. Tuition, nonresident: part-time $880 per credit hour. Tuition and fees vary according to program. *Financial support:* In 2007–08, 7 fellowships (averaging $18,000 per year), 2 research assistantships with full tuition reimbursements (averaging $18,000 per year) were awarded; Federal Work-Study, institutionally sponsored loans, scholarships/grants, health care benefits, and unspecified assistantships also available. *Faculty research:* Learning disabilities, phonological processing, psychology of reading, emergent literacy, aging. *Unit head:* Dr. Richard Wagner, Director, 850-644-1033, Fax: 850-644-7739, E-mail: rkwagner@psy.fsu.edu. *Application contact:* Cherie P. Miller, Graduate Program Assistant, 850-644-2499, Fax: 850-644-7739, E-mail: grad-info@psy.fsu.edu.

Fordham University, Graduate School of Arts and Sciences, Department of Psychology, Program in Applied Developmental Psychology, New York, NY 10458. Offers PhD. *Students:* 25 full-time (20 women), 11 part-time (9 women); includes 8 minority (3 African Americans, 2 Asian Americans or Pacific Islanders, 3 Hispanic Americans), 4 international. Average age 29. 27 applicants, 41% accepted, 6 enrolled. In 2007, 1 degree awarded. *Degree requirements:* For doctorate, comprehensive exam, thesis/dissertation. *Entrance requirements:* For doctorate, GRE General Test, GRE Subject Test. Additional exam requirements/recommendations for international students: Required—TOEFL (minimum score 600 paper-based; 250 computer-based). *Application deadline:* For fall admission, 12/14 for domestic students. Application fee: $70. Electronic applications accepted. *Expenses:* Tuition: Full-time $23,880; part-time $995 per credit. *Financial support:* In 2007–08, 13 students received support, including 2 fellowships with tuition reimbursements available (averaging $19,100 per year), 11 research assistantships with tuition reimbursements available (averaging $18,336 per year); teaching assistantships with tuition reimbursements available, career-related internships or fieldwork, institutionally sponsored loans, tuition waivers (full and partial), and unspecified assistantships also available. Financial award application deadline: 12/14. *Faculty research:* Development of citizenship, impact of participation in community service, impact of poverty on children, development of moral reasoning and behavior. Total annual research expenditures: $1.4 million. *Unit head:* Dr. Ann D'Allesandro, Director, 718-817-3789, Fax: 718-817-3785, E-mail: sherrod@fordham.edu. *Application contact:* Charlene Dundie, Director of Graduate Admissions, 718-817-4420, Fax: 718-817-3566, E-mail: dundie@fordham.edu.

Gallaudet University, The Graduate School, College of Arts and Sciences, Department of Psychology, Program in School Psychology, Washington, DC 20002-3625. Offers developmental psychology (MA); school psychology (Psy S). *Accreditation:* NCATE. *Degree requirements:* For master's, thesis optional. *Entrance requirements:* For master's, GRE General Test or MAT. *Application deadline:* For fall admission, 2/15 priority date for domestic students. Applications are processed on a rolling basis. Application fee: $50. Electronic applications accepted. *Expenses:* Tuition: Full-time $5,790. Required fees: $1,886. *Financial support:* Unspecified assistantships and stipends available. Financial award application deadline: 8/1. *Unit head:* Dr. Lynne Blennerhassett, Director, 202-651-5540. *Application contact:* Wednesday Luria, Coordinator of Prospective Graduate Student Services, 202-651-5647, Fax: 202-651-5295, E-mail: wednesday.luria@gallaudet.edu.

George Mason University, College of Humanities and Social Sciences, Department of Psychology, Fairfax, VA 22030. Offers applied developmental psychology (MA, PhD); biopsychology (MA, PhD); clinical psychology (MA, PhD); human factors engineering psychology (MA, PhD); industrial/organizational psychology (MA, PhD); psychology (MA, PhD); school psychology (MA). *Accreditation:* APA. *Faculty:* 44 full-time (17 women), 16 part-time/adjunct (10 women). *Students:* 101 full-time (80 women), 135 part-time (88 women); includes 30 minority (6 African Americans, 13 Asian Americans or Pacific Islanders, 11 Hispanic Americans), 14 international. Average age 27. 734 applicants, 22% accepted, 86 enrolled. In 2007, 49 master's, 17 doctorates awarded. Terminal master's awarded for partial completion of doctoral program. *Median time to degree:* Of those who began their doctoral program in fall 1999, 97% received their degree in 8 years or less. *Degree requirements:* For master's, thesis (for applied developmental psychology and biopsychology); for doctorate, comprehensive exam, thesis/dissertation or alternative. *Entrance requirements:* For master's, GRE General Test, minimum GPA of 3.0 in last 60 hours of course work, undergraduate course work in psychology; for doctorate, GRE General Test, minimum undergraduate GPA of 3.0, 3.3 in major. Additional exam requirements/recommendations for international students: Required—TOEFL (minimum score 575 paper-based; 230 computer-based; 88 iBT), IELTS (minimum score 6). Application fee: $60 ($75 for international students). Electronic applications accepted. *Financial support:* In 2007–08, 15 fellowships with partial tuition reimbursements (averaging $2,300 per year), 33 research assistantships with partial tuition reimbursements (averaging $12,200 per year), 21 teaching assistantships with partial tuition reimbursements (averaging $12,200 per year) were awarded; career-related internships or fieldwork, scholarships/grants, traineeships, tuition waivers (partial), and unspecified assistantships also available. Financial award application deadline: 3/1; financial award applicants required to submit FAFSA. *Unit head:* Dr. Deborah Boehm-Davis, Chairperson, 703-993-1398, Fax: 703-993-1359, E-mail: bsmith@gmu.edu. *Application contact:* Dr. James Maddux, Information Contact, 703-993-3590, Fax: 703-993-1355, E-mail: psycgrad@gmu.edu.

Graduate School and University Center of the City University of New York, Graduate Studies, Program in Psychology, New York, NY 10016-4039. Offers basic applied neurocognition (PhD); biopsychology (PhD); clinical psychology (PhD); developmental psychology (PhD); environmental psychology (PhD); experimental psychology (PhD); industrial psychology (PhD); learning processes (PhD); neuropsychology (PhD); psychology (PhD); social personality (PhD). *Faculty:* 119 full-time (40 women). *Students:* 510 full-time (379 women), 1 (woman) part-time; includes 98 minority (39 African Americans, 1 American Indian/Alaska Native, 21 Asian Americans or Pacific Islanders, 37 Hispanic Americans), 63 international. Average age 33. 747 applicants, 17% accepted, 78 enrolled. In 2007, 59 degrees awarded. *Degree requirements:* For doctorate, one foreign language, thesis/dissertation. *Entrance requirements:* For doctorate, GRE General Test. Additional exam requirements/recommendations for international students: Required—TOEFL. *Application deadline:* For fall admission, 12/15 for domestic students. Application fee: $125. Electronic applications accepted. *Financial support:* In 2007–08, 371 students received support, including 308 fellowships, 34 research assistantships, 33 teaching assistantships; career-related internships or fieldwork, Federal Work-Study, institutionally sponsored loans, and tuition waivers (full and partial) also available. Financial award application deadline: 2/1; financial award applicants required to submit FAFSA. *Unit head:* Dr. Joseph Glick, Executive Officer, 212-817-8706, Fax: 212-817-1533, E-mail: jglick@gc.cuny.edu.

Harvard University, Graduate School of Arts and Sciences, Department of Psychology, Cambridge, MA 02138. Offers psychology (PhD), including behavior and decision analysis, cognition, developmental psychology, experimental psychology, personality, psychobiology, psychopathology; social psychology (PhD). *Degree requirements:* For doctorate, thesis/dissertation, general exams. *Entrance requirements:* For doctorate, GRE General Test. Additional exam requirements/recommendations for international students: Required—TOEFL. *Expenses:* Tuition: Full-time $31,456. Full-time tuition and fees vary according to program and student level.

Howard University, Graduate School, Department of Psychology, Washington, DC 20059-0002. Offers clinical psychology (PhD); developmental psychology (PhD); experimental psychology (PhD); neuropsychology (PhD); personality psychology (PhD); psychology (MS); social psychology (PhD). *Accreditation:* APA (one or more programs are accredited). Part-time programs available. *Degree requirements:* For master's, thesis; for doctorate, comprehensive exam, thesis/dissertation, qualifying exam. *Entrance requirements:* For master's, GRE General Test, minimum GPA of 2.5, bachelor's degree in psychology or related field; for doctorate, GRE General Test, minimum GPA of 3.0. *Expenses:* Tuition: Full-time $16,175; part-time $899 per credit hour. Required fees: $805. *Faculty research:* Personality and psychophysiology, educational and social development of African-American children, child and adult psychopathology.

Illinois State University, Graduate School, College of Arts and Sciences, Department of Psychology, Normal, IL 61790-2200. Offers psychology (MA, MS), including clinical psychology, counseling psychology, developmental psychology, educational psychology, experimental psychology, measurement-evaluation, organizational-industrial psychology; school psychology (PhD, SSP). *Accreditation:* APA. *Faculty:* 36 full-time (14 women). *Students:* 49 full-time (37 women), 19 part-time (14 women); includes 3 minority (all Asian Americans or Pacific Islanders), 7 international. 91 applicants, 43% accepted. In 2007, 24 degrees awarded. *Degree requirements:* For master's, thesis or alternative; for doctorate, variable foreign language requirement, thesis/dissertation, 2 terms of residency, internship, practicum. *Entrance requirements:* For master's, GRE General Test, GRE Subject Test, minimum GPA of 3.0 in last 60 hours of course work; for doctorate, GRE General Test. *Application deadline:* Applications are processed on a rolling basis. Application fee: $40. *Expenses:* Tuition, state resident: full-time $3,492; part-time $194 per credit hour. Tuition, nonresident: full-time $7,272; part-time $404 per credit hour. Required fees: $1,024; $57 per credit hour. *Financial support:* In 2007–08, 33 research assistantships (averaging $6,252 per year), 49 teaching assistantships (averaging $4,217 per year) were awarded; tuition waivers (full) and unspecified assistantships also available. Financial award application deadline: 4/1. *Faculty research:* Comprehensive evaluation system for the central region professional development grant, Illinois school psychology internship consortium, for children's sake. Total annual research expenditures: $292,085. *Unit head:* Dr. Neil Skaggs, Acting Chairperson, 309-438-8651.

Indiana University Bloomington, University Graduate School, College of Arts and Sciences, Department of Psychological and Brain Sciences, Bloomington, IN 47405-7000. Offers biology and behavior (PhD); clinical science (PhD); cognitive psychology (PhD); developmental psychology (PhD); psychological and brain sciences (MA); social psychology (PhD). *Accreditation:* APA (one or more programs are accredited). *Faculty:* 53 full-time (16 women). *Students:* 79 full-time (42 women), 14 part-time (7 women); includes 10 minority (3 African Americans, 3 Asian Americans or Pacific Islanders, 4 Hispanic Americans), 16 international. Average age 28. 240 applicants, 10% accepted, 20 enrolled. In 2007, 5 master's, 15 doctorates awarded. *Median time to degree:* Of those who began their doctoral program in fall 1999, 86% received their degree in 8 years or less. *Degree requirements:* For doctorate, comprehensive exam, thesis/dissertation, 1st and 2nd year projects, 1 year as associate instructor, qualifying exam, teaching. *Entrance requirements:* For doctorate, GRE. Additional exam requirements/recommendations for international students: Required—TOEFL (minimum score 550 paper-based; 213 computer-based). *Application deadline:* For fall admission, 12/15 for domestic students, 12/1 for international students. Application fee: $50 ($60 for international students). Electronic applications accepted. *Financial support:* Fellowships with full tuition reimbursements, research assistantships with full tuition reimbursements, teaching assistantships with full tuition reimbursements, scholarships/grants, health care benefits, and unspecified assistantships available. *Unit head:* Dr. Linda B. Smith, Chair, 812-855-3991, Fax: 812-855-4691, E-mail: smith4@indiana.edu. *Application contact:* Patricia G. Crouch, Academic Services Coordinator, 812-855-4528, Fax: 812-855-4691, E-mail: pcrouch@indiana.edu.

Louisiana State University and Agricultural and Mechanical College, Graduate School, College of Arts and Sciences, Department of Psychology, Baton Rouge, LA 70803. Offers biological psychology (MA, PhD); clinical psychology (MA, PhD); cognitive psychology (MA, PhD); developmental psychology (MA, PhD); industrial/organizational psychology (MA, PhD); school psychology (MA, PhD). *Accreditation:* APA (one or more programs are accredited). *Faculty:* 25 full-time (9 women). *Students:* 81 full-time (60 women), 23 part-time (15 women); includes 15 minority (6 African Americans, 4 American Indian/Alaska Native, 2 Asian Americans or Pacific Islanders, 3 Hispanic Americans), 3 international. Average age 28. 199 applicants, 15% accepted, 23 enrolled. In 2007, 11 master's, 13 doctorates awarded. Terminal master's awarded for partial completion of doctoral program. *Degree requirements:* For master's, thesis; for doctorate, thesis/dissertation, 1 year internship. *Entrance requirements:* For master's and doctorate, GRE General Test, minimum GPA of 3.0. Additional exam requirements/recommendations for international students: Required—TOEFL (minimum score 550 paper-based; 213 computer-based; 79 iBT). *Application deadline:* For fall admission, 1/15 for domestic and international students. Applications are processed on a rolling basis. Application fee: $25. Electronic applications accepted. *Financial support:* In 2007–08, 101 students received support, including 5 fellowships (averaging $26,557 per year), 55 teaching assistantships with partial tuition reimbursements available (averaging $13,218 per year); research assistantships with partial tuition reimbursements available, career-related internships or fieldwork, Federal Work-Study, institutionally sponsored loans, scholarships/grants, health care benefits, and tuition waivers (full and partial) also available. Financial award applicants required to submit FAFSA. *Faculty research:* Clinical psychology, autism, anxiety, addition, neuro-psychology, school psychology, cognitive psychology, experimental psychology. Total annual research expenditures: $582,678. *Unit head:* Dr. Alan Baumeister, Chair, 225-578-4099, Fax: 225-578-4125, E-mail: abaumei@lsu.edu. *Application contact:* Dr. Janet McDonald, Coordinator of Graduate Studies, 225-578-4116, Fax: 225-578-4125, E-mail: psmcdo@lsu.edu.

Loyola University Chicago, Graduate School, Department of Psychology, Program in Developmental Psychology, Chicago, IL 60611-2196. Offers PhD. *Faculty:* 6 full-time (4 women),

Developmental Psychology

Loyola University Chicago (continued)
1 (woman) part-time/adjunct. *Students:* 11 full-time (10 women); includes 3 minority (1 African American, 1 American Indian/Alaska Native, 1 Hispanic American). Average age 24. 18 applicants, 17% accepted, 3 enrolled. In 2007, 2 doctorates awarded. *Degree requirements:* For doctorate, comprehensive exam, thesis/dissertation, internship or teaching. *Entrance requirements:* For doctorate, GRE General Test, GRE Subject Test. Additional exam requirements/recommendations for international students: Required—TOEFL (minimum score 500 paper-based). *Application deadline:* For fall admission, 2/1 for domestic students. Application fee: $50. Electronic applications accepted. *Expenses:* Tuition: Full-time $12,780; part-time $710 per credit hour. Required fees: $55 per semester. Full-time tuition and fees vary according to program. *Financial support:* In 2007–08, 5 students received support, including fellowships with full tuition reimbursements available (averaging $14,000 per year), research assistantships with full tuition reimbursements available (averaging $14,000 per year), teaching assistantships with full tuition reimbursements available (averaging $14,000 per year); career-related internships or fieldwork, scholarships/grants, and unspecified assistantships also available. Financial award application deadline: 2/1; financial award applicants required to submit FAFSA. *Faculty research:* Cognitive development, parenting, bilingualism, memory development, emotion development, aggression and violence, racism stereotyping. Total annual research expenditures: $10,000. *Unit head:* Dr. Denise Davidson, Director, 773-508-3008, Fax: 773-508-2813, E-mail: ddavids@luc.edu.

McGill University, Faculty of Graduate and Postdoctoral Studies, Faculty of Education, Department of Educational and Counseling Psychology, Montréal, QC H3A 2T5, Canada. Offers counseling psychology (MA, PhD); educational psychology (M Ed, MA, PhD); school/applied child psychology and applied developmental psychology (M Ed, MA, PhD, Diploma), including school psychology. *Accreditation:* APA. *Faculty:* 33 full-time (19 women), 36 part-time/adjunct (23 women). *Students:* 198 full-time (172 women), 70 part-time (61 women). 327 applicants, 37% accepted, 92 enrolled. In 2007, 78 master's, 16 doctorates awarded.

New York University, Steinhardt School of Culture, Education and Human Development, Department of Applied Psychology, Program in Educational and Developmental Psychology, New York, NY 10012-1019. Offers educational psychology (MA), including general educational psychology, psychological measurement and evaluation, psychology of parenthood; psychological development (PhD); school psychology (PhD). *Accreditation:* APA (one or more programs are accredited). Part-time and evening/weekend programs available. *Faculty:* 28 full-time (18 women). *Students:* 65 full-time (57 women), 60 part-time (58 women); includes 38 minority (17 African Americans, 7 Asian Americans or Pacific Islanders, 14 Hispanic Americans), 16 international. 159 applicants, 60% accepted, 27 enrolled. In 2007, 21 master's, 10 doctorates awarded. Terminal master's awarded for partial completion of doctoral program. *Degree requirements:* For master's, thesis (for some programs); for doctorate, thesis/dissertation. *Entrance requirements:* For doctorate, GRE General Test, interview. Additional exam requirements/recommendations for international students: Required—TOEFL. *Application deadline:* For fall admission, 12/15 priority date for domestic and international students; for spring admission, 11/1 for domestic and international students. Applications are processed on a rolling basis. Application fee: $50. *Financial support:* Teaching assistantships with partial tuition reimbursements, career-related internships or fieldwork, Federal Work-Study, institutionally sponsored loans, and tuition waivers (partial) available. Support available to part-time students. Financial award application deadline: 2/1; financial award applicants required to submit FAFSA. *Faculty research:* High risk children and youth; child and adolescent developments; families and schooling; infant cognition; exploration, language, and symbolic play in toddlerhood. *Unit head:* Dr. Barbara Hummel-Rossi, Director, 212-998-5360, Fax: 212-995-4358. *Application contact:* 212-998-5030, Fax: 212-995-4328, E-mail: steinhardt.gradadmissions@nyu.edu.

North Carolina State University, Graduate School, College of Humanities and Social Sciences, Department of Psychology, Raleigh, NC 27695. Offers developmental psychology (PhD); ergonomics and experimental psychology (PhD); industrial/organizational psychology (PhD); psychology in the public interest (PhD); school psychology (PhD). *Accreditation:* APA. *Degree requirements:* For doctorate, comprehensive exam, thesis/dissertation. *Entrance requirements:* For doctorate, GRE General Test, GRE Subject Test (industrial/organizational psychology), MAT (recommended), minimum GPA of 3.0 in major. Electronic applications accepted. *Faculty research:* Cognitive and social development (human factors, families, the workplace, community issues and health, aging).

The Ohio State University, Graduate School, College of Social and Behavioral Sciences, School of Social and Behavioral Science, Department of Psychology, Columbus, OH 43210. Offers behavioral neuroscience (PhD); clinical psychology (PhD); cognitive psychology (PhD); developmental psychology (PhD); mental retardation and developmental disabilities (PhD); psychology (MA); quantitative psychology (PhD); social psychology (PhD). *Accreditation:* APA (one or more programs are accredited). *Faculty:* 60. *Students:* 111 full-time (78 women), 6 part-time (4 women); includes 19 minority (6 African Americans, 1 American Indian/Alaska Native, 3 Asian Americans or Pacific Islanders, 9 Hispanic Americans), 16 international. Average age 27. In 2007, 17 master's, 41 doctorates awarded. *Degree requirements:* For doctorate, thesis/dissertation. *Entrance requirements:* For master's and doctorate, GRE General Test. Additional exam requirements/recommendations for international students: Required—TOEFL (minimum score 600 paper-based; 250 computer-based). *Application deadline:* For fall admission, 12/31 for domestic students, 11/30 for international students. Applications are processed on a rolling basis. Application fee: $40 ($50 for international students). Electronic applications accepted. *Financial support:* Fellowships, research assistantships, teaching assistantships available. *Unit head:* Marilynn B. Brewer, Graduate Studies Committee Chair, 614-292-3038, Fax: 614-292-4537. *Application contact:* 614-292-9444, Fax: 614-292-3895, E-mail: domestic.grad@osu.edu.

Penn State University Park, Graduate School, College of the Liberal Arts, Department of Psychology, State College, University Park, PA 16802-1503. Offers clinical psychology (MS, PhD); cognitive psychology (MS, PhD); developmental psychology (MS, PhD); industrial/organizational psychology (MS, PhD); psychobiology (MS, PhD); social psychology (MS, PhD). *Accreditation:* APA (one or more programs are accredited). *Expenses:* Tuition, state resident: full-time $14,738; part-time $614 per credit. Tuition, nonresident: full-time $26,050; part-time $1,085 per credit. Tuition and fees vary according to course load, program and student level. *Unit head:* Dr. Melvin M. Mark, Interim Head, 814-865-9515, Fax: 814-863-7002, E-mail: m5m@psu.edu.

Queen's University at Kingston, School of Graduate Studies and Research, Faculty of Arts and Sciences, Department of Psychology, Kingston, ON K7L 3N6, Canada. Offers brain behavior and cognitive science (MA, PhD); clinical psychology (MA, PhD); developmental psychology (MA, PhD); social personality psychology (MA, PhD). *Accreditation:* APA (one or more programs are accredited). *Degree requirements:* For master's, thesis; for doctorate, comprehensive exam, thesis/dissertation. *Entrance requirements:* For master's and doctorate, GRE General Test. Additional exam requirements/recommendations for international students: Required—TOEFL. *Faculty research:* Human development, social, personality, behavioral neuroscience, forensic.

Stanford University, School of Education, Program in Psychological Studies in Education, Stanford, CA 94305-9991. Offers child and adolescent development (PhD); counseling psychology (PhD); educational psychology (PhD). *Degree requirements:* For doctorate, thesis/dissertation. *Entrance requirements:* For doctorate, GRE General Test. Electronic applications accepted.

Suffolk University, College of Arts and Sciences, Department of Psychology, Boston, MA 02108-2770. Offers clinical-developmental psychology (PhD). *Accreditation:* APA. *Faculty:* 16 full-time (11 women). *Students:* 36 full-time (31 women), 15 part-time (11 women); includes 5 minority (2 African Americans, 2 Asian Americans or Pacific Islanders, 1 Hispanic American), 2 international. Average age 28. 315 applicants, 10% accepted, 13 enrolled. In 2007, 16 degrees awarded. *Degree requirements:* For doctorate, thesis/dissertation, practicum. *Entrance requirements:* For doctorate, GRE General Test or MAT. Additional exam requirements/recommendations for international students: Required—TOEFL (minimum score 550 paper-based; 213 computer-based; 80 iBT). *Application deadline:* For fall admission, 12/15 for domestic and international students. Applications are processed on a rolling basis. Application fee: $50. Electronic applications accepted. *Expenses:* Contact institution. *Financial support:* In 2007–08, 46 students received support, including 36 fellowships with full and partial tuition reimbursements available (averaging $16,747 per year); career-related internships or fieldwork, Federal Work-Study, and institutionally sponsored loans also available. Support available to part-time students. Financial award application deadline: 4/1; financial award applicants required to submit FAFSA. *Faculty research:* Olfaction decision-making in substance-dependent individuals, ego development, experiential avoidance in generalized anxiety disorder. *Unit head:* Dr. Robert Webb, Chair, 617-573-8293, Fax: 617-367-2924, E-mail: rwebb@suffolk.edu. *Application contact:* Judith Reynolds, Director of Graduate Admissions, 617-573-8302, Fax: 617-523-0116, E-mail: grad.admission@suffolk.edu.

Teachers College, Columbia University, Graduate Faculty of Education, Department of Human Development, Program in Developmental Psychology, New York, NY 10027-6696. Offers MA, Ed D, PhD. *Faculty:* 6 full-time (5 women). *Students:* 40 full-time (35 women), 39 part-time (31 women); includes 21 minority (5 African Americans, 8 Asian Americans or Pacific Islanders, 8 Hispanic Americans), 13 international. Average age 28. 88 applicants, 93% accepted, 39 enrolled. In 2007, 25 master's, 3 doctorates awarded. *Degree requirements:* For doctorate, thesis/dissertation, integrative project. *Entrance requirements:* For doctorate, GRE General Test. *Application deadline:* For fall admission, 5/15 for domestic students. Application fee: $70. *Financial support:* Research assistantships, teaching assistantships, career-related internships or fieldwork, Federal Work-Study, institutionally sponsored loans, and tuition waivers (full and partial) available. Support available to part-time students. Financial award application deadline: 2/1. *Faculty research:* Language development in infants, psychology of mathematics education, intellectual development, testing and assessment, cognitive development. *Unit head:* Office of Admissions, 212-678-3710, Fax: 212-678-4171. *Application contact:* Melba Remice, Assistant Director of Admission, 212-678-4035, Fax: 212-678-4171, E-mail: ms2545@columbia.edu.

See Close-Up on page 1503.

Temple University, Graduate School, College of Liberal Arts, Department of Psychology, Program in Developmental Psychology, Philadelphia, PA 19122-6096. Offers PhD. *Degree requirements:* For doctorate, thesis/dissertation. *Entrance requirements:* For doctorate, GRE General Test, minimum GPA of 3.0. Additional exam requirements/recommendations for international students: Required—TOEFL (minimum score 550 paper-based; 213 computer-based; 79 iBT). Electronic applications accepted. *Faculty research:* Social development, cognitive development, emotional development, research methodology.

Texas A&M University, College of Liberal Arts, Department of Psychology, College Station, TX 77843. Offers behavioral and cellular neuroscience (MS, PhD); clinical psychology (MS, PhD); cognitive psychology (MS, PhD); developmental psychology (MS, PhD); industrial/organizational psychology (MS, PhD); social psychology (MS, PhD). *Accreditation:* APA (one or more programs are accredited). *Faculty:* 33. *Students:* 69 full-time (46 women), 14 part-time (10 women); includes 27 minority (7 African Americans, 1 American Indian/Alaska Native, 5 Asian Americans or Pacific Islanders, 14 Hispanic Americans), 8 international. 274 applicants, 11% accepted, 15 enrolled. In 2007, 11 master's, 7 doctorates awarded. *Degree requirements:* For master's, thesis; for doctorate, comprehensive exam (for some programs), thesis/dissertation. *Entrance requirements:* For master's and doctorate, GRE General Test. Additional exam requirements/recommendations for international students: Required—TOEFL. *Application deadline:* For fall admission, 1/5 for domestic and international students. Application fee: $50 ($75 for international students). Electronic applications accepted. *Expenses:* Tuition, state resident: full-time $6,129. Tuition, nonresident: full-time $11,689. Tuition and fees vary according to course load. *Financial support:* Fellowships with partial tuition reimbursements, research assistantships with partial tuition reimbursements, teaching assistantships with partial tuition reimbursements, career-related internships or fieldwork, institutionally sponsored loans, health care benefits, and unspecified assistantships available. Financial award application deadline: 1/5; financial award applicants required to submit FAFSA. *Unit head:* Dr. Steve Rholes, Head, 979-845-2581, Fax: 979-845-4727, E-mail: wsr@psyc.tamu.edu. *Application contact:* Sharon Starr, Graduate Admissions Supervisor, 979-458-1710, Fax: 979-845-4727, E-mail: gradadv@psyc.tamu.edu.

Tufts University, Graduate School of Arts and Sciences, Department of Child Development, Medford, MA 02155. Offers applied developmental psychology (PhD); child development (MA, CAGS); early childhood education (MAT). Part-time programs available. *Faculty:* 15 full-time, 8 part-time/adjunct. *Students:* 102 (89 women); includes 17 minority (7 African Americans, 5 Asian Americans or Pacific Islanders, 5 Hispanic Americans) 12 international. 123 applicants, 64% accepted, 35 enrolled. In 2007, 70 master's, 6 doctorates, 2 other advanced degrees awarded. *Degree requirements:* For master's, thesis (for some programs); for doctorate, thesis/dissertation. *Entrance requirements:* For master's and doctorate, GRE General Test. Additional exam requirements/recommendations for international students: Required—TOEFL (minimum score 550 paper-based; 213 computer-based; 80 iBT). *Application deadline:* For fall admission, 1/15 for domestic and international students. Applications are processed on a rolling basis. Application fee: $70. Electronic applications accepted. *Expenses:* Tuition: Full-time $35,052. *Financial support:* Fellowships, research assistantships with full and partial tuition reimbursements, teaching assistantships with full and partial tuition reimbursements, career-related internships or fieldwork, Federal Work-Study, scholarships/grants, and tuition waivers (partial) available. Support available to part-time students. Financial award application deadline: 1/15; financial award applicants required to submit FAFSA. *Unit head:* Ellen Pinderhughes, Chair, 617-628-5000.

Université de Montréal, Faculty of Arts and Sciences, School of Psychoeducation, Montréal, QC H3C 3J7, Canada. Offers M Sc, PhD, Certificate. Part-time programs available. *Faculty:* 15 full-time (5 women), 4 part-time/adjunct (2 women). *Students:* 94 full-time (89 women), 6 part-time (5 women). 103 applicants, 37% accepted, 34 enrolled. In 2007, 35 degrees awarded. *Degree requirements:* For master's, one foreign language, thesis. *Application deadline:* For fall admission, 2/1 priority date for domestic students; for winter admission, 11/1 priority date for domestic students; for spring admission, 2/1 priority date for domestic students. Application fee: $100. Electronic applications accepted. *Financial support:* Fellowships, research assistantships, teaching assistantships, career-related internships or fieldwork and institutionally sponsored loans available. Support available to part-time students. *Faculty research:* Child maladjustment, family, prevention, treatment, antisocial behavior. *Unit head:* Sophie Parent, Chairperson, 514-343-7421, Fax: 514-343-6951, E-mail: sophie.parent@umontreal.ca. *Application contact:* Lyse Turgeon, Graduate Chairperson, 514-343-6111 Ext. 2559, Fax: 514-343-6951, E-mail: lyse.turgeon@umontreal.ca.

The University of British Columbia, Faculty of Arts and Faculty of Graduate Studies, Department of Psychology, Vancouver, BC V6T 1Z1, Canada. Offers behavioral neuroscience (MA, PhD); clinical psychology (MA, PhD); cognitive science (MA, PhD); developmental psychology (MA, PhD); forensic psychology (PhD); health psychology (MA, PhD); quantitative methods (MA, PhD); social/personality psychology (MA, PhD). *Accreditation:* APA (one or more programs are accredited). *Faculty:* 46 full-time (20 women), 26 part-time/adjunct (13 women). *Students:* 102 full-time (69 women). Average age 29. 247 applicants, 14% accepted, 18 enrolled. In 2007, 14 master's, 11 doctorates awarded. Terminal master's awarded for partial completion of doctoral program. *Median time to degree:* Of those who began their doctoral program in fall 1999, 91% received their degree in 8 years or less. *Degree requirements:* For master's, thesis; for doctorate, comprehensive exam, thesis/dissertation. *Entrance requirements:* For master's and doctorate, GRE General Test, GRE Subject Test. Additional exam requirements/recommendations for international students: Required—TOEFL (minimum score 550 paper-based; 230 computer-based; 80 iBT). *Application deadline:* For fall admission, 1/15 for domestic and international students. Applications are processed on a rolling basis. Application fee: $90 Canadian dollars ($150 Canadian dollars for international students). Electronic applications accepted. *Financial support:* In 2007–08, 95 students received support, including 27 fellowships with full and partial tuition reimbursements available (averaging $16,500 per year), 50 research assistantships with full and partial tuition reimbursements available (averaging $6,775 per year), 80 teaching assistantships with full and partial tuition reimbursements available (averaging $8,065 per year); career-related internships or fieldwork, Federal Work-Study, institutionally sponsored loans, scholarships/grants, health care benefits, tuition waivers (full and partial), and unspecified assistantships also available. Financial award application deadline: 1/15. *Faculty research:* Clinical, developmental, social/personality, cognition, behavioral neuroscience. Total annual research expenditures: $5.5 million Canadian dollars. *Unit head:* Dr. Eric Eich, Head, 604-822-3078, Fax: 604-822-6923, E-mail: ee@psych.ubc.ca. *Application contact:* Rose Tam, Graduate Secretary, 604-822-3144, Fax: 604-822-6923, E-mail: gradsec@psych.ubc.ca.

University of California, Santa Barbara, Graduate Division, Gevirtz Graduate School of Education, Santa Barbara, CA 93106. Offers counseling, clinical and school psychology (PhD), including clinical psychology, counseling psychology; education (MA, PhD), including child and adolescent development, cultural perspectives and comparative education, educational leadership and organizations, research methodology, special education disabilities and risk studies (MA), special education, disabilities and risk studies (PhD), teaching and learning; educational leadership (Ed D); school psychology (M Ed); MA/PhD. *Accreditation:* APA (one or more programs are accredited). Postbaccalaureate distance learning degree programs offered (minimal on-campus study). *Faculty:* 36 full-time (18 women), 7 part-time/adjunct (3 women). *Students:* 400 full-time (308 women); includes 119 minority (11 African Americans, 6 American Indian/Alaska Native, 46 Asian Americans or Pacific Islanders, 56 Hispanic Americans), 18 international. Average age 31. 721 applicants, 41% accepted, 189 enrolled. In 2007, 157 master's, 35 doctorates awarded. Terminal master's awarded for partial completion of doctoral program. *Median time to degree:* Of those who began their doctoral program in fall 1999, 60% received their degree in 8 years or less. *Degree requirements:* For master's, comprehensive exam (for some programs), thesis (for some programs); for doctorate, comprehensive exam (for some programs), thesis/dissertation, qualifying exam. *Entrance requirements:* For master's, GRE, MAT (M Ed); for doctorate, GRE. Additional exam requirements/recommendations for international students: Required—TOEFL (minimum score 550 paper-based; 213 computer-based; 80 iBT). *Application deadline:* For fall admission, 12/15 priority date for domestic and international students. Application fee: $60. Electronic applications accepted. *Expenses:* Tuition, nonresident: full-time $14,888. Required fees: $10,108. *Financial support:* In 2007–08, 292 students received support, including 170 fellowships with full and partial tuition reimbursements available (averaging $5,200 per year), 80 research assistantships with full and partial tuition reimbursements available, 124 teaching assistantships with full and partial tuition reimbursements available; career-related internships or fieldwork, Federal Work-Study, institutionally sponsored loans, scholarships/grants, traineeships, health care benefits, and unspecified assistantships also available. Financial award applicants required to submit FAFSA. *Faculty research:* Professional development, early childhood development, school violence, literacy, science/math initiative. Total annual research expenditures: $4.2 million. *Unit head:* Carol Dixon, Associate Dean of Students, 805-893-2137, Fax: 805-893-7264, E-mail: sao@education.ucsb.edu. *Application contact:* Katie Tucciarone, Student Affairs Officer, 805-893-2137, Fax: 805-893-2588, E-mail: katiet@education.ucsb.edu.

University of Connecticut, Graduate School, College of Liberal Arts and Sciences, Department of Psychology, Field of Psychology, Storrs, CT 06269. Offers behavioral neuroscience (PhD); biopsychology (PhD); clinical psychology (MA, PhD); cognition and instruction (PhD); developmental psychology (MA, PhD); ecological psychology (PhD); experimental psychology (PhD); general psychology (MA, PhD); health psychology (Graduate Certificate); industrial/organizational psychology (PhD); language and cognition (PhD); neuroscience (PhD); occupational health psychology (Graduate Certificate); social psychology (MA, PhD). *Accreditation:* APA (one or more programs are accredited). *Faculty:* 52 full-time (23 women). *Students:* 130 full-time (94 women), 25 part-time (11 women); includes 24 minority (8 African Americans, 6 Asian Americans or Pacific Islanders, 10 Hispanic Americans), 18 international. Average age 28. 531 applicants, 7% accepted, 35 enrolled. In 2007, 19 master's, 20 doctorates, 2 other advanced degrees awarded. Terminal master's awarded for partial completion of doctoral program. *Degree requirements:* For master's, comprehensive exam; for doctorate, thesis/dissertation. *Entrance requirements:* For master's and doctorate, GRE General Test, GRE Subject Test. Additional exam requirements/recommendations for international students: Required—TOEFL (minimum score 550 paper-based; 213 computer-based). *Application deadline:* For fall admission, 2/1 priority date for domestic and international students; for spring admission, 11/1 for domestic students, 10/1 for international students. Applications are processed on a rolling basis. Application fee: $55. Electronic applications accepted. *Expenses:* Tuition, state resident: part-time $469 per credit hour. Tuition, nonresident: part-time $1,218 per credit hour. *Financial support:* In 2007–08, 54 research assistantships with full tuition reimbursements, 69 teaching assistantships with full tuition reimbursements were awarded; fellowships, career-related internships or fieldwork, Federal Work-Study, scholarships/grants, health care benefits, and unspecified assistantships also available. Financial award application deadline: 2/1; financial award applicants required to submit FAFSA. *Application contact:* Deborah Doucette, Administrative Assistant, 860-486-2057, Fax: 860-486-2760, E-mail: futuregr@psych.psy.uconn.edu.

University of Florida, Graduate School, College of Liberal Arts and Sciences, Department of Psychology, Gainesville, FL 32611. Offers behavior analysis (PhD); behavioral neuroscience (MS, PhD); cognitive and sensory processes (PhD); counseling psychology (PhD); developmental psychology (PhD); social psychology (MS, PhD); JD/PhD. *Faculty:* 42 full-time (12 women), 3 part-time/adjunct (1 woman). *Students:* 136 (90 women); includes 22 minority (7 African Americans, 1 American Indian/Alaska Native, 5 Asian Americans or Pacific Islanders, 9 Hispanic Americans) 22 international. In 2007, 25 master's, 14 doctorates awarded. *Degree requirements:* For master's, thesis or alternative; for doctorate, thesis/dissertation. *Entrance requirements:* For master's and doctorate, GRE General Test, minimum GPA of 3.0. Additional exam requirements/recommendations for international students: Required—TOEFL (minimum score 550 paper-based; 213 computer-based). *Application deadline:* For fall admission, 1/15 priority date for domestic students. Applications are processed on a rolling basis. Application fee: $30. Electronic applications accepted. *Expenses:* Tuition, state resident: full-time $7,478. Tuition, nonresident: full-time $22,603. *Financial support:* In 2007–08, 33 research assistantships (averaging $16,597 per year), 64 teaching assistantships (averaging $16,703 per year) were awarded; fellowships, career-related internships or fieldwork and unspecified assistantships also available. Financial award application deadline: 1/15. *Faculty research:* Experimental analysis of behavior, psychobiology, cognition and sensory processes, counseling psychology, social psychology, developmental psychology. *Unit head:* Dr. Martin Heesacker, Chair, 352-392-0601 Ext. 200, Fax: 352-392-7985, E-mail: heesack@ufl.edu. *Application contact:* Dr. Gregory Neimeyer, Coordinator, 352-392-0601 Ext. 259, Fax: 352-392-7985, E-mail: neimeyer@ufl.edu.

University of Kansas, Research and Graduate Studies, College of Liberal Arts and Sciences, Department of Applied Behavioral Science, Lawrence, KS 66045. Offers applied behavioral science (MA); behavioral psychology (PhD); clinical child psychology (PhD); developmental and child psychology (PhD); human development (MA). *Faculty:* 18. *Students:* 38 full-time (27 women), 9 part-time (8 women); includes 7 minority (2 African Americans, 2 Asian Americans or Pacific Islanders, 3 Hispanic Americans), 2 international. Average age 33. 41 applicants, 17% accepted, 3 enrolled. In 2007, 7 master's, 9 doctorates awarded. Terminal master's awarded for partial completion of doctoral program. *Degree requirements:* For master's, thesis; for doctorate, thesis/dissertation, comprehensive oral and written exams, journal reviews. *Entrance requirements:* Additional exam requirements/recommendations for international students: Required—TOEFL, TWE. *Application deadline:* For fall admission, 1/15 priority date for domestic and international students. Application fee: $55 ($60 for international students). Electronic applications accepted. *Expenses:* Tuition, state resident: full-time $5,838. Tuition, nonresident: full-time $13,409. Tuition and fees vary according to program. *Financial support:* Fellowships, research assistantships with full and partial tuition reimbursements, teaching assistantships with full and partial tuition reimbursements, career-related internships or fieldwork, traineeships, tuition waivers (full), and unspecified assistantships available. Financial award application deadline: 2/1. *Faculty research:* Early childhood, developmental disabilities, community health and development, adults with disabilities, applied behavior analysis. *Unit head:* Edward K. Morris, Chair, 785-864-4840, Fax: 785-864-5202, E-mail: ekm@ku.edu. *Application contact:* Gregory J. Madden, Graduate Director, 785-864-4840, Fax: 785-864-5202, E-mail: gmadden@ku.edu.

University of Kansas, Research and Graduate Studies, College of Liberal Arts and Sciences, Program in Child Language, Lawrence, KS 66045. Offers MA, PhD. *Faculty:* 22. *Students:* 6 full-time (5 women). Average age 26. 8 applicants, 50% accepted, 3 enrolled. In 2007, 2 degrees awarded. *Degree requirements:* For master's, thesis; for doctorate, comprehensive exam, thesis/dissertation, written preliminary exam. *Entrance requirements:* For master's and doctorate, GRE, minimum GPA of 3.5, 3 letters of reference. Additional exam requirements/recommendations for international students: Required—TOEFL. *Application deadline:* For fall admission, 2/1 priority date for domestic and international students; for spring admission, 11/1 for domestic and international students. Applications are processed on a rolling basis. Application fee: $55 ($60 for international students). Electronic applications accepted. *Expenses:* Tuition, state resident: full-time $5,838. Tuition, nonresident: full-time $13,409. Tuition and fees vary according to program. *Financial support:* Fellowships with full tuition reimbursements, research assistantships with full tuition reimbursements, career-related internships or fieldwork, traineeships, and unspecified assistantships available. Financial award application deadline: 2/1. *Faculty research:* Etiology of language impairments, word recognition processes, cultural context and linguistic patterns, language acquisition. *Unit head:* Mabel Rice, Director, 785-864-4570, E-mail: mabel@ku.edu. *Application contact:* Susan Kemper, Graduate Adviser, 785-864-0748, E-mail: skemper@ku.edu.

University of Maine, Graduate School, College of Liberal Arts and Sciences, Department of Psychology, Orono, ME 04469. Offers clinical psychology (PhD); developmental psychology (MA); experimental psychology (MA, PhD); social psychology (MA). *Accreditation:* APA (one or more programs are accredited). *Faculty:* 24. *Students:* 28 full-time (17 women), 10 part-time (6 women); includes 2 minority (1 American Indian/Alaska Native, 1 Hispanic American), 1 international. Average age 29. 129 applicants, 9% accepted, 8 enrolled. In 2007, 5 master's, 2 doctorates awarded. *Degree requirements:* For master's, thesis; for doctorate, thesis/dissertation. *Entrance requirements:* For master's and doctorate, GRE General Test, GRE Subject Test. Additional exam requirements/recommendations for international students: Required—TOEFL. *Application deadline:* For fall admission, 2/1 priority date for domestic students. Applications are processed on a rolling basis. Application fee: $60. Electronic applications accepted. *Financial support:* In 2007–08, 3 research assistantships with tuition reimbursements (averaging $13,400 per year), 21 teaching assistantships with tuition reimbursements (averaging $9,010 per year) were awarded; fellowships with tuition reimbursements, Federal Work-Study, institutionally sponsored loans, and tuition waivers (full and partial) also available. Financial award application deadline: 3/1. *Faculty research:* Social development, hypertension and aging, attitude change, self-confidence in achievement situations, health psychology. *Unit head:* Dr. Jeffrey Hecker, Chair, 207-581-2032, Fax: 207-581-6128. *Application contact:* Scott G. Delcourt, Associate Dean of the Graduate School, 207-581-3219, Fax: 207-581-3232, E-mail: graduate@maine.edu.

University of Maryland, Baltimore County, Graduate School, College of Arts, Humanities and Social Sciences, Department of Psychology, Program in Applied Developmental Psychology, Baltimore, MD 21250. Offers PhD. *Faculty:* 10 full-time (5 women), 11 part-time/adjunct (2 women). *Students:* 24 full-time (22 women), 9 part-time (8 women); includes 6 minority (3 African Americans, 2 Asian Americans or Pacific Islanders, 1 Hispanic American), 4 international. Average age 32. 29 applicants, 31% accepted, 3 enrolled. In 2007, 2 degrees awarded. *Median time to degree:* Of those who began their doctoral program in fall 1999, 50% received their degree in 8 years or less. *Degree requirements:* For doctorate, comprehensive exam, thesis/dissertation. *Entrance requirements:* For doctorate, GRE General Test, GRE Subject Test, minimum GPA of 3.0. Additional exam requirements/recommendations for international students: Required—TOEFL. *Application deadline:* For fall admission, 1/9 for domestic and international students. Application fee: $50. Electronic applications accepted. *Financial support:* In 2007–08, 1 fellowship with partial tuition reimbursement (averaging $15,000 per year), 4 research assistantships with full and partial tuition reimbursements (averaging $14,566 per year), 16 teaching assistantships with full and partial tuition reimbursements (averaging $14,566 per year) were awarded; career-related internships or fieldwork, Federal Work-Study, health care benefits, and unspecified assistantships also available. Financial award application deadline: 3/1; financial award applicants required to submit FAFSA. *Faculty research:* Early intervention and development, schooling and development, cultural aspects of development, development in high risk children, social-emotional development. Total annual research expenditures: $2.5 million. *Unit head:* Dr. Susan Sonnenschein, Director, 410-455-2361, Fax: 410-455-1055, E-mail: sonnenschein@umbc.edu. *Application contact:* Cara Lane, Program Management Specialist, 410-455-2567, Fax: 410-455-1055, E-mail: psycdept@umbc.edu.

University of Maryland, College Park, Graduate Studies, College of Behavioral and Social Sciences, Department of Psychology, College Park, MD 20742. Offers clinical psychology (PhD); developmental psychology (PhD); experimental psychology (PhD); industrial psychology (MA, MS, PhD); social psychology (PhD). *Accreditation:* APA (one or more programs are accredited). *Faculty:* 53 full-time (23 women), 12 part-time/adjunct (6 women). *Students:* 92 full-time (70 women), 4 part-time (3 women); includes 15 minority (2 African Americans, 1 American Indian/Alaska Native, 6 Asian Americans or Pacific Islanders, 6 Hispanic Americans), 12 international. 609 applicants, 4% accepted, 13 enrolled. In 2007, 13 master's, 18 doctorates awarded. *Median time to degree:* Of those who began their doctoral program in fall 1999, 71% received their degree in 8 years or less. *Degree requirements:* For master's, thesis; for doctorate, variable foreign language requirement, comprehensive exam, thesis/dissertation. *Entrance requirements:* For master's and doctorate, GRE General Test, GRE Subject Test, minimum GPA of 3.5, research and/or work experience, 3 letters of recommendation. *Application deadline:* For fall admission, 12/15 for domestic students, 2/1 for international students. Applications are processed on a rolling basis. Application fee: $60. Electronic applications accepted. *Financial support:* In 2007–08, 11 fellowships with full tuition reimbursements (averaging $15,736 per year), 9 research assistantships (averaging $15,312 per year), 56 teaching assistantships with tuition reimbursements (averaging $15,292 per year) were awarded; career-related internships or fieldwork, Federal Work-Study, and scholarships/grants also available. Support available to part-time students. Financial award applicants required to submit FAFSA. *Faculty research:* Social stereotyping and prejudice, anxiety disorders, auditory neuroethology, counseling and social psychology. Total annual research expenditures: $4.4 million. *Unit head:* Thomas S. Wallsten, Chair, 301-405-5862, Fax: 301-314-9566, E-mail: twallsten@psyc.umd.edu. *Application contact:* Dean of Graduate School, 301-405-0358, Fax: 301-314-9305.

University of Miami, Graduate School, College of Arts and Sciences, Department of Psychology, Coral Gables, FL 33124. Offers adult clinical (PhD); behavioral neuroscience (PhD); child clinical (PhD); developmental psychology (PhD); health clinical (PhD); psychology (MS). *Accreditation:* APA (one or more programs are accredited). *Faculty:* 27 full-time (13 women). *Students:* 88 full-time (69 women); includes 28 minority (5 African Americans, 7 Asian Americans or Pacific Islanders, 16 Hispanic Americans), 5 international. Average age 27. 340 applicants, 6% accepted, 14 enrolled. In 2007, 13 master's, 15 doctorates awarded. *Median time to degree:* Of those who began their doctoral program in fall 1999, 88% received their degree in 8 years or less. *Degree requirements:* For doctorate, comprehensive exam, thesis/dissertation. *Entrance requirements:* For doctorate, GRE General Test, minimum GPA of 3.5. Additional

Developmental Psychology

University of Miami (continued)

exam requirements/recommendations for international students: Required—TOEFL. *Application deadline:* For fall admission, 12/1 for domestic and international students. Application fee: $50. Electronic applications accepted. *Financial support:* In 2007–08, 88 students received support, including 9 fellowships with full tuition reimbursements available (averaging $22,000 per year), 24 research assistantships with full tuition reimbursements available (averaging $22,000 per year), 18 teaching assistantships with full tuition reimbursements available (averaging $16,500 per year); career-related internships or fieldwork, institutionally sponsored loans, scholarships/grants, and traineeships also available. Financial award applicants required to submit FAFSA. *Faculty research:* Behavioral factors in cardiovascular disease and cancer adult psychopathology, developmental disabilities, social and emotional development, mechanisms of coping. Total annual research expenditures: $12.4 million. *Unit head:* Dr. A. Rodney Wellens, Chairman, 305-284-2814, Fax: 305-284-3402. *Application contact:* Prof. Phil McCabe, Director of Graduate Studies, 305-284-2814, Fax: 305-284-3402, E-mail: inquire@psy.miami.edu.

University of Michigan, Horace H. Rackham School of Graduate Studies, College of Literature, Science, and the Arts, Department of Psychology, Ann Arbor, MI 48109. Offers biopsychology (PhD); clinical psychology (PhD); cognition and perception (PhD); developmental psychology (PhD); personality and social contexts (PhD); social psychology (PhD). *Accreditation:* APA. *Faculty:* 86 full-time, 69 part-time/adjunct. *Students:* 157 full-time (112 women); includes 51 minority (21 African Americans, 1 American Indian/Alaska Native, 17 Asian Americans or Pacific Islanders, 12 Hispanic Americans), 32 international. Average age 25. 698 applicants, 9% accepted, 29 enrolled. In 2007, 25 degrees awarded. *Degree requirements:* For doctorate, comprehensive exam, thesis/dissertation, oral defense of dissertation, preliminary exam. *Entrance requirements:* For doctorate, GRE General Test (optional), GRE Subject Test (optional). Additional exam requirements/recommendations for international students: Required—TOEFL. *Application deadline:* For fall admission, 12/15 for domestic students. Application fee: $60 ($75 for international students). Electronic applications accepted. *Financial support:* Fellowships with full tuition reimbursements, research assistantships with full tuition reimbursements, teaching assistantships with full tuition reimbursements, career-related internships or fieldwork available. Financial award application deadline: 4/15. *Unit head:* Theresa Lee, Chair, 734-764-7429. *Application contact:* Laurie Brannan, Psychology Student Academic Affairs, 731-764-2580, Fax: 734-615-7584, E-mail: psych.saa@umich.edu.

The University of Montana, Graduate School, College of Arts and Sciences, Department of Psychology, Missoula, MT 59812-0002. Offers clinical psychology (PhD); experimental psychology (PhD), including animal behavior psychology, developmental psychology; school psychology (MA, PhD, Ed S). *Accreditation:* APA (one or more programs are accredited). Terminal master's awarded for partial completion of doctoral program. *Degree requirements:* For master's, thesis; for doctorate, thesis/dissertation. *Entrance requirements:* For master's, doctorate, and Ed S, GRE General Test. Additional exam requirements/recommendations for international students: Required—TOEFL.

University of Nebraska at Omaha, Graduate Studies and Research, College of Arts and Sciences, Department of Psychology, Omaha, NE 68182. Offers developmental psychology (PhD); industrial/organizational psychology (MS, PhD); psychobiology (PhD); psychology (MA); school psychology (MS, Ed S). Part-time programs available. *Faculty:* 17 full-time (8 women). *Students:* 33 full-time (24 women), 32 part-time (26 women); includes 4 minority (2 African Americans, 1 Asian American or Pacific Islander, 1 Hispanic American), 3 international. Average age 28. 89 applicants, 56% accepted, 25 enrolled. In 2007, 16 master's, 5 other advanced degrees awarded. *Degree requirements:* For master's, comprehensive exam, thesis (for some programs). *Entrance requirements:* For master's, GRE General Test, GRE Subject Test, previous course work in psychology, including statistics and a laboratory course; minimum GPA of 3.0, 3 letters of recommendation; for doctorate, GRE General Test. Additional exam requirements/recommendations for international students: Required—TOEFL (minimum score 500 paper-based; 173 computer-based; 61 iBT). *Application deadline:* For fall admission, 1/5 for domestic students. Application fee: $45. Electronic applications accepted. *Financial support:* In 2007–08, 55 students received support; fellowships, research assistantships with tuition reimbursements available, teaching assistantships with tuition reimbursements available, career-related internships or fieldwork, Federal Work-Study, institutionally sponsored loans, scholarships/grants, tuition waivers (partial), and unspecified assistantships available. Support available to part-time students. Financial award application deadline: 3/1; financial award applicants required to submit FAFSA. *Unit head:* Dr. Kenneth Deffenbacher, Chairperson, 402-554-2592. *Application contact:* Dr. Joseph Brown, Student Contact, 402-554-2592.

The University of North Carolina at Chapel Hill, Graduate School, College of Arts and Sciences, Department of Psychology, Chapel Hill, NC 27599. Offers biological psychology (PhD); clinical psychology (PhD); cognitive psychology (PhD); developmental psychology (PhD); quantitative psychology (PhD); social psychology (PhD). *Accreditation:* APA. *Degree requirements:* For doctorate, comprehensive exam, thesis/dissertation. *Entrance requirements:* For doctorate, GRE General Test, minimum GPA of 3.0. Electronic applications accepted. *Faculty research:* Expressed emotion, cognitive development, social cognitive neuroscience, human memory personality.

The University of North Carolina at Greensboro, Graduate School, College of Arts and Sciences, Department of Psychology, Greensboro, NC 27412-5001. Offers clinical psychology (MA, PhD); cognitive psychology (MA, PhD); developmental psychology (MA, PhD); social psychology (MA, PhD). *Accreditation:* APA (one or more programs are accredited). *Faculty:* 23 full-time (8 women). *Students:* 46 full-time (31 women), 13 part-time (10 women); includes 7 minority (3 African Americans, 1 American Indian/Alaska Native, 1 Asian American or Pacific Islander, 2 Hispanic Americans). 218 applicants, 7% accepted.Terminal master's awarded for partial completion of doctoral program. *Degree requirements:* For master's, comprehensive exam, thesis; for doctorate, one foreign language, thesis/dissertation, preliminary exam. *Entrance requirements:* For master's and doctorate, GRE General Test. Additional exam requirements/recommendations for international students: Required—TOEFL. *Application deadline:* For fall admission, 2/1 for domestic students. Application fee: $45. Electronic applications accepted. *Financial support:* Fellowships with full tuition reimbursements, research assistantships with full tuition reimbursements, teaching assistantships with full tuition reimbursements, unspecified assistantships available. *Faculty research:* Sensory and perceptual determinants; evoked potential: disorders, deafness, and development. *Unit head:* Dr. George Michel, Head, 336-336-5013, E-mail: gfmichel@uncg.edu. *Application contact:* Michelle Harkleroad, Director of Graduate Admissions, 336-334-4884, Fax: 336-334-4424, E-mail: mbharkle@uncg.edu.

University of Notre Dame, Graduate School, College of Arts and Letters, Division of Social Science, Department of Psychology, Notre Dame, IN 46556. Offers cognitive psychology (PhD); counseling psychology (PhD); developmental psychology (PhD); quantitative psychology (PhD). *Accreditation:* APA. *Faculty:* 28 full-time (11 women), 5 part-time/adjunct (4 women). *Students:* 62 full-time (43 women); includes 9 minority (3 African Americans, 2 Asian Americans or Pacific Islanders, 4 Hispanic Americans), 9 international. 166 applicants, 15% accepted, 8 enrolled. In 2007, 13 doctorates awarded. *Degree requirements:* For doctorate, comprehensive exam, thesis/dissertation, candidacy exam. *Entrance requirements:* For doctorate, GRE General Test, GRE Subject Test (strongly recommended). Additional exam requirements/recommendations for international students: Required—TOEFL (minimum score 600 paper-based; 250 computer-based; 80 iBT). *Application deadline:* For fall admission, 1/2 for domestic and international students. Application fee: $50. Electronic applications accepted. *Financial support:* In 2007–08, 4 fellowships with full tuition reimbursements (averaging $22,000 per year), 14 research assistantships with full tuition reimbursements (averaging $16,000 per year), 41 teaching assistantships with full tuition reimbursements (averaging $16,000 per year) were awarded; career-related internships or fieldwork and tuition waivers (full) also available. Financial award application deadline: 1/2. *Faculty research:* Cognitive and socio-emotional development, statistical methods and quantitative models applicable to psychology, interpersonal relations, life span development and developmental delay, childhood depression, structural equation and dynamical systems. *Unit head:* Dr. Dawn Gondoli, Director of Graduate Studies, 574-631-6650, Fax: 574-631-8883. *Application contact:* Dr. Jarren Gonzales, Director of Graduate Admissions, 574-631-7706, Fax: 574-631-4183.

University of Oregon, Graduate School, College of Arts and Sciences, Department of Psychology, Eugene, OR 97403. Offers clinical psychology (PhD); cognitive psychology (MA, MS, PhD); developmental psychology (MA, MS, PhD); physiological psychology (MA, MS, PhD); psychology (MA, MS, PhD); social/personality psychology (MA, MS, PhD). *Accreditation:* APA (one or more programs are accredited). *Faculty:* 27 full-time (11 women), 11 part-time/adjunct (8 women). *Students:* 76 full-time (48 women), 10 part-time (7 women); includes 11 minority (1 African American, 7 Asian Americans or Pacific Islanders, 3 Hispanic Americans), 15 international. 320 applicants, 8% accepted. In 2007, 21 master's, 11 doctorates awarded. Terminal master's awarded for partial completion of doctoral program. *Degree requirements:* For doctorate, thesis/dissertation. *Entrance requirements:* For master's, GRE General Test, minimum GPA of 3.0; for doctorate, GRE General Test. Additional exam requirements/recommendations for international students: Required—TOEFL. *Application deadline:* For fall admission, 12/1 for domestic students. Application fee: $50. *Financial support:* In 2007–08, 48 teaching assistantships were awarded; research assistantships, career-related internships or fieldwork also available. *Unit head:* Louis Moses, Head, 541-346-4918, Fax: 541-346-4911. *Application contact:* Lori Olsen, Admissions Contact, 541-346-5060, Fax: 541-346-4911, E-mail: gradsec@psych.uoregon.edu.

University of Pittsburgh, School of Education, Department of Psychology in Education, Program in Applied Developmental Psychology, Pittsburgh, PA 15260. Offers MS, PhD. Part-time and evening/weekend programs available. *Students:* 40 full-time (36 women), 69 part-time (62 women); includes 18 minority (10 African Americans, 7 Asian Americans or Pacific Islanders, 1 Hispanic American), 7 international. 107 applicants, 66% accepted, 48 enrolled. In 2007, 26 master's, 5 doctorates awarded. *Degree requirements:* For master's, thesis. *Entrance requirements:* For doctorate, GRE. Additional exam requirements/recommendations for international students: Required—TOEFL. *Application deadline:* For fall admission, 2/1 for domestic students, 2/1 priority date for international students; for spring admission, 7/1 priority date for international students. Applications are processed on a rolling basis. Application fee: $50. Electronic applications accepted. *Financial support:* Tuition waivers (partial) available. Support available to part-time students. Financial award applicants required to submit FAFSA. *Application contact:* Dr. Marjorie K. Schermer, Enrollment Manager, 412-648-2230, Fax: 412-648-1899, E-mail: soeinfo@pitt.edu.

University of Rochester, The College, Arts and Sciences, Department of Clinical and Social Sciences in Psychology, Rochester, NY 14627-0250. Offers clinical psychology (PhD); developmental psychology (PhD); psychology (MA); social-personality psychology (PhD). *Accreditation:* APA (one or more programs are accredited). Terminal master's awarded for partial completion of doctoral program. *Degree requirements:* For doctorate, thesis/dissertation, qualifying exam. *Entrance requirements:* For doctorate, GRE General Test. Additional exam requirements/recommendations for international students: Required—TOEFL.

University of Victoria, Faculty of Graduate Studies, Faculty of Social Sciences, Department of Psychology, Victoria, BC V8W 2Y2, Canada. Offers clinical psychology (PhD); clinical psychology (neuropsychology) (M Sc); cognition and brain science (M Sc, PhD); experimental neuropsychology (M Sc, PhD); individualized study (M Sc, PhD); life span development psychology (PhD); life span developmental psychology (M Sc); social psychology (M Sc, PhD). *Accreditation:* APA (one or more programs are accredited). *Faculty:* 24 full-time (12 women), 14 part-time/adjunct (7 women). *Students:* 26, 4 international. Average age 25. 146 applicants, 21% accepted, 14 enrolled. In 2007, 36 master's, 2 doctorates awarded. *Degree requirements:* For master's, thesis; for doctorate, thesis/dissertation, candidacy exam. *Entrance requirements:* For master's and doctorate, GRE General Test. Additional exam requirements/recommendations for international students: Required—TOEFL (minimum score 600 paper-based; 250 computer-based). *Application deadline:* For fall admission, 1/1 for domestic students, 12/15 priority date for international students. Applications are processed on a rolling basis. Application fee: $65 ($100 for international students). Electronic applications accepted. *Expenses:* Tuition, state resident: full-time $3,110. International tuition: $3,700 full-time. Tuition and fees vary according to program. *Financial support:* In 2007–08, 4 fellowships (averaging $13,000 per year), 23 research assistantships, 22 teaching assistantships (averaging $2,750 per year) were awarded; career-related internships or fieldwork and institutionally sponsored loans also available. Financial award application deadline: 1/15. *Faculty research:* Life span development psychology and aging, behavioral neuroscience, cognitive psychology, behavioral psychology, environmental psychology. *Unit head:* Dr. Elizabeth Brimacombe, Chair, 250-721-7547, Fax: 250-721-8929, E-mail: psychair@uvic.ca. *Application contact:* Paul Taylor, Graduate Secretary, 250-721-6109, Fax: 250-721-8929, E-mail: ptaylor@uvic.ca.

University of Wisconsin–Madison, Graduate School, College of Letters and Science, Department of Psychology, Program in Developmental Psychology, Madison, WI 53706-1380. Offers PhD. *Degree requirements:* For doctorate, comprehensive exam, thesis/dissertation. *Entrance requirements:* For doctorate, GRE General Test, minimum undergraduate GPA of 3.0. Additional exam requirements/recommendations for international students: Required—TOEFL. Electronic applications accepted.

Virginia Polytechnic Institute and State University, Graduate School, College of Science, Department of Psychology, Blacksburg, VA 24061. Offers bio-behavioral sciences (PhD); clinical psychology (PhD); developmental psychology (PhD); industrial/organizational psychology (PhD); psychology (MS). *Accreditation:* APA (one or more programs are accredited). *Entrance requirements:* For master's and doctorate, GRE General Test. Additional exam requirements/recommendations for international students: Required—TOEFL (minimum score 550 paper-based; 213 computer-based). Electronic applications accepted. *Faculty research:* Infant development from electrophysical point of view, work motivation and personnel selection, EEG, ERP and hypnosis with reference to chronic pain, intimate violence.

Walden University, Graduate Programs, School of Psychology, Minneapolis, MN 55401. Offers clinical assessment (Post-Doctoral Certificate); clinical child psychology (Post-Doctoral Certificate); clinical psychology (PhD, Post-Doctoral Certificate); counseling psychology (PhD, Post-Doctoral Certificate); general psychology (MS, PhD, Post-Doctoral Certificate); health psychology (PhD, Post-Doctoral Certificate); organizational psychology (PhD, Post-Doctoral Certificate); organizational psychology and development (MS); school psychology (PhD, Post-Doctoral Certificate); teaching online (Post-Doctoral Certificate). Part-time and evening/weekend programs available. Postbaccalaureate distance learning degree programs offered (minimal on-campus study). *Students:* 1,428 full-time (1,130 women), 1,933 part-time (1,483 women); includes 959 minority (737 African Americans, 35 American Indian/Alaska Native, 53 Asian Americans or Pacific Islanders, 134 Hispanic Americans), 39 international. Average age 40. 1,254 applicants, 75% accepted, 548 enrolled. In 2007, 182 master's, 43 doctorates awarded. *Degree requirements:* For master's, thesis; for doctorate, thesis/dissertation, brief dispersed residency sessions. *Entrance requirements:* For master's, minimum GPA of 3.0; for doctorate, 3 years of professional experience, master's degree; for Post-Doctoral Certificate, PhD in related field, 3 years of professional experience. Additional exam requirements/recommendations for international students: Required—TOEFL (minimum score 550 paper-based; 213 computer-based), IELTS (minimum score 7). *Application deadline:* For fall admission, 8/15 priority date for domestic and international students; for winter admission, 11/15 priority date for domestic and international students; for spring admission, 12/15 priority date for domestic and international students. Applications are processed on a rolling basis. Application fee: $50. Electronic applications accepted. *Financial support:* Fellowships with partial tuition reimbursements, career-related internships or fieldwork, Federal Work-Study, institutionally sponsored loans, scholarships/grants, tuition waivers (partial), and unspecified assistantships available. Support available to part-time students. Financial award applicants required to submit FAFSA. *Faculty research:* Clinical psychology, organizational psychology, forensic psychology, group processes, educational psychology. *Unit head:* Dr. Nina Nabors, Associate Dean, 800-925-3368. *Application contact:* 866-4-WALDEN, Fax: 410-843-8780, E-mail: request@waldenu.edu.

Wayne State University, College of Liberal Arts and Sciences, Department of Psychology, Program in Psychology, Detroit, MI 48202. Offers behavioral and cognitive neuroscience (PhD); clinical psychology (PhD); cognitive and social psychology (PhD); industrial/organizational psychology (PhD); psychology (MA, MS). *Accreditation:* APA (one or more programs are accredited). *Students:* 99 full-time (74 women), 20 part-time (16 women); includes 14 minority (7 African Americans, 4 Asian Americans or Pacific Islanders, 3 Hispanic Americans), 13 international. Average age 27. 219 applicants, 17% accepted, 23 enrolled. In 2007, 13 master's, 12 doctorates awarded. *Degree requirements:* For doctorate, thesis/dissertation. *Entrance requirements:* For doctorate, GRE General Test, GRE Subject Test. Additional exam requirements/recommendations for international students: Required—TOEFL (minimum score 550 paper-based; 213 computer-based); Recommended—TWE (minimum score 6). *Application deadline:* For fall admission, 2/1 for domestic students, 6/1 for international students; for winter admission, 10/1 for international students; for spring admission, 2/1 for international students. Applications are processed on a rolling basis. Application fee: $30 ($50 for international students). Electronic applications accepted. *Expenses:* Tuition, state resident: part-time $403 per credit hour. Tuition, nonresident: part-time $890 per credit hour. *Financial support:* Application deadline:2/1. *Application contact:* Dr. Melissa Kaplan-Estrin, Graduate Director, 313-577-2824, Fax: 313-577-7636, E-mail: mkestrin@sun.science.wayne.edu.

West Virginia University, Eberly College of Arts and Sciences, Department of Psychology, Morgantown, WV 26506. Offers behavior analysis (PhD); clinical psychology (MA, PhD); development psychology (PhD); psychology (MS). *Accreditation:* APA (one or more programs are accredited). Part-time programs available. *Faculty:* 21 full-time (10 women), 2 part-time/adjunct (both women). *Students:* 67 full-time (41 women), 6 part-time (all women); includes 4 minority (2 African Americans, 1 Asian American or Pacific Islander, 1 Hispanic American), 8 international. Average age 27. 195 applicants, 10% accepted, 20 enrolled. In 2007, 7 master's, 12 doctorates awarded. Terminal master's awarded for partial completion of doctoral program. *Degree requirements:* For master's, thesis optional; for doctorate, comprehensive exam, thesis/dissertation. *Entrance requirements:* For master's and doctorate, GRE General Test, minimum GPA of 3.0. Additional exam requirements/recommendations for international students: Required—TOEFL. *Application deadline:* For fall admission, 1/15 for domestic students. Application fee: $45. *Expenses:* Tuition, state resident: full-time $5,196; part-time $292 per credit hour. Tuition, nonresident: full-time $15,064; part-time $840 per credit hour. Tuition and fees vary according to program. *Financial support:* In 2007–08, 73 students received support, including 28 research assistantships (averaging $13,000 per year), 34 teaching assistantships (averaging $10,000 per year); fellowships, career-related internships or fieldwork, Federal Work-Study, institutionally sponsored loans, and tuition waivers (full and partial) also available. Financial award application deadline: 1/15; financial award applicants required to submit FAFSA. *Faculty research:* Adult and child clinical psychology, behavioral assessment and therapy, child and adolescent behavior, life span development, experimental and applied behavior analysis. Total annual research expenditures: $415,123. *Unit head:* Dr. Michael T. Perone, Chair, 304-293-2001 Ext. 31604, Fax: 304-293-6606, E-mail: michael.perone@mail.wvu.edu. *Application contact:* Dr. Barry Edelstein, Director, Graduate Training, 304-293-2001 Ext. 31661, Fax: 304-293-6606, E-mail: barry.edelstein@mail.wvu.edu.

Wilfrid Laurier University, Faculty of Graduate Studies, Faculty of Science, Department of Psychology, Waterloo, ON N2L 3C5, Canada. Offers brain and cognition (M Sc, PhD); community psychology (MA, PhD); social and developmental psychology (MA, PhD). *Faculty:* 32 full-time, 3 part-time/adjunct. *Students:* 61 full-time, 4 part-time. 129 applicants, 27% accepted, 27 enrolled. In 2007, 3 degrees awarded. *Degree requirements:* For master's, thesis; for doctorate, thesis/dissertation. *Entrance requirements:* For master's, honors BA or the equivalent in psychology, minimum B average in undergraduate course work, GRE (General Test); for doctorate, master's degree, minimum A- average, GRE (General Test). Additional exam requirements/recommendations for international students: Required—TOEFL (minimum score 230 computer-based; 89 iBT). *Application deadline:* For fall admission, 2/1 priority date for domestic students. Application fee: $75. Electronic applications accepted. *Financial support:* Fellowships, research assistantships, teaching assistantships available. *Faculty research:* Brain and cognition, community psychology, social and developmental psychology. *Unit head:* Dr. Mark Pancer, Chairperson, 619-884-1970 Ext. 3149. *Application contact:* Jennifer Poppe, Student Contact, 519-884-0710 Ext. 3536, Fax: 519-884-1020, E-mail: gradstudies@wlu.ca.

Experimental Psychology

American University, College of Arts and Sciences, Department of Psychology, Program in Psychology, Washington, DC 20016-8001. Offers experimental/biological psychology (MA); general psychology (MA); personality/social psychology (MA). Part-time programs available. *Students:* 42 full-time (35 women), 18 part-time (15 women); includes 11 minority (5 African Americans, 3 Asian Americans or Pacific Islanders, 3 Hispanic Americans), 1 international. Average age 26. In 2007, 28 degrees awarded. *Degree requirements:* For master's, comprehensive exam, thesis or alternative. *Entrance requirements:* For master's, GRE General Test, GRE Subject Test. *Application deadline:* For fall admission, 3/1 for domestic students. Applications are processed on a rolling basis. Application fee: $50. *Expenses:* Tuition: Full-time $19,998; part-time $1,111 per credit hour. Required fees: $380. Tuition and fees vary according to program. *Financial support:* Research assistantships, teaching assistantships available. Financial award application deadline: 2/1. *Faculty research:* Behavior therapy, cognitive behavior modification, pro-social behavior, conditioning and learning, olfaction.

Appalachian State University, Cratis D. Williams Graduate School, Department of Psychology, Boone, NC 28608. Offers clinical health psychology (MA); general experimental psychology (MA); industrial and organizational psychology (MA). Part-time programs available. *Faculty:* 31 full-time (11 women). *Students:* 43 full-time (31 women), 37 part-time (30 women); includes 4 minority (3 African Americans, 1 Asian American or Pacific Islander), 4 international. 197 applicants, 30% accepted, 30 enrolled. In 2007, 23 master's, 6 other advanced degrees awarded. *Degree requirements:* For master's and MS/SSP, comprehensive exam, thesis optional, GRE Subject Test exit exam. *Entrance requirements:* For master's, GRE General Test, 3 letters of recommendation. Additional exam requirements/recommendations for international students: Required—TOEFL (minimum score 550 paper-based; 230 computer-based; 79 iBT), IELTS (minimum score 7). *Application deadline:* For fall admission, 3/1 for domestic students, 1/1 for international students. Applications are processed on a rolling basis. Application fee: $50. *Expenses:* Tuition, state resident: part-time $127 per semester hour. Tuition, nonresident: part-time $597 per semester hour. Required fees: $18 per semester. *Financial support:* In 2007–08, 34 research assistantships (averaging $3,500 per year), 25 teaching assistantships (averaging $3,500 per year) were awarded; fellowships, career-related internships or fieldwork, Federal Work-Study, scholarships/grants, and unspecified assistantships also available. Financial award application deadline: 4/1. *Faculty research:* Eating disorders, school-based consultations, organizational behavior management, brain mechanisms of sound localization, parenting styles. Total annual research expenditures: $158,688. *Unit head:* Dr. Paul Fox, Chair, 828-262-2272, Fax: 828-262-2974, E-mail: foxpa@appstate.edu. *Application contact:* Dr. Denise Martz, Graduate Coordinator, 828-262-2715, E-mail: martzdm@appstate.edu.

Auburn University, Graduate School, College of Liberal Arts, Department of Psychology, Auburn University, AL 36849. Offers applied behavior analysis in developmental disabilities (MS); clinical psychology (PhD); experimental psychology (PhD); industrial/organizational psychology (PhD). *Accreditation:* APA (one or more programs are accredited). Part-time programs available. *Faculty:* 22 full-time (5 women). *Students:* 30 full-time (18 women), 65 part-time (44 women); includes 10 minority (5 African Americans, 1 American Indian/Alaska Native, 2 Asian Americans or Pacific Islanders, 2 Hispanic Americans), 2 international. Average age 28. 298 applicants, 15% accepted, 27 enrolled. In 2007, 15 master's, 3 doctorates awarded. *Degree requirements:* For doctorate, thesis/dissertation. *Entrance requirements:* For master's, GRE General Test, GRE Subject Test, minimum GPA of 3.25 in psychology, 3.0 overall; for doctorate, GRE General Test, GRE Subject Test. *Application deadline:* For fall admission, 7/7 for domestic students; for spring admission, 11/24 for domestic students. Applications are processed on a rolling basis. Application fee: $25 ($50 for international students). Electronic applications accepted. *Financial support:* Research assistantships, teaching assistantships, Federal Work-Study available. Support available to part-time students. Financial award application deadline: 3/15. *Faculty research:* Clinical psychology, learning, industrial psychology, organizational psychology. Total annual research expenditures: $200,000. *Unit head:* Dr. Barry Burkhart, Chair, 334-844-4412. *Application contact:* Dr. Joe Pittman, Interim Dean of the Graduate School, 334-844-4700.

Bowling Green State University, Graduate College, College of Arts and Sciences, Department of Psychology, Bowling Green, OH 43403. Offers clinical psychology (MA, PhD); developmental psychology (MA, PhD); experimental psychology (MA, PhD); industrial/organizational psychology (MA, PhD); quantitative psychology (MA, PhD). *Accreditation:* APA (one or more programs are accredited). *Faculty:* 29 full-time (9 women), 14 part-time/adjunct (5 women). *Students:* 88 full-time (61 women), 27 part-time (19 women); includes 10 minority (5 Asian Americans or Pacific Islanders, 5 Hispanic Americans), 12 international. Average age 27. 225 applicants, 15% accepted, 19 enrolled. In 2007, 22 master's, 14 doctorates awarded. *Degree requirements:* For doctorate, thesis/dissertation. *Entrance requirements:* For doctorate, GRE General Test, GRE Subject Test. Additional exam requirements/recommendations for international students: Required—TOEFL. *Application deadline:* For fall admission, 1/1 for domestic students. Application fee: $30. Electronic applications accepted. *Financial support:* In 2007–08, 5 fellowships with full tuition reimbursements (averaging $16,187 per year), 50 research assistantships with full tuition reimbursements (averaging $11,844 per year), 29 teaching assistantships with full tuition reimbursements (averaging $11,805 per year) were awarded; career-related internships or fieldwork, Federal Work-Study, institutionally sponsored loans, tuition waivers (full), and unspecified assistantships also available. Financial award applicants required to submit FAFSA. *Faculty research:* Personnel psychology, developmental-mathematical models, behavioral medication, brain process, child/adolescent social cognition. *Unit head:* Dr. Dale Klopfer, Chair, 419-372-2733.

Brooklyn College of the City University of New York, Division of Graduate Studies, Department of Psychology, Brooklyn, NY 11210-2889. Offers experimental psychology (MA); industrial and organizational psychology (MA), including industrial and organizational psychology-human relations, psychology-organizational psychology and behavior; mental health counseling (MA); psychology (PhD). The City University doctoral program in experimental psychology is based at Brooklyn College; candidates who complete the MA may apply for admission to the doctoral program. MA programs in industrial and organizational psychology and mental health counseling are fall admissions only. Part-time programs available. *Students:* 57 full-time (49 women), 91 part-time (73 women); includes 67 minority (39 African Americans, 1 American Indian/Alaska Native, 13 Asian Americans or Pacific Islanders, 14 Hispanic Americans), 9 international. 207 applicants, 60% accepted, 77 enrolled. In 2007, 37 degrees awarded. *Degree requirements:* For master's, comprehensive exam, thesis (for some programs). *Entrance requirements:* For master's, minimum GPA of 3.0, 2 letters of recommendation, essay; for doctorate, GRE. Additional exam requirements/recommendations for international students: Required—TOEFL. *Application deadline:* For fall admission, 3/1 for domestic students, 2/1 for international students; for spring admission, 11/1 for domestic students, 10/1 for international students. Applications are processed on a rolling basis. Application fee: $125. Electronic applications accepted. *Financial support:* Career-related internships or fieldwork, Federal Work-Study, institutionally sponsored loans, scholarships/grants, and tuition waivers (partial) available. Support available to part-time students. Financial award application deadline: 5/1; financial award applicants required to submit FAFSA. *Unit head:* Dr. Glen Hass, Chairperson, 718-951-5601, Fax: 718-951-4814, E-mail: ghass@brooklyn.cuny.edu. *Application contact:* Hernan Sierra, Graduate Admissions Coordinator, 718-951-4536, Fax: 718-951-4506, E-mail: grads@brooklyn.cuny.edu.

California State University, Northridge, Graduate Studies, College of Social and Behavioral Sciences, Department of Psychology, Northridge, CA 91330. Offers clinical psychology (MA); general-experimental psychology (MA); human factors and applied experimental psychology (MA). *Faculty:* 26 full-time (17 women), 32 part-time/adjunct (15 women). *Students:* 51 full-time (29 women), 18 part-time (13 women); includes 21 minority (1 African American, 4 Asian Americans or Pacific Islanders, 16 Hispanic Americans), 9 international. Average age 28. 102 applicants, 48% accepted, 38 enrolled. In 2007, 13 degrees awarded. *Degree requirements:* For master's, thesis. *Entrance requirements:* For master's, GRE General Test, GRE Subject Test, minimum GPA of 3.0, letters of recommendation. Additional exam requirements/recommendations for international students: Required—TOEFL. *Application deadline:* For fall admission, 11/30 for domestic students. Application fee: $55. *Financial support:* Application deadline: 3/1. *Unit head:* Dr. Paul Skolnick, Chair, 818-677-2827.

California State University, San Bernardino, Graduate Studies, College of Social and Behavioral Sciences, Department of Psychology, Program in General/Experimental Psychology, San Bernardino, CA 92407-2397. Offers MA. *Students:* 33 full-time (24 women), 12 part-time (8 women); includes 12 minority (1 African American, 11 Hispanic Americans), 1 international. Average age 26. 31 applicants, 39% accepted, 11 enrolled. In 2007, 8 degrees awarded. *Entrance requirements:* For master's, minimum GPA of 3.0 in major. *Application deadline:* For fall admission, 4/1 for domestic students; for spring admission, 3/1 for domestic students. Application fee: $55. *Financial support:* Unspecified assistantships available. *Unit head:* Dr. Sanders McDougall, Head, 909-537-5581, Fax: 909-537-7003, E-mail: smcdouga@csusb.edu. *Application contact:* Stacy Brooks, Graduate Secretary, 909-537-5570, Fax: 909-537-7003, E-mail: sbrooks@csusb.edu.

Case Western Reserve University, School of Graduate Studies, Department of Psychology, Program in Experimental Psychology, Cleveland, OH 44106. Offers PhD. *Faculty:* 9 full-time (4 women). *Students:* 8 full-time (5 women); includes 1 minority (Asian American or Pacific Islander) *Degree requirements:* For doctorate, thesis/dissertation, internship. *Entrance requirements:* For doctorate, GRE General Test, GRE Subject Test. Additional exam requirements/recommendations for international students: Required—TOEFL. *Application deadline:* For fall admission, 1/15 for domestic students. Application fee: $50. Electronic applications accepted. *Financial support:* Fellowships, teaching assistantships available. *Faculty research:* Memory and intelligence, brain function in rats. *Application contact:* Dr. James C. Overholser, Director of Clinical Training, 216-368-2686, Fax: 216-368-4891, E-mail: overholser@case.edu.

The Catholic University of America, School of Arts and Sciences, Department of Psychology, Program in Applied Experimental Psychology, Washington, DC 20064. Offers MA, PhD. *Students:*

Experimental Psychology

The Catholic University of America (continued)
3 full-time (2 women), 4 part-time (2 women), 1 international. Average age 31. 13 applicants, 31% accepted, 1 enrolled. In 2007, 1 degree awarded. Terminal master's awarded for partial completion of doctoral program. *Degree requirements:* For master's, comprehensive exam, thesis (for some programs); for doctorate, comprehensive exam, thesis/dissertation. *Entrance requirements:* For master's, GRE General Test, 3 letters of recommendation; for doctorate, GRE General Test, GRE Subject Test, 3 letters of recommendation. Additional exam requirements/recommendations for international students: Required—TOEFL (minimum score 580 paper-based; 237 computer-based). *Application deadline:* For fall admission, 2/1 priority date for domestic students; for spring admission, 11/15 priority date for domestic students. Applications are processed on a rolling basis. Application fee: $55. Electronic applications accepted. *Financial support:* Fellowships, research assistantships, teaching assistantships, career-related internships or fieldwork, Federal Work-Study, scholarships/grants, tuition waivers (full and partial), and unspecified assistantships available. Support available to part-time students. Financial award application deadline: 2/1; financial award applicants required to submit FAFSA. *Faculty research:* Aviation human factors, human perception and cognition, cognitive science, artificial intelligence, attention and vigilance. *Unit head:* Dr. Deborah Clawson, Director, 202-319-5750, Fax: 202-319-6263, E-mail: clawson@cua.edu.

Central Michigan University, College of Graduate Studies, College of Humanities and Social and Behavioral Sciences, Department of Psychology, Program in General, Applied, and Experimental Psychology, Mount Pleasant, MI 48859. Offers applied experimental psychology (PhD); general/experimental psychology (MS). *Degree requirements:* For master's, thesis or alternative. *Entrance requirements:* For doctorate, GRE.

Central Washington University, Graduate Studies, Research and Continuing Education, College of the Sciences, Department of Psychology, Program in Experimental Psychology, Ellensburg, WA 98926. Offers MS. *Faculty:* 27 full-time (13 women). *Students:* 9 full-time (8 women), 8 part-time (4 women); includes 5 minority (3 American Indian/Alaska Native, 2 Hispanic Americans). 9 applicants, 44% accepted, 4 enrolled. In 2007, 7 degrees awarded. *Degree requirements:* For master's, thesis. *Entrance requirements:* For master's, GRE General Test, minimum GPA of 3.0. Additional exam requirements/recommendations for international students: Required—TOEFL (minimum score 550 paper-based; 213 computer-based; 79 iBT). *Application deadline:* For fall admission, 4/1 priority date for domestic students. Applications are processed on a rolling basis. Application fee: $50. *Expenses:* Tuition, state resident: full-time $2,209; part-time $221 per credit. Tuition, nonresident: full-time $4,939; part-time $442 per credit. Required fees: $207 per quarter. Tuition and fees vary according to degree level. *Financial support:* Research assistantships with partial tuition reimbursements, teaching assistantships, career-related internships or fieldwork, Federal Work-Study, health care benefits, and unspecified assistantships available. Financial award application deadline: 3/1. *Unit head:* Dr. Warren Street, Chair, 509-963-3674. *Application contact:* Justine Eason, Admissions Program Coordinator, 509-963-3103, Fax: 509-963-1799, E-mail: masters@cwu.edu.

City College of the City University of New York, Graduate School, College of Liberal Arts and Science, Division of Social Science, Department of Psychology, New York, NY 10031-9198. Offers clinical psychology (PhD); experimental cognition (PhD); general psychology (MA); mental health counseling (MA). *Accreditation:* APA (one or more programs are accredited). Part-time programs available. *Students:* 17 full-time (12 women), 98 part-time (72 women); includes 79 minority (28 African Americans, 13 Asian Americans or Pacific Islanders, 38 Hispanic Americans), 23 international. 40 applicants, 55% accepted, 30 enrolled. In 2007, 43 degrees awarded. *Degree requirements:* For master's, one foreign language, comprehensive exam, thesis. *Entrance requirements:* For master's, GRE. Additional exam requirements/recommendations for international students: Required—TOEFL (minimum score 550 paper-based; 213 computer-based). *Application deadline:* For fall admission, 4/15 for domestic students; for spring admission, 11/15 for domestic students. Application fee: $125. *Financial support:* Fellowships, teaching assistantships, career-related internships or fieldwork, Federal Work-Study, and tuition waivers (full and partial) available. Support available to part-time students. Financial award application deadline: 5/1. *Faculty research:* Social/personality psychology, physiological psychology, cognition and development. *Unit head:* Vivien Tartter, Graduate Adviser, 212-650-5709, Fax: 212-650-5865, E-mail: vtartter@ccny.cuny.edu.

Cleveland State University, College of Graduate Studies, College of Science, Department of Psychology, Cleveland, OH 44115. Offers clinical psychology (MA); consumer/industrial research (MA); diversity management (MA); experimental research psychology (MA); school psychology (Psy S). Part-time programs available. *Faculty:* 17 full-time (5 women), 16 part-time/adjunct (10 women). *Students:* 76 full-time (52 women), 44 part-time (37 women); includes 19 minority (15 African Americans, 1 American Indian/Alaska Native, 2 Asian Americans or Pacific Islanders, 1 Hispanic American), 3 international. Average age 29. 153 applicants, 27% accepted, 37 enrolled. In 2007, 26 master's, 9 other advanced degrees awarded. *Degree requirements:* For master's, thesis (for some programs). *Entrance requirements:* For master's, GRE General Test. Additional exam requirements/recommendations for international students: Required—TOEFL (minimum score 525 paper-based; 197 computer-based). *Application deadline:* For fall admission, 2/1 priority date for domestic and international students. Applications are processed on a rolling basis. Application fee: $30. Electronic applications accepted. *Financial support:* In 2007–08, 45 students received support. Career-related internships or fieldwork, Federal Work-Study, tuition waivers (partial), and unspecified assistantships available. Financial award applicants required to submit FAFSA. Total annual research expenditures: $112,607. *Unit head:* Dr. David M. Grilly, Chairperson, 216-687-2545, Fax: 216-687-9294, E-mail: d.grilly@csuohio.edu. *Application contact:* Karen Colston, Administrative Coordinator, 216-687-2552, E-mail: k.colston@csuohio.edu.

The College of William and Mary, Faculty of Arts and Sciences, Department of Psychology, Program in General Experimental Psychology, Williamsburg, VA 23187-8795. Offers MA. *Faculty:* 9 full-time (3 women), 1 part-time/adjunct (0 women). *Students:* 14 full-time (13 women); includes 2 minority (1 African American, 1 Asian American or Pacific Islander). Average age 24. 93 applicants, 11% accepted, 7 enrolled. In 2007, 6 degrees awarded. *Degree requirements:* For master's, comprehensive exam, thesis, oral exams. *Entrance requirements:* For master's, GRE, passed previous course work in statistics and experimental psychology. Additional exam requirements/recommendations for international students: Required—TOEFL. *Application deadline:* For fall admission, 2/15 for domestic and international students. Application fee: $45. Electronic applications accepted. *Expenses:* Tuition, state resident: full-time $6,250; part-time $275 per credit hour. Tuition, nonresident: part-time $760 per credit hour. Required fees: $3,550. Tuition and fees vary according to program. *Financial support:* In 2007–08, 14 students received support, including 1 research assistantship with full tuition reimbursement available (averaging $9,000 per year), 13 teaching assistantships with full tuition reimbursements available (averaging $9,000 per year); institutionally sponsored loans, scholarships/grants, and unspecified assistantships also available. Financial award application deadline: 2/15; financial award applicants required to submit FAFSA. *Faculty research:* Personality, developmental, professional development, applied decision theory, social psychology. *Unit head:* Dr. Peter M. Vishton, Graduate Director, 757-221-3879, Fax: 757-221-3896, E-mail: vishton@wm.edu. *Application contact:* Barbara B. Pumilia, Graduate Administrator, 757-221-3872, Fax: 757-221-3872, E-mail: bbpumi@wm.edu.

Columbia University, Graduate School of Arts and Sciences, Division of Natural Sciences, Department of Psychology, New York, NY 10027. Offers experimental psychology (M Phil, MA, PhD); psychobiology (M Phil, MA, PhD); social psychology (M Phil, MA, PhD); JD/MA; JD/PhD; MD/PhD. *Faculty:* 23 full-time. *Students:* 35 full-time (19 women), 2 part-time. Average age 28. 156 applicants, 7% accepted. In 2007, 7 master's, 6 doctorates awarded. *Degree requirements:* For master's, thesis; for doctorate, thesis/dissertation. *Entrance requirements:* For master's and doctorate, GRE General Test. Additional exam requirements/recommendations for international students: Required—TOEFL. Application fee: $90. *Expenses:* Tuition: Part-time $1,452 per credit. Required fees: $152 per term. One-time fee: $75 part-time. Full-time tuition and fees vary according to course level, course load, degree level and program. *Financial support:* Fellowships, teaching assistantships, Federal Work-Study and institutionally sponsored loans available. Support available to part-time students. Financial award application deadline: 1/5; financial award applicants required to submit FAFSA. *Unit head:* Norma Graham, Chair, 212-854-5591, Fax: 212-854-3609, E-mail: nb2229@columbia.edu.

Cornell University, Graduate School, Graduate Fields of Arts and Sciences, Field of Psychology, Ithaca, NY 14853-0001. Offers biopsychology (PhD); human experimental psychology (PhD); personality and social psychology (PhD). *Faculty:* 42 full-time (15 women). *Students:* 33 full-time (18 women); includes 5 minority (2 African Americans, 2 Asian Americans or Pacific Islanders, 1 Hispanic American), 10 international. Average age 29. 175 applicants, 8% accepted, 8 enrolled. In 2007, 4 doctorates awarded. *Degree requirements:* For doctorate, comprehensive exam, thesis/dissertation, 2 semesters of teaching experience. *Entrance requirements:* For doctorate, GRE General Test, 3 letters of recommendation. Additional exam requirements/recommendations for international students: Required—TOEFL (minimum score 550 paper-based; 213 computer-based; 77 iBT). *Application deadline:* For fall admission, 12/15 for domestic students. Application fee: $70. Electronic applications accepted. *Financial support:* In 2007–08, 33 students received support, including 11 fellowships with full tuition reimbursements available, 22 teaching assistantships with full tuition reimbursements available; research assistantships with full tuition reimbursements available, institutionally sponsored loans, scholarships/grants, health care benefits, tuition waivers (full and partial), and unspecified assistantships also available. Financial award applicants required to submit FAFSA. *Faculty research:* Sensory and perceptual systems, social cognition, cognitive development, quantitative and computational modeling, behavioral neuroscience. *Unit head:* Director of Graduate Studies, 607-255-6364, Fax: 607-255-8433. *Application contact:* Graduate Field Assistant, 607-255-3834, Fax: 607-255-8433, E-mail: psychapp@cornell.edu.

Dallas Baptist University, Gary Cook School of Leadership and Christian Education, Program in Christian Education, Dallas, TX 75211-9299. Offers adult ministry (MA); business ministry (MA); childhood ministry (MA); collegiate ministry (MA); communication ministry (MA); counseling ministry (MA); education ministry (MA); general ministry (MA); missions ministry (MA); student ministry (MA); worship ministry (MA). Part-time and evening/weekend programs available. *Faculty:* 55 full-time (22 women), 114 part-time/adjunct (44 women). *Students:* 20 full-time, 52 part-time. 29 applicants, 52% accepted, 13 enrolled. In 2007, 34 degrees awarded. *Entrance requirements:* For master's, minimum GPA of 3.0. Additional exam requirements/recommendations for international students: Required—TOEFL. *Application deadline:* Applications are processed on a rolling basis. Application fee: $25. Electronic applications accepted. *Expenses:* Tuition: Full-time $9,144; part-time $508 per credit hour. *Financial support:* Federal Work-Study, institutionally sponsored loans, scholarships/grants, and tuition waivers (full and partial) available. Support available to part-time students. Financial award applicants required to submit FAFSA. *Unit head:* Dr. Judy Morris, Director, 214-333-5246, Fax: 214-333-5115, E-mail: graduate@dbu.edu. *Application contact:* Kit P. Montgomery, Director of Graduate Programs, 214-333-5242, Fax: 214-333-5579, E-mail: graduate@dbu.edu.

DePaul University, College of Liberal Arts and Sciences, Department of Psychology, Chicago, IL 60604-2287. Offers clinical psychology (MA, PhD), including child clinical psychology, community clinical psychology; experimental psychology (MA, PhD); general psychology (MS); industrial/organizational psychology (MA, PhD); MA/PhD. *Accreditation:* APA (one or more programs are accredited). *Faculty:* 31 full-time (19 women), 6 part-time/adjunct (4 women). *Students:* 57 full-time (36 women), 53 part-time (36 women); includes 24 minority (14 African Americans, 1 American Indian/Alaska Native, 3 Asian Americans or Pacific Islanders, 6 Hispanic Americans), 1 international. Average age 28. 332 applicants, 14% accepted, 23 enrolled. In 2007, 14 master's, 17 doctorates awarded. *Median time to degree:* Of those who began their doctoral program in fall 1999, 60% received their degree in 8 years or less. *Degree requirements:* For master's, thesis, oral exam; for doctorate, comprehensive exam, thesis/dissertation, oral and written exams. *Entrance requirements:* For master's and doctorate, GRE General Test, GRE Subject Test, 32 quarter hours of course work in psychology, 3 letters of recommendation. Additional exam requirements/recommendations for international students: Required—TOEFL. Application fee: $40. Electronic applications accepted. *Financial support:* In 2007–08, 48 students received support, including 35 research assistantships with full tuition reimbursements available (averaging $11,800 per year), 13 teaching assistantships with full tuition reimbursements available (averaging $11,800 per year); career-related internships or fieldwork, scholarships/grants, traineeships, tuition waivers (full and partial), and unspecified assistantships also available. Financial award application deadline: 1/10. *Faculty research:* Adolescent stress and depression, minority adolescents sexuality, public policy, community influences in child adjustment. *Unit head:* Dr. Christopher B Keys, Chairman, 773-325-7887, Fax: 773-325-7888. *Application contact:* Alison Pereida Knapp, Graduate Admissions Assistant, 773-325-7887, Fax: 773-325-7888.

Duke University, Graduate School, Department of Psychology, Durham, NC 27708-0586. Offers biological psychology (PhD); clinical psychology (PhD); cognitive psychology (PhD); developmental psychology (PhD); experimental psychology (PhD); health psychology (PhD); human social development (PhD); JD/MA. *Accreditation:* APA (one or more programs are accredited). *Faculty:* 40 full-time. *Students:* 91 full-time (71 women); includes 15 minority (9 African Americans, 1 Asian American or Pacific Islander, 5 Hispanic Americans), 13 international. 468 applicants, 7% accepted, 19 enrolled. In 2007, 14 doctorates awarded. *Degree requirements:* For doctorate, thesis/dissertation. *Entrance requirements:* For doctorate, GRE General Test. Additional exam requirements/recommendations for international students: Required—TOEFL (minimum score 550 paper-based; 213 computer-based; 83 iBT), IELTS (minimum score 7). *Application deadline:* For fall admission, 12/15 priority date for domestic and international students. Application fee: $75. Electronic applications accepted. *Financial support:* Fellowships, research assistantships, teaching assistantships, career-related internships or fieldwork and Federal Work-Study available. Financial award application deadline: 12/31. *Unit head:* Amy Needham, Co-Director of Graduate Studies, 919-660-5715, Fax: 919-660-5726, E-mail: morrell@duke.edu.

Fairleigh Dickinson University, Metropolitan Campus, University College: Arts, Sciences, and Professional Studies, School of Psychology, Program in General-Theoretical Psychology, Teaneck, NJ 07666-1914. Offers MA, Certificate. *Students:* 17 full-time (11 women), 13 part-time (9 women), 2 international. Average age 29. 31 applicants, 94% accepted, 17 enrolled. In 2007, 26 degrees awarded. *Application deadline:* Applications are processed on a rolling basis. Application fee: $40. *Expenses:* Tuition: Part-time $869 per credit. Tuition and fees vary according to degree level, campus/location and program.

Graduate School and University Center of the City University of New York, Graduate Studies, Program in Psychology, New York, NY 10016-4039. Offers basic applied neurocognition (PhD); biopsychology (PhD); clinical psychology (PhD); developmental psychology (PhD); environmental psychology (PhD); experimental psychology (PhD); industrial psychology (PhD); learning processes (PhD); neuropsychology (PhD); psychology (PhD); social personality (PhD). *Faculty:* 119 full-time (40 women). *Students:* 510 full-time (379 women), 1 (woman) part-time; includes 98 minority (39 African Americans, 1 American Indian/Alaska Native, 21 Asian Americans or Pacific Islanders, 37 Hispanic Americans), 63 international. Average age 33. 747 applicants, 17% accepted, 78 enrolled. In 2007, 59 degrees awarded. *Degree requirements:* For doctorate, one foreign language, thesis/dissertation. *Entrance requirements:* For doctorate, GRE General Test. Additional exam requirements/recommendations for international students: Required—TOEFL. *Application deadline:* For fall admission, 12/15 for domestic students. Application fee: $125. Electronic applications accepted. *Financial support:* In 2007–08, 371 students received support, including 308 fellowships, 34 research assistantships, 33 teaching assistantships; career-related internships or fieldwork, Federal Work-Study, institutionally sponsored loans, and tuition waivers (full and partial) also available. Financial award application deadline: 2/1; financial award applicants required to submit FAFSA. *Unit head:* Dr. Joseph Glick, Executive Officer, 212-817-8706, Fax: 212-817-1533, E-mail: jglick@gc.cuny.edu.

Harvard University, Graduate School of Arts and Sciences, Department of Psychology, Cambridge, MA 02138. Offers psychology (PhD), including behavior and decision analysis, cognition, developmental psychology, experimental psychology, personality, psychobiology, psychopathology; social psychology (PhD). *Degree requirements:* For doctorate, thesis/dissertation, general exams. *Entrance requirements:* For doctorate, GRE General Test. Additional exam requirements/recommendations for international students: Required—TOEFL. *Expenses:* Tuition: Full-time $31,456. Full-time tuition and fees vary according to program and student level.

Howard University, Graduate School, Department of Psychology, Washington, DC 20059-0002. Offers clinical psychology (PhD); developmental psychology (PhD); experimental psychology (PhD); neuropsychology (PhD); personality psychology (PhD); psychology (MS); social psychology (PhD). *Accreditation:* APA (one or more programs are accredited). Part-time programs available. *Degree requirements:* For master's, thesis; for doctorate, comprehensive exam, thesis/dissertation, qualifying exam. *Entrance requirements:* For master's, GRE General Test, minimum GPA of 2.5, bachelor's degree in psychology or related field; for doctorate, GRE General Test, minimum GPA of 3.0. *Expenses:* Tuition: Full-time $16,175; part-time $899 per credit hour. Required fees: $805. *Faculty research:* Personality and psychophysiology, educational and social development of African-American children, child and adult psychopathology.

Illinois State University, Graduate School, College of Arts and Sciences, Department of Psychology, Normal, IL 61790-2200. Offers psychology (MA, MS), including clinical psychology, counseling psychology, developmental psychology, educational psychology, experimental psychology, measurement-evaluation, organizational-industrial psychology; school psychology (PhD, SSP). *Accreditation:* APA. *Faculty:* 36 full-time (14 women). *Students:* 49 full-time (37 women), 19 part-time (14 women); includes 3 minority (all Asian Americans or Pacific Islanders), 7 international. 91 applicants, 43% accepted. In 2007, 24 degrees awarded. *Degree requirements:* For master's, thesis or alternative; for doctorate, variable foreign language requirement, thesis/dissertation, 2 terms of residency, internship, practicum. *Entrance requirements:* For master's, GRE General Test, GRE Subject Test, minimum GPA of 3.0 in last 60 hours of course work; for doctorate, GRE General Test. *Application deadline:* Applications are processed on a rolling basis. Application fee: $40. *Expenses:* Tuition, state resident: full-time $3,492; part-time $194 per credit hour. Tuition, nonresident: full-time $7,272; part-time $404 per credit hour. Required fees: $1,024; $57 per credit hour. *Financial support:* In 2007–08, 33 research assistantships (averaging $6,252 per year), 49 teaching assistantships (averaging $4,217 per year) were awarded; tuition waivers (full) and unspecified assistantships also available. Financial award application deadline: 4/1. *Faculty research:* Comprehensive evaluation system for the central region professional development grant, Illinois school psychology internship consortium, for children's sake. Total annual research expenditures: $292,085. *Unit head:* Dr. Neil Skaggs, Acting Chairperson, 309-438-8651.

Iona College, School of Arts and Science, Department of Psychology, New Rochelle, NY 10801-1890. Offers experimental psychology (MA); industrial-organizational psychology (MA); mental health counseling (MA); psychology (MA); school psychology (MA). Part-time and evening/weekend programs available. *Faculty:* 12 full-time (6 women), 5 part-time/adjunct (2 women). *Students:* 77 full-time (62 women), 21 part-time (19 women); includes 19 minority (5 African Americans, 2 Asian Americans or Pacific Islanders, 12 Hispanic Americans). Average age 25. 105 applicants, 66% accepted, 33 enrolled. In 2007, 29 degrees awarded. *Degree requirements:* For master's, thesis. *Entrance requirements:* For master's, GRE or minimum GPA of 3.0. Additional exam requirements/recommendations for international students: Required—TOEFL (minimum score 550 paper-based; 213 computer-based). *Application deadline:* Applications are processed on a rolling basis. Application fee: $50. Electronic applications accepted. *Expenses:* Tuition: Part-time $712 per credit. Required fees: $150 per term. *Financial support:* Career-related internships or fieldwork, tuition waivers (partial), and unspecified assistantships available. Support available to part-time students. *Unit head:* Dr. Pauline Jirik-Babb, Chair, 914-633-2191, E-mail: pjirikbabb@iona.edu. *Application contact:* Veronica Jarek-Prinz, Director of Graduate Admissions, 914-633-2420, Fax: 914-633-2277, E-mail: vjarekprinz@iona.edu.

Kent State University, College of Arts and Sciences, Department of Psychology, Kent, OH 44242-0001. Offers clinical psychology (MA, PhD); experimental psychology (MA, PhD). *Accreditation:* APA (one or more programs are accredited). *Faculty:* 28 full-time (12 women). *Students:* 119 full-time (87 women). 324 applicants, 7% accepted. In 2007, 16 master's, 16 doctorates awarded. *Degree requirements:* For master's, thesis; for doctorate, thesis/dissertation. *Entrance requirements:* For master's, GRE, minimum GPA of 3.0, minimum 18 semester hours in psychology with one course in statistics and one experimental course with a lab component; for doctorate, GRE, minimum GPA of 3.0. Additional exam requirements/recommendations for international students: Required—TOEFL (minimum score 525 paper-based), Michigan English Language Assessment Battery (minimum score: 77). *Application deadline:* For fall admission, 1/1 for domestic and international students. Application fee: $30. *Financial support:* Fellowships, research assistantships, teaching assistantships, career-related internships or fieldwork, Federal Work-Study, institutionally sponsored loans, health care benefits, and tuition waivers (full) available. Financial award application deadline: 1/1. *Unit head:* Dr. Mary Ann Parris Stephens, Chair, 330-672-2027, Fax: 330-672-3786, E-mail: mstephen@kent.edu. *Application contact:* Jack Graham, Coordinator of Graduate Studies, E-mail: jgraham@kent.edu.

Lakehead University, Graduate Studies, Department of Psychology, Thunder Bay, ON P7B 5E1, Canada. Offers clinical psychology (MA, PhD); experimental psychology (MA). Part-time and evening/weekend programs available. *Degree requirements:* For master's, thesis optional; for doctorate, thesis/dissertation, 2 comprehensive exams, internship. *Entrance requirements:* For master's, GRE, honors degree in psychology, advanced course work in statistics, minimum B average; for doctorate, GRE, minimum B average. Additional exam requirements/recommendations for international students: Required—TOEFL. *Faculty research:* Chaos theory, health psychology, counseling psychology, gerontology, women's studies.

McGill University, Faculty of Graduate and Postdoctoral Studies, Faculty of Science, Department of Psychology, Montréal, QC H3A 2T5, Canada. Offers clinical psychology (PhD); experimental psychology (M Sc, MA, PhD). *Accreditation:* APA (one or more programs are accredited). *Faculty:* 45 full-time (17 women), 67 part-time/adjunct (38 women). *Students:* 100 full-time (72 women), 2 part-time (both women). 256 applicants, 11% accepted, 26 enrolled. In 2007, 3 master's, 12 doctorates awarded.

Memorial University of Newfoundland, School of Graduate Studies, Department of Psychology, St. John's, NL A1C 5S7, Canada. Offers applied social psychology (MASP); experimental psychology (M Sc, PhD). Part-time programs available. *Degree requirements:* For master's, workterms (MASP), thesis (M Sc); for doctorate, comprehensive exam, thesis/dissertation, oral thesis defense. *Entrance requirements:* For master's, GRE, honors bachelor's degree of high second class standing or equivalent; for doctorate, GRE, master's or honors degree. Electronic applications accepted. *Faculty research:* Behavioral neuroscience, cognition, theory and research on abnormal behavior.

Miami University, Graduate School, College of Arts and Sciences, Department of Psychology, Oxford, OH 45056. Offers clinical psychology (PhD); experimental psychology (PhD); social psychology (PhD). *Accreditation:* APA. *Degree requirements:* For doctorate, comprehensive exam, thesis/dissertation, final exams. *Entrance requirements:* For doctorate, GRE General Test, GRE Subject Test, minimum GPA of 2.75 (undergraduate), 3.0 (graduate). Additional exam requirements/recommendations for international students: Required—TOEFL (minimum score 550 paper-based; 213 computer-based), TWE (minimum score 4). Electronic applications accepted.

Mississippi State University, College of Arts and Sciences, Department of Psychology, Mississippi State, MS 39762. Offers clinical psychology (MS); cognitive science (PhD); experimental psychology (MS). *Faculty:* 16 full-time (7 women), 2 part-time/adjunct (1 woman). *Students:* 31 full-time (21 women), 14 part-time (7 women); includes 2 minority (1 African American, 1 American Indian/Alaska Native), 2 international. Average age 26. 32 applicants, 47% accepted, 8 enrolled. In 2007, 8 master's awarded. Terminal master's awarded for partial completion of doctoral program. *Degree requirements:* For master's, comprehensive exam, thesis; for doctorate, thesis/dissertation, qualifying exam, comprehensive written and oral exam. *Entrance requirements:* For master's, GRE General Test, minimum GPA of 2.75; for doctorate, GRE General Test, proficiency in at least 1 computer language. Additional exam requirements/recommendations for international students: Required—TOEFL. *Application deadline:* For fall admission, 7/1 priority date for domestic students; for spring admission, 11/1 for domestic students. Applications are processed on a rolling basis. Application fee: $30. *Expenses:* Tuition, state resident: full-time $4,978; part-time $274 per hour. Tuition, nonresident: full-time $11,469; part-time $635 per hour. *Financial support:* In 2007–08, 13 teaching assistantships with full tuition reimbursements (averaging $8,877 per year) were awarded; research assistantships with full tuition reimbursements, career-related internships or fieldwork, Federal Work-Study, institutionally sponsored loans, scholarships/grants, and unspecified assistantships also available. Financial award applicants required to submit FAFSA. *Faculty research:* Personality type, alcoholism, blindness and low vision, mental retardation, language comprehension. Total annual research expenditures: $4.5 million. *Unit head:* Dr. Stephen B. Klein, Head, 662-325-3202, Fax: 662-325-7212, E-mail: sbkl@ra.msstate.edu. *Application contact:* Dr. William A. Person, Interim Associate Vice President for Academic Affairs/Interim Dean of Graduate Studies, 662-325-7400, Fax: 662-325-1967, E-mail: grad@grad.msstate.edu.

Morehead State University, Graduate Programs, College of Science and Technology, Department of Psychology, Morehead, KY 40351. Offers clinical psychology (MA); counseling psychology (MA); experimental/general psychology (MA). Part-time programs available. *Faculty:* 7 full-time (3 women), 3 part-time/adjunct (1 woman). *Students:* 21 full-time (18 women), 4 part-time (1 woman); includes 1 minority (African American) Average age 26. In 2007, 12 degrees awarded. *Degree requirements:* For master's, comprehensive exam, thesis optional. *Entrance requirements:* For master's, GRE General Test, 18 undergraduate hours in psychology, minimum GPA of 3.0. Additional exam requirements/recommendations for international students: Required—TOEFL (minimum score 500 paper-based; 173 computer-based). *Application deadline:* For fall admission, 8/1 priority date for domestic and international students; for spring admission, 12/1 for domestic students, 12/1 priority date for international students. Applications are processed on a rolling basis. Application fee: $0 ($55 for international students). Electronic applications accepted. *Financial support:* In 2007–08, 19 research assistantships (averaging $6,000 per year) were awarded; career-related internships or fieldwork, Federal Work-Study, and institutionally sponsored loans also available. Financial award application deadline: 4/1; financial award applicants required to submit FAFSA. *Faculty research:* Mood induction effects, serotonin receptor activity, stress, perceptual processes. *Application contact:* Michelle Barber, Graduate Admissions Counselor, 606-783-2039, Fax: 606-783-5061, E-mail: m.barber@moreheadstate.edu.

North Carolina State University, Graduate School, College of Humanities and Social Sciences, Department of Psychology, Raleigh, NC 27695. Offers developmental psychology (PhD); ergonomics and experimental psychology (PhD); industrial/organizational psychology (PhD); psychology in the public interest (PhD); school psychology (PhD). *Accreditation:* APA. *Degree requirements:* For doctorate, comprehensive exam, thesis/dissertation. *Entrance requirements:* For doctorate, GRE General Test, GRE Subject Test (industrial/organizational psychology), MAT (recommended), minimum GPA of 3.0 in major.. Electronic applications accepted. *Faculty research:* Cognitive and social development (human factors, families, the workplace, community issues and health, aging).

Northeastern University, College of Arts and Sciences, Department of Psychology, Boston, MA 02115-5096. Offers experimental psychology (MA, PhD). *Faculty:* 22 full-time (6 women). *Students:* 115 applicants, 4% accepted. In 2007, 2 master's, 9 doctorates awarded. *Degree requirements:* For doctorate, thesis/dissertation. *Entrance requirements:* For doctorate, GRE General Test. Additional exam requirements/recommendations for international students: Required—TOEFL. *Application deadline:* For fall admission, 1/15 for domestic students. Applications are processed on a rolling basis. Application fee: $50. *Financial support:* In 2007–08, 24 teaching assistantships with full tuition reimbursements (averaging $16,760 per year) were awarded; fellowships with full tuition reimbursements, research assistantships with full tuition reimbursements, career-related internships or fieldwork and traineeships also available. Financial award application deadline: 1/15; financial award applicants required to submit FAFSA. *Faculty research:* Behavioral, neuroscience language and cognition, perception, personality and social. *Unit head:* Dr. Rhea Eskew, Chair, 617-373-3076, Fax: 617-373-8714, E-mail: psychology@neu.edu. *Application contact:* Rhonda Johnson, Graduate Coordinator, 617-373-3076, Fax: 617-373-8714, E-mail: psychology@neu.edu.

Ohio University, Graduate College, College of Arts and Sciences, Department of Psychology, Program in Experimental Psychology, Athens, OH 45701-2979. Offers PhD. *Faculty:* 12 full-time (4 women). *Students:* 19 full-time (11 women), 4 part-time; includes 1 minority (Asian American or Pacific Islander), 6 international. Average age 28. 32 applicants, 44% accepted, 6 enrolled. In 2007, 2 degrees awarded. *Degree requirements:* For doctorate, one foreign language, comprehensive exam, thesis/dissertation. *Entrance requirements:* For doctorate, GRE General Test, GRE Subject Test, minimum graduate GPA of 3.4. Additional exam requirements/recommendations for international students: Required—TOEFL. *Application deadline:* For fall admission, 1/1 for domestic students. Application fee: $50 ($55 for international students). *Financial support:* In 2007–08, 14 students received support, including 5 fellowships with full tuition reimbursements available (averaging $16,400 per year), research assistantships with full tuition reimbursements available (averaging $13,200 per year), 8 teaching assistantships with full tuition reimbursements available (averaging $13,200 per year); Federal Work-Study, institutionally sponsored loans, tuition waivers (full), and unspecified assistantships also available. Financial award application deadline: 1/15. *Faculty research:* Cognitive psychology, quantitative psychology, social psychology, judgment and decision making, health psychology. Total annual research expenditures: $3.8 million. *Unit head:* Jeffrey Vancouver, Director of Experimental Studies, 740-593-1071, Fax: 740-593-0579. *Application contact:* Karyl Jones, Administrative Secretary, 740-593-1090, Fax: 740-593-0579, E-mail: psychology@ohio.edu.

Oklahoma State University, College of Arts and Sciences, Department of Psychology, Stillwater, OK 74078. Offers clinical psychology (PhD); experimental psychology (PhD); general psychology (MS). *Accreditation:* APA (one or more programs are accredited). *Faculty:* 24 full-time (13 women), 1 part-time/adjunct (0 women). *Students:* 36 full-time (20 women), 13 part-time (10 women); includes 13 minority (2 African Americans, 5 American Indian/Alaska Native, 2 Asian Americans or Pacific Islanders, 4 Hispanic Americans), 2 international. Average age 28. 154 applicants, 7% accepted, 10 enrolled. In 2007, 12 master's, 7 doctorates awarded. *Degree requirements:* For doctorate, thesis/dissertation. *Entrance requirements:* For master's and doctorate, GRE General Test or GMAT. Additional exam requirements/recommendations for international students: Required—TOEFL. *Application deadline:* For fall admission, 3/1 priority date for international students; for spring admission, 8/1 priority date for international students. Applications are processed on a rolling basis. Application fee: $40 ($75 for international students). Electronic applications accepted. *Expenses:* Tuition, state resident: full-time $4,993; part-time $148 per credit hour. Tuition, nonresident: full-time $14,755; part-time $555 per credit hour. Tuition and fees vary according to program. *Financial support:* In 2007–08, 12 research assistantships (averaging $13,222 per year), 34 teaching assistantships (averaging $14,372 per year) were awarded; career-related internships or fieldwork, Federal Work-Study, scholarships/grants, health care benefits, tuition waivers (partial), and unspecified assistantships also available. Support available to part-time students. Financial award application deadline: 3/1. *Unit head:* Dr. Maureen A. Sullivan, Head, 405-744-6028.

Old Dominion University, College of Sciences, Doctoral Program in Psychology, Norfolk, VA 23529. Offers applied experimental psychology (PhD); human factors psychology (PhD); industrial/organizational psychology (PhD). *Faculty:* 17 full-time (7 women), 1 part-time/adjunct (0 women). *Students:* 15 full-time (12 women), 16 part-time (10 women); includes 3 minority (1 African American, 1 Asian American or Pacific Islander, 1 Hispanic American). Average age 29. 42 applicants, 29% accepted, 6 enrolled. In 2007, 5 degrees awarded.

Experimental Psychology

Old Dominion University (continued)

Degree requirements: For doctorate, thesis/dissertation, qualifying exam. *Entrance requirements:* For doctorate, GRE, GRE Subject Test, 3 recommendation letters. Additional exam requirements/recommendations for international students: Required—TOEFL (minimum score 550 paper-based). *Application deadline:* For winter admission, 1/15 for domestic and international students. Application fee: $40. *Expenses:* Tuition, state resident: part-time $304 per credit hour. Tuition, nonresident: part-time $761 per credit hour. *Financial support:* In 2007–08, 6 students received support, including 2 fellowships with full tuition reimbursements available (averaging $18,000 per year), research assistantships with full tuition reimbursements available (averaging $12,000 per year), 3 teaching assistantships with full tuition reimbursements available (averaging $12,000 per year). Financial award application deadline: 1/15. *Faculty research:* Human-computer interaction, simulation, neuroergonomics, attention and workload. Total annual research expenditures: $399,161. *Unit head:* Dr. James Bliss, Graduate Program Director, 757-683-4051, Fax: 757-683-5087, E-mail: psychppd@odu.edu.

Radford University, Graduate College, College of Humanities and Behavioral Sciences, Department of Psychology, Radford, VA 24142. Offers clinical psychology (MA, MS); counseling psychology (Psy D); experimental psychology (MA); industrial-organizational psychology (MA, MS); school psychology (Ed S). Part-time programs available. *Faculty:* 24 full-time (10 women). *Students:* 38 full-time (31 women), 52 part-time (39 women); includes 5 minority (4 African Americans, 1 Asian American or Pacific Islander), 2 international. Average age 25. 128 applicants, 64% accepted, 38 enrolled. In 2007, 45 degrees awarded. *Degree requirements:* For master's, comprehensive exam, thesis (for some programs); for doctorate, comprehensive exam, thesis/dissertation; for Ed S, comprehensive exam. *Entrance requirements:* For master's, GRE, minimum GPA 3.0; for doctorate, GRE; for Ed S, GMAT, GRE General Test, MAT, NTE. Additional exam requirements/recommendations for international students: Required—TOEFL. *Application deadline:* For fall admission, 3/1 priority date for domestic students, 12/1 for international students; for spring admission, 10/1 for domestic students, 7/1 for international students. Applications are processed on a rolling basis. Application fee: $40. Electronic applications accepted. *Financial support:* In 2007–08, 42 research assistantships with partial tuition reimbursements (averaging $8,000 per year), 12 teaching assistantships with partial tuition reimbursements (averaging $8,700 per year) were awarded; career-related internships or fieldwork, Federal Work-Study, institutionally sponsored loans, scholarships/grants, and unspecified assistantships also available. Financial award application deadline: 3/1; financial award applicants required to submit FAFSA. *Unit head:* Dr. Hilary M. Lips, Chair, 540-831-5387, Fax: 540-831-6113, E-mail: hlips@radford.edu.

St. John's University, St. John's College of Liberal Arts and Sciences, Department of Psychology, Program in General Experimental Psychology, Queens, NY 11439. Offers MA. Part-time and evening/weekend programs available. *Students:* 5 full-time (3 women), 12 part-time (10 women); includes 4 minority (1 African American, 2 Asian Americans or Pacific Islanders, 1 Hispanic American), 1 international. Average age 29. 33 applicants, 58% accepted, 6 enrolled. In 2007, 8 degrees awarded. *Degree requirements:* For master's, comprehensive exam, thesis optional. *Entrance requirements:* For master's, minimum GPA of 3.0, 2 writing samples. Additional exam requirements/recommendations for international students: Required—TOEFL (minimum score 500 paper-based; 173 computer-based; 61 iBT), IELTS (minimum score 6). *Application deadline:* For fall admission, 5/1 priority date for domestic and international students; for spring admission, 11/1 priority date for domestic and international students. Applications are processed on a rolling basis. Application fee: $40. Electronic applications accepted. *Financial support:* Research assistantships, career-related internships or fieldwork, scholarships/grants, and unspecified assistantships available. Support available to part-time students. Financial award application deadline: 3/1; financial award applicants required to submit FAFSA. *Faculty research:* Learning and memory neuropsychology, perception, social psychology, developmental psychology. *Unit head:* Dr. Leonard Brosgole, Director, 718-990-1552, E-mail: brosgoll@stjohns.edu. *Application contact:* Beth Evans, Associate Vice President and Executive Director, Enrollment Management, 718-990-6999, Fax: 718-990-5686, E-mail: gradhelp@stjohns.edu.

Saint Louis University, Graduate School, College of Arts and Sciences and Graduate School, Department of Psychology, St. Louis, MO 63103-2097. Offers clinical psychology (MS-R, PhD); experimental psychology (MS-R, PhD); industrial-organizational psychology (PhD); psychology (PhD). *Accreditation:* APA (one or more programs are accredited). Part-time programs available. *Faculty:* 18 full-time (7 women). *Students:* 77 full-time (53 women), 8 part-time (5 women); includes 14 minority (12 African Americans, 1 American Indian/Alaska Native, 1 Asian American or Pacific Islander). Average age 27. 234 applicants, 11% accepted, 20 enrolled. In 2007, 11 master's, 10 doctorates awarded. *Median time to degree:* Of those who began their doctoral program in fall 1999, 90% received their degree in 8 years or less. *Degree requirements:* For master's, comprehensive exam, thesis; for doctorate, thesis/dissertation, clinical internship (for clinical psychology PhD). *Entrance requirements:* For master's and doctorate, GRE General Test, interview, letters of recommendation, resumé, transcripts, goal statement. Additional exam requirements/recommendations for international students: Required—TOEFL (minimum score 550 paper-based; 213 computer-based). *Application deadline:* For fall admission, 1/1 for domestic and international students. Application fee: $40. Electronic applications accepted. *Expenses:* Tuition: Part-time $845 per credit hour. Required fees: $105 per semester. *Financial support:* In 2007–08, 71 students received support, including 16 research assistantships with full tuition reimbursements available (averaging $14,000 per year), 14 teaching assistantships with full tuition reimbursements available (averaging $12,000 per year); career-related internships or fieldwork, Federal Work-Study, scholarships/grants, traineeships, health care benefits, tuition waivers, and unspecified assistantships also available. Support available to part-time students. Financial award application deadline: 2/1; financial award applicants required to submit FAFSA. *Faculty research:* Violence and trauma; neural basis of learning and memory function; eating disorders; body image and health behavior; prejudice, stereotyping, and victimization; memory, cognitive aging and language processing. Total annual research expenditures: $514,559. *Unit head:* Dr. Donna J. LaVoie, Chairperson, 314-977-3676, Fax: 314-977-3679, E-mail: lavoiedj@slu.edu. *Application contact:* Gary U. Behrman, Associate Dean of Graduate School Admissions, 314-977-3827, Fax: 314-977-3943, E-mail: behrmang@slu.edu.

San Jose State University, Graduate Studies and Research, College of Social Sciences, Department of Psychology, San Jose, CA 95192-0001. Offers clinical psychology (MS); experimental psychology (MA); industrial/organizational psychology (MS); psychology (MA). *Students:* 53 full-time (41 women), 16 part-time (11 women); includes 18 minority (11 Asian Americans or Pacific Islanders, 7 Hispanic Americans), 7 international. Average age 27. 124 applicants, 34% accepted, 38 enrolled. In 2007, 27 degrees awarded. *Degree requirements:* For master's, comprehensive exam, thesis (for some programs). *Entrance requirements:* For master's, GRE General Test, minimum GPA of 3.0. *Application deadline:* For fall admission, 6/29 for domestic students; for spring admission, 11/30 for domestic students. Applications are processed on a rolling basis. Application fee: $59. Electronic applications accepted. *Financial support:* In 2007–08, 15 teaching assistantships were awarded; career-related internships or fieldwork and institutionally sponsored loans also available. Financial award application deadline: 3/1; financial award applicants required to submit FAFSA. *Faculty research:* Drug and alcohol abuse, neurohormonal mechanisms in motion sickness, behavior modification, sleep research, genetics. *Unit head:* Dr. Sheila Bienenfeld, Chair, 408-924-5600, Fax: 408-924-5605, E-mail: sheila.bienenfeld@sjsu.edu.

Seton Hall University, College of Arts and Sciences, Department of Psychology, South Orange, NJ 07079-2697. Offers experimental psychology (MS), including behavioral neuroscience. *Entrance requirements:* Additional exam requirements/recommendations for international students: Required—TOEFL. Electronic applications accepted. *Faculty research:* Behavioral neuroscience, cognitive psychology, social psychology, perception/motor skills, memory.

See Close-Up on page 1477.

Southern Illinois University Carbondale, Graduate School, College of Liberal Arts, Department of Psychology, Carbondale, IL 62901-4701. Offers clinical psychology (MA, MS, PhD); counseling psychology (MA, MS, PhD); experimental psychology (MA, MS, PhD). *Accreditation:* APA (one or more programs are accredited). *Faculty:* 27 full-time (14 women), 1 part-time/adjunct (0 women). *Students:* 81 full-time (54 women), 43 part-time (32 women); includes 25 minority (13 African Americans, 1 American Indian/Alaska Native, 6 Asian Americans or Pacific Islanders, 5 Hispanic Americans), 13 international. 291 applicants, 9% accepted, 13 enrolled. In 2007, 17 master's, 15 doctorates awarded. *Degree requirements:* For master's, thesis; for doctorate, thesis/dissertation. *Entrance requirements:* For master's, GRE General Test, GRE Subject Test, minimum GPA of 2.7; for doctorate, GRE General Test, GRE Subject Test, minimum GPA of 3.25. Additional exam requirements/recommendations for international students: Required—TOEFL. *Application deadline:* For fall admission, 3/1 priority date for domestic students. Applications are processed on a rolling basis. Application fee: $20. *Financial support:* In 2007–08, 82 students received support, including 14 fellowships with full tuition reimbursements available, 23 research assistantships with full tuition reimbursements available, 22 teaching assistantships with full tuition reimbursements available; Federal Work-Study, institutionally sponsored loans, and tuition waivers (full) also available. *Faculty research:* Developmental neuropsychology; smoking, affect, and cognition; personality measurement; vocational psychology; program evaluation. *Unit head:* Dr. Jane Swanson, Chair, 618-453-3529, E-mail: swanson@siu.edu. *Application contact:* Connie Childers, Office Specialist, 618-453-3564, E-mail: childers@siu.edu.

See Close-Up on page 1479.

Stony Brook University, State University of New York, Graduate School, College of Arts and Sciences, Department of Psychology, Program in Cognitive/Experimental Psychology, Stony Brook, NY 11794. Offers PhD. *Students:* 16 full-time (10 women); includes 3 minority (1 African American, 2 Hispanic Americans), 3 international. Average age 28. 36 applicants, 28% accepted. In 2007, 1 degree awarded. *Degree requirements:* For doctorate, thesis/dissertation. *Entrance requirements:* For doctorate, GRE General Test, GRE Subject Test. Additional exam requirements/recommendations for international students: Required—TOEFL. *Application deadline:* For fall admission, 1/15 for domestic students. Application fee: $60. *Unit head:* Dr. Nancy Franklin, Head, 631-632-7840, E-mail: nancy.franklin@stonybrook.edu.

Announcement: Cognitive/Experimental Psychology faculty members play a prominent role in running major journals in the field. In recent years, they have served as editor or associate editor at the *Journal of Memory & Language, Psychological Science, Psychonomic Bulletin and Review,* and *Discourse Processes.* Consulting editorships among faculty include *Psychological Science, Cognition, Memory & Cognition, Journal of Memory & Language, Journal of Experimental Psychology: Learning, Memory & Cognition, Journal of Experimental Psychology: Human Perception & Performance, Perception & Psychophysics, Computational Linguistics, Discourse Processes, Poetics,* and *Metaphor and Symbol.*

See Close-Up on page 1497.

Syracuse University, Graduate School, College of Arts and Sciences, Department of Psychology, Program in Experimental Psychology, Syracuse, NY 13244. Offers PhD. Part-time programs available. *Students:* 7 full-time (5 women), 1 (woman) part-time, 1 international. 13 applicants, 23% accepted, 1 enrolled. *Degree requirements:* For doctorate, thesis/dissertation. *Entrance requirements:* For doctorate, GRE General Test. Additional exam requirements/recommendations for international students: Required—TOEFL. *Application deadline:* For fall admission, 1/10 for domestic students. Applications are processed on a rolling basis. Application fee: $75. *Expenses:* Tuition: Full-time $18,216; part-time $1,012 per credit. Required fees: $980. Tuition and fees vary according to program. *Financial support:* Fellowships with full tuition reimbursements, research assistantships with full tuition reimbursements, teaching assistantships with full tuition reimbursements, tuition waivers available. *Unit head:* Dr. William Hoyer, Graduate Director, 315-443-3663. *Application contact:* Sue Bova, Information Contact, 315-443-1050, E-mail: skbova@syr.edu.

Texas Tech University, Graduate School, College of Arts and Sciences, Department of Psychology, Lubbock, TX 79409. Offers clinical psychology (PhD); counseling psychology (MA, PhD); experimental psychology (MA, PhD); psychology (MA, PhD). *Accreditation:* APA (one or more programs are accredited). Part-time programs available. *Faculty:* 25 full-time (11 women). *Students:* 91 full-time (59 women), 11 part-time (8 women); includes 16 minority (6 African Americans, 2 Asian Americans or Pacific Islanders, 8 Hispanic Americans), 4 international. Average age 28. 264 applicants, 10% accepted, 17 enrolled. In 2007, 15 master's, 16 doctorates awarded. *Degree requirements:* For doctorate, thesis/dissertation. *Entrance requirements:* For master's and doctorate, GRE General Test, GRE Subject Test. Additional exam requirements/recommendations for international students: Required—TOEFL (minimum score 550 paper-based; 213 computer-based). *Application deadline:* For fall admission, 3/1 priority date for international students; for spring admission, 11/1 priority date for international students. Applications are processed on a rolling basis. Application fee: $50 ($60 for international students). Electronic applications accepted. *Expenses:* Tuition, state resident: part-time $373 per credit hour. Tuition, nonresident: part-time $651 per credit hour. Tuition and fees vary according to program. *Financial support:* In 2007–08, 99 students received support, including 8 research assistantships with partial tuition reimbursements available (averaging $11,462 per year), 64 teaching assistantships with partial tuition reimbursements available (averaging $11,759 per year); career-related internships or fieldwork, Federal Work-Study, and institutionally sponsored loans also available. Support available to part-time students. Financial award application deadline: 4/15; financial award applicants required to submit FAFSA. *Faculty research:* Failure/success in relationships, peer rejection in school, stress and coping, group processes, clinical and health psychology. Total annual research expenditures: $459,933. *Unit head:* Dr. M. David Rudd, Chair, 806-742-3711 Ext. 224, Fax: 806-742-0818, E-mail: david.rudd@ttu.edu. *Application contact:* Dr. Steve Richards, Graduate Advisor, 806-742-3711 Ext. 254, Fax: 806-742-0818, E-mail: steven.richards@ttu.edu.

University at Albany, State University of New York, College of Arts and Sciences, Department of Psychology, Albany, NY 12222-0001. Offers autism (Certificate); biopsychology (PhD); clinical psychology (PhD); general/experimental psychology (PhD); industrial/organizational psychology (PhD); psychology (MA); social/personality psychology (PhD). *Accreditation:* APA (one or more programs are accredited). *Students:* 51 full-time (32 women), 47 part-time (40 women). Average age 30. In 2007, 8 master's, 15 doctorates, 7 other advanced degrees awarded. *Degree requirements:* For doctorate, thesis/dissertation. *Entrance requirements:* For doctorate, GRE General Test, GRE Subject Test. Additional exam requirements/recommendations for international students: Required—TOEFL (minimum score 550 paper-based; 213 computer-based). *Application deadline:* For fall admission, 1/15 for domestic and international students. Application fee: $75. Electronic applications accepted. *Expenses:* Tuition, state resident: part-time $576 per credit. Tuition, nonresident: part-time $910 per credit. Tuition and fees vary according to program. *Financial support:* Fellowships, research assistantships, teaching assistantships, career-related internships or fieldwork available. Financial award application deadline: 2/1. *Unit head:* Kevin J. Williams, Chair, 518-442-4820.

The University of Alabama, Graduate School, College of Arts and Sciences, Department of Psychology, Tuscaloosa, AL 35487. Offers clinical psychology (PhD); experimental psychology (PhD). *Accreditation:* APA. *Faculty:* 23 full-time (10 women), 1 part-time/adjunct (0 women). *Students:* 74 full-time (57 women), 12 part-time (11 women); includes 14 minority (8 African Americans, 3 Asian Americans or Pacific Islanders, 3 Hispanic Americans), 4 international. Average age 27. 231 applicants, 11% accepted, 15 enrolled. In 2007, 14 doctorates awarded. *Median time to degree:* Of those who began their doctoral program in fall 1999, 64% received their degree in 8 years or less. *Degree requirements:* For doctorate, thesis/dissertation. *Entrance requirements:* For doctorate, GRE. Additional exam requirements/recommendations for international students: Required—TOEFL (minimum score 550 paper-based). *Application deadline:* For fall admission, 12/1 for domestic and international students. Application fee: $30. Electronic applications accepted. *Expenses:* Tuition, state resident: full-time $5,700. Tuition, nonresident: full-time $16,518. *Financial support:* In 2007–08, 73 students received support, including 12 fellowships with full tuition reimbursements available (averaging $15,000 per year), 34 research assistantships with full and partial tuition reimbursements available (averaging $11,142 per year), 26 teaching assistantships with tuition reimbursements available (averaging $11,142 per year); career-related internships or fieldwork, institutionally sponsored loans, scholarships/grants, health care benefits, and unspecified assistantships also available. Financial award application deadline: 12/1. *Faculty research:* Cognitive development/disability, child clinical, psychology and law, health/aging, social psychology. Total annual research expenditures: $2.5 million. *Unit head:* Dr. Kenneth Lichstein, Chair, 205-348-4962, Fax: 205-348-8648, E-mail: lichstein@ua.edu. *Application contact:* Mary Beth Hubbard, Information Contact, 205-348-1919, Fax: 205-348-8648, E-mail: mbhubbard@as.ua.edu.

University of Central Florida, College of Sciences, Department of Psychology, Program in Applied Experimental and Human Factors Psychology, Orlando, FL 32816. Offers MA, PhD. *Accreditation:* APA. In 2007, 8 degrees awarded. *Degree requirements:* For doctorate, thesis/dissertation, departmental candidacy exam. *Entrance requirements:* For doctorate, GRE General Test, minimum GPA of 3.2 in last 60 hours or master's qualifying exam. Additional exam requirements/recommendations for international students: Required—TOEFL. *Application deadline:* For fall admission, 2/1 for domestic students. Application fee: $30. Electronic applications accepted. *Expenses:* Tuition, state resident: full-time $6,484. Tuition, nonresident: full-time $23,938. Tuition and fees vary according to program. *Financial support:* Fellowships with partial tuition reimbursements, research assistantships with partial tuition reimbursements, teaching assistantships with partial tuition reimbursements, career-related internships or fieldwork, Federal Work-Study, institutionally sponsored loans, tuition waivers (partial), and unspecified assistantships available. Financial award application deadline: 3/1; financial award applicants required to submit FAFSA. *Faculty research:* Visual performance, team training, controls/displays, synthetic speech, alarms/warning. *Unit head:* Dr. Edward Rinalducci, Coordinator, 407-823-5860, Fax: 407-823-5862, E-mail: erinaldu@mail.ucf.edu.

University of Cincinnati, Graduate School, McMicken College of Arts and Sciences, Department of Psychology, Cincinnati, OH 45221. Offers clinical psychology (PhD); experimental psychology (PhD). *Accreditation:* APA. *Faculty:* 26 full-time (8 women), 5 part-time/adjunct (2 women). *Students:* 66 full-time (45 women), 6 part-time (3 women); includes 15 minority (8 African Americans, 4 Asian Americans or Pacific Islanders, 3 Hispanic Americans), 6 international. Average age 28. 274 applicants, 5% accepted, 9 enrolled. In 2007, 16 doctorates awarded. *Median time to degree:* Of those who began their doctoral program in fall 1999, 100% received their degree in 8 years or less. *Degree requirements:* For doctorate, comprehensive exam, thesis/dissertation. *Entrance requirements:* For doctorate, GRE General Test. Additional exam requirements/recommendations for international students: Required—TOEFL. *Application deadline:* For fall admission, 1/3 for domestic and international students. Application fee: $35. *Financial support:* Fellowships with full tuition reimbursements, research assistantships with full tuition reimbursements, teaching assistantships with full tuition reimbursements, scholarships/grants, traineeships, tuition waivers (partial), and unspecified assistantships available. Financial award application deadline: 5/1. *Faculty research:* Neuropsychology, human factors, health. Total annual research expenditures: $509,418. *Unit head:* Dr. Steven J. Howe, Head, 513-556-5572, Fax: 513-556-1904, E-mail: steven.howe@uc.edu. *Application contact:* Dr. Paula K. Shear, Graduate Program Director, 513-556-5577, Fax: 513-556-1904, E-mail: paula.shear@uc.edu.

University of Connecticut, Graduate School, College of Liberal Arts and Sciences, Department of Psychology, Field of Psychology, Storrs, CT 06269. Offers behavioral neuroscience (PhD); biopsychology (PhD); clinical psychology (MA, PhD); cognition and instruction (PhD); developmental psychology (MA, PhD); ecological psychology (PhD); experimental psychology (PhD); general psychology (MA, PhD); health psychology (Graduate Certificate); industrial/organizational psychology (PhD); language and cognition (PhD); neuroscience (PhD); occupational health psychology (Graduate Certificate); social psychology (MA, PhD). *Accreditation:* APA (one or more programs are accredited). *Faculty:* 52 full-time (23 women). *Students:* 130 full-time (94 women), 25 part-time (11 women); includes 24 minority (8 African Americans, 6 Asian Americans or Pacific Islanders, 10 Hispanic Americans), 18 international. Average age 28. 531 applicants, 7% accepted, 35 enrolled. In 2007, 19 master's, 20 doctorates, 2 other advanced degrees awarded. Terminal master's awarded for partial completion of doctoral program. *Degree requirements:* For master's, comprehensive exam; for doctorate, thesis/dissertation. *Entrance requirements:* For master's and doctorate, GRE General Test, GRE Subject Test. Additional exam requirements/recommendations for international students: Required—TOEFL (minimum score 550 paper-based; 213 computer-based). *Application deadline:* For fall admission, 2/1 priority date for domestic and international students; for spring admission, 11/1 for domestic students, 10/1 for international students. Applications are processed on a rolling basis. Application fee: $55. Electronic applications accepted. *Expenses:* Tuition, state resident: part-time $469 per credit hour. Tuition, nonresident: part-time $1,218 per credit hour. *Financial support:* In 2007–08, 54 research assistantships with full tuition reimbursements, 69 teaching assistantships with full tuition reimbursements were awarded; fellowships, career-related internships or fieldwork, Federal Work-Study, scholarships/grants, health care benefits, and unspecified assistantships also available. Financial award application deadline: 2/1; financial award applicants required to submit FAFSA. *Application contact:* Deborah Doucette, Administrative Assistant, 860-486-2057, Fax: 860-486-2760, E-mail: futuregr@psych.psy.uconn.edu.

University of Hartford, College of Arts and Sciences, Department of Psychology, Program in General Experimental Psychology, West Hartford, CT 06117-1599. Offers MA. Part-time programs available. *Faculty:* 1 (woman) full-time, 1 (woman) part-time/adjunct. *Students:* 4 full-time (3 women), 4 part-time (3 women). Average age 27. 13 applicants, 92% accepted, 3 enrolled. In 2007, 8 degrees awarded. *Degree requirements:* For master's, comprehensive exam, thesis or alternative. *Entrance requirements:* For master's, GRE General Test, GRE Subject Test, minimum GPA of 3.0, 3 letters of recommendation. Additional exam requirements/recommendations for international students: Required—TOEFL (minimum score 550 paper-based; 213 computer-based). *Application deadline:* For fall admission, 2/25 priority date for domestic students. Applications are processed on a rolling basis. Application fee: $45. Electronic applications accepted. *Expenses:* Tuition: Part-time $595 per credit. Required fees: $200 per term. *Financial support:* In 2007–08, 1 research assistantship (averaging $2,000 per year), 4 teaching assistantships (averaging $2,600 per year) were awarded. Financial award application deadline: 6/1; financial award applicants required to submit FAFSA. *Faculty research:* Decision making, social judgment and stereotyping, stress and health. *Unit head:* Dr. Jack Powell, Director, 860-768-4720, E-mail: powell@hartford.edu. *Application contact:* Reneé Murphy, Assistant Director of Graduate Admissions, 860-768-4371, Fax: 860-768-5160, E-mail: rmurphy@hartford.edu.

University of Kentucky, Graduate School, College of Arts and Sciences, Program in Psychology, Lexington, KY 40506-0032. Offers clinical psychology (MA); experimental psychology (MA). *Accreditation:* APA (one or more programs are accredited). *Faculty:* 39 full-time (12 women), 1 part-time/adjunct (0 women). *Students:* 73 full-time (58 women), 6 part-time (4 women); includes 9 minority (4 African Americans, 1 American Indian/Alaska Native, 4 Hispanic Americans), 2 international. Average age 29. 286 applicants, 5% accepted, 14 enrolled. In 2007, 10 master's, 9 doctorates awarded. *Median time to degree:* Of those who began their doctoral program in fall 1999, 87% received their degree in 8 years or less. *Degree requirements:* For master's, comprehensive exam, thesis; for doctorate, comprehensive exam, thesis/dissertation. *Entrance requirements:* For master's, GRE General Test, minimum undergraduate GPA of 2.75; for doctorate, GRE General Test, minimum graduate GPA of 3.0. Additional exam requirements/recommendations for international students: Required—TOEFL (minimum score 550 paper-based; 213 computer-based). *Application deadline:* For fall admission, 7/17 for domestic students, 2/1 priority date for international students; for spring admission, 12/13 for domestic students, 6/15 priority date for international students. Application fee: $50 ($65 for international students). Electronic applications accepted. *Expenses:* Tuition, state resident: part-time $437 per credit hour. Tuition, nonresident: part-time $931 per credit hour. *Financial support:* In 2007–08, 64 students received support, including 20 fellowships with full tuition reimbursements available (averaging $3,461 per year), 30 research assistantships with full tuition reimbursements available (averaging $14,000 per year), 24 teaching assistantships with full tuition reimbursements available (averaging $14,000 per year); career-related internships or fieldwork, Federal Work-Study, institutionally sponsored loans, scholarships/grants, traineeships, health care benefits, tuition waivers (partial), and unspecified assistantships also available. Support available to part-time students. Financial award application deadline: 3/15; financial award applicants required to submit FAFSA. *Faculty research:* Psychopharmacology and teratology, behavioral neuroscience, social psychology, cognitive psychology, development and developmental psychobiology. *Unit head:* Dr. David Berry, Director of Graduate Studies, 859-257-5451, Fax: 859-323-1979, E-mail: dtrb@pop.uky.edu. *Application contact:* Dr. Brian Jackson, Senior Associate Dean, 859-257-4667, Fax: 859-257-4676, E-mail: brian.jackson@uky.edu.

University of Louisville, Graduate School, College of Arts and Sciences, Department of Psychological and Brain Sciences, Program in Experimental Psychology, Louisville, KY 40292-0001. Offers PhD. *Students:* 37 full-time (26 women); includes 3 minority (1 African American, 1 Asian American or Pacific Islander, 1 Hispanic American), 6 international. Average age 28. In 2007, 2 degrees awarded. *Degree requirements:* For doctorate, thesis/dissertation. *Entrance requirements:* For doctorate, GRE General Test. *Application deadline:* Applications are processed on a rolling basis. Application fee: $50. *Unit head:* Dr. John Pani, Head, 502-852-3956, Fax: 502-852-8904, E-mail: jrpani@louisville.edu.

University of Maine, Graduate School, College of Liberal Arts and Sciences, Department of Psychology, Orono, ME 04469. Offers clinical psychology (PhD); developmental psychology (MA); experimental psychology (MA, PhD); social psychology (MA). *Accreditation:* APA (one or more programs are accredited). *Faculty:* 24. *Students:* 28 full-time (17 women), 10 part-time (6 women); includes 2 minority (1 American Indian/Alaska Native, 1 Hispanic American), 1 international. Average age 29. 129 applicants, 9% accepted, 8 enrolled. In 2007, 5 master's, 2 doctorates awarded. *Degree requirements:* For master's, thesis; for doctorate, thesis/dissertation. *Entrance requirements:* For master's and doctorate, GRE General Test, GRE Subject Test. Additional exam requirements/recommendations for international students: Required—TOEFL. *Application deadline:* For fall admission, 2/1 priority date for domestic students. Applications are processed on a rolling basis. Application fee: $60. Electronic applications accepted. *Financial support:* In 2007–08, 3 research assistantships with tuition reimbursements (averaging $13,400 per year), 21 teaching assistantships with tuition reimbursements (averaging $9,010 per year) were awarded; fellowships with tuition reimbursements, Federal Work-Study, institutionally sponsored loans, and tuition waivers (full and partial) also available. Financial award application deadline: 3/1. *Faculty research:* Social development, hypertension and aging, attitude change, self-confidence in achievement situations, health psychology. *Unit head:* Dr. Jeffrey Hecker, Chair, 207-581-2032, Fax: 207-581-6128. *Application contact:* Scott G. Delcourt, Associate Dean of the Graduate School, 207-581-3219, Fax: 207-581-3232, E-mail: graduate@maine.edu.

University of Maryland, College Park, Graduate Studies, College of Behavioral and Social Sciences, Department of Psychology, College Park, MD 20742. Offers clinical psychology (PhD); developmental psychology (PhD); experimental psychology (PhD); industrial psychology (MA, MS, PhD); social psychology (PhD). *Accreditation:* APA (one or more programs are accredited). *Faculty:* 53 full-time (23 women), 12 part-time/adjunct (6 women). *Students:* 92 full-time (70 women), 4 part-time (3 women); includes 15 minority (2 African Americans, 1 American Indian/Alaska Native, 6 Asian Americans or Pacific Islanders, 6 Hispanic Americans), 12 international. 609 applicants, 4% accepted, 13 enrolled. In 2007, 13 master's, 18 doctorates awarded. *Median time to degree:* Of those who began their doctoral program in fall 1999, 71% received their degree in 8 years or less. *Degree requirements:* For master's, thesis; for doctorate, variable foreign language requirement, comprehensive exam, thesis/dissertation. *Entrance requirements:* For master's and doctorate, GRE General Test, GRE Subject Test, minimum GPA of 3.5, research and/or work experience, 3 letters of recommendation. *Application deadline:* For fall admission, 12/15 for domestic students, 2/1 for international students. Applications are processed on a rolling basis. Application fee: $60. Electronic applications accepted. *Financial support:* In 2007–08, 11 fellowships with full tuition reimbursements (averaging $15,736 per year), 9 research assistantships (averaging $15,312 per year), 56 teaching assistantships with tuition reimbursements (averaging $15,292 per year) were awarded; career-related internships or fieldwork, Federal Work-Study, and scholarships/grants also available. Support available to part-time students. Financial award applicants required to submit FAFSA. *Faculty research:* Social stereotyping and prejudice, anxiety disorders, auditory neuroethology, counseling and social psychology. Total annual research expenditures: $4.4 million. *Unit head:* Thomas S. Wallsten, Chair, 301-405-5862, Fax: 301-314-9566, E-mail: twallsten@psyc.umd.edu. *Application contact:* Dean of Graduate School, 301-405-0358, Fax: 301-314-9305.

University of Memphis, Graduate School, College of Arts and Sciences, Department of Psychology, Memphis, TN 38152. Offers clinical psychology (PhD); experimental psychology (PhD); general psychology (MS); school psychology (MA, PhD). Part-time programs available. *Faculty:* 29 full-time (8 women), 4 part-time/adjunct (1 woman). *Students:* 92 full-time (56 women), 29 part-time (19 women); includes 18 minority (11 African Americans, 3 Asian Americans or Pacific Islanders, 4 Hispanic Americans), 10 international. Average age 28. 269 applicants, 16% accepted, 37 enrolled. In 2007, 14 master's, 8 doctorates awarded. Terminal master's awarded for partial completion of doctoral program. *Degree requirements:* For master's, comprehensive exam, thesis (for some programs), oral exam (MS); for doctorate, thesis/dissertation, internship. *Entrance requirements:* For master's, GRE General Test, 18 undergraduate hours in psychology, minimum GPA of 2.5; for doctorate, GRE General Test, GRE Subject Test. *Application deadline:* For fall admission, 2/1 for domestic students. Applications are processed on a rolling basis. Application fee: $35 ($60 for international students). *Expenses:* Tuition, state resident: full-time $6,990; part-time $377 per hour. Tuition, nonresident: full-time $17,818; part-time $830 per hour. Tuition and fees vary according to course load and program. *Financial support:* In 2007–08, 75 research assistantships with full tuition reimbursements (averaging $4,500 per year), 13 teaching assistantships with full tuition reimbursements (averaging $4,600 per year) were awarded; fellowships with full tuition reimbursements, tuition waivers (partial) and unspecified assistantships also available. *Faculty research:* Psychotherapy and psychopathology, behavioral medicine and community psychology, child and family studies, cognitive and social processes, neuropsychology and behavioral neuroscience. *Unit head:* Dr. Arthur C. Graesser, Chair, 901-678-2146, Fax: 901-678-2579, E-mail: a-graesser@memphis.edu. *Application contact:* Dr. Robert Cohen, Graduate Studies Coordinator, 901-678-2146.

University of Michigan, Horace H. Rackham School of Graduate Studies, College of Literature, Science, and the Arts, Department of Psychology, Ann Arbor, MI 48109. Offers biopsychology (PhD); clinical psychology (PhD); cognition and perception (PhD); developmental psychology (PhD); personality and social contexts (PhD); social psychology (PhD). *Accreditation:* APA. *Faculty:* 86 full-time, 69 part-time/adjunct. *Students:* 157 full-time (112 women); includes 51 minority (21 African Americans, 1 American Indian/Alaska Native, 17 Asian Americans or Pacific Islanders, 12 Hispanic Americans), 32 international. Average age 25. 698 applicants, 9% accepted, 29 enrolled. In 2007, 25 degrees awarded. *Degree requirements:* For doctorate, comprehensive exam, thesis/dissertation, oral defense of dissertation, preliminary exam. *Entrance requirements:* For doctorate, GRE General Test (optional), GRE Subject Test (optional). Additional exam requirements/recommendations for international students: Required—TOEFL. *Application deadline:* For fall admission, 12/15 for domestic students. Application fee: $60 ($75 for international students). Electronic applications accepted. *Financial support:* Fellowships with full tuition reimbursements, research assistantships with full tuition reimbursements, teaching assistantships with full tuition reimbursements, career-related internships or fieldwork available. Financial award application deadline: 4/15. *Unit head:* Theresa Lee, Chair, 734-764-7429. *Application contact:* Laurie Brannan, Psychology Student Academic Affairs, 731-764-2580, Fax: 734-615-7584, E-mail: psych.saa@umich.edu.

Experimental Psychology

University of Mississippi, Graduate School, College of Liberal Arts, Department of Psychology, Oxford, University, MS 38677. Offers clinical psychology (PhD); experimental psychology (PhD); psychology (MA). *Accreditation:* APA (one or more programs are accredited). *Faculty:* 16 full-time (7 women), 5 part-time/adjunct (3 women). *Students:* 45 full-time (34 women), 8 part-time (6 women); includes 11 minority (8 African Americans, 1 American Indian/Alaska Native, 2 Hispanic Americans). In 2007, 6 master's, 13 doctorates awarded. *Degree requirements:* For master's, thesis; for doctorate, thesis/dissertation. *Entrance requirements:* For master's, GRE General Test, minimum GPA of 3.0; for doctorate, GRE General Test. Additional exam requirements/recommendations for international students: Required—TOEFL. *Application deadline:* For fall admission, 1/15 for domestic students; for spring admission, 10/1 for domestic students. Applications are processed on a rolling basis. Application fee: $25. Electronic applications accepted. *Expenses:* Tuition, state resident: full-time $4,932. Tuition, nonresident: full-time $11,436. *Financial support:* Scholarships/grants available. Financial award application deadline: 3/1; financial award applicants required to submit FAFSA. *Unit head:* Dr. Michael T. Allen, Chairman, 662-915-5190, Fax: 662-915-5398, E-mail: mta1@olemiss.edu.

The University of Montana, Graduate School, College of Arts and Sciences, Department of Psychology, Missoula, MT 59812-0002. Offers clinical psychology (PhD); experimental psychology (PhD), including animal behavior psychology, developmental psychology; school psychology (MA, PhD, Ed S). *Accreditation:* APA (one or more programs are accredited). Terminal master's awarded for partial completion of doctoral program. *Degree requirements:* For master's, thesis; for doctorate, thesis/dissertation. *Entrance requirements:* For master's, doctorate, and Ed S, GRE General Test. Additional exam requirements/recommendations for international students: Required—TOEFL.

University of Nevada, Las Vegas, Graduate College, College of Liberal Arts, Department of Psychology, Las Vegas, NV 89154-9900. Offers clinical psychology (PhD); experimental psychology (PhD); general psychology (MA). *Accreditation:* APA. Part-time programs available. *Faculty:* 24 full-time (7 women), 2 part-time/adjunct (both women). *Students:* 63 full-time (48 women), 16 part-time (10 women); includes 11 minority (4 African Americans, 1 Asian American or Pacific Islander, 6 Hispanic Americans), 3 international. 89 applicants, 13% accepted, 11 enrolled. In 2007, 11 master's, 9 doctorates awarded. *Degree requirements:* For master's, comprehensive exam, thesis, oral exam; for doctorate, comprehensive exam, thesis/dissertation, oral exam. *Entrance requirements:* For master's, GRE General Test, GRE Subject Test, minimum GPA of 3.2; for doctorate, GRE General Test, GRE Subject Test, minimum undergraduate GPA of 3.2, graduate 3.5. Additional exam requirements/recommendations for international students: Required—TOEFL (minimum score 550 paper-based; 213 computer-based; 80 iBT). *Application deadline:* For fall admission, 1/15 for domestic and international students. Application fee: $60 ($75 for international students). Electronic applications accepted. *Expenses:* Tuition, state resident: part-time $198 per credit. Tuition, nonresident: part-time $416 per credit. Required fees: $256 per semester. Tuition and fees vary according to course load and reciprocity agreements. *Financial support:* In 2007–08, 24 research assistantships with full and partial tuition reimbursements (averaging $12,000 per year), 25 teaching assistantships with partial tuition reimbursements (averaging $12,000 per year) were awarded; career-related internships or fieldwork, Federal Work-Study, institutionally sponsored loans, scholarships/grants, health care benefits, and unspecified assistantships also available. Support available to part-time students. Financial award application deadline: 3/1. *Unit head:* Dr. Mark Ashcraft, Chair, 702-895-0195. *Application contact:* Graduate College Admissions Evaluator, 702-895-3320, Fax: 702-895-4180, E-mail: gradcollege@unlv.edu.

University of New Brunswick Fredericton, School of Graduate Studies, Faculty of Arts, Department of Psychology, Fredericton, NB E3B 5A3, Canada. Offers clinical psychology (PhD); experimental and applied psychology (MA). *Accreditation:* APA. Part-time programs available. *Faculty:* 14 full-time (9 women). *Students:* 43 full-time (38 women), 1 (woman) part-time. In 2007, 4 doctorates awarded. *Degree requirements:* For doctorate, thesis/dissertation. *Entrance requirements:* For master's, GRE, minimum GPA of 3.5; for doctorate, GRE, minimum GPA of 3.7. Additional exam requirements/recommendations for international students: Required—TOEFL, TWE. *Application deadline:* For fall admission, 1/15 priority date for domestic and international students. Applications are processed on a rolling basis. Application fee: $50 Canadian dollars. *Financial support:* In 2007–08, 4 fellowships (averaging $3,750 per year), 11 research assistantships, 11 teaching assistantships were awarded. Financial award application deadline: 1/15. *Faculty research:* Depression, adolescence, human sexuality, family violence, autism. *Unit head:* Dr. Janet Stoppard, Acting Director of Graduate Studies, 506-458-7994, Fax: 506-447-3063, E-mail: stoppard@unb.ca. *Application contact:* Theresa Mills, Graduate Secretary, 506-453-4707, Fax: 506-447-3063, E-mail: tmills@unb.ca.

University of New Brunswick Saint John, Faculty of Arts, Saint John, NB E2L 4L5, Canada. Offers applied and experimental psychology (PhD); clinical psychology (PhD); experimental psychology (MA). *Faculty:* 9 full-time (4 women), 1 part-time/adjunct (0 women). *Students:* 5 full-time (4 women). Average age 23. 4 applicants, 75% accepted, 2 enrolled. In 2007, 2 master's, 1 doctorate awarded. *Degree requirements:* For master's, thesis. *Entrance requirements:* For master's, GRE General Test. Additional exam requirements/recommendations for international students: Required—TOEFL (minimum score 550 paper-based). *Application deadline:* For fall admission, 2/1 for domestic students. Application fee: $50. Electronic applications accepted. *Financial support:* In 2007–08, 7 research assistantships (averaging $2,550 per year), 5 teaching assistantships (averaging $3,600 per year) were awarded; fellowships, unspecified assistantships also available. Support available to part-time students. Financial award application deadline: 2/1. *Faculty research:* Psychopharmacology and addictions; forensic psychology and criminal justice; interpersonal relations; perception and graphical perception; lie detection. *Unit head:* Dr. Enrico DiTommaso, Director of Graduate Studies, 506-648-5636, Fax: 506-648-5780, E-mail: rico@unb.ca. *Application contact:* Frances Stevens, Secretary, 506-648-5640, Fax: 506-648-5780, E-mail: fstevens@unb.ca.

The University of North Carolina at Chapel Hill, Graduate School, College of Arts and Sciences, Department of Psychology, Chapel Hill, NC 27599. Offers biological psychology (PhD); clinical psychology (PhD); cognitive psychology (PhD); developmental psychology (PhD); quantitative psychology (PhD); social psychology (PhD). *Accreditation:* APA. *Degree requirements:* For doctorate, comprehensive exam, thesis/dissertation. *Entrance requirements:* For doctorate, GRE General Test, minimum GPA of 3.0. Electronic applications accepted. *Faculty research:* Expressed emotion, cognitive development, social cognitive neuroscience, human memory personality.

University of North Dakota, Graduate School, College of Arts and Sciences, Department of Psychology, Grand Forks, ND 58202. Offers clinical psychology (PhD); counseling psychology (PhD); experimental psychology (PhD); forensic psychology (MA, MS); psychology (MA). *Accreditation:* APA (one or more programs are accredited). *Faculty:* 15 full-time (3 women). *Students:* 79 full-time (60 women), 15 part-time (11 women); includes 19 minority (2 African Americans, 15 American Indian/Alaska Native, 2 Asian Americans or Pacific Islanders), 9 international. 168 applicants, 24% accepted, 32 enrolled. In 2007, 4 master's, 16 doctorates awarded. *Degree requirements:* For master's, thesis, final exam; for doctorate, comprehensive exam, thesis/dissertation, internship, final exam. *Entrance requirements:* For master's, GRE General Test, GRE Subject Test, minimum GPA of 3.0; for doctorate, GRE General Test, GRE Subject Test, minimum GPA of 3.5. Additional exam requirements/recommendations for international students: Required—TOEFL (minimum score 550 paper-based; 213 computer-based; 79 iBT), IELTS (minimum score 7). *Application deadline:* For fall admission, 1/15 for domestic and international students. Application fee: $35. Electronic applications accepted. *Expenses:* Tuition, state resident: full-time $4,050; part-time $225 per credit. Tuition, nonresident: full-time $10,818; part-time $601 per credit. Required fees: $110 per semester. Tuition and fees vary according to class time, campus/location, program and reciprocity agreements. *Financial support:* In 2007–08, 34 students received support, including 8 research assistantships with full tuition reimbursements available (averaging $11,476 per year), 23 teaching assistantships with full tuition reimbursements available (averaging $8,993 per year); fellowships with full and partial tuition reimbursements available, career-related internships or fieldwork, Federal Work-Study, institutionally sponsored loans, scholarships/grants, health care benefits, tuition waivers (full and partial), and unspecified assistantships also available. Support available to part-time students. Financial award application deadline: 3/15; financial award applicants required to submit FAFSA. *Faculty research:* Developmental psychology, clinical social psychology, educational psychology, personality disorders. *Unit head:* Dr. Jeffrey N. Weatherly, Chairperson, 701-777-3470, E-mail: jeffrey.weatherly@und.nodak.edu. *Application contact:* Brenda Halle, Admissions Specialist, 701-777-2947, Fax: 701-777-3619, E-mail: brendahalle@mail.und.edu.

University of North Texas, Robert B. Toulouse School of Graduate Studies, College of Arts and Sciences, Department of Psychology, Denton, TX 76203. Offers clinical psychology (PhD); counseling psychology (MA, MS, PhD); experimental psychology (MA, MS, PhD); health psychology and behavioral medicine (PhD). *Accreditation:* APA (one or more programs are accredited). *Faculty:* 26 full-time (8 women). *Students:* 101 full-time (74 women), 105 part-time (77 women); includes 27 minority (8 African Americans, 1 American Indian/Alaska Native, 5 Asian Americans or Pacific Islanders, 13 Hispanic Americans), 7 international. Average age 29. 472 applicants, 9% accepted, 36 enrolled. In 2007, 28 master's, 23 doctorates awarded. Terminal master's awarded for partial completion of doctoral program. *Degree requirements:* For master's, comprehensive exam, thesis or alternative; for doctorate, one foreign language, comprehensive exam, thesis/dissertation. *Entrance requirements:* For master's and doctorate, GRE General Test, interview. Additional exam requirements/recommendations for international students: Required—proof of English language proficiency required for non-native English speakers; Recommended—TOEFL (minimum score 550 paper-based; 213 computer-based). *Application deadline:* For fall admission, 7/15 for domestic students; for spring admission, 11/15 for domestic students. Application fee: $50 ($75 for international students). *Financial support:* In 2007–08, 2 fellowships (averaging $20,000 per year), 18 research assistantships (averaging $9,000 per year), 38 teaching assistantships (averaging $9,000 per year) were awarded; career-related internships or fieldwork, Federal Work-Study, and institutionally sponsored loans also available. Financial award application deadline: 8/1. *Faculty research:* Very broad range of topics and approaches. *Unit head:* Dr. Linda Marshall, Chair, 940-565-2339, Fax: 940-546-4682, E-mail: psychair@unt.edu. *Application contact:* Amy Mayfield, Graduate Coordinator, 940-565-2671, Fax: 940-565-4682, E-mail: amym@unt.edu.

University of Regina, Faculty of Graduate Studies and Research, Faculty of Arts, Department of Psychology, Regina, SK S4S 0A2, Canada. Offers clinical psychology (MA, PhD); experimental and applied psychology (MA, PhD). *Faculty:* 18 full-time (10 women). *Students:* 45 full-time (37 women), 6 part-time (all women). 66 applicants, 32% accepted. In 2007, 6 master's, 2 doctorates awarded. *Degree requirements:* For master's, thesis; for doctorate, comprehensive exam, thesis/dissertation. *Entrance requirements:* For master's, GRE General Test, GRE Subject Test; for doctorate, GRE General Test, GRE Subject Test (optional for students who hold a master's degree from a Canadian university). Additional exam requirements/recommendations for international students: Required—TOEFL (minimum score 580 paper-based; 237 computer-based; 88 iBT). *Application deadline:* For fall admission, 2/15 for domestic students. Application fee: $85 ($100 for international students). Electronic applications accepted. *Financial support:* In 2007–08, 19 fellowships (averaging $15,750 per year), 4 research assistantships (averaging $13,875 per year), 10 teaching assistantships (averaging $13,060 per year) were awarded; career-related internships or fieldwork and scholarships/grants also available. Financial award application deadline: 6/15. *Faculty research:* Clinical and experimental and applied psychology. *Unit head:* Dr. William E. Smythe, Head, 306-585-4157, Fax: 306-585-5429, E-mail: william.smythe@uregina.ca.

University of South Carolina, The Graduate School, College of Arts and Sciences, Department of Psychology, Program in Experimental Psychology, Columbia, SC 29208. Offers MA, PhD. *Faculty:* 13 full-time (5 women), 5 part-time/adjunct (4 women). *Students:* 16 full-time (10 women), 2 international. Average age 29. 28 applicants, 39% accepted, 7 enrolled. In 2007, 3 master's, 4 doctorates awarded. Terminal master's awarded for partial completion of doctoral program. *Median time to degree:* Of those who began their doctoral program in fall 1999, 80% received their degree in 8 years or less. *Degree requirements:* For master's, comprehensive exam, thesis; for doctorate, comprehensive exam, thesis/dissertation. *Entrance requirements:* For master's and doctorate, GRE General Test. Additional exam requirements/recommendations for international students: Required—TOEFL. *Application deadline:* For fall admission, 2/1 priority date for domestic students. Applications are processed on a rolling basis. Application fee: $35. Electronic applications accepted. *Expenses:* Tuition, state resident: part-time $440 per hour. Tuition, nonresident: part-time $936 per hour. Required fees: $17 per hour. Tuition and fees vary according to program. *Financial support:* In 2007–08, 3 fellowships with full tuition reimbursements (averaging $16,000 per year), 5 research assistantships with full tuition reimbursements (averaging $12,000 per year), 4 teaching assistantships with full tuition reimbursements (averaging $12,000 per year) were awarded; Federal Work-Study and institutionally sponsored loans also available. Support available to part-time students. *Faculty research:* Cognition, development, neuroscience. *Unit head:* Dr. Gordon Baylis, Director, 803-777-5480, Fax: 803-777-9558, E-mail: gordon@sc.edu. *Application contact:* Marti Brown, Student Services Program Coordinator, 803-777-9482, Fax: 803-777-0670, E-mail: marthab@gwm.sc.edu.

University of Southern Mississippi, Graduate School, College of Education and Psychology, Department of Psychology, Hattiesburg, MS 39406-0001. Offers clinical psychology (MA, PhD); counseling psychology (PhD); experimental psychology (MA, PhD); psychology (MS); school psychology (MA, PhD). *Accreditation:* ACA; APA (one or more programs are accredited). *Faculty:* 33 full-time (12 women), 1 (woman) part-time/adjunct. *Students:* 111 full-time (87 women), 32 part-time (22 women); includes 11 minority (6 African Americans, 3 Asian Americans or Pacific Islanders, 2 Hispanic Americans), 8 international. Average age 28. 201 applicants, 21% accepted, 33 enrolled. In 2007, 32 master's, 15 doctorates awarded. Terminal master's awarded for partial completion of doctoral program. *Degree requirements:* For master's, comprehensive exam, thesis; for doctorate, comprehensive exam, thesis/dissertation. *Entrance requirements:* For master's, GRE General Test, minimum GPA of 3.0; for doctorate, GRE General Test, interview, minimum GPA of 3.0. Additional exam requirements/recommendations for international students: Required—TOEFL. *Application deadline:* For fall admission, 3/1 priority date for domestic students, 3/1 for international students. Applications are processed on a rolling basis. Application fee: $30. *Financial support:* In 2007–08, 46 research assistantships with full tuition reimbursements (averaging $7,731 per year), 49 teaching assistantships with full tuition reimbursements (averaging $7,731 per year) were awarded; career-related internships or fieldwork, Federal Work-Study, and institutionally sponsored loans also available. Financial award application deadline: 3/15. *Faculty research:* Dolphin cognition, sleep, neuropsychology, health-related behaviors, psychopathology. Total annual research expenditures: $101,200. *Unit head:* Dr. Stan Kuczaj, Chair, 601-266-4177, Fax: 601-266-5580. *Application contact:* Dr. Heather Sterling-Tairner, Graduate Coordinator, 601-266-4177, Fax: 601-266-5580.

The University of Tennessee, Graduate School, College of Arts and Sciences, Department of Psychology, Knoxville, TN 37996. Offers clinical psychology (PhD); experimental psychology (MA, PhD); psychology (MA). *Accreditation:* APA (one or more programs are accredited). Terminal master's awarded for partial completion of doctoral program. *Degree requirements:* For master's, thesis; for doctorate, thesis/dissertation. *Entrance requirements:* For master's and doctorate, GRE General Test, GRE Subject Test, minimum GPA of 2.7. Additional exam requirements/recommendations for international students: Required—TOEFL. Electronic applications accepted.

The University of Tennessee at Chattanooga, Graduate School, College of Arts and Sciences, Department of Psychology, Program in Research Psychology, Chattanooga, TN 37403-2598. Offers MS. Part-time and evening/weekend programs available. *Faculty:* 5 full-time (1 woman). *Students:* 9 full-time (8 women), 5 part-time (4 women); includes 4 minority (2 African Americans, 2 Hispanic Americans), 1 international. Average age 27. 18 applicants, 78%

accepted, 8 enrolled. In 2007, 6 degrees awarded. *Degree requirements:* For master's, thesis. *Entrance requirements:* For master's, GRE General Test. Additional exam requirements/recommendations for international students: Required—TOEFL (minimum score 550 paper-based; 213 computer-based; 79 iBT); Recommended—IELTS (minimum score 6). *Application deadline:* For fall admission, 8/1 priority date for domestic students, 6/1 for international students; for spring admission, 12/1 priority date for domestic students, 10/1 for international students. Applications are processed on a rolling basis. Application fee: $30 ($35 for international students). *Expenses:* Tuition, state resident: full-time $5,854; part-time $393 per hour. Tuition, nonresident: full-time $15,816; part-time $946 per hour. Required fees: $1,090; $256 per hour. *Financial support:* In 2007–08, 4 fellowships with full and partial tuition reimbursements (averaging $4,125 per year) were awarded; career-related internships or fieldwork, Federal Work-Study, institutionally sponsored loans, scholarships/grants, tuition waivers (partial), and unspecified assistantships also available. Support available to part-time students. Financial award application deadline: 4/1; financial award applicants required to submit FAFSA. *Faculty research:* Cognition; psychology of religion; self-esteem; abnormal psychology; child development. *Unit head:* Dr. David Ross, Coordinator, 423-425-5288, Fax: 423-425-4284, E-mail: david-ross@utc.edu. *Application contact:* Dr. Deborah E. Arfken, Dean of Graduate Studies, 423-425-4666, Fax: 423-425-5223, E-mail: deborah-arfken@utc.edu.

The University of Texas at Arlington, Graduate School, College of Science, Department of Psychology, Arlington, TX 76019. Offers experimental psychology (PhD); health psychology (PhD); psychology (MS). Part-time programs available. *Faculty:* 8 full-time (2 women), 1 (woman) part-time/adjunct. *Students:* 60 full-time (45 women), 6 part-time (4 women); includes 8 minority (2 African Americans, 1 Asian American or Pacific Islander, 5 Hispanic Americans), 18 international. 51 applicants, 29% accepted, 17 enrolled. In 2007, 13 master's, 3 doctorates awarded. Terminal master's awarded for partial completion of doctoral program. *Median time to degree:* Of those who began their doctoral program in fall 1999, 100% received their degree in 8 years or less. *Degree requirements:* For master's, comprehensive exam or thesis; for doctorate, thesis/dissertation (for some programs). *Entrance requirements:* For master's and doctorate, GRE General Test, minimum GPA of 3.0 in last 60 hours of course work. Additional exam requirements/recommendations for international students: Required—TOEFL (minimum score 550 paper-based; 213 computer-based). *Application deadline:* For fall admission, 6/16 for domestic students. Applications are processed on a rolling basis. Application fee: $35 ($50 for international students). *Expenses:* Tuition, state resident: full-time $5,934. Tuition, nonresident: full-time $10,938. *Financial support:* In 2007–08, 4 fellowships (averaging $1,000 per year), 2 research assistantships with tuition reimbursements (averaging $15,000 per year), 28 teaching assistantships with tuition reimbursements (averaging $15,000 per year) were awarded; career-related internships or fieldwork, Federal Work-Study, institutionally sponsored loans, scholarships/grants, traineeships, tuition waivers (partial), and unspecified assistantships also available. Financial award application deadline: 6/1; financial award applicants required to submit FAFSA. *Unit head:* Dr. Robert Gatchel, Chair, 817-272-2281, Fax: 817-272-2364, E-mail: gatchel@uta.edu. *Application contact:* Dr. Jared Kenworthy, Graduate Advisor, 817-272-2281, Fax: 817-272-2364, E-mail: kenworthy@uta.edu.

The University of Texas at El Paso, Graduate School, College of Liberal Arts, Department of Psychology, El Paso, TX 79968-0001. Offers clinical psychology (MA); experimental psychology (MA); psychology (PhD). Part-time and evening/weekend programs available. *Degree requirements:* For master's, thesis; for doctorate, thesis/dissertation. *Entrance requirements:* For master's and doctorate, GRE General Test. Additional exam requirements/recommendations for international students: Required—TOEFL. Electronic applications accepted.

The University of Texas–Pan American, College of Social and Behavioral Sciences, Department of Psychology and Anthropology, Edinburg, TX 78541-2999. Offers psychology (MA), including clinical psychology, experimental psychology. Part-time and evening/weekend programs available. *Faculty:* 10 full-time (2 women). *Students:* 24 full-time (17 women), 12 part-time (7 women); includes 29 minority (all Hispanic Americans) Average age 29. 15 applicants, 60% accepted, 9 enrolled. In 2007, 3 degrees awarded. *Degree requirements:* For master's, comprehensive exam, thesis optional, internship. *Entrance requirements:* For master's, GRE, letters of recommendation. Additional exam requirements/recommendations for international students: Required—TOEFL. *Application deadline:* For fall admission, 7/1 priority date for domestic and international students; for spring admission, 11/1 priority date for domestic and international students. Application fee: $0. Electronic applications accepted. *Financial support:* In 2007–08, 1 research assistantship (averaging $10,000 per year), 3 teaching assistantships (averaging $6,000 per year) were awarded; career-related internships or fieldwork, Federal Work-Study, and institutionally sponsored loans also available. *Faculty research:* Biofeedback, acculturation, health, stress/trauma, neuropsychological assessment, false memories, children's theory of mind. Total annual research expenditures: $60,000. *Unit head:* Dr. Philip G. Gasquoine, Director, 956-381-2155, Fax: 956-381-3333, E-mail: pgasquoine@panam.edu.

The University of Toledo, College of Graduate Studies, College of Arts and Sciences, Department of Psychology, Toledo, OH 43606-3390. Offers behavioral (PhD), including cognitive, psychobiology and learning, social; clinical psychology (PhD); experimental psychology (MA). *Accreditation:* APA. *Faculty:* 22. *Students:* 34 full-time (24 women), 4 part-time (2 women); includes 2 minority (1 Asian American or Pacific Islander, 1 Hispanic American), 4 international. Average age 26. 150 applicants, 13% accepted, 9 enrolled. In 2007, 9 master's, 7 doctorates awarded. *Degree requirements:* For master's, thesis; for doctorate, one foreign language, thesis/dissertation. *Entrance requirements:* For master's and doctorate, GRE General Test, GRE Subject Test. *Application deadline:* For fall admission, 1/15 priority date for domestic students. Application fee: $45. *Financial support:* In 2007–08, 13 research assistantships (averaging $8,400 per year), 18 teaching assistantships (averaging $11,000 per year) were awarded; career-related internships or fieldwork, Federal Work-Study, institutionally sponsored loans, scholarships/grants, and unspecified assistantships also available. Support available to part-time students. Financial award application deadline: 1/15; financial award applicants required to submit FAFSA. *Faculty research:* Neural taste response. *Unit head:* Dr. Joseph Hovey, Chair, 419-530-2693, Fax: 419-530-8479.

See Close-Up on page 1509.

University of Victoria, Faculty of Graduate Studies, Faculty of Social Sciences, Department of Psychology, Victoria, BC V8W 2Y2, Canada. Offers clinical psychology (PhD); clinical psychology (neuropsychology) (M Sc); cognition and brain science (M Sc, PhD); experimental neuropsychology (M Sc, PhD); individualized study (M Sc, PhD); life span development psychology (PhD); life span developmental psychology (M Sc); social psychology (M Sc, PhD). *Accreditation:* APA (one or more programs are accredited). *Faculty:* 24 full-time (12 women), 14 part-time/adjunct (7 women). *Students:* 26, 4 international. Average age 25. 146 applicants, 21% accepted, 14 enrolled. In 2007, 36 master's, 2 doctorates awarded. *Degree requirements:* For master's, thesis; for doctorate, thesis/dissertation, candidacy exam. *Entrance requirements:* For master's and doctorate, GRE General Test. Additional exam requirements/recommendations for international students: Required—TOEFL (minimum score 600 paper-based; 250 computer-based). *Application deadline:* For fall admission, 1/1 for domestic students, 12/15 priority date for international students. Applications are processed on a rolling basis. Application fee: $65 ($100 for international students). Electronic applications accepted. *Expenses:* Tuition, state resident: full-time $3,110. International tuition: $3,700 full-time. Tuition and fees vary according to program. *Financial support:* In 2007–08, 4 fellowships (averaging $13,000 per year), 23 research assistantships, 22 teaching assistantships (averaging $2,750 per year) were awarded; career-related internships or fieldwork and institutionally sponsored loans also available. Financial award application deadline: 1/15. *Faculty research:* Life span development psychology and aging, behavioral neuroscience, cognitive psychology, behavioral psychology, environmental psychology. *Unit head:* Dr. Elizabeth Brimacombe, Chair, 250-721-7547, Fax: 250-721-8929, E-mail: psychair@uvic.ca. *Application contact:* Paul Taylor, Graduate Secretary, 250-721-6109, Fax: 250-721-8929, E-mail: ptaylor@uvic.ca.

University of Wisconsin–Oshkosh, The Office of Graduate Studies, College of Letters and Science, Department of Psychology, Oshkosh, WI 54901. Offers experimental psychology (MS); industrial/organizational psychology (MS). *Faculty:* 10 full-time (3 women). *Students:* 27. Average age 26. 22 applicants, 100% accepted. In 2007, 9 degrees awarded. *Degree requirements:* For master's, thesis. *Entrance requirements:* For master's, GRE, 10 semester hours of undergraduate course work in psychology. Additional exam requirements/recommendations for international students: Required—TOEFL (minimum score 550 paper-based; 213 computer-based; 79 iBT). *Application deadline:* For fall admission, 4/1 priority date for domestic students. Applications are processed on a rolling basis. Application fee: $45. Electronic applications accepted. *Financial support:* Fellowships, research assistantships with partial tuition reimbursements, career-related internships or fieldwork, institutionally sponsored loans, scholarships/grants, tuition waivers (partial), and unspecified assistantships available. Financial award application deadline: 3/15; financial award applicants required to submit FAFSA. *Faculty research:* Performance evaluation, training, biological bases of behavior, tactile perception, aging. *Unit head:* Dr. Jim Koch, Chair, 920-424-2303, E-mail: kochj@uwosh.edu. *Application contact:* Dr. Gary Adams, Graduate Program Coordinator, 920-424-2300, E-mail: psychology@uwosh.edu.

Washington State University, Graduate School, College of Liberal Arts, Department of Psychology, Pullman, WA 99164. Offers clinical psychology (PhD); experimental psychology (PhD); psychology (MS). *Accreditation:* APA (one or more programs are accredited). *Faculty:* 28. *Students:* 58 full-time (37 women), 2 part-time (1 woman); includes 9 minority (1 African American, 1 Asian American or Pacific Islander, 7 Hispanic Americans), 7 international. Average age 29. 238 applicants, 6% accepted, 12 enrolled. In 2007, 4 master's, 8 doctorates awarded. *Degree requirements:* For master's, comprehensive exam (for some programs), thesis (for some programs), oral exam; for doctorate, comprehensive exam, thesis/dissertation, oral exam, written exam. *Entrance requirements:* For master's, GRE General Test, minimum GPA of 3.0, research or clinical experience, 3 letters of recommendation; for doctorate, GRE General Test, minimum GPA of 3.0, 1 course in statistics and research methodology, research or clinical experience, 3 letters of recommendation. *Application deadline:* For fall admission, 1/1 for domestic students. Applications are processed on a rolling basis. Application fee: $50. *Financial support:* In 2007–08, 47 students received support, including 5 research assistantships with full and partial tuition reimbursements available (averaging $13,917 per year), 39 teaching assistantships with full and partial tuition reimbursements available (averaging $13,056 per year); fellowships, career-related internships or fieldwork, Federal Work-Study, institutionally sponsored loans, and unspecified assistantships also available. Financial award application deadline: 4/1; financial award applicants required to submit FAFSA. *Faculty research:* Childhood conduct disorders, etiology of depression, treatment of reading disorders, applied behavior analysis, selective attention. Total annual research expenditures: $240,986. *Unit head:* Dr. John Hinson, Chair, 509-335-2631, E-mail: hinson@mail.wsu.edu. *Application contact:* Graduate School Admissions, 800-GRADWSU, Fax: 509-335-16949, E-mail: gradsch@wsu.edu.

Washington University in St. Louis, Graduate School of Arts and Sciences, Department of Psychology, St. Louis, MO 63130-4899. Offers clinical psychology (PhD); general experimental psychology (MA, PhD); social psychology (MA, PhD). *Accreditation:* APA (one or more programs are accredited). Terminal master's awarded for partial completion of doctoral program. *Degree requirements:* For master's, thesis or alternative; for doctorate, thesis/dissertation. *Entrance requirements:* For master's and doctorate, GRE General Test. Electronic applications accepted.

Western Michigan University, Graduate College, College of Arts and Sciences, Department of Psychology, Kalamazoo, MI 49008-5202. Offers applied behavior analysis (MA, PhD); clinical psychology (MA, PhD); experimental analysis of behavior (PhD); experimental psychology (MA); industrial/organizational psychology (MA); school psychology (PhD, Ed S). *Accreditation:* APA (one or more programs are accredited). *Degree requirements:* For master's, variable foreign language requirement, thesis, oral exams; for doctorate, 2 foreign languages, comprehensive exam, thesis/dissertation, oral exams; for Ed S, thesis, oral exams. *Entrance requirements:* For master's, doctorate, and Ed S, GRE General Test.

Western Washington University, Graduate School, College of Humanities and Social Sciences, Department of Psychology, Program in Experimental Psychology, Bellingham, WA 98225-5996. Offers MS. *Students:* 17 full-time (10 women), 4 part-time (1 woman); includes 2 minority (1 Asian American or Pacific Islander, 1 Hispanic American). 28 applicants, 57% accepted, 13 enrolled. In 2007, 5 degrees awarded. *Degree requirements:* For master's, thesis. *Entrance requirements:* For master's, GRE General Test, minimum GPA of 3.0 in last 60 semester hours or last 90 quarter hours. Additional exam requirements/recommendations for international students: Required—TOEFL (minimum score 567 paper-based; 227 computer-based). *Application deadline:* For fall admission, 2/1 priority date for domestic students. Application fee: $50. Electronic applications accepted. *Expenses:* Tuition, state resident: part-time $208 per credit. Tuition, nonresident: part-time $541 per credit. Required fees: $241 per quarter. One-time fee: $250 part-time. *Financial support:* In 2007–08, 3 teaching assistantships with partial tuition reimbursements (averaging $9,339 per year) were awarded; career-related internships or fieldwork, Federal Work-Study, institutionally sponsored loans, scholarships/grants, tuition waivers (partial), and unspecified assistantships also available. Support available to part-time students. Financial award application deadline: 2/15; financial award applicants required to submit FAFSA. *Unit head:* Dr. Kristi Lemm, Adviser, 360-650-3187, E-mail: kristi.lemm@wwu.edu. *Application contact:* Lynn Graham, Graduate Coordinator, 360-650-3184, E-mail: lynn.graham@wwu.edu.

Xavier University, College of Social Sciences, Health and Education, Department of Psychology, Cincinnati, OH 45207. Offers clinical psychology (Psy D); psychology (MA), including general experimental, industrial-organizational. *Accreditation:* APA (one or more programs are accredited). *Faculty:* 16 full-time (8 women), 10 part-time/adjunct (5 women). *Students:* 83 full-time (62 women), 27 part-time (20 women); includes 9 minority (4 African Americans, 4 Asian Americans or Pacific Islanders, 1 Hispanic American), 2 international. Average age 29. 275 applicants, 28% accepted, 27 enrolled. In 2007, 27 master's, 12 doctorates awarded. Terminal master's awarded for partial completion of doctoral program. *Median time to degree:* Of those who began their doctoral program in fall 1999, 100% received their degree in 8 years or less. *Degree requirements:* For master's, one foreign language, comprehensive exam, thesis, internship; for doctorate, one foreign language, comprehensive exam, thesis/dissertation, internship, practicum. *Entrance requirements:* For master's, GRE, minimum GPA of 3.0, 18 hours of course work in psychology; for doctorate, GRE, 18 hours of course work in psychology or a master's degree in clinical psychology, minimum GPA of 3.0. Additional exam requirements/recommendations for international students: Required—TOEFL (minimum score 550 paper-based; 213 computer-based). *Application deadline:* For fall admission, 1/15 priority date for domestic students. Application fee: $35. Electronic applications accepted. *Expenses:* Contact institution. *Financial support:* In 2007–08, 50 students received support, including 16 research assistantships with partial tuition reimbursements available, 4 teaching assistantships with partial tuition reimbursements available; career-related internships or fieldwork, traineeships, health care benefits, and unspecified assistantships also available. Financial award application deadline: 3/1; financial award applicants required to submit FAFSA. *Faculty research:* Cognitive development in children, weight management, psychodiagnostics, psychotherapy, gerontology I-O psychology. *Unit head:* Dr. Christine M. Dacey, Chair, 513-745-3533, Fax: 513-745-3327, E-mail: dacey@xavier.edu. *Application contact:* Margaret Maybury, Assistant Director-Enrollment and Student Services, 513-745-1053, Fax: 513-745-3327, E-mail: maybury@xavier.edu.

Forensic Psychology

Alliant International University–Fresno, Center for Forensic Studies, Fresno, CA 93727. Offers forensic psychology (PhD, Psy D). *Degree requirements:* For doctorate, thesis/dissertation. *Entrance requirements:* For doctorate, interview; master's degree in psychology, forensic psychology, criminology, criminal justice, social work or law; minimum GPA of 3.0 in psychology and overall. Additional exam requirements/recommendations for international students: Required—TOEFL (minimum score 600 paper-based; 250 computer-based), TWE (minimum score 5). Electronic applications accepted. *Faculty research:* Domestic violence, serial killers, court evaluations, drug and alcohol abuse.

See Close-Up on page 1371.

Alliant International University–Los Angeles, Center for Forensic Studies, Alhambra, CA 91803-1360. Offers forensic psychology (Psy D). *Degree requirements:* For doctorate, thesis/dissertation. *Entrance requirements:* For doctorate, interview; master's degree in psychology, forensic psychology, criminology, criminal justice, social work or law; minimum GPA of 3.0 in psychology and overall. Additional exam requirements/recommendations for international students: Required—TOEFL (minimum score 600 paper-based; 250 computer-based), TWE (minimum score 5). *Faculty research:* Court testimony.

See Close-Up on page 1371.

American International College, School of Arts, Education and Science, Department of Psychology, Program in Forensic Psychology, Springfield, MA 01109-3189. Offers MS. Part-time and evening/weekend programs available. *Faculty:* 2 full-time (0 women), 1 part-time/adjunct (0 women). *Students:* 28 full-time (27 women), 14 part-time (13 women); includes 7 minority (3 African Americans, 1 American Indian/Alaska Native, 1 Asian American or Pacific Islander, 2 Hispanic Americans). Average age 34. In 2007, 19 degrees awarded. *Degree requirements:* For master's, comprehensive exam (for some programs), thesis optional. *Entrance requirements:* For master's, minimum B- average in undergraduate course work, BS or BA. Additional exam requirements/recommendations for international students: Required—TOEFL. *Application deadline:* For fall admission, 4/15 for domestic and international students. Applications are processed on a rolling basis. Application fee: $50. Electronic applications accepted. *Expenses:* Tuition: Part-time $615 per credit hour. Full-time tuition and fees vary according to degree level, campus/location and program. *Financial support:* Career-related internships or fieldwork, Federal Work-Study, and unspecified assistantships available. Financial award applicants required to submit FAFSA. *Application contact:* Barbara Z. Benoit, Director of Graduate Admissions, 413-205-3700, Fax: 413-205-3051, E-mail: barbara.benoit@aic.edu.

Argosy University, Chicago, College of Psychology and Behavioral Sciences, Doctoral Program in Clinical Psychology, Chicago, IL 60654. Offers child and adolescent psychology (Psy D); client-centered and experiential psychotherapies (Psy D); diversity and multicultural psychology (Psy D); family psychology (Psy D); forensic psychology (Psy D); health psychology (Psy D); psychoanalytic psychology (Psy D); psychology and spirituality (Psy D). *Accreditation:* APA.

See Close-Up on page 1379.

Argosy University, Denver, College of Psychology and Behavioral Sciences, Denver, CO 80203. Offers clinical psychology (MA, Psy D); community counseling (MA); counseling psychology (Ed D), including counselor education and supervision; counselor education and supervision (Ed D); forensic psychology (MA); marriage and family therapy (MA); organizational leadership (Ed D).

See Close-Up on page 1383.

Argosy University, Inland Empire, College of Psychology and Behavioral Sciences, San Bernardino, CA 92408. Offers clinical psychology/marriage and family therapy (MA); counseling psychology (MA, Ed D); counseling psychology/marriage and family therapy (MA); forensic psychology (MA).

See Close-Up on page 1387.

Argosy University, Orange County, College of Psychology and Behavioral Sciences, Program in Forensic Psychology, Santa Ana, CA 92704. Offers MA. *Application contact:* Mark Betz, Director of Admissions, 800-716-9598, Fax: 714-437-1697, E-mail: mbetz@argosy.edu.

See Close-Up on page 1393.

Argosy University, Phoenix, College of Psychology and Behavioral Sciences, Program in Forensic Psychology, Phoenix, AZ 85021. Offers MA.

See Close-Up on page 1395.

Argosy University, San Francisco Bay Area, College of Psychology and Behavioral Sciences, Program in Forensic Psychology, Alameda, CA 94501. Offers MA.

See Close-Up on page 1401.

Argosy University, Sarasota, College of Psychology and Behavioral Sciences, Sarasota, FL 34235. Offers community counseling (MA); counseling psychology (Ed D); counselor education and supervision (Ed D); forensic psychology (MA); marriage and family therapy (MA); mental health counseling (MA); organizational leadership (Ed D); pastoral community counseling (Ed D); school counseling (MA, Ed S); school psychology (MA).

See Close-Up on page 1403.

Argosy University, Schaumburg, College of Psychology and Behavioral Sciences, Schaumburg, IL 60173-5403. Offers clinical health psychology (Post-Graduate Certificate); clinical psychology (MA, Psy D), including child and family psychology (Psy D), clinical health psychology (Psy D), diversity and multicultural psychology (Psy D), forensic psychology (Psy D); community counseling (MA); counseling psychology (Ed D), including counselor education and supervision; counselor education and supervision (Ed D); forensic psychology (Post-Graduate Certificate); organizational leadership (Ed D). *Accreditation:* ACA; APA.

See Close-Up on page 1405.

Argosy University, Twin Cities, College of Psychology and Behavioral Sciences, Eagan, MN 55121. Offers clinical psychology (MA, Psy D), including child and family psychology (Psy D), forensic psychology (Psy D), health psychology (Psy D), marriage/couples and family therapy (Psy D), neuropsychology (Psy D); forensic counseling (Post-Graduate Certificate); forensic psychology (MA); marriage and family therapy (MA, DMFT), including forensic counseling (MA); organizational leadership (Ed D). *Accreditation:* APA.

See Close-Up on page 1411.

Argosy University, Washington DC, College of Psychology and Behavioral Sciences, Arlington, VA 22209. Offers clinical psychology (MA, Psy D), including child and family psychology (Psy D), diversity and multicultural psychology (Psy D), forensic psychology (Psy D), health and neuropsychology (Psy D); community counseling (MA); counseling psychology (Ed D), including counselor education and supervision; counselor education and supervision (Ed D); forensic psychology (MA); organizational leadership (Ed D). *Accreditation:* APA.

See Close-Up on page 1413.

California Baptist University, Program in Forensic Psychology, Riverside, CA 92504-3206. Offers MA. *Faculty:* 2 full-time (both women), 1 part-time/adjunct (0 women). *Students:* 5 full-time (all women), 2 part-time (1 woman); includes 2 minority (1 Asian American or Pacific Islander, 1 Hispanic American). 17 applicants, 59% accepted. *Entrance requirements:* Additional exam requirements/recommendations for international students: Required—TOEFL (minimum score 575 paper-based; 230 computer-based), IELTS (minimum score 7). *Application deadline:* For fall admission, 9/1 for domestic students, 7/1 for international students; for spring admission, 1/3 for domestic students, 10/15 for international students. Application fee: $45. *Expenses:* Tuition: Full-time $7,992; part-time $444 per semester hour. Required fees: $510; $125 per semester. *Unit head:* Dr. Anne-Marie Larsen, Director, 951-343-4761. *Application contact:* Gail Ronveaux, Dean of Graduate Enrollment, 951-343-5045, Fax: 951-343-5095, E-mail: graduateadmissions@calbaptist.edu.

Castleton State College, Division of Graduate Studies, Department of Psychology, Castleton, VT 05735. Offers forensic psychology (MA). *Degree requirements:* For master's, thesis. *Entrance requirements:* For master's, GRE General Test, minimum undergraduate GPA of 3.5, previous course work in research methodology and statistics. Additional exam requirements/recommendations for international students: Required—TOEFL. *Faculty research:* Psychology and law, juvenile delinquency, criminal psychology, correctional psychology, police psychology.

The Chicago School of Professional Psychology, Graduate School, Program in Forensic Psychology, Chicago, IL 60610. Offers MA. *Students:* 294. Average age 25. *Degree requirements:* For master's, thesis optional. *Entrance requirements:* For master's, GRE (highly recommended), 1 course in research methods, statistics, 1 course in psychology. Additional exam requirements/recommendations for international students: Required—TOEFL (minimum score 550 paper-based; 213 computer-based; 79 iBT). *Application deadline:* For fall admission, 2/15 priority date for domestic students, 4/15 for international students. Application fee: $50. *Financial support:* Federal Work-Study and scholarships/grants available. Financial award applicants required to submit FAFSA. *Unit head:* Dr. Michael Fogel, Director, 312-329-6600, E-mail: mfogel@thechicagoschool.edu. *Application contact:* Yarelli Meza, Director of Admission, 312-329-6666, Fax: 312-644-3333, E-mail: admissions@thechicagoschool.edu.

See Close-Up on page 1427.

College of Saint Elizabeth, Department of Psychology, Morristown, NJ 07960-6989. Offers counseling psychology (MA); forensic psychology (MA); student affairs in higher education (Certificate). Part-time and evening/weekend programs available. *Faculty:* 5 full-time (2 women), 6 part-time/adjunct (4 women). *Students:* 7 full-time (all women), 61 part-time (58 women); includes 21 minority (7 African Americans, 2 Asian Americans or Pacific Islanders, 12 Hispanic Americans), 2 international. Average age 30. In 2007, 8 degrees awarded. *Degree requirements:* For master's, thesis or alternative, portfolio. *Entrance requirements:* For master's, minimum GPA of 3.0, BA in psychology (preferred), 12 credits of course work in psychology. *Application deadline:* For fall admission, 4/14 priority date for domestic students; for spring admission, 11/15 for domestic students. Applications are processed on a rolling basis. Application fee: $35. Electronic applications accepted. *Expenses:* Tuition: Full-time $17,016; part-time $709 per credit. Required fees: $1,300; $370 per term. Full-time tuition and fees vary according to program and student's religious affiliation. Part-time tuition and fees vary according to campus/location and student's religious affiliation. *Financial support:* Career-related internships or fieldwork, tuition waivers (partial), and unspecified assistantships available. Support available to part-time students. Financial award application deadline: 3/15; financial award applicants required to submit FAFSA. *Faculty research:* Family systems, dissociative identity disorder, multicultural counseling, outcomes assessment. *Unit head:* Dr. Valerie Scott, Director of the Graduate Program in Counseling Psychology, 973-290-4102, Fax: 973-290-4676, E-mail: vscott@cse.edu. *Application contact:* Michael Szarek, Director of Enrollment Management, 973-290-4112, Fax: 973-290-4167, E-mail: mszarek@cse.edu.

Drexel University, College of Arts and Sciences, Department of Psychology, Clinical Psychology Program, Philadelphia, PA 19104-2875. Offers clinical psychology (MA, MS); forensic psychology (PhD); health psychology (PhD); neuropsychology (PhD). *Accreditation:* APA. Terminal master's awarded for partial completion of doctoral program. *Degree requirements:* For master's, comprehensive exam, thesis; for doctorate, thesis/dissertation, qualifying exam. *Entrance requirements:* For master's, GRE General Test, minimum GPA of 3.0; for doctorate, GRE General Test, GRE Subject Test, minimum GPA of 3.0. Electronic applications accepted. Expenses: Contact institution. *Faculty research:* Cognitive behavioral therapy, stress and coping, eating disorders, substance abuse, developmental disabilities.

Fairleigh Dickinson University, Metropolitan Campus, University College: Arts, Sciences, and Professional Studies, School of Psychology, Program in Forensic Psychology, Teaneck, NJ 07666-1914. Offers MA. *Expenses:* Tuition: Part-time $869 per credit. Tuition and fees vary according to degree level, campus/location and program. *Unit head:* Dr. Christopher Capuano, Director, School of Psychology, 201-692-2000.

Holy Names University, Graduate Division, Department of Counseling Psychology, Oakland, CA 94619-1699. Offers counseling psychology (MA); forensic psychology (MA, Certificate); pastoral counseling (MA, Certificate). Part-time and evening/weekend programs available. *Faculty:* 3 full-time (1 woman), 11 part-time/adjunct (6 women). *Students:* 36 full-time (33 women), 16 part-time (15 women); includes 32 minority (23 African Americans, 3 Asian Americans or Pacific Islanders, 6 Hispanic Americans), 2 international. Average age 35. 21 applicants, 81% accepted, 16 enrolled. In 2007, 13 master's awarded. *Degree requirements:* For master's, comprehensive paper, seminars. *Entrance requirements:* For master's, minimum undergraduate GPA of 2.6 overall, 3.0 in major. Additional exam requirements/recommendations for international students: Required—TOEFL. *Application deadline:* For fall admission, 8/1 priority date for domestic students; for spring admission, 12/1 priority date for domestic students. Applications are processed on a rolling basis. Application fee: $65. *Expenses:* Tuition: Part-time $635 per unit. One-time fee: $340 part-time. Tuition and fees vary according to program. *Financial support:* In 2007–08, 34 students received support. Available to part-time students. Application deadline: 3/2; *Faculty research:* Cognitive psychology, anger management, grief and grief counseling, post-modernism and psychotherapy, spirituality and psychology. *Unit head:* Helen Shoemaker, Program Director, 510-436-1543, E-mail: shoemaker@hnu.edu. *Application contact:* 800-430-1351, Fax: 510-436-1325, E-mail: admissions@hnu.edu.

John Jay College of Criminal Justice of the City University of New York, Graduate Studies, Program in Forensic Psychology, New York, NY 10019-1093. Offers MA, PhD. Part-time and evening/weekend programs available. *Degree requirements:* For master's, thesis or alternative, externship. *Entrance requirements:* For master's, GRE General Test, minimum B average in major. Additional exam requirements/recommendations for international students: Required—TOEFL (minimum score 500 paper-based; 173 computer-based).

John Jay College of Criminal Justice of the City University of New York, Graduate Studies, Programs in Criminal Justice, New York, NY 10019-1093. Offers criminal justice (MA, PhD); criminology and deviance (PhD); forensic psychology (PhD); forensic science (PhD); law and philosophy (PhD); organizational behavior (PhD); public policy (PhD). Part-time and evening/weekend programs available. Terminal master's awarded for partial completion of doctoral program. *Degree requirements:* For master's, thesis or alternative; for doctorate, one foreign language, thesis/dissertation. *Entrance requirements:* For master's, GRE General Test, minimum B average; for doctorate, GRE General Test. Additional exam requirements/recommendations for international students: Required—TOEFL (minimum score 500 paper-based; 173 computer-based).

Marymount University, School of Education and Human Services, Program in Community Counseling and Forensic Psychology, Arlington, VA 22207-4299. Offers MS/MA. Part-time and evening/weekend programs available. *Students:* 17 full-time (all women), 6 part-time (all women); includes 8 minority (all African Americans) Average age 26. 1 applicant, 0% accepted. *Entrance requirements:* Additional exam requirements/recommendations for international students: Required—TOEFL (minimum score 600 paper-based; 250 computer-based; 100

iBT). *Application deadline:* For fall admission, 2/15 for domestic students. Application fee: $40. *Expenses:* Tuition: Full-time $11,790; part-time $655 per credit. Required fees: $121; $6.7 per credit. *Financial support:* Research assistantships with full tuition reimbursements, career-related internships or fieldwork, scholarships/grants, and unspecified assistantships available. Support available to part-time students. Financial award applicants required to submit FAFSA. *Unit head:* Dr. Wayne Lesko, Dean, School of Education and Human Services, 703-284-1620, Fax: 703-284-1631, E-mail: wayne.lesko@marymount.edu.

Marymount University, School of Education and Human Services, Program in Forensic Psychology, Arlington, VA 22207-4299. Offers MA. Part-time and evening/weekend programs available. *Faculty:* 3 full-time (2 women), 7 part-time/adjunct (5 women). *Students:* 116 full-time (99 women), 36 part-time (29 women); includes 19 minority (10 African Americans, 1 American Indian/Alaska Native, 4 Asian Americans or Pacific Islanders, 4 Hispanic Americans), 3 international. Average age 25. 210 applicants, 78% accepted, 86 enrolled. In 2007, 84 degrees awarded. *Degree requirements:* For master's, thesis or alternative. *Entrance requirements:* For master's, GRE, 2 letters of recommendation, resumé. Additional exam requirements/recommendations for international students: Required—TOEFL (minimum score 600 paper-based; 250 computer-based). *Application deadline:* For fall admission, 2/15 for domestic students. Applications are processed on a rolling basis. Application fee: $40. Electronic applications accepted. *Expenses:* Tuition: Full-time $11,790; part-time $655 per credit. Required fees: $121; $6.7 per credit. *Financial support:* Research assistantships with full tuition reimbursements, career-related internships or fieldwork, scholarships/grants, and unspecified assistantships available. Support available to part-time students. Financial award applicants required to submit FAFSA. *Unit head:* Dr. Mary Lindahl, Chair, 703-526-6825, Fax: 703-284-5708, E-mail: mary.lindahl@marymount.edu.

Massachusetts School of Professional Psychology, Graduate Programs, Boston, MA 02132. Offers clinical psychology (Psy D); clinical psychopharmacology (Post-Doctoral MS); counseling psychology (MA); executive coaching (Graduate Certificate); forensic psychology (MA); organizational psychology (MA); respecialization in clinical psychology (Certificate); MA/CAGS. *Accreditation:* APA. *Faculty:* 24 full-time (11 women), 13 part-time/adjunct (9 women). *Students:* 223 full-time (177 women), 81 part-time (68 women); includes 22 minority (3 African Americans, 8 Asian Americans or Pacific Islanders, 11 Hispanic Americans), 9 international. Average age 28. 415 applicants, 42% accepted, 77 enrolled. In 2007, 14 master's, 37 doctorates awarded. *Degree requirements:* For master's, comprehensive exam; for doctorate, thesis/dissertation. *Entrance requirements:* For doctorate, GRE General Test. Additional exam requirements/recommendations for international students: Required—TOEFL (minimum score 550 paper-based; 213 computer-based). *Application deadline:* For fall admission, 1/3 for domestic and international students. Application fee: $50. Electronic applications accepted. *Expenses:* Tuition: Full-time $25,952; part-time $811 per credit. Required fees: $200. *Financial support:* In 2007–08, 20 teaching assistantships (averaging $3,300 per year) were awarded; career-related internships or fieldwork also available. Financial award applicants required to submit FAFSA. *Unit head:* Dr. Nicholas A. Covino, President, 617-327-6777, Fax: 617-327-4447. *Application contact:* 617-327-6777 Ext. 210, Fax: 617-327-4447, E-mail: admissions@mspp.edu.

See Close-Up on page 1447.

Oklahoma State University Center for Health Sciences, Graduate Program in Forensic Sciences, Tulsa, OK 74107-1898. Offers forensic DNA/molecular biology (MS); forensic examination of questioned documents (MFSA, Certificate); forensic pathology (MS); forensic psychology (MS); forensic sciences (MFSA); forensic toxicology (MS). Part-time and evening/weekend programs available. Postbaccalaureate distance learning degree programs offered (no on-campus study). *Faculty:* 2 full-time (0 women), 14 part-time/adjunct (5 women). *Students:* 3 full-time (1 woman), 21 part-time (14 women); includes 6 minority (4 African Americans, 1 Asian American or Pacific Islander, 1 Hispanic American), 1 international. Average age 34. 27 applicants, 63% accepted, 8 enrolled. In 2007, 12 master's, 1 other advanced degree awarded. *Degree requirements:* For master's, comprehensive exam (for some programs), thesis (for some programs). *Entrance requirements:* For master's, MAT (MFSA) or GRE General Test, professional experience (MFSA). Additional exam requirements/recommendations for international students: Required—TOEFL (minimum score 600 paper-based; 250 computer-based), TWE (minimum score 5). *Application deadline:* For fall admission, 3/1 for domestic and international students; for spring admission, 10/1 for domestic and international students. Application fee: $40 ($75 for international students). *Financial support:* In 2007–08, 10 students received support, including 10 research assistantships (averaging $29,000 per year); career-related internships or fieldwork, Federal Work-Study, and tuition waivers (partial) also available. Support available to part-time students. *Faculty research:* DNA typing, DNA polymorphism, identification through DNA, disease transmission, forensic dentistry, neurotoxicity of HIV, forensic toxicology method development, toxin detection and characterization. Total annual research expenditures: $58,000. *Unit head:* Dr. Robert T. Allen, Director, 918-561-1108, Fax: 918-561-8414. *Application contact:* Cathy Newsome, Coordinator, 918-699-8608, Fax: 918-561-8414, E-mail: cathy.newsome@okstate.edu.

Prairie View A&M University, College of Juvenile Justice and Psychology, Prairie View, TX 77446-0519. Offers clinical adolescent psychology (PhD); juvenile forensic psychology (MSJFP); juvenile justice (MSJJ, PhD). Part-time and evening/weekend programs available. *Faculty:* 11 full-time (5 women), 2 part-time/adjunct (1 woman). *Students:* 45 full-time (37 women), 54 part-time (42 women); includes 76 minority (70 African Americans, 2 Asian Americans or Pacific Islanders, 4 Hispanic Americans), 4 international. Average age 30. 55 applicants, 60% accepted, 33 enrolled. In 2007, 5 master's, 5 doctorates awarded. *Degree requirements:* For master's, comprehensive exam (for some programs), thesis (for some programs); for doctorate, comprehensive exam, thesis/dissertation. *Entrance requirements:* For master's, GRE, minimum GPA of 2.75; for doctorate, GRE, previous course work in clinical adolescent psychology, minimum GPA of 3.5. Additional exam requirements/recommendations for international students: Required—TOEFL. *Application deadline:* For fall admission, 3/1 for domestic and international students; for spring admission, 10/1 for domestic and international students. Applications are processed on a rolling basis. Application fee: $50. *Financial support:* In 2007–08, 18 students received support; research assistantships, teaching assistantships, career-related internships or fieldwork, Federal Work-Study, institutionally sponsored loans, tuition waivers (full and partial), and unspecified assistantships available. Support available to part-time students. Financial award application deadline: 3/1; financial award applicants required to submit FAFSA. *Faculty research:* Juvenile justice, juvenile forensic psychology, teen court, graduate education, capital punishment. Total annual research expenditures: $2,888. *Unit head:* Dr. Elaine Rodney, Dean, 936-261-520, Fax: 936-261-5252, E-mail: ehrodney@pvamu.edu. *Application contact:* Sandy Siegmund, Executive Secretary, Graduate Program, 936-857-5234, Fax: 936-857-5249, E-mail: sisiegmund@pvamu.edu.

Roger Williams University, Feinstein College of Arts and Sciences, Program in Forensic Psychology, Bristol, RI 02809. Offers MA. Part-time programs available. *Faculty:* 4 full-time (1 woman), 1 part-time/adjunct (0 women). *Students:* 28 full-time (19 women), 1 part-time; includes 1 minority (Hispanic American) Average age 24. 45 applicants, 78% accepted, 16 enrolled. *Degree requirements:* For master's, thesis optional. *Entrance requirements:* For master's, GRE. *Application deadline:* Applications are processed on a rolling basis. Application fee: $50. Electronic applications accepted. *Financial support:* In 2007–08, 29 students received support. *Unit head:* Dr. Donald Whitworth, Professor of Psychology, 401-254-3509, E-mail: dwhitworth@rwu.edu. *Application contact:* Suzanne Faubl, Director of Graduate Admissions, 401-254-3809, Fax: 401-254-3557, E-mail: sfaubl@rwu.edu.

Announcement: The master's degree in forensic psychology is designed to prepare students to provide assessment and treatment services in a forensic setting or to pursue further training at the doctoral level. Students are trained in psychological testing, treatment, research methodology, and psychopathology. For more information, students should visit the Web site at www.rwu.edu/admission/graduate/.

See Close-Up on page 1473.

Sage Graduate School, Graduate School, Department of Psychology, Program in Forensic Psychology, Troy, NY 12180-4115. Offers Certificate. Part-time and evening/weekend programs available. *Faculty:* 4 full-time (all women), 4 part-time/adjunct (1 woman). *Students:* 6 full-time (all women), 7 part-time (5 women). Average age 26. 1 applicant, 100% accepted, 0 enrolled. In 2007, 2 Certificates awarded. *Entrance requirements:* Additional exam requirements/recommendations for international students: Required—TOEFL (minimum score 550 paper-based; 213 computer-based). *Application deadline:* Applications are processed on a rolling basis. Application fee: $40. *Expenses:* Tuition: Full-time $9,720; part-time $540 per credit hour. *Financial support:* Fellowships, research assistantships, Federal Work-Study, scholarships/grants, and unspecified assistantships available. Support available to part-time students. Financial award application deadline: 3/1; financial award applicants required to submit FAFSA. *Unit head:* Dr. Bronna Romanoff, Director, 518-244-2260, E-mail: romanb@sage.edu. *Application contact:* Shannon K. Easton, Director of Graduate and Adult Admission, 518-244-2443, Fax: 518-244-6880, E-mail: sgsadm@sage.edu.

Sage Graduate School, Graduate School, Department of Sociology and Criminal Justice, Program in Forensic Mental Health, Troy, NY 12180-4115. Offers MS, Certificate. Part-time and evening/weekend programs available. *Faculty:* 2 part-time/adjunct (both women). *Students:* 3 full-time (all women), 4 part-time (all women); includes 1 minority (African American) Average age 31. 12 applicants, 58% accepted, 7 enrolled. *Entrance requirements:* Additional exam requirements/recommendations for international students: Required—TOEFL (minimum score 550 paper-based; 213 computer-based). *Application deadline:* Applications are processed on a rolling basis. Application fee: $40. *Expenses:* Tuition: Full-time $9,720; part-time $540 per credit hour. *Financial support:* Fellowships, research assistantships, Federal Work-Study, scholarships/grants, and unspecified assistantships available. Support available to part-time students. *Unit head:* Lisa Callahan, Director, Graduate Program in Forensic Mental Health, 518-244-2245, E-mail: fmhp@sage.edu. *Application contact:* Shannon K. Easton, Director of Graduate and Adult Admission, 518-244-2443, Fax: 518-244-6880, E-mail: sgsadm@sage.edu.

Tiffin University, Program in Criminal Justice, Tiffin, OH 44883-2161. Offers crime analysis (MSCJ); criminal behavior (MSCJ); forensic psychology (MSCJ); homeland security administration (MSCJ); justice administration (MSCJ). Part-time and evening/weekend programs available. Postbaccalaureate distance learning degree programs offered (no on-campus study). *Degree requirements:* For master's, thesis optional. *Entrance requirements:* For master's, minimum undergraduate GPA of 2.5, work experience. Additional exam requirements/recommendations for international students: Required—TOEFL (minimum score 550 paper-based; 213 computer-based). Electronic applications accepted. *Faculty research:* Terrorism, intelligence, homeland security, guns and crime.

Universidad de Iberoamerica, Graduate School, San Jose, Costa Rica. Offers clinical psychology (M Psych); educational psychology (M Psych); forensic psychology (M Psych); hospital and health services management (MHA); intensive care nursing (MN); medicine (MD). *Entrance requirements:* For master's, 2 letters of recommendation, interview.

The University of British Columbia, Faculty of Arts and Faculty of Graduate Studies, Department of Psychology, Vancouver, BC V6T 1Z1, Canada. Offers behavioral neuroscience (MA, PhD); clinical psychology (MA, PhD); cognitive science (MA, PhD); developmental psychology (MA, PhD); forensic psychology (PhD); health psychology (MA, PhD); quantitative methods (MA, PhD); social/personality psychology (MA, PhD). *Accreditation:* APA (one or more programs are accredited). *Faculty:* 46 full-time (20 women), 26 part-time/adjunct (13 women). *Students:* 102 full-time (69 women). Average age 29. 247 applicants, 14% accepted, 18 enrolled. In 2007, 14 master's, 11 doctorates awarded. Terminal master's awarded for partial completion of doctoral program. *Median time to degree:* Of those who began their doctoral program in fall 1999, 91% received their degree in 8 years or less. *Degree requirements:* For master's, thesis; for doctorate, comprehensive exam, thesis/dissertation. *Entrance requirements:* For master's and doctorate, GRE General Test, GRE Subject Test. Additional exam requirements/recommendations for international students: Required—TOEFL (minimum score 550 paper-based; 230 computer-based; 80 iBT). *Application deadline:* For fall admission, 1/15 for domestic and international students. Applications are processed on a rolling basis. Application fee: $90 Canadian dollars ($150 Canadian dollars for international students). Electronic applications accepted. *Financial support:* In 2007–08, 95 students received support, including 27 fellowships with full and partial tuition reimbursements available (averaging $16,500 per year), 50 research assistantships with full and partial tuition reimbursements available (averaging $6,775 per year), 80 teaching assistantships with full and partial tuition reimbursements available (averaging $8,065 per year); career-related internships or fieldwork, Federal Work-Study, institutionally sponsored loans, scholarships/grants, health care benefits, tuition waivers (full and partial), and unspecified assistantships also available. Financial award application deadline: 1/15. *Faculty research:* Clinical, developmental, social/personality, cognition, behavioral neuroscience. Total annual research expenditures: $5.5 million Canadian dollars. *Unit head:* Dr. Eric Eich, Head, 604-822-3078, Fax: 604-822-6923, E-mail: ee@psych.ubc.ca. *Application contact:* Rose Tam, Graduate Secretary, 604-822-3144, Fax: 604-822-6923, E-mail: gradsec@psych.ubc.ca.

University of Massachusetts Boston, Office of Graduate Studies, Graduate College of Education, Counseling and School Psychology Department, Program in Mental Health Counseling, Boston, MA 02125-3393. Offers forensic counseling (M Ed, CAGS).

University of North Dakota, Graduate School, College of Arts and Sciences, Department of Psychology, Grand Forks, ND 58202. Offers clinical psychology (PhD); counseling psychology (PhD); experimental psychology (PhD); forensic psychology (MA, MS); psychology (MA). *Accreditation:* APA (one or more programs are accredited). *Faculty:* 15 full-time (3 women). *Students:* 79 full-time (60 women), 15 part-time (11 women); includes 19 minority (2 African Americans, 15 American Indian/Alaska Native, 2 Asian Americans or Pacific Islanders), 9 international. 168 applicants, 24% accepted, 32 enrolled. In 2007, 4 master's, 16 doctorates awarded. *Degree requirements:* For master's, thesis, final exam; for doctorate, comprehensive exam, thesis/dissertation, internship, final exam. *Entrance requirements:* For master's, GRE General Test, GRE Subject Test, minimum GPA of 3.0; for doctorate, GRE General Test, GRE Subject Test, minimum GPA of 3.5. Additional exam requirements/recommendations for international students: Required—TOEFL (minimum score 550 paper-based; 213 computer-based; 79 iBT), IELTS (minimum score 7). *Application deadline:* For fall admission, 1/15 for domestic and international students. Application fee: $35. Electronic applications accepted. *Expenses:* Tuition, state resident: full-time $4,050; part-time $225 per credit. Tuition, nonresident: full-time $10,818; part-time $601 per credit. Required fees: $110 per semester. Tuition and fees vary according to class time, campus/location, program and reciprocity agreements. *Financial support:* In 2007–08, 34 students received support, including 8 research assistantships with full tuition reimbursements available (averaging $11,476 per year), 23 teaching assistantships with full tuition reimbursements available (averaging $8,993 per year); fellowships with full and partial tuition reimbursements available, career-related internships or fieldwork, Federal Work-Study, institutionally sponsored loans, scholarships/grants, health care benefits, tuition waivers (full and partial), and unspecified assistantships also available. Support available to part-time students. Financial award application deadline: 3/15; financial award applicants required to submit FAFSA. *Faculty research:* Developmental psychology, clinical social psychology, educational psychology, personality disorders. *Unit head:* Dr. Jeffrey N. Weatherly, Chairperson, 701-777-3470, E-mail: jeffrey.weatherly@und.nodak.edu. *Application contact:* Brenda Halle, Admissions Specialist, 701-777-2947, Fax: 701-777-3619, E-mail: brendahalle@mail.und.edu.

Genetic Counseling

Arcadia University, Graduate Studies, Program in Genetic Counseling, Glenside, PA 19038-3295. Offers MSGC. *Degree requirements:* For master's, thesis. *Entrance requirements:* For master's, GRE. Additional exam requirements/recommendations for international students: Required—TOEFL. Expenses: Contact institution.

Brandeis University, Graduate School of Arts and Sciences, Program in Genetic Counseling, Waltham, MA 02454-9110. Offers MS. *Faculty:* 4 full-time (1 woman), 8 part-time/adjunct (7 women). *Students:* 21 full-time (20 women); includes 2 minority (1 African American, 1 Asian American or Pacific Islander), 2 international. Average age 28. 77 applicants, 49% accepted, 12 enrolled. In 2007, 8 degrees awarded. *Degree requirements:* For master's, thesis. *Entrance requirements:* For master's, GRE General Test, resumé, 3 letters of recommendation, statement of purpose. Additional exam requirements/recommendations for international students: Required—TOEFL (minimum score 600 paper-based; 250 computer-based; 100 iBT), IELTS (minimum score 7). *Application deadline:* For fall admission, 2/1 for domestic and international students. Application fee: $55. Electronic applications accepted. *Expenses: Contact institution. Financial support:* In 2007–08, 20 students received support. Career-related internships or fieldwork, scholarships/grants, and tuition waivers (partial) available. Financial award application deadline: 4/15; financial award applicants required to submit CSS PROFILE or FAFSA. *Unit head:* Dr. Judith Tsipis, Director, 781-736-3179, Fax: 781-736-3107, E-mail: tsipis@brandeis.edu.

California State University, Stanislaus, College of Natural Sciences, Department of Biological Sciences, Turlock, CA 95382. Offers ecology and sustainability (MS); genetic counseling (MS); marine sciences (MS). Part-time programs available. *Faculty:* 20 full-time, 5 part-time/adjunct. *Students:* 3 full-time (2 women), 6 part-time (all women); includes 1 minority (Hispanic American), 1 international. Average age 34. 1 applicant, 100% accepted, 1 enrolled. *Degree requirements:* For master's, thesis. *Entrance requirements:* For master's, GRE General Test, GRE Subject Test, minimum GPA of 3.0, 3 letters of reference, personal statement. Additional exam requirements/recommendations for international students: Required—TOEFL (minimum score 550 paper-based; 213 computer-based). *Application deadline:* For fall admission, 2/15 for domestic and international students; for spring admission, 9/15 for domestic and international students. Application fee: $55. Electronic applications accepted. *Expenses:* Tuition, nonresident: full-time $10,170; part-time $339 per unit. Required fees: $3,972; $2,538 per term. $1,165 per semester. *Financial support:* Fellowships, career-related internships or fieldwork, Federal Work-Study, and scholarships/grants available. Support available to part-time students. Financial award application deadline: 3/2; financial award applicants required to submit FAFSA. *Faculty research:* Long-term smoking and pregnancy rate, vertebrate paleobiology, terrestrial animals, benthic invertebrates of central California coastline. *Application contact:* Dr. Mark Grobner, Chair, 209-667-3476, E-mail: pmartin@csustan.edu.

Case Western Reserve University, School of Medicine and School of Graduate Studies, Graduate Programs in Medicine, Department of Genetics, Program in Genetic Counseling, Cleveland, OH 44106. Offers MS. *Faculty:* 24 full-time (14 women). *Students:* 7 full-time (all women), 1 international. Average age 24. 41 applicants, 10% accepted, 4 enrolled. In 2007, 4 degrees awarded. *Degree requirements:* For master's, thesis. *Entrance requirements:* For master's, GRE General Test. Additional exam requirements/recommendations for international students: Required—TOEFL. *Application deadline:* For fall admission, 2/1 for domestic students. Application fee: $50. *Financial support:* In 2007–08, 8 fellowships (averaging $10,000 per year) were awarded. Financial award application deadline: 2/28. *Faculty research:* Genetic testing, ethical issues in genetics, cancer genetics, reproductive genetics, prenatal diagnosis. *Unit head:* Dr. Anne L. Matthews, Director, 216-368-1821, Fax: 216-368-3432, E-mail: alm14@po.cwru.edu. *Application contact:* Dianne R. Austin, Administrative Assistant, 216-368-3433, Fax: 216-368-3432, E-mail: dra3@po.cwru.edu.

The Johns Hopkins University, Bloomberg School of Public Health, Department of Health, Behavior and Society, Baltimore, MD 21218-2699. Offers behavioral sciences and health education (MHS); genetic counseling (Sc M); social and behavioral sciences (PhD, Sc D). *Faculty:* 36 full-time (27 women), 35 part-time/adjunct (24 women). *Students:* 79 full-time (74 women), 9 part-time (8 women); includes 24 minority (11 African Americans, 1 American Indian/Alaska Native, 8 Asian Americans or Pacific Islanders, 4 Hispanic Americans), 10 international. Average age 27. 197 applicants, 41% accepted, 33 enrolled. In 2007, 8 master's, 4 doctorates awarded. *Degree requirements:* For master's, comprehensive exam (for some programs), thesis (for some programs); for doctorate, comprehensive exam, thesis/dissertation. *Entrance requirements:* For master's and doctorate, GRE, transcripts, curriculum vitae, statement, 3 recommendation letters. Additional exam requirements/recommendations for international students: Required—TOEFL (minimum score 250 computer-based; 100 iBT). *Application deadline:* For fall admission, 12/1 for domestic and international students. Electronic applications accepted. *Financial support:* In 2007–08, 89 students received support, including 2 fellowships with tuition reimbursements available (averaging $24,000 per year), 7 teaching assistantships (averaging $4,770 per year); career-related internships or fieldwork, Federal Work-Study, scholarships/grants, traineeships, health care benefits, and unspecified assistantships also available. Financial award application deadline: 3/15. *Faculty research:* Structural and community-level inventions to improve health communication and health education behavioral and social aspects of genetic counseling. Total annual research expenditures: $4.6 million. *Unit head:* Georgean Smith, Administrator, 410-502-3715, Fax: 410-502-4333, E-mail: gesmith@jhsph.edu. *Application contact:* Barbara W. Diehl, Senior Academic Program Coordinator, 410-502-4415, Fax: 410-502-4333, E-mail: bdiehl@jhsph.edu.

McGill University, Faculty of Graduate and Postdoctoral Studies, Faculty of Medicine, Department of Human Genetics, Montréal, QC H3A 2T5, Canada. Offers genetic counseling (M Sc); human genetics (M Sc, PhD). *Faculty:* 17 full-time (8 women), 19 part-time/adjunct (12 women). *Students:* 86 full-time (54 women), 2 part-time (both women). 101 applicants, 20% accepted, 17 enrolled. In 2007, 12 master's, 8 doctorates awarded. *Unit head:* Dr. David Rosenblatt, Chair, 514-398-3600, Fax: 514-398-2430, E-mail: david.rosenblatt@mcgill.ca. *Application contact:* Laura Benner, Graduate Program Assistant, 514-398-3600, Fax: 514-398-2430, E-mail: laura.benner@mcgill.ca.

Mount Sinai School of Medicine of New York University, Graduate School of Biological Sciences, New York, NY 10029-6504. Offers bioethics (MS); community medicine (MPH); genetic counseling (MS); neurosciences (PhD); MD/PhD. *Faculty:* 126 full-time (40 women). *Students:* 283 full-time (147 women); includes 57 minority (11 African Americans, 2 American Indian/Alaska Native, 31 Asian Americans or Pacific Islanders, 13 Hispanic Americans), 89 international. 623 applicants, 20% accepted, 59 enrolled. In 2007, 12 master's, 25 doctorates awarded. Terminal master's awarded for partial completion of doctoral program. *Degree requirements:* For master's, thesis; for doctorate, comprehensive exam, thesis/dissertation. *Entrance requirements:* For doctorate, GRE General Test, GRE Subject Test, 3 years of college pre-med course work. Additional exam requirements/recommendations for international students: Required—TOEFL. *Application deadline:* For fall admission, 1/1 for domestic students. Applications are processed on a rolling basis. Application fee: $75. Electronic applications accepted. *Financial support:* In 2007–08, fellowships with full tuition reimbursements (averaging $27,000 per year), research assistantships with full tuition reimbursements (averaging $27,000 per year) were awarded; Federal Work-Study, institutionally sponsored loans, scholarships/grants, health care benefits, and unspecified assistantships also available. Financial award application deadline: 4/30; financial award applicants required to submit FAFSA. *Faculty research:* Cancer, gene therapy, minimally invasive surgery, cardiac translational research. Total annual research expenditures: $275 million. *Unit head:* Dr. John Morrison, Dean, 212-241-6546, Fax: 212-241-0651, E-mail: john.morrison@mssm.edu. *Application contact:* Lily Recanati, Manager, 212-241-2793, Fax: 212-241-0651, E-mail: lily.recantati@mssm.edu.

Northwestern University, The Graduate School, Program in Genetic Counseling, Evanston, IL 60208. Offers MS. *Degree requirements:* For master's, thesis. *Entrance requirements:* For master's, GRE General Test, interview. Additional exam requirements/recommendations for international students: Required—TOEFL. *Faculty research:* Preimplantation genetic diagnosis, gene expression in preimplantation embryos, fetal cells in maternal blood: first trimester prenatal screening for Down's Syndrome, genetic counseling efficacy and counseling issues in prenatal diagnosis.

Sarah Lawrence College, Graduate Studies, Program in Genetic Counseling, Bronxville, NY 10708-5999. Offers human genetics (MS). Part-time programs available. *Faculty:* 21 part-time/adjunct (16 women). *Students:* 37 full-time (33 women), 7 part-time (6 women); includes 3 minority (1 African American, 2 Asian Americans or Pacific Islanders), 18 international. Average age 28. 110 applicants, 44% accepted, 23 enrolled. In 2007, 19 degrees awarded. *Degree requirements:* For master's, thesis, fieldwork. *Entrance requirements:* For master's, previous course work in biology, chemistry, developmental biology, genetics, probability and statistics. *Application deadline:* For fall admission, 1/15 for domestic students. Application fee: $60. *Expenses: Contact institution.* Tuition and fees vary according to program. *Financial support:* In 2007–08, 30 fellowships (averaging $7,500 per year) were awarded; career-related internships or fieldwork, Federal Work-Study, scholarships/grants, and unspecified assistantships also available. Support available to part-time students. Financial award application deadline: 3/1. *Unit head:* Caroline Lieber, Director, 914-395-2371. *Application contact:* Susan Guma, Dean of Graduate Studies, 914-395-2373, E-mail: sguma@mail.slc.edu.

Simmons College, School for Health Studies, Program in Clinical Genetics, Boston, MA 02115. Offers CAGS, Certificate. Part-time programs available. Postbaccalaureate distance learning degree programs offered (no on-campus study). *Faculty:* 1 (woman) full-time, 3 part-time/adjunct (all women). *Students:* Average age 43. 10 applicants, 70% accepted, 6 enrolled. In 2007, 5 degrees awarded. *Entrance requirements:* Additional exam requirements/recommendations for international students: Required—TOEFL (minimum score 570 paper-based; 230 computer-based; 88 iBT). *Application deadline:* For fall admission, 6/1 for domestic students. Application fee: $50. *Expenses: Contact institution. Financial support:* Application deadline: 3/1; *Faculty research:* Genetic counseling, DNA patenting. *Unit head:* Vilma Torres, Administrative Assistant II, 617-521-2654, Fax: 617-521-3137, E-mail: shs@simmons.edu.

University of Arkansas for Medical Sciences, Graduate School, Program in Genetic Counseling, Little Rock, AR 72205-7199. Offers MS. *Faculty:* 18 full-time (11 women). *Students:* 9 full-time. *Unit head:* Bruce Haas, Chairman, 501-526-7701, E-mail: brhaas@uams.edu.

University of California, Irvine, School of Medicine, Department of Pediatrics, Program in Genetic Counseling, Irvine, CA 92697. Offers MS. *Students:* 10 full-time (8 women); includes 6 minority (all Asian Americans or Pacific Islanders), 1 international. In 2007, 8 degrees awarded. *Degree requirements:* For master's, thesis. *Entrance requirements:* For master's, GRE General Test, minimum GPA of 3.0. Additional exam requirements/recommendations for international students: Required—TOEFL (minimum score 550 paper-based; 213 computer-based). *Application deadline:* For fall admission, 2/1 priority date for domestic students; for winter admission, 10/15 priority date for domestic students. Applications are processed on a rolling basis. Application fee: $60. Electronic applications accepted. *Financial support:* In 2007–08, 3 students received support; research assistantships with full tuition reimbursements available, teaching assistantships, career-related internships or fieldwork, institutionally sponsored loans, traineeships, health care benefits, and unspecified assistantships available. Financial award application deadline: 3/1; financial award applicants required to submit FAFSA. *Faculty research:* Gene mapping and linkage analysis, delineation of new malformation and chromosomal syndromes, ethical and counseling issues in genetics. *Unit head:* Dr. Ann P. Walker, Director, 714-456-5789, Fax: 714-456-5330, E-mail: awalker@uci.edu. *Application contact:* Evelyn Hohlfeld, Administrative Assistant, 714-456-8520, Fax: 714-456-5330, E-mail: eahohlfe@uci.edu.

University of Cincinnati, Graduate School, College of Allied Health Sciences, Program in Genetic Counseling, Cincinnati, OH 45221. Offers medical genetics (MS). Part-time programs available. *Faculty:* 30 full-time (15 women). *Students:* 9 full-time (8 women). Average age 23. 100 applicants, 19% accepted, 9 enrolled. In 2007, 9 degrees awarded. *Degree requirements:* For master's, thesis. *Entrance requirements:* For master's, GRE General Test. Additional exam requirements/recommendations for international students: Required—TOEFL. *Application deadline:* For fall admission, 2/1 for domestic and international students. Application fee: $40. Electronic applications accepted. *Financial support:* In 2007–08, 1 student received support, including 1 fellowship with full tuition reimbursement available (averaging $7,000 per year), 10 teaching assistantships with partial tuition reimbursements available (averaging $5,000 per year); tuition waivers (partial) and unspecified assistantships also available. Financial award application deadline: 2/1. *Faculty research:* Lysosomal disease, Tourette's syndrome, epidemiology of Down syndrome, genetic counseling, genetic disease treatment. *Unit head:* Nancy Steinberg Warren, Program Director, 513-636-8448, Fax: 513-636-7297, E-mail: nancy.warren@uc.edu. *Application contact:* Carol Turner, Graduate Program Secretary, 513-636-8448, Fax: 513-636-0543, E-mail: gcprog@chmcc.org.

University of Colorado Denver, Graduate School, Program in Genetic Counseling, Denver, CO 80217-3364. Offers MS. *Students:* 12 full-time (11 women); includes 1 minority (Asian American or Pacific Islander) In 2007, 6 degrees awarded. *Degree requirements:* For master's, comprehensive exam, thesis optional. *Entrance requirements:* For master's, GRE General Test, minimum GPA of 3.0, 4 letters of recommendation. Additional exam requirements/recommendations for international students: Required—TOEFL (minimum score 550 paper-based; 213 computer-based). *Application deadline:* For fall admission, 1/2 for domestic students. Application fee: $50. *Expenses: Contact institution. Financial support:* Application deadline: 3/15; *Unit head:* Carol Walton, Director, 303-861-6395, E-mail: walton.carol@tchden.org.

University of Minnesota, Twin Cities Campus, Graduate School, Program in Molecular, Cellular, Developmental Biology and Genetics, Minneapolis, MN 55455-0213. Offers genetic counseling (MS); molecular, cellular, developmental biology and genetics (PhD). Part-time programs available. *Faculty:* 83 full-time (28 women), 15 part-time/adjunct (13 women). *Students:* 106 full-time (66 women), 2 part-time (1 woman); includes 4 minority (1 American Indian/Alaska Native, 3 Asian Americans or Pacific Islanders), 40 international. Average age 24. 179 applicants, 11% accepted, 19 enrolled. In 2007, 13 master's, 16 doctorates awarded. Terminal master's awarded for partial completion of doctoral program. *Median time to degree:* Of those who began their doctoral program in fall 1999, 100% received their degree in 8 years or less. *Degree requirements:* For master's, thesis optional; for doctorate, thesis/dissertation. *Entrance requirements:* For master's and doctorate, GRE General Test. Additional exam requirements/recommendations for international students: Required—TOEFL (minimum score 625 paper-based; 263 computer-based; 80 iBT). *Application deadline:* For fall admission, 1/2 priority date for domestic and international students. Applications are processed on a rolling basis. Application fee: $55 ($75 for international students). Electronic applications accepted. *Financial support:* In 2007–08, 10 fellowships with full tuition reimbursements (averaging $23,000 per year), 79 research assistantships with full tuition reimbursements (averaging $24,500 per year), 11 teaching assistantships with partial tuition reimbursements (averaging $9,236 per year) were awarded; scholarships/grants, traineeships, and health care benefits also available. Financial award application deadline: 1/2. *Faculty research:* Membrane receptors and membrane transport, cell interactions, cytoskeleton and cell mobility, regulation of gene expression, plant cell and molecular biology. Total annual research expenditures: $9.1 million. *Unit head:* Jocelyn Shaw, Director of Graduate Studies, 612-625-1912, Fax: 612-626-6140, E-mail: shawx005@umn.edu. *Application contact:* Sue Knoblauch, Student Support Coordinator, 612-624-7470, Fax: 612-626-6140, E-mail: mcdbg@cbs.umn.edu.

The University of North Carolina at Greensboro, Graduate School, Program in Genetic Counseling, Greensboro, NC 27412-5001. Offers MS. *Students:* 16 full-time (all women); includes 1 minority (Hispanic American) 56 applicants, 14% accepted. *Application deadline:*

For fall admission, 1/1 for domestic students. Application fee: $45. Electronic applications accepted. *Unit head:* Nancy Callanan, Director, 336-256-0175, Fax: 336-256-0174, E-mail: nancy_callanan@uncg.edu. *Application contact:* Michelle Harkleroad, Director of Graduate Admissions, 336-334-4884, Fax: 336-334-4424, E-mail: mbharkle@uncg.edu.

University of Oklahoma Health Sciences Center, College of Medicine and Graduate College, Department of Genetic Counseling, Oklahoma City, OK 73190. Offers MS. *Faculty:* 7 full-time (1 woman), 1 (woman) part-time/adjunct. *Students:* 6 full-time (all women); includes 1 minority (Hispanic American) Average age 24. 14 applicants, 29% accepted, 4 enrolled. In 2007, 4 master's awarded. *Entrance requirements:* For master's, GRE General Test, 3 letters of recommendation. *Application deadline:* For fall admission, 3/1 for domestic students. *Expenses:* Tuition, area resident: Part-time $144 per hour. Tuition, state resident: part-time $144 per hour. Tuition, nonresident: part-time $374 per hour. Required fees: $500 per semester. Tuition and fees vary according to campus/location and program. *Unit head:* Dr. John Mulvihill, Head, 405-271-8685. *Application contact:* Susan I. Hassed, Information Contact, 405-271-8685.

University of Pittsburgh, Graduate School of Public Health, Department of Human Genetics, Program in Genetic Counseling, Pittsburgh, PA 15260. Offers MS. *Students:* 11 full-time (10 women), 9 part-time (all women); includes 2 minority (both Asian Americans or Pacific Islanders), 2 international. Average age 27. 66 applicants, 29% accepted, 10 enrolled. In 2007, 9 degrees awarded. *Degree requirements:* For master's, comprehensive exam, thesis, clinical internship. *Entrance requirements:* For master's, GRE General Test, previous course work in biochemistry, calculus, and genetics. Additional exam requirements/recommendations for international students: Required—TOEFL (minimum score 550 paper-based; 213 computer-based; 80 iBT). *Application deadline:* For fall admission, 2/1 for domestic students, 4/1 for international students; for winter admission, 9/1 for international students; for spring admission, 2/1 for international students. Application fee: $50 ($60 for international students). Electronic applications accepted. *Financial support:* In 2007–08, 19 students received support, including 19 research assistantships with tuition reimbursements available (averaging $25,740 per year). *Faculty research:* Statistical genetics, molecular genetics, cytogenetics, gene therapy. *Unit head:* Elizabeth A. Gettig, Director, 412-624-3018, Fax: 412-624-3020, E-mail: bgettig@pitt.edu. *Application contact:* Jeanette Norbut, Administrative Secretary, 412-624-3018, Fax: 412-624-3020, E-mail: jeanette.norbut@hgen.pitt.edu.

University of South Carolina, School of Medicine and The Graduate School, Graduate Programs in Medicine, Program in Genetic Counseling, Columbia, SC 29208. Offers MS. *Faculty:* 8 full-time (5 women), 30 part-time/adjunct (20 women). *Students:* 13 full-time (12 women); includes 1 minority (Asian American or Pacific Islander) Average age 24. 80 applicants, 13% accepted, 7 enrolled. In 2007, 6 degrees awarded. *Degree requirements:* For master's, comprehensive exam, internship, practicum. *Entrance requirements:* For master's, GRE General Test. *Application deadline:* For fall admission, 1/15 for domestic students. Application fee: $40. Electronic applications accepted. *Expenses: Contact institution.* Tuition and fees vary according to program. *Financial support:* Unspecified assistantships available. Financial award application deadline: 4/15. *Faculty research:* Genetic counseling, international, transition, prenatal diagnosis. *Unit head:* Janice G. Edwards, Director, 803-779-4928 Ext. 227, Fax: 803-434-4596, E-mail: jedwards@medpark.sc.edu.

The University of Texas Health Science Center at Houston, Graduate School of Biomedical Sciences, Program in Genetic Counseling, Houston, TX 77225-0036. Offers MS. *Faculty:* 17 full-time (15 women). *Students:* 12 full-time (11 women); includes 1 minority (Hispanic American) Average age 24. 46 applicants, 15% accepted, 7 enrolled. In 2007, 6 degrees awarded. *Degree requirements:* For master's, thesis. *Entrance requirements:* For master's, GRE General Test. Additional exam requirements/recommendations for international students: Required—TOEFL, TWE. *Application deadline:* For fall admission, 2/1 for domestic students. Application fee: $10. Electronic applications accepted. *Financial support:* Institutionally sponsored loans available. Financial award application deadline: 1/15. *Faculty research:* Genetics, molecular genetics, ctyogenetics, psychosocial issues associated with genetics counseling, research aspects of the practice of medical genetics. *Unit head:* Claire Singletary, Director, 713-500-5195, Fax: 713-500-5689, E-mail: claire.n.@singletary@uth.tmc.edu. *Application contact:* Dr. Victoria P. Knutson, Associate Dean of Admissions, 713-500-9860, Fax: 713-500-9877, E-mail: victoria.p.knutson@uth.tmc.edu.

University of Toronto, School of Graduate Studies, Life Sciences Division, Department of Molecular and Medical Genetics, Toronto, ON M5S 1A1, Canada. Offers genetic counseling (M Sc); molecular and medical genetics (M Sc, PhD). *Faculty:* 81 full-time, 28 part-time/adjunct. *Students:* 281 full-time (156 women), 25 international. 330 applicants, 31% accepted. In 2007, 14 master's, 18 doctorates awarded. *Degree requirements:* For master's, thesis; for doctorate, thesis/dissertation. *Entrance requirements:* For master's, B Sc or equivalent, minimum B+ average; for doctorate, M Sc or equivalent, minimum B+ average. Additional exam requirements/recommendations for international students: Required—TOEFL, IELTS (minimum score: 7), MELAB (minimum score: 85) or COPE (minimum score: 4). *Application deadline:* For fall admission, 2/2 priority date for domestic students; for winter admission, 10/1 for domestic students. Application fee: $100 Canadian dollars. *Faculty research:* Structural biology, developmental genetics, molecular medicine, genetic counseling. *Unit head:* Prof. Howard Lipshitz, Chair, 416-978-7145, Fax: 416-978-6885. *Application contact:* Iliana Sztainbok, Program Administrator, 416-978-7145, Fax: 416-978-6885, E-mail: molecular.medgen@utoronto.ca.

Health Psychology

American University of Beirut, Graduate Programs, Faculty of Health Sciences, Beirut, Lebanon. Offers environmental sciences (MSES), including environmental health; epidemiology (MS); epidemiology and biostatistics (MPH); health behavior and education (MPH); population health (MS); public health (MPH). Part-time programs available. *Faculty:* 26 full-time (19 women), 10 part-time/adjunct (4 women). *Students:* 42 full-time (32 women), 56 part-time (49 women). Average age 28. 159 applicants, 65% accepted, 36 enrolled. In 2007, 51 degrees awarded. *Degree requirements:* For master's, one foreign language, comprehensive exam, thesis (for some programs). *Entrance requirements:* For master's, 2 letters of recommendation, personal statement, transcripts. Additional exam requirements/recommendations for international students: Required—TOEFL (minimum score 573 paper-based; 230 computer-based; 98 iBT), IELTS (minimum score 8). *Application deadline:* For fall admission, 4/30 for domestic and international students; for spring admission, 11/1 for domestic and international students. Application fee: $50. Electronic applications accepted. *Expenses:* Tuition: Full-time $9,954; part-time $553 per credit. Tuition and fees vary according to course load and program. *Financial support:* In 2007–08, 56 students received support. Scholarships/grants, health care benefits, and unspecified assistantships available. Financial award application deadline: 4/30. *Faculty research:* Urban health, childbirth, tobacco control, HIV/AIDS surveillance, health finance and policies. *Unit head:* Huda Zurayk, Dean, 961-1340119 Ext. 4600, Fax: 961-1744470, E-mail: hzurayk@aub.edu.lb.

Appalachian State University, Cratis D. Williams Graduate School, Department of Psychology, Boone, NC 28608. Offers clinical health psychology (MA); general experimental psychology (MA); industrial and organizational psychology (MA). Part-time programs available. *Faculty:* 31 full-time (11 women). *Students:* 43 full-time (31 women), 37 part-time (30 women); includes 4 minority (3 African Americans, 1 Asian American or Pacific Islander), 4 international. 197 applicants, 30% accepted, 30 enrolled. In 2007, 23 master's, 6 other advanced degrees awarded. *Degree requirements:* For master's and MS/SSP, comprehensive exam, thesis optional, GRE Subject Test exit exam. *Entrance requirements:* For master's, GRE General Test, 3 letters of recommendation. Additional exam requirements/recommendations for international students: Required—TOEFL (minimum score 550 paper-based; 230 computer-based; 79 iBT), IELTS (minimum score 7). *Application deadline:* For fall admission, 3/1 for domestic students, 1/1 for international students. Applications are processed on a rolling basis. Application fee: $50. *Expenses:* Tuition, state resident: part-time $127 per semester hour. Tuition, nonresident: part-time $597 per semester hour. Required fees: $18 per semester. *Financial support:* In 2007–08, 34 research assistantships (averaging $3,500 per year), 25 teaching assistantships (averaging $3,500 per year) were awarded; fellowships, career-related internships or fieldwork, Federal Work-Study, scholarships/grants, and unspecified assistantships also available. Financial award application deadline: 4/1. *Faculty research:* Eating disorders, school-based consultations, organizational behavior management, brain mechanisms of sound localization, parenting styles. Total annual research expenditures: $158,688. *Unit head:* Dr. Paul Fox, Chair, 828-262-2272, Fax: 828-262-2974, E-mail: foxpa@appstate.edu. *Application contact:* Dr. Denise Martz, Graduate Coordinator, 828-262-2715, E-mail: martzdm@appstate.edu.

Argosy University, Atlanta, College of Psychology and Behavioral Sciences, Atlanta, GA 30328. Offers clinical psychology (MA, Psy D, Postdoctoral Respecialization Certificate), including child and family psychology (Psy D), general adult clinical (Psy D), health psychology (Psy D), neuropsychology/geropsychology (Psy D); community counseling (MA), including marriage and family therapy; counselor education and supervision (Ed D); marriage and family therapy (Certificate). *Accreditation:* APA.

See Close-Up on page 1377.

Argosy University, Chicago, College of Psychology and Behavioral Sciences, Doctoral Program in Clinical Psychology, Chicago, IL 60654. Offers child and adolescent psychology (Psy D); client-centered and experiential psychotherapies (Psy D); diversity and multicultural psychology (Psy D); family psychology (Psy D); forensic psychology (Psy D); health psychology (Psy D); psychoanalytic psychology (Psy D); psychology and spirituality (Psy D). *Accreditation:* APA.

See Close-Up on page 1379.

Argosy University, Schaumburg, College of Psychology and Behavioral Sciences, Schaumburg, IL 60173-5403. Offers clinical health psychology (Post-Graduate Certificate); clinical psychology (MA, Psy D), including child and family psychology (Psy D), clinical health psychology (Psy D), diversity and multicultural psychology (Psy D), forensic psychology (Psy D); community counseling (MA); counseling psychology (Ed D), including counselor education and supervision; counselor education and supervision (Ed D); forensic psychology (Post-Graduate Certificate); organizational leadership (Ed D). *Accreditation:* ACA; APA.

See Close-Up on page 1405.

Argosy University, Twin Cities, College of Psychology and Behavioral Sciences, Eagan, MN 55121. Offers clinical psychology (MA, Psy D), including child and family psychology (Psy D), forensic psychology (Psy D), health psychology (Psy D), marriage/couples and family therapy (Psy D), neuropsychology (Psy D); forensic counseling (Post-Graduate Certificate); forensic psychology (MA); marriage and family therapy (MA, DMFT), including forensic counseling (MA); organizational leadership (Ed D). *Accreditation:* APA.

See Close-Up on page 1411.

Argosy University, Washington DC, College of Psychology and Behavioral Sciences, Arlington, VA 22209. Offers clinical psychology (MA, Psy D), including child and family psychology (Psy D), diversity and multicultural psychology (Psy D), forensic psychology (Psy D), health and neuropsychology (Psy D); community counseling (MA); counseling psychology (Ed D), including counselor education and supervision; counselor education and supervision (Ed D); forensic psychology (MA); organizational leadership (Ed D). *Accreditation:* APA.

See Close-Up on page 1413.

Bastyr University, Graduate and Professional Programs, School of Nutrition and Exercise Science, Kenmore, WA 98028-4966. Offers nutrition (MS); nutrition and clinical health psychology (MS). Part-time programs available. *Students:* 101 (93 women); includes 7 minority (1 African American, 3 Asian Americans or Pacific Islanders, 3 Hispanic Americans) 5 international. Average age 30. In 2007, 35 degrees awarded. *Degree requirements:* For master's, thesis optional. *Entrance requirements:* For master's, BS with 1 year of course work in chemistry, biochemistry, physiology and nutrition. Additional exam requirements/recommendations for international students: Required—TOEFL (minimum score 550 paper-based; 213 computer-based; 79 iBT). *Application deadline:* For fall admission, 3/15 priority date for domestic and international students. Applications are processed on a rolling basis. Application fee: $75. *Financial support:* Career-related internships or fieldwork, Federal Work-Study, and scholarships/grants available. Support available to part-time students. Financial award application deadline: 4/15; financial award applicants required to submit FAFSA. *Unit head:* Dr. Mark Kestin, Dean, 425-823-1300, Fax: 425-823-6222. *Application contact:* Admissions Office, 425-602-3330, Fax: 425-602-3090, E-mail: admiss@bastyr.edu.

California Institute of Integral Studies, Graduate Programs, School of Consciousness and Transformation, San Francisco, CA 94103. Offers cultural anthropology and social transformation (MA); East-West psychology (MA, PhD); integrative health studies (MA); philosophy and religion (MA, PhD), including Asian and comparative studies, philosophy, cosmology, and consciousness, social and cultural anthropology (PhD), transformative leadership (MA), transformative studies (PhD), women's spirituality, women's spirituality flex format; social and cultural anthropology (PhD); transformative leadership (MA); transformative studies (PhD). Part-time and evening/weekend programs available. Postbaccalaureate distance learning degree programs offered (minimal on-campus study). *Faculty:* 30 full-time, 28 part-time/adjunct. *Students:* 456; includes 92 minority (32 African Americans, 3 American Indian/Alaska Native, 40 Asian Americans or Pacific Islanders, 17 Hispanic Americans), 1 international. Average age 37. 206 applicants, 93% accepted, 114 enrolled. In 2007, 26 degrees awarded. Terminal master's awarded for partial completion of doctoral program. *Degree requirements:* For master's, comprehensive exam (for some programs), thesis optional; for doctorate, comprehensive exam, thesis/dissertation. *Entrance requirements:* For master's, minimum GPA of 3.0, letters of recommendation, writing sample; for doctorate, master's degree, minimum GPA of 3.0, letters of recommendation, writing sample. Additional exam requirements/recommendations for international students: Required—TOEFL. *Application deadline:* For fall admission, 2/15 priority date for domestic and international students; for spring admission, 10/15 priority date for domestic and international students. Applications are processed on a rolling basis. Application fee: $65. Electronic applications accepted. *Expenses:* Tuition: Full-time $16,930; part-time $780 per unit. Tuition and fees vary according to course load and program. *Financial support:* In 2007–08, 292 students received support; research assistantships, teaching assistantships, career-related internships or fieldwork, Federal Work-Study, institutionally sponsored

Health Psychology

California Institute of Integral Studies (continued)
loans, scholarships/grants, and tuition waivers (partial) available. Support available to part-time students. Financial award application deadline: 3/15; financial award applicants required to submit FAFSA. *Faculty research:* Altered states of consciousness, dreams, cosmology, postcolonial studies, integrative health studies. *Application contact:* Allyson Werner, Senior Admissions Counselor, 415-575-6155, Fax: 415-575-1268.

See Close-Up on page 445.

California Institute of Integral Studies, Graduate Programs, School of Professional Psychology, San Francisco, CA 94103. Offers clinical psychology (Psy D); community mental health (MA); drama therapy (MA); expressive arts therapy (MA); integral counseling psychology (MA); integral counseling, psychology-weekend (MA); psychology (Psy D), including clinical psychology; somatic psychology (MA). *Accreditation:* APA. Part-time programs available. *Faculty:* 28 full-time, 54 part-time/adjunct. *Students:* 591; includes 113 minority (19 African Americans, 3 American Indian/Alaska Native, 48 Asian Americans or Pacific Islanders, 43 Hispanic Americans). Average age 37. 383 applicants, 75% accepted, 155 enrolled. In 2007, 109 master's, 20 doctorates awarded. *Degree requirements:* For master's, comprehensive exam; for doctorate, comprehensive exam, thesis/dissertation. *Entrance requirements:* For master's, minimum GPA of 3.0, letters of recommendation, writing sample; for doctorate, GRE, MA in psychology or social work with appropriate practical experience for advanced standing, or BA with a minimum GPA of 3.1; letters of recommendation; writing sample. Additional exam requirements/recommendations for international students: Required—TOEFL. *Application deadline:* For fall admission, 2/1 priority date for domestic and international students; for spring admission, 10/15 priority date for domestic and international students. Applications are processed on a rolling basis. Application fee: $65. Electronic applications accepted. *Expenses:* Tuition: Full-time $16,930; part-time $780 per unit. Tuition and fees vary according to course load and program. *Financial support:* In 2007–08, 393 students received support; research assistantships with tuition reimbursements available, teaching assistantships with tuition reimbursements available, career-related internships or fieldwork, Federal Work-Study, institutionally sponsored loans, scholarships/grants, and tuition waivers (partial) available. Support available to part-time students. Financial award application deadline: 3/15; financial award applicants required to submit FAFSA. *Faculty research:* Somatic psychology, comparative psychology, art therapy, transpersonal psychology, eco-psychology. *Application contact:* David Townes, Senior Admissions Counselor, 415-575-6152, Fax: 415-575-1268, E-mail: dtownes@ciis.edu.

See Close-Up on page 1421.

Central Connecticut State University, School of Graduate Studies, School of Arts and Sciences, Department of Psychology, New Britain, CT 06050-4010. Offers community psychology (MA); general psychology (MA); health psychology (MA). Part-time and evening/weekend programs available. *Faculty:* 21 full-time (11 women), 22 part-time/adjunct (10 women). *Students:* 21 full-time (13 women), 20 part-time (15 women); includes 5 minority (1 African American, 4 Hispanic Americans), 3 international. Average age 29. 42 applicants, 40% accepted, 11 enrolled. In 2007, 11 degrees awarded. *Degree requirements:* For master's, thesis, comprehensive exam or special project. *Entrance requirements:* For master's, minimum GPA of 2.7. Additional exam requirements/recommendations for international students: Required—TOEFL. *Application deadline:* For fall admission, 4/25 for domestic students; for spring admission, 12/1 for domestic students. Applications are processed on a rolling basis. Application fee: $50. Electronic applications accepted. *Expenses:* Tuition, area resident: Full-time $4,169. Tuition, state resident: full-time $6,253. Tuition, nonresident: full-time $11,614; part-time $400 per credit. Required fees: $3,322. One-time fee: $62 part-time. Tuition and fees vary according to degree level and program. *Financial support:* In 2007–08, 3 students received support, including 6 research assistantships; career-related internships or fieldwork, Federal Work-Study, scholarships/grants, and unspecified assistantships also available. Support available to part-time students. Financial award application deadline: 3/1; financial award applicants required to submit FAFSA. *Faculty research:* Clinical psychology, general psychology, child development, cognitive development, drugs/behavior. *Unit head:* Dr. Bradley M. Waite, Chair, 860-832-3100.

Claremont Graduate University, Graduate Programs, School of Behavioral and Organizational Sciences, Department of Psychology, Claremont, CA 91711-6160. Offers advanced study in evaluation (Certificate); cognitive psychology (MA, PhD); developmental psychology (MA, PhD); evaluation and applied research methods (MA, PhD); health behavior research and evaluation (MA, PhD); human resource development and evaluation (MA); industrial/organizational psychology (MA, PhD); organizational behavior (MA, PhD); organizational psychology (MA, PhD); social psychology (MA, PhD); MBA/PhD. Part-time programs available. *Faculty:* 15 full-time (7 women), 4 part-time/adjunct (2 women). *Students:* 184 full-time (137 women), 24 part-time (20 women); includes 51 minority (13 African Americans, 1 American Indian/Alaska Native, 26 Asian Americans or Pacific Islanders, 11 Hispanic Americans), 12 international. Average age 29. In 2007, 42 master's, 10 doctorates, 2 other advanced degrees awarded. Terminal master's awarded for partial completion of doctoral program. *Degree requirements:* For master's, thesis (for some programs); for doctorate, comprehensive exam, thesis/dissertation. *Entrance requirements:* For master's and doctorate, GRE General Test. *Application deadline:* For fall admission, 2/15 priority date for domestic students. Applications are processed on a rolling basis. Electronic applications accepted. *Expenses:* Tuition: Full-time $31,640; part-time $1,376 per unit. Required fees: $145 per semester. Tuition and fees vary according to course load, degree level and program. *Financial support:* Fellowships, research assistantships, teaching assistantships, career-related internships or fieldwork, Federal Work-Study, institutionally sponsored loans, and tuition waivers (full and partial) available. Support available to part-time students. Financial award application deadline: 2/15; financial award applicants required to submit FAFSA. *Faculty research:* Social intervention, diversity in organizations, eyewitness memory, aging and cognition, drug policy. *Unit head:* Natalie Brown, Program Coordinator, 909-621-8084, Fax: 909-621-8905, E-mail: natalie.brown@cgu.edu.

Drexel University, College of Arts and Sciences, Department of Psychology, Clinical Psychology Program, Philadelphia, PA 19104-2875. Offers clinical psychology (MA, MS); forensic psychology (PhD); health psychology (PhD); neuropsychology (PhD). *Accreditation:* APA. Terminal master's awarded for partial completion of doctoral program. *Degree requirements:* For master's, comprehensive exam, thesis; for doctorate, thesis/dissertation, qualifying exam. *Entrance requirements:* For master's, GRE General Test, minimum GPA of 3.0; for doctorate, GRE General Test, GRE Subject Test, minimum GPA of 3.0. Electronic applications accepted. Expenses: Contact institution. *Faculty research:* Cognitive behavioral therapy, stress and coping, eating disorders, substance abuse, developmental disabilities.

Drexel University, College of Arts and Sciences, Department of Psychology, Program in Law-Psychology, Philadelphia, PA 19104-2875. Offers PhD, JD/PhD. *Degree requirements:* For doctorate, thesis/dissertation, qualifying exam. *Entrance requirements:* For doctorate, GRE General Test, GRE Subject Test, minimum GPA of 3.0. Electronic applications accepted. Expenses: Contact institution. *Faculty research:* Mental health law issues, professional ethics, social science applications to law.

Duke University, Graduate School, Department of Psychology, Durham, NC 27708-0586. Offers biological psychology (PhD); clinical psychology (PhD); cognitive psychology (PhD); developmental psychology (PhD); experimental psychology (PhD); health psychology (PhD); human social development (PhD); JD/MA. *Accreditation:* APA (one or more programs are accredited). *Faculty:* 40 full-time. *Students:* 91 full-time (71 women); includes 15 minority (9 African Americans, 1 Asian American or Pacific Islander, 5 Hispanic Americans), 13 international. 468 applicants, 7% accepted, 19 enrolled. In 2007, 14 doctorates awarded. *Degree requirements:* For doctorate, thesis/dissertation. *Entrance requirements:* For doctorate, GRE General Test. Additional exam requirements/recommendations for international students: Required—TOEFL (minimum score 550 paper-based; 213 computer-based; 83 iBT), IELTS (minimum score 7). *Application deadline:* For fall admission, 12/15 priority date for domestic and international students. Application fee: $75. Electronic applications accepted. *Financial support:* Fellowships, research assistantships, teaching assistantships, career-related internships or fieldwork and Federal Work-Study available. Financial award application deadline: 12/31. *Unit head:* Amy Needham, Co-Director of Graduate Studies, 919-660-5715, Fax: 919-660-5726, E-mail: morrell@duke.edu.

East Carolina University, Graduate School, Thomas Harriot College of Arts and Sciences, Department of Psychology, Program in Health Psychology, Greenville, NC 27858-4353. Offers PhD. *Students:* 1 (woman) full-time. Average age 20. *Entrance requirements:* For doctorate, GRE. *Financial support:* Fellowships, research assistantships, teaching assistantships available. *Application contact:* Dr. Larry Bolen, Chair, 252-328-6634, Fax: 252-328-6283, E-mail: bolenl@ecu.edu.

The George Washington University, School of Public Health and Health Services, Doctoral Program in Public Health, Washington, DC 20052. Offers environmental and occupational health (Dr PH); health behavior (Dr PH); health policy (Dr PH). *Accreditation:* CEPH. *Faculty research:* Community organization, tele-medicine, long-term care, financing for vulnerable populations, quantitative analysis in public health policy.

John F. Kennedy University, Graduate School of Holistic Studies, Department of Counseling Psychology, Program in Counseling Psychology, Pleasant Hill, CA 94523-4817. Offers holistic studies (MA); somatic psychology (MA); transpersonal psychology (MA). Part-time and evening/weekend programs available. *Degree requirements:* For master's, thesis or alternative. *Entrance requirements:* For master's, interview. Additional exam requirements/recommendations for international students: Required—TOEFL.

Lesley University, Graduate School of Arts and Social Sciences, Self-Designed Master's Program in Interdisciplinary Studies, Cambridge, MA 02138-2790. Offers individualized studies (MA); integrative holistic health (MA); women's studies (MA). Part-time and evening/weekend programs available. Postbaccalaureate distance learning degree programs offered (no on-campus study). *Faculty:* 3 full-time (all women), 5 part-time/adjunct (3 women). *Students:* 12 full-time (11 women), 14 part-time (12 women); includes 3 minority (2 African Americans, 1 Hispanic American), 1 international. Average age 35. 10 applicants, 100% accepted, 9 enrolled. In 2007, 20 degrees awarded. *Entrance requirements:* For master's, 3 letters of recommendation. Additional exam requirements/recommendations for international students: Required—TOEFL (minimum score 550 paper-based; 213 computer-based; 80 iBT). Application fee: $50. *Financial support:* In 2007–08, 1 student received support, including research assistantships (averaging $3,400 per year), teaching assistantships (averaging $3,400 per year); Federal Work-Study, scholarships/grants, and unspecified assistantships also available. Support available to part-time students. Financial award application deadline: 4/15; financial award applicants required to submit FAFSA. *Unit head:* Sharlene Cochrane, Director, 617-349-8477, E-mail: cochrane@lesley.edu. *Application contact:* Lisa Lombardi, Assistant Director, Advising and Student Services, 617-349-8454, E-mail: lombardi@lesley.edu.

National-Louis University, College of Arts and Sciences, Program in Psychology, Chicago, IL 60603. Offers cultural psychology (MA); health psychology (MA); human development (MA); organizational psychology (MA); psychology (Certificate). Part-time and evening/weekend programs available. *Students:* 37 full-time (33 women), 147 part-time (127 women); includes 99 minority (79 African Americans, 1 American Indian/Alaska Native, 6 Asian Americans or Pacific Islanders, 13 Hispanic Americans). Average age 38. *Degree requirements:* For master's, thesis, internship (health psychology). *Entrance requirements:* For master's, GRE, MAT, or Watson-Glaser Critical Thinking Appraisal, interview, minimum GPA of 3.0; for Certificate, GRE, MAT, or Watson-Glaser Critical Thinking Appraisal, interview, minimum GPA of 3.0, undergraduate course work in psychology. *Application deadline:* Applications are processed on a rolling basis. *Expenses:* Tuition: Full-time $18,900; part-time $630 per credit hour. Required fees: $20 per term. One-time fee: $40 part-time. Tuition and fees vary according to course load, campus/location and program. *Financial support:* Federal Work-Study, institutionally sponsored loans, scholarships/grants, and tuition waivers available. Support available to part-time students. Financial award applicants required to submit FAFSA. *Faculty research:* Human development, personality theory, abnormal psychology. *Unit head:* Dr. Edward Risinger, Professor, 224-233-2533, Fax: 224-233-2533, E-mail: erisinger@nl.edu. *Application contact:* David McCulloch, Vice President for University Services, 800-443-5522 Ext. 5151, Fax: 847-465-0593, E-mail: dmcc@wheeling1.nl.edu.

North Dakota State University, College of Graduate and Interdisciplinary Studies, College of Science and Mathematics, Department of Psychology, Fargo, ND 58105. Offers clinical psychology (MS); cognitive and visual neuroscience (PhD); health and social psychology (PhD); psychology (MS). *Faculty:* 18 full-time (4 women), 2 part-time/adjunct (1 woman). *Students:* 36 full-time (27 women); includes 4 minority (1 African American, 2 Asian Americans or Pacific Islanders, 1 Hispanic American), 1 international. Average age 24. 48 applicants, 33% accepted, 10 enrolled. In 2007, 3 master's, 1 doctorate awarded. *Degree requirements:* For master's, thesis; for doctorate, thesis/dissertation. *Entrance requirements:* For master's and doctorate, GRE General Test, GRE Subject Test. Additional exam requirements/recommendations for international students: Required—TOEFL (minimum score 525 paper-based; 197 computer-based; 71 iBT). *Application deadline:* For fall admission, 3/1 for domestic and international students. Application fee: $45 ($60 for international students). Electronic applications accepted. *Expenses:* Tuition, state resident: full-time $5,376; part-time $224 per credit. Tuition, nonresident: full-time $14,354; part-time $598 per credit. Required fees: $962; $40 per credit. Part-time tuition and fees vary according to course load and reciprocity agreements. *Financial support:* In 2007–08, 36 students received support, including 2 fellowships with full tuition reimbursements available (averaging $16,000 per year), 23 research assistantships with full tuition reimbursements available (averaging $16,000 per year), 11 teaching assistantships with full tuition reimbursements available (averaging $6,000 per year); career-related internships or fieldwork, Federal Work-Study, institutionally sponsored loans, tuition waivers (full and partial), and unspecified assistantships also available. Support available to part-time students. Financial award application deadline: 3/1. *Faculty research:* Cognition science, neuropsychology, group behavior, applied behavior analysis, behavior therapy. Total annual research expenditures: $2 million. *Unit head:* Dr. Paul D. Rokke, Chair, 701-231-8622, Fax: 701-231-8426, E-mail: paul.rokke@ndsu.edu.

Northern Arizona University, Graduate College, College of Social and Behavioral Sciences, Department of Psychology, Flagstaff, AZ 86011. Offers applied health psychology (MA); general (MA). Part-time programs available. *Degree requirements:* For master's, thesis, oral defense. *Entrance requirements:* For master's, GRE General Test.

Northern Kentucky University, Office of Graduate Programs, College of Arts and Sciences, Program in Industrial-Organizational Psychology, Highland Heights, KY 41099. Offers industrial psychology (Certificate); industrial-organizational psychology (MSIO); occupational health psychology (Certificate); organizational psychology (Certificate). Part-time and evening/weekend programs available. *Faculty:* 4 full-time (1 woman), 3 part-time/adjunct (1 woman). *Students:* 20 full-time (16 women), 30 part-time (20 women); includes 6 minority (3 African Americans, 2 Asian Americans or Pacific Islanders, 1 Hispanic American), 1 international. Average age 29. 36 applicants, 39% accepted, 13 enrolled. In 2007, 7 degrees awarded. *Degree requirements:* For master's, thesis optional. *Entrance requirements:* For master's, GRE, minimum GPA of 3.0, at least 9 semester hours of undergraduate psychology, 1 course in statistics. Additional exam requirements/recommendations for international students: Required—TOEFL (minimum score 550 paper-based; 213 computer-based; 79 iBT), Michigan English Language Assessment Battery (must be taken at NKU). *Application deadline:* For fall admission, 6/1 priority date for domestic students, 6/1 for international students; for spring admission, 11/1 priority date for domestic students, 10/1 for international students. Application fee: $40. Electronic applications accepted. *Financial support:* Unspecified assistantships available. *Faculty research:* Bullying in the workplace, consumer and social dilemma research, self efficiency and goal orientations. *Unit head:* Dr. Jeffrey Smith, Director, 859-572-5317, Fax: 859-572-6085, E-mail: smithj@nku.edu. *Application contact:* Dr. Peg Griffin, Director of Graduate Programs, 859-572-1555, Fax: 859-572-6670, E-mail: gradprog@nku.edu.

Philadelphia College of Osteopathic Medicine, Graduate and Professional Programs, Department of Psychology, Philadelphia, PA 19131-1694. Offers clinical psychology (Psy D); counseling and clinical health psychology (MS); organizational leadership and development (MS); psychology (Certificate); school psychology (MS, Psy D, Ed S). *Accreditation:* APA. *Degree requirements:* For master's, thesis; for doctorate, comprehensive exam, thesis/dissertation, final project, fieldwork. *Entrance requirements:* For master's, GRE or MAT, minimum GPA of 3.0; course work in biology, chemistry, English, physics; for other advanced degree, PRAXIS. *Faculty research:* Depression in primary care, integrated primary care, geriatric mental health.

See Close-Up on page 1469.

Rutgers, The State University of New Jersey, New Brunswick, Graduate School, Program in Psychology, New Brunswick, NJ 08901-1281. Offers behavioral neuroscience (PhD); clinical psychology (PhD); cognitive psychology (PhD); interdisciplinary health psychology (PhD); social psychology (PhD). *Accreditation:* APA. *Degree requirements:* For doctorate, thesis/dissertation. *Entrance requirements:* For doctorate, GRE General Test, 3 letters of recommendation. Additional exam requirements/recommendations for international students: Required—TOEFL (minimum score 577 paper-based; 233 computer-based). Electronic applications accepted. *Faculty research:* Learning and memory, behavioral ecology, hormones and behavior, psychopharmacology, anxiety disorders.

San Diego State University, Graduate and Research Affairs, College of Health and Human Services, Graduate School of Public Health, San Diego, CA 92182. Offers environmental health (MPH); epidemiology (MPH, PhD), including biostatistics (MPH); global emergency preparedness and response (MS); global health (PhD); health behavior (PhD); health promotion (MPH); health services administration (MPH); toxicology (MS); MPH/MA; MSW/MPH. *Accreditation:* ABET (one or more programs are accredited); CAHME (one or more programs are accredited); CEPH (one or more programs are accredited). Part-time programs available. *Faculty:* 30 full-time (14 women), 99 part-time/adjunct (44 women). *Students:* 274 full-time (204 women), 94 part-time (70 women); includes 131 minority (23 African Americans, 1 American Indian/Alaska Native, 59 Asian Americans or Pacific Islanders, 48 Hispanic Americans), 41 international. 517 applicants, 59% accepted, 109 enrolled. In 2007, 103 master's, 6 doctorates awarded. *Degree requirements:* For master's, comprehensive exam (for some programs), thesis (for some programs); for doctorate, thesis/dissertation. *Entrance requirements:* For master's, GMAT (health services administration MPH), GRE General Test; for doctorate, GRE General Test. Additional exam requirements/recommendations for international students: Required—TOEFL. *Application deadline:* For fall admission, 5/1 for domestic and international students; for spring admission, 11/1 for domestic students, 10/1 for international students. Applications are processed on a rolling basis. Application fee: $55. *Financial support:* Research assistantships, teaching assistantships, career-related internships or fieldwork, Federal Work-Study, and traineeships available. Financial award applicants required to submit FAFSA. *Faculty research:* Evaluation of tobacco, AIDS prevalence and prevention, mammography, infant death project, Alzheimer's in elderly Chinese. *Unit head:* Dr. Carleen Stoskopf, Director, 619-594-6317. *Application contact:* Brenda Fass-Holmes, Coordinator, Admissions and Student Affairs, 619-594-6317, E-mail: brenda.fass-holmes@sdsu.edu.

Saybrook Graduate School and Research Center, Programs in Psychology, Human Science and Organizational Systems, San Francisco, CA 94111-1920. Offers clinical psychology (PhD); creativity studies (MA); human science (MA, PhD), including consciousness and spirituality, individualized (PhD), integrative health studies, organizational systems, social transformation; marriage and family therapy (MA); organizational systems (MA, PhD), including individualized (PhD), organizational systems; psychology (MA, PhD), including consciousness and spirituality, humanistic and transpersonal psychology, individualized (PhD), integrative health studies, licensure track (MA), organizational systems, social transformation. Postbaccalaureate distance learning degree programs offered (minimal on-campus study). Terminal master's awarded for partial completion of doctoral program. *Degree requirements:* For master's, thesis or alternative; for doctorate, thesis/dissertation. Electronic applications accepted. *Faculty research:* Humanistic theory, health studies, organizational systems, consciousness and spirituality, social transformation.

Southwestern College, Program in Integral Somatic Psychology, Santa Fe, NM 87502-4788. Offers Certificate. *Faculty:* 1 (woman) full-time. *Students:* 9 applicants, 100% accepted, 9 enrolled. *Entrance requirements:* For degree, applic, & certificate refeence program interview. Application fee: $25. *Expenses:* Tuition: Full-time $16,416.

Stony Brook University, State University of New York, Graduate School, College of Arts and Sciences, Department of Psychology, Program in Social and Health Psychology, Stony Brook, NY 11794. Offers PhD. *Students:* 30 full-time (26 women); includes 4 minority (1 Asian American or Pacific Islander, 3 Hispanic Americans), 4 international. Average age 28. 74 applicants, 11% accepted. In 2007, 3 degrees awarded. *Degree requirements:* For doctorate, thesis/dissertation. *Entrance requirements:* For doctorate, GRE General Test, GRE Subject Test. Additional exam requirements/recommendations for international students: Required—TOEFL. *Application deadline:* For fall admission, 1/15 for domestic students. Application fee: $60. *Unit head:* Dr. Marci Lobel, Head, 631-632-7651, E-mail: marci.lobel@stonybrook.edu.

See Close-Up on page 1499.

Texas State University–San Marcos, Graduate School, College of Liberal Arts, Department of Psychology, San Marcos, TX 78666. Offers health psychology (MA). *Faculty:* 6 full-time (2 women), 1 part-time/adjunct (0 women). *Students:* 29 full-time (22 women), 5 part-time (2 women); includes 8 minority (2 African Americans, 6 Hispanic Americans), 3 international. Average age 28. 35 applicants, 91% accepted, 21 enrolled. In 2007, 10 degrees awarded. *Degree requirements:* For master's, thesis, 450 hours of practicum courses. *Entrance requirements:* For master's, GRE General Test, minimum GPA of 3.0 in last 60 hours and in psychology, 3 letters of rec, 3.0 GPA in psy core courses, statement of purpose. Additional exam requirements/recommendations for international students: Required—TOEFL (minimum score 550 paper-based; 213 computer-based). *Application deadline:* For fall admission, 3/15 for domestic and international students. Applications are processed on a rolling basis. Application fee: $40 ($90 for international students). Electronic applications accepted. *Expenses:* Tuition, state resident: full-time $3,780; part-time $210 per credit hour. Tuition, nonresident: full-time $8,784; part-time $488 per credit hour. Required fees: $493 per semester. Full-time tuition and fees vary according to course load. *Financial support:* In 2007–08, 29 students received support, including 1 research assistantship (averaging $4,928 per year), 7 teaching assistantships (averaging $3,444 per year). Financial award application deadline: 4/1. *Unit head:* Dr. Francisco Barrios, Chair, 512-245-2526, Fax: 512-245-3153, E-mail: fb12@txstate.edu.

The University of British Columbia, Faculty of Arts and Faculty of Graduate Studies, Department of Psychology, Vancouver, BC V6T 1Z1, Canada. Offers behavioral neuroscience (MA, PhD); clinical psychology (MA, PhD); cognitive science (MA, PhD); developmental psychology (MA, PhD); forensic psychology (PhD); health psychology (MA, PhD); quantitative methods (MA, PhD); social/personality psychology (MA, PhD). *Accreditation:* APA (one or more programs are accredited). *Faculty:* 46 full-time (20 women), 26 part-time/adjunct (13 women). *Students:* 102 full-time (69 women). Average age 29. 247 applicants, 14% accepted, 18 enrolled. In 2007, 14 master's, 11 doctorates awarded. Terminal master's awarded for partial completion of doctoral program. *Median time to degree:* Of those who began their doctoral program in fall 1999, 91% received their degree in 8 years or less. *Degree requirements:* For master's, thesis; for doctorate, comprehensive exam, thesis/dissertation. *Entrance requirements:* For master's and doctorate, GRE General Test, GRE Subject Test. Additional exam requirements/recommendations for international students: Required—TOEFL (minimum score 550 paper-based; 230 computer-based; 80 iBT). *Application deadline:* For fall admission, 1/15 for domestic and international students. Applications are processed on a rolling basis. Application fee: $90 Canadian dollars ($150 Canadian dollars for international students). Electronic applications accepted. *Financial support:* In 2007–08, 95 students received support, including 27 fellowships with full and partial tuition reimbursements available (averaging $16,500 per year), 50 research assistantships with full and partial tuition reimbursements available (averaging $6,775 per year), 80 teaching assistantships with full and partial tuition reimbursements available (averaging $8,065 per year); career-related internships or fieldwork, Federal Work-Study, institutionally sponsored loans, scholarships/grants, health care benefits, tuition waivers (full and partial), and unspecified assistantships also available. Financial award application deadline: 1/15. *Faculty research:* Clinical, developmental, social/personality, cognition, behavioral neuroscience. Total annual research expenditures: $5.5 million Canadian dollars. *Unit head:* Dr. Eric Eich, Head, 604-822-3078, Fax: 604-822-6923, E-mail: ee@psych.ubc.ca. *Application contact:* Rose Tam, Graduate Secretary, 604-822-3144, Fax: 604-822-6923, E-mail: gradsec@psych.ubc.ca.

University of Connecticut, Graduate School, College of Liberal Arts and Sciences, Department of Psychology, Field of Psychology, Storrs, CT 06269. Offers behavioral neuroscience (PhD); biopsychology (PhD); clinical psychology (MA, PhD); cognition and instruction (PhD); developmental psychology (MA, PhD); ecological psychology (PhD); experimental psychology (PhD); general psychology (MA, PhD); health psychology (Graduate Certificate); industrial/organizational psychology (PhD); language and cognition (PhD); neuroscience (PhD); occupational health psychology (Graduate Certificate); social psychology (MA, PhD). *Accreditation:* APA (one or more programs are accredited). *Faculty:* 52 full-time (23 women). *Students:* 130 full-time (94 women), 25 part-time (11 women); includes 24 minority (8 African Americans, 6 Asian Americans or Pacific Islanders, 10 Hispanic Americans), 18 international. Average age 28. 531 applicants, 7% accepted, 35 enrolled. In 2007, 19 master's, 20 doctorates, 2 other advanced degrees awarded. Terminal master's awarded for partial completion of doctoral program. *Degree requirements:* For master's, comprehensive exam; for doctorate, thesis/dissertation. *Entrance requirements:* For master's and doctorate, GRE General Test, GRE Subject Test. Additional exam requirements/recommendations for international students: Required—TOEFL (minimum score 550 paper-based; 213 computer-based). *Application deadline:* For fall admission, 2/1 priority date for domestic and international students; for spring admission, 11/1 for domestic students, 10/1 for international students. Applications are processed on a rolling basis. Application fee: $55. Electronic applications accepted. *Expenses:* Tuition, state resident: part-time $469 per credit hour. Tuition, nonresident: part-time $1,218 per credit hour. *Financial support:* In 2007–08, 54 research assistantships with full tuition reimbursements, 69 teaching assistantships with full tuition reimbursements were awarded; fellowships, career-related internships or fieldwork, Federal Work-Study, scholarships/grants, health care benefits, and unspecified assistantships also available. Financial award application deadline: 2/1; financial award applicants required to submit FAFSA. *Application contact:* Deborah Doucette, Administrative Assistant, 860-486-2057, Fax: 860-486-2760, E-mail: futuregr@psych.psy.uconn.edu.

University of Florida, Graduate School, College of Public Health and Health Professions, Department of Clinical and Health Psychology, Gainesville, FL 32611. Offers PhD. *Accreditation:* APA. *Faculty:* 19 full-time (10 women), 1 part-time/adjunct (0 women). *Students:* 87 (69 women); includes 14 minority (5 African Americans, 6 Asian Americans or Pacific Islanders, 3 Hispanic Americans) 4 international. In 2007, 9 doctorates awarded. *Degree requirements:* For doctorate, thesis/dissertation. *Entrance requirements:* For doctorate, GRE General Test, minimum GPA of 3.0. Additional exam requirements/recommendations for international students: Required—TOEFL (minimum score 550 paper-based; 213 computer-based). *Application deadline:* For fall admission, 12/1 for domestic students. Application fee: $30. Electronic applications accepted. *Expenses:* Tuition, state resident: full-time $7,478. Tuition, nonresident: full-time $22,603. *Financial support:* In 2007–08, 53 research assistantships with partial tuition reimbursements (averaging $10,164 per year) were awarded; fellowships with partial tuition reimbursements, teaching assistantships with partial tuition reimbursements, career-related internships or fieldwork, Federal Work-Study, institutionally sponsored loans, scholarships/grants, and unspecified assistantships also available. Financial award application deadline: 12/1. *Faculty research:* Child psychology, pediatric psychology, health/medical psychology, neuropsychology. *Unit head:* Dr. Ronald H. Rozensky, Chair, 352-273-6033, Fax: 352-273-6156, E-mail: rrozensky@phhp.ufl.edu. *Application contact:* Dr. Russell M. Bauer, Coordinator, 352-273-6455, Fax: 352-273-6156, E-mail: rbauer@phhp.ufl.edu.

University of Michigan–Dearborn, College of Arts, Sciences, and Letters, Department of Behavioral Sciences, Dearborn, MI 48128-1491. Offers clinical health psychology (MS); health psychology (MS). Part-time programs available. *Faculty:* 8 full-time (4 women), 1 part-time/adjunct (0 women). *Students:* 15 full-time (11 women), 13 part-time (10 women); includes 9 minority (2 African Americans, 1 American Indian/Alaska Native, 4 Asian Americans or Pacific Islanders, 2 Hispanic Americans). Average age 34. 57 applicants, 35% accepted, 16 enrolled. In 2007, 9 degrees awarded. *Degree requirements:* For master's, thesis or alternative, oral defense of thesis. *Entrance requirements:* For master's, GRE, 3 letters of recommendation, statement of purpose. Additional exam requirements/recommendations for international students: Required—TOEFL (minimum score 560 paper-based; 220 computer-based). *Application deadline:* For fall admission, 3/15 for domestic and international students. Application fee: $60 ($75 for international students). *Expenses:* Tuition, state resident: part-time $318 per credit hour. Tuition, nonresident: part-time $722 per credit hour. Tuition and fees vary according to course load and program. *Financial support:* In 2007–08, 4 students received support. Scholarships/grants available. *Faculty research:* Cardiovascular reactivity, coping, addiction, psychoneuroimmunology. *Unit head:* Dr. Pam McAuslan, Program Director, 313-593-5376, E-mail: pmcausla@umd.umich.edu. *Application contact:* Carol Ligienza, Administrative Coordinator, CASL Graduate Programs, 313-593-1183, Fax: 313-583-6498, E-mail: caslgrad@umd.umich.edu.

The University of North Carolina at Charlotte, Graduate School, College of Arts and Sciences, Department of Psychology, Program in Health Psychology, Charlotte, NC 28223-0001. Offers PhD. *Students:* 20 full-time (16 women), 1 (woman) part-time; includes 1 African American, 2 Hispanic Americans. Average age 29. 35 applicants, 23% accepted, 7 enrolled. *Entrance requirements:* For doctorate, GRE, minimum GPA of 3.0 in undergraduate major. Additional exam requirements/recommendations for international students: Required—TOEFL (minimum score 557 paper-based; 220 computer-based). *Application deadline:* For fall admission, 12/1 for domestic and international students. Application fee: $55. *Expenses:* Tuition, state resident: full-time $2,855. Tuition, nonresident: full-time $13,062. Required fees: $1,692. *Financial support:* In 2007–08, 14 research assistantships (averaging $12,179 per year), 5 teaching assistantships (averaging $9,000 per year) were awarded; fellowships, career-related internships or fieldwork, Federal Work-Study, institutionally sponsored loans, scholarships/grants, and unspecified assistantships also available. Support available to part-time students. Financial award application deadline: 4/1; financial award applicants required to submit FAFSA. *Unit head:* Dr. Art W. Blume, IV, Director, 704-687-4789, Fax: 704-687-3096, E-mail: awblume@email.uncc.edu. *Application contact:* Kathy B. Giddings, Director of Graduate Admissions, 704-687-3366, Fax: 704-687-3279, E-mail: agidding@uncc.edu.

University of North Texas, Robert B. Toulouse School of Graduate Studies, College of Arts and Sciences, Department of Psychology, Denton, TX 76203. Offers clinical psychology (PhD); counseling psychology (MA, MS, PhD); experimental psychology (MA, MS, PhD); health psychology and behavioral medicine (PhD). *Accreditation:* APA (one or more programs are accredited). *Faculty:* 26 full-time (8 women). *Students:* 101 full-time (74 women), 105 part-time (77 women); includes 27 minority (8 African Americans, 1 American Indian/Alaska Native, 5 Asian Americans or Pacific Islanders, 13 Hispanic Americans), 7 international. Average age 29. 472 applicants, 9% accepted, 36 enrolled. In 2007, 28 master's, 23 doctorates awarded. Terminal master's awarded for partial completion of doctoral program. *Degree requirements:* For master's, comprehensive exam, thesis or alternative; for doctorate, one foreign language, comprehensive exam, thesis/dissertation. *Entrance requirements:* For master's and doctorate, GRE General Test, interview. Additional exam requirements/recommendations for international students: Required—proof of English language proficiency required for non-native English speakers; Recommended—TOEFL (minimum score 550 paper-based; 213 computer-based). *Application deadline:* For fall admission, 7/15 for domestic students; for spring admission, 11/15 for domestic students. Application fee: $50 ($75 for

Health Psychology

University of North Texas (continued)
international students). *Financial support:* In 2007–08, 2 fellowships (averaging $20,000 per year), 18 research assistantships (averaging $9,000 per year), 38 teaching assistantships (averaging $9,000 per year) were awarded; career-related internships or fieldwork, Federal Work-Study, and institutionally sponsored loans also available. Financial award application deadline: 8/1. *Faculty research:* Very broad range of topics and approaches. *Unit head:* Dr. Linda Marshall, Chair, 940-565-2339, Fax: 940-546-4682, E-mail: psychair@unt.edu. *Application contact:* Amy Mayfield, Graduate Coordinator, 940-565-2671, Fax: 940-565-4682, E-mail: amym@unt.edu.

The University of Texas at Arlington, Graduate School, College of Science, Department of Psychology, Arlington, TX 76019. Offers experimental psychology (PhD); health psychology (PhD); psychology (MS). Part-time programs available. *Faculty:* 8 full-time (2 women), 1 (woman) part-time/adjunct. *Students:* 60 full-time (45 women), 6 part-time (4 women); includes 8 minority (2 African Americans, 1 Asian American or Pacific Islander, 5 Hispanic Americans), 18 international. 51 applicants, 29% accepted, 17 enrolled. In 2007, 13 master's, 3 doctorates awarded. Terminal master's awarded for partial completion of doctoral program. *Median time to degree:* Of those who began their doctoral program in fall 1999, 100% received their degree in 8 years or less. *Degree requirements:* For master's, comprehensive exam or thesis; for doctorate, thesis/dissertation (for some programs). *Entrance requirements:* For master's and doctorate, GRE General Test, minimum GPA of 3.0 in last 60 hours of course work. Additional exam requirements/recommendations for international students: Required—TOEFL (minimum score 550 paper-based; 213 computer-based). *Application deadline:* For fall admission, 6/16 for domestic students. Applications are processed on a rolling basis. Application fee: $35 ($50 for international students). *Expenses:* Tuition, state resident: full-time $5,934. Tuition, nonresident: full-time $10,938. *Financial support:* In 2007–08, 4 fellowships (averaging $1,000 per year), 2 research assistantships with tuition reimbursements (averaging $15,000 per year), 28 teaching assistantships with tuition reimbursements (averaging $15,000 per year) were awarded; career-related internships or fieldwork, Federal Work-Study, institutionally sponsored loans, scholarships/grants, traineeships, tuition waivers (partial), and unspecified assistantships also available. Financial award application deadline: 6/1; financial award applicants required to submit FAFSA. *Unit head:* Dr. Robert Gatchel, Chair, 817-272-2281, Fax: 817-272-2364, E-mail: gatchel@uta.edu. *Application contact:* Dr. Jared Kenworthy, Graduate Advisor, 817-272-2281, Fax: 817-272-2364, E-mail: kenworthy@uta.edu.

University of the Sciences in Philadelphia, College of Graduate Studies, Program in Health Psychology, Philadelphia, PA 19104-4495. Offers MS. *Faculty:* 7 full-time (2 women), 1 (woman) part-time/adjunct. *Students:* 14 full-time (13 women), 11 part-time (8 women); includes 4 minority (1 African American, 2 Asian Americans or Pacific Islanders, 1 Hispanic American), 1 international. Average age 25. In 2007, 8 degrees awarded. *Entrance requirements:* For master's, bachelor's degree in related field, minimum GPA of 3.0 in major. Additional exam requirements/recommendations for international students: Required—TOEFL, TWE. *Application deadline:* For fall admission, 5/1 for international students; for winter admission, 10/1 for international students; for spring admission, 3/1 for international students. Applications are processed on a rolling basis. Application fee: $50. *Expenses: Contact institution. Financial support:* In 2007–08, 9 students received support, including 3 fellowships (averaging $3,080 per year), 1 research assistantship; tuition waivers (partial) also available. Financial award application deadline: 5/1. *Faculty research:* Stress and immune system, women's health and breast cancer, memory, health care policy. *Unit head:* Dr. Philip Gehrman, Acting Program Director, 215-596-8517, E-mail: pgehrma@usp.edu. *Application contact:* Joyce D'Angelo, Administrative Assistant, 215-596-8937, E-mail: j.dangel@usp.edu.

Walden University, Graduate Programs, School of Psychology, Minneapolis, MN 55401. Offers clinical assessment (Post-Doctoral Certificate); clinical child psychology (Post-Doctoral Certificate); clinical psychology (PhD, Post-Doctoral Certificate); counseling psychology (PhD, Post-Doctoral Certificate); general psychology (MS, PhD, Post-Doctoral Certificate); health psychology (PhD, Post-Doctoral Certificate); organizational psychology (PhD, Post-Doctoral Certificate); organizational psychology and development (MS); school psychology (PhD, Post-Doctoral Certificate); teaching online (Post-Doctoral Certificate). Part-time and evening/weekend programs available. Postbaccalaureate distance learning degree programs offered (minimal on-campus study). *Students:* 1,428 full-time (1,130 women), 1,933 part-time (1,483 women); includes 959 minority (737 African Americans, 35 American Indian/Alaska Native, 53 Asian Americans or Pacific Islanders, 134 Hispanic Americans), 39 international. Average age 40. 1,254 applicants, 75% accepted, 548 enrolled. In 2007, 182 master's, 43 doctorates awarded. *Degree requirements:* For master's, thesis; for doctorate, thesis/dissertation, brief dispersed residency sessions. *Entrance requirements:* For master's, minimum GPA of 3.0; for doctorate, 3 years of professional experience, master's degree; for Post-Doctoral Certificate, PhD in related field, 3 years of professional experience. Additional exam requirements/recommendations for international students: Required—TOEFL (minimum score 550 paper-based; 213 computer-based), IELTS (minimum score 7). *Application deadline:* For fall admission, 8/15 priority date for domestic and international students; for winter admission, 11/15 priority date for domestic and international students; for spring admission, 12/15 priority date for domestic and international students. Applications are processed on a rolling basis. Application fee: $50. Electronic applications accepted. *Financial support:* Fellowships with partial tuition reimbursements, career-related internships or fieldwork, Federal Work-Study, institutionally sponsored loans, scholarships/grants, tuition waivers (partial), and unspecified assistantships available. Support available to part-time students. Financial award applicants required to submit FAFSA. *Faculty research:* Clinical psychology, organizational psychology, forensic psychology, group processes, educational psychology. *Unit head:* Dr. Nina Nabors, Associate Dean, 800-925-3368. *Application contact:* 866-4-WALDEN, Fax: 410-843-8780, E-mail: request@waldenu.edu.

West Chester University of Pennsylvania, Office of Graduate Studies and Extended Education, College of Health Sciences, Department of Health, West Chester, PA 19383. Offers emergency preparedness (Certificate); gerontology (MS); health care administration (Certificate); integrative health (Certificate); public health (MPH, MS); school health (M Ed). *Accreditation:* CEPH.Part-time and evening/weekend programs available. *Students:* 47 full-time (23 women), 65 part-time (48 women); includes 20 minority (18 African Americans, 2 Asian Americans or Pacific Islanders), 26 international. Average age 30. 120 applicants, 95% accepted, 38 enrolled. In 2007, 58 degrees awarded. *Degree requirements:* For master's, comprehensive exam, thesis (for some programs). *Entrance requirements:* For master's, GRE. Additional exam requirements/recommendations for international students: Required—TOEFL (minimum score 550 paper-based; 213 computer-based; 80 iBT). *Application deadline:* For fall admission, 4/15 priority date for domestic students; for spring admission, 10/15 for domestic students. Applications are processed on a rolling basis. Application fee: $35. *Expenses:* Tuition, state resident: part-time $345 per credit. Tuition, nonresident: part-time $552 per credit. Tuition and fees vary according to course load. *Financial support:* In 2007–08, 10 research assistantships with full and partial tuition reimbursements (averaging $5,000 per year) were awarded; unspecified assistantships also available. Support available to part-time students. Financial award application deadline: 2/15; financial award applicants required to submit FAFSA. *Faculty research:* HIV/AIDS education, teacher preparation, water quality. *Unit head:* Dr. Roger Mustalish, Chair, 610-436-2931, E-mail: rmustalish@wcupa.edu. *Application contact:* Dr. Bethann Cinelli, Graduate Coordinator, 610-436-2267, E-mail: bcinelli@wcupa.edu.

Yeshiva University, Ferkauf Graduate School of Psychology, Program in Clinical Health Psychology, New York, NY 10033-3201. Offers PhD. *Accreditation:* APA. Part-time programs available. *Degree requirements:* For doctorate, comprehensive exam, thesis/dissertation. *Entrance requirements:* For doctorate, GRE General Test. *Faculty research:* Dieting, substance abuse, adolescent depression and suicide, cancer research, MS research.

Human Development

Argosy University, Chicago, College of Psychology and Behavioral Sciences, Doctoral Program in Clinical Psychology, Chicago, IL 60654. Offers child and adolescent psychology (Psy D); client-centered and experiential psychotherapies (Psy D); diversity and multicultural psychology (Psy D); family psychology (Psy D); forensic psychology (Psy D); health psychology (Psy D); psychoanalytic psychology (Psy D); psychology and spirituality (Psy D). *Accreditation:* APA.

See Close-Up on page 1379.

Arizona State University, Graduate College, College of Liberal Arts and Sciences, Division of Social Sciences, Department of Family and Human Development, Tempe, AZ 85287. Offers family and human development (MS); family science (PhD). *Degree requirements:* For master's, thesis or alternative; for doctorate, thesis/dissertation. *Entrance requirements:* For master's and doctorate, GRE.

Auburn University, Graduate School, College of Human Sciences, Department of Human Development and Family Studies, Auburn University, AL 36849. Offers MS, PhD. *Accreditation:* AAMFT/COAMFTE (one or more programs are accredited). Part-time programs available. *Faculty:* 12 full-time (7 women). *Students:* 26 full-time (24 women), 20 part-time (18 women); includes 7 minority (4 African Americans, 3 Asian Americans or Pacific Islanders), 11 international. Average age 26. 49 applicants, 59% accepted, 15 enrolled. In 2007, 18 master's, 7 doctorates awarded. *Degree requirements:* For master's, thesis, oral exam; for doctorate, thesis/dissertation. *Entrance requirements:* For master's, GRE General Test; for doctorate, GRE General Test, master's degree. *Application deadline:* For fall admission, 7/7 for domestic students; for spring admission, 11/24 for domestic students. Applications are processed on a rolling basis. Application fee: $25 ($50 for international students). *Financial support:* Research assistantships, teaching assistantships, Federal Work-Study available. Support available to part-time students. Financial award application deadline: 3/15. *Faculty research:* Family influences on personality and social development, parent-child relations, infancy, day care, parent education. *Unit head:* Dr. Leanne K. Lamke, Head, 334-844-4151, E-mail: mbradbar@humsci.auburn.edu. *Application contact:* Dr. Joe Pittman, Interim Dean of the Graduate School, 334-844-4700.

Boston University, School of Education, Department of Literacy and Language, Counseling and Development, Program in Developmental Studies, Boston, MA 02215. Offers Ed M, Ed D, CAGS. *Students:* 12 full-time (10 women), 19 part-time (16 women); includes 2 minority (1 African American, 1 Hispanic American), 7 international. Average age 37. 53 applicants, 75% accepted. In 2007, 7 master's, 6 doctorates, 2 CAGSs awarded. *Degree requirements:* For doctorate, comprehensive exam, thesis/dissertation; for CAGS, comprehensive exam. *Entrance requirements:* For master's, doctorate, and CAGS, GRE General Test or MAT. Additional exam requirements/recommendations for international students: Required—TOEFL. *Application deadline:* For fall admission, 2/15 priority date for domestic students; for winter admission, 10/1 priority date for domestic students. Applications are processed on a rolling basis. Application fee: $70. Electronic applications accepted. *Expenses:* Tuition: Full-time $34,930; part-time $1,092 per credit. Tuition and fees vary according to class time, course level and program. *Financial support:* Application deadline: 2/15. *Faculty research:* Moral development, social and cognitive development, language and literacy development, cross-cultural development. *Unit head:* Dr. Deborah Youngman, Coordinator, 617-353-7107, E-mail: drdjy@bu.edu. *Application contact:* 617-353-4237, Fax: 617-353-8937, E-mail: sedgrad@bu.edu.

Bowling Green State University, Graduate College, College of Education and Human Development, School of Family and Consumer Sciences, Bowling Green, OH 43403. Offers food and nutrition (MFCS); human development and family studies (MFCS). Part-time programs available. *Faculty:* 20 full-time (15 women), 4 part-time/adjunct (2 women). *Students:* 10 full-time (8 women), 23 part-time (all women); includes 4 minority (all Hispanic Americans), 2 international. Average age 28. 29 applicants, 69% accepted, 20 enrolled. In 2007, 4 degrees awarded. *Degree requirements:* For master's, thesis. *Entrance requirements:* For master's, GRE General Test, minimum GPA of 3.0. Additional exam requirements/recommendations for international students: Required—TOEFL. *Application deadline:* For fall admission, 3/1 priority date for domestic students. Application fee: $30. Electronic applications accepted. *Financial support:* In 2007–08, 1 research assistantship with full tuition reimbursement (averaging $8,404 per year), 9 teaching assistantships with full tuition reimbursements (averaging $7,089 per year) were awarded; career-related internships or fieldwork and unspecified assistantships also available. Financial award applicants required to submit FAFSA. *Faculty research:* Public health, wellness, social issues and policies, ethnic foods, nutrition and aging. *Unit head:* Dr. Deborah Wooldridge, Director, 419-372-7823. *Application contact:* Dr. Dawn Anderson, Graduate Coordinator, 419-372-8090.

Bradley University, Graduate School, College of Education and Health Sciences, Department of Educational Leadership and Human Development, Peoria, IL 61625-0002. Offers human development counseling (MA), including community and agency counseling, school counseling; leadership in educational administration (MA); leadership in human service administration (MA). *Accreditation:* ACA; NCATE. Part-time and evening/weekend programs available. *Students:* 27 full-time (20 women), 95 part-time (68 women); includes 7 minority (6 Asian Americans or Pacific Islanders, 1 Hispanic American), 1 international. 46 applicants, 80% accepted, 34 enrolled. In 2007, 42 degrees awarded. *Degree requirements:* For master's, comprehensive exam, thesis optional. *Entrance requirements:* For master's, GRE General Test or MAT, interview, 3 letters of recommendation. Additional exam requirements/recommendations for international students: Required—TOEFL (minimum score 550 paper-based; 213 computer-based; 79 iBT). *Application deadline:* For fall admission, 5/15 priority date for domestic and international students; for spring admission, 10/15 priority date for domestic and international students. Applications are processed on a rolling basis. Application fee: $40 ($50 for international students). *Financial support:* Research assistantships, scholarships/grants, tuition waivers (partial), and unspecified assistantships available. Financial award application deadline: 4/1. *Unit head:* Dr. Christopher Rybak, Chairperson, 309-677-3171, E-mail: cjr@bradley.edu.

Brigham Young University, Graduate Studies, College of Family, Home, and Social Sciences, Program in Marriage, Family and Human Development, Provo, UT 84602-1001. Offers MS, PhD. *Accreditation:* AAMFT/COAMFTE. *Faculty:* 24 full-time (5 women). *Students:* 28 full-time (19 women); includes 1 minority (Asian American or Pacific Islander), 2 international. Average age 28. 22 applicants, 36% accepted, 6 enrolled. In 2007, 4 master's awarded. *Degree requirements:* For master's, thesis; for doctorate, comprehensive exam, thesis/dissertation, 2 publishable papers. *Entrance requirements:* For master's and doctorate, GRE General Test, minimum GPA of 3.0 in last 60 semester hours, letters of recommendation. Additional exam requirements/recommendations for international students: Required—TOEFL (minimum score 580 paper-based; 237 computer-based; 85 iBT), IELTS (minimum score 7). *Application deadline:* For fall admission, 1/10 for domestic and international students.

Application fee: $50. Electronic applications accepted. *Financial support:* In 2007–08, 20 research assistantships with full and partial tuition reimbursements (averaging $5,096 per year), 5 teaching assistantships with full and partial tuition reimbursements (averaging $5,096 per year) were awarded; scholarships/grants and unspecified assistantships also available. Financial award application deadline: 1/10. *Faculty research:* Early childhood education, family process, family life education. *Unit head:* Dr. Richard Miller, Director, School of Life, 801-422-2069, Fax: 801-422-0230, E-mail: rick_miller@byu.edu.

Brock University, Faculty of Graduate Studies, Faculty of Social Sciences, Program in Psychology, St. Catharines, ON L2S 3A1, Canada. Offers behavioral neuroscience (MA, PhD); life span development (MA, PhD); social personality (MA, PhD). Part-time programs available. *Degree requirements:* For master's, thesis; for doctorate, thesis/dissertation. *Entrance requirements:* For master's, GRE, honors degree; for doctorate, GRE, master's degree. Additional exam requirements/recommendations for international students: Required—TOEFL (minimum score 550 paper-based; 213 computer-based; 80 iBT), IELTS (minimum score 7), TWE (minimum score 4). Electronic applications accepted. *Faculty research:* Social personality, behavioral neuroscience, life-span development.

California State University, San Bernardino, Graduate Studies, College of Social and Behavioral Sciences, Department of Psychology, Program in Child Development, San Bernardino, CA 92407-2397. Offers MA. *Students:* 17 full-time (14 women), 14 part-time (13 women); includes 10 minority (1 African American, 1 Asian American or Pacific Islander, 8 Hispanic Americans). Average age 27. 32 applicants, 44% accepted, 7 enrolled. In 2007, 6 degrees awarded. *Entrance requirements:* For master's, minimum GPA of 3.0 in major. *Application deadline:* For fall admission, 8/31 priority date for domestic students. Application fee: $55. *Unit head:* Dr. Sharon Ward, Head, 909-537-7304, E-mail: sward@csusb.edu. *Application contact:* Stacy Brooks, Graduate Secretary, 909-537-5570, Fax: 909-537-7003, E-mail: sbrooks@csusb.edu.

The Catholic University of America, School of Arts and Sciences, Department of Psychology, Program in Human Development, Washington, DC 20064. Offers PhD. *Degree requirements:* For doctorate, comprehensive exam, thesis/dissertation. *Entrance requirements:* For doctorate, GRE General Test, GRE Subject Test, 3 letters of recommendation. Additional exam requirements/recommendations for international students: Required—TOEFL (minimum score 580 paper-based; 237 computer-based). *Application deadline:* For fall admission, 2/1 priority date for domestic students; for spring admission, 11/15 priority date for domestic students. Applications are processed on a rolling basis. Application fee: $55. Electronic applications accepted. *Financial support:* Fellowships, research assistantships, teaching assistantships, career-related internships or fieldwork, Federal Work-Study, institutionally sponsored loans, scholarships/grants, and tuition waivers (full and partial) available. Support available to part-time students. Financial award application deadline: 2/1; financial award applicants required to submit FAFSA. *Faculty research:* Social interaction, adolescent development, social and intellectual development, adult development. *Unit head:* Dr. James E. Youniss, Director, 202-319-5750, Fax: 202-319-6263, E-mail: youniss@cua.edu.

Central Michigan University, College of Graduate Studies, College of Education and Human Services, Department of Human Environmental Studies, Mount Pleasant, MI 48859. Offers human development and family studies (MA); nutrition and dietetics (MS). *Degree requirements:* For master's, thesis or alternative. *Entrance requirements:* For master's, GRE (MA), minimum GPA of 3.0 in last 60 hours, 15 credits of course work in human development and family studies or related area (MA). *Faculty research:* Human growth and development, family studies and human sexuality, nutritional food science/food services, apparel and textile retailing, computer-aided design for apparel and interior design.

Claremont Graduate University, Graduate Programs, School of Educational Studies, Claremont, CA 91711-6160. Offers Africana education (Certificate); education and policy (MA, PhD); higher education/student affairs (MA, PhD); human development (MA, PhD); public school administration (MA, PhD); quantitative evaluation (MA, PhD); special education (MA, PhD); teacher education (MA); teaching and learning (MA, PhD); urban leadership (PhD); MBA/PhD. Part-time programs available. *Faculty:* 17 full-time (11 women), 22 part-time/adjunct (14 women). *Students:* 272 full-time (182 women), 172 part-time (115 women); includes 171 minority (39 African Americans, 1 American Indian/Alaska Native, 38 Asian Americans or Pacific Islanders, 93 Hispanic Americans), 8 international. Average age 37. In 2007, 79 master's, 28 doctorates awarded. Terminal master's awarded for partial completion of doctoral program. *Degree requirements:* For master's, comprehensive exam (for some programs), thesis or alternative; for doctorate, comprehensive exam, thesis/dissertation. *Entrance requirements:* For master's and doctorate, GRE General Test. *Application deadline:* For fall admission, 2/15 priority date for domestic students. Applications are processed on a rolling basis. Electronic applications accepted. *Expenses:* Tuition: Full-time $31,640; part-time $1,376 per unit. Required fees: $145 per semester. Tuition and fees vary according to course load, degree level and program. *Financial support:* Fellowships, research assistantships, Federal Work-Study and institutionally sponsored loans available. Support available to part-time students. Financial award application deadline: 2/15; financial award applicants required to submit FAFSA. *Faculty research:* Education administration, K–12 and higher education, multicultural education, education policy, diversity in higher education, faculty issues. *Unit head:* Barbara Hart, Interim Dean, 909-621-8317, Fax: 909-621-8734, E-mail: barbara.hart@cgu.edu. *Application contact:* Cece Gaddy, Administrative Director, 909-621-8317, Fax: 909-621-8734, E-mail: cece.gaddy@cgu.edu.

Clemson University, Graduate School, College of Health, Education, and Human Development, Program in Youth Development, Clemson, SC 29634. Offers MS. *Faculty:* 1 full-time (0 women). *Students:* 1 full-time (0 women), 29 part-time (17 women); includes 9 minority (8 African Americans, 1 Asian American or Pacific Islander). 9 applicants, 56% accepted, 3 enrolled. *Unit head:* Dr. William Quinn, Coordinator, 864-656-1501, Fax: 864-656-5488, E-mail: wquinn@clemson.edu.

Colorado State University, Graduate School, College of Applied Human Sciences, Department of Human Development and Family Studies, Fort Collins, CO 80523-0015. Offers MS. *Accreditation:* AAMFT/COAMFTE. Part-time programs available. *Faculty:* 13 full-time (9 women). *Students:* 21 full-time (20 women), 18 part-time (all women); includes 1 minority (Asian American or Pacific Islander), 2 international. Average age 32. 102 applicants, 27% accepted, 15 enrolled. In 2007, 8 degrees awarded. *Degree requirements:* For master's, thesis. *Entrance requirements:* For master's, GRE General Test, minimum GPA of 3.0; course work in human development, family studies, and statistics, letters of recommendation forms, additional departmental application, interview. Additional exam requirements/recommendations for international students: Required—TOEFL (minimum score 550 paper-based; 220 computer-based); Recommended—TWE. *Application deadline:* For fall admission, 1/15 for domestic and international students. Application fee: $50. Electronic applications accepted. *Expenses:* Tuition, state resident: full-time $4,887; part-time $272 per credit. Tuition, nonresident: full-time $16,425; part-time $913 per credit. Required fees: $1,379; $75 per credit. *Financial support:* In 2007–08, 12 students received support, including 2 research assistantships with partial tuition reimbursements available (averaging $8,915 per year), 12 teaching assistantships with partial tuition reimbursements available (averaging $8,420 per year); fellowships, career-related internships or fieldwork, Federal Work-Study, institutionally sponsored loans, scholarships/grants, and unspecified assistantships also available. Financial award application deadline: 1/15; financial award applicants required to submit FAFSA. *Faculty research:* Promoting resiliency and optimal development; gender, culture and diversity; intervention programming and evaluation; gerontology/aging. Total annual research expenditures: $733,061. *Unit head:* Dr. Lise Youngblade, Interim Department Head, 970-491-5558, Fax: 970-491-7975, E-mail: lise.youngblade@colostate.edu. *Application contact:* Dr. Karen C. Barrett, Graduate Chair, 970-491-7382, Fax: 970-491-7975, E-mail: barrett@cahs.colostate.edu.

Cornell University, Graduate School, Graduate Fields of Human Ecology, Field of Human Development, Ithaca, NY 14853-0001. Offers developmental psychology (PhD), including cognitive development, developmental psychopathology, ecology of human development, social and personality development; human development and family studies (PhD), including ecology of human development, family studies and the life course. *Faculty:* 35 full-time (12 women). *Students:* 29 full-time (22 women); includes 4 minority (2 Asian Americans or Pacific Islanders, 2 Hispanic Americans), 10 international. Average age 27. 63 applicants, 19% accepted, 5 enrolled. In 2007, 5 doctorates awarded. *Degree requirements:* For doctorate, comprehensive exam, thesis/dissertation, pre-doctoral research project, teaching experience. *Entrance requirements:* For doctorate, GRE General Test, 2 letters of recommendation. Additional exam requirements/recommendations for international students: Required—TOEFL (minimum score 550 paper-based; 213 computer-based; 77 iBT). *Application deadline:* For fall admission, 1/15 for domestic students. Application fee: $70. Electronic applications accepted. *Financial support:* In 2007–08, 28 students received support, including 6 fellowships with full tuition reimbursements available, 6 research assistantships with full tuition reimbursements available, 16 teaching assistantships with full tuition reimbursements available; institutionally sponsored loans, scholarships/grants, health care benefits, tuition waivers (full and partial), and unspecified assistantships also available. Financial award applicants required to submit FAFSA. *Faculty research:* Cognitive development, developmental psychopathology, ecology of human development, family studies and the life course, social and personality development. *Unit head:* Director of Graduate Studies, 607-255-3181, Fax: 607-255-9856. *Application contact:* Graduate Field Assistant, 607-255-3181, Fax: 607-255-9856, E-mail: hdfs@cornell.edu.

DePaul University, School of Education, Chicago, IL 60604-2287. Offers bilingual and bicultural education (M Ed, MA); curriculum studies (M Ed, MA); education (Ed D), including curriculum studies, educational leadership; educational leadership (M Ed, MA), including administration and supervision, Catholic school leadership, physical education; human development and learning (MA); human services and counseling (M Ed, MA), including agencies, family concerns, and higher education, elementary schools, human services management, secondary schools; reading and learning disabilities (M Ed, MA); social culture studies in education and development (M Ed, MA), including curriculum studies/development; teaching and learning (early childhood, elementary and secondary) (M Ed), including elementary education (M Ed, MA), secondary education (M Ed, MA); teaching and learning (early childhood, elementary, and secondary) (MA), including elementary education (M Ed, MA), secondary education (M Ed, MA). *Accreditation:* NCATE. Part-time and evening/weekend programs available. *Faculty:* 61 full-time (40 women), 76 part-time/adjunct (46 women). *Students:* 803 full-time (654 women), 379 part-time (287 women); includes 201 minority (81 African Americans, 3 American Indian/Alaska Native, 43 Asian Americans or Pacific Islanders, 74 Hispanic Americans), 11 international. Average age 30. 993 applicants, 80% accepted, 617 enrolled. In 2007, 324 master's, 7 doctorates awarded. *Degree requirements:* For doctorate, thesis/dissertation. *Entrance requirements:* For master's, interview, minimum GPA of 2.75, 2 letters of recommendation; for doctorate, interview, master's degree, 2 years of work experience (recommended), writing sample, 3 letters of recommendation. Application fee: $25. Electronic applications accepted. *Financial support:* In 2007–08, 16 research assistantships with tuition reimbursements (averaging $4,370 per year), 1 teaching assistantship (averaging $6,000 per year) were awarded; career-related internships or fieldwork also available. *Faculty research:* Reflective teaching, children at risk, loss, ethnicity, urban education. Total annual research expenditures: $556,194. *Unit head:* Dr. Clara Jennings, Dean, 773-325-7581, Fax: 773-325-7728, E-mail: cjennings@depaul.edu. *Application contact:* Dr. John Bollwark, Data Project Manager, 773-325-7582, Fax: 773-325-7713, E-mail: jbollwar@depaul.edu.

Dowling College, Graduate Programs in Education, Oakdale, NY 11769-1999. Offers educational administration (Ed D, PD), including computers in education (PD), educational administration (Ed D), school administration and supervision (PD), school district administration (PD); human development and learning (MS Ed); literacy (MS Ed); literacy/special education (MS Ed); secondary education (MS Ed); special education (MS Ed). *Accreditation:* NCATE. Part-time and evening/weekend programs available. Postbaccalaureate distance learning degree programs offered. *Faculty:* 28 full-time (13 women), 94 part-time/adjunct (60 women). *Students:* 528 full-time (361 women), 981 part-time (765 women); includes 136 minority (43 African Americans, 1 American Indian/Alaska Native, 17 Asian Americans or Pacific Islanders, 75 Hispanic Americans). Average age 38. 462 applicants, 76% accepted, 248 enrolled. In 2007, 585 master's, 14 doctorates, 39 other advanced degrees awarded. *Degree requirements:* For master's and PD, comprehensive exam; for doctorate, thesis/dissertation. *Entrance requirements:* For master's, minimum GPA of 3.0; for doctorate, GRE, master's degree; for PD, teaching certificate. Additional exam requirements/recommendations for international students: Required—TOEFL (minimum score 550 paper-based). *Application deadline:* For fall admission, 9/1 priority date for domestic students; for winter admission, 1/1 priority date for domestic students; for spring admission, 2/1 priority date for domestic students. Applications are processed on a rolling basis. Application fee: $25. Electronic applications accepted. *Expenses:* Tuition: Full-time $17,452; part-time $606 per credit. Required fees: $2,908; $538 per term. One-time fee: $55. *Financial support:* In 2007–08, 176 students received support, including 19 research assistantships with tuition reimbursements available (averaging $6,008 per year); career-related internships or fieldwork, Federal Work-Study, scholarships/grants, tuition waivers (partial), and unspecified assistantships also available. Support available to part-time students. Financial award application deadline: 6/30; financial award applicants required to submit FAFSA. *Faculty research:* Natural readers, Korean styles and learning strategies, mothers of children with disabilities, computers in instruction, cultural background and organizational roadblocks to problem solving. *Unit head:* Dr. Clyde Payne, Associate Provost, 631-244-3404, Fax: 631-589-6644, E-mail: paynec@dowling.edu. *Application contact:* Frank S. Pizzardi, Director of Admissions Operations, 631-244-3227, Fax: 631-244-1059, E-mail: pizzardf@dowling.edu.

Duke University, Graduate School, Department of Psychology, Durham, NC 27708-0586. Offers biological psychology (PhD); clinical psychology (PhD); cognitive psychology (PhD); developmental psychology (PhD); experimental psychology (PhD); health psychology (PhD); human social development (PhD); JD/MA. *Accreditation:* APA (one or more programs are accredited). *Faculty:* 40 full-time. *Students:* 91 full-time (71 women); includes 15 minority (9 African Americans, 1 Asian American or Pacific Islander, 5 Hispanic Americans), 13 international. 468 applicants, 7% accepted, 19 enrolled. In 2007, 14 doctorates awarded. *Degree requirements:* For doctorate, thesis/dissertation. *Entrance requirements:* For doctorate, GRE General Test. Additional exam requirements/recommendations for international students: Required—TOEFL (minimum score 550 paper-based; 213 computer-based; 83 iBT), IELTS (minimum score 7). *Application deadline:* For fall admission, 12/15 priority date for domestic and international students. Application fee: $75. Electronic applications accepted. *Financial support:* Fellowships, research assistantships, teaching assistantships, career-related internships or fieldwork and Federal Work-Study available. Financial award application deadline: 12/31. *Unit head:* Amy Needham, Co-Director of Graduate Studies, 919-660-5715, Fax: 919-660-5726, E-mail: morrell@duke.edu.

East Tennessee State University, School of Graduate Studies, College of Education, Department of Human Development and Learning, Johnson City, TN 37614. Offers advanced practitioner (M Ed); community agency counseling (M Ed, MA); comprehensive concentration (M Ed); counseling (M Ed, MA); early childhood education (M Ed, MA); early childhood general (M Ed); early childhood special education (M Ed); early childhood teaching (M Ed); elementary and secondary (school counseling) (M Ed, MA); marriage and family therapy (M Ed, MA); modified concentration (M Ed). *Accreditation:* ACA; NCATE. Part-time programs available. *Degree requirements:* For master's, comprehensive exam, thesis (for some programs). *Entrance requirements:* For master's, GRE General Test, minimum GPA of 3.0. Additional exam requirements/recommendations for international students: Required—TOEFL (minimum score 550 paper-based; 213 computer-based). *Faculty research:* Drug and alcohol abuse, marriage and family counseling, severe mental retardation, parenting of children with disabilities.

Erikson Institute, Academic Programs, Chicago, IL 60611-5627. Offers administration (Certificate); bilingual/ESL (Certificate); child development (MS); early childhood education (MS); infant mental health (Certificate); infant studies (Certificate); MS/MSW. Part-time and evening/weekend programs available. *Degree requirements:* For master's, comprehensive

Human Development

Erikson Institute (continued)

exam, internship; for Certificate, internship. *Entrance requirements:* For master's and Certificate, minimum GPA of 2.75. Additional exam requirements/recommendations for international students: Required—TOEFL. *Faculty research:* Assessment strategies from early childhood through elementary years; language, literacy, and the arts in children's development; inclusive special education; parent-child relationships; cognitive development.

Fielding Graduate University, Graduate Programs, School of Human and Organization Development, Santa Barbara, CA 93105-3538. Offers evidence-based coaching (Certificate); human and organizational systems (PhD); human development (PhD); integral studies (Certificate); organization management and development (MA). Evening/weekend programs available. *Faculty:* 30 full-time (14 women), 32 part-time/adjunct (13 women). *Students:* 503 full-time (347 women), 121 part-time (76 women); includes 131 minority (75 African Americans, 4 American Indian/Alaska Native, 22 Asian Americans or Pacific Islanders, 30 Hispanic Americans), 19 international. Average age 47. 268 applicants, 85% accepted, 168 enrolled. In 2007, 29 master's, 36 doctorates, 61 other advanced degrees awarded. *Degree requirements:* For doctorate, comprehensive exam, thesis/dissertation. *Entrance requirements:* For doctorate, 2 letters of recommendation, writing sample, resumé, self-assessment statement. *Application deadline:* For fall admission, 3/1 for domestic and international students; for spring admission, 9/1 for domestic and international students. Application fee: $75. Electronic applications accepted. *Expenses:* Contact institution. *Financial support:* In 2007–08, 303 students received support, including 3 research assistantships (averaging $1,875 per year); career-related internships or fieldwork, institutionally sponsored loans, and scholarships/grants also available. Financial award application deadline: 3/1; financial award applicants required to submit FAFSA. *Unit head:* Dr. Charles McClintock, Dean, 805-898-2930, Fax: 805-687-4590, E-mail: cmcclintock@fielding.edu. *Application contact:* Carmen Kuchera, Admission Counselor, 800-340-1099, Fax: 805-687-9793, E-mail: ckuchera@fielding.edu.

The George Washington University, Columbian College of Arts and Sciences, Program in Human Sciences, Washington, DC 20052. Offers PhD. Part-time programs available. *Degree requirements:* For doctorate, 2 foreign languages, thesis/dissertation, general exam. *Entrance requirements:* For doctorate, GRE General Test, interview, minimum GPA of 3.0. Additional exam requirements/recommendations for international students: Required—TOEFL (minimum score 550 paper-based; 213 computer-based). Electronic applications accepted.

The George Washington University, Graduate School of Education and Human Development, Individualized Master's Program in Educational Human Development, Washington, DC 20052. Offers MA Ed. *Degree requirements:* For master's, comprehensive exam. *Entrance requirements:* For master's, GRE General Test or MAT, minimum GPA of 2.75.

Harvard University, Graduate School of Education, Doctoral Program in Education, Cambridge, MA 02138. Offers culture, communities and education (Ed D); education policy, leadership and instructional practice (Ed D); higher education (Ed D); human development and education (Ed D); quantitative policy analysis in education (Ed D); urban superintendency (Ed D). Part-time programs available. *Faculty:* 67 full-time (34 women), 31 part-time/adjunct (15 women). *Students:* 293 full-time (206 women), 29 part-time (21 women); includes 91 minority (37 African Americans, 2 American Indian/Alaska Native, 35 Asian Americans or Pacific Islanders, 17 Hispanic Americans), 38 international. Average age 31. 502 applicants, 12% accepted, 43 enrolled. In 2007, 53 degrees awarded. Terminal master's awarded for partial completion of doctoral program. *Degree requirements:* For doctorate, thesis/dissertation. *Entrance requirements:* For doctorate, GRE General Test, 3 letters of recommendation, official transcripts, statement of purpose. Additional exam requirements/recommendations for international students: Required—TOEFL (minimum score 600 paper-based; 250 computer-based; 100 iBT), TWE (minimum score 5). *Application deadline:* For fall admission, 12/14 for domestic and international students. Application fee: $85. Electronic applications accepted. *Expenses:* Contact institution. Full-time tuition and fees vary according to program and student level. *Financial support:* In 2007–08, 191 students received support, including 114 fellowships with full and partial tuition reimbursements available (averaging $11,655 per year), 59 research assistantships (averaging $9,087 per year), 142 teaching assistantships (averaging $8,776 per year); career-related internships or fieldwork, Federal Work-Study, institutionally sponsored loans, scholarships/grants, health care benefits, tuition waivers (full and partial), and unspecified assistantships also available. Support available to part-time students. Financial award application deadline: 2/1; financial award applicants required to submit FAFSA. *Faculty research:* Learning and development; educational leadership and organizations; education policy analysis. Total annual research expenditures: $16.7 million. *Unit head:* Dr. Shu-Ling Chen, Assistant Dean for Doctoral Studies, 617-496-4406. *Application contact:* Information Contact, 617-495-3414, Fax: 617-496-3577, E-mail: gseadmissions@harvard.edu.

Harvard University, Graduate School of Education, Master's Programs in Education, Cambridge, MA 02138. Offers arts in education (Ed M); education policy and management (Ed M); higher education (Ed M); human development and psychology (Ed M); international education policy (Ed M); language and literacy (Ed M); learning and teaching (Ed M); mid-career mathematics and science (teaching certificate) (Ed M); mind brain and education (Ed M); risk and prevention (Ed M); school leadership (Ed M); special studies (Ed M); teaching and curriculum (teaching certificate) (Ed M); technology innovation and education (Ed M). Part-time programs available. *Faculty:* 67 full-time (34 women), 31 part-time/adjunct (15 women). *Students:* 515 full-time (395 women), 71 part-time (55 women); includes 135 minority (46 African Americans, 1 American Indian/Alaska Native, 55 Asian Americans or Pacific Islanders, 33 Hispanic Americans), 72 international. Average age 28. 1,219 applicants, 61% accepted, 537 enrolled. In 2007, 610 degrees awarded. *Entrance requirements:* For master's, GRE General Test, 3 letters of recommendation, official transcripts, statement of purpose. Additional exam requirements/recommendations for international students: Required—TOEFL (minimum score 600 paper-based; 250 computer-based; 100 iBT), TWE (minimum score 5). *Application deadline:* For fall admission, 1/4 for domestic and international students. Application fee: $85. Electronic applications accepted. *Expenses:* Contact institution. *Financial support:* In 2007–08, 375 students received support, including 31 fellowships with full and partial tuition reimbursements available (averaging $17,189 per year); career-related internships or fieldwork, Federal Work-Study, institutionally sponsored loans, scholarships/grants, health care benefits, tuition waivers (full and partial), and unspecified assistantships also available. Support available to part-time students. Financial award application deadline: 2/1; financial award applicants required to submit FAFSA. *Faculty research:* Learning and development; educational leadership and organizations; educational policy analysis. Total annual research expenditures: $16.7 million. *Unit head:* Jennifer L. Petrallia, Assistant Dean for Master's Studies, 617-495-8445. *Application contact:* Information Contact, 617-495-3414, Fax: 617-496-3577, E-mail: gseadmissions@harvard.edu.

Hood College, Graduate School, Programs in Human Sciences, Frederick, MD 21701-8575. Offers human sciences (MA); thanatology (MA, Certificate). Part-time and evening/weekend programs available. *Degree requirements:* For master's, comprehensive exam, thesis or alternative. *Entrance requirements:* For master's, minimum GPA of 2.5. *Faculty research:* Mind-body medicine and multicultural healing, the New Orleans jazz funeral, death practices in African-American culture, bereavement theories and gender differences, Piaget's theory of cognitive development as a formal mathematical model.

Howard University, School of Education, Department of Human Development and Psychoeducational Studies, Program in Human Development, Washington, DC 20059-0002. Offers MS. Offered through the Graduate School of Arts and Sciences. Part-time programs available. *Faculty:* 5 full-time (4 women). *Students:* 1 (woman) full-time, 2 part-time (both women); all minorities (all African Americans) Average age 25. 1 applicant, 0% accepted. *Degree requirements:* For master's, comprehensive exam, thesis, expository writing exam. *Entrance requirements:* For master's, GRE General Test, minimum GPA of 2.7. *Application deadline:* For fall admission, 4/1 priority date for domestic students; for spring admission, 11/1 for domestic students. Applications are processed on a rolling basis. Application fee: $45. *Expenses:* Tuition: Full-time $16,175; part-time $899 per credit hour. Required fees: $805. *Financial support:* Fellowships, research assistantships, teaching assistantships, career-related internships or fieldwork, Federal Work-Study, institutionally sponsored loans, scholarships/grants, tuition waivers (full and partial), and unspecified assistantships available. Financial award application deadline: 3/15. *Faculty research:* Overweight and obesity in black youth, diabetes, sickle–cell anemia. *Unit head:* Dr. Sylvan Alleyne, Professor/Coordinator, 202-806-7522, Fax: 202-806-5205, E-mail: salleyne@howard.edu.

Indiana University Bloomington, School of Health, Physical Education and Recreation, Department of Applied Health Science, Bloomington, IN 47405-7000. Offers health behavior (PhD); health promotion (MS); human development/family studies (MS); nutrition science (MS); public health (MPH); safety management (MS); school and college health programs (MS). PhD offered through the University Graduate School. *Accreditation:* CEPH (one or more programs are accredited). *Faculty:* 23 full-time (12 women). *Students:* 84 full-time (64 women), 51 part-time (36 women); includes 16 minority (12 African Americans, 1 American Indian/Alaska Native, 2 Asian Americans or Pacific Islanders, 1 Hispanic American), 26 international. Average age 30. 94 applicants, 88% accepted, 54 enrolled. In 2007, 36 master's, 4 doctorates awarded. *Degree requirements:* For master's, thesis optional; for doctorate, thesis/dissertation. *Entrance requirements:* For master's, GRE (MS in nutrition science), 3 recommendations; for doctorate, GRE, 3 recommendations. Additional exam requirements/recommendations for international students: Required—TOEFL (minimum score 550 paper-based; 213 computer-based; 79 iBT). *Application deadline:* For fall admission, 4/30 priority date for domestic students, 12/1 priority date for international students; for spring admission, 11/15 priority date for domestic students, 9/1 priority date for international students. Application fee: $50 ($60 for international students). *Financial support:* In 2007–08, 80 students received support, including 12 fellowships (averaging $2,316 per year), 50 research assistantships (averaging $7,536 per year), 27 teaching assistantships with full and partial tuition reimbursements available (averaging $11,251 per year); career-related internships or fieldwork, Federal Work-Study, institutionally sponsored loans, scholarships/grants, tuition waivers (partial), and fee remissions also available. Financial award application deadline: 3/1. *Faculty research:* Cancer education, HIV/AIDS and drug education, public health, parent-child interactions, safety education. *Unit head:* Dr. Mohammad R. Torabi, Chair, 812-855-4808, Fax: 812-855-3936, E-mail: torabi@indiana.edu.

Iowa State University of Science and Technology, Graduate College, College of Human Sciences, Department of Human Development and Family Studies, Ames, IA 50011. Offers human development and family studies (MFCS, MS, PhD); marriage and family therapy (PhD). *Accreditation:* AAMFT/COAMFTE. *Faculty:* 26 full-time (19 women), 7 part-time/adjunct (5 women). *Students:* 53 full-time (45 women), 17 part-time (15 women); includes 4 minority (2 Asian Americans or Pacific Islanders, 2 Hispanic Americans), 10 international. 50 applicants, 78% accepted, 22 enrolled. In 2007, 14 master's, 7 doctorates awarded. *Degree requirements:* For master's, thesis; for doctorate, thesis/dissertation. *Entrance requirements:* For master's and doctorate, GRE General Test. Additional exam requirements/recommendations for international students: Required—TOEFL (paper-based 550; computer-based 213; iBT 79) or IELTS (6.0). *Application deadline:* For fall admission, 12/1 priority date for domestic students. Application fee: $30 ($70 for international students). Electronic applications accepted. *Financial support:* In 2007–08, 31 research assistantships with full and partial tuition reimbursements (averaging $17,019 per year), 10 teaching assistantships with full and partial tuition reimbursements (averaging $20,457 per year) were awarded; fellowships, scholarships/grants also available. *Faculty research:* Child development, early childhood education, family resource management and housing, life span studies. *Unit head:* Dr. Maurice M. MacDonald, Chair, 515-294-6316, Fax: 515-294-2502, E-mail: hdfs-grad-adm@iastate.edu. *Application contact:* Dr. Dee Draper, Director of Graduate Education, 515-294-4024, Fax: 515-294-2502, E-mail: hdfs-grad-adm@iastate.edu.

Kansas State University, Graduate School, College of Human Ecology, Program in Human Ecology, Manhattan, KS 66506. Offers apparel and textiles (PhD); family life education and consultation (PhD); food service, hospitality management, and administrative dietetics (PhD); institutional management (PhD); lifespan and human development (PhD); marriage and family therapy (PhD). *Students:* 44 full-time (29 women), 23 part-time (12 women); includes 12 minority (9 African Americans, 1 American Indian/Alaska Native, 2 Asian Americans or Pacific Islanders), 14 international. 39 applicants, 54% accepted, 6 enrolled. In 2007, 14 degrees awarded. *Application deadline:* For fall admission, 2/1 priority date for domestic and international students; for spring admission, 8/1 priority date for domestic and international students. Application fee: $30 ($55 for international students). *Unit head:* Elizabeth McCullough, Director, 785-532-2284, Fax: 785-532-3796, E-mail: lizm@ksu.edu.

Kent State University, Graduate School of Education, Health, and Human Services, Department of Adult, Counseling, Health and Vocational Education, Program in Counseling and Human Development Services, Kent, OH 44242-0001. Offers PhD. *Accreditation:* ACA; NCATE. *Faculty:* 9 full-time (3 women), 2 part-time/adjunct (both women). *Students:* 56 full-time (44 women), 13 part-time (8 women); includes 12 minority (10 African Americans, 1 Asian American or Pacific Islander, 1 Hispanic American), 4 international. 17 applicants, 65% accepted. In 2007, 6 degrees awarded. *Degree requirements:* For doctorate, comprehensive exam, thesis/dissertation. *Entrance requirements:* For doctorate, GRE General Test. Additional exam requirements/recommendations for international students: Required—TOEFL. *Application deadline:* For fall admission, 2/15 for domestic students. Application fee: $30. Electronic applications accepted. *Financial support:* In 2007–08, fellowships with full tuition reimbursements (averaging $11,055 per year), research assistantships with full tuition reimbursements (averaging $11,055 per year) were awarded; teaching assistantships with full tuition reimbursements, career-related internships or fieldwork, Federal Work-Study, institutionally sponsored loans, scholarships/grants, health care benefits, and unspecified assistantships also available. Support available to part-time students. Financial award application deadline: 4/1; financial award applicants required to submit FAFSA. *Faculty research:* Family/child therapy, clinical supervision, group work, experiential training methods. *Unit head:* Dr. Martin Jencius, Interim Coordinator, 330-672-2662, Fax: 330-672-5396, E-mail: mjencius@kent.edu. *Application contact:* Nancy Miller, Academic Program Coordinator, Office of Graduate Student Services, 330-672-2576, Fax: 330-672-9162, E-mail: ogs@kent.edu.

Kent State University, Graduate School of Education, Health, and Human Services, School of Family and Consumer Studies, Program in Family Studies, Kent, OH 44242-0001. Offers gerontology (MA); human development and family studies (MA). *Faculty:* 17 full-time (10 women). *Students:* 3 full-time (all women), 4 part-time (all women). 3 applicants, 0% accepted. In 2007, 1 degree awarded. Application fee: $30. *Financial support:* In 2007–08, research assistantships (averaging $8,313 per year). *Unit head:* Dr. Rhonda Richardson, Coordinator, 330-672-2197, E-mail: rrichard@kent.edu. *Application contact:* Nancy Miller, Academic Program Coordinator, 330-672-2576, Fax: 330-672-9162, E-mail: ogs@kent.edu.

Laurentian University, School of Graduate Studies and Research, Programme in Human Development, Sudbury, ON P3E 2C6, Canada. Offers M Sc, MA. Interdisciplinary program consisting of the Departments of Psychology, Sociology, and Human Movement. Part-time programs available. *Degree requirements:* For master's, thesis or alternative. *Entrance requirements:* For master's, honors degree with second class or better. *Faculty research:* Aging and well-being, physical, social and cognitive development of children, social cognition and social relationships including peers and family, education and schooling.

Lehigh University, College of Arts and Sciences, Department of Psychology, Bethlehem, PA 18015-3094. Offers human cognition and development (MS, PhD). *Faculty:* 10 full-time (7 women). *Students:* 17 full-time (12 women), 17 part-time (12 women), 4 international. Average age 25. 57 applicants, 21% accepted, 4 enrolled. In 2007, 4 master's, 1 doctorate awarded. *Degree requirements:* For doctorate, comprehensive exam, thesis/dissertation. *Entrance requirements:* For doctorate, GRE General Test. Additional exam requirements/recommendations for international students: Required—TOEFL. *Application deadline:* For fall admission, 1/15 for domestic and international students. Application fee: $65. Electronic applications accepted. *Expenses:* Contact institution. *Financial support:* In 2007–08, 1 fellowship with full tuition reimbursement (averaging $20,000 per year), 4 research assistantships with full tuition reimbursements (averaging $15,100 per year), 11 teaching assistantships with full tuition reimbursements (averaging $15,100 per year) were awarded; scholarships/grants, tuition waivers (full and partial), and unspecified assistantships also available. Financial award application deadline: 1/15. *Faculty research:* Social-cognitive developmental psychology, cognition and language, social cognition. Total annual research expenditures: $258,519. *Unit head:* Diane Hyland, Chairperson, 610-758-3631, Fax: 610-758-6277, E-mail: dthl@lehigh.edu. *Application contact:* Dr. Ageliki Nicolopoulu, Program Director, 610-758-3630, Fax: 610-758-6277, E-mail: inpsy@lehigh.edu.

Lindsey Wilson College, School of Professional Counseling, Columbia, KY 42728-1298. Offers counseling and human development (M Ed). *Accreditation:* ACA. Part-time and evening/weekend programs available.

Marywood University, Academic Affairs, College of Education and Human Development, Department of Human Development, Doctoral Program in Human Development, Scranton, PA 18509-1598. Offers PhD. *Expenses:* Tuition: Full-time $15,290; part-time $695 per credit. Required fees: $990; $370 per term. Tuition and fees vary according to degree level. *Unit head:* Dr. Marie Loftus, Director, 570-348-6211.

Montana State University, College of Graduate Studies, College of Education, Health, and Human Development, Department of Health and Human Development, Bozeman, MT 59717. Offers MS. *Accreditation:* ACA. Part-time programs available. Postbaccalaureate distance learning degree programs offered. *Faculty:* 25 full-time (18 women), 10 part-time/adjunct (7 women). *Students:* 56 full-time (43 women), 38 part-time (29 women); includes 3 minority (2 American Indian/Alaska Native, 1 Hispanic American), 3 international. Average age 29. 35 applicants, 51% accepted, 21 enrolled. In 2007, 37 degrees awarded. *Degree requirements:* For master's, comprehensive exam. *Entrance requirements:* For master's, GRE General Test. Additional exam requirements/recommendations for international students: Required—TOEFL (minimum score 550 paper-based; 213 computer-based). *Application deadline:* For fall admission, 7/15 priority date for domestic students, 5/15 priority date for international students; for spring admission, 12/1 priority date for domestic students, 10/1 priority date for international students. Applications are processed on a rolling basis. Application fee: $30. Electronic applications accepted. *Expenses:* Tuition, state resident: full-time $5,176. Tuition, nonresident: full-time $13,070. *Financial support:* In 2007–08, 24 students received support, including 7 research assistantships (averaging $1,000 per year), 17 teaching assistantships with full tuition reimbursements available (averaging $8,000 per year). Financial award application deadline: 3/1; financial award applicants required to submit FAFSA. *Faculty research:* Gait analysis, cancer prevention, obesity prevention, energy expenditure, decision making. Total annual research expenditures: $2.6 million. *Unit head:* Dr. Tim Dunnagan, Head, 404-994-3242, Fax: 404-994-2013, E-mail: dunnagan@montana.edu.

Morehead State University, Graduate Programs, College of Science and Technology, Department of Agricultural and Human Sciences, Morehead, KY 40351. Offers career/technical education (MS), including agriculture, human sciences, industrial education. *Accreditation:* NCATE. Part-time and evening/weekend programs available. *Students:* 3 full-time (2 women), 17 part-time (8 women). Average age 38. In 2007, 11 degrees awarded. *Degree requirements:* For master's, thesis optional, oral and/or written final exam. *Entrance requirements:* For master's, GRE General Test, minimum GPA of 3.0 in major, 2.5 overall. Additional exam requirements/recommendations for international students: Required—TOEFL (minimum score 500 paper-based; 173 computer-based). *Application deadline:* For fall admission, 8/1 priority date for domestic and international students; for spring admission, 12/1 priority date for domestic and international students. Applications are processed on a rolling basis. Application fee: $0. Electronic applications accepted. *Financial support:* In 2007–08, teaching assistantships (averaging $6,000 per year); career-related internships or fieldwork and Federal Work-Study also available. Financial award application deadline: 4/1; financial award applicants required to submit FAFSA. *Faculty research:* Robotics, herbicide safeness and forage grass species, computer-animated learning modules. *Unit head:* Dr. Lane Cowsert, Chair, 606-783-2662, E-mail: l.cowser@moreheadstate.edu. *Application contact:* Michelle Barber, Graduate Admissions Counselor, 606-783-2039, Fax: 606-783-5061, E-mail: m.barber@moreheadstate.edu.

National-Louis University, College of Arts and Sciences, Program in Psychology, Chicago, IL 60603. Offers cultural psychology (MA); health psychology (MA); human development (MA); organizational psychology (MA); psychology (Certificate). Part-time and evening/weekend programs available. *Students:* 37 full-time (33 women), 147 part-time (127 women); includes 99 minority (79 African Americans, 1 American Indian/Alaska Native, 6 Asian Americans or Pacific Islanders, 13 Hispanic Americans). Average age 38. *Degree requirements:* For master's, thesis, internship (health psychology). *Entrance requirements:* For master's, GRE, MAT, or Watson-Glaser Critical Thinking Appraisal, interview, minimum GPA of 3.0; for Certificate, GRE, MAT, or Watson-Glaser Critical Thinking Appraisal, interview, minimum GPA of 3.0, undergraduate course work in psychology. *Application deadline:* Applications are processed on a rolling basis. *Expenses:* Tuition: Full-time $18,900; part-time $630 per credit hour. Required fees: $20 per term. One-time fee: $40 part-time. Tuition and fees vary according to course load, campus/location and program. *Financial support:* Federal Work-Study, institutionally sponsored loans, scholarships/grants, and tuition waivers available. Support available to part-time students. Financial award applicants required to submit FAFSA. *Faculty research:* Human development, personality theory, abnormal psychology. *Unit head:* Dr. Edward Risinger, Professor, 224-233-2533, Fax: 224-233-2533, E-mail: erisinger@nl.edu. *Application contact:* David McCulloch, Vice President for University Services, 800-443-5522 Ext. 5151, Fax: 847-465-0593, E-mail: dmcc@wheeling1.nl.edu.

National-Louis University, National College of Education, Doctoral Programs in Education, Program in Human Learning and Development, Chicago, IL 60603. Offers Ed D. Part-time and evening/weekend programs available. *Students:* 1 (woman) full-time, 5 part-time (2 women); includes 3 minority (1 African American, 1 Asian American or Pacific Islander, 1 Hispanic American). Average age 40. In 2007, 1 degree awarded. *Degree requirements:* For doctorate, comprehensive exam, thesis/dissertation, internship. *Entrance requirements:* For doctorate, GRE General Test, minimum GPA of 3.25, interview, resumé, writing sample. *Application deadline:* For fall admission, 5/1 for domestic students; for spring admission, 1/15 for domestic students. *Expenses:* Tuition: Full-time $18,900; part-time $630 per credit hour. Required fees: $20 per term. One-time fee: $40 part-time. Tuition and fees vary according to course load, campus/location and program. *Financial support:* Fellowships, research assistantships, teaching assistantships, career-related internships or fieldwork, Federal Work-Study, institutionally sponsored loans, and scholarships/grants available. Support available to part-time students. Financial award application deadline: 4/15; financial award applicants required to submit FAFSA. *Application contact:* Dr. Larry Poselli, Vice President of Enrollment and Student Services, 800-443-5522 Ext. 5718, Fax: 312-261-.3550, E-mail: larry.polselli@nl.edu.

National-Louis University, National College of Education, Program in Educational Psychology/Human Learning and Development, Chicago, IL 60603. Offers educational psychology (CAS, Ed S); educational psychology/human learning and development (M Ed, MS Ed). Part-time and evening/weekend programs available. *Students:* 36 full-time (34 women), 44 part-time (40 women); includes 9 minority (2 African Americans, 7 Hispanic Americans). Average age 33. In 2007, 10 master's, 1 CAS awarded. *Degree requirements:* For master's, thesis (for some programs). *Entrance requirements:* For master's, MAT or GRE, minimum GPA of 3.0, teaching certificate; for other advanced degree, master's degree, teaching certificate. *Application deadline:* Applications are processed on a rolling basis. Electronic applications accepted. *Expenses:* Tuition: Full-time $18,900; part-time $630 per credit hour. Required fees: $20 per term. One-time fee: $40 part-time. Tuition and fees vary according to course load, campus/location and program. *Financial support:* Fellowships, career-related internships or fieldwork, Federal Work-Study, institutionally sponsored loans, and scholarships/grants available. Support available to part-time students. Financial award applicants required to submit FAFSA.

New York Institute of Technology, Graduate Division, School of Allied Health and Life Sciences, Program in Human Relations, Old Westbury, NY 11568-8000. Offers MPS. Part-time and evening/weekend programs available. Postbaccalaureate distance learning degree programs offered. *Students:* 2 full-time (1 woman), 11 part-time (8 women); includes 5 minority (3 African Americans, 2 Asian Americans or Pacific Islanders), 2 international. Average age 36. 49 applicants, 27% accepted, 7 enrolled. In 2007, 15 degrees awarded. *Degree requirements:* For master's, thesis or alternative. *Entrance requirements:* For master's, minimum QPA of 2.85. Additional exam requirements/recommendations for international students: Required—TOEFL (minimum score 550 paper-based; 213 computer-based). *Application deadline:* For fall admission, 7/1 priority date for domestic students; for spring admission, 12/1 priority date for domestic students. Applications are processed on a rolling basis. Application fee: $50. Electronic applications accepted. *Expenses:* Tuition: Part-time $739 per credit. Required fees: $75 per semester. *Financial support:* Fellowships, research assistantships with partial tuition reimbursements, institutionally sponsored loans, tuition waivers (full and partial), and unspecified assistantships available. Support available to part-time students. Financial award applicants required to submit FAFSA. *Faculty research:* Distance learning delivery systems. *Unit head:* Dr. Maria LaPadula, Coordinator, 516-686-3869, E-mail: mlapadul@nyit.edu. *Application contact:* Jacquelyn Nealon, Dean of Admissions and Financial Aid, 516-686-7925, Fax: 516-686-7613, E-mail: jnealon@nyit.edu.

New York University, Steinhardt School of Culture, Education and Human Development, New York, NY 10012-1019. Offers MA, MFA, MM, MPH, MS, DA, DPS, DPT, Ed D, PhD, Advanced Certificate. *Accreditation:* Teacher Education Accreditation Council. Part-time and evening/weekend programs available. *Faculty:* 261 full-time (156 women), 687 part-time/adjunct (369 women). *Students:* 2,076 full-time (1,665 women), 1,446 part-time (1,131 women); includes 740 minority (242 African Americans, 5 American Indian/Alaska Native, 280 Asian Americans or Pacific Islanders, 213 Hispanic Americans), 559 international. Average age 32. 5,422 applicants, 52% accepted, 1251 enrolled. In 2007, 1,330 master's, 93 doctorates, 22 other advanced degrees awarded. *Degree requirements:* For doctorate, comprehensive exam (for some programs), thesis/dissertation. *Entrance requirements:* For doctorate, GRE General Test, interview. Additional exam requirements/recommendations for international students: Required—TOEFL. *Application deadline:* For fall admission, 2/1 priority date for domestic students, 2/1 for international students; for spring admission, 12/1 for domestic and international students. Applications are processed on a rolling basis. Application fee: $50. *Expenses:* Contact institution. *Financial support:* In 2007–08, fellowships with full and partial tuition reimbursements (averaging $15,000 per year); research assistantships with full and partial tuition reimbursements, teaching assistantships with full and partial tuition reimbursements, career-related internships or fieldwork, Federal Work-Study, institutionally sponsored loans, scholarships/grants, traineeships, tuition waivers (partial), and unspecified assistantships also available. Support available to part-time students. Financial award application deadline: 2/1; financial award applicants required to submit FAFSA. *Faculty research:* Equity, urban adolescents, arts in education, globalization, community and public health. Total annual research expenditures: $21.3 million. *Unit head:* Dr. Mary Brabeck, Dean, 212-998-5000. *Application contact:* 212-998-5030, Fax: 212-995-4328, E-mail: steinhardt.gradadmissions@nyu.edu.

North Dakota State University, College of Graduate and Interdisciplinary Studies, College of Human Development and Education, Program in Human Development, Fargo, ND 58105. Offers PhD. *Degree requirements:* For doctorate, comprehensive exam, thesis/dissertation. *Entrance requirements:* Additional exam requirements/recommendations for international students: Required—TOEFL (minimum score 525 paper-based; 197 computer-based; 71 iBT). *Application deadline:* For fall admission, 2/1 priority date for domestic and international students. Applications are processed on a rolling basis. Application fee: $45 ($60 for international students). *Expenses:* Tuition, state resident: full-time $5,376; part-time $224 per credit. Tuition, nonresident: full-time $14,354; part-time $598 per credit. Required fees: $962; $40 per credit. Part-time tuition and fees vary according to course load and reciprocity agreements. *Financial support:* In 2007–08, 12 students received support; research assistantships with full tuition reimbursements available, teaching assistantships with full tuition reimbursements available, scholarships/grants, tuition waivers (partial), and unspecified assistantships available. *Faculty research:* Gerontology, wellness, counselor education. Total annual research expenditures: $1.3 million. *Unit head:* Dr. Greg Sanders, Coordinator, 701-231-8211, E-mail: greg.sanders@ndsu.edu.

Northwestern University, The Graduate School, School of Education and Social Policy, Program in Human Development and Social Policy, Evanston, IL 60208. Offers PhD. Admissions and degrees offered through The Graduate School. *Faculty:* 13 full-time (5 women), 7 part-time/adjunct (2 women). *Students:* 32 full-time (31 women); includes 5 minority (3 African Americans, 2 Hispanic Americans), 1 international. Average age 30. 93 applicants, 11% accepted, 5 enrolled. In 2007, 1 degree awarded. *Degree requirements:* For doctorate, comprehensive exam, thesis/dissertation. *Entrance requirements:* For doctorate, GRE General Test, writing sample. Additional exam requirements/recommendations for international students: Required—TOEFL (minimum score 600 paper-based; 250 computer-based; 100 iBT). *Application deadline:* For fall admission, 12/31 priority date for domestic and international students. Application fee: $75. Electronic applications accepted. *Financial support:* In 2007–08, 31 students received support, including 5 fellowships with full tuition reimbursements available; research assistantships with full tuition reimbursements available, teaching assistantships with full tuition reimbursements available, institutionally sponsored loans, scholarships/grants, and unspecified assistantships also available. Financial award application deadline: 12/31; financial award applicants required to submit FAFSA. *Faculty research:* Social context of development; social policy issues affecting children, adolescents, adults, and families. *Unit head:* Dr. Dan McAdams, Coordinator, 847-491-4329. *Application contact:* Mary Lou Manning, Department Assistant, 847-491-4329, Fax: 847-491-8999, E-mail: mmanning@northwestern.edu.

See Close-Up on page 1613.

The Ohio State University, Graduate School, College of Education and Human Ecology, Department of Human Development and Family Science, Columbus, OH 43210. Offers M Ed, MS, PhD. *Faculty:* 24. *Students:* 18 full-time (16 women), 17 part-time (13 women); includes 3 minority (all African Americans), 10 international. Average age 29. In 2007, 10 master's, 7 doctorates awarded. *Degree requirements:* For master's, thesis optional; for doctorate, thesis/dissertation. *Entrance requirements:* For master's and doctorate, GRE General Test. Additional exam requirements/recommendations for international students: Required—TOEFL (minimum score 577 paper-based; 233 computer-based). *Application deadline:* For fall admission, 8/15 priority date for domestic students, 7/1 priority date for international students; for winter admission, 12/1 priority date for domestic students, 11/1 priority date for international students; for spring admission, 3/1 priority date for domestic students, 2/1 priority date for international students. Applications are processed on a rolling basis. Application fee: $40 ($50 for international students). Electronic applications accepted. *Financial support:* Fellowships, research assistantships, teaching assistantships, Federal Work-Study and institutionally sponsored loans available. Support available to part-time students. *Unit head:* Suzanne Bartle-Haring, Graduate Studies Committee Chair, 614-292-5685, Fax: 614-292-2581, E-mail: haring.19@osu.edu. *Application contact:* 614-292-9444, Fax: 614-292-3895, E-mail: domestic.grad@osu.edu.

Oregon State University, Graduate School, College of Health and Human Sciences, Department of Human Development and Family Sciences, Corvallis, OR 97331. Offers gerontology (MAIS); human development and family studies (MS, PhD). *Faculty:* 17 full-time (11 women), 6 part-time/adjunct (all women). *Students:* 30 full-time (25 women), 4 part-time (all women); includes 4 minority (3 Asian Americans or Pacific Islanders, 1 Hispanic American), 9 international. Average age 37. In 2007, 3 master's, 1 doctorate awarded. *Degree requirements:* For doctorate, thesis/dissertation. *Entrance requirements:* For master's and doctorate, GRE, minimum GPA of 3.0 in last 90 hours. Additional exam requirements/recommendations for

Human Development

Oregon State University (continued)

international students: Required—TOEFL. *Application deadline:* Applications are processed on a rolling basis. Application fee: $50. *Expenses:* Tuition, state resident: full-time $9,126; part-time $338 per credit. Tuition, nonresident: full-time $14,796; part-time $548 per credit. Required fees: $1,447. *Financial support:* Research assistantships, teaching assistantships, career-related internships or fieldwork, Federal Work-Study, and institutionally sponsored loans available. Support available to part-time students. Financial award application deadline: 2/1. *Unit head:* Dr. Carolyn Aldwin, Chair, 541-737-2024, Fax: 541-737-1076, E-mail: carolyn.aldwin@oregonstate.edu.

Our Lady of the Lake University of San Antonio, School of Education and Clinical Studies, Program in Human Sciences, San Antonio, TX 78207-4689. Offers MA. Part-time and evening/weekend programs available. *Entrance requirements:* For master's, GRE General Test or MAT, interview. Additional exam requirements/recommendations for international students: Required—TOEFL. Electronic applications accepted.

Pacific Oaks College, Graduate School, Program in Human Development, Pasadena, CA 91103. Offers MA. Part-time and evening/weekend programs available. Postbaccalaureate distance learning degree programs offered (minimal on-campus study). *Degree requirements:* For master's, thesis. *Entrance requirements:* Additional exam requirements/recommendations for international students: Required—TOEFL (minimum score 550 paper-based; 213 computer-based). *Faculty research:* Bicultural development, teaching adults, art education, literacy development, adolescent development.

Penn State University Park, Graduate School, College of Health and Human Development, Department of Human Development and Family Studies, State College, University Park, PA 16802-1503. Offers MS, PhD. *Expenses:* Tuition, state resident: full-time $14,738; part-time $614 per credit. Tuition, nonresident: full-time $26,050; part-time $1,085 per credit. Tuition and fees vary according to course load, program and student level. *Unit head:* Dr. Steven H. Zarit, Head, 814-865-5260, Fax: 814-863-7963, E-mail: z67@psu.edu. *Application contact:* Dr. Douglas M. Teti, Professor in Charge of Graduate Program, 814-865-2644, E-mail: dmt16@psu.edu.

Purdue University, Graduate School, College of Consumer and Family Sciences, Department of Child Development and Family Studies, West Lafayette, IN 47907. Offers developmental studies (MS, PhD); family studies (MS, PhD); marriage and family therapy (MS, PhD). *Accreditation:* AAMFT/COAMFTE (one or more programs are accredited). Part-time programs available. Terminal master's awarded for partial completion of doctoral program. *Degree requirements:* For master's, thesis; for doctorate, thesis/dissertation. *Entrance requirements:* For master's and doctorate, GRE General Test. Additional exam requirements/recommendations for international students: Required—TWE. Electronic applications accepted. *Faculty research:* Inclusion of children with special needs, families as learning environments, relationships in child care, work-family relations, AIDS prevention.

Saint Joseph College, Graduate Division, Institute in Gerontology, West Hartford, CT 06117-2700. Offers human development/gerontology (Certificate). Part-time and evening/weekend programs available. Electronic applications accepted. *Faculty research:* Education, aging, public health.

St. Lawrence University, Department of Education, Program in Counseling and Human Development, Canton, NY 13617-1455. Offers M Ed, CAS. Part-time and evening/weekend programs available. *Entrance requirements:* For master's, GRE General Test. *Faculty research:* Defense mechanisms and mediation.

Saint Louis University, Graduate School, College of Education and Public Service and Graduate School, Department of Counseling and Family Therapy, St. Louis, MO 63103-2097. Offers counseling and family therapy (PhD); human development counseling (MA); marriage and family therapy (Certificate); school counseling (MA, MA-R). *Accreditation:* NCATE. Part-time programs available. *Faculty:* 4 full-time (2 women), 4 part-time/adjunct (all women). *Students:* 61 full-time (56 women), 33 part-time (25 women); includes 16 minority (9 African Americans, 1 American Indian/Alaska Native, 4 Asian Americans or Pacific Islanders, 2 Hispanic Americans), 1 international. Average age 33. 60 applicants, 38% accepted, 14 enrolled. In 2007, 10 master's, 3 doctorates awarded. *Degree requirements:* For master's, comprehensive exam, thesis (for some programs); for doctorate, comprehensive exam, thesis/dissertation, preliminary oral and written exams. *Entrance requirements:* For master's and doctorate, GRE General Test, letters of recommendation, resumé, transcripts, goal statement. Additional exam requirements/recommendations for international students: Required—TOEFL (minimum score 550 paper-based; 213 computer-based). *Application deadline:* For fall admission, 1/15 for domestic and international students. Applications are processed on a rolling basis. Application fee: $40. Electronic applications accepted. *Expenses:* Tuition: Part-time $845 per credit hour. Required fees: $105 per semester. *Financial support:* In 2007–08, 32 students received support, including 4 research assistantships with full tuition reimbursements available (averaging $13,000 per year), 2 teaching assistantships with full tuition reimbursements available (averaging $13,000 per year); Federal Work-Study, scholarships/grants, traineeships, health care benefits, tuition waivers (partial), and unspecified assistantships also available. Support available to part-time students. Financial award application deadline: 2/1; financial award applicants required to submit FAFSA. *Faculty research:* Medical family therapy/collaborative health care multicultural counseling, mental health needs of diverse, minority, or Immigrant/refugee populations, divorce, aging families. *Unit head:* Dr. Craig W. Smith, Chairperson, 314-997-2507, Fax: 314-977-3214, E-mail: csmit112@slu.edu. *Application contact:* Gary U. Behrman, Associate Dean of Graduate School Admissions, 314-977-3827, Fax: 314-977-3943, E-mail: behrmang@slu.edu.

Saint Mary's University of Minnesota, Schools of Graduate and Professional Programs, Graduate School of Business and Technology, Human Development Program, Winona, MN 55987-1399. Offers MA. *Unit head:* Dr. Priscilla Herbison, Director, 612-728-5103, Fax: 612-728-5121, E-mail: pherbiso@smumn.edu.

South Dakota State University, Graduate School, College of Family and Consumer Sciences, Department of Human Development, Consumer and Family Sciences, Brookings, SD 57007. Offers MFCS. *Entrance requirements:* For master's, resumé. Additional exam requirements/recommendations for international students: Required—TOEFL (minimum score 525 paper-based).

Southern Illinois University Carbondale, Graduate School, College of Education, Department of Educational Psychology and Special Education, Program in Educational Psychology, Carbondale, IL 62901-4701. Offers counselor education (MS Ed, PhD); educational psychology (PhD); human learning and development (MS Ed); measurement and statistics (PhD). *Accreditation:* NCATE. *Faculty:* 19 full-time (9 women), 7 part-time/adjunct (2 women). *Students:* 40 full-time (33 women), 52 part-time (36 women); includes 72 minority (70 African Americans, 1 Asian American or Pacific Islander, 1 Hispanic American), 13 international. Average age 36. 37 applicants, 35% accepted, 3 enrolled. In 2007, 25 master's, 3 doctorates awarded. *Degree requirements:* For master's, thesis; for doctorate, thesis/dissertation. *Entrance requirements:* For master's, GRE General Test, minimum GPA of 2.7; for doctorate, minimum GPA of 3.25. Additional exam requirements/recommendations for international students: Required—TOEFL. *Application deadline:* For fall admission, 6/15 priority date for domestic students. Applications are processed on a rolling basis. Application fee: $20. *Financial support:* In 2007–08, 36 students received support, including 2 fellowships with full tuition reimbursements available, 4 research assistantships with full tuition reimbursements available; teaching assistantships with full tuition reimbursements available, career-related internships or fieldwork, Federal Work-Study, institutionally sponsored loans, and tuition waivers (full) also available. Support available to part-time students. Financial award application deadline: 5/1. *Faculty research:* Career development, problem solving, learning and instruction, cognitive development, family assessment. Total annual research expenditures: $10,000. *Application contact:* Cathy Earnhart, Administrative Clerk, 618-453-6932, E-mail: pern@siu.edu.

Texas A&M University, College of Education and Human Development, Department of Educational Psychology, College Station, TX 77843. Offers counseling psychology (PhD); educational psychology (PhD); educational technology (M Ed); gifted and talented education (M Ed, MS); Hispanic bilingual education (M Ed, PhD); human learning and development (MS); intelligence, creativity, and giftedness (PhD); learning, development, and instruction (PhD); research, measurement and statistics (MS); research, measurement, and statistics (PhD); school counseling (M Ed); school psychology (PhD); special education (M Ed, PhD). *Accreditation:* APA (one or more programs are accredited); NCATE. Part-time and evening/weekend programs available. Postbaccalaureate distance learning degree programs offered (no on-campus study). *Faculty:* 43. *Students:* 140 full-time (109 women), 153 part-time (129 women); includes 77 minority (27 African Americans, 1 American Indian/Alaska Native, 7 Asian Americans or Pacific Islanders, 42 Hispanic Americans), 41 international. 222 applicants, 61% accepted, 90 enrolled. In 2007, 42 master's, 24 doctorates awarded. *Median time to degree:* Of those who began their doctoral program in fall 1999, 89% received their degree in 8 years or less. *Degree requirements:* For master's, thesis optional; for doctorate, thesis/dissertation. *Entrance requirements:* For master's and doctorate, GRE General Test. Additional exam requirements/recommendations for international students: Required—TOEFL. Application fee: $50 ($75 for international students). Electronic applications accepted. *Expenses:* Tuition, state resident: full-time $6,129. Tuition, nonresident: full-time $11,689. Tuition and fees vary according to course load. *Financial support:* In 2007–08, fellowships (averaging $12,000 per year), research assistantships (averaging $9,000 per year), teaching assistantships (averaging $9,000 per year) were awarded; career-related internships or fieldwork, institutionally sponsored loans, scholarships/grants, and unspecified assistantships also available. Financial award applicants required to submit FAFSA. *Unit head:* Dr. Michael R. Benz, Head, 979-845-1394, Fax: 979-862-1256, E-mail: mbanz@tamu.edu. *Application contact:* Carol A. Wagner, Director of Advising, 979-845-1833, Fax: 979-862-1256, E-mail: c-wagner@tamu.edu.

Texas Tech University, Graduate School, College of Human Sciences, Department of Human Development and Family Studies, Lubbock, TX 79409. Offers gerontology (MS); human development and family studies (MS, PhD). *Accreditation:* AAMFT/COAMFTE (one or more programs are accredited). Part-time programs available. *Faculty:* 20 full-time (16 women). *Students:* 45 full-time (38 women), 16 part-time (12 women); includes 9 minority (1 African American, 1 American Indian/Alaska Native, 3 Asian Americans or Pacific Islanders, 4 Hispanic Americans), 13 international. Average age 34. 44 applicants, 75% accepted, 16 enrolled. In 2007, 2 master's, 2 doctorates awarded. *Degree requirements:* For master's, thesis; for doctorate, thesis/dissertation. *Entrance requirements:* For master's and doctorate, GRE General Test. Additional exam requirements/recommendations for international students: Required—TOEFL (minimum score 550 paper-based; 213 computer-based). *Application deadline:* For fall admission, 3/1 priority date for international students; for spring admission, 11/1 priority date for international students. Applications are processed on a rolling basis. Application fee: $50 ($60 for international students). Electronic applications accepted. *Expenses:* Tuition, state resident: part-time $373 per credit hour. Tuition, nonresident: part-time $651 per credit hour. Tuition and fees vary according to program. *Financial support:* In 2007–08, 50 students received support, including 11 research assistantships with partial tuition reimbursements available (averaging $12,849 per year), 35 teaching assistantships with partial tuition reimbursements available (averaging $12,986 per year); career-related internships or fieldwork, Federal Work-Study, institutionally sponsored loans, and scholarships/grants also available. Support available to part-time students. Financial award application deadline: 4/15; financial award applicants required to submit FAFSA. *Faculty research:* Parenting, marital and premarital relationships, adolescent drug abuse, life span; child development. Total annual research expenditures: $72,657. *Unit head:* Anisa Zvonkovic, Interim Chair, 806-742-3000 Ext. 279, Fax: 806-742-0285, E-mail: anisa.zvonkovic@ttu.edu. *Application contact:* Judy McMurry, Graduate Secretary, 806-742-3000, Fax: 806-742-0285.

The University of Alabama, Graduate School, College of Human Environmental Sciences, Department of Human Development and Family Studies, Tuscaloosa, AL 35487. Offers MSHES. *Faculty:* 6 full-time (4 women). *Students:* 19 full-time (all women), 9 part-time (all women); includes 4 minority (all African Americans) Average age 29. 25 applicants, 64% accepted, 10 enrolled. In 2007, 6 degrees awarded. *Degree requirements:* For master's, thesis (for some programs). *Entrance requirements:* For master's, GRE General Test or MAT, minimum GPA of 3.0. Additional exam requirements/recommendations for international students: Required—TOEFL. *Application deadline:* For fall admission, 7/6 for domestic students. Applications are processed on a rolling basis. Application fee: $30. Electronic applications accepted. *Expenses:* Tuition, state resident: full-time $5,700. Tuition, nonresident: full-time $16,518. *Financial support:* In 2007–08, 2 students received support, including research assistantships with full tuition reimbursements available (averaging $10,908 per year), teaching assistantships with full tuition reimbursements available (averaging $10,908 per year); career-related internships or fieldwork, Federal Work-Study, scholarships/grants, and health care benefits also available. Financial award application deadline: 3/15. *Faculty research:* Parent/child relationships, psychosocial care of hospitalized children, family strengths and adolescent wildness, depression in mothers and infants. *Unit head:* Dr. Carroll M. Tingle, Chair, 205-348-6158, Fax: 205-348-8153, E-mail: ctingle@ches.ua.edu. *Application contact:* Dr. Mary Elizabeth Curtner-Smith, Associate Professor, 205-348-8151, E-mail: mcurtner@ches.ua.edu.

The University of Arizona, Graduate College, College of Agriculture and Life Sciences, School of Family and Consumer Sciences, Division of Family Studies and Human Development, Tucson, AZ 85721. Offers family and consumer sciences education (MS); family studies and human development (PhD). In 2007, 3 master's, 5 doctorates awarded. Terminal master's awarded for partial completion of doctoral program. *Entrance requirements:* For master's, GRE General Test, minimum undergraduate GPA of 3.0, personal resumé, personal statement, 3 letters of recommendation. Additional exam requirements/recommendations for international students: Required—TOEFL. *Application deadline:* For fall admission, 1/15 for domestic and international students. Applications are processed on a rolling basis. Application fee: $50. *Unit head:* Dr. Angela R. Taylor, Division Chair, 520-621-7129, Fax: 520-621-3401, E-mail: artaylor@u.arizona.edu. *Application contact:* Mary Helen Scott, Administrative Assistant, 520-621-5884, Fax: 520-621-3401, E-mail: mhscott@ag.arizona.edu.

The University of British Columbia, Faculty of Graduate Studies, Faculty of Education, Department of Educational and Counseling Psychology, and Special Education, Vancouver, BC V6T 1Z1, Canada. Offers counseling psychology (M Ed, MA, PhD); development, learning and culture (PhD); guidance studies (Diploma); human development, learning and culture (M Ed, MA); measurement and evaluation and research methodology (M Ed); measurement, evaluation and research methodology (MA); measurement, evaluation, and research methodology (PhD); school psychology (M Ed, MA, PhD); special education (M Ed, MA, PhD, Diploma). Part-time programs available. *Faculty:* 37 full-time (25 women). *Students:* 293 full-time (237 women), 102 part-time (86 women). 269 applicants, 41% accepted, 108 enrolled. In 2007, 91 master's, 17 doctorates awarded. *Median time to degree:* Of those who began their doctoral program in fall 1999, 95% received their degree in 8 years or less. *Degree requirements:* For master's, thesis (for some programs); for doctorate, comprehensive exam, thesis/dissertation. *Entrance requirements:* For master's, GRE General Test (counseling psychology MA); for doctorate, GRE General Test. Additional exam requirements/recommendations for international students: Required—TOEFL. *Application deadline:* For fall admission, 12/1 for domestic and international students. Application fee: $90 Canadian dollars ($150 Canadian dollars for international students). Electronic applications accepted. *Financial support:* In 2007–08, 14 fellowships (averaging $35,000 per year), 50 research assistantships (averaging $12,000 per year), 40 teaching assistantships (averaging $5,000 per year) were awarded; career-related internships or fieldwork, Federal Work-Study, institutionally sponsored loans, scholarships/grants, health care benefits, tuition waivers (full and partial), and unspecified assistantships also available. *Faculty research:* Women, family, social problems, career transition, stress and coping problems. *Unit head:* Dr. Shelley Hymel, Head, 604-822-6022, Fax: 604-822-3302, E-mail: shelley.hymel@ubc.ca. *Application contact:* Karen Yan, Graduate Program Assistant, 604-822-6371, Fax: 604-822-3302, E-mail: karen.yan@ubc.ca.

University of Calgary, Faculty of Graduate Studies, Faculty of Education, Division of Applied Psychology, Calgary, AB T2N 1N4, Canada. Offers counseling psychology (M Ed, M Sc, PhD); human development and learning (M Ed, M Sc, PhD); school psychology (M Ed, M Sc, PhD); special education (M Ed, M Sc, PhD). Part-time programs available. *Degree requirements:* For master's, thesis (for some programs), final oral exam; for doctorate, thesis/dissertation, candidacy exam, final oral exam. *Entrance requirements:* For master's, minimum GPA of 3.0, 3 letters of reference; for doctorate, minimum GPA of 3.5, 3 letters of reference. *Faculty research:* Counselor education, family life studies, learning and cognition.

University of California, Berkeley, Graduate Division, School of Education, Division of Cognition and Development, Program in Human Development and Education, Berkeley, CA 94720-1500. Offers MA, PhD, PhD/MA. *Application deadline:* For fall admission, 12/1 for domestic students. Application fee: $70 ($90 for international students). Electronic applications accepted. *Financial support:* Unspecified assistantships available. *Application contact:* Admissions Office, 510-642-0841, Fax: 510-642-4808, E-mail: gse_info@uclink.berkeley.edu.

University of California, Davis, Graduate Studies, Graduate Group in Human Development, Davis, CA 95616. Offers PhD. *Degree requirements:* For doctorate, thesis/dissertation. *Entrance requirements:* For doctorate, GRE General Test, GRE Subject Test, minimum GPA of 3.0. Additional exam requirements/recommendations for international students: Required—TOEFL (minimum score 550 paper-based; 213 computer-based). Electronic applications accepted. *Faculty research:* Life span socioemotional and cognitive development, individual differences, relationship between biological and behavioral development, cross-cultural and cross-generational development.

University of California, Santa Barbara, Graduate Division, College of Letters and Sciences, Division of Humanities and Fine Arts, Department of Linguistics, Santa Barbara, CA 93106. Offers linguistics (PhD), including applied linguistics, cognitive science, human development, language interaction, social organizations; MA/PhD. *Faculty:* 27 full-time (20 women). *Students:* 27 full-time (20 women); includes 3 minority (2 Asian Americans or Pacific Islanders, 1 Hispanic American), 3 international. Average age 32. 46 applicants, 22% accepted, 4 enrolled. In 2007, 3 doctorates awarded. *Median time to degree:* Of those who began their doctoral program in fall 1999, 40% received their degree in 8 years or less. *Degree requirements:* For doctorate, one foreign language, thesis/dissertation, 48 units of coursework, minimum GPA of 3.7. *Entrance requirements:* For doctorate, GRE. Additional exam requirements/recommendations for international students: Required—TOEFL (minimum score 550 paper-based; 213 computer-based; 80 iBT). *Application deadline:* For fall admission, 12/1 for domestic and international students. Application fee: $60. Electronic applications accepted. *Expenses:* Tuition, nonresident: full-time $14,888. Required fees: $10,108. *Financial support:* In 2007–08, 27 students received support, including 18 fellowships with full tuition reimbursements available (averaging $10,500 per year), 4 research assistantships with full tuition reimbursements available (averaging $15,000 per year), 22 teaching assistantships (averaging $10,310 per year); Federal Work-Study, institutionally sponsored loans, scholarships/grants, health care benefits, and unspecified assistantships also available. Financial award application deadline: 12/1; financial award applicants required to submit FAFSA. *Faculty research:* Syntax, sociolinguistics, discourse and grammar, phonetics and phonology, corpus linguistics. *Unit head:* Prof. Patricia M. Clancy, Chair, 805-893-8658, E-mail: pclancy@linguistics.ucsb.edu. *Application contact:* Prof. Matthew K. Gordon, Information Contact, 805-893-5954, Fax: 805-893-7769, E-mail: mgordon@linguistics.ucsb.edu.

University of California, Santa Barbara, Graduate Division, College of Letters and Sciences, Division of Social Sciences, Department of Anthropology, Santa Barbara, CA 93106. Offers anthropology (MA, PhD), including global studies (PhD), human development (PhD), quantitative methods in social sciences (PhD), technology and society (PhD), women's studies (PhD); North American archaeology (MA); MA/PhD. *Faculty:* 13 full-time (2 women), 2 part-time/adjunct (both women). *Students:* 55 full-time (29 women); includes 10 minority (3 Asian Americans or Pacific Islanders, 7 Hispanic Americans), 10 international. Average age 32. 73 applicants, 25% accepted, 6 enrolled. In 2007, 9 master's, 8 doctorates awarded. Terminal master's awarded for partial completion of doctoral program. *Median time to degree:* Of those who began their doctoral program in fall 1999, 38% received their degree in 8 years or less. *Degree requirements:* For master's, comprehensive exam, thesis; for doctorate, comprehensive exam, thesis/dissertation. *Entrance requirements:* For master's and doctorate, GRE General Test, sample of written work, statement of purpose with completed coversheets (2 copies), post-secondary institutions attended. Additional exam requirements/recommendations for international students: Required—TOEFL (minimum score 550 paper-based; 213 computer-based; 80 iBT). *Application deadline:* For fall admission, 12/1 for domestic and international students. Application fee: $60. Electronic applications accepted. *Expenses:* Tuition, nonresident: full-time $14,888. Required fees: $10,108. *Financial support:* In 2007–08, 56 students received support, including 14 fellowships with full and partial tuition reimbursements available (averaging $9,623 per year), 13 research assistantships with full and partial tuition reimbursements available (averaging $10,000 per year), 32 teaching assistantships with partial tuition reimbursements available (averaging $19,988 per year); career-related internships or fieldwork, Federal Work-Study, institutionally sponsored loans, scholarships/grants, traineeships, health care benefits, and unspecified assistantships also available. Financial award application deadline: 12/1; financial award applicants required to submit FAFSA. *Faculty research:* Evolutionary psychology, archaeology, sociocultural anthropology, biosocial anthropology, evolutionary ecology, bioarchaeology. *Unit head:* Prof. Barbara Voorhies, Chair, 805-896-2519, Fax: 805-893-8707, E-mail: voorhies@anth.oesb.edu. *Application contact:* Larisa Traga, Graduate Program Assistant, 805-893-2516, Fax: 805-893-8707, E-mail: traga@anth.ucsb.edu.

University of Central Arkansas, Graduate School, College of Business Administration, Program in Community and Economic Development, Conway, AR 72035-0001. Offers MS. *Students:* 15 full-time (4 women), 16 part-time (9 women); includes 3 minority (2 African Americans, 1 Hispanic American), 7 international. 17 applicants, 94% accepted, 16 enrolled. In 2007, 6 degrees awarded. *Degree requirements:* For master's, comprehensive exam, thesis. *Entrance requirements:* For master's, GRE General Test, minimum GPA of 2.7. Additional exam requirements/recommendations for international students: Required—TOEFL (minimum score 550 paper-based; 213 computer-based). *Application deadline:* For fall admission, 3/1 priority date for domestic students; for spring admission, 10/1 priority date for domestic students. Applications are processed on a rolling basis. Application fee: $25 ($40 for international students). *Expenses:* Contact institution. *Financial support:* Career-related internships or fieldwork, Federal Work-Study, and unspecified assistantships available. Financial award applicants required to submit FAFSA. *Unit head:* Dr. Lauren Maxwell, Coordinator, 501-450-5349. *Application contact:* Brenda Herring, Admissions Assistant, 501-450-5065, Fax: 501-450-5678, E-mail: bherring@uca.edu.

University of Central Oklahoma, College of Graduate Studies and Research, College of Education, Department of Human Environmental Sciences, Edmond, OK 73034-5209. Offers family and child studies (MS); family and consumer science education (MS); interior design (MS); nutrition-food management (MS). Part-time programs available. *Faculty:* 5 full-time (all women), 5 part-time/adjunct (3 women). *Students:* 38 full-time (32 women), 57 part-time (54 women); includes 24 minority (13 African Americans, 4 American Indian/Alaska Native, 3 Asian Americans or Pacific Islanders, 4 Hispanic Americans), 4 international. Average age 30. 21 applicants, 95% accepted. In 2007, 20 degrees awarded. *Entrance requirements:* Additional exam requirements/recommendations for international students: Required—TOEFL (minimum score 550 paper-based; 213 computer-based). *Application deadline:* For fall admission, 7/1 for international students; for spring admission, 11/1 for international students. Applications are processed on a rolling basis. Application fee: $25. Electronic applications accepted. *Expenses:* Tuition, state resident: full-time $3,516; part-time $147 per hour. Tuition, nonresident: full-time $9,054; part-time $377 per hour. Required fees: $433; $18 per hour. *Financial support:* Career-related internships or fieldwork and unspecified assistantships available. Financial award application deadline: 3/31; financial award applicants required to submit FAFSA. *Faculty research:* Dietetics and food science. *Unit head:* Dr. Kaye Sears, Chairperson, 405-974-5786.

University of Chicago, Division of Social Sciences, Department of Comparative Human Development, Chicago, IL 60637-1513. Offers PhD. *Students:* 63. In 2007, 3 degrees awarded. *Degree requirements:* For doctorate, one foreign language, thesis/dissertation, pre-doctoral written exams. *Entrance requirements:* For doctorate, GRE General Test, GRE Subject Test. Additional exam requirements/recommendations for international students: Required—TOEFL, IELTS (minimum score 7). *Application deadline:* For fall admission, 12/10 for domestic and international students. Application fee: $55. Electronic applications accepted. *Financial support:* Fellowships, research assistantships, teaching assistantships, Federal Work-Study, institutionally sponsored loans, scholarships/grants, traineeships, health care benefits, and unspecified assistantships available. Financial award application deadline: 12/10; financial award applicants required to submit FAFSA. *Unit head:* Prof. Richard P. Taub, Chair, 773-702-3971. *Application contact:* Office of the Dean of Students, 773-702-8415.

University of Connecticut, Graduate School, College of Liberal Arts and Sciences, Department of Human Development and Family Studies, Field of Human Development and Family Studies, Storrs, CT 06269. Offers culture, health and human development (Graduate Certificate); human development and family studies (MA, PhD). *Accreditation:* AAMFT/COAMFTE. *Faculty:* 25 full-time (16 women). *Students:* 47 full-time (42 women), 9 part-time (8 women); includes 10 minority (3 African Americans, 3 Asian Americans or Pacific Islanders, 4 Hispanic Americans), 7 international. Average age 33. 79 applicants, 25% accepted, 18 enrolled. In 2007, 11 master's, 2 doctorates awarded. Terminal master's awarded for partial completion of doctoral program. *Degree requirements:* For master's, comprehensive exam; for doctorate, thesis/dissertation. *Entrance requirements:* For master's and doctorate, GRE General Test. Additional exam requirements/recommendations for international students: Required—TOEFL (minimum score 550 paper-based; 213 computer-based). *Application deadline:* For fall admission, 2/1 priority date for domestic and international students; for spring admission, 11/1 for domestic students, 10/1 for international students. Applications are processed on a rolling basis. Application fee: $55. Electronic applications accepted. *Expenses:* Tuition, state resident: part-time $469 per credit hour. Tuition, nonresident: part-time $1,218 per credit hour. *Financial support:* In 2007–08, 6 research assistantships with full tuition reimbursements, 34 teaching assistantships with full tuition reimbursements were awarded; fellowships, career-related internships or fieldwork, Federal Work-Study, scholarships/grants, health care benefits, and unspecified assistantships also available. Financial award application deadline: 2/1; financial award applicants required to submit FAFSA. *Application contact:* Liz Little, Administrative Assistant, 860-486-4721, Fax: 860-486-3452, E-mail: elizabeth.little@uconn.edu.

University of Dayton, Graduate School, School of Education and Allied Professions, Department of Counselor Education and Human Services, Dayton, OH 45469-1300. Offers college student personnel (MS Ed); community counseling (MS Ed); higher education administration (MS Ed); human development services (MS Ed); school counseling (MS Ed); school psychology (MS Ed, Ed S); teacher as child/youth development specialist (MS Ed). *Accreditation:* NCATE. Part-time and evening/weekend programs available. *Faculty:* 11 full-time (7 women), 32 part-time/adjunct (17 women). *Students:* 269 full-time (218 women), 305 part-time (255 women); includes 82 minority (66 African Americans, 4 Asian Americans or Pacific Islanders, 12 Hispanic Americans), 8 international. Average age 32. 403 applicants, 49% accepted, 117 enrolled. In 2007, 267 degrees awarded. *Degree requirements:* For master's, thesis optional, exit exam. *Entrance requirements:* For master's, MAT or GRE (if GPA is below 2.75), interview. Additional exam requirements/recommendations for international students: Required—TOEFL (minimum score 550 paper-based; 213 computer-based; 80 iBT). *Application deadline:* For fall admission, 4/10 for domestic students, 3/1 priority date for international students; for winter admission, 9/10 for domestic students, 7/1 priority date for international students; for spring admission, 1/10 for domestic students, 1/1 priority date for international students. Applications are processed on a rolling basis. Application fee: $0 ($50 for international students). Electronic applications accepted. *Financial support:* In 2007–08, 1 research assistantship with partial tuition reimbursement (averaging $7,400 per year), 4 teaching assistantships with partial tuition reimbursements (averaging $7,600 per year) were awarded; career-related internships or fieldwork, institutionally sponsored loans, health care benefits, and unspecified assistantships also available. Financial award applicants required to submit FAFSA. *Faculty research:* Anger as part of the grief process, inclusion of children with severe disabilities, comparisons of school counselors in Bosnia and the U. S., graduate and professional student socialization, use of cohort groups in doctoral programs. *Unit head:* Dr. Alan Demmitt, Chairperson, 937-229-3644, Fax: 937-229-1055. *Application contact:* Angela Jones-Glukhov, Associate Director of Graduate Admissions, 937-229-4305, Fax: 937-229-4729.

University of Delaware, College of Human Services, Education and Public Policy, Department of Individual and Family Studies, Newark, DE 19716. Offers human development and family studies (MS, PhD). Part-time programs available. *Faculty:* 21 full-time (15 women). *Students:* 20 full-time (19 women), 3 part-time (2 women); includes 2 minority (both Asian Americans or Pacific Islanders), 4 international. Average age 32. 16 applicants, 19% accepted, 3 enrolled. In 2007, 10 master's, 1 doctorate awarded. Terminal master's awarded for partial completion of doctoral program. *Median time to degree:* Of those who began their doctoral program in fall 1999, 99% received their degree in 8 years or less. *Degree requirements:* For master's, thesis or alternative; for doctorate, comprehensive exam, thesis/dissertation. *Entrance requirements:* For master's and doctorate, GRE General Test, 3 letters of recommendation. Additional exam requirements/recommendations for international students: Required—TOEFL. *Application deadline:* For fall admission, 2/1 for domestic and international students. Application fee: $60. Electronic applications accepted. *Financial support:* In 2007–08, 20 students received support, including 1 fellowship with full tuition reimbursement available (averaging $11,000 per year), 16 research assistantships with full tuition reimbursements available (averaging $11,000 per year), 3 teaching assistantships with full tuition reimbursements available (averaging $11,000 per year); career-related internships or fieldwork and institutionally sponsored loans also available. Financial award application deadline: 2/1. *Faculty research:* Early childhood inclusive education, relationships, family risk and resilience, disability issues, program development and evaluation. Total annual research expenditures: $2.5 million. *Unit head:* Dr. Donald G. Unger, Acting Chair, 302-831-1922, Fax: 302-831-8776. *Application contact:* Dr. John Bishop, Associate Professor, Graduate Coordinator, 302-831-6500, Fax: 302-831-8776, E-mail: jbbishop@udel.edu.

University of Guelph, Graduate Program Services, College of Social and Applied Human Sciences, Department of Family Relations and Applied Nutrition, Guelph, ON N1G 2W1, Canada. Offers applied nutrition (MAN); family relations and human development (M Sc, PhD), including applied human nutrition, couple and family therapy (M Sc), family relations and human development. *Accreditation:* AAMFT/COAMFTE (one or more programs are accredited). Part-time programs available. *Faculty:* 23 full-time (16 women). *Students:* 56 full-time (51 women), 5 part-time (all women); includes 4 minority (2 African Americans, 1 Asian American or Pacific Islander, 1 Hispanic American), 2 international. Average age 30. 153 applicants, 32% accepted, 33 enrolled. In 2007, 9 master's, 3 doctorates awarded. *Median time to degree:* Of those who began their doctoral program in fall 1999, 100% received their degree in 8 years or less. *Degree requirements:* For master's, thesis (for some programs); for doctorate, comprehensive exam, thesis/dissertation. *Entrance requirements:* For master's, minimum B+ average; for doctorate, master's degree in family relations and human development or related field with a minimum B+ average or master's degree in applied human nutrition. Additional exam requirements/recommendations for international students: Required—TOEFL (minimum score 600 paper-based; 250 computer-based). *Application deadline:* For fall admission, 1/2 priority date for domestic and international students. Application fee: $85. Electronic applications accepted. *Financial support:* In 2007–08, 54 students received support; fellowships, research assistantships, teaching assistantships, career-related internships or fieldwork and health care benefits available. *Faculty research:* Child and adolescent development, social gerontology, family roles and relations, couple and family therapy, applied human nutrition. Total annual research expenditures: $500,000. *Unit head:* Dr. Susan Lollis, Interim Chair, 519-824-4120 Ext. 56326, Fax: 519-766-0691, E-mail: slollis@uoguelph.ca. *Application contact:* Jo Anne Waechter, Graduate Secretary, 519-824-4120 Ext. 53968, Fax: 519-766-0691, E-mail: jwaechte@uoguelph.ca.

Human Development

University of Houston, College of Technology, Department of Human Development and Consumer Science, Houston, TX 77204. Offers MS. *Faculty:* 2 full-time (1 woman), 1 (woman) part-time/adjunct. *Students:* 17 full-time (12 women), 26 part-time (14 women); includes 12 minority (5 African Americans, 2 American Indian/Alaska Native, 4 Asian Americans or Pacific Islanders, 1 Hispanic American), 6 international. Average age 36. 25 applicants, 88% accepted, 15 enrolled. In 2007, 7 degrees awarded. *Expenses:* Tuition, state resident: full-time $6,297; part-time $262 per credit. Tuition, nonresident: full-time $12,969; part-time $540 per credit. Required fees: $2,696. *Unit head:* Carole Goodson, Chairperson, 713-743-4046, Fax: 713-743-4033.

University of Illinois at Chicago, Graduate College, College of Applied Health Sciences, Department of Disability, Disability Studies, and Human Development, Chicago, IL 60607-7128. Offers disability and human development (MS); disability studies (PhD). *Accreditation:* AOTA. Part-time programs available. *Degree requirements:* For master's, thesis optional; for doctorate, thesis/dissertation. *Entrance requirements:* For master's and doctorate, GRE General Test. Additional exam requirements/recommendations for international students: Required—TOEFL. Electronic applications accepted. *Faculty research:* Emerging trends in disability, demography and financial structure of disability services, aging and disability, empowerment of people with disabilities, health promotion in disabilities.

University of Illinois at Springfield, Graduate Programs, College of Education and Human Services, Program in Human Development Counseling, Springfield, IL 62703-5407. Offers MA. *Accreditation:* ACA. Part-time and evening/weekend programs available. *Faculty:* 4 full-time (2 women), 4 part-time/adjunct (3 women). *Students:* 28 full-time (25 women), 35 part-time (29 women); includes 6 minority (4 African Americans, 1 Asian American or Pacific Islander, 1 Hispanic American). Average age 35. 36 applicants, 22% accepted, 8 enrolled. In 2007, 9 degrees awarded. *Degree requirements:* For master's, project or comprehensive exam. *Entrance requirements:* For master's, minimum undergraduate GPA of 3.0 in last 60 hours of course work, course work in psychology, 3 letters of reference, interview, a supervised written essay. Additional exam requirements/recommendations for international students: Required—TOEFL (minimum score 550 paper-based; 213 computer-based). *Application deadline:* For fall admission, 3/15 for domestic and international students; for spring admission, 10/15 for domestic and international students. Application fee: $50 ($60 for international students). Electronic applications accepted. *Expenses:* Tuition, state resident: full-time $5,424; part-time $226 per credit hour. Tuition, nonresident: part-time $553 per credit hour. Required fees: $618 per term. *Financial support:* In 2007–08, research assistantships with full tuition reimbursements (averaging $7,988 per year), teaching assistantships with full tuition reimbursements (averaging $7,988 per year) were awarded; career-related internships or fieldwork, Federal Work-Study, scholarships/grants, health care benefits, and unspecified assistantships also available. Support available to part-time students. Financial award application deadline: 11/15; financial award applicants required to submit FAFSA. *Unit head:* Dr. William Abler, Program Administrator, 217-206-7567, Fax: 217-206-6775, E-mail: abler.william@uis.edu.

University of Illinois at Urbana–Champaign, Graduate College, College of Agricultural, Consumer and Environmental Sciences, Department of Human and Community Development, Champaign, IL 61820. Offers agricultural education (MS); human and community development (MS, PhD); MS/MSW. *Faculty:* 16 full-time (9 women), 1 part-time/adjunct (0 women). *Students:* 26 full-time (22 women), 10 part-time (6 women); includes 9 minority (5 African Americans, 3 Asian Americans or Pacific Islanders, 1 Hispanic American), 5 international. 28 applicants, 46% accepted, 9 enrolled. In 2007, 22 master's, 8 doctorates awarded. *Degree requirements:* For doctorate, thesis/dissertation. *Entrance requirements:* For master's, GRE, minimum GPA of 3.0. *Application deadline:* For fall admission, 1/16 for domestic students; for spring admission, 12/1 for domestic students. Applications are processed on a rolling basis. Application fee: $60 ($75 for international students). Electronic applications accepted. *Financial support:* In 2007–08, 12 fellowships, 16 research assistantships, 16 teaching assistantships were awarded; tuition waivers (full and partial) also available. Financial award application deadline: 2/15. *Unit head:* Robert Hughes, Head, 217-333-3790, Fax: 217-244-7877, E-mail: hughesro@uiuc.edu. *Application contact:* Leann Topol, Clerk, 217-333-3869, Fax: 217-244-7877, E-mail: ltopol@uiuc.edu.

University of Kansas, Research and Graduate Studies, College of Liberal Arts and Sciences, Department of Applied Behavioral Science, Lawrence, KS 66045. Offers applied behavioral science (MA); behavioral psychology (PhD); clinical child psychology (PhD); developmental and child psychology (PhD); human development (MA). *Faculty:* 18. *Students:* 38 full-time (27 women), 9 part-time (8 women); includes 7 minority (2 African Americans, 2 Asian Americans or Pacific Islanders, 3 Hispanic Americans), 2 international. Average age 33. 41 applicants, 17% accepted, 3 enrolled. In 2007, 7 master's, 9 doctorates awarded. Terminal master's awarded for partial completion of doctoral program. *Degree requirements:* For master's, thesis; for doctorate, thesis/dissertation, comprehensive oral and written exams, journal reviews. *Entrance requirements:* Additional exam requirements/recommendations for international students: Required—TOEFL, TWE. *Application deadline:* For fall admission, 1/15 priority date for domestic and international students. Application fee: $55 ($60 for international students). Electronic applications accepted. *Expenses:* Tuition, state resident: full-time $5,838. Tuition, nonresident: full-time $13,409. Tuition and fees vary according to program. *Financial support:* Fellowships, research assistantships with full and partial tuition reimbursements, teaching assistantships with full and partial tuition reimbursements, career-related internships or fieldwork, traineeships, tuition waivers (full), and unspecified assistantships available. Financial award application deadline: 2/1. *Faculty research:* Early childhood, developmental disabilities, community health and development, adults with disabilities, applied behavior analysis. *Unit head:* Edward K. Morris, Chair, 785-864-4840, Fax: 785-864-5202, E-mail: ekm@ku.edu. *Application contact:* Gregory J. Madden, Graduate Director, 785-864-4840, Fax: 785-864-5202, E-mail: gmadden@ku.edu.

University of Maine, Graduate School, College of Education and Human Development, Department of Human Development and Family Relations, Orono, ME 04469. Offers human development (MS). Part-time programs available. *Faculty:* 11 full-time (5 women). *Students:* 11 full-time (10 women), 2 part-time (1 woman); includes 1 minority (African American) Average age 33. 9 applicants, 67% accepted, 3 enrolled. *Degree requirements:* For master's, thesis. *Entrance requirements:* For master's, GRE General Test. Additional exam requirements/recommendations for international students: Required—TOEFL. *Application deadline:* For fall admission, 2/1 priority date for domestic students. Applications are processed on a rolling basis. Application fee: $60. Electronic applications accepted. *Financial support:* In 2007–08, 5 teaching assistantships with tuition reimbursements (averaging $9,010 per year) were awarded; research assistantships with tuition reimbursements, career-related internships or fieldwork, Federal Work-Study, institutionally sponsored loans, tuition waivers (full and partial), and unspecified assistantships also available. Financial award application deadline: 3/1. *Faculty research:* Methods to assess nutrient intake and risk, carnitine-supplemented diets for protein-calorie malnutrition, nutrition education, grandfathers' perceptions of relations to grandchildren, social participation of spouses in distressed and nondistressed marriages. *Unit head:* Dr. Sandra Caron, Coordinator, 207-581-3138, Fax: 207-581-3120. *Application contact:* Scott G. Delcourt, Associate Dean of the Graduate School, 207-581-3219, Fax: 207-581-3232, E-mail: graduate@maine.edu.

University of Maryland, College Park, Graduate Studies, College of Arts and Humanities, School of Languages, Literature, and Cultures, Program in Second Language Acquisition and Application, College Park, MD 20742. Offers French (MA); German (MA); Japanese (MA); Russian (MA); second language instruction (PhD); second language learning (PhD); second language measurement and assessment (PhD); second language use (PhD); Spanish (MA). *Students:* 1 (woman) full-time, 1 international. 50 applicants, 14% accepted. *Entrance requirements:* For master's, BA or BS in related field, demonstrated language competency, 3 letters of reference. *Application deadline:* For fall admission, 1/15 for domestic students, 2/1 for international students; for spring admission, 9/15 for domestic students, 6/1 for international students. Applications are processed on a rolling basis. Application fee: $60. Electronic applications accepted. *Financial support:* In 2007–08, 1 research assistantship (averaging $20,450 per year) was awarded; fellowships also available. *Faculty research:* Second language acquisition, pedagogical perspectives, technological applications, language use in professional contexts. *Unit head:* Dr. Cynthia L. Martin, Acting Chair, 301-405-4244, E-mail: cmartin@umd.edu. *Application contact:* Dean of Graduate School, 301-405-0358, Fax: 301-314-9305.

University of Maryland, College Park, Graduate Studies, College of Education, Department of Human Development, College Park, MD 20742. Offers early childhood/elementary education (M Ed, MA, Ed D, PhD); human development (M Ed, MA, Ed D, PhD). *Accreditation:* NCATE. Part-time and evening/weekend programs available. Postbaccalaureate distance learning degree programs offered. *Faculty:* 44 full-time (38 women), 13 part-time/adjunct (7 women). *Students:* 62 full-time (55 women), 35 part-time (31 women); includes 18 minority (9 African Americans, 6 Asian Americans or Pacific Islanders, 3 Hispanic Americans), 9 international. 99 applicants, 39% accepted, 27 enrolled. In 2007, 11 master's, 14 doctorates awarded. *Median time to degree:* Of those who began their doctoral program in fall 1999, 57% received their degree in 8 years or less. *Degree requirements:* For master's, comprehensive exam, thesis optional; for doctorate, comprehensive exam, thesis/dissertation, essay, exam, research paper. *Entrance requirements:* For master's, GRE General Test, minimum GPA of 3.0, 3 letters of recommendation; for doctorate, GRE General Test or MAT, minimum undergraduate GPA of 3.0, graduate 3.5; 3 letters of recommendation. Additional exam requirements/recommendations for international students: Required—TOEFL. *Application deadline:* For fall admission, 5/1 for domestic students, 11/15 for international students. Applications are processed on a rolling basis. Application fee: $60. Electronic applications accepted. *Financial support:* In 2007–08, 14 fellowships with full tuition reimbursements (averaging $14,337 per year), 2 research assistantships with tuition reimbursements (averaging $17,256 per year), 37 teaching assistantships with tuition reimbursements (averaging $16,102 per year) were awarded; Federal Work-Study and scholarships/grants also available. Support available to part-time students. Financial award applicants required to submit FAFSA. *Faculty research:* Developmental science, educational psychology, cognitive development, language development. Total annual research expenditures: $3.2 million. *Unit head:* Dr. Allan L. Wigfield, Chair, 301-405-1659, Fax: 301-405-2891, E-mail: awigfield@umd.edu. *Application contact:* Dean of Graduate School, 301-405-0358, Fax: 301-314-9305.

University of Missouri–Columbia, Graduate School, College of Human Environmental Science, Department of Human Development and Family Studies, Columbia, MO 65211. Offers MA, MS, PhD. *Entrance requirements:* For master's, GRE General Test, minimum GPA of 3.0. Additional exam requirements/recommendations for international students: Required—TOEFL (minimum score 550 paper-based; 220 computer-based).

University of Nevada, Reno, Graduate School, College of Health and Human Sciences, Department of Human Development and Family Studies, Reno, NV 89557. Offers MS. *Faculty:* 14. *Students:* 6 full-time (all women), 12 part-time (10 women); includes 5 minority (1 African American, 2 Asian Americans or Pacific Islanders, 2 Hispanic Americans), 1 international. Average age 33. 11 applicants, 45% accepted, 4 enrolled. In 2007, 3 degrees awarded. *Degree requirements:* For master's, thesis. *Entrance requirements:* For master's, GRE General Test, minimum GPA of 3.0. Additional exam requirements/recommendations for international students: Required—TOEFL. *Application deadline:* For fall admission, 3/30 for domestic students; for spring admission, 10/1 for domestic students. Application fee: $60 ($95 for international students). *Expenses:* Tuition, state resident: full-time $2,774; part-time $154 per credit. Tuition, nonresident: full-time $13,578; part-time $330 per credit. Required fees: $49 per semester. *Financial support:* In 2007–08, 10 research assistantships, 2 teaching assistantships were awarded; tuition waivers (full) also available. Financial award application deadline: 3/30. *Unit head:* Dr. Karen Kopera–Frye, Graduate Program Director, 775-784-7010, E-mail: kfrye@unr.edu.

The University of North Carolina at Greensboro, Graduate School, School of Human Environmental Sciences, Department of Human Development and Family Studies, Greensboro, NC 27412-5001. Offers M Ed, MS, PhD. *Faculty:* 21 full-time (17 women), 9 part-time/adjunct (7 women). *Students:* 44 full-time (42 women), 9 part-time (7 women); includes 12 minority (5 African Americans, 1 American Indian/Alaska Native, 5 Asian Americans or Pacific Islanders, 1 Hispanic American). 58 applicants, 29% accepted. *Degree requirements:* For master's, one foreign language; for doctorate, one foreign language, thesis/dissertation. *Entrance requirements:* For master's and doctorate, GRE General Test. Additional exam requirements/recommendations for international students: Required—TOEFL. *Application deadline:* For fall admission, 3/15 for domestic students. Application fee: $45. Electronic applications accepted. *Expenses:* Contact institution. *Financial support:* Fellowships with full tuition reimbursements, research assistantships with full tuition reimbursements, teaching assistantships with full tuition reimbursements, career-related internships or fieldwork, Federal Work-Study, scholarships/grants, traineeships, and unspecified assistantships available. Support available to part-time students. *Faculty research:* Adolescent mothers, multi-handicapped, older adults. *Unit head:* Dr. Dan Perlman, Chair, 336-334-5307, Fax: 336-334-5076, E-mail: d_perlma@uncg.edu. *Application contact:* Michelle Harkleroad, Director of Graduate Admissions, 336-334-4884, Fax: 336-334-4424, E-mail: mbharkle@uncg.edu.

University of North Texas, Robert B. Toulouse School of Graduate Studies, College of Education, Department of Educational Psychology, Program in Development and Family Studies, Denton, TX 76203. Offers MS. Evening/weekend programs available. *Students:* 9 full-time (8 women), 12 part-time (all women); includes 2 minority (1 African American, 1 Hispanic American), 2 international. Average age 29. 12 applicants, 58% accepted, 3 enrolled. In 2007, 5 master's awarded. *Degree requirements:* For master's, comprehensive exam, thesis optional. *Entrance requirements:* For master's, GRE General Test, letter of application, resumè, references. Additional exam requirements/recommendations for international students: Required—proof of English language proficiency required for non-native English speakers; Recommended—TOEFL (minimum score 550 paper-based; 213 computer-based). *Application deadline:* For fall admission, 7/15 for domestic students; for spring admission, 11/15 for domestic students. Application fee: $50 ($75 for international students). *Financial support:* Teaching assistantships, career-related internships or fieldwork, Federal Work-Study, and institutionally sponsored loans available. Financial award application deadline: 4/1. *Faculty research:* Parent-child issues, cognitive development, social development. *Application contact:* Dr. Rebecca Glover, Graduate Advisor, 940-565-2000, E-mail: bglover@unt.edu.

University of Pennsylvania, Graduate School of Education, Division of Applied Psychology and Human Development, Interdisciplinary Studies in Human Development, Philadelphia, PA 19104. Offers MS Ed, PhD. Part-time programs available. Terminal master's awarded for partial completion of doctoral program. *Degree requirements:* For master's, exam; for doctorate, thesis/dissertation, exam. *Entrance requirements:* For master's, GRE General Test; for doctorate, GRE General Test, GRE Subject Test. Electronic applications accepted. Expenses: Contact institution. *Faculty research:* Child development, risk and resilience among vulnerable youth in high-risk environments.

University of Puerto Rico, Medical Sciences Campus, Graduate School of Public Health, Department of Human Development, San Juan, PR 00936-5067. Offers developmental disabilities-early intervention (Certificate); gerontology (MPH, Certificate); health science nutrition (MS); mother and child health (MPH); nurse midwifery (MPH, Certificate). Part-time programs available. *Entrance requirements:* For master's, GRE, previous course work in algebra.

University of St. Thomas, Graduate Studies, School of Education, Program in Organization Learning and Development, St. Paul, MN 55105-1096. Offers MA, Ed D, Certificate. Part-time and evening/weekend programs available. Postbaccalaureate distance learning degree programs offered (minimal on-campus study). *Degree requirements:* For doctorate, comprehensive exam, thesis/dissertation. *Entrance requirements:* For master's, minimum GPA of 2.75, 3 letters of reference; for doctorate, MAT, minimum GPA of 3.5, interview; for Certificate, minimum graduate GPA of 3.25. Additional exam requirements/recommendations for international students:

Required—TOEFL (minimum score 550 paper-based; 213 computer-based). Expenses: Contact institution. *Faculty research:* Workplace conflict, physician leaders, entrepreneurship education, mentoring.

University of South Africa, College of Human Sciences, Pretoria, South Africa. Offers adult education (M Ed); African languages (MA, PhD); African politics (MA, PhD); Afrikaans (MA, PhD); ancient history (MA, PhD); ancient Near Eastern studies (MA, PhD); anthropology (MA, PhD); applied linguistics (MA); Arabic (MA, PhD); archaeology (MA); art history (MA); Biblical archaeology (MA); Biblical studies (M Th, D Th, PhD); Christian spirituality (M Th, D Th); church history (M Th, D Th); classical studies (MA, PhD); clinical psychology (MA); communication (MA, PhD); comparative education (M Ed, Ed D); consulting psychology (D Admin, D Com, PhD); curriculum studies (M Ed, Ed D); development studies (M Admin, MA, D Admin, PhD); didactics (M Ed, Ed D); education (M Tech); education management (M Ed, Ed D); educational psychology (M Ed); English (MA); environmental education (M Ed); French (MA, PhD); German (MA, PhD); Greek (MA); guidance and counseling (M Ed); health studies (MA, PhD), including health sciences education (MA), health services management (MA), medical and surgical nursing science (critical care general) (MA), midwifery and neonatal nursing science (MA), trauma and emergency care (MA); history (MA, PhD); history of education (Ed D); inclusive education (M Ed, Ed D); information and communications technology policy and regulation (MA); information science (MA, MIS, PhD); international politics (MA, PhD); Islamic studies (MA, PhD); Italian (MA, PhD); Judaica (MA, PhD); linguistics (MA, PhD); mathematical education (M Ed); mathematics education (MA); missiology (M Th, D Th); modern Hebrew (MA, PhD); musicology (MA, MMus, D Mus, PhD); natural science education (M Ed); New Testament (M Th, D Th); Old Testament (D Th); pastoral therapy (M Th, D Th); philosophy (MA); philosophy of education (M Ed, Ed D); politics (MA, PhD); Portuguese (MA, PhD); practical theology (M Th, D Th); psychology (MA, MS, PhD); psychology of education (M Ed, Ed D); public health (MA); religious studies (MA, D Th, PhD); Romance languages (MA); Russian (MA, PhD); Semitic languages (MA, PhD); social behavior studies in HIV/AIDS (MA); social science (mental health) (MA); social science in development studies (MA); social science in psychology (MA); social science in social work (MA); social science in sociology (MA); social work (MSW, DSW, PhD); socio-education (M Ed, Ed D); sociolinguistics (MA); sociology (MA, PhD); Spanish (MA, PhD); systematic theology (M Th, D Th); TESOL (teaching English to speakers of other languages) (MA); theological ethics (M Th, D Th); theory of literature (MA, PhD); urban ministries (D Th); urban ministry (M Th).

The University of Texas at Austin, Graduate School, College of Education, Department of Educational Psychology, Austin, TX 78712-1111. Offers academic educational psychology (M Ed, MA); counseling education (M Ed); counseling psychology (PhD); human development and education (PhD); learning cognition and instruction (PhD); quantitative methods (PhD); school psychology (PhD). *Accreditation:* APA (one or more programs are accredited). *Degree requirements:* For master's, thesis optional; for doctorate, thesis/dissertation. *Entrance requirements:* For master's and doctorate, GRE General Test, 3 letters of recommendation. Additional exam requirements/recommendations for international students: Required—TOEFL.

University of Victoria, Faculty of Graduate Studies, Faculty of Education, Department of Educational Psychology and Leadership Studies, Victoria, BC V8W 2Y2, Canada. Offers aboriginal communities counseling (M Ed); counseling (M Ed, MA); educational psychology (M Ed, MA, PhD), including counseling psychology (M Ed, MA), leadership studies (PhD), learning and development (MA, PhD), measurement and evaluation, special education (M Ed, MA); leadership studies (M Ed, MA). Part-time programs available. *Faculty:* 18 full-time (10 women), 4 part-time/adjunct (2 women). *Students:* 133, 8 international. Average age 30. In 2007, 48 master's, 2 doctorates awarded. *Degree requirements:* For master's, thesis (for some programs), comprehensive exam (M Ed); for doctorate, comprehensive exam, thesis/dissertation, candidacy exam. *Entrance requirements:* For master's, 2 years of work experience in a relevant field, minimum B average; for doctorate, GRE, 2 years of work experience in a relevant field, minimum B average. Additional exam requirements/recommendations for international students: Required—TOEFL (minimum score 575 paper-based; 233 computer-based), IELTS (minimum score 7). *Application deadline:* Applications are processed on a rolling basis. Application fee: $75 ($125 for international students). *Expenses:* Tuition, state resident: full-time $3,110. International tuition: $3,700 full-time. Tuition and fees vary according to program. *Financial support:* In 2007–08, 29 students received support; fellowships, research assistantships, teaching assistantships, institutionally sponsored loans available. Financial award application deadline: 2/15. *Faculty research:* Learning and development (child, adolescent and adult), special education and exceptional children. *Unit head:* Dr. John Walsh, Chair, 250-721-7799, Fax: 250-721-6190. *Application contact:* Gloria F. Bennett, Graduate Program Assistant, 250-472-5005, Fax: 250-721-6190, E-mail: gbennett@uvic.ca.

University of Victoria, Faculty of Graduate Studies, Faculty of Human and Social Development, Studies in Policy and Practice Program, Victoria, BC V8W 2Y2, Canada. Offers MA. Part-time programs available. *Faculty:* 5 full-time (4 women). *Students:* 8 full-time (all women). Average age 28. 10 applicants, 60% accepted, 5 enrolled. In 2007, 1 degree awarded. *Degree requirements:* For master's, thesis. *Entrance requirements:* For master's, resumé. Additional exam requirements/recommendations for international students: Required—TOEFL (minimum score 575 paper-based; 233 computer-based), IELTS (minimum score 7). *Application deadline:* For fall admission, 12/1 for domestic and international students. Application fee: $75 ($125 for international students). Electronic applications accepted. *Expenses:* Tuition, state resident: full-time $3,110. International tuition: $3,700 full-time. Tuition and fees vary according to program. *Financial support:* In 2007–08, fellowships (averaging $13,500 per year), research assistantships (averaging $4,000 per year) were awarded; career-related internships or fieldwork, scholarships/grants, and health care benefits also available. Financial award application deadline: 2/15. *Faculty research:* Women's issues, public policy formation and implementation, health promotion and education, children, youth and families. *Unit head:* Dr. Pamela Moss, Graduate Advisor, 250-721-6297, Fax: 250-721-7067, E-mail: pamelam@uvic.ca. *Application contact:* Daisy Williams, Program Assistant, 250-721-8204, Fax: 250-721-7067, E-mail: sppgrad@uvic.ca.

University of Washington, Graduate School, College of Education, Program in Educational Psychology, Seattle, WA 98195. Offers human development and cognition (M Ed, PhD); measurement and research (M Ed, PhD); school counseling (M Ed, PhD); school psychology (M Ed, PhD). *Accreditation:* APA. *Degree requirements:* For master's, thesis optional; for doctorate, thesis/dissertation. *Entrance requirements:* For master's and doctorate, GRE General Test, minimum GPA of 3.0. Additional exam requirements/recommendations for international students: Required—TOEFL.

University of Wisconsin–Madison, Graduate School, School of Human Ecology, Program in Human Development and Family Studies, Madison, WI 53706-1380. Offers MS, PhD. Part-time programs available. Terminal master's awarded for partial completion of doctoral program. *Degree requirements:* For master's, thesis; for doctorate, comprehensive exam, thesis/dissertation. *Entrance requirements:* For master's, GRE General Test, 3 letters of recommendation; for doctorate, GRE General Test, MS or MA, 3 letters of recommendation. Additional exam requirements/recommendations for international students: Required—TOEFL. Electronic applications accepted. *Faculty research:* Human development, adolescence, adulthood, prevention, intervention.

University of Wisconsin–Stevens Point, College of Professional Studies, School of Health Promotion and Human Development, Stevens Point, WI 54481-3897. Offers human and community resources (MS); nutritional sciences (MS). Part-time programs available. *Degree requirements:* For master's, thesis or alternative. *Entrance requirements:* For master's, minimum GPA of 2.75. *Application deadline:* For fall admission, 5/1 priority date for domestic students. Applications are processed on a rolling basis. Application fee: $45. *Expenses:* Tuition, state resident: full-time $6,161. Tuition, nonresident: full-time $16,771. Required fees: $884. Tuition and fees vary according to course load. *Financial support:* Research assistantships, teaching assistantships, career-related internships or fieldwork, Federal Work-Study, and unspecified assistantships available. Support available to part-time students. Financial award application deadline: 5/1; financial award applicants required to submit FAFSA. *Unit head:* Dr. Marty Loy, Head, 715-346-2830, Fax: 715-346-2720. *Application contact:* Dr. Jasia Steinmetz, Information Contact, 715-346-2830, Fax: 715-346-2720, E-mail: jsteinme@uwsp.edu.

University of Wisconsin–Stout, Graduate School, College of Human Development, Program in Family Studies and Human Development, Menomonie, WI 54751. Offers MS. Part-time programs available. *Faculty:* 2 full-time (1 woman). *Students:* 1 (woman) full-time, 15 part-time (14 women); includes 1 minority (African American), 1 international. Average age 35. 4 applicants, 100% accepted, 1 enrolled. In 2007, 4 degrees awarded. *Degree requirements:* For master's, thesis. *Entrance requirements:* For master's, minimum GPA of 2.75. Additional exam requirements/recommendations for international students: Required—TOEFL (minimum score 500 paper-based; 173 computer-based; 61 iBT). *Application deadline:* Applications are processed on a rolling basis. Application fee: $45. Electronic applications accepted. *Expenses:* Tuition, state resident: part-time $332 per credit. Tuition, nonresident: part-time $553 per credit. *Financial support:* In 2007–08, 2 research assistantships with partial tuition reimbursements (averaging $8,712 per year) were awarded; teaching assistantships with partial tuition reimbursements, Federal Work-Study, scholarships/grants, tuition waivers (partial), and unspecified assistantships also available. Support available to part-time students. Financial award application deadline: 4/1; financial award applicants required to submit FAFSA. *Faculty research:* Diversity, work and family medical ethics, family policy, dementia and families. *Unit head:* Dr. Dale Hawley, Director, 715-232-1273, E-mail: hawleyd@uwstout.edu. *Application contact:* Anne E. Johnson, Graduate Student Evaluator, 715-232-1322, Fax: 715-232-2413, E-mail: johnsona@uwstout.edu.

Utah State University, School of Graduate Studies, College of Education and Human Services, Department of Family, Consumer, and Human Development, Logan, UT 84322. Offers family and human development (MFHD); family, consumer, and human development (MS, PhD), including adolescence/youth (MS), adult development/aging (MS), consumer science (MS), infancy/childhood (MS), marriage and family relations (MS), marriage and family therapy (MS). *Accreditation:* AAMFT/COAMFTE (one or more programs are accredited). Part-time and evening/weekend programs available. Postbaccalaureate distance learning degree programs offered (minimal on-campus study). *Degree requirements:* For master's, thesis; for doctorate, comprehensive exam, thesis/dissertation, competencies. *Entrance requirements:* For master's, GRE General Test or MAT, minimum GPA of 3.0, 3 letters of recommendation; for doctorate, GRE, minimum GPA of 3.0, 3 letters of recommendation. Additional exam requirements/recommendations for international students: Required—TOEFL. Electronic applications accepted. *Faculty research:* Marriage and family relations, adolescent problem behavior, family financial management, early literacy, mental health in the elderly, parent child attachment.

Vanderbilt University, Peabody College, Department of Human and Organizational Development, Nashville, TN 37240-1001. Offers community development action (M Ed); human development counseling (M Ed). *Accreditation:* ACA; NCATE. Part-time programs available. *Faculty:* 19 full-time (9 women), 14 part-time/adjunct (11 women). *Students:* 55 full-time (49 women), 4 part-time (3 women); includes 17 minority (12 African Americans, 5 Hispanic Americans), 2 international. Average age 27. 106 applicants, 55% accepted, 32 enrolled. In 2007, 30 degrees awarded. *Degree requirements:* For master's, comprehensive exam, thesis optional. *Entrance requirements:* For master's, GRE General Test, MAT. Additional exam requirements/recommendations for international students: Required—TOEFL (minimum score 550 paper-based; 213 computer-based). *Application deadline:* For fall admission, 12/31 priority date for domestic and international students; for spring admission, 11/1 priority date for domestic and international students. Applications are processed on a rolling basis. Application fee: $0. Electronic applications accepted. *Financial support:* In 2007–08, 41 students received support, including 11 fellowships with full and partial tuition reimbursements available, 10 research assistantships with full and partial tuition reimbursements available, 20 teaching assistantships with full and partial tuition reimbursements available; Federal Work-Study, institutionally sponsored loans, scholarships/grants, tuition waivers (partial), and unspecified assistantships also available. Support available to part-time students. Financial award application deadline: 2/1; financial award applicants required to submit FAFSA. *Faculty research:* Community psychology, community development and urban policy, counseling and mental health services, organizational development and institutional change; youth physical and behavioral health in schools and communities. *Unit head:* Joseph Cunningham, Chair, 615-322-6881, Fax: 615-322-1141, E-mail: joe.cunningham@vanderbilt.edu. *Application contact:* Sherrie Lane, Office Assistant, 615-322-8484, Fax: 615-322-1141, E-mail: sherrie.a.lane@vanderbilt.edu.

Virginia Polytechnic Institute and State University, Graduate School, College of Liberal Arts and Human Sciences, Department of Human Development, Blacksburg, VA 24061. Offers adult development and aging (MS, PhD); adult learning and human resource development (MS, PhD); child development (MS, PhD); family studies (MS, PhD); marriage and family therapy (MS, PhD). *Accreditation:* AAMFT/COAMFTE (one or more programs are accredited). *Entrance requirements:* For master's and doctorate, GRE General Test. Additional exam requirements/recommendations for international students: Required—TOEFL (minimum score 600 paper-based; 250 computer-based). Electronic applications accepted. *Faculty research:* Stress management, children's play, dual-career families, social cognition, relationships of elderly.

Washington State University, Graduate School, College of Agricultural, Human, and Natural Resource Sciences, Department of Human Development, Pullman, WA 99164. Offers MA. Part-time programs available. *Faculty:* 12 full-time (9 women). *Students:* 12 full-time (11 women), 1 (woman) part-time; includes 1 minority (Hispanic American), 2 international. Average age 25. 14 applicants, 57% accepted, 6 enrolled. In 2007, 6 degrees awarded. *Degree requirements:* For master's, comprehensive exam (for some programs), thesis (for some programs), oral exam. *Entrance requirements:* For master's, GRE General Test, minimum GPA of 3.0, 3 letters of recommendation. Additional exam requirements/recommendations for international students: Required—TOEFL. *Application deadline:* For fall admission, 2/15 priority date for domestic students, 1/1 for international students; for spring admission, 6/1 for international students. Application fee: $50. Electronic applications accepted. *Financial support:* In 2007–08, 12 students received support, including 1 research assistantship with partial tuition reimbursement available (averaging $13,917 per year), 11 teaching assistantships with partial tuition reimbursements available (averaging $13,056 per year); Federal Work-Study, institutionally sponsored loans, tuition waivers (partial), and teaching associateships also available. Financial award application deadline: 2/15; financial award applicants required to submit FAFSA. *Faculty research:* Family processes, social development of children, quality child care, community collaborations, parent-child relationships. Total annual research expenditures: $290,253. *Unit head:* Dr. Thomas G. Power, Chair, 509-355-9540, Fax: 509-335-2456, E-mail: tompower@wsu.edu. *Application contact:* Graduate School Admissions, 800-GRADWSU, Fax: 509-335-1949, E-mail: gradsch@wsu.edu.

Wayne State University, College of Liberal Arts and Sciences, Department of Psychology, Program in Human Development, Detroit, MI 48202. Offers MA. *Students:* 4 full-time (all women), 6 part-time (all women); includes 1 minority (African American) Average age 31. 15 applicants, 40% accepted, 4 enrolled. In 2007, 3 degrees awarded. *Entrance requirements:* For master's, GRE General Test. Additional exam requirements/recommendations for international students: Required—TOEFL (minimum score 550 paper-based; 213 computer-based); Recommended—TWE (minimum score 6). *Application deadline:* For fall admission, 6/15 for domestic students, 6/1 for international students; for winter admission, 10/1 for international students; for spring admission, 10/15 for domestic students, 2/1 for international students. Applications are processed on a rolling basis. Application fee: $30 ($50 for international students). Electronic applications accepted. *Expenses:* Tuition, state resident: part-time $403 per credit hour. Tuition, nonresident: part-time $890 per credit hour. *Financial support:* Application deadline: 2/1. *Faculty research:* Emotional expression, peer influence in adolescence, preschool concept formation and memory, mother-infant interaction. *Unit head:* Dr. Melissa

Human Development

Wayne State University (continued)

Kaplan-Estrin, Graduate Director, 313-577-2824, Fax: 313-577-7636, E-mail: mkestrin@sun.science.wayne.edu.

West Virginia University, Davis College of Agriculture, Forestry and Consumer Sciences, Division of Resource Management and Sustainable Development, Morgantown, WV 26506. Offers agricultural and extension education (MS, PhD), including agricultural and extension education, teaching vocational-agriculture (MS); agricultural and resource economics (MS); human and community development (PhD); natural resource economics (PhD); resource management (PhD); resource management and sustainable development (PhD). Part-time programs available. *Faculty:* 19 full-time (5 women), 8 part-time/adjunct (3 women). *Students:* 30 full-time (15 women), 11 part-time (5 women); includes 4 minority (3 African Americans, 1 Asian American or Pacific Islander), 15 international. Average age 33. 35 applicants, 77% accepted, 11 enrolled. In 2007, 1 degree awarded. *Degree requirements:* For master's, thesis; for doctorate, comprehensive exam, thesis/dissertation. *Entrance requirements:* For master's, GRE General Test. Additional exam requirements/recommendations for international students: Required—TOEFL. *Application deadline:* Applications are processed on a rolling basis. Application fee: $50. *Expenses:* Tuition, state resident: full-time $5,196; part-time $292 per credit hour. Tuition, nonresident: full-time $15,064; part-time $840 per credit hour. Tuition and fees vary according to program. *Financial support:* In 2007–08, 32 students received support, including 28 research assistantships (averaging $11,700 per year); teaching assistantships, Federal Work-Study, institutionally sponsored loans, and tuition waivers (full and partial) also available. Financial award application deadline: 2/1; financial award applicants required to submit FAFSA. *Faculty research:* Environmental economics, energy economics, agriculture. Total annual research expenditures: $1.3 million. *Unit head:* Dr. Timothy T. Phipps, Director, 304-293-6253 Ext. 2474, Fax: 304-293-3752, E-mail: tphipps@mail.wvu.edu.

Wheelock College, Graduate Programs, Division of Arts and Sciences, Boston, MA 02215-4176. Offers human development (MS). *Entrance requirements:* Additional exam requirements/recommendations for international students: Required—TOEFL. Electronic applications accepted.

Industrial and Organizational Psychology

Adler Graduate School, Program in Adlerian Studies, Richfield, MN 55423. Offers art therapy specialization (MA); clinical counseling track (MA); coaching and consulting in organizations (Certificate); management consulting and organizational leadership (MA); marriage and family track (MA); non-clinical Adlerian studies track (MA); personal and professional life coaching (Certificate); school counseling (MA). Part-time and evening/weekend programs available. *Faculty:* 4 full-time (1 woman), 44 part-time/adjunct (27 women). *Students:* Average age 37. 46 applicants, 96% accepted, 44 enrolled. In 2007, 37 degrees awarded. *Degree requirements:* For master's, thesis or alternative, 500-700 hour internship, depending on license choice. *Entrance requirements:* For master's, minimum undergraduate GPA of 3.0, 12 credits of course work in psychology or related field. *Application deadline:* For fall admission, 10/1 priority date for domestic students; for winter admission, 1/1 priority date for domestic students; for spring admission, 4/1 priority date for domestic students. Applications are processed on a rolling basis. Application fee: $50. *Expenses:* Tuition: Part-time $430 per credit. Required fees: $85 per term. *Financial support:* In 2007–08, 121 students received support. Career-related internships or fieldwork and tuition waivers available. Support available to part-time students. Financial award applicants required to submit FAFSA. *Unit head:* Dr. Dennis Rislove, President, 612-861-7554 Ext. 106, Fax: 612-861-7559, E-mail: rislove@alfredadler.edu. *Application contact:* Evelyn B. Haas, Director of Student Services and Admissions, 612-861-7554 Ext. 103, Fax: 612-861-7559, E-mail: ev@alfredadler.edu.

Adler School of Professional Psychology, Programs in Psychology, Chicago, IL 60601-7203. Offers art therapy (Certificate); clinical hypnosis (Certificate); clinical psychology (Psy D); counseling psychology (MACP); counseling psychology/art therapy (MACAT); gerontology (MAGP); marriage and family counseling (MAMFC); marriage and family therapy (Certificate); organizational psychology (MAO); substance abuse counseling (MASAC, Certificate); Psy D/Certificate; Psy D/MACAT; Psy D/MACP; Psy D/MAMFC; Psy D/MASAC. *Accreditation:* APA. Part-time and evening/weekend programs available. Terminal master's awarded for partial completion of doctoral program. *Degree requirements:* For master's, thesis or alternative, oral exam, practicum; for doctorate, thesis/dissertation, clinical exam, internship, oral exam, practicum, written qualifying exam. *Entrance requirements:* For master's, 12 semester hours in psychology, minimum GPA of 3.0; for doctorate, 18 semester hours in psychology, minimum GPA of 3.25; for Certificate, appropriate master's or doctoral degree.

See Close-Up on page 1363.

Alliant International University–Fresno, Marshall Goldsmith School of Management, Organizational Psychology Division, Fresno, CA 93727. Offers organizational behavior (MA); organizational development (Psy D); MA/PhD; Psy D/MA. Part-time and evening/weekend programs available. *Degree requirements:* For doctorate, thesis/dissertation. *Entrance requirements:* For doctorate, interview, minimum GPA of 3.0. Additional exam requirements/recommendations for international students: Required—TOEFL (minimum score 600 paper-based; 250 computer-based), TWE (minimum score 5). Electronic applications accepted. *Faculty research:* Leadership, ethics and management, career development, human resources management.

Alliant International University–Los Angeles, Marshall Goldsmith School of Management, Organizational Psychology Division, Alhambra, CA 91803-1360. Offers industrial/organizational psychology (MA, PhD). Part-time programs available. Terminal master's awarded for partial completion of doctoral program. *Degree requirements:* For doctorate, thesis/dissertation. *Entrance requirements:* For master's and doctorate, interview, minimum GPA of 3.0 in both psychology and overall. Additional exam requirements/recommendations for international students: Required—TOEFL (minimum score 600 paper-based; 250 computer-based), TWE (minimum score 5). Electronic applications accepted. *Faculty research:* Organizational transitions, productivity, work force demographics, management technology, comparative and international research.

Alliant International University–Sacramento, Marshall Goldsmith School of Management, Program in Organizational Development, Sacramento, CA 95825. Offers Psy D. *Entrance requirements:* For doctorate, minimum GPA of 3.0, interview, letters of recommendation.

Alliant International University–San Diego, Marshall Goldsmith School of Management, Organizational Psychology Division, San Diego, CA 92131-1799. Offers clinical/industrial organizational psychology (PhD); consulting psychology (PhD); industrial/organizational psychology (MA, MS, PhD); organizational behavior (MA). Part-time and evening/weekend programs available. Terminal master's awarded for partial completion of doctoral program. *Degree requirements:* For doctorate, thesis/dissertation. *Entrance requirements:* For master's and doctorate, interview, minimum GPA of 3.0 in both psychology and overall. Additional exam requirements/recommendations for international students: Required—TOEFL (minimum score 600 paper-based; 250 computer-based), TWE (minimum score 5). Electronic applications accepted. *Faculty research:* Cultural diversity in the workplace, work motivation, personnel, performance management.

Alliant International University–San Francisco, Marshall Goldsmith School of Management, Organizational Psychology Division, San Francisco, CA 94133-1221. Offers organization development (MA); organizational psychology (MA, PhD). Part-time and evening/weekend programs available. Terminal master's awarded for partial completion of doctoral program. *Degree requirements:* For doctorate, thesis/dissertation. *Entrance requirements:* For master's and doctorate, interview, minimum GPA of 3.0. Additional exam requirements/recommendations for international students: Required—TOEFL (minimum score 650 paper-based; 250 computer-based), TWE (minimum score 5). Electronic applications accepted. *Faculty research:* Leadership, ethics and management, career development, organizational behavior, strategic change.

American InterContinental University Online, Program in Business Administration, Hoffman Estates, IL 60192. Offers accounting and finance (MBA); finance (MBA); healthcare management (MBA); human resource management (MBA); international business (MBA); management (MBA); marketing (MBA); operations management (MBA); organizational psychology and development (MBA); project management (MBA). Evening/weekend programs available. Postbaccalaureate distance learning degree programs offered (no on-campus study). *Students:* 1,513 full-time (948 women); includes 725 minority (562 African Americans, 14 American Indian/Alaska Native, 42 Asian Americans or Pacific Islanders, 107 Hispanic Americans). Average age 36. In 2007, 1298 degrees awarded. *Entrance requirements:* Additional exam requirements/recommendations for international students: Required—TOEFL (minimum score 550 paper-based; 213 computer-based). *Application deadline:* Applications are processed on a rolling basis. Application fee: $50. Electronic applications accepted. *Expenses:* Tuition: Full-time $30,976; part-time $645 per credit hour. *Financial support:* Institutionally sponsored loans and scholarships/grants available. Financial award applicants required to submit FAFSA. *Unit head:* Kerri J Holloway, Vice President of Academic Affairs, 847-851-5000 Ext. 15399, Fax: 847-586-6309, E-mail: kholloway@aivonline.edu. *Application contact:* 877-701-3800, E-mail: info@aiuonline.edu.

Angelo State University, College of Graduate Studies, College of Liberal and Fine Arts, Department of Psychology and Sociology, San Angelo, TX 76909. Offers psychology (MS), including counseling psychology, general psychology, industrial and organizational psychology. Part-time and evening/weekend programs available. *Faculty:* 8 full-time (2 women). *Students:* 11 full-time (8 women), 39 part-time (21 women); includes 8 minority (2 African Americans, 1 American Indian/Alaska Native, 5 Hispanic Americans), 1 international. Average age 26. 35 applicants, 66% accepted, 17 enrolled. In 2007, 27 degrees awarded. *Degree requirements:* For master's, comprehensive exam, thesis optional. *Entrance requirements:* For master's, GRE General Test. Additional exam requirements/recommendations for international students: Required—TOEFL or IELTS. *Application deadline:* For fall admission, 7/15 priority date for domestic students, 6/10 for international students; for spring admission, 12/8 for domestic students, 11/1 for international students. Applications are processed on a rolling basis. Application fee: $40 ($50 for international students). Electronic applications accepted. *Financial support:* In 2007–08, 44 students received support, including 3 teaching assistantships (averaging $10,251 per year); career-related internships or fieldwork, Federal Work-Study, scholarships/grants, and unspecified assistantships also available. Support available to part-time students. Financial award application deadline: 3/1; financial award applicants required to submit FAFSA. *Faculty research:* Toddlers use of actors' intentions to learn verbs. Total annual research expenditures: $116,915. *Unit head:* Dr. William B. Davidson, Department Head, 325-942-2068 Ext. 248, E-mail: bill.davidson@angelo.edu.

Antioch University Seattle, Graduate Programs, Center for Creative Change, Seattle, WA 98121-1814. Offers environment and community (MA); management (MS); organizational psychology (MA); strategic communications (MA); whole system design (MA). Evening/weekend programs available. Electronic applications accepted. Expenses: Contact institution.

Appalachian State University, Cratis D. Williams Graduate School, Department of Psychology, Boone, NC 28608. Offers clinical health psychology (MA); general experimental psychology (MA); industrial and organizational psychology (MA). Part-time programs available. *Faculty:* 31 full-time (11 women). *Students:* 43 full-time (31 women), 37 part-time (30 women); includes 4 minority (3 African Americans, 1 Asian American or Pacific Islander), 4 international. 197 applicants, 30% accepted, 30 enrolled. In 2007, 23 master's, 6 other advanced degrees awarded. *Degree requirements:* For master's and MS/SSP, comprehensive exam, thesis optional, GRE Subject Test exit exam. *Entrance requirements:* For master's, GRE General Test, 3 letters of recommendation. Additional exam requirements/recommendations for international students: Required—TOEFL (minimum score 550 paper-based; 230 computer-based; 79 iBT), IELTS (minimum score 7). *Application deadline:* For fall admission, 3/1 for domestic students, 1/1 for international students. Applications are processed on a rolling basis. Application fee: $50. *Expenses:* Tuition, state resident: part-time $127 per semester hour. Tuition, nonresident: part-time $597 per semester hour. Required fees: $18 per semester. *Financial support:* In 2007–08, 34 research assistantships (averaging $3,500 per year), 25 teaching assistantships (averaging $3,500 per year) were awarded; fellowships, career-related internships or fieldwork, Federal Work-Study, scholarships/grants, and unspecified assistantships also available. Financial award application deadline: 4/1. *Faculty research:* Eating disorders, school-based consultations, organizational behavior management, brain mechanisms of sound localization, parenting styles. Total annual research expenditures: $158,688. *Unit head:* Dr. Paul Fox, Chair, 828-262-2272, Fax: 828-262-2974, E-mail: foxpa@appstate.edu. *Application contact:* Dr. Denise Martz, Graduate Coordinator, 828-262-2715, E-mail: martzdm@appstate.edu.

Auburn University, Graduate School, College of Liberal Arts, Department of Psychology, Auburn University, AL 36849. Offers applied behavior analysis in developmental disabilities (MS); clinical psychology (PhD); experimental psychology (PhD); industrial/organizational psychology (PhD). *Accreditation:* APA (one or more programs are accredited). Part-time programs available. *Faculty:* 22 full-time (5 women). *Students:* 30 full-time (18 women), 65 part-time (44 women); includes 10 minority (5 African Americans, 1 American Indian/Alaska Native, 2 Asian Americans or Pacific Islanders, 2 Hispanic Americans), 2 international. Average age 28. 298 applicants, 15% accepted, 27 enrolled. In 2007, 15 master's, 3 doctorates awarded. *Degree requirements:* For doctorate, thesis/dissertation. *Entrance requirements:* For master's, GRE General Test, GRE Subject Test, minimum GPA of 3.25 in psychology, 3.0 overall; for doctorate, GRE General Test, GRE Subject Test. *Application deadline:* For fall admission, 7/7 for domestic students; for spring admission, 11/24 for domestic students. Applications are processed on a rolling basis. Application fee: $25 ($50 for international students). Electronic applications accepted. *Financial support:* Research assistantships, teaching assistantships, Federal Work-Study available. Support available to part-time students. Financial award application deadline: 3/15. *Faculty research:* Clinical psychology, learning, industrial psychology, organizational psychology. Total annual research expenditures: $200,000. *Unit head:* Dr. Barry Burkhart, Chair, 334-844-4412. *Application contact:* Dr. Joe Pittman, Interim Dean of the Graduate School, 334-844-4700.

Bernard M. Baruch College of the City University of New York, Weissman School of Arts and Sciences, Program in Industrial Organizational Psychology, New York, NY 10010-5585. Offers MS.

Bernard M. Baruch College of the City University of New York, Zicklin School of Business, Program in Industrial and Organizational Psychology, New York, NY 10010-5585. Offers MBA,

MS, PhD, Certificate. Part-time and evening/weekend programs available. *Degree requirements:* For master's, thesis or alternative; for doctorate, comprehensive exam, thesis/dissertation. *Entrance requirements:* For master's, GMAT or GRE General Test, 2 letters of recommendation, resumé, 2 years of work experience; for doctorate, GMAT or GRE General Test. Additional exam requirements/recommendations for international students: Required—TOEFL (minimum score 590 paper-based; 243 computer-based), TWE. *Faculty research:* Job attitudes, power and leadership in organizations, measurement issues in organizational behavior, work motivation, fair employment practices.

Bowling Green State University, Graduate College, College of Arts and Sciences, Department of Psychology, Bowling Green, OH 43403. Offers clinical psychology (MA, PhD); developmental psychology (MA, PhD); experimental psychology (MA, PhD); industrial/organizational psychology (MA, PhD); quantitative psychology (MA, PhD). *Accreditation:* APA (one or more programs are accredited). *Faculty:* 29 full-time (9 women), 14 part-time/adjunct (5 women). *Students:* 88 full-time (61 women), 27 part-time (19 women); includes 10 minority (5 Asian Americans or Pacific Islanders, 5 Hispanic Americans), 12 international. Average age 27. 225 applicants, 15% accepted, 19 enrolled. In 2007, 22 master's, 14 doctorates awarded. *Degree requirements:* For doctorate, thesis/dissertation. *Entrance requirements:* For doctorate, GRE General Test, GRE Subject Test. Additional exam requirements/recommendations for international students: Required—TOEFL. *Application deadline:* For fall admission, 1/1 for domestic students. Application fee: $30. Electronic applications accepted. *Financial support:* In 2007–08, 5 fellowships with full tuition reimbursements (averaging $16,187 per year), 50 research assistantships with full tuition reimbursements (averaging $11,844 per year), 29 teaching assistantships with full tuition reimbursements (averaging $11,805 per year) were awarded; career-related internships or fieldwork, Federal Work-Study, institutionally sponsored loans, tuition waivers (full), and unspecified assistantships also available. Financial award applicants required to submit FAFSA. *Faculty research:* Personnel psychology, developmental-mathematical models, behavioral medication, brain process, child/adolescent social cognition. *Unit head:* Dr. Dale Klopfer, Chair, 419-372-2733.

Brooklyn College of the City University of New York, Division of Graduate Studies, Department of Psychology, Brooklyn, NY 11210-2889. Offers experimental psychology (MA); industrial and organizational psychology (MA), including industrial and organizational psychology-human relations, psychology-organizational psychology and behavior; mental health counseling (MA); psychology (PhD). The City University doctoral program in experimental psychology is based at Brooklyn College; candidates who complete the MA may apply for admission to the doctoral program. MA programs in industrial and organizational psychology and mental health counseling are fall admissions only. Part-time programs available. *Students:* 57 full-time (49 women), 91 part-time (73 women); includes 67 minority (39 African Americans, 1 American Indian/Alaska Native, 13 Asian Americans or Pacific Islanders, 14 Hispanic Americans), 9 international. 207 applicants, 60% accepted, 77 enrolled. In 2007, 37 degrees awarded. *Degree requirements:* For master's, comprehensive exam, thesis (for some programs). *Entrance requirements:* For master's, minimum GPA of 3.0, 2 letters of recommendation, essay; for doctorate, GRE. Additional exam requirements/recommendations for international students: Required—TOEFL. *Application deadline:* For fall admission, 3/1 for domestic students, 2/1 for international students; for spring admission, 11/1 for domestic students, 10/1 for international students. Applications are processed on a rolling basis. Application fee: $125. Electronic applications accepted. *Financial support:* Career-related internships or fieldwork, Federal Work-Study, institutionally sponsored loans, scholarships/grants, and tuition waivers (partial) available. Support available to part-time students. Financial award application deadline: 5/1; financial award applicants required to submit FAFSA. *Unit head:* Dr. Glen Hass, Chairperson, 718-951-5601, Fax: 718-951-4814, E-mail: ghass@brooklyn.cuny.edu. *Application contact:* Hernan Sierra, Graduate Admissions Coordinator, 718-951-4536, Fax: 718-951-4506, E-mail: grads@brooklyn.cuny.edu.

California State University, San Bernardino, Graduate Studies, College of Social and Behavioral Sciences, Department of Psychology, Program in Industrial/Organizational Psychology, San Bernardino, CA 92407-2397. Offers MS. *Students:* 22 full-time (14 women), 9 part-time (3 women); includes 10 minority (1 African American, 4 Asian Americans or Pacific Islanders, 5 Hispanic Americans), 2 international. Average age 24. 37 applicants, 43% accepted, 12 enrolled. In 2007, 12 degrees awarded. *Entrance requirements:* For master's, minimum GPA of 3.0 in major. *Application deadline:* For fall admission, 8/31 priority date for domestic students. Application fee: $55. *Unit head:* Dr. Mark Agars, Head, 909-537-5433, Fax: 909-537-7003, E-mail: magars@csusb.edu. *Application contact:* Stacy Brooks, Graduate Secretary, 909-537-5570, Fax: 909-537-7003, E-mail: sbrooks@csusb.edu.

Capella University, Harold Abel School of Psychology, Minneapolis, MN 55402. Offers clinical psychology (MS); counseling psychology (MS); educational psychology (MS, PhD); general psychology (MS, PhD); industrial/organizational psychology (MS, PhD); school psychology (MS, Certificate); sport psychology (MS). Part-time and evening/weekend programs available. Postbaccalaureate distance learning degree programs offered (minimal on-campus study). Terminal master's awarded for partial completion of doctoral program. *Degree requirements:* For master's, thesis optional, project; for doctorate, thesis/dissertation. *Entrance requirements:* For degree, master's degree in school psychology. Additional exam requirements/recommendations for international students: Required—TOEFL (minimum score 550 paper-based; 213 computer-based), TWE (minimum score 4). Electronic applications accepted. *Faculty research:* Correctional mental health delivery, community mental health, attachment and caregiving in adult and family relationships, influence of encouragement on motivation, and moral dilemmas in business.

Carlos Albizu University, Graduate Programs in Psychology, San Juan, PR 00901. Offers clinical psychology (MS, PhD, Psy D); general psychology (PhD); industrial/organizational psychology (MS, PhD); speech and language pathology (MS). *Accreditation:* APA (one or more programs are accredited). Part-time and evening/weekend programs available. *Degree requirements:* For master's, one foreign language, comprehensive exam, thesis; for doctorate, one foreign language, comprehensive exam, thesis/dissertation, written qualifying exams. *Entrance requirements:* For master's, GRE General Test or EXADEP, interview, minimum GPA of 3.0; for doctorate, GRE General Test or EXADEP, interview, minimum GPA of 3.0 (industrial/organizational psychology), minimum GPA of 3.25 (clinical psychology). *Faculty research:* Psychotherapeutic techniques for Hispanics, psychology of the aged, school dropouts, stress, violence.

Carlos Albizu University, Miami Campus, Graduate Programs, Miami, FL 33172-2209. Offers clinical psychology (Psy D); entrepreneurship (MBA); exceptional student education (MS); industrial/organizational psychology (MS); marriage and family therapy (MS); mental health counseling (MS); nonprofit management (MBA); organizational management (MBA); psychology (MS); school counseling (MS); teaching English as a second language (MS). *Accreditation:* APA. Part-time and evening/weekend programs available. *Faculty:* 20 full-time (13 women), 65 part-time/adjunct (39 women). *Students:* 514 full-time (409 women), 143 part-time (119 women); includes 465 minority (54 African Americans, 1 American Indian/Alaska Native, 4 Asian Americans or Pacific Islanders, 406 Hispanic Americans). Average age 35. 194 applicants, 73% accepted, 130 enrolled. In 2007, 208 master's, 37 doctorates awarded. Terminal master's awarded for partial completion of doctoral program. *Median time to degree:* Of those who began their doctoral program in fall 1999, 65% received their degree in 8 years or less. *Degree requirements:* For master's, one foreign language, comprehensive exam, integrative project (MBA), research project (MSESE and MSTESOL); for doctorate, one foreign language, comprehensive exam, internship, doctoral project. *Entrance requirements:* For master's, 3 letters of recommendation, interview, minimum GPA of 3.0, resumé, statement of purpose, official transcripts; for doctorate, 3 letters of recommendation, minimum GPA of 3.0, resumé, interview. *Application deadline:* For fall admission, 8/1 priority date for domestic students; for spring admission, 11/30 priority date for domestic students. Applications are processed on a rolling basis. Application fee: $50. *Expenses:* Tuition: Full-time $9,090; part-time $505 per credit. Required fees: $298 per term. Tuition and fees vary according to course load and degree level. *Financial support:* In 2007–08, 37 students received support. Federal Work-Study and scholarships/grants available. Financial award application deadline: 6/1; financial award applicants required to submit FAFSA. *Faculty research:* Psychotherapy, forensic psychology, neuropsychology, marketing strategy, entrepreneurship, special education. *Unit head:* Dr. Carmen S. Roca, Interim Chancellor, 305-593-1223 Ext. 120, Fax: 305-629-8052, E-mail: croca@albizu.edu. *Application contact:* Barbara De la Cruz, Admission Officer, 305-593-1223 Ext. 218, Fax: 305-593-1854, E-mail: bdelacruz@albizu.edu.

Central Michigan University, College of Graduate Studies, College of Humanities and Social and Behavioral Sciences, Department of Psychology, Program in Industrial/Organizational Psychology, Mount Pleasant, MI 48859. Offers MA, PhD. *Degree requirements:* For master's, thesis or alternative; for doctorate, thesis/dissertation or alternative. *Entrance requirements:* For master's and doctorate, GRE. *Faculty research:* Work stress, personnel selection.

The Chicago School of Professional Psychology, Graduate School, Program in Industrial and Organizational Psychology, Chicago, IL 60610. Offers business psychology (Psy D); industrial and organizational psychology (MA). Part-time and evening/weekend programs available. *Students:* 191. Average age 25. *Degree requirements:* For master's, internship; for doctorate, thesis/dissertation, internship. *Entrance requirements:* For master's, 1 course in psychology and statistics and research methods; for doctorate, GRE, writing test, 12 hours of psychology credit including a course in statistics and research methods. Additional exam requirements/recommendations for international students: Required—TOEFL (minimum score 550 paper-based; 213 computer-based; 79 iBT). *Application deadline:* For fall admission, 2/15 priority date for domestic students, 4/15 for international students; for spring admission, 10/30 for domestic students, 10/1 for international students. Application fee: $50. Electronic applications accepted. *Financial support:* Federal Work-Study and scholarships/grants available. Financial award application deadline: 4/1; financial award applicants required to submit FAFSA. *Application contact:* Director of Admissions, 312-329-6666, Fax: 312-644-3333, E-mail: admissions@thechicagoschool.edu.

See Close-Up on page 1423.

Claremont Graduate University, Graduate Programs, School of Behavioral and Organizational Sciences, Department of Psychology, Claremont, CA 91711-6160. Offers advanced study in evaluation (Certificate); cognitive psychology (MA, PhD); developmental psychology (MA, PhD); evaluation and applied research methods (MA, PhD); health behavior research and evaluation (MA, PhD); human resource development and evaluation (MA); industrial/organizational psychology (MA, PhD); organizational behavior (MA, PhD); organizational psychology (MA, PhD); social psychology (MA, PhD); MBA/PhD. Part-time programs available. *Faculty:* 15 full-time (7 women), 4 part-time/adjunct (2 women). *Students:* 184 full-time (137 women), 24 part-time (20 women); includes 51 minority (13 African Americans, 1 American Indian/Alaska Native, 26 Asian Americans or Pacific Islanders, 11 Hispanic Americans), 12 international. Average age 29. In 2007, 42 master's, 10 doctorates, 2 other advanced degrees awarded. Terminal master's awarded for partial completion of doctoral program. *Degree requirements:* For master's, thesis (for some programs); for doctorate, comprehensive exam, thesis/dissertation. *Entrance requirements:* For master's and doctorate, GRE General Test. *Application deadline:* For fall admission, 2/15 priority date for domestic students. Applications are processed on a rolling basis. Electronic applications accepted. *Expenses:* Tuition: Full-time $31,640; part-time $1,376 per unit. Required fees: $145 per semester. Tuition and fees vary according to course load, degree level and program. *Financial support:* Fellowships, research assistantships, teaching assistantships, career-related internships or fieldwork, Federal Work-Study, institutionally sponsored loans, and tuition waivers (full and partial) available. Support available to part-time students. Financial award application deadline: 2/15; financial award applicants required to submit FAFSA. *Faculty research:* Social intervention, diversity in organizations, eyewitness memory, aging and cognition, drug policy. *Unit head:* Natalie Brown, Program Coordinator, 909-621-8084, Fax: 909-621-8905, E-mail: natalie.brown@cgu.edu.

Clemson University, Graduate School, College of Business and Behavioral Science, Department of Psychology, Program in Industrial/Organizational Psychology, Clemson, SC 29634. Offers PhD. *Students:* 20 full-time (12 women), 8 part-time (5 women); includes 3 minority (2 African Americans, 1 Hispanic American), 1 international. 90 applicants, 11% accepted, 7 enrolled. *Degree requirements:* For doctorate, thesis/dissertation. *Entrance requirements:* For doctorate, GRE General Test. Additional exam requirements/recommendations for international students: Required—TOEFL. *Application deadline:* For fall admission, 3/15 for domestic students. Application fee: $55. *Financial support:* In 2007–08, 7 research assistantships were awarded. Financial award application deadline: 3/15; financial award applicants required to submit FAFSA. *Unit head:* Chris Pagano, Coordinator, 864-656-4984, Fax: 864-656-0358, E-mail: cpagano@clemson.edu.

Cleveland State University, College of Graduate Studies, College of Science, Department of Psychology, Cleveland, OH 44115. Offers clinical psychology (MA); consumer/industrial research (MA); diversity management (MA); experimental research psychology (MA); school psychology (Psy S). Part-time programs available. *Faculty:* 17 full-time (5 women), 16 part-time/adjunct (10 women). *Students:* 76 full-time (52 women), 44 part-time (37 women); includes 19 minority (15 African Americans, 1 American Indian/Alaska Native, 2 Asian Americans or Pacific Islanders, 1 Hispanic American), 3 international. Average age 29. 153 applicants, 27% accepted, 37 enrolled. In 2007, 26 master's, 9 other advanced degrees awarded. *Degree requirements:* For master's, thesis (for some programs). *Entrance requirements:* For master's, GRE General Test. Additional exam requirements/recommendations for international students: Required—TOEFL (minimum score 525 paper-based; 197 computer-based). *Application deadline:* For fall admission, 2/1 priority date for domestic and international students. Applications are processed on a rolling basis. Application fee: $30. Electronic applications accepted. *Financial support:* In 2007–08, 45 students received support. Career-related internships or fieldwork, Federal Work-Study, tuition waivers (partial), and unspecified assistantships available. Financial award applicants required to submit FAFSA. Total annual research expenditures: $112,607. *Unit head:* Dr. David M. Grilly, Chairperson, 216-687-2545, Fax: 216-687-9294, E-mail: d.grilly@csuohio.edu. *Application contact:* Karen Colston, Administrative Coordinator, 216-687-2552, E-mail: k.colston@csuohio.edu.

DePaul University, College of Liberal Arts and Sciences, Department of Psychology, Chicago, IL 60604-2287. Offers clinical psychology (MA, PhD), including child clinical psychology, community clinical psychology; experimental psychology (MA, PhD); general psychology (MS); industrial/organizational psychology (MA, PhD); MA/PhD. *Accreditation:* APA (one or more programs are accredited). *Faculty:* 31 full-time (19 women), 6 part-time/adjunct (4 women). *Students:* 57 full-time (36 women), 53 part-time (36 women); includes 24 minority (14 African Americans, 1 American Indian/Alaska Native, 3 Asian Americans or Pacific Islanders, 6 Hispanic Americans), 1 international. Average age 28. 332 applicants, 14% accepted, 23 enrolled. In 2007, 14 master's, 17 doctorates awarded. *Median time to degree:* Of those who began their doctoral program in fall 1999, 60% received their degree in 8 years or less. *Degree requirements:* For master's, thesis, oral exam; for doctorate, comprehensive exam, thesis/dissertation, oral and written exams. *Entrance requirements:* For master's and doctorate, GRE General Test, GRE Subject Test, 32 quarter hours of course work in psychology, 3 letters of recommendation. Additional exam requirements/recommendations for international students: Required—TOEFL. Application fee: $40. Electronic applications accepted. *Financial support:* In 2007–08, 48 students received support, including 35 research assistantships with full tuition reimbursements available (averaging $11,800 per year), 13 teaching assistantships with full tuition reimbursements available (averaging $11,800 per year); career-related internships or fieldwork, scholarships/grants, traineeships, tuition waivers (full and partial), and unspecified assistantships also available. Financial award application deadline: 1/10. *Faculty research:* Adolescent stress and depression, minority adolescents sexuality, public policy, community influences in child adjustment. *Unit head:* Dr. Christopher B Keys, Chairman, 773-325-7887, Fax: 773-325-7888. *Application contact:* Alison Pereida Knapp, Graduate Admissions Assistant, 773-325-7887, Fax: 773-325-7888.

Industrial and Organizational Psychology

Eastern Kentucky University, The Graduate School, College of Arts and Sciences, Department of Psychology, Richmond, KY 40475-3102. Offers clinical psychology (MS); industrial/organizational psychology (MS); school psychology (Psy S). Part-time programs available. *Faculty:* 11 full-time (5 women). *Students:* 64 full-time (47 women), 10 part-time (8 women); includes 5 minority (4 African Americans, 1 Asian American or Pacific Islander). Average age 25. 166 applicants, 31% accepted, 18 enrolled. In 2007, 32 master's, 11 other advanced degrees awarded. *Entrance requirements:* For master's and Psy S, GRE General Test, minimum GPA of 2.5. *Application deadline:* For fall admission, 3/15 priority date for domestic students. Applications are processed on a rolling basis. Application fee: $35. *Financial support:* In 2007–08, 30 students received support, including research assistantships (averaging $10,000 per year), teaching assistantships (averaging $10,000 per year); career-related internships or fieldwork and Federal Work-Study also available. Support available to part-time students. *Faculty research:* Autism, social psychology, parenting, assessment of depression/anxiety, reading. Total annual research expenditures: $40,000. *Unit head:* Dr. Robert Brubaker, Chair, 859-622-1105, Fax: 859-622-5871, E-mail: robert.brubaker@eku.edu.

Elmhurst College, Graduate Programs, Program in Industrial/Organizational Psychology, Elmhurst, IL 60126-3296. Offers MA. Part-time and evening/weekend programs available. *Faculty:* 1 full-time (0 women), 3 part-time/adjunct (1 woman). *Students:* Average age 24. 54 applicants, 69% accepted, 12 enrolled. In 2007, 8 degrees awarded. *Degree requirements:* For master's, thesis optional. *Entrance requirements:* For master's, GRE General Test, 3 recommendations. Additional exam requirements/recommendations for international students: Required—TOEFL (minimum score 550 paper-based; 213 computer-based). *Application deadline:* Applications are processed on a rolling basis. Application fee: $25. Electronic applications accepted. *Financial support:* In 2007–08, 12 students received support. Federal Work-Study and scholarships/grants available. Support available to part-time students. Financial award application deadline: 6/1; financial award applicants required to submit FAFSA. *Application contact:* Elizabeth D. Kuebler, Director of Adult and Graduate Admission, 630-617-3069, Fax: 630-617-5501, E-mail: betsyk@elmhurst.edu.

Emporia State University, School of Graduate Studies, The Teachers College, Department of Psychology and Special Education, Program in Psychology, Emporia, KS 66801-5087. Offers general psychology (MS); industrial/organizational psychology (MS). Part-time programs available. *Students:* 11 full-time (5 women), 20 part-time (15 women); includes 1 minority (Hispanic American), 3 international. 16 applicants, 69% accepted, 11 enrolled. In 2007, 10 degrees awarded. *Degree requirements:* For master's, comprehensive exam or thesis, internship. *Entrance requirements:* For master's, GRE General Test or MAT, graduate essay exam, appropriate bachelor's degree, letters of recommendation. Additional exam requirements/recommendations for international students: Required—TOEFL. *Application deadline:* For fall admission, 6/1 priority date for domestic students; for spring admission, 10/1 for domestic students. Applications are processed on a rolling basis. Application fee: $30 ($75 for international students). Electronic applications accepted. *Expenses:* Tuition, state resident: part-time $157 per credit hour. Tuition, nonresident: part-time $475 per credit hour. Required fees: $47 per credit hour. Tuition and fees vary according to campus/location. *Financial support:* Career-related internships or fieldwork, Federal Work-Study, institutionally sponsored loans, health care benefits, and unspecified assistantships available. Financial award application deadline: 3/15; financial award applicants required to submit FAFSA. *Faculty research:* Driving under the influence (DUI) personality, lifestyles and imposter phenomenon. *Unit head:* Dr. Kenneth A. Weaver, Chair, Department of Psychology and Special Education, 620-341-5317, E-mail: kweaver@emporia.edu.

Fairleigh Dickinson University, College at Florham, Maxwell Becton College of Arts and Sciences, Department of Psychology, Program in Industrial/Organizational Psychology, Madison, NJ 07940-1099. Offers MA, MA/MBA. *Students:* 12 full-time (11 women), 3 part-time (all women), 2 international. Average age 24. 20 applicants, 70% accepted, 8 enrolled. In 2007, 3 degrees awarded. *Entrance requirements:* For master's, GRE General Test. *Application deadline:* Applications are processed on a rolling basis. Application fee: $40. *Expenses:* Tuition: Part-time $869 per credit.

Florida Institute of Technology, Graduate Programs, College of Psychology and Liberal Arts, School of Psychology, Melbourne, FL 32901-6975. Offers applied behavior analysis (MS); clinical psychology (Psy D); industrial/organizational psychology (MS, PhD). *Accreditation:* APA (one or more programs are accredited). Part-time programs available. *Faculty:* 17 full-time (7 women), 8 part-time/adjunct (2 women). *Students:* 188 full-time (145 women), 14 part-time (9 women); includes 24 minority (8 African Americans, 4 Asian Americans or Pacific Islanders, 12 Hispanic Americans), 14 international. Average age 27. 304 applicants, 50% accepted, 72 enrolled. In 2007, 62 master's, 21 doctorates awarded. *Degree requirements:* For master's, comprehensive exam (for some programs), thesis (for some programs); for doctorate, comprehensive exam, thesis/dissertation (for some programs), internship. *Entrance requirements:* For master's, GRE General Test, 3 letters of recommendation, minimum GPA of 3.0, resumé; for doctorate, GRE General Test, GRE Subject Test, 3 letters of recommendation, minimum GPA of 3.2, resumé. Additional exam requirements/recommendations for international students: Required—TOEFL (minimum score 550 paper-based; 213 computer-based). *Application deadline:* For fall admission, 3/15 for domestic students. Applications are processed on a rolling basis. Application fee: $50. Electronic applications accepted. *Expenses:* Tuition: Part-time $945 per credit. *Financial support:* In 2007–08, 12 students received support, including 5 research assistantships with full and partial tuition reimbursements available (averaging $7,575 per year), 7 teaching assistantships with full and partial tuition reimbursements available (averaging $5,926 per year); career-related internships or fieldwork, institutionally sponsored loans, tuition waivers (partial), unspecified assistantships, and tuition remissions also available. Financial award application deadline: 3/1; financial award applicants required to submit FAFSA. *Faculty research:* Addictions, neuropsychology, child abuse, assessment, psychological trauma. Total annual research expenditures: $69,032. *Application contact:* Thomas M. Shea, Director of Graduate Admissions, 321-674-7577, Fax: 321-723-9468, E-mail: tshea@fit.edu.

See Close-Up on page 1435.

George Mason University, College of Humanities and Social Sciences, Department of Psychology, Fairfax, VA 22030. Offers applied developmental psychology (MA, PhD); biopsychology (MA, PhD); clinical psychology (MA, PhD); human factors engineering psychology (MA, PhD); industrial/organizational psychology (MA, PhD); psychology (MA, PhD); school psychology (MA). *Accreditation:* APA. *Faculty:* 44 full-time (17 women), 16 part-time/adjunct (10 women). *Students:* 101 full-time (80 women), 135 part-time (88 women); includes 30 minority (6 African Americans, 13 Asian Americans or Pacific Islanders, 11 Hispanic Americans), 14 international. Average age 27. 734 applicants, 22% accepted, 86 enrolled. In 2007, 49 master's, 17 doctorates awarded. Terminal master's awarded for partial completion of doctoral program. *Median time to degree:* Of those who began their doctoral program in fall 1999, 97% received their degree in 8 years or less. *Degree requirements:* For master's, thesis (for applied developmental psychology and biopsychology); for doctorate, comprehensive exam, thesis/dissertation or alternative. *Entrance requirements:* For master's, GRE General Test, minimum GPA of 3.0 in last 60 hours of course work, undergraduate course work in psychology; for doctorate, GRE General Test, minimum undergraduate GPA of 3.0, 3.3 in major. Additional exam requirements/recommendations for international students: Required—TOEFL (minimum score 575 paper-based; 230 computer-based; 88 iBT), IELTS (minimum score 6). Application fee: $60 ($75 for international students). Electronic applications accepted. *Financial support:* In 2007–08, 15 fellowships with partial tuition reimbursements (averaging $2,300 per year), 33 research assistantships with partial tuition reimbursements (averaging $12,200 per year), 21 teaching assistantships with partial tuition reimbursements (averaging $12,200 per year) were awarded; career-related internships or fieldwork, scholarships/grants, traineeships, tuition waivers (partial), and unspecified assistantships also available. Financial award application deadline: 3/1; financial award applicants required to submit FAFSA. *Unit head:* Dr. Deborah Boehm-Davis, Chairperson, 703-993-1398, Fax: 703-993-1359, E-mail: bsmith@gmu.edu. *Application contact:* Dr. James Maddux, Information Contact, 703-993-3590, Fax: 703-993-1355, E-mail: psycgrad@gmu.edu.

The George Washington University, Columbian College of Arts and Sciences, Department of Psychology, Washington, DC 20052. Offers applied social psychology (PhD); clinical psychology (PhD); cognitive neuropsychology (PhD); industrial-organizational psychology (PhD). *Accreditation:* APA. Part-time and evening/weekend programs available. *Degree requirements:* For doctorate, thesis/dissertation or alternative, general exam. *Entrance requirements:* For doctorate, GRE General Test, minimum GPA of 3.0. Additional exam requirements/recommendations for international students: Required—TOEFL (minimum score 550 paper-based; 213 computer-based).

Goddard College, Graduate Program, Program in Psychology and Counseling, Plainfield, VT 05667-9432. Offers organizational development (MA); psychology and counseling (MA). Postbaccalaureate distance learning degree programs offered (minimal on-campus study). *Faculty:* 7 part-time/adjunct (4 women). *Students:* 54 full-time. Average age 42. 18 applicants, 94% accepted, 17 enrolled. *Degree requirements:* For master's, thesis. *Entrance requirements:* For master's, previous coursework in psychology. *Application deadline:* Applications are processed on a rolling basis. Application fee: $40. Electronic applications accepted. *Expenses:* Tuition: Full-time $14,038. *Financial support:* In 2007–08, 44 students received support. Applicants required to submit FAFSA. *Unit head:* Dr. Steve James, Director, 802-454-8311 Ext. 247, Fax: 802-454-8017, E-mail: jamess@goddard.edu. *Application contact:* David DeLucca, Admissions Counselor, 800-906-8312 Ext. 248, Fax: 802-454-1029, E-mail: david.delucca@goddard.edu.

Graduate School and University Center of the City University of New York, Graduate Studies, Program in Psychology, New York, NY 10016-4039. Offers basic applied neurocognition (PhD); biopsychology (PhD); clinical psychology (PhD); developmental psychology (PhD); environmental psychology (PhD); experimental psychology (PhD); industrial psychology (PhD); learning processes (PhD); neuropsychology (PhD); psychology (PhD); social personality (PhD). *Faculty:* 119 full-time (40 women). *Students:* 510 full-time (379 women), 1 (woman) part-time; includes 98 minority (39 African Americans, 1 American Indian/Alaska Native, 21 Asian Americans or Pacific Islanders, 37 Hispanic Americans), 63 international. Average age 33. 747 applicants, 17% accepted, 78 enrolled. In 2007, 59 degrees awarded. *Degree requirements:* For doctorate, one foreign language, thesis/dissertation. *Entrance requirements:* For doctorate, GRE General Test. Additional exam requirements/recommendations for international students: Required—TOEFL. *Application deadline:* For fall admission, 12/15 for domestic students. Application fee: $125. Electronic applications accepted. *Financial support:* In 2007–08, 371 students received support, including 308 fellowships, 34 research assistantships, 33 teaching assistantships; career-related internships or fieldwork, Federal Work-Study, institutionally sponsored loans, and tuition waivers (full and partial) also available. Financial award application deadline: 2/1; financial award applicants required to submit FAFSA. *Unit head:* Dr. Joseph Glick, Executive Officer, 212-817-8706, Fax: 212-817-1533, E-mail: jglick@gc.cuny.edu.

Hofstra University, College of Liberal Arts and Sciences, Department of Psychology, Program in Applied Organizational Psychology, Hempstead, NY 11549. Offers PhD. *Students:* 14 full-time (10 women), 18 part-time (8 women); includes 5 minority (2 African Americans, 3 Asian Americans or Pacific Islanders). Average age 34. 13 applicants, 38% accepted, 4 enrolled. In 2007, 2 degrees awarded. *Degree requirements:* For doctorate, comprehensive exam, thesis/dissertation. *Entrance requirements:* For doctorate, GRE, 2 letters of recommendation, essay, interview. Additional exam requirements/recommendations for international students: Required—TOEFL (minimum score 550 paper-based; 213 computer-based). *Application deadline:* For fall admission, 4/1 for domestic and international students. Application fee: $60. Electronic applications accepted. *Expenses:* Tuition: Full-time $14,220; part-time $820 per credit. Required fees: $970; $165 per term. Tuition and fees vary according to program. *Financial support:* In 2007–08, 23 students received support, including 22 fellowships with tuition reimbursements available (averaging $5,932 per year), 1 research assistantship with full and partial tuition reimbursement available (averaging $13,320 per year); career-related internships or fieldwork, Federal Work-Study, institutionally sponsored loans, scholarships/grants, tuition waivers (full and partial), and unspecified assistantships also available. Support available to part-time students. Financial award applicants required to submit FAFSA. *Faculty research:* Customer satisfaction, personal selection, faking and personality, performance management; organizational health. Total annual research expenditures: $130,000. *Unit head:* Dr. William Metlay, Program Director, 516-463-6344, Fax: 516-463-4664, E-mail: psyzm@hofstra.edu. *Application contact:* Carol Drummer, Dean of Graduate Admissions, 516-463-4876, Fax: 516-463-4664, E-mail: gradstudent@hofstra.edu.

Hofstra University, College of Liberal Arts and Sciences, Department of Psychology, Program in Industrial/Organizational Psychology, Hempstead, NY 11549. Offers MA. Part-time and evening/weekend programs available. *Students:* 50 full-time (26 women), 8 part-time (4 women); includes 8 minority (6 African Americans, 1 Asian American or Pacific Islander, 1 Hispanic American). Average age 24. 97 applicants, 59% accepted, 26 enrolled. In 2007, 19 degrees awarded. Terminal master's awarded for partial completion of doctoral program. *Degree requirements:* For master's, comprehensive exam, thesis optional, internship. *Entrance requirements:* For master's, GRE General Test, minimum GPA of 3.0, essay, interview. Additional exam requirements/recommendations for international students: Required—TOEFL (minimum score 550 paper-based; 213 computer-based). *Application deadline:* Applications are processed on a rolling basis. Application fee: $60. Electronic applications accepted. *Expenses:* Tuition: Full-time $14,220; part-time $820 per credit. Required fees: $970; $165 per term. Tuition and fees vary according to program. *Financial support:* In 2007–08, 17 students received support, including 13 fellowships with tuition reimbursements available (averaging $4,692 per year), 3 research assistantships with full and partial tuition reimbursements available (averaging $12,570 per year); career-related internships or fieldwork, Federal Work-Study, institutionally sponsored loans, scholarships/grants, tuition waivers (full and partial), and unspecified assistantships also available. Support available to part-time students. Financial award applicants required to submit FAFSA. *Faculty research:* Customer satisfaction, personnel selection, faking and personality, performance management; organizational health. *Unit head:* Dr. Camila Shahani-Denning, Director, 516-463-6343, Fax: 516-463-6354, E-mail: psyc2s@hofstra.edu. *Application contact:* Carol Drummer, Dean of Graduate Admissions, 516-463-4876, Fax: 516-463-4664, E-mail: gradstudent@hofstra.edu.

Illinois Institute of Technology, Graduate College, Institute of Psychology, Chicago, IL 60616-3793. Offers clinical psychology (PhD); industrial/organizational psychology (PhD); personnel/human resource development (MS); psychology (MS); rehabilitation counseling (MS); rehabilitation counselor education (PhD). *Accreditation:* APA (one or more programs are accredited); CORE. Evening/weekend programs available. *Faculty:* 18 full-time (8 women), 4 part-time/adjunct (2 women). *Students:* 122 full-time (95 women), 66 part-time (45 women); includes 44 minority (15 African Americans, 1 American Indian/Alaska Native, 17 Asian Americans or Pacific Islanders, 11 Hispanic Americans), 22 international. Average age 29. 261 applicants, 34% accepted, 32 enrolled. In 2007, 31 master's, 12 doctorates awarded. Terminal master's awarded for partial completion of doctoral program. *Degree requirements:* For master's, comprehensive exam, thesis (for some programs); for doctorate, comprehensive exam, thesis/dissertation, qualifying exams. *Entrance requirements:* For master's, GRE General Test, minimum GPA of 3.0; for doctorate, GRE General Test, minimum GPA of 3.2. Additional exam requirements/recommendations for international students: Required—TOEFL (minimum score 550 paper-based; 213 computer-based; 80 iBT). *Application deadline:* For fall admission, 1/15 for domestic and international students. Application fee: $40. Electronic applications accepted. *Expenses:* Tuition: Full-time $14,004; part-time $778 per credit. Required fees: $7 per credit. $235 per term. Tuition and fees vary according to class time, course level, course load, program and student level. *Financial support:* In 2007–08, 39 fellowships with partial tuition reimbursements (averaging $2,798 per year), 1 research assistantship with partial tuition reimbursement, 24 teaching assistantships with partial tuition reimbursements (averaging $4,405 per year) were awarded; career-related internships or fieldwork, Federal Work-Study, institutionally sponsored loans, scholarships/grants, traineeships, health care benefits, tuition waivers (partial), and unspecified assistantships also available. Support available to part-time students. Financial award applicants required to submit FAFSA. *Faculty research:* Stigma and mental illness, depression, couples communication, leadership, psychometric theory. Total annual research expenditures: $636,382. *Unit head:* Dr. M. Ellen Mitchell, Dean, 312-567-3362, Fax: 312-567-3493, E-mail: mitchelle@itt.edu. *Application contact:* Application Contact, 312-567-3500, Fax: 312-567-3493, E-mail: psychology@iit.edu.

Illinois State University, Graduate School, College of Arts and Sciences, Department of Psychology, Normal, IL 61790-2200. Offers psychology (MA, MS), including clinical psychology, counseling psychology, developmental psychology, educational psychology, experimental psychology, measurement-evaluation, organizational-industrial psychology; school psychology (PhD, SSP). *Accreditation:* APA. *Faculty:* 36 full-time (14 women). *Students:* 49 full-time (37 women), 19 part-time (14 women); includes 3 minority (all Asian Americans or Pacific Islanders), 7 international. 91 applicants, 43% accepted. In 2007, 24 degrees awarded. *Degree requirements:* For master's, thesis or alternative; for doctorate, variable foreign language requirement, thesis/dissertation, 2 terms of residency, internship, practicum. *Entrance requirements:* For master's, GRE General Test, GRE Subject Test, minimum GPA of 3.0 in last 60 hours of course work; for doctorate, GRE General Test. *Application deadline:* Applications are processed on a rolling basis. Application fee: $40. *Expenses:* Tuition, state resident: full-time $3,492; part-time $194 per credit hour. Tuition, nonresident: full-time $7,272; part-time $404 per credit hour. Required fees: $1,024; $57 per credit hour. *Financial support:* In 2007–08, 33 research assistantships (averaging $6,252 per year), 49 teaching assistantships (averaging $4,217 per year) were awarded; tuition waivers (full) and unspecified assistantships also available. Financial award application deadline: 4/1. *Faculty research:* Comprehensive evaluation system for the central region professional development grant, Illinois school psychology internship consortium, for children's sake. Total annual research expenditures: $292,085. *Unit head:* Dr. Neil Skaggs, Acting Chairperson, 309-438-8651.

Indiana University–Purdue University Indianapolis, School of Science, Department of Psychology, Program in Industrial/Organizational Psychology, Indianapolis, IN 46202-2896. Offers MS. *Faculty:* 5 full-time (3 women). *Students:* 12 full-time (10 women); includes 1 minority (Asian American or Pacific Islander) Average age 26. *Entrance requirements:* For master's, GRE General Test (minimum combined verbal and quantitative score: 1100, including quantitative score of 550), minimum undergraduate GPA of 3.0 on a 4.0 scale. Application fee: $50 ($60 for international students). *Expenses:* Tuition, state resident: full-time $5,818; part-time $242 per credit hour. Tuition, nonresident: full-time $17,106; part-time $713 per credit hour. Required fees: $629. Tuition and fees vary according to course load, campus/location and program. *Financial support:* In 2007–08, 12 students received support; fellowships with partial tuition reimbursements available, research assistantships with partial tuition reimbursements available, teaching assistantships with partial tuition reimbursements available, career-related internships or fieldwork, Federal Work-Study, and institutionally sponsored loans available. Financial award application deadline: 3/1; financial award applicants required to submit FAFSA. *Faculty research:* Stereotyping and prejudice biases, performance feedback, personnel psychology, organizational decision making, counterproductive behaviors.

Iona College, School of Arts and Science, Department of Psychology, New Rochelle, NY 10801-1890. Offers experimental psychology (MA); industrial-organizational psychology (MA); mental health counseling (MA); psychology (MA); school psychology (MA). Part-time and evening/weekend programs available. *Faculty:* 12 full-time (6 women), 5 part-time/adjunct (2 women). *Students:* 77 full-time (62 women), 21 part-time (19 women); includes 19 minority (5 African Americans, 2 Asian Americans or Pacific Islanders, 12 Hispanic Americans). Average age 25. 105 applicants, 66% accepted, 33 enrolled. In 2007, 29 degrees awarded. *Degree requirements:* For master's, thesis. *Entrance requirements:* For master's, GRE or minimum GPA of 3.0. Additional exam requirements/recommendations for international students: Required—TOEFL (minimum score 550 paper-based; 213 computer-based). *Application deadline:* Applications are processed on a rolling basis. Application fee: $50. Electronic applications accepted. *Expenses:* Tuition: Part-time $712 per credit. Required fees: $150 per term. *Financial support:* Career-related internships or fieldwork, tuition waivers (partial), and unspecified assistantships available. Support available to part-time students. *Unit head:* Dr. Pauline Jirik-Babb, Chair, 914-633-2191, E-mail: pjirikbabb@iona.edu. *Application contact:* Veronica Jarek-Prinz, Director of Graduate Admissions, 914-633-2420, Fax: 914-633-2277, E-mail: vjarekprinz@iona.edu.

John F. Kennedy University, Graduate School of Professional Psychology, Program in Organizational Psychology, Pleasant Hill, CA 94523-4817. Offers MA, Certificate. *Accreditation:* APA. Part-time and evening/weekend programs available. *Degree requirements:* For master's, thesis or alternative. *Entrance requirements:* For master's, interview. Additional exam requirements/recommendations for international students: Required—TOEFL.

Kean University, College of Humanities and Social Sciences, Program in Behavioral Sciences, Union, NJ 07083. Offers human behavior and organizational psychology (MA); psychological services (MA). Part-time and evening/weekend programs available. *Faculty:* 20 full-time (13 women). *Students:* 22 full-time (19 women), 21 part-time (20 women); includes 8 African Americans, 2 Asian Americans or Pacific Islanders, 4 Hispanic Americans, 4 international. Average age 27. 32 applicants, 78% accepted, 17 enrolled. In 2007, 16 degrees awarded. *Degree requirements:* For master's, comprehensive exam, thesis, research. *Entrance requirements:* For master's, GRE General Test, 2 letters of recommendation, interview, prerequisite courses in behavioral sciences. *Application deadline:* For fall admission, 5/1 for domestic students; for spring admission, 11/1 for domestic students. Application fee: $60 ($150 for international students). Electronic applications accepted. *Expenses:* Tuition, state resident: full-time $9,384; part-time $391 per credit. Tuition, nonresident: full-time $12,720; part-time $530 per credit. Required fees: $2,382; $99 per credit. Part-time tuition and fees vary according to course load. *Financial support:* In 2007–08, 4 research assistantships with full tuition reimbursements (averaging $3,217 per year) were awarded; unspecified assistantships also available. *Unit head:* Dr. Henry L. Kaplowitz, Program Coordinator, 908-737-4018, E-mail: hkaplowi@kean.edu. *Application contact:* Joanne Morris, Director of Graduate Admissions, 908-737-3355, Fax: 908-737-3354, E-mail: grad-adm@kean.edu.

Lamar University, College of Graduate Studies, College of Arts and Sciences, Department of Psychology, Beaumont, TX 77710. Offers community/clinical psychology (MS); industrial/organizational psychology (MS). Part-time programs available. *Faculty:* 6 full-time (3 women). *Students:* 19 full-time (11 women), 10 part-time (8 women); includes 6 minority (2 African Americans, 1 Asian American or Pacific Islander, 3 Hispanic Americans), 1 international. Average age 25. 37 applicants, 43% accepted, 10 enrolled. In 2007, 6 degrees awarded. *Degree requirements:* For master's, thesis, practicum. *Entrance requirements:* For master's, GRE General Test, minimum GPA of 2.75 in last 60 hours of undergraduate course work. Additional exam requirements/recommendations for international students: Required—TOEFL. *Application deadline:* For fall admission, 8/1 for domestic students; for spring admission, 12/1 for domestic students. Application fee: $25 ($50 for international students). *Expenses:* Tuition, state resident: part-time $348 per semester hour. Tuition, nonresident: part-time $626 per semester hour. Tuition and fees vary according to course load. *Financial support:* In 2007–08, 12 students received support, including 3 teaching assistantships (averaging $4,500 per year); fellowships, research assistantships, career-related internships or fieldwork, Federal Work-Study, scholarships/grants, and tuition waivers (partial) also available. Support available to part-time students. Financial award application deadline: 4/1. *Faculty research:* Groupthink, health psychology, school psychology, behavioral neuroscience. *Unit head:* Dr. Oney D. Fitzpatrick, Chair, 409-880-8285, Fax: 409-880-1779, E-mail: fitzpatrod@hal.lamar.edu.

Louisiana State University and Agricultural and Mechanical College, Graduate School, College of Arts and Sciences, Department of Psychology, Baton Rouge, LA 70803. Offers biological psychology (MA, PhD); clinical psychology (MA, PhD); cognitive psychology (MA, PhD); developmental psychology (MA, PhD); industrial/organizational psychology (MA, PhD); school psychology (MA, PhD). *Accreditation:* APA (one or more programs are accredited). *Faculty:* 25 full-time (9 women). *Students:* 81 full-time (60 women), 23 part-time (15 women); includes 15 minority (6 African Americans, 4 American Indian/Alaska Native, 2 Asian Americans or Pacific Islanders, 3 Hispanic Americans), 3 international. Average age 28. 199 applicants, 15% accepted, 23 enrolled. In 2007, 11 master's, 13 doctorates awarded. Terminal master's awarded for partial completion of doctoral program. *Degree requirements:* For master's, thesis; for doctorate, thesis/dissertation, 1 year internship. *Entrance requirements:* For master's and doctorate, GRE General Test, minimum GPA of 3.0. Additional exam requirements/recommendations for international students: Required—TOEFL (minimum score 550 paper-based; 213 computer-based; 79 iBT). *Application deadline:* For fall admission, 1/15 for domestic and international students. Applications are processed on a rolling basis. Application fee: $25. Electronic applications accepted. *Financial support:* In 2007–08, 101 students received support, including 5 fellowships (averaging $26,557 per year), 55 teaching assistantships with partial tuition reimbursements available (averaging $13,218 per year); research assistantships with partial tuition reimbursements available, career-related internships or fieldwork, Federal Work-Study, institutionally sponsored loans, scholarships/grants, health care benefits, and tuition waivers (full and partial) also available. Financial award applicants required to submit FAFSA. *Faculty research:* Clinical psychology, autism, anxiety, addition, neuro-psychology, school psychology, cognitive psychology, experimental psychology. Total annual research expenditures: $582,678. *Unit head:* Dr. Alan Baumeister, Chair, 225-578-4099, Fax: 225-578-4125, E-mail: abaumei@lsu.edu. *Application contact:* Dr. Janet McDonald, Coordinator of Graduate Studies, 225-578-4116, Fax: 225-578-4125, E-mail: psmcdo@lsu.edu.

Louisiana Tech University, Graduate School, College of Education, Department of Behavioral Sciences and Psychology, Ruston, LA 71272. Offers counseling (MA); counseling psychology (PhD); industrial/organizational psychology (MA); special education (MA). *Accreditation:* APA (one or more programs are accredited). Part-time programs available. *Degree requirements:* For master's, thesis or alternative; for doctorate, thesis/dissertation. *Entrance requirements:* For master's and doctorate, GRE General Test. *Application deadline:* For fall admission, 7/29 for domestic students; for spring admission, 2/3 for domestic students. Application fee: $20 ($30 for international students). *Financial support:* Fellowships, research assistantships, teaching assistantships, career-related internships or fieldwork available. Financial award application deadline: 2/1. *Unit head:* Dr. Tilman Sheets, Head, 318-257-4315, Fax: 318-257-2379. *Application contact:* Dr. Cathy Stockton, Director of Graduate Studies, 318-257-3229, Fax: 318-257-2379, E-mail: cstock@latech.edu.

Marshall University, Academic Affairs Division, College of Liberal Arts, Department of Psychology, Huntington, WV 25755. Offers clinical psychology (MA); general psychology (MA); industrial and organizational psychology (MA); psychology (Psy D). *Accreditation:* APA. *Faculty:* 20 full-time (8 women), 1 part-time/adjunct (0 women). *Students:* 94 full-time (60 women), 31 part-time (23 women); includes 3 minority (1 Asian American or Pacific Islander, 2 Hispanic Americans), 4 international. Average age 29. In 2007, 26 master's, 3 doctorates awarded. *Degree requirements:* For master's, thesis optional. *Entrance requirements:* For master's, GRE General Test or MAT. *Application deadline:* For fall admission, 3/1 for domestic students; for spring admission, 11/1 for domestic students. Application fee: $40. *Financial support:* Teaching assistantships with tuition reimbursements available. *Unit head:* Dr. Martin Amerikaner, Chairperson, 304-696-2783, E-mail: amerikan@marshall.edu. *Application contact:* Information Contact, 304-746-1900, Fax: 304-746-1902, E-mail: services@marshall.edu.

Massachusetts School of Professional Psychology, Graduate Programs, Boston, MA 02132. Offers clinical psychology (Psy D); clinical psychopharmacology (Post-Doctoral MS); counseling psychology (MA); executive coaching (Graduate Certificate); forensic psychology (MA); organizational psychology (MA); respecialization in clinical psychology (Certificate); MA/CAGS. *Accreditation:* APA. *Faculty:* 24 full-time (11 women), 13 part-time/adjunct (9 women). *Students:* 223 full-time (177 women), 81 part-time (68 women); includes 22 minority (3 African Americans, 8 Asian Americans or Pacific Islanders, 11 Hispanic Americans), 9 international. Average age 28. 415 applicants, 42% accepted, 77 enrolled. In 2007, 14 master's, 37 doctorates awarded. *Degree requirements:* For master's, comprehensive exam; for doctorate, thesis/dissertation. *Entrance requirements:* For doctorate, GRE General Test. Additional exam requirements/recommendations for international students: Required—TOEFL (minimum score 550 paper-based; 213 computer-based). *Application deadline:* For fall admission, 1/3 for domestic and international students. Application fee: $50. Electronic applications accepted. *Expenses:* Tuition: Full-time $25,952; part-time $811 per credit. Required fees: $200. *Financial support:* In 2007–08, 20 teaching assistantships (averaging $3,300 per year) were awarded; career-related internships or fieldwork also available. Financial award applicants required to submit FAFSA. *Unit head:* Dr. Nicholas A. Covino, President, 617-327-6777, Fax: 617-327-4447. *Application contact:* 617-327-6777 Ext. 210, Fax: 617-327-4447, E-mail: admissions@mspp.edu.

See Close-Up on page 1447.

Middle Tennessee State University, College of Graduate Studies, College of Education and Behavioral Science, Department of Psychology, Murfreesboro, TN 37132. Offers industrial/organizational psychology (MA); professional counseling (M Ed, Ed S), including curriculum and instruction (Ed S), school counseling (M Ed); psychology (MA); school psychology (Ed S). Part-time and evening/weekend programs available. Postbaccalaureate distance learning degree programs offered. *Faculty:* 36 full-time (16 women), 2 part-time/adjunct (0 women). *Students:* 18 full-time (14 women), 153 part-time (117 women); includes 25 minority (15 African Americans, 9 Asian Americans or Pacific Islanders, 1 Hispanic American). Average age 26. 243 applicants, 58% accepted. In 2007, 41 master's, 12 other advanced degrees awarded. *Entrance requirements:* Additional exam requirements/recommendations for international students: Required—TOEFL (paper-based 525; computer-based 195; IBT 71) or IELTS (6.0). *Application deadline:* For fall admission, 8/1 priority date for domestic students. Applications are processed on a rolling basis. Application fee: $25. Electronic applications accepted. *Financial support:* In 2007–08, 16 students received support. Career-related internships or fieldwork and institutionally sponsored loans available. Support available to part-time students. Financial award application deadline: 5/1; financial award applicants required to submit FAFSA. *Faculty research:* Industrial/organizational, social/personality/sports, counseling/clinical/school, cognitive/language/learning/perception, developmental/aging. *Unit head:* Dr. Dennis Papini, Interim Chair, 615-898-2706, Fax: 615-898-5027.

Minnesota State University Mankato, College of Graduate Studies, College of Social and Behavioral Sciences, Department of Psychology, Mankato, MN 56001. Offers clinical psychology (MA); industrial/organizational psychology (MA); psychology (MT). Part-time programs available. *Students:* 43 full-time (26 women), 5 part-time (3 women). Average age 26. In 2007, 11 degrees awarded. *Degree requirements:* For master's, one foreign language, comprehensive exam, thesis (for some programs). *Entrance requirements:* For master's, GRE General Test, GRE Subject Test (clinical psychology), minimum GPA of 3.0 during previous 2 years, 3 letters of reference. Additional exam requirements/recommendations for international students: Required—TOEFL. *Application deadline:* For fall admission, 3/1 for domestic students; for spring admission, 11/27 for domestic students. Applications are processed on a rolling basis. Application fee: $40. Electronic applications accepted. *Financial support:* Research assistantships, teaching assistantships with full tuition reimbursements, career-related internships or fieldwork, Federal Work-Study, institutionally sponsored loans, and unspecified assistantships available. Support available to part-time students. Financial award application deadline: 3/15; financial award applicants required to submit FAFSA. *Faculty research:* Professional competency in hospitals, mood disturbance, 360-degree feedback, employee selection, planning fallacy. *Unit head:* Dr. Rosemary Krawczyk, Chairperson, 507-389-2724. *Application contact:* 507-389-2321, E-mail: grad@mnsu.edu.

Montclair State University, The Office of Graduate Admissions and Support Services, College of Humanities and Social Sciences, Department of Psychology, Montclair, NJ 07043-1624. Offers educational psychology (MA), including child/adolescent clinical psychology, clinical psychology for Spanish/English bilinguals; psychology (MA, Certificate), including industrial

Industrial and Organizational Psychology

Montclair State University (continued)
and organizational psychology (MA); school psychologist (Certificate). Part-time and evening/weekend programs available. *Faculty:* 27 full-time (11 women), 27 part-time/adjunct (20 women). *Students:* 27 full-time (21 women), 39 part-time (32 women); includes 26 minority (7 African Americans, 4 Asian Americans or Pacific Islanders, 15 Hispanic Americans), 3 international. 86 applicants, 21% accepted, 13 enrolled. In 2007, 22 master's, 11 other advanced degrees awarded. *Degree requirements:* For master's, comprehensive exam, thesis or alternative. *Entrance requirements:* For master's, GRE General Test, GRE Subject Test, previous course work in psychology, interview, 2 letters of recommendation. Additional exam requirements/recommendations for international students: Required—TOEFL (minimum score 83 computer-based). *Application deadline:* For fall admission, 2/1 for domestic and international students; for spring admission, 10/1 for domestic and international students. Applications are processed on a rolling basis. Application fee: $60. Electronic applications accepted. *Financial support:* In 2007–08, 10 research assistantships with full tuition reimbursements (averaging $7,000 per year) were awarded; Federal Work-Study, scholarships/grants, and unspecified assistantships also available. Support available to part-time students. Financial award application deadline: 3/1; financial award applicants required to submit FAFSA. *Faculty research:* Engaged learning, academic and civic development. Total annual research expenditures: $10,000. *Unit head:* Dr. Peter Vietze, Chairperson, 973-655-5201.

National-Louis University, College of Arts and Sciences, Program in Psychology, Chicago, IL 60603. Offers cultural psychology (MA); health psychology (MA); human development (MA); organizational psychology (MA); psychology (Certificate). Part-time and evening/weekend programs available. *Students:* 37 full-time (33 women), 147 part-time (127 women); includes 99 minority (79 African Americans, 1 American Indian/Alaska Native, 6 Asian Americans or Pacific Islanders, 13 Hispanic Americans). Average age 38. *Degree requirements:* For master's, thesis, internship (health psychology). *Entrance requirements:* For master's, GRE, MAT, or Watson-Glaser Critical Thinking Appraisal, interview, minimum GPA of 3.0; for Certificate, GRE, MAT, or Watson-Glaser Critical Thinking Appraisal, interview, minimum GPA of 3.0, undergraduate course work in psychology. *Application deadline:* Applications are processed on a rolling basis. *Expenses:* Tuition: Full-time $18,900; part-time $630 per credit hour. Required fees: $20 per term. One-time fee: $40 part-time. Tuition and fees vary according to course load, campus/location and program. *Financial support:* Federal Work-Study, institutionally sponsored loans, scholarships/grants, and tuition waivers available. Support available to part-time students. Financial award applicants required to submit FAFSA. *Faculty research:* Human development, personality theory, abnormal psychology. *Unit head:* Dr. Edward Risinger, Professor, 224-233-2533, Fax: 224-233-2533, E-mail: erisinger@nl.edu. *Application contact:* David McCulloch, Vice President for University Services, 800-443-5522 Ext. 5151, Fax: 847-465-0593, E-mail: dmcc@wheeling1.nl.edu.

New York University, Graduate School of Arts and Science, Department of Psychology, New York, NY 10012-1019. Offers cognition and perception (PhD); community psychology (PhD); general psychology (MA); industrial/organizational psychology (MA); psychotherapy and psychoanalysis (Advanced Certificate); social/personality psychology (PhD). Part-time programs available. *Faculty:* 38 full-time (13 women), 78 part-time/adjunct. *Students:* 155 full-time (115 women), 305 part-time (218 women); includes 77 minority (24 African Americans, 29 Asian Americans or Pacific Islanders, 24 Hispanic Americans), 53 international. Average age 32. 767 applicants, 46% accepted, 112 enrolled. In 2007, 80 master's, 15 doctorates awarded. Terminal master's awarded for partial completion of doctoral program. *Degree requirements:* For master's, comprehensive exam, thesis or alternative; for doctorate, thesis/dissertation. *Entrance requirements:* For master's, GRE General Test, minimum GPA of 3.0; for doctorate, GRE General Test, GRE Subject Test; for Advanced Certificate, doctoral degree, minimum GPA of 3.0. Additional exam requirements/recommendations for international students: Required—TOEFL. *Application deadline:* For fall admission, 12/18 for domestic students. Application fee: $85. *Financial support:* Fellowships with tuition reimbursements, research assistantships with tuition reimbursements, teaching assistantships with tuition reimbursements, career-related internships or fieldwork, Federal Work-Study, institutionally sponsored loans, scholarships/grants, traineeships, health care benefits, and unspecified assistantships available. Financial award application deadline: 12/18; financial award applicants required to submit FAFSA. *Faculty research:* Vision, memory, social cognition, social and cognitive development, relationships. *Unit head:* Marisa Carrasco, Chair, 212-998-7900, Fax: 212-995-4018, E-mail: psychq@psych.nyu.edu. *Application contact:* Laurence Maloney, Director of Graduate Studies, 212-998-7900, Fax: 212-995-4018, E-mail: psychq@psych.nyu.edu.

North Carolina State University, Graduate School, College of Humanities and Social Sciences, Department of Psychology, Raleigh, NC 27695. Offers developmental psychology (PhD); ergonomics and experimental psychology (PhD); industrial/organizational psychology (PhD); psychology in the public interest (PhD); school psychology (PhD). *Accreditation:* APA. *Degree requirements:* For doctorate, comprehensive exam, thesis/dissertation. *Entrance requirements:* For doctorate, GRE General Test, GRE Subject Test (industrial/organizational psychology), MAT (recommended), minimum GPA of 3.0 in major. Electronic applications accepted. *Faculty research:* Cognitive and social development (human factors, families, the workplace, community issues and health, aging).

Northern Kentucky University, Office of Graduate Programs, College of Arts and Sciences, Program in Industrial-Organizational Psychology, Highland Heights, KY 41099. Offers industrial psychology (Certificate); industrial-organizational psychology (MSIO); occupational health psychology (Certificate); organizational psychology (Certificate). Part-time and evening/weekend programs available. *Faculty:* 4 full-time (1 woman), 3 part-time/adjunct (1 woman). *Students:* 20 full-time (16 women), 30 part-time (20 women); includes 6 minority (3 African Americans, 2 Asian Americans or Pacific Islanders, 1 Hispanic American), 1 international. Average age 29. 36 applicants, 39% accepted, 13 enrolled. In 2007, 7 degrees awarded. *Degree requirements:* For master's, thesis optional. *Entrance requirements:* For master's, GRE, minimum GPA of 3.0, at least 9 semester hours of undergraduate psychology, 1 course in statistics. Additional exam requirements/recommendations for international students: Required—TOEFL (minimum score 550 paper-based; 213 computer-based; 79 iBT), Michigan English Language Assessment Battery (must be taken at NKU). *Application deadline:* For fall admission, 6/1 priority date for domestic students, 6/1 for international students; for spring admission, 11/1 priority date for domestic students, 10/1 for international students. Application fee: $40. Electronic applications accepted. *Financial support:* Unspecified assistantships available. *Faculty research:* Bullying in the workplace, consumer and social dilemma research, self efficiency and goal orientations. *Unit head:* Dr. Jeffrey Smith, Director, 859-572-5317, Fax: 859-572-6085, E-mail: smithj@nku.edu. *Application contact:* Dr. Peg Griffin, Director of Graduate Programs, 859-572-1555, Fax: 859-572-6670, E-mail: gradprog@nku.edu.

Ohio University, Graduate College, College of Arts and Sciences, Department of Psychology, Program in Organizational Psychology, Athens, OH 45701-2979. Offers PhD. *Faculty:* 3 full-time (1 woman). *Students:* 3 full-time (1 woman), 2 part-time. 18 applicants, 17% accepted, 3 enrolled. In 2007, 2 degrees awarded. *Degree requirements:* For doctorate, one foreign language, comprehensive exam, thesis/dissertation. *Entrance requirements:* For doctorate, GRE General Test, GRE Subject Test. Additional exam requirements/recommendations for international students: Required—TOEFL. *Application deadline:* For fall admission, 1/1 for domestic students. Application fee: $50 ($55 for international students). *Financial support:* In 2007–08, 1 fellowship with full tuition reimbursement (averaging $16,400 per year), 2 teaching assistantships with full tuition reimbursements (averaging $12,000 per year) were awarded; research assistantships with full tuition reimbursements, career-related internships or fieldwork, Federal Work-Study, institutionally sponsored loans, tuition waivers (full), and unspecified assistantships also available. Financial award application deadline: 1/15. *Faculty research:* Performance appraisal, job satisfaction, organizational entry, sexual harassment. *Unit head:* Rodger Griffeth, Coordinator of Organizational Studies, 740-593-1069, Fax: 740-593-0579. *Application contact:* Karyl Jones, Administrative Secretary, 740-593-1090, Fax: 740-593-0579, E-mail: psychology@ohio.edu.

Old Dominion University, College of Sciences, Doctoral Program in Psychology, Norfolk, VA 23529. Offers applied experimental psychology (PhD); human factors psychology (PhD); industrial/organizational psychology (PhD). *Faculty:* 17 full-time (7 women), 1 part-time/adjunct (0 women). *Students:* 15 full-time (12 women), 16 part-time (10 women); includes 3 minority (1 African American, 1 Asian American or Pacific Islander, 1 Hispanic American). Average age 29. 42 applicants, 29% accepted, 6 enrolled. In 2007, 5 degrees awarded. *Degree requirements:* For doctorate, thesis/dissertation, qualifying exam. *Entrance requirements:* For doctorate, GRE, GRE Subject Test, 3 recommendation letters. Additional exam requirements/recommendations for international students: Required—TOEFL (minimum score 550 paper-based). *Application deadline:* For winter admission, 1/15 for domestic and international students. Application fee: $40. *Expenses:* Tuition, state resident: part-time $304 per credit hour. Tuition, nonresident: part-time $761 per credit hour. *Financial support:* In 2007–08, 6 students received support, including 2 fellowships with full tuition reimbursements available (averaging $18,000 per year), research assistantships with full tuition reimbursements available (averaging $12,000 per year), 3 teaching assistantships with full tuition reimbursements available (averaging $12,000 per year). Financial award application deadline: 1/15. *Faculty research:* Human-computer interaction, simulation, neuroergonomics, attention and workload. Total annual research expenditures: $399,161. *Unit head:* Dr. James Bliss, Graduate Program Director, 757-683-4051, Fax: 757-683-5087, E-mail: psychppd@odu.edu.

Penn State University Park, Graduate School, College of the Liberal Arts, Department of Psychology, State College, University Park, PA 16802-1503. Offers clinical psychology (MS, PhD); cognitive psychology (MS, PhD); developmental psychology (MS, PhD); industrial/organizational psychology (MS, PhD); psychobiology (MS, PhD); social psychology (MS, PhD). *Accreditation:* APA (one or more programs are accredited). *Expenses:* Tuition, state resident: full-time $14,738; part-time $614 per credit. Tuition, nonresident: full-time $26,050; part-time $1,085 per credit. Tuition and fees vary according to course load, program and student level. *Unit head:* Dr. Melvin M. Mark, Interim Head, 814-865-9515, Fax: 814-863-7002, E-mail: m5m@psu.edu.

Philadelphia College of Osteopathic Medicine, Graduate and Professional Programs, Department of Psychology, Philadelphia, PA 19131-1694. Offers clinical psychology (Psy D); counseling and clinical health psychology (MS); organizational leadership and development (MS); psychology (Certificate); school psychology (MS, Psy D, Ed S). *Accreditation:* APA. *Degree requirements:* For master's, thesis; for doctorate, comprehensive exam, thesis/dissertation, final project, fieldwork. *Entrance requirements:* For master's, GRE or MAT, minimum GPA of 3.0; course work in biology, chemistry, English, physics; for other advanced degree, PRAXIS. *Faculty research:* Depression in primary care, integrated primary care, geriatric mental health.

See Close-Up on page 1469.

Pontifical Catholic University of Puerto Rico, Institute of Graduate Studies in Behavioral Science and Community Affairs, Program in Industrial Psychology (Doctorate), Ponce, PR 00717-0777. Offers PhD. Part-time and evening/weekend programs available. *Entrance requirements:* For doctorate, EXADEP, minimum GPA of 2.75.

Pontifical Catholic University of Puerto Rico, Institute of Graduate Studies in Behavioral Science and Community Affairs, Program in Industrial Psychology (Master's), Ponce, PR 00717-0777. Offers MS. Part-time and evening/weekend programs available. *Degree requirements:* For master's, thesis. *Entrance requirements:* For master's, EXADEP, 3 letters of recommendation, interview, minimum GPA of 2.75.

Radford University, Graduate College, College of Humanities and Behavioral Sciences, Department of Psychology, Radford, VA 24142. Offers clinical psychology (MA, MS); counseling psychology (Psy D); experimental psychology (MA); industrial-organizational psychology (MA, MS); school psychology (Ed S). Part-time programs available. *Faculty:* 24 full-time (10 women). *Students:* 38 full-time (31 women), 52 part-time (39 women); includes 5 minority (4 African Americans, 1 Asian American or Pacific Islander), 2 international. Average age 25. 128 applicants, 64% accepted, 38 enrolled. In 2007, 45 degrees awarded. *Degree requirements:* For master's, comprehensive exam, thesis (for some programs); for doctorate, comprehensive exam, thesis/dissertation; for Ed S, comprehensive exam. *Entrance requirements:* For master's, GRE, minimum GPA 3.0; for doctorate, GRE; for Ed S, GMAT, GRE General Test, MAT, NTE. Additional exam requirements/recommendations for international students: Required—TOEFL. *Application deadline:* For fall admission, 3/1 priority date for domestic students, 12/1 for international students; for spring admission, 10/1 for domestic students, 7/1 for international students. Applications are processed on a rolling basis. Application fee: $40. Electronic applications accepted. *Financial support:* In 2007–08, 42 research assistantships with partial tuition reimbursements (averaging $8,000 per year), 12 teaching assistantships with partial tuition reimbursements (averaging $8,700 per year) were awarded; career-related internships or fieldwork, Federal Work-Study, institutionally sponsored loans, scholarships/grants, and unspecified assistantships also available. Financial award application deadline: 3/1; financial award applicants required to submit FAFSA. *Unit head:* Dr. Hilary M. Lips, Chair, 540-831-5387, Fax: 540-831-6113, E-mail: hlips@radford.edu.

Rice University, Graduate Programs, School of Social Sciences, Department of Psychology, Houston, TX 77251-1892. Offers cognitive sciences (MA, PhD); industrial-organizational/social psychology (MA, PhD); psychology (MA, PhD). Terminal master's awarded for partial completion of doctoral program. *Degree requirements:* For master's, thesis; for doctorate, thesis/dissertation. *Entrance requirements:* For doctorate, GRE General Test, minimum GPA of 3.0. Additional exam requirements/recommendations for international students: Required—TOEFL. Electronic applications accepted. *Faculty research:* Learning and memory, information processing, decision theory.

Roosevelt University, Graduate Division, College of Arts and Sciences, Department of Psychology, Program in Industrial/Organizational Psychology, Chicago, IL 60605-1394. Offers MA. *Students:* 43 full-time (34 women), 44 part-time (33 women); includes 27 minority (12 African Americans, 12 Asian Americans or Pacific Islanders, 3 Hispanic Americans), 3 international. Average age 29. 77 applicants, 53% accepted, 26 enrolled. In 2007, 18 degrees awarded. *Unit head:* Michael Helford, Director, 847-619-8543. *Application contact:* Joanne Canyon-Heller, Coordinator of Graduate Admission, 877-APPLY RU, Fax: 312-281-3356, E-mail: applyru@roosevelt.edu.

Rutgers, The State University of New Jersey, New Brunswick, Graduate School of Applied and Professional Psychology, Program in Organizational Psychology, New Brunswick, NJ 08901-1281. Offers Psy M, Psy D. *Degree requirements:* For doctorate, comprehensive exam, thesis/dissertation, 1 year internship. *Entrance requirements:* For doctorate, GRE General Test, GRE Subject Test (psychology), BA in psychology or equivalent. Additional exam requirements/recommendations for international students: Required—TOEFL. Electronic applications accepted. Expenses: Contact institution. *Faculty research:* Organizational assessment, managerial and organizational practice, consultation, organizational development, decision making.

St. Cloud State University, School of Graduate Studies, College of Social Sciences, Program in Industrial-Organizational Psychology, St. Cloud, MN 56301-4498. Offers MS. *Faculty:* 11 full-time (6 women). *Students:* 22 (13 women); includes 1 minority (African American) 8 international. 27 applicants, 48% accepted. In 2007, 6 degrees awarded. *Degree requirements:* For master's, thesis or alternative. *Entrance requirements:* For master's, GRE General Test, minimum GPA of 2.75. Additional exam requirements/recommendations for international students: Required—MELAB; Recommended—TOEFL (minimum score 550 paper-based; 213 computer-based), IELTS (minimum score 7). *Application deadline:* For fall admission, 3/1 for domestic and international students. Electronic applications accepted. *Expenses:* Tuition, state resident: part-time $267 per credit. Tuition, nonresident: part-time $418 per credit. Required fees: $28 per credit. *Financial support:* Federal Work-Study, scholarships/grants, and unspecified assistantships available. *Unit head:* Dr. Daren Protolipac, Coordinator, 320-308-4157, E-mail:

dsprotolipac@stcloudstate.edu. *Application contact:* Linda Lou Krueger, School of Graduate Studies, 320-308-2113, Fax: 320-308-5371, E-mail: lekrueger@stcloudstate.edu.

Saint Joseph's University, College of Arts and Sciences, Programs in Training and Organizational Development, Philadelphia, PA 19131-1395. Offers adult learning and training (MS, Certificate); organization dynamics and leadership (MS, Certificate); organizational psychology and development (MS, Certificate). *Students:* 1 full-time (0 women), 64 part-time (47 women); includes 20 minority (18 African Americans, 1 Asian American or Pacific Islander, 1 Hispanic American), 4 international. Average age 37. In 2007, 18 degrees awarded. *Entrance requirements:* For master's, GRE (if GPA is below 2.7), application, official transcripts, minimum GPA of 2.7, personal statement, 2 letters of recommendation. Additional exam requirements/recommendations for international students: Required—TOEFL (minimum score 550 paper-based; 213 computer-based; 79 iBT). *Application deadline:* For fall admission, 7/15 priority date for domestic students, 4/15 for international students; for winter admission, 1/15 for international students; for spring admission, 11/15 priority date for domestic students, 10/15 for international students. Applications are processed on a rolling basis. Application fee: $35. Electronic applications accepted. *Expenses:* Tuition: Part-time $738 per credit. Tuition and fees vary according to degree level and program. *Unit head:* John Thinnes, Director, 610-660-1575.

Saint Louis University, Graduate School, College of Arts and Sciences and Graduate School, Department of Psychology, St. Louis, MO 63103-2097. Offers clinical psychology (MS-R, PhD); experimental psychology (MS-R, PhD); industrial-organizational psychology (PhD); psychology (PhD). *Accreditation:* APA (one or more programs are accredited). Part-time programs available. *Faculty:* 18 full-time (7 women). *Students:* 77 full-time (53 women), 8 part-time (5 women); includes 14 minority (12 African Americans, 1 American Indian/Alaska Native, 1 Asian American or Pacific Islander). Average age 27. 234 applicants, 11% accepted, 20 enrolled. In 2007, 11 master's, 10 doctorates awarded. *Median time to degree:* Of those who began their doctoral program in fall 1999, 90% received their degree in 8 years or less. *Degree requirements:* For master's, comprehensive exam, thesis; for doctorate, thesis/dissertation, clinical internship (for clinical psychology PhD). *Entrance requirements:* For master's and doctorate, GRE General Test, interview, letters of recommendation, resumé, transcripts, goal statement. Additional exam requirements/recommendations for international students: Required—TOEFL (minimum score 550 paper-based; 213 computer-based). *Application deadline:* For fall admission, 1/1 for domestic and international students. Application fee: $40. Electronic applications accepted. *Expenses:* Tuition: Part-time $845 per credit hour. Required fees: $105 per semester. *Financial support:* In 2007–08, 71 students received support, including 16 research assistantships with full tuition reimbursements available (averaging $14,000 per year), 14 teaching assistantships with full tuition reimbursements available (averaging $12,000 per year); career-related internships or fieldwork, Federal Work-Study, scholarships/grants, traineeships, health care benefits, tuition waivers, and unspecified assistantships also available. Support available to part-time students. Financial award application deadline: 2/1; financial award applicants required to submit FAFSA. *Faculty research:* Violence and trauma; neural basis of learning and memory function; eating disorders; body image and health behavior; prejudice, stereotyping, and victimization; memory, cognitive aging and language processing. Total annual research expenditures: $514,559. *Unit head:* Dr. Donna J. LaVoie, Chairperson, 314-977-3676, Fax: 314-977-3679, E-mail: lavoiedj@slu.edu. *Application contact:* Gary U. Behrman, Associate Dean of Graduate School Admissions, 314-977-3827, Fax: 314-977-3943, E-mail: behrmang@slu.edu.

Saint Mary's University, Faculty of Science, Department of Psychology, Halifax, NS B3H 3C3, Canada. Offers applied psychology (M Sc), including clinical psychology, industrial/organizational psychology. M Sc (clinical psychology) offered jointly with Dalhousie University. Part-time programs available. *Degree requirements:* For master's, thesis, internship. *Entrance requirements:* For master's, GRE General Test, honors degree, minimum QPA of 3.25. *Faculty research:* Assessment, health psychology, social psychology, cognition.

St. Mary's University, Graduate School, Department of Psychology, Program in Industrial/Organizational Psychology, San Antonio, TX 78228-8507. Offers MA, MS. *Students:* 14 full-time (8 women), 7 part-time (6 women); includes 4 minority (1 African American, 3 Hispanic Americans). Average age 29. In 2007, 17 degrees awarded. *Degree requirements:* For master's, comprehensive exam, thesis optional. *Entrance requirements:* For master's, GRE General Test. Additional exam requirements/recommendations for international students: Required—TOEFL (minimum score 550 paper-based; 213 computer-based). Application fee: $0. *Financial support:* Career-related internships or fieldwork, Federal Work-Study, institutionally sponsored loans, scholarships/grants, health care benefits, and unspecified assistantships available. Financial award application deadline: 3/31; financial award applicants required to submit FAFSA. *Unit head:* Dr. Gregory Pool, Director, 210-436-3314, Fax: 210-431-4301, E-mail: gpool@stmarytx.edu.

San Diego State University, Graduate and Research Affairs, College of Sciences, Department of Psychology, San Diego, CA 92182. Offers clinical psychology (MS, PhD); industrial and organizational psychology (MS); program evaluation (MS); psychology (MA). *Accreditation:* APA (one or more programs are accredited). *Students:* 141 full-time (108 women), 32 part-time (24 women); includes 41 minority (4 African Americans, 1 American Indian/Alaska Native, 14 Asian Americans or Pacific Islanders, 22 Hispanic Americans), 8 international. Average age 25. 445 applicants, 20% accepted, 63 enrolled. In 2007, 52 master's, 14 doctorates awarded. Terminal master's awarded for partial completion of doctoral program. *Degree requirements:* For master's, thesis, oral exam; for doctorate, thesis/dissertation. *Entrance requirements:* For master's, GRE General Test, GRE Subject Test, 3 letters of recommendation; for doctorate, GRE General Test, GRE Subject Test, minimum GPA of 3.0, 3 letters of recommendation. Additional exam requirements/recommendations for international students: Required—TOEFL. *Application deadline:* For fall admission, 2/1 for domestic students, 2/1 priority date for international students. Application fee: $55. Electronic applications accepted. *Financial support:* Fellowships, research assistantships, teaching assistantships, career-related internships or fieldwork, scholarships/grants, and unspecified assistantships available. Financial award applicants required to submit FAFSA. Total annual research expenditures: $8 million. *Unit head:* Dr. Claire Murphy, Chair, 619-594-4559, Fax: 619-594-1332, E-mail: cmurphy@sunstroke.sdsu.edu. *Application contact:* Judy Price, Graduate Advisor, 619-594-5401, Fax: 619-594-1332, E-mail: judyprice@sunstroke.sdsu.edu.

San Jose State University, Graduate Studies and Research, College of Social Sciences, Department of Psychology, San Jose, CA 95192-0001. Offers clinical psychology (MS); experimental psychology (MA); industrial/organizational psychology (MS); psychology (MA). *Students:* 53 full-time (41 women), 16 part-time (11 women); includes 18 minority (11 Asian Americans or Pacific Islanders, 7 Hispanic Americans), 7 international. Average age 27. 124 applicants, 34% accepted, 38 enrolled. In 2007, 27 degrees awarded. *Degree requirements:* For master's, comprehensive exam, thesis (for some programs). *Entrance requirements:* For master's, GRE General Test, minimum GPA of 3.0. *Application deadline:* For fall admission, 6/29 for domestic students; for spring admission, 11/30 for domestic students. Applications are processed on a rolling basis. Application fee: $59. Electronic applications accepted. *Financial support:* In 2007–08, 15 teaching assistantships were awarded; career-related internships or fieldwork and institutionally sponsored loans also available. Financial award application deadline: 3/1; financial award applicants required to submit FAFSA. *Faculty research:* Drug and alcohol abuse, neurohormonal mechanisms in motion sickness, behavior modification, sleep research, genetics. *Unit head:* Dr. Sheila Bienenfeld, Chair, 408-924-5600, Fax: 408-924-5605, E-mail: sheila.bienenfeld@sjsu.edu.

Seattle Pacific University, Graduate School, School of Psychology, Family and Community, Program in Organizational Psychology, Seattle, WA 98119-1997. Offers MA, PhD. *Students:* 22 full-time (20 women), 24 part-time (16 women); includes 12 minority (4 African Americans, 7 Asian Americans or Pacific Islanders, 1 Hispanic American), 2 international. 49 applicants, 29% accepted, 14 enrolled. In 2007, 9 degrees awarded. Application fee: $50. *Expenses:* Tuition: Part-time $522 per credit hour. Tuition and fees vary according to program. *Unit head:* Dr. Robert B McKenna, Chair, 206-281-2629, E-mail: rmckenna@spu.edu. *Application contact:* Smruti Desai, Coordinator, 206-281-2312, E-mail: smruti@spu.edu.

Southern Illinois University Edwardsville, Graduate Studies and Research, School of Education, Department of Psychology, Program in Industrial-Organizational Psychology, Edwardsville, IL 62026-0001. Offers MA. *Students:* 17 full-time (14 women), 9 part-time (5 women); includes 3 minority (all African Americans) In 2007, 9 degrees awarded. *Degree requirements:* For master's, thesis. *Application deadline:* For fall admission, 3/1 for domestic and international students. Applications are processed on a rolling basis. Application fee: $30. Electronic applications accepted. *Unit head:* Dr. Lynn Bartels, Director, 618-650-2202, E-mail: lbartel@siue.edu.

Springfield College, Graduate Programs, Programs in Psychology and Counseling, Springfield, MA 01109-3797. Offers athletic counseling (M Ed, MS, CAGS); industrial/organizational psychology (M Ed, MS, CAGS); marriage and family therapy (M Ed, MS, CAGS); mental health counseling (M Ed, MS, CAGS); school guidance and counseling (M Ed, MS, CAGS); student personnel in higher education (M Ed, MS, CAGS). Part-time and evening/weekend programs available. *Faculty:* 14 full-time (8 women), 17 part-time/adjunct (7 women). *Students:* 157 full-time, 44 part-time. Average age 28. 220 applicants, 72% accepted, 97 enrolled. In 2007, 93 master's, 1 other advanced degree awarded. *Degree requirements:* For master's, comprehensive exam, thesis (for some programs), research project, internship. *Entrance requirements:* For master's and CAGS, interview. Additional exam requirements/recommendations for international students: Required—TOEFL (minimum score 550 paper-based; 213 computer-based). *Application deadline:* For fall admission, 1/15 priority date for domestic students; for winter admission, 11/1 for domestic students; for spring admission, 12/1 for domestic students. Applications are processed on a rolling basis. Application fee: $50. Electronic applications accepted. *Expenses:* Tuition: Full-time $12,942; part-time $719 per semester hour. Required fees: $25. Tuition and fees vary according to program. *Financial support:* In 2007–08, 8 fellowships with partial tuition reimbursements (averaging $2,000 per year), 2 research assistantships (averaging $4,000 per year), 7 teaching assistantships (averaging $1,800 per year) were awarded; career-related internships or fieldwork, Federal Work-Study, institutionally sponsored loans, scholarships/grants, and tuition waivers (full and partial) also available. Financial award application deadline: 3/1. *Faculty research:* Sport psychology, leadership and emotional intelligence, violence and terrorism, performance enhancement, cognitive function. Total annual research expenditures: $715,109. *Unit head:* Dr. Anna L. Moriarty, Director, 413-748-3322, Fax: 413-748-3854, E-mail: anna_l_moriarty@spfldcol.edu. *Application contact:* Donald James Shaw, Director of Graduate Admissions, 413-748-3060, Fax: 413-748-3069, E-mail: donald_shaw_jr@spfldcol.edu.

Teachers College, Columbia University, Graduate Faculty of Education, Department of Organization and Leadership, Program in Social and Organizational Psychology, New York, NY 10027-6696. Offers organizational psychology (MA, Ed D, PhD); social psychology (Ed D, PhD). *Faculty:* 8 full-time (5 women), 5 part-time/adjunct. *Students:* 121 full-time (78 women), 106 part-time (76 women); includes 47 minority (14 African Americans, 22 Asian Americans or Pacific Islanders, 11 Hispanic Americans), 25 international. Average age 32. 216 applicants, 59% accepted, 67 enrolled. In 2007, 121 master's, 6 doctorates awarded. Terminal master's awarded for partial completion of doctoral program. *Degree requirements:* For master's, comprehensive exam; for doctorate, thesis/dissertation. *Entrance requirements:* For master's, minimum GPA of 3.0; for doctorate, GRE General Test. *Application deadline:* For fall admission, 5/15 for domestic students; for spring admission, 12/1 for domestic students. Application fee: $70. *Financial support:* Fellowships, research assistantships, career-related internships or fieldwork, Federal Work-Study, institutionally sponsored loans, and tuition waivers (full and partial) available. Support available to part-time students. Financial award application deadline: 2/1. *Faculty research:* Conflict resolution, human resource and organization development, management competence, organizational culture, leadership. *Application contact:* Debbie Lesperance, Assistant Director of Admission, 212-678-3710, Fax: 212-678-4171.

Temple University, Graduate School, College of Education, Department of Psychological Studies in Education, Program in Adult and Organizational Development, Philadelphia, PA 19122-6096. Offers Ed M. Part-time and evening/weekend programs available. *Degree requirements:* For master's, thesis or alternative. *Entrance requirements:* For master's, GRE General Test or MAT, minimum GPA of 3.0. Additional exam requirements/recommendations for international students: Required—TOEFL (minimum score 550 paper-based; 213 computer-based; 79 iBT). Electronic applications accepted.

Texas A&M University, College of Liberal Arts, Department of Psychology, College Station, TX 77843. Offers behavioral and cellular neuroscience (MS, PhD); clinical psychology (MS, PhD); cognitive psychology (MS, PhD); developmental psychology (MS, PhD); industrial/organizational psychology (MS, PhD); social psychology (MS, PhD). *Accreditation:* APA (one or more programs are accredited). *Faculty:* 33. *Students:* 69 full-time (46 women), 14 part-time (10 women); includes 27 minority (7 African Americans, 1 American Indian/Alaska Native, 5 Asian Americans or Pacific Islanders, 14 Hispanic Americans), 8 international. 274 applicants, 11% accepted, 15 enrolled. In 2007, 11 master's, 7 doctorates awarded. *Degree requirements:* For master's, thesis; for doctorate, comprehensive exam (for some programs), thesis/dissertation. *Entrance requirements:* For master's and doctorate, GRE General Test. Additional exam requirements/recommendations for international students: Required—TOEFL. *Application deadline:* For fall admission, 1/5 for domestic and international students. Application fee: $50 ($75 for international students). Electronic applications accepted. *Expenses:* Tuition, state resident: full-time $6,129. Tuition, nonresident: full-time $11,689. Tuition and fees vary according to course load. *Financial support:* Fellowships with partial tuition reimbursements, research assistantships with partial tuition reimbursements, teaching assistantships with partial tuition reimbursements, career-related internships or fieldwork, institutionally sponsored loans, health care benefits, and unspecified assistantships available. Financial award application deadline: 1/5; financial award applicants required to submit FAFSA. *Unit head:* Dr. Steve Rholes, Head, 979-845-2581, Fax: 979-845-4727, E-mail: wsr@psyc.tamu.edu. *Application contact:* Sharon Starr, Graduate Admissions Supervisor, 979-458-1710, Fax: 979-845-4727, E-mail: gradadv@psyc.tamu.edu.

University at Albany, State University of New York, College of Arts and Sciences, Department of Psychology, Albany, NY 12222-0001. Offers autism (Certificate); biopsychology (PhD); clinical psychology (PhD); general/experimental psychology (PhD); industrial/organizational psychology (PhD); psychology (MA); social/personality psychology (PhD). *Accreditation:* APA (one or more programs are accredited). *Students:* 51 full-time (32 women), 47 part-time (40 women). Average age 30. In 2007, 8 master's, 15 doctorates, 7 other advanced degrees awarded. *Degree requirements:* For doctorate, thesis/dissertation. *Entrance requirements:* For doctorate, GRE General Test, GRE Subject Test. Additional exam requirements/recommendations for international students: Required—TOEFL (minimum score 550 paper-based; 213 computer-based). *Application deadline:* For fall admission, 1/15 for domestic and international students. Application fee: $75. Electronic applications accepted. *Expenses:* Tuition, state resident: part-time $576 per credit. Tuition, nonresident: part-time $910 per credit. Tuition and fees vary according to program. *Financial support:* Fellowships, research assistantships, teaching assistantships, career-related internships or fieldwork available. Financial award application deadline: 2/1. *Unit head:* Kevin J. Williams, Chair, 518-442-4820.

The University of Akron, Graduate School, Buchtel College of Arts and Sciences, Department of Psychology, Program in Industrial/Organizational Psychology, Akron, OH 44325. Offers MA, PhD. *Students:* 30 full-time (19 women), 11 part-time (5 women); includes 6 minority (3 African Americans, 3 Asian Americans or Pacific Islanders), 4 international. Average age 28. 29 applicants, 24% accepted, 6 enrolled. In 2007, 5 degrees awarded. Terminal master's awarded for partial completion of doctoral program. *Degree requirements:* For master's, thesis optional, thesis or specialty exam; for doctorate, one foreign language, comprehensive exam, thesis/dissertation. *Entrance requirements:* For master's, GRE General Test, GRE Subject Test,

Industrial and Organizational Psychology

The University of Akron (continued)

minimum GPA of 2.75, letters of recommendation; for doctorate, GRE General Test, GRE Subject Test, minimum graduate GPA of 3.25, letters of recommendation, personal statement. Additional exam requirements/recommendations for international students: Required—TOEFL (minimum score 550 paper-based; 213 computer-based; 79 iBT). *Application deadline:* For fall admission, 1/15 for domestic and international students. Applications are processed on a rolling basis. Application fee: $30 ($40 for international students). Electronic applications accepted. *Expenses:* Tuition, state resident: full-time $6,164; part-time $342 per credit. Tuition, nonresident: full-time $10,575; part-time $588 per credit. Required fees: $806; $43 per credit. $12 per term. Tuition and fees vary according to course load, degree level and program. *Financial support:* Fellowships with full tuition reimbursements, research assistantships with full tuition reimbursements, teaching assistantships with full tuition reimbursements available. *Faculty research:* Personnel selection, performance management, leadership, self-regulation, affect. *Unit head:* Dr. Rosalie Hall, Coordinator, 330-972-8375, E-mail: rhall@uakron.edu.

University of Baltimore, Graduate School, The Yale Gordon College of Liberal Arts, Division of Applied Sciences, Baltimore, MD 21201-5779. Offers applied psychology (MS), including counseling, industrial and organizational psychology, psychological applications; human services (MS). Part-time and evening/weekend programs available. *Faculty:* 7 full-time (5 women), 7 part-time/adjunct (2 women). *Students:* 61 full-time (49 women), 43 part-time (34 women); includes 30 minority (23 African Americans, 5 Asian Americans or Pacific Islanders, 2 Hispanic Americans), 6 international. Average age 28. 112 applicants, 64% accepted, 27 enrolled. In 2007, 31 degrees awarded. *Degree requirements:* For master's, thesis optional. *Entrance requirements:* For master's, GRE, minimum GPA of 3.0. Additional exam requirements/recommendations for international students: Required—TOEFL (minimum score 550 paper-based; 213 computer-based). *Application deadline:* For fall admission, 8/1 for domestic students, 6/1 for international students; for spring admission, 12/1 for domestic students, 11/1 for international students. Applications are processed on a rolling basis. Application fee: $45. Electronic applications accepted. *Expenses: Contact institution.* Tuition and fees vary according to program. *Financial support:* In 2007–08, 5 research assistantships with full and partial tuition reimbursements were awarded; fellowships, career-related internships or fieldwork and Federal Work-Study also available. Support available to part-time students. Financial award application deadline: 4/1; financial award applicants required to submit FAFSA. *Faculty research:* Participatory decision making, counter productive workplace behavior, organizational consulting, substance abuse treatment, cognitive functioning in head injured. Total annual research expenditures: $93,146. *Unit head:* Dr. Thomas Mitchell, Director of Program in Applied Psychology, 410-837-5348, Fax: 410-837-4793, E-mail: tmitchell@ubalt.edu. *Application contact:* Wendy Bolyard.

See Close-Up on page 1505.

University of Central Florida, College of Sciences, Department of Psychology, Program in Industrial/Organizational Psychology, Orlando, FL 32816. Offers MS, PhD. *Accreditation:* APA. Part-time and evening/weekend programs available. *Students:* Average age 28. *Degree requirements:* For master's, comprehensive exam, thesis, practicum. *Entrance requirements:* For master's, GRE General Test, minimum GPA of 3.0 in last 60 hours, resumé. Additional exam requirements/recommendations for international students: Required—TOEFL. *Application deadline:* For fall admission, 2/1 for domestic students. Application fee: $30. Electronic applications accepted. *Expenses:* Tuition, state resident: full-time $6,484. Tuition, nonresident: full-time $23,938. Tuition and fees vary according to program. *Financial support:* Fellowships with partial tuition reimbursements, research assistantships with partial tuition reimbursements, teaching assistantships with partial tuition reimbursements, career-related internships or fieldwork, Federal Work-Study, institutionally sponsored loans, tuition waivers (partial), and unspecified assistantships available. Financial award application deadline: 3/1; financial award applicants required to submit FAFSA. *Faculty research:* Sports psychology, electronic selection systems, team training, stress effects, psychometrics. *Unit head:* Dr. Barbara Fritzsche, Director, 407-823-3919, E-mail: bfritzsc@mail.ucf.edu.

University of Connecticut, Graduate School, College of Liberal Arts and Sciences, Department of Psychology, Field of Psychology, Storrs, CT 06269. Offers behavioral neuroscience (PhD); biopsychology (PhD); clinical psychology (MA, PhD); cognition and instruction (PhD); developmental psychology (MA, PhD); ecological psychology (PhD); experimental psychology (PhD); general psychology (MA, PhD); health psychology (Graduate Certificate); industrial/organizational psychology (PhD); language and cognition (PhD); neuroscience (PhD); occupational health psychology (Graduate Certificate); social psychology (MA, PhD). *Accreditation:* APA (one or more programs are accredited). *Faculty:* 52 full-time (23 women). *Students:* 130 full-time (94 women), 25 part-time (11 women); includes 24 minority (8 African Americans, 6 Asian Americans or Pacific Islanders, 10 Hispanic Americans), 18 international. Average age 28. 531 applicants, 7% accepted, 35 enrolled. In 2007, 19 master's, 20 doctorates, 2 other advanced degrees awarded. Terminal master's awarded for partial completion of doctoral program. *Degree requirements:* For master's, comprehensive exam; for doctorate, thesis/dissertation. *Entrance requirements:* For master's and doctorate, GRE General Test, GRE Subject Test. Additional exam requirements/recommendations for international students: Required—TOEFL (minimum score 550 paper-based; 213 computer-based). *Application deadline:* For fall admission, 2/1 priority date for domestic and international students; for spring admission, 11/1 for domestic students, 10/1 for international students. Applications are processed on a rolling basis. Application fee: $55. Electronic applications accepted. *Expenses:* Tuition, state resident: part-time $469 per credit hour. Tuition, nonresident: part-time $1,218 per credit hour. *Financial support:* In 2007–08, 54 research assistantships with full tuition reimbursements, 69 teaching assistantships with full tuition reimbursements were awarded; fellowships, career-related internships or fieldwork, Federal Work-Study, scholarships/grants, health care benefits, and unspecified assistantships also available. Financial award application deadline: 2/1; financial award applicants required to submit FAFSA. *Application contact:* Deborah Doucette, Administrative Assistant, 860-486-2057, Fax: 860-486-2760, E-mail: futuregr@psych.psy.uconn.edu.

University of Detroit Mercy, College of Liberal Arts and Education, Department of Psychology, Program in Industrial/Organizational Psychology, Detroit, MI 48221. Offers MA. *Entrance requirements:* For master's, GRE General Test, minimum GPA of 3.0.

University of Guelph, Graduate Program Services, College of Social and Applied Human Sciences, Department of Psychology, Guelph, ON N1G 2W1, Canada. Offers applied social psychology (MA, PhD); clinical psychology applied development emphasis (PhD); clinical psychology applied developmental emphasis (MA); industrial/organizational psychology (MA, PhD); neuroscience and applied cognitive science (MA, PhD). *Faculty:* 34 full-time (14 women). *Students:* 95 full-time (72 women), 6 part-time (all women); includes 6 minority (2 African Americans, 4 Asian Americans or Pacific Islanders). 230 applicants, 28% accepted, 35 enrolled. In 2007, 8 master's, 2 doctorates awarded. *Median time to degree:* Of those who began their doctoral program in fall 1999, 100% received their degree in 8 years or less. *Degree requirements:* For master's, thesis; for doctorate, comprehensive exam, thesis/dissertation. *Entrance requirements:* For master's, GRE General Test, GRE Subject Test, minimum B+ average during previous 2 years of course work; for doctorate, GRE General Test, GRE Subject Test, minimum A- average. Additional exam requirements/recommendations for international students: Required—TOEFL (minimum score 89 iBT). *Application deadline:* For fall admission, 12/15 priority date for domestic students, 1/15 priority date for international students; for spring admission, 12/15 priority date for domestic students. Application fee: $85. Electronic applications accepted. *Financial support:* In 2007–08, 108 teaching assistantships with partial tuition reimbursements (averaging $10,213 per year) were awarded. *Faculty research:* Organizational psychology, reading comprehension and mathematical ability, drug addiction and relapse, gender issues and culture, memory, clinical psychology. *Unit head:* Dr. Harvey Marmurek, Chair, 519-824-4120 Ext. 53673, Fax: 519-837-8629, E-mail: marmurek@psy.uoguelph.ca. *Application contact:* Dr. Ian Newby-Clark, Graduate Coordinator, 519-824-4120 Ext. 53307, Fax: 519-837-8629, E-mail: newby-clark@psy.uoguelph.ca.

University of Houston, College of Liberal Arts and Social Sciences, Department of Psychology, Houston, TX 77204. Offers clinical psychology (PhD); industrial/organizational psychology (PhD); psychology (MA); social psychology (PhD). *Accreditation:* APA (one or more programs are accredited). *Faculty:* 24 full-time (9 women), 3 part-time/adjunct (1 woman). *Students:* 102 full-time (77 women), 16 part-time (12 women); includes 22 minority (4 African Americans, 8 Asian Americans or Pacific Islanders, 10 Hispanic Americans), 8 international. Average age 27. 187 applicants, 13% accepted, 22 enrolled. In 2007, 10 master's, 12 doctorates awarded. *Degree requirements:* For doctorate, thesis/dissertation. *Entrance requirements:* For doctorate, GRE General Test, minimum GPA of 3.0. *Application deadline:* For fall admission, 1/1 for domestic students. Application fee: $40 ($75 for international students). *Expenses:* Tuition, state resident: full-time $6,297; part-time $262 per credit. Tuition, nonresident: full-time $12,969; part-time $540 per credit. Required fees: $2,696. *Financial support:* In 2007–08, 12 fellowships with full tuition reimbursements (averaging $11,200 per year), 13 research assistantships with full tuition reimbursements (averaging $10,050 per year), 74 teaching assistantships with full tuition reimbursements (averaging $10,250 per year) were awarded; career-related internships or fieldwork, Federal Work-Study, institutionally sponsored loans, scholarships/grants, health care benefits, and unspecified assistantships also available. Support available to part-time students. Financial award application deadline: 2/1; financial award applicants required to submit FAFSA. *Faculty research:* Health psychology, depression, child/family process, organizational effectiveness, close relationships. *Unit head:* Dr. David Francis, Chairperson, 713-743-7036, Fax: 713-743-8588, E-mail: dfrancis@uh.edu. *Application contact:* Sherry A. Berun, Coordinator—Academic Affairs, 713-743-8508, Fax: 713-743-8588, E-mail: sherryr@uh.edu.

University of Maryland, Baltimore County, Graduate School, College of Arts, Humanities and Social Sciences, Department of Psychology, Baltimore, MD 21250. Offers applied developmental psychology (PhD); human services psychology (MA, PhD), including applied behavioral analysis (MA), human services psychology/clinical (PhD); industrial and organizational psychology (MPS); psychology (MPS). *Accreditation:* APA (one or more programs are accredited). *Faculty:* 28 full-time (12 women), 11 part-time/adjunct (2 women). *Students:* 100 full-time (85 women), 23 part-time (21 women); includes 29 minority (13 African Americans, 1 American Indian/Alaska Native, 7 Asian Americans or Pacific Islanders, 8 Hispanic Americans). Average age 30. 207 applicants, 27% accepted, 32 enrolled. In 2007, 23 master's, 13 doctorates awarded. Terminal master's awarded for partial completion of doctoral program. *Degree requirements:* For master's, thesis or alternative; for doctorate, comprehensive exam, thesis/dissertation. *Entrance requirements:* For master's, GRE General Test; for doctorate, GRE General Test, GRE Subject Test. Additional exam requirements/recommendations for international students: Required—TOEFL. *Application deadline:* For fall admission, 12/1 for domestic and international students. Application fee: $50. Electronic applications accepted. *Financial support:* In 2007–08, 2 fellowships (averaging $22,000 per year), 32 research assistantships with full and partial tuition reimbursements (averaging $14,566 per year), 28 teaching assistantships with full and partial tuition reimbursements (averaging $14,566 per year) were awarded; career-related internships or fieldwork, Federal Work-Study, health care benefits, and tuition waivers (full and partial) also available. Financial award application deadline: 3/1; financial award applicants required to submit FAFSA. *Faculty research:* Prevention and treatment of behavior problems, early intervention, cultural contexts, applications to education, behavioral medicine. Total annual research expenditures: $2.5 million. *Unit head:* Dr. Linda Baker, Chair, 410-455-2415, Fax: 410-455-1055, E-mail: baker@umbc.edu. *Application contact:* Cara Lane, Program Management Specialist, 410-455-2567, Fax: 410-455-1055, E-mail: psycdept@umbc.edu.

University of Maryland, College Park, Graduate Studies, College of Behavioral and Social Sciences, Department of Psychology, College Park, MD 20742. Offers clinical psychology (PhD); developmental psychology (PhD); experimental psychology (PhD); industrial psychology (MA, MS, PhD); social psychology (PhD). *Accreditation:* APA (one or more programs are accredited). *Faculty:* 53 full-time (23 women), 12 part-time/adjunct (6 women). *Students:* 92 full-time (70 women), 4 part-time (3 women); includes 15 minority (2 African Americans, 1 American Indian/Alaska Native, 6 Asian Americans or Pacific Islanders, 6 Hispanic Americans), 12 international. 609 applicants, 4% accepted, 13 enrolled. In 2007, 13 master's, 18 doctorates awarded. *Median time to degree:* Of those who began their doctoral program in fall 1999, 71% received their degree in 8 years or less. *Degree requirements:* For master's, thesis; for doctorate, variable foreign language requirement, comprehensive exam, thesis/dissertation. *Entrance requirements:* For master's and doctorate, GRE General Test, GRE Subject Test, minimum GPA of 3.5, research and/or work experience, 3 letters of recommendation. *Application deadline:* For fall admission, 12/15 for domestic students, 2/1 for international students. Applications are processed on a rolling basis. Application fee: $60. Electronic applications accepted. *Financial support:* In 2007–08, 11 fellowships with full tuition reimbursements (averaging $15,736 per year), 9 research assistantships (averaging $15,312 per year), 56 teaching assistantships with tuition reimbursements (averaging $15,292 per year) were awarded; career-related internships or fieldwork, Federal Work-Study, and scholarships/grants also available. Support available to part-time students. Financial award applicants required to submit FAFSA. *Faculty research:* Social stereotyping and prejudice, anxiety disorders, auditory neuroethology, counseling and social psychology. Total annual research expenditures: $4.4 million. *Unit head:* Thomas S. Wallsten, Chair, 301-405-5862, Fax: 301-314-9566, E-mail: twallsten@psyc.umd.edu. *Application contact:* Dean of Graduate School, 301-405-0358, Fax: 301-314-9305.

University of Minnesota, Twin Cities Campus, Graduate School, College of Liberal Arts, Department of Psychology, Program in Industrial/Organizational Psychology, Minneapolis, MN 55455-0213. Offers PhD. *Faculty:* 4 full-time (1 woman). *Students:* 22 full-time (12 women); includes 2 minority (1 African American, 1 Asian American or Pacific Islander), 2 international. 80 applicants, 9% accepted, 5 enrolled. In 2007, 4 degrees awarded. *Median time to degree:* Of those who began their doctoral program in fall 1999, 50% received their degree in 8 years or less. *Degree requirements:* For doctorate, comprehensive exam, thesis/dissertation. *Entrance requirements:* For doctorate, GRE General Test, GRE Subject Test (recommended), 12 credits of upper-level psychology courses, including a course in statistics or psychological measurement. Additional exam requirements/recommendations for international students: Required—TOEFL (minimum score 550 paper-based; 213 computer-based; 79 iBT). *Application deadline:* For fall admission, 12/1 for domestic and international students. Application fee: $55 ($75 for international students). *Financial support:* In 2007–08, fellowships with full tuition reimbursements (averaging $21,000 per year), research assistantships with full tuition reimbursements (averaging $12,254 per year), teaching assistantships with full tuition reimbursements (averaging $12,254 per year) were awarded; career-related internships or fieldwork and tuition waivers (partial) also available. Financial award application deadline: 12/1. *Unit head:* Paul Sackett, Area Director, 612-624-9842. *Application contact:* Coordinator, 612-624-4181, Fax: 612-626-2079, E-mail: psyapply@tc.umn.edu.

University of Missouri–St. Louis, College of Arts and Sciences, Department of Psychology, St. Louis, MO 63121. Offers behavioral neuroscience (PhD); clinical psychology respecialization (Certificate); community psychology (PhD); general psychology (MA); industrial/organizational psychology (PhD). *Accreditation:* APA (one or more programs are accredited). Evening/weekend programs available. *Faculty:* 20 full-time (9 women), 2 part-time/adjunct (both women). *Students:* 51 full-time (40 women), 22 part-time (16 women); includes 5 minority (1 African American, 3 Asian Americans or Pacific Islanders, 1 Hispanic American), 2 international. Average age 29. In 2007, 11 master's, 8 doctorates awarded. Terminal master's awarded for partial completion of doctoral program. *Degree requirements:* For doctorate, thesis/dissertation. *Entrance requirements:* For master's and doctorate, GRE General Test, GRE Subject Test, 3 letters of recommendation. Additional exam requirements/recommendations for international students: Required—TOEFL (minimum score 550 paper-based; 213 computer-based). *Application deadline:* For fall admission, 2/1 priority date for domestic students. Applications are processed on a rolling basis. Application fee: $35 ($40 for international students). Electronic applications accepted. *Financial support:* In 2007–08, 11 research assistantships with full and partial tuition reimbursements (averaging $11,333 per year), 18 teaching assistantships with full and partial tuition reimbursements (averaging $10,525 per year) were awarded; fellowships with full tuition reimbursements also available. *Faculty research:* Bereavement and loss, neuroscience, post-traumatic stress disorder, conflict and negotiation, social psychology. *Unit head:* Dr. Robert Calsyn, Chair, 314-516-5391, Fax: 314-516-5392, E-mail: umslpsychology@msx.umsl.edu. *Application contact:* 314-516-5458, Fax: 314-516-6996, E-mail: gradadm@umsl.edu.

University of Nebraska at Omaha, Graduate Studies and Research, College of Arts and Sciences, Department of Psychology, Omaha, NE 68182. Offers developmental psychology (PhD); industrial/organizational psychology (MS, PhD); psychobiology (PhD); psychology (MA); school psychology (MS, Ed S). Part-time programs available. *Faculty:* 17 full-time (8 women). *Students:* 33 full-time (24 women), 32 part-time (26 women); includes 4 minority (2 African Americans, 1 Asian American or Pacific Islander, 1 Hispanic American), 3 international. Average age 28. 89 applicants, 56% accepted, 25 enrolled. In 2007, 16 master's, 5 other advanced degrees awarded. *Degree requirements:* For master's, comprehensive exam, thesis (for some programs). *Entrance requirements:* For master's, GRE General Test, GRE Subject Test, previous course work in psychology, including statistics and a laboratory course; minimum GPA of 3.0, 3 letters of recommendation; for doctorate, GRE General Test. Additional exam requirements/recommendations for international students: Required—TOEFL (minimum score 500 paper-based; 173 computer-based; 61 iBT). *Application deadline:* For fall admission, 1/5 for domestic students. Application fee: $45. Electronic applications accepted. *Financial support:* In 2007–08, 55 students received support; fellowships, research assistantships with tuition reimbursements available, teaching assistantships with tuition reimbursements available, career-related internships or fieldwork, Federal Work-Study, institutionally sponsored loans, scholarships/grants, tuition waivers (partial), and unspecified assistantships available. Support available to part-time students. Financial award application deadline: 3/1; financial award applicants required to submit FAFSA. *Unit head:* Dr. Kenneth Deffenbacher, Chairperson, 402-554-2592. *Application contact:* Dr. Joseph Brown, Student Contact, 402-554-2592.

University of New Haven, Graduate School, College of Arts and Sciences, Program in Industrial and Organizational Psychology, West Haven, CT 06516-1916. Offers MA, Certificate. Part-time and evening/weekend programs available. *Students:* 69 full-time (52 women), 18 part-time (13 women); includes 8 minority (4 African Americans, 2 Asian Americans or Pacific Islanders, 2 Hispanic Americans), 10 international. In 2007, 45 degrees awarded. *Degree requirements:* For master's, thesis or alternative. *Application deadline:* Applications are processed on a rolling basis. Application fee: $50. *Expenses:* Tuition: Part-time $630 per credit. Required fees: $40 per term. *Financial support:* Career-related internships or fieldwork and Federal Work-Study available. Support available to part-time students. Financial award application deadline: 5/1; financial award applicants required to submit FAFSA. *Unit head:* Dr. Stuart Sidle, Coordinator, 203-932-7341. *Application contact:* Information Contact, 800-DIAL-UNH Ext. 7341, Fax: 203-931-6032.

See Close-Up on page 1507.

The University of North Carolina at Charlotte, Graduate School, College of Arts and Sciences, Department of Psychology, Program in Industrial/Organizational Psychology, Charlotte, NC 28223-0001. Offers MA. *Students:* 13 full-time (10 women), 9 part-time (8 women); includes 1 African American, 1 Hispanic American. Average age 24. 86 applicants, 10% accepted, 6 enrolled. In 2007, 9 degrees awarded. *Degree requirements:* For master's, comprehensive exam, thesis. *Entrance requirements:* For master's, GRE General Test, GRE Subject Test, minimum undergraduate GPA of 3.0 in major, 2.8 overall. Additional exam requirements/recommendations for international students: Required—TOEFL (minimum score 557 paper-based; 220 computer-based). *Application deadline:* For fall admission, 2/1 for domestic and international students. Application fee: $55. Electronic applications accepted. *Expenses:* Tuition, state resident: full-time $2,855. Tuition, nonresident: full-time $13,062. Required fees: $1,692. *Financial support:* In 2007–08, 1 fellowship (averaging $10,000 per year), 10 research assistantships (averaging $5,270 per year), 2 teaching assistantships (averaging $9,000 per year) were awarded; career-related internships or fieldwork, Federal Work-Study, institutionally sponsored loans, scholarships/grants, and unspecified assistantships also available. Support available to part-time students. Financial award application deadline: 4/1; financial award applicants required to submit FAFSA. *Unit head:* Dr. Steven G. Rogelberg, Coordinator, 704-687-4731, Fax: 704-687-3096, E-mail: sgrogelb@uncc.edu. *Application contact:* Kathy B. Giddings, Director of Graduate Admissions, 704-687-3366, Fax: 704-687-3279, E-mail: agidding@uncc.edu.

The University of North Carolina at Charlotte, Graduate School, College of Arts and Sciences, Department of Psychology, Program in Organizational Science, Charlotte, NC 28223-0001. Offers PhD. *Students:* 10 full-time (6 women), 1 international. Average age 24. 51 applicants, 35% accepted, 5 enrolled. *Expenses:* Tuition, state resident: full-time $2,855. Tuition, nonresident: full-time $13,062. Required fees: $1,692. *Financial support:* In 2007–08, 2 fellowships (averaging $20,000 per year), 5 research assistantships (averaging $15,000 per year) were awarded. *Unit head:* Dr. Steven G. Rogelberg, Coordinator, 704-687-4731, Fax: 704-687-3096, E-mail: sgrogelb@uncc.edu.

University of Puerto Rico, Río Piedras, College of Social Sciences, Department of Psychology, San Juan, PR 00931-3300. Offers clinical psychology (MA); industrial organizational psychology (MA); investigative academic psychology (MA); psychology (PhD). Part-time programs available. *Students:* 177 full-time (136 women), 55 part-time (42 women). Average age 30. In 2007, 18 master's, 21 doctorates awarded. *Degree requirements:* For master's, comprehensive exam, thesis; for doctorate, comprehensive exam, thesis/dissertation, internship. *Entrance requirements:* For master's, GRE or PAEG, interview, minimum GPA of 3.0; for doctorate, GRE or PAEG, interview, master's degree, minimum GPA of 3.0. *Application deadline:* For fall admission, 2/1 for domestic and international students. Application fee: $17. *Expenses:* Tuition, state resident: full-time $1,808; part-time $113 per credit. Tuition, nonresident: full-time $5,248; part-time $328 per credit. Required fees: $72 per term. *Financial support:* Fellowships, research assistantships, teaching assistantships, career-related internships or fieldwork, Federal Work-Study, institutionally sponsored loans, and tuition waivers (partial) available. Financial award application deadline: 5/31. *Faculty research:* Intervention on Depressed Latino Youth, biosychosocial training. *Unit head:* Dr. Dolores Miranda, Director, 787-764-0000 Ext. 2094. *Application contact:* Information Contact, 787-764-0000, Fax: 787-763-4599.

University of South Africa, College of Economic and Management Sciences, Pretoria, South Africa. Offers accounting (D Admin, D Com); accounting science (DA); auditing (D Admin, D Com); business administration (M Tech); business economics (D Admin); business leadership (DBL); business management (D Admin, D Com); economic management analysis (M Tech); economics (D Admin, D Com, PhD); human resource development (M Tech); industrial psychology (D Admin, D Com, PhD); logistics (D Com); marketing (M Tech); public administration (D Admin, D Com, DPA, PhD); public management (M Tech); quantitative management (D Admin, D Com); real estate (M Tech); statistics (D Admin, PhD); tourism management (D Admin, D Com); transport economics (D Admin, D Com).

University of South Africa, College of Human Sciences, Pretoria, South Africa. Offers adult education (M Ed); African languages (MA, PhD); African politics (MA, PhD); Afrikaans (MA, PhD); ancient history (MA, PhD); ancient Near Eastern studies (MA, PhD); anthropology (MA, PhD); applied linguistics (MA); Arabic (MA, PhD); archaeology (MA); art history (MA); Biblical archaeology (MA); Biblical studies (M Th, D Th, PhD); Christian spirituality (M Th, D Th); church history (M Th, D Th); classical studies (MA, PhD); clinical psychology (MA); communication (MA, PhD); comparative education (M Ed, Ed D); consulting psychology (D Admin, D Com, PhD); curriculum studies (M Ed, Ed D); development studies (M Admin, MA, D Admin, PhD); didactics (M Ed, Ed D); education (M Tech); education management (M Ed, Ed D); educational psychology (M Ed); English (MA); environmental education (M Ed); French (MA, PhD); German (MA, PhD); Greek (MA); guidance and counseling (M Ed); health studies (MA, PhD), including health sciences education (MA), health services management (MA), medical and surgical nursing science (critical care general) (MA), midwifery and neonatal nursing science (MA), trauma and emergency care (MA); history (MA, PhD); history of education (Ed D); inclusive education (M Ed, Ed D); information and communications technology policy and regulation (MA); information science (MA, MIS, PhD); international politics (MA, PhD); Islamic studies (MA, PhD); Italian (MA, PhD); Judaica (MA, PhD); linguistics (MA, PhD); mathematical education (M Ed); mathematics education (MA); missiology (M Th, D Th); modern Hebrew (MA, PhD); musicology (MA, MMus, D Mus, PhD); natural science education (M Ed); New Testament (M Th, D Th); Old Testament (D Th); pastoral therapy (M Th, D Th); philosophy (MA); philosophy of education (M Ed, Ed D); politics (MA, PhD); Portuguese (MA, PhD); practical theology (M Th, D Th); psychology (MA, MS, PhD); psychology of education (M Ed, Ed D); public health (MA); religious studies (MA, D Th, PhD); Romance languages (MA); Russian (MA, PhD); Semitic languages (MA, PhD); social behavior studies in HIV/AIDS (MA); social science (mental health) (MA); social science in development studies (MA); social science in psychology (MA); social science in social work (MA); social science in sociology (MA); social work (MSW, DSW, PhD); socio-education (M Ed, Ed D); sociolinguistics (MA); sociology (MA, PhD); Spanish (MA, PhD); systematic theology (M Th, D Th); TESOL (teaching English to speakers of other languages) (MA); theological ethics (M Th, D Th); theory of literature (MA, PhD); urban ministries (D Th); urban ministry (M Th).

University of South Florida, Graduate School, College of Arts and Sciences, Department of Psychology, Tampa, FL 33620-9951. Offers clinical psychology (MA, PhD); cognitive and neural sciences (MA, PhD); industrial-organizational psychology (MA, PhD). *Accreditation:* APA (one or more programs are accredited). *Faculty:* 32 full-time (8 women), 1 (woman) part-time/adjunct. *Students:* 106 full-time (65 women), 21 part-time (16 women); includes 17 minority (4 African Americans, 4 Asian Americans or Pacific Islanders, 9 Hispanic Americans), 17 international. 398 applicants, 6% accepted, 22 enrolled. In 2007, 16 master's, 21 doctorates awarded. *Degree requirements:* For master's, thesis; for doctorate, comprehensive exam, thesis/dissertation. *Entrance requirements:* For master's and doctorate, GRE General Test, minimum GPA of 3.0 in last 60 hours of course work. Application fee: $30. Electronic applications accepted. *Expenses: Contact institution. Financial support:* In 2007–08, 13 fellowships with full and partial tuition reimbursements (averaging $17,500 per year), 50 research assistantships with partial tuition reimbursements (averaging $13,000 per year), 50 teaching assistantships with partial tuition reimbursements (averaging $13,000 per year) were awarded; career-related internships or fieldwork, scholarships/grants, tuition waivers (partial), and unspecified assistantships also available. Financial award applicants required to submit FAFSA. *Faculty research:* Human memory; job analysis; stress, drug and alcohol abuse; neuroscience. *Unit head:* Michael T. Brannick, Director of Graduate Program, 813-974-0478, Fax: 813-974-4617, E-mail: mbrannick@cas.usf.edu. *Application contact:* Laura Pierce, Program Assistant, 813-974-0497, Fax: 813-974-4617, E-mail: lpierce@cas.usf.edu.

The University of Tennessee, Graduate School, College of Business Administration, Program in Industrial and Organizational Psychology, Knoxville, TN 37996. Offers PhD. *Degree requirements:* For doctorate, thesis/dissertation. *Entrance requirements:* For doctorate, GRE General Test, minimum GPA of 2.7. Additional exam requirements/recommendations for international students: Required—TOEFL. Electronic applications accepted.

The University of Tennessee at Chattanooga, Graduate School, College of Arts and Sciences, Department of Psychology, Program in Industrial/Organizational Psychology, Chattanooga, TN 37403-2598. Offers MS. Part-time and evening/weekend programs available. *Faculty:* 4 full-time (0 women), 1 (woman) part-time/adjunct. *Students:* 31 full-time (20 women), 3 part-time (all women); includes 5 minority (2 African Americans, 3 Asian Americans or Pacific Islanders), 1 international. Average age 24. 70 applicants, 87% accepted, 20 enrolled. In 2007, 21 degrees awarded. *Degree requirements:* For master's, comprehensive exam, practicum. *Entrance requirements:* For master's, GRE General Test. Additional exam requirements/recommendations for international students: Required—TOEFL (minimum score 550 paper-based; 213 computer-based; 79 iBT); Recommended—IELTS (minimum score 6). *Application deadline:* For fall admission, 8/1 priority date for domestic students, 6/1 for international students; for spring admission, 12/1 priority date for domestic students, 10/1 for international students. Applications are processed on a rolling basis. Application fee: $30 ($35 for international students). *Expenses:* Tuition, state resident: full-time $5,854; part-time $393 per hour. Tuition, nonresident: full-time $15,816; part-time $946 per hour. Required fees: $1,090; $256 per hour. *Financial support:* In 2007–08, 8 fellowships with full and partial tuition reimbursements (averaging $3,094 per year) were awarded; career-related internships or fieldwork, Federal Work-Study, institutionally sponsored loans, scholarships/grants, tuition waivers (partial), and unspecified assistantships also available. Support available to part-time students. Financial award application deadline: 4/1; financial award applicants required to submit FAFSA. *Faculty research:* Employee selection; group dynamics; compensation and benefits; statistical models; organizational methods. *Unit head:* Dr. Michael D. Biderman, Coordinator, 423-425-4268, Fax: 423-425-4284, E-mail: michael-biderman@utc.edu. *Application contact:* Dr. Deborah E. Arfken, Dean of Graduate Studies, 423-425-4666, Fax: 423-425-5223, E-mail: deborah-arfken@utc.edu.

University of Tulsa, Graduate School, College of Arts and Sciences, Department of Psychology, Program in Industrial/Organizational Psychology, Tulsa, OK 74104-3189. Offers MA, PhD, JD/MA. Part-time programs available. *Faculty:* 3 full-time (2 women). *Students:* 13 full-time (8 women), 7 part-time (3 women); includes 2 minority (both African Americans), 2 international. Average age 28. 47 applicants, 49% accepted, 7 enrolled. In 2007, 6 master's, 1 doctorate awarded. Terminal master's awarded for partial completion of doctoral program. *Degree requirements:* For master's, comprehensive exam, thesis (for some programs), 200 hour internship; for doctorate, comprehensive exam, thesis/dissertation. *Entrance requirements:* For master's and doctorate, GRE General Test. Additional exam requirements/recommendations for international students: Required—TOEFL (minimum score 575 paper-based; 231 computer-based; 91 iBT), IELTS (minimum score 7). *Application deadline:* For fall admission, 1/15 for domestic and international students. Application fee: $40. Electronic applications accepted. *Expenses:* Tuition: Full-time $14,004; part-time $778 per credit hour. Required fees: $60; $30 per term. Tuition and fees vary according to course load. *Financial support:* In 2007–08, 11 students received support, including 2 research assistantships with full and partial tuition reimbursements available (averaging $8,050 per year), 10 teaching assistantships with full and partial tuition reimbursements available (averaging $10,734 per year); fellowships with full and partial tuition reimbursements available, career-related internships or fieldwork, Federal Work-Study, scholarships/grants, tuition waivers (full and partial), and unspecified assistantships also available. Support available to part-time students. Financial award application deadline: 2/1; financial award applicants required to submit FAFSA. *Faculty research:* Evaluation and e-learning, personnel assessment and selection, training, industrial gerontology, personality factors in organizational performance. Total annual research expenditures: $24,237. *Unit head:* Dr. John McNulty, Director, 918-631-2835, Fax: 918-631-2833, E-mail: john-mcnulty@utulsa.edu. *Application contact:* Information Contact, E-mail: grad@utulsa.edu.

University of West Florida, College of Arts and Sciences: Arts, Department of Psychology, Pensacola, FL 32514-5750. Offers counseling (MA); counseling-licensed mental health counselor (MA); general (MA); industrial-organizational (MA). Part-time programs available. *Faculty:* 14 full-time (5 women), 1 (woman) part-time/adjunct. *Students:* 52 full-time (41 women), 29 part-time (23 women); includes 18 minority (10 African Americans, 2 American Indian/Alaska Native, 2 Asian Americans or Pacific Islanders, 4 Hispanic Americans), 3 international. Average age 29. 120 applicants, 53% accepted, 26 enrolled. In 2007, 18 degrees awarded. *Degree requirements:* For master's, thesis (for some programs). *Entrance requirements:* For master's, GRE General Test, GRE Subject Test, minimum GPA of 3.0. Additional exam requirements/recommendations for international students: Required—TOEFL (minimum score 550 paper-based; 213 computer-based). *Application deadline:* For fall admission, 6/1 for domestic students, 5/15 for international students; for spring admission, 11/1 for domestic students, 10/1 for international students. Applications are processed on a rolling basis. Application fee: $30. *Expenses:* Tuition, state resident: full-time $6,054; part-time $252 per credit. Tuition, nonresident:

Industrial and Organizational Psychology

University of West Florida (continued)
full-time $21,886; part-time $912 per credit. *Financial support:* In 2007–08, 3 research assistantships with partial tuition reimbursements (averaging $17,440 per year), 2 teaching assistantships with partial tuition reimbursements (averaging $4,948 per year) were awarded; fellowships with partial tuition reimbursements, career-related internships or fieldwork and Federal Work-Study also available. Financial award application deadline: 4/15; financial award applicants required to submit FAFSA. *Faculty research:* Prose recall, brain imaging, peak performance, biofeedback and pain control, comparable worth. Total annual research expenditures: $15,000. *Unit head:* Dr. Laura Koppes, Chairperson, 850-474-3493.

University of Wisconsin–Oshkosh, The Office of Graduate Studies, College of Letters and Science, Department of Psychology, Oshkosh, WI 54901. Offers experimental psychology (MS); industrial/organizational psychology (MS). *Faculty:* 10 full-time (3 women). *Students:* 27. Average age 26. 22 applicants, 100% accepted. In 2007, 9 degrees awarded. *Degree requirements:* For master's, thesis. *Entrance requirements:* For master's, GRE, 10 semester hours of undergraduate course work in psychology. Additional exam requirements/recommendations for international students: Required—TOEFL (minimum score 550 paper-based; 213 computer-based; 79 iBT). *Application deadline:* For fall admission, 4/1 priority date for domestic students. Applications are processed on a rolling basis. Application fee: $45. Electronic applications accepted. *Financial support:* Fellowships, research assistantships with partial tuition reimbursements, career-related internships or fieldwork, institutionally sponsored loans, scholarships/grants, tuition waivers (partial), and unspecified assistantships available. Financial award application deadline: 3/15; financial award applicants required to submit FAFSA. *Faculty research:* Performance evaluation, training, biological bases of behavior, tactile perception, aging. *Unit head:* Dr. Jim Koch, Chair, 920-424-2303, E-mail: kochj@uwosh.edu. *Application contact:* Dr. Gary Adams, Graduate Program Coordinator, 920-424-2300, E-mail: psychology@uwosh.edu.

Valdosta State University, Graduate School, College of Education, Department of Psychology and Counseling, Valdosta, GA 31698. Offers clinical/counseling psychology (MS); industrial/organizational psychology (MS); school counseling (M Ed, Ed S); school psychology (Ed S). Part-time and evening/weekend programs available. *Faculty:* 16 full-time (2 women). *Students:* 61 full-time (48 women), 38 part-time (31 women); includes 22 minority (19 African Americans, 1 American Indian/Alaska Native, 1 Asian American or Pacific Islander, 1 Hispanic American). Average age 27. 103 applicants, 31% accepted, 22 enrolled. In 2007, 25 degrees awarded. *Degree requirements:* For master's, thesis or alternative, comprehensive written and/or oral exams; for Ed S, thesis. *Entrance requirements:* For master's and Ed S, GRE General Test or MAT. Additional exam requirements/recommendations for international students: Required—TOEFL (minimum score 523 paper-based; 193 computer-based). *Application deadline:* For fall admission, 7/1 for domestic and international students; for spring admission, 11/15 for domestic and international students. Applications are processed on a rolling basis. Application fee: $40. Electronic applications accepted. *Expenses:* Tuition, state resident: part-time $147 per hour. Tuition, nonresident: part-time $586 per hour. Required fees: $520 per semester. Tuition and fees vary according to course level, course load, campus/location and program. *Financial support:* In 2007–08, 2 students received support, including 2 research assistantships with full tuition reimbursements available (averaging $2,452 per year); institutionally sponsored loans and unspecified assistantships also available. Support available to part-time students. Financial award application deadline: 7/1; financial award applicants required to submit FAFSA. *Faculty research:* Using Bender-Gestalt to predict graphomotor dimensions of the draw-a-person test, neurobehavioral hemispheric dominance. *Unit head:* Dr. Robert Bauer, Chair, 229-333-5930, Fax: 229-259-5576, E-mail: bbauer@valdosta.edu.

Virginia Polytechnic Institute and State University, Graduate School, College of Science, Department of Psychology, Blacksburg, VA 24061. Offers bio-behavioral sciences (PhD); clinical psychology (PhD); developmental psychology (PhD); industrial/organizational psychology (PhD); psychology (MS). *Accreditation:* APA (one or more programs are accredited). *Entrance requirements:* For master's and doctorate, GRE General Test. Additional exam requirements/recommendations for international students: Required—TOEFL (minimum score 550 paper-based; 213 computer-based). Electronic applications accepted. *Faculty research:* Infant development from electrophysical point of view, work motivation and personnel selection, EEG, ERP and hypnosis with reference to chronic pain, intimate violence.

Walden University, Graduate Programs, School of Psychology, Minneapolis, MN 55401. Offers clinical assessment (Post-Doctoral Certificate); clinical child psychology (Post-Doctoral Certificate); clinical psychology (PhD, Post-Doctoral Certificate); counseling psychology (PhD, Post-Doctoral Certificate); general psychology (MS, PhD, Post-Doctoral Certificate); health psychology (PhD, Post-Doctoral Certificate); organizational psychology (PhD, Post-Doctoral Certificate); organizational psychology and development (MS); school psychology (PhD, Post-Doctoral Certificate); teaching online (Post-Doctoral Certificate). Part-time and evening/weekend programs available. Postbaccalaureate distance learning degree programs offered (minimal on-campus study). *Students:* 1,428 full-time (1,130 women), 1,933 part-time (1,483 women); includes 959 minority (737 African Americans, 35 American Indian/Alaska Native, 53 Asian Americans or Pacific Islanders, 134 Hispanic Americans), 39 international. Average age 40. 1,254 applicants, 75% accepted, 548 enrolled. In 2007, 182 master's, 43 doctorates awarded. *Degree requirements:* For master's, thesis; for doctorate, thesis/dissertation, brief dispersed residency sessions. *Entrance requirements:* For master's, minimum GPA of 3.0; for doctorate, 3 years of professional experience, master's degree; for Post-Doctoral Certificate, PhD in related field, 3 years of professional experience. Additional exam requirements/recommendations for international students: Required—TOEFL (minimum score 550 paper-based; 213 computer-based), IELTS (minimum score 7). *Application deadline:* For fall admission, 8/15 priority date for domestic and international students; for winter admission, 11/15 priority date for domestic and international students; for spring admission, 12/15 priority date for domestic and international students. Applications are processed on a rolling basis. Application fee: $50. Electronic applications accepted. *Financial support:* Fellowships with partial tuition reimbursements, career-related internships or fieldwork, Federal Work-Study, institutionally sponsored loans, scholarships/grants, tuition waivers (partial), and unspecified assistantships available. Support available to part-time students. Financial award applicants required to submit FAFSA. *Faculty research:* Clinical psychology, organizational psychology, forensic psychology, group processes, educational psychology. *Unit head:* Dr. Nina Nabors, Associate Dean, 800-925-3368. *Application contact:* 866-4-WALDEN, Fax: 410-843-8780, E-mail: request@waldenu.edu.

Wayne State University, College of Liberal Arts and Sciences, Department of Psychology, Program in Psychology, Detroit, MI 48202. Offers behavioral and cognitive neuroscience (PhD); clinical psychology (PhD); cognitive and social psychology (PhD); industrial/organizational psychology (PhD); psychology (MA, MS). *Accreditation:* APA (one or more programs are accredited). *Students:* 99 full-time (74 women), 20 part-time (16 women); includes 14 minority (7 African Americans, 4 Asian Americans or Pacific Islanders, 3 Hispanic Americans), 13 international. Average age 27. 219 applicants, 17% accepted, 23 enrolled. In 2007, 13 master's, 12 doctorates awarded. *Degree requirements:* For doctorate, thesis/dissertation. *Entrance requirements:* For doctorate, GRE General Test, GRE Subject Test. Additional exam requirements/recommendations for international students: Required—TOEFL (minimum score 550 paper-based; 213 computer-based); Recommended—TWE (minimum score 6). *Application deadline:* For fall admission, 2/1 for domestic students, 6/1 for international students; for winter admission, 10/1 for international students; for spring admission, 2/1 for international students. Applications are processed on a rolling basis. Application fee: $30 ($50 for international students). Electronic applications accepted. *Expenses:* Tuition, state resident: part-time $403 per credit hour. Tuition, nonresident: part-time $890 per credit hour. *Financial support:* Application deadline: 2/1. *Application contact:* Dr. Melissa Kaplan-Estrin, Graduate Director, 313-577-2824, Fax: 313-577-7636, E-mail: mkestrin@sun.science.wayne.edu.

West Chester University of Pennsylvania, Office of Graduate Studies and Extended Education, College of Arts and Sciences, Department of Psychology, West Chester, PA 19383. Offers clinical mental health (Certificate); clinical psychology (MA); general psychology (MA); industrial organizational psychology (MA). Part-time and evening/weekend programs available. *Students:* 61 full-time (44 women), 29 part-time (18 women); includes 6 minority (4 African Americans, 1 Asian American or Pacific Islander, 1 Hispanic American), 2 international. Average age 27. 177 applicants, 68% accepted, 37 enrolled. In 2007, 22 degrees awarded. *Degree requirements:* For master's, comprehensive exam, thesis (for some programs). *Entrance requirements:* For master's, GRE General Test or MAT, interview. Additional exam requirements/recommendations for international students: Required—TOEFL (minimum score 550 paper-based; 213 computer-based; 80 iBT). *Application deadline:* For fall admission, 4/15 priority date for domestic students; for spring admission, 10/15 for domestic students. Applications are processed on a rolling basis. Application fee: $35. *Expenses:* Tuition, state resident: part-time $345 per credit. Tuition, nonresident: part-time $552 per credit. Tuition and fees vary according to course load. *Financial support:* In 2007–08, 13 research assistantships with full and partial tuition reimbursements (averaging $5,000 per year) were awarded; unspecified assistantships also available. Support available to part-time students. Financial award application deadline: 2/15; financial award applicants required to submit FAFSA. *Faculty research:* Animal learning and cognition. *Unit head:* Dr. Sandra Kerr, Chair, 610-436-2945, E-mail: skerr@wcupa.edu. *Application contact:* Dr. Loretta Rieser-Danner, Graduate Coordinator, 610-436-3106, E-mail: lriserdanner@wcupa.edu.

Western Michigan University, Graduate College, College of Arts and Sciences, Department of Psychology, Kalamazoo, MI 49008-5202. Offers applied behavior analysis (MA, PhD); clinical psychology (MA, PhD); experimental analysis of behavior (PhD); industrial/organizational psychology (MA); school psychology (PhD, Ed S). *Accreditation:* APA (one or more programs are accredited). *Degree requirements:* For master's, variable foreign language requirement, thesis, oral exams; for doctorate, 2 foreign languages, comprehensive exam, thesis/dissertation, oral exams; for Ed S, thesis, oral exams. *Entrance requirements:* For master's, doctorate, and Ed S, GRE General Test.

Wright State University, School of Graduate Studies, College of Science and Mathematics, Department of Psychology, Program in Human Factors and Industrial/Organizational Psychology, Dayton, OH 45435. Offers MS, PhD. *Degree requirements:* For master's, thesis; for doctorate, thesis/dissertation.

Xavier University, College of Social Sciences, Health and Education, Department of Psychology, Cincinnati, OH 45207. Offers clinical psychology (Psy D); psychology (MA), including general experimental, industrial-organizational. *Accreditation:* APA (one or more programs are accredited). *Faculty:* 16 full-time (8 women), 10 part-time/adjunct (5 women). *Students:* 83 full-time (62 women), 27 part-time (20 women); includes 9 minority (4 African Americans, 4 Asian Americans or Pacific Islanders, 1 Hispanic American), 2 international. Average age 29. 275 applicants, 28% accepted, 27 enrolled. In 2007, 27 master's, 12 doctorates awarded. Terminal master's awarded for partial completion of doctoral program. *Median time to degree:* Of those who began their doctoral program in fall 1999, 100% received their degree in 8 years or less. *Degree requirements:* For master's, one foreign language, comprehensive exam, thesis, internship; for doctorate, one foreign language, comprehensive exam, thesis/dissertation, internship, practicum. *Entrance requirements:* For master's, GRE, minimum GPA of 3.0, 18 hours of course work in psychology; for doctorate, GRE, 18 hours of course work in psychology or a master's degree in clinical psychology, minimum GPA of 3.0. Additional exam requirements/recommendations for international students: Required—TOEFL (minimum score 550 paper-based; 213 computer-based). *Application deadline:* For fall admission, 1/15 priority date for domestic students. Application fee: $35. Electronic applications accepted. *Expenses:* Contact institution. *Financial support:* In 2007–08, 50 students received support, including 16 research assistantships with partial tuition reimbursements available, 4 teaching assistantships with partial tuition reimbursements available; career-related internships or fieldwork, traineeships, health care benefits, and unspecified assistantships also available. Financial award application deadline: 3/1; financial award applicants required to submit FAFSA. *Faculty research:* Cognitive development in children, weight management, psychodiagnostics, psychotherapy, gerontology I-O psychology. *Unit head:* Dr. Christine M. Dacey, Chair, 513-745-3533, Fax: 513-745-3327, E-mail: dacey@xavier.edu. *Application contact:* Margaret Maybury, Assistant Director-Enrollment and Student Services, 513-745-1053, Fax: 513-745-3327, E-mail: maybury@xavier.edu.

Marriage and Family Therapy

Abilene Christian University, Graduate School, College of Biblical Studies, Program in Marriage and Family Therapy, Abilene, TX 79699-9100. Offers MMFT. *Accreditation:* AAMFT/COAMFTE. *Faculty:* 3 full-time (2 women), 5 part-time/adjunct (2 women). *Students:* 33 full-time (20 women), 1 (woman) part-time; includes 3 minority (2 African Americans, 1 Asian American or Pacific Islander), 1 international. 40 applicants, 50% accepted, 15 enrolled. In 2007, 19 degrees awarded. *Degree requirements:* For master's, comprehensive exam. *Entrance requirements:* For master's, GRE General Test, interview. *Application deadline:* For fall admission, 4/1 priority date for domestic students; for spring admission, 11/1 for domestic students. Applications are processed on a rolling basis. Application fee: $40 ($45 for international students). Electronic applications accepted. *Expenses:* Tuition: Full-time $13,368; part-time $557 per hour. Required fees: $700; $34 per hour. $10 per semester. Tuition and fees vary according to degree level and campus/location. *Financial support:* Teaching assistantships, career-related internships or fieldwork available. Support available to part-time students. Financial award application deadline: 4/1. *Faculty research:* Overeating variables, family systems, intervention strategies. *Unit head:* Dr. Jackie Halstead, Chairperson, 325-674-3778, Fax: 325-674-3749, E-mail: halsteadj@acu.edu. *Application contact:* William Horn, Graduate Admissions Counselor, 325-674-2656, Fax: 325-674-6717, E-mail: gradinfo@acu.edu.

Adler Graduate School, Program in Adlerian Studies, Richfield, MN 55423. Offers art therapy specialization (MA); clinical counseling track (MA); coaching and consulting in organizations (Certificate); management consulting and organizational leadership (MA); marriage and family track (MA); non-clinical Adlerian studies track (MA); personal and professional life coaching (Certificate); school counseling (MA). Part-time and evening/weekend programs available. *Faculty:* 4 full-time (1 woman), 44 part-time/adjunct (27 women). *Students:* Average age 37. 46 applicants, 96% accepted, 44 enrolled. In 2007, 37 degrees awarded. *Degree requirements:* For master's, thesis or alternative, 500-700 hour internship, depending on license choice. *Entrance requirements:* For master's, minimum undergraduate GPA of 3.0, 12 credits of course work in psychology or related field. *Application deadline:* For fall admission, 10/1 priority date for domestic students; for winter admission, 1/1 priority date for domestic students; for spring admission, 4/1 priority date for domestic students. Applications are processed on a rolling basis. Application fee: $50. *Expenses:* Tuition: Part-time $430 per credit. Required fees: $85 per term. *Financial support:* In 2007–08, 121 students received support. Career-related internships or fieldwork and tuition waivers available. Support available to part-time students. Financial award applicants required to submit FAFSA. *Unit head:* Dr. Dennis Rislove, President, 612-861-7554 Ext. 106, Fax: 612-861-7559, E-mail: rislove@alfredadler.edu. *Application contact:* Evelyn B. Haas, Director of Student Services and Admissions, 612-861-7554 Ext. 103, Fax: 612-861-7559, E-mail: ev@alfredadler.edu.

Adler School of Professional Psychology, Programs in Psychology, Chicago, IL 60601-7203. Offers art therapy (Certificate); clinical hypnosis (Certificate); clinical psychology (Psy D); counseling psychology (MACP); counseling psychology/art therapy (MACAT); gerontology (MAGP); marriage and family counseling (MAMFC); marriage and family therapy (Certificate); organizational psychology (MAO); substance abuse counseling (MASAC, Certificate); Psy D/Certificate; Psy D/MACAT; Psy D/MACP; Psy D/MAMFC; Psy D/MASAC. *Accreditation:* APA. Part-time and evening/weekend programs available. Terminal master's awarded for partial completion of doctoral program. *Degree requirements:* For master's, thesis or alternative, oral exam, practicum; for doctorate, thesis/dissertation, clinical exam, internship, oral exam, practicum, written qualifying exam. *Entrance requirements:* For master's, 12 semester hours in psychology, minimum GPA of 3.0; for doctorate, 18 semester hours in psychology, minimum GPA of 3.25; for Certificate, appropriate master's or doctoral degree.

See Close-Up on page 1363.

Alliant International University–Irvine, California School of Professional Psychology, Program in Marital and Family Therapy, Irvine, CA 92612. Offers MA, Psy D. *Accreditation:* AAMFT/COAMFTE. Part-time programs available. *Degree requirements:* For doctorate, thesis/dissertation. *Entrance requirements:* For master's, minimum GPA of 3.0, letters of recommendation, interview; for doctorate, letters of recommendation, minimum GPA of 3.0, interview. Additional exam requirements/recommendations for international students: Required—TOEFL (minimum score 600 paper-based; 250 computer-based), TWE (minimum score 5). Electronic applications accepted. *Faculty research:* Chemical dependency, observational research.

See Close-Up on page 1373.

Alliant International University–Los Angeles, California School of Professional Psychology, Program in Marital and Family Therapy, Alhambra, CA 91803-1360. Offers biofeedback (MA); chemical dependency (MA); gerontology (MA); Latin American family therapy (MA). *Accreditation:* AAMFT/COAMFTE.

See Close-Up on page 1373.

Alliant International University–Sacramento, California School of Professional Psychology, Program in Marital and Family Therapy, Sacramento, CA 95825. Offers MA. *Accreditation:* AAMFT/COAMFTE. *Entrance requirements:* For master's, minimum GPA of 3.0, letters of recommendation, interview. Additional exam requirements/recommendations for international students: Required—TOEFL (minimum score 600 paper-based; 250 computer-based), TWE (minimum score 5). Electronic applications accepted. *Faculty research:* Couples therapy, marital myths, cross-cultural issues.

See Close-Up on page 1373.

Alliant International University–San Diego, California School of Professional Psychology, Program in Marital and Family Therapy, San Diego, CA 92131-1799. Offers MA, Psy D. *Accreditation:* AAMFT/COAMFTE. Part-time programs available. *Degree requirements:* For doctorate, thesis/dissertation. *Entrance requirements:* For master's and doctorate, minimum GPA of 3.0, letters of recommendation, interview. Additional exam requirements/recommendations for international students: Required—TOEFL (minimum score 600 paper-based; 250 computer-based), TWE (minimum score 5). Electronic applications accepted. *Faculty research:* Chemical dependency, women's issues, emotionally focused therapy, couple relationships, work/family/parenting.

See Close-Up on page 1373.

Amridge University, Graduate and Professional Programs, Montgomery, AL 36117. Offers behavioral leadership and management (MA); biblical studies (MA, D Min, PhD); Christian ministry (M Div); family therapy (D Min, PhD), including marriage and family therapy (PhD), professional counseling (PhD); leadership and management (MS); marriage and family therapy (M Div, MA); ministerial leadership (M Div, MS); pastoral counseling (M Div, MS); practical theology (MA); professional counseling (M Div, MA). *Accreditation:* ATS. Part-time and evening/weekend programs available. Postbaccalaureate distance learning degree programs offered (no on-campus study). *Faculty:* 50 full-time (12 women), 36 part-time/adjunct (10 women). *Students:* 165 full-time (85 women), 212 part-time (111 women); includes 174 minority (164 African Americans, 1 American Indian/Alaska Native, 1 Asian American or Pacific Islander, 8 Hispanic Americans). Average age 35. In 2007, 8 first professional degrees, 35 master's, 5 doctorates awarded. *Degree requirements:* For master's, one foreign language, comprehensive exam (for some programs), thesis (for some programs); for doctorate, comprehensive exam (for some programs), thesis/dissertation; for M Div, comprehensive exam (for some programs). *Entrance requirements:* For M Div, master's, and doctorate, GRE General Test or MAT. Additional exam requirements/recommendations for international students: Required—TOEFL. *Application deadline:* For fall admission, 9/1 priority date for domestic students; for spring admission, 1/1 priority date for domestic students. Applications are processed on a rolling basis. Application fee: $50. Electronic applications accepted. *Expenses:* Tuition: Full-time $9,180; part-time $510 per semester hour. Required fees: $400 per term. Tuition and fees vary according to course load and degree level. *Financial support:* Federal Work-Study and scholarships/grants available. Support available to part-time students. Financial award applicants required to submit FAFSA. *Faculty research:* Homiletics, hermeneutics, ancient Near Eastern history. *Unit head:* Rick Johnson, Director of Enrollment Management, 800-351-4040 Ext. 7513, Fax: 334-387-3878, E-mail: rickjohnson@amridgeuniversity.edu. *Application contact:* Ora Davis, Admissions Officer, 334-387-3877 Ext. 7524, Fax: 334-387-3878, E-mail: oradavis@amridgeuniversity.edu.

Antioch University New England, Graduate School, Department of Applied Psychology, Program in Marriage and Family Therapy, Keene, NH 03431-3552. Offers MA, PhD. *Accreditation:* AAMFT/COAMFTE. *Faculty:* 9 full-time (7 women), 14 part-time/adjunct (9 women). *Students:* 20 full-time (17 women), 1 (woman) part-time; includes 1 minority (African American), 1 international. Average age 34. 25 applicants, 92% accepted, 14 enrolled. In 2007, 18 degrees awarded. *Degree requirements:* For master's, internship, practicum. *Entrance requirements:* For master's, previous course work and work experience in psychology; resumé; essay; official transcripts; 3 letters of recommendation. Additional exam requirements/recommendations for international students: Required—TOEFL (minimum score 600 paper-based; 250 computer-based). *Application deadline:* For fall admission, 5/1 for domestic and international students. Applications are processed on a rolling basis. Application fee: $50. Electronic applications accepted. *Expenses: Contact institution.* Tuition and fees vary according to degree level, program and student level. *Financial support:* In 2007–08, 3 fellowships (averaging $1,667 per year) were awarded; career-related internships or fieldwork, Federal Work-Study, and scholarships/grants also available. Financial award applicants required to submit FAFSA. *Faculty research:* Use of reflective team model in case teaching and in organizational consulting, executive mentoring and coaching. *Unit head:* Dr. Kevin Lyness, Director, 603-283-2149, Fax: 603-357-0718, E-mail: kevin_lyness@antiochne.edu. *Application contact:* Leatrice A. Oram, Co-Director of Admissions, 800-490-3310, Fax: 603-357-0718, E-mail: admissions@antiochne.edu.

See Close-Up on page 1375.

Appalachian State University, Cratis D. Williams Graduate School, Department of Human Development and Psychological Counseling, Boone, NC 28608. Offers community counseling (MA); marriage and family therapy (MA); school counseling (MA); student development (MA). *Accreditation:* AAMFT/COAMFTE; ACA; NCATE. Part-time programs available. *Faculty:* 28 full-time (15 women). *Students:* 77 full-time (58 women), 91 part-time (71 women); includes 16 minority (15 African Americans, 1 Asian American or Pacific Islander), 1 international. 152 applicants, 63% accepted, 57 enrolled. In 2007, 52 master's awarded. *Degree requirements:* For master's, comprehensive exam (for some programs), thesis optional, internships. *Entrance requirements:* Additional exam requirements/recommendations for international students: Required—TOEFL (minimum score 570 paper-based; 230 computer-based). *Application deadline:* For fall admission, 2/1 priority date for domestic students, 1/1 for international students; for spring admission, 6/1 for international students. Applications are processed on a rolling basis. Application fee: $50. *Expenses:* Tuition, state resident: part-time $127 per semester hour. Tuition, nonresident: part-time $597 per semester hour. Required fees: $18 per semester. *Financial support:* In 2007–08, 20 research assistantships (averaging $6,000 per year), 7 teaching assistantships (averaging $7,000 per year) were awarded; fellowships, career-related internships or fieldwork, Federal Work-Study, scholarships/grants, and unspecified assistantships also available. Financial award application deadline: 4/1. *Faculty research:* Multicultural counseling, addictions counseling, play therapy, expressive arts, child and adolescent therapy, sexual abuse counseling. *Unit head:* Dr. Lee Baruth, Chairman, 828-262-2055, E-mail: baruthlg@appstate.edu.

Argosy University, Atlanta, College of Psychology and Behavioral Sciences, Atlanta, GA 30328. Offers clinical psychology (MA, Psy D, Postdoctoral Respecialization Certificate), including child and family psychology (Psy D), general adult clinical (Psy D), health psychology (Psy D), neuropsychology/geropsychology (Psy D); community counseling (MA), including marriage and family therapy; counselor education and supervision (Ed D); marriage and family therapy (Certificate). *Accreditation:* APA.

See Close-Up on page 1377.

Argosy University, Chicago, College of Psychology and Behavioral Sciences, Doctoral Program in Clinical Psychology, Chicago, IL 60654. Offers child and adolescent psychology (Psy D); client-centered and experiential psychotherapies (Psy D); diversity and multicultural psychology (Psy D); family psychology (Psy D); forensic psychology (Psy D); health psychology (Psy D); psychoanalytic psychology (Psy D); psychology and spirituality (Psy D). *Accreditation:* APA.

See Close-Up on page 1379.

Argosy University, Denver, College of Psychology and Behavioral Sciences, Denver, CO 80203. Offers clinical psychology (MA, Psy D); community counseling (MA); counseling psychology (Ed D), including counselor education and supervision; counselor education and supervision (Ed D); forensic psychology (MA); marriage and family therapy (MA); organizational leadership (Ed D).

See Close-Up on page 1383.

Argosy University, Hawai'i, College of Psychology and Behavioral Sciences, Program in Marriage and Family Therapy, Honolulu, HI 96813. Offers MA.

See Close-Up on page 1385.

Argosy University, Inland Empire, College of Psychology and Behavioral Sciences, San Bernardino, CA 92408. Offers clinical psychology/marriage and family therapy (MA); counseling psychology (MA, Ed D); counseling psychology/marriage and family therapy (MA); forensic psychology (MA).

See Close-Up on page 1387.

Argosy University, Los Angeles, College of Psychology and Behavioral Sciences, Santa Monica, CA 90405. Offers clinical psychology/marriage and family therapy (MA); counseling psychology (Ed D); counseling psychology/marriage and family therapy (MA); organizational leadership (Ed D).

See Close-Up on page 1389.

Argosy University, Orange County, College of Psychology and Behavioral Sciences, Program in Clinical Psychology, Santa Ana, CA 92704. Offers child and adolescent psychology (Psy D); forensic psychology (Psy D); marriage and family therapy (MA).

See Close-Up on page 1393.

Argosy University, Orange County, College of Psychology and Behavioral Sciences, Program in Counseling Psychology, Santa Ana, CA 92704. Offers counseling psychology (Ed D); marriage and family therapy (MA).

See Close-Up on page 1393.

Argosy University, Salt Lake City, College of Psychology and Behavioral Sciences, Draper, UT 84020. Offers counseling psychology (Ed D); marriage and family therapy (MA).

See Close-Up on page 1397.

Argosy University, San Diego, College of Psychology and Behavioral Sciences, San Diego, CA 92108. Offers clinical psychology/marriage and family therapy (MA); counseling psychology (MA, Ed D); counseling psychology/marriage and family therapy (MA).

See Close-Up on page 1399.

Argosy University, Sarasota, College of Psychology and Behavioral Sciences, Sarasota, FL 34235. Offers community counseling (MA); counseling psychology (Ed D); counselor education and supervision (Ed D); forensic psychology (MA); marriage and family therapy (MA); mental health counseling (MA); organizational leadership (Ed D); pastoral community counseling (Ed D); school counseling (MA, Ed S); school psychology (MA).

See Close-Up on page 1403.

Argosy University, Schaumburg, College of Psychology and Behavioral Sciences, Schaumburg, IL 60173-5403. Offers clinical health psychology (Post-Graduate Certificate); clinical psychology (MA, Psy D), including child and family psychology (Psy D), clinical health psychology (Psy D), diversity and multicultural psychology (Psy D), forensic psychology (Psy D); community counseling (MA); counseling psychology (Ed D), including counselor education and supervision; counselor education and supervision (Ed D); forensic psychology (Post-Graduate Certificate); organizational leadership (Ed D). *Accreditation:* ACA; APA.

See Close-Up on page 1405.

Argosy University, Tampa, College of Psychology and Behavioral Sciences, Program in Clinical Psychology, Tampa, FL 33614. Offers clinical psychology (MA, Psy D), including child and adolescent psychology (Psy D), geropsychology (Psy D), marriage/couples and family therapy (Psy D), neuropsychology (Psy D). *Accreditation:* APA.

See Close-Up on page 1409.

Argosy University, Twin Cities, College of Psychology and Behavioral Sciences, Eagan, MN 55121. Offers clinical psychology (MA, Psy D), including child and family psychology (Psy D), forensic psychology (Psy D), health psychology (Psy D), marriage/couples and family therapy (Psy D), neuropsychology (Psy D); forensic counseling (Post-Graduate Certificate); forensic psychology (MA); marriage and family therapy (MA, DMFT), including forensic counseling (MA); organizational leadership (Ed D). *Accreditation:* APA.

See Close-Up on page 1411.

Argosy University, Washington DC, College of Psychology and Behavioral Sciences, Arlington, VA 22209. Offers clinical psychology (MA, Psy D), including child and family psychology (Psy D), diversity and multicultural psychology (Psy D), forensic psychology (Psy D), health

Marriage and Family Therapy

Argosy University, Washington DC (continued)
and neuropsychology (Psy D); community counseling (MA); counseling psychology (Ed D), including counselor education and supervision; counselor education and supervision (Ed D); forensic psychology (MA); organizational leadership (Ed D). *Accreditation:* APA.

See Close-Up on page 1413.

Azusa Pacific University, School of Behavioral and Applied Sciences, Department of Graduate Psychology, Azusa, CA 91702-7000. Offers clinical psychology (MA, Psy D), including family therapy (MA). *Accreditation:* APA (one or more programs are accredited). Part-time and evening/weekend programs available. *Degree requirements:* For master's, comprehensive exam, 250 hours of clinical experience, individual and group therapy. *Entrance requirements:* For master's, interview, minimum GPA of 3.0, Minnesota Multiphasic Personality Inventory. Additional exam requirements/recommendations for international students: Required—TOEFL (minimum score 600 paper-based).

Barry University, School of Education, Program in Marital, Couple and Family Counseling/Therapy, Miami Shores, FL 33161-6695. Offers MS, Ed S. Part-time and evening/weekend programs available. *Degree requirements:* For master's, comprehensive exam, scholarly paper; for Ed S, comprehensive exam. *Entrance requirements:* For master's, GRE General Test or MAT, minimum GPA of 3.0; for Ed S, GRE General Test, minimum GPA of 3.0. *Application deadline:* For fall admission, 5/1 priority date for domestic students. Applications are processed on a rolling basis. Application fee: $30. Electronic applications accepted. *Unit head:* Dr. James Rudes, Program Coordinator, 305-899-3714, Fax: 305-899-4708, E-mail: jrudes@mail.barry.edu. *Application contact:* Dave Fletcher, Director of Graduate Admissions, 305-899-3113, Fax: 305-899-2971, E-mail: dfletcher@mail.barry.edu.

Bethel Seminary, Graduate and Professional Programs, St. Paul, MN 55112-6998. Offers adult developments and generativity (Certificate); biblical studies (MATS, Certificate); children's and family ministry (MACFM); Christian education (MACE); Christian thought (M Div, MACT); church leadership (D Min); congregation and family care (D Min); global and contextual studies (MA); global missions (Certificate); lay ministry (Certificate); marriage and family studies (M Div); marriage and family therapy (MAMFT); missions (MATS); pastoral counseling (Certificate); pastoral ministries (M Div); spiritual formation (Certificate); theological studies (MATS, Certificate); transformational leadership (MATL); youth ministries (MACE). *Accreditation:* ACIPE; ATS (one or more programs are accredited). Part-time and evening/weekend programs available. Postbaccalaureate distance learning degree programs offered (minimal on-campus study). *Faculty:* 26 full-time (3 women), 73 part-time/adjunct (21 women). *Students:* 374 full-time (115 women), 669 part-time (268 women); includes 183 minority (90 African Americans, 2 American Indian/Alaska Native, 65 Asian Americans or Pacific Islanders, 26 Hispanic Americans). Average age 36. 417 applicants, 86% accepted, 223 enrolled. In 2007, 62 first professional degrees, 102 master's, 14 doctorates awarded. *Degree requirements:* For master's, variable foreign language requirement, thesis (for some programs); for doctorate, thesis/dissertation; for M Div, one foreign language. *Entrance requirements:* For M Div, letters of reference; for master's, letters of reference, transcripts, personal statement; for doctorate, M Div, letters of reference, essays, organizational support. Additional exam requirements/recommendations for international students: Required—TOEFL (minimum score 550 paper-based; 213 computer-based). *Application deadline:* For fall admission, 8/1 priority date for domestic students, 3/1 for international students; for winter admission, 12/1 priority date for domestic students; for spring admission, 3/1 priority date for domestic students. Applications are processed on a rolling basis. Application fee: $20. Electronic applications accepted. *Expenses:* Tuition: Part-time $325 per credit. Required fees: $10 per quarter. *Financial support:* In 2007–08, 661 students received support, including 20 teaching assistantships; career-related internships or fieldwork, Federal Work-Study, scholarships/grants, and tuition waivers (full) also available. Financial award application deadline: 7/15; financial award applicants required to submit FAFSA. *Faculty research:* Nature of theology, ethics, biblical commentaries, nature of God, science and theology. *Unit head:* Dr. Leland Eliason, Executive Vice President and Provost, 651-638-6182. *Application contact:* Joseph V. Dworak, Director of Admissions, 651-638-6288, Fax: 651-638-6002, E-mail: j-dworak@bethel.edu.

Briercrest Seminary, Graduate Programs, Program in Christian Ministries, Caronport, SK S0H 0S0, Canada. Offers leadership (MA); marriage and family counseling (MA); missions (MA); pastoral counseling (MA); worship (MA); youth and family ministry (MA). Part-time programs available. *Degree requirements:* For master's, comprehensive exam, thesis optional. *Entrance requirements:* Additional exam requirements/recommendations for international students: Required—TOEFL (minimum score 550 paper-based; 213 computer-based).

Brigham Young University, Graduate Studies, College of Family, Home, and Social Sciences, Program of Marriage and Family Therapy, Provo, UT 84602-1001. Offers MS, PhD. *Faculty:* 9 full-time (1 woman), 6 part-time/adjunct (3 women). *Students:* 50 full-time (22 women); includes 10 minority (1 African American, 1 American Indian/Alaska Native, 3 Asian Americans or Pacific Islanders, 5 Hispanic Americans), 1 international. Average age 30. 75 applicants, 23% accepted, 15 enrolled. In 2007, 9 master's, 2 doctorates awarded. *Median time to degree:* Of those who began their doctoral program in fall 1999, 100% received their degree in 8 years or less. *Degree requirements:* For master's, comprehensive exam, thesis; for doctorate, comprehensive exam, thesis/dissertation. *Entrance requirements:* For master's and doctorate, GRE General Test, GRE Writing Test, minimum GPA of 3.0 in last 60 hours of course work. Additional exam requirements/recommendations for international students: Required—TOEFL. *Application deadline:* For fall admission, 1/10 for domestic and international students. Application fee: $50. Electronic applications accepted. *Financial support:* In 2007–08, 38 students received support, including 28 research assistantships with full and partial tuition reimbursements available (averaging $12,900 per year); fellowships, teaching assistantships, career-related internships or fieldwork, scholarships/grants, and tuition waivers (partial) also available. Financial award application deadline: 1/10. *Faculty research:* Therapy process and outcome, preparation for marriage, family relationships across the life cycle, marriage and family therapy, healthcare costs. Total annual research expenditures: $37,018. *Unit head:* Dr. Leslie L. Feinauer, Program Director, 801-422-7750, Fax: 801-422-0163, E-mail: leslie_feinauer@byu.edu. *Application contact:* Linda Kader, Program Secretary, 801-422-5680, Fax: 801-422-0163, E-mail: linda_kader@byu.edu.

California Baptist University, Program in Marriage and Family Therapy, Riverside, CA 92504-3206. Offers counseling psychology (MS). Part-time programs available. *Faculty:* 8 full-time (3 women), 7 part-time/adjunct (2 women). *Students:* 82 full-time (68 women), 53 part-time (43 women); includes 61 minority (21 African Americans, 6 American Indian/Alaska Native, 4 Asian Americans or Pacific Islanders, 30 Hispanic Americans), 2 international. 96 applicants, 43% accepted, 34 enrolled. In 2007, 66 degrees awarded. *Degree requirements:* For master's, comprehensive exam, 24 hours (individual) or 50 hours (group) psychotherapy. *Entrance requirements:* For master's, Minnesota Multiphasic Personality Inventory and Myers-Briggs Type Inventory, course work in developmental psychology, theories of personality, and statistics; minimum undergraduate GPA of 2.75. Additional exam requirements/recommendations for international students: Required—TOEFL (minimum score 575 paper-based; 230 computer-based), IELTS (minimum score 7). *Application deadline:* For fall admission, 9/1 for domestic students, 7/1 priority date for international students; for spring admission, 1/3 for domestic students, 10/15 priority date for international students. Applications are processed on a rolling basis. Application fee: $45. Electronic applications accepted. *Expenses:* Contact institution. *Financial support:* Career-related internships or fieldwork and Federal Work-Study available. Support available to part-time students. Financial award applicants required to submit FAFSA. *Unit head:* Dr. Gary Collins, Director and Associate Dean, School of Business, 951-343-4304, Fax: 951-343-4569, E-mail: gcollins@calbaptist.edu. *Application contact:* Gail Ronveaux, Dean of Graduate Enrollment, 951-343-5045, Fax: 951-343-5095, E-mail: graduateadmissions@calbaptist.edu.

California Lutheran University, Graduate Studies, Department of Psychology, Thousand Oaks, CA 91360-2787. Offers clinical psychology (MS); marital and family therapy (MS). Part-time programs available. *Degree requirements:* For master's, thesis or comprehensive exams. *Entrance requirements:* For master's, GRE General Test, interview, minimum GPA of 3.0.

California State University, Chico, Graduate School, College of Behavioral and Social Sciences, Department of Psychology, Program in Marriage and Family Therapy, Chico, CA 95929-0722. Offers MS. *Students:* 28 full-time (25 women), 6 part-time (3 women); includes 6 minority (1 American Indian/Alaska Native, 2 Asian Americans or Pacific Islanders, 3 Hispanic Americans). Average age 32. 36 applicants, 69% accepted, 15 enrolled. In 2007, 21 degrees awarded. *Degree requirements:* For master's, thesis or alternative. *Entrance requirements:* For master's, GRE General Test or MAT, 3 letters of recommendation on departmental form, statement of purpose. Additional exam requirements/recommendations for international students: Required—TOEFL (minimum score 550 paper-based; 213 computer-based; 80 iBT), IELTS (minimum score 7). *Application deadline:* For fall admission, 3/1 for domestic and international students. Application fee: $55. *Unit head:* Dr. Linda Kline, Graduate Coordinator, 530-898-6263.

California State University, Dominguez Hills, College of Health and Human Services, Program in Marital and Family Therapy, Carson, CA 90747-0001. Offers MS. Part-time and evening/weekend programs available. *Faculty:* 2 full-time (both women), 5 part-time/adjunct (4 women). *Students:* 60 full-time (50 women), 20 part-time (17 women); includes 52 minority (33 African Americans, 5 Asian Americans or Pacific Islanders, 14 Hispanic Americans), 2 international. Average age 37. 43 applicants, 81% accepted, 31 enrolled. In 2007, 30 degrees awarded. *Degree requirements:* For master's, comprehensive exam. *Entrance requirements:* For master's, minimum GPA of 3.0. *Application deadline:* For fall admission, 8/1 for domestic students; for spring admission, 12/15 for domestic students. Applications are processed on a rolling basis. Application fee: $55. Electronic applications accepted. *Faculty research:* Sociology of the family, clinical psychology theory, employee assistance programs, race and sport, secondary trauma. *Unit head:* Dr. Michele Linden, Coordinator, 310-243-2693, E-mail: mlinden@csudh.edu.

California State University, Fresno, Division of Graduate Studies, School of Education and Human Development, Department of Counseling and Special Education, Program in Marriage and Family Therapy, Fresno, CA 93740-8027. Offers MS. *Accreditation:* ACA. Part-time and evening/weekend programs available. *Students:* 423; includes 224 minority (18 African Americans, 5 American Indian/Alaska Native, 40 Asian Americans or Pacific Islanders, 161 Hispanic Americans), 9 international. Average age 28. 10 applicants. In 2007, 133 degrees awarded. *Degree requirements:* For master's, thesis or alternative. *Entrance requirements:* For master's, GRE General Test, MAT, minimum GPA of 3.0. Additional exam requirements/recommendations for international students: Required—TOEFL. *Application deadline:* For fall admission, 5/1 for domestic and international students; for spring admission, 10/1 for domestic and international students. Applications are processed on a rolling basis. Application fee: $55. Electronic applications accepted. *Financial support:* Career-related internships or fieldwork, Federal Work-Study, scholarships/grants, and research awards available. Support available to part-time students. Financial award application deadline: 3/1; financial award applicants required to submit FAFSA. *Faculty research:* Child abuse prevention, early childhood education. *Unit head:* Claire Sham Choy, Head, 559-278-0328, Fax: 559-278-0045, E-mail: cshamchoy@csufresno.edu.

California State University, Northridge, Graduate Studies, College of Education, Department of Educational Psychology and Counseling, Northridge, CA 91330. Offers counseling (MS), including career counseling, college counseling and student services, marriage and family therapy, school counseling, school psychology; educational psychology (MA Ed), including development, learning, and instruction, early childhood education. *Accreditation:* ACA (one or more programs are accredited); NCATE. Part-time and evening/weekend programs available. *Faculty:* 17 full-time (10 women), 50 part-time/adjunct (29 women). *Students:* 358 full-time (312 women), 120 part-time (102 women); includes 216 minority (27 African Americans, 2 American Indian/Alaska Native, 41 Asian Americans or Pacific Islanders, 146 Hispanic Americans), 9 international. Average age 31. 284 applicants, 60% accepted, 148 enrolled. In 2007, 142 degrees awarded. *Entrance requirements:* For master's, GRE General Test or minimum GPA of 3.0. Additional exam requirements/recommendations for international students: Required—TOEFL. *Application deadline:* For fall admission, 11/30 for domestic students. Application fee: $55. *Financial support:* Scholarships/grants available. Support available to part-time students. Financial award application deadline: 3/1. *Unit head:* Dr. Beverly Cabello, Chair, 818-677-2599.

Capella University, School of Human Services, Minneapolis, MN 55402. Offers addictions counseling (Certificate); counseling studies (MS, PhD); criminal justice (MS, PhD, Certificate); diversity studies (Certificate); general human services (MS, PhD); health care administration (MS, PhD, Certificate); management of nonprofit agencies (MS, PhD, Certificate); marital, couple and family counseling/therapy (MS); marriage and family services (Certificate); mental health counseling (MS); professional counseling (Certificate); social and community services (MS, PhD, Certificate). Part-time and evening/weekend programs available. Postbaccalaureate distance learning degree programs offered (minimal on-campus study). Terminal master's awarded for partial completion of doctoral program. *Degree requirements:* For master's, thesis optional, integrative project; for doctorate, comprehensive exam, thesis/dissertation. *Entrance requirements:* Additional exam requirements/recommendations for international students: Required—TOEFL (minimum score 550 paper-based; 213 computer-based), TWE (minimum score 4). Electronic applications accepted. *Faculty research:* Compulsive and addictive behaviors, substance abuse, assessment of psychopathology and neuropsychology.

Carlos Albizu University, Miami Campus, Graduate Programs, Miami, FL 33172-2209. Offers clinical psychology (Psy D); entrepreneurship (MBA); exceptional student education (MS); industrial/organizational psychology (MS); marriage and family therapy (MS); mental health counseling (MS); nonprofit management (MBA); organizational management (MBA); psychology (MS); school counseling (MS); teaching English as a second language (MS). *Accreditation:* APA. Part-time and evening/weekend programs available. *Faculty:* 20 full-time (13 women), 65 part-time/adjunct (39 women). *Students:* 514 full-time (409 women), 143 part-time (119 women); includes 465 minority (54 African Americans, 1 American Indian/Alaska Native, 4 Asian Americans or Pacific Islanders, 406 Hispanic Americans). Average age 35. 194 applicants, 73% accepted, 130 enrolled. In 2007, 208 master's, 37 doctorates awarded. Terminal master's awarded for partial completion of doctoral program. *Median time to degree:* Of those who began their doctoral program in fall 1999, 65% received their degree in 8 years or less. *Degree requirements:* For master's, one foreign language, comprehensive exam, integrative project (MBA), research project (MSESE and MSTESOL); for doctorate, one foreign language, comprehensive exam, internship, doctoral project. *Entrance requirements:* For master's, 3 letters of recommendation, interview, minimum GPA of 3.0, résumé, statement of purpose, official transcripts; for doctorate, 3 letters of recommendation, minimum GPA of 3.0, resumé, interview. *Application deadline:* For fall admission, 8/1 priority date for domestic students; for spring admission, 11/30 priority date for domestic students. Applications are processed on a rolling basis. Application fee: $50. *Expenses:* Tuition: Full-time $9,090; part-time $505 per credit. Required fees: $298 per term. Tuition and fees vary according to course load and degree level. *Financial support:* In 2007–08, 37 students received support. Federal Work-Study and scholarships/grants available. Financial award application deadline: 6/1; financial award applicants required to submit FAFSA. *Faculty research:* Psychotherapy, forensic psychology, neuropsychology, marketing strategy, entrepreneurship, special education. *Unit head:* Dr. Carmen S. Roca, Interim Chancellor, 305-593-1223 Ext. 120, Fax: 305-629-8052, E-mail: croca@albizu.edu. *Application contact:* Barbara De la Cruz, Admission Officer, 305-593-1223 Ext. 218, Fax: 305-593-1854, E-mail: bdelacruz@albizu.edu.

Central Connecticut State University, School of Graduate Studies, School of Education and Professional Studies, Department of Counseling and Family Therapy, New Britain, CT 06050-4010. Offers marriage and family therapy (MS); professional counseling (MS, Certificate); school counseling (MS); student development in higher education (MS). *Accreditation:* AAMFT/

COAMFTE. Part-time and evening/weekend programs available. *Faculty:* 6 full-time (4 women), 14 part-time/adjunct (8 women). *Students:* 112 full-time (89 women), 175 part-time (147 women); includes 43 minority (20 African Americans, 1 American Indian/Alaska Native, 3 Asian Americans or Pacific Islanders, 19 Hispanic Americans), 3 international. Average age 33. 199 applicants, 45% accepted, 69 enrolled. In 2007, 64 master's, 5 other advanced degrees awarded. *Degree requirements:* For master's, thesis or alternative, special project. *Entrance requirements:* For master's, minimum GPA of 2.7. Additional exam requirements/recommendations for international students: Required—TOEFL. *Application deadline:* For fall admission, 5/1 for domestic students. Applications are processed on a rolling basis. Application fee: $50. Electronic applications accepted. *Expenses:* Tuition, area resident: Full-time $4,169. Tuition, state resident: full-time $6,253. Tuition, nonresident: full-time $11,614; part-time $400 per credit. Required fees: $3,322. One-time fee: $62 part-time. Tuition and fees vary according to degree level and program. *Financial support:* In 2007–08, 11 students received support, including 15 research assistantships; career-related internships or fieldwork, Federal Work-Study, scholarships/grants, and unspecified assistantships also available. Support available to part-time students. Financial award application deadline: 3/1; financial award applicants required to submit FAFSA. *Faculty research:* Elementary/secondary school counseling, marriage/family therapy, rehabilitation counseling, counseling in higher educational settings. *Unit head:* Dr. Connie Tait, Chair, 860-832-2154.

Chapman University, Graduate Studies, Wilkinson College of Social Sciences and Humanities, Department of Psychology, Orange, CA 92866. Offers marriage and family therapy (MA). Part-time and evening/weekend programs available. *Faculty:* 12 full-time (4 women), 4 part-time/adjunct (3 women). *Students:* 44 full-time (39 women), 22 part-time (19 women); includes 14 minority (5 Asian Americans or Pacific Islanders, 9 Hispanic Americans), 4 international. Average age 29. 72 applicants, 57% accepted, 16 enrolled. In 2007, 16 degrees awarded. *Degree requirements:* For master's, comprehensive exam. *Entrance requirements:* For master's, GRE General Test, minimum undergraduate GPA of 3.0. Additional exam requirements/recommendations for international students: Required—TOEFL (minimum score 550 paper-based). *Application deadline:* Applications are processed on a rolling basis. Application fee: $55. Electronic applications accepted. *Expenses: Contact institution. Financial support:* Fellowships, Federal Work-Study and scholarships/grants available. Financial award application deadline: 6/30; financial award applicants required to submit FAFSA. *Unit head:* Dr. Georg Eifert, Chair, 714-997-6776, E-mail: eifert@chapman.edu. *Application contact:* Susan Read-Weil, Coordinator, 714-744-7837, E-mail: sreadwei@chapman.edu.

Christian Theological Seminary, Graduate and Professional Programs, Indianapolis, IN 46208-3301. Offers marriage and family (MA); pastoral care and counseling (D Min); practical theology (D Min); psychotherapy and faith (MA); sacred theology (STM); specialized ministries (MA); theological studies (MTS); theology (M Div). *Accreditation:* AAMFT/COAMFTE (one or more programs are accredited); ACIPE; ATS. Part-time programs available. Terminal master's awarded for partial completion of doctoral program. *Degree requirements:* For master's, comprehensive exam (for some programs), thesis (for some programs); for doctorate, comprehensive exam, thesis/dissertation; for M Div, comprehensive exam, thesis/dissertation (for some programs), missionary and cross-cultural experience. *Entrance requirements:* For master's, GRE General Test, MAT; for doctorate, M Div or BD. Electronic applications accepted. *Faculty research:* Faith formation, peer learning post graduation.

The College of New Jersey, Graduate Division, School of Education, Department of Counselor Education, Program in Marriage and Family Therapy, Ewing, NJ 08628. Offers Ed S. Part-time and evening/weekend programs available. *Students:* 6 applicants, 100% accepted. In 2007, 7 degrees awarded. *Entrance requirements:* For degree, GRE, minimum GPA of 3.0 in field or 2.75 overall. Additional exam requirements/recommendations for international students: Required—TOEFL. *Application deadline:* For fall admission, 4/15 for domestic students; for spring admission, 10/15 for domestic students. Application fee: $60. Electronic applications accepted. *Financial support:* Unspecified assistantships available. Financial award application deadline: 5/1; financial award applicants required to submit FAFSA. *Unit head:* Dr. Charlene Alderfer, Coordinator, 609-771-2136, Fax: 609-637-5116, E-mail: alderfer@tcnj.edu. *Application contact:* Susan L. Hydro, Office of Graduate Studies, Assistant Dean, 609-771-2300, Fax: 609-637-5105, E-mail: graduate@tcnj.edu.

The College of William and Mary, School of Education, Program in Counselor Education, Williamsburg, VA 23187-8795. Offers community and addictions counseling (M Ed); community counseling (M Ed); educational counseling (PhD); family counseling (M Ed); school counseling (M Ed). *Accreditation:* ACA; NCATE. Part-time and evening/weekend programs available. *Faculty:* 5 full-time (2 women), 5 part-time/adjunct (3 women). *Students:* 62 full-time (49 women), 13 part-time (12 women); includes 7 minority (4 African Americans, 1 American Indian/Alaska Native, 2 Hispanic Americans), 1 international. Average age 32. 112 applicants, 50% accepted, 35 enrolled. In 2007, 37 master's, 2 doctorates awarded. *Degree requirements:* For doctorate, comprehensive exam, thesis/dissertation. *Entrance requirements:* For master's, GRE, minimum GPA of 2.5; for doctorate, GRE, minimum GPA of 3.5. Additional exam requirements/recommendations for international students: Required—TOEFL. *Application deadline:* For fall admission, 1/15 for domestic and international students. Application fee: $45. Electronic applications accepted. *Expenses:* Tuition, state resident: full-time $6,250; part-time $275 per credit hour. Tuition, nonresident: part-time $760 per credit hour. Required fees:$3,550. Tuition and fees vary according to program. *Financial support:* In 2007–08, 1 fellowship with full tuition reimbursement (averaging $20,000 per year), 43 research assistantships with full tuition reimbursements (averaging $9,000 per year) were awarded; career-related internships or fieldwork, Federal Work-Study, institutionally sponsored loans, scholarships/grants, and unspecified assistantships also available. Financial award application deadline: 1/15; financial award applicants required to submit FAFSA. *Faculty research:* Sexuality, multicultural education, substance abuse, transpersonal psychology. *Unit head:* Dr. Charles McAdams, Area Coordinator, 757-221-2338, E-mail: crmcad@wm.edu. *Application contact:* Dorothy Smith Osborne, Director of Admissions, 757-221-2317, Fax: 757-221-2293, E-mail: dsosbo@wm.edu.

Converse College, School of Education and Graduate Studies, Education Specialist Program, Spartanburg, SC 29302-0006. Offers administration and supervision (Ed S); curriculum and instruction (Ed S); marriage and family therapy (Ed S). *Accreditation:* AAMFT/COAMFTE. Part-time programs available. *Entrance requirements:* For degree, GRE or MAT (marriage and family therapy), minimum GPA of 3.0. Electronic applications accepted.

Denver Seminary, Graduate and Professional Programs, Littleton, CO 80120. Offers apologetics (Certificate); biblical studies (MA); Christian formation and soul care (MA, Certificate); Christian studies (MA, Certificate); church and parachurch leadership (D Min); counseling licensure (MA); counseling ministry (MA); intercultural ministry (Certificate); leadership (MA, Certificate); marriage and family counseling (D Min); pastoral ministry (D Min); philosophy of religion (MA); spiritual guidance (Certificate); theology (M Div, Certificate); worship (Certificate); youth and family ministry (MA). *Accreditation:* ACA; ACIPE; ATS (one or more programs are accredited). Part-time and evening/weekend programs available. Postbaccalaureate distance learning degree programs offered. *Faculty:* 23 full-time (4 women), 94 part-time/adjunct (39 women). *Students:* 517 full-time (154 women), 283 part-time (130 women); includes 47 minority (15 African Americans, 1 American Indian/Alaska Native, 22 Asian Americans or Pacific Islanders, 9 Hispanic Americans), 43 international. Average age 34. 333 applicants, 76% accepted, 166 enrolled. In 2007, 41 first professional degrees, 77 master's, 8 doctorates, 9 other advanced degrees awarded. *Degree requirements:* For master's, 2 foreign languages, thesis (for some programs); for doctorate, 2 foreign languages, thesis/dissertation; for M Div, 2 foreign languages. *Entrance requirements:* For M Div, minimum undergraduate GPA of 2.5; for master's, minimum undergraduate GPA of 3.0; for doctorate, M Div, 3 years of ministry experience. Additional exam requirements/recommendations for international students: Required—TOEFL (minimum score 575 paper-based; 233 computer-based; 90 iBT). *Application deadline:* For fall admission, 7/15 priority date for domestic students; for spring admission, 12/15 priority date for domestic students. Applications are processed on a rolling basis. Application fee: $35. Electronic applications accepted. *Expenses:* Tuition: Part-time $495 per semester hour. One-time fee: $150 part-time. Part-time tuition and fees vary according to course load. *Financial support:* In 2007–08, 220 students received support. Career-related internships or fieldwork, Federal Work-Study, scholarships/grants, and unspecified assistantships available. Support available to part-time students. Financial award application deadline: 4/1; financial award applicants required to submit FAFSA. *Unit head:* Dr. Randy MacFarland, Vice President and Dean, 303-762-6980, Fax: 303-761-8020, E-mail: randy.macfarland@denverseminary.edu. *Application contact:* Nathan Lamb, Director of Admissions, 303-357-5801, Fax: 303-783-3122, E-mail: info@denverseminary.edu.

Drexel University, College of Nursing and Health Professions, Program in Couples and Family Therapy, Philadelphia, PA 19104-2875. Offers couples and family therapy (PhD); family therapy (MFT). *Accreditation:* AAMFT/COAMFTE (one or more programs are accredited). Part-time programs available. Terminal master's awarded for partial completion of doctoral program. *Degree requirements:* For master's, comprehensive exam, thesis; for doctorate, thesis/dissertation, qualifying exam. *Entrance requirements:* For master's, GRE General Test or MAT, minimum GPA of 2.75; for doctorate, GRE General Test, minimum GPA of 3.0. Electronic applications accepted. *Faculty research:* Family assessment, gender issues, chronic illness, early intervention.

East Carolina University, Graduate School, College of Human Ecology, Department of Child Development and Family Relations, Greenville, NC 27858-4353. Offers child development and family relations (MS); marriage and family therapy (MS). *Accreditation:* AAMFT/COAMFTE. Part-time programs available. *Students:* 45 full-time (38 women), 17 part-time (all women); includes 13 minority (8 African Americans, 1 American Indian/Alaska Native, 1 Asian American or Pacific Islander, 3 Hispanic Americans). Average age 27. 30 applicants, 3% accepted, 1 enrolled. In 2007, 21 degrees awarded. *Degree requirements:* For master's, comprehensive exam, thesis optional. *Application deadline:* For fall admission, 1/15 for domestic students; for spring admission, 10/15 for domestic students. Applications are processed on a rolling basis. Application fee: $50. *Financial support:* In 2007–08, 18 students received support, including 10 research assistantships, 8 teaching assistantships; career-related internships or fieldwork, Federal Work-Study, institutionally sponsored loans, and scholarships/grants also available. Support available to part-time students. Financial award application deadline: 6/1. *Faculty research:* Child care quality, mental health delivery systems for children, family violence. *Unit head:* Dr. Cynthia Johnson, Chairperson, 252-328-4273, E-mail: johnsoncy@ecu.edu.

Eastern Nazarene College, Adult and Graduate Studies, Program in Family Counseling, Quincy, MA 02170-2999. Offers marriage and family therapy (MS). Part-time and evening/weekend programs available. *Entrance requirements:* For master's, 3 letters of recommendation, resumé. Additional exam requirements/recommendations for international students: Required—TOEFL (minimum score 550 paper-based).

Eastern University, Palmer Theological Seminary, Program in Ministry, St. Davids, PA 19087-3696. Offers marriage and family (D Min). *Accreditation:* ACIPE. Part-time programs available. *Degree requirements:* For doctorate, thesis/dissertation. *Entrance requirements:* For doctorate, 3 years of experience, involvement in ministry, church endorsement. Expenses: Contact institution.

East Tennessee State University, School of Graduate Studies, College of Education, Department of Human Development and Learning, Johnson City, TN 37614. Offers advanced practitioner (M Ed); community agency counseling (M Ed, MA); comprehensive concentration (M Ed); counseling (M Ed, MA); early childhood education (M Ed, MA); early childhood general (M Ed); early childhood special education (M Ed); early childhood teaching (M Ed); elementary and secondary (school counseling) (M Ed, MA); marriage and family therapy (M Ed, MA); modified concentration (M Ed). *Accreditation:* ACA; NCATE. Part-time programs available. *Degree requirements:* For master's, comprehensive exam, thesis (for some programs). *Entrance requirements:* For master's, GRE General Test, minimum GPA of 3.0. Additional exam requirements/recommendations for international students: Required—TOEFL (minimum score 550 paper-based; 213 computer-based). *Faculty research:* Drug and alcohol abuse, marriage and family counseling, severe mental retardation, parenting of children with disabilities.

Edgewood College, Program in Marriage and Family Therapy, Madison, WI 53711-1997. Offers MS. Part-time and evening/weekend programs available. *Students:* 12 full-time (all women), 20 part-time (17 women); includes 3 minority (1 African American, 2 Hispanic Americans). Average age 32. In 2007, 13 degrees awarded. *Degree requirements:* For master's, research project. *Entrance requirements:* For master's, minimum GPA of 2.75, 2 letters of reference, personal statement, interviews. Additional exam requirements/recommendations for international students: Required—TOEFL (minimum score 213 computer-based). *Application deadline:* For fall admission, 3/1 for domestic students. Application fee: $25. Electronic applications accepted. *Expenses:* Tuition: Part-time $655 per credit. *Unit head:* Dr. Peter Fabian, Director, 608-663-2233, Fax: 608-663-3291, E-mail: fabian@edgewood.edu. *Application contact:* Paula O'Malley, Director of Graduate and Professional Studies, 608-663-2217, Fax: 608-663-3496, E-mail: gps@edgewood.edu.

Evangelical Theological Seminary, Graduate and Professional Programs, Myerstown, PA 17067-1212. Offers divinity (M Div); marriage and family therapy (MA); ministry (Certificate); religion (MA). *Accreditation:* ATS (one or more programs are accredited). Part-time programs available. Postbaccalaureate distance learning degree programs offered (minimal on-campus study). *Faculty:* 7 full-time (2 women), 21 part-time/adjunct (3 women). *Students:* 22 full-time (0 women), 152 part-time (66 women). Average age 33. 60 applicants, 77% accepted, 46 enrolled. In 2007, 11 first professional degrees, 22 master's awarded. *Degree requirements:* For master's, 2 foreign languages; for M Div, 2 foreign languages, ministry internship. *Entrance requirements:* For M Div and master's, minimum GPA of 2.5. Additional exam requirements/recommendations for international students: Required—TOEFL (minimum score 550 paper-based; 213 computer-based). *Application deadline:* For fall admission, 6/1 priority date for domestic students, 4/1 priority date for international students; for spring admission, 11/1 priority date for domestic students, 9/1 priority date for international students. Applications are processed on a rolling basis. Application fee: $35. *Expenses:* Tuition: Full-time $10,440; part-time $435 per credit. Required fees: $25 per semester. One-time fee: $125. *Financial support:* Career-related internships or fieldwork, scholarships/grants, and tuition waivers (full) available. Support available to part-time students. Financial award application deadline: 6/1; financial award applicants required to submit FAFSA. *Faculty research:* Literary form and structure within the Hebrew and Greek scriptures, Wesley studies, esoteric biblical languages, the Mosaic law and the Christian, ethics. *Unit head:* Rev. Dr. John V. Tornfelt, Vice President, Academic Affairs, 717-866-5775 Ext. 140, Fax: 717-866-4667, E-mail: jtornfelt@evangelical.edu. *Application contact:* Tom M. Maiello, Dean of Admissions, 800-532-5775 Ext. 109, Fax: 717-866-4667, E-mail: admissions@evangelical.edu.

Fairfield University, Graduate School of Education and Allied Professions, Department of Marriage and Family Therapy, Fairfield, CT 06824-5195. Offers MA. *Accreditation:* AAMFT/COAMFTE. Part-time and evening/weekend programs available. *Faculty:* 3 full-time (2 women), 5 part-time/adjunct (3 women). *Students:* 21 full-time (18 women), 44 part-time (40 women). 26 applicants, 46% accepted, 8 enrolled. In 2007, 20 degrees awarded. *Degree requirements:* For master's, comprehensive exam. *Entrance requirements:* For master's, minimum QPA of 2.67, 2 recommendations, resumè, essay. Additional exam requirements/recommendations for international students: Required—TOEFL (minimum score 550 paper-based; 213 computer-based; 79 iBT). *Application deadline:* For fall admission, 4/1 for domestic students; for spring admission, 10/15 for domestic students. Application fee: $60. Electronic applications accepted. *Financial support:* Tuition waivers (partial) and unspecified assistantships available. Financial award applicants required to submit FAFSA. *Faculty research:* Couple therapy, professional ethics, multicultural issues in counseling, alcoholism and family structure. *Unit head:* Dr. Rona Preli, Chair, 203-254-4000 Ext. 2475, Fax: 203-254-4047. *Application contact:* Marianne Gumpper, Director of Graduate and Continuing Studies Admissions, 203-254-4184, Fax: 203-254-4073, E-mail: gradadmis@mail.fairfield.edu.

Marriage and Family Therapy

Fitchburg State College, Division of Graduate and Continuing Education, Programs in Counseling, Fitchburg, MA 01420-2697. Offers elementary school guidance counseling (MS); marriage and family therapy (Certificate); mental health counseling (MS); secondary school guidance counseling (MS). *Accreditation:* NCATE. Part-time and evening/weekend programs available. *Students:* 16 full-time (13 women), 65 part-time (55 women); includes 6 minority (1 African American, 1 American Indian/Alaska Native, 4 Hispanic Americans), 2 international. Average age 31. 20 applicants, 85% accepted, 15 enrolled. In 2007, 17 degrees awarded. *Entrance requirements:* For master's, GRE General Test or MAT, letters of recommendation, resumé; for Certificate, master's degree. Additional exam requirements/recommendations for international students: Required—TOEFL (minimum score 550 paper-based; 213 computer-based; 79 iBT). *Application deadline:* Applications are processed on a rolling basis. Application fee: $25 ($50 for international students). *Expenses:* Tuition, nonresident: part-time $150 per credit. Required fees: $109 per credit. *Financial support:* In 2007–08, research assistantships with partial tuition reimbursements (averaging $5,500 per year); Federal Work-Study, scholarships/grants, and unspecified assistantships also available. Support available to part-time students. Financial award application deadline: 3/1; financial award applicants required to submit FAFSA. *Unit head:* Dr. John Hancock, Chair, 978-665-3604, Fax: 978-665-3658, E-mail: gce@fsc.edu. *Application contact:* Director of Admissions, 978-665-3144, Fax: 978-665-4540, E-mail: admissions@fsc.edu.

Florida Atlantic University, College of Education, Department of Counselor Education, Boca Raton, FL 33431-0991. Offers counselor education (M Ed); family counseling (Ed S); mental health counseling (M Ed, Ed S); rehabilitation counseling (M Ed); school counseling (Ed S). *Accreditation:* ACA; NCATE. Part-time and evening/weekend programs available. *Degree requirements:* For Ed S, departmental qualifying exam. *Entrance requirements:* For master's, GRE General Test, minimum GPA of 3.0 during previous 2 years; for Ed S, GRE General Test, minimum graduate GPA of 3.25. Additional exam requirements/recommendations for international students: Required—TOEFL. *Faculty research:* Brief therapy, psychological type, marriage and family counseling, international programs, integrated services.

Florida State University, Graduate Studies, College of Human Sciences, Department of Family and Child Sciences, Tallahassee, FL 32306. Offers child development (MS, PhD); family relations (MS, PhD); marriage and family therapy (PhD). *Accreditation:* AAMFT/COAMFTE. Part-time programs available. *Faculty:* 16 full-time (9 women). *Students:* 29 full-time (20 women), 38 part-time (32 women); includes 20 minority (14 African Americans, 2 Asian Americans or Pacific Islanders, 4 Hispanic Americans), 2 international. 47 applicants, 30% accepted, 10 enrolled. In 2007, 4 master's, 10 doctorates awarded. *Degree requirements:* For master's, comprehensive exam, thesis optional; for doctorate, thesis/dissertation. *Entrance requirements:* For master's and doctorate, GRE General Test, minimum GPA of 3.0. Additional exam requirements/recommendations for international students: Required—TOEFL (minimum score 80 iBT). *Application deadline:* For fall admission, 7/1 for domestic students, 5/1 for international students; for spring admission, 11/1 for domestic students, 12/1 for international students. Application fee: $30. Electronic applications accepted. *Expenses:* Tuition, state resident: part-time $248 per credit hour. Tuition, nonresident: part-time $880 per credit hour. Tuition and fees vary according to program. *Financial support:* In 2007–08, 31 students received support, including 1 fellowship (averaging $10,000 per year), research assistantships with partial tuition reimbursements available (averaging $5,000 per year), teaching assistantships with partial tuition reimbursements available (averaging $5,000 per year); career-related internships or fieldwork, Federal Work-Study, institutionally sponsored loans, scholarships/grants, and unspecified assistantships also available. Financial award application deadline: 1/15; financial award applicants required to submit FAFSA. *Faculty research:* Addictions, family therapy, sexuality, parent-child relations, adolescent development. *Unit head:* Dr. Kay Pasley, Chair, 850-644-3217, Fax: 850-644-3439, E-mail: kpasley@admin.fsu.edu. *Application contact:* Suzi Hyacinthe, Academic Support Assistant, 850-644-3217, Fax: 850-644-3439, E-mail: shyacinthe@admin.fsu.edu.

See Close-Up on page 1073.

Friends University, Graduate School, Division of Science, Arts, and Education, Program in Family Therapy, Wichita, KS 67213. Offers MSFT. *Accreditation:* AAMFT/COAMFTE. Evening/weekend programs available. *Faculty:* 5 full-time (2 women), 10 part-time/adjunct (3 women). *Students:* 107 full-time. In 2007, 47 degrees awarded. *Entrance requirements:* Additional exam requirements/recommendations for international students: Required—TOEFL (minimum score 560 paper-based; 220 computer-based). *Application deadline:* For winter admission, 2/23 priority date for domestic and international students; for spring admission, 4/30 priority date for domestic and international students. Applications are processed on a rolling basis. Application fee: $45 ($65 for international students). Electronic applications accepted. *Unit head:* Dr. Steve Rathbun, Director, 800-794-6945 Ext. 5621. *Application contact:* Craig Davis, Executive Director of Recruitment-Adult and Graduate Studies, 800-794-6945 Ext. 5573, Fax: 316-295-5050, E-mail: cdavis@friends.edu.

Fuller Theological Seminary, Graduate School of Psychology, Department of Marriage and Family Therapy, Pasadena, CA 91182. Offers marital/family therapy (MS). *Degree requirements:* For master's, practicum. *Entrance requirements:* For master's, GRE General Test. Additional exam requirements/recommendations for international students: Required—TOEFL. Expenses: Contact institution. *Faculty research:* Marital intimacy, sex-roles, psychoanalytical theory, men's issues.

Geneva College, Program in Counseling, Beaver Falls, PA 15010-3599. Offers marriage and family (MA); mental health (MA); school counseling (MA). *Accreditation:* ACA. Part-time and evening/weekend programs available. *Degree requirements:* For master's, internship. *Entrance requirements:* For master's, GRE General Test or MAT, minimum GPA of 3.0, letters of recommendation, faith statement, 12 credits in undergraduate psychology. Additional exam requirements/recommendations for international students: Required—TOEFL. Electronic applications accepted.

George Fox University, School of Education, Graduate Department of Counseling, Newberg, OR 97132-2697. Offers counseling (MA); marriage and family therapy (MA, Certificate); mental health trauma (Certificate); school counseling (MA); school psychology (MS, Certificate). Part-time programs available. *Faculty:* 10 full-time (7 women), 12 part-time/adjunct (8 women). *Students:* 101 full-time (82 women), 134 part-time (111 women); includes 19 minority (3 African Americans, 2 American Indian/Alaska Native, 8 Asian Americans or Pacific Islanders, 6 Hispanic Americans), 1 international. Average age 36. 86 applicants, 65% accepted, 56 enrolled. In 2007, 60 master's, 4 other advanced degrees awarded. *Degree requirements:* For master's, thesis optional. *Application deadline:* For fall admission, 5/30 for domestic students. Applications are processed on a rolling basis. Application fee: $40. Electronic applications accepted. *Expenses: Contact institution. Financial support:* Career-related internships or fieldwork available. *Unit head:* Dr. Richard Shaw, Director, 503-554-6142, E-mail: rshaw@georgefox.edu. *Application contact:* Carol Namburi, Admissions Counselor, 800-631-0921, Fax: 503-554-6111, E-mail: counseling@georgefox.edu.

Harding University, College of Bible and Religion, Program in Marriage and Family Therapy, Searcy, AR 72149-0001. Offers marriage and family therapy (MS); mental health counseling (MS). Part-time programs available. *Faculty:* 4 full-time (0 women), 4 part-time/adjunct (2 women). *Students:* 25 full-time (12 women), 2 part-time; includes 1 minority (African American), 2 international. Average age 27. 19 applicants, 79% accepted, 14 enrolled. In 2007, 8 degrees awarded. *Degree requirements:* For master's, comprehensive exam, 15-month practicum. *Entrance requirements:* For master's, GRE General Test, minimum undergraduate GPA of 2.75, graduate 3.0. *Application deadline:* For fall admission, 4/1 priority date for domestic students. Applications are processed on a rolling basis. Application fee: $25. *Expenses:* Tuition: Part-time $485 per credit hour. Required fees: $21 per credit hour. *Financial support:* Career-related internships or fieldwork, Federal Work-Study, institutionally sponsored loans, and scholarships/grants available. Financial award application deadline: 4/1. *Faculty research:* Forgiveness, substance abuse, PTSD. *Unit head:* Dr. Lewis L. Moore, Chairman, 501-279-4347, Fax: 501-279-4417, E-mail: lmoore@harding.edu. *Application contact:* Ruth Ann Dawson, Office Manager, 501-279-4347, Fax: 501-279-4417, E-mail: radawson@harding.edu.

Hardin-Simmons University, Graduate School, Cynthia Ann Parker College of Liberal Arts, Department of Psychology, Program in Family Psychology, Abilene, TX 79698-0001. Offers MA. Part-time programs available. *Faculty:* 5 full-time (1 woman), 1 (woman) part-time/adjunct. *Students:* 18 full-time (12 women), 10 part-time (5 women); includes 3 minority (1 African American, 2 Hispanic Americans). Average age 27. 18 applicants, 67% accepted, 11 enrolled. In 2007, 8 degrees awarded. *Degree requirements:* For master's, comprehensive exam, clinical experience, project. *Entrance requirements:* For master's, minimum undergraduate GPA of 3.0 in major, 2.7 overall; 21 semester hours of course work in psychology, 18 of those in upper division classes; writing sample; letters of recommendation. Additional exam requirements/recommendations for international students: Required—TOEFL (minimum score 550 paper-based; 213 computer-based). *Application deadline:* For fall admission, 8/15 priority date for domestic students; for spring admission, 1/5 priority date for domestic students. Applications are processed on a rolling basis. Application fee: $50 ($100 for international students). *Expenses:* Tuition: Full-time $9,810; part-time $545 per hour. Required fees: $590; $75 per semester. One-time fee: $50 part-time. *Financial support:* In 2007–08, 25 students received support, including 20 fellowships (averaging $690 per year); career-related internships or fieldwork and scholarships/grants also available. Support available to part-time students. Financial award application deadline: 6/30; financial award applicants required to submit FAFSA. *Faculty research:* Family stress management, spirituality in marriage, intimacy and sexuality in marriage, sex education in the church, role of faith in marital satisfaction. *Unit head:* Dr. Sue Lucas, Director, 325-670-1538, Fax: 325-670-1458, E-mail: slucas@hsutx.edu. *Application contact:* Dr. Gary Stanlake, Dean of Graduate Studies, 325-670-1298, Fax: 325-670-1564, E-mail: gradoff@hsutx.edu.

Hofstra University, School of Education and Allied Human Services, Department of Health Professions and Family Studies, Program in Marriage and Family Therapy, Hempstead, NY 11549. Offers addiction studies (Advanced Certificate); marriage and family therapy (MA, PD). Part-time programs available. *Students:* 35 full-time (32 women), 15 part-time (all women); includes 10 minority (6 African Americans, 1 Asian American or Pacific Islander, 3 Hispanic Americans), 1 international. Average age 27. 50 applicants, 94% accepted, 19 enrolled. In 2007, 17 master's, 9 other advanced degrees awarded. *Degree requirements:* For master's, comprehensive exam, internship, clinic hours. *Entrance requirements:* For master's, GRE General Test, interview, letters of recommendation; for other advanced degree, 3 letters of recommendation, interview, resumé, essay, masters degree. Additional exam requirements/recommendations for international students: Required—TOEFL (minimum score 550 paper-based; 213 computer-based). *Application deadline:* Applications are processed on a rolling basis. Application fee: $60. Electronic applications accepted. *Expenses:* Tuition: Full-time $14,220; part-time $820 per credit. Required fees: $970; $165 per term. Tuition and fees vary according to program. *Financial support:* In 2007–08, 19 students received support, including 1 fellowship with tuition reimbursement available (averaging $3,000 per year), 2 research assistantships with full and partial tuition reimbursements available (averaging $11,100 per year); career-related internships or fieldwork, Federal Work-Study, institutionally sponsored loans, scholarships/grants, tuition waivers (full and partial), and unspecified assistantships also available. Support available to part-time students. Financial award applicants required to submit FAFSA. *Faculty research:* Marriage and family therapy, addiction studies, divorce mediation, human sexuality. *Unit head:* Prof. Lauren B. Mangino, Program Director, 516-463-5224. *Application contact:* Carol Drummer, Dean of Graduate Admissions, 516-463-4876, Fax: 516-463-4664, E-mail: gradstudent@hofstra.edu.

Hope International University, School of Graduate Studies, Program in Marriage and Family Therapy, Fullerton, CA 92831-3138. Offers MA, MFT. *Faculty:* 24. *Students:* 63 full-time (51 women), 26 part-time (21 women); includes 35 minority (10 African Americans, 1 American Indian/Alaska Native, 5 Asian Americans or Pacific Islanders, 19 Hispanic Americans), 5 international. Average age 38. 59 applicants, 81% accepted, 45 enrolled. In 2007, 29 degrees awarded. *Degree requirements:* For master's, comprehensive exam, thesis (for some programs), final exam, practicum. *Entrance requirements:* For master's, minimum GPA of 3.0, comprehensive career statement, interview, bachelor's degree, official transcripts, application, 2 references. Additional exam requirements/recommendations for international students: Required—TOEFL (minimum score 550 paper-based; 213 computer-based; 86 iBT); Recommended—IELTS (minimum score 7). *Application deadline:* For fall admission, 8/3 priority date for domestic and international students; for winter admission, 12/14 priority date for domestic and international students; for spring admission, 1/4 priority date for domestic and international students. Applications are processed on a rolling basis. Application fee: $75. Electronic applications accepted. *Expenses: Contact institution. Financial support:* Scholarships/grants and health care benefits available. Support available to part-time students. Financial award applicants required to submit FAFSA. *Unit head:* Dr. Laura Steele, Chair, 800-762-1294 Ext. 1235, E-mail: llsteele@hiu.edu. *Application contact:* Teresa Smith, Director of Graduate and Adult Admissions, 714-879-3901, Fax: 714-681-7450, E-mail: sgsadmissions@hiu.edu.

Idaho State University, Office of Graduate Studies, Kasiska College of Health Professions, Department of Counseling, Pocatello, ID 83209. Offers counseling (M Coun, Ed S, Post-baccalaureate Certificate), including family-centered practice (Postbaccalaureate Certificate), marriage and family counseling (M Coun), mental health counseling (M Coun), school counseling (M Coun), student affairs and college counseling (M Coun); counselor education and counseling (PhD). *Accreditation:* ACA (one or more programs are accredited). *Faculty:* 6 full-time (3 women). *Students:* 62 full-time (40 women), 28 part-time (21 women); includes 6 minority (1 American Indian/Alaska Native, 1 Asian American or Pacific Islander, 4 Hispanic Americans). Average age 34. In 2007, 28 master's, 2 doctorates awarded. *Degree requirements:* For master's, comprehensive exam, thesis; for doctorate, comprehensive exam, thesis/dissertation, internship; for other advanced degree, comprehensive exam, thesis, case studies, oral exam. *Entrance requirements:* For master's, GRE General Test, MAT, minimum GPA of 3.0; for doctorate, GRE General Test, MAT, minimum graduate GPA of 3.0, resumé, interview, counseling license; for other advanced degree, GRE General Test, minimum graduate GPA of 3.0, master's degree in counseling, 3 letters of recommendation, 2 years work experience. Additional exam requirements/recommendations for international students: Required—TOEFL (minimum score 600 paper-based; 213 computer-based; 80 iBT). *Application deadline:* For fall admission, 7/1 for domestic students, 6/1 for international students; for spring admission, 12/1 for domestic students, 11/1 for international students. Applications are processed on a rolling basis. Application fee: $55. *Expenses:* Tuition, state resident: full-time $2,882; part-time $259 per credit hour. Tuition, nonresident: full-time $11,566; part-time $379 per credit hour. Required fees: $2,278. Full-time tuition and fees vary according to program. Part-time tuition and fees vary according to course load. *Financial support:* In 2007–08, 14 teaching assistantships with full and partial tuition reimbursements (averaging $9,128 per year) were awarded; career-related internships or fieldwork, Federal Work-Study, institutionally sponsored loans, scholarships/grants, traineeships, health care benefits, tuition waivers (full), and unspecified assistantships also available. Financial award application deadline: 1/1; financial award applicants required to submit FAFSA. *Faculty research:* Group counseling, multicultural counseling, family counseling, child therapy, supervision. *Unit head:* Dr. Stephen Feit, Chair, 208-282-3663, Fax: 208-282-2583, E-mail: feitstep@isu.edu. *Application contact:* Ellen Combs, Graduate School Technical Records Specialist, 208-282-2150, Fax: 208-282-4847.

Indiana Wesleyan University, College of Graduate Studies, Program in Counseling, Marion, IN 46953-4974. Offers community counseling (MS); marriage and family counseling (MS); school counseling (MS). *Accreditation:* ACA. Part-time programs available. *Faculty:* 3 full-time (1 woman), 3 part-time/adjunct (2 women). *Students:* 41 full-time (31 women), 62 part-time (47 women); includes 5 minority (4 African Americans, 1 Hispanic American). Average age 32. In 2007, 23 degrees awarded. *Degree requirements:* For master's, thesis or alternative. *Entrance requirements:* For master's, GRE General Test. *Application deadline:* For fall admission, 4/1 priority date for domestic students; for spring admission, 10/1 priority date for domestic students. Application fee: $25. Electronic applications accepted. *Expenses: Contact institution.*

Financial support: In 2007–08, 1 research assistantship with tuition reimbursement, 1 teaching assistantship with partial tuition reimbursement (averaging $1,000 per year) were awarded. Financial award application deadline: 3/1; financial award applicants required to submit FAFSA. *Unit head:* Dr. Mark Gerig, Director of Graduate Counseling Studies, 765-677-2995, Fax: 765-677-2504, E-mail: mark.gerig@indwes.edu. *Application contact:* David McMillan, Assistant Director of Enrollment Management, 765-677-2688, E-mail: david.mcmillan@indwes.edu.

Iona College, School of Arts and Science, Department of Family and Pastoral Counseling, New Rochelle, NY 10801-1890. Offers family counseling (MS, Certificate); pastoral counseling (MS). Part-time and evening/weekend programs available. *Faculty:* 7 full-time (2 women), 1 (woman) part-time/adjunct. *Students:* 30 full-time (23 women), 21 part-time (16 women); includes 13 minority (8 African Americans, 5 Hispanic Americans), 1 international. Average age 33. 27 applicants, 74% accepted, 13 enrolled. In 2007, 5 degrees awarded. *Degree requirements:* For master's, thesis, project. *Entrance requirements:* For master's, draw-a-person test, sentence completion test, interview, minimum GPA of 3.0. *Application deadline:* Applications are processed on a rolling basis. Application fee: $50. Electronic applications accepted. *Expenses:* Contact institution. *Financial support:* Career-related internships or fieldwork, tuition waivers (partial), and unspecified assistantships available. Support available to part-time students. *Faculty research:* Marriage counseling. *Unit head:* Dr. Robert Burns, Chair, 914-633-2418, E-mail: rburns@iona.edu. *Application contact:* Veronica Jarek-Prinz, Director of Graduate Admissions, 914-633-2420, Fax: 914-633-2277, E-mail: vjarekprinz@iona.edu.

Iowa State University of Science and Technology, Graduate College, College of Human Sciences, Department of Human Development and Family Studies, Ames, IA 50011. Offers human development and family studies (MFCS, MS, PhD); marriage and family therapy (PhD). *Accreditation:* AAMFT/COAMFTE. *Faculty:* 26 full-time (19 women), 7 part-time/adjunct (5 women). *Students:* 53 full-time (45 women), 17 part-time (15 women); includes 4 minority (2 Asian Americans or Pacific Islanders, 2 Hispanic Americans), 10 international. 50 applicants, 78% accepted, 22 enrolled. In 2007, 14 master's, 7 doctorates awarded. *Degree requirements:* For master's, thesis; for doctorate, thesis/dissertation. *Entrance requirements:* For master's and doctorate, GRE General Test. Additional exam requirements/recommendations for international students: Required—TOEFL (paper-based 550; computer-based 213; iBT 79) or IELTS (6.0). *Application deadline:* For fall admission, 12/1 priority date for domestic students. Application fee: $30 ($70 for international students). Electronic applications accepted. *Financial support:* In 2007–08, 31 research assistantships with full and partial tuition reimbursements (averaging $17,019 per year), 10 teaching assistantships with full and partial tuition reimbursements (averaging $20,457 per year) were awarded; fellowships, scholarships/grants also available. *Faculty research:* Child development, early childhood education, family resource management and housing, life span studies. *Unit head:* Dr. Maurice M. MacDonald, Chair, 515-294-6316, Fax: 515-294-2502, E-mail: hdfs-grad-adm@iastate.edu. *Application contact:* Dr. Dee Draper, Director of Graduate Education, 515-294-4024, Fax: 515-294-2502, E-mail: hdfs-grad-adm@iastate.edu.

John Brown University, Graduate Studies Division of Counseling, Siloam Springs, AR 72761-2121. Offers community counseling (MS); marriage and family therapy (MS); school counseling (MS). *Accreditation:* NCATE. Part-time and evening/weekend programs available. *Faculty:* 4 full-time (1 woman), 9 part-time/adjunct (2 women). *Students:* 65 full-time (53 women), 110 part-time (78 women); includes 15 minority (5 African Americans, 6 American Indian/Alaska Native, 2 Asian Americans or Pacific Islanders, 2 Hispanic Americans), 1 international. Average age 34. 47 applicants, 100% accepted, 41 enrolled. In 2007, 9 degrees awarded. *Degree requirements:* For master's, practica or internships. *Entrance requirements:* For master's, GRE General Test, MAT, minimum GPA of 3.0. Additional exam requirements/recommendations for international students: Required—TOEFL (minimum score 550 paper-based; 173 computer-based). *Application deadline:* For fall admission, 8/11 priority date for domestic students; for spring admission, 1/12 for domestic students. Applications are processed on a rolling basis. Application fee: $35 ($100 for international students). Electronic applications accepted. *Financial support:* In 2007–08, 3 research assistantships (averaging $6,210 per year) were awarded; scholarships/grants, tuition waivers (full), and unspecified assistantships also available. Financial award application deadline: 3/1; financial award applicants required to submit FAFSA. *Unit head:* Dr. John V. Carmack, Program Director, 479-524-7460, Fax: 479-524-9548, E-mail: jcarmack@jbu.edu. *Application contact:* Chris Ray, Associate Director of Graduate Recruitment, 479-631-4665, E-mail: cray@jbu.edu.

Johnson Bible College, Department of Marriage and Family Therapy, Knoxville, TN 37998-1001. Offers marriage and family therapy/professional counseling (MA). *Faculty:* 3 full-time (0 women), 2 part-time/adjunct (0 women). *Students:* 25 (11 women); includes 2 minority (1 African American, 1 Asian American or Pacific Islander). Average age 30. 10 applicants, 80% accepted, 8 enrolled. In 2007, 10 degrees awarded. *Degree requirements:* For master's, variable foreign language requirement, comprehensive exam, thesis (for some programs), internship (500 client contact hours). *Entrance requirements:* For master's, interview, minimum GPA of 3.0, 20 credits of course work in psychology, 15 credits of course work in Bible. Additional exam requirements/recommendations for international students: Required—TOEFL. *Application deadline:* For fall admission, 3/1 for domestic students. Application fee: $50. *Financial support:* In 2007–08, 11 students received support. Scholarships/grants available. Financial award application deadline: 8/1; financial award applicants required to submit FAFSA. *Unit head:* Dr. Rick Townsend, Chair, 865-573-4517, Fax: 865-251-2435, E-mail: rtownsen@jbc.edu. *Application contact:* Anita Rankin, Office Coordinator, 865-251-3402, Fax: 865-251-2435.

Kansas State University, Graduate School, College of Human Ecology, Program in Human Ecology, Manhattan, KS 66506. Offers apparel and textiles (PhD); family life education and consultation (PhD); food service, hospitality management, and administrative dietetics (PhD); institutional management (PhD); lifespan and human development (PhD); marriage and family therapy (PhD). *Students:* 44 full-time (29 women), 23 part-time (12 women); includes 12 minority (9 African Americans, 1 American Indian/Alaska Native, 2 Asian Americans or Pacific Islanders), 14 international. 39 applicants, 54% accepted, 6 enrolled. In 2007, 14 degrees awarded. *Application deadline:* For fall admission, 2/1 priority date for domestic and international students; for spring admission, 8/1 priority date for domestic and international students. Application fee: $30 ($55 for international students). *Unit head:* Elizabeth McCullough, Director, 785-532-2284, Fax: 785-532-3796, E-mail: lizm@ksu.edu.

Kean University, College of Humanities and Social Sciences, Program in Marriage and Family Therapy, Union, NJ 07083. Offers Diploma. Part-time and evening/weekend programs available. *Faculty:* 20 full-time (13 women). *Students:* 13 full-time (10 women), 20 part-time (17 women); includes 3 African Americans, 1 Asian American or Pacific Islander, 6 Hispanic Americans, 2 international. Average age 29. 9 applicants, 67% accepted, 4 enrolled. In 2007, 5 degrees awarded. *Degree requirements:* For Diploma, comprehensive exam, thesis, internship, practicum. *Entrance requirements:* For degree, GRE General Test, 3 letters of recommendation, 12 credits in psychology, minimum 3.0 GPA, interview. *Application deadline:* For fall admission, 5/1 for domestic students; for spring admission, 11/1 for domestic students. Application fee: $60 ($150 for international students). Electronic applications accepted. *Expenses:* Tuition, state resident: full-time $9,384; part-time $391 per credit. Tuition, nonresident: full-time $12,720; part-time $530 per credit. Required fees: $2,382; $99 per credit. Part-time tuition and fees vary according to course load. *Financial support:* In 2007–08, 1 research assistantship with full tuition reimbursement (averaging $3,217 per year) was awarded; unspecified assistantships also available. *Unit head:* Dr. Muriel B. Singer, Program Coordinator, 908-737-4025, E-mail: msinger@kean.edu. *Application contact:* Joanne Morris, Director of Graduate Admissions, 908-737-3355, Fax: 908-737-3354, E-mail: grad-adm@kean.edu.

Kutztown University of Pennsylvania, College of Graduate Studies and Extended Learning, Program in Counseling Psychology, Kutztown, PA 19530-0730. Offers agency counseling (MA); marriage and family therapy (MA). Part-time and evening/weekend programs available. *Faculty:* 5 full-time (2 women). *Students:* 28 full-time (22 women), 21 part-time (18 women); includes 2 minority (1 African American, 1 Hispanic American). Average age 29. 45 applicants, 67% accepted, 14 enrolled. In 2007, 16 degrees awarded. *Degree requirements:* For master's, comprehensive exam, thesis optional. *Entrance requirements:* For master's, GRE General Test, interview. Additional exam requirements/recommendations for international students: Required—TOEFL. *Application deadline:* For fall admission, 3/1 for domestic students; for spring admission, 9/1 for domestic students. Application fee: $35. Electronic applications accepted. *Expenses:* Tuition, state resident: full-time $6,214; part-time $345 per credit. Tuition, nonresident: full-time $9,944; part-time $552 per credit. Required fees: $1,536; $78 per credit. $65 per semester. *Financial support:* Career-related internships or fieldwork, Federal Work-Study, scholarships/grants, and unspecified assistantships available. Financial award application deadline: 3/15; financial award applicants required to submit FAFSA. *Faculty research:* Addicted families. *Unit head:* Dr. Margaret Herrick, Chairperson, 610-683-4204, Fax: 610-683-1585, E-mail: herrick@kutztown.edu.

La Salle University, School of Arts and Sciences, Program in Psychology, Philadelphia, PA 19141-1199. Offers clinical psychology (Psy D); family psychology (Psy D); rehabilitation psychology (Psy D). Part-time and evening/weekend programs available. *Faculty:* 8 full-time (4 women), 5 part-time/adjunct (2 women). *Students:* 91 full-time (80 women), 18 part-time (11 women); includes 13 minority (6 African Americans, 4 Asian Americans or Pacific Islanders, 3 Hispanic Americans), 1 international. Average age 27. 111 applicants, 48% accepted, 23 enrolled. In 2007, 21 doctorates awarded. *Entrance requirements:* For doctorate, GRE, minimum GPA of 3.0. *Application deadline:* For fall admission, 3/1 for domestic students. Application fee: $35. *Expenses:* Contact institution. Tuition and fees vary according to program. *Financial support:* In 2007–08, 94 students received support. Scholarships/grants available. Financial award applicants required to submit FAFSA. *Faculty research:* Cognitive therapy, attribution theory, treatment of addiction. *Unit head:* Dr. Frank Gardner, Director, 215-951-5016, Fax: 215-951-1351.

Lewis & Clark College, Graduate School of Education and Counseling, Department of Counseling Psychology, Program in Marriage, Couple and Family Therapy, Portland, OR 97219-7899. Offers MA. Part-time and evening/weekend programs available. *Faculty:* 8 full-time (5 women), 18 part-time/adjunct (10 women). *Students:* 33 full-time (28 women), 9 part-time (8 women); includes 5 minority (2 African Americans, 3 Hispanic Americans). Average age 29. 45 applicants, 67% accepted, 19 enrolled. In 2007, 7 degrees awarded. *Entrance requirements:* For master's, GRE General Test, minimum undergraduate GPA of 2.75. Additional exam requirements/recommendations for international students: Required—TOEFL (minimum score 575 paper-based; 233 computer-based). *Application deadline:* For fall admission, 2/1 priority date for domestic and international students; for spring admission, 10/1 priority date for domestic and international students. Application fee: $50. Electronic applications accepted. *Expenses:* Tuition: Part-time $645 per credit. Tuition and fees vary according to campus/location. *Financial support:* In 2007–08, 39 students received support, including fellowships (averaging $22,000 per year); career-related internships or fieldwork, Federal Work-Study, institutionally sponsored loans, scholarships/grants, health care benefits, and tuition waivers (partial) also available. Support available to part-time students. Financial award applicants required to submit FAFSA. *Unit head:* Dr. Teresa McDowell, Program Coordinator, 503-768-6060, Fax: 503-768-6005, E-mail: teresamc@lclark.edu. *Application contact:* Becky Haas, Director of Admissions, 503-768-6200, Fax: 503-768-6205, E-mail: gseadmit@lclark.edu.

Loyola Marymount University, Graduate Division, Department of Marital and Family Therapy, Los Angeles, CA 90045-2659. Offers MA. Part-time programs available. *Faculty:* 2 full-time (both women), 9 part-time/adjunct (7 women). *Students:* 44 full-time (42 women); includes 12 minority (6 Asian Americans or Pacific Islanders, 6 Hispanic Americans), 3 international. Average age 32. 38 applicants, 53% accepted, 20 enrolled. In 2007, 29 degrees awarded. *Degree requirements:* For master's, thesis, project. *Entrance requirements:* For master's, MAT, interview, course work in art and psychology. Additional exam requirements/recommendations for international students: Required—TOEFL (minimum score 600 paper-based; 250 computer-based). *Application deadline:* Applications are processed on a rolling basis. Application fee: $50. Electronic applications accepted. *Expenses:* Contact institution. *Financial support:* In 2007–08, 37 students received support, including 1 research assistantship (averaging $12,370 per year); career-related internships or fieldwork and scholarships/grants also available. Support available to part-time students. Financial award application deadline: 6/1; financial award applicants required to submit FAFSA. *Unit head:* Dr. Debra Linesch, Chair, 310-338-7674, Fax: 310-338-4518, E-mail: dlinesch@lmu.edu.

Maryville University of Saint Louis, School of Health Professions, Program in Rehabilitation Counseling, St. Louis, MO 63141-7299. Offers marriage and family therapy (MARC); music therapy (MARC); substance abuse (MARC). *Accreditation:* CORE. Part-time and evening/weekend programs available. *Degree requirements:* For master's, internship, seminar. *Entrance requirements:* For master's, minimum cumulative GPA of 3.0, 2 letters of recommendation, interview. *Application deadline:* For fall admission, 1/15 for domestic students; for spring admission, 10/1 for domestic students. Application fee: $35. Electronic applications accepted. *Expenses:* Tuition: Full-time $18,600; part-time $580 per credit. Required fees: $75 per semester. *Financial support:* Career-related internships or fieldwork, Federal Work-Study, and campus employment available. Financial award application deadline: 7/31. *Unit head:* Barbara Parker, Director, 314-529-9437.

Mennonite Brethren Biblical Seminary, School of Theology, Program in Marriage, Family, and Child Counseling, Fresno, CA 93727-5097. Offers MAMFCC, Diploma. *Students:* Average age 36. 16 applicants, 88% accepted, 12 enrolled. In 2007, 4 degrees awarded. *Degree requirements:* For master's, thesis or alternative. *Entrance requirements:* For master's, GRE General Test, MAT. Additional exam requirements/recommendations for international students: Required—TOEFL (minimum score 550 paper-based; 213 computer-based). *Application deadline:* For fall admission, 8/1 for domestic students; for spring admission, 12/1 for domestic students. Application fee: $35. *Financial support:* Career-related internships or fieldwork, institutionally sponsored loans, scholarships/grants, and tuition waivers (partial) available. Support available to part-time students. Financial award application deadline: 5/1; financial award applicants required to submit FAFSA. *Unit head:* Delores Friesen, Head, 559-452-1711. *Application contact:* Andy Johnson, Director of Recruitment, 559-452-1714, Fax: 559-251-7212, E-mail: ajohnson@mbseminary.edu.

Mercy College, Division of Social and Behavioral Sciences, Program in Counseling, Dobbs Ferry, NY 10522-1189. Offers alcohol and substance abuse counseling (AC); counseling (MS); family counseling (AC); retirement counseling (AC). *Students:* 85 full-time (79 women), 213 part-time (174 women); includes 202 minority (94 African Americans, 1 Asian American or Pacific Islander, 107 Hispanic Americans). Average age 34. In 2007, 74 master's, 14 other advanced degrees awarded. *Entrance requirements:* For master's, interview, letters of recommendation, minimum undergraduate GPA of 3.0. *Expenses:* Tuition: Part-time $575 per credit. Required fees: $220 per semester. Tuition and fees vary according to program. *Unit head:* Dr. Fernando Cabrera, Program Director, 914-674-7334, E-mail: fcabrera@mercy.edu.

Mercy College, Division of Social and Behavioral Sciences, Program in Marriage and Family Therapy, Dobbs Ferry, NY 10522-1189. Offers MS. *Students:* 24 full-time (21 women), 25 part-time (22 women); includes 14 African Americans, 11 Hispanic Americans. Average age 34. In 2007, 1 degree awarded. *Expenses:* Tuition: Part-time $575 per credit. Required fees: $220 per semester. Tuition and fees vary according to program. *Unit head:* Barbara Melamed, Director, 914-674-7345, E-mail: bmelamed@mercy.edu.

Michigan State University, The Graduate School, College of Social Science, Department of Family and Child Ecology, East Lansing, MI 48824. Offers child development (MA); community services (MS); family and child ecology (PhD); family studies (MA); marriage and family therapy (MA); youth development (MA). *Accreditation:* AAMFT/COAMFTE (one or more programs are accredited). *Entrance requirements:* For master's, GRE General Test, minimum GPA of 3.0 in last 2 years of undergraduate course work, 3 letters of recommendation; for doctorate, GRE General Test, minimum GPA of 3.0, 3 letters of recommendation, background

Marriage and Family Therapy

Michigan State University (continued)

in behavioral sciences. Additional exam requirements/recommendations for international students: Required—TOEFL. Electronic applications accepted. *Expenses:* Tuition, state resident: part-time $379 per credit hour. Tuition, nonresident: part-time $800 per credit hour. Tuition and fees vary according to program.

Minnesota State University Mankato, College of Graduate Studies, College of Education, Department of Counseling and Student Personnel, Mankato, MN 56001. Offers college student affairs (MS); counselor education and supervision (Ed D); marriage and family counseling (Certificate); professional community counseling (MS); professional school counseling (MS). *Accreditation:* ACA (one or more programs are accredited); NCATE. *Students:* 65 full-time (55 women), 36 part-time (31 women). Average age 30. In 2007, 49 degrees awarded. *Degree requirements:* For master's, comprehensive exam, thesis or alternative. *Entrance requirements:* For master's, GRE General Test or MAT (if GPA is below 3.0 for last 2 years), minimum GPA of 3.0 during previous 2 years, 3 letters of reference. Additional exam requirements/recommendations for international students: Required—TOEFL. *Application deadline:* For fall admission, 3/15 priority date for domestic students; for spring admission, 11/20 for domestic students. Applications are processed on a rolling basis. Application fee: $40. Electronic applications accepted. *Financial support:* Research assistantships with full tuition reimbursements, teaching assistantships with full tuition reimbursements, career-related internships or fieldwork, Federal Work-Study, institutionally sponsored loans, and unspecified assistantships available. Support available to part-time students. Financial award application deadline: 3/15; financial award applicants required to submit FAFSA. *Unit head:* Dr. Richard Auger, Chairperson, 507-389-5658. *Application contact:* 507-389-2321, E-mail: grad@mnsu.edu.

Mississippi College, Graduate School, School of Education, Department of Psychology and Counseling, Clinton, MS 39058. Offers counseling (Ed S); marriage and family counseling (MS); mental health counseling (MS); school counseling (M Ed). Part-time programs available. *Faculty:* 8 full-time (3 women), 4 part-time/adjunct (0 women). *Students:* 27 full-time (24 women), 64 part-time (56 women); includes 35 minority (33 African Americans, 2 American Indian/Alaska Native), 5 international. Average age 31. In 2007, 31 degrees awarded. *Degree requirements:* For master's and Ed S, comprehensive exam, thesis optional. *Entrance requirements:* For master's, GRE or NTE. Additional exam requirements/recommendations for international students: Recommended—IELTS. *Application deadline:* Applications are processed on a rolling basis. Application fee: $25. Electronic applications accepted. *Expenses:* Tuition: Full-time $7,470; part-time $415 per hour. Required fees: $1,160 per term. Part-time tuition and fees vary according to course load and degree level. *Financial support:* Career-related internships or fieldwork, Federal Work-Study, and unspecified assistantships available. Support available to part-time students. Financial award applicants required to submit FAFSA. *Unit head:* Dr. Buddy Wagner, Interim Chair, 601-925-3354, E-mail: bwagner@mc.edu.

Montclair State University, The Office of Graduate Admissions and Support Services, College of Humanities and Social Sciences, Center for Child Advocacy, Montclair, NJ 07043-1624. Offers child advocacy (MA, Certificate); public child welfare (MA). *Faculty:* 9 full-time (8 women), 9 part-time/adjunct (3 women). *Students:* 10 full-time (9 women), 67 part-time (61 women); includes 29 minority (22 African Americans, 7 Hispanic Americans), 2 international. 67 applicants, 61% accepted, 38 enrolled. In 2007, 14 master's, 20 other advanced degrees awarded. Application fee: $60. *Financial support:* In 2007–08, 2 research assistantships (averaging $7,000 per year) were awarded. *Unit head:* Dr. Robert McCormick, Head, 973-655-4188.

Montclair State University, The Office of Graduate Admissions and Support Services, College of Humanities and Social Sciences, Department of Psychology, Montclair, NJ 07043-1624. Offers educational psychology (MA), including child/adolescent clinical psychology, clinical psychology for Spanish/English bilinguals; psychology (MA, Certificate), including industrial and organizational psychology (MA); school psychologist (Certificate). Part-time and evening/weekend programs available. *Faculty:* 27 full-time (11 women), 27 part-time/adjunct (20 women). *Students:* 27 full-time (21 women), 39 part-time (32 women); includes 26 minority (7 African Americans, 4 Asian Americans or Pacific Islanders, 15 Hispanic Americans), 3 international. 86 applicants, 21% accepted, 13 enrolled. In 2007, 22 master's, 11 other advanced degrees awarded. *Degree requirements:* For master's, comprehensive exam, thesis or alternative. *Entrance requirements:* For master's, GRE General Test, GRE Subject Test, previous course work in psychology, interview, 2 letters of recommendation. Additional exam requirements/recommendations for international students: Required—TOEFL (minimum score 83 computer-based). *Application deadline:* For fall admission, 2/1 for domestic and international students; for spring admission, 10/1 for domestic and international students. Applications are processed on a rolling basis. Application fee: $60. Electronic applications accepted. *Financial support:* In 2007–08, 10 research assistantships with full tuition reimbursements (averaging $7,000 per year) were awarded; Federal Work-Study, scholarships/grants, and unspecified assistantships also available. Support available to part-time students. Financial award application deadline: 3/1; financial award applicants required to submit FAFSA. *Faculty research:* Engaged learning, academic and civic development. Total annual research expenditures: $10,000. *Unit head:* Dr. Peter Vietze, Chairperson, 973-655-5201.

North Dakota State University, College of Graduate and Interdisciplinary Studies, College of Human Development and Education, Department of Child Development and Family Science, Fargo, ND 58105. Offers child development and family science (MS); couple and family therapy (MS); family financial planning (MS); gerontology (MS, PhD). *Accreditation:* AAMFT/COAMFTE. Part-time and evening/weekend programs available. Postbaccalaureate distance learning degree programs offered (no on-campus study). *Faculty:* 12 full-time (7 women). *Students:* 39 full-time (35 women), 14 part-time (13 women); includes 5 minority (1 African American, 2 American Indian/Alaska Native, 2 Asian Americans or Pacific Islanders), 1 international. 22 applicants, 64% accepted, 12 enrolled. In 2007, 6 degrees awarded. *Degree requirements:* For master's, thesis or alternative; for doctorate, thesis/dissertation. *Entrance requirements:* Additional exam requirements/recommendations for international students: Required—TOEFL (minimum score 525 paper-based; 197 computer-based; 71 iBT). *Application deadline:* For fall admission, 2/1 for domestic and international students; for spring admission, 10/1 for domestic and international students. Application fee: $45 ($60 for international students). *Expenses:* Tuition, state resident: full-time $5,376; part-time $224 per credit. Tuition, nonresident: full-time $14,354; part-time $598 per credit. Required fees: $962; $40 per credit. Part-time tuition and fees vary according to course load and reciprocity agreements. *Financial support:* In 2007–08, 17 students received support, including research assistantships with full tuition reimbursements available (averaging $3,000 per year), 17 teaching assistantships with full tuition reimbursements available (averaging $3,000 per year); career-related internships or fieldwork, Federal Work-Study, institutionally sponsored loans, and tuition waivers (full) also available. Financial award application deadline: 4/1. *Faculty research:* Family therapy, resilience, parenting, adolescent development, mental health. Total annual research expenditures:$333,582. *Unit head:* Dr. James Deal, Head, 701-231-7568, Fax: 701-231-9645, E-mail: jim_deal@ndsu.edu. *Application contact:* Theresa Anderson, Administrative Assistant, 701-231-8628, Fax: 701-231-9645, E-mail: theresa.anderson@ndsu.edu.

Northwestern University, The Graduate School, Program in Marital and Family Therapy, Evanston, IL 60208. Offers MS. *Accreditation:* AAMFT/COAMFTE. *Entrance requirements:* For master's, GRE General Test. *Faculty research:* Marital and family therapy training, gender, psychotherapy outcome, adolescents and pre-school children at risk, families.

Northwest Nazarene University, Graduate Studies, Program in Counselor Education, Nampa, ID 83686-5897. Offers community counseling (MS); marriage and family counseling (MS); school counseling (MS). *Faculty:* 3 full-time (1 woman), 10 part-time/adjunct (6 women). *Students:* 69 full-time (52 women), 12 part-time (8 women); includes 4 minority (1 American Indian/Alaska Native, 3 Hispanic Americans). In 2007, 19 degrees awarded. Application fee: $25. *Unit head:* Dr. Brenda Freeman, Chair, 208-467-8428, Fax: 208-467-8339.

Notre Dame de Namur University, Division of Academic Affairs, School of Sciences, Department of Clinical Psychology and Gerontology, Program in Marital and Family Therapy, Belmont, CA 94002-1908. Offers MAMFT. *Application contact:* Helen Valine, Director of Graduate Admissions, 650-508-3534, Fax: 650-508-3426, E-mail: grad.admit@ndnu.edu.

Nova Southeastern University, Graduate School of Humanities and Social Sciences, Department of Family Therapy, Doctor of Marriage and Family Therapy Program, Fort Lauderdale, FL 33314-7796. Offers DMFT. Part-time and evening/weekend programs available. *Faculty:* 10 full-time (5 women), 16 part-time/adjunct (13 women). *Students:* 9 full-time (all women), 5 part-time (4 women); includes 5 minority (4 African Americans, 1 Hispanic American), 1 international. 2 applicants, 50% accepted, 1 enrolled. In 2007, 2 degrees awarded. *Degree requirements:* For doctorate, thesis/dissertation or alternative, qualifying exams. *Entrance requirements:* For doctorate, minimum GPA of 3.0, interview, master's degree in related field. Additional exam requirements/recommendations for international students: Required—TOEFL. *Application deadline:* For fall admission, 7/1 priority date for domestic and international students; for winter admission, 11/1 priority date for domestic and international students; for spring admission, 3/1 priority date for domestic and international students. Applications are processed on a rolling basis. Application fee: $50. Electronic applications accepted. *Financial support:* In 2007–08, 1 research assistantship (averaging $10,000 per year) was awarded; career-related internships or fieldwork, Federal Work-Study, scholarships/grants, and unspecified assistantships also available. Financial award applicants required to submit CSS PROFILE. *Faculty research:* Diversity, family business, brief therapy, medical family therapy, human sexuality. *Application contact:* Marcia Arango, Student Recruitment Coordinator, 954-262-3006, Fax: 954-262-3968, E-mail: marango@nsu.nova.edu.

Nova Southeastern University, Graduate School of Humanities and Social Sciences, Department of Family Therapy, Master's Program in Family Therapy, Fort Lauderdale, FL 33314-7796. Offers family ministry (Certificate); family studies (Certificate); family systems healthcare (Certificate); family therapy (MS). *Accreditation:* AAMFT/COAMFTE (one or more programs are accredited). Part-time programs available. *Faculty:* 10 full-time (5 women), 16 part-time/adjunct (13 women). *Students:* 86 full-time (74 women), 32 part-time (30 women); includes 51 minority (25 African Americans, 7 Asian Americans or Pacific Islanders, 19 Hispanic Americans), 4 international. 85 applicants, 89% accepted, 48 enrolled. In 2007, 59 degrees awarded. *Degree requirements:* For master's, comprehensive exam. *Entrance requirements:* For master's, minimum GPA of 3.0, interview, writing sample. Additional exam requirements/recommendations for international students: Required—TOEFL. *Application deadline:* For fall admission, 6/1 priority date for domestic students; for winter admission, 11/1 priority date for domestic students; for spring admission, 3/1 priority date for domestic students. Applications are processed on a rolling basis. Application fee: $50. Electronic applications accepted. *Financial support:* Career-related internships or fieldwork, Federal Work-Study, and scholarships/grants available. Financial award application deadline: 4/1; financial award applicants required to submit CSS PROFILE. *Faculty research:* Cross-cultural counseling, family business, medical family therapy, brief therapy, diversity. *Application contact:* Marcia Arango, Student Recruitment Coordinator, 954-262-3006, Fax: 954-262-3968, E-mail: marango@nsu.nova.edu.

See Close-Up on page 953.

Nova Southeastern University, Graduate School of Humanities and Social Sciences, Department of Family Therapy, PhD Program in Family Therapy, Fort Lauderdale, FL 33314-7796. Offers PhD. *Accreditation:* AAMFT/COAMFTE. Part-time and evening/weekend programs available. *Faculty:* 9 full-time (5 women), 16 part-time/adjunct (13 women). *Students:* 58 full-time (51 women), 22 part-time (17 women); includes 34 minority (19 African Americans, 1 Asian American or Pacific Islander, 14 Hispanic Americans), 6 international. 17 applicants, 100% accepted, 13 enrolled. In 2007, 9 degrees awarded. *Degree requirements:* For doctorate, thesis/dissertation, qualifying exam. *Entrance requirements:* For doctorate, master's degree in related field, minimum GPA of 3.0, interview, writing sample. Additional exam requirements/recommendations for international students: Required—TOEFL. *Application deadline:* For fall admission, 7/1 priority date for domestic and international students; for winter admission, 11/1 priority date for domestic and international students; for spring admission, 3/1 priority date for domestic and international students. Applications are processed on a rolling basis. Application fee: $50. Electronic applications accepted. *Financial support:* In 2007–08, 63 students received support, including 2 research assistantships (averaging $10,000 per year); career-related internships or fieldwork, Federal Work-Study, scholarships/grants, and unspecified assistantships also available. Financial award application deadline: 4/1. *Faculty research:* Medical family therapy, brief therapy, family business, diversity, human sexuality and therapy. *Application contact:* Marcia Arango, Student Recruitment Coordinator, 954-262-3006, Fax: 954-262-3968, E-mail: marango@nsu.nova.edu.

See Close-Up on page 953.

Oral Roberts University, School of Theology and Missions, Tulsa, OK 74171-0001. Offers biblical literature (MA), including advanced languages, Judaic-Christian studies; Christian counseling (MA), including marriage and family therapy; Christian education (MA); divinity (M Div); missions (MA); practical theology (MA); theological/historical studies (MA); theology (D Min). *Accreditation:* ATS; NASM. Part-time programs available. Postbaccalaureate distance learning degree programs offered (minimal on-campus study). *Faculty:* 17 full-time (2 women). *Students:* 371 full-time (156 women), 110 part-time (65 women); includes 177 minority (127 African Americans, 5 American Indian/Alaska Native, 20 Asian Americans or Pacific Islanders, 25 Hispanic Americans), 82 international. Average age 36. 159 applicants, 95% accepted, 124 enrolled. In 2007, 38 first professional degrees, 52 master's, 10 doctorates awarded. *Degree requirements:* For master's, thesis (for some programs), practicum/internship; for doctorate, thesis/dissertation, applied research project; for M Div, one foreign language, field experience. *Entrance requirements:* For M Div and master's, GRE General Test or MAT, minimum GPA of 2.5; for doctorate, M Div, minimum GPA of 3.0, 3 years of full-time ministry experience. Additional exam requirements/recommendations for international students: Required—TOEFL (minimum score 500 paper-based; 213 computer-based; 79 iBT). *Application deadline:* For fall admission, 7/1 priority date for domestic and international students; for spring admission, 12/1 priority date for domestic students, 10/1 priority date for international students. Applications are processed on a rolling basis. Application fee: $35. Electronic applications accepted. *Expenses:* Tuition: Part-time $450 per hour. Required fees: $125 per semester. Tuition and fees vary according to class time, degree level and program. *Financial support:* In 2007–08, teaching assistantships (averaging $3,600 per year); scholarships/grants and employment assistantships also available. Financial award application deadline: 6/1; financial award applicants required to submit FAFSA. *Unit head:* Dr. Thomson K. Mathew, Dean, 918-495-7016, Fax: 918-495-6259, E-mail: tmathew@oru.edu. *Application contact:* Debra E. Watkins, Graduate Theology Representative, 918-495-6618, Fax: 918-495-7965, E-mail: owatkins@oru.edu.

Ottawa University, Graduate Studies-Arizona, Program in Professional Counseling, Ottawa, KS 66067-3399. Offers Christian counseling (MA); expressive arts therapy (MA); marriage and family therapy (MA); treatment of trauma, abuse and deprivation (MA). Programs offered in Mesa, Phoenix, Tempe and West Valley, AZ. Part-time and evening/weekend programs available. Postbaccalaureate distance learning degree programs offered. *Degree requirements:* For master's, comprehensive exam, thesis or alternative, field experience, practicum. *Entrance requirements:* For master's, minimum undergraduate GPA of 3.0; course work in theories of personality, abnormal psychology, and human growth and development. Additional exam requirements/recommendations for international students: Required—TOEFL (minimum score 550 paper-based; 213 computer-based).

Our Lady of Holy Cross College, Program in Education and Counseling, New Orleans, LA 70131-7399. Offers administration and supervision (M Ed); curriculum and instruction (M Ed); marriage and family counseling (MA); school counseling (M Ed, MA). *Accreditation:* ACA; NCATE. Part-time and evening/weekend programs available. *Degree requirements:* For master's, thesis. *Entrance requirements:* For master's, GRE General Test, minimum GPA of 2.7.

Our Lady of the Lake University of San Antonio, School of Education and Clinical Studies, Program in Counseling Psychology, San Antonio, TX 78207-4689. Offers counseling psychology (MS, Psy D); marriage and family therapy (MS); school psychology (MS). *Accreditation:* APA (one or more programs are accredited). Part-time and evening/weekend programs available. *Degree requirements:* For master's, comprehensive exam, thesis optional, practicum; for doctorate, thesis/dissertation, internship, qualifying exam. *Entrance requirements:* For master's and doctorate, GRE General Test or MAT, interview. Additional exam requirements/recommendations for international students: Required—TOEFL. Electronic applications accepted. *Faculty research:* Marriage and family therapy, supervision, cross-cultural counseling, violence.

Pacific Lutheran University, Division of Graduate Studies, Division of Social Sciences, Program in Marriage and Family Therapy, Tacoma, WA 98447. Offers MA. *Accreditation:* AAMFT/COAMFTE. *Faculty:* 4 full-time (0 women), 3 part-time/adjunct (all women). *Students:* 38 full-time (31 women), 9 part-time (6 women); includes 7 minority (2 African Americans, 4 Asian Americans or Pacific Islanders, 1 Hispanic American), 1 international. Average age 28. 59 applicants, 58% accepted, 20 enrolled. In 2007, 16 degrees awarded. *Degree requirements:* For master's, thesis optional, clinical competency. *Entrance requirements:* For master's, GRE, interview (selected applicants). Additional exam requirements/recommendations for international students: Required—TOEFL (minimum score 550 paper-based; 213 computer-based). *Application deadline:* For fall admission, 1/31 priority date for domestic and international students; for spring admission, 3/1 priority date for domestic students. Application fee: $40. Electronic applications accepted. *Expenses:* Tuition: Full-time $18,816; part-time $784 per semester hour. Tuition and fees vary according to course load and program. *Financial support:* In 2007–08, 39 students received support, including 13 fellowships (averaging $1,870 per year); Federal Work-Study, scholarships/grants, and unspecified assistantships also available. Financial award application deadline: 3/1; financial award applicants required to submit FAFSA. *Unit head:* Dr. Charles York, Chair, 253-535-7747, Fax: 253-536-5139, E-mail: yorkcd@plu.edu. *Application contact:* Linda DuBay, Senior Office Assistant, 253-535-7151, Fax: 253-536-5136, E-mail: admissions@plu.edu.

Pacific Oaks College, Graduate School, Program in Marriage and Family Therapy, Pasadena, CA 91103. Offers marriage, family and child counseling (MA). Part-time and evening/weekend programs available. *Degree requirements:* For master's, thesis. *Entrance requirements:* For master's, interview. Additional exam requirements/recommendations for international students: Required—TOEFL (minimum score 550 paper-based; 213 computer-based). *Faculty research:* Family systems, cross-cultural development, therapeutic intervention and Latino families, battered women.

Palm Beach Atlantic University, School of Education and Behavioral Studies, West Palm Beach, FL 33416-4708. Offers counseling psychology (MSCP), including addictions/mental health, marriage and family therapy, mental health counseling, school guidance counseling; elementary education (M Ed). Part-time and evening/weekend programs available. *Faculty:* 11 full-time (5 women), 10 part-time/adjunct (5 women). *Students:* 223 full-time (178 women), 65 part-time (48 women); includes 114 minority (62 African Americans, 5 Asian Americans or Pacific Islanders, 47 Hispanic Americans), 9 international. Average age 36. 145 applicants, 60% accepted, 73 enrolled. In 2007, 56 degrees awarded. *Entrance requirements:* For master's, GRE General Test, minimum GPA of 3.0 in last 60 hours of course work. Additional exam requirements/recommendations for international students: Required—TOEFL (minimum score 550 paper-based; 213 computer-based). *Application deadline:* For fall admission, 7/15 priority date for domestic students; for spring admission, 11/15 priority date for domestic students. Applications are processed on a rolling basis. Application fee: $45. Electronic applications accepted. *Expenses:* Tuition: Full-time $7,560; part-time $420 per credit. Required fees: $260; $95 per semester. Tuition and fees vary according to degree level, campus/location and program. *Financial support:* Career-related internships or fieldwork and unspecified assistantships available. Support available to part-time students. Financial award applicants required to submit FAFSA. *Unit head:* Dr. Melise Bunker, Dean, 561-803-2350, Fax: 561-803-2186, E-mail: melise_bunker@pba.edu. *Application contact:* Myra Santiago, Assistant Director of Graduate and Evening Admissions, 888-468-6722, Fax: 561-803-2115, E-mail: grad@pba.edu.

Phillips Graduate Institute, Program in Clinical Family Psychology and Organizational Consulting, Encino, CA 91316-1509. Offers clinical psychology (Psy D); organizational consulting (Psy D). Evening/weekend programs available. *Faculty:* 13 full-time, 30 part-time/adjunct. *Students:* 39 full-time (32 women), 30 part-time (22 women); includes 19 minority (4 African Americans, 1 American Indian/Alaska Native, 2 Asian Americans or Pacific Islanders, 12 Hispanic Americans). *Degree requirements:* For doctorate, thesis/dissertation. *Entrance requirements:* For doctorate, minimum GPA of 3.0, interview. *Application deadline:* For fall admission, 6/1 priority date for domestic students; for spring admission, 12/1 priority date for domestic students. Applications are processed on a rolling basis. Application fee: $75. *Expenses:* Tuition: Part-time $820 per unit. Required fees: $300 per semester. Tuition and fees vary according to course load, degree level and program. *Financial support:* Tuition waivers (full and partial) available. *Application contact:* Kim Bell, Assistant Director of Admission, 818-386-5639, Fax: 818-386-5699, E-mail: admit@pgi.edu.

Phillips Graduate Institute, Programs in Marriage and Family Therapy, School Counseling and School Psychology, Encino, CA 91316-1509. Offers marital and family therapy (MA); organizational consulting (MA); school counseling (MA). Evening/weekend programs available. *Faculty:* 13 full-time, 30 part-time/adjunct. *Students:* 175 full-time (143 women), 63 part-time (56 women); includes 64 minority (21 African Americans, 1 American Indian/Alaska Native, 26 Asian Americans or Pacific Islanders, 16 Hispanic Americans), 1 international. Average age 39. In 2007, 122 degrees awarded. *Degree requirements:* For master's, comprehensive exam, thesis. *Entrance requirements:* For master's, minimum GPA of 2.5. *Application deadline:* For fall admission, 8/15 priority date for domestic students; for spring admission, 12/15 for domestic students. Applications are processed on a rolling basis. Application fee: $75. *Expenses:* Tuition: Part-time $820 per unit. Required fees: $300 per semester. Tuition and fees vary according to course load, degree level and program. *Financial support:* Federal Work-Study and tuition waivers (full and partial) available. Financial award application deadline: 8/15; financial award applicants required to submit FAFSA. *Faculty research:* Integration of interpersonal psychological theory, systems approach, firsthand experiential learning. *Application contact:* Kim Bell, Assistant Director of Admission, 818-386-5639, Fax: 818-386-5699, E-mail: admit@pgi.edu.

Purdue University, Graduate School, College of Consumer and Family Sciences, Department of Child Development and Family Studies, West Lafayette, IN 47907. Offers developmental studies (MS, PhD); family studies (MS, PhD); marriage and family therapy (MS, PhD). *Accreditation:* AAMFT/COAMFTE (one or more programs are accredited). Part-time programs available. Terminal master's awarded for partial completion of doctoral program. *Degree requirements:* For master's, thesis; for doctorate, thesis/dissertation. *Entrance requirements:* For master's and doctorate, GRE General Test. Additional exam requirements/recommendations for international students: Required—TWE. Electronic applications accepted. *Faculty research:* Inclusion of children with special needs, families as learning environments, relationships in child care, work-family relations, AIDS prevention.

Purdue University Calumet, Graduate School, School of Liberal Arts and Sciences, Department of Behavioral Sciences, Hammond, IN 46323-2094. Offers marriage and family therapy (MS). *Accreditation:* AAMFT/COAMFTE. Part-time programs available. *Degree requirements:* For master's, thesis. *Entrance requirements:* For master's, GRE, interview. Additional exam requirements/recommendations for international students: Required—TOEFL. *Faculty research:* Substance abuse, sexual abuse, couple therapy, professional issues, adolescent therapy.

Reformed Theological Seminary–Jackson Campus, Graduate and Professional Programs, Jackson, MS 39209-3099. Offers Bible, theology, and missions (Certificate); biblical studies (MA); Christian education (M Div, MA); counseling (M Div); divinity (M Div, Diploma); marriage and family therapy (MA); ministry (D Min); missions (M Div, MA, D Min); New Testament (Th M); Old Testament (Th M); theological studies (MA); theology (Th M); M Div/MA. *Accreditation:* AAMFT/COAMFTE (one or more programs are accredited); ATS (one or more programs are accredited). *Degree requirements:* For master's, thesis (for some programs), fieldwork; for doctorate, 2 foreign languages, thesis/dissertation; for M Div, 2 foreign languages, thesis/dissertation (for some programs). *Entrance requirements:* For M Div and master's, minimum GPA of 2.6; for doctorate, minimum GPA of 3.0. Additional exam requirements/recommendations for international students: Required—TOEFL.

Regis University, College for Professional Studies, Graduate Counseling Program, Denver, CO 80221-1099. Offers community counseling (MAC); counseling children and adolescents (Post-Graduate Certificate); marriage and family therapy (Post-Graduate Certificate). Program offered in Henderson and Las Vegas (Summerlin), NV. *Accreditation:* ACA. Part-time and evening/weekend programs available. *Faculty:* 18. *Students:* 231 (189 women). In 2007, 50 degrees awarded. *Degree requirements:* For master's, internships, practicum. *Entrance requirements:* For master's, 2 admissions essays, interview, 2 recommendations, resumé, criminal background check. Additional exam requirements/recommendations for international students: Required—TOEFL (minimum score 213 computer-based), TWE (minimum score 5). *Application deadline:* For fall admission, 8/6 for domestic students, 7/6 for international students; for spring admission, 12/14 for domestic students, 11/14 for international students. Application fee: $75. *Expenses:* Contact institution. *Faculty research:* Group Development, Counselor Education, Counsel and Therapy, Influence of Technology on Psychology, Dream finding groups, Adult Development, Depression. *Unit head:* Dr. Jolynne Reynolds, Head, 303-458-4100.

St. Cloud State University, School of Graduate Studies, College of Education, Department of Educational Leadership and Community Psychology, Program in Marriage and Family Therapy, St. Cloud, MN 56301-4498. Offers MS. *Faculty:* 2 full-time (1 woman). *Students:* 20 full-time (17 women), 8 part-time (7 women); includes 2 minority (1 African American, 1 Asian American or Pacific Islander), 2 international. 29 applicants, 69% accepted. In 2007, 4 degrees awarded. *Entrance requirements:* Additional exam requirements/recommendations for international students: Required—MELAB; Recommended—TOEFL (minimum score 550 paper-based; 213 computer-based), IELTS (minimum score 7). Electronic applications accepted. *Expenses:* Tuition, state resident: part-time $267 per credit. Tuition, nonresident: part-time $418 per credit. Required fees: $28 per credit. *Financial support:* Federal Work-Study, scholarships/grants, and unspecified assistantships available. *Unit head:* Dr. Manijeh Daneshpour, Coordinator, 320-308-0121.

Saint Joseph College, Graduate Division, Department of Marriage and Family Therapy, West Hartford, CT 06117-2700. Offers MA, Certificate. *Accreditation:* AAMFT/COAMFTE. Part-time and evening/weekend programs available. *Degree requirements:* For master's, comprehensive exam, thesis or alternative. *Entrance requirements:* For master's, GRE or MAT, 2 letters of recommendation, interview. Electronic applications accepted. *Faculty research:* Communication in organizations, adoptive family development, therapeutic services for adoptive families.

Saint Louis University, Graduate School, College of Education and Public Service and Graduate School, Department of Counseling and Family Therapy, St. Louis, MO 63103-2097. Offers counseling and family therapy (PhD); human development counseling (MA); marriage and family therapy (Certificate); school counseling (MA, MA-R). *Accreditation:* NCATE.Part-time programs available. *Faculty:* 4 full-time (2 women), 4 part-time/adjunct (all women). *Students:* 61 full-time (56 women), 33 part-time (25 women); includes 16 minority (9 African Americans, 1 American Indian/Alaska Native, 4 Asian Americans or Pacific Islanders, 2 Hispanic Americans), 1 international. Average age 33. 60 applicants, 38% accepted, 14 enrolled. In 2007, 10 master's, 3 doctorates awarded. *Degree requirements:* For master's, comprehensive exam, thesis (for some programs); for doctorate, comprehensive exam, thesis/dissertation, preliminary oral and written exams. *Entrance requirements:* For master's and doctorate, GRE General Test, letters of recommendation, resumé, transcripts, goal statement. Additional exam requirements/recommendations for international students: Required—TOEFL (minimum score 550 paper-based; 213 computer-based). *Application deadline:* For fall admission, 1/15 for domestic and international students. Applications are processed on a rolling basis. Application fee: $40. Electronic applications accepted. *Expenses:* Tuition: Part-time $845 per credit hour. Required fees: $105 per semester. *Financial support:* In 2007–08, 32 students received support, including 4 research assistantships with full tuition reimbursements available (averaging $13,000 per year), 2 teaching assistantships with full tuition reimbursements available (averaging $13,000 per year); Federal Work-Study, scholarships/grants, traineeships, health care benefits, tuition waivers (partial), and unspecified assistantships also available. Support available to part-time students. Financial award application deadline: 2/1; financial award applicants required to submit FAFSA. *Faculty research:* Medical family therapy/collaborative health care multi-cultural counseling, mental health needs of diverse, minority, or Immigrant/refugee populations, divorce, aging families. *Unit head:* Dr. Craig W. Smith, Chairperson, 314-997-2507, Fax: 314-977-3214, E-mail: csmit112@slu.edu. *Application contact:* Gary U. Behrman, Associate Dean of Graduate School Admissions, 314-977-3827, Fax: 314-977-3943, E-mail: behrmang@slu.edu.

Saint Mary's College of California, Kalmanovitz School of Education, Program in Counseling, Moraga, CA 94575. Offers general counseling (MA); marital and family therapy (MA); school counseling (MA). Part-time and evening/weekend programs available. *Faculty:* 4 full-time (3 women), 25 part-time/adjunct (20 women). *Students:* 62 full-time (49 women), 119 part-time (95 women); includes 55 minority (13 African Americans, 1 American Indian/Alaska Native, 14 Asian Americans or Pacific Islanders, 27 Hispanic Americans), 9 international. Average age 35. 69 applicants, 63 enrolled. In 2007, 31 degrees awarded. *Degree requirements:* For master's, thesis or alternative. *Entrance requirements:* For master's, interview, minimum GPA of 3.0. *Application deadline:* Applications are processed on a rolling basis. Application fee: $50. *Financial support:* In 2007–08, 5 students received support. Career-related internships or fieldwork and Federal Work-Study available. Support available to part-time students. Financial award application deadline: 2/15; financial award applicants required to submit FAFSA. *Faculty research:* Counselor training effectiveness, multicultural development, empathy, the interface of spirituality and psychotherapy, gender issues. *Unit head:* Dr. Laura Heid, Director, 925-631-4293, Fax: 925-376-8379, E-mail: lheid@stmarys.ca.edu.

St. Mary's University, Graduate School, Department of Counseling and Human Services, Program in Marriage and Family Therapy, San Antonio, TX 78228-8507. Offers MA, PhD. *Students:* 36 full-time (26 women), 30 part-time (23 women); includes 19 minority (2 African Americans, 2 Asian Americans or Pacific Islanders, 15 Hispanic Americans), 7 international. Average age 33. In 2007, 17 master's, 2 doctorates awarded. *Degree requirements:* For master's, thesis optional, internship; for doctorate, thesis/dissertation, internship. *Entrance requirements:* For master's, GRE; for doctorate, GRE, master's degree, work experience, letters of recommendation. Additional exam requirements/recommendations for international students: Required—TOEFL (minimum score 550 paper-based; 213 computer-based). Application fee: $0. *Financial support:* Career-related internships or fieldwork, Federal Work-Study, institutionally sponsored loans, scholarships/grants, health care benefits, and unspecified assistantships available. Financial award application deadline: 3/31; financial award applicants required to submit FAFSA. *Unit head:* Dr. Becky Davenport, Director, 210-436-3226, Fax: 210-431-6886, E-mail: bdavenport@stmarytx.edu.

Saint Mary's University of Minnesota, Schools of Graduate and Professional Programs, Graduate School of Health and Human Services, Marriage and Family Therapy Program, Winona, MN 55987-1399. Offers MA, Certificate. *Unit head:* Dr. Steve W. Peltier, Director, 612-728-5140, Fax: 612-728-5121, E-mail: speltier@smumn.edu.

Saint Paul University, Faculty of Human Sciences, Program in Counseling and Spirituality, Ottawa, ON K1S 1C4, Canada. Offers individual or marital/couple counseling (MA); spiritual care (MA). Part-time programs available. *Students:* 57 applicants, 72% accepted, 32 enrolled. In 2007, 18 degrees awarded. *Degree requirements:* For master's, research project or thesis. *Entrance requirements:* For master's, honors BA in human sciences, minimum B average, 12 theology credits. *Application deadline:* For fall admission, 3/31 priority date for domestic and international students; for spring admission, 5/1 priority date for domestic students.

Marriage and Family Therapy

Saint Paul University (continued)

Application fee: $60. *Unit head:* Manal Guirguis-Younger, Head, 613-236-1393 Ext. 2390, E-mail: jlowe@ustpaul.ca. *Application contact:* Diane Boudreault, Head, 613-236-1393 Ext. 2292, E-mail: dboudreault@ustpaul.ca.

St. Thomas University, Biscayne College, Department of Social Sciences and Counseling, Program in Marriage and Family Therapy, Miami Gardens, FL 33054-6459. Offers MS, Post-Master's Certificate. Part-time and evening/weekend programs available. *Students:* 11 full-time (8 women), 35 part-time (27 women); includes 38 minority (26 African Americans, 1 Asian American or Pacific Islander, 11 Hispanic Americans), 5 international. Average age 37. In 2007, 15 degrees awarded. *Degree requirements:* For master's, comprehensive exam. *Entrance requirements:* For master's, interview, minimum GPA of 3.0 or GRE. Additional exam requirements/recommendations for international students: Required—TOEFL. *Application deadline:* For fall admission, 6/15 priority date for domestic students; for spring admission, 11/15 for domestic students. Applications are processed on a rolling basis. Application fee: $40. Electronic applications accepted. *Financial support:* Unspecified assistantships available. Support available to part-time students. Financial award application deadline: 4/15; financial award applicants required to submit FAFSA. *Unit head:* Dr. Barbara Buzzi, Coordinator, 305-628-6584, Fax: 305-628-6510, E-mail: bbuzzi@stu.edu. *Application contact:* Marilyn Carballosa, Assistant Director of Admissions, 305-628-6546, Fax: 305-628-6591, E-mail: graduate@stu.edu.

San Francisco State University, Division of Graduate Studies, College of Health and Human Services, Department of Counseling, San Francisco, CA 94132-1722. Offers counseling (MS); marriage, family, and child counseling (MSC); rehabilitation counseling (MS). *Accreditation:* ACA (one or more programs are accredited). Part-time programs available. *Application deadline:* Applications are processed on a rolling basis. *Unit head:* Dr. Robert Chope, Chair, 415-338-2005. *Application contact:* Couryll Pineda, Academic Office Coordinator, 415-338-2005, E-mail: counsel@sfsu.edu.

Saybrook Graduate School and Research Center, Programs in Psychology, Human Science and Organizational Systems, San Francisco, CA 94111-1920. Offers clinical psychology (PhD); creativity studies (MA); human science (MA, PhD), including consciousness and spirituality, individualized (PhD), integrative health studies, organizational systems, social transformation; marriage and family therapy (MA); organizational systems (MA, PhD), including individualized (PhD), organizational systems; psychology (MA, PhD), including consciousness and spirituality, humanistic and transpersonal psychology, individualized (PhD), integrative health studies, licensure track (MA), organizational systems, social transformation. Postbaccalaureate distance learning degree programs offered (minimal on-campus study). Terminal master's awarded for partial completion of doctoral program. *Degree requirements:* For master's, thesis or alternative; for doctorate, thesis/dissertation. Electronic applications accepted. *Faculty research:* Humanistic theory, health studies, organizational systems, consciousness and spirituality, social transformation.

Seattle Pacific University, Graduate School, School of Psychology, Family and Community, Program in Marriage and Family Therapy, Seattle, WA 98119-1997. Offers MS. *Accreditation:* AAMFT/COAMFTE. Part-time programs available. *Students:* 54 full-time (40 women), 21 part-time (14 women); includes 10 minority (1 African American, 1 American Indian/Alaska Native, 6 Asian Americans or Pacific Islanders, 2 Hispanic Americans), 3 international. 107 applicants, 28% accepted, 30 enrolled. In 2007, 28 degrees awarded. *Degree requirements:* For master's, thesis optional, internship. *Entrance requirements:* For master's, GRE General Test or MAT, interview. *Application deadline:* For fall admission, 3/1 for domestic students. Application fee: $50. *Expenses: Contact institution.* Tuition and fees vary according to program. *Financial support:* Career-related internships or fieldwork and unspecified assistantships available. Financial award applicants required to submit FAFSA. *Faculty research:* Roles of therapists, models of collaboration, medical and mental health theories of marriage and family therapy. *Unit head:* Dr. Claudia Grauf-Grounds, Chair, 206-281-2632, Fax: 206-281-2695, E-mail: claudiagg@spu.edu. *Application contact:* Amanda Smith, Program Coordinator, 206-281-2762, E-mail: amanda@spu.edu.

Seton Hall University, College of Education and Human Services, Department of Professional Psychology and Family Therapy, Program in Marriage and Family Therapy, South Orange, NJ 07079-2697. Offers MS, PhD, Ed S. *Accreditation:* AAMFT/COAMFTE. *Faculty:* 5 full-time (3 women). *Students:* 18 full-time (16 women), 30 part-time (24 women); includes 2 African Americans, 3 Hispanic Americans, 3 international. Average age 35. 16 applicants, 94% accepted, 4 enrolled. In 2007, 3 doctorates, 5 other advanced degrees awarded. *Degree requirements:* For master's, comprehensive exam, case study; for Ed S, comprehensive exam, internship. *Entrance requirements:* For master's, GRE; for Ed S, GRE or MAT, interview. *Application deadline:* For fall admission, 2/15 for domestic students. Application fee: $50. *Financial support:* In 2007–08, 1 research assistantship with full tuition reimbursement (averaging $4,500 per year), 1 teaching assistantship with full tuition reimbursement (averaging $4,500 per year) were awarded. Financial award application deadline: 2/1. *Faculty research:* Family systems. *Unit head:* Dr. Robert Massey, Director, 973-761-9591, E-mail: masseyro@shu.edu. *Application contact:* Information Contact, 973-761-9451.

Seton Hill University, Program in Marriage and Family Therapy, Greensburg, PA 15601. Offers MA. *Accreditation:* AAMFT/COAMFTE. Part-time and evening/weekend programs available. *Faculty:* 3 full-time (2 women), 4 part-time/adjunct (3 women). *Students:* 28 full-time (26 women), 15 part-time (13 women); includes 5 minority (4 African Americans, 1 Asian American or Pacific Islander), 2 international. Average age 31. 40 applicants, 63% accepted, 16 enrolled. In 2007, 13 degrees awarded. *Entrance requirements:* For master's, minimum GPA of 3.0, 12 credits of course work in psychology. Additional exam requirements/recommendations for international students: Required—TOEFL (minimum score 600 paper-based; 250 computer-based). *Application deadline:* For fall admission, 8/15 priority date for domestic students; for spring admission, 12/15 for domestic students. Applications are processed on a rolling basis. Application fee: $35. Electronic applications accepted. *Expenses:* Tuition: Full-time $17,955; part-time $665 per credit. Tuition and fees vary according to program. *Financial support:* In 2007–08, 30 students received support. Scholarships/grants, tuition waivers (partial), and unspecified assistantships available. Support available to part-time students. Financial award application deadline: 8/15; financial award applicants required to submit FAFSA. *Faculty research:* Social cognition, feminist psychology, psychology of gender, developmental psychology, systemic theory. *Unit head:* Dr. Susan Cooley, Director, 724-838-7816, E-mail: cooley@setonhill.edu. *Application contact:* Dane Zimmer, Advisor, 724-838-4209, Fax: 724-830-1891, E-mail: zimmer@setonhill.edu.

Shippensburg University of Pennsylvania, School of Graduate Studies, College of Education and Human Services, Department of Counseling, Shippensburg, PA 17257-2299. Offers Adlerian studies (Certificate); advanced study in counseling (Certificate); counseling (MS); couple and family counseling (Certificate); guidance and counseling (M Ed). *Accreditation:* ACA (one or more programs are accredited); NCATE. Part-time and evening/weekend programs available. *Faculty:* 9 full-time (4 women), 1 (woman) part-time/adjunct. *Students:* 86 full-time (70 women), 100 part-time (80 women); includes 21 minority (16 African Americans, 3 Asian Americans or Pacific Islanders, 2 Hispanic Americans), 3 international. Average age 29. 156 applicants, 42% accepted, 49 enrolled. In 2007, 58 degrees awarded. *Degree requirements:* For master's, fieldwork, research project, internship, candidacy. *Entrance requirements:* For master's, minimum GPA of 2.75 (3.0 for M Ed), interview, resumé, 3 letters of reference, 1 year of relevant work experience, MAT or GRE if GPA less than 2.75. Additional exam requirements/recommendations for international students: Required—TOEFL (minimum score 560 paper-based; 220 computer-based). *Application deadline:* For fall admission, 3/1 for international students; for spring admission, 7/1 for international students. Applications are processed on a rolling basis. Application fee: $30. Electronic applications accepted. *Expenses:* Tuition, state resident: part-time $345 per credit. Tuition, nonresident: part-time $552 per credit. Required fees: $28 per credit. Tuition and fees vary according to course load. *Financial support:* In 2007–08, 47 research assistantships with full tuition reimbursements (averaging $3,575 per year) were awarded; career-related internships or fieldwork, scholarships/grants, and unspecified assistantships also available. Support available to part-time students. Financial award application deadline: 3/1; financial award applicants required to submit FAFSA. *Unit head:* Dr. Jan Arminio, Chairperson, 717-477-1668, Fax: 717-477-4016, E-mail: jlarmi@ship.edu. *Application contact:* Renee Payne, Associate Dean of Graduate Admissions, 717-477-1231, Fax: 717-477-4016, E-mail: rmpayn@ship.edu.

Sioux Falls Seminary, Graduate and Professional Programs, Program in Marriage and Family Therapy, Sioux Falls, SD 57105-1599. Offers MA. *Students:* 12 full-time (9 women). *Entrance requirements:* For master's, minimum GPA of 3.0. *Application deadline:* For fall admission, 8/1 priority date for domestic students; for spring admission, 1/1 priority date for domestic students. Applications are processed on a rolling basis. Application fee: $35. *Financial support:* Scholarships/grants available. *Unit head:* Dr. Del Donaldson, Professor of Marriage and Family Therapy, 605-336-6588, Fax: 605-335-9090. *Application contact:* Bryce H. Eben, Director of Enrollment Development, 605-336-6588, Fax: 605-335-9090, E-mail: beben@sfseminary.edu.

Sonoma State University, School of Social Sciences, Department of Counseling, Rohnert Park, CA 94928-3609. Offers counseling (MA); marriage, family, and child counseling (MA); pupil personnel services (MA). *Accreditation:* ACA. Part-time programs available. *Faculty:* 6 full-time (4 women), 3 part-time/adjunct (2 women). *Students:* 86 full-time (66 women), 6 part-time (all women); includes 14 minority (3 African Americans, 2 American Indian/Alaska Native, 4 Asian Americans or Pacific Islanders, 5 Hispanic Americans). Average age 33. 111 applicants, 40% accepted, 40 enrolled. In 2007, 26 degrees awarded. *Degree requirements:* For master's, internship. *Entrance requirements:* For master's, minimum GPA of 3.0. *Application deadline:* For fall admission, 11/30 for domestic students. Application fee: $55. *Financial support:* Career-related internships or fieldwork available. Financial award application deadline: 3/2. *Faculty research:* Self-esteem, relationship of emotion and health, at-risk youth, feminist issues, supervision strategies. *Unit head:* Maureen Buckley, Chair, 707-664-2544, E-mail: maureen.buckley@sonoma.edu. *Application contact:* Stephanie Wilkinson, Administrative Analyst, 707-664-2544, Fax: 707-664-2038, E-mail: stephanie.wilkinson@sonoma.edu.

Southern Connecticut State University, School of Graduate Studies, School of Health and Human Services, Program in Marriage and Family Therapy, New Haven, CT 06515-1355. Offers MFT. *Accreditation:* AAMFT/COAMFTE. *Faculty:* 3 full-time. *Students:* 36 full-time (32 women), 9 part-time (8 women); includes 10 minority (6 African Americans, 3 Asian Americans or Pacific Islanders, 1 Hispanic American). 29 applicants, 79% accepted, 15 enrolled. In 2007, 10 degrees awarded. *Degree requirements:* For master's, internship. *Entrance requirements:* For master's, minimum undergraduate QPA of 3.0 in graduate major field or 2.5 overall, interview. *Application deadline:* For fall admission, 7/15 priority date for domestic students. Applications are processed on a rolling basis. Application fee: $50. Electronic applications accepted. *Financial support:* Application deadline: 4/15; *Unit head:* Dr. Edward Lynch, Chairperson, 203-392-6411, Fax: 203-392-6441, E-mail: lynch_j@southernct.edu.

Southern Nazarene University, Graduate College, School of Psychology, Bethany, OK 73008. Offers counseling psychology (MSCP); marriage and family therapy (MA). *Degree requirements:* For master's, thesis optional. *Entrance requirements:* For master's, English proficiency exam, minimum GPA of 3.0 in last 60 hours/major, 2.7 overall.

Springfield College, Graduate Programs, Programs in Psychology and Counseling, Springfield, MA 01109-3797. Offers athletic counseling (M Ed, MS, CAGS); industrial/organizational psychology (M Ed, MS, CAGS); marriage and family therapy (M Ed, MS, CAGS); mental health counseling (M Ed, MS, CAGS); school guidance and counseling (M Ed, MS, CAGS); student personnel in higher education (M Ed, MS, CAGS). Part-time and evening/weekend programs available. *Faculty:* 14 full-time (8 women), 17 part-time/adjunct (7 women). *Students:* 157 full-time, 44 part-time. Average age 28. 220 applicants, 72% accepted, 97 enrolled. In 2007, 93 master's, 1 other advanced degree awarded. *Degree requirements:* For master's, comprehensive exam, thesis (for some programs), research project, internship. *Entrance requirements:* For master's and CAGS, interview. Additional exam requirements/recommendations for international students: Required—TOEFL (minimum score 550 paper-based; 213 computer-based). *Application deadline:* For fall admission, 1/15 priority date for domestic students; for winter admission, 11/1 for domestic students; for spring admission, 12/1 for domestic students. Applications are processed on a rolling basis. Application fee: $50. Electronic applications accepted. *Expenses:* Tuition: Full-time $12,942; part-time $719 per semester hour. Required fees: $25. Tuition and fees vary according to program. *Financial support:* In 2007–08, 8 fellowships with partial tuition reimbursements (averaging $2,000 per year), 2 research assistantships (averaging $4,000 per year), 7 teaching assistantships (averaging $1,800 per year) were awarded; career-related internships or fieldwork, Federal Work-Study, institutionally sponsored loans, scholarships/grants, and tuition waivers (full and partial) also available. Financial award application deadline: 3/1. *Faculty research:* Sport psychology, leadership and emotional intelligence, violence and terrorism, performance enhancement, cognitive function. Total annual research expenditures: $715,109. *Unit head:* Dr. Anna L. Moriarty, Director, 413-748-3322, Fax: 413-748-3854, E-mail: anna_l_moriarty@spfldcol.edu. *Application contact:* Donald James Shaw, Director of Graduate Admissions, 413-748-3060, Fax: 413-748-3069, E-mail: donald_shaw_jr@spfldcol.edu.

Stetson University, College of Arts and Sciences, Division of Education, Department of Counselor Education, DeLand, FL 32723. Offers marriage and family therapy (MS); mental health counseling (MS); school guidance and family consultation (MS). *Accreditation:* ACA. Evening/weekend programs available. *Students:* 76 full-time (67 women), 8 part-time (all women); includes 6 African Americans, 1 Asian American or Pacific Islander, 9 Hispanic Americans, 2 international. Average age 33. In 2007, 16 degrees awarded. *Entrance requirements:* For master's, GRE General Test. *Application deadline:* For fall admission, 3/1 priority date for domestic students; for spring admission, 11/1 for domestic students. Applications are processed on a rolling basis. Application fee: $25. *Unit head:* Dr. Brigid Noonan-Klima, Chair, 386-822-8992. *Application contact:* Diana Belian, Office of Graduate Studies, 386-822-7075, Fax: 386-822-7388, E-mail: dbelian@stetson.edu.

Syracuse University, Graduate School, College of Human Ecology, Marriage and Family Therapy Program, Syracuse, NY 13244. Offers MA, PhD. *Accreditation:* AAMFT/COAMFTE. Part-time programs available. *Students:* 37 full-time (28 women), 6 part-time (3 women); includes 16 minority (9 African Americans, 2 Asian Americans or Pacific Islanders, 5 Hispanic Americans), 5 international. 81 applicants, 52% accepted, 11 enrolled. In 2007, 14 master's, 7 doctorates awarded. *Degree requirements:* For doctorate, thesis/dissertation. *Entrance requirements:* For master's, GRE General Test. Additional exam requirements/recommendations for international students: Required—TOEFL. *Application deadline:* For fall admission, 3/15 for domestic students. Application fee: $75. Electronic applications accepted. *Expenses:* Tuition: Full-time $18,216; part-time $1,012 per credit. Required fees: $980. Tuition and fees vary according to program. *Financial support:* Fellowships with tuition reimbursements, research assistantships with full and partial tuition reimbursements, teaching assistantships with full and partial tuition reimbursements, tuition waivers (partial) available. *Unit head:* Thomas DeLara, Chair, 315-443-9403, E-mail: inquire@hshp.syr.edu. *Application contact:* Amy Pangborn, Information Contact, 315-443-5555, E-mail: inquire@hshp.syr.edu.

Texas Tech University, Graduate School, College of Human Sciences, Department of Applied and Professional Studies, Lubbock, TX 79409. Offers family and consumer sciences education (MS, PhD); marriage and family therapy (MS, PhD); personal financial planning (MS); JD/MS. Part-time programs available. *Faculty:* 13 full-time (8 women). *Students:* 66 full-time (28 women), 47 part-time (27 women); includes 14 minority (4 African Americans, 2 American Indian/Alaska Native, 2 Asian Americans or Pacific Islanders, 6 Hispanic Americans), 5 international. Average age 30. 120 applicants, 67% accepted, 26 enrolled. In 2007, 18 master's, 11 doctorates awarded. Terminal master's awarded for partial completion of doctoral program. *Degree requirements:* For master's, thesis (for some programs); for doctorate, thesis/dissertation. *Entrance requirements:* For master's and doctorate, GRE General Test. Additional exam requirements/recommendations for international students: Required—TOEFL (minimum score 550 paper-based; 213 computer-based). *Application deadline:* For fall admission, 3/1 priority date for international students; for spring admission, 11/1 priority date for international students. Applications are processed on a rolling basis. Application fee: $50 ($60 for international students). *Expenses:* Tuition, state resident: part-time $373 per credit hour. Tuition, nonresident: part-time $651 per credit hour. Tuition and fees vary according to program. *Financial support:* In 2007–08, 77 students received support, including 20 research assistantships with partial tuition reimbursements available (averaging $13,531 per year), 33 teaching assistantships with partial tuition reimbursements available (averaging $13,583 per year); career-related internships or fieldwork, Federal Work-Study, institutionally sponsored loans, and tuition waivers (partial) also available. Support available to part-time students. Financial award application deadline: 4/15; financial award applicants required to submit FAFSA. *Faculty research:* Functional interior design applications for special needs populations; retirement planning and income/expenditure patterns for teachers; surface design, purchase, and consumption of leather products; financial counseling outcome and assessment of college students; multicultural housing environments and behavior correlations. Total annual research expenditures: $939,769. *Unit head:* Dr. Sterling Shumway, Chair, 806-742-5050, Fax: 806-742-5033, E-mail: sterling.shumway@ttu.edu.

Texas Woman's University, Graduate School, College of Professional Education, Department of Family Sciences, Denton, TX 76201. Offers child development (MS, PhD); counseling and development (MS); early childhood education (M Ed, MA, MS, Ed D); family studies (MS, PhD); family therapy (MS, PhD). *Accreditation:* ACA (one or more programs are accredited). Part-time and evening/weekend programs available. *Students:* 100 full-time (93 women), 336 part-time (308 women); includes 134 minority (89 African Americans, 5 American Indian/Alaska Native, 11 Asian Americans or Pacific Islanders, 29 Hispanic Americans), 15 international. Average age 36. In 2007, 79 master's, 11 doctorates awarded. *Median time to degree:* Of those who began their doctoral program in fall 1999, 50% received their degree in 8 years or less. *Degree requirements:* For doctorate, comprehensive exam, thesis/dissertation. *Entrance requirements:* For master's, interview, writing sample, minimum GPA of 3.25 may be required; for doctorate, interview, writing sample may be required, GPA 3.25 last 60 hours of course work. Additional exam requirements/recommendations for international students: Required—TOEFL (minimum score 550 paper-based; 213 computer-based; 79 iBT). *Application deadline:* For fall admission, 2/15 for domestic students, 4/15 for international students; for spring admission, 9/15 for domestic students, 8/1 for international students. Applications are processed on a rolling basis. Application fee: $30 ($50 for international students). Electronic applications accepted. *Expenses:* Tuition, state resident: full-time $3,294; part-time $183 per credit. Tuition, nonresident: full-time $8,298; part-time $461 per credit. Required fees: $985; $55 per credit. Tuition and fees vary according to degree level. *Financial support:* In 2007–08, 3 research assistantships (averaging $10,746 per year), 20 teaching assistantships (averaging $10,746 per year) were awarded; career-related internships or fieldwork, Federal Work-Study, institutionally sponsored loans, scholarships/grants, traineeships, health care benefits, and unspecified assistantships also available. Support available to part-time students. Financial award application deadline: 3/1; financial award applicants required to submit FAFSA. *Faculty research:* Parenting/parent education, distance education, play therapy, family sexuality, diversity. *Unit head:* Dr. Larry LeFlore, Chair, 940-898-2685, Fax: 940-898-2676, E-mail: lleflore@twu.edu. *Application contact:* Samuel Wheeler, Assistant Director of Admissions, 940-898-3188, Fax: 940-898-3081, E-mail: wheelersr@twu.edu.

Thomas Jefferson University, Jefferson College of Health Professions, Couple and Family Therapy Department, Philadelphia, PA 19107. Offers family therapy (MS). *Expenses:* Tuition: Full-time $20,340. Required fees: $400. Tuition and fees vary according to course load, degree level and program.

Trevecca Nazarene University, Graduate Division, Graduate Psychology Programs, Major in Marriage and Family Therapy, Nashville, TN 37210-2877. Offers MMFT. Part-time and evening/weekend programs available. *Students:* 46 full-time (36 women), 9 part-time (7 women); includes 8 minority (7 African Americans, 1 Hispanic American). In 2007, 17 degrees awarded. *Degree requirements:* For master's, comprehensive exam, practicum. *Entrance requirements:* For master's, GRE General Test or MAT, minimum GPA of 2.7, letters of reference. Additional exam requirements/recommendations for international students: Required—TOEFL (minimum score 500 paper-based; 173 computer-based). *Application deadline:* Applications are processed on a rolling basis. Application fee: $25. *Expenses: Contact institution.* Tuition and fees vary according to degree level and program. *Financial support:* Applicants required to submit FAFSA. *Application contact:* Heather Ambrefe, Department Secretary, 615-248-1384, Fax: 615-248-1662, E-mail: admissions_psy@trevecca.edu.

Universidad de las Americas, A.C., Program in Psychology, Mexico City, Mexico. Offers family therapy (MA).

The University of Akron, Graduate School, College of Education, Department of Counseling, Program in Marriage and Family Therapy, Akron, OH 44325. Offers MA, MS. *Accreditation:* AAMFT/COAMFTE; ACA. *Students:* 30 full-time (27 women), 31 part-time (28 women); includes 8 minority (6 African Americans, 1 Asian American or Pacific Islander, 1 Hispanic American), 1 international. Average age 30. 20 applicants, 70% accepted, 9 enrolled. In 2007, 9 degrees awarded. *Degree requirements:* For master's, comprehensive exam. *Entrance requirements:* For master's, minimum GPA of 2.75, interview, letters of recommendation, supplemental form. Additional exam requirements/recommendations for international students: Required—TOEFL (minimum score 550 paper-based; 213 computer-based; 79 iBT). *Application deadline:* For fall admission, 3/15 for domestic and international students; for spring admission, 10/1 for domestic and international students. Applications are processed on a rolling basis. Application fee: $30 ($40 for international students). Electronic applications accepted. *Expenses:* Tuition, state resident: full-time $6,164; part-time $342 per credit. Tuition, nonresident: full-time $10,575; part-time $588 per credit. Required fees: $806; $43 per credit. $12 per term. Tuition and fees vary according to course load, degree level and program. *Unit head:* Dr. Patricia Parr, Coordinator, 330-972-8151, E-mail: pparr@uakron.edu.

University of Arkansas at Little Rock, Graduate School, College of Professional Studies, School of Social Work, Program in Marriage and Family Therapy, Little Rock, AR 72204-1099. Offers Graduate Certificate. *Application contact:* Amy G. Angel, Coordinator, E-mail: aegarland@ualr.edu.

University of Central Florida, College of Education, Department of Child, Family and Community Sciences, Program in Marriage and Family Therapy, Orlando, FL 32816. Offers MA, Certificate. *Expenses:* Tuition, state resident: full-time $6,484. Tuition, nonresident: full-time $23,938. Tuition and fees vary according to program. *Unit head:* Dr. Mark Young, Coordinator, 407-823-6314, E-mail: meyoung@mail.ucf.edu.

University of Florida, Graduate School, College of Education, Department of Counselor Education, Gainesville, FL 32611. Offers marriage and family counseling (M Ed, MAE, Ed D, PhD, Ed S); mental health counseling (M Ed, MAE, Ed D, PhD, Ed S); school counseling and guidance (M Ed, MAE, Ed D, PhD, Ed S). *Accreditation:* ACA (one or more programs are accredited); NCATE. Part-time programs available. *Faculty:* 12 full-time (7 women). *Students:* 177 (138 women); includes 37 minority (12 African Americans, 9 Asian Americans or Pacific Islanders, 16 Hispanic Americans) 4 international. In 2007, 84 master's, 7 doctorates awarded. Terminal master's awarded for partial completion of doctoral program. *Degree requirements:* For master's, thesis optional; for doctorate, thesis/dissertation. *Entrance requirements:* For master's and doctorate, GRE General Test, minimum GPA of 3.0 (undergraduate), 3.5 (graduate); for Ed S, GRE General Test. Additional exam requirements/recommendations for international students: Required—TOEFL (minimum score 550 paper-based; 213 computer-based). *Application deadline:* For fall admission, 2/27 priority date for domestic students. Applications are processed on a rolling basis. Application fee: $30. Electronic applications accepted. *Expenses:* Tuition, state resident: full-time $7,478. Tuition, nonresident: full-time $22,603. *Financial support:* In 2007–08, 1 research assistantship (averaging $8,775 per year), 9 teaching assistantships (averaging $8,883 per year) were awarded; fellowships, career-related internships or fieldwork and unspecified assistantships also available. *Unit head:* Dr. Harry M. Daniels, Chairman, 352-392-0731 Ext. 226, Fax: 352-846-2697, E-mail: harryd@coe.ufl.edu. *Application contact:* Dr. Peter Sherrard, Coordinator, 352-392-0731 Ext. 234, Fax: 352-846-2697, E-mail: psherrard@coe.ufl.edu.

University of Guelph, Graduate Program Services, College of Social and Applied Human Sciences, Department of Family Relations and Applied Nutrition, Guelph, ON N1G 2W1, Canada. Offers applied nutrition (MAN); family relations and human development (M Sc, PhD), including applied human nutrition, couple and family therapy (M Sc), family relations and human development. *Accreditation:* AAMFT/COAMFTE (one or more programs are accredited). Part-time programs available. *Faculty:* 23 full-time (16 women). *Students:* 56 full-time (51 women), 5 part-time (all women); includes 4 minority (2 African Americans, 1 Asian American or Pacific Islander, 1 Hispanic American), 2 international. Average age 30. 153 applicants, 32% accepted, 33 enrolled. In 2007, 9 master's, 3 doctorates awarded. *Median time to degree:* Of those who began their doctoral program in fall 1999, 100% received their degree in 8 years or less. *Degree requirements:* For master's, thesis (for some programs); for doctorate, comprehensive exam, thesis/dissertation. *Entrance requirements:* For master's, minimum B+ average; for doctorate, master's degree in family relations and human development or related field with a minimum B+ average or master's degree in applied human nutrition. Additional exam requirements/recommendations for international students: Required—TOEFL (minimum score 600 paper-based; 250 computer-based). *Application deadline:* For fall admission, 1/2 priority date for domestic and international students. Application fee: $85. Electronic applications accepted. *Financial support:* In 2007–08, 54 students received support; fellowships, research assistantships, teaching assistantships, career-related internships or fieldwork and health care benefits available. *Faculty research:* Child and adolescent development, social gerontology, family roles and relations, couple and family therapy, applied human nutrition. Total annual research expenditures: $500,000. *Unit head:* Dr. Susan Lollis, Interim Chair, 519-824-4120 Ext. 56326, Fax: 519-766-0691, E-mail: slollis@uoguelph.ca. *Application contact:* Jo Anne Waechter, Graduate Secretary, 519-824-4120 Ext. 53968, Fax: 519-766-0691, E-mail: jwaechte@uoguelph.ca.

University of Houston–Clear Lake, School of Human Sciences and Humanities, Programs in Human Sciences, Houston, TX 77058-1098. Offers behavioral sciences (MA), including behavioral sciences-general, behavioral sciences-psychology, behavioral sciences-sociology; clinical psychology (MA); criminology (MA); cross-cultural studies (MA); family therapy (MA); fitness and human performance (MA); school psychology (MA). *Accreditation:* AAMFT/COAMFTE. Part-time and evening/weekend programs available. Postbaccalaureate distance learning degree programs offered (minimal on-campus study). *Degree requirements:* For master's, thesis or alternative. *Entrance requirements:* For master's, GRE General Test. Additional exam requirements/recommendations for international students: Required—TOEFL (minimum score 550 paper-based; 213 computer-based). Electronic applications accepted. *Faculty research:* Smoking cessation, adolescent sexuality, white collar crime, serial murder, human factors/human computer interaction.

University of La Verne, College of Arts and Sciences, Department of Psychology, Programs in Counseling, La Verne, CA 91750-4443. Offers general counseling (MS); higher education counseling (MS); marriage and family therapy (MS). Part-time programs available. *Faculty:* 2 full-time (1 woman), 9 part-time/adjunct (8 women). *Students:* 32 full-time (30 women), 64 part-time (56 women); includes 64 minority (12 African Americans, 4 Asian Americans or Pacific Islanders, 48 Hispanic Americans). Average age 30. In 2007, 24 degrees awarded. *Degree requirements:* For master's, thesis, competency exam, personal psychotherapy. *Entrance requirements:* For master's, minimum undergraduate GPA of 3.0, 3 recommendations, interview. Additional exam requirements/recommendations for international students: Required—TOEFL (minimum score 600 paper-based; 250 computer-based). *Application deadline:* Applications are processed on a rolling basis. Application fee: $50. *Expenses: Contact institution.* Tuition and fees vary according to course load and program. *Financial support:* Career-related internships or fieldwork, institutionally sponsored loans, and scholarships/grants available. Financial award application deadline: 3/2; financial award applicants required to submit FAFSA. *Application contact:* Connie Hamlow, Admissions Information Specialist, 909-593-3511 Ext. 4244, Fax: 909-392-2761, E-mail: gradadmission@ulv.edu.

University of Louisiana at Monroe, Graduate Studies and Research, College of Education and Human Development, Department of Educational Leadership and Counseling, Program in Marriage and Family Therapy, Monroe, LA 71209-0001. Offers MA, PhD. *Accreditation:* AAMFT/COAMFTE (one or more programs are accredited); ACA. Part-time and evening/weekend programs available. *Students:* 38 full-time (24 women), 14 part-time (10 women); includes 8 minority (7 African Americans, 1 Asian American or Pacific Islander). Average age 30. In 2007, 15 master's, 5 doctorates awarded. *Degree requirements:* For master's, comprehensive exam; for doctorate, thesis/dissertation. *Entrance requirements:* For master's, GRE General Test, interview, minimum GPA of 2.8; for doctorate, GRE General Test. Additional exam requirements/recommendations for international students: Required—TOEFL (minimum score 500 paper-based; 173 computer-based; 61 iBT). *Application deadline:* For fall admission, 8/22 priority date for domestic students, 7/1 for international students; for winter admission, 12/12 priority date for domestic students; for spring admission, 1/17 for domestic students, 11/1 for international students. Applications are processed on a rolling basis. Application fee: $20 ($30 for international students). Electronic applications accepted. *Expenses:* Tuition, state resident: full-time $2,220. Tuition, nonresident: full-time $8,172. *Financial support:* Research assistantships with full tuition reimbursements, teaching assistantships with full tuition reimbursements, career-related internships or fieldwork, Federal Work-Study, and unspecified assistantships available. Financial award application deadline: 4/1; financial award applicants required to submit FAFSA. *Faculty research:* Family systems, substance abuse. Total annual research expenditures: $20,000. *Unit head:* Dr. Lamar Woodham, Program Director, 318-362-3008, Fax: 318-342-3131, E-mail: woodham@ulm.edu. *Application contact:* Dr. Harper Gaushell, Admissions Coordinator, 318-343-8441, Fax: 318-342-3131, E-mail: gaushell@ulm.edu.

University of Louisville, Graduate School, Raymond A. Kent School of Social Work, Louisville, KY 40292-0001. Offers marriage and family therapy (PMC); social work (MSSW, PhD). *Accreditation:* AAMFT/COAMFTE; CSWE (one or more programs are accredited). *Faculty:* 23 full-time (15 women), 38 part-time/adjunct (21 women). *Students:* 308 full-time (251 women), 92 part-time (76 women); includes 88 minority (83 African Americans, 1 American Indian/Alaska Native, 3 Asian Americans or Pacific Islanders, 1 Hispanic American), 6 international. Average age 32. In 2007, 152 master's, 8 doctorates, 4 other advanced degrees awarded. *Degree requirements:* For doctorate, thesis/dissertation. *Entrance requirements:* For master's, GRE or minimum GPA of 2.75; for doctorate, GRE General Test, interview, writing sample. *Application deadline:* Applications are processed on a rolling basis. Application fee: $50. *Financial support:* In 2007–08, 2 fellowships with full tuition reimbursements (averaging $19,000 per year), 7 research assistantships with full tuition reimbursements (averaging $19,000 per year) were awarded; tuition waivers (full) also available. Financial award application deadline: 4/1. *Faculty research:* Child welfare, substance abuse, gerontology, family functioning, health behavior. *Unit head:* Dr. Terry Singer, Dean, 502-852-6402, Fax: 502-852-0422, E-mail: terry.singer@louisville.edu.

University of Mary Hardin-Baylor, College of Sciences and Humanities, Department of Psychology, Belton, TX 76513. Offers community counseling (MA); marriage and family Christian counseling (MA); psychology and counseling (MA); school counseling and psychology (MA). Part-time and evening/weekend programs available. *Degree requirements:* For master's, comprehensive exam. *Entrance requirements:* For master's, GRE General Test, minimum GPA of 3.0 in last 60 hours or 2.75 overall. Electronic applications accepted.

University of Maryland, College Park, Graduate Studies, School of Public Health, Department of Family Science, College Park, MD 20742. Offers family studies (PhD); marriage and family therapy (MS). *Accreditation:* AAMFT/COAMFTE. Part-time and evening/weekend

Marriage and Family Therapy

University of Maryland, College Park (continued)
programs available. *Faculty:* 15 full-time (12 women), 14 part-time/adjunct (11 women). *Students:* 40 full-time (35 women), 1 (woman) part-time; includes 10 minority (8 African Americans, 1 Asian American or Pacific Islander, 1 Hispanic American), 2 international. 91 applicants, 24% accepted, 17 enrolled. In 2007, 17 master's, 9 doctorates awarded. *Degree requirements:* For master's, thesis or alternative; for doctorate, comprehensive exam, thesis/dissertation, oral defense. *Entrance requirements:* For master's, GRE General Test, minimum GPA of 3.0, 3 letters of recommendation; for doctorate, GRE General Test, minimum GPA of 3.0, 3 letters of recommendation, research sample. *Application deadline:* For fall admission, 1/15 for domestic students, 2/1 for international students. Applications are processed on a rolling basis. Application fee: $60. Electronic applications accepted. *Financial support:* In 2007–08, 8 fellowships with full tuition reimbursements (averaging $7,450 per year), 1 research assistantship with tuition reimbursement (averaging $15,126 per year), 28 teaching assistantships with tuition reimbursements (averaging $14,911 per year) were awarded; career-related internships or fieldwork, Federal Work-Study, and scholarships/grants also available. Support available to part-time students. Financial award applicants required to submit FAFSA. *Faculty research:* Family life quality, interracial couples, child support, homeless families, family and child well-being. Total annual research expenditures: $291,811. *Unit head:* Dr. Sally Koblinsky, Chairman, 301-405-1377, Fax: 301-314-9161, E-mail: koblinsk@umd.edu. *Application contact:* Dean of Graduate School, 301-405-0358, Fax: 301-314-9305.

See Close-Up on page 1075.

University of Massachusetts Boston, Office of Graduate Studies, Graduate College of Education, Counseling and School Psychology Department, Program in Family Therapy, Boston, MA 02125-3393. Offers M Ed, CAGS. *Accreditation:* AAMFT/COAMFTE.

University of Miami, Graduate School, School of Education, Department of Educational and Psychological Studies, Program in Counseling, Coral Gables, FL 33124. Offers bilingual and bicultural counseling (Certificate); marriage and family therapy (MS Ed); mental health counseling (MS Ed). Part-time programs available. *Faculty:* 9 full-time (4 women), 10 part-time/adjunct (8 women). *Students:* 30 full-time (26 women), 23 part-time (21 women); includes 23 minority (1 African American, 1 Asian American or Pacific Islander, 21 Hispanic Americans), 1 international. Average age 27. 76 applicants, 47% accepted, 22 enrolled. In 2007, 19 degrees awarded. *Degree requirements:* For master's, comprehensive exam. *Entrance requirements:* For master's, GRE General Test; for Certificate, master's degree in a mental health field. Additional exam requirements/recommendations for international students: Required—TOEFL (minimum score 550 paper-based; 212 computer-based). *Application deadline:* For fall admission, 3/15 priority date for domestic and international students. Applications are processed on a rolling basis. Application fee: $50. Electronic applications accepted. *Financial support:* In 2007–08, 49 students received support; research assistantships, teaching assistantships, Federal Work-Study, institutionally sponsored loans, scholarships/grants, unspecified assistantships, and employee benefits available. Support available to part-time students. Financial award application deadline: 3/15; financial award applicants required to submit FAFSA. *Faculty research:* Cocaine recidivism, HIV, non-traditional families, health psychology, diversity. *Unit head:* Dr. Margaret Crosbie-Burnett, Visiting Associate Professor, 305-284-2802, Fax: 305-284-3003, E-mail: mcrosbur@miami.edu. *Application contact:* Shelley Lue Foung, Senior Administrative Assistant, 305-284-3001, Fax: 305-284-3003, E-mail: sluefoung@miami.edu.

University of Minnesota, Twin Cities Campus, Graduate School, College of Education and Human Development, Department of Family Social Science, Minneapolis, MN 55455-0213. Offers marriage and family therapy (MA, PhD). *Accreditation:* AAMFT/COAMFTE (one or more programs are accredited). *Faculty:* 18 full-time (13 women). *Students:* 52 full-time (42 women), 14 part-time (11 women); includes 11 minority (3 African Americans, 2 American Indian/Alaska Native, 5 Asian Americans or Pacific Islanders, 1 Hispanic American), 15 international. Average age 36. 24 applicants, 67% accepted, 10 enrolled. In 2007, 3 master's, 6 doctorates awarded. *Median time to degree:* Of those who began their doctoral program in fall 1999, 86% received their degree in 8 years or less. *Degree requirements:* For master's, thesis; for doctorate, thesis/dissertation. *Entrance requirements:* For master's and doctorate, GRE General Test, minimum undergraduate GPA of 3.0 (preferred). Additional exam requirements/recommendations for international students: Required—TOEFL. *Application deadline:* For fall admission, 12/15 for domestic students. Application fee: $55 ($75 for international students). *Financial support:* In 2007–08, 41 research assistantships (averaging $25,212 per year), 13 teaching assistantships (averaging $26,543 per year) were awarded; fellowships, career-related internships or fieldwork, Federal Work-Study, institutionally sponsored loans, and tuition waivers (partial) also available. Financial award application deadline: 6/30; financial award applicants required to submit FAFSA. *Faculty research:* Families and diversity, families and health, families and economic well-being, individuals and relationships across the lifespan. Total annual research expenditures: $1.3 million. *Unit head:* Dr. Jan McCulloch, Head, 612-624-1208, Fax: 612-625-4227, E-mail: jmccullo@che.umn.edu. *Application contact:* Roberta Daigle, Information Contact, 612-625-3116, E-mail: rdaigle@che.umn.edu.

University of Mobile, Graduate Programs, Program in Religious Studies, Mobile, AL 36613. Offers biblical/theological studies (MA); marriage and family counseling (MA). Part-time and evening/weekend programs available. *Faculty:* 6 full-time (0 women), 2 part-time/adjunct (0 women). *Students:* 18 full-time (16 women), 35 part-time (18 women); includes 15 minority (13 African Americans, 2 American Indian/Alaska Native). Average age 27. In 2007, 15 degrees awarded. *Degree requirements:* For master's, one foreign language, comprehensive exam, thesis optional. *Entrance requirements:* For master's, GRE General Test. Additional exam requirements/recommendations for international students: Required—TOEFL. *Application deadline:* For fall admission, 8/3 priority date for domestic students; for spring admission, 12/23 for domestic students. Applications are processed on a rolling basis. Application fee: $40 ($50 for international students). *Financial support:* Federal Work-Study available. Support available to part-time students. Financial award application deadline: 8/1. *Unit head:* Dr. Cecil Taylor, Dean, School of Christian Studies, 251-442-2255, Fax: 251-442-2523, E-mail: ctaylor@mail.umobile.edu. *Application contact:* Tammy C. Eubanks, Administrative Assistant to Dean of Graduate Programs, 251-442-2270, Fax: 251-442-2523, E-mail: teubanks@umobile.edu.

University of Montevallo, College of Education, Program in Counseling, Montevallo, AL 35115. Offers community counseling (M Ed); marriage and family (M Ed); school counseling (M Ed). *Accreditation:* ACA; NCATE. Part-time and evening/weekend programs available. *Entrance requirements:* For master's, GRE General Test or MAT, minimum undergraduate GPA of 2.75 in last 60 hours or 2.5 overall, interview. Additional exam requirements/recommendations for international students: Required—TOEFL (minimum score 550 paper-based).

University of Nevada, Las Vegas, Graduate College, Greenspun College of Urban Affairs, Department of Marriage and Family Therapy, Las Vegas, NV 89154-9900. Offers community agency counseling (MS); marriage and family counseling (MS); marriage and family therapy (Certificate); rehabilitation counseling (MS). *Accreditation:* ACA. Part-time programs available. *Faculty:* 4 full-time (2 women), 3 part-time/adjunct (2 women). *Students:* 17 full-time (all women), 25 part-time (22 women); includes 6 minority (4 African Americans, 2 Hispanic Americans). 28 applicants, 36% accepted, 10 enrolled. In 2007, 12 degrees awarded. *Degree requirements:* For master's, comprehensive exam (for some programs), thesis (for some programs). *Entrance requirements:* For master's, GRE General Test, minimum GPA of 3.0 during previous 2 years, 2.75 overall. Additional exam requirements/recommendations for international students: Required—TOEFL (minimum score 550 paper-based; 213 computer-based; 80 iBT). *Application deadline:* For winter admission, 2/1 for domestic and international students. Application fee: $60 ($75 for international students). Electronic applications accepted. *Expenses:* Tuition, state resident: part-time $198 per credit. Tuition, nonresident: part-time $416 per credit. Required fees: $256 per semester. Tuition and fees vary according to course load and reciprocity agreements. *Financial support:* In 2007–08, 4 research assistantships with partial tuition reimbursements (averaging $10,000 per year) were awarded; career-related internships or fieldwork, Federal Work-Study, institutionally sponsored loans, scholarships/grants, health care benefits, and unspecified assistantships also available. Support available to part-time students. Financial award application deadline: 3/1. *Unit head:* Dr. Gerald Weeks, Chair, 702-895-1867. *Application contact:* Graduate College Admissions Evaluator, 702-895-3320, Fax: 702-895-4180, E-mail: gradcollege@unlv.edu.

University of New Hampshire, Graduate School, School of Health and Human Services, Department of Family Studies, Durham, NH 03824. Offers family studies (MS); marriage and family therapy (MS). *Accreditation:* AAMFT/COAMFTE. Part-time programs available. *Faculty:* 8 full-time. *Students:* 15 full-time (12 women), 7 part-time (6 women); includes 3 minority (2 African Americans, 1 Asian American or Pacific Islander), 1 international. Average age 30. 25 applicants, 48% accepted, 8 enrolled. In 2007, 6 degrees awarded. *Degree requirements:* For master's, thesis or alternative. *Entrance requirements:* For master's, GRE General Test. Additional exam requirements/recommendations for international students: Required—TOEFL (minimum score 550 paper-based; 213 computer-based; 80 iBT). *Application deadline:* For fall admission, 4/1 priority date for domestic students, 4/1 for international students; for winter admission, 12/1 for domestic students. Applications are processed on a rolling basis. Application fee: $60. Electronic applications accepted. *Financial support:* In 2007–08, 1 research assistantship, 5 teaching assistantships were awarded; fellowships, career-related internships or fieldwork, Federal Work-Study, scholarships/grants, and tuition waivers (full and partial) also available. Support available to part-time students. Financial award application deadline: 2/15. *Unit head:* Dr. Elizabeth Dolan, Chairperson, 603-862-2137. *Application contact:* Mary Leighton, Administrative Assistant, 603-862-5021, E-mail: family.studies@unh.edu.

The University of North Carolina at Greensboro, Graduate School, School of Education, Department of Counseling and Educational Development, Greensboro, NC 27412-5001. Offers advanced school counseling (PMC); counseling and counselor education (PhD); counseling and educational development (MS); couple and family counseling (PMC); school counseling (PMC); MS/Ed S. *Accreditation:* ACA (one or more programs are accredited); NCATE. *Faculty:* 10 full-time (5 women), 1 part-time/adjunct (0 women). *Students:* 106 full-time (92 women), 18 part-time (14 women); includes 21 minority (12 African Americans, 1 American Indian/Alaska Native, 4 Asian Americans or Pacific Islanders, 4 Hispanic Americans). 314 applicants, 22% accepted. *Degree requirements:* For master's, comprehensive exam, practicum, internship; for doctorate, comprehensive exam, thesis/dissertation. *Entrance requirements:* For master's, doctorate, and PMC, GRE General Test. Additional exam requirements/recommendations for international students: Required—TOEFL. *Application deadline:* For fall admission, 2/15 for domestic students. Application fee: $45. Electronic applications accepted. *Financial support:* In 2007–08, 57 students received support; fellowships with full tuition reimbursements available, research assistantships with full tuition reimbursements, teaching assistantships with full tuition reimbursements available, career-related internships or fieldwork, Federal Work-Study, scholarships/grants, traineeships, and unspecified assistantships available. Support available to part-time students. *Faculty research:* Gerontology, invitational theory, career development, marriage and family therapy, drug and alcohol abuse prevention. *Unit head:* Dr. DiAnne Borders, Chair and Director of Graduate Studies, 336-334-3425, Fax: 336-334-4120, E-mail: borders@uncg.edu. *Application contact:* Michelle Harkleroad, Director of Graduate Admissions, 336-334-4884, Fax: 336-334-4424, E-mail: mbharkle@uncg.edu.

University of Phoenix–Bay Area Campus, The Artemis School, College of Health and Human Services, Pleasanton, CA 94588-3677. Offers administration of justice and security (MS); family nurse practitioner (MSN); health care management (MBA); marriage, family and child therapy (MSC). Evening/weekend programs available. *Degree requirements:* For master's, thesis (for some programs). *Entrance requirements:* For master's, minimum undergraduate GPA of 2.5, 3 years of work experience, RN license. Additional exam requirements/recommendations for international students: Required—TOEFL (minimum score 550 paper-based; 213 computer-based; 79 iBT). Electronic applications accepted.

University of Phoenix–Central Valley Campus, College of Social and Behavioral Science, Fresno, CA 93720-1562. Offers marriage, family and child therapy (MSC).

University of Phoenix–Denver Campus, The Artemis School, College of Health and Human Services, Lone Tree, CO 80124-5453. Offers community counseling (MSC); health care management (MBA); marriage, family and child therapy (MSC); nursing (MSN). Evening/weekend programs available. *Degree requirements:* For master's, thesis (for some programs). *Entrance requirements:* For master's, minimum undergraduate GPA of 2.5, 3 years work experience, RN license. Additional exam requirements/recommendations for international students: Required—TOEFL (minimum score 550 paper-based; 213 computer-based; 79 iBT). Electronic applications accepted.

University of Phoenix–Hawaii Campus, The Artemis School, College of Health and Human Services, Honolulu, HI 96813-4317. Offers administration of justice and security (MS); community counseling (MSC); family nurse practitioner (MSN); health administration (MHA); health care management (MBA); marriage, family and child therapy (MSC); nursing (MSN); psychology (MS). Evening/weekend programs available. *Degree requirements:* For master's, thesis (for some programs). *Entrance requirements:* For master's, minimum undergraduate GPA of 2.5, 3 years of work experience, RN license. Additional exam requirements/recommendations for international students: Required—TOEFL (minimum score 550 paper-based; 213 computer-based; 79 iBT). Electronic applications accepted.

University of Phoenix–Las Vegas Campus, The Artemis School, College of Health and Human Services, Las Vegas, NV 89128. Offers marriage, family, and child therapy (MSC); mental health counseling (MSC). *Entrance requirements:* For master's, minimum undergraduate GPA of 2.5, 3 years of work experience. Additional exam requirements/recommendations for international students: Required—TOEFL (minimum score 550 paper-based; 213 computer-based; 79 iBT). Electronic applications accepted.

University of Phoenix–New Mexico Campus, The Artemis School, College of Health and Human Services, Albuquerque, NM 87109-4645. Offers health care management (MBA); marriage and family therapy (MSC). Evening/weekend programs available. *Degree requirements:* For master's, thesis (for some programs). *Entrance requirements:* For master's, minimum undergraduate GPA of 2.5, 3 years of work experience, RN license. Additional exam requirements/recommendations for international students: Required—TOEFL (minimum score 550 paper-based; 213 computer-based; 79 iBT). Electronic applications accepted.

University of Phoenix–Northern Nevada Campus, College of Social and Behavioral Science, Reno, NV 89511. Offers administration of justice and security (MS); marriage, family and child therapy (MSC); psychology (MS); school counseling (MSC).

University of Phoenix–Puerto Rico Campus, The Artemis School, College of Health and Human Services, Guaynabo, PR 00968. Offers marriage, family and child therapy (MSC); mental health counseling (MSC). Evening/weekend programs available. *Degree requirements:* For master's, thesis (for some programs). *Entrance requirements:* For master's, Counselor Preparation Comprehensive Examination, minimum undergraduate GPA of 2.5, 3 years work experience. Additional exam requirements/recommendations for international students: Required—TOEFL (minimum score 550 paper-based; 213 computer-based; 79 iBT). Electronic applications accepted.

University of Phoenix–Sacramento Valley Campus, The Artemis School, College of Health and Human Services, Sacramento, CA 95833-3632. Offers administration of justice and security (MS); family nurse practitioner (MSN); health care management (MBA); marriage, family and child counseling (MSC); nursing (MSN); nursing education (MSN). Evening/weekend programs available. *Degree requirements:* For master's, thesis (for some programs). *Entrance requirements:* For master's, RN license, minimum undergraduate GPA of 2.5, 3 years work experience. Additional exam requirements/recommendations for international students: Required—TOEFL (minimum score 550 paper-based; 213 computer-based; 79 iBT). Electronic applications accepted.

University of Phoenix–San Diego Campus, The Artemis School, College of Health and Human Services, San Diego, CA 92123. Offers administration of justice and security (MS); marriage, family and child counseling (MSC); marriage, family and child therapy (MSC); nursing (MSN); MSN/MBA. Evening/weekend programs available. *Degree requirements:* For master's, thesis (for some programs). *Entrance requirements:* For master's, minimum undergraduate GPA of 2.5, 3 years work experience, RN license. Additional exam requirements/recommendations for international students: Required—TOEFL (minimum score 550 paper-based; 213 computer-based; 79 iBT). Electronic applications accepted.

University of Phoenix–Southern Arizona Campus, The Artemis School, College of Health and Human Services, Tucson, AZ 85711. Offers administration of justice and security (MS); family nurse practitioner (Certificate); health administration (MHA); marriage, family and child therapy (MSC); nursing (MSN). Evening/weekend programs available. *Degree requirements:* For master's, thesis (for some programs). *Entrance requirements:* For master's, minimum undergraduate GPA of 2.5, 3 years of work experience, RN license. Additional exam requirements/recommendations for international students: Required—TOEFL (minimum score 550 paper-based; 213 computer-based; 79 iBT). Electronic applications accepted.

University of Phoenix–Southern California Campus, The Artemis School, College of Health and Human Services, Costa Mesa, CA 92626. Offers family nurse practitioner (MSN, Certificate); health care education (MSN); health care management (MBA); marriage, family and child therapy (MSC); nursing (MSN). Evening/weekend programs available. *Degree requirements:* For master's, thesis (for some programs). *Entrance requirements:* For master's, minimum undergraduate GPA of 2.5, 3 years work experience, RN license. Additional exam requirements/recommendations for international students: Required—TOEFL (minimum score 550 paper-based; 213 computer-based; 79 iBT). Electronic applications accepted.

University of Phoenix–Southern Colorado Campus, The Artemis School, College of Health and Human Services, Colorado Springs, CO 80919-2335. Offers community counseling (MSC); health care management (MBA); marriage, family and child therapy (MSC); nursing (MSN). Evening/weekend programs available. *Degree requirements:* For master's, thesis (for some programs). *Entrance requirements:* For master's, minimum undergraduate GPA of 2.5, 3 years of work experience, RN license. Additional exam requirements/recommendations for international students: Required—TOEFL (minimum score 550 paper-based; 213 computer-based; 79 iBT). Electronic applications accepted.

University of Rochester, School of Medicine and Dentistry, Graduate Programs in Medicine and Dentistry, Department of Psychiatry, Rochester, NY 14627-0250. Offers marriage and family therapy (MS). *Accreditation:* AAMFT/COAMFTE. Part-time programs available. *Degree requirements:* For master's, projects. *Entrance requirements:* For master's, GRE General Test.

University of St. Thomas, Graduate Studies, Graduate School of Professional Psychology, St. Paul, MN 55105-1096. Offers counseling psychology (MA, Psy D); family psychology (Certificate). *Accreditation:* APA. Part-time and evening/weekend programs available. *Degree requirements:* For master's, comprehensive exam, practicum; for doctorate, comprehensive exam, thesis/dissertation, qualifying exam, practicum, internship. *Entrance requirements:* For master's, MAT or GRE, minimum GPA of 2.75, letters of recommendation; for doctorate, GRE, minimum GPA of 3.2, letters of recommendation. Additional exam requirements/recommendations for international students: Required—TOEFL. Expenses: Contact institution. *Faculty research:* Elderly, eating disorders, anxiety.

University of San Diego, School of Leadership and Education Sciences, Program in Marital and Family Therapy, San Diego, CA 92110-2492. Offers MA. *Accreditation:* AAMFT/COAMFTE. Part-time and evening/weekend programs available. *Faculty:* 4 full-time (2 women), 9 part-time/adjunct (7 women). *Students:* 59 full-time (54 women), 6 part-time (4 women); includes 13 minority (3 African Americans, 4 Asian Americans or Pacific Islanders, 6 Hispanic Americans), 5 international. Average age 26. 110 applicants, 40% accepted, 27 enrolled. In 2007, 22 degrees awarded. *Degree requirements:* For master's, comprehensive exam. *Entrance requirements:* For master's, GRE General Test or MAT, minimum GPA of 3.0, interview with faculty, 3 letters of recommendation, resumé. Additional exam requirements/recommendations for international students: Required—TOEFL (minimum score 580 paper-based; 237 computer-based), TWE. *Application deadline:* For fall admission, 3/1 for domestic students. Application fee: $45. *Expenses:* Tuition: Part-time $1,095 per unit. Tuition and fees vary according to degree level and program. *Financial support:* Career-related internships or fieldwork, Federal Work-Study, institutionally sponsored loans, scholarships/grants, tuition waivers (partial), unspecified assistantships, and stipends available. Support available to part-time students. Financial award application deadline: 4/1; financial award applicants required to submit FAFSA. *Unit head:* Dr. Todd M. Edwards, Director, 619-260-5963, Fax: 619-260-6835, E-mail: tedwards@sandiego.edu. *Application contact:* Brandina Morrison, Program Specialist, 619-260-7548, Fax: 619-260-4158, E-mail: bmorrison@sandiego.edu.

University of San Francisco, School of Education, Department of Counseling Psychology, San Francisco, CA 94117-1080. Offers counseling (MA), including educational counseling, life transitions counseling, marital and family therapy; counseling psychology (Ed D). *Faculty:* 7 full-time (3 women), 34 part-time/adjunct (25 women). *Students:* 240 full-time (206 women), 38 part-time (29 women); includes 92 minority (21 African Americans, 4 American Indian/Alaska Native, 30 Asian Americans or Pacific Islanders, 37 Hispanic Americans), 7 international. Average age 33. 345 applicants, 82% accepted, 131 enrolled. In 2007, 133 master's awarded. *Degree requirements:* For doctorate, thesis/dissertation. *Entrance requirements:* For doctorate, GRE General Test. Application fee: $55 ($65 for international students). *Expenses:* Tuition: Part-time $1,005 per unit. Tuition and fees vary according to degree level, campus/location and program. *Financial support:* In 2007–08, 211 students received support; fellowships, research assistantships, teaching assistantships available. Financial award application deadline: 3/2; financial award applicants required to submit FAFSA. *Unit head:* Dr. Brian Gerrard, Chair, 415-422-6868.

University of Southern California, Graduate School, School of Education, Master's Programs in Education, Los Angeles, CA 90089. Offers counseling psychology (ME); curriculum and teaching (MS); instructional technology (MS); marriage, family and child counseling (MMFT); postsecondary administration and student affairs [PASA] (ME); school counseling (ME); teaching and teaching credential program (MAT); teaching English as a foreign language (ME); teaching English to speakers of other languages (MS). Part-time and evening/weekend programs available. *Faculty:* 24 full-time (17 women), 21 part-time/adjunct (13 women). *Students:* 364 full-time (289 women), 80 part-time (57 women); includes 201 minority (34 African Americans, 1 American Indian/Alaska Native, 90 Asian Americans or Pacific Islanders, 76 Hispanic Americans), 68 international. 427 applicants, 72% accepted. In 2007, 268 degrees awarded. *Entrance requirements:* For master's, GRE. Application fee: $85. *Financial support:* Career-related internships or fieldwork, Federal Work-Study, and scholarships/grants available. Support available to part-time students. *Unit head:* Dr. Kristan Venegas, Head, 213-740-2311.

University of Southern Mississippi, Graduate School, College of Education and Psychology, Department of Child and Family Studies, Hattiesburg, MS 39406-0001. Offers child and family studies (MS); early intervention (MS); marriage and family therapy (MS). *Accreditation:* AAMFT/COAMFTE. Part-time programs available. *Faculty:* 8 full-time (4 women). *Students:* 29 full-time (27 women), 19 part-time (18 women); includes 15 minority (13 African Americans, 1 Asian American or Pacific Islander, 1 Hispanic American), 1 international. Average age 28. 51 applicants, 51% accepted, 22 enrolled. In 2007, 20 master's awarded. *Degree requirements:* For master's, comprehensive exam, thesis optional. *Entrance requirements:* For master's, GRE General Test, minimum GPA of 2.75 in last 60 hours. Additional exam requirements/recommendations for international students: Required—TOEFL. *Application deadline:* For fall admission, 3/1 priority date for domestic students, 3/1 for international students. Applications are processed on a rolling basis. Application fee: $30. Electronic applications accepted. *Financial support:* In 2007–08, 21 students received support, including 1 research assistantship with full tuition reimbursement available (averaging $5,164 per year), teaching assistantships with full tuition reimbursements available (averaging $5,458 per year); fellowships, career-related internships or fieldwork, Federal Work-Study, institutionally sponsored loans, scholarships/grants, and unspecified assistantships also available. Financial award application deadline: 3/15. *Faculty research:* School food service, teen pregnancy, diet and cholesterol metabolism. *Unit head:* Dr. Ann Blackwell, Chair, 601-266-5661, Fax: 601-266-4680.

The University of Texas at Tyler, College of Education and Psychology, Department of Psychology, Tyler, TX 75799-0001. Offers clinical psychology (MS), including neuropsychology, school psychology; counseling psychology (MA), including general, marriage and family; interdisciplinary studies (MSIS); school counseling (MA). Part-time and evening/weekend programs available. *Faculty:* 10 full-time (2 women), 8 part-time/adjunct (5 women). *Students:* 67 full-time (50 women), 60 part-time (50 women); includes 12 minority (4 African Americans, 1 American Indian/Alaska Native, 2 Asian Americans or Pacific Islanders, 5 Hispanic Americans). 37 applicants, 97% accepted, 32 enrolled. In 2007, 16 degrees awarded. *Degree requirements:* For master's, comprehensive exam, thesis optional. *Entrance requirements:* For master's, GRE General Test, minimum GPA of 3.0. *Application deadline:* For fall admission, 2/1 for domestic students; for spring admission, 10/1 for domestic students. Application fee: $0 ($50 for international students). Electronic applications accepted. *Expenses:* Tuition, state resident: part-time $627 per semester hour. Tuition, nonresident: part-time $908 per semester hour. Required fees: $107 per semester hour. Tuition and fees vary according to course load. *Financial support:* In 2007–08, fellowships with partial tuition reimbursements (averaging $3,000 per year), research assistantships (averaging $5,000 per year), teaching assistantships (averaging $1,500 per year) were awarded; career-related internships or fieldwork, Federal Work-Study, and institutionally sponsored loans also available. Support available to part-time students. Financial award application deadline: 7/1. *Faculty research:* Neuropsychology, child abuse, psychometric properties of psychological instruments, maternal behavior, clinical practice issues, victimization of women, post-traumatic stress disorder. *Unit head:* Dr. Charles B. Barke, Interim Chair, 903-565-5875, Fax: 903-565-5560, E-mail: cbarke@uttyler.edu. *Application contact:* Pam Morrow, Assistant to Dean for Enrollment Management, 903-566-7205, Fax: 903-566-7068, E-mail: pmorrow@uttyler.edu.

The University of Winnipeg, Faculty of Theology, Winnipeg, MB R3B 2E9, Canada. Offers marriage and family therapy (MMFT, Certificate); sacred theology (STM); theology (M Div). *Accreditation:* AAMFT/COAMFTE; ATS. Part-time programs available. *Degree requirements:* For M Div, thesis/dissertation optional.

University of Wisconsin–Stout, Graduate School, College of Human Development, Program in Marriage and Family Therapy, Menomonie, WI 54751. Offers MS. *Accreditation:* AAMFT/COAMFTE. Part-time programs available. *Faculty:* 9 full-time (2 women). *Students:* 23 full-time (17 women); includes 2 minority (1 African American, 1 Asian American or Pacific Islander). Average age 36. 49 applicants, 22% accepted, 8 enrolled. In 2007, 10 degrees awarded. *Degree requirements:* For master's, thesis or alternative. *Entrance requirements:* For master's, minimum GPA of 2.75. Additional exam requirements/recommendations for international students: Required—TOEFL (minimum score 500 paper-based; 173 computer-based; 61 iBT). *Application deadline:* For fall admission, 2/1 for domestic and international students. Application fee: $45. *Expenses:* Tuition, state resident: part-time $332 per credit. Tuition, nonresident: part-time $553 per credit. *Financial support:* In 2007–08, 1 research assistantship (averaging $4,979 per year) was awarded; Federal Work-Study, scholarships/grants, tuition waivers (partial), and unspecified assistantships also available. Support available to part-time students. Financial award application deadline: 4/1; financial award applicants required to submit FAFSA. *Faculty research:* Abuse, addiction, resilience, diversity, narrative therapy. *Unit head:* Dr. Bruce Kuehl, Director, 715-232-2194, E-mail: kuehlb@uwstout.edu. *Application contact:* Anne E. Johnson, Graduate Student Evaluator, 715-232-1322, Fax: 715-232-2413, E-mail: johnsona@uwstout.edu.

Utah State University, School of Graduate Studies, College of Education and Human Services, Department of Family, Consumer, and Human Development, Logan, UT 84322. Offers family and human development (MFHD); family, consumer, and human development (MS, PhD), including adolescence/youth (MS), adult development/aging (MS), consumer science (MS), infancy/childhood (MS), marriage and family relations (MS), marriage and family therapy (MS). *Accreditation:* AAMFT/COAMFTE (one or more programs are accredited). Part-time and evening/weekend programs available. Postbaccalaureate distance learning degree programs offered (minimal on-campus study). *Degree requirements:* For master's, thesis; for doctorate, comprehensive exam, thesis/dissertation, competencies. *Entrance requirements:* For master's, GRE General Test or MAT, minimum GPA of 3.0, 3 letters of recommendation; for doctorate, GRE, minimum GPA of 3.0, 3 letters of recommendation. Additional exam requirements/recommendations for international students: Required—TOEFL. Electronic applications accepted. *Faculty research:* Marriage and family relations, adolescent problem behavior, family financial management, early literacy, mental health in the elderly, parent child attachment.

Valdosta State University, Graduate School, College of Arts and Sciences, Department of Sociology, Anthropology, and Criminal Justice, Valdosta, GA 31698. Offers criminal justice (MS); marriage and family therapy (MS); sociology (MS). *Accreditation:* AAMFT/COAMFTE. Part-time and evening/weekend programs available. *Faculty:* 19 full-time (7 women). *Students:* 51 full-time (39 women), 20 part-time (14 women); includes 24 minority (19 African Americans, 4 Asian Americans or Pacific Islanders, 1 Hispanic American). Average age 27. 62 applicants, 47% accepted, 26 enrolled. In 2007, 29 degrees awarded. *Degree requirements:* For master's, thesis or alternative, comprehensive written and/or oral exams. *Entrance requirements:* For master's, GRE General Test or MAT (sociology, marriage and family therapy), minimum GPA of 2.5. Additional exam requirements/recommendations for international students: Required—TOEFL (minimum score 523 paper-based; 193 computer-based). *Application deadline:* For fall admission, 7/1 for domestic and international students; for spring admission, 11/15 for domestic and international students. Applications are processed on a rolling basis. Application fee: $40. Electronic applications accepted. *Expenses:* Tuition, state resident: part-time $147 per hour. Tuition, nonresident: part-time $586 per hour. Required fees: $520 per semester. Tuition and fees vary according to course level, course load, campus/location and program. *Financial support:* In 2007–08, 5 students received support, including 5 research assistantships with full tuition reimbursements available (averaging $2,452 per year); career-related internships or fieldwork, institutionally sponsored loans, scholarships/grants, and unspecified assistantships also available. Support available to part-time students. Financial award application deadline: 7/1; financial award applicants required to submit FAFSA. *Faculty research:* Police-civilian ride-along project. *Unit head:* Dr. Mike Capece, Acting Head, 229-333-5943, Fax: 229-333-5492.

Virginia Polytechnic Institute and State University, Graduate School, College of Liberal Arts and Human Sciences, Department of Human Development, Blacksburg, VA 24061. Offers adult development and aging (MS, PhD); adult learning and human resource development (MS, PhD); child development (MS, PhD); family studies (MS, PhD); marriage and family therapy (MS, PhD). *Accreditation:* AAMFT/COAMFTE (one or more programs are accredited). *Entrance requirements:* For master's and doctorate, GRE General Test. Additional exam requirements/recommendations for international students: Required—TOEFL (minimum score 600 paper-based; 250 computer-based). Electronic applications accepted. *Faculty research:* Stress management, children's play, dual-career families, social cognition, relationships of elderly.

Wesley Biblical Seminary, Graduate Programs, Jackson, MS 39206. Offers Biblical literature (MA); Christian studies (MA); evangelism (M Div); family life ministry (M Div); honors research (M Div); missions (M Div); pastoral ministry (M Div); teaching (M Div); theology (MA). *Accreditation:* ATS. Part-time programs available. *Degree requirements:* For master's, thesis. *Entrance requirements:* Additional exam requirements/recommendations for international students: Required—TOEFL. *Application deadline:* For fall admission, 7/1 priority date for domestic students; for spring admission, 12/1 priority date for domestic students. Applications are processed on a rolling basis. Application fee: $25. Electronic applications accepted. *Financial support:* Scholarships/grants available. Support available to part-time students. *Faculty*

Marriage and Family Therapy

Wesley Biblical Seminary (continued)
research: Patristics, missiology, culture, hermeneutics. *Unit head:* Dr. Ray R. Easley, Vice President for Academic Affairs, 601-366-8880 Ext. 112, Fax: 601-366-8832. *Application contact:* Megan Tirrill, Assistant to the Vice President for Student Development, 800-366-8880 Ext. 110, Fax: 601-366-8832, E-mail: mtirrill@wbs.edu.

Western Michigan University, Graduate College, College of Education, Department of Counselor Education and Counseling Psychology, Kalamazoo, MI 49008-5202. Offers counseling psychology (PhD); counselor education (MA, Ed D, PhD); counselor education and counseling psychology (MA, PhD); counselor psychology (MA); marriage and family therapy (MA). *Accreditation:* ACA (one or more programs are accredited); APA (one or more programs are accredited); CORE; NCATE. *Degree requirements:* For doctorate, thesis/dissertation, oral exams. *Entrance requirements:* For doctorate, GRE General Test.

Western Seminary, Graduate Programs, Program in Marriage and Family Counseling, Portland, OR 97215-3367. Offers MA, MFT. Offered at San Jose campus only. *Degree requirements:* For master's, practicum.

Western Seminary–Sacramento Campus, Graduate Programs, Sacramento, CA 95821. Offers exegetical theology (MA); marital and family therapy (MA); ministry (M Div); specialized ministry (MA). Postbaccalaureate distance learning degree programs offered. *Entrance requirements:* For M Div, minimum GPA of 2.5; for master's, minimum GPA of 3.0.

Western Seminary–San Jose Campus, Graduate Programs, Los Gatos, CA 95032-4520. Offers exegetical theology (MA); expositional ministry (M Div); marital and family therapy (MA); ministry (M Div); pastoral ministry (M Div); specialized ministry (MA). Postbaccalaureate distance learning degree programs offered. *Degree requirements:* For master's, 2 foreign languages; for M Div, 3 foreign languages. *Entrance requirements:* For M Div, minimum GPA of 2.5; for master's, minimum GPA of 3.0.

Psychoanalysis and Psychotherapy

Adler Graduate School, Program in Adlerian Studies, Richfield, MN 55423. Offers art therapy specialization (MA); clinical counseling track (MA); coaching and consulting in organizations (Certificate); management consulting and organizational leadership (MA); marriage and family track (MA); non-clinical Adlerian studies track (MA); personal and professional life coaching (Certificate); school counseling (MA). Part-time and evening/weekend programs available. *Faculty:* 4 full-time (1 woman), 44 part-time/adjunct (27 women). *Students:* Average age 37. 46 applicants, 96% accepted, 44 enrolled. In 2007, 37 degrees awarded. *Degree requirements:* For master's, thesis or alternative, 500-700 hour internship, depending on license choice. *Entrance requirements:* For master's, minimum undergraduate GPA of 3.0, 12 credits of course work in psychology or related field. *Application deadline:* For fall admission, 10/1 priority date for domestic students; for winter admission, 1/1 priority date for domestic students; for spring admission, 4/1 priority date for domestic students. Applications are processed on a rolling basis. Application fee: $50. *Expenses:* Tuition: Part-time $430 per credit. Required fees: $85 per term. *Financial support:* In 2007–08, 121 students received support. Career-related internships or fieldwork and tuition waivers available. Support available to part-time students. Financial award applicants required to submit FAFSA. *Unit head:* Dr. Dennis Rislove, President, 612-861-7554 Ext. 106, Fax: 612-861-7559, E-mail: rislove@alfredadler.edu. *Application contact:* Evelyn B. Haas, Director of Student Services and Admissions, 612-861-7554 Ext. 103, Fax: 612-861-7559, E-mail: ev@alfredadler.edu.

Argosy University, Chicago, College of Psychology and Behavioral Sciences, Doctoral Program in Clinical Psychology, Chicago, IL 60654. Offers child and adolescent psychology (Psy D); client-centered and experiential psychotherapies (Psy D); diversity and multicultural psychology (Psy D); family psychology (Psy D); forensic psychology (Psy D); health psychology (Psy D); psychoanalytic psychology (Psy D); psychology and spirituality (Psy D). *Accreditation:* APA.

See Close-Up on page 1379.

Boston Graduate School of Psychoanalysis, Master's, Certificate, and Doctoral Programs, Brookline, MA 02446-4602. Offers MA, Psya D, Certificate. Part-time programs available. *Faculty:* 11 full-time (7 women), 16 part-time/adjunct (8 women). *Students:* 17 full-time (14 women), 80 part-time (59 women); includes 13 minority (2 African Americans, 5 Asian Americans or Pacific Islanders, 6 Hispanic Americans), 14 international. 9 applicants, 78% accepted, 7 enrolled. In 2007, 9 master's, 1 other advanced degree awarded. Terminal master's awarded for partial completion of doctoral program. *Degree requirements:* For master's and Certificate, thesis. *Entrance requirements:* For master's and doctorate, interview, writing sample; for Certificate, interview, MA. *Application deadline:* For fall admission, 5/19 priority date for domestic students, 5/15 priority date for international students; for spring admission, 11/15 priority date for domestic and international students. Applications are processed on a rolling basis. Application fee: $100. Electronic applications accepted. *Expenses:* Tuition: Full-time $5,400; part-time $1,350 per course. Required fees: $460 per semester. Tuition and fees vary according to course load, campus/location and program. *Financial support:* In 2007–08, 17 students received support. Career-related internships or fieldwork and unspecified assistantships available. Financial award applicants required to submit FAFSA. *Faculty research:* The effect of extra-analytic contact on the analysis, psychoanalytic intervention with schizophrenia, emotional learning in the classroom, psychoanalytic techniques in the geriatric setting, addictions research. *Unit head:* Dr. Jane Snyder, Provost, 617-277-3915, Fax: 617-277-0312, E-mail: snyderj@bgsp.edu. *Application contact:* Caroline Egnaczyk, Admissions Coordinator, 617-277-3915, Fax: 617-277-0312, E-mail: bgsp@bgsp.edu.

See Close-Up on page 1417.

Boston Graduate School of Psychoanalysis, Master's Program—New York, New York, NY 10011. Offers MA. Part-time programs available. *Faculty:* 12 full-time (10 women), 11 part-time/adjunct (7 women). *Students:* 8 full-time (7 women), 13 part-time (6 women), 1 international. In 2007, 5 degrees awarded. *Entrance requirements:* For master's, interview, writing sample. *Application deadline:* Applications are processed on a rolling basis. Application fee: $100. *Expenses:* Tuition: Full-time $5,400; part-time $1,350 per course. Required fees: $460 per semester. Tuition and fees vary according to course load, campus/location and program. *Financial support:* Career-related internships or fieldwork available. Financial award applicants required to submit FAFSA. *Unit head:* Dr. Mimi Crowell, Dean, 212-260-7050, Fax: 212-228-6410, E-mail: bgsp-ny.registrar@bgsp.edu. *Application contact:* Stephen Guttman, Registrar, 212-260-7050, Fax: 212-228-6410, E-mail: bgsp-ny.registrar@bgsp.edu.

See Close-Up on page 1417.

Boston Graduate School of Psychoanalysis, Program in the Study of Violence, Brookline, MA 02446-4602. Offers Psya D. Evening/weekend programs available. *Faculty:* 2 full-time (1 woman), 20 part-time/adjunct (6 women). *Students:* 2 full-time (1 woman), 12 part-time (7 women); includes 1 minority (African American), 2 international. 6 applicants, 100% accepted. *Degree requirements:* For doctorate, thesis/dissertation. *Entrance requirements:* For doctorate, interview, master's degree or equivalent, writing sample. *Application deadline:* For fall admission, 5/15 priority date for domestic and international students; for spring admission, 11/15 priority date for domestic and international students. Applications are processed on a rolling basis. Application fee: $100. Electronic applications accepted. *Expenses:* Tuition: Full-time $5,400; part-time $1,350 per course. Required fees: $460 per semester. Tuition and fees vary according to course load, campus/location and program. *Financial support:* In 2007–08, 3 students received support. Unspecified assistantships available. Financial award applicants required to submit FAFSA. *Faculty research:* Institutional violence, developmental impulse control, psychodynamics of murderers, community violence, psychodynamics in the Salem Witch Trials. *Unit head:* Dr. Siamak Movahedi, Program Director, Institute for the Study of Violence, 617-277-3915, E-mail: bgsp@bgsp.edu. *Application contact:* Dr. Jane Snyder, Co-Director, Institute for the Study of Violence, 617-277-3915, Fax: 617-277-0312, E-mail: bgsp@bgsp.edu.

Naropa University, Graduate Programs, Program in Contemplative Psychotherapy, Boulder, CO 80302-6697. Offers MA. *Faculty:* 1 (woman) full-time, 19 part-time/adjunct (12 women). *Students:* 67 full-time (44 women), 1 part-time; includes 5 minority (1 African American, 4 Hispanic Americans), 1 international. Average age 32. 72 applicants, 58% accepted, 27 enrolled. In 2007, 21 degrees awarded. *Degree requirements:* For master's, thesis, internship. *Entrance requirements:* For master's, in-person interview; supplemental application. Additional exam requirements/recommendations for international students: Required—TOEFL (minimum score 600 paper-based; 250 computer-based). *Application deadline:* For fall admission, 1/15 priority date for domestic and international students; for spring admission, 10/15 priority date for domestic students. Applications are processed on a rolling basis. Application fee: $60. Electronic applications accepted. *Expenses:* Tuition: Full-time $15,070; part-time $685 per credit. Required fees: $250 per semester. Tuition and fees vary according to course load. *Financial support:* In 2007–08, 38 students received support, including 4 research assistantships with partial tuition reimbursements available (averaging $3,000 per year), 1 teaching assistantship with partial tuition reimbursement available (averaging $3,000 per year); career-related internships or fieldwork, Federal Work-Study, scholarships/grants, tuition waivers (partial), and unspecified assistantships also available. Support available to part-time students. Financial award application deadline: 3/1; financial award applicants required to submit FAFSA. *Unit head:* Lauren Casalino, Chair, 303-245-4778. *Application contact:* Donna McIntyre, Admissions Counselor, 303-546-3555, Fax: 303-546-3583, E-mail: donna@naropa.edu.

See Close-Up on page 1449.

Naropa University, Graduate Programs, Program in Somatic Counseling Psychotherapy, Concentration in Body Psychotherapy, Boulder, CO 80302-6697. Offers MA. Part-time programs available. *Faculty:* 3 full-time (2 women), 11 part-time/adjunct (8 women). *Students:* 19 full-time (16 women), 3 part-time (2 women), 1 international. Average age 25. 33 applicants, 61% accepted, 10 enrolled. In 2007, 11 degrees awarded. *Degree requirements:* For master's, comprehensive exam, thesis, internship. *Entrance requirements:* For master's, interview; body-mind discipline; course work in psychology, anatomy. Additional exam requirements/recommendations for international students: Required—TOEFL (minimum score 600 paper-based; 250 computer-based). *Application deadline:* For fall admission, 1/15 priority date for domestic and international students. Applications are processed on a rolling basis. Application fee: $60. Electronic applications accepted. *Expenses:* Tuition: Full-time $15,070; part-time $685 per credit. Required fees: $250 per semester. Tuition and fees vary according to course load. *Financial support:* In 2007–08, 7 students received support, including 1 research assistantship with partial tuition reimbursement available (averaging $3,000 per year); career-related internships or fieldwork, Federal Work-Study, scholarships/grants, tuition waivers (partial), and unspecified assistantships also available. Support available to part-time students. Financial award application deadline: 3/1; financial award applicants required to submit FAFSA. *Unit head:* Ryan Kennedy, Co-Chair, 303-245-4759. *Application contact:* Donna McIntyre, Admissions Counselor, 303-546-3555, Fax: 303-546-3583, E-mail: donna@naropa.edu.

See Close-Up on page 1449.

New York University, Graduate School of Arts and Science, Department of Psychology, New York, NY 10012-1019. Offers cognition and perception (PhD); community psychology (PhD); general psychology (MA); industrial/organizational psychology (MA); psychotherapy and psychoanalysis (Advanced Certificate); social/personality psychology (PhD). Part-time programs available. *Faculty:* 38 full-time (13 women), 78 part-time/adjunct. *Students:* 155 full-time (115 women), 305 part-time (218 women); includes 77 minority (24 African Americans, 29 Asian Americans or Pacific Islanders, 24 Hispanic Americans), 53 international. Average age 32. 767 applicants, 46% accepted, 112 enrolled. In 2007, 80 master's, 15 doctorates awarded. Terminal master's awarded for partial completion of doctoral program. *Degree requirements:* For master's, comprehensive exam, thesis or alternative; for doctorate, thesis/dissertation. *Entrance requirements:* For master's, GRE General Test, minimum GPA of 3.0; for doctorate, GRE General Test, GRE Subject Test; for Advanced Certificate, doctoral degree, minimum GPA of 3.0. Additional exam requirements/recommendations for international students: Required—TOEFL. *Application deadline:* For fall admission, 12/18 for domestic students. Application fee: $85. *Financial support:* Fellowships with tuition reimbursements, research assistantships with tuition reimbursements, teaching assistantships with tuition reimbursements, career-related internships or fieldwork, Federal Work-Study, institutionally sponsored loans, scholarships/grants, traineeships, health care benefits, and unspecified assistantships available. Financial award application deadline: 12/18; financial award applicants required to submit FAFSA. *Faculty research:* Vision, memory, social cognition, social and cognitive development, relationships. *Unit head:* Marisa Carrasco, Chair, 212-998-7900, Fax: 212-995-4018, E-mail: psychq@psych.nyu.edu. *Application contact:* Laurence Maloney, Director of Graduate Studies, 212-998-7900, Fax: 212-995-4018, E-mail: psychq@psych.nyu.edu.

Rehabilitation Counseling

Arkansas State University, Graduate School, College of Education, Department of Psychology and Counseling, Jonesboro, State University, AR 72467. Offers college student personnel services (MS); counselor education (Ed S), including college student personnel services, psychoeducational diagnosis, school counseling; rehabilitation counseling (MRC); school counseling (MSE); student affairs (Certificate). *Accreditation:* ACA (one or more programs are accredited); CORE (one or more programs are accredited); NCATE. Part-time programs available. *Faculty:* 11 full-time (6 women), 6 part-time/adjunct (2 women). *Students:* 69 full-time (54 women), 71 part-time (58 women); includes 27 minority (24 African Americans, 3 Hispanic Americans). Average age 32. 53 applicants, 66% accepted, 32 enrolled. In 2007, 17 master's, 6 other advanced degrees awarded. *Degree requirements:* For master's and other advanced degree, comprehensive exam, thesis or alternative. *Entrance requirements:* For master's, GRE General Test or MAT (MSE), appropriate bachelor's degree, interview, letters of reference, official transcript; for other advanced degree, GRE General Test, interview, master's degree, letters of reference, official transcript. Additional exam requirements/recommendations for international students: Required—TOEFL (minimum score 213 computer-based). *Application deadline:* Applications are processed on a rolling basis. Application fee: $30 ($40 for international students). Electronic applications accepted. *Expenses:* Tuition, state resident: full-time $3,528; part-time $196 per hour. Tuition, nonresident: full-time $8,928; part-time $496 per hour. Required fees: $842; $44 per hour. $25 per term. Tuition and fees vary according to course load and program. *Financial support:* Teaching assistantships, career-related internships or fieldwork, scholarships/grants, and unspecified assistantships available. Financial award application deadline: 7/1; financial award applicants required to submit FAFSA. *Faculty research:* Abuse issues in children and adolescents, career counseling, children's learning and memory, crisis intervention, drug use and addition. *Unit head:* Dr. Loretta McGregor, Chair, 870-972-3064, Fax: 870-972-3962, E-mail: lmcgregor@astate.edu.

Assumption College, Graduate School, Rehabilitation Counseling Program, Worcester, MA 01609-1296. Offers MA, CAGS. *Accreditation:* CORE. Part-time and evening/weekend programs available. Postbaccalaureate distance learning degree programs offered (minimal on-campus study). *Faculty:* 2 full-time (0 women), 13 part-time/adjunct (7 women). *Students:* 56 full-time (41 women), 31 part-time (18 women); includes 8 minority (3 African Americans, 3 Asian Americans or Pacific Islanders, 2 Hispanic Americans). Average age 31. 55 applicants, 93% accepted. In 2007, 22 master's, 8 other advanced degrees awarded. *Degree requirements:* For master's, comprehensive exam, internship, practicum. *Entrance requirements:* For master's and CAGS, 3 letters of recommendation, resumé, interview, essay. Additional exam requirements/recommendations for international students: Required—TOEFL, IELTS. *Application deadline:* For fall admission, 6/1 priority date for domestic students, 5/1 priority date for international students; for spring admission, 11/1 priority date for domestic students, 10/1 priority date for international students. Applications are processed on a rolling basis. Application fee: $30. Electronic applications accepted. *Expenses:* Tuition: Part-time $450 per credit. Required fees: $20 per semester. *Financial support:* In 2007–08, 81 students received support, including 45 fellowships with full and partial tuition reimbursements available (averaging $5,124 per year), 1 teaching assistantship (averaging $19,860 per year); scholarships/grants and traineeships also available. Financial award application deadline: 6/1; financial award applicants required to submit FAFSA. *Faculty research:* Job placement for severe disabilities, vocational counseling, conflict resolution, health issues in mental illness. *Unit head:* A. Lee Pearson, Director, 508-767-7063, Fax: 508-767-7030, E-mail: lpearson@assumption.edu. *Application contact:* Adrian O. Dumas, Director of Graduate Enrollment Management and Services, 508-767-7365, Fax: 508-767-7030, E-mail: adumas@assumption.edu.

Auburn University, Graduate School, College of Education, Department of Rehabilitation and Special Education, Auburn University, AL 36849. Offers collaborative teacher special education (M Ed, MS); early childhood special education (M Ed, MS); rehabilitation counseling (M Ed, MS, PhD). *Accreditation:* CORE; NCATE. Part-time programs available. *Faculty:* 12 full-time (6 women). *Students:* 85 full-time (68 women), 45 part-time (36 women); includes 30 minority (24 African Americans, 3 American Indian/Alaska Native, 2 Asian Americans or Pacific Islanders, 1 Hispanic American). Average age 32. 69 applicants, 77% accepted, 41 enrolled. In 2007, 64 master's, 1 doctorate awarded. *Degree requirements:* For master's, thesis (for some programs); for doctorate, thesis/dissertation. *Entrance requirements:* For master's, GRE General Test; for doctorate, GRE General Test, interview. *Application deadline:* For fall admission, 7/17 for domestic students; for spring admission, 11/24 for domestic students. Applications are processed on a rolling basis. Application fee: $25 ($50 for international students). Electronic applications accepted. *Financial support:* Research assistantships, teaching assistantships, Federal Work-Study available. Support available to part-time students. Financial award application deadline: 3/15. *Faculty research:* Emotional conflict/behavior disorders, gifted and talented, learning disabilities, mental retardation, multi-handicapped. *Unit head:* Dr. Philip L. Browning, Head, 334-844-5943. *Application contact:* Dr. Joe Pittman, Interim Dean of the Graduate School, 334-844-4700.

Barry University, School of Education, Program in Rehabilitation Counseling, Miami Shores, FL 33161-6695. Offers MS, Ed S. Part-time and evening/weekend programs available. *Students:* Average age 35. *Degree requirements:* For master's, comprehensive exam, scholarly paper; for Ed S, comprehensive exam. *Entrance requirements:* For master's, GRE General Test or MAT, minimum GPA of 3.0; for Ed S, GRE General Test, minimum GPA of 3.0. *Application deadline:* For fall admission, 5/1 priority date for domestic students. Applications are processed on a rolling basis. Application fee: $30. Electronic applications accepted. *Financial support:* Application deadline: 5/1; *Unit head:* Dr. Jeffrey Guterman, Chair, 305-899-3862, Fax: 305-899-4708, E-mail: jguterman@mail.barry.edu. *Application contact:* Dave Fletcher, Director of Graduate Admissions, 305-899-3113, Fax: 305-899-2971, E-mail: dfletcher@mail.barry.edu.

Bowling Green State University, Graduate College, College of Education and Human Development, School of Education and Intervention Services, Intervention Services Division, Program in Rehabilitation Counseling, Bowling Green, OH 43403. Offers MRC. *Accreditation:* CORE. Part-time programs available. *Students:* 23 full-time (16 women), 15 part-time (11 women); includes 6 minority (4 African Americans, 2 Hispanic Americans), 5 international. Average age 35. 23 applicants, 65% accepted, 11 enrolled. In 2007, 9 degrees awarded. *Degree requirements:* For master's, thesis or alternative. *Entrance requirements:* For master's, GRE General Test, interview. Additional exam requirements/recommendations for international students: Required—TOEFL. *Application deadline:* For fall admission, 3/1 priority date for domestic students. Applications are processed on a rolling basis. Application fee: $30. Electronic applications accepted. *Financial support:* In 2007–08, 7 research assistantships with full tuition reimbursements (averaging $4,202 per year) were awarded; teaching assistantships with full tuition reimbursements, career-related internships or fieldwork, institutionally sponsored loans, tuition waivers (full), and unspecified assistantships also available. Financial award applicants required to submit FAFSA. *Faculty research:* Depression, disability management, schizophrenia, job analysis, rehabilitation counseling curriculum. *Application contact:* Dr. Jay Stewart, Graduate Coordinator, 419-372-7301.

California State University, Fresno, Division of Graduate Studies, School of Education and Human Development, Department of Counseling and Special Education, Rehabilitation Counseling Program, Fresno, CA 93740-8027. Offers MS. *Accreditation:* CORE. Part-time and evening/weekend programs available. *Faculty:* 2 full-time (0 women). *Students:* 423; includes 224 minority (18 African Americans, 5 American Indian/Alaska Native, 40 Asian Americans or Pacific Islanders, 161 Hispanic Americans), 9 international. Average age 28. 15 applicants. In 2007, 133 degrees awarded. *Degree requirements:* For master's, thesis optional. *Entrance requirements:* For master's, GRE General Test, MAT, minimum GPA of 2.75. Additional exam requirements/recommendations for international students: Required—TOEFL. *Application deadline:* For fall admission, 5/1 for domestic and international students; for spring admission, 10/1 for domestic and international students. Applications are processed on a rolling basis. Application fee: $55. Electronic applications accepted. *Financial support:* Career-related internships or fieldwork, Federal Work-Study, scholarships/grants, and research awards available. Support available to part-time students. Financial award application deadline: 3/1; financial award applicants required to submit FAFSA. *Faculty research:* Aging, career development, job retention, rehabilitation administration. *Unit head:* Dr. Charles Arokiasamy, Coordinator, 559-278-0340, Fax: 559-278-0045, E-mail: charlesa@csufresno.edu.

California State University, Los Angeles, Graduate Studies, Charter College of Education, Division of Special Education and Counseling, Major in Counseling, Los Angeles, CA 90032-8530. Offers applied behavior analysis (MS); community college counseling (MS); rehabilitation counseling (MS); school counseling and school psychology (MS). *Accreditation:* ACA; CORE; NCATE. Part-time and evening/weekend programs available. *Students:* 200 full-time (157 women), 144 part-time (119 women); includes 205 minority (25 African Americans, 1 American Indian/Alaska Native, 32 Asian Americans or Pacific Islanders, 147 Hispanic Americans), 46 international. Average age 32. In 2007, 106 degrees awarded. *Degree requirements:* For master's, comprehensive exam, project or thesis. *Entrance requirements:* For master's, interview, minimum GPA of 2.75 in last 90 units of course work, teaching certificate. Additional exam requirements/recommendations for international students: Required—TOEFL. *Application deadline:* For fall admission, 6/30 for domestic students; for spring admission, 2/1 for domestic students. Applications are processed on a rolling basis. Application fee: $55. *Financial support:* Career-related internships or fieldwork and Federal Work-Study available. Support available to part-time students. Financial award application deadline: 3/1. *Unit head:* Dr. Randy Campbell, Chair, Division of Special Education and Counseling, 323-343-4400 Ext. 34257, Fax: 323-343-5605, E-mail: rcampbe@calstatela.edu.

California State University, San Bernardino, Graduate Studies, College of Education, Program in Educational Psychology and Counseling, San Bernardino, CA 92407-2397. Offers counseling and guidance (MS); rehabilitation counseling (MA). *Accreditation:* NCATE. Part-time and evening/weekend programs available. *Faculty:* 19 full-time, 20 part-time/adjunct. *Students:* 110 full-time (87 women), 5 part-time (4 women); includes 80 minority (13 African Americans, 1 American Indian/Alaska Native, 7 Asian Americans or Pacific Islanders, 59 Hispanic Americans), 2 international. Average age 28. 29 applicants, 66% accepted, 2 enrolled. In 2007, 26 degrees awarded. *Degree requirements:* For master's, thesis or alternative. *Entrance requirements:* For master's, minimum GPA of 3.0 in education. *Application deadline:* For fall admission, 8/31 priority date for domestic students. Application fee: $55. *Financial support:* Career-related internships or fieldwork and Federal Work-Study available. Support available to part-time students. *Unit head:* Dr. Ruth Ann Sandlin, Chair, 909-537-5641, Fax: 909-537-7040, E-mail: rsandlin@csusb.edu.

California State University, San Bernardino, Graduate Studies, College of Education, Programs in Special Education and Rehabilitation Counseling, San Bernardino, CA 92407-2397. Offers rehabilitation counseling (MA); special education (MA). *Accreditation:* CORE; NCATE. Part-time and evening/weekend programs available. *Students:* 211 full-time (161 women), 104 part-time (75 women); includes 152 minority (60 African Americans, 5 American Indian/Alaska Native, 9 Asian Americans or Pacific Islanders, 78 Hispanic Americans), 1 international. Average age 38. 108 applicants, 78% accepted, 50 enrolled. In 2007, 93 degrees awarded. *Degree requirements:* For master's, thesis or alternative. *Entrance requirements:* For master's, minimum GPA of 3.0 in education. *Application deadline:* For fall admission, 8/31 priority date for domestic students. Application fee: $55. *Financial support:* Career-related internships or fieldwork and Federal Work-Study available. Support available to part-time students. *Unit head:* Dr. Ruth Ann Sandlin, Chair, 909-537-5641, Fax: 909-537-7040, E-mail: rsandlin@csusb.edu.

Central Connecticut State University, School of Graduate Studies, School of Education and Professional Studies, Department of Counseling and Family Therapy, New Britain, CT 06050-4010. Offers marriage and family therapy (MS); professional counseling (MS, Certificate); school counseling (MS); student development in higher education (MS). *Accreditation:* AAMFT/COAMFTE. Part-time and evening/weekend programs available. *Faculty:* 6 full-time (4 women), 14 part-time/adjunct (8 women). *Students:* 112 full-time (89 women), 175 part-time (147 women); includes 43 minority (20 African Americans, 1 American Indian/Alaska Native, 3 Asian Americans or Pacific Islanders, 19 Hispanic Americans), 3 international. Average age 33. 199 applicants, 45% accepted, 69 enrolled. In 2007, 64 master's, 5 other advanced degrees awarded. *Degree requirements:* For master's, thesis or alternative, special project. *Entrance requirements:* For master's, minimum GPA of 2.7. Additional exam requirements/recommendations for international students: Required—TOEFL. *Application deadline:* For fall admission, 5/1 for domestic students. Applications are processed on a rolling basis. Application fee: $50. Electronic applications accepted. *Expenses:* Tuition, area resident: Full-time $4,169. Tuition, state resident: full-time $6,253. Tuition, nonresident: full-time $11,614; part-time $400 per credit. Required fees: $3,322. One-time fee: $62 part-time. Tuition and fees vary according to degree level and program. *Financial support:* In 2007–08, 11 students received support, including 15 research assistantships; career-related internships or fieldwork, Federal Work-Study, scholarships/grants, and unspecified assistantships also available. Support available to part-time students. Financial award application deadline: 3/1; financial award applicants required to submit FAFSA. *Faculty research:* Elementary/secondary school counseling, marriage/family therapy, rehabilitation counseling, counseling in higher educational settings. *Unit head:* Dr. Connie Tait, Chair, 860-832-2154.

Coppin State University, Division of Graduate Studies, Division of Arts and Sciences, Department of Applied Psychology and Rehabilitation Counseling, Program in Rehabilitation Counseling, Baltimore, MD 21216-3698. Offers M Ed. *Accreditation:* CORE. Part-time programs available. *Students:* 55 full-time (40 women), 40 part-time (29 women); includes 91 minority (89 African Americans, 1 American Indian/Alaska Native, 1 Hispanic American), 3 international. Average age 43. 40 applicants, 88% accepted, 20 enrolled. In 2007, 12 degrees awarded. *Degree requirements:* For master's, comprehensive exam (for some programs), thesis optional, internship, clinical requirements. *Entrance requirements:* For master's, GRE General Test, interview, minimum GPA of 3.0. *Application deadline:* For fall admission, 8/15 for domestic students; for spring admission, 12/15 for domestic students. Application fee: $45. *Expenses:* Tuition, state resident: part-time $217 per credit. Tuition, nonresident: part-time $400 per credit. *Financial support:* Career-related internships or fieldwork available. Financial award application deadline: 6/30; financial award applicants required to submit FAFSA. *Unit head:* Dr. Janet D. Spry, Coordinator, 410-951-3514, E-mail: jspry@coppin.edu.

Drake University, School of Education, Department of Leadership, Counseling and Adult Development, Program in Rehabilitation Counseling, Des Moines, IA 50311-4516. Offers rehabilitation administration (MS); rehabilitation counseling (MS); réhabilitation placement (MS). Part-time and evening/weekend programs available. *Faculty:* 10 full-time (3 women), 28 part-time/adjunct (16 women). *Students:* 17 applicants, 53% accepted. In 2007, 4 degrees awarded. *Degree requirements:* For master's, comprehensive exam, thesis (for some programs), internships (for some programs). *Entrance requirements:* For master's, GRE General Test, MAT or Drake SOE writing assessment, resumé, 2 letters of recommendation. Additional exam requirements/recommendations for international students: Required—TOEFL (minimum score 550 paper-based; 213 computer-based). *Application deadline:* For fall admission, 7/1 priority date for domestic students, 6/1 priority date for international students; for spring admission, 11/1 priority date for domestic students, 10/1 priority date for international students. Applications are processed on a rolling basis. Application fee: $25. Electronic applications accepted. *Expenses:* Tuition: Full-time $26,030; part-time $370 per credit hour. Required fees: $406; $40 per semester. Tuition and fees vary according to program. *Financial support:* Career-related internships or fieldwork available. Support available to part-time students. *Faculty research:* Counseling and rehabilitation, behavioral supports, inquiry-based science methods, teacher quality enhancement. Total annual research expenditures: $1.5 million. *Unit head:* Dr. Matt

Rehabilitation Counseling

Drake University (continued)
Bruinekool, Director, 515-271-3992, E-mail: matt.bruinekool@drake.edu. *Application contact:* Ann J. Martin, Graduate Coordinator, 515-271-2034, Fax: 515-271-2831, E-mail: ann.martin@drake.edu.

East Carolina University, Graduate School, School of Allied Health Sciences, Program in Rehabilitation Studies, Greenville, NC 27858-4353. Offers rehabilitation counseling (MS); substance abuse and clinical counseling (MS); vocational evaluation (MS). *Accreditation:* CORE. Part-time and evening/weekend programs available. *Students:* 61 full-time (45 women), 10 part-time (8 women); includes 9 minority (8 African Americans, 1 American Indian/Alaska Native), 2 international. Average age 31. 22 applicants, 14% accepted, 3 enrolled. In 2007, 21 degrees awarded. *Degree requirements:* For master's, comprehensive exam, thesis or alternative, internship. *Entrance requirements:* For master's, GRE General Test or MAT. Additional exam requirements/recommendations for international students: Required—TOEFL. *Application deadline:* For fall admission, 3/1 priority date for domestic students; for spring admission, 10/1 priority date for domestic students. Applications are processed on a rolling basis. Application fee: $50. *Financial support:* Research assistantships with partial tuition reimbursements, teaching assistantships with partial tuition reimbursements, Federal Work-Study and scholarships/grants available. Support available to part-time students. Financial award application deadline: 3/1. *Unit head:* Dr. Paul Alston, Chair, 252-744-6290, Fax: 252-328-0725, E-mail: alstonp@ecu.edu. *Application contact:* Dean of Graduate School, 252-328-6012, Fax: 252-328-6071, E-mail: gradschool@ecu.edu.

East Central University, School of Graduate Studies, Department of Human Resources, Ada, OK 74820-6899. Offers administration (MSHR); counseling (MSHR); criminal justice (MSHR); rehabilitation counseling (MSHR). *Accreditation:* CORE. Part-time and evening/weekend programs available. *Faculty:* 7 part-time/adjunct (3 women). *Students:* 83 full-time (71 women), 103 part-time (73 women); includes 54 minority (11 African Americans, 38 American Indian/Alaska Native, 1 Asian American or Pacific Islander, 4 Hispanic Americans). Average age 37. 125 applicants, 90% accepted. In 2007, 60 degrees awarded. *Degree requirements:* For master's, thesis optional. *Entrance requirements:* For master's, GRE General Test, MAT, minimum GPA of 2.5. *Application deadline:* Applications are processed on a rolling basis. Application fee: $0 ($50 for international students). Electronic applications accepted. *Expenses:* Tuition, state resident: full-time $2,784. Required fees: $53. *Financial support:* In 2007–08, 1 teaching assistantship was awarded. *Unit head:* Dr. James Burke, Chairman, 580-332-8000 Ext. 481, E-mail: jburke@ecok.edu. *Application contact:* Juanita L. Pratt, Secretary, 580-310-5708, Fax: 580-282-8691, E-mail: jpratt@ecok.edu.

Edinboro University of Pennsylvania, Graduate Studies and Research, School of Education, Department of Professional Studies, Program in Counseling, Edinboro, PA 16444. Offers community counseling (MA); elementary guidance (MA); rehabilitation counseling (MA); secondary guidance (MA); student personnel services (MA). *Accreditation:* ACA; CORE. Part-time and evening/weekend programs available. *Students:* 79 full-time (63 women), 53 part-time (41 women); includes 16 minority (12 African Americans, 2 Asian Americans or Pacific Islanders, 2 Hispanic Americans). Average age 29. In 2007, 43 degrees awarded. *Degree requirements:* For master's, thesis or alternative, competency exam. *Entrance requirements:* For master's, GRE or MAT, minimum QPA of 2.5. *Application deadline:* Applications are processed on a rolling basis. Application fee: $30. Electronic applications accepted. *Expenses:* Tuition, state resident: full-time $6,214; part-time $345 per credit. Tuition, nonresident: full-time $9,944; part-time $552 per credit. Required fees: $46 per credit. *Financial support:* In 2007–08, 26 research assistantships with full and partial tuition reimbursements (averaging $3,850 per year) were awarded; career-related internships or fieldwork, Federal Work-Study, scholarships/grants, and unspecified assistantships also available. Support available to part-time students. Financial award application deadline: 2/15; financial award applicants required to submit FAFSA. *Unit head:* Dr. Susan Norton, Head, 814-732-2260, E-mail: snorton@edinboro.edu. *Application contact:* Dr. R. Scott Baldwin, Dean, 814-732-2752, Fax: 814-732-2268, E-mail: sbaldwin@edinboro.edu.

Emporia State University, School of Graduate Studies, The Teachers College, Department of Counselor Education and Rehabilitation Programs, Program in Rehabilitation Counseling, Emporia, KS 66801-5087. Offers MS. *Accreditation:* CORE. Part-time programs available. *Students:* 3 full-time (all women), 11 part-time (10 women); includes 1 minority (African American) 1 applicant, 100% accepted, 1 enrolled. In 2007, 9 degrees awarded. *Degree requirements:* For master's, comprehensive exam or thesis, practicum. *Entrance requirements:* For master's, GRE or MAT, graduate essay exam, appropriate bachelor's degree, interview, letters of recommendation. *Application deadline:* For fall admission, 8/15 priority date for domestic students. Applications are processed on a rolling basis. Application fee: $30 ($75 for international students). Electronic applications accepted. *Expenses:* Tuition, state resident: part-time $157 per credit hour. Tuition, nonresident: part-time $475 per credit hour. Required fees: $47 per credit hour. Tuition and fees vary according to campus/location. *Financial support:* Career-related internships or fieldwork, Federal Work-Study, institutionally sponsored loans, health care benefits, and unspecified assistantships available. Financial award application deadline: 3/15; financial award applicants required to submit FAFSA. *Unit head:* Dr. Colleen Etzbach, Graduate Co-Coordinator, 620-341-5220, E-mail: cetzbach@emporia.edu. *Application contact:* Dr. James Costello, Graduate Co-Coordinator, 620-341-5220, E-mail: jcostell@emporia.edu.

Florida Atlantic University, College of Education, Department of Counselor Education, Boca Raton, FL 33431-0991. Offers counselor education (M Ed); family counseling (Ed S); mental health counseling (M Ed, Ed S); rehabilitation counseling (M Ed); school counseling (Ed S). *Accreditation:* ACA; NCATE. Part-time and evening/weekend programs available. *Degree requirements:* For Ed S, departmental qualifying exam. *Entrance requirements:* For master's, GRE General Test, minimum GPA of 3.0 during previous 2 years; for Ed S, GRE General Test, minimum graduate GPA of 3.25. Additional exam requirements/recommendations for international students: Required—TOEFL. *Faculty research:* Brief therapy, psychological type, marriage and family counseling, international programs, integrated services.

Florida International University, College of Education, Department of Educational and Psychological Studies, Program in Counselor Education, Miami, FL 33199. Offers mental health counseling (MS); rehabilitation counseling (MS); school counseling (MS). *Accreditation:* ACA; NCATE. Part-time and evening/weekend programs. available. *Entrance requirements:* For master's, General Knowledge test, College Level Academic Skills Test, GRE or PRAXIS (school counseling track), minimum GPA of 3.0, interview. Additional exam requirements/recommendations for international students: Required—TOEFL (minimum score 550 paper-based; 213 computer-based; 80 iBT), IELTS (minimum score 6). Electronic applications accepted. *Expenses:* Tuition, state resident: full-time $6,106. Tuition, nonresident: full-time $15,528. Required fees: $284.

Florida State University, Graduate Studies, College of Education, Department of Childhood Education, Reading, and Disability Services, Program in Special Education, Tallahassee, FL 32306. Offers emotional disturbance/learning disabilities (MS); mental retardation (MS); rehabilitation counseling (MS, PhD, Ed S); special education (PhD, Ed S); visual disabilities (MS). *Accreditation:* CORE. *Faculty:* 5 full-time (4 women), 1 (woman) part-time/adjunct. *Students:* 45 full-time (39 women), 108 part-time (103 women); includes 38 minority (27 African Americans, 6 Asian Americans or Pacific Islanders, 5 Hispanic Americans). 111 applicants, 67% accepted, 44 enrolled. In 2007, 37 master's, 3 doctorates, 1 other advanced degree awarded. *Degree requirements:* For master's, comprehensive exam, thesis optional; for doctorate, comprehensive exam, thesis/dissertation; for Ed S, comprehensive exam. *Entrance requirements:* For master's, doctorate, and Ed S, GRE General Test, minimum GPA of 3.0. *Application deadline:* For fall admission, 7/1 for domestic students; for spring admission, 11/1 for domestic students. Applications are processed on a rolling basis. Application fee: $20. *Expenses:* Tuition, state resident: part-time $248 per credit hour. Tuition, nonresident: part-time $880 per credit hour. Tuition and fees vary according to program. *Financial support:* In 2007–08, 5 research assistantships, 7 teaching assistantships were awarded; fellowships, career-related internships or fieldwork and traineeships also available. Financial award applicants required to submit FAFSA. *Unit head:* Dr. Mary Frances Hanline, Chair, 850-644-4880, Fax: 850-644-8715, E-mail: hanline@mail.coe.fsu.edu. *Application contact:* Timolin Lynette Bodison-Baker, Program Assistant, 850-644-5458, Fax: 850-644-7736, E-mail: bodison@coe.fsu.edu.

Fort Valley State University, College of Graduate Studies and Extended Education, Department of Counseling Psychology, Program in Rehabilitation Counseling, Fort Valley, GA 31030-4313. Offers MS. *Accreditation:* CORE. Part-time programs available. *Faculty:* 3 full-time (1 woman), 1 (woman) part-time/adjunct. *Students:* 31 full-time (23 women), 20 part-time (13 women); all minorities (all African Americans) In 2007, 3 degrees awarded. *Degree requirements:* For master's, comprehensive exam (for some programs), thesis optional. *Entrance requirements:* For master's, GRE General Test or MAT. *Application deadline:* For fall admission, 8/23 for domestic students. Application fee: $20. *Expenses:* Tuition, state resident: full-time $3,390; part-time $142 per credit hour. Tuition, nonresident: full-time $13,550; part-time $565 per credit hour. Required fees: $920; $50 per credit hour. *Financial support:* Federal Work-Study available. Support available to part-time students. Financial award application deadline: 5/1; financial award applicants required to submit FAFSA. *Unit head:* Dr. Teri Kulkosky, Department Head, 478-825-6232, Fax: 478-825-6161, E-mail: kulkoskyt@fvsu.edu. *Application contact:* Donovan Coley, Director of Admissions, 478-825-6672, E-mail: coleyd@fvsu.edu.

The George Washington University, Graduate School of Education and Human Development, Department of Counseling/Human and Organizational Studies, Programs in Counseling: School, Community and Rehabilitation, Washington, DC 20052. Offers MA Ed. School counseling program also offered in Alexandria, VA. *Accreditation:* ACA; CORE; NCATE. *Degree requirements:* For master's, comprehensive exam. *Entrance requirements:* For master's, GRE General Test or MAT, minimum GPA of 2.75. *Faculty research:* Adjustment to disability, head injury rehabilitation, cross-cultural counseling.

Georgia State University, College of Education, Department of Counseling and Psychological Services, Program in Rehabilitation Counseling, Atlanta, GA 30303-3083. Offers MS. *Accreditation:* CORE. Part-time and evening/weekend programs available. *Students:* 27 applicants, 96% accepted. In 2007, 12 degrees awarded. *Degree requirements:* For master's, comprehensive exam. *Entrance requirements:* For master's, GRE General Test, minimum GPA of 2.5. *Application deadline:* For fall admission, 3/1 for domestic students. Application fee: $50. *Expenses:* Tuition, state resident: part-time $221 per credit hour. *Financial support:* Career-related internships or fieldwork and scholarships/grants available. Financial award application deadline: 4/1. *Faculty research:* Catastrophic injuries, private sector rehabilitation, closed head injuries, persons with multiple handicaps. *Unit head:* Dr. Joanna White, Chairperson, Department of Counseling and Psychological Services, 404-413-8010, E-mail: cpsjfw@langate.gsu.edu.

Hofstra University, School of Education and Allied Human Services, Department of Counseling, Research, Special Education and Rehabilitation, Program in Rehabilitation Counseling, Hempstead, NY 11549. Offers rehabilitation administration (PD); rehabilitation counseling (MS Ed); rehabilitation counseling in mental health (MS Ed). *Accreditation:* CORE. Part-time and evening/weekend programs available. *Students:* 25 full-time (20 women), 3 part-time (all women); includes 12 minority (10 African Americans, 2 Hispanic Americans), 2 international. Average age 33. 9 applicants, 78% accepted, 7 enrolled. In 2007, 10 degrees awarded. *Degree requirements:* For master's, comprehensive exam, 600 hour internship and 100 hour practicum; for PD, internship in rehabilitation administration. *Entrance requirements:* For master's, 4 letters of recommendation, interview, essay, professional experience; for PD, 3 letters of recommendation, masters degree in related field, CRC/CRC elig. professional experience. Additional exam requirements/recommendations for international students: Required—TOEFL (minimum score 550 paper-based; 213 computer-based). *Application deadline:* Applications are processed on a rolling basis. Application fee: $60. Electronic applications accepted. *Expenses:* Tuition: Full-time $14,220; part-time $820 per credit. Required fees: $970; $165 per term. Tuition and fees vary according to program. *Financial support:* In 2007–08, 44 students received support, including 3 fellowships with tuition reimbursements available (averaging $3,083 per year), 2 research assistantships with full and partial tuition reimbursements available (averaging $12,210 per year); career-related internships or fieldwork, Federal Work-Study, institutionally sponsored loans, scholarships/grants, traineeships, tuition waivers (full and partial), and unspecified assistantships also available. Support available to part-time students. Financial award applicants required to submit FAFSA. *Faculty research:* Workplace socialization and individuals with disabilities; collaboration among rehabilitation agencies and consumer outcomes; job retention among rehabilitation counseling professionals; transition services for youth with disabilities. Total annual research expenditures: $90,000. *Unit head:* Dr. Jamie Mitus, Director, 516-463-7453, Fax: 516-463-6184, E-mail: cprjsm@hofstra.edu. *Application contact:* Carol Drummer, Dean of Graduate Admissions, 516-463-4876, Fax: 516-463-4664, E-mail: gradstudent@hofstra.edu.

Hunter College of the City University of New York, Graduate School, School of Education, Department of Educational Foundations and Counseling Programs, Program in Rehabilitation Counseling, New York, NY 10021-5085. Offers MS Ed. *Accreditation:* CORE. *Faculty:* 1 (woman) full-time. *Students:* 38 full-time (30 women), 39 part-time (35 women); includes 20 minority (8 African Americans, 4 Asian Americans or Pacific Islanders, 8 Hispanic Americans). Average age 35. 69 applicants, 61% accepted, 33 enrolled. In 2007, 34 degrees awarded. *Degree requirements:* For master's, thesis, seminar. *Entrance requirements:* For master's, interview, minimum GPA of 2.7, recommendations. Additional exam requirements/recommendations for international students: Required—TOEFL, TWE. *Application deadline:* For fall admission, 4/1 for domestic students, 2/1 for international students; for spring admission, 11/1 for domestic students, 9/1 for international students. Applications are processed on a rolling basis. Application fee: $125. *Expenses:* Tuition, state resident: full-time $6,400; part-time $270 per credit. Tuition, nonresident: part-time $500 per credit. One-time fee: $125 full-time. Tuition and fees vary according to program. *Financial support:* Federal Work-Study and tuition waivers (partial) available. Support available to part-time students. *Unit head:* Dr. John O'Neill, Coordinator, 212-772-5188, E-mail: joneil@hunter.cuny.edu. *Application contact:* William Zlata, Director for Graduate Admissions, 212-772-4482, Fax: 212-650-3336, E-mail: admissions@hunter.cuny.edu.

Illinois Institute of Technology, Graduate College, Institute of Psychology, Chicago, IL 60616-3793. Offers clinical psychology (PhD); industrial/organizational psychology (PhD); personnel/human resource development (MS); psychology (MS); rehabilitation counseling (MS); rehabilitation counselor education (PhD). *Accreditation:* APA (one or more programs are accredited); CORE. Evening/weekend programs available. *Faculty:* 18 full-time (8 women), 4 part-time/adjunct (2 women). *Students:* 122 full-time (95 women), 66 part-time (45 women); includes 44 minority (15 African Americans, 1 American Indian/Alaska Native, 17 Asian Americans or Pacific Islanders, 11 Hispanic Americans), 22 international. Average age 29. 261 applicants, 34% accepted, 32 enrolled. In 2007, 31 master's, 12 doctorates awarded. Terminal master's awarded for partial completion of doctoral program. *Degree requirements:* For master's, comprehensive exam, thesis (for some programs); for doctorate, comprehensive exam, thesis/dissertation, qualifying exams. *Entrance requirements:* For master's, GRE General Test, minimum GPA of 3.0; for doctorate, GRE General Test, minimum GPA of 3.2. Additional exam requirements/recommendations for international students: Required—TOEFL (minimum score 550 paper-based; 213 computer-based; 80 iBT). *Application deadline:* For fall admission, 1/15 for domestic and international students. Application fee: $40. Electronic applications accepted. *Expenses:* Tuition: Full-time $14,004; part-time $778 per credit. Required fees: $7 per credit. $235 per term. Tuition and fees vary according to class time, course level, course load, program and student level. *Financial support:* In 2007–08, 39 fellowships with partial tuition reimbursements (averaging $2,798 per year), 1 research assistantship with partial tuition reimbursement, 24 teaching assistantships with partial tuition reimbursements (averaging $4,405 per year) were awarded; career-related internships or fieldwork, Federal Work-Study, institutionally sponsored loans, scholarships/grants, traineeships, health care benefits, tuition waivers (partial), and unspecified assistantships also available. Support available to part-time students. Financial award applicants required to submit FAFSA. *Faculty research:* Stigma and mental illness, depression, couples communication, leadership, psychometric theory. Total annual research expenditures: $636,382. *Unit head:* Dr. M. Ellen Mitchell, Dean, 312-567-3362, Fax: 312-567-3493, E-mail: mitchelle@iit.edu. *Application contact:* Application Contact, 312-567-3500, Fax: 312-567-3493, E-mail: psychology@iit.edu.

Indiana University–Purdue University Indianapolis, School of Science, Department of Psychology, Indianapolis, IN 46202-3275. Offers clinical rehabilitation psychology (MS); industrial/organizational psychology (MS); psychobiology of addictions (MS, PhD). *Accreditation:* APA (one or more programs are accredited). *Faculty:* 10 full-time (2 women). *Students:* 21 full-time (19 women), 5 part-time (all women); includes 4 minority (2 African Americans, 2 Asian Americans or Pacific Islanders). Average age 26. In 2007, 7 degrees awarded. Terminal master's awarded for partial completion of doctoral program. *Degree requirements:* For master's, thesis; for doctorate, thesis/dissertation. *Entrance requirements:* For master's, GRE General Test, minimum undergraduate GPA of 3.0; for doctorate, GRE General Test, GRE Subject Test (clinical rehabilitation psychology), minimum undergraduate GPA of 3.2. *Application deadline:* For fall admission, 1/1 priority date for domestic students. Application fee: $50 ($60 for international students). *Expenses:* Tuition, state resident: full-time $5,818; part-time $242 per credit hour. Tuition, nonresident: full-time $17,106; part-time $713 per credit hour. Required fees: $629. Tuition and fees vary according to course load, campus/location and program. *Financial support:* In 2007–08, 5 fellowships with partial tuition reimbursements (averaging $12,218 per year), 23 teaching assistantships with partial tuition reimbursements (averaging $7,553 per year) were awarded; research assistantships with partial tuition reimbursements, career-related internships or fieldwork, Federal Work-Study, and institutionally sponsored loans also available. Financial award application deadline: 3/1; financial award applicants required to submit FAFSA. *Faculty research:* Psychiatric rehabilitation, chronic stress, neurological research, language and cognitive development in infants. alcoholism and psychopathology. *Unit head:* Dr. J. Gregor Fetterman, Chairman, 317-274-6945, Fax: 317-274-6756, E-mail: gfetter@iupui.edu.

Jackson State University, Graduate School, School of Education, Department of Counseling and Human Resource Education, Jackson, MS 39217. Offers community and agency counseling (MS); guidance and counseling (MS, MS Ed, Ed S); rehabilitative counseling (MS Ed). *Accreditation:* ACA; CORE (one or more programs are accredited); NCATE. Part-time and evening/weekend programs available. *Degree requirements:* For master's, comprehensive exam, thesis. *Entrance requirements:* For master's, GRE General Test. Additional exam requirements/recommendations for international students: Required—TOEFL.

Jackson State University, Graduate School, School of Education, Department of Special Education and Rehabilitative Services, Jackson, MS 39217. Offers rehabilitative counseling service (MS Ed); special education (MS Ed, Ed S). *Accreditation:* NCATE. Evening/weekend programs available. *Degree requirements:* For master's, comprehensive exam, thesis or alternative. *Entrance requirements:* For master's, GRE General Test. Additional exam requirements/recommendations for international students: Required—TOEFL.

Kent State University, Graduate School of Education, Health, and Human Services, Department of Educational Foundations and Special Services, Program in Rehabilitation Counseling, Kent, OH 44242-0001. Offers M Ed, MA, Ed S. *Accreditation:* CORE (one or more programs are accredited). *Faculty:* 3 full-time (1 woman), 5 part-time/adjunct (3 women). *Students:* 23 full-time (17 women), 13 part-time (8 women); includes 6 minority (4 African Americans, 1 Asian American or Pacific Islander, 1 Hispanic American), 3 international. 11 applicants, 64% accepted. In 2007, 14 degrees awarded. *Degree requirements:* For master's, thesis (for some programs). *Entrance requirements:* For degree, GRE General Test. Additional exam requirements/recommendations for international students: Required—TOEFL. *Application deadline:* Applications are processed on a rolling basis. Application fee: $30. Electronic applications accepted. *Financial support:* In 2007–08, research assistantships with full tuition reimbursements (averaging $8,313 per year); fellowships with full tuition reimbursements, teaching assistantships with full tuition reimbursements, career-related internships or fieldwork, Federal Work-Study, institutionally sponsored loans, scholarships/grants, health care benefits, and unspecified assistantships also available. Support available to part-time students. Financial award application deadline: 4/1; financial award applicants required to submit FAFSA. *Unit head:* Dr. Phillip Rumrill, Coordinator, 330-672-2294, E-mail: prumrill@kent.edu. *Application contact:* Nancy Miller, Academic Program Coordinator, Office of Graduate Student Services, 330-672-2576, Fax: 330-672-9162, E-mail: ogs@kent.edu.

Langston University, School of Education and Behavioral Sciences, Langston, OK 73050-0907. Offers bilingual/multicultural (M Ed); elementary education (M Ed); English as a second language (M Ed); rehabilitation counseling (M Sc); urban education (M Ed). *Accreditation:* CORE; NCATE (one or more programs are accredited). Part-time programs available. *Degree requirements:* For master's, comprehensive exam, thesis optional. *Entrance requirements:* For master's, GRE, writing skills test, minimum GPA of 2.5, 3 letters of recommendation. Additional exam requirements/recommendations for international students: Required—TOEFL, TWE. *Faculty research:* Bilingual/multicultural education, financing post-secondary education.

La Salle University, School of Arts and Sciences, Program in Psychology, Philadelphia, PA 19141-1199. Offers clinical psychology (Psy D); family psychology (Psy D); rehabilitation psychology (Psy D). Part-time and evening/weekend programs available. *Faculty:* 8 full-time (4 women), 5 part-time/adjunct (2 women). *Students:* 91 full-time (80 women), 18 part-time (11 women); includes 13 minority (6 African Americans, 4 Asian Americans or Pacific Islanders, 3 Hispanic Americans), 1 international. Average age 27. 111 applicants, 48% accepted, 23 enrolled. In 2007, 21 doctorates awarded. *Entrance requirements:* For doctorate, GRE, minimum GPA of 3.0. *Application deadline:* For fall admission, 3/1 for domestic students. Application fee: $35. *Expenses: Contact institution.* Tuition and fees vary according to program. *Financial support:* In 2007–08, 94 students received support. Scholarships/grants available. Financial award applicants required to submit FAFSA. *Faculty research:* Cognitive therapy, attribution theory, treatment of addiction. *Unit head:* Dr. Frank Gardner, Director, 215-951-5016, Fax: 215-951-1351.

Louisiana State University Health Sciences Center, School of Allied Health Professions, Department of Rehabilitation Counseling, New Orleans, LA 70112-2262. Offers MHS. *Accreditation:* CORE. Part-time programs available. *Faculty:* 5 full-time (2 women), 2 part-time/adjunct (1 woman). *Students:* 15 full-time (14 women), 5 part-time (all women); includes 4 minority (all African Americans) Average age 29. 9 applicants, 100% accepted, 8 enrolled. In 2007, 19 degrees awarded. *Degree requirements:* For master's, clinical internship. *Entrance requirements:* For master's, GRE General Test, minimum GPA of 2.5, Bachelor degree, 2 letters recommendation, written essay. *Application deadline:* For fall admission, 4/15 priority date for domestic students. Applications are processed on a rolling basis. Application fee: $50. *Financial support:* In 2007–08, 20 students received support, including 9 fellowships with full tuition reimbursements available (averaging $6,000 per year). Financial award application deadline: 4/15. *Faculty research:* Job placement, clinical judgement, counseling process, consumer satisfaction, vocational assessment. Total annual research expenditures: $10,000. *Unit head:* Dr. John Dolan, Head, 504-568-4315, Fax: 504-568-4324, E-mail: jdolan@lsuhsc.edu. *Application contact:* Yudralys Delgado, Student Affairs Director, 504-568-4254, Fax: 504-568-3185, E-mail: ydelga@lsuhsc.edu.

Maryville University of Saint Louis, School of Health Professions, Program in Rehabilitation Counseling, St. Louis, MO 63141-7299. Offers marriage and family therapy (MARC); music therapy (MARC); substance abuse (MARC). *Accreditation:* CORE. Part-time and evening/weekend programs available. *Degree requirements:* For master's, internship, seminar. *Entrance requirements:* For master's, minimum cumulative GPA of 3.0, 2 letters of recommendation, interview. *Application deadline:* For fall admission, 1/15 for domestic students; for spring admission, 10/1 for domestic students. Application fee: $35. Electronic applications accepted. *Expenses:* Tuition: Full-time $18,600; part-time $580 per credit. Required fees: $75 per semester. *Financial support:* Career-related internships or fieldwork, Federal Work-Study, and campus employment available. Financial award application deadline: 7/31. *Unit head:* Barbara Parker, Director, 314-529-9437.

Michigan State University, The Graduate School, College of Education, Department of Counseling, Educational Psychology and Special Education, East Lansing, MI 48824. Offers counseling (MA); educational psychology and educational technology (PhD); educational technology (MA); measurement and quantitative methods (PhD); rehabilitation counseling (MA); rehabilitation counselor education (PhD); school psychology (MA, PhD, Ed S); special education (MA, PhD). *Accreditation:* APA (one or more programs are accredited); CORE (one or more programs are accredited). Part-time programs available. *Entrance requirements:* Additional exam requirements/recommendations for international students: Required—TOEFL. Electronic applications accepted. *Expenses:* Tuition, state resident: part-time $379 per credit hour. Tuition, nonresident: part-time $800 per credit hour. Tuition and fees vary according to program.

Minnesota State University Mankato, College of Graduate Studies, College of Allied Health and Nursing, Program in Rehabilitation Counseling, Mankato, MN 56001. Offers MS. *Accreditation:* CORE. *Students:* 15 full-time (12 women), 7 part-time (2 women). Average age 33. In 2007, 4 degrees awarded. *Degree requirements:* For master's, comprehensive exam. *Entrance requirements:* For master's, GRE General Test, minimum GPA of 3.0 during previous 2 years. *Application deadline:* For fall admission, 2/1 priority date for domestic students; for spring admission, 11/27 for domestic students. Applications are processed on a rolling basis. Application fee: $40. *Financial support:* Research assistantships with full tuition reimbursements, teaching assistantships with full tuition reimbursements available. Financial award application deadline: 3/15; financial award applicants required to submit FAFSA. *Unit head:* Dr. Bonnie Lund, Graduate Coordinator, 507-389-5841. *Application contact:* 507-389-2321, E-mail: grad@mnsu.edu.

Montana State University–Billings, College of Allied Health Professions, Department of Rehabilitation and Human Services, Billings, MT 59101-0298. Offers MSRC. *Accreditation:* CORE. Part-time programs available. *Students:* 56. 9 applicants, 100% accepted, 9 enrolled. In 2007, 10 degrees awarded. *Degree requirements:* For master's, thesis optional, thesis or professional paper and/or field experience. *Entrance requirements:* For master's, GRE General Test or MAT, minimum GPA of 3.0. *Application deadline:* For fall admission, 7/15 for international students; for spring admission, 12/1 for international students. Applications are processed on a rolling basis. Application fee: $40. *Expenses:* Tuition, state resident: full-time $4,665. Tuition, nonresident: full-time $11,096. *Financial support:* Teaching assistantships, career-related internships or fieldwork, Federal Work-Study, institutionally sponsored loans, scholarships/grants, tuition waivers (partial), and unspecified assistantships available. Support available to part-time students. Financial award application deadline: 5/1; financial award applicants required to submit FAFSA. *Unit head:* Dr. Kyle Colling, Acting Chairperson, 406-657-5830, E-mail: kcolling@msubillings.edu. *Application contact:* David M. Sullivan, Graduate Studies Counselor, 406-657-2053, Fax: 406-657-2299, E-mail: dsullivan@msubillings.edu.

Northeastern University, Bouvé College of Health Sciences Graduate School, Department of Counseling and Applied Educational Psychology, Program in Applied Behavior Analysis, Boston, MA 02115-5096. Offers MS. Part-time programs available. *Degree requirements:* For master's, thesis. *Entrance requirements:* For master's, GRE General Test or MAT. *Faculty research:* Stimulus control, failure-to-thrive children, severe behavior disorders, autism.

Ohio University, Graduate College, College of Education, Department of Counseling and Higher Education, Athens, OH 45701-2979. Offers college student personnel (M Ed); community/agency counseling (M Ed); counselor education (PhD); higher education (M Ed, PhD); rehabilitation counseling (M Ed); school counseling (M Ed). *Accreditation:* ACA; CORE. Part-time and evening/weekend programs available. *Faculty:* 12 full-time (6 women), 7 part-time/adjunct (1 woman). *Students:* 123 full-time (89 women), 111 part-time (73 women); includes 20 minority (18 African Americans, 2 Hispanic Americans), 42 international. 209 applicants, 62% accepted, 106 enrolled. In 2007, 40 master's, 7 doctorates awarded. *Median time to degree:* Of those who began their doctoral program in fall 1999, 92% received their degree in 8 years or less. *Degree requirements:* For master's, thesis or alternative; for doctorate, comprehensive exam, thesis/dissertation. *Entrance requirements:* For master's, GRE General Test or MAT (if GPA is below 2.9), 3 letters of reference, 5-page biography, statement of purpose; for doctorate, GRE General Test, work experience, minimum GPA of 3.4. Additional exam requirements/recommendations for international students: Required—TOEFL (minimum score 550 paper-based; 213 computer-based). *Application deadline:* For fall admission, 2/15 for domestic and international students. Applications are processed on a rolling basis. Application fee: $50 ($55 for international students). Electronic applications accepted. *Financial support:* In 2007–08, 78 students received support, including 35 research assistantships with full tuition reimbursements available (averaging $8,469 per year), 6 teaching assistantships with full tuition reimbursements available (averaging $8,469 per year); Federal Work-Study, institutionally sponsored loans, tuition waivers (partial), and unspecified assistantships also available. Financial award application deadline: 3/15. *Faculty research:* Youth violence, gender studies, student affairs, chemical dependency, disabilities issues. Total annual research expenditures: $527,983. *Unit head:* Dr. Jerry Olsheski, Chair, 740-593-0032, Fax: 740-593-0477, E-mail: olsheski@ohio.edu. *Application contact:* Floyd J. Doney, Director of Student Affairs, 740-593-4400, Fax: 740-593-9310, E-mail: doney@ohio.edu.

Pontifical Catholic University of Puerto Rico, Institute of Graduate Studies in Behavioral Science and Community Affairs, Program in Vocational Rehabilitation Counseling, Ponce, PR 00717-0777. Offers MSS. Part-time programs available. *Degree requirements:* For master's, thesis. *Entrance requirements:* For master's, EXADEP, GRE, 3 letters of recommendation, interview, minimum GPA of 2.75.

St. Cloud State University, School of Graduate Studies, College of Education, Department of Counselor Education and Educational Psychology, Program in Rehabilitation Counseling, St. Cloud, MN 56301-4498. Offers MS. *Accreditation:* CORE. *Faculty:* 12 full-time (5 women). *Students:* 37 full-time (28 women), 15 part-time (all women); includes 1 minority (Hispanic American), 4 international. 9 applicants, 100% accepted. In 2007, 10 degrees awarded. *Degree requirements:* For master's, comprehensive exam (for some programs), thesis or alternative. *Entrance requirements:* For master's, GRE General Test, minimum GPA of 2.75. Additional exam requirements/recommendations for international students: Required—MELAB; Recommended—TOEFL (minimum score 550 paper-based; 213 computer-based), IELTS (minimum score 7). *Application deadline:* For fall admission, 3/1 for domestic and international students. Application fee: $35. Electronic applications accepted. *Expenses:* Tuition, state resident: part-time $267 per credit. Tuition, nonresident: part-time $418 per credit. Required fees: $28 per credit. *Financial support:* Career-related internships or fieldwork, Federal Work-Study, scholarships/grants, and unspecified assistantships available. Financial award application deadline: 3/1. *Unit head:* Dr. Bradley Kuhlman, Coordinator, 320-308-2240, E-mail: bkuhlman@stcloudstate.edu. *Application contact:* Linda Lou Krueger, School of Graduate Studies, 320-308-2113, Fax: 320-308-5371, E-mail: lekrueger@stcloudstate.edu.

St. John's University, The School of Education, Department of Human Services and Counseling, Queens, NY 11439. Offers bilingual school counseling (MS Ed, PD); bilingual/multicultural education/teaching English to speakers of other languages (MS Ed); literacy (MS Ed, Ed D, PhD), including literacy (Ed D), teaching literacy 5-12 (MS Ed), teaching literacy B-12 (MS Ed), teaching literacy B-6 (MS Ed); mental health counseling (MS Ed); school counseling (MS Ed, PD); teaching children with disabilities in childhood education (MS Ed). Part-time and evening/weekend programs available. *Faculty:* 15 full-time (5 women), 28 part-time/adjunct (18 women). *Students:* 52 full-time (46 women), 286 part-time (253 women); includes 91 minority (20 African Americans, 9 Asian Americans or Pacific Islanders, 62 Hispanic Americans), 8 international. Average age 30. 204 applicants, 86% accepted, 97 enrolled. In 2007, 147 degrees awarded. *Degree requirements:* For master's, comprehensive exam. *Entrance requirements:* For master's and PD, application and fee, statement of goals, official transcripts showing conferral of degree and B or better average, 2 reference letters, interview;

Rehabilitation Counseling

St. John's University (continued)
for doctorate, Miller Analogies Test, GRE General Test (analytical), application and fee, statement of goals, official transcript showing conferral of degree and B+ or better average, 2 reference letters, interview, professional resumè, teaching experience. Additional exam requirements/recommendations for international students: Required—TOEFL (minimum score 500 paper-based; 173 computer-based; 61 iBT), IELTS (minimum score 6). *Application deadline:* For fall admission, 4/1 for domestic students, 6/1 for international students; for spring admission, 11/1 for domestic and international students. Applications are processed on a rolling basis. Application fee: $40. Electronic applications accepted. *Financial support:* Research assistantships, career-related internships or fieldwork and scholarships/grants available. Support available to part-time students. Financial award application deadline: 3/1; financial award applicants required to submit FAFSA. *Faculty research:* Assisting troubled children and teens with substance abuse, truancy, and coping skills, literacy development for ESL learners, investigating Caribbean and Creole language and culture. *Unit head:* Dr. Richard Sinatra, Chair, 718-990-1557, Fax: 718-990-1614, E-mail: sinatrar@stjohns.edu. *Application contact:* Kelly K. Ronayne, Assistant Dean, 718-990-2303, Fax: 718-990-2343, E-mail: graded@stjohns.edu.

Salve Regina University, Graduate Studies, Program in Rehabilitation Counseling, Newport, RI 02840-4192. Offers mental health counseling (CAGS); rehabilitation counseling (MA). Part-time programs available. Postbaccalaureate distance learning degree programs offered. *Entrance requirements:* For master's, GMAT, GRE General Test or MAT. Additional exam requirements/recommendations for international students: Required—TOEFL or IELTS. Electronic applications accepted.

San Diego State University, Graduate and Research Affairs, College of Education, Department of Administration, Rehabilitation and Post-Secondary Education, San Diego, CA 92182. Offers educational leadership in post-secondary education (MA); rehabilitation counseling (MS), including deafness. Evening/weekend programs available. Postbaccalaureate distance learning degree programs offered. *Students:* 61 full-time (47 women), 4 part-time (3 women); includes 19 minority (10 African Americans, 1 American Indian/Alaska Native, 1 Asian American or Pacific Islander, 7 Hispanic Americans), 2 international. 63 applicants, 67% accepted, 23 enrolled. In 2007, 47 degrees awarded. *Degree requirements:* For master's, comprehensive exam (for some programs), thesis (for some programs). *Entrance requirements:* For master's, GRE General Test, letters of reference. Additional exam requirements/recommendations for international students: Required—TOEFL. *Application deadline:* For fall admission, 5/1 for domestic and international students; for spring admission, 11/1 for domestic students, 10/1 for international students. Applications are processed on a rolling basis. Application fee: $55. Electronic applications accepted. *Financial support:* Career-related internships or fieldwork available. Financial award applicants required to submit FAFSA. *Faculty research:* Rehabilitation in cultural diversity, distance learning technology. Total annual research expenditures: $3.3 million. *Unit head:* Fred McFarlane, Chair, 619-594-6115, Fax: 619-594-4208, E-mail: fmcfarla@mail.sdsu.edu.

San Francisco State University, Division of Graduate Studies, College of Health and Human Services, Department of Counseling, San Francisco, CA 94132-1722. Offers counseling (MS); marriage, family, and child counseling (MSC); rehabilitation counseling (MS). *Accreditation:* ACA (one or more programs are accredited). Part-time programs available. *Application deadline:* Applications are processed on a rolling basis. *Unit head:* Dr. Robert Chope, Chair, 415-338-2005. *Application contact:* Couryll Pineda, Academic Office Coordinator, 415-338-2005, E-mail: counsel@sfsu.edu.

South Carolina State University, School of Graduate Studies, Department of Human Services, Orangeburg, SC 29117-0001. Offers elementary counselor education (M Ed); rehabilitation counseling (MA); secondary counselor education (M Ed). *Accreditation:* CORE. Part-time and evening/weekend programs available. *Faculty:* 9 full-time (6 women), 2 part-time/adjunct (1 woman). *Students:* 113 full-time (88 women), 31 part-time (28 women); includes 136 minority (all African Americans) Average age 33. 77 applicants, 69% accepted, 41 enrolled. In 2007, 69 degrees awarded. *Degree requirements:* For master's, thesis optional, departmental qualifying exam, internship. *Entrance requirements:* For master's, GRE, MAT, minimum GPA of 2.7. *Application deadline:* For fall admission, 6/15 priority date for domestic students, 6/15 for international students; for spring admission, 11/1 for domestic and international students. Applications are processed on a rolling basis. Application fee: $25. Electronic applications accepted. *Financial support:* In 2007–08, 35 students received support; fellowships, research assistantships, career-related internships or fieldwork, institutionally sponsored loans, and unspecified assistantships available. Financial award application deadline: 6/1. *Faculty research:* Handicap, disability, rehabilitation evaluation, vocation. *Unit head:* Dr. David Staten, Chair, 803-533-3968, Fax: 803-533-3666, E-mail: dstaten@scsu.edu. *Application contact:* Annette Hazzard-Jones, Program Coordinator II, 803-536-8809, Fax: 803-536-8812, E-mail: zs_ahazzard@scsu.edu.

Southern Illinois University Carbondale, Graduate School, College of Education, Rehabilitation Institute, Carbondale, IL 62901-4701. Offers behavioral analysis and therapy (MS); communication disorders and sciences (MS); rehabilitation (Rh D); rehabilitation administration and services (MS); rehabilitation counseling (MS). *Accreditation:* CORE. Part-time programs available. *Faculty:* 12 full-time (2 women), 1 part-time/adjunct (0 women). *Students:* 55 full-time (36 women), 67 part-time (46 women); includes 36 minority (28 African Americans, 2 Asian Americans or Pacific Islanders, 6 Hispanic Americans), 12 international. 58 applicants, 33% accepted, 7 enrolled. In 2007, 28 master's, 2 doctorates awarded. *Degree requirements:* For master's, thesis; for doctorate, thesis/dissertation. *Entrance requirements:* For master's, GRE; for doctorate, GRE or MAT, minimum GPA of 3.25. Additional exam requirements/recommendations for international students: Required—TOEFL. Application fee: $20. *Financial support:* In 2007–08, 2 fellowships with full tuition reimbursements, 48 research assistantships with full tuition reimbursements, 43 teaching assistantships with full tuition reimbursements were awarded; career-related internships or fieldwork, Federal Work-Study, institutionally sponsored loans, traineeships, and tuition waivers (full) also available. Support available to part-time students. *Faculty research:* Professional ethics. *Unit head:* Dr. John Benshoff, Director, 618-453-8281, E-mail: jbenshof@siu.edu. *Application contact:* Mary Falaster, Administrative Clerk, 618-453-8274, E-mail: mfalast@siu.edu.

Announcement: The Rehabilitation Institute offers four Master of Science programs: Behavior Analysis and Therapy, Communication Disorders and Sciences, Rehabilitation Administration and Services, and Rehabilitation Counseling. Graduates are prepared to work in the multidisciplinary field of rehabilitation. The Institute also offers a program leading to the PhD in Rehabilitation. This 96-hour program prepares graduates to function effectively as rehabilitation educators, researchers, and administrators.

See Close-Up on page 1481.

Southern University and Agricultural and Mechanical College, Graduate School, College of Sciences, Department of Psychology, Program in Rehabilitation Counseling, Baton Rouge, LA 70813. Offers MS. *Accreditation:* CORE. *Faculty:* 7 full-time (5 women). *Students:* 16 full-time (13 women), 29 part-time (21 women); includes 32 minority (28 African Americans, 1 American Indian/Alaska Native, 3 Asian Americans or Pacific Islanders), 1 international. Average age 32. 6 applicants, 67% accepted, 4 enrolled. *Degree requirements:* For master's, comprehensive exam, thesis optional. *Entrance requirements:* For master's, GMAT or GRE General Test. Additional exam requirements/recommendations for international students: Required—TOEFL. *Application deadline:* For fall admission, 6/1 priority date for domestic students; for spring admission, 11/1 for domestic students. Applications are processed on a rolling basis. Application fee: $25. *Financial support:* Research assistantships, scholarships/grants available. Financial award application deadline: 4/15. *Faculty research:* Cultural diversity, professional preparation and participation of minorities, needs and satisfaction of students with disabilities, prediction model for rehabilitation outcome, diabetes. *Unit head:* Dr. Madan Kundu, Coordinator, 225-771-2990, Fax: 225-771-2082, E-mail: kundusubr@aol.com.

See Close-Up on page 1483.

Springfield College, Graduate Programs, Programs in Rehabilitation Counseling and Services, Springfield, MA 01109-3797. Offers alcohol rehabilitation/substance abuse counseling (M Ed, MS, CAS); deaf counseling (M Ed, MS, CAS); developmental disabilities (M Ed, MS, CAS); general counseling and casework (M Ed, MS, CAS); psychiatric rehabilitation/mental health counseling (M Ed, MS, CAS); special services (M Ed, MS, CAS). *Accreditation:* CORE (one or more programs are accredited). Part-time and evening/weekend programs available. *Faculty:* 8 full-time (2 women), 4 part-time/adjunct (3 women). *Students:* 31 full-time, 9 part-time. Average age 31. 27 applicants, 89% accepted, 16 enrolled. In 2007, 13 degrees awarded. *Degree requirements:* For master's, comprehensive exam, thesis (for some programs). *Entrance requirements:* For master's and CAS, interview. Additional exam requirements/recommendations for international students: Required—TOEFL (minimum score 550 paper-based; 213 computer-based). *Application deadline:* For fall admission, 1/15 for domestic students; for winter admission, 11/1 for domestic students; for spring admission, 12/1 for domestic students. Applications are processed on a rolling basis. Application fee: $50. Electronic applications accepted. *Expenses:* Tuition: Full-time $12,942; part-time $719 per semester hour. Required fees: $25. Tuition and fees vary according to program. *Financial support:* In 2007–08, 4 teaching assistantships with partial tuition reimbursements were awarded; fellowships with partial tuition reimbursements, career-related internships or fieldwork, Federal Work-Study, institutionally sponsored loans, traineeships, and tuition waivers (full and partial) also available. Financial award application deadline: 3/1. *Faculty research:* Mental health, multicultural counseling, alcohol and substance abuse, developmental disabilities, families and disabilities, rehabilitation treatment outcomes. *Unit head:* Thomas J. Ruscio, Director, 413-748-3318, E-mail: thomas_ruscio@spfldcol.edu. *Application contact:* Donald James Shaw, Director of Graduate Admissions, 413-748-3060, Fax: 413-748-3069, E-mail: donald_shaw_jr@spfldcol.edu.

Syracuse University, Graduate School, School of Education, Counseling and Human Services Program, Program in Rehabilitation and Community Counseling, Syracuse, NY 13244. Offers MS. *Students:* 2 full-time (both women), 2 part-time (1 woman), 1 international. 2 applicants, 0% accepted. In 2007, 1 degree awarded. *Entrance requirements:* For master's, GRE General Test or MAT, interview. Additional exam requirements/recommendations for international students: Required—TOEFL. *Application deadline:* For fall admission, 2/1 priority date for domestic students; for spring admission, 10/15 priority date for domestic students. Application fee: $75. *Expenses:* Tuition: Full-time $18,216; part-time $1,012 per credit. Required fees: $980. Tuition and fees vary according to program. *Unit head:* Dr. Janine Bernard, Chair, 315-443-5266, Fax: 315-443-5732, E-mail: bernard@syr.edu. *Application contact:* Traci Washburn, Graduate Recruiter, School of Education, 315-443-2505, E-mail: e-gradrcrt@syr.edu.

Syracuse University, Graduate School, School of Education, Counseling and Human Services Program, Program in Rehabilitation Counseling, Syracuse, NY 13244. Offers MS. *Accreditation:* CORE. Part-time programs available. *Students:* 5 full-time (all women), 3 part-time (all women), 6 international. 4 applicants, 50% accepted, 1 enrolled. In 2007, 2 master's awarded. *Degree requirements:* For master's, thesis or alternative. *Entrance requirements:* For master's, GRE or MAT, interview. Additional exam requirements/recommendations for international students: Required—TOEFL. *Application deadline:* For fall admission, 2/1 priority date for domestic students; for spring admission, 10/15 priority date for domestic students. Applications are processed on a rolling basis. Application fee: $75. Electronic applications accepted. *Expenses:* Tuition: Full-time $18,216; part-time $1,012 per credit. Required fees: $980. Tuition and fees vary according to program. *Financial support:* Fellowships with full tuition reimbursements, teaching assistantships with full tuition reimbursements available. *Unit head:* Dr. Dennis D. Gilbride, Head, 315-443-5264, E-mail: ddgilbri@syr.edu. *Application contact:* Traci Washburn, Graduate Recruiter, School of Education, 315-443-2505, E-mail: e-gradrcrt@syr.edu.

Texas Tech University Health Sciences Center, School of Allied Health Sciences, Program in Rehabilitation Counseling, Lubbock, TX 79430. Offers MRC. *Accreditation:* CORE. Part-time programs available. *Faculty:* 4 full-time (3 women). *Students:* 52 full-time (41 women), 3 part-time (1 woman); includes 13 African Americans, 1 Asian American or Pacific Islander, 8 Hispanic Americans. Average age 38. 41 applicants, 88% accepted, 36 enrolled. In 2007, 22 degrees awarded. *Entrance requirements:* Additional exam requirements/recommendations for international students: Required—TOEFL. *Application deadline:* For fall admission, 6/1 for domestic students; for spring admission, 10/1 for domestic students. Application fee: $35. Electronic applications accepted. *Financial support:* Career-related internships or fieldwork and institutionally sponsored loans available. *Unit head:* Dr. Robin Satterwhite, Chair, 806-743-2263, Fax: 806-743-3249, E-mail: robin.satterwhite@ttuhsc.edu. *Application contact:* Jeri Moravcik, Assistant Director of Admissions and Student Affairs, 806-743-3220, Fax: 806-743-2994, E-mail: jeri.moravcik@ttuhsc.edu.

Thomas University, Department of Human Services, Thomasville, GA 31792-7499. Offers community counseling (MSCC); rehabilitation counseling (MRC). *Accreditation:* CORE.Part-time programs available. *Entrance requirements:* For master's, resumé, 3 academic/professional references. Additional exam requirements/recommendations for international students: Required—TOEFL (minimum score 600 paper-based; 250 computer-based). Electronic applications accepted.

Troy University, Graduate School, College of Education, Program in School Counseling, Troy, AL 36082. Offers community counseling (Ed S); counselor education (MS); guidance services (MS); rehabilitation counseling (Ed S); school counseling (Ed S). *Accreditation:* ACA; CORE; NCATE. Part-time and evening/weekend programs available. *Students:* 21 full-time (18 women), 78 part-time (70 women); includes 59 minority (58 African Americans, 1 Hispanic American). Average age 36. In 2007, 10 master's, 10 other advanced degrees awarded. *Degree requirements:* For master's, comprehensive exam, thesis. *Entrance requirements:* For master's, minimum GPA of 2.5, teaching certification, 2 years of teaching experience. Additional exam requirements/recommendations for international students: Required—TOEFL (minimum score 523 paper-based; 200 computer-based). *Application deadline:* Applications are processed on a rolling basis. Application fee: $50. Electronic applications accepted. *Unit head:* Dr. Andrew Creamer, Chair, 334-670-3350, Fax: 334-670-32961, E-mail: drcreamer@troy.edu. *Application contact:* Brenda K. Campbell, Director of Graduate Admissions, 334-670-3178, Fax: 334-670-3733, E-mail: bcamp@troy.edu.

Université de Montréal, Faculty of Medicine, Program in Specialized Studies, Montréal, QC H3C 3J7, Canada. Offers anesthesia (DESS); diagnostic radiology (DESS); family medicine (DESS); medical biochemistry (DESS); medical genetics (DESS); medicine (DESS); microbiology and infectious diseases (DESS); nuclear medicine (DESS); obstetrics and gynecology (DESS); ophthalmology (DESS); pediatrics (DESS); psychiatry (DESS); radiology-oncology (DESS); surgery (DESS). *Faculty:* 154 full-time (40 women), 333 part-time/adjunct (100 women). *Entrance requirements:* For degree, proficiency in French. *Application deadline:* For fall admission, 2/1 priority date for domestic students; for winter admission, 11/1 priority date for domestic students; for spring admission, 2/1 priority date for domestic students. Application fee: $100. Electronic applications accepted. *Unit head:* Dr. Pierre Boyle, Vice Dean of Studies, 514-343-6300, Fax: 514-343-5751, E-mail: pierre.boyle@umontreal.ca.

University at Albany, State University of New York, School of Education, Department of Educational and Counseling Psychology, Program in Rehabilitation Counseling, Albany, NY 12222-0001. Offers counseling psychology (MS). *Accreditation:* CORE. Evening/weekend programs available. *Entrance requirements:* For master's, GRE General Test. Additional exam requirements/recommendations for international students: Required—TOEFL (minimum score 550 paper-based; 213 computer-based). *Application deadline:* For fall admission, 2/15 for domestic and international students. Application fee: $75. Electronic applications accepted. *Expenses:* Tuition, state resident: part-time $576 per credit. Tuition, nonresident: part-time $910 per credit. Tuition and fees vary according to program. *Financial support:* Career-related internships or fieldwork available. *Unit head:* Sheldon Grand, Coordinator, 518-442-5041.

University at Buffalo, the State University of New York, Graduate School, Graduate School of Education, Department of Counseling, School, and Educational Psychology, Buffalo, NY

14260. Offers counseling/school psychology (PhD); counselor education (PhD); educational psychology (MA, PhD); mental health counseling (MS); rehabilitation counseling (MS); school counseling (Ed M, Certificate); school psychology (MA). *Accreditation:* CORE (one or more programs are accredited). *Degree requirements:* For master's, comprehensive exam (for some programs), thesis (for some programs); for doctorate, comprehensive exam, thesis/dissertation. *Entrance requirements:* For master's and doctorate, GRE General Test, interview, letters of reference. Additional exam requirements/recommendations for international students: Required—TOEFL. Electronic applications accepted. *Faculty research:* Multicultural counseling, class size effects, quality of life, eating disorders, outcome assessment.

The University of Arizona, Graduate College, College of Education, Department of Special Education, Rehabilitation and School Psychology, Tucson, AZ 85721. Offers M Ed, MA, MS, Ed D, PhD, Ed S. *Accreditation:* CORE. Part-time programs available. *Faculty:* 17. *Students:* 166 full-time (131 women), 119 part-time (98 women); includes 72 minority (10 African Americans, 13 American Indian/Alaska Native, 5 Asian Americans or Pacific Islanders, 44 Hispanic Americans), 16 international. Average age 37. 109 applicants, 59% accepted, 56 enrolled. In 2007, 82 master's, 10 doctorates, 12 other advanced degrees awarded. Terminal master's awarded for partial completion of doctoral program. *Degree requirements:* For master's, comprehensive exam, thesis optional; for doctorate, comprehensive exam, thesis/dissertation. *Entrance requirements:* For doctorate, GRE General Test or MAT. Additional exam requirements/recommendations for international students: Required—TOEFL (minimum score 550 paper-based; 213 computer-based). *Application deadline:* For fall admission, 2/15 for domestic students, 2/1 for international students; for spring admission, 9/1 priority date for domestic students, 10/1 for international students. Applications are processed on a rolling basis. Application fee: $50. *Financial support:* In 2007–08, 83 students received support, including 11 fellowships with partial tuition reimbursements available (averaging $2,379 per year), 2 teaching assistantships with partial tuition reimbursements available (averaging $9,414 per year); research assistantships, career-related internships or fieldwork, institutionally sponsored loans, and tuition waivers (full) also available. Financial award applicants required to submit FAFSA. *Faculty research:* Teacher assistant teams, self-advocacy, language development in preschool, the deaf, comprehension of the learning disabled. Total annual research expenditures: $4.1 million. *Unit head:* Dr. Lawrence M. Aleamoni, Head, 520-621-7822, Fax: 520-621-3821. *Application contact:* Cecilia Carlon, Coordinator, 520-621-7822, Fax: 520-621-3821, E-mail: sergrad@mail.ed.arizona.edu.

University of Arkansas, Graduate School, College of Education and Health Professions, Department of Rehabilitation, Human Resources and Communication Disorders, Program in Rehabilitation, Fayetteville, AR 72701-1201. Offers MS, PhD. *Accreditation:* CORE (one or more programs are accredited). Part-time programs available. *Students:* 19 full-time (13 women), 19 part-time (14 women); includes 3 minority (all African Americans), 2 international. In 2007, 8 master's, 2 doctorates awarded. *Degree requirements:* For doctorate, thesis/dissertation. *Entrance requirements:* For doctorate, GRE General Test. Application fee: $40 ($50 for international students). *Financial support:* In 2007–08, 2 fellowships with tuition reimbursements, 4 research assistantships were awarded; teaching assistantships, career-related internships or fieldwork and Federal Work-Study also available. Support available to part-time students. Financial award application deadline: 4/1; financial award applicants required to submit FAFSA. *Application contact:* Faye Turner, Graduate Coordinator, 479-575-6411, E-mail: fturner@uark.edu.

University of Arkansas at Little Rock, Graduate School, College of Education, Department of Counseling and Rehabilitation Education, Little Rock, AR 72204-1099. Offers adult education (M Ed); counselor education (M Ed), including school counseling; orientation and mobility of the blind (Graduate Certificate); rehabilitation counseling (MA, Graduate Certificate); rehabilitation of the blind (MA). *Accreditation:* CORE; NCATE. Part-time programs available. *Students:* Average age 36. *Entrance requirements:* For master's, interview, minimum GPA of 2.75. *Application deadline:* Applications are processed on a rolling basis. *Financial support:* Research assistantships with tuition reimbursements, teaching assistantships with tuition reimbursements, career-related internships or fieldwork, Federal Work-Study, and institutionally sponsored loans available. Support available to part-time students. Financial award application deadline: 6/30. *Faculty research:* Low vision, orientation and mobility instruction. *Unit head:* Dr. Patricia B. Smith, Chairperson, 501-569-3169, E-mail: pbsmith@ualr.edu.

University of Florida, Graduate School, College of Public Health and Health Professions, Department of Behavioral Science and Community Health, Gainesville, FL 32611. Offers rehabilitation counseling (MHS). *Accreditation:* CORE. Part-time programs available. *Faculty:* 7 full-time (5 women). *Students:* 75 (50 women); includes 12 minority (3 African Americans, 5 Asian Americans or Pacific Islanders, 4 Hispanic Americans) 20 international. Average age 27. In 2007, 18 master's awarded. *Entrance requirements:* For master's, GRE General Test, minimum GPA of 3.0. *Application deadline:* For fall admission, 6/1 priority date for domestic students. Applications are processed on a rolling basis. Application fee: $30. Electronic applications accepted. *Expenses:* Tuition, state resident: full-time $7,478. Tuition, nonresident: full-time $22,603. *Financial support:* In 2007–08, 1 teaching assistantship (averaging $9,360 per year) was awarded; fellowships with full tuition reimbursements, research assistantships also available. *Faculty research:* Overcoming mental, physical, or emotional handicaps toward personal/vocational independence. *Unit head:* Dr. Linda R. Shaw, Acting Chair, 352-273-6745, Fax: 352-273-6048, E-mail: lshaw@phhp.ufl.edu.

The University of Iowa, Graduate College, College of Education, Department of Counseling, Rehabilitation, and Student Development, Iowa City, IA 52242-1316. Offers administration and research (PhD); counselor education and supervision (PhD); rehabilitation counseling (MA); rehabilitation counselor education (PhD); school counseling (MA); student development (MA, PhD). *Accreditation:* ACA (one or more programs are accredited); CORE (one or more programs are accredited). *Faculty:* 14 full-time, 14 part-time/adjunct. *Students:* 102 full-time (84 women), 19 part-time (13 women); includes 21 minority (16 African Americans, 2 Asian Americans or Pacific Islanders, 3 Hispanic Americans), 11 international. 68 applicants, 65% accepted, 28 enrolled. In 2007, 30 master's, 5 doctorates awarded. *Degree requirements:* For master's, thesis optional, exam; for doctorate, comprehensive exam, thesis/dissertation. *Entrance requirements:* For master's and doctorate, GRE General Test, minimum GPA of 3.0. Additional exam requirements/recommendations for international students: Required—TOEFL (minimum score 550 paper-based; 213 computer-based; 81 iBT). Application fee: $60 ($85 for international students). Electronic applications accepted. *Expenses:* Tuition, state resident: part-time $349 per hour. Tuition, nonresident: part-time $349 per hour. Tuition and fees vary according to course load and program. *Financial support:* In 2007–08, 13 research assistantships with partial tuition reimbursements, 23 teaching assistantships with partial tuition reimbursements were awarded; fellowships also available. Financial award applicants required to submit FAFSA. *Unit head:* Dr. Dennis R. Maki, Chair, 319-335-5275, Fax: 319-335-5291.

University of Kentucky, Graduate School, College of Education, Program in Special Education, Lexington, KY 40506-0032. Offers early childhood special education (MS Ed); rehabilitation counseling (MRC); special education (MS Ed); special education leadership personnel preparation (Ed D). *Accreditation:* CORE; NCATE. *Faculty:* 32 full-time (16 women), 3 part-time/adjunct (2 women). *Students:* 125 full-time (95 women), 46 part-time (42 women); includes 36 minority (29 African Americans, 2 American Indian/Alaska Native, 5 Hispanic Americans), 1 international. Average age 36. 130 applicants, 48% accepted, 43 enrolled. In 2007, 55 master's, 1 doctorate awarded. Terminal master's awarded for partial completion of doctoral program. *Median time to degree:* Of those who began their doctoral program in fall 1999, 68% received their degree in 8 years or less. *Degree requirements:* For master's, comprehensive exam, thesis optional; for doctorate, comprehensive exam, thesis/dissertation. *Entrance requirements:* For master's, GRE General Test, minimum undergraduate GPA of 2.75; for doctorate, GRE General Test, minimum graduate GPA of 3.0. Additional exam requirements/recommendations for international students: Required—TOEFL (minimum score 550 paper-based; 213 computer-based). *Application deadline:* For fall admission, 7/17 priority date for domestic students, 2/1 priority date for international students; for spring admission, 12/13 priority date for domestic students, 6/15 priority date for international students. Application fee: $50 ($65 for international students). Electronic applications accepted. *Expenses:* Tuition, state resident: part-time $437 per credit hour. Tuition, nonresident: part-time $931 per credit hour. *Financial support:* In 2007–08, 14 students received support, including 8 fellowships with full tuition reimbursements available, 3 research assistantships with full tuition reimbursements available (averaging $13,000 per year), 3 teaching assistantships with full tuition reimbursements available (averaging $12,000 per year); career-related internships or fieldwork, Federal Work-Study, institutionally sponsored loans, scholarships/grants, traineeships, health care benefits, tuition waivers (partial), and unspecified assistantships also available. Support available to part-time students. Financial award application deadline: 3/15. *Faculty research:* Applied behavior analysis applications in special education, single subject research design in classroom settings, transition research across life span, rural special education personnel. Total annual research expenditures: $1.6 million. *Unit head:* Dr. John Schuster, Director of Graduate Studies, 859-257-8594, Fax: 859-257-1325. *Application contact:* Dr. Brian Jackson, Senior Associate Dean, 859-257-4667, Fax: 859-257-4676, E-mail: brian.jackson@uky.edu.

University of Louisiana at Lafayette, Graduate School, College of Liberal Arts, Department of Psychology, Program in Rehabilitation Counseling, Lafayette, LA 70504. Offers MS. *Entrance requirements:* For master's, GRE General Test, minimum GPA of 3.0. Additional exam requirements/recommendations for international students: Required—TOEFL (minimum score 550 paper-based; 213 computer-based). Electronic applications accepted. *Faculty research:* Vocational assessment, psychology.

University of Maryland, College Park, Graduate Studies, College of Education, Department of Counseling and Personnel Services, College Park, MD 20742. Offers college student personnel (M Ed, MA); college student personnel administration (PhD); community counseling (CAGS); community/career counseling (M Ed, MA); counseling and personnel services (M Ed, MA, PhD); counseling psychology (PhD); counselor education (PhD); rehabilitation counseling (M Ed, MA, AGSC); school counseling (M Ed, MA); school psychology (M Ed, MA, PhD). *Accreditation:* ACA (one or more programs are accredited); APA (one or more programs are accredited); CORE (one or more programs are accredited); NCATE. Part-time and evening/weekend programs available. Postbaccalaureate distance learning degree programs offered (no on-campus study). *Faculty:* 41 full-time (29 women), 2 part-time/adjunct (both women). *Students:* 157 full-time (114 women), 19 part-time (13 women); includes 63 minority (34 African Americans, 3 American Indian/Alaska Native, 14 Asian Americans or Pacific Islanders, 12 Hispanic Americans), 11 international. 375 applicants, 20% accepted, 48 enrolled. In 2007, 44 master's, 6 doctorates, 4 other advanced degrees awarded. *Degree requirements:* For master's, thesis (for some programs); for doctorate, thesis/dissertation. *Entrance requirements:* For master's, GRE General Test or MAT, minimum GPA of 3.0, 3 letters of recommendation; for doctorate, GRE General Test or MAT, minimum GPA of 3.5, 3 letters of recommendation. Additional exam requirements/recommendations for international students: Required—TOEFL. *Application deadline:* For fall admission, 3/1 for domestic students, 2/1 for international students; for spring admission, 9/1 for domestic students, 6/1 for international students. Applications are processed on a rolling basis. Application fee: $60. Electronic applications accepted. *Financial support:* In 2007–08, 20 fellowships with full tuition reimbursements (averaging $8,362 per year), 5 research assistantships (averaging $14,192 per year), 105 teaching assistantships with tuition reimbursements (averaging $14,702 per year) were awarded; career-related internships or fieldwork, Federal Work-Study, and scholarships/grants also available. Support available to part-time students. Financial award applicants required to submit FAFSA. *Faculty research:* Educational psychology, counseling, health. Total annual research expenditures: $2.1 million. *Unit head:* Dr. Ruth Fassingel, Dean, 301-405-2860, Fax: 301-405-9995, E-mail: rfassing@umd.edu. *Application contact:* Dean of Graduate School, 301-405-0358, Fax: 301-314-9305.

University of Maryland Eastern Shore, Graduate Programs, Department of Rehabilitation Services, Princess Anne, MD 21853-1299. Offers rehabilitation counseling (MS). *Accreditation:* CORE. Part-time and evening/weekend programs available. *Faculty:* 4 full-time (2 women), 4 part-time/adjunct (2 women). *Students:* 21 full-time (13 women), 6 part-time (5 women); includes 18 minority (17 African Americans, 1 Hispanic American), 4 international. Average age 23. 13 applicants, 85% accepted, 11 enrolled. In 2007, 6 degrees awarded. *Degree requirements:* For master's, internship. *Entrance requirements:* For master's, interview. Additional exam requirements/recommendations for international students: Required—TOEFL (minimum score 213 computer-based; 80 iBT). *Application deadline:* For fall admission, 5/1 priority date for domestic and international students. Application fee: $30. Electronic applications accepted. *Financial support:* In 2007–08, 6 students received support, including 3 research assistantships with full tuition reimbursements available (averaging $13,000 per year); scholarships/grants and unspecified assistantships also available. Financial award application deadline: 3/1. *Faculty research:* Long-term rehabilitation training. Total annual research expenditures: $149,062. *Unit head:* Dr. William Talley, Chair, 410-651-6261, Fax: 410-651-6736, E-mail: wbtalley@umes.edu. *Application contact:* Dr. MaryAnn Rahimi, Coordinator, 410-651-6514, Fax: 410-651-6736, E-mail: merahimi@umes.edu.

University of Massachusetts Boston, Office of Graduate Studies, Graduate College of Education, Counseling and School Psychology Department, Program in Rehabilitation Counseling, Boston, MA 02125-3393. Offers M Ed, CAGS. *Accreditation:* CORE.

University of Medicine and Dentistry of New Jersey, School of Health Related Professions, Department of Psychiatric Rehabilitation and Counseling Professions, Program in Psychiatric Rehabilitation, Newark, NJ 07107-1709. Offers MS, PhD. *Accreditation:* CORE. *Entrance requirements:* For doctorate, GRE General Test. Additional exam requirements/recommendations for international students: Required—TOEFL. *Application deadline:* For fall admission, 6/1 for domestic students; for spring admission, 11/15 for domestic students. Applications are processed on a rolling basis. Application fee: $50. Electronic applications accepted. *Financial support:* Traineeships available. *Unit head:* Dr. Carlos W. Pratt, Program Director, 908-889-2461, E-mail: pratt@umdnj.edu.

University of Medicine and Dentistry of New Jersey, School of Health Related Professions, Department of Psychiatric Rehabilitation and Counseling Professions, Program in Rehabilitation Counseling, Newark, NJ 07107-1709. Offers psychiatric rehabilitation (MS); vocational rehabilitation (MS). Programs offered at Scotch Plains and Stratford campuses. *Accreditation:* CORE. *Degree requirements:* For master's, internship, practicum. *Entrance requirements:* For master's, minimum 2 years of psychiatric rehabilitation or related professional experience or GRE General Test, interview. Additional exam requirements/recommendations for international students: Required—TOEFL. *Application deadline:* For fall admission, 6/15 for domestic students; for spring admission, 11/15 for domestic students. Applications are processed on a rolling basis. Application fee: $50. Electronic applications accepted. *Unit head:* Dr. Janice Oursler, Director, 908-889-2462, Fax: 908-889-2432, E-mail: ms-crc@umdnj.edu. *Application contact:* Francis W. Ulrich, Information Contact, Stratford Campus, 856-566-6455, E-mail: ulrichfw@umdnj.edu.

University of Memphis, Graduate School, College of Education, Department of Counseling, Educational Psychology and Research, Memphis, TN 38152. Offers counseling (MS, Ed D), including community counseling (MS), rehabilitation counseling (MS), school counseling (MS); counseling psychology (PhD); educational psychology and research (MS, PhD), including educational psychology, educational research. *Accreditation:* ACA (one or more programs are accredited); APA (one or more programs are accredited); CORE (one or more programs are accredited); NCATE. *Faculty:* 35 full-time (17 women), 9 part-time/adjunct (5 women). *Students:* 9 full-time (6 women), 29 part-time (25 women); includes 10 African Americans, 1 American Indian/Alaska Native, 2 international. Average age 32. 77 applicants, 51% accepted, 35 enrolled. In 2007, 49 master's, 16 doctorates awarded. *Degree requirements:* For master's, comprehensive exam, thesis or alternative; for doctorate, comprehensive exam, thesis/dissertation. *Entrance requirements:* For master's, GRE General Test or MAT, minimum GPA of 2.5; for doctorate, GRE General Test. *Application deadline:* For fall admission, 10/1 for domestic students; for spring admission, 4/1 for domestic students. Application fee: $35 ($60

Rehabilitation Counseling

University of Memphis (continued)

for international students). *Expenses:* Tuition, state resident: full-time $6,990; part-time $377 per hour. Tuition, nonresident: full-time $17,818; part-time $830 per hour. Tuition and fees vary according to course load and program. *Financial support:* In 2007–08, 15 research assistantships with full tuition reimbursements (averaging $6,650 per year), 4 teaching assistantships with full tuition reimbursements (averaging $6,000 per year) were awarded; fellowships with full tuition reimbursements, career-related internships or fieldwork also available. *Faculty research:* Anger management, aging and disability, supervision, multicultural counseling. *Unit head:* Dr. Douglas C. Strohmer, Chair, 901-678-2841, Fax: 901-678-5114.

University of Nevada, Las Vegas, Graduate College, College of Education, Department of Counselor Education, Las Vegas, NV 89154-9900. Offers addiction studies (Certificate); community mental health (MS); rehabilitation counseling (Certificate); school counseling (M Ed). *Faculty:* 7 full-time (4 women). *Students:* 27 full-time (24 women), 20 part-time (all women); includes 12 minority (2 African Americans, 3 Asian Americans or Pacific Islanders, 7 Hispanic Americans). 26 applicants, 38% accepted, 9 enrolled. In 2007, 21 master's, 2 other advanced degrees awarded. *Entrance requirements:* Additional exam requirements/recommendations for international students: Required—TOEFL (minimum score 550 paper-based; 213 computer-based; 80 iBT). *Application deadline:* For fall and winter admission, 2/1 for domestic and international students. Electronic applications accepted. *Expenses:* Tuition, state resident: part-time $198 per credit. Tuition, nonresident: part-time $416 per credit. Required fees: $256 per semester. Tuition and fees vary according to course load and reciprocity agreements. *Financial support:* In 2007–08, 4 research assistantships with partial tuition reimbursements (averaging $10,000 per year), 5 teaching assistantships with partial tuition reimbursements (averaging $10,000 per year) were awarded. *Unit head:* Dr. Pat Markos, Chair, 702-895-5994. *Application contact:* Graduate College Admissions Evaluator, 702-895-3320, E-mail: gradcollege@unlv.edu.

University of Nevada, Las Vegas, Graduate College, Greenspun College of Urban Affairs, Department of Marriage and Family Therapy, Las Vegas, NV 89154-9900. Offers community agency counseling (MS); marriage and family counseling (MS); marriage and family therapy (Certificate); rehabilitation counseling (MS). *Accreditation:* ACA. Part-time programs available. *Faculty:* 4 full-time (2 women), 3 part-time/adjunct (2 women). *Students:* 17 full-time (all women), 25 part-time (22 women); includes 6 minority (4 African Americans, 2 Hispanic Americans). 28 applicants, 36% accepted, 10 enrolled. In 2007, 12 degrees awarded. *Degree requirements:* For master's, comprehensive exam (for some programs), thesis (for some programs). *Entrance requirements:* For master's, GRE General Test, minimum GPA of 3.0 during previous 2 years, 2.75 overall. Additional exam requirements/recommendations for international students: Required—TOEFL (minimum score 550 paper-based; 213 computer-based; 80 iBT). *Application deadline:* For winter admission, 2/1 for domestic and international students. Application fee: $60 ($75 for international students). Electronic applications accepted. *Expenses:* Tuition, state resident: part-time $198 per credit. Tuition, nonresident: part-time $416 per credit. Required fees: $256 per semester. Tuition and fees vary according to course load and reciprocity agreements. *Financial support:* In 2007–08, 4 research assistantships with partial tuition reimbursements (averaging $10,000 per year) were awarded; career-related internships or fieldwork, Federal Work-Study, institutionally sponsored loans, scholarships/grants, health care benefits, and unspecified assistantships also available. Support available to part-time students. Financial award application deadline: 3/1. *Unit head:* Dr. Gerald Weeks, Chair, 702-895-1867. *Application contact:* Graduate College Admissions Evaluator, 702-895-3320, Fax: 702-895-4180, E-mail: gradcollege@unlv.edu.

The University of North Carolina at Chapel Hill, School of Medicine and Graduate School, Graduate Programs in Medicine, Chapel Hill, NC 27599. Offers allied health sciences (MPT, MS, Au D, DPT, PhD), including human movement science (MS, PhD), occupational science (MS, PhD), physical therapy (MPT, MS, DPT), rehabilitation counseling and psychology (MS), speech and hearing sciences (MS, Au D, PhD); biochemistry and biophysics (MS, PhD); biomedical engineering (MS, PhD); cell and developmental biology (PhD); cell and molecular physiology (PhD); genetics and molecular biology (PhD); microbiology and immunology (MS, PhD), including immunology, microbiology; neurobiology (PhD); pathology and laboratory medicine (PhD), including experimental pathology; pharmacology (PhD); MD/PhD. Post-baccalaureate distance learning degree programs offered. *Faculty:* 498 full-time (175 women), 119 part-time/adjunct (37 women). *Students:* 723 full-time (450 women), 48 part-time (39 women); includes 130 minority (46 African Americans, 2 American Indian/Alaska Native, 66 Asian Americans or Pacific Islanders, 16 Hispanic Americans), 46 international. In 2007, 73 master's, 62 doctorates awarded. Terminal master's awarded for partial completion of doctoral program. *Degree requirements:* For master's, comprehensive exam; for doctorate, thesis/dissertation. *Application deadline:* Applications are processed on a rolling basis. Application fee: $65. Electronic applications accepted. *Expenses: Contact institution. Financial support:* In 2007–08, 77 fellowships with full and partial tuition reimbursements, 309 research assistantships with full tuition reimbursements, 23 teaching assistantships with full tuition reimbursements were awarded; career-related internships or fieldwork, Federal Work-Study, institutionally sponsored loans, traineeships, tuition waivers (full and partial), and unspecified assistantships also available. Support available to part-time students. Financial award applicants required to submit FAFSA. *Unit head:* Dr. William I. Roper, Dean, 919-966-4161, Fax: 919-966-6354.

The University of North Carolina at Chapel Hill, School of Medicine and Graduate School, Graduate Programs in Medicine, Department of Allied Health Sciences, Division of Rehabilitation Counseling and Psychology, Chapel Hill, NC 27599. Offers MS. *Accreditation:* CORE. *Faculty:* 3 full-time (2 women), 2 part-time/adjunct (both women). *Students:* 21 full-time (17 women); includes 3 minority (all African Americans) Average age 27. 20 applicants, 75% accepted, 12 enrolled. In 2007, 5 degrees awarded. *Degree requirements:* For master's, comprehensive exam, thesis or alternative, internship. *Entrance requirements:* For master's, GRE. Additional exam requirements/recommendations for international students: Required—TOEFL (minimum score 550 paper-based; 79 computer-based). *Application deadline:* For fall admission, 4/1 for domestic students, 1/1 for international students. Application fee: $73. *Financial support:* In 2007–08, 2 research assistantships (averaging $4,800 per year) were awarded; teaching assistantships, Federal Work-Study, institutionally sponsored loans, traineeships, and unspecified assistantships also available. Financial award application deadline: 1/1. *Faculty research:* Motor development, motor control; treatment of sports/orthopedic patient problems; movement in older adults; postural control across the lifespan; research in clinical practice; fetal, preterm, and infant movement; functional assessment across the lifespan. *Unit head:* Charles Bernacchio, EdD, CRC, Director, 919-843-4730, Fax: 919-966-9007, E-mail: cbernacchio@med.unc.edu. *Application contact:* Holly Kathryn Maguire, Program Assistant, 919-966-8788, Fax: 919-966-9007, E-mail: holly_maguire@med.unc.edu.

University of Northern Colorado, Graduate School, College of Natural and Health Sciences, School of Human Sciences, Program in Rehabilitation, Greeley, CO 80639. Offers human rehabilitation (PhD); rehabilitation counseling (MA). *Accreditation:* CORE (one or more programs are accredited). Part-time programs available. *Faculty:* 3 full-time (1 woman). *Students:* 16 full-time (13 women), 6 part-time (5 women); includes 1 minority (African American), 4 international. Average age 35. 11 applicants, 91% accepted, 10 enrolled. In 2007, 3 master's, 8 doctorates awarded. *Degree requirements:* For master's, comprehensive exam, thesis or alternative; for doctorate, comprehensive exam, thesis/dissertation. *Entrance requirements:* For master's, GRE General Test or MAT, 2 letters of recommendation; for doctorate, GRE General Test, 2 letters of recommendation. *Application deadline:* Applications are processed on a rolling basis. Application fee: $50 ($60 for international students). Electronic applications accepted. *Expenses:* Tuition, state resident: part-time $222 per credit. Tuition, nonresident: part-time $627 per credit. Required fees: $36 per credit. *Financial support:* In 2007–08, 2 research assistantships (averaging $4,917 per year) were awarded; fellowships, teaching assistantships, unspecified assistantships also available. Financial award application deadline: 3/1; financial award applicants required to submit FAFSA. *Unit head:* Dr. Joe Ososkre, Program Coordinator, 970-351-2403.

University of North Florida, College of Health, Department of Public Health, Jacksonville, FL 32224-2645. Offers community health (MPH); geriatric management (MSH); health administration (MHA); health behavior research and evaluation (Certificate); nutrition (MSH); rehabilitation counseling (MS). *Accreditation:* CORE. Part-time and evening/weekend programs available. *Faculty:* 23 full-time (18 women). *Students:* 75 full-time (59 women), 55 part-time (47 women); includes 30 minority (20 African Americans, 4 Asian Americans or Pacific Islanders, 6 Hispanic Americans), 8 international. Average age 30. 171 applicants, 52% accepted, 50 enrolled. In 2007, 49 degrees awarded. *Degree requirements:* For master's, thesis optional. *Entrance requirements:* For master's, GRE General Test (MSH, MS, MPH), GMAT or GRE General Test (MHA), minimum GPA of 3.0 in last 60 hours. Additional exam requirements/recommendations for international students: Required—TOEFL (minimum score 500 paper-based; 173 computer-based). *Application deadline:* For fall admission, 7/1 priority date for domestic students, 5/1 for international students; for spring admission, 11/10 priority date for domestic students, 10/1 for international students. Applications are processed on a rolling basis. Application fee: $30. Electronic applications accepted. *Expenses:* Tuition, state resident: part-time $266 per credit hour. Tuition, nonresident: part-time $858 per credit hour. One-time fee: $35 part-time. Tuition and fees vary according to program. *Financial support:* In 2007–08, 66 students received support; research assistantships, teaching assistantships, career-related internships or fieldwork, Federal Work-Study, scholarships/grants, and tuition waivers (partial) available. Support available to part-time students. Financial award application deadline: 4/1; financial award applicants required to submit FAFSA. *Faculty research:* Dietary supplements; alcohol, tobacco, and other drug use prevention; turnover among health professionals; aging; psychosocial aspects of disabilities. Total annual research expenditures:$412,026. *Unit head:* Dr. Judith Perkin, Chair, 904-620-2840, Fax: 904-620-2848, E-mail: jperkin@unf.edu. *Application contact:* Rachel Broderick, Director of Advising, 904-620-2817, Fax: 904-620-1770, E-mail: rbroderi@unf.edu.

University of North Texas, Robert B. Toulouse School of Graduate Studies, College of Public Affairs and Community Service, Department of Rehabilitation, Social Work, and Addictions, Denton, TX 76203. Offers rehabilitation counseling (MS). *Accreditation:* CORE. Part-time programs available. *Faculty:* 16 full-time (8 women). *Students:* 19 full-time (16 women), 55 part-time (37 women); includes 28 minority (15 African Americans, 1 American Indian/Alaska Native, 12 Hispanic Americans). Average age 41. 51 applicants, 39% accepted, 11 enrolled. In 2007, 47 degrees awarded. *Degree requirements:* For master's, comprehensive exam, thesis optional, 600-hour internship. *Entrance requirements:* For master's, GRE General Test or 2 years experience, minimum overall GPA of 2.8, 3.0 in last 60 hours. Additional exam requirements/recommendations for international students: Required—proof of English language proficiency required for non-native English speakers; Recommended—TOEFL (minimum score 550 paper-based; 213 computer-based). *Application deadline:* For fall admission, 7/15 for domestic students; for spring admission, 11/15 for domestic students. Applications are processed on a rolling basis. Application fee: $50 ($75 for international students). *Financial support:* Career-related internships or fieldwork, Federal Work-Study, institutionally sponsored loans, and scholarships/grants available. Financial award application deadline: 4/1. *Faculty research:* Resiliency, multiculturalism, substance abuse and co-existing disabilities, social work pedagogy, spiritual aspects of disability and aging. Total annual research expenditures: $1.2 million. *Unit head:* Dr. Linda Holloway, Interim Chair, 940-565-2488, Fax: 940-565-3960, E-mail: holloway@pacs.unt.edu.

University of Pittsburgh, School of Health and Rehabilitation Sciences, Program in Health and Rehabilitation Sciences, Pittsburgh, PA 15260. Offers dietetics (MS); health and rehabilitation sciences (MS), including clinical dietetics, coordinated with dietetics, health care supervision and management, health information systems, occupational therapy, physical therapy, rehabilitation counseling, rehabilitation science and technology, sports medicine; wellness and human performance (MS). *Accreditation:* APTA. Part-time and evening/weekend programs available. *Faculty:* 29 full-time (14 women), 5 part-time/adjunct (3 women). *Students:* 76 full-time (46 women), 43 part-time (27 women); includes 16 minority (9 African Americans, 6 Asian Americans or Pacific Islanders, 1 Hispanic American), 32 international. Average age 30. 217 applicants, 76% accepted, 80 enrolled. In 2007, 57 degrees awarded. *Entrance requirements:* For master's, minimum GPA of 3.0. Additional exam requirements/recommendations for international students: Required—TOEFL, IELTS. *Application deadline:* For fall admission, 1/31 for domestic students. Applications are processed on a rolling basis. Application fee: $50. Electronic applications accepted. *Financial support:* In 2007–08, 10 research assistantships with full tuition reimbursements (averaging $18,672 per year) were awarded; teaching assistantships, Federal Work-Study, institutionally sponsored loans, traineeships, and unspecified assistantships also available. Support available to part-time students. Financial award applicants required to submit FAFSA. *Faculty research:* Assistive technology, seating and wheeled mobility, cellular neurophysiology, low back syndrome, augmentative communication. Total annual research expenditures: $666,046. *Application contact:* Shameem Gangjee, Director of Admissions, 412-383-6558, Fax: 412-383-6535, E-mail: admissions@shrs.pitt.edu.

University of Puerto Rico, Río Piedras, College of Social Sciences, Graduate School of Rehabilitation Counseling, San Juan, PR 00931-3300. Offers MRC. *Accreditation:* CORE. Part-time programs available. *Students:* 112 full-time (89 women), 7 part-time (4 women); includes 100 minority (all Hispanic Americans) Average age 31. In 2007, 21 degrees awarded. *Degree requirements:* For master's, comprehensive exam, thesis, internship. *Entrance requirements:* For master's, GRE or PAEG, interview, minimum GPA of 3.0, letter of recommendation. *Application deadline:* For fall admission, 2/1 for domestic and international students. Application fee: $17. *Expenses:* Tuition, state resident: full-time $1,808; part-time $113 per credit. Tuition, nonresident: full-time $5,248; part-time $328 per credit. Required fees: $72 per term. *Financial support:* Fellowships, research assistantships, teaching assistantships, career-related internships or fieldwork, Federal Work-Study, institutionally sponsored loans, and tuition waivers (partial) available. Financial award application deadline: 5/31. *Unit head:* Dr. Marilyn Mendoza-Lugo, Director, 787-764-0000 Ext. 87419, Fax: 787-764-0000. *Application contact:* Information Contact, 787-764-0000 Ext. 2177, Fax: 787-764-0000 Ext.1212.

The University of Scranton, Graduate School, Department of Counseling and Human Services, Program in Rehabilitation Counseling, Scranton, PA 18510. Offers MS. *Accreditation:* CORE. Part-time and evening/weekend programs available. *Degree requirements:* For master's, comprehensive exam, capstone experience. *Entrance requirements:* For master's, minimum GPA of 2.75. Additional exam requirements/recommendations for international students: Required—TOEFL (minimum score 500 paper-based; 173 computer-based), IELTS (minimum score 6).

University of South Alabama, Graduate School, College of Education, Department of Professional Studies, Mobile, AL 36688-0002. Offers community counseling (MS); educational media (M Ed, MS); instructional design and development (MS, PhD); rehabilitation counseling (MS); school counseling (M Ed); school psychometry (M Ed). *Accreditation:* NCATE. Part-time programs available. *Faculty:* 12 full-time (5 women), 7 part-time/adjunct (5 women). *Students:* 146 full-time (121 women), 178 part-time (150 women); includes 84 minority (77 African Americans, 3 American Indian/Alaska Native, 2 Asian Americans or Pacific Islanders, 2 Hispanic Americans), 14 international. 98 applicants, 69% accepted, 38 enrolled. In 2007, 30 master's, 10 doctorates awarded. *Degree requirements:* For master's, comprehensive exam. *Entrance requirements:* For master's, GRE General Test or MAT, minimum GPA of 3.0. *Application deadline:* For fall admission, 9/1 priority date for domestic students. Applications are processed on a rolling basis. Application fee: $25. *Expenses:* Tuition, state resident: full-time $4,224; part-time $176 per credit hour. Tuition, nonresident: full-time $8,448; part-time $352 per credit hour. Required fees: $802. Full-time tuition and fees vary according to program and student level. *Financial support:* In 2007–08, 5 research assistantships were awarded; career-related internships or fieldwork also available. Support available to part-time students. Financial award application deadline: 4/1. *Faculty research:* Agency counseling, rehabilitation counseling, school psychometry. *Unit head:* Dr. Charles Guest, Chair, 251-380-2861.

University of South Carolina, School of Medicine and The Graduate School, Graduate Programs in Medicine, Program in Rehabilitation Counseling, Columbia, SC 29208. Offers psychiatric rehabilitation (Certificate); rehabilitation counseling (MRC). *Accreditation:* CORE. Part-time and evening/weekend programs available. *Faculty:* 3 full-time (2 women), 2 part-time/adjunct (1 woman). *Students:* 21 full-time (19 women), 12 part-time (5 women); includes 4 minority (all African Americans), 1 international. Average age 34. 35 applicants, 40% accepted. In 2007, 9 degrees awarded. *Degree requirements:* For master's, comprehensive exam, internship, practicum. *Entrance requirements:* For master's and Certificate, GRE General Test or GMAT. *Application deadline:* For fall admission, 5/30 priority date for domestic students. Application fee: $35. Electronic applications accepted. *Expenses: Contact institution.* Tuition and fees vary according to program. *Financial support:* In 2007–08, 10 fellowships with full tuition reimbursements (averaging $4,800 per year), 5 research assistantships with partial tuition reimbursements (averaging $6,000 per year) were awarded; career-related internships or fieldwork, institutionally sponsored loans, and unspecified assistantships also available. *Faculty research:* Quality of life, alcohol dependency, technology for disabled, psychiatric rehabilitation, women with disabilities. *Unit head:* Dr. Linda L. Leech, Graduate Director, 803-434-4296, Fax: 803-434-4231, E-mail: lleech@richmed.medpark.sc.edu. *Application contact:* Linda Howell, Administrative Support Specialist, 803-434-4296, Fax: 803-434-4231, E-mail: linda@richmed.medpark.sc.edu.

University of South Florida, Graduate School, College of Arts and Sciences, Department of Rehabilitation and Mental Health Counseling, Tampa, FL 33620-9951. Offers MA. *Accreditation:* CORE. Part-time and evening/weekend programs available. *Faculty:* 8 full-time (2 women), 3 part-time/adjunct (all women). *Students:* 55 full-time (47 women), 50 part-time (43 women); includes 23 minority (12 African Americans, 1 Asian American or Pacific Islander, 10 Hispanic Americans), 1 international. 65 applicants, 57% accepted, 33 enrolled. In 2007, 30 degrees awarded. *Entrance requirements:* For master's, GRE General Test, minimum GPA of 3.0 in last 60 hours. Additional exam requirements/recommendations for international students: Required—TWE. *Application deadline:* For fall admission, 3/30 for domestic students; for spring admission, 10/15 for domestic students. Application fee: $30. Electronic applications accepted. *Financial support:* Application deadline: 6/30. *Faculty research:* Allied health, multiculturalism, couples therapy, addictions. *Unit head:* Charotte Dixon, Chairperson, 813-974-0973, Fax: 813-974-8080, E-mail: dixon@cas.usf.edu. *Application contact:* Shari Allen, Office Manager, 813-974-0970, Fax: 813-974-8080, E-mail: allen@chuma1.cas.usf.edu.

The University of Tennessee, Graduate School, College of Education, Health and Human Sciences, Department of Educational Psychology and Counseling, Knoxville, TN 37996. Offers adult education (MS); applied educational psychology (MS); collaborative learning (Ed D); college student personnel (MS); mental health counseling (MS); rehabilitation counseling (MS); school counseling (MS). *Accreditation:* ACA (one or more programs are accredited); CORE (one or more programs are accredited); NCATE. Part-time and evening/weekend programs available. *Degree requirements:* For master's, thesis optional. *Entrance requirements:* For master's, GRE General Test, minimum GPA of 2.7. Additional exam requirements/recommendations for international students: Required—TOEFL. Electronic applications accepted.

The University of Texas–Pan American, College of Health Sciences and Human Services, Department of Rehabilitation, Edinburg, TX 78541-2999. Offers rehabilitation counseling (MS). *Accreditation:* CORE. Part-time and evening/weekend programs available. *Faculty:* 9 full-time (4 women). *Students:* 26 full-time (19 women), 24 part-time (21 women); includes 45 minority (1 African American, 44 Hispanic Americans). Average age 28. 21 applicants, 100% accepted, 17 enrolled. In 2007, 15 degrees awarded. *Degree requirements:* For master's, comprehensive exam, thesis optional. *Entrance requirements:* For master's, minimum GPA of 3.0. *Application deadline:* For fall admission, 4/1 priority date for domestic students; for winter admission, 11/1 priority date for domestic students; for spring admission, 11/1 for domestic students. Application fee: $35. *Financial support:* In 2007–08, 4 students received support, including 1 research assistantship (averaging $10,000 per year), 3 teaching assistantships (averaging $10,000 per year); career-related internships or fieldwork, Federal Work-Study, institutionally sponsored loans, and scholarships/grants also available. *Faculty research:* Attitudes and disability, substance abuse, multicultural counseling, Hispanics and disability, Social Security beneficiary characteristics. *Unit head:* Thomas Shefcik, Interim Chair, 956-316-7036 Ext. 7038, Fax: 956-318-5237, E-mail: tshefcik@panam.edu. *Application contact:* Dr. Shawn P. Saladin, Assistant Professor and Graduate Coordinator, 956-316-7036, Fax: 956-318-5237, E-mail: ssaladin@utpa.edu.

The University of Texas Southwestern Medical Center at Dallas, Southwestern Graduate School of Biomedical Sciences, Division of Clinical Science, Rehabilitation Counseling Psychology Program, Dallas, TX 75390. Offers MS. *Accreditation:* CORE. *Faculty:* 19 full-time (14 women), 10 part-time/adjunct (3 women). *Students:* 21 full-time (15 women); includes 5 minority (1 African American, 1 American Indian/Alaska Native, 3 Hispanic Americans), 1 international. Average age 30. 16 applicants, 31% accepted, 5 enrolled. In 2007, 15 degrees awarded. *Degree requirements:* For master's, thesis. *Entrance requirements:* For master's, GRE General Test, minimum GPA of 3.0. *Application deadline:* For fall admission, 5/1 for domestic students. Applications are processed on a rolling basis. Application fee: $0. Electronic applications accepted. *Financial support:* Career-related internships or fieldwork and institutionally sponsored loans available. Financial award application deadline: 3/1; financial award applicants required to submit FAFSA. *Faculty research:* Psychophysiology of stress and emotion, psychosocial rehabilitation, assessment of learning disabilities. *Unit head:* Dr. Cheryl Silver, Chair, 214-648-1750, Fax: 214-648-1076, E-mail: cheryl.silver@utsouthwestern.edu. *Application contact:* Wanda Madyun, Administrative Assistant, 214-648-1544, Fax: 214-648-1076, E-mail: wanda.madyun@utsouthwestern.edu.

University of Wisconsin–Madison, Graduate School, School of Education, Department of Rehabilitation Psychology and Special Education, Program in Rehabilitation Psychology, Madison, WI 53706-1380. Offers MA, MS, PhD. *Accreditation:* CORE (one or more programs are accredited). *Degree requirements:* For doctorate, thesis/dissertation. *Application deadline:* For fall admission, 2/15 for domestic and international students; for spring admission, 10/15 for domestic and international students. Application fee: $45. *Financial support:* Fellowships with full tuition reimbursements, research assistantships with full tuition reimbursements, teaching assistantships with full tuition reimbursements, project assistantships available. *Unit head:* Dr. David Rosenthal, Chair, Department of Rehabilitation Psychology and Special Education, 608-262-5860.

University of Wisconsin–Stout, Graduate School, College of Human Development, Program in Vocational Rehabilitation, Menomonie, WI 54751. Offers MS. *Accreditation:* CORE.Part-time programs available. Postbaccalaureate distance learning degree programs offered (no on-campus study). *Faculty:* 13 full-time (6 women). *Students:* 35 full-time (24 women), 49 part-time (44 women); includes 6 minority (5 African Americans, 1 American Indian/Alaska Native), 5 international. Average age 36. 46 applicants, 83% accepted, 27 enrolled. In 2007, 21 degrees awarded. *Degree requirements:* For master's, comprehensive exam or thesis. *Entrance requirements:* For master's, minimum GPA of 2.75. Additional exam requirements/recommendations for international students: Required—TOEFL (minimum score 500 paper-based; 173 computer-based; 61 iBT). *Application deadline:* For fall admission, 3/15 for domestic and international students. Applications are processed on a rolling basis. Application fee: $45. Electronic applications accepted. *Expenses:* Tuition, state resident: part-time $332 per credit. Tuition, nonresident: part-time $553 per credit. *Financial support:* In 2007–08, 6 research assistantships with partial tuition reimbursements (averaging $4,283 per year) were awarded; teaching assistantships, Federal Work-Study, scholarships/grants, and tuition waivers (partial) also available. Support available to part-time students. Financial award application deadline: 4/1; financial award applicants required to submit FAFSA. *Faculty research:* Aging/gerontology, athletics, neuropsychology, recreation, transition to work. *Unit head:* Dr. Michelle Hamilton, Director, 715-232-1895, E-mail: hamiltonmi@uwstout.edu. *Application contact:* Information Contact, 715-232-1983.

Utah State University, School of Graduate Studies, College of Education and Human Services, Department of Special Education and Rehabilitation, Program in Rehabilitation Counselor Education, Logan, UT 84322. Offers MRC. *Accreditation:* CORE. Part-time programs available. Postbaccalaureate distance learning degree programs offered (minimal on-campus study). *Degree requirements:* For master's, internship. *Entrance requirements:* For master's, GRE General Test, minimum GPA of 3.0. Additional exam requirements/recommendations for international students: Required—TOEFL (minimum score 550 paper-based; 213 computer-based). Electronic applications accepted. Expenses: Contact institution. *Faculty research:* Distance education, Hispanic rehabilitation, transition from school to work.

Virginia Commonwealth University, Graduate School, School of Allied Health Professions, Department of Rehabilitation Counseling, Richmond, VA 23284-9005. Offers MS, CPC. *Accreditation:* CORE (one or more programs are accredited). *Faculty:* 6 full-time (2 women). *Students:* 51 full-time (42 women), 35 part-time (25 women); includes 30 minority (25 African Americans, 1 American Indian/Alaska Native, 1 Asian American or Pacific Islander, 3 Hispanic Americans), 1 international. 49 applicants, 73% accepted, 25 enrolled. In 2007, 24 master's, 8 other advanced degrees awarded. *Entrance requirements:* For master's, GRE General Test or MAT. *Application deadline:* For fall admission, 8/1 for domestic students; for spring admission, 12/1 for domestic students. Applications are processed on a rolling basis. Application fee: $50. *Expenses:* Tuition, state resident: full-time $7,224; part-time $401 per credit. Tuition, nonresident: full-time $16,072; part-time $891 per credit. Required fees: $1,679; $63 per credit. Tuition and fees vary according to campus/location. *Financial support:* Fellowships, research assistantships, teaching assistantships, career-related internships or fieldwork and tuition waivers (full and partial) available. Financial award application deadline: 3/1. *Faculty research:* Substance abuse/addictions, lifelong disabilities, consumer empowerment, counseling models, adjustment to disability. *Unit head:* Dr. Christine A. Reid, Chairman, 804-827-0915, Fax: 801-828-1321, E-mail: careid@vcu.edu.

Wayne State University, College of Education, Division of Theoretical and Behavioral Foundations, Detroit, MI 48202. Offers counseling (M Ed, MA, Ed D, PhD, Ed S); education evaluation and research (M Ed, Ed D, PhD); educational psychology (M Ed, Ed D, PhD, Ed S); educational sociology (M Ed, Ed D, PhD, Ed S); history and philosophy of education (M Ed, Ed D, PhD); rehabilitation counseling and community inclusion (MA, Ed S); school and community psychology (MA, Ed S); school clinical psychology (Ed S). *Accreditation:* ACA (one or more programs are accredited); CORE (one or more programs are accredited). Evening/weekend programs available. *Students:* 166 full-time (135 women), 215 part-time (173 women); includes 141 minority (127 African Americans, 3 American Indian/Alaska Native, 6 Asian Americans or Pacific Islanders, 5 Hispanic Americans), 17 international. Average age 35. 149 applicants, 50% accepted, 58 enrolled. In 2007, 90 master's, 16 doctorates, 2 other advanced degrees awarded. *Degree requirements:* For doctorate, thesis/dissertation. *Entrance requirements:* For master's, GRE; for doctorate, GRE, interview, minimum GPA of 3.0, curriculum vitae, references. Additional exam requirements/recommendations for international students: Required—TOEFL (minimum score 550 paper-based; 213 computer-based), TWE (minimum score 6). *Application deadline:* For fall admission, 7/1 for domestic students, 6/1 for international students; for winter admission, 10/1 for international students; for spring admission, 2/1 for international students. Application fee: $20 ($30 for international students). Electronic applications accepted. *Expenses:* Tuition, state resident: part-time $403 per credit hour. Tuition, nonresident: part-time $890 per credit hour. *Financial support:* In 2007–08, 1 fellowship with tuition reimbursement (averaging $14,201 per year), 2 research assistantships with tuition reimbursements (averaging $13,627 per year) were awarded; career-related internships or fieldwork, Federal Work-Study, and institutionally sponsored loans also available. *Faculty research:* Adolescents at risk, supervision of counseling. *Unit head:* Dr. JoAnne Holbert, Assistant Dean, 313-577-1721, E-mail: jholbert@wayne.edu.

Wayne State University, Graduate School, Interdisciplinary Program in Developmental Disabilities, Detroit, MI 48202. Offers Certificate. *Entrance requirements:* For degree, master's degree; reference; goal statement. Additional exam requirements/recommendations for international students: Required—TOEFL (minimum score 550 paper-based; 213 computer-based); Recommended—TWE (minimum score 6). *Application deadline:* For fall admission, 6/1 for international students; for winter admission, 10/1 for international students; for spring admission, 2/1 for international students. Applications are processed on a rolling basis. Application fee: $30 ($50 for international students). Electronic applications accepted. *Expenses:* Tuition, state resident: part-time $403 per credit hour. Tuition, nonresident: part-time $890 per credit hour. *Unit head:* Dr. Barbara Leroy, Director, 313-577-0334, Fax: 313-577-3770.

Western Michigan University, Graduate College, College of Health and Human Services, Department of Blindness and Low Vision Studies, Kalamazoo, MI 49008-5202. Offers MA. *Accreditation:* CORE.

Western Oregon University, Graduate Programs, College of Education, Division of Special Education, Program in Rehabilitation Counseling, Monmouth, OR 97361-1394. Offers MS. *Accreditation:* CORE. *Faculty:* 2 full-time (both women), 4 part-time/adjunct (3 women). *Students:* 27 full-time (23 women); includes 8 minority (1 African American, 2 American Indian/Alaska Native, 1 Asian American or Pacific Islander, 4 Hispanic Americans), 1 international. Average age 36. 21 applicants, 67% accepted, 13 enrolled. In 2007, 13 degrees awarded. *Degree requirements:* For master's, thesis optional, oral exam, portfolio. *Entrance requirements:* For master's, interview, minimum GPA of 3.0. Additional exam requirements/recommendations for international students: Required—TOEFL (minimum score 550 paper-based; 213 computer-based; 79 iBT), IELTS (minimum score 7). *Application deadline:* For fall admission, 4/15 priority date for domestic students. Applications are processed on a rolling basis. Application fee: $50. *Expenses:* Tuition, state resident: full-time $9,648; part-time $346 per quarter. Tuition, nonresident: full-time $15,588; part-time $526 per quarter. Required fees: $374 per quarter. Tuition and fees vary according to course level and course load. *Financial support:* In 2007–08, 5 research assistantships with full tuition reimbursements (averaging $1,057 per year), 1 teaching assistantship with full tuition reimbursement (averaging $837 per year) were awarded; career-related internships or fieldwork, Federal Work-Study, scholarships/grants, and tuition waivers (full and partial) also available. Support available to part-time students. Financial award application deadline: 3/1; financial award applicants required to submit FAFSA. *Faculty research:* Deafness, rehabilitation counseling. *Unit head:* Dr. Julia Smith, Coordinator, 503-838-8444, Fax: 503-838-8228, E-mail: smithj@wou.edu. *Application contact:* Dr. David McDonald, Associate Provost for Retention and Enrollment Management, 503-838-8919, Fax: 503-838-8067, E-mail: mcdonald@wou.edu.

Western Washington University, Graduate School, Woodring College of Education, Program in Rehabilitation Counseling, Bellingham, WA 98225-5996. Offers MA. *Accreditation:* CORE. Part-time and evening/weekend programs available. Postbaccalaureate distance learning degree programs offered (minimal on-campus study). *Faculty:* 1. *Students:* 24 full-time (18 women), 28 part-time (22 women); includes 11 minority (5 African Americans, 2 American Indian/Alaska Native, 3 Asian Americans or Pacific Islanders, 1 Hispanic American). 19 applicants, 79% accepted, 13 enrolled. In 2007, 20 degrees awarded. *Degree requirements:* For master's, research project. *Entrance requirements:* For master's, GRE General Test or MAT, minimum GPA of 3.0 in last 60 semester hours or last 90 quarter hours of course work. Additional exam requirements/recommendations for international students: Required—TOEFL (minimum score 567 paper-based; 227 computer-based). *Application deadline:* For fall admission, 6/1 for domestic students; for winter admission, 10/1 for domestic students; for spring admission, 2/1 for domestic students. Applications are processed on a rolling basis. Application fee: $50. Electronic applications accepted. *Expenses:* Tuition, state resident: part-time $208 per credit. Tuition, nonresident: part-time $541 per credit. Required fees: $241 per quarter. One-time fee: $250 part-time. *Financial support:* Career-related internships or fieldwork, Federal Work-Study, institutionally sponsored loans, and scholarships/grants available. Support available to part-time students. Financial award application deadline: 2/15. *Faculty research:* Employment issues for

Rehabilitation Counseling

Western Washington University (continued)
individuals with significant disabilities, research and statistics techniques, rehabilitation counselor education. *Unit head:* Dr. Elizabeth Swett, Director, 425-774-7424, E-mail: elizabeth.swett@wwu.edu. *Application contact:* Alex Burns, Graduate Program Coordinator, 425-771-7429, E-mail: alex.burns@wwu.edu.

West Virginia University, College of Human Resources and Education, Department of Counseling, Rehabilitation Counseling, and Counseling Psychology, Program in Rehabilitation Counseling, Morgantown, WV 26506. Offers MS. *Accreditation:* CORE. Part-time programs available. Postbaccalaureate distance learning degree programs offered (minimal on-campus study). *Students:* 40 full-time (31 women), 14 part-time (9 women); includes 4 minority (2 African Americans, 2 Asian Americans or Pacific Islanders), 1 international. Average age 36. 19 applicants, 53% accepted, 8 enrolled. In 2007, 22 degrees awarded. *Degree requirements:* For master's, content exams. *Entrance requirements:* For master's, GRE General Test, minimum GPA of 2.5, interview. Additional exam requirements/recommendations for international students: Required—TOEFL (minimum score 550 paper-based; 213 computer-based; 65 iBT). *Application deadline:* For fall admission, 3/15 priority date for domestic and international students. Application fee: $50. Electronic applications accepted. *Expenses:* Tuition, state resident: full-time $5,196; part-time $292 per credit hour. Tuition, nonresident: full-time $15,064; part-time $840 per credit hour. Tuition and fees vary according to program. *Financial support:* In 2007–08, 39 students received support, including 2 research assistantships with full tuition reimbursements available (averaging $8,864 per year), 2 teaching assistantships with full tuition reimbursements available (averaging $8,864 per year); career-related internships or fieldwork, Federal Work-Study, institutionally sponsored loans, traineeships, tuition waivers (full and partial), and unspecified assistantships also available. Financial award application deadline: 2/1; financial award applicants required to submit FAFSA. *Faculty research:* Work adjustment, job modification for the handicapped, computer resource networks, vocational evaluation. *Unit head:* Dr. Margaret Glenn, Interim Chair, Department of Counseling, Rehabilitation Counseling, and Counseling Psychology, 304-293-2276, Fax: 304-293-4082, E-mail: margaret.glenn@mail.wvu.edu.

Winston-Salem State University, Program in Rehabilitation Counseling, Winston-Salem, NC 27110-0003. Offers MRC. *Accreditation:* CORE. Part-time programs available. Postbaccalaureate distance learning degree programs offered (minimal on-campus study). *Faculty:* 5 full-time (3 women). *Students:* 29 full-time (23 women), 32 part-time (24 women); includes 52 minority (all African Americans) 33 applicants, 27% accepted, 9 enrolled. In 2007, 18 degrees awarded. *Degree requirements:* For master's, thesis optional. *Entrance requirements:* For master's, GRE, 3 letters of recommendation. *Application deadline:* For fall admission, 4/15 for domestic and international students. Applications are processed on a rolling basis. Application fee: $40. Electronic applications accepted. *Financial support:* In 2007–08, 9 students received support, including 5 research assistantships (averaging $2,500 per year), 1 teaching assistantship (averaging $5,000 per year); career-related internships or fieldwork, institutionally sponsored loans, scholarships/grants, and tuition waivers (partial) also available. *Faculty research:* Drug addiction, recovery, HIV/AIDS interventions. *Unit head:* Dr. Cynthia Williams-Brown, Chair, 336-750-2589, Fax: 336-750-2591, E-mail: williamsc@wssu.edu. *Application contact:* Graduate Studies and Research, 336-750-2102, Fax: 336-750-3042, E-mail: graduate@wssu.edu.

Wright State University, School of Graduate Studies, College of Education and Human Services, Department of Human Services, Program in Rehabilitation Counseling, Dayton, OH 45435. Offers chemical dependency (MRC); severe disabilities (MRC). *Accreditation:* CORE. *Degree requirements:* For master's, comprehensive exam. *Entrance requirements:* For master's, GRE General Test, MAT, interview. Additional exam requirements/recommendations for international students: Required—TOEFL.

School Psychology

Abilene Christian University, Graduate School, College of Arts and Sciences, Department of Psychology, Program in School Psychology, Abilene, TX 79699-9100. Offers MS. *Students:* 13 full-time (12 women), 4 part-time (2 women). 14 applicants, 79% accepted, 9 enrolled. In 2007, 3 degrees awarded. *Degree requirements:* For master's, comprehensive exam, thesis optional. *Entrance requirements:* For master's, GRE General Test. *Application deadline:* For fall admission, 4/1 priority date for domestic students; for spring admission, 11/1 for domestic students. Applications are processed on a rolling basis. Application fee: $40 ($45 for international students). Electronic applications accepted. *Expenses:* Tuition: Full-time $13,368; part-time $557 per hour. Required fees: $700; $34 per hour. $10 per semester. Tuition and fees vary according to degree level and campus/location. *Financial support:* Federal Work-Study available. Support available to part-time students. Financial award application deadline: 4/1. *Unit head:* Dr. Jennifer Shewmaker, Graduate Advisor, 325-674-2381, Fax: 325-674-6968, E-mail: jennifer.shewmaker@acu.edu. *Application contact:* William Horn, Graduate Admissions Counselor, 325-674-2656, Fax: 325-674-6717, E-mail: gradinfo@acu.edu.

Adelphi University, Derner Institute of Advanced Psychological Studies, Program in School Psychology, Garden City, NY 11530-0701. Offers MA. Part-time and evening/weekend programs available. *Students:* 43 full-time (36 women), 35 part-time (33 women); includes 7 minority (4 African Americans, 1 Asian American or Pacific Islander, 2 Hispanic Americans). Average age 26. In 2007, 23 degrees awarded. *Degree requirements:* For master's, comprehensive exam. *Entrance requirements:* For master's, minimum GPA of 3.0; 15 credits of course work in psychology including general psychology, developmental child or adolescent psychology, abnormal personality in school psychology, tests and measurements, statistics; 3 letters of recommendation. Additional exam requirements/recommendations for international students: Required—TOEFL (minimum score 550 paper-based; 213 computer-based). *Application deadline:* For fall admission, 3/1 for domestic students, 5/1 for international students. Application fee: $50. Electronic applications accepted. *Financial support:* Research assistantships with full and partial tuition reimbursements, career-related internships or fieldwork, Federal Work-Study, institutionally sponsored loans, and unspecified assistantships available. *Unit head:* Dr. Patrick Grehan, Director, 516-877-4749, E-mail: grehan@adelphi.edu. *Application contact:* Christine Murphy, Director of Admissions, 516-877-3050, Fax: 516-877-3039, E-mail: graduateadmissions@adelphi.edu.

Alabama Agricultural and Mechanical University, School of Graduate Studies, School of Education, Department of Counseling and Special Education, Huntsville, AL 35811. Offers communicative disorders (M Ed, MS); psychology and counseling (MS, Ed S), including clinical psychology (MS), counseling and guidance, counseling psychology (MS), personnel management (MS), psychometry (MS), school psychology (MS); special education (M Ed, MS). *Accreditation:* CORE; NCATE. Part-time and evening/weekend programs available. *Faculty:* 4 full-time (3 women), 3 part-time/adjunct (1 woman). *Students:* 24 full-time (16 women), 58 part-time (48 women); includes 59 minority (56 African Americans, 1 American Indian/Alaska Native, 2 Hispanic Americans), 2 international. In 2007, 55 master's, 2 other advanced degrees awarded. *Degree requirements:* For master's, comprehensive exam. *Entrance requirements:* For master's, GRE General Test. *Application deadline:* For fall admission, 5/1 for domestic students. Application fee: $15 ($20 for international students). *Financial support:* Career-related internships or fieldwork available. Support available to part-time students. Financial award application deadline: 4/1. *Faculty research:* Increasing numbers of minorities in special education and speech-language pathology. Total annual research expenditures: $300,000. *Unit head:* Dr. Shirley King, Chair, 256-372-5520, Fax: 256-372-5526.

Alfred University, Graduate School, Program in School Psychology, Alfred, NY 14802-1205. Offers school counseling (MS Ed, CAS); school psychology (MA, Psy D, CAS). *Accreditation:* APA. *Students:* 90 full-time (69 women), 56 part-time (47 women). Average age 23. 107 applicants, 44% accepted, 36 enrolled. In 2007, 43 master's, 5 doctorates, 27 other advanced degrees awarded. *Degree requirements:* For master's, internship; for doctorate, thesis/dissertation, internship. *Entrance requirements:* For master's and doctorate, GRE General Test. Additional exam requirements/recommendations for international students: Required—TOEFL (minimum score 590 paper-based; 243 computer-based; 90 iBT); Recommended—IELTS (minimum score 7). *Application deadline:* For fall admission, 1/15 priority date for domestic and international students. Application fee: $50. Electronic applications accepted. *Expenses:* Tuition: Full-time $32,016; part-time $680 per credit hour. Required fees: $850; $140 per year. *Financial support:* In 2007–08, 77 students received support, including research assistantships (averaging $15,280 per year); career-related internships or fieldwork, tuition waivers (full and partial), and unspecified assistantships also available. Financial award applicants required to submit FAFSA. *Faculty research:* Family processes, alternative assessment approaches, behavior disorders in children, parent involvement, school psychology training issues. *Unit head:* Dr. Nancy Evangelista, Chair, 607-871-2212, E-mail: fevangel@alfred.edu. *Application contact:* Valerie Stephens, Coordinator of Graduate Admissions, 607-871-2141, Fax: 607-871-2198, E-mail: gradinquiry@alfred.edu.

See Close-Up on page 1365.

Alliant International University–Irvine, Graduate School of Education, Educational Psychology Programs, Irvine, CA 92612. Offers educational psychology (Psy D); pupil personnel services (Credential); school psychology (MA). Part-time programs available. *Degree requirements:* For doctorate, thesis/dissertation. *Entrance requirements:* For master's, minimum GPA of 3.0, letters of recommendation; for doctorate, interview, minimum GPA of 3.0, letters of recommendation. Additional exam requirements/recommendations for international students: Required—TOEFL (minimum score 550 paper-based; 213 computer-based), TWE (minimum score 5). *Faculty research:* School based mental health.

Alliant International University–Los Angeles, Graduate School of Education, Educational Psychology Programs, Alhambra, CA 91803-1360. Offers educational psychology (Psy D); pupil personnel services (Credential); school psychology (MA). Part-time programs available. *Degree requirements:* For doctorate, thesis/dissertation. *Entrance requirements:* For master's, minimum GPA of 3.0, letters of recommendation; for doctorate, interview, minimum GPA of 3.0, letters of recommendation. Additional exam requirements/recommendations for international students: Required—TOEFL (minimum score 550 paper-based; 213 computer-based), TWE (minimum score 5). Electronic applications accepted. *Faculty research:* Early identification and intervention with high-risk preschoolers, pediatric neuropsychology, interpersonal violence, ADHD, learning theories.

Alliant International University–San Diego, Graduate School of Education, Educational Psychology Programs, San Diego, CA 92131-1799. Offers educational psychology (Psy D); pupil personnel services (Credential); school psychology (MA); student personnel services (Certificate). Part-time programs available. *Degree requirements:* For doctorate, thesis/dissertation. *Entrance requirements:* For master's, minimum GPA of 3.0, letters of recommendation; for doctorate, interview, letters of recommendation. Additional exam requirements/recommendations for international students: Required—TOEFL (minimum score 550 paper-based; 213 computer-based), TWE (minimum score 5). Electronic applications accepted.

Alliant International University–San Francisco, Graduate School of Education, Educational Psychology Programs, San Francisco, CA 94133-1221. Offers educational psychology (Psy D); pupil personnel services (Credential); school psychology (MA). Part-time programs available. *Degree requirements:* For doctorate, thesis/dissertation. *Entrance requirements:* For master's, minimum GPA of 3.0, letters of recommendation; for doctorate, interview, minimum GPA of 3.0, letters of recommendation. Additional exam requirements/recommendations for international students: Required—TOEFL (minimum score 550 paper-based; 213 computer-based), TWE (minimum score 5). Electronic applications accepted. *Faculty research:* Social skills, ADHD, effects of sightedness on areas of knowledge.

Andrews University, School of Graduate Studies, School of Education, Department of Educational and Counseling Psychology, Program in School Counseling, Berrien Springs, MI 49104. Offers MA. *Degree requirements:* For master's, thesis optional.

Andrews University, School of Graduate Studies, School of Education, Department of Educational and Counseling Psychology, Program in School Psychology, Berrien Springs, MI 49104. Offers Ed S. Part-time programs available.

Appalachian State University, Cratis D. Williams Graduate School, Department of Human Development and Psychological Counseling, Boone, NC 28608. Offers community counseling (MA); marriage and family therapy (MA); school counseling (MA); student development (MA). *Accreditation:* AAMFT/COAMFTE; ACA; NCATE. Part-time programs available. *Faculty:* 28 full-time (15 women). *Students:* 77 full-time (58 women), 91 part-time (71 women); includes 16 minority (15 African Americans, 1 Asian American or Pacific Islander), 1 international. 152 applicants, 63% accepted, 57 enrolled. In 2007, 52 master's awarded. *Degree requirements:* For master's, comprehensive exam (for some programs), thesis optional, internships. *Entrance requirements:* Additional exam requirements/recommendations for international students: Required—TOEFL (minimum score 570 paper-based; 230 computer-based). *Application deadline:* For fall admission, 2/1 priority date for domestic students, 1/1 for international students; for spring admission, 6/1 for international students. Applications are processed on a rolling basis. Application fee: $50. *Expenses:* Tuition, state resident: part-time $127 per semester hour. Tuition, nonresident: part-time $597 per semester hour. Required fees: $18 per semester. *Financial support:* In 2007–08, 20 research assistantships (averaging $6,000 per year), 7 teaching assistantships (averaging $7,000 per year) were awarded; fellowships, career-related internships or fieldwork, Federal Work-Study, scholarships/grants, and unspecified assistantships also available. Financial award application deadline: 4/1. *Faculty research:* Multicultural counseling, addictions counseling, play therapy, expressive arts, child and adolescent therapy, sexual abuse counseling. *Unit head:* Dr. Lee Baruth, Chairman, 828-262-2055, E-mail: baruthlg@appstate.edu.

Arcadia University, Graduate Studies, Department of Psychology, Glenside, PA 19038-3295. Offers community counseling (MACP); school counseling (MACP). Part-time programs available. *Degree requirements:* For master's, practicum. *Entrance requirements:* For master's, GRE General Test or MAT.

Argosy University, Hawai'i, College of Psychology and Behavioral Sciences, Program in School Psychology, Honolulu, HI 96813. Offers MA.

See Close-Up on page 1385.

Argosy University, Phoenix, College of Psychology and Behavioral Sciences, Program in School Psychology, Phoenix, AZ 85021. Offers MA, Psy D.

See Close-Up on page 1395.

Argosy University, Sarasota, College of Psychology and Behavioral Sciences, Sarasota, FL 34235. Offers community counseling (MA); counseling psychology (Ed D); counselor education and supervision (Ed D); forensic psychology (MA); marriage and family therapy (MA); mental health counseling (MA); organizational leadership (Ed D); pastoral community counseling (Ed D); school counseling (MA, Ed S); school psychology (MA).

See Close-Up on page 1403.

Arkansas State University, Graduate School, College of Education, Department of Psychology and Counseling, Jonesboro, State University, AR 72467. Offers college student personnel services (MS); counselor education (Ed S), including college student personnel services, psychoeducational diagnosis, school counseling; rehabilitation counseling (MRC); school counseling (MSE); student affairs (Certificate). *Accreditation:* ACA (one or more programs are accredited); CORE (one or more programs are accredited); NCATE. Part-time programs available. *Faculty:* 11 full-time (6 women), 6 part-time/adjunct (2 women). *Students:* 69 full-time (54 women), 71 part-time (58 women); includes 27 minority (24 African Americans, 3 Hispanic Americans). Average age 32. 53 applicants, 66% accepted, 32 enrolled. In 2007, 17 master's, 6 other advanced degrees awarded. *Degree requirements:* For master's and other advanced degree, comprehensive exam, thesis or alternative. *Entrance requirements:* For master's, GRE General Test or MAT (MSE), appropriate bachelor's degree, interview, letters of reference, official transcript; for other advanced degree, GRE General Test, interview, master's degree, letters of reference, official transcript. Additional exam requirements/recommendations for international students: Required—TOEFL (minimum score 213 computer-based). *Application deadline:* Applications are processed on a rolling basis. Application fee: $30 ($40 for international students). Electronic applications accepted. *Expenses:* Tuition, state resident: full-time $3,528; part-time $196 per hour. Tuition, nonresident: full-time $8,928; part-time $496 per hour. Required fees: $842; $44 per hour. $25 per term. Tuition and fees vary according to course load and program. *Financial support:* Teaching assistantships, career-related internships or fieldwork, scholarships/grants, and unspecified assistantships available. Financial award application deadline: 7/1; financial award applicants required to submit FAFSA. *Faculty research:* Abuse issues in children and adolescents, career counseling, children's learning and memory, crisis intervention, drug use and addition. *Unit head:* Dr. Loretta McGregor, Chair, 870-972-3064, Fax: 870-972-3962, E-mail: lmcgregor@astate.edu.

Assumption College, Graduate School, School Counseling Program, Worcester, MA 01609-1296. Offers MA, CAGS. Part-time and evening/weekend programs available. *Faculty:* 3 full-time (1 woman), 5 part-time/adjunct (2 women). *Students:* 43 full-time (36 women), 19 part-time (16 women); includes 1 minority (Hispanic American), 1 international. Average age 24. 40 applicants, 90% accepted. In 2007, 10 degrees awarded. *Degree requirements:* For master's and CAGS, comprehensive exam. *Entrance requirements:* For master's, 3 letters of recommendation, resumé, interview, essay; for CAGS, 3 letters of recommendation, resumé, essay, interview. Additional exam requirements/recommendations for international students: Required—TOEFL, IELTS. *Application deadline:* For fall admission, 6/1 priority date for domestic students, 5/1 priority date for international students; for spring admission, 11/1 priority date for domestic students, 10/1 priority date for international students. Applications are processed on a rolling basis. Application fee: $30. Electronic applications accepted. *Expenses:* Tuition: Part-time $450 per credit. Required fees: $20 per semester. *Financial support:* In 2007–08, 47 students received support. Tuition waivers (partial) available. Financial award application deadline: 6/1; financial award applicants required to submit FAFSA. *Unit head:* Dr. Mary Ann Mariani, Director, 508-767-7087, Fax: 508-767-7263, E-mail: mmariani@assumption.edu. *Application contact:* Adrian O. Dumas, Director of Graduate Enrollment Management and Services, 508-767-7365, Fax: 508-767-7030, E-mail: adumas@assumption.edu.

Auburn University, Graduate School, College of Education, Department of Counseling and Counseling Psychology, Auburn University, AL 36849. Offers community agency counseling (M Ed, MS, Ed D, PhD, Ed S); counseling psychology (PhD); counselor education (Ed D, PhD); school counseling (M Ed, MS, Ed D, PhD, Ed S); school psychometry (M Ed, MS, Ed D, PhD, Ed S). *Accreditation:* ACA (one or more programs are accredited); APA (one or more programs are accredited); NCATE. Part-time programs available. *Faculty:* 10 full-time (6 women). *Students:* 51 full-time (35 women), 41 part-time (33 women); includes 27 minority (26 African Americans, 1 Hispanic American), 5 international. Average age 31. 140 applicants, 42% accepted, 30 enrolled. In 2007, 20 master's, 9 doctorates, 4 other advanced degrees awarded. *Degree requirements:* For master's, thesis (for some programs); for doctorate, thesis/dissertation; for Ed S, thesis or alternative. *Entrance requirements:* For master's and Ed S, GRE General Test; for doctorate, GRE General Test, GRE Subject Test. *Application deadline:* For fall admission, 5/15 for domestic students. Application fee: $25 ($50 for international students). Electronic applications accepted. *Financial support:* Research assistantships, Federal Work-Study and traineeships available. Support available to part-time students. Financial award application deadline: 3/15. *Faculty research:* At-risk students, substance abuse, gender roles, AIDS, professional ethics. *Unit head:* Dr. Holly Stadler, Head, 334-844-5160. *Application contact:* Dr. Joe Pittman, Interim Dean of the Graduate School, 334-844-4700.

Azusa Pacific University, School of Education, Department of School Counseling and School Psychology, Program in Educational Psychology, Azusa, CA 91702-7000. Offers MA.

Ball State University, Graduate School, Teachers College, Department of Educational Psychology, Program in School Psychology, Muncie, IN 47306-1099. Offers MA, PhD, Ed S. *Accreditation:* APA (one or more programs are accredited); NCATE. *Students:* 28 full-time (19 women), 29 part-time (19 women); includes 3 minority (2 African Americans, 1 Asian American or Pacific Islander), 3 international. Average age 26. 132 applicants, 28% accepted, 12 enrolled. In 2007, 13 master's, 4 doctorates, 5 other advanced degrees awarded. *Degree requirements:* For doctorate, thesis/dissertation; for Ed S, thesis. *Entrance requirements:* For master's and Ed S, GRE General Test; for doctorate, GRE General Test, interview, minimum graduate GPA of 3.2. Application fee: $25 ($35 for international students). *Expenses:* Tuition, state resident: full-time $6,864. Tuition, nonresident: full-time $17,932. Required fees: $1,866. *Financial support:* Research assistantships, teaching assistantships available. Financial award application deadline: 3/1. *Unit head:* Raymond Dean, Head, 785-285-8500, Fax: 785-285-3653.

Barry University, School of Arts and Sciences, Department of Psychology, Miami Shores, FL 33161-6695. Offers clinical psychology (MS); school psychology (MS, SSP). Part-time and evening/weekend programs available. *Students:* 6 full-time (0 women), 56 part-time (52 women); includes 34 minority (14 African Americans, 2 Asian Americans or Pacific Islanders, 18 Hispanic Americans), 8 international. *Degree requirements:* For master's, thesis, practicum. *Entrance requirements:* For master's, GRE General Test, minimum GPA of 3.0, course work in psychology. *Application deadline:* Applications are processed on a rolling basis. Application fee: $30. Electronic applications accepted. *Financial support:* In 2007–08, 5 research assistantships with partial tuition reimbursements (averaging $3,000 per year) were awarded; career-related internships or fieldwork and tuition waivers (partial) also available. Support available to part-time students. Financial award application deadline: 5/1; financial award applicants required to submit FAFSA. *Faculty research:* Closed head injury, memory and aging, infant/mother interaction, evolutionary aspects of behavior, gender roles. *Unit head:* Dr. Lenore Szuchman, Chair, 305-899-3278, Fax: 305-899-3279, E-mail: lszuchman@mail.barry.edu. *Application contact:* Dave Fletcher, Director of Graduate Admissions, 305-899-3113, Fax: 305-899-2971, E-mail: dfletcher@mail.barry.edu.

See Close-Up on page 1415.

Bowling Green State University, Graduate College, College of Education and Human Development, School of Education and Intervention Services, Intervention Services Division, Program in School Psychology, Bowling Green, OH 43403. Offers M Ed, Sp Ed. *Accreditation:* NCATE. Part-time programs available. *Students:* 27 full-time (24 women); includes 1 minority (Asian American or Pacific Islander) Average age 26. 40 applicants, 58% accepted, 0 enrolled. In 2007, 10 master's, 12 other advanced degrees awarded. *Degree requirements:* For master's, thesis or alternative, internship. *Entrance requirements:* For master's, GRE General Test. Additional exam requirements/recommendations for international students: Required—TOEFL. *Application deadline:* For fall admission, 2/1 priority date for domestic students. Applications are processed on a rolling basis. Application fee: $30. Electronic applications accepted. *Financial support:* In 2007–08, 16 research assistantships with full tuition reimbursements (averaging $4,202 per year), 1 teaching assistantship with full tuition reimbursement (averaging $4,202 per year) were awarded; career-related internships or fieldwork, Federal Work-Study, and unspecified assistantships also available. Financial award applicants required to submit FAFSA. *Faculty research:* Family therapists/multicultural issues, pre-school readiness skills, family relations, multifaceted evaluation, multidisciplinary decision-making. *Application contact:* Dr. Audrey Ellenwood, Graduate Coordinator, 419-372-9848.

Brigham Young University, Graduate Studies, David O. McKay School of Education, Department of Counseling Psychology and Special Education, Provo, UT 84602-1001. Offers counseling psychology (PhD); school psychology (Ed S); special education (MS). *Accreditation:* NCATE. Part-time programs available. *Faculty:* 13 full-time (8 women), 10 part-time/adjunct (2 women). *Students:* 72 full-time (47 women), 15 part-time (14 women); includes 19 minority (1 African American, 3 American Indian/Alaska Native, 8 Asian Americans or Pacific Islanders, 7 Hispanic Americans), 5 international. Average age 31. 82 applicants, 45% accepted, 26 enrolled. In 2007, 3 master's, 4 doctorates, 11 other advanced degrees awarded. *Degree requirements:* For master's, comprehensive exam, thesis; for doctorate, comprehensive exam, thesis/dissertation. *Entrance requirements:* For master's and doctorate, GRE General Test, minimum GPA of 3.0 in last 60 hours of undergrad coursework. Additional exam requirements/recommendations for international students: Required—TOEFL (minimum score 580 paper-based; 237 computer-based), IELTS (minimum score 7). *Application deadline:* For fall admission, 1/15 for domestic and international students. Application fee: $50. Electronic applications accepted. *Financial support:* In 2007–08, 51 students received support, including 30 research assistantships with partial tuition reimbursements available (averaging $4,500 per year), 3 teaching assistantships with partial tuition reimbursements available (averaging $5,140 per year); career-related internships or fieldwork, institutionally sponsored loans, and tuition waivers (partial) also available. Financial award application deadline: 4/30. *Faculty research:* Gender issues in education, psychotherapy progress and outcome, and behavior disorders and ABA. Total annual research expenditures: $195,507. *Unit head:* Dr. Mary Anne Prater, Chair, 801-422-3857, Fax: 801-422-0198, E-mail: prater@byu.edu. *Application contact:* Diane E. Hancock, Department Secretary, 801-422-3859, Fax: 801-422-0198, E-mail: diane_hancock@byu.edu.

Brooklyn College of the City University of New York, Division of Graduate Studies, School of Education, Program in School Psychologist, Brooklyn, NY 11210-2889. Offers school psychologist (MS Ed, CAS); school psychologist-bilingual (CAS). Part-time and evening/weekend programs available. *Students:* 28 full-time (23 women), 61 part-time (56 women); includes 32 minority (19 African Americans, 1 American Indian/Alaska Native, 2 Asian Americans or Pacific Islanders, 10 Hispanic Americans). 127 applicants, 82% accepted, 27 enrolled. In 2007, 32 master's, 27 CASs awarded. *Degree requirements:* For master's, internship. *Entrance requirements:* For master's, interview, previous course work in education and psychology, teaching certificate, resumé, 2 letters of recommendation; for CAS, master's degree, teaching experience. Additional exam requirements/recommendations for international students: Required—TOEFL. *Application deadline:* For fall admission, 3/1 for domestic students, 2/1 for international students. Application fee: $125. Electronic applications accepted. *Financial support:* Career-related internships or fieldwork, Federal Work-Study, institutionally sponsored loans, and scholarships/grants available. Support available to part-time students. Financial award application deadline: 5/1; financial award applicants required to submit FAFSA. *Unit head:* Dr. Paul McCabe, Program Head, 718-951-5214, Fax: 718-951-4816, E-mail: paulmc@brooklyn.cuny.edu. *Application contact:* Hernan Sierra, Graduate Admissions Coordinator, 718-951-4536, Fax: 718-951-4506, E-mail: grads@brooklyn.cuny.edu.

Bucknell University, Graduate Studies, College of Arts and Sciences, Department of Education, Specialization in School Psychology, Lewisburg, PA 17837. Offers MS Ed. *Degree requirements:* For master's, thesis or alternative. *Entrance requirements:* For master's, GRE General Test, minimum GPA of 2.8. Additional exam requirements/recommendations for international students: Required—TOEFL. *Application deadline:* For fall admission, 6/1 priority date for domestic students; for spring admission, 12/1 priority date for domestic students. Applications are processed on a rolling basis. Application fee: $25. *Expenses:* Tuition: Full-time $16,660; part-time $1,041 per credit hour. *Financial support:* Unspecified assistantships available. Financial award application deadline: 3/1.

California State University, Los Angeles, Graduate Studies, Charter College of Education, Division of Special Education and Counseling, Major in Counseling, Los Angeles, CA 90032-8530. Offers applied behavior analysis (MS); community college counseling (MS); rehabilitation counseling (MS); school counseling and school psychology (MS). *Accreditation:* ACA; CORE; NCATE. Part-time and evening/weekend programs available. *Students:* 200 full-time (157 women), 144 part-time (119 women); includes 205 minority (25 African Americans, 1 American Indian/Alaska Native, 32 Asian Americans or Pacific Islanders, 147 Hispanic Americans), 46 international. Average age 32. In 2007, 106 degrees awarded. *Degree requirements:* For master's, comprehensive exam, project or thesis. *Entrance requirements:* For master's, interview, minimum GPA of 2.75 in last 90 units of course work, teaching certificate. Additional exam requirements/recommendations for international students: Required—TOEFL. *Application deadline:* For fall admission, 6/30 for domestic students; for spring admission, 2/1 for domestic students. Applications are processed on a rolling basis. Application fee: $55. *Financial support:* Career-related internships or fieldwork and Federal Work-Study available. Support available to part-time students. Financial award application deadline: 3/1. *Unit head:* Dr. Randy Campbell, Chair, Division of Special Education and Counseling, 323-343-4400 Ext. 34257, Fax: 323-343-5605, E-mail: rcampbe@calstatela.edu.

California State University, Northridge, Graduate Studies, College of Education, Department of Educational Psychology and Counseling, Northridge, CA 91330. Offers counseling (MS), including career counseling, college counseling and student services, marriage and family therapy, school counseling, school psychology; educational psychology (MA Ed), including development, learning, and instruction, early childhood education. *Accreditation:* ACA (one or more programs are accredited); NCATE. Part-time and evening/weekend programs available. *Faculty:* 17 full-time (10 women), 50 part-time/adjunct (29 women). *Students:* 358 full-time (312 women), 120 part-time (102 women); includes 216 minority (27 African Americans, 2 American Indian/Alaska Native, 41 Asian Americans or Pacific Islanders, 146 Hispanic Americans), 9 international. Average age 31. 284 applicants, 60% accepted, 148 enrolled. In 2007, 142 degrees awarded. *Entrance requirements:* For master's, GRE General Test or minimum GPA of 3.0. Additional exam requirements/recommendations for international students: Required—TOEFL. *Application deadline:* For fall admission, 11/30 for domestic students. Application fee: $55. *Financial support:* Scholarships/grants available. Support available to part-time students. Financial award application deadline: 3/1. *Unit head:* Dr. Beverly Cabello, Chair, 818-677-2599.

California State University, Sacramento, Graduate Studies, College of Education, Department of Special Education, Rehabilitation, and School Psychology, Sacramento, CA 95819-6048. Offers school psychology (MS); special education (MA); vocational rehabilitation (MS). *Accreditation:* CORE. Part-time programs available. *Students:* 37 full-time (29 women), 72 part-time (62 women); includes 18 minority (5 African Americans, 1 American Indian/Alaska Native, 3 Asian Americans or Pacific Islanders, 9 Hispanic Americans), 2 international. Average

School Psychology

California State University, Sacramento (continued)
age 36. 168 applicants, 77% accepted, 90 enrolled. *Degree requirements:* For master's, thesis or alternative, writing proficiency exam. *Entrance requirements:* For master's, minimum GPA of 2.5. Additional exam requirements/recommendations for international students: Required—TOEFL. *Application deadline:* Applications are processed on a rolling basis. Application fee: $55. Electronic applications accepted. *Expenses:* Tuition, state resident: full-time $3,414. Tuition, nonresident: full-time $13,584; part-time $339 per unit. Required fees: $786; $393 per semester. *Financial support:* Career-related internships or fieldwork and Federal Work-Study available. Support available to part-time students. Financial award application deadline: 3/1. *Unit head:* Bernice Bassde Martinez, Chair, 916-278-6622, Fax: 916-278-3498.

California University of Pennsylvania, School of Graduate Studies and Research, School of Education, Program in School Psychology, California, PA 15419-1394. Offers MS. *Accreditation:* NCATE. Part-time and evening/weekend programs available. *Degree requirements:* For master's, comprehensive exam, thesis optional, internship. *Entrance requirements:* For master's, MAT or GRE, minimum GPA of 3.0, work experience in psychology, letters of reference. Additional exam requirements/recommendations for international students: Required—TOEFL (minimum score 550 paper-based; 213 computer-based; 80 iBT). Electronic applications accepted.

Canisius College, Graduate Division, School of Education and Human Services, Department of Counseling and Human Services, Buffalo, NY 14208-1098. Offers community mental health counseling (MS); general counseling (MS); school counseling (MS). Part-time and evening/weekend programs available. *Faculty:* 5 full-time (3 women), 6 part-time/adjunct (2 women). *Students:* 93 full-time (79 women), 50 part-time (45 women); includes 16 minority (11 African Americans, 1 Asian American or Pacific Islander, 4 Hispanic Americans), 5 international. Average age 29. 93 applicants, 90% accepted, 35 enrolled. In 2007, 48 degrees awarded. *Degree requirements:* For master's, thesis, research project. *Entrance requirements:* For master's, interview, minimum GPA of 2.5. *Application deadline:* Applications are processed on a rolling basis. Application fee: $25. Electronic applications accepted. *Expenses:* Tuition: Full-time $32,574; part-time $651 per credit. Required fees: $222; $19 per credit. Tuition and fees vary according to program. *Financial support:* In 2007–08, 2 research assistantships with partial tuition reimbursements (averaging $8,500 per year) were awarded; career-related internships or fieldwork, Federal Work-Study, institutionally sponsored loans, health care benefits, and unspecified assistantships also available. Support available to part-time students. Financial award applicants required to submit FAFSA. *Faculty research:* Positive psychology, wellness, school violence prevention, chronic pain. *Unit head:* Dr. David L. Farrugia, Chairman, 716-888-2393, Fax: 716-888-3290, E-mail: farrugia@canisius.edu. *Application contact:* James D. Bagwell, Director of Graduate Recruitment and Admissions, 716-888-2544, Fax: 716-888-3290, E-mail: bagwellj@canisius.edu.

Capella University, Harold Abel School of Psychology, Minneapolis, MN 55402. Offers clinical psychology (MS); counseling psychology (MS); educational psychology (MS, PhD); general psychology (MS, PhD); industrial/organizational psychology (MS, PhD); school psychology (MS, Certificate); sport psychology (MS). Part-time and evening/weekend programs available. Postbaccalaureate distance learning degree programs offered (minimal on-campus study). Terminal master's awarded for partial completion of doctoral program. *Degree requirements:* For master's, thesis optional, project; for doctorate, thesis/dissertation. *Entrance requirements:* For degree, master's degree in school psychology. Additional exam requirements/recommendations for international students: Required—TOEFL (minimum score 550 paper-based; 213 computer-based), TWE (minimum score 4). Electronic applications accepted. *Faculty research:* Correctional mental health delivery, community mental health, attachment and caregiving in adult and family relationships, influence of encouragement on motivation, and moral dilemmas in business.

Carlos Albizu University, Miami Campus, Graduate Programs, Miami, FL 33172-2209. Offers clinical psychology (Psy D); entrepreneurship (MBA); exceptional student education (MS); industrial/organizational psychology (MS); marriage and family therapy (MS); mental health counseling (MS); nonprofit management (MBA); organizational management (MBA); psychology (MS); school counseling (MS); teaching English as a second language (MS). *Accreditation:* APA. Part-time and evening/weekend programs available. *Faculty:* 20 full-time (13 women), 65 part-time/adjunct (39 women). *Students:* 514 full-time (409 women), 143 part-time (119 women); includes 465 minority (54 African Americans, 1 American Indian/Alaska Native, 4 Asian Americans or Pacific Islanders, 406 Hispanic Americans). Average age 35. 194 applicants, 73% accepted, 130 enrolled. In 2007, 208 master's, 37 doctorates awarded. Terminal master's awarded for partial completion of doctoral program. *Median time to degree:* Of those who began their doctoral program in fall 1999, 65% received their degree in 8 years or less. *Degree requirements:* For master's, one foreign language, comprehensive exam, integrative project (MBA), research project (MSESE and MSTESOL); for doctorate, one foreign language, comprehensive exam, internship, doctoral project. *Entrance requirements:* For master's, 3 letters of recommendation, interview, minimum GPA of 3.0, resumé, statement of purpose, official transcripts; for doctorate, 3 letters of recommendation, minimum GPA of 3.0, resumé, interview. *Application deadline:* For fall admission, 8/1 priority date for domestic students; for spring admission, 11/30 priority date for domestic students. Applications are processed on a rolling basis. Application fee: $50. *Expenses:* Tuition: Full-time $9,090; part-time $505 per credit. Required fees: $298 per term. Tuition and fees vary according to course load and degree level. *Financial support:* In 2007–08, 37 students received support. Federal Work-Study and scholarships/grants available. Financial award application deadline: 6/1; financial award applicants required to submit FAFSA. *Faculty research:* Psychotherapy, forensic psychology, neuropsychology, marketing strategy, entrepreneurship, special education. *Unit head:* Dr. Carmen S. Roca, Interim Chancellor, 305-593-1223 Ext. 120, Fax: 305-629-8052, E-mail: croca@albizu.edu. *Application contact:* Barbara De la Cruz, Admission Officer, 305-593-1223 Ext. 218, Fax: 305-593-1854, E-mail: bdelacruz@albizu.edu.

Central Connecticut State University, School of Graduate Studies, School of Education and Professional Studies, Department of Counseling and Family Therapy, New Britain, CT 06050-4010. Offers marriage and family therapy (MS); professional counseling (MS, Certificate); school counseling (MS); student development in higher education (MS). *Accreditation:* AAMFT/COAMFTE. Part-time and evening/weekend programs available. *Faculty:* 6 full-time (4 women), 14 part-time/adjunct (8 women). *Students:* 112 full-time (89 women), 175 part-time (147 women); includes 43 minority (20 African Americans, 1 American Indian/Alaska Native, 3 Asian Americans or Pacific Islanders, 19 Hispanic Americans), 3 international. Average age 33. 199 applicants, 45% accepted, 69 enrolled. In 2007, 64 master's, 5 other advanced degrees awarded. *Degree requirements:* For master's, thesis or alternative, special project. *Entrance requirements:* For master's, minimum GPA of 2.7. Additional exam requirements/recommendations for international students: Required—TOEFL. *Application deadline:* For fall admission, 5/1 for domestic students. Applications are processed on a rolling basis. Application fee: $50. Electronic applications accepted. *Expenses:* Tuition, area resident: Full-time $4,169. Tuition, state resident: full-time $6,253. Tuition, nonresident: full-time $11,614; part-time $400 per credit. Required fees: $3,322. One-time fee: $62 part-time. Tuition and fees vary according to degree level and program. *Financial support:* In 2007–08, 11 students received support, including 15 research assistantships; career-related internships or fieldwork, Federal Work-Study, scholarships/grants, and unspecified assistantships also available. Support available to part-time students. Financial award application deadline: 3/1; financial award applicants required to submit FAFSA. *Faculty research:* Elementary/secondary school counseling, marriage/family therapy, rehabilitation counseling, counseling in higher educational settings. *Unit head:* Dr. Connie Tait, Chair, 860-832-2154.

Central Michigan University, College of Graduate Studies, College of Humanities and Social and Behavioral Sciences, Department of Psychology, Program in School Psychology, Mount Pleasant, MI 48859. Offers PhD, S Psy S. *Accreditation:* APA; NCATE. *Degree requirements:* For doctorate, thesis/dissertation or alternative; for S Psy S, thesis. *Entrance requirements:* For doctorate, GRE. *Faculty research:* Psychology and education foundations, psychology and education assessment, intervention strategies.

Central Washington University, Graduate Studies, Research and Continuing Education, College of the Sciences, Department of Psychology, Program in School Psychology, Ellensburg, WA 98926. Offers M Ed. *Faculty:* 27 full-time (13 women). *Students:* 9 full-time (all women), 7 part-time (all women); includes 1 minority (Hispanic American) 17 applicants, 47% accepted, 8 enrolled. In 2007, 8 degrees awarded. *Degree requirements:* For master's, thesis, internship. *Entrance requirements:* For master's, GRE General Test, minimum GPA of 3.0. Additional exam requirements/recommendations for international students: Required—TOEFL (minimum score 550 paper-based; 213 computer-based; 79 iBT). *Application deadline:* For fall admission, 4/1 priority date for domestic students. Applications are processed on a rolling basis. Application fee: $50. Electronic applications accepted. *Expenses:* Tuition, state resident: full-time $2,209; part-time $221 per credit. Tuition, nonresident: full-time $4,939; part-time $442 per credit. Required fees: $207 per quarter. Tuition and fees vary according to degree level. *Financial support:* Research assistantships with partial tuition reimbursements, career-related internships or fieldwork, Federal Work-Study, health care benefits, and unspecified assistantships available. Financial award application deadline: 3/1; financial award applicants required to submit FAFSA. *Application contact:* Justine Eason, Admissions Program Coordinator, 509-963-3103, Fax: 509-963-1799, E-mail: masters@cwu.edu.

Chapman University, Graduate Studies, School of Education, Program in Educational Psychology, Orange, CA 92866. Offers educational psychology (MA); school psychology (Ed S). Part-time and evening/weekend programs available. *Faculty:* 19 full-time (13 women), 20 part-time/adjunct (12 women). *Students:* 48 full-time (41 women), 9 part-time (5 women); includes 16 minority (1 African American, 3 Asian Americans or Pacific Islanders, 12 Hispanic Americans). Average age 27. 65 applicants, 35% accepted, 17 enrolled. In 2007, 42 degrees awarded. *Degree requirements:* For master's, comprehensive exam. *Entrance requirements:* For master's, GRE General Test, MAT, or California Subject Examinations for Teachers, minimum undergraduate GPA of 2.75. Additional exam requirements/recommendations for international students: Required—TOEFL (minimum score 550 paper-based). *Application deadline:* Applications are processed on a rolling basis. Application fee: $55. Electronic applications accepted. *Expenses:* Contact institution. *Financial support:* Fellowships, Federal Work-Study and scholarships/grants available. Financial award application deadline: 6/30; financial award applicants required to submit FAFSA. *Unit head:* Dr. Michael Hass, Coordinator, 714-997-6781, E-mail: hass@chapman.edu. *Application contact:* Rika Judd, Information Contact, 714-997-6786, Fax: 714-997-6713, E-mail: rjudd@chapman.edu.

Chapman University, Graduate Studies, School of Education, Program in Education: School Psychology, Orange, CA 92866. Offers PhD. *Faculty:* 19 full-time (13 women), 20 part-time/adjunct (12 women). *Students:* Average age 38. 9 applicants, 89% accepted, 8 enrolled. *Degree requirements:* For doctorate, thesis/dissertation. *Financial support:* Federal Work-Study and scholarships/grants available. *Unit head:* Dr. Joel Colbert, Director, 714-744-7076.

The Chicago School of Professional Psychology, Graduate School, Program in School Psychology, Chicago, IL 60610. Offers Ed S. *Accreditation:* APA. Part-time programs available. *Students:* 79. *Entrance requirements:* For degree, GRE (recommended), minimum GPA of 3.2 (recommended); completion of one course in statistics or research methods and one course in psychology. Additional exam requirements/recommendations for international students: Required—TOEFL (minimum score 550 paper-based; 213 computer-based; 79 iBT). *Application deadline:* For fall admission, 2/15 priority date for domestic students. *Financial support:* Federal Work-Study and scholarships/grants available. *Unit head:* Dr. Ellis Copeland, Department Chair, 312-329-6600, E-mail: ecopeland@thechicagoschool.edu.

See Close-Up on page 1429.

The Citadel, The Military College of South Carolina, Citadel Graduate College, School of Education, Program in School Psychology, Charleston, SC 29409. Offers MA, Ed S. *Accreditation:* NCATE. Part-time and evening/weekend programs available. *Students:* 21 full-time (20 women), 28 part-time (25 women); includes 2 minority (both African Americans) Average age 27. In 2007, 15 master's, 13 other advanced degrees awarded. *Entrance requirements:* For degree, GRE General Test. Additional exam requirements/recommendations for international students: Required—TOEFL (minimum score 550 paper-based; 213 computer-based). *Application deadline:* For fall admission, 3/15 for domestic students; for spring admission, 10/15 for domestic students. Applications are processed on a rolling basis. Application fee: $30. *Expenses:* Tuition, state resident: part-time $280 per credit hour. Tuition, nonresident: part-time $503 per credit hour. *Financial support:* In 2007–08, 5 students received support; research assistantships, teaching assistantships, career-related internships or fieldwork available. Financial award application deadline: 7/1; financial award applicants required to submit FAFSA. *Faculty research:* Childhood depression, violence against women, developmental disorders, eyewitness testimony. *Unit head:* Dr. Kerry Lassiter, Coordinator, 843-953-5098, Fax: 843-953-7084, E-mail: kerry.lassiter@citadel.edu. *Application contact:* Dr. Raymond S. Jones, Associate Dean, Citadel Graduate College, 843-953-5089, Fax: 843-953-7630, E-mail: ray.jones@citadel.edu.

City University of Seattle, Graduate Division, Gordon Albright School of Education, Bellevue, WA 98005. Offers curriculum and instruction (M Ed); educational leadership (M Ed); educational leadership: administrator certification (Certificate); executive leadership: superintendent certification (Certificate); guidance and counseling (M Ed); leadership (M Ed); leadership and school counseling (M Ed); professional certification for teachers (Certificate); reading and literacy (M Ed); reading and literacy in education (M Ed); teacher certification (elementary K-8) (MIT); teacher certification (special education K-12) (MIT); technology, curriculum, and instruction (M Ed). Part-time and evening/weekend programs available. Postbaccalaureate distance learning degree programs offered (no on-campus study). *Faculty:* 23 full-time (13 women), 345 part-time/adjunct (212 women). *Students:* 798; includes 93 minority (39 African Americans, 12 American Indian/Alaska Native, 24 Asian Americans or Pacific Islanders, 18 Hispanic Americans). Average age 36. 692 applicants, 100% accepted, 165 enrolled. In 2007, 450 degrees awarded. *Entrance requirements:* Additional exam requirements/recommendations for international students: Required—TOEFL (minimum score 540 paper-based; 207 computer-based); Recommended—IELTS. *Application deadline:* For fall admission, 9/1 for international students; for winter admission, 12/1 for international students; for spring admission, 3/1 for international students. Applications are processed on a rolling basis. Application fee: $50. Electronic applications accepted. *Expenses:* Contact institution. *Financial support:* In 2007–08, 40 students received support. Federal Work-Study and scholarships/grants available. Support available to part-time students. Financial award applicants required to submit FAFSA. *Unit head:* Judy Hinrichs, Interim Dean, 425-637-101 Ext. 5465, Fax: 425-709-5363, E-mail: jhinrichs@cityu.edu. *Application contact:* 800-426-5596, Fax: 425-709-5363, E-mail: info@cityu.edu.

Cleveland State University, College of Graduate Studies, College of Science, Department of Psychology, Cleveland, OH 44115. Offers clinical psychology (MA); consumer/industrial research (MA); diversity management (MA); experimental research psychology (MA); school psychology (Psy S). Part-time programs available. *Faculty:* 17 full-time (5 women), 16 part-time/adjunct (10 women). *Students:* 76 full-time (52 women), 44 part-time (37 women); includes 19 minority (15 African Americans, 1 American Indian/Alaska Native, 2 Asian Americans or Pacific Islanders, 1 Hispanic American), 3 international. Average age 29. 153 applicants, 27% accepted, 37 enrolled. In 2007, 26 master's, 9 other advanced degrees awarded. *Degree requirements:* For master's, thesis (for some programs). *Entrance requirements:* For master's, GRE General Test. Additional exam requirements/recommendations for international students: Required—TOEFL (minimum score 525 paper-based; 197 computer-based). *Application deadline:* For fall admission, 2/1 priority date for domestic and international students. Applications are processed on a rolling basis. Application fee: $30. Electronic applications accepted. *Financial support:* In 2007–08, 45 students received support. Career-related internships or fieldwork, Federal Work-Study, tuition waivers (partial), and unspecified assistantships available.

Financial award applicants required to submit FAFSA. Total annual research expenditures: $112,607. *Unit head:* Dr. David M. Grilly, Chairperson, 216-687-2545, Fax: 216-687-9294, E-mail: d.grilly@csuohio.edu. *Application contact:* Karen Colston, Administrative Coordinator, 216-687-2552, E-mail: k.colston@csuohio.edu.

The College of New Rochelle, Graduate School, Division of Human Services, Program in Community-School Psychology, New Rochelle, NY 10805-2308. Offers MS. *Faculty:* 7 full-time (3 women), 6 part-time/adjunct (2 women). *Students:* 23 full-time (20 women), 40 part-time (32 women); includes 19 minority (13 African Americans, 1 Asian American or Pacific Islander, 5 Hispanic Americans). Average age 32. In 2007, 18 degrees awarded. *Degree requirements:* For master's, comprehensive exam, clinical fieldwork, journal. *Entrance requirements:* For master's, interview, minimum GPA of 3.0, course work in psychology, sample of written work. *Application deadline:* For fall admission, 8/1 priority date for domestic students. Applications are processed on a rolling basis. Application fee: $35. *Expenses:* Tuition: Part-time $650 per credit. Required fees: $90 per term. *Financial support:* Career-related internships or fieldwork and scholarships/grants available. *Unit head:* Dr. Marie Ribarich, Associate Dean, Division of Human Services, 914-654-5561, Fax: 914-654-5593, E-mail: mribarich@cnr.edu.

College of St. Joseph, Graduate Programs, Division of Psychology and Human Services, Program in School Guidance Counseling, Rutland, VT 05701-3899. Offers MS. Part-time and evening/weekend programs available. *Faculty:* 4 full-time (1 woman), 8 part-time/adjunct (4 women). *Students:* 6 full-time (all women), 5 part-time (4 women). Average age 33. 4 applicants, 100% accepted, 3 enrolled. In 2007, 2 degrees awarded. *Degree requirements:* For master's, comprehensive exam, thesis optional. *Entrance requirements:* For master's, PRAXIS I, 2 letters of reference, interview. *Application deadline:* Applications are processed on a rolling basis. Application fee: $35. Electronic applications accepted. *Expenses:* Tuition: Full-time $12,000; part-time $325 per credit. Required fees: $45 per semester. *Financial support:* Unspecified assistantships available. Financial award application deadline: 3/1. *Application contact:* Tracy Gallipo, Director of Admissions, 802-773-5900 Ext. 3262, Fax: 802-773-5900, E-mail: tracygallipo@csj.edu.

The College of Saint Rose, Graduate Studies, School of Education, Educational and School Psychology Department, Albany, NY 12203-1419. Offers applied technology education (MS Ed); educational psychology (MS Ed); school psychology (MS, Certificate). Part-time and evening/weekend programs available. *Faculty:* 15 full-time (7 women), 16 part-time/adjunct (8 women). *Students:* 7 full-time (5 women), 20 part-time (18 women); includes 2 minority (both African Americans) Average age 33. 2 applicants, 50% accepted, 0 enrolled. In 2007, 23 master's awarded. *Entrance requirements:* For master's, minimum undergraduate GPA of 3.0. Additional exam requirements/recommendations for international students: Required—TOEFL (minimum score 550 paper-based; 213 computer-based). *Application deadline:* For fall admission, 7/15 priority date for domestic and international students; for spring admission, 11/15 priority date for domestic and international students. Applications are processed on a rolling basis. Application fee: $35. Electronic applications accepted. *Financial support:* Career-related internships or fieldwork, scholarships/grants, tuition waivers (partial), and unspecified assistantships available. Support available to part-time students. Financial award application deadline: 3/1; financial award applicants required to submit FAFSA. *Unit head:* Dr. Richard Brody, Chair, 518-458-5352, Fax: 518-454-2083, E-mail: brodyr@strose.edu. *Application contact:* Susan Patterson, Assistant Vice President for Graduate Admission, 518-454-5136, Fax: 518-458-5479, E-mail: ace@strose.edu.

The College of William and Mary, School of Education, Program in School Psychology, Williamsburg, VA 23187-8795. Offers M Ed, Ed S. *Accreditation:* NCATE. *Faculty:* 4 full-time (2 women), 2 part-time/adjunct (both women). *Students:* 23 full-time (21 women), 14 part-time (12 women); includes 8 minority (5 African Americans, 3 Asian Americans or Pacific Islanders). Average age 26. 83 applicants, 45% accepted, 24 enrolled. In 2007, 13 master's, 12 Ed Ss awarded. *Degree requirements:* For Ed S, internship. *Entrance requirements:* For master's, GRE, minimum GPA of 3.0; for Ed S, GRE, minimum GPA of 3.5. Additional exam requirements/recommendations for international students: Required—TOEFL. *Application deadline:* For fall admission, 1/15 for domestic and international students. Application fee: $45. Electronic applications accepted. *Expenses:* Tuition, state resident: full-time $6,250; part-time $275 per credit hour. Tuition, nonresident: part-time $760 per credit hour. Required fees: $3,550. Tuition and fees vary according to program. *Financial support:* In 2007–08, 20 research assistantships (averaging $7,500 per year) were awarded; career-related internships or fieldwork, Federal Work-Study, institutionally sponsored loans, scholarships/grants, and unspecified assistantships also available. Financial award application deadline: 1/15; financial award applicants required to submit FAFSA. *Faculty research:* Home schooling, gifted preschoolers, inclusive schools, ability testing. *Unit head:* Dr. Thomas J. Ward, Associate Dean, 757-221-2358, E-mail: tjward@wm.edu. *Application contact:* Dorothy Smith Osborne, Director of Admissions, 757-221-2317, Fax: 757-221-2293, E-mail: dsosbo@wm.edu.

Duquesne University, School of Education, Department of Counseling, Psychology, and Special Education, Program in School Psychology, Pittsburgh, PA 15282-0001. Offers child psychology (MS Ed); school psychology (PhD, CAGS). Part-time and evening/weekend programs available. *Faculty:* 6 full-time (4 women), 2 part-time/adjunct (0 women). *Students:* 87. Average age 31. 29 applicants, 83% accepted, 18 enrolled. In 2007, 13 master's, 4 doctorates, 5 other advanced degrees awarded. *Degree requirements:* For master's, thesis optional; for doctorate, thesis/dissertation. *Entrance requirements:* For master's, MAT, minimum GPA of 3.0; for doctorate, 3 letters of reference; for CAGS, MAT, interview. Additional exam requirements/recommendations for international students: Required—TOEFL. *Application deadline:* For fall admission, 8/1 for domestic students; for spring admission, 12/1 for domestic students. Applications are processed on a rolling basis. Application fee: $50. *Expenses:* Tuition: Part-time $774 per credit. Required fees: $74 per credit. Tuition and fees vary according to program. *Financial support:* In 2007–08, 1 research assistantship with full and partial tuition reimbursement (averaging $5,200 per year) was awarded; Federal Work-Study also available. Support available to part-time students. *Faculty research:* Neuropsychology. *Unit head:* Dr. Kara McGoey, Director, 412-396-4105, Fax: 412-396-5585, E-mail: mcgeoyk@duq.edu.

East Carolina University, Graduate School, Thomas Harriot College of Arts and Sciences, Department of Psychology, Program in School Psychology, Greenville, NC 27858-4353. Offers MA/CAS. *Accreditation:* NCATE. Part-time and evening/weekend programs available. *Students:* 12 full-time (all women), 7 part-time (all women); includes 2 minority (1 African American, 1 Asian American or Pacific Islander), 1 international. Average age 24. 10 applicants, 80% accepted, 0 enrolled. *Application deadline:* For fall admission, 3/15 priority date for domestic students. Applications are processed on a rolling basis. Application fee: $50. *Financial support:* Available to part-time students. Application deadline: 6/1. *Unit head:* Dr. Michael Brown, Director, 252-328-4170. *Application contact:* Dean of Graduate School, 252-328-6012, Fax: 252-328-6071, E-mail: gradschool@ecu.edu.

Eastern Illinois University, Graduate School, College of Sciences, Charleston, IL 61920-3099. Offers biological sciences (MS); chemistry (MS); communication disorders and sciences (MS); economics (MA); mathematics and computer science (MA), including mathematics, mathematics education; natural sciences (MS); political science (MA); psychology (MA, SSP), including clinical psychology (MA), school psychology (SSP). Part-time programs available. *Faculty:* 193 full-time (40 women). In 2007, 83 master's, 11 other advanced degrees awarded. *Degree requirements:* For SSP, thesis. *Entrance requirements:* For degree, GRE General Test. *Application deadline:* For fall admission, 7/31 priority date for domestic students. Applications are processed on a rolling basis. Application fee: $30. *Expenses:* Tuition, state resident: part-time $218 per hour. Tuition, nonresident: part-time $654 per hour. *Financial support:* In 2007–08, research assistantships with tuition reimbursements (averaging $7,200 per year), teaching assistantships with tuition reimbursements (averaging $7,200 per year) were awarded; career-related internships or fieldwork and Federal Work-Study also available. Support available to part-time students. *Unit head:* Dr. Mary Ann Hanner, Dean, 217-581-3328, Fax: 217-581-7110, E-mail: mahanner@eiu.edu.

Eastern Illinois University, Graduate School, College of Sciences, Department of Psychology, Program in School Psychology, Charleston, IL 61920-3099. Offers SSP. *Accreditation:* NCATE. In 2007, 11 degrees awarded. *Degree requirements:* For SSP, thesis. *Entrance requirements:* For degree, GRE General Test. *Application deadline:* For fall admission, 7/31 priority date for domestic students. Applications are processed on a rolling basis. Application fee: $30. *Expenses:* Tuition, state resident: part-time $218 per hour. Tuition, nonresident: part-time $654 per hour. *Financial support:* In 2007–08, research assistantships with tuition reimbursements (averaging $7,200 per year), 4 teaching assistantships with tuition reimbursements (averaging $7,200 per year) were awarded; career-related internships or fieldwork also available. *Unit head:* Dr. J. Michael Havey, Coordinator, 217-581-2127, Fax: 217-581-6764, E-mail: jmhavey@eiu.edu.

Eastern Kentucky University, The Graduate School, College of Arts and Sciences, Department of Psychology, Richmond, KY 40475-3102. Offers clinical psychology (MS); industrial/organizational psychology (MS); school psychology (Psy S). Part-time programs available. *Faculty:* 11 full-time (5 women). *Students:* 64 full-time (47 women), 10 part-time (8 women); includes 5 minority (4 African Americans, 1 Asian American or Pacific Islander). Average age 25. 166 applicants, 31% accepted, 18 enrolled. In 2007, 32 master's, 11 other advanced degrees awarded. *Entrance requirements:* For master's and Psy S, GRE General Test, minimum GPA of 2.5. *Application deadline:* For fall admission, 3/15 priority date for domestic students. Applications are processed on a rolling basis. Application fee: $35. *Financial support:* In 2007–08, 30 students received support, including research assistantships (averaging $10,000 per year), teaching assistantships (averaging $10,000 per year); career-related internships or fieldwork and Federal Work-Study also available. Support available to part-time students. *Faculty research:* Autism, social psychology, parenting, assessment of depression/anxiety, reading. Total annual research expenditures: $40,000. *Unit head:* Dr. Robert Brubaker, Chair, 859-622-1105, Fax: 859-622-5871, E-mail: robert.brubaker@eku.edu.

Eastern Washington University, Graduate Studies, College of Education and Human Development, Department of Counseling, Educational, and Developmental Psychology, Program in School Psychology, Cheney, WA 99004-2431. Offers MS. *Degree requirements:* For master's, comprehensive exam, thesis or alternative. *Entrance requirements:* For master's, GRE General Test, minimum GPA of 3.0.

Eastern Washington University, Graduate Studies, College of Social and Behavioral Sciences, Department of Psychology, Cheney, WA 99004-2431. Offers psychology (MS); school psychology (MS). *Degree requirements:* For master's, comprehensive exam, thesis or alternative. *Entrance requirements:* For master's, GRE General Test, minimum GPA of 3.0.

Emporia State University, School of Graduate Studies, The Teachers College, Department of Psychology and Special Education, Program in School Psychology, Emporia, KS 66801-5087. Offers MS, Ed S. *Accreditation:* NCATE. Part-time programs available. *Students:* 2 full-time (both women), 20 part-time (13 women). 13 applicants, 54% accepted, 7 enrolled. In 2007, 9 master's, 7 other advanced degrees awarded. *Degree requirements:* For master's, comprehensive exam or thesis, internship; for Ed S, comprehensive exam, thesis or alternative, internship. *Entrance requirements:* For master's, GRE General Test or MAT, graduate essay exam, appropriate bachelor's degree, teacher certification, letters of recommendation; for Ed S, GRE, graduate essay exam, letters of recommendation, teacher certification. Additional exam requirements/recommendations for international students: Required—TOEFL. *Application deadline:* For fall admission, 8/15 priority date for domestic students. Applications are processed on a rolling basis. Application fee: $30 ($75 for international students). Electronic applications accepted. *Expenses:* Tuition, state resident: part-time $157 per credit hour. Tuition, nonresident: part-time $475 per credit hour. Required fees: $47 per credit hour. Tuition and fees vary according to campus/location. *Financial support:* Career-related internships or fieldwork, Federal Work-Study, institutionally sponsored loans, health care benefits, and unspecified assistantships available. Financial award application deadline: 3/15; financial award applicants required to submit FAFSA. *Unit head:* Dr. Kenneth A. Weaver, Chair, Department of Psychology and Special Education, 620-341-5317, E-mail: kweaver@emporia.edu.

Evangel University, School Counseling Program, Springfield, MO 65802-2191. Offers MS. Part-time and evening/weekend programs available. *Faculty:* 2 full-time (both women), 3 part-time/adjunct (2 women). *Students:* 3 full-time (all women), 36 part-time (27 women). Average age 32. 17 applicants, 94% accepted, 14 enrolled. In 2007, 4 degrees awarded. *Degree requirements:* For master's, comprehensive exam, thesis optional. *Entrance requirements:* For master's, MAT, teaching certificate. Additional exam requirements/recommendations for international students: Required—TOEFL (minimum score 550 paper-based; 213 computer-based). *Application deadline:* For fall admission, 7/15 priority date for domestic and international students; for spring admission, 11/15 priority date for domestic and international students. Application fee: $25. *Financial support:* In 2007–08, 2 students received support. Career-related internships or fieldwork, institutionally sponsored loans, scholarships/grants, and unspecified assistantships available. Support available to part-time students. Financial award application deadline: 3/1; financial award applicants required to submit FAFSA. *Unit head:* Debbie Bicket, Chair, 417-865-8567 Ext. 8618, Fax: 417-575-5484, E-mail: bicketd@evangel.edu. *Application contact:* Charity H. Fahlstrom, Admissions Representative, Graduate and Professional Studies Admissions, 417-865-2811 Ext. 7227, Fax: 417-575-5484.

Fairfield University, Graduate School of Education and Allied Professions, Department of Psychology and Special Education, Fairfield, CT 06824-5195. Offers applied psychology (MA); school psychology (MA, CAS); special education (MA, CAS). Part-time and evening/weekend programs available. *Faculty:* 7 full-time (4 women), 7 part-time/adjunct (4 women). *Students:* 44 full-time (39 women), 114 part-time (87 women). 74 applicants, 46% accepted, 26 enrolled. In 2007, 40 master's, 17 other advanced degrees awarded. *Degree requirements:* For master's, comprehensive exam, thesis optional, educational technology course. *Entrance requirements:* For master's, PRAXIS I (PPST), minimum QPA of 2.67, 2 recommendations, resumé, essay. Additional exam requirements/recommendations for international students: Required—TOEFL (minimum score 550 paper-based; 213 computer-based; 79 iBT). *Application deadline:* For fall admission, 2/15 for domestic students; for spring admission, 10/15 for domestic students. Applications are processed on a rolling basis. Application fee: $60. Electronic applications accepted. *Financial support:* Scholarships/grants, tuition waivers (partial), and unspecified assistantships available. Financial award applicants required to submit FAFSA. *Faculty research:* School university collaboration, special education consultation, child neuropsychology, disabilities, effect of pretreatment orientation on treatment. *Unit head:* Dr. Daniel Geller, Chair, 203-254-4000 Ext. 2324, Fax: 203-254-4047, E-mail: dgeller@mail.fairfield.edu. *Application contact:* Marianne Gumpper, Director of Graduate and Continuing Studies Admissions, 203-254-4184, Fax: 203-254-4073, E-mail: gradadmis@mail.fairfield.edu.

Fairleigh Dickinson University, Metropolitan Campus, University College: Arts, Sciences, and Professional Studies, School of Psychology, Program in School Psychology, Teaneck, NJ 07666-1914. Offers MA, Psy D. *Students:* 63 full-time (47 women), 3 part-time (1 woman). Average age 32. 61 applicants, 46% accepted, 15 enrolled. In 2007, 18 master's, 14 doctorates awarded. *Application deadline:* Applications are processed on a rolling basis. Application fee: $40. *Expenses:* Tuition: Part-time $869 per credit. Tuition and fees vary according to degree level, campus/location and program.

Florida Agricultural and Mechanical University, Division of Graduate Studies, Research, and Continuing Education, College of Arts and Sciences, Department of Psychology, Program in School Psychology, Tallahassee, FL 32307-3200. Offers MS. *Accreditation:* NCATE. *Degree requirements:* For master's, thesis. *Entrance requirements:* For master's, GRE General Test, minimum GPA of 3.0, letters of recommendation (3). Additional exam requirements/recommendations for international students: Required—TOEFL.

School Psychology

Florida International University, College of Education, Department of Educational and Psychological Studies, Program in Counselor Education, Miami, FL 33199. Offers mental health counseling (MS); rehabilitation counseling (MS); school counseling (MS). *Accreditation:* ACA; NCATE. Part-time and evening/weekend programs available. *Entrance requirements:* For master's, General Knowledge test, College Level Academic Skills Test, GRE or PRAXIS (school counseling track), minimum GPA of 3.0, interview. Additional exam requirements/recommendations for international students: Required—TOEFL (minimum score 550 paper-based; 213 computer-based; 80 iBT), IELTS (minimum score 6). Electronic applications accepted. *Expenses:* Tuition, state resident: full-time $6,106. Tuition, nonresident: full-time $15,528. Required fees: $284.

Florida International University, College of Education, Department of Educational and Psychological Studies, Program in School Psychology, Miami, FL 33199. Offers Ed S. *Accreditation:* NCATE. Part-time and evening/weekend programs available. *Degree requirements:* For Ed S, internship. *Entrance requirements:* For degree, General Knowledge test, College Level Academic Skills Test, GRE or PRAXIS I, minimum GPA of 3.0 in last 60 undergraduate credits. Additional exam requirements/recommendations for international students: Required—TOEFL (minimum score 550 paper-based; 213 computer-based; 80 iBT), IELTS (minimum score 6). Electronic applications accepted. *Expenses:* Tuition, state resident: full-time $6,106. Tuition, nonresident: full-time $15,528. Required fees: $284. *Faculty research:* Incidence assessment, personality evaluation, psychopathology in children and adolescents, school psychology licensure, biased assessment.

Florida State University, Graduate Studies, College of Education, Department of Educational Psychology and Learning Systems, Program in School Psychology, Tallahassee, FL 32306. Offers MS, Ed S. *Faculty:* 9 full-time (3 women), 2 part-time/adjunct (both women). *Students:* 23 full-time (19 women), 15 part-time (11 women); includes 8 minority (3 African Americans, 1 Asian American or Pacific Islander, 4 Hispanic Americans). Average age 20. 56 applicants, 39% accepted, 12 enrolled. In 2007, 10 master's, 10 other advanced degrees awarded. *Degree requirements:* For master's, comprehensive exam; for Ed S, comprehensive exam, thesis. *Entrance requirements:* For master's and Ed S, GRE General Test, minimum GPA of 3.0. *Application deadline:* For fall admission, 7/1 priority date for domestic students; for spring admission, 11/1 for domestic students. Applications are processed on a rolling basis. Application fee: $30. *Expenses:* Tuition, state resident: part-time $248 per credit hour. Tuition, nonresident: part-time $880 per credit hour. Tuition and fees vary according to program. *Financial support:* In 2007–08, fellowships with partial tuition reimbursements (averaging $5,000 per year), research assistantships with partial tuition reimbursements (averaging $18,000 per year), teaching assistantships with partial tuition reimbursements (averaging $18,000 per year) were awarded; career-related internships or fieldwork also available. Financial award applicants required to submit FAFSA. *Unit head:* Dr. Briley Proctor, Program Leader, 850-644-3742, Fax: 850-644-8776, E-mail: proctor@coe.fsu.edu. *Application contact:* Sally Gadson, Program Assistant, 850-644-8046, Fax: 850-644-5067, E-mail: gadson@coe.fsu.edu.

Fordham University, Graduate School of Education, Division of Psychological and Educational Services, New York, NY 10023. Offers counseling and personnel services (MSE, Adv C); counseling psychology (PhD); educational psychology (MSE, PhD); school psychology (PhD); urban and urban bilingual school psychology (Adv C). *Accreditation:* APA (one or more programs are accredited); NCATE. *Degree requirements:* For doctorate, thesis/dissertation. *Entrance requirements:* For doctorate, GRE General Test. *Expenses:* Tuition: Full-time $23,880; part-time $995 per credit.

Fort Hays State University, Graduate School, College of Arts and Sciences, Department of Psychology, Program in School Psychology, Hays, KS 67601-4099. Offers Ed S. *Accreditation:* NCATE. *Faculty:* 7 full-time (1 woman). *Students:* 3 full-time (all women), 5 part-time (4 women). Average age 33. 8 applicants, 100% accepted. In 2007, 5 degrees awarded. *Degree requirements:* For Ed S, comprehensive exam, thesis. *Entrance requirements:* Additional exam requirements/recommendations for international students: Required—TOEFL (minimum score 550 paper-based; 213 computer-based). *Application deadline:* For fall admission, 3/1 priority date for domestic students. Applications are processed on a rolling basis. Application fee: $35. Electronic applications accepted. *Expenses:* Tuition, state resident: part-time $155 per credit hour. Tuition, nonresident: part-time $409 per credit hour. Tuition and fees vary according to class time, course level, course load, degree level, campus/location and program. *Financial support:* Research assistantships, teaching assistantships available.

Francis Marion University, Graduate Programs, Department of Psychology, Florence, SC 29501-0547. Offers applied clinical psychology (MS); applied community psychology (MS); school psychology (MS). Part-time and evening/weekend programs available. *Faculty:* 10 full-time (3 women), 6 part-time/adjunct (3 women). *Students:* 12 full-time (all women), 34 part-time (31 women); includes 5 minority (all African Americans), 1 international. Average age 28. 34 applicants, 100% accepted, 9 enrolled. In 2007, 9 degrees awarded. *Degree requirements:* For master's, internship. *Entrance requirements:* For master's, GRE General Test. *Application deadline:* For fall admission, 4/15 for domestic students; for spring admission, 10/15 for domestic students. Applications are processed on a rolling basis. Application fee: $30. *Expenses:* Tuition, state resident: full-time $7,547; part-time $377 per credit hour. Tuition, nonresident: full-time $15,094; part-time $755 per credit hour. Required fees: $285; $10 per credit hour. $45 per term. *Financial support:* In 2007–08, 2 research assistantships (averaging $7,000 per year), 3 teaching assistantships (averaging $8,000 per year) were awarded; career-related internships or fieldwork and unspecified assistantships also available. Support available to part-time students. Financial award application deadline: 3/1; financial award applicants required to submit FAFSA. *Faculty research:* Critical thinking, spatial localization, cognition and aging, family psychology. *Unit head:* Dr. John R. Hester, Chair, 843-661-1635, Fax: 843-661-1628. *Application contact:* Jennifer Taylor, Administrative Assistant, 843-661-1378, Fax: 843-661-1628.

Fresno Pacific University, Graduate Programs, School of Education, Fresno, CA 93702-4709. Offers administration (MA Ed), including administrative services; foundations, curriculum and teaching (MA Ed), including curriculum and teaching, school library and information technology; language, literacy, and culture (MA Ed), including bilingual/cross-cultural education, language development, multilingual contexts, reading; mathematics/science/computer education (MA Ed), including educational technology, integrated mathematics/science education, mathematics education; pupil personnel services (MA Ed), including school counseling, school psychology; special education (MA Ed), including mild/moderate, moderate/severe, physical and health impairments. Part-time and evening/weekend programs available. *Faculty:* 13 full-time (6 women), 14 part-time/adjunct (7 women). *Students:* Average age 39. 101 applicants, 75% accepted, 11 enrolled. In 2007, 81 degrees awarded. *Degree requirements:* For master's, thesis (for some programs). *Entrance requirements:* For master's, interview; GMAT, GRE, MAT, or 6 units of course work with a faculty recommendation. Additional exam requirements/recommendations for international students: Required—TOEFL (minimum score 550 paper-based; 213 computer-based). *Application deadline:* For fall admission, 7/15 for domestic and international students; for spring admission, 11/15 for domestic and international students. Applications are processed on a rolling basis. Application fee: $90. Electronic applications accepted. *Expenses:* Tuition: Full-time $7,470; part-time $415 per unit. *Financial support:* In 2007–08, 275 students received support. Career-related internships or fieldwork, scholarships/grants, and tuition waivers (full and partial) available. Support available to part-time students. Financial award applicants required to submit FAFSA. *Unit head:* Jo Ellen Priest Misakian, Interim Director, 559-453-2000, Fax: 559-453-2001, E-mail: jmisakian@fresno.edu.

Fresno Pacific University, Graduate Programs, School of Education, Division of Pupil Personnel Services, Program in School Psychology, Fresno, CA 93702-4709. Offers MA Ed. Part-time and evening/weekend programs available. *Students:* Average age 33. 8 applicants, 75% accepted, 1 enrolled. In 2007, 13 degrees awarded. *Degree requirements:* For master's, thesis or alternative. *Entrance requirements:* Additional exam requirements/recommendations for international students: Required—TOEFL (minimum score 550 paper-based; 213 computer-based). *Application deadline:* For fall admission, 7/15 for domestic and international students; for spring admission, 11/15 for domestic and international students. Applications are processed on a rolling basis. Application fee: $90. *Expenses:* Tuition: Full-time $7,470; part-time $415 per unit. *Financial support:* In 2007–08, 59 students received support. Scholarships/grants and tuition waivers (full and partial) available. Support available to part-time students. Financial award applicants required to submit FAFSA. *Unit head:* Dr. Dale M. Matson, Director, 559-453-2096, Fax: 559-453-2001, E-mail: dematson@fresno.edu.

Gallaudet University, The Graduate School, College of Arts and Sciences, Department of Psychology, Program in School Psychology, Washington, DC 20002-3625. Offers developmental psychology (MA); school psychology (Psy S). *Accreditation:* NCATE. *Degree requirements:* For master's, thesis optional. *Entrance requirements:* For master's, GRE General Test or MAT. *Application deadline:* For fall admission, 2/15 priority date for domestic students. Applications are processed on a rolling basis. Application fee: $50. Electronic applications accepted. *Expenses:* Tuition: Full-time $5,790. Required fees: $1,886. *Financial support:* Unspecified assistantships and stipends available. Financial award application deadline: 8/1. *Unit head:* Dr. Lynne Blennerhassett, Director, 202-651-5540. *Application contact:* Wednesday Luria, Coordinator of Prospective Graduate Student Services, 202-651-5647, Fax: 202-651-5295, E-mail: wednesday.luria@gallaudet.edu.

Gardner-Webb University, Graduate School, School of Psychology, Program in School Counseling, Boiling Springs, NC 28017. Offers MA. *Accreditation:* NCATE. Part-time and evening/weekend programs available. *Faculty:* 7 full-time (4 women), 1 part-time/adjunct (0 women). *Students:* 2 full-time (both women), 41 part-time (32 women); includes 10 minority (9 African Americans, 1 Asian American or Pacific Islander). Average age 32. In 2007, 6 degrees awarded. *Degree requirements:* For master's, comprehensive exam. *Entrance requirements:* For master's, GRE General Test, MAT, minimum GPA of 2.7. *Application deadline:* For fall admission, 7/1 priority date for domestic students. Applications are processed on a rolling basis. Application fee: $25. Electronic applications accepted. *Expenses:* Tuition: Part-time $275 per hour. *Financial support:* Unspecified assistantships available. *Unit head:* Dr. Pat Partin, Coordinator, 704-406-4242, Fax: 704-406-4329, E-mail: ppartin@gardner-webb.edu.

George Fox University, School of Education, Graduate Department of Counseling, Newberg, OR 97132-2697. Offers counseling (MA); marriage and family therapy (MA, Certificate); mental health trauma (Certificate); school counseling (MA); school psychology (MS, Certificate). Part-time programs available. *Faculty:* 10 full-time (7 women), 12 part-time/adjunct (8 women). *Students:* 101 full-time (82 women), 134 part-time (111 women); includes 19 minority (3 African Americans, 2 American Indian/Alaska Native, 8 Asian Americans or Pacific Islanders, 6 Hispanic Americans), 1 international. Average age 36. 86 applicants, 65% accepted, 56 enrolled. In 2007, 60 master's, 4 other advanced degrees awarded. *Degree requirements:* For master's, thesis optional. *Application deadline:* For fall admission, 5/30 for domestic students. Applications are processed on a rolling basis. Application fee: $40. Electronic applications accepted. *Expenses:* Contact institution. *Financial support:* Career-related internships or fieldwork available. *Unit head:* Dr. Richard Shaw, Director, 503-554-6142, E-mail: rshaw@georgefox.edu. *Application contact:* Carol Namburi, Admissions Counselor, 800-631-0921, Fax: 503-554-6111, E-mail: counseling@georgefox.edu.

George Mason University, College of Humanities and Social Sciences, Department of Psychology, Program in School Psychology, Fairfax, VA 22030. Offers MA. *Accreditation:* NCATE. *Faculty:* 44 full-time (17 women), 15 part-time/adjunct (11 women). *Students:* 16 full-time (all women). Average age 27. 70 applicants, 24% accepted, 9 enrolled. *Degree requirements:* For master's, thesis optional, internship. *Entrance requirements:* For master's, GRE General Test, minimum GPA of 3.0 in last 60 hours, previous undergraduate course work in psychology. *Application deadline:* For fall admission, 4/15 for domestic students; for spring admission, 11/1 for domestic students. Application fee: $60 ($75 for international students). Electronic applications accepted. *Financial support:* Available to part-time students. Application deadline: 3/1; *Unit head:* Dr. Jack Naglieri, Coordinator, 703-993-3811, Fax: 703-993-1359, E-mail: jnaglier@gmu.edu.

Georgia Southern University, Jack N. Averitt College of Graduate Studies, College of Education, Department of Leadership, Technology, and Human Development, Program in School Psychology, Statesboro, GA 30460. Offers M Ed, Ed S. *Accreditation:* NCATE.Part-time and evening/weekend programs available. *Students:* 36 full-time (34 women), 30 part-time (25 women); includes 18 minority (17 African Americans, 1 Hispanic American). Average age 30. 27 applicants, 78% accepted, 13 enrolled. In 2007, 12 master's, 16 Ed Ss awarded. *Degree requirements:* For master's and Ed S, comprehensive exam. *Entrance requirements:* For master's, GRE General Test or MAT, minimum GPA of 2.5, letters of reference, interview; for Ed S, GRE General Test or MAT, minimum graduate GPA of 3.25, letters of reference, interview. Additional exam requirements/recommendations for international students: Required—TOEFL (minimum score 550 paper-based; 213 computer-based; 80 iBT). *Application deadline:* For fall admission, 3/1 priority date for domestic and international students; for spring admission, 10/1 priority date for domestic students, 10/1 for international students. Applications are processed on a rolling basis. Application fee: $50. Electronic applications accepted. *Expenses:* Tuition, state resident: full-time $3,516; part-time $147 per semester hour. Tuition, nonresident: full-time $14,060; part-time $586 per semester hour. Required fees: $562 per term. *Financial support:* In 2007–08, 40 students received support, including research assistantships with partial tuition reimbursements available (averaging $6,850 per year), teaching assistantships with partial tuition reimbursements available (averaging $6,850 per year); career-related internships or fieldwork, Federal Work-Study, scholarships/grants, tuition waivers (partial), and unspecified assistantships also available. Support available to part-time students. Financial award application deadline: 4/15; financial award applicants required to submit FAFSA. *Unit head:* Dr. Terry Diamanduros, Coordinator, 912-478-1548, Fax: 912-478-7104, E-mail: tdiamanduros@georgiasouthern.edu. *Application contact:* 912-478-5384, Fax: 912-478-0740, E-mail: gradadmissions@georgiasouthern.edu.

Georgia State University, College of Education, Department of Counseling and Psychological Services, Program in School Psychology, Atlanta, GA 30303-3083. Offers M Ed, PhD, Ed S. *Accreditation:* APA (one or more programs are accredited); NCATE. *Students:* 91 applicants, 34% accepted. In 2007, 14 master's, 1 doctorate, 11 other advanced degrees awarded. *Degree requirements:* For master's, comprehensive exam; for doctorate, comprehensive exam, thesis/dissertation. *Entrance requirements:* For master's, GRE General Test, minimum GPA of 2.5; for doctorate, GRE General Test, minimum GPA of 3.3; for Ed S, GRE General Test, minimum graduate GPA of 3.25. Application fee: $50. *Expenses:* Tuition, state resident: part-time $221 per credit hour. *Financial support:* Career-related internships or fieldwork and scholarships/grants available. Financial award application deadline: 4/1. *Faculty research:* School reform, reading (early intervention), school violence. *Unit head:* Dr. Joanna White, Chairperson, Department of Counseling and Psychological Services, 404-413-8010, E-mail: cpsjfw@langate.gsu.edu.

Grand Canyon University, College of Education, Phoenix, AZ 85017-1097. Offers curriculum and instruction (M Ed); education administration (M Ed); elementary education (M Ed); school counseling (M Ed); secondary education (M Ed); special education (M Ed); teaching (MAT); teaching English as a second language (MA). Part-time and evening/weekend programs available. Postbaccalaureate distance learning degree programs offered (no on-campus study). *Faculty:* 3 full-time (2 women), 271 part-time/adjunct (214 women). *Students:* 685 full-time (529 women), 6,239 part-time (4,792 women); includes 266 minority (158 African Americans, 5 American Indian/Alaska Native, 16 Asian Americans or Pacific Islanders, 87 Hispanic Americans), 1 international. Average age 38. In 2007, 2694 degrees awarded. *Degree requirements:* For master's, publishable research paper (M Ed), e-portfolio, minimum GPA of 3.0. *Entrance requirements:* Additional exam requirements/recommendations for international students: Required—TOEFL (minimum score 550 paper-based; 213 computer-based; 79 iBT), IELTS (minimum score 6). *Application deadline:* Applications are processed on a rolling basis. Application fee: $100. *Expenses:* Tuition: Part-time $645 per credit. *Financial support:* Federal

Work-Study available. Support available to part-time students. Financial award applicants required to submit FAFSA. *Unit head:* Cheri St. Arnauld, Interim Dean, 602-639-6985, E-mail: cstarnauld@gcu.edu. *Application contact:* Becky Schildt, Online Enrollment Manager, 800-557-9551, Fax: 888-695-6316, E-mail: bschildt@online.gcu.edu.

Grand Valley State University, College of Education, Program in School Counseling, Allendale, MI 49401-9403. Offers M Ed. Part-time programs available. *Faculty:* 3 full-time (2 women). *Students:* 29 full-time (13 women), 64 part-time (48 women); includes 10 minority (6 African Americans, 1 Asian American or Pacific Islander, 3 Hispanic Americans). Average age 30. 34 applicants, 94% accepted, 17 enrolled. In 2007, 36 degrees awarded. *Degree requirements:* For master's, thesis or project. *Entrance requirements:* For master's, GRE General Test or minimum GPA of 3.0. Additional exam requirements/recommendations for international students: Required—TOEFL. *Application deadline:* Applications are processed on a rolling basis. Application fee: $30. Electronic applications accepted. *Financial support:* In 2007–08, 5 students received support, including research assistantships with full and partial tuition reimbursements available (averaging $8,000 per year); career-related internships or fieldwork also available. *Faculty research:* Multicultural issues in counselor education, use of technology in counseling programs. *Unit head:* Dr. Claudia Sowa-Wojciakowski, Chair of Community Outreach, 616-331-6706, E-mail: sowac@gvsu.edu. *Application contact:* Stephen Worst, Student Information and Services Center, 616-331-6650, Fax: 616-331-2000, E-mail: worsts@gvsu.edu.

Hofstra University, College of Liberal Arts and Sciences, Department of Psychology, Program in School-Community Psychology, Hempstead, NY 11549. Offers MS, Psy D, CAS. *Accreditation:* NCATE. *Students:* 41 full-time (33 women), 15 part-time (9 women); includes 6 minority (1 African American, 3 Asian Americans or Pacific Islanders, 2 Hispanic Americans). Average age 27. 119 applicants, 24% accepted, 12 enrolled. In 2007, 10 master's, 13 doctorates, 8 other advanced degrees awarded. *Degree requirements:* For master's, comprehensive exam; for doctorate, comprehensive exam, thesis/dissertation. *Entrance requirements:* For doctorate, GRE General Test, GRE Subject Test (psychology), interview, 3 letters of recommendation, essay. Additional exam requirements/recommendations for international students: Required—TOEFL (minimum score 550 paper-based; 213 computer-based). *Application deadline:* For fall admission, 1/15 for domestic and international students. Application fee: $60. Electronic applications accepted. *Expenses:* Tuition: Full-time $14,220; part-time $820 per credit. Required fees: $970; $165 per term. Tuition and fees vary according to program. *Financial support:* In 2007–08, 46 students received support, including 22 fellowships with tuition reimbursements available (averaging $4,591 per year), 2 research assistantships with full and partial tuition reimbursements available (averaging $13,320 per year); career-related internships or fieldwork, Federal Work-Study, institutionally sponsored loans, scholarships/grants, and tuition waivers (full and partial) also available. Support available to part-time students. Financial award applicants required to submit FAFSA. *Faculty research:* Cross-cultural psychology, school psychology, childhood & adult trauma, positive psychology, autism spectrum disorders. *Unit head:* Dr. Robert Motta, Program Director, 516-463-5029, Fax: 516-463-6052, E-mail: psyrwm@hofstra.edu. *Application contact:* Carol Drummer, Dean of Graduate Admissions, 516-463-4876, Fax: 516-463-4664, E-mail: gradstudent@hofstra.edu.

Howard University, School of Education, Department of Human Development and Psychoeducational Studies, Program in School Psychology, Washington, DC 20059-0002. Offers M Ed, MA, Ed D, PhD, CAGS. MA and PhD offered through the Graduate School of Arts and Sciences. *Accreditation:* NCATE. *Faculty:* 2 full-time (0 women), 1 part-time/adjunct (0 women). *Students:* 18 full-time (15 women), 10 part-time (4 women); includes 27 minority (all African Americans) Average age 32. 29 applicants, 59% accepted, 4 enrolled. In 2007, 6 master's, 1 other advanced degree awarded. *Degree requirements:* For master's, comprehensive exam, thesis (MA), expository writing exam, practicum; for doctorate, one foreign language, comprehensive exam, thesis/dissertation, expository writing exam, internship. *Entrance requirements:* For master's, GRE General Test, minimum GPA of 2.7; for doctorate, GRE General Test, minimum GPA of 3.4; for CAGS, GRE General Test, minimum graduate GPA of 3.0, master's degree. *Application deadline:* For fall admission, 4/1 priority date for domestic students; for spring admission, 11/1 for domestic students. Applications are processed on a rolling basis. Application fee: $45. *Expenses:* Tuition: Full-time $16,175; part-time $899 per credit hour. Required fees: $805. *Financial support:* In 2007–08, fellowships (averaging $12,000 per year), research assistantships (averaging $10,000 per year), teaching assistantships with full tuition reimbursements (averaging $13,000 per year) were awarded; career-related internships or fieldwork, Federal Work-Study, institutionally sponsored loans, scholarships/grants, and unspecified assistantships also available. Financial award application deadline: 3/15. *Faculty research:* Psychopathology, maltreatment abuse and neglect, children exposed to political unrest, family conflict and community violence. *Unit head:* Dr. Salman M. Elbedour, Professor/Coordinator, 202-806-7345, Fax: 202-806-5205, E-mail: selbedour@howard.edu.

Idaho State University, Office of Graduate Studies, College of Education, Department of Educational Learning and Development, Pocatello, ID 83209. Offers human exceptionality (M Ed); school psychology (Ed S); special education (Ed S). Part-time programs available. *Faculty:* 4 full-time (1 woman). *Students:* 22 full-time (15 women), 20 part-time (17 women); includes 1 minority (Hispanic American), 3 international. Average age 40. In 2007, 14 master's, 5 Ed Ss awarded. *Degree requirements:* For master's, thesis (for some programs), oral thesis defense or written comprehensive exam and oral exam; for Ed S, comprehensive exam, thesis (for some programs), oral exam, minimum GPA of 3.0, specialist paper or portfolio. *Entrance requirements:* For master's, GRE or MAT, minimum undergraduate GPA of 3.0; for Ed S, master's degree. Additional exam requirements/recommendations for international students: Required—TOEFL (minimum score 550 paper-based; 213 computer-based; 80 iBT). *Application deadline:* For fall admission, 7/1 for domestic students, 6/1 for international students; for spring admission, 12/1 for domestic students, 11/1 for international students. Applications are processed on a rolling basis. Application fee: $55. Electronic applications accepted. *Expenses:* Tuition, state resident: full-time $2,882; part-time $259 per credit hour. Tuition, nonresident: full-time $11,566; part-time $379 per credit hour. Required fees: $2,278. Full-time tuition and fees vary according to program. Part-time tuition and fees vary according to course load. *Financial support:* In 2007–08, teaching assistantships with full and partial tuition reimbursements (averaging $9,128 per year); career-related internships or fieldwork, Federal Work-Study, institutionally sponsored loans, scholarships/grants, health care benefits, and unspecified assistantships also available. Support available to part-time students. Financial award application deadline: 1/1; financial award applicants required to submit FAFSA. *Faculty research:* Literacy, School Psychology, Special Education. *Unit head:* Dr. Stephanie Peterson, Chairman, 208-282-3552, Fax: 208-282-4697, E-mail: petestе4@isu.edu. *Application contact:* Dr. Peter Denner, Assistant Dean, 208-282-3807, Fax: 208-282-4697, E-mail: dennpete@isu.edu.

Idaho State University, Office of Graduate Studies, Kasiska College of Health Professions, Department of Counseling, Pocatello, ID 83209. Offers counseling (M Coun, Ed S, Post-baccalaureate Certificate), including family-centered practice (Postbaccalaureate Certificate), marriage and family counseling (M Coun), mental health counseling (M Coun), school counseling (M Coun), student affairs and college counseling (M Coun); counselor education and counseling (PhD). *Accreditation:* ACA (one or more programs are accredited). *Faculty:* 6 full-time (3 women). *Students:* 62 full-time (40 women), 28 part-time (21 women); includes 6 minority (1 American Indian/Alaska Native, 1 Asian American or Pacific Islander, 4 Hispanic Americans). Average age 34. In 2007, 28 master's, 2 doctorates awarded. *Degree requirements:* For master's, comprehensive exam, thesis; for doctorate, comprehensive exam, thesis/dissertation, internship; for other advanced degree, comprehensive exam, thesis, case studies, oral exam. *Entrance requirements:* For master's, GRE General Test, MAT, minimum GPA of 3.0; for doctorate, GRE General Test, MAT, minimum graduate GPA of 3.0, resumé, interview, counseling license; for other advanced degree, GRE General Test, minimum graduate GPA of 3.0, master's degree in counseling, 3 letters of recommendation, 2 years work experience. Additional exam requirements/recommendations for international students: Required—TOEFL (minimum score 600 paper-based; 213 computer-based; 80 iBT). *Application deadline:* For fall admission, 7/1 for domestic students, 6/1 for international students; for spring admission, 12/1 for domestic students, 11/1 for international students. Applications are processed on a rolling basis. Application fee: $55. *Expenses:* Tuition, state resident: full-time $2,882; part-time $259 per credit hour. Tuition, nonresident: full-time $11,566; part-time $379 per credit hour. Required fees: $2,278. Full-time tuition and fees vary according to program. Part-time tuition and fees vary according to course load. *Financial support:* In 2007–08, 14 teaching assistantships with full and partial tuition reimbursements (averaging $9,128 per year) were awarded; career-related internships or fieldwork, Federal Work-Study, institutionally sponsored loans, scholarships/grants, traineeships, health care benefits, tuition waivers (full), and unspecified assistantships also available. Financial award application deadline: 1/1; financial award applicants required to submit FAFSA. *Faculty research:* Group counseling, multicultural counseling, family counseling, child therapy, supervision. *Unit head:* Dr. Stephen Feit, Chair, 208-282-3663, Fax: 208-282-2583, E-mail: feitstep@isu.edu. *Application contact:* Ellen Combs, Graduate School Technical Records Specialist, 208-282-2150, Fax: 208-282-4847.

Illinois State University, Graduate School, College of Arts and Sciences, Department of Psychology, Program in School Psychology, Normal, IL 61790-2200. Offers PhD, SSP. *Accreditation:* APA (one or more programs are accredited); NCATE (one or more programs are accredited). *Students:* 32 full-time (27 women), 26 part-time (21 women); includes 7 minority (2 African Americans, 1 American Indian/Alaska Native, 2 Asian Americans or Pacific Islanders, 2 Hispanic Americans), 1 international. 766 applicants, 4% accepted. In 2007, 7 doctorates, 7 other advanced degrees awarded. *Degree requirements:* For doctorate, variable foreign language requirement, thesis/dissertation, 2 terms of residency, internship, practicum. *Entrance requirements:* For doctorate, GRE General Test. *Application deadline:* Applications are processed on a rolling basis. Application fee: $40. *Expenses:* Tuition, state resident: full-time $3,492; part-time $194 per credit hour. Tuition, nonresident: full-time $7,272; part-time $404 per credit hour. Required fees: $1,024; $57 per credit hour. *Financial support:* Tuition waivers (full) available. Financial award application deadline: 4/1. *Unit head:* Dr. Neil Skaggs, Acting Chairperson, Department of Psychology, 309-438-8651.

Immaculata University, College of Graduate Studies, Department of Psychology, Immaculata, PA 19345. Offers clinical psychology (Psy D); counseling psychology (MA, Certificate), including school guidance counselor (Certificate), school psychologist (Certificate). *Accreditation:* APA. Part-time and evening/weekend programs available. *Students:* 106 full-time (71 women), 207 part-time (194 women); includes 30 minority (20 African Americans, 6 Asian Americans or Pacific Islanders, 4 Hispanic Americans). Average age 34. 182 applicants, 62% accepted, 56 enrolled. In 2007, 38 master's, 10 doctorates awarded. *Degree requirements:* For master's, comprehensive exam, thesis optional; for doctorate, comprehensive exam, thesis/dissertation. *Entrance requirements:* For master's, GRE General Test or MAT, minimum GPA of 3.0; for doctorate, GRE General Test, minimum GPA of 3.5. Additional exam requirements/recommendations for international students: Required—TOEFL, IELTS. *Application deadline:* Applications are processed on a rolling basis. Application fee: $35. *Financial support:* Application deadline: 5/1. *Faculty research:* Supervision ethics, psychology of teaching, gender. *Unit head:* Dr. Jed A. Yalof, Chair, 610-647-4400 Ext. 3503, Fax: 610-993-8550, E-mail: jyalof@immaculata.edu. *Application contact:* Office of Graduate Admission, 610-647-4400 Ext. 3211, Fax: 610-993-8550, E-mail: graduate@immaculata.edu.

Indiana State University, School of Graduate Studies, College of Education, Department of Communication Disorders, Counseling and School and Educational Psychology, Terre Haute, IN 47809-1401. Offers counseling psychology (MS, PhD); counselor education (PhD); mental health counseling (MS); school counseling (M Ed); school psychology (PhD, Ed S); MA/MS. *Accreditation:* ACA; NCATE. Part-time and evening/weekend programs available. *Faculty:* 10 full-time (5 women), 9 part-time/adjunct (8 women). *Students:* 104 full-time (82 women), 88 part-time (70 women); includes 29 minority (22 African Americans, 1 American Indian/Alaska Native, 2 Asian Americans or Pacific Islanders, 4 Hispanic Americans), 4 international. Average age 30. 154 applicants, 38% accepted, 40 enrolled. In 2007, 75 master's, 12 doctorates, 8 other advanced degrees awarded. *Degree requirements:* For master's, thesis optional; for doctorate, thesis/dissertation, research tools proficiency tests. *Entrance requirements:* For master's, GRE General Test or MAT, minimum undergraduate GPA of 2.75; for doctorate, GRE General Test, master's degree, minimum undergraduate GPA of 3.5. *Application deadline:* For fall admission, 2/15 for domestic students. Applications are processed on a rolling basis. Application fee: $35. Electronic applications accepted. *Expenses:* Tuition, state resident: full-time $7,056; part-time $294 per semester hour. Tuition, nonresident: full-time $14,016; part-time $584 per semester hour. Required fees: $175 per semester. *Financial support:* In 2007–08, 37 research assistantships with partial tuition reimbursements (averaging $6,300 per year) were awarded; teaching assistantships, career-related internships or fieldwork and tuition waivers (partial) also available. Financial award application deadline: 3/1; financial award applicants required to submit FAFSA. *Faculty research:* Vocational development supervision. *Unit head:* Dr. Michele Boyer, Chairperson, 812-237-2832.

Indiana University Bloomington, School of Education, Department of Counseling and Educational Psychology, Bloomington, IN 47405-7000. Offers counseling (MS, PhD, Ed S); counseling psychology (PhD); counselor education (MS, Ed S); educational psychology (MS, PhD); learning and developmental sciences (MS, PhD); school psychology (PhD, Ed S). PhD offered through the University Graduate School. *Accreditation:* ACA (one or more programs are accredited); APA (one or more programs are accredited); NCATE. *Students:* 96 full-time (72 women), 79 part-time (56 women); includes 16 minority (10 African Americans, 4 Asian Americans or Pacific Islanders, 2 Hispanic Americans), 38 international. Average age 29. In 2007, 50 degrees awarded. Terminal master's awarded for partial completion of doctoral program. *Degree requirements:* For master's, thesis optional; for doctorate, thesis/dissertation; for Ed S, comprehensive exam or project. *Entrance requirements:* For master's, doctorate, and Ed S, GRE General Test. *Application deadline:* For fall admission, 6/1 for domestic students, 3/1 for international students; for winter admission, 11/1 for domestic students; for spring admission, 9/1 for international students. Applications are processed on a rolling basis. Application fee: $50 ($60 for international students). Electronic applications accepted. *Financial support:* Fellowships with partial tuition reimbursements, research assistantships with partial tuition reimbursements, teaching assistantships with partial tuition reimbursements, career-related internships or fieldwork, Federal Work-Study, institutionally sponsored loans, tuition waivers (full and partial), and unspecified assistantships available. Support available to part-time students. *Faculty research:* Affective and maturational factors in learning complex cognitive tasks, children's strategies for representing depth, prime time evaluation, rural school psychology. *Unit head:* Dr. Joyce Alexander, Chairperson, 812-856-8300.

Indiana University of Pennsylvania, School of Graduate Studies and Research, College of Education and Educational Technology, Department of Educational and School Psychology, Program in School Psychology, Indiana, PA 15705-1087. Offers D Ed, Certificate. *Accreditation:* NCATE. Part-time programs available. *Faculty:* 9 full-time (4 women), 1 part-time/adjunct (0 women). *Students:* 6 full-time (5 women), 49 part-time (35 women); includes 5 minority (4 African Americans, 1 Hispanic American). Average age 30. 36 applicants, 69% accepted, 13 enrolled. In 2007, 5 doctorates, 10 Certificates awarded. *Degree requirements:* For doctorate, comprehensive exam, thesis/dissertation. *Entrance requirements:* For doctorate, GRE General Test, GRE Subject Test, 2 letters of recommendation. Additional exam requirements/recommendations for international students: Required—TOEFL. *Application deadline:* For fall admission, 1/10 for domestic students. Applications are processed on a rolling basis. Application fee: $30. *Expenses:* Tuition, state resident: full-time $6,214; part-time $345 per credit. Tuition, nonresident: full-time $9,944; part-time $552 per credit. Required fees: $43 per credit. One-time fee: $140 part-time. Tuition and fees vary according to course load. *Financial support:* In 2007–08, 3 fellowships (averaging $2,500 per year), 16 research assistantships with full and partial tuition reimbursements (averaging $6,180 per year), 6 teaching assistantships with partial tuition reimbursements (averaging $17,001 per year) were awarded; career-related internships or fieldwork and Federal Work-Study also available. Support available to part-time students. Financial award application deadline: 3/15; financial award applicants required to submit FAFSA. *Unit head:* Dr. John Quirk, Graduate Coordinator, 724-357-3785.

Inter American University of Puerto Rico, San Germán Campus, Graduate Studies Center, Program in Psychology, San Germán, PR 00683-5008. Offers counseling psychology (MA,

School Psychology

Inter American University of Puerto Rico, San Germán Campus (continued)

PhD); school psychology (MA, PhD). Part-time and evening/weekend programs available. *Faculty:* 8 full-time, 24 part-time/adjunct. *Students:* 223. In 2007, 51 master's, 2 doctorates awarded. *Degree requirements:* For master's, comprehensive exam, thesis; for doctorate, comprehensive exam, thesis/dissertation. *Entrance requirements:* For master's, GRE General Test or EXADEP, minimum GPA of 3.0; for doctorate, GRE, EXADEP or MAT, minimum GPA of 3.0. *Application deadline:* For fall admission, 4/30 priority date for domestic students; for spring admission, 11/15 for domestic students. Applications are processed on a rolling basis. Application fee: $31. *Expenses:* Tuition: Full-time $3,258; part-time $181 per credit. Required fees: $258 per semester. Tuition and fees vary according to degree level. *Financial support:* Teaching assistantships, unspecified assistantships available. *Application contact:* Dr. Ines Canabel, Program Coordinator, 787-264-1912 Ext. 7646, Fax: 787-892-7510, E-mail: icanabal@sg.intev.edu.

Iona College, School of Arts and Science, Department of Psychology, New Rochelle, NY 10801-1890. Offers experimental psychology (MA); industrial-organizational psychology (MA); mental health counseling (MA); psychology (MA); school psychology (MA). Part-time and evening/weekend programs available. *Faculty:* 12 full-time (6 women), 5 part-time/adjunct (2 women). *Students:* 77 full-time (62 women), 21 part-time (19 women); includes 19 minority (5 African Americans, 2 Asian Americans or Pacific Islanders, 12 Hispanic Americans). Average age 25. 105 applicants, 66% accepted, 33 enrolled. In 2007, 29 degrees awarded. *Degree requirements:* For master's, thesis. *Entrance requirements:* For master's, GRE or minimum GPA of 3.0. Additional exam requirements/recommendations for international students: Required—TOEFL (minimum score 550 paper-based; 213 computer-based). *Application deadline:* Applications are processed on a rolling basis. Application fee: $50. Electronic applications accepted. *Expenses:* Tuition: Part-time $712 per credit. Required fees: $150 per term. *Financial support:* Career-related internships or fieldwork, tuition waivers (partial), and unspecified assistantships available. Support available to part-time students. *Unit head:* Dr. Pauline Jirik-Babb, Chair, 914-633-2191, E-mail: pjirikbabb@iona.edu. *Application contact:* Veronica Jarek-Prinz, Director of Graduate Admissions, 914-633-2420, Fax: 914-633-2277, E-mail: vjarekprinz@iona.edu.

James Madison University, The Graduate School, College of Integrated Science and Technology, Department of Graduate Psychology, Program in Combined-Integrated Clinical and School Psychology, Harrisonburg, VA 22807. Offers Psy D. Part-time and evening/weekend programs available. *Students:* 19 full-time (16 women), 3 part-time (2 women); includes 2 minority (1 African American, 1 Asian American or Pacific Islander), 4 international. Average age 27. In 2007, 2 degrees awarded. *Degree requirements:* For doctorate, thesis/dissertation, 12-month internship. *Entrance requirements:* For doctorate, GRE General Test, GRE Subject Test (advanced psychology), 3 letters of recommendation. Additional exam requirements/recommendations for international students: Required—TOEFL. *Application deadline:* For fall admission, 2/1 for domestic students. Applications are processed on a rolling basis. Application fee: $55. Electronic applications accepted. *Expenses:* Tuition, state resident: full-time $6,720; part-time $280 per credit hour. Tuition, nonresident: full-time $19,104; part-time $796 per credit hour. *Financial support:* In 2007–08, 12 students received support. 12 doctoral assistantships ($14,216) available. Financial award application deadline: 3/1; financial award applicants required to submit FAFSA. *Unit head:* Dr. Gregg R. Henriques, Program Director, 540-568-7857.

James Madison University, The Graduate School, College of Integrated Science and Technology, Department of Graduate Psychology, Program in School Psychology, Harrisonburg, VA 22807. Offers school counseling (M Ed, Ed S); school psychology (MA, Ed S). *Accreditation:* APA (one or more programs are accredited); NCATE (one or more programs are accredited). Part-time and evening/weekend programs available. *Students:* 17 full-time (13 women), 11 part-time (8 women); includes 4 minority (1 African American, 2 Asian Americans or Pacific Islanders, 1 Hispanic American). Average age 27. In 2007, 10 master's, 5 other advanced degrees awarded. *Degree requirements:* For master's, comprehensive exam; for Ed S, thesis, research project, 10-month internship. *Entrance requirements:* For master's, GRE General Test, interview, 3 letters of recommendation. Additional exam requirements/recommendations for international students: Required—TOEFL. *Application deadline:* For fall admission, 2/1 priority date for domestic students. Applications are processed on a rolling basis. Application fee: $55. Electronic applications accepted. *Expenses:* Tuition, state resident: full-time $6,720; part-time $280 per credit hour. Tuition, nonresident: full-time $19,104; part-time $796 per credit hour. *Financial support:* In 2007–08, 14 students received support, including 1 teaching assistantship with full tuition reimbursement available (averaging $8,494 per year); career-related internships or fieldwork, Federal Work-Study, unspecified assistantships, and 13 graduate assistantships ($7,237) also available. Financial award application deadline: 3/1; financial award applicants required to submit FAFSA. *Unit head:* Dr. Patricia J. Warner, Program Director, 540-568-3358.

Kean University, College of Humanities and Social Sciences, Program in School Psychology, Union, NJ 07083. Offers Diploma. Part-time and evening/weekend programs available. *Faculty:* 20 full-time (13 women). *Students:* 19 full-time (16 women), 13 part-time (12 women); includes 1 African American, 2 Hispanic Americans. Average age 26. 52 applicants, 27% accepted, 10 enrolled. In 2007, 9 degrees awarded. *Degree requirements:* For Diploma, comprehensive exam, practicum, externship. *Entrance requirements:* For degree, GRE General Test, interview, minimum GPA of 3.0, 3 letters of recommendation, prerequisites in psychology. *Application deadline:* For fall admission, 3/15 for domestic students. Application fee: $60 ($150 for international students). Electronic applications accepted. *Expenses:* Tuition, state resident: full-time $9,384; part-time $391 per credit. Tuition, nonresident: full-time $12,720; part-time $530 per credit. Required fees: $2,382; $99 per credit. Part-time tuition and fees vary according to course load. *Financial support:* In 2007–08, 1 research assistantship with full tuition reimbursement (averaging $3,217 per year) was awarded; unspecified assistantships also available. *Unit head:* Dr. Dennis Finger, Program Coordinator, 908-737-4024, E-mail: dfinger@kean.edu. *Application contact:* Joanne Morris, Director of Graduate Admissions, 908-737-3355, Fax: 908-737-3354, E-mail: grad-adm@kean.edu.

Kent State University, Graduate School of Education, Health, and Human Services, Department of Educational Foundations and Special Services, Program in School Psychology, Kent, OH 44242-0001. Offers M Ed, PhD, Ed S. *Accreditation:* APA; NCATE. *Faculty:* 4 full-time (2 women), 2 part-time/adjunct (both women). *Students:* 63 full-time (54 women), 6 part-time (5 women); includes 3 minority (1 African American, 2 Hispanic Americans). 30 applicants, 43% accepted. In 2007, 23 master's, 13 other advanced degrees awarded. *Degree requirements:* For doctorate, comprehensive exam, thesis/dissertation. *Entrance requirements:* For master's and doctorate, GRE General Test; for Ed S, GRE General Test, MAT or minimum graduate GPA of 3.5. Additional exam requirements/recommendations for international students: Required—TOEFL. *Application deadline:* For fall admission, 6/15 for domestic students; for spring admission, 10/15 for domestic students. Application fee: $30. Electronic applications accepted. *Financial support:* In 2007–08, fellowships with full tuition reimbursements (averaging $10,952 per year), research assistantships with full tuition reimbursements (averaging $9,632 per year) were awarded; teaching assistantships with full tuition reimbursements, career-related internships or fieldwork, Federal Work-Study, institutionally sponsored loans, scholarships/grants, health care benefits, and unspecified assistantships also available. Support available to part-time students. Financial award application deadline: 4/1; financial award applicants required to submit FAFSA. *Faculty research:* Special education policy and practice, treatment fidelity, school-based consultation. *Unit head:* Dr. Richard Cowan, Coordinator, 330-672-2294, E-mail: rcowan1@kent.edu. *Application contact:* Nancy Miller, Academic Program Coordinator, Office of Graduate Student Services, 330-672-2576, Fax: 330-672-9162, E-mail: ogs@kent.edu.

La Sierra University, School of Education, Department of Educational Psychology and Counseling, Riverside, CA 92515. Offers counseling (MA); educational psychology (Ed S); school psychology (Ed S). Part-time and evening/weekend programs available. *Degree requirements:* For master's, thesis optional; for Ed S, practicum (educational psychology). *Entrance requirements:* For master's, California Basic Educational Skills Test, NTE, minimum GPA of 3.0; for Ed S, minimum GPA of 3.3. *Faculty research:* Equivalent score scales, self perception.

Lehigh University, College of Education, Program in School Psychology, Bethlehem, PA 18015-3094. Offers PhD, Ed S. *Accreditation:* APA (one or more programs are accredited). Part-time and evening/weekend programs available. *Faculty:* 5 full-time (3 women), 2 part-time/adjunct (1 woman). *Students:* 38 full-time (34 women), 12 part-time (10 women); includes 4 minority (3 African Americans, 1 Hispanic American), 1 international. Average age 27. 90 applicants, 22% accepted, 10 enrolled. In 2007, 4 doctorates awarded. *Median time to degree:* Of those who began their doctoral program in fall 1999, 100% received their degree in 8 years or less. *Degree requirements:* For doctorate, comprehensive exam, internship, research qualifying exam; for Ed S, internship. *Entrance requirements:* For doctorate, GRE General Test, minimum GPA of 3.0, 2 letters of recommendation, supplemental application, essay; for Ed S, GRE General Test, minimum GPA of 3.0. Additional exam requirements/recommendations for international students: Required—TOEFL (minimum score 600 paper-based; 250 computer-based; 93 iBT). *Application deadline:* For fall admission, 1/1 for domestic and international students. Application fee: $65. Electronic applications accepted. *Financial support:* Fellowships, research assistantships, career-related internships or fieldwork, Federal Work-Study, institutionally sponsored loans, and tuition waivers (full and partial) available. Financial award application deadline: 1/31. *Faculty research:* Applied behavior, analysis development disabilities, psychology of the mildly handicapped. *Unit head:* Dr. Christine L. Cole, Coordinator, 610-758-3256, Fax: 610-758-6223, E-mail: clc2@lehigh.edu.

Lenoir-Rhyne College, Graduate Programs, School of Social and Behavioral Sciences, Program in School Counseling, Hickory, NC 28601. Offers MA. Part-time and evening/weekend programs available. *Faculty:* 2 part-time/adjunct (1 woman). *Students:* 3 full-time (all women), 13 part-time (11 women); includes 1 minority (Hispanic American) Average age 32. In 2007, 2 degrees awarded. *Degree requirements:* For master's, comprehensive exam, thesis optional. *Entrance requirements:* For master's, GRE General Test, minimum undergraduate GPA of 2.7, graduate 3.0; writing sample. Additional exam requirements/recommendations for international students: Required—TOEFL (minimum score 600 paper-based). *Application deadline:* Applications are processed on a rolling basis. Application fee: $35. Electronic applications accepted. *Expenses:* Tuition: Full-time $6,930; part-time $385 per credit. Required fees: $50; $25 per term. *Financial support:* Application deadline: 3/1; *Unit head:* Dr. Amy Wood, Coordinator, 828-328-7728, Fax: 828-328-7368, E-mail: amy.wood@lrc.edu. *Application contact:* 828-328-7300, Fax: 828-328-7378, E-mail: admission@lrc.edu.

Lesley University, Graduate School of Arts and Social Sciences, Program in Counseling Psychology, Cambridge, MA 02138-2790. Offers professional counseling (MA); school counseling (MA). Part-time and evening/weekend programs available. Postbaccalaureate distance learning degree programs offered (no on-campus study). *Faculty:* 11 full-time (8 women), 40 part-time/adjunct (26 women). *Students:* 143 full-time (132 women), 140 part-time (121 women); includes 15 minority (8 African Americans, 2 Asian Americans or Pacific Islanders, 5 Hispanic Americans), 5 international. Average age 33. 108 applicants, 84% accepted, 63 enrolled. In 2007, 90 master's awarded. Terminal master's awarded for partial completion of doctoral program. *Degree requirements:* For master's, internship, practicum. *Entrance requirements:* For master's, MAT. Additional exam requirements/recommendations for international students: Required—TOEFL (minimum score 550 paper-based; 213 computer-based; 80 iBT). Application fee: $50. *Financial support:* In 2007–08, 5 students received support, including research assistantships (averaging $3,400 per year), teaching assistantships (averaging $3,400 per year); Federal Work-Study, scholarships/grants, and unspecified assistantships also available. Support available to part-time students. Financial award application deadline: 4/15; financial award applicants required to submit FAFSA. *Unit head:* Dr. Susan Gere, Associate Professor and Division Director, 617-349-8342, E-mail: sgere@lesley.edu. *Application contact:* John Gearin, Assistant Director of Advising and Student Services, 617-349-8339, E-mail: jgearin@mail.lesley.edu.

See Close-Up on page 1441.

Lewis & Clark College, Graduate School of Education and Counseling, Department of Counseling Psychology, Program in School Psychology, Portland, OR 97219-7899. Offers MS, Ed S. Part-time and evening/weekend programs available. *Faculty:* 4 full-time (1 woman), 14 part-time/adjunct (7 women). *Students:* 10 full-time (8 women), 32 part-time (27 women); includes 5 minority (1 African American, 3 Asian Americans or Pacific Islanders, 1 Hispanic American). Average age 29. 33 applicants, 70% accepted, 11 enrolled. In 2007, 14 degrees awarded. *Entrance requirements:* For master's, GRE General Test, minimum undergraduate GPA of 2.75. Additional exam requirements/recommendations for international students: Required—TOEFL (minimum score 575 paper-based; 233 computer-based). *Application deadline:* For fall admission, 2/1 for domestic and international students; for spring admission, 10/1 for domestic and international students. Application fee: $50. Electronic applications accepted. *Expenses:* Tuition: Part-time $645 per credit. Tuition and fees vary according to campus/location. *Financial support:* In 2007–08, 35 students received support. Career-related internships or fieldwork, Federal Work-Study, institutionally sponsored loans, scholarships/grants, health care benefits, and tuition waivers (partial) available. Support available to part-time students. Financial award applicants required to submit FAFSA. *Unit head:* Dr. Peter Mortola, Program Coordinator, 503-768-6060, Fax: 503-768-6065, E-mail: cpsy@lclark.edu. *Application contact:* Becky Haas, Director of Admissions, 503-768-6200, Fax: 503-768-6205, E-mail: gseadmit@lclark.edu.

Lewis & Clark College, Graduate School of Education and Counseling, Department of Education, Program in School Counseling, Portland, OR 97219-7899. Offers M Ed. Part-time and evening/weekend programs available. *Faculty:* 1 (woman) full-time, 8 part-time/adjunct (4 women). *Students:* 25 full-time (19 women), 24 part-time (22 women); includes 11 minority (1 African American, 2 American Indian/Alaska Native, 1 Asian American or Pacific Islander, 7 Hispanic Americans). Average age 30. 42 applicants, 55% accepted, 16 enrolled. In 2007, 18 degrees awarded. *Degree requirements:* For master's, thesis. *Entrance requirements:* For master's, minimum undergraduate GPA of 2.75. Additional exam requirements/recommendations for international students: Required—TOEFL (minimum score 575 paper-based; 233 computer-based). *Application deadline:* For fall admission, 2/26 for domestic and international students; for spring admission, 11/26 for domestic and international students. Applications are processed on a rolling basis. Application fee: $50. Electronic applications accepted. *Expenses:* Tuition: Part-time $645 per credit. Tuition and fees vary according to campus/location. *Financial support:* In 2007–08, 38 students received support. Career-related internships or fieldwork, Federal Work-Study, institutionally sponsored loans, scholarships/grants, health care benefits, and tuition waivers (partial) available. Support available to part-time students. Financial award applicants required to submit FAFSA. *Faculty research:* Peer rejection, social skills, consultation, sexual abuse. *Unit head:* Dr. Laura Pedersen, Coordinator, 503-768-6140, Fax: 503-768-6085, E-mail: schcoun@lclark.edu. *Application contact:* Becky Haas, Director of Admissions, 503-768-6200, Fax: 503-768-6205, E-mail: gseadmit@lclark.edu.

Lindenwood University, Graduate Programs, Division of Education, St. Charles, MO 63301-1695. Offers education (MA); educational administration (MA, Ed D, Ed S); instructional leadership (Ed D, Ed S); library media (MA); professional and school counseling (MA); professional counseling (MA); school counseling (MA); teaching (MA). Part-time and evening/weekend programs available. *Faculty:* 29 full-time (18 women), 185 part-time/adjunct (110 women). *Students:* 556 full-time (445 women), 1,952 part-time (1,502 women); includes 624 minority (594 African Americans, 5 American Indian/Alaska Native, 13 Asian Americans or Pacific Islanders, 12 Hispanic Americans), 9 international. Average age 37. In 2007, 869 master's, 3 doctorates, 39 other advanced degrees awarded. *Degree requirements:* For master's, thesis (for some programs), minimum GPA of 3.0; for doctorate, thesis/dissertation, minimum GPA of 3.0; for Ed S, specialist project, minimum GPA of 3.0. *Entrance requirements:*

For master's, interview, minimum GPA of 3.0, writing sample; for Ed S, master's degree in education, relevant work experience. Additional exam requirements/recommendations for international students: Required—TOEFL (minimum score 550 paper-based; 213 computer-based; 80 iBT). *Application deadline:* For fall admission, 8/30 priority date for domestic and international students; for spring admission, 12/30 priority date for domestic and international students. Applications are processed on a rolling basis. Application fee: $30 ($100 for international students). Electronic applications accepted. *Expenses:* Tuition: Full-time $12,400; part-time $350 per hour. Full-time tuition and fees vary according to degree level and program. *Financial support:* Career-related internships or fieldwork, institutionally sponsored loans, tuition waivers (partial), and unspecified assistantships available. Financial award applicants required to submit FAFSA. *Unit head:* Dr. John Dougherty, Dean of Education, 636-949-4937, Fax: 636-949-4197, E-mail: jdougherty@lindenwood.edu. *Application contact:* Brett Barger, Dean of Evening Admissions and Extension Campuses, 636-949-4934, Fax: 636-949-4109, E-mail: adultadmissions@lindenwood.edu.

Long Island University, Brooklyn Campus, School of Education, Department of Human Development and Leadership, Program in School Psychology, Brooklyn, NY 11201-8423. Offers MS Ed. Part-time and evening/weekend programs available. *Degree requirements:* For master's, thesis optional. *Entrance requirements:* For master's, 2 letters of recommendation. Additional exam requirements/recommendations for international students: Required—TOEFL (minimum score 500 paper-based; 173 computer-based). Electronic applications accepted.

Long Island University, Westchester Graduate Campus, Programs in Education-School Counselor and School Psychology, Purchase, NY 10577. Offers school counselor (MS Ed); school psychologist (MS Ed). Part-time and evening/weekend programs available. *Faculty:* 2 full-time (both women), 12 part-time/adjunct (8 women). *Students:* 84 (72 women). 40 applicants, 73% accepted, 21 enrolled. In 2007, 21 degrees awarded. *Application deadline:* Applications are processed on a rolling basis. Application fee: $30. *Financial support:* In 2007–08, 22 students received support. Scholarships/grants, tuition waivers (partial), and unspecified assistantships available. *Unit head:* Prof. Beth Weiner, Director, 914-831-2717, Fax: 914-251-5959, E-mail: beth.weiner@liu.edu. *Application contact:* Cindy Doctor, Enrollment Specialist, 914-831-2701, Fax: 914-251-5959, E-mail: cindy.doctor@liu.edu.

Louisiana State University and Agricultural and Mechanical College, Graduate School, College of Arts and Sciences, Department of Psychology, Baton Rouge, LA 70803. Offers biological psychology (MA, PhD); clinical psychology (MA, PhD); cognitive psychology (MA, PhD); developmental psychology (MA, PhD); industrial/organizational psychology (MA, PhD); school psychology (MA, PhD). *Accreditation:* APA (one or more programs are accredited). *Faculty:* 25 full-time (9 women). *Students:* 81 full-time (60 women), 23 part-time (15 women); includes 15 minority (6 African Americans, 4 American Indian/Alaska Native, 2 Asian Americans or Pacific Islanders, 3 Hispanic Americans), 3 international. Average age 28. 199 applicants, 15% accepted, 23 enrolled. In 2007, 11 master's, 13 doctorates awarded. Terminal master's awarded for partial completion of doctoral program. *Degree requirements:* For master's, thesis; for doctorate, thesis/dissertation, 1 year internship. *Entrance requirements:* For master's and doctorate, GRE General Test, minimum GPA of 3.0. Additional exam requirements/recommendations for international students: Required—TOEFL (minimum score 550 paper-based; 213 computer-based; 79 iBT). *Application deadline:* For fall admission, 1/15 for domestic and international students. Applications are processed on a rolling basis. Application fee: $25. Electronic applications accepted. *Financial support:* In 2007–08, 101 students received support, including 5 fellowships (averaging $26,557 per year), 55 teaching assistantships with partial tuition reimbursements available (averaging $13,218 per year); research assistantships with partial tuition reimbursements available, career-related internships or fieldwork, Federal Work-Study, institutionally sponsored loans, scholarships/grants, health care benefits, and tuition waivers (full and partial) also available. Financial award applicants required to submit FAFSA. *Faculty research:* Clinical psychology, autism, anxiety, addition, neuro-psychology, school psychology, cognitive psychology, experimental psychology. Total annual research expenditures: $582,678. *Unit head:* Dr. Alan Baumeister, Chair, 225-578-4099, Fax: 225-578-4125, E-mail: abaumei@lsu.edu. *Application contact:* Dr. Janet McDonald, Coordinator of Graduate Studies, 225-578-4116, Fax: 225-578-4125, E-mail: psmcdo@lsu.edu.

Louisiana State University in Shreveport, College of Education and Human Development, Program in School Psychology, Shreveport, LA 71115-2399. Offers SSP. *Faculty:* 6 full-time (3 women), 1 (woman) part-time/adjunct. *Students:* 17 full-time (13 women), 2 part-time (both women); includes 1 minority (African American) Average age 27. 8 applicants, 75% accepted, 6 enrolled. In 2007, 2 degrees awarded. *Entrance requirements:* For degree, GRE General Test, minimum GPA of 2.75. Additional exam requirements/recommendations for international students: Required—TOEFL (minimum score 500 paper-based; 173 computer-based; 61 iBT). *Application deadline:* For fall admission, 6/30 for domestic and international students; for spring admission, 11/30 for domestic and international students. Applications are processed on a rolling basis. Application fee: $10. *Financial support:* In 2007–08, 2 research assistantships with partial tuition reimbursements (averaging $10,000 per year) were awarded. Financial award applicants required to submit FAFSA. *Unit head:* Dr. Rebecca Nolan, Program Director, 318-797-5050, E-mail: rnolan@lsus.edu.

Loyola Marymount University, Graduate Division, School of Education, Program in Educational Psychology, Los Angeles, CA 90045-2659. Offers school psychology (MA). Part-time and evening/weekend programs available. *Students:* 38 full-time (35 women), 2 part-time (both women); includes 24 minority (5 African Americans, 4 Asian Americans or Pacific Islanders, 15 Hispanic Americans). Average age 25. In 2007, 17 degrees awarded. *Degree requirements:* For master's, comprehensive exam. *Entrance requirements:* For master's, GRE General Test, interview. Additional exam requirements/recommendations for international students: Required—TOEFL (minimum score 600 paper-based; 250 computer-based). *Application deadline:* For fall admission, 7/15 for domestic students; for spring admission, 11/15 for domestic students. Application fee: $50. Electronic applications accepted. *Financial support:* In 2007–08, 37 students received support. Scholarships/grants available. Support available to part-time students. Financial award application deadline: 6/1; financial award applicants required to submit FAFSA. *Unit head:* Dr. Brian Leung, Coordinator, 310-338-1707, E-mail: bleung@lmu.edu.

Loyola University Chicago, School of Education, Program in School Psychology, Chicago, IL 60611-2196. Offers M Ed, PhD, Ed S. PhD offered through the Graduate School. Part-time and evening/weekend programs available. *Faculty:* 6 full-time (4 women), 11 part-time/adjunct (8 women). *Students:* 71. Average age 28. 141 applicants, 45% accepted, 25 enrolled. In 2007, 2 doctorates, 15 other advanced degrees awarded. Terminal master's awarded for partial completion of doctoral program. *Degree requirements:* For master's, comprehensive exam; for doctorate, comprehensive exam, thesis/dissertation. *Entrance requirements:* For doctorate, GRE, interview, letters of recommendation, transcripts, minimum GPA of 3.0. Additional exam requirements/recommendations for international students: Required—TOEFL (minimum score 550 paper-based; 213 computer-based; 79 iBT). *Application deadline:* For fall admission, 12/15 for domestic and international students. Application fee: $40. Electronic applications accepted. *Expenses:* Tuition: Full-time $12,780; part-time $710 per credit hour. Required fees: $55 per semester. Full-time tuition and fees vary according to program. *Financial support:* In 2007–08, 2 fellowships (averaging $14,000 per year), 12 research assistantships with full tuition reimbursements (averaging $11,000 per year) were awarded; institutionally sponsored loans, scholarships/grants, and tuition waivers (full and partial) also available. Financial award application deadline: 2/15. *Faculty research:* Learning theory and teaching, school reform, instructional intervention, violence prevention, mental health programming in schools and communities. *Unit head:* Dr. Pamela Fenning, Director, 312-915-6803, E-mail: pfennin@luc.edu. *Application contact:* Marie Rosin-Dittmar, Information Contact, 312-915-6800, E-mail: schleduc@luc.edu.

Marist College, Graduate Programs, School of Social and Behavioral Sciences, Poughkeepsie, NY 12601-1387. Offers counseling psychology (MA); education (M Ed); education psychology (MA); school psychology (MA, Adv C). Part-time and evening/weekend programs available. *Faculty:* 20 full-time (10 women), 18 part-time/adjunct (7 women). *Students:* 98 full-time (82 women), 121 part-time (97 women); includes 23 minority (7 African Americans, 3 Asian Americans or Pacific Islanders, 13 Hispanic Americans), 4 international. Average age 29. 100 applicants, 56% accepted, 45 enrolled. In 2007, 87 master's, 3 other advanced degrees awarded. *Degree requirements:* For master's, thesis optional. *Entrance requirements:* For master's, GRE General Test, letters of recommendation, minimum undergraduate GPA of 3.0, interview, essay, official transcript. Additional exam requirements/recommendations for international students: Required—TOEFL (minimum score 550 paper-based; 213 computer-based; 80 iBT); Recommended—IELTS (minimum score 7). *Application deadline:* For fall admission, 8/1 for domestic students, 6/1 for international students; for spring admission, 12/1 for domestic students, 10/31 for international students. Applications are processed on a rolling basis. Application fee: $50. Electronic applications accepted. *Expenses:* Tuition: Part-time $665 per credit. *Financial support:* In 2007–08, 130 students received support. Career-related internships or fieldwork, scholarships/grants, and unspecified assistantships available. Support available to part-time students. Financial award application deadline: 8/15; financial award applicants required to submit FAFSA. *Faculty research:* AIDS prevention, educational intervention, humanistic counseling research, aging and development, neuroimaging. *Unit head:* Margaret Calista, Dean, 845-575-3000 Ext. 2960, E-mail: margaret.calista@marist.edu. *Application contact:* Kelly Holmes, Director of Admissions, 845-575-3800, Fax: 845-575-3166, E-mail: graduate@marist.edu.

Marshall University, Academic Affairs Division, College of Education and Human Services, Graduate School of Education and Professional Development, Program in School Psychology, Huntington, WV 25755. Offers Ed S. *Accreditation:* NCATE. Part-time and evening/weekend programs available. *Faculty:* 2 full-time (1 woman), 4 part-time/adjunct (1 woman). *Students:* 22 full-time (18 women), 11 part-time (10 women). Average age 32. In 2007, 8 degrees awarded. *Entrance requirements:* For degree, master's degree in psychology. Application fee: $40. *Financial support:* Career-related internships or fieldwork and tuition waivers (full) available. Support available to part-time students. Financial award applicants required to submit FAFSA. *Unit head:* Dr. Fred Kreig, Program Director, 304-746-2067, E-mail: fkreig@marshall.edu. *Application contact:* Information Contact, 304-746-1900, Fax: 304-746-1902, E-mail: services@marshall.edu.

Marywood University, Academic Affairs, College of Education and Human Development, Department of Psychology and Counseling, Program in Psychology, Scranton, PA 18509-1598. Offers child/clinical school psychology (MA); clinical services (MA); general theoretical psychology (MA). Part-time and evening/weekend programs available. *Students:* 41 full-time (34 women), 15 part-time (11 women); includes 5 minority (2 African Americans, 3 Asian Americans or Pacific Islanders). Average age 28. 62 applicants, 66% accepted. In 2007, 24 degrees awarded. *Degree requirements:* For master's, comprehensive exam, thesis or alternative, internship/practicum. *Entrance requirements:* For master's, GRE or MAT. Additional exam requirements/recommendations for international students: Required—TOEFL (minimum score 550 paper-based; 213 computer-based). *Application deadline:* For fall admission, 4/15 priority date for domestic and international students; for spring admission, 11/15 priority date for domestic and international students. Applications are processed on a rolling basis. Application fee: $30. Electronic applications accepted. *Expenses:* Tuition: Full-time $15,290; part-time $695 per credit. Required fees: $990; $370 per term. Tuition and fees vary according to degree level. *Financial support:* Research assistantships with tuition reimbursements, career-related internships or fieldwork, scholarships/grants, tuition waivers (partial), and unspecified assistantships available. Support available to part-time students. Financial award application deadline: 2/15; financial award applicants required to submit FAFSA. *Faculty research:* Personality disorders, counselor training, preschool development, self-esteem measurement, family dynamics. *Unit head:* Dr. Edward J. O'Brien, Chairperson, 570-348-6211 Ext. 2459, E-mail: obrien@es.marywood.edu. *Application contact:* Tammy Manka, Assistant Director of Graduate Admissions, 570-340-6002, E-mail: tmanka@marywood.edu.

Marywood University, Academic Affairs, College of Education and Human Development, Department of Psychology and Counseling, Program in School Psychology, Scranton, PA 18509-1598. Offers Ed S. *Students:* 7 full-time (4 women), 17 part-time (13 women); includes 1 minority (Asian American or Pacific Islander) Average age 27. *Expenses:* Tuition: Full-time $15,290; part-time $695 per credit. Required fees: $990; $370 per term. Tuition and fees vary according to degree level. *Unit head:* Dr. Edward J. O'Brien, Chairperson, 570-348-6211 Ext. 2459, E-mail: obrien@es.marywood.edu.

Massachusetts School of Professional Psychology, Graduate Programs, Boston, MA 02132. Offers clinical psychology (Psy D); clinical psychopharmacology (Post-Doctoral MS); counseling psychology (MA); executive coaching (Graduate Certificate); forensic psychology (MA); organizational psychology (MA); respecialization in clinical psychology (Certificate); MA/CAGS. *Accreditation:* APA. *Faculty:* 24 full-time (11 women), 13 part-time/adjunct (9 women). *Students:* 223 full-time (177 women), 81 part-time (68 women); includes 22 minority (3 African Americans, 8 Asian Americans or Pacific Islanders, 11 Hispanic Americans), 9 international. Average age 28. 415 applicants, 42% accepted, 77 enrolled. In 2007, 14 master's, 37 doctorates awarded. *Degree requirements:* For master's, comprehensive exam; for doctorate, thesis/dissertation. *Entrance requirements:* For doctorate, GRE General Test. Additional exam requirements/recommendations for international students: Required—TOEFL (minimum score 550 paper-based; 213 computer-based). *Application deadline:* For fall admission, 1/3 for domestic and international students. Application fee: $50. Electronic applications accepted. *Expenses:* Tuition: Full-time $25,952; part-time $811 per credit. Required fees: $200. *Financial support:* In 2007–08, 20 teaching assistantships (averaging $3,300 per year) were awarded; career-related internships or fieldwork also available. Financial award applicants required to submit FAFSA. *Unit head:* Dr. Nicholas A. Covino, President, 617-327-6777, Fax: 617-327-4447. *Application contact:* 617-327-6777 Ext. 210, Fax: 617-327-4447, E-mail: admissions@mspp.edu.

See Close-Up on page 1447.

McGill University, Faculty of Graduate and Postdoctoral Studies, Faculty of Education, Department of Educational and Counseling Psychology, Montréal, QC H3A 2T5, Canada. Offers counseling psychology (MA, PhD); educational psychology (M Ed, MA, PhD); school/applied child psychology and applied developmental psychology (M Ed, MA, PhD, Diploma), including school psychology. *Accreditation:* APA. *Faculty:* 33 full-time (19 women), 36 part-time/adjunct (23 women). *Students:* 198 full-time (172 women), 70 part-time (61 women). 327 applicants, 37% accepted, 92 enrolled. In 2007, 78 master's, 16 doctorates awarded.

McNeese State University, Graduate School, College of Education, Department of Teacher Education, Program in School Counseling, Lake Charles, LA 70609. Offers M Ed. *Accreditation:* NCATE. Evening/weekend programs available. *Faculty:* 2 full-time (both women). *Students:* 2 full-time (both women), 17 part-time (16 women); includes 1 minority (African American) In 2007, 1 degree awarded. *Entrance requirements:* For master's, GRE, teaching certificate, 18 hours in professional education. *Application deadline:* For fall admission, 5/15 priority date for domestic students. Applications are processed on a rolling basis. Application fee: $20 ($30 for international students). *Expenses:* Tuition, state resident: full-time $2,226; part-time $193 per hour. Required fees: $935; $110 per hour. Tuition and fees vary according to course load. *Financial support:* Application deadline: 5/1. *Unit head:* Dr. Royce Zant, Head, Department of Teacher Education, 337-475-5404, Fax: 337-475-5398, E-mail: rzant@mcneese.edu.

Mercy College, Division of Social and Behavioral Sciences, Program in Psychology, Dobbs Ferry, NY 10522-1189. Offers psychology (MS); school psychology (MS). *Students:* 28 full-time (22 women), 40 part-time (30 women); includes 35 minority (12 African Americans, 2 American Indian/Alaska Native, 1 Asian American or Pacific Islander, 20 Hispanic Americans), 1 international. Average age 32. In 2007, 17 degrees awarded. *Entrance requirements:* For master's, BA in psychology, sociology, behavioral science or education; interview; letters of recommendation. *Expenses:* Tuition: Part-time $575 per credit. Required fees: $220

School Psychology

Mercy College (continued)

per semester. Tuition and fees vary according to program. *Unit head:* Dr. Barbara Melamed, Program Director, 914-674-7345, E-mail: bmelamed@mercy.edu.

Miami University, Graduate School, School of Education and Allied Professions, Department of Educational Psychology, Program in School Psychology, Oxford, OH 45056. Offers MS, Ed S. *Accreditation:* NCATE. *Degree requirements:* For master's, thesis or alternative, oral or written exam; for Ed S, oral or written exam. *Entrance requirements:* For master's, GRE General Test or MAT, minimum undergraduate GPA of 3.0 during previous 2 years or 2.75 overall; for Ed S, GRE General Test or MAT.

Michigan State University, The Graduate School, College of Education, Department of Counseling, Educational Psychology and Special Education, East Lansing, MI 48824. Offers counseling (MA); educational psychology and educational technology (PhD); educational technology (MA); measurement and quantitative methods (PhD); rehabilitation counseling (MA); rehabilitation counselor education (PhD); school psychology (MA, PhD, Ed S); special education (MA, PhD). *Accreditation:* APA (one or more programs are accredited); CORE (one or more programs are accredited). Part-time programs available. *Entrance requirements:* Additional exam requirements/recommendations for international students: Required—TOEFL. Electronic applications accepted. *Expenses:* Tuition, state resident: part-time $379 per credit hour. Tuition, nonresident: part-time $800 per credit hour. Tuition and fees vary according to program.

Middle Tennessee State University, College of Graduate Studies, College of Education and Behavioral Science, Department of Psychology, Program in Professional Counseling, Murfreesboro, TN 37132. Offers curriculum and instruction (Ed S), including school psychology; school counseling (M Ed). *Accreditation:* ACA; NCATE. Part-time and evening/weekend programs available. Postbaccalaureate distance learning degree programs offered. *Students:* 1 (woman) full-time, 53 part-time (48 women); includes 9 minority (7 African Americans, 2 Asian Americans or Pacific Islanders). 58 applicants, 64% accepted. In 2007, 10 master's, 12 Ed Ss awarded. *Degree requirements:* For master's, one foreign language, comprehensive exam. *Entrance requirements:* For master's, GRE or MAT. Additional exam requirements/recommendations for international students: Required—TOEFL (paper-based 525; computer-based 195; IBT 71) or IELTS (6.0). *Application deadline:* For fall admission, 8/1 priority date for domestic students. Applications are processed on a rolling basis. Application fee: $25. Electronic applications accepted. *Financial support:* Career-related internships or fieldwork, institutionally sponsored loans, and scholarships/grants available. Financial award application deadline: 5/1.

Millersville University of Pennsylvania, Graduate School, School of Education, Department of Psychology, Program in Psychology, Millersville, PA 17551-0302. Offers clinical psychology (MS); school psychology (MS). Part-time and evening/weekend programs available. *Faculty:* 20 full-time (14 women), 13 part-time/adjunct (9 women). *Students:* 47 full-time (37 women), 44 part-time (34 women); includes 6 minority (5 African Americans, 1 Hispanic American), 1 international. Average age 28. 53 applicants, 75% accepted, 30 enrolled. In 2007, 33 degrees awarded. *Degree requirements:* For master's, thesis optional, departmental exam. *Entrance requirements:* For master's, GRE General Test, minimum undergraduate GPA of 2.75, 18 undergraduate hours of course work in psychology, group interview, letters of recommendation, writing sample. Additional exam requirements/recommendations for international students: Required—TOEFL (minimum score 500 paper-based; 183 computer-based). *Application deadline:* For fall admission, 2/29 for domestic students; for winter admission, 10/1 for domestic students; for spring admission, 10/1 for domestic students. Application fee: $40. Electronic applications accepted. *Expenses:* Tuition, state resident: full-time $6,214; part-time $345 per credit. Tuition, nonresident: full-time $9,944; part-time $552 per credit. Required fees: $1,442. Tuition and fees vary according to course load. *Financial support:* In 2007–08, 33 students received support, including 33 research assistantships with full and partial tuition reimbursements available (averaging $5,200 per year); institutionally sponsored loans and unspecified assistantships also available. Support available to part-time students. Financial award application deadline: 3/15; financial award applicants required to submit FAFSA. *Faculty research:* Childhood disorders, family stress, anxiety and worry treatments, solution focused counseling, creativity and personality correlates. *Application contact:* Dr. Victor S. DeSantis, Dean of Graduate Studies, 717-872-3099, Fax: 717-871-2022, E-mail: victor.desantis@millersville.edu.

Millersville University of Pennsylvania, Graduate School, School of Education, Department of Psychology, Program in School Counseling, Millersville, PA 17551-0302. Offers M Ed. *Accreditation:* NCATE. Part-time and evening/weekend programs available. *Faculty:* 20 full-time (14 women), 13 part-time/adjunct (9 women). *Students:* 8 full-time (all women), 40 part-time (35 women); includes 1 minority (African American) Average age 29. 17 applicants, 35% accepted, 3 enrolled. In 2007, 15 degrees awarded. *Degree requirements:* For master's, thesis optional, departmental exam. *Entrance requirements:* For master's, GRE General Test, group interview, minimum undergraduate GPA of 2.75, 6 undergraduate hours of course work in education and psychology, letters of recommendation, writing sample. Additional exam requirements/recommendations for international students: Required—TOEFL (minimum score 500 paper-based; 183 computer-based). *Application deadline:* For fall admission, 2/29 for domestic students; for winter admission, 10/1 for domestic students; for spring admission, 10/1 for domestic students. Application fee: $40. Electronic applications accepted. *Expenses:* Tuition, state resident: full-time $6,214; part-time $345 per credit. Tuition, nonresident: full-time $9,944; part-time $552 per credit. Required fees: $1,442. Tuition and fees vary according to course load. *Financial support:* In 2007–08, 14 students received support, including 14 research assistantships with full and partial tuition reimbursements available (averaging $5,200 per year); institutionally sponsored loans and unspecified assistantships also available. Support available to part-time students. Financial award application deadline: 3/15; financial award applicants required to submit FAFSA. *Unit head:* Dr. Nadine E. Garner, Director, 717-872-3097, Fax: 717-871-2480, E-mail: nadine.garner@millersville.edu. *Application contact:* Dr. Victor S. DeSantis, Dean of Graduate Studies, 717-872-3099, Fax: 717-871-2022, E-mail: victor.desantis@millersville.edu.

Minnesota State University Moorhead, Graduate Studies, College of Social and Natural Sciences, Program in School Psychology, Moorhead, MN 56563-0002. Offers MS, Psy S. *Accreditation:* NCATE (one or more programs are accredited). *Degree requirements:* For master's, thesis, final oral and written comprehensive exams. *Entrance requirements:* For master's, GRE General Test, interview, minimum GPA of 3.0, 3 letters of recommendation; for Psy S, MS in school psychology. Additional exam requirements/recommendations for international students: Required—TOEFL (minimum score 550 paper-based; 213 computer-based). Electronic applications accepted.

Minot State University, Graduate School, Program in School Psychology, Minot, ND 58707-0002. Offers Ed Sp. *Faculty:* 5 full-time (2 women), 3 part-time/adjunct (1 woman). *Students:* Average age 31. 13 applicants, 69% accepted. In 2007, 7 degrees awarded. *Entrance requirements:* For degree, GRE General Test, minimum GPA of 3.0. Additional exam requirements/recommendations for international students: Required—TOEFL. *Application deadline:* For fall admission, 3/1 for domestic students. Applications are processed on a rolling basis. Application fee: $35. *Expenses:* Tuition, state resident: full-time $5,264. Tuition, nonresident: full-time $14,053. Required fees: $700. *Financial support:* In 2007–08, 11 teaching assistantships with partial tuition reimbursements were awarded; research assistantships with partial tuition reimbursements, career-related internships or fieldwork, institutionally sponsored loans, scholarships/grants, traineeships, tuition waivers (partial), and unspecified assistantships also available. Support available to part-time students. Financial award application deadline: 4/1. *Faculty research:* Oppositional defiance disorder and autism, experimental psychology, statistical genetics, adults with developmental disabilities, psychopharmacology. *Unit head:* Dr. Donald Burke, Chairperson, 701-858-3138. *Application contact:* Brenda Anderson, Administrative Assistant, 701-858-3250, Fax: 701-858-4286, E-mail: brenda.anderson@minotstateu.edu.

Montclair State University, The Office of Graduate Admissions and Support Services, College of Humanities and Social Sciences, Department of Psychology, Montclair, NJ 07043-1624. Offers educational psychology (MA), including child/adolescent clinical psychology, clinical psychology for Spanish/English bilinguals; psychology (MA, Certificate), including industrial and organizational psychology (MA); school psychologist (Certificate). Part-time and evening/weekend programs available. *Faculty:* 27 full-time (11 women), 27 part-time/adjunct (20 women). *Students:* 27 full-time (21 women), 39 part-time (32 women); includes 26 minority (7 African Americans, 4 Asian Americans or Pacific Islanders, 15 Hispanic Americans), 3 international. 86 applicants, 21% accepted, 13 enrolled. In 2007, 22 master's, 11 other advanced degrees awarded. *Degree requirements:* For master's, comprehensive exam, thesis or alternative. *Entrance requirements:* For master's, GRE General Test, GRE Subject Test, previous course work in psychology, interview, 2 letters of recommendation. Additional exam requirements/recommendations for international students: Required—TOEFL (minimum score 83 computer-based). *Application deadline:* For fall admission, 2/1 for domestic and international students; for spring admission, 10/1 for domestic and international students. Applications are processed on a rolling basis. Application fee: $60. Electronic applications accepted. *Financial support:* In 2007–08, 10 research assistantships with full tuition reimbursements (averaging $7,000 per year) were awarded; Federal Work-Study, scholarships/grants, and unspecified assistantships also available. Support available to part-time students. Financial award application deadline: 3/1; financial award applicants required to submit FAFSA. *Faculty research:* Engaged learning, academic and civic development. Total annual research expenditures: $10,000. *Unit head:* Dr. Peter Vietze, Chairperson, 973-655-5201.

Mount Saint Vincent University, Graduate Programs, Faculty of Education, Program in School Psychology, Halifax, NS B3M 2J6, Canada. Offers MASP. *Degree requirements:* For master's, thesis, 500 hour practicum. *Entrance requirements:* For master's, bachelor's degree in psychology or equivalent, related work experience. Electronic applications accepted. *Faculty research:* Relationship between cognitive and emotional development, expression of emotions, cognitive-behavioral constituents of racism.

National-Louis University, National College of Education, Doctoral Programs in Education, Program in Educational Psychology/School Psychology, Chicago, IL 60603. Offers Ed D. Part-time and evening/weekend programs available. *Students:* 6 full-time (all women), 10 part-time (all women); includes 3 minority (1 African American, 2 Hispanic Americans). Average age 37. *Degree requirements:* For doctorate, comprehensive exam, thesis/dissertation, internship. *Entrance requirements:* For doctorate, GRE General Test, minimum GPA of 3.25, interview, resumé, writing sample. *Application deadline:* For fall admission, 5/1 for domestic students; for spring admission, 1/15 for domestic students. *Expenses:* Tuition: Full-time $18,900; part-time $630 per credit hour. Required fees: $20 per term. One-time fee: $40 part-time. Tuition and fees vary according to course load, campus/location and program. *Financial support:* Fellowships, research assistantships, teaching assistantships, career-related internships or fieldwork, Federal Work-Study, institutionally sponsored loans, and scholarships/grants available. Support available to part-time students. Financial award application deadline: 4/15; financial award applicants required to submit FAFSA. *Application contact:* Dr. Larry Poselli, Vice President of Enrollment and Student Services, 800-443-5522 Ext. 5718, Fax: 312-261-.3550, E-mail: larry.polselli@nl.edu.

National-Louis University, National College of Education, Programs in School Psychology, Chicago, IL 60603. Offers M Ed, Ed S. *Students:* 18 full-time (17 women), 34 part-time (31 women); includes 6 minority (1 African American, 5 Hispanic Americans). Average age 32. In 2007, 20 degrees awarded. *Degree requirements:* For master's and Ed S, internship. *Entrance requirements:* For master's, MAT or GRE, minimum GPA of 3.0; for Ed S, GRE, interview, master's degree, writing sample. *Application deadline:* Applications are processed on a rolling basis. *Expenses:* Tuition: Full-time $18,900; part-time $630 per credit hour. Required fees: $20 per term. One-time fee: $40 part-time. Tuition and fees vary according to course load, campus/location and program. *Financial support:* Fellowships, career-related internships or fieldwork, Federal Work-Study, scholarships/grants, and tuition waivers available. Support available to part-time students. *Unit head:* Dr. Diane Salmon, Coordinator, 224-233-2726. *Application contact:* Dr. Larry Poselli, Vice President of Enrollment and Student Services, 800-443-5522 Ext. 5718, Fax: 312-261-.3550, E-mail: larry.polselli@nl.edu.

National University, Academic Affairs, School of Education, Department of School Counseling and Psychology, La Jolla, CA 92037-1011. Offers educational counseling (MS); school psychology (MS). Part-time and evening/weekend programs available. Postbaccalaureate distance learning degree programs offered (no on-campus study). *Faculty:* 11 full-time (4 women), 190 part-time/adjunct (114 women). *Students:* 470 full-time (383 women), 596 part-time (460 women); includes 389 minority (93 African Americans, 6 American Indian/Alaska Native, 56 Asian Americans or Pacific Islanders, 234 Hispanic Americans), 1 international. Average age 34. 737 applicants, 636 enrolled. In 2007, 172 degrees awarded. *Degree requirements:* For master's, thesis (for some programs). *Entrance requirements:* For master's, interview, minimum GPA of 2.5. Additional exam requirements/recommendations for international students: Required—TOEFL (minimum score 550 paper-based; 213 computer-based; 80 iBT), IELTS (minimum score 6). *Application deadline:* Applications are processed on a rolling basis. Application fee: $60 ($65 for international students). Electronic applications accepted. *Expenses:* Tuition: Full-time $8,262; part-time $306 per unit. One-time fee: $60. *Financial support:* Career-related internships or fieldwork, institutionally sponsored loans, scholarships/grants, and tuition waivers (partial) available. Support available to part-time students. Financial award application deadline: 6/30; financial award applicants required to submit FAFSA. *Unit head:* Dr. Susan Eldred, Chair, 858-642-8372, Fax: 858-642-8724, E-mail: seldred@nu.edu. *Application contact:* Dominick Giovanniello, Associate Regional Dean—San Diego, 800-NAT-UNIV, Fax: 858-642-8709, E-mail: dgiovann@nu.edu.

New Jersey City University, Graduate Studies and Continuing Education, College of Arts and Sciences, Department of Psychology, Program in Educational Psychology, Jersey City, NJ 07305-1597. Offers educational psychology (MA); school psychology (PD). *Faculty:* 9. *Students:* 7 full-time (all women), 31 part-time (22 women); includes 10 minority (4 African Americans, 2 Asian Americans or Pacific Islanders, 4 Hispanic Americans), 1 international. Average age 30. In 2007, 33 master's, 5 other advanced degrees awarded. *Degree requirements:* For PD, summer internship or externship. *Entrance requirements:* For master's, GRE General Test or MAT; for PD, GRE General Test. Additional exam requirements/recommendations for international students: Required—TOEFL. *Application deadline:* For fall admission, 8/1 priority date for domestic students; for spring admission, 12/1 for domestic students. Applications are processed on a rolling basis. Application fee: $0. *Expenses:* Tuition, state resident: full-time $7,462. Tuition, nonresident: full-time $13,762. Required fees: $1,296. *Financial support:* Unspecified assistantships available. *Unit head:* Dr. James Lennon, Director, 201-200-3309, E-mail: jlennon@njcu.edu.

New Mexico State University, Graduate School, College of Education, Department of Counseling and Educational Psychology, Las Cruces, NM 88003-8001. Offers counseling and guidance (MA); counseling psychology (PhD); school psychology (Ed S). *Accreditation:* ACA; APA (one or more programs are accredited); NCATE. Part-time programs available. *Faculty:* 7 full-time (4 women). *Students:* 70 full-time (52 women), 23 part-time (14 women); includes 48 minority (5 African Americans, 1 American Indian/Alaska Native, 1 Asian American or Pacific Islander, 41 Hispanic Americans), 4 international. Average age 33. 35 applicants, 46% accepted, 11 enrolled. In 2007, 15 master's, 6 doctorates, 6 other advanced degrees awarded. *Degree requirements:* For master's, comprehensive exam, thesis optional, internship; for doctorate, comprehensive exam, thesis/dissertation, internship; for Ed S, thesis or alternative, internship. *Entrance requirements:* For master's, doctorate, and Ed S, GRE General Test, 3.0 GPA. *Application deadline:* For fall admission, 12/15 for domestic students; for spring admission, 4/1 priority date for domestic students. Application fee: $30 ($50 for international students). Electronic applications accepted. *Expenses:* Tuition, state resident: full-time $3,602; part-time $199 per credit. Tuition, nonresident: full-time $13,380; part-time $607 per credit. Required fees: $1,178. *Financial support:* In 2007–08, 30 students received support, including 8 fellowships with partial tuition reimbursements available, 10 research assistantships, 25 teaching assistantships with partial tuition reimbursements available; career-related internships or fieldwork, Federal Work-Study, institutionally sponsored loans, scholarships/grants, traineeships, health care benefits, and unspecified assistantships also available. Support available to part-time students. Financial award application deadline: 4/1. *Faculty research:* Multicultural counseling, integrative health psychology group, career development school counseling. *Unit head:* Dr. Eve Adams, Head, 575-646-2121, Fax: 575-646-8035, E-mail: eadams@nmsu.edu.

New York University, Steinhardt School of Culture, Education and Human Development, Department of Applied Psychology, Program in Educational and Developmental Psychology, New York, NY 10012-1019. Offers educational psychology (MA), including general educational psychology, psychological measurement and evaluation, psychology of parenthood; psychological development (PhD); school psychology (PhD). *Accreditation:* APA (one or more programs are accredited). Part-time and evening/weekend programs available. *Faculty:* 28 full-time (18 women). *Students:* 65 full-time (57 women), 60 part-time (58 women); includes 38 minority (17 African Americans, 7 Asian Americans or Pacific Islanders, 14 Hispanic Americans), 16 international. 159 applicants, 60% accepted, 27 enrolled. In 2007, 21 master's, 10 doctorates awarded. Terminal master's awarded for partial completion of doctoral program. *Degree requirements:* For master's, thesis (for some programs); for doctorate, thesis/dissertation. *Entrance requirements:* For doctorate, GRE General Test, interview. Additional exam requirements/recommendations for international students: Required—TOEFL. *Application deadline:* For fall admission, 12/15 priority date for domestic and international students; for spring admission, 11/1 for domestic and international students. Applications are processed on a rolling basis. Application fee: $50. *Financial support:* Teaching assistantships with partial tuition reimbursements, career-related internships or fieldwork, Federal Work-Study, institutionally sponsored loans, and tuition waivers (partial) available. Support available to part-time students. Financial award application deadline: 2/1; financial award applicants required to submit FAFSA. *Faculty research:* High risk children and youth; child and adolescent developments; families and schooling; infant cognition; exploration, language, and symbolic play in toddlerhood. *Unit head:* Dr. Barbara Hummel-Rossi, Director, 212-998-5360, Fax: 212-995-4358. *Application contact:* 212-998-5030, Fax: 212-995-4328, E-mail: steinhardt.gradadmissions@nyu.edu.

Niagara University, Graduate Division of Education, Concentration in School Psychology, Niagara Falls, Niagara University, NY 14109. Offers MS, Certificate. *Students:* 20 full-time (15 women), 10 part-time (all women), 2 international. In 2007, 8 master's, 8 other advanced degrees awarded. *Expenses:* Tuition: Full-time $11,790; part-time $655 per credit. Required fees: $50; $25 per term. *Unit head:* Dr. Shannon Hodges, Chair, 716-286-8328.

Nicholls State University, Graduate Studies, College of Education, Department of Psychology and Counselor Education, Thibodaux, LA 70310. Offers psychological counseling (MA); school psychology (SSP). *Accreditation:* NCATE. Part-time and evening/weekend programs available. *Faculty:* 8 full-time (2 women). *Students:* 29 full-time (25 women), 20 part-time (16 women); includes 16 minority (13 African Americans, 2 American Indian/Alaska Native, 1 Hispanic American), 1 international. Average age 27. In 2007, 15 master's, 7 other advanced degrees awarded. *Degree requirements:* For master's, comprehensive exam; for SSP, comprehensive exam, internship. *Entrance requirements:* For master's, GRE General Test. *Application deadline:* For fall admission, 6/17 priority date for domestic students; for spring admission, 11/15 priority date for domestic students. Applications are processed on a rolling basis. Application fee: $20 ($30 for international students). Electronic applications accepted. *Financial support:* In 2007–08, 12 teaching assistantships with tuition reimbursements (averaging $7,000 per year) were awarded; research assistantships with tuition reimbursements. Financial award application deadline: 6/17. *Unit head:* Dr. J. Steven Welsh, Head, 985-448-4371, Fax: 985-448-4435, E-mail: steven.welsh@nicholls.edu.

North Carolina State University, Graduate School, College of Humanities and Social Sciences, Department of Psychology, Raleigh, NC 27695. Offers developmental psychology (PhD); ergonomics and experimental psychology (PhD); industrial/organizational psychology (PhD); psychology in the public interest (PhD); school psychology (PhD). *Accreditation:* APA. *Degree requirements:* For doctorate, comprehensive exam, thesis/dissertation. *Entrance requirements:* For doctorate, GRE General Test, GRE Subject Test (industrial/organizational psychology), MAT (recommended), minimum GPA of 3.0 in major. Electronic applications accepted. *Faculty research:* Cognitive and social development (human factors, families, the workplace, community issues and health, aging).

Northeastern University, Bouvé College of Health Sciences Graduate School, Department of Counseling and Applied Educational Psychology, Program in Applied Educational Psychology, Boston, MA 02115-5096. Offers school counseling (MS); school psychology (MS). Part-time programs available. *Entrance requirements:* For master's, GRE General Test or MAT. Additional exam requirements/recommendations for international students: Required—TOEFL. *Faculty research:* Multicultural issues, assessment, early intervention, bilingual education.

Northeastern University, Bouvé College of Health Sciences Graduate School, Department of Counseling and Applied Educational Psychology, Program in School Psychology, Boston, MA 02115-5096. Offers PhD, CAGS. *Accreditation:* APA (one or more programs are accredited). Part-time programs available. *Degree requirements:* For doctorate, comprehensive exam, thesis/dissertation, qualifying exams; for CAGS, comprehensive exam. *Entrance requirements:* For doctorate, GRE General Test, school psychologist certificate; for CAGS, GRE General Test or MAT, MS in school psychology or related field. Additional exam requirements/recommendations for international students: Required—TOEFL. *Faculty research:* Multicultural education, early intervention.

Northern Arizona University, Graduate College, College of Education, Program in Educational Psychology, Flagstaff, AZ 86011. Offers counseling psychology (Ed D); learning and instruction (Ed D); school psychology (Ed D). *Degree requirements:* For doctorate, comprehensive exam, thesis/dissertation, internship. *Entrance requirements:* For doctorate, GRE General Test.

Northern Arizona University, Graduate College, College of Education, Program in School Psychology, Flagstaff, AZ 86011. Offers MA. *Degree requirements:* For master's, internship. *Entrance requirements:* For master's, GRE General Test.

Northwest Nazarene University, Graduate Studies, Program in Counselor Education, Nampa, ID 83686-5897. Offers community counseling (MS); marriage and family counseling (MS); school counseling (MS). *Faculty:* 3 full-time (1 woman), 10 part-time/adjunct (6 women). *Students:* 69 full-time (52 women), 12 part-time (8 women); includes 4 minority (1 American Indian/Alaska Native, 3 Hispanic Americans). In 2007, 19 degrees awarded. Application fee: $25. *Unit head:* Dr. Brenda Freeman, Chair, 208-467-8428, Fax: 208-467-8339.

Nova Southeastern University, Center for Psychological Studies, Specialist Program in School Psychology, Fort Lauderdale, FL 33314-7796. Offers Psy S. Evening/weekend programs available. Postbaccalaureate distance learning degree programs offered. *Faculty:* 6 full-time (3 women), 16 part-time/adjunct (10 women). *Students:* 59 full-time (54 women), 70 part-time (65 women); includes 63 minority (35 African Americans, 5 Asian Americans or Pacific Islanders, 23 Hispanic Americans), 2 international. 110 applicants, 50% accepted, 37 enrolled. In 2007, 34 degrees awarded. *Degree requirements:* For Psy S, comprehensive exam, internship. *Entrance requirements:* Additional exam requirements/recommendations for international students: Required—TOEFL (minimum score 530 paper-based; 213 computer-based). *Application deadline:* For fall admission, 2/22 priority date for domestic and international students; for winter admission, 6/30 priority date for domestic and international students. Applications are processed on a rolling basis. Application fee: $50. Electronic applications accepted. *Financial support:* In 2007–08, 1 teaching assistantship was awarded; research assistantships, career-related internships or fieldwork, Federal Work-Study, scholarships/grants, and unspecified assistantships also available. *Unit head:* Karen S. Grosby, Dean, 954-262-5701, Fax: 954-262-3859. *Application contact:* Carlos Perez, Enrollment Management, 954-262-5790, Fax: 954-262-3893, E-mail: cpsinfo@cps.nova.edu.

See Close-Up on page 1457.

Oregon State University–Cascades, Program in Counseling, Bend, OR 97701. Offers community counseling (MS); school counseling (MS).

Ottawa University, Graduate Studies-Arizona, Program in Education, Ottawa, KS 66067-3399. Offers community college counseling (MA); curriculum and instruction (MA); early childhood (MA); education intervention (MA); education leadership (MA); education technology (MA); Montessori early childhood education (MA); Montessori elementary education (MA); professional development (MA); school guidance counseling (MA); special education—cross categorical (MA). Programs offered in Mesa, Phoenix, Tempe and West Valley, AZ. *Accreditation:* NCATE. Part-time programs available. *Degree requirements:* For master's, thesis or alternative. *Entrance requirements:* For master's, minimum undergraduate GPA of 3.0, copy of current state certification or teaching license. Additional exam requirements/recommendations for international students: Required—TOEFL (minimum score 550 paper-based; 213 computer-based). Electronic applications accepted. Expenses: Contact institution.

Our Lady of the Lake University of San Antonio, School of Education and Clinical Studies, Program in Counseling Psychology, San Antonio, TX 78207-4689. Offers counseling psychology (MS, Psy D); marriage and family therapy (MS); school psychology (MS). *Accreditation:* APA (one or more programs are accredited). Part-time and evening/weekend programs available. *Degree requirements:* For master's, comprehensive exam, thesis optional, practicum; for doctorate, thesis/dissertation, internship, qualifying exam. *Entrance requirements:* For master's and doctorate, GRE General Test or MAT, interview. Additional exam requirements/recommendations for international students: Required—TOEFL. Electronic applications accepted. *Faculty research:* Marriage and family therapy, supervision, cross-cultural counseling, violence.

Pace University, Dyson College of Arts and Sciences, Department of Psychology, Program in School Psychology, New York, NY 10038. Offers MS Ed. *Students:* 3 full-time (all women). Average age 28. 42 applicants, 14% accepted, 1 enrolled. In 2007, 18 degrees awarded. *Application deadline:* For fall admission, 7/31 priority date for domestic students; for spring admission, 11/30 for domestic students. Applications are processed on a rolling basis. Application fee: $65. Electronic applications accepted. *Expenses:* Tuition: Part-time $856 per credit. Tuition and fees vary according to degree level and program. *Unit head:* Dr. Barbara Mowder, Director, 212-346-1506. *Application contact:* Joanna Broda, Director of Admissions, 212-346-1652, Fax: 212-346-1585, E-mail: gradnyc@pace.edu.

Penn State University Park, Graduate School, College of Education, Department of Educational and School Psychology and Special Education, State College, University Park, PA 16802-1503. Offers educational psychology (MS, PhD); school psychology (M Ed, MS, PhD); special education (M Ed, MS, PhD). *Expenses:* Tuition, state resident: full-time $14,738; part-time $614 per credit. Tuition, nonresident: full-time $26,050; part-time $1,085 per credit. Tuition and fees vary according to course load, program and student level. *Unit head:* Dr. Kathy L. Ruhl, Head, 814-865-6072, Fax: 814-865-7066, E-mail: klr3@psu.edu. *Application contact:* Bobbi Jo Robison, Department Head Secretary, 814-863-4450, E-mail: bjb9@psu.edu.

Philadelphia College of Osteopathic Medicine, Graduate and Professional Programs, Department of Psychology, Philadelphia, PA 19131-1694. Offers clinical psychology (Psy D); counseling and clinical health psychology (MS); organizational leadership and development (MS); psychology (Certificate); school psychology (MS, Psy D, Ed S). *Accreditation:* APA. *Degree requirements:* For master's, thesis; for doctorate, comprehensive exam, thesis/dissertation, final project, fieldwork. *Entrance requirements:* For master's, GRE or MAT, minimum GPA of 3.0; course work in biology, chemistry, English, physics; for other advanced degree, PRAXIS. *Faculty research:* Depression in primary care, integrated primary care, geriatric mental health.

See Close-Up on page 1469.

Pittsburg State University, Graduate School, College of Education, Department of Psychology and Counseling, Program in School Psychology, Pittsburg, KS 66762. Offers Ed S. *Accreditation:* NCATE. *Degree requirements:* For Ed S, thesis or alternative. *Entrance requirements:* For degree, GRE General Test, minimum GPA of 3.0.

Queens College of the City University of New York, Division of Graduate Studies, Division of Education, Department of Educational and Community Programs, Program in School Psychology, Flushing, NY 11367-1597. Offers MS Ed, AC. Part-time programs available. *Faculty:* 4 full-time (3 women). *Students:* 29 full-time (26 women), 62 part-time (54 women). 136 applicants, 48% accepted, 33 enrolled. In 2007, 22 degrees awarded. *Degree requirements:* For master's, internship, research project; for AC, thesis optional, internship. *Entrance requirements:* For master's, minimum GPA of 3.0; for AC, master's degree or equivalent. Additional exam requirements/recommendations for international students: Required—TOEFL. *Application deadline:* For fall admission, 4/1 for domestic students; for spring admission, 11/1 for domestic students. Applications are processed on a rolling basis. Application fee: $125. *Financial support:* Career-related internships or fieldwork, Federal Work-Study, institutionally sponsored loans, and tuition waivers (partial) available. Support available to part-time students. Financial award application deadline: 4/1; financial award applicants required to submit FAFSA. *Unit head:* Dr. Marion Fish, Coordinator/Graduate Adviser, 718-997-5230. *Application contact:* Mario Caruso, Director of Graduate Admissions, 718-997-5200, Fax: 718-997-5193, E-mail: graduate_admissions@qc.edu.

Radford University, Graduate College, College of Humanities and Behavioral Sciences, Department of Psychology, Program in School Psychology, Radford, VA 24142. Offers Ed S. *Accreditation:* NCATE. Part-time programs available. *Faculty:* 15 full-time (7 women), 1 part-time/adjunct (0 women). *Students:* 15 full-time (13 women), 13 part-time (all women); includes 1 minority (African American) Average age 28. 25 applicants, 44% accepted, 9 enrolled. In 2007, 9 degrees awarded. *Degree requirements:* For Ed S, comprehensive exam. *Entrance requirements:* For degree, GRE. Additional exam requirements/recommendations for international students: Required—TOEFL. *Application deadline:* For fall admission, 3/1 priority date for domestic students, 12/1 for international students; for spring admission, 10/1 for domestic students, 7/1 for international students. Applications are processed on a rolling basis. Application fee: $40. Electronic applications accepted. *Financial support:* In 2007–08, 13 students received support, including research assistantships with partial tuition reimbursements available (averaging $8,000 per year), teaching assistantships with partial tuition reimbursements available (averaging $8,700 per year); career-related internships or fieldwork, Federal Work-Study, institutionally sponsored loans, scholarships/grants, and unspecified assistantships also available. Financial award application deadline: 3/1; financial award applicants required to submit FAFSA. *Unit head:* Dr. Jayne Bucy, Coordinator, 540-831-5341, E-mail: jebucy@radford.edu.

Regent University, Graduate School, School of Psychology and Counseling, Virginia Beach, VA 23464-9800. Offers clinical psychology (Psy D); counseling (MA), including clinical psychology, community counseling, human services counseling, school guidance; counseling studies (CAGS); counselor education and supervision (PhD); M Div/MA; M Ed/MA; MBA/MA. PhD program offered online only. *Accreditation:* ACA; APA (one or more programs are accredited). Part-time programs available. Postbaccalaureate distance learning degree programs offered. *Faculty:* 25 full-time (14 women), 17 part-time/adjunct (7 women). *Students:* 223 full-time (176 women), 187 part-time (141 women); includes 110 minority (89 African Americans, 2 American Indian/Alaska Native, 9 Asian Americans or Pacific Islanders, 10 Hispanic Americans), 11 international. Average age 31. 293 applicants, 58% accepted, 99 enrolled. In 2007, 79 master's, 23 doctorates awarded. *Degree requirements:* For master's, thesis or alternative, internship, practicum, written competency exam; for doctorate, thesis/dissertation or alternative. *Entrance requirements:* For master's, GRE General Test including

School Psychology

Regent University (continued)

writing exam, minimum undergraduate GPA of 2.75, 3 recommendations, resumé, transcripts, writing sample; for doctorate, GRE General Test including writing exam, GRE Subject Test, minimum undergraduate GPA of 3.0, 3.5 (PhD), 10-15 minute VHS tape demonstrating counseling skills, writing sample, 3 recommendations, resumé, transcripts. Additional exam requirements/recommendations for international students: Required—TOEFL (minimum score 577 paper-based; 233 computer-based). *Application deadline:* For fall admission, 4/1 priority date for domestic students; for spring admission, 11/1 priority date for domestic students. Applications are processed on a rolling basis. Application fee: $50. Electronic applications accepted. *Expenses: Contact institution. Financial support:* In 2007–08, 362 students received support, including 15 research assistantships with full and partial tuition reimbursements available (averaging $4,439 per year), 6 teaching assistantships with full and partial tuition reimbursements available (averaging $12,699 per year); career-related internships or fieldwork, scholarships/grants, and tuition waivers (full and partial) also available. Support available to part-time students. Financial award application deadline: 9/1. *Faculty research:* Marriage enrichment, AIDS counseling, troubled youth. Total annual research expenditures: $12,000. *Unit head:* Dr. Rosemarie Hughes, Dean, 757-226-4269, Fax: 757-226-4282, E-mail: rosehug@regent.edu. *Application contact:* Althea Bishard, Registrar and Executive Director of Enrollment and Academic Services, 800-373-5504, Fax: 757-226-4381, E-mail: admissions@regent.edu.

Rider University, Department of Graduate Education, Leadership and Counseling, Program in School Psychology, Lawrenceville, NJ 08648-3001. Offers Certificate, Ed S. *Faculty:* 3 full-time (1 woman), 4 part-time/adjunct (2 women). *Students:* 18 full-time (15 women), 17 part-time (14 women); includes 3 minority (1 African American, 1 Asian American or Pacific Islander, 1 Hispanic American). Average age 27. 44 applicants, 32% accepted, 7 enrolled. In 2007, 11 degrees awarded. *Entrance requirements:* For degree, GRE or MAT, resumé, 2 professional references, interview, 1 year of counseling experience. Additional exam requirements/recommendations for international students: Required—TOEFL (minimum score 550 paper-based; 213 computer-based). Application fee: $50. *Expenses:* Tuition: Full-time $25,650; part-time $472 per credit. Required fees: $22 per credit. Tuition and fees vary according to program. *Financial support:* In 2007–08, 20 students received support. Career-related internships or fieldwork, Federal Work-Study, institutionally sponsored loans, and unspecified assistantships available. Support available to part-time students. Financial award applicants required to submit FAFSA. *Faculty research:* Prenatal factors on child development, child abuse developmental assessments. *Unit head:* Dr. Stefan Dombrowski, Program Coordinator, 609-895-5448.

Roberts Wesleyan College, Division of Social Sciences, Rochester, NY 14624-1997. Offers counseling in ministry (MA); school counseling (MS); school psychology (MS).

Rochester Institute of Technology, Graduate Enrollment Services, College of Liberal Arts, Department of Behavioral Science, Program in School Psychology, Rochester, NY 14623-5603. Offers MS, AC. *Students:* 47 full-time (45 women), 3 part-time (all women); includes 1 minority (Asian American or Pacific Islander), 1 international. 60 applicants, 30% accepted, 17 enrolled. In 2007, 30 master's, 14 other advanced degrees awarded. *Degree requirements:* For master's, comprehensive exam. *Entrance requirements:* For master's, GRE General Test, minimum GPA of 3.0. Additional exam requirements/recommendations for international students: Required—TOEFL (minimum score 580 paper-based; 237 computer-based; 92 iBT). *Application deadline:* For fall admission, 3/1 priority date for domestic students. Applications are processed on a rolling basis. Electronic applications accepted. *Expenses:* Tuition: Full-time $28,491; part-time $800 per credit hour. Required fees: $201; $67 per term. *Financial support:* Career-related internships or fieldwork, institutionally sponsored loans, scholarships/grants, and unspecified assistantships available. Support available to part-time students. Financial award applicants required to submit FAFSA. *Unit head:* Dr. Scott Merydith, Director, 585-475-7980, E-mail: spmgsp@rit.edu.

Rowan University, Graduate School, College of Education, Department of Special Educational Services/Instruction, Program in School Psychology, Glassboro, NJ 08028-1701. Offers MA, Ed S. *Accreditation:* NCATE. Part-time and evening/weekend programs available. *Faculty:* 15 full-time (6 women), 4 part-time/adjunct (1 woman). *Students:* 22 full-time (18 women), 31 part-time (30 women); includes 3 minority (2 Asian Americans or Pacific Islanders, 1 Hispanic American). Average age 29. 18 applicants, 6% accepted, 1 enrolled. In 2007, 18 degrees awarded. *Degree requirements:* For master's, comprehensive exam, thesis; for Ed S, thesis or alternative. *Entrance requirements:* For master's and Ed S, GRE General Test, GRE Subject Test, interview, minimum GPA of 3.0. Additional exam requirements/recommendations for international students: Required—TOEFL. *Application deadline:* For winter admission, 12/1 priority date for domestic students; for spring admission, 4/1 priority date for domestic students. Applications are processed on a rolling basis. Application fee: $50. Electronic applications accepted. *Expenses:* Tuition, nonresident: full-time $9,882; part-time $549 per credit. Required fees: $104,385 per credit. *Financial support:* Career-related internships or fieldwork, Federal Work-Study, and unspecified assistantships available. Support available to part-time students. *Unit head:* Charles Brett, Adviser, 856-256-4787, E-mail: brett@rowan.edu.

Rutgers, The State University of New Jersey, New Brunswick, Graduate School of Applied and Professional Psychology, Program in School Psychology, New Brunswick, NJ 08901-1281. Offers Psy M, Psy D. *Accreditation:* APA (one or more programs are accredited). *Degree requirements:* For doctorate, comprehensive exam, thesis/dissertation, 1 year internship. *Entrance requirements:* For doctorate, GRE General Test, GRE Subject Test, bachelor's degree in psychology or equivalent. Additional exam requirements/recommendations for international students: Required—TOEFL. Electronic applications accepted. Expenses: Contact institution. *Faculty research:* Consultation, program evaluation, applied educational psychology, exceptional children, crisis intervention.

St. John's University, St. John's College of Liberal Arts and Sciences, Department of Psychology, Program in School Psychology, Queens, NY 11439. Offers MS, Psy D. Part-time programs available. *Students:* 115 full-time (105 women), 58 part-time (51 women); includes 17 minority (6 African Americans, 5 Asian Americans or Pacific Islanders, 6 Hispanic Americans), 1 international. Average age 28. 150 applicants, 43% accepted, 42 enrolled. In 2007, 32 master's, 24 doctorates awarded. *Median time to degree:* Of those who began their doctoral program in fall 1999, 71% received their degree in 8 years or less. *Degree requirements:* For master's, comprehensive exam, thesis optional; for doctorate, comprehensive exam, thesis/dissertation, internship. *Entrance requirements:* For master's, GRE General Test, GRE Subject Test, minimum GPA of 3.0, 2 writing samples; for doctorate, GRE General Test, GRE Subject Test, interview, minimum GPA of 3.0. Additional exam requirements/recommendations for international students: Required—TOEFL (minimum score 500 paper-based; 173 computer-based; 61 iBT), IELTS (minimum score 6). *Application deadline:* For fall admission, 2/1 for domestic students, 5/1 priority date for international students; for spring admission, 11/1 priority date for international students. Applications are processed on a rolling basis. Application fee: $40. Electronic applications accepted. *Expenses: Contact institution. Financial support:* Fellowships, research assistantships, career-related internships or fieldwork, scholarships/grants, and unspecified assistantships available. Support available to part-time students. Financial award application deadline: 3/1; financial award applicants required to submit FAFSA. *Faculty research:* Therapeutic alliance, intelligence testing, multicultural assessment, neuropsychological assessment, adolescent suicide. *Unit head:* Dr. Mark Terjesen, Director, 718-990-5860, E-mail: terjesem@stjohns.edu. *Application contact:* Beth Evans, Associate Vice President and Executive Director, Enrollment Management, 718-990-6999, Fax: 718-990-5686, E-mail: gradhelp@stjohns.edu.

St. Mary's University, Graduate School, Department of Psychology, San Antonio, TX 78228-8507. Offers clinical psychology (MA, MS); industrial/organizational psychology (MA, MS); school psychology (MA). Part-time programs available. *Students:* 30 full-time (20 women), 15 part-time (12 women); includes 13 minority (2 African Americans, 11 Hispanic Americans). Average age 28. In 2007, 25 degrees awarded. *Degree requirements:* For master's, comprehensive exam, thesis optional. *Entrance requirements:* For master's, GRE General Test, letters of recommendation, work experience. Additional exam requirements/recommendations for international students: Required—TOEFL (minimum score 550 paper-based; 213 computer-based). *Application deadline:* Applications are processed on a rolling basis. Application fee: $0. Electronic applications accepted. *Financial support:* Research assistantships, career-related internships or fieldwork, Federal Work-Study, institutionally sponsored loans, scholarships/grants, and health care benefits available. Financial award application deadline: 3/31; financial award applicants required to submit FAFSA. *Unit head:* Dr. Patricia Owen, Director, 210-436-3314, Fax: 210-431-4301, E-mail: psycpat@stmarytx.edu.

Sam Houston State University, College of Humanities and Social Sciences, Department of Psychology and Philosophy, Huntsville, TX 77341. Offers clinical psychology (MA, PhD); psychology (MA); school psychology (MA). *Accreditation:* APA. Part-time programs available. *Faculty:* 22 full-time (6 women). *Students:* 59 full-time (47 women), 36 part-time (35 women); includes 15 minority (4 African Americans, 2 American Indian/Alaska Native, 3 Asian Americans or Pacific Islanders, 6 Hispanic Americans), 2 international. Average age 27. In 2007, 25 master's, 6 doctorates awarded. *Degree requirements:* For master's, thesis. *Entrance requirements:* For master's, GRE General Test or MAT, minimum GPA of 3.0. *Application deadline:* For fall admission, 8/1 for domestic students; for spring admission, 12/1 for domestic students. Applications are processed on a rolling basis. Application fee: $20. *Expenses:* Tuition, state resident: full-time $5,026; part-time $184 per semester hour. Tuition, nonresident: full-time $10,586; part-time $462 per semester hour. Required fees: $494 per semester. *Financial support:* Research assistantships, teaching assistantships, career-related internships or fieldwork and institutionally sponsored loans available. Support available to part-time students. Financial award application deadline: 5/31; financial award applicants required to submit FAFSA. *Unit head:* Dr. Donna M. Desforges, Chair, 936-294-1178, Fax: 936-294-3798. *Application contact:* Dr. Rowland Miller, Graduate Coordinator, 936-294-1176, Fax: 936-294-3798, E-mail: psy_rsm@shsu.edu.

San Diego State University, Graduate and Research Affairs, College of Education, Department of Counseling and School Psychology, San Diego, CA 92182. Offers MS. *Accreditation:* NCATE. Evening/weekend programs available. *Students:* 165 full-time (120 women), 3 part-time (all women); includes 107 minority (16 African Americans, 6 American Indian/Alaska Native, 26 Asian Americans or Pacific Islanders, 59 Hispanic Americans), 8 international. Average age 30. 351 applicants, 25% accepted, 80 enrolled. In 2007, 135 degrees awarded. *Degree requirements:* For master's, comprehensive exam (for some programs), thesis (for some programs). *Entrance requirements:* For master's, GRE General Test, interview, letters of reference. Additional exam requirements/recommendations for international students: Required—TOEFL. *Application deadline:* For fall admission, 2/1 priority date for domestic and international students; for spring admission, 11/1 for domestic students, 10/1 for international students. Applications are processed on a rolling basis. Application fee: $55. Electronic applications accepted. *Financial support:* In 2007–08, 7 teaching assistantships were awarded; career-related internships or fieldwork also available. Financial award applicants required to submit FAFSA. *Faculty research:* Multicultural and cross-cultural counseling and training, AIDS counseling. Total annual research expenditures: $626,857. *Unit head:* Carol Robinson-Zañartu, Chair, 619-594-7725, Fax: 619-594-7025, E-mail: crobinsn@mail.sdsu.edu.

Seattle University, College of Education, Program in Counseling and School Psychology, Seattle, WA 98122-1090. Offers MA, Certificate, Ed S. *Accreditation:* NCATE. Part-time and evening/weekend programs available. *Degree requirements:* For master's, comprehensive exam. *Entrance requirements:* For master's, interview; GRE, MAT, or minimum GPA of 3.0; related work experience. Additional exam requirements/recommendations for international students: Required—TOEFL.

Seton Hall University, College of Education and Human Services, Department of Professional Psychology and Family Therapy, Program in School Psychology, South Orange, NJ 07079-2697. Offers Ed S. *Faculty:* 2 full-time (1 woman). *Students:* 7 full-time (all women), 36 part-time (34 women); includes 3 minority (2 African Americans, 1 Hispanic American). Average age 27. 10 applicants, 70% accepted, 0 enrolled. In 2007, 9 degrees awarded. *Degree requirements:* For Ed S, comprehensive exam, thesis, internship. *Entrance requirements:* For degree, GRE or MAT, interview. *Application deadline:* Applications are processed on a rolling basis. Application fee: $50. *Financial support:* In 2007–08, 1 research assistantship with full tuition reimbursement (averaging $4,500 per year) was awarded. Financial award application deadline: 2/1. *Faculty research:* Family systems, ethical behavior, childhood depression. *Unit head:* Dr. Thomas Masserelli, Director, 973-275-2503. *Application contact:* Information Contact, 973-761-9451.

Southeast Missouri State University, School of Graduate Studies, Department of Educational Leadership and Counseling, Program in Guidance and Counseling, Cape Girardeau, MO 63701-4799. Offers community counseling (MA); counseling education (Ed S); school counseling (MA), including elementary counseling, secondary counseling. *Accreditation:* ACA; NCATE. Part-time and evening/weekend programs available. *Faculty:* 6 full-time (3 women). *Students:* 21 full-time (18 women), 50 part-time (45 women); includes 4 minority (3 African Americans, 1 Asian American or Pacific Islander), 1 international. Average age 33. 16 applicants, 63% accepted. In 2007, 16 master's, 4 other advanced degrees awarded. *Degree requirements:* For master's, thesis or alternative. *Entrance requirements:* For master's, GRE General Test, MAT, minimum GPA of 3.0; for Ed S, GRE General Test or MAT, minimum graduate GPA of 3.5. Additional exam requirements/recommendations for international students: Required—TOEFL (minimum score 550 paper-based; 213 computer-based). *Application deadline:* For fall admission, 8/1 for domestic students, 6/1 for international students; for spring admission, 11/21 for domestic students, 10/1 for international students. Applications are processed on a rolling basis. Application fee: $25 ($100 for international students). Electronic applications accepted. *Expenses:* Tuition, state resident: part-time $224 per credit hour. Tuition, nonresident: part-time $395 per credit hour. Tuition and fees vary according to course load and program. *Financial support:* In 2007–08, 29 students received support, including 13 research assistantships with full tuition reimbursements available (averaging $7,600 per year), 1 teaching assistantship (averaging $7,600 per year); career-related internships or fieldwork and unspecified assistantships also available. Financial award applicants required to submit FAFSA. *Application contact:* Marsha L. Arant, Senior Administrative Assistant, Office of Graduate Studies, 573-651-2192, Fax: 573-651-2001, E-mail: marant@semo.edu.

Southern Connecticut State University, School of Graduate Studies, School of Education, Department of Counseling and School Psychology, New Haven, CT 06515-1355. Offers community counseling (MS); counseling (Diploma); school counseling (MS); school psychology (MS, Diploma). *Accreditation:* ACA (one or more programs are accredited); NCATE. *Faculty:* 8 full-time, 10 part-time/adjunct. *Students:* 87 full-time (74 women), 77 part-time (67 women); includes 24 minority (18 African Americans, 6 Hispanic Americans), 3 international. 179 applicants, 27% accepted, 45 enrolled. In 2007, 44 master's, 12 other advanced degrees awarded. *Degree requirements:* For master's, comprehensive exam. *Entrance requirements:* For master's, interview, previous course work in behavioral sciences, minimum QPA of 2.7. *Application deadline:* For fall admission, 1/15 for domestic students; for spring admission, 10/15 for domestic students. Application fee: $50. Electronic applications accepted. *Financial support:* Teaching assistantships, career-related internships or fieldwork available. Financial award application deadline: 4/15; financial award applicants required to submit FAFSA. *Unit head:* Dr. Norris Haynes, Chairperson, 203-392-5912, E-mail: haynesn1@southernct.edu. *Application contact:* Dr. Uchenna Nwachuku, Graduate Coordinator, Community Counseling Program, 203-392-5914, E-mail: nwachuku@southernct.edu.

Southern Illinois University Edwardsville, Graduate Studies and Research, School of Education, Department of Psychology, Program in School Psychology, Edwardsville, IL 62026-0001. Offers SD. *Accreditation:* NCATE. Part-time programs available. *Students:* Average age 33. 9 applicants, 0% accepted. In 2007, 8 degrees awarded. *Degree requirements:* For SD, thesis. *Application deadline:* For fall admission, 3/1 for domestic and international students. Applications are processed on a rolling basis. Application fee: $30. Electronic applications accepted. *Financial support:* Fellowships, research assistantships, teaching assistantships, career-related internships or fieldwork, Federal Work-Study, institutionally sponsored loans, traineeships, and unspecified assistantships available. Financial award application deadline: 3/1; financial award applicants required to submit FAFSA. *Unit head:* Dr. Lynn Bartels, Director, 618-650-2202, E-mail: lbartel@siue.edu. *Application contact:* Dr. Lynn Bartels, Director, 618-650-2202, E-mail: lbartel@siue.edu.

Southwestern Oklahoma State University, College of Professional and Graduate Studies, School of Behavioral Sciences and Education, Specialization in School Psychology, Weatherford, OK 73096-3098. Offers MS.

State University of New York at Oswego, Graduate Studies, School of Education, Department of Counseling and Psychological Services, Program in School Psychology, Oswego, NY 13126. Offers MS, CAS, MS/CAS. *Faculty:* 6 full-time, 8 part-time/adjunct. *Students:* 26 full-time (22 women), 14 part-time (11 women); includes 2 minority (both African Americans) Average age 31. 46 applicants, 52% accepted. In 2007, 15 master's, 1 other advanced degree awarded. *Degree requirements:* For master's, comprehensive exam, fieldwork; for CAS, thesis, fieldwork. *Entrance requirements:* For master's, GRE General Test, interview, minimum GPA of 3.0; for CAS, GRE General Test, interview, MA or MS, minimum GPA of 3.0. Additional exam requirements/recommendations for international students: Required—TOEFL (minimum score 560 paper-based; 220 computer-based). *Application deadline:* For fall admission, 2/1 for domestic students. Application fee: $50. *Expenses:* Tuition, state resident: full-time $6,900; part-time $288 per credit. Tuition, nonresident: full-time $10,920; part-time $455 per credit. Required fees: $607; $32 per credit. $225 per term. Tuition and fees vary according to degree level. *Financial support:* In 2007–08, 2 students received support, including 2 fellowships with full tuition reimbursements available (averaging $5,100 per year); teaching assistantships, career-related internships or fieldwork, Federal Work-Study, institutionally sponsored loans, scholarships/grants, health care benefits, and unspecified assistantships also available. Support available to part-time students. Financial award application deadline: 4/1; financial award applicants required to submit FAFSA. *Faculty research:* Psychological applications in education and human services, evaluation of standard tests for admissions criteria. *Unit head:* Thomas Cushman, Coordinator, 315-312-3282.

State University of New York at Plattsburgh, Faculty of Arts and Science, Department of Psychology, Plattsburgh, NY 12901-2681. Offers school psychology (MA, CAS). Part-time programs available. *Faculty:* 2 full-time (1 woman), 3 part-time/adjunct (2 women). *Students:* 18 full-time (13 women), 14 part-time (10 women); includes 4 minority (1 African American, 3 Hispanic Americans). Average age 26. 22 applicants, 86% accepted, 11 enrolled. In 2007, 4 master's, 4 other advanced degrees awarded. *Degree requirements:* For master's, thesis, internship. *Entrance requirements:* For master's, GRE General Test, minimum GPA of 3.0. Additional exam requirements/recommendations for international students: Required—TOEFL (minimum score 550 paper-based). *Application deadline:* For fall admission, 3/1 priority date for domestic students. Applications are processed on a rolling basis. Application fee: $50. *Expenses:* Tuition, state resident: full-time $6,900; part-time $288 per credit hour. Tuition, nonresident: full-time $10,920; part-time $455 per credit hour. Required fees: $1,036. *Financial support:* Federal Work-Study available. Support available to part-time students. Financial award application deadline: 4/15; financial award applicants required to submit FAFSA. *Faculty research:* Alzheimer's disease, adolescent behavior, intellectual assessment, learning disabilities, reading skill acquisition. *Unit head:* Dr. Jeanne Ryan, Chair, 518-564-3380. *Application contact:* Dr. Ronald Dumont, Chair, Graduate Admissions Committee, 518-564-2000.

Stephen F. Austin State University, Graduate School, College of Education, Department of Human Services, Nacogdoches, TX 75962. Offers counseling (MA); school psychology (MA); special education (M Ed); speech pathology (MS). *Accreditation:* ACA (one or more programs are accredited); ASHA (one or more programs are accredited); CORE; NCATE. *Degree requirements:* For master's, comprehensive exam, thesis (for some programs). *Entrance requirements:* For master's, GRE General Test, minimum GPA of 2.8. Additional exam requirements/recommendations for international students: Required—TOEFL.

Syracuse University, Graduate School, College of Arts and Sciences, Department of Psychology, Program in School Psychology, Syracuse, NY 13244. Offers PhD. *Accreditation:* APA. *Students:* 16 full-time (14 women), 1 (woman) part-time; includes 1 minority (Hispanic American), 2 international. 29 applicants, 14% accepted, 3 enrolled. In 2007, 5 degrees awarded. *Degree requirements:* For doctorate, thesis/dissertation. *Entrance requirements:* For doctorate, GRE General Test, GRE Subject Test. Additional exam requirements/recommendations for international students: Required—TOEFL. *Application deadline:* For fall admission, 1/1 for domestic students. Application fee: $75. Electronic applications accepted. *Expenses:* Tuition: Full-time $18,216; part-time $1,012 per credit. Required fees: $980. Tuition and fees vary according to program. *Financial support:* Fellowships with full tuition reimbursements, research assistantships with full tuition reimbursements, teaching assistantships with full tuition reimbursements available. *Unit head:* Dr. Brian Martens, Graduate Director, 315-443-3835, Fax: 315-443-4085, E-mail: bkmarten@syr.edu. *Application contact:* Sue Bova, Information Contact, 315-443-1050, E-mail: skbova@syr.edu.

Syracuse University, Graduate School, School of Education, Counseling and Human Services Program, Program in School Counseling, Syracuse, NY 13244. Offers MS, CAS. *Students:* 18 full-time (15 women), 11 part-time (9 women); includes 1 African American, 1 American Indian/Alaska Native, 1 Asian American or Pacific Islander. 33 applicants, 52% accepted, 7 enrolled. In 2007, 24 degrees awarded. *Entrance requirements:* For master's, GRE General Test or MAT, interview. Additional exam requirements/recommendations for international students: Required—TOEFL. *Application deadline:* For fall admission, 2/1 for domestic students; for spring admission, 10/15 for domestic students. Application fee: $75. *Expenses:* Tuition: Full-time $18,216; part-time $1,012 per credit. Required fees: $980. Tuition and fees vary according to program. *Unit head:* Dr. Janine Bernard, Chair, 315-443-5266, Fax: 315-443-5732, E-mail: bernard@syr.edu. *Application contact:* Traci Washburn, Graduate Recruiter, School of Education, 315-443-2505, E-mail: e-gradrcrt@syr.edu.

Tarleton State University, College of Graduate Studies, College of Education, Department of Psychology and Counseling, Stephenville, TX 76402. Offers counseling and psychology (M Ed), including counseling, counseling psychology, educational psychology; educational administration (M Ed); secondary education (Certificate); special education (Certificate). Part-time and evening/weekend programs available. Postbaccalaureate distance learning degree programs offered (minimal on-campus study). *Faculty:* 14 full-time (6 women), 7 part-time/adjunct (3 women). *Students:* 52 full-time (43 women), 223 part-time (199 women); includes 64 minority (49 African Americans, 1 American Indian/Alaska Native, 2 Asian Americans or Pacific Islanders, 12 Hispanic Americans). Average age 37. 127 applicants, 86% accepted, 71 enrolled. In 2007, 53 degrees awarded. *Degree requirements:* For master's, comprehensive exam, thesis optional. *Entrance requirements:* For master's, GRE General Test, minimum GPA of 3.0. Additional exam requirements/recommendations for international students: Required—TOEFL (minimum score 550 paper-based; 213 computer-based). *Application deadline:* For fall admission, 8/5 priority date for domestic students; for spring admission, 12/1 for domestic students. Applications are processed on a rolling basis. Application fee: $25 ($125 for international students). Electronic applications accepted. *Expenses:* Tuition, state resident: full-time $2,520; part-time $140 per credit hour. Tuition, nonresident: full-time $7,344; part-time $408 per credit hour. Required fees: $948; $39 per credit hour. *Financial support:* Research assistantships, teaching assistantships, career-related internships or fieldwork, Federal Work-Study, institutionally sponsored loans, and tuition waivers (partial) available. Support available to part-time students. Financial award application deadline: 5/1; financial award applicants required to submit FAFSA. *Unit head:* Dr. Robert Newby, Head, 254-968-9945, Fax: 254-968-1991, E-mail: newby@tarleton.edu.

Teachers College, Columbia University, Graduate Faculty of Education, Department of Health and Behavioral Studies, Program in Applied Educational Psychology–School Psychology, New York, NY 10027-6696. Offers Ed M, MA, Ed D, PhD. *Accreditation:* APA (one or more programs are accredited). *Faculty:* 2 full-time (1 woman), 3 part-time/adjunct. *Students:* 53 full-time (50 women), 36 part-time (31 women); includes 16 minority (5 African Americans, 8 Asian Americans or Pacific Islanders, 3 Hispanic Americans), 1 international. Average age 31. 201 applicants, 28% accepted, 26 enrolled. In 2007, 27 master's, 8 doctorates awarded. *Degree requirements:* For master's, integrative paper; for doctorate, thesis/dissertation, integrative project. *Entrance requirements:* For doctorate, GRE General Test. *Application deadline:* For fall admission, 5/15 for domestic students. Application fee: $70. *Financial support:* Fellowships, research assistantships, career-related internships or fieldwork, Federal Work-Study, institutionally sponsored loans, and tuition waivers (full and partial) available. Support available to part-time students. Financial award application deadline: 2/1. *Faculty research:* Psychoeducational assessment, observation and concept acquisition in young children, reading, mathematical thinking, memory. *Application contact:* Peter Shon, Assistant Director of Admission, 212-678-3305, Fax: 212-678-4171, E-mail: shon@exchange.tc.columbia.edu.

Temple University, Graduate School, College of Education, Department of Psychological Studies in Education, Program in School Psychology, Philadelphia, PA 19122-6096. Offers Ed M, PhD. *Accreditation:* APA (one or more programs are accredited). Part-time and evening/weekend programs available. Terminal master's awarded for partial completion of doctoral program. *Degree requirements:* For master's, thesis or alternative; for doctorate, thesis/dissertation. *Entrance requirements:* For master's and doctorate, GRE General Test, GRE Subject Test, minimum GPA of 3.0. Additional exam requirements/recommendations for international students: Required—TOEFL (minimum score 550 paper-based; 213 computer-based; 79 iBT). Electronic applications accepted.

Tennessee State University, The School of Graduate Studies and Research, College of Education, Department of Psychology, Nashville, TN 37209-1561. Offers counseling and guidance (MS), including counseling, elementary school counseling, organizational counseling, secondary school counseling; counseling psychology (PhD); psychology (MS, PhD); school psychology (MS, PhD). *Accreditation:* APA. *Faculty:* 15 full-time (9 women), 1 (woman) part-time/adjunct. *Students:* 91 full-time (74 women), 114 part-time (91 women); includes 141 minority (136 African Americans, 1 American Indian/Alaska Native, 3 Asian Americans or Pacific Islanders, 1 Hispanic American), 2 international. Average age 33. 205 applicants, 45% accepted, 44 enrolled. In 2007, 17 master's, 10 doctorates awarded. *Degree requirements:* For doctorate, thesis/dissertation (for some programs). *Entrance requirements:* For master's, GRE General Test or MAT; for doctorate, GRE General Test or MAT, minimum GPA of 3.25, work experience. Application fee: $25. *Expenses:* Tuition, state resident: full-time $6,271; part-time $490 per hour. Tuition, nonresident: full-time $16,550; part-time $936 per hour. *Unit head:* Dr. Linda Guthrie, Head, 615-963-2920, Fax: 615-963-5140, E-mail: lguthrie@tnstate.edu.

Texas A&M University, College of Education and Human Development, Department of Educational Psychology, College Station, TX 77843. Offers counseling psychology (PhD); educational psychology (PhD); educational technology (M Ed); gifted and talented education (M Ed, MS); Hispanic bilingual education (M Ed, PhD); human learning and development (MS); intelligence, creativity, and giftedness (PhD); learning, development, and instruction (PhD); research, measurement and statistics (MS); research, measurement, and statistics (PhD); school counseling (M Ed); school psychology (PhD); special education (M Ed, PhD). *Accreditation:* APA (one or more programs are accredited); NCATE. Part-time and evening/weekend programs available. Postbaccalaureate distance learning degree programs offered (no on-campus study). *Faculty:* 43. *Students:* 140 full-time (109 women), 153 part-time (129 women); includes 77 minority (27 African Americans, 1 American Indian/Alaska Native, 7 Asian Americans or Pacific Islanders, 42 Hispanic Americans), 41 international. 222 applicants, 61% accepted, 90 enrolled. In 2007, 42 master's, 24 doctorates awarded. *Median time to degree:* Of those who began their doctoral program in fall 1999, 89% received their degree in 8 years or less. *Degree requirements:* For master's, thesis optional; for doctorate, thesis/dissertation. *Entrance requirements:* For master's and doctorate, GRE General Test. Additional exam requirements/recommendations for international students: Required—TOEFL. Application fee: $50 ($75 for international students). Electronic applications accepted. *Expenses:* Tuition, state resident: full-time $6,129. Tuition, nonresident: full-time $11,689. Tuition and fees vary according to course load. *Financial support:* In 2007–08, fellowships (averaging $12,000 per year), research assistantships (averaging $9,000 per year), teaching assistantships (averaging $9,000 per year) were awarded; career-related internships or fieldwork, institutionally sponsored loans, scholarships/grants, and unspecified assistantships also available. Financial award applicants required to submit FAFSA. *Unit head:* Dr. Michael R. Benz, Head, 979-845-1394, Fax: 979-862-1256, E-mail: mbanz@tamu.edu. *Application contact:* Carol A. Wagner, Director of Advising, 979-845-1833, Fax: 979-862-1256, E-mail: c-wagner@tamu.edu.

Texas State University–San Marcos, Graduate School, College of Education, Department of Educational Administration and Psychological Services, Program in School Psychology, San Marcos, TX 78666. Offers MA. Part-time programs available. *Faculty:* 2 full-time (both women), 7 part-time/adjunct (6 women). *Students:* 35 full-time (28 women), 20 part-time (18 women); includes 22 minority (4 African Americans, 1 Asian American or Pacific Islander, 17 Hispanic Americans), 1 international. Average age 28. 30 applicants, 57% accepted, 11 enrolled. In 2007, 24 degrees awarded. *Degree requirements:* For master's, comprehensive exam. *Entrance requirements:* For master's, GRE General Test, interview, minimum GPA of 2.75 in last 60 hours of course work. Additional exam requirements/recommendations for international students: Required—TOEFL (minimum score 550 paper-based; 213 computer-based). *Application deadline:* For fall admission, 2/15 for domestic and international students; for spring admission, 10/15 for domestic students, 10/1 for international students. Applications are processed on a rolling basis. Application fee: $40 ($90 for international students). Electronic applications accepted. *Expenses:* Tuition, state resident: full-time $3,780; part-time $210 per credit hour. Tuition, nonresident: full-time $8,784; part-time $488 per credit hour. Required fees: $493 per semester. Full-time tuition and fees vary according to course load. *Financial support:* In 2007–08, 39 students received support, including 4 research assistantships (averaging $3,880 per year), 10 teaching assistantships (averaging $2,791 per year); career-related internships or fieldwork, Federal Work-Study, and institutionally sponsored loans also available. Support available to part-time students. Financial award application deadline: 4/1; financial award applicants required to submit FAFSA. *Unit head:* Dr. Cynthia Plotts, Graduate Advisor, 512-245-3083, Fax: 512-245-8872, E-mail: cp11@txstate.edu.

Texas Woman's University, Graduate School, College of Arts and Sciences, Department of Psychology and Philosophy, Denton, TX 76201. Offers counseling psychology (MA, PhD); school psychology (PhD, SSP). *Accreditation:* APA (one or more programs are accredited). *Students:* 74 full-time (66 women), 50 part-time (46 women); includes 22 minority (7 African Americans, 7 Asian Americans or Pacific Islanders, 8 Hispanic Americans), 3 international. Average age 29. In 2007, 18 master's, 5 doctorates awarded. Terminal master's awarded for partial completion of doctoral program. *Median time to degree:* Of those who began their doctoral program in fall 1999, 25% received their degree in 8 years or less. *Degree requirements:* For master's, thesis; for doctorate, comprehensive exam, thesis/dissertation, internship, residency. *Entrance requirements:* For master's, 2 letters of reference, resumé, interview; for doctorate, 3 letters of reference; resumé; interview; minimum overall GPA of 3.0, 3.5 for all undergraduate psychology courses; autobiographical statement; BS/BA in psychology or 18 hours of required psychology classes. Additional exam requirements/recommendations for international students: Required—TOEFL (minimum score 550 paper-based; 213 computer-based; 79 iBT). *Application deadline:* For fall admission, 12/15 for domestic and international students. Applications are processed on a rolling basis. Application fee: $30 ($50 for international students). Electronic applications accepted. *Expenses:* Tuition, state resident: full-time $3,294; part-time $183 per credit. Tuition, nonresident: full-time $8,298; part-time $461 per credit. Required fees: $985; $55 per credit. Tuition and fees vary according to degree level. *Financial support:* In 2007–08, 1 teaching assistantship (averaging $10,746 per year) was awarded; career-related internships or fieldwork, Federal Work-Study, institutionally sponsored loans, scholarships/grants,

School Psychology

Texas Woman's University (continued)

traineeships, health care benefits, and unspecified assistantships also available. Support available to part-time students. Financial award application deadline: 3/1; financial award applicants required to submit FAFSA. *Faculty research:* Women's anger, pre-school assessments, body image dysfunction, traumatic stress, classical ethics. *Unit head:* Dr. Dan Miller, Chair, 940-898-2303, Fax: 940-898-2301, E-mail: dmiller@twu.edu. *Application contact:* Samuel Wheeler, Assistant Director of Admissions, 940-898-3188, Fax: 940-898-3081, E-mail: wheelersr@twu.edu.

Towson University, College of Graduate Studies and Research, Program in School Psychology, Towson, MD 21252-0001. Offers CAS. Part-time and evening/weekend programs available. *Faculty:* 6 full-time (4 women). *Students:* Average age 26. In 2007, 15 CASs awarded. *Application deadline:* For fall admission, 1/15 for domestic students. Application fee: $50. Electronic applications accepted. *Expenses:* Tuition, state resident: part-time $286 per credit. Tuition, nonresident: part-time $600 per credit. Required fees: $75 per credit. *Financial support:* In 2007–08, 5 students received support, including 5 fellowships with full tuition reimbursements available (averaging $4,000 per year); Federal Work-Study and unspecified assistantships also available. Financial award application deadline: 4/1; financial award applicants required to submit FAFSA. *Faculty research:* Cognitive behavior, issues affecting the aging, relaxation hypnosis and imagery, lesbian and gay issues. *Unit head:* Dr. Susan Bartels, Graduate Program Director, 410-704-3070, Fax: 410-704-3800, E-mail: sbartels@towson.edu. *Application contact:* 410-704-2501, Fax: 410-704-4675, E-mail: grads@towson.edu.

Trinity University, Department of Education, Program in School Psychology, San Antonio, TX 78212-7200. Offers MA. *Accreditation:* NCATE. *Faculty:* 10 full-time (8 women), 14 part-time/adjunct (8 women). *Students:* 23 full-time (20 women), 11 part-time (7 women); includes 11 minority (1 Asian American or Pacific Islander, 10 Hispanic Americans). Average age 30. In 2007, 13 degrees awarded. *Entrance requirements:* For master's, GRE General Test, minimum GPA of 3.0, interview. *Application deadline:* For fall admission, 4/1 for domestic students. Applications are processed on a rolling basis. Application fee: $30. *Expenses:* Tuition: Full-time $24,864; part-time $1,036 per credit. One-time fee: $18 full-time. *Financial support:* Fellowships, research assistantships, career-related internships or fieldwork, Federal Work-Study, and institutionally sponsored loans available. Support available to part-time students. Financial award application deadline: 4/1. *Unit head:* Dr. Terry Robertson, Director, 210-999-7595, Fax: 210-999-7592, E-mail: terry.robertson@trinity.edu.

Troy University, Graduate School, College of Education, Program in Counseling and Psychology, Troy, AL 36082. Offers clinical mental health (MS); community counseling (MS); school psychology (MS); student affairs counseling (MS). *Accreditation:* ACA; CORE; NCATE. Part-time and evening/weekend programs available. *Students:* 355 full-time (303 women), 555 part-time (461 women); includes 598 minority (550 African Americans, 20 American Indian/Alaska Native, 6 Asian Americans or Pacific Islanders, 22 Hispanic Americans). Average age 32. In 2007, 328 degrees awarded. *Degree requirements:* For master's, comprehensive exam, thesis. *Entrance requirements:* For master's, MAT, minimum GPA of 2.5. Additional exam requirements/recommendations for international students: Required—TOEFL (minimum score 523 paper-based; 200 computer-based). *Application deadline:* Applications are processed on a rolling basis. Application fee: $50. Electronic applications accepted. *Unit head:* Dr. Andrew Creamer, Chair, 334-670-3350, Fax: 334-670-32961, E-mail: drcreamer@troy.edu. *Application contact:* Brenda K. Campbell, Director of Graduate Admissions, 334-670-3178, Fax: 334-670-3733, E-mail: bcamp@troy.edu.

Tufts University, Graduate School of Arts and Sciences, Department of Education, Program in School Psychology, Medford, MA 02155. Offers MA, CAGS. *Faculty:* 13 full-time, 9 part-time/adjunct. *Students:* 50 (43 women); includes 7 minority (2 African Americans, 1 American Indian/Alaska Native, 3 Asian Americans or Pacific Islanders, 1 Hispanic American) 1 international. 96 applicants, 34% accepted, 18 enrolled. In 2007, 3 master's, 16 other advanced degrees awarded. *Entrance requirements:* For master's, GRE General Test. Additional exam requirements/recommendations for international students: Required—TOEFL (minimum score 550 paper-based; 213 computer-based; 80 iBT). *Application deadline:* For fall admission, 2/1 for domestic students, 12/30 for international students. Applications are processed on a rolling basis. Application fee: $70. Electronic applications accepted. *Expenses:* Tuition: Full-time $35,052. *Financial support:* Federal Work-Study, scholarships/grants, and tuition waivers (full and partial) available. Financial award application deadline: 2/1.

Universidad del Turabo, Graduate Programs, School of Social Sciences and Humanities, Programs in Psychology, Program in School Psychology, Gurabo, PR 00778-3030. Offers MSS. *Students:* 23 full-time (19 women); all minorities (all Hispanic Americans) Average age 28. In 2007, 1 degree awarded. *Expenses:* Tuition: Full-time $5,560.

University at Albany, State University of New York, School of Education, Department of Educational and Counseling Psychology, Albany, NY 12222-0001. Offers counseling psychology (MS, PhD, CAS); educational psychology (Ed D); educational psychology and statistics (MS); measurements and evaluation (Ed D); rehabilitation counseling (MS), including counseling psychology; school counselor (CAS); school psychology (Psy D, CAS); special education (MS); statistics and research design (Ed D). *Accreditation:* APA (one or more programs are accredited). Evening/weekend programs available. *Students:* 121 full-time (101 women), 79 part-time (61 women). Average age 28. In 2007, 86 master's, 13 doctorates, 13 other advanced degrees awarded. *Degree requirements:* For doctorate, thesis/dissertation. *Entrance requirements:* For doctorate, GRE General Test. Additional exam requirements/recommendations for international students: Required—TOEFL (minimum score 550 paper-based; 213 computer-based). Application fee: $75. Electronic applications accepted. *Expenses:* Tuition, state resident: part-time $576 per credit. Tuition, nonresident: part-time $910 per credit. Tuition and fees vary according to program. *Financial support:* Fellowships, career-related internships or fieldwork available. *Unit head:* Kevin Quinn, Chair, 518-442-5050.

University at Buffalo, the State University of New York, Graduate School, Graduate School of Education, Department of Counseling, School, and Educational Psychology, Buffalo, NY 14260. Offers counseling/school psychology (PhD); counselor education (PhD); educational psychology (MA, PhD); mental health counseling (MS); rehabilitation counseling (MS); school counseling (Ed M, Certificate); school psychology (MA). *Accreditation:* CORE (one or more programs are accredited). *Degree requirements:* For master's, comprehensive exam (for some programs), thesis (for some programs); for doctorate, comprehensive exam, thesis/dissertation. *Entrance requirements:* For master's and doctorate, GRE General Test, interview, letters of reference. Additional exam requirements/recommendations for international students: Required—TOEFL. Electronic applications accepted. *Faculty research:* Multicultural counseling, class size effects, quality of life, eating disorders, outcome assessment.

The University of Akron, Graduate School, College of Education, Department of Counseling, Program in Classroom Guidance for Teachers, Akron, OH 44325. Offers MA, MS. *Accreditation:* NCATE. *Students:* Average age 42. 1 applicant, 0% accepted. In 2007, 4 degrees awarded. *Degree requirements:* For master's, comprehensive exam. *Entrance requirements:* For master's, minimum GPA of 2.75, interview, letters of recommendation, criminal background check, resumé, supplemental form. Additional exam requirements/recommendations for international students: Required—TOEFL (minimum score 550 paper-based; 213 computer-based; 79 iBT). *Application deadline:* For fall admission, 3/15 for domestic and international students; for spring admission, 10/1 for domestic and international students. Applications are processed on a rolling basis. Application fee: $30 ($40 for international students). Electronic applications accepted. *Expenses:* Tuition, state resident: full-time $6,164; part-time $342 per credit. Tuition, nonresident: full-time $10,575; part-time $588 per credit. Required fees: $806; $43 per credit. $12 per term. Tuition and fees vary according to course load, degree level and program. *Unit head:* Dr. Cynthia Reynolds, Coordinator, 330-972-6748, E-mail: creynol@uakron.edu.

University of Alberta, Faculty of Graduate Studies and Research, Department of Educational Psychology, Edmonton, AB T6G 2E1, Canada. Offers counseling psychology (M Ed, PhD); educational psychology (M Ed, PhD); instructional technology (M Ed); school counseling (M Ed); school psychology (M Ed, PhD); special education (M Ed, PhD); special education-deafness studies (M Ed); teaching English as a second language (M Ed). Part-time programs available. *Degree requirements:* For master's, thesis optional; for doctorate, comprehensive exam, thesis/dissertation. *Entrance requirements:* For master's and doctorate, minimum GPA of 3.0. Additional exam requirements/recommendations for international students: Required—TOEFL. *Faculty research:* Human learning, development and assessment.

The University of British Columbia, Faculty of Graduate Studies, Faculty of Education, Department of Educational and Counseling Psychology, and Special Education, Vancouver, BC V6T 1Z1, Canada. Offers counseling psychology (M Ed, MA, PhD); development, learning and culture (PhD); guidance studies (Diploma); human development, learning and culture (M Ed, MA); measurement and evaluation and research methodology (M Ed); measurement, evaluation and research methodology (MA); measurement, evaluation, and research methodology (PhD); school psychology (M Ed, MA, PhD); special education (M Ed, MA, PhD, Diploma). Part-time programs available. *Faculty:* 37 full-time (25 women). *Students:* 293 full-time (237 women), 102 part-time (86 women). 269 applicants, 41% accepted, 108 enrolled. In 2007, 91 master's, 17 doctorates awarded. *Median time to degree:* Of those who began their doctoral program in fall 1999, 95% received their degree in 8 years or less. *Degree requirements:* For master's, thesis (for some programs); for doctorate, comprehensive exam, thesis/dissertation. *Entrance requirements:* For master's, GRE General Test (counseling psychology MA); for doctorate, GRE General Test. Additional exam requirements/recommendations for international students: Required—TOEFL. *Application deadline:* For fall admission, 12/1 for domestic and international students. Application fee: $90 Canadian dollars ($150 Canadian dollars for international students). Electronic applications accepted. *Financial support:* In 2007–08, 14 fellowships (averaging $35,000 per year), 50 research assistantships (averaging $12,000 per year), 40 teaching assistantships (averaging $5,000 per year) were awarded; career-related internships or fieldwork, Federal Work-Study, institutionally sponsored loans, scholarships/grants, health care benefits, tuition waivers (full and partial), and unspecified assistantships also available. *Faculty research:* Women, family, social problems, career transition, stress and coping problems. *Unit head:* Dr. Shelley Hymel, Head, 604-822-6022, Fax: 604-822-3302, E-mail: shelley.hymel@ubc.ca. *Application contact:* Karen Yan, Graduate Program Assistant, 604-822-6371, Fax: 604-822-3302, E-mail: karen.yan@ubc.ca.

University of Calgary, Faculty of Graduate Studies, Faculty of Education, Division of Applied Psychology, Calgary, AB T2N 1N4, Canada. Offers counseling psychology (M Ed, M Sc, PhD); human development and learning (M Ed, M Sc, PhD); school psychology (M Ed, M Sc, PhD); special education (M Ed, M Sc, PhD). Part-time programs available. *Degree requirements:* For master's, thesis (for some programs), final oral exam; for doctorate, thesis/dissertation, candidacy exam, final oral exam. *Entrance requirements:* For master's, minimum GPA of 3.0, 3 letters of reference; for doctorate, minimum GPA of 3.5, 3 letters of reference. *Faculty research:* Counselor education, family life studies, learning and cognition.

University of California, Berkeley, Graduate Division, School of Education, Division of Cognition and Development, Program in School Psychology, Berkeley, CA 94720-1500. Offers Ph D/Credential, PhD/MA. *Accreditation:* APA. *Application deadline:* For fall admission, 12/1 for domestic students. Application fee: $70 ($90 for international students). Electronic applications accepted. *Financial support:* Fellowships, research assistantships, teaching assistantships, unspecified assistantships available. *Application contact:* Admissions Office, 510-642-0841, Fax: 510-642-4808, E-mail: gse_info@uclink.berkeley.edu.

University of California, Santa Barbara, Graduate Division, Gevirtz Graduate School of Education, Santa Barbara, CA 93106. Offers counseling, clinical and school psychology (PhD), including clinical psychology, counseling psychology; education (MA, PhD), including child and adolescent development, cultural perspectives and comparative education, educational leadership and organizations, research methodology, special education disabilities and risk studies (MA), special education, disabilities and risk studies (PhD), teaching and learning; educational leadership (Ed D); school psychology (M Ed); MA/PhD. *Accreditation:* APA (one or more programs are accredited). Postbaccalaureate distance learning degree programs offered (minimal on-campus study). *Faculty:* 36 full-time (18 women), 7 part-time/adjunct (3 women). *Students:* 400 full-time (308 women); includes 119 minority (11 African Americans, 6 American Indian/Alaska Native, 46 Asian Americans or Pacific Islanders, 56 Hispanic Americans), 18 international. Average age 31. 721 applicants, 41% accepted, 189 enrolled. In 2007, 157 master's, 35 doctorates awarded. Terminal master's awarded for partial completion of doctoral program. *Median time to degree:* Of those who began their doctoral program in fall 1999, 60% received their degree in 8 years or less. *Degree requirements:* For master's, comprehensive exam (for some programs), thesis (for some programs); for doctorate, comprehensive exam (for some programs), thesis/dissertation, qualifying exam. *Entrance requirements:* For master's, GRE, MAT (M Ed); for doctorate, GRE. Additional exam requirements/recommendations for international students: Required—TOEFL (minimum score 550 paper-based; 213 computer-based; 80 iBT). *Application deadline:* For fall admission, 12/15 priority date for domestic and international students. Application fee: $60. Electronic applications accepted. *Expenses:* Tuition, nonresident: full-time $14,888. Required fees: $10,108. *Financial support:* In 2007–08, 292 students received support, including 170 fellowships with full and partial tuition reimbursements available (averaging $5,200 per year), 80 research assistantships with full and partial tuition reimbursements available, 124 teaching assistantships with full and partial tuition reimbursements available; career-related internships or fieldwork, Federal Work-Study, institutionally sponsored loans, scholarships/grants, traineeships, health care benefits, and unspecified assistantships also available. Financial award applicants required to submit FAFSA. *Faculty research:* Professional development, early childhood development, school violence, literacy, science/math initiative. Total annual research expenditures: $4.2 million. *Unit head:* Carol Dixon, Associate Dean of Students, 805-893-2137, Fax: 805-893-7264, E-mail: sao@education.ucsb.edu. *Application contact:* Katie Tucciarone, Student Affairs Officer, 805-893-2137, Fax: 805-893-2588, E-mail: katiet@education.ucsb.edu.

University of Central Arkansas, Graduate School, College of Health and Behavioral Sciences, Department of Counseling and Psychology, Program in School Psychology, Conway, AR 72035-0001. Offers MS, PhD. *Accreditation:* APA; NCATE. *Students:* 23 full-time (22 women), 12 part-time (all women); includes 4 minority (2 African Americans, 2 American Indian/Alaska Native), 2 international. 11 applicants, 91% accepted, 10 enrolled. In 2007, 11 degrees awarded. Terminal master's awarded for partial completion of doctoral program. *Degree requirements:* For master's, comprehensive exam, thesis optional; for doctorate, comprehensive exam, thesis/dissertation. *Entrance requirements:* For master's, GRE General Test, minimum GPA of 2.7; for doctorate, GRE General Test. Additional exam requirements/recommendations for international students: Required—TOEFL (minimum score 550 paper-based; 213 computer-based). *Application deadline:* For fall admission, 3/1 priority date for domestic and international students; for spring admission, 10/1 for domestic and international students. Applications are processed on a rolling basis. Application fee: $25 ($50 for international students). *Expenses:* Tuition, state resident: full-time $4,513; part-time $240 per credit. Tuition, nonresident: full-time $8,805; part-time $440 per credit. International tuition: $9,700 full-time. Required fees: $100 per term. *Financial support:* Career-related internships or fieldwork, Federal Work-Study, scholarships/grants, tuition waivers (partial), and unspecified assistantships available. Financial award application deadline: 2/15; financial award applicants required to submit FAFSA. *Unit head:* Dr. Ron Bramlett, Coordinator, 501-450-5405. *Application contact:* Patti Hornor, Administrative Assistant, 501-450-5063, Fax: 501-450-5678, E-mail: pattih@uca.edu.

University of Central Florida, College of Education, Department of Child, Family and Community Sciences, Program in School Psychology, Orlando, FL 32816. Offers Ed S. Part-time and evening/weekend programs available. *Degree requirements:* For Ed S, thesis or alternative, practicum, internship. *Entrance requirements:* For degree, GRE General Test, minimum GPA of 3.0, resumé, interview. Additional exam requirements/recommendations for international students: Required—TOEFL. *Application deadline:* For fall admission, 3/1 for domestic students. Application fee: $30. Electronic applications accepted. *Expenses:* Tuition, state resident: full-time $6,484. Tuition, nonresident: full-time $23,938. Tuition and fees vary according to program. *Financial support:* Fellowships with partial tuition reimbursements, research assistantships with partial tuition reimbursements, teaching assistantships with partial tuition reimbursements, career-related internships or fieldwork, Federal Work-Study, institutionally sponsored loans, tuition waivers (partial), and unspecified assistantships available. Financial award application deadline: 3/1; financial award applicants required to submit FAFSA. *Unit head:* Dr. Gordon Taub, Coordinator, 407-823-0373, E-mail: gtaub@mail.ucf.edu.

University of Cincinnati, Graduate School, College of Education, Criminal Justice, and Human Services, Division of Human Services, Program in School Psychology, Cincinnati, OH 45221. Offers PhD, Ed S. *Accreditation:* NCATE. Part-time programs available. *Faculty:* 5 full-time (2 women), 5 part-time/adjunct (4 women). *Students:* 35 full-time (31 women), 16 part-time (all women); includes 3 minority (1 African American, 1 American Indian/Alaska Native, 1 Hispanic American), 1 international. In 2007, 2 doctorates awarded. *Degree requirements:* For doctorate, comprehensive exam, thesis/dissertation. *Entrance requirements:* For doctorate, GRE General Test, GRE Subject Test. Additional exam requirements/recommendations for international students: Required—TOEFL (minimum score 520 paper-based; 190 computer-based; 68 iBT), OEPT. *Application deadline:* For fall admission, 1/15 for domestic students. Application fee: $40. Electronic applications accepted. *Financial support:* Fellowships, research assistantships with full tuition reimbursements, career-related internships or fieldwork, scholarships/grants, tuition waivers (partial), and unspecified assistantships available. *Faculty research:* School psychology services delivery, direct assessment and intervention. *Application contact:* Linda Pelton, Student Contact, 513-556-3335, Fax: 513-556-3898, E-mail: linda.pelton@uc.edu.

University of Colorado Denver, School of Education and Human Development, Program in Counseling Psychology and Counselor Education, Denver, CO 80217-3364. Offers counseling psychology and counselor education (MA); school psychology (Ed S). *Accreditation:* ACA (one or more programs are accredited); NCATE. Part-time and evening/weekend programs available. *Faculty:* 11 full-time (8 women). *Students:* 71 full-time (62 women), 147 part-time (129 women); includes 21 minority (7 African Americans, 2 American Indian/Alaska Native, 2 Asian Americans or Pacific Islanders, 10 Hispanic Americans), 1 international. Average age 33. 154 applicants, 27% accepted, 33 enrolled. In 2007, 59 master's, 21 other advanced degrees awarded. *Degree requirements:* For master's, comprehensive exam, thesis optional. *Entrance requirements:* For master's, GRE or MAT, minimum GPA of 2.75, 4 letters of recommendation, interview, resumé. Additional exam requirements/recommendations for international students: Required—TOEFL (minimum score 525 paper-based; 197 computer-based). *Application deadline:* For fall admission, 2/15 for domestic students; for spring admission, 9/15 for domestic students. Applications are processed on a rolling basis. Application fee: $50 ($75 for international students). Electronic applications accepted. *Financial support:* Research assistantships, teaching assistantships, Federal Work-Study available. Financial award application deadline: 4/1; financial award applicants required to submit FAFSA. *Faculty research:* Spiritual issues in counseling, multicultural and diversity issues in counseling, adolescent suicide, career development. *Unit head:* Dr. Marsha Wiggins-Frame, Division Coordinator, 303-556-6032, Fax: 303-556-4479, E-mail: marsha.frame@cudenver.edu. *Application contact:* Lori Sisneros, Student Services Coordinator, 303-556-8854, Fax: 303-556-4479, E-mail: bri.sisneros@cudenver.edu.

University of Connecticut, Graduate School, Neag School of Education, Department of Educational Psychology, Storrs, CT 06269. Offers educational psychology (MA, PhD, Post-Master's Certificate), including cognition and instruction, counseling psychology, gifted and talented education, learning technology, measurement, evaluation, and assessment, school psychology, special education. *Faculty:* 39 full-time (17 women). *Students:* 163 full-time (119 women), 141 part-time (104 women); includes 40 minority (18 African Americans, 1 American Indian/Alaska Native, 8 Asian Americans or Pacific Islanders, 13 Hispanic Americans), 18 international. Average age 34. 348 applicants, 38% accepted, 126 enrolled. In 2007, 65 master's, 24 doctorates, 19 other advanced degrees awarded. *Degree requirements:* For master's, comprehensive exam; for doctorate, thesis/dissertation. *Entrance requirements:* For doctorate, GRE General Test. Additional exam requirements/recommendations for international students: Required—TOEFL (minimum score 550 paper-based; 213 computer-based). *Application deadline:* For fall admission, 2/1 priority date for domestic and international students; for spring admission, 11/1 for domestic students, 10/1 for international students. Applications are processed on a rolling basis. Application fee: $55. Electronic applications accepted. *Expenses:* Tuition, state resident: part-time $469 per credit hour. Tuition, nonresident: part-time $1,218 per credit hour. *Financial support:* In 2007–08, 80 research assistantships with full tuition reimbursements, 3 teaching assistantships with full tuition reimbursements were awarded; fellowships, Federal Work-Study, scholarships/grants, health care benefits, and unspecified assistantships also available. Financial award application deadline: 2/1; financial award applicants required to submit FAFSA. *Unit head:* Hariharan Swaminathan, Head, 860-486-4031, Fax: 860-486-0210, E-mail: hariharan.swaminathan@uconn.edu. *Application contact:* Lisa Rasicot, Graduate Coordinator, 860-486-3065, Fax: 860-486-0210, E-mail: l.rasicot@uconn.edu.

University of Connecticut, Graduate School, Neag School of Education, Department of Educational Psychology, Field of Educational Psychology, Program in School Psychology, Storrs, CT 06269. Offers MA, PhD, Post-Master's Certificate. *Accreditation:* NCATE. *Faculty:* 17 full-time (7 women). *Students:* 20 full-time (17 women), 10 part-time (5 women); includes 4 minority (2 African Americans, 1 Asian American or Pacific Islander, 1 Hispanic American). Average age 28. 96 applicants, 14% accepted, 11 enrolled. In 2007, 5 master's, 7 doctorates, 9 other advanced degrees awarded. Terminal master's awarded for partial completion of doctoral program. *Degree requirements:* For master's, comprehensive exam, thesis or alternative; for doctorate, thesis/dissertation. *Entrance requirements:* For doctorate, GRE General Test. Additional exam requirements/recommendations for international students: Required—TOEFL (minimum score 550 paper-based; 213 computer-based). *Application deadline:* For fall admission, 2/1 priority date for domestic and international students; for spring admission, 11/1 for domestic students, 10/1 for international students. Applications are processed on a rolling basis. Application fee: $55. Electronic applications accepted. *Expenses:* Tuition, state resident: part-time $469 per credit hour. Tuition, nonresident: part-time $1,218 per credit hour. *Financial support:* In 2007–08, 15 research assistantships with full tuition reimbursements were awarded; fellowships, teaching assistantships with full tuition reimbursements, Federal Work-Study, scholarships/grants, health care benefits, and unspecified assistantships also available. Financial award application deadline: 2/1; financial award applicants required to submit FAFSA. *Application contact:* Lisa Rasicot, Graduate Coordinator, 860-486-3065, Fax: 860-486-0210, E-mail: l.rasicot@uconn.edu.

University of Dayton, Graduate School, School of Education and Allied Professions, Department of Counselor Education and Human Services, Dayton, OH 45469-1300. Offers college student personnel (MS Ed); community counseling (MS Ed); higher education administration (MS Ed); human development services (MS Ed); school counseling (MS Ed); school psychology (MS Ed, Ed S); teacher as child/youth development specialist (MS Ed). *Accreditation:* NCATE. Part-time and evening/weekend programs available. *Faculty:* 11 full-time (7 women), 32 part-time/adjunct (17 women). *Students:* 269 full-time (218 women), 305 part-time (255 women); includes 82 minority (66 African Americans, 4 Asian Americans or Pacific Islanders, 12 Hispanic Americans), 8 international. Average age 32. 403 applicants, 49% accepted, 117 enrolled. In 2007, 267 degrees awarded. *Degree requirements:* For master's, thesis optional, exit exam. *Entrance requirements:* For master's, MAT or GRE (if GPA is below 2.75), interview. Additional exam requirements/recommendations for international students: Required—TOEFL (minimum score 550 paper-based; 213 computer-based; 80 iBT). *Application deadline:* For fall admission, 4/10 for domestic students, 3/1 priority date for international students; for winter admission, 9/10 for domestic students, 7/1 priority date for international students; for spring admission, 1/10 for domestic students, 1/1 priority date for international students. Applications are processed on a rolling basis. Application fee: $0 ($50 for international students). Electronic applications accepted. *Financial support:* In 2007–08, 1 research assistantship with partial tuition reimbursement (averaging $7,400 per year), 4 teaching assistantships with partial tuition reimbursements (averaging $7,600 per year) were awarded; career-related internships or fieldwork, institutionally sponsored loans, health care benefits, and unspecified assistantships also available. Financial award applicants required to submit FAFSA. *Faculty research:* Anger as part of the grief process, inclusion of children with severe disabilities, comparisons of school counselors in Bosnia and the U. S., graduate and professional student socialization, use of cohort groups in doctoral programs. *Unit head:* Dr. Alan Demmitt, Chairperson, 937-229-3644, Fax: 937-229-1055. *Application contact:* Angela Jones-Glukhov, Associate Director of Graduate Admissions, 937-229-4305, Fax: 937-229-4729.

University of Delaware, College of Human Services, Education and Public Policy and Department of Individual and Family Studies, Program in Counseling in Higher Education, Newark, DE 19716. Offers M Ed, MA. *Accreditation:* NCATE. *Faculty:* 14 part-time/adjunct (7 women). *Students:* 27 full-time (17 women), 1 part-time; includes 8 minority (6 African Americans, 2 Hispanic Americans), 1 international. Average age 30. 37 applicants, 41% accepted, 8 enrolled. In 2007, 12 degrees awarded. *Degree requirements:* For master's, comprehensive exam. *Entrance requirements:* For master's, GRE (quantitative and verbal), on-campus interview, letters of recommendation. Additional exam requirements/recommendations for international students: Required—TOEFL (minimum score 600 paper-based). *Application deadline:* For fall admission, 2/15 priority date for domestic and international students; for spring admission, 11/15 priority date for domestic and international students. Applications are processed on a rolling basis. Application fee: $60. Electronic applications accepted. *Financial support:* In 2007–08, 25 teaching assistantships with full tuition reimbursements (averaging $13,000 per year) were awarded; career-related internships or fieldwork and unspecified assistantships also available. *Faculty research:* Counseling outcomes, student culture, group counseling. *Unit head:* Charles L. Beale, Director, 302-831-8107, Fax: 302-831-2148.

University of Delaware, College of Human Services, Education and Public Policy, School of Education, Newark, DE 19716. Offers education (PhD); educational leadership (Ed D); higher education (M Ed); instruction (MI); reading (M Ed); school leadership (M Ed); school psychology (MA, Ed S); teaching English as a second language (TESL) (MA). *Accreditation:* NCATE. Part-time and evening/weekend programs available. *Faculty:* 47 full-time (27 women), 1 part-time/adjunct (0 women). *Students:* 149 full-time (103 women), 250 part-time (188 women); includes 53 minority (29 African Americans, 1 American Indian/Alaska Native, 9 Asian Americans or Pacific Islanders, 14 Hispanic Americans), 26 international. Average age 34. 307 applicants, 40% accepted, 88 enrolled. In 2007, 100 master's, 40 doctorates awarded. Terminal master's awarded for partial completion of doctoral program. *Degree requirements:* For master's, comprehensive exam (for some programs), thesis (for some programs); for doctorate, comprehensive exam (for some programs), thesis/dissertation. *Entrance requirements:* For master's and doctorate, GRE, 3 letters of recommendation. Additional exam requirements/recommendations for international students: Required—TOEFL (minimum score 600 paper-based; 250 computer-based). *Application deadline:* For fall admission, 7/1 for domestic students; for spring admission, 2/1 for domestic students. Applications are processed on a rolling basis. Application fee: $60. Electronic applications accepted. *Financial support:* In 2007–08, 95 students received support, including 4 fellowships with full tuition reimbursements available (averaging $14,600 per year), 78 research assistantships with full tuition reimbursements available (averaging $14,600 per year), 12 teaching assistantships with full tuition reimbursements available (averaging $14,600 per year); scholarships/grants, health care benefits, and tuition waivers (full) also available. Financial award application deadline: 2/1. *Faculty research:* Teacher education; curriculum theory and development; community based education models, educational leadership. Total annual research expenditures: $12.5 million. *Unit head:* Dr. Nancy W. Brickhouse, Director, 302-831-2573, Fax: 302-831-4421. *Application contact:* Dr. Gail S. Rys, Assistant Director, 302-831-1165, Fax: 302-831-4421, E-mail: gailrys@udel.edu.

University of Denver, College of Education, Denver, CO 80208. Offers counseling psychology (MA, PhD); curriculum and instruction (MA, PhD, Certificate), including curriculum leadership (MA, PhD); educational administration and policy studies (Certificate); educational psychology (MA, PhD, Ed S), including child and family studies (MA, PhD), quantitative research methods (MA, PhD), school psychology (PhD, Ed S); higher education and adult studies (MA, PhD); library and information science (MLIS); library and information sciences (Certificate); school administration (PhD). *Accreditation:* ALA; APA (one or more programs are accredited). Part-time and evening/weekend programs available. Postbaccalaureate distance learning degree programs offered (no on-campus study). *Faculty:* 26 full-time (18 women). *Students:* 327 full-time (260 women), 438 part-time (343 women); includes 119 minority (31 African Americans, 7 American Indian/Alaska Native, 14 Asian Americans or Pacific Islanders, 67 Hispanic Americans), 15 international. Average age 34. 778 applicants, 76% accepted, 368 enrolled. In 2007, 183 master's, 29 doctorates, 54 other advanced degrees awarded. Terminal master's awarded for partial completion of doctoral program. *Degree requirements:* For master's, comprehensive exam; for doctorate, 2 foreign languages, comprehensive exam, thesis/dissertation. *Entrance requirements:* For master's and doctorate, GRE General Test or MAT. *Application deadline:* Applications are processed on a rolling basis. Application fee: $50. Electronic applications accepted. *Financial support:* In 2007–08, 58 teaching assistantships with full and partial tuition reimbursements (averaging $6,300 per year) were awarded; career-related internships or fieldwork, Federal Work-Study, institutionally sponsored loans, and scholarships/grants also available. Support available to part-time students. Financial award application deadline: 3/1; financial award applicants required to submit FAFSA. *Faculty research:* Parkinson's disease, personnel training, development and assessments, gifted education, service learning, transportation, public schools. Total annual research expenditures: $340,000. *Unit head:* Dr. Virginia Maloney, Dean, 303-871-2509. *Application contact:* Linda McCarthy, Student Services Coordinator, 303-871-2509, E-mail: edinfo@du.edu.

University of Detroit Mercy, College of Liberal Arts and Education, Department of Psychology, Program in School Psychology, Detroit, MI 48221. Offers Spec.

University of Florida, Graduate School, College of Education, Department of Educational Psychology, Gainesville, FL 32611. Offers educational psychology (M Ed, MAE, Ed D, PhD, Ed S); research and evaluation methodology (M Ed, MAE, Ed D, PhD, Ed S); school psychology (M Ed, MAE, Ed D, PhD, Ed S). *Accreditation:* NCATE. *Faculty:* 16 full-time (7 women). *Students:* 95 (74 women); includes 22 minority (6 African Americans, 1 American Indian/Alaska Native, 4 Asian Americans or Pacific Islanders, 11 Hispanic Americans) 17 international. In 2007, 16 master's, 10 doctorates awarded. Terminal master's awarded for partial completion of doctoral program. *Degree requirements:* For master's, thesis (MAE); for doctorate, variable foreign language requirement, thesis/dissertation. *Entrance requirements:* For master's and doctorate, GRE General Test, minimum GPA of 3.0; for Ed S, GRE General Test. Additional exam requirements/recommendations for international students: Required—TOEFL (minimum score 550 paper-based; 213 computer-based). *Application deadline:* For fall admission, 6/1 priority date for domestic students. Applications are processed on a rolling basis. Application fee: $30. Electronic applications accepted. *Expenses:* Tuition, state resident: full-time $7,478. Tuition, nonresident: full-time $22,603. *Financial support:* In 2007–08, 13 teaching assistantships (averaging $8,858 per year) were awarded; fellowships, research assistantships, career-related internships or fieldwork and unspecified assistantships also available. Financial award application deadline: 4/30. *Faculty research:* School improvement, teaching and learning, item response theory. *Unit head:* Tina Smith-Bonahue, Interim Chair, 352-392-0725 Ext. 224. *Application contact:* Dr. Bridget Franks, Coordinator, 352-395-0723 Ext. 234, Fax: 352-392-5929, E-mail: bfranks@coe.ufl.edu.

University of Hartford, College of Arts and Sciences, Department of Psychology, Program in School Psychology, West Hartford, CT 06117-1599. Offers MS. *Accreditation:* NCATE. Part-time programs available. *Faculty:* 2 full-time (1 woman). *Students:* 23 full-time (18 women), 10 part-time (9 women); includes 4 minority (1 African American, 1 American Indian/Alaska

School Psychology

University of Hartford (continued)

Native, 2 Hispanic Americans). Average age 26. 37 applicants, 65% accepted, 23 enrolled. In 2007, 7 master's awarded. *Degree requirements:* For master's, comprehensive exam. *Entrance requirements:* For master's, GRE General Test, GRE Subject Test, minimum GPA of 3.0, 3 letters of recommendation. Additional exam requirements/recommendations for international students: Required—TOEFL (minimum score 550 paper-based; 213 computer-based). *Application deadline:* For fall admission, 2/15 priority date for domestic students. Application fee: $45. Electronic applications accepted. *Expenses:* Tuition: Part-time $595 per credit. Required fees: $200 per term. *Financial support:* In 2007–08, 1 research assistantship (averaging $2,000 per year), 5 teaching assistantships (averaging $2,600 per year) were awarded; Federal Work-Study also available. Support available to part-time students. Financial award application deadline: 6/1; financial award applicants required to submit FAFSA. *Faculty research:* Family therapy, child developments, clinical supervision. *Unit head:* Dr. Tony Crespi, Director, 860-768-5081, Fax: 860-768-5292, E-mail: crespi@hartford.edu. *Application contact:* Reneé Murphy, Assistant Director of Graduate Admissions, 860-768-4371, Fax: 860-768-5160, E-mail: gettoknow@hartford.edu.

University of Houston–Clear Lake, School of Human Sciences and Humanities, Programs in Human Sciences, Houston, TX 77058-1098. Offers behavioral sciences (MA), including behavioral sciences-general, behavioral sciences-psychology, behavioral sciences-sociology; clinical psychology (MA); criminology (MA); cross-cultural studies (MA); family therapy (MA); fitness and human performance (MA); school psychology (MA). *Accreditation:* AAMFT/COAMFTE. Part-time and evening/weekend programs available. Postbaccalaureate distance learning degree programs offered (minimal on-campus study). *Degree requirements:* For master's, thesis or alternative. *Entrance requirements:* For master's, GRE General Test. Additional exam requirements/recommendations for international students: Required—TOEFL (minimum score 550 paper-based; 213 computer-based). Electronic applications accepted. *Faculty research:* Smoking cessation, adolescent sexuality, white collar crime, serial murder, human factors/human computer interaction.

University of Houston–Victoria, School of Arts and Sciences, Program in Psychology, Victoria, TX 77901-4450. Offers counseling psychology (MA); school psychology (MA). Part-time and evening/weekend programs available. Postbaccalaureate distance learning degree programs offered. *Faculty:* 4 full-time (2 women). *Students:* 18 full-time (15 women), 47 part-time (36 women); includes 18 minority (3 African Americans, 2 Asian Americans or Pacific Islanders, 13 Hispanic Americans). In 2007, 8 degrees awarded. *Degree requirements:* For master's, project or thesis. *Entrance requirements:* For master's, GRE General Test. Additional exam requirements/recommendations for international students: Required—TOEFL (minimum score 550 paper-based; 213 computer-based). *Application deadline:* Applications are processed on a rolling basis. Application fee: $0. Electronic applications accepted. *Expenses:* Tuition, state resident: full-time $3,492; part-time $194 per semester hour. Tuition, nonresident: full-time $7,596; part-time $422 per semester hour. Required fees: $774; $43 per semester hour. Tuition and fees vary according to course load. *Financial support:* In 2007–08, research assistantships with partial tuition reimbursements (averaging $2,000 per year), teaching assistantships with partial tuition reimbursements (averaging $2,000 per year) were awarded; career-related internships or fieldwork, Federal Work-Study, scholarships/grants, and unspecified assistantships also available. Support available to part-time students. Financial award application deadline: 4/15. *Unit head:* Dr. Rick Harrington, Head, 361-570-4205, Fax: 361-570-4229, E-mail: harringtonr@unh.edu. *Application contact:* Admissions and Records, E-mail: admissions@uhv.edu.

University of Idaho, College of Graduate Studies, College of Education, Department of Counseling and School Psychology, Special Education, and Educational Leadership, Program in School Psychology, Moscow, ID 83844-2282. Offers Ed S. *Accreditation:* NCATE. *Students:* 41 (32 women). Average age 40. In 2007, 22 degrees awarded. *Application deadline:* For fall admission, 8/1 for domestic students; for spring admission, 12/15 for domestic students. Application fee: $55 ($60 for international students). *Financial support:* Application deadline: 2/15. *Unit head:* Dr. Russell A. Joki, Chair, Department of Counseling and School Psychology, Special Education, and Educational Leadership, 208-364-4099, E-mail: rjoki@uidaho.edu.

The University of Iowa, Graduate College, College of Education, Department of Psychological and Quantitative Foundations, Iowa City, IA 52242-1316. Offers counseling psychology (PhD); educational measurement and statistics (MA, PhD); educational psychology (MA, PhD); school psychology (PhD, Ed S); JD/PhD. *Accreditation:* APA. *Faculty:* 23 full-time, 21 part-time/adjunct. *Students:* 85 full-time (59 women), 81 part-time (61 women); includes 23 minority (8 African Americans, 8 Asian Americans or Pacific Islanders, 7 Hispanic Americans), 39 international. 147 applicants, 31% accepted, 23 enrolled. In 2007, 7 master's, 16 doctorates, 3 other advanced degrees awarded. *Degree requirements:* For master's, thesis optional, exam; for doctorate, comprehensive exam, thesis/dissertation; for Ed S, exam. *Entrance requirements:* For master's, doctorate, and Ed S, GRE General Test, minimum GPA of 3.0. Additional exam requirements/recommendations for international students: Required—TOEFL (minimum score 550 paper-based; 213 computer-based; 81 iBT). Application fee: $60 ($85 for international students). Electronic applications accepted. *Expenses:* Tuition, state resident: part-time $349 per hour. Tuition, nonresident: part-time $349 per hour. Tuition and fees vary according to course load and program. *Financial support:* In 2007–08, 9 fellowships, 61 research assistantships with partial tuition reimbursements, 15 teaching assistantships with partial tuition reimbursements were awarded. Financial award applicants required to submit FAFSA. *Unit head:* Timothy Ansley, Chair, 319-335-5579, Fax: 319-335-6145.

University of Kansas, Research and Graduate Studies, School of Education, Department of Psychology and Research in Education, School Psychology Program, Lawrence, KS 66045. Offers PhD, Ed S. *Accreditation:* APA (one or more programs are accredited); NCATE. *Faculty:* 3. *Students:* 24 full-time (23 women), 1 (woman) part-time; includes 1 minority (Hispanic American), 1 international. Average age 27. 48 applicants, 52% accepted, 9 enrolled. In 2007, 2 doctorates, 11 other advanced degrees awarded. *Degree requirements:* For doctorate, comprehensive exam, thesis/dissertation; for Ed S, comprehensive exam. *Entrance requirements:* For doctorate, GRE General Test; for Ed S, GRE General Test, minimum GPA of 3.0. Additional exam requirements/recommendations for international students: Required—TOEFL. *Application deadline:* For fall admission, 1/15 for domestic students. Application fee: $55 ($60 for international students). Electronic applications accepted. *Expenses:* Tuition, state resident: full-time $5,838. Tuition, nonresident: full-time $13,409. Tuition and fees vary according to program. *Financial support:* Fellowships, research assistantships with full and partial tuition reimbursements, teaching assistantships with full and partial tuition reimbursements available. Financial award application deadline: 2/1. *Faculty research:* Classroom management, anxiety in children and youth, child behavior and learning problems, behavioral and personality assessment, and home/school/community partnerships. *Unit head:* Patricia A. Lowe, Director of Training, 785-864-9710, Fax: 785-864-3820, E-mail: tlowe@ku.edu. *Application contact:* Admissions Coordinator, 785-864-3931, Fax: 785-864-3820, E-mail: preadmit@ku.edu.

University of Kentucky, Graduate School, College of Education, Program in Educational and Counseling Psychology, Lexington, KY 40506-0032. Offers counseling psychology (MS Ed, PhD, Ed S); educational and counseling psychology (MS Ed); educational psychology (Ed D, PhD, Ed S); school psychometrist and school psychology (MA Ed). *Accreditation:* APA (one or more programs are accredited); NCATE. *Faculty:* 14 full-time (8 women), 1 part-time/adjunct (0 women). *Students:* 123 full-time (103 women), 16 part-time (12 women); includes 23 minority (19 African Americans, 4 Hispanic Americans), 7 international. Average age 31. 250 applicants, 20% accepted, 37 enrolled. In 2007, 20 master's, 14 doctorates, 12 other advanced degrees awarded. *Degree requirements:* For master's, comprehensive exam, thesis optional; for doctorate, comprehensive exam, thesis/dissertation; for Ed S, comprehensive exam. *Entrance requirements:* For master's, GRE General Test, minimum undergraduate GPA of 2.75; for doctorate, GRE General Test, minimum graduate GPA of 3.0; for Ed S, GRE General Test. Additional exam requirements/recommendations for international students: Required—TOEFL (minimum score 550 paper-based; 213 computer-based). *Application deadline:* For fall admission, 7/17 priority date for domestic students, 2/1 priority date for international students; for spring admission, 12/13 priority date for domestic students, 6/15 priority date for international students. Application fee: $50 ($65 for international students). Electronic applications accepted. *Expenses:* Tuition, state resident: part-time $437 per credit hour. Tuition, nonresident: part-time $931 per credit hour. *Financial support:* In 2007–08, 73 students received support, including 16 fellowships with full tuition reimbursements available (averaging $2,250 per year), 38 research assistantships with full tuition reimbursements available (averaging $12,874 per year), 31 teaching assistantships with full tuition reimbursements available (averaging $9,700 per year); career-related internships or fieldwork, Federal Work-Study, institutionally sponsored loans, scholarships/grants, traineeships, health care benefits, tuition waivers (partial), and unspecified assistantships also available. Support available to part-time students. Financial award application deadline: 3/15. *Unit head:* Dr. Lynley Anderman, Director of Graduate Studies, 859-257-8647, Fax: 859-257-5662, E-mail: lynley.anderman@uky.edu. *Application contact:* Dr. Brian Jackson, Senior Associate Dean, 859-257-4667, Fax: 859-257-4676, E-mail: brian.jackson@uky.edu.

University of Louisiana at Monroe, Graduate Studies and Research, College of Education and Human Development, Department of Psychology, Program in School Psychology, Monroe, LA 71209-0001. Offers SSP. *Accreditation:* NCATE. *Students:* 2 full-time (both women), 10 part-time (9 women); includes 2 minority (both African Americans) Average age 28. In 2007, 1 SSP awarded. *Degree requirements:* For SSP, thesis. *Entrance requirements:* For degree, GRE General Test, minimum GPA of 2.75. Additional exam requirements/recommendations for international students: Required—TOEFL (minimum score 500 paper-based; 173 computer-based; 61 iBT). *Application deadline:* For fall admission, 8/22 priority date for domestic students, 7/1 for international students; for winter admission, 12/12 priority date for domestic students; for spring admission, 1/17 for domestic students, 11/1 for international students. Applications are processed on a rolling basis. Application fee: $20 ($30 for international students). Electronic applications accepted. *Expenses:* Tuition, state resident: full-time $2,220. Tuition, nonresident: full-time $8,172. *Financial support:* Research assistantships with full tuition reimbursements, teaching assistantships with full tuition reimbursements, career-related internships or fieldwork, Federal Work-Study, and unspecified assistantships available. Financial award application deadline: 4/1; financial award applicants required to submit FAFSA. *Unit head:* Dr. Veronica Lewis, Coordinator, 818-342-1332, E-mail: vlewis@ulm.edu.

University of Mary Hardin-Baylor, College of Sciences and Humanities, Department of Psychology, Belton, TX 76513. Offers community counseling (MA); marriage and family Christian counseling (MA); psychology and counseling (MA); school counseling and psychology (MA). Part-time and evening/weekend programs available. *Degree requirements:* For master's, comprehensive exam. *Entrance requirements:* For master's, GRE General Test, minimum GPA of 3.0 in last 60 hours or 2.75 overall. Electronic applications accepted.

University of Maryland, College Park, Graduate Studies, College of Education, Department of Counseling and Personnel Services, College Park, MD 20742. Offers college student personnel (M Ed, MA); college student personnel administration (PhD); community counseling (CAGS); community/career counseling (M Ed, MA); counseling and personnel services (M Ed, MA, PhD); counseling psychology (PhD); counselor education (PhD); rehabilitation counseling (M Ed, MA, AGSC); school counseling (M Ed, MA); school psychology (M Ed, MA, PhD). *Accreditation:* ACA (one or more programs are accredited); APA (one or more programs are accredited); CORE (one or more programs are accredited); NCATE. Part-time and evening/weekend programs available. Postbaccalaureate distance learning degree programs offered (no on-campus study). *Faculty:* 41 full-time (29 women), 2 part-time/adjunct (both women). *Students:* 157 full-time (114 women), 19 part-time (13 women); includes 63 minority (34 African Americans, 3 American Indian/Alaska Native, 14 Asian Americans or Pacific Islanders, 12 Hispanic Americans), 11 international. 375 applicants, 20% accepted, 48 enrolled. In 2007, 44 master's, 6 doctorates, 4 other advanced degrees awarded. *Degree requirements:* For master's, thesis (for some programs); for doctorate, thesis/dissertation. *Entrance requirements:* For master's, GRE General Test or MAT, minimum GPA of 3.0, 3 letters of recommendation; for doctorate, GRE General Test or MAT, minimum GPA of 3.5, 3 letters of recommendation. Additional exam requirements/recommendations for international students: Required—TOEFL. *Application deadline:* For fall admission, 3/1 for domestic students, 2/1 for international students; for spring admission, 9/1 for domestic students, 6/1 for international students. Applications are processed on a rolling basis. Application fee: $60. Electronic applications accepted. *Financial support:* In 2007–08, 20 fellowships with full tuition reimbursements (averaging $8,362 per year), 5 research assistantships (averaging $14,192 per year), 105 teaching assistantships with tuition reimbursements (averaging $14,702 per year) were awarded; career-related internships or fieldwork, Federal Work-Study, and scholarships/grants also available. Support available to part-time students. Financial award applicants required to submit FAFSA. *Faculty research:* Educational psychology, counseling, health. Total annual research expenditures: $2.1 million. *Unit head:* Dr. Ruth Fassingel, Dean, 301-405-2860, Fax: 301-405-9995, E-mail: rfassing@umd.edu. *Application contact:* Dean of Graduate School, 301-405-0358, Fax: 301-314-9305.

University of Massachusetts Amherst, Graduate School, School of Education, Program in School Psychology, Amherst, MA 01003. Offers PhD. *Accreditation:* APA; NCATE. *Students:* 25 full-time (21 women), 6 part-time (5 women); includes 5 minority (2 African Americans, 3 Asian Americans or Pacific Islanders), 1 international. Average age 30. 43 applicants, 19% accepted, 5 enrolled. In 2007, 2 degrees awarded. *Degree requirements:* For doctorate, thesis/dissertation. *Entrance requirements:* For doctorate, 3 letters of recommendation. Additional exam requirements/recommendations for international students: Required—TOEFL (minimum score 530 paper-based; 197 computer-based). *Application deadline:* For fall admission, 1/15 for domestic and international students. Applications are processed on a rolling basis. Application fee: $50 ($65 for international students). *Expenses:* Tuition, state resident: full-time $2,640; part-time $110 per credit. Tuition, nonresident: full-time $9,936; part-time $414 per credit. Required fees: $7,455. One-time fee: $332. Tuition and fees vary according to course load, campus/location, program and reciprocity agreements. *Financial support:* Fellowships with full tuition reimbursements, research assistantships with full tuition reimbursements, teaching assistantships with full tuition reimbursements, career-related internships or fieldwork, Federal Work-Study, scholarships/grants, traineeships, and unspecified assistantships available. Support available to part-time students. Financial award application deadline: 1/15. *Unit head:* Gary Stoner, Professor, 413-545-2062.

University of Massachusetts Boston, Office of Graduate Studies, Graduate College of Education, Counseling and School Psychology Department, Program in School Guidance Counseling, Boston, MA 02125-3393. Offers M Ed, CAGS.

University of Massachusetts Boston, Office of Graduate Studies, Graduate College of Education, Counseling and School Psychology Department, Program in School Psychology, Boston, MA 02125-3393. Offers M Ed, CAGS. Part-time and evening/weekend programs available. *Degree requirements:* For master's, comprehensive exam, practicum, final project; for CAGS, comprehensive exam. *Entrance requirements:* For master's, GRE General Test or MAT, minimum GPA of 3.0; for CAGS, minimum GPA of 2.75. *Faculty research:* School psychology services, assessment of children, cultural and gender differences on psychological adjustment to disabilities.

University of Memphis, Graduate School, College of Arts and Sciences, Department of Psychology, Memphis, TN 38152. Offers clinical psychology (PhD); experimental psychology (PhD); general psychology (MS); school psychology (MA, PhD). Part-time programs available. *Faculty:* 29 full-time (8 women), 4 part-time/adjunct (1 woman). *Students:* 92 full-time (56 women), 29 part-time (19 women); includes 18 minority (11 African Americans, 3 Asian Americans or Pacific Islanders, 4 Hispanic Americans), 10 international. Average age 28. 269 applicants, 16% accepted, 37 enrolled. In 2007, 14 master's, 8 doctorates awarded. Terminal master's awarded for partial completion of doctoral program. *Degree requirements:* For master's, comprehensive exam, thesis (for some programs), oral exam (MS); for doctorate, thesis/dissertation, internship. *Entrance requirements:* For master's, GRE General Test, 18 undergraduate hours in psychology, minimum GPA of 2.5; for doctorate, GRE General Test, GRE Subject Test. *Application deadline:* For fall admission, 2/1 for domestic students. Applications are processed on a rolling basis. Application fee: $35 ($60 for international students). *Expenses:* Tuition, state resident: full-time $6,990; part-time $377 per hour. Tuition, nonresident: full-time $17,818; part-time $830 per hour. Tuition and fees vary according to course load and program. *Financial support:* In 2007–08, 75 research assistantships with full tuition reimbursements (averaging $4,500 per year), 13 teaching assistantships with full tuition reimbursements (averaging $4,600 per year) were awarded; fellowships with full tuition reimbursements, tuition waivers (partial) and unspecified assistantships also available. *Faculty research:* Psychotherapy and psychopathology, behavioral medicine and community psychology, child and family studies, cognitive and social processes, neuropsychology and behavioral neuroscience. *Unit head:* Dr. Arthur C. Graesser, Chair, 901-678-2146, Fax: 901-678-2579, E-mail: a-graesser@memphis.edu. *Application contact:* Dr. Robert Cohen, Graduate Studies Coordinator, 901-678-2146.

University of Minnesota, Twin Cities Campus, Graduate School, College of Education and Human Development, Department of Educational Psychology, Program in School Psychology, Minneapolis, MN 55455-0213. Offers MA, PhD, Ed S. *Accreditation:* APA. *Students:* 44 full-time (37 women), 21 part-time (all women); includes 6 minority (2 African Americans, 1 American Indian/Alaska Native, 2 Asian Americans or Pacific Islanders, 1 Hispanic American), 4 international. Average age 28. 46 applicants, 33% accepted, 10 enrolled. In 2007, 14 master's, 5 doctorates, 5 other advanced degrees awarded. *Application contact:* Dr. Mary Bents, Associate Dean, 612-625-6501, Fax: 612-626-1580, E-mail: mbents@tc.umn.edu.

University of Minnesota, Twin Cities Campus, Graduate School, College of Education and Human Development, Institute of Child Development, Minneapolis, MN 55455-0213. Offers child psychology (MA, PhD); early childhood education (M Ed, MA, PhD); school psychology (MA, PhD). *Faculty:* 20 full-time (8 women). *Students:* 85 full-time (76 women), 48 part-time (45 women); includes 12 minority (4 African Americans, 1 American Indian/Alaska Native, 3 Asian Americans or Pacific Islanders, 4 Hispanic Americans), 10 international. Average age 31. 131 applicants, 38% accepted, 38 enrolled. In 2007, 45 master's, 7 doctorates awarded. *Financial support:* In 2007–08, 26 fellowships (averaging $22,938 per year), 25 research assistantships with full tuition reimbursements (averaging $25,212 per year), 27 teaching assistantships with full tuition reimbursements (averaging $26,543 per year) were awarded. *Faculty research:* Developmental affective and cognitive neuroscience; developmental psychopathology; intervention and prevention science; social and emotional development; cognitive, language, and perceptual development. Total annual research expenditures: $2.8 million. *Unit head:* Dr. Nicki Crick, Director, 612-625-8879, Fax: 612-624-6373, E-mail: crick001@umn.edu. *Application contact:* Claudia Johnston, Information Contact, 612-624-2576, Fax: 612-624-6373, E-mail: johnstc@staff.tc.umn.edu.

University of Minnesota, Twin Cities Campus, Graduate School, College of Liberal Arts, Department of Psychology, Minneapolis, MN 55455-0213. Offers biological psychopathology (PhD); clinical psychology (PhD); cognitive and biological psychology (PhD); counseling psychology (PhD); industrial/organizational psychology (PhD); personality, individual differences, and behavior genetics (PhD); quantitative/psychometric methods (PhD); school psychology (PhD); social psychology (PhD). *Accreditation:* APA. *Faculty:* 44 full-time (10 women), 40 part-time/adjunct (11 women). *Students:* 134 full-time (71 women), 16 part-time (11 women); includes 30 minority (2 African Americans, 25 Asian Americans or Pacific Islanders, 3 Hispanic Americans), 18 international. 509 applicants, 5% accepted, 16 enrolled. In 2007, 19 doctorates awarded. *Median time to degree:* Of those who began their doctoral program in fall 1999, 54% received their degree in 8 years or less. *Degree requirements:* For doctorate, comprehensive exam, thesis/dissertation. *Entrance requirements:* For doctorate, GRE General Test, GRE Subject Test (recommended), 12 credits of upper-level psychology courses, including a course in statistics or psychological measurement. Additional exam requirements/recommendations for international students: Required—TOEFL (minimum score 550 paper-based; 213 computer-based; 79 iBT). *Application deadline:* For fall admission, 12/1 for domestic and international students. Application fee: $55 ($75 for international students). *Financial support:* In 2007–08, fellowships with full tuition reimbursements (averaging $21,000 per year), research assistantships with full tuition reimbursements (averaging $12,254 per year), teaching assistantships with full tuition reimbursements (averaging $12,254 per year) were awarded; career-related internships or fieldwork, traineeships, and tuition waivers (partial) also available. Financial award application deadline: 12/1. Total annual research expenditures: $6.5 million. *Unit head:* Gordon Legge, Chair, 612-625-0846, Fax: 612-626-2079. *Application contact:* Coordinator, 612-624-4181, Fax: 612-626-2079, E-mail: psyapply@tc.umn.edu.

University of Missouri–Columbia, Graduate School, College of Education, Department of Educational, School, and Counseling Psychology, Columbia, MO 65211. Offers counseling psychology (M Ed, MA, PhD, Ed S); educational psychology (M Ed, MA, PhD, Ed S); learning and instruction (M Ed); school psychology (M Ed, MA, PhD, Ed S). *Accreditation:* APA (one or more programs are accredited); CORE. Part-time programs available. *Degree requirements:* For doctorate, thesis/dissertation. *Entrance requirements:* For master's, doctorate, and Ed S, GRE General Test, minimum GPA of 3.0.

University of Missouri–St. Louis, College of Education, Division of Educational Psychology, Research, and Evaluation, St. Louis, MO 63121. Offers education (Ed D); educational psychology (PhD); school psychology (Certificate, Ed S). *Faculty:* 12 full-time (3 women), 3 part-time/adjunct (1 woman). *Students:* 19 full-time (all women), 12 part-time (10 women); includes 1 minority (African American) Average age 31. In 2007, 1 doctorate, 2 other advanced degrees awarded. *Degree requirements:* For doctorate, thesis/dissertation. *Entrance requirements:* For doctorate, GRE General Test, 3 letters of recommendation. Additional exam requirements/recommendations for international students: Required—TOEFL (minimum score 550 paper-based; 213 computer-based). *Application deadline:* For fall admission, 2/15 for domestic students; for spring admission, 9/15 for domestic students. Application fee: $35 ($40 for international students). Electronic applications accepted. *Financial support:* Research assistantships, teaching assistantships available. *Faculty research:* Child/adolescent psychology, quantitative and qualitative methodology, evaluation processes, measurement and assessment. *Unit head:* Dr. Matthew Keefer, Chairperson, 314-516-5783, Fax: 314-516-5784, E-mail: keefer@umsl.edu. *Application contact:* 314-516-5458, Fax: 314-516-6996, E-mail: gradadm@umsl.edu.

The University of Montana, Graduate School, College of Arts and Sciences, Department of Psychology, Program in School Psychology, Missoula, MT 59812-0002. Offers MA, PhD, Ed S. *Degree requirements:* For master's, oral exam, professional paper; for Ed S, thesis. *Entrance requirements:* For master's, GRE General Test, GRE Subject Test, minimum GPA of 3.25 during previous 2 years; for Ed S, GRE General Test. Additional exam requirements/recommendations for international students: Required—TOEFL. *Faculty research:* Child development and creativity, psychological measurement.

University of Nebraska at Kearney, College of Graduate Study, College of Education, Department of Counseling and School Psychology, Kearney, NE 68849-0001. Offers counseling (MS Ed, Ed S); school psychology (Ed S). *Accreditation:* ACA; NCATE. Part-time and evening/weekend programs available. *Degree requirements:* For master's, thesis optional; for Ed S, thesis. *Entrance requirements:* For master's and Ed S, interview. Additional exam requirements/recommendations for international students: Required—TOEFL (minimum score 550 paper-based; 213 computer-based). Electronic applications accepted. *Faculty research:* Multicultural counseling and diversity issues, team decision making, adult development, women's issues, brief therapy.

University of Nebraska at Omaha, Graduate Studies and Research, College of Arts and Sciences, Department of Psychology, Omaha, NE 68182. Offers developmental psychology (PhD); industrial/organizational psychology (MS, PhD); psychobiology (PhD); psychology (MA); school psychology (MS, Ed S). Part-time programs available. *Faculty:* 17 full-time (8 women). *Students:* 33 full-time (24 women), 32 part-time (26 women); includes 4 minority (2 African Americans, 1 Asian American or Pacific Islander, 1 Hispanic American), 3 international. Average age 28. 89 applicants, 56% accepted, 25 enrolled. In 2007, 16 master's, 5 other advanced degrees awarded. *Degree requirements:* For master's, comprehensive exam, thesis (for some programs). *Entrance requirements:* For master's, GRE General Test, GRE Subject Test, previous course work in psychology, including statistics and a laboratory course; minimum GPA of 3.0, 3 letters of recommendation; for doctorate, GRE General Test. Additional exam requirements/recommendations for international students: Required—TOEFL (minimum score 500 paper-based; 173 computer-based; 61 iBT). *Application deadline:* For fall admission, 1/5 for domestic students. Application fee: $45. Electronic applications accepted. *Financial support:* In 2007–08, 55 students received support; fellowships, research assistantships with tuition reimbursements available, teaching assistantships with tuition reimbursements available, career-related internships or fieldwork, Federal Work-Study, institutionally sponsored loans, scholarships/grants, tuition waivers (partial), and unspecified assistantships available. Support available to part-time students. Financial award application deadline: 3/1; financial award applicants required to submit FAFSA. *Unit head:* Dr. Kenneth Deffenbacher, Chairperson, 402-554-2592. *Application contact:* Dr. Joseph Brown, Student Contact, 402-554-2592.

University of Nevada, Las Vegas, Graduate College, College of Education, Department of Educational Psychology, Las Vegas, NV 89154-9900. Offers education psychology (MS); educational psychology (PhD); learning and technology (PhD); school counselor education (PhD); school psychology (PhD, Ed S). *Accreditation:* ACA (one or more programs are accredited); NCATE. Part-time and evening/weekend programs available. *Faculty:* 25 full-time (12 women), 2 part-time/adjunct (both women). *Students:* 57 full-time (40 women), 68 part-time (42 women); includes 27 minority (14 African Americans, 6 Asian Americans or Pacific Islanders, 7 Hispanic Americans), 6 international. 77 applicants, 49% accepted, 29 enrolled. In 2007, 19 master's, 4 doctorates, 20 other advanced degrees awarded. *Degree requirements:* For master's, comprehensive exam (for some programs), thesis (for some programs); for doctorate, comprehensive exam, thesis/dissertation, oral exam. *Entrance requirements:* For master's, GRE General Test, minimum GPA of 3.0 during previous 2 years, 2.75 overall; for doctorate, GRE General Test, minimum GPA of 3.0. Additional exam requirements/recommendations for international students: Required—TOEFL (minimum score 550 paper-based; 213 computer-based; 80 iBT). *Application deadline:* For fall admission, 2/1 for domestic and international students. Application fee: $60 ($75 for international students). Electronic applications accepted. *Expenses:* Tuition, state resident: part-time $198 per credit. Tuition, nonresident: part-time $416 per credit. Required fees: $256 per semester. Tuition and fees vary according to course load and reciprocity agreements. *Financial support:* In 2007–08, 20 research assistantships with partial tuition reimbursements (averaging $11,000 per year), 8 teaching assistantships with partial tuition reimbursements (averaging $12,000 per year) were awarded; career-related internships or fieldwork, Federal Work-Study, institutionally sponsored loans, scholarships/grants, health care benefits, and unspecified assistantships also available. Support available to part-time students. Financial award application deadline: 3/1. *Unit head:* Dr. Ralph E. Reynolds, Chair, 702-895-3787, E-mail: ralph.reynolds@unlv.edu. *Application contact:* Graduate College Admissions Evaluator, 702-895-3320, Fax: 702-895-4180, E-mail: gradcollege@unlv.edu.

The University of North Carolina at Chapel Hill, Graduate School, School of Education, Program in School Psychology, Chapel Hill, NC 27599. Offers M Ed, MA, PhD. *Accreditation:* APA (one or more programs are accredited); NCATE. *Degree requirements:* For master's, comprehensive exam, thesis (for some programs); for doctorate, comprehensive exam, thesis/dissertation. *Entrance requirements:* For master's and doctorate, GRE General Test, minimum GPA of 3.0 during last 2 years of undergraduate course work. Additional exam requirements/recommendations for international students: Required—TOEFL (minimum score 550 paper-based; 213 computer-based). Electronic applications accepted.

The University of North Carolina at Greensboro, Graduate School, School of Education, Department of Counseling and Educational Development, Greensboro, NC 27412-5001. Offers advanced school counseling (PMC); counseling and counselor education (PhD); counseling and educational development (MS); couple and family counseling (PMC); school counseling (PMC); MS/Ed S. *Accreditation:* ACA (one or more programs are accredited); NCATE. *Faculty:* 10 full-time (5 women), 1 part-time/adjunct (0 women). *Students:* 106 full-time (92 women), 18 part-time (14 women); includes 21 minority (12 African Americans, 1 American Indian/Alaska Native, 4 Asian Americans or Pacific Islanders, 4 Hispanic Americans). 314 applicants, 22% accepted. *Degree requirements:* For master's, comprehensive exam, practicum, internship; for doctorate, comprehensive exam, thesis/dissertation. *Entrance requirements:* For master's, doctorate, and PMC, GRE General Test. Additional exam requirements/recommendations for international students: Required—TOEFL. *Application deadline:* For fall admission, 2/15 for domestic students. Application fee: $45. Electronic applications accepted. *Financial support:* In 2007–08, 57 students received support; fellowships with full tuition reimbursements available, research assistantships with full tuition reimbursements available, teaching assistantships with full tuition reimbursements available, career-related internships or fieldwork, Federal Work-Study, scholarships/grants, traineeships, and unspecified assistantships available. Support available to part-time students. *Faculty research:* Gerontology, invitational theory, career development, marriage and family therapy, drug and alcohol abuse prevention. *Unit head:* Dr. DiAnne Borders, Chair and Director of Graduate Studies, 336-334-3425, Fax: 336-334-4120, E-mail: borders@uncg.edu. *Application contact:* Michelle Harkleroad, Director of Graduate Admissions, 336-334-4884, Fax: 336-334-4424, E-mail: mbharkle@uncg.edu.

University of Northern Colorado, Graduate School, College of Education and Behavioral Sciences, School of Applied Psychology and Counselor Education, Program in School Psychology, Greeley, CO 80639. Offers PhD, Ed S. *Accreditation:* APA (one or more programs are accredited); NCATE. Part-time and evening/weekend programs available. *Faculty:* 5 full-time (3 women). *Students:* 28 full-time (22 women), 26 part-time (19 women); includes 5 minority (1 African American, 1 Asian American or Pacific Islander, 3 Hispanic Americans). Average age 29. 50 applicants, 78% accepted, 8 enrolled. In 2007, 4 doctorates, 11 other advanced degrees awarded. *Degree requirements:* For doctorate, comprehensive exam, thesis/dissertation; for Ed S, comprehensive exam. *Entrance requirements:* For doctorate, GRE General Test, curriculum vitae, 3 letters of recommendation. *Application deadline:* For fall admission, 1/1 for domestic and international students. Applications are processed on a rolling basis. Application fee: $50 ($60 for international students). Electronic applications accepted. *Expenses:* Tuition, state resident: part-time $222 per credit. Tuition, nonresident: part-time $627 per credit. Required fees: $36 per credit. *Financial support:* In 2007–08, 16 research assistantships (averaging $10,978 per year) were awarded; fellowships, teaching assistantships, unspecified assistantships also available. Financial award application deadline: 3/1; financial award applicants required to submit FAFSA. *Unit head:* Dr. Michelle Athanasiou, Program Coordinator, 970-351-2731, Fax: 970-351-2625.

University of Northern Iowa, Graduate College, College of Education, Department of Educational Psychology and Foundations, Cedar Falls, IA 50614. Offers educational psychology (MAE); professional development for teachers (MAE); school psychology (Ed S). Part-time and evening/weekend programs available. *Students:* 21 full-time (15 women), 48 part-time (39 women); includes 4 minority (all African Americans), 3 international. 43 applicants, 47% accepted, 8 enrolled. In 2007, 18 degrees awarded. *Degree requirements:* For master's, comprehensive exam (for some programs), thesis or alternative; for Ed S, thesis or alternative. *Entrance requirements:* For master's, GRE General Test, minimum GPA of 3.0; for Ed S, GRE General Test. Additional exam requirements/recommendations for international students: Required—TOEFL (minimum score 500 paper-based; 180 computer-based; 61 iBT). *Application deadline:* For fall admission, 8/1 priority date for domestic students. Applications are processed on a rolling basis. Application fee: $30 ($50 for international students). Electronic applications accepted. *Expenses:* Tuition, state resident: full-time $6,246; part-time $694 per credit hour. Tuition, nonresident: full-time $14,554; part-time $694 per credit hour. Required fees: $838; $119 per semester. *Financial support:* Career-related internships or fieldwork, Federal Work-Study, scholarships/grants, and tuition waivers (full and partial) available. Support available to part-time students. Financial award application deadline: 2/1. *Unit head:* Dr. Radhi Al-Mabuk, Interim Head, 319-273-2609, Fax: 319-273-5175, E-mail: radhi.al-mabuk@uni.edu.

School Psychology

University of North Texas, Robert B. Toulouse School of Graduate Studies, College of Education, Department of Educational Psychology, Program in School Psychology, Denton, TX 76203. Offers MS. *Students:* 1 (woman) full-time, 1 (woman) part-time. Average age 37. 2 applicants, 50% accepted, 1 enrolled. *Degree requirements:* For master's, comprehensive exam, thesis optional, school psychology licensure. *Entrance requirements:* For master's, GRE General Test, undergraduate major in psychology; minimum GPA of 2.8, 3.0 in psychology. Additional exam requirements/recommendations for international students: Required—proof of English language proficiency required for non-native English speakers; Recommended—TOEFL (minimum score 550 paper-based; 213 computer-based). *Application deadline:* For fall admission, 7/15 for domestic students; for spring admission, 11/15 for domestic students. Application fee: $50 ($75 for international students). *Faculty research:* Resirience in minority families, behavioral assessment in natural settings. *Application contact:* Alica Panning, Administrative Assistant, 940-565-3486.

University of Oklahoma, Graduate College, College of Education, Department of Educational Psychology, Norman, OK 73019-0390. Offers community counseling (M Ed); counseling psychology (PhD); instructional psychology (M Ed, PhD); school counseling (M Ed); special education (M Ed, PhD). *Accreditation:* NCATE. Part-time programs available. *Faculty:* 26 full-time (16 women), 3 part-time/adjunct (1 woman). *Students:* 105 full-time (75 women), 77 part-time (54 women); includes 41 minority (17 African Americans, 15 American Indian/Alaska Native, 2 Asian Americans or Pacific Islanders, 7 Hispanic Americans), 16 international. 50 applicants, 34% accepted, 9 enrolled. In 2007, 37 master's, 13 doctorates awarded. Terminal master's awarded for partial completion of doctoral program. *Degree requirements:* For doctorate, thesis/dissertation. *Entrance requirements:* For master's, minimum GPA of 3.0, 12 hours of course work in education; for doctorate, GRE General Test, master's degree, minimum graduate GPA of 3.25. Additional exam requirements/recommendations for international students: Required—TOEFL (minimum score 550 paper-based; 213 computer-based). *Application deadline:* For fall admission, 6/1 for domestic students, 4/1 for international students; for spring admission, 11/1 for domestic students, 9/1 for international students. Applications are processed on a rolling basis. Application fee: $40 ($90 for international students). Electronic applications accepted. *Expenses:* Tuition, state resident: full-time $3,451; part-time $144 per credit hour. Tuition, nonresident: full-time $12,432; part-time $518 per credit hour. Required fees: $1,925; $70 per credit hour. $122 per semester. *Financial support:* In 2007–08, 102 students received support, including 11 fellowships with full tuition reimbursements available (averaging $3,945 per year), 17 research assistantships with partial tuition reimbursements available (averaging $11,154 per year), 16 teaching assistantships with partial tuition reimbursements available (averaging $10,596 per year); career-related internships or fieldwork, Federal Work-Study, institutionally sponsored loans, health care benefits, and unspecified assistantships also available. Financial award applicants required to submit FAFSA. *Faculty research:* Motivation, cognition and instruction; epistemic cognition and critical thinking; instructional design; computer learning environment. Total annual research expenditures: $267,154. *Unit head:* Dr. Barbara Greene, Chair, 405-325-5974, Fax: 405-325-6655, E-mail: barbara@ou.edu. *Application contact:* Applications Officer, 405-325-4525, Fax: 405-325-6655, E-mail: gpoedpsych@ou.edu.

University of Pennsylvania, Graduate School of Education, Division of Applied Psychology and Human Development, Program in School, Community, and Clinical Child Psychology, Philadelphia, PA 19104. Offers PhD. *Degree requirements:* For doctorate, thesis/dissertation, exams. *Entrance requirements:* For doctorate, GRE General Test, GRE Subject Test. Electronic applications accepted. Expenses: Contact institution. *Faculty research:* Therapeutic interventions at a preschool level, childhood stress, college psychology, school and community psychology.

University of Phoenix–Denver Campus, The Artemis School, College of Education, Lone Tree, CO 80124-5453. Offers administration and supervision (MAEd); curriculum instruction (MAEd); elementary teacher education (MAEd); school counseling (MSC); secondary teacher education (MAEd). Evening/weekend programs available. *Degree requirements:* For master's, thesis (for some programs). *Entrance requirements:* For master's, minimum undergraduate GPA of 2.5, 3 years work experience. Additional exam requirements/recommendations for international students: Required—TOEFL (minimum score 550 paper-based; 213 computer-based; 79 iBT). Electronic applications accepted.

University of Phoenix–Las Vegas Campus, The Artemis School, College of Education, Las Vegas, NV 89128. Offers administration and supervision (MA Ed); curriculum and instruction (MA Ed); school counseling (MSC); teacher education-elementary licensure (MA Ed). Evening/weekend programs available. *Degree requirements:* For master's, thesis (for some programs). *Entrance requirements:* For master's, minimum undergraduate GPA of 2.5, 3 years of work experience. Additional exam requirements/recommendations for international students: Required—TOEFL (minimum score 550 paper-based; 213 computer-based; 79 iBT). Electronic applications accepted.

University of Phoenix–Northern Nevada Campus, College of Social and Behavioral Science, Reno, NV 89511. Offers administration of justice and security (MS); marriage, family and child therapy (MSC); psychology (MS); school counseling (MSC).

University of Phoenix–Puerto Rico Campus, The Artemis School, College of Education, Guaynabo, PR 00968. Offers administration and supervision (MA Ed); early childhood education (MA Ed); school counselor (MSC). Evening/weekend programs available. *Degree requirements:* For master's, thesis (for some programs). *Entrance requirements:* For master's, minimum undergraduate GPA of 2.5, 3 years work experience. Additional exam requirements/recommendations for international students: Required—TOEFL (minimum score 550 paper-based; 213 computer-based; 79 iBT). Electronic applications accepted.

University of Phoenix–Southern Colorado Campus, The Artemis School, College of Education, Colorado Springs, CO 80919-2335. Offers administration and supervision (MA Ed); curriculum and instruction (MA Ed); elementary licensure (MA Ed); principal licensure certification (Certificate); school counseling (MSC); secondary licensure (MA Ed). Evening/weekend programs available. *Degree requirements:* For master's, thesis (for some programs). *Entrance requirements:* For master's, minimum undergraduate GPA of 2.5, 3 years of work experience. Additional exam requirements/recommendations for international students: Required—TOEFL (minimum score 550 paper-based; 213 computer-based; 79 iBT). Electronic applications accepted.

University of Phoenix–Utah Campus, The Artemis School, College of Education, Salt Lake City, UT 84123-4617. Offers administration and supervision (MA Ed); curriculum and instruction (MA Ed); elementary education (MA Ed); school counseling (MSC); secondary education (MA Ed). Evening/weekend programs available. *Degree requirements:* For master's, thesis (for some programs). *Entrance requirements:* For master's, minimum undergraduate GPA of 2.5, 3 years work experience. Additional exam requirements/recommendations for international students: Required—TOEFL (minimum score 550 paper-based; 213 computer-based; 79 iBT). Electronic applications accepted.

University of Rhode Island, Graduate School, College of Arts and Sciences, Department of Psychology, Program in School Psychology, Kingston, RI 02881. Offers MS, PhD. *Accreditation:* APA (one or more programs are accredited); NCATE. In 2007, 3 master's, 6 doctorates awarded. *Application deadline:* For spring admission, 2/15 for domestic students. Application fee: $35. *Expenses:* Tuition, state resident: full-time $6,936; part-time $385 per credit. Tuition, nonresident: full-time $19,044; part-time $1,058 per credit. Required fees: $1,508; $48 per credit. $30 per semester. One-time fee: $80 part-time. *Unit head:* Dr. Paul Bueno de Mesquita, Director, 401-874-4216.

University of South Alabama, Graduate School, College of Education, Department of Professional Studies, Mobile, AL 36688-0002. Offers community counseling (MS); educational media (M Ed, MS); instructional design and development (MS, PhD); rehabilitation counseling (MS); school counseling (M Ed); school psychometry (M Ed). *Accreditation:* NCATE. Part-time programs available. *Faculty:* 12 full-time (5 women), 7 part-time/adjunct (5 women). *Students:* 146 full-time (121 women), 178 part-time (150 women); includes 84 minority (77 African Americans, 3 American Indian/Alaska Native, 2 Asian Americans or Pacific Islanders, 2 Hispanic Americans), 14 international. 98 applicants, 69% accepted, 38 enrolled. In 2007, 30 master's, 10 doctorates awarded. *Degree requirements:* For master's, comprehensive exam. *Entrance requirements:* For master's, GRE General Test or MAT, minimum GPA of 3.0. *Application deadline:* For fall admission, 9/1 priority date for domestic students. Applications are processed on a rolling basis. Application fee: $25. *Expenses:* Tuition, state resident: full-time $4,224; part-time $176 per credit hour. Tuition, nonresident: full-time $8,448; part-time $352 per credit hour. Required fees: $802. Full-time tuition and fees vary according to program and student level. *Financial support:* In 2007–08, 5 research assistantships were awarded; career-related internships or fieldwork also available. Support available to part-time students. Financial award application deadline: 4/1. *Faculty research:* Agency counseling, rehabilitation counseling, school psychometry. *Unit head:* Dr. Charles Guest, Chair, 251-380-2861.

University of South Carolina, The Graduate School, College of Arts and Sciences, Department of Psychology, Program in School Psychology, Columbia, SC 29208. Offers PhD. *Accreditation:* APA; NCATE. *Faculty:* 5 full-time (1 woman), 4 part-time/adjunct (2 women). *Students:* 24 full-time (20 women), 11 part-time (9 women); includes 5 minority (1 African American, 3 Asian Americans or Pacific Islanders, 1 Hispanic American), 1 international. Average age 27. 65 applicants, 11% accepted. In 2007, 5 doctorates awarded. *Degree requirements:* For doctorate, thesis/dissertation. *Entrance requirements:* For doctorate, GRE General Test, minimum GPA of 3.0. Additional exam requirements/recommendations for international students: Required—TOEFL. *Application deadline:* For fall admission, 2/1 priority date for domestic students. Applications are processed on a rolling basis. Application fee: $35. Electronic applications accepted. *Expenses:* Tuition, state resident: part-time $440 per hour. Tuition, nonresident: part-time $936 per hour. Required fees: $17 per hour. Tuition and fees vary according to program. *Financial support:* In 2007–08, 3 fellowships (averaging $16,000 per year), 5 research assistantships (averaging $9,400 per year), 4 teaching assistantships (averaging $9,400 per year) were awarded; career-related internships or fieldwork, Federal Work-Study, institutionally sponsored loans, traineeships, and unspecified assistantships also available. Support available to part-time students. *Faculty research:* Preschool services, families and diversity life satisfaction, ADHD intervention, attachment. *Unit head:* Dr. E. Scott Huebner, Director, 803-777-4137, Fax: 803-777-9558, E-mail: huebner@sc.edu. *Application contact:* Marti Brown, Student Services Program Coordinator, 803-777-9482, Fax: 803-777-0670, E-mail: marthab@gwm.sc.edu.

University of Southern Maine, College of Education and Human Development, Program in School Psychology, Portland, ME 04104-9300. Offers applied behavior analysis (Certificate); school psychology (MS, Psy D). *Accreditation:* NCATE. Part-time and evening/weekend programs available. *Faculty:* 4 full-time (1 woman), 4 part-time/adjunct (3 women). *Students:* 21 full-time (17 women), 20 part-time (15 women). 40 applicants, 50% accepted, 17 enrolled. In 2007, 7 degrees awarded. *Degree requirements:* For master's, comprehensive exam, thesis or alternative, portfolio; for doctorate, comprehensive exam, thesis/dissertation or alternative, portfolio. *Entrance requirements:* For master's, GRE General Test or MAT, interview; for doctorate, GRE General Test. *Application deadline:* For fall admission, 12/1 for domestic students. Application fee: $50. Electronic applications accepted. *Financial support:* In 2007–08, 7 students received support, including 4 research assistantships with tuition reimbursements available (averaging $4,500 per year), 2 teaching assistantships with tuition reimbursements available (averaging $5,000 per year); career-related internships or fieldwork, Federal Work-Study, institutionally sponsored loans, scholarships/grants, and unspecified assistantships also available. Support available to part-time students. Financial award application deadline: 3/1; financial award applicants required to submit FAFSA. *Unit head:* Dr. E. Michael Brady, Chair, Human Resource Development Department, 207-780-5316, Fax: 207-780-5043, E-mail: mbrady@usm.maine.edu. *Application contact:* Robin Audesse, Associate Director of Graduate Admissions, 207-780-5306, Fax: 207-780-5193, E-mail: raudesse@usm.maine.edu.

University of Southern Mississippi, Graduate School, College of Education and Psychology, Department of Psychology, Hattiesburg, MS 39406-0001. Offers clinical psychology (MA, PhD); counseling psychology (PhD); experimental psychology (MA, PhD); psychology (MS); school psychology (MA, PhD). *Accreditation:* ACA; APA (one or more programs are accredited). *Faculty:* 33 full-time (12 women), 1 (woman) part-time/adjunct. *Students:* 111 full-time (87 women), 32 part-time (22 women); includes 11 minority (6 African Americans, 3 Asian Americans or Pacific Islanders, 2 Hispanic Americans), 8 international. Average age 28. 201 applicants, 21% accepted, 33 enrolled. In 2007, 32 master's, 15 doctorates awarded. Terminal master's awarded for partial completion of doctoral program. *Degree requirements:* For master's, comprehensive exam, thesis; for doctorate, comprehensive exam, thesis/dissertation. *Entrance requirements:* For master's, GRE General Test, minimum GPA of 3.0; for doctorate, GRE General Test, interview, minimum GPA of 3.0. Additional exam requirements/recommendations for international students: Required—TOEFL. *Application deadline:* For fall admission, 3/1 priority date for domestic students, 3/1 for international students. Applications are processed on a rolling basis. Application fee: $30. *Financial support:* In 2007–08, 46 research assistantships with full tuition reimbursements (averaging $7,731 per year), 49 teaching assistantships with full tuition reimbursements (averaging $7,731 per year) were awarded; career-related internships or fieldwork, Federal Work-Study, and institutionally sponsored loans also available. Financial award application deadline: 3/15. *Faculty research:* Dolphin cognition, sleep, neuropsychology, health-related behaviors, psychopathology. Total annual research expenditures: $101,200. *Unit head:* Dr. Stan Kuczaj, Chair, 601-266-4177, Fax: 601-266-5580. *Application contact:* Dr. Heather Sterling-Tairner, Graduate Coordinator, 601-266-4177, Fax: 601-266-5580.

University of South Florida, Graduate School, College of Education, Department of Psychological and Social Foundations of Education, Tampa, FL 33620-9951. Offers college student affairs (M Ed); counselor education (MA, PhD); interdisciplinary education (PhD, Ed S); school psychology (PhD, Ed S). Part-time and evening/weekend programs available. *Faculty:* 24 full-time (13 women), 3 part-time/adjunct (2 women). *Students:* 161 full-time (125 women), 102 part-time (84 women); includes 77 minority (40 African Americans, 1 American Indian/Alaska Native, 6 Asian Americans or Pacific Islanders, 30 Hispanic Americans), 6 international. 278 applicants, 55% accepted, 90 enrolled. In 2007, 56 master's, 11 doctorates awarded. *Degree requirements:* For doctorate, thesis/dissertation. *Entrance requirements:* For master's, GRE General Test, minimum GPA of 3.5 in last 60 hours of course work; for doctorate, GRE General Test, minimum GPA of 3.5 in last 60 hours of coursework; for Ed S, GRE General Test. *Application deadline:* For fall admission, 1/15 for domestic and international students. Application fee: $30. Electronic applications accepted. *Financial support:* Career-related internships or fieldwork, scholarships/grants, and unspecified assistantships available. Financial award applicants required to submit CSS PROFILE. Total annual research expenditures: $2.2 million. *Unit head:* Dr. Harold R. Keller, Chairperson, 813-974-6709, Fax: 813-974-5814, E-mail: hkeller@tempest.coedu.usf.edu. *Application contact:* Dr. Kathy Bradley, Faculty Program Coordinator, 813-974-9486, Fax: 813-974-5814, E-mail: kbradley@tempest.coedu.usf.edu.

The University of Tennessee, Graduate School, College of Education, Health and Human Sciences, Program in Education, Knoxville, TN 37996. Offers art education (MS); counseling education (PhD); cultural studies in education (PhD); curriculum (MS, Ed S); curriculum, educational research and evaluation (Ed D, PhD); early childhood education (PhD); early childhood special education (MS); education of deaf and hard of hearing (MS); educational administration and policy studies (Ed D, PhD); educational administration and supervision (Ed S); educational psychology (Ed D, PhD); elementary education (MS, Ed S); elementary teaching (MS); English education (MS, Ed S); exercise science (PhD); foreign language/ESL education (MS, Ed S); instructional technology (MS, Ed D, PhD, Ed S); literacy, language and ESL education (PhD); literacy, language education, and ESL education (Ed D); mathematics education (MS, Ed S); modified and comprehensive special education (MS); reading education (MS, Ed S); school counseling (Ed S); school psychology (PhD, Ed S); science education (MS, Ed S); secondary teaching (MS); social foundations (MS); social science education (MS, Ed S); socio-cultural foundations of sports and education (PhD); special education (Ed S);

teacher education (Ed D, PhD). *Accreditation:* NCATE. Part-time and evening/weekend programs available. *Degree requirements:* For master's and Ed S, thesis optional; for doctorate, variable foreign language requirement, thesis/dissertation. *Entrance requirements:* For master's, minimum GPA of 2.7; for doctorate and Ed S, GRE General Test, minimum GPA of 2.7. Additional exam requirements/recommendations for international students: Required—TOEFL. Electronic applications accepted.

The University of Tennessee at Chattanooga, Graduate School, College of Health, Education and Professional Studies, Graduate Studies Division of Education, Program for Educational Specialist, Chattanooga, TN 37403-2598. Offers educational technology (Ed S); school psychology (Ed S). Part-time and evening/weekend programs available. Postbaccalaureate distance learning degree programs offered (no on-campus study). *Faculty:* 4 full-time (2 women), 2 part-time/adjunct (0 women). *Students:* 25 full-time (20 women), 20 part-time (18 women); includes 2 minority (both African Americans) Average age 38. 19 applicants, 100% accepted, 13 enrolled. In 2007, 10 degrees awarded. *Degree requirements:* For Ed S, internship. *Entrance requirements:* For degree, GRE, letters of reference. Additional exam requirements/ recommendations for international students: Required—TOEFL (minimum score 550 paper-based; 213 computer-based; 79 iBT); Recommended—IELTS (minimum score 6). *Application deadline:* For fall admission, 8/1 priority date for domestic students, 6/1 for international students; for spring admission, 12/1 priority date for domestic students, 10/1 for international students. Applications are processed on a rolling basis. Application fee: $30 ($35 for international students). Electronic applications accepted. *Expenses:* Tuition, state resident: full-time $5,854; part-time $393 per hour. Tuition, nonresident: full-time $15,816; part-time $946 per hour. Required fees: $1,090; $256 per hour. *Financial support:* Career-related internships or fieldwork, Federal Work-Study, institutionally sponsored loans, scholarships/grants, and unspecified assistantships available. Support available to part-time students. Financial award application deadline: 4/1; financial award applicants required to submit FAFSA. *Faculty research:* Educational technology; using technology in the classroom; interactive media; distance learning; instructional design technological implementation. *Unit head:* Dr. Lloyd D. Davis, Coordinator, 423-425-4161, Fax: 423-425-5380, E-mail: lloyd-davis@utc.edu. *Application contact:* Dr. Deborah E. Arfken, Dean of Graduate Studies, 423-425-4666, Fax: 423-425-5223, E-mail: deborah-arfken@utc.edu.

The University of Texas at Austin, Graduate School, College of Education, Department of Educational Psychology, Austin, TX 78712-1111. Offers academic educational psychology (M Ed, MA); counseling education (M Ed); counseling psychology (PhD); human development and education (PhD); learning cognition and instruction (PhD); quantitative methods (PhD); school psychology (PhD). *Accreditation:* APA (one or more programs are accredited). *Degree requirements:* For master's, thesis optional; for doctorate, thesis/dissertation. *Entrance requirements:* For master's and doctorate, GRE General Test, 3 letters of recommendation. Additional exam requirements/recommendations for international students: Required—TOEFL.

The University of Texas at Tyler, College of Education and Psychology, Department of Psychology, Tyler, TX 75799-0001. Offers clinical psychology (MS), including neuropsychology, school psychology; counseling psychology (MA), including general, marriage and family; interdisciplinary studies (MSIS); school counseling (MA). Part-time and evening/weekend programs available. *Faculty:* 10 full-time (2 women), 8 part-time/adjunct (5 women). *Students:* 67 full-time (50 women), 60 part-time (50 women); includes 12 minority (4 African Americans, 1 American Indian/Alaska Native, 2 Asian Americans or Pacific Islanders, 5 Hispanic Americans). 37 applicants, 97% accepted, 32 enrolled. In 2007, 16 degrees awarded. *Degree requirements:* For master's, comprehensive exam, thesis optional. *Entrance requirements:* For master's, GRE General Test, minimum GPA of 3.0. *Application deadline:* For fall admission, 2/1 for domestic students; for spring admission, 10/1 for domestic students. Application fee: $0 ($50 for international students). Electronic applications accepted. *Expenses:* Tuition, state resident: part-time $627 per semester hour. Tuition, nonresident: part-time $908 per semester hour. Required fees: $107 per semester hour. Tuition and fees vary according to course load. *Financial support:* In 2007–08, fellowships with partial tuition reimbursements (averaging $3,000 per year), research assistantships (averaging $5,000 per year), teaching assistantships (averaging $1,500 per year) were awarded; career-related internships or fieldwork, Federal Work-Study, and institutionally sponsored loans also available. Support available to part-time students. Financial award application deadline: 7/1. *Faculty research:* Neuropsychology, child abuse, psychometric properties of psychological instruments, maternal behavior, clinical practice issues, victimization of women, post-traumatic stress disorder. *Unit head:* Dr. Charles B. Barke, Interim Chair, 903-565-5875, Fax: 903-565-5560, E-mail: cbarke@uttyler.edu. *Application contact:* Pam Morrow, Assistant to Dean for Enrollment Management, 903-566-7205, Fax: 903-566-7068, E-mail: pmorrow@uttyler.edu.

The University of Texas–Pan American, College of Education, Department of Educational Psychology, Edinburg, TX 78541-2999. Offers counseling (M Ed); educational diagnostician (M Ed); gifted education (M Ed); school psychology (MA); special education (M Ed). Part-time and evening/weekend programs available. *Degree requirements:* For master's, comprehensive exam (for some programs), thesis (for some programs). *Entrance requirements:* For master's, GRE General Test, interview. *Faculty research:* Reading instruction, assessment practice, behavior interventions consultation, mental retardation.

University of the Pacific, School of Education, Department of Educational and School Psychology, Stockton, CA 95211-0197. Offers educational psychology (MA, Ed D); school psychology (Ed S). *Accreditation:* NCATE. *Faculty:* 4 full-time (3 women), 3 part-time/ adjunct (2 women). *Students:* 11 full-time (10 women), 13 part-time (11 women); includes 11 minority (4 Asian Americans or Pacific Islanders, 7 Hispanic Americans). Average age 29. 11 applicants, 27% accepted, 3 enrolled. In 2007, 15 master's, 3 doctorates awarded. *Degree requirements:* For master's, thesis (for some programs); for doctorate, thesis/dissertation. *Entrance requirements:* For master's and doctorate, GRE General Test, GRE Subject Test. Additional exam requirements/recommendations for international students: Required—TOEFL (minimum score 475 paper-based; 150 computer-based). *Application deadline:* For fall admission, 3/1 priority date for domestic students; for spring admission, 10/1 priority date for domestic students. Applications are processed on a rolling basis. Application fee: $75. *Financial support:* In 2007–08, 6 teaching assistantships were awarded. Financial award application deadline: 3/1; financial award applicants required to submit FAFSA. *Unit head:* Dr. Linda Webster, Chairperson, 209-946-2559, E-mail: lwebster@pacific.edu.

The University of Toledo, College of Graduate Studies, College of Health Science and Human Service, Division of Human Services, Toledo, OH 43606-3390. Offers counselor education and school psychology (MA, PhD, Ed S), including counselor education, guidance/ counselor education (PhD), school psychology (MA, Ed S); criminal justice (MA, Certificate), including criminal justice (MA), juvenile justice (Certificate), severe behavioral spectrum (Certificate); health and rehabilitative services (MA), including speech language pathology; health education (PhD); kinesiology (MSX, PhD), including exercise science; recreation and leisure (MA); social work (MSW); speech-language pathology (MA). *Faculty:* 47. *Students:* 197 full-time (149 women), 156 part-time (126 women); includes 56 minority (50 African Americans, 1 Asian American or Pacific Islander, 5 Hispanic Americans), 9 international. Average age 31. 307 applicants, 64% accepted, 119 enrolled. In 2007, 103 master's, 12 doctorates, 11 other advanced degrees awarded. *Application deadline:* For fall admission, 1/15 priority date for domestic students. Application fee: $45. *Financial support:* In 2007–08, 7 research assistantships with full tuition reimbursements (averaging $11,000 per year), 32 teaching assistantships with full tuition reimbursements (averaging $10,600 per year) were awarded; Federal Work-Study, scholarships/grants, and unspecified assistantships also available. *Unit head:* Dr. Margaret F. Traband, Interim Dean, College of Health Science and Human Service, E-mail: margaret.traband@utoledo.edu.

The University of Toledo, College of Graduate Studies, College of Health Science and Human Service, Division of Human Services, Department of Counselor Education and School Psychology, Program in School Psychology, Toledo, OH 43606-3390. Offers school counseling (MA); school psychology (Ed S). *Students:* 14 full-time (11 women), 9 part-time (all women); includes 2 minority (1 African American, 1 Hispanic American). Average age 25. 35 applicants, 46% accepted, 15 enrolled. In 2007, 10 master's, 8 other advanced degrees awarded. *Entrance requirements:* For master's, GRE. *Application deadline:* For fall admission, 1/15 priority date for domestic students. Application fee: $45. *Financial support:* Research assistantships with tuition reimbursements, teaching assistantships with tuition reimbursements, Federal Work-Study, scholarships/grants, tuition waivers, and unspecified assistantships available. *Application contact:* Wendy Luellen, Information Contact, 419-530-2013, E-mail: wendy.luellen@utoledo.edu.

University of Utah, The Graduate School, College of Education, Department of Educational Psychology, Salt Lake City, UT 84112-1107. Offers counseling psychology (PhD); educational psychology (MA); professional counseling (MS); professional psychology (M Ed); school counseling (M Ed, MS); school psychology (MS, PhD); statistics (M Stat). *Accreditation:* APA (one or more programs are accredited). Evening/weekend programs available. *Faculty:* 18 full-time (7 women), 8 part-time/adjunct (3 women). *Students:* 79 full-time (47 women), 85 part-time (57 women); includes 17 minority (1 African American, 3 American Indian/Alaska Native, 5 Asian Americans or Pacific Islanders, 8 Hispanic Americans), 5 international. Average age 32. 193 applicants, 32% accepted, 62 enrolled. In 2007, 41 master's, 15 doctorates awarded. *Degree requirements:* For master's, variable foreign language requirement, comprehensive exam, thesis (for some programs); for doctorate, variable foreign language requirement, thesis/dissertation, oral exam. *Entrance requirements:* For master's and doctorate, GRE General Test, minimum GPA of 3.0. Additional exam requirements/recommendations for international students: Required—TOEFL (minimum score 500 paper-based; 173 computer-based). *Application deadline:* For fall admission, 4/1 for domestic and international students; for spring admission, 11/1 for domestic and international students. Application fee: $45 ($65 for international students). *Financial support:* In 2007–08, 20 fellowships with full tuition reimbursements (averaging $10,000 per year), 5 research assistantships with full tuition reimbursements (averaging $10,000 per year), 32 teaching assistantships with full and partial tuition reimbursements (averaging $10,000 per year) were awarded; career-related internships or fieldwork, Federal Work-Study, institutionally sponsored loans, scholarships/grants, and unspecified assistantships also available. Financial award application deadline: 2/1; financial award applicants required to submit FAFSA. *Faculty research:* Autism, computer technology and instruction, cognitive behavior, aging, group counseling 50728. Total annual research expenditures:$50,728. *Unit head:* Dr. Elaine Clark, Chair, 801-581-7148, Fax: 801-581-5566, E-mail: clark@ed.utah.edu. *Application contact:* Sherrill Christensen, Academic Program Specialist, 801-581-7148, Fax: 801-581-5566, E-mail: sherrill.christensen@ed.utah.edu.

University of Virginia, Curry School of Education, Department of Human Services, Charlottesville, VA 22903. Offers clinical and school psychology (Ed D, PhD); communication disorders (M Ed); counselor education (M Ed, Ed D, Ed S); health and physical education (M Ed, Ed D), including kinesiology. *Accreditation:* APA (one or more programs are accredited). *Faculty:* 28 full-time (15 women), 1 (woman) part-time/adjunct. *Students:* 130 full-time (109 women), 9 part-time (7 women); includes 12 minority (5 African Americans, 7 Asian Americans or Pacific Islanders), 3 international. Average age 25. 238 applicants, 48% accepted, 48 enrolled. In 2007, 83 master's, 1 doctorate awarded. *Entrance requirements:* For master's, doctorate, and Ed S, GRE General Test. Additional exam requirements/recommendations for international students: Required—TOEFL (minimum score 600 paper-based; 250 computer-based). *Application deadline:* Applications are processed on a rolling basis. Application fee: $60. *Financial support:* Fellowships with tuition reimbursements, research assistantships with tuition reimbursements, teaching assistantships with tuition reimbursements available. Financial award applicants required to submit FAFSA. *Unit head:* Ronald E. Reeve, Chair, 434-924-6254. *Application contact:* Lynn Renfroe, Information Contact, 434-924-6254, E-mail: ldr9t@virginia.edu.

University of Washington, Graduate School, College of Education, Program in Educational Psychology, Seattle, WA 98195. Offers human development and cognition (M Ed, PhD); measurement and research (M Ed, PhD); school counseling (M Ed, PhD); school psychology (M Ed, PhD). *Accreditation:* APA. *Degree requirements:* For master's, thesis optional; for doctorate, thesis/dissertation. *Entrance requirements:* For master's and doctorate, GRE General Test, minimum GPA of 3.0. Additional exam requirements/recommendations for international students: Required—TOEFL.

University of Wisconsin–Eau Claire, College of Arts and Sciences, Department of Psychology, Eau Claire, WI 54702-4004. Offers school psychology (MSE, Ed S). *Faculty:* 13 full-time (7 women). *Students:* 14 full-time (12 women), 9 part-time (7 women), 1 international. Average age 25. 42 applicants, 36% accepted, 14 enrolled. In 2007, 17 degrees awarded. *Degree requirements:* For master's, comprehensive exam, thesis. *Entrance requirements:* For master's, GRE, minimum undergraduate GPA of 3.07. *Application deadline:* For fall admission, 3/1 for domestic students. Applications are processed on a rolling basis. Application fee: $45. Electronic applications accepted. *Expenses:* Tuition, state resident: full-time $6,870; part-time $381 per credit. Tuition, nonresident: full-time $17,480; part-time $971 per credit. Tuition and fees vary according to reciprocity agreements. *Financial support:* In 2007–08, 15 students received support, including 6 teaching assistantships (averaging $3,600 per year); Federal Work-Study also available. Financial award application deadline: 4/15; financial award applicants required to submit FAFSA. *Unit head:* Dr. Barbara Lozar, Program Director, 715-836-5733, Fax: 715-836-2214, E-mail: lozarb@uwec.edu.

University of Wisconsin–La Crosse, Office of University Graduate Studies, College of Liberal Studies, Department of Psychology, Program in School Psychology, La Crosse, WI 54601-3742. Offers MS Ed, Ed S. *Faculty:* 9 full-time (6 women), 6 part-time/adjunct (4 women). *Students:* 15 full-time (12 women), 28 part-time (23 women). Average age 25. 47 applicants, 89% accepted, 6 enrolled. In 2007, 19 degrees awarded. *Degree requirements:* For master's, comprehensive exam, thesis. *Entrance requirements:* For master's, GRE, 3 letters of recommendation, writing sample, resumé. *Financial support:* In 2007–08, 3 research assistantships (averaging $6,516 per year) were awarded. *Faculty research:* Substance use in children, parent tutoring, crisis management in schools, life satisfaction, hope and optimism in children. *Unit head:* Dr. Rob Dixon, School Psychology Program Director, 608-785-6893, Fax: 608-785-8443, E-mail: dixon.rob@uwlax.edu. *Application contact:* Kathryn Kiefer, Associate Director of Admissions, 608-785-8939, E-mail: admissions@uwlac.edu.

University of Wisconsin–Milwaukee, Graduate School, School of Education, Program in School Psychology, Milwaukee, WI 53201-0413. Offers Ed S. *Accreditation:* APA. *Students:* 4 full-time (3 women), 6 part-time (all women); includes 1 minority (Hispanic American) 6 applicants, 50% accepted, 0 enrolled. *Expenses:* Tuition, state resident: part-time $530 per credit. Tuition, nonresident: part-time $1,428 per credit. Required fees: $19 per credit. $229 per term. Tuition and fees vary according to course load and program. *Unit head:* Alfonzo Thurman, Dean, School of Education, 414-229-4181, E-mail: athurman@uwm.edu.

University of Wisconsin–River Falls, Outreach and Graduate Studies, College of Education and Professional Studies, Department of Counseling and School Psychology, River Falls, WI 54022-5001. Offers counseling (MSE); school psychology (MSE, Ed S). *Accreditation:* NCATE. Part-time programs available. *Faculty:* 5 full-time (1 woman). *Students:* 104. In 2007, 29 master's, 8 other advanced degrees awarded. *Entrance requirements:* For master's, minimum GPA of 2.75, resumé, 3 letters of reference, vita. Additional exam requirements/recommendations for international students: Required—TOEFL (minimum score 500 paper-based; 65 iBT), IELTS (minimum score 6). *Application deadline:* For fall admission, 2/1 for domestic students. Application fee: $45. Electronic applications accepted. *Financial support:* Research assistantships, Federal Work-Study available. Financial award application deadline: 3/1. *Unit head:* Dr. Donald Lee Stovall, Chair, 715-425-3291, Fax: 715-425-3242, E-mail: donald.lee.stovall@uwrf.edu. *Application contact:* Kristine Tappe, Program Assistant II, 715-425-3843, Fax: 715-425-3185, E-mail: kristine.tappe@uwrf.edu.

University of Wisconsin–Stout, Graduate School, School of Education, Program in School Psychology, Menomonie, WI 54751. Offers MS Ed, Ed S. Part-time programs available. *Faculty:*

School Psychology

University of Wisconsin–Stout (continued)
18 full-time (10 women). *Students:* 23 full-time (19 women), 8 part-time (6 women); includes 3 minority (1 African American, 2 Hispanic Americans). Average age 26. 43 applicants, 33% accepted, 9 enrolled. In 2007, 11 master's, 7 Ed Ss awarded. *Degree requirements:* For master's and Ed S, thesis. *Entrance requirements:* For master's, minimum GPA of 3.0; for Ed S, minimum GPA of 3.25. Additional exam requirements/recommendations for international students: Required—TOEFL (minimum score 500 paper-based; 173 computer-based; 61 iBT). *Application deadline:* For fall admission, 1/15 priority date for domestic and international students. Applications are processed on a rolling basis. Application fee: $45. Electronic applications accepted. *Expenses:* Tuition, state resident: part-time $332 per credit. Tuition, nonresident: part-time $553 per credit. *Financial support:* In 2007–08, 9 research assistantships with partial tuition reimbursements (averaging $6,979 per year) were awarded; Federal Work-Study, scholarships/grants, health care benefits, tuition waivers (partial), and unspecified assistantships also available. Support available to part-time students. Financial award application deadline: 4/1; financial award applicants required to submit FAFSA. *Faculty research:* Intelligence assessment, eating disorders, intervention models, resilience, school violence. *Unit head:* Dr. Jacalyn Weissenburger, Director, 715-232-1326, E-mail: weissenburgj@uwstout.edu. *Application contact:* Anne E. Johnson, Graduate Student Evaluator, 715-232-1322, Fax: 715-232-2413, E-mail: johnsona@uwstout.edu.

University of Wisconsin–Whitewater, School of Graduate Studies, College of Education, Department of Counselor Education, Whitewater, WI 53190-1790. Offers community counseling (MS Ed); higher education (MS Ed); school counseling (MS Ed). *Accreditation:* ACA; NCATE. Part-time and evening/weekend programs available. *Students:* 31 full-time (25 women), 96 part-time (80 women); includes 9 minority (1 African American, 1 Asian American or Pacific Islander, 7 Hispanic Americans). Average age 32. 39 applicants, 92% accepted, 18 enrolled. In 2007, 30 degrees awarded. *Degree requirements:* For master's, thesis or alternative. *Entrance requirements:* For master's, resumé, 2 letters of reference. Additional exam requirements/recommendations for international students: Required—TOEFL (minimum score 550 paper-based; 213 computer-based). *Application deadline:* For fall admission, 2/1 for domestic and international students. Application fee: $45. Electronic applications accepted. *Expenses:* Tuition, state resident: full-time $3,451; part-time $244 per credit. Tuition, nonresident: full-time $8,756; part-time $560 per credit. *Financial support:* In 2007–08, 1 research assistantship (averaging $9,875 per year) was awarded; Federal Work-Study, unspecified assistantships, and out of state fee waiver also available. Support available to part-time students. Financial award application deadline: 3/15; financial award applicants required to submit FAFSA. *Faculty research:* Alcohol and other drugs, counseling effectiveness, teacher mentoring. *Unit head:* Dr. Brenda O'Beirne, Coordinator, 262-472-1452, Fax: 262-472-2841, E-mail: obeirneneb@uww.edu. *Application contact:* Sally A. Lange, School of Graduate Studies, 262-472-1006, Fax: 262-472-5027, E-mail: gradschl@uww.edu.

University of Wisconsin–Whitewater, School of Graduate Studies, College of Letters and Sciences, Department of Psychology, Program in School Psychology, Whitewater, WI 53190-1790. Offers Ed S. Part-time and evening/weekend programs available. Postbaccalaureate distance learning degree programs offered (no on-campus study). *Students:* 21 full-time (17 women), 13 part-time (10 women); includes 4 minority (1 African American, 1 American Indian/Alaska Native, 2 Asian Americans or Pacific Islanders). Average age 26. 21 applicants, 90% accepted, 18 enrolled. *Degree requirements:* For Ed S, specialist project. *Entrance requirements:* For degree, master's degree in school psychology from an accredited school. Additional exam requirements/recommendations for international students: Required—TOEFL (minimum score 550 paper-based; 213 computer-based). *Application deadline:* For fall and spring admission, 3/1 for domestic and international students. Applications are processed on a rolling basis. Application fee: $45. Electronic applications accepted. *Expenses:* Tuition, state resident: full-time $3,451; part-time $244 per credit. Tuition, nonresident: full-time $8,756; part-time $560 per credit. *Financial support:* Research assistantships available. *Unit head:* Dr. James Larson, Coordinator, 262-472-5412, Fax: 262-472-1863, E-mail: larsonj@uww.edu. *Application contact:* Sally A. Lange, School of Graduate Studies, 262-472-1006, Fax: 262-472-5027, E-mail: gradschl@uww.edu.

Utah State University, School of Graduate Studies, College of Education and Human Services, Department of Psychology, Logan, UT 84322. Offers clinical/counseling/school psychology (PhD); research and evaluation methodology (PhD); school counseling (MS); school psychology (MS). *Accreditation:* APA (one or more programs are accredited). Part-time and evening/weekend programs available. Postbaccalaureate distance learning degree programs offered (no on-campus study). Terminal master's awarded for partial completion of doctoral program. *Degree requirements:* For master's, thesis (for some programs); for doctorate, thesis/dissertation. *Entrance requirements:* For master's, GRE General Test (school psychology), MAT (school counseling), minimum GPA of 3.5; for doctorate, GRE General Test, minimum GPA of 3.5. Additional exam requirements/recommendations for international students: Required—TOEFL. *Faculty research:* Hearing loss detection in infancy, ADHD, eating disorders, domestic violence, neuropsychology, bilingual/Spanish speaking students/parents.

Valdosta State University, Graduate School, College of Education, Department of Psychology and Counseling, Valdosta, GA 31698. Offers clinical/counseling psychology (MS); industrial/organizational psychology (MS); school counseling (M Ed, Ed S); school psychology (Ed S). Part-time and evening/weekend programs available. *Faculty:* 16 full-time (2 women). *Students:* 61 full-time (48 women), 38 part-time (31 women); includes 22 minority (19 African Americans, 1 American Indian/Alaska Native, 1 Asian American or Pacific Islander, 1 Hispanic American). Average age 27. 103 applicants, 31% accepted, 22 enrolled. In 2007, 25 degrees awarded. *Degree requirements:* For master's, thesis or alternative, comprehensive written and/or oral exams; for Ed S, thesis. *Entrance requirements:* For master's and Ed S, GRE General Test or MAT. Additional exam requirements/recommendations for international students: Required—TOEFL (minimum score 523 paper-based; 193 computer-based). *Application deadline:* For fall admission, 7/1 for domestic and international students; for spring admission, 11/15 for domestic and international students. Applications are processed on a rolling basis. Application fee: $40. Electronic applications accepted. *Expenses:* Tuition, state resident: part-time $147 per hour. Tuition, nonresident: part-time $586 per hour. Required fees: $520 per semester. Tuition and fees vary according to course level, course load, campus/location and program. *Financial support:* In 2007–08, 2 students received support, including 2 research assistantships with full tuition reimbursements available (averaging $2,452 per year); institutionally sponsored loans and unspecified assistantships also available. Support available to part-time students. Financial award application deadline: 7/1; financial award applicants required to submit FAFSA. *Faculty research:* Using Bender-Gestalt to predict graphomotor dimensions of the draw-a-person test, neurobehavioral hemispheric dominance. *Unit head:* Dr. Robert Bauer, Chair, 229-333-5930, Fax: 229-259-5576, E-mail: bbauer@valdosta.edu.

Valparaiso University, Graduate Division, Department of Education, Program in School Psychology, Valparaiso, IN 46383. Offers M Ed/Ed S. Part-time and evening/weekend programs available. *Students:* 20 full-time (16 women), 10 part-time (all women). Average age 27. *Entrance requirements:* Additional exam requirements/recommendations for international students: Required—TOEFL (minimum score 550 paper-based; 213 computer-based). *Application deadline:* Applications are processed on a rolling basis. Application fee: $30 ($50 for international students). Electronic applications accepted. *Financial support:* Unspecified assistantships available. Support available to part-time students. Financial award applicants required to submit FAFSA.

Walden University, Graduate Programs, School of Psychology, Minneapolis, MN 55401. Offers clinical assessment (Post-Doctoral Certificate); clinical child psychology (Post-Doctoral Certificate); clinical psychology (PhD, Post-Doctoral Certificate); counseling psychology (PhD, Post-Doctoral Certificate); general psychology (MS, PhD, Post-Doctoral Certificate); health psychology (PhD, Post-Doctoral Certificate); organizational psychology (PhD, Post-Doctoral Certificate); organizational psychology and development (MS); school psychology (PhD, Post-Doctoral Certificate); teaching online (Post-Doctoral Certificate). Part-time and evening/weekend programs available. Postbaccalaureate distance learning degree programs offered (minimal on-campus study). *Students:* 1,428 full-time (1,130 women), 1,933 part-time (1,483 women); includes 959 minority (737 African Americans, 35 American Indian/Alaska Native, 53 Asian Americans or Pacific Islanders, 134 Hispanic Americans), 39 international. Average age 40. 1,254 applicants, 75% accepted, 548 enrolled. In 2007, 182 master's, 43 doctorates awarded. *Degree requirements:* For master's, thesis; for doctorate, thesis/dissertation, brief dispersed residency sessions. *Entrance requirements:* For master's, minimum GPA of 3.0; for doctorate, 3 years of professional experience, master's degree; for Post-Doctoral Certificate, PhD in related field, 3 years of professional experience. Additional exam requirements/recommendations for international students: Required—TOEFL (minimum score 550 paper-based; 213 computer-based), IELTS (minimum score 7). *Application deadline:* For fall admission, 8/15 priority date for domestic and international students; for winter admission, 11/15 priority date for domestic and international students; for spring admission, 12/15 priority date for domestic and international students. Applications are processed on a rolling basis. Application fee: $50. Electronic applications accepted. *Financial support:* Fellowships with partial tuition reimbursements, career-related internships or fieldwork, Federal Work-Study, institutionally sponsored loans, scholarships/grants, tuition waivers (partial), and unspecified assistantships available. Support available to part-time students. Financial award applicants required to submit FAFSA. *Faculty research:* Clinical psychology, organizational psychology, forensic psychology, group processes, educational psychology. *Unit head:* Dr. Nina Nabors, Associate Dean, 800-925-3368. *Application contact:* 866-4-WALDEN, Fax: 410-843-8780, E-mail: request@waldenu.edu.

Washington State University, Graduate School, College of Education, Department of Educational Leadership and Counseling Psychology, Program in Counseling Psychology, Pullman, WA 99164. Offers counseling psychology (Ed M, MA, PhD); school psychologist (Certificate). *Accreditation:* APA (one or more programs are accredited). *Faculty:* 15. *Students:* 49 full-time (34 women), 17 part-time (13 women); includes 24 minority (4 African Americans, 2 American Indian/Alaska Native, 8 Asian Americans or Pacific Islanders, 10 Hispanic Americans), 4 international. Average age 27. 113 applicants, 28% accepted, 16 enrolled. In 2007, 20 master's, 8 doctorates awarded. Terminal master's awarded for partial completion of doctoral program. *Degree requirements:* For master's, comprehensive exam (for some programs), thesis (for some programs), oral or written exam; for doctorate, comprehensive exam, thesis/dissertation, oral and written exam. *Entrance requirements:* For master's and doctorate, GRE General Test, minimum GPA of 3.0, 3 letters of recommendation. Additional exam requirements/recommendations for international students: Required—TOEFL (minimum score 550 paper-based; 213 computer-based). *Application deadline:* For fall admission, 2/1 for domestic and international students. Application fee: $50. Electronic applications accepted. *Financial support:* In 2007–08, research assistantships with partial tuition reimbursements (averaging $13,917 per year), teaching assistantships with partial tuition reimbursements (averaging $13,056 per year) were awarded; career-related internships or fieldwork, Federal Work-Study, institutionally sponsored loans, scholarships/grants, tuition waivers (partial), and unspecified assistantships also available. Financial award application deadline: 4/1; financial award applicants required to submit FAFSA. *Faculty research:* Hypnosis supervision, multicultural counseling, American Indian mental health, eating disorders. *Unit head:* Dr. Marianne Barabasz, Director of Training, 509-335-3416, Fax: 509-335-7977, E-mail: mbarabasz@wsu.edu. *Application contact:* Graduate School Admissions, 800-GRADWSU, Fax: 509-335-1949, E-mail: gradsch@wsu.edu.

Wayne State University, College of Education, Division of Theoretical and Behavioral Foundations, Detroit, MI 48202. Offers counseling (M Ed, MA, Ed D, PhD, Ed S); education evaluation and research (M Ed, Ed D, PhD); educational psychology (M Ed, Ed D, PhD, Ed S); educational sociology (M Ed, Ed D, PhD, Ed S); history and philosophy of education (M Ed, Ed D, PhD); rehabilitation counseling and community inclusion (MA, Ed S); school and community psychology (MA, Ed S); school clinical psychology (Ed S). *Accreditation:* ACA (one or more programs are accredited); CORE (one or more programs are accredited). Evening/weekend programs available. *Students:* 166 full-time (135 women), 215 part-time (173 women); includes 141 minority (127 African Americans, 3 American Indian/Alaska Native, 6 Asian Americans or Pacific Islanders, 5 Hispanic Americans), 17 international. Average age 35. 149 applicants, 50% accepted, 58 enrolled. In 2007, 90 master's, 16 doctorates, 2 other advanced degrees awarded. *Degree requirements:* For doctorate, thesis/dissertation. *Entrance requirements:* For master's, GRE; for doctorate, GRE, interview, minimum GPA of 3.0, curriculum vitae, references. Additional exam requirements/recommendations for international students: Required—TOEFL (minimum score 550 paper-based; 213 computer-based), TWE (minimum score 6). *Application deadline:* For fall admission, 7/1 for domestic students, 6/1 for international students; for winter admission, 10/1 for international students; for spring admission, 2/1 for international students. Application fee: $20 ($30 for international students). Electronic applications accepted. *Expenses:* Tuition, state resident: part-time $403 per credit hour. Tuition, nonresident: part-time $890 per credit hour. *Financial support:* In 2007–08, 1 fellowship with tuition reimbursement (averaging $14,201 per year), 2 research assistantships with tuition reimbursements (averaging $13,627 per year) were awarded; career-related internships or fieldwork, Federal Work-Study, and institutionally sponsored loans also available. *Faculty research:* Adolescents at risk, supervision of counseling. *Unit head:* Dr. JoAnne Holbert, Assistant Dean, 313-577-1721, E-mail: jholbert@wayne.edu.

Western Carolina University, Graduate School, College of Education and Allied Professions, Department of Human Services, Program in Counseling, Cullowhee, NC 28723. Offers community counseling (M Ed, MS); school counseling (MA Ed). *Accreditation:* ACA. Part-time and evening/weekend programs available. *Faculty:* 14 full-time (7 women), 5 part-time/adjunct (2 women). *Students:* 58 full-time (38 women), 37 part-time (27 women); includes 10 minority (8 African Americans, 2 Hispanic Americans), 2 international. Average age 30. 67 applicants, 72% accepted, 37 enrolled. In 2007, 37 degrees awarded. *Degree requirements:* For master's, comprehensive exam, thesis or alternative. *Entrance requirements:* For master's, GRE General Test, appropriate undergraduate with 3.0 GPA, 3 recommendations, writing sample, resume. Additional exam requirements/recommendations for international students: Required—TOEFL (minimum score 550 paper-based; 270 computer-based; 79 iBT). *Application deadline:* For fall admission, 2/1 for domestic students. Application fee: $40. *Expenses:* Tuition, state resident: full-time $2,314. Tuition, nonresident: full-time $11,899. Required fees: $2,033. Tuition and fees vary according to course load. *Financial support:* In 2007–08, 33 students received support, including 25 research assistantships with full and partial tuition reimbursements available (averaging $6,880 per year), 8 teaching assistantships with full and partial tuition reimbursements available (averaging $7,000 per year); fellowships, career-related internships or fieldwork, institutionally sponsored loans, scholarships/grants, and unspecified assistantships also available. Financial award application deadline: 3/31; financial award applicants required to submit FAFSA. *Faculty research:* Marital and family development, spirituality in counseling, home school law, sexuality education, family functioning models. *Application contact:* Admissions Specialist for Counseling, 828-227-7398, Fax: 828-227-6280, E-mail: gradsch@email.wcu.edu.

Western Carolina University, Graduate School, College of Education and Allied Professions, Department of Psychology, Cullowhee, NC 28723. Offers general psychology (MA); school psychology (MA). Part-time programs available. *Faculty:* 20 full-time (6 women). *Students:* 41 full-time (28 women), 1 part-time; includes 3 minority (2 African Americans, 1 Asian American or Pacific Islander). Average age 25. 60 applicants, 45% accepted, 13 enrolled. In 2007, 10 degrees awarded. *Degree requirements:* For master's, comprehensive exam, thesis. *Entrance requirements:* For master's, GRE General Test, appropriate undergraduate, interview, 3 letters of recommendation, personal statement. Additional exam requirements/recommendations for international students: Required—TOEFL (minimum score 550 paper-based; 270 computer-based; 79 iBT). *Application deadline:* For fall admission, 2/1 for domestic students. Application fee: $40. *Expenses:* Tuition, state resident: full-time $2,314. Tuition, nonresident: full-time $11,899. Required fees: $2,033. Tuition and fees vary according to course load. *Financial support:* In 2007–08, 32 students received support, including 32 teaching assistantships with full and partial tuition reimbursements available (averaging $7,000 per year);

fellowships, research assistantships with full and partial tuition reimbursements available, career-related internships or fieldwork, institutionally sponsored loans, scholarships/grants, and unspecified assistantships also available. Financial award application deadline: 3/31; financial award applicants required to submit FAFSA. *Faculty research:* Five-factor model of personality, evolutionary psychology, stress and worry, body image and physical attractiveness, moral decision-making, memory, learning styles. *Unit head:* Dr. David McCord, Head, 828-227-7361, Fax: 828-227-7005, E-mail: mccord@email.wcu.edu. *Application contact:* Admissions Specialist for Psychology, 828-227-7398, Fax: 828-227-7480, E-mail: gradsch@email.wcu.edu.

Western Illinois University, School of Graduate Studies, College of Arts and Sciences, Department of Psychology, Macomb, IL 61455-1390. Offers clinical/community mental health (MS); general psychology (MS); psychology (MS, SSP); school psychology (SSP). Part-time programs available. *Students:* 40 full-time (24 women), 18 part-time (10 women); includes 1 minority (Asian American or Pacific Islander), 1 international. Average age 25. 78 applicants, 35% accepted. In 2007, 15 master's, 8 other advanced degrees awarded. *Degree requirements:* For master's, comprehensive exam (for some programs), thesis or alternative. *Entrance requirements:* For master's and SSP, GRE General Test. Additional exam requirements/recommendations for international students: Required—TOEFL (minimum score 550 paper-based; 213 computer-based; 80 iBT). *Application deadline:* Applications are processed on a rolling basis. Application fee: $30. Electronic applications accepted. *Expenses:* Tuition, state resident: part-time $217 per credit hour. Tuition, nonresident: part-time $433 per credit hour. Required fees: $54 per credit hour. *Financial support:* In 2007–08, 38 students received support, including 38 research assistantships with full tuition reimbursements available (averaging $6,800 per year). Financial award applicants required to submit FAFSA. *Unit head:* Dr. Virginia Diehl, Chairperson, 309-298-1593. *Application contact:* Dr. Barbara Baily, Director of Graduate Studies/Associate Provost, 309-298-1806, Fax: 309-298-2345, E-mail: grad-office@wiu.edu.

Western Kentucky University, Graduate Studies, College of Education and Behavioral Sciences, Department of Psychology, Bowling Green, KY 42101. Offers psychology (MA); school psychology (Ed S). *Degree requirements:* For master's, comprehensive exam, thesis (for some programs); for Ed S, thesis, oral exam. *Entrance requirements:* For master's, GRE General Test; for Ed S, GRE General Test, minimum GPA of 3.5. Additional exam requirements/recommendations for international students: Required—TOEFL (minimum score 555 paper-based; 213 computer-based; 79 iBT). *Faculty research:* Neural regeneration, enhancing mobility in the elderly, improvement in visual processing in older adults, lifespan development.

Western Michigan University, Graduate College, College of Arts and Sciences, Department of Psychology, Kalamazoo, MI 49008-5202. Offers applied behavior analysis (MA, PhD); clinical psychology (MA, PhD); experimental analysis of behavior (PhD); experimental psychology (MA); industrial/organizational psychology (MA); school psychology (PhD, Ed S). *Accreditation:* APA (one or more programs are accredited). *Degree requirements:* For master's, variable foreign language requirement, thesis, oral exams; for doctorate, 2 foreign languages, comprehensive exam, thesis/dissertation, oral exams; for Ed S, thesis, oral exams. *Entrance requirements:* For master's, doctorate, and Ed S, GRE General Test.

Western New Mexico University, Graduate Division, School of Education, Silver City, NM 88062-0680. Offers bilingual education (MAT); counseling (MA); educational leadership (MA); elementary education (MAT); reading (MAT); school psychology (MA); secondary education (MAT); special education (MAT); TESOL (teaching English to speakers of other languages) (MAT). *Accreditation:* NCATE. *Faculty:* 15 full-time (8 women), 2 part-time/adjunct (both women). *Degree requirements:* For master's, comprehensive exam. *Entrance requirements:* For master's, GRE General Test, GRE Subject Test, minimum GPA of 3.2 in last 64 hours of undergraduate study. Additional exam requirements/recommendations for international students: Required—TOEFL (minimum score 550 paper-based; 213 computer-based). *Application deadline:* For fall admission, 6/1 priority date for domestic and international students; for spring admission, 10/1 priority date for domestic and international students. Applications are processed on a rolling basis. Application fee: $0. Electronic applications accepted. *Financial support:* Fellowships, research assistantships, tuition waivers (partial) available. Financial award application deadline: 4/1; financial award applicants required to submit FAFSA. *Unit head:* Dr. Patricia Manzanares-Gonzales, Dean, 505-538-6416, Fax: 505-538-6417, E-mail: manzanaresgonzalesp@wnmu.edu. *Application contact:* Dan Tressler, Director of Admissions, 505-538-6106, Fax: 505-538-6127, E-mail: tresslerd@wnmu.edu.

Wichita State University, Graduate School, College of Education, Department of Administration, Counseling, Educational and School Psychology, Wichita, KS 67260. Offers counseling (M Ed); education administration (M Ed, Ed D); educational psychology (M Ed); school psychology (Ed S). *Accreditation:* NCATE. Part-time and evening/weekend programs available. *Degree requirements:* For master's, comprehensive exam, thesis optional; for doctorate, one foreign language, thesis/dissertation; for Ed S, internship, practicum. *Entrance requirements:* For master's, minimum GPA of 2.75; for doctorate, GRE General Test. Additional exam requirements/recommendations for international students: Required—TOEFL. Electronic applications accepted.

Worcester State College, Graduate Studies, Program in School Psychology, Worcester, MA 01602-2597. Offers M Ed, CAGS. *Students:* 14 full-time (11 women), 5 part-time (4 women). Average age 29. 22 applicants, 77% accepted, 10 enrolled. *Degree requirements:* For master's, comprehensive exam (for some programs), thesis optional. *Entrance requirements:* Additional exam requirements/recommendations for international students: Required—TOEFL (minimum score 550 paper-based; 213 computer-based). *Application deadline:* For fall admission, 3/15 priority date for domestic and international students. *Expenses:* Tuition, state resident: full-time $4,230; part-time $235 per credit. Tuition, nonresident: full-time $4,230; part-time $235 per credit. *Financial support:* Career-related internships or fieldwork, scholarships/grants, and unspecified assistantships available. Financial award application deadline: 3/1; financial award applicants required to submit FAFSA. *Unit head:* Drane Tighe Cooke, Coordinator, 508-929-8673, Fax: 508-929-8164, E-mail: dcooke@worcester.edu. *Application contact:* Nicole Brown, Assistant Dean of Graduate and Continuing Education, 508-929-8787, Fax: 508-929-8100, E-mail: nbrown@worcester.edu.

Yeshiva University, Ferkauf Graduate School of Psychology, Program in School/Clinical-Child Psychology, New York, NY 10033-3201. Offers Psy D. *Accreditation:* APA. Part-time programs available. *Degree requirements:* For doctorate, comprehensive exam, thesis/dissertation. *Entrance requirements:* For doctorate, GRE General Test. *Faculty research:* Testing, early childhood intervention, child and adolescent psychotherapy, clinical child psychology.

Social Psychology

Alvernia College, Graduate and Continuing Studies, Department of Psychology, Reading, PA 19607-1799. Offers community counseling (MA). *Entrance requirements:* For master's, GRE or MAT.

American University, College of Arts and Sciences, Department of Psychology, Program in Psychology, Washington, DC 20016-8001. Offers experimental/biological psychology (MA); general psychology (MA); personality/social psychology (MA). Part-time programs available. *Students:* 42 full-time (35 women), 18 part-time (15 women); includes 11 minority (5 African Americans, 3 Asian Americans or Pacific Islanders, 3 Hispanic Americans), 1 international. Average age 26. In 2007, 28 degrees awarded. *Degree requirements:* For master's, comprehensive exam, thesis or alternative. *Entrance requirements:* For master's, GRE General Test, GRE Subject Test. *Application deadline:* For fall admission, 3/1 for domestic students. Applications are processed on a rolling basis. Application fee: $50. *Expenses:* Tuition: Full-time $19,998; part-time $1,111 per credit hour. Required fees: $380. Tuition and fees vary according to program. *Financial support:* Research assistantships, teaching assistantships available. Financial award application deadline: 2/1. *Faculty research:* Behavior therapy, cognitive behavior modification, pro-social behavior, conditioning and learning, olfaction.

Andrews University, School of Graduate Studies, School of Education, Department of Educational and Counseling Psychology, Program in Community Counseling, Berrien Springs, MI 49104. Offers MA. *Degree requirements:* For master's, thesis optional.

Appalachian State University, Cratis D. Williams Graduate School, Department of Human Development and Psychological Counseling, Boone, NC 28608. Offers community counseling (MA); marriage and family therapy (MA); school counseling (MA); student development (MA). *Accreditation:* AAMFT/COAMFTE; ACA; NCATE. Part-time programs available. *Faculty:* 28 full-time (15 women). *Students:* 77 full-time (58 women), 91 part-time (71 women); includes 16 minority (15 African Americans, 1 Asian American or Pacific Islander), 1 international. 152 applicants, 63% accepted, 57 enrolled. In 2007, 52 master's awarded. *Degree requirements:* For master's, comprehensive exam (for some programs), thesis optional, internships. *Entrance requirements:* Additional exam requirements/recommendations for international students: Required—TOEFL (minimum score 570 paper-based; 230 computer-based). *Application deadline:* For fall admission, 2/1 priority date for domestic students, 1/1 for international students; for spring admission, 6/1 for international students. Applications are processed on a rolling basis. Application fee: $50. *Expenses:* Tuition, state resident: part-time $127 per semester hour. Tuition, nonresident: part-time $597 per semester hour. Required fees: $18 per semester. *Financial support:* In 2007–08, 20 research assistantships (averaging $6,000 per year), 7 teaching assistantships (averaging $7,000 per year) were awarded; fellowships, career-related internships or fieldwork, Federal Work-Study, scholarships/grants, and unspecified assistantships also available. Financial award application deadline: 4/1. *Faculty research:* Multicultural counseling, addictions counseling, play therapy, expressive arts, child and adolescent therapy, sexual abuse counseling. *Unit head:* Dr. Lee Baruth, Chairman, 828-262-2055, E-mail: baruthlg@appstate.edu.

Arcadia University, Graduate Studies, Department of Psychology, Glenside, PA 19038-3295. Offers community counseling (MACP); school counseling (MACP). Part-time programs available. *Degree requirements:* For master's, practicum. *Entrance requirements:* For master's, GRE General Test or MAT.

Argosy University, Atlanta, College of Psychology and Behavioral Sciences, Atlanta, GA 30328. Offers clinical psychology (MA, Psy D, Postdoctoral Respecialization Certificate), including child and family psychology (Psy D), general adult clinical (Psy D), health psychology (Psy D), neuropsychology/geropsychology (Psy D); community counseling (MA), including marriage and family therapy; counselor education and supervision (Ed D); marriage and family therapy (Certificate). *Accreditation:* APA.

See Close-Up on page 1377.

Argosy University, Chicago, College of Psychology and Behavioral Sciences, Chicago, IL 60654. Offers clinical psychology (MA, Psy D), including child and adolescent psychology (Psy D), client-centered and experiential psychotherapies (Psy D), diversity and multicultural psychology (Psy D), family psychology (Psy D), forensic psychology (Psy D), health psychology (Psy D), psychoanalytic psychology (Psy D), psychology and spirituality (Psy D); community counseling (MA); counseling psychology (Ed D), including counselor education and supervision; counselor education and supervision (Ed D); organizational leadership (Ed D). *Accreditation:* APA (one or more programs are accredited). Postbaccalaureate distance learning degree programs offered (minimal on-campus study).

See Close-Up on page 1379.

Argosy University, Dallas, College of Psychology and Behavioral Sciences, Program in Community Counseling, Dallas, TX 75231. Offers MA.

See Close-Up on page 1381.

Argosy University, Denver, College of Psychology and Behavioral Sciences, Denver, CO 80203. Offers clinical psychology (MA, Psy D); community counseling (MA); counseling psychology (Ed D), including counselor education and supervision; counselor education and supervision (Ed D); forensic psychology (MA); marriage and family therapy (MA); organizational leadership (Ed D).

See Close-Up on page 1383.

Argosy University, Sarasota, College of Psychology and Behavioral Sciences, Sarasota, FL 34235. Offers community counseling (MA); counseling psychology (Ed D); counselor education and supervision (Ed D); forensic psychology (MA); marriage and family therapy (MA); mental health counseling (MA); organizational leadership (Ed D); pastoral community counseling (Ed D); school counseling (MA, Ed S); school psychology (MA).

See Close-Up on page 1403.

Argosy University, Schaumburg, College of Psychology and Behavioral Sciences, Schaumburg, IL 60173-5403. Offers clinical health psychology (Post-Graduate Certificate); clinical psychology (MA, Psy D), including child and family psychology (Psy D), clinical health psychology (Psy D), diversity and multicultural psychology (Psy D), forensic psychology (Psy D); community counseling (MA); counseling psychology (Ed D), including counselor education and supervision; counselor education and supervision (Ed D); forensic psychology (Post-Graduate Certificate); organizational leadership (Ed D). *Accreditation:* ACA; APA.

See Close-Up on page 1405.

Argosy University, Washington DC, College of Psychology and Behavioral Sciences, Arlington, VA 22209. Offers clinical psychology (MA, Psy D), including child and family psychology (Psy D), diversity and multicultural psychology (Psy D), forensic psychology (Psy D), health and neuropsychology (Psy D); community counseling (MA); counseling psychology (Ed D), including counselor education and supervision; counselor education and supervision (Ed D); forensic psychology (MA); organizational leadership (Ed D). *Accreditation:* APA.

See Close-Up on page 1413.

Arizona State University, Graduate College, College of Liberal Arts and Sciences, Division of Natural Sciences and Mathematics, Department of Psychology, Tempe, AZ 85287. Offers behavioral neuroscience (PhD); clinical psychology (PhD); cognitive/behavioral systems (PhD); developmental psychology (PhD); environmental psychology (PhD); quantitative research methods (PhD); social psychology (PhD). *Accreditation:* APA. *Degree requirements:* For doctorate, thesis/dissertation. *Entrance requirements:* For doctorate, GRE General Test, GRE Subject Test.

Social Psychology

Auburn University, Graduate School, College of Education, Department of Counseling and Counseling Psychology, Auburn University, AL 36849. Offers community agency counseling (M Ed, MS, Ed D, PhD, Ed S); counseling psychology (PhD); counselor education (Ed D, PhD); school counseling (M Ed, MS, Ed D, PhD, Ed S); school psychometry (M Ed, MS, Ed D, PhD, Ed S). *Accreditation:* ACA (one or more programs are accredited); APA (one or more programs are accredited); NCATE. Part-time programs available. *Faculty:* 10 full-time (6 women). *Students:* 51 full-time (35 women), 41 part-time (33 women); includes 27 minority (26 African Americans, 1 Hispanic American), 5 international. Average age 31. 140 applicants, 42% accepted, 30 enrolled. In 2007, 20 master's, 9 doctorates, 4 other advanced degrees awarded. *Degree requirements:* For master's, thesis (for some programs); for doctorate, thesis/dissertation; for Ed S, thesis or alternative. *Entrance requirements:* For master's and Ed S, GRE General Test; for doctorate, GRE General Test, GRE Subject Test. *Application deadline:* For fall admission, 5/15 for domestic students. Application fee: $25 ($50 for international students). Electronic applications accepted. *Financial support:* Research assistantships, Federal Work-Study and traineeships available. Support available to part-time students. Financial award application deadline: 3/15. *Faculty research:* At-risk students, substance abuse, gender roles, AIDS, professional ethics. *Unit head:* Dr. Holly Stadler, Head, 334-844-5160. *Application contact:* Dr. Joe Pittman, Interim Dean of the Graduate School, 334-844-4700.

Ball State University, Graduate School, Teachers College, Department of Counseling Psychology and Guidance Services, Program in Social Psychology, Muncie, IN 47306-1099. Offers MA. *Faculty:* 12. *Students:* 5 full-time (4 women), 3 part-time (1 woman); includes 1 minority (African American), 1 international. Average age 24. 20 applicants, 60% accepted, 1 enrolled. In 2007, 3 degrees awarded. *Entrance requirements:* For master's, GRE General Test. Application fee: $25 ($35 for international students). *Expenses:* Tuition, state resident: full-time $6,864. Tuition, nonresident: full-time $17,932. Required fees: $1,866. *Financial support:* Application deadline: 3/1. *Unit head:* Dr. Michael White, Head, 765-285-8040, Fax: 765-285-2067, E-mail: 00mjwhite@bsu.edu.

Bowling Green State University, Graduate College, College of Arts and Sciences, Department of Sociology, Bowling Green, OH 43403. Offers demography and population studies (MA); social psychology (MA); sociology (PhD). Part-time programs available. *Faculty:* 21 full-time (11 women). *Students:* 40 full-time (27 women), 8 part-time (all women); includes 4 minority (3 African Americans, 1 Hispanic American), 6 international. Average age 30. 46 applicants, 85% accepted, 11 enrolled. In 2007, 8 master's, 3 doctorates awarded. *Degree requirements:* For master's, thesis or alternative; for doctorate, comprehensive exam, thesis/dissertation. *Entrance requirements:* For master's and doctorate, GRE General Test. Additional exam requirements/recommendations for international students: Required—TOEFL. *Application deadline:* For fall admission, 1/15 priority date for domestic students. Application fee: $30. Electronic applications accepted. *Financial support:* In 2007–08, 1 fellowship with full tuition reimbursement (averaging $16,598 per year), 33 research assistantships with full tuition reimbursements (averaging $12,064 per year), 1 teaching assistantship with full tuition reimbursement (averaging $13,278 per year) were awarded; career-related internships or fieldwork, Federal Work-Study, institutionally sponsored loans, and unspecified assistantships also available. Financial award applicants required to submit FAFSA. *Faculty research:* Applied demography, criminology and deviance, family studies, population studies, social psychology. *Unit head:* Dr. Gary Lee, Chair, 419-372-2292. *Application contact:* Dr. Steve Cernkovich, Graduate Coordinator, 419-372-2743.

Brandeis University, Graduate School of Arts and Sciences, Department of Psychology, Waltham, MA 02454-9110. Offers cognitive neuroscience (PhD); general psychology (MA); social/developmental psychology (PhD). MA program offered to students enrolled in PhD program only. *Faculty:* 16 full-time (3 women), 3 part-time/adjunct (all women). *Students:* 26 full-time (19 women), 8 international. Average age 26. 44 applicants, 20% accepted, 5 enrolled. In 2007, 5 master's, 3 doctorates awarded. *Median time to degree:* Of those who began their doctoral program in fall 1999, 100% received their degree in 8 years or less. *Degree requirements:* For doctorate, comprehensive exam, thesis/dissertation. *Entrance requirements:* For doctorate, GRE General Test, GRE Subject Test (recommended), 3 letters of recommendation. Additional exam requirements/recommendations for international students: Required—TOEFL (minimum score 600 paper-based; 250 computer-based). *Application deadline:* For fall admission, 1/15 for domestic and international students. Application fee: $55. Electronic applications accepted. *Financial support:* In 2007–08, 21 fellowships with full tuition reimbursements (averaging $18,000 per year), teaching assistantships with full tuition reimbursements (averaging $3,000 per year) were awarded; institutionally sponsored loans, scholarships/grants, traineeships, health care benefits, tuition waivers (full), and unspecified assistantships also available. *Faculty research:* Development, cognition, social aging, perception. Total annual research expenditures: $5.1 million. *Unit head:* Paul DiZio, Director of Graduate Studies, 781-736-3300, Fax: 781-736-3291, E-mail: dizio@brandeis.edu. *Application contact:* Donna J. Coletti, Graduate Admissions Coordinator, 781-736-3303, Fax: 781-736-3291, E-mail: coletti@brandeis.edu.

Brigham Young University, Graduate Studies, College of Family, Home, and Social Sciences, Department of Psychology, Provo, UT 84602-1001. Offers clinical psychology (PhD); general psychology (MS); psychology (PhD), including applied social psychology, behavioral neurobiology, theoretical/philosophical psychology. *Accreditation:* APA (one or more programs are accredited). *Faculty:* 30 full-time (7 women), 10 part-time/adjunct (4 women). *Students:* 99 full-time (30 women); includes 11 minority (3 African Americans, 6 Asian Americans or Pacific Islanders, 2 Hispanic Americans), 7 international. Average age 24. 107 applicants, 23% accepted, 25 enrolled. In 2007, 9 master's, 14 doctorates awarded. *Degree requirements:* For master's, thesis; for doctorate, thesis/dissertation, publishable paper. *Entrance requirements:* For master's and doctorate, GRE General Test, minimum GPA of 3.0 in last 60 hours of course work. Additional exam requirements/recommendations for international students: Required—TOEFL. *Application deadline:* For fall admission, 1/1 for domestic students. Application fee: $50. Electronic applications accepted. *Financial support:* In 2007–08, 85 students received support, including 13 research assistantships with partial tuition reimbursements available (averaging $3,000 per year), 26 teaching assistantships with partial tuition reimbursements available (averaging $3,000 per year); fellowships, career-related internships or fieldwork, scholarships/grants, tuition waivers (partial), and unspecified assistantships also available. Financial award application deadline: 5/31. *Faculty research:* Psychotherapy process, Alzheimer's disease/dementia, psychology and law, health, psychology. Total annual research expenditures: $533,878. *Unit head:* Dr. Ramona Hopkins, Chair, 801-422-1170, Fax: 801-422-0602, E-mail: ramona_hopkins@byu.edu. *Application contact:* Karen A. Christensen, Coordinator of Student Programs, 801-422-4560, Fax: 801-422-0602, E-mail: karen_christensen@byu.edu.

Brock University, Faculty of Graduate Studies, Faculty of Social Sciences, Program in Psychology, St. Catharines, ON L2S 3A1, Canada. Offers behavioral neuroscience (MA, PhD); life span development (MA, PhD); social personality (MA, PhD). Part-time programs available. *Degree requirements:* For master's, thesis; for doctorate, thesis/dissertation. *Entrance requirements:* For master's, GRE, honors degree; for doctorate, GRE, master's degree. Additional exam requirements/recommendations for international students: Required—TOEFL (minimum score 550 paper-based; 213 computer-based; 80 iBT), IELTS (minimum score 7), TWE (minimum score 4). Electronic applications accepted. *Faculty research:* Social personality, behavioral neuroscience, life-span development.

Brooklyn College of the City University of New York, Division of Graduate Studies, Department of Psychology, Brooklyn, NY 11210-2889. Offers experimental psychology (MA); industrial and organizational psychology (MA), including industrial and organizational psychology-human relations, psychology-organizational psychology and behavior; mental health counseling (MA); psychology (PhD). The City University doctoral program in experimental psychology is based at Brooklyn College; candidates who complete the MA may apply for admission to the doctoral program. MA programs in industrial and organizational psychology and mental health counseling are fall admissions only. Part-time programs available. *Students:* 57 full-time (49 women), 91 part-time (73 women); includes 67 minority (39 African Americans, 1 American Indian/Alaska Native, 13 Asian Americans or Pacific Islanders, 14 Hispanic Americans), 9 international. 207 applicants, 60% accepted, 77 enrolled. In 2007, 37 degrees awarded. *Degree requirements:* For master's, comprehensive exam, thesis (for some programs). *Entrance requirements:* For master's, minimum GPA of 3.0, 2 letters of recommendation, essay; for doctorate, GRE. Additional exam requirements/recommendations for international students: Required—TOEFL. *Application deadline:* For fall admission, 3/1 for domestic students, 2/1 for international students; for spring admission, 11/1 for domestic students, 10/1 for international students. Applications are processed on a rolling basis. Application fee: $125. Electronic applications accepted. *Financial support:* Career-related internships or fieldwork, Federal Work-Study, institutionally sponsored loans, scholarships/grants, and tuition waivers (partial) available. Support available to part-time students. Financial award application deadline: 5/1; financial award applicants required to submit FAFSA. *Unit head:* Dr. Glen Hass, Chairperson, 718-951-5601, Fax: 718-951-4814, E-mail: ghass@brooklyn.cuny.edu. *Application contact:* Hernan Sierra, Graduate Admissions Coordinator, 718-951-4536, Fax: 718-951-4506, E-mail: grads@brooklyn.cuny.edu.

California Institute of Integral Studies, Graduate Programs, School of Professional Psychology, San Francisco, CA 94103. Offers clinical psychology (Psy D); community mental health (MA); drama therapy (MA); expressive arts therapy (MA); integral counseling psychology (MA); integral counseling, psychology-weekend (MA); psychology (Psy D), including clinical psychology; somatic psychology (MA). *Accreditation:* APA. Part-time programs available. *Faculty:* 28 full-time, 54 part-time/adjunct. *Students:* 591; includes 113 minority (19 African Americans, 3 American Indian/Alaska Native, 48 Asian Americans or Pacific Islanders, 43 Hispanic Americans). Average age 37. 383 applicants, 75% accepted, 155 enrolled. In 2007, 109 master's, 20 doctorates awarded. *Degree requirements:* For master's, comprehensive exam; for doctorate, comprehensive exam, thesis/dissertation. *Entrance requirements:* For master's, minimum GPA of 3.0, letters of recommendation, writing sample; for doctorate, GRE, MA in psychology or social work with appropriate practical experience for advanced standing, or BA with a minimum GPA of 3.1; letters of recommendation; writing sample. Additional exam requirements/recommendations for international students: Required—TOEFL. *Application deadline:* For fall admission, 2/1 priority date for domestic and international students; for spring admission, 10/15 priority date for domestic and international students. Applications are processed on a rolling basis. Application fee: $65. Electronic applications accepted. *Expenses:* Tuition: Full-time $16,930; part-time $780 per unit. Tuition and fees vary according to course load and program. *Financial support:* In 2007–08, 393 students received support; research assistantships with tuition reimbursements available, teaching assistantships with tuition reimbursements available, career-related internships or fieldwork, Federal Work-Study, institutionally sponsored loans, scholarships/grants, and tuition waivers (partial) available. Support available to part-time students. Financial award application deadline: 3/15; financial award applicants required to submit FAFSA. *Faculty research:* Somatic psychology, comparative psychology, art therapy, transpersonal psychology, eco-psychology. *Application contact:* David Townes, Senior Admissions Counselor, 415-575-6152, Fax: 415-575-1268, E-mail: dtownes@ciis.edu.

See Close-Up on page 1421.

California State University, Fullerton, Graduate Studies, College of Humanities and Social Sciences, Department of Psychology, Fullerton, CA 92834-9480. Offers clinical/community psychology (MS); psychology (MA). Part-time programs available. *Students:* 56 full-time (43 women), 11 part-time (5 women); includes 22 minority (2 African Americans, 6 Asian Americans or Pacific Islanders, 14 Hispanic Americans), 6 international. Average age 28. 138 applicants, 28% accepted, 34 enrolled. In 2007, 22 degrees awarded. *Degree requirements:* For master's, thesis. *Entrance requirements:* For master's, GRE General Test, GRE Subject Test, undergraduate major in psychology or related field. *Application deadline:* For fall admission, 3/15 for domestic students. Application fee: $55. *Financial support:* Teaching assistantships, career-related internships or fieldwork, Federal Work-Study, institutionally sponsored loans, and scholarships/grants available. Support available to part-time students. Financial award application deadline: 3/1. *Unit head:* Dr. Daniel Kee, Chair, 714-278-3514.

Canisius College, Graduate Division, School of Education and Human Services, Department of Counseling and Human Services, Buffalo, NY 14208-1098. Offers community mental health counseling (MS); general counseling (MS); school counseling (MS). Part-time and evening/weekend programs available. *Faculty:* 5 full-time (3 women), 6 part-time/adjunct (2 women). *Students:* 93 full-time (79 women), 50 part-time (45 women); includes 16 minority (11 African Americans, 1 Asian American or Pacific Islander, 4 Hispanic Americans), 5 international. Average age 29. 93 applicants, 90% accepted, 35 enrolled. In 2007, 48 degrees awarded. *Degree requirements:* For master's, thesis, research project. *Entrance requirements:* For master's, interview, minimum GPA of 2.5. *Application deadline:* Applications are processed on a rolling basis. Application fee: $25. Electronic applications accepted. *Expenses:* Tuition: Full-time $32,574; part-time $651 per credit. Required fees: $222; $19 per credit. Tuition and fees vary according to program. *Financial support:* In 2007–08, 2 research assistantships with partial tuition reimbursements (averaging $8,500 per year) were awarded; career-related internships or fieldwork, Federal Work-Study, institutionally sponsored loans, health care benefits, and unspecified assistantships also available. Support available to part-time students. Financial award applicants required to submit FAFSA. *Faculty research:* Positive psychology, wellness, school violence prevention, chronic pain. *Unit head:* Dr. David L. Farrugia, Chairman, 716-888-2393, Fax: 716-888-3290, E-mail: farrugia@canisius.edu. *Application contact:* James D. Bagwell, Director of Graduate Recruitment and Admissions, 716-888-2544, Fax: 716-888-3290, E-mail: bagwellj@canisius.edu.

Carnegie Mellon University, College of Humanities and Social Sciences, Department of Psychology, Program in Social/Personality/Health Psychology, Pittsburgh, PA 15213-3891. Offers PhD. *Degree requirements:* For doctorate, comprehensive exam, thesis/dissertation. *Entrance requirements:* For doctorate, GRE General Test. Additional exam requirements/recommendations for international students: Required—TOEFL.

Central Connecticut State University, School of Graduate Studies, School of Arts and Sciences, Department of Psychology, New Britain, CT 06050-4010. Offers community psychology (MA); general psychology (MA); health psychology (MA). Part-time and evening/weekend programs available. *Faculty:* 21 full-time (11 women), 22 part-time/adjunct (10 women). *Students:* 21 full-time (13 women), 20 part-time (15 women); includes 5 minority (1 African American, 4 Hispanic Americans), 3 international. Average age 29. 42 applicants, 40% accepted, 11 enrolled. In 2007, 11 degrees awarded. *Degree requirements:* For master's, thesis, comprehensive exam or special project. *Entrance requirements:* For master's, minimum GPA of 2.7. Additional exam requirements/recommendations for international students: Required—TOEFL. *Application deadline:* For fall admission, 4/25 for domestic students; for spring admission, 12/1 for domestic students. Applications are processed on a rolling basis. Application fee: $50. Electronic applications accepted. *Expenses:* Tuition, area resident: Full-time $4,169. Tuition, state resident: full-time $6,253. Tuition, nonresident: full-time $11,614; part-time $400 per credit. Required fees: $3,322. One-time fee: $62 part-time. Tuition and fees vary according to degree level and program. *Financial support:* In 2007–08, 3 students received support, including 6 research assistantships; career-related internships or fieldwork, Federal Work-Study, scholarships/grants, and unspecified assistantships also available. Support available to part-time students. Financial award application deadline: 3/1; financial award applicants required to submit FAFSA. *Faculty research:* Clinical psychology, general psychology, child development, cognitive development, drugs/behavior. *Unit head:* Dr. Bradley M. Waite, Chair, 860-832-3100.

Claremont Graduate University, Graduate Programs, School of Behavioral and Organizational Sciences, Department of Psychology, Claremont, CA 91711-6160. Offers advanced study in evaluation (Certificate); cognitive psychology (MA, PhD); developmental psychology (MA, PhD); evaluation and applied research methods (MA, PhD); health behavior research and evaluation (MA, PhD); human resource development and evaluation (MA); industrial/organizational psychology (MA, PhD); organizational behavior (MA, PhD); organizational psychology (MA, PhD); social psychology (MA, PhD); MBA/PhD. Part-time programs available.

Faculty: 15 full-time (7 women), 4 part-time/adjunct (2 women). *Students:* 184 full-time (137 women), 24 part-time (20 women); includes 51 minority (13 African Americans, 1 American Indian/Alaska Native, 26 Asian Americans or Pacific Islanders, 11 Hispanic Americans), 12 international. Average age 29. In 2007, 42 master's, 10 doctorates, 2 other advanced degrees awarded. Terminal master's awarded for partial completion of doctoral program. *Degree requirements:* For master's, thesis (for some programs); for doctorate, comprehensive exam, thesis/dissertation. *Entrance requirements:* For master's and doctorate, GRE General Test. *Application deadline:* For fall admission, 2/15 priority date for domestic students. Applications are processed on a rolling basis. Electronic applications accepted. *Expenses:* Tuition: Full-time $31,640; part-time $1,376 per unit. Required fees: $145 per semester. Tuition and fees vary according to course load, degree level and program. *Financial support:* Fellowships, research assistantships, teaching assistantships, career-related internships or fieldwork, Federal Work-Study, institutionally sponsored loans, and tuition waivers (full and partial) available. Support available to part-time students. Financial award application deadline: 2/15; financial award applicants required to submit FAFSA. *Faculty research:* Social intervention, diversity in organizations, eyewitness memory, aging and cognition, drug policy. *Unit head:* Natalie Brown, Program Coordinator, 909-621-8084, Fax: 909-621-8905, E-mail: natalie.brown@cgu.edu.

Clark University, Graduate School, Department of Psychology, Program in Social-Personality Psychology, Worcester, MA 01610-1477. Offers PhD. *Degree requirements:* For doctorate, thesis/dissertation. *Entrance requirements:* For doctorate, GRE General Test. Additional exam requirements/recommendations for international students: Required—TOEFL. *Application deadline:* For fall admission, 1/1 priority date for domestic students. Applications are processed on a rolling basis. Application fee: $55. *Expenses:* Tuition: Full-time $32,600; part-time $1,019 per credit. Required fees: $30. Tuition and fees vary according to program. *Financial support:* In 2007–08, fellowships with full tuition reimbursements (averaging $15,700 per year), research assistantships with full tuition reimbursements (averaging $15,700 per year), teaching assistantships with full tuition reimbursements (averaging $15,700 per year) were awarded. *Unit head:* Dr. Joseph deRivera, Director, 508-793-7274. *Application contact:* Peggy Moskowitz, Graduate School Secretary, 508-793-7274, Fax: 508-793-7265, E-mail: psychology@clarku.edu.

The College of New Rochelle, Graduate School, Division of Human Services, Program in Community-School Psychology, New Rochelle, NY 10805-2308. Offers MS. *Faculty:* 7 full-time (3 women), 6 part-time/adjunct (2 women). *Students:* 23 full-time (20 women), 40 part-time (32 women); includes 19 minority (13 African Americans, 1 Asian American or Pacific Islander, 5 Hispanic Americans). Average age 32. In 2007, 18 degrees awarded. *Degree requirements:* For master's, comprehensive exam, clinical fieldwork, journal. *Entrance requirements:* For master's, interview, minimum GPA of 3.0, course work in psychology, sample of written work. *Application deadline:* For fall admission, 8/1 priority date for domestic students. Applications are processed on a rolling basis. Application fee: $35. *Expenses:* Tuition: Part-time $650 per credit. Required fees: $90 per term. *Financial support:* Career-related internships or fieldwork and scholarships/grants available. *Unit head:* Dr. Marie Ribarich, Associate Dean, Division of Human Services, 914-654-5561, Fax: 914-654-5593, E-mail: mribarich@cnr.edu.

College of St. Joseph, Graduate Programs, Division of Psychology and Human Services, Program in Community Counseling, Rutland, VT 05701-3899. Offers MS. Part-time and evening/weekend programs available. *Faculty:* 4 full-time (1 woman), 8 part-time/adjunct (4 women). *Students:* 3 full-time (2 women), 6 part-time (2 women). Average age 35. 5 applicants, 100% accepted, 5 enrolled. In 2007, 1 degree awarded. *Degree requirements:* For master's, comprehensive exam, thesis optional. *Entrance requirements:* For master's, 2 letters of reference, interview. *Application deadline:* Applications are processed on a rolling basis. Application fee: $35. Electronic applications accepted. *Expenses:* Tuition: Full-time $12,000; part-time $325 per credit. Required fees: $45 per semester. *Financial support:* Career-related internships or fieldwork, Federal Work-Study, and unspecified assistantships available. Support available to part-time students. Financial award application deadline: 3/1. *Application contact:* Tracy Gallipo, Director of Admissions, 802-773-5900 Ext. 3262, Fax: 802-773-5900, E-mail: tracygallipo@csj.edu.

Columbia University, Graduate School of Arts and Sciences, Division of Natural Sciences, Department of Psychology, New York, NY 10027. Offers experimental psychology (M Phil, MA, PhD); psychobiology (M Phil, MA, PhD); social psychology (M Phil, MA, PhD); JD/MA; JD/PhD; MD/PhD. *Faculty:* 23 full-time. *Students:* 35 full-time (19 women), 2 part-time. Average age 28. 156 applicants, 7% accepted. In 2007, 7 master's, 6 doctorates awarded. *Degree requirements:* For master's, thesis; for doctorate, thesis/dissertation. *Entrance requirements:* For master's and doctorate, GRE General Test. Additional exam requirements/recommendations for international students: Required—TOEFL. Application fee: $90. *Expenses:* Tuition: Part-time $1,452 per credit. Required fees: $152 per term. One-time fee: $75 part-time. Full-time tuition and fees vary according to course level, course load, degree level and program. *Financial support:* Fellowships, teaching assistantships, Federal Work-Study and institutionally sponsored loans available. Support available to part-time students. Financial award application deadline: 1/5; financial award applicants required to submit FAFSA. *Unit head:* Norma Graham, Chair, 212-854-5591, Fax: 212-854-3609, E-mail: nb2229@columbia.edu.

Cornell University, Graduate School, Graduate Fields of Arts and Sciences, Field of Psychology, Ithaca, NY 14853-0001. Offers biopsychology (PhD); human experimental psychology (PhD); personality and social psychology (PhD). *Faculty:* 42 full-time (15 women). *Students:* 33 full-time (18 women); includes 5 minority (2 African Americans, 2 Asian Americans or Pacific Islanders, 1 Hispanic American), 10 international. Average age 29. 175 applicants, 8% accepted, 8 enrolled. In 2007, 4 doctorates awarded. *Degree requirements:* For doctorate, comprehensive exam, thesis/dissertation, 2 semesters of teaching experience. *Entrance requirements:* For doctorate, GRE General Test, 3 letters of recommendation. Additional exam requirements/recommendations for international students: Required—TOEFL (minimum score 550 paper-based; 213 computer-based; 77 iBT). *Application deadline:* For fall admission, 12/15 for domestic students. Application fee: $70. Electronic applications accepted. *Financial support:* In 2007–08, 33 students received support, including 11 fellowships with full tuition reimbursements available, 22 teaching assistantships with full tuition reimbursements available; research assistantships with full tuition reimbursements available, institutionally sponsored loans, scholarships/grants, health care benefits, tuition waivers (full and partial), and unspecified assistantships also available. Financial award applicants required to submit FAFSA. *Faculty research:* Sensory and perceptual systems, social cognition, cognitive development, quantitative and computational modeling, behavioral neuroscience. *Unit head:* Director of Graduate Studies, 607-255-6364, Fax: 607-255-8433. *Application contact:* Graduate Field Assistant, 607-255-3834, Fax: 607-255-8433, E-mail: psychapp@cornell.edu.

Cornell University, Graduate School, Graduate Fields of Arts and Sciences, Field of Sociology, Ithaca, NY 14853-0001. Offers economy and society (MA, PhD); gender and life course (MA, PhD); methodology (MA, PhD); organizations (MA, PhD); policy analysis (MA, PhD); political sociology/social movements (MA, PhD); racial and ethnic relations (MA, PhD); social networks (MA, PhD); social psychology (MA, PhD); social stratification (MA, PhD). *Faculty:* 37 full-time (12 women). *Students:* 46 full-time (20 women); includes 10 minority (2 African Americans, 6 Asian Americans or Pacific Islanders, 2 Hispanic Americans), 10 international. Average age 30. 149 applicants, 7% accepted, 5 enrolled. In 2007, 4 master's, 6 doctorates awarded. Terminal master's awarded for partial completion of doctoral program. *Degree requirements:* For master's, thesis; for doctorate, thesis/dissertation, 1 year of teaching experience. *Entrance requirements:* For master's and doctorate, GRE General Test, 2 letters of recommendation, writing sample. Additional exam requirements/recommendations for international students: Required—TOEFL (minimum score 550 paper-based; 213 computer-based; 77 iBT). *Application deadline:* For fall admission, 1/15 for domestic students. Application fee: $70. Electronic applications accepted. *Financial support:* In 2007–08, 40 students received support, including 16 fellowships with full tuition reimbursements available, 8 research assistantships with full tuition reimbursements available, 16 teaching assistantships with full tuition reimbursements available; institutionally sponsored loans, scholarships/grants, health care benefits, tuition waivers (full and partial), and unspecified assistantships also available. Financial award applicants required to submit FAFSA. *Faculty research:* Comparative societal analysis, work and family, simulations, social class and mobility, racial segregation and inequality. *Unit head:* Director of Graduate Studies, 607-255-4266. *Application contact:* Graduate Field Assistant, 607-255-4266, E-mail: sociology@cornell.edu.

DePaul University, College of Liberal Arts and Sciences, Department of Psychology, Chicago, IL 60604-2287. Offers clinical psychology (MA, PhD), including child clinical psychology, community clinical psychology; experimental psychology (MA, PhD); general psychology (MS); industrial/organizational psychology (MA, PhD); MA/PhD. *Accreditation:* APA (one or more programs are accredited). *Faculty:* 31 full-time (19 women), 6 part-time/adjunct (4 women). *Students:* 57 full-time (36 women), 53 part-time (36 women); includes 24 minority (14 African Americans, 1 American Indian/Alaska Native, 3 Asian Americans or Pacific Islanders, 6 Hispanic Americans), 1 international. Average age 28. 332 applicants, 14% accepted, 23 enrolled. In 2007, 14 master's, 17 doctorates awarded. *Median time to degree:* Of those who began their doctoral program in fall 1999, 60% received their degree in 8 years or less. *Degree requirements:* For master's, thesis, oral exam; for doctorate, comprehensive exam, thesis/dissertation, oral and written exams. *Entrance requirements:* For master's and doctorate, GRE General Test, GRE Subject Test, 32 quarter hours of course work in psychology, 3 letters of recommendation. Additional exam requirements/recommendations for international students: Required—TOEFL. Application fee: $40. Electronic applications accepted. *Financial support:* In 2007–08, 48 students received support, including 35 research assistantships with full tuition reimbursements available (averaging $11,800 per year), 13 teaching assistantships with full tuition reimbursements available (averaging $11,800 per year); career-related internships or fieldwork, scholarships/grants, traineeships, tuition waivers (full and partial), and unspecified assistantships also available. Financial award application deadline: 1/10. *Faculty research:* Adolescent stress and depression, minority adolescents sexuality, public policy, community influences in child adjustment. *Unit head:* Dr. Christopher B Keys, Chairman, 773-325-7887, Fax: 773-325-7888. *Application contact:* Alison Pereida Knapp, Graduate Admissions Assistant, 773-325-7887, Fax: 773-325-7888.

Eastern Michigan University, Graduate School, College of Education, Department of Leadership and Counseling, Programs in Counseling, Ypsilanti, MI 48197. Offers college counseling (MA); community counseling (MA); helping interventions in a multicultural society (Graduate Certificate); school counseling (MA); school counselor (MA); school counselor licensure (Post Master's Certificate). Part-time and evening/weekend programs available. Postbaccalaureate distance learning degree programs offered (minimal on-campus study). *Students:* 13 full-time (all women), 129 part-time (107 women); includes 39 minority (32 African Americans, 4 Asian Americans or Pacific Islanders, 3 Hispanic Americans), 2 international. Average age 33. In 2007, 49 degrees awarded. *Entrance requirements:* Additional exam requirements/recommendations for international students: Required—TOEFL. *Application deadline:* Applications are processed on a rolling basis. Application fee: $35. *Expenses:* Tuition, state resident: full-time $8,952; part-time $373 per credit hour. Tuition, nonresident: full-time $17,634; part-time $735 per credit hour. Required fees: $896; $34 per credit hour. Tuition and fees vary according to course level, degree level and program. *Financial support:* Fellowships, research assistantships with full tuition reimbursements, teaching assistantships with full tuition reimbursements, career-related internships or fieldwork, Federal Work-Study, institutionally sponsored loans, scholarships/grants, tuition waivers (partial), and unspecified assistantships available. Support available to part-time students. Financial award applicants required to submit FAFSA. *Application contact:* Dr. Dibya Choudhuri, Advisor, 734-487-0255, Fax: 734-487-4608, E-mail: dibya.chouduri@emich.edu.

Florida Agricultural and Mechanical University, Division of Graduate Studies, Research, and Continuing Education, College of Arts and Sciences, Department of Psychology, Program in Community Psychology, Tallahassee, FL 32307-3200. Offers MS. *Degree requirements:* For master's, thesis, internship. *Entrance requirements:* For master's, GRE General Test, minimum GPA of 3.0, letters of recommendation (3). Additional exam requirements/recommendations for international students: Required—TOEFL. *Faculty research:* African-American personality and mental health, racism in the socialization of black children.

Florida State University, Graduate Studies, College of Arts and Sciences, Department of Psychology, Program in Social Psychology, Tallahassee, FL 32306. Offers PhD. *Faculty:* 5 full-time (3 women). *Students:* 18 full-time (7 women); includes 2 minority (1 Asian American or Pacific Islander, 1 Hispanic American). Average age 24. 88 applicants, 6% accepted, 5 enrolled. In 2007, 5 doctorates awarded. *Median time to degree:* Of those who began their doctoral program in fall 1999, 100% received their degree in 8 years or less. *Degree requirements:* For doctorate, thesis/dissertation, preliminary exam. *Entrance requirements:* For doctorate, GRE, minimum GPA of 3.0, research experience, letters of recommendation. Additional exam requirements/recommendations for international students: Required—TOEFL (minimum score 550 paper-based; 213 computer-based; 80 iBT). *Application deadline:* For fall admission, 12/15 for domestic and international students. Application fee: $30. *Expenses:* Tuition, state resident: part-time $248 per credit hour. Tuition, nonresident: part-time $880 per credit hour. Tuition and fees vary according to program. *Financial support:* In 2007–08, 1 fellowship with full tuition reimbursement (averaging $18,000 per year), 5 research assistantships with full tuition reimbursements (averaging $15,000 per year), 12 teaching assistantships with full tuition reimbursements (averaging $15,000 per year) were awarded; Federal Work-Study, institutionally sponsored loans, scholarships/grants, traineeships, and unspecified assistantships also available. *Faculty research:* The self, prejudice, stereotyping. Total annual research expenditures: $333,390. *Unit head:* Dr. Roy Baumeister, Director, 850-644-4200, Fax: 850-644-7739, E-mail: baumeister@psy.fsu.edu. *Application contact:* Cherie P. Miller, Graduate Program Assistant, 850-644-2499, Fax: 850-644-7739, E-mail: grad-info@psy.fsu.edu.

Francis Marion University, Graduate Programs, Department of Psychology, Florence, SC 29501-0547. Offers applied clinical psychology (MS); applied community psychology (MS); school psychology (MS). Part-time and evening/weekend programs available. *Faculty:* 10 full-time (3 women), 6 part-time/adjunct (3 women). *Students:* 12 full-time (all women), 34 part-time (31 women); includes 5 minority (all African Americans), 1 international. Average age 28. 34 applicants, 100% accepted, 9 enrolled. In 2007, 9 degrees awarded. *Degree requirements:* For master's, internship. *Entrance requirements:* For master's, GRE General Test. *Application deadline:* For fall admission, 4/15 for domestic students; for spring admission, 10/15 for domestic students. Applications are processed on a rolling basis. Application fee: $30. *Expenses:* Tuition, state resident: full-time $7,547; part-time $377 per credit hour. Tuition, nonresident: full-time $15,094; part-time $755 per credit hour. Required fees: $285; $10 per credit hour. $45 per term. *Financial support:* In 2007–08, 2 research assistantships (averaging $7,000 per year), 3 teaching assistantships (averaging $8,000 per year) were awarded; career-related internships or fieldwork and unspecified assistantships also available. Support available to part-time students. Financial award application deadline: 3/1; financial award applicants required to submit FAFSA. *Faculty research:* Critical thinking, spatial localization, cognition and aging, family psychology. *Unit head:* Dr. John R. Hester, Chair, 843-661-1635, Fax: 843-661-1628. *Application contact:* Jennifer Taylor, Administrative Assistant, 843-661-1378, Fax: 843-661-1628.

The George Washington University, Columbian College of Arts and Sciences, Department of Psychology, Washington, DC 20052. Offers applied social psychology (PhD); clinical psychology (PhD); cognitive neuropsychology (PhD); industrial-organizational psychology (PhD). *Accreditation:* APA. Part-time and evening/weekend programs available. *Degree requirements:* For doctorate, thesis/dissertation or alternative, general exam. *Entrance requirements:* For doctorate, GRE General Test, minimum GPA of 3.0. Additional exam requirements/recommendations for international students: Required—TOEFL (minimum score 550 paper-based; 213 computer-based).

Graduate School and University Center of the City University of New York, Graduate Studies, Program in Psychology, New York, NY 10016-4039. Offers basic applied neurocognition

Social Psychology

Graduate School and University Center of the City University of New York (continued)

(PhD); biopsychology (PhD); clinical psychology (PhD); developmental psychology (PhD); environmental psychology (PhD); experimental psychology (PhD); industrial psychology (PhD); learning processes (PhD); neuropsychology (PhD); psychology (PhD); social personality (PhD). *Faculty:* 119 full-time (40 women). *Students:* 510 full-time (379 women), 1 (woman) part-time; includes 98 minority (39 African Americans, 1 American Indian/Alaska Native, 21 Asian Americans or Pacific Islanders, 37 Hispanic Americans), 63 international. Average age 33. 747 applicants, 17% accepted, 78 enrolled. In 2007, 59 degrees awarded. *Degree requirements:* For doctorate, one foreign language, thesis/dissertation. *Entrance requirements:* For doctorate, GRE General Test. Additional exam requirements/recommendations for international students: Required—TOEFL. *Application deadline:* For fall admission, 12/15 for domestic students. Application fee: $125. Electronic applications accepted. *Financial support:* In 2007–08, 371 students received support, including 308 fellowships, 34 research assistantships, 33 teaching assistantships; career-related internships or fieldwork, Federal Work-Study, institutionally sponsored loans, and tuition waivers (full and partial) also available. Financial award application deadline: 2/1; financial award applicants required to submit FAFSA. *Unit head:* Dr. Joseph Glick, Executive Officer, 212-817-8706, Fax: 212-817-1533, E-mail: jglick@gc.cuny.edu.

Harvard University, Graduate School of Arts and Sciences, Department of Psychology, Cambridge, MA 02138. Offers psychology (PhD), including behavior and decision analysis, cognition, developmental psychology, experimental psychology, personality, psychobiology, psychopathology; social psychology (PhD). *Degree requirements:* For doctorate, thesis/dissertation, general exams. *Entrance requirements:* For doctorate, GRE General Test. Additional exam requirements/recommendations for international students: Required—TOEFL. *Expenses:* Tuition: Full-time $31,456. Full-time tuition and fees vary according to program and student level.

Henderson State University, Graduate Studies, School of Education, Department of Counselor Education, Arkadelphia, AR 71999-0001. Offers community counseling (MS); elementary school counseling (MSE); secondary school counseling (MSE). *Accreditation:* ACA; NCATE. Part-time programs available. *Entrance requirements:* For master's, GRE General Test or MAT, letters of recommendation, minimum GPA of 2.7, teacher certification. Additional exam requirements/recommendations for international students: Required—TOEFL (minimum score 550 paper-based; 213 computer-based).

Hofstra University, College of Liberal Arts and Sciences, Department of Psychology, Program in School-Community Psychology, Hempstead, NY 11549. Offers MS, Psy D, CAS. *Accreditation:* NCATE. *Students:* 41 full-time (33 women), 15 part-time (9 women); includes 6 minority (1 African American, 3 Asian Americans or Pacific Islanders, 2 Hispanic Americans). Average age 27. 119 applicants, 24% accepted, 12 enrolled. In 2007, 10 master's, 13 doctorates, 8 other advanced degrees awarded. *Degree requirements:* For master's, comprehensive exam; for doctorate, comprehensive exam, thesis/dissertation. *Entrance requirements:* For doctorate, GRE General Test, GRE Subject Test (psychology), interview, 3 letters of recommendation, essay. Additional exam requirements/recommendations for international students: Required—TOEFL (minimum score 550 paper-based; 213 computer-based). *Application deadline:* For fall admission, 1/15 for domestic and international students. Application fee: $60. Electronic applications accepted. *Expenses:* Tuition: Full-time $14,220; part-time $820 per credit. Required fees: $970; $165 per term. Tuition and fees vary according to program. *Financial support:* In 2007–08, 46 students received support, including 22 fellowships with tuition reimbursements available (averaging $4,591 per year), 2 research assistantships with full and partial tuition reimbursements available (averaging $13,320 per year); career-related internships or fieldwork, Federal Work-Study, institutionally sponsored loans, scholarships/grants, and tuition waivers (full and partial) also available. Support available to part-time students. Financial award applicants required to submit FAFSA. *Faculty research:* Cross-cultural psychology, school psychology, childhood & adult trauma, positive psychology, autism spectrum disorders. *Unit head:* Dr. Robert Motta, Program Director, 516-463-5029, Fax: 516-463-6052, E-mail: psyrwm@hofstra.edu. *Application contact:* Carol Drummer, Dean of Graduate Admissions, 516-463-4876, Fax: 516-463-4664, E-mail: gradstudent@hofstra.edu.

Howard University, Graduate School, Department of Psychology, Washington, DC 20059-0002. Offers clinical psychology (PhD); developmental psychology (PhD); experimental psychology (PhD); neuropsychology (PhD); personality psychology (PhD); psychology (MS); social psychology (PhD). *Accreditation:* APA (one or more programs are accredited). Part-time programs available. *Degree requirements:* For master's, thesis; for doctorate, comprehensive exam, thesis/dissertation, qualifying exam. *Entrance requirements:* For master's, GRE General Test, minimum GPA of 2.5, bachelor's degree in psychology or related field; for doctorate, GRE General Test, minimum GPA of 3.0. *Expenses:* Tuition: Full-time $16,175; part-time $899 per credit hour. Required fees: $805. *Faculty research:* Personality and psychophysiology, educational and social development of African-American children, child and adult psychopathology.

Hunter College of the City University of New York, Graduate School, School of Arts and Sciences, Department of Psychology, New York, NY 10021-5085. Offers applied and evaluative psychology (MA); biopsychology and comparative psychology (MA); social, cognitive, and developmental psychology (MA). Part-time and evening/weekend programs available. *Faculty:* 8 full-time (2 women), 4 part-time/adjunct (2 women). *Students:* 7 full-time (5 women), 68 part-time (57 women); includes 10 minority (2 African Americans, 1 Asian American or Pacific Islander, 7 Hispanic Americans). Average age 29. 100 applicants, 47% accepted, 21 enrolled. In 2007, 30 degrees awarded. *Degree requirements:* For master's, comprehensive exam, thesis. *Entrance requirements:* For master's, GRE General Test, minimum 12 credits of course work in psychology, including statistics and experimental psychology; 2 letters of recommendation. Additional exam requirements/recommendations for international students: Required—TOEFL. *Application deadline:* For fall admission, 4/1 for domestic students, 2/1 for international students; for spring admission, 11/1 for domestic students, 9/1 for international students. Applications are processed on a rolling basis. Application fee: $125. *Expenses:* Tuition, state resident: full-time $6,400; part-time $270 per credit. Tuition, nonresident: part-time $500 per credit. One-time fee: $125 full-time. Tuition and fees vary according to program. *Financial support:* Federal Work-Study, scholarships/grants, and tuition waivers (partial) available. Support available to part-time students. *Faculty research:* Personality, cognitive and linguistic development, hormonal and neural control of behavior, gender and culture, social cognition of health and attitudes. *Unit head:* Dr. Gordon A. Barr, Acting Chair, 212-772-5550. *Application contact:* William Zlata, Director for Graduate Admissions, 212-772-4482, Fax: 212-650-3336, E-mail: admissions@hunter.cuny.edu.

Indiana University Bloomington, University Graduate School, College of Arts and Sciences, Department of Psychological and Brain Sciences, Bloomington, IN 47405-7000. Offers biology and behavior (PhD); clinical science (PhD); cognitive psychology (PhD); developmental psychology (PhD); psychological and brain sciences (MA); social psychology (PhD). *Accreditation:* APA (one or more programs are accredited). *Faculty:* 53 full-time (16 women). *Students:* 79 full-time (42 women), 14 part-time (7 women); includes 10 minority (3 African Americans, 3 Asian Americans or Pacific Islanders, 4 Hispanic Americans), 16 international. Average age 28. 240 applicants, 10% accepted, 20 enrolled. In 2007, 5 master's, 15 doctorates awarded. *Median time to degree:* Of those who began their doctoral program in fall 1999, 86% received their degree in 8 years or less. *Degree requirements:* For doctorate, comprehensive exam, thesis/dissertation, 1st and 2nd year projects, 1 year as associate instructor, qualifying exam, teaching. *Entrance requirements:* For doctorate, GRE. Additional exam requirements/recommendations for international students: Required—TOEFL (minimum score 550 paper-based; 213 computer-based). *Application deadline:* For fall admission, 12/15 for domestic students, 12/1 for international students. Application fee: $50 ($60 for international students). Electronic applications accepted. *Financial support:* Fellowships with full tuition reimbursements, research assistantships with full tuition reimbursements, teaching assistantships with full tuition reimbursements, scholarships/grants, health care benefits, and unspecified assistantships available. *Unit head:* Dr. Linda B. Smith, Chair, 812-855-3991, Fax: 812-855-4691, E-mail: smith4@indiana.edu. *Application contact:* Patricia G. Crouch, Academic Services Coordinator, 812-855-4528, Fax: 812-855-4691, E-mail: pcrouch@indiana.edu.

Indiana Wesleyan University, College of Graduate Studies, Program in Counseling, Marion, IN 46953-4974. Offers community counseling (MS); marriage and family counseling (MS); school counseling (MS). *Accreditation:* ACA. Part-time programs available. *Faculty:* 3 full-time (1 woman), 3 part-time/adjunct (2 women). *Students:* 41 full-time (31 women), 62 part-time (47 women); includes 5 minority (4 African Americans, 1 Hispanic American). Average age 32. In 2007, 23 degrees awarded. *Degree requirements:* For master's, thesis or alternative. *Entrance requirements:* For master's, GRE General Test. *Application deadline:* For fall admission, 4/1 priority date for domestic students; for spring admission, 10/1 priority date for domestic students. Application fee: $25. Electronic applications accepted. *Expenses: Contact institution. Financial support:* In 2007–08, 1 research assistantship with tuition reimbursement, 1 teaching assistantship with partial tuition reimbursement (averaging $1,000 per year) were awarded. Financial award application deadline: 3/1; financial award applicants required to submit FAFSA. *Unit head:* Dr. Mark Gerig, Director of Graduate Counseling Studies, 765-677-2995, Fax: 765-677-2504, E-mail: mark.gerig@indwes.edu. *Application contact:* David McMillan, Assistant Director of Enrollment Management, 765-677-2688, E-mail: david.mcmillan@indwes.edu.

Iowa State University of Science and Technology, Graduate College, College of Liberal Arts and Sciences, Department of Psychology, Ames, IA 50011. Offers cognitive psychology (PhD); counseling psychology (PhD); social psychology (PhD). *Accreditation:* APA. *Faculty:* 25 full-time (8 women), 8 part-time/adjunct (4 women). *Students:* 63 full-time (43 women); includes 10 minority (3 African Americans, 7 Asian Americans or Pacific Islanders), 4 international. Average age 26. 117 applicants, 14% accepted, 11 enrolled. In 2007, 8 doctorates awarded. Terminal master's awarded for partial completion of doctoral program. *Median time to degree:* Of those who began their doctoral program in fall 1999, 100% received their degree in 8 years or less. *Degree requirements:* For doctorate, thesis/dissertation. *Entrance requirements:* For doctorate, GRE General Test, GRE Subject Test (psychology). Additional exam requirements/recommendations for international students: Required—TOEFL (minimum score 560 paper-based; 220 computer-based). *Application deadline:* For fall admission, 1/5 priority date for domestic and international students. Application fee: $30 ($70 for international students). Electronic applications accepted. *Financial support:* In 2007–08, 45 students received support, including 2 fellowships with full tuition reimbursements available (averaging $14,055 per year), 13 research assistantships with full tuition reimbursements available (averaging $12,200 per year), 30 teaching assistantships with full tuition reimbursements available (averaging $12,200 per year); scholarships/grants, health care benefits, and unspecified assistantships also available. *Faculty research:* Counseling psychology, cognitive psychology, social psychology, health psychology, psychology and public policy. Total annual research expenditures: $2 million. *Unit head:* Dr. David L Vogel, Director of Graduate Education, 515-294-1742, Fax: 515-294-6424, E-mail: dvogel@iastate.edu. *Application contact:* Ann K Schmidt, Graduate Admissions Secretary, 515-294-1743, Fax: 515-294-6424, E-mail: psychadm@iastate.edu.

Lamar University, College of Graduate Studies, College of Arts and Sciences, Department of Psychology, Beaumont, TX 77710. Offers community/clinical psychology (MS); industrial/organizational psychology (MS). Part-time programs available. *Faculty:* 6 full-time (3 women). *Students:* 19 full-time (11 women), 10 part-time (8 women); includes 6 minority (2 African Americans, 1 Asian American or Pacific Islander, 3 Hispanic Americans), 1 international. Average age 25. 37 applicants, 43% accepted, 10 enrolled. In 2007, 6 degrees awarded. *Degree requirements:* For master's, thesis, practicum. *Entrance requirements:* For master's, GRE General Test, minimum GPA of 2.75 in last 60 hours of undergraduate course work. Additional exam requirements/recommendations for international students: Required—TOEFL. *Application deadline:* For fall admission, 8/1 for domestic students; for spring admission, 12/1 for domestic students. Application fee: $25 ($50 for international students). *Expenses:* Tuition, state resident: part-time $348 per semester hour. Tuition, nonresident: part-time $626 per semester hour. Tuition and fees vary according to course load. *Financial support:* In 2007–08, 12 students received support, including 3 teaching assistantships (averaging $4,500 per year); fellowships, research assistantships, career-related internships or fieldwork, Federal Work-Study, scholarships/grants, and tuition waivers (partial) also available. Support available to part-time students. Financial award application deadline: 4/1. *Faculty research:* Groupthink, health psychology, school psychology, behavioral neuroscience. *Unit head:* Dr. Oney D. Fitzpatrick, Chair, 409-880-8285, Fax: 409-880-1779, E-mail: fitzpatrod@hal.lamar.edu.

Lenoir-Rhyne College, Graduate Programs, School of Social and Behavioral Sciences, Programs in Counseling, Hickory, NC 28601. Offers agency counseling (MA); community counseling (MA). Part-time and evening/weekend programs available. *Faculty:* 1 (woman) full-time. *Students:* 8 full-time (7 women), 37 part-time (31 women); includes 3 minority (all African Americans) Average age 37. In 2007, 2 degrees awarded. *Degree requirements:* For master's, comprehensive exam, thesis optional. *Entrance requirements:* For master's, GRE General Test, writing sample, minimum undergraduate GPA of 2.7, minimum graduate GPA of 3.0. Additional exam requirements/recommendations for international students: Required—TOEFL (minimum score 600 paper-based). *Application deadline:* Applications are processed on a rolling basis. Application fee: $35. Electronic applications accepted. *Expenses:* Tuition: Full-time $6,930; part-time $385 per credit. Required fees: $50; $25 per term. *Financial support:* Career-related internships or fieldwork available. Financial award application deadline: 3/1; financial award applicants required to submit FAFSA. *Unit head:* Dr. Amy Wood, Coordinator, 828-328-7728, Fax: 828-328-7368, E-mail: amy.wood@lrc.edu. *Application contact:* 828-328-7300, Fax: 828-328-7378, E-mail: admission@lrc.edu.

Lesley University, Graduate School of Arts and Social Sciences, Cambridge, MA 02138-2790. Offers clinical mental health counseling (MA), including expressive therapies counseling, holistic counseling, school and community counseling; counseling psychology (MA, CAGS), including professional counseling (MA), school counseling (MA); creative arts in learning (CAGS); creative writing (MFA); ecological teaching and learning (MS); environmental education (MS); expressive therapies (MA, PhD, CAGS), including art (MA), dance (MA), expressive therapies, music (MA); independent studies (CAGS); independent study (MA); intercultural relations (MA, CAGS); interdisciplinary studies (MA), including individualized studies, integrative holistic health, women's studies; visual arts (MFA). Part-time and evening/weekend programs available. Postbaccalaureate distance learning degree programs offered (minimal on-campus study). *Faculty:* 49 full-time (41 women), 185 part-time/adjunct (137 women). *Students:* 653 full-time (580 women), 1,972 part-time (1,795 women); includes 191 minority (103 African Americans, 11 American Indian/Alaska Native, 19 Asian Americans or Pacific Islanders, 58 Hispanic Americans), 61 international. Average age 37. 1,011 applicants, 87% accepted, 645 enrolled. In 2007, 1,107 master's, 1 doctorate, 3 other advanced degrees awarded. *Degree requirements:* For master's, internship, practicum, thesis (expressive therapies); for doctorate, thesis/dissertation, arts apprenticeship, field placement; for CAGS, thesis, internship (counseling psychology, expressive therapies). *Entrance requirements:* For master's, MAT (counseling psychology), interview, writing samples, art portfolio; for doctorate, GRE or MAT; for CAGS, interview, master's degree. Additional exam requirements/recommendations for international students: Required—TOEFL (minimum score 550 paper-based; 213 computer-based; 80 iBT). *Application deadline:* Applications are processed on a rolling basis. Application fee: $50. Electronic applications accepted. *Financial support:* In 2007–08, 64 students received support, including research assistantships (averaging $3,400 per year), 1 teaching assistantship (averaging $7,298 per year); career-related internships or fieldwork, Federal Work-Study, scholarships/grants, and unspecified assistantships also available. Support available to part-time students. Financial award application deadline: 4/15; financial award applicants required to submit FAFSA. *Faculty research:* Psychotherapy and culture; psychotherapy and psychological trauma; women's issues in art, teaching and psychotherapy; community based art, psycho-spiritual inquiry. *Unit head:* Dr. Julia Halevy, Dean, 617-349-8317, Fax: 617-349-8366, E-mail: jhalevy@lesley.edu. *Application contact:* Christina Murray, Senior Assistant Director, On-Campus Admissions, 617-349-8827, Fax: 617-349-8313, E-mail: cmurray3@lesley.edu.

Loyola University Chicago, Graduate School, Department of Psychology, Program in Applied Social Psychology, Chicago, IL 60611-2196. Offers MA, PhD. *Faculty:* 7 full-time (3 women), 2 part-time/adjunct (1 woman). *Students:* 42 full-time (33 women), 3 part-time (2 women); includes 6 minority (2 African Americans, 4 Asian Americans or Pacific Islanders), 4 international. Average age 27. 79 applicants, 20% accepted, 6 enrolled. In 2007, 5 master's, 4 doctorates awarded. Terminal master's awarded for partial completion of doctoral program. *Degree requirements:* For master's, thesis; for doctorate, comprehensive exam, thesis/dissertation, internship. *Entrance requirements:* For master's and doctorate, GRE General Test, GRE Subject Test, sample of written work. *Application deadline:* For fall admission, 1/15 for domestic students. Applications are processed on a rolling basis. Application fee: $50. *Expenses:* Tuition: Full-time $12,780; part-time $710 per credit hour. Required fees: $55 per semester. Full-time tuition and fees vary according to program. *Financial support:* In 2007–08, 1 fellowship with tuition reimbursement (averaging $14,000 per year), 5 research assistantships with tuition reimbursements (averaging $14,000 per year), 1 teaching assistantship (averaging $14,000 per year) were awarded; career-related internships or fieldwork, Federal Work-Study, and scholarships/grants also available. Financial award application deadline: 1/15; financial award applicants required to submit FAFSA. *Faculty research:* Program evaluation, attitudes and prejudice, psychological well-being, mass media, groups and organizations and communities. Total annual research expenditures: $200,000.

Martin University, Division of Psychology, Indianapolis, IN 46218-3867. Offers community psychology (MS). Part-time and evening/weekend programs available. *Degree requirements:* For master's, thesis. *Entrance requirements:* For master's, GRE General Test, GRE Subject Test.

Marymount University, School of Education and Human Services, Program in Community Counseling and Forensic Psychology, Arlington, VA 22207-4299. Offers MA/MA. Part-time and evening/weekend programs available. *Students:* 17 full-time (all women), 6 part-time (all women); includes 8 minority (all African Americans) Average age 26. 1 applicant, 0% accepted. *Entrance requirements:* Additional exam requirements/recommendations for international students: Required—TOEFL (minimum score 600 paper-based; 250 computer-based; 100 iBT). *Application deadline:* For fall admission, 2/15 for domestic students. Application fee: $40. *Expenses:* Tuition: Full-time $11,790; part-time $655 per credit. Required fees: $121; $6.7 per credit. *Financial support:* Research assistantships with full tuition reimbursements, career-related internships or fieldwork, scholarships/grants, and unspecified assistantships available. Support available to part-time students. Financial award applicants required to submit FAFSA. *Unit head:* Dr. Wayne Lesko, Dean, School of Education and Human Services, 703-284-1620, Fax: 703-284-1631, E-mail: wayne.lesko@marymount.edu.

Memorial University of Newfoundland, School of Graduate Studies, Department of Psychology, St. John's, NL A1C 5S7, Canada. Offers applied social psychology (MASP); experimental psychology (M Sc, PhD). Part-time programs available. *Degree requirements:* For master's, workterms (MASP), thesis (M Sc); for doctorate, comprehensive exam, thesis/dissertation, oral thesis defense. *Entrance requirements:* For master's, GRE, honors bachelor's degree of high second class standing or equivalent; for doctorate, GRE, master's or honors degree. Electronic applications accepted. *Faculty research:* Behavioral neuroscience, cognition, theory and research on abnormal behavior.

Miami University, Graduate School, College of Arts and Sciences, Department of Psychology, Oxford, OH 45056. Offers clinical psychology (PhD); experimental psychology (PhD); social psychology (PhD). *Accreditation:* APA. *Degree requirements:* For doctorate, comprehensive exam, thesis/dissertation, final exams. *Entrance requirements:* For doctorate, GRE General Test, GRE Subject Test, minimum GPA of 2.75 (undergraduate), 3.0 (graduate). Additional exam requirements/recommendations for international students: Required—TOEFL (minimum score 550 paper-based; 213 computer-based), TWE (minimum score 4). Electronic applications accepted.

Minnesota State University Mankato, College of Graduate Studies, College of Education, Department of Counseling and Student Personnel, Mankato, MN 56001. Offers college student affairs (MS); counselor education and supervision (Ed D); marriage and family counseling (Certificate); professional community counseling (MS); professional school counseling (MS). *Accreditation:* ACA (one or more programs are accredited); NCATE. *Students:* 65 full-time (55 women), 36 part-time (31 women). Average age 30. In 2007, 49 degrees awarded. *Degree requirements:* For master's, comprehensive exam, thesis or alternative. *Entrance requirements:* For master's, GRE General Test or MAT (if GPA is below 3.0 for last 2 years), minimum GPA of 3.0 during previous 2 years, 3 letters of reference. Additional exam requirements/recommendations for international students: Required—TOEFL. *Application deadline:* For fall admission, 3/15 priority date for domestic students; for spring admission, 11/20 for domestic students. Applications are processed on a rolling basis. Application fee: $40. Electronic applications accepted. *Financial support:* Research assistantships with full tuition reimbursements, teaching assistantships with full tuition reimbursements, career-related internships or fieldwork, Federal Work-Study, institutionally sponsored loans, and unspecified assistantships available. Support available to part-time students. Financial award application deadline: 3/15; financial award applicants required to submit FAFSA. *Unit head:* Dr. Richard Auger, Chairperson, 507-389-5658. *Application contact:* 507-389-2321, E-mail: grad@mnsu.edu.

Montclair State University, The Office of Graduate Admissions and Support Services, College of Education and Human Services, Department of Counseling, Human Development, and Educational Leadership, Montclair, NJ 07043-1624. Offers administration and supervision (MA), including administration and supervision, educator/trainer; advanced counseling (Certificate); counseling and guidance (MA), including addictions counseling, community counseling, student affairs; principal (Certificate); school administrator (Certificate); school business administrator (Certificate); school counselor (Certificate); substance awareness coordinator (Certificate). *Accreditation:* NCATE. Part-time and evening/weekend programs available. *Faculty:* 19 full-time (14 women), 18 part-time/adjunct (8 women). *Students:* 119 full-time (98 women), 582 part-time (427 women); includes 131 minority (68 African Americans, 14 Asian Americans or Pacific Islanders, 49 Hispanic Americans), 3 international. Average age 33. 581 applicants, 54% accepted, 270 enrolled. In 2007, 187 master's, 25 other advanced degrees awarded. *Degree requirements:* For master's, comprehensive exam, thesis or alternative. *Entrance requirements:* For master's, GRE General Test, interview, 2 letters of recommendation. Additional exam requirements/recommendations for international students: Required—TOEFL (minimum score 83 computer-based). *Application deadline:* For fall admission, 6/1 for international students; for spring admission, 10/1 for international students. Applications are processed on a rolling basis. Application fee: $60. Electronic applications accepted. *Financial support:* In 2007–08, 15 research assistantships with full tuition reimbursements (averaging $7,000 per year) were awarded; Federal Work-Study, scholarships/grants, and unspecified assistantships also available. Support available to part-time students. Financial award application deadline: 3/1; financial award applicants required to submit FAFSA. *Faculty research:* K-12 education, data collection. *Unit head:* Dr. Catherine Roland, Chairperson, 973-655-7216, E-mail: rolandc@mail.montclair.edu.

Montclair State University, The Office of Graduate Admissions and Support Services, College of Humanities and Social Sciences, Department of Psychology, Montclair, NJ 07043-1624. Offers educational psychology (MA), including child/adolescent clinical psychology, clinical psychology for Spanish/English bilinguals; psychology (MA, Certificate), including industrial and organizational psychology (MA); school psychologist (Certificate). Part-time and evening/weekend programs available. *Faculty:* 27 full-time (11 women), 27 part-time/adjunct (20 women). *Students:* 27 full-time (21 women), 39 part-time (32 women); includes 26 minority (7 African Americans, 4 Asian Americans or Pacific Islanders, 15 Hispanic Americans), 3 international. 86 applicants, 21% accepted, 13 enrolled. In 2007, 22 master's, 11 other advanced degrees awarded. *Degree requirements:* For master's, comprehensive exam, thesis or alternative. *Entrance requirements:* For master's, GRE General Test, GRE Subject Test, previous course work in psychology, interview, 2 letters of recommendation. Additional exam requirements/recommendations for international students: Required—TOEFL (minimum score 83 computer-based). *Application deadline:* For fall admission, 2/1 for domestic and international students; for spring admission, 10/1 for domestic and international students. Applications are processed on a rolling basis. Application fee: $60. Electronic applications accepted. *Financial support:* In 2007–08, 10 research assistantships with full tuition reimbursements (averaging $7,000 per year) were awarded; Federal Work-Study, scholarships/grants, and unspecified assistantships also available. Support available to part-time students. Financial award application deadline: 3/1; financial award applicants required to submit FAFSA. *Faculty research:* Engaged learning, academic and civic development. Total annual research expenditures: $10,000. *Unit head:* Dr. Peter Vietze, Chairperson, 973-655-5201.

Naropa University, Graduate Programs, Program in Transpersonal Psychology, Ecopsychology Concentration, Boulder, CO 80302-6697. Offers MA. *Faculty:* 2 full-time (0 women). *Students:* Average age 38. 27 applicants, 74% accepted, 14 enrolled. In 2007, 11 degrees awarded. *Degree requirements:* For master's, thesis. *Entrance requirements:* For master's, interview (by phone or in-person), technology form. *Application deadline:* For fall admission, 1/15 for domestic students; for spring admission, 10/15 for domestic students. Applications are processed on a rolling basis. Application fee: $60. Electronic applications accepted. *Expenses:* Tuition: Full-time $15,070; part-time $685 per credit. Required fees: $250 per semester. Tuition and fees vary according to course load. *Financial support:* In 2007–08, 2 students received support. Career-related internships or fieldwork, scholarships/grants, and tuition waivers (partial) available. Support available to part-time students. Financial award application deadline: 3/1; financial award applicants required to submit FAFSA. *Unit head:* Jed Swift, Assistant Director, 303-245-4837. *Application contact:* Kate Levene, Assistant Director of Admissions, 303-245-4657, Fax: 303-546-3583, E-mail: klevene@naropa.edu.

National-Louis University, College of Arts and Sciences, Department of Counseling and Human Services, Chicago, IL 60603. Offers addictions counseling (Certificate); addictions treatment (Certificate); career counseling and development studies (Certificate); community counseling (MS); community wellness and prevention (Certificate); counseling (Certificate); eating disorders counseling (Certificate); employee assistance programs (MS, Certificate); gerontology administration (Certificate); gerontology counseling (MS, Certificate); human services administration (MS, Certificate); long-term care administration (Certificate); school counseling (MS). Part-time programs available. *Students:* 15 full-time (11 women), 229 part-time (187 women); includes 69 minority (56 African Americans, 1 American Indian/Alaska Native, 2 Asian Americans or Pacific Islanders, 10 Hispanic Americans). Average age 38. In 2007, 53 master's, 6 other advanced degrees awarded. *Degree requirements:* For master's and Certificate, internship. *Entrance requirements:* For master's and Certificate, GRE, MAT, or Watson-Glaser Critical Thinking Appraisal, interview, minimum GPA of 3.0. *Application deadline:* Applications are processed on a rolling basis. *Expenses:* Tuition: Full-time $18,900; part-time $630 per credit hour. Required fees: $20 per term. One-time fee: $40 part-time. Tuition and fees vary according to course load, campus/location and program. *Financial support:* Federal Work-Study, institutionally sponsored loans, scholarships/grants, and tuition waivers available. Support available to part-time students. Financial award applicants required to submit FAFSA. *Faculty research:* Religion and aging, drug abuse prevention, hunger, homelessness, multicultural diversity. *Unit head:* Dr. Susan Thorne-Devin, Assistant Professor, 630-874-4560, E-mail: stdevin@nl.edu. *Application contact:* Dr. Larry Poselli, Vice President of Enrollment and Student Services, 800-443-5522 Ext. 5718, Fax: 312-261-.3550, E-mail: larry.polselli@nl.edu.

New York University, Graduate School of Arts and Science, Department of Psychology, New York, NY 10012-1019. Offers cognition and perception (PhD); community psychology (PhD); general psychology (MA); industrial/organizational psychology (MA); psychotherapy and psychoanalysis (Advanced Certificate); social/personality psychology (PhD). Part-time programs available. *Faculty:* 38 full-time (13 women), 78 part-time/adjunct. *Students:* 155 full-time (115 women), 305 part-time (218 women); includes 77 minority (24 African Americans, 29 Asian Americans or Pacific Islanders, 24 Hispanic Americans), 53 international. Average age 32. 767 applicants, 46% accepted, 112 enrolled. In 2007, 80 master's, 15 doctorates awarded. Terminal master's awarded for partial completion of doctoral program. *Degree requirements:* For master's, comprehensive exam, thesis or alternative; for doctorate, thesis/dissertation. *Entrance requirements:* For master's, GRE General Test, minimum GPA of 3.0; for doctorate, GRE General Test, GRE Subject Test; for Advanced Certificate, doctoral degree, minimum GPA of 3.0. Additional exam requirements/recommendations for international students: Required—TOEFL. *Application deadline:* For fall admission, 12/18 for domestic students. Application fee: $85. *Financial support:* Fellowships with tuition reimbursements, research assistantships with tuition reimbursements, teaching assistantships with tuition reimbursements, career-related internships or fieldwork, Federal Work-Study, institutionally sponsored loans, scholarships/grants, traineeships, health care benefits, and unspecified assistantships available. Financial award application deadline: 12/18; financial award applicants required to submit FAFSA. *Faculty research:* Vision, memory, social cognition, social and cognitive development, relationships. *Unit head:* Marisa Carrasco, Chair, 212-998-7900, Fax: 212-995-4018, E-mail: psychq@psych.nyu.edu. *Application contact:* Laurence Maloney, Director of Graduate Studies, 212-998-7900, Fax: 212-995-4018, E-mail: psychq@psych.nyu.edu.

Norfolk State University, School of Graduate Studies, School of Liberal Arts, Department of Psychology, Program in Community/Clinical Psychology, Norfolk, VA 23504. Offers MA. *Degree requirements:* For master's, comprehensive exam, thesis or alternative. *Entrance requirements:* For master's, minimum GPA of 2.7.

North Carolina State University, Graduate School, College of Education, Department of Educational Research, Leadership and Counselor Education, Program in Agency Counseling, Raleigh, NC 27695. Offers M Ed, MS. *Degree requirements:* For master's, thesis optional. *Entrance requirements:* For master's, GRE General Test or MAT, minimum GPA of 3.0 in major. Electronic applications accepted. *Faculty research:* Cross-cultural issues, non-cognitive variables, achievement gaps, identity development, counseling supervision.

North Dakota State University, College of Graduate and Interdisciplinary Studies, College of Science and Mathematics, Department of Psychology, Fargo, ND 58105. Offers clinical psychology (MS); cognitive and visual neuroscience (PhD); health and social psychology (PhD); psychology (MS). *Faculty:* 18 full-time (4 women), 2 part-time/adjunct (1 woman). *Students:* 36 full-time (27 women); includes 4 minority (1 African American, 2 Asian Americans or Pacific Islanders, 1 Hispanic American), 1 international. Average age 24. 48 applicants, 33% accepted, 10 enrolled. In 2007, 3 master's, 1 doctorate awarded. *Degree requirements:* For master's, thesis; for doctorate, thesis/dissertation. *Entrance requirements:* For master's and doctorate, GRE General Test, GRE Subject Test. Additional exam requirements/recommendations for international students: Required—TOEFL (minimum score 525 paper-based; 197 computer-based; 71 iBT). *Application deadline:* For fall admission, 3/1 for domestic and international students. Application fee: $45 ($60 for international students). Electronic applications accepted. *Expenses:* Tuition, state resident: full-time $5,376; part-time $224 per credit. Tuition, nonresident: full-time $14,354; part-time $598 per credit. Required fees: $962; $40 per credit. Part-time tuition and fees vary according to course load and reciprocity agreements. *Financial support:* In 2007–08, 36 students received support, including 2 fellowships with full tuition reimbursements available (averaging $16,000 per year), 23 research assistantships with full tuition reimbursements available (averaging $16,000 per year), 11 teaching assistantships with full tuition reimbursements available (averaging $6,000 per year); career-related internships or fieldwork, Federal Work-Study, institutionally sponsored loans, tuition waivers (full and partial), and unspecified assistantships also available. Support available to part-time students. Financial award application deadline: 3/1. *Faculty research:* Cognition science, neuropsychology, group behavior, applied behavior analysis, behavior therapy. Total annual research expenditures: $2 million. *Unit head:* Dr. Paul D. Rokke, Chair, 701-231-8622, Fax: 701-231-8426, E-mail: paul.rokke@ndsu.edu.

Northern Kentucky University, Office of Graduate Programs, College of Education and Human Services, Program in Community Counseling, Highland Heights, KY 41099. Offers MSCC. *Faculty:* 5 full-time (1 woman), 1 (woman) part-time/adjunct. *Students:* 17 full-time (16 women),

Social Psychology

Northern Kentucky University (continued)
23 part-time (21 women); includes 2 minority (both African Americans) Average age 28. 46 applicants, 48% accepted, 18 enrolled. *Degree requirements:* For master's, comprehensive exam, internship. *Entrance requirements:* For master's, GRE, minimum GPA of 2.75, essay, 3 letters of reference, criminal background check. Additional exam requirements/recommendations for international students: Required—TOEFL (minimum score 550 paper-based; 213 computer-based; 79 iBT), Michigan English Language Assessment Battery (must be taken at NKU). *Application deadline:* For fall admission, 8/1 for domestic students, 5/1 priority date for international students; for spring admission, 10/1 priority date for international students. Applications are processed on a rolling basis. Application fee: $40. Electronic applications accepted. *Faculty research:* Family assessment, counselor development, counselor supervision, counseling preferences. *Unit head:* Dr. Jacqueline Smith, Director, 859-572-6149, E-mail: smithjac@nku.edu. *Application contact:* Dr. Peg Griffin, Director, Graduate Programs, 859-572-6364, Fax: 859-572-6670, E-mail: gradprog@nku.edu.

North Georgia College & State University, Graduate Studies, Program in Community Counseling, Dahlonega, GA 30597. Offers MS. Part-time and evening/weekend programs available. *Degree requirements:* For master's, one foreign language, thesis optional. *Entrance requirements:* For master's, GRE General Test, minimum GPA of 3.0, 3 letters of recommendation, interview. Electronic applications accepted.

Northwestern University, The Graduate School, Judd A. and Marjorie Weinberg College of Arts and Sciences, Department of Psychology, Evanston, IL 60208. Offers brain, behavior and cognition (PhD); clinical psychology (PhD); cognitive psychology (PhD); personality (PhD); social psychology (PhD); JD/PhD. Admissions and degrees offered through The Graduate School. *Accreditation:* APA (one or more programs are accredited). Part-time programs available. *Degree requirements:* For doctorate, thesis/dissertation. *Entrance requirements:* For doctorate, GRE General Test, GRE Subject Test. Additional exam requirements/recommendations for international students: Required—TOEFL. Electronic applications accepted. *Faculty research:* Memory and higher order cognition, anxiety and depression, effectiveness of psychotherapy, social cognition, molecular basis of memory.

Northwest Nazarene University, Graduate Studies, Program in Counselor Education, Nampa, ID 83686-5897. Offers community counseling (MS); marriage and family counseling (MS); school counseling (MS). *Faculty:* 3 full-time (1 woman), 10 part-time/adjunct (6 women). *Students:* 69 full-time (52 women), 12 part-time (8 women); includes 4 minority (1 American Indian/Alaska Native, 3 Hispanic Americans). In 2007, 19 degrees awarded. Application fee: $25. *Unit head:* Dr. Brenda Freeman, Chair, 208-467-8428, Fax: 208-467-8339.

The Ohio State University, Graduate School, College of Social and Behavioral Sciences, School of Social and Behavioral Science, Department of Psychology, Columbus, OH 43210. Offers behavioral neuroscience (PhD); clinical psychology (PhD); cognitive psychology (PhD); developmental psychology (PhD); mental retardation and developmental disabilities (PhD); psychology (MA); quantitative psychology (PhD); social psychology (PhD). *Accreditation:* APA (one or more programs are accredited). *Faculty:* 60. *Students:* 111 full-time (78 women), 6 part-time (4 women); includes 19 minority (6 African Americans, 1 American Indian/Alaska Native, 3 Asian Americans or Pacific Islanders, 9 Hispanic Americans), 16 international. Average age 27. In 2007, 17 master's, 41 doctorates awarded. *Degree requirements:* For doctorate, thesis/dissertation. *Entrance requirements:* For master's and doctorate, GRE General Test. Additional exam requirements/recommendations for international students: Required—TOEFL (minimum score 600 paper-based; 250 computer-based). *Application deadline:* For fall admission, 12/31 for domestic students, 11/30 for international students. Applications are processed on a rolling basis. Application fee: $40 ($50 for international students). Electronic applications accepted. *Financial support:* Fellowships, research assistantships, teaching assistantships available. *Unit head:* Marilynn B. Brewer, Graduate Studies Committee Chair, 614-292-3038, Fax: 614-292-4537. *Application contact:* 614-292-9444, Fax: 614-292-3895, E-mail: domestic.grad@osu.edu.

Oregon State University–Cascades, Program in Counseling, Bend, OR 97701. Offers community counseling (MS); school counseling (MS).

Penn State Harrisburg, Graduate School, School of Behavioral Sciences and Education, Middletown, PA 17057-4898. Offers adult education (D Ed); applied behavior analysis (MA); applied clinical psychology (MA); applied psychological research (MA); community psychology and social change (MA); health education (M Ed); teaching and curriculum (M Ed); training and development (M Ed). Part-time and evening/weekend programs available. *Financial support:* Career-related internships or fieldwork available. *Unit head:* Dr. William D. Milheim, Director, 717-948-6205, Fax: 717-948-6209, E-mail: wdm2@psu.edu.

Penn State University Park, Graduate School, College of the Liberal Arts, Department of Psychology, State College, University Park, PA 16802-1503. Offers clinical psychology (MS, PhD); cognitive psychology (MS, PhD); developmental psychology (MS, PhD); industrial/organizational psychology (MS, PhD); psychobiology (MS, PhD); social psychology (MS, PhD). *Accreditation:* APA (one or more programs are accredited). *Expenses:* Tuition, state resident: full-time $14,738; part-time $614 per credit. Tuition, nonresident: full-time $26,050; part-time $1,085 per credit. Tuition and fees vary according to course load, program and student level. *Unit head:* Dr. Melvin M. Mark, Interim Head, 814-865-9515, Fax: 814-863-7002, E-mail: m5m@psu.edu.

Pittsburg State University, Graduate School, College of Education, Department of Psychology and Counseling, Program in Counselor Education, Pittsburg, KS 66762. Offers community counseling (MS); school counseling (MS). *Accreditation:* ACA; NCATE. *Degree requirements:* For master's, thesis or alternative. *Entrance requirements:* For master's, GRE General Test, minimum GPA of 2.8.

Prescott College, Graduate Programs, Program in Environmental Studies, Prescott, AZ 86301. Offers agroecology (MA); ecopsychology (MA); environmental education (MA); environmental studies (MA); sustainability (MA). MA in environmental education offered jointly with Teton Science School. Part-time programs available. Postbaccalaureate distance learning degree programs offered (minimal on-campus study). *Faculty:* 1 full-time (0 women), 37 part-time/adjunct (15 women). *Students:* 31 full-time (19 women), 19 part-time (9 women); includes 6 minority (1 African American, 3 American Indian/Alaska Native, 2 Hispanic Americans), 1 international. Average age 35. 21 applicants, 90% accepted, 13 enrolled. In 2007, 12 degrees awarded. *Degree requirements:* For master's, thesis, fieldwork or internship, practicum. *Entrance requirements:* For master's, 2 letters of recommendation, resumé. Additional exam requirements/recommendations for international students: Required—TOEFL (minimum score 550 paper-based; 213 computer-based). *Application deadline:* For fall admission, 5/1 priority date for domestic and international students; for spring admission, 11/1 priority date for domestic and international students. Applications are processed on a rolling basis. Application fee: $40. Electronic applications accepted. *Expenses:* Tuition: Full-time $6,480; part-time $540 per credit. *Financial support:* Career-related internships or fieldwork and Federal Work-Study available. Financial award applicants required to submit FAFSA. *Unit head:* Dr. Richard Cellarius, Interim Chair, 928-350-3204. *Application contact:* Kerstin Alicki, Admissions Counselor, 877-350-2102, Fax: 928-776-5242, E-mail: admissions@prescott.edu.

Queen's University at Kingston, School of Graduate Studies and Research, Faculty of Arts and Sciences, Department of Psychology, Kingston, ON K7L 3N6, Canada. Offers brain behavior and cognitive science (MA, PhD); clinical psychology (MA, PhD); developmental psychology (MA, PhD); social personality psychology (MA, PhD). *Accreditation:* APA (one or more programs are accredited). *Degree requirements:* For master's, thesis; for doctorate, comprehensive exam, thesis/dissertation. *Entrance requirements:* For master's and doctorate, GRE General Test. Additional exam requirements/recommendations for international students: Required—TOEFL. *Faculty research:* Human development, social, personality, behavioral neuroscience, forensic.

Regent University, Graduate School, School of Psychology and Counseling, Virginia Beach, VA 23464-9800. Offers clinical psychology (Psy D); counseling (MA), including clinical psychology, community counseling, human services counseling, school guidance; counseling studies (CAGS); counselor education and supervision (PhD); M Div/MA; M Ed/MA; MBA/MA. PhD program offered online only. *Accreditation:* ACA; APA (one or more programs are accredited). Part-time programs available. Postbaccalaureate distance learning degree programs offered. *Faculty:* 25 full-time (14 women), 17 part-time/adjunct (7 women). *Students:* 223 full-time (176 women), 187 part-time (141 women); includes 110 minority (89 African Americans, 2 American Indian/Alaska Native, 9 Asian Americans or Pacific Islanders, 10 Hispanic Americans), 11 international. Average age 31. 293 applicants, 58% accepted, 99 enrolled. In 2007, 79 master's, 23 doctorates awarded. *Degree requirements:* For master's, thesis or alternative, internship, practicum, written competency exam; for doctorate, thesis/dissertation or alternative. *Entrance requirements:* For master's, GRE General Test including writing exam, minimum undergraduate GPA of 2.75, 3 recommendations, resumé, transcripts, writing sample; for doctorate, GRE General Test including writing exam, GRE Subject Test, minimum undergraduate GPA of 3.0, 3.5 (PhD), 10-15 minute VHS tape demonstrating counseling skills, writing sample, 3 recommendations, resumé, transcripts. Additional exam requirements/recommendations for international students: Required—TOEFL (minimum score 577 paper-based; 233 computer-based). *Application deadline:* For fall admission, 4/1 priority date for domestic students; for spring admission, 11/1 priority date for domestic students. Applications are processed on a rolling basis. Application fee: $50. Electronic applications accepted. *Expenses:* Contact institution. *Financial support:* In 2007–08, 362 students received support, including 15 research assistantships with full and partial tuition reimbursements available (averaging $4,439 per year), 6 teaching assistantships with full and partial tuition reimbursements available (averaging $12,699 per year); career-related internships or fieldwork, scholarships/grants, and tuition waivers (full and partial) also available. Support available to part-time students. Financial award application deadline: 9/1. *Faculty research:* Marriage enrichment, AIDS counseling, troubled youth. Total annual research expenditures: $12,000. *Unit head:* Dr. Rosemarie Hughes, Dean, 757-226-4269, Fax: 757-226-4282, E-mail: rosehug@regent.edu. *Application contact:* Althea Bishard, Registrar and Executive Director of Enrollment and Academic Services, 800-373-5504, Fax: 757-226-4381, E-mail: admissions@regent.edu.

Regis University, College for Professional Studies, Graduate Counseling Program, Denver, CO 80221-1099. Offers community counseling (MAC); counseling children and adolescents (Post-Graduate Certificate); marriage and family therapy (Post-Graduate Certificate). Program offered in Henderson and Las Vegas (Summerlin), NV. *Accreditation:* ACA. Part-time and evening/weekend programs available. *Faculty:* 18. *Students:* 231 (189 women). In 2007, 50 degrees awarded. *Degree requirements:* For master's, internships, practicum. *Entrance requirements:* For master's, 2 admissions essays, interview, 2 recommendations, resumé, criminal background check. Additional exam requirements/recommendations for international students: Required—TOEFL (minimum score 213 computer-based), TWE (minimum score 5). *Application deadline:* For fall admission, 8/6 for domestic students, 7/6 for international students; for spring admission, 12/14 for domestic students, 11/14 for international students. Application fee: $75. *Expenses:* Contact institution. *Faculty research:* Group Development, Counselor Education, Counsel and Therapy, Influence of Technology on Psychology, Dream finding groups, Adult Development, Depression. *Unit head:* Dr. Jolynne Reynolds, Head, 303-458-4100.

Rutgers, The State University of New Jersey, Newark, Graduate School, Program in Psychology, Newark, NJ 07102. Offers cognitive neuroscience (PhD); cognitive science (PhD); perception (PhD); psychobiology (PhD); social cognition (PhD). *Degree requirements:* For doctorate, comprehensive exam, thesis/dissertation. *Entrance requirements:* For doctorate, GRE General Test, GRE Subject Test, minimum undergraduate B average. Electronic applications accepted. *Faculty research:* Visual perception (luminance, motion), neuroendocrine mechanisms in behavior (reproduction, pain), attachment theory, connectionist modeling of cognition.

See Close-Up on page 1475.

Rutgers, The State University of New Jersey, New Brunswick, Graduate School, Program in Psychology, New Brunswick, NJ 08901-1281. Offers behavioral neuroscience (PhD); clinical psychology (PhD); cognitive psychology (PhD); interdisciplinary health psychology (PhD); social psychology (PhD). *Accreditation:* APA. *Degree requirements:* For doctorate, thesis/dissertation. *Entrance requirements:* For doctorate, GRE General Test, 3 letters of recommendation. Additional exam requirements/recommendations for international students: Required—TOEFL (minimum score 577 paper-based; 233 computer-based). Electronic applications accepted. *Faculty research:* Learning and memory, behavioral ecology, hormones and behavior, psychopharmacology, anxiety disorders.

Sage Graduate School, Graduate School, Department of Psychology, Program in Community Psychology, Troy, NY 12180-4115. Offers child care and children's services (MA); community counseling (MA); community health education (MA); general psychology (MA). Part-time and evening/weekend programs available. *Faculty:* 4 full-time (all women), 4 part-time/adjunct (1 woman). *Students:* 38 full-time (36 women), 65 part-time (60 women); includes 13 minority (8 African Americans, 2 American Indian/Alaska Native, 1 Asian American or Pacific Islander, 2 Hispanic Americans). Average age 29. 66 applicants, 50% accepted, 19 enrolled. In 2007, 33 degrees awarded. *Degree requirements:* For master's, thesis or alternative. *Entrance requirements:* For master's, minimum GPA of 2.75, official transcripts, 2 letters of reference, undergraduate courses in statistics, history and systems of psychology, three other courses in behavioral scince, personel prospectus statement, current resum&e, completed application. Additional exam requirements/recommendations for international students: Required—TOEFL (minimum score 550 paper-based; 213 computer-based). *Application deadline:* Applications are processed on a rolling basis. Application fee: $40. *Expenses:* Tuition: Full-time $9,720; part-time $540 per credit hour. *Financial support:* Fellowships, research assistantships, teaching assistantships, Federal Work-Study, scholarships/grants, and unspecified assistantships available. Support available to part-time students. Financial award application deadline: 3/1; financial award applicants required to submit FAFSA. *Unit head:* Dr. Bronna Romanoff, Director, 518-244-2260, E-mail: romanb@sage.edu. *Application contact:* Shannon K. Easton, Director of Graduate and Adult Admission, 518-244-2443, Fax: 518-244-6880, E-mail: sgsadm@sage.edu.

St. Cloud State University, School of Graduate Studies, College of Education, Department of Educational Leadership and Community Psychology, Program in Community Counseling, St. Cloud, MN 56301-4498. Offers MS. *Faculty:* 7 full-time (3 women), 3 part-time/adjunct (all women). *Students:* 18 full-time (14 women), 5 part-time (4 women); includes 2 minority (both Asian Americans or Pacific Islanders) 84 applicants, 24% accepted. In 2007, 8 degrees awarded. *Degree requirements:* For master's, comprehensive exam (for some programs), thesis or alternative. *Entrance requirements:* For master's, GRE General Test, minimum GPA of 2.75. Additional exam requirements/recommendations for international students: Required—MELAB; Recommended—TOEFL (minimum score 550 paper-based; 213 computer-based), IELTS (minimum score 7). *Application deadline:* For fall admission, 4/1 for domestic and international students. Applications are processed on a rolling basis. Application fee: $35. Electronic applications accepted. *Expenses:* Tuition, state resident: part-time $267 per credit. Tuition, nonresident: part-time $418 per credit. Required fees: $28 per credit. *Financial support:* Federal Work-Study, scholarships/grants, and unspecified assistantships available. *Unit head:* Dr. LeeAnn Jorgensen, Coordinator, 320-308-4915, E-mail: lsjorgensen@stcloudstate.edu. *Application contact:* Linda Lou Krueger, School of Graduate Studies, 320-308-2113, Fax: 320-308-5371, E-mail: lekrueger@stcloudstate.edu.

Saint Joseph College, Graduate Division, Department of Counselor Education, West Hartford, CT 06117-2700. Offers community counseling (MA), including child welfare, pastoral counseling, school counseling; spirituality (Certificate). Part-time and evening/weekend programs available. *Degree requirements:* For master's, comprehensive exam, thesis optional, Capstone project.

Entrance requirements: For master's, PRAXIS I (school counseling), 2 letters of recommendation. Electronic applications accepted.

Saint Martin's University, Graduate Programs, Program in Counseling Psychology, Lacey, WA 98503-1297. Offers MAC. Part-time and evening/weekend programs available. *Faculty:* 3 full-time (2 women), 3 part-time/adjunct (all women). *Students:* 40 full-time (29 women), 58 part-time (52 women); includes 14 minority (3 African Americans, 1 American Indian/Alaska Native, 6 Asian Americans or Pacific Islanders, 4 Hispanic Americans), 1 international. Average age 36. 24 applicants, 79% accepted, 18 enrolled. In 2007, 17 degrees awarded. *Degree requirements:* For master's, clinical experience, interview. *Entrance requirements:* For master's, BA in psychology or related field, clinical experience. Additional exam requirements/recommendations for international students: Required—TOEFL. *Application deadline:* For fall admission, 7/1 for domestic students, 2/15 for international students; for spring admission, 11/1 priority date for domestic students, 7/1 for international students. Applications are processed on a rolling basis. Application fee: $35. *Expenses:* Tuition: Part-time $742 per credit. Tuition and fees vary according to course level, campus/location and program. *Financial support:* In 2007–08, 97 students received support. Career-related internships or fieldwork, Federal Work-Study, and institutionally sponsored loans available. Support available to part-time students. Financial award application deadline: 3/1. *Faculty research:* Alcohol studies, clinical effectiveness, social justice, parent adolescent interaction. *Unit head:* Dr. Godfrey J. Ellis, Director, 360-438-4560, E-mail: gellis@stmartin.edu. *Application contact:* Sandy Brandt, Administrative Assistant, 360-438-4560, E-mail: sbrandt@stmartin.edu.

St. Mary's University, Graduate School, Department of Counseling and Human Services, Program in Community Counseling, San Antonio, TX 78228-8507. Offers MA. *Students:* 19 full-time (12 women), 18 part-time (14 women); includes 16 minority (6 African Americans, 1 Asian American or Pacific Islander, 9 Hispanic Americans), 1 international. Average age 35. In 2007, 8 degrees awarded. *Degree requirements:* For master's, thesis optional, internship. *Entrance requirements:* For master's, GRE. Additional exam requirements/recommendations for international students: Required—TOEFL (minimum score 550 paper-based; 213 computer-based). Application fee: $0. *Financial support:* Career-related internships or fieldwork, Federal Work-Study, institutionally sponsored loans, scholarships/grants, health care benefits, and unspecified assistantships available. Financial award application deadline: 3/31; financial award applicants required to submit FAFSA. *Unit head:* Dr. Ray Wooten, Director, 210-436-3226, Fax: 210-431-6886, E-mail: hrwooten@stmarytx.edu.

Southeast Missouri State University, School of Graduate Studies, Department of Educational Leadership and Counseling, Program in Guidance and Counseling, Cape Girardeau, MO 63701-4799. Offers community counseling (MA); counseling education (Ed S); school counseling (MA), including elementary counseling, secondary counseling. *Accreditation:* ACA; NCATE. Part-time and evening/weekend programs available. *Faculty:* 6 full-time (3 women). *Students:* 21 full-time (18 women), 50 part-time (45 women); includes 4 minority (3 African Americans, 1 Asian American or Pacific Islander), 1 international. Average age 33. 16 applicants, 63% accepted. In 2007, 16 master's, 4 other advanced degrees awarded. *Degree requirements:* For master's, thesis or alternative. *Entrance requirements:* For master's, GRE General Test, MAT, minimum GPA of 3.0; for Ed S, GRE General Test or MAT, minimum graduate GPA of 3.5. Additional exam requirements/recommendations for international students: Required—TOEFL (minimum score 550 paper-based; 213 computer-based). *Application deadline:* For fall admission, 8/1 for domestic students, 6/1 for international students; for spring admission, 11/21 for domestic students, 10/1 for international students. Applications are processed on a rolling basis. Application fee: $25 ($100 for international students). Electronic applications accepted. *Expenses:* Tuition, state resident: part-time $224 per credit hour. Tuition, nonresident: part-time $395 per credit hour. Tuition and fees vary according to course load and program. *Financial support:* In 2007–08, 29 students received support, including 13 research assistantships with full tuition reimbursements available (averaging $7,600 per year), 1 teaching assistantship (averaging $7,600 per year); career-related internships or fieldwork and unspecified assistantships also available. Financial award applicants required to submit FAFSA. *Application contact:* Marsha L. Arant, Senior Administrative Assistant, Office of Graduate Studies, 573-651-2192, Fax: 573-651-2001, E-mail: marant@semo.edu.

Southwestern College, Program in Transformational Ecopsychology, Santa Fe, NM 87502-4788. Offers Certificate. *Faculty:* 1 (woman) full-time, 4 part-time/adjunct (all women). *Students:* 18 applicants, 100% accepted, 18 enrolled. *Entrance requirements:* For degree, application, reference, interview. Application fee: $25. *Expenses:* Tuition: Full-time $16,416. *Unit head:* Dr. Carol Parker, Program Director, 505-471-5756. *Application contact:* Dru Phoenix, Director of Admissions, 505-471-5756 Ext. 26, Fax: 505-471-4071, E-mail: admissions@swc.edu.

Springfield College, Graduate Programs, Program in Human Services, Springfield, MA 01109-3797. Offers human services (MS), including community counseling psychology, mental health counseling, organizational management and leadership. Part-time and evening/weekend programs available. *Faculty:* 28 full-time (19 women), 74 part-time/adjunct (41 women). *Students:* 464; includes 339 minority (250 African Americans, 5 American Indian/Alaska Native, 5 Asian Americans or Pacific Islanders, 79 Hispanic Americans). Average age 39. 335 applicants, 53% accepted, 160 enrolled. In 2007, 245 degrees awarded. *Degree requirements:* For master's, project. *Entrance requirements:* Additional exam requirements/recommendations for international students: Required—TOEFL (minimum score 550 paper-based; 213 computer-based). *Application deadline:* For fall admission, 8/15 priority date for domestic students; for winter admission, 12/15 for domestic students; for spring admission, 4/15 priority date for domestic students. Applications are processed on a rolling basis. Application fee: $40. Electronic applications accepted. *Expenses: Contact institution.* Tuition and fees vary according to program. *Financial support:* Federal Work-Study and scholarships/grants available. Support available to part-time students. Financial award application deadline: 7/15. *Faculty research:* Social justice, organizational management and leadership, counseling, education and criminal justice. *Unit head:* Dr. Robert J. Willey, Dean, 413-748-3985, Fax: 413-748-3557, E-mail: rwilley@spfldcol.edu. *Application contact:* Joanna Marie Lenfest, Associate Director of Admissions, 413-748-3972, Fax: 413-748-3557, E-mail: jlenfest@spfldcol.edu.

Stony Brook University, State University of New York, Graduate School, College of Arts and Sciences, Department of Psychology, Program in Social and Health Psychology, Stony Brook, NY 11794. Offers PhD. *Students:* 30 full-time (26 women); includes 4 minority (1 Asian American or Pacific Islander, 3 Hispanic Americans), 4 international. Average age 28. 74 applicants, 11% accepted. In 2007, 3 degrees awarded. *Degree requirements:* For doctorate, thesis/dissertation. *Entrance requirements:* For doctorate, GRE General Test, GRE Subject Test. Additional exam requirements/recommendations for international students: Required—TOEFL. *Application deadline:* For fall admission, 1/15 for domestic students. Application fee: $60. *Unit head:* Dr. Marci Lobel, Head, 631-632-7651, E-mail: marci.lobel@stonybrook.edu.

Announcement: The Social and Health Psychology Program conducts basic research with real-world applications on topics that include stress, behavior and health, attachment, relationships, prejudice, and social cognition. All faculty members are active researchers who publish in leading journals. Faculty members have won wide recognition for their research, teaching, and mentoring of graduate students.

See Close-Up on page 1499.

Syracuse University, Graduate School, College of Arts and Sciences, Department of Psychology, Program in Social Psychology, Syracuse, NY 13244. Offers PhD. Part-time programs available. *Students:* 4 full-time (3 women), 1 (woman) part-time; includes 1 minority (Hispanic American), 1 international. 49 applicants, 10% accepted, 1 enrolled. *Degree requirements:* For doctorate, thesis/dissertation. *Entrance requirements:* For doctorate, GRE General Test, GRE Subject Test (recommended). Additional exam requirements/recommendations for international students: Required—TOEFL. *Application deadline:* For fall admission, 1/10 for domestic students. Application fee: $75. *Expenses:* Tuition: Full-time $18,216; part-time $1,012 per credit. Required fees: $980. Tuition and fees vary according to program. *Financial support:* Fellowships, research assistantships, teaching assistantships available. *Unit head:* Dr. Joshua Smyth, Director, 315-443-3723, Fax: 315-443-4085, E-mail: jmsmyth@syr.edu. *Application contact:* Sue Bova, Information Contact, 315-443-1050, E-mail: skbova@syr.edu.

Syracuse University, Graduate School, School of Education, Counseling and Human Services Program, Program in Community Counseling, Syracuse, NY 13244. Offers MS. *Students:* 10 full-time (9 women), 5 part-time (4 women), 1 international. 14 applicants, 71% accepted, 9 enrolled. In 2007, 4 degrees awarded. *Entrance requirements:* For master's, GRE General Test or MAT. *Application deadline:* For fall admission, 2/1 priority date for domestic students. Application fee: $75. *Expenses:* Tuition: Full-time $18,216; part-time $1,012 per credit. Required fees: $980. Tuition and fees vary according to program. *Unit head:* Dr. Janine Bernard, Chair, 315-443-5266, Fax: 315-443-5732, E-mail: bernard@syr.edu. *Application contact:* Traci Washburn, Graduate Recruiter, School of Education, 315-443-2505, E-mail: e-gradrcrt@syr.edu.

Syracuse University, Graduate School, School of Education, Counseling and Human Services Program, Program in Rehabilitation and Community Counseling, Syracuse, NY 13244. Offers MS. *Students:* 2 full-time (both women), 2 part-time (1 woman), 1 international. 2 applicants, 0% accepted. In 2007, 1 degree awarded. *Entrance requirements:* For master's, GRE General Test or MAT, interview. Additional exam requirements/recommendations for international students: Required—TOEFL. *Application deadline:* For fall admission, 2/1 priority date for domestic students; for spring admission, 10/15 priority date for domestic students. Application fee: $75. *Expenses:* Tuition: Full-time $18,216; part-time $1,012 per credit. Required fees: $980. Tuition and fees vary according to program. *Unit head:* Dr. Janine Bernard, Chair, 315-443-5266, Fax: 315-443-5732, E-mail: bernard@syr.edu. *Application contact:* Traci Washburn, Graduate Recruiter, School of Education, 315-443-2505, E-mail: e-gradrcrt@syr.edu.

Teachers College, Columbia University, Graduate Faculty of Education, Department of Organization and Leadership, Program in Social and Organizational Psychology, New York, NY 10027-6696. Offers organizational psychology (MA, Ed D, PhD); social psychology (Ed D, PhD). *Faculty:* 8 full-time (5 women), 5 part-time/adjunct. *Students:* 121 full-time (78 women), 106 part-time (76 women); includes 47 minority (14 African Americans, 22 Asian Americans or Pacific Islanders, 11 Hispanic Americans), 25 international. Average age 32. 216 applicants, 59% accepted, 67 enrolled. In 2007, 121 master's, 6 doctorates awarded. Terminal master's awarded for partial completion of doctoral program. *Degree requirements:* For master's, comprehensive exam; for doctorate, thesis/dissertation. *Entrance requirements:* For master's, minimum GPA of 3.0; for doctorate, GRE General Test. *Application deadline:* For fall admission, 5/15 for domestic students; for spring admission, 12/1 for domestic students. Application fee: $70. *Financial support:* Fellowships, research assistantships, career-related internships or fieldwork, Federal Work-Study, institutionally sponsored loans, and tuition waivers (full and partial) available. Support available to part-time students. Financial award application deadline: 2/1. *Faculty research:* Conflict resolution, human resource and organization development, management competence, organizational culture, leadership. *Application contact:* Debbie Lesperance, Assistant Director of Admission, 212-678-3710, Fax: 212-678-4171.

Temple University, Graduate School, College of Liberal Arts, Department of Psychology, Program in Social Psychology, Philadelphia, PA 19122-6096. Offers PhD. *Degree requirements:* For doctorate, thesis/dissertation, preliminary exam. *Entrance requirements:* For doctorate, GRE General Test, minimum GPA of 3.0. Additional exam requirements/recommendations for international students: Required—TOEFL (minimum score 550 paper-based; 213 computer-based; 79 iBT). Electronic applications accepted. *Faculty research:* Power and technology, organizational behavior, interpersonal dynamics, belief, consumer behavior.

Texas A&M University, College of Liberal Arts, Department of Psychology, College Station, TX 77843. Offers behavioral and cellular neuroscience (MS, PhD); clinical psychology (MS, PhD); cognitive psychology (MS, PhD); developmental psychology (MS, PhD); industrial/organizational psychology (MS, PhD); social psychology (MS, PhD). *Accreditation:* APA (one or more programs are accredited). *Faculty:* 33. *Students:* 69 full-time (46 women), 14 part-time (10 women); includes 27 minority (7 African Americans, 1 American Indian/Alaska Native, 5 Asian Americans or Pacific Islanders, 14 Hispanic Americans), 8 international. 274 applicants, 11% accepted, 15 enrolled. In 2007, 11 master's, 7 doctorates awarded. *Degree requirements:* For master's, thesis; for doctorate, comprehensive exam (for some programs), thesis/dissertation. *Entrance requirements:* For master's and doctorate, GRE General Test. Additional exam requirements/recommendations for international students: Required—TOEFL. *Application deadline:* For fall admission, 1/5 for domestic and international students. Application fee: $50 ($75 for international students). Electronic applications accepted. *Expenses:* Tuition, state resident: full-time $6,129. Tuition, nonresident: full-time $11,689. Tuition and fees vary according to course load. *Financial support:* Fellowships with partial tuition reimbursements, research assistantships with partial tuition reimbursements, teaching assistantships with partial tuition reimbursements, career-related internships or fieldwork, institutionally sponsored loans, health care benefits, and unspecified assistantships available. Financial award application deadline: 1/5; financial award applicants required to submit FAFSA. *Unit head:* Dr. Steve Rholes, Head, 979-845-2581, Fax: 979-845-4727, E-mail: wsr@psyc.tamu.edu. *Application contact:* Sharon Starr, Graduate Admissions Supervisor, 979-458-1710, Fax: 979-845-4727, E-mail: gradadv@psyc.tamu.edu.

Thomas University, Department of Human Services, Thomasville, GA 31792-7499. Offers community counseling (MSCC); rehabilitation counseling (MRC). *Accreditation:* CORE. Part-time programs available. *Entrance requirements:* For master's, resumé, 3 academic/professional references. Additional exam requirements/recommendations for international students: Required—TOEFL (minimum score 600 paper-based; 250 computer-based). Electronic applications accepted.

Université du Québec à Rimouski, Graduate Programs, Program in Psychosocial Studies, Rimouski, QC G5L 3A1, Canada. Offers MA. *Students:* 8 full-time, 24 part-time. Application fee: $50. *Unit head:* Pascal Galvani, Director, 418-724-1647, Fax: 418-724-1525, E-mail: pascal_galvani@uqar.ca. *Application contact:* Office of Admission, 418-724-1433, Fax: 418-724-1525, E-mail: marc_berube@uqar.qc.ca.

Université Laval, Faculty of Social Sciences, School of Psychology, Programs in Psychology, Québec, QC G1K 7P4, Canada. Offers clinical psychology (PhD); community psychology (PhD); psychology (PhD, Psy D). *Degree requirements:* For doctorate, comprehensive exam, thesis/dissertation. *Entrance requirements:* For doctorate, comprehension of written English, knowledge of French, interview. Electronic applications accepted.

University at Albany, State University of New York, College of Arts and Sciences, Department of Psychology, Albany, NY 12222-0001. Offers autism (Certificate); biopsychology (PhD); clinical psychology (PhD); general/experimental psychology (PhD); industrial/organizational psychology (PhD); psychology (MA); social/personality psychology (PhD). *Accreditation:* APA (one or more programs are accredited). *Students:* 51 full-time (32 women), 47 part-time (40 women). Average age 30. In 2007, 8 master's, 15 doctorates, 7 other advanced degrees awarded. *Degree requirements:* For doctorate, thesis/dissertation. *Entrance requirements:* For doctorate, GRE General Test, GRE Subject Test. Additional exam requirements/recommendations for international students: Required—TOEFL (minimum score 550 paper-based; 213 computer-based). *Application deadline:* For fall admission, 1/15 for domestic and international students. Application fee: $75. Electronic applications accepted. *Expenses:* Tuition, state resident: part-time $576 per credit. Tuition, nonresident: part-time $910 per credit. Tuition and fees vary according to program. *Financial support:* Fellowships, research assistantships, teaching assistantships, career-related internships or fieldwork available. Financial award application deadline: 2/1. *Unit head:* Kevin J. Williams, Chair, 518-442-4820.

Social Psychology

University at Buffalo, the State University of New York, Graduate School, College of Arts and Sciences, Department of Psychology, Buffalo, NY 14260. Offers behavioral neuroscience (PhD); clinical psychology (PhD); cognitive psychology (PhD); general psychology (MA); social-personality psychology (PhD). *Accreditation:* APA (one or more programs are accredited). Terminal master's awarded for partial completion of doctoral program. *Degree requirements:* For master's, project; for doctorate, thesis/dissertation. *Entrance requirements:* For master's and doctorate, GRE General Test. Additional exam requirements/recommendations for international students: Required—TOEFL (minimum score 550 paper-based; 213 computer-based; 79 iBT). Electronic applications accepted. *Faculty research:* Neural, endocrine, and molecular bases of behavior; adult mood and anxiety disorders; relationship dysfunction; attention deficit/hyperactivity disorder; psycho-linguistics.

University of Alaska Anchorage, College of Arts and Sciences, Department of Psychology, Anchorage, AK 99508-8060. Offers clinical psychology (MS); clinical-community psychology with rural-indigenous emphasis (PhD). Part-time programs available. *Degree requirements:* For master's, thesis. *Entrance requirements:* For master's, GRE General Test, GRE Subject Test, interview, references; for doctorate, interview, bachelor's or master's degree in psychology. Additional exam requirements/recommendations for international students: Required—TOEFL (minimum score 550 paper-based; 213 computer-based). *Faculty research:* Substance abuse, childhood autism, biofeedback, psychological assessment, mental health in Native Alaskans.

University of Alaska Fairbanks, College of Liberal Arts, Department of Psychology, Fairbanks, AK 99775-7520. Offers clinical-community psychology (PhD), including rural cross-cultural emphasis. *Degree requirements:* For doctorate, comprehensive exam, thesis/dissertation. *Entrance requirements:* For doctorate, GRE General Test, minimum GPA of 3.0, letters of reference. Additional exam requirements/recommendations for international students: Required—TOEFL (minimum score 550 paper-based; 213 computer-based). *Faculty research:* Clinical and community psychology, rural, indigenous, and cultural psychology.

The University of British Columbia, Faculty of Arts and Faculty of Graduate Studies, Department of Psychology, Vancouver, BC V6T 1Z1, Canada. Offers behavioral neuroscience (MA, PhD); clinical psychology (MA, PhD); cognitive science (MA, PhD); developmental psychology (MA, PhD); forensic psychology (PhD); health psychology (MA, PhD); quantitative methods (MA, PhD); social/personality psychology (MA, PhD). *Accreditation:* APA (one or more programs are accredited). *Faculty:* 46 full-time (20 women), 26 part-time/adjunct (13 women). *Students:* 102 full-time (69 women). Average age 29. 247 applicants, 14% accepted, 18 enrolled. In 2007, 14 master's, 11 doctorates awarded. Terminal master's awarded for partial completion of doctoral program. *Median time to degree:* Of those who began their doctoral program in fall 1999, 91% received their degree in 8 years or less. *Degree requirements:* For master's, thesis; for doctorate, comprehensive exam, thesis/dissertation. *Entrance requirements:* For master's and doctorate, GRE General Test, GRE Subject Test. Additional exam requirements/recommendations for international students: Required—TOEFL (minimum score 550 paper-based; 230 computer-based; 80 iBT). *Application deadline:* For fall admission, 1/15 for domestic and international students. Applications are processed on a rolling basis. Application fee: $90 Canadian dollars ($150 Canadian dollars for international students). Electronic applications accepted. *Financial support:* In 2007–08, 95 students received support, including 27 fellowships with full and partial tuition reimbursements available (averaging $16,500 per year), 50 research assistantships with full and partial tuition reimbursements available (averaging $6,775 per year), 80 teaching assistantships with full and partial tuition reimbursements available (averaging $8,065 per year); career-related internships or fieldwork, Federal Work-Study, institutionally sponsored loans, scholarships/grants, health care benefits, tuition waivers (full and partial), and unspecified assistantships also available. Financial award application deadline: 1/15. *Faculty research:* Clinical, developmental, social/personality, cognition, behavioral neuroscience. Total annual research expenditures: $5.5 million Canadian dollars. *Unit head:* Dr. Eric Eich, Head, 604-822-3078, Fax: 604-822-6923, E-mail: ee@psych.ubc.ca. *Application contact:* Rose Tam, Graduate Secretary, 604-822-3144, Fax: 604-822-6923, E-mail: gradsec@psych.ubc.ca.

University of Central Arkansas, Graduate School, College of Health and Behavioral Sciences, Department of Counseling and Psychology, Program in Community Service Counseling, Conway, AR 72035-0001. Offers MS. *Students:* 29 full-time (22 women), 11 part-time (7 women); includes 4 minority (3 African Americans, 1 American Indian/Alaska Native), 1 international. 17 applicants, 100% accepted, 17 enrolled. *Degree requirements:* For master's, comprehensive exam, thesis optional. *Entrance requirements:* For master's, GRE General Test, minimum GPA of 2.7. Additional exam requirements/recommendations for international students: Required—TOEFL (minimum score 550 paper-based; 213 computer-based). *Application deadline:* For fall admission, 3/1 priority date for domestic students; for spring admission, 10/1 priority date for domestic students. Applications are processed on a rolling basis. Application fee: $25 ($50 for international students). *Expenses:* Tuition, state resident: full-time $4,513; part-time $240 per credit. Tuition, nonresident: full-time $8,805; part-time $440 per credit. International tuition: $9,700 full-time. Required fees: $100 per term. *Financial support:* Career-related internships or fieldwork, Federal Work-Study, scholarships/grants, tuition waivers (partial), and unspecified assistantships available. Support available to part-time students. Financial award application deadline: 2/15; financial award applicants required to submit FAFSA. *Unit head:* Dr. Art Gillaspy, Coordinator, 501-450-5410, Fax: 501-450-5424, E-mail: artg@uca.edu. *Application contact:* Patti Hornor, Administrative Assistant, 501-450-5063, Fax: 501-450-5678, E-mail: pattih@uca.edu.

University of Connecticut, Graduate School, College of Liberal Arts and Sciences, Department of Psychology, Field of Psychology, Storrs, CT 06269. Offers behavioral neuroscience (PhD); biopsychology (PhD); clinical psychology (MA, PhD); cognition and instruction (PhD); developmental psychology (MA, PhD); ecological psychology (PhD); experimental psychology (PhD); general psychology (MA, PhD); health psychology (Graduate Certificate); industrial/organizational psychology (PhD); language and cognition (PhD); neuroscience (PhD); occupational health psychology (Graduate Certificate); social psychology (MA, PhD). *Accreditation:* APA (one or more programs are accredited). *Faculty:* 52 full-time (23 women). *Students:* 130 full-time (94 women), 25 part-time (11 women); includes 24 minority (8 African Americans, 6 Asian Americans or Pacific Islanders, 10 Hispanic Americans), 18 international. Average age 28. 531 applicants, 7% accepted, 35 enrolled. In 2007, 19 master's, 20 doctorates, 2 other advanced degrees awarded. Terminal master's awarded for partial completion of doctoral program. *Degree requirements:* For master's, comprehensive exam; for doctorate, thesis/dissertation. *Entrance requirements:* For master's and doctorate, GRE General Test, GRE Subject Test. Additional exam requirements/recommendations for international students: Required—TOEFL (minimum score 550 paper-based; 213 computer-based). *Application deadline:* For fall admission, 2/1 priority date for domestic and international students; for spring admission, 11/1 for domestic students, 10/1 for international students. Applications are processed on a rolling basis. Application fee: $55. Electronic applications accepted. *Expenses:* Tuition, state resident: part-time $469 per credit hour. Tuition, nonresident: part-time $1,218 per credit hour. *Financial support:* In 2007–08, 54 research assistantships with full tuition reimbursements, 69 teaching assistantships with full tuition reimbursements were awarded; fellowships, career-related internships or fieldwork, Federal Work-Study, scholarships/grants, health care benefits, and unspecified assistantships also available. Financial award application deadline: 2/1; financial award applicants required to submit FAFSA. *Application contact:* Deborah Doucette, Administrative Assistant, 860-486-2057, Fax: 860-486-2760, E-mail: futuregr@psych.psy.uconn.edu.

University of Dayton, Graduate School, School of Education and Allied Professions, Department of Counselor Education and Human Services, Dayton, OH 45469-1300. Offers college student personnel (MS Ed); community counseling (MS Ed); higher education administration (MS Ed); human development services (MS Ed); school counseling (MS Ed); school psychology (MS Ed, Ed S); teacher as child/youth development specialist (MS Ed). *Accreditation:* NCATE. Part-time and evening/weekend programs available. *Faculty:* 11 full-time (7 women), 32 part-time/adjunct (17 women). *Students:* 269 full-time (218 women), 305 part-time (255 women); includes 82 minority (66 African Americans, 4 Asian Americans or Pacific Islanders, 12 Hispanic Americans), 8 international. Average age 32. 403 applicants, 49% accepted, 117 enrolled. In 2007, 267 degrees awarded. *Degree requirements:* For master's, thesis optional, exit exam. *Entrance requirements:* For master's, MAT or GRE (if GPA is below 2.75), interview. Additional exam requirements/recommendations for international students: Required—TOEFL (minimum score 550 paper-based; 213 computer-based; 80 iBT). *Application deadline:* For fall admission, 4/10 for domestic students, 3/1 priority date for international students; for winter admission, 9/10 for domestic students, 7/1 priority date for international students; for spring admission, 1/10 for domestic students, 1/1 priority date for international students. Applications are processed on a rolling basis. Application fee: $0 ($50 for international students). Electronic applications accepted. *Financial support:* In 2007–08, 1 research assistantship with partial tuition reimbursement (averaging $7,400 per year), 4 teaching assistantships with partial tuition reimbursements (averaging $7,600 per year) were awarded; career-related internships or fieldwork, institutionally sponsored loans, health care benefits, and unspecified assistantships also available. Financial award applicants required to submit FAFSA. *Faculty research:* Anger as part of the grief process, inclusion of children with severe disabilities, comparisons of school counselors in Bosnia and the U. S., graduate and professional student socialization, use of cohort groups in doctoral programs. *Unit head:* Dr. Alan Demmitt, Chairperson, 937-229-3644, Fax: 937-229-1055. *Application contact:* Angela Jones-Glukhov, Associate Director of Graduate Admissions, 937-229-4305, Fax: 937-229-4729.

University of Delaware, College of Arts and Sciences, Department of Psychology, Newark, DE 19716. Offers behavioral neuroscience (PhD); clinical psychology (PhD); cognitive psychology (PhD); social psychology (PhD). *Accreditation:* APA. *Faculty:* 28 full-time (10 women), 3 part-time/adjunct (1 woman). *Students:* 46 full-time (32 women), 3 part-time (2 women); includes 5 minority (4 African Americans, 1 Asian American or Pacific Islander), 3 international. Average age 27. 252 applicants, 8% accepted, 7 enrolled. In 2007, 6 doctorates awarded. *Degree requirements:* For doctorate, thesis/dissertation. *Entrance requirements:* For doctorate, GRE General Test. Additional exam requirements/recommendations for international students: Required—TOEFL (minimum score 600 paper-based; 250 computer-based). *Application deadline:* For fall admission, 1/7 priority date for domestic students. Application fee: $60. Electronic applications accepted. *Financial support:* In 2007–08, 47 students received support, including 7 fellowships with full tuition reimbursements available (averaging $16,000 per year), 14 research assistantships with full tuition reimbursements available (averaging $15,500 per year), 20 teaching assistantships with full tuition reimbursements available (averaging $16,000 per year); career-related internships or fieldwork, Federal Work-Study, institutionally sponsored loans, scholarships/grants, and tuition waivers (full and partial) also available. Financial award application deadline: 1/7. *Faculty research:* Emotion development, neural and cognitive aspects of memory, neural control of feeding, intergroup relations, social cognition and communication. Total annual research expenditures: $2.5 million. *Unit head:* Dr. Thomas M. DiLorenzo, Chair, 302-831-2271, Fax: 302-831-3645. *Application contact:* Linda Scarpitti, Information Contact, 302-831-2271, Fax: 302-831-3645, E-mail: linnie@udel.edu.

University of Florida, Graduate School, College of Liberal Arts and Sciences, Department of Psychology, Gainesville, FL 32611. Offers behavior analysis (PhD); behavioral neuroscience (MS, PhD); cognitive and sensory processes (PhD); counseling psychology (PhD); developmental psychology (PhD); social psychology (MS, PhD); JD/PhD. *Faculty:* 42 full-time (12 women), 3 part-time/adjunct (1 woman). *Students:* 136 (90 women); includes 22 minority (7 African Americans, 1 American Indian/Alaska Native, 5 Asian Americans or Pacific Islanders, 9 Hispanic Americans) 22 international. In 2007, 25 master's, 14 doctorates awarded. *Degree requirements:* For master's, thesis or alternative; for doctorate, thesis/dissertation. *Entrance requirements:* For master's and doctorate, GRE General Test, minimum GPA of 3.0. Additional exam requirements/recommendations for international students: Required—TOEFL (minimum score 550 paper-based; 213 computer-based). *Application deadline:* For fall admission, 1/15 priority date for domestic students. Applications are processed on a rolling basis. Application fee: $30. Electronic applications accepted. *Expenses:* Tuition, state resident: full-time $7,478. Tuition, nonresident: full-time $22,603. *Financial support:* In 2007–08, 33 research assistantships (averaging $16,597 per year), 64 teaching assistantships (averaging $16,703 per year) were awarded; fellowships, career-related internships or fieldwork and unspecified assistantships also available. Financial award application deadline: 1/15. *Faculty research:* Experimental analysis of behavior, psychobiology, cognition and sensory processes, counseling psychology, social psychology, developmental psychology. *Unit head:* Dr. Martin Heesacker, Chair, 352-392-0601 Ext. 200, Fax: 352-392-7985, E-mail: heesack@ufl.edu. *Application contact:* Dr. Gregory Neimeyer, Coordinator, 352-392-0601 Ext. 259, Fax: 352-392-7985, E-mail: neimeyer@ufl.edu.

University of Guelph, Graduate Program Services, College of Social and Applied Human Sciences, Department of Psychology, Guelph, ON N1G 2W1, Canada. Offers applied social psychology (MA, PhD); clinical psychology applied development emphasis (PhD); clinical psychology applied developmental emphasis (MA); industrial/organizational psychology (MA, PhD); neuroscience and applied cognitive science (MA, PhD). *Faculty:* 34 full-time (14 women). *Students:* 95 full-time (72 women), 6 part-time (all women); includes 6 minority (2 African Americans, 4 Asian Americans or Pacific Islanders). 230 applicants, 28% accepted, 35 enrolled. In 2007, 8 master's, 2 doctorates awarded. *Median time to degree:* Of those who began their doctoral program in fall 1999, 100% received their degree in 8 years or less. *Degree requirements:* For master's, thesis; for doctorate, comprehensive exam, thesis/dissertation. *Entrance requirements:* For master's, GRE General Test, GRE Subject Test, minimum B+ average during previous 2 years of course work; for doctorate, GRE General Test, GRE Subject Test, minimum A- average. Additional exam requirements/recommendations for international students: Required—TOEFL (minimum score 89 iBT). *Application deadline:* For fall admission, 12/15 priority date for domestic students, 1/15 priority date for international students; for spring admission, 12/15 priority date for domestic students. Application fee: $85. Electronic applications accepted. *Financial support:* In 2007–08, 108 teaching assistantships with partial tuition reimbursements (averaging $10,213 per year) were awarded. *Faculty research:* Organizational psychology, reading comprehension and mathematical ability, drug addiction and relapse, gender issues and culture, memory, clinical psychology. *Unit head:* Dr. Harvey Marmurek, Chair, 519-824-4120 Ext. 53673, Fax: 519-837-8629, E-mail: marmurek@psy.uoguelph.ca. *Application contact:* Dr. Ian Newby-Clark, Graduate Coordinator, 519-824-4120 Ext. 53307, Fax: 519-837-8629, E-mail: newby-clark@psy.uoguelph.ca.

University of Hawaii at Manoa, Graduate Division, Colleges of Arts and Sciences, College of Social Sciences, Department of Psychology, Honolulu, HI 96822. Offers clinical psychology (PhD); community and cultural psychology (PhD); community and culture (MA); psychology (MA, PhD, Graduate Certificate). *Accreditation:* APA (one or more programs are accredited). Part-time programs available. *Faculty:* 35 full-time (13 women), 8 part-time/adjunct (1 woman). *Students:* 86 full-time (61 women), 7 part-time (5 women); includes 30 minority (1 African American, 1 American Indian/Alaska Native, 26 Asian Americans or Pacific Islanders, 2 Hispanic Americans), 11 international. 199 applicants, 14% accepted, 16 enrolled. Terminal master's awarded for partial completion of doctoral program. *Median time to degree:* Of those who began their doctoral program in fall 1999, 83% received their degree in 8 years or less. *Degree requirements:* For master's, comprehensive exam, thesis; for doctorate, comprehensive exam, thesis/dissertation. *Entrance requirements:* For master's and doctorate, GRE General Test, GRE Subject Test. Additional exam requirements/recommendations for international students: Required—TOEFL (minimum score 600 paper-based; 250 computer-based; 100 iBT), IELTS (minimum score 7). *Application deadline:* For fall admission, 1/1 for domestic and international students. Application fee: $50. *Financial support:* In 2007–08, 44 research assistantships (averaging $16,926 per year), 18 teaching assistantships (averaging $14,042 per year) were awarded; career-related internships or fieldwork, institutionally sponsored loans, and tuition waivers (full and partial) also available. Financial award application deadline: 1/1. *Faculty research:* Cross-cultural psychology, health psychology, marine mammals, child/adult psychopathology. Total annual research expenditures: $1.1 million. *Application contact:* Catherine Sophian, Graduate Chair, 808-956-8414, Fax: 808-956-4700, E-mail: csophian@hawaii.edu.

University of Houston, College of Liberal Arts and Social Sciences, Department of Psychology, Houston, TX 77204. Offers clinical psychology (PhD); industrial/organizational psychology (PhD); psychology (MA); social psychology (PhD). *Accreditation:* APA (one or more programs are accredited). *Faculty:* 24 full-time (9 women), 3 part-time/adjunct (1 woman). *Students:* 102 full-time (77 women), 16 part-time (12 women); includes 22 minority (4 African Americans, 8 Asian Americans or Pacific Islanders, 10 Hispanic Americans), 8 international. Average age 27. 187 applicants, 13% accepted, 22 enrolled. In 2007, 10 master's, 12 doctorates awarded. *Degree requirements:* For doctorate, thesis/dissertation. *Entrance requirements:* For doctorate, GRE General Test, minimum GPA of 3.0. *Application deadline:* For fall admission, 1/1 for domestic students. Application fee: $40 ($75 for international students). *Expenses:* Tuition, state resident: full-time $6,297; part-time $262 per credit. Tuition, nonresident: full-time $12,969; part-time $540 per credit. Required fees: $2,696. *Financial support:* In 2007–08, 12 fellowships with full tuition reimbursements (averaging $11,200 per year), 13 research assistantships with full tuition reimbursements (averaging $10,050 per year), 74 teaching assistantships with full tuition reimbursements (averaging $10,250 per year) were awarded; career-related internships or fieldwork, Federal Work-Study, institutionally sponsored loans, scholarships/grants, health care benefits, and unspecified assistantships also available. Support available to part-time students. Financial award application deadline: 2/1; financial award applicants required to submit FAFSA. *Faculty research:* Health psychology, depression, child/family process, organizational effectiveness, close relationships. *Unit head:* Dr. David Francis, Chairperson, 713-743-7036, Fax: 713-743-8588, E-mail: dfrancis@uh.edu. *Application contact:* Sherry A. Berun, Coordinator—Academic Affairs, 713-743-8508, Fax: 713-743-8588, E-mail: sherryr@uh.edu.

University of La Verne, College of Arts and Sciences, Department of Psychology, Program in Clinical-Community Psychology, La Verne, CA 91750-4443. Offers Psy D. Part-time programs available. *Faculty:* 8 full-time (1 woman), 5 part-time/adjunct (1 woman). *Students:* 47 full-time (38 women), 22 part-time (19 women); includes 40 minority (7 African Americans, 11 American Indian/Alaska Native, 4 Asian Americans or Pacific Islanders, 18 Hispanic Americans). Average age 29. In 2007, 20 degrees awarded. *Degree requirements:* For doctorate, thesis/dissertation, clinical internship, competency exams, practicum, personal psychotherapy. *Entrance requirements:* For doctorate, minimum GPA of 3.25 undergraduate, 3.65 graduate; 3 recommendations; interview; curriculum vitae. Additional exam requirements/recommendations for international students: Required—TOEFL (minimum score 600 paper-based; 250 computer-based). *Application deadline:* For fall admission, 1/15 for domestic and international students. Application fee: $75. *Expenses:* Contact institution. Tuition and fees vary according to course load and program. *Financial support:* Career-related internships or fieldwork, institutionally sponsored loans, scholarships/grants, and unspecified assistantships available. Financial award application deadline: 3/2; financial award applicants required to submit FAFSA. *Unit head:* Dr. Raymond Scott, Chairperson, 909-593-3511 Ext. 4181, E-mail: rscott@ulv.edu. *Application contact:* Connie Hamlow, Admissions Information Specialist, 909-593-3511 Ext. 4244, Fax: 909-392-2761, E-mail: gradadmission@ulv.edu.

University of Maine, Graduate School, College of Liberal Arts and Sciences, Department of Psychology, Orono, ME 04469. Offers clinical psychology (PhD); developmental psychology (MA); experimental psychology (MA, PhD); social psychology (MA). *Accreditation:* APA (one or more programs are accredited). *Faculty:* 24. *Students:* 28 full-time (17 women), 10 part-time (6 women); includes 2 minority (1 American Indian/Alaska Native, 1 Hispanic American), 1 international. Average age 29. 129 applicants, 9% accepted, 8 enrolled. In 2007, 5 master's, 2 doctorates awarded. *Degree requirements:* For master's, thesis; for doctorate, thesis/dissertation. *Entrance requirements:* For master's and doctorate, GRE General Test, GRE Subject Test. Additional exam requirements/recommendations for international students: Required—TOEFL. *Application deadline:* For fall admission, 2/1 priority date for domestic students. Applications are processed on a rolling basis. Application fee: $60. Electronic applications accepted. *Financial support:* In 2007–08, 3 research assistantships with tuition reimbursements (averaging $13,400 per year), 21 teaching assistantships with tuition reimbursements (averaging $9,010 per year) were awarded; fellowships with tuition reimbursements, Federal Work-Study, institutionally sponsored loans, and tuition waivers (full and partial) also available. Financial award application deadline: 3/1. *Faculty research:* Social development, hypertension and aging, attitude change, self-confidence in achievement situations, health psychology. *Unit head:* Dr. Jeffrey Hecker, Chair, 207-581-2032, Fax: 207-581-6128. *Application contact:* Scott G. Delcourt, Associate Dean of the Graduate School, 207-581-3219, Fax: 207-581-3232, E-mail: graduate@maine.edu.

University of Mary Hardin-Baylor, College of Sciences and Humanities, Department of Psychology, Belton, TX 76513. Offers community counseling (MA); marriage and family Christian counseling (MA); psychology and counseling (MA); school counseling and psychology (MA). Part-time and evening/weekend programs available. *Degree requirements:* For master's, comprehensive exam. *Entrance requirements:* For master's, GRE General Test, minimum GPA of 3.0 in last 60 hours or 2.75 overall. Electronic applications accepted.

University of Maryland, College Park, Graduate Studies, College of Behavioral and Social Sciences, Department of Psychology, College Park, MD 20742. Offers clinical psychology (PhD); developmental psychology (PhD); experimental psychology (PhD); industrial psychology (MA, MS, PhD); social psychology (PhD). *Accreditation:* APA (one or more programs are accredited). *Faculty:* 53 full-time (23 women), 12 part-time/adjunct (6 women). *Students:* 92 full-time (70 women), 4 part-time (3 women); includes 15 minority (2 African Americans, 1 American Indian/Alaska Native, 6 Asian Americans or Pacific Islanders, 6 Hispanic Americans), 12 international. 609 applicants, 4% accepted, 13 enrolled. In 2007, 13 master's, 18 doctorates awarded. *Median time to degree:* Of those who began their doctoral program in fall 1999, 71% received their degree in 8 years or less. *Degree requirements:* For master's, thesis; for doctorate, variable foreign language requirement, comprehensive exam, thesis/dissertation. *Entrance requirements:* For master's and doctorate, GRE General Test, GRE Subject Test, minimum GPA of 3.5, research and/or work experience, 3 letters of recommendation. *Application deadline:* For fall admission, 12/15 for domestic students, 2/1 for international students. Applications are processed on a rolling basis. Application fee: $60. Electronic applications accepted. *Financial support:* In 2007–08, 11 fellowships with full tuition reimbursements (averaging $15,736 per year), 9 research assistantships (averaging $15,312 per year), 56 teaching assistantships with tuition reimbursements (averaging $15,292 per year) were awarded; career-related internships or fieldwork, Federal Work-Study, and scholarships/grants also available. Support available to part-time students. Financial award applicants required to submit FAFSA. *Faculty research:* Social stereotyping and prejudice, anxiety disorders, auditory neuroethology, counseling and social psychology. Total annual research expenditures: $4.4 million. *Unit head:* Thomas S. Wallsten, Chair, 301-405-5862, Fax: 301-314-9566, E-mail: twallsten@psyc.umd.edu. *Application contact:* Dean of Graduate School, 301-405-0358, Fax: 301-314-9305.

University of Massachusetts Lowell, College of Arts and Sciences, Department of Psychology, Lowell, MA 01854-2881. Offers community social psychology (MA). Part-time programs available. *Faculty:* 22. *Degree requirements:* For master's, thesis optional. *Entrance requirements:* For master's, GRE General Test or MAT. *Application deadline:* For fall admission, 4/1 priority date for domestic students; for spring admission, 10/1 for domestic students. Applications are processed on a rolling basis. Application fee: $20 ($35 for international students). Electronic applications accepted. *Financial support:* Research assistantships with full tuition reimbursements, teaching assistantships with full tuition reimbursements, career-related internships or fieldwork, Federal Work-Study, scholarships/grants, and traineeships available. Financial award application deadline: 4/1. *Faculty research:* Domestic violence, youth sports, teen pregnancy, substance abuse, family and work roles. *Unit head:* Dr. Nina Coppens, Chair, 978-934-3954, E-mail: nina_coppens@uml.edu. *Application contact:* Dr. Khanh T. Dinh, Graduate Coordinator, 978-934-3916, E-mail: khanh_dinh@uml.edu.

University of Michigan, Horace H. Rackham School of Graduate Studies, College of Literature, Science, and the Arts, Department of Psychology, Ann Arbor, MI 48109. Offers biopsychology (PhD); clinical psychology (PhD); cognition and perception (PhD); developmental psychology (PhD); personality and social contexts (PhD); social psychology (PhD). *Accreditation:* APA. *Faculty:* 86 full-time, 69 part-time/adjunct. *Students:* 157 full-time (112 women); includes 51 minority (21 African Americans, 1 American Indian/Alaska Native, 17 Asian Americans or Pacific Islanders, 12 Hispanic Americans), 32 international. Average age 25. 698 applicants, 9% accepted, 29 enrolled. In 2007, 25 degrees awarded. *Degree requirements:* For doctorate, comprehensive exam, thesis/dissertation, oral defense of dissertation, preliminary exam. *Entrance requirements:* For doctorate, GRE General Test (optional), GRE Subject Test (optional). Additional exam requirements/recommendations for international students: Required—TOEFL. *Application deadline:* For fall admission, 12/15 for domestic students. Application fee: $60 ($75 for international students). Electronic applications accepted. *Financial support:* Fellowships with full tuition reimbursements, research assistantships with full tuition reimbursements, teaching assistantships with full tuition reimbursements, career-related internships or fieldwork available. Financial award application deadline: 4/15. *Unit head:* Theresa Lee, Chair, 734-764-7429. *Application contact:* Laurie Brannan, Psychology Student Academic Affairs, 731-764-2580, Fax: 734-615-7584, E-mail: psych.saa@umich.edu.

University of Minnesota, Twin Cities Campus, Graduate School, College of Liberal Arts, Department of Psychology, Program in Social Psychology, Minneapolis, MN 55455-0213. Offers PhD. *Faculty:* 8 full-time (3 women). *Students:* 23 full-time (12 women); includes 4 minority (3 Asian Americans or Pacific Islanders, 1 Hispanic American), 2 international. 101 applicants, 9% accepted, 3 enrolled. In 2007, 4 degrees awarded. *Median time to degree:* Of those who began their doctoral program in fall 1999, 50% received their degree in 8 years or less. *Degree requirements:* For doctorate, comprehensive exam, thesis/dissertation. *Entrance requirements:* For doctorate, GRE General Test, GRE Subject Test (recommended), 12 credits of upper-level psychology courses, including a course in statistics or psychological measurement. Additional exam requirements/recommendations for international students: Required—TOEFL (minimum score 550 paper-based; 213 computer-based; 79 iBT). *Application deadline:* For fall admission, 12/1 for domestic and international students. Application fee: $55 ($75 for international students). *Financial support:* In 2007–08, fellowships with full tuition reimbursements (averaging $21,000 per year), research assistantships with full tuition reimbursements (averaging $12,254 per year), teaching assistantships with full tuition reimbursements (averaging $12,254 per year) were awarded; career-related internships or fieldwork and tuition waivers (partial) also available. Financial award application deadline: 12/1. *Unit head:* Mark Snyder, Area Director, 612-625-1507. *Application contact:* Coordinator, 612-624-4181, Fax: 612-626-2079, E-mail: psyapply@tc.umn.edu.

University of Missouri–Kansas City, College of Arts and Sciences, Department of Psychology, Kansas City, MO 64110-2499. Offers psychology (MA, PhD), including clinical psychology (PhD), community psychology (PhD). *Accreditation:* APA. *Faculty:* 16 full-time (12 women). *Students:* 14 full-time (10 women), 10 part-time (8 women); includes 2 minority (1 African American, 1 Hispanic American). Average age 31. 72 applicants, 6% accepted, 3 enrolled. In 2007, 4 master's, 4 doctorates awarded. Terminal master's awarded for partial completion of doctoral program. *Degree requirements:* For master's, thesis; for doctorate, comprehensive exam, thesis/dissertation, residency. *Entrance requirements:* For master's, GRE, minimum GPA of 3.5, letter of recommendation; for doctorate, GRE, minimum GPA of 3.25. Additional exam requirements/recommendations for international students: Required—TOEFL. *Application deadline:* For fall admission, 1/15 for domestic and international students. Applications are processed on a rolling basis. Application fee: $35 ($50 for international students). Electronic applications accepted. *Expenses:* Tuition, state resident: part-time $287 per hour. Tuition, nonresident: part-time $741 per hour. Required fees: $31 per hour. Tuition and fees vary according to program. *Financial support:* In 2007–08, 10 research assistantships (averaging $13,294 per year), 9 teaching assistantships (averaging $12,083 per year) were awarded; career-related internships or fieldwork, Federal Work-Study, and institutionally sponsored loans also available. Support available to part-time students. Financial award application deadline: 3/1; financial award applicants required to submit FAFSA. *Faculty research:* HIV/AIDS research group, psycho-oncology, sensory and cognitive neuroscience, cognitive psychophysiology, obesity and related metabolic disorders. Total annual research expenditures: $666,164. *Unit head:* Dr. Diane Filion, Chairperson, 816-235-1061. *Application contact:* 816-235-1111.

University of Missouri–St. Louis, College of Arts and Sciences, Department of Psychology, St. Louis, MO 63121. Offers behavioral neuroscience (PhD); clinical psychology respecialization (Certificate); community psychology (PhD); general psychology (MA); industrial/organizational psychology (PhD). *Accreditation:* APA (one or more programs are accredited). Evening/weekend programs available. *Faculty:* 20 full-time (9 women), 2 part-time/adjunct (both women). *Students:* 51 full-time (40 women), 22 part-time (16 women); includes 5 minority (1 African American, 3 Asian Americans or Pacific Islanders, 1 Hispanic American), 2 international. Average age 29. In 2007, 11 master's, 8 doctorates awarded. Terminal master's awarded for partial completion of doctoral program. *Degree requirements:* For doctorate, thesis/dissertation. *Entrance requirements:* For master's and doctorate, GRE General Test, GRE Subject Test, 3 letters of recommendation. Additional exam requirements/recommendations for international students: Required—TOEFL (minimum score 550 paper-based; 213 computer-based). *Application deadline:* For fall admission, 2/1 priority date for domestic students. Applications are processed on a rolling basis. Application fee: $35 ($40 for international students). Electronic applications accepted. *Financial support:* In 2007–08, 11 research assistantships with full and partial tuition reimbursements (averaging $11,333 per year), 18 teaching assistantships with full and partial tuition reimbursements (averaging $10,525 per year) were awarded; fellowships with full tuition reimbursements also available. *Faculty research:* Bereavement and loss, neuroscience, post-traumatic stress disorder, conflict and negotiation, social psychology. *Unit head:* Dr. Robert Calsyn, Chair, 314-516-5391, Fax: 314-516-5392, E-mail: umslpsychology@msx.umsl.edu. *Application contact:* 314-516-5458, Fax: 314-516-6996, E-mail: gradadm@umsl.edu.

University of Missouri–St. Louis, College of Education, Division of Counseling, St. Louis, MO 63121. Offers community counseling (M Ed); counseling (PhD); elementary school counseling (M Ed); secondary school counseling (M Ed). *Accreditation:* ACA; NCATE. *Faculty:* 7 full-time (3 women). *Students:* 55 full-time (46 women), 157 part-time (130 women); includes 33 minority (30 African Americans, 1 Asian American or Pacific Islander, 2 Hispanic Americans), 6 international. Average age 32. In 2007, 57 master's, 2 doctorates awarded. *Entrance requirements:* For master's, 3 letters of recommendation, supplemental application; for doctorate, GRE General Test, 3 letters of recommendation. Additional exam requirements/recommendations for international students: Required—TOEFL (minimum score 550 paper-based; 213 computer-based). *Application deadline:* Applications are processed on a rolling basis. Application fee: $35 ($40 for international students). Electronic applications accepted. *Financial support:* In 2007–08, 2 research assistantships with full and partial tuition reimbursements (averaging $18,000 per year) were awarded. *Faculty research:* Vocational interests, self-concept, decision-making factors, developmental differences. *Unit head:* Dr. Mark Pope, Chair, 314-516-5782. *Application contact:* 314-516-5458, Fax: 314-516-6996, E-mail: gradadm@umsl.edu.

University of Montevallo, College of Education, Program in Counseling, Montevallo, AL 35115. Offers community counseling (M Ed); marriage and family (M Ed); school counseling (M Ed). *Accreditation:* ACA; NCATE. Part-time and evening/weekend programs available. *Entrance requirements:* For master's, GRE General Test or MAT, minimum undergraduate GPA of 2.75 in last 60 hours or 2.5 overall, interview. Additional exam requirements/recommendations for international students: Required—TOEFL (minimum score 550 paper-based).

University of Nevada, Reno, Graduate School, Interdisciplinary Program in Social Psychology, Reno, NV 89557. Offers PhD. *Faculty:* 9. *Students:* 27 full-time (20 women), 13 part-time (11 women); includes 6 minority (2 Asian Americans or Pacific Islanders, 4 Hispanic Americans), 5 international. Average age 31. 39 applicants, 36% accepted, 10 enrolled. In 2007, 4 doctorates awarded. *Degree requirements:* For doctorate, one foreign language, thesis/dissertation. *Entrance requirements:* For doctorate, GRE General Test, GRE Subject Test (psychology or sociology), minimum GPA of 3.0. Additional exam requirements/recommendations for international students: Required—TOEFL. *Application deadline:* For fall admission, 2/1

Social Psychology

University of Nevada, Reno (continued)
priority date for domestic students. Applications are processed on a rolling basis. Application fee: $60 ($95 for international students). *Expenses:* Tuition, state resident: full-time $2,774; part-time $154 per credit. Tuition, nonresident: full-time $13,578; part-time $330 per credit. Required fees: $49 per semester. *Financial support:* In 2007–08, 2 research assistantships, 2 teaching assistantships were awarded; unspecified assistantships also available. Financial award application deadline: 3/1. *Faculty research:* Social psychological theory, social psychology of law. *Unit head:* Dr. Colleen Murray, Director, 775-784-7006, E-mail: gpg@scs.unr.edu.

University of New Haven, Graduate School, College of Arts and Sciences, Program in Community Psychology, West Haven, CT 06516-1916. Offers MA, Certificate. *Students:* 4 full-time (3 women), 7 part-time (6 women); includes 3 minority (all African Americans), 1 international. In 2007, 9 degrees awarded. *Degree requirements:* For master's, thesis or alternative. *Application deadline:* Applications are processed on a rolling basis. Application fee: $50. *Expenses:* Tuition: Part-time $630 per credit. Required fees: $40 per term. *Financial support:* Career-related internships or fieldwork and Federal Work-Study available. Support available to part-time students. Financial award application deadline: 5/1; financial award applicants required to submit FAFSA. *Unit head:* Dr. Michael Morris, Coordinator, 203-932-7281.

The University of North Carolina at Chapel Hill, Graduate School, College of Arts and Sciences, Department of Psychology, Chapel Hill, NC 27599. Offers biological psychology (PhD); clinical psychology (PhD); cognitive psychology (PhD); developmental psychology (PhD); quantitative psychology (PhD); social psychology (PhD). *Accreditation:* APA. *Degree requirements:* For doctorate, comprehensive exam, thesis/dissertation. *Entrance requirements:* For doctorate, GRE General Test, minimum GPA of 3.0. Electronic applications accepted. *Faculty research:* Expressed emotion, cognitive development, social cognitive neuroscience, human memory personality.

The University of North Carolina at Charlotte, Graduate School, College of Arts and Sciences, Department of Psychology, Program in Community/Clinical Psychology, Charlotte, NC 28223-0001. Offers MA. *Students:* 10 full-time (9 women), 18 part-time (16 women); includes 8 minority (4 African Americans, 1 Asian American or Pacific Islander, 3 Hispanic Americans), 2 international. Average age 26. 94 applicants, 5% accepted, 5 enrolled. In 2007, 12 degrees awarded. *Degree requirements:* For master's, comprehensive exam, thesis. *Entrance requirements:* For master's, GRE General Test, GRE Subject Test, minimum GPA of 3.0 in undergraduate major, 2.8 overall. Additional exam requirements/recommendations for international students: Required—TOEFL (minimum score 557 paper-based; 220 computer-based). *Application deadline:* For fall admission, 3/1 for domestic and international students. Application fee: $55. Electronic applications accepted. *Expenses:* Tuition, state resident: full-time $2,855. Tuition, nonresident: full-time $13,062. Required fees: $1,692. *Financial support:* In 2007–08, 1 research assistantship (averaging $9,000 per year), 2 teaching assistantships (averaging $9,000 per year) were awarded; fellowships, career-related internships or fieldwork, Federal Work-Study, institutionally sponsored loans, scholarships/grants, and unspecified assistantships also available. Support available to part-time students. Financial award application deadline: 4/1; financial award applicants required to submit FAFSA. *Unit head:* Dr. Richard G. Tedeschi, Coordinator, 704-687-4754, Fax: 704-687-3096, E-mail: rtedesch@email.uncc.edu. *Application contact:* Kathy B. Giddings, Director of Graduate Admissions, 704-687-3366, Fax: 704-687-3279, E-mail: agidding@uncc.edu.

The University of North Carolina at Greensboro, Graduate School, College of Arts and Sciences, Department of Psychology, Greensboro, NC 27412-5001. Offers clinical psychology (MA, PhD); cognitive psychology (MA, PhD); developmental psychology (MA, PhD); social psychology (MA, PhD). *Accreditation:* APA (one or more programs are accredited). *Faculty:* 23 full-time (8 women). *Students:* 46 full-time (31 women), 13 part-time (10 women); includes 7 minority (3 African Americans, 1 American Indian/Alaska Native, 1 Asian American or Pacific Islander, 2 Hispanic Americans). 218 applicants, 7% accepted.Terminal master's awarded for partial completion of doctoral program. *Degree requirements:* For master's, comprehensive exam, thesis; for doctorate, one foreign language, thesis/dissertation, preliminary exam. *Entrance requirements:* For master's and doctorate, GRE General Test. Additional exam requirements/recommendations for international students: Required—TOEFL. *Application deadline:* For fall admission, 2/1 for domestic students. Application fee: $45. Electronic applications accepted. *Financial support:* Fellowships with full tuition reimbursements, research assistantships with full tuition reimbursements, teaching assistantships with full tuition reimbursements, unspecified assistantships available. *Faculty research:* Sensory and perceptual determinants; evoked potential: disorders, deafness, and development. *Unit head:* Dr. George Michel, Head, 336-336-5013, E-mail: gfmichel@uncg.edu. *Application contact:* Michelle Harkleroad, Director of Graduate Admissions, 336-334-4884, Fax: 336-334-4424, E-mail: mbharkle@uncg.edu.

University of Oklahoma, Graduate College, College of Education, Department of Educational Psychology, Program in Community Counseling, Norman, OK 73019-0390. Offers M Ed. *Students:* 28 full-time (24 women); includes 5 minority (4 American Indian/Alaska Native, 1 Asian American or Pacific Islander). In 2007, 13 degrees awarded. Terminal master's awarded for partial completion of doctoral program. *Degree requirements:* For master's, comprehensive exam. *Entrance requirements:* For master's, GRE General Test, minimum GPA of 3.0. Additional exam requirements/recommendations for international students: Required—TOEFL (minimum score 550 paper-based; 213 computer-based). *Application deadline:* For fall admission, 1/31 for domestic students, 4/1 for international students; for spring admission, 11/1 for domestic students, 9/1 for international students. Applications are processed on a rolling basis. Application fee: $40 ($90 for international students). Electronic applications accepted. *Expenses:* Tuition, state resident: full-time $3,451; part-time $144 per credit hour. Tuition, nonresident: full-time $12,432; part-time $518 per credit hour. Required fees: $1,925; $70 per credit hour. $122 per semester. *Financial support:* Institutionally sponsored loans, scholarships/grants, health care benefits, tuition waivers (partial), and unspecified assistantships available. Financial award application deadline: 3/1; financial award applicants required to submit FAFSA. *Faculty research:* Marriage and family counseling assessment; process and outcome; diversity issues; health psychology; education, training and supervision. *Application contact:* Rindi Ledo, Applications Officer, 405-325-4525, Fax: 405-325-6655, E-mail: gpoedpsych@ou.edu.

University of Oregon, Graduate School, College of Arts and Sciences, Department of Psychology, Eugene, OR 97403. Offers clinical psychology (PhD); cognitive psychology (MA, MS, PhD); developmental psychology (MA, MS, PhD); physiological psychology (MA, MS, PhD); psychology (MA, MS, PhD); social/personality psychology (MA, MS, PhD). *Accreditation:* APA (one or more programs are accredited). *Faculty:* 27 full-time (11 women), 11 part-time/adjunct (8 women). *Students:* 76 full-time (48 women), 10 part-time (7 women); includes 11 minority (1 African American, 7 Asian Americans or Pacific Islanders, 3 Hispanic Americans), 15 international. 320 applicants, 8% accepted. In 2007, 21 master's, 11 doctorates awarded. Terminal master's awarded for partial completion of doctoral program. *Degree requirements:* For doctorate, thesis/dissertation. *Entrance requirements:* For master's, GRE General Test, minimum GPA of 3.0; for doctorate, GRE General Test. Additional exam requirements/recommendations for international students: Required—TOEFL. *Application deadline:* For fall admission, 12/1 for domestic students. Application fee: $50. *Financial support:* In 2007–08, 48 teaching assistantships were awarded; research assistantships, career-related internships or fieldwork also available. *Unit head:* Louis Moses, Head, 541-346-4918, Fax: 541-346-4911. *Application contact:* Lori Olsen, Admissions Contact, 541-346-5060, Fax: 541-346-4911, E-mail: gradsec@psych.uoregon.edu.

University of Pennsylvania, Graduate School of Education, Division of Applied Psychology and Human Development, Program in School, Community, and Clinical Child Psychology, Philadelphia, PA 19104. Offers PhD. *Degree requirements:* For doctorate, thesis/dissertation, exams. *Entrance requirements:* For doctorate, GRE General Test, GRE Subject Test. Electronic applications accepted. Expenses: Contact institution. *Faculty research:* Therapeutic interventions at a preschool level, childhood stress, college psychology, school and community psychology.

University of Phoenix–Denver Campus, The Artemis School, College of Health and Human Services, Lone Tree, CO 80124-5453. Offers community counseling (MSC); health care management (MBA); marriage, family and child therapy (MSC); nursing (MSN). Evening/weekend programs available. *Degree requirements:* For master's, thesis (for some programs). *Entrance requirements:* For master's, minimum undergraduate GPA of 2.5, 3 years work experience, RN license. Additional exam requirements/recommendations for international students: Required—TOEFL (minimum score 550 paper-based; 213 computer-based; 79 iBT). Electronic applications accepted.

University of Phoenix–Hawaii Campus, The Artemis School, College of Health and Human Services, Honolulu, HI 96813-4317. Offers administration of justice and security (MS); community counseling (MSC); family nurse practitioner (MSN); health administration (MHA); health care management (MBA); marriage, family and child therapy (MSC); nursing (MSN); psychology (MS). Evening/weekend programs available. *Degree requirements:* For master's, thesis (for some programs). *Entrance requirements:* For master's, minimum undergraduate GPA of 2.5, 3 years of work experience, RN license. Additional exam requirements/recommendations for international students: Required—TOEFL (minimum score 550 paper-based; 213 computer-based; 79 iBT). Electronic applications accepted.

University of Phoenix–Kansas City Campus, The Artemis School, College of Health and Human Services, Kansas City, MO 64131-4517. Offers administration of justice and security (MS); community counseling (MSC); health administration (MHA); health care management (MBA); nursing (MSN). Evening/weekend programs available. *Degree requirements:* For master's, thesis (for some programs). *Entrance requirements:* For master's, 3 years work experience, minimum undergraduate GPA or 2.5. Additional exam requirements/recommendations for international students: Required—TOEFL (minimum score 550 paper-based; 213 computer-based).

University of Phoenix–Phoenix Campus, The Artemis School, College of Health and Human Services, Phoenix, AZ 85040-1958. Offers community counseling (MSC); family nurse practitioner (MSN); health care management (MBA); nurse practitioner (Certificate); nursing (MSN); nursing health care education (Certificate). Evening/weekend programs available. *Degree requirements:* For master's, thesis (for some programs). *Entrance requirements:* For master's, 3 years of work experience in field, minimum undergraduate GPA of 2.5, RN license. Additional exam requirements/recommendations for international students: Required—TOEFL (minimum score 550 paper-based; 213 computer-based; 79 iBT). Electronic applications accepted.

University of Phoenix–Southern Colorado Campus, The Artemis School, College of Health and Human Services, Colorado Springs, CO 80919-2335. Offers community counseling (MSC); health care management (MBA); marriage, family and child therapy (MSC); nursing (MSN). Evening/weekend programs available. *Degree requirements:* For master's, thesis (for some programs). *Entrance requirements:* For master's, minimum undergraduate GPA of 2.5, 3 years of work experience, RN license. Additional exam requirements/recommendations for international students: Required—TOEFL (minimum score 550 paper-based; 213 computer-based; 79 iBT). Electronic applications accepted.

University of Puget Sound, Graduate Studies, School of Education, Program in Counseling, Tacoma, WA 98416. Offers agency counseling (M Ed); pastoral counseling (M Ed); school counseling (M Ed). *Accreditation:* NCATE. Part-time programs available. *Faculty:* 2 full-time (both women), 1 (woman) part-time/adjunct. *Students:* 2 full-time (both women), 19 part-time (13 women); includes 4 minority (3 African Americans, 1 American Indian/Alaska Native), 1 international. Average age 32. 27 applicants, 59% accepted, 7 enrolled. In 2007, 19 degrees awarded. *Entrance requirements:* For master's, GRE General Test, minimum GPA of 3.0. Additional exam requirements/recommendations for international students: Required—TOEFL (minimum score 550 paper-based; 213 computer-based; 80 iBT). *Application deadline:* For fall admission, 3/1 priority date for domestic and international students. Applications are processed on a rolling basis. Application fee: $65. Electronic applications accepted. *Expenses:* Contact institution. Tuition and fees vary according to course load. *Financial support:* In 2007–08, 1 teaching assistantship with tuition reimbursement (averaging $14,204 per year) was awarded; career-related internships or fieldwork and tuition waivers (full) also available. Financial award application deadline: 3/31; financial award applicants required to submit FAFSA. *Faculty research:* Cross-role professional preparation, suicide prevention. *Application contact:* Dr. George H. Mills, Vice President for Enrollment, 253-879-3211, Fax: 253-879-3993, E-mail: admission@ups.edu.

University of Rochester, The College, Arts and Sciences, Department of Clinical and Social Sciences in Psychology, Rochester, NY 14627-0250. Offers clinical psychology (PhD); developmental psychology (PhD); psychology (MA); social-personality psychology (PhD). *Accreditation:* APA (one or more programs are accredited). Terminal master's awarded for partial completion of doctoral program. *Degree requirements:* For doctorate, thesis/dissertation, qualifying exam. *Entrance requirements:* For doctorate, GRE General Test. Additional exam requirements/recommendations for international students: Required—TOEFL.

The University of Scranton, Graduate School, Department of Counseling and Human Services, Program in Community Counseling, Scranton, PA 18510. Offers MS. *Accreditation:* ACA.Part-time and evening/weekend programs available. *Degree requirements:* For master's, comprehensive exam, capstone experience. *Entrance requirements:* For master's, minimum GPA of 2.75. Additional exam requirements/recommendations for international students: Required—TOEFL (minimum score 500 paper-based; 173 computer-based), IELTS (minimum score 6).

University of South Carolina, The Graduate School, College of Arts and Sciences, Department of Psychology, Program in Clinical/Community Psychology, Columbia, SC 29208. Offers clinical/community psychology (PhD); general psychology (MA). *Accreditation:* APA. *Faculty:* 14 full-time (6 women), 2 part-time/adjunct (both women). *Students:* 31 full-time (23 women), 18 part-time (13 women); includes 14 minority (10 African Americans, 2 Asian Americans or Pacific Islanders, 2 Hispanic Americans), 2 international. Average age 31. 110 applicants, 8% accepted, 5 enrolled. In 2007, 9 master's, 8 doctorates awarded. *Median time to degree:* Of those who began their doctoral program in fall 1999, 77% received their degree in 8 years or less. *Degree requirements:* For master's, comprehensive exam, thesis; for doctorate, comprehensive exam, thesis/dissertation. *Entrance requirements:* For doctorate, GRE General Test, minimum GPA of 3.2. Additional exam requirements/recommendations for international students: Required—TOEFL. *Application deadline:* For fall admission, 1/4 priority date for domestic students. Applications are processed on a rolling basis. Application fee: $35. Electronic applications accepted. *Expenses:* Tuition, state resident: part-time $440 per hour. Tuition, nonresident: part-time $936 per hour. Required fees: $17 per hour. Tuition and fees vary according to program. *Financial support:* In 2007–08, 43 students received support, including 3 fellowships with full tuition reimbursements available (averaging $16,000 per year), 6 research assistantships with full tuition reimbursements available (averaging $12,000 per year), 6 teaching assistantships with full tuition reimbursements available (averaging $12,000 per year); career-related internships or fieldwork, Federal Work-Study, and institutionally sponsored loans also available. Support available to part-time students. *Faculty research:* Developmental psychopathology, health disparities, community-level interventions for psychological well being. *Unit head:* Jeffrey C. Schatz, Director, 803-777-8439, Fax: 803-777-9558, E-mail: schatz@sc.edu. *Application contact:* Marti Brown, Student Services Program Coordinator, 803-777-9482, Fax: 803-777-0670, E-mail: marthab@gwm.sc.edu.

The University of Tennessee at Martin, Graduate Programs, College of Education and Behavioral Sciences, Programs in Counseling, Martin, TN 38238-1000. Offers community counseling (MS Ed); school counseling (MS Ed). *Accreditation:* NCATE. Part-time programs available. *Students:* 50 (43 women). 16 applicants, 100% accepted, 15 enrolled. In 2007, 10 degrees awarded. *Degree requirements:* For master's, comprehensive exam. *Entrance* *requirements:* For master's, GRE General Test, minimum GPA of 2.5, resumé, letters of reference. Additional exam requirements/recommendations for international students: Required—TOEFL (minimum score 525 paper-based; 197 computer-based). *Application deadline:* For fall admission, 8/1 priority date for domestic students, 8/1 for international students; for spring admission, 1/1 priority date for domestic students, 1/1 for international students. Applications are processed on a rolling basis. Application fee: $30 ($50 for international students). Electronic applications accepted. *Expenses:* Tuition, state resident: full-time $2,893; part-time $323 per credit hour. Tuition, nonresident: full-time $7,913; part-time $881 per credit hour. Required fees: $220 per credit hour. *Financial support:* Career-related internships or fieldwork, scholarships/grants, tuition waivers (partial), and unspecified assistantships available. Support available to part-time students. Financial award application deadline: 3/1. *Unit head:* Crystal Whitlow, Coordinator, 731-881-7163, Fax: 731-881-7975, E-mail: cwhitlow@utm.edu.

University of the Incarnate Word, School of Graduate Studies and Research, College of Humanities, Arts, and Social Sciences, Program in Community Psychology, San Antonio, TX 78209-6397. Offers MS. *Expenses:* Tuition: Part-time $605 per credit hour. Required fees: $58 per credit hour. Tuition and fees vary according to degree level. *Application contact:* Andrea Cyterski-Acosta, Dean of Enrollment, 210-829-6005, Fax: 210-829-3921, E-mail: admis@uiwtx.edu.

The University of Toledo, College of Graduate Studies, College of Arts and Sciences, Department of Psychology, Toledo, OH 43606-3390. Offers behavioral (PhD), including cognitive, psychobiology and learning, social; clinical psychology (PhD); experimental psychology (MA). *Accreditation:* APA. *Faculty:* 22. *Students:* 34 full-time (24 women), 4 part-time (2 women); includes 2 minority (1 Asian American or Pacific Islander, 1 Hispanic American), 4 international. Average age 26. 150 applicants, 13% accepted, 9 enrolled. In 2007, 9 master's, 7 doctorates awarded. *Degree requirements:* For master's, thesis; for doctorate, one foreign language, thesis/dissertation. *Entrance requirements:* For master's and doctorate, GRE General Test, GRE Subject Test. *Application deadline:* For fall admission, 1/15 priority date for domestic students. Application fee: $45. *Financial support:* In 2007–08, 13 research assistantships (averaging $8,400 per year), 18 teaching assistantships (averaging $11,000 per year) were awarded; career-related internships or fieldwork, Federal Work-Study, institutionally sponsored loans, scholarships/grants, and unspecified assistantships also available. Support available to part-time students. Financial award application deadline: 1/15; financial award applicants required to submit FAFSA. *Faculty research:* Neural taste response. *Unit head:* Dr. Joseph Hovey, Chair, 419-530-2693, Fax: 419-530-8479.

See Close-Up on page 1509.

The University of Toledo, College of Graduate Studies, College of Health Science and Human Service, Division of Human Services, Department of Counselor Education and School Psychology, Program in Counselor Education, Toledo, OH 43606-3390. Offers community counseling (MA); counselor education (Ed S); counselor education and supervision (PhD). *Students:* 23 full-time (17 women), 61 part-time (52 women); includes 13 minority (all African Americans) Average age 34. 49 applicants, 78% accepted, 19 enrolled. In 2007, 24 master's, 5 doctorates awarded. *Application deadline:* For fall admission, 1/15 priority date for domestic students. Application fee: $45. *Financial support:* Research assistantships with full tuition reimbursements, teaching assistantships with full tuition reimbursements, Federal Work-Study, scholarships/grants, tuition waivers, and unspecified assistantships available. *Unit head:* Dr. Martin Ritchie, Chair, Department of Counselor Education and School Psychology, 419-530-4775, E-mail: martin.ritchie@utoledo.edu.

University of Victoria, Faculty of Graduate Studies, Faculty of Education, Department of Educational Psychology and Leadership Studies, Victoria, BC V8W 2Y2, Canada. Offers aboriginal communities counseling (M Ed); counseling (M Ed, MA); educational psychology (M Ed, MA, PhD), including counseling psychology (M Ed, MA), leadership studies (PhD), learning and development (MA, PhD), measurement and evaluation, special education (M Ed, MA); leadership studies (M Ed, MA). Part-time programs available. *Faculty:* 18 full-time (10 women), 4 part-time/adjunct (2 women). *Students:* 133, 8 international. Average age 30. In 2007, 48 master's, 2 doctorates awarded. *Degree requirements:* For master's, thesis (for some programs), comprehensive exam (M Ed); for doctorate, comprehensive exam, thesis/dissertation, candidacy exam. *Entrance requirements:* For master's, 2 years of work experience in a relevant field, minimum B average; for doctorate, GRE, 2 years of work experience in a relevant field, minimum B average. Additional exam requirements/recommendations for international students: Required—TOEFL (minimum score 575 paper-based; 233 computer-based), IELTS (minimum score 7). *Application deadline:* Applications are processed on a rolling basis. Application fee: $75 ($125 for international students). *Expenses:* Tuition, state resident: full-time $3,110. International tuition: $3,700 full-time. Tuition and fees vary according to program. *Financial support:* In 2007–08, 29 students received support; fellowships, research assistantships, teaching assistantships, institutionally sponsored loans available. Financial award application deadline: 2/15. *Faculty research:* Learning and development (child, adolescent and adult), special education and exceptional children. *Unit head:* Dr. John Walsh, Chair, 250-721-7799, Fax: 250-721-6190. *Application contact:* Gloria F. Bennett, Graduate Program Assistant, 250-472-5005, Fax: 250-721-6190, E-mail: gbennett@uvic.ca.

University of Victoria, Faculty of Graduate Studies, Faculty of Social Sciences, Department of Psychology, Victoria, BC V8W 2Y2, Canada. Offers clinical psychology (PhD); clinical psychology (neuropsychology) (M Sc); cognition and brain science (M Sc, PhD); experimental neuropsychology (M Sc, PhD); individualized study (M Sc, PhD); life span development psychology (PhD); life span developmental psychology (M Sc); social psychology (M Sc, PhD). *Accreditation:* APA (one or more programs are accredited). *Faculty:* 24 full-time (12 women), 14 part-time/adjunct (7 women). *Students:* 26, 4 international. Average age 25. 146 applicants, 21% accepted, 14 enrolled. In 2007, 36 master's, 2 doctorates awarded. *Degree requirements:* For master's, thesis; for doctorate, thesis/dissertation, candidacy exam. *Entrance requirements:* For master's and doctorate, GRE General Test. Additional exam requirements/recommendations for international students: Required—TOEFL (minimum score 600 paper-based; 250 computer-based). *Application deadline:* For fall admission, 1/1 for domestic students, 12/15 priority date for international students. Applications are processed on a rolling basis. Application fee: $65 ($100 for international students). Electronic applications accepted. *Expenses:* Tuition, state resident: full-time $3,110. International tuition: $3,700 full-time. Tuition and fees vary according to program. *Financial support:* In 2007–08, 4 fellowships (averaging $13,000 per year), 23 research assistantships, 22 teaching assistantships (averaging $2,750 per year) were awarded; career-related internships or fieldwork and institutionally sponsored loans also available. Financial award application deadline: 1/15. *Faculty research:* Life span development psychology and aging, behavioral neuroscience, cognitive psychology, behavioral psychology, environmental psychology. *Unit head:* Dr. Elizabeth Brimacombe, Chair, 250-721-7547, Fax: 250-721-8929, E-mail: psychair@uvic.ca. *Application contact:* Paul Taylor, Graduate Secretary, 250-721-6109, Fax: 250-721-8929, E-mail: ptaylor@uvic.ca.

University of Windsor, Faculty of Graduate Studies, Faculty of Arts and Social Sciences, Department of Psychology, Windsor, ON N9B 3P4, Canada. Offers adult clinical (MA, PhD); applied social psychology (MA, PhD); child clinical (MA, PhD); clinical neuropsychology (MA, PhD). *Accreditation:* APA (one or more programs are accredited). *Faculty:* 30 full-time (12 women). *Students:* 106 full-time (89 women). 183 applicants, 19% accepted. In 2007, 19 master's, 10 doctorates awarded. *Degree requirements:* For master's, thesis; for doctorate, comprehensive exam, thesis/dissertation. *Entrance requirements:* For master's, GRE General Test, GRE Subject Test in psychology, minimum B average; for doctorate, GRE General Test, GRE Subject Test in psychology, master's degree. Additional exam requirements/recommendations for international students: Required—TOEFL (minimum score 600 paper-based; 250 computer-based). *Application deadline:* For fall admission, 1/15 for domestic students. Application fee: $55. Electronic applications accepted. *Financial support:* In 2007–08, 67 teaching assistantships (averaging $9,409 per year) were awarded; Federal Work-Study, scholarships/grants, tuition waivers (full and partial), unspecified assistantships, and bursaries also available. Financial award application deadline: 2/15. *Faculty research:* Gambling, suicidology, emotional competence, psychotherapy and trauma. *Unit head:* Dr. Shelagh Towson, Head, 519-253-3000 Ext. 2215, Fax: 519-973-7021, E-mail: towson@uwindsor.ca. *Application contact:* Applicant Services, 519-253-3000 Ext. 6459, Fax: 519-971-3653, E-mail: gradadmit@uwindsor.ca.

University of Wisconsin–Madison, Graduate School, College of Letters and Science, Department of Psychology, Program in Social and Personality Psychology, Madison, WI 53706-1380. Offers PhD. *Degree requirements:* For doctorate, comprehensive exam, thesis/dissertation. *Entrance requirements:* For doctorate, GRE General Test, minimum undergraduate GPA of 3.0. Additional exam requirements/recommendations for international students: Required—TOEFL. Electronic applications accepted.

University of Wisconsin–Superior, Graduate Division, Department of Counseling and Psychological Professions, Superior, WI 54880-4500. Offers community counseling (MSE); elementary school counseling (MSE); human relations (MSE); secondary school counseling (MSE). Part-time and evening/weekend programs available. *Degree requirements:* For master's, position paper, practicum. *Entrance requirements:* For master's, California Psychological Inventory, GRE and/or MAT, minimum GPA of 2.75. *Faculty research:* Women and power, intrafamily dynamics.

University of Wisconsin–Whitewater, School of Graduate Studies, College of Education, Department of Counselor Education, Whitewater, WI 53190-1790. Offers community counseling (MS Ed); higher education (MS Ed); school counseling (MS Ed). *Accreditation:* ACA; NCATE. Part-time and evening/weekend programs available. *Students:* 31 full-time (25 women), 96 part-time (80 women); includes 9 minority (1 African American, 1 Asian American or Pacific Islander, 7 Hispanic Americans). Average age 32. 39 applicants, 92% accepted, 18 enrolled. In 2007, 30 degrees awarded. *Degree requirements:* For master's, thesis or alternative. *Entrance requirements:* For master's, resumé, 2 letters of reference. Additional exam requirements/recommendations for international students: Required—TOEFL (minimum score 550 paper-based; 213 computer-based). *Application deadline:* For fall admission, 2/1 for domestic and international students. Application fee: $45. Electronic applications accepted. *Expenses:* Tuition, state resident: full-time $3,451; part-time $244 per credit. Tuition, nonresident: full-time $8,756; part-time $560 per credit. *Financial support:* In 2007–08, 1 research assistantship (averaging $9,875 per year) was awarded; Federal Work-Study, unspecified assistantships, and out of state fee waiver also available. Support available to part-time students. Financial award application deadline: 3/15; financial award applicants required to submit FAFSA. *Faculty research:* Alcohol and other drugs, counseling effectiveness, teacher mentoring. *Unit head:* Dr. Brenda O'Beirne, Coordinator, 262-472-1452, Fax: 262-472-2841, E-mail: obeirneb@uww.edu. *Application contact:* Sally A. Lange, School of Graduate Studies, 262-472-1006, Fax: 262-472-5027, E-mail: gradschl@uww.edu.

Washington State University, Graduate School, College of Liberal Arts, Department of Sociology, Pullman, WA 99164. Offers crime and deviance (MA, PhD); environments, community and demographics (MA, PhD); institutions and social organizations (MA, PhD); political sociology (MA, PhD); social inequality (MA, PhD); social psychology and life course (MA, PhD). *Faculty:* 22 full-time (14 women), 8 part-time/adjunct (3 women). *Students:* 42 full-time (23 women), 2 part-time (both women); includes 2 minority (1 African American, 1 American Indian/Alaska Native), 4 international. Average age 30. 71 applicants, 13% accepted, 9 enrolled. In 2007, 7 master's, 4 doctorates awarded. Terminal master's awarded for partial completion of doctoral program. *Degree requirements:* For master's, thesis; for doctorate, comprehensive exam, thesis/dissertation. *Entrance requirements:* For master's, GRE General Test, minimum GPA of 3.0; for doctorate, GRE General Test, MA in sociology, minimum GPA of 3.0. Additional exam requirements/recommendations for international students: Required—TOEFL (minimum score 550 paper-based). *Application deadline:* For fall admission, 1/15 priority date for domestic students, 1/15 for international students. Application fee: $50. Electronic applications accepted. *Financial support:* In 2007–08, 5 research assistantships with tuition reimbursements (averaging $12,749 per year), 36 teaching assistantships with tuition reimbursements (averaging $12,749 per year) were awarded; fellowships with tuition reimbursements, Federal Work-Study, institutionally sponsored loans, scholarships/grants, health care benefits, and unspecified assistantships also available. Support available to part-time students. Financial award application deadline: 4/1; financial award applicants required to submit FAFSA. *Faculty research:* Crime/deviance, environmental sociology, social inequality, social psychology, gender. Total annual research expenditures: $101,888. *Unit head:* Dr. Gregory Hooks, Chair, 509-335-4595, Fax: 509-335-6419, E-mail: hooks@mail.wsu.edu. *Application contact:* Dr. Tom Rotolo, Director of Graduate Studies, 509-335-4595, Fax: 509-335-6419, E-mail: rotolo@wsu.edu.

Washington University in St. Louis, Graduate School of Arts and Sciences, Department of Psychology, St. Louis, MO 63130-4899. Offers clinical psychology (PhD); general experimental psychology (MA, PhD); social psychology (MA, PhD). *Accreditation:* APA (one or more programs are accredited). Terminal master's awarded for partial completion of doctoral program. *Degree requirements:* For master's, thesis or alternative; for doctorate, thesis/dissertation. *Entrance requirements:* For master's and doctorate, GRE General Test. Electronic applications accepted.

Western Carolina University, Graduate School, College of Education and Allied Professions, Department of Human Services, Program in Counseling, Cullowhee, NC 28723. Offers community counseling (M Ed, MS); school counseling (MA Ed). *Accreditation:* ACA. Part-time and evening/weekend programs available. *Faculty:* 14 full-time (7 women), 5 part-time/adjunct (2 women). *Students:* 58 full-time (38 women), 37 part-time (27 women); includes 10 minority (8 African Americans, 2 Hispanic Americans), 2 international. Average age 30. 67 applicants, 72% accepted, 37 enrolled. In 2007, 37 degrees awarded. *Degree requirements:* For master's, comprehensive exam, thesis or alternative. *Entrance requirements:* For master's, GRE General Test, appropriate undergraduate with 3.0 GPA, 3 recommendations, writing sample, resume. Additional exam requirements/recommendations for international students: Required—TOEFL (minimum score 550 paper-based; 270 computer-based; 79 iBT). *Application deadline:* For fall admission, 2/1 for domestic students. Application fee: $40. *Expenses:* Tuition, state resident: full-time $2,314. Tuition, nonresident: full-time $11,899. Required fees: $2,033. Tuition and fees vary according to course load. *Financial support:* In 2007–08, 33 students received support, including 25 research assistantships with full and partial tuition reimbursements available (averaging $6,880 per year), 8 teaching assistantships with full and partial tuition reimbursements available (averaging $7,000 per year); fellowships, career-related internships or fieldwork, institutionally sponsored loans, scholarships/grants, and unspecified assistantships also available. Financial award application deadline: 3/31; financial award applicants required to submit FAFSA. *Faculty research:* Marital and family development, spirituality in counseling, home school law, sexuality education, family functioning models. *Application contact:* Admissions Specialist for Counseling, 828-227-7398, Fax: 828-227-6280, E-mail: gradsch@email.wcu.edu.

Western Connecticut State University, Division of Graduate Studies, School of Professional Studies, Department of Education and Educational Psychology, Program in Community Counseling, Danbury, CT 06810-6885. Offers MS. *Accreditation:* ACA. Part-time and evening/weekend programs available. *Students:* 9 full-time (8 women), 34 part-time (30 women); includes 4 minority (2 Asian Americans or Pacific Islanders, 2 Hispanic Americans). Average age 37. 16 applicants, 88% accepted, 9 enrolled. In 2007, 8 degrees awarded. *Degree requirements:* For master's, practicum, internship. *Entrance requirements:* For master's, minimum GPA of 2.8, 3 letters of reference, interview, 9 hours of psychology. *Application deadline:* For fall admission, 8/5 priority date for domestic students; for spring admission, 1/5 for domestic students. Applications are processed on a rolling basis. Application fee: $50. *Expenses:* Tuition, state resident: full-time $4,169. Tuition, nonresident: full-time $11,614. Required fees: $3,278. *Financial support:* Fellowships, career-related internships or fieldwork available. Support available to part-time students. Financial award application deadline: 5/1; financial award applicants required to submit FAFSA. *Unit head:* Dr. Mike Gilles, Assistant Professor, 203-837-8513. *Application contact:* Chris Shankle, Associate Director of Graduate Admissions, 203-837-8244, Fax: 203-837-8338, E-mail: shanklec@wcsu.edu.

Social Psychology

Western Illinois University, School of Graduate Studies, College of Arts and Sciences, Department of Psychology, Macomb, IL 61455-1390. Offers clinical/community mental health (MS); general psychology (MS); psychology (MS, SSP); school psychology (SSP). Part-time programs available. *Students:* 40 full-time (24 women), 18 part-time (10 women); includes 1 minority (Asian American or Pacific Islander), 1 international. Average age 25. 78 applicants, 35% accepted. In 2007, 15 master's, 8 other advanced degrees awarded. *Degree requirements:* For master's, comprehensive exam (for some programs), thesis or alternative. *Entrance requirements:* For master's and SSP, GRE General Test. Additional exam requirements/recommendations for international students: Required—TOEFL (minimum score 550 paper-based; 213 computer-based; 80 iBT). *Application deadline:* Applications are processed on a rolling basis. Application fee: $30. Electronic applications accepted. *Expenses:* Tuition, state resident: part-time $217 per credit hour. Tuition, nonresident: part-time $433 per credit hour. Required fees: $54 per credit hour. *Financial support:* In 2007–08, 38 students received support, including 38 research assistantships with full tuition reimbursements available (averaging $6,800 per year). Financial award applicants required to submit FAFSA. *Unit head:* Dr. Virginia Diehl, Chairperson, 309-298-1593. *Application contact:* Dr. Barbara Baily, Director of Graduate Studies/Associate Provost, 309-298-1806, Fax: 309-298-2345, E-mail: grad-office@wiu.edu.

Wichita State University, Graduate School, Fairmount College of Liberal Arts and Sciences, Department of Psychology, Wichita, KS 67260. Offers community/clinical psychology (PhD); human factors (PhD); psychology (MA). *Accreditation:* APA. Part-time programs available. *Degree requirements:* For doctorate, thesis/dissertation. *Entrance requirements:* For doctorate, GRE. Additional exam requirements/recommendations for international students: Required—TOEFL. Electronic applications accepted. *Faculty research:* Behavioral evolution, women and alcohol, behavioral medicine, delinquency prevention.

Wilfrid Laurier University, Faculty of Graduate Studies, Faculty of Science, Department of Psychology, Waterloo, ON N2L 3C5, Canada. Offers brain and cognition (M Sc, PhD); community psychology (MA, PhD); social and developmental psychology (MA, PhD). *Faculty:* 32 full-time, 3 part-time/adjunct. *Students:* 61 full-time, 4 part-time. 129 applicants, 27% accepted, 27 enrolled. In 2007, 3 degrees awarded. *Degree requirements:* For master's, thesis; for doctorate, thesis/dissertation. *Entrance requirements:* For master's, honors BA or the equivalent in psychology, minimum B average in undergraduate course work, GRE (General Test); for doctorate, master's degree, minimum A- average, GRE (General Test). Additional exam requirements/recommendations for international students: Required—TOEFL (minimum score 230 computer-based; 89 iBT). *Application deadline:* For fall admission, 2/1 priority date for domestic students. Application fee: $75. Electronic applications accepted. *Financial support:* Fellowships, research assistantships, teaching assistantships available. *Faculty research:* Brain and cognition, community psychology, social and developmental psychology. *Unit head:* Dr. Mark Pancer, Chairperson, 519-884-1970 Ext. 3149. *Application contact:* Jennifer Poppe, Student Contact, 519-884-0710 Ext. 3536, Fax: 519-884-1020, E-mail: gradstudies@wlu.ca.

Wilmington University, Division of Behavioral Science, New Castle, DE 19720-6491. Offers administration of human services (MS); administration of justice (MS); community counseling (MS). *Accreditation:* ACA. Part-time and evening/weekend programs available. *Faculty:* 3 full-time (1 woman). *Students:* 68 full-time (48 women), 196 part-time (148 women); includes 41 minority (35 African Americans, 1 American Indian/Alaska Native, 1 Asian American or Pacific Islander, 4 Hispanic Americans). Average age 35. 146 applicants, 88% accepted, 99 enrolled. In 2007, 64 degrees awarded. *Entrance requirements:* Additional exam requirements/recommendations for international students: Required—TOEFL (minimum score 500 paper-based; 173 computer-based). *Application deadline:* Applications are processed on a rolling basis. Application fee: $25. Electronic applications accepted. *Expenses:* Tuition: Full-time $6,246; part-time $1,041 per course. Tuition and fees vary according to degree level and campus/location. *Financial support:* Applicants required to submit FAFSA. *Unit head:* Christian Trowbridge, Chair, 302-295-1151, Fax: 302-328-5164. *Application contact:* Chris Ferguson, Director of Admissions, 302-356-4636 Ext. 256, Fax: 302-328-5164, E-mail: inquire@wilmcoll.edu.

Sport Psychology

Argosy University, Orange County, College of Psychology and Behavioral Sciences, Program in Sport-Exercise Psychology, Santa Ana, CA 92704. Offers MA. *Application contact:* Mark Betz, Director of Admissions, 800-716-9598, Fax: 714-437-1697, E-mail: mbetz@argosy.edu.

See Close-Up on page 1393.

Argosy University, Phoenix, College of Psychology and Behavioral Sciences, Program in Clinical Psychology, Phoenix, AZ 85021. Offers clinical psychology (MA); sports-exercise psychology (Psy D). *Accreditation:* APA (one or more programs are accredited).

See Close-Up on page 1395.

Argosy University, Phoenix, College of Psychology and Behavioral Sciences, Program in Sport–Exercise Psychology, Phoenix, AZ 85021. Offers MA.

See Close-Up on page 1395.

Barry University, School of Human Performance and Leisure Sciences, Programs in Movement Science, Specialization in Sport and Exercise Psychology, Miami Shores, FL 33161-6695. Offers MS. *Students:* 7 full-time (6 women), 9 part-time (5 women); includes 3 minority (all African Americans), 3 international. 28 applicants, 36% accepted, 5 enrolled. In 2007, 6 degrees awarded. *Entrance requirements:* For master's, GRE. *Unit head:* Dr. Gualberto Cremades, Coordinator, 305-899-4846, Fax: 305-899-3556, E-mail: gcremades@mail.barry.edu. *Application contact:* Dave Fletcher, Director of Graduate Admissions, 305-899-3113, Fax: 305-899-2971, E-mail: dfletcher@mail.barry.edu.

California State University, Fresno, Division of Graduate Studies, College of Health and Human Services, Department of Kinesiology, Fresno, CA 93740-8027. Offers exercise science (MA); sport psychology (MA). Part-time and evening/weekend programs available. *Faculty:* 10 full-time (3 women). *Students:* 66; includes 22 minority (2 African Americans, 1 American Indian/Alaska Native, 7 Asian Americans or Pacific Islanders, 12 Hispanic Americans), 7 international. Average age 31. 9 applicants. In 2007, 10 degrees awarded. *Degree requirements:* For master's, thesis or alternative. *Entrance requirements:* For master's, GRE General Test, minimum GPA of 2.7. Additional exam requirements/recommendations for international students: Required—TOEFL. *Application deadline:* For fall admission, 5/1 for domestic and international students; for spring admission, 10/1 for domestic and international students. Applications are processed on a rolling basis. Application fee: $55. Electronic applications accepted. *Financial support:* In 2007–08, 9 teaching assistantships were awarded; career-related internships or fieldwork, Federal Work-Study, and scholarships/grants also available. Support available to part-time students. Financial award application deadline: 3/1; financial award applicants required to submit FAFSA. *Faculty research:* Refugee education, homeless, geriatrics, fitness. *Unit head:* Dr. Tim Anderson, Chair, 559-278-2016, Fax: 559-278-7010, E-mail: tima@csufresno.edu. *Application contact:* Dr. Jenelle Gilbert, Coordinator, 559-278-5165, Fax: 559-278-7010, E-mail: jgilbert@csufresno.edu.

California University of Pennsylvania, School of Graduate Studies and Research, School of Education, Department of Athletic Training, Program in Exercise Science and Health Promotion, California, PA 15419-1394. Offers fitness and wellness (MS); performance enhancement and injury prevention (MS); rehabilitation sciences (MS); sport management (MS); sport psychology (MS). Part-time and evening/weekend programs available. Postbaccalaureate distance learning degree programs offered (no on-campus study). *Degree requirements:* For master's, comprehensive exam, thesis optional. *Entrance requirements:* For master's, minimum QPA of 3.0. Additional exam requirements/recommendations for international students: Required—TOEFL (minimum score 550 paper-based; 213 computer-based; 80 iBT). Electronic applications accepted. Expenses: Contact institution. *Faculty research:* Reducing obesity in children, sport performance, creating unique biomechanical assessment techniques, Web-based training for fitness professionals, Webcams.

Capella University, Harold Abel School of Psychology, Minneapolis, MN 55402. Offers clinical psychology (MS); counseling psychology (MS); educational psychology (MS, PhD); general psychology (MS, PhD); industrial/organizational psychology (MS, PhD); school psychology (MS, Certificate); sport psychology (MS). Part-time and evening/weekend programs available. Postbaccalaureate distance learning degree programs offered (minimal on-campus study). Terminal master's awarded for partial completion of doctoral program. *Degree requirements:* For master's, thesis optional, project; for doctorate, thesis/dissertation. *Entrance requirements:* For degree, master's degree in school psychology. Additional exam requirements/recommendations for international students: Required—TOEFL (minimum score 550 paper-based; 213 computer-based), TWE (minimum score 4). Electronic applications accepted. *Faculty research:* Correctional mental health delivery, community mental health, attachment and caregiving in adult and family relationships, influence of encouragement on motivation, and moral dilemmas in business.

Cleveland State University, College of Graduate Studies, College of Education and Human Services, Department of Health, Physical Education, Recreation and Dance, Cleveland, OH 44115. Offers community health education (M Ed); exercise science (M Ed); human performance (M Ed); physical education pedagogy (M Ed); public health (MPH); school health education (M Ed); sport and exercise psychology (M Ed); sports management (M Ed). Part-time programs available. *Faculty:* 10 full-time (7 women), 2 part-time/adjunct (0 women). *Students:* 19 full-time (11 women), 80 part-time (50 women); includes 23 minority (21 African Americans, 2 Hispanic Americans), 6 international. Average age 34. 52 applicants, 52% accepted, 19 enrolled. In 2007, 36 degrees awarded. *Degree requirements:* For master's, comprehensive exam, thesis optional. *Entrance requirements:* For master's, GRE General Test or MAT (if undergraduate GPA is below 2.75), minimum undergraduate GPA of 2.75. Additional exam requirements/recommendations for international students: Required—TOEFL (minimum score 525 paper-based; 197 computer-based), IELTS (minimum score 6). *Application deadline:* For fall admission, 7/15 priority date for domestic students; for spring admission, 12/15 priority date for domestic students. Applications are processed on a rolling basis. Application fee: $30. Electronic applications accepted. *Financial support:* In 2007–08, 6 research assistantships with full and partial tuition reimbursements (averaging $3,480 per year), 1 teaching assistantship with full and partial tuition reimbursement (averaging $3,480 per year) were awarded; career-related internships or fieldwork, tuition waivers (full), and unspecified assistantships also available. Financial award application deadline: 3/15. *Faculty research:* Bone density, marketing fitness centers, motor development of disabled, online learning and survey research. *Unit head:* Dr. Sheila M. Patterson, Chairperson, 216-687-4870, Fax: 216-687-5410, E-mail: s.m.patterson@csuohio.edu.

Florida State University, Graduate Studies, College of Education, Department of Educational Psychology and Learning Systems, Program in Educational Psychology, Tallahassee, FL 32306. Offers learning and cognition (MS, PhD); sports psychology (MS, PhD). *Faculty:* 6 full-time (3 women), 4 part-time/adjunct (2 women). *Students:* 33 full-time (20 women), 25 part-time (14 women); includes 13 minority (5 African Americans, 4 Asian Americans or Pacific Islanders, 4 Hispanic Americans). Average age 20. 82 applicants, 43% accepted, 16 enrolled. In 2007, 2 master's, 2 doctorates awarded. *Degree requirements:* For master's, comprehensive exam, thesis optional; for doctorate, comprehensive exam, thesis/dissertation. *Entrance requirements:* For master's and doctorate, GRE General Test, minimum GPA of 3.0. *Application deadline:* For fall admission, 7/1 priority date for domestic students; for spring admission, 11/1 for domestic students. Applications are processed on a rolling basis. Application fee: $30. *Expenses:* Tuition, state resident: part-time $248 per credit hour. Tuition, nonresident: part-time $880 per credit hour. Tuition and fees vary according to program. *Financial support:* In 2007–08, fellowships with partial tuition reimbursements (averaging $5,000 per year), research assistantships with partial tuition reimbursements (averaging $18,000 per year), teaching assistantships with partial tuition reimbursements (averaging $18,000 per year) were awarded; career-related internships or fieldwork also available. Financial award applicants required to submit FAFSA. *Unit head:* Dr. Susan Losh, Program Leader, 850-644-8776, Fax: 850-644-8776, E-mail: slosh@coe.fsu.edu. *Application contact:* Sally Gadson, Program Assistant, 850-644-8046, Fax: 850-644-5067, E-mail: gadson@coe.fsu.edu.

John F. Kennedy University, Graduate School of Professional Psychology, Program in Sport Psychology, Pleasant Hill, CA 94523-4817. Offers MA. *Accreditation:* APA. Part-time and evening/weekend programs available. *Degree requirements:* For master's, thesis or alternative. *Entrance requirements:* For master's, interview. Additional exam requirements/recommendations for international students: Required—TOEFL.

Memorial University of Newfoundland, School of Graduate Studies, School of Human Kinetics and Recreation, St. John's, NL A1C 5S7, Canada. Offers administration, curriculum and supervision (MPE); biomechanics/ergonomics (MS Kin); exercise and work physiology (MS Kin); sport psychology (MS Kin). Part-time programs available. *Degree requirements:* For master's, thesis optional, seminars, thesis presentations. *Entrance requirements:* For master's, bachelor's degree in a related field, minimum B average. Electronic applications accepted. *Faculty research:* Administration, sociology of sports, kinesiology, physiology/recreation.

Purdue University, Graduate School, College of Liberal Arts, Department of Health and Kinesiology, West Lafayette, IN 47907. Offers exercise, human physiology of movement and sport (PhD); health and fitness (MS); health promotion (MS); health promotion and disease prevention (PhD); movement and sport science (MS); pedagogy and administration (MS); pedagogy of physical activity and health (PhD); psychology of sport and exercise, and motor behavior (PhD). Part-time programs available. *Degree requirements:* For master's, thesis (for some programs); for doctorate, thesis/dissertation. *Entrance requirements:* For master's and doctorate, GRE General Test. Additional exam requirements/recommendations for international students: Required—TOEFL. Electronic applications accepted. *Faculty research:* Wellness, motivation, teaching effectiveness, learning and development.

Queen's University at Kingston, School of Graduate Studies and Research, School of Physical and Health Education, Kingston, ON K7L 3N6, Canada. Offers applied exercise science (PhD); biomechanics/ergonomics (M Sc); exercise physiology rehabilitation (M Sc); social psychology of sport and exercise rehabilitation (MA); sociology of sport (MA). Part-time programs available. *Degree requirements:* For master's, thesis (for some programs); for doctorate, comprehensive exam, thesis/dissertation. *Entrance requirements:* For master's and doctorate, minimum B+ average. Additional exam requirements/recommendations for international students: Required—TOEFL. Electronic applications accepted. *Faculty research:* Expert performance ergonomics, obesity research, pregnancy and exercise, gender and sport participation.

Southern Connecticut State University, School of Graduate Studies, School of Education, Department of Exercise Science, New Haven, CT 06515-1355. Offers human performance (MS); physical education (MS); school health education (MS); sport psychology (MS). Part-time and evening/weekend programs available. *Faculty:* 8 full-time. *Students:* 28 full-time (13 women), 54 part-time (28 women); includes 6 minority (2 African Americans, 4 Hispanic Americans), 1 international. 20 applicants, 55% accepted, 10 enrolled. In 2007, 18 degrees awarded. *Degree requirements:* For master's, thesis or alternative. *Entrance requirements:* For master's, interview. *Application deadline:* For fall admission, 7/15 priority date for domestic students. Applications are processed on a rolling basis. Application fee: $50. Electronic applications accepted. *Financial support:* In 2007–08, 8 teaching assistantships were awarded. Financial award application deadline: 4/15; financial award applicants required to submit FAFSA. *Unit head:* Dr. David Martens, Chairperson, 203-392-6094, Fax: 203-392-6911. *Application contact:* Dr. Robert Axtell, Coordinator, 203-392-6037, Fax: 203-392-6093, E-mail: axtell@southernct.edu.

Springfield College, Graduate Programs, Programs in Exercise Science and Sports Studies, Springfield, MA 01109-3797. Offers athletic training (MS); exercise physiology (MS, DPE), including clinical exercise physiology (MS), science and research (MS); health promotion and disease prevention (MS); sport psychology (MS, DPE). Part-time programs available. *Faculty:* 3 full-time (0 women), 4 part-time/adjunct (1 woman). *Students:* 48 full-time, 8 part-time. Average age 26. 74 applicants, 74% accepted, 24 enrolled. In 2007, 31 master's, 1 doctorate awarded. *Degree requirements:* For master's, thesis. *Entrance requirements:* For master's, GRE General Test. Additional exam requirements/recommendations for international students: Required—TOEFL (minimum score 550 paper-based; 213 computer-based). *Application deadline:* For fall admission, 1/15 for domestic students; for winter admission, 11/1 for domestic students; for spring admission, 12/1 for domestic students. Applications are processed on a rolling basis. Application fee: $50. Electronic applications accepted. *Expenses:* Tuition: Full-time $12,942; part-time $719 per semester hour. Required fees: $25. Tuition and fees vary according to program. *Financial support:* In 2007–08, 6 teaching assistantships with partial tuition reimbursements were awarded; fellowships with partial tuition reimbursements, career-related internships or fieldwork, Federal Work-Study, institutionally sponsored loans, and tuition waivers (full and partial) also available. Financial award application deadline: 3/1. *Faculty research:* Fitness in renal disease, environmental exercise physiology. *Unit head:* Dr. Tracey F. Matthews, Director, 413-748-3397, Fax: 413-748-3371, E-mail: tmatthews@spfldcol.edu. *Application contact:* Donald James Shaw, Director of Graduate Admissions, 413-748-3060, Fax: 413-748-3069, E-mail: donald_shaw_jr@spfldcol.edu.

Springfield College, Graduate Programs, Programs in Psychology and Counseling, Springfield, MA 01109-3797. Offers athletic counseling (M Ed, MS, CAGS); industrial/organizational psychology (M Ed, MS, CAGS); marriage and family therapy (M Ed, MS, CAGS); mental health counseling (M Ed, MS, CAGS); school guidance and counseling (M Ed, MS, CAGS); student personnel in higher education (M Ed, MS, CAGS). Part-time and evening/weekend programs available. *Faculty:* 14 full-time (8 women), 17 part-time/adjunct (7 women). *Students:* 157 full-time, 44 part-time. Average age 28. 220 applicants, 72% accepted, 97 enrolled. In 2007, 93 master's, 1 other advanced degree awarded. *Degree requirements:* For master's, comprehensive exam, thesis (for some programs), research project, internship. *Entrance requirements:* For master's and CAGS, interview. Additional exam requirements/recommendations for international students: Required—TOEFL (minimum score 550 paper-based; 213 computer-based). *Application deadline:* For fall admission, 1/15 priority date for domestic students; for winter admission, 11/1 for domestic students; for spring admission, 12/1 for domestic students. Applications are processed on a rolling basis. Application fee: $50. Electronic applications accepted. *Expenses:* Tuition: Full-time $12,942; part-time $719 per semester hour. Required fees: $25. Tuition and fees vary according to program. *Financial support:* In 2007–08, 8 fellowships with partial tuition reimbursements (averaging $2,000 per year), 2 research assistantships (averaging $4,000 per year), 7 teaching assistantships (averaging $1,800 per year) were awarded; career-related internships or fieldwork, Federal Work-Study, institutionally sponsored loans, scholarships/grants, and tuition waivers (full and partial) also available. Financial award application deadline: 3/1. *Faculty research:* Sport psychology, leadership and emotional intelligence, violence and terrorism, performance enhancement, cognitive function. Total annual research expenditures: $715,109. *Unit head:* Dr. Anna L. Moriarty, Director, 413-748-3322, Fax: 413-748-3854, E-mail: anna_l_moriarty@spfldcol.edu. *Application contact:* Donald James Shaw, Director of Graduate Admissions, 413-748-3060, Fax: 413-748-3069, E-mail: donald_shaw_jr@spfldcol.edu.

University of Florida, Graduate School, College of Health and Human Performance, Department of Applied Physiology and Kinesiology, Gainesville, FL 32611. Offers athletic training/sport medicine (MS, PhD); biomechanics (MS, PhD); clinical exercise physiology (MS); exercise physiology (MS, PhD); health and human performance (PhD); human performance (MS); motor learning/control (MS, PhD); sport and exercise psychology (MS). *Faculty:* 13 full-time (1 woman), 1 part-time/adjunct (0 women). *Students:* 147 (74 women); includes 17 minority (4 African Americans, 1 American Indian/Alaska Native, 6 Asian Americans or Pacific Islanders, 6 Hispanic Americans) 39 international. In 2007, 43 master's, 16 doctorates awarded. *Degree requirements:* For doctorate, thesis/dissertation. *Entrance requirements:* For doctorate, GRE General Test. *Application deadline:* For fall admission, 6/1 priority date for domestic students. Applications are processed on a rolling basis. Application fee: $20. Electronic applications accepted. *Expenses:* Tuition, state resident: full-time $7,478. Tuition, nonresident: full-time $22,603. *Financial support:* In 2007–08, 15 research assistantships (averaging $13,152 per year), 24 teaching assistantships (averaging $1,917 per year) were awarded; fellowships, unspecified assistantships also available. *Unit head:* Dr. Steven Dodd, Chair, 352-392-0584 Ext. 1342, E-mail: sdodd@hhp.ufl.edu. *Application contact:* Dr. Paul A. Borsa, Coordinator, 352-392-0584 Ext. 1261, Fax: 352-392-5262, E-mail: pborsa@hhp.ufl.edu.

The University of Iowa, Graduate College, College of Liberal Arts and Sciences, Department of Health and Sport Studies, Iowa City, IA 52242-1316. Offers psychology of sport and physical activity (MA, PhD); sports studies (MA, PhD). *Faculty:* 6 full-time, 18 part-time/adjunct. *Students:* 23 full-time (18 women), 7 part-time (6 women); includes 4 minority (3 African Americans, 1 American Indian/Alaska Native). 38 applicants, 29% accepted, 5 enrolled. In 2007, 6 master's, 1 doctorate awarded. *Degree requirements:* For master's, thesis optional, exam; for doctorate, comprehensive exam, thesis/dissertation. *Entrance requirements:* For master's and doctorate, GRE General Test, minimum GPA of 3.0. Additional exam requirements/recommendations for international students: Required—TOEFL (minimum score 600 paper-based; 250 computer-based; 100 iBT). *Application deadline:* For fall admission, 3/1 for domestic and international students. Application fee: $60 ($85 for international students). Electronic applications accepted. *Expenses:* Tuition, state resident: part-time $349 per hour. Tuition, nonresident: part-time $349 per hour. Tuition and fees vary according to course load and program. *Financial support:* In 2007–08, 2 research assistantships with partial tuition reimbursements, 19 teaching assistantships with partial tuition reimbursements were awarded; fellowships also available. Financial award applicants required to submit FAFSA. *Unit head:* Beth Pelton, Chair, 319-335-9337, Fax: 319-335-6669.

University of Rhode Island, Graduate School, College of Human Science and Services, Department of Kinesiology, Kingston, RI 02881. Offers adapted physical education (MS); cultural studies of sport and physical culture (MS); exercise science (MS); physical education pedagogy (MS); physical therapy (DPT); psychosocial/behavioral aspects of physical activity (MS). *Accreditation:* NCATE (one or more programs are accredited). In 2007, 14 degrees awarded. *Entrance requirements:* For master's, MAT or GRE. *Application deadline:* For fall admission, 4/15 priority date for domestic students; for spring admission, 11/15 for domestic students. Applications are processed on a rolling basis. Application fee: $35. *Expenses:* Tuition, state resident: full-time $6,936; part-time $385 per credit. Tuition, nonresident: full-time $19,044; part-time $1,058 per credit. Required fees: $1,508; $48 per credit. $30 per semester. One-time fee: $80 part-time. *Financial support:* Career-related internships or fieldwork available. *Unit head:* Dr. Deborah Riebe, Chair, 401-874-5444.

West Virginia University, School of Physical Education, Morgantown, WV 26506. Offers athletic coaching education (MS); athletic training (MS); physical education/teacher education (MS, PhD), including curriculum and instruction (PhD), motor behavior (PhD), physical education supervision (PhD); sport and exercise psychology (PhD); sport management (MS). *Faculty:* 20 full-time (6 women), 16 part-time/adjunct (7 women). *Students:* 119 full-time (46 women), 128 part-time (45 women); includes 16 minority (14 African Americans, 1 American Indian/Alaska Native, 1 Asian American or Pacific Islander), 11 international. Average age 28. 382 applicants, 41% accepted, 100 enrolled. In 2007, 91 master's, 3 doctorates awarded. *Degree requirements:* For doctorate, comprehensive exam, thesis/dissertation, oral exam. *Entrance requirements:* For master's, GRE or MAT, minimum GPA of 3.0; for doctorate, GRE General Test or MAT, minimum GPA of 3.5. Additional exam requirements/recommendations for international students: Required—TOEFL (minimum score 550 paper-based; 213 computer-based). *Application deadline:* For fall admission, 12/15 for domestic students, 10/1 for international students. Application fee: $50. Electronic applications accepted. *Expenses:* Tuition, state resident: full-time $5,196; part-time $292 per credit hour. Tuition, nonresident: full-time $15,064; part-time $840 per credit hour. Tuition and fees vary according to program. *Financial support:* In 2007–08, 4 research assistantships, 67 teaching assistantships were awarded; career-related internships or fieldwork, Federal Work-Study, institutionally sponsored loans, tuition waivers (full and partial), and graduate administrative assistantships also available. Support available to part-time students. Financial award application deadline: 2/1; financial award applicants required to submit FAFSA. *Faculty research:* Sport psychosociology, teacher education, exercise psychology, counseling. Total annual research expenditures: $569,668. *Unit head:* Dr. Dana D. Brooks, Dean, 304-293-3295 Ext. 5285, Fax: 304-293-4641, E-mail: dana.brooks@mail.wvu.edu. *Application contact:* Carol Straight, Student Records Assistant, 304-293-3295 Ext. 5265, Fax: 304-293-4641, E-mail: cstraig@mail.wvu.edu.

Thanatology

Brooklyn College of the City University of New York, Division of Graduate Studies, Department of Health and Nutrition Science, Program in Community Health, Brooklyn, NY 11210-2889. Offers community health education (MA); computer science and health science (MS); health care management (MPH); health care policy and administration (MPH); thanatology (MA). *Accreditation:* CEPH. *Students:* 1 (woman) full-time, 32 part-time (27 women); includes 19 minority (14 African Americans, 3 Asian Americans or Pacific Islanders, 2 Hispanic Americans), 5 international. 18 applicants, 100% accepted, 10 enrolled. In 2007, 11 degrees awarded. *Degree requirements:* For master's, thesis or alternative. *Entrance requirements:* For master's, 18 credits, 2 letters of recommendation, essay. Additional exam requirements/recommendations for international students: Required—TOEFL. *Application deadline:* For fall admission, 3/1 priority date for domestic students, 2/1 priority date for international students; for spring admission, 11/1 priority date for domestic students, 10/1 priority date for international students. Applications are processed on a rolling basis. Application fee: $125. Electronic applications accepted. *Financial support:* Federal Work-Study, institutionally sponsored loans, and scholarships/grants available. Support available to part-time students. Financial award application deadline: 5/1; financial award applicants required to submit FAFSA. *Faculty research:* Diet restriction, religious practices in bereavement, diabetes, stress management, palliative care. *Unit head:* Dr. Jean Grassman, Graduate Deputy Chairperson, 718-951-5026, Fax: 718-951-4670, E-mail: grassman@brooklyn.cuny.edu. *Application contact:* Hernan Sierra, Graduate Admissions Coordinator, 718-951-4536, Fax: 718-951-4506, E-mail: grads@brooklyn.cuny.edu.

Hood College, Graduate School, Programs in Human Sciences, Frederick, MD 21701-8575. Offers human sciences (MA); thanatology (MA, Certificate). Part-time and evening/weekend programs available. *Degree requirements:* For master's, comprehensive exam, thesis or alternative. *Entrance requirements:* For master's, minimum GPA of 2.5. *Faculty research:* Mind-body medicine and multicultural healing, the New Orleans jazz funeral, death practices in African-American culture, bereavement theories and gender differences, Piaget's theory of cognitive development as a formal mathematical model.

Southwestern College, Program in Grief, Loss and Trauma Counseling, Santa Fe, NM 87502-4788. Offers MA, Certificate. Part-time and evening/weekend programs available. Post-baccalaureate distance learning degree programs offered (minimal on-campus study). *Faculty:* 1 (woman) full-time, 7 part-time/adjunct (4 women). *Students:* 12 full-time (9 women), 6 part-time (5 women); includes 1 American Indian/Alaska Native, 1 Asian American or Pacific Islander, 1 Hispanic American. Average age 37. 12 applicants, 58% accepted, 6 enrolled. In 2007, 11 degrees awarded. *Entrance requirements:* For master's, personal statement of 3 pages, interview, references, resumé; for Certificate, 3 letters of reference, interview. *Application deadline:* For fall admission, 6/1 priority date for domestic students; for winter admission, 10/15 priority date for domestic students; for spring admission, 1/30 priority date for domestic students. Applications are processed on a rolling basis. Application fee: $50. *Expenses:* Tuition: Full-time $16,416. *Unit head:* Dr. Janet Schreiber, Director, Fax: 877-471-4071. *Application contact:* Dru Phoenix, Director of Admissions, 505-471-5756 Ext. 26, Fax: 505-471-4071, E-mail: admissions@swc.edu.

Transpersonal and Humanistic Psychology

Atlantic University, Program in Transpersonal Studies, Virginia Beach, VA 23451-2061. Offers MA. Part-time and evening/weekend programs available. Postbaccalaureate distance learning degree programs offered (no on-campus study). *Faculty:* 16 part-time/adjunct (5 women). *Students:* Average age 45. 70 applicants, 81% accepted. In 2007, 15 degrees awarded. *Degree requirements:* For master's, thesis. *Entrance requirements:* For master's, minimum undergraduate GPA of 2.5. Additional exam requirements/recommendations for international students: Required—TOEFL (minimum score 550 paper-based; 213 computer-based). *Application deadline:* Applications are processed on a rolling basis. Application fee: $50. Electronic applications accepted. *Expenses:* Tuition: Full-time $4,320; part-time $720 per course. One-time fee: $75 full-time. *Unit head:* Kevin J. Todeschi, Chief Executive Officer, 757-631-8101, Fax: 757-631-8096, E-mail: info@atlanticuniv.edu. *Application contact:* R. Gregory Deming, Director of Admissions, 757-631-8101, Fax: 757-631-8096, E-mail: admissions@atlanticuniv.edu.

Atlantic University, Program in Visionary Art and Consciousness, Virginia Beach, VA 23451-2061. Offers MFA. Part-time and evening/weekend programs available. Postbaccalaureate distance learning degree programs offered (no on-campus study). *Faculty:* 2 part-time/adjunct (1 woman). *Degree requirements:* For master's, thesis. *Entrance requirements:* For master's, BFA or BA or BS in Studio Art with 40 studio credits or more. Additional exam requirements/recommendations for international students: Required—TOEFL (minimum score 550 paper-based; 213 computer-based). *Application deadline:* For fall admission, 3/31 for domestic and international students. Application fee: $50. *Expenses: Contact institution. Unit head:* Kevin J. Todeschi, Chief Executive Officer, 757-631-8101, Fax: 757-631-8096, E-mail: info@atlanticuniv.edu. *Application contact:* R. Gregory Deming, Director of Admissions, 757-631-8101, Fax: 757-631-8096, E-mail: admissions@atlanticuniv.edu.

Institute of Transpersonal Psychology, Global Programs, Palo Alto, CA 94303. Offers psychology (PhD); transpersonal psychology (MTP); transpersonal studies (Certificate). Postbaccalaureate distance learning degree programs offered (minimal on-campus study). *Faculty:* 8 full-time (4 women), 26 part-time/adjunct (19 women). *Students:* 154 full-time (123 women), 32 part-time (25 women); includes 29 minority (9 African Americans, 2 American Indian/Alaska Native, 5 Asian Americans or Pacific Islanders, 13 Hispanic Americans), 20 international. Average age 44. 112 applicants, 88% accepted, 80 enrolled. In 2007, 19 master's, 8 doctorates awarded. Terminal master's awarded for partial completion of doctoral program. *Degree requirements:* For master's, thesis (for some programs); for doctorate, thesis/dissertation. *Entrance requirements:* For master's and doctorate, bachelor's degree. Additional exam requirements/recommendations for international students: Required—TOEFL. *Application deadline:* Applications are processed on a rolling basis. Application fee: $55. *Expenses: Contact institution.* Tuition and fees vary according to degree level and student level. *Financial support:* In 2007–08, 68 students received support. Federal Work-Study and scholarships/grants available. Support available to part-time students. Financial award application deadline: 6/30; financial award applicants required to submit FAFSA. *Unit head:* Dr. Paul Roy, Academic Vice President, 650-493-4430 Ext. 243, Fax: 650-493-6835, E-mail: proy@itp.edu. *Application contact:* Hana Schneider, Admissions Assistant, 650-493-4430 Ext. 240, Fax: 650-493-6835, E-mail: itpinfo@itp.edu.

Institute of Transpersonal Psychology, Residential Programs, Palo Alto, CA 94303. Offers clinical psychology (PhD); counseling psychology (MA); transpersonal psychology (MA, PhD); women's spirituality (PhD). Part-time and evening/weekend programs available. *Faculty:* 17 full-time (9 women), 31 part-time/adjunct (18 women). *Students:* 239 full-time (164 women), 48 part-time (33 women); includes 46 minority (8 African Americans, 4 American Indian/Alaska Native, 18 Asian Americans or Pacific Islanders, 16 Hispanic Americans), 16 international. Average age 38. 132 applicants, 80% accepted, 79 enrolled. In 2007, 47 master's, 16 doctorates awarded. Terminal master's awarded for partial completion of doctoral program. *Degree requirements:* For doctorate, thesis/dissertation. *Entrance requirements:* For master's and doctorate, bachelor's degree. *Application deadline:* For fall admission, 2/15 priority date for domestic students. Applications are processed on a rolling basis. Application fee: $55. *Expenses:* Tuition: Full-time $11,877; part-time $3,959 per quarter. Tuition and fees vary according to degree level and student level. *Financial support:* In 2007–08, 178 students received support; teaching assistantships, career-related internships or fieldwork, Federal Work-Study, and scholarships/grants available. Support available to part-time students. Financial award application deadline: 7/1; financial award applicants required to submit FAFSA. *Unit head:* Dr. Paul Roy, Academic Vice President, 650-493-4430 Ext. 243, Fax: 650-493-6835, E-mail: proy@itp.edu. *Application contact:* 650-493-4430 Ext. 16, Fax: 650-493-6835, E-mail: itpinfo@itp.edu.

See Close-Up on page 1439.

John F. Kennedy University, Graduate School of Holistic Studies, Department of Counseling Psychology, Program in Counseling Psychology, Pleasant Hill, CA 94523-4817. Offers holistic studies (MA); somatic psychology (MA); transpersonal psychology (MA). Part-time and evening/weekend programs available. *Degree requirements:* For master's, thesis or alternative. *Entrance requirements:* For master's, interview. Additional exam requirements/recommendations for international students: Required—TOEFL.

Michigan School of Professional Psychology, Programs in Humanistic and Clinical Psychology, Farmington Hills, MI 48334. Offers humanistic and clinical psychology (MA, Psy D). *Faculty:* 3 full-time (1 woman), 20 part-time/adjunct (11 women). *Students:* 109 full-time (86 women); includes 20 minority (13 African Americans, 7 Asian Americans or Pacific Islanders). Average age 38. 200 applicants, 40% accepted, 69 enrolled. In 2007, 39 master's, 11 doctorates awarded. *Median time to degree:* Of those who began their doctoral program in fall 1999, 100% received their degree in 8 years or less. *Degree requirements:* For master's, thesis, practicum; for doctorate, thesis/dissertation, internship, practicum. *Entrance requirements:* For master's, 1 year of work experience, interview, minimum GPA of 3.0, curriculum vitae, personal essay, Bachelor's completion; for doctorate, 3 years of work experience, 2 interviews, minimum graduate GPA of 3.0, scholarly writing sample, curriculum vitae, personal essay, MA degree completion. Additional exam requirements/recommendations for international students: Required—TOEFL. *Application deadline:* For fall admission, 1/15 priority date for domestic students. Applications are processed on a rolling basis. Application fee: $75. Electronic applications accepted. *Expenses:* Tuition: Full-time $21,255. One-time fee: $200 full-time. *Financial support:* In 2007–08, 39 students received support. Application deadline: 6/30. *Faculty research:* Qualitative research, existential-phenomenological psychology, applications to clinical practice. *Unit head:* Dr. Kerry Moustakas, President, 248-476-1122, Fax: 248-476-1125, E-mail: kmoustakas@mispp.edu. *Application contact:* Linda Potter-Gallant, Admissions Advisor, 248-476-1122 Ext. 117, Fax: 248-476-1125, E-mail: lpgallant@mispp.edu.

Naropa University, Graduate Programs, Program in Transpersonal Counseling Psychology, Boulder, CO 80302-6697. Offers art therapy (MA); counseling psychology (MA); wilderness therapy (MA). *Faculty:* 10 full-time (6 women), 40 part-time/adjunct (29 women). *Students:* 130 full-time (97 women), 71 part-time (54 women); includes 14 minority (3 African Americans, 3 Asian Americans or Pacific Islanders, 8 Hispanic Americans), 18 international. Average age 33. 123 applicants, 50% accepted, 38 enrolled. In 2007, 37 degrees awarded. *Degree requirements:* For master's, internship. *Entrance requirements:* For master's, in-person interview, course work in psychology. Additional exam requirements/recommendations for international students: Required—TOEFL (minimum score 600 paper-based; 250 computer-based). *Application deadline:* For fall admission, 1/15 priority date for domestic and international students; for spring admission, 10/15 priority date for domestic students. Applications are processed on a rolling basis. Application fee: $60. Electronic applications accepted. *Expenses:* Tuition: Full-time $15,070; part-time $685 per credit. Required fees: $250 per semester. Tuition and fees vary according to course load. *Financial support:* In 2007–08, 41 students received support, including 3 research assistantships with partial tuition reimbursements available (averaging $3,000 per year), 1 teaching assistantship with partial tuition reimbursement available (averaging $3,000 per year); career-related internships or fieldwork, Federal Work-Study, scholarships/grants, and tuition waivers (partial) also available. Support available to part-time students. Financial award application deadline: 3/1; financial award applicants required to submit FAFSA. *Unit head:* Carla Clements, Chair, 303-546-3577. *Application contact:* Alice Di Tullio, Admissions Counselor, 303-546-3598, Fax: 303-546-3583, E-mail: aliced@naropa.edu.

See Close-Up on page 1449.

Naropa University, Graduate Programs, Program in Transpersonal Psychology, Boulder, CO 80302-6697. Offers ecopsychology (MA); transpersonal psychology (MA). *Faculty:* 2 full-time (0 women). *Students:* Average age 40. 45 applicants, 71% accepted, 23 enrolled. In 2007, 23 degrees awarded. *Degree requirements:* For master's, thesis. *Entrance requirements:* For master's, interview (by phone or in-person), technology form. Additional exam requirements/recommendations for international students: Required—TOEFL (minimum score 600 paper-based). *Application deadline:* For fall admission, 1/15 for domestic and international students; for spring admission, 10/15 for domestic students. Applications are processed on a rolling basis. Application fee: $60. Electronic applications accepted. *Expenses:* Tuition: Full-time $15,070; part-time $685 per credit. Required fees: $250 per semester. Tuition and fees vary according to course load. *Financial support:* In 2007–08, 2 students received support. Career-related internships or fieldwork, Federal Work-Study, scholarships/grants, health care benefits, and tuition waivers (partial) available. Support available to part-time students. Financial award application deadline: 3/1; financial award applicants required to submit FAFSA. *Unit head:* Dr. John Davis, Director, 303-245-4654, Fax: 303-546-4044, E-mail: jdavis@naropa.edu. *Application contact:* Kate Levene, Assistant Director of Admissions, 303-245-4657, Fax: 303-546-3583, E-mail: klevene@naropa.edu.

See Close-Up on page 1449.

Saybrook Graduate School and Research Center, Programs in Psychology, Human Science and Organizational Systems, San Francisco, CA 94111-1920. Offers clinical psychology (PhD); creativity studies (MA); human science (MA, PhD), including consciousness and spirituality, individualized (PhD), integrative health studies, organizational systems, social transformation; marriage and family therapy (MA); organizational systems (MA, PhD), including individualized (PhD), organizational systems; psychology (MA, PhD), including consciousness and spirituality, humanistic and transpersonal psychology, individualized (PhD), integrative health studies, licensure track (MA), organizational systems, social transformation. Postbaccalaureate distance learning degree programs offered (minimal on-campus study). Terminal master's awarded for partial completion of doctoral program. *Degree requirements:* For master's, thesis or alternative; for doctorate, thesis/dissertation. Electronic applications accepted. *Faculty research:* Humanistic theory, health studies, organizational systems, consciousness and spirituality, social transformation.

Seattle University, College of Arts and Sciences, Department of Psychology, Seattle, WA 98122-1090. Offers existential and phenomenological therapeutic psychology (MA Psych). *Degree requirements:* For master's, thesis. *Entrance requirements:* For master's, interview, minimum GPA of 3.0, previous undergraduate course work in psychology. *Faculty research:* Healing, transformations in relationships, therapy, dialogical research.

Cross-Discipline Announcement

Northwestern University, The Graduate School, School of Education and Social Policy, Program in Human Development and Social Policy, Evanston, IL 60208.

Students interested in developmental psychology (including life-span), personality, or community psychology may wish to pursue a PhD in this interdisciplinary program, which brings together scholars from psychology, sociology, economics, policy studies, and human development. The HDSP program focuses on how various social contexts—including families, schools, communities, and social policies—shape individual lives as they develop from infancy to old age. HDSP graduates obtain teaching and research positions in colleges and universities or work as policy analysts and program directors in the public or private sectors.

ADELPHI UNIVERSITY

Derner Institute of Advanced Psychological Studies

Programs of Study

The Gordon F. Derner Institute of Advanced Psychological Studies offers a Ph.D. program in clinical psychology and Master of Arts programs in general psychology, school psychology, and mental health counseling. There are also several postgraduate programs.

The Ph.D. program in clinical psychology emphasizes a psychodynamic approach to human behavior and prepares graduates for community practice. The program encompasses research; theory; psychological, biological, and social bases of behavior; and extensive clinical practice in psychodiagnostics and psychotherapy. Four years of full-time study, supervised research, a one-year full-time internship, and a dissertation are required. The clinical psychology program has been accredited by the American Psychological Association (APA) since 1957.

The Master of Arts in general psychology enables students to advance their exploration of human personality, psychodynamics, developmental and social psychology, and psychoanalytic theory. It requires the completion of a 36-credit course of study, which can be completed in one year of full-time study or two years of part-time study. Concentrations are offered in preclinical, forensic psychology, or industrial organizational psychology.

The Master of Arts in school psychology is a 72-credit program that can be completed in three years of full-time study or four years of part-time study. The program enables students to practice in a school setting using integrated skills, such as providing comprehensive psychoeducational evaluations and school consultations. The school practice core culminates with a full-time internship in a public school working under the supervision of a certified school psychologist.

The Master of Arts in mental health counseling is a graduate training program designed to help students acquire knowledge and the clinical skills to become competent mental health counselors. The program is designed to help students acquire competency in the diagnosis and treatment of mental disorders, the ability to facilitate client growth, development, and respect for the ethics and standards of practice endorsed by the mental health counseling profession. The 60-credit curriculum, including an internship, is designed to be completed in two years. The program complies with all standards for state and national accrediting groups. After licensure, mental health counselors may work in a variety of settings, such as hospitals, clinics, and private practice.

The Respecialization Certificate Program in clinical psychology equips doctoral-level psychologists to make a career shift into clinical psychology for community practice. The program focuses on academic work and intensive clinical training, and requires two years of full-time study, supervised clinical practice, and a one-year full-time internship. Graduates of this program earn a Certificate of Respecialization in Clinical Psychology, which is recognized by the American Psychological Association.

Postgraduate programs are available for students who have already earned a Ph.D. in clinical psychology or are licensed mental health professionals—psychiatrists, social workers, and psychiatric nurses—who wish to expand the focus of their practice. Adelphi's postgraduate programs include psychoanalysis and psychotherapy; child, adolescent, and family psychotherapy; group psychotherapy; marriage and couple therapy; and psychodynamic school psychology.

Research Facilities

Clinical facilities on campus include the Psychological Services Center and the Postgraduate Psychotherapy Center. Clinical facilities are also located in many neighboring hospitals, public schools, and agencies. Research facilities include the University library and computing center and a number of Institute research laboratories.

Financial Aid

Adelphi University offers a wide variety of federal aid programs; state grants; scholarship and fellowship programs; on- and off-campus employment; teaching, research, and clinical assistantships; and paid field placements.

Cost of Study

In 2007–08, tuition for full-time study (12–17 credits) was $29,900 per year for doctoral study in the Derner Institute of Advanced Psychological Studies. Tuition for part-time study (1–11 credits) was $755 per credit hour for master's degree programs. University fees ranged from about $300 to $500 per semester.

Living and Housing Costs

The University assists single and married students in finding suitable accommodations whenever possible. The cost of living is dependent upon location and the number of rooms rented.

Location

Adelphi University is located in Nassau County on Long Island, part of the New York City metropolitan area. Students can draw upon the city's cultural and social resources as well as the University's own extensive program in the arts.

The University

Adelphi University is set within a beautifully landscaped campus of 75 acres in the attractive residential community of Garden City, Long Island.

Applying

Application requirements can be found at http://derner.adelphi.edu/graduate (master's programs), http://derner.adelphi.edu/doctoral (doctoral program), http://derner.adelphi.edu/postgraduate (postgraduate programs), and http://derner.adelphi.edu/respecialization (respecialization program).

Correspondence and Information

Office of the Dean
Derner Institute of Advanced Psychological Studies
Adelphi University
Garden City, New York 11530
Phone: 800-ADELPHI (toll-free)
Fax: 516-877-3093
E-mail: admissions@adelphi.edu
Web site: http://derner.adelphi.edu

Adelphi University

FULL-TIME FACULTY AND THEIR RESEARCH

Jean Lau Chin, Professor and Dean; Ed.D., Columbia Teachers College. School psychology.
Robert Bornstein, Professor; Ph.D., SUNY at Buffalo. Personality disorders and assessment, unconscious processes, interpersonal dependency.
Wilma S. Bucci, Professor; Ph.D., NYU. Psychoanalytic and psycholinguistic research.
Francine Conway, Assistant Professor; Ph.D., Adelphi. Aging, emotions, and health studies.
Rebecca C. Curtis, Professor; Ph.D., Columbia. Social/clinical interface, psychotherapy research, self-defeating behavior.
Laura M. DeRose, Assistant Professor; Ph.D., Columbia. Developmental psychology, pubertal development and adjustment during early adolescence.
Rosemary Flanagan, Assistant Professor and Director of the M.A. Program in School Psychology; Ph.D., Hofstra; ABPP. School psychology.
Jerold Gold, Chair of Undergraduate Psychology; Ph.D., Adelphi. Interpersonal psychoanalysis, personality theory, psychotheory integration.
Patrick Grehan, Assistant Professor; Ph.D., Hofstra. School psychology, emotional intelligence, psychotherapy integration.
Lenore Heller, Assistant Dean; Ph.D., St. John's (New York). Clinical intervention, domestic abuse.
Mark Hilsenroth, Associate Professor; Ph.D., Tennessee. Psychodiagnostics.
Jonathan Jackson, Director of Clinical Training and Director, Psychological Services Clinic; Ph.D., NYU. Psychotherapy and psychoanalysis.
Lawrence Josephs, Professor; Ph.D., Tennessee; ABPP. Psychoanalysis, psychotherapy, self-psychology.
Morton Kissen, Professor; Ph.D., New School; ABPP. Object relations theory, projective testing, diagnostic issues.
Karen Lombardi, Professor; Ph.D., NYU. Child clinical psychology, psychoanalytic-developmental psychology, fairy tales and myths.
Robert Mendelsohn, Professor; Ph.D., Massachusetts; ABPP. Short-term psychotherapy, psychoanalytic theory.
Joseph W. Newirth, Professor; Ph.D., Massachusetts; ABPP. Psychoanalysis, object relations theory, disorders of self.
Coleman Paul, Professor; Ph.D., Wayne State. Behavior modification, stimulus control, computer technology in psychology.
Susan Petry, Professor; Ph.D., Columbia. Sensation and perception.
Louis H. Primavera, Professor; Ph.D., CUNY. Psychological studies, personality.
Barry Protter, Assistant Professor; Ph.D., Purdue. Forensic psychological consultation.
Patrick L. Ross, Professor and Special Assistant to the Dean; Ph.D., Johns Hopkins. Statistics, data processing.
Carolyn Springer, Assistant Professor; Ph.D., NYU. Statistics.
Janice M. Steil, Professor; Ph.D., Columbia. Social psychology, psychology of injustice and women's issues.
Kate A. Szymanski, Associate Professor; Ph.D., Northeastern. Small groups, social loafing, intrinsic/extrinsic motivation.
Joel Weinberger, Professor; Ph.D., New School. Human motivation.

ADLER SCHOOL OF PROFESSIONAL PSYCHOLOGY

Graduate Programs

Programs of Study

The Adler School of Professional Psychology is the oldest independent school of psychology in the U.S. Founded in 1952, the School continues the work of Alfred Adler, the first community psychologist. It educates socially responsible professionals, provides holistic service to individuals and communities, and promotes social justice. The School includes a home campus in the Chicago Loop and a growing campus in downtown Vancouver, British Columbia, Canada. The School offers a doctoral program in clinical psychology and several master's programs in behavioral sciences and services, including a recently launched master's program in policy psychology, which is the first in the country.

The Adler School pursues social responsibility through service to communities as well as service to diverse and marginalized populations. The School trains a diverse population of students and offers opportunities for students to reach out to these groups through community service practicum and internship opportunities at its on-site clinic, the Dreikurs Psychological Services Center (PSC). In the PSC, students gain real-world skills with a variety of diverse and underserved populations.

The Doctor of Psychology in Clinical Psychology program prepares students for the general practice of professional clinical psychology. The program follows the practitioner model of training developed by the National Council of Schools and Programs of Professional Psychology. This model aims to develop the knowledge, skills, and values in six core competency areas: relationship, assessment, intervention, research and evaluation, consultation and education, and management and supervision.

The Master of Arts in Counseling Psychology program provides students with a foundation in the theories and methods of counseling psychology with hands-on, practical, supervised training in counseling psychology techniques with an emphasis on Adlerian psychology. This broad-based program usually takes two years to complete. Graduates of the program are prepared for entry-level professional work in a variety of human services agencies and organizations in the public and private sectors.

The Master of Arts in Marriage and Family Counseling program prepares entry-level counselors to specialize in working with couples and families. Students complete course work and practicum experiences focused on the understanding and integration of individual lifestyle dynamics with marital and family systems. Graduates have a theoretical understanding of individual marital and family systems, including developmental issues and major variations, assessment skills in lifestyle and systemic diagnosis, and intervention skills based on major models of martial and family therapy, with the theory and methods of individual psychology as the foundation.

The Master of Arts in Counseling Psychology: Art Therapy Program combines the theories and techniques of individual psychology with education and clinical training in the field of art therapy. The program is approved by the American Art Therapy Association. It requires 65 credit hours of courses, including 700 hours of clinical practicum experience under at least partial supervision of a registered art therapist (ATR). The program provides students with the academic and predegree clinical experiences required to apply for registration as an art therapist as well as sit for the Licensed Professional Counselor (LPC) examination in the state of Illinois.

The Master of Arts in Counseling & Organizational Psychology program combines the theories and skills of counseling psychology with organizational theory, design, and development in order to prepare graduates for positions in business and industry, especially in organizational psychology and the related areas of personnel management, team building, performance enhancement, executive coaching, organizational development, training, and employee assistance programs. The program is one of a kind, because it prepares graduates to sit for state-level licensure as a master's-level counselor. Graduates are trained and qualified to be entry-level counselors with skills in assessing and providing counseling services to individuals, couples, and families. Graduates also receive training in assessing and providing intervention in organizational settings on the level of the individual (personal selection, leadership development, executive coaching, career assessment, and counseling) and the work group (team assessment, team issue resolution, and team building) and at the organizational level (talent audits, needs analysis, strategic planning, and organizational design and development). Courses are offered on an alternate weekend schedule, or on Friday evenings, Saturdays, or Sundays.

The Master of Arts in Police Psychology program is designed for field officers, supervisory personnel, command members, and those interested in a career in law enforcement. The program blends numerous areas within the discipline of psychology with pragmatic applications to patrol, operational, and managerial concerns that arise daily in the field of law enforcement. This degree is not designed to teach students to conduct therapy or engage in psychological testing. There are no clinical hours required or practicum to complete. Rather, the program teaches students the practical applications of psychology to the field of law enforcement. Core professors and adjunct faculty members all have extensive experience in clinical psychology and/or law enforcement. Many courses are team taught, combining expertise from both fields, and are offered in the evening or on weekends.

Research Facilities

The Sol and Elaine Mosak Library provides resources and services in an atmosphere that fosters the educational and intellectual inquiry of students and faculty members. In addition to its major holdings in Adlerian-oriented materials, the library also contains a wide variety of materials in mental health and related disciplines. The library has a collection of more than 12,000 volumes and subscribes to more than 150 professional journals. It also has an extensive collection of more than 1,000 audiotapes and videotapes.

The library's CD-ROM indexes facilitate research by extending its reach to the larger research community. Through interlibrary loans, cooperative agreements with local libraries, and membership in ILLINET, OCLC, and NLM-Docline, students have computer access to learning materials from all over the country.

Financial Aid

Adler School is approved by the U.S. Department of Education to participate in the Federal Family Education Loan Program. A limited number of Federal Work-Study positions are available. The School also offers a number of scholarships to students based on financial need, academic achievement, service to the community, and availability of funds.

Cost of Study

Tuition on the Chicago campus for 2007–08 was $740 per credit hour. The M.A. degree in police psychology was $890 per credit hour. Student activity and library fees are $170 per term. Tuition costs for each year vary depending on whether the student enrolls full-time or part-time. Full-time students enroll for 8 or more credit hours per term. Courses are offered during fall, spring, and summer semesters.

Living and Housing Costs

The School does not provide housing but assists students in securing off-campus housing. Students typically live in apartments in the Chicago area. Living expenses vary considerably according to standard of living, housing, and transportation.

Student Group

Adler School's commitment to social responsibility draws students from all over the world who wish to study in a collaborative atmosphere with accomplished faculty members. The School attracts both recent college graduates and working professionals and offers significant cultural diversity by attracting the best students the world has to offer. The Adler Student Association represents many different countries and encourages students to celebrate their heritage through on- and off-campus learning activities.

There are 518 students enrolled in the psychology programs, 103 of whom are part-time and 386 of whom are women. There are 37 international students and 96 members of minority groups. The average age is 27.

Location

Located in the heart of downtown Chicago, Adler School occupies four floors of a modern office building overlooking the Chicago River. Easy accessibility by car or public transportation makes this an ideal setting for students commuting not only from the greater Chicago area but from throughout the United States and Canada as well. Several major colleges and universities, public libraries, lakefront parks, museums, and shopping districts are located near the School.

The School

Founded in 1952 by Rudolf Dreikurs, M.D., the Adler School is the oldest independent psychology school in the United States. The School is named after Alfred Adler (1870–1937), the first community psychologist, whose theories and teachings of psychology emphasize the uniqueness of every individual's relationship and connection with society. Adler School is committed to continuing the work of Alfred Adler by producing socially responsible graduates, by providing holistic services to individuals and communities, and by promoting social justice. In addition to preparing individuals for the general practice of clinical psychology, Adler School also offers a Community Service Practicum—an exciting new educational experience for students. Available in the first-year curriculum, this unique practicum allows students to get involved in community organizing, volunteer projects, political initiatives, advocacy, and public policy analysis.

Applying

All applicants for admission to the degree programs offered at the Adler School must have at least a bachelor's degree from an accredited college or university. Applicants to the master's programs should ideally have a GPA of 3.0 or higher (on a 4.0 scale) and at least 12 credits of course work in psychology. Applicants to the doctoral program preferably have a GPA of 3.25 or higher (on a 4.0 scale) and at least 18 credits of course work in psychology. Applications are accepted for the fall and winter terms on a rolling basis. The priority deadline for the Psy.D. program is February 15. Admitted students may begin taking classes in the fall or winter term. Applicants are strongly encouraged to begin the preliminary application process at least three months before they plan to begin taking classes. Additional information can be obtained from the Office of Admissions.

Correspondence and Information

Adler School of Professional Psychology
Admissions Office
65 East Wacker Place, Suite 2100
Chicago, Illinois 60601-7203
Phone: 312-201-5900 Ext. 222
Fax: 312-201-5917
E-mail: admissions@adler.edu
Web site: http://www.adler.edu

Adler School of Professional Psychology

THE FACULTY

Dr. Robert Baker is a member of the core faculty and is the Clinical Director of the Psychological Services Center's Prison Aftercare Program in Chicago. He is also the Coordinator of the Sex Offender Treatment Program. Dr. Baker earned his B.A. in economics at Michigan State University and his M.A. in counseling psychology and Psy.D. in clinical psychology at the Adler School of Professional Psychology. He is a licensed clinical psychologist. Dr. Baker teaches courses in psychophysiology, cognitive psychology, and clinical skills seminars. His additional interests include gerontology, forensics and correctional psychology, neuropsychology, clinical hypnosis, and psychotherapy with children, adolescents, and adults.

Dr. Dan Barnes is a member of the core faculty and serves as the Director and Chief Psychologist of the Dreikurs Psychological Services Center (PSC). He is also the Director of Clinical Training and in that capacity oversees the PSC's training programs, which include the Pre-Doctoral Internship in Professional Psychology, the therapy and assessment practicums, and the Post-Doctoral Residency in the PSC's Prison Aftercare Program. He received his B.S. in psychology from Loyola University Chicago and M.A. and Ph.D. degrees in clinical psychology from the University of Kentucky. He is a licensed clinical psychologist and has maintained a clinical practice since 1972. He teaches courses in systems of psychotherapy and constructivist cognitive psychotherapy.

Dr. Neil Bockian is a member of the core faculty. He earned his Ph.D. from the University of Miami, where he studied personality disorders with Dr. Theodore Millon and mindfulness meditation with Jon Kabat-Zinn. Dr. Bockian has research and clinical interests in the areas of personality disorders, health psychology, meditation, treatment planning, and behavioral medicine. He has written two books on personality disorders, and he has extensive experience treating individuals with spinal cord injuries and patients with chronic pain. He has employed individual therapy, group therapy, hypnosis, relaxation training, and mindfulness meditation in his practice.

Dr. Wendy Bostwick is the Director of Community Engagement and a member of the core faculty. She received her M.P.H. and Ph.D. in public health from the University of Illinois at Chicago and recently completed a National Institute on Drug Abuse postdoctoral fellowship at the University of Michigan Substance Abuse Research Center. Some of her research interests include sexual minority women's health; substance use and mental health issues among women; the health effects of stigma, discrimination, and marginalization; bisexuality; measurement of sexual orientation and sexual identity; and research with hidden and hard-to-reach populations. Her work has appeared in the *Journal of Studies on Alcohol* and the *Journal of Lesbian Studies,* among others. Her community work most recently entailed volunteering as a housing crisis counselor for a social service agency in Michigan.

Dr. Julie Chodacki is a member of the core faculty in the MAC Program. She earned her B.A. at Harvard, her M.A. at University of Illinois at Chicago, and her Doctor of Psychology degree from the Illinois School of Professional Psychology, Chicago Campus. After completing an internship in adult psychology at Cambridge Hospital, Harvard Medical School, she received specialized training and clinical experience in family systems and health during her postdoctoral fellowship the Chicago Center for Family Health and MacNeal Medical Center, University of Chicago affiliates. She is licensed in clinical psychology. Prior to teaching at the Adler School, Dr. Chodacki was the Coordinator of Behavioral Health at the Family Practice Residency Program at Saint Elizabeth Hospital.

Dr. Cristina Cox is a member of the core faculty. Dr. Cox earned her B.S. in psychology at Michigan State University and her M.A. and Ph.D. in clinical psychology at Loyola University. She is a licensed clinical psychologist. Dr. Cox teaches courses in child and adolescent therapy, ethnocultural diversity, gender diversity, and psychological assessment of children and clinical seminars. Her additional interests include models of intervention and assessment with children, integrative psychotherapy, bilingual/bicultural and language issues, learning disabilities and cognitive deficits, development and temperament, and consultation in educational settings.

Dr. Raymond E. Crossman is President of the Adler School and a member of the doctoral core faculty. Dr. Crossman completed his B.S. in psychology and fine arts at Fordham University and his Ph.D. in clinical psychology at Temple University. He is President of the National Council of Schools and Programs in Professional Psychology, and he is the Chair of the Council of Chairs of Training Councils of the American Psychological Association. He has taught courses, presented, written about, and developed programs and initiatives in diversity education, psychology training, family therapy and family diversity, and HIV disease prevention and coping.

Dr. Vida Dyson is a member of the core faculty. Dr. Dyson earned her B.A. in psychology at DePaul University and her M.A. and Ph.D. in psychology/personality process at the University of Chicago. She is a licensed clinical psychologist. Dr. Dyson teaches courses in ethnocultural diversity and gender issues and clinical seminars. Her interests include substance abuse assessment and treatment, schizophrenia, and the professional development of women, blacks, and other minorities.

Dr. Frank Gruba-McCallister is a member of the core faculty and Vice President of Academic Affairs. Dr. Gruba-McCallister received his B.S. in psychology from Loyola University and his M.A. and Ph.D. in clinical psychology from Purdue University. He is a licensed clinical psychologist. He teaches courses in history and systems, theories of psychotherapy, advanced psychotherapy, existential psychotherapy, and psychology and advocacy. His interests include health psychology, the integration of psychology and spirituality, transpersonal psychology, peace studies, and the role of psychology in advocacy and activism for social change.

Dr. Peter Liu is a member of the core faculty and the Program Director for the Master of Arts in Counseling and Organizational Psychology Program. He completed his B.Sc. and Ph.D. degrees at the University of Toronto and also holds a Certificate in Management (C.M.) from Harvard University. His academic training in cross-cultural educational psychology is complemented with clinical training at CHEO (Children's Hospital of Eastern Ontario) in Ottawa, Canada, and a postdoctoral clinical internship at The University of Zurich, Switzerland. He has taught psychology and management courses for international college students, adult learners, and corporate executives. In addition, he has been active in conducting organizational projects, talent assessment, and leadership development initiatives for major global corporations. He is a licensed industrial psychologist and specializes in executive coaching, organizational change, emotional intelligence, life span development, and career counseling.

Dr. Erik Mansager is a member of the core faculty. Dr. Mansager earned his B.A. in humanities from St. Thomas Seminary College in Denver, his M.A. in marriage and family counseling at the University of Arizona, and his Ph.D. in depth psychology at the Catholic University of Leuven in Belgium. Previously he was the Director of the Counseling Center at the University of North Dakota. Dr. Mansager is currently president of NASAP and has extensive publications and presentations on Adlerian psychology. He has particular interest in parenting and the integration of psychology and spirituality, and he has more than twenty years' experience providing therapy and education to abused children, adolescent substance abusers, and their parents, as well as mediating acrimonious divorces.

Dr. Larry Maucieri is a member of the core faculty and serves as the Director of the Clinical Neuropsychology Certificate Program. Dr. Maucieri received his Ph.D. in clinical psychology from Fordham University and did his clinical internship at Yale University School of Medicine. He recently completed a two year postdoctoral fellowship in clinical neuropsychology at Northwestern University, Feinberg School of Medicine. Dr. Maucieri will be teaching courses in the neuropsychology program in addition to courses in biological bases and assessment.

Dr. Steven Migalski is a member of the doctoral core faculty and a licensed clinical psychologist. He is also the Coordinator of Psychological Assessment at Adler's Psychological Services Center. He received his B.S. in psychology from Loyola University Chicago and both his master's and doctorate from the Illinois School of Professional Psychology. He completed a postdoctoral fellowship in clinical child psychology at the Josselyn Center for Mental Health, where he served as Director of Psychology for four years. Dr. Migalski's areas of concentration include clinical interviewing, personality assessment, mood disorders across the lifespan, assessment of ADHD and learning disabilities, multimodal and constructivist psychotherapies, primary and secondary prevention of HIV-risk behavior, and sexual orientation diversity in clinical practice. In his clinical work and in supervision, Dr. Migalski draws heavily upon the cognitive-behavioral and interpersonal traditions. Dr. Migalski is presently the consulting psychologist for Lawrence Hall Youth Services, and he maintains a very active private practice in Chicago's Lincoln Square neighborhood.

Dr. Nataka Moore is a member of the core faculty and serves as the Associate Director of Training. Dr. Moore earned her B.S. in chemistry at the University of Illinois at Urbana-Champaign. She earned her M.A. and Psy.D. in clinical psychology at the Illinois School of Professional Psychology. Dr. Moore currently teaches cognitive behavioral therapy, professional development seminar, and assessment practicum seminar. Her professional interests include school psychology and consultation, mother-daughter relationships, multicultural psychology, and public health issues.

Dr. Harold Mosak is a Distinguished Service Professor and serves as Chair of the Doctoral Scholars in Clinical Psychology Program. Dr. Mosak earned his A.B. in psychology and Ph.D. in clinical psychology at the University of Chicago. He is a diplomate in clinical psychology of the American Board of Professional Psychology, a life member and fellow of the APA, and a licensed clinical psychologist. Dr. Mosak teaches courses in Adlerian theory and methods and a year-long "Adler from Scratch" series as well as clinical seminars. His additional interests include the use of humor, the role of the spiritual in psychotherapy, multiple psychotherapy, and group and couples therapy.

Dr. John Newbauer is a member of the core faculty and Coordinator of the Fort Wayne campus Doctoral Program. Dr. Newbauer earned his B.A. and M.S.Ed. in psychology and his M.S. in preclinical psychology at St. Francis College, his Ed.D. in counseling and guidance (cognates: psychology and educational psychology) at Ball State University, a certificate in rehabilitation administration at DePaul University, and a postgraduate certificate in Adlerian psychology at the Alfred Adler Institute of Chicago. Dr. Newbauer is a licensed clinical psychologist, a diplomate and fellow of the College of Forensic Examiners, a licensed marriage and family therapist, and a certified clinical mental health counselor. Dr. Newbauer teaches courses in Adlerian theory and methods, psychological assessment, and gender issues as well as clinical seminars. His additional interests include correctional and forensic psychology, juvenile delinquency, sexual offenders, clinical hypnosis, custody and parenting issues, and gender and multicultural issues.

Dr. Wendy Paszkiewicz is a member of the core faculty and serves as Director of Training and Community Service. Dr. Paszkiewicz earned her B.S. in psychology at Michigan State University and her Psy.D. in clinical psychology at the Illinois School of Professional Psychology/Chicago. She is a licensed clinical psychologist and maintains a private practice serving children, adolescents, and families. Dr. Paszkiewicz teaches practicum and internship seminars. Her additional interests include managerial psychology, social interest and responsibility, diversity issues, the professional development of psychologists, and issues of education and training in professional psychology.

Dr. Victoria Priola-Surowiec joined the Adler faculty in July 2006 and serves as Director of the Police Psychology Program. She earned her B.S. in psychology at the University of Illinois-Champaign-Urbana and her M.A in counseling psychology and Psy.D. in clinical psychology from the Adler School of Professional Psychology. She is a licensed clinical psychologist and maintains a private practice in Chicago serving police officers and their families. Formerly, she was the Director of Training at Safe Alternatives, an inpatient treatment program for individuals who engage in self-destructive behaviors, including self-injury. Dr. Priola-Surowiec teaches courses in Adlerian theory and methods, basic assessment and interviewing, and professional development. Her additional interests include psychoanalysis, mentoring, attachment theory, and parenting.

Dr. Nancy Slater is a member of the core faculty and serves as Director of the Art Therapy Program. Dr. Slater earned her B.A. in psychology at the University of Michigan, her M.A. in art therapy at the University of Louisville, and her Ph.D. in psychology at the Union Institute. She is a registered, board certified art therapist of the American Art Therapy Association. Dr. Slater is the coordinator of the International Networking Group of Art Therapists. Currently she is the chair of the American Art Therapy Association Ethics Committee. Dr. Slater has taught and directed graduate art therapy programs in Melbourne, Australia, and in Beer Sheva, Israel. She has given conference presentations and consultation in other countries. Dr. Slater's teaching interests include art therapy ethics, art therapy addressing the effects of trauma, multicultural approaches to art therapy, and clinical supervision. Her additional interests include art therapy research, international collaborative training and research, and multicultural art therapy intervention in response to domestic violence and sexual assault, to substance abuse, and to the effects of interpersonal violence and war.

Dr. Thomas Todd is a member of the core faculty and serves as Program Director of the Marriage and Family Program. Dr. Todd earned his B.A. in psychology at Princeton University and his Ph.D. in clinical psychology at New York University. He is a diplomate of the American Board of Family Psychology, a fellow of the Division of Family Psychology (APA) and of the American Association for Marriage and Family Therapy, a licensed clinical psychologist, and an AAMFT Approved Supervisor. Dr. Todd teaches courses in marriage and family therapy, clinical supervision, and practicum seminars. His additional interests include qualitative research, substance abuse, eating disorders, supervision, and outcome assessment.

Lynn C. Todman is the Director of the Adler Institute on Social Exclusion (ISE), a member of the core faculty, and a member of the School's Leadership Team. She earned a B.A. from Wellesley College and a master's and a Ph.D. in city and regional planning from MIT. Dr. Todman's research and teaching interests center on problems of social marginalization, isolation, and exclusion experienced by urban communities. Her work focuses especially on the ways in which the structures and systems that comprise and organize American society cause disadvantage in urban communities. Dr. Todman's approach to her work is highly multidimensional, drawing on such diverse disciplines as law, political science, economics, sociology, community and urban development, psychology, medicine, public health, and systems' dynamics. She has spoken at numerous national and international conferences on the problem of urban disadvantage. Her recent research and writings include working papers that explore the relevance of the concept of social exclusion to the American social policy context and the development of a transdisciplinary discourse on social exclusion.

Dr. Jerry Westermeyer is a member of the doctoral core faculty and serves as Dean of Clinical Training. Dr. Westermeyer earned his B.A. in social studies at St. Mary's College and his M.A. in international relations and Ph.D. (Committee on Human Development) at the University of Chicago. He is a licensed clinical psychologist. Dr. Westermeyer teaches courses in psychopathology, human development, and research methodology. His additional interests include successful aging across the lifespan, the course and outcome of psychopathology, positive mental health, political psychology, and children's issues in developing countries.

Dr. Ian Wickramasekera II is a member of the core faculty and Coordinator of the Clinical Hypnosis Certificate Program. Dr. Wickramasekera earned his B.S. in psychology with Honors Distinction from the University of Illinois at Champaign-Urbana and his Psy.D. from the Illinois School of Professional Psychology at Chicago. He is licensed in clinical psychology and has worked in a variety of health psychology settings such as pain management and mind/body medicine. In his clinical work he draws upon his background in Buddhism, cognitive neuroscience, humanistic/transpersonal psychology, and mind/body medicine. His major clinical and research interests involve the application of techniques in mind/body medicine such as hypnosis, meditation, and biofeedback to a wide variety of health problems such as chronic pain. He is the current Secretary of the APA's Division of Psychological Hypnosis (Division 30). His research has appeared in the *International Journal of Clinical and Experimental Hypnosis, Journal of Humanistic Psychology,* and in *Dissociation.* Dr. Wickramasekera is also an associate editor of the *American Journal of Clinical Hypnosis.*

Dr. Torrey Wilson is a member of the core faculty and the Program Director for the Psy.D. program. He earned his Ph.D. in counseling psychology from Loyola University. Dr. Wilson served as the program director at Gilda's Club, a cancer support center. He has also held administrative positions at the American Medical Association and Rush-Presbyterian-St. Luke's Medical Center-Rush University. He has been involved in teaching and training at Rush and as a faculty member at Northeastern Illinois, Loyola, and Aurora Universities, as well as providing management and diversity training to corporations and organizations as a consultant. Dr Wilson is a former president of the Chicago Chapter of the Association of Black Psychologists (2003–04) and serves on several nonprofit and organizational boards. Dr. Wilson's interests include multicultural psychology, health psychology/behavioral medicine, and public health.

ALFRED UNIVERSITY

Division of School Psychology

Programs of Study Alfred University's Master of Arts/Certificate of Advanced Studies (M.A./C.A.S.) degree is a 79-credit-hour, NASP-approved program (two years of course work, one year of internship) that satisfies the academic component of the New York State Education Department's requirements for permanent certification in school psychology and for national certification. Training emphases include a knowledge base in psychology and education, assessment, intervention and remediation, family systems, child counseling techniques, consultation, and professional identification and functioning.

The Doctor of Psychology (Psy.D.) degree is a 120-credit-hour program accredited by the American Psychological Association that leads to state and national certification as well as to New York State license eligibility. This program requires a minimum of four years, which includes three years of course work, one year of supervised internship, and completion of a research dissertation. The course work balances scientific bases with academic and applied professional psychology. Students may develop a specialty area through course work, research, and field experience. As in the M.A./C.A.S. program, all students must pass written comprehensive examinations, participate in practicums, and complete an internship. In addition, a doctoral qualifying examination and a dissertation are required. In order to meet the requirements for NASP approval, all students are required to take the Praxis examination in school psychology, administered by Educational Testing Service, prior to completing their internship.

Research Facilities Herrick Memorial Library contains more than 328,000 volumes, 1,500 periodical titles in house, more than 95,000 units of microforms, 4,200 units of audiovisual materials, 170,000 slides, and more than 14,000 titles available through electronic subscriptions. Internet access to databases such as PSYCHINFO and ERIC is available throughout the campus. The library's interlibrary loan service connects students to information resources worldwide. Microcomputer labs are conveniently located across campus and within the Division and provide Internet-connected PC and Mac workstations. The Lea R. Powell Institute for Children and Families is an organizing entity for the Division's research, training, and service missions. The Institute provides start-up research funding for faculty members, students, and practitioners in addition to pursuing sources of external funding for research and training programs of the Division. The Center for Rural School Psychology, the training arm of the Institute, offers continuing professional development for current practitioners. The Child and Family Services Center (CFSC), the service entity of the Institute, is a spacious, renovated facility with a state-of-the-art audiovisual, communication/observation system. In addition to their work in the schools, all students gain experience working under supervision in this community clinic. The research conducted by students is applied research—searching for solutions to behavior, academic, or organizational problems or seeking ways to deliver new psychological research or services to children and their families, organizations, and groups.

Financial Aid Graduate assistantships (partial tuition remission) are available to all students. In addition, paid internships (averaging $15,000) are sought for students in their final year in the program. The Financial Aid Office assists graduate students in obtaining additional forms of assistance.

Cost of Study Tuition for the 2007–08 academic year was $30,784. Tuition for students on a paid internship was $15,392.

Living and Housing Costs Most students live in apartments off campus. For assistance in locating housing, students may contact the Division of School Psychology or write to the Director of Residence Life.

Student Group Alfred University has approximately 2,000 undergraduate and 300 graduate students drawn from forty states and fifteen countries. There are 55 full-time graduate students and 30 students on internship in the Division of School Psychology, allowing for close interaction between students and faculty. Seven percent of students self-identify as African American, Hispanic, or Asian. Seventy-five percent are women. Although the average age is 26, students range in age from 22 to their mid-50s. Students may come directly from undergraduate school, with master's degrees and many years of experience, or with prior careers in different fields.

Location Alfred University is located in Alfred, New York, a college town 70 miles south of Rochester, 90 miles southeast of Buffalo, and 60 miles west of Corning. Nestled among the pine-sheltered foothills of the Allegheny Mountains, this popular recreation area is close to ski slopes and the water sports and fishing of the Finger Lakes region. New York City is 6 hours away by car via the Southern Tier Expressway/I-86.

The University Founded in 1836, Alfred University is the oldest coeducational institution in New York State and the second oldest in the nation. Alfred grants bachelor's, master's, and doctoral degrees. The fifty-nine-building, 232-acre hillside campus adjoins the village of Alfred. The University comprises the College of Business, the College of Liberal Arts and Sciences, and the New York State College of Ceramics, which houses the School of Art and Design as well as the Inamori School of Engineering. In addition to the graduate programs in each of these colleges and schools, the graduate programs in school psychology are administered by the Division of School Psychology within the Graduate School.

Applying To be eligible for admission, an applicant must hold a baccalaureate degree from an accredited college or university, and the undergraduate record must clearly indicate ability to perform credibly at the graduate level. The student must have successfully completed undergraduate work in introduction to psychology, statistical and/or experimental methods, and developmental psychology (child and adolescent psychology), personality, or abnormal psychology. Other relevant courses and practical experiences in psychology or education are looked upon favorably. To apply, students must send to the graduate admission office a completed application form and fee, three letters of recommendation, official transcripts of all undergraduate and graduate course work, GRE General Test results, and a brief personal statement of objectives; Psy.D. applicants must also submit a statement of research interest. The application deadline for the Psy.D. program is January 15. Review of applications for the M.A./C.A.S. program begins on February 15 and continues until the class is filled. Early application is encouraged. Official TOEFL scores are required of international students who have not received a baccalaureate degree from an institution in the U.S. The TSE is recommended. An application fee of $50 is charged, but the fee is waived if the student applies using the online application.

Correspondence and Information

For additional information:

Nancy Evangelista, Ph.D., Chair,
Division of School Psychology
Alfred University
One Saxon Drive
Alfred, New York 14802-1232

Phone: 607-871-2212

For applications:

Office of Graduate Admissions
Alfred University
One Saxon Drive
Alfred, New York 14802-1232

Phone: 607-871-2115
800-541-9229 (toll-free)
E-mail: gradinquiry@alfred.edu
Web site: http://www.alfred.edu/gradschool

Alfred University

THE FACULTY AND THEIR RESEARCH

Division of School Psychology

Nancy Evangelista, Associate Professor of School Psychology and Chairperson, Division of School Psychology; Ph.D., Syracuse, 1986; licensed psychologist, certified school psychologist. Autism, pervasive developmental disorders, developmental assessment, school psychology, special education, preschool/early childhood.

Jana Atlas, Associate Professor of School Psychology; Ph.D., Wayne State, 1988; licensed psychologist. Clinical psychology, developmental psychology, psychotherapy, psychopathology, eating disorders.

Robert Bitting, Associate Professor of Counseling; Ph.D., Buffalo, SUNY, 1988; licensed mental health counselor. College counseling, higher education administration, group methods.

John D. Cerio, Professor of School Psychology and Director, Child and Family Services Center and Center for Rural School Psychology; Ph.D., Boston College, 1988; licensed psychologist, certified school psychologist and school counselor. Counseling psychology, school psychology, family therapy, play therapy, personality assessment, cultural diversity.

Ellen Faherty, Clinical Assistant Professor of School Psychology and Director, Lea R. Powell Institute for Children and Families; Psy.D., SUNY Albany; licensed psychologist, certified school psychologist and teacher. School psychology, special education, early childhood/preschool, consultation, psychotherapy, grant development.

Mark Fugate, Associate Professor of Psychology; Ph.D., Lehigh, 1993; licensed psychologist, certified school psychologist. Preschool assessment and intervention, applied behavior analysis, educational assessment, alternative approaches to assessment.

Edward Gaughan, Powell Professor of Psychology and Schooling and Professor of School Psychology; Ph.D., Temple, 1985; licensed psychologist, certified school psychologist. School psychology, direct and indirect intervention, family assessment, psychopathology, professional preparation issues.

Chris Lauback, Assistant Professor of School Psychology; Psy.D., Alfred, 1996; certified school psychologist. School psychology, consultation, preschool screening, prereferral teams, family systems psychology.

Lynn O'Connell, Assistant Professor of School Psychology; Psy.D., Alfred, 2001; licensed psychologist, certified school psychologist. School psychology, reading development and assessment, consultation, rural schools.

Terry Taggart, Clinical Assistant Professor of School Psychology and Director, Office of Special Academic Services; Psy.D., Alfred; licensed psychologist, certified school psychologist, registered nurse. School psychology, play therapy, family therapy, postsecondary disabilities.

Division of Psychology

Nancy E. Furlong, Professor of Psychology and Chairperson, Division of Psychology; Ph.D., Pittsburgh, 1983. Cognition and social development of children, research design and statistics.

Gordon D. Atlas, Professor of Psychology; Ph.D., Michigan, 1987. Defense mechanisms, depression, sensitivity to criticism.

Danielle Gagne, Assistant Professor of Psychology; Ph.D., New Hampshire, 2004. Discourse and aging, role of self-efficacy beliefs.

Louis J. Lichtman, Professor of Psychology; Ph.D., Maine, 1971. Neuropsychology, parenting, eating disorders.

Robert J. Maiden, Professor of Psychology; Ph.D., New School, 1980; licensed psychologist. Clinical psychology, aging, marital and family therapy, drug and alcohol abuse, medical psychology.

ALLIANT INTERNATIONAL UNIVERSITY

California School of Professional Psychology
Ph.D. in Clinical Psychology

Programs of Study

The Doctor of Philosophy in Clinical Psychology (Ph.D.) programs at the California School of Professional Psychology (CSPP) follow a scholar-practitioner model to prepare students to become effective professional psychologists who are skilled at evaluating psychological functioning and provide effective interventions with diverse clients across a range of settings. Equally important, the programs prepare students to conduct applied research in clinical psychology and to contribute actively to the knowledge base in the field. The program's training philosophies promote the view that research training and professional skill development should be closely intertwined and based on a core body of knowledge in scientific psychology.

In the first and second years, all programs provide an extensive background in the foundations of psychology; they develop students' basic scientific understanding and practice skills. Students participate in clerkship or practicum experiences requiring 8–20 hours of student time per week in their second and/or third years. At this level, students receive training in specific skills, such as psychological assessment, evaluation of clients and programs, and intervention and psychotherapeutic techniques. They are also introduced to the roles and ethical practices of professional psychologists.

During the second or third year, students must pass formal evaluations, which may include written comprehensive or preliminary examinations, in order to be advanced to doctoral candidacy. Each program establishes specific methods and procedures for evaluating students. Evaluations focus on a student's demonstrated academic ability, expected competency in research, interpersonal competencies, and understanding of the basic theoretical foundations of psychology.

The curriculum for third-, fourth-, and fifth-year students includes advanced training in the analysis and performance of applied research, theoretical issues, psychological intervention techniques, professional ethics and issues, psychopharmacology, and supervision. Students also participate in the dissertation, field placements, growth experiences, and elective courses.

While required course work is substantial, in the final years there is also time to develop special interests. Internships occupy 20 to 40 hours per week, intensifying students' mastery of professional skills and providing supervisory experience. Clinical internship requirements meet, and in some programs exceed, the 1,500 hours of predoctoral internship accepted by the California Board of Psychology for licensure. CSPP doctoral course requirements at all campuses are designed to fulfill all of the state licensing requirements of California, and in some cases they exceed the requirements.

In content, the clinical psychology curricula reflect four areas of study—applied research, professional skills, professional concepts, and personal growth. A student's course work each year consists of required courses and electives from each of these areas.

Research Facilities

The Alliant library system is a distributed collection of print, media, and electronic resources with primary strengths in psychology (clinical, forensic, organizational, and educational), business administration, global liberal studies, and education. The collections have a multicultural and international focus.

Alliant's largest library facility is in San Diego on the Scripps Ranch Campus, but comprehensive specialized collections are also available in San Francisco, Los Angeles, and Fresno. The collections at California locations are represented in the Web-based library catalog and total over 200,000 physical volumes, 640 current print journal subscriptions, and 1,200 videos.

The Alliant libraries share access to online resources, including 28 research databases, full-text content from over 16,000 journals, and 5,200 e-books. Resources that are not available on site may be requested from other Alliant libraries via the shared online catalog or from LINK+, a network of thirty-eight California and Nevada libraries with over 6 million titles.

An accomplished staff of librarians and support personnel provide services across the University and to distance learners. Services include reference, bibliographic research consultation, information literacy instruction, interlibrary loan, document delivery, and course reserves.

In each library, computers are available to access the Internet, electronic books and journals, and online research database resources, such as PsycINFO, Lexis-Nexis, OCLC FirstSearch, Digital Dissertations, Social Science Citation Index, Medline, ERIC, and Criminal Justice Periodical Index. Most of these online resources may also be accessed from home or office.

Financial Aid

Alliant offers financial aid to qualified students in the form of loans, scholarships, grants, and part-time employment. The federal government, state government, Alliant, and private sources finance these programs. Federal and state financial aid funds are only available to students who are United States citizens or permanent residents of the United States.

Financial aid packages, although predominantly in the form of loans, may also include scholarships and student employment. Most students interested in school-based financial aid pursue college work-study. A limited number of teaching and research assistantships are available. In addition, students can work on campus in a number of departments, including admissions and field placement. Stipends generally average about $1000 per assistantship per semester. For more information, students should e-mail finaid@alliant.edu.

Cost of Study

CSPP doctoral program tuition is $865 per semester unit. A full-time student averages 30 units per year. Students completing an internship in one full-time year or in two years of half-time rotations pay $3850 and $2400 per semester, respectively. Fees are additional.

Living and Housing Costs

Students can expect to pay between $700 and $1500 per month plus utilities (gas and electricity) for an off-campus, unfurnished, one-bedroom apartment. On-campus housing is available on the San Diego campus; the cost of room and board for an academic year is $15,480 for a 2-person suite, $11,700 for a 1-person suite, $10,800 for a private room, and $8250 for double occupancy.

Student Group

Alliant prides itself on the diversity of its student body. The University has students from almost every state and international students from sixty-four countries, including Cameroon, Botswana, Greece, Iceland, Portugal, and Turkey. There are 2,626 full-time and 1,284 part-time students at Alliant International University, of whom 76 percent are women and approximately 46 percent are from groups underrepresented in higher education. Within the California School of Professional Psychology, there are 2,148 students.

Location

The Ph.D. in Clinical Psychology is offered at four of Alliant's campuses in California: Fresno, Los Angeles, San Diego, and San Francisco.

The University and The School

Alliant International University focuses on preparing students for professional careers. Formed in July 2001 through the combination of the California School of Professional Psychology and United States International University (USIU), Alliant is an independent, not-for-profit institution of higher education with a history distinguished by innovation. The University's mission is to educate citizens of the world, ensuring the acquisition of knowledge and competencies that are essential to live, lead, and solve problems in a global society.

CSPP, the largest of the five schools and centers at Alliant, prepares students for careers as clinical psychologists, marital and family therapists, and other mental health professionals. While earning their degrees, students work in a wide variety of settings, establishing themselves in the professional community as experienced practitioners. By the time students earn their degrees, they have already developed a network of colleagues and professional affiliations that make them exceptionally attractive to employers as vital contributors to their field.

Applying

Applicants should have a bachelor's or master's degree in psychology (preferred), with a minimum GPA of 3.0. Students must submit the completed application, the application fee, official transcripts from all institutions attended, a personal statement, and letters of recommendation. An interview is required. International students must also submit TOEFL/TWE scores. The application deadline is January 15. Submitting a complete application by January 15 guarantees notification by April 1. Applications submitted after January 15 are welcome, but are reviewed on a space-available basis.

Correspondence and Information

Central Contact Center
Alliant International University
10455 Pomerado Road
San Diego, California 92131

Phone: 866-U-ALLIANT (toll-free)
Fax: 858-635-4555
E-mail: admissions@alliant.edu
Web site: http://www.alliant.edu/cspp

Alliant International University

THE FACULTY AND THEIR RESEARCH

Fresno Campus

Sue Ammen, Professor; Ph.D., California School of Professional Psychology–Fresno 1989. Parent-child attachment, infant mental health, pediatric psychology, cross-cultural assessment and issues with children and families, gay/lesbian issues, qualitative research methods.

Manuel Figueroa-Unda, Professor; Ph.D., Stanford, 1985; ABPP-Diplomate in Clinical Psychology. Multicultural research and topics in learning and motivation, social bases of behavior, multicultural studies, adolescent self-image, eating disorders.

Paul Lebby, Associate Professor; Ph.D., Berkeley, 1994. Neuropsychological assessment, medical rehabilitation, child and adolescent brain injury, forensic neuropsychology.

Kevin J. O'Connor, Professor, Program Director, and Coordinator, Ecosystemic Clinical Psychology Emphasis Area; Ph.D., Toledo, 1980. Parent-child attachment, child psychotherapy process, play therapy, attachment disorders, child abuse, impact of parental narcissism, child development, sex role socialization, Ecosystemic child psychotherapy, art therapy, Theraplay.

Siobhan O'Toole, Assistant Professor and Assistant Program Director; Ph.D., California School of Professional Psychology, 2000. Evaluating cultural competence in clinicians; child abuse, primarily physical and verbal; body image.

Los Angeles Campus

Linda Beckman, Distinguished Professor; Ph.D., UCLA, 1969. Women's health, substance abuse, population psychology, social-psychological models in health promotion.

Terece S. Bell, Principal Lecturer; Ph.D., USC, 1982. Cognitive development in children, neuropsychological assessment, Asian values.

Ellin L. Bloch, Professor, Program Director, and Director of Professional Field Training; Ph.D., Cincinnati, 1972. Post-traumatic stress disorder, trauma and crisis intervention.

Ron E. F. Duran, Associate Professor; Ph.D., UCLA, 1994. Group-based interventions for persons living with chronic and life-threatening medical conditions, collaboration with community-based agencies to improve health-related service delivery, measurement of social and academic adjustment of nontraditional undergraduate and graduate students.

Tracy L. Heller, Associate Professor and Associate Dean, CSPP; Ph.D., UCLA, 1994. Children with attention-deficit/hyperactivity disorder; behavioral, social, and cognitive components of ADHD; multimodal treatments of ADHD.

Derek K. Iwamoto, Assistant Professor; Ph.D., Nebraska–Lincoln, 2007. Racial and ethnic identity, intergenerational conflict, masculinity and gender role strain to positive psychological well-being, depression and substance use among Asian Americans.

Paula Johnson, Professor; Ph.D., UCLA, 1974. Peace studies, values related to war, gender roles and power, community psychology models of system interventions, social policy research using social and community psychology models, values and methodology.

Richard Mendoza, Professor; Ph.D., California, Irvine, 1980. Acculturation among refugees and immigrant individuals; implications for mental health, psychopathology, and psychotherapy.

Nicholas Noviello, Associate Professor; Ph.D., California, Irvine, 1985. Personality traits and emotional expressiveness, content analysis of speech and text, personal belief systems, well-being.

Susan J. Regas, Professor; Ph.D., Purdue, 1983. Sex, intimacy and relationship problems, differentiation assessment, couple therapy effectiveness.

Kathryn White, Professor; Ph.D., North Carolina at Chapel Hill, 1982; D.H.M., Hahnemann, 1995; M.T.D.M., Emperor's College of Traditional Oriental Medicine, 1995. Psychotherapy and complementary and alternative medicine, psychotherapy East-West, psychology and meditation, clinical health psychology, somatic therapies, sexual and physical abuse, women's issues, object relations, self psychology.

San Diego Campus

Kristi Alexander, Associate Professor; Ph.D., Alabama, 1992. Pediatric and child clinical psychology, with special interest in social skills and children's injuries.

Milton Z. Brown, Assistant Professor; Ph.D., Washington (Seattle), 2002. Personality disorders; chronic suicidality and self-injury; PTSD; cognitive-behavior therapy, in particular, exposure therapy and dialectical behavior therapy.

Joanne E. Callan, Distinguished Professor; Ph.D., Texas, 1970. Child and adolescent development, adjustment, and psychopathology (including gender development); parenting and school support—preschool through high school; life-span development—female development and psychology; psychoanalysis and psychoanalytic theory and psychotherapy; training in professional psychology; ethics.

Constance J. Dalenberg, Professor; Ph.D., Denver, 1983. Countertransference, child abuse, trauma, PTSD, repressed memory, ethics and standards in psychology, empirical foundations of psychoanalytic concepts, trauma related to racism and discrimination.

Sharon L. Foster, Distinguished Professor; Ph.D., SUNY at Stony Brook, 1978. Childhood social competence and peer relations, family conflict in adolescence, behavioral assessment.

Richard N. Gevirtz, Distinguished Professor; Ph.D., DePaul, 1971. Physiological patterning in stress-related disorders, clinical protocols for biofeedback training, mediators of autonomic control, anxiety disorders.

Alan J. Lincoln, Professor; Ph.D., California School of Professional Psychology–San Diego, 1980. Early childhood psychopathology, biological and neuropsychological basis of autism and neurodevelopmental disorders, neurodevelopmental effects of child abuse, attention-deficit/hyperactivity and severe language disorders, assessment of children, differential diagnosis and treatment of childhood psychopathology.

Fernando Ortiz, Assistant Professor; Ph.D., Washington State, 2005. Cross-cultural and multicultural issues, personality assessment and personality structure, mental health and minority populations.

Adele S. Rabin, Professor and Interim Program Director; Ph.D., Houston, 1984. Women's health, comparative psychotherapy outcomes, unipolar depression, psychological factors affecting physical health.

Irwin S. Rosenfarb, Professor; Ph.D., North Carolina at Greensboro, 1986. Schizophrenia, mood disorders, role of the family in the course and treatment of severe psychopathology.

Erika E. Swift, Assistant Professor; Ph.D., Case Western Reserve, 2002. Pediatric psychology and child community psychology, health-promoting behaviors and beliefs, quality of life among pediatric patients, obesity, type 1 and 2 diabetes, sleep disorders.

Donald J. Viglione Jr., Professor; Ph.D., LIU, 1981. Rorschach and personality assessment; malingering; assessment of child psychopathology; trauma, dangerousness, and sexual offenses.

San Francisco Campus

Shannon Casey-Cannon, Assistant Professor; Ph.D., Stanford, 2002. Adolescents within diverse family and school contexts, multicultural identity and women's issues, depression, eating disorders.

Dalia Ducker, Professor and Program Director; Ph.D., CUNY, 1974. Psychology of women, including role strain, work, and health; gender roles; issues relevant to the practice of professional psychology; graduate education.

Robert Jay Green, Distinguished Professor and Executive Director, Rockway Institute for LGBT Research and Public Policy; Ph.D., Michigan State, 1975. Lesbian, gay, bisexual, and transgender (LGBT) research and public policy in the fields of couple/family relations, mental health care, education, and the work place; family psychology; male gender roles.

Davis Ying Ja, Professor; Ph.D., Washington (Seattle), 1981. Substance abuse and AIDS treatment and prevention in multicultural communities; program evaluation in behavioral health systems, including managed-care systems; juvenile and adult justice systems, including drug courts and alternative community approaches in juvenile probation; organizational systems with a focus on managed behavioral health policy, evaluation, and analysis; early childhood prevention and intervention; multicultural influences in family therapy; cost analysis; studies in programs for assertive community treatment (PACT).

Eduardo Morales, Professor; Ph.D., Texas Tech, 1976. HIV, substance abuse, intervention for adolescents, community prevention, ethnic and sexual minorities, drug exposed infants and parents, juvenile delinquency.

Natalie Porter, Professor; Ph.D., Delaware, 1981. Feminist and antiracist models of clinical training and supervision, cognitive and emotional developmental changes in individuals abused or traumatized as children, feminist therapy supervision and ethics.

Kristin Samuelson, Assistant Professor; Ph.D., Virginia, 1998. Trauma/post-traumatic stress disorder, neuropsychological and psychodiagnostic assessment, pediatric psychology.

Paul D. Werner, Professor; Ph.D., Berkeley, 1976. Personality and family assessment, research on violent behavior, gender roles, psychology of social change, psychology of population and family planning, aesthetics, clinical research.

ALLIANT INTERNATIONAL UNIVERSITY

California School of Professional Psychology
Psy.D. in Clinical Psychology

Programs of Study

The Doctor of Psychology in Clinical Psychology (Psy.D.) programs at the California School of Professional Psychology (CSPP) provide a strong foundation in clinical psychology, emphasizing the applications of theory and research to clinical practice and addressing the societal need for professionals who deliver or facilitate the delivery of psychological services to diverse populations, including underserved and poorly served populations. The programs are designed to develop professional clinical psychologists who bring critical-thinking and active problem-solving skills to bear on human problems and who have acquired the skills necessary to deliver a variety of clinical services to people from diverse backgrounds within many types of settings and institutions. Students are educated and trained to be able to intervene effectively using multiple methods of assessment and intervention, working with diverse populations, across many settings, and in changing and evolving contexts.

In the first and second years, all programs provide an extensive background in the foundations of psychology; they develop students' basic scientific understanding and practice skills. Students participate in clerkship or practicum experiences requiring 8–20 hours of student time per week in their first and/or second years. At this level, students receive training in specific skills, such as psychological assessment, evaluation of clients and programs, and intervention and psychotherapeutic techniques. They are also introduced to the roles and ethical practices of professional psychologists.

During the second or third year, students must pass formal evaluations, which may include written comprehensive or preliminary examinations, in order to be advanced to doctoral candidacy. Each program establishes specific methods and procedures for evaluating students. Evaluations focus on a student's demonstrated academic ability, expected competency in research, interpersonal competencies, and understanding of the basic theoretical foundations of psychology.

The curriculum for third and fourth year students includes advanced training in theoretical issues, psychological intervention techniques, professional ethics and issues, psychopharmacology, and supervision. Students also participate in the dissertation or doctoral project, field placements, growth experiences, and elective courses.

While required course work is substantial, in the final years there is also time to develop special interests. Internships occupy 20 to 40 hours per week, intensifying students' mastery of professional skills and providing supervisory experience. Clinical internship requirements meet and, in some programs, exceed the 1,500 hours of predoctoral internship accepted by the California Board of Psychology for licensure. CSPP doctoral course requirements at all campuses are designed to fulfill all of the state licensing requirements of California, and, in some cases, they exceed the requirements.

In content, the clinical psychology curricula reflect four areas of study—applied research, professional skills, professional concepts, and personal growth. A student's course work each year consists of required courses and electives from each of these areas.

Research Facilities

The Alliant library system is a distributed collection of print, media, and electronic resources with primary strengths in psychology (clinical, forensic, organizational, and educational), business administration, global liberal studies, and education. The collections have a multicultural and international focus.

Alliant's largest library facility is in San Diego on the Scripps Ranch Campus, but comprehensive specialized collections are also available in San Francisco, Los Angeles, and Fresno. The collections at California locations are represented in the Web-based library catalog and total over 200,000 physical volumes, 640 current print journal subscriptions, and 1,200 videos.

The Alliant libraries share access to online resources, including 28 research databases, full-text content from over 16,000 journals, and 5,200 e-books. Resources that are not available on site may be requested from other Alliant libraries via the shared online catalog or from LINK+, a network of thirty-eight California and Nevada libraries with over 6 million titles.

An accomplished staff of librarians and support personnel provide services across the University and to distance learners. Services include reference, bibliographic research consultation, information literacy instruction, interlibrary loan, document delivery, and course reserves.

In each library, computers are available to access the Internet, electronic books and journals, and online research database resources, such as PsycINFO, Lexis-Nexis, OCLC FirstSearch, Digital Dissertations, Social Science Citation Index, Medline, ERIC, and Criminal Justice Periodical Index. Most of these online resources may also be accessed from home or office.

Financial Aid

Alliant offers financial aid to qualified students in the form of loans, scholarships, grants, and part-time employment. The federal government, state government, Alliant, and private sources finance these programs. Federal and state financial aid funds are only available to students who are United States citizens or permanent residents of the United States.

Financial aid packages, although predominantly in the form of loans, may also include scholarships and student employment. Most students interested in school-based financial aid pursue college work-study. A limited number of teaching and research assistantships are available. In addition, students can work on campus in a number of departments, including admissions and field placement. Stipends generally average about $1000 per assistantship per semester. For more information, students should e-mail finaid@alliant.edu.

Cost of Study

CSPP doctoral program tuition is $865 per semester unit. A full-time student averages 30 units per year. Students completing an internship in one full-time year or in two years of half-time rotations pay $3850 and $2400 per semester, respectively. Fees are additional.

Living and Housing Costs

Students can expect to pay between $700 and $1500 per month plus utilities (gas and electricity) for an off-campus, unfurnished, one-bedroom apartment. On-campus housing is available on the San Diego campus; the cost of room and board for an academic year is $15,480 for a two-person suite, $11,700 for a one-person suite, $10,800 for a private room, and $8250 for double occupancy.

Student Group

Alliant prides itself on the diversity of its student body. The University has students from almost every state and international students from sixty-four countries, including Cameroon, Botswana, Greece, Iceland, Portugal, and Turkey. There are 2,626 full-time and 1,284 part-time students at Alliant International University, of whom 76 percent are women and approximately 46 percent are from groups underrepresented in higher education. Within the California School of Professional Psychology, there are 2,148 students.

Location

The Psy.D. in Clinical Psychology is offered at five of Alliant's campuses in California: Fresno, Los Angeles, Sacramento, San Diego, and San Francisco. The Clinical Psychology Psy.D. program is also offered in Hong Kong, in association with the School of Continuing and Professional Education (SCOPE), City University of Hong Kong.

The University and The School

Alliant International University focuses on preparing students for professional careers. Formed in July 2001 through the combination of the California School of Professional Psychology (CSPP) and United States International University (USIU), Alliant is an independent, not-for-profit institution of higher education with a history distinguished by innovation. The University's mission is to educate citizens of the world, ensuring the acquisition of knowledge and competencies that are essential to live, lead, and solve problems in a global society.

CSPP, the largest of the five schools and centers at Alliant, prepares students for careers as clinical psychologists, marital and family therapists, and other mental health professionals. While earning their degree, students work in a wide variety of settings, establishing themselves in the professional community as experienced practitioners. By the time students earn their degrees, they have already developed a network of colleagues and professional affiliations that make them exceptionally attractive to employers as vital contributors to their field.

Applying

Applicants should have a bachelor's or master's degree in psychology (preferred), with a minimum GPA of 3.0. Students must submit the completed application, the application fee, official transcripts from all institutions attended, a personal statement, and letters of recommendation. An interview is required. International students must also submit TOEFL/TWE scores. The application deadline is January 15. Submission of a complete application by the January 15 deadline guarantees notification by April 1. Applications submitted after January 15 are welcome, but are reviewed on a space-available basis.

Correspondence and Information

Central Contact Center
Alliant International University
10455 Pomerado Road
San Diego, California 92131
Phone: 866-U-ALLIANT (toll-free)
Fax: 858-635-4555
E-mail: admissions@alliant.edu
Web site: http://www.alliant.edu/cspp

Alliant International University

THE FACULTY AND THEIR RESEARCH

Fresno and Sacramento Campuses

Lynette E. Bassman, Associate Professor, Fresno; Assistant Program Director; and Coordinator of the Health Psychology Emphasis Area; Ph.D., NYU, 1990. Alternative treatments for mental health, psychodynamic correlates of self-care behavior, defense mechanisms and health.

Wesley T. Forbes, Professor, Fresno, and Director of Clinical Field Placement; Ed.D., Massachusetts Amherst, 1983. Child/family, adolescents, delinquency/corrections, multicultural issues in psychology, ban on IQ testing of African Americans and other ethnic minorities in California, system of multipluralistic assessment.

Ronald L. Gandolfo, Professor, Fresno, and Coordinator of the Clinical Forensic Emphasis Area; Ph.D., LSU, 1970; ABPP Diplomat in Clinical Psychology. Individual therapy, intellectual and personality assessment, child custody, process of supervision, delivery of psychological services, clinical diagnostic studies, marital issues.

Sue A. Kuba, Professor, Fresno, and Associate Program Director, Online Psy.D. Option; Ph.D., California School of Professional Psychology–Fresno, 1981. Women's health, eating disorders in multicultural populations, phenomenology, sister relationships, women's development, gay and lesbian issues.

Elizabeth Limberg, Assistant Professor, Sacramento, and Assistant Program Director; Ph.D., California School of Professional Psychology–Fresno, 1999. Infant-preschool mental health, family therapy, play therapy, community mental health.

Kevin J. O'Connor, Professor, Fresno/Sacramento; Program Director; and Coordinator, Ecosystemic Clinical Psychology Emphasis Area; Ph.D., Toledo, 1980. Parent-child attachment, child psychotherapy process, play therapy, attachment disorders, child abuse, impact of parental narcissism, child development, sex role socialization, Ecosystemic child psychotherapy, art therapy, and Theraplay.

Suni Peterson, Assistant Professor, Sacramento; Ph.D., Florida, 1997. Health psychology with minority populations, evidence-based interventions, health promotion, cardiovascular disease, cancer.

John D. Preston, Professor, Fresno/Sacramento; Psy.D., Baylor, 1979. Psychopharmacology, neuropsychology, trauma, aging.

Ronald W. Teague, Professor, Fresno; Ph.D., California School of Professional Psychology–Berkeley, 1973; ABPP, Diplomate in Clinical Psychology. Psychology of antiquity, psychohistory phenomenology, Jungian psychology, psychoanalysis, psychoanthropology, psychology and the humanities, history of psychology.

Los Angeles Campus

John Bakaly, Associate Professor; Ph.D., USC, 1988. Clinical intervention with children and adolescents and their families; treatment of depression, anxiety, and general childhood disorders.

Leena Banerjee Brown, Professor; Ph.D., Virginia Tech, 1985. Presence and self-awareness, multicultural psychology interfaces with family systems therapy, infant family mental health, paradigms of knowledge.

Walter Brown, Assistant Professor; Ph.D., UCLA, 1995. Pediatric psychology, substance abuse, working with at-risk juveniles, training of health and mental health professionals.

Elaine Burke, Associate Professor; Psy.D., Denver, 1989. Pediatric and adult neuropsychology, assessment and culture, health and culture, gender and culture.

John V. Caffaro, Professor; Ph.D., Fielding Institute, 1989. Child maltreatment, sibling relationships, post-traumatic stress disorder, group psychotherapy.

William Chien, Assistant Professor; Psy.D., California School of Professional Psychology–Los Angeles, 1996. Asian American mental health issues, psychotherapy with Asian Americans, bereavement, depression.

Victor Cohen, Associate Professor; Ph.D., Michigan, 1981. Counter transference phenomenon and the interpersonal processes in therapist-client psychotherapy relationships, psychotherapist self-development and teaching and training of clinical skills, alternative paradigms for studying subjective and experiential aspects of the psychotherapy process.

Judith Holloway, Assistant Professor; Ph.D., California School of Professional Psychology–Los Angeles, 1991. Ecopsychology, adventure therapy, relationship to nature and healing the natural environment, LGBTQ issues.

Dennis S. Klos, Professor; Ph.D., Harvard, 1974. Interpersonal conflict resolution, assessment and intervention with couples, professional development, academic administration.

Richard R. Kopp, Distinguished Professor; Ph.D., Chicago, 1972. Use of metaphor in psychotherapy, Adlerian psychology, psychotherapy integration, resolving interpersonal and intrapersonal power conflicts.

Glenn Isoa Masuda, Associate Professor; Ph.D., Washington (Seattle), 1988. Asian American mental health, community mental health service delivery, interventions with adolescents, diversity competency training.

Randy Noblitt, Professor and Program Director, Los Angeles Psy.D. Program; Ph.D., North Texas, 1978. Cult and ritual abuse, child abuse, trauma and dissociation, dissociative identity disorder, psychopharmacology.

Jeffrey Tirengel, Professor; Psy.D., California School of Professional Psychology–Los Angeles, 1991. Positive psychology in diverse cultural communities, resilience, strength-based approaches, attachment, couples, emotionally focused interventions, evidence-based practice and practice-based evidence.

San Diego Campus

Anabel Bejarano, Assistant Professor; Ph.D., CUNY, 2000. Childhood trauma, Latino mental health, child development and attachment, multicultural psychology.

Steven F. Bucky, Professor and Director of Professional Training; Ph.D., Cincinnati, 1970. Childhood psychopathology, chemical dependency, forensic psychology, ethics, alcoholic family, children of alcoholics, sports psychology.

Joanne E. Callan, Distinguished Professor; Ph.D., Texas, 1970. Child and adolescent development, adjustment, and psychopathology (including gender development); parenting and school support: preschool through high school; life-span development: female development and psychology; psychoanalysis and psychoanalytic theory and psychotherapy; training in professional psychology; ethics.

David J. Diamond, Associate Professor; Ph.D., Michigan, 1983. Reproductive trauma, psychoanalytic theory and psychopathology, clinical inference process and other psychotherapy topics, child and adolescent development.

Marina Dorian, Assistant Professor; Ph.D., Illinois at Urbana-Champagne, 2007. Couple and family intervention, gender roles in marriage, couples communication, cross-cultural studies, intimacy.

Donald Eulert, Professor; Ph.D., New Mexico, 1968. C. G. Jung's theories, postmodern cultural and spirituality issues, moral development, creativity, integrative psychology.

Veronica Gutierrez, Assistant Professor; Ph.D., California, Santa Barbara, 2004. Issues of multiculturalism; lesbian, gay, and bisexual issues; therapist competence in multicultural issues; therapeutic process and outcome. Dr. Gutierrez' professional background includes work with diverse student populations, specifically Latinos.

Debra Kawahara, Assistant Professor; Ph.D., California School of Professional Psychology–Los Angeles, 1994. Multicultural and cross-cultural psychology, Asian American mental health, women's issues, cultural competency, qualitative research methodology.

Mojgan Khademi, Assistant Professor; Psy.D., Indiana of Pennsylvania, 1992. Psychodynamic theory and treatment. Dr. Khademi's work at several university counseling centers has led to interest in psychotherapy intervention and treatment outcome studies; he supervises dissertations in treatment outcomes, eating disorders, suicide, and multicultural issues and teaches first-year psychotherapy sequence and advanced seminars in feminism and eating disorders.

Gary W. Lawson, Professor; Ph.D., Southern Illinois, 1975. Clinical psychology, marriage and family therapy, chemical dependency.

James N. Madero, Professor; Ph.D., Catholic University, 1975. Projective tests, differential diagnoses, workplace violence prevention, school violence prevention.

Neil G. Ribner, Professor and Program Director; Ph.D., Cincinnati, 1971. Family studies, divorce, stepfamilies, custody, parenting, siblings.

Ronald Stolberg, Assistant Professor; Ph.D., Pacific Graduate School of Psychology, 2001. Personality assessment instruments with an emphasis on the MMPI-2/MMPI-A, assessment instruments use among practicing clinicians, standard of care practices, suicide, clinical work with adolescents.

San Francisco Campus

Diane M. Adams, Associate Professor and Associate Dean, CSPP; Ph.D., Wright Institute, 1983. Adult development; psychotherapy; biographical interviewing; case histories and theoretical or conceptual analytic thesis; clinical and theoretical issues involving ethnic minority populations, particularly African American; application of psychoanalytic theory in practice and research.

Stephen Blum, Professor; Ph.D., Berkeley, 1973. Ethical issues in health, community psychology, health policy and administration, birth and death of persons and programs, managed (mental) health care.

Edward F. Bourg, Professor; Ph.D., California School of Professional Psychology–Berkeley, 1973. Family and marital therapy and process, prevention and rehabilitation in chronic and acute illness, roles of relaxation and meditation in health psychology.

Tai Chang, Assistant Professor; Ph.D., Illinois at Urbana-Champaign, 1999. Acculturation and identity development processes as well as their relations to adjustment and help-seeking, particularly among Asian Americans; interface of counseling and the Internet, including online support and online information regarding mental illness and psychology.

Eddie Chiu, Assistant Professor and Director, Psychological Service Center; Ph.D., California School of Professional Psychology–Los Angeles, 1996. Ethnic minority stress and coping, immigrant and refugee mental health, cultural-specific assessment and intervention, problem gambling, child and family issues.

Harriet Curtis-Boles, Associate Professor; Ph.D., Berkeley, 1984. Issues related to multiculturalism and peoples of color, psychotherapy process and outcome with African American clients, influence of violence exposure on children and families in the inner cities, African American women and substance abuse.

Samuel Gerson, Professor; Ph.D., Texas at Austin, 1978. Intersubjectivity, gender, and sexuality; interaction of affect and clinical judgment; the process of therapeutic interactions; schools of psychodynamic psychotherapy.

Frederick J. Heide, Associate Professor; Ph.D., Penn State, 1981. Charismatic communication, using humor in psychotherapy, constructivist therapies, transpersonal psychology, cognitive therapy, psychedelics.

Valata Jenkins-Monroe, Professor; Ph.D., California School of Professional Psychology–Berkeley, 1978. Cognitive styles and problem-solving abilities of Third World children, development of children of substance abusive mothers, child sexual abuse treatment, African American women and substance abuse, intergenerational study of black teen parenting, race and racism, special needs children, forensic psychology.

Gerald Y. Michaels, Associate Professor and Director of the PSC Child/Family Program; Ph.D., Michigan, 1981. Developmental psychopathology, transition to parenthood, adolescent pregnancy, parents' and children's social perceptions in the family, children of divorce, primary prevention strategies in mental health.

Valory Mitchell, Professor and Coordinator of the Gender Studies Emphasis Area; Ph.D., Berkeley, 1983. Psychology of women; development of personality across the lifespan; lesbian/gay issues; interface of feminist, self, relational, and psychodynamic theory; spirituality and religion.

Rhoda Olkin, Distinguished Professor; Ph.D., California, Santa Barbara, 1981. Social model of disability; disability rights activism; marriage and family therapy; psychopathology, diagnosis, and case formulation; cognitive behavioral therapy.

Elena Padron, Assistant Professor and Director of Professional Training; Ph.D., Minnesota, 2003. Developmental psychopathology and attachment theory, social-emotional development and psychopathology, early childhood development, child and family psychotherapy, culturally sensitive therapeutic models for use with Latino families.

Patrick Petti, Assistant Professor; Ph.D., California School of Professional Psychology–Alameda, 1991. Education and training in psychology, clinical competency evaluation, child development, treatment approaches in child therapy.

Julie Shulman, Assistant Professor; Ph.D., Memphis, 2003. Sexual and gender identity, same-sex couples, feminist theory and practice, gender issues in therapy, experiential therapy, multiculturally competent therapy, supervision/training.

Alan J. Swope, Professor; Ph.D., Columbia, 1969. Psychoanalytic psychotherapy, core curriculum in professional psychology, psychology and technology, theories of culture, evaluation of clinical competency, music and personality.

Daniel O. Taube, Professor and Program Director; J.D., Villanova, 1985; Ph.D., Hahnemann, 1987. Ethical and legal issues for mental health professionals, child maltreatment, substance abuse.

Christopher D. Tori, Professor Emeritus; Ph.D., Kentucky, 1971. Psychotherapy methods, cross-cultural psychology, Buddhism, religion and spirituality, addictions, psycholinguistics, psychometrics and statistics, international studies.

Diane Zelman, Associate Professor and Coordinator of the Health Psychology Emphasis Area; Ph.D., Wisconsin–Madison, 1989. Health psychology, families and chronic illness, anxiety disorders, neuropsychology, addictions, psychopharmacology.

ALLIANT INTERNATIONAL UNIVERSITY

Center for Forensic Studies

Programs of Study

Forensic psychology is the application of the science and profession of psychology to questions and issues relating to law and the legal system. At Alliant, the practitioner-scholar programs at the Center for Forensic Studies (CFS) prepare professionals with both the academic background and the real-world skill they need to contribute to the field of forensic psychology. By studying forensic psychology at Alliant, students are part of a rapidly growing field.

Specializations available to Center for Forensic Studies students include assessment and treatment of sex offenders, child custody, child neglect and abuse, clergy and teacher sex abuse, competence to receive death penalty, correctional psychology, criminal profiling, expert witness, investigative psychology, jury selection, neuropsychology, police psychology, school violence, terrorism, and violence prevention in schools and in the workplace.

Programs are associated with a wide range of government, community, legal, and nonprofit organizations, and, as such, students are able to select internships in a wide range of settings, including federal, state, and local law enforcement; prisons; government agencies; juvenile halls; and others. Students not only learn about their chosen professional field, but also develop a network of business contacts.

The Doctor of Psychology (Psy.D.) in forensic psychology is offered at Fresno, Irvine, Los Angeles, Sacramento, and San Diego. With an emphasis on the application of forensic psychological theory and practice, this degree prepares students for a career in one of the fastest growing fields in the country. Course topics include police stress, neuropsychology, addiction, sex offending, domestic violence, serial and mass murder, juvenile delinquency, and stalking. Course work also emphasizes rules of evidence and discovery, examination and cross-examination, and expert witness testimony. Beyond receiving rigorous academic training, students acquire experience in treatment and assessment through field training in a variety of settings. For full-time students, the Psy.D. program can be completed in four years.

The Ph.D. in forensic psychology, offered only in Fresno, focuses on research and theory. The degree prepares students for a wide range of positions, from university professor to professional researcher to practicing forensic psychologist. In the clinical track, students are trained as forensic clinicians, with an emphasis on obtaining clinical licensure. Course work focuses on the integration between forensic clinical psychology, forensic research, criminology, and law. In the policy and justice track, with an emphasis on psychologeal research, courses focus on the legal and justice system, organization development, expert witness testimony, human trafficking, torture, war crimes, genocide, civil rights, federal administration, international treaties, and forensic psychology. For full-time students, the Ph.D. program can be completed in five years.

Research Facilities

The Alliant library system is a distributed collection of print, media, and electronic resources with primary strengths in psychology (clinical, forensic, organizational, and educational), business administration, global liberal studies, and education. The collections have a multicultural and international focus.

Alliant's largest library facility is in San Diego on the Scripps Ranch Campus, but comprehensive specialized collections are also available in San Francisco, Los Angeles, and Fresno. The collections at California locations are represented in the Web-based library catalog and total over 200,000 physical volumes, 640 current print journal subscriptions, and 1,200 videos.

The Alliant libraries share access to online resources, including 28 research databases, full-text content from over 16,000 journals, and 5,200 e-books. Resources that are not available on site may be requested from other Alliant libraries via the shared online catalog or from LINK+, a network of thirty-eight California and Nevada libraries with over 6 million titles.

An accomplished staff of librarians and support personnel provide services across the University and to distance learners. Services include reference, bibliographic research consultation, information literacy instruction, interlibrary loan, document delivery, and course reserves.

In each library, computers are available to access the Internet, electronic books and journals, and online research database resources, such as PsycINFO, Lexis-Nexis, OCLC FirstSearch, Digital Dissertations, Social Science Citation Index, Medline, ERIC, and Criminal Justice Periodical Index. Most of these online resources may also be accessed from home or office.

Financial Aid

Alliant offers financial aid to qualified students in the form of loans, scholarships, grants, and part-time employment. The federal government, state government, Alliant, and private sources finance these programs. Federal and state financial aid funds are only available to students who are United States citizens or permanent residents of the United States.

Financial aid packages, although predominantly in the form of loans, may also include scholarships and student employment. Most students interested in school-based financial aid pursue college work-study. A limited number of teaching and research assistantships are available. In addition, students can work on campus in a number of departments, including admissions and field placement. Stipends generally average about $1000 per assistantship per semester. For more information, students should e-mail finaid@alliant.edu.

Cost of Study

Doctoral programs cost $915 per semester unit.

Living and Housing Costs

Students can expect to pay between $700 and $1500 per month plus utilities (gas and electricity) for an off-campus, unfurnished, one-bedroom apartment. On-campus housing is available on the San Diego campus; the cost of room and board for an academic year is $15,480 for a 2 -person suite, $11,700 for a 1-person suite, $10,800 for a private room, and $8250 for double occupancy.

Student Outcomes

Center for Forensic Studies graduates hold positions such as staff psychologist/condemned coordinator (death row) for San Quentin State Prison. Many work for the court system, district attorneys, or public defenders. Others are critical incident specialists or psychologists with police departments. The California Department of Corrections and Rehabilitation (CDC) is one of the largest employers of forensic psychologists in the state, and many CFS graduates secure positions with the CDC. Other graduates are in private practice as expert witnesses. In addition, many choose to become faculty members and instruct at the undergraduate and graduate levels.

Location

Center for Forensic Studies programs are located on Alliant's Fresno, Irvine, Los Angeles, Sacramento, and San Diego campuses.

The University

Founded in 2001, Alliant International University is a nonprofit university that prepares students for professional careers in psychology, education, business, and forensics. Alliant offers mentored field experiences and individual coaching that allow students to develop hands-on professional skills and practical experience with clients. An exceptionally diverse faculty and student body helps graduates learn to work productively with colleagues and clients from different cultural and international backgrounds. *U.S. News & World Report* ranked Alliant number one in international diversity among national doctoral universities. According to *Diverse* magazine, Alliant awarded more doctorate degrees to minority students than any other U.S. university. With headquarters in San Francisco and San Diego, Alliant also has campuses in Fresno, Los Angeles, Irvine, and Sacramento, California. Alliant also hosts accredited programs in Mexico City, Mexico; Hong Kong, China; and Tokyo, Japan.

Applying

Applicants must have a bachelor's or master's degree in psychology, forensic psychology, criminology, criminal justice, social work, or law, with a minimum GPA of 3.0 both in psychology courses and overall. Students with lower GPAs may apply but must submit the GPA exemption form in the application. Students must submit the completed application, the $70 application fee, and official transcripts from all institutions attended. An interview is required. Applicants are strongly encouraged to submit GRE scores, but they are not required. International students must also submit TOEFL scores. Applications are considered on a rolling admissions basis (no deadline). Classes may close, so early applications are encouraged.

Correspondence and Information

Alliant Admissions
Alliant International University
Phone: 866—U-ALLIANT (866-825-5426, toll-free)
E-mail: admissions@alliant.edu

5130 East Clinton Way
Fresno, California 93727-2014

2500 Michelson Drive
Irvine, California 92612-1548

(Los Angeles metro area)
1000 South Fremont Avenue
Alhambra, California 91803

425 University Avenue
Sacramento, California 95825-6509

10455 Pomerado Road
San Diego, California 92131-1799

Alliant International University–Fresno

THE FACULTY AND THEIR RESEARCH

Core Faculty

Diane M. Beneventi, Regional Field Training Director; Ph.D., CSPP at Alliant, 1996. Neuropsychology.
Kyle Boone, Associate Professor and Program Director, Los Angeles; Ph.D., California School of Professional Psychology, 1984. Malingering and neuropsychology.
Peter English, Coordinator, Ph.D. Clinical Track; Ph.D., Arizona, 2003. Criminology, policy and law.
Valerie Forward, Assistant Professor; Ph.D., California School of Professional Psychology, 1984.
Eric Hickey, Professor and Systemwide Director, Center for Forensic Studies; Ph.D., Brigham Young, 1990. Etiology of violence and serial crime.
William Holcomb, Program Director, Fresno; Ph.D., Missouri–Columbia, 1979. Abnormal psychology, human relations in organizations.
Robert A. Leark, Associate Professor and Interim Program Director, San Diego; Ph.D., US International, 1982. Neuropsychology, test construction, malingering and ADHD.
James N. Madero, Professor; Psy.D., Catholic University, 1975. Projective tests, differential diagnoses, workplace violence prevention, school violence prevention.
Eva McKenzie, Assistant Professor; Ph.D., Fuller Theological Seminary. Forensic evaluations: family, dependency, and criminal courts; victimology: child maltreatment, intimate partner violence.
Jana Price-Sharps, Assistant Professor; Ph.D., University of the Pacific, 1999. Drug and alcohol abuse and its behavioral and neurological consequences, attention deficit hyperactivity disorder.
Sherry Skidmore, Assistant Professor; Ph.D., US International, 1975. Neuropsychology and abnormal psychology.
Sean Sterling, Interim Program Director, Irvine; Ph.D., California School of Professional Psychology, 1996. Cultural competency; behavioral, cognitive, and social learning.
Lenore Artie Tate, Associate Professor and Assistant Program Director, Sacramento; Ph.D., California School of Professional Psychology. Geriatrics, neuropsychology, social and cultural psychology.
Dale White, Assistant Professor; Ph.D., California School of Professional Psychology, 1996. Foster children and social problem solving, treatment variables and inpatient mental health, factors underlying academic success.

Adjunct Faculty

Burton Alperson, Ph.D., Michigan State, 1967.
Robert Briones, Psy.D., California School of Professional Psychology, 2005.
Lynn O. Bundy, Ph.D., University of the Pacific, 1988.
Natalie Claussen-Rogers, Psy.D., Alliant International, 2003.
Phillip Corrado, Ph.D., Alliant International, 1997.
Dennis Dixon, Ph.D., Louisiana State, 2006.
Annette Lorene Ermshar, Ph.D., Loma Linda, 2000.
Debra F. Glaser, Ph.D., California School of Professional Psychology, 1983.
Adam K. Herdina, Psy.D., La Verne, 2004.
James Kelly Jr., J.D., California, Hastings Law, 1992.
Gerard Labuschagne, Ph.D., Pretoria (South Africa).
Rachel Latter, Ph.D., Alliant International, 2003.
Theresa Lu, Ph.D., Southern Illinois, 1997.
William V. McTaggart Jr., J.D., Loyola, 1978.
Deborah S. Miora, Ph.D., California School of Professional Psychology, 1987.
Douglas Noll, J.D., University of the Pacific, 1977.
Gaetano Pascale, Ph.D., Bologna (Italy).
Michael Reid, J.D., San Joaquin College of Law, 1992.
Matthew Sharps, Ph.D., Colorado, 1986.
David Tanner, Ph.D., Texas A&M, 1984.
Amy Tillery, Ph.D., Alliant International.

ALLIANT INTERNATIONAL UNIVERSITY

California School of Professional Psychology
Programs in Marital and Family Therapy

Programs of Study

The California School of Professional Psychology (CSPP) at Alliant offers two graduate programs in Marital and Family Therapy (MFT)—the Master of Arts (M.A.) and the Doctor of Psychology (Psy.D.). The M.A. program is offered at the Irvine, Los Angeles, Sacramento, and San Diego campuses, and the Psy.D. program is available at the Irvine, Sacramento, and San Diego campuses.

The programs provide students with the essential training needed to pursue a career as a professional marital and family therapist. Graduates become skilled in theory, research, and clinical practice, with the ability to integrate individual and systemic therapeutic models in an international, multicultural environment.

Students in both the master's and doctoral MFT programs are trained to treat relational mental health issues with individuals, couples, families, and larger organizations from a systemic perspective. As such, attention is directed to relationships and interaction patterns. Students develop skills in the mental health assessment, diagnosis, and treatment of individuals and relationship systems. The programs provide an integrative approach to the major systemic theories and interventions.

To prepare students for the clinical practicum experience, the MFT programs provide intensive theoretical and practical skill-based training. The programs place students in community-based practicum and internship sites where students get real-world training experiences with a diverse clientele.

The master's program contains the same course work as the first two years of the doctoral program. Consequently, all of the master's program requirements transfer into the doctoral program. Those students entering the doctoral program with a bachelor's degree can earn a licensable marital and family therapy master's degree as part of their doctoral studies upon completion of the requirements for that degree.

In addition to the program course work and practicum experiences, students may choose to specialize in select areas of concentration offered at their campus, including biofeedback, chemical dependency counseling, gerontology, and Latin American family therapy.

Classes are typically held in the evenings to allow students to work during the day. Daytime classes are also held in San Diego and Irvine for students who prefer to attend during the day.

Research Facilities

The Alliant library system is a distributed collection of print, media, and electronic resources with primary strengths in psychology (clinical, forensic, organizational, and educational), business administration, global liberal studies, and education. The collections have a multicultural and international focus.

Alliant's largest library facility is in San Diego on the Scripps Ranch Campus, but comprehensive specialized collections are also available in San Francisco, Los Angeles, and Fresno. The collections at California locations are represented in the Web-based library catalog and total over 200,000 physical volumes, 640 current print journal subscriptions, and 1,200 videos.

The Alliant libraries share access to online resources, including 28 research databases, full-text content from over 16,000 journals, and 5,200 e-books. Resources that are not available on site may be requested from other Alliant libraries via the shared online catalog or from LINK+, a network of thirty-eight California and Nevada libraries with over 6 million titles.

An accomplished staff of librarians and support personnel provide services across the University and to distance learners. Services include reference, bibliographic research consultation, information literacy instruction, interlibrary loan, document delivery, and course reserves.

In each library, computers are available to access the Internet, electronic books and journals, and online research database resources, such as PsycINFO, Lexis-Nexis, OCLC FirstSearch, Digital Dissertations, Social Science Citation Index, Medline, ERIC, and Criminal Justice Periodical Index. Most of these online resources may also be accessed from home or office.

Financial Aid

Alliant offers financial aid to qualified students in the form of loans, scholarships, grants, and part-time employment. The federal government, state government, Alliant, and private sources finance these programs. Federal and state financial aid funds are only available to students who are United States citizens or permanent residents of the United States.

Financial aid packages, although predominantly in the form of loans, may also include scholarships and student employment. Most students interested in school-based financial aid pursue college work-study. A limited number of teaching and research assistantships are available. In addition, students can work on campus in a number of departments, including admissions and field placement. Stipends generally average about $1000 per assistantship per semester. For more information, students should e-mail finaid@alliant.edu.

Cost of Study

CSPP master's and doctoral program tuition is $865 per semester unit. A full-time student averages 30 units per year. Fees are additional.

Living and Housing Costs

Students can expect to pay between $700 and $1500 per month plus utilities (gas and electricity) for an off-campus, unfurnished, one-bedroom apartment. On-campus housing is available on the San Diego campus; the cost of room and board for an academic year is $15,480 for a 2-person suite, $11,700 for a 1-person suite, $10,800 for a private room, and $8250 for double occupancy.

Student Group

Alliant prides itself on the diversity of its student body. The University has students from almost every state and international students from sixty-four countries, including Cameroon, Botswana, Greece, Iceland, Portugal, and Turkey. There are 2,626 full-time and 1,284 part-time students at Alliant International University, of whom 76 percent are women and approximately 46 percent are from groups underrepresented in higher education. Within the California School of Professional Psychology, there are 2,148 students.

Location

Among the safest cities in America, Irvine has a strong base of technology industries along with a wealth of community entertainment, recreation, and educational resources. Irvine is within easy driving distance of beautiful Corona Del Mar and the sun-drenched sand of Laguna Beach and Newport Beach. With more than 9 million people in the over 4,000 square miles of Los Angeles County, Los Angeles is California's largest city and the second-largest in the nation. One of the premier cities in the Pacific Rim, it is a center for culture and commerce. The Sacramento campus is easily accessible from all major thoroughfares in the metropolitan Sacramento area. Sacramento is California's capital, providing many great cultural and recreational opportunities and activities. San Diego is a vibrant, metropolitan city with a laid-back, small-town feel. The area is filled with an incredible selection of activities and attractions that make San Diego one of the most popular spots in the United States.

The University and The School

Alliant International University focuses on preparing students for professional careers. Formed in July 2001 through the combination of the California School of Professional Psychology and United States International University (USIU), Alliant is an independent, not-for-profit institution of higher education with a history distinguished by innovation. The University's mission is to educate citizens of the world, ensuring the acquisition of knowledge and competencies that are essential to live, lead, and solve problems in a global society.

CSPP, the largest of the five schools and centers at Alliant, prepares students for careers as clinical psychologists, marital and family therapists, and other mental health professionals. While earning their degrees, students work in a wide variety of settings, establishing themselves in the professional community as experienced practitioners. By the time students earn their degrees, they have already developed a network of colleagues and professional affiliations that make them exceptionally attractive to employers as vital contributors to their field.

Applying

Applicants should have a bachelor's degree in psychology (preferred), with a minimum GPA of 3.0. Students must submit the completed application, the application fee, official transcripts from all institutions attended, a personal statement, and letters of recommendation. An interview is required for doctoral applicants. International students must also submit TOEFL/TWE scores. The application deadlines are January 15 (priority deadline), March 1, and April 16. Applications submitted after the priority deadline are welcome but are reviewed on a space-available basis.

Correspondence and Information

Central Contact Center
Alliant International University
10455 Pomerado Road
San Diego, California 92131

Phone: 866-U-ALLIANT (toll-free)
Fax: 858-635-4555
E-mail: admissions@alliant.edu
Web site: http://mft.alliant.edu

Alliant International University

THE FACULTY AND THEIR RESEARCH

Stephen Brown, Associate Professor, Irvine; Ph.D., USC, 1996. Quantitative and qualitative research design in MFT, measurement and evaluation in MFT, statistical analysis, professional education and teaching, performance improvement and quality assurance in mental health service delivery.

Robin Denise Bullette, Assistant Professor, Irvine; Psy.D., US International, 2000. MFT teaching, training, and supervision; courtship, marital therapy, and family systems.

Benjamin Caldwell, Assistant Professor and Site Director, Sacramento; Psy.D., Alliant International, 2004. Marital myths, couples therapy outcome, sex education, MFT cost-effectiveness research.

Janice W. Cone, Associate Professor and Site Director, Irvine; Ph.D., Pittsburgh, 1984. Chronic illnesses and family systems, AIDS, sexual abuse, sexuality, family and couple violence, MFT process and outcome research.

Sean Davis, Assistant Professor and Clinical Training Coordinator, Sacramento; Ph.D., Syracuse, 2005. Common factors across effective MFT models, MFT training and supervision, commonalities of healthy and distressed couples, process and outcome research, observational research, bridging the scientist/practitioner gap in MFT.

Janice Ewing, Assistant Professor, San Diego; Ph.D., Virginia Tech, 1997. Postmodern family therapy, clinical training, emotion and physical health, supervision, gender issues in therapy.

Darryl Freeland, Associate Professor, San Diego and Irvine; Ph.D., USC, 1972. Family dynamics, epistemology, chaos theory, women's issues, imagination and the therapy process.

Susan Johnson, Research Professor, San Diego; Ed.D., British Columbia, 1984. Emotionally focused therapy, process and outcome research. Dr. Johnson is the primary developer of emotionally focused therapy and is an internationally recognized leader in the area of couples therapy, theory, and research. Dr. Johnson resides in Ottawa, Canada, and visits Alliant's San Diego campus to lecture and engage in research activities.

Ann Lawson, Professor, San Diego; Ph.D., US International, 1988. Family chemical dependency, intergenerational family processes, family therapy evaluation.

Marianne Miller, Assistant Professor, San Diego; Ph.D., Texas Tech, 2003. Spirituality in therapy and MFT training, supervision, gender, diversity, MFT theories, chronic pain.

Rajeswari Natrajan, Assistant Professor, Irvine; Ph.D., Purdue, 2004. Family interventions and therapy, children in therapy, therapeutic outcome assessments, families in multicultural societies, family therapy training and evaluation, supervision, multicultural issues.

Jason J. Platt, Assistant Professor, Irvine; and Site Director and Program Director, M.A. in Counseling Psychology, Mexico; Ph.D., Syracuse, 1986. Clinical competency, evaluation, supervision, and family therapy training practices; gender and multiculturalism; clinical outcome research; brief family therapy.

Brandon C. Silverthorn, Assistant Professor, Irvine; Ph.D., Michigan State, 2005. Contextual family therapy, client suicide, MFT professional development, therapist well-being, fatherhood, cross-cultural issues.

Narumi Taniguchi, Assistant Professor, San Diego; Ph.D., Texas Tech, 2006. Cross-cultural issues, family of origin, couples therapy, work/family/parenting issues, statistics, quantitative methodology.

H. Luis Vargas, Assistant Professor, San Diego; Ph.D., Loma Linda, 2005. Cross-cultural family therapy, therapy process.

Linna Wang, Associate Professor and Site Director, San Diego; Ph.D., Brigham Young, 1996. Native American studies, cross-cultural issues, women's issues, marriage and family evaluation, survey research, impact of family factors on children.

Scott R. Woolley, Professor, San Diego; and Systemwide Director, Marital and Family Therapy Programs; Ph.D., Texas Tech, 1995. Emotionally focused therapy; courtship, marriage, couples therapy; MFT process and outcome research; observational research; cultural issues in couple relationships; MFT supervision processes; MFT therapy training; chemical dependency.

ANTIOCH UNIVERSITY NEW ENGLAND

Department of Applied Psychology
Master's in Marriage and Family Therapy

Program of Study

The mission of the Marriage and Family Therapy master's program is to provide students with the academic preparation and experience needed to become highly competent marriage and family therapy professionals. The program's goals and philosophy parallel the standards set by the Commission on Accreditation for Marriage and Family Therapy Education (COAMFTE) of the American Association for Marriage and Family Therapy (AAMFT). The Marriage and Family Therapy master's program is designed to be a full-time, concentrated, integrated experience, with students completing the course work and clinical hours in six semesters over two years.

Students enter this two-year program in the summer semester. Classes are held one day a week during fall and spring semesters and two days per week during summer semesters at Antioch New England. There are occasionally other short courses available as electives.

In the first year, students are introduced to systems thinking and to the basic theories of individual and family process, professional ethics, approaches to family assessment and treatment, practical skills in observing and intervening in family and larger systems, and issues of diversity. Students also complete an eight-month 450-hour practicum concurrent with a professional seminar experience.

In the second year, students work on advanced topics including human sexuality and sex therapy, family violence, MFT research methods, groups and larger systems, and substance abuse and enroll in a second year-long professional seminar. A twelve-month, 1,000-hour clinical internship is also required. Through their practicum and internship placements, students complete a minimum of 500 face-to-face clinical hours during the program, at least 250 of which are with couples or families.

There is also a Ph.D. in Marriage and Family Therapy at Antioch New England (see http://www.antiochne.edu/ap/mftphd).

Research Facilities

The librarians at Antioch New England offer professional and personalized reference service for graduate research. Extensive class and research support is available via the library Web site. Access to the library catalog is available through Horace, the library's automated catalog system. Also available are specialized online reference pages for classes and key topics, access to many online bibliographic databases, reserve reading, and links to scholarly Internet resources with full Internet access. In addition, detailed reference instruction, specific research information, an electronic book collection, and specific class support resources are available on the library Web site. All library services, such as book requests, renewals, reference help, and interlibrary loan requests, are available online.

Antioch New England's focused library collection includes print and electronic books and journals, dissertations and theses, audiovisual materials, and government documents. This collection is enhanced by the large collection of more than 300,000 books and 13,000 journal titles at Antioch College Antioch New England's partner in the larger Antioch University Library system. Recent additions include OhioLINK, which offers more than 100 electronic research databases, including a variety of full-text resources and RefWORKS, a bibliographic management program. The Antioch New England Library also participates in local, regional, and national interlibrary loan services.

Financial Aid

Approximately 70 percent of students receive some type of aid, usually in the form of federal loans and work-study. The Jonathan Daniels Scholarship, established in 2003, strives to increase the diversity of the student body in its racial, ethnic, cultural, international, and socioeconomic makeup and to encourage service to underserved groups. All full-time Antioch New England students are eligible, although funding is limited. The completed scholarship form, along with relevant information from the Office of Financial Aid, is forwarded to each academic department for decisions. Awards range from $500 to 50 percent of tuition for a given year.

Cost of Study

Tuition per semester is approximately $7050 for the M.A. in marriage and family therapy with a $350 fee each semester.

Living and Housing Costs

The University's location enables a majority of students to commute to classes from their established homes in various parts of New England. Other students move close to Antioch New England, where they have a varied selection of settings—urban, rural, semi-rural, mountains, or valley—in which to live.

Student Group

About 1,200 students attend Antioch New England. The average age ranges between 25 and 55; women make up 69 percent of the population.

Location

Located in Keene, New Hampshire, Antioch New England is in the heart of the Monadnock region, a picturesque area that has been described as the "Currier & Ives" corner of New Hampshire. The school is geographically situated so that students also have easy access to several popular metropolitan areas, including Boston and Montreal. With a population of nearly 23,000, Keene has been named by the National Trust for Historic Preservation as one of "America's Dozen Distinctive Destinations."

The School and The Department

Antioch University New England offers a rich array of master's and doctoral-level academic programming and institutional activities. The University's values-driven mission and focus on experiential learning, peer interaction, and reflective practice make the Antioch New England experience unique for each individual who is part of this learning community. The Department of Applied Psychology is committed to fostering a multicultural environment and promoting social justice in marriage and family therapy and the mental health field. The programs focus on an examination of the practitioner's role in the larger systems and contexts of society and the global village and encourage students to develop a personal philosophy of psychological, social, and cultural change.

Applying

Students must submit the completed application form, including a resume and an essay; a nonrefundable application fee of $50; an official transcript from each accredited college or university attended, indicating courses taken and degree(s) earned; and three letters of recommendation (four letters for Alternative Admissions Process applicants who do not have a bachelor's degree), preferably from persons who are, or have been, in a position to evaluate the applicant's work. An interview with a department faculty member is required. Antioch New England does not require applicants to the Marriage and Family Therapy master's program to take the Graduate Record Examinations (GRE) or similar written examinations. The GRE is required for applicants to the Ph.D. program.

The application deadline is May 1 for the Marriage and Family Therapy program.

Correspondence and Information

Office of Admissions
Antioch University New England
40 Avon Street
Keene, New Hampshire 03431-3516

Phone: 800-490-3310 (toll-free)
Fax: 603-357-0718
E-mail: petersons@antiochne.edu
Web site: http://www.antiochne.edu

Antioch University New England

THE FACULTY AND THEIR RESEARCH

Kendall F. Bacon, Senior Associate Professor and Director of Clinical Training for the Clinical Mental Health Counseling Program; M.S.W., Simmons. Couples and solution-focused counseling.

Katherine Clarke, Professor and Chairperson; Ph.D., Loyola Chicago; M.B.A., Simmons. Meaning-making in individuals and organizations, leadership and spirituality.

William T. Griffith, Professor of Interdisciplinary Studies; Ph.D. (philosophy), Boston College; Ph.D. (psychology), Massachusetts Amherst. Information technology and systems, postmodernism and social criticism, models of communication, technology and culture, and applications of narrative.

Phyllis K. Jeswald, Senior Associate Professor and Assistant Director of the Dance/Movement Therapy and Counseling Program; M.Ed., Massachusetts; LMHC, ADTR. Integration of verbal and nonverbal elements in the therapeutic process.

Diane Kurinsky, Professor, Associate Chairperson, and Director of the Clinical Mental Health Counseling Program; Ed.D., Massachusetts Amherst. Addictions and marriage and family therapy.

Susan Loman, Professor, Associate Chairperson, and Director of the Dance/Movement Therapy and Counseling Program; M.A., Goddard; ADTR, NCC. Kestenberg Movement Profile (KMP).

Walter Lowe, Assistant Professor; Ph.D. (marriage and family therapy), Purdue. Investigating problems families face after long separations, either as the result of military service or incarceration; development of a model of reunification therapy that can be adapted to various ethnic and economic populations; development of a model of Common Factors supervision, which is not model-based, but rather based on certain basic principles that inform all successful therapies, regardless of the model practiced.

Anne Prouty Lyness, Associate Professor and Director of Clinical Training for the Marriage and Family Therapy Program; Ph.D. (child development and family studies), Purdue. How families deal with health and illness; belief systems that create resilient families; human diversity and how it informs couple and family life; how current and emerging family public policies, laws, and politics influence families based on gender, ethnicity, social class, age, and country of origin.

Kevin P. Lyness, Associate Professor, Associate Chairperson, and Director of the Marriage and Family Therapy Program; Ph.D. (marriage and family therapy), Purdue. Adolescent development in family context, interface between family variables and adolescent resiliency and ability to face risks; critical issues facing couple and family therapists.

Carlotta J. Willis, Professor and Director of Academic Affairs; Ed.D., Massachusetts Amherst; NCC. Role of nonverbal communication in counseling and creative approaches to career development.

ARGOSY UNIVERSITY

ARGOSY UNIVERSITY, ATLANTA

College of Psychology and Behavioral Sciences

Programs of Study

Argosy University, Atlanta, offers the Master of Arts (M.A.) degree in clinical psychology, community counseling, and forensic psychology; the Doctor of Education (Ed.D.) degree in counselor education and supervision; and the Doctor of Psychology (Psy.D.) degree in clinical psychology. Students completing a program may wish to become licensed professionals. As master's-level licensure varies from state to state, students should verify the current licensing requirements for the state in which they plan to practice.

The M.A. in Clinical Psychology program prepares students with the clinical knowledge and skills required to serve the mental health needs of individuals and groups. Students develop proficiency in clinical observation, assessment, appropriate intervention, and evaluation. The program emphasizes a practitioner-oriented philosophy and integrates applied theory, research, and field experience. It is designed for students who are interested in a terminal degree and practice as a master's-level clinician, or for students planning to transfer to the Psy.D. program.

The M.A. in Community Counseling program prepares students to enter the counseling profession as ethical, effective, skilled, and culturally competent practitioners. It provides a multifaceted focus on developmental and preventive mental health services. Students gain the knowledge and skills required for individual, group, family, and organizational interventions. Curriculum integrates foundational counseling skills and theories with clinical field experience. An optional concentration in marriage and family therapy is available.

The M.A. in Forensic Psychology program provides course work in forensic psychology for application to law enforcement, legal and organizational consultation, and program analysis. The program is designed to meet growing needs of the legal and criminal justice systems for professional counseling within victim assistance programs, probation and parole offices, court-mandated treatment programs, jails, and prisons. With the exception of the practicum component, courses are offered on weekends, allowing students to continue full-time employment while enrolled in this program.

The Ed.D. in Counselor Education and Supervision program is designed to develop the advanced skills and knowledge necessary for leadership and advocacy roles in a variety of settings. The field is dedicated to both the academic preparation and comprehensive supervision of counselors across multiple settings. This course of study aligns with the Master of Arts in Community Counseling program to encourage entry-level counseling students to work toward becoming doctoral-level advanced practitioners, educators, and supervisors.

The Psy.D. in Clinical Psychology program prepares students to deliver basic diagnostic and therapeutic services to diverse populations, including individuals, groups, and families. By integrating theory, training, research, and practice, students develop and apply the clinical skills of observation, assessment, intervention, and evaluation. Optional concentrations are available in child and family psychology, general adult clinical, health psychology, or neuropsychology/geropsychology. The program prepares graduates for positions in traditional settings, including, but not limited to, independent practice, mental health centers, hospitals, medical centers, and managed-care systems. Graduates are encouraged to utilize clinical skills in innovative ways to become more competitive. Eventual positions may include consulting in various corporate, governmental, academic, multimedia, law, scientific, marketing, and industrial settings. The Doctor of Psychology in Clinical Psychology program at Argosy University, Atlanta, is accredited by the Committee on Accreditation of the American Psychological Association (APA, 750 First Street, NE, Washington, D.C. 20002-4242; 202-336-5510).

Research Facilities

Argosy University libraries provide curriculum support and educational resources, including current text materials, diagnostic training documents, reference materials and databases, journals and dissertations, and major and current titles in program areas. There is an online public-access catalog of library resources available throughout the Argosy University system. Students have full remote access to the campus library database, enabling them to study and conduct research at home. Academic databases offer dissertation abstracts, academic journals, and professional periodicals. All library computers are Internet accessible. Software applications include Word, Excel, PowerPoint, SPSS, and various test-scoring programs.

Financial Aid

A wide range of financial aid options is available to students who qualify. Argosy University, Atlanta, offers access to federal and state aid programs, merit-based awards, grants, loans, and a work-study program. As a first step, students should complete the Free Application for Federal Student Aid (FAFSA). Prospective students can apply electronically at http://www.fafsa.ed.gov or at the campus. To receive consideration for the maximum amount of aid and ensure timely receipt of funds, students should submit an application promptly.

Cost of Study

Tuition varies by program. Students should contact Argosy University, Atlanta, for tuition information.

Living and Housing Costs

Students typically live in apartments in the metropolitan Atlanta area. Living expenses vary according to each student's preferred standard of living, housing, and transportation. The University does not offer or operate student housing. Most Argosy University students are full-time working professionals who live within driving distance of the campus. Several nearby hotels offer special rates for those who commute from long distances. The Admissions Department also maintains a list of housing options, including contact information for University students who wish to share housing. For more information, students should contact the Admissions Department.

Student Group

Admission to Argosy University, Atlanta, is selective to ensure a highly qualified student body. The University encourages diversity in academic and employment backgrounds and promotes integration of the student body into professional life through established connections with local and national professional associations. Argosy University offers a professionally oriented education with rich opportunities to gain practical experience in class, field placements, and internships. Full-time students and working professionals gain the extensive knowledge and range of skills necessary for effective performance in their chosen field.

Student Outcomes

Students can register with Argosy University's online career-services system and use select services from a distance, such as degree-specific career e-mail lists, national job posts, and virtual job fairs. Students should contact the University for more information.

Location

Argosy University, Atlanta, is housed in a modern building in Sandy Springs, a northern suburb of Atlanta. The campus features a café and outdoor lakeside terrace. Beyond the college, students will find a wide selection of affordable housing options. This major metropolitan area offers many social and recreational opportunities, from clubs and concerts to galleries and museums, from a growing restaurant scene to Braves baseball games and rollerblading in Piedmont Park. The many hospitals, clinics, agencies, and educational institutions in the Atlanta area provide excellent opportunities for student training. Atlanta's thriving business environment includes high-technology companies such as EarthLink and Macquarium as well as corporate giants such as the Coca-Cola Company, CNN, Delta Air Lines, AT&T, and Georgia Pacific.

The University

Argosy University is a private institution with nineteen locations across the nation. Argosy University, Atlanta, provides a career resources office, an academic resources center, and extensive information access for research. It offers the resources of a large university plus the friendliness and personal attention of a small campus. The innovative programs feature dynamic, relevant, and practical curricula delivered in flexible class formats. Students enjoy scheduling options that make it easier to fit school into their busy lives, choosing from day and evening courses, on campus or online. Many students find a combination of class formats to be an ideal way of continuing their education while meeting family and professional demands.

Argosy University is accredited by the Higher Learning Commission and is a member of the North Central Association (NCA, 30 North LaSalle Street, Suite 2400, Chicago, Illinois 60602; 800-621-7440 (toll-free); http://www.ncahlc.org).

Applying

Argosy University, Atlanta, accepts students year-round on a rolling admissions basis, depending on availability of required courses. Applications for admission are available online or by contacting the campus.

Correspondence and Information

Argosy University, Atlanta
990 Hammond Drive, Suite 100
Atlanta, Georgia 30328

Phone: 770-671-1200
888-671-4777 (toll-free)
Fax: 770-671-0476
E-mail: auadmissions@argosy.edu
Web site: http://www.argosy.edu/atlanta

Argosy University, Atlanta

THE FACULTY

The Argosy University faculty comprises working professionals who are eager to help students succeed. Members bring real-world experience and the latest practice innovations to the academic setting. The diverse faculty members of the College of Psychology and Behavioral Sciences are widely recognized for contributions to the field. Many are published scholars, and most hold doctoral degrees. They provide a substantive education that combines comprehensive knowledge with critical skills and practical workplace relevance. Above all, faculty members are committed to their students' personal and professional development.

ARGOSY UNIVERSITY.

ARGOSY UNIVERSITY, CHICAGO

College of Psychology and Behavioral Sciences

Programs of Study

Argosy University, Chicago, offers the Master of Arts (M.A.) degree in clinical psychology and community counseling; the Doctor of Education (Ed.D.) degree in counseling psychology, counselor education and supervision, and organizational leadership; and the Doctor of Psychology (Psy.D.) degree in clinical psychology. Students completing a program may wish to become licensed professionals. As master's-level licensure varies from state to state, students should determine licensing requirements for the state in which they plan to practice.

The M.A. in Clinical Psychology program prepares students with the clinical knowledge and skills required to serve the mental health needs of individuals and groups. Students develop proficiency in clinical observation, assessment, appropriate intervention, and evaluation. The program emphasizes a practitioner-oriented philosophy and integrates applied theory, research, and field experience. It is designed for students who are interested in a terminal degree and practice as a master's-level clinician or for students planning to transfer to the Psy.D. program.

The M.A. in Community Counseling program provides a multifaceted focus on developmental and preventive mental health services. Students gain the knowledge and skills required for individual, group, family, and organizational interventions. The curriculum integrates foundational counseling skills and theories with clinical field experience.

The Ed.D. in Counseling Psychology program prepares counselors with the skills and credentials necessary to pursue leadership, supervision, training, and teaching positions. Students develop new interests and levels of competency through an applied, research-practitioner approach to the role of professional counselor. An optional concentration in counselor education and supervision is available. The challenges of a changing society and the diversity of roles available to the mental health practitioner require a lifelong commitment to continuing education.

The Ed.D. in Counselor Education & Supervision program is designed to develop the advanced skills and knowledge necessary for leadership and advocacy roles in a variety of settings. The field is dedicated to both the academic preparation and comprehensive supervision of counselors across multiple settings. This course of study aligns with the Master of Arts in Professional Counseling program to encourage entry-level counseling students to work toward becoming doctoral-level advanced practitioners, educators, and supervisors.

The Ed.D. in Organizational Leadership program is designed for working professionals who wish to develop the knowledge and skills required to hold leadership positions in complex organizations. The program focuses on transformational leadership skills in addition to managerial attributes. This approach prepares students for strategic challenges such as increasing globalization, changing economies, societal shifts, and individual-organizational relationships. Leaders prepared in this manner can become visionaries and innovators, leading viable organizations capable of meeting the challenges of the future.

The Psy.D. in Clinical Psychology program prepares students to deliver basic diagnostic and therapeutic services to diverse populations, including individuals, groups, and families. By integrating theory, training, research, and practice, students develop and apply the clinical skills of observation, assessment, intervention, and evaluation. Optional concentrations are available in child and adolescent psychology, client-centered and experiential psychotherapies, diversity and multicultural psychology, family psychology, forensic psychology, health psychology, psychoanalytic psychology, or psychology and spirituality. The program prepares graduates for positions in traditional settings including, but not limited to, independent practice, mental health centers, hospitals, medical centers, and managed-care systems. Graduates are also encouraged to utilize clinical skills in innovative ways to become more competitive. Eventual positions may include consulting in various corporate, governmental, academic, multimedia, law, scientific, marketing, and industrial settings.

The Doctor of Psychology in Clinical Psychology program at Argosy University, Chicago, is accredited by the Committee on Accreditation of the American Psychological Association (APA, 750 First Street NE, Washington, D.C. 20002-4242; 202-336-5510).

Research Facilities

Argosy University libraries provide curriculum support and educational resources, including current text materials, diagnostic training documents, reference materials and databases, journals and dissertations, and major and current titles in program areas. There is an online public-access catalog of library resources available throughout the Argosy University system. Students have full remote access to the campus library database, enabling them to study and conduct research at home. Academic databases offer dissertation abstracts, academic journals, and professional periodicals. All library computers are Internet accessible. Software applications include Word, Excel, PowerPoint, SPSS, and various test-scoring programs.

Financial Aid

A wide range of financial aid options is available to students who qualify. Argosy University, Chicago, offers access to federal and state aid programs, merit-based awards, grants, loans, and a work-study program. As a first step, students should complete the Free Application for Federal Student Aid (FAFSA). Prospective students can apply electronically at http://www.fafsa.ed.gov or at the campus. To receive consideration for the maximum amount of aid and ensure timely receipt of funds, it is best to submit an application promptly.

Cost of Study

Tuition varies by program. Students should contact Argosy University, Chicago, for tuition information.

Living and Housing Costs

Students typically live in apartments in the metropolitan Chicago area. Living expenses vary according to each student's preferred standard of living, housing, and transportation. The University does not offer or operate student housing. Most of the students are full-time working professionals who live within driving distance of the campus. Several nearby hotels offer special rates for those who commute from long distances. The Admissions Department also maintains a list of housing options, including contact information for university students who wish to share housing. For more information, students should contact the Admissions Department.

Student Group

Admission to Argosy University, Chicago, is selective to ensure a highly qualified student body. The University encourages diversity in academic and employment backgrounds and promotes integration of the student body into professional life through established connections with local and national professional associations. Argosy University offers a professionally oriented education with rich opportunities to gain practical experience in class, field placements, and internships. Full-time students and working professionals gain the extensive knowledge and range of skills necessary for effective performance in their chosen fields.

Student Outcomes

Students can register with the University's online career-services system and use select services from a distance, such as degree-specific career e-mail lists, national job posts, and virtual job fairs. Students should contact the University for more information.

Location

Chicago is a city of world-class status and beauty, drawing visitors from around the globe. Argosy University, Chicago, sits in the heart of The Loop, the city's business and entertainment center. Located on the shores of Lake Michigan, Chicago is home to world-champion sports teams, an internationally acclaimed symphony orchestra, renowned architecture, and a variety of history and art museums. Recreational opportunities include hiking and cycling on miles of lakefront trails, golfing, and shopping. Chicago's thriving business environment includes a broad array of companies including Boeing and Pepsi America. The commercial banking headquarters of JP Morgan Chase is also located in Chicago.

The University

Argosy University is a private institution with nineteen locations across the nation. Argosy University, Chicago, provides a career services office, an academic resources center, and extensive information access for research. It offers the resources of a large university plus the friendliness and personal attention of a small campus. Argosy University, Chicago, is closely associated with the Schaumburg, Illinois, campus, located 45 minutes from downtown Chicago.

The innovative programs feature dynamic, relevant, and practical curricula delivered in flexible class formats. Students enjoy scheduling options that make it easier to fit school into their busy lives, choosing from day and evening courses, on campus or online. Many students find a combination of class formats to be an ideal way of continuing their education while meeting family and professional demands.

Argosy University is accredited by the Higher Learning Commission and is a member of the North Central Association (NCA, 30 North LaSalle Street, Suite 2400, Chicago, Illinois 60602; 800-621-7440 (toll-free); http://www.ncahlc.org).

Applying

Argosy University, Chicago, accepts students year-round on a rolling admissions basis, depending on availability of required courses. Applications for admission are available online or by contacting the campus.

Correspondence and Information

Argosy University, Chicago
225 North Michigan Avenue, Suite 1300
Chicago, Illinois 60601

Phone: 312-777-7600
800-626-4123 (toll-free)
Fax: 312-777-7748
E-mail: auadmissions@argosy.edu
Web site: http://www.argosy.edu/chicago

Argosy University, Chicago

THE FACULTY

The Argosy University faculty comprises working professionals who are eager to help students succeed. Members bring real-world experience and the latest practice innovations to the academic setting. The diverse faculty members of the College of Psychology and Behavioral Sciences are widely recognized for contributions to the field. Many are published scholars, and most hold doctoral degrees. They provide a substantive education that combines comprehensive knowledge with critical skills and practical workplace relevance. Above all, faculty members are committed to their students' personal and professional development.

ARGOSY UNIVERSITY

ARGOSY UNIVERSITY, DALLAS

College of Psychology and Behavioral Sciences

Programs of Study

Argosy University, Dallas, offers the Master of Arts (M.A.) degree in clinical psychology, community counseling, forensic psychology, and school psychology and the Doctor of Psychology (Psy.D.) degree in clinical psychology. Students completing a program may wish to become licensed professionals. As master's-level licensure varies from state to state, students should determine licensing requirements for the state in which they plan to practice.

The M.A. in Clinical Psychology program prepares students with the clinical knowledge and skills required to serve the mental health needs of individuals and groups. Students develop proficiency in clinical observation, assessment, appropriate intervention, and evaluation. The program emphasizes a practitioner-oriented philosophy and integrates applied theory, research, and field experience. It is designed for students who are interested in a terminal degree and practice as a master's-level clinician or for students planning to transfer to the Psy.D. program.

The M.A. in Community Counseling program provides a multifaceted focus on developmental and preventive mental health services. Students gain the knowledge and skills required for individual, group, family, and organizational interventions. The curriculum integrates foundational counseling skills and theories with clinical field experience.

The M.A. in Forensic Psychology program provides course work in forensic psychology for application to law enforcement, legal and organizational consultation, and program analysis. The program is designed to meet growing needs of the legal and criminal justice systems for professional counseling within victim assistance programs, probation and parole offices, court-mandated treatment programs, jails, and prisons. With the exception of the practicum component, courses are offered on weekends, allowing students to continue full-time employment while enrolled in this program.

The M.A. in School Psychology program is dedicated to producing ethical, responsible, and competent school psychologists. Students develop core competencies in psychological assessment, intervention, and consultation as well as cultural and individual diversity. The curriculum provides for the meaningful integration of theory, training, and practice. Graduates of the program may be eligible for Department of Education certification and are prepared for employment as school psychologists. Students are also prepared to work toward certification by the Nationally Certified School Psychologists in accordance with criteria developed by the National Association of School Psychologists (NASP).

The Psy.D. in Clinical Psychology program prepares students to deliver basic diagnostic and therapeutic services to diverse populations, including individuals, groups, and families. By integrating theory, training, research, and practice, students develop and apply the clinical skills of observation, assessment, intervention, and evaluation. The program prepares graduates for positions in traditional settings, including, but not limited to, independent practice, mental health centers, hospitals, medical centers, and managed-care systems. Argosy also encourages graduates to utilize clinical skills in innovative ways to become more competitive. Eventual positions may include consulting in various corporate, governmental, academic, multimedia, law, scientific, marketing, and industrial settings.

Research Facilities

Argosy University libraries provide curriculum support and educational resources, including current text materials, diagnostic training documents, reference materials and databases, journals and dissertations, and major and current titles in program areas. There is an online public-access catalog of library resources available throughout the Argosy University system. Students have full remote access to the campus library database, enabling them to study and conduct research at home. Academic databases offer dissertation abstracts, academic journals, and professional periodicals. All library computers are Internet accessible. Software applications include Word, Excel, PowerPoint, SPSS, and various test-scoring programs.

Financial Aid

A wide range of financial aid options is available to students who qualify. Argosy University, Dallas, offers access to federal and state aid programs, merit-based awards, grants, loans, and a work-study program. As a first step, students should complete the Free Application for Federal Student Aid (FAFSA). Prospective students can apply electronically at http://www.fafsa.ed.gov or at the campus. To receive consideration for the maximum amount of aid and ensure timely receipt of funds, it is best to submit an application promptly.

Cost of Study

Tuition varies by program. Students should contact Argosy University, Dallas, for tuition information.

Living and Housing Costs

Students typically live in apartments in the metropolitan Dallas area. Living expenses vary according to each student's preferred standard of living, housing, and transportation. The University does not offer or operate student housing. Most of the students are full-time working professionals who live within driving distance of the campus. Several nearby hotels offer special rates for those who commute from long distances. The Admissions Department also maintains a list of housing options, including contact information, for University students who wish to share housing. For more information, students should contact the Admissions Department.

Student Group

Admission to Argosy University, Dallas, is selective to ensure a highly qualified student body. The University encourages diversity in academic and employment backgrounds and promotes integration of the student body into professional life through established connections with local and national professional associations. Argosy University offers a professionally oriented education with rich opportunities to gain practical experience in class, field placements, and internships. Full-time students and working professionals gain the extensive knowledge and range of skills necessary for effective performance in their chosen fields.

Student Outcomes

Students can register with the University's online career-services system and use select services from a distance, such as degree-specific career e-mail lists, national job posts, and virtual job fairs. Students should contact the University for more information.

Location

Argosy University, Dallas, offers a north-central location in Dallas, with easy access to freeways, neighboring colleges and universities, libraries, shops, restaurants, theaters, art museums, and other tourist attractions. The thriving business environment in the Dallas–Fort Worth metropolitan area includes a broad array of companies, such as Lockheed Martin Corporation, Baylor University Medical System, and Southwest Airlines.

The University

Argosy University is a private institution with nineteen locations across the nation. Argosy University, Dallas, provides a career resources office, an academic resources center, and extensive information access for research. It offers the resources of a large university, plus the friendliness and personal attention of a small campus.

Argosy University, Dallas, offers the unique opportunity to take one class at a time, with each class lasting for one month. Students are never required to study for multiple exams at the same time. New classes start each month. This flexible format lets students begin working on a graduate degree without waiting for the traditional semester to start.

Argosy University is accredited by the Higher Learning Commission and is a member of the North Central Association (NCA, 30 North LaSalle Street, Suite 2400, Chicago, Illinois 60602; 800-621-7440 (toll-free); http://www.ncahlc.org).

Applying

Argosy University, Dallas, accepts students year-round on a rolling admissions basis, depending on availability of required courses. Applications for admission are available online or by contacting the campus.

Correspondence and Information

Argosy University, Dallas
8080 Park Lane, Suite 500
Dallas, Texas 75231

Phone: 214-890-9900
866-954-9900 (toll-free)
Fax: 214-696-3900
E-mail: http://auadmissions@argosy.edu
Web site: http://www.argosy.edu/dallas

Argosy University, Dallas

THE FACULTY

The Argosy University faculty comprises working professionals who are eager to help students succeed. Members bring real-world experience and the latest practice innovations to the academic setting. The diverse faculty members of the College of Psychology and Behavioral Sciences are widely recognized for contributions to the field. Many are published scholars, and most hold doctoral degrees. They provide a substantive education that combines comprehensive knowledge with critical skills and practical workplace relevance. Above all, faculty members are committed to their students' personal and professional development.

ARGOSY UNIVERSITY

ARGOSY UNIVERSITY, DENVER

College of Psychology and Behavioral Sciences

Programs of Study

Argosy University, Denver, offers the Master of Arts (M.A.) degree in clinical psychology, community counseling, forensic psychology, and marriage and family therapy; the Master of Arts in Industrial Organizational Psychology (M.A.I.O.) degree; the Doctor of Marriage and Family Therapy (D.M.F.T.) degree; the Doctor of Education (Ed.D.) degree in counseling psychology, counselor education and supervision, and organizational leadership; and the Doctor of Psychology (Psy.D.) degree in clinical psychology. Students completing a program may wish to become licensed professionals. As master's-level licensure varies from state to state, students should verify the current licensing requirements for the state in which they plan to practice.

The M.A. in Clinical Psychology program prepares students with the clinical knowledge and skills required to serve the mental health needs of individuals and groups. Students develop proficiency in clinical observation, assessment, appropriate intervention, and evaluation. The program emphasizes a practitioner-oriented philosophy and integrates applied theory, research, and field experience. It is designed for students who are interested in a terminal degree and practice as a master's-level clinician or for students planning to transfer to the Psy.D. program.

The M.A. in Community Counseling program prepares students to enter the counseling profession as ethical, effective, skilled, and culturally competent practitioners. It provides a multifaceted focus on developmental and preventive mental health services. Students gain the knowledge and skills required for individual, group, family, and organizational interventions. The curriculum integrates foundational counseling skills and theories with clinical field experience.

The M.A. in Forensic Psychology program provides course work in forensic psychology for application to law enforcement, legal and organizational consultation, and program analysis. The program is designed to meet growing needs of the legal and criminal justice systems for professional counseling within victim assistance programs, probation and parole offices, court-mandated treatment programs, jails, and prisons. With the exception of the practicum component, courses are offered on weekends, allowing students to continue full-time employment while enrolled in this program.

The M.A. in Industrial Organizational Psychology program is designed to apply the knowledge of industrial organizational psychology to issues involving individuals and groups in organizational and work settings. This program prepares students for careers in areas such as compensation, training, data analysis, consultation, statistical decision making, organizational development, leadership, and human resource management positions. The curriculum is competency based, focusing on the outcomes of training and on the knowledge, skills, and behavior necessary to function as a master's-level professional in industrial organizational psychology. This is an interdisciplinary program that combines the expertise of the faculty in the Colleges of Psychology and Behavioral Sciences and Business.

The M.A. in Marriage & Family Therapy program develops the theoretical and clinical elements required to provide effective counseling to individuals, couples, families, and groups. The program introduces basic counseling skills that incorporate foundations of applied psychology and systems theory into the development of appropriate clinical relationships. Course work in addiction studies and substance-abuse counseling prepares students to work with families affected by this burgeoning problem. Marriage and family therapy is recognized by the Public Health Service Act as one of the five core mental health professions, and the National Institute of Mental Health accepts marriage and family therapists as qualified mental health professionals. The program is offered through weekend courses to allow concurrent employment.

The Doctor of Marriage and Family Therapy is a practice-oriented degree for licensed marriage and family therapists or professionals who can meet state requirements for licensure as a marriage and family therapist (meeting the Commission on Accreditation of Marriage and Family Therapy Education (COAMFTE) criteria for clinical practice prior to admission). The program seeks to build upon students' prior learning and professional experience by expanding and deepening their knowledge of human development, family dynamics, systemic thinking, interactional theories, traditional and contemporary marriage and family therapy theories and practices, and the cultural contexts within which these are embedded.

The Ed.D. in Counseling Psychology program prepares counselors with the skills and credentials necessary to pursue leadership, supervision, training, and teaching positions. Students develop new interests and levels of competency through an applied research-practitioner approach to the role of professional counselor. An optional concentration in counselor education and supervision is available. The challenges of a changing society and the diversity of roles available to the mental health practitioner require a lifelong commitment to continuing education.

The Ed.D. in Counselor Education & Supervision program is designed to develop the advanced skills and knowledge necessary for leadership and advocacy roles in a variety of settings. The field is dedicated to both the academic preparation and comprehensive supervision of counselors across multiple settings. This course of study aligns with the Master of Arts in Professional Counseling program to encourage entry-level counseling students to work toward becoming doctoral-level advanced practitioners, educators, and supervisors.

The Ed.D. in Organizational Leadership program is designed for working professionals who wish to develop the knowledge and skills required to hold leadership positions in complex organizations. The program focuses on transformational leadership skills in addition to managerial attributes. This approach prepares students for strategic challenges such as increasing globalization, changing economies, societal shifts, and individual-organizational relationships. Leaders prepared in this manner can become visionaries and innovators, leading viable organizations capable of meeting the challenges of the future.

The Psy.D. in Clinical Psychology program prepares students to deliver basic diagnostic and therapeutic services to diverse populations, including individuals, groups, and families. By integrating theory, training, research, and practice, students develop and apply the clinical skills of observation, assessment, intervention, and evaluation. Optional concentrations are available in child and family psychology, general adult clinical, health psychology, or neuropsychology/geropsychology. The program prepares graduates for positions in traditional settings, including, but not limited to, independent practice, mental health centers, hospitals, medical centers, and managed-care systems. Graduates are encouraged to utilize clinical skills in innovative ways to become more competitive. Eventual positions may include consulting in various corporate, governmental, academic, multimedia, law, scientific, marketing, and industrial settings.

Research Facilities

Argosy University libraries provide curriculum support and educational resources, including current text materials, diagnostic training documents, reference materials and databases, journals and dissertations, and major and current titles in program areas. There is an online public-access catalog of library resources available throughout the Argosy University system. Students have full remote access to the campus library database, enabling them to study and conduct research at home. Academic databases offer dissertation abstracts, academic journals, and professional periodicals. All library computers are Internet accessible. Software applications include Word, Excel, PowerPoint, SPSS, and various test-scoring programs.

Financial Aid

A wide range of financial aid options is available to students who qualify. Argosy University, Denver, offers access to federal and state aid programs, merit-based awards, grants, loans, and a work-study program. As a first step, students should complete the Free Application for Federal Student Aid (FAFSA). Prospective students can apply electronically at http://www.fafsa.ed.gov or at the campus. To receive consideration for the maximum amount of aid and ensure timely receipt of funds, it is best to submit an application promptly.

Cost of Study

Tuition varies by program. Students should contact Argosy University, Denver, for tuition information.

Living and Housing Costs

Students typically live in apartments in the metropolitan Denver area. Living expenses vary according to each student's preferred standard of living, housing, and transportation. The University does not offer or operate student housing. Most of the students are full-time working professionals who live within driving distance of the campus. Several nearby hotels offer special rates for those who commute from long distances. The Admissions Department also maintains a list of housing options, including contact information for University students who wish to share housing. For more information, students should contact the Admissions Department.

Student Group

Admission to Argosy University, Denver, is selective to ensure a highly qualified student body. The University encourages diversity in academic and employment backgrounds and promotes integration of the student body into professional life through established connections with local and national professional associations. Argosy University offers a professionally oriented education with rich opportunities to gain practical experience in class, field placements, and internships. Full-time students and working professionals gain the extensive knowledge and range of skills necessary for effective performance in their chosen fields.

Student Outcomes

Students can register with the University's online career-services system and use select services from a distance, such as degree-specific career e-mail lists, national job posts, and virtual job fairs. Students should contact the University for more information.

Location

Argosy University, Denver, is located at 1200 Lincoln Street in Denver, Colorado. The ten-story downtown facility includes classrooms, computer labs, a resource center with Internet access, a student lounge, staff and faculty offices, and other amenities. The campus is close to a variety of local libraries, shops, restaurants, theaters, and art museums. Denver's thriving professional organizations, major corporations, high-tech companies, hospitals, schools, clinics, and social service agencies can also provide outstanding training opportunities for students.

The University

Argosy University is a private institution with nineteen locations across the nation. Argosy University, Denver, provides a career resources office, an academic resources center, and extensive information access for research. It offers the resources of a large university plus the friendliness and personal attention of a small campus.

The innovative programs feature dynamic, relevant, and practical curricula delivered in flexible class formats. Students enjoy scheduling options that make it easier to fit school into their busy lives, choosing from day and evening courses, on campus or online. Many students find a combination of class formats to be an ideal way of continuing their education while meeting family and professional demands.

Argosy University is accredited by the Higher Learning Commission and is a member of the North Central Association (NCA, 30 North LaSalle Street, Suite 2400, Chicago, Illinois 60602; 800-621-7440 (toll-free); http://www.ncahlc.org).

Applying

Argosy University, Denver, accepts students year-round on a rolling admissions basis, depending on availability of required courses. Applications for admission are available online or by contacting the campus.

Correspondence and Information

Argosy University, Denver
1200 Lincoln Street
Denver, Colorado 80203

Phone: 303-248-2700
866-431-5981 (toll-free)
Fax: 303-248-2600
E-mail: auadmissions@argosy.edu
Web site: http://www.argosy.edu/denver

Argosy University, Denver

THE FACULTY

The Argosy University faculty comprises working professionals who are eager to help students succeed. Members bring real-world experience and the latest practice innovations to the academic setting. The diverse faculty members of the College of Psychology and Behavioral Sciences are widely recognized for contributions to the field. Many are published scholars, and most hold doctoral degrees. They provide a substantive education that combines comprehensive knowledge with critical skills and practical workplace relevance. Above all, faculty members are committed to their students' personal and professional development.

ARGOSY UNIVERSITY.

ARGOSY UNIVERSITY, HAWAI'I

College of Psychology and Behavioral Sciences

Programs of Study

Argosy University, Hawai'i, offers the Master of Arts (M.A.) degree in clinical psychology, marriage and family therapy, and school psychology; the Master of Science (M.S.) in psychopharmacology; the Doctor of Education (Ed.D.) degree in counseling psychology and organizational leadership; and the Doctor of Psychology (Psy.D.) degree in clinical psychology. Students completing a program may wish to become licensed professionals. As master's-level licensure varies from state to state, students should verify the current licensing requirements for the state in which they plan to practice.

The M.A. in Clinical Psychology program prepares students with the clinical knowledge and skills required to serve the mental health needs of individuals and groups. Students develop proficiency in clinical observation, assessment, appropriate intervention, and evaluation. The program emphasizes a practitioner-oriented philosophy and integrates applied theory, research, and field experience. It is designed for students who are interested in a terminal degree and practice as a master's-level clinician or for students planning to transfer to the Psy.D. program.

The M.A. in Marriage & Family Therapy program develops the theoretical and clinical elements required to provide effective counseling to individuals, couples, families, and groups. The program introduces basic counseling skills that incorporate foundations of applied psychology and systems theory into the development of appropriate clinical relationships. Course work in addiction studies and substance-abuse counseling prepares students to work with families affected by this burgeoning problem. Marriage and family therapy is recognized by the Public Health Service Act as one of the five core mental health professions, and the National Institute of Mental Health accepts marriage and family therapists as qualified mental health professionals. The program is offered through weekend courses to allow concurrent employment.

The M.A. in School Psychology program is dedicated to producing ethical, responsible, and competent school psychologists. Students develop core competencies in psychological assessment, intervention, and consultation as well as cultural and individual diversity. The curriculum provides for the meaningful integration of theory, training, and practice. Graduates of the program may be eligible for Department of Education certification and are prepared for employment as school psychologists. Students are also prepared to work toward certification by the Nationally Certified School Psychologists in accordance with criteria developed by the National Association of School Psychologists (NASP).

The M.S. in Psychopharmacology incorporates course work and clinical practice to comprehensively train postdoctoral psychologists to prescribe medications independently, appropriately, effectively, and safely. It is a 32-credit-hour program with a practicum component requiring treatment of 100 patients. Upon successful completion of the program, students have the education and experience to prescribe psychopharmacological medications consistent with state and federal laws and work collaboratively with physicians, nurses, and other health-care providers to coordinate care. This program is intended to prepare students for the Psychopharmacology Exam for Psychologists (PEP).

The Ed.D. in Counseling Psychology program prepares counselors with the skills and credentials necessary to pursue leadership, supervision, training, and teaching positions. Students develop new interests and levels of competency through an applied, research-practitioner approach to the role of professional counselor. An optional concentration in counselor education and supervision is available. The challenges of a changing society and the diversity of roles available to the mental health practitioner require a lifelong commitment to continuing education.

The Ed.D. in Organizational Leadership program is designed for working professionals who wish to develop the knowledge and skills required to hold leadership positions in complex organizations. The program focuses on transformational leadership skills in addition to managerial attributes. This approach prepares students for strategic challenges such as increasing globalization, changing economies, societal shifts, and individual-organizational relationships. Leaders prepared in this manner can become visionaries and innovators, leading viable organizations capable of meeting the challenges of the future.

The Psy.D. in Clinical Psychology program prepares students to deliver basic diagnostic and therapeutic services to diverse populations, including individuals, groups, and families. By integrating theory, training, research, and practice, students develop and apply the clinical skills of observation, assessment, intervention, and evaluation. Optional concentrations are available in child and family clinical practice and diversity in clinical practice. The program prepares graduates for positions in traditional settings including, but not limited to, independent practice, mental health centers, hospitals, medical centers, and managed-care systems. Graduates are also encouraged to utilize clinical skills in innovative ways to become more competitive. Eventual positions may include consulting in various corporate, governmental, academic, multimedia, law, scientific, marketing, and industrial settings. The Doctor of Psychology in clinical psychology program at Argosy University, Hawai'i, is accredited by the Committee on Accreditation of the American Psychological Association (APA, 750 First Street NE, Washington, D.C. 20002-4242; 202-336-5510).

Research Facilities

Argosy University libraries provide curriculum support and educational resources, including current text materials, diagnostic training documents, reference materials and databases, journals and dissertations, and major and current titles in program areas. There is an online public-access catalog of library resources available throughout the Argosy University system. Students have full remote access to the campus library database, enabling them to study and conduct research at home. Academic databases offer dissertation abstracts, academic journals, and professional periodicals. All library computers are Internet accessible. Software applications include Word, Excel, PowerPoint, SPSS, and various test-scoring programs.

Financial Aid

A wide range of financial aid options is available to students who qualify. Argosy University, Hawai'i, offers access to federal and state aid programs, merit-based awards, grants, loans, and a work-study program. As a first step, students should complete the Free Application for Federal Student Aid (FAFSA). Prospective students can apply electronically at http://www.fafsa.ed.gov or at the campus. To receive consideration for the maximum amount of aid and ensure timely receipt of funds, it is best to submit an application promptly.

Cost of Study

Tuition varies by program. Students should contact Argosy University, Hawai'i, for tuition information.

Living and Housing Costs

Students typically live in apartments in the metropolitan Honolulu area. Living expenses vary according to each student's preferred standard of living, housing, and transportation. The University does not offer or operate student housing. Most of the students are full-time working professionals who live within driving distance of the campus. Several nearby hotels offer special rates for those who commute from long distances. The Admissions Department also maintains a list of housing options, including contact information for University students who wish to share housing. For more information, students should contact the Admissions Department.

Student Group

Admission to Argosy University, Hawai'i, is selective to ensure a highly qualified student body. The University encourages diversity in academic and employment backgrounds and promotes integration of the student body into professional life through established connections with local and national professional associations. Argosy University offers a professionally oriented education with rich opportunities to gain practical experience in class, field placements, and internships. Full-time students and working professionals gain the extensive knowledge and range of skills necessary for effective performance in their chosen fields.

Student Outcomes

Students can register with the University's online career-services system and use select services from a distance, such as degree-specific career e-mail lists, national job posts, and virtual job fairs. Students should contact the University for more information.

Location

Argosy University, Hawai'i, is located in downtown Honolulu on Oahu. Additional satellite locations on Maui and in Hilo on the island of Hawaii offer programs to communities on the neighboring islands. These locations connect the campus to Hawaii and to the local and native communities of the Pacific Islands and the Pacific Rim. Students enjoy the cultural and recreational opportunities that these locations provide. University faculty and staff members often work in cooperation with the Hawaiian community to create an educational focus on social issues, human diversity, and programs that make a difference to underserved populations.

Honolulu's thriving business environment includes a broad array of companies. The area's largest employers include Bank of Hawaii, Queens Medical Center, and the U.S. government. Many businesses in the metropolitan area provide excellent, varied opportunities for student training.

The University

Argosy University is a private institution with nineteen locations across the nation. Argosy University, Hawai'i, provides a career resources office, an academic resources center, and extensive information access for research. It offers the resources of a large university plus the friendliness and personal attention of a small campus.

The innovative programs feature dynamic, relevant, and practical curricula delivered in flexible class formats. Students enjoy scheduling options that make it easier to fit school into their busy lives, choosing from day and evening courses, on campus or online. Many students find a combination of class formats to be an ideal way of continuing their education while meeting family and professional demands.

Argosy University is accredited by the Higher Learning Commission and is a member of the North Central Association (NCA, 30 North LaSalle Street, Suite 2400, Chicago, Illinois 60602; 800-621-7440 (toll-free); http://www.ncahlc.org).

Applying

Argosy University, Hawai'i, accepts students year-round on a rolling admissions basis, depending on availability of required courses. Applications for admission are available online or by contacting the campus.

Correspondence and Information

Argosy University, Hawai'i
400 ASB Tower
1001 Bishop Street
Honolulu, Hawaii 96813

Phone: 808-536-5555
888-323-2777 (toll-free)
Fax: 808-536-5505
E-mail: auadmissions@argosy.edu
Web site: http://www.argosy.edu/hawaii

Argosy University, Hawai'i

THE FACULTY

The Argosy University faculty comprises working professionals who are eager to help students succeed. Members bring real-world experience and the latest practice innovations to the academic setting. The diverse faculty members of the College of Psychology and Behavioral Sciences are widely recognized for contributions to the field. Many are published scholars, and most hold doctoral degrees. They provide a substantive education that combines comprehensive knowledge with critical skills and practical workplace relevance. Above all, faculty members are committed to their students' personal and professional development.

Argosy University

ARGOSY UNIVERSITY, INLAND EMPIRE

College of Psychology and Behavioral Sciences

Programs of Study

Argosy University, Inland Empire, offers the Master of Arts (M.A.) degree in clinical psychology/marriage and family therapy, counseling psychology/marriage and family therapy, and forensic psychology and the Doctor of Education (Ed.D.) degree in counseling psychology and in organizational leadership. Students completing a program may wish to become licensed professionals. As master's-level licensure varies from state to state, students should verify the current licensing requirements for the state in which they plan to practice.

The M.A. in Clinical Psychology/Marriage & Family Therapy program provides an opportunity for students to pursue the clinical psychology track while receiving graduate-level training in core curricular areas, including supervised clinical practice. The program emphasizes a practitioner-oriented philosophy and integrates applied theory and field experience. The curriculum shares a common core with most of the first- and second-year course offerings of the doctoral program in clinical psychology. The program is designed to meet requirements for licensure as a marriage and family therapist in the state of California.

The M.A. in Counseling Psychology/Marriage & Family Therapy program emphasizes a practitioner-oriented philosophy, integrating applied theory and field experience. It is designed for students who wish to pursue the counseling psychology track while receiving graduate-level training in the core curricular areas, including supervised clinical practice. The curriculum shares a common core with most of the first- and second-year course offerings of the doctoral program in clinical psychology. The program is designed to meet requirements for licensure as a marriage and family therapist in the state of California.

The M.A. in Forensic Psychology program provides course work in forensic psychology for application to law enforcement, legal and organizational consultation, and program analysis. The program is designed to meet the growing needs of the legal and criminal justice systems for professional counseling within victim assistance programs, probation and parole offices, court-mandated treatment programs, jails, and prisons. With the exception of the practicum component, courses are offered on weekends, allowing students to continue full-time employment while enrolled in this program.

The Ed.D. in Counseling Psychology program prepares counselors with the skills and credentials necessary to pursue leadership, supervision, training, and teaching positions. Students develop new interests and levels of competency through an applied, research-practitioner approach to the role of professional counselor. The challenges of a changing society and the diversity of roles available to the mental health practitioner require a lifelong commitment to continuing education.

The Ed.D. in Organizational Leadership program is designed for working professionals who wish to develop the knowledge and skills required to hold leadership positions in complex organizations. The program focuses on transformational leadership skills in addition to managerial attributes. This approach prepares students for strategic challenges such as increasing globalization, changing economies, societal shifts, and individual-organizational relationships. Leaders prepared in this manner can become visionaries and innovators, leading viable organizations capable of meeting the challenges of the future.

Research Facilities

Argosy University libraries provide curriculum support and educational resources, including current text materials, diagnostic training documents, reference materials and databases, journals and dissertations, and major and current titles in program areas. There is an online public-access catalog of library resources available throughout the Argosy University system. Students have full remote access to the campus library database, enabling them to study and conduct research at home. Academic databases offer dissertation abstracts, academic journals, and professional periodicals. All library computers are Internet accessible. Software applications include Word, Excel, PowerPoint, SPSS, and various test-scoring programs.

Financial Aid

A wide range of financial aid options is available to students who qualify. Argosy University, Inland Empire, offers access to federal and state aid programs, merit-based awards, grants, loans, and a work-study program. As a first step, students should complete the Free Application for Federal Student Aid (FAFSA). Prospective students can apply electronically at http://www.fafsa.ed.gov or at the campus. To receive consideration for the maximum amount of aid and ensure timely receipt of funds, it is best to submit an application promptly.

Cost of Study

Tuition varies by program. Students should contact Argosy University, Inland Empire, for tuition information.

Living and Housing Costs

Students typically live in apartments in the San Bernardino metropolitan area. Living expenses vary according to each student's preferred standard of living, housing, and transportation. The University does not offer or operate student housing. Most of the students are full-time working professionals who live within driving distance of the campus. Several nearby hotels offer special rates for those who commute from long distances. The Admissions Department also maintains a list of housing options, including contact information for University students who wish to share housing. For more information, students should contact the Admissions Department.

Student Group

Admission to Argosy University, Inland Empire, is selective to ensure a highly qualified student body. The University encourages diversity in academic and employment backgrounds and promotes integration of the student body into professional life through established connections with local and national professional associations. Argosy University offers a professionally oriented education with rich opportunities to gain practical experience in class, field placements, and internships. Full-time students and working professionals gain the extensive knowledge and range of skills necessary for effective performance in their chosen field.

Student Outcomes

Students can register with the University's online career-services system and use select services from a distance, such as degree-specific career e-mail lists, national job posts, and virtual job fairs. Students should contact the University for more information.

Location

Argosy University, Inland Empire, is conveniently located in the Hospitality Lane section of San Bernardino, California. The facility features classrooms, computer labs, a resource center with Internet access, a student lounge, staff and faculty offices, and proximity to the region's many cultural and recreational attractions. The University provides a supportive educational environment with convenient class options that enable students to earn a degree while fulfilling other life responsibilities. All of the programs are thoroughly oriented to the real working world. Argosy University focuses on developing technical proficiency in each student's field as well as an overall professional career approach.

The University

Argosy University is a private institution with nineteen locations across the nation. Argosy University, Inland Empire, provides a career resources office, an academic resources center, and extensive information access for research. It offers the resources of a large university plus the friendliness and personal attention of a small campus.

The innovative programs feature dynamic, relevant, and practical curricula delivered in flexible class formats. Students enjoy scheduling options that make it easier to fit school into their busy lives, choosing from day and evening courses, on campus or online. Many students find a combination of class formats to be an ideal way of continuing their education while meeting family and professional demands.

Argosy University is accredited by the Higher Learning Commission and is a member of the North Central Association (NCA, 30 North LaSalle Street, Suite 2400, Chicago, Illinois 60602; 800-621-7440 (toll-free); http://www.ncahlc.org).

Applying

Argosy University, Inland Empire, accepts students year-round on a rolling admissions basis, depending on availability of required courses. Applications for admission are available online or by contacting the campus.

Correspondence and Information

Argosy University, Inland Empire
636 East Brier Drive, Suite 120
San Bernardino, California 92408

Phone: 909-915-3800
866-217-9075 (toll-free)
Fax: 909-915-3810
E-mail: auadmissions@argosy.edu
Web site: http://www.argosy.edu/inlandempire

Argosy University, Inland Empire

THE FACULTY

The Argosy University faculty comprises working professionals who are eager to help students succeed. Members bring real-world experience and the latest practice innovations to the academic setting. The diverse faculty members of the College of Psychology and Behavioral Sciences are widely recognized for contributions to the field. Many are published scholars, and most hold doctoral degrees. They provide a substantive education that combines comprehensive knowledge with critical skills and practical workplace relevance. Above all, faculty members are committed to their students' personal and professional development.

ARGOSY UNIVERSITY

ARGOSY UNIVERSITY, LOS ANGELES

College of Psychology and Behavioral Sciences

Programs of Study

Argosy University, Los Angeles, offers the Master of Arts (M.A.) degree in clinical psychology/marriage and family therapy and counseling psychology/marriage and family therapy and the Doctor of Education (Ed.D.) degree in counseling psychology and organizational leadership. Students completing a program may wish to become licensed professionals. As master's-level licensure varies from state to state, students should verify the current licensing requirements for the state in which they plan to practice.

The M.A. in Clinical Psychology/Marriage & Family Therapy program provides an opportunity for students to pursue the clinical psychology track while receiving graduate-level training in core curricular areas, including supervised clinical practice. The program emphasizes a practitioner-oriented philosophy and integrates applied theory and field experience. The curriculum shares a common core with most of the first- and second-year course offerings of the doctorate in clinical psychology. The program is designed to meet requirements for licensure as a marriage and family therapist (MFT) in the state of California.

The M.A. in Counseling Psychology/Marriage & Family Therapy program emphasizes a practitioner-oriented philosophy, integrating applied theory and field experience. It is designed for students who wish to pursue the counseling psychology track while receiving graduate-level training in the core curricular areas, including supervised clinical practice. The curriculum shares a common core with most of the first- and second-year course offerings of the doctorate in clinical psychology. The program is designed to meet requirements for licensure as a marriage and family therapist (MFT) in the state of California.

The Ed.D. in Counseling Psychology program prepares counselors with the skills and credentials necessary to pursue leadership, supervision, training, and teaching positions. Students develop new interests and levels of competency through an applied research-practitioner approach to the role of professional counselor. The challenges of a changing society and the diversity of roles available to the mental health practitioner require a lifelong commitment to continuing education.

The Ed.D. in Organizational Leadership program is designed for working professionals who wish to develop the knowledge and skills required to hold leadership positions in complex organizations. The program focuses on transformational leadership skills in addition to managerial attributes. This approach prepares students for such strategic challenges as increasing globalization, changing economies, societal shifts, and individual-organizational relationships.

Research Facilities

Argosy University libraries provide curriculum support and educational resources, including current text materials, diagnostic training documents, reference materials and databases, journals and dissertations, and major and current titles in program areas. There is an online public-access catalog of library resources available throughout the Argosy University system. Students have full remote access to the campus library database, enabling them to study and conduct research at home. Academic databases offer dissertation abstracts, academic journals, and professional periodicals. All library computers are Internet accessible. Software applications include Word, Excel, PowerPoint, SPSS, and various test-scoring programs.

Financial Aid

A wide range of financial aid options is available to students who qualify. Argosy University, Los Angeles, offers access to federal and state aid programs, merit-based awards, grants, loans, and a work-study program. As a first step, students should complete the Free Application for Federal Student Aid (FAFSA). Prospective students can apply electronically at http://www.fafsa.ed.gov or at the campus. To receive consideration for the maximum amount of aid and ensure timely receipt of funds, students should submit an application promptly.

Cost of Study

Tuition varies by program. Students should contact Argosy University, Los Angeles, for tuition information.

Living and Housing Costs

Students typically live in apartments in the metropolitan Santa Monica area. Living expenses vary according to each student's preferred standard of living, housing, and transportation. The University does not offer or operate student housing. Most Argosy University students are full-time working professionals who live within driving distance of the campus. Several nearby hotels offer special rates for those who commute from long distances. The Admissions Department also maintains a list of housing options, including contact information for University students who wish to share housing. For more information, students should contact the Admissions Department.

Student Group

Admission to Argosy University, Los Angeles, is selective to ensure a highly qualified student body. The University encourages diversity in academic and employment backgrounds and promotes integration of the student body into professional life through established connections with local and national professional associations. Argosy University offers a professionally oriented education with rich opportunities to gain practical experience in class, field placements, and internships. Full-time students and working professionals gain the extensive knowledge and range of skills necessary for effective performance in their chosen fields.

Student Outcomes

Students can register with the University's online career-services system and use select services from a distance, such as degree-specific career e-mail lists, national job posts, and virtual job fairs. Students should contact the University for more information.

Location

Argosy University, Los Angeles, is located in the beach community of Santa Monica, California. This undeniably sophisticated urban environment is coupled with the charm of the famous Santa Monica Pier, beautiful beaches, and farmer's markets. On campus, the main facility covers approximately 107,000 square feet and houses classrooms, laboratories, offices, a student lounge, and a library. Many educational institutions and agencies in the area provide excellent opportunities for student training. The thriving business environment in Santa Monica includes a broad array of companies, including a proliferation of entertainment, high tech, and software firms. Principal employers in the area include Yahoo, MTV Networks, RAND Corporation, and Symantec Corporation.

The University

Argosy University is a private institution with nineteen locations across the nation. Argosy University, Los Angeles, provides students with a career resources office, an academic resources center, and extensive information access for research. It offers the resources of a large university plus the friendliness and personal attention of a small campus.

The innovative programs feature dynamic, relevant, and practical curricula delivered in flexible class formats. Students enjoy scheduling options that make it easier to fit school into their busy lives, choosing from day and evening courses, on campus or online. Many students find a combination of class formats to be an ideal way of continuing their education while meeting family and professional demands.

Argosy University is accredited by the Higher Learning Commission and is a member of the North Central Association (NCA, 30 North LaSalle Street, Suite 2400, Chicago, Illinois 60602; 800-621-7440 (toll-free); http://www.ncahlc.org).

Applying

Argosy University, Los Angeles, accepts students year-round on a rolling admissions basis, depending on availability of required courses. Applications for admission are available online or by contacting the campus.

Correspondence and Information

Argosy University, Los Angeles
2950 31st Street
Santa Monica, California 90405
Phone: 310-866-4000
866-505-0332 (toll-free)
Fax: 310-399-1804
E-mail: auadmissions@argosy.edu
Web site: http://www.argosy.edu/losangeles

Argosy University, Los Angeles

THE FACULTY

The Argosy University faculty comprises working professionals who are eager to help students succeed. Members bring real-world experience and the latest practice innovations to the academic setting. The diverse faculty members of the College of Psychology and Behavioral Sciences are is widely recognized for contributions to the field. Many are published scholars, and most hold doctoral degrees. They provide a substantive education that combines comprehensive knowledge with critical skills and practical workplace relevance. Above all, faculty members are committed to their students' personal and professional development.

ARGOSY UNIVERSITY.

ARGOSY UNIVERSITY, NASHVILLE

College of Psychology and Behavioral Sciences

Programs of Study

Argosy University, Nashville, offers the Master of Arts (M.A.) degree in mental health counseling and the Doctor of Education (Ed.D.) degree in counselor education and supervision. Students completing a program may wish to become licensed professionals. As master's-level licensure varies from state to state, students should verify the current licensing requirements for the state in which they plan to practice.

The M.A. in Mental Health Counseling program offers practicing health-services providers and those planning to enter the field extensive knowledge and the broad range of skills required to provide effective counseling to diverse patient populations. The curriculum was developed using standards set by the Council for Accreditation of Counseling and Related Educational Programs (CACREP). Course objectives meet the standards of practice of the American Counseling Association (ACA).The course work and practicum are also designed to meet current requirements for master's-level licensure in the state of Tennessee.

The Ed.D. in Counselor Education & Supervision program is designed to develop the advanced skills and knowledge necessary for leadership and advocacy roles in a variety of settings. The field is dedicated to both the academic preparation and comprehensive supervision of counselors across multiple settings. This course of study aligns with the M.A. in Professional Counseling Program to encourage entry-level counseling students to work toward becoming doctoral-level advanced practitioners, educators, and supervisors.

Research Facilities

Argosy University libraries provide curriculum support and educational resources, including current text materials, diagnostic training documents, reference materials and databases, journals and dissertations, and major and current titles in program areas. There is an online public-access catalog of library resources available throughout the Argosy University system. Students have full remote access to the campus library database, enabling them to study and conduct research at home. Academic databases offer dissertation abstracts, academic journals, and professional periodicals. All library computers are Internet accessible. Software applications include Word, Excel, PowerPoint, SPSS, and various test-scoring programs.

Financial Aid

A wide range of financial aid options is available to students who qualify. Argosy University, Nashville, offers access to federal and state aid programs, merit-based awards, grants, loans, and a work-study program. As a first step, students should complete the Free Application for Federal Student Aid (FAFSA). Prospective students can apply electronically at http://www.fafsa.ed.gov or at the campus. To receive consideration for the maximum amount of aid and ensure timely receipt of funds, it is best to submit an application promptly.

Cost of Study

Tuition varies by program. Students should contact Argosy University, Nashville, for tuition information.

Living and Housing Costs

Students typically live in apartments in the metropolitan Nashville area. Living expenses vary according to each student's preferred standard of living, housing, and transportation. The University does not offer or operate student housing. Most of the students are full-time working professionals who live within driving distance of the campus. Several nearby hotels offer special rates for those who commute from long distances. The Admissions Department also maintains a list of housing options, including contact information for University students who wish to share housing. For more information, students should contact the Admissions Department.

Student Group

Admission to Argosy University, Nashville, is selective to ensure a highly qualified student body. The University encourages diversity in academic and employment backgrounds and promotes integration of the student body into professional life through established connections with local and national professional associations. Argosy University offers a professionally oriented education with rich opportunities to gain practical experience in class, field placements, and internships. Full-time students and working professionals gain the extensive knowledge and range of skills necessary for effective performance in their chosen field.

Student Outcomes

Students can register with the University's online career-services system and use select services from a distance, such as degree-specific career e-mail lists, national job posts, and virtual job fairs. Students should contact the University for more information.

Location

Argosy University, Nashville, is located at 100 Centerview Drive in Nashville, Tennessee. This growing city offers a variety of recreational activities, including the ballet and symphony, the newly established Frist Museum of Art, and professional sports. Nashville is known as Music City, USA, and is home to the Country Music Hall of Fame. The thriving business environment includes companies such as Moses Cone Health Systems, Inc., and Novant Health, Inc.

The University

Argosy University is a private institution with nineteen locations across the nation. Argosy University, Nashville, provides a career resources office, an academic resources center, and extensive information access for research. It offers the resources of a large university plus the friendliness and personal attention of a small campus. Argosy University, Nashville, is an approved degree site that is closely associated with Argosy University, Atlanta.

The innovative programs feature dynamic, relevant, and practical curricula delivered in flexible class formats. Students enjoy scheduling options that make it easier to fit school into their busy lives, choosing from day and evening courses, on campus or online. Many students find a combination of class formats to be an ideal way of continuing their education while meeting family and professional demands.

Argosy University, Nashville, is authorized by the Tennessee Higher Education Commission (Parkway Towers, Suite 1900, 404 James Robertson Parkway, Nashville, Tennessee 37243; 615-741-3605). This authorization must be renewed each year and is based on an evaluation against minimum standards concerning quality of education, ethical business practices, health and safety, and fiscal responsibility. Argosy University is accredited by the Higher Learning Commission and is a member of the North Central Association (NCA, 30 North LaSalle Street, Suite 2400, Chicago, Illinois 60602; 800-621-7440 (toll-free); http://www.ncahlc.org).

Applying

Argosy University, Nashville, accepts students year-round on a rolling admissions basis, depending on availability of required courses. Applications for admission are available online or by contacting the campus.

Correspondence and Information

Argosy University, Nashville
100 Centerview Drive, Suite 225
Nashville, Tennessee 37214
Phone: 615-525-2800
866-833-6598 (toll-free)
Fax: 615-525-2900
E-mail: auadmissions@argosy.edu
Web site: http://www. argosy.edu/nashville

Argosy University, Nashville

THE FACULTY

The Argosy University faculty comprises working professionals who are eager to help students succeed. Members bring real-world experience and the latest practice innovations to the academic setting. The diverse faculty members of the College of Psychology and Behavioral Sciences are widely recognized for contributions to the field. Many are published scholars, and most hold doctoral degrees. They provide a substantive education that combines comprehensive knowledge with critical skills and practical workplace relevance. Above all, faculty members are committed to their students' personal and professional development.

ARGOSY UNIVERSITY

ARGOSY UNIVERSITY, ORANGE COUNTY

College of Psychology and Behavioral Sciences

Programs of Study

Argosy University, Orange County, offers the Master of Arts (M.A.) degree in clinical psychology/marriage and family therapy, counseling psychology/marriage and family therapy, forensic psychology, and sport-exercise psychology; the Doctor of Education (Ed.D.) degree in counseling psychology and organizational leadership; and the Doctor of Psychology (Psy.D.) degree in clinical psychology. Students completing a program may wish to become licensed professionals. As master's-level licensure varies from state to state, students should verify the current licensing requirements for the state in which they plan to practice.

The M.A. in clinical psychology/marriage and family therapy program provides an opportunity for students to pursue the clinical psychology track while receiving graduate-level training in core curricular areas, including supervised clinical practice. The program emphasizes a practitioner-oriented philosophy and integrates applied theory and field experience. The curriculum shares a common core with most of the first- and second-year course offerings of the doctorate in clinical psychology. The program is designed to meet requirements for licensure as a marriage and family therapist (MFT) in the state of California.

The M.A. in counseling psychology/marriage and family therapy program emphasizes a practitioner-oriented philosophy, integrating applied theory and field experience. It is designed for students who wish to pursue the counseling psychology track while receiving graduate-level training in core curricular areas, including supervised clinical practice. The curriculum shares a common core with most of the first- and second-year course offerings of the doctorate in clinical psychology. The program is designed to meet requirements for licensure as a marriage and family therapist (MFT) in the state of California.

The M.A. in forensic psychology program provides coursework in forensic psychology for application to law enforcement, legal and organizational consultation, and program analysis. The program is designed to meet growing needs of the legal and criminal justice systems for professional counseling within victim assistance programs, probation and parole offices, court-mandated treatment programs, jails, and prisons. With the exception of the practicum component, courses are offered on weekends, allowing students to continue full-time employment while enrolled in this program.

The M.A. in sport-exercise psychology program is designed to educate and train capable and ethical performance-enhancement specialists. This two-year degree is intended to meet the needs of students seeking employment in a variety of settings, including private practice, athletic departments, coaching, exercise/health, and education, as well as those planning to ultimately pursue their doctorate. The program provides a thorough grounding in both theory and practice. Based on the educational requirements outlined by the Association for the Advancement of Applied Sport Psychology (AAASP), the curriculum provides a foundation in applied sport psychology, an understanding of normal and abnormal psychological functioning, and a knowledge base in the physiological, motor, and psychosocial aspects of sport behavior. A supervised practicum provides experience in working directly with athletes or performers in applied settings.

The Ed.D. in counseling psychology program prepares counselors with the skills and credentials necessary to pursue leadership, supervision, training, and teaching positions. Students develop new interests and levels of competency through an applied research-practitioner approach to the role of professional counselor. The challenges of a changing society and the diversity of roles available to the mental health practitioner require a lifelong commitment to continuing education.

The Ed.D. in organizational leadership program is designed for working professionals who wish to develop the knowledge and skills required to hold leadership positions in complex organizations. The program focuses on transformational leadership skills in addition to managerial attributes. This approach prepares students for such strategic challenges as increasing globalization, changing economies, societal shifts, and individual-organizational relationships. Leaders prepared in this manner can become visionaries and innovators, leading viable organizations capable of meeting the challenges of the future.

The Psy.D. in clinical psychology program prepares students to deliver basic diagnostic and therapeutic services to diverse populations, including individuals, groups, and families. By integrating theory, training, research, and practice, students develop and apply the clinical skills of observation, assessment, intervention, and evaluation. Optional concentrations are available in child and family psychology, general adult clinical psychology, health psychology, or neuropsychology/geropsychology. The program prepares graduates for positions in traditional settings, including, but not limited to, independent practice, mental health centers, hospitals, medical centers, and managed-care systems. Graduates are encouraged to utilize clinical skills in innovative ways to become more competitive. Eventual positions may include consulting in various corporate, governmental, academic, multimedia, law, scientific, marketing, and industrial settings.

Research Facilities

Argosy University libraries provide curriculum support and educational resources, including current text materials, diagnostic training documents, reference materials and databases, journals and dissertations, and major and current titles in program areas. There is an online public-access catalog of library resources available throughout the Argosy University system. Students have full remote access to the campus library database, enabling them to study and conduct research at home. Academic databases offer dissertation abstracts, academic journals, and professional periodicals. All library computers are Internet accessible. Software applications include Word, Excel, PowerPoint, SPSS, and various test-scoring programs.

Financial Aid

A wide range of financial aid options is available to students who qualify. Argosy University, Orange County, offers access to federal and state aid programs, merit-based awards, grants, loans, and a work-study program. As a first step, students should complete the Free Application for Federal Student Aid (FAFSA). Prospective students can apply electronically at http://www.fafsa.ed.gov or at the campus. To receive consideration for the maximum amount of aid and ensure timely receipt of funds, students should submit an application promptly.

Cost of Study

Tuition varies by program. Students should contact Argosy University, Orange County, for tuition information.

Living and Housing Costs

Students typically live in apartments in the Santa Ana metropolitan area. Living expenses vary according to each student's preferred standard of living, housing, and transportation. The University does not offer or operate student housing. Most Argosy University students are full-time working professionals who live within driving distance of the campus. Several nearby hotels offer special rates for those who commute from long distances. The Admissions Department also maintains a list of housing options, including contact information for University students who wish to share housing. For more information, students should contact the Admissions Department.

Student Group

Admission to Argosy University, Orange County, is selective to ensure a highly qualified student body. The University encourages diversity in academic and employment backgrounds and promotes integration of the student body into professional life through established connections with local and national professional associations. Argosy University offers a professionally oriented education with rich opportunities to gain practical experience in class, field placements, and internships. Full-time students and working professionals gain the extensive knowledge and range of skills necessary for effective performance in their chosen field.

Student Outcomes

Students can register with Argosy University's online career-services system and use select services from a distance, such as degree-specific career e-mail lists, national job posts, and virtual job fairs. Students should contact the University for more information.

Location

Argosy University, Orange County, attracts students from Southern California as well as around the country and the world. Orange County features a temperate climate, sunny beaches, and a host of cultural and entertainment options. The campus is located approximately 30 miles south of downtown Los Angeles, 90 miles north of San Diego, and just minutes from one of the many freeways that connect the Southern California basin. Regional parks and preserved lands provide opportunities for hiking, biking, riding, and other recreational activities. Whether it's ultra-chic Newport Beach, artsy Laguna Beach, or unspoiled Catalina Island, Orange County's oceanside personalities are as varied as the people who visit the area.

Orange County's thriving business environment includes a broad array of companies. The area's largest employers include Ingram Micro Inc., Orange County Register, ITT Industries, and OneSource.

The University

Argosy University is a private institution with nineteen locations across the nation. Argosy University, Orange County, provides a career resources office, an academic resources center, and extensive information access for research. It offers the resources of a large university plus the friendliness and personal attention of a small campus. The innovative programs feature dynamic, relevant, and practical curricula delivered in flexible class formats. Students enjoy scheduling options that make it easier to fit school into their busy lives, choosing from day and evening courses, on campus or online. Many students find a combination of class formats to be an ideal way of continuing their education while meeting family and professional demands.

Argosy University is accredited by the Higher Learning Commission and is a member of the North Central Association (NCA, 30 North LaSalle Street, Suite 2400, Chicago, Illinois 60602; 800-621-7440 (toll-free); http://www.ncahlc.org).

Applying

Argosy University, Orange County, accepts students year-round on a rolling admissions basis, depending on availability of required courses. Applications for admission are available online or by contacting the campus.

Correspondence and Information

Argosy University, Orange County
3501 West Sunflower Avenue, Suite 110
Santa Ana, California 92704

Phone: 714-338-6200
800-716-9598 (toll-free)
Fax: 714-4437-1697
E-mail: auadmissions@argosy.edu
Web site: http://www.argosy.edu/orangecounty/

Argosy University, Orange County

THE FACULTY

The Argosy University faculty comprises working professionals who are eager to help students succeed. Members bring real-world experience and the latest practice innovations to the academic setting. The diverse faculty members of the College of Psychology and Behavioral Sciences are widely recognized for contributions to the field. Many are published scholars, and most hold doctoral degrees. They provide a substantive education that combines comprehensive knowledge with critical skills and practical workplace relevance. Above all, faculty members are committed to their students' personal and professional development.

ARGOSY UNIVERSITY.

ARGOSY UNIVERSITY, PHOENIX

College of Psychology and Behavioral Sciences

Programs of Study

Argosy University, Phoenix, offers the Master of Arts (M.A.) degree in clinical psychology, forensic psychology, mental health counseling, school psychology, and sport-exercise psychology; the Master of Arts in industrial organizational psychology (MAIO); and the Doctor of Psychology (Psy.D.) degree in clinical psychology or school psychology. Students completing a program may wish to become licensed. As master's-level licensure varies from state to state, students should verify the current licensing requirements for the state in which they plan to practice.

The M.A. in clinical psychology program prepares students with the clinical knowledge and skills required to serve the mental health needs of individuals and groups. Students develop proficiency in clinical observation, assessment, appropriate intervention, and evaluation. The program emphasizes a practitioner-oriented philosophy and integrates applied theory, research, and field experience. It is designed for students who are interested in a terminal degree and practice as a master's-level clinician, or for students planning to transfer to the Psy.D. program.

The M.A. in forensic psychology program provides coursework in forensic psychology for application to law enforcement, legal and organizational consultation, and program analysis. The program is designed to meet growing needs of the legal and criminal justice systems for professional counseling within victim assistance programs, probation and parole offices, court-mandated treatment programs, jails, and prisons. With the exception of the practicum component, courses are offered on weekends, allowing students to continue full-time employment while enrolled in this program.

The M.A. in mental health counseling program offers practicing health-services providers and those planning to enter the field extensive knowledge and the broad range of skills required to provide effective counseling to diverse patient populations. The curriculum was developed using standards set by the Council for Accreditation of Counseling and Related Educational Programs (CACREP). Course objectives meet the standards of practice of the American Counseling Association (ACA). The course work and practicum are also designed to meet current requirements for master's-level licensure in the state of Arizona.

The M.A. in school psychology program is dedicated to producing ethical, responsible, and competent school psychologists who can serve effectively in a number of professional roles. Students develop core competencies in psychological assessment, intervention, and consultation as well as cultural and individual diversity. The curriculum offers meaningful integration of theory, training, and practice. Graduates of the program may be eligible for Department of Education certification and are prepared for employment as school psychologists. Students are also prepared to work toward certification by the Nationally Certified School Psychologists in accordance with criteria developed by the National Association of School Psychologists (NASP).

The M.A. in sport-exercise psychology Program is designed to educate and train capable and ethical performance-enhancement specialists. This two-year degree is intended to meet the needs of students seeking employment in a variety of settings, including private practice, athletic departments, coaching, exercise/health, and education, as well as those planning to ultimately pursue their doctorate. The program provides a thorough grounding in both theory and practice. Based on the educational requirements outlined by the Association for the Advancement of Applied Sport Psychology (AAASP), the curriculum provides a foundation in applied sport psychology, an understanding of normal and abnormal psychological functioning, and a knowledge base in the physiological, motor, and psychosocial aspects of sport behavior. A supervised practicum provides experience in working directly with athletes or performers in applied settings.

The M.A. in industrial organizational psychology is designed to apply the knowledge of industrial organizational psychology to issues involving individuals and groups in organizational and work settings. This program prepares students for careers in areas such as compensation, training, data analysis, consultation, statistical decision making, organizational development, leadership, and human resource management. The curriculum is competency-based, focusing on the outcomes of training and on the knowledge, skills, and behavior necessary to function as a master's-level professional in industrial organizational psychology. This is an interdisciplinary program that combines the expertise of the faculty in the Colleges of Psychology and Behavioral Sciences and Business.

The Psy.D. in clinical psychology program prepares students to deliver basic diagnostic and therapeutic services to diverse populations, including individuals, groups, and families. By integrating theory, training, research, and practice, students develop and apply the clinical skills of observation, assessment, intervention, and evaluation. Students may choose an optional concentration in sport-exercise psychology. The program prepares graduates for positions in traditional settings, including, but not limited to, independent practice, mental health centers, hospitals, medical centers, and managed-care systems. The University encourages graduates to utilize clinical skills in innovative ways to become more competitive. Eventual positions may include consulting in various corporate, governmental, academic, multimedia, law, scientific, marketing, and industrial settings. The Doctor of Psychology in clinical psychology program at Argosy University, Phoenix, is accredited by the Committee on Accreditation of the American Psychological Association (APA, 750 First Street, N.E., Washington, D.C. 20002-4242, 202-336-5510).

The Psy.D. in school psychology program prepares students to become nationally certified school psychologists in accordance with the National Association of School Psychologists (NASP). It is designed for students who plan to become leaders in district psychology departments or trainers in programs at the university level. Graduates of the program display competence in the following areas: cognitive, academic, and personality assessment; practicum experiences; professional school psychology course work; psychological and educational foundations; interventions; research initiatives; and statistics and research methodology. Graduates may also be eligible for licensure as psychologists at the state level as well as certified school psychologists, which may enable them to provide school psychology services as independent consultants in private practice.

Research Facilities

Argosy University libraries provide curriculum support and educational resources, including current text materials, diagnostic training documents, reference materials and databases, journals and dissertations, and major and current titles in program areas. There is an online public-access catalog of library resources available throughout the Argosy University system. Students have full remote access to the campus library database, enabling them to study and conduct research at home. Academic databases offer dissertation abstracts, academic journals, and professional periodicals. All library computers are Internet accessible. Software applications include Word, Excel, PowerPoint, SPSS, and various test-scoring programs.

Financial Aid

A wide range of financial aid options is available to students who qualify. Argosy University, Phoenix, offers access to federal and state aid programs, merit-based awards, grants, loans, and a work-study program. As a first step, students should complete the Free Application for Federal Student Aid (FAFSA). Prospective students can apply electronically at http://www.fafsa.ed.gov or at the campus. To receive consideration for the maximum amount of aid and ensure timely receipt of funds, students should submit an application promptly.

Cost of Study

Tuition varies by program. Students should contact Argosy University, Phoenix, for tuition information.

Living and Housing Costs

Students typically live in apartments in the metropolitan Phoenix area. Living expenses vary according to each student's preferred standard of living, housing, and transportation. The University does not offer or operate student housing. Most Argosy University students are full-time working professionals who live within driving distance of the campus. Several nearby hotels offer special rates for those who commute from long distances. The Admissions Department also maintains a list of housing options, including contact information for University students who wish to share housing. For more information, students should contact the Admissions Department.

Student Group

Admission to Argosy University, Phoenix, is selective to ensure a highly qualified student body. The University encourages diversity in academic and employment backgrounds and promotes integration of the student body into professional life through established connections with local and national professional associations. Argosy University offers a professionally oriented education with rich opportunities to gain practical experience in class, field placements, and internships. Full-time students and working professionals gain the extensive knowledge and range of skills necessary for effective performance in their chosen field.

Student Outcomes

Students can register with Argosy University's online career-services system and use select services from a distance, such as degree-specific career e-mail lists, national job posts, and virtual job fairs. Students should contact the University for more information.

Location

Argosy University, Phoenix, offers a high quality education in an intimate, small-group setting. The campus is located near I-17, close to shops, restaurants, and recreational areas. Phoenix is home to several major league sports teams, and the city offers an array of cultural activities ranging from opera and theatre to science museums. The multi-cultural environment of Arizona, coupled with Argosy University's professional training affiliations throughout the state, creates an exciting opportunity for students to work with urban, rural, and culturally diverse populations.

The thriving business environment in Phoenix includes a wide variety of companies such as Intel and Go Daddy Group, an internet company. Wells Fargo, Home Depot, Lowe's, and Wal-Mart also represent some of the area's largest employers.

The University

Argosy University is a private institution with nineteen locations across the nation. Argosy University, Phoenix, provides a career resources office, an academic resources center, and extensive information access for research. It offers the resources of a large university plus the friendliness and personal attention of a small campus. The innovative programs feature dynamic, relevant, and practical curricula delivered in flexible class formats. Students enjoy scheduling options that make it easier to fit school into their busy lives, choosing from day and evening courses, on campus or online. Many students find a combination of class formats to be an ideal way of continuing their education while meeting family and professional demands.

Argosy University is accredited by the Higher Learning Commission and is a member of the North Central Association (NCA, 30 North LaSalle Street, Suite 2400, Chicago, Illinois 60602; 800-621-7440 (toll-free); http://www.ncahlc.org).

Applying

Argosy University, Phoenix, accepts students year-round on a rolling admissions basis, depending on availability of required courses. Applications for admission are available online or by contacting the campus.

Correspondence and Information

Argosy University, Phoenix
2233 West Dunlap Avenue
Phoenix, Arizona 85021
Phone: 602-216-2600
866-216-2777 (toll-free)
Fax: 602-216-2601
E-mail: auadmissions@argosy.edu
Web site: http://www.argosy.edu/phoenix/

Argosy University, Phoenix

THE FACULTY

The Argosy University faculty comprises working professionals who are eager to help students succeed. Members bring real-world experience and the latest practice innovations to the academic setting. The diverse faculty members of the College of Psychology and Behavioral Sciences are widely recognized for contributions to the field. Many are published scholars, and most hold doctoral degrees. They provide a substantive education that combines comprehensive knowledge with critical skills and practical workplace relevance. Above all, faculty members are committed to their students' personal and professional development.

ARGOSY UNIVERSITY

ARGOSY UNIVERSITY, SALT LAKE CITY

College of Psychology and Behavioral Sciences

Programs of Study

Argosy University, Salt Lake City, offers the Master of Arts (M.A.) degree in marriage and family therapy and the Doctor of Education (Ed.D.) degree in counseling psychology. Students completing a program may wish to become licensed professionals. As master's-level licensure varies from state to state, students should verify the current licensing requirements for the state in which they plan to practice.

The M.A. in marriage and family therapy program develops the theoretical and clinical elements required to provide effective counseling to individuals, couples, families, and groups. The program introduces basic counseling skills that incorporate foundations of applied psychology and systems theory into the development of appropriate clinical relationships. Course work in addiction studies and substance-abuse counseling prepares students to work with families affected by this burgeoning problem. An optional concentration in forensic counseling is available. Marriage and family therapy is recognized by the Public Health Service Act as one of the five core mental health professions, and the National Institute of Mental Health accepts marriage and family therapists as qualified mental health professionals. The program is offered through weekend courses to allow concurrent employment.

The Ed.D. in Counseling Psychology program prepares counselors with the skills and credentials necessary to pursue leadership, supervision, training, and teaching positions. Students develop new interests and levels of competency through an applied, research-practitioner approach to the role of professional counselor. An optional concentration in counselor education and supervision is available. The challenges of a changing society and the diversity of roles available to the mental health practitioner require a lifelong commitment to continuing education.

Research Facilities

Argosy University libraries provide curriculum support and educational resources, including current text materials, diagnostic training documents, reference materials and databases, journals and dissertations, and major and current titles in program areas. There is an online public-access catalog of library resources available throughout the Argosy University system. Students have full remote access to their campus library database, enabling them to study and conduct research at home. Academic databases offer dissertation abstracts, academic journals, and professional periodicals. All library computers are Internet accessible. Software applications include Word, Excel, PowerPoint, SPSS, and various test-scoring programs.

Financial Aid

A wide range of financial aid options is available to students who qualify. Argosy University, Salt Lake City, offers access to federal and state aid programs, merit-based awards, grants, loans, and a work-study program. As a first step, students should complete the Free Application for Federal Student Aid (FAFSA). Prospective students can apply electronically at http://www.fafsa.ed.gov or at the campus. To receive consideration for the maximum amount of aid and ensure timely receipt of funds, students should submit an application promptly.

Cost of Study

Tuition varies by program. Students should contact Argosy University, Salt Lake City, for tuition information.

Living and Housing Costs

Students typically live in apartments in the metropolitan Salt Lake City area. Living expenses vary according to each student's preferred standard of living, housing, and transportation. The University does not offer or operate student housing. Most of the students are full-time working professionals who live within driving distance of the campus. Several nearby hotels offer special rates for those who commute from long distances. The Admissions Department also maintains a list of housing options, including contact information for University students who wish to share housing. For more information, students should contact the Admissions Department.

Student Group

Admission to Argosy University, Salt Lake City, is selective to ensure a highly qualified student body. The University encourages diversity in academic and employment backgrounds and promotes integration of the student body into professional life through established connections with local and national professional associations. Argosy University offers a professionally oriented education with rich opportunities to gain practical experience in class, field placements, and internships. Full-time students and working professionals gain the extensive knowledge and range of skills necessary for effective performance in their chosen field.

Student Outcomes

Students can register with Argosy University's online career-services system and use select services from a distance, such as degree-specific career e-mail lists, national job posts, and virtual job fairs. Students should contact the University for more information.

Location

Argosy University, Salt Lake City, offers a high-quality education in an intimate, small-group setting. Argosy University, Salt Lake City, is conveniently located in Draper, Utah, nestled in the Wasatch Mountains about 20 miles south of Salt Lake City. The area's thriving business climate and numerous hospitals, schools, clinics, and social service agencies can provide many exciting training opportunities for students.

The University

Argosy University is a private institution with nineteen locations across the nation. Argosy University, Salt Lake City, provides a career resources office, an academic resources center, and extensive information access for research. It offers the resources of a large university plus the friendliness and personal attention of a small campus. The innovative programs feature dynamic, relevant, and practical curricula delivered in flexible class formats. Students enjoy scheduling options that make it easier to fit school into their busy lives, choosing from day and evening courses, on campus or online. Many students find a combination of class formats to be an ideal way of continuing their education while meeting family and professional demands.

Argosy University is accredited by the Higher Learning Commission and is a member of the North Central Association (NCA, 30 North LaSalle Street, Suite 2400, Chicago, Illinois 60602; 800-621-7440 (toll-free); http://www.ncahlc.org).

Applying

Argosy University, Salt Lake City, accepts students on a rolling admissions basis year-round, depending on availability of required courses. Applications for admission may be obtained online or by contacting the campus.

Correspondence and Information

Argosy University, Salt Lake City
121 Election Road, Suite 300
Draper, Utah 84020

Phone: 801-601-5000
888-639-4756 (toll-free)
Fax: 801-601-4990
E-mail: auadmissions@argosy.edu
Web site: http://www.argosy.edu/saltlakecity

Argosy University, Salt Lake City

THE FACULTY

The Argosy University faculty comprises working professionals who are eager to help students succeed. Members bring real-world experience and the latest practice innovations to the academic setting. The diverse faculty members of the College of Psychology and Behavioral Sciences are widely recognized for contributions to the field. Many are published scholars, and most hold doctoral degrees. They provide a substantive education that combines comprehensive knowledge with critical skills and practical workplace relevance. Above all, faculty members are committed to their students' personal and professional development.

ARGOSY UNIVERSITY

ARGOSY UNIVERSITY, SAN DIEGO

College of Psychology and Behavioral Sciences

Programs of Study

Argosy University, San Diego, offers the Master of Arts (M.A.) degree in clinical psychology/marriage and family therapy and in counseling psychology/marriage and family therapy and the Doctor of Education (Ed.D.) degree in counseling psychology. Students completing a program may wish to become licensed professionals. As master's-level licensure varies from state to state, students should verify the current licensing requirements for the state in which they plan to practice.

The M.A. in clinical psychology/marriage and family therapy program provides an opportunity for students to pursue the clinical psychology track while receiving graduate-level training in core curricular areas, including supervised clinical practice. The program emphasizes a practitioner-oriented philosophy and integrates applied theory and field experience. The curriculum shares a common core with most of the first- and second-year course offerings of the doctorate in clinical psychology. The program is designed to meet requirements for licensure as a marriage and family therapist (MFT) in the state of California.

The M.A. in counseling psychology/marriage & family therapy program emphasizes a practitioner-oriented philosophy, integrating applied theory and field experience. It is designed for students who wish to pursue the counseling psychology track while receiving graduate-level training in the core curricular areas, including supervised clinical practice. The curriculum shares a common core with most of the first- and second-year course offerings of the doctoral program in clinical psychology. The program is designed to meet requirements for licensure as a marriage and family therapist (MFT) in the state of California.

The Ed.D. in counseling psychology program prepares counselors with the skills and credentials necessary to pursue leadership, supervision, training, and teaching positions. Students develop new interests and levels of competency through an applied, research-practitioner approach to the role of professional counselor. The challenges of a changing society and the diversity of roles available to the mental health practitioner require a lifelong commitment to continuing education.

Research Facilities

Argosy University libraries provide curriculum support and educational resources, including current text materials, diagnostic training documents, reference materials and databases, journals and dissertations, and major and current titles in program areas. There is an online public-access catalog of library resources available throughout the Argosy University system. Students have full remote access to the campus library database, enabling them to study and conduct research at home. Academic databases offer dissertation abstracts, academic journals, and professional periodicals. All library computers are Internet accessible. Software applications include Word, Excel, PowerPoint, SPSS, and various test-scoring programs.

Financial Aid

A wide range of financial aid options is available to students who qualify. Argosy University, San Diego, offers access to federal and state aid programs, merit-based awards, grants, loans, and a work-study program. As a first step, students should complete the Free Application for Federal Student Aid (FAFSA). Prospective students can apply electronically at http://www.fafsa.ed.gov or at the campus. To receive consideration for the maximum amount of aid and ensure timely receipt of funds, it is best to submit an application promptly.

Cost of Study

Tuition varies by program. Students should contact Argosy University, San Diego, for tuition information.

Living and Housing Costs

Students typically live in apartments in the San Diego metropolitan area. Living expenses vary according to each student's preferred standard of living, housing, and transportation. The University does not offer or operate student housing. Most of the students are full-time working professionals who live within driving distance of the campus. Several nearby hotels offer special rates for those who commute from long distances. The Admissions Department also maintains a list of housing options, including contact information for University students who wish to share housing. For more information, students should contact the Admissions Department.

Student Group

Admission to Argosy University, San Diego, is selective to ensure a highly qualified student body. The University encourages diversity in academic and employment backgrounds and promotes integration of the student body into professional life through established connections with local and national professional associations. Argosy University offers a professionally oriented education with rich opportunities to gain practical experience in class, field placements, and internships. Full-time students and working professionals gain the extensive knowledge and range of skills necessary for effective performance in their chosen field.

Student Outcomes

Students can register with the University's online career-services system and use select services from a distance, such as degree-specific career e-mail lists, national job posts, and virtual job fairs. Students should contact the University for more information.

Location

San Diego, southern California's second-largest city, offers an ideal climate year-round, 70 miles of beautiful beaches, colorful neighborhoods, and a dynamic downtown district. Argosy University, San Diego, provides classrooms, a library resource center, a student lounge, staff and faculty offices, and other amenities. The area offers numerous attractions, including the famous San Diego Zoo, San Diego Wild Animal Park, and SeaWorld. San Diego's thriving business environment includes several Fortune 500 companies such as QUALCOMM and Pfizer, Inc., and a concentration of high-tech companies.

The University

Argosy University is a private institution with nineteen locations across the nation. Argosy University, San Diego, provides a career resources office, an academic resources center, and extensive information access for research. It offers the resources of a large university plus the friendliness and personal attention of a small campus.

The innovative programs feature dynamic, relevant, and practical curricula delivered in flexible class formats. Students enjoy scheduling options that make it easier to fit school into their busy lives, choosing from day and evening courses, on campus or online. Many students find a combination of class formats to be an ideal way of continuing their education while meeting family and professional demands.

Argosy University is accredited by the Higher Learning Commission and is a member of the North Central Association (NCA) (30 North LaSalle Street, Suite 2400, Chicago, Illinois 60602; 800-621-7440 (toll-free); http://www.ncahlc.org).

Applying

Argosy University, San Diego, accepts students year-round on a rolling admissions basis, depending on availability of required courses. Applications for admission are available online or by contacting the campus.

Correspondence and Information

Argosy University, San Diego
7650 Mission Valley Road
San Diego, California 92108

Phone: 858-598-1900
866-505-0333 (toll-free)
Fax: 619-291-0553
E-mail: auadmissions@argosy.edu
Web site: http://www.argosy.edu/sandiego/

Argosy University, San Diego

THE FACULTY

The Argosy University faculty comprises working professionals who are eager to help students succeed. Members bring real-world experience and the latest practice innovations to the academic setting. The diverse faculty members of the College of Psychology and Behavioral Sciences are widely recognized for contributions to the field. Many are published scholars, and most hold doctoral degrees. They provide a substantive education that combines comprehensive knowledge with critical skills and practical workplace relevance. Above all, faculty members are committed to their students' personal and professional development.

ARGOSY UNIVERSITY

ARGOSY UNIVERSITY, SAN FRANCISCO BAY AREA

College of Psychology and Behavioral Sciences

Programs of Study

Argosy University, San Francisco Bay Area, offers the Master of Arts (M.A.) degree in clinical psychology, clinical psychology/marriage and family therapy, counseling psychology, counseling psychology/marriage and family therapy, forensic psychology, and sport-exercise psychology; the Doctor of Education (Ed.D.) degree in counseling psychology and organizational leadership; and the Doctor of Psychology (Psy.D.) degree in clinical psychology. Students completing a program may wish to become licensed professionals. As master's-level licensure varies from state to state, students should verify the current licensing requirements for the state in which they plan to practice.

The M.A. in Clinical Psychology program prepares students with the clinical knowledge and skills required to serve the mental health needs of individuals and groups. Students develop proficiency in clinical observation, assessment, appropriate intervention, and evaluation. The program emphasizes a practitioner-oriented philosophy and integrates applied theory, research, and field experience. It is designed for students who are interested in a terminal degree and practice as a master's-level clinician or for students planning to transfer to the Psy.D. program.

The M.A. in Clinical Psychology/Marriage and Family Therapy program provides an opportunity for students to pursue the clinical psychology track while receiving graduate-level training in core curricular areas, including supervised clinical practice. The program emphasizes a practitioner-oriented philosophy and integrates applied theory and field experience. The curriculum shares a common core with most of the first- and second-year course offerings of the doctorate in clinical psychology. The program is designed to meet requirements for licensure as a marriage and family therapist (MFT) in the state of California.

The M.A. in Counseling Psychology program provides the necessary theoretical and practical elements required to serve effectively as a licensed marriage family therapist (MFT). The curriculum is designed to develop the attitudes, knowledge, and skills essential to becoming thoughtful, ethical professionals who can serve as counselors in a wide variety of government, community, and private settings. This two-year degree can lead to licensure and independent counseling practice. Graduates meet the academic requirements for the Licensed Mental Health Counselor (LMHC) examination in the state of California.

The M.A. in Counseling Psychology/Marriage and Family Therapy program emphasizes a practitioner-oriented philosophy, integrating applied theory and field experience. It is designed for students who wish to pursue the counseling psychology track while receiving graduate-level training in the core curricular areas, including supervised clinical practice. The curriculum shares a common core with most of the first- and second-year course offerings of the doctorate in clinical psychology. The program is designed to meet requirements for licensure as a marriage and family therapist (MFT) in the state of California.

The M.A. in Forensic Psychology program provides course work in forensic psychology for application to law enforcement, legal and organizational consultation, and program analysis. The program is designed to meet growing needs of the legal and criminal justice systems for professional counseling within victim assistance programs, probation and parole offices, court-mandated treatment programs, jails, and prisons. With the exception of the practicum component, courses are offered on weekends, allowing students to continue full-time employment while enrolled in this program.

The M.A. in Sport-Exercise Psychology program is designed to educate and train capable and ethical performance-enhancement specialists. This two-year degree is intended to meet the needs of students seeking employment in a variety of settings, including private practice, athletic departments, coaching, exercise/health, and education, as well as those planning to ultimately pursue their doctorate. The program provides a thorough grounding in both theory and practice. Based on the educational requirements outlined by the Association for the Advancement of Applied Sport Psychology (AAASP), the curriculum provides a foundation in applied sport psychology, an understanding of normal and abnormal psychological functioning, and a knowledge base in the physiological, motor, and psychosocial aspects of sport behavior. A supervised practicum provides experience in working directly with athletes or performers in applied settings.

The Ed.D. in Counseling Psychology program prepares counselors with the skills and credentials necessary to pursue leadership, supervision, training, and teaching positions. Students develop new interests and levels of competency through an applied research-practitioner approach to the role of professional counselor. An optional concentration in forensic counseling is available. The challenges of a changing society and the diversity of roles available to the mental health practitioner require a lifelong commitment to continuing education.

The Ed.D. in Organizational Leadership program is designed for working professionals who wish to develop the knowledge and skills required to hold leadership positions in complex organizations. The program focuses on transformational leadership skills in addition to managerial attributes. This approach prepares students for such strategic challenges as increasing globalization, changing economies, societal shifts, and individual-organizational relationships. Leaders prepared in this manner can become visionaries and innovators, leading viable organizations capable of meeting the challenges of the future.

The Psy.D. in Clinical Psychology program prepares students to deliver basic diagnostic and therapeutic services to diverse populations, including individuals, groups, and families. By integrating theory, training, research, and practice, students develop and apply the clinical skills of observation, assessment, intervention, and evaluation. The program prepares graduates for positions in traditional settings, including, but not limited to, independent practice, mental health centers, hospitals, medical centers, and managed-care systems. Graduates are encouraged to utilize clinical skills in innovative ways to become more competitive. Eventual positions may include consulting in various corporate, governmental, academic, multimedia, law, scientific, marketing, and industrial settings. The Doctor of Psychology in Clinical Psychology program at Argosy University, San Francisco Bay Area, is accredited by the Committee on Accreditation of the American Psychological Association (APA, 750 First Street, N.E., Washington, D.C. 20002-4242; 202-336-5510).

Research Facilities

Argosy University libraries provide curriculum support and educational resources, including current text materials, diagnostic training documents, reference materials and databases, journals and dissertations, and major and current titles in program areas. There is an online public-access catalog of library resources available throughout the Argosy University system. Students have full remote access to the campus library database, enabling them to study and conduct research at home. Academic databases offer dissertation abstracts, academic journals, and professional periodicals. All library computers are Internet accessible. Software applications include Word, Excel, PowerPoint, SPSS, and various test-scoring programs.

Financial Aid

A wide range of financial aid options is available to students who qualify. Argosy University, San Francisco Bay Area, offers access to federal and state aid programs, merit-based awards, grants, loans, and a work-study program. As a first step, students should complete the Free Application for Federal Student Aid (FAFSA). Prospective students can apply electronically at http://www.fafsa.ed.gov or at the campus. To receive consideration for the maximum amount of aid and ensure timely receipt of funds, students should submit an application promptly.

Cost of Study

Tuition varies by program. Students should contact Argosy University, San Francisco Bay Area, for tuition information.

Living and Housing Costs

Students typically live in apartments in the San Francisco metropolitan area. Living expenses vary according to each student's preferred standard of living, housing, and transportation. The University does not offer or operate student housing. Most Argosy University students are full-time working professionals who live within driving distance of the campus. Several nearby hotels offer special rates for those who commute from long distances. The Admissions Department also maintains a list of housing options, including contact information for University students who wish to share housing. For more information, students should contact the Admissions Department.

Student Group

Admission to Argosy University, San Francisco Bay Area, is selective to ensure a highly qualified student body. The University encourages diversity in academic and employment backgrounds and promotes integration of the student body into professional life through established connections with local and national professional associations. Argosy University offers a professionally oriented education with rich opportunities to gain practical experience in class, field placements, and internships. Full-time students and working professionals gain the extensive knowledge and range of skills necessary for effective performance in their chosen field.

Student Outcomes

Students can register with Argosy University's online career-services system and use select services from a distance, such as degree-specific career e-mail lists, national job posts, and virtual job fairs. Students should contact the University for more information.

Location

Located in northern California, Argosy University, San Francisco Bay Area, attracts students from the immediate area as well as from around the country and the world. In July 2007, the University moved to its new location at 1005 Atlantic Avenue, Alameda, California. The energy in San Francisco is contagious. Numerous surveys rank San Francisco as the most wired city in the world, thanks to its high concentration of computer-savvy citizens and businesses.

Many educational institutions and agencies in the area provide excellent opportunities for student training. The Bay Area and nearby Silicon Valley are home to leading new media companies such as Pixar, ILM, and Sega. A who's who of technology companies call the Bay Area home, including Apple, Cisco, Hewlett-Packard, Intel, Oracle, and Sun Microsystems. The Bay Area also is the home of traditional companies such as BankAmerica, Chevron, Levi-Strauss, Safeway, and Wells Fargo.

The University

Argosy University is a private institution with nineteen locations across the nation. Argosy University, San Francisco Bay Area, provides a career resources office, an academic resources center, and extensive information access for research. It offers the resources of a large university plus the friendliness and personal attention of a small campus. The innovative programs feature dynamic, relevant, and practical curricula delivered in flexible class formats. Students enjoy scheduling options that make it easier to fit school into their busy lives, choosing from day and evening courses, on campus or online. Many students find a combination of class formats to be an ideal way of continuing their education while meeting family and professional demands.

Argosy University is accredited by the Higher Learning Commission and is a member of the North Central Association (NCA, 30 North LaSalle Street, Suite 2400, Chicago, Illinois 60602; 800-621-7440 (toll-free); http://www.ncahlc.org).

Applying

Argosy University, San Francisco Bay Area, accepts students year-round on a rolling admissions basis, depending on availability of required courses. Applications for admission are available online or by contacting the campus.

Correspondence and Information

Argosy University, San Francisco Bay Area
1005 Atlantic Avenue
Alameda, California 94501

Phone: 510-215-0277
866-215-2777 (toll free)
Fax: 510-215-0299
E-mail: auadmissions@argosy.edu
Web site: http://www.argosy.edu/sanfrancisco

Argosy University, San Francisco Bay Area

THE FACULTY

The Argosy University faculty comprises working professionals who are eager to help students succeed. Members bring real-world experience and the latest practice innovations to the academic setting. The diverse faculty members of the College of Psychology and Behavioral Sciences are widely recognized for contributions to the field. Many are published scholars, and most hold doctoral degrees. They provide a substantive education that combines comprehensive knowledge with critical skills and practical workplace relevance. Above all, faculty members are committed to their students' personal and professional development.

ARGOSY UNIVERSITY

ARGOSY UNIVERSITY, SARASOTA

College of Psychology and Behavioral Sciences

Programs of Study

Argosy University, Sarasota, offers the Master of Arts (M.A.) degree in community counseling, forensic psychology, marriage and family therapy, mental health counseling, school counseling, and school psychology; the Education Specialist (Ed.S.) degree in school counseling; and the Doctor of Education (Ed.D.) degree in counseling psychology, counselor education and supervision, organizational leadership, and pastoral community counseling. Students completing a program may wish to become licensed professionals. As master's-level licensure varies from state to state, students should verify the current licensing requirements for the state in which they plan to practice.

The M.A. in Community Counseling program provides a multifaceted focus on developmental and preventive mental health services. Students gain the knowledge and skills required for individual, group, family, and organizational interventions. The curriculum integrates foundational counseling skills and theories with clinical field experience.

The M.A. in Forensic Psychology program provides course work in forensic psychology for application to law enforcement, legal and organizational consultation, and program analysis. The program is designed to meet the growing needs of the legal and criminal justice systems for professional counseling within victim assistance programs, probation and parole offices, court-mandated treatment programs, jails, and prisons. With the exception of the practicum component, courses are offered on weekends, allowing students to continue full-time employment while enrolled in this program.

The M.A. in Marriage & Family Therapy program develops the theoretical and clinical elements required to provide effective counseling to individuals, couples, families, and groups. The program introduces basic counseling skills that incorporate foundations of applied psychology and systems theory into the development of appropriate clinical relationships. Course work in addiction studies and substance-abuse counseling prepares students to work with families affected by this burgeoning problem. Marriage and family therapy is recognized by the Public Health Service Act as one of the five core mental health professions, and the National Institute of Mental Health accepts marriage and family therapists as qualified mental health professionals. The program is offered through weekend courses to allow concurrent employment.

The M.A. in Mental Health Counseling program offers practicing health services providers and those planning to enter the field extensive knowledge and the broad range of skills required to provide effective counseling to diverse patient populations. The curriculum was developed using standards set by the Council for Accreditation of Counseling and Related Educational Programs (CACREP, 599 Stevenson Avenue, Alexandria, Virginia 22304; 703-823-9800; http://www.cacrep.org). CACREP, a specialized accrediting body recognized by the Council for Higher Education Accreditation (CHEA), has granted accreditation to the M.A. in Mental Health Counseling program at Argosy University, Sarasota. Course objectives meet the standards of practice of the American Counseling Association (ACA). The course work and practicum are also designed to meet current requirements for master's-level licensure in the state of Florida.

The M.A. in School Counseling program integrates theoretical foundations of counseling with fundamental counseling skills and field experience for the application of appropriate interaction and intervention in a school setting. The curriculum focuses on behavior management, wellness, career and personal growth, and pathology. Graduates of the program can serve as effective and ethical professionals with a demonstrated knowledge of social and cultural diversity in adherence to the principles of the American School Counselor Association.

The M.A. in School Psychology program is dedicated to producing ethical, responsible, and competent school psychologists. Students develop core competencies in psychological assessment, intervention, and consultation as well as cultural and individual diversity. The curriculum provides for the meaningful integration of theory, training, and practice. Graduates of the program may be eligible for Department of Education certification and are prepared for employment as school psychologists. Students are also prepared to work toward certification by the Nationally Certified School Psychologists in accordance with criteria developed by the National Association of School Psychologists (NASP).

The Ed.S. in School Counseling program is intended for teaching professionals with a master's degree who wish to continue their professional development. The program focuses students on a specialty area applicable to the public school setting. The curriculum helps students meet the specialization requirements for certification in guidance and counseling (K–12) in the state of Florida.

The Ed.D. in Counseling Psychology program prepares counselors with the skills and credentials necessary to pursue leadership, supervision, training, and teaching positions. Students develop new interests and levels of competency through an applied, research-practitioner approach to the role of professional counselor. The challenges of a changing society and the diversity of roles available to the mental health practitioner require a lifelong commitment to continuing education.

The Ed.D. in Counselor Education & Supervision program is designed to develop the advanced skills and knowledge necessary for leadership and advocacy roles in a variety of settings. The field is dedicated to both the academic preparation and comprehensive supervision of counselors across multiple settings. This course of study aligns with the Master of Arts in Professional Counseling program to encourage entry-level counseling students to work toward becoming doctoral-level advanced practitioners, educators, and supervisors.

The Ed.D. in Organizational Leadership program is designed for working professionals who wish to develop the knowledge and skills required to hold leadership positions in complex organizations. Argosy focuses on transformational leadership skills in addition to managerial attributes. This approach prepares students for strategic challenges such as increasing globalization, changing economies, societal shifts, and individual-organizational relationships.

The Ed.D. in Pastoral Community Counseling program is based on the fundamental belief that religious and spiritual communities provide a unique opportunity for human growth and development. The program integrates extensive knowledge with advanced skills, reflective practice, and research to aid individual and communal development. It affords students the opportunity to pursue doctoral study while maintaining active participation in professional service.

Research Facilities

Argosy University libraries provide curriculum support and educational resources, including current text materials, diagnostic training documents, reference materials and databases, journals and dissertations, and major and current titles in program areas. There is an online public-access catalog of library resources available throughout the Argosy University system. Students have full remote access to the campus library database, enabling them to study and conduct research at home. Academic databases offer dissertation abstracts, academic journals, and professional periodicals. All library computers are Internet accessible. Software applications include Word, Excel, PowerPoint, SPSS, and various test-scoring programs.

Financial Aid

A wide range of financial aid options is available to students who qualify. Argosy University, Sarasota, offers access to federal and state aid programs, merit-based awards, grants, loans, and a work-study program. As a first step, students should complete the Free Application for Federal Student Aid (FAFSA). Prospective students can apply electronically at http://www.fafsa.ed.gov or at the campus. To receive consideration for the maximum amount of aid and ensure timely receipt of funds, it is best to submit an application promptly.

Cost of Study

Tuition varies by program. Students should contact Argosy University, Sarasota, for tuition information.

Living and Housing Costs

Students typically live in apartments in the metropolitan Sarasota area. Living expenses vary according to each student's preferred standard of living, housing, and transportation. The University does not offer or operate student housing. Most of the students are full-time working professionals who live within driving distance of the campus. Several nearby hotels offer special rates for those who commute from long distances to attend scheduled weeklong in-residence sessions. The Admissions Department also maintains a list of housing options, including contact information for University students who wish to share housing. For more information, students should contact the Admissions Department.

Student Group

Admission to Argosy University, Sarasota, is selective to ensure a highly qualified student body. The University encourages diversity in academic and employment backgrounds and promotes integration of the student body into professional life through established connections with local and national professional associations. Argosy University offers a professionally oriented education with rich opportunities to gain practical experience in class, field placements, and internships. Full-time students and working professionals gain the extensive knowledge and range of skills necessary for effective performance in their chosen fields.

Student Outcomes

Students can register with the University's online career-services system and use select services from a distance, such as degree-specific career e-mail lists, national job posts, and virtual job fairs. Students should contact the University for more information.

Location

Located in northeast Sarasota, the campus is specifically designed for postsecondary and graduate-level instruction through a unique combination of in-residence course work, tutorials, and online study courses. Several programs are off-site tutorials and intensive one-week classroom sessions. Students may also complete up to 49 percent of the work in some degree programs via online courses that allow interaction with faculty members and classmates from any Internet connection.

Sarasota is recognized as Florida's cultural coast and is home to a professional symphony, ballet, and opera as well as dozens of theaters and art galleries. Well-known vacation attractions such as Disney World, Busch Gardens–Tampa, and the city of Miami are within a few hours' drive. The area enjoys mild winters and endless summer beauty.

The growing business sector in the Gulf Coast community helps make it one of the top 20 places to live and work. ASO Corporation, Nelson Publishing, and Select Technology Group are among the numerous companies headquartered in Sarasota County. The area's top employers include Sarasota Memorial Hospital and Publix Supermarkets.

The University

Argosy University is a private institution with nineteen locations across the nation. Argosy University, Sarasota, provides a career resources office, an academic resources center, and extensive information access for research. It offers the resources of a large university plus the friendliness and personal attention of a small campus.

The innovative programs feature dynamic, relevant, and practical curricula delivered in flexible class formats. Students enjoy scheduling options that make it easier to fit school into their busy lives, choosing from day and evening courses, on campus or online. Many students find a combination of class formats to be an ideal way of continuing their education while meeting family and professional demands.

Argosy University is accredited by the Higher Learning Commission and is a member of the North Central Association (NCA, 30 North LaSalle Street, Suite 2400, Chicago, Illinois 60602; 800-621-7440 (toll-free); http://www.ncahlc.org).

Applying

Argosy University, Sarasota, accepts students year-round on a rolling admissions basis, depending on availability of required courses. Applications for admission are available online or by contacting the campus.

Correspondence and Information

Argosy University, Sarasota
5250 17th Street
Sarasota, Florida 34235

Phone: 941-379-0404
800-331-5995 (toll-free)
Fax: 941-371-8910
E-mail: auadmissions@argosy.edu
Web site: http://www.argosy.edu/sarasota

Argosy University, Sarasota

THE FACULTY

The Argosy University faculty comprises working professionals who are eager to help students succeed. Members bring real-world experience and the latest practice innovations to the academic setting. The diverse faculty members of the College of Psychology and Behavioral Sciences are widely recognized for contributions to the field. Many are published scholars, and most hold doctoral degrees. They provide a substantive education that combines comprehensive knowledge with critical skills and practical workplace relevance. Above all, faculty members are committed to their students' personal and professional development.

ARGOSY UNIVERSITY

ARGOSY UNIVERSITY, SCHAUMBURG

College of Psychology and Behavioral Sciences

Programs of Study

Argosy University, Schaumburg, offers the Master of Arts (M.A.) degree in clinical psychology and community counseling; the Doctor of Education (Ed.D.) degree in counseling psychology, counselor education and supervision, and organizational leadership; and the Doctor of Psychology (Psy.D.) degree in clinical psychology. Students completing a program may wish to become licensed professionals. As master's-level licensure varies from state to state, students should verify the current licensing requirements for the state in which they plan to practice.

The M.A. in Clinical Psychology program prepares students with the clinical knowledge and skills required to serve the mental health needs of individuals and groups. Students develop proficiency in clinical observation, assessment, appropriate intervention, and evaluation. The program emphasizes a practitioner-oriented philosophy and integrates applied theory, research, and field experience. It is designed for students who are interested in a terminal degree and practice as a master's-level clinician or for students planning to transfer to the Psy.D. program.

The M.A. in Community Counseling program prepares students to enter the counseling profession as ethical, effective, skilled, and culturally competent practitioners. It provides a multifaceted focus on developmental and preventive mental health services. Students gain the knowledge and skills required for individual, group, family, and organizational interventions. The curriculum integrates foundational counseling skills and theories with clinical field experience. The Council for Accreditation of Counseling and Related Educational Programs (CACREP, 599 Stevenson Avenue, Alexandria, Virginia 22304; 703-823-9800; http://www.cacrep.org), a specialized accrediting body recognized by the Council for Higher Education Accreditation (CHEA), has granted accreditation to the M.A. in Community Counseling program at Argosy University, Schaumburg.

The Ed.D. in Counseling Psychology program prepares counselors with the skills and credentials necessary to pursue leadership, supervision, training, and teaching positions. Students develop new interests and levels of competency through an applied research-practitioner approach to the role of professional counselor. An optional concentration in counselor education and supervision is available. The challenges of a changing society and the diversity of roles available to the mental health practitioner require a lifelong commitment to continuing education.

The Ed.D. in Counselor Education and Supervision program is designed to develop the advanced skills and knowledge necessary for leadership and advocacy roles in a variety of settings. The field is dedicated to both the academic preparation and comprehensive supervision of counselors across multiple settings. This course of study aligns with the Master of Arts in Community Counseling program to encourage entry-level counseling students to work toward becoming doctoral-level advanced practitioners, educators, and supervisors.

The Ed.D. in Organizational Leadership program is designed for working professionals who wish to develop the knowledge and skills required to hold leadership positions in complex organizations. The program focuses on transformational leadership skills in addition to managerial attributes. This approach prepares students for such strategic challenges as increasing globalization, changing economies, societal shifts, and individual-organizational relationships.

The Psy.D. in Clinical Psychology program prepares students to deliver basic diagnostic and therapeutic services to diverse populations, including individuals, groups, and families. By integrating theory, training, research, and practice, students develop and apply the clinical skills of observation, assessment, intervention, and evaluation. Optional concentrations are available in child and family psychology, clinical health psychology, diversity and multicultural psychology, or forensic psychology. The program prepares graduates for positions in traditional settings, including, but not limited to, independent practice, mental health centers, hospitals, medical centers, and managed-care systems. Graduates are encouraged to utilize clinical skills in innovative ways to become more competitive. Eventual positions may include consulting in various corporate, governmental, academic, multimedia, law, scientific, marketing, and industrial settings. The Doctor of Psychology in Clinical Psychology program at Argosy University, Schaumburg, is accredited by the Committee on Accreditation of the American Psychological Association (APA, 750 First Street, NE, Washington, D.C. 20002-4242; 202-336-5510).

Research Facilities

Argosy University libraries provide curriculum support and educational resources, including current text materials, diagnostic training documents, reference materials and databases, journals and dissertations, and major and current titles in program areas. There is an online public-access catalog of library resources available throughout the Argosy University system. Students have full remote access to the campus library database, enabling them to study and conduct research at home. Academic databases offer dissertation abstracts, academic journals, and professional periodicals. All library computers are Internet accessible. Software applications include Word, Excel, PowerPoint, SPSS, and various test-scoring programs.

Financial Aid

A wide range of financial aid options is available to students who qualify. Argosy University, Schaumburg, offers access to federal and state aid programs, merit-based awards, grants, loans, and a work-study program. As a first step, students should complete the Free Application for Federal Student Aid (FAFSA). Prospective students can apply electronically at http://www.fafsa.ed.gov or at the campus. To receive consideration for the maximum amount of aid and ensure timely receipt of funds, students should submit an application promptly.

Cost of Study

Tuition varies by program. Students should contact Argosy University, Schaumburg, for tuition information.

Living and Housing Costs

Students typically live in apartments in the metropolitan Chicago area. Living expenses vary according to each student's preferred standard of living, housing, and transportation. The University does not offer or operate student housing. Most Argosy University students are full-time working professionals who live within driving distance of the campus. Several nearby hotels offer special rates for those who commute from long distances. The Admissions Department also maintains a list of housing options, including contact information for University students who wish to share housing. For more information, students should contact the Admissions Department.

Student Group

Admission to Argosy University, Schaumburg, is selective to ensure a highly qualified student body. The University encourages diversity in academic and employment backgrounds and promotes integration of the student body into professional life through established connections with local and national professional associations. Argosy University offers a professionally oriented education with rich opportunities to gain practical experience in class, field placements, and internships. Full-time students and working professionals gain the extensive knowledge and range of skills necessary for effective performance in their chosen field.

Student Outcomes

Students can register with Argosy University's online career-services system and use select services from a distance, such as degree-specific career e-mail lists, national job posts, and virtual job fairs. Students should contact the University for more information.

Location

Argosy University, Schaumburg, is located in the northwest suburban area, approximately 45 minutes from downtown Chicago. The University's small size offers a highly personal atmosphere and flexible programs tailored to students' needs. Visitors to Chicago experience a range of attractions to stimulate both intellectual and recreational pursuits. Located on the shores of Lake Michigan in the Midwest, Chicago is home to world-champion sports teams, an internationally acclaimed symphony orchestra, renowned architecture, and nearly 3 million residents. Among the variety of history and art museums in the city, the Chicago Cultural Center offers more than 600 art programs and exhibits each year. Recreational opportunities include hiking and cycling on miles of lakefront trails, golfing, and shopping

Many facilities and agencies in the area provide excellent opportunities for student training. Schaumburg's thriving business environment includes 5,000 businesses that employ 80,000 people. The area's largest employers are Motorola, Experian, Cingular, and IBM.

The University

Argosy University is a private institution with nineteen locations across the nation. Argosy University, Schaumburg, provides a career resources office, an academic resources center, and extensive information access for research. It offers the resources of a large university plus the friendliness and personal attention of a small campus. Argosy University, Schaumburg, is an approved degree site that is closely associated with the University's Chicago campus. The innovative programs feature dynamic, relevant, and practical curricula delivered in flexible class formats. Students enjoy scheduling options that make it easier to fit school into their busy lives, choosing from day and evening courses, on campus or online. Many students find a combination of class formats to be an ideal way of continuing their education while meeting family and professional demands.

Argosy University is accredited by the Higher Learning Commission and is a member of the North Central Association (NCA, 30 North LaSalle Street, Suite 2400, Chicago, Illinois 60602; 800-621-7440 (toll-free); http://www.ncahlc.org).

Applying

Argosy University, Schaumburg, accepts students year-round on a rolling admissions basis, depending on availability of required courses. Applications for admission are available online or by contacting the campus.

Correspondence and Information

Argosy University, Schaumburg
999 North Plaza Drive, Suite 111
Schaumburg, Illinois 60173-5403

Phone: 847-969-7400
866-290-2777 (toll-free)
Fax: 847-969-4998
E-mail: auadmissions@argosy.edu
Web site: http://www.argosy.edu/schaumburg

Argosy University, Schaumburg

THE FACULTY

The Argosy University faculty comprises working professionals who are eager to help students succeed. Members bring real-world experience and the latest practice innovations to the academic setting. The diverse faculty members of the College of Psychology and Behavioral Sciences are widely recognized for contributions to the field. Many are published scholars, and most hold doctoral degrees. They provide a substantive education that combines comprehensive knowledge with critical skills and practical workplace relevance. Above all, faculty members are committed to their students' personal and professional development.

ARGOSY UNIVERSITY.

ARGOSY UNIVERSITY, SEATTLE

College of Psychology and Behavioral Sciences

Programs of Study

Argosy University, Seattle, offers the Master of Arts (M.A.) degree in clinical psychology and counseling psychology, the Doctor of Education (Ed.D.) degree in counseling psychology, and the Doctor of Psychology (Psy.D.) degree in clinical psychology. Students completing a program may wish to become licensed professionals. As master's-level licensure varies from state to state, students should verify the current licensing requirements for the state in which they plan to practice.

The M.A. in Clinical Psychology program prepares students with the clinical knowledge and skills required to serve the mental health needs of individuals and groups. Students develop proficiency in clinical observation, assessment, appropriate intervention, and evaluation. The program emphasizes a practitioner-oriented philosophy and integrates applied theory, research, and field experience. It is designed for students who are interested in a terminal degree and practice as a master's-level clinician or for students planning to transfer to the Psy.D. program.

The M.A. in Counseling Psychology program provides the necessary theoretical and practical elements required to serve effectively as a licensed marriage family therapist (MFT). The curriculum is designed to develop the attitudes, knowledge, and skills essential to becoming thoughtful, ethical professionals who can serve as counselors in a wide variety of government, community, and private settings. This two-year degree can lead to licensure for independent counseling practice. Graduates meet the academic requirements for the Licensed Mental Health Counselor (LMHC) examination in the state of Washington.

The Ed.D. in Counseling Psychology program prepares counselors with the skills and credentials necessary to pursue leadership, supervision, training, and teaching positions. Students develop new interests and levels of competency through an applied, research-practitioner approach to the role of professional counselor. The challenges of a changing society and the diversity of roles available to the mental health practitioner require a lifelong commitment to continuing education.

The Psy.D. in Clinical Psychology program prepares students to deliver basic diagnostic and therapeutic services to diverse populations, including individuals, groups, and families. By integrating theory, training, research, and practice, students develop and apply the clinical skills of observation, assessment, intervention, and evaluation. The program prepares graduates for positions in traditional settings, including, but not limited to, independent practice, mental health centers, hospitals, medical centers, and managed-care systems. Argosy also encourages graduates to utilize clinical skills in innovative ways to become more competitive. Eventual positions may include consulting in various corporate, governmental, academic, multimedia, law, scientific, marketing, and industrial settings.

Research Facilities

Argosy University libraries provide curriculum support and educational resources, including current text materials, diagnostic training documents, reference materials and databases, journals and dissertations, and major and current titles in program areas. There is an online public-access catalog of library resources available throughout the Argosy University system. Students have full remote access to the campus library database, enabling them to study and conduct research at home. Academic databases offer dissertation abstracts, academic journals, and professional periodicals. All library computers are Internet accessible. Software applications include Word, Excel, PowerPoint, SPSS, and various test-scoring programs.

Financial Aid

A wide range of financial aid options is available to students who qualify. Argosy University, Seattle, offers access to federal and state aid programs, merit-based awards, grants, loans, and a work-study program. As a first step, students should complete the Free Application for Federal Student Aid (FAFSA). Prospective students can apply electronically at http://www.fafsa.ed.gov or at the campus. To receive consideration for the maximum amount of aid and ensure timely receipt of funds, it is best to submit an application promptly.

Cost of Study

Tuition varies by program. Students should contact Argosy University, Seattle, for tuition information.

Living and Housing Costs

Students typically live in apartments in the metropolitan Seattle area. Living expenses vary according to each student's preferred standard of living, housing, and transportation. The University does not offer or operate student housing. Most of the students are full-time working professionals who live within driving distance of the campus. Several nearby hotels offer special rates for those who commute from long distances. The Admissions Department also maintains a list of housing options, including contact information, for University students who wish to share housing. For more information, students should contact the Admissions Department.

Student Group

Admission to Argosy University, Seattle, is selective to ensure a highly qualified student body. The University encourages diversity in academic and employment backgrounds and promotes integration of the student body into professional life through established connections with local and national professional associations. Argosy University offers a professionally oriented education with rich opportunities to gain practical experience in class, field placements, and internships. Full-time students and working professionals gain the extensive knowledge and range of skills necessary for effective performance in their chosen fields.

Student Outcomes

Students can register with the University's online career-services system and use select services from a distance, such as degree-specific career e-mail lists, national job posts, and virtual job fairs. Students should contact the University for more information.

Location

Argosy University, Seattle, aspires to provide a supportive, collaborative, and engaging yet challenging learning environment. Easily reached through the King County Public Transportation System, the campus sits in proximity to local libraries, shops, restaurants, theaters, and art museums. Seattle offers numerous historical and multicultural museums, a symphony, ballet, and many theater companies. The city is home to several major-league sports teams and offers a myriad of outdoor recreational opportunities, such as camping, hiking, fishing, skiing, and rock climbing. Seattle's thriving business environment encompasses a wide range of industries and features such giants as Microsoft, Boeing, and Alaska Air Group. The Port of Seattle and the University of Washington are also among the area's largest employers.

The University

Argosy University is a private institution with nineteen locations across the nation. Argosy University, Seattle, provides a career resources office, an academic resources center, and extensive information access for research. It offers the resources of a large university, plus the friendliness and personal attention of a small campus.

The innovative programs feature dynamic, relevant, and practical curricula delivered in flexible class formats. Students enjoy scheduling options that make it easier to fit school into their busy lives, choosing from day and evening courses, on campus or online. Many students find a combination of class formats to be an ideal way of continuing their education while meeting family and professional demands.

Argosy University is accredited by the Higher Learning Commission and is a member of the North Central Association (NCA, 30 North LaSalle Street, Suite 2400, Chicago, Illinois 60602; 800-621-7440 (toll-free); http://www.ncahlc.org).

Applying

Argosy University, Seattle, accepts students year-round on a rolling admissions basis, depending on availability of required courses. Applications for admission are available online or by contacting the campus.

Correspondence and Information

Argosy University, Seattle
2601-A Elliott Avenue
Seattle, Washington 98121

Phone: 206-283-4500
866-283-2777 (toll-free)
Fax: 206-283-5777
E-mail: auadmissions@argosy.edu
Web site: http://www.argosy.edu/seattle

Argosy University, Seattle

THE FACULTY

The Argosy University faculty comprises working professionals who are eager to help students succeed. Members bring real-world experience and the latest practice innovations to the academic setting. The diverse faculty members of the College of Psychology and Behavioral Sciences are widely recognized for contributions to the field. Many are published scholars, and most hold doctoral degrees. They provide a substantive education that combines comprehensive knowledge with critical skills and practical workplace relevance. Above all, faculty members are committed to their students' personal and professional development.

ARGOSY UNIVERSITY

ARGOSY UNIVERSITY, TAMPA

College of Psychology and Behavioral Sciences

Programs of Study

Argosy University, Tampa, offers the Master of Arts (M.A.) degree in clinical psychology, marriage and family therapy, mental health counseling, and school counseling; the Doctor of Education (Ed.D.) degree in counselor education and supervision and organizational leadership; and the Doctor of Psychology (Psy.D.) degree in clinical psychology. Students completing a program may wish to become licensed professionals. As master's-level licensure varies from state to state, students should verify the current licensing requirements for the state in which they plan to practice.

The M.A. in Clinical Psychology program prepares students with the clinical knowledge and skills required to serve the mental health needs of individuals and groups. Students develop proficiency in clinical observation, assessment, appropriate intervention, and evaluation. The program emphasizes a practitioner-oriented philosophy and integrates applied theory, research, and field experience. It is designed for students who are interested in a terminal degree and practice as a master's-level clinician or for students planning to transfer to the Psy.D. program.

The M.A. in Marriage & Family Therapy program develops the theoretical and clinical elements required to provide effective counseling to individuals, couples, families, and groups. The program introduces basic counseling skills that incorporate foundations of applied psychology and systems theory into the development of appropriate clinical relationships. Course work in addiction studies and substance-abuse counseling prepares students to work with families affected by this burgeoning problem. Marriage and family therapy is recognized by the Public Health Service Act as one of the five core mental health professions, and the National Institute of Mental Health accepts marriage and family therapists as qualified mental health professionals. The program is offered through weekend courses to allow concurrent employment.

The M.A. in Mental Health Counseling program offers practicing health services providers and those planning to enter the field extensive knowledge and the broad range of skills required to provide effective counseling to diverse patient populations. The curriculum was developed using standards set by the Council for Accreditation of Counseling and Related Educational Programs (CACREP). Course objectives meet the standards of practice of the American Counseling Association (ACA).The course work and practicum are also designed to meet current requirements for master's-level licensure in the state of Florida.

The M.A. in School Counseling program integrates theoretical foundations of counseling with fundamental counseling skills and field experience for the application of appropriate interaction and intervention in a school setting. The curriculum focuses on behavior management, wellness, career and personal growth, and pathology. Graduates of the program can serve as effective and ethical professionals with a demonstrated knowledge of social and cultural diversity in adherence to the principles of the American School Counselor Association.

The Ed.D. in Counselor Education & Supervision program is designed to develop the advanced skills and knowledge necessary for leadership and advocacy roles in a variety of settings. The field is dedicated to both the academic preparation and comprehensive supervision of counselors across multiple settings. This course of study aligns with the Master of Arts in Professional Counseling program to encourage entry-level counseling students to work toward becoming doctoral-level advanced practitioners, educators, and supervisors.

The Ed.D. in Organizational Leadership program is designed for working professionals who wish to develop the knowledge and skills required to hold leadership positions in complex organizations. Argosy focuses on transformational leadership skills in addition to managerial attributes. This approach prepares students for strategic challenges such as increasing globalization, changing economies, societal shifts, and individual-organizational relationships.

The Psy.D. in Clinical Psychology program prepares students to deliver basic diagnostic and therapeutic services to diverse populations, including individuals, groups, and families. By integrating theory, training, research, and practice, students develop and apply the clinical skills of observation, assessment, intervention, and evaluation. Students may choose an optional concentration in child and adolescent psychology, geropsychology, marriage/couples and family therapy, or neuropsychology. The program prepares graduates for positions in traditional settings, including, but not limited to, independent practice, mental health centers, hospitals, medical centers, and managed-care systems. Argosy also encourages graduates to utilize clinical skills in innovative ways to become more competitive. Eventual positions may include consulting in various corporate, governmental, academic, multimedia, law, scientific, marketing, and industrial settings.

The Doctor of Psychology in Clinical Psychology program at Argosy University, Tampa, is accredited by the Committee on Accreditation of the American Psychological Association (APA, 750 First Street, N.E., Washington, D.C. 20002-4242; 202-336-5510).

Research Facilities

Argosy University libraries provide curriculum support and educational resources, including current text materials, diagnostic training documents, reference materials and databases, journals and dissertations, and major and current titles in program areas. There is an online public-access catalog of library resources available throughout the Argosy University system. Students have full remote access to the campus library database, enabling them to study and conduct research at home. Academic databases offer dissertation abstracts, academic journals, and professional periodicals. All library computers are Internet accessible. Software applications include Word, Excel, PowerPoint, SPSS, and various test-scoring programs.

Financial Aid

A wide range of financial aid options is available to students who qualify. Argosy University, Tampa, offers access to federal and state aid programs, merit-based awards, grants, loans, and a work-study program. As a first step, students should complete the Free Application for Federal Student Aid (FAFSA). Prospective students can apply electronically at http://www.fafsa.ed.gov or at the campus. To receive consideration for the maximum amount of aid and ensure timely receipt of funds, it is best to submit an application promptly.

Cost of Study

Tuition varies by program. Students should contact Argosy University, Tampa, for tuition information.

Living and Housing Costs

Students typically live in apartments in the metropolitan Tampa area. Living expenses vary according to each student's preferred standard of living, housing, and transportation. The University does not offer or operate student housing. Most of the students are full-time working professionals who live within driving distance of the campus. Several nearby hotels offer special rates for those who commute from long distances. The Admissions Department also maintains a list of housing options, including contact information, for University students who wish to share housing. For more information, students should contact the Admissions Department.

Student Group

Admission to Argosy University, Tampa, is selective to ensure a highly qualified student body. The University encourages diversity in academic and employment backgrounds and promotes integration of the student body into professional life through established connections with local and national professional associations. Argosy University offers a professionally oriented education with rich opportunities to gain practical experience in class, field placements, and internships. Full-time students and working professionals gain the extensive knowledge and range of skills necessary for effective performance in their chosen fields.

Student Outcomes

Students can register with the University's online career-services system and use select services from a distance, such as degree-specific career e-mail lists, national job posts, and virtual job fairs. Students should contact the University for more information.

Location

Located in sunny Florida, Argosy University, Tampa, attracts a diverse student population from throughout the United States, the Caribbean, Europe, Africa, and Asia. Tampa's central location affords students the opportunity to work for major corporations and hear speakers of international acclaim. The school offers rigorous programs of study in a supportive, collaborative environment. The campus sits within an hour's drive of some of the most popular tourist destinations in the world, including the Disney theme parks, Busch Gardens, and the Florida Gulf Coast beaches. Major-league sporting events, concerts, theaters, world-renowned restaurants, recreational facilities, and a cosmopolitan social scene are all within easy reach. The University's location provides easy access to I-4 and I-75. Tampa combines the opportunities of a large city with the friendliness of a small town.

The Tampa-St. Petersburg-Clearwater metropolitan area offers a diversified economic base fueled by a broad array of companies, including Verizon Communications and JP Morgan Chase. In addition, Tampa serves as headquarters for three Fortune 100 companies—OSI Restaurant Partners; TECO, an energy provider; and Raymond James Financial.

The University

Argosy University is a private institution with nineteen locations across the nation. Argosy University, Tampa, provides a network of resources, including a career resources office, an academic resources center, and extensive information access for research. It offers the resources of a large university, plus the friendliness and personal attention of a small campus.

The innovative programs feature dynamic, relevant, and practical curricula delivered in flexible class formats. Students enjoy scheduling options that make it easier to fit school into their busy lives, choosing from day and evening courses, on campus or online. Many students find a combination of class formats to be an ideal way of continuing their education while meeting family and professional demands.

Argosy University is accredited by the Higher Learning Commission and is a member of the North Central Association (NCA, 30 North LaSalle Street, Suite 2400, Chicago, Illinois 60602; 800-621-7440 (toll-free); http://www.ncahlc.org).

Applying

Argosy University, Tampa, accepts students year-round on a rolling admissions basis, depending on availability of required courses. Applications for admission are available online or by contacting the campus.

Correspondence and Information

Argosy University, Tampa
Parkside at Tampa Bay Park
4401 North Himes Avenue, Suite 150
Tampa, Florida 33614

Phone: 813-393-5290
800-850-6488 (toll-free)
Fax: 813-874-1989
E-mail: auadmissions@argosy.edu
Web site: http://www.argosy.edu/tampa

Argosy University, Tampa

THE FACULTY

The Argosy University faculty comprises working professionals who are eager to help students succeed. Members bring real-world experience and the latest practice innovations to the academic setting. The diverse faculty members of the College of Psychology and Behavioral Sciences are widely recognized for contributions to the field. Many are published scholars, and most hold doctoral degrees. They provide a substantive education that combines comprehensive knowledge with critical skills and practical workplace relevance. Above all, faculty members are committed to their students' personal and professional development.

ARGOSY UNIVERSITY

ARGOSY UNIVERSITY, TWIN CITIES

College of Psychology and Behavioral Sciences

Programs of Study

Argosy University, Twin Cities, offers the Master of Arts (M.A.) degree in clinical psychology, forensic psychology, and marriage and family therapy; the Doctor of Marriage and Family Therapy (D.M.F.T.); the Doctor of Education (Ed.D.) degree in organizational leadership; and the Doctor of Psychology (Psy.D.) degree in clinical psychology. Students completing a program may wish to become licensed professionals. As master's-level licensure varies from state to state, students should verify the current licensing requirements for the state in which they plan to practice.

The M.A. in Clinical Psychology program prepares students with the clinical knowledge and skills required to serve the mental health needs of individuals and groups. Students develop proficiency in clinical observation, assessment, appropriate intervention, and evaluation. The program emphasizes a practitioner-oriented philosophy and integrates applied theory, research, and field experience. It is designed for students who are interested in a terminal degree and practice as a master's-level clinician, or for students planning to transfer to the Psy.D. program.

The M.A. in Forensic Psychology program provides course work in forensic psychology for application to law enforcement, legal and organizational consultation, and program analysis. The program is designed to meet growing needs of the legal and criminal justice systems for professional counseling within victim assistance programs, probation and parole offices, court-mandated treatment programs, jails, and prisons. With the exception of the practicum component, courses are offered on weekends, allowing students to continue full-time employment while enrolled in this program.

The M.A. in Marriage and Family Therapy program develops the theoretical and clinical elements required to provide effective counseling to individuals, couples, families, and groups. The program introduces basic counseling skills that incorporate foundations of applied psychology and systems theory into the development of appropriate clinical relationships. Course work in addiction studies and substance-abuse counseling prepares students to work with families affected by this burgeoning problem. An optional concentration in forensic counseling is available. Marriage and family therapy is recognized by the Public Health Service Act as one of the five core mental health professions, and the National Institute of Mental Health accepts marriage and family therapists as qualified mental health professionals. The program is offered through weekend courses to allow concurrent employment.

The Doctor of Marriage and Family Therapy is a practice-oriented degree for licensed marriage and family therapists or professionals who can meet state requirements for licensure as a marriage and family therapist (meeting the Commission on Accreditation of Marriage and Family Therapy Education (COAMFTE) criteria for clinical practice prior to admission). The program seeks to build upon students' prior learning and professional experience by expanding and deepening their knowledge of human development, family dynamics, systemic thinking, interactional theories, traditional and contemporary marriage and family therapy theories and practices, and the cultural contexts within which these are embedded.

The Ed.D. in Organizational Leadership program is designed for working professionals who wish to develop the knowledge and skills required to hold leadership positions in complex organizations. The program focuses on transformational leadership skills in addition to managerial attributes. This approach prepares students for such strategic challenges as increasing globalization, changing economies, societal shifts, and individual-organizational relationships.

The Psy.D. in Clinical Psychology program prepares students to deliver basic diagnostic and therapeutic services to diverse populations, including individuals, groups, and families. By integrating theory, training, research, and practice, students develop and apply the clinical skills of observation, assessment, intervention, and evaluation. Optional concentrations are available in child and family psychology, forensic psychology, health psychology, marriage/couple and family therapy, or neuropsychology. The program prepares graduates for positions in traditional settings, including, but not limited to, independent practice, mental health centers, hospitals, medical centers, and managed-care systems. Graduates are encouraged to utilize clinical skills in innovative ways to become more competitive. Eventual positions may include consulting in various corporate, governmental, academic, multimedia, law, scientific, marketing, and industrial settings. The Doctor of Psychology in Clinical Psychology program at Argosy University, Twin Cities, is accredited by the Committee on Accreditation of the American Psychological Association (APA) (750 First Street, N.E., Washington, D.C. 20002-4242, 202-336-5510).

Research Facilities

Argosy University libraries provide curriculum support and educational resources, including current text materials, diagnostic training documents, reference materials and databases, journals and dissertations, and major and current titles in program areas. There is an online public-access catalog of library resources available throughout the Argosy University system. Students have full remote access to the campus library database, enabling them to study and conduct research at home. Academic databases offer dissertation abstracts, academic journals, and professional periodicals. All library computers are Internet accessible. Software applications include Word, Excel, PowerPoint, SPSS, and various test-scoring programs.

Financial Aid

A wide range of financial aid options is available to students who qualify. Argosy University, Twin Cities, offers access to federal and state aid programs, merit-based awards, grants, loans, and a work-study program. As a first step, students should complete the Free Application for Federal Student Aid (FAFSA). Prospective students can apply electronically at http://www.fafsa.ed.gov or at the campus. To receive consideration for the maximum amount of aid and ensure timely receipt of funds, students should submit an application promptly.

Cost of Study

Tuition varies by program. Students should contact Argosy University, Twin Cities, for tuition information.

Living and Housing Costs

Students typically live in apartments in the metropolitan Twin Cities area. Living expenses vary according to each student's preferred standard of living, housing, and transportation. The University does not offer or operate student housing. Most Argosy University students are full-time working professionals who live within driving distance of the campus. Several nearby hotels offer special rates for those who commute from long distances. The Admissions Department also maintains a list of housing options, including contact information for University students who wish to share housing. For more information, students should contact the Admissions Department.

Student Group

Admission to Argosy University, Twin Cities, is selective to ensure a highly qualified student body. The University encourages diversity in academic and employment backgrounds and promotes integration of the student body into professional life through established connections with local and national professional associations. Argosy University offers a professionally oriented education with rich opportunities to gain practical experience in class, field placements, and internships. Full-time students and working professionals gain the extensive knowledge and range of skills necessary for effective performance in their chosen field.

Student Outcomes

Students can register with Argosy University's online career-services system and use select services from a distance, such as degree-specific career e-mail lists, national job posts, and virtual job fairs. Students should contact the University for more information.

Location

Argosy University, Twin Cities, offers rigorous academics in a supportive environment. The campus is nestled in a parklike suburban setting within 10 miles of the airport and the Mall of America. Students enjoy the convenience of nearby shops, restaurants, and housing and easy freeway access. The neighboring Eagan Community Center offers many amenities, including walking paths, a fitness center, meeting rooms, and an outdoor amphitheater. The twin cities of Minneapolis and St. Paul have been rated by popular magazines as one of the most livable metropolitan areas in the country. With a population of 2.5 million, the area offers an abundance of recreational activities. Year-round outdoor activities and nationally acclaimed venues for theater, art, music, and professional sports teams attract residents and visitors alike. The Minneapolis-St. Paul metropolitan area offers a diversified economic base fueled by a broad array of companies. Among the numerous publicly traded companies headquartered in the area are Target, UnitedHealth Group, 3M, General Mills, and US Bancorp.

The University

Argosy University is a private institution with nineteen locations across the nation. Argosy University, Twin Cities, provides a career resources office, an academic resources center, and extensive information access for research. It offers the resources of a large university plus the friendliness and personal attention of a small campus. The innovative programs feature dynamic, relevant, and practical curricula delivered in flexible class formats. Students enjoy scheduling options that make it easier to fit school into their busy lives, choosing from day and evening courses, on campus or online. Many students find a combination of class formats to be an ideal way of continuing their education while meeting family and professional demands.

Argosy University is accredited by the Higher Learning Commission and is a member of the North Central Association (NCA, 30 North LaSalle Street, Suite 2400, Chicago, Illinois 60602; 800-621-7440 (toll-free); http://www.ncahlc.org).

Applying

Argosy University, Twin Cities, accepts students on a rolling admissions basis year-round, depending on availability of required courses. Applications for admission may be obtained online or by contacting the campus.

Correspondence and Information

Argosy University, Twin Cities
1515 Central Parkway
Eagan, Minnesota 55121

Phone: 651-846-2882
888-844-2004 (toll-free)
Fax: 651-994-7956
E-mail: auadmissions@argosy.edu
Web site: http://www.argosy.edu/twincities

Argosy University, Twin Cities

THE FACULTY

The Argosy University faculty comprises working professionals who are eager to help students succeed. Members bring real-world experience and the latest practice innovations to the academic setting. The diverse faculty members of the College of Psychology and Behavioral Sciences are widely recognized for contributions to the field. Many are published scholars, and most hold doctoral degrees. They provide a substantive education that combines comprehensive knowledge with critical skills and practical workplace relevance. Above all, faculty members are committed to their students' personal and professional development.

ARGOSY UNIVERSITY

ARGOSY UNIVERSITY, WASHINGTON DC

College of Psychology and Behavioral Sciences

Programs of Study

Argosy University, Washington DC, offers the Master of Arts (M.A.) degree in clinical psychology, community counseling, and forensic psychology; the Doctor of Education (Ed.D.) degree in counselor education and supervision, counseling psychology, and organizational leadership; and the Doctor of Psychology (Psy.D.) degree in clinical psychology. Students completing a program may wish to become licensed professionals. As master's-level licensure varies from state to state, students should determine licensing requirements for the state in which they plan to practice.

The M.A. in Clinical Psychology program prepares students with the clinical knowledge and skills required to serve the mental health needs of individuals and groups. Students develop proficiency in clinical observation, assessment, appropriate intervention, and evaluation. The program emphasizes a practitioner-oriented philosophy and integrates applied theory, research, and field experience. It is designed for students who are interested in a terminal degree and practice as a master's-level clinician, or for students planning to transfer to the Psy.D. program.

The M.A. in Community Counseling program provides a multifaceted focus on developmental and preventive mental health services. Students gain the knowledge and skills required for individual, group, family, and organizational interventions. Curriculum integrates foundational counseling skills and theories with clinical field experience.

The M.A. in Forensic Psychology program provides coursework in forensic psychology for application to law enforcement, legal and organizational consultation, and program analysis. The program is designed to meet growing needs of the legal and criminal justice systems for professional counseling within victim assistance programs, probation and parole offices, court-mandated treatment programs, jails, and prisons. With the exception of the practicum component, courses are offered on weekends to allow concurrent employment.

The Ed.D. in Counselor Education and Supervision program is designed to develop the advanced skills and knowledge necessary for leadership and advocacy roles in a variety of settings. The field is dedicated to both the academic preparation and comprehensive supervision of counselors across multiple settings. This course of study aligns with the Master of Arts in Professional Counseling program to encourage entry-level counseling students to work toward becoming doctoral-level advanced practitioners, educators, and supervisors.

The Ed.D. in Counseling Psychology program prepares counselors with the skills and credentials necessary to pursue leadership, supervision, training, and teaching positions. Students develop new interests and levels of competency through an applied research-practitioner approach to the role of professional counselor. An optional concentration in counselor education and supervision is available. The challenges of a changing society and the diversity of roles available to the mental health practitioner require a lifelong commitment to continuing education.

The Ed.D. in Organizational Leadership program is designed for working professionals who wish to develop the knowledge and skills required to hold leadership positions in complex organizations. The program focuses on transformational leadership skills in addition to managerial attributes. This approach prepares students for strategic challenges such as increasing globalization, changing economies, societal shifts, and individual-organizational relationships.

The Psy.D. in Clinical Psychology Program prepares students to deliver basic diagnostic and therapeutic services to diverse populations, including individuals, groups, and families. By integrating theory, training, research, and practice, students develop and apply the clinical skills of observation, assessment, intervention, and evaluation. Optional concentrations are available in child and family psychology, diversity and multicultural psychology, forensic psychology, or health and neuropsychology. The program prepares graduates for positions in traditional settings, including, but not limited to, independent practice, mental health centers, hospitals, medical centers, and managed-care systems. Graduates are encouraged to utilize clinical skills in innovative ways to become more competitive. Eventual positions may include consulting in various corporate, governmental, academic, multimedia, law, scientific, marketing, and industrial settings. The Doctor of Psychology in Clinical Psychology program at Argosy University, Washington DC, is accredited by the Committee on Accreditation of the American Psychological Association (APA, 750 First Street, N.E., Washington, D.C. 20002-4242; 202-336-5510).

Research Facilities

Argosy University libraries provide curriculum support and educational resources, including current text materials, diagnostic training documents, reference materials and databases, journals and dissertations, and major and current titles in program areas. There is an online public-access catalog of library resources available throughout the Argosy University system. Students have full remote access to the campus library database, enabling them to study and conduct research at home. Academic databases offer dissertation abstracts, academic journals, and professional periodicals. All library computers are Internet accessible. Software applications include Word, Excel, PowerPoint, SPSS, and various test-scoring programs.

Financial Aid

A wide range of financial aid options is available to students who qualify. Argosy University, Washington DC, offers access to federal and state aid programs, merit-based awards, grants, loans, and a work-study program. As a first step, students should complete the Free Application for Federal Student Aid (FAFSA). Prospective students can apply electronically at http://www.fafsa.ed.gov or at the campus. To receive consideration for the maximum amount of aid and ensure timely receipt of funds, students should submit an application promptly.

Cost of Study

Tuition varies by program. Students should contact Argosy University, Washington DC, for tuition information.

Living and Housing Costs

Students typically live in apartments in the metropolitan Washington, D.C., area. Living expenses vary according to each student's preferred standard of living, housing, and transportation. The University does not offer or operate student housing. Most Argosy University students are full-time working professionals who live within driving distance of the campus. Several nearby hotels offer special rates for those who commute from long distances. The Admissions Department also maintains a list of housing options, including contact information for University students who wish to share housing. For more information, students should contact the Admissions Department.

Student Group

Admission to Argosy University, Washington DC, is selective to ensure a highly qualified student body. The University encourages diversity in academic and employment backgrounds and promotes integration of the student body into professional life through established connections with local and national professional associations. Argosy University offers a professionally oriented education with rich opportunities to gain practical experience in class, field placements, and internships. Full-time students and working professionals gain the extensive knowledge and range of skills necessary for effective performance in their chosen field.

Student Outcomes

Students can register with Argosy University's online career-services system and use select services from a distance, such as degree-specific career e-mail lists, national job posts, and virtual job fairs. Students should contact the University for more information.

Location

Argosy University, Washington DC, is located in suburban Arlington, Virginia. The school provides easy access to most major highways in area and is accessible by public transportation. With its proximity to Georgetown, students enjoy access to the many diverse attractions of the D.C. area. Additional campus space is located at the Art Institute of Washington Building (1820 Fort Myer Drive). The university houses administrative space and seven classrooms at this location. Perhaps best known as the home of the Pentagon and Arlington National Cemetery, Arlington, Virginia, is one of the most highly educated areas in the nation. It is also one of the most diverse. Major employers in the region include MCI Telecommunications Corporation; Bell Atlantic Network Services, Inc.; and Gannett/USA Today Company, Inc.

The University

Argosy University is a private institution with nineteen locations across the nation. Argosy University, Washington DC, provides a career resources office, an academic resources center, and extensive information access for research. It offers the resources of a large university plus the friendliness and personal attention of a small campus. The innovative programs feature dynamic, relevant, and practical curricula delivered in flexible class formats. Students enjoy scheduling options that make it easier to fit school into their busy lives, choosing from day and evening courses, on campus or online. Many students find a combination of class formats to be an ideal way of continuing their education while meeting family and professional demands.

Argosy University is accredited by the Higher Learning Commission and is a member of the North Central Association (NCA, 30 North LaSalle Street, Suite 2400, Chicago, Illinois 60602; 800-621-7440 (toll-free); http://www.ncahlc.org).

Applying

Argosy University, Washington DC, accepts students year-round on a rolling admissions basis, depending on availability of required courses. Applications for admission are available online or by contacting the campus.

Correspondence and Information

Argosy University, Washington DC
1550 Wilson Boulevard, Suite 600
Arlington, Virginia 22209

Phone: 703-526-5800
866-703-2777 (toll-free)
Fax: 703-243-8973
E-mail: auadmissions@argosy.edu
Web site: http://www.argosy.edu/washingtondc

Argosy University, Washington DC

THE FACULTY

The Argosy University faculty comprises working professionals who are eager to help students succeed. Members bring real-world experience and the latest practice innovations to the academic setting. The diverse faculty members of the College of Psychology and Behavioral Sciences is widely recognized for contributions to the field. Many are published scholars, and most hold doctoral degrees. They provide a substantive education that combines comprehensive knowledge with critical skills and practical workplace relevance. Above all, faculty members are committed to their students' personal and professional development.

BARRY UNIVERSITY

Department of Psychology

Programs of Study

The Department of Psychology at Barry University offers a Master of Science in Clinical Psychology degree program and a School Psychology Program comprising the Master of Science in Psychology and Specialist in School Psychology (S.S.P.) degrees.

The Master of Science in Clinical Psychology program employs the scientist/practitioner model of training with faculty actively involved in research and clinical practice. This offers students the opportunity to obtain the theoretical, scientific, technical, and personal experience necessary to enter into the practice of mental health evaluation and treatment of diverse populations with appropriate guidance and supervision. The program also prepares students for doctoral-level training. Training is provided in an environment that promotes knowledge of the discipline, basic clinical skills, and the establishment of an identity as a professional in the field of psychology.

Clinical psychology students can choose from two tracks. The 36-credit option prepares students for application to doctoral programs, while the 60-credit option prepares students to sit for licensing as mental health counselors. The latter qualifies students to engage in private practice and to seek employment with public or private mental health organizations, social service agencies, government and private research teams, and community colleges. The program provides high-quality academic instruction, research experience, and supervised clinical training at a variety of mental health centers. Students are trained to master the traditional clinical skills of evaluation, diagnosis, and treatment. The theoretical orientation of the program is eclectic, with emphasis on the clinical assessment and treatment of the mentally ill. All courses are offered in the evening. The 165-hour clinical psychology practicum requires one day per week of supervised clinical work in a mental health setting, with a minimum of 40 client contact hours. Diagnostic and therapeutic skills are practiced, and basic documentation skills are learned. The clinical psychology internship offered in the third year of the 60-credit option is a full-time, supervised clinical experience that requires a minimum of 1,000 hours. Under supervision in a mental health facility, students perform a variety of clinically related activities that a licensed professional with a master's degree in clinical psychology would be expected to perform. The clinical experience includes a minimum of 240 hours of direct client contact hours.

Barry's School Psychology Program includes both the Master of Science in Psychology degree and Specialist in School Psychology degree (equivalent to an Ed.S. degree). The School Psychology Program is designed to meet the needs of a broad group of students, including recent graduates with bachelor's degrees and teachers and mental health professionals with years of experience who are interested in a career upgrade. The student is awarded an M.S. degree after completion of 30 credits and can advance to the specialist program. The master's is a prerequisite for the specialist degree, and many students earn both at Barry. However, for students who already have a master's in psychology or a related field, a program adviser can customize a course sequence, which requires the completion of 38 credits.

Completion of the School Psychology Program requires 71 credits and satisfies the academic requirements in accordance with standards set by the National Association of School Psychologists (NASP). Following the internship, students are prepared to meet licensure requirements for the private practice of school psychology as set forth by the state of Florida, as well as certification requirements as set forth by the Florida State Board of Education. The School Psychology Program is approved by the Florida Department of Education and by the National Association of School Psychologists.

All graduate courses in the Department of Psychology at Barry University are offered in the evening to accommodate working professionals. Field placement and internship courses, which occur near the completion of training, require daytime availability.

Research Facilities

The Monsignor William Barry Memorial Library provides materials and services in support of educational and cultural objectives of the University. Students have access in open stacks to a collection exceeding 700,000 items, including more than 2,500 periodical titles. The Barry library participates in a number of library networks. The Southeast Florida Library Information Network (SEFLIN) provides, by courier service and fax, access to more than 12 million items and 30,000 periodical titles held by larger academic and public libraries of Dade, Broward, and Palm Beach Counties. Materials not readily available at this level are obtained through the Florida Library Information Network (FLIN), which provides for the delivery of materials based in the major libraries of the state of Florida, including those in the state university system. The psychology department also has a testing library and computer lab access.

Financial Aid

A limited number of graduate assistantships are available. Compensation each semester includes $1500 and tuition remission for one course. Normally, positions are awarded for a full academic year.

Barry University participates in the federal and state financial aid programs. In addition to these government-funded programs, there are a number of scholarships for graduate students as well as professional tuition discounts. All full-time Florida teachers receive at least a 30 percent tuition discount under the Professional Recognition Scholarship Program.

Cost of Study

Graduate tuition is $765 per credit. Course fees may be required, depending on the program of study.

Living and Housing Costs

Campus housing is available for full-time graduate students, space permitting. Barry University provides assistance in locating off-campus housing.

Student Group

The 2006–07 programs comprised 36 full-time and 25 part-time students. This included 53 women, 30 students who are members of minority groups, and 9 international students.

Location

The University's 122-acre campus is located in Miami Shores, which is between the cities of Miami and Fort Lauderdale. This ideal location provides students with access to one of the nation's most dynamic multicultural environments and all of its business, cultural, and recreational opportunities.

The University

Barry University is an independent, coeducational university with a history of distinguished graduate programs. Founded in 1940 by the Adrian Dominican Sisters, the University embodies the Catholic liberal arts tradition. It has grown steadily in size and diversity while maintaining a low student-faculty ratio of 14:1. With small classes, students can count on personal attention from experienced faculty.

Applying

Applicants must have a bachelor's degree in psychology or a related field. Completion of the following five undergraduate psychology courses is required: developmental psychology, abnormal psychology, tests and measurements (psychological testing), physiological psychology (biological bases of behavior), and theories of personality. Students with an M.S. in psychology or a related field may apply to the S.S.P. program directly. To apply, students must submit the completed application, the nonrefundable $30 application fee, official transcripts from all universities and colleges attended, a statement of purpose, letters of recommendation, and GRE scores. International students must also submit TOEFL scores. The application and all credentials should be received at least thirty days before the published first day of registration.

Correspondence and Information

Dr. Lenore Szuchman, Chair
Department of Psychology
School of Arts and Sciences
Barry University
11300 NE Second Avenue
Miami Shores, Florida 33161-6695

Phone: 305-899-3278
Fax: 305-899-3279
E-mail: lszuchman@mail.barry.edu
Web site: http://www.barry.edu/psychology

Barry University

THE FACULTY AND THEIR RESEARCH

Laura Ferrer-Wreder, Associate Professor; Ph.D., Florida International, 1998. Design, implementation, and evaluation of prevention/intervention initiatives; youth development programs (adolescent-adulthood transition); prevention of youth problem behaviors; identity development; parent-/school-level influences in relation to youth development and problem behaviors; gender/ethnicity considerations in intervention development and dissemination.

Gladys Ibañez, Research Assistant Professor; PhD, Georgia State. HIV prevention, community intervention, health psychology, health disparities, adolescent development.

Stephen W. Koncsol, Associate Professor; Ph.D., Rutgers, 1976. Psychological well-being and culture, dyadic communication failures, marital satisfaction/dissatisfaction.

Maria R. Lopez, Visiting Assistant Professor; Ph.D., Nova Southeastern, 2003. Child maltreatment, parental stress, culture and assessment.

Frank Muscarella, Professor and Director of the Clinical Psychology Program; Ph.D., Louisville, 1991. Evolutionary psychology, human sexuality.

Michelle Major Sanabria, Assistant Professor; S.S.P., Ph.D., Barry; NCSP. Children with autism, with a focus on the effectiveness of behavioral intervention and special education; stress, attribution, and life satisfaction of parents with children with autism; cognitive processes of children with autism and Asperger syndrome.

Agnes E. Shine, Associate Professor and Director of the School Psychology Program; Ph.D., Ball State, 1990. Neuropsychological issues with children, traumatic brain injury, training issues in school psychology, low-incidence handicaps in children, learning disabilities.

Lenore Szuchman, Professor and Department Chair; Ph.D., Florida International, 1990. Cognition and social cognition in older adults, advice.

Manuel J. Tejeda, Associate Professor; Ph.D., Miami. Leadership, organizational behavior, diversity in the workplace, research methods, structural equation modeling, random regression, substance abuse.

Guillermo Wated, Assistant Professor; Ph.D., Florida International, 2002. Employee attitudes, counterproductive behavior in organizations, cultures and organizations.

BOSTON GRADUATE SCHOOL OF PSYCHOANALYSIS

Master's, Certificate, and Doctoral Programs

Programs of Study

The Boston Graduate School of Psychoanalysis (BGSP) awards the Master of Arts (M.A.) in psychoanalysis, the Master of Arts in psychoanalytic counseling, the Certificate in Psychoanalysis, the Doctor of Psychoanalysis (Psya.D.), and the Master of Arts in psychoanalysis and culture, and the Doctor of Psychoanalysis in psychoanalysis and culture. BGSP's main campus is in Brookline, Massachusetts, with a branch campus, New York Graduate School of Psychoanalysis (NYGSP), in Manhattan, New York. The Doctor of Psychoanalysis, the Master of Arts and the Doctor of Psychoanalysis in Psychoanalysis and Culture, the Master of Arts in Psychoanalysis, the Master of Arts in Psychoanalytic Counseling, and the Certificate in Psychoanalysis programs are offered in Brookline. The Master of Arts in Psychoanalysis program is also offered at NYGSP.

The 48-credit Master of Arts in Psychoanalysis program grounds students in academic psychoanalysis and prepares them for advanced clinical and research studies. Courses are structured to facilitate intellectual and emotional learning. A three-semester fieldwork externship offers training in the understanding of psychosis and primitive emotional states. A master's paper is developed demonstrating an understanding of unconscious dynamics. The M.A. program is equivalent to the first two years of the doctoral and certificate programs.

The 68-credit Master of Arts in Psychoanalytic Counseling program provides students with comprehensive master's-level training in mental health counseling, with a specialization in psychoanalytic studies. Graduates meet the educational requirements for licensure in mental health counseling in Massachusetts and many other states. The program may be completed over two years (two academic years plus one summer semester) and includes nineteen 3-credit courses, a 100-hour practicum, and a 600-hour internship. Most students complete a research paper at the culmination of the program. This program is equivalent to the first two years of the doctoral and certificate programs.

The certificate and Doctor of Psychoanalysis programs are designed to provide full clinical training leading to certification as a psychoanalyst as well as a solid foundation in psychoanalytic theory and research. Following the fieldwork externship, the advanced student undertakes supervised clinical training through the School's Therapy Center, while engaging in advanced course work. Clinical training includes the completion of two control analyses (individual supervisions). The doctoral and certificate programs combine intellectual and emotional education for the purpose of developing the therapeutic aspects of each student's personality. In the certificate program, a final project integrates research and clinical training in a single case study. In the doctoral program, the student has a range of options for the dissertation research project, including the single case study. Both programs take at least 5½ to six years to complete.

All students in the master's, certificate, and Doctor of Psychoanalysis programs engage in a training analysis.

The Doctor of Psychoanalysis and Master of Arts in Psychoanalysis and Culture programs promote systematic dialogue between psychoanalysis, critical social theory, and cultural analysis. The distinctive character of the programs are their emphasis on crafting new theoretical and methodological links between psychoanalysis, social sciences, humanities, and cultural studies. Students in the programs are exposed to new conceptions of psychoanalysis and culture and to new methods for their interdisciplinary study. Students may choose to concentrate on the study of psychoanalysis in relation to culture, on cultural analysis of psychoanalytic thinking, on psychoanalytic readings, or interpretations of cultural representation, such as media, literature, or arts. Students may also choose to focus on interdisciplinary work responsive to the contemporary issues of national and international violence, conflicts, terrorism, and culture wars.

On the main campus in Brookline, classes are scheduled on every other Thursday evening, Friday, and Saturday. Classes for the Master of Arts in Psychoanalytic Counseling program meet once a week in the evening or Saturday morning and during the day on Friday. At NYGSP, classes are scheduled in the evening during the week and meet weekly. Many students maintain regular employment during their course of study.

Research Facilities

BGSP and NYGSP branches have extensive libraries of psychoanalytic and related literature, including electronic databases with remote access. Resources are available to support student and faculty research in psychoanalysis, the study of violence, and important related fields. Students may take advantage of interlibrary loan services and affiliations with nearby academic libraries.

Financial Aid

Federal Stafford Student Loans are available for most programs, and a limited number of graduate assistantships are available to students seeking financial aid. Assistantships are not available to first-year students.

Cost of Study

The annual cost for the master's programs is approximately $14,910, an average fee depending on the cost of the training analysis.

The costs for the certificate program are averages, depending on the fees for training analysis and supervision. The cost for years one and two is $12,550 annually; for year three, $16,150; for year four, $20,530; and for year five, $14,875 (years four and five include the additional expense of control analyses; year five is based on directed research, supervision, and analytic fees.

The cost for the Doctor of Psychoanalysis in Psychoanalysis and Culture program is $11,320 in the first year and $12,100 in years two and three (additional research supervision costs).

The costs for the Doctor of Psychoanalysis program are averages, depending on the fees for the training analysis and supervision. The cost for years one and two is $14,910 annually; for years three and four, $21,085 annually; and for year five, $14,875 (research supervisors replace course tuition).

Living and Housing Costs

Students at the Brookline campus live off campus in the greater Boston area. The cost of living is approximately $17,785 for ten months.

Student Group

Current enrollment in programs on the main campus numbers 97 students (56 women). Most of the master's students are enrolled full-time. One third are international students. Most doctoral students enroll full time. Most certificate students enroll half-time. Half of the Institute for the Study of Violence doctoral students are enrolled full-time. At the NYGSP campus, there are 19 students, most of whom are enrolled full-time.

Student Outcomes

Graduates of the master's programs work in mental health, education, and human services or continue their graduate education. Certified and doctoral-level psychoanalysts function as private practitioners of psychoanalysis, supervise, teach, and work in applied fields.

Location

The main campus of BGSP is located in Washington Square in Brookline, Massachusetts. NYGSP is located in the west village in Manhattan, New York.

The School

The mission of BGSP is to train students in understanding emotional and mental functioning so that they may respond to society's need for understanding individual character development and human motivation. Individuals are prepared to use this understanding in clinical and other professional settings and to conduct research contributing to the development of the field of psychoanalysis. BGSP is also committed to integrating psychoanalytic knowledge with that of other disciplines in order to understand and address the problem of violence through the doctoral program in the Institute for the Study of Violence.

Applying

Students are admitted on a rolling basis. Specific academic requirements vary by program. Applicants from all backgrounds are selected who demonstrate academic ability and motivation for training. Nonnative speakers of English must submit TOEFL scores.

Correspondence and Information

Mara Wagner, Psy.D.
Admissions Director
Boston Graduate School of Psychoanalysis
1581 Beacon Street
Brookline, Massachusetts 02446
Phone: 617-277-3915
Fax: 617-277-0312
E-mail: bgsp@bgsp.edu
Web site: http://www.bgsp.edu

Mr. Ronald Lieber, Administrative Director
New York Graduate School of Psychoanalysis
16 West Tenth Street
New York, New York 10011
Phone: 212-260-7050
E-mail: nygsp@bgsp.edu
Web site: http://nygsp.bgsp.edu

Boston Graduate School of Psychoanalysis

THE FACULTY

Rodrigo Barahona, Psya.D., Boston Graduate School of Psychoanalysis.
June Bernstein, Ph.D., Florida Tech.
Frances Bigda-Peyton, Ed.D., Boston University.
Jorge Capetillo-Ponce, Ph.D., New School.
Elizabeth Dorsey, M.S.W., Illinois at Chicago.
Susan Fleischer, Ph.D., Columbia.
Carl Fulwiler, Ph.D., M.D., Harvard.
James Gilligan, M.D., Case Western Reserve.
Eugene Goldwater, M.D., Columbia.
Robin Gomolin, Psya.D., Boston Graduate School of Psychoanalysis.
Audrey Jones, Ph.D., Clark.
Marjorie Kettell, Ph.D., Boston University.
Wayne Klein, Ph.D., Florida.
Theodore Laquercia, Ph.D., California Graduate Institute.
Charles Lemert, Ph.D., Harvard.
Evelyn Liegner, Ph.D., California Graduate Institute.
Nigel Mackay, D.Phil., Oxford.
John Madonna, Ed.D., Clark.
Robert Marshall, Ph.D., SUNY at Buffalo.
James Morrell, M.A., Boston Graduate School of Psychoanalysis.
Siamak Movahedi, Ph.D., Washington State.
Faye Newsome, M.A., California Graduate Institute.
Vincent Panetta, Ph.D., Greenwich (England).
Lynn Perlman, Ph.D., CUNY.
Stephen C. Price, Ph.D., Brandeis.
Kenneth Rogers, Ed.D., Boston University.
Maureen Ryan, Ed.M., Harvard.
Mary Shepherd, M.A., Yale.
Lorraine Smithberg, Ph.D., Union (Ohio).
Jane Snyder, Ph.D., Boston University.
Stephen Soldz, Ph.D., Boston University.
Thomas Twyman, M.S.W., Boston University.
Mara Wagner, Psy.D., Massachusetts School of Professional Psychology.
Douglas Watt, Ph.D., Boston College.
Dolores Welber, Ph.D., California Graduate Institute.
Joanne White, Psya.D., Illinois.

BOSTON UNIVERSITY

School of Medicine
Division of Graduate Medical Sciences
Master of Arts in Mental Health and Behavioral Medicine

Program of Study The Master of Arts (M.A.) in mental health and behavioral medicine at the Boston University School of Medicine is an intensive 60-credit degree program designed to meet the requirements for an independent mental health-care license in Massachusetts and other states. The primary objective is to prepare individuals in mental health counseling interventions with a complementary background in behavioral medicine and neuroscience. Graduates of the Mental Health and Behavioral Medicine Program (MHBM) provide a range of assessment, diagnostic, and treatment-focused counseling services to clients in mental health, medical, research, and independent practice settings.

The program can be completed in two years of full-time study. The curriculum consists of a combination of academic course work and substantial clinical experiences in a diverse medical school/hospital environment. Special emphasis is placed on areas of intervention, which integrate mental health and physical health care across the lifespan. Students may have an opportunity to work with people with severe mental disorders, children at risk for mental disorders, HIV/AIDS, morbid obesity, sports injuries, and other health issues. During the first year, students take a total of 30 credits, of which 24 are core courses required for licensure and 6 for the supervised practicum. The first-year practicum consists primarily of closely supervised and observed emergency, individual, group, and family interventions conducted in a number of clinical settings primarily within the medical campus. Students review their experiences with faculty members in weekly seminars. During the second year, students complete the remainder of the 60-credit-hour academic requirements by successfully passing 30 credit hours—18 hours of class work and 12 hours of internship. The post-practicum internship field placement must total a minimum of 900 clock hours, of which 360 are direct service. The internship field placements are prearranged based upon the student's area of specialization.

Research Facilities The Boston University Medical Center Campus is home to a Clinical Research Center, Pulmonary Center, Arthritis Center, Cardiovascular Institute, Cancer Center, Center of Human Genetics, Gerontology Center, and Center for Research in Women's Health as well as the Mallory Institute of Pathology, the Thorndike Memorial Laboratory, the Maxwell Finland Laboratory for Infectious Diseases, and the Sloan Epidemiology Unit.

To accommodate the growth in these areas and in research emanating from the basic science departments, significant additions to the school's physical plant have been made, including the 35,000-square-foot Dermatology Research Facility and the 180,000-square-foot Center for Advanced Biomedical Research. The state-of-the-art McNary Learning Center contains lecture halls, seminar rooms, and a highly sophisticated computerized teaching lab. Boston's largest biomedical research park continues to grow as construction has begun on the third laboratory building of Bio-Square, the 14-acre research and business park in Boston's South End—a joint venture by Boston University and Boston Medical Center.

Financial Aid The University participates in the Federal Direct Stafford/Ford Program. Graduate students receive their direct loans through this program, which has the same loan limits, interest rates, and fees as the Federal Stafford Loan Program. Subsidized and Unsubsidized Direct Loans and Work-Study Programs are also available to all qualifying students.

Cost of Study In 2008–09, full-time students (12–18 credits) pay $36,540 in tuition and $50 in fees per year; part-time students pay $1142 per credit (up to 11 credits) and $25 in activity fees.

Living and Housing Costs Most graduate students choose to live in off-campus apartments. The Office of Off-Campus Services provides listings of available apartments in the area. Although most graduate students do live off campus, the Office of Rental Property Management offers University-owned furnished and unfurnished apartments in various neighborhoods. Monthly rents start at $400 for a room, $800 for studios, $1000 for one-bedroom apartments, and $1400 for two-bedroom apartments. Most rents include heat and hot water.

Student Group With more than 29,000 students from all fifty states and 143 countries, Boston University is the fourth-largest independent university in the United States. For over 150 years, the University has anticipated the changing needs of its students while serving the greater needs of the society. There are approximately 650 students pursuing graduate degrees on the medical school campus.

Location Boston is rich in history, old-world charm, and modern vitality. Home to more than sixty colleges and universities, it is an intellectual and cultural center that is diverse in its people and stimulating in its opportunities, yet relaxed and accessible. Boston is the largest city in New England and the site of many significant events in early American Colonial and Revolutionary history. Much of that early flavor remains today in its cobbled streets, in its historic landmarks that bring alive Paul Revere's ride and the Boston Tea Party, and in the Federalist row houses on Beacon Hill. A historic seaport that grew to prominence in the days of the China trade and the whaling industry, the city maintains a thriving and picturesque waterfront.

The University and The Program One of the largest independent universities in the United States, Boston University—independent, coeducational, and nonsectarian—is an internationally recognized institution of higher education and research. As one of the nation's premier research universities, Boston University believes that all students benefit by learning from dedicated teachers who are actively engaged in original research. The University's learning environment is further enriched by an extraordinary array of direct involvements with the broader artistic, economic, social, intellectual, and educational life of the community. These relationships provide a distinctly practical edge to the University's educational and research programs, while enhancing the life and vitality of one of the world's great cities. The M.A. program in mental health counseling and behavioral medicine is the first of its kind in the United States, making Boston University a leader in preparing master's-level mental health clinicians.

Applying All applicants are required to have a background in psychology. If psychology prerequisites are not fulfilled, the student must take these courses before entering the program or in the first semester of matriculation. All applicants are required to have a baccalaureate degree from an accredited college, to submit the results of the Graduate Record Examination or MCATS, and to demonstrate an interest in or a background in mental health counseling. The application fee for electronic applications is $60 and $50 by mail. Each student must complete the Free Application for Federal Student Aid (FAFSA) form when applying for institutional financial aid; the complete packet must be received no later than March 31 for fall admission and October 15 for spring admission. Late applications are considered with prior approval of the Program Director. Students are also required to attend an open house and interview session before a final decision is made. The dates and times can be found on the program's Web site (http://www.bumc.bu.edu/mhbm).

Correspondence and Information

For program information:
Dr. Stephen Brady, Program Director
Mental Health and Behavioral Medicine Program
Division of Graduate Medical Sciences
Robinson Building, Suite B-2903
Boston University School of Medicine
715 Albany Street
Boston, Massachusetts 02118
E-mail: sbrady@bu.edu
Web site: http://www.bumc.bu.edu/mhbm

For general information:
Bernice R. Mark, Program Administrator
Mental Health and Behavioral Medicine Program
Division of Graduate Medical Sciences
Robinson Building, Suite B-2903
Boston University School of Medicine
715 Albany Street
Boston, Massachusetts 02118
Phone: 617-414-2320
Fax: 617-414-2323
E-mail: nicey@bu.edu

Boston University

THE CORE FACULTY AND THEIR RESEARCH

Stephen Brady, Associate Professor of Psychiatry and Graduate Medical Sciences and Director, Mental Health and Behavioral Medicine Program; Ph.D. (counseling psychology), California, Santa Barbara. A licensed psychologist, Dr. Brady is integrally involved in all aspects of the development of the Mental Health and Behavioral Medicine Program. He currently teaches courses in counseling techniques, group psychotherapy, and clinical supervision and is also responsible for all day-to-day operations of the program. He received a B.A. in sociology from the University of Florida and M.A. and Ph.D. degrees in counseling psychology from the University of California, Santa Barbara. He is currently licensed as a psychologist in Massachusetts. He has been a member of the faculty since 1991 with numerous responsibilities as a senior administrator, clinician, teacher, and researcher in the School of Medicine's Division of Psychiatry and Graduate Medical Sciences. His principal areas of clinical, research, and teaching interests include HIV/AIDS, serious mental disorders, trauma, and gay/lesbian identity formation. Dr. Brady has been the recipient of NIMH Training Grants for HIV/AIDS Mental Health and more recently the Co-Principal Investigator for a study examining HIV/AIDS, trauma, substance abuse, and cost. He anticipates funding as the principle investigator for an NIMH study examining HIV prevention for mentally ill adults. Dr. Brady has presented at numerous conferences and has numerous publications relevant to his area of interest.

Rachel J. Levy, Director of Clinical Training; Psy.D., Chicago School of Professional Psychology. A licensed clinical psychologist, Dr. Levy's doctoral dissertation examined the relationship between coping style and spirituality as it related to adaptation to HIV disease in African American women. Dr. Levy was an intern at Cook County Hospital's Women & Children's HIV Clinic and completed her residency training at Temple University Hospital, with a specific focus on assessment and therapy with cardiac and pulmonary transplant candidates and inpatient psychiatry. Dr. Levy's postdoctoral training was conducted at Boston University Medical Center's Dr. Solomon Carter Fuller Mental Health Center. Her clinical and research experiences are in the areas of HIV disease in multicultural populations, cross-cultural psychology, organ transplant assessments, and disaster psychology. Over the past several years, Dr. Levy has provided several consultations through the Massachusetts Department of Mental Health on training professional clinical staff members on how to perform HIV risk assessments with the chronically mentally ill population. Dr. Levy has been a consultant on HIV prevention and mental health treatment to various community-based agencies and school systems. She was also a clinician for the Federal Emergency Management Team through the Department of Mental Health's Crisis Counseling network, working with airline staff and crew members and families affected by the occurrences of September 11.

Jori Berger-Greenstein, Assistant Professor; Ph.D. (clinical psychology), Bowling Green State. Dr. Berger-Greenstein, a licensed clinical psychologist, completed her predoctoral internship at the Boston Consortium, where she completed rotations in medical psychology, substance abuse, and pediatrics. Dr. Berger-Greenstein's clinical and research interests are in the areas of general behavioral medicine and health psychology, substance abuse and dependence, motivational interviewing, and ethics. She is currently the Project Director for a federally funded HIV prevention study for people with serious and persistent mental illness, in collaboration with Dr. Stephen Brady. She spent five years serving as a clinician in a federally funded, multisite intervention study designed to investigate the effect of a motivational interviewing intervention on adherence for people living with HIV/AIDS. She has published several articles on the topic of HIV/AIDS and has presented at numerous professional conferences. Dr. Berger-Greenstein has taught with the Mental Health and Behavioral Medicine Program since its inception in 2001 and joined the staff as a member of the core faculty in the fall of 2004.

Jane O'Hern, Professor Emeritus; Ed.D., Boston University. A practicing psychologist for the past forty years, Dr. O'Hern's academic training at Michigan State University and Boston University was followed by a career that included: teaching; administration, including being the chairman of programs in counselor education and counseling psychology at Boston University and Director of International Education; Peace Corps assessment; and a small private practice. In addition, Dr. O'Hern has worked in Europe and Asia. Her research interests are in interdisciplinary program development and the measurement of counselor sensitivity. She has received numerous grants from the U.S. Departments of Education and Defense as well as from the National Institute of Mental Health.

Len Zaichkowsky, Professor of Education; Ph.D., Toronto. Dr. Zaichkowsky is a licensed psychologist who specializes in sport and exercise psychology. He has a joint appointment in the School of Education and School of Medicine, Division of Psychiatry, and Division of Graduate Medical Sciences and is very active professionally. He is a past president of the Association for the Advancement of Applied Sport Psychology (1997–99), a member of the editorial board of the *Journal of Applied Sport Psychology,* and currently is section editor on psychology for the *International Journal of Sport and Health Science.* He has authored and edited six books, with the most recent being *Medical and Psychological Aspects of Sport and Exercise* (FIT Publishing, 2002). He has published over ninety papers on sport psychology, research design, and related topics in scholarly journals or books as well as numerous magazine and newspaper columns. Dr. Zaichkowsky has made more than 300 professional presentations worldwide. His current research interests are in psychophysiological self-regulation of performance stress and the development of "expert" performance. He has consulted with the U.S., Canadian, and Australian Olympic Organizations; the NBA (Boston Celtics); the Major League Baseball Players Association; the NFL; the NHL Players Association and the Calgary Flames; and most recently with Spain's World Cup Soccer Team.

CALIFORNIA INSTITUTE OF INTEGRAL STUDIES

School of Professional Psychology

Programs of Study

The School of Professional Psychology at California Institute of Integral Studies (CIIS) balances traditional clinical training with a concern for contemporary social, cultural, and spiritual issues. Courses of study encourage integration of new and alternative approaches to psychological health while adhering to rigorous standards of scholarship, research, and practice. Depending upon the course of study, psychology programs provide comprehensive training in the foundation areas of clinical skills, ethics, psychology, and research design and statistics. Clinical training is integrated through the use of practicums prior to internship. Many students train in one of the School's five clinics, drawing upon the rich opportunities for clinical experience in the San Francisco Bay Area. The School of Professional Psychology also supports ongoing research in the study of biofeedback and states of consciousness, promoting the interdisciplinary study of psychology, meditation, and alternative interventions. These resources, combined with innovative psychotherapeutic approaches and with faculty members who are scholar/practitioners, provide CIIS psychology students with a competitive advantage with state and national licensure and professional examinations. Recent state marriage and family therapy (MFT) licensing test results revealed that 93 percent of CIIS psychology graduates who took the exam passed. All graduate programs include some elective study in the Institute's rich palate of disciplines, including Asian and comparative studies, cosmology and consciousness studies, East-West psychology, philosophy, social and cultural anthropology, transformation studies, and women's spirituality studies.

Clinical Psychology: doctorate in Clinical Psychology, Psy.D. degree. The primary objective of the clinical psychology doctoral program is to produce competent, well-rounded psychologists whose practice of professional psychology is rooted in a depth of self-knowledge, breadth of worldviews, and an abiding commitment to honoring and exploring the diverse dimensions of human experience. The program offers an emphasis in analytical psychology, child and family therapy, ecopsychology, health psychology, and transformative psychotherapy.

Community Mental Health: Master of Arts in Counseling Psychology with a concentration in community mental health; Advanced Certificate in Community Mental Health. To begin in fall 2008, this groundbreaking program integrates the fundamentals of intensive and supplemental case management with an emphasis on counseling and cultural competence and public sector practicum. Students receive thorough training in psychological theory and practice and learn to understand the various public health and community mental health programs available and specific methods to help clients negotiate the system. Students develop expertise in case management, teamwork with multidisciplinary care providers, treatment of complex and multidiagnosis patients, and cross-cultural counseling.

Drama Therapy: Master of Arts in Counseling Psychology with a concentration in drama therapy. One of only two approved graduate training programs in the United States, the drama therapy program offers a broad and thorough background in counseling psychology as well as specialized training in the systematic use of drama and theater processes as means of furthering emotional growth and psychological integration. Graduates work in diverse settings, including mental-health facilities, hospitals, schools, community centers, prisons, senior centers, industry, and private practice.

Expressive Arts Therapy: Master of Arts in Counseling Psychology with a concentration in expressive arts therapy. One of only a handful of fully accredited expressive arts therapy graduate-level programs in the world, the expressive arts program at CIIS integrates a thorough training in theories and methods of psychotherapy with intensive training in expressive arts therapy, which is a multimodal approach to psychotherapy that incorporates painting, drawing, sculpture, dance/movement, drama, music, ritual, poetry, and prose.

Integral Counseling Psychology: Master of Arts in Counseling Psychology with a concentration in integral counseling. The integral counseling psychology program at CIIS was the first accredited, transpersonally oriented, East-West psychology program in the U.S. It maintains a vision of psychotherapy practice that draws upon the major spiritual traditions of the East and West, recent cultural and social sciences research, and the innovations made by contemporary psychoanalytic, humanistic, systemic, and transpersonal psychologies. This program offers a flexible weekend option designed for working adults and students who plan on completing the degree within two and a half years.

Somatic Psychology: Master of Arts in Counseling Psychology with a concentration in somatic psychology. The CIIS somatic psychology program is one of only three accredited graduate programs in somatic psychology in the U.S. Somatics is a movement-oriented, body-centered psychotherapy that integrates Western and non-Western knowledge of the ways in which the body is formed in social, cultural, psychological, ecological, and spiritual environments. Its counseling center is the only academically based community somatics clinic in the U.S.

Research Facilities

The Laurance S. Rockefeller Library has collections of approximately 35,000 volumes (including numerous e-books), 290 periodicals (including electronic journals), 1,000 audiovisual materials (audiocassettes, videotapes, compact disks), and almost 1,000 CIIS dissertations and master's theses. The collections are especially strong in the areas of transpersonal and multicultural psychology, spirituality (particularly women's spirituality, Buddhism, Hinduism, Taoism, Confucianism, and wisdom traditions), integral studies, and studies of consciousness. Among these materials are special collections: Alan Watts' and Haridas Chaudhuri's personal collections, the Langley-Porter collection of psychology and psychiatry, the Rogo collection of parapsychology, and a CIIS Institute Authors' collection.

Financial Aid

Financial assistance is awarded primarily on the basis of need. Financial aid consists of scholarships, loans, grants, and Federal Work-Study. Veterans who qualify may receive full benefits under the G. I. Bill. International students may obtain nonimmigrant visas and are eligible for part-time employment on the campus. Students enrolling in the new Community Mental Health Counseling Program for fall 2008 will receive a $5000 scholarship for the first year of the program ($2500 per semester, applied to tuition only). For details about this scholarship, students should contact the Office of Admissions (415-575-6154).

Cost of Study

In 2007–08, full-time annual tuition and fees were $16,930 for M.A. programs and $20,070 for doctoral programs.

Living and Housing Costs

There is no campus housing. Living expenses (rent, travel, and food) in the Bay Area are around $1200 per month. Information about living and housing costs can be found on the CIIS Web site at http://www.ciis.edu/students/housing.

Student Group

Total enrollment in 2007–08 was 1,149. About 20 percent of the students are people of color; about 9 percent are international students. Seventy-five percent of the students are women.

The Institute

Founded in 1968 by the Indian philosopher, educator, and humanist Haridas Chaudhuri, the California Institute of Integral Studies is a regionally accredited institution of higher learning and research dedicated to integrating mind, body, and spirit in service to individuals, communities, and the earth. This small, urban, student-centered academic community is situated in central San Francisco. Classes are offered during the day, in the evening, on weekends, and online to accommodate working professionals. Certain programs offer distance learning options or a combination of online and monthly weekend meetings. The Institute is defined by its value of cultural diversity as well as cultural coherence, multiple ways of knowing, spiritual development, a sense of community, emancipatory ideals, and ecological sustainability.

Applying

Decisions regarding admission are based on the potential for success in the chosen field of study by considering past academic achievement and motivation for educational and personal development and the congruence of the applicant's worldview with the Institute's mission and vision. Applicants to the M.A. programs must have earned a bachelor's degree from a regionally accredited institution, with a grade point average of 3.0 or higher. Applicants to the Ph.D. and Psy.D. programs must have earned an M.A., preferably in a related discipline, with a minimum 3.1 GPA. Academic transcripts, the autobiographical and goal statements, a writing sample (if required), letters of recommendation (if required), and an interview are all considered in the admissions committee decision. The Graduate Record Examinations (GRE) test is required only for the Psy.D. program.

Correspondence and Information

Office of Admissions
California Institute of Integral Studies
1453 Mission Street
San Francisco, California 94103

Phone: 415-575-6154
Fax: 415-575-1268
E-mail: admissions@ciis.edu
Web site: http://www.ciis.edu

California Institute of Integral Studies

THE FACULTY AND THEIR RESEARCH

Philip Brooks, Ed.D., Massachusetts, 1975. Psychosynthesis, existential-humanistic, experiential learning, guided imagery.
Padma Catell, Ph.D., Psychology, California Institute of Integral Studies, 1984. Synthesis of the biochemical, the spiritual, and the psychological.
Brant Cortright, Ph.D., Union (Ohio), 1976. Sri Aurobindo's philosophy as a transpersonal framework for psychotherapy.
Frank Echenhofer, Program Director; Ph.D., Temple, 1985. Physiology and phenomenology of meditation, integrating developmental and transpersonal psychologies.
Renée Emunah, Program Director, Clinical Psychology; Ph.D., Union (Ohio), 1996. Drama therapy group process, drama therapy with adolescents, self-revelatory performance.
Judith Glass, Ph.D., California School of Professional Psychology–San Diego, 1995. Drama therapy, psychodrama, sociometry, and group.
Ian J. Grand, Ph.D., Jungian Institute, 1999. Somatic aspects of interpersonal and intercultural relations, psychodynamic theory.
Lucanna Grey, M.A., Santa Clara, 1981. MFT, existential and Gestalt approaches to psychotherapy.
Judye Hess, Ph.D., Rhode Island, l975. Family systems, Gestalt, experiential learning, and interpersonal dynamics. Private practice specializing in couples, families, and groups.
Michael Kahn, Ph.D., Harvard, 1960. Psychotherapeutic practice, small-group practice, design of higher education.
Don Hanlon Johnson, Ph.D., Yale, 1971. Bodily experience in society, spirituality, and psychology; efficacy of specific somatics practices; psychotherapy; specialization in using action methods with posttraumatic stress disorder (PTSD).
Katharine McGovern, Ph.D., Minnesota, 1981. Consciousness, feeling and emotion, false memory.
Sanjen Miedzinski, Ph.D., CUNY Graduate Center, 1980. Imagery-in-movement process, expressive arts, transpersonal psychology and spiritual practice.
Esther Nzewi, Ph.D., NYU, 1978. Cross-cultural perspectives in personality assessment, women's roles, child welfare.
Janis Phelps, Ph.D., Connecticut, 1986. Child development, clinical studies in enhanced expectancies and treatment, mind-body wellness, Eastern disciplines, interaction of meditation and creativity.
Kaisa Puhakka, Ph.D., Adelphi, 1983. Zen and psychotherapy, knowing, spirituality and psychotherapy, cognition, gender, meditation.
Benjamin Tong, Ph.D., California School of Professional Psychology, 1974. Cross-cultural issues, critical social thought, existential psychoanalysis, stress and trauma.
Leland van den Daele, Ph.D., Purdue, 1967. Psychology and psychoanalysis, moral judgment, cognition, dreams, music, imagery.
Barbara Vivino, Director, Clinical Training; Ph.D., Maryland, 1998. Dream interpretation, marriage and family counseling, acupuncture.
Harrison Voigt, Ph.D., Ohio, 1969. Eastern and Western growth models and psychotherapy, group process, sexuality.
Armand Volkas, M.A., Antioch, 1986. Cultural conflict resolution, drama therapy and social change, Playback Theater.
Jack S. Weller, M.A., California, Santa Barbara, 1968. Buddhism and Buddhist art, spirituality (Eastern, Western, and shamanic), expressive arts.
Tanya Wilkinson, Ph.D., California School of Professional Psychology–Berkeley, 1979. Feminism and Jungian theory/practice, psychological effects of mythological systems.

THE CHICAGO SCHOOL OF PROFESSIONAL PSYCHOLOGY

Business Psychology and Industrial/Organizational Psychology Programs

Programs of Study

The Chicago School of Professional Psychology offers an innovative doctoral degree (Psy.D.) in business psychology and a Master of Arts (M.A.) degree in industrial and organizational (I/O) psychology. The programs provide students with the necessary skill sets in I/O psychology theory and research to lead personnel selection, development, organizational assessment, and interventions as well as the necessary skills in research and statistical methods to become educated consumers of professional literature. Students learn to draw upon research methods in design intervention and to critically approach problems in the appropriate setting. The program also aims to provide students with the personal and interpersonal skills needed in the business environment, such as effective communication, conflict negotiation, and influence strategies. The business psychology and I/O psychology programs at The Chicago School are distinctive in that they apply the discipline's assessment skills and feedback mechanisms in the program itself. Students not only learn how to design and implement assessment centers and feedback tools, but they also benefit by participating in these very same practices to identify their own strengths and improve developmental areas.

The business psychology doctoral program integrates I/O, business, and individual intervention, emphasizing the skills and knowledge needed to assume professional responsibilities in human resource, consulting, organization development, and management positions. Courses provide students with the scientific and theoretical principles of psychology and the application of these principles to a variety of work settings in which I/O psychologists are employed. Internship training ensures that students are able to transfer classroom knowledge to the real world of work.

The Master of Arts (M.A.) in industrial and organizational (I/O) psychology program has a curriculum that enables students to gain the essential diagnostic and consultative skills to help organizations and the individuals within them solve problems; perform effectively; work in a global, multicultural environment; and grow professionally. The Chicago School focuses not just on theory and research but on teaching its students the applied skills necessary to succeed in the business world. Intensive course work that balances theory and practice is accompanied by two supervised internships. Students must successfully complete 46 credit hours, 6 of which are electives, to graduate.

The Chicago School, in cooperation with Lake Forest Graduate School of Management (LFGSM), also offers its M.A. alumni the option of earning an accelerated M.B.A. degree. This program is designed to facilitate additional graduate level education for actively employed professionals who receive their M.A. in industrial/organizational psychology. The Chicago School graduates who enroll at LFGSM through this educational alliance receive transfer credit for three graduate-level courses toward the completion of an M.B.A. degree.

Students have secured internships and jobs at such organizations as the Chicago Board of Trade, U.S. Navy, *Chicago Tribune*, ACNielsen, Red Cross, Allstate, Tapestry Resources, Rush Health Medical Systems, GM Electromotive Division, Buck Consulting, YMCA, United Health Care, and Bank of America.

Research Facilities

The Chicago School maintains an on-site library with a wide range of books and journals in psychology and related fields. Library holdings include approximately 10,000 volumes, subscriptions to more than 235 core psychology journals, and access to more than 50 electronic databases, including PsycInfo, PsyArticles, MEDLINE, and several online library networks that allow students to borrow from worldwide libraries, which hold more than 35 million items. Library consortia and reciprocal networking agreements, coupled with the library's interlibrary loan and document locator services, provide access to the collections of major public, private, and academic libraries worldwide. The library also offers Internet access and maintains its own research-reference-links Web page to psychology-related databases and Web sites throughout the world.

Financial Aid

Just as the field of psychology is a helping profession, The Chicago School believes in helping its students afford the expenses associated with graduate education. The Office of Financial Aid assists all students with managing resources and securing the financial assistance they need. The Chicago School offers numerous types of assistance to eligible students, including federal student aid, scholarships and assistantships, and employment. Students may also qualify for tuition assistance through an employer, a fellowship, and outside scholarships. For additional information on these and other available programs, students should visit The Chicago School's Web site or e-mail the Office of Financial Aid at finaid@thechicagoschool.edu.

Cost of Study

Tuition for the doctoral program for the 2007–08 academic year was $940 per hour; for the master's programs, $780 per hour. Other fees included registration, $85; late registration, $85; drop/add fee per course, $25; and an annual student services fee (per term) of $530 for full-time students or $265 for part-time students.

Living and Housing Costs

On-campus housing is not provided by The Chicago School of Professional Psychology. Students can find ample rental housing within a short walking distance or commute, utilizing Chicago public transportation or suburban Metra trains. The cost of living in or near Chicago is above the median for larger Midwestern cities.

Student Group

Enrolled students are successful graduates of some of the nation's top undergraduate psychology programs. More than 1,000 students are currently enrolled in The Chicago School. The students are ethnically and culturally diverse and come from a wide variety of educational and occupational backgrounds. The Chicago School attracts students from across the country and around the world.

Location

The Chicago School of Professional Psychology is centrally located in the River North neighborhood of downtown Chicago.

The School

The Chicago School of Professional Psychology is an independent, nonprofit graduate school that provides students with an outstanding education in a student-centered environment. Integrating theory, professional practice, and innovation, The Chicago School provides an excellent education for careers in psychology and related behavioral and health sciences. The Chicago School is committed to service, embraces the diverse communities of society, and educates professionals whose practices exemplify a commitment to understand and respect individual and cultural differences. The curriculum and training opportunities prepare students to deliver outstanding professional services, emphasizing the need to understand diversity and the importance of working with underserved populations.

Applying

Application to The Chicago School is open to anyone who has earned a bachelor's degree from an accredited institution. Because admission requirements differ by program, prospective students should contact the Office of Admission or visit the Web site for details on their program of interest.

Doctoral and master's application deadlines for fall admission are as follows: early consideration, February 15, and general consideration, April 1 (international students must have a completed application by April 1 for admission into the fall term in order to allow sufficient time to obtain the additional documentation required to study in the U.S.). After the April 1 deadline, students should contact the Office of Admission at http://www.admissions@thechicagoschool.edu regarding space availability.

Correspondence and Information

Office of Admission
Chicago School of Professional Psychology
325 North Wells Street
Chicago, Illinois 60610

Phone: 312-329-6666
E-mail: admissions@thechicagoschool.edu
Web site: http://www.thechicagoschool.edu

The Chicago School of Professional Psychology

THE FACULTY AND THEIR RESEARCH

Jaleel Abdul-Adil, Program Faculty; Ph.D., DePaul. Evidence-based, culturally sensitive family therapy for urban youth; conduct disorder and oppositional defiant disorder; gang involvement; inner-city violence.
Michael Barr, Program Faculty and Director of Corporate Education and Consulting Services; Ph.D., IIT. Job satisfaction, employee motivation and loyalty, leadership development, stress, trends, team building, 360-degree feedback, work/life balance.
John C. Benitez, Program Faculty and Consultant with the Department of Children and Family Services; Ph.D., Northwestern. Issues related to clergy and mental health, supervision, and diversity.
Larisa Buhin, Program Faculty; Ph.D., Loyola Chicago. Training for multicultural competence, ethnic identity development, and social justice.
Marie Ciavarella, Program Faculty and Director of Career Services; Psy.D., Illinois School of Professional Psychology. How the complexities of culture affect the provision of mental health and educational services.
Ellis Copeland, Program Faculty and Department Chair of the School Psychology Program; Ph.D., Texas at Austin. Measurement, research methods, community psychology, health psychology, child psychopathology, consultation.
Gail Berger Darlow, Program Faculty and Director of Industrial and Organizational Internships; Ph.D., Northwestern. Negotiation and conflict resolution, teamwork, organizational communication, decision making, power.
Nancy Davis, Program Faculty; Ph.D., Fielding Graduate Institute. Cultural change in an organization, strategic planning, executive coaching, team development, organizational assessment and reorganization, competency modeling, conflict resolution.
Chanté D. DeLoach, Program Faculty; Psy.D., Azusa Pacific. Racism, racialized sexism, health disparities, African psychology, sociocultural consciousness and hip-hop music.
Michael DiDomenico, Program Faculty; Psy.D., Illinois School of Professional Psychology. Aging disorders, organic brain syndromes, forensic issues, social issues and policies that affect mental health, ADHD, learning disabilities, developmental disabilities.
Todd DuBose, Program Faculty; Ph.D., Duquesne. Working with persons and families under extreme stress across the life span; trauma; loss and mourning; interpersonal violence; severe physical, neurological, and disease-related limitations in the areas of psychosomatics.
Kelly Ducheny, Program Faculty and Department Chair of the Clinical Psychology Doctoral Program; Psy.D., Wright State. Cultural competence and multicultural psychology; gay, lesbian, bisexual, and transgendered issues; assessment; professional development; gender roles and race in Disney animation; qualitative research; cognitive-behavioral, existential, and feminist psychotherapies.
Ken Fogel, Program Faculty; Psy.D., Chicago School of Professional Psychology. ADHD, anxiety, child abuse, depression, mood and personality disorders, posttraumatic stress, psychotherapy, sexually abused children, stress, trauma.
Michael Fogel, Program Faculty and Associate Department Chair of the Forensic Psychology Master's Program; Psy.D., Illinois School of Professional Psychology. Sex offender evaluations, competency/sanity evaluations, dangerous/violence evaluations, testamentary capacity.
Michael Gaubatz, Program Faculty; Ph.D., Loyola Chicago. Clinical training issues, especially formalized student review procedures and trainees' and practitioners' awareness of the cultural embeddedness of mental health interventions.
Grant Gautreaux, Program Faculty; Ph.D., Columbia. Applied behavior analysis, autism, developmental disabilities, disability issues, learning disabilities.
Enrique Gonzalez, Program Faculty; Ph.D., Loyola Chicago. Health psychology, pain management, psychosocial oncology, cultural issues related to psychology.
Kevin Gyoerkoe, Program Faculty; Psy.D., Nova Southeastern. Anxiety, cognitive-behavior therapy, depression, mood disorders, obsessive-compulsive disorder, stress.
Bridget Scott Hagood, Program Faculty; Psy.D., Argosy. Eating and mood disorders, diversity issues, meditative practices in psychotherapy.
Bianka Hardin, Program Faculty; Psy.D., Chicago School of Professional Psychology. Trauma, cultural issues.
Evan Harrington, Program Faculty; Ph.D., Temple. Nocebo (negative placebo) effect, psychology of terrorism, accuracy of child-abuse accusations.
Michael Horowitz, Program Faculty and President of the Chicago School of Professional Psychology; Ph.D., Northwestern. Organizational leadership, political advocacy, parenting, graduate education and the expansion of professional psychology practice.
Michelle Hoy-Watkins, Program Faculty; Psy.D., California School of Professional Psychology, Alameda. Criminal forensic evaluations, social security disability claims, pre-employment law-enforcement screenings, fitness-for-duty evaluations, cross-cultural assessment.
Jordan Jacobowitz, Program Faculty; Ph.D., Hebrew (Jerusalem). Applying and developing the psychoanalytic orientation to understand and treat psychopathology, examining life-span psychology, educating students to become clinicians.
Mark Kassel, Program Faculty; Psy.D., Adler School of Professional Psychology. Addiction, mood disorders, diversity issues, stress, anxiety.
Tiffany Keller, Program Faculty; Psy.D., Argosy. Personality assessment, child and adolescent assessment, neuropsychological assessment, feminist psychology, adolescent peer relation.
Ken H. Kessler, Program Faculty; Ph.D., University of Health Sciences. Ethics and professional issues, forensic assessment, professional and practice development.
Michael Komie, Program Faculty; Ph.D., Northwestern. Health psychology, life and work transitions, disability issues, attachment and loss, psychoanalytic therapies, work stress in minority and immigrant populations, gender issues, work/vocational issues.
Kin Ching Kong, Program Faculty; Ph.D., DePaul. ADHD, anxiety, behavior therapy, child psychology, cultural and diversity issues, family therapy, immigrant populations, marriage and divorce, parenting, psychotherapy, stress.
Lukasz Konopka, Program Faculty and Director of Neurophysiology and Pharmacology at Hines VA Hospital; Ph.D., Loyola Chicago. Adolescent psychology.
Paul Larson, Program Faculty; Ph.D., Utah; J.D., DePaul. Inpatient, residential, and outpatient veterans with severe and chronic disabilities, including a variety of physical and medical conditions and mental illness.
Christoph Leonhard, Program Faculty; Ph.D., Nevada, Reno. Behavior therapy with a variety of adult populations, including persons with mental retardation, severe mental illness, mood and anxiety disorders, and substance addiction.
Tiffany Mason, Program Faculty; Psy.D., Alliant International. Adolescence and child psychology, child abuse, family therapy, forensic psychology, gender issues, parenting, juvenile delinquency, sexually abused children and trauma.
Charles Merbitz, Program Faculty and Department Chair of the Clinical Psychology–Applied Behavior Analysis Specialization Master's Program; Ph.D., Florida. Objective process measures for relating clinical interventions in rehabilitation to outcomes and outcome measures.
Perry C. Meyers, Program Faculty and Department Chair of the Forensic Psychology Master's Program; Ph.D., IIT. Juvenile justice, adult criminal forensics, child protection, child-custody assessment, psychodynamic psychotherapy.
John Murray, Program Faculty; Psy.D., Illinois School of Professional Psychology. Clinical and forensic psychology, clinical training, role of psychology in justice system.
Michele Nealon-Woods, Program Faculty; Psy.D., Chicago School of Professional Psychology. Development and improvement of treatment interventions for children and adolescents, improving the application of clinical approaches with diverse populations.
Noelle Newhouse, Program Faculty; M.S., IIT. Leadership, testing, workplace issues.
Nancy A. Newton, Program Faculty; Ph.D., Wayne State. Life span, psychology and psychogeriatrics, women's issues, mediation and psychotherapy, executive coaching, workplace failure as a developmental experience.
Richard Niolon, Program Faculty; Ph.D., Saint Louis. Couples therapy (straight, gay, lesbian, married, or unmarried), divorce/remarriage/Gottman Theory/Technique, Bowenian Theory/Technique, stepparenting/stepfamilies, marital satisfaction.
Joyce Nugent-Hirschbeck, Program Faculty; Psy.D., Chicago School of Professional Psychology. Schizophrenia, family therapy, staff barriers and burnout, chronic mental illness, borderline personality disorders.
Shelly O'Neal-Benson, Program Faculty; Ph.D., Union (Ohio). Forensic psychology.
David Pyles, Program Faculty and Associate Department Chair of the Clinical Psychology–Applied Behavior Analysis Specialization Master's Program; Ph.D., Florida State. Developmental disabilities, behavioral diagnostics/functional assessment of behavior, behavioral psychopharmacology, behavioral systems management, behavior analysis in business and industry, dual diagnosis.
Virginia G. Quiñonez, Program Faculty and Department Chair of the Clinical Psychology–Counseling Specialization Master's Program; Psy.D., Illinois School of Professional Psychology. Multicultural psychology; trauma theory; minority students in higher education; gay, lesbian, and bisexual issues; HIV mental health.
Deane Rabe, Program Faculty and Associate Vice President of Academic Affairs; Psy.D., Illinois School of Professional Psychology. Psychological assessment, forensic evaluation, supervision and training, sex therapy, corporate consultation.
Karen Randall, Program Faculty; Ph.D., Loyola Chicago. Self-injury, women's health, managed-care issues, professional development and identity, psychoanalytic models of treatment, supervision, trauma, assessment, treatment of adult and adolescent clients.
Meghan Roekle, Program Faculty; Psy.D., Chicago School of Professional Psychology. Constructivist and feminist-relational thinking, philosophical roots and practical applications of clinical theory.
Kerri Rönne, Program Faculty; Ph.D., Iowa. Personality assessment, transgendered and transsexual populations, creativity and the visual arts, female-based religions.
Ted Rubenstein, Program Faculty; Psy.D., Chicago School of Professional Psychology. Creative arts therapy and the psychology of music, art, dance, and theater.
Susan Sances, Program Faculty and Vice President of Academic Affairs; Psy.D., Illinois School of Professional Psychology. Academic programs, including the Center for Multicultural and Diversity Studies and the Academic Support Services.
Paul Sanders, Program Faculty; Ph.D., Minnesota. Schizophrenic and borderline psychopathology, interfaith dimensions in treatment, diagnostic interviewing.
Shaifali Sandhya, Program Faculty; Ph.D., Chicago. Well-being, intimate relationships, conflict and negotiation, culture and social change.
Gale Sargeant, Program Faculty and Associate Department Chair of the Clinical Psychology–Counseling Specialization Master's Program; Ph.D., DePaul. HIV mental health, health psychology.
Wendy Schiffman, Program Faculty; Psy.D., Illinois School of Professional Psychology. Juvenile delinquency and criminal forensic evaluation.
John Shustitzky, Program Faculty; Ph.D., Illinois at Chicago. Community psychology and domestic violence.
Sandra Siegel, Program Faculty; Psy.D., Adler School of Professional Psychology. Community mental health, mentally ill substance-abuse clients, mentally ill prisoners in jail and prison systems.
Michael Smith, Program Faculty and Associate Department Chair of the Clinical Psychology Doctoral Program; Ph.D., IIT. Adjustment of immigrants and refugees, particularly examination of multigenerational issues; child and adolescent psychology; health psychology.
Drake Spaeth, Program Faculty; Psy.D., Chicago School of Professional Psychology. Aging; child abuse; cultural issues; depression; domestic violence; forensic psychology; gay, lesbian, and bisexual issues; racism; schizophrenia.
Jennifer Thompson, Program Faculty and Department Chair of the Industrial and Organizational Psychology Master's Program and Business Psychology Doctoral Program; Ph.D., IIT. Legal issues, affirmative action, attitudes, stereotypes, program evaluation, selection in education, gender bias.
Emily Trolley, Program Faculty; M.A., Chicago School of Professional Psychology. Work/life balance, workplace interests, job satisfaction, leadership.
Marla Gal Vannucci, Program Faculty; Ph.D., Northwestern. Training and developmental relationships, philosophy of psychology, consultation, smoking cessation.
Diana Walker, Program Faculty; Ph.D., Florida. Autism, cultural and diversity issues, education, learning disabilities, schizophrenia.
Gary Walls, Program Faculty; Ph.D., Miami (Ohio). Contemporary relational psychoanalysis; transference and countertransference; history of ideas; philosophy of science; hermeneutics; issues of class, gender, race, politics, and culture in the teaching and practice of psychology.
James Walsh, Program Faculty; Ph.D., Texas at Austin. ADHD, adolescent psychology, anxiety, behavior therapy, depression, child and family therapy, learning disabilities, mood disorders, obsessive-compulsive disorder, psychotherapy.
Grant White, Program Faculty; Psy.D., Chicago School of Professional Psychology. Assessment, disability issues, parenting, race, racism.

THE CHICAGO SCHOOL OF PROFESSIONAL PSYCHOLOGY

Clinical Psychology Programs

Programs of Study

The Chicago School's APA-accredited doctoral program in clinical psychology (Psy.D.) provides an outstanding and innovative curriculum, taught by experienced practitioner faculty members with an emphasis on innovation, community, diversity, and multicultural awareness. Students develop essential diagnostic, therapeutic, and consultative skills through immersion in intensive course work, field placements, and internship. The program awards a master's degree after successful completion of required course work and an assessment practicum. A clinical dissertation is completed during the program.

The program does not advocate any single theoretical orientation. Students receive an excellent generalist-based education in theory, conceptualization, and technique and then choose a theoretical orientation in which to specialize. Students following this generalist track choose an area of special interest from seven concentrations, including child/adolescent, forensic, generalist, health, multicultural/community, organizational, and school psychology. The clinical psychology doctoral program also offers a child and adolescent track and a certificate in applied behavior analysis.

The doctoral program in clinical psychology bases its training on the practitioner-scholar model of education, integrating the core competencies endorsed by the National Council of Schools and Programs of Professional Psychology (NCSPP) for professional psychologists. The incorporation of issues of individual/cultural difference is a required component of all learning activities and the program has been nationally recognized for its training in culturally competent service provision.

The clinical psychology programs also offer Master of Arts (M.A.) degrees, which include two areas of specialization: counseling and applied behavior analysis. Through these full-time programs, students learn the essential skills needed to become competent, professional psychologists. They develop essential diagnostic, therapeutic, and consultative skills in order to work with a variety of clients with a wide range of psychological conditions. Students learn significant theoretical frameworks and the scientific bases of clinical psychology at the graduate level as well as the necessary research methodologies. Students also learn the ethical and professional guidelines of clinical psychology and gain an understanding of the impact of diversity and clinical issues in this dynamic field.

The master's program in clinical counseling teaches the essential consultative and therapeutic skills needed to work with a variety of clients, from children to the elderly, who have a wide range of emotional and psychological conditions. Graduates have the training necessary to work in a variety of settings, including hospitals, mental health services, schools, family counseling centers, group homes, and correctional facilities as well as establishing successful private practices. Students may choose from among five concentrations to fulfill the elective requirements: child and adolescent treatment, health psychology, Latino mental health, supervision and leadership in community mental health, and treatment of addiction disorders. The program also offers two certificates related to Latino mental health.

The master's program in applied behavior analysis incorporates the content areas and practicum requirements to make graduates eligible for National Board Certification by the Behavior Analysis Certification Board. The program's aim is to prepare students for a rewarding career in the rapidly growing field of applied behavior analysis, working in residential-, school-, and community-based settings with children, adults, and seniors diagnosed with developmental disabilities, behavioral difficulties, major mental illness, and a variety of geriatric conditions.

Research Facilities

The Chicago School maintains an on-site library with a wide range of books and journals in psychology and related fields. Library holdings include approximately 10,000 volumes, subscriptions to more than 235 core psychology journals, and access to more than 50 electronic databases, including PsycInfo, PsyArticles, MEDLINE, and several online library networks that allow students to borrow from worldwide libraries, which hold more than 35 million items. Library consortia and reciprocal networking agreements, coupled with the library's interlibrary loan and document locator services, provide access to the collections of major public, private, and academic libraries worldwide. The library also offers Internet access and maintains its own research-reference-links Web page to psychology-related databases and Web sites throughout the world.

Financial Aid

Just as the field of psychology is a helping profession, The Chicago School believes in helping its students afford the expenses associated with graduate education. The Office of Financial Aid assists all students with managing resources and securing the financial assistance they need. The Chicago School offers numerous types of assistance to eligible students, including federal student aid, scholarships and assistantships, and employment. Students may also qualify for tuition assistance through an employer, a fellowship, and outside scholarships. For additional information on these and other available programs, students should visit The Chicago School's Web site or e-mail the Office of Financial Aid at finaid@thechicagoschool.edu.

Cost of Study

Tuition for the doctoral program for the 2007–08 academic year was $940 per hour; for the master's programs, $780 per hour. Other fees included registration, $85; late registration, $85; drop/add fee per course, $25; and an annual student services fee (per term) of $530 for full-time students or $265 for part-time students.

Living and Housing Costs

On-campus housing is not provided by The Chicago School of Professional Psychology. Students can find ample rental housing within a short walking distance or commute, utilizing Chicago public transportation or suburban Metra. The cost of living in or near Chicago is above the median for larger Midwestern cities.

Student Group

Enrolled students are successful graduates of some of the nation's top undergraduate psychology programs. More than1,000 students are currently enrolled in The Chicago School. The students are ethnically and culturally diverse and come from a wide variety of educational and occupational backgrounds. The Chicago School attracts students from across the country and around the world.

Location

The Chicago School of Professional Psychology is centrally located in the River North neighborhood of downtown Chicago.

The School

The Chicago School of Professional Psychology is an independent, nonprofit graduate school that provides students with an outstanding education in a student-centered environment. Integrating theory, professional practice, and innovation, The Chicago School provides an excellent education for careers in psychology and related behavioral and health sciences. The Chicago School is committed to service, embraces the diverse communities of society, and educates professionals whose practices exemplify a commitment to understand and respect individual and cultural differences. The curriculum and training opportunities prepare students to deliver outstanding professional services, emphasizing the need to understand diversity and the importance of working with underserved populations.

Applying

Application to The Chicago School is open to anyone who has earned a bachelor's degree from an accredited institution. Because admission requirements differ by program, prospective students should contact the Office of Admission or visit the Web site for details on their program of interest.

Doctoral application deadlines for fall admission are as follows: early consideration, December 15, and general, February 15 (international students must have a completed application by February 15 for admission into the fall term in order to allow sufficient time to obtain the additional documentation required to study in the U.S.). After the February 15 deadline, students should contact the Office of Admission at http://www.admissions@thechicagoschool.edu regarding space availability.

Master's application deadlines for fall admission are as follows: early consideration, February 15, and general consideration, April 1 (international students must have a completed application by April 1 for admission into the fall term in order to allow sufficient time to obtain the additional documentation required to study in the U.S.). After the April 1 deadline, students should contact the Office of Admission at http://www.admissions@thechicagoschool.edu regarding space availability.

Correspondence and Information

Office of Admission
Chicago School of Professional Psychology
325 North Wells Street
Chicago, Illinois 60610
Phone: 312-329-6666
E-mail: admissions@thechicagoschool.edu
Web site: http://www.thechicagoschool.edu

The Chicago School of Professional Psychology

THE FACULTY AND THEIR RESEARCH

Jaleel Abdul-Adil, Program Faculty; Ph.D., DePaul. Evidence-based, culturally sensitive family therapy for urban youth; conduct disorder and oppositional defiant disorder; gang involvement; inner-city violence.

Michael Barr, Program Faculty and Director of Corporate Education and Consulting Services; Ph.D., IIT. Job satisfaction, employee motivation and loyalty, leadership development, stress, trends, team building, 360-degree feedback, work/life balance.

John C. Benitez, Program Faculty and Consultant with the Department of Children and Family Services; Ph.D., Northwestern. Issues related to clergy and mental health, supervision, and diversity.

Larisa Buhin, Program Faculty; Ph.D., Loyola Chicago. Training for multicultural competence, ethnic identity development, and social justice.

Marie Ciavarella, Program Faculty and Director of Career Services; Psy.D., Illinois School of Professional Psychology. How the complexities of culture affect the provision of mental health and educational services.

Ellis Copeland, Program Faculty and Department Chair of the School Psychology Program; Ph.D., Texas at Austin. Measurement, research methods, community psychology, health psychology, child psychopathology, consultation.

Gail Berger Darlow, Program Faculty and Director of Industrial and Organizational Internships; Ph.D., Northwestern. Negotiation and conflict resolution, teamwork, organizational communication, decision making, power.

Nancy Davis, Program Faculty; Ph.D., Fielding Graduate Institute. Cultural change in an organization, strategic planning, executive coaching, team development, organizational assessment and reorganization, competency modeling, conflict resolution.

Chanté D. DeLoach, Program Faculty; Psy.D., Azusa Pacific. Racism, racialized sexism, health disparities, African psychology, sociocultural consciousness and hip-hop music.

Michael DiDomenico, Program Faculty; Psy.D., Illinois School of Professional Psychology. Aging disorders, organic brain syndromes, forensic issues, social issues and policies that affect mental health, ADHD, learning disabilities, developmental disabilities.

Todd DuBose, Program Faculty; Ph.D., Duquesne. Working with persons and families under extreme stress across the life span; trauma; loss and mourning; interpersonal violence; severe physical, neurological, and disease-related limitations in the areas of psychosomatics.

Kelly Ducheny, Program Faculty and Department Chair of the Clinical Psychology Doctoral Program; Psy.D., Wright State. Cultural competence and multicultural psychology; gay, lesbian, bisexual, and transgendered issues; assessment; professional development; gender roles and race in Disney animation; qualitative research; cognitive-behavioral, existential, and feminist psychotherapies.

Ken Fogel, Program Faculty; Psy.D., Chicago School of Professional Psychology. ADHD, anxiety, child abuse, depression, mood and personality disorders, posttraumatic stress, psychotherapy, sexually abused children, stress, trauma.

Michael Fogel, Program Faculty and Associate Department Chair of the Forensic Psychology Master's Program; Psy.D., Illinois School of Professional Psychology. Sex offender evaluations, competency/sanity evaluations, dangerous/violence evaluations, testamentary capacity.

Michael Gaubatz, Program Faculty; Ph.D., Loyola Chicago. Clinical training issues, especially formalized student review procedures and trainees' and practitioners' awareness of the cultural embeddedness of mental health interventions.

Grant Gautreaux, Program Faculty; Ph.D., Columbia. Applied behavior analysis, autism, developmental disabilities, disability issues, learning disabilities.

Enrique Gonzalez, Program Faculty; Ph.D., Loyola Chicago. Health psychology, pain management, psychosocial oncology, cultural issues related to psychology.

Kevin Gyoerkoe, Program Faculty; Psy.D., Nova Southeastern. Anxiety, cognitive-behavior therapy, depression, mood disorders, obsessive-compulsive disorder, stress.

Bridget Scott Hagood, Program Faculty; Psy.D., Argosy. Eating and mood disorders, diversity issues, meditative practices in psychotherapy.

Bianka Hardin, Program Faculty; Psy.D., Chicago School of Professional Psychology. Trauma, cultural issues.

Evan Harrington, Program Faculty; Ph.D., Temple. Nocebo (negative placebo) effect, psychology of terrorism, accuracy of child-abuse accusations.

Michael Horowitz, Program Faculty and President of the Chicago School of Professional Psychology; Ph.D., Northwestern. Organizational leadership, political advocacy, parenting, graduate education and the expansion of professional psychology practice.

Michelle Hoy-Watkins, Program Faculty; Psy.D., California School of Professional Psychology, Alameda. Criminal forensic evaluations, social security disability claims, pre-employment law-enforcement screenings, fitness-for-duty evaluations, cross-cultural assessment.

Jordan Jacobowitz, Program Faculty; Ph.D., Hebrew (Jerusalem). Applying and developing the psychoanalytic orientation to understand and treat psychopathology, examining life-span psychology, educating students to become clinicians.

Mark Kassel, Program Faculty; Psy.D., Adler School of Professional Psychology. Addiction, mood disorders, diversity issues, stress, anxiety.

Tiffany Keller, Program Faculty; Psy.D., Argosy. Personality assessment, child and adolescent assessment, neuropsychological assessment, feminist psychology, adolescent peer relation.

Ken H. Kessler, Program Faculty; Ph.D., University of Health Sciences. Ethics and professional issues, forensic assessment, professional and practice development.

Michael Komie, Program Faculty; Ph.D., Northwestern. Health psychology, life and work transitions, disability issues, attachment and loss, psychoanalytic therapies, work stress in minority and immigrant populations, gender issues, work/vocational issues.

Kin Ching Kong, Program Faculty; Ph.D., DePaul. ADHD, anxiety, behavior therapy, child psychology, cultural and diversity issues, family therapy, immigrant populations, marriage and divorce, parenting, psychotherapy, stress.

Lukasz Konopka, Program Faculty and Director of Neurophysiology and Pharmacology at Hines VA Hospital; Ph.D., Loyola Chicago. Adolescent psychology.

Paul Larson, Program Faculty; Ph.D., Utah; J.D., DePaul. Inpatient, residential, and outpatient veterans with severe and chronic disabilities, including a variety of physical and medical conditions and mental illness.

Christoph Leonhard, Program Faculty; Ph.D., Nevada, Reno. Behavior therapy with a variety of adult populations, including persons with mental retardation, severe mental illness, mood and anxiety disorders, and substance addiction.

Tiffany Mason, Program Faculty; Psy.D., Alliant International. Adolescence and child psychology, child abuse, family therapy, forensic psychology, gender issues, parenting, juvenile delinquency, sexually abused children and trauma.

Charles Merbitz, Program Faculty and Department Chair of the Clinical Psychology–Applied Behavior Analysis Specialization Master's Program; Ph.D., Florida. Objective process measures for relating clinical interventions in rehabilitation to outcomes and outcome measures.

Perry C. Meyers, Program Faculty and Department Chair of the Forensic Psychology Master's Program; Ph.D., IIT. Juvenile justice, adult criminal forensics, child protection, child-custody assessment, psychodynamic psychotherapy.

John Murray, Program Faculty; Psy.D., Illinois School of Professional Psychology. Clinical and forensic psychology, clinical training, role of psychology in justice system.

Michele Nealon-Woods, Program Faculty; Psy.D., Chicago School of Professional Psychology. Development and improvement of treatment interventions for children and adolescents, improving the application of clinical approaches with diverse populations.

Noelle Newhouse, Program Faculty; M.S., IIT. Leadership, testing, workplace issues.

Nancy A. Newton, Program Faculty; Ph.D., Wayne State. Life span, psychology and psychogeriatrics, women's issues, mediation and psychotherapy, executive coaching, workplace failure as a developmental experience.

Richard Niolon, Program Faculty; Ph.D., Saint Louis. Couples therapy (straight, gay, lesbian, married, or unmarried), divorce/remarriage/Gottman Theory/Technique, Bowenian Theory/Technique, stepparenting/stepfamilies, marital satisfaction.

Joyce Nugent-Hirschbeck, Program Faculty; Psy.D., Chicago School of Professional Psychology. Schizophrenia, family therapy, staff barriers and burnout, chronic mental illness, borderline personality disorders.

Shelly O'Neal-Benson, Program Faculty; Ph.D., Union (Ohio). Forensic psychology.

David Pyles, Program Faculty and Associate Department Chair of the Clinical Psychology–Applied Behavior Analysis Specialization Master's Program; Ph.D., Florida State. Developmental disabilities, behavioral diagnostics/functional assessment of behavior, behavioral psychopharmacology, behavioral systems management, behavior analysis in business and industry, dual diagnosis.

Virginia G. Quiñonez, Program Faculty and Department Chair of the Clinical Psychology–Counseling Specialization Master's Program; Psy.D., Illinois School of Professional Psychology. Multicultural psychology; trauma theory; minority students in higher education; gay, lesbian, and bisexual issues; HIV mental health.

Deane Rabe, Program Faculty and Associate Vice President of Academic Affairs; Psy.D., Illinois School of Professional Psychology. Psychological assessment, forensic evaluation, supervision and training, sex therapy, corporate consultation.

Karen Randall, Program Faculty; Ph.D., Loyola Chicago. Self-injury, women's health, managed-care issues, professional development and identity, psychoanalytic models of treatment, supervision, trauma, assessment, treatment of adult and adolescent clients.

Meghan Roekle, Program Faculty; Psy.D., Chicago School of Professional Psychology. Constructivist and feminist-relational thinking, philosophical roots and practical applications of clinical theory.

Kerri Rönne, Program Faculty; Ph.D., Iowa. Personality assessment, transgendered and transsexual populations, creativity and the visual arts, female-based religions.

Ted Rubenstein, Program Faculty; Psy.D., Chicago School of Professional Psychology. Creative arts therapy and the psychology of music, art, dance, and theater.

Susan Sances, Program Faculty and Vice President of Academic Affairs; Psy.D., Illinois School of Professional Psychology. Academic programs, including the Center for Multicultural and Diversity Studies and the Academic Support Services.

Paul Sanders, Program Faculty; Ph.D., Minnesota. Schizophrenic and borderline psychopathology, interfaith dimensions in treatment, diagnostic interviewing.

Shaifali Sandhya, Program Faculty; Ph.D., Chicago. Well-being, intimate relationships, conflict and negotiation, culture and social change.

Gale Sargeant, Program Faculty and Associate Department Chair of the Clinical Psychology–Counseling Specialization Master's Program; Ph.D., DePaul. HIV mental health, health psychology.

Wendy Schiffman, Program Faculty; Psy.D., Illinois School of Professional Psychology. Juvenile delinquency and criminal forensic evaluation.

John Shustitzky, Program Faculty; Ph.D., Illinois at Chicago. Community psychology and domestic violence.

Sandra Siegel, Program Faculty; Psy.D., Adler School of Professional Psychology. Community mental health, mentally ill substance-abuse clients, mentally ill prisoners in jail and prison systems.

Michael Smith, Program Faculty and Associate Department Chair of the Clinical Psychology Doctoral Program; Ph.D., IIT. Adjustment of immigrants and refugees, particularly examination of multigenerational issues; child and adolescent psychology; health psychology.

Drake Spaeth, Program Faculty; Psy.D., Chicago School of Professional Psychology. Aging; child abuse; cultural issues; depression; domestic violence; forensic psychology; gay, lesbian, and bisexual issues; racism; schizophrenia.

Jennifer Thompson, Program Faculty and Department Chair of the Industrial and Organizational Psychology Master's Program and Business Psychology Doctoral Program; Ph.D., IIT. Legal issues, affirmative action, attitudes, stereotypes, program evaluation, selection in education, gender bias.

Emily Trolley, Program Faculty; M.A., Chicago School of Professional Psychology. Work/life balance, workplace interests, job satisfaction, leadership.

Marla Gal Vannucci, Program Faculty; Ph.D., Northwestern. Training and developmental relationships, philosophy of psychology, consultation, smoking cessation.

Diana Walker, Program Faculty; Ph.D., Florida. Autism, cultural and diversity issues, education, learning disabilities, schizophrenia.

Gary Walls, Program Faculty; Ph.D., Miami (Ohio). Contemporary relational psychoanalysis; transference and countertransference; history of ideas; philosophy of science; hermeneutics; issues of class, gender, race, politics, and culture in the teaching and practice of psychology.

James Walsh, Program Faculty; Ph.D., Texas at Austin. ADHD, adolescent psychology, anxiety, behavior therapy, depression, child and family therapy, learning disabilities, mood disorders, obsessive-compulsive disorder, psychotherapy.

Grant White, Program Faculty; Psy.D., Chicago School of Professional Psychology. Assessment, disability issues, parenting, race, racism.

THE CHICAGO SCHOOL OF PROFESSIONAL PSYCHOLOGY

Master of Arts in Forensic Psychology Program

Program of Study

The Chicago School of Professional Psychology's Master of Arts in Forensic Psychology Program focuses on the application of the science and profession of psychology to questions and issues relating to law and the legal system. The program has three objectives: to prepare master's-level specialists to bring psychology into the legal arena; to prepare master's-level specialists to contribute services (i.e., supervision, assessment, intervention, and treatment planning) to address problems and issues of various populations; and to provide students with the necessary interpersonal, behavioral, academic, and technical skills needed in a variety of forensic settings. Students are required to complete 60 semester hours of course work, which includes practicum experience (licensure or nonlicensure options) or a master's thesis.

In consultation with the student's adviser, the course work is customized to meet an individual's needs and educational and professional goals. This program provides the academic requirements to enable a student to take the Illinois master-level licensure exams (LPC and LCPC), pursue a doctoral degree, or further his or her career through specific promotion opportunities that require a graduate degree.

The curriculum is designed to prepare graduates to work in a variety of areas, including community mental health centers, jails or prisons, probation services, court service units, protective services, secure forensics units, violence risk assessment, specialized agencies, and law enforcement.

Research Facilities

The Chicago School maintains an on-site library with a wide range of books and journals in psychology and related fields. Library holdings include approximately 10,000 volumes, subscriptions to more than 235 core psychology journals, and access to more than 50 electronic databases, including PsycInfo, PsyArticles, and MEDLINE, and several online library networks that allow students to borrow from worldwide libraries, which hold more than 35 million items. Library consortia and reciprocal networking agreements, coupled with the library's interlibrary loan and document-locator services, provide access to the collections of major public, private, and academic libraries worldwide. The library also offers Internet access and maintains its own research-reference-links Web page to psychology-related databases and Web sites throughout the world.

Financial Aid

Just as the field of psychology is a helping profession, The Chicago School believes in helping its students afford the expenses associated with graduate education. The Office of Financial Aid assists all students with managing resources and securing the financial assistance needed. The Chicago School offers numerous types of assistance to eligible students, including federal student aid, scholarships and assistantships, and employment. Students may also qualify for tuition assistance through an employer, a fellowship, and outside scholarships. For additional information on these and other available programs, students should visit The Chicago School's Web site or e-mail the Office of Financial Aid at finaid@thechicagoschool.edu.

Cost of Study

Tuition for the Master of Arts programs for the 2007–08 academic year was $780 per hour. Other fees included registration, $85; late registration, $85; drop/add fee per course, $25; and an annual student services fee (per term) of $530 for full-time students or $265 for part-time students.

Living and Housing Costs

On-campus housing is not provided by The Chicago School of Professional Psychology. Students can find ample rental housing within a short walking distance or commute on Chicago public transportation or suburban Metra. The cost of living in or near Chicago is above the median for large Midwestern cities.

Student Group

Enrolled students are successful graduates of some of the nation's top undergraduate psychology programs. More than 1,000 students are currently enrolled in The Chicago School. The students are ethnically and culturally diverse and come from a wide variety of educational and occupational backgrounds. The Chicago School attracts students from across the country and from around the world.

Location

The Chicago School of Professional Psychology is centrally located in the River North neighborhood of downtown Chicago.

The School

The Chicago School of Professional Psychology is an independent, nonprofit graduate school that provides students with an outstanding education in a student-centered environment. Integrating theory, professional practice, and innovation, The Chicago School provides an excellent education for careers in psychology and related behavioral and health sciences. The Chicago School is committed to service, embraces the diverse communities of society, and educates professionals whose practices exemplify a commitment to understanding and respecting individual and cultural differences. The curriculum and training opportunities prepare students to deliver outstanding professional services, emphasizing the need to understand diversity and the importance of working with underserved populations.

Applying

Application to The Chicago School is open to any person who has earned a bachelor's degree from an accredited institution. Because admission requirements differ by program, prospective students should contact the Office of Admission or visit the Web site for details on their program of interest.

Students applying to the Master of Arts in Forensic Psychology Program must submit a completed application, which includes the application form, appropriate transcripts, essay question response, a resume, three letters of recommendation, and a $50 nonrefundable application fee. All required undergraduate courses must be completed prior to enrollment, with a grade earned of C or better.

Application deadlines for fall admission are as follows: early consideration, February 15; general consideration, April 1. (International students must have a completed application by April 1 for admission into the fall term in order to allow sufficient time to obtain the additional documentation required to study in the U.S.) After the April 1 deadline, students should contact the Office of Admission at admissions@thechicagoschool.edu regarding space availability.

Correspondence and Information

Office of Admission
Chicago School of Professional Psychology
325 North Wells Street
Chicago, Illinois 60610

Phone: 312-329-6666
E-mail: admissions@thechicagoschool.edu
Web site: http://www.thechicagoschool.edu

The Chicago School of Professional Psychology

THE FACULTY AND THEIR RESEARCH

Jaleel Abdul-Adil, Program Faculty; Ph.D., DePaul. Evidence-based, culturally sensitive family therapy for urban youth; conduct disorder and oppositional defiant disorder; gang involvement; inner-city violence.
Michael Barr, Program Faculty and Director of Corporate Education and Consulting Services; Ph.D., IIT. Job satisfaction, employee motivation and loyalty, leadership development, stress, trends, team building, 360-degree feedback, work/life balance.
John C. Benitez, Program Faculty and Consultant with the Department of Children and Family Services; Ph.D., Northwestern. Issues related to clergy and mental health, supervision, and diversity.
Larisa Buhin, Program Faculty; Ph.D., Loyola Chicago. Training for multicultural competence, ethnic identity development, and social justice.
Marie Ciavarella, Program Faculty and Director of Career Services; Psy.D., Illinois School of Professional Psychology. How the complexities of culture affect the provision of mental health and educational services.
Ellis Copeland, Program Faculty and Department Chair of the School Psychology Program; Ph.D., Texas at Austin. Measurement, research methods, community psychology, health psychology, child psychopathology, consultation.
Gail Berger Darlow, Program Faculty and Director of Industrial and Organizational Internships; Ph.D., Northwestern. Negotiation and conflict resolution, teamwork, organizational communication, decision making, power.
Nancy Davis, Program Faculty; Ph.D., Fielding Graduate Institute. Cultural change in an organization, strategic planning, executive coaching, team development, organizational assessment and reorganization, competency modeling, conflict resolution.
Chanté D. DeLoach, Program Faculty; Psy.D., Azusa Pacific. Racism, racialized sexism, health disparities, African psychology, sociocultural consciousness and hip-hop music.
Michael DiDomenico, Program Faculty; Psy.D., Illinois School of Professional Psychology. Aging disorders, organic brain syndromes, forensic issues, social issues and policies that affect mental health, ADHD, learning disabilities, developmental disabilities.
Todd DuBose, Program Faculty; Ph.D., Duquesne. Working with persons and families under extreme stress across the life span; trauma; loss and mourning; interpersonal violence; severe physical, neurological, and disease-related limitations in the areas of psychosomatics.
Kelly Ducheny, Program Faculty and Department Chair of the Clinical Psychology Doctoral Program; Psy.D., Wright State. Cultural competence and multicultural psychology; gay, lesbian, bisexual, and transgendered issues; assessment; professional development; gender roles and race in Disney animation; qualitative research; cognitive-behavioral, existential, and feminist psychotherapies.
Ken Fogel, Program Faculty; Psy.D., Chicago School of Professional Psychology. ADHD, anxiety, child abuse, depression, mood and personality disorders, posttraumatic stress, psychotherapy, sexually abused children, stress, trauma.
Michael Fogel, Program Faculty and Associate Department Chair of the Forensic Psychology Master's Program; Psy.D., Illinois School of Professional Psychology. Sex offender evaluations, competency/sanity evaluations, dangerous/violence evaluations, testamentary capacity.
Michael Gaubatz, Program Faculty; Ph.D., Loyola Chicago. Clinical training issues, especially formalized student review procedures and trainees' and practitioners' awareness of the cultural embeddedness of mental health interventions.
Grant Gautreaux, Program Faculty; Ph.D., Columbia. Applied behavior analysis, autism, developmental disabilities, disability issues, learning disabilities.
Enrique Gonzalez, Program Faculty; Ph.D., Loyola Chicago. Health psychology, pain management, psychosocial oncology, cultural issues related to psychology.
Kevin Gyoerkoe, Program Faculty; Psy.D., Nova Southeastern. Anxiety, cognitive-behavior therapy, depression, mood disorders, obsessive-compulsive disorder, stress.
Bridget Scott Hagood, Program Faculty; Psy.D., Argosy. Eating and mood disorders, diversity issues, meditative practices in psychotherapy.
Bianka Hardin, Program Faculty; Psy.D., Chicago School of Professional Psychology. Trauma, cultural issues.
Evan Harrington, Program Faculty; Ph.D., Temple. Nocebo (negative placebo) effect, psychology of terrorism, accuracy of child-abuse accusations.
Michael Horowitz, Program Faculty and President of the Chicago School of Professional Psychology; Ph.D., Northwestern. Organizational leadership, political advocacy, parenting, graduate education and the expansion of professional psychology practice.
Michelle Hoy-Watkins, Program Faculty; Psy.D., California School of Professional Psychology, Alameda. Criminal forensic evaluations, social security disability claims, pre-employment law-enforcement screenings, fitness-for-duty evaluations, cross-cultural assessment.
Jordan Jacobowitz, Program Faculty; Ph.D., Hebrew (Jerusalem). Applying and developing the psychoanalytic orientation to understand and treat psychopathology, examining life-span psychology, educating students to become clinicians.
Mark Kassel, Program Faculty; Psy.D., Adler School of Professional Psychology. Addiction, mood disorders, diversity issues, stress, anxiety.
Tiffany Keller, Program Faculty; Psy.D., Argosy. Personality assessment, child and adolescent assessment, neuropsychological assessment, feminist psychology, adolescent peer relation.
Ken H. Kessler, Program Faculty; Ph.D., University of Health Sciences. Ethics and professional issues, forensic assessment, professional and practice development.
Michael Komie, Program Faculty; Ph.D., Northwestern. Health psychology, life and work transitions, disability issues, attachment and loss, psychoanalytic therapies, work stress in minority and immigrant populations, gender issues, work/vocational issues.
Kin Ching Kong, Program Faculty; Ph.D., DePaul. ADHD, anxiety, behavior therapy, child psychology, cultural and diversity issues, family therapy, immigrant populations, marriage and divorce, parenting, psychotherapy, stress.
Lukasz Konopka, Program Faculty and Director of Neurophysiology and Pharmacology at Hines VA Hospital; Ph.D., Loyola Chicago. Adolescent psychology.
Paul Larson, Program Faculty; Ph.D., Utah; J.D., DePaul. Inpatient, residential, and outpatient veterans with severe and chronic disabilities, including a variety of physical and medical conditions and mental illness.
Christoph Leonhard, Program Faculty; Ph.D., Nevada, Reno. Behavior therapy with a variety of adult populations, including persons with mental retardation, severe mental illness, mood and anxiety disorders, and substance addiction.
Tiffany Mason, Program Faculty; Psy.D., Alliant International. Adolescence and child psychology, child abuse, family therapy, forensic psychology, gender issues, parenting, juvenile delinquency, sexually abused children and trauma.
Charles Merbitz, Program Faculty and Department Chair of the Clinical Psychology–Applied Behavior Analysis Specialization Master's Program; Ph.D., Florida. Objective process measures for relating clinical interventions in rehabilitation to outcomes and outcome measures.
Perry C. Meyers, Program Faculty and Department Chair of the Forensic Psychology Master's Program; Ph.D., IIT. Juvenile justice, adult criminal forensics, child protection, child-custody assessment, psychodynamic psychotherapy.
John Murray, Program Faculty; Psy.D., Illinois School of Professional Psychology. Clinical and forensic psychology, clinical training, role of psychology in justice system.
Michele Nealon-Woods, Program Faculty; Psy.D., Chicago School of Professional Psychology. Development and improvement of treatment interventions for children and adolescents, improving the application of clinical approaches with diverse populations.
Noelle Newhouse, Program Faculty; M.S., IIT. Leadership, testing, workplace issues.
Nancy A. Newton, Program Faculty; Ph.D., Wayne State. Life span, psychology and psychogeriatrics, women's issues, mediation and psychotherapy, executive coaching, workplace failure as a developmental experience.
Richard Niolon, Program Faculty; Ph.D., Saint Louis. Couples therapy (straight, gay, lesbian, married, or unmarried), divorce/remarriage/Gottman Theory/Technique, Bowenian Theory/Technique, stepparenting/stepfamilies, marital satisfaction.
Joyce Nugent-Hirschbeck, Program Faculty; Psy.D., Chicago School of Professional Psychology. Schizophrenia, family therapy, staff barriers and burnout, chronic mental illness, borderline personality disorders.
Shelly O'Neal-Benson, Program Faculty; Ph.D., Union (Ohio). Forensic psychology.
David Pyles, Program Faculty and Associate Department Chair of the Clinical Psychology–Applied Behavior Analysis Specialization Master's Program; Ph.D., Florida State. Developmental disabilities, behavioral diagnostics/functional assessment of behavior, behavioral psychopharmacology, behavioral systems management, behavior analysis in business and industry, dual diagnosis.
Virginia G. Quiñonez, Program Faculty and Department Chair of the Clinical Psychology–Counseling Specialization Master's Program; Psy.D., Illinois School of Professional Psychology. Multicultural psychology; trauma theory; minority students in higher education; gay, lesbian, and bisexual issues; HIV mental health.
Deane Rabe, Program Faculty and Associate Vice President of Academic Affairs; Psy.D., Illinois School of Professional Psychology. Psychological assessment, forensic evaluation, supervision and training, sex therapy, corporate consultation.
Karen Randall, Program Faculty; Ph.D., Loyola Chicago. Self-injury, women's health, managed-care issues, professional development and identity, psychoanalytic models of treatment, supervision, trauma, assessment, treatment of adult and adolescent clients.
Meghan Roekle, Program Faculty; Psy.D., Chicago School of Professional Psychology. Constructivist and feminist-relational thinking, philosophical roots and practical applications of clinical theory.
Kerri Rönne, Program Faculty; Ph.D., Iowa. Personality assessment, transgendered and transsexual populations, creativity and the visual arts, female-based religions.
Ted Rubenstein, Program Faculty; Psy.D., Chicago School of Professional Psychology. Creative arts therapy and the psychology of music, art, dance, and theater.
Susan Sances, Program Faculty and Vice President of Academic Affairs; Psy.D., Illinois School of Professional Psychology. Academic programs, including the Center for Multicultural and Diversity Studies and the Academic Support Services.
Paul Sanders, Program Faculty; Ph.D., Minnesota. Schizophrenic and borderline psychopathology, interfaith dimensions in treatment, diagnostic interviewing.
Shaifali Sandhya, Program Faculty; Ph.D., Chicago. Well-being, intimate relationships, conflict and negotiation, culture and social change.
Gale Sargeant, Program Faculty and Associate Department Chair of the Clinical Psychology–Counseling Specialization Master's Program; Ph.D., DePaul. HIV mental health, health psychology.
Wendy Schiffman, Program Faculty; Psy.D., Illinois School of Professional Psychology. Juvenile delinquency and criminal forensic evaluation.
John Shustitzky, Program Faculty; Ph.D., Illinois at Chicago. Community psychology and domestic violence.
Sandra Siegel, Program Faculty; Psy.D., Adler School of Professional Psychology. Community mental health, mentally ill substance-abuse clients, mentally ill prisoners in jail and prison systems.
Michael Smith, Program Faculty and Associate Department Chair of the Clinical Psychology Doctoral Program; Ph.D., IIT. Adjustment of immigrants and refugees, particularly examination of multigenerational issues; child and adolescent psychology; health psychology.
Drake Spaeth, Program Faculty; Psy.D., Chicago School of Professional Psychology. Aging; child abuse; cultural issues; depression; domestic violence; forensic psychology; gay, lesbian, and bisexual issues; racism; schizophrenia.
Jennifer Thompson, Program Faculty and Department Chair of the Industrial and Organizational Psychology Master's Program and Business Psychology Doctoral Program; Ph.D., IIT. Legal issues, affirmative action, attitudes, stereotypes, program evaluation, selection in education, gender bias.
Emily Trolley, Program Faculty; M.A., Chicago School of Professional Psychology. Work/life balance, workplace interests, job satisfaction, leadership.
Marla Gal Vannucci, Program Faculty; Ph.D., Northwestern. Training and developmental relationships, philosophy of psychology, consultation, smoking cessation.
Diana Walker, Program Faculty; Ph.D., Florida. Autism, cultural and diversity issues, education, learning disabilities, schizophrenia.
Gary Walls, Program Faculty; Ph.D., Miami (Ohio). Contemporary relational psychoanalysis; transference and countertransference; history of ideas; philosophy of science; hermeneutics; issues of class, gender, race, politics, and culture in the teaching and practice of psychology.
James Walsh, Program Faculty; Ph.D., Texas at Austin. ADHD, adolescent psychology, anxiety, behavior therapy, depression, child and family therapy, learning disabilities, mood disorders, obsessive-compulsive disorder, psychotherapy.
Grant White, Program Faculty; Psy.D., Chicago School of Professional Psychology. Assessment, disability issues, parenting, race, racism.

THE CHICAGO SCHOOL OF PROFESSIONAL PSYCHOLOGY

School Psychology Ed.S. Program

Program of Study

School psychologists help students—as well as teachers, administrators, and parents—overcome obstacles to learning and personal development, which include learning disabilities, academic difficulties, family disruptions, and mental health problems. Significant shortages of qualified school psychologists, both nationally and in Illinois, served as a compelling reason for the Chicago School's decision to begin an Educational Specialist (Ed.S.) degree program in school psychology. School psychologists are in high demand for positions in public and private schools, and projections show the demand increasing.

Students develop essential diagnostic, therapeutic, and consultative skills in order to work with a variety of clinical populations and with a variety of emotional and psychological conditions. They also learn the theoretical frameworks and scientific bases of school psychology, the ethical and professional guidelines of school psychology, and research methodologies, critically evaluating research as it relates to school psychology. The program helps students understand and appreciate the impact of diversity and cultural issues in the field of school psychology.

The Ed.S. is a full- or part-time program requiring 65 credits, including 56 credits of classroom-based course work and 9 credits of practicum/field learning. The program, which is designed to prepare students for endorsement as a school psychologist, includes 120 hours of shadowing a school psychologist, 600 or more hours of practicum training, and 1,200 or more hours of internship (full-time) in a school setting. The maximum duration of the program is five years. The School Psychology Ed.S. Program prepares students to take the Type 73 examination for Illinois endorsement as a school psychologist and the Nationally Certified School Psychology examination (Praxis II) administered by the Educational Testing Service. The Praxis examination is a required component to become a Nationally Certified School Psychologist (NCSP).

Research Facilities

The Chicago School maintains an on-site library with a wide range of books and journals in psychology and related fields. Library holdings include approximately 10,000 volumes, subscriptions to more than 235 core psychology journals, and access to more than 50 electronic databases, including PsycInfo, PsyArticles, and MEDLINE, and several online library networks that allow students to borrow from worldwide libraries, which hold more than 35 million items. Library consortia and reciprocal networking agreements, coupled with the library's interlibrary loan and document-locator services, provide access to the collections of major public, private, and academic libraries worldwide. The library also offers Internet access and maintains its own research-reference-links Web page to psychology-related databases and Web sites throughout the world.

Financial Aid

Just as the field of psychology is a helping profession, The Chicago School believes in helping its students afford the expenses associated with graduate education. The Office of Financial Aid assists all students with managing resources and securing the financial assistance needed. The Chicago School offers numerous types of assistance to eligible students, including federal student aid, scholarships and assistantships, and employment. Students may also qualify for tuition assistance through an employer, a fellowship, and outside scholarships. For additional information on these and other available programs, students should visit The Chicago School's Web site or e-mail the Office of Financial Aid at finaid@thechicagoschool.edu.

Cost of Study

Tuition for the Ed.S. program in 2007–08 was $780 per credit. Other fees included registration, $85; late registration, $85; drop/add fee per course, $25; and an annual student services fee (per term) of $530 for full-time students or $265 for part-time students.

Living and Housing Costs

On-campus housing is not provided by The Chicago School of Professional Psychology. Students can find ample rental housing within a short walking distance or commute on Chicago public transportation or suburban Metra. The cost of living in or near Chicago is above the median for large Midwestern cities.

Student Group

The Chicago School's geographically diverse population consists of students from thirty-eight states and nineteen countries. About 80 percent of students are women; the average age is 26.

Location

The Chicago School of Professional Psychology is centrally located in the River North neighborhood of downtown Chicago. One of the most ethnically diverse cities in the world, Chicago offers students the opportunity to fully immerse themselves in myriad multifaceted cultures. From Bronzeville to Chinatown, Little Italy to Pilsen, Chicago's vibrant neighborhoods offer students unique experiences beyond the classroom walls, which are unrivaled by most other graduate psychology programs in the country. Chicago School students enjoy unlimited city amenities that are just blocks from the School's main campus in the River North neighborhood. The Merchandise Mart, which is located directly across the street, provides CTA transportation, postal service, a food court, and a salon. Students are known to spot local celebrities coming to and from the Mart's Q101 radio station.

The School

The Chicago School of Professional Psychology is an independent, nonprofit graduate school that provides students with an outstanding education in a student-centered environment. Integrating theory, professional practice, and innovation, The Chicago School provides an excellent education for careers in psychology and related behavioral and health sciences. The Chicago School is committed to service, embraces the diverse communities of society, and educates professionals whose practices exemplify a commitment to understanding and respecting individual and cultural differences. The curriculum and training opportunities prepare students to deliver outstanding professional services, emphasizing the need to understand diversity and the importance of working with underserved populations.

Applying

Generally, applicants should have a bachelor's degree from an accredited institution and a combined undergraduate and graduate GPA of 3.2 or higher. One course in statistics or research methods and at least one course in psychology should have been completed. Students must submit the completed application, the $50 nonrefundable application fee, official college transcripts, a 500-word essay, a resume or curriculum vitae, and three letters of recommendation. The GRE is not required, but a combined verbal and qualitative score of 900 or higher enhances a student's application. Students whose primary language is not English must send in TOEFL scores. The fall semester deadlines are February 15 for early consideration and April 1 for general consideration. Spring semester applications are due by November 1.

Correspondence and Information

Office of Admission
Chicago School of Professional Psychology
325 North Wells Street
Chicago, Illinois 60610

Phone: 312-329-6666
E-mail: admissions@thechicagoschool.edu
Web site: http://www.thechicagoschool.edu/content.cfm/school_psychology_eds

The Chicago School of Professional Psychology

THE FACULTY AND THEIR RESEARCH

Jaleel Abdul-Adil, Program Faculty; Ph.D., DePaul. Evidence-based, culturally sensitive family therapy for urban youth; conduct disorder and oppositional defiant disorder; gang involvement; inner-city violence.

Michael Barr, Program Faculty and Director of Corporate Education and Consulting Services; Ph.D., IIT. Job satisfaction, employee motivation and loyalty, leadership development, stress, trends, team building, 360-degree feedback, work/life balance.

John C. Benitez, Program Faculty and Consultant with the Department of Children and Family Services; Ph.D., Northwestern. Issues related to clergy and mental health, supervision, and diversity.

Larisa Buhin, Program Faculty; Ph.D., Loyola Chicago. Training for multicultural competence, ethnic identity development, and social justice.

Marie Ciavarella, Program Faculty and Director of Career Services; Psy.D., Illinois School of Professional Psychology. How the complexities of culture affect the provision of mental health and educational services.

Ellis Copeland, Program Faculty and Department Chair of the School Psychology Program; Ph.D., Texas at Austin. Measurement, research methods, community psychology, health psychology, child psychopathology, consultation.

Gail Berger Darlow, Program Faculty and Director of Industrial and Organizational Internships; Ph.D., Northwestern. Negotiation and conflict resolution, teamwork, organizational communication, decision making, power.

Nancy Davis, Program Faculty; Ph.D., Fielding Graduate Institute. Cultural change in an organization, strategic planning, executive coaching, team development, organizational assessment and reorganization, competency modeling, conflict resolution.

Chanté D. DeLoach, Program Faculty; Psy.D., Azusa Pacific. Racism, racialized sexism, health disparities, African psychology, sociocultural consciousness and hip-hop music.

Michael DiDomenico, Program Faculty; Psy.D., Illinois School of Professional Psychology. Aging disorders, organic brain syndromes, forensic issues, social issues and policies that affect mental health, ADHD, learning disabilities, developmental disabilities.

Todd DuBose, Program Faculty; Ph.D., Duquesne. Working with persons and families under extreme stress across the life span; trauma; loss and mourning; interpersonal violence; severe physical, neurological, and disease-related limitations in the areas of psychosomatics.

Kelly Ducheny, Program Faculty and Department Chair of the Clinical Psychology Doctoral Program; Psy.D., Wright State. Cultural competence and multicultural psychology; gay, lesbian, bisexual, and transgendered issues; assessment; professional development; gender roles and race in Disney animation; qualitative research; cognitive-behavioral, existential, and feminist psychotherapies.

Ken Fogel, Program Faculty; Psy.D., Chicago School of Professional Psychology. ADHD, anxiety, child abuse, depression, mood and personality disorders, posttraumatic stress, psychotherapy, sexually abused children, stress, trauma.

Michael Fogel, Program Faculty and Associate Department Chair of the Forensic Psychology Master's Program; Psy.D., Illinois School of Professional Psychology. Sex offender evaluations, competency/sanity evaluations, dangerous/violence evaluations, testamentary capacity.

Michael Gaubatz, Program Faculty; Ph.D., Loyola Chicago. Clinical training issues, especially formalized student review procedures and trainees' and practitioners' awareness of the cultural embeddedness of mental health interventions.

Grant Gautreaux, Program Faculty; Ph.D., Columbia. Applied behavior analysis, autism, developmental disabilities, disability issues, learning disabilities.

Enrique Gonzalez, Program Faculty; Ph.D., Loyola Chicago. Health psychology, pain management, psychosocial oncology, cultural issues related to psychology.

Kevin Gyoerkoe, Program Faculty; Psy.D., Nova Southeastern. Anxiety, cognitive-behavior therapy, depression, mood disorders, obsessive-compulsive disorder, stress.

Bridget Scott Hagood, Program Faculty; Psy.D., Argosy. Eating and mood disorders, diversity issues, meditative practices in psychotherapy.

Bianka Hardin, Program Faculty; Psy.D., Chicago School of Professional Psychology. Trauma, cultural issues.

Evan Harrington, Program Faculty; Ph.D., Temple. Nocebo (negative placebo) effect, psychology of terrorism, accuracy of child-abuse accusations.

Michael Horowitz, Program Faculty and President of the Chicago School of Professional Psychology; Ph.D., Northwestern. Organizational leadership, political advocacy, parenting, graduate education and the expansion of professional psychology practice.

Michelle Hoy-Watkins, Program Faculty; Psy.D., California School of Professional Psychology, Alameda. Criminal forensic evaluations, social security disability claims, pre-employment law-enforcement screenings, fitness-for-duty evaluations, cross-cultural assessment.

Jordan Jacobowitz, Program Faculty; Ph.D., Hebrew (Jerusalem). Applying and developing the psychoanalytic orientation to understand and treat psychopathology, examining life-span psychology, educating students to become clinicians.

Mark Kassel, Program Faculty; Psy.D., Adler School of Professional Psychology. Addiction, mood disorders, diversity issues, stress, anxiety.

Tiffany Keller, Program Faculty; Psy.D., Argosy. Personality assessment, child and adolescent assessment, neuropsychological assessment, feminist psychology, adolescent peer relation.

Ken H. Kessler, Program Faculty; Ph.D., University of Health Sciences. Ethics and professional issues, forensic assessment, professional and practice development.

Michael Komie, Program Faculty; Ph.D., Northwestern. Health psychology, life and work transitions, disability issues, attachment and loss, psychoanalytic therapies, work stress in minority and immigrant populations, gender issues, work/vocational issues.

Kin Ching Kong, Program Faculty; Ph.D., DePaul. ADHD, anxiety, behavior therapy, child psychology, cultural and diversity issues, family therapy, immigrant populations, marriage and divorce, parenting, psychotherapy, stress.

Lukasz Konopka, Program Faculty and Director of Neurophysiology and Pharmacology at Hines VA Hospital; Ph.D., Loyola Chicago. Adolescent psychology.

Paul Larson, Program Faculty; Ph.D., Utah; J.D., DePaul. Inpatient, residential, and outpatient veterans with severe and chronic disabilities, including a variety of physical and medical conditions and mental illness.

Christoph Leonhard, Program Faculty; Ph.D., Nevada, Reno. Behavior therapy with a variety of adult populations, including persons with mental retardation, severe mental illness, mood and anxiety disorders, and substance addiction.

Tiffany Mason, Program Faculty; Psy.D., Alliant International. Adolescence and child psychology, child abuse, family therapy, forensic psychology, gender issues, parenting, juvenile delinquency, sexually abused children and trauma.

Charles Merbitz, Program Faculty and Department Chair of the Clinical Psychology–Applied Behavior Analysis Specialization Master's Program; Ph.D., Florida. Objective process measures for relating clinical interventions in rehabilitation to outcomes and outcome measures.

Perry C. Meyers, Program Faculty and Department Chair of the Forensic Psychology Master's Program; Ph.D., IIT. Juvenile justice, adult criminal forensics, child protection, child-custody assessment, psychodynamic psychotherapy.

John Murray, Program Faculty; Psy.D., Illinois School of Professional Psychology. Clinical and forensic psychology, clinical training, role of psychology in justice system.

Michele Nealon-Woods, Program Faculty; Psy.D., Chicago School of Professional Psychology. Development and improvement of treatment interventions for children and adolescents, improving the application of clinical approaches with diverse populations.

Noelle Newhouse, Program Faculty; M.S., IIT. Leadership, testing, workplace issues.

Nancy A. Newton, Program Faculty; Ph.D., Wayne State. Life span, psychology and psychogeriatrics, women's issues, mediation and psychotherapy, executive coaching, workplace failure as a developmental experience.

Richard Niolon, Program Faculty; Ph.D., Saint Louis. Couples therapy (straight, gay, lesbian, married, or unmarried), divorce/remarriage/Gottman Theory/Technique, Bowenian Theory/Technique, stepparenting/stepfamilies, marital satisfaction.

Joyce Nugent-Hirschbeck, Program Faculty; Psy.D., Chicago School of Professional Psychology. Schizophrenia, family therapy, staff barriers and burnout, chronic mental illness, borderline personality disorders.

Shelly O'Neal-Benson, Program Faculty; Ph.D., Union (Ohio). Forensic psychology.

David Pyles, Program Faculty and Associate Department Chair of the Clinical Psychology–Applied Behavior Analysis Specialization Master's Program; Ph.D., Florida State. Developmental disabilities, behavioral diagnostics/functional assessment of behavior, behavioral psychopharmacology, behavioral systems management, behavior analysis in business and industry, dual diagnosis.

Virginia G. Quiñonez, Program Faculty and Department Chair of the Clinical Psychology–Counseling Specialization Master's Program; Psy.D., Illinois School of Professional Psychology. Multicultural psychology; trauma theory; minority students in higher education; gay, lesbian, and bisexual issues; HIV mental health.

Deane Rabe, Program Faculty and Associate Vice President of Academic Affairs; Psy.D., Illinois School of Professional Psychology. Psychological assessment, forensic evaluation, supervision and training, sex therapy, corporate consultation.

Karen Randall, Program Faculty; Ph.D., Loyola Chicago. Self-injury, women's health, managed-care issues, professional development and identity, psychoanalytic models of treatment, supervision, trauma, assessment, treatment of adult and adolescent clients.

Meghan Roekle, Program Faculty; Psy.D., Chicago School of Professional Psychology. Constructivist and feminist-relational thinking, philosophical roots and practical applications of clinical theory.

Kerri Rönne, Program Faculty; Ph.D., Iowa. Personality assessment, transgendered and transsexual populations, creativity and the visual arts, female-based religions.

Ted Rubenstein, Program Faculty; Psy.D., Chicago School of Professional Psychology. Creative arts therapy and the psychology of music, art, dance, and theater.

Susan Sances, Program Faculty and Vice President of Academic Affairs; Psy.D., Illinois School of Professional Psychology. Academic programs, including the Center for Multicultural and Diversity Studies and the Academic Support Services.

Paul Sanders, Program Faculty; Ph.D., Minnesota. Schizophrenic and borderline psychopathology, interfaith dimensions in treatment, diagnostic interviewing.

Shaifali Sandhya, Program Faculty; Ph.D., Chicago. Well-being, intimate relationships, conflict and negotiation, culture and social change.

Gale Sargeant, Program Faculty and Associate Department Chair of the Clinical Psychology–Counseling Specialization Master's Program; Ph.D., DePaul. HIV mental health, health psychology.

Wendy Schiffman, Program Faculty; Psy.D., Illinois School of Professional Psychology. Juvenile delinquency and criminal forensic evaluation.

John Shustitzky, Program Faculty; Ph.D., Illinois at Chicago. Community psychology and domestic violence.

Sandra Siegel, Program Faculty; Psy.D., Adler School of Professional Psychology. Community mental health, mentally ill substance-abuse clients, mentally ill prisoners in jail and prison systems.

Michael Smith, Program Faculty and Associate Department Chair of the Clinical Psychology Doctoral Program; Ph.D., IIT. Adjustment of immigrants and refugees, particularly examination of multigenerational issues; child and adolescent psychology; health psychology.

Drake Spaeth, Program Faculty; Psy.D., Chicago School of Professional Psychology. Aging; child abuse; cultural issues; depression; domestic violence; forensic psychology; gay, lesbian, and bisexual issues; racism; schizophrenia.

Jennifer Thompson, Program Faculty and Department Chair of the Industrial and Organizational Psychology Master's Program and Business Psychology Doctoral Program; Ph.D., IIT. Legal issues, affirmative action, attitudes, stereotypes, program evaluation, selection in education, gender bias.

Emily Trolley, Program Faculty; M.A., Chicago School of Professional Psychology. Work/life balance, workplace interests, job satisfaction, leadership.

Marla Gal Vannucci, Program Faculty; Ph.D., Northwestern. Training and developmental relationships, philosophy of psychology, consultation, smoking cessation.

Diana Walker, Program Faculty; Ph.D., Florida. Autism, cultural and diversity issues, education, learning disabilities, schizophrenia.

Gary Walls, Program Faculty; Ph.D., Miami (Ohio). Contemporary relational psychoanalysis; transference and countertransference; history of ideas; philosophy of science; hermeneutics; issues of class, gender, race, politics, and culture in the teaching and practice of psychology.

James Walsh, Program Faculty; Ph.D., Texas at Austin. ADHD, adolescent psychology, anxiety, behavior therapy, depression, child and family therapy, learning disabilities, mood disorders, obsessive-compulsive disorder, psychotherapy.

Grant White, Program Faculty; Psy.D., Chicago School of Professional Psychology. Assessment, disability issues, parenting, race, racism.

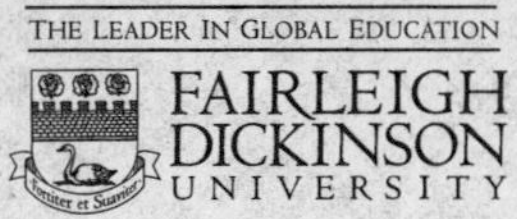

FAIRLEIGH DICKINSON UNIVERSITY

Psychology Programs

Programs of Study

Fairleigh Dickinson University offers a broad spectrum of psychology programs at its two northern New Jersey locations: the Metropolitan Campus in Teaneck and the College at Florham in Madison. Several of these programs are offered during evenings and weekends for the convenience of the working professional.

At the College at Florham, the Master of Arts (M.A.) in psychology is offered through the Maxwell Becton College of Arts and Sciences in the following areas: counseling with specializations in addictions and career and a licensed professional counselor (LPC) option, industrial/organizational psychology, and organizational behavior.

Housed in University College: Arts, Sciences, Professional Studies on the Metropolitan Campus, graduate psychology offerings include a postbaccalaureate respecialization certificate program in psychology, an M.A. program in general/theoretical psychology, an M.A. plus certificate program in school psychology, an M.A. program in forensic psychology, a postdoctoral M.S. program in clinical psychopharmacology (online), a Psy.D. program in school psychology, and an APA-approved Ph.D. program in clinical psychology.

The Ph.D. in clinical psychology is a five-year, full-time program—including an internship. This program follows the scientist-practitioner model, in which both the internship and dissertation are combined with individual areas of specialization.

The Psy.D. in school psychology is a year-round, full-time program, although it is possible to both work and pursue the degree, since classes are held in late afternoons and evenings. Individuals entering the program with school psychology certification typically complete the course work portion of the program in two years.

In addition, a second postdoctoral program is available through the University in the area of psychoanalytic training.

Research Facilities

The University provides extensive facilities to support education, research, and training in psychology, including excellent library resources, research laboratories, and computer facilities. At the College at Florham, research efforts emphasize industrial/organizational psychology and counseling. Research interests include attachment theory, career development in women, crisis counseling and intervention, the effects of constant work accessibility, female adolescent issues, organizational effectiveness, psychoanalytic thought and therapy, psychopharmacology, substance-abuse issues, and work/life balance issues. The Department of Psychology sponsors the Corporate Alliance Center for Organizational Resources, a consulting arm that provides academic expertise to local organizations and relevant work experience for students. In addition, the counseling program provides facilities for in vivo practice of counseling techniques. On the Metropolitan Campus, student and faculty research spans a variety of areas, including psychological assessment; neuropsychological assessment; childhood anxiety disorders; ADHD; play therapy; attachment theory; stress, trauma, and coping; jury selection; women's issues; men's issues; minority issues; spinal cord injury; data analytic techniques; MMPI; Rorschach; and behavioral medicine.

The Metropolitan Campus features a Center for Psychological Services, providing psychological counseling, psychotherapy, and psychodiagnostics to the general and University communities. The center offers graduate psychology students extensive observation and faculty-mentored experiences. It includes a child anxiety disorders clinic and a child and adult ADHD clinic.

The *Journal of Psychology and the Behavioral Sciences* (JPBS) is an annual periodical published by the Department of Psychology at the College at Florham. JPBS offers undergraduate and graduate students and their sponsoring faculty members an opportunity to be published in a recognized academic journal.

Financial Aid

A limited number of research, honors research, and teaching scholarships and graduate assistantships are available at Fairleigh Dickinson University. In the clinical psychology Ph.D. program, fellowships are provided to full-time students; teaching and other assistantships are also available. A Johnson & Johnson Scholarship is available to minority doctoral students.

An international scholarship program is offered for non-U.S., full-time graduate students. The University's application, available through the Office of International Admissions, evaluates the student on both academic merit and financial need.

Eligible domestic students may borrow up to $20,500 annually in subsidized and unsubsidized loans under the Federal Stafford Student Loan program. The University also offers students several attractive flexible financing programs.

Cost of Study

Tuition for master's-level studies in 2008–09 is $921 per credit for either full- or part-time students. Both doctoral-level programs in psychology carry an inclusive full-program fee. An annual technology fee of $308 for part-time students or $648 for full-time students is also assessed. Full details on doctoral program costs can be obtained by contacting the School of Psychology at the Metropolitan Campus at 201-692-2300 or by visiting the University's Web site at http://www.fdu.edu.

Living and Housing Costs

The University currently offers only limited on-campus housing for graduate students, offered on a first-come, first-served basis. The annual costs at the Metropolitan Campus are $6900 for a standard double room and $3614 for the standard eleven-meal plan, which includes $300 in flex dollars. At the College at Florham, the annual charge is $6534 for a standard double room and $3614 for the standard eleven-meal plan, which includes $300 in flex dollars. International students should contact the University's international student organizations for assistance in locating housing. Proof of health insurance is required of all full-time students, and coverage can be obtained through the University if needed.

Student Group

Students generally come from the Eastern Seaboard, although the Ph.D. program in clinical psychology draws from a more national and international base. The University's proximity to New York draws students from diverse ethnic, cultural, and experiential backgrounds. Classes are small and intimate, and students are afforded individual attention from assigned faculty advisers. In addition to numerous on-site courses across many specialized fields in psychology, independent, cooperative, field, and practicum courses are also available in many programs.

Location

The University has two locations in northern New Jersey. The Metropolitan Campus is located less than 10 miles from New York City on a modern, 88-acre site in Teaneck. The College at Florham is situated in the heart of New Jersey's growing corporate center near Madison and Morristown. The campus's stately, Georgian-style buildings span 166 acres of wooded ground on what once was a private estate.

The strategic location of each campus offers students majoring in graduate psychology access to a wide range of experiences in community, mental health, medical, pharmaceutical, and corporate settings. The faculty members of the programs are actively involved as leaders in their fields and maintain close networking relationships in the community that lead to invaluable opportunities for students. The Metropolitan Campus's proximity to New York City is especially appealing to students intending to pursue a career in a more urban setting.

The University

Founded in 1942, Fairleigh Dickinson is New Jersey's largest private university, with more than 12,000 students. In addition to its two major New Jersey campuses, the University offers many programs throughout the state and operates its own international campuses in Wroxton, England, and Vancouver, British Columbia, Canada.

Applying

Students seeking admission to any graduate program offered at Fairleigh Dickinson University must formally apply for admission before registering for graduate courses. Applications should be sent to the Admissions Office at the campus the student wishes to attend (College at Florham or Metropolitan Campus) during the semester preceding the one in which the student plans to enroll. Candidates may apply for admission to one campus only. The test results of the Graduate Record Examinations (GRE), college transcripts, a personal statement of interest, and three letters of recommendation are required for master's-level programs in psychology.

Applications for the master's-level programs are processed on a rolling basis, except for the M.A. in school psychology and M.A. in forensic psychology programs. Students are encouraged to apply at the earliest opportunity to allow ample time to complete the application process. Personal interviews are not normally required (except for the M.A. in school psychology and M.A. in counseling programs) but may be requested as part of the admissions process. Students interested in either the Ph.D. or Psy.D. programs should consult the appropriate Web pages for application deadlines and criteria on these competitive programs.

For applicants whose native language is not English and who have not completed a baccalaureate degree at an English language institution, a satisfactory score on the Test of English as a Foreign Language (TOEFL) is required.

Correspondence and Information

College at Florham:

Dr. Yolanda Hawkins-Rodgers, Chair
Department of Psychology
Fairleigh Dickinson University
285 Madison Avenue, M-AB2-01
Madison, New Jersey 07940

Phone: 973-443-8554
E-mail: hrodgers@fdu.edu
Web site: http://www.fdu.edu

Metropolitan Campus:

Dr. Christopher A. Capuano, Director
School of Psychology
Fairleigh Dickinson University
1000 River Road, T-WH1-01
Teaneck, New Jersey 07666

Phone: 201-692-2811
E-mail: capuano@fdu.edu
Web site: http://www.fdu.edu

Fairleigh Dickinson University

THE FACULTY AND THEIR RESEARCH

College at Florham
Yolanda Hawkins-Rodgers, Associate Professor and Department Chair; Ed.D., Rutgers. Counseling psychology.

Donalee Brown, Assistant Professor; Ph.D., Seton Hall. Counseling psychology.
Daniel J. Calcagnetti, Associate Professor; Ph.D., Temple. Behavioral neuroscience.
Jane Cooper, Lecturer; M.A., Fairleigh Dickinson. Industrial and organizational psychology.
John Duryee, Professor; Ph.D., Columbia. Clinical psychology.
Ketrin Saud-Maxwell, Assistant Professor; Ph.D., Fordham. Counseling psychology.
Jakob Steinberg, Professor; Ph.D., Vermont. Social psychology.
Paul Strauss, Professor; Ph.D., NYU. Industrial and organizational psychology.
Anthony Tasso, Assistant Professor; Ph.D., Tennessee. Clinical psychology.
Judith A. Waters, Professor; Ph.D., CUNY, Brooklyn. Social psychology.
Diane Keyser Wentworth, Professor; Ph.D., Wayne State. Industrial and organizational psychology.
Lona Whitmarsh, Associate Professor; Ed.D., Boston University. Counseling psychology.

Metropolitan Campus
Christopher A. Capuano, Associate Professor and Director of the School of Psychology; Ph.D., CUNY Graduate Center. Biopsychology.

Stephen R. Armeli, Associate Professor; Ph.D., Delaware. Social psychology.
Jane Braden-Maguire, Professor; Ph.D., Columbia. Experimental psychology.
Kathleen M. Davis, Assistant Professor; Ph.D., Ball State. School psychology.
Ron Dumont, Associate Professor and Director, Graduate Programs in School Psychology; Ed.D., Boston University; NCSP. School psychology.
Andrew R. Eisen, Associate Professor; Ph.D., SUNY at Albany. Clinical psychology.
Samuel Feinberg, Associate Professor; Ph.D., NYU. Educational psychology.
Margaret S. Gibbs, Professor Emeritus; Ph.D., Harvard. Clinical psychology.
Louis M. Hsu, Professor Emeritus; Ph.D., Fordham. Psychometrics.
Judith Kaufman, Professor; Ph.D., Yeshiva. School psychology.
Juliana Rasic Lachenmeyer, Professor; Ph.D., Columbia. Psychology.
Katharine Loeb, Associate Professor; Ph.D., Rutgers. Clinical psychology.
Neil A. Massoth, Professor; Ph.D., Washington (St. Louis). Clinical psychology.
Robert McGrath, Professor; Ph.D., Auburn. Clinical psychology.
David L. Pogge, Senior Clinical Lecturer; Ph.D., New Mexico. Clinical psychology.
Robert A. Prentky, Associate Professor; Ph.D., Northwestern. Forensic psychology.
Cynthia L. Radnitz, Professor; Ph.D., SUNY at Albany. Clinical psychology.
John C. Santelli, Professor; Ph.D., CUNY Graduate Center. Neuropsychology.
Charles E. Schaefer, Professor Emeritus; Ph.D., Fordham. Clinical psychology.
Janet Sigal, Professor; Ph.D., Northwestern. Social psychology.
Lana A. Tiersky, Associate Professor; Ph.D., California School of Professional Psychology–Los Angeles. Clinical psychology.

FIELDING GRADUATE UNIVERSITY

School of Psychology

Programs of Study

The School of Psychology offers doctoral (Ph.D.) degrees in clinical psychology and media psychology, a master's degree in media psychology and social change, a postdoctoral respecialization in clinical psychology certificate, and a postdoctoral certificate in neuropsychology.

In both Ph.D. programs, students pursue their course of study in their geographical area. These distributed learning programs combine face-to-face faculty-student contact with a Web-based learning environment. The clinical psychology Ph.D. is the only distributed doctoral program accredited by the American Psychological Association (APA). Students may earn a generalist degree or choose a concentration in parent-infant mental health, forensic psychology, neuropsychology, health psychology, or the prevention and control of violence. In the media psychology Ph.D. program, students are encouraged to embrace theory, research, and their own experiences in relation to the production of mass communications and media messages and their impact on individuals, groups, and societies. Students begin the Ph.D. programs by attending a required face-to-face orientation session; they then continue to work independently, with groups, and online. Intensive, face-to-face contact takes place at local cluster meetings, research sessions, psychological assessment labs, and national sessions. Structured online activities deepen the interactions among students and faculty members. Utilizing these resources, students maintain their professional careers and family responsibilities while simultaneously undertaking advanced studies.

The master's degree in media psychology and social change is offered by the School of Psychology in cooperation with UCLA Extension. Students study the specific benefits of understanding human behavior when working with media applications, how media affects individuals and cultures, and how media can be used for socially constructive purposes. Offered entirely online, the program allows for great flexibility and attention to individual goals; carefully planned activities to allow students to maintain their professional careers while in the program.

The postdoctoral respecialization program in clinical psychology enables professionals to maintain their current work commitments while in attendance. Students take advantage of individualized, self-paced, time-efficient offerings that provide the required course work and clinical training to allow them to qualify for examination to become licensed clinical psychologists in most states.

The postdoctoral neuropsychology certificate program allows students to continue working in their current positions while gaining both the theoretical grounding and applied clinical experience needed to develop proficiency in neuropsychological assessment and intervention. The program is designed to meet the needs of professional psychologists who seek an alternative to residency programs that take them away from their work.

Research Facilities

Fielding's library services are designed to serve the complex needs of busy professionals by offering substantial research tools via the Web. The library collection and services include a database of Internet resources, a subsidized document delivery service, a catalog of available dissertations and electronic books, and access to numerous online library databases and journals.

Financial Aid

Fielding Graduate University participates in the Federal Stafford Student Loan program, which makes subsidized and unsubsidized loans available based on financial need. Clinical psychology students are also eligible to borrow HEAL student loans, an additional, unsubsidized Stafford Student Loan separate from the traditional yearly maximum of $18,500. Fielding also participates in Veterans Assistance Programs. In 2007–08, Fielding Graduate University administered approximately $18 million in aid to about 75 percent of its graduate students.

Cost of Study

The 2007–08 tuition for the Ph.D. programs was $19,695. Tuition for the master's program was $12,000, the neuropsychology program was $7970, and the respecialization program was $18,614. Tuition and fee rates are subject to change each academic year. Current tuition information can be found at http://www.fielding.edu/tuition.

Living and Housing Costs

Because Fielding Graduate University psychology students work independently and live in various parts of the United States and Canada, costs in addition to tuition vary. Considerations include computer equipment, books and materials, travel to regional cluster meetings, and optional travel to research, clinical, and national sessions. There may be other costs related to the specific course of study.

Student Group

Fielding Graduate University's student community consists of adult learners who have chosen a self-directed, independent learning program and are geographically dispersed, as are the members of the faculty. Fielding's total student population numbers more than 1,500. The approximately 500 students in the School of Psychology are a diverse group of individuals who form a worldwide professional network. The average student age at Fielding Graduate University is 46, with a range from 22 to 74 years of age.

Location

Fielding's administrative offices are located in Santa Barbara, California. The students and faculty members create the Fielding community. The psychology community resides in the forty-eight contiguous United States and Canada.

The University and The School

Founded in 1974, Fielding Graduate University is a global leader in graduate-level networked education for professionals. Fielding is dedicated to providing high-quality, accredited programs through a combination of face-to-face and online interactions between accomplished students and nationally recognized faculty members. The School of Psychology's community of scholar-practitioners embraces diverse approaches to theory, research, and practice. The School's student-centered faculty members serve as partners in the quest for knowledge, collaborating with students in a remarkably collegial atmosphere.

Applying

Students enter the Ph.D. and master's programs in the School of Psychology twice a year (March and September). Applicants to the respecialization program are considered for July and January admission. Neuropsychology applications are considered for the fall term only. Applicants must submit a $75 nonrefundable fee, an application form, and additional materials specific to their program of interest.

Correspondence and Information

Admission Office
Fielding Graduate University
2112 Santa Barbara Street
Santa Barbara, California 93105

Phone: 800-340-1099 (toll-free)
E-mail: admission@fielding.edu
Web site: http://www.fielding.edu

Fielding Graduate University

THE FACULTY

Each faculty member's cluster location is in parentheses.

SCHOOL OF PSYCHOLOGY

Core Faculty
Raymond J. Trybus, Ph.D., Dean
Joseph P. Bush, Ph.D., Associate Dean
Nancy H. Leffert, Ph.D., Associate Dean
Gilbert Reyes, Ph.D., Associate Dean
Kjell E. Rudestam, Ph.D., ABPP, Associate Dean

Nancy Baker, Ph.D., ABPP (San Francisco, CA)
Margaret Cramer, Ph.D. (Melrose, MA)
Sanford Drob, Ph.D. (New York, NY)
Charles Elliot, Ph.D. (Albuquerque, NM)
Debra Bendell Estroff, Ph.D. (Los Angeles, CA)
April Fallon, Ph.D. (Philadelphia, PA)
Tiffani Field, Ph.D. (Miami, FL)
Marilyn Freimuth, Ph.D. (New York, NY)
William Friedman, Ph.D. (Chapel Hill, NC)
Ronald A. Giannetti, Ph.D. (Santa Barbara, CA)
John Gladfelter, Ph.D., ABPP (Dallas, TX)
Anthony F. Greene, Ph.D. (Gainesville, FL)
Erik Gregory, Ph.D. (Boston, MA)
Nancy Hansen, Ph.D. (Fort Collins, CO)
Garry Hare, Ph.D. (Corte Madera, CA)
Sherry L. Hatcher, Ph.D., ABPP (Ann Arbor, MI)
Raymond Hawkins, Ph.D. (Austin, TX)
Patricia M. Hodges, Ph.D. (Claremont, CA)
Jean Pierre Isbouts, D. Litt. (Santa Monica, CA)
Ruthellen Josselson, Ph.D. (Baltimore, MD)
Maureen Kirby Lassen, Ph.D. (Phoenix, AZ)
Bernard Luskin, Ed.D. (Los Angeles, CA)
Sandra McPherson, Ph.D., ABPP (Cleveland, OH)
Gregory Jay Murrey, Ph.D. (Minneapolis, MN)
Jerry Nims, Ph.D., J.D. (Reno, NV; Sacramento, CA)
Samuel D. Osherson, Ph.D. (Cambridge, MA)
Nolan E. Penn, Ph.D., ABPP (San Diego, CA)
Katherine VanDusen Randazzo, Ph.D. (San Diego, CA)
Joan Read, Ph.D. (Atlanta, GA)
Stephen A. Ruffins, Ph.D. (New York, NY)
Lynne Saba, Ph.D. (Santa Barbara, CA)
Judith Schoenholtz-Read, Ed.D. (Seattle, WA)
Daniel Sewell, Ph.D. (Santa Barbara, CA)
Henry Soper, Ph.D. (Camarillo, CA)
Ed Tronick, Ph.D. (New York, NY)
Paul Wright, Esq. (Malibu, CA)

Adjunct and Consulting Faculty
David Blustein, Ph.D. (Arlington, MA)
Jodi De Luca, Ph.D. (Daytona Beach, FL)
Pamela Drury, Ph.D. (Durham, NC)
Elizabeth E. Green, Ph.D. (San Diego, CA)
Michele Harway, Ph.D. (Los Angeles, CA)
Marti Kranzberg, Ph.D. (Dallas, TX)
Kenneth Milles, Ph.D. (Edinboro, PA)
Rae Newton, Ph.D. (Capistrano Beach, CA)
Donald J. Polkinghorne, Ph.D. (Pasadena, CA)
Janice R. Rudestam, Ph.D. (Santa Barbara, CA)
Jason Ohler, Ph.D. (Anchorage, AK)
Jack Saporta, Ph.D., ABPP (Huntley, IL)
Gary I. Schulman, Ph.D. (Santa Barbara, CA)
Laura Smith, Ph.D. (Albuquerque, NM)
Leann Stadtlander, Ph.D. (Bozeman, MT)
Sandra L. Webster, Ph.D. (Olmsted Falls, OH)

NEUROPSYCHOLOGY PROGRAM
Elkhonon Goldberg, Ph.D., ABPP/ABCN (Boston, MA; New York, NY)
Leonard F. Koziol, Psy.D., ABPN (Chicago, IL)
Allan F. Mirsky, Ph.D., ABPP/ABCN (Bethesda, MD)
Arnold D. Purisch, Ph.D., ABPP/ABCN, ABPN, ABAP (Irvine, CA)

FLORIDA INSTITUTE OF TECHNOLOGY

School of Psychology

Programs of Study The School of Psychology offers Master of Science (M.S.) and Ph.D. degrees in the field of industrial/organizational psychology, an M.S. in applied behavior analysis, and a Psy.D. degree in the field of clinical psychology.

The Clinical Doctor of Psychology, APA-accredited program is a practitioner-scientist model, emphasizing assessment, diagnosis, intervention, and evaluation skills, along with training in consultation, supervision, education, administration, and diversity. A strong generalist predoctoral focus is emphasized, with particular training opportunities in neuropsychology, child and family, forensic psychology, primary-care psychology, sexual abuse, and multiculturalism. Practicum placements occur across inpatient and outpatient sites, with a variety of populations and presenting issues. Students enter their internships possessing a wide variety of clinical skills and knowledge of the major treatment modalities. Program requirements include 104 semester hours for postbaccalaureate students, with a possible 18 semester hours of doctoral transfer credit for students with master's degrees in psychology or related disciplines; four years of residence; completion of a doctoral research project; completion of comprehensive and clinical qualification examinations; and completion of a one-year, 2,000-hour internship at an approved site.

The M.S. program in industrial/organizational psychology prepares graduate students to either continue their education in a doctoral program or to work in any of the broad human resource functions of business and industry. The program is based on the scientist-practitioner models in which students are encouraged to collect data while participating in organizational interventions. Scholarly works such as journal and conference submissions are encouraged and supported by the I/O faculty. Practical training is required as part of this 45-semester-hour program. Either the completion of a master's thesis or a nonthesis written summary of the student practicum is required. The Ph.D. program requires students to actively participate in academic research and provides students with opportunities to polish their consulting skills. Advanced statistical courses, electives, and research credits round out this 90-semester-hour program. Students can explore specific areas of concentration, including multicultural I/O psychology. Comprehensive examinations take place at the end of the third year. Dissertation research is begun immediately after successful completion of the comprehensive exam. Ph.D. students are encouraged to finish the program in four years. Both programs prepare I/O psychology graduates for a wide variety of careers in academics, management, human resources, and consulting.

The M.S. degree in applied behavior analysis has two tracks: clinical and organizational behavior management. The core curriculum is based on the *Behavior Analysis Task List and Knowledge, Skills, and Ability Statements*, which are used as the basis for board certification examinations in behavior analysis. The Behavior Analyst Certification Board has approved the Florida Institute of Technology course sequence (as listed in the University catalog) as meeting the course work requirements for eligibility to take the Board Certified Behavior Analyst examination. A minimum of 42 credit hours are required, including core ABA classes, specialized track classes, electives, a practicum, and either a capstone project or a thesis. Students may enroll on either a part-time or full-time basis. Passing a comprehensive exam is also required prior to graduation. Full-time students typically finish the degree in four semesters. The program is offered in Melbourne, Florida, and in the Institute's Orlando Graduate Center.

Research Facilities The School of Psychology includes the Psychology Building, the Community Psychological Services Clinic, the Applied Research Lab, and the Country Club Lane Research Labs. The East Central Florida Memory Disorder Clinic, Family Learning Program, Center for Professional Services, and the Applied Behavioral Service Center provide service and research opportunities.

Financial Aid A limited number of research and teaching assistantships are available to graduate students, providing yearly stipends and tuition remission packages ranging from $1800 to $7200. University Graduate Scholarships provide tuition remission for incoming students. A number of work-study positions, as well as various loan programs, are available to students who qualify. Advanced field placement sites usually provide student stipends.

Cost of Study Graduate tuition for the 2008–09 academic year is $9015 per semester for the Psy.D. program and $980 per credit hour for the M.S. and Ph.D. programs. Books and testing materials cost about $1800 for the first year of the clinical program.

Living and Housing Costs Room and board on campus are approximately $4000 per semester in 2008–09. On-campus housing is available for full-time students. Many apartment complexes and rental houses are available near the campus.

Student Group The School's graduate population averages 170 to 190 students. Approximately two thirds of the students are women, and about 12 percent are members of minority groups.

Twenty students are admitted into the clinical program each year, 8 to 12 into the industrial/organizational psychology master's program, 2 to 4 into the industrial/organizational Ph.D. program, and 30 into the applied behavior analysis program.

Student Outcomes Graduates from the Psy.D. program secure positions across a number of settings, including psychiatric hospitals, VA medical centers, community mental health centers, rehabilitation hospitals, and private practice. Graduates of the industrial/organizational program find positions in the following areas: employee selection and placement, performance appraisal, training and evaluation, career counseling, management development, organizational development, and employee relations. Graduates of the applied behavioral analysis program find positions in schools, residential programs, group homes, foster- care programs, and consulting firms.

Location Melbourne is located on the central east coast of Florida, a short drive from the John F. Kennedy Space Center and the city of Orlando.

The Institute In response to a need for specialized and advanced educational opportunities, Florida Institute of Technology was founded in 1958 by a group of scientists and engineers pioneering America's space program at Cape Canaveral. Florida Tech has rapidly developed into a residential institution that is the second-largest private university in the state of Florida. The faculty and administration are committed to the pursuit of academic excellence in teaching and research in the sciences, engineering, aeronautics, management, and psychology.

Applying All applicants must possess a bachelor's degree from an accredited institution. Although the degree need not be in psychology, no less than 18 hours of psychology course work must have been completed (including courses in statistics, personality, learning, social, abnormal, and physiological psychology for the clinical applicants). These prerequisite courses may be completed before admission outside of a degree program.

Applicants are expected to have a grade point average of 3.0 or higher on a scale where A = 4.0. All applicants must submit three letters of recommendation, provide a statement of career objectives, and arrange for GRE General Test scores to be sent. The GRE Subject Test in psychology is required for application to the Psy.D. clinical program. Official transcripts of all undergraduate and graduate courses attempted must be submitted. Fall term application deadlines are January 15 for clinical, February 1 for industrial/organizational psychology, and March 1 for applied behavior analysis applicants.

Correspondence and Information

School of Psychology
Florida Institute of Technology
150 West University Boulevard
Melbourne, Florida 32901-6988

Phone: 321-674-8105
Fax: 321-674-7105
E-mail: lsorum@fit.edu
Web site: http://www.fit.edu

Florida Institute of Technology

THE FACULTY AND THEIR RESEARCH

Juanita Baker, Associate Professor of Psychology; Ph.D., Illinois. Behavioral change (grieving, trauma); evaluation of teaching, training, program effectiveness; child sexual abuse.
Felipa T. Chavez, Assistant Professor of Psychology; Ph.D., SUNY at Buffalo. Multiculturalism, parenting, child development, family dysfunction, impact of substance abuse on child maltreatment in different sociocultural contexts, social support networks as a buffer to stress and family dysfunction, parent-child interaction therapy treatment effectiveness with minority populations and recovering families.
Patrick D. Converse, Assistant Professor; Ph.D., Michigan. Motivation, self-regulatory processes, personality measurement and cognitive ability, ability requirements of occupations.
Richard T. Elmore Jr., Associate Professor of Psychology and Director of Clinical Training; Ph.D., Georgia State. Clinical hypnosis, marital and sex therapy, traumatology, occupational health psychology.
Philip D. Farber, Associate Professor of Psychology; Ph.D., Wisconsin–Milwaukee. Psychological assessment, clinical training issues, competencies in professional psychology training, health psychology.
William K. Gabrenya, Associate Professor of Psychology and Chair, Undergraduate Program; Ph.D., Missouri. Cross-cultural psychology, Chinese culture, social class and modernization, indigenous psychology, sex, work psychology.
Rich Griffith, Assistant Professor of Psychology and Director, Industrial/Organizational Psychology Program; Ph.D., Akron. Response distortion on noncognitive selection procedures, advanced measurement issues, organizational innovation, cognitive process of work teams.
Arthur Gutman, Professor of Psychology; Ph.D., Syracuse. Personnel law, applied statistics, program evaluation, personnel psychology, research design.
Thomas H. Harrell, Professor of Psychology; Ph.D., Georgia. Psychometrics and computerized psychological assessment, use of the MMPI-2 in clinical evaluation, cognitive-behavioral approaches to assessment and therapy, adaptation to aging.
Mark T. Harvey, Assistant Professor of Psychology; Ph.D., Oregon; BCBA. Applied behavior analysis, developmental disabilities, behavioral strategies in educational settings, sleep architecture, integration of biomedical and behavioral indices.
Marshall Jones, Instructor and Coordinator, Undergraduate Forensic Psychology; M.S., Alabama. Law enforcement leadership, law enforcement recruiting and retention, training technology, promotional assessment, racial profiling.
Mary Beth Kenkel, Professor of Psychology and Dean; Ph.D., Miami (Ohio). Clinical/community psychology, integrated care models, women and leadership, rural mental health, psychology and technology, prevention activities in psychology, feminization of psychology, future of professional psychology.
Radhika Krishnamurthy, Associate Professor of Psychology and Director, Clinical Training; Psy.D., Virginia Consortium for Professional Psychology. Personality assessment with the MMPI-2/MMPI-A and Rorschach, child and adolescent development, interface between personality and neuropsychological functioning.
Jose Martinez-Diaz, Assistant Professor and Chair, Applied Behavioral Analysis Program; Ph.D., West Virginia. Professional and conceptual issues, verbal behavior, antecedent events in the treatment of problem behavior, treatment of persons with developmental disabilities and with schizophrenia.
Matthew P. Normand, Assistant Professor of Psychology; Ph.D., Florida State; BCBA. Application of basic behavioral principles to problems of social significance (including autism, obesity, and other community health issues), verbal behavior.
Thomas H. Peake, Professor of Psychology; Ph.D., Memphis; ABPP. Brief psychotherapies, couples therapy, healthy aging, clinical training, neuropsychology, behavioral medicine.
Erin M. Richard, Assistant Professor; Ph.D., LSU. Emotional regulation in the workplace, individual differences related to work motivation.
Lisa Steelman, Associate Professor of Psychology; Ph.D., Akron. Feedback processes, multirater feedback, performance appraisal, work-related attitudes, employee commitment and engagement.
Frank M. Webbe, Professor of Psychology; Ph.D., Florida. Aging and technology, sport neuropsychology.
David A. Wilder, Associate Professor of Psychology; Ph.D., Nevada, Reno. Functional analysis and function-based intervention in children with disruptive behavior, organizational behavior management (assessment in OBM, feedback), stimulus preference assessment methods.

Adjunct Faculty
W. Abernathy, Ph.D., Ohio State; Abernathy & Associates, Memphis, Tennessee.
J. Beltran, Psy.D., Florida Tech; Beltran Behavioral Health, Kissimmee, Florida.
D. Bersoff, Ph.D., NYU; J.D., Yale; Professor and Director, Law and Psychology Program, Hahnemann.
C. Binder, Ph.D., Columbia Pacific; Binder Reha Associates, Santa Rosa, California.
E. Blakley, Ph.D., Western Michigan; Director of Behavioral Analysis, Quest Kids, Orlando, Florida.
V. J. Carbone, Ph.D., Nova Southeastern; private practice, New York.
E. Cipani, Ph.D., Florida State; Professor, Alliant International University, Fresno, California.
W. E. Eyring III, Psy.D., Florida Tech; clinical psychologist, Circles of Care, Melbourne, Florida.
P. W. Gorman, Psy.D., Florida Tech; private practice, Orlando, Florida.
B. Hensel, Ph.D., Toledo; Circles of Care, Melbourne, Florida.
S. Howze, Psy.D., Florida Tech; private practice, Melbourne, Florida.
F. Kaslow, Visiting Professor of Psychology; Ph.D., Bryn Mawr; marital family, divorce and marriage-dynamics and treatment.
E. Levine, Ph.D., NYU; Associate Chairman and Director, Industrial/Organizational Psychology Program, University of South Florida.
P. McGreevy, Ph.D., Kansas; Private practice, Winter Park, Florida.
K. Murdock, Ph.D., South Florida; Hillsborough County Public Schools, Florida.
T. Rogers, Ph.D., Florida; Florida Department of Children and Families, Florida.
H. Schlinger, Ph.D., Western Michigan; California State University, Northridge, California.
C. Stevens, Psy.D., Florida Tech; private practice, Melbourne, Florida.
M. Stoutimore, Ph.D., Florida; Florida Department of Children and Families.

RECENT FACULTY PUBLICATIONS AND PRESENTATIONS

Lenzen-Roth, Y., and **J. N. Baker.** After-Disclosure Factors as Mediators and Moderators of Child Sexual Abuse and Its Impact. Poster presented at the 113th Annual Convention American Psychological Association, August 17, 2005, Washington, D.C.
Baker, J. N. A Comprehensive Approach to Sexual Offending? A review of *Attachment and Sexual Offending: Understanding and Applying Attachment Theory to the Treatment of Juvenile Sexual Offenders* by Phil Rich. *Contemporary Psychology: American Psychological Association Review of Books,* in press.
Levenson, J.S., T. Fortney, T., Y. Brannon, and **J. N. Baker.** Public perceptions about sex offenders and community protection policies. *Analyses of Social Issues and Public Policy.* 7(1):1–25, 2007.
Baker, J. N., F. T. Chavez, and R. Krishnamurthy. Advanced training workshop for sexual abuse treatment program providers on assessment, diagnosis, and treatment of children traumatized by sexual abuse. Sponsored by the State of Florida, Department of Health, Children's Medical Services, and Florida Tech and supported by the Florida Office for Victims of Crime, Office of Justice Programs, April 3–5, 2006, Jacksonville.
Eiden, R. D., K. E. Leonard, R. H. Hoyle, and **F. T. Chavez.** A transactional model of parent-infant interactions in alcoholic families. *Psychol. Addict. Behav.* 18(4):350–61, 2004.
Cavasos, P., **F. T. Chavez,** M. A. Zevon, and D. M. Green. Impact of surviving canter on locus of control and reproductive concerns. A poster at American Psychological Association Annual Convention, Toronto, Canada, 2003.
Converse, P. D., et al. Forcing choices in personality measurement: Benefits and limitations. In *A closer examination of applicant faking behavior,* ed. R. Griffith. Greenwich, CT: Information Age Publishing, in press.
Converse, P. D., and F. L. Oswald. General Aptitude Test Battery. In *Encyclopedia of Career Development,* eds. J. Greenhaus and C. Callanan. Thousand Oaks, CA: Sage, in press.
Oswald, F. L., and **P. D. Converse.** Job typologies. In *Encyclopedia of Industrial/Organizational Psychology,* ed. S. Rogelberg. Thousand Oaks, CA: Sage, in press.
Janner, R., and **R. Elmore.** Coping resources of ROTC cadets: PTSD risk factors for combat deployment. Presented at the Southeastern Psychological Association, Atlanta, Georgia, 2006.
Cimino, A., and **R. Elmore.** Hurricanes Francis and Jeanne: Perceptions of stress among college students. Presented at the Southeastern Psychological Association, Atlanta, Georgia, 2006.
Fernandez, M., and **R. Elmore.** Differential trust and religiosity levels among premarital cohabiters and non-cohabiters. Presented at the Southeastern Psychological Association, Atlanta, Georgia, 2006.
Van Sickle, K. S., and **P. D. Farber.** Measured versus self-reported personality traits: Testing for prediction bias. Poster presented at the meeting of the Florida Psychological Association, Naples, Florida, 2004.
Gabrenya, W. K., Jr., M.-C. Kung, and L.-Y. Chen. Understanding the Taiwan indigenous psychology movement: A sociology of science approach. *J. Cross-Cultural Psych.,* in press.
Gabrenya, W. K., Jr. A sociology of science approach to understanding indigenous psychologies. In *Ongoing Themes on Cross-Cultural Psychology,* eds. B. Setiadia, A. Supratiknya, W. Lonner, and Y. Poortinga. Jakarta, Indonesia: International Association for Cross-Cultural Psychology, 2004.
Griffith, R. L., and M. Peterson. *A Closer Examination of Applicant Faking Behavior.* Greenwich, CT: Information Age Publishing, 2006.
Comeau, D., and **R .L. Griffith.** Structural interdependence, personality, and organizational citizenship behavior: An examination of person-environment interaction. *Personnel Rev.,* in press.
English, A., **R. L. Griffith,** and **L. A. Steelman.** Team performance: The impact of conscientiousness and task type. *Small Group Res.* 35(6):643–65, 2004.
Gutman, A. The administration's position on Gratz and Grutter: Too many inconsistencies. *Ind.-Organ. Psychol..,* in press.
Gutman, A. Adverse Impact: Why is it so difficult to understand? *Ind.-Organ. Psychol.* 40(2).
Gutman, A. *EEO Law and Personnel Pract.,* 2nd ed. Thousand Oaks, Calif., Sage Publishers, 2000.
Malow, B. A., et al. **(M. T. Harvey).** Impact of treating sleep apnea in a child with autism spectrum disorder. *Pediatric Neurology,* in press.
Doran, S. M., **M. T. Harvey,** and R. H. Horner. Sleep and developmental disorders: Assessment, treatment, and outcome measures. *Mental Retardation* 44, 13–27, 2006.
Kenkel, M. B., P. H. DeLeon, E. O. Mantell, and A. Steep. Divided no more: Psychology's role in integrated health care. *Canadian Psychology/Psychologie Canadienne* 189–202, November 2005.
DeLeon, P. H., B. Giesting, and **M. B. Kenkel.** Community health centers: Exciting opportunities for the twenty-first century. *Professional Psychol.: Res. Pract.* 34:579–85, 2003.
Kenkel, M. B., P. H. DeLeon, J. A. Albino, and N. Porter. Challenges to professional psychology in the twenty-first century: Response to Peterson. *Am. Psychol.* 58:801–5, 2003.
Krishnamurthy, R. Review of the Minnesota multiphasic personality inventory-adolescent. In *Test Critiques,* ed. D. J. Keyser, vol. 11, pp. 281–90. Austin, Tex.: Pro-Ed, 2005.
Krishnamurthy, R., K. Bolinskey, and R. P. Archer. MMPI-A structural summary: Integrating new scales and subscales. In *MMPI/MMPI-A,* chairs R. Krishnamurthy and R. P. Archer. Paper presented at the annual meeting of the Society for Personality Assessment, Chicago, Illinois, 2005.
Krishnamurthy, R., et al. Achieving competency in psychological assessment: Directions for education and training. *J. Clin. Psychol.* 60(7):725–39, 2004.
Martinez-Diaz, J. A., T. R. Freeman, **M. P. Normand,** and T. E. Heron. The ethical practice of applied behavior analysis. Invited chapter in J. O. Cooper, T. E. Heron, and W. L. Heward, *Applied Behavioral Analysis,* 2nd ed. Upper Saddle River, N.J.: Merrill/Prentice Hall, in press.
Martinez-Diaz, J. A., and **D. A. Wilder.** Behavior, not symptoms: A behavior analytic interpretation of schizophrenia and other severe and persistent mental disorders. Invited presentation for Continuing Education Units, Gainesville, Fla., 2004.
Martinez-Diaz, J. A., P. Osnes, and C. Peeler. Master's level graduate training programs in applied behavior analysis in Florida. Panel presented at the Florida Association for Behavior Analysis, Daytona Beach, Florida, 2002.
Martinez-Diaz, J. A. Providing home- and community-based behavior analysis services to persons diagnosed with mental retardation and other developmental disabilities. Invited workshop presented at the Alabama Association for Behavior Analysis, Birmingham, Alabama, 2003.
Palmer, D., et al. **(M. P. Normand).** Dialogue on private events. *Anal. Verbal Behav.,* in press.
Normand, M. P., and J. S. Bailey. The effects of celeration lines on visual analysis. *Behav. Modif.,* in press.
Peake, T. H., and A. Steep. Therapy with older couples: Love stories-The good, the bad and the movies. In *Handbook of Couples Therapy,* ed. Michele Harway. Indianapolis: John Wiley & Sons, 2005.
Peake, T. H. *Cinema and life development: Healing lives & training therapists.* Westport, CT: Praeger/Greenwood, 2004.
Richard, E. M., J. M. Diefendorff, and J. H. Martin. Revisiting the within-person self-efficacy and performance relationship. *Human Performance* 19(1):67–87, 2006.
Diefendorff, J. M., and **E. M. Richard.** Antecedents and consequences of emotional display rule perceptions. *J. Appl. Psychol.* 88:284–95, 2003.
Domagalski, T., and **L. A. Steelman.** The impact of work events and disposition on the experience and expression of employee anger. *Organ. Anal.* 13(1):31–52, 2005.
Rutkowski, K. A., and **L. A. Steelman.** Testing a path model for antecedents of accountability. *J. Managerial Dev.* 24(5):473–86, 2005.
Steelman, L. A., P. E. Levy, and A. F. Snell. The feedback environment scale: Construct definition, measurement and validation. *Educ. Psychol. Meas.* 64:(1):165–84, 2004.
Webbe, F. M. Definition, Physiology, and Severity of Cerebral Concussion. In *Sports neuropsychology: Assessment and management of traumatic brain injury,* ed. R. J. Echemendia. New York: The Guilford Press, 2006.
Becker, S. A., and **F. M. Webbe.** Designing for older adult users of handheld technology. Proceedings of the 28th IEEE Engineering in Medicine and Biology Society Annual International Conference. 3297–300, 2006.
Lichtenberg, P. A., et al. **(F. M. Webbe).** Enhancing cognitive screening in geriatric care: Use of an internet-based system. *Int. J. Health Information Systems Informatics* 1:47–57, 2006.
Wilder, D. A., et al. Further analysis of antecedent interventions on preschooler's compliance. *J. Appl. Behav. Anal.,* in press.
Wilder, D. A., C. Harris, R. Reagan, and A. Rasey. Functional analysis and treatment of noncompliance by preschool children. *J. Appl. Behav. Anal.,* in press.
Wilder, D. A., et al. Brief functional analysis and treatment of tantrums associated with transitions in preschool children. *J. Appl. Behav. Anal.* 39:103–7, 2006.
Wilder, D. A., and J. Atwell. Evaluation of a guided compliance procedure to reduce noncompliance among preschool children. *Behav. Interventions* 21:265–72, 2006.

GEORGE FOX UNIVERSITY

Doctor of Psychology Program

Programs of Study

The Doctor of Psychology (Psy.D.) degree emphasizes the practitioner-scholar model, which puts more emphasis on clinical skills than the more traditional research-oriented, scientist-practitioner model leading to the Ph.D. Nonetheless, within the George Fox University Psy.D. degree program, training in empirical research skills is an important part of the program, and it is common for students and faculty members to present and publish empirical research findings at regional and national conferences. The Psy.D. degree prepares students for internships and subsequent professional practices in a variety of settings. A Master of Arts (M.A.) degree in psychology is conferred on the way to the Psy.D. degree.

The Psy.D. degree program typically consists of four years of full-time study followed by a year of full-time internship. More than 90 percent of recent internships obtained have been accredited by the American Psychological Association and/or meet standards of the Association of Psychology Postdoctoral and Internship Centers. The curriculum, consisting of 125 semester hours, includes courses in scientific foundations of psychology, psychological research, assessment and psychotherapy, Bible and religion, and integration of psychology and Christian faith. Required courses encourage students to become well-rounded, skilled clinicians, and electives allow students to explore areas of special interest. A research-based or theoretical dissertation also is required. The program is accredited by the Northwest Association of Schools and Colleges and the American Psychological Association (Committee on Accreditation, Office of Program Consultation and Accreditation, American Psychological Association, 750 First Street NE, Washington, D.C., 20002-4242; telephone: 202-336-5979; http://www.apa.org/ed/accred.html). Distinctives of the program include its emphasis on mentoring (using clinical team and research team models), its inclusion of a Christian worldview, and a university setting in a nonurban location.

Research Facilities

The Newberg campus library and the Portland Center library house a combined total of nearly 200,000 print volumes and receive more than 1,100 print journal subscriptions. Thousands of journal titles are available in electronic format. The University is a member of the Portland Area Library System (PORTALS) and the Orbis Cascade Alliance, a consortium of twenty-six college and university libraries in Oregon and Washington. The Orbis Cascade union catalog enables users to make requests from millions of books held in member libraries as well as obtain full-text recent journal articles electronically. Students may use many other academic libraries in the Northwest. A computer lab also is available; it provides most word processing, spreadsheet, slide-making, and statistical software for graduate student use. An on-campus health and counseling center serves as a clinical training facility. Classrooms, faculty offices, a computer lab, café, and a student lounge are all conveniently located in the Villa Academic Complex on the east side of campus.

Financial Aid

The University participates in the Federal Direct Student Loan Program for the Federal Subsidized Stafford Loan and the Federal Unsubsidized Stafford Loan. Scholarship aid is available for those contributing to ethnic diversity within the program. Teaching and research assistantships are available after the first year.

Cost of Study

The Psy.D. program cost $695 per semester hour for the 2007–08 school year. The amount was billed per semester. An interest-free monthly payment plan was available. Additional fees applied to items such as books and assessment lab materials.

Living and Housing Costs

A wide variety of housing is available in Newberg and throughout the Portland metropolitan area. On-campus housing is not available for graduate students, but off-campus housing resources are available on the University's Web site. Rent for off-campus private rooms range from $275 to $400 a month; one-bedroom apartments range from $425 to $650 per month; and two-bedroom apartments range from $500 to $800 per month. Rentals of two-bedroom homes start at $850.

Meals may be purchased at a bristo-like café at the program's principal location, or an on-campus cafeteria, which provides menu items ranging from sandwiches to pizza. Students may pay for meals individually or by purchasing a declining-balance card from the food services department. Many eating establishments also exist near the campus.

Student Group

Alumni of the Graduate Department of Clinical Psychology (GDCP) are licensed psychologists in numerous states throughout the United States. They work in a variety of practice settings, including independent and group practices, hospitals, community and public-health agencies, military and veteran administration facilities, correctional institutions, as well as church and parachurch organizations. Graduates also teach in a variety of settings, including colleges and seminaries. The GDCP Student Council represents on-campus student interests to the faculty and administration. The student council is composed of elected officers from each cohort of the GDCP student body.

Location

George Fox University's main campus covers 85 tree-shaded acres in a residential neighborhood of Newberg, a friendly community of 22,000 located 23 miles from Portland, Oregon. The Pacific Ocean is just a 60-minute drive to the west, and the year-round ski slopes and hiking trails of Mt. Hood are 90 minutes to the east. A grass campus quad bordered by academic buildings, a library, gymnasium, and the student commons surrounds the Centennial Tower. Running through campus is Hess Creek Canyon, a natural setting of trees, ferns, and wildflowers.

The University

George Fox University is the only evangelical Christian university in the Pacific Northwest classified by *U.S. News & World Report* as a national university. The University was founded in 1891 by Quaker pioneers. From the beginning, the University's purpose has been to demonstrate the meaning of Jesus Christ by offering a caring educational community in which each individual can achieve the highest intellectual and personal growth and participate responsibly in world concerns.

Applying

The Psy.D. program begins at the end of August. To apply for admission, the following is required: a baccalaureate degree from a regionally accredited college or university, with a GPA of at least 3.0 (on a 4.0 scale) in the last two years of course work; submission of scores for the General Test and the Psychology Subject Test of the Graduate Record Examinations (scores must be less than five years old); and an interview with the program faculty members. Completion of at least 18 semester hours in undergraduate psychology is preferred. Applicants may apply to the program online or request printed materials. The application deadline for admission materials is January 15.

Correspondence and Information

For correspondence and information, contact:

Graduate Admission Office
George Fox University
414 North Meridian Street, #6149
Newberg, Oregon 97132

Phone: 800-631-0921 (toll-free)
503-554-2263 (Adina McConaughey; Graduate Admission Counselor)
503-554-2761 (Wayne Adams, Ph.D., ABPP; Program Chairperson)
E-mail: psyd@georgefox.edu
Web site: http://psyd.georgefox.edu

George Fox University

THE FACULTY AND THEIR RESEARCH

Wayne V. Adams, Professor and Program Chairperson; Ph.D., Syracuse; ABPP(CL). Research interests: Child memory and its assessment, child/adolescent cognitive assessment, hospital-based pediatric psychology, learning disorders, school consultation, childhood and adolescent behavior disorders. Clinical interests: learning and related behavior disorders, pediatric neuropsychological assessment, neurodevelopmental disorders.

Robert E. Buckler, Professor; M.P.H., Johns Hopkins; M.D., Georgetown. Research interests: Medical psychology; corrections; community mental health; epidemiology; religious variables and mental health; organization, administration, and delivery of mental health services in religious settings; selected religious, family, and demographic variables as they relate to social adaptation status of first-grade children (a longitudinal study); psychosomatic patterns in families.

Roger K. Bufford, Professor; Ph.D., Illinois. Research interests: Religious/spiritual issues in psychotherapy, spiritual outcomes of psychotherapy, theoretical and applied issues related to relationship of psychology and Christian faith, spiritual well-being and spiritual maturity, assessment of mental health treatment outcomes in managed-care settings.

William Buhrow, Director of Health and Counseling Services; Psy.D., George Fox. Research interests: University student alcohol use, premarital counseling, short-term solution-focused therapy, university health-care issues and systems.

Clark D. Campbell, Professor and Director of Clinical Training; Ph.D., Western Seminary; ABPP(CL). Research interests: Development and maintenance of professional relationships between disciplines, assessment of family health and dysfunction, rural psychology. Clinical interests: Interpersonal and cognitive therapies.

Kathleen A. Gathercoal, Professor and Director of Research; Ph.D., Case Western Reserve. Research interests: Effects of postmodernism on the discipline of psychology and psychological phenomena (including spiritual development, problem solving, and identity development), cognitive, or social developmental psychology.

Christopher J. Koch, Associate Professor; Ph.D., Georgia. Research interests: Attention, Stroop effect, analysis of error rates, sports medicine, individual differences, visual perception.

Mark R. McMinn. Professor and Director of Integration; Ph.D., Vanderbilt; ABPP (CL). Research interests: Integration of psychology and Christianity, clergy health and prayer. Clinical interests: Cognitive therapy.

Mary Peterson, Assistant Professor and Associate Director of Clinical Training; Ph.D., California School of Professional Psychology. Research interests: Outcome research in clinical interventions for the adult severely mentally ill population, adjudicated minors and adolescents. Clinical interests: Health psychology and family therapy.

Patrick Stone, Adjunct Professor; Ph.D., Biola. Research interests: Effects of political and social advocacy, multicultural psychology, post-war mental-health effects. Clinical interests: PTSD and related disorders.

Nancy S. Thurston, Professor; Psy.D., Central Michigan. Research interests: Shame, validity of the Thurston-Cradock Test of Shame; psychological assessment. Clinical interests: Clergy evaluation.

INSTITUTE OF TRANSPERSONAL PSYCHOLOGY

Program of Study

The Institute of Transpersonal Psychology (ITP) is a private nonsectarian graduate school accredited by the Western Association of Schools and Colleges. Residential programs include a Ph.D. in Clinical Psychology; a Ph.D. in Transpersonal Psychology; a Master of Arts in Counseling Psychology, which leads to clinical licensure (both daytime and evening cohorts); a Master of Arts in Women's Spirituality; and a Master of Arts in Transpersonal Psychology. Global (distance learning) programs include a Ph.D. in Psychology, a Master of Transpersonal Psychology, a one-year Certificate in Transpersonal Studies, and Professional Training in Transformational Life Coaching.

Transpersonal psychology is the extension of traditional psychology into the areas of consciousness studies, spiritual inquiry, body-mind relationships, and personal transformation. ITP supports a broad range of ideas, spiritual traditions, cultural perspectives, and professional backgrounds. The Institute's whole-person education provides the foundation for professional training, personal growth, and continuing education. The Institute's programs encourage students to develop as individuals within the larger professional community through research, formal presentations, and published writing.

The low faculty-student ratio is designed to provide an ideal container for students to work closely with leaders in the field.

The residential Ph.D. in Clinical Psychology requires three years of full-time course work, one year of full-time internship, and one year of dissertation writing. The Ph.D. in Transpersonal Psychology requires three years of full-time course work and one year of dissertation writing. The Master of Arts in Counseling Psychology requires three years of part-time course work for the evening program and two years of full-time course work for the daytime program, both of which include a supervised practicum. The Master of Arts in Women's Spirituality consists of one or two weekends per month for two years and includes a community service project and a thesis. The Master of Arts in Transpersonal Psychology requires two years of part-time course work. The global Ph.D. in Psychology requires four years of part-time course work and one year of dissertation writing. The global master's degrees require two years of part-time course work and offer specializations in spiritual psychology, creative expression and innovation, and transpersonal health and wellness, while the certificate requires one year of part-time study. Students with a master's in psychology or a related degree can apply for advanced standing in any of the residential or global Ph.D. programs.

Research Facilities

Named in honor of the pioneering American psychologist, philosopher, and writer, the William James Center was established in 1994 as the main research arm of the Institute of Transpersonal Psychology. The aim of the center is to encourage and support a broad range of studies of consciousness and of the mind that have clear implications for the field of transpersonal psychology. Research at the center encourages the development, initiation, and evaluation of possible practical applications of the principles that emerge from the research, e.g., in education, business, wellness, counseling, therapy, and spiritual guidance. Research projects are designed and conducted primarily by Institute faculty members and students. However, the center also provides an umbrella for work by adjunct researchers and outside investigators.

The Institute will soon add to its facilities a neuro-phenomenological lab, which is expected to add even greater breadth to its research studies.

ITP is expanding its counseling center into a Community Health & Wellness Center with several offerings: affordable psychological therapy; spiritual guidance; trauma, forgiveness, and reconciliation services; and an opportunity for both master's and doctoral-level students to learn how to develop their private practice.

Financial Aid

Financial aid is available to all eligible students and is awarded to 95 percent of them. The Institute participates in the Federal Stafford Student Loan Program. The Stafford loans are the primary source of financial assistance available to Institute students and are available to all eligible students who are U.S. citizens or permanent residents enrolled at least half-time in a residential or global program. ITP also participates in the Federal Work-Study Program. Through this program qualified students are allowed to work on campus and receive payment for their services.

Cost of Study

Residential program tuition for 2008–09 is $24,543 per year for the doctoral programs and $12,591 to $19,655 per year for the master's programs. Global program tuition is $16,248 per year for years one and two and $20,412 per year for years three, four, and five for the distance learning Ph.D. program; $12,268 per year for the master's program; and $12,268 per year for the one-year certificate program. Tuition for the Professional Training in Transformational Life Coaching program is a total of $6,135 for four courses. All Global programs require additional fees for online services.

Living and Housing Costs

There is no on-campus housing. Students live in the community at large. If students are in need of housing, they may contact the Admissions Office at 650-493-4430 Ext. 216 for a list of local housing resources and contacts.

Student Group

Of the 371 students enrolled at ITP, 28 percent are men, 7 percent are international, 95 percent are full-time, and 5 percent are part-time.

Student Outcomes

Graduates of ITP's programs pursue careers as psychotherapists, counselors, school psychologists and counselors, educators, teachers, trainers, spiritual directors, business consultants, coaches, and community activists. Many also introduce transpersonal principles, such as mindfulness, compassion, discernment, and an appreciation of differences, into business administration and organizational development.

Location

ITP is located in Palo Alto, near Stanford University, just south of San Francisco, northwest of Santa Cruz, and across the bay from Berkeley. Palo Alto is noted for its access to a diverse mix of cultural, educational, and recreational resources. Students enjoy the benefits of living in a dynamic residential community, just minutes from two major urban areas.

The Institute

The Institute was founded in 1975, and it has remained at the cutting edge of psychological research, clinical training, and education for more than thirty years. ITP's unique curriculum focuses on six core areas of inquiry: the intellectual, emotional, spiritual, physical, social, and creative aspects of life. This whole-person education model incorporates the tenets of transpersonal psychology and offers students not only a solid intellectual foundation, but also an extraordinary opportunity for deep growth and personal experience of the subject matter.

Applying

The ITP admissions faculty members look for mature students who have a strong connection to the philosophy, values, and vision of transpersonal psychology. Faculty members also seek students who will approach their graduate studies with discipline, professionalism, and a commitment to their own intellectual, spiritual, and emotional growth.

The application priority deadline for the campus programs and the Global Ph.D. is February 1. Applications received after this date are processed, and admission is granted on a space-available basis. The global certificate and master's programs admit students each quarter and accept applications until four weeks prior to the beginning of the quarter. ITP does not require the GRE. Interviews in person or by telephone are required. Applicants are notified of their admission within two weeks of their interview.

Correspondence and Information

Admissions Office
Institute of Transpersonal Psychology
1069 East Meadow Circle
Palo Alto, California 94303

Phone: 650-493-4430 Ext. 216
Fax: 650-493-6835
E-mail: itpinfo@itp.edu
Web site: http://www.itp.edu

Institute of Transpersonal Psychology

THE FACULTY AND THEIR RESEARCH

Rosemarie Anderson, Professor; Ph.D. (psychology), Nebraska, 1973. Dr. Anderson's current scholarly interests include the symbolic and oracular dimensions of indigenous spiritualities, particularly Celtic spirituality; the phenomenology of sacred weeping; and the research methods for transpersonal psychology. She is the author of numerous research articles in social psychology and the psychology of women.

William Braud, Professor; Ph.D. (experimental psychology), Iowa, 1967. Dr. Braud's research interests include studies in parapsychology and the effects of psychological exercises, such as relaxation, attention, intention, and visualization, on the immune system, behavior, and experience. He is studying and researching exceptional human experiences (psychic, mystical, and intuitive) and their meanings and life impacts; personal and spiritual change and transformation; alternative ways of knowing; and the development and promotion of more complete and inclusive methodologies for transpersonal studies. He has written numerous articles, including more than ninety original research reports featured in professional journals, and has produced tapes on mind-body relationships.

Christopher Dryer, Associate Professor; Ph.D. (clinical psychology), 1993. Dr. Dryer is a former Chair of the Residential Ph.D. Program and a member of the core faculty. He is an experienced management consultant and industrial psychologist, having served many of Silicon Valley's leading companies, including IBM, Adobe Systems, and Microsoft. His scholarly interests include research methods, transcendent experiences, team dynamics, human-computer interactions, and leadership and service. He has received two international patents for his innovations in interface technologies. He has taught at Santa Clara University, UCLA, and Stanford University, where he also studied as a postdoctoral fellow at the School of Medicine and the Center for Language and Information.

Jan Fisher, Assistant Professor; Ph.D. (transpersonal psychology), 1996. Dr. Fisher is the Chair of the Residential Ph.D. in Clinical Psychology and Assistant Professor in the Residential Program. In addition, she has a private practice in Mountain View, working with individual adults and groups as a transpersonally oriented psychologist and expressive-arts therapist. Dr. Fisher supports clients in the practice of Authentic Movement, long-term depth work, and working with issues of shyness, anxiety, depression, trauma recovery, relationship concerns, caregiver demands, and spiritual exploration. A graduate of ITP, Dr. Fisher explored the experience of dance as a spiritual practice in her dissertation. She continues her exploration of authentic movement and creative expression in her individual work and is a Certified Dance Leader for the Dances of Universal Peace. Areas of research interest include creative expression, movement/dance, and clinical psychology. Her expertise in methodologies includes phenomenology, organic inquiry, feminist, integral inquiry, intuitive inquiry, and using creative expression in data collection, analysis, or presentation.

Robert Frager, Professor; Ph.D. (social psychology), Harvard, 1967. Dr. Frager was the founder of ITP and its first President. He was trained in aikido in Japan and holds a seventh-degree black belt. He is a transpersonal psychologist, consultant, educator, and a spiritual teacher in the Sufi tradition and is currently Director of the Spiritual Guidance Program.

Arthur Hastings, Professor; Ph.D. (public address and small-group communication), Northwestern, 1962. Prior to his arrival to ITP in 1975, Dr. Hastings taught at Stanford University, the University of Nevada, and the University of California, Santa Barbara. His recent work includes research studies on remote viewing, hypnosis and non-drug altered states, dreams, and facilitated reunions in a Psychomanteum chamber.

Olga Louchakova, Assistant Professor; Ph.D. (neuroimmunology), USSR Academy of Sciences, 1989. Dr. Louchakova is the Director of the Transpersonal Education & Research specialization. After completing her career as a senior medical scientist at the Pavlov Institute of the Academy of Sciences in St. Petersburg, Russia, Dr. Louchakova became an educator and spiritual guide in Kundalini yoga/Vedanta tradition and Prayer of the Heart. Her interest now is in studies in culture and consciousness, engaged spirituality and awakening, human development, Kundalini yoga, and Sufism. She has maintained a private practice in Kundalini process, coaching in the Bay Area since 1994.

Fred Luskin, Associate Professor; Ph.D. (counseling and health psychology), Stanford, 1999. Dr. Luskin is the Director of the Stanford Forgiveness Project, a series of research projects affirming his forgiveness training methodology. He has taught and lectured on forgiveness worldwide and has been featured for his forgiveness work on most major media outlets. In addition, he is a licensed marriage and family counselor and a nationally certified school psychologist. He also holds a California license as an educational psychologist.

Genie Palmer, Assistant Professor; Ph.D. (transpersonal psychology), Institute of Transpersonal Psychology, 1999. Dr. Palmer is the Director of Dissertations and is also actively involved in the Institute's Spiritual Guidance Certificate program, assisting in the facilitation of the Spiritual Guidance Council and serving as a supervisor for spiritual guidance interns. Her research interests include the study of the meanings and life impacts of nonordinary and transcendent experiences and other exceptional human experiences; the connection between psychology and spirituality; spiritual development, change, and transformation; and group spiritual guidance, particularly from cross-cultural and cross-traditional perspectives.

Kartikeya Patel, Assistant Professor; Ph.D. (philosophy and religion), California Institute of Integral Studies, 1998. Dr. Patel is proficient in Sanskrit, Pali, Dhodafu (an Indian tribal language), Hindi, and Gujarati as well as Web-based languages. His current research includes cross-cultural issues in transpersonal psychology, Eastern spiritual traditions (notably Hinduism and Buddhism), and the Internet and education.

Ana Perez-Chisti, Associate Professor; Ph.D. (philosophy and religion), California Institute of Integral Studies, 1998. Dr. Perez-Chisti is both the Chair and a core faculty member of ITP's Global Ph.D. Program. She also is a professor at Naropa University in Boulder, Colorado, teaching in the Distant Learning Program in the Department of Religion and Philosophy. Dr. Perez-Chisti specializes in such subjects as comparative world religions, the mystical traditions, ethics, Eastern and Western philosophy, women saints and prophets–East and West, Jungian psychology, psycho-spiritual synthesis, culture and consciousness, and contemporary and wisdom psychologies. She has worked as a counselor in the field of homeless-shelter support, hospice care, prison reform, and emergency food distribution in areas of the world where extreme conditions of natural disaster, war, and political upheaval have occurred. Dr. Perez-Chisti is an ordained minister, lineage teacher (Murshida), and National Representative of the Sufi Movement International of the U.S.A. (http://www.sufimovement.net). Her latest academic interest is to publish her two major texts this year: *Foundations of the Buddha's Teachings—Abhidhamma and its Causation, Correlation, and Liberation* and *Sufi Akbar-The First Mogul Interfaith King.*

Henry Poon, Assistant Professor; Ph.D. (East-West psychology), California Institute of Integral Studies, 1995. Dr. Poon is Chair of the Global Master's and Certificate programs. His research interests include cross-cultural psychology and counseling, integrative life psychology, East-West approaches to self-cultivation, and transpersonal psychology and psychotherapy.

Shani Robins, Assistant Professor; Ph.D. (clinical psychology), California School of Professional Psychology, 2003. Dr. Robins' research and personal interests focus on the development of wisdom across the lifespan, the emotion-cognition interactions associated with wisdom, an instrument for measuring wisdom, and the applications of this research to clinical settings and organizational consulting. He is also investigating metaphor as a tool for cognitive reframing.

Nancy Rowe, Assistant Professor; Ph.D. (educational curriculum and instruction), Texas A&M, 1982. Dr. Rowe's current interests include creative process, eco-spirituality, earth consciousness, arts as meditation, intuition, the imagination, alternative ways of knowing, shamanism, and pilgrimage. She is most interested in helping others to reconnect to Earth, to their imaginations, and to their creative, intuitive selves. Her devotion to Earth is expressed through her spiritual practice, in the retreats and workshops that she facilitates, in her writing and photography, and through her work with the Woodstock Land Conservancy.

Paul J. Roy, Academic Vice President; Ph.D. (clinical psychology), California School of Professional Psychology, 1985. Prior to receiving his Ph.D., Dr. Roy was Assistant Professor of Pastoral Counseling at the Weston Jesuit School of Theology in Cambridge, Massachusetts. He has an extensive theological background and more than twenty-five years of experience as a spiritual director. His interests have focused on the connection between spirituality and psychology, the integration of spiritual development, and work for justice, peacemaking, and mind-body healing.

Judy Schavrien, Associate Professor; Ph.D. (psychology history and systems), Chicago, 1973. Dr. Schavrien's scholarly interests include women's spirituality, the body-centered focusing techniques of Eugene Gendlin, feminist transpersonal psychology, and the psychology of trauma.

Patricia Sohl, Associate Professor; M.P.H., Harvard, 1975. Dr. Sohl is a certified Jungian Analyst (graduate of the C.G. Jung Institute, Zurich, Switzerland, and a member of IAAP) whose special interest is in the role of symbolic expression in healing. She is curator of the ARAS collection (Archive for Research in Archetypal Symbolism) at the C.G. Jung Institute in San Francisco, where she also serves as Associate Director of the clinic. She has broad international teaching experience, and for thirteen years, she was Visiting Lecturer in Health Policy and Ethics at Harvard University's School of Public Health. Scholarly interests include the aesthetic response as an aspect of the transcendent function; the spiritual aspects of archetypal images as they appear in the dreams of individuals and in the arts and rituals of cultures; the deeply unconscious nature of somatic symptoms; and the use of "landscapes of childhood" in healing trauma. Dr. Sohl is the Director of the Creative Expression Program.

Charles Tart, Professor; Ph.D. (psychology), North Carolina, 1963. A student of meditation, Dr. Tart has studied Tibetan Buddhism, G. I. Gurdjieff's work, and other psychological and spiritual disciplines. His primary goal is to build bridges between the scientific and spiritual communities and to bring about a refinement and integration of Western and Eastern approaches for knowing the world for personal and social growth.

Jenny Wade, Associate Professor; Ph.D. (human development), Fielding Institute, 1993. Dr. Wade's teaching specialties include developmental psychology, pre- and perinatal psychology, consciousness studies, transpersonal psychology, altered states, sex, systems theory as applied to epistemological and consciousness studies, organization development, applications of consciousness studies and spirituality to business, and qualitative research.

Kathleen Wall, Assistant Professor; Ph.D. (counseling psychology), Miami (Florida), 1977. Dr. Wall is a licensed psychologist and a certified mental health administrator. She was the Founding Executive Director of the Mental Health Resource Center, Jacksonville, Florida, and she was the Director of Counseling Services at San Jose State University. A student of integral yoga (Sri Aurobindo and the Mother), her expertise is in spiritual integration in psychotherapy.

Kate Wolf-Pizor, Associate Professor; M.A. (marriage and family therapy), Santa Clara, 1986. Kate Wolf-Pizor has been a licensed marriage and family therapist in California for thirteen years and is Chair of the Residential Master's Program. She is currently the President of the California State Division of the American Association for Marriage and Family Therapy. She has a strong interest in ritual and works with the labyrinth as a healing practice and has a background in Western mystical traditions.

LESLEY UNIVERSITY

Graduate School of Arts and Social Sciences
Division of Counseling and Psychology

Programs of Study

Since their founding in 1975, Lesley University's graduate programs in counseling and psychology have advanced a philosophy of education grounded in a strong foundation of psychology-based, rigorous theoretical study; an emphasis on field experience in a variety of professional settings; and the personal development of each student as a reflective practitioner. This philosophy, with its integrative holistic approach to training in counseling and psychology, its footing in reality, and its emphasis on the student's personal development, has given Lesley a unique and highly regarded position in graduate education. The counseling and psychology programs lead to two types of credentials—licensure as mental health counselors and initial licensure as school counselors.

The Master of Arts (M.A.) in Clinical Mental Health Counseling Program (60 credits) is intended for graduates who wish to have the most comprehensive training available at the master's level to support mental health counseling practice. The program meets the educational requirements for master's-level counseling licensure in Massachusetts and most other states. This program is offered on the Cambridge campus and can be completed in three academic years of full-time study, with 1,300 hours of required field experience. In this program, students have the opportunity to specialize in one of three areas in which Lesley has built a distinguished reputation: holistic studies, trauma studies, and school and community counseling.

The M.A. in counseling psychology with the professional counseling specialization is a 60-credit program designed for individuals who wish to practice professional counseling in the community. This program meets the educational requirements for licensure as a mental health counselor in Massachusetts and many other states. Offered in Cambridge and at off-campus sites in Massachusetts, this program can be completed in three academic years of full-time study on campus or approximately four years of part-time study on campus and at Massachusetts off-campus sites. A minimum of 700 hours of field experience is required.

The 48-credit M.A. program in counseling psychology with the school counseling specialization provides the required graduate training for individuals who wish to work as guidance counselors in primary and secondary school settings. Graduates are eligible for initial licensure in school guidance counseling from the Massachusetts Department of Education at grade levels pre-K–8 or 5–12. Both programs can be completed in two academic years of full-time study, and a minimum of 700 hours of field experience is required.

The M.A. in counseling psychology with no specialization is a 48-credit program designed for individuals who wish to practice counseling interventions and consultation skills with children and adults in community settings or who intend to continue on to doctoral studies in psychology. The program allows students to become generalists in the field. To be eligible for licensure in mental health counseling in Massachusetts, graduates of this program must complete 12 additional credits of graduate course work in counseling.

Candidates who already hold a master's degree in psychology or a related field may pursue a Certificate of Advanced Graduate Study (C.A.G.S.). This 36-credit certificate option is for experienced professionals who wish to expand their clinical skills, engage in scholarly reflection, and enhance theoretical understanding. On-campus enrollment is required.

The Advanced Professional Certificate in Trauma Studies Program offers the opportunity for post-master's professional counselors and other post-master's practitioners to develop expertise in psychosocial trauma work. The curriculum includes an overview of trauma theory and practice as well as a focus on specific client populations and topics.

The Division of Counseling and Psychology offers school guidance counseling and school adjustment counseling master's degree programs that are approved by the Massachusetts Department of Education (leading to initial licensure). The M.A. in counseling psychology programs are accredited by the Masters in Psychology Accreditation Council (MPAC). The Division of Counseling and Psychology is approved by the Council of Applied Masters Programs in Psychology (CAMPP).

Research Facilities

The Ludcke Library maintains a working collection of books, periodicals, microfilm and microfiches, curriculum materials, nonprint materials, and software resources. The Library provides Internet resources and database access to general and subject-specific resources appropriate to the subject focuses of the University. The Kresge Center for Teaching Resources provides instructional resources for individual and group instruction, and the Microcomputer Center houses the instructional computing activities of the University, including a collection of educational software. Through the Fenway Consortium students can access thirteen other libraries in the Boston-Cambridge area.

Financial Aid

The Lesley University Financial Aid Office administers all federal financial aid programs. There are opportunities in college teaching, advising, and research activities, as well as field placements. A limited number of assistantships are awarded by semester or academic year. Most positions require about 10 to 15 hours of work per week.

Cost of Study

Tuition for on-campus graduate students is $765 per credit for 2008–09; tuition for off-campus graduate cohort students ranges from $430 to $550 per credit.

Living and Housing Costs

Housing is not available for graduate students on campus. Information on local housing and housing assistance are available upon request from the Residence Life Office of Student Affairs.

Student Group

Students in the Division of Counseling and Psychology vary in age, academic background, and life and professional experiences—a heterogeneity that contributes to the vitality and real-world flavor of the programs. In its admission practices, Lesley is strongly committed to assembling a student body that reflects the diversity in society.

Location

Lesley University occupies a campus near Harvard Square in Cambridge, an area that benefits from the many advantages of the cities of Boston and Cambridge. The University is connected to downtown Boston by public transportation. Within a 6-mile radius are numerous historical sites and cultural attractions, including theaters, museums, and concerts.

The University

Lesley University, founded in 1909 as a women's teaching college, continues its commitment to educating undergraduates while also offering graduate and Ph.D. programs in the fields of education, environmental studies, human services, counseling and psychology, and the arts. With today's student in mind, Lesley University has successfully pioneered a wide variety of flexible programs for adult learners that share a commitment to quality, innovation, and the integration of theory with practice.

Lesley offers degree programs for learners at all levels. The University also supports several centers and hosts a variety of academic and professional conferences and institutes. Lesley programs operate throughout Massachusetts and in twenty-three other states as well as at an affiliated site in Israel.

Applying

Requirements for admission to graduate degree programs are a bachelor's degree (for the M.A. programs) or a master's degree (for the C.A.G.S. program) from a regionally accredited college or university as well as a satisfactory grade point average, official transcripts of undergraduate and graduate work, scores from the Miller Analogies Test, three letters of recommendation, a three- to five-page personal statement, and the nonrefundable $50 application fee. An interview is required once all application materials are received. Application packets are available from the Office of Admissions for Graduate and Adult Bachelor's Programs. Applications are processed on a rolling basis. International students not residing in the United States should apply by May 1 for the fall semester and October 1 for the spring semester.

Correspondence and Information

Office of Graduate and Adult Bachelor's Admissions
Lesley University
29 Everett Street
Cambridge, Massachusetts 02138-2790

Phone: 617-349-8300
888-LESLEY.U (toll-free)
E-mail: info@lesley.edu
Web site: http://www.lesley.edu/oncampus

Lesley University

THE FACULTY AND THEIR RESEARCH

Core Faculty

Paul Crowley, Professor Emeritus; Ph.D., Catholic University. Group therapy and counseling and spirituality.

Priscilla Dass-Brailsford, Associate Professor; Ed.D., Harvard. Resiliency across the life span, with a focus on longitudinal research designs and comparative studies; impact of the stressors of community violence and political violence on different communities and understanding community coping styles; effects of racism, discrimination, and poverty and the sustaining factors.

Susan Gere, Professor and Division Director; Ph.D., Simmons. Adult and child psychopathology, trauma recovery, community consultation.

Lisa Tsoi Hoshmand, Professor; Ph.D., Hawaii. Philosophical and theoretical psychology, qualitative methodology and action research, cross-cultural issues, professional education in counseling and psychology.

Jared Kass, Professor; Ph.D., Union (Ohio). Contributions of spiritual development to health-promoting behaviors, pro-social behaviors, psychological maturation.

Dalia Llera, Associate Professor; Ed.D., Harvard. Mental health and community agencies, with a focus on women, Spanish-speaking minorities, children, and adolescent victims of violence and oppression.

Sue Motulsky, Assistant Professor; Ph.D., Harvard. Career planning and development.

Rick Reinkraut, Associate Professor and Supervisor of Academic Affairs; Ed.D., Harvard; Ph.D., Connecticut. Therapist use of self, empathy, the healing power of relationships.

Eleanor Roffman, Professor and Director of Field Training; Ed.D., Boston University. Transformative education.

Rakhshanda Saleem, Assistant Professor; Ph.D., Colorado State. Neuropsychology and assessments.

LONG ISLAND UNIVERSITY, ROCKLAND GRADUATE CAMPUS

Counseling and Development Programs

Programs of Study

The Department of Counseling and Development provides an educational environment that fosters the personal and professional growth of future counselors, while upholding the highest ethical standards and respect for individual differences. The department's goal is to prepare students to be professional and competent and to take leadership roles in the counseling profession, both in the Greater New York area and nationwide. Graduates are skilled in the latest counseling techniques and the technology available to counselors. They become advocates for the diverse population they serve.

The school counseling program is designed to prepare students to enter the profession of school counseling. All courses, from theory to practicum, are approached from a developmental and wellness perspective. The program leads to provisional certification as a school counselor in New York and consists of 48 credits of study. On completion of this Master of Science degree in school counseling, a student may submit an application for New York State certification. Students interested in obtaining New Jersey certification are responsible for applying to New Jersey on their own.

The mental health counseling program integrates mental health counseling theories and approaches with carefully supervised practical experiences in state-of-the-art appropriate field settings. The training comprises individual counseling as well as family, group, and other systemic modalities within the developmental model and brief therapy framework. This is an individualized program emphasizing self-development and the integration of individual and group counseling theories and techniques with supervised clinical experiences. The approved 60-credit plan of study leads to a Master of Science degree in mental health counseling.

Graduates of the mental health counseling program are eligible to take the National Counselor Examination. Successful completion of this examination qualifies the student to become a national certified counselor (NCC). This program prepares students to fulfill the educational requirements for licensure as a mental health counselor in New York State.

Research Facilities

Students are involved in two or more practicums that consist of working at either public schools or client-based mental health facilities. In addition, students have access to a modern library and extensive online databases to perform research and in-depth studies.

Financial Aid

The Rockland Graduate Campus offers a variety of scholarships based on past academic achievement as well as current employment. Students may apply for federal financial aid for graduate study by completing an online FAFSA application. For further information about available scholarships or financial aid, students should contact the Graduate Admissions Office. More than 80 percent of campus graduate students receive either scholarships or federal financial aid.

Cost of Study

Graduate tuition for 2007–08 was $835 per credit. In addition, students were responsible for certain registration fees.

Living and Housing Costs

Most students are local professionals who attend evening or weekend classes, generally on a part-time basis; therefore, there are no additional expenses for housing and food.

Student Outcomes

Graduates of the school counseling program become certified counselors in school systems, and graduates of the mental health counseling program are prepared for careers as agency counselor, mental health professional, or human resource counselor in public/private agencies or outpatient clinics.

Location

The Rockland Graduate Campus is a regional campus of Long Island University and is located in a two-story building in a suburban environment. The campus has a modern library, two student computer centers, a student lobby lounge, and attractive classrooms. The campus is located in Orangeburg, a town located in Rockland County approximately 18 miles from New York City, and is easily accessible from the Palisades Parkway and New York State Thruway. Safe student parking is available adjacent to the campus building.

The University

Long Island University is an accredited undergraduate, graduate, and doctoral degree–granting university with major residential campuses located in Brookville and Brooklyn, New York. The Rockland Graduate Campus is one of five regional campuses serving suburban student populations. Long Island University is entering its ninth decade of providing access to the American dream through excellence in higher education. It is one of the largest and most comprehensive universities in the country. It offers more than 600 undergraduate, graduate, and doctoral degree programs and certificates. The Rockland Campus has an active chapter of Chi Sigma Iota Counseling Academic and Professional Honor Society.

Applying

The campus offers rolling admissions for students who wish to begin their graduate studies in the fall, spring, or summer semester. The counseling programs require the completion of an admission application; two letters of recommendation; undergraduate transcripts from all colleges previously attended, showing an undergraduate grade point average of 3.0 or higher; and an interview with the Counseling and Development Program Director.

Correspondence and Information

Graduate Admissions Office
Long Island University, Rockland Campus
70 Route 340
Orangeburg, New York 10962
Phone: 845-359-7200 Ext. 5403
E-mail: rockland@liu.edu
Web site: http://www.liu.edu/rockland

Dr. Kathleen Keefe-Cooperman
Counseling Program Director
Phone: 845-359-7200 Ext. 5406
E-mail: kathleen.keefe-cooperman@liu.edu

Long Island University, Rockland Graduate Campus

THE FACULTY

Department of Counseling and Development
Kathleen Keefe-Cooperman, Program Director; Psy.D., Hartford.

David Drassner, Adjunct Professor of Education; Ph.D., NYU.
A. Scott McGowan, Professor of Education; Ph.D., Fordham.
Thomas Nardi, Adjunct Professor of Education; Ph.D., St. John's (New York).
David J. Parr, Adjunct Professor of Mental Health Counseling Program; Psy.D., Illinois School of Professional Psychology; Licensed Clinical Psychologist (New York).
Cindy Roland, Adjunct Professor of Education; M.S., Vermont.
Mindy Ross, Assistant Professor of Education; M.S., CUNY, City College.
Donald Schneider, Adjunct Professor of Education; M.A., CUNY, Brooklyn; M.A., NYU; M.S.W., Yeshiva.

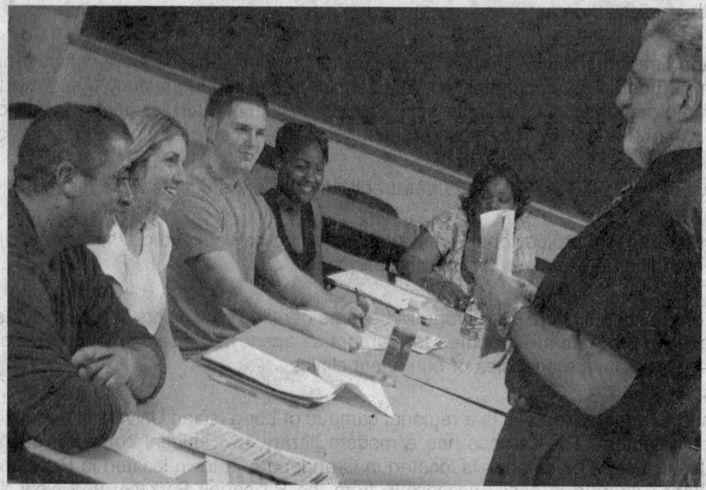

Classroom at Long Island University, Rockland Graduate Campus.

LOYOLA COLLEGE IN MARYLAND

Graduate Programs in Psychology

Programs of Study

The graduate programs offered by Loyola College's Department of Psychology prepare students to obtain licensure or to enter careers in the field of psychology, in both research and counseling capacities. The programs combine course work in both theory and skill development with clinical field experiences at numerous sites throughout Baltimore.

The Doctor of Psychology (Psy.D.) degree emphasizes clinical training and a foundation of psychological theory and knowledge. The degree requires completion of 124 credits, including dissertation, field placement, and course work. During the first four years, students take 4–5 courses per semester and devote 10–16 hours per week to clinical training at the Loyola clinical centers, hospitals, and university research centers. The fifth year is a full-time clinical internship, which may or may not be located in the Baltimore area. Additional information about the Psy.D. degree is available at http://www.loyola.edu/psychology/psyd/index.html.

Master of Science (M.S.) degree programs are offered in clinical psychology and in counseling psychology, with thesis and practitioner tracks for each degree. Both degrees require completion of 45 credits, including 18 credits in core courses and 27 credits in electives and externships. Students in the thesis tracks must pass a comprehensive examination and complete a thesis project; students in the practitioner tracks complete an externship and must pass a comprehensive examination.

For practitioners who already hold master's degrees and want to practice independently, the Licensed Clinical Professional Counselor (LCPC) Program provides the course work needed to become licensed professional counselors in the state of Maryland. For licensure eligibility, students must complete a total of 60 credits in an individualized program of study.

The Certificate of Advanced Study (CAS) is open to students who hold a master's degree and wish to supplement their studies with additional courses. The certificate requires completion of 30 credits.

Students can find further information about the M.S., LCPC, and CAS programs, including course requirements, at http://www.loyola.edu/psychology/mastersdegree/index.html.

Research Facilities

Departmental facilities are available for research and clinical training experience. The department also maintains a behavioral medicine laboratory for research and training. In addition, computers, with helpful tools such as SPSS, PsycINFO, and Internet access, are available for student research.

The Loyola Notre Dame Library contains approximately 463,000 books and bound periodical volumes; over 11,000 videos, DVDs, and CDs; and 989 print periodical subscriptions. The library's Web site serves as a gateway to a variety of Internet resources, including numerous databases such as ERIC, Lexis-Nexis Academic Universe, Maryland Digital Library, Cambridge Scientific, and Business Source Premier, as well as full-text articles from over 23,000 periodicals.

Financial Aid

A variety of financial assistance is available to graduate students. Graduate assistants work 10–20 hours per week in faculty and administrative departments in exchange for a stipend and tuition remission. A number of scholarships are available from the College; award amounts, entry requirements, and eligibility criteria vary. Federal Stafford Loans provide up to $8500 per year in subsidized loans or $20,500 in unsubsidized loans. The Federal Graduate PLUS Loan Program allows students to borrow up to the full cost of attendance, less other aid received. Other loans may be available from alternative sources. Some students may be eligible for federal work-study.

Cost of Study

In 2007-08, tuition is $535 per credit for most psychology students. Students in the Doctor of Psychology program spend $22,800 during the first and second years and smaller amounts in subsequent years. Other costs include a $25 registration fee, a $75 laboratory fee, and a $300 field experience fee.

Living and Housing Costs

The College does not offer on-campus housing for graduate students, except those who work as resident assistants as part of their financial aid package. However, off-campus housing is available. Students can expect to spend $400–$1000 per month for a 1-bedroom apartment and $850–$1300 for a 2-bedroom apartment, depending on size and location.

Student Group

Approximately 200 students are enrolled in the master's programs in any given year, including 125 in the clinical psychology program and 75 in the counseling psychology program. Approximately 35 students are enrolled in the Doctor of Psychology program each year. These students come from a wide range of backgrounds, but all are expected to hold an undergraduate degree in psychology or in an allied field.

Student Outcomes

Graduates of the program enter into a wide variety of careers in the field of psychology. Some enter into private practice, working with the general population or within a specialized area. Others work at hospitals, research centers, universities, and other organizations.

Location

Baltimore is one of the most visited cities in the nation, with 12 million visitors each year. The city has a variety of museums, art galleries, theaters, and music venues, as well as annual festivals. The Inner Harbor, a popular waterfront attraction, is surrounded by historic neighborhoods with unique shops and restaurants for every style and taste.

The University

Founded by Jesuits in 1852, Loyola College remains committed to the ideals embodied by the priests and brothers of the Society of Jesus, which include an emphasis on academic excellence, the importance of the liberal arts, and the education of the whole person. The College enrolls approximately 6,100 students in a broad spectrum of programs that are practitioner-oriented and designed for professionals seeking a greater level of expertise and satisfaction in their careers.

Applying

Applicants to all programs offered by the Department of Psychology must submit a completed application form and a nonrefundable $50 application fee. In addition to the program-specific information outlined below, interested students can find further information about application requirements at http://www.loyola.edu/psychology/index.html.

Applicants to the Psy.D. program must possess a bachelor's or master's degree from an accredited institution. Students with a bachelor's degree must have earned a minimum GPA of 3.0 (on a 4.0 scale) over the last two years of undergraduate study. Students with a master's must have at least a 3.2 GPA at the graduate level. Applicants must also submit three letters of recommendation, a personal essay, their current vitae, official GRE scores, and official transcripts from all colleges and universities attended. Other criteria to be considered include previous work and life experiences and extracurricular activities.

Admission to the M.S. practitioner tracks is selective and requires students to present a strong academic background. Successful applicants typically present undergraduate GPAs of 3.2 or higher and scores above 500 on each GRE subtest. Professional accomplishments, personal statements, and references are also taken into consideration.

As with the practitioner tracks, admission to the M.S. thesis tracks is selective and the standards are similar. However, strength in quantitative areas is viewed favorably in the successful thesis track applicant.

When applying to the Certificate of Advanced Study Program, students must submit official graduate and undergraduate transcripts, three letters of recommendation, and an essay or personal statement describing the applicant's professional goals and reason for applying to Loyola College. GRE scores are not required.

Individuals who possess a master's degree from an accredited college or university are eligible for the LCPC option.

Correspondence and Information

Office of Graduate Admission
Loyola College in Maryland
4501 North Charles Street
Baltimore, Maryland 21210
Phone: 410-617-2587
800-221-9107 Ext. 5020 (toll-free)
Fax: 410-617-2002
E-mail: graduate@loyola.edu
Web site: http://graduate.loyola.edu/psychgrad.info

Loyola College in Maryland

THE FACULTY AND THEIR RESEARCH

Jeffrey E. Barnett, Affiliate Professor; Psy.D., Yeshiva. Legal and ethical issues, cognitive and personality assessment, cognitive psychotherapy, assessment and treatment of children, psychotherapy process and outcome, professional development, therapist distress and impairment.

Carolyn McNamara Barry, Assistant Professor; Ph.D., Maryland, College Park. Social and self development within childhood, adolescence, and emerging adulthood, including peer relationships, friendships, peer influence, academic and social motivation, and issues concerning the transition to adulthood.

Gilbert Clapperton, Professor Emeritus; Ph.D., Baylor. Validation of projective techniques, executive selection and employment screening, psychotherapy outcome and process, aggression, ethics, psychopathology.

Mary Jo Coiro, Assistant Professor; Ph.D., Virginia. Effects of maternal depression on children's mental health and the family environment, risk and protective factors in the development of child psychopathology, prevention of child psychopathology, cognitive-behavioral therapy with adolescents, policy issues affecting children.

David G. Crough, Associate Professor; Ph.D., Catholic University. Pupillometry, sensation seeking, pace of living, animal research, physiology of behavior, aggressive behavior, educational research, drug abuse.

George S. Everly Jr., Affiliate Professor; Ph.D., Maryland, College Park. Health psychology; behavioral medicine; biofeedback; psychophysiology; cognitive behavior therapy; post-traumatic stress disorder, human stress, and stress management.

Faith M. Gilroy, Professor Emerita; Ph.D., Saint Louis. Business applications of psychology, attribution theory, conformity, attitudinal measurement, women's issues, gerontology, career patterns, gender choice of offspring.

Kerri A. Goodwin, Assistant Professor; Ph.D., Florida State. Encoding and retrieval factors in the creation of false memories, social factors as they relate to eyewitness memory, memory and problem solving, psychology and law.

Sharon Green-Hennessy, Associate Professor and Director of Master's Education, Practitioner Track; Ph.D., Rochester. Access to mental health care, attachment theory, child maltreatment, child and adolescent psychopathology, child and adolescent assessment.

Rachel L. Grover, Assistant Professor; Ph.D., Maine. Development and quality of adolescent friendships and romantic relationships, defining social competence, social skills development and training in adolescence, assessment and treatment of childhood anxiety.

Deborah Haskins, Non-tenure Professor and Director of Undergraduate and Master's Field Education; Ph.D., Loyola (Baltimore). Spirituality and mental health; cross-cultural issues in supervision, therapy, and personality; trauma psychology; sexual abuse; women's issues; career/life transitions; drug abuse.

Christopher Higginson, Assistant Professor; Ph.D., Washington State. The degree to which cognitive measures are predictive of daily function; degenerative diseases in general, and the cognitive deficits associated with Parkinson's disease and its surgical treatment.

Matthew W. Kirkhart, Associate Professor; Ph.D., North Carolina at Greensboro. Medical/health psychology, psychological and medical barriers to adaptation, learning and cognition, adult psychopathology, functional analysis of language, interpersonal psychotherapy, psychological assessment, teaching of psychology.

Beth Kotchick, Assistant Professor; Ph.D., Georgia. Parenting and family processes, child and adolescent psychopathology, adolescent sexual and health behavior, cognitive-behavioral theory and therapy with children and adolescents.

Jeffery M. Lating, Professor, Associate Chair, and Director of Clinical Training; Ph.D., Georgia. Post-traumatic stress disorder, coronary-prone risk factors, behavioral medicine.

Charles T. LoPresto, Associate Professor; Ph.D., Howard. Homophobia, sexual orientation and sexual minority issues, adolescent treatment issues, cognitive-behavioral approaches to treatment, cross-cultural psychology, men's issues.

Jen L. Lowry, Associate Professor and Chair; Ph.D., Saint Louis. Factors influencing duration of psychotherapy, psychotherapy outcomes, ethics and professional issues, medical psychology, forensic psychology, managed care issues.

Heather Lyons, Assistant Professor; Ph.D., Maryland, College Park. Culture, discrimination, and person-organization fit in the workplace; social, cognitive, and cultural influences on career expectations; training issues in multicultural psychology.

Elizabeth E. MacDougall, Non-tenure Professor; Ph.D., Fairleigh Dickinson. Clinical geropsychology, geriatric neuropsychology/assessment of dementia syndromes, rehabilitation psychology, cognitive/intellectual assessment, psychometrics.

Alison Papadakis, Assistant Professor; Ph.D., Duke. The emergence of gender differences in depression during adolescence, gender roles, self-regulation, self-discrepancy, stress and coping, eating disorders.

Anthony S. Parente, Affiliate Professor; M.A., Loyola (Baltimore). Mental health and substance abuse treatment, stress management, group process, interpersonal relations, addiction recovery issues, adolescent development, employee assistance and workplace issues, the therapeutic relationship.

David V. Powers, Associate Professor; Ph.D., Washington (St. Louis). Gerontology, caregiving for dementia patients, death and dying issues, common factors in psychotherapy research, geriatric depression.

Martin F. Sherman, Professor and Director of Master's Education, Thesis Track; Ph.D., Maine. Disgust sensitivity, personality research (locus of control, silencing the self), survey and attitude research, gender role research, addictions, terror management theory.

Jeffrey D. Strain, Assistant Professor; Ph.D., Indiana State. Diverse expressions of gender and sexual identity, correctional psychology, community/ecological approaches to counseling.

Amanda McCombs Thomas, Professor and Associate Dean, College of Arts and Sciences; Ph.D., Georgia. Obsessive-compulsive spectrum disorders, trichotillomania, anxiety problems in children and adolescents.

Angelita M. Yu, Assistant Professor and Director of Doctoral Field Education; Ph.D., Utah. Psychotherapy, training, supervision.

MASSACHUSETTS SCHOOL OF PROFESSIONAL PSYCHOLOGY

Graduate Programs

Programs of Study

The Massachusetts School of Professional Psychology (MSPP) integrates rigorous academic instruction with extensive field education and close attention to professional development. MSPP assumes an ongoing social responsibility to create programs that educate specialists of many disciplines to meet the evolving mental health needs of society. The curriculum honors the best academic traditions of psychology and provides a thorough and comprehensive grounding in the knowledge base and in the breadth and depth of applications that define the discipline. At the same time, it is reflective of the latest trends in the field, is flexible and responsive to continuing developments in the profession, and prepares graduates for a strong position in the marketplace for psychological services. MSPP offers the following degree programs of study: Doctor in Clinical Psychology (Psy.D.), School Psychology (M.A./CAGS), Counseling Psychology (M.A.), Forensic Psychology (M.A.), Organizational Psychology (M.A.), and the Postdoctoral (M.S.) Program in Clinical Psychopharmacology. Certificate programs in Professional Executive Coaching and Respecialization in Clinical Psychology for Psychologists are also available.

Throughout the doctoral, school psychology, and counseling programs, course work is closely coordinated with field experiences, and together they provide for the academic and experiential base for understanding and treating human problems. In the doctoral program, beginning in the third year, students may continue the generalist training or select a predoctoral concentration track in forensic, health, or childhood, adolescence, and family studies. The counseling psychology program offers concentration tracks in community psychology, substance abuse, trauma, child and adolescent psychology, and spirituality.

The innovative and one-of-a-kind Latino Mental Health Program (LMHT) has been created to train students across programs in the cultural and linguistic aspects of serving Spanish-speaking populations. The Postdoctoral M.S. in Clinical Psychopharmacology Program trains psychologists, social workers, pharmacists, physician assistants, and nurse practitioners to work in collaboration with medical doctors who have patients requiring mental health medicine. This program affords an online option.

Research Facilities

The library at MSPP is an information service and referral center that maintains a core collection of books, periodicals, newsletters, and audiovisual materials. Also available are statistical data processing facilities, microcomputers, computerized bibliographic search facilities, and interlibrary loans. Supplementing services offered by the MSPP library is a formal affiliation agreement between MSPP and the Countway Medical Library at the Harvard Medical School and the Boston Library Consortium. The MSPP librarian also educates users about other large, accessible university libraries in the local area that have extensive resources reflective of the rich academic environment in the Boston area.

Financial Aid

The Financial Services Office at MSPP offers three types of student financial assistance: the Federal Stafford Student Loan program, alternative commercial loan programs, and institutional grants. Other sources of educational funding include a limited amount of paid field stipends, teaching assistantships, and campus employment. MSPP has been approved by the Department of Veterans Affairs for the purpose of training veterans and eligible persons.

Cost of Study

Tuition for the 2007–08 academic year was $811 per credit.

Living and Housing Costs

Students live off campus within the Boston metropolitan and suburban areas, as there is no on-campus housing available. The cost of attending MSPP (including tuition, books, housing, food, transportation, and personal expenses) for a ten-month period is estimated to be $46,700.

Student Group

MSPP seeks a diverse group of students who demonstrate academic and clinical aptitude, with personal qualities that would enable them to function creatively and effectively in working toward the amelioration of a variety of human problems. They range in age from the early twenties to the late fifties, from people holding master's degrees in psychology and related fields with years of professional experience to recent college graduates. They all share a very real commitment to the field of psychology through a practitioner-based model of education.

Student Outcomes

MSPP alumni are engaged in a variety of professional affiliations, such as outpatient clinics, community mental health centers, hospitals, private practice, schools, colleges, universities, and corporate environments. The most recent survey of alumni found that individual psychotherapy accounted for 42 percent of their work, followed by assessment, clinical supervision, family therapy, and administrative work.

Location

MSPP is conveniently located in the West Roxbury section of Boston, just minutes from the heart of downtown and from many field placement sites. Yet, it is only 4 miles from Route 128, the primary circumferential highway linking Boston's major routes, including the Massachusetts Turnpike. The building is located on an attractive site adjacent to the Charles River, with ample free parking and comfortable classrooms. Public transportation via the MBTA surface lines is available.

The School

In 1974, MSPP opened its doors as a nonprofit training institution in response to society's need for psychologists to be able to function in a variety of practitioner roles. The school received authority to grant the Doctor of Psychology (Psy.D.) degree in 1980 by the Board of Regents of Higher Education of the Commonwealth of Massachusetts. In 1984, MSPP was accredited by the New England Association of Schools and Colleges, with full accreditation by the American Psychological Association secured in 1991. As of 2006, more than 780 students have received the Psy.D. degree. MSPP also has an extensive offering of continuing education and professional development programs available and a selection of nonmatriculating courses for either academic or continuing education credit.

Applying

Applicants to the doctoral (Psy.D.) and master's programs in school psychology and counseling must have successfully earned a baccalaureate degree from an accredited institution of higher learning with basic course work in psychology. Prospective students are invited to view all program-specific application requirements, application forms, and instructions on the MSPP Web site. Applicants must submit official GRE (and/or TOEFL for those whose first language is not English) scores, three letters of recommendation, and a variety of writing samples by the set deadlines. Finalists are selected to interview with the Admissions Committee in February and March, depending on the program. Both the M.A. in Clinical Psychopharmacology and the Respecialization Programs are on a rolling admissions basis. The Professional Executive Coaching Program admits entering classes in January.

Correspondence and Information

Mario Murga, Director of Admissions
Massachusetts School of Professional Psychology
221 Rivermoor Street
Boston, Massachusetts 02132

Phone: 617-327-6777
888-664-MSPP (toll-free)
Fax: 617-327-4447
E-mail: admissions@mspp.edu
Web site: http://www.mspp.edu

Massachusetts School of Professional Psychology

THE FACULTY AND THEIR RESEARCH

Alan Dodge Beck, Ph.D., SUNY at Buffalo, 1976. Dr. Beck is a clinical psychologist whose interests include child and adolescent assessment and treatment, transitions to fathering, the role of parenting in life-cycle development, student training, and supervision and professional development. He is also the Dean of the Doctoral Program.

Hilary E. Bender, Ph.D., Pittsburgh, 1971; Th.D., Catholic University, 1969. Dr. Bender focuses on the scientifically documented, nonmaterial aspects of the human psyche, on consciousness in its various levels and dynamics, and on how this phenomenon affects psychological healing and growth. His latest interest is exploring the cross-cultural perspectives between Western medicine and Chinese medicine.

Stanley J. Berman, Ph.D., Temple, 1982. Dr. Berman is the Director of the Institute for Clinical Health Psychology, the Clinical Health Psychology Specialty Track, and the Master's Program in Clinical Psychopharmacology.

Jill Bloom, Ph.D., Boston College, 1981. Dr. Bloom is a member of the American Psychological Association, the Massachusetts Psychological Association, and the National Women's Studies Association. Her areas of interest are eating disorders; bereavement research; the study of women's psychological issues in terms of broad historical, political, and social contexts; and women treating women.

Terrie M. Burda, Psy.D., Massachusetts School of Professional Psychology, 1991. As a forensic psychologist, Dr. Burda is involved with the treatment and assessment of seriously mentally ill patients. She has also developed an assessment and treatment program for mentally ill patients with sex offending behaviors.

Haskel Cohen, Ph.D., Boston University, 1957. Dr. Cohen is known for his work as a codeveloper of the Tasks of Emotional Development (TED) Test and has written a book and manual about this test. It is a unique projective test using photographic representations of key developmental issues. Dr. Cohen has a special interest in testing and how this relates to the therapeutic process. He is currently a fellow of APA.

Linda Daniels, Psy.D., LIU, C.W. Post, 1995. Dr. Daniels is a specialist in traumatic stress and crisis response. She is the Associate Director of the Forensic Concentration Track.

Edward De Vos, Ed.D., Harvard, 1983. Dr. De Vos is a research psychologist with a long-standing commitment to violence issues, from both a research and social policy perspective. His approach to research and evaluation emphasizes responsive methodology, frequently combining both quantitative and qualitative methods.

Elena J. Eisman, Ed.D., Boston University, 1975. Dr. Eisman focuses on psychotherapy with adolescents, adults, couples, families, and groups; consultation; and training. She also has interest in women's issues, professional practice and policy issues, and professional advocacy.

Claire Fialkov, Ph.D., Boston University, 1985. Dr. Fialkov is devoted to individual and family therapy, providing collaborative consultations to schools, hospitals, and community agencies. Current academic interests include the development of the self of the therapist and its relation to clinical practice and the use of reflecting teams in supervision.

Kenneth J. Hopkins, Psy.D., Massachusetts School of Professional Psychology, 1982. Dr. Hopkins focuses on individual, couples, family, and group psychotherapy; psychological and educational testing; consultation to business, community agencies, and schools; supervision and consultation to community staff and Head Start; training seminars for teachers; and specialized foster parents programs.

Robert M. Jampel, Ph.D., Adelphi, 1973. Dr. Jampel is involved in individual and group therapy. His areas of interest are inpatient treatment, group psychotherapy, and psychological testing.

Robert Kinscherff, Ph.D., CUNY, 1988; J.D., Harvard, 1992. Dr. Kinscherff is currently the Director of the Forensic Specialization Track. He is a forensic psychologist and attorney whose research and professional practice areas include juvenile forensic mental health, juvenile and adult sexual offenders, serious delinquency and juvenile homicide, violence risk assessment and management, and severe forms of child maltreatment.

Jodie Kliman, Ph.D., Wright Institute, 1979. Dr. Kliman is a social-clinical psychologist and family therapist who teaches and directs at MSPP's practicum site. She focuses on the interplay of culture, class, race, and gender in family and therapeutic relationships; culturally respectful clinical practice; social constructionist approaches to therapy; multicultural families; social networks; and trauma.

Amaro J. Laria, Ph.D., Massachusetts Boston, 1997. Dr. Laria is a clinical psychologist with primary expertise in the areas of behavioral medicine, culture and mental health, and trauma and dissociation. He is founder and director of the Medical Consultation and Multicultural Competence Training Program, an MSPP internship housed at the Joseph M. Smith Community Health Center in Allston and Waltham.

Frances V. Mervyn, Ph.D., Boston College, 1978. Dr. Mervyn is a psychologist who is especially interested in the roles of the psychologist in the community. Dr. Mervyn's work has focused on the need for psychologists to extend themselves from the solely clinical role of treating already defined emotional disorders. In addition, she is concerned with health psychology issues over the life span.

Samuel J. Moncata, Psy.D., Hartford, 1990. Dr. Moncata's areas of interest are psychological assessment, diagnosis, and treatment of children, adolescents, and young adults. His specialty areas include learning style issues and differences, adolescent depression, trauma, educating troubled youth, pervasive developmental disorders, and Asperger's syndrome.

Brian D. Ott, Ph.D., Hofstra, 1980. Dr. Ott specializes in cognitive-behavioral therapies and health psychology. His primary area of clinical practice is the application of exposure and response prevention and cognitive restructuring to anxiety disorders. The majority of his practice is devoted to patients suffering from panic disorder and obsessive-compulsive disorder.

Ethan Pollack, Ph.D., Massachusetts, 1968. Dr. Pollack's professional interests include provision of clinical services to children, adolescents, couples, and families. In addition, he has specialty training in clinical work with stepfamilies. Dr. Pollack has a longstanding interest in ethics and has published articles in that area.

Sanford M. Portnoy, Ph.D., Massachusetts, 1970. Dr. Portnoy's interests are in assessment and treatment of individual adults, adolescents, families, and couples with specializations in couples therapy and divorce. He is a consultant on impasse resolution to divorcing individuals and consults to matrimonial attorneys on lawyer-client relationships during divorce.

Erlene Rosowsky, Psy.D., Massachusetts School of Professional Psychology, 1988. Dr. Rosowsky specializes in the assessment and treatment of emotional problems at middle age through later life. Specific interests are personality in older age, health and aging, and the older couple. She is the Director of MSPP's Center for Mental Health and Aging.

Wynn Schwartz, Ph.D., Colorado at Boulder, 1976. Dr. Schwartz is a clinical and experimental psychologist and research psychoanalyst. He has been primarily interested in clarifying fundamental aspects of the subject matters of psychotherapy, psychoanalysis, dreaming, and hypnosis. His published work has been both conceptual and experimental.

Marsha Vannicelli, Ph.D., Tufts, 1970. Dr. Vannicelli focuses on couples, group and individual therapy, women's issues, and substance abuse.

Shyamala Venkataraman, Ph.D., Clark, 1986. Dr. Venkataraman sees the parallels between the individual life cycle and the family cycle, both of which can punctuate developmental changes at crucial moments. In her clinical work, she sees developmental psychology and clinical psychology as intricately interwoven, thus looking for signs of both normality and pathology in her developmental assessments of individuals.

Laurel Wainwright, Ph.D., Boston University, 1988. Dr. Wainwright has been involved with the Autism and Language Disorders Nosology Project for several years. Currently, she is evaluating aspects of problem solving and social interaction in language-disordered and autistic children at ages 7 and 9.

Anne Waters, Psy.D., Massachusetts School of Professional Psychology, 1987. Dr. Waters is interested in comparative psychoanalytic theory and making psychoanalytic principles applicable to a diversity of patient populations and treatment settings. She is a qualified administrator of the Myers-Briggs Type Inventory (MBTI) and has done MBTI trainings in both business and human service settings.

Elana Weiner, Psy.D., Massachusetts School of Professional Psychology, 1995. Dr. Weiner has had extensive experience working with adult survivors of trauma and abuse. She has a special interest in psychoanalytic theory. Dr. Weiner is originally from South Africa, where she worked with children and families as a psychologist. Her major research interests are trauma, parent development, and psychoanalytic theory.

NAROPA UNIVERSITY

Graduate Programs

Programs of Study

Naropa University offers graduate degrees in the arts, education, environmental leadership, psychology, and religious studies. Inspired by its Buddhist educational heritage and its mission of contemplative education, Naropa offers students a highly individualized and transformative learning path that brings both academic rigor and a spiritual component to a student's educational life.

The Graduate School of Psychology consists of three departments and offers several distinct graduate programs at the cutting-edge of psychology. The Psychology: Contemplative Psychotherapy program (M.A.) combines the wisdom of Buddhism and Shambhala with Western humanistic psychotherapy. The Somatic Counseling Psychology program (M.A.) trains students in body-centered psychotherapy, offering concentrations in body psychotherapy and dance/movement therapy. The Transpersonal Psychology program (M.A.) is a low-residency degree that combines psychology and spirituality. The Transpersonal Psychology program (M.A.) with a concentration in ecopsychology integrates psychology and ecology in the study of human-nature relationships. The Transpersonal Counseling Psychology program (M.A.) brings together psychology and spirituality, with concentrations in art therapy, wilderness therapy, and counseling psychology. Naropa's Art Therapy program is approved by the American Art Therapy Association.

Naropa offers five graduate degree programs in the field of religious studies: Religious Studies (M.A.), Religious Studies with Sanskrit or Tibetan Language (M.A.), Indo-Tibetan Buddhism (M.A.), Indo-Tibetan Buddhism with Tibetan or Sanskrit Language (M.A.), and the Master of Divinity degree (M.Div.). Naropa's M.Div. degree program offers an in-depth theological study of the Buddhist tradition integrated with a thorough grounding in contemplative approaches to community work, spiritual care giving, and interfaith chaplaincy.

Employing an integrated, whole-systems perspective, the Environmental Leadership program (M.A.) offers a balance of theory, skills, and practical application infused with perspectives from ecopsychology and contemplative traditions. The Contemplative Education program (M.A.) offers a low-residency, professional-development degree program that combines the wisdom and skillful means of Eastern meditative traditions with Western holistic educational methods and insights.

Naropa offers four graduate degree programs in the arts. The Writing and Poetics program (M.F.A.) has a curriculum that balances writing workshops with literary studies requirements and offers concentrations in poetry and prose and translation as well as additional course work in letterpress printing and outreach. In cooperation with the London International School of Performing Arts, Naropa offers a Lecoq Based Actor Created Theater program (M.F.A.) that is based in London. The Contemporary Performance program (M.F.A.) is based in Boulder and brings together contemporary physical theater, Viewpoints theory and practice, and traditional contemplative practices. The low-residency Creative Writing program (M.F.A.) balances online writing workshops and literature seminars.

Research Facilities

The Allen Ginsberg Library contains approximately 30,000 volumes in areas that support Naropa's unique academic curriculum and is particularly strong in the fields of Buddhist studies, contemporary American poetry, and psychology. The library also subscribes to approximately seventy-five print periodicals and has access to more than 13,000 periodicals online through a variety of electronic databases. In addition, Naropa students have access to the Norlin Library at the University of Colorado, an institution with more than 2 million volumes.

Financial Aid

Naropa University makes every attempt to assist students who do not have the financial resources to accomplish their educational objectives. Naropa offers institutional grants and scholarships as well as all types of federal student aid. Some financial aid for international students is available. Approximately 70 percent of Naropa's degree-seeking students receive financial assistance in the form of loans, student employment, scholarships, assistantships, and grants.

Cost of Study

Graduate tuition for the 2007–08 academic year was $685 per semester credit. In addition, there is a registration fee of $250 per semester, and low-residency programs require a technology fee of $120 per 3-credit course.

Living and Housing Costs

The cost of living in Boulder, Colorado, is relatively high, and housing is competitive. Approximate rent begins at $575 for a one-bedroom apartment and $400 for one bedroom in a shared house. Off-campus living expenses for a single student are estimated to be $1300 to $1400 per month. Some students choose to live in less expensive towns surrounding Boulder.

Student Group

Naropa seeks resourceful students who have a strong appetite for learning and enjoy experiential education in a rigorous academic setting. The faculty and student body form a close-knit community, and this relationship is an integral part of the educational experience. Drawn from forty-eight states and twenty-four countries, Naropa students represent a wide range of life experiences, spiritual traditions, backgrounds, and ages (ranging from 18 to 65). Total enrollment at Naropa University in fall 2007 was 1,083 students: 627 graduates and 456 undergraduates.

Student Outcomes

Naropa University's graduate counseling programs prepare students to become private practitioners, to become therapists in mental-health agencies or social-service agencies, or to serve in a variety of other positions that provide direct service to individuals, clients, or groups. Students in the M.F.A. in Writing and Poetics and Creative Writing programs are trained in creative writing, publishing, editing, translation, and the teaching of writing workshops. Naropa's other graduate programs prepare students for leadership positions in the environmental arena, chaplaincy in hospice and other institutional settings, and doctoral work.

Location

Naropa University is located in Boulder, Colorado, a city of 100,000 nestled at the base of the majestic Rocky Mountains' foothills. Boulder is located 25 miles northwest of Denver and is home to many theater, dance, and music companies as well as the University of Colorado.

The University

Accredited by the Higher Learning Commission of the North Central Association of Colleges and Schools, Naropa University is a private, nonprofit, nonsectarian, liberal arts institution dedicated to advancing contemplative education. This approach to learning integrates the best of Eastern and Western educational traditions, helping students know themselves more deeply and engage constructively with others. Founded in 1974 by Tibetan meditation master and scholar Chögyam Trungpa Rinpoche, Naropa University grew out of an educational philosophy that dates back to Nalanda University, a major center of learning founded in India in the sixth century.

Applying

The suggested deadline for receiving completed applications is January 15 for the fall and summer semester and October 15 for the spring semester. Applications received after the suggested deadline are reviewed on a space-available basis. Most graduate programs require that students enter only in the fall; however, the Department of Writing and Poetics also accepts students in the spring and summer semesters. Programs that only accept students in the summer include the M.A. in Contemplative Education program, the M.F.A. in Creative Writing program, and the M.A. in Transpersonal Psychology program. Many departments require supplemental application materials and telephone or on-site interviews. GRE scores are not required.

Correspondence and Information

Office of Admissions
Naropa University
2130 Arapahoe Avenue
Boulder, Colorado 80302-6697

Phone: 303-546-3572
800-772-6951 (toll-free)
Fax: 303-546-3583
E-mail: admissions@naropa.edu
Web site: http://www.naropa.edu

Naropa University

CORE FACULTY AND THEIR RESEARCH

Contemplative Education

Richard C. Brown, Department Chair; M.A., Naropa. Contemplative educational practices and competencies, contemplative observation, emotional awareness in teachers, Nalanda University curriculum.

Lee Worley, Co-Chair, Contemplative Education; M.A., Naropa. Basic acting and theater studies and application to education, presence of teaching, space, Buddhist approaches to mind/body. Author of *Coming from Nothing: The Sacred Art of Acting* (Turquoise Dragon Press, 2001).

Deborah Young, Co-Chair, Early Childhood Education; Ph.Ed. candidate, Colorado. Peace studies in education, poverty, multiculturalism.

Contemplative Psychotherapy

Lauren Casalino, Department Chair; M.A., Naropa. Private practice working with adults, specializing in life-changing transitions, the process of aging, grief work, and fertility and adoption issues. Co-founder of Windhorse Family and Elder Services, specializing in intensive home-based team treatment. International workshop leader: "Buddhism and Healing."

MacAndrew Jack, Ph.D., Temple. Private practice with individuals and couples integrating psychodynamic, cognitive behavioral, and mind/body orientations. Research has explored psychophysiological processes involved in panic, breathing, and the parasympathetic nervous system as well as personal and interpersonal effects of meditation and contemplative training.

Sherri L. Kimbell, M.A., Naropa. Senior clinician and clinical supervisor, Windhorse Community Services, Inc. Private contemplative psychotherapy practice specializing in diversity, social justice, and community engagement dynamics. Meditation practitioner in the Theravadin Vipassana and Tibetan Shambhala Buddhist traditions.

Karen Kissel Wegela, Ph.D., Union (Ohio). Licensed psychologist with experience working with a variety of populations. Author of *How to Be a Help Instead of a Nuisance* as well as several articles and chapters in the field of Buddhist psychology. Presented contemplative psychotherapy in Europe, Australia, Canada, Mexico, and Chile. Former director, Contemplative Psychotherapy.

Contemporary Performance

Wendell Beavers, Department Chair; B.A., Boston University. Founding faculty member and early director of NYU's Experimental Theater Wing (1979–2003). Named master teacher at Tisch School of the Arts (1996). Noted choreographer, teacher, and developer of The Viewpoints. Co-founder and early director of Movement Research, Inc.

Barbara Dilley, B.A., Mount Holyoke. Toured internationally with Merce Cunningham Dance Company (1963–68). Participated in Judson Dance Theater and, in 1970, became part of the dance/theater collaboration Grand Union. Choreographed and performed solo and group works internationally. Contemplative dance art.

Ethelyn Friend, M.F.A., Brandeis. Actor/singer, writer, solo performance artist and teacher. Acted in professional theaters in San Francisco, Boston, and Denver/Boulder, including Merrimack Repertory Theatre and New Repertory Theatre. Extensive work with Roy Hart Theatre of France. Private voice workshops. Artistic director of Colorado Shakespeare Festival's Education Outreach Program.

Environmental Leadership

Suzanne Benally, M.A., Colorado. Associate Vice President for Academic Affairs and Senior Diversity Officer. Extensive experience in higher education policy, assessment, and diversity. Research focuses on American Indian relationship between land and place as expressed through written and oral literature. Tribal affiliation is Navajo and Santa Clara Tewa.

Jeanine Canty, Ph.D., California Institute of Integral Studies. Cultural and ecological awareness, ecopsychology, transformative learning, social and environmental justice, consciousness studies and ecological healing.

Sherry Ellms, M.A., Naropa. Buddhism, meditation, wilderness rights of passage, ecopsychology.

Anne Parker, Ph.D., Oregon. Geography, Inner Asian studies, environmental studies, pilgrimage and sacred landscape. Fulbright Scholar and National Science Foundation grant recipient for study of indigenous agriculture in Nepal, Bhutan, and India. Australian Institute for Aboriginal Studies grant recipient for ethnobotanical study of traditional Aboriginal plant use.

Lecoq Based Actor Created Theater

Amy Russell, Department Chair; M.F.A., Tennessee. Graduate of Ecole Jacques Lecoq. Certified by the late Jacques Lecoq as a teacher of his pedagogy. Wrote five professionally produced original plays. Trained in Balinese topeng with I Made Djimat and mask creation with Donato Sartori.

Religious Studies

Thomas B. Coburn, Naropa University President; Ph.D., Harvard. Renowned scholar and academician in the field of religious studies. Widely published author, specializing in South and East Asia and Islamic world. Visiting scholar for a year at Harvard Divinity School. Author of *Devi-Mahatmya: The Crystallization of the Goddess Tradition* (Motilal Banarsdass and South Asian Books, 1984) and *Encountering the Goddess* (State University of New York Press, 1991). One of the world's leading experts on Hindu tradition of the great goddess.

Roger Dorris, Ph.D., Union (Ohio). Engaged Buddhist studies, with a focus on community building and large group transformation. Ordained as a Buddhist minister. Works with marginalized populations, including homeless and incarcerated.

Acharya Tenpa Gyaltsen, Khenpo degree from Karma Shri Nalanda Institute (Sikkim). Senior director and senior teacher of Nitartha Institute. Former resident teacher of Thegsum Tashi Chöling in Hamburg, Germany.

Sarah Harding, B.A., Naropa. Lama in the Shangpa Kagyu tradition of Tibetan Buddhism; teacher and oral interpreter; translator with the Tsadra Foundation. Books include *Creation and Completion* and *Machik's Complete Explanation*.

Victoria Howard, Ph.D., Union (Ohio). Buddhist minister in Shambhala tradition. Co-founder and co-director, Dana Home Care, national nonprofit organization providing in-home care for seniors. Consultant, elder-care agencies and facilities in Denver-metro area.

Reginald A. Ray, Ph.D., Chicago. Indian Mahasiddhas (Tantric Buddhist saints) and practices traditions of Tibetan Buddhism. Recipient of Fulbright-Hays Fellowship and two N.E.H. Senior Research Fellowships. Member of Nalanda Translation Committee. Author of *Buddhist Saints in India, Indestructible Truth*, and *Secret of the Vajra World*.

Judith Simmer-Brown, Ph.D., Walden; Ph.D. candidate, Columbia. Acharya in the Shambhala Buddhist tradition; Director of Ngedon School of Higher Learning. Trained in South Asian Religious Studies and Sanskrit. Steering committee, Buddhist Critical-Constructive Reflection Group of American Academy of Religion. Tibetan Buddhism, women and Buddhism, Buddhist-Christian dialogue, American Buddhism. Author of *Dakini's Warm Breath: The Feminine Principle in Tibetan Buddhism* (Shambhala, 2001) and *Benedict's Dharma: Buddhists Comment on the Rule of St. Benedict* Riverhead, 2001 (with Brother David Steindl-Rast et al.).

D. Philip Stanley, Department Co-Chair; Ph.D. candidate, Virginia. Recipient of Fulbright-Hays Fellowship for doctoral research analyzing Tibetan Buddhist canon and of a National Endowment for the Humanities grant to place his Tibetan canon catalog database online in conjunction with the Tibetan and Himalayan Digital Library, the Library of Congress, and the British Library. Board member of the International Association of Buddhist Universities. Co-director of Nitartha Institute. Member of Nalanda Translation Committee.

Somatic Counseling Psychology

Zoë Avstreih, Department Co-Chair; M.S., CUNY, Hunter. Founder/Director, Center for the Study of Authentic Movement. International lecturer and teacher, published widely.

Christine Caldwell, Ph.D., Union (Ohio). Dance therapy, Aston Patterning and Gestalt, body-centered Healing Cycle. Her work emphasizes the pre- and perinatal time, the transformational effect of movement processes, and the opportunities in addiction.

J. Ryan Kennedy, Department Co-Chair; Psy.D., Capella. Private psychotherapy practice. Chronic and persistent mental illness, trauma and dissociative disorders, addiction and recovery, domestic/family violence.

Transpersonal Counseling Psychology

Dale Asrael, B.S., Northwestern. Teacher certification. Acharya in the Shambhala Buddhist lineage and Buddhist minister. Leads meditation retreats internationally and trains meditation instructors. Contemplative education.

Deborah Bowman, Ph.D., Union (Ohio). Co-founder, M.A. TCP program. Initiated and developed Wilderness Therapy program. Faculty member and Interim President of Boulder Graduate School. A licensed psychologist, certified Gestalt therapist in private practice. Instructor with the National Outdoor Leadership School and former river guide. Dream-painting process: combining art therapy, Jungian, transpersonal, and Gestalt therapy.

Barbara Catbagan, M.Ed., Colorado State. Director, Counseling Psychology; Coordinator of multicultural courses. Certified mediator and consultant with businesses, organizations, and educational institutions to facilitate growth of dynamic working teams. Diversity, social justice, issues of human and civil rights.

David Chernikoff, M.S.W., Denver; M.Div., Graduate Theological Union. Meditation teacher, psychotherapist, and life and business coach. Founder of Boulder College of Massage Therapy. Guiding teacher of Insight Meditation Community of Colorado. Private practice.

John Davis, Ph.D., Colorado. Director, M.A. in Transpersonal Psychology program; Teacher of transpersonal psychology, ecopsychology, and wilderness therapy. Ordained teacher of the Diamond Approach of A. H. Almaas and faculty member in the School of Lost Borders, a training facility for guides of wilderness rites of passage.

Michael Franklin, M.A., George Washington. Director, Art Therapy program. Teacher and lecturer of art therapy in various academic and clinical settings. Research focus is on the relationship between art therapy, yoga philosophy, and meditation.

Duey Freeman, M.A., Northern Colorado. Director and founder, Gestalt Institute of the Rockies and Equine Journeys. Psychotherapist, professor, consultant, and clinical supervisor. Coordinator, Gestalt and Family and Child programs. Gestalt therapy, family therapy, bioenergetics and therapy with children; fostering equine assistance in work with children, adults, and families.

Deborah Piranian, Ph.D., Washington (Seattle). Director, Wilderness Therapy. Private psychotherapy practice and counselor in a variety of settings. Consultant with for-profit and nonprofit organizations. Outward Bound senior course director, specializing in wilderness therapy and multinational mountaineering programs.

Laurie Rugenstein, M.M.T., SMU. Founder and former director, Music Therapy. Developed and implemented a music therapy program for HospiceCare of Boulder and Broomfield Counties. Private practice in music therapy. Primary trainer in Bonny Method of Guided Imagery and Music. Use of expressive arts to access human potential and create viable social structures.

Sue Wallingford, M.A., Naropa. Experience includes work in various psychiatric facilities, a prison, a home for abused children, nursing homes, and hospice. Private practice, offering consulting, supervision, counseling, and art-therapy services. Use of art therapy with various populations.

Writing and Poetics

Keith Abbott, M.A., Western Washington. Fiction, poetry, nonfiction, screenwriting. Author of a Richard Brautigan memoir, *Downstream From Trout Fishing in America* (Capra, 1989). His fourth novel, *Racer* (DTV, 2006), was short-listed for a 2007 Berlinale award. Abbott co-wrote the screenplay for "Spanish Castle" from *The First Thing Coming* (Coffee House, 1987), optioned by Ziji Productions (2005). Articles on Brautigan, Kerouac, Snyder, Whalen, and Raymond Carver appeared in 2007.

Junior Burke, Department Chair and Director, M.F.A. in Creative Writing; M.F.A., Naropa. Fiction, screenplay writing, literary studies. Prose writer, dramatist, and lyricist. His song cycle, *Someone Else's Dream*, was performed at Boulder Museum of Contemporary Art (2004). Author of *Something Gorgeous* (Farfalla/McMillan & Parrish, 2005) and a CD of original songs, *While You Were Gone* (Red Thread Records, 2007).

Reed Bye, Ph.D., Colorado. Poetry, contemplative poetics, contemporary and classic literature, prosody, Shakespeare, William Blake. Songwriter and poet. Author of new and selected poems, *Join the Planets*, (United Artists Books, 2005). CD of original songs, *Long Way Around*, (Farfalla/ McMillan & Parrish, 2005).

Indira Ganesan, M.F.A., Iowa. Fiction, memoir, essay writing. Author of *The Journey* and *Inheritance*, both published by Alfred A. Knopf. Two-time fellow at the Fine Arts Work Center in Provincetown. Fellowships from Radcliffe College, the MacDowell Colony, and the Paden Institute.

Bobbie Louise Hawkins, Associate Professor. Fiction, literary studies, performance monologues. Recipient of NEA Fellowship in Fiction. Author of more than ten books of fiction, performance monologues, and poetry; most recently, *Bijou* (Farfalla/ McMillan & Parrish, 2005). Work performed in New York, England, Holland, and Germany.

Anselm Hollo, Professor. Poetry, translation, literary studies. Recipient of the NEA Fellowship in Poetry, grants from the Fund for Poetry, and Finland's Distinguished Foreign Translator's Award. Author of thirty books of poetry; most recently, *Notes on the Possibilities and Attractions of Existence: Selected Poems 1965–2000* (Coffee House, 2001) and *Guests of Space* (Coffee House, 2007). Translations include the work of Paul Klee, Bertolt Brecht, and Jean Genet.

Bhanu Kapil, M.A., SUNY at Brockport. Author of three full-length collections: *The Vertical Interrogation of Strangers* (Kelsey Street Press, 2001), *Incubation: a space for monsters* (Leon Works), and *Humanimal: a project for future children* (forthcoming from Kelsey Street Press). She is currently researching cross-cultural approaches to treating schizophrenia in the Indian and Pakistani populations of northwest London. Her project, a cross-genre work, "Schizophrene," is also a tracing of transgenerational trauma from the time of Partition in 1947 in India to the present time.

Andrew Schelling, B.A., California, Santa Cruz. Poetry, translation, ecopoetics, Sanskrit, literary studies. Recipient of the Academy of American Poets translation award and two Witter Bynner Foundation for Poetry grants. Author of a dozen books, including *Two Elk: A High Country Notebook* (Bootstrap Productions, 2005) and *The Wisdom Anthology of North American Buddhist Poetry* (Wisdom, 2005).

Steven Taylor, Ph.D., Brown. Musician and writer. Collaborations on concert works, performances, recordings, and theater works with artists such as Allen Ginsberg, Anne Waldman, and the seminal poetry rock group The Fugs. Author of *Loveland* (Bootstrap Press, 2001) and *False Prophet: Fieldnotes from the Punk Underground* (Wesleyan University Press, 2003), recordings and compositions for theater and concert stage. Critical theory, poetry, and music.

Anne Waldman, B.A., Bennington. Distinguished Professor of Poetics and Chair of Naropa's Summer Writing Program. Co-founder of Jack Kerouac School of Disembodied Poetics. Poetry, experimental writing, performance poetics. Recipient of NEA award and the Shelley prize for poetry. Author and editor of more than forty books of poetry, including *Structure of the World Compared to a Bubble* (Penguin, 2004).

NORTHWESTERN UNIVERSITY

Master's Program in Counseling Psychology

Program of Study

The Master's Program in Counseling Psychology is a counselor training program designed to prepare professional counselors to intervene in relation to both individual and social system functioning within family, work, academic, and community settings. The program, jointly administered by the Graduate School at Northwestern University and The Family Institute, is strongly committed to ensuring that every student achieves the highest standards of excellence as a clinically skilled and theoretically sophisticated practitioner. The program leads to a terminal master's degree with specializations in general psychological counseling (individual, group, and family), career counseling, human services in the corporate sector, or child assessment and intervention. Students are prepared for clinical positions in mental health, special service, educational, and industrial settings including, but not limited to, hospitals, community mental health centers, specialized social service agencies, college/university counseling services, employee assistance programs, government agencies, and business consulting firms. Graduates are also competitive for high-quality counseling or clinical psychology Ph.D. or Psy.D. programs.

Intensive supervised clinical training and the rigorous and ongoing integration of theoretical knowledge and applied practice are hallmarks of the program. The program continually screens and evaluates clinical training settings throughout the greater Chicago area and selects settings of the highest quality for students' clinical placements. In addition, the selection of courses and training settings is customized to meet each student's needs and interests to the fullest extent possible within the parameters of the basic requirements.

The faculty members represent diverse backgrounds and scholarly interests, and all are strongly committed to a life-course developmental perspective and to a personality and social systems approach to the study of human behavior, psychopathology, and the adaptational aspects of individuals, groups, families, and organizational systems. Beyond the program curriculum, students can also take courses in the Clinical Psychology Program at the Medical School, the Kellogg School of Management, and other Northwestern University departments.

Twenty-five students typically enter the program each year, including some with undergraduate majors in psychology and others from an array of different academic and professional backgrounds. Prior course work in psychology and human development is desirable but not required. One basic course in personality and one in abnormal psychology are required for matriculation, but not admission. Students may enroll on a full-time basis (register for three courses every quarter) and complete the program in two years or on a part-time basis (register for fewer than three courses each quarter) and complete the degree in three to five years. Mid-year matriculation is possible, although fall quarter matriculation is encouraged. Students are not expected to register for courses during summer quarter but may do so when suitable courses are offered.

A special alternative curriculum called Two-Plus is available for qualified students with a minimal psychology background, and the program welcomes applicants who are shifting to counseling from other fields. Both the standard curriculum and the Two-Plus curriculum satisfy the requirements for licensure as a clinical professional counselor in Illinois and efforts are made to tailor curricula to satisfy counselor licensure requirements in other states.

Research Facilities

Research libraries contain approximately 3.9 million volumes, 3.4 million microfilm units, and 40,000 serial publications. Research and teaching activities are supported by a state-of-the-art multimedia computing network with full Internet access. The program is housed in and has a formal affiliation with the Family Institute, an institution that provides extensive Chicago-area clinical services, training, and research. Master's students may also become involved in research programs sponsored by the Center for Urban School Research, the Department of Psychiatry and Behavioral Sciences, the Center for Talent Development, and the Center for the Study of Lives, as well as individual faculty research projects.

Financial Aid

Information on student loans is available from the Graduate School. A limited number of teaching assistantships with program faculty members are available to master's students. Special opportunities for research assistantships and other employment also exist within the Center's and the University's many research programs.

Cost of Study

Tuition for full-time study for the 2008–09 academic year (at least three courses per quarter) is $12,252 per quarter.

Living and Housing Costs

The University operates two graduate student residences in Evanston. Information and assistance in securing off-campus housing is also available.

Student Group

There are currently 65 students in the program. Approximately 25 students are typically admitted to the program each year, including some with undergraduate majors in psychology and others from an array of different academic, professional, and work backgrounds.

Location

Northwestern University's Evanston campus is located on Lake Michigan, 12 miles north of the city of Chicago. The beautiful lakefront campus offers a rich cultural environment through a wealth of theatrical, musical, and athletic events. The extensive cultural resources of Chicago are readily accessible via public transportation.

The University

Established in 1851, Northwestern University is recognized as one of the most distinguished private universities in the United States.

Applying

Applications for admission are reviewed and acted upon as they are received, beginning in October for the following fall quarter. Applications may only be submitted online.

Correspondence and Information

Marina Elyash, M.A. Education Programs Coordinator
Master's Program in Counseling Psychology
Center for Applied Psychological and Family Studies
Northwestern University
618 Library Place
Evanston, Illinois 60201-4103
Phone: 847-733-4300 Ext. 205
Fax: 847-773-0390
E-mail: counseling-psychology@northwestern.edu
Web site: http://www.tgs.northwestern.edu/

Northwestern University

THE FACULTY AND THEIR RESEARCH

Amy Anson, Ph.D., Northwestern. Child/adolescent therapy, counselor education and training.
Jayne M. Bazos, Psy.D., Illinois School of Professional Psychology. Marital and family therapy.
Lenore S. Blum, Program Director; Ph.D., Northwestern. Health psychology; stress and coping; clinical education, training and supervision.
Ava Carn-Watkins, Assistant Program Director; Ph.D., Northwestern. Gifted adolescents, psychosocial development, counselor education.
Don Catherall, Ph.D., Northwestern. Trauma.
Joseph Cullen, Psy.D., Mansfield. Counseling theory.
Solomon Cytrynbaum, Ph.D., Michigan. Psychodynamic theory and psychopathology, group and organization dynamics, gender and group relations, adult development, evaluation of school reform.
James Dod, Ph.D., Illinois at Chicago. Cognitive-behavioral therapy.
John Dunkle, Ph.D., SUNY at Albany. Professional ethics.
Linda Edelstein, Ph.D., Northwestern. Psychology of adult development, female development.
Jordan Jacobowitz, Ph.D., Hebrew (Jerusalem). Psychodiagnostics, personality assessment, personality and aging.
Jelani Mandara, Ph.D., California, Riverside. Research methodology, statistics, adolescent and family studies.
Donald McDevitt, M.A., George Williams. Psychodynamic psychotherapy.
Derek McNeil, Ph.D., Northwestern. Cultural diversity.
Martin Parker, Psy.D., Adler School of Professional Psychology. Substance abuse assessment and management.
Richard Rotberg, M.A., Roosevelt. Career counseling and job placement.
Vicki Seglin, Ph.D., Northwestern. Women's roles and personal authority, mentoring and training.
Patricia Shafer, Ph.D., Northwestern. Child development.

NOVA SOUTHEASTERN UNIVERSITY

Center for Psychological Studies
Doctoral Programs in Clinical Psychology

Program of Study

The Doctor of Philosophy (Ph.D.) in Clinical Psychology program at Nova Southeastern University (NSU) is based on a model of the scientist-practitioner in support of the proposition that the clinical psychologist will contribute most to society when educated for the roles of both scientist and practitioner. The focus of the program is on the development of sophistication in applied clinical research. Much of the research conducted within the program involves the development and rigorous investigation of innovative assessment and intervention for clinical problems. From this base, the student proceeds through research training that culminates in a dissertation.

The Doctor of Psychology (Psy.D.) in Clinical Psychology program at NSU is based on a model of the practitioner informed by science. Traditionally, the training model for clinical psychologists has focused on the graduate student as scientist first and practitioner second. However, with the growing need in society for practitioners, many graduate students have elected to enter the clinical services arena rather than the academic or research arena. The primary goal of the Psy.D. program is to offer academic, practicum, internship, and research experiences directly relevant to the practice of clinical psychology. The training retains the important scientific base upon which professional competence and knowledge rest, has students participate in ongoing research, and prepares them to be lifelong consumers of research. Clinical expertise is molded by a sequence of courses on assessment and intervention, both theory and technique, supplemented by practicum experiences with clients in a variety of settings under intensive supervision.

The program curriculum is anchored in the cumulative body of psychological knowledge and provides a firm basis in statistics, research design, and experimental research methodology. Through these experiences and a sequence of formal courses and graded exposure to clinical populations in supervised practicums, the program imparts the knowledge and skills required for the student to assume the role of academician, researcher, or practicing clinical psychologist. The required clinical training includes clinical practicums, the clinical competency exam, and a 2,000-hour predoctoral internship at a site where the student has applied and been accepted.

Beyond the required courses and experiences of the program, individual interests in psychology are accommodated through elective course offerings. Students have the option of seeking admission to a concentration, in which a series of electives are taken in a single specialty area. Each concentration accepts a limited number of students at admission or during the first or second year of study; therefore, a student is not guaranteed a slot in a particular concentration. Each concentration consists of a set of electives, a practicum in an approved clinical program related to the concentration, and research activities with faculty in the concentration. Areas of concentration in this program are clinical forensic psychology, clinical health psychology, clinical neuropsychology, psychodynamic psychology, and psychology of long-term mental illness. In addition to the concentrations, students may select a track in child, adolescent, and family psychology or in multicultural diversity through a number of elective courses. Students are also able to gain admission to a joint clinical psychology (Ph.D. or Psy.D.) and Master of Business Administration (M.B.A.) program simultaneously by fulfilling the clinical psychology admissions process and indicating the interest to be admitted to the joint psychology and M.B.A. program during their first year.

Ph.D. students must complete a minimum of 119 credits, successfully pass the Clinical Competency Examination, and complete a one-year internship to be eligible for the degree. The students are expected to be actively involved in research throughout their graduate training. First they complete a series of four research practicums, which provide the opportunity to sample research under different faculty members or continue under one. Then they plan and conduct research under faculty mentorship: the Major Paper. The culmination is a dissertation of publishable quality, defended before a faculty committee as a contribution to the field.

Psy.D. students must complete a minimum of 118 credits, successfully pass the Clinical Competency Examination, and complete a one-year internship to be eligible for the degree. Students in the program complete Directed Study: Research, which provides an opportunity to participate in faculty research or pursue their own interests.

Research Facilities

In addition to training persons to provide care and treatment for those with psychological problems, the Center is equally committed to applied research. Areas of research in which the Center is currently engaged can be found in the section listing the faculty members and their research interests. The Center is uniquely organized so that one faculty, full-time and adjunct, services all programs. Access to all of the specialty interests and clinical skills of the full-time faculty members is available to all students in the school.

Research in the Center is supported by extensive computer facilities, including mainframe, workstation, and microcomputer environments. Methodological, statistical, and computing consultation is available to faculty members and students engaged in research or related course work. In addition, all students, regardless of location, have access to hundreds of databases and online resources through the University's electronic library.

Financial Aid

Nova Southeastern University's Office of Student Financial Services and Registration administers comprehensive federal, state, institutional, and private financial aid, which includes grants, loans, and student employment. The purpose of these programs is to provide monetary assistance to qualified students to meet their educational objectives. In addition, professional financial aid counselors can help students plan the most efficient use of financial resources for their education. Students do not have to be admitted to apply for financial aid; however, they must be registered in order for financial aid funds to be distributed.

Cost of Study

In 2008–09, tuition is $815 per credit hour, and there are miscellaneous fees. There is a seat deposit of $1000 (nonrefundable), payable after acceptance and credited toward first semester's tuition.

Living and Housing Costs

The University offers graduate on-campus housing in Fort Lauderdale. Graduate apartments and rooms in shared apartments are available. Costs range from $7344 to $13,300 per academic year. For more information, students should contact the Office of Residential Life and Housing at 954-262-7052 or visit http://www.nova.edu/reslife.

Student Group

The traditional format program enjoys a diverse student population, with participants from across the United States as well as from many other countries.

Location

The main campus is located in a parklike setting consisting of royal palm trees, a lake, and large expanses of open lawn space. The surrounding community is suburban. The campus is within 10 miles of Fort Lauderdale, and Miami is 25 miles to the south. There are two international airports within 25 miles of the campus.

The University and The Center

Nova Southeastern University is Florida's largest independent university. NSU is known throughout Florida and the United States as a university dedicated to educational excellence, technology, and community service. The Center for Psychological Studies is dedicated to providing the highest-quality education to its students, superior mental-health-care services to the community, and research contributions to mental health sciences. The Center has become a national leader in providing education and cutting-edge services to the public.

Applying

The application deadline is January 8. Scores on the General Test of the GRE are required. A combined score of at least 1000 is preferred. The GRE Subject Test in psychology is recommended but not required. Three semester hours in statistics are required. Applicants must have a bachelor's degree in psychology from a regionally accredited institution and a minimum 3.0 GPA on a 4.0 scale or 3.5 graduate-level GPA based on a 4.0 scale. An interview is required. There is a $50 nonrefundable application fee.

Correspondence and Information

Carlos Perez
Enrollment Processing Services (EPS)
Attention: Center for Psychological Studies
Nova Southeastern University
P.O. Box 299000
Fort Lauderdale, Florida 33329-9905

Phone: 954-262-5790
800-541-6682 Ext. 25790 (toll-free)
Fax: 954-262-3893
E-mail: cpsinfo@nova.edu
Web site: http://www.cps.nova.edu

Nova Southeastern University

THE FULL-TIME FACULTY AND THEIR RESEARCH

Nathan H. Azrin, Ph.D., Harvard; ABPP; Professor. Conduct disorder, oppositional defiant disorder (ODD), youth, drug addiction, behavior therapy, depression, marital and couple counseling, muscular tics, self-injurious behavior, vocational counseling and placement, alcoholism, retardation, rehabilitation of the brain injured, insomnia.

Stephen N. Campbell, Ph.D., Howard; Associate Professor. General clinical/community psychology, psychology of social change, dual diagnosed, program design and consultation, conduct disorder.

Ralph E. (Gene) Cash, Ph.D., NYU; NCSP; Associate Professor. School psychology; psychoeducational assessment, diagnosis, and treatment; depression; anxiety disorders; suicide prevention; individual, marital, and group psychotherapy; forensics, including child custody, wrongful death effects, and disability; stress management; psychology and public policy.

Christian DeLucia, Ph.D., Arizona State; Assistant Professor. Emergence of problem behaviors during adolescence, with a particular emphasis on adolescent substance use and abuse; statistical methods for the analysis of longitudinal data; methodological issues relevant for the design and analysis of psychosocial interventions.

Frank A. DePiano, Ph.D., South Carolina; Vice President for Academic Affairs, University-Wide Faculty Appointments. Hypnosis, community psychology, health and medicine, development of models for professional training of psychologists.

William Dorfman, Ph.D., Ohio State; ABPP; Professor. Community mental health, short-term approaches to psychotherapy, eclectic approaches to individual and marital psychotherapy, psychodiagnosis, objective personality measurement with the MMPI-2 and MMPI-A, role of families and primary caretakers in the treatment and rehabilitation of the chronically and severely mentally ill.

Jan Faust, Ph.D., Georgia; Professor. Child-clinical and pediatric psychology: child abuse (sexual and physical) and neglect, child treatment outcome research, PTSD in children and adolescents, child adjustment to acute and chronic medical conditions, life span psychosis.

Ana Imia Fins, Ph.D., Miami (Florida); Associate Professor. Health psychology, sleep medicine, insomnia, chronic fatigue syndrome, post-traumatic stress disorder, periodic limb movement disorder.

Diana Formoso, Ph.D., Arizona State; Assistant Professor. Risk and protective factors that shape youth development within low-income, ethnic minority families; family conflict, parenting, and child outcome and how they are impacted by families' ecological and cultural contexts (e.g., economic hardship, neighborhood risk, immigration, and acculturation); intervention development for ethnic minority children and families experiencing adversity; the family lives and school experiences of immigrant youth.

Steven N. Gold, Ph.D., Michigan State; Professor. Adult survivors of childhood sexual abuse; dissociative disorders; post-traumatic stress disorder; doctoral-level clinical training; hypnotherapy; psychological assessment; interpersonal, family, and systems theory and intervention; psychotherapy case conceptualization and treatment planning; psychological defenses; personality theory.

Charles Golden, Ph.D., Hawaii; ABPP/ABCN/ABAP; Professor. Neuropsychology of head injury, stroke, and multiple sclerosis; neuropsychological and personality assessment, rehabilitation, and community reintegration following brain injury; neuropsychology in childhood and in school settings; learning disabilities; hyperactivity; general assessment.

Alan D. Katell, Ph.D., West Virginia; Professor. Assessment and treatment of eating disorders, psychological factors in cardiac rehabilitation, exercise promotion and maintenance, health psychology, coping with chronic illnesses and other physical challenges.

Jeffrey L. Kibler, Ph.D., Miami (Florida); Associate Professor. Cognitive-behavior regulation of emotion/mood disorders; behavioral medicine; biobehavioral aspects of post-traumatic stress, psychosocial stress, and pain; psychosocial risks for illness (e.g., heart disease); health risk reduction; psychophysiology; minority health; predictors of biobehavioral research participation for individuals of racial minorities.

Stacey Lambert, Psy.D., Nova Southeastern; Associate Professor. Community mental health, schizophrenia, the impact of social factors on serious mental illness, recovery, empowerment, psychosocial rehabilitation for people with serious psychiatric disabilities, behavior therapy.

Robert C. Lane, Ph.D., NYU; ABPP; Clinical Professor. Psychopathology, diagnosis, difficult patients, psychoanalysis, psychotherapy, supervision.

John E. Lewis, Ph.D., Syracuse; Professor. Intercultural psychotherapy and assessment, counseling and psychotherapy with prison populations, educational and vocational assessment and counseling, school psychology, international perspectives.

Craig D. Marker, Ph.D., Chicago Medical School; Assistant Professor. Anxiety disorders, with a particular emphasis on obsessive-compulsive disorder, panic disorder, and social anxiety; longitudinal data analysis, with an emphasis on intra-individual variability and change methods.

Wiley Mittenberg, Ph.D., University of Health Sciences (Chicago); ABPP/ABCN; Professor. Neuropsychology of head injury in adults and children, malingering, forensic neuropsychology, neuropsychology of cortical and subcortical dementias, professional issues in clinical neuropsychology.

Timothy R. Moragne, Psy.D., Wright State; Professor. Minority issues, health psychology, community psychology, human sexuality, psychological aspects of AIDS, AIDS and minorities.

Barry Nierenberg, Ph.D., Tennessee; ABPP; Associate Professor. Rehabilitation and health psychology: psychological factors in chronic illness, biopsychosocial aspects of wellness and disease, health-care disparities, pediatric psychology, and child and family adaptations to acute and chronic medical conditions; the business of psychology and professional credentialing.

Helen Orvaschel, Ph.D., New School; Professor. Mood disorders, genetic contributions to psychopathology, risk factors for child psychiatric disorders, psychiatric epidemiology, differential diagnostic assessment of child and adolescent psychopathology.

Scott Poland, Ed.D., Ball State; Associate Professor. Crisis intervention, youth violence, suicide, clinical interventions, administration and delivery of school psychological services.

Bady Quintar, Ph.D., Kentucky; ABPP; Professor. Projective techniques, psychoanalytic psychotherapy, ego psychology, postdoctoral training.

Shannon Ray, Ph.D., Central Florida; Assistant Professor. Community mental health, chronic pain, eating disorders, domestic violence, child and adolescent treatment, post-traumatic stress disorder.

David Reitman, Ph.D., Mississippi; Associate Professor. Cross-setting (home and school) problems involving children and adolescents, with emphasis on disruptive behavior (e.g., attention deficit/hyperactivity disorder, oppositional defiant disorder, conduct disorder); interventions are behaviorally based, empirical, and focus on parent disciplinary practices, problem solving, and skills building.

Stephen A. Russo, Ph.D., Nova Southeastern; Assistant Professor. Sport psychology; sports medicine, physical rehabilitation, and recovery from injury; performance enhancement and coaching consultation; anxiety, anger, and emotional regulation; counseling college student-athletes, performance artists, and athletes of all ability levels.

Barry A. Schneider, Ph.D., Columbia; Professor. Psychodiagnosis and personality evaluation, integrated psychotherapy, medical psychotherapy, rare neurological disorders.

David Shapiro, Ph.D., Michigan; ABPP; Professor. Forensic psychology, mental health law, forensic and clinical assessment, expert witness testimony, malingering, legal and ethical issues.

Edward R. Simco, Ph.D., Nova Southeastern; Professor. Applied and computational statistics, research design and evaluation, cluster analysis, psychometrics.

Linda C. Sobell, Ph.D., California, Irvine; ABPP; Professor. Alcohol, tobacco, and other drug use disorders; cognitive-behavior therapy; research dissemination; assessment and treatment evaluation; natural recovery; motivational interventions; professional issues.

Mark B. Sobell, Ph.D., California, Riverside; ABPP; Professor. Substance use disorders, especially alcohol use disorders; behavior therapy; motivational interventions; treatment outcome evaluation; public health approach; processes of persuasion and behavior change; philosophy of science.

Mercedes B. ter Maat, Ph.D., Virginia Tech; LPC, ATR-BC; Associate Professor. School counseling and guidance, professional training, and supervision; multicultural counseling; community mental health; art therapy.

Sarah Valley-Gray, Psy.D., Nova; Associate Professor. Neuropsychological, psychological, and psychoeducational assessment; pediatric neuropsychological disorders; psychological services within the schools; infancy and child development.

Vincent B. Van Hasselt, Ph.D., Pittsburgh; Professor. Interpersonal violence, police psychology, criminal investigative analysis (psychological profiling) and apprehension, interviewing and interrogation techniques, intervention with juvenile offenders, behavioral forensics.

Angela Waguespack, Ph.D., LSU; Associate Professor. Psychological, psychoeducational, and functional behavior assessments; school-based consultation; psychological services within schools; behavioral interventions with children and adolescents.

Lenore Walker, Ed.D., Rutgers; ABPP; Professor. Forensic psychology, expert witness testimony, battered woman syndrome, violence against women, family and interpersonal violence, sexual harassment, impact of trauma, post-traumatic stress disorder, feminist theory.

NOVA SOUTHEASTERN UNIVERSITY

Center for Psychological Studies
Master's Programs in Mental Health Counseling and School Guidance and Counseling

Programs of Study The Master of Science in Mental Health Counseling program at Nova Southeastern University (NSU) is designed for the continued professional development of persons who currently serve or will serve their communities in a variety of counseling capacities. Master's degree training is based on a developmental model that emphasizes interdisciplinary collaboration, prevention of dysfunction, and direct service. Classes offered on the main campus in Fort Lauderdale are in traditional format with late afternoon and evening classes. The program is offered in an intensive weekend format at NSU Student Educational Centers in Jacksonville, Miami, Orlando, West Palm Beach, and Tampa, Florida. The program requires 60 semester hours, including three consecutive semesters of practicum and a comprehensive examination. The on-campus program is typically completed in two to three years; the off-campus program takes approximately three years to complete.

The Master of Science in Counseling program at Nova Southeastern University is designed for individuals who have demanding schedules and require a flexible, accessible approach to high-quality education. The M.S. in Counseling is offered online with concentrations available applied behavior analysis, advanced applied behavior analysis, mental health counseling, substance abuse counseling, and substance abuse counseling and education. The M.S. in Counseling program takes approximately two to three years to complete.

The Master of Science in School Guidance and Counseling program at Nova Southeastern University, which is based on a developmental model, prepares students to function as guidance counselors in school systems. While the role of the school counselor varies within and across schools, districts, and states, counselors increasingly serve in multiple roles, interacting and consulting with parents, teachers, school psychologists, and agencies to provide effective services to students (pre-kindergarten through grade 12). The School Guidance and Counseling program is offered in a weekend format for working adults on both the main campus and at NSU Student Educational Centers in Jacksonville, Miami, Orlando, West Palm Beach, and Tampa, Florida. The program requires 46 semester hours, including two semesters of practicum and a comprehensive examination. The program takes approximately 2½ years to complete.

Research Facilities In addition to training persons to provide care and treatment for those with psychological problems, the Center is equally committed to applied research. Areas of research in which the Center is currently engaged can be found in the section listing the faculty and their research interests. The Center is uniquely organized so that one faculty, full-time and adjunct, services all programs. Access to all of the specialty interests and clinical skills of full-time faculty members is available to all students in the school.

Research in the Center is supported by extensive computer facilities, including mainframe, workstation, and microcomputer environments. Methodological, statistical, and computing consultation is available to faculty members and students engaged in research or related course work. In addition, all students, regardless of location, have access to hundreds of databases and online resources through the University's electronic library.

Financial Aid The Office of Student Financial Assistance administers comprehensive federal, state, institutional, and private financial aid, which includes grants, loans, and student employment. In addition, professional financial aid counselors can help students plan the most efficient use of financial resources for their education. Students do not have to be admitted to apply for financial aid; however, they must be registered in order for financial aid to be distributed.

Cost of Study In 2008–09, tuition is $525 per credit, and there are other miscellaneous fees.

Living and Housing Costs The University offers graduate on-campus housing in Fort Lauderdale. Graduate apartments and rooms in shared apartments are available. Costs range from $7344 to $13,300 per academic year. For more information, students should contact the Office of Residential Life and Housing at 954-262-7052 or visit http://www.nova.edu/reslife.

Student Group Both traditional and nontraditional students participate in this program.

Location The main campus is located in a parklike setting consisting of royal palm trees, a lake, and large expanses of open lawn space. The surrounding community is suburban. The campus is within 10 miles of Fort Lauderdale, and Miami is 25 miles to the south. The off-campus locations are in Jacksonville, Miami, Orlando, West Palm Beach, and Tampa, Florida.

The University and The Center Nova Southeastern University is Florida's largest independent university. NSU is known throughout Florida and the United States as a university dedicated to educational excellence, technology, and community service. The Center for Psychological Studies is dedicated to providing the highest-quality education to its students, superior mental-health-care services to the community, and research contributions to mental health sciences.

Applying Applicants must have a bachelor's degree from a regionally accredited institution. Students are admitted to the main campus program in the fall, winter, and summer semesters and either for fall or winter at the off-campus locations. Application deadlines are generally in June for the fall and in October for the winter semester. Students who are going to participate in the off-campus programs must register at least four weeks before the first weekend of classes. Students are admitted with a minimum GPA of 2.5 on the condition that they achieve a minimum 3.0 GPA on their completion of four specific courses. There is a $50 nonrefundable application fee.

Correspondence and Information

Carlos Perez
Enrollment Processing Services (EPS)
Attention: Center for Psychological Studies
Nova Southeastern University
P.O. Box 299000
Fort Lauderdale, Florida 33329-9905

Phone: 954-262-5790
800-541-6682 Ext. 25790 (toll-free)
Fax: 954-262-3893
E-mail: cpsinfo@nova.edu
Web site: http://www.cps.nova.edu

Nova Southeastern University

THE FULL-TIME FACULTY AND THEIR RESEARCH

Nathan H. Azrin, Ph.D., Harvard; ABPP; Professor. Conduct disorder, oppositional defiant disorder (ODD), youth, drug addiction, behavior therapy, depression, marital and couple counseling, muscular tics, self-injurious behavior, vocational counseling and placement, alcoholism, retardation, rehabilitation of the brain injured, insomnia.

Stephen N. Campbell, Ph.D., Howard; Associate Professor. General clinical/community psychology, psychology of social change, dual diagnosed, program design and consultation, conduct disorder.

Ralph E. (Gene) Cash, Ph.D., NYU; NCSP; Associate Professor. School psychology; psychoeducational assessment, diagnosis, and treatment; depression; anxiety disorders; suicide prevention; individual, marital, and group psychotherapy; forensics, including child custody, wrongful death effects, and disability; stress management; psychology and public policy.

Christian DeLucia, Ph.D., Arizona State; Assistant Professor. Emergence of problem behaviors during adolescence, with a particular emphasis on adolescent substance use and abuse; statistical methods for the analysis of longitudinal data; methodological issues relevant for the design and analysis of psychosocial interventions.

Frank A. DePiano, Ph.D., South Carolina; Vice President for Academic Affairs, University-Wide Faculty Appointments. Hypnosis, community psychology, health and medicine, development of models for professional training of psychologists.

William Dorfman, Ph.D., Ohio State; ABPP; Professor. Community mental health, short-term approaches to psychotherapy, eclectic approaches to individual and marital psychotherapy, psychodiagnosis, objective personality measurement with the MMPI-2 and MMPI-A, role of families and primary caretakers in the treatment and rehabilitation of the chronically and severely mentally ill.

Jan Faust, Ph.D., Georgia; Professor. Child-clinical and pediatric psychology: child abuse (sexual and physical) and neglect, child treatment outcome research, PTSD in children and adolescents, child adjustment to acute and chronic medical conditions, life span psychosis.

Ana Imia Fins, Ph.D., Miami (Florida); Associate Professor. Health psychology, sleep medicine, insomnia, chronic fatigue syndrome, post-traumatic stress disorder, periodic limb movement disorder.

Diana Formoso, Ph.D., Arizona State; Assistant Professor. Risk and protective factors that shape youth development within low-income, ethnic minority families; family conflict, parenting, and child outcome and how they are impacted by families' ecological and cultural contexts (e.g., economic hardship, neighborhood risk, immigration, and acculturation); intervention development for ethnic minority children and families experiencing adversity; the family lives and school experiences of immigrant youth.

Steven N. Gold, Ph.D., Michigan State; Professor. Adult survivors of childhood sexual abuse; dissociative disorders; post-traumatic stress disorder; doctoral-level clinical training; hypnotherapy; psychological assessment; interpersonal, family, and systems theory and intervention; psychotherapy case conceptualization and treatment planning; psychological defenses; personality theory.

Charles Golden, Ph.D., Hawaii; ABPP/ABCN/ABAP; Professor. Neuropsychology of head injury, stroke, and multiple sclerosis; neuropsychological and personality assessment, rehabilitation, and community reintegration following brain injury; neuropsychology in childhood and in school settings; learning disabilities; hyperactivity; general assessment.

Alan D. Katell, Ph.D., West Virginia; Professor. Assessment and treatment of eating disorders, psychological factors in cardiac rehabilitation, exercise promotion and maintenance, health psychology, coping with chronic illnesses and other physical challenges.

Jeffrey L. Kibler, Ph.D., Miami (Florida); Associate Professor. Cognitive-behavior regulation of emotion/mood disorders; behavioral medicine; biobehavioral aspects of post-traumatic stress, psychosocial stress, and pain; psychosocial risks for illness (e.g., heart disease); health risk reduction; psychophysiology; minority health; predictors of biobehavioral research participation for individuals of racial minorities.

Stacey Lambert, Psy.D., Nova Southeastern; Associate Professor. Community mental health, schizophrenia, the impact of social factors on serious mental illness, recovery, empowerment, psychosocial rehabilitation for people with serious psychiatric disabilities, behavior therapy.

Robert C. Lane, Ph.D., NYU; ABPP; Clinical Professor. Psychopathology, diagnosis, difficult patients, psychoanalysis, psychotherapy, supervision.

John E. Lewis, Ph.D., Syracuse; Professor. Intercultural psychotherapy and assessment, counseling and psychotherapy with prison populations, educational and vocational assessment and counseling, school psychology, international perspectives.

Craig D. Marker, Ph.D., Chicago Medical School; Assistant Professor. Anxiety disorders, with a particular emphasis on obsessive-compulsive disorder, panic disorder, and social anxiety; longitudinal data analysis, with an emphasis on intra-individual variability and change methods.

Wiley Mittenberg, Ph.D., University of Health Sciences (Chicago); ABPP/ABCN; Professor. Neuropsychology of head injury in adults and children, malingering, forensic neuropsychology, neuropsychology of cortical and subcortical dementias, professional issues in clinical neuropsychology.

Timothy R. Moragne, Psy.D., Wright State; Professor. Minority issues, health psychology, community psychology, human sexuality, psychological aspects of AIDS, AIDS and minorities.

Barry Nierenberg, Ph.D., Tennessee; ABPP; Associate Professor. Rehabilitation and health psychology: psychological factors in chronic illness, biopsychosocial aspects of wellness and disease, health-care disparities, pediatric psychology, and child and family adaptations to acute and chronic medical conditions; the business of psychology and professional credentialing.

Helen Orvaschel, Ph.D., New School; Professor. Mood disorders, genetic contributions to psychopathology, risk factors for child psychiatric disorders, psychiatric epidemiology, differential diagnostic assessment of child and adolescent psychopathology.

Scott Poland, Ed.D., Ball State; Associate Professor. Crisis intervention, youth violence, suicide, clinical interventions, administration and delivery of school psychological services.

Bady Quintar, Ph.D., Kentucky; ABPP; Professor. Projective techniques, psychoanalytic psychotherapy, ego psychology, postdoctoral training.

Shannon Ray, Ph.D., Central Florida; Assistant Professor. Community mental health, chronic pain, eating disorders, domestic violence, child and adolescent treatment, post-traumatic stress disorder.

David Reitman, Ph.D., Mississippi; Associate Professor. Cross-setting (home and school) problems involving children and adolescents, with emphasis on disruptive behavior (e.g., attention deficit/hyperactivity disorder, oppositional defiant disorder, conduct disorder); interventions are behaviorally based, empirical, and focus on parent disciplinary practices, problem solving, and skills building.

Stephen A. Russo, Ph.D., Nova Southeastern; Assistant Professor. Sport psychology; sports medicine, physical rehabilitation, and recovery from injury; performance enhancement and coaching consultation; anxiety, anger, and emotional regulation; counseling college student-athletes, performance artists, and athletes of all ability levels.

Barry A. Schneider, Ph.D., Columbia; Professor. Psychodiagnosis and personality evaluation, integrated psychotherapy, medical psychotherapy, rare neurological disorders.

David Shapiro, Ph.D., Michigan; ABPP; Professor. Forensic psychology, mental health law, forensic and clinical assessment, expert witness testimony, malingering, legal and ethical issues.

Edward R. Simco, Ph.D., Nova Southeastern; Professor. Applied and computational statistics, research design and evaluation, cluster analysis, psychometrics.

Linda C. Sobell, Ph.D., California, Irvine; ABPP; Professor. Alcohol, tobacco, and other drug use disorders; cognitive-behavior therapy; research dissemination; assessment and treatment evaluation; natural recovery; motivational interventions; professional issues.

Mark B. Sobell, Ph.D., California, Riverside; ABPP; Professor. Substance use disorders, especially alcohol use disorders; behavior therapy; motivational interventions; treatment outcome evaluation; public health approach; processes of persuasion and behavior change; philosophy of science.

Mercedes B. ter Maat, Ph.D., Virginia Tech; LPC, ATR-BC; Associate Professor. School counseling and guidance, professional training, and supervision; multicultural counseling; community mental health; art therapy.

Sarah Valley-Gray, Psy.D., Nova; Associate Professor. Neuropsychological, psychological, and psychoeducational assessment; pediatric neuropsychological disorders; psychological services within the schools; infancy and child development.

Vincent B. Van Hasselt, Ph.D., Pittsburgh; Professor. Interpersonal violence, police psychology, criminal investigative analysis (psychological profiling) and apprehension, interviewing and interrogation techniques, intervention with juvenile offenders, behavioral forensics.

Angela Waguespack, Ph.D., LSU; Associate Professor. Psychological, psychoeducational, and functional behavior assessments; school-based consultation; psychological services within schools; behavioral interventions with children and adolescents.

Lenore Walker, Ed.D., Rutgers; ABPP; Professor. Forensic psychology, expert witness testimony, battered woman syndrome, violence against women, family and interpersonal violence, sexual harassment, impact of trauma, post-traumatic stress disorder, feminist theory.

NOVA SOUTHEASTERN UNIVERSITY

Center for Psychological Studies
Specialist in School Psychology

Program of Study

The Specialist in School Psychology (Psy.S.) program at Nova Southeastern University (NSU) was developed in response to the national and state shortage of school psychologists and the increased public attention being paid to the important role that psychologists play in the schools. The program is designed to meet the National Association of School Psychologists (NASP) Standards for Training Programs in School Psychology and to meet the current educational requirements for the Florida Department of Education (DOE) certification and for licensure as a school psychologist under Chapter 490, Florida Statutes.

The program consists of 79 semester hours that span three years of course work (including two practicums) and one year of internship, for a total of four years. The format is designed for the working professional, with courses offered primarily on weekends and evenings. A thirty-week, full-time, 40-hour-a-week internship is required, so participants must anticipate this requirement and make appropriate arrangements. This program is offered on the main campus and at NSU Student Educational Centers in Jacksonville, Tampa, and West Palm Beach, Florida.

The program is offered by the Center for Psychological Studies, a graduate school that is enriched by its more than 30 nationally renowned full-time faculty members.

Research Facilities

In addition to training persons to provide care and treatment for those with psychological problems, the Center is equally committed to applied research. Areas of research in which the Center is currently engaged can be found in the section listing the faculty members and their research interests. The Center is uniquely organized so that one faculty, full-time and adjunct, services all programs. Access to all of the specialty interests and clinical skills of the full-time faculty members is available to all students in the school.

Research in the Center is supported by extensive computer facilities, including mainframe, workstation, and microcomputer environments. Methodological, statistical, and computing consultation is available to faculty members and students engaged in research or related course work. In addition, all students, regardless of location, have access to hundreds of databases and online resources through the University's electronic library.

Financial Aid

Nova Southeastern University's Office of Student Financial Services and Registration administers comprehensive federal, state, institutional, and private financial aid, which includes grants, loans, and student employment. The purpose of these programs is to provide monetary assistance to qualified students to meet their educational objectives. In addition, professional financial aid counselors can help students plan the most efficient use of financial resources for their education. Students do not have to be admitted to apply for financial aid; however, they must be registered in order for financial aid funds to be distributed.

Cost of Study

In 2008–09, tuition is $580 per credit, and there are miscellaneous fees.

Living and Housing Costs

The University offers graduate on-campus housing in Fort Lauderdale. Graduate apartments and rooms in shared apartments are available. Costs range from $7344 to $13,300 per academic year. For more information, students should contact the Office of Residential Life and Housing at 954-262-7052 or visit http://www.nova.edu/reslife.

Student Group

Participants in this program are both traditional and nontraditional students. Many are employed in education, psychology, or a related field.

Location

The main campus is located in a parklike setting consisting of royal palm trees, a lake, and large expanses of open lawn space. The surrounding community is suburban. The campus is within 10 miles of Fort Lauderdale, and Miami is 25 miles to the south. There are two international airports within 25 miles of the campus. The off-campus locations are in Jacksonville, Tampa, and West Palm Beach, Florida.

The University and The Center

Nova Southeastern University is Florida's largest independent university. NSU is known throughout Florida and the United States as a university dedicated to educational excellence, technology, and community service. The Center for Psychological Studies is dedicated to providing the highest-quality education to its students, superior mental-health-care services to the community, and research contributions to mental health sciences. The Center has become a national leader in providing education and cutting-edge services to the public.

Applying

The specialist program is open to individuals with a bachelor's or master's degree in psychology, education, counseling, or a related field who demonstrate the scholastic ability and interpersonal skills to be an effective psychological practitioner in the schools.

Applicants must submit scores of 1000 or higher on the GRE General Test or a 40th percentile score or better on the Miller Analogies Test (MAT). Transcripts must show evidence a GPA of 3.0 or higher for the last two years of undergraduate course work or a minimum 3.4 GPA from a regionally accredited graduate program in psychology, education, or a related field based on a minimum of 18 credit hours. In addition, an interview is required. There is a $50 nonrefundable application fee. Applicants not meeting the above criteria may apply on the basis of relevant, professional, or exceptional experience or accomplishment.

Programs at each location post early and regular admission deadlines. Enrollment is limited. As such, prospective students are advised to apply at the earliest possible date.

Correspondence and Information

Carlos Perez
Enrollment Processing Services (EPS)
Attention: Center for Psychological Studies
Nova Southeastern University
P.O. Box 299000
Fort Lauderdale, Florida 33329-9905

Phone: 954-262-5790
800-541-6682 Ext. 25790 (toll-free)
Fax: 954-262-3893
E-mail: cpsinfo@nova.edu
Web site: http://www.cps.nova.edu

Nova Southeastern University

THE FULL-TIME FACULTY AND THEIR RESEARCH

Nathan H. Azrin, Ph.D., Harvard; ABPP; Professor. Conduct disorder, oppositional defiant disorder (ODD), youth, drug addiction, behavior therapy, depression, marital and couple counseling, muscular tics, self-injurious behavior, vocational counseling and placement, alcoholism, retardation, rehabilitation of the brain injured, insomnia.

Stephen N. Campbell, Ph.D., Howard; Associate Professor. General clinical/community psychology, psychology of social change, dual diagnosed, program design and consultation, conduct disorder.

Ralph E. (Gene) Cash, Ph.D., NYU; NCSP; Associate Professor. School psychology; psychoeducational assessment, diagnosis, and treatment; depression; anxiety disorders; suicide prevention; individual, marital, and group psychotherapy; forensics, including child custody, wrongful death effects, and disability; stress management; psychology and public policy.

Christian DeLucia, Ph.D., Arizona State; Assistant Professor. Emergence of problem behaviors during adolescence, with a particular emphasis on adolescent substance use and abuse; statistical methods for the analysis of longitudinal data; methodological issues relevant for the design and analysis of psychosocial interventions.

Frank A. DePiano, Ph.D., South Carolina; Vice President for Academic Affairs, University-Wide Faculty Appointments. Hypnosis, community psychology, health and medicine, development of models for professional training of psychologists.

William Dorfman, Ph.D., Ohio State; ABPP; Professor. Community mental health, short-term approaches to psychotherapy, eclectic approaches to individual and marital psychotherapy, psychodiagnosis, objective personality measurement with the MMPI-2 and MMPI-A, role of families and primary caretakers in the treatment and rehabilitation of the chronically and severely mentally ill.

Jan Faust, Ph.D., Georgia; Professor. Child-clinical and pediatric psychology: child abuse (sexual and physical) and neglect, child treatment outcome research, PTSD in children and adolescents, child adjustment to acute and chronic medical conditions, life span psychosis.

Ana Imia Fins, Ph.D., Miami (Florida); Associate Professor. Health psychology, sleep medicine, insomnia, chronic fatigue syndrome, post-traumatic stress disorder, periodic limb movement disorder.

Diana Formoso, Ph.D., Arizona State; Assistant Professor. Risk and protective factors that shape youth development within low-income, ethnic minority families; family conflict, parenting, and child outcome and how they are impacted by families' ecological and cultural contexts (e.g., economic hardship, neighborhood risk, immigration, and acculturation); intervention development for ethnic minority children and families experiencing adversity; the family lives and school experiences of immigrant youth.

Steven N. Gold, Ph.D., Michigan State; Professor. Adult survivors of childhood sexual abuse; dissociative disorders; post-traumatic stress disorder; doctoral-level clinical training; hypnotherapy; psychological assessment; interpersonal, family, and systems theory and intervention; psychotherapy case conceptualization and treatment planning; psychological defenses; personality theory.

Charles Golden, Ph.D., Hawaii; ABPP/ABCN/ABAP; Professor. Neuropsychology of head injury, stroke, and multiple sclerosis; neuropsychological and personality assessment, rehabilitation, and community reintegration following brain injury; neuropsychology in childhood and in school settings; learning disabilities; hyperactivity; general assessment.

Alan D. Katell, Ph.D., West Virginia; Professor. Assessment and treatment of eating disorders, psychological factors in cardiac rehabilitation, exercise promotion and maintenance, health psychology, coping with chronic illnesses and other physical challenges.

Jeffrey L. Kibler, Ph.D., Miami (Florida); Associate Professor. Cognitive-behavior regulation of emotion/mood disorders; behavioral medicine; biobehavioral aspects of post-traumatic stress, psychosocial stress, and pain; psychosocial risks for illness (e.g., heart disease); health risk reduction; psychophysiology; minority health; predictors of biobehavioral research participation for individuals of racial minorities.

Stacey Lambert, Psy.D., Nova Southeastern; Associate Professor. Community mental health, schizophrenia, the impact of social factors on serious mental illness, recovery, empowerment, psychosocial rehabilitation for people with serious psychiatric disabilities, behavior therapy.

Robert C. Lane, Ph.D., NYU; ABPP; Clinical Professor. Psychopathology, diagnosis, difficult patients, psychoanalysis, psychotherapy, supervision.

John E. Lewis, Ph.D., Syracuse; Professor. Intercultural psychotherapy and assessment, counseling and psychotherapy with prison populations, educational and vocational assessment and counseling, school psychology, international perspectives.

Craig D. Marker, Ph.D., Chicago Medical School; Assistant Professor. Anxiety disorders, with a particular emphasis on obsessive-compulsive disorder, panic disorder, and social anxiety; longitudinal data analysis, with an emphasis on intra-individual variability and change methods.

Wiley Mittenberg, Ph.D., University of Health Sciences (Chicago); ABPP/ABCN; Professor. Neuropsychology of head injury in adults and children, malingering, forensic neuropsychology, neuropsychology of cortical and subcortical dementias, professional issues in clinical neuropsychology.

Timothy R. Moragne, Psy.D., Wright State; Professor. Minority issues, health psychology, community psychology, human sexuality, psychological aspects of AIDS, AIDS and minorities.

Barry Nierenberg, Ph.D., Tennessee; ABPP; Associate Professor. Rehabilitation and health psychology: psychological factors in chronic illness, biopsychosocial aspects of wellness and disease, health-care disparities, pediatric psychology, and child and family adaptations to acute and chronic medical conditions; the business of psychology and professional credentialing.

Helen Orvaschel, Ph.D., New School; Professor. Mood disorders, genetic contributions to psychopathology, risk factors for child psychiatric disorders, psychiatric epidemiology, differential diagnostic assessment of child and adolescent psychopathology.

Scott Poland, Ed.D., Ball State; Associate Professor. Crisis intervention, youth violence, suicide, clinical interventions, administration and delivery of school psychological services.

Bady Quintar, Ph.D., Kentucky; ABPP; Professor. Projective techniques, psychoanalytic psychotherapy, ego psychology, postdoctoral training.

Shannon Ray, Ph.D., Central Florida; Assistant Professor. Community mental health, chronic pain, eating disorders, domestic violence, child and adolescent treatment, post-traumatic stress disorder.

David Reitman, Ph.D., Mississippi; Associate Professor. Cross-setting (home and school) problems involving children and adolescents, with emphasis on disruptive behavior (e.g., attention deficit/hyperactivity disorder, oppositional defiant disorder, conduct disorder); interventions are behaviorally based, empirical, and focus on parent disciplinary practices, problem solving, and skills building.

Stephen A. Russo, Ph.D., Nova Southeastern; Assistant Professor. Sport psychology; sports medicine, physical rehabilitation, and recovery from injury; performance enhancement and coaching consultation; anxiety, anger, and emotional regulation; counseling college student-athletes, performance artists, and athletes of all ability levels.

Barry A. Schneider, Ph.D., Columbia; Professor. Psychodiagnosis and personality evaluation, integrated psychotherapy, medical psychotherapy, rare neurological disorders.

David Shapiro, Ph.D., Michigan; ABPP; Professor. Forensic psychology, mental health law, forensic and clinical assessment, expert witness testimony, malingering, legal and ethical issues.

Edward R. Simco, Ph.D., Nova Southeastern; Professor. Applied and computational statistics, research design and evaluation, cluster analysis, psychometrics.

Linda C. Sobell, Ph.D., California, Irvine; ABPP; Professor. Alcohol, tobacco, and other drug use disorders; cognitive-behavior therapy; research dissemination; assessment and treatment evaluation; natural recovery; motivational interventions; professional issues.

Mark B. Sobell, Ph.D., California, Riverside; ABPP; Professor. Substance use disorders, especially alcohol use disorders; behavior therapy; motivational interventions; treatment outcome evaluation; public health approach; processes of persuasion and behavior change; philosophy of science.

Mercedes B. ter Maat, Ph.D., Virginia Tech; LPC, ATR-BC; Associate Professor. School counseling and guidance, professional training, and supervision; multicultural counseling; community mental health; art therapy.

Sarah Valley-Gray, Psy.D., Nova; Associate Professor. Neuropsychological, psychological, and psychoeducational assessment; pediatric neuropsychological disorders; psychological services within the schools; infancy and child development.

Vincent B. Van Hasselt, Ph.D., Pittsburgh; Professor. Interpersonal violence, police psychology, criminal investigative analysis (psychological profiling) and apprehension, interviewing and interrogation techniques, intervention with juvenile offenders, behavioral forensics.

Angela Waguespack, Ph.D., LSU; Associate Professor. Psychological, psychoeducational, and functional behavior assessments; school-based consultation; psychological services within schools; behavioral interventions with children and adolescents.

Lenore Walker, Ed.D., Rutgers; ABPP; Professor. Forensic psychology, expert witness testimony, battered woman syndrome, violence against women, family and interpersonal violence, sexual harassment, impact of trauma, post-traumatic stress disorder, feminist theory.

PACE UNIVERSITY

Dyson College of Arts and Sciences
Master of Science in Counseling

Program of Study

The Department of Psychology on the Pleasantville campus offers a Master of Science in counseling program to provide specialized knowledge and skill development to individuals who wish to pursue professional careers in this area. Students choose from four areas of specialization: substance abuse counseling, grief and loss counseling, general counseling, and mental health counseling. Courses in the counseling core provide a foundation of advanced psychology and basic counseling theories, research, and practices. The degree program emphasizes hands-on skills development through role-playing, group exercise, and extensive use of videotaping and other tools. All students take part in a supervised counseling internship. With additional paid work experience in the field, graduates are eligible for New York State certification in substance abuse counseling. Graduates of the mental health counseling program are eligible for mental health counseling certification in New York State.

Research Facilities

The Pace University Library is a comprehensive teaching library and student-learning center, a virtual library that combines strong core collections with ubiquitous access to global Internet resources to support broad and diversified curricula. Reciprocal borrowing and access accords, traditional interlibrary loan services, and commercial document delivery options supplement the aggregate holdings of the library. Pace offers Instructional Services Librarians, a state-of-the-art electronic classroom, digital reference services, and multimedia applications. Pace's computer resource centers are linked to high-speed data networks and feature sophisticated hardware and software to facilitate active learning. Recognized as one of America's most wired universities, Pace supports high-speed Internet and Internet2 access on every campus, resident facilities are wired, and most public areas are enabled for wireless connectivity. Full-motion videoconference facilities enable remote delivery of instruction between campus sites for synchronous learning applications. Many courses are Web assisted with state-of-the-art software, and some courses and programs are completely Web based.

Financial Aid

Pace's comprehensive student financial aid assistance program includes scholarships, graduate assistantships, student loans, and tuition payment plans. Scholarships are awarded to students in recognition of academic achievement and are available for full- and part-time study. Highly qualified students may be eligible for assistantships awarded by departments, which pay stipends of up to $5100 and provide tuition remission for up to 24 credits during the 2008–09 academic year. Pace participates in all major federal and state financial aid programs, such as Federal Direct Loans, the New York State Tuition Assistance Program (TAP), and Federal Perkins Loans. All students are encouraged to apply for these programs by filing the Free Application for Federal Student Aid (FAFSA).

Cost of Study

Tuition for graduate courses is $890 per credit in 2008–09.

Living and Housing Costs

Residence facilities are available on campus in both New York City and Westchester. Double-occupancy rooms ranged from approximately $8500 to $12,000 for 2007–08. University-operated, off-campus housing is available in proximity of the New York City campus.

Student Group

Pace students represent diversified personal, cultural, and educational backgrounds. Many students are employed and pursue graduate study for personal growth and career advancement, and 52 percent are enrolled part-time in evening classes. Current enrollment in the graduate counseling program is approximately 100 students.

Location

Pace University is a multicampus institution with campuses in both New York City and Westchester County, New York. All locations are within reach of cultural, business, and social resources and opportunities. The downtown Manhattan campus is adjacent to Wall Street and City Hall. Pace's Midtown Center is a short distance from Times Square, theaters, and Grand Central Station. The Pleasantville/Briarcliff campus is in a suburban setting, surrounded by towns offering various forms of recreation. The Graduate Center and the School of Law are located in White Plains among major retail districts and many corporate headquarters. All locations are accessible by public transportation. The graduate counseling program is available at the Westchester campus.

The University

Founded in 1906, Pace University is a private, nonsectarian, coeducational institution. Originally founded as a school of accounting, Pace Institution was designated Pace College in 1973. Through growth and various successes, it was renamed Pace University as approved by the New York State Board of Regents. Today, Pace offers comprehensive undergraduate, graduate, doctoral, and professional programs at several campus locations through six schools and colleges.

Applying

Admission to Pace University requires successful completion of a U.S. baccalaureate degree, or its equivalent, from an accredited institution. Students must submit a completed application, an application fee, official transcripts from all postsecondary institutions attended, a personal statement, a resume, and two letters of recommendation. International students must submit official TOEFL scores and official transcripts in the native language with a professional English translation. Applications should be submitted by August 1 for the fall semester, December 1 for the spring semester, and May 1 for summer sessions. International applications should be submitted five months prior to these dates.

Correspondence and Information

Office of Graduate Admission
Pace University
1 Martine Avenue
White Plains, New York 10606
Phone: 914-422-4283
Fax: 914-422-4287
E-mail: gradwp@pace.edu
Web site: http://www.pace.edu

Pace University

THE FACULTY

Sheila Chiffriller, Assistant Professor of Psychology; Ph.D., Fordham.
Frances Delahanty, Associate Professor; Ph.D., Fordham.
Harold Ford, Lecturer of Psychology; M.S.Ed., Fordham.
David Geiber, Adjunct Professor; M.Ed., Georgia.
Abigail Gleason, Adjunct Assistant Professor; Ph.D., Michigan State.
Paul Griffin, Adjunct Lecturer of Psychology; M.S., Pace.
Lisa Hauptner, Adjunct Lecturer of Psychology; M.S., Pace.
Sharon Kelly, Adjunct Professor; M.S., Columbia.
Barbara Kutcher, Adjunct Professor; Ph.D., Pace.
Alma McManus, Assistant Professor and Coordinator, M.S. in Counseling Program; Ph.D., Fordham.
Thomas Nardi, Adjunct Professor; Ph.D., St. John's (New York).
Florence Poole, Adjunct Professor; M.S., LIU.
Rostyslaw Robak, Associate Professor and Department Chair; Ph.D., Hofstra.
Evan Stern, Adjunct Instructor of Psychology; M.S., Pace.
Al Ward, Associate Professor of Psychology; Ph.D., Fordham.

PACE UNIVERSITY

Dyson College of Arts and Sciences
Psychology Department

Programs of Study The Department of Psychology offers on the New York City campus of Pace University four distinguished graduate programs: the Doctor of Psychology (Psy.D.) program in school-clinical psychology, the Master of Science in Education (M.S.Ed.) in school psychology, the M.S.Ed. in bilingual school psychology with a bilingual extension certificate, and the Master of Arts (M.A.) in psychology. The M.A. in psychology curriculum contains 18 credits in basic psychology principles and 18 credits of electives. The program seeks to fill a gap between the training and the changing professional preparation in human service organizations. Courses are offered in areas such as advanced research, multicultural issues, developmental disabilities, program evaluation, and community mental health. The M.S.Ed. in school psychology (69 credits) and the M.S.Ed. in bilingual school psychology (78 credits) train students to provide psychoeducational services in the school setting and balance basic science and foundation psychology courses. Students receive training in a variety of University and field settings and complete a 1200-clock-hour school psychology internship. Graduates are recommended for New York State school psychology certification. The program may be completed on a full- or part-time basis. The Psy.D. program in school-clinical child psychology trains psychologists, who consult with teachers, school administrators, parents, and social service agencies on matters affecting children's learning and development. The program prepares professionals to plan, develop, and evaluate research and testing programs and to offer assessment, consultation, and intervention services for youth in schools and community agencies. Students gain a firm foundation in psychology and also take courses in areas such as assessment, consultation, psychotherapy, and intervention techniques. The doctoral program is fully accredited as a school/clinical combined program by the American Psychological Association (APA) and is approved by the National Association of School Psychologists (NASP). In addition to the internship, students complete a doctoral project and three years of practicum experience in Pace University's Thomas J. McShane Center for Psychological Services, where they receive training in areas such as applied research, assessment, biofeedback, consultation, counseling and therapy, parent-infant interaction, and program development and evaluation. The program culminates in a full-time, one-year doctoral internship. Graduates are eligible to apply for New York State licensure for the professional practice of psychology.

Research Facilities The Pace University Library is a comprehensive teaching library and student-learning center, a virtual library that combines strong core collections with ubiquitous access to global Internet resources to support broad and diversified curricula. Reciprocal borrowing and access accords, traditional interlibrary loan services, and commercial document delivery options supplement the aggregate holdings of the library. Pace offers Instructional Services Librarians, a state-of-the-art electronic classroom, digital reference services, and multimedia applications. Pace's computer resource centers are linked to high-speed data networks and feature sophisticated hardware and software to facilitate active learning. Recognized as one of America's most wired universities, Pace supports high-speed Internet and Internet2 access on every campus, resident facilities are wired, and most public areas are enabled for wireless connectivity. Full-motion videoconference facilities enable remote delivery of instruction between campus sites for synchronous learning applications.

Financial Aid Pace's comprehensive student financial aid assistance program includes scholarships, graduate assistantships, student loans, and tuition payment plans. Scholarships are awarded to students in recognition of academic achievement and are available for full- and part-time study. Highly qualified students may be eligible for assistantships awarded by departments, which pay stipends of up to $5100 and tuition remission of up to 24 credits during the 2008–09 academic year. Pace participates in all major federal and state financial aid programs, such as Federal Direct Loans, the New York State Tuition Assistance Program (TAP), and Federal Perkins Loans. All students are encouraged to apply for these programs by filing the Free Application for Federal Student Aid (FAFSA).

Cost of Study Tuition for graduate courses is $890 per credit for 2008–09.

Living and Housing Costs Residence facilities are available on campus in both New York City and Westchester. Double-occupancy rooms ranged from approximately $8500 to $12,000 for the 2007–08 academic year. University-operated off-campus housing is available in proximity of the New York City campus. A wide variety of rooms and apartments are also available for students.

Student Group Pace students represent diversified personal, cultural, and educational backgrounds. Many students are employed and pursue graduate study for personal growth and career advancement. Most graduate psychology students attend on a full-time basis. Courses are typically offered late afternoon and early evenings. Current enrollment in the graduate psychology programs is 109 students.

Location Pace University is a multicampus institution with campuses in both New York City and Westchester County. All locations are within reach of cultural, business, and social resources and opportunities. The downtown Manhattan campus is adjacent to Wall Street and City Hall. Pace's Midtown Center is a short distance from Times Square, theaters, and Grand Central Station. The Pleasantville/Briarcliff campus is in a suburban setting surrounded by towns offering various forms of recreation. The Graduate Center and the School of Law are located in White Plains among major retail districts and many corporate headquarters. All locations are accessible by public transportation. Graduate psychology programs are available at the New York City campus only.

The University Founded in 1906, Pace University is a private, nonsectarian, coeducational institution. Originally founded as a school of accounting, Pace Institute was designated Pace College in 1973. Through growth and various successes, Pace College was renamed Pace University as approved by the New York State Board of Regents. Today, Pace offers comprehensive undergraduate, graduate, doctoral, and professional-level programs at several campus locations, through six schools and colleges.

Applying Admission to Pace University requires successful completion of a U.S. baccalaureate degree, or its equivalent, from an accredited institution. Students must submit a completed application, an application fee, official transcripts from all postsecondary institutions, a personal statement, a resume, and three letters of recommendation. International students must submit official TOEFL scores and official transcripts in the native language with a professional English translation.

Applicants to the M.S.Ed. and Psy.D. programs must demonstrate satisfactory performance on both the GRE General Test and the Subject Test in Psychology. Students are only admitted for the fall semester. Completed applications should be submitted by February 1. International applications should be submitted one month prior to these dates.

Applicants to the M.A. program must demonstrate satisfactory performance on the GRE General Test and are expected to have 12 credits of undergraduate preparation in psychology. Applications should be submitted by August 1 for the fall semester, December 1 for the spring semester, and May 1 for summer sessions. International applications should be submitted five months prior to these dates.

Correspondence and Information

Office of Graduate Admission
Pace University
1 Pace Plaza
New York, New York 10038
Phone: 212-346-1531
Fax: 212-346-1585
E-mail: gradnyc@pace.edu
Web site: http://www.pace.edu.

For information regarding APA accreditation:
Committee on Accreditation
American Psychological Association
750 First Street, NE
Washington, D.C. 20002-4242
Phone: 202-336-5979

Pace University

THE FACULTY

Stephen Armeli, Assistant Professor; Ph.D., Delaware, 1998.
Leonard Bart, Adjunct Professor; Ph.D., St. John's (New York), 1971.
June Chisholm, Professor; Ph.D., Massachusetts Amherst, 1978.
Florence Denmark, Adjunct Professor; Ph.D., Pennsylvania, 1968.
Paul Echandia, Adjunct Professor Emeritus in Residence; Ph.D., NYU, 1963.
Madeline Fernandez, Assistant Professor; Psy.D, Pace, 2004.
Beth Hart, Professor and Director of the Center for Psychological Services; Ph.D., Yeshiva, 1981.
Jack L. Herman, Adjunct Professor; Ph.D., NYU, 1957.
Janice Jackson, Professor; Ph.D., Fordham, 1974.
Herbert Krauss, Professor and Chairperson; Ph.D., Northwestern, 1966.
Barbara Mowder, Professor and Director of Graduate Psychology Programs; Ph.D., Indiana, 1976.
Weihua Niu, Assistant Professor; Ph.D., Yale, 2003.
Yvonne Rafferty, Professor; Ph.D., SUNY at Stony Brook, 1993.
Mark Sossin, Associate Professor; Ph.D., Yeshiva, 1996.
John Stokes, Professor; Ph.D., Fordham, 1983.
Richard Velayo, Professor; Ph.D., Michigan, 1994.
Alfred Ward, Associate Professor; Ph.D., Fordham, 1985.
Anastasia Yasik, Assistant Professor; Ph.D., CUNY Graduate Center, 1998.

PACIFIC GRADUATE SCHOOL OF PSYCHOLOGY

Ph.D. Program in Clinical Psychology

Program of Study

Pacific Graduate School of Psychology (PGSP) offers the Ph.D. in clinical psychology. The primary goals are to train psychologists whose work is firmly grounded in theory and is informed by current research, who can function effectively as independent practitioners, and who can critically evaluate and perform research that contributes to the academic discipline of scientific psychology. PGSP places a high value on scholarship and an equal emphasis on research and clinical training.

The PGSP curriculum includes intensive study in five areas: basic theoretical concepts in psychology, psychological evaluation, psychotherapy theory and process, clinical field experience, and research. Academic schedules in each year of study include required and elective course work in each of these areas. Students also have the opportunity to focus their course work in specific areas of individual and group psychotherapy. The program also offers two specialized training certificates in forensic psychology and neuropsychological assessment. All students are required to complete 16 hours of personal psychotherapy; PGSP believes that the personal psychotherapy experience is critical to the ability to work therapeutically with others.

Research Facilities

The Pacific Graduate School of Psychology's Research Library's collections include books, journals, assessment materials, dissertations, audiotapes, and videotapes. The on-site computer network is accessible to library users at home via the Internet. The computer network features access to the PGSP library catalog as well as PsycINFO, Medline, ERIC, and the American Psychiatric Association's database of full-text journals and books.

Financial Aid

Financial assistance is available to eligible PGSP students in the form of fellowships, scholarships, loans (repayable with interest), and on-campus employment. While independent professional schools have neither state support nor extensive endowments, some type of government-subsidized and/or alternative student loan funding is available to almost all students. PGSP is a HEALTH-approved program. Prospective students who wish to be considered for a PGSP fellowship must submit a completed application to the Admissions department.

Cost of Study

Quarterly tuition for the Ph.D. program in 2008–09 is $10,529, the per-unit rate is $1190, the dissertation flat rate is $8431, and the internship flat rate is $2108. Other fees add up to $1190 per quarter.

Living and Housing Costs

The cost of living in the Palo Alto, California, area is comparable to the cost of living in other larger California communities. On-campus housing is not available, although ample off-campus housing is available within a short distance of the campus.

Student Group

PGSP averages 38 graduates from its program each year. With a student-faculty ratio of 10:1, students enjoy a close working relationship with faculty members. The institution actively seeks and encourages diversity on its campus and within its intellectual community.

Location

Located 35 miles south of San Francisco, in the heart of Silicon Valley, Pacific Graduate School of Psychology is just minutes away from Stanford University and downtown Palo Alto and is across the scenic San Francisco Bay from the University of California, Berkeley campus. Situated between a suburban neighborhood and a thriving business park, PGSP lies within easy reach of the best that northern California has to offer, including Lake Tahoe skiing, Yosemite National Park, San Francisco, the Napa Valley wine country, and Monterey Bay.

The School

The Pacific Graduate School of Psychology is a private, free-standing professional school, training doctoral students since 1975. The School offers a Master of Science (M.S.) degree in psychology, a Ph.D. in psychology, and joint degrees of Ph.D./J.D. and Ph.D./M.B.A. In addition, there is a distance learning M.S. in psychology program, which is offered to students via the Web; courses are taken throughout a two-year period. Pacific Graduate School of Psychology also offers the PGSP-STANFORD Psy.D. Consortium Program. This innovative program emphasizes the biopsychosocial model and empirically supported treatments for psychological disorders.

PGSP is accredited by the Western Association of Schools and Colleges. The Ph.D. program is accredited by the American Psychological Association (APA), and it brings together highly talented faculty members and graduate students working closely together to bridge scientific rigor and theoretical knowledge to the analysis and practice of clinical psychology. Its community supports broad cultural and professional backgrounds and a wide range of alternative perspectives. In so doing, PGSP trains students to work in a wide range of settings and with a broad spectrum of clients. The highly skilled faculty, low student-faculty ratio, and rigorous academic program ensure the high-quality teaching and mentoring necessary to produce outstanding graduates.

Applying

The completed application packet is due by mid-January if students wish to be considered for a fellowship. Applicants are encouraged to apply as early as possible. Late applications may be considered and are evaluated on a case-by-case basis, if space is available. The nonrefundable application fee is $50. All applicants must also include a resume or curriculum vitae that lists all employment, training, and any volunteer work relevant to the field of psychology; GRE scores; and official transcripts from undergraduate and graduate schools attended, even if a degree was not awarded. Each applicant must also include a written statement that includes a brief biographical profile, details of goals and reasons for applying to PGSP, strengths and accomplishments, and qualities that the student thinks are important assets as a practicing clinical psychologist.

Correspondence and Information

Office of Admissions
Pacific Graduate School of Psychology
405 Broadway Street
Redwood City, California 94063

Phone: 800-818-6136 (toll-free)
E-mail: admissions@pgsp.edu
Web site: http://www.pgsp.edu

Pacific Graduate School of Psychology

THE FACULTY AND THEIR RESEARCH

Professors
Leonard Beckum, Ph.D. Cultural issues and education.
Larry E. Beutler, Ph.D. Psychotherapy outcomes, depression, chemical abuse.
Bruce Bongar, Ph.D. Suicide.
Jim Breckenridge. Depression, health psychology, research design and methodology, health care policy.
Allison Briscoe-Smith, Ph.D. Child trauma and child diversity.
William J. Froming, Ph.D. Personality.
Peter Goldblum, Ph.D. HIV and gay/lesbian/bisexual psychology.
Roger L. Greene, Ph.D. Assessment.
James Moses, Ph.D. Diagnostic neuropsychology, psychopathology assessment.
Amy Wisniewski, Ph.D. Neuropsychology.

Associate Professors
Nigel Field, Ph.D. Bereavement, psychotherapy.
Shelley Fleming, Ph.D. Cognitive therapy and women's issues.
Robert Reiser, Assistant Professor; Ph.D. Evidence-based treatment of serious mental health in community mental health.
Lynn C. Waelde, Ph.D. Meditation and psychotherapy, post-traumatic stress disorder (PTSD).

Assistant Professors
Matthew J. Cordova, Ph.D. Health psychology, oncology, trauma.
Rowena Gomez, Ph.D. Aging, neuropsychology and depression.
Rebecca Jackson, Ph.D. Forensic psychology.
Steve Lovett, Ph.D. Clinical geropsychology.
Sandra Macias, Ph.D. Couples and children.
Wendy Packman, J.D., Ph.D. Pediatric psychology.

Research Faculty Members
Theodore Jacob, Professor; Ph.D.
Alvin Cooper, Associate Professor; Ph.D.

PACIFIC GRADUATE SCHOOL OF PSYCHOLOGY

PGSP-STANFORD Psy.D. Consortium
Doctor of Psychology Program

Program of Study

The Doctor of Psychology (Psy.D.) Program is a consortium between the Stanford University School of Medicine's Department of Psychiatry and Behavioral Sciences and the Pacific Graduate School of Psychology (PGSP), with the purpose of expanding training opportunities for students in the field of clinical psychology.

The PGSP-STANFORD Doctor of Psychology consortium training program is a full-time, five-year program. The APA-accredited program is broken down into three years of academic course work, one year for a clinical dissertation, and one year for a full-time, pre-doctoral internship. The nine-month academic year runs on the quarter system, with only a limited number of courses offered during the summer quarter. Students are not expected to attend during the summer quarter. Students are enrolled in intensive practicum training throughout the course of the first four years, followed by a one-year internship in clinical psychology.

A sampling of courses includes the following: Research Methods and Statistics; Psychological Assessment; Ethics and Professional Issues; Empirically-based Psychotherapies; Psychopathology Across the Life Span; Critical Evaluation of Psychological Research; Health Psychology and Behavioral Medicine; Clinical Emergencies and Crises; Family, Group, and Individual Psychotherapy; Neurobiologic Bases of Psychiatric Disorders; Diversity Issues in Clinical Psychology; Nature and Treatment of Personality Disorders, Mood Disorders, Eating Disorders, Anxiety Disorders, and Sleep Disorders.

Research Facilities

PGSP-STANFORD Psy.D. students have full access to Stanford libraries, along with the Pacific Graduate School of Psychology's Research Library's collections that include books, journals, assessment materials, dissertations, audiotapes, and videotapes. The on-site computer network is accessible to library users at home via the Internet. The computer network features access to the PGSP library catalog as well as PsycINFO, Medline, ERIC, and the American Psychiatric Association's database of full-text journals and books.

Financial Aid

Financial assistance is available to eligible PGSP-STANFORD students in the form of grants, fellowships, scholarships, loans (repayable with interest), and on-campus employment. While independent professional schools have neither state support nor extensive endowments, some type of government-subsidized and/or alternative student loan funding is available to almost all students. PGSP-STANFORD Psy.D is a HEALTH-approved program. Prospective students who wish to be considered for a PGSP fellowship must submit a completed application to the Admissions department. A majority of students in the PGSP-STANFORD Psy.D. program have paid research assistant positions at Stanford Medical School and the National Center on Disaster Psychology and Terrorism (NCDPT), teaching assistantships, and other graduate student assistant positions. There is an extensive merit-based graduate student fellowship program for entering students.

Cost of Study

Quarterly tuition for the Doctor of Psychology Program is $11,035. The consortium fee is $1420 per quarter.

Living and Housing Costs

The Palo Alto, California, area is amenable to students' lifestyles and budgets. Because it is a college town (Stanford University), the Palo Alto community offers many affordable dining, shopping, and entertainment options. Full- and part-time employment opportunities in the community are plentiful. On-campus housing is not available, although ample off-campus housing is available within a short distance of the campus.

Student Group

The PGSP-STANFORD Psy.D. program can accept up to 30 students. The class of 2005 had 22 students; the class of 2006 had 26 students. With more than 25 faculty members from the Stanford Department of Psychiatry and PGSP, students enjoy a close working relationship with faculty members. The institution enjoys and promotes diversity on its campus and within its intellectual community.

Location

Located 35 miles south of San Francisco, in the heart of Silicon Valley, the PGSP-STANFORD Psy.D. program is just minutes away from Stanford University and downtown Palo Alto and across the scenic San Francisco Bay from the University of California, Berkeley campus. It lies within easy reach of the best that northern California has to offer, including Lake Tahoe skiing, Yosemite National Park, San Francisco, the Napa Valley wine country, and Monterey Bay.

The Schools

The Department of Psychiatry and Behavioral Sciences at Stanford University School of Medicine is ranked as one of the top ten departments of psychiatry in the United States. The department is on the cutting edge of clinical research and practice in numerous nationally ranked studies in mood disorders, eating disorders, anxiety disorders, thought disorders, and psychological and psychiatric approaches to working with patients with a variety of medical conditions.

The Pacific Graduate School of Psychology is a private, free-standing professional school, training doctoral students since 1975. The School offers a Master of Science (M.S.) degree in psychology, an APA-accredited Ph.D. in clinical psychology, and joint degrees of Ph.D./J.D. and Ph.D./M.B.A. It is accredited by the Western Association of Schools and Colleges. The Psy.D. program brings together highly talented faculty members and graduate students working closely together to bridge scientific rigor and theoretical knowledge to the analysis and practice of clinical psychology. Its community supports broad cultural and professional backgrounds and a wide range of alternative perspectives. The PGSP-STANFORD Psy.D. Consortium trains students to work in a wide range of settings and with a broad spectrum of clients. The highly skilled faculty members, low student-faculty ratio, and rigorous academic program ensure the high-quality teaching and mentoring necessary to produce outstanding graduates.

Applying

The completed application packet is due by January 15. Highly qualified applications may be considered on a case-by-case basis after this date if the maximum class enrollment has not yet been reached. Due to the high caliber of applicants and the selective nature of the PGSP-STANFORD program, applicants are strongly encouraged to apply as early as possible. The nonrefundable application fee is $50. All applicants must also submit the following: a resume or curriculum vitae that lists all employment, training, and any volunteer work relevant to the field of psychology; GRE scores and official transcripts from undergraduate and graduate schools attended, even if a degree was not awarded; and a written statement that includes a brief biographical profile, details of goals and reasons for applying to the PGSP-STANFORD program, strengths and accomplishments, and qualities that the student thinks are important assets as a practicing clinical psychologist. A personal interview with the directors of the training program is an essential part of the selection process for qualified applicants.

Correspondence and Information

Office of Admissions
PGSP-STANFORD Psy.D. Consortium
405 Broadway Street
Redwood City, California 94063
Phone: 800-818-6136 (toll-free)
E-mail: admissions@pgsp.edu
Web site: http://www.pgsp.edu

Pacific Graduate School of Psychology

THE FACULTY AND THEIR RESEARCH

Directors

Bruce Arnow, Ph.D. Utilization of medical services, treatment of chronic depression.
James Breckenridge, Ph.D. Terrorism, homeland security, political violence.

Faculty

John J. Barry, M.D.
Leonard Beckum, Ph.D.
Christine Blasey, Ph.D.
Allison Briscoe-Smith, Ph.D.
Brenda Brownlow, Ph.D.
David Burns, M.D.
Betsy Corrin, Ph.D.
Charles DeBattista, Ph.D., D.M.H., M.D.
Katherine DeWitt, Ph.D.
Kathleen Eldredge, Ph.D.
Shelley Fleming, Ph.D.
Elizabeth Gifford, Ph.D.
Cheryl Gore-Felton, Ph.D.
Roger Greene, Ph.D.
Tamara Hartl, Ph.D.
Chris Hayward, M.D., M.P.H.
Kimberly Hill, Ph.D.
Keith Humphreys, Ph.D.
Jennifer Keller, Ph.D.
Roy King, M.D., Ph.D.
Cheryl Koopman, Ph.D.
Kristine Luce, Ph.D.
Rachel Manber, Ph.D.
Meg Marnell, Ph.D.
Louis Moffett, Ph.D.
Yvonne Morris, Ph.D.
Wendy Packman, J.D., Ph.D.
Thomas Plante, Ph.D.; ABPP.
Lisa Post, Ph.D.
Douglas Rait, Ph.D.
Craig Rosen, Ph.D.
Debra Safer, M.D.
Brent Solvason, Ph.D., M.D.
Hans Steiner, M.D.
Margo Thienemann, M.D.
Kim Wilson, Ph.D.
Toni Wroolie, Ph.D.
Phil Zimbardo, Ph.D.

PEPPERDINE UNIVERSITY

Graduate School of Education and Psychology
Psychology and Counseling Programs

Programs of Study

As more and more Americans understand the importance of mental health and the psychological underpinnings of marriage and family, teamwork, organizational change, and multicultural relationships, therapists and specialists in human behavior are enjoying a widening range of career options in the business world, the private sector, and private practice. Pepperdine University's Graduate School of Education and Psychology offers degree and credential programs designed to educate psychologists and counselors, mental health administrators, consultants, and change agents. Since its founding, Pepperdine University has maintained a values-based commitment to improving the lives of others. At the Graduate School of Education and Psychology, students benefit from the University's academic dedication to purpose, service, and leadership.

Psychology degree programs include a Master of Arts in psychology; a Master of Arts in clinical psychology, with an emphasis in marriage and family therapy; and a Doctor of Psychology (Psy.D.). The master's programs are designed for serious students seeking advanced learning in the research foundations and clinical applications of many current and emerging fields in psychology. Students may work at their own pace, with evening classes available for working professionals and a daytime program offered for full-time students.

The Doctor of Psychology in clinical psychology embodies the practitioner-scholar model of professional training. The University considers the practice of clinical psychology to be a healing art and professional discipline that is based upon the principles obtained from psychology as a science. The program, which is fully accredited by the American Psychological Association, offers both a generalist orientation as well as opportunities to study with experts in the major theoretical schools. Doctoral students learn research methods for application in professional practice and in advancing scientific knowledge. The Psy.D. program consists of three years of course work and an internship. A dissertation is required.

Research Facilities

A computer network links each of the University's libraries, which collectively contain more than 800,000 books, bound journals, and microforms. Each facility is fully supported with library services, wireless networking, and a computer center. The West Los Angeles Graduate Campus houses a multimedia center.

Pepperdine also offers psychology students the opportunity to work in one of the four University clinics where they receive both generalist and specialist training to serve children, adolescents, adults, and families. Also included in the wide array of clinical training venues are the unique partnership training programs administered by the University on public school campuses and at community agencies, such as the Union Rescue Mission.

Financial Aid

Scholarships, grants, and loans are available to qualified students. Veterans should follow regular admission procedures and secure the certificate of eligibility from the Veterans Administration or the state of California. More than 85 percent of students qualify for federal loans, and close to 70 percent are eligible for Pepperdine-funded assistance. Current information and all forms necessary to apply for financial aid are available on the financial aid Web site at http://gsep.pepperdine.edu/financialaid. For additional information, students should contact the Financial Aid Office at 310-568-5775 or gsepfaid@pepperdine.edu.

Cost of Study

Charges for one unit of instruction in 2007–08 varied from $840 to $1055, depending upon the program.

Living and Housing Costs

While there is a limited amount of graduate housing available for clinical M.A. students at Malibu, the other campuses are in proximity to apartment buildings and residential areas. Students are assisted in finding housing near the campus at which they are enrolled, whether the housing is an apartment, a town house, a condominium, or a guest room.

Student Group

Total University enrollment is approximately 7,356, and enrollment at the Graduate School of Education and Psychology is 1,600. Students range in age and experience, with many returning to the workforce or changing their careers and others entering the programs upon completing their undergraduate degree.

Location

The headquarters for the Graduate School of Education and Psychology is the West Los Angeles Graduate Campus, located 30 minutes west of downtown Los Angeles. The Drescher Graduate Campus in Malibu overlooks the Pacific Ocean from the Santa Monica Mountains. The Encino Graduate Campus is located in the San Fernando Valley. The Irvine Graduate Campus is in Orange County near the John Wayne Airport. The Westlake Village Graduate Campus is in Ventura County. Program offerings vary by location.

The University

Pepperdine, an independent, medium-sized Christian university, has two major campuses. Headquarters for the Graduate School of Education and Psychology and the Graziadio School of Business and Management is in West Los Angeles. On an 830-acre campus overlooking the Pacific Ocean at Malibu are Seaver College, the undergraduate residential college of letters, arts, and sciences; the School of Public Policy; and the School of Law.

Applying

Admission requirements vary by program. For more information, prospective students should contact the Graduate School of Education and Psychology.

Correspondence and Information

Office of Admissions
Graduate School of Education and Psychology
Pepperdine University
6100 Center Drive
Los Angeles, California 90045
Phone: 800-347-4849 (toll-free)
Web site: http://www.pepperdine.edu/GSEP

Pepperdine University

THE FACULTY

Joy Keiko Asamen, Professor; Ph.D., UCLA.
Aaron Aviera, Clinical Faculty and Clinic Director, West Los Angeles; Ph.D., UCLA.
Thema Bryant-Davis, Assistant Professor; Ph.D., Duke.
Anat Cohen, Clinical Faculty; Ph.D., California School of Professional Psychology.
Louis John Cozolino, Professor; Ph.D., UCLA.
Robert deMayo, Associate Dean of Psychology and Professor; Ph.D., UCLA.
Kathleen Eldridge, Assistant Professor; Ph.D., UCLA.
Drew Erhardt, Professor; Ph.D., UCLA.
David Foy, Professor; Ph.D., Southern Mississippi.
Miguel Gallardo, Assistant Professor; Psy.D., California School of Professional Psychology.
Susan Hall, Assistant Professor; J.D., Ph.D., Arizona.
Pamela Harmell, Lecturer; Ph.D., California School of Professional Psychology.
Shelly Prillerman Harrell, Professor; Ph.D., UCLA.
Joanne Hedgespeth, Professor; Ph.D., Biola.
Susan Himelstein, Lecturer; Ph.D., UCLA.
Robert Hohenstein, Visiting Faculty; Ph.D., American Commonwealth.
Barbara Ingram, Professor; Ph.D., USC.
Caroline Keatinge, Lecturer; Ph.D., Illinois at Chicago.
David Levy, Professor; Ph.D., UCLA.
Dennis Lowe, Professor; Ph.D., Florida State.
Tomas Martinez, Professor; Ph.D., Michigan.
Cary Mitchell, Professor; Ph.D., Kentucky.
Frances Neely, Emeritus Professor; Ph.D., Kansas.
Daryl Rowe, Professor; Ph.D., Ohio State.
Edward Shafranske, Professor; Ph.D., US International; Ph.D., Southern California Psychoanalytic Institute.
Amy R. Tuttle, Assistant Professor; Ph.D., Loma Linda.
Duncan Wigg, Clinical Faculty and Clinic Director, Irvine; Ph.D., California School of Professional Psychology.
Stephanie Woo, Associate Professor; Ph.D., UCLA.

Pepperdine University Malibu Campus.

The headquarters for the Graduate School of Education and Psychology in West Los Angeles.

PHILADELPHIA COLLEGE OF OSTEOPATHIC MEDICINE

Graduate Programs in Clinical Psychology, Counseling and Clinical Health Psychology, and School Psychology

Programs of Study

Philadelphia College of Osteopathic Medicine (PCOM) offers eight graduate programs taught by an internationally renowned, highly credentialed faculty. All faculty members in PCOM's psychology department are teaching faculty members who work closely with students to help them achieve their professional goals. Students often have the opportunity to coauthor scholarly papers, books, and professional presentations with faculty members. PCOM has one of the only psychology departments in the country that provides a standardized patient program. The standardized patient program presents authentic clinical learning and skills situations in which "patients" simulate mental health conditions. Students conduct sessions with the patients, which are videotaped and reviewed by the faculty members to help train and assess students' skills. Students in the psychology program also have the opportunity for clinical experience at any of the College's urban health-care centers.

The 85-credit Psy.D. in clinical psychology program takes five to seven years to complete, including course work, practicum, internship, and dissertation. Graduates of this program are prepared to assume responsibilities in a broad range of clinical settings. Post-doctoral certificates in clinical health psychology and clinical neuropsychology will each provide one year (16 and 19 credits respectively) of post-doctoral specialty training to doctoral-level psychologists. The 57-credit Psy.D. in school psychology program takes three to five years to complete. The fourteen-month, 33-credit M.S. in school psychology program prepares paraprofessionals in community and school settings to provide mental health services to children, youth, and families. This program, taken in sequence with the Ed.S. degree program, leads to certification in school psychology. The three-year, 45-credit Ed.S. program provides students with the knowledge and skills to assume the role of a school psychologist in diverse settings. The two-year, 48-credit M.S. in counseling and clinical health psychology program trains graduates to provide evaluation, counseling, and therapy services to clients in a variety of clinical settings. There is also a 60-credit addictions and offenders counseling track for the M.S. degree. M.S. graduates may also take 12 additional credits offered by PCOM and earn a Certificate of Advanced Graduate Study to meet the education requirements of the licensed professional counseling (LPC) credential in Pennsylvania and New Jersey. Designed for the working professional, all classes for the M.S., Ed.S., and Psy.D. programs are held in the evening and on weekends.

Research Facilities

The academic facilities at PCOM include state-of-the-art amphitheaters and classroom facilities; computer laboratories with extensive software, including PsycLIT and SPSS; a comfortable, sophisticated library with online access to electronic textbooks, journals, databases, and Internet guides; and access to the digital library and statistical programs through the Internet.

Financial Aid

The Financial Aid Office at PCOM offers financial assistance to students through the Federal Stafford Student Loan program, institutional grants, and various alternative private loan programs.

Cost of Study

In 2007–08, the direct cost of attending PCOM (including tuition, fees, required health insurance, books, and supplies) for the year was approximately $19,825 for counseling and clinical health psychology M.S. students, $19,825 for school psychology M.S. students, $16,225 for Ed.S. students, $27,145 for clinical psychology Psy.D. students, and $27,785 for school psychology Psy.D. students.

Living and Housing Costs

Students live off-campus within the Philadelphia metropolitan and suburban areas, as there is no on-campus housing. Room and board costs vary by each student's individual preferences.

Student Group

The programs seek a diverse group of students who are committed to excellence. The Psy.D. in clinical psychology program recruits in-practice professionals who have earned master's degrees in psychology, social work, counseling, psychiatric nursing, or a related field and are working in human services. This population brings to their studies a high level of maturity, established skills, diverse backgrounds, and a strong motivation to succeed. The Psy.D. in school psychology program recruits working school psychologists who want to be leaders in psychoeducational and mental health services to children, youth, and families. For 2007, the applicant pool for the clinical psychology Psy.D. class included 153 applicants. The average age of the 28 entering Psy.D. students was 29, with 82 percent women and 29 percent members of minority groups. For 2007, the Psy.D. in school psychology program enrolled a class of 16 with 69 percent women and 13 percent members of minority groups, with an average age of 35. The M.S. program in counseling and clinical health psychology enrolled a class of 33 students, 76 percent of whom were women and 9 percent of whom were members of minority groups, with an average age of 24. The M.S. program in school psychology enrolled a class of 19: 84 percent women and 11 percent members of minority groups, with an average age of 24. The Ed.S. program in school psychology enrolled a class of 20, 85 percent women and 30 percent members of minority groups, with an average age of 30.

Location

Located on City Avenue in Philadelphia, PCOM's 21-acre campus is minutes away from Fairmount Park, Philadelphia's historic district, art museums, theaters, restaurants, and professional sports complexes. Its renovated facilities include two large lecture halls, small classrooms, labs for teaching and research, and scenic landscaping, all in a suburban setting. PCOM also has four health-care centers in Philadelphia and one in LaPorte, Pennsylvania.

The College and The Programs

PCOM, which was chartered in 1899, enrolls approximately 2,090 students in its various programs. The clinical and teaching facility makes an ideal home for psychology graduate programs. The graduate psychology programs at PCOM are accredited by the Department of Education of the Commonwealth of Pennsylvania and the Middle States Association of Colleges and Schools. The clinical psychology Psy.D. program is accredited by the American Psychological Association and fulfills the requirements of the National Register for Healthcare Providers in Psychology. Clinical Psy.D. graduates qualify to take the Examination for Professional Practice of Psychology Licensure in Pennsylvania and New Jersey. The curriculum provides school psychology Psy.D. students with the knowledge and skills to assume the role of a school psychologist, practice in a variety of settings, and be prepared for eligibility for National Certification and for Pennsylvania licensure. The school psychology Psy.D. program has been granted approval by the National Association of School Psychologists. The M.S. program plus 12 credits has been designed to fulfill the Licensed Professional Counselor curriculum requirements in Pennsylvania and New Jersey.

Applying

Clinical psychology M.S. applicants need to have a baccalaureate degree from a regionally accredited institution, with basic psychology course work (introduction to psychology, abnormal psychology or psychopathology, and statistics). Psy.D. in clinical psychology applicants must have completed a master's degree in psychology or a related field at a regionally accredited institution and also completed developmental psychology, theories of personality, abnormal psychology or psychopathology, and statistics. Candidates for the post-doctoral certificate programs must have completed a doctoral degree in clinical psychology at a regionally accredited institution. Applicants to the M.S. in school psychology need to have a baccalaureate degree in psychology, education, or a related field from a regionally accredited institution and must have completed 6 credits each of English and math, abnormal psychology/psychopathology, or exceptional children and child psychology/adolescent psychology. Nine additional credits in psychology must also have been completed. Applicants to either M.S. program must have taken the GRE or MAT exam. Applicants to the Ed.S. program must have a master's degree in school psychology or a related field and must submit test scores from the GRE Psychology Subtest #81 and have successfully passed the Praxis I exam. Applicants to the Psy.D. in school psychology program must have a master's and specialist degree in school psychology and must be a licensed school psychologist. Candidates must also submit scores from the Praxis II School Psychology Specialty exam. All applicants must submit all college transcripts and three letters of recommendation with accompanying recommendation forms. The M.S., Ed.S., and Psy.D. programs utilize a rolling admissions policy. Finalists for all programs interview with the Admissions Committee and are then notified in writing of the committee's decision.

Correspondence and Information

Office of Admissions
Philadelphia College of Osteopathic Medicine
4170 City Avenue
Philadelphia, Pennsylvania 19131-1694
Phone: 215-871-6700
800-999-6998 (toll-free)
Fax: 215-871-6719
E-mail: gradadmissions@pcom.edu
Web site: http://www.pcom.edu

Philadelphia College of Osteopathic Medicine

THE FACULTY AND THEIR RESEARCH

Robert A. DiTomasso, Professor; Chair, Department of Psychology; and Director, Outcomes Assessment Research; Ph.D., Pennsylvania; ABPP (clinical psychology). Dr. DiTomasso has extensive teaching experience and has published dozens of chapters, articles, and reviews and a book on anxiety disorders. He specializes in behavioral medicine, the cognitive behavioral treatment of anxiety and stress-related medical disorders, research design, psychometrics, methodology, program evaluation, and primary-care consultation. He also specializes in patient nonadherence to medical advice and instrument development for cognitive distortions, anger, health risk behaviors, and patient satisfaction with medical services.

Stephanie Felgoise, Associate Professor; Vice Chair, Department of Psychology; and Director, Clinical Psy.D. Program; Ph.D., Hahnemann; ABPP. Dr. Felgoise has coauthored numerous national conference presentations and publications in psycho-oncology, sexual health and dysfunction, and coping and adjustment with chronic medical illness. Other interests include behavioral medicine, social problem solving, caregiver issues, and diversity issues in health care.

Michael Ascher, Clinical Professor; Ph.D., Pittsburgh. Dr. Ascher has done extensive research on the treatment of anxiety disorders (particularly agoraphobia, obsessive compulsive disorder, panic disorders, and phobias) within the context of behavior therapy. In addition, he has researched investor anxiety, including the emotional difficulties experienced by the average retail stock market investor, and the psychogenic disorders of sleep.

Stuart Badner, Clinical Assistant Professor; Psy.D., Wright State. Dr. Badner's research interests include critical incident stress management and debriefing, working with difficult clients, behavior management systems for children and adolescents, quality assurance/outcomes, family and organizational systems and program development, design, and staff training and development.

Virginia Burks-Salzer, Assistant Professor; Ph.D., Illinois. Dr. Salzer's research interests include social information processing in the development of children's aggressive behavior, linkages between family and children's peer systems, comorbidity of children's externalizing and internalizing disorders, and impact of parental psychopathology and the development of childhood disorders.

Stacey C. Cahn, Assistant Professor; Ph.D., Rutgers. Dr. Cahn's area of expertise is broadly clinical health psychology, including eating disorders, as well as the areas of sleep, depression in heart disease, and aging.

Ray W. Christner, Clinical Assistant Professor; Psy.D., Philadelphia College of Osteopathic Medicine; NCSP. Dr. Christner has published and presented on topics such as cognitive behavioral therapy (CBT) for various populations, crisis intervention, school psychology, consultation, and school violence. He has presented locally, statewide, nationally, and internationally. His research interests also include improving school climate and training and preparation of school psychologists and mental health professionals as well as crisis and trauma response.

William Clinton, Program Director, Organizational Development and Leadership Program; M.A., Bastyr. Mr. Clinton has extensive experience in organizational consultation and has held various leadership positions. His specialty is in training practitioners to become effective leaders who implement change in organizational settings.

Terri Erbacher, Clinical Assistant Professor; Ph.D., Temple. Dr. Erbacher is a certified school psychologist and licensed psychologist. Her specific population and program expertise includes nonpublic elementary and secondary schools, autistic support, learning support, early intervention, and supervision of school psychology interns.

Arthur Freeman, Professor; Ed.D., Columbia; ABPP. An internationally renowned expert on cognitive behavioral therapy, Dr. Freeman holds diplomas in clinical and behavioral psychology from the American Board of Professional Psychology and is a Fellow of the American Psychological Association. He has published extensively on cognitive behavioral therapy and is a past President of the Association for Advancement of Behavior Therapy.

Barbara Golden, Associate Professor and Director, Clinical Services; Psy.D., Loyola; ABPP. Dr. Golden's experience includes clinical service, administration, supervision, consultation, and education. Her primary areas of interest and research are in behavioral medicine, including nonpharmacological pain management, stress management, and somatization disorder, as well as in psychology and primary-care medicine.

Elizabeth Gosch, Associate Professor and Director, M.S. Program in Clinical Health Psychology; Ph.D., Temple; ABPP. One of Dr. Gosch's primary areas of expertise is psychotherapy with children and adolescents. Her major research interest concerns the processes and effectiveness of psychotherapy with differing populations. She has published and lectured internationally on the cognitive behavioral treatment of anxiety in children.

James B. Hale, Associate Professor and Associate Director, Clinical Training–School Psychology Program; Ph.D., Loyola. Trained in clinical neuropsychology, Dr. Hale has research interests in such areas as language and psychosocial functions associated with right-hemisphere dysfunction, challenging assumptions about standardized cognitive assessment and the validity of global IQ scores for children with disabilities, and frontal-subcortical circuit dysfunction in ADHD and medication response.

Dan Ingram, Clinical Instructor; Psy.D., Philadelphia College of Osteopathic Medicine. Dr. Ingram teaches in the school psychology M.S. program. He is a certified school psychologist with more than twenty-five years' experience. His research interests are in the area of autism.

Donald Masey, Clinical Associate Professor; Psy.D., Indiana of Pennsylvania. Dr. Masey's research interests include memory and aging, psychological assessment, hospital practice for psychologists, practice models and issues in professional psychology, medical psychology, adult learning disabilities, and adult ADHD.

George McCloskey, Associate Professor and Co-Director, Research; Ph.D., Penn State. Dr. McCloskey has accumulated a broad range of work experiences in the field of psychology over the last twenty-five years, including research, clinical work, administration, teaching, and business. His research and interests include neuropsychological process and learning, psychological and educational assessment and intervention, reading achievement, ADHD, executive dysfunction, memory problems, and expression disability.

Rosemary Mennuti, Clinical Professor and Director, School Psychology Program; Ed.D., Virginia Tech/Philadelphia College of Osteopathic Medicine; NCSP. Dr. Mennuti has extensive experience as a school psychologist and in teaching. She has lectured and published in the areas of moral development, eating disorders, and therapist self-disclosure. Other areas of interest include female development, CBT in schools, and relational cultural theory in practice.

Bradley Rosenfield, Clinical Assistant Professor; Psy.D., Philadelphia College of Osteopathic Medicine. Dr. Rosenfield's current research interests include cognitive behavioral therapy for adult ADHD, human-animal interactions, depressive disorders, somatic disorders, anxiety disorders, single session treatment for panic attacks, the social psychology of terrorism, multicultural counseling, communication skills, and treating difficult patients.

Frederick Rotgers, Clinical Associate Professor; Psy.D., Rutgers; ABPP. Dr. Rotgers' research interests include substance-use disorders, motivation and change in addictions, brief interventions for substance use in primary-care settings, efficacy of correctional addictions treatment, self-change of substance-use disorders, training nonspecialists in identification and intervention with substance-use disorders, and efficacy of non-12-step support groups for persons with alcohol/drug problems.

Christopher Royer, Clinical Assistant Professor; Psy.D., Widener. Dr. Royer's research interests include brain injury evaluation and/or treatment, cognitive disorders in psychiatric conditions, personality assessment, clinical outcomes, medical psychology, test construction/validation, assessment and intervention in geriatric populations, evaluation of model clinical approaches, and anxiety disorders.

Matthew Schure, President and Chief Executive Officer; Ph.D., Columbia. Dr. Schure's major areas of interest include personality correlates of learning, such as self-esteem, level of aspiration, and locus of control. In addition, he has done extensive research on community mental health interventions and family dynamics, including the outcome of dysfunctional parenting and parental rejection.

Marsha S. Singer, Clinical Assistant Professor and Associate Director, M.S. Program in Counseling and Clinical Health Psychology; Ph.D., Pennsylvania. Dr. Singer's main professional interest is clinical health psychology. She is very interested in the role of cultural, spiritual, and other psychosocial factors in health behavior and patient attitudes. She is also interested in the role of family members as social supports in medical and mental health settings.

Diane Smallwood, Associate Professor and Director, Training; Psy.D., Rutgers; NCSP. In addition to school-based work experience, for the past twenty years, Dr. Smallwood has been involved in leadership activities at both the state and national levels. Her professional interests include school crisis prevention, intervention, and response; social-emotional learning; classroom resiliency; bullying and violence in schools; and translating research to practice.

Takako Suzuki, Ph.D. Dr. Suzuki's major areas of interest include CBT of mood and anxiety disorders; multicultural issues such as development of cultural identity, acculturation process, and issues with expatriates; religion and spirituality; and emotional intelligence and development of empathy.

Yuma I. Tomes, Assistant Professor and Director, M.S. Program in School Psychology; Ph.D., Virginia Commonwealth/Medical College of Virginia. Dr. Tomes has accumulated a diverse range of work experiences in the field of psychology and education over the last ten years. He brings a unique perspective of clinical, teaching, research, and administrative experience to his position at PCOM. Dr. Tomes has worked as a psychologist in urban school districts. His major areas of interest are cross-cultural psychology, multicultural assessment, cognitive/learning styles, cognition and learning theories, psychological/educational assessments, consultation, and developmental issues.

Beverly White, Clinical Assistant Professor; Psy.D., Philadelphia College of Osteopathic Medicine. Dr. White has worked extensively with traumatized children and adolescents. She has published and has research interests in the areas of psychological assessment, dreams in CBT-oriented treatment, and crisis/trauma, post-traumatic stress, and CBT interventions. Other research interests include right/left-hemisphere performance and malfunction and multicultural issues.

Carrie Yurica, Clinical Assistant Professor; Psy.D., Philadelphia College of Osteopathic Medicine. Dr. Yurica is a certified school psychologist and half-time core faculty member at PCOM. She specializes in cognitive behavioral treatment for children, adolescents, and adults. Her research involves the relationship between cognitive distortions and various forms of psychotherapy.

Bruce Zahn, Assistant Professor and Clinical Training Director; Ed.D., Temple; ABPP. Dr. Zahn has published on cognitive behavioral therapy, childhood sexual abuse, multimodal therapy programs for adolescents, and psychological functioning in survivors of traumatic brain injury. His areas of expertise include geropsychology, behavioral medicine, cognitive behavioral therapy, self-esteem, group therapy, and supervision. Dr. Zahn's mentoring and research interests are in the areas of psychological testing (including projective personality assessment), post-traumatic stress disorder, managed-care issues, and chronic mental illness.

RENSSELAER POLYTECHNIC INSTITUTE

Cognitive Science Department

Program of Study

The doctoral program in Cognitive Science was launched in 2003 with the aim of training the next generation of world-class cognitive scientists, and making seminal contributions to the field. In keeping with the interdisciplinary nature of cognitive science, this program trains students to integrate theories, methods, and tools from a variety of fields. Students become engaged in research from the beginning of their first semester in the program, working closely with individual faculty members whose research interests include computational cognitive modeling, artificial intelligence, human and machine reasoning, computational linguistics, perception and action, theoretical neuroscience, cognitive robotics, cognitive engineering, and advanced synthetic characters. There is a strong emphasis on building models of natural and artificial cognitive systems using formal, quantitative, and mathematical tools. The Department has excellent research facilities, such as eye tracking equipment, a robotic arm, and a large-scale immersive virtual environment lab.

The general requirements for completion of the Ph.D. in cognition science consist of a combination of research and other scholarly activities, course work, and attendance at and participation in the Department's colloquia series. Individual and team-taught seminars are offered on a range of topics, from low-level perception-and-action to high-level reasoning and problem-solving. The program prepares students to become modelers, experimentalists, and theorists and to apply their research to solving real-world problems.

Research Facilities

Research is supported by state-of-the-art facilities and equipment including the Rensselaer Libraries, whose electronic information system provides access to collections, databases, and the Internet from campus and remote terminals; the Rensselaer Computing System, which permeates the campus with a coherent array of more than 7,000 nodes of distributed laptops, desktops, advanced workstations, and servers; a shared toolkit of applications for interactive learning and research and high-speed Internet connectivity; one of the country's largest academically based, class 100 clean room facilities; high-performance campuswide computing facilities that allow for serial or parallel computation; and five core laboratories for molecular biology, proteomics, bio-imaging, and tissue engineering.

Rensselaer's research capabilities have been enhanced with the addition of the Computational Center for Nanotechnology Innovations (CCNI). The result of a $100-million collaboration with IBM and New York State, the CCNI is the world's most powerful university-based supercomputing center and a top ten supercomputing center of any kind in the world. The CCNI is made up of massively parallel Blue Gene supercomputers, POWER-based Linux clusters, and Opteron-based clusters, providing more than 100 teraflops of computational muscle and approximately a petabyte of shared online storage.

Other facilities and research centers include the Center for Biotechnology and Interdisciplinary Studies; the George M. Low Center for Industrial Innovation; research centers for integrated electronics, terahertz science, nanotechnology, fuel cell and hydrogen research, lighting research, science and technology policy, and infrastructure and transportation studies; the Geotechnical Centrifuge Research Center; the Darrin Fresh Water Institute; and the Scientific Computation Research Center. In addition, academic departments and faculty laboratories have extensive discipline-specific research capabilities and equipment.

Within the Cognitive Science Department, research is conducted in the following labs: the CogWorks Laboratory, the Rensselaer Artificial Intelligence and Reasoning (RAIR) Laboratory, the PandA Labs, the Human-Level Intelligence Laboratory, and the Cognitive Architecture Laboratory (CogArch Lab).

At the CogWorks Laboratory, researchers conduct basic and applied research focused on understanding the interplay of cognition, perception, and action in interactive behavior. These interests entail understanding top-down versus bottom-up control of behavior, the role of implicit versus explicit knowledge, internal versus external representations, and knowledge in-the-head versus knowledge in-the-world.

Research and development in the RAIR Lab ranges across a number of applied projects as well as across many of the fundamental questions AI raises (e.g., Are we machines ourselves? If so, what sort of machines?). Everything is unified to a high degree by the fact that the formalisms, tools, techniques, systems, etc., that underlie the lab's R&D are invariably based on reasoning.

Research in the PandA Labs is aimed at understanding intelligence by studying the tight linkage between perception and action. Basic questions about visual perception and motor control and coordination are addressed by investigating routine and skilled perceptual-motor tasks, with a specific focus on visually guided actions. Experimental research is conducted in real and virtual environments, and mathematical models are developed using tools from dynamical systems theory and artificial intelligence.

The goal of the Human-Level Intelligence Laboratory is to explain human intelligence and design machines with human-level intelligence. Research is conducted in the integration of reasoning and learning, language understanding, metacognition, and physical reasoning.

The CogArch Lab is focused on research developing comprehensive models of human cognition, that is, cognitive architectures. Research is ongoing investigating the fundamental interaction of implicit and explicit cognition and the interaction of motivation, metacognition, and cognition, consciousness, and computation, as well as cognitive social simulation.

Financial Aid

Financial aid is available in the forms of teaching and research assistantships and fellowships, which include tuition scholarships and stipends. Rensselaer assistantships cover the academic year, with summer support available in many departments. University, corporate, or national fellowships fund many of Rensselaer's full-time graduate students. Outstanding students may qualify for university-sponsored Rensselaer Graduate Fellowship Awards, which carry a minimum stipend of $22,000 and a full tuition and fees scholarship. All fellowship awards are calendar-year awards for full-time graduate students. Low-interest, deferred-repayment graduate loans are available to U.S. citizens with demonstrated need.

Cost of Study

Full-time graduate tuition for the 2008–09 academic year is $36,950. Other costs (estimated living expenses, insurance, etc.) are projected to be about $13,680. Therefore, the cost of attendance for full-time graduate study is approximately $50,630. Part-time study and cohort programs are priced differently. Students should contact Rensselaer for specific cost information related to the programs they wish to study.

Living and Housing Costs

Graduate students at Rensselaer may choose from a variety of housing options. On campus, students can select one of the many residence halls and immerse themselves in campus life or choose from a select number of apartments designed for graduate students only. There are abundant, affordable options off campus as well, many within easy walking distance.

Student Group

Of the 1,176 graduate students, 29 percent are women and 92 percent are full-time, with 75 percent of full-time graduate students studying at the doctoral level.

Student Outcomes

Rensselaer's graduate students are hired in a variety of industries and sectors of the economy and by private and public organizations, the government, and institutions of higher education. Their starting salaries average $74,807 for master's degree recipients and $82,750 for Ph.D. recipients.

Location

Located just 10 miles northeast of Albany, New York State's capital city, Rensselaer's historic 275-acre campus sits on a hill overlooking the city of Troy, New York, and the Hudson River. The area offers a relaxed lifestyle with many cultural and recreational opportunities, with easy access to both the high-energy metropolitan centers of the Northeast—such as Boston, New York City, and Montreal, Canada—and the quiet beauty of the neighboring Adirondack Mountains.

The Institute

Recognized as a leader in interactive learning and interdisciplinary research, Rensselaer continues a tradition of excellence and technological innovation dating back to 1824. Rensselaer has five schools—Architecture, Engineering, Management, Science, and Humanities and Social Sciences—that offer more than 100 graduate programs in over forty-eight disciplines that attract top students, researchers, and professors. The discovery of new scientific concepts and technologies, especially in emerging interdisciplinary fields, is the lifeblood of Rensselaer's culture and a core goal for the faculty, staff, and students. Fueled by significant support from government, industry, and private donors, Rensselaer provides a world-class education in an environment tailored to the individual.

Applying

The admission deadline for the fall semester is January 1. Basic admission requirements are the submission of a completed application form (available online), the required application fee ($75), a statement of background and goals, official transcripts, official scores on the GRE General Test, TOEFL or IELTS scores (if applicable), and two recommendations.

Correspondence and Information

Cognitive Science Department
Carnegie 108
Rensselaer Polytechnic Institute
110 8th Street
Troy, New York 12180

Phone: 518-276-6472
E-mail: osgane@rpi.edu
Web site: http://www.cogsci.rpi.edu/index.shtml

Rensselaer Polytechnic Institute

THE FACULTY AND THEIR RESEARCH

Selmer Bringsjord, Professor and Chair; Ph.D., Brown. Artificial intelligence and cognitive science, including reasoning (computational, empirical, logico-mathematical, educational dimensions), logico-mathematical foundations of AI and Cog Sci, and computational creativity (especially literary), narrative, story generation; philosophy of mind, including philosophical and psychological foundations of AI & Cog Sci. (selmer@rpi.edu)
Toward a general logicist methodology for engineering ethically correct robots. *IEEE Intel. Syst.* 21.4:38–44, 2006.
A new Godelian argument for hypercomputing minds based on the busy beaver problem. *J. Appl. Math. Comput.* 176:516–30, 2006. With Yang.
Advanced synthetic characters, evil, and e. In *Sixth International Conference on Intelligent Games and Simulation,* pp. 31–9, Ghent-Zwijnaarde, Belgium: European Simulation Society, 2005.

Nick Cassimatis, Assistant Professor; Ph.D., MIT. Understanding and creating human-level intelligence. (cassin@rpi.edu)
A cognitive substrate for human-level intelligence. *AI Magazine* 27(2), 2006.
A model of syntactic parsing based on domain-general cognitive mechanisms. In *Proceedings of 28th Annual Conference of the Cognitive Science Society,* 2006.

Mark A. Changizi, Assistant Professor; Ph.D., Maryland. Theoretical and evolutionary neurobiology and cognitive science: understanding the design principles underlying the organization of organisms, cultural artifacts, and ourselves. (changizi@rpi.edu)
Scaling the brain and its connections. In *Evolution of Nervous Systems,* ed. J. H. Kaas. Oxford: Elsevier, 2007.
The structures of letters and symbols throughout human history are selected to match those found in objects in natural scenes. *Am. Nat.* 167:E117–39, 2006. With Zhang and Shimojo.
Bare skin, blood, and the evolution of primate color vision. *Biol. Lett.* 2:217–21, 2006. With Zhang and Shimojo.

Brett Fajen, Associate Professor; Ph.D., Connecticut. Perception and action, visual perception, motor control, virtual environments, ecological psychology, dynamical systems modeling. (fajenb@rpi.edu)
The scaling of information to action in visually guided braking. *J. Exp. Psych. Hum. Percept. Perform.* 31(5):1107–23, 2005.
Perceiving possibilities for action: On the necessity of calibration and perceptual learning for the visual guidance of action. *Perception* 34(6):741–55, 2005.
The behavioral dynamics of steering, obstacle avoidance, and route selection. *Journal of Experimental Psychology: Human Perception and Performance* 29(2):362, 2003.

Wayne D. Gray, Professor; Ph.D., Berkeley. Integrated cognitive systems, computational cognitive modeling, cognitive engineering: understanding the interplay of cognition, perception, and action in routine interactive behavior. (grayw@rpi.edu)
Integrated Models of Cognitive Systems. W. D. Gray, ed. New York: Oxford University Press, 2007.
The soft constraints hypothesis: A rational analysis approach to resource allocation for interactive behavior. *Psych. Rev.* 113(3):461–82, 2006.
Project Ernestine: Validating a GOMS analysis for predicting and explaining real-world performance. *Human-Computer Interaction* 8(3):237–309, 1993.

Mike Kalsher, Associate Professor; Ph.D., Virginia Tech. Human factors, industrial/organizational psychology, applied experimental psychology. (kalshm@rpi.edu)
Human factors design considerations for on-product medical device labels. In *Human Factors in Medical Device Design: A Handbook for Designers,* eds. M. Wiklund, D. Gardner-Bonneau, and M. B. Weinger. Mahwah, New Jersey: Lawrence Erlbaum & Associates, in press.
Psychology: From Science to Practice, Needham Heights, Massachusetts: Allyn & Bacon, 2005. With Baron.
Behavioral compliance and methodology. In *Handbook of Warnings,* ed. M. Wogalter. Mahwah, New Jersey: Lawrence Erlbaum & Associates, 2005.

Ralph G. Noble, Associate Professor; Ph.D., Berkeley. Psychobiology of choice and decision making. (nobler@rpi.edu)

Bill Puka, Professor; Ph.D., Harvard. Ethics and moral development, cognitive science: ethical problem-solving processes using protocol analysis. (pukab@rpi.edu)
Supporting ethical problem solving: An exploratory investigation. *Proceedings of the 2004 SIGMIS Conference on Computer Personnel Research: Careers, Culture, and Ethics in a Networked Environment,* pp.134–43. New York: ACM Press, 2004.
Fundamental Research in Moral Development. New York: Garland, 1994.

Larry Reid, Professor; Ph.D., Utah. Physiological psychology of reinforcement, drug and alcohol addiction. (reidl@rpi.edu)
Periodic naltrexone and propensity to take alcoholic beverage. *Alcoholism: Clinical and Experimental Research* 20:1329, 1996.

Ron Sun, Professor; Ph.D., Brandeis. Cognitive science and artificial intelligence, cognitive architectures, learning and skill acquisition, cognitive social simulation and multiagent systems, everyday commonsense reasoning, computational studies of consciousness, connectionist models and hybrid systems. (rsun@rpi.edu)
The interaction of the explicit and the implicit in skill learning: A dual-process approach. *Psychol. Rev.* 112(1):159–92, 2005.
From implicit skills to explicit knowledge: A bottom-up model of skill learning. *Cog. Sci.* 25(2):203–44, 2001.
Robust reasoning: Integrating rule-based and similarity-based reasoning. *Artif. Intell.* 75(2):241–96, 1995.

Yingrui Yang, Associate Professor; Ph.D., NYU. Cognitive psychology; thinking, reasoning, and decision making; cognitive science. (yangyri@rpi.edu)
Mental possible world mechanism: A new method for analyzing logical reasoning problems on the GRE. *J. Exp. Theo. Artif. Intell.* I18(2):157–68, 2006. With Bringsjord.
Strategies in sentential reasoning. *Cognitive Sci.* 26:425–68, 2002.
Some empirical justifications of one mental predicate-logic model. In *Mental Logic,* pp. 333–65, eds. M. D. S. Braine and D. P. O'Brien. Mahwah, New Jersey: Lawrence Erlbaum Associates, 1998.

Michael Zenzen, Professor; Ph.D., Rensselaer. Philosophy of science and foundations of physics, especially the use of mathematics in the construction of physical theory; general relation between rationality and intuition, specifically, the use of formalism to extend intuitive understanding. (zenzem@rpi.edu)
Superminds: People Harness Hypercomputation, and More. Dordrecht, The Netherlands: Kluwer, 2003. With Bringsjord.
Toward a formal philosophy of hypercomputation. *Minds and Machines* 12(2):241–58, 2002. With Bringsjord.
Cognition is not computation: The argument from irreversibility. *Synthese* 113(2):285–320. 1997. With Bringsjord.

ROGER WILLIAMS UNIVERSITY

Program in Forensic Psychology

Program of Study

Roger Williams is one of only a handful of academic institutions offering degrees specifically focused on the field of forensic psychology. The Master of Arts in Forensic Psychology Program at Roger Williams University prepares students in either a thesis or nonthesis track. Graduates are trained to conduct assessments and provide treatment services in a variety of forensic settings or pursue advanced training at the doctoral level. Students learn how to conduct psychological tests, explore various treatment methods, strengthen their research methodology skills, and become knowledgeable in psychopathology and clinical diagnosis.

In their second year of study, students are placed at a variety of internships and practicum sites. Students complete practical experiences in areas including group psychotherapy, sex offender treatment, individual psychotherapy, psychological testing, and specialized assessment techniques. Research-based internships are also possible for those students who are interested in preparing for further study at the doctoral level. The University strives to educate all students to become productive citizens of the social and professional communities in which they will live and build their careers, and faculty members are committed to fostering a strong sense of intellectual curiosity in all students, regardless of the intended career path.

Research Facilities

The Main Library has an extensive book collection, including access to more than 4,500,000 volumes in the HELIN library consortium, over 2,500 periodicals, and a wide selection of research tools, including twenty-nine new wireless computer workstations. The Law Library offers an impressive collection of legal research materials, including 270,000 volumes and volume equivalents in print and microform. In addition, the library subscribes to a variety of online and Web-based databases, including PsycArticles, PsycINFO, LexisNexis, and Westlaw.

The Justice System Training and Research Institute within the School of Justice Studies serves as a national model for integrating current research methodologies and state-of-the-art technology with the programmatic needs of the justice system. Work at the institute provides replicable models to strengthen the ability of state and local governments to provide more comprehensive and efficient programs designed to deliver a modern, fair, and equitable justice system to the communities and citizens served.

Financial Aid

Roger Williams University recognizes the need on the part of some students for financial assistance to meet the cost of higher education. Students who file the necessary paperwork may be able to receive funds available through federal student loan programs. Students fully accepted and maintaining a minimum of 6 credit hours per semester are eligible to receive loans that potentially cover the cost of graduate education. In order to be considered for the Federal Loan Program, students must submit the Free Application for Federal student Aid (FAFSA), which is available at http://www.fafsa.ed.gov.

Cost of Study

In 2007–08, graduate tuition for the Program in Forensic Psychology was $600 per credit. Each 3-credit course cost $1800. A slight increase is expected for the 2008–09 academic year. Some additional feels may apply.

Living and Housing Costs

The Department of Housing has designated a select group of University apartments as graduate housing. However, University housing is not guaranteed for graduate students, and the majority of graduate students seek a variety of off-campus housing options. In 2006–07, the average cost for graduate housing was $7150 per academic year. Off-campus housing costs vary depending on the size and location of the unit.

Student Group

The program is designed for students with an undergraduate degree in psychology, criminal justice, or another related field who are interested in contributing to the treatment of forensic populations.

Student Outcomes

Graduates of the program will be trained to serve forensic populations, including juveniles and sex offenders, in prisons or specialized treatment settings, through group and individualized psychotherapy, psychological testing, specialized testing with specific populations, specialized treatment or psycho-educational groups, work with families of juveniles, and work with psychiatrists and other clinical staff members in treatment and discharge planning. Program graduates may go on to act as trial consultants, work for family courts, research violent crimes for the FBI, become psychologists for the police department and federal government, and conduct psychological testing with prison populations.

Location

The University is located on 140 beautiful acres of waterfront campus in historic Bristol, Rhode Island. The location offers the comfort of a small, local community, and it is only 20 minutes from scenic Newport. The campus is an hour from Boston and approximately 3 hours from New York City. Bristol's streets are lined with historic homes, restaurants, great shops, and museums. Bristol Harbor offers sailing and kayaking, and bike riders can take advantage of the East Bay Bike Path or Colt State Park.

The University

Roger Williams University is an independent liberal arts university that strives to educate its 5,000 students to become productive citizens of the social and professional communities in which they live and work. The University was named for Roger Williams, the first major figure in colonial America to argue forcefully for the need for democracy and religious freedom. It is consistently rated in the top tier of private liberal arts colleges in the region by *U.S. News & World Report.*

Applying

A completed application includes a bachelor's degree in psychology, criminal justice, or a related field, with a 3.0 GPA and course work in statistics and research methods; a two-page personal statement describing the student's interest in forensic psychology and career goals and how the student can positively contribute to the graduate program; official college transcripts; minimum GRE scores of 1000; three letters of recommendation; and a $50 application fee. Applications are accepted for fall admission only; the application deadline date is March 15.

Correspondence and Information

Donald R. Whitworth, Ph.D.
Professor and Chair, Department of Psychology
Feinstein College of Arts and Sciences
Roger Williams University
One Old Ferry Road
Bristol, Rhode Island 02809
E-mail: dwhitworth@rwu.edu
Web site: http://www.rwu.edu/fcas/

Roger Williams University

THE FACULTY

Garrett L Berman, Associate Professor of Psychology; Ph.D., Florida International.
Bonita Cade, Assistant Professor of Psychology; Ph.D., Iowa State; J.D., Washington (St. Louis).
Frank DiCataldo, Assistant Professor of Psychology; Ph.D., St. Louis.
Kim Knight, Professor of Psychology; Ph.D., Boston University.
Judith Platania, Assistant Professor of Psychology; Ph.D., Florida International.
Becky L. Spritz, Assistant Professor of Psychology; Ph.D., Penn State.
Charles Trimbach, Professor of Psychology; Ph.D., Princeton.
Laura L. Turner, Assistant Professor of Psychology. Ph.D., Penn State.
Donald Whitworth, Professor of Psychology; Ph.D., Rhode Island.
Matt Zaitchik, Associate Professor of Psychology; Ph.D., Connecticut.

RUTGERS, THE STATE UNIVERSITY OF NEW JERSEY, NEWARK

Graduate Program in Psychology
Concentrations in Cognitive Science, Cognitive Neuroscience, Perception, Biopsychology, and Social Psychology

Programs of Study

Students entering the graduate program in psychology can take courses of study leading to a Ph.D. in psychology with specializations in biopsychology, cognitive neuroscience, cognitive science, perception, and social psychology. Current research in the biopsychology of emotion and adaptive behavior focuses on the motivational, evolutionary, and developmental mechanisms underlying behavior. Research in cognitive neuroscience offers training in neuroimaging methods, concepts, and experimental paradigms. The neuroimaging research focus includes studies in motion and event perception, learning and memory, and how humans process rewards and punishments. Research in the area of cognitive science offers training in the computational and experimental study of cognitive processes. The curriculum provides basic instruction in computational and mathematical modeling methods, with a focus on connectionist systems, learning, memory, and categorization. The perception specialization offers training in the experimental study of motion and color perception as well as many advanced areas within vision science. The social psychology concentration focuses on attachment theory, the mediation of social and interpersonal conflict, aggression, violence and bullying, interracial feedback, social support, and the methods and techniques used most commonly in these areas.

Students are encouraged to take advantage of training opportunities in the adjacent Center for Molecular and Behavioral Neuroscience, the College of Business (Information Sciences), the College of Nursing, the Department of Biological Sciences, the University of Medicine and Dentistry of New Jersey (UMDNJ), and the New Jersey Institute of Technology as well as adjunct courses listed in related areas (such as linguistics, philosophy, or cognitive science) on the New Brunswick campus. A written qualifying examination is given after the completion of basic course work at the end of the second year. Upon satisfactory completion of these requirements, students advance to candidacy for the Ph.D. degree and must submit a thesis proposal, carry out their thesis research, and then defend their dissertation.

Research Facilities

The Department of Psychology occupies about 42,000 square feet on the first, third, fourth, and fifth floors of Smith Hall. The department has its own servers (http://psychology.rutgers.edu, http://www.psych.rutgers.edu), computing laboratory, and a series of individual laboratories for neurophysiological, neuroanatomical, and neuropharmacological research. There are more than 16,000 square feet for animal holding and testing. The Psychology Department with UMDNJ supports the Advanced Imaging Center with a state-of-the-art Siemens 3T Allegra head-only magnet (more information can be found at http://www.rutgers-newark.rutgers.edu/fmri) and 64-channel EEG (Neuroscan) and 32-channel EEG (Digital ANT) systems.

Additional equipment includes an optical motion capture system for the perception of biological movement, a variety of human observation and testing rooms, one-way observation rooms, video equipment, high-speed graphics computers, and access to a Hewlett Packard Itanium II Workstation linked to the department's 28-node Opteron computer cluster and storage system, which can hold one trillion bytes of data.

Financial Aid

Students accepted into the program receive a full stipend and tuition remission through one of the wide range of scholarships, fellowships, and assistantships offered by the Rutgers Graduate School to full-time Ph.D. students whose records demonstrate superior academic achievement and scholarly promise. Stipends range up to $18,000 plus tuition remission for fellowships and $21,400 for teaching or graduate assistantships. They may be renewed for one or more years depending on the availability of funds and the academic standing of the student.. Students who are members of minority groups may also be eligible to receive additional support through the Minority Biomedical Research Support Program and other programs. Students also receive financial support from the Department of Psychology to attend conferences.

Cost of Study

Tuition for the 2008–09 academic year is about $14,500 (for New Jersey residents) and about $22,000 for out-of-state residents; graduate students receive tuition remission along with their source of support.

Living and Housing Costs

Graduate student housing is available in Talbott Apartments and University Square Apartments. Costs range from $7300 for an academic year lease to $10,500 for a calendar year lease. All options are single rooms in either a 3-person or 4-person shared apartment. A limited number of family apartment options are available for married/domestic partners and students with children in University-owned brownstones.

Student Group

There are currently 25 full-time graduate doctoral students carrying out research in the Department of Psychology. The faculty-student ratio of 1:2 affords ample opportunity for students to interact with faculty members. Students in the Department of Psychology are represented in policy decisions and are actively involved in the selection of new students.

Location

Rutgers' Newark campus is conveniently located in the center of a diverse and thriving educational, professional, and cultural community in the downtown area of New Jersey's largest city. Newark is also at the center of the nation's largest concentration of pharmaceutical industries. The campus is a modern complex serving more than 10,000 students and 500 faculty members. Rutgers-Newark is easily accessible by car or mass transit and is approximately 30 minutes by road or rail from midtown Manhattan. A free campus shuttle bus links the campus with the city's mass transit centers during the evening hours. The Department of Psychology is located one block from the University's jogging track, fully equipped gymnasium, and swimming pool.

The University

Rutgers, The State University of New Jersey, with more than 47,000 students on campuses in Camden, Newark, and New Brunswick, is one of the major state universities in the nation. The Newark campus is part of a complex of higher education institutions that includes the New Jersey Institute of Technology and the University of Medicine and Dentistry of New Jersey.

Applying

Students apply to enter the program on a full-time basis. Students should apply to the Department of Psychology and mention the area of study they are most interested in. Applications can be submitted at http://gradstudy.rutgers.edu/. The application deadline for the fall semester is January 15 and for the spring semester, November 1. Students should include scores for the General GRE and the Subject GRE in their area of interest.

Correspondence and Information

Kenneth Kressel, Ph.D., Director of Graduate Programs in Psychology
Department of Psychology
301 Smith Hall
Rutgers, The State University of New Jersey
101 Warren Street
Newark, New Jersey 07102
Phone: 973-353-5440 Ext. 232
Fax: 973-353-1171
E-mail: gradprogram@psychology.rutgers.edu
Web site: http://www.psych.rutgers.edu

Rutgers, The State University of New Jersey, Newark

THE FACULTY AND THEIR RESEARCH

Colin G. Beer, D.Phil., Oxford. Ethology, communication, and social development of birds; historical and philosophical aspects of ethology; comparative psychology.
Paul Boxer, Ph.D., Bowling Green. Aggression and violence, social development, contextual influences on behavior.
Mei-Fang Cheng, Ph.D., Bryn Mawr. Neuroethology; neurobiological study of vocal behavior and self-stimulation; mechanism and function of brain injury–induced neurogenesis in adult animals.
Mauricio Delgado, Ph.D., Pittsburgh. Behavioral and neural correlates of reward-related processing, with an emphasis on how the affective properties of outcomes or feedback influence choice behavior; using neuroimaging and behavioral and psychophysiological methods.
Alan Gilchrist, Ph.D., Rutgers. Visual cognition; surface-color perception.
Stephen José Hanson, Ph.D., Arizona State. Learning and memory, connectionist models, categorization, cognitive science.
Kent D. Harber, Ph.D., Stanford. Interracial feedback biases; social support and coping; emotion and social perception.
Barry R. Komisaruk, Ph.D., Rutgers. Neurophysiological, functional neuroanatomical, and neuropharmacological study of endogenous pain-blocking mechanisms related to sexual behavior and parturition in mammals, including humans; brain, spinal cord, autonomic, and peripheral nerve mechanisms, using functional magnetic resonance imaging (fMRI).
Ken Kressel, Ph.D., Columbia. Social and interpersonal conflict, mediation of conflict, conflict dynamics in organizational settings.
Lillian Robbins, Ph.D., NYU. Improving educational practices (K–16) for the disadvantaged, sex discrimination in academe, parental attitudes and practices, environmental factors in health and safety.
Maggie Shiffrar, Ph.D., Stanford. Visual motion perception; object recognition.
Harold I. Siegel, Ph.D., Rutgers. Attachment theory; adult attachment; attitudes toward mother and other adult relationships, attachment and sexual offenders.
Elizabeth Tricomi, Ph.D., Pittsburgh. Functional neuroimaging of learning and decision making, social and affective influences on reward processing and valuation, neural basis of goal-directed behavior.
Gretchen Van de Walle, Ph.D., Cornell. Conceptual understanding of physical objects and numbers and the interaction between conceptual development and linguistic abilities, particularly the relationship between children's ability to categorize and label classes of objects.

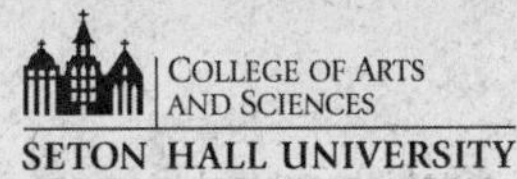

SETON HALL UNIVERSITY

Department of Psychology
Master of Science in Experimental Psychology

Program of Study

The Department of Psychology offers the Master of Science (M.S.) in experimental psychology, with concentrations in general psychology and behavioral neuroscience. The M.S. degree program is designed specifically for students seeking to gain a solid foundation in empirical research for eventual entry into Ph.D. programs in clinical or counseling psychology, experimental psychology, or neuroscience. Graduates also go directly to related areas of employment as laboratory assistants, market researchers, science writers, or community college teachers.

The program consists of 36 credits, or twelve courses (two courses in research design and analysis, four semesters of independent research, and either six experimental psychology electives or six required neuroscience courses), to be completed in two years. The courses offered include biological bases of behavior, foundations of neuropsychology, developmental psychology, conditioning and behavior, and many others. Those in the general psychology concentration must consult an adviser on elective course selections.

For additional information about the program, including details about faculty research and graduate student research, students should visit http://www.shu.edu/academics/artsci/ms-psychology/index.cfm.

Research Facilities

The University libraries have notable resources, including extensive holdings of almost 523,000 book volumes, 1,127 current periodical subscriptions, back-files of more than 6,500 serial titles, electronic access to full text articles in 11,500 journals, a broad selection of indexing and abstracting services in both digital and print formats, various microform collections, music CDs, and audiovisual aids.

The Department of Psychology is housed in Jubilee Hall, one of the newest academic buildings at Seton Hall University. The department facilities include two wireless classrooms with adjacent support areas (for instructional equipment and media production). The department maintains a Behavioral Neuroscience Laboratory for surgery, histology, and computerized monitoring of rodent behaviors to conduct modern behavioral neuroscience research. Research space for Human Experimental Psychology includes eleven research cubicles and a three-room Perception Laboratory suite.

Financial Aid

Graduate assistantships, which include tuition benefits and stipend, are available on a competitive basis. The online application for graduate assistantships can be found at http://www.shu.edu/applying/graduate/grad-finaid.cfm. Students should contact the Department at psych@shu.edu for further information about graduate assistantships.

Cost of Study

In 2008–09, tuition is $875 per credit. Full-time students pay $305 in University and technology fees; part-time students pay $185.

Living and Housing Costs

Housing and living costs in South Orange and the surrounding towns are comparable to most suburban cities, with studio and one-bedroom apartments renting for $750 to $1000 per month. Some students have also opted to share apartments with roommates.

Student Group

The M.S. in Experimental Psychology program enrolls about 8 to 10 new students each year. Overall, Seton Hall has approximately 4,500 graduate students.

Location

Seton Hall University is located in South Orange, New Jersey, only 14 miles by car, bus, or direct train to New York City. The University's proximity to New York allows students to take advantage of all the city has to offer, while still living in a suburban area.

The University and The Department

Seton Hall University's diverse academic program is characterized by a strong teaching faculty and a wide range of academic choices. At Seton Hall, students find people who are willing to listen, offer support, and help them get the most out of their education.

The Department of Psychology is a part of the College of Arts and Sciences, home to more than 4,000 students and faculty members engaged in one of the most rewarding of all human endeavors—the pursuit of knowledge. Rooted in tradition, yet looking to the future through innovative use of technology and a commitment to providing students with co-curricular and professional opportunities, the College of Arts and Sciences offers a rich array of graduate programs.

Applying

In addition to the general University requirements for admission to graduate studies, the Department of Psychology requires applicants to have a baccalaureate degree that reflects the completion of a minimum of 18 credits in psychology with at least a 3.0 grade point average. All applicants must have completed Introduction to Psychology, Psychological Statistics, and Research Methods courses. Students considering a concentration in behavioral neuroscience must have completed Physiological Psychology or the equivalent. Applicants should submit official transcripts of all previous academic work, official scores on the Graduate Record Examination (GRE), three letters of recommendation from individuals familiar with the applicant's academic and research ability, and a personal statement of 300 to 400 words that outlines the student's academic achievements, research interests, and career goals.

Applications are available online at http://www.shu.edu/academics/artsci/apply-graduate.cfm. Applications completed before April 1 for fall admissions and before November 1 for spring admissions are given top priority. Applications after these dates are reviewed on a rolling basis. This process continues until no openings are left.

Correspondence and Information

Dr. Janine P. Buckner, Director of Graduate Studies
Department of Psychology
College of Arts and Sciences
Jubilee Hall, Room 339
Seton Hall University
400 South Orange Avenue
South Orange, New Jersey 07079
Phone: 973-761-9484
Fax: 973-275-5829
E-mail: artsci@shu.edu
psych@shu.edu
Web site: http://www.shu.edu/academics/artsci/ms-psychology/

Seton Hall University

THE FACULTY AND THEIR RESEARCH

Janine P. Buckner, Associate Professor and Director of Graduate Studies; Ph.D., Emory, 2000. Gender differences in autobiographical memory narratives; personal, social, and contextual factors shaping gender disparities in science fields.

Gregory Burton, Professor; Ph.D., Connecticut, 1990. Touch perception of and with tools.

Paige Fisher, Assistant Professor; Ph.D., Massachusetts Amherst, 2005. Anxiety and mood disorders in children.

Kelly Goedert, Assistant Professor; Ph.D., Virginia, 2001. Statistical, heuristic, and memory processes in causal reasoning from contingency information; characteristics of memory for motor skills and perceptual-motor adaptations.

John Hovancik, Associate Professor; Ph.D., Purdue, 1975. Computer applications in psychology.

Jeffrey Levy, Associate Professor; Ph.D., Adelphi, 1972. Teaching of psychology, outcomes assessment.

Marianne Lloyd, Assistant Professor; Ph.D., Binghamton, 2005. Memory illusions, metacognition, geography learning.

Susan A. Nolan, Associate Professor and Chair; Ph.D., Northwestern, 1998. Interpersonal dynamics of depression and anxiety, gender issues in the sciences, teaching of statistics.

Amy Silvestri, Associate Professor; Ph.D., Vermont, 1997. Interactions between sleep and learning in experimental animals, how REM sleep deprivation can impair memory for a previously learned event and the biochemical mechanisms that underlie this phenomenon.

Andrew Simon, Associate Professor; Ph.D., Psy.D., Rutgers. Organizational dynamics, with a focus on leadership and decision making and work-teams.

Susan Teague, Associate Professor; Ph.D., Georgia, 1987. Attitude change and persuasion processes, especially as related to promotion of preventive health behaviors; aggressive and violent behavior.

Michael Vigorito, Associate Professor; Ph.D., Massachusetts Amherst, 1988. Animal learning and motivation, behavioral pharmacology, technology-enhanced curriculum development.

SOUTHERN ILLINOIS UNIVERSITY CARBONDALE

Department of Psychology

Programs of Study The Southern Illinois University Carbondale (SIUC) Department of Psychology offers doctoral training in four areas: applied psychology (AP), brain and cognitive sciences (BCS), clinical psychology, and counseling psychology. The clinical and counseling programs are accredited by the American Psychological Association (APA). All programs involve a full-time course of study, typically four years on campus, with an additional internship year for both the clinical and counseling programs. Students complete Departmental course requirements (primarily methodology), a carefully developed program curriculum, an empirical M.A. thesis, and a doctoral dissertation. The Department does not admit students seeking a terminal master's degree; students earn the M.A. en route to a Ph.D. Rarely, students earn a terminal M.A. or nonempirical M.S. when they or the faculty members reconsider their suitability for doctoral study. The Department has a strong collegial atmosphere, and students benefit from access to faculty members from all programs. Throughout their studies, students are engaged in diverse preprofessional training assignments appropriate to their program, involving wide-ranging activities related to teaching, basic and applied research, and clinical or counseling services.

Research Facilities The Department maintains extensive and quite comprehensive research facilities. Active human laboratories permit the use of methodologies such as eye tracking, single-unit recording, computer presentation of stimuli, controlled delivery of substances, recording and coding of child behavior, three-dimensional animation, neural network modeling, EEG recording, evoked potential recording, and human genotyping of individual differences related to personality, psychopathology, and substance use. Animal laboratories permit studies of animal learning (operant chambers and mazes), recovery of function, specific nerve stimulation, experimental surgery, contingent delivery of substances, psychopharmacology, and other areas of neuroscience. Diverse field research opportunities are available; collaborative sites include the campus Clinical Center, Student Health Service, the Department's Career Development and Resource Clinic, and local mental health and human service agencies, in addition to access to equipment necessary for survey development and scanning, telephone and in-person interviewing, computer-assisted interviewing and data collection, and still and video recording. Students also have access to state-of-the-art computer labs, including a small lab dedicated to psychology graduate students.

Financial Aid The SIUC Department of Psychology has a very strong record of supporting students. All students in good standing are guaranteed support for their first academic year (nine months), and they typically receive nine to ten months of support for four or more academic years. Assistantship support comes from diverse sources such as college teaching assistantships, Graduate School fellowships, research grants, and service contracts with campus and local agencies, providing valuable preprofessional training opportunities. Assistantships include tuition waivers.

Cost of Study In-state graduate tuition is $313.90 per credit hour in 2008–09. Out-of-state tuition is 2.5 times the in-state tuition rate ($784.75 per credit hour). Graduate students with at least a 25 percent appointment as a graduate assistant receive a tuition scholarship. Fees vary from $511.26 (1 credit hour) to $1416.05 (12 credit hours). Students with a graduate assistantship receive a 25 percent reduction in the Primary Care Medical Fee.

Living and Housing Costs For married couples, students with families, and single graduate students, the University has 690 efficiency and one-, two-, three-, and four-bedroom apartments that rent for $484 to $686 per month in 2008–09. Residence halls for single graduate students are also available, as are accessible residence hall rooms and apartments for students with disabilities.

Student Group The program usually admits approximately 20 students per year. Typically, the program has approximately 80 students, of whom roughly 65 percent are women, 20 percent are members of minority groups, and 5 to 10 percent are international.

Location SIUC is 350 miles south of Chicago and 100 miles southeast of St. Louis. Nestled in rolling hills bordered by the Ohio and Mississippi Rivers and enhanced by a mild climate, the area has state parks, national forests and wildlife refuges, and large lakes for outdoor recreation. Cultural offerings include theater, opera, concerts, art exhibits, and cinema. Educational facilities for the families of students are excellent.

The University Southern Illinois University Carbondale is a comprehensive public university with a variety of general and professional education programs. The University offers associate, bachelor's, master's, and doctoral degrees; the J.D. degree; and the M.D. degree. The University is fully accredited by the North Central Association of Colleges and Schools. The Graduate School has an essential role in the development and coordination of graduate instruction and research programs. The Graduate Council has academic responsibility for determining graduate standards, recommending new graduate programs and research centers, and establishing policies to facilitate the research effort. Southern Illinois University Carbondale is a state-funded university founded in 1869.

Applying Applications are accepted once a year (December 15 and February 1 application deadlines, depending on the program) for admission the following fall. Applications are available on the Department's Web site or may be requested via e-mail or phone or by mail. All application materials should be sent to the Psychology Graduate Program Office. A complete application includes the Departmental application form; the Graduate School application form, which must be completed online; a personal statement; a summary of research/professional experience; three letters of recommendation; two copies of official transcripts of all college work; official GRE scores; the official Advanced Psychology GRE score (not required, but preferred); and a $50 application fee.

Correspondence and Information

Graduate Program Office
Department of Psychology
Room 281A
Southern Illinois University Carbondale
Carbondale, Illinois 62901-6502

Phone: 618-453-3564
E-mail: gradpsyc@siu.edu
Web site: http://www.psychology.siu.edu

Southern Illinois University Carbondale

THE FACULTY AND THEIR RESEARCH

Mary Louise Cashel, Ph.D., North Texas, 1997. Clinical: Child and adolescent assessment, juvenile delinquency and preventative interventions, post-traumatic stress disorder (PTSD).
Kathleen Chwalisz, Ph.D., Iowa, 1992. Counseling: Health psychology, neuropsychology, group process and intervention, personality.
M. H. Clark, Ph.D., Memphis, 2004. Experimental–Applied Psychology: Methodology, quasi-experimentation, meta-analysis, statistics.
David DiLalla, Ph.D., Virginia, 1989. Clinical: Personality and psychopathology, personality assessment, computer-assisted assessment, behavioral genetics, sexual violence, social development.
*Lisabeth DiLalla, Ph.D., Virginia, 1987. Experimental–Brain and Cognitive Sciences: Behavioral genetics, social cognition.
Stephanie Clancy Dollinger, Ph.D., Syracuse, 1989. Experimental–Brain and Cognitive Sciences: Aging and cognition, identity development and cognition across the lifespan.
Stephen Dollinger, Director of Clinical Training; Ph.D., Missouri, 1977. Psychotherapy, personality, child-clinical.
Paul E. Etcheverry, Ph.D., Purdue, 2004. Experimental-Applied Psychology: Interpersonal relationships and health, social network influence on relationship outcomes and substance use.
Ann R. Fischer, Ph.D., Missouri–Columbia, 1995. Counseling: Counseling, gender issues, multicultural issues.
Brenda Gilbert, Ph.D., Florida, 1983. Clinical: Child behavior therapy, pediatric psychology, child abuse.
David Gilbert, Ph.D., Florida State, 1978. Clinical: State-dependent motivation, marital research, substance use, smoking, psychophysiology, personality, emotions, cerebral asymmetries.
Reza Habib, Ph.D., Toronto, 2000. Experimental–Brain and Cognitive Sciences: Cognitive neuroscience, brain imaging, cognition and memory.
Michael R. Hoane, Ph.D., Texas Christian, 1996. Experimental–Brain and Cognitive Sciences: Effects of vita-nutrients in brain injury and neurodegenerative diseases.
Eric A. Jacobs, Ph.D., Florida, 1997. Experimental–Applied Psychology and Brain and Cognitive Sciences: Experimental analysis of behavior, human operant behavior, verbal behavior, choice and self-control, behavioral ecology, behavioral economics, behavioral pharmacology, contingency management, radical behaviorism, cultural materialism.
Michelle Y. Kibby, Ph.D., Memphis, 1998. Clinical: Child assessment, clinical neuropsychology, reading disorders.
Meera Komarraju, Ph.D., Osmania (India), 1982; Ph.D., Cincinnati, 1987. Experimental–Applied Psychology: Life-stages and career-stages, work-family interface, cross-cultural influences on work values, academic motivation and dual-career phenomena, management of health-care quality.
Usha Lakshmanan, Ph.D., Michigan, 1989. Psycholinguistics, bilingualism, child first-language acquisition (monolingual and bilingual), child and adult second-language acquisition, language and cognition.
Benjamin F. Rodriguez, Ph.D., Catholic University, 2001. Clinical: Anxiety disorders, PTSD, religion and coping, epidemiology.
Patrick J. Rottinghaus, Ph.D. Iowa State, 2004. Counseling: Vocational psychology, counseling psychology.
Matthew Schlesinger, Ph.D., Berkeley, 1993. Experimental–Brain and Cognitive Sciences: Early cognitive development, problem solving, motor control, computational models of sensorimotor cognition.
Douglas Smith, Ph.D., Kansas State, 1977. Experimental–Brain and Cognitive Sciences: Biopsychology, neurophysiology, vision, development, learning and memory, recovery of function, epilepsy, psychoactive drugs.
Margaret Stockdale, Ph.D., Kansas State, 1990. Experimental–Applied Psychology: Industrial/organizational, gender bias in personnel decision, sexual harassment, workplace violence.
Jane Swanson, Ph.D., Minnesota, 1986. Counseling: Career choice and development, career assessment, adolescent career exploration.
Alan Vaux, Ph.D., Trinity College (Dublin), 1979; Ph.D., California, Irvine, 1981. Clinical and Experimental–Applied Psychology: Community psychology, social support and stress, close relationships and personality, violence, prevention, social interventions.
Yu-Wei Wang, Ph.D., Missouri–Columbia. Counseling: Stress, trauma, and coping/problem solving; sexual abuse/assault; multicultural and international issues; research methodology.
Rebecca Weston, Ph.D., North Texas, 2001. Experimental–Applied Psychology: Interpersonal relationships, violence, psychological abuse, sexual assault, and relational outcomes; advanced multivariate statistics.
Michael Young, Ph.D., Minnesota, Twin Cities, 1995. Experimental–Brain and Cognitive Sciences: Learning (of causal and temporal relationships and of categories), abstract concepts, judgment and decision making, computational modeling of learning processes (with a focus on radial basis function neural network models).

Emerita/Emeritus Faculty

Linda Gannon, Ph.D., Wisconsin, 1975. Clinical: Psychology of women, feminist therapy, behavior medicine, depression, cognitive styles.
Robert Jensen, Ph.D., Northern Illinois, 1976. Experimental–Brain and Cognitive Sciences: Neurobiology of learning and memory, psychopharmacology, drug dependence, behavioral development.
Jack McKillip, Ph.D., Loyola of Chicago, 1994. Experimental–Applied Psychology: Program evaluation, training and certification program development and evaluation, needs assessment, secondary data analysis.
James O'Donnell, Ph.D., Pittsburgh, 1965. Clinical: Child psychopathology, clinical neuropsychology, child and adult learning disabilities, attention deficit disorders.
Robert Radtke, Ph.D., Iowa, 1963. Experimental: Memory, cognitive processes.
Nerella Ramanaiah, Ph.D., Oregon, 1971. Experimental and Clinical: Personality and prediction, test theory, quantitative methods.
Thomas Schill, Ph.D., Oklahoma State, 1963. Clinical: Personality theory and dynamics, personality evaluation, rational emotive psychotherapy.
Ronald Schmeck, Ph.D., Ohio, 1969. Experimental: Teaching methods, individual differences in learning, learning style, cognitive style.
John Snyder, Ph.D., Loyola Chicago, 1965; ABPP. Counseling: Disaster intervention; American Red Cross Mental Health professional.
Barbara Yanico, Ph.D., Ohio State, 1977. Counseling: Gender roles and stereotyping, preferences for and expectations of counselors, stress and coping, racial/ethnic identity, personality and attitude measurement.

**Cross-appointed faculty member*

SOUTHERN ILLINOIS UNIVERSITY CARBONDALE

Rehabilitation Institute

Programs of Study

Recent census data estimate that approximately 50 million American adults have a chronic health condition and/or disability that prevent them from achieving personal or vocational independence. The Rehabilitation Institute at Southern Illinois University Carbondale (SIUC) is dedicated to improving the lives of people with disability. This mission is pursued through the teaching, research, and service activities of the Institute's faculty and staff members. A Doctor of Philosophy in Rehabilitation degree and four Master of Science degrees (behavior analysis and therapy, communication disorders and sciences, rehabilitation administration and services, rehabilitation counseling) are offered. To date, there are more than 3,200 graduates of the academic programs. They are found in every state of the nation and, with the exception of Antarctica, on every continent of the world. Graduates work in such varied settings as universities, hospitals, schools, mental health facilities, substance-abuse centers, geriatric agencies, correctional facilities, public vocational rehabilitation programs, rehabilitation centers, and private rehabilitation. Examples of direct service job titles held by Institute graduates include rehabilitation counselor, substance abuse counselor, behavior analyst, speech-language pathologist, case manager, job-placement specialist, vocational evaluator, work-adjustment specialist, community-based training instructor, job coach, and developmental trainer. In short, the Rehabilitation Institute is one of the largest, most comprehensive and respected rehabilitation training programs in the United States.

Research Facilities

The Institute currently has several community-service programs that offer training and research experiences for students. For example, the Evaluation and Developmental Center provides vocational rehabilitation, adult education, and independent living services to adolescents and adults with disabilities. Project 12-Ways offers a behavioral intervention program to prevent child neglect and abuse. Speech and Hearing Services assess and treat people with communication disorders. This Institute's Center for Autism Spectrum Disorders has been recently added to enhance the language and social skills of preschool children with autism. The service programs provide lifelong benefits to people with different rehabilitation needs, serving hundreds of citizens of Southern Illinois yearly. They also provide excellent real-world training and research opportunities for students.

Financial Aid

Financial assistance is available to students through graduate assistantships, traineeships, and tuition scholarships. Students with outstanding qualifications may be considered for graduate fellowships. The University Financial Aid office is also a source of assistance.

Cost of Study

In-state graduate tuition is $313.90 per credit hour in 2008–09. Out-of-state tuition is 2.5 times the in-state tuition rate ($784.75 per credit hour). Graduate students with at least a 25 percent appointment as a graduate assistant receive a tuition scholarship. Fees vary from $511.26 (1 credit hour) to $1416.05 (12 credit hours). Students with a graduate assistantship receive a 25 percent reduction in the Primary Care Medical Fee.

Living and Housing Costs

For married couples, students with families, and single graduate students, the University has 690 efficiency and one-, two-, three-, and four-bedroom apartments that rent for $484 to $686 per month in 2008–09. Residence halls for single graduate students are also available, as are accessible residence hall rooms and apartments for students with disabilities.

Student Group

Approximately 25 students enter each master's program per year. About half of the M.S. students enter just after receiving their bachelor's degree. Others enter after having worked and are seeking a career change or advancement. The students are a diverse group and enjoy close working relations with faculty members and each other.

Location

SIUC is 350 miles south of Chicago and 100 miles southeast of St. Louis. Nestled in rolling hills bordered by the Ohio and Mississippi Rivers and enhanced by a mild climate, the area has state parks, national forests and wildlife refuges, and large lakes for outdoor recreation. Much of the area is a part of the 240,000-acre Shawnee National Forest. Cultural offerings include theater, opera, concerts, art exhibits, and cinema. Educational facilities for the families of students are excellent.

The University

Southern Illinois University Carbondale is a comprehensive public university, founded in 1869, with a variety of general and professional education programs. The University offers associate, bachelor's, master's, and doctoral degrees, in addition to the J.D. degree and the M.D. degree. The University is fully accredited by the North Central Association of Colleges and Schools. The Graduate School has an essential role in the development and coordination of graduate instruction and research programs. The Graduate Council has academic responsibility for determining graduate standards, recommending new graduate programs and research centers, and establishing policies to facilitate the research effort.

Applying

Applications should be requested from the address given in the Correspondence and Information section. Each application must include the standards forms, transcripts from all colleges and universities previously attended, three letters of academic reference, and a personal statement of career goals. Applicants are considered for both fall and spring semesters. Rh.D. applicants must also provide GRE scores.

Correspondence and Information

Director
Rehabilitation Institute, Mail Code 4609
Southern Illinois University Carbondale
Carbondale, Illinois 62901-4609
Phone: 618-536-7704
E-mail: bordieri@siu.edu
Web site: http://www.siu.edu/~rehab

Southern Illinois University Carbondale

THE FACULTY AND THEIR RESEARCH

The Rehabilitation Institute is led by a group of nationally recognized faculty members. In addition to being dedicated teachers, many of the faculty members have received national research and professional awards. They serve in leadership roles in professional organizations and on editorial boards of major journals. Faculty members consult on disability-related issues to private and public organizations regionally, nationally, and internationally. In recent years, faculty members have developed partnerships with rehabilitation professionals in Australia, Brazil, China, Ireland, Italy, Mexico, and Russia.

John J. Benshoff, Professor; Ph.D.; CRC. Substance abuse, rehabilitation counseling, gerontology.
James E. Bordieri, Professor and Director; Ph.D. Vocational evaluation, rehabilitation psychology, job placement.
William Crimando, Professor; Ph.D. Staff training and development, placement of persons with severe disabilities, computers in rehabilitation.
Anthony J. Cuvo, Professor; Ph.D. Behavior analysis, developmental disabilities, evaluation research.
Paula K. Davis, Professor; Ph.D. Developmental disabilities, behavior analysis.
Mark R. Dixon, Associate Professor; Ph.D. Behavior medicine/behavioral therapy, organizational management.
Carl R. Flowers, Associate Professor; Rh.D.; CRC. Diversity management, fiscal management, leadership.
Irene Gallenbach, Clinical Supervisor; CCS/SLP. Communications disorders and sciences.
Brandon F. Greene, Professor; Ph.D. Politics of developmental disabilities, child abuse/neglect, consumer affairs.
Diana Muzio, Instructor; CCS/SLP. Communication disorders and sciences.
Ruth Anne Rehfeldt, Associate Professor; Ph.D. Autism, supported employment, applied behavior analysis.
Ted F. Riggar, Professor; Ed.D. Rehabilitation administration and supervision.
Kenneth O. Simpson, Associate Professor; Ph.D.; CCC/SLP. Augmentative and alternative communication, interaction analysis, neurogenic communication disorders.
Linda McCabe Smith, Associate Professor; Ph.D.; CCC/SLP. Language development/language disorders in children, assessment of language in children from multicultural populations.
Darrell W. Taylor, Associate Professor; Ph.D.; CVE, CRC. Vocational evaluation and assessment, job development and placement, private section rehabilitation.
Rebecca Trammel, Clinical Instructor; M.S.; CCS/SLP. Communication disorders and sciences.
Thomas D. Upton, Associate Professor; Ph.D.; CRC. Brain injury, disabilities attitudes, vocational rehabilitation.
April Worsdell, Assistant Professor; Ph.D. Applied behavior analysis, severe behavior disorders, autism.

SOUTHERN UNIVERSITY AND AGRICULTURAL AND MECHANICAL COLLEGE

Department of Rehabilitation and Disability Studies
Master of Science in Rehabilitation Counseling

Program of Study

The Rehabilitation Counseling Program (RCP), established in 1983, has the distinguished honor of becoming the first nationally accredited program in the state of Louisiana. In recognition of the quality of its academic pursuits, it has been reaccredited for eight years (2002–2010) by the Council on Rehabilitation Education (CORE). In 1998, the program received Honorable Mention from the Commissioner of Rehabilitation Services Administration, U.S. Department of Education, Washington, D.C.

The mission of the program is to educate and train individuals at the master's level to satisfy the qualified personnel needs of the rehabilitation profession and to enhance the quality of services offered to individuals with disabilities. The objectives of the program are to develop the skills, knowledge, and competencies required to provide high-quality services to people with disabilities; to prepare the students to conduct rehabilitation research and participate in scholarly activities; to prepare the students to become effective advocates for individuals with disabilities; and to provide continuing education to the professionals in the rehabilitation community for further skills development and attainment/maintenance of national certification/state licensure.

The graduation requirements are completion of at least 48 semester hours of core courses, including 100 hours of practicum, and 600 hours of internship. Graduation requirements can be attained through the following options—Option A: a minimum of 48 hours and passing the comprehensive examination; Option B: a minimum of 48 hours (including REHB 599), completion of a research paper/project, and passing the comprehensive examination; or Option C: a minimum of 48 hours (including REHB 599 and REHB 600) and completion of a thesis instead of taking the comprehensive examination. The program offers three specialty tracks, Assistive Technology (RC-AT), Rehabilitation of Ethnic Minorities (REM), and Vocational Evaluation and Work Adjustment (VEWA), under three long-term training grants from the Rehabilitation Services Administration (RSA) of the U.S. Department of Education. The curriculum incorporates the knowledge and competencies necessary to serve in a variety of rehabilitation counseling and related positions through both classroom and practical experiences. Upon completion of 75 percent of the course work, the students are eligible to take the national certification examinations, such as Certified Rehabilitation Counselor (CRC) and Certified Vocational Evaluator (CVE). The Department is a member of the National Council on Rehabilitation Education (NCRE). The program houses the National Student Rehabilitation Counseling Association (NSRCA), the Southern University Student Rehabilitation Association (SUSRA), and the Sigma Upsilon Chi Chapter of the Chi Sigma Iota Counseling Academic and Professional Honor Society International (SUC-CSI).

The Department offers an online M.S. in Rehabilitation Counseling program. This program is designed to offer professional-development training opportunities to practicing rehabilitation counselors of state or federal rehabilitation agencies, culminating in a master's degree. The project responds to the Comprehensive System of Personnel Development (CSPD) as mandated by the RSA of the U.S. Department of Education.

Research Facilities

The Rehabilitation Research Institute for Underrepresented Populations (RRIUP), a Disability Rehabilitation Research Project (DRRP), is funded by the National Institute on Disability and Rehabilitation Research (NIDRR), U.S. Department of Education. The goal of the institute is to develop and incorporate culturally appropriate research techniques in rehabilitation and implement targeted dissemination methods for the fullest utilization of research findings by culturally diverse groups.

The University's John B. Cade Library is committed to supporting instructional and research objectives in all subject areas. This fully accessible library has more than 1 million volumes, including books, journals, manuscripts, and computer software. Research support is provided by several outstanding facilities, such as the Center for Energy and Environmental Studies, the Health Research Center, the Center for Social Research, the National Plant Data Center, the Research Institute for Pure and Applied Sciences, and the Office of Grants and Sponsored Programs. Computers for student use are available throughout the campus.

The Rehabilitation Capacity Building Project (RCBP) is designed to offer technical assistance to faculty members of minority-serving institutions in the areas of disability awareness; rehabilitation legislation; long-term training in rehabilitation program development at the associate, undergraduate, and graduate levels; the Field Initiated Project (FIP) and Fellowship for the National Institute on Disability and Rehabilitation Research (NIDRR); techniques of writing effective proposals for submission to RSA-NIDRR; and methods of managing federally funded projects. In addition, the American Indian Vocational Rehabilitation Programs receive consultation in the development of such proposals as Section 121, Projects with Industry, and Special Demonstration Projects. This project is funded by the RSA, U.S. Department of Education.

Financial Aid

Thirty highly qualified students in the program receive $12,500 per year in Rehabilitation Services Administration scholarships and $5500 in assistantships from the Graduate School. Other student loans and financial opportunities are also available, such as stipends from the Diversity Graduate Scholars Program.

Cost of Study

Tuition for the 2008–09 academic year for a full-time graduate student is $1962 per semester for Louisiana residents and $4545 per semester for out-of-state students. Tuition and fees are subject to change without notice.

Living and Housing Costs

The University has no separate graduate housing. For single graduate students, limited accommodations may be available in on-campus residence halls. A variety of rooms in private residences in Baton Rouge are available for student rental.

Student Group

Total enrollment in fall 2007 was 8,288, of whom 1,314 were graduate students. Of these graduate students, 993 were women, 321 were men, and 96 were international students. The Rehabilitation Counseling Program has about 60 graduate students.

Student Outcomes

Students have a broad range of opportunities available to them upon completion of the program due to the critical shortage of rehabilitation counselors available to serve 54 million Americans with disabilities at the state, regional, and national levels. The most qualified students are prepared for doctoral programs in rehabilitation or related fields.

Location

The University is located in northeast Baton Rouge, the capital of Louisiana. The campus is on the scenic Scott's Bluff, overlooking the Mississippi River.

The University

Southern University and Agricultural and Mechanical College is a publicly supported land-grant institution that, since its chartering in 1880, has been focused on teaching. Founded in New Orleans, the University moved to Baton Rouge in 1914. Southern University and Agricultural and Mechanical College is part of the Southern University system, the only Historically Black College and University (HBCU) system in the United States, and is accredited by the Southern Association of Colleges and Schools (SACS).

Applying

A prerequisite for admission to the program is an undergraduate degree in rehabilitation services, psychology, sociology, criminal justice, counseling, mental health counseling, nursing, speech pathology and audiology, therapeutic recreation, physical and occupational therapy, or another related field from an accredited institution. However, students in other majors are both encouraged to apply and accepted into the program. Upon review of the Rehabilitation Counseling Program and Graduate School applications, the official transcript, Graduate Record Examinations (GRE) scores, and three letters of recommendation by the Graduate Admission Committee, the eligible applicants are called for a personal interview. Admission is granted in two statuses: an applicant with a cumulative undergraduate/graduate GPA of 3.0 or above receives regular admission status, and an applicant with a cumulative undergraduate/graduate GPA of 2.7 to 2.9 receives conditional admission status. A student admitted under conditional status is required to complete the first 12 semester hours of core courses with a minimum cumulative GPA of 3.0. Application packets can be obtained by calling, faxing, or e-mailing the coordinator of the program; applications are also available online at http://www.subr.edu/science/rehabcounsel/. New students are admitted only in the fall, and the application deadline is April 15.

Correspondence and Information

Madan M. Kundu, Ph.D., FNRCA, CRC, NCC, LRC
Chair and Professor
Department of Rehabilitation and Disability Studies
229 A. C. Blanks Hall
Southern University
Baton Rouge, Louisiana 70813
Phone: 225-771-2667, 2819, or 3020 Ext. 201
Fax: 225-771-2293
E-mail: kundusubr@aol.com
Web site: http://www.subr.edu/science/rehabcounsel/

Southern University and Agricultural and Mechanical College

THE FACULTY

Alo Dutta, Assistant Professor; Ph.D., Illinois at Urbana-Champaign; CRC.
Madan M. Kundu, Professor and Chair; Ph.D., Michigan State; FNRCA, CRC, NCC, LRC.
Doreen Miller, Professor; Rh.D., Southern Illinois; CRC, LPC.
Frank Puckett, Associate Professor and Coordinator, Distance Education; Ph.D., Southern Illinois; CRC, ATP.
Carliss Y. Washington, Associate Professor; Rh.D., Southern Illinois; CRC.
Michael Welch, Adjunct Professor; Ed.D., Auburn; CVE, CVS.

SouthUniversity℠

SOUTH UNIVERSITY

Columbia Campus
Professional Counseling Program

Program of Study

The Master of Arts in Professional Counseling degree program at South University is intended to meet the local and regional need for qualified professional counselors. The emphasis of the program is on counseling in a community setting. The program is designed to enable graduates to obtain all initial eligibility criteria to become licensed as a professional counselor in the state of South Carolina. The delivery structure of the program gives students the ability to balance the rigors of work and home while pursuing their master's degree. Students can complete one or two courses each term, with each quarter lasting ten weeks. Students select from the convenient Saturday sessions that meet once per week or attend two evenings during the week.

Students are taught via two primary modes of instruction. The majority of the program involves didactic and experiential classroom instruction, supplemented by computer-based assignments, including the use of Internet technology. The second mode of instruction focuses on supervised field experiences. Students are placed in community counseling settings (while on internship) and practice counseling under the supervision of an on-site supervisor. Students in field placements also receive weekly individual and group supervision from qualified faculty supervisors.

Research Facilities

Along with classrooms and offices, the campus includes a bookstore, student lounge, and career services center. Students may retrieve periodicals in paper or electronic form. The South University Library provides in-library and remote access to electronic databases. Both bibliographic and full-text databases are available via EBSCOhost (e.g., Academic Search Premier, SocINDEX, PsycINFO, PsycARTICLES, and Mental Measurements Yearbook), the search and retrieval system of EBSCO Information Services, and via the Library and Information Resources Network (e.g., Infotrac and ProQuest databases). Infotrac databases include counseling sources such as Expanded Academic ASAP, Academic OneFile, and InfotracOneFile, and ProQuest databases include counseling sources such as ProQuest Psychology Journals and ProQuest Research Library. Internet access is available on all computers throughout the campus.

Financial Aid

A wide range of financial aid options is available to students who qualify. The Columbia campus of South University offers access to federal and state programs, including grants, loans, and work-study programs. Eligible students may apply for veterans' educational benefits and are encouraged to investigate the availability of grants and scholarships through community resources. As a first step, students should complete the Free Application for Federal Student Aid (FAFSA) and add South University's campus code, 004922. Students may apply electronically at http://www.fafsa.ed.gov or through the campus Director of Student Financial Services. Applications should be submitted promptly to receive consideration for the maximum amount of aid.

Cost of Study

Tuition information for the Professional Counseling Program may be obtained by contacting the Admissions Department at South University's Columbia campus.

Living and Housing Costs

South University does not offer or operate student housing. Professional Counseling Program students typically live in apartments in the Columbia area. Students who commute from long distances can arrange to stay at nearby hotels that offer long-term rates. More information is available by contacting the Admissions Department.

Student Group

The Columbia campus of South University has a diverse student body enrolled in both day and evening classes. Students are primarily commuters who live within 50 miles of the city.

Student Outcomes

The South University Career Services Department has been established to assist currently enrolled students in developing their career plans and reaching their employment goals. Career services include, but are not limited to, one-on-one career counseling, special career-related workshops and programs, coaching for resume and cover letter development, and resume referral to employers.

Location

South University recently relocated its Columbia campus to the growing east side of Columbia, just minutes from downtown. The new campus is conveniently located off of I-77 at Farrow Road and Parklane.

The campus surroundings are highlighted by a natural wooded landscape and vast greenspace featuring a tranquil campus courtyard. Convenient to malls, shopping, and the growing east side of Columbia, the new campus location provides easier access to students from throughout the greater Columbia area.

The University

South University is accredited by the Commission on Colleges of the Southern Association of Colleges and Schools (SACS) to award associate, bachelor's, master's, and doctoral degrees. Students should contact the Commission on Colleges at 1866 Southern Lane, Decatur, Georgia 30033-4097 or call 404-679-4500 for questions about the accreditation of South University.

Applying

Students are accepted into the Master of Arts in Professional Counseling degree program every academic quarter. Entrance into the program is gained through a formal application review and interview process. Acceptance is competitive and based on the admission committee's evaluation of the applicant's academic background and personal motivation. Application packets are available by contacting the South University Admissions Department (866-629-3031, toll-free) or visiting the University's Web site (http://www.southuniversity.edu).

Correspondence and Information

Applications for admission to the South University Master of Arts in Professional Counseling program are available by contacting:

Professional Counseling Program
South University
9 Science Court
Columbia, South Carolina 29203

Phone: 803-799-9082
866-629-3031 (toll-free)
Fax: 803-935-4382
E-mail: coladmis@southuniversity.edu
Web site: http://www.southuniversity.edu

South University

THE FACULTY

One of the most outstanding aspects of South University's Professional Counseling Program is the dedication of the faculty members and their ability to cultivate a supportive learning environment. Faculty members are committed to their roles as mentors, teachers, and colearners. They are also dedicated to the training of students who can assume positions of leadership within the counseling field. A current list of program faculty members appears in the South University catalog, which is available on the South University Web site (http://www.southuniversity.edu).

SouthUniversity℠

SOUTH UNIVERSITY

Montgomery Campus
Professional Counseling Program

Program of Study

The Master of Arts in Professional Counseling degree program at South University is intended to meet the local and regional need for qualified professional counselors. The emphasis of the program is on counseling in a community setting. The program is designed to enable graduates to obtain all initial eligibility criteria to become licensed as professional counselors in the state of Alabama. The delivery structure of the program gives students the ability to balance the rigors of work and home while pursuing their master's degree. Students can complete two courses each term, with each quarter lasting eleven weeks. Classes meet on Saturdays from 8:30 a.m. to 5 p.m.

Students are taught via two primary modes of instruction. The majority of the program involves didactic and experiential classroom instruction, supplemented by computer-based assignments, including the use of Internet technology. The second mode of instruction focuses on supervised field experiences. Students are placed in community counseling settings (during practicum and internship) and practice counseling under the supervision of an on-site supervisor. Students in field placements also receive weekly individual and group supervision from qualified faculty supervisors.

Research Facilities

South University in Montgomery is located in a modern 26,000-square-foot, two-story building on a 3¾-acre campus. This building houses computer and health professions labs, classrooms, a library, a student lounge, a bookstore, and faculty and administrative offices.

The South University library has wireless technology throughout, comfortable seating, and quiet study space. The South University library provides in-library and remote access to electronic databases. Both bibliographic and full-text databases are available via EBSCOhost (e.g., Academic Search Premier, SocINDEX, PsycINFO, PsycARTICLES, and Mental Measurements Yearbook), the search and retrieval system of EBSCO Information Services, and via the Library and Information Resources Network (e.g., Infotrac and ProQuest databases). Infotrac databases include counseling sources such as Expanded Academic ASAP, Academic OneFile, and InfotracOneFile, and ProQuest databases include counseling sources such as ProQuest Psychology Journals and ProQuest Research Library. Also for student use, the library has a modern computer lab with eleven workstations, each with Internet access, online database services, an office suite, tutorials, and class-support software.

Financial Aid

A wide range of financial aid options is available to students who qualify. South University offers access to federal and state programs, including grants, loans, and work-study programs. Eligible students may apply for veterans' educational benefits and are encouraged to investigate the availability of grants and scholarships through community resources. As a first step, students should complete the Free Application for Federal Student Aid (FAFSA). Students may apply electronically at http://www.fafsa.ed.gov or through the campus Director of Financial Aid. Applications should be submitted promptly to receive consideration for the maximum amount of aid.

Cost of Study

Tuition information for the Professional Counseling program may be obtained by contacting the admissions department at South University.

Living and Housing Costs

South University does not offer or operate student housing. Professional Counseling program students typically live in private housing in the Montgomery area. Students who commute from long distances can arrange to stay at nearby hotels that offer long-term rates. More information is available by contacting the admissions department.

Student Group

South University in Montgomery has a diverse student body enrolled in both day and evening classes. Students are primarily commuters who live within 50 miles of the city.

Student Outcomes

The South University career services department has been established to assist currently enrolled students in developing their career plans and reaching their employment goals. Career services include, but are not limited to, one-on-one career counseling, special career-related workshops and programs, coaching for resume and cover letter development, and resume referral to employers.

Location

South University is located on the rapidly growing east side of Alabama's capital city. As the state capital, Montgomery is a hub of government, banking, and law as well as a state center for culture and entertainment. Montgomery is situated in the middle of the southeastern U.S. and is less than a 3-hour drive from Atlanta and the Gulf of Mexico.

The University

South University is accredited by the Commission on Colleges of the Southern Association of Colleges and Schools (SACS) to award associate, bachelor's, master's, and doctoral degrees. Students should contact the Commission on Colleges at 1866 Southern Lane, Decatur, Georgia 30033-4097 or call 404-679-4500 with questions about the accreditation of South University.

Applying

Students may be accepted into the Master of Arts in Professional Counseling degree program every academic quarter. Entrance into the program is gained through a formal application review and interview process. Acceptance is competitive and based on the admission committee's evaluation of the applicant's academic background (completed bachelor's degree with a cumulative minimum GPA of 2.6 or a minimum score of 3.5 on the Graduate Record Examinations writing exam) and personal motivation. Application packets are available by contacting the South University admissions department or visiting the University's Web site.

Correspondence and Information

Applications for admission to the South University Master of Arts in Professional Counseling program are available by contacting:

Professional Counseling Program
South University
5355 Vaughn Road
Montgomery, Alabama 36116

Phone: 334-395-8800
866-629-2962 (toll-free)
Fax: 334-395-8859
E-mail: mtgadmis@southuniversity.edu
Web site: http://www.southuniversity.edu

South University

THE FACULTY

One of the most outstanding aspects of South University's Professional Counseling program is the dedication of the faculty members and their ability to cultivate a supportive learning environment. Faculty members are committed to their roles as mentors, teachers, and colearners. They are also dedicated to the education of students who can assume positions of leadership within the counseling field. A current list of program faculty members is available at the South University Web site (http://www.southuniversity.edu).

SouthUniversity℠

SOUTH UNIVERSITY

Savannah Campus
Professional Counseling Program

Program of Study

The Master of Arts in Professional Counseling degree program at South University is intended to meet the local and regional need for qualified professional counselors. The emphasis of the program is on counseling in a community setting. The program is designed to enable graduates to obtain all initial eligibility criteria to become licensed as a professional counselor in the state of Georgia. The delivery structure of the program gives students the ability to balance the rigors of work and home while pursuing their master's degree. Students can complete two courses each term (or more with approval), with each quarter lasting ten weeks. Class meetings are held mostly on Saturdays between 8:30 a.m. and 12 noon and some weeknights from 6 to 9:30 p.m.

Students are taught via two primary modes of instruction. The majority of the program involves didactic and experiential classroom instruction, supplemented by computer-based assignments, including the use of Internet technology. The second mode of instruction focuses on supervised field experiences. Students are placed in community counseling settings (during internship) and practice counseling under the supervision of an on-site supervisor. Students in field placements also receive weekly individual and group supervision from qualified faculty supervisors.

Research Facilities

In 2000, the 25,000-square-foot Health Professions building was opened on the Savannah campus to house classroom, computer, and lab facilities for graduate programs within the School of Health Professions Also in this building are the student lounge and administrative offices. In 2007, a new library facility was opened that provides comfortable study space for students, wireless capabilities for laptop network connectivity, and reference and interlibrary loan services. The South University Library also provides in-library and remote access to electronic databases. Both bibliographic and full-text databases are available via EBSCOhost (e.g., Academic Search Premier, SocINDEX, PsycINFO, PsycARTICLES, and Mental Measurements Yearbook), the search and retrieval system of EBSCO Information Services, and via the Library and Information Resources Network (e.g., Infotrac and ProQuest databases). Infotrac databases include counseling sources such as Expanded Academic ASAP, Academic OneFile, and InfotracOneFile, and ProQuest databases include counseling sources such as ProQuest Psychology Journals and ProQuest Research Library.

Financial Aid

A wide range of financial aid options is available to students who qualify. The Savannah campus of South University offers access to federal and state programs, including grants, loans, and work-study programs. Eligible students may apply for veterans' educational benefits and are encouraged to investigate the availability of grants and scholarships through community resources. As a first step, students should complete the Free Application for Federal Student Aid (FAFSA). Students may apply electronically at http://www.fafsa.ed.gov or through the campus Director of Financial Aid. Applications should be submitted promptly to receive consideration for the maximum amount of aid.

Cost of Study

Tuition information for the Professional Counseling Program may be obtained by contacting the Admissions Department at South University's Savannah campus.

Living and Housing Costs

South University offers school-sponsored student housing at its Savannah, Georgia, campus in conjunction with a local apartment complex. Students who commute from long distances can arrange to stay at nearby hotels that offer long-term rates. More information is available by contacting the Director of Student Housing at 912-201-8000.

Student Group

The Savannah campus of South University has a diverse student body enrolled in both day and evening classes. Students consist of commuters who live within 50 miles of the city or students from other portions of the United States (e.g., California, Ohio, Pennsylvania, Connecticut) who have moved to Savannah to pursue the degree in professional counseling.

Student Outcomes

The South University Career Services Department has been established to assist currently enrolled students in developing their career plans and reaching their employment goals. Career services include, but are not limited to, one-on-one career counseling, special career-related workshops and programs, coaching for resume and cover letter development, and resume referral to employers.

Location

Located on the south side of the historic city of Savannah, the campus is situated on 9 acres of land. It is convenient to the city's bustling midtown section and a full range of educational and cultural activities. The Atlantic Ocean and recreational amenities of Tybee Island, including beaches and numerous outdoor activities, are just a short drive away. In addition, the campus is located just a short drive from Hilton Head Island and Charleston, South Carolina.

The University

South University is accredited by the Commission on Colleges of the Southern Association of Colleges and Schools (SACS) to award associate, bachelor's, master's, and doctoral degrees. Students should contact the Commission on Colleges at 1866 Southern Lane, Decatur, Georgia 30033-4097 or call 404-679-4500 with questions about the accreditation of South University.

Applying

Students are accepted into the Master of Arts in Professional Counseling degree program twice per year (fall and spring quarters). Entrance into the program is gained through a formal application review and interview process. Acceptance is competitive and based on the admission committee's evaluation of the applicant's academic background (completed bachelor's degree with a cumulative minimum GPA of 2.6 or a minimum score of 3.5 on the Graduate Record Examinations writing exam) and personal motivation. Application packets are available by contacting the South University Admissions Department or visiting the University's Web site.

Correspondence and Information

Applications for admission to the South University Master of Arts in Professional Counseling program are available by contacting:

Professional Counseling Program
South University
709 Mall Boulevard
Savannah, Georgia 31406-4805

Phone: 912-201-8000
866-629-2901 (toll-free)
Fax: 912-201-8070
E-mail: savadmis@southuniversity.edu
Web site: http://www.southuniversity.edu

South University

THE FACULTY

One of the most outstanding aspects of South University's Professional Counseling Program is the dedication of the faculty members and their ability to cultivate a supportive learning environment. Faculty members are committed to their roles as mentors, teachers, and colearners. They are also dedicated to the training of students who can assume positions of leadership within the counseling field. A current list of program faculty members is available at the South University Web site (http://www.southuniversity.edu).

SouthUniversity℠

SOUTH UNIVERSITY

West Palm Beach Campus
Professional Counseling Program

Program of Study

The Master of Arts in Professional Counseling degree program at South University is intended to meet the local and regional need for qualified professional counselors. The emphasis of the program is on counseling in a community setting. The program is designed to enable graduates to obtain all initial eligibility criteria to become licensed as a professional counselor in the state of Florida. The delivery structure of the program gives students the ability to balance the rigors of work and home while pursuing their master's degree. Students can complete two to three courses each term, with each quarter lasting ten weeks. Class meetings are held mostly on Saturdays between 8:30 a.m. and 5 p.m. and some weeknights from 6 to 9:30.

Students are taught via two primary modes of instruction. The majority of the program involves didactic and experiential classroom instruction, supplemented by computer-based assignments, including the use of Internet technology. The second mode of instruction focuses on supervised field experiences. Students are placed in community counseling settings (during practicum and internship) and practice counseling under the supervision of an on-site supervisor. Students in field placements also receive weekly individual and group supervision from qualified faculty supervisors.

Research Facilities

The South University library has wireless technology throughout, comfortable seating, and quiet study space. The South University library provides in-library and remote access to electronic databases. Both bibliographic and full-text databases are available via EBSCOhost (e.g., Academic Search Premier, SocINDEX, PsycINFO, PsycARTICLES, and Mental Measurements Yearbook), the search and retrieval system of EBSCO Information Services, and via the Library and Information Resources Network (e.g., Infotrac and ProQuest databases). Infotrac databases include counseling sources such as Expanded Academic ASAP, Academic OneFile, and InfotracOneFile, and ProQuest databases include counseling sources such as ProQuest Psychology Journals and ProQuest Research Library. Also for student use, the library has a modern computer lab with ten workstations, each with Internet access, online database services, an office suite, tutorials, and class-support software.

Financial Aid

A wide range of financial aid options is available to students who qualify. The West Palm Beach campus of South University offers access to federal and state programs, including grants, loans, and work-study programs. Eligible students may apply for veterans' educational benefits and are encouraged to investigate the availability of grants and scholarships through community resources. As a first step, students should complete the Free Application for Federal Student Aid (FAFSA). Students may apply electronically at http://www.fafsa.ed.gov or through the campus Director of Financial Aid. Applications should be submitted promptly to receive consideration for the maximum amount of aid.

Cost of Study

Tuition information for the Professional Counseling Program may be obtained by contacting the Admissions Department at South University's West Palm Beach campus.

Living and Housing Costs

South University does not offer or operate student housing at its West Palm Beach campus. Professional Counseling Program students typically live in homes or apartments in or near the West Palm Beach area. Students who commute from long distances may arrange to stay at nearby hotels that offer long-term rates. More information is available by contacting the Admissions Department.

Student Group

The West Palm Beach campus of South University has a diverse student body enrolled in both day and evening classes. Students are primarily commuters who live within 50 miles of the city.

Student Outcomes

The South University Career Services Department has been established to assist currently enrolled students in developing their career plans and reaching their employment goals. Career services include, but are not limited to, one-on-one career counseling, special career-related workshops and programs, coaching for resume and cover letter development, and resume referral to employers.

Location

South University in West Palm Beach is centrally located near the heart of Palm Beach County. Midway between Palm Beach International Airport and heavily traveled Okeechobee Boulevard, the campus is just minutes west of both Interstate 95 and downtown West Palm Beach.

The University

South University is accredited by the Commission on Colleges of the Southern Association of Colleges and Schools (SACS) to award associate, bachelor's, master's, and doctoral degrees. Students should contact the Commission on Colleges at 1866 Southern Lane, Decatur, Georgia 30033-4097 or call 404-679-4500 with questions about the accreditation of South University.

Applying

Students are accepted into the Master of Arts in Professional Counseling degree program every academic quarter. Entrance into the program is gained through a formal application review and interview process. Acceptance is competitive and based on the admission committee's evaluation of the applicant's academic background (completed bachelor's degree with a cumulative minimum GPA of 2.6 or a minimum score of 3.5 on the Graduate Record Examinations writing exam) and personal motivation. Application packets are available by contacting the South University Admissions Department or visiting the University's Web site.

Correspondence and Information

Applications for admission to the South University Master of Arts in Professional Counseling program are available by contacting:

Professional Counseling Program
South University
1760 North Congress Avenue
West Palm Beach, Florida 33409

Phone: 561-697-9200
866-629-2902 (toll-free)
Fax: 561-697-9944
Web site: http://www.southuniversity.edu

South University

THE FACULTY

One of the most outstanding aspects of South University's Professional Counseling Program is the dedication of the faculty members and their ability to cultivate a supportive learning environment. Faculty members are committed to their roles as mentors, teachers, and colearners. They are also dedicated to the training of students who can assume positions of leadership within the counseling field. A current list of program faculty members appears in the South University catalog, which is available on the South University Web site (http://www.southuniversity.edu).

SOUTHWESTERN COLLEGE

Program in Counseling

Programs of Study

The purpose of the master's programs at Southwestern College is to prepare mental health professionals in counseling, art therapy, and grief, loss, and trauma counseling. Graduate degrees at Southwestern College are based on the attainment of educational objectives in three areas: theoretical knowledge, applied skills, and character strength. All master's programs are two academic years in length. In year one, the emphasis is on students' exploration of their personal psychological transformation. This reflective emphasis provides insight into the nature of character development and the human condition. A foundation is laid for understanding the nature of change and its application in the helping professions. In year two, the emphasis is on students' professional identity and the development of clinical skills. Students acquire the competencies needed for working in the mental health professions.

The master's program in counseling integrates effective modes of counseling, incorporating all levels of psychological functioning: imaginal, emotional, mental, and spiritual. This holistic approach fosters a creative sense of self and the potential for change.

The master's program in art therapy emphasizes the use of the visual arts as a therapeutic approach in clinical, educational, forensic, community, and rehabilitation settings. While visual art is the primary therapeutic modality, the creative process is supported by classroom instruction and experiences in the use of drama, movement, and music.

The master's program in counseling with a concentration in grief, loss, and trauma integrates effective modes of counseling through the incorporation of all levels of psychological functioning–imaginal, emotional, mental, and spiritual–to deal with the accumulated losses of a lifetime. In addition, there is an emphasis on creative expression and the transformation of bonds that continue after death. Certificates in grief counseling, psychodrama and action methods, ecopsychology, and somatic studies are also offered.

Research Facilities

The Quimby Memorial Library supports teaching and research in counseling, art therapy, applied psychology, and experiential education. The library contains approximately 20,000 books, journals, and audiovisual materials. Patrons have access to interlibrary loan through the New Mexico State Library. Behavioral and social sciences indexes can be accessed through the College's database. The Quimby Memorial Library also houses the second-largest metaphysical collection in the United States.

Financial Aid

Financial aid programs include Subsidized and Unsubsidized Federal Direct Student Loans, scholarships, and payment plans. A Free Application for Federal Student Aid (FAFSA) must be submitted at least three months before admission in order to have a loan guarantee in place at the time of registration. For the 2007–08 academic year, the maximum amount potentially awarded to a student in combined Subsidized and Unsubsidized Federal Direct Student Loans was $20,500. Students and their families should investigate local sources, such as service organizations, churches, Native American tribal affiliations, corporations, and foundations for scholarship and loan funds. A limited number of scholarships are available, including the quarterly Southwestern College Scholarship.

Cost of Study

The current cost is $342 per quarter unit. The cost of study is dependent upon the number of units taken each quarter. Full-time study is $16,416 per year. Additional expenses for books and supplies are approximately $1200 per year. A graduation fee of $80 is required.

Living and Housing Costs

There is no on-campus housing. There are numerous apartment complexes nearby with rentals from the $550 to $800 price range. Several property managers are available to help students find housing in the area. For more information, students should contact the Director of Admissions.

Student Group

Students select Southwestern College because of the unique nature of the programs offered. The age of students ranges from the early 20s to students in their 60s. Younger students tend to come directly from undergraduate programs and are preparing to enter their first profession. Older students have often had one or more careers and a wealth of life experience. The unifying characteristic of all students at the College is the commitment to self-knowledge and the desire to be of service to others.

Student Outcomes

Southwestern College graduates are uniquely qualified to take their place as transformational leaders in the world. Counseling graduates are well prepared to fulfill licensure requirements in mental health counseling. Graduates of all of the counseling and art therapy programs pursue successful careers in educational, mental health, and residential treatment settings and private practice. Graduates are able to apply for licensure in the state of New Mexico and other states. Art therapy graduates are eligible to apply for registration with the Art Therapy Credentials Board (ATCB) of the American Art Therapy Association as well as for licensure in counseling.

Location

Southwestern College's campus is located in Santa Fe, the capital of New Mexico. At an altitude of 7,000 feet, Santa Fe offers stunning high-desert vistas and breathtaking sunsets. A mild four-season climate boasts 300 days of sunshine each year. This tricultural area offers outdoor recreation, museums, stage productions, the Santa Fe Opera, and Indian and Spanish markets.

The College

The roots of Southwestern College can be traced to 1945, when a group of forward-thinking individuals began a collection of metaphysical books to establish the Quimby Memorial Library. The collection included the manuscripts of Phineas Parkhurst Quimby, an American Transcendentalist. Quimby believed that the mind had great healing powers in regard to physical illness and that maintaining the mind/body connection could bring a person into balance. In 1976, Southwestern College, then called Quimby College, was dedicated. Today, the College continues to teach in a holistic and experiential way. The College is accredited by the Higher Learning Commission and is a member of the North Central Association of Colleges and Schools (NCA). The art therapy program is approved by the American Art Therapy Association.

Applying

Southwestern College accepts students who have the motivation for self-discovery, a love of learning, and a quest for deeper meaning in their lives. Applicants are required to submit an application, $50 application fee, personal statement, current resume, transcripts from each college previously attended, and three letters of recommendation. An admissions interview is required. In addition, art therapy applicants must submit a portfolio of twelve to fifteen slides of recent work. Students may be admitted during the fall, winter, and spring quarters.

Correspondence and Information

Admissions Office
Southwestern College
P.O. Box 4788
Santa Fe, New Mexico 87502-4788

Phone: 505-471-5756 Ext. 26
877-471-5756 Ext. 26 (toll-free)
E-mail: admissions@swc.edu
Web site: http://www.swc.edu

Southwestern College

THE FACULTY AND THEIR RESEARCH

Christopher Alexander, Ph.D.
Susan Benjamin, LPAT, ATR-BC.
Diane Berman, M.A., LMFT.
Rosvita Botkin, Ph.D., ATR, LPAT, LPCC. Jungian and expressive art therapy.
Yolanda Briscoe, Ph.D.
Connie Buck, Ph.D.
Marylou Butler, Ph.D. Licensed psychologist.
Wendy Chapin, M.A. Performing arts.
Robert Colby, LPCC.
Kate Cook, M.A., LPCC, CPP, TEP. Psychodrama.
Amy Cortese, M.S. Shamanic studies.
Jim Ficky, Ph.D., LPCC.
Helaine Foster, Ph.D., RMHC.
Kate Greenway, M.S., LPCC.
Gary Grimm, M.A., LPCC.
Diane Haug, M.A.
Deborah John, LPCC.
Carla Kleefeld, LPCC.
Michael Maestas, LPCC.
Catherine Monserrat, M.A.
Katherine M. Ninos, M.A., LPC. Consciousness studies and transpersonal psychology.
James Nolan, Ph.D.
Antonio Nunez, Ph.D.
Ruth Omlin, M.P.S., LPAT, ATR-BC.
Carol Parker, Ph.D., LPCC.
Beth Prothro, Ph.D., LPCC. Gestalt psychology.
Kate Rogers, M.A., LPAT, LPCC, ATR-BC.
Karen Sands, M.A., LMSW, LPCC.
Ernesto Santistevan, Ph.D.
Janet Schreiber, Ph.D. Grief counseling and death education.
Deborah Schroder, M.A., ATR-BC.
Alexander Shaia, Ph.D.
Megan Sturges, M.A., LPAT, LPC.
George Tate, Th.D. Multicultural issues.
Robert Waterman, Ed.D., LPCC.

STONY BROOK UNIVERSITY, STATE UNIVERSITY OF NEW YORK

Department of Psychology
Graduate Training Program in Clinical Psychology

Program of Study

The Department of Psychology includes four graduate training programs: clinical, biopsychology, cognitive/experimental, and social and health. Students must be admitted to one of these four areas. The Graduate Training Program in Clinical Psychology offers courses and research training leading to the degree of Doctor of Philosophy in clinical psychology. The program is accredited by the American Psychological Association (APA).

The clinical program trains students to expand the scientific understanding of behavior problems and psychopathology and to apply this knowledge as skilled clinicians. A mentorship model of research training is employed. Students are involved in active research laboratories from the time of admission, and a second-year research paper is required. Within the first three years, required courses are completed. These include statistics, first-year lectures, a sequence of required courses within the clinical area, and three breadth courses. A quantitative minor is available. Students receive practice in teaching that typically involves at least two semesters of substantial direct instruction of undergraduates. Students are expected to complete a specialties examination and advance to candidacy for the Ph.D. at the end of the third year. Clinical preparation includes work with individuals and families from the community in the Psychological Center under the supervision of the faculty during each year of the program. After advancing to candidacy, students complete a dissertation and a one-year internship. Students can meet New York State's licensure requirements with careful course selection. Additional information about requirements and training opportunities may be obtained by writing to the Graduate Program Coordinator or the Director of Clinical Training.

Research Facilities

Faculty members maintain active laboratories for research and graduate training. Clinical facilities include the Psychological Center, a training, research, and service unit that provides psychological services and consultation to the community as well as a site for graduate practicum and internships. The Department-sponsored University Preschool enrolls children from eighteen months to five years of age, permitting both research and observation. The University Marital Therapy Clinic provides therapy for couples and individuals in the community who are experiencing relationship difficulties. It also provides forensic evaluations regarding custody and visitation for the Supreme Court of Suffolk County, New York. The Autism Help Center is a private local agency that deals with school and family issues for children with autism and related developmental disabilities. The Developmental Disabilities Institute, another local agency, also offers services for people with a variety of disabilities. Affiliations have been established with the University's Health Sciences Center, local public schools, an agency for the mentally retarded, private psychiatric hospitals, and a nearby VA hospital.

Financial Aid

Ph.D. students are normally admitted with financial support, which is at least $17,145 for the 2008–09 academic (nine-month) year. This funding is associated with teaching or research responsibilities. Clinical students making good progress receive additional summer funding from sources such as summer teaching assignments, work-study, and faculty research grants; summer support currently averages more than $4000. A fifth year of support is available on a competitive basis. Some students receive competitive fellowships from the Graduate Council and the W. Burghardt Turner Foundation. Such fellows receive a total stipend of $18,572 with an additional year of guaranteed funding.

Cost of Study

In 2008–09, full-time tuition at 12 credits for entering in-state residents is $3450 per semester, while out-of-state residents and international students pay $5460. Additional fees for each semester, including (but not limited to) the infirmary, activity, technology, and transportation fees, total about $875. International students also pay a service fee of approximately $35 per semester and an orientation fee of $50. Fees for the mandatory Student Health Insurance Plan vary depending on citizenship and employment status.

Living and Housing Costs

For 2008–09, Stony Brook calculates the cost of education excluding tuition, fees, and insurance at $14,228 per year. On-campus apartments range in cost from approximately $336 per month to approximately $1456 per month, depending on the size of the unit and the number of students sharing the space. Off-campus housing options include rooms, houses, and apartments that can be rented from approximately $350 to $2500 per month. Costs including books, food, and transportation may vary depending on academic program and/or personal circumstances.

Student Group

The Department of Psychology, one of Stony Brook's largest graduate departments, has awarded more than 600 Ph.D. degrees since its inception more than forty years ago. In 2007–08, 36 graduate students were enrolled in the clinical program (86 percent women, 3 percent black or Hispanic). For the class entering in fall 2008, there were 33 applications; 9 were accepted, yielding an entering class of 5. The program seeks bright, socially skilled students with strong research backgrounds and interests compatible with those of core clinical faculty members.

Student Outcomes

The clinical program has an outstanding placement record; almost 80 percent of recent graduates have taken academic or research positions in universities, colleges, medical schools, and research institutes. In a recent study examining which clinical psychology programs have trained the most faculty members in other doctoral programs across the country, Stony Brook ranked second. Over the past ten years, Stony Brook has trained more faculty members in APA-approved clinical psychology doctoral programs than any other program in North America or Europe.

Location

Stony Brook is located on the North Shore of Long Island, in a region of beaches and small historic villages. It is 60 miles east of New York City, conveniently connected by the Long Island Railroad, which stops at the edge of the campus. Nearby research facilities at Cold Spring Harbor Laboratory and Brookhaven National Laboratory provide additional advantages for the scientific community.

The University

Stony Brook University, the flagship campus of the SUNY system, is a world-class, student-centered research university. Stony Brook is one of the top fifteen research institutions in the U.S. and one of the top three public research universities (Graham and Diamond, 1997). Stony Brook's new responsibility for the management of Brookhaven National Laboratory is testimony to the high quality of its programs in science, engineering, and health sciences. The University has more than 20,000 students, including nearly 7,000 graduate students.

Applying

For the fall application deadline, visit the Departmental Web site. The GRE General Test is required; the Subject Test in psychology is optional. For more information, students should visit http://www.psychology.sunysb.edu. Online applications are required. They may be submitted to the Graduate School online at http://www.grad.sunysb.edu/applying/applying.htm. The Department of Psychology requires an additional supplementary recommendation form available at the Departmental Web page.

Correspondence and Information

Graduate Program Coordinator
Clinical Graduate Program
Department of Psychology
Stony Brook University, State University of New York
Stony Brook, New York 11794-2500
E-mail: psychgradprogram@notes.cc.sunysb.edu

Stony Brook University, State University of New York

THE FACULTY AND THEIR RESEARCH

Stony Brook's faculty members are nationally recognized for their contributions to research and training in cognitive and behavioral approaches to clinical problems and remain committed to developing, evaluating, and implementing empirically based assessment and treatment of adults, children, couples, and families. Their research programs are well funded by federal and other granting agencies. The research interests of the core faculty members include depression and dysthymia, spouse abuse and marital discord, psychotherapy process and integration, substance abuse, pain perception, developmental disabilities, parenting, language disorders, child abuse, and close relationships.

Edward G. Carr, Professor; Ph.D., California, San Diego, 1973. Applied behavior analysis, positive behavior support, developmental disabilities, child problem behavior, family and school intervention, biological factors in intervention.
Joanne Davila, Associate Professor; Ph.D., UCLA, 1993. Interpersonal functioning and psychopathology, depression, maladaptive personality styles, close relationships, attachment processes.
Marvin Goldfried, Professor; Ph.D., Buffalo, 1961. Gay, lesbian, and bisexual issues; psychotherapy process research; cognitive behavior therapy.
Greg Hajcak, Assistant Professor; Ph.D., Delaware, 2006. Psychophysiological approaches to studying cognition, emotion, and psychopathology; etiology, maintenance, and treatment of adult and childhood anxiety disorders.
Richard Heyman, Research Associate Professor; Ph.D., Oregon, 1992. Escalation and de-escalation of marital conflict, observation of marital interactions, assessment and treatment of spouse abuse, prevalence of partner abuse.
Daniel N. Klein, Professor; Ph.D., SUNY at Buffalo, 1983. Psychopathology; mood and personality disorders; assessment, classification, course, development, familial transmission, and treatment of depression.
E. David Klonsky, Assistant Professor; Ph.D., Virginia, 2005. Self-injurious behaviors, borderline personality traits, emotion regulation and psychopathology, classification and assessment of normal and pathological personality traits, validity of psychological tests.
K. Daniel O'Leary, Distinguished Professor and Director of Clinical Training; Ph.D., Illinois, 1967. Etiology and treatment of marital discord and spouse abuse, marital discord models of depression, treatment of coexisting depression and marital discord, effects of marital discord on childhood problems.
Amy Smith Slep, Research Assistant Professor; Ph.D., SUNY at Stony Brook, 1995. Affect regulation in parent-child and marital dyads, etiology of parental and partner aggression/abuse, connections between parenting and marital functioning.
Dina Vivian, Research Associate Professor; Ph.D., SUNY at Stony Brook, 1986. Marital therapy, communication skills in maritally discordant couples, communication and problem solving in physically abusive couples, cognitive and affective processes in physically abusive and maritally discordant couples.
Grover J. Whitehurst, Professor; Director, Institute of Education Sciences; and Assistant Secretary, Education Research and Improvement; Ph.D., Illinois, 1970. Language disorders, emergent literacy, early interventions to enhance child development and reduce the effects of poverty.

Associated Faculty in Other Stony Brook Departments
Janet Fischel, Associate Professor of Pediatrics; Ph.D., SUNY at Stony Brook, 1978. Behavioral and developmental pediatrics, developmental language disorders and emergent literacy skills, psychological management of disorders of elimination.
Joyce Sprafkin, Associate Professor of Psychiatry; Ph.D., SUNY at Stony Brook, 1975. Child psychopathology, ADHD, tic disorders, effects of television on child behavior.
Arthur Stone, Professor of Psychiatry; Ph.D., SUNY at Stony Brook, 1978. Stress, coping, and illness; immune system functioning and health.

Adjunct Faculty
Anne Peterson, Professor and Associate Director, University Counseling Center; Ph.D., Ohio, 1980. Psychopathology, assessment, psychodynamic psychotherapy, women's issues, couple's therapy, multicultural issues.

STONY BROOK UNIVERSITY, STATE UNIVERSITY OF NEW YORK

Department of Psychology
Graduate Training Program in Cognitive/Experimental Psychology

Program of Study

The Department of Psychology includes four graduate training programs: Cognitive/Experimental, Clinical, Social and Health Psychology, and Biopsychology. Students are admitted to one of these areas. The Graduate Training Program in Cognitive/Experimental Psychology offers courses and research training leading to the degree of Doctor of Philosophy in experimental psychology.

Students in the program conduct research from the beginning of graduate training, in close collaboration with a faculty mentor. First- and second-year research papers are required. Required courses include statistics courses, First Year Lectures, three depth courses within the Cognitive/Experimental Area, and three breadth courses. In conjunction with the Departments of Linguistics and Computer Science, interdisciplinary training is offered in cognitive science. In cooperation with the Biopsychology Area, the Department of Neurobiology and Behavior, and Brookhaven National Laboratory's Medical Department, interdisciplinary training is offered in cognitive neuroscience. A quantitative minor is available. Graduate students and faculty members meet weekly to present their work in a supportive "brown bag" setting. A journal club provides opportunities to discuss current literature within cognitive psychology. Mentoring includes topics such as grant writing and taking articles through the publication process. All second- and fourth-year Ph.D. students present their work at a formal research symposium designed to provide experience in speaking in a conference-style environment. Students are encouraged to conduct research projects with more than 1 faculty member, which broadens their professional opportunities. Students receive practice in undergraduate teaching that involves at least two semesters of substantial direct instruction. A specialties examination is completed, with advancement to candidacy for the Ph.D. at the end of the third year. The dissertation is completed in the fourth or fifth year. Additional information about requirements and training opportunities may be obtained by writing to the Department's Graduate Program Coordinator.

Research Facilities

The Cognitive/Experimental Area maintains active laboratories with state-of-the-art equipment for research and graduate training. Laboratory facilities include one Purkinje and several Eyelink II and head-free eyetrackers for psycholinguistics and visual cognition studies; rooms equipped to study electronic communication and human-computer interaction; sound-isolated chambers for perception and psycholinguistics experiments; multimedia workstations for presenting stimuli and collecting data; and computer-controlled choice stations for testing humans and pigeons. Faculty members, students, and postdoctoral associates rely largely on the Department of Psychology's large volunteer pool of human subjects; some studies are conducted on patients with memory disorders. Ample office and laboratory space is available for all graduate students. The area is affiliated with the Departments of Linguistics, Computer Science, and Neurology as well as Brookhaven National Laboratory and the Northport Veterans' Administration Medical Center. The Language, Mind, and Brain Initiative regularly sponsors interdisciplinary seminars, with participation from the Departments of Psychology, Linguistics, Computer Science, Philosophy, and Biology.

Financial Aid

Ph.D. students are normally admitted with financial support, which is at least $17,145 for the 2008–09 academic year (nine months); tuition costs are also normally covered by the Department. This funding is associated with teaching or research responsibilities. In addition, for the past thirteen years, all Cognitive/Experimental students making good progress have received summer funding from sources such as faculty research grants; summer support currently averages more than $4000. A fifth year of support is available on a competitive basis. Some students receive competitive fellowships from the National Science Foundation, the W. Burghardt Turner Foundation, or other sources.

Cost of Study

In 2008–09, full-time tuition at 12 credits for entering in-state residents is $3450 per semester, while out-of-state residents and international students pay $5460. Additional fees for each semester, including (but not limited to) the infirmary, activity, technology, and transportation fees, total about $875. International students also pay a service fee of approximately $35 per semester and an orientation fee of $50. Fees for the mandatory Student Health Insurance Plan vary depending on citizenship and employment status.

Living and Housing Costs

For 2008–09, Stony Brook calculates the cost of education excluding tuition, fees, and insurance at $14,228 per year. On-campus apartments range in cost from approximately $336 per month to approximately $1456 per month, depending on the size of the unit and the number of students sharing the space. Off-campus housing options include rooms, houses, and apartments that can be rented from approximately $350 to $2500 per month. Costs including books, food, and transportation may vary depending on academic program and/or personal circumstances.

Student Group

The Department of Psychology is one of Stony Brook's largest graduate departments. More than 600 Ph.D. degrees have been awarded since the program began more than forty years ago. Recent demographics show the department has about 77 percent women, 7 percent students from underrepresented groups, and 11 percent international students. During the 2007–08 academic year, there were 96 graduate students enrolled in psychology's four training programs; 18 of these were enrolled in the Graduate Training Program in Cognitive/Experimental Psychology.

Student Outcomes

In recent years, graduates of the program have achieved excellent placement in academic and industry positions. Recent placements include tenure-track assistant professor positions at the University of Minnesota, Texas A&M University, Northwestern University, Central China Normal University, Illinois Institute of Technology, Southern Minnesota State University, and the University of Minnesota, as well as postdoctoral positions at University of Chicago, Beckman Institute for Advanced Science and Technology (University of Illinois, Champaign-Urbana), University of Vermont, Arizona State University, University of Massachusetts, Carnegie Mellon University, Washington University in St. Louis, Johns Hopkins University, Brown University, and Tufts University.

Location

Stony Brook is located on the North Shore of Long Island in a region of beaches and small historic villages. It is 60 miles east of New York City, conveniently connected by the Long Island Railroad (which stops at the edge of campus). Nearby research facilities at Cold Spring Harbor and Brookhaven National Laboratories provide additional advantages for the scientific community.

The University

The University at Stony Brook, flagship campus of the SUNY system, is a world-class, student-centered research university. Stony Brook is one of the top fifteen research institutions in the United States and one of the top three public research universities (Graham and Diamond, 1997). Stony Brook's new responsibility for the management of Brookhaven National Laboratory is testimony to the high quality of its programs in science, engineering, and health sciences. The University has more than 20,000 students, including nearly 7,000 graduate students.

Applying

The current fall application deadline can be found on the Department's Web site. The GRE General Test is required; the Subject Test in psychology is optional. For more information, prospective students can visit http://www.psychology.sunysb.edu. Online applications are required. They may be submitted to the Graduate School at http://www.grad.sunysb.edu/applying/applying.htm. The Department of Psychology requires an additional application page, available on the Web site or via postal mail.

Correspondence and Information

Graduate Program Coordinator
Cognitive/Experimental Graduate Program
Department of Psychology
Stony Brook University, State University of New York
Stony Brook, New York 11794-2500
E-mail: psychgradprogram@notes.cc.sunysb.edu

Stony Brook University, State University of New York

THE FACULTY AND THEIR RESEARCH

Cognitive/Experimental Area faculty members are well represented on the editorial boards of major journals. Most area research programs are funded by agencies such as the National Science Foundation and the National Institutes of Health.

Susan E. Brennan, Associate Professor; Ph.D., Stanford, 1990. Language production and comprehension, speech disfluencies, human-computer interaction, computational linguistics, eye gaze as a measure of language processing and as a cue in conversation.

Nancy Franklin, Associate Professor and Head, Cognitive/Experimental Area; Ph.D., Stanford, 1989. Human memory, spatial cognition, mental models of physical systems, reality monitoring.

Richard Gerrig, Professor; Ph.D., Stanford, 1984. Psycholinguistics, text understanding and representation, nonconventional language, cognitive experiences of narrative worlds.

Christian C. Luhmann, Assistant Professor; Ph.D., Vanderbilt, 2006. High-level cognition, causal and statistical learning, probabilistic reasoning, economic and perceptual decision making, neuroimaging and computational modeling.

Howard Rachlin, Distinguished Professor; Ph.D., Harvard, 1965. Choice, decision making, behavioral economics, self-control, addiction, gambling, time allocation in humans and other animals.

Suparna Rajaram, Professor; Ph.D., Rice, 1991. Human memory and amnesia, implicit and explicit memory distinctions, new learning in amnesia, inhibitory processes in memory, priming, experimental investigation of remembering and knowing the past.

Arthur G. Samuel, Professor; Ph.D., California, San Diego, 1979. Perception, psycholinguistics, attention, and memory; perception of speech and music as domains of study in cognitive psychology.

Gregory Zelinsky, Associate Professor; Ph.D., Brown, 1994. Visual cognition; search, attention, eye movements, working memory, and scene perception; computational models of visuospatial behaviors.

Associated Faculty in Biopsychology

Nancy K. Squires, Professor and Chairperson; Ph.D., California, San Diego, 1972. Neuropsychology; neurophysiological measures of sensory and cognitive functions of the human brain, both in normal and clinical populations.

Turhan Canli, Assistant Professor; Ph.D., Yale, 1993. Neural basis of personality and emotion, social phobia, and depression.

Hoi-Chung Leung, Assistant Professor; Ph.D., Northwestern, 1997. Prefrontal and parietal function in human cognition, neural mechanisms underlying spatial information processing and eye-movement control, fMRI applications in cognitive neuroscience.

Associated Faculty in Clinical Psychology

K. Daniel O'Leary, Professor and Director, Clinical Training; Ph.D., Illinois, 1967. Etiology and treatment of marital discord and spouse abuse, effects of marital discord on childhood problems.

Associated Faculty in Other Stony Brook Departments

Mark Aronoff, Professor of Linguistics; Ph.D., MIT, 1974. Morphology, orthography.

Ellen Broselow, Professor of Linguistics; Ph.D., Massachusetts Amherst, 1976. Phonology, phonetics, second-language acquisition.

Marie K. Huffman, Associate Professor of Linguistics; Ph.D., UCLA, 1989. Phonetics, phonology.

Amanda Stent, Assistant Professor of Computer Science; Ph.D., Rochester, 2001. Spoken and multimodal dialogue systems, natural language generation, theories of discourse, information extraction.

STONY BROOK UNIVERSITY, STATE UNIVERSITY OF NEW YORK

Department of Psychology
Graduate Training Program in Social and Health Psychology

Program of Study The Department of Psychology includes four graduate training programs: social and health, biopsychology, clinical, and cognitive/experimental. Students must be admitted to one of these four areas. The Graduate Training Program in Social and Health Psychology offers courses and research training leading to the degree of Doctor of Philosophy in social and health psychology.

The social and health program is a good choice for students who are interested in a research career in social psychology, health psychology, or the interface between these two disciplines (e.g., application of social psychology theory to health problems such as adherence to medical regimens). Social psychology focuses on the influences of the social environment and relationships on behavior, cognition, and emotion throughout the life span. Health psychology focuses on identifying, evaluating, and enhancing the psychosocial and behavioral factors that promote health and prevent disease. Students also have the opportunity to participate in a Departmental close relationships concentration that includes faculty members and students in other areas. Students in the program work collaboratively with the faculty members on research projects of mutual interest. The course curriculum is extremely flexible and can be tailored to each student's interests and needs. A second-year research paper is required. Within the first three years, required courses are completed; these include statistics, core courses within the Social and Health Area, and three Departmental breadth courses. In addition, students have the opportunity to receive training in such methodological and quantitative techniques as multivariate statistics, structural equation modeling, and meta-analysis and may elect to complete a quantitative minor. Students are also welcome to take courses in other departments, such as the medical school. A noteworthy feature of the program is that considerable emphasis is placed on professional socialization. Seminars are offered on such topics as career issues, teaching methods, and grant writing. Students receive practice in teaching that typically involves at least two semesters of direct instruction of undergraduates. Students are expected to complete a specialties project (e.g., literature review, grant proposal, or meta-analysis) and to advance to candidacy for the Ph.D. at the end of the third year. The dissertation is ordinarily completed in the fourth or fifth year. Additional information about requirements and training opportunities may be obtained by writing to the Graduate Program Coordinator at the address listed in the correspondence and information section.

Research Facilities Students in the program have the opportunity to conduct research in both laboratory and field settings. The Social and Health Area maintains active laboratories with state-of-the-art facilities for research and graduate training. Facilities include laboratories for cross-sectional and longitudinal studies of attachment, pregnancy, close relationships, social neuroscience, stress and coping, social/cognitive development, prejudice, social cognition, volunteerism, tobacco dependence, meta-analysis, and medical decision making. The Social and Health Area faculty members have affiliations with a number of departments within Stony Brook University Medical School.

Financial Aid Ph.D. students are normally admitted with financial support, which is at least $17,145 for the 2008–09 academic year (nine months). This funding is associated with teaching or research responsibilities. Social and health students making good progress receive additional summer funding from sources such as summer teaching assignments, work-study programs, and faculty research grants; summer support currently averages more than $4000. A fifth year of support is available on a competitive basis. Some students receive competitive fellowships from the W. Burghardt Turner Foundation or other sources.

Cost of Study In 2008–09, full-time tuition at 12 credits for entering in-state residents is $3450 per semester, while out-of-state residents and international students pay $5460. Additional fees for each semester, including (but not limited to) the infirmary, activity, technology, and transportation fees, total about $875. International students also pay a service fee of approximately $35 per semester and an orientation fee of $50. Fees for the mandatory Student Health Insurance Plan vary depending on citizenship and employment status.

Living and Housing Costs For 2008–09, Stony Brook calculates the cost of education excluding tuition, fees, and insurance at $14,228 per year. On-campus apartments range in cost from approximately $336 per month to approximately $1456 per month, depending on the size of the unit and the number of students sharing the space. Off-campus housing options include rooms, houses, and apartments that can be rented from approximately $350 to $2500 per month. Costs including books, food, and transportation may vary depending on academic program and/or personal circumstances.

Student Group The Department of Psychology is one of Stony Brook's largest graduate departments. More than 600 Ph.D. degrees have been awarded since the program began more than forty years ago. Recent demographics show the program has about 77 percent women, 7 percent students from underrepresented groups, and 11 percent international students. During the 2007–08 academic year, there were 96 graduate students enrolled in psychology's four training programs, 27 of whom were enrolled in the Graduate Training Program in Social and Health Psychology.

Student Outcomes The social and health program prepares students who are highly competitive for top research and teaching positions in academic institutions, research organizations, policy institutes, government agencies, and health-care settings. Most students graduate with publications in top journals, including *Psychological Bulletin, Journal of Personality and Social Psychology, Health Psychology,* and *Personality and Social Psychology Bulletin.* Recent placements include assistant professor positions at Case Western Reserve University, the University of Maryland, University of Vermont, Syracuse University, Cornell Medical School, and the City College of the City University of New York, as well as postdoctoral or research positions at Ohio State University, Yale University, Mt. Sinai School of Medicine, the Fred Hutchinson Cancer Center, the National Institutes of Health, and other institutions.

Location Stony Brook is located on the North Shore of Long Island in a region of beaches and small historic villages. It is 60 miles east of New York City, conveniently connected by the Long Island Railroad (which stops at the edge of campus). Nearby research facilities at Cold Spring Harbor Laboratory and Brookhaven National Laboratory provide additional advantages for the scientific community.

The University The University at Stony Brook, flagship campus of the SUNY system, is a world-class, student-centered research university. Stony Brook is one of the top fifteen research institutions in the United States and one of the top three public research universities (Graham and Diamond, 1997). Stony Brook's new responsibility for the management of Brookhaven National Laboratory is testimony to the high quality of its programs in science, engineering, and health sciences. The University has more than 20,000 students, including nearly 7,000 graduate students.

Applying For the fall application deadline, visit the Departmental Web site. The GRE General Test is required; the Subject Test in psychology is optional. For more information, prospective students should visit http://www.psychology.sunysb.edu. Online applications are required. They may be submitted online to the Graduate School at http://www.grad.sunysb.edu/applying/applying.htm. The Department of Psychology requires an additional application page, available at the Web site or via postal mail.

Correspondence and Information
Graduate Program Coordinator
Social and Health Graduate Program
Department of Psychology
Stony Brook University, State University of New York
Stony Brook, New York 11794-2500
E-mail: psychgradprogram@notes.cc.sunysb.edu
Web site: http://www. psychology.sunysb.edu

Stony Brook University, State University of New York

THE FACULTY AND THEIR RESEARCH

Areas of particular strength in the faculty's research in social psychology include the study of close relationships in adults and children; prejudice, racism, and stereotyping; and the representation and processing of social experience. Research topics in health psychology include the impact of stress on health, the role of social support in dealing with health problems, and women's health issues, such as coping with breast cancer, pregnancy, or the loss of a spouse.

Arthur Aron, Professor; Ph.D., Toronto, 1970. Motivation and cognition in close relationships, social neuroscience, intergroup relations, and prejudice; methodology.

Antonio Freitas, Assistant Professor; Ph.D., Yale, 2002. Social cognition, motivation, self-regulation.

Joan Kuchner, Lecturer; Ph.D., Chicago, 1981. Life-span development, cross-cultural parent-infant interactions, motherhood, learning environments for young children, child care, children's play.

Sheri Levy, Associate Professor; Ph.D., Columbia, 1998. Development, maintenance, and reduction of prejudice among adults and children; social cognition and prosocial behavior.

Marci Lobel, Associate Professor and Head, Social and Health Area; Ph.D., UCLA, 1989. Stress, coping, and physical health; psychosocial factors in women's reproductive health; social comparison processes.

Bonita London, Assistant Professor; Ph.D., Columbia, 2006. Social identity, stereotyping and prejudice, gender- and race-based marginalization, stress and coping, social and motivational factors in academic engagement.

Anne Moyer, Assistant Professor; Ph.D., Yale, 1995. Psychosocial issues surrounding cancer risk and treatment, women's health, research synthesis and research methodology.

Everett Waters, Professor; Ph.D., Minnesota, 1977. Social and personality development, parent-child and adult-adult attachment relationships.

Harriet Salatas Waters, Professor; Ph.D., Minnesota, 1976. Social cognitive development, parent-child co-construction of event representations, representation of early experience in memory.

Camille Wortman, Professor; Ph.D., Duke, 1972. Reactions to stressful life experiences, particularly bereavement; role of social support and coping strategies in ameliorating the impact of life stress; others' reactions to those who experience life crisis.

Associated Faculty in Other Areas of Psychology

Turhan Canli, Associate Professor; Ph.D., Yale, 1993. Neural basis of personality and emotion, social phobia, depression.

Edward Carr, Professor; Ph.D., California, San Diego, 1973. Autism, developmental disabilities, applied behavior analysis, positive behavior support with families and schools, health and illness in disabilities.

Associated Faculty in Other Stony Brook Departments

Judith A. Crowell, Associate Professor of Psychiatry; M.D., Vermont, 1978. Child and adolescent psychiatry, attachment system across the life span, parent-child and adult-adult interactions.

Joyce Sprafkin, Associate Professor of Psychiatry; Ph.D., SUNY at Stony Brook, 1975. Child psychopathology, ADHD, tic disorders, effects of television on child behavior.

Arthur Stone, Professor of Psychiatry; Ph.D., SUNY at Stony Brook, 1978. Stress, coping, and illness; immune system functioning and health.

Adjunct Faculty

Barbara Burkhard, Assistant Professor and Director, Child Treatment Program, North Suffolk Center; Ph.D., SUNY at Stony Brook, 1976. Child abuse and neglect.

Sarah Sternglanz, Assistant Professor, Social Sciences Interdisciplinary Program; Ph.D., Stanford, 1973. Human ethology, sex roles, social learning theory, female academic and career success.

TEACHERS COLLEGE, COLUMBIA UNIVERSITY

Department of Counseling and Clinical Psychology

Programs of Study

The Department of Counseling and Clinical Psychology at Teachers College, Columbia University, prepares students to investigate and address the psychological needs of individuals, families, groups, organizations/institutions, and communities. Counseling psychology provides rigorous training focusing on normal and optimal development across the life span. Particular attention is paid to expanding knowledge and skills in occupational choice and transitions and multicultural competencies as applied to individual, group, and family counseling; program development; and systemwide settings.

The Clinical Psychology Program provides rigorous training in both contemporary clinical science and intervention. Increasingly, both aspects of this training have been focused on the needs of at-risk children and adolescents. The clinical component of the program reflects an ongoing psychodynamic tradition with additional opportunities for training in other theoretical models.

Students in this Department are trained to become knowledgeable and proficient researchers, to provide psychological and educational leadership, and to be effective practitioners. Specifically, graduates from these programs seek positions in teaching, research, policy, administration, psychotherapy, and counseling.

Research Facilities

The Gottesman Libraries, with more than a million books and materials, is one of the nation's largest and most comprehensive research libraries in education, psychology, and health services. Students also have access to the 9.5 million volumes in the Columbia University library system. Organized research and service activities at Teachers College, in addition to being carried out by individual professors, are conducted through special projects and major institutes.

Financial Aid

Each year, Teachers College awards approximately $5 million of its own funds in scholarship and stipend aid and $2 million of endowed funds to new and continuing students. Most scholarship awards are made on the basis of academic merit. Scholarships are applied to tuition only, and students should expect to provide additional funds for the tuition balance, fees, medical insurance, academic, and living expenses.

Cost of Study

For the 2008–09 academic year, tuition is $1085 per point, with 12 or more points considered full-time. Fees include the Teachers College, $358; Teachers College research, $358; health service, $387; continuous doctoral advisement registration, $3255; and Ph.D. oral defense, $4581. The tuition deposit is $300. Medical insurance ranges from about $591 to $1303.

Living and Housing Costs

Teachers College offers a variety of on-campus housing options that are unique to the area and convenient to the campus. Housing for a single student ranges from $3600 to $8750 per semester, depending on the type of setting selected. Family housing ranges from $7200 to $8600 per semester. Teachers College has approximately 705 spaces available for single students and 150 apartments for students with families. The buildings are located in the vibrant and historic urban neighborhood of Morningside Heights. Current residence halls are historic buildings similar to other apartment-style buildings that were in New York City in the early 1900s.

Student Group

There are approximately 5,000 students enrolled at Teachers College. About 77 percent are women, 10 percent are African American, 13 percent are Asian American, and 7 percent are Latino/a. The student body is composed of 15 percent international students from eighty different countries and 87 percent domestic students from all fifty states. While about one third of TC students are working toward or developing their teaching career, the balance of the TC student community are pursuing careers in a wide range of fields, including educational policy, educational administration and leadership, arts administration, technology, psychology, social and behavioral sciences, health, communication, and international and comparative education.

Location

The College is located in the Morningside Heights section of Manhattan's Upper West Side, home to such venerable New York landmarks as Lincoln Center, the Cathedral of St. John the Divine, Grant's Tomb, Morningside Park, and the Manhattan School of Music. The Upper West Side is bounded by Central Park on the east and the Hudson River on the west. Because the College is located in New York City, students have access to an outstanding array of learning organizations, including museums, libraries, galleries, corporate learning centers, and K–12 schools.

The College and The University

Teachers College was founded in 1887 to provide a new form of schooling for the teachers of children from low-income families of New York—one that combined a humanitarian concern to help others with a scientific approach to human development. For more than 100 years, Teachers College has conducted research on the central issues facing education, prepared generations of education leaders, and shaped debate and public policy in education. The College provides programs of study in administration, counseling, curriculum development, and school health care and continues its efforts to strengthen teaching skills, prepare leaders to develop and administer psychological and health-care programs, and develop new teaching software. In 1898, Teachers College became affiliated with Columbia University.

Columbia University was founded in 1754 as King's College by royal charter of King George II of England. It is the oldest institution of higher learning in the state of New York and the fifth-oldest in the United States. From its beginnings in a schoolhouse in lower Manhattan, the University has grown to encompass two principal campuses: the historic, neoclassical campus in Morningside Heights and the modern Medical Center in Washington Heights. Today, Columbia is one of the top academic and research institutions in the world, conducting research in medicine, science, the arts, and the humanities. It includes three undergraduate schools, thirteen graduate and professional schools, and a school of continuing education. Sixty-four Nobel laureates have taught or studied at Columbia. Each year, the faculty of approximately 4,000 teaches more than 24,000 students from more than 150 countries.

Applying

Teachers College welcomes applicants who wish to pursue graduate study associated with the education, psychological, and health-service professions. All applicants receive consideration for admission without regard to race, color, creed, religion, sex, national origin, age, or disability. In order to be considered for scholarships, students must meet the early deadline. Admissions applications received after the early deadline may be considered on a space-available basis. Certain programs have special application deadlines. The 2008–09 early deadline for Ph.D. and all psychology doctoral programs is December 15. The early deadline for Ed.D. programs is January 2, with a final deadline of April 1. The early deadline for master's programs is January 15, with a final deadline of April 15. For the spring semester, the early deadline is November 1.

Teachers College requests that applicants collect the required documents for the application process and submit the complete application to the Office of Admission at one time. Admission application deadlines always refer to the date by which the Teachers College Office of Admissions must have received the application components and any other supporting material required by the Department. For more information on applying to Teachers College and for an online application, prospective students may visit the College's Web site at http://www.tc.columbia.edu/admissions.

Correspondence and Information

Teachers College, Columbia University
525 West 120th Street, Box 302
New York, New York 10027

Phone: 212-678-3710
Web site: http://www.tc.columbia.edu/discover
http://www.tc.columbia.edu/ccp

Teachers College Columbia University

THE FACULTY AND THEIR RESEARCH

The following is a brief listing of current Teachers College faculty members. For a complete listing and more detailed information, including profiles, selected publications, news, and photos, students should visit the Web site at http//www.tc.columbia.edu/faculty.

Professors
George Bonanno (Clinical).
Robert T. Carter (Counseling).
Madonna G. Constantine (Counseling).
Barry A. Farber (Clinical).
Suniya Luthar (Clinical and Developmental).
Elizabeth Midlarsky (Clinical).
Derald Wing Sue (Counseling).

Adjunct Professors
Xavier Amador (Clinical).
Jesse D. Geller (Clinical).
Jerome W. Kosseff (Clinical).
Judith Kuriansky (Clinical).
Arnold W. Wolf (Counseling).

Associate Professors
George Gushue (Counseling).
Lisa Miller (Clinical).
Marie L. Miville (Counseling).

Adjunct Associate Professors
Ghislaine Boulanger (Clinical).
Patti Cox (Counseling).
Valentina Harrell (Clinical).
Lisa Kentgen (Clinical).
Billie Pivnick (Clinical).
Dinelia Rosa (Clinical/Counseling).
Roni Beth Tower (Clinical).

Assistant Professors
Jill Hill (Counseling).
Michael Lau (Counseling).
Laura Smith (Counseling).
Helena Verdeli (Clinical).

Adjunct Assistant Professors
Edith Cooper (Clinical).
Jeptha Tausig Edwards (Clinical).
Motoni Fong-Hodges (Counseling).
Elizabeth Fraga (Counseling).
David Greenan (Counseling).
Merav Gur (Clinical).
Stephanie Fagin Jones (Clinical).
Richard Keller (Counseling).
Shamir Khan (Clinical).
Michael J. Koski (Counseling).
Samuel E. Menahem (Clinical).
Nancy Nereo (Clinical).
Elizabeth Owen (Clinical).
Jason Rudolph (Clinical).
Andrea Safirstein (Counseling).
Gil Tunnell (Counseling).
Teraesa Vinson (Counseling).
Anika Warren (Counseling).
A. Jordan Wright (Clinical).

Instructor
Margaret Brady-Amoon (Counseling).

TEACHERS COLLEGE, COLUMBIA UNIVERSITY

Department of Human Development

Programs of Study

The Department of Human Development at Teachers College, Columbia University, offers four programs: cognitive studies in education; developmental psychology; measurement, evaluation, and statistics; and sociology and education.

Students in the cognitive studies in education program may earn M.A., Ed.M., Ph.D., or Ed.D degrees. After completing a set of core courses, they select one of five concentrations: cognition and learning, intelligent technologies, reading research, cognitive studies of educational practice, and creativity and cognition. Students may also design their own concentration in consultation with their adviser. Those pursuing doctorates take more advanced classes, including a statistics sequence. All students must register for research practicum seminars that culminate in a substantive project.

The program in development psychology offers the M.A. and the Ph.D. degrees. Master's students have the option of concentrating in risk, resilience, and prevention; developmental psychology for educators; or creativity and cognition or may follow a more general course of study in developmental psychology. The M.A. mandates that students complete a special project; the Ph.D. requires students to take four courses in general psychology, advanced courses in developmental psychology, a proseminar, and a one-year statistics sequence; pass a certification examination; and write theoretical and empirical papers to qualify for dissertation status.

Students in the measurement, evaluation, and statistics program can earn an M.S. in applied statistics or an Ed.M., Ed.D., or Ph.D. in measurement and evaluation. The M.S. takes about a year to complete, while the Ed.M. culminates in an evaluation project. For the Ph.D., students must complete two years of full-time study, an empirical and a research paper, a certification exam, and an approved dissertation. The Ed.D. degree program has requirements similar to those of the Ph.D.

In the sociology and education program, students may pursue the M.A., Ed.M., Ed.D., and Ph.D. A concentration in policy studies in sociology is available to master's candidates. Both master's degrees culminate in either a comprehensive exam or an essay and successful completion of an advanced research methods class. Students develop their doctoral programs in consultation with their respective advisers. The *Academic Catalog,* which can be found online, offers more detailed program information.

Research Facilities

The Gottesman Libraries, with more than a million books and materials, is one of the nation's largest and most comprehensive research libraries in education, psychology, and health services. Students also have access to the 9.5 million volumes in the Columbia University library system. Organized research and service activities at Teachers College, in addition to being carried out by individual professors, are conducted through special projects and major institutes.

Financial Aid

Each year, Teachers College awards approximately $5 million of its own funds in scholarship and stipend aid and $2 million of endowed funds to new and continuing students. Most scholarship awards are made on the basis of academic merit. Scholarships are applied to tuition only, and students should expect to provide additional funds for the tuition balance, fees, medical insurance, academic, and living expenses.

Cost of Study

For the 2008–09 academic year, tuition is $1085 per point, with 12 or more points considered full-time. Fees include the Teachers College, $358; Teachers College research, $358; health service, $387; continuous doctoral advisement registration, $3255; and Ph.D. oral defense, $4581. The tuition deposit is $300. Medical insurance ranges from about $591 to $1303.

Living and Housing Costs

Teachers College offers a variety of on-campus housing options that are unique to the area and convenient to the campus. Housing for a single student ranges from $3600 to $8750 per semester, depending on the type of setting selected. Family housing ranges from $7200 to $8600 per semester. Teachers College has approximately 705 spaces available for single students and 150 apartments for students with families. The buildings are located in the vibrant and historic urban neighborhood of Morningside Heights. Current residence halls are historic buildings similar to other apartment-style buildings that were in New York City in the early 1900s.

Student Group

There are approximately 5,000 students enrolled at Teachers College. About 77 percent are women, 10 percent are African American, 13 percent are Asian American, and 7 percent are Latino/a. The student body is composed of 15 percent international students from eighty different countries and 87 percent domestic students from all fifty states. While about one third of TC students are working toward or developing their teaching career, the balance of the TC student community are pursuing careers in a wide range of fields, including educational policy, educational administration and leadership, arts administration, technology, psychology, social and behavioral sciences, health, communication, and international and comparative education.

Location

The College is located in the Morningside Heights section of Manhattan's Upper West Side, home to such venerable New York landmarks as Lincoln Center, the Cathedral of St. John the Divine, Grant's Tomb, Morningside Park, and the Manhattan School of Music. The Upper West Side is bounded by Central Park on the east and the Hudson River on the west. Located in New York City, students have access to an outstanding array of learning organizations, including museums, libraries, galleries, corporate learning centers, and K–12 schools.

The College and The University

Teachers College was founded in 1887 to provide a new form of schooling for the teachers of children from low-income families of New York, one that combined a humanitarian concern to help others with a scientific approach to human development. For more than 100 years, Teachers College has conducted research on the central issues facing education, prepared generations of education leaders, and shaped debate and public policy in education. The College provides programs of study in administration, counseling, curriculum development, and school health care and continues its efforts to strengthen teaching skills, prepare leaders to develop and administer psychological and health-care programs, and develop new teaching software. In 1898, Teachers College became affiliated with Columbia University.

Columbia University was founded in 1754 as King's College by royal charter of King George II of England. It is the oldest institution of higher learning in the state of New York and the fifth oldest in the United States. From its beginnings in a schoolhouse in lower Manhattan, the University has grown to encompass two principal campuses: the historic, neoclassical campus in Morningside Heights and the modern Medical Center in Washington Heights. Today, Columbia is one of the top academic and research institutions in the world, conducting research in medicine, science, the arts, and the humanities. It includes three undergraduate schools, thirteen graduate and professional schools, and a school of continuing education. Sixty-four Nobel laureates have taught or studied at Columbia. Each year, the faculty of approximately 4,000 teaches more than 24,000 students from more than 150 countries.

Applying

Teachers College welcomes applicants who wish to pursue graduate study associated with the education, psychology, and health-related professions. All applicants receive consideration for admission without regard to race, color, creed, religion, sex, national origin, age, or disability. In order to be considered for scholarships, students must meet the early deadline. Admissions applications received after the early deadline may be considered on a space-available basis. Certain programs have special application deadlines. The 2008–09 early deadline for Ph.D. and all psychology doctoral programs is December 15. The early deadline for Ed.D. programs is January 2, with a final deadline of April 1. The early deadline for master's programs is January 15, with a final deadline of April 15. For the spring semester, the early deadline is November 1.

Teachers College requests that applicants collect the required documents for the application process and submit the complete application to the Office of Admission at one time. Admission application deadlines always refer to the date by which the Teachers College Office of Admissions must have received the application components and any other supporting material required by the Department. For more information on applying to Teachers College and for an online application, prospective students may visit the College's Web site at http://www.tc.columbia.edu/admissions.

Correspondence and Information

Teachers College, Columbia University
525 West 120th Street, Box 302
New York, New York 10027

Phone: 212-678-3710
Web site: http://www.tc.columbia.edu/discover
http://www.tc.columbia.edu/hud

Teachers College Columbia University

THE FACULTY AND THEIR RESEARCH

Professors
The following is a brief listing of current Teachers College faculty members. For a complete listing and more detailed information, including profiles, selected publications, news, and photos, students should visit the Web site at http://www.tc.columbia.edu/faculty.

Professors
John B. Black (Cognitive Studies in Education/Instructional Technology and Media).
Jeanne Brooks-Gunn (Developmental Psychology).
James E. Corter (Measurement, Evaluation, and Statistics/Cognitive Studies in Education).
Herbert P. Ginsburg (Developmental Psychology/Cognitive Studies in Education).
Deanna Kuhn (Developmental Psychology/Cognitive Studies in Education).
Suniya S. Luthar (Developmental Psychology/Clinical Psychology).
Gary Natriello (Sociology and Education).
Aaron M. Pallas (Sociology and Education).
Barbara G. Tversky (Cognitive Studies in Education).
Amy Stuart Wells (Sociology and Education).
Joanna P. Williams (Cognitive Studies in Education).

Adjunct Professors
Hugh F. Cline (Sociology and Education).
Linda M. Hirsch (Cognitive Studies in Education).

Associate Professors
Lawrence T. DeCarlo (Measurement, Evaluation, and Statistics/Cognitive Studies in Education).
Peter Gordon (Developmental Psychology/Speech-Language Pathology).
Jane A. Monroe (Measurement, Evaluation, and Statistics).

Adjunct Associate Professors
Joseph R. Lao (Developmental Psychology).
Judith Miller (Developmental Psychology).

Assistant Professor
Young-Sun Lee (Measurement, Evaluation, and Statistics).

Adjunct Assistant Professors
Janet F. Alperstein (Sociology and Education).
Ann Cami (Developmental Psychology).
David Guralnick (Cognitive Studies in Education).
Alyse C. Hachey (Cognitive Studies in Education).
Michael Hanchett Hanson (Developmental Psychology/Cognitive Studies in Education).
Sari Locker (Developmental Psychology).

UNIVERSITY OF BALTIMORE

Yale Gordon College of Liberal Arts
Division of Applied Behavioral Sciences

Programs of Study

The Division of Applied Behavioral Sciences offers a wide range of psychology-related courses of study, including Master of Science (M.S.) degree programs in Applied Psychology (APPL) and Human Services Administration (HSAD). The APPL program prepares students for immediate employment, career advancement, or admission to doctoral programs in several areas of professional psychology specialization. The HSAD program is a collaborative effort between the University of Baltimore (UB) and Coppin State University, allowing students to take courses at both campuses. This program prepares students for careers in the field of human services administration in a variety of settings, including corporate, government, nonprofit, and community environments. The Yale Gordon College of Liberal Arts' emphasis on professional applications of the liberal arts provides an environment for unusually flexible programs that offer a rewarding mix of academic and practical experiences.

All APPL students are required to complete 12 credits of core psychology and methodology courses. As a result, all students acquire a fundamental background for pursuing Ph.D. or Psy.D. degrees. In addition, APPL students choose a specialization in counseling psychology, industrial/organizational (I/O) psychology, or psychological applications. Each specialization includes a combination of required applications courses and electives—48 total credits for counseling psychology and 42 credits for the other two specializations. Elective credits permit students to combine aspects of several areas of specialization or to create customized, cross-disciplinary degrees that support careers in many professional settings. A variety of internship opportunities are available. Counseling students often plan for careers as licensed, master's-level counselors. The APPL program offers all course work required for the National Certified Counselor credential, including the eight content areas tested in the National Counselor Exam required for licensure. Through UB's participation in a special program, students can take the exam at UB as a master's student after completing as few as 45–48 credits (as opposed to the otherwise required 60). Students also begin accumulating the hours of supervised psychotherapy experience required by the state of Maryland to become a licensed clinical professional counselor. This track is ideally paired with UB's post-master's Certificate in Professional Counseling Studies, which allows students to complete the 60 credits of graduate study necessary for licensure. APPL students within the specialization area of I/O psychology develop skills they can apply to employment at businesses, consulting firms, and government agencies. Students seeking careers in human resources can specialize in I/O psychology with a focus on human resource development. APPL students in the psychological applications track select an area of interest other than counseling or I/O psychology (communication, conflict management, forensics, or health-care management). Assessment, program evaluation, and courses from other departments prepare students for employment in psychology or related areas.

The M.S. in Human Services Administration program focuses on identification of organizational and client needs as well as on leadership skills required to design and administer effective human services programs. Through classroom and fieldwork experiences, students develop skills in program planning, implementation, and evaluation; grant writing and administration; fund raising; personnel and fiscal administration; and community outreach. All HSAD students complete 36 credits of graduate course work, encompassing 24 credits of required core courses (including a student's choice of an internship or research option) and 12 credits of course work in one of the program's eight elective content areas. These elective content areas allow students to individualize their courses of study and include addictions counseling, applied psychology, family counseling, gerontology, health-care delivery systems, negotiations and conflict management, rehabilitation counseling, and special education.

Research Facilities

The University is completely wireless, and its computing facilities include several large labs with up-to-date, networked PCs with Internet access for research.

The William and Althea Wagman Applied Psychology Laboratory is a gift from Professor Emeritus William Wagman and his wife and includes a computer Intranet system, a sensory deprivation room, a group testing facility, an assessment library, an individual testing room, and a wet lab.

The University's Langsdale Library houses hundreds of books and dozens of periodicals in the areas of applied psychology and human services administration. Students also have full access to several million volumes and thousands of journals throughout the University System of Maryland. Langsdale Library subscribes to more than 70 online databases that provide on- and off-campus access to full-text journal articles from almost 12,000 titles.

Financial Aid

The UB Office of Financial Aid assists graduate students in obtaining loans, scholarships, and other means of assistance. Many students participate in internships or work on independent or contractual projects. A limited number of graduate assistantships, which provide tuition remission and a stipend, are available.

Cost of Study

In 2007–08, tuition for liberal arts graduate students who are Maryland residents was $498 per credit hour. Nonresident graduate students paid $751 per credit hour. All students pay a University flat fee ($70 for students taking 1–11 credits; $422.50 for students taking 12 or more credits), a University per-credit fee of $56 (not to exceed $309.50), and a technology fee ($6 per credit from 1–11; $72.50 for 12 credits or more). Web-based classes are an additional $88 per credit for in-state students and $86 per credit for students from out-of-state. Students may pay tuition and fees with cash, check, Visa, MasterCard, or Discover.

Living and Housing Costs

UB is a commuter campus and does not presently offer student housing on campus; however, University-affiliated housing is located within walking distance, and assistance in locating affordable housing is provided by the Center for Student Involvement. UB is located in midtown Baltimore's cultural district, off the Jones Falls Expressway (I-83) and across the street from Pennsylvania Station, which provides MARC commuter and Amtrak service. The University is accessible by major bus routes and its own light rail stop, making the campus an easy commute from a variety of neighborhoods within the Baltimore area.

Student Group

More than 100 students are enrolled in the APPL program, half of whom are studying full-time. They come from all over the country and from a variety of backgrounds. Many are back in school after several years of working in some aspect of applied psychology and are seeking advancement in their careers. Others come directly from undergraduate study and are preparing to enter the field or to move on to doctoral programs. Many APPL students are active in the program's chapter of Psi Chi and in a local chapter of the Society for Human Resource Management.

More than 50 students are enrolled in UB's component of the collaborative HSAD program, with a comparable number enrolled through Coppin State University. The typical student pursuing an M.S. in Human Services Administration is a working professional from the Baltimore metropolitan area who is either new to the field or seeking career advancement. Many hold bachelor's degrees in human services, social science, or related disciplines and have previously attended either UB or Coppin State. The collaborative nature of the program furthers both institutions' goals of meeting the needs of minority students and generally increasing diversity in higher education.

Location

Baltimore is both a big city and a small town. UB is nestled in the Mount Vernon Cultural District—home to art galleries, theaters, the symphony and opera, and historic architecture. The neighborhood serves as the backdrop for First Thursdays, a monthly event that includes the likes of outdoor concerts and wine tasting in nearby art galleries. Within 2 miles of campus is the bustling Inner Harbor, with its shops and waterfront activities, including the National Aquarium, Maryland Science Center, Oriole Park at Camden Yards, and the Ravens' M&T Bank Stadium. The city also offers a museum for nearly every interest and specialty—from the legendary histories told at the Babe Ruth Birthplace and Museum, Edgar Allan Poe House Museum, Eubie Blake Museum, and Great Blacks in Wax Museum to the world-class art found at the Walters Art Museum, Baltimore Museum of Art, and the American Visionary Art Museum. Baltimore is also full of friendly neighborhoods, including Little Italy, Fells Point, Canton, and Hampden. Nighttime pub crawls, vintage shops, steamed crabs, and bocce ball along with street fairs, ethnic festivals, and unique markets make Baltimore a city like few others for those of all ages.

The University of Baltimore and Coppin State University are located 3 miles apart; a free shuttle bus service connects the campuses.

The University

UB offers undergraduate and graduate education in three unique schools: the Yale Gordon College of Liberal Arts, the Merrick School of Business, and the School of Law. The University of Baltimore was founded as a private institution in 1925 and is now part of the University System of Maryland. Total student enrollment is approximately 5,400, and the student-faculty ratio is 16:1.

Applying

All candidates for admission to either program must have a bachelor's degree from a regionally accredited institution. Unconditional admission to the APPL program requires a minimum grade point average of 3.0, an undergraduate degree in psychology, and grades of B or better in statistics and research methods courses. Applicants to the HSAD program should have a strong career interest in a human services field; unconditional admission requires a minimum undergraduate GPA of 3.0. Conditional admission to both programs may be possible and is evaluated on an individual basis.

Admission for both fall and spring semesters is possible. APPL applicants must submit an official transcript from each higher-education institution attended, an application and the appropriate application fee, GRE scores, a letter of recommendation, and a statement of personal interest in the program of study. HSAD applicants must submit the transcript(s), application and fee, a resume, and a statement of personal interest in the program of study.

Correspondence and Information

Office of Graduate Admissions
University of Baltimore
1420 North Charles Street
Baltimore, Maryland 21201-5779
Phone: 410-837-6565
Fax: 410-837-4774
E-mail: gradadmissions@ubalt.edu
Web site: http://www.ubalt.edu/cla

Dr. Tom Mitchell
Program Director
M.S. in Applied Psychology
Phone: 410-837-5348
E-mail: gradadmissions@ubalt.edu
Web site: http://www.ubalt.edu/appliedpsychology

Dr. Bridal Pearson
Program Director
M.S. in Human Services Administration
Phone: 410-837-5251
E-mail: gradadmissions@ubalt.edu
Web site: http://www.ubalt.edu/humanservices

University of Baltimore

THE FACULTY

John A. Bates, Professor and Chair; Ph.D., Massachusetts. The nature and evolution of consciousness, learning outcomes assessment.
Brenda Cartwright, Assistant Professor (Coppin State University); Ed.D., George Washington. Rehabilitation counseling.
Courtney E. Gasser, Clinical Assistant Professor; Ph.D., Iowa State. Counseling, clinical supervision and training, eating disorders, women's issues.
Theresa Harris, Associate Professor (Coppin State University); Ph.D., Howard. General and adult education.
John Hudgins, Associate Professor (Coppin State University); Ph.D., Duke. Race and ethnicity, family studies, leadership, social intervention.
Elaine Johnson, Clinical Associate Professor; Ph.D., Iowa State. Counselor training and supervision, gender issues, Gestalt therapy.
Deborah Kohl, Associate Professor; Ph.D., Johns Hopkins. Neuropsychology of memory, work and family issues, critical thinking.
Thomas E. Mitchell, Associate Professor; Ph.D., Virginia Commonwealth. Social psychology, organizational assessment, employee selection, personality research.
Bridal Pearson, Clinical Assistant Professor; Ph.D., Morgan State. Stereotype threat and standardized testing outcomes, multicultural issues in counseling, diversity in the global community.
Thaddeus Phillips, Assistant Professor (Coppin State University); Ph.D., Southern Illinois at Carbondale. Special education.
Margaret J. Potthast, Associate Professor; Ph.D., Maryland. Statistics and assessment.
Janet Spry, Associate Professor (Coppin State University); Ed.D., George Washington. Rehabilitation counseling.
George Taylor, Professor (Coppin State University); Ed.D., Maryland. General and adult education.
DeVance Walker Jr., Adjunct Assistant Professor; Ph.D., Howard. Program planning, program evaluation, policy analysis.
Helga S. Walz, Assistant Professor; Ph.D., Johns Hopkins. Gerontology, aging, statistics.
Janet Yun, Assistant Professor; Ph.D., George Mason. Personnel selection, performance appraisal, employee training/development, workplace diversity issues.

UNIVERSITY OF NEW HAVEN

Master of Arts in Industrial and Organizational Psychology

Programs of Study

The practice of industrial and organizational psychology enhances the effectiveness and functioning of organizations by applying psychological principles to human work behavior. The Master of Arts in Industrial and Organizational Psychology (MAIOP) program at the University of New Haven (UNH) provides students with the knowledge and experience necessary to improve the satisfaction and productivity of people at work.

The MAIOP curriculum is strengthened by ongoing, active relationships with local and regional human resource and applied psychological associations. Students are actively involved with the campus chapter of the Society for Human Resources Management (SHRM-UNH) and supplement their classroom education by participating in a variety of professional workshops and seminars in the field.

A total of 48 credit hours are required for the degree, including 24 credit hours of required courses in the core curriculum and 24 credit hours in concentrations, program options, and elective courses. Students may not complete more than 9 credit hours of electives until they have satisfied the core requirements. Up to 9 elective credit hours may be taken in other departments.

Students may develop a program that meets their particular needs and interests. The thesis option is intended for students who wish to continue their education in doctoral-level programs. The internship/practicum option allows students to acquire special skills through an internship or practicum in an organizational setting. The approved electives option consists of elective courses that provide students with a broad interdisciplinary background, complementing the student's own academic training and interest. A comprehensive examination covering material from the required core psychology courses is required under this option.

Within each option, students may concentrate in one of three areas: industrial–human resources, organizational development and consultation, or conflict management. A concentration requires 12 credit hours of specific elective courses within the 24 credit hours required in the elective option.

The industrial and organizational psychology program at UNH conforms to the standards set by the Council of Applied Master's Programs in Psychology (CAMPP).

Research Facilities

The Marvin K. Peterson Library contains more than 500,000 volumes, subscribes to hundreds of journals, and is a U.S. government documents depository library. Computer workstations are available in the library to access online subscription databases, CDs, and DVDs. In addition, there are more than a dozen computer labs for student use and teaching on campus.

The Center for Dispute Resolution offers mediation services to UNH students and faculty and staff members as well as providing training in mediation and negotiation.

Financial Aid

About 75 percent of all University students receive some form of financial aid. Graduate students may borrow up to $18,500 in both subsidized and unsubsidized Federal Stafford Student Loans. Teaching, research, or administrative assistantships are available to full-time students. Compensation includes $7.65 per hour as well as a 50 percent tuition reduction; student typically work 15 to 20 hours per week.

Cost of Study

Tuition for both full-time and part-time students is $750 per credit hour, or $2250 per 3-credit course. Other fees include a Graduate Student Council fee of $20 and a technology fee of $20 per trimester. Laboratory fees range from $25 and up depending on the course.

Living and Housing Costs

On-campus housing for graduate students is not available. However, off-campus housing is available in the area at a cost of $575 to $1000 per month for a one-bedroom apartment or $775 to $1200 for a two-bedroom unit.

Student Group

Students in the program come from a wide variety of educational backgrounds and work experiences. Some students arrive directly from undergraduate school, others arrive after working for a few years, and some are busy professionals interested in augmenting their careers with a graduate degree. They come from large and small schools, from all points in the United States, and from numerous countries around the globe.

Student Outcomes

Graduates of the program typically obtain related positions in organizational development and human resources management functions at Fortune 500 companies, consulting firms, government agencies, and applied research institutions. Activities include training design and implementation, compensation and benefits, job analysis, talent management, recruiting, employee development, company surveys, and conflict management.

Location

The UNH campus is in West Haven, Connecticut, which is contiguous to New Haven. New Haven has numerous art museums, a deepwater harbor and beaches, fine restaurants, parks and walking trails, and three Tony award–winning regional theaters. New Haven is served by a local airport and major railroads, and its location at the junction of two interstate highways places the University within easy driving distance of New York, Boston, Cape Cod, and the ski areas of New England.

The University

The University of New Haven was founded on the Yale campus in 1920 and became New Haven College in 1926. Today, it includes five undergraduate schools and a Graduate School, with a combined population of 4,500 students. Its programs prepare students to advance in their careers and meet the ever-changing demands of their respective fields. The University offers thirty master's degrees as well as a number of graduate certificates.

Applying

To apply to the program, prospective students must submit a completed application form, transcripts from all colleges and universities previously attended, two letters of recommendation, GRE scores (if taken within the past five years), and a $50 application fee. In addition, applicants must complete an I/O program questionnaire and submit it directly to the Graduate School. For applicants whose native language is not English, TOEFL scores are required. ESL certification may also be submitted. An undergraduate major in psychology is not specifically required, but students are expected to have at least an introductory-level understanding of psychological concepts, principles, and methods before entering the program.

Correspondence and Information

Dr. Stuart Sidle
Program Coordinator
College of Arts and Sciences
University of New Haven
300 Boston Post Road
West Haven, Connecticut 06516
Phone: 800-DIAL-UNH Ext. 7339 (toll-free)
Fax: 203-931-6032
E-mail: ssidle@newhaven.edu
Web site: http://www.newhaven.edu/academics/

Eloise Gormley
Director of Graduate Admissions
University of New Haven
300 Boston Post Road
West Haven, Connecticut 06516
Phone: 203-932-7448
Fax: 203-932-7137
E-mail: gradinfo@newhaven.edu
Web site: http://www.newhaven.edu

University of New Haven

THE FACULTY AND THEIR RESEARCH

The full- and part-time faculty members at the University of New Haven are qualified through education and experience in the subareas of industrial and organizational (I/O) psychology. They have had many years of experience as practicing I/O psychologists in consulting, government, and industry as well as academia. In addition, students in the program enjoy an excellent student-faculty relationship. Faculty members are willing to take the time to help students make UNH a very positive experience.

Full-Time Faculty

Stuart Sidle, Graduate Program Coordinator; Ph.D. (industrial and organizational psychology), DePaul. Employee surveys, job motivation, job stress, leadership styles, workplace humor, gender stereotypes.

Tara L'Heureux-Barrett, Associate Professor; Ph.D. (industrial and organizational psychology), Connecticut, 1991. Performance management, worker well-being, training competencies for master's-level I/O psychologists.

Dennis McGough, Practitioner in Residence; Ph.D. (industrial and organizational psychology), Union (Ohio). Evaluation of training program effectiveness, leadership development, executive coaching, incentive compensation programs.

Michael Morris, Professor; Ph.D. (community-social psychology), Boston College. Ethical challenges faced by program evaluators in their work.

Gordon R. Simerson, Associate Professor and Associate Dean, College of Arts and Sciences; Ph.D. (industrial and organizational psychology), Wayne State, 1984. Management of employees in creative functions, applying the "Big 5" model of personality to understanding work-related attitudes, procedural justice and organizational ethics, spirituality in the workplace.

Adjunct Faculty

Martin Anderson, Adjunct Professor; Ph.D. (school psychology and psychometrics), Oklahoma State. Test development and validation; job analysis; statistical investigations and organizational research; survey development, administration, and analysis; performance appraisal system development and administration.

Robert Beaudoin, Adjunct Professor; Ed.D. (adult learning and organizational behavior). Employee motivation, training and development, leadership development.

Marilyn Kendrix, Adjunct Professor; E.M.B.A., 1997, M.A. (industrial and organizational psychology), 2000, New Haven. Effects of downsizing, conflict resolution.

Donna Morris, Adjunct Professor; J.D., Yale, 1979. Employment discrimination law, conflict management.

UNIVERSITY OF TOLEDO

Department of Psychology

Programs of Study

The Department of Psychology at the University of Toledo offers the Doctor of Philosophy degree in two areas of concentration, behavioral science and clinical psychology, and the Master of Arts degree in general psychology. Training in behavioral science includes the following areas of student specialization: behavioral neuroscience and learning, cognitive psychology, developmental psychology, and social psychology. Training in clinical psychology provides students with a broad educational foundation in the science and the practice of clinical psychology. The purpose of the doctoral program is to prepare students for careers in academia (teaching, research, clinical work), in mental health programs, in clinical intervention settings, as well as in other settings. Each student must complete specific course-related requirements, a master's thesis, doctoral examinations, a doctoral dissertation; and the Department's foreign language requirement.

The **behavioral science** concentration involves a systematic course of study and research. It provides the comprehensive background in basic psychological science that is necessary for those interested in academic and research careers and the growing number of nonacademic careers that draw on and apply the basic principles of psychology. Student programs are tailored to meet each student's career interests and provide opportunities for student specialization in behavioral neuroscience and learning, cognitive psychology, developmental psychology, or social psychology. In addition, all students receive in-depth training in quantitative methods and research methodology. Faculty members and graduate students carry out research in such diverse areas as nonverbal communication, group behavior processes, cognitive processes in infants and young children, comparative differences in hearing processes, the effects of effort and secondary reinforcement on learning, and cerebral lateralization of perceptual, motor, and cognitive functions.

The concentration in **clinical psychology** develops clinical psychologists capable of serving within a wide range of professional contexts and provides a broad and flexible view of the discipline of psychology that enables graduates to engage in new fields of interest and emerging specializations. The three traditional functions of clinical research, diagnostic assessment, and psychotherapy are emphasized. Training in research conceptualization and methodology is an integral part of the educational sequence. On the continuum between practitioner and researcher, the clinical psychology concentration at the University of Toledo strives for an equal balance between research and practice.

Research Facilities

Behavioral neuroscience and animal learning facilities accommodate the latest anatomical, chemical, and physiological techniques for research investigating the neuroanatomical basis of behavior and the evolution of the nervous system. They also accommodate behavioral techniques for assessing sensory processes and perceptual abilities of animals. Learning laboratories for instrumental and classical conditioning studies are equipped with computer-controlled operant chambers and other appropriate apparatus. Cognitive psychology labs contain an extensive collection of computer hardware and software designed to study lower and higher order cognitive processes and to analyze data. Laptop and Web technologies are available for those interested in collecting data on-site. Rooms are available for individuals and small groups and are used for a variety of purposes, including survey and index data collection. A 3,700-square-foot developmental psychology facility includes laboratories for studying cognitive processes in infants and young children. Infant labs contain observation chambers and are equipped with computers as well as equipment for displaying visual and auditory stimuli. Preschool labs are equipped with one-way observation capability. Research facilities in social psychology include customized observation rooms with one-way windows and the latest audiovisual recording devices. The Center for the Study of Anxiety Disorders and Depression is a clinical research center specializing in assessment and treatment of depression and anxiety disorders for children, adolescents, and adults. The Program for the Study of Immigration and Mental Health is devoted to the study of mental-health-related issues among immigrant/ethnic groups, refugees, and other acculturating individuals.

Financial Aid

The out-of-state tuition surcharge normally charged to out-of-state and international students is waived for students whose permanent address is within one of the following Michigan counties: Hillsdale, Lenawee, Macomb, Oakland, Washtenaw, and Wayne. In addition, the University of Toledo offers an out-of-state tuition surcharge waiver to cities and regions that are a part of the Sister Cities Agreement. These regions include Toledo, Spain; Londrina, Brazil; Qinhuangdao, China; Csongrad County, Hungary; Delmenhorst, Germany; Toyohashi, Japan; Tanga, Tanzania; Bekaa Valley, Lebanon; and Poznan, Poland. The University of Toledo Graduate College offers a variety of memorial scholarship awards, including the Ronald E. McNair Postbaccalaureate Achievement Scholarship, the Graduate Opportunity Assistantship Award, and two full University fellowships.

Cost of Study

The graduate tuition rate for the 2008–09 academic year is $434.05 per semester credit hour for in-state students. For nonresidents, the out-of-state surcharge is $389 per semester credit hour. Additional fees are required and include the general fee, technology fee, and mandatory insurance.

Living and Housing Costs

The University of Toledo has a diverse offering of student housing options, including suite-style and traditional residential halls. Housing is offered to graduate students through Residence Life or contracted individually by the student. Affordable, high-quality off-campus apartment-style housing within walking distance of campus is abundant.

Student Group

There are approximately 20,000 students at the University of Toledo. About 4,000 are graduate and professional students. The University has a rich diversity of student organizations. Students join groups that are organized around common cultural, religious, athletic, and educational interests.

Student Outcomes

The purpose of the doctoral program is to prepare students for careers in academia (teaching, research, and clinical work), mental health programs, clinical intervention settings, and the growing number of nonacademic careers that draw on and apply basic principles of psychology.

Location

The University of Toledo has several campus sites in the city of Toledo. Most graduate students take classes on the Main campus, which is located in suburban western Toledo. With a population of more than 330,000, Toledo is the fiftieth-largest city in the United States. It is located on the western shores of Lake Erie, within a 2-hour drive of Cleveland and Detroit.

The University

The University of Toledo was founded by Jessup W. Scott in 1872 as a municipal institution and became part of the state of Ohio's system of higher education in 1967. On July 1, 2006, the University of Toledo merged with the Medical University of Ohio becoming one of only seventeen American universities to offer professional and graduate academic programs in medicine, law, pharmacy, nursing, health sciences, engineering, and business.

Applying

Applicants must satisfy admission requirements of the Graduate School (http://www.utoledo.edu/graduate). The Department requires that each applicant submit an application, transcripts of previous academic work, three letters of recommendation, and scores from the Graduate Record Examinations (including the advanced psychology test). A brief biographical sketch is also required from each applicant in clinical psychology.

Correspondence and Information

Dr. Joseph D. Hovey, Department Chair
Department of Psychology, Mail Stop 948
University of Toledo
Toledo, Ohio 43606

Phone: 419-530-2717
E-mail: grdsch@utoledo.edu
Web site: http://www.utoledo.edu/psychology

University of Toledo

THE FACULTY AND THEIR RESEARCH INTERESTS

Harvard L. Armus. Learning and conditioning in animals; the effect of physical and cognitive effort on subjective reward value; factors influencing symbolic reward; conditioning in unicellular organisms.

Wesley A. Bullock. Public mental health issues and the application of the mental health recovery paradigm within the public mental health arena, including forensic settings.

Michael Caruso. Teaching methods, technology and teaching, aging, memory.

Stephen D. Christman. Understanding different information-processing abilities of the cerebral hemispheres in humans by presenting visual and auditory information to each hemisphere and comparing the performance of right- and left-handers.

Alexander M. Czopp. Prejudice and stereotypes, social cognition, attitude formation and attitude change.

Robert K. Elliott. Evaluation of humanistic-experiential psychotherapies: emotion focused, growth oriented, and egalitarian.

Jeanne B. Funk. Factors influencing children's preference for violent electronic games, e.g., their experiences of game playing, their attitudes toward violence, violence prevention, autistic disorders.

Andrew L. Geers. The influence of expectations on affect, emotion, and social judgment; optimism-pessimism in social interaction; perception of ongoing behavior; psychology and law.

Henry E. Heffner. Role of primate auditory cortex on hearing, comparative study of mammalian hearing.

Rickye Heffner. Hearing sensitivity and sound localization in animals, how characteristics of other senses affect hearing in animals.

Joseph D. Hovey. Mental health of acculturating individuals; anxiety, depression, and suicide risk factors; evaluation of prevention activities in the community.

John D. Jasper. Cognitive processes involved in judgment and decision making, consumer behavior, health attitudes and beliefs.

Gregory J. Meyer. Cognitive assessment, personality assessment, neuropsychological testing.

Joni L. Mihura. Personality assessment, reliability and validity of the Rorschach, psychodynamic theory and therapy.

Lisa A. Neff. Interpersonal relationships, social cognition, cognitive processes involved in close relationship maintenance and deterioration.

Laura D. Seligman. Anxiety and depression in youth; issues of comorbidity in childhood psychopathology; cognitive-behavioral treatments for children, adolescents, and families.

Alice Skeens. Gender research, assessment of teaching methods.

P. Hull Smith. Infant cognitive processes, early language acquisition and conceptual development, temperament and cognition.

Mojisola Tiamiyu (Center for Applied Psychology). Community psychology, University-community collaboration and human services.

VILLANOVA UNIVERSITY

Department of Psychology

Program of Study The Villanova Department of Psychology has offered a Master of Science (M.S.) degree in general psychology since 1961. This M.S. degree program is particularly well suited to provide a strong foundation for individuals seeking entry into Ph.D. programs in most subfields of psychology. In addition, the program serves the needs of students who are unsure of their future professional goals, of individuals who want a more gradual transition between undergraduate and Ph.D.-level work, and of those seeking a terminal master's degree.

The two-year curriculum is designed to provide excellent training in research skills. Students gain expertise in the formulation of research designs and in the acquisition, analysis, and interpretation of data. Laboratory courses in cognitive psychology, statistics, and physiological psychology are complemented by electives in many of the other subfields of psychology. In addition, students may elect to take a graduate course in a department other than psychology to round out their area of special interest. Biology, chemistry, computer science, human organization science, and statistics have been of particular interest in this regard. Students are required to complete a total of eight courses, including statistics and at least two laboratory courses, and to conduct an original piece of research under faculty supervision in the form of a thesis. The elective courses are designed to allow students the flexibility to tailor the program to their particular goals. The master's thesis is required, and additional independent research is strongly encouraged. There is no comprehensive examination or foreign language requirement.

The psychology faculty has maintained a consistently strong record for productivity and scholarly research. During a recent three-year period, seventy-seven journal articles, fourteen book chapters, three books, and fifty-eight convention presentations emerged from the Department of Psychology. Graduate students frequently coauthor the research published by their mentors, thereby enhancing their graduate education and preparation for a top-quality doctoral program. Villanova's master's program in psychology has been ranked among the top ten M.S.-only–granting departments (95th percentile) in the United States and Canada with regard to research productivity. Several of the Department's faculty members hold research grants from various government agencies.

Research Facilities The University library contains more than 780,000 volumes and 5,600 current periodicals. Public computing facilities that consist of networked Windows-based microcomputers are available in a number of campus locations, including Tolentine Hall (the location of the Department of Psychology). All facilities are available to University students and faculty members. Computer facilities that are dedicated to the Department of Psychology and laboratories within the Department are also available.

Financial Aid A limited number of University-funded assistantships and tuition scholarships are awarded to psychology graduate students on a competitive basis. These include research/teaching assistantships that carry a remission of tuition and fees and, in some instances, a monthly stipend. Students with assistantships and tuition scholarships are assigned to faculty members to help with their teaching and/or research efforts. Depending on the type of award, assistants and tuition scholars are expected to work from 7 to 20 hours per week under the supervision of their faculty mentor. Additional research assistantships, supported by extramural grants, are awarded by faculty members who hold the grants. Villanova University also has a number of additional scholarships and graduate assistantship, for which psychology program students may be eligible.

Cost of Study Graduate tuition was $610 per credit hour in 2007–08.

Living and Housing Costs The University does not maintain accommodations for graduate students, but second-year students are eligible for positions as resident counselors in the dormitories. The area has a wide selection of living quarters that are convenient to the campus.

Student Group Approximately 20 students representing all geographical sections of the United States are selected for admission each year from approximately 150 applications. About 30 percent of the class comes from the Philadelphia area. The majority (58 percent) of students come from out of state, and a large proportion are from outside the Mid-Atlantic region (e.g., California, Arizona, Texas, Missouri, Kansas, Florida, Georgia, and Virginia).

Student Outcomes While the program is not specifically designed to provide terminal training for mental health professionals, some graduates continue on to Ph.D. programs in clinical or counseling psychology. Others accept positions in the private sector as science writers, lab technicians, data analysts, and marketing researchers. The program enjoys a strong national reputation, thereby contributing to the success that a large proportion of graduates have in gaining admission to some of the top Ph. D. programs in psychology (e.g., Brown; Columbia; Cornell; Tufts University; University of California, Berkeley; University of California, San Diego; University of Colorado; University of Illinois; and Johns Hopkins). Additional information about graduates of the program can be found on the Web at the address given in this description.

Location Located in the heart of the Philadelphia Region's Main Line suburbs, the University occupies more than 200 handsomely landscaped acres in the town of Villanova, 12 miles west of Philadelphia. The location combines the advantages of a tranquil suburban setting with proximity to a large metropolitan city known for its outstanding contributions in the areas of culture, education, history, recreation, religion, and sport.

The University Villanova University is a private institution founded in 1842 by the Augustinian Fathers. Graduate programs were first administered separately in 1931. Currently, there are five academic units—the Colleges of Arts and Sciences, Engineering, and Nursing; the Villanova School of Business; and the School of Law.

Applying Application forms and the *Graduate Studies Viewbook* may be obtained from the Graduate Studies Office. There is a $50 application fee. Additional information about the psychology program may be obtained by contacting the Department of Psychology. In addition to forwarding the completed application form, GRE scores, and official college transcripts, applicants must also arrange to have three letters of recommendation submitted on their behalf. Submission of a personal statement, describing the nature of the applicant's interest in psychology and in the Villanova program, is also suggested. Most successful applicants have an undergraduate GPA of at least 3.0 (with an average of 3.5) and above-average GRE scores (average verbal, 540; quantitative, 640; analytic writing, 5.0; Subject Test in psychology (optional), 620; statistics taken from the most recent three years).

Applications are accepted for fall admission only. Admissions are on a rolling basis, and applications are accepted for the following fall throughout the year. However, to receive full consideration for financial aid, completed applications should be received before March 1.

Correspondence and Information

For applications:

Graduate Studies Office
Kennedy Hall, 2nd Floor
Villanova University
800 Lancaster Avenue
Villanova, Pennsylvania 19085-1699
Phone: 610-519-7090
Fax: 610-519-7096

For further information about the M.S. program in psychology:

Graduate Admissions Committee
Department of Psychology
Villanova University
Villanova, Pennsylvania 19085-1699
Phone: 610-519-4720
Fax: 610-519-4269
E-mail: Visit Web site
Web site: http://www.villanova.edu/artsci/psychology

Villanova University

THE FACULTY AND THEIR RESEARCH

The Department of Psychology comprises 16 full-time faculty members, most of whom maintain active research laboratories in their specialties. Strong research specializations within the Department are provided in animal learning, clinical, cognition, developmental, human factors, organizational, perception, personality, physiological, and social psychology.

Cognitive Psychology/Cognitive Neuroscience/Human Factors

Dr. Diego Fernandez-Duque's research spans cognitive and social neuroscience. Within cognitive neuroscience, he studies how different aspects of attention change due to aging and pathology and why visual perception sometimes occurs in the absence of awareness. Within social neuroscience, he investigates impairments in social cognition brought about by brain insult, using frontotemporal dementia as a model disease in which to explore empathy and metacognition.

Dr. Charles Folk has been studying the nature of visual distractibility. What kinds of events capture attention, and to what degree is such capture under voluntary control? The outcome of his work has important implications for applied settings, such as aircraft cockpits, as well as for theoretical models of selective attention.

Dr. Irene Kan's general research interest is the cognitive architecture and neural bases of human memory. Combining cognitive neuroscientific, neuropsychological, and behavioral approaches, research in her laboratory is focused on understanding how semantic memory and episodic memory are organized and retrieved.

Dr. Thomas Toppino investigates human cognitive processes and the development of those processes in children. Most recently, he has studied fundamental factors underlying the effects of repetition and order of presentation in learning and memory. He also investigates the relationship between sensory and higher cognitive processes in visual perception, focusing especially on factors affecting the perception of ambiguous patterns.

Developmental Psychology

Dr. Pamela Blewitt studies both the cognitive and social/interactive processes involved in word learning. She examines how young children approach the word learning task, traces changes in children's word meanings over time, and assesses the relationships between word learning and logical thinking. Her studies also examine parents' and teachers' contributions to children's vocabulary growth, including conversational, word defining, and book-reading strategies.

Dr. Rebecca Brand is interested in infants' knowledge acquisition across several domains. In the language domain, she has recently been investigating the development of inhibitory control and its role in early vocabulary development. In the action domain, she has been investigating the specialized action adults present toward infants ("motionese") and its role in infants' understanding of new action sequences.

Dr. Nicole Else-Quest studies psychological development across the lifespan, with special focus on gender roles and emotions. Her recent projects include an investigation of the roles of emotions, scaffolding and social relationships in mathematics learning, meta-analyses of gender differences in temperament and emotion, and a study of emotional adaptation to disease later in life.

Clinical/Social/Personality and Organizational Psychology

Dr. David Bush investigates gender differences in work-related issues such as gender stereotyping of jobs, performance appraisal, compensation, and negotiating strategies. He also conducts research on organizational changes related to downsizing and reorganization and their consequences for the organizational culture.

Dr. Deborah Kendzierski's social psychology research program focuses on the links between intentions and behavior in the context of adherence to health-behavior regimens. She is interested in the role of self-concept in linking intentions and such health behaviors as exercising and dieting.

Dr. Douglas Klieger's research program focuses on establishing an empirical basis for the measurement of anxiety, fear, and phobias. Secondary to this, he is interested in developing new measurement techniques that apply generally to questionnaires, inventories, and personality scales.

Dr. Steven Krauss examines normal and disordered mood expression and personality across cultures. He also investigates the relationships between values, moral reasoning, relationship models, and individualism/collectivism from a cross-cultural perspective.

Dr. John Kurtz studies issues and techniques related to psychological assessment and the diagnosis of mental disorders. His recent research is concerned with factors related to change versus stability in personality traits during adulthood and the use of informants in personality assessment.

Dr. Patrick Markey's research program is focused on two broad issues: How people differ and if these differences are related to how they actually behave. Much of this research has related personality attributes to behaviors in diverse contexts, including Internet chat rooms, marital interactions, face-to-face communications among college students, and interactions between preadolescent children and their mothers.

Sensation/Perception

Dr. Gerald Long has focused on the validity and reliability of various visual assessment tasks that are often used to screen our visual abilities, including color vision, contrast sensitivity, and dynamic visual acuity. Another productive line of research has involved examination of the processes underlying certain classes of visual illusions. These illusions have proven to be useful research tools in identifying sensory and cognitive effects in perception.

Dr. Paul Sheldon's interests lie in cutaneous sensitivity. He has studied the relationship between pain sensitivity and personality characteristics and, most recently, the effect of interpersonal interactions upon tickle sensitivity.

Comparative/Physiological Psychology

Dr. Michael Brown's laboratory has been concerned with understanding basic cognitive processes by studying the behavior of nonhuman animals. Most recently, this research has centered on spatial abilities and decision processes in rats and spatial memory in honey bees.

Dr. Matthew Matell is interested in the cognitive and neural mechanisms underlying the perception of time and sequence. Primary techniques include ensemble electrophysiological recordings, pharmacology, and lesion techniques in rats, with a current focus on the role of cortical-striatal-thalamic interactions. Computational models of timing are also being developed.

WIDENER UNIVERSITY

Institute for Graduate Clinical Psychology

Programs of Study

The Institute for Graduate Clinical Psychology at Widener University offers nine programs: the Doctor of Psychology degree (Psy.D.), a postdoctoral respecialization program, a post-master's option, and dual-degree programs with business (Psy.D./M.B.A.), criminal justice (Psy.D./M.A. in criminal justice), education (Psy.D./M.Ed. in human sexuality education), health administration (Psy.D./M.B.A.–HMSA), law (J.D./Psy.D.), and public administration (Psy.D./M.P.A.).

The Doctor of Psychology degree (Psy.D.) is fully accredited by the American Psychological Association. The program offers five years of intensive professional training in psychology. The content of the program is designed to help students retain the basic skills and knowledge of traditional clinical psychology, such as psychodiagnostic testing and psychotherapy, while simultaneously exposing them to new ideas and practices in the field. Following a scholar-professional model, the philosophy of the program is grounded in the belief that both scholarship and practical supervised experience are essential to clinical applications. Within the program, students may pursue the following areas of concentration: brief psychotherapies, cognitive/behavioral therapy, cross-cultural psychology, family therapy, forensic psychology, group psychotherapy, health psychology, neuropsychology, organizational psychology, psychoanalytic psychology, and school psychology. The program provides extensive practical experience in a wide variety of service settings. An integrated internship, which is fully accredited by the American Psychological Association, is an important aspect of the program.

The law/psychology six-year program leads to an award of the J.D. degree by Widener University School of Law and the Psy.D. degree by Widener's Institute for Graduate Clinical Psychology. It trains lawyers–clinical psychologists to integrate the two fields and deal more effectively with issues related to the rights of mental health patients, families and children, expert testimony, and other areas.

The postdoctoral respecialization program is a three-year, full-time program leading to a Certificate of Respecialization. The program is intended to help doctoral-level psychologists in other fields, including developmental, experimental, and social psychology, acquire the additional training necessary to practice clinical psychology.

Research Facilities

The Wolfgram Memorial Library has a fine collection that numbers more than 240,000 printed volumes, 175,000 microforms, and close to 2,000 periodical titles. Services include online access to bibliographic information and electronic databases (such as PsychINFO), audiovisual media collections and facilities, and access to other libraries' resources through interlibrary loans. State-of-the-art computing facilities are available to meet students' needs.

The School of Law library maintains a collection of more than 600,000 volumes. Contained in the collection are legal publications and journals, treatises, reports, and statutes. Access to a wide range of supporting materials is available through LexisNexis and Westlaw online legal research services.

Financial Aid

Students may apply for federal loans and work-study through the Financial Aid Office on the Main Campus. Stipends associated with internships are available to fourth-year and fifth-year students. Some academically based grants and scholarships are also available.

Cost of Study

Tuition for the Doctor of Psychology program is $21,900 for the 2008–09 academic year. Students pay a Psy.D. joint-program fee of $325 per semester of joint enrollment, excluding the J.D./Psy.D. and respecialization programs.

Living and Housing Costs

Affordable rental apartments are available within a 3-mile radius of all three campuses.

Student Group

Approximately 175 students are enrolled in the clinical psychology program. The students are drawn from areas throughout the United States and are heterogeneous in terms of age, academic background, and clinical experience. The total University enrollment is approximately 6,500 students. Enrollment in all graduate programs is approximately 3,200 students; about 57 percent are women.

Location

The Institute for Graduate Clinical Psychology is located on Widener's Main Campus in Chester, Pennsylvania. The campus occupies more than 100 acres and is easily accessible from Interstate 95. Located in Delaware County, one of the oldest counties in Pennsylvania, the campus is near Philadelphia, which lies just 15 miles to the north, and other historic and commercial areas.

The 40-acre Delaware Campus, 15 miles southwest of the Main Campus, is located on Route 202 (Concord Pike) north of Wilmington and is only a short distance from Interstate 95. It houses the School of Law and is a course site for the School of Business Administration. A branch of the School of Law is also located on the 21-acre Harrisburg Campus in central Pennsylvania.

The University

Widener University is a multicampus, independent, metropolitan institution located in and accredited by the commonwealth of Pennsylvania and the state of Delaware. Founded in 1821, Widener offers doctoral, master's, baccalaureate, and associate degrees through its eight schools and colleges. The University distinguishes itself by connecting curricula to societal issues through civic engagement and by inspiring its students to be citizens of character as well as professional and civic leaders.

Applying

The applicant must possess a B.A. or B.S. degree from an accredited institution. A major in psychology is desirable but not essential. Students must have had courses in statistics, abnormal psychology (or psychopathology), and research design (or experimental psychology) by the time they matriculate into the program. Evaluation of the student's ability to do graduate work is based upon academic performance and scores on the Graduate Record Examinations (GRE). Personal character and attributes of emotional maturity and stability are major factors in reviewing applicants, along with a capacity for relating to and working with other people. Evidence for these attributes is sought from records of past performance, letters of reference, work history, and a personal interview. Applications must be submitted by December 31 for admission the next fall. Spring or summer admission is not possible.

Correspondence and Information

For the Psy.D. and respecialization programs:
Dr. Virginia Brabender, Director
Institute for Graduate Clinical Psychology
Widener University
Chester, Pennsylvania 19013
Phone: 610-499-1206
E-mail: graduate.psychology@widener.edu
Web site: http://www.widener.edu

For the law/psychology program:
Dr. Amiram Elwork
Institute for Graduate Clinical Psychology
Widener University
Chester, Pennsylvania 19013
Phone: 610-499-1217
E-mail: amiram.elwork@widener.edu

Widener University

THE FACULTY AND THEIR RESEARCH

Jules C. Abrams, Professor; Ph.D.; ABPP (Clinical). Learning disabilities, psychoanalysis, psychoanalytically oriented psychotherapy, professional issues, psychological and neuropsychological assessment (phone: 610-499-1205).

Bret A. Boyer, Assistant Professor; Ph.D. Health psychology, pediatric psychology, developmental psychopathology, development throughout the life-span, family and couple therapy, integrative approaches to therapy (phone: 610-499-1220).

Virginia Brabender, Professor, Associate Dean, and Director; Ph.D.; ABPP (Clinical). Group psychotherapy, personality assessment, professional issues, live events of the therapist (phone: 610-499-1208).

Patricia M. Bricklin, Professor; Ph.D. Reading and learning disabilities, professional issues and ethics, school psychology (phone: 610-499-1212).

Dennis Debiak, Clinical Associate Professor; Psy.D. Psychoanalytic psychotherapy; gay, lesbian, and bisexual issues; gender identity development (phone: 610-499-1219).

Clifford M. DeCato, Professor; Ph.D.; ABPP (Clinical). Diagnostic psychological assessment, clinical and teaching applications, Rorschach perceptanalytic system (phone: 610-499-1207).

Amiram Elwork, Professor; Ph.D. Law/psychology, professional issues, cognitive psychotherapy, stress management (phone: 610-499-1217).

Elisabeth N. Gibbings, Director of Admissions and Practicum; Psy.D. Supervision, professional training in assessment (phone: 610-499-1221).

Kenneth B. Goldberg, Associate Professor; Psy.D. Neuropsychology treatment and assessment, learning disabilities, professional training in neuropsychology (phone: 610-499-1222).

Linda Knauss, Associate Professor and Director of Internship Training; Ph.D.; ABPP (Clinical). Professional ethics, development, family therapy, assessment (phone: 610-499-1211).

Geoffrey R. Marcyk, Assistant Professor; J.D., Ph.D. Law and psychology, correctional psychology, forensic assessment, organizational assessment and intervention (phone: 610-499-4598).

Frank Masterpasqua, Professor; Ph.D. Development, constructivism, nonlinear dynamics, community psychology and prevention, neurofeedback (phone: 610-499-1234).

Sanjay Nath, Assistant Professor; Ph.D. Ethnic diversity formation, narrative studies, qualitative research methodology, identity formation, cross-cultural psychology, immigration/acculturation, interracial relationships, arranged marriages, postpartum adjustment (phone: 610-499-1214).

Maurice Prout, Professor; Ph.D.; ABPP (Clinical). Cognitive and behavioral psychotherapy of Axis I and II disorders, psychosomatics and behavioral medicine (phone: 610-499-1216).

Stephen C. Wilhite, Professor; D.Phil. Learning and memory and research methods (phone: 610-499-4351).

Professor Bret Boyer, of Widener's Institute for Graduate Clinical Psychology, teaches health psychology.

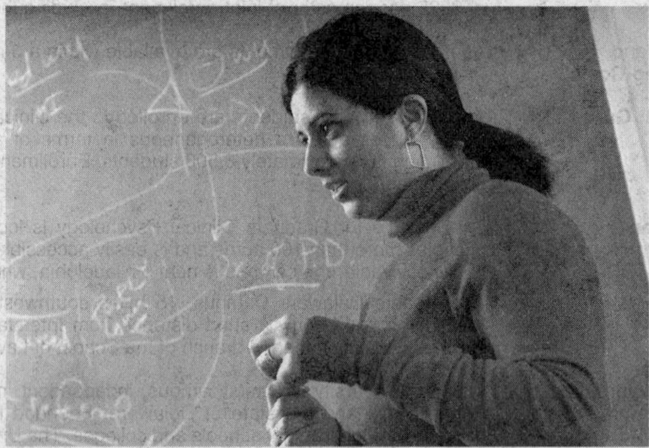

Varsha Reddy, clinical psychology student.

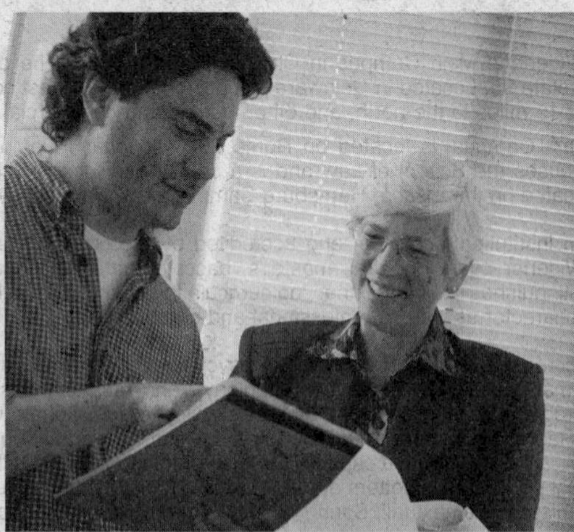

Dr. Linda Knauss, Director of Internship Training, provides supervision on a psychological assessment.

Section 25
Public, Regional, and Industrial Affairs

This section contains a directory of institutions offering graduate work in public, regional, and industrial affairs, followed by in-depth entries submitted by institutions that chose to prepare detailed program descriptions. Additional information about programs listed in the directory but not augmented by an in-depth entry may be obtained by writing directly to the dean of a graduate school or chair of a department at the address given in the directory.

For programs offering related work, see also in this book *Architecture, Area and Cultural Studies, Criminology and Forensics, Economics, Humanities, Political Science and International Affairs,* and *Sociology, Anthropology, and Archaeology.* In the other guides in this series:

Graduate Programs in the Physical Sciences, Mathematics, Agricultural Sciences, the Environment & Natural Resources

See *Environmental Sciences and Management*

Graduate Programs in Engineering & Applied Sciences

See *Management of Engineering and Technology*

Graduate Programs in Business, Education, Health, Information Studies, Law & Social Work

See *Business Administration and Management, Law,* and *Public Health*

CONTENTS

Program Directories

Announcements

Cross-Discipline Announcement

Close-Ups

See also:

Disability Studies

Brandeis University, The Heller School for Social Policy and Management, Program in Social Policy, Waltham, MA 02454-9110. Offers aging (MPP); assets and inequalities (PhD); behavioral health (MPP); children, youth and families (MPP, PhD); general social policy (MPP); health (MPP); health and behavioral health (PhD); poverty alleviation and development (MPP). Part-time programs available. *Degree requirements:* For doctorate, thesis/dissertation, qualifying paper, 2 year residency. *Entrance requirements:* For doctorate, GRE General Test. Additional exam requirements/recommendations for international students: Required—TOEFL (minimum score 600 paper-based). Electronic applications accepted. *Faculty research:* Health policy, child and family policy, mental health policy, disability policy, aging policy, substance abuse, work, inequality and social change.

See Close-Ups on pages 1579 and 1581.

Brock University, Faculty of Graduate Studies, Faculty of Social Sciences, Program in Applied Disability Studies, St. Catharines, ON L2S 3A1, Canada. Offers MA, MADS, Diploma. Part-time programs available. *Degree requirements:* For master's, thesis (for some programs). *Entrance requirements:* For master's, honors degree. Additional exam requirements/recommendations for international students: Required—TOEFL (minimum score 550 paper-based; 213 computer-based; 80 iBT), IELTS (minimum score 7). Electronic applications accepted.

Chapman University, Graduate Studies, School of Education, Program in Education: Disability Studies, Orange, CA 92866. Offers PhD. *Faculty:* 19 full-time (13 women), 20 part-time/adjunct (12 women). *Students:* Average age 41. 17 applicants, 53% accepted, 7 enrolled. *Degree requirements:* For doctorate, thesis/dissertation. *Financial support:* Federal Work-Study and scholarships/grants available. *Unit head:* Dr. Joel Colbert, Director, 714-744-7076.

New York Medical College, School of Public Health, Department of Disability and Human Development, Valhalla, NY 10595-1691. Offers MPH. Part-time and evening/weekend programs available. *Degree requirements:* For master's, thesis. *Entrance requirements:* For master's, minimum undergraduate GPA of 3.0. Additional exam requirements/recommendations for international students: Required—TOEFL (minimum score 600 paper-based; 250 computer-based; 100 iBT), IELTS (minimum score 7). *Application deadline:* For fall admission, 8/1 priority date for domestic students, 5/15 for international students; for spring admission, 12/1 priority date for domestic students, 10/15 for international students. Applications are processed on a rolling basis. Application fee: $50 ($100 for international students). Electronic applications accepted. *Financial support:* Research assistantships with full and partial tuition reimbursements, teaching assistantships with full and partial tuition reimbursements, career-related internships or fieldwork, Federal Work-Study, institutionally sponsored loans, health care benefits, tuition waivers (partial), and tuition reimbursements available. Support available to part-time students. Financial award applicants required to submit FAFSA. *Unit head:* Dr. Ansley Bacon, Chair, 914-493-8204, Fax: 914-493-7899, E-mail: abacon@wihd.org. *Application contact:* Marian F. McGowan, Assistant Dean for Admissions, 914-594-4510, Fax: 914-594-4292, E-mail: sph_admissions@nymc.edu.

Suffolk University, Sawyer Business School, Department of Public Administration, Boston, MA 02108-2770. Offers disability studies (MPA); health administration (MPA); nonprofit management (MPA); public administration (CASPA); public finance and human resources (MPA); state and local government (MPA); JD/MPA; MPA/MS. *Accreditation:* NASPAA (one or more programs are accredited). Part-time and evening/weekend programs available. *Faculty:* 11 full-time (6 women), 7 part-time/adjunct (2 women). *Students:* 39 full-time (21 women), 117 part-time (79 women); includes 18 minority (10 African Americans, 4 Asian Americans or Pacific Islanders, 4 Hispanic Americans), 7 international. Average age 31. 86 applicants, 83% accepted, 42 enrolled. In 2007, 63 degrees awarded. *Entrance requirements:* Additional exam requirements/recommendations for international students: Required—TOEFL (minimum score 550 paper-based; 213 computer-based; 80 iBT). *Application deadline:* For fall admission, 6/15 priority date for domestic students, 6/15 for international students; for spring admission, 11/1 priority date for domestic students, 11/1 for international students. Applications are processed on a rolling basis. Application fee: $50. Electronic applications accepted. *Expenses:* Contact institution. *Financial support:* In 2007–08, 114 students received support, including 71 fellowships with full and partial tuition reimbursements available (averaging $7,661 per year); career-related internships or fieldwork and Federal Work-Study also available. Support available to part-time students. Financial award application deadline: 4/1; financial award applicants required to submit FAFSA. *Faculty research:* Local government, health care, federal policy, mental health, HIV/AIDS. Total annual research expenditures: $200,000. *Unit head:* Dr. Michael Lavin, Chair, 617-573-8062, E-mail: mlavin@suffolk.edu. *Application contact:* Judith Reynolds, Director of Graduate Admissions, 617-573-8302, Fax: 617-523-0116, E-mail: grad.admission@suffolk.edu.

Syracuse University, Graduate School, School of Education, Program in Disabilities Studies, Syracuse, NY 13244. Offers CAS. Part-time and evening/weekend programs available. *Students:* 1 (woman) full-time, 1 (woman) part-time; includes 1 minority (Asian American or Pacific Islander) 3 applicants, 100% accepted, 2 enrolled. In 2007, 7 degrees awarded. *Entrance requirements:* Additional exam requirements/recommendations for international students: Required—TOEFL. Application fee: $75. *Expenses:* Tuition: Full-time $18,216; part-time $1,012 per credit. Required fees: $980. Tuition and fees vary according to program. *Unit head:* Dr. Steve Taylor, Program Coordinator, 315-443-4484. *Application contact:* Traci Washburn, Graduate Recruiter, School of Education, 315-443-2505, E-mail: e-gradrcrt@syr.edu.

University of Hawaii at Manoa, Graduate Division, College of Education, Center on Disability Studies, Honolulu, HI 96822. Offers Graduate Certificate. Part-time programs available. *Faculty:* 5 full-time (2 women). *Students:* 7 full-time (5 women), 11 part-time (9 women); includes 8 minority (1 African American, 7 Asian Americans or Pacific Islanders), 2 international. 3 applicants, 67% accepted, 1 enrolled. *Entrance requirements:* Additional exam requirements/recommendations for international students: Required—TOEFL (minimum score 500 paper-based; 173 computer-based; 61 iBT), IELTS (minimum score 5). *Application deadline:* For fall admission, 3/1 for domestic and international students; for spring admission, 10/1 for domestic and international students. Application fee: $50. *Financial support:* In 2007–08, 2 research assistantships (averaging $15,552 per year) were awarded. *Application contact:* Norma Jean Stodden, Director, 808-956-4454, Fax: 808-956-3162, E-mail: nhemphil@hawaii.edu.

University of Illinois at Chicago, Graduate College, College of Applied Health Sciences, Department of Disability, Disability Studies, and Human Development, Chicago, IL 60607-7128. Offers disability and human development (MS); disability studies (PhD). *Accreditation:* AOTA. Part-time programs available. *Degree requirements:* For master's, thesis optional; for doctorate, thesis/dissertation. *Entrance requirements:* For master's and doctorate, GRE General Test. Additional exam requirements/recommendations for international students: Required—TOEFL. Electronic applications accepted. *Faculty research:* Emerging trends in disability, demography and financial structure of disability services, aging and disability, empowerment of people with disabilities, health promotion in disabilities.

University of Manitoba, Faculty of Graduate Studies, Interdisciplinary Programs, Department of Disability Studies, Winnipeg, MB R3T 2N2, Canada. Offers M Sc, MA.

University of Northern British Columbia, Office of Graduate Studies, Prince George, BC V2N 4Z9, Canada. Offers business administration (Diploma); community health science (M Sc); disability management (MA); education (M Ed); first nations studies (MA); gender studies (MA); history (MA); interdisciplinary studies (MA); international studies (MA); mathematical, computer and physical sciences (M Sc); natural resources and environmental studies (M Sc, MA, MNRES, PhD); political science (MA); psychology (M Sc, PhD); social work (MSW). Part-time and evening/weekend programs available. Postbaccalaureate distance learning degree programs offered (no on-campus study). *Degree requirements:* For master's, thesis; for doctorate, thesis/dissertation. *Entrance requirements:* For master's, GRE, minimum B average in undergraduate course work; for doctorate, candidacy exam, minimum A average in graduate course work.

University of Pittsburgh, School of Health and Rehabilitation Sciences, Disability Studies Program, Pittsburgh, PA 15260. Offers Certificate. *Application contact:* Shameem Gangjee, Director of Admissions, 412-383-6558, Fax: 412-383-6535, E-mail: admissions@shrs.pitt.edu.

Utah State University, School of Graduate Studies, College of Education and Human Services, Department of Special Education and Rehabilitation, Logan, UT 84322. Offers disability disciplines (PhD); rehabilitation counselor education (MRC); special education (M Ed, MS, Ed S). *Accreditation:* NCATE (one or more programs are accredited). Part-time programs available. Postbaccalaureate distance learning degree programs offered (minimal on-campus study). *Degree requirements:* For master's, thesis (for some programs), internships (for some programs); for doctorate, comprehensive exam, thesis/dissertation. *Entrance requirements:* For master's and doctorate, GRE General Test, minimum GPA of 3.0. Additional exam requirements/recommendations for international students: Required—TOEFL (minimum score 550 paper-based; 213 computer-based). Electronic applications accepted. *Faculty research:* Applied behavior analysis, effective instructional practices, early childhood teacher training research, distance education, multicultural rehabilitation.

York University, Faculty of Graduate Studies, Faculty of Health, Program in Critical Disability Studies, Toronto, ON M3J 1P3, Canada. Offers MA, PhD. *Degree requirements:* For master's, thesis or alternative. *Entrance requirements:* Additional exam requirements/recommendations for international students: Required—TOEFL (minimum score 600 paper-based; 250 computer-based). Electronic applications accepted.

Emergency Management

Adelphi University, Graduate School of Arts and Sciences, Department of Emergency Management, Garden City, NY 11530-0701. Offers Certificate. Part-time and evening/weekend programs available. *Students:* Average age 47. *Application deadline:* For fall admission, 5/1 for international students; for spring admission, 12/1 for international students. Applications are processed on a rolling basis. Application fee: $50. Electronic applications accepted. *Financial support:* Research assistantships with partial tuition reimbursements, Federal Work-Study and institutionally sponsored loans available. *Faculty research:* Emergency nursing, disaster management, disaster preparedness. *Unit head:* Dr. John Vetter, Chairperson, 516-877-4110, E-mail: vetter@adelphi.edu. *Application contact:* Christine Murphy, Director of Admissions, 516-877-3050, Fax: 516-877-3039, E-mail: graduateadmissions@adelphi.edu.

American Public University System, AMU/APU Graduate Programs, Charles Town, WV 25414. Offers air warfare (MA Military Studies); American Revolution (MA Military Studies); business administration (MBA); Civil War (MA Military Studies); criminal justice (MA); defense management (MA Military Studies); emergency and disaster management (MA); environmental policy and management (MS); fire science management (MA); global engagement (MA); history (MA); homeland security (MA); humanities (MA); intelligence (MA Military Studies, MA Strategic Intelligence); international peace and conflict resolution (MA); international relations and conflict resolution (MA); joint warfare (MA Military Studies); land warfare international perspective (MA Military Studies); management (MA); military history (MA); military leadership (MA Military Studies); national security studies (MA); naval warfare international (MA Military Studies); naval warfare US (MA Military Studies); political science (MA); public administration (MA); public health (MA); security management (MA); space studies (MS); special ops/LIC (MA Military Studies); sports management (MA); transportation and logistics management (MA); transportation management (MA); unconventional warfare (MA Military Studies); World War II (MA Military Studies). Programs offered via distance learning only. Part-time and evening/weekend programs available. Postbaccalaureate distance learning degree programs offered (no on-campus study). *Faculty:* 10 full-time (3 women), 188 part-time/adjunct (57 women). *Students:* 340 full-time (98 women), 3,567 part-time (790 women); includes 615 minority (317 African Americans, 28 American Indian/Alaska Native, 85 Asian Americans or Pacific Islanders, 185 Hispanic Americans), 20 international. Average age 36. 2,123 applicants, 100% accepted, 893 enrolled. In 2007, 829 degrees awarded. *Degree requirements:* For master's, comprehensive exam. *Entrance requirements:* For master's, bachelor's degree or equivalent, minimum GPA of 2.7 in last 60 hours of course work. *Application deadline:* Applications are processed on a rolling basis. Application fee: $0. Electronic applications accepted. *Expenses:* Tuition: Part-time $275 per semester hour. *Financial support:* Applicants required to submit FAFSA. *Faculty research:* Military history, criminal justice, management performance, national security. *Unit head:* Dr. Frank McCluskey, Provost, 877-468-6268, Fax: 304-724-3780. *Application contact:* Terry Grant, Director of Enrollment Management, 877-468-6268, Fax: 304-724-3780, E-mail: info@apus.edu.

Anna Maria College, Graduate Division, Program in Emergency Management, Paxton, MA 01612. Offers MS, Graduate Certificate. Part-time and evening/weekend programs available. *Faculty:* 1 (woman) full-time, 3 part-time/adjunct (0 women). *Students:* 3 full-time (0 women), 14 part-time (5 women); includes 1 minority (African American), 1 international. Average age 36. In 2007, 2 master's, 5 other advanced degrees awarded. *Degree requirements:* For master's, thesis. *Entrance requirements:* For master's, minimum GPA of 2.7. Additional exam requirements/recommendations for international students: Required—TOEFL (minimum score 500 paper-based). *Application deadline:* For fall admission, 3/1 priority date for domestic and international students; for spring admission, 11/1 priority date for domestic and international students. Applications are processed on a rolling basis. Application fee: $40. Electronic applications accepted. *Expenses:* Tuition: Part-time $1,272 per course. *Financial support:* Applicants required to submit FAFSA. *Unit head:* Dr. Susan Swedis, Director, 508-849-3382, E-mail: sswedis@annamaria.edu. *Application contact:* Dennis Braun, Director, Graduate and Continuing Education Recruitment, 508-849-3293, Fax: 508-819-3362, E-mail: dbraun@annamaria.edu.

Arkansas Tech University, Graduate School, School of Community Education, Russellville, AR 72801. Offers emergency management and homeland security (MS). Part-time programs available. *Students:* 18 full-time (4 women), 23 part-time (14 women); includes 4 minority (1 African American, 1 American Indian/Alaska Native, 1 Asian American or Pacific Islander, 1 Hispanic American). Average age 30. *Entrance requirements:* For master's, GRE General Test or MAT. Additional exam requirements/recommendations for international students: Required—TOEFL (minimum score 500 paper-based; 173 computer-based; 61 iBT). *Application deadline:*

For fall admission, 3/1 priority date for domestic students, 5/1 priority date for international students; for winter admission, 10/1 priority date for international students; for spring admission, 10/1 priority date for domestic and international students. Applications are processed on a rolling basis. Application fee: $0 ($30 for international students). Electronic applications accepted. *Expenses:* Tuition, state resident: full-time $3,150; part-time $175 per hour. Tuition, nonresident: full-time $6,300; part-time $350 per hour. Required fees: $384; $8 per hour. $120 per term. Tuition and fees vary according to course load. *Financial support:* In 2007–08, teaching assistantships with full tuition reimbursements (averaging $4,000 per year); career-related internships or fieldwork, Federal Work-Study, scholarships/grants, health care benefits, and unspecified assistantships also available. Support available to part-time students. Financial award application deadline: 4/15; financial award applicants required to submit FAFSA. *Unit head:* Dr. Mary Ann Rollans, Dean, 479-968-0234 Ext. 479, E-mail: maryann.rollans@atu.edu. *Application contact:* Dr. Eldon G. Clary, Dean of Graduate School, 479-968-0398, Fax: 479-964-0542, E-mail: graduate.school@atu.edu.

Benedictine University, Graduate Programs, Program in Public Health, Lisle, IL 60532-0900. Offers administration of health care institutions (MPH); dietetics (MPH); disaster management (MPH); health education (MPH); health information systems (MPH); MBA/MPH; MPH/MS. Part-time and evening/weekend programs available. Postbaccalaureate distance learning degree programs offered. *Faculty:* 2 full-time (0 women), 8 part-time/adjunct (3 women). *Students:* 28 full-time (23 women), 65 part-time (52 women); includes 35 minority (16 African Americans, 1 American Indian/Alaska Native, 14 Asian Americans or Pacific Islanders, 4 Hispanic Americans). Average age 33. 71 applicants, 61% accepted, 31 enrolled. In 2007, 39 degrees awarded. *Entrance requirements:* For master's, MAT, GRE, or GMAT. Additional exam requirements/recommendations for international students: Required—TOEFL (minimum score 550 paper-based; 213 computer-based). *Application deadline:* For fall admission, 9/1 for domestic students; for winter admission, 12/1 for domestic students; for spring admission, 2/15 for domestic students. Application fee: $40. *Expenses:* Tuition: Full-time $12,825; part-time $475 per credit hour. *Financial support:* Career-related internships or fieldwork and health care benefits available. Support available to part-time students. *Unit head:* Dr. Alan Gorr, Director, 630-829-6566, Fax: 630-960-1126, E-mail: agorr@ben.edu. *Application contact:* Kari Gibbons, Director, Admissions, 630-829-6200, Fax: 630-829-6584, E-mail: kgibbons@ben.edu.

California State University, Long Beach, Graduate Studies, College of Health and Human Services, Department of Professional Studies, Long Beach, CA 90840. Offers emergency services administration (MS); occupational studies (MA). *Accreditation:* NCATE. Part-time and evening/weekend programs available. Postbaccalaureate distance learning degree programs offered (no on-campus study). *Faculty:* 3 full-time (0 women), 17 part-time/adjunct (10 women). *Students:* Average age 44. *Degree requirements:* For master's, comprehensive exam or thesis. *Application deadline:* For fall admission, 7/1 for domestic students; for spring admission, 12/1 for domestic students. Applications are processed on a rolling basis. Application fee: $55. Electronic applications accepted. *Financial support:* Federal Work-Study, institutionally sponsored loans, and scholarships/grants available. Financial award application deadline: 3/2. *Faculty research:* Special needs, leadership, training and development. *Unit head:* Dr. Paul Bott, Chair, 562-985-5633, Fax: 562-985-8815, E-mail: pbott@csulb.edu. *Application contact:* Dr. Peter Kreysa, Graduate Coordinator, 562-985-8111, Fax: 562-985-8815, E-mail: pkreysa@csulb.edu.

Drexel University, College of Nursing and Health Professions, Emergency and Public Safety Services Program, Philadelphia, PA 19104-2875. Offers MS. Part-time and evening/weekend programs available. *Degree requirements:* For master's, comprehensive exam. *Entrance requirements:* For master's, GRE General Test, minimum GPA of 2.75.

The George Washington University, School of Medicine and Health Sciences, Health Sciences Programs, Washington, DC 20052. Offers adult nurse practitioner (MSN, Post Master's Certificate); advanced family nurse practitioner (Post Master's Certificate); clinical practice management (MSHS); clinical research administration (MSHS); clinical research administration for nurses (MSN); emergency services management (MSHS); end-of-life care (MSHS, MSN); family nurse practitioner (MSN); immunohematology (MSHS); nursing leadership and management (MSN); oral biology (MSHS); physical therapy (DPT); physician assistant (MSHS); MSHS/MPH. Postbaccalaureate distance learning degree programs offered (no on-campus study). *Entrance requirements:* Additional exam requirements/recommendations for international students: Required—TOEFL (minimum score 550 paper-based; 213 computer-based). Expenses: Contact institution.

The George Washington University, School of Public Health and Health Services, Department of Prevention and Community Health, Washington, DC 20052. Offers community-oriented primary care (MPH); health promotion (MPH); maternal and child health (MPH); public health and emergency management (Certificate). *Accreditation:* CEPH. *Entrance requirements:* For master's, GRE or GMAT, 2 letters of recommendation, resumé. Additional exam requirements/recommendations for international students: Required—TOEFL.

Georgia State University, Andrew Young School of Policy Studies, Department of Public Administration and Urban Studies, Atlanta, GA 30303-3083. Offers disaster management (Certificate); non-profit management (Certificate); planning and economic development (Certificate); public administration (MPA); public policy (PhD); urban policy studies (MS); JD/MPA. *Accreditation:* NASPAA (one or more programs are accredited). Part-time and evening/weekend programs available. *Faculty:* 15 full-time (5 women). *Students:* 131 full-time (82 women), 91 part-time (58 women); includes 83 minority (73 African Americans, 7 Asian Americans or Pacific Islanders, 3 Hispanic Americans), 32 international. Average age 32. 250 applicants, 49% accepted, 74 enrolled. In 2007, 51 master's, 1 doctorate, 7 other advanced degrees awarded. Terminal master's awarded for partial completion of doctoral program. *Degree requirements:* For master's, thesis optional; for doctorate, comprehensive exam, thesis/dissertation. *Entrance requirements:* For master's and doctorate, GRE General Test. Additional exam requirements/recommendations for international students: Required—TOEFL. *Application deadline:* For fall admission, 4/1 for domestic students; for spring admission, 10/1 for domestic students. Applications are processed on a rolling basis. Application fee: $50. Electronic applications accepted. *Expenses:* Tuition, state resident: part-time $221 per credit hour. *Financial support:* In 2007–08, 34 research assistantships with full tuition reimbursements were awarded; fellowships, teaching assistantships with full tuition reimbursements, career-related internships or fieldwork, Federal Work-Study, institutionally sponsored loans, scholarships/grants, and tuition waivers (partial) also available. Support available to part-time students. Financial award applicants required to submit FAFSA. *Faculty research:* Public management, urban policy, policy analysis, public finance, public involvement. *Unit head:* Dr. Greg Streib, Chair, 404-413-0116, E-mail: gstreib@gsu.edu. *Application contact:* Sue Fagan, Office of Academic Assistance Director, 404-413-0021, Fax: 404-413-0023, E-mail: suefagan@gsu.edu.

Jacksonville State University, College of Graduate Studies and Continuing Education, College of Arts and Sciences, Department of Emergency Management, Jacksonville, AL 36265-1602. Offers MS. *Faculty:* 4 full-time (1 woman). *Students:* 3 full-time (1 woman), 90 part-time (34 women); includes 21 minority (17 African Americans, 1 American Indian/Alaska Native, 1 Asian American or Pacific Islander, 2 Hispanic Americans). In 2007, 26 degrees awarded. Application fee: $20. *Financial support:* Available to part-time students. Application deadline: 4/1. *Unit head:* Dr. Barry Cox, Head, 256-782-5926, E-mail: graduate@jsu.edu. *Application contact:* 256-782-5329, Fax: 256-782-5321, E-mail: graduate@jsu.edu.

The Johns Hopkins University, School of Nursing, Nurse Practitioner Program, Baltimore, MD 21218-2699. Offers adult acute/critical care (MSN, Certificate); adult and pediatric primary care (MSN); adult or pediatric primary care (Certificate); emergency preparedness/disaster response (Certificate); family primary care (MSN, Certificate); women's health (Certificate). *Accreditation:* AACN; NLN (one or more programs are accredited). Part-time programs available. *Faculty:* 12 full-time (all women), 6 part-time/adjunct (5 women). *Students:* 26 full-time (25 women), 72 part-time (69 women); includes 25 minority (6 African Americans, 1 American Indian/Alaska Native, 12 Asian Americans or Pacific Islanders, 6 Hispanic Americans), 2 international. Average age 31. 183 applicants, 91% accepted, 27 enrolled. In 2007, 26 master's, 2 other advanced degrees awarded. *Degree requirements:* For master's, thesis optional, scholarly project or portfolio. *Entrance requirements:* For master's, GRE, interview, minimum GPA of 3.0, BSN, Maryland RN license. Additional exam requirements/recommendations for international students: Required—TOEFL (minimum score 550 paper-based; 230 computer-based). *Application deadline:* For fall admission, 3/1 priority date for domestic and international students; for spring admission, 7/1 priority date for domestic and international students. Application fee: $75. *Expenses: Contact institution. Financial support:* In 2007–08, 53 students received support. Federal Work-Study, scholarships/grants, traineeships, and tuition waivers (partial) available. Support available to part-time students. Financial award application deadline: 3/1; financial award applicants required to submit FAFSA. *Faculty research:* Community outreach, primary care of underserved populations, substance abusing individuals, childhood violence, women's health. *Unit head:* Dr. Kathleen M. White, Director, Master's Programs, 410-614-4664, Fax: 410-955-7463, E-mail: kwhite@son.jhmi.edu. *Application contact:* Mary O'Rourke, Director of Admissions/Student Services, 410-955-7548, Fax: 410-614-7086, E-mail: orourke@son.jhmi.edu.

Lynn University, College of Arts and Sciences, Boca Raton, FL 33431-5598. Offers applied psychology (MS); criminal justice administration (MS); emergency planning and administration (MS, Certificate). Part-time and evening/weekend programs available. Postbaccalaureate distance learning degree programs offered. *Entrance requirements:* For master's, GRE, resumé, 2 letters of recommendation, minimum undergraduate GPA of 3.0. Additional exam requirements/recommendations for international students: Required—TOEFL (minimum score 550 paper-based; 213 computer-based). *Faculty research:* Terrorism, criminological theory, corrections, emergency planning.

Massachusetts Maritime Academy, Program in Emergency Management, Buzzards Bay, MA 02532-1803. Offers MS. *Unit head:* Lianne Boas, Dean, Graduate and Continuing Education, 508-830-5096, Fax: 508-830-5018, E-mail: lboas@maritime.edu. *Application contact:* Kristine Esdale, Media Specialist, 508-830-5019, Fax: 508-830-5018, E-mail: dce@maritime.edu.

Millersville University of Pennsylvania, Graduate School, School of Humanities and Social Sciences, Center for Disaster Research and Education, Program in Emergency Management, Millersville, PA 17551-0302. Offers MS. Part-time programs available. Postbaccalaureate distance learning degree programs offered (no on-campus study). *Faculty:* 11 full-time (5 women). *Students:* 1 (woman) full-time, 18 part-time (8 women), 1 international. Average age 33. 15 applicants, 87% accepted, 13 enrolled. *Entrance requirements:* For master's, GRE or MAT, work experience in emergency management or related job or volunteer experience in an emergency management position, telephone interview. Additional exam requirements/recommendations for international students: Required—TOEFL (minimum score 550 paper-based; 213 computer-based). *Application deadline:* For fall admission, 2/1 for domestic students. Application fee: $40. Electronic applications accepted. *Expenses: Contact institution. Financial support:* Available to part-time students. Application deadline: 3/15; *Unit head:* Dr. Henry W. Fischer, Program Director of Emergency Management, 717-8721-3568, Fax: 717-872-2429. *Application contact:* Dr. Victor S. DeSantis, Dean of Graduate Studies and Research, 717-872-3099, Fax: 717-872-3453, E-mail: victor.desantis@millersville.edu.

North Dakota State University, College of Graduate and Interdisciplinary Studies, College of Arts, Humanities and Social Sciences, Department of Sociology, Anthropology, and Emergency Management, Fargo, ND 58105. Offers emergency management (MS, PhD); social science (MA, MS); sociology (MS). Part-time programs available. *Faculty:* 8 full-time (3 women), 5 part-time/adjunct (2 women). *Students:* 20 full-time (13 women), 14 part-time (8 women); includes 1 minority (American Indian/Alaska Native), 3 international. Average age 27. 15 applicants, 60% accepted, 7 enrolled. In 2007, 7 degrees awarded. *Degree requirements:* For master's, thesis; for doctorate, comprehensive exam, thesis/dissertation. *Entrance requirements:* For master's, GRE (emergency management), course work in sociology, minimum GPA of 3.2; for doctorate, GRE, minimum GPA of 3.2. Additional exam requirements/recommendations for international students: Required—TOEFL. *Application deadline:* For fall admission, 4/1 priority date for domestic students. Applications are processed on a rolling basis. Application fee: $45 ($60 for international students). *Expenses:* Tuition, state resident: full-time $5,376; part-time $224 per credit. Tuition, nonresident: full-time $14,354; part-time $598 per credit. Required fees: $962; $40 per credit. Part-time tuition and fees vary according to course load and reciprocity agreements. *Financial support:* In 2007–08, 7 research assistantships with full tuition reimbursements (averaging $6,156 per year), 7 teaching assistantships with full tuition reimbursements (averaging $3,078 per year) were awarded; fellowships, career-related internships or fieldwork, Federal Work-Study, institutionally sponsored loans, and tuition waivers (full) also available. Support available to part-time students. Financial award application deadline: 4/15. *Faculty research:* Medical sociology, demography, ethnology, archaeology. Total annual research expenditures: $75,000. *Unit head:* Dr. Daniel J. Klenow, Chair, 701-231-8657, Fax: 701-231-1047, E-mail: daniel.klenow@ndsu.edu.

Oklahoma State University, College of Arts and Sciences, Department of Political Science, Interdisciplinary Program in Fire and Emergency Management Administration, Stillwater, OK 74078. Offers MS. *Entrance requirements:* For master's, minimum GPA of 3.0. Additional exam requirements/recommendations for international students: Required—TOEFL. *Application deadline:* For fall admission, 3/1 for international students; for spring admission, 8/1 for international students. Applications are processed on a rolling basis. Application fee: $40 ($75 for international students). Electronic applications accepted. *Expenses:* Tuition, state resident: full-time $4,993; part-time $148 per credit hour. Tuition, nonresident: full-time $14,755; part-time $555 per credit hour. Tuition and fees vary according to program. *Financial support:* Teaching assistantships available. Financial award application deadline: 3/1. *Unit head:* Dr. Anthony Brown, Director, 405-744-5606. *Application contact:* Dr. Anthony Brown, Director, 405-744-5606.

Park University, College of Graduate and Professional Studies, Kansas City, MO 54105. Offers adult education (M Ed); at-risk students (M Ed); disaster and emergency management (MPA); educational administration (M Ed); entrepreneurship (MBA); general business (MBA); general education (M Ed); government/business relations (MPA); healthcare/services management (MBA, MPA); international business (MBA); K-12 certification (MAT); management information systems (MBA); management of information systems (MPA); middle school certification (MAT); multi-cultural education (M Ed); nonprofit management (MPA); public management (MPA); school law (M Ed); secondary school certification (MAT); special education (M Ed). Part-time and evening/weekend programs available. Postbaccalaureate distance learning degree programs offered (no on-campus study). *Degree requirements:* For master's, comprehensive exam, thesis (for some programs). *Entrance requirements:* For master's, GRE, GMAT, teacher certification (M Ed). Additional exam requirements/recommendations for international students: Required—TOEFL (minimum score 550 paper-based). Electronic applications accepted. *Faculty research:* Literacy, leadership, brain based research, multicultural education, diversity.

San Diego State University, Graduate and Research Affairs, College of Health and Human Services, Graduate School of Public Health, San Diego, CA 92182. Offers environmental health (MPH); epidemiology (MPH, PhD), including biostatistics (MPH); global emergency preparedness and response (MS); global health (PhD); health behavior (PhD); health promotion (MPH); health services administration (MPH); toxicology (MS); MPH/MA; MSW/MPH. *Accreditation:* ABET (one or more programs are accredited); CAHME (one or more programs are accredited); CEPH (one or more programs are accredited). Part-time programs available. *Faculty:* 30 full-time (14 women), 99 part-time/adjunct (44 women). *Students:* 274 full-time (204 women), 94 part-time (70 women); includes 131 minority (23 African Americans, 1 American Indian/Alaska Native, 59 Asian Americans or Pacific Islanders, 48 Hispanic Americans), 41 international. 517 applicants, 59% accepted, 109 enrolled. In 2007, 103 master's, 6 doctorates awarded. *Degree requirements:* For master's, comprehensive exam (for some programs), thesis (for some programs); for doctorate, thesis/dissertation. *Entrance requirements:* For master's, GMAT (health services administration MPH), GRE General Test; for doctorate, GRE General Test. Additional exam requirements/recommendations for international students:

Emergency Management

San Diego State University (continued)
Required—TOEFL. *Application deadline:* For fall admission, 5/1 for domestic and international students; for spring admission, 11/1 for domestic students, 10/1 for international students. Applications are processed on a rolling basis. Application fee: $55. *Financial support:* Research assistantships, teaching assistantships, career-related internships or fieldwork, Federal Work-Study, and traineeships available. Financial award applicants required to submit FAFSA. *Faculty research:* Evaluation of tobacco, AIDS prevalence and prevention, mammography, infant death project, Alzheimer's in elderly Chinese. *Unit head:* Dr. Carleen Stoskopf, Director, 619-594-6317. *Application contact:* Brenda Fass-Holmes, Coordinator, Admissions and Student Affairs, 619-594-6317, E-mail: brenda.fass-holmes@sdsu.edu.

TUI University, College of Health Sciences, Program in Health Sciences, Cypress, CA 90630. Offers clinical research administration (MS, Certificate); emergency and disaster management (MS, Certificate); environmental health science (Certificate); health care administration (PhD); health care management (MS), including health informatics; health education (MS, Certificate); health informatics (Certificate); health sciences (PhD); international health (MS); international health: educator or researcher option (PhD); international health: practitioner option (PhD); law and expert witness studies (MS, Certificate); public health (MS); quality assurance (Certificate). Part-time and evening/weekend programs available. Postbaccalaureate distance learning degree programs offered (no on-campus study). In 2007, 366 master's, 29 doctorates awarded. *Degree requirements:* For doctorate, comprehensive exam, thesis/dissertation, defense of dissertation. *Entrance requirements:* For master's, minimum GPA of 2.5 (students with GPA 3.0 or greater may transfer up to 30% of graduate level credits); for doctorate, minimum GPA of 3.4, curriculum vitae, course work in research methods or statistics. Additional exam requirements/recommendations for international students: Required—TOEFL. *Unit head:* Dr. Michaela Tanasescu, Dean, College of Health Sciences, 714-816-0366, Fax: 714-226-9844, E-mail: infocoe@tuiu.edu.

University of Central Florida, College of Health and Public Affairs, Department of Public Administration, Orlando, FL 32816. Offers emergency management and homeland security (Certificate); non-profit management (MNM, Certificate); public administration (MPA, Certificate); urban and regional planning (Certificate). *Accreditation:* NASPAA. Part-time and evening/weekend programs available. *Faculty:* 11 full-time (2 women), 9 part-time/adjunct (3 women). *Degree requirements:* For master's, comprehensive exam, thesis or alternative, research report. *Entrance requirements:* For master's, GRE General Test. *Application deadline:* For fall admission, 7/1 for domestic students; for spring admission, 12/1 for domestic students. Application fee: $30. Electronic applications accepted. *Expenses:* Tuition, state resident: full-time $6,484. Tuition, nonresident: full-time $23,938. Tuition and fees vary according to program. *Financial support:* Fellowships with partial tuition reimbursements, research assistantships with partial tuition reimbursements, teaching assistantships with partial tuition reimbursements, career-related internships or fieldwork, Federal Work-Study, institutionally sponsored loans, tuition waivers (partial), and unspecified assistantships available. Financial award application deadline: 3/1; financial award applicants required to submit FAFSA. *Unit head:* Dr. MaryAnn Feldheim, Chair, 407-823-3693, Fax: 407-823-5651.

University of Nevada, Las Vegas, Graduate College, Greenspun College of Urban Affairs, Department of Public Administration, Las Vegas, NV 89154-9900. Offers crisis and emergency management (MS); public administration (MPA); public affairs (PhD); public management (Certificate). *Accreditation:* NASPAA. Part-time and evening/weekend programs available. *Faculty:* 7 full-time (1 woman), 6 part-time/adjunct (3 women). *Students:* 31 full-time (16 women), 113 part-time (66 women); includes 40 minority (23 African Americans, 1 American Indian/Alaska Native, 2 Asian Americans or Pacific Islanders, 14 Hispanic Americans), 3 international. 86 applicants, 55% accepted, 40 enrolled. In 2007, 36 master's, 1 doctorate, 22 other advanced degrees awarded. *Degree requirements:* For master's, comprehensive exam, professional paper. *Entrance requirements:* For master's, GMAT or GRE General Test, minimum GPA of 3.0 during previous 2 years, 2.75 overall; minimum 1 year of work experience; resumé. Additional exam requirements/recommendations for international students: Required—TOEFL (minimum score 550 paper-based; 213 computer-based; 80 iBT). *Application deadline:* For fall admission, 4/10 for domestic and international students; for spring admission, 11/15 for domestic students, 10/1 for international students. Application fee: $60 ($75 for international students). Electronic applications accepted. *Expenses:* Tuition, state resident: part-time $198 per credit. Tuition, nonresident: part-time $416 per credit. Required fees: $256 per semester. Tuition and fees vary according to course load and reciprocity agreements. *Financial support:* In 2007–08, 7 research assistantships (averaging $11,000 per year), 1 teaching assistantship with partial tuition reimbursement (averaging $10,000 per year) were awarded; career-related internships or fieldwork, Federal Work-Study, institutionally sponsored loans, scholarships/grants, health care benefits, and unspecified assistantships also available. Support available to part-time students. Financial award application deadline: 3/1. *Unit head:* Dr. Lee Bernick, Chair, 702-895-4828. *Application contact:* Graduate College Admissions Evaluator, 702-895-3320, Fax: 702-895-4180, E-mail: gradcollege@unlv.edu.

University of Pittsburgh, Graduate School of Public Health, Department of Environmental and Occupational Health, Pittsburgh, PA 15260. Offers environmental and occupational health (MPH, MS, PhD); occupational medicine (MPH); public health awareness and disaster response (Certificate); risk assessment (Certificate); MD/MPH. *Accreditation:* CEPH (one or more programs are accredited). Part-time programs available. *Faculty:* 26 full-time (7 women), 33 part-time/adjunct (7 women). *Students:* 26 full-time (19 women), 17 part-time (9 women); includes 5 minority (3 African Americans, 2 Hispanic Americans), 6 international. Average age 32. 66 applicants, 55% accepted, 15 enrolled. In 2007, 3 master's awarded. *Degree requirements:* For master's, comprehensive exam, thesis; for doctorate, comprehensive exam, thesis/dissertation, preliminary exams. *Entrance requirements:* For master's and Certificate, GRE General Test; for doctorate, GRE General Test, minimum GPA of 3.4; background in biology, physics, chemistry and calculus. Additional exam requirements/recommendations for international students: Required—TOEFL (minimum score 550 paper-based; 213 computer-based; 80 iBT). *Application deadline:* For fall admission, 2/15 priority date for domestic students, 2/15 for international students; for winter admission, 9/1 for international students; for spring admission, 2/1 for international students. Applications are processed on a rolling basis. Application fee: $50 ($60 for international students). Electronic applications accepted. *Financial support:* In 2007–08, 8 students received support, including 8 research assistantships with full tuition reimbursements available (averaging $22,800 per year); scholarships/grants and unspecified assistantships also available. *Faculty research:* Molecular toxicology, redox signaling, gene environment interaction, progenitor-progeny lineage, occupational and pulmonary medicine. Total annual research expenditures: $6.7 million. *Unit head:* Dr. Bruce R. Pitt, Chairman, 412-383-8400, Fax: 412-383-7658, E-mail: brucep@pitt.edu. *Application contact:* Eileen Penny Weiss, Student Affairs Administrator, 412-383-7297, Fax: 412-383-7658, E-mail: pweiss@pitt.edu.

Virginia Commonwealth University, Graduate School, College of Humanities and Sciences, Wilder School of Government and Public Affairs, Program in Homeland Security and Emergency Preparedness, Richmond, VA 23284-9005. Offers MA, Graduate Certificate. Postbaccalaureate distance learning degree programs offered. *Students:* 5 full-time (1 woman), 5 part-time (1 woman); includes 3 minority (all African Americans) 45 applicants, 58% accepted. *Expenses:* Tuition, state resident: full-time $7,224; part-time $401 per credit. Tuition, nonresident: full-time $16,072; part-time $891 per credit. Required fees: $1,679; $63 per credit. Tuition and fees vary according to campus/location. *Unit head:* Dr. Susan Gooden, Head, 804-827-7078, E-mail: stgooden@vcu.edu.

West Chester University of Pennsylvania, Office of Graduate Studies and Extended Education, College of Health Sciences, Department of Health, West Chester, PA 19383. Offers emergency preparedness (Certificate); gerontology (MS); health care administration (Certificate); integrative health (Certificate); public health (MPH, MS); school health (M Ed). *Accreditation:* CEPH.Part-time and evening/weekend programs available. *Students:* 47 full-time (23 women), 65 part-time (48 women); includes 20 minority (18 African Americans, 2 Asian Americans or Pacific Islanders), 26 international. Average age 30. 120 applicants, 95% accepted, 38 enrolled. In 2007, 58 degrees awarded. *Degree requirements:* For master's, comprehensive exam, thesis (for some programs). *Entrance requirements:* For master's, GRE. Additional exam requirements/recommendations for international students: Required—TOEFL (minimum score 550 paper-based; 213 computer-based; 80 iBT). *Application deadline:* For fall admission, 4/15 priority date for domestic students; for spring admission, 10/15 for domestic students. Applications are processed on a rolling basis. Application fee: $35. *Expenses:* Tuition, state resident: part-time $345 per credit. Tuition, nonresident: part-time $552 per credit. Tuition and fees vary according to course load. *Financial support:* In 2007–08, 10 research assistantships with full and partial tuition reimbursements (averaging $5,000 per year) were awarded; unspecified assistantships also available. Support available to part-time students. Financial award application deadline: 2/15; financial award applicants required to submit FAFSA. *Faculty research:* HIV/AIDS education, teacher preparation, water quality. *Unit head:* Dr. Roger Mustalish, Chair, 610-436-2931, E-mail: rmustalish@wcupa.edu. *Application contact:* Dr. Bethann Cinelli, Graduate Coordinator, 610-436-2267, E-mail: bcinelli@wcupa.edu.

York University, Faculty of Graduate Studies, Atkinson Faculty of Liberal and Professional Studies, Program in Disaster and Emergency Management, Toronto, ON M3J 1P3, Canada. Offers MA.

Homeland Security

American Public University System, AMU/APU Graduate Programs, Charles Town, WV 25414. Offers air warfare (MA Military Studies); American Revolution (MA Military Studies); business administration (MBA); Civil War (MA Military Studies); criminal justice (MA); defense management (MA Military Studies); emergency and disaster management (MA); environmental policy and management (MS); fire science management (MA); global engagement (MA); history (MA); homeland security (MA); humanities (MA); intelligence (MA Military Studies, MA Strategic Intelligence); international peace and conflict resolution (MA); international relations and conflict resolution (MA); joint warfare (MA Military Studies); land warfare international perspective (MA Military Studies); management (MA); military history (MA); military leadership (MA Military Studies); national security studies (MA); naval warfare international (MA Military Studies); naval warfare US (MA Military Studies); political science (MA); public administration (MA); public health (MA); security management (MA); space studies (MS); special ops/LIC (MA Military Studies); sports management (MA); transportation and logistics management (MA); transportation management (MA); unconventional warfare (MA Military Studies); World War II (MA Military Studies). Programs offered via distance learning only. Part-time and evening/weekend programs available. Postbaccalaureate distance learning degree programs offered (no on-campus study). *Faculty:* 10 full-time (3 women), 188 part-time/adjunct (57 women). *Students:* 340 full-time (98 women), 3,567 part-time (790 women); includes 615 minority (317 African Americans, 28 American Indian/Alaska Native, 85 Asian Americans or Pacific Islanders, 185 Hispanic Americans), 20 international. Average age 36. 2,123 applicants, 100% accepted, 893 enrolled. In 2007, 829 degrees awarded. *Degree requirements:* For master's, comprehensive exam. *Entrance requirements:* For master's, bachelor's degree or equivalent, minimum GPA of 2.7 in last 60 hours of course work. *Application deadline:* Applications are processed on a rolling basis. Application fee: $0. Electronic applications accepted. *Expenses:* Tuition: Part-time $275 per semester hour. *Financial support:* Applicants required to submit FAFSA. *Faculty research:* Military history, criminal justice, management performance, national security. *Unit head:* Dr. Frank McCluskey, Provost, 877-468-6268, Fax: 304-724-3780. *Application contact:* Terry Grant, Director of Enrollment Management, 877-468-6268, Fax: 304-724-3780, E-mail: info@apus.edu.

Arkansas Tech University, Graduate School, School of Community Education, Russellville, AR 72801. Offers emergency management and homeland security (MS). Part-time programs available. *Students:* 18 full-time (4 women), 23 part-time (14 women); includes 4 minority (1 African American, 1 American Indian/Alaska Native, 1 Asian American or Pacific Islander, 1 Hispanic American). Average age 30. *Entrance requirements:* For master's, GRE General Test or MAT. Additional exam requirements/recommendations for international students: Required—TOEFL (minimum score 500 paper-based; 173 computer-based; 61 iBT). *Application deadline:* For fall admission, 3/1 priority date for domestic students, 5/1 priority date for international students; for winter admission, 10/1 priority date for international students; for spring admission, 10/1 priority date for domestic and international students. Applications are processed on a rolling basis. Application fee: $0 ($30 for international students). Electronic applications accepted. *Expenses:* Tuition, state resident: full-time $3,150; part-time $175 per hour. Tuition, nonresident: full-time $6,300; part-time $350 per hour. Required fees: $384; $8 per hour. $120 per term. Tuition and fees vary according to course load. *Financial support:* In 2007–08, teaching assistantships with full tuition reimbursements (averaging $4,000 per year); career-related internships or fieldwork, Federal Work-Study, scholarships/grants, health care benefits, and unspecified assistantships also available. Support available to part-time students. Financial award application deadline: 4/15; financial award applicants required to submit FAFSA. *Unit head:* Dr. Mary Ann Rollans, Dean, 479-968-0234 Ext. 479, E-mail: maryann.rollans@atu.edu. *Application contact:* Dr. Eldon G. Clary, Dean of Graduate School, 479-968-0398, Fax: 479-964-0542, E-mail: graduate.school@atu.edu.

Chaminade University of Honolulu, Graduate Services, Program in Criminal Justice Administration, Honolulu, HI 96816-1578. Offers criminal justice administration (MSCJA); homeland security (Certificate). Part-time and evening/weekend programs available. Postbaccalaureate distance learning degree programs offered (no on-campus study). *Faculty:* 3 full-time (1 woman), 12 part-time/adjunct (6 women). *Students:* 41 full-time (25 women), 10 part-time (6 women); includes 39 minority (7 African Americans, 30 Asian Americans or Pacific Islanders, 2 Hispanic Americans), 1 international. Average age 29. 36 applicants, 81% accepted, 14 enrolled. In 2007, 28 degrees awarded. *Degree requirements:* For master's, thesis optional. *Entrance requirements:* For master's, minimum undergraduate GPA of 3.0, 3 letters of recommendation. Additional exam requirements/recommendations for international students: Required—TOEFL (minimum score 550 paper-based). *Application deadline:* For fall admission, 9/1 priority date for domestic students; for winter admission, 12/1 for domestic students; for spring admission, 3/1 for domestic students. Applications are processed on a rolling basis. Application fee: $50. Electronic applications accepted. *Expenses:* Tuition: Part-time $490 per credit hour. *Financial support:* In 2007–08, 36 students received support. Career-related internships or fieldwork, Federal Work-Study, and scholarships/grants available. Financial award application deadline: 3/1; financial award applicants required to submit FAFSA. *Faculty research:* Penology, juvenile delinquency, multicultural and ethnic diversity in criminology, law enforcement administration and training, homeland security. *Unit head:* Ronald Becker, Director, 808-735-4873, Fax: 808-739-4614, E-mail: rbecker@chaminade.edu. *Application contact:* Melissa Hangai, Assistant to the Director, 808-735-4703, Fax: 808-739-4614, E-mail: mscja@chaminade.edu.

Fairleigh Dickinson University, Metropolitan Campus, Anthony J. Petrocelli College of Continuing Studies, School of Administrative Science, Program in Homeland Security, Teaneck, NJ 07666-1914. Offers MSHS. Application fee: $40. *Expenses:* Tuition: Part-time $869 per credit. Tuition and fees vary according to degree level, campus/location and program. *Unit head:* Dr. Paulette Laubsch, Head, 201-692-2000.

George Mason University, College of Humanities and Social Sciences, Department of Public and International Affairs, Fairfax, VA 22030. Offers biodefense (MS, PhD); political science (MA, PhD); public administration (MPA). *Accreditation:* NASPAA (one or more programs are accredited). *Faculty:* 40 full-time (14 women), 48 part-time/adjunct (11 women). *Students:* 59 full-time (41 women), 214 part-time (146 women); includes 46 minority (18 African Americans, 1 American Indian/Alaska Native, 15 Asian Americans or Pacific Islanders, 12 Hispanic Americans), 7 international. Average age 30. 492 applicants, 55% accepted, 172 enrolled. In 2007, 99 degrees awarded. *Entrance requirements:* For master's, GRE General Test, minimum GPA of 3.0 in last 60 hours of course work. *Application deadline:* For fall admission, 5/1 for domestic students; for spring admission, 11/1 for domestic students. Application fee: $60 ($75 for international students). Electronic applications accepted. *Financial support:* Fellowships, research assistantships, teaching assistantships available. Support available to part-time students. Financial award application deadline: 3/1; financial award applicants required to submit FAFSA. *Unit head:* Dr. Robert Dudley, Chair, 703-993-1400, Fax: 703-993-1399, E-mail: rdudley@gmu.edu. *Application contact:* Dr. Ming Wan, Information Contact, 703-993-2955, Fax: 703-993-1399, E-mail: mpa@gmu.edu.

The Johns Hopkins University, School of Education, Division of Public Safety Leadership, Baltimore, MD 21218-2699. Offers homeland security (MS); intelligence analysis (MS); management (MS). Part-time and evening/weekend programs available. *Students:* 133 full-time (36 women), 12 part-time (5 women); includes 55 minority (48 African Americans, 5 Asian Americans or Pacific Islanders, 2 Hispanic Americans). Average age 37. 70 applicants, 90% accepted, 60 enrolled. In 2007, 96 degrees awarded. *Entrance requirements:* For master's, minimum GPA of 3.0, interview, resumé, letters of recommendation. Additional exam requirements/recommendations for international students: Required—TOEFL (minimum score 600 paper-based; 250 computer-based; 100 iBT). *Application deadline:* For fall admission, 5/1 for international students; for spring admission, 10/15 for international students. Applications are processed on a rolling basis. Application fee: $60. *Financial support:* Scholarships/grants available. Support available to part-time students. Financial award application deadline: 6/1; financial award applicants required to submit FAFSA. *Faculty research:* Ethics and integrity, counter terrorism, school safety, Homeland Security, identity theft. *Unit head:* Dr. Sheldon Greenberg, Associate Dean, 410-312-4401, Fax: 410-290-1061, E-mail: greenberg@jhu.edu. *Application contact:* Kelly Williams, Academic Administrator, 410-312-4409, Fax: 410-290-1061, E-mail: kelly.williams@jhu.edu.

The Johns Hopkins University, Zanvyl Krieger School of Arts and Sciences, Advanced Academic Programs, Program in Government, Washington, DC 20036. Offers government (MA); national securities study (Certificate); MA/MBA. Part-time and evening/weekend programs available. *Faculty:* 8 full-time, 16 part-time/adjunct. *Students:* 132 applicants, 73% accepted, 91 enrolled. *Degree requirements:* For master's, thesis. *Entrance requirements:* For master's, minimum GPA of 3.0. Additional exam requirements/recommendations for international students: Required—TOEFL (minimum score 250 computer-based; 100 iBT). *Application deadline:* For fall admission, 5/31 priority date for domestic students, 4/30 priority date for international students; for spring admission, 10/31 priority date for domestic and international students. Applications are processed on a rolling basis. Application fee: $70. Electronic applications accepted. *Financial support:* Applicants required to submit FAFSA. *Unit head:* Dr. Kathy Hill, Associate Program Chair, 202-452-1953, E-mail: kathyhill@jhu.edu. *Application contact:* Rachel C. Jenkins, Admissions Manager, 202-452-1941, Fax: 202-452-1970, E-mail: aapadmissions@jhu.edu.

See Close-Up on page 1153.

Long Island University at Riverhead, Homeland Security Management Institute, Riverhead, NY 11901. Offers MS, Advanced Certificate. *Faculty:* 2 full-time (0 women), 4 part-time/adjunct (1 woman). *Students:* 14 full-time (2 women), 88 part-time (19 women). 88 applicants, 81% accepted, 65 enrolled. In 2007, 7 degrees awarded. *Degree requirements:* For master's, thesis. *Entrance requirements:* For master's, minimum GPA of 3.0, 2 letters of reference. *Application deadline:* For fall admission, 5/30 priority date for domestic students; for winter admission, 11/30 priority date for domestic students; for spring admission, 11/30 priority date for domestic students. Application fee: $30. *Expenses:* Tuition: Part-time $835 per credit. Tuition and fees vary according to program. *Financial support:* Career-related internships or fieldwork and scholarships/grants available. Support available to part-time students. *Unit head:* Dr. Vincent E. Henry, Unit Head, 631-287-8010, Fax: 631-287-8130, E-mail: vincent.henry@liu.edu. *Application contact:* Joyce Tuttle, Director of Graduate Admissions and Program Administration, 631-287-8010, Fax: 631-287-8253, E-mail: joyce.tuttle@liu.edu.

National University, Academic Affairs, School of Engineering and Technology, Department of Applied Engineering, La Jolla, CA 92037-1011. Offers database administration (MS); engineering management (MS); environmental engineering (MS); homeland security and safety engineering (MS); system engineering (MS); wireless communications (MS). Part-time and evening/weekend programs available. Postbaccalaureate distance learning degree programs offered (no on-campus study). *Faculty:* 7 full-time (1 woman), 90 part-time/adjunct (14 women). *Students:* 41 full-time (11 women), 92 part-time (18 women); includes 29 minority (9 African Americans, 12 Asian Americans or Pacific Islanders, 8 Hispanic Americans), 59 international. Average age 31. 128 applicants, 103 enrolled. In 2007, 22 degrees awarded. *Degree requirements:* For master's, thesis. *Entrance requirements:* For master's, interview, minimum GPA of 2.5. Additional exam requirements/recommendations for international students: Required—TOEFL (minimum score 550 paper-based; 213 computer-based; 80 iBT), IELTS (minimum score 6). *Application deadline:* Applications are processed on a rolling basis. Application fee: $60 ($65 for international students). Electronic applications accepted. *Expenses:* Tuition: Full-time $8,262; part-time $306 per unit. One-time fee: $60. *Financial support:* Career-related internships or fieldwork, institutionally sponsored loans, scholarships/grants, and tuition waivers (partial) available. Support available to part-time students. Financial award application deadline: 6/30; financial award applicants required to submit FAFSA. *Unit head:* Dr. Shekar Viswanathan, Chair and Associate Professor, 858-642-8416, Fax: 858-642-8486, E-mail: sviswana@nu.edu. *Application contact:* Dominick Giovanniello, Associate Regional Dean—San Diego, 800-NAT-UNIV, Fax: 858-642-8709, E-mail: dgiovann@nu.edu.

Regent University, Graduate School, Robertson School of Government, Virginia Beach, VA 23464-9800. Offers health care policy and administration (MA); international politics (MA); law and public policy (MA); political leadership and management (MA); political management (MA); public administration (MA); public policy (MA); terrorism and homeland defense (MA); world economies and political development (MA); JD/MA; M Div/MA; M Ed/MA; MBA/MA. Part-time programs available. *Faculty:* 6 full-time (2 women), 11 part-time/adjunct (1 woman). *Students:* 50 full-time (31 women), 67 part-time (32 women); includes 31 minority (20 African Americans, 1 American Indian/Alaska Native, 2 Asian Americans or Pacific Islanders, 8 Hispanic Americans), 2 international. Average age 31. 147 applicants, 50% accepted, 28 enrolled. In 2007, 47 degrees awarded. *Degree requirements:* For master's, thesis optional, internship. *Entrance requirements:* For master's, GRE General Test or LSAT, minimum undergraduate GPA of 3.0, writing sample, resumé, interview, references, transcripts. Additional exam requirements/recommendations for international students: Required—TOEFL (minimum score 577 paper-based; 233 computer-based). *Application deadline:* For fall admission, 5/1 priority date for domestic students; for spring admission, 11/1 priority date for domestic students. Applications are processed on a rolling basis. Application fee: $50. Electronic applications accepted. *Expenses:* Contact institution. *Financial support:* In 2007–08, 123 students received support. Career-related internships or fieldwork, scholarships/grants, tuition waivers (full and partial), and unspecified assistantships available. Support available to part-time students. Financial award application deadline: 9/1; financial award applicants required to submit FAFSA. *Faculty research:* Education reform, political character issues, social capital concerns, administrative ethics, biblical law and public policy. *Unit head:* Dr. Charles W. Dunn, Dean, 757-226-4322, Fax: 757-226-4643, E-mail: cwdunn@regent.edu. *Application contact:* Althea Bishard, Registrar and Executive Director of Enrollment and Academic Services, 800-373-5504, Fax: 757-226-4381, E-mail: admissions@regent.edu.

Saint Joseph's University, College of Arts and Sciences, Programs in Public Safety and Management, Philadelphia, PA 19131-1395. Offers homeland security (MS, Certificate); public safety management (MS, Certificate). *Students:* Average age 40. *Entrance requirements:* For master's, GRE (if GPA is below 2.75), application, official transcripts, minimum GPA of 2.75, personal statemetn, 2 letters of recommendation. Additional exam requirements/recommendations for international students: Required—TOEFL (minimum score 550 paper-based; 213 computer-based; 79 iBT). *Application deadline:* For fall admission, 7/15 priority date for domestic students, 4/15 for international students; for winter admission, 1/15 for international students; for spring admission, 11/15 priority date for domestic students, 10/15 for international students. Applications are processed on a rolling basis. Application fee: $35. Electronic applications accepted. *Expenses:* Tuition: Part-time $738 per credit. Tuition and fees vary according to degree level and program. *Unit head:* Dr. Vincent P. McNally, Director, 610-660-1641, Fax: 610-660-2903, E-mail: vmcnally@sju.edu.

Salve Regina University, Graduate Studies, Program in International Relations, Newport, RI 02840-4192. Offers homeland security (Certificate); international relations (MA, Certificate). Part-time and evening/weekend programs available. Postbaccalaureate distance learning degree programs offered (minimal on-campus study). *Entrance requirements:* For master's, GMAT, GRE General Test, MAT or LSAT. Additional exam requirements/recommendations for international students: Required—TOEFL or IELTS. Electronic applications accepted.

Salve Regina University, Graduate Studies, Programs in Administration of Justice, Newport, RI 02840-4192. Offers justice and homeland security (MS); law enforcement leadership (MS, MSM).

Texas A&M University, George Bush School of Government and Public Service, College Station, TX 77843. Offers advanced international affairs (Certificate); homeland security (Certificate); international affairs (MPIA), including international economics and development, national security affairs; nonprofit management (Certificate); public service and administration (MPSA), including public management, public policy analysis. *Accreditation:* NASPAA. *Faculty:* 39. *Students:* 155 full-time (67 women), 97 part-time (27 women); includes 37 minority (8 African Americans, 2 American Indian/Alaska Native, 4 Asian Americans or Pacific Islanders, 23 Hispanic Americans), 18 international. Average age 24. 249 applicants, 57% accepted, 88 enrolled. In 2007, 69 degrees awarded. *Degree requirements:* For master's, summer internship. *Entrance requirements:* For master's, GRE (preferred) or GMAT. *Application deadline:* For fall admission, 1/24 for domestic and international students. Application fee: $50 ($75 for international students). Electronic applications accepted. *Expenses:* Tuition, state resident: full-time $6,129. Tuition, nonresident: full-time $11,689. Tuition and fees vary according to course load. *Financial support:* In 2007–08, fellowships (averaging $11,000 per year), research assistantships (averaging $11,250 per year) were awarded; career-related internships or fieldwork, Federal Work-Study, and institutionally sponsored loans also available. Financial award application deadline: 2/1; financial award applicants required to submit FAFSA. *Faculty research:* Public policy, Presidential studies, public leadership, economic policy, social policy. *Unit head:* Richard A. Chilcoat, Dean, 979-862-8007, Fax: 979-862-7953, E-mail: bushschool@tamu.edu. *Application contact:* Kathryn Meyer, Recruitment/Placement Officer, 979-458-4767, Fax: 979-845-4155, E-mail: admissions@bushschool.tamu.edu.

See Close-Up on page 1623.

Thomas Edison State College, Heavin School of Arts and Sciences, Program in Homeland Security, Trenton, NJ 08608-1176. Offers Graduate Certificate. Part-time programs available. Postbaccalaureate distance learning degree programs offered (no on-campus study). *Students:* Average age 37. 10 applicants, 1 enrolled. In 2007, 1 degree awarded. *Entrance requirements:* Additional exam requirements/recommendations for international students: Required—TOEFL (minimum score 550 paper-based; 213 computer-based; 79 iBT). *Application deadline:* For fall admission, 8/15 priority date for domestic and international students; for winter admission, 11/15 priority date for domestic and international students; for spring admission, 2/15 priority date for domestic and international students. Applications are processed on a rolling basis. Application fee: $75. Electronic applications accepted. *Expenses:* Tuition, state resident: part-time $440 per credit. Tuition, nonresident: part-time $440 per credit. Part-time tuition and fees vary according to program. *Financial support:* Applicants required to submit FAFSA. *Application contact:* David Hoftiezer, Director of Admissions, 888-442-8372, Fax: 609-984-8447, E-mail: admissions@tesc.edu.

Thomas Edison State College, Heavin School of Arts and Sciences, Program in Liberal Studies, Trenton, NJ 08608-1176. Offers homeland security (MALS); human resource management (MALS); online learning and teaching (MALS); organizational leadership (MALS). Part-time programs available. Postbaccalaureate distance learning degree programs offered (no on-campus study). *Students:* Average age 45. 16 applicants, 26 enrolled. In 2007, 13 degrees awarded. *Degree requirements:* For master's, capstone project. *Entrance requirements:* Additional exam requirements/recommendations for international students: Required—TOEFL (minimum score 550 paper-based; 213 computer-based; 79 iBT). *Application deadline:* For fall admission, 8/15 priority date for domestic and international students; for winter admission, 11/15 priority date for domestic and international students; for spring admission, 2/15 priority date for domestic and international students. Applications are processed on a rolling basis. Application fee: $75. Electronic applications accepted. *Expenses:* Tuition, state resident: part-time $440 per credit. Tuition, nonresident: part-time $440 per credit. Part-time tuition and fees vary according to program. *Financial support:* Applicants required to submit FAFSA. *Application contact:* David Hoftiezer, Director of Admissions, 888-442-8372, Fax: 609-984-8447, E-mail: admissions@tesc.edu.

Tiffin University, Program in Criminal Justice, Tiffin, OH 44883-2161. Offers crime analysis (MSCJ); criminal behavior (MSCJ); forensic psychology (MSCJ); homeland security administration (MSCJ); justice administration (MSCJ). Part-time and evening/weekend programs available. Postbaccalaureate distance learning degree programs offered (no on-campus study). *Degree requirements:* For master's, thesis optional. *Entrance requirements:* For master's, minimum undergraduate GPA of 2.5, work experience. Additional exam requirements/recommendations for international students: Required—TOEFL (minimum score 550 paper-based; 213 computer-based). Electronic applications accepted. *Faculty research:* Terrorism, intelligence, homeland security, guns and crime.

Towson University, College of Graduate Studies and Research, Program in Integrated Homeland Security Management, Towson, MD 21252-0001. Offers integrated homeland security management (MS); security assessment and management (Certificate). Part-time and evening/weekend programs available. *Students:* 7 full-time (2 women), 22 part-time (8 women); includes 9 minority (7 African Americans, 1 American Indian/Alaska Native, 1 Hispanic American). Average age 32. 17 applicants, 94% accepted, 9 enrolled. *Entrance requirements:* For master's, BA in related field 3 yrs related work experience admission essay, resumè, transcripts. Application fee: $50. *Expenses:* Tuition, state resident: part-time $286 per credit. Tuition, nonresident: part-time $600 per credit. Required fees: $75 per credit. *Financial support:* Application deadline: 4/1. *Unit head:* Sharma Pillutla, Graduate Program Director, 410-704-3136, E-mail: spillutla@towson.edu. *Application contact:* The Graduate School, 410-704-2501, Fax: 410-704-4675, E-mail: grads@towson.edu.

Homeland Security

University of Central Florida, College of Health and Public Affairs, Department of Public Administration, Orlando, FL 32816. Offers emergency management and homeland security (Certificate); non-profit management (MNM, Certificate); public administration (MPA, Certificate); urban and regional planning (Certificate). *Accreditation:* NASPAA. Part-time and evening/weekend programs available. *Faculty:* 11 full-time (2 women), 9 part-time/adjunct (3 women). *Degree requirements:* For master's, comprehensive exam, thesis or alternative, research report. *Entrance requirements:* For master's, GRE General Test. *Application deadline:* For fall admission, 7/1 for domestic students; for spring admission, 12/1 for domestic students. Application fee: $30. Electronic applications accepted. *Expenses:* Tuition, state resident: full-time $6,484. Tuition, nonresident: full-time $23,938. Tuition and fees vary according to program. *Financial support:* Fellowships with partial tuition reimbursements, research assistantships with partial tuition reimbursements, teaching assistantships with partial tuition reimbursements, career-related internships or fieldwork, Federal Work-Study, institutionally sponsored loans, tuition waivers (partial), and unspecified assistantships available. Financial award application deadline: 3/1; financial award applicants required to submit FAFSA. *Unit head:* Dr. MaryAnn Feldheim, Chair, 407-823-3693, Fax: 407-823-5651.

University of Connecticut, Graduate School, Center for Continuing Studies, Program in Homeland Security Leadership, Storrs, CT 06269. Offers MPS. *Faculty:* 4 full-time (0 women). *Students:* Average age 42. 25 applicants, 28% accepted, 0 enrolled. In 2007, 23 degrees awarded. *Expenses:* Tuition, state resident: part-time $469 per credit hour. Tuition, nonresident: part-time $1,218 per credit hour.

The University of Toledo, College of Graduate Studies, College of Medicine, Department of Public Health and Homeland Security, Toledo, OH 43606-3390. Offers occupational health (MSOH, Certificate); public health (MPH, Certificate), including biostatistics and epidemiology (Certificate), emergency response (Certificate), global health (Certificate), public health (MPH); MD/MPH. Part-time programs available. *Students:* 38 full-time (27 women), 59 part-time (45 women); includes 23 minority (17 African Americans, 5 Asian Americans or Pacific Islanders, 1 Hispanic American), 8 international. 64 applicants, 83% accepted, 38 enrolled. In 2007, 40 degrees awarded. *Degree requirements:* For master's, thesis, qualifying exam. *Entrance requirements:* For master's, GRE. Application fee: $45. *Financial support:* In 2007–08, 6 research assistantships with full tuition reimbursements (averaging $9,000 per year) were awarded; fellowships with full tuition reimbursements, Federal Work-Study, institutionally sponsored loans, scholarships/grants, tuition waivers (full), and unspecified assistantships also available. Financial award applicants required to submit FAFSA. *Faculty research:* Hypertension, endocrinology, molecular biology. Total annual research expenditures: $754,479. *Unit head:* Dr. Michael S. Bisesi, Chair, 419-383-4112, Fax: 419-383-6140, E-mail: michael.bisesi@utoledo.edu. *Application contact:* Theresa Langenderfer, Secretary, 419-383-4160, Fax: 419-383-6140, E-mail: mcogradschool@mco.edu.

Upper Iowa University, Online Master's Programs, Fayette, IA 52142-1857. Offers accounting (MBA); corporate financial management (MBA); global business (MBA); health and human services (MPA); homeland security (MPA); human resources management (MBA); justice administration (MPA); organizational development (MBA); public personnel management (MPA); quality management (MBA). MBA also available at Madison, Wisconsin campus. Part-time programs available. Postbaccalaureate distance learning degree programs offered (no on-campus study). *Faculty:* 1 full-time (0 women), 25 part-time/adjunct (12 women). *Students:* 255 full-time (170 women); includes 58 minority (44 African Americans, 1 American Indian/Alaska Native, 7 Asian Americans or Pacific Islanders, 6 Hispanic Americans), 3 international. 127 applicants, 85% accepted, 64 enrolled. In 2007, 72 degrees awarded. *Degree requirements:* For master's, research project. *Entrance requirements:* For master's, GMAT, GRE, or minimum GPA of 2.7 during last 60 hours. Additional exam requirements/recommendations for international students: Required—TOEFL (minimum score 570 paper-based; 230 computer-based). *Application deadline:* Applications are processed on a rolling basis. Application fee: $50. Electronic applications accepted. *Financial support:* In 2007–08, 153 students received support. Available to part-time students. Applicants required to submit FAFSA. *Faculty research:* Total quality management, CQI, teams, organization culture and climate, management. *Application contact:* David Hannum, Online Program Recruiter/Advisor, 866-225-2208, E-mail: hannumd@uiu.edu.

Virginia Commonwealth University, Graduate School, College of Humanities and Sciences, Wilder School of Government and Public Affairs, Program in Homeland Security and Emergency Preparedness, Richmond, VA 23284-9005. Offers MA, Graduate Certificate. Postbaccalaureate distance learning degree programs offered. *Students:* 5 full-time (1 woman), 5 part-time (1 woman); includes 3 minority (all African Americans) 45 applicants, 58% accepted. *Expenses:* Tuition, state resident: full-time $7,224; part-time $401 per credit. Tuition, nonresident: full-time $16,072; part-time $891 per credit. Required fees: $1,679; $63 per credit. Tuition and fees vary according to campus/location. *Unit head:* Dr. Susan Gooden, Head, 804-827-7078, E-mail: stgooden@vcu.edu.

Walden University, Graduate Programs, School of Public Policy and Administration, Minneapolis, MN 55401. Offers criminal justice (MPA, PhD); health services (MPA, PhD); homeland security policy and coordination (MPA, PhD); international nongovernmental organizations (MPA, PhD); knowledge management (MPA, PhD); nonprofit management and leadership (MPA, PhD); public management and leadership (MPA, PhD); public policy (MPA, PhD); public safety management (MPA, PhD). Part-time and evening/weekend programs available. Postbaccalaureate distance learning degree programs offered (minimal on-campus study). *Students:* 433 full-time (228 women), 148 part-time (79 women); includes 265 minority (234 African Americans, 6 American Indian/Alaska Native, 11 Asian Americans or Pacific Islanders, 14 Hispanic Americans), 4 international. Average age 42. 475 applicants, 76% accepted, 220 enrolled. In 2007, 71 master's, 7 doctorates awarded. *Degree requirements:* For doctorate, thesis/dissertation. *Entrance requirements:* For master's, minimum GPA of 3.0; for doctorate, 3 years of professional experience, master's degree. Additional exam requirements/recommendations for international students: Required—TOEFL (minimum score 550 paper-based; 213 computer-based), IELTS (minimum score 7). *Application deadline:* For fall admission, 8/15 priority date for domestic and international students; for winter admission, 11/15 priority date for domestic and international students; for spring admission, 12/15 priority date for domestic and international students. Applications are processed on a rolling basis. Application fee: $50. Electronic applications accepted. *Financial support:* Fellowships with partial tuition reimbursements, Federal Work-Study, institutionally sponsored loans, scholarships/grants, and unspecified assistantships available. Financial award application deadline: 6/1; financial award applicants required to submit FAFSA. *Unit head:* Gary Kelsey, Associate Dean, 800-925-3368, Fax: 612-338-5092. *Application contact:* 866-4-WALDEN, Fax: 410-843-8780, E-mail: request@waldenu.edu.

Wilmington University, Division of Business, New Castle, DE 19720-6491. Offers business administration (MBA); finance (MBA); health care administration (MBA, MS); homeland security (MBA, MS); human resource management (MS); management (MS); management information systems (MBA); organizational leadership (MS); public administration (MS); transportation and logistics (MBA, MS). Part-time and evening/weekend programs available. *Faculty:* 4 full-time (0 women). *Students:* 232 full-time (117 women), 503 part-time (326 women); includes 97 minority (83 African Americans, 6 Asian Americans or Pacific Islanders, 8 Hispanic Americans). Average age 34. 396 applicants, 100% accepted, 259 enrolled. In 2007, 290 degrees awarded. *Entrance requirements:* Additional exam requirements/recommendations for international students: Required—TOEFL (minimum score 500 paper-based; 173 computer-based). *Application deadline:* Applications are processed on a rolling basis. Application fee: $25. Electronic applications accepted. *Expenses:* Tuition: Full-time $6,246; part-time $1,041 per course. Tuition and fees vary according to degree level and campus/location. *Financial support:* Applicants required to submit FAFSA. *Unit head:* Dr. Robert Edelson, Chair, 302-295-1147, Fax: 302-328-7021, E-mail: robert.e.edelson@wilmcoll.edu. *Application contact:* Chris Ferguson, Director of Admissions, 302-356-4636 Ext. 256, Fax: 302-328-5164, E-mail: inquire@wilmcoll.edu.

Industrial and Labor Relations

Bernard M. Baruch College of the City University of New York, Zicklin School of Business, Zicklin Executive Programs, Baruch Executive Master of Science in Industrial and Labor Relations Program, New York, NY 10010-5585. Offers MS. Part-time and evening/weekend programs available. *Entrance requirements:* For master's, professional experience in HR or labor relations. Additional exam requirements/recommendations for international students: Required—TOEFL. Expenses: Contact institution.

Case Western Reserve University, Weatherhead School of Management, Department of Marketing and Policy Studies, Division of Labor and Human Resource Policy, Cleveland, OH 44106. Offers MBA. Part-time and evening/weekend programs available. *Entrance requirements:* For master's, GMAT. *Application deadline:* Applications are processed on a rolling basis. Application fee: $50. *Financial support:* Career-related internships or fieldwork, Federal Work-Study, institutionally sponsored loans, and tuition waivers (full and partial) available. Financial award application deadline: 5/1. *Faculty research:* Strategic human resource management, negotiations and conflict management, human resources in high performance organizations, international human resources management, union management relations and collective bargaining. *Unit head:* Dr. Paul F. Gerhart, Head, 216-368-2045, E-mail: pfg2@po.cwru.edu.

Cleveland State University, College of Graduate Studies, Nance College of Business Administration, Department of Management and Labor Relations, Cleveland, OH 44115. Offers labor relations and human resources (MLRHR). Part-time programs available. *Faculty:* 10 full-time (3 women), 4 part-time/adjunct (2 women). *Students:* 24 full-time (15 women), 35 part-time (27 women); includes 12 minority (10 African Americans, 2 American Indian/Alaska Native), 7 international. Average age 29. 57 applicants, 60% accepted, 16 enrolled. In 2007, 22 degrees awarded. *Entrance requirements:* For master's, GMAT or GRE. Additional exam requirements/recommendations for international students: Required—TOEFL (minimum score 525 paper-based; 197 computer-based). *Application deadline:* For fall admission, 7/15 for domestic students; for spring admission, 12/15 for domestic students. Applications are processed on a rolling basis. Application fee: $30. Electronic applications accepted. *Financial support:* In 2007–08, 3 research assistantships with full and partial tuition reimbursements (averaging $6,960 per year) were awarded; career-related internships or fieldwork, tuition waivers (full), and unspecified assistantships also available. Financial award applicants required to submit FAFSA. *Unit head:* Dr. Jeffrey C. Susbauer, Chairperson, 216-687-4747, Fax: 216-687-4708, E-mail: j.susbauer@csuohio.edu.

Cornell University, Graduate School, Graduate Fields of Industrial and Labor Relations, Ithaca, NY 14853-0001. Offers collective bargaining, labor law and labor history (MILR, MPS, MS, PhD); economic and social statistics (MILR); human resource studies (MILR, MPS, MS, PhD); industrial and labor relations problems (MILR, MPS, MS, PhD); international and comparative labor (MILR, MPS, MS, PhD); labor economics (MILR, MPS, MS, PhD); organizational behavior (MILR, MPS, MS, PhD). *Faculty:* 49 full-time (11 women). *Students:* 137 full-time (76 women); includes 23 minority (8 African Americans, 1 American Indian/Alaska Native, 8 Asian Americans or Pacific Islanders, 6 Hispanic Americans), 58 international. Average age 30. 205 applicants, 40% accepted, 62 enrolled. In 2007, 53 master's, 4 doctorates awarded. *Degree requirements:* For master's, thesis (MS); for doctorate, comprehensive exam, thesis/dissertation, teaching experience. *Entrance requirements:* For master's and doctorate, GMAT or GRE General Test, 2 academic recommendations. Additional exam requirements/recommendations for international students: Required—TOEFL (minimum score 550 paper-based; 213 computer-based; 77 iBT). Application fee: $70. Electronic applications accepted. *Expenses: Contact institution. Financial support:* In 2007–08, 80 students received support, including 22 fellowships with full tuition reimbursements available, 18 research assistantships with full tuition reimbursements available, 40 teaching assistantships with full tuition reimbursements available; institutionally sponsored loans, scholarships/grants, health care benefits, tuition waivers (full and partial), and unspecified assistantships also available. Financial award applicants required to submit FAFSA. *Unit head:* Director of Graduate Studies, 607-255-1522. *Application contact:* Graduate Field Assistant, 607-255-1522, E-mail: ilrgradapplicant@cornell.edu.

See Close-Up on page 1591.

Indiana University of Pennsylvania, School of Graduate Studies and Research, College of Health and Human Services, Department of Industrial and Labor Relations, Indiana, PA 15705-1087. Offers MA. Part-time and evening/weekend programs available. *Faculty:* 5 full-time (1 woman). *Students:* 31 full-time (12 women), 17 part-time (11 women); includes 7 minority (5 African Americans, 1 Asian American or Pacific Islander, 1 Hispanic American), 1 international. Average age 29. 69 applicants, 68% accepted, 27 enrolled. In 2007, 41 degrees awarded. *Degree requirements:* For master's, thesis optional. *Entrance requirements:* For master's, 2 letters of recommendation. Additional exam requirements/recommendations for international students: Required—TOEFL. *Application deadline:* For fall admission, 7/1 priority date for domestic students; for spring admission, 11/1 for domestic students. Applications are processed on a rolling basis. Application fee: $30. *Expenses:* Tuition, state resident: full-time $6,214; part-time $345 per credit. Tuition, nonresident: full-time $9,944; part-time $552 per credit. Required fees: $43 per credit. One-time fee: $140 part-time. Tuition and fees vary according to course load. *Financial support:* In 2007–08, 18 research assistantships with full and partial tuition reimbursements (averaging $2,955 per year) were awarded; fellowships, career-related internships or fieldwork and Federal Work-Study also available. Support available to part-time students. Financial award application deadline: 3/15; financial award applicants required to submit FAFSA. *Faculty research:* Conflict resolution, labor-management cooperation, unemployment compensation, public sector labor relations, employee discipline. *Unit head:* Dr. Jennie K. Bullard, Chairperson and Graduate Coordinator, 724-357-4470, E-mail: jbullard@iup.edu.

Inter American University of Puerto Rico, Metropolitan Campus, Faculty of Economics and Administrative Sciences, School of Management, Program in Labor Relations, San Juan, PR 00919-1293. Offers MA. *Degree requirements:* For master's, comprehensive exam. *Entrance requirements:* For master's, GRE or EXADEP, interview. Electronic applications accepted.

Inter American University of Puerto Rico, San Germán Campus, Graduate Studies Center, Program in Business Administration, San Germán, PR 00683-5008. Offers accounting (MBA); finance (MBA); human resources (MBA, PhD); industrial relations (MBA); international business

(PhD); labor relations (PhD); management information systems (MBA); marketing (MBA); quality organizational design (MBA). Part-time and evening/weekend programs available. *Faculty:* 10 full-time, 3 part-time/adjunct. *Students:* 192. Average age 27. In 2007, 57 master's, 4 doctorates awarded. *Degree requirements:* For master's, comprehensive exam. *Entrance requirements:* For master's, GRE General Test or EXADEP, minimum GPA of 3.0. *Application deadline:* For fall admission, 4/30 priority date for domestic students; for spring admission, 11/15 for domestic students. Applications are processed on a rolling basis. Application fee: $31. *Expenses:* Tuition: Full-time $3,258; part-time $181 per credit. Required fees: $258 per semester. Tuition and fees vary according to degree level. *Financial support:* Teaching assistantships, Federal Work-Study and unspecified assistantships available. *Application contact:* Prof. Duay Rivera, Graduate Coordinator, 787-264-1912 Ext. 7218, Fax: 787-892-7510, E-mail: durivera@sg.inter.edu.

Inter American University of Puerto Rico, San Germán Campus, Graduate Studies Center, Program in Entrepreneurial and Managerial Development, San Germán, PR 00683-5008. Offers human resources (PhD); interregional and international business (PhD); labor relations (PhD). Part-time and evening/weekend programs available. *Faculty:* 10 full-time, 3 part-time/adjunct. *Students:* 47. Average age 41. In 2007, 4 degrees awarded. *Degree requirements:* For doctorate, comprehensive exam, thesis/dissertation. *Entrance requirements:* For doctorate, EXADEP or GMAT, minimum graduate GPA of 3.25. *Application deadline:* For fall admission, 4/30 priority date for domestic students; for spring admission, 11/15 for domestic students. Applications are processed on a rolling basis. Application fee: $75. *Expenses:* Tuition: Full-time $3,258; part-time $181 per credit. Required fees: $258 per semester. Tuition and fees vary according to degree level. *Financial support:* Teaching assistantships, unspecified assistantships available. *Application contact:* Dr. Carlos E. Irizarry, Director of Graduate Studies Center, 787-264-1912 Ext. 7357, Fax: 787-892-6350, E-mail: carlos.irizarry@sg.inter.edu.

Loyola University Chicago, Graduate School of Business, Institute of Human Resources and Employee Relations, Chicago, IL 60611-2196. Offers MSHR. Part-time programs available. *Faculty:* 6 full-time (3 women), 1 part-time/adjunct (0 women). *Students:* 16 full-time (13 women), 56 part-time (43 women); includes 17 minority (8 African Americans, 5 Asian Americans or Pacific Islanders, 4 Hispanic Americans). In 2007, 25 degrees awarded. *Entrance requirements:* For master's, GMAT or GRE General Test, personal statement, letters of recommendation. Additional exam requirements/recommendations for international students: Required—TOEFL (minimum score 550 paper-based; 213 computer-based; 80 iBT). *Application deadline:* For fall admission, 7/15 for domestic and international students; for winter admission, 10/1 for domestic and international students; for spring admission, 1/15 for domestic and international students. Applications are processed on a rolling basis. Application fee: $50. *Expenses: Contact institution.* Full-time tuition and fees vary according to program. *Financial support:* In 2007–08, 3 research assistantships were awarded; career-related internships or fieldwork and Federal Work-Study also available. Support available to part-time students. Financial award applicants required to submit FAFSA. *Faculty research:* Human resource management, labor relations, global human resource management, organizational development, compensation. *Unit head:* Dr. Suzy Fox, Chair, 312-915-7518, Fax: 312-915-6231, E-mail: avarma@luc.edu. *Application contact:* Olivia Heath, Enrollment Advisor, 312-915-8908, Fax: 312-915-7207, E-mail: oheath@luc.edu.

McMaster University, School of Graduate Studies, Faculty of Social Sciences, Program in Labour Studies, Hamilton, ON L8S 4M2, Canada. Offers work and society (MA). *Faculty:* 6 full-time. *Students:* 18 full-time, 4 part-time. Application fee: $90. *Unit head:* Dr. Charlotte Yates, Director, 905-525-9140 Ext. 27061, Fax: 905-528-1228, E-mail: yatesch@mcmaster.ca. *Application contact:* Sharon Molnar, Administrative Secretary, 905-525-9140 Ext. 24692, Fax: 905-528-1228, E-mail: molnars@mcmaster.ca.

Memorial University of Newfoundland, School of Graduate Studies, Interdisciplinary Program in Employment Relations, St. John's, NL A1C 5S7, Canada. Offers MER. Part-time programs available. *Degree requirements:* For master's, major supervised paper. *Entrance requirements:* For master's, undergraduate degree in related field, minimum B average. Electronic applications accepted.

Michigan State University, The Graduate School, College of Social Science, School of Labor and Industrial Relations, East Lansing, MI 48824. Offers human resources and labor relations (MLRHR); industrial relations and human resources (PhD). *Entrance requirements:* Additional exam requirements/recommendations for international students: Required—TOEFL. *Expenses:* Tuition, state resident: part-time $379 per credit hour. Tuition, nonresident: part-time $800 per credit hour. Tuition and fees vary according to program.

New York Institute of Technology, Graduate Division, School of Management, Program in Human Resources Management and Labor Relations, Old Westbury, NY 11568-8000. Offers human resources administration (Advanced Certificate); human resources management and labor relations (MS); labor relations (Advanced Certificate). Part-time and evening/weekend programs available. *Students:* 29 full-time (21 women), 55 part-time (44 women); includes 24 minority (13 African Americans, 9 Asian Americans or Pacific Islanders, 2 Hispanic Americans), 19 international. Average age 32. 45 applicants, 76% accepted, 22 enrolled. In 2007, 41 master's, 1 other advanced degree awarded. *Degree requirements:* For master's, comprehensive exam, thesis optional. *Entrance requirements:* For master's, GRE, minimum QPA of 2.85, interview, 2 letters of recommendation. *Application deadline:* For fall admission, 7/1 priority date for domestic students; for spring admission, 12/1 priority date for domestic students. Applications are processed on a rolling basis. Application fee: $50. Electronic applications accepted. *Expenses:* Tuition: Part-time $739 per credit. Required fees: $75 per semester. *Financial support:* Fellowships, research assistantships, career-related internships or fieldwork, institutionally sponsored loans, and tuition waivers (full and partial) available. Support available to part-time students. Financial award applicants required to submit FAFSA. *Faculty research:* Ethics in industrial relations, employee relations, public sector labor relations, benefits. *Unit head:* Dr. Richard Dibble, Chair, 516-686-7722. *Application contact:* Jacquelyn Nealon, Dean of Admissions and Financial Aid, 516-686-7925, Fax: 516-686-7613, E-mail: jnealon@nyit.edu.

The Ohio State University, Graduate School, Max M. Fisher College of Business, Program in Labor and Human Resources, Columbus, OH 43210. Offers MLHR, PhD. *Faculty:* 28. *Students:* 70 full-time (48 women), 43 part-time (33 women); includes 21 minority (10 African Americans, 2 American Indian/Alaska Native, 6 Asian Americans or Pacific Islanders, 3 Hispanic Americans), 16 international. In 2007, 37 master's, 1 doctorate awarded. *Degree requirements:* For master's, thesis optional; for doctorate, thesis/dissertation. *Entrance requirements:* For master's and doctorate, GRE General Test. Additional exam requirements/recommendations for international students: Recommended—TOEFL (minimum score 600 paper-based; 250 computer-based). *Application deadline:* For fall admission, 8/15 priority date for domestic students, 7/1 priority date for international students; for winter admission, 12/1 priority date for domestic students, 11/1 priority date for international students; for spring admission, 3/1 priority date for domestic students, 2/1 priority date for international students. Applications are processed on a rolling basis. Application fee: $40 ($50 for international students). Electronic applications accepted. *Financial support:* Fellowships, research assistantships, teaching assistantships, Federal Work-Study and institutionally sponsored loans available. Support available to part-time students. *Unit head:* Robert L. Heneman, Graduate Studies Committee Chair, 614-292-4587, Fax: 614-292-9006, E-mail: heneman.1@osu.edu. *Application contact:* 614-292-9444, Fax: 614-292-3895, E-mail: domestic.grad@osu.edu.

Penn State University Park, Graduate School, College of the Liberal Arts, Department of Labor Studies and Industrial Relations, State College, University Park, PA 16802-1503. Offers industrial relations and human resources (MS). *Expenses:* Tuition, state resident: full-time $14,738; part-time $614 per credit. Tuition, nonresident: full-time $26,050; part-time $1,085 per credit. Tuition and fees vary according to course load, program and student level. *Unit head:* Dr. Paul Clark, Department Head, 814-865-0752, Fax: 814-863-3578, E-mail: pfc2@psu.edu.

Pontificia Universidad Catolica Madre y Maestra, Graduate School, Santiago, Dominican Republic. Offers administration (M Adm, M Ed); architecture of interiors (M Arch); architecture of tourist lodgings (M Arch); construction administration (ME); convergent networks (ME); corporate business law (LL M); criminal procedure law (LL M); earthquake-resistant engineering (ME); environmental engineering (MEE); finance (M Mgmt); human resources (EMBA); international business (M Mgmt); international relations (LL M); labor law and Social Security (M Mgmt); logistics management (ME); marketing (M Mgmt); urban planning (M Urb). *Entrance requirements:* For master's, curriculum vitae, interview.

Queen's University at Kingston, School of Graduate Studies and Research, School of Industrial Relations, Kingston, ON K7L 3N6, Canada. Offers MIR. Part-time programs available. *Degree requirements:* For master's, research essay, skill seminars and modules. *Entrance requirements:* For master's, course work in micro-economics, macro-economics, and quantitative statistics. Additional exam requirements/recommendations for international students: Required—TOEFL (minimum score 600 paper-based; 250 computer-based). *Faculty research:* Collective bargaining and labor law, personnel and human relations, labor market analysis and policy, change management, teams.

Rutgers, The State University of New Jersey, New Brunswick, School of Management and Labor Relations, Program in Industrial Relations and Human Resources, New Brunswick, NJ 08901-1281. Offers PhD. *Degree requirements:* For doctorate, comprehensive exam, thesis/dissertation. *Entrance requirements:* For doctorate, GMAT, GRE. Electronic applications accepted. *Faculty research:* Strategic human resource management, international human resource management, labor economics, collective bargaining, teams and diversity.

Announcement: MHRM program focuses on strategic positioning of human resources management principally in business and government organizations. MLER allows students to focus on labor relations, organizational change, employee diversity, and/or public policy. PhD prepares students for academic careers.

Rutgers, The State University of New Jersey, New Brunswick, School of Management and Labor Relations, Program in Labor and Employment Relations, New Brunswick, NJ 08901-1281. Offers MLER. Part-time and evening/weekend programs available. *Degree requirements:* For master's, thesis optional. *Entrance requirements:* For master's, GRE General Test. Additional exam requirements/recommendations for international students: Required—TOEFL. Electronic applications accepted. Expenses: Contact institution. *Faculty research:* Labor history, women and work, labor education, comparative labor movements, labor involvement and corporate decision making.

State University of New York Empire State College, Graduate Studies, Program in Labor and Policy Studies, Saratoga Springs, NY 12866-4391. Offers MA. Part-time and evening/weekend programs available. Postbaccalaureate distance learning degree programs offered (minimal on-campus study). *Degree requirements:* For master's, thesis, exam. *Entrance requirements:* Additional exam requirements/recommendations for international students: Required—TOEFL (minimum score 600 paper-based; 280 computer-based). Electronic applications accepted. *Faculty research:* Work and technology, collective bargaining, labor law, human resources management, trade union governance.

Université de Montréal, Faculty of Arts and Sciences, School of Industrial Relations, Montréal, QC H3C 3J7, Canada. Offers M Sc, PhD, DESS. Part-time programs available. *Faculty:* 22 full-time (5 women), 2 part-time/adjunct (1 woman). *Students:* 134 full-time (103 women), 55 part-time (39 women). 154 applicants, 39% accepted, 45 enrolled. In 2007, 19 master's, 2 doctorates awarded. *Degree requirements:* For master's, thesis; for doctorate, thesis/dissertation, general exam. *Entrance requirements:* For master's, BS in industrial relations. *Application deadline:* For fall admission, 2/1 priority date for domestic students; for winter admission, 11/1 priority date for domestic students; for spring admission, 2/1 priority date for domestic students. Application fee: $100. Electronic applications accepted. *Financial support:* Fellowships, research assistantships, teaching assistantships, tuition waivers (full) available. *Faculty research:* Labor law, health and safety at work, stress, job satisfaction, labor economics. *Unit head:* Reynald Bourque, Director, 514-343-7039, Fax: 514-343-5764, E-mail: reynald.bourque@umontreal.ca. *Application contact:* Marcel Simard, Responsible for PhD, 514-343-2484, Fax: 514-343-5764, E-mail: marcel.simard@umontreal.ca.

Université du Québec à Trois-Rivières, Graduate Programs, Program in Labor Relations, Trois-Rivières, QC G9A 5H7, Canada. Offers DESS.

Université du Québec en Outaouais, Graduate Programs, Department of Industrial Relations, Gatineau, QC J8X 3X7, Canada. Offers M Sc, MA, PhD, Diploma. Part-time programs available. *Students:* 17 full-time, 70 part-time, 6 international. *Degree requirements:* For master's, thesis (for some programs); for doctorate, thesis/dissertation. *Entrance requirements:* For master's, appropriate bachelor's degree, proficiency in French; for doctorate, appropriate master's degree, proficiency in French. *Application deadline:* For fall admission, 6/1 for domestic students, 3/1 for international students; for winter admission, 11/1 for domestic students, 10/1 for international students. Application fee: $30 Canadian dollars. *Financial support:* Fellowships, research assistantships, teaching assistantships available. *Unit head:* Eric Gosselin, Director, 819-595-3900 Ext. 1777, Fax: 819-773-1788, E-mail: eric.gosselin@uqo.ca. *Application contact:* Registrar's Office, 819-773-1850, Fax: 819-773-1835, E-mail: registraire@uqo.ca.

Université Laval, Faculty of Social Sciences, Department of Industrial Relations, Programs in Industrial Relations, Québec, QC G1K 7P4, Canada. Offers MA, PhD. Terminal master's awarded for partial completion of doctoral program. *Degree requirements:* For master's, thesis (for some programs); for doctorate, comprehensive exam, thesis/dissertation. *Entrance requirements:* For master's and doctorate, knowledge of French, comprehension of written English. Electronic applications accepted.

University of Alberta, Faculty of Graduate Studies and Research, Doctoral Program in Business, Edmonton, AB T6G 2E1, Canada. Offers accounting (PhD); finance (PhD); human resources/industrial relations (PhD); management science (PhD); marketing (PhD); organizational analysis (PhD); MBA/PhD. *Accreditation:* AACSB. Part-time programs available. *Degree requirements:* For doctorate, comprehensive exam, thesis/dissertation. *Entrance requirements:* For doctorate, GMAT. Additional exam requirements/recommendations for international students: Required—TOEFL (minimum score 550 paper-based; 213 computer-based). Electronic applications accepted. *Faculty research:* Accounting, capital markets and corporate finance, organizational change and human resource management, marketing, strategic management.

University of California, Berkeley, Graduate Division, Haas School of Business, Program in Business, Berkeley, CA 94720-1500. Offers accounting (PhD); business and public policy (PhD); finance (PhD); marketing (PhD); organizational behavior and industrial relations (PhD); real estate (PhD). *Accreditation:* AACSB. *Students:* 77 full-time (22 women); includes 21 minority (17 Asian Americans or Pacific Islanders, 4 Hispanic Americans), 23 international. Average age 31. 401 applicants, 8% accepted, 15 enrolled. In 2007, 14 doctorates awarded. *Median time to degree:* Of those who began their doctoral program in fall 1999, 100% received their degree in 8 years or less. *Degree requirements:* For doctorate, comprehensive exam, thesis/dissertation, oral exam, written preliminary exams. *Entrance requirements:* For doctorate, GMAT or GRE, minimum GPA of 3.0. Additional exam requirements/recommendations for international students: Required—TOEFL (minimum score 570 paper-based; 230 computer-based; 68 iBT), IELTS (minimum score 7). *Application deadline:* For fall admission, 12/15 for domestic and international students. Application fee: $60 ($80 for international students). Electronic applications accepted. *Financial support:* Fellowships with full and partial tuition reimbursements, research assistantships with full and partial tuition reimbursements, teaching assistantships with full and partial tuition reimbursements, career-related internships or fieldwork, Federal Work-Study, scholarships/grants, health care benefits, tuition waivers (full), unspecified

Industrial and Labor Relations

University of California, Berkeley (continued)
assistantships, and transit pass, travel grants available. Financial award application deadline: 12/15; financial award applicants required to submit FAFSA. *Unit head:* Miguel Villas-Boas, Director, 510-642-1409, Fax: 510-643-4255, E-mail: kimg@haas.berkeley.edu. *Application contact:* Kim Guilfoyle, Administrative Director, 510-642-3944, Fax: 510-643-4255, E-mail: kimg@haas.berkeley.edu.

University of Cincinnati, Graduate School, McMicken College of Arts and Sciences, Center for Organizational Leadership, Program in Labor and Employment Relations, Cincinnati, OH 45221. Offers MALER. Part-time and evening/weekend programs available. *Faculty:* 2 full-time (1 woman). *Students:* 15 full-time (11 women), 32 part-time (28 women); includes 8 minority (6 African Americans, 1 American Indian/Alaska Native, 1 Asian American or Pacific Islander), 2 international. Average age 37. In 2007, 25 degrees awarded. *Degree requirements:* For master's, thesis or alternative, final experience project. *Entrance requirements:* For master's, minimum undergraduate GPA of 3.0. Additional exam requirements/recommendations for international students: Required—TOEFL (minimum score 560 paper-based). *Application deadline:* Applications are processed on a rolling basis. Application fee: $50. Electronic applications accepted. *Financial support:* In 2007–08, 6 students received support, including research assistantships with full tuition reimbursements available (averaging $9,648 per year), teaching assistantships with full tuition reimbursements available (averaging $9,648 per year); career-related internships or fieldwork, tuition waivers (partial), and unspecified assistantships also available. Financial award application deadline: 3/1. *Faculty research:* Human resource management, diversity, leadership. *Unit head:* Dr. Joseph Gallo, Head, 513-556-2605, E-mail: joseph.gallo@uc.edu. *Application contact:* Donna Chrobot-Mason, Director, 513-556-2659, E-mail: donna.chrobot-mason@uc.edu.

University of Cincinnati, Graduate School, McMicken College of Arts and Sciences, Department of Economics, Cincinnati, OH 45221. Offers applied economics (MA); labor and employment relations (MALER). Part-time and evening/weekend programs available. *Faculty:* 16 full-time (2 women). *Students:* 41 full-time (22 women), 34 part-time (28 women); includes 10 minority (7 African Americans, 1 American Indian/Alaska Native, 2 Asian Americans or Pacific Islanders), 17 international. 43 applicants, 44% accepted. In 2007, 39 degrees awarded. *Application deadline:* For fall admission, 4/1 priority date for domestic students. Applications are processed on a rolling basis. Application fee: $30. Electronic applications accepted. *Financial support:* In 2007–08, 20 students received support; fellowships with full tuition reimbursements available, research assistantships with full tuition reimbursements available, teaching assistantships with full tuition reimbursements available, career-related internships or fieldwork, scholarships/grants, tuition waivers (partial), and unspecified assistantships available. Financial award application deadline: 4/1. *Unit head:* Dr. Wolfgang Mayer, Head, 513-556-2618, E-mail: wolfgang.mayer@uc.edu.

University of Illinois at Urbana–Champaign, Graduate College, Institute of Labor and Industrial Relations, Champaign, IL 61820. Offers human resources (MHRIR, PhD); human resources and industrial relations (MHRIR, PhD); MHRIR/JD; MHRIR/MBA. Part-time programs available. *Faculty:* 13 full-time (4 women). *Students:* 167 full-time (114 women), 12 part-time (10 women); includes 33 minority (16 African Americans, 1 American Indian/Alaska Native, 12 Asian Americans or Pacific Islanders, 4 Hispanic Americans), 39 international. Average age 25. 230 applicants, 50% accepted, 77 enrolled. In 2007, 82 master's, 2 doctorates awarded. Terminal master's awarded for partial completion of doctoral program. *Degree requirements:* For doctorate, thesis/dissertation. *Entrance requirements:* For master's, GRE General Test, minimum GPA of 3.0; for doctorate, GRE General Test, research experience. *Application deadline:* For fall admission, 2/1 for domestic students; for spring admission, 11/1 for domestic students. Application fee: $60 ($75 for international students). Electronic applications accepted. *Financial support:* In 2007–08, 47 fellowships, 11 research assistantships, 5 teaching assistantships were awarded; career-related internships or fieldwork, Federal Work-Study, scholarships/grants, and tuition waivers (full) also available. Support available to part-time students. Financial award application deadline: 2/1. *Unit head:* Dr. Joe Cutcher Gershenfeld, Director, 217-333-1480, Fax: 217-244-9290, E-mail: joelcg@uiuc.edu. *Application contact:* Becky Barker, Graduate Admissions, 217-333-2381, Fax: 217-244-9290, E-mail: ebarker@uiuc.edu.

University of Louisville, Graduate School, College of Arts and Sciences, Department of Urban and Public Affairs, Program in Public Administration, Louisville, KY 40292-0001. Offers labor and public management (MPA); public policy and administration (MPA); urban and regional development (MPA). *Accreditation:* NASPAA. *Students:* 21 full-time (14 women), 22 part-time (12 women); includes 6 minority (4 African Americans, 1 Asian American or Pacific Islander, 1 Hispanic American), 1 international. Average age 30. In 2007, 15 degrees awarded. *Degree requirements:* For master's, practicum or thesis. *Entrance requirements:* For master's, GRE General Test, minimum GPA of 3.25, resumé. *Application deadline:* For fall admission, 7/1 priority date for domestic students; for spring admission, 12/1 priority date for domestic students. Applications are processed on a rolling basis. Application fee: $50. *Unit head:* Dr. Steve Koven, Director, 502-852-7906, Fax: 502-852-4558, E-mail: sgkove01@louisville.edu.

University of Massachusetts Amherst, Graduate School, College of Social and Behavioral Sciences, The Labor Center, Amherst, MA 01003. Offers labor studies (MS). Part-time programs available. *Faculty:* 3 full-time (2 women). *Students:* 26 full-time (9 women), 55 part-time (21 women); includes 12 minority (6 African Americans, 1 Asian American or Pacific Islander, 5 Hispanic Americans), 1 international. Average age 39. 13 applicants, 85% accepted, 7 enrolled. In 2007, 17 degrees awarded. *Degree requirements:* For master's, thesis or alternative. *Entrance requirements:* Additional exam requirements/recommendations for international students: Required—TOEFL (minimum score 530 paper-based; 197 computer-based). *Application deadline:* For fall admission, 2/1 priority date for domestic and international students; for spring admission, 10/1 for domestic and international students. Applications are processed on a rolling basis. Application fee: $50 ($65 for international students). Electronic applications accepted. *Expenses:* Tuition, state resident: full-time $2,640; part-time $110 per credit. Tuition, nonresident: full-time $9,936; part-time $414 per credit. Required fees: $7,455. One-time fee: $332. Tuition and fees vary according to course load, campus/location, program and reciprocity agreements. *Financial support:* In 2007–08, 1 research assistantship with full tuition reimbursement (averaging $3,468 per year), 10 teaching assistantships with full tuition reimbursements (averaging $5,157 per year) were awarded; fellowships with full tuition reimbursements, career-related internships or fieldwork, Federal Work-Study, scholarships/grants, traineeships, and unspecified assistantships also available. Support available to part-time students. Financial award application deadline: 2/1. *Unit head:* Dr. Thomas Juravich, Director, 413-545-5986, Fax: 413-545-0110, E-mail: juravich@lrrc.umass.edu.

University of Minnesota, Twin Cities Campus, Carlson School of Management, Program in Human Resources and Industrial Relations, Minneapolis, MN 55455-0213. Offers MA, PhD. *Accreditation:* AACSB. Part-time and evening/weekend programs available. *Faculty:* 16 full-time (5 women), 8 part-time/adjunct (3 women). *Students:* 148 full-time (100 women), 78 part-time (63 women); includes 19 minority (9 African Americans, 6 Asian Americans or Pacific Islanders, 4 Hispanic Americans), 71 international. Average age 26. 177 applicants, 79% accepted, 70 enrolled. In 2007, 97 master's, 1 doctorate awarded. Terminal master's awarded for partial completion of doctoral program. *Degree requirements:* For master's, thesis optional; for doctorate, thesis/dissertation. *Entrance requirements:* For master's, GMAT or GRE General Test; for doctorate, GRE General Test. Additional exam requirements/recommendations for international students: Required—TOEFL (minimum score 580 paper-based). *Application deadline:* For fall admission, 6/15 for domestic and international students; for spring admission, 10/15 for domestic and international students. Applications are processed on a rolling basis. Application fee: $55 ($75 for international students). *Expenses:* Contact institution. *Financial support:* In 2007–08, 39 fellowships with partial tuition reimbursements (averaging $6,000 per year), 17 research assistantships with full and partial tuition reimbursements (averaging $10,500 per year), 7 teaching assistantships with full tuition reimbursements (averaging $8,000 per year) were awarded; career-related internships or fieldwork, Federal Work-Study, institutionally sponsored loans, and tuition waivers (full and partial) also available. Support available to part-time students. Financial award application deadline: 2/1. *Faculty research:* Staffing, training, and development; compensation and benefits; organization theory; collective bargaining. Total annual research expenditures: $200,000. *Unit head:* John Budd, Director of Graduate Studies, 612-624-0357, Fax: 612-624-8360, E-mail: jbudd@umn.edu. *Application contact:* Celeste Pape, Admissions Coordinator, 612-624-5704, Fax: 612-624-8360, E-mail: cpape@umn.edu.

University of New Haven, Graduate School, School of Business, Program in Industrial Relations, West Haven, CT 06516-1916. Offers MS. *Students:* 19 full-time (11 women), 17 part-time (9 women); includes 9 minority (7 African Americans, 2 Hispanic Americans), 3 international. In 2007, 9 degrees awarded. *Degree requirements:* For master's, thesis or alternative. *Application deadline:* Applications are processed on a rolling basis. Application fee: $50. *Expenses:* Tuition: Part-time $630 per credit. Required fees: $40 per term. *Financial support:* Federal Work-Study available. Support available to part-time students. Financial award application deadline: 5/1; financial award applicants required to submit FAFSA. *Unit head:* Charles Coleman, Coordinator, 203-932-7375.

University of New Haven, Graduate School, School of Business, Program in Public Administration, West Haven, CT 06516-1916. Offers health care management (MPA); personnel and labor relations (MPA); MBA/MPA. Part-time and evening/weekend programs available. *Students:* 30 full-time (20 women), 24 part-time (16 women); includes 3 minority (1 African American, 1 Asian American or Pacific Islander, 1 Hispanic American), 1 international. 28 applicants, 36% accepted, 8 enrolled. In 2007, 13 degrees awarded. *Degree requirements:* For master's, thesis or alternative. *Application deadline:* Applications are processed on a rolling basis. Application fee: $60. *Expenses:* Tuition: Part-time $630 per credit. Required fees: $40 per term. *Financial support:* Federal Work-Study available. Support available to part-time students. Financial award application deadline: 5/1; financial award applicants required to submit FAFSA. *Unit head:* Charles Coleman, Chairman, 203-932-7375.

University of North Texas, Robert B. Toulouse School of Graduate Studies, College of Arts and Sciences, Department of Economics, Denton, TX 76203. Offers economic research (MS); economics (MA, MS); labor and industrial relations (MS). Part-time programs available. *Faculty:* 16 full-time (7 women). *Students:* 32 full-time (11 women), 11 part-time (3 women); includes 6 minority (2 African Americans, 1 Asian American or Pacific Islander, 3 Hispanic Americans), 19 international. Average age 28. 26 applicants, 73% accepted, 9 enrolled. In 2007, 4 degrees awarded. *Degree requirements:* For master's, comprehensive exam, thesis (for some programs). *Entrance requirements:* For master's, GMAT, GRE General Test, 3.0 GPA, 2 letters of recommendation, 500 word essay. Additional exam requirements/recommendations for international students: Required—proof of English language proficiency required for non-native English speakers; Recommended—TOEFL (minimum score 550 paper-based; 213 computer-based). *Application deadline:* For fall admission, 7/15 for domestic students; for spring admission, 11/15 for domestic students. Application fee: $50 ($75 for international students). *Financial support:* In 2007–08, 3 fellowships with partial tuition reimbursements (averaging $10,740 per year), 9 research assistantships with partial tuition reimbursements (averaging $9,060 per year), 5 teaching assistantships with partial tuition reimbursements (averaging $9,060 per year) were awarded; career-related internships or fieldwork, Federal Work-Study, and institutionally sponsored loans also available. Support available to part-time students. Financial award application deadline: 4/1. *Faculty research:* Resource economics, international trade and development, immigration, telecommunications, micro enterprise development. Total annual research expenditures: $150,000. *Unit head:* Dr. Steven L. Cobb, Chair, 940-565-2573, Fax: 940-565-4426, E-mail: cobb@econ.unt.edu. *Application contact:* Dr. Margie A. Tieslau, Graduate Adviser, 940-565-3442, Fax: 940-565-4426, E-mail: tieslau@unt.edu.

University of Rhode Island, Graduate School, Labor Research Center, Kingston, RI 02881. Offers labor relations and human resources (MS). Part-time and evening/weekend programs available. *Students:* Average age 32. In 2007, 4 degrees awarded. *Degree requirements:* For master's, core exams. *Entrance requirements:* For master's, GMAT, GRE, or MAT. *Application deadline:* For fall admission, 4/15 priority date for domestic students; for spring admission, 11/15 for domestic students. Applications are processed on a rolling basis. Application fee: $35. *Expenses:* Tuition, state resident: full-time $6,936; part-time $385 per credit. Tuition, nonresident: full-time $19,044; part-time $1,058 per credit. Required fees: $1,508; $48 per credit. $30 per semester. One-time fee: $80 part-time. *Financial support:* Fellowships, research assistantships, teaching assistantships, career-related internships or fieldwork, Federal Work-Study, institutionally sponsored loans, and tuition waivers (full and partial) available. Support available to part-time students. *Unit head:* Dr. Richard Scholl, Director, 401-874-4347.

University of Saskatchewan, College of Graduate Studies and Research, Edwards School of Business, Department of Industrial Relations and Organizational Behavior, Saskatoon, SK S7N 5A2, Canada. Offers M Sc. Part-time programs available. *Degree requirements:* For master's, thesis. *Entrance requirements:* For master's, GMAT. Additional exam requirements/recommendations for international students: Required—TOEFL.

University of Toronto, School of Graduate Studies, Social Sciences Division, Centre for Industrial Relations and Human Resources, Toronto, ON M5S 1A1, Canada. Offers MHRIR, PhD. Part-time programs available. *Faculty:* 22 full-time, 16 part-time/adjunct. *Students:* 89 full-time (64 women), 34 part-time, 5 international. 212 applicants, 36% accepted. In 2007, 1 master's, 1 doctorate awarded. *Degree requirements:* For doctorate, thesis/dissertation. *Entrance requirements:* For master's, GRE or GMAT (for applicants who completed degree outside of Canada), minimum B+ in final 2 years of bachelor's degree completion, 2 letters of reference, resumé; for doctorate, GRE or GMAT, MIR degree or equivalent, minimum B+ average, 3 letters of reference, resumé. Additional exam requirements/recommendations for international students: Required—TOEFL (minimum score 600 paper-based; 250 computer-based), TWE (minimum score 5), MELAB, IELTS, or COPE. *Application deadline:* For fall admission, 2/1 priority date for domestic students. Application fee: $100 Canadian dollars. *Expenses:* Contact institution. *Financial support:* Fellowships available. *Unit head:* Prof. Frank J. Reid, Director, 416-978-5693, Fax: 416-978-5696. *Application contact:* Anna Sousa, Graduate Administrator, 416-978-3181, Fax: 416-978-3305, E-mail: cir.info@utoronto.ca.

University of Wisconsin–Madison, Graduate School, College of Letters and Science, Industrial Relations Research Institute, Madison, WI 53706-1380. Offers MA, MS, PhD. Part-time programs available. *Degree requirements:* For master's, thesis or alternative; for doctorate, variable foreign language requirement, thesis/dissertation. *Entrance requirements:* For master's, GRE General Test, GRE writing assessment, minimum GPA of 3.0, 1 course each in economics and statistics; for doctorate, GRE General Test, GRE writing assessment, master's degree in related field. Electronic applications accepted. *Faculty research:* Comparative industrial relations, unions and economic competitiveness, dispute resolution in the public sector, merit pay practices.

University of Wisconsin–Milwaukee, Graduate School, College of Letters and Sciences, Interdepartmental Program in Human Resources and Labor Relations, Milwaukee, WI 53201-0413. Offers MHRLR, Certificate. Part-time programs available. *Faculty:* 17 full-time (7 women). *Students:* 14 full-time (10 women), 37 part-time (31 women); includes 8 minority (5 African Americans, 1 Asian American or Pacific Islander, 2 Hispanic Americans), 2 international. 47 applicants, 57% accepted, 11 enrolled. In 2007, 15 degrees awarded. *Entrance requirements:* For master's, GMAT or GRE General Test. *Application deadline:* For fall admission, 1/1 priority date for domestic students; for spring admission, 9/1 for domestic students. Applications are processed on a rolling basis. Application fee: $45 ($75 for international students). *Expenses:* Tuition, state resident: part-time $530 per credit. Tuition, nonresident: part-time $1,428 per credit. Required fees: $19 per credit. $229 per term. Tuition and fees vary according to course load and program. *Financial support:* Fellowships, research assistantships, teaching assistantships, career-related internships or fieldwork available. Support available to part-time students.

Financial award application deadline: 4/15. *Unit head:* Susan M. Donohue-Davies, Representative, 414-299-4009, Fax: 414-229-5915, E-mail: suedono@uwm.edu.

Wayne State University, College of Liberal Arts and Sciences, Interdisciplinary Program in Industrial Relations, Detroit, MI 48202. Offers MAIR. Part-time and evening/weekend programs available. *Students:* 3 full-time (1 woman), 28 part-time (17 women); includes 16 minority (14 African Americans, 2 Hispanic Americans), 1 international. Average age 33. 23 applicants, 70% accepted, 5 enrolled. In 2007, 13 degrees awarded. *Degree requirements:* For master's, thesis optional. *Entrance requirements:* For master's, GMAT, GRE General Test. Additional exam requirements/recommendations for international students: Required—TOEFL (minimum score 550 paper-based; 213 computer-based); Recommended—TWE (minimum score 6). *Application deadline:* For fall admission, 7/1 for domestic students, 6/1 for international students; for winter admission, 10/1 for international students; for spring admission, 2/1 for international students. Applications are processed on a rolling basis. Application fee: $30 ($50 for international students). Electronic applications accepted. *Expenses:* Tuition, state resident: part-time $403 per credit hour. Tuition, nonresident: part-time $890 per credit hour. *Financial support:* In 2007–08, 2 students received support. Career-related internships or fieldwork, institutionally sponsored loans, and scholarships/grants available. Support available to part-time students. *Faculty research:* Two-tier wage system, affirmative action practices in higher education; employment relations in China. *Unit head:* Dr. Hal Stack, Academic Director, 313-577-8828, Fax: 313-577-9969, E-mail: h.stack@wayne.edu.

West Virginia University, College of Business and Economics, Program in Industrial Relations, Morgantown, WV 26506. Offers MSIR. *Accreditation:* AACSB. *Students:* 43 full-time (25 women), 1 (woman) part-time; includes 6 minority (3 African Americans, 1 American Indian/Alaska Native, 1 Asian American or Pacific Islander, 1 Hispanic American), 2 international. Average age 24. 80 applicants, 66% accepted, 39 enrolled. In 2007, 43 degrees awarded. *Entrance requirements:* For master's, GRE or GMAT, GPA 3.0 or better. Additional exam requirements/recommendations for international students: Required—TOEFL. *Application deadline:* For fall admission, 3/1 for domestic students. Applications are processed on a rolling basis. Application fee: $50. Electronic applications accepted. *Expenses:* Tuition, state resident: full-time $5,196; part-time $292 per credit hour. Tuition, nonresident: full-time $15,064; part-time $840 per credit hour. Tuition and fees vary according to program. *Financial support:* In 2007–08, 32 students received support, including 2 research assistantships, 1 teaching assistantship; fellowships, career-related internships or fieldwork, institutionally sponsored loans, scholarships/grants, tuition waivers (full and partial), unspecified assistantships, and graduate administrative assistantships also available. Financial award application deadline: 3/1. *Faculty research:* Labor relations, mediation, leadership, benefits. *Unit head:* Dr. Jeff Houghton, Director, 304-293-7933, Fax: 304-293-2385, E-mail: jeff.houghton@mail.wvu.edu. *Application contact:* Bonnie Anderson, Associate Director, 304-293-7812, Fax: 304-293-2385, E-mail: bonnie.anderson@mail.wvu.edu.

Philanthropic Studies

Indiana University–Purdue University Indianapolis, School of Liberal Arts, Center on Philanthropy, Indianapolis, IN 46202. Offers philanthropic studies (MA, PhD); MA/MA; MPA/MA; MSN/MA. Part-time and evening/weekend programs available. Postbaccalaureate distance learning degree programs offered (minimal on-campus study). In 2007, 28 degrees awarded. *Degree requirements:* For master's, thesis optional. *Entrance requirements:* For master's, GRE General Test or equivalent, minimum undergraduate GPA of 3.0. Application fee: $50 ($60 for international students). *Expenses:* Tuition, state resident: full-time $5,818; part-time $242 per credit hour. Tuition, nonresident: full-time $17,106; part-time $713 per credit hour. Required fees: $629. Tuition and fees vary according to course load, campus/location and program. *Financial support:* Fellowships with full and partial tuition reimbursements, research assistantships with full and partial tuition reimbursements, career-related internships or fieldwork, Federal Work-Study, institutionally sponsored loans, and scholarships/grants available. Financial award applicants required to submit FAFSA. *Unit head:* Dr. Eugene Tempel, Executive Director, 317-274-4200. *Application contact:* Marsha Currin-McGriff, Director of Student Services, 317-278-8927, E-mail: mcurrin@iupui.edu.

Indiana University–Purdue University Indianapolis, School of Liberal Arts, Department of Philanthropic Studies, Indianapolis, IN 46202. Offers MA, XMA, PhD. *Faculty:* 52 full-time, 10 part-time/adjunct. *Students:* 25 full-time (21 women), 49 part-time (37 women); includes 17 minority (9 African Americans, 1 American Indian/Alaska Native, 6 Asian Americans or Pacific Islanders, 1 Hispanic American), 6 international. Average age 33. *Degree requirements:* For master's, thesis optional; for doctorate, thesis/dissertation. *Entrance requirements:* For master's, GRE General Test (minimum score: 500 quantitative, 500 verbal, 4.5 analytical writing), 3.0 undergraduate GPA; for doctorate, GRE General Test (minimum score: 500 quantitative, 500 verbal, 4.5 analytical writing), 3.0 GPA, master's. *Application deadline:* For fall admission, 1/15 for domestic students, 1/1 for international students. Application fee: $50 ($60 for international students). *Expenses:* Tuition, state resident: full-time $5,818; part-time $242 per credit hour. Tuition, nonresident: full-time $17,106; part-time $713 per credit hour. Required fees: $629. Tuition and fees vary according to course load, campus/location and program. *Financial support:* In 2007–08, 1 fellowship with partial tuition reimbursement (averaging $16,500 per year), 3 teaching assistantships (averaging $5,567 per year) were awarded; research assistantships with partial tuition reimbursements, career-related internships or fieldwork, Federal Work-Study, institutionally sponsored loans, and scholarships/grants also available. Financial award application deadline: 3/1; financial award applicants required to submit FAFSA. *Application contact:* Student Services, 317-274-4200, E-mail: maphil@iupui.edu.

Saint Mary's University of Minnesota, Schools of Graduate and Professional Programs, Graduate School of Business and Technology, Philanthropy and Development Program, Winona, MN 55987-1399. Offers MA. *Unit head:* Dr. Gary Kelsey, Director, 651-275-0206, E-mail: gkelsey@smumn.edu. *Application contact:* Jami Spitzer, Information Contact, 507-457-7500, E-mail: jspitzer@smumn.edu.

Public Administration

Adelphi University, Graduate School of Arts and Sciences, Department of Emergency Management, Garden City, NY 11530-0701. Offers Certificate. Part-time and evening/weekend programs available. *Students:* Average age 47. *Application deadline:* For fall admission, 5/1 for international students; for spring admission, 12/1 for international students. Applications are processed on a rolling basis. Application fee: $50. Electronic applications accepted. *Financial support:* Research assistantships with partial tuition reimbursements, Federal Work-Study and institutionally sponsored loans available. *Faculty research:* Emergency nursing, disaster management, disaster preparedness. *Unit head:* Dr. John Vetter, Chairperson, 516-877-4110, E-mail: vetter@adelphi.edu. *Application contact:* Christine Murphy, Director of Admissions, 516-877-3050, Fax: 516-877-3039, E-mail: graduateadmissions@adelphi.edu.

Albany State University, College of Arts and Sciences, Department of History, Political Science and Public Administration, Albany, GA 31705-2717. Offers community and economic development (MPA); criminal justice (MPA); fiscal management (MPA); general management (MPA); health administration and policy (MPA); human resources management (MPA); public policy (MPA); water resource management and policy (MPA). *Accreditation:* NASPAA. Part-time programs available. *Degree requirements:* For master's, comprehensive exam, thesis. *Entrance requirements:* For master's, GRE General Test, minimum GPA of 2.5. Electronic applications accepted. *Faculty research:* Transportation, urban affairs, political economy.

American International College, School of Business Administration, Program in Public Administration, Springfield, MA 01109-3189. Offers MPA. Part-time and evening/weekend programs available. *Faculty:* 1 full-time (0 women), 4 part-time/adjunct (2 women). *Students:* 6 full-time (4 women), 5 part-time (1 woman). Average age 36. In 2007, 10 degrees awarded. *Degree requirements:* For master's, comprehensive exam (for some programs), thesis (for some programs), oral exam, practicum. *Entrance requirements:* For master's, BS or BA . Additional exam requirements/recommendations for international students: Required—TOEFL. *Application deadline:* For fall admission, 7/1 priority date for domestic and international students; for spring admission, 12/1 priority date for domestic and international students. Applications are processed on a rolling basis. Application fee: $50. Electronic applications accepted. *Expenses:* Tuition: Part-time $615 per credit hour. Full-time tuition and fees vary according to degree level, campus/location and program. *Financial support:* In 2007–08, 3 students received support. Career-related internships or fieldwork available. Support available to part-time students. Financial award applicants required to submit FAFSA. *Application contact:* Barbara Z. Benoit, Director of Graduate Admissions, 413-205-3700, Fax: 413-205-3051, E-mail: barbara.benoit@aic.edu.

American Public University System, AMU/APU Graduate Programs, Charles Town, WV 25414. Offers air warfare (MA Military Studies); American Revolution (MA Military Studies); business administration (MBA); Civil War (MA Military Studies); criminal justice (MA); defense management (MA Military Studies); emergency and disaster management (MA); environmental policy and management (MS); fire science management (MA); global engagement (MA); history (MA); homeland security (MA); humanities (MA); intelligence (MA Military Studies, MA Strategic Intelligence); international peace and conflict resolution (MA); international relations and conflict resolution (MA); joint warfare (MA Military Studies); land warfare international perspective (MA Military Studies); management (MA); military history (MA); military leadership (MA Military Studies); national security studies (MA); naval warfare international (MA Military Studies); naval warfare US (MA Military Studies); political science (MA); public administration (MA); public health (MA); security management (MA); space studies (MS); special ops/LIC (MA Military Studies); sports management (MA); transportation and logistics management (MA); transportation management (MA); unconventional warfare (MA Military Studies); World War II (MA Military Studies). Programs offered via distance learning only. Part-time and evening/weekend programs available. Postbaccalaureate distance learning degree programs offered (no on-campus study). *Faculty:* 10 full-time (3 women), 188 part-time/adjunct (57 women). *Students:* 340 full-time (98 women), 3,567 part-time (790 women); includes 615 minority (317 African Americans, 28 American Indian/Alaska Native, 85 Asian Americans or Pacific Islanders, 185 Hispanic Americans), 20 international. Average age 36. 2,123 applicants, 100% accepted, 893 enrolled. In 2007, 829 degrees awarded. *Degree requirements:* For master's, comprehensive exam. *Entrance requirements:* For master's, bachelor's degree or equivalent, minimum GPA of 2.7 in last 60 hours of course work. *Application deadline:* Applications are processed on a rolling basis. Application fee: $0. Electronic applications accepted. *Expenses:* Tuition: Part-time $275 per semester hour. *Financial support:* Applicants required to submit FAFSA. *Faculty research:* Military history, criminal justice, management performance, national security. *Unit head:* Dr. Frank McCluskey, Provost, 877-468-6268, Fax: 304-724-3780. *Application contact:* Terry Grant, Director of Enrollment Management, 877-468-6268, Fax: 304-724-3780, E-mail: info@apus.edu.

American University, School of Public Affairs, Department of Public Administration, Program in Public Administration, Washington, DC 20016-8001. Offers MPA, PhD, Certificate. *Accreditation:* NASPAA (one or more programs are accredited). Part-time and evening/weekend programs available. *Students:* 80 full-time (55 women), 124 part-time (76 women); includes 45 minority (30 African Americans, 2 American Indian/Alaska Native, 6 Asian Americans or Pacific Islanders, 7 Hispanic Americans), 24 international. Average age 31. In 2007, 84 master's, 4 doctorates awarded. *Degree requirements:* For master's, comprehensive exam; for doctorate, comprehensive exam, thesis/dissertation. *Entrance requirements:* For master's, GRE General Test, statement of purpose; 2 recommendations; for doctorate, GRE General Test, statement of purpose; 3 recommendations; for Certificate, Bachelor's Degree. *Application deadline:* For fall admission, 2/1 for domestic students; for spring admission, 11/1 for domestic students. Application fee: $50. *Expenses:* Tuition: Full-time $19,998; part-time $1,111 per credit hour. Required fees: $380. Tuition and fees vary according to program. *Financial support:* Fellowships, teaching assistantships, career-related internships or fieldwork, Federal Work-Study, and institutionally sponsored loans available. Financial award application deadline: 2/1.

American University of Beirut, Graduate Programs, Faculty of Arts and Sciences, Beirut, Lebanon. Offers anthropology (MA); Arabic language and literature (MA); archaeology (MA); biology (MS); chemistry (MS); computer science (MS); economics (MA); education (MA); English language (MA); English literature (MA); environmental policy planning (MSES); financial economics (MAFE); geology (MS); history (MA); mathematics (MA, MS); Middle Eastern studies (MA); philosophy (MA); physics (MS); political studies (MA); psychology (MA); public administration (MA); sociology (MA); statistics (MA, MS). Part-time programs available. *Faculty:* 108 full-time (29 women), 5 part-time/adjunct (3 women). *Students:* 134 full-time (92 women), 228 part-time (167 women). Average age 25. 319 applicants, 67% accepted, 91 enrolled. In 2007, 144 degrees awarded. *Degree requirements:* For master's, one foreign language, comprehensive exam, thesis (for some programs). *Entrance requirements:* For master's, GRE, letter of recommendation. Additional exam requirements/recommendations for international students: Required—TOEFL (minimum score 600 paper-based; 250 computer-based; 100 iBT), IELTS (minimum score 8). *Application deadline:* For fall admission, 4/30 for

Public Administration

American University of Beirut (continued)
domestic and international students; for spring admission, 11/1 for domestic and international students. Application fee: $50. *Expenses:* Tuition: Full-time $9,954; part-time $553 per credit. Tuition and fees vary according to course load and program. *Financial support:* In 2007–08, 28 students received support. Career-related internships or fieldwork, institutionally sponsored loans, scholarships/grants, health care benefits, and unspecified assistantships available. Financial award application deadline: 2/4; financial award applicants required to submit FAFSA. *Faculty research:* String theory and supergravity; computer graphics; algebra and number theory; popular Arabic literature; marine and freshwater biology; integrating science, math and technology. Total annual research expenditures: $132,270. *Unit head:* Khalil Bitar, Dean, 961-1374374 Ext. 3800, Fax: 961-1744461, E-mail: kmb@aub.edu.lb. *Application contact:* Dr. Salim Kanaan, Director, Admissions Office, 961-1350000 Ext. 2594, Fax: 961-1750775, E-mail: sk00@aub.edu.lb.

The American University of Paris, Graduate Programs, Paris, France. Offers finance (MSF); global communications (MAGC); international affairs, conflict resolution and civil society development (MA); Middle Eastern and Islamic studies (MA); public administration (MPA). *Degree requirements:* For master's, thesis. *Entrance requirements:* For master's, minimum undergraduate GPA of 3.0.

Andrew Jackson University, Jeffrey D. Rubenstein College of Criminal Justice, Program in Public Administration, Birmingham, AL 35244. Offers MPA. Part-time and evening/weekend programs available. Postbaccalaureate distance learning degree programs offered (no on-campus study). *Faculty:* 10 part-time/adjunct (0 women). In 2007, 4 degrees awarded. *Entrance requirements:* For master's, course work in calculus, statistics. Additional exam requirements/recommendations for international students: Required—TOEFL (minimum score 550 paper-based; 213 computer-based). *Application deadline:* Applications are processed on a rolling basis. Application fee: $75. Electronic applications accepted. *Financial support:* Scholarships/grants available. *Application contact:* Tammy Kassner, Senior Admissions Coordinator, 205-271-9288 Ext. 107, Fax: 205-871-9294, E-mail: tkassner@aju.edu.

Angelo State University, College of Graduate Studies, College of Liberal and Fine Arts, Department of Government, San Angelo, TX 76909. Offers public administration (MPA). Part-time and evening/weekend programs available. *Faculty:* 3 full-time (0 women). *Students:* 1 (woman) full-time, 8 part-time (3 women); includes 2 African Americans, 2 Hispanic Americans. Average age 30. 9 applicants, 78% accepted, 6 enrolled. In 2007, 6 degrees awarded. *Degree requirements:* For master's, comprehensive exam. *Entrance requirements:* For master's, GRE General Test. Additional exam requirements/recommendations for international students: Required—TOEFL or IELTS. *Application deadline:* For fall admission, 7/15 priority date for domestic students, 6/10 for international students; for spring admission, 12/8 for domestic students, 11/1 for international students. Applications are processed on a rolling basis. Application fee: $40 ($50 for international students). Electronic applications accepted. *Financial support:* In 2007–08, 7 students received support. Career-related internships or fieldwork, Federal Work-Study, and scholarships/grants available. Support available to part-time students. Financial award application deadline: 3/1; financial award applicants required to submit FAFSA. *Unit head:* Dr. Edward C. Olson, Department Head, 325-942-2262 Ext. 275, E-mail: ed.olson@angelo.edu. *Application contact:* Dr. Jack Barbour, Graduate Advisor, 325-942-2262 Ext. 282, E-mail: jack.barbour@angelo.edu.

Appalachian State University, Cratis D. Williams Graduate School, Department of Government and Justice Studies, Boone, NC 28608. Offers criminal justice (MS); political science (MA); public administration (MPA). Part-time programs available. *Faculty:* 26 full-time (5 women). *Students:* 51 full-time (20 women), 71 part-time (30 women); includes 11 minority (8 African Americans, 1 American Indian/Alaska Native, 2 Asian Americans or Pacific Islanders), 4 international. 77 applicants, 77% accepted, 47 enrolled. In 2007, 45 degrees awarded. *Degree requirements:* For master's, variable foreign language requirement, comprehensive exam, thesis optional. *Entrance requirements:* For master's, GRE General Test. Additional exam requirements/recommendations for international students: Required—TOEFL (minimum score 570 paper-based; 230 computer-based; 79 iBT), IELTS (minimum score 7), TOEFL or IELTS. *Application deadline:* For fall admission, 7/1 for domestic students, 1/1 for international students; for spring admission, 11/1 for domestic students, 6/1 for international students. Applications are processed on a rolling basis. Application fee: $50. Electronic applications accepted. *Expenses:* Tuition, state resident: part-time $127 per semester hour. Tuition, nonresident: part-time $597 per semester hour. Required fees: $18 per semester. *Financial support:* In 2007–08, 35 research assistantships (averaging $7,000 per year) were awarded; fellowships, teaching assistantships, career-related internships or fieldwork, Federal Work-Study, scholarships/grants, and unspecified assistantships also available. Financial award application deadline: 4/1. *Faculty research:* Campaign finance, emerging democracies, bureaucratic politics, judicial behavior, administration of justice. Total annual research expenditures: $43,054. *Unit head:* Dr. Brian Ellison, Chairperson, 828-262-3085, E-mail: ellisonba@appstate.edu.

Argosy University, Orange County, College of Business, Santa Ana, CA 92704. Offers accounting (DBA, Adv C); customized professional concentration (MBA, DBA); finance (MBA, Certificate); healthcare administration (MBA); information systems (DBA, Adv C); information systems management (MBA); international business (MBA, DBA, Adv C, Certificate); management (MBA, MSM, DBA, Adv C); marketing (MBA, DBA, Adv C, Certificate); public administration (MBA, Certificate).

Argosy University, Tampa, College of Business, Tampa, FL 33614. Offers accounting (DBA); customized professional concentration (MBA, DBA); finance (MBA); healthcare administration (MBA); information systems (DBA); information systems management (MBA); international business (MBA, DBA); management (MBA, MSM, DBA); marketing (MBA, DBA); public administration (MBA).

Arkansas State University, Graduate School, College of Humanities and Social Sciences, Department of Political Science, Jonesboro, State University, AR 72467. Offers political science (MA); political science education (SCCT); public administration (MPA). *Accreditation:* NASPAA (one or more programs are accredited). Part-time programs available. *Faculty:* 8 full-time (3 women), 1 (woman) part-time/adjunct. *Students:* 25 full-time (11 women), 21 part-time (14 women); includes 9 minority (all African Americans), 3 international. Average age 30. 22 applicants, 91% accepted, 17 enrolled. In 2007, 15 degrees awarded. *Degree requirements:* For master's, comprehensive exam, thesis or alternative; for SCCT, comprehensive exam. *Entrance requirements:* For master's, GRE General Test or MAT, GMAT, appropriate bachelor's degree, letters of reference, official transcript; for SCCT, GRE General Test or MAT, GMAT, interview, master's degree, official transcript. Additional exam requirements/recommendations for international students: Required—TOEFL (minimum score 213 computer-based). *Application deadline:* Applications are processed on a rolling basis. Application fee: $30 ($40 for international students). Electronic applications accepted. *Expenses:* Tuition, state resident: full-time $3,528; part-time $196 per hour. Tuition, nonresident: full-time $8,928; part-time $496 per hour. Required fees: $842; $44 per hour. $25 per term. Tuition and fees vary according to course load and program. *Financial support:* Teaching assistantships, career-related internships or fieldwork, scholarships/grants, and unspecified assistantships available. Financial award application deadline: 7/1; financial award applicants required to submit FAFSA. *Faculty research:* Peace Corps, political communication, political psychology, public opinion, elections. *Unit head:* Dr. Richard Wang, Chair, 870-972-3048, Fax: 870-972-2720, E-mail: rwang@astate.edu.

Auburn University, Graduate School, College of Liberal Arts, Department of Political Science, Program in Public Administration, Auburn University, AL 36849. Offers MPA, PhD, MPA/MCP. *Accreditation:* NASPAA (one or more programs are accredited). Part-time programs available. *Faculty:* 15 full-time (4 women). *Students:* 24 full-time (9 women), 36 part-time (22 women); includes 18 minority (16 African Americans, 2 Hispanic Americans), 2 international. Average age 35. 69 applicants, 54% accepted, 18 enrolled. In 2007, 19 master's, 5 doctorates awarded. *Degree requirements:* For master's, internship or research project; for doctorate, thesis/dissertation. *Entrance requirements:* For master's, GRE General Test, sample of written work; for doctorate, GRE General Test. *Application deadline:* For fall admission, 7/7 for domestic students; for spring admission, 11/24 for domestic students. Applications are processed on a rolling basis. Application fee: $25 ($50 for international students). Electronic applications accepted. *Financial support:* Fellowships, research assistantships, teaching assistantships, career-related internships or fieldwork and Federal Work-Study available. Support available to part-time students. Financial award application deadline: 3/15. *Faculty research:* Privatization studies, policy evolution, water resources, election administration. *Unit head:* Dr. Caleb Clark, Head, 334-844-5371. *Application contact:* Dr. Joe Pittman, Interim Dean of the Graduate School, 334-844-4700.

Announcement: A unique 2-track PhD in public administration and public policy. Common core; electives; policy track: (3 of 5) comparative, American, international, law and policy, theory and policy; and/or administration track: organization theory, budgeting, human resource management. Graduates successfully placed in academic and public sector positions. Master's-level degree required. Web site: http://www.auburn.edu/academic/liberal_arts/poli_sci.

Auburn University Montgomery, School of Sciences, Department of Public Administration and Political Science, Montgomery, AL 36124-4023. Offers MPA, MPS, PhD. *Accreditation:* NASPAA (one or more programs are accredited). Part-time and evening/weekend programs available. *Faculty:* 4 full-time (0 women), 4 part-time/adjunct (1 woman). *Students:* 20 full-time (8 women), 90 part-time (54 women); includes 42 minority (37 African Americans, 2 Asian Americans or Pacific Islanders, 3 Hispanic Americans). Average age 34. In 2007, 16 degrees awarded. *Degree requirements:* For master's, comprehensive exam; for doctorate, thesis/dissertation. *Entrance requirements:* For master's, GRE General Test or MAT; for doctorate, GRE General Test. *Application deadline:* Applications are processed on a rolling basis. Application fee: $25. Electronic applications accepted. *Expenses:* Tuition, state resident: full-time $4,536; part-time $189 per credit hour. Tuition, nonresident: full-time $13,608; part-time $567 per credit hour. Required fees: $234. *Financial support:* In 2007–08, 1 research assistantship was awarded; career-related internships or fieldwork and scholarships/grants also available. Support available to part-time students. Financial award application deadline: 3/1; financial award applicants required to submit FAFSA. *Unit head:* Dr. Thomas Vocino, Head, 334-244-3696, Fax: 334-244-3826, E-mail: vocino@mail.aum.edu.

Ball State University, Graduate School, College of Sciences and Humanities, Department of Political Science, Program in Public Administration, Muncie, IN 47306-1099. Offers MPA. *Faculty:* 16. *Students:* 8 full-time (4 women), 16 part-time (6 women); includes 8 minority (7 African Americans, 1 Hispanic American). Average age 28. 15 applicants, 87% accepted, 5 enrolled. In 2007, 6 degrees awarded. *Entrance requirements:* For master's, GRE General Test. Application fee: $25 ($35 for international students). *Expenses:* Tuition, state resident: full-time $6,864. Tuition, nonresident: full-time $17,932. Required fees: $1,866. *Financial support:* Career-related internships or fieldwork available. Financial award application deadline: 3/1. *Faculty research:* Employment training programs, personnel and labor relations, planning. *Unit head:* Dr. Roger Hollands, Director, 765-285-8800, Fax: 765-285-5345.

Barry University, School of Adult and Continuing Education, Program in Public Administration, Miami Shores, FL 33161-6695. Offers MPA. Part-time and evening/weekend programs available. *Entrance requirements:* For master's, GMAT, GRE or MAT, recommendations. *Application deadline:* Applications are processed on a rolling basis. Application fee: $30. Electronic applications accepted. *Financial support:* Applicants required to submit FAFSA. *Unit head:* Dr. Richard Orman, Professor of Public Administration, 561-622-9000, Fax: 561-622-0158, E-mail: rorman@mail.barry.edu. *Application contact:* Dave Fletcher, Director of Graduate Admissions, 305-899-3113, Fax: 305-899-2971, E-mail: dfletcher@mail.barry.edu.

Baylor University, Graduate School, College of Arts and Sciences, Department of Political Science, Waco, TX 76798. Offers international studies (MA); political science (MA, PhD); public policy and administration (MPPA); JD/MPPA. *Students:* 24 full-time (8 women), 3 part-time (2 women); includes 1 minority (Hispanic American), 3 international. In 2007, 11 degrees awarded. *Entrance requirements:* For master's, GRE General Test. *Application deadline:* Applications are processed on a rolling basis. Application fee: $25. *Financial support:* Research assistantships, career-related internships or fieldwork, Federal Work-Study, and institutionally sponsored loans available. Financial award application deadline: 3/1. *Unit head:* Dr. Dwight Allman, Graduate Program Director, 254-710-3161, Fax: 254-710-3122, E-mail: dwight_allman@baylor.edu. *Application contact:* Suzanne Keener, Administrative Assistant, 254-710-3588, Fax: 254-710-3870.

Belhaven College, School of Business, Jackson, MS 39202-1789. Offers business administration (MBA); business management (MSM); public administration (MPA). MBA program also offered in Houston, TX; Memphis, TN; and Orlando, FL. Evening/weekend programs available. *Faculty:* 12 full-time (3 women), 8 part-time/adjunct (1 woman). *Students:* 233 full-time (159 women); includes 132 minority (127 African Americans, 1 Asian American or Pacific Islander, 4 Hispanic Americans). Average age 33. 64 applicants, 94% accepted, 35 enrolled. In 2007, 86 degrees awarded. *Degree requirements:* For master's, comprehensive exam (for some programs). *Entrance requirements:* For master's, GMAT, GRE General Test or MAT, minimum GPA of 2.8. *Application deadline:* Applications are processed on a rolling basis. Application fee: $25. Electronic applications accepted. *Financial support:* In 2007–08, 2 students received support, including 2 research assistantships. Financial award applicants required to submit FAFSA. *Unit head:* Dr. Ralph Mason, Dean, School of Business, 601-968-8949, Fax: 601-968-8951, E-mail: cmason@belhaven.edu. *Application contact:* Dr. Audrey Kelleher, Vice President Adult and Graduate Marketing and Development, 407-804-1424, Fax: 407-620-5210, E-mail: akelleher@belhaven.edu.

Bernard M. Baruch College of the City University of New York, School of Public Affairs, Program in Public Administration, New York, NY 10010-5585. Offers MPA, MS/MPA. *Accreditation:* NASPAA. Part-time and evening/weekend programs available. *Students:* 91 full-time (59 women), 402 part-time (295 women); includes 198 minority (111 African Americans, 27 Asian Americans or Pacific Islanders, 60 Hispanic Americans). Average age 33. 395 applicants, 58% accepted, 175 enrolled. In 2007, 234 degrees awarded. *Degree requirements:* For master's, thesis, capstone. *Entrance requirements:* For master's, GRE General Test. Additional exam requirements/recommendations for international students: Required—TOEFL (minimum score 650 paper-based; 247 computer-based). *Application deadline:* For fall admission, 4/1 priority date for domestic and international students; for spring admission, 11/1 priority date for domestic and international students. Applications are processed on a rolling basis. Application fee: $125. Electronic applications accepted. *Expenses:* Contact institution. *Financial support:* In 2007–08, 34 students received support, including 8 fellowships (averaging $1,500 per year), 26 research assistantships (averaging $12,000 per year); career-related internships or fieldwork, Federal Work-Study, scholarships/grants, tuition waivers (partial), and unspecified assistantships also available. Support available to part-time students. Financial award application deadline: 5/30; financial award applicants required to submit FAFSA. *Faculty research:* Child health, nonprofit administration, health economics, welfare reform, urban population distribution, transnationalism, urban service delivery, community health improvement. Total annual research expenditures: $2.6 million. *Application contact:* Michael J. Lovaglio, Director of Student Affairs and Graduate Admissions, 646-660-6750, Fax: 646-660-6751, E-mail: michael_lovaglio@baruch.cuny.edu.

Birmingham-Southern College, Program in Public and Private Management, Birmingham, AL 35254. Offers MPPM. *Accreditation:* AACSB. Part-time and evening/weekend programs available. *Degree requirements:* For master's, thesis optional. *Entrance requirements:* For master's, GMAT, GRE, or MAT.

Boise State University, Graduate College, College of Social Sciences and Public Affairs, Department of Public Policy and Administration, Boise, ID 83725-0399. Offers environmental and natural resources policy and administration (MPA); general public administration (MPA); state and local government policy and administration (MPA). *Accreditation:* NASPAA. Part-time programs available. *Degree requirements:* For master's, comprehensive exam, directed research project, internship. *Entrance requirements:* For master's, GRE General Test, minimum GPA of 3.0. Additional exam requirements/recommendations for international students: Required—TOEFL. Electronic applications accepted.

Boston University, School of Management, Master of Business Administration Program, Boston, MA 02215. Offers advanced accounting (Certificate); general management (MBA); healthcare management (MBA); public and nonprofit management (MBA); JD/MBA; MBA/MA; MBA/MPH; MBA/MS; MBA/MSIS; MS/MBA. Part-time and evening/weekend programs available. *Faculty:* 69 full-time (9 women), 33 part-time/adjunct (8 women). *Students:* 294 full-time (112 women), 582 part-time (221 women); includes 126 minority (13 African Americans, 2 American Indian/Alaska Native, 91 Asian Americans or Pacific Islanders, 20 Hispanic Americans), 130 international. Average age 27. 1,725 applicants, 43% accepted, 380 enrolled. In 2007, 283 degrees awarded. *Entrance requirements:* For master's, GMAT. *Application deadline:* For fall admission, 5/1 for domestic students. Applications are processed on a rolling basis. Application fee: $125. Electronic applications accepted. *Expenses:* Tuition: Full-time $34,930; part-time $1,092 per credit. Tuition and fees vary according to class time, course level and program. *Financial support:* Career-related internships or fieldwork, Federal Work-Study, institutionally sponsored loans, and tuition waivers (partial) available. Support available to part-time students. Financial award applicants required to submit FAFSA. *Unit head:* Dr. John Chalykoff, Associate Dean, Academic Program, 617-353-4157, Fax: 617-353-5003, E-mail: chalykof@bu.edu. *Application contact:* Hayden Estrada, Assistant Dean, Admissions, 617-353-2670, Fax: 617-353-7368, E-mail: mba@bu.edu.

Bowie State University, Graduate Programs, Program in Public Administration, Bowie, MD 20715-9465. Offers MPA. Part-time and evening/weekend programs available. *Degree requirements:* For master's, comprehensive exam. *Entrance requirements:* For master's, undergraduate GPA 2.5. Electronic applications accepted.

Bowling Green State University, Graduate College, College of Arts and Sciences, Department of Political Science, Program in Public Administration, Bowling Green, OH 43403. Offers MPA. *Students:* 31 full-time (14 women), 5 part-time (3 women); includes 4 minority (1 African American, 3 Hispanic Americans), 14 international. Average age 28. 22 applicants, 77% accepted, 10 enrolled. In 2007, 18 degrees awarded. *Degree requirements:* For master's, comprehensive exam or thesis, experiential paper for all non-thesis students. *Entrance requirements:* For master's, GRE General Test. Additional exam requirements/recommendations for international students: Required—TOEFL. *Application deadline:* For fall admission, 3/1 for domestic students. Application fee: $30. Electronic applications accepted. *Financial support:* In 2007–08, 7 research assistantships with full tuition reimbursements (averaging $7,677 per year), 12 teaching assistantships with full tuition reimbursements (averaging $4,643 per year) were awarded; unspecified assistantships also available. Financial award applicants required to submit FAFSA. *Faculty research:* Public sector labor relations, administrative law, sexual harassment and violence in the public workplace.

Bridgewater State College, School of Graduate Studies, School of Arts and Sciences, Department of Political Science, Program in Public Administration, Bridgewater, MA 02325-0001. Offers MPA. *Entrance requirements:* For master's, GRE General Test. *Application deadline:* For fall admission, 4/1 priority date for domestic students; for spring admission, 10/1 priority date for domestic students. Application fee: $50. *Financial support:* Career-related internships or fieldwork, health care benefits, and unspecified assistantships available. Support available to part-time students. *Application contact:* Dr. Raymond Charles Guillette, Assistant Dean School of Graduate Studies-Enrollment Management, 508-531-2919, Fax: 508-531-6162, E-mail: rguillette@bridgew.edu.

Brigham Young University, Graduate Studies, Marriott School of Management, George W. Romney Institute of Public Management, Program in Public Administration, Provo, UT 84602-1001. Offers MPA, EMPA. *Students:* 111 full-time (46 women), 123 part-time (42 women); includes 23 minority (1 African American, 4 American Indian/Alaska Native, 8 Asian Americans or Pacific Islanders, 10 Hispanic Americans), 17 international. 195 applicants, 75% accepted, 114 enrolled. In 2007, 90 degrees awarded. *Entrance requirements:* For master's, minimum GPA of 3.0. Application fee: $50. *Financial support:* Scholarships/grants available. Support available to part-time students. Financial award application deadline: 4/15; financial award applicants required to submit FAFSA. *Faculty research:* Taxes, budgeting, nonprofit, ethics, decision modeling, work balance, organizational behavior. *Application contact:* Catherine Cooper, Director of Student Services.

Brock University, Faculty of Graduate Studies, Faculty of Social Sciences, Program in Political Science, St. Catharines, ON L2S 3A1, Canada. Offers Canadian politics (MA); international and comparative politics (MA); political philosophy (MA); public administration (MA). Part-time programs available. *Degree requirements:* For master's, thesis optional. *Entrance requirements:* For master's, honors degree. Additional exam requirements/recommendations for international students: Required—TOEFL (minimum score 550 paper-based; 213 computer-based; 80 iBT), IELTS (minimum score 7), TWE (minimum score 4). Electronic applications accepted. *Faculty research:* Public administration reform, economic and social justice, politics of societies, Canadian politics, international relations.

California Baptist University, Program in Public Administration, Riverside, CA 92504-3206. Offers MPA. Part-time programs available. *Faculty:* 4 full-time (1 woman). *Students:* 14 full-time (6 women), 12 part-time (7 women); includes 13 minority (7 African Americans, 6 Hispanic Americans), 2 international. 27 applicants, 56% accepted, 11 enrolled. *Entrance requirements:* Additional exam requirements/recommendations for international students: Required—TOEFL (minimum score 575 paper-based; 230 computer-based), IELTS (minimum score 7). *Application deadline:* For fall admission, 9/1 for domestic students, 7/1 priority date for international students; for spring admission, 1/3 for domestic students, 10/15 priority date for international students. Applications are processed on a rolling basis. Application fee: $45. Electronic applications accepted. *Expenses:* Tuition: Full-time $7,992; part-time $444 per semester hour. Required fees: $510; $125 per semester. *Financial support:* Federal Work-Study available. Support available to part-time students. Financial award applicants required to submit FAFSA. *Unit head:* Dr. Patricia Kircher, Director, 951-343-4306, Fax: 951-343-4661, E-mail: pkircher@calbaptist.edu. *Application contact:* Gail Ronveaux, Dean of Graduate Enrollment, 951-343-5045, Fax: 951-343-5095, E-mail: graduateadmissions@calbaptist.edu.

California Lutheran University, Graduate Studies, Program in Public Policy and Administration, Thousand Oaks, CA 91360-2787. Offers MPPA. *Degree requirements:* For master's, comprehensive exam, thesis or project, internship. *Entrance requirements:* For master's, GMAT or GRE General Test, interview, minimum GPA of 3.0. Expenses: Contact institution.

California State Polytechnic University, Pomona, Academic Affairs, College of Letters, Arts, and Social Sciences, Program in Public Administration, Pomona, CA 91768-2557. Offers MPA. *Accreditation:* NASPAA. *Students:* Average age 27. 47 applicants, 70% accepted, 16 enrolled. In 2007, 10 degrees awarded. *Degree requirements:* For master's, thesis or alternative. *Entrance requirements:* For master's, GRE General Test. *Application deadline:* For fall admission, 5/1 priority date for domestic students; for winter admission, 10/15 priority date for domestic students; for spring admission, 1/20 priority date for domestic students. Applications are processed on a rolling basis. Application fee: $55. Electronic applications accepted. *Expenses:* Tuition, nonresident: full-time $7,232; part-time $226 per unit. Required fees: $3,920. One-time fee: $2,486 part-time. *Unit head:* Dr. Sandra M. Emerson, Director, 909-869-3879, E-mail: smemerson@csupomona.edu.

California State University, Bakersfield, Division of Graduate Studies, School of Business and Public Administration, Program in Public Administration, Bakersfield, CA 93311-1022. Offers MPA. *Accreditation:* NASPAA. *Degree requirements:* For master's, thesis or alternative. *Entrance requirements:* For master's, GRE, minimum GPA of 2.75.

California State University, Chico, Graduate School, College of Behavioral and Social Sciences, Department of Political Science, Program in Public Administration, Chico, CA 95929-0722. Offers health administration (MPA); local government management (MPA); public administration (MPA). *Accreditation:* NASPAA. Part-time programs available. *Students:* 13 full-time (3 women), 27 part-time (16 women); includes 12 minority (2 African Americans, 1 American Indian/Alaska Native, 4 Asian Americans or Pacific Islanders, 5 Hispanic Americans). Average age 32. 40 applicants, 70% accepted, 9 enrolled. In 2007, 5 degrees awarded. *Entrance requirements:* For master's, 2 letters of recommendation, statement of purpose. Additional exam requirements/recommendations for international students: Required—TOEFL (minimum score 550 paper-based; 213 computer-based; 80 iBT), IELTS (minimum score 7). *Application deadline:* For fall admission, 3/1 priority date for domestic students, 3/1 for international students; for spring admission, 9/15 priority date for domestic students, 9/15 for international students. Applications are processed on a rolling basis. Application fee: $55. Electronic applications accepted. *Financial support:* Fellowships, career-related internships or fieldwork available. *Unit head:* Dr. Donna Kemp, Graduate Coordinator, 530-898-5734.

California State University, Dominguez Hills, College of Business Administration and Public Policy, Program in Public Administration, Carson, CA 90747-0001. Offers MPA. *Accreditation:* NASPAA. Part-time and evening/weekend programs available. Postbaccalaureate distance learning degree programs offered (no on-campus study). *Faculty:* 4 full-time (1 woman), 5 part-time/adjunct (1 woman). *Students:* 75 full-time (53 women), 237 part-time (151 women); includes 191 minority (114 African Americans, 2 American Indian/Alaska Native, 26 Asian Americans or Pacific Islanders, 49 Hispanic Americans), 8 international. Average age 36. 278 applicants, 74% accepted, 81 enrolled. In 2007, 74 degrees awarded. *Degree requirements:* For master's, thesis or alternative, capstone project. *Entrance requirements:* For master's, GRE, minimum GPA of 2.75. Additional exam requirements/recommendations for international students: Required—TOEFL (minimum score 550 paper-based; 213 computer-based; 79 iBT). *Application deadline:* For fall admission, 4/1 for domestic and international students; for spring admission, 11/1 for domestic students, 10/1 for international students. Application fee: $55. *Faculty research:* Applied public management. *Unit head:* Dr. Iris Baxter, Coordinator, 310-243-3661, E-mail: lbaxter@csudh.edu. *Application contact:* Eileen Hall, Graduate Advisor, 310-243-3465, E-mail: ehall@csudh.edu.

California State University, East Bay, Academic Programs and Graduate Studies, College of Letters, Arts, and Social Sciences, Department of Public Affairs and Administration, Hayward, CA 94542-3000. Offers health care administration (MS); public administration (MPA). *Accreditation:* NASPAA. Part-time and evening/weekend programs available. *Faculty:* 6 full-time (1 woman), 10 part-time/adjunct (2 women). *Students:* 71 full-time (50 women), 232 part-time (179 women); includes 170 minority (78 African Americans, 64 Asian Americans or Pacific Islanders, 28 Hispanic Americans), 19 international. Average age 34. 127 applicants, 71% accepted, 54 enrolled. In 2007, 103 degrees awarded. *Degree requirements:* For master's, comprehensive exam or thesis. *Entrance requirements:* For master's, minimum GPA of 3.0. Additional exam requirements/recommendations for international students: Required—TOEFL (minimum score 550 paper-based; 213 computer-based). *Application deadline:* For fall admission, 5/31 for domestic students, 4/30 for international students; for winter admission, 9/30 for domestic and international students; for spring admission, 12/31 for domestic students, 11/30 for international students. Applications are processed on a rolling basis. Application fee: $55. Electronic applications accepted. *Expenses:* Required fees: $3,987; $851 per quarter. *Financial support:* Fellowships, teaching assistantships, career-related internships or fieldwork, Federal Work-Study, institutionally sponsored loans, and scholarships/grants available. Support available to part-time students. Financial award application deadline: 3/2. *Unit head:* Dr. Jay Umeh, Head, 510-885-3282, Fax: 510-885-3726. *Application contact:* My Huynh, Graduate Prospect Specialist, 510-885-2989, Fax: 510-885-4059, E-mail: my.huynh@csueastbay.edu.

California State University, Fresno, Division of Graduate Studies, College of Social Sciences, Department of Political Science, Program in Public Administration, Fresno, CA 93740-8027. Offers MPA. *Accreditation:* NASPAA. Part-time and evening/weekend programs available. *Students:* 61; includes 20 minority (3 African Americans, 1 American Indian/Alaska Native, 5 Asian Americans or Pacific Islanders, 11 Hispanic Americans), 5 international. Average age 28. 2 applicants. In 2007, 22 degrees awarded. *Degree requirements:* For master's, thesis or alternative. *Entrance requirements:* For master's, GRE General Test or GMAT, minimum GPA of 3.0. Additional exam requirements/recommendations for international students: Required—TOEFL. *Application deadline:* For fall admission, 5/1 for domestic and international students; for spring admission, 10/1 for domestic and international students. Applications are processed on a rolling basis. Application fee: $55. Electronic applications accepted. *Financial support:* Career-related internships or fieldwork, Federal Work-Study, scholarships/grants, and unspecified assistantships available. Support available to part-time students. Financial award application deadline: 3/1; financial award applicants required to submit FAFSA. *Unit head:* Dr. Kurt Cline, Coordinator, 559-278-2988, Fax: 559-278-5230, E-mail: kcline@csufresno.edu.

California State University, Fullerton, Graduate Studies, College of Humanities and Social Sciences, Division of Politics, Administration, and Justice, Fullerton, CA 92834-9480. Offers political science (MA); public administration (MPA). *Accreditation:* NASPAA (one or more programs are accredited). Part-time programs available. *Students:* 61 full-time (35 women), 158 part-time (79 women); includes 112 minority (10 African Americans, 38 Asian Americans or Pacific Islanders, 64 Hispanic Americans), 7 international. Average age 30. 179 applicants, 78% accepted, 91 enrolled. In 2007, 30 degrees awarded. *Degree requirements:* For master's, comprehensive exam, project or thesis. *Entrance requirements:* For master's, minimum GPA of 2.5 in last 60 units of course work, 12 units of course work in social sciences. Application fee: $55. *Financial support:* Teaching assistantships, career-related internships or fieldwork, Federal Work-Study, institutionally sponsored loans, and scholarships/grants available. Support available to part-time students. Financial award application deadline: 3/1. *Faculty research:* Emergency management plans. *Unit head:* Dr. Phil Gianos, Chair, 714-278-3521.

California State University, Long Beach, Graduate Studies, College of Health and Human Services, Center for Public Policy and Administration, Long Beach, CA 90840. Offers MPA. *Accreditation:* NASPAA. Part-time and evening/weekend programs available. *Faculty:* 5 full-time (1 woman), 12 part-time/adjunct (5 women). *Students:* 52 full-time (33 women), 224 part-time (135 women); includes 179 minority (46 African Americans, 1 American Indian/Alaska Native, 53 Asian Americans or Pacific Islanders, 79 Hispanic Americans). Average age 33. *Degree requirements:* For master's, comprehensive exam. *Entrance requirements:* For master's, minimum GPA of 2.75. *Application deadline:* For fall admission, 7/1 for domestic students; for spring admission, 12/1 for domestic students. Applications are processed on a rolling basis. Application fee: $55. Electronic applications accepted. *Financial support:* Fellowships, career-related internships or fieldwork, Federal Work-Study, institutionally sponsored loans, and scholarships/grants available. Financial award application deadline: 3/2. *Faculty research:* Transportation access, air quality controls, coastal issues, intergovernmental relations. *Unit head:* Dr. Martha J Dede, Director, 562-985-4178, Fax: 562-985-4672, E-mail: mdede@csulb.edu. *Application contact:* Dr. Frank Barber, Graduate Adviser, 562-985-5747, Fax: 562-985-4672.

California State University, Los Angeles, Graduate Studies, College of Natural and Social Sciences, Department of Political Science, Major in Public Administration, Los Angeles, CA 90032-8530. Offers MS. *Accreditation:* NASPAA. Part-time and evening/weekend programs available. *Students:* 5 full-time (4 women), 60 part-time (42 women); includes 40 minority (4 African Americans, 10 Asian Americans or Pacific Islanders, 26 Hispanic Americans), 14 international. Average age 33. In 2007, 23 degrees awarded. *Degree requirements:* For master's, comprehensive exam or thesis. *Entrance requirements:* For master's, minimum GPA of 2.5. Additional exam requirements/recommendations for international students: Required—TOEFL. *Application deadline:* For fall admission, 6/30 for domestic students; for spring admission,

Public Administration

California State University, Los Angeles (continued)

2/1 for domestic students. Applications are processed on a rolling basis. Application fee: $55. *Financial support:* Career-related internships or fieldwork and Federal Work-Study available. Support available to part-time students. Financial award application deadline: 3/1. *Faculty research:* Finance, state and local administration, organization and development. *Unit head:* Dr. Naomi Caiden, Acting Chair, Department of Political Science, 323-343-2230, Fax: 323-343-6452, E-mail: ncaiden@calstatela.edu.

California State University, Northridge, Graduate Studies, The Tseng College of Extended Learning, Northridge, CA 91330. Offers knowledge management (MKM); public administration (MPA); taxation (MS). *Entrance requirements:* For master's, GRE if cumulative undergraduate GPA below 3.0. *Unit head:* Joyce Feucht-Haviar, Dean, 866-873-6439.

California State University, Sacramento, Graduate Studies, College of Social Sciences and Interdisciplinary Studies, Program in Public Policy and Administration, Sacramento, CA 95819-6048. Offers MPPA. Part-time programs available. *Students:* 16 full-time (12 women), 78 part-time (51 women); includes 24 minority (4 African Americans, 1 American Indian/Alaska Native, 6 Asian Americans or Pacific Islanders, 13 Hispanic Americans). Average age 33. 80 applicants, 76% accepted, 45 enrolled. *Degree requirements:* For master's, thesis or alternative, writing proficiency exam. *Entrance requirements:* For master's, GRE General Test. Additional exam requirements/recommendations for international students: Required—TOEFL. *Application deadline:* Applications are processed on a rolling basis. Application fee: $55. Electronic applications accepted. *Expenses:* Tuition, state resident: full-time $3,414. Tuition, nonresident: full-time $13,584; part-time $339 per unit. Required fees: $786; $393 per semester. *Financial support:* Career-related internships or fieldwork and Federal Work-Study available. Support available to part-time students. Financial award application deadline: 3/1. *Unit head:* Dr. Rob Wassmer, Chair, 916-278-557, Fax: 916-278-6544.

California State University, San Bernardino, Graduate Studies, College of Business and Public Administration, Program in Public Administration, San Bernardino, CA 92407-2397. Offers MPA. *Accreditation:* NASPAA. Part-time and evening/weekend programs available. *Faculty:* 6 full-time, 7 part-time/adjunct. *Students:* 59 full-time (36 women), 81 part-time (52 women); includes 74 minority (20 African Americans, 4 American Indian/Alaska Native, 7 Asian Americans or Pacific Islanders, 43 Hispanic Americans), 2 international. Average age 33. 106 applicants, 78% accepted, 54 enrolled. In 2007, 46 degrees awarded. *Application deadline:* For fall admission, 8/31 priority date for domestic students. Applications are processed on a rolling basis. Application fee: $55. *Financial support:* Career-related internships or fieldwork, Federal Work-Study, and institutionally sponsored loans available. Support available to part-time students. Financial award application deadline: 3/1. *Unit head:* Dr. Montgomery Vanwart, Director, 909-537-5759, Fax: 909-537-7517, E-mail: dbellis@csusb.edu.

California State University, Stanislaus, College of Humanities and Social Sciences, Department of Politics and Public Administration, Turlock, CA 95382. Offers public administration (MPA). *Accreditation:* NASPAA. Part-time and evening/weekend programs available. *Students:* 13 full-time (8 women), 76 part-time (39 women); includes 37 minority (2 African Americans, 2 American Indian/Alaska Native, 9 Asian Americans or Pacific Islanders, 24 Hispanic Americans). Average age 32. 31 applicants, 100% accepted, 27 enrolled. In 2007, 13 degrees awarded. *Degree requirements:* For master's, comprehensive exam, thesis or alternative. *Entrance requirements:* For master's, minimum GPA of 2.7, 3 letters of reference, personal statement. Additional exam requirements/recommendations for international students: Required—TOEFL (minimum score 550 paper-based; 213 computer-based), ELPT (minimum score: 954). *Application deadline:* For fall admission, 6/30 for domestic students; for winter admission, 11/30 for domestic students; for spring admission, 11/30 for domestic students. Application fee: $55. Electronic applications accepted. *Expenses:* Tuition, nonresident: full-time $10,170; part-time $339 per unit. Required fees: $3,972; $2,538 per term. $1,165 per semester. *Financial support:* Fellowships, career-related internships or fieldwork and Federal Work-Study available. Financial award application deadline: 3/2; financial award applicants required to submit FAFSA. *Faculty research:* Blogging in the Middle East, incumbency and electoral competitiveness, legislative acceptance of gubernatorial budget proposals. *Application contact:* Dr. Jason C. Myers, Chair, 209-667-3388, Fax: 209-667-3724, E-mail: lriddell@csustan.edu.

Carleton University, Faculty of Graduate Studies, Faculty of Public Affairs and Management, School of Public Policy and Administration, Ottawa, ON K1S 5B6, Canada. Offers public administration (MA, DPA); public policy (PhD). Part-time programs available. *Degree requirements:* For master's, thesis optional; for doctorate, one foreign language, comprehensive exam, thesis/dissertation. *Entrance requirements:* For master's, GRE, honors degree; for doctorate, master's degree. Additional exam requirements/recommendations for international students: Required—TOEFL. *Application deadline:* Applications are processed on a rolling basis. Application fee: $77 Canadian dollars. *Financial support:* Fellowships, research assistantships, teaching assistantships, institutionally sponsored loans, scholarships/grants, and unspecified assistantships available. *Faculty research:* Canadian public administration and policy, development administration, public policy analysis, public management. *Unit head:* Susan Phillips, Director, 613-520-2600 Ext. 2547, Fax: 613-520-2551, E-mail: public_administration@carleton.ca. *Application contact:* Nicole Enouy, Graduate Secretary, 613-520-2600 Ext. 2548, Fax: 613-520-2551, E-mail: public_administration@carleton.ca.

Carnegie Mellon University, H. John Heinz III School of Public Policy and Management, Program in Public Management, Pittsburgh, PA 15213-3891. Offers MPM. Part-time and evening/weekend programs available. *Degree requirements:* For master's, internship.

See Close-Up on page 1585.

Central Michigan University, Central Michigan University Off-Campus Programs, Program in Administration, Mount Pleasant, MI 48859. Offers acquisitions administration (MSA, Certificate); general administration (MSA, Certificate); health services administration (MSA, Certificate); human resources administration (MSA, Certificate); information resource management (MSA, Certificate); international administration (MSA, Certificate); leadership (MSA, Certificate); public administration (MSA, Certificate); software engineering administration (MSA); vehicle design and manufacturing administration (MSA, Certificate). Part-time and evening/weekend programs available. Postbaccalaureate distance learning degree programs offered (no on-campus study). *Students:* Average age 38. *Entrance requirements:* For master's, minimum GPA of 2.7 in major. *Application deadline:* Applications are processed on a rolling basis. Application fee: $50. Electronic applications accepted. *Financial support:* Scholarships/grants available. Support available to part-time students. Financial award applicants required to submit FAFSA. *Unit head:* Dr. Scott J. Smith, Head, 989-774-2859, E-mail: smith5sj@cmich.edu. *Application contact:* 877-268-4636, E-mail: cmuoffcampus@cmich.edu.

Central Michigan University, Central Michigan University Off-Campus Programs, Program in Public Administration, Mount Pleasant, MI 48859. Offers MPA. Part-time and evening/weekend programs available. *Entrance requirements:* For master's, minimum GPA of 2.8. Additional exam requirements/recommendations for international students: Required—TOEFL. Electronic applications accepted. *Financial support:* Scholarships/grants available. Support available to part-time students. *Unit head:* Dr. Lawrence Sych, Program Director, 989-774-3316, E-mail: sych1l@cmich.edu. *Application contact:* 877-268-4636, E-mail: cmuoffcampus@cmich.edu.

Central Michigan University, College of Graduate Studies, College of Humanities and Social and Behavioral Sciences, Department of Political Science, Program in Public Administration, Mount Pleasant, MI 48859. Offers MPA. *Degree requirements:* For master's, thesis or alternative. *Entrance requirements:* For master's, GRE.

Central Michigan University, College of Graduate Studies, Program in Administration, Mount Pleasant, MI 48859. Offers acquisitions administration (MSA); general administration (MSA); health services administration (MSA); hospitality and tourism administration (MSA); human resources administration (MSA); information resource management (MSA); international administration (MSA); leadership (MSA); long-term care administration (MSA); organizational communication (MSA); public administration (MSA); recreation and park administration (MSA); sport administration (MSA). *Accreditation:* AACSB. *Degree requirements:* For master's, thesis or alternative. *Entrance requirements:* For master's, minimum undergraduate GPA of 2.5.

Cheyney University of Pennsylvania, School of Education, Program in Public Administration, Cheyney, PA 19319-0200. Offers MPA. *Faculty:* 8 full-time (1 woman), 5 part-time/adjunct (3 women). *Students:* 15 full-time (8 women), 5 part-time (4 women); includes 19 minority (all African Americans) Average age 37. *Expenses:* Tuition, state resident: full-time $6,214; part-time $345 per credit. Tuition, nonresident: full-time $9,944; part-time $552 per credit. Required fees: $645; $161 per semester. *Unit head:* Dr. O. Denis Ekwerike, Chair, 215-560-3891, Fax: 215-560-3893. *Application contact:* Dr. John Williams, Executive Dean of Graduate Studies, 215-560-7034, Fax: 215-560-3893, E-mail: jwilliams@cheyney.edu.

Clark Atlanta University, School of Arts and Sciences, Department of Public Administration, Atlanta, GA 30314. Offers MPA. *Accreditation:* NASPAA. Part-time programs available. *Faculty:* 3 full-time (1 woman), 1 part-time/adjunct (0 women). *Students:* 11 full-time (10 women), 24 part-time (17 women); includes 28 minority (27 African Americans, 1 Hispanic American), 1 international. Average age 28. 12 applicants, 100% accepted, 8 enrolled. In 2007, 9 degrees awarded. *Degree requirements:* For master's, one foreign language, thesis. *Entrance requirements:* For master's, GRE General Test, minimum GPA of 2.5. Additional exam requirements/recommendations for international students: Required—TOEFL (minimum score 500 paper-based; 173 computer-based). *Application deadline:* For fall admission, 4/1 for domestic and international students; for spring admission, 11/1 for domestic and international students. Applications are processed on a rolling basis. Application fee: $40 ($55 for international students). *Expenses:* Tuition: Full-time $11,664; part-time $648 per credit hour. Required fees: $550; $275 per semester. *Financial support:* Fellowships, career-related internships or fieldwork, Federal Work-Study, scholarships/grants, and unspecified assistantships available. Support available to part-time students. Financial award application deadline: 4/30; financial award applicants required to submit FAFSA. *Faculty research:* Nutrition education, Africa. *Unit head:* Dr. Ron Finnell, Chairperson, 404-880-6651, E-mail: rfinell@cau.edu. *Application contact:* Michelle Clark-Davis, Graduate Program Admissions, 404-880-8709, E-mail: mdowis@cau.edu.

Clark University, Graduate School, College of Professional and Continuing Education, Program in Public Administration, Worcester, MA 01610-1477. Offers MPA, Certificate. Part-time and evening/weekend programs available. *Students:* 19 full-time (14 women), 25 part-time (19 women); includes 4 minority (2 African Americans, 2 Asian Americans or Pacific Islanders), 3 international. Average age 29. 16 applicants, 100% accepted, 16 enrolled. In 2007, 26 degrees awarded. *Degree requirements:* For master's, thesis optional. *Entrance requirements:* For master's, GMAT or GRE General Test. *Application deadline:* For fall admission, 2/15 for domestic students. Applications are processed on a rolling basis. Application fee: $40. Electronic applications accepted. *Expenses:* Tuition: Full-time $32,600; part-time $1,019 per credit. Required fees: $30. Tuition and fees vary according to program. *Financial support:* Career-related internships or fieldwork available. Support available to part-time students. *Unit head:* Max E. Hess, Director of Graduate Studies, 508-793-7217, Fax: 508-793-7232. *Application contact:* Julia Parent, Director of Marketing, Communications, and Admissions, 508-793-7217, Fax: 508-793-7232, E-mail: jparent@clarku.edu.

Clemson University, Graduate School, College of Business and Behavioral Science, Department of Political Science, Program in Public Administration, Clemson, SC 29634. Offers MPA. *Students:* 9 full-time (8 women), 13 part-time (7 women); includes 1 minority (African American), 1 international. 16 applicants, 63% accepted, 5 enrolled. In 2007, 12 degrees awarded. *Entrance requirements:* For master's, GRE, 2 letters of recommendation. *Application deadline:* For fall admission, 7/1 for domestic students; for spring admission, 11/1 for domestic students. Application fee: $55. Electronic applications accepted. *Unit head:* Dr. Robert Smith, Coordinator, 864-656-3550, Fax: 864-656-0690, E-mail: rws@clemson.edu. *Application contact:* Angela Guido, Information Contact, 864-656-3233, E-mail: nangela@clemson.edu.

Cleveland State University, College of Graduate Studies, Maxine Goodman Levin College of Urban Affairs, Program in Public Administration, Cleveland, OH 44115. Offers geographic information systems (Certificate); local and urban management (Certificate); non-profit management (Certificate); public administration (MPA); research administration (Certificate); JD/MPA. *Accreditation:* NASPAA. Part-time and evening/weekend programs available. *Faculty:* 26 full-time (10 women), 14 part-time/adjunct (8 women). *Students:* 36 full-time (17 women), 108 part-time (76 women); includes 46 minority (43 African Americans, 1 Asian American or Pacific Islander, 2 Hispanic Americans), 1 international. Average age 35. 45 applicants, 78% accepted, 23 enrolled. In 2007, 1 degree awarded. *Degree requirements:* For master's, thesis or alternative, capstone course. *Entrance requirements:* For master's, GRE General Test (minimum score: verbal and quantitative 40th percentile, analytical writing 4.0), minimum GPA of 3.0. Additional exam requirements/recommendations for international students: Required—TOEFL (minimum score 525 paper-based; 197 computer-based). *Application deadline:* For fall admission, 7/15 priority date for domestic students, 5/15 for international students; for spring admission, 11/1 for international students. Applications are processed on a rolling basis. Application fee: $30. Electronic applications accepted. *Financial support:* In 2007–08, 17 students received support, including 10 research assistantships with full and partial tuition reimbursements available (averaging $6,960 per year); career-related internships or fieldwork, institutionally sponsored loans, tuition waivers (full and partial), and unspecified assistantships also available. Financial award application deadline: 3/1. *Faculty research:* Health care, public management, economic development, city management. *Unit head:* Dr. Vera Vogelsang-Coombs, Director, 216-687-9223, Fax: 216-687-5398, E-mail: v.vogelsang-coombs@csuohio.edu. *Application contact:* Graduate Advisor, 216-523-7522, Fax: 216-687-5398, E-mail: urbanprograms@csuohio.edu.

The College at Brockport, State University of New York, School of Professions, Department of Public Administration, Brockport, NY 14420-2997. Offers MPA. *Accreditation:* NASPAA. Part-time and evening/weekend programs available. *Students:* 27 full-time (20 women), 93 part-time (56 women); includes 18 minority (14 African Americans, 1 American Indian/Alaska Native, 3 Hispanic Americans). 31 applicants, 97% accepted, 27 enrolled. In 2007, 26 degrees awarded. *Degree requirements:* For master's, thesis or alternative. *Entrance requirements:* For master's, GRE or minimum GPA of 3.0, letters of recommendation. Additional exam requirements/recommendations for international students: Required—TOEFL (minimum score 550 paper-based; 213 computer-based; 79 iBT). *Application deadline:* For fall admission, 3/1 for domestic and international students; for spring admission, 10/1 for domestic and international students. Application fee: $50. *Expenses:* Tuition, state resident: full-time $6,900; part-time $288 per credit. Tuition, nonresident: full-time $10,920; part-time $455 per credit. Required fees: $738; $31 per credit. *Financial support:* In 2007–08, 1 fellowship with tuition reimbursement (averaging $7,500 per year) was awarded; Federal Work-Study, scholarships/grants, and unspecified assistantships also available. Support available to part-time students. Financial award application deadline: 3/15; financial award applicants required to submit FAFSA. *Faculty research:* Public safety administration, ethic, integrity and professionalism in public safety, E-government; complexity theories of public management; Medicaid and disabilities. *Unit head:* Dr. James Fatula, Chairperson, 585-395-2375, Fax: 585-395-2172, E-mail: jfatula@brockport.edu.

College of Charleston, Graduate School, School of Humanities and Social Sciences, Program in Public Administration, Charleston, SC 29424-0001. Offers MPA. *Accreditation:* NASPAA. Part-time programs available. *Faculty:* 27 full-time (11 women), 3 part-time/adjunct (1 woman). *Students:* 30 full-time (22 women), 24 part-time (16 women); includes 6 minority (5 African Americans, 1 Asian American or Pacific Islander), 2 international. Average age 27. 43 applicants, 65% accepted, 21 enrolled. In 2007, 16 degrees awarded. *Degree requirements:* For master's, internship, capstone seminar. *Entrance requirements:* For master's, GRE General Test, previous course work in statistics, 3 letters of recommendation, minimum GPA of 3.0. Additional exam requirements/recommendations for international students: Required—TOEFL. *Application* *deadline:* For fall admission, 7/1 for domestic students; for spring admission, 11/1 for domestic students. Applications are processed on a rolling basis. Application fee: $35. Electronic applications accepted. *Expenses:* Tuition, state resident: full-time $7,778; part-time $324 per hour. Tuition, nonresident: full-time $18,732; part-time $781 per hour. *Financial support:* Research assistantships, career-related internships or fieldwork, Federal Work-Study, and unspecified assistantships available. Support available to part-time students. Financial award application deadline: 4/1; financial award applicants required to submit FAFSA. *Faculty research:* Local government, environmental policy, budgeting, ethics. *Unit head:* Dr. Philip Jos, Acting Director, 843-953-6105, Fax: 843-953-8140, E-mail: jos@cofc.edu. *Application contact:* Susan Hallatt, Assistant Director of Graduate Admissions, 843-953-5614, Fax: 843-953-1434, E-mail: hallatts@cofc.edu.

Columbia University, School of International and Public Affairs, Program in Public Policy and Administration, New York, NY 10027. Offers MPA, JD/MPA, MPA/MS, MPH/MPA. *Faculty:* 70 full-time (18 women), 203 part-time/adjunct (80 women). *Students:* 241 full-time (157 women). Average age 27. 659 applicants, 50% accepted, 126 enrolled. In 2007, 104 degrees awarded. *Entrance requirements:* For master's, GRE General Test. Additional exam requirements/recommendations for international students: Required—TOEFL (minimum score 600 paper-based; 250 computer-based; 100 iBT). *Application deadline:* For fall admission, 1/5 for domestic students; for spring admission, 10/1 for domestic students. Application fee: $85. Electronic applications accepted. *Expenses:* Tuition: Part-time $1,452 per credit. Required fees: $152 per term. One-time fee: $75 part-time. Full-time tuition and fees vary according to course level, course load, degree level and program. *Financial support:* In 2007–08, 81 students received support, including 80 fellowships with full and partial tuition reimbursements available (averaging $14,692 per year), 9 teaching assistantships with full tuition reimbursements available (averaging $25,701 per year); research assistantships, career-related internships or fieldwork, Federal Work-Study, institutionally sponsored loans, and unspecified assistantships also available. Financial award application deadline: 1/5; financial award applicants required to submit FAFSA. *Unit head:* Director, 212-854-8690, Fax: 212-854-8059, E-mail: sipa_admission@columbia.edu. *Application contact:* Matt Clemons, Director of Admissions and Financial Aid, 212-854-6216, Fax: 212-854-3010, E-mail: mc2793@columbia.edu.

Columbus State University, Graduate Studies, College of Arts and Letters, Program in Public Administration, Columbus, GA 31907-5645. Offers justice administration (MPA). Part-time and evening/weekend programs available. *Faculty:* 7 full-time (3 women), 10 part-time/adjunct (0 women). *Students:* 110 full-time (38 women), 230 part-time (88 women); includes 117 minority (111 African Americans, 1 Asian American or Pacific Islander, 5 Hispanic Americans), 3 international. Average age 36. 102 applicants, 81% accepted, 69 enrolled. In 2007, 114 degrees awarded. *Degree requirements:* For master's, comprehensive exam. *Entrance requirements:* For master's, GRE General Test, GMAT, MAT. Additional exam requirements/recommendations for international students: Required—TOEFL (minimum score 550 paper-based; 213 computer-based). *Application deadline:* For fall admission, 5/1 priority date for domestic students, 5/1 for international students; for spring admission, 11/1 for domestic and international students. Applications are processed on a rolling basis. Application fee: $25. Electronic applications accepted. *Expenses:* Tuition, state resident: part-time $143 per semester hour. Tuition, nonresident: part-time $569 per semester hour. Required fees: $273 per term. Tuition and fees vary according to course load. *Financial support:* In 2007–08, 78 students received support, including 7 research assistantships with partial tuition reimbursements available (averaging $3,000 per year); career-related internships or fieldwork, Federal Work-Study, institutionally sponsored loans, scholarships/grants, tuition waivers (full), and unspecified assistantships also available. Support available to part-time students. Financial award application deadline: 5/1; financial award applicants required to submit FAFSA. *Unit head:* Dr. William Chappell, Program Director, 706-568-2055, E-mail: chappell_william@colstate.edu. *Application contact:* Katie Thornton, Graduate Admissions Specialist, 706-568-2035, Fax: 706-568-2462, E-mail: thornton_katie@colstate.edu.

Concordia University, School of Graduate Studies, Faculty of Arts and Science, Department of Political Science, Montréal, QC H3G 1M8, Canada. Offers political science (PhD); public policy and public administration (MA), including geography. *Degree requirements:* For master's, one foreign language, comprehensive exam, thesis optional, internship. *Entrance requirements:* For master's, honors degree or equivalent. Additional exam requirements/recommendations for international students: Required—TOEFL. *Faculty research:* International public policy and administration, Quebec public administration, public policy and social/political theory, geography and public policy, public administration and decision making.

Concordia University Wisconsin, Graduate Programs, School of Business and Legal Studies, MBA Program, Mequon, WI 53097-2402. Offers finance (MBA); health care administration (MBA); human resource management (MBA); international business (MBA); international business-bilingual English/Chinese (MBA); management (MBA); management information systems (MBA); managerial communications (MBA); marketing (MBA); public administration (MBA); risk management (MBA). Postbaccalaureate distance learning degree programs offered (minimal on-campus study). *Degree requirements:* For master's, comprehensive exam, thesis or alternative. *Entrance requirements:* Additional exam requirements/recommendations for international students: Required—TOEFL. Expenses: Contact institution.

Cumberland University, Program in Public Service Administration, Lebanon, TN 37087-3408. Offers MS. Part-time and evening/weekend programs available. *Faculty:* 2 full-time (0 women), 3 part-time/adjunct (2 women). *Students:* Average age 37. 40 applicants, 88% accepted, 35 enrolled. In 2007, 36 degrees awarded. *Degree requirements:* For master's, comprehensive exam. *Entrance requirements:* For master's, MAT, 3 letters of recommendation. Additional exam requirements/recommendations for international students: Required—TOEFL (minimum score 500 paper-based; 173 computer-based). Application fee: $50. *Expenses:* Tuition: Full-time $15,240; part-time $635 per hour. *Financial support:* Scholarships/grants and unspecified assistantships available. Financial award application deadline: 8/1; financial award applicants required to submit FAFSA. *Unit head:* Dr. C. William McKee, Professor, 615-444-2562 Ext. 1111, Fax: 615-444-2569, E-mail: bmckee@cumberland.edu. *Application contact:* Karen Hobson, Assistant to Executive Vice President and Dean, 615-444-2562 Ext. 1139, Fax: 615-444-2569, E-mail: khobson@cumberland.edu.

Dalhousie University, Faculty of Management, School of Public Administration, Halifax, NS B3H 4R2, Canada. Offers MPA, LL B/MPA, MLIS/MPA. Part-time programs available. *Faculty:* 9 full-time (1 woman), 6 part-time/adjunct (1 woman). *Students:* 59 full-time (36 women), 25 part-time (13 women). 58 applicants, 79% accepted. *Entrance requirements:* For master's, GMAT. Additional exam requirements/recommendations for international students: Required—TOEFL. *Application deadline:* For fall admission, 6/1 for domestic students. Applications are processed on a rolling basis. Application fee: $60. *Expenses: Contact institution. Financial support:* Fellowships, teaching assistantships, career-related internships or fieldwork available. *Faculty research:* Municipal management, policy and program management, environmental policy, economic and social policy, business and government. *Unit head:* Dr. Fazley Siddiq, Director, 902-494-3743, Fax: 902-494-7023, E-mail: dalmpa@dal.ca. *Application contact:* Dr. Keith Sullivan, Administrative Secretary, 902-494-1097, Fax: 902-494-7023, E-mail: keith.sullivan@dal.ca.

DePaul University, School of Public Service, Chicago, IL 60604-2287. Offers financial administration management (Certificate); health administration (Certificate); health law and policy (MS); international public services (MS); metropolitan planning (Certificate); public administration (MS); public service management (MS), including association management, fundraising and philanthropy, healthcare administration, higher education administration, metropolitan planning, non-profit administration, public administration, public policy; public services (Certificate); JD/MS; MA/MS. Part-time and evening/weekend programs available. Postbaccalaureate distance learning degree programs offered (minimal on-campus study). *Faculty:* 11 full-time (2 women), 19 part-time/adjunct (16 women). *Students:* 139 full-time (108 women), 245 part-time (178 women); includes 121 minority (76 African Americans, 2 American Indian/Alaska Native, 15 Asian Americans or Pacific Islanders, 28 Hispanic Americans), 11 international. 140 applicants, 96% accepted, 96 enrolled. In 2007, 89 degrees awarded. *Degree requirements:* For master's, thesis or integrative seminar. *Entrance requirements:* For master's, minimum GPA of 2.7. Additional exam requirements/recommendations for international students: Required—TOEFL (minimum score 550 paper-based; 213 computer-based; 80 iBT), IELTS (minimum score 7). *Application deadline:* Applications are processed on a rolling basis. Application fee: $25. Electronic applications accepted. *Financial support:* In 2007–08, 28 students received support, including 3 research assistantships with full tuition reimbursements available (averaging $7,000 per year); career-related internships or fieldwork, Federal Work-Study, institutionally sponsored loans, scholarships/grants, and tuition waivers (partial) also available. Support available to part-time students. Financial award application deadline: 7/1; financial award applicants required to submit FAFSA. *Faculty research:* Government financing, transportation, leadership, health care, volunteerism and organizational behavior, non-profit organizations. Total annual research expenditures: $20,000. *Unit head:* Dr. J. Patrick Murphy, Director, 312-362-5608, Fax: 312-362-5506, E-mail: jpmurphy@depaul.edu. *Application contact:* Megan B. Balderston, Director of Admissions and Marketing, 312-362-5565, Fax: 312-362-5506, E-mail: pubserv@depaul.edu.

DeVry University, Keller Graduate School of Management, Oakbrook Terrace, IL 60181. Offers accounting and financial management (MAFM); business administration (MBA); human resources management (MHRM); information systems management (MISM); network and communications management (MNCM); project management (MPM); public administration (MPA). *Faculty:* 22 full-time, 425 part-time/adjunct. *Unit head:* Dr. Sherril Hoel, Academic Dean of Administration and Accreditation, 630-574-1894. *Application contact:* Student Application Contact, 630-571-7700.

Drake University, College of Business and Public Administration, Des Moines, IA 50311-4516. Offers M Acc, MBA, MFM, MPA, JD/MBA, JD/MPA, Pharm D/MBA, Pharm D/MPA. *Accreditation:* AACSB. Part-time and evening/weekend programs available. *Faculty:* 19 full-time (4 women), 2 part-time/adjunct (0 women). *Students:* 81 full-time (59 women), 461 part-time (253 women); includes 52 minority (21 African Americans, 26 Asian Americans or Pacific Islanders, 5 Hispanic Americans), 31 international. Average age 26. 276 applicants, 64% accepted, 119 enrolled. In 2007, 188 degrees awarded. *Degree requirements:* For master's, comprehensive exam (for some programs), thesis (for some programs), internships. *Entrance requirements:* For master's, GMAT, letters of recommendation, resumé. Additional exam requirements/recommendations for international students: Required—TOEFL (minimum score 550 paper-based; 213 computer-based). *Application deadline:* For fall admission, 8/15 priority date for domestic students; for winter admission, 12/20 priority date for domestic students; for spring admission, 12/1 priority date for domestic students. Applications are processed on a rolling basis. Application fee: $25. Electronic applications accepted. *Expenses: Contact institution.* Tuition and fees vary according to program. *Financial support:* Fellowships with tuition reimbursements, teaching assistantships, career-related internships or fieldwork and institutionally sponsored loans available. Support available to part-time students. Financial award application deadline: 3/1; financial award applicants required to submit FAFSA. *Faculty research:* Venture capital, online commerce, professional ethics, process improvement, project management. *Unit head:* Dr. Charles Edwards, Dean, 515-271-2871, Fax: 515-271-4518, E-mail: charles.edwards@drake.edu. *Application contact:* Danette Kenne, Director of Graduate Programs, 515-271-2188, Fax: 515-271-4518, E-mail: cbpa.gradprograms@drake.edu.

Duquesne University, Graduate School of Liberal Arts, Graduate Center for Social and Public Policy, Pittsburgh, PA 15282-1750. Offers conflict resolution and peace studies (Certificate); social and public policy (MA, Certificate). Programs are a collaboration between the Departments of Political Science and Sociology. Part-time and evening/weekend programs available. *Faculty:* 15 full-time (3 women), 1 (woman) part-time/adjunct. *Students:* 25 full-time (13 women), 17 part-time (12 women). Average age 27. In 2007, 11 degrees awarded. *Degree requirements:* For master's, thesis. *Entrance requirements:* For master's, GRE General Test. Additional exam requirements/recommendations for international students: Required—TOEFL. *Application deadline:* For fall admission, 4/30 priority date for domestic and international students; for spring admission, 10/31 priority date for domestic and international students. Applications are processed on a rolling basis. Application fee: $50. *Expenses:* Tuition: Part-time $774 per credit. Required fees: $74 per credit. Tuition and fees vary according to program. *Financial support:* In 2007–08, 20 students received support, including 12 research assistantships with full and partial tuition reimbursements available (averaging $9,000 per year), 4 teaching assistantships with full and partial tuition reimbursements available (averaging $9,000 per year); career-related internships or fieldwork, institutionally sponsored loans, scholarships/grants, tuition waivers (full and partial), and unspecified assistantships also available. Support available to part-time students. Financial award application deadline: 5/1. *Faculty research:* Program evaluation, environmental policy, criminal justice policy, health care policy. Total annual research expenditures: $30,000. *Unit head:* Dr. Joseph Yenerall, Director, 412-396-6485, Fax: 412-396-5265, E-mail: socialpolicy@duq.edu.

East Carolina University, Graduate School, Thomas Harriot College of Arts and Sciences, Department of Political Science, Greenville, NC 27858-4353. Offers public administration (MPA). *Accreditation:* NASPAA. Part-time and evening/weekend programs available. *Faculty:* 21 full-time (7 women). *Students:* 23 full-time (16 women), 28 part-time (11 women); includes 9 minority (7 African Americans, 2 Asian Americans or Pacific Islanders), 3 international. Average age 28. 49 applicants, 53% accepted. In 2007, 22 degrees awarded. *Degree requirements:* For master's, one foreign language, comprehensive exam. *Entrance requirements:* For master's, GRE General Test. Additional exam requirements/recommendations for international students: Required—TOEFL. *Application deadline:* For fall admission, 6/1 priority date for domestic students; for spring admission, 10/15 for domestic students. Applications are processed on a rolling basis. Application fee: $50. *Financial support:* Research assistantships with partial tuition reimbursements, teaching assistantships with partial tuition reimbursements, Federal Work-Study available. Support available to part-time students. Financial award application deadline: 6/1. *Unit head:* Dr. Robert J. Thompson, Interim Chair, 252-328-4134, E-mail: thompsonr@ecu.edu. *Application contact:* Dean of Graduate School, 252-328-6012, Fax: 252-328-6071, E-mail: gradschool@ecu.edu.

Eastern Kentucky University, The Graduate School, College of Arts and Sciences, Department of Government, Program in General Public Administration, Richmond, KY 40475-3102. Offers community development (MPA); community health administration (MPA); general public administration (MPA). *Accreditation:* NASPAA. Part-time and evening/weekend programs available. *Students:* 17 full-time (10 women), 30 part-time (15 women); includes 5 minority (4 African Americans, 1 American Indian/Alaska Native), 4 international. Average age 31. 23 applicants, 83% accepted, 11 enrolled. In 2007, 12 degrees awarded. *Entrance requirements:* For master's, GRE General Test, minimum GPA of 2.5. Application fee: $30. *Unit head:* Dr. Sara Zeigler, Chair, Department of Government, 859-622-5931.

Eastern Michigan University, Graduate School, College of Arts and Sciences, Department of Political Science, Program in Public Administration, Ypsilanti, MI 48197. Offers local government management (Graduate Certificate); management of public healthcare services (Graduate Certificate); public administration (MPA, Graduate Certificate); public budget management (Graduate Certificate); public land planning (Graduate Certificate); public management (Graduate Certificate); public personnel management (Graduate Certificate); public policy analysis (Graduate Certificate). *Accreditation:* NASPAA. *Students:* 19 full-time (8 women), 97 part-time (57 women); includes 43 minority (34 African Americans, 3 American Indian/Alaska Native, 3 Asian Americans or Pacific Islanders, 3 Hispanic Americans), 7 international. Average age 32. In 2007, 42 master's, 35 other advanced degrees awarded. Application fee: $35. *Expenses:* Tuition, state resident: full-time $8,952; part-time $373 per credit hour. Tuition, nonresident: full-time $17,634; part-time $735 per credit hour. Required fees: $896; $34 per credit hour. Tuition and fees vary according to course level, degree level and program. *Unit head:* Dr. Joseph Ohren, Director, 734-487-2522, Fax: 734-487-3340, E-mail: joseph.ohren@emich.edu.

Public Administration

Eastern Michigan University (continued)

Application contact: Dr. Dogan Koyluoglu, Program Coordinator, 734-487-0063, E-mail: sukru.koyuoglu@emich.edu.

Eastern Washington University, Graduate Studies, College of Business and Public Administration, Program in Public Administration, Cheney, WA 99004-2431. Offers MPA, MBA/MPA, MPA/MSW, MPA/MURP. Part-time and evening/weekend programs available. *Degree requirements:* For master's, comprehensive exam, thesis optional. *Entrance requirements:* For master's, minimum GPA of 3.0.

The Evergreen State College, Graduate Programs, Program in Public Administration, Olympia, WA 98505. Offers MPA, MES/MPA. Part-time and evening/weekend programs available. *Faculty:* 5 full-time (3 women), 7 part-time/adjunct (4 women). *Students:* 36 full-time (19 women), 104 part-time (78 women); includes 42 minority (11 African Americans, 22 American Indian/Alaska Native, 5 Asian Americans or Pacific Islanders, 4 Hispanic Americans), 2 international. Average age 37. 71 applicants, 89% accepted, 50 enrolled. In 2007, 59 degrees awarded. *Degree requirements:* For master's, thesis optional. *Entrance requirements:* For master's, minimum GPA of 3.0 in last 90 quarter hours toward BA/BS; 4 quarter credits in statistics within past 5 years; evidence of writing, analytical, and general communication skills at appropriate level for graduate study. Additional exam requirements/recommendations for international students: Required—TOEFL (minimum score 600 paper-based; 250 computer-based). *Application deadline:* For fall admission, 2/15 priority date for domestic and international students. Applications are processed on a rolling basis. Application fee: $50. Electronic applications accepted. *Expenses:* Tuition, state resident: full-time $6,570; part-time $218 per credit. Tuition, nonresident: full-time $20,004; part-time $666 per credit. Required fees: $377; $8 per credit. $47 per quarter. Tuition and fees vary according to course load. *Financial support:* Fellowships with full and partial tuition reimbursements, research assistantships with partial tuition reimbursements, career-related internships or fieldwork, Federal Work-Study, scholarships/grants, tuition waivers (full and partial), and unspecified assistantships available. Support available to part-time students. Financial award application deadline: 3/15; financial award applicants required to submit FAFSA. *Faculty research:* Public policy, organizational theory, public health, tribal governance, nonprofit administration, leadership, healthcare reform. *Unit head:* Dr. Cheryl Simrell King, MPA Program Director, 360-867-5541, E-mail: kingcs@evergreen.edu. *Application contact:* Randee Gibbons, Assistant Director MPA Program, 360-867-6554, E-mail: graduatestudies@evergreen.edu.

Fairleigh Dickinson University, College at Florham, Anthony J. Petrocelli College of Continuing Studies, Public Administration Institute, Program in Public Administration, Madison, NJ 07940-1099. Offers MPA. *Students:* 1 full-time (0 women), 1 international. Average age 26. 2 applicants, 50% accepted, 1 enrolled. In 2007, 1 degree awarded. Application fee: $40. *Expenses:* Tuition: Part-time $869 per credit. *Unit head:* Dr. William Roberts, Head, Public Administration Institute, 973-443-8500.

Fairleigh Dickinson University, Metropolitan Campus, Anthony J. Petrocelli College of Continuing Studies, Public Administration Institute, Program in Public Administration, Teaneck, NJ 07666-1914. Offers MPA, Certificate. *Students:* 86 full-time (41 women), 116 part-time (59 women), 77 international. Average age 34. 196 applicants, 69% accepted, 56 enrolled. In 2007, 44 degrees awarded. *Application deadline:* Applications are processed on a rolling basis. Application fee: $40. *Expenses:* Tuition: Part-time $869 per credit. Tuition and fees vary according to degree level, campus/location and program.

Florida Agricultural and Mechanical University, Division of Graduate Studies, Research, and Continuing Education, College of Arts and Sciences, Division of History and Political Sciences, Program in Applied Social Science, Tallahassee, FL 32307-3200. Offers African American history (MASS); criminal justice (MASS); economics (MASS); history (MASS); political science (MASS); public administration (MASS); public management (MASS); social work (MASS); sociology (MASS). Part-time programs available. *Degree requirements:* For master's, thesis optional. *Entrance requirements:* For master's, GRE General Test, minimum GPA of 3.0. *Faculty research:* Southern history, black history, election trends, presidential history.

Florida Atlantic University, College of Architecture, Urban and Public Affairs, School of Public Administration, Boca Raton, FL 33431-0991. Offers MNM, MPA, PhD. *Accreditation:* NASPAA (one or more programs are accredited). Part-time and evening/weekend programs available. *Degree requirements:* For master's, thesis optional; for doctorate, comprehensive exam, thesis/dissertation. *Entrance requirements:* For master's, GRE General Test, minimum GPA of 3.0; for doctorate, GRE General Test, faculty reference, scholarly writing samples, letters of recommendation. Additional exam requirements/recommendations for international students: Required—TOEFL. *Faculty research:* Public finance and budgeting, public management, evaluation, criminal justice, postmodern public administration.

Florida Gulf Coast University, College of Professional Studies, Program in Public Administration, Fort Myers, FL 33965-6565. Offers criminal justice (MPA); environmental policy (MPA); general public administration (MPA); management (MPA). Part-time programs available. *Faculty:* 30 full-time (12 women), 24 part-time/adjunct (8 women). *Students:* 40 full-time (27 women), 16 part-time (11 women); includes 9 minority (2 African Americans, 2 American Indian/Alaska Native, 2 Asian Americans or Pacific Islanders, 3 Hispanic Americans). Average age 35. 26 applicants, 88% accepted, 17 enrolled. In 2007, 8 degrees awarded. *Entrance requirements:* For master's, GRE General Test, MAT, minimum GPA of 3.0. Additional exam requirements/recommendations for international students: Required—TOEFL (minimum score 550 paper-based; 213 computer-based). *Application deadline:* For fall admission, 7/1 priority date for domestic students; for spring admission, 11/15 for domestic students. Applications are processed on a rolling basis. Application fee: $30. Electronic applications accepted. *Expenses:* Tuition, state resident: full-time $4,542. Tuition, nonresident: full-time $19,449. Required fees: $1,297. *Financial support:* In 2007–08, 5 research assistantships were awarded; career-related internships or fieldwork and tuition waivers (full and partial) also available. Support available to part-time students. *Faculty research:* Personnel, public policy, public finance, housing policy. *Unit head:* Terry Busson, Chair, 239-590-7704, E-mail: tbusson@fgcu.edu. *Application contact:* Roger Green, Information Contact, 239-590-7838, Fax: 239-590-7846.

Florida Institute of Technology, Graduate Programs, University College, Melbourne, FL 32901-6975. Offers accounting and finance (MBA); acquisition and contract management (MS, PMBA); aerospace engineering (MS); business administration (PMBA); computer information systems (MS); computer science (MS); e-business (PMBA); electrical engineering (MS); engineering management (MS); healthcare management (MBA); human resource management (PMBA); human resources management (MS); information systems (PMBA); information technology (MS); logistics management (MS); management (MBA, MS), including acquisition and contract management (MS), e-business (MS), human resource management (MS), information systems (MS), logistics management (MS), transportation management (MS); marketing (MBA); materiel acquisition management (MS); mechanical engineering (MS); operations research (MS); project management (MS), including information systems, operations research; public administration (MPA); software engineering (MS); space systems (MS); space systems management (MS); systems management (MS), including information systems, operations research. Part-time and evening/weekend programs available. Postbaccalaureate distance learning degree programs offered (no on-campus study). *Faculty:* 16 full-time (3 women), 130 part-time/adjunct (19 women). *Students:* 102 full-time (40 women), 1,320 part-time (522 women); includes 394 minority (262 African Americans, 11 American Indian/Alaska Native, 56 Asian Americans or Pacific Islanders, 65 Hispanic Americans), 27 international. Average age 36. 533 applicants, 58% accepted, 293 enrolled. In 2007, 418 degrees awarded. *Entrance requirements:* For master's, minimum GPA of 3.0. Additional exam requirements/recommendations for international students: Required—TOEFL (minimum score 550 paper-based; 213 computer-based). *Application deadline:* Applications are processed on a rolling basis. Application fee: $50. Electronic applications accepted. *Expenses:* Tuition: Part-time $945 per credit. *Financial support:* Institutionally sponsored loans available. Financial award application deadline: 3/1; financial award applicants required to submit FAFSA. *Unit head:* Dr. Clifford Bragdon, Dean, 321-674-8821, Fax: 321-674-7597, E-mail: cbragdon@fit.edu. *Application contact:* Thomas M. Shea, Director of Graduate Admissions, 321-674-7577, Fax: 321-723-9468, E-mail: tshea@fit.edu.

Florida International University, College of Social Work, Justice and Public Affairs, School of Public Administration, Miami, FL 33199. Offers MPA, PhD. *Accreditation:* NASPAA (one or more programs are accredited). Part-time and evening/weekend programs available. *Faculty:* 10 full-time (3 women). *Students:* 70 full-time (44 women), 106 part-time (64 women); includes 139 minority (48 African Americans, 2 Asian Americans or Pacific Islanders, 89 Hispanic Americans), 7 international. Average age 33. 94 applicants, 56% accepted, 43 enrolled. In 2007, 55 degrees awarded. *Degree requirements:* For doctorate, comprehensive exam, thesis/dissertation. *Entrance requirements:* For master's, minimum GPA of 3.0, letters of recommendation; for doctorate, GRE General Test, minimum GPA of 3.0, letters of recommendation. Additional exam requirements/recommendations for international students: Required—TOEFL (minimum score 550 paper-based; 213 computer-based). *Application deadline:* For fall admission, 6/1 for domestic students, 4/1 for international students; for spring admission, 10/1 for domestic students, 9/1 for international students. Applications are processed on a rolling basis. Application fee: $30. Electronic applications accepted. *Expenses:* Tuition, state resident: full-time $6,106. Tuition, nonresident: full-time $15,528. Required fees: $284. *Financial support:* Research assistantships, teaching assistantships, career-related internships or fieldwork, Federal Work-Study, institutionally sponsored loans, and scholarships/grants available. *Unit head:* Dr. Meredith Newman, Director, 305-348-5890, Fax: 305-348-5848, E-mail: meredith.newman@fiu.edu.

Florida State University, Graduate Studies, College of Social Sciences, Reubin O'D. Askew School of Public Administration and Policy, Tallahassee, FL 32306. Offers MPA, PhD, Certificate, JD/MPA, MPA/MSC, MPA/MSP, MPA/MSW. *Accreditation:* NASPAA (one or more programs are accredited). Part-time and evening/weekend programs available. *Faculty:* 11 full-time (2 women), 9 part-time/adjunct (5 women). *Students:* 55 full-time (22 women), 105 part-time (65 women); includes 42 minority (31 African Americans, 2 Asian Americans or Pacific Islanders, 9 Hispanic Americans), 34 international. Average age 25. 191 applicants, 73% accepted, 80 enrolled. In 2007, 31 master's, 4 doctorates awarded. *Median time to degree:* Of those who began their doctoral program in fall 1999, 98% received their degree in 8 years or less. *Degree requirements:* For master's, action report; for doctorate, comprehensive exam, thesis/dissertation. *Entrance requirements:* For master's, GRE General Test, minimum GPA of 3.0; for doctorate, GRE General Test, minimum undergraduate GPA of 3.0, graduate 3.5. Additional exam requirements/recommendations for international students: Required—TOEFL (minimum score 550 paper-based; 213 computer-based; 80 iBT). *Application deadline:* For fall admission, 7/1 for domestic students, 5/1 for international students; for spring admission, 11/1 for domestic students, 9/1 for international students. Applications are processed on a rolling basis. Application fee: $30. Electronic applications accepted. *Expenses:* Tuition, state resident: part-time $248 per credit hour. Tuition, nonresident: part-time $880 per credit hour. Tuition and fees vary according to program. *Financial support:* In 2007–08, 37 students received support, including 6 fellowships with full tuition reimbursements available (averaging $15,000 per year), 29 research assistantships with full tuition reimbursements available (averaging $10,000 per year), 3 teaching assistantships with full tuition reimbursements available (averaging $9,000 per year); career-related internships or fieldwork, Federal Work-Study, institutionally sponsored loans, scholarships/grants, tuition waivers (full), and unspecified assistantships also available. Support available to part-time students. Financial award application deadline: 2/1. *Faculty research:* Financial management, human resource management, policy, strategic management, organizations, nonprofit management. *Unit head:* Dr. Frances S. Berry, Director, 850-644-3525, Fax: 850-644-7617, E-mail: fberry@fsu.edu. *Application contact:* Velda Williams, Academic Program Specialist, 850-644-3060, Fax: 850-644-7617, E-mail: vwilliams3@fsu.edu.

Framingham State College, Division of Graduate and Continuing Education, Program in Public Administration, Framingham, MA 01701-9101. Offers MA. Part-time and evening/weekend programs available. *Faculty:* 2 full-time, 3 part-time/adjunct. *Students:* 46. In 2007, 14 degrees awarded. *Unit head:* Dr. George Jarnis, Coordinator, 508-626-4550, Fax: 508-626-4030, E-mail: gjarnis@frc.mass.edu. *Application contact:* 508-626-4550, Fax: 508-626-4030, E-mail: dgce@frc.mass.edu.

Gannon University, School of Graduate Studies, College of Humanities, Business, and Education, School of Business, Program in Public Administration, Erie, PA 16541-0001. Offers MPA, Certificate. Part-time and evening/weekend programs available. *Students:* 9 full-time (2 women), 10 part-time (5 women); includes 2 minority (both African Americans) Average age 31. 15 applicants, 73% accepted, 8 enrolled. In 2007, 9 degrees awarded. *Degree requirements:* For master's, comprehensive exam, thesis, internship. *Entrance requirements:* For master's, GMAT. Additional exam requirements/recommendations for international students: Required—TOEFL. *Application deadline:* Applications are processed on a rolling basis. Application fee: $25. *Expenses:* Tuition: Full-time $13,050; part-time $725 per credit. Required fees: $502; $16 per credit. Tuition and fees vary according to course load, degree level, campus/location and program. *Financial support:* Career-related internships or fieldwork and unspecified assistantships available. Support available to part-time students. Financial award application deadline: 7/1; financial award applicants required to submit FAFSA. *Unit head:* Dr. Rick Prokop, Co-Director, 814-871-7576, E-mail: prokop001@gannon.edu. *Application contact:* Debra Meszaros, Director of Graduate Recruitment, 814-871-5819, Fax: 814-871-5827, E-mail: cfal@gannon.edu.

The George Washington University, Columbian College of Arts and Sciences, School of Public Policy and Public Administration, Washington, DC 20052. Offers public policy (MA, MPP), including environmental and resource policy (MA), philosophy and social policy (MA), women's studies (MA); public policy and administration (PhD); public policy and public administration (MPA), including budget and public finance, federal policy, politics, and management, international development management, managing public organizations, managing state and local governments and urban policy, nonprofit management, policy analysis and evaluation, public administration; JD/MPP; MPA/JD; PhD/MPP. Part-time and evening/weekend programs available. *Degree requirements:* For doctorate, thesis/dissertation, general exam. *Entrance requirements:* For master's, GRE General Test, minimum GPA of 3.0; for doctorate, GRE General Test, interview, minimum GPA of 3.0. Additional exam requirements/recommendations for international students: Required—TOEFL (minimum score 550 paper-based; 213 computer-based). Electronic applications accepted.

Georgia College & State University, Graduate School, School of Liberal Arts and Sciences, Department of Government and Sociology, Program in Public Administration and Public Affairs, Milledgeville, GA 31061. Offers MPA. *Accreditation:* NASPAA. Part-time and evening/weekend programs available. *Students:* 30 full-time (19 women), 52 part-time (28 women); includes 23 minority (21 African Americans, 2 Asian Americans or Pacific Islanders), 3 international. Average age 29. 54 applicants, 61% accepted, 26 enrolled. In 2007, 29 degrees awarded. *Degree requirements:* For master's, thesis optional, capstone project. *Entrance requirements:* For master's, GRE. Additional exam requirements/recommendations for international students: Required—TOEFL. *Application deadline:* For fall admission, 7/1 priority date for domestic students. Applications are processed on a rolling basis. Application fee: $25. Electronic applications accepted. *Expenses:* Tuition, state resident: full-time $3,726. Tuition, nonresident: full-time $14,868. Required fees: $858. Tuition and fees vary according to campus/location. *Financial support:* In 2007–08, 11 research assistantships were awarded; career-related internships or fieldwork, Federal Work-Study, and unspecified assistantships also available. Support available to part-time students. Financial award application deadline: 3/1; financial award applicants required to submit FAFSA. *Unit head:* Dr. Jerry Herbel, Coordinator of MPA Program, 478-445-7393, E-mail: jerry.herbel@gcsu.edu.

Georgia Southern University, Jack N. Averitt College of Graduate Studies, College of Liberal Arts and Social Sciences, Department of Political Science, Program in Public Administration,

Statesboro, GA 30460. Offers MPA. *Accreditation:* NASPAA. Part-time and evening/weekend programs available. *Students:* 29 full-time (13 women), 27 part-time (16 women); includes 19 minority (16 African Americans, 2 Asian Americans or Pacific Islanders, 1 Hispanic American), 2 international. Average age 27. 22 applicants, 86% accepted, 15 enrolled. In 2007, 17 degrees awarded. *Degree requirements:* For master's, comprehensive exam, internship, terminal exam. *Entrance requirements:* For master's, GRE General Test, minimum GPA of 2.5, resumé, undergraduate major appropriate to field, letters of reference. Additional exam requirements/recommendations for international students: Required—TOEFL (minimum score 550 paper-based; 213 computer-based; 80 iBT). *Application deadline:* For fall admission, 3/1 priority date for domestic and international students; for spring admission, 10/1 priority date for domestic students, 10/1 for international students. Applications are processed on a rolling basis. Application fee: $50. Electronic applications accepted. *Expenses:* Tuition, state resident: full-time $3,516; part-time $147 per semester hour. Tuition, nonresident: full-time $14,060; part-time $586 per semester hour. Required fees: $562 per term. *Financial support:* In 2007–08, 41 students received support, including research assistantships with partial tuition reimbursements available (averaging $6,850 per year), teaching assistantships with partial tuition reimbursements available (averaging $6,850 per year); career-related internships or fieldwork, Federal Work-Study, scholarships/grants, tuition waivers (partial), and unspecified assistantships also available. Support available to part-time students. Financial award application deadline: 4/15; financial award applicants required to submit FAFSA. *Faculty research:* Comparative public administration, equal employment policies, gangs, environmental policy, AIDS policy. *Unit head:* Dr. George Cox, Professor, 912-478-5573, Fax: 912-478-5348, E-mail: gcox@georgiasouthern.edu. *Application contact:* 912-478-5384, Fax: 912-478-0740, E-mail: gradadmissions@georgiasouthern.edu.

Georgia State University, Andrew Young School of Policy Studies, Department of Public Administration and Urban Studies, Program in Public Administration, Atlanta, GA 30303-3083. Offers MPA, JD/MPA. Part-time and evening/weekend programs available. *Students:* Average age 32. *Degree requirements:* For master's, thesis optional. *Entrance requirements:* For master's, GRE General Test. Additional exam requirements/recommendations for international students: Required—TOEFL. *Application deadline:* For fall admission, 4/1 for domestic and international students; for spring admission, 10/1 for domestic and international students. Applications are processed on a rolling basis. Application fee: $50. *Expenses:* Tuition, state resident: part-time $221 per credit hour. *Financial support:* In 2007–08, research assistantships with full tuition reimbursements (averaging $9,000 per year). *Faculty research:* Public management, nonprofit, policy. *Application contact:* AYSPS Office of Academic Assistance, E-mail: ayspsacademicassist@gsu.edu.

Governors State University, College of Business and Public Administration, Program in Public Administration, University Park, IL 60466-0975. Offers MPA. *Accreditation:* NASPAA. Part-time and evening/weekend programs available. *Students:* 38 full-time, 142 part-time. Average age 37. *Degree requirements:* For master's, comprehensive exam, thesis or alternative, internship or previous work in field. *Entrance requirements:* For master's, minimum GPA of 2.5. *Application deadline:* For fall admission, 7/15 priority date for domestic students; for spring admission, 11/10 for domestic students. Applications are processed on a rolling basis. Application fee: $25. *Financial support:* Fellowships, research assistantships, career-related internships or fieldwork, Federal Work-Study, institutionally sponsored loans, and tuition waivers (full and partial) available. Support available to part-time students. Financial award application deadline: 5/1. *Faculty research:* State and local politics.

Grambling State University, School of Graduate Studies and Research, College of Arts and Sciences, Program in Public Administration, Grambling, LA 71245. Offers MPA. *Accreditation:* NASPAA. Part-time programs available. *Faculty:* 3 full-time (0 women), 2 part-time/adjunct (1 woman). *Students:* 44 full-time (32 women), 30 part-time (20 women); includes 71 minority (all African Americans), 2 international. Average age 28. In 2007, 37 degrees awarded. *Degree requirements:* For master's, comprehensive exam (for some programs), thesis optional. *Entrance requirements:* For master's, GRE, minimum GPA of 2.75 on last degree. Additional exam requirements/recommendations for international students: Required—TOEFL. *Application deadline:* For fall admission, 7/1 for domestic students; for spring admission, 12/1 for domestic students. Applications are processed on a rolling basis. Application fee: $20 ($30 for international students). *Expenses:* Tuition, state resident: full-time $1,729. Tuition, nonresident: full-time $3,736. *Financial support:* In 2007–08, 10 research assistantships (averaging $3,440 per year) were awarded; institutionally sponsored loans and unspecified assistantships also available. Financial award application deadline: 5/31. *Unit head:* Dr. Rose Harris, Director, 318-274-2714, Fax: 318-274-3427, E-mail: harrisr@gram.edu. *Application contact:* Sarah Dennis, Admissions Coordinator, 318-274-2319, Fax: 318-274-3427, E-mail: denniss@alpha0.gram.edu.

Grand Valley State University, College of Community and Public Service, School of Public and Nonprofit Administration, Allendale, MI 49401-9403. Offers MHA, MPA. *Accreditation:* NASPAA. Part-time and evening/weekend programs available. *Faculty:* 11 full-time (4 women), 15 part-time/adjunct (5 women). *Students:* 66 full-time (38 women), 143 part-time (87 women); includes 30 minority (17 African Americans, 1 American Indian/Alaska Native, 5 Asian Americans or Pacific Islanders, 7 Hispanic Americans), 17 international. Average age 32. 87 applicants, 91% accepted, 57 enrolled. In 2007, 53 degrees awarded. *Application deadline:* For fall admission, 5/1 priority date for domestic students; for winter admission, 11/1 priority date for domestic students. Applications are processed on a rolling basis. Application fee: $30. Electronic applications accepted. *Financial support:* In 2007–08, 28 students received support, including 13 research assistantships with partial tuition reimbursements available (averaging $8,000 per year); career-related internships or fieldwork, Federal Work-Study, scholarships/grants, and unspecified assistantships also available. Financial award application deadline: 5/1. *Faculty research:* Comparative urban systems, ethics and public management, local economic development, public and nonprofit boards and governance. *Unit head:* Dr. Mark Hoffman, Director, 616-331-6575, Fax: 616-331-7120, E-mail: hoffman@gvsu.edu.

Hamline University, School of Business, St. Paul, MN 55104-1284. Offers business (MBA); nonprofit management (MANM); public administration (MPA, DPA); JD/MAM; JD/MANM; JD/MAPA. Part-time and evening/weekend programs available. *Faculty:* 9 full-time (3 women), 28 part-time/adjunct (11 women). *Students:* 227 full-time (127 women), 170 part-time (105 women); includes 55 minority (26 African Americans, 4 American Indian/Alaska Native, 19 Asian Americans or Pacific Islanders, 6 Hispanic Americans), 71 international. Average age 32. 249 applicants, 78% accepted, 160 enrolled. In 2007, 98 master's, 4 doctorates awarded. *Degree requirements:* For master's, thesis; for doctorate, thesis/dissertation. *Entrance requirements:* For master's and doctorate, personal statement, curriculum vitae, official transcripts, letters of recommendation, writing sample. Additional exam requirements/recommendations for international students: Required—TOEFL (minimum score 550 paper-based; 213 computer-based). *Application deadline:* For fall admission, 3/30 priority date for domestic students. Applications are processed on a rolling basis. Application fee: $30. Electronic applications accepted. *Expenses:* Tuition: Full-time $6,336; part-time $396 per credit. Required fees: $5 per credit. One-time fee: $175 part-time. *Financial support:* Federal Work-Study available. Financial award applicants required to submit FAFSA. *Unit head:* Julian Schuster, Dean, 651-523-2284, Fax: 651-523-3098, E-mail: jschuster01@hamline.edu. *Application contact:* Rae A. Lenway, Director, Graduate Recruitment and Admission, 651-523-2900, Fax: 651-523-3058, E-mail: rlenway@hamline.edu.

Harvard University, John F. Kennedy School of Government, Lucius N. Littauer Mid-Career Program in Public Administration, Cambridge, MA 02138. Offers MPA. *Students:* 187 full-time (80 women); includes 18 minority (7 African Americans, 1 American Indian/Alaska Native, 4 Asian Americans or Pacific Islanders, 6 Hispanic Americans), 93 international. Average age 38. 479 applicants, 61% accepted, 187 enrolled. *Entrance requirements:* For master's, GMAT or GRE General Test, minimum 7 years of professional experience. Additional exam requirements/recommendations for international students: Required—TOEFL (minimum score 600 paper-based; 250 computer-based; 100 iBT), TWE. *Application deadline:* For fall admission, 3/7 for domestic students, 12/5 for international students. Applications are processed on a rolling basis. Application fee: $80. Electronic applications accepted. *Expenses: Contact institution. Financial support:* Fellowships, Federal Work-Study, institutionally sponsored loans, scholarships/grants, health care benefits, and unspecified assistantships available. Financial award application deadline: 3/7; financial award applicants required to submit CSS PROFILE or FAFSA. *Unit head:* Judy Kugel, Acting Director, 617-496-1100, E-mail: judy_kugel@harvard.edu. *Application contact:* 617-495-1155.

Harvard University, John F. Kennedy School of Government, Master in Public Administration/International Development Program, Cambridge, MA 02138. Offers MPAID. *Students:* 60 full-time (30 women); includes 4 minority (1 African American, 2 Asian Americans or Pacific Islanders, 1 Hispanic American), 40 international. Average age 26. 351 applicants, 27% accepted, 60 enrolled. *Entrance requirements:* For master's, GMAT or GRE General Test (for joint Business School applicants only), one course each in microeconomics and macroeconomics; two college-level calculus courses (one must contain multivariable calculus); bachelor's degree; 2-3 years of professional experience in development (strongly encouraged). Additional exam requirements/recommendations for international students: Required—TOEFL (minimum score 600 paper-based; 250 computer-based; 100 iBT). *Application deadline:* For fall admission, 1/9 for domestic students. Application fee: $80. Electronic applications accepted. *Expenses:* Tuition: Full-time $31,456. Full-time tuition and fees vary according to program and student level. *Financial support:* Fellowships, research assistantships, teaching assistantships, career-related internships or fieldwork, Federal Work-Study, institutionally sponsored loans, scholarships/grants, health care benefits, and unspecified assistantships available. Financial award application deadline: 2/2; financial award applicants required to submit CSS PROFILE or FAFSA. *Unit head:* Carol Finney, Director, 617-495-7799, E-mail: carol_finney@harvard.edu. *Application contact:* 617-495-2133.

Harvard University, John F. Kennedy School of Government, Two-year Program in Public Administration, Cambridge, MA 02138. Offers MPA. *Students:* 57 full-time (17 women); includes 8 minority (1 African American, 5 Asian Americans or Pacific Islanders, 2 Hispanic Americans), 31 international. Average age 28. 131 applicants, 66% accepted, 57 enrolled. *Entrance requirements:* For master's, GMAT or GRE General Test, minimum of 3 years of work experience, relevant graduate work. Additional exam requirements/recommendations for international students: Required—TOEFL (minimum score 600 paper-based; 250 computer-based; 100 iBT), TWE. *Application deadline:* For fall admission, 1/5 for domestic students. Application fee: $80. Electronic applications accepted. *Expenses:* Tuition: Full-time $31,456. Full-time tuition and fees vary according to program and student level. *Financial support:* Fellowships, research assistantships, teaching assistantships, career-related internships or fieldwork, Federal Work-Study, institutionally sponsored loans, scholarships/grants, health care benefits, and unspecified assistantships available. Financial award application deadline: 2/2; financial award applicants required to submit CSS PROFILE or FAFSA. *Unit head:* Judy Kugel, Acting Director, 617-496-1100, E-mail: judy_kugel@harvard.edu. *Application contact:* 617-495-1155.

Hodges University, Graduate Programs, Naples, FL 34119. Offers business administration (MBA); computer information technology (MS); criminal justice (MCJ); education (MPS); information systems management (MIS); interdisciplinary (MPS); law (MPS); management (MSM); professional studies (MPS); psychology (MPS); public administration (MPA). Part-time and evening/weekend programs available. Postbaccalaureate distance learning degree programs offered (no on-campus study). *Faculty:* 16 full-time (4 women), 2 part-time/adjunct (1 woman). *Students:* 37 full-time (25 women), 175 part-time (104 women); includes 64 minority (29 African Americans, 2 Asian Americans or Pacific Islanders, 33 Hispanic Americans). Average age 36. In 2007, 75 degrees awarded. *Degree requirements:* For master's, comprehensive exam (for some programs). *Entrance requirements:* For master's, in-house entrance exam. *Application deadline:* Applications are processed on a rolling basis. Application fee: $50. Electronic applications accepted. *Expenses:* Tuition: Full-time $10,260; part-time $570 per credit hour. Required fees: $190 per trimester. *Financial support:* In 2007–08, 181 students received support. Federal Work-Study and scholarships/grants available. Financial award application deadline: 7/8; financial award applicants required to submit FAFSA. *Unit head:* Terry McMahan, President, 239-513-1122, Fax: 239-598-6253, E-mail: tmcmahan@hodges.edu. *Application contact:* Rita Lampus, Vice President of Student Enrollment Management, 239-513-1122, Fax: 239-598-6253, E-mail: rlampus@internationalcollege.edu.

Howard University, Graduate School, Department of Political Science, Program in Public Administration, Washington, DC 20059-0002. Offers MAPA. *Accreditation:* NASPAA. Part-time programs available. *Degree requirements:* For master's, comprehensive exam. *Entrance requirements:* For master's, GRE General Test, minimum GPA of 3.0. *Expenses:* Tuition: Full-time $16,175; part-time $899 per credit hour. Required fees: $805.

Idaho State University, Office of Graduate Studies, College of Arts and Sciences, Department of Political Science, Program in Public Administration, Pocatello, ID 83209. Offers MPA. Part-time programs available. *Students:* 15 full-time (8 women), 13 part-time (9 women); includes 3 minority (all Hispanic Americans) Average age 31. In 2007, 17 degrees awarded. *Degree requirements:* For master's, comprehensive exam, thesis optional, public service internship. *Entrance requirements:* For master's, GRE General Test, course work in humanities and social sciences, 3 letters of recommendation. Additional exam requirements/recommendations for international students: Required—TOEFL (minimum score 550 paper-based; 213 computer-based; 80 iBT). *Application deadline:* For fall admission, 7/1 for domestic students, 6/1 for international students; for spring admission, 12/1 for domestic students, 11/1 for international students. Applications are processed on a rolling basis. Application fee: $55. Electronic applications accepted. *Expenses:* Tuition, state resident: full-time $2,882; part-time $259 per credit hour. Tuition, nonresident: full-time $11,566; part-time $379 per credit hour. Required fees: $2,278. Full-time tuition and fees vary according to program. Part-time tuition and fees vary according to course load. *Financial support:* Teaching assistantships with full and partial tuition reimbursements, career-related internships or fieldwork, Federal Work-Study, institutionally sponsored loans, scholarships/grants, health care benefits, and unspecified assistantships available. Support available to part-time students. Financial award application deadline: 1/1; financial award applicants required to submit FAFSA. *Faculty research:* Constitutional law, policy theory, public administration, international affairs. *Application contact:* Ellen Combs, Graduate School Technical Records Specialist, 208-282-2150, Fax: 208-282-4847.

Illinois Institute of Technology, Graduate College, College of Science and Letters, Department of Social Sciences, Chicago, IL 60616-3793. Offers nonprofit management (MPA); public administration (MPA); public safety and crisis management (MPA); JD/MPA; MBA/MPA. Part-time and evening/weekend programs available. *Faculty:* 10 full-time (2 women), 18 part-time/adjunct (4 women). *Students:* 12 full-time (7 women), 40 part-time (25 women); includes 20 minority (15 African Americans, 1 American Indian/Alaska Native, 1 Asian American or Pacific Islander, 3 Hispanic Americans), 10 international. Average age 34. 167 applicants, 81% accepted, 21 enrolled. In 2007, 62 master's awarded. *Degree requirements:* For master's, comprehensive exam, capstone course (practicum). *Entrance requirements:* For master's, minimum undergraduate GPA of 3.0, 2 letters of recommendation. Additional exam requirements/recommendations for international students: Required—TOEFL (minimum score 550 paper-based; 213 computer-based; 80 iBT). *Application deadline:* For fall admission, 5/1 for domestic and international students; for spring admission, 1/5 for domestic and international students. Applications are processed on a rolling basis. Application fee: $40. Electronic applications accepted. *Expenses:* Tuition: Full-time $14,004; part-time $778 per credit. Required fees: $7 per credit. $235 per term. Tuition and fees vary according to class time, course level, course load, program and student level. *Financial support:* Federal Work-Study, institutionally sponsored loans, scholarships/grants, and health care benefits available. Support available to part-time students. Financial award applicants required to submit FAFSA. *Faculty research:* Comparative public administration and policy, migration and ethnic politics, social dimension and impact of science and technology, urban politics, urban ethnography. *Unit head:* Dr. Patrick R. Ireland, Professor and Chairman, 312-567-5128, Fax: 312-567-6821, E-mail: socscience@iit.edu. *Application contact:* Lawerence Ruffolo, Assistant Director, Graduate

Public Administration

Illinois Institute of Technology (continued)
Program in Public Administration, 312-906-5197, Fax: 312-906-5199, E-mail: lruffolo@kentlaw.edu.

Indiana State University, School of Graduate Studies, College of Arts and Sciences, Department of Political Science, Terre Haute, IN 47809-1401. Offers political science (MA, MS); public administration (MPA). *Faculty:* 6 full-time (1 woman), 6 part-time/adjunct (2 women). *Students:* 14 full-time (7 women), 31 part-time (14 women); includes 9 minority (5 African Americans, 2 Asian Americans or Pacific Islanders, 2 Hispanic Americans), 4 international. Average age 34. 40 applicants, 75% accepted, 18 enrolled. In 2007, 9 degrees awarded. *Degree requirements:* For master's, thesis (for some programs). *Entrance requirements:* For master's, GRE or minimum undergraduate GPA of 2.75, 18 semester hours of course work in political science. Additional exam requirements/recommendations for international students: Required—TOEFL (minimum score 550 paper-based). *Application deadline:* For fall admission, 7/1 priority date for domestic students; for spring admission, 11/1 priority date for domestic students. Applications are processed on a rolling basis. Application fee: $20. Electronic applications accepted. *Expenses:* Tuition, state resident: full-time $7,056; part-time $294 per semester hour. Tuition, nonresident: full-time $14,016; part-time $584 per semester hour. Required fees: $175 per semester. *Financial support:* In 2007–08, 1 research assistantship with partial tuition reimbursement (averaging $7,000 per year), 6 teaching assistantships (averaging $7,000 per year) were awarded; career-related internships or fieldwork, Federal Work-Study, institutionally sponsored loans, and tuition waivers (partial) also available. Support available to part-time students. Financial award application deadline: 3/1; financial award applicants required to submit FAFSA. *Unit head:* Dr. Michael Chambers, Interim Chairperson, 812-237-2429.

Indiana University Bloomington, School of Public and Environmental Affairs, Public Affairs Programs, Bloomington, IN 47405-7000. Offers nonprofit management (Certificate); public affairs (MPA, PhD); public management (Certificate); public policy (PhD); JD/MPA; MPA/MA; MPA/MIS; MPA/MLS; MSES/MPA. *Accreditation:* NASPAA (one or more programs are accredited). Part-time programs available. Terminal master's awarded for partial completion of doctoral program. *Degree requirements:* For doctorate, thesis/dissertation. *Entrance requirements:* For master's, GMAT or GRE, LSAT; for doctorate, GRE General Test. *Application deadline:* For fall admission, 2/1 priority date for domestic students, 1/15 for international students; for spring admission, 9/1 for international students. Applications are processed on a rolling basis. Application fee: $50 ($60 for international students). *Financial support:* Fellowships, research assistantships, teaching assistantships, career-related internships or fieldwork, Federal Work-Study, institutionally sponsored loans, and unspecified assistantships available. Financial award application deadline: 2/1; financial award applicants required to submit FAFSA. *Faculty research:* Comparative and international affairs, environmental policy and resource management, policy analysis, public finance, public management, urban management, nonprofit management. *Application contact:* Charles A. Johnson, Coordinator of Student Recruitment, 800-765-7755, Fax: 812-855-7802, E-mail: speainfo@indiana.edu.

See Close-Up on page 1597.

Indiana University Kokomo, School of Public and Environmental Affairs, Kokomo, IN 46904-9003. Offers public management (MS, Graduate Certificate). *Students:* 4 full-time (1 woman), 11 part-time (7 women); includes 3 minority (all African Americans) Average age 40. In 2007, 1 degree awarded. *Application deadline:* For fall admission, 8/1 priority date for domestic students; for spring admission, 12/9 priority date for domestic students. Application fee: $40 ($50 for international students). *Expenses:* Tuition, state resident: full-time $4,698; part-time $196 per credit hour. Tuition, nonresident: full-time $10,746; part-time $448 per credit hour. Required fees: $397; $397 per year. Full-time tuition and fees vary according to course load, campus/location and program. *Unit head:* Dr. Robert Dibie, Assistant Dean, 765-455-9417, Fax: 765-455-9537, E-mail: iuadmis@iuk.edu. *Application contact:* Susan Wilson, Information Contact, 765-455-9330.

Indiana University Northwest, School of Public and Environmental Affairs, Gary, IN 46408-1197. Offers criminal justice (MPA); environmental affairs (Graduate Certificate); health services administration (MPA); human services administration (MPA); nonprofit management (Graduate Certificate); public management (MPA, Graduate Certificate). *Accreditation:* NASPAA (one or more programs are accredited). Part-time programs available. *Faculty:* 5 full-time (3 women). *Students:* 28 full-time (21 women), 98 part-time (78 women); includes 82 minority (71 African Americans, 1 American Indian/Alaska Native, 1 Asian American or Pacific Islander, 9 Hispanic Americans). Average age 38. In 2007, 29 master's, 27 other advanced degrees awarded. *Entrance requirements:* For master's, GRE General Test or GMAT, letters of recommendation. *Application deadline:* For fall admission, 8/15 priority date for domestic students. Applications are processed on a rolling basis. Application fee: $25. *Expenses:* Tuition, state resident: full-time $4,636; part-time $193 per credit hour. Tuition, nonresident: full-time $10,787; part-time $449 per credit hour. Required fees: $436; $436 per year. Full-time tuition and fees vary according to course load, campus/location and program. *Financial support:* Career-related internships or fieldwork, Federal Work-Study, and tuition waivers (partial) available. Support available to part-time students. Financial award application deadline: 3/1. *Faculty research:* Employment in income security policies, evidence in criminal justice, equal employment law, social welfare policy and welfare reform, public finance in developing countries. *Unit head:* George Assibey-Mensah, Interim Dean/Division Director, 219-980-6695, Fax: 219-980-6737. *Application contact:* Sandra Hall Smith, Secretary, 219-980-6695, Fax: 219-980-6737, E-mail: shsmith@iun.edu.

Indiana University–Purdue University Indianapolis, School of Public and Environmental Affairs, Indianapolis, IN 46202-2896. Offers health administration (MHA); public affairs (MPA), including criminal justice, environmental management, nonprofit management, policy analysis, public management; JD/MHA; MBA/MHA; MLS/NMC; MLS/PMC; MSN/MHA. *Accreditation:* CAHME (one or more programs are accredited). Part-time and evening/weekend programs available. *Faculty:* 17 full-time (6 women). *Students:* 108 full-time (67 women), 291 part-time (159 women); includes 74 minority (43 African Americans, 1 American Indian/Alaska Native, 25 Asian Americans or Pacific Islanders, 5 Hispanic Americans), 10 international. Average age 35. In 2007, 77 degrees awarded. *Entrance requirements:* For master's, GRE General Test, minimum GPA of 3.0 (preferred). Additional exam requirements/recommendations for international students: Required—TOEFL. *Application deadline:* For fall admission, 7/15 priority date for domestic students; for spring admission, 11/15 for domestic students. Applications are processed on a rolling basis. Application fee: $50 ($60 for international students). *Expenses:* Tuition, state resident: full-time $5,818; part-time $242 per credit hour. Tuition, nonresident: full-time $17,106; part-time $713 per credit hour. Required fees: $629. Tuition and fees vary according to course load, campus/location and program. *Financial support:* In 2007–08, 11 fellowships with full and partial tuition reimbursements (averaging $5,890 per year), 10 teaching assistantships (averaging $9,900 per year) were awarded; research assistantships with full and partial tuition reimbursements, career-related internships or fieldwork, Federal Work-Study, institutionally sponsored loans, and scholarships/grants also available. Support available to part-time students. Financial award application deadline: 3/1. *Faculty research:* Economic development, water and air quality, ethics, financing, organization design and structure. Total annual research expenditures: $1.9 million. *Unit head:* Dr. Greg Lindsey, Associate Dean, 317-274-4656, Fax: 317-274-5153. *Application contact:* 317-274-4656, Fax: 317-274-5153, E-mail: speainfo@speanet.iupui.edu.

See Close-Up on page 1599.

Indiana University South Bend, School of Public and Environmental Affairs, South Bend, IN 46634-7111. Offers health systems administration and policy (MPA); health systems management (Certificate); nonprofit management (Certificate); public and community services administration and policy (MPA); public management (Certificate); urban affairs (Certificate). *Accreditation:* NASPAA. Part-time and evening/weekend programs available. *Faculty:* 4 full-time (1 woman). *Students:* 11 full-time (8 women), 32 part-time (23 women); includes 6 minority (4 African Americans, 2 Hispanic Americans), 2 international. Average age 35. In 2007, 9 degrees awarded. *Entrance requirements:* For master's, GRE General Test, minimum undergraduate GPA of 2.5. *Application deadline:* For fall admission, 7/1 priority date for domestic students; for spring admission, 11/1 for domestic students. Applications are processed on a rolling basis. Application fee: $46 ($58 for international students). *Expenses:* Tuition, state resident: full-time $4,762; part-time $198 per credit hour. Tuition, nonresident: full-time $11,720; part-time $488 per credit hour. Required fees: $422; $422 per year. Full-time tuition and fees vary according to course load, campus/location and program. *Financial support:* Fellowships, research assistantships, career-related internships or fieldwork, Federal Work-Study, and institutionally sponsored loans available. Support available to part-time students. Financial award application deadline: 3/1; financial award applicants required to submit FAFSA. *Unit head:* Leda M. Hall, Dean, 574-520-4803.

Institute of Public Administration, Programs in Public Administration, Dublin, Ireland. Offers healthcare management (MA); local government management (MA); public management (MA, Diploma).

Iowa State University of Science and Technology, Graduate College, College of Liberal Arts and Sciences, Department of Political Science, Ames, IA 50011. Offers political science (MA); public administration (MPA); JD/MA. *Accreditation:* NASPAA. *Faculty:* 12 full-time (4 women), 2 part-time/adjunct (1 woman). *Students:* 26 full-time (12 women), 33 part-time (10 women); includes 3 minority (2 African Americans, 1 Asian American or Pacific Islander), 5 international. 31 applicants, 77% accepted, 15 enrolled. In 2007, 16 degrees awarded. *Degree requirements:* For master's, thesis (for some programs). *Entrance requirements:* For master's, GRE General Test or GMAT or LSAT. Additional exam requirements/recommendations for international students: Required—TOEFL (paper-based 570; computer-based 230; iBT 80) or IELTS (6.0). *Application deadline:* For fall admission, 1/1 priority date for domestic and international students; for spring admission, 10/1 for domestic and international students. Applications are processed on a rolling basis. Application fee: $30 ($70 for international students). Electronic applications accepted. *Financial support:* In 2007–08, 18 research assistantships with full and partial tuition reimbursements (averaging $16,052 per year) were awarded; fellowships, teaching assistantships with full and partial tuition reimbursements, scholarships/grants, health care benefits, and unspecified assistantships also available. *Unit head:* Dr. James M. McCormick, Chair, 515-294-8682, Fax: 515-294-1003, E-mail: polsc@iastate.edu. *Application contact:* Dr. Richard Mansback, Director of Graduate Education, 515-294-3764, E-mail: polsci@iastate.edu.

Jackson State University, Graduate School, School of Liberal Arts, Department of Public Policy and Administration, Jackson, MS 39217. Offers MPPA, PhD. *Accreditation:* NASPAA (one or more programs are accredited). Evening/weekend programs available. *Degree requirements:* For master's, comprehensive exam, thesis optional; for doctorate, comprehensive exam, thesis/dissertation. *Entrance requirements:* For master's, GRE General Test; for doctorate, GRE, GMAT, MAT. Additional exam requirements/recommendations for international students: Required—TOEFL.

James Madison University, The Graduate School, College of Arts and Letters, Department of Political Science, Harrisonburg, VA 22807. Offers public administration (MPA). Part-time programs available. *Faculty:* 4 full-time (0 women), 1 part-time/adjunct (0 women). *Students:* 14 full-time (5 women), 23 part-time (12 women); includes 3 minority (2 African Americans, 1 Asian American or Pacific Islander), 1 international. Average age 27. In 2007, 5 degrees awarded. *Degree requirements:* For master's, comprehensive exam. *Entrance requirements:* For master's, GMAT or GRE General Test, Prospective applicants should contact MPA Director prior to applying to The Graduate School. Additional exam requirements/recommendations for international students: Required—TOEFL. *Application deadline:* For fall admission, 5/1 priority date for domestic students; for spring admission, 9/1 priority date for domestic students. Applications are processed on a rolling basis. Application fee: $55. Electronic applications accepted. *Expenses:* Tuition, state resident: full-time $6,720; part-time $280 per credit hour. Tuition, nonresident: full-time $19,104; part-time $796 per credit hour. *Financial support:* In 2007–08, 9 students received support. Unspecified assistantships and 9 graduate assistantships ($7,237) available. Financial award application deadline: 3/1; financial award applicants required to submit FAFSA. *Unit head:* Dr. Kay Knickrehm, Academic Unit Head, 540-568-6149. *Application contact:* Dr. B. Douglas Skelley, Graduate Coordinator, 540-568-6149.

John Jay College of Criminal Justice of the City University of New York, Graduate Studies, Program in Public Administration, New York, NY 10019-1093. Offers MPA. *Accreditation:* NASPAA. Part-time and evening/weekend programs available. *Degree requirements:* For master's, thesis or alternative. *Entrance requirements:* For master's, minimum B average. Additional exam requirements/recommendations for international students: Required—TOEFL (minimum score 500 paper-based; 173 computer-based).

Kansas State University, Graduate School, College of Arts and Sciences, Department of Political Science, Program in Public Administration, Manhattan, KS 66506. Offers MPA. *Accreditation:* NASPAA. Part-time programs available. *Students:* 19 full-time (7 women), 3 part-time (all women); includes 1 minority (Asian American or Pacific Islander), 2 international. Average age 33. In 2007, 7 degrees awarded. *Degree requirements:* For master's, thesis or alternative, comprehensive written and oral exams. *Entrance requirements:* For master's, GRE (recommended), minimum GPA of 3.0. Additional exam requirements/recommendations for international students: Required—TOEFL (minimum score 550 paper-based; 213 computer-based). *Application deadline:* For fall admission, 2/1 priority date for domestic and international students; for spring admission, 10/1 for domestic students, 8/1 for international students. Applications are processed on a rolling basis. Application fee: $30 ($55 for international students). *Financial support:* Fellowships, research assistantships, teaching assistantships, career-related internships or fieldwork, institutionally sponsored loans, and scholarships/grants available. Support available to part-time students. Financial award application deadline: 3/1; financial award applicants required to submit FAFSA. *Faculty research:* Comparative administration, comparative affirmative action, tourism, agricultural policy, state and local government. *Application contact:* Prof. Krishna Tummala, Director, 785-532-0452, Fax: 785-532-2339, E-mail: tummala@ksu.edu.

Kean University, College of Business and Public Administration, Program in Public Administration, Union, NJ 07083. Offers criminal justice (MPA); environmental management (MPA); health services administration (MPA); non-profit management (MPA); public administration (MPA). *Accreditation:* NASPAA. Part-time and evening/weekend programs available. *Faculty:* 7 full-time (4 women). *Students:* 63 full-time (37 women), 82 part-time (52 women); includes 68 African Americans, 6 Asian Americans or Pacific Islanders, 17 Hispanic Americans, 14 international. Average age 32. 64 applicants, 73% accepted, 25 enrolled. In 2007, 58 degrees awarded. *Degree requirements:* For master's, thesis, internship, research seminar. *Entrance requirements:* For master's, 2 letters of recommendation, interview, essay. *Application deadline:* For fall admission, 5/1 for domestic students; for spring admission, 11/1 for domestic students. Application fee: $60 ($150 for international students). Electronic applications accepted. *Expenses:* Tuition, state resident: full-time $9,384; part-time $391 per credit. Tuition, nonresident: full-time $12,720; part-time $530 per credit. Required fees: $2,382; $99 per credit. Part-time tuition and fees vary according to course load. *Financial support:* In 2007–08, 15 research assistantships with full tuition reimbursements (averaging $3,217 per year) were awarded; unspecified assistantships also available. *Faculty research:* Fiscal impact of New Federalism, New Jersey state and local government, computer application in public management. *Unit head:* Dr. Craig P. Donovan, Program Coordinator, 908-737-4307, E-mail: cpdonova@kean.edu. *Application contact:* Joanne Morris, Director of Graduate Admissions, 908-737-3355, Fax: 908-737-3354, E-mail: grad-adm@kean.edu.

Kean University, College of Natural, Applied and Health Sciences, Program in Nursing and Public Administration, Union, NJ 07083. Offers MSN/MPA. *Accreditation:* NLN. Part-time and evening/weekend programs available. *Faculty:* 9 full-time (all women). *Students:* 4 full-time (all women), 7 part-time (5 women); includes 9 minority (8 African Americans, 1 Hispanic American), 1 international. Average age 44. 2 applicants, 100% accepted, 1 enrolled. *Application deadline:* For fall admission, 5/1 for domestic students; for spring admission, 11/1 for domestic students. Application fee: $60 ($150 for international students). Electronic applications accepted. *Expenses:* Tuition, state resident: full-time $9,384; part-time $391 per credit. Tuition, nonresident: full-time $12,720; part-time $530 per credit. Required fees: $2,382; $99 per credit. Part-time tuition and fees vary according to course load. *Financial support:* In 2007–08, research assistantships with full tuition reimbursements (averaging $3,217 per year); unspecified assistantships also available. *Unit head:* Dr. Estelle A. Pisani, Program Coordinator, 908-737-3386, E-mail: episani@kean.edu. *Application contact:* Joanne Morris, Director of Graduate Admissions, 908-737-3355, Fax: 908-737-3354, E-mail: grad-adm@kean.edu.

Kennesaw State University, College of Humanities and Social Sciences, Program in Public Administration, Kennesaw, GA 30144-5591. Offers MPA. *Accreditation:* NASPAA. Part-time and evening/weekend programs available. *Faculty:* 11 full-time (7 women), 4 part-time/adjunct (1 woman). *Students:* 25 full-time (13 women), 49 part-time (30 women); includes 23 minority (22 African Americans, 1 Asian American or Pacific Islander), 10 international. Average age 33. 30 applicants, 83% accepted, 21 enrolled. In 2007, 21 degrees awarded. *Entrance requirements:* For master's, GRE General Test, minimum GPA of 2.75. Additional exam requirements/recommendations for international students: Required—TOEFL (minimum score 550 paper-based; 213 computer-based; 80 iBT), IELTS (minimum score 6). *Application deadline:* For fall admission, 7/1 for domestic and international students; for spring admission, 10/1 for domestic and international students. Applications are processed on a rolling basis. Application fee: $50. Electronic applications accepted. *Financial support:* In 2007–08, 2 research assistantships with full tuition reimbursements (averaging $15,000 per year) were awarded; Federal Work-Study also available. Support available to part-time students. Financial award application deadline: 6/15; financial award applicants required to submit FAFSA. *Unit head:* Dr. Martha Griffith, Director, 770-423-6631, E-mail: mgriffith@kennesaw.edu. *Application contact:* Vilma Marquez, Admissions Counselor, 770-420-4377, Fax: 770-423-6885, E-mail: ksugrad@kennesaw.edu.

Kent State University, College of Arts and Sciences, Department of Political Science, Program in Public Administration, Kent, OH 44242-0001. Offers MPA. *Accreditation:* NASPAA. *Faculty:* 4 full-time (1 woman), 3 part-time/adjunct (2 women). *Students:* 7 full-time (4 women), 23 part-time (10 women); includes 3 minority (all African Americans) Average age 33. 50 applicants, 38% accepted, 5 enrolled. In 2007, 1 degree awarded. *Degree requirements:* For master's, thesis optional, public sector internship. *Entrance requirements:* For master's, GRE General Test, minimum GPA of 2.75. Additional exam requirements/recommendations for international students: Required—TOEFL. *Application deadline:* For fall admission, 7/12 for domestic students; for spring admission, 11/29 for domestic students. Applications are processed on a rolling basis. Application fee: $30. Electronic applications accepted. *Financial support:* In 2007–08, 4 research assistantships with full tuition reimbursements (averaging $9,000 per year) were awarded; teaching assistantships with full tuition reimbursements, career-related internships or fieldwork, Federal Work-Study, institutionally sponsored loans, and tuition waivers (full) also available. Financial award application deadline: 2/1. *Unit head:* Dr. Joseph Drew, Associate Professor and MPA Coordinator, 330-672-3239, E-mail: jdrew@kent.edu.

Kentucky State University, College of Professional Studies, Frankfort, KY 40601. Offers business (MBA); public administration (MPA); special education (MA). Part-time and evening/weekend programs available. *Faculty:* 11 full-time (2 women). *Students:* 44 full-time (26 women), 69 part-time (40 women); includes 67 minority (64 African Americans, 1 Asian American or Pacific Islander, 2 Hispanic Americans), 1 international. Average age 32. 70 applicants, 74% accepted, 41 enrolled. In 2007, 26 degrees awarded. *Degree requirements:* For master's, comprehensive exam, thesis optional. *Entrance requirements:* For master's, GMAT. Additional exam requirements/recommendations for international students: Required—TOEFL. *Application deadline:* For fall admission, 7/1 priority date for domestic students, 4/1 priority date for international students; for spring admission, 11/15 priority date for domestic students, 8/15 priority date for international students. Applications are processed on a rolling basis. Application fee: $30 ($100 for international students). Electronic applications accepted. *Financial support:* In 2007–08, 4 research assistantships (averaging $613 per year) were awarded. Financial award application deadline: 4/15; financial award applicants required to submit FAFSA. *Unit head:* Dr. Gashaw Lake, Dean, E-mail: gashaw.lake@kysu.edu. *Application contact:* James Burrell, Director of Admission, 502-597-6322, Fax: 502-597-5814, E-mail: james.burrell@kysu.edu.

Kutztown University of Pennsylvania, College of Graduate Studies and Extended Learning, College of Liberal Arts and Sciences, Program in Public Administration, Kutztown, PA 19530-0730. Offers MPA. Part-time and evening/weekend programs available. *Faculty:* 3 full-time (2 women). *Students:* 7 full-time (3 women), 14 part-time (8 women); includes 3 minority (all African Americans) Average age 29. 15 applicants, 67% accepted, 5 enrolled. In 2007, 8 degrees awarded. *Degree requirements:* For master's, comprehensive exam, thesis optional. *Entrance requirements:* For master's, GRE General Test. Additional exam requirements/recommendations for international students: Required—TOEFL. *Application deadline:* Applications are processed on a rolling basis. Application fee: $35. Electronic applications accepted. *Expenses:* Tuition, state resident: full-time $6,214; part-time $345 per credit. Tuition, nonresident: full-time $9,944; part-time $552 per credit. Required fees: $1,536; $78 per credit. $65 per semester. *Financial support:* Career-related internships or fieldwork, Federal Work-Study, scholarships/grants, and unspecified assistantships available. Financial award application deadline: 3/15; financial award applicants required to submit FAFSA. *Faculty research:* Structure of code enforcement offices in smaller developing communities. *Unit head:* Dr. Jack Treadway, Chairperson, 610-683-4449, Fax: 610-683-4603, E-mail: treadway@kutztown.edu.

Lamar University, College of Graduate Studies, College of Arts and Sciences, Department of Political Science, Beaumont, TX 77710. Offers public administration (MPA). Part-time programs available. *Faculty:* 6 full-time (1 woman), 1 part-time/adjunct (0 women). *Students:* 3 full-time (0 women), 3 part-time (2 women); includes 2 minority (1 African American, 1 Asian American or Pacific Islander), 1 international. Average age 26. 11 applicants, 36% accepted, 3 enrolled. In 2007, 5 degrees awarded. *Entrance requirements:* For master's, GRE General Test. Additional exam requirements/recommendations for international students: Required—TOEFL. *Application deadline:* For fall admission, 8/1 for domestic students; for spring admission, 12/1 for domestic students. Applications are processed on a rolling basis. Application fee: $25 ($50 for international students). *Expenses:* Tuition, state resident: part-time $348 per semester hour. Tuition, nonresident: part-time $626 per semester hour. Tuition and fees vary according to course load. *Financial support:* Fellowships, research assistantships, teaching assistantships, career-related internships or fieldwork, Federal Work-Study, and institutionally sponsored loans available. Financial award application deadline: 4/1. *Faculty research:* Political activities of administrators, administrative response to Hurricane Rita, budgeting, environmental politics, urban planning. *Unit head:* Dr. Glenn Utter, Chair, 409-880-8526, Fax: 409-880-8710. *Application contact:* Dr. Terri Davis, Director, 409-880-8533, Fax: 409-880-1710, E-mail: davistb@hal.lamar.edu.

Lewis University, College of Arts and Sciences, Program in Organizational Leadership, Romeoville, IL 60446. Offers higher education/student services (MA); organizational management (MA); public administration (MA); training and development (MA). Part-time and evening/weekend programs available. *Students:* 21 full-time (12 women), 115 part-time (92 women); includes 35 minority (30 African Americans, 1 Asian American or Pacific Islander, 4 Hispanic Americans), 1 international. Average age 38. 64 applicants, 89% accepted, 57 enrolled. *Entrance requirements:* For master's, bachelor's degree, at least 25 years of age, minimum of 3 years of work experience, minimum GPA of 3.0 (provisional admission possible), letter of recommendation, interview. Additional exam requirements/recommendations for international students: Required—TOEFL (minimum score 550 paper-based; 213 computer-based). *Application deadline:* For fall admission, 5/1 priority date for international students; for spring admission, 11/15 priority date for international students. Applications are processed on a rolling basis. Application fee: $40. Electronic applications accepted. *Financial support:* Federal Work-Study, scholarships/grants, tuition waivers, and unspecified assistantships available. Financial award application deadline: 5/1; financial award applicants required to submit FAFSA. *Unit head:* Dr. Rich Walsh, Director, 815-838-0500, E-mail: walshri@lewisu.edu. *Application contact:* Bernadette Valderrama, Information Contact, 815-838-0500 Ext. 5629.

Lincoln University, School of Graduate Studies and Continuing Education, College of Business and Professional Studies, Department of Business and Economics, Jefferson City, MO 65102. Offers business administration (MBA), including accounting, entrepreneurship, management, public administration and policy. *Accreditation:* ACBSP. Part-time and evening/weekend programs available. *Faculty:* 1 full-time (0 women), 6 part-time/adjunct (1 woman). *Students:* 26 full-time (11 women), 22 part-time (17 women); includes 16 minority (all African Americans), 10 international. Average age 33. 20 applicants, 95% accepted, 13 enrolled. In 2007, 38 degrees awarded. *Degree requirements:* For master's, comprehensive exam, thesis optional, portfolio. *Entrance requirements:* For master's, GMAT, undergraduate prerequisite courses; see parent units for general requirements. Additional exam requirements/recommendations for international students: Required—TOEFL (minimum score 500 paper-based; 173 computer-based; 61 iBT). *Application deadline:* For fall admission, 7/1 priority date for domestic and international students; for spring admission, 12/1 priority date for domestic and international students. Applications are processed on a rolling basis. Application fee: $20. *Expenses:* Tuition, state resident: full-time $5,400; part-time $225 per credit hour. Tuition, nonresident: full-time $10,020; part-time $417 per credit hour. Required fees: $360; $15 per credit hour. $20 per semester. *Financial support:* Federal Work-Study and scholarships/grants available. Financial award application deadline: 4/1; financial award applicants required to submit FAFSA. *Unit head:* Dr. Kylar Broadus, Interim Department Head, 573-681-5487, Fax: 573-681-6085, E-mail: broadusk@lincolnu.edu.

Lindenwood University, Graduate Programs, Division of Management, St. Charles, MO 63301-1695. Offers accounting (MBA, MS); business administration (MBA); entrepreneurial studies (MBA, MS); finance (MBA, MS); human resource management (MBA); human resources (MS); international business (MBA, MS); management (MBA, MS); management information systems (MBA, MS); marketing (MBA, MS); public management (MBA, MS); sport management (MA). Part-time and evening/weekend programs available. *Faculty:* 27 full-time (12 women), 12 part-time/adjunct (7 women). *Students:* 221 full-time (106 women), 142 part-time (73 women); includes 37 minority (26 African Americans, 2 American Indian/Alaska Native, 6 Asian Americans or Pacific Islanders, 3 Hispanic Americans), 124 international. Average age 31. In 2007, 153 degrees awarded. *Degree requirements:* For master's, thesis (for some programs), minimum GPA of 3.0. *Entrance requirements:* For master's, interview, minimum GPA of 3.0. Additional exam requirements/recommendations for international students: Required—TOEFL (minimum score 550 paper-based; 213 computer-based; 80 iBT). *Application deadline:* For fall admission, 7/30 priority date for domestic students, 9/30 priority date for international students; for winter admission, 12/30 priority date for domestic and international students; for spring admission, 3/30 priority date for domestic and international students. Application fee: $30 ($100 for international students). *Expenses:* Tuition: Full-time $12,400; part-time $350 per hour. Full-time tuition and fees vary according to degree level and program. *Financial support:* Career-related internships or fieldwork, Federal Work-Study, institutionally sponsored loans, and tuition waivers (partial) available. Financial award application deadline: 6/30; financial award applicants required to submit FAFSA. *Unit head:* Ed Morris, Dean of Enrollment Division, 636-949-4832, E-mail: emorris@lindenwood.edu. *Application contact:* Brett Barger, Dean of Evening Admissions and Extension Campuses, 636-949-4934, Fax: 636-949-4109, E-mail: adultadmissions@lindenwood.edu.

Long Island University, Brooklyn Campus, School of Business, Public Administration and Information Sciences, Program in Public Administration, Brooklyn, NY 11201-8423. Offers MPA. *Accreditation:* NASPAA. Part-time and evening/weekend programs available. *Entrance requirements:* For master's, GMAT or GRE Subject Test, 2 letters of recommendation. Additional exam requirements/recommendations for international students: Required—TOEFL (minimum score 500 paper-based; 173 computer-based). Electronic applications accepted.

Long Island University, C.W. Post Campus, College of Management, Department of Health Care and Public Administration, Brookville, NY 11548-1300. Offers gerontology (Certificate); health care administration (MPA); health care administration/gerontology (MPA); nonprofit management (MPA, Certificate); public administration (MPA). *Accreditation:* NASPAA (one or more programs are accredited). Part-time and evening/weekend programs available. *Faculty:* 8 full-time (4 women), 14 part-time/adjunct (4 women). *Students:* 51 full-time (31 women), 65 part-time (43 women); includes 41 minority (19 African Americans, 15 Asian Americans or Pacific Islanders, 7 Hispanic Americans), 5 international. Average age 32. 232 applicants, 69% accepted, 26 enrolled. In 2007, 44 degrees awarded. *Degree requirements:* For master's, thesis. *Entrance requirements:* For master's, GMAT, minimum GPA of 2.5; for Certificate, minimum GPA of 2.5. *Application deadline:* Applications are processed on a rolling basis. Application fee: $30. Electronic applications accepted. *Expenses:* Tuition: Part-time $825 per credit. Tuition and fees vary according to course load. *Financial support:* In 2007–08, 10 students received support, including 3 research assistantships with partial tuition reimbursements available; Federal Work-Study and unspecified assistantships also available. Support available to part-time students. Financial award application deadline: 5/15; financial award applicants required to submit CSS PROFILE or FAFSA. *Faculty research:* Critical issues in sexuality, social work in religious communities, gerontological social work. *Unit head:* Dr. Linda Vila, Chair, 516-299-2578, E-mail: linda.vila@liu.edu.

Long Island University, Rockland Graduate Campus, Graduate School, Programs in Health and Public Administration, Orangeburg, NY 10962. Offers gerontology (Advanced Certificate); health administration (MPA); public administration (MPA). *Faculty:* 1 full-time (0 women), 3 part-time/adjunct (1 woman). *Students:* 3 full-time (1 woman), 27 part-time (19 women). In 2007, 9 degrees awarded. *Entrance requirements:* For master's, GRE General Test. *Application deadline:* Applications are processed on a rolling basis. Application fee: $30. *Expenses:* Tuition: Part-time $835 per credit. Required fees: $100 per term. *Unit head:* Prof. Patricia Latona, Program Director, 845-359-7200 Ext. 5410, Fax: 845-359-7248, E-mail: patricia.latona@liu.edu. *Application contact:* Peter S. Reiner, Director of Admissions and Marketing, 845-359-7200, Fax: 845-359-7248, E-mail: peter.reiner@liu.edu.

See Close-Up on page 1603.

Louisiana State University and Agricultural and Mechanical College, Graduate School, E. J. Ourso College of Business, Public Administration Institute, Baton Rouge, LA 70803. Offers MPA, JD/MPA. Part-time programs available. *Faculty:* 9 full-time (2 women). *Students:* 39 full-time (27 women), 64 part-time (35 women); includes 26 minority (21 African Americans, 2 American Indian/Alaska Native, 1 Asian American or Pacific Islander, 2 Hispanic Americans), 2 international. Average age 32. 44 applicants, 82% accepted, 29 enrolled. In 2007, 32 degrees awarded. *Degree requirements:* For master's, comprehensive exam. *Entrance requirements:* For master's, GRE General Test, minimum GPA of 3.0. Additional exam requirements/recommendations for international students: Required—TOEFL (minimum score 550 paper-based; 213 computer-based; 79 iBT). *Application deadline:* For fall admission, 1/25 priority date for domestic students, 5/15 for international students; for spring admission, 10/15 for international students. Applications are processed on a rolling basis. Application fee: $25. Electronic applications accepted. *Financial support:* In 2007–08, 82 students received support, including 12 research assistantships with full and partial tuition reimbursements available (averaging $9,750 per year), 3 teaching assistantships with partial tuition reimbursements available (averaging $9,832 per year); Federal Work-Study, scholarships/grants, health care benefits, and unspecified assistantships also available. Support available to part-time students. Financial award applicants required to submit FAFSA. *Faculty research:* Policy analysis, health care policy, financial and budget analysis. Total annual research expenditures: $1,956. *Unit head:* Dr. James A. Richardson, Director, 225-578-6745, Fax: 225-578-9078, E-mail: parich@lsu.edu.

Public Administration

Louisiana State University and Agricultural and Mechanical College, Graduate School, Manship School of Mass Communication, Baton Rouge, LA 70803. Offers MMC, PhD. *Accreditation:* ACEJMC. Part-time programs available. Postbaccalaureate distance learning degree programs offered (minimal on-campus study). *Faculty:* 25 full-time (13 women). *Students:* 39 full-time (24 women), 14 part-time (12 women); includes 6 minority (5 African Americans, 1 Hispanic American), 14 international. Average age 31. 61 applicants, 39% accepted, 17 enrolled. In 2007, 8 master's, 1 doctorate awarded. *Degree requirements:* For master's, thesis. *Entrance requirements:* For master's, GRE General Test, minimum GPA of 3.0. Additional exam requirements/recommendations for international students: Required—TOEFL (minimum score 550 paper-based; 213 computer-based; 79 iBT). *Application deadline:* For fall admission, 1/25 priority date for domestic students, 5/15 for international students; for spring admission, 10/15 for international students. Applications are processed on a rolling basis. Application fee: $25. Electronic applications accepted. *Financial support:* In 2007–08, 44 students received support, including 26 research assistantships with full and partial tuition reimbursements available (averaging $15,415 per year), 4 teaching assistantships with full and partial tuition reimbursements available (averaging $20,250 per year); fellowships, career-related internships or fieldwork, Federal Work-Study, institutionally sponsored loans, scholarships/grants, health care benefits, tuition waivers (full and partial), and unspecified assistantships also available. Support available to part-time students. Financial award application deadline: 3/1; financial award applicants required to submit FAFSA. *Faculty research:* Media effects, political communication, new media technologies, persuasive communication, journalism processes and practice. Total annual research expenditures: $85,046. *Unit head:* Dr. John Maxwell Hamilton, Dean, 225-578-2002, Fax: 225-578-2125, E-mail: jhamilt@lsu.edu. *Application contact:* Dr. Margaret DeFleur, Associate Dean of Graduate Studies and Research, 225-578-9294, Fax: 225-578-2125, E-mail: defleur@lsu.edu.

See Close-Up on page 905.

Marist College, Graduate Programs, School of Management, Program in Public Administration, Poughkeepsie, NY 12601-1387. Offers MPA. Part-time and evening/weekend programs available. Postbaccalaureate distance learning degree programs offered (no on-campus study). *Faculty:* 5 full-time (1 woman), 4 part-time/adjunct (1 woman). *Students:* 17 full-time (7 women), 236 part-time (127 women); includes 53 minority (33 African Americans, 3 Asian Americans or Pacific Islanders, 17 Hispanic Americans). Average age 38. 115 applicants, 70% accepted, 64 enrolled. In 2007, 87 degrees awarded. *Entrance requirements:* For master's, GRE General Test, resumé, personal statement, transcript. Additional exam requirements/recommendations for international students: Required—TOEFL (minimum score 550 paper-based; 213 computer-based; 80 iBT); Recommended—IELTS (minimum score 7). *Application deadline:* For fall admission, 7/1 for domestic students, 6/15 for international students; for spring admission, 12/1 for domestic students, 10/31 for international students. Applications are processed on a rolling basis. Application fee: $30. Electronic applications accepted. *Expenses:* Tuition: Part-time $665 per credit. *Financial support:* In 2007–08, 71 students received support. Scholarships/grants available. Support available to part-time students. Financial award application deadline: 8/15; financial award applicants required to submit FAFSA. *Faculty research:* Public policy analysis, health administration. *Unit head:* Dr. James Melitski, Director, 845-575-3225, E-mail: james.melitski@marist.edu. *Application contact:* Kelly Holmes, Director of Admissions, 845-575-3800, Fax: 845-575-3166, E-mail: graduate@marist.edu.

Marquette University, Graduate School, Program in Public Service, Milwaukee, WI 53201-1881. Offers MAPS. *Faculty:* 2 full-time (0 women). *Students:* 34 full-time (26 women), 98 part-time (63 women); includes 25 minority (15 African Americans, 2 American Indian/Alaska Native, 2 Asian Americans or Pacific Islanders, 6 Hispanic Americans), 1 international. Average age 36. 100 applicants, 76% accepted, 29 enrolled. *Unit head:* Dr. Johnette Caulfield, Adjunct Assistant Professor and Director of Graduate Programs, 414-288-5556, E-mail: jay.caulfield@marquette.edu.

Marywood University, Academic Affairs, College of Health and Human Services, Department of Nursing and Public Administration, Program in Public Administration, Scranton, PA 18509-1598. Offers criminal justice (MPA); public administration (MPA); MPA/MSW. *Students:* 4 full-time (all women), 11 part-time (5 women); includes 2 minority (both African Americans) Average age 30. In 2007, 8 degrees awarded. *Degree requirements:* For master's, thesis or alternative, internship/practicum. *Entrance requirements:* Additional exam requirements/recommendations for international students: Required—TOEFL (minimum score 550 paper-based; 213 computer-based). *Application deadline:* For fall admission, 4/15 priority date for domestic and international students; for spring admission, 11/15 priority date for domestic and international students. Applications are processed on a rolling basis. Application fee: $30. Electronic applications accepted. *Expenses:* Tuition: Full-time $15,290; part-time $695 per credit. Required fees: $990; $370 per term. Tuition and fees vary according to degree level. *Financial support:* Research assistantships with tuition reimbursements, career-related internships or fieldwork, scholarships/grants, tuition waivers (partial), and unspecified assistantships available. Support available to part-time students. Financial award application deadline: 2/15; financial award applicants required to submit FAFSA. *Application contact:* Tammy Manka, Assistant Director of Graduate Admissions, 570-340-6002, E-mail: tmanka@marywood.edu.

McMaster University, School of Graduate Studies, Faculty of Social Sciences, Department of Political Science, Hamilton, ON L8S 4M2, Canada. Offers international relations (PhD); political science (MA); public and the global economy (MA); public policy (PhD); public policy and administration (MA). Part-time programs available. *Faculty:* 21 full-time. *Students:* 63 full-time, 6 part-time. 140 applicants, 20% accepted. *Degree requirements:* For master's, thesis or alternative. *Entrance requirements:* For master's, minimum B+ average. Additional exam requirements/recommendations for international students: Required—TOEFL (minimum score 580 paper-based; 237 computer-based). *Application deadline:* For fall admission, 2/15 priority date for domestic students. Applications are processed on a rolling basis. Application fee: $90. *Financial support:* In 2007–08, 27 teaching assistantships (averaging $8,440 per year) were awarded; scholarships/grants also available. *Faculty research:* Organizational theory, internationalization of public policy, water resource policies, political interest intermediation, comparative politics. *Unit head:* Dr. Robert O'Brien, Chair, 905-525-9140 Ext. 23705, Fax: 905-527-3071, E-mail: obrienr@mcmaster.ca. *Application contact:* Manuela Dozzi, Administrative Secretary, 905-525-9140 Ext. 24742, Fax: 905-527-3071, E-mail: dozzim@mcmaster.ca.

Metropolitan College of New York, Program in Public Administration, New York, NY 10013. Offers MPA. Evening/weekend programs available. *Degree requirements:* For master's, thesis. *Entrance requirements:* For master's, appropriate work experience, interview, minimum GPA of 2.7, internship or job in administrative setting. Additional exam requirements/recommendations for international students: Required—TOEFL (minimum score 600 paper-based; 220 computer-based). Electronic applications accepted. Expenses: Contact institution. *Faculty research:* Transnational politics and culture, women and social policy, confidentiality in the human services, concepts of marginality, ethics in social policy.

Metropolitan State University, College of Management, St. Paul, MN 55106-5000. Offers business administration (MBA); information management (MMIS); MIS generalist (Graduate Certificate); MIS systems analysis (Graduate Certificate); nonprofit management (MPNA); project management (Graduate Certificate); public administration (MPNA); systems management (MMIS). Part-time and evening/weekend programs available. *Faculty:* 18 full-time (2 women), 26 part-time/adjunct (9 women). *Students:* 125 full-time (61 women), 184 part-time (87 women); includes 34 minority (18 African Americans, 1 American Indian/Alaska Native, 14 Asian Americans or Pacific Islanders, 1 Hispanic American), 42 international. Average age 36. 137 applicants, 83% accepted, 93 enrolled. In 2007, 104 degrees awarded. *Degree requirements:* For master's, thesis optional, computer language (MMIS). *Entrance requirements:* For master's, GMAT (MBA), resumé. Additional exam requirements/recommendations for international students: Required—TOEFL (minimum score 550 paper-based; 213 computer-based). *Application deadline:* For fall admission, 7/15 for international students; for winter admission, 11/15 for international students; for spring admission, 3/15 for international students. Applications are processed on a rolling basis. Application fee: $20. *Expenses:* Tuition, state resident: full-time $5,080; part-time $254 per credit. Tuition, nonresident: full-time $10,160; part-time $508 per credit. Required fees: $189; $34 per credit. *Financial support:* In 2007–08, 31 students received support, including 11 research assistantships with partial tuition reimbursements available (averaging $7,200 per year); career-related internships or fieldwork and Federal Work-Study also available. Support available to part-time students. Financial award applicants required to submit FAFSA. *Faculty research:* Yugoslav economic system, workers' cooperatives, participative management and job enrichment, global business systems. *Unit head:* Dr. Carol Bormann-Young, Graduate Director, 612-659-7287, Fax: 612-659-7268, E-mail: carol.bormann.young@metrostate.edu. *Application contact:* Gloria B. Marcus, Recruiter/Admissions Adviser, 612-659-7258, Fax: 612-659-7268, E-mail: gloria.marcus@metrostate.edu.

Midwestern State University, Graduate Studies, College of Health Sciences and Human Services, Program in Health Services and Public Administration, Wichita Falls, TX 76308. Offers health services administration (MHA); public administration (MPA); public administration (administrative justice) (MPA); public administration (health services administration) with certificate (MPA); public administration (health services) (MPA). Part-time and evening/weekend programs available. *Degree requirements:* For master's, comprehensive exam, thesis. *Entrance requirements:* For master's, GRE. Additional exam requirements/recommendations for international students: Required—TOEFL (minimum score 550 paper-based; 213 computer-based). Electronic applications accepted.

Minnesota State University Mankato, College of Graduate Studies, College of Social and Behavioral Sciences, Department of Political Science and Law Enforcement, Program in Public Administration, Mankato, MN 56001. Offers MAPA, MAPA/MA. *Students:* 10 full-time (3 women), 27 part-time (12 women). Average age 33. In 2007, 14 degrees awarded. *Degree requirements:* For master's, one foreign language, comprehensive exam, thesis or alternative. *Entrance requirements:* For master's, minimum GPA of 3.0 during previous 2 years. Additional exam requirements/recommendations for international students: Required—TOEFL. *Application deadline:* For fall admission, 7/1 priority date for domestic students; for spring admission, 11/1 for domestic students. Applications are processed on a rolling basis. Application fee: $40. Electronic applications accepted. *Financial support:* Research assistantships with full tuition reimbursements, teaching assistantships with full tuition reimbursements, unspecified assistantships available. Financial award application deadline: 3/15; financial award applicants required to submit FAFSA. *Unit head:* Dr. Scott Granberg-Rademacker, Graduate Coordinator, 507-389-6939. *Application contact:* 507-389-2321, E-mail: grad@mnsu.edu.

Minnesota State University Moorhead, Graduate Studies, College of Social and Natural Sciences, Program in Public, Human Services, and Health Administration, Moorhead, MN 56563-0002. Offers MS. Part-time and evening/weekend programs available. *Degree requirements:* For master's, final oral exam, final project paper or thesis. *Entrance requirements:* For master's, GRE General Test, minimum GPA of 2.75. Additional exam requirements/recommendations for international students: Required—TOEFL (minimum score 550 paper-based; 213 computer-based). Electronic applications accepted.

Mississippi State University, College of Arts and Sciences, Department of Political Science and Public Administration, Mississippi State, MS 39762. Offers political science (MA); public policy and administration (MPPA, PhD). *Accreditation:* NASPAA (one or more programs are accredited). Evening/weekend programs available. *Faculty:* 13 full-time (3 women), 2 part-time/adjunct (both women). *Students:* 47 full-time (24 women), 34 part-time (19 women); includes 25 minority (22 African Americans, 3 Hispanic Americans), 2 international. Average age 32. 33 applicants, 76% accepted, 20 enrolled. In 2007, 23 master's, 3 doctorates awarded. *Degree requirements:* For master's, comprehensive oral or written exam; for doctorate, thesis/dissertation, comprehensive oral and written exam. *Entrance requirements:* For master's, minimum GPA of 3.0; for doctorate, GRE General Test, minimum graduate GPA of 3.35. Additional exam requirements/recommendations for international students: Required—TOEFL. *Application deadline:* For fall admission, 8/1 priority date for domestic students; for spring admission, 12/1 priority date for domestic students. Applications are processed on a rolling basis. Application fee: $30. *Expenses:* Tuition, state resident: full-time $4,978; part-time $274 per hour. Tuition, nonresident: full-time $11,469; part-time $635 per hour. *Financial support:* In 2007–08, 8 teaching assistantships with full tuition reimbursements (averaging $9,044 per year) were awarded; Federal Work-Study, institutionally sponsored loans, and unspecified assistantships also available. Financial award application deadline: 4/15. *Faculty research:* American politics, international relations, state and local government, comparative government, public administration. Total annual research expenditures: $890,000. *Unit head:* Dr. David A. Breaux, Head, 662-325-2711, Fax: 662-325-2716, E-mail: dab1@ps.msstate.edu. *Application contact:* Dr. William A. Person, Interim Associate Vice President for Academic Affairs/Interim Dean of Graduate Studies, 662-325-7400, Fax: 662-325-1967, E-mail: grad@grad.msstate.edu.

Missouri State University, Graduate College, College of Humanities and Public Affairs, Department of Political Science, Program in Public Administration, Springfield, MO 65804-0094. Offers MPA. *Accreditation:* NASPAA. Part-time programs available. *Students:* 14 full-time (7 women), 8 part-time (4 women); includes 2 minority (1 African American, 1 Asian American or Pacific Islander), 3 international. Average age 30. 9 applicants, 100% accepted, 5 enrolled. In 2007, 6 degrees awarded. *Degree requirements:* For master's, comprehensive exam, thesis or alternative, internship. *Entrance requirements:* For master's, GRE, minimum GPA of 3.0. Additional exam requirements/recommendations for international students: Required—TOEFL (minimum score 550 paper-based; 213 computer-based; 79 iBT). *Application deadline:* For fall admission, 7/20 priority date for domestic students; for spring admission, 12/20 priority date for domestic students. Applications are processed on a rolling basis. Application fee: $35. *Expenses:* Tuition, state resident: full-time $3,708; part-time $206 per credit hour. Tuition, nonresident: full-time $7,236; part-time $206 per credit hour. Required fees: $622. Full-time tuition and fees vary according to course level, course load, program and reciprocity agreements. *Financial support:* Research assistantships with full tuition reimbursements, teaching assistantships with full tuition reimbursements, career-related internships or fieldwork, Federal Work-Study, and unspecified assistantships available. Support available to part-time students. Financial award application deadline: 3/31; financial award applicants required to submit FAFSA. *Faculty research:* Health care, global environmental problems, legislatures. *Unit head:* Dr. James Kaatz, Graduate Director, 417-836-6424, Fax: 417-836-6655, E-mail: jameskaatz@missouristate.edu.

Missouri State University, Graduate College, Interdisciplinary Program in Administrative Studies, Springfield, MO 65804-0094. Offers applied communication (MSAS); criminal justice (MSAS); environmental management (MSAS); project management (MSAS); sports management (MSAS). Part-time programs available. Postbaccalaureate distance learning degree programs offered (no on-campus study). *Students:* 21 full-time (10 women), 64 part-time (35 women); includes 5 minority (4 African Americans, 1 Hispanic American), 1 international. Average age 35. 17 applicants, 94% accepted, 13 enrolled. In 2007, 21 degrees awarded. *Degree requirements:* For master's, comprehensive exam, thesis or alternative. *Entrance requirements:* For master's, GRE, GMAT, 3 years of work experience. Additional exam requirements/recommendations for international students: Required—TOEFL (minimum score 550 paper-based; 213 computer-based; 79 iBT). *Application deadline:* For fall admission, 7/20 priority date for domestic students; for spring admission, 12/20 priority date for domestic students. Applications are processed on a rolling basis. Application fee: $35. Electronic applications accepted. *Expenses:* Tuition, state resident: full-time $3,708; part-time $206 per credit hour. Tuition, nonresident: full-time $7,236; part-time $206 per credit hour. Required fees: $622. Full-time tuition and fees vary according to course level, course load, program and reciprocity agreements. *Financial support:* In 2007–08, 4 teaching assistantships (averaging $7,050 per year) were awarded; research assistantships, career-related internships or fieldwork, Federal Work-Study, institutionally sponsored loans, scholarships/grants, and unspecified assistantships also available. Support available to part-time students. Financial award application deadline: 3/31; financial award applicants required to submit FAFSA. *Unit head:* John Bourhis, Director, 417-836-6390, E-mail: johnbourhis@missouristate.edu.

Montana State University, College of Graduate Studies, College of Letters and Science, Department of Political Science, Bozeman, MT 59717. Offers public administration (MPA). Part-time programs available. *Faculty:* 6 full-time (3 women), 3 part-time/adjunct (1 woman). *Students:* 5 full-time (4 women), 15 part-time (11 women), 3 international. Average age 30. 43 applicants, 40% accepted, 12 enrolled. In 2007, 12 degrees awarded. *Degree requirements:* For master's, comprehensive exam, thesis (for some programs). *Entrance requirements:* For master's, GRE General Test. Additional exam requirements/recommendations for international students: Required—TOEFL (minimum score 550 paper-based; 213 computer-based). *Application deadline:* For fall admission, 7/15 priority date for domestic students, 5/15 priority date for international students; for spring admission, 12/1 priority date for domestic students, 10/1 priority date for international students. Applications are processed on a rolling basis. Application fee: $30. Electronic applications accepted. *Expenses:* Tuition, state resident: full-time $5,176. Tuition, nonresident: full-time $13,070. *Financial support:* In 2007–08, 8 students received support, including research assistantships with full tuition reimbursements available (averaging $6,000 per year), 1 teaching assistantship with tuition reimbursement available (averaging $6,000 per year); career-related internships or fieldwork, tuition waivers (full and partial), and unspecified assistantships also available. Support available to part-time students. Financial award application deadline: 3/1; financial award applicants required to submit FAFSA. *Faculty research:* Natural resources policy, civil society, new west economics, organization development, media analysis. Total annual research expenditures: $351,240. *Unit head:* Dr. Jerry Johnson, Head, 406-994-5164, Fax: 406-994-6692, E-mail: jdj@montana.edu.

Montana State University–Billings, College of Arts and Sciences, Program in Public Administration, Billings, MT 59101-0298. Offers MPA. *Students:* 13. 5 applicants, 100% accepted, 5 enrolled. *Application deadline:* For fall admission, 7/15 for domestic students; for spring admission, 12/1 for domestic students. Application fee: $40. *Expenses:* Tuition, state resident: full-time $4,665. Tuition, nonresident: full-time $11,096. *Unit head:* Dr. David Hood, Chair, 406-657-2997. *Application contact:* David M. Sullivan, Graduate Studies Counselor, 406-657-2053, Fax: 406-657-2299, E-mail: dsullivan@msubillings.edu.

Monterey Institute of International Studies, Graduate School of International Policy Studies, Program in International Public Administration, Monterey, CA 93940-2691. Offers international management (MPA). *Students:* 61 full-time (41 women), 1 (woman) part-time; includes 4 minority (1 Asian American or Pacific Islander, 3 Hispanic Americans), 23 international. Average age 28. 53 applicants, 94% accepted, 24 enrolled. In 2007, 33 degrees awarded. *Degree requirements:* For master's, one foreign language. *Entrance requirements:* For master's, minimum GPA of 3.0, proficiency in a foreign language. Additional exam requirements/recommendations for international students: Required—TOEFL (minimum score 550 paper-based; 213 computer-based; 80 iBT). *Application deadline:* For fall admission, 3/15 priority date for domestic students; for spring admission, 10/1 priority date for domestic students. Applications are processed on a rolling basis. Application fee: $50. Electronic applications accepted. *Expenses:* Tuition: Full-time $27,750; part-time $1,250 per credit. Required fees: $200. *Financial support:* Career-related internships or fieldwork, Federal Work-Study, and institutionally sponsored loans available. Support available to part-time students. Financial award application deadline: 3/15; financial award applicants required to submit FAFSA. *Application contact:* 831-647-4123, Fax: 831-647-6405, E-mail: admit@miis.edu.

See Close-Up on page 1157.

Morehead State University, Graduate Programs, Institute for Regional Analysis and Public Policy, Morehead, KY 40351. Offers public administration (MPA). *Faculty:* 5 full-time (1 woman). *Students:* 13 full-time (4 women), 14 part-time (7 women); includes 2 minority (both African Americans), 1 international. Average age 32. *Entrance requirements:* For master's, GRE. Additional exam requirements/recommendations for international students: Required—TOEFL (minimum score 500 paper-based). *Application deadline:* For fall admission, 8/1 priority date for domestic and international students; for spring admission, 12/1 priority date for domestic and international students. Applications are processed on a rolling basis. Electronic applications accepted. *Financial support:* In 2007–08, 10 teaching assistantships (averaging $6,000 per year) were awarded. *Unit head:* Dr. David Rudy, Dean, 606-783-5419, Fax: 606-783-5092, E-mail: d.rudy@moreheadstate.edu. *Application contact:* Michelle Barber, Graduate Admissions Counselor, 606-783-2039, Fax: 606-783-5061, E-mail: m.barber@moreheadstate.edu.

National University, Academic Affairs, College of Letters and Sciences, Department of Professional Studies, La Jolla, CA 92037-1011. Offers forensic science (MFS); public administration (MPA). Part-time and evening/weekend programs available. Postbaccalaureate distance learning degree programs offered (no on-campus study). *Faculty:* 8 full-time (2 women), 147 part-time/adjunct (42 women). *Students:* 128 full-time (61 women), 176 part-time (86 women); includes 123 minority (48 African Americans, 21 Asian Americans or Pacific Islanders, 54 Hispanic Americans), 2 international. Average age 37. 540 applicants. In 2007, 272 degrees awarded. *Degree requirements:* For master's, thesis. *Entrance requirements:* For master's, interview, minimum GPA of 2.5. Additional exam requirements/recommendations for international students: Required—TOEFL (minimum score 550 paper-based; 213 computer-based; 80 iBT), IELTS (minimum score 6). *Application deadline:* Applications are processed on a rolling basis. Application fee: $60 ($65 for international students). Electronic applications accepted. *Expenses:* Tuition: Full-time $8,262; part-time $306 per unit. One-time fee: $60. *Financial support:* Career-related internships or fieldwork, institutionally sponsored loans, scholarships/grants, and tuition waivers (partial) available. Support available to part-time students. Financial award application deadline: 6/30; financial award applicants required to submit FAFSA. *Unit head:* Chandrika M. Kelso, Associate Professor and Chair, 858-642-8433, Fax: 858-642-8715, E-mail: ckelso@nu.edu. *Application contact:* Dominick Giovanniello, Associate Regional Dean—San Diego, 800-NAT-UNIV, Fax: 858-642-8709, E-mail: dgiovann@nu.edu.

National University of Singapore, Lee Kuan Yew School of Public Policy, Singapore, Singapore. Offers MPA, MPM, MPP, PhD.

See Close-Up on page 1605.

New York University, Robert F. Wagner Graduate School of Public Service, Program in Public Administration, New York, NY 10012-1019. Offers public administration (PhD); public and nonprofit management and policy (MPA, Advanced Certificate), including developmental administration (Advanced Certificate), financial management and public finance, human resources management (Advanced Certificate), international administration (Advanced Certificate), management (MPA), management for public and nonprofit organizations (Advanced Certificate), public policy analysis, quantitative analysis and computer applications (Advanced Certificate), urban public policy (Advanced Certificate); JD/MPA; MBA/MPA; MPA/MA. *Accreditation:* NASPAA (one or more programs are accredited). Part-time and evening/weekend programs available. *Faculty:* 16 full-time (10 women), 52 part-time/adjunct (28 women). *Students:* 318 full-time (229 women), 245 part-time (183 women); includes 105 minority (34 African Americans, 43 Asian Americans or Pacific Islanders, 28 Hispanic Americans), 66 international. Average age 28. 803 applicants, 61% accepted, 175 enrolled. In 2007, 206 master's, 3 doctorates awarded. *Degree requirements:* For master's, thesis or alternative, capstone/end event; for doctorate, one foreign language, thesis/dissertation. *Entrance requirements:* For master's, minimum undergraduate GPA of 3.0; for doctorate, GMAT or GRE General Test, minimum GPA of 3.5. Additional exam requirements/recommendations for international students: Required—TOEFL (minimum score 600 paper-based; 250 computer-based; 100 iBT), TWE (minimum score 4). *Application deadline:* For fall admission, 6/1 for domestic students, 1/15 for international students; for spring admission, 11/15 for domestic students, 10/1 for international students. Applications are processed on a rolling basis. Application fee: $70. Electronic applications accepted. *Expenses:* Contact institution. *Financial support:* In 2007–08, 160 fellowships (averaging $9,051 per year), 4 research assistantships with full tuition reimbursements (averaging $16,000 per year) were awarded; career-related internships or fieldwork, Federal Work-Study, institutionally sponsored loans, scholarships/grants, health care benefits, and unspecified assistantships also available. Support available to part-time students. Financial award application deadline: 12/1; financial award applicants required to submit FAFSA. *Unit head:* Prof. Katherine O'Regan, Director, 212-998-7400, Fax: 212-995-4161. *Application contact:* Bethany Godsoe, Assistant Dean, Enrollment and Student Services, 212-998-7414, Fax: 212-995-4164, E-mail: wagner.admissions@nyu.edu.

See Close-Up on page 1611.

North Carolina Central University, Division of Academic Affairs, College of Arts and Sciences, Public Administration Program, Durham, NC 27707-3129. Offers MPA. Part-time and evening/weekend programs available. *Degree requirements:* For master's, one foreign language, comprehensive exam, thesis or alternative. *Entrance requirements:* For master's, GRE, minimum GPA of 3.0 in major, 2.5 overall. Additional exam requirements/recommendations for international students: Required—TOEFL. *Faculty research:* Racial diversity and community policing, economic development, issues in urban transportation.

North Carolina State University, Graduate School, College of Humanities and Social Sciences, Department of Political Science and Public Administration, Program in Public Administration, Raleigh, NC 27695. Offers MPA, PhD. *Accreditation:* NASPAA. *Degree requirements:* For master's, thesis optional; for doctorate, thesis/dissertation. *Entrance requirements:* For master's, GRE General Test, minimum GPA of 3.0 during previous 2 years; for doctorate, GRE General Test. Electronic applications accepted. *Faculty research:* Public budgeting, human resources, public information technology, nonprofit management, environmental policy.

Northeastern University, College of Arts and Sciences, Department of Political Science, Program in Public Administration, Boston, MA 02115-5096. Offers development administration (MPA); health administration and policy (MPA); state and local government (MPA); urban studies (Certificate). *Accreditation:* NASPAA (one or more programs are accredited). Part-time and evening/weekend programs available. *Faculty:* 22 full-time (4 women), 3 part-time/adjunct. *Students:* 19 full-time (8 women), 19 part-time (14 women). In 2007, 11 degrees awarded. *Degree requirements:* For master's, thesis optional. *Entrance requirements:* For master's, GRE General Test. Additional exam requirements/recommendations for international students: Required—TOEFL. *Application deadline:* For fall admission, 2/1 priority date for domestic students, 5/1 for international students. Applications are processed on a rolling basis. Application fee: $50. *Financial support:* Research assistantships with tuition reimbursements, teaching assistantships with tuition reimbursements, career-related internships or fieldwork, Federal Work-Study, tuition waivers (full and partial), and unspecified assistantships available. Support available to part-time students. Financial award application deadline: 2/1; financial award applicants required to submit FAFSA. *Faculty research:* National health care, Third World development, leadership and ethics, science and technology, budgeting. *Unit head:* Dr. Ronald D. Hedlund, Graduate Coordinator, 617-373-2796, Fax: 617-373-5311, E-mail: gradpolisci@neu.edu. *Application contact:* Brynn Thompson, Graduate Programs Assistant, 617-373-4404, Fax: 617-373-5311, E-mail: gradpolisci@neu.edu.

Northern Arizona University, Graduate College, College of Social and Behavioral Sciences, Department of Political Science, Program in Political Science, Flagstaff, AZ 86011. Offers political science (MA); public management (Certificate); public policy (PhD). *Degree requirements:* For master's, thesis optional; for doctorate, one foreign language, thesis/dissertation. *Entrance requirements:* For doctorate, GRE General Test.

Northern Arizona University, Graduate College, College of Social and Behavioral Sciences, Department of Political Science, Program in Public Administration, Flagstaff, AZ 86011. Offers MPA. *Degree requirements:* For master's, internship.

Northern Illinois University, Graduate School, College of Liberal Arts and Sciences, Department of Political Science, Division of Public Administration, De Kalb, IL 60115-2854. Offers MPA. *Accreditation:* NASPAA. Part-time and evening/weekend programs available. *Faculty:* 5 full-time (1 woman), 3 part-time/adjunct (1 woman). *Students:* 38 full-time (11 women), 50 part-time (17 women); includes 6 minority (5 African Americans, 1 Asian American or Pacific Islander), 1 international. Average age 29. 59 applicants, 69% accepted, 26 enrolled. In 2007, 36 degrees awarded. *Degree requirements:* For master's, comprehensive exam, internship, research paper. *Entrance requirements:* For master's, GRE General Test, minimum GPA of 2.75, 9 hours in social science. Additional exam requirements/recommendations for international students: Required—TOEFL (minimum score 550 paper-based; 213 computer-based). *Application deadline:* For fall admission, 3/1 priority date for domestic students, 5/1 for international students; for spring admission, 10/1 priority date for domestic students, 10/1 for international students. Applications are processed on a rolling basis. Application fee: $30. Electronic applications accepted. *Expenses:* Tuition, area resident: Part-time $226 per credit hour. Tuition, state resident: full-time $5,424; part-time $225 per credit hour. Tuition, nonresident: full-time $10,848. Required fees: $2,416; $64 per credit hour. *Financial support:* Fellowships with full tuition reimbursements, research assistantships with full tuition reimbursements, teaching assistantships, career-related internships or fieldwork, Federal Work-Study, scholarships/grants, tuition waivers (full), and unspecified assistantships available. Support available to part-time students. Financial award applicants required to submit FAFSA. *Faculty research:* Urban service and management, manpower public policy, performance appraisal, bureaucratic politics. *Unit head:* Dr. Gerald Gabris, Acting Director, 815-753-6140, Fax: 815-753-2539, E-mail: ggabris@niu.edu. *Application contact:* Dr. Vicki Clarke, Program Coordinator, 815-753-6149, E-mail: vclarke@niu.edu.

Northern Kentucky University, Office of Graduate Programs, College of Arts and Sciences, Program in Public Administration, Highland Heights, KY 41099. Offers non-profit management (Certificate); public administration (MPA). *Accreditation:* NASPAA. Part-time and evening/weekend programs available. *Faculty:* 5 full-time (3 women), 8 part-time/adjunct (5 women). *Students:* 7 full-time (3 women), 79 part-time (43 women); includes 7 minority (6 African Americans, 1 Hispanic American). Average age 35. 39 applicants, 72% accepted, 21 enrolled. In 2007, 34 degrees awarded. *Degree requirements:* For master's, capstone course. *Entrance requirements:* For master's, GRE, GMAT or MAT, 2 letters of recommendation, writing sample, minimum GPA of 2.75, 2 supportive letters, current resumé, narrative essay of academic and career goals, portfolio demonstrating professional activities. Additional exam requirements/recommendations for international students: Required—TOEFL (minimum score 550 paper-based; 213 computer-based; 79 iBT), Michigan English Language Assessment Battery (must be taken at NKU). *Application deadline:* For fall admission, 7/1 priority date for domestic students, 6/1 for international students; for spring admission, 12/1 priority date for domestic students, 10/1 for international students. Applications are processed on a rolling basis. Application fee: $40. Electronic applications accepted. *Financial support:* Unspecified assistantships available. *Faculty research:* Local government, non-profit, public safety, human resources. *Unit head:* Dr. Shamima Ahmed, Director, 859-572-6402, Fax: 859-572-6184, E-mail: ahmed@nku.edu. *Application contact:* Beth Devantier, MPA Coordinator, 859-572-5326, Fax: 859-572-6184.

Northern Michigan University, College of Graduate Studies, College of Arts and Sciences, Department of Political Science, Marquette, MI 49855-5301. Offers administrative services (MA); public administration (MPA). Part-time programs available. *Degree requirements:* For master's, thesis or alternative. *Entrance requirements:* For master's, minimum GPA of 3.0.

North Georgia College & State University, Graduate Studies, Program in Public Administration, Dahlonega, GA 30597. Offers MPA. Part-time and evening/weekend programs available. Postbaccalaureate distance learning degree programs offered. *Degree requirements:* For master's, thesis optional, internship. *Entrance requirements:* For master's, GMAT or GRE General Test, minimum undergraduate GPA of 2.75, 3 letters of recommendation. Electronic applications accepted.

Norwich University, School of Graduate Studies, Program in Public Administration, Northfield, VT 05663. Offers MPA. Evening/weekend programs available. *Faculty:* 6 part-time/adjunct (2 women). *Students:* 57 full-time (26 women); includes 10 minority (5 African Americans,

Public Administration

Norwich University (continued)

2 Asian Americans or Pacific Islanders, 3 Hispanic Americans). Average age 37. 33 applicants, 100% accepted, 29 enrolled. *Entrance requirements:* Additional exam requirements/recommendations for international students: Required—TOEFL (minimum score 550 paper-based). *Application deadline:* For fall admission, 8/10 for domestic and international students; for winter admission, 11/7 for domestic and international students; for spring admission, 2/6 for domestic and international students. Application fee: $50. *Expenses:* Tuition: Full-time $15,768; part-time $657 per credit. Tuition and fees vary according to program. *Financial support:* Scholarships/grants available. Financial award applicants required to submit FAFSA. *Unit head:* Donal Hartman, Program Director, 802-485-2730, E-mail: dhartman@norwich.edu. *Application contact:* Chris Ormsby, Administrative Director, 802-485-2730, Fax: 802-485-2533, E-mail: cormsby@norwich.edu.

Notre Dame de Namur University, Division of Academic Affairs, School of Business and Management, Department of Public Administration, Belmont, CA 94002-1908. Offers MPA. Part-time and evening/weekend programs available. *Faculty:* 2 full-time (1 woman), 4 part-time/adjunct (2 women). *Students:* 3 full-time (2 women), 37 part-time (28 women); includes 21 minority (5 Asian Americans or Pacific Islanders, 16 Hispanic Americans). Average age 36. 20 applicants, 100% accepted, 11 enrolled. In 2007, 20 degrees awarded. *Entrance requirements:* For master's, interview, minimum GPA of 2.5. Additional exam requirements/recommendations for international students: Required—TOEFL. *Application deadline:* For fall admission, 8/1 priority date for domestic students; for spring admission, 12/1 priority date for domestic students. Applications are processed on a rolling basis. Application fee: $50. Electronic applications accepted. *Financial support:* Career-related internships or fieldwork available. Support available to part-time students. Financial award applicants required to submit FAFSA. *Unit head:* Dr. C. J. Kalin, Director, 650-508-3721, E-mail: cjkalin@ndnu.edu. *Application contact:* Helen Valine, Director of Graduate Admissions, 650-508-3534, Fax: 650-508-3426, E-mail: grad.admit@ndnu.edu.

Nova Southeastern University, H. Wayne Huizenga School of Business and Entrepreneurship, Program in Public Administration, Fort Lauderdale, FL 33314-7796. Offers MPA, DPA. Part-time and evening/weekend programs available. *Students:* 14 full-time (11 women), 180 part-time (109 women); includes 125 minority (94 African Americans, 4 Asian Americans or Pacific Islanders, 27 Hispanic Americans), 2 international. In 2007, 57 master's, 4 doctorates awarded. *Degree requirements:* For master's, thesis or alternative; for doctorate, comprehensive exam, thesis/dissertation. *Entrance requirements:* For master's, GMAT, GRE General Test, work experience; for doctorate, GMAT or GRE, master's degree; work experience in field; course work in accounting, finance, and economics; computer literacy. *Application deadline:* For fall admission, 8/15 priority date for domestic students; for spring admission, 2/10 for domestic students. Applications are processed on a rolling basis. Application fee: $50. *Financial support:* Career-related internships or fieldwork, Federal Work-Study, and institutionally sponsored loans available. *Unit head:* Steve Harvey, Assistant Dean, 954-262-5047, Fax: 954-262-3829, E-mail: harvey@nsu.nova.edu. *Application contact:* Karen Goldberg, Assistant Director, 954-262-5039, Fax: 954-262-3822, E-mail: karen@nova.edu.

Oakland University, Graduate Study and Lifelong Learning, College of Arts and Sciences, Department of Political Science, Rochester, MI 48309-4401. Offers public administration (MPA). *Accreditation:* NASPAA. Part-time and evening/weekend programs available. *Faculty:* 4 full-time (2 women), 3 part-time/adjunct (1 woman). *Students:* 36 full-time (22 women), 32 part-time (25 women); includes 16 minority (14 African Americans, 1 Asian American or Pacific Islander, 1 Hispanic American). Average age 30. 31 applicants, 90% accepted, 23 enrolled. In 2007, 17 degrees awarded. *Entrance requirements:* For master's, minimum GPA of 3.0 for unconditional admission. Additional exam requirements/recommendations for international students: Required—TOEFL (minimum score 550 paper-based; 213 computer-based). *Application deadline:* For fall admission, 7/15 priority date for domestic students, 5/1 priority date for international students; for winter admission, 12/1 priority date for domestic students, 9/1 priority date for international students; for spring admission, 3/15 priority date for domestic students. Applications are processed on a rolling basis. Application fee: $35. Electronic applications accepted. *Expenses:* Tuition, state resident: full-time $9,936; part-time $414 per credit. Tuition, nonresident: full-time $17,202; part-time $716 per credit. *Financial support:* Federal Work-Study, institutionally sponsored loans, and tuition waivers (full) available. Financial award application deadline: 3/1; financial award applicants required to submit FAFSA. *Unit head:* Dr. John S. Klemanski, Program Coordinator, 248-370-2352, Fax: 248-370-2355, E-mail: klemanski@oakland.edu. *Application contact:* Dr. Dale K. Nesbary, MPA Director, 248-370-2375, Fax: 248-370-4299, E-mail: nesbary@oakland.edu.

Ohio University, Graduate College, College of Arts and Sciences, Department of Political Science, Athens, OH 45701-2979. Offers political science (MA); public administration (MPA). Part-time programs available. *Faculty:* 24 full-time (8 women). *Students:* 39 full-time (12 women), 29 part-time (11 women); includes 4 minority (3 African Americans, 1 American Indian/Alaska Native), 15 international. 54 applicants, 76% accepted, 31 enrolled. In 2007, 31 degrees awarded. *Degree requirements:* For master's, comprehensive exam, thesis or alternative. *Entrance requirements:* For master's, GRE General Test, minimum GPA of 3.0. Additional exam requirements/recommendations for international students: Required—TOEFL. *Application deadline:* For fall admission, 3/1 priority date for domestic students. Applications are processed on a rolling basis. Application fee: $50 ($55 for international students). Electronic applications accepted. *Financial support:* In 2007–08, 30 students received support, including 10 research assistantships with full tuition reimbursements available (averaging $8,000 per year), 6 teaching assistantships with full tuition reimbursements available (averaging $8,000 per year); career-related internships or fieldwork, Federal Work-Study, institutionally sponsored loans, and tuition waivers (full and partial) also available. Financial award application deadline: 2/15. *Faculty research:* International relations, Latin American politics, public policy, economic development, political theory. *Unit head:* Dr. John Gilliom, Chair, 740-593-4368, Fax: 740-593-0394. *Application contact:* Dr. Judith Millesen, Graduate Director, 740-593-4381, Fax: 740-593-0394.

Old Dominion University, College of Business and Public Administration, Doctoral Program in Public Administration and Urban Policy, Norfolk, VA 23529. Offers PhD. Part-time and evening/weekend programs available. Postbaccalaureate distance learning degree programs offered. *Faculty:* 7 full-time (1 woman), 3 part-time/adjunct (2 women). *Students:* 3 full-time (all women), 25 part-time (11 women); includes 8 minority (6 African Americans, 1 American Indian/Alaska Native, 1 Asian American or Pacific Islander), 2 international. Average age 39. 5 applicants, 80% accepted, 4 enrolled. In 2007, 4 degrees awarded. *Degree requirements:* For doctorate, comprehensive exam, thesis/dissertation. *Entrance requirements:* For doctorate, GMAT, GRE General Test, master's degree, minimum graduate GPA of 3.0. Additional exam requirements/recommendations for international students: Required—TOEFL (minimum score 550 paper-based; 213 computer-based; 79 iBT). *Application deadline:* For fall admission, 7/1 priority date for domestic students; for spring admission, 10/1 priority date for domestic students. Applications are processed on a rolling basis. Application fee: $40. *Expenses:* Tuition, state resident: part-time $304 per credit hour. Tuition, nonresident: part-time $761 per credit hour. *Financial support:* In 2007–08, 6 students received support, including 6 research assistantships with tuition reimbursements available (averaging $12,908 per year); fellowships, teaching assistantships, career-related internships or fieldwork, scholarships/grants, and tuition waivers (partial) also available. Support available to part-time students. Financial award application deadline: 2/15; financial award applicants required to submit FAFSA. *Faculty research:* Educational needs and program development, policy analysis and administration, excellence norms for cooperative education programs. Total annual research expenditures: $60,000. *Unit head:* Dr. John C. Morris, Graduate Program Director, 757-683-3961, Fax: 757-683-5639, E-mail: jcmorris@odu.edu. *Application contact:* Megan S. Jones, Graduate Program Manager, 757-683-3961, Fax: 757-683-4886, E-mail: mmjones@odu.edu.

Old Dominion University, College of Business and Public Administration, Master's Program in Business Administration, Norfolk, VA 23529. Offers business and economic forecasting (MBA); financial analysis and valuation (MBA); information technology and enterprise integration (MBA); international business (MBA); maritime and port management (MBA); public administration (MBA). *Accreditation:* AACSB. Part-time and evening/weekend programs available. *Faculty:* 66 full-time (15 women), 6 part-time/adjunct (1 woman). *Students:* 86 full-time (38 women), 201 part-time (86 women); includes 53 minority (33 African Americans, 1 American Indian/Alaska Native, 16 Asian Americans or Pacific Islanders, 3 Hispanic Americans), 36 international. Average age 31. 235 applicants, 71% accepted, 114 enrolled. In 2007, 83 degrees awarded. *Entrance requirements:* For master's, GMAT, letters of reference, resumé, essay, transcripts, calculus. Additional exam requirements/recommendations for international students: Required—TOEFL (minimum score 550 paper-based; 213 computer-based; 80 iBT). *Application deadline:* For fall admission, 6/1 priority date for domestic students, 4/15 priority date for international students; for spring admission, 11/1 priority date for domestic students, 10/1 priority date for international students. Applications are processed on a rolling basis. Application fee: $40. Electronic applications accepted. *Expenses:* Tuition, state resident: part-time $304 per credit hour. Tuition, nonresident: part-time $761 per credit hour. *Financial support:* In 2007–08, 46 students received support, including 31 research assistantships with partial tuition reimbursements available (averaging $7,000 per year), 3 teaching assistantships with partial tuition reimbursements available (averaging $6,300 per year); career-related internships or fieldwork, scholarships/grants, and unspecified assistantships also available. Support available to part-time students. Financial award application deadline: 2/15; financial award applicants required to submit FAFSA. *Faculty research:* International business, buyer behavior, financial markets, strategy, operations research. *Unit head:* Dr. Bruce Rubin, Graduate Program Director, 757-683-3585, E-mail: mbainfo@odu.edu. *Application contact:* Shanna Wood, MBA Program Manager, 757-683-3585, Fax: 757-683-5750, E-mail: mbainfo@odu.edu.

Old Dominion University, College of Business and Public Administration, Program in Public Administration, Norfolk, VA 23529. Offers MPA. *Accreditation:* NASPAA. Part-time and evening/weekend programs available. *Faculty:* 7 full-time (1 woman), 6 part-time/adjunct (3 women). *Students:* 24 full-time (16 women), 111 part-time (71 women); includes 43 minority (37 African Americans, 3 Asian Americans or Pacific Islanders, 3 Hispanic Americans), 4 international. Average age 34. 66 applicants, 91% accepted. In 2007, 34 degrees awarded. *Degree requirements:* For master's, thesis optional, capstone seminar. *Entrance requirements:* For master's, GRE or GMAT. Additional exam requirements/recommendations for international students: Required—TOEFL (minimum score 550 paper-based; 213 computer-based; 79 iBT). *Application deadline:* For fall admission, 7/15 for domestic students; for spring admission, 11/15 for domestic students. Applications are processed on a rolling basis. Application fee: $40. Electronic applications accepted. *Expenses:* Tuition, state resident: part-time $304 per credit hour. Tuition, nonresident: part-time $761 per credit hour. *Financial support:* In 2007–08, 25 students received support, including 2 research assistantships with partial tuition reimbursements available (averaging $5,000 per year); fellowships, teaching assistantships, career-related internships or fieldwork, scholarships/grants, tuition waivers (partial), and unspecified assistantships also available. Financial award application deadline: 2/15; financial award applicants required to submit FAFSA. *Faculty research:* Environmental administration, personnel policy analysis, urban administration. Total annual research expenditures: $15,000. *Unit head:* Dr. William M. Leavitt, Graduate Program Director, 757-683-5695, Fax: 757-683-5639, E-mail: padmgpd@odu.edu. *Application contact:* Megan S. Jones, Graduate Program Manager, 757-683-3961, Fax: 757-683-4886, E-mail: mmjones@odu.edu.

Pace University, Dyson College of Arts and Sciences, Department of Public Administration, New York, NY 10038. Offers government management (MPA); health care administration (MPA); nonprofit management (MPA); JD/MPA. Offered at White Plains, NY location only. Part-time and evening/weekend programs available. *Faculty:* 4 full-time, 6 part-time/adjunct. *Students:* 33 full-time (21 women), 77 part-time (51 women); includes 47 minority (31 African Americans, 2 Asian Americans or Pacific Islanders, 14 Hispanic Americans), 6 international. Average age 32. 65 applicants, 89% accepted, 33 enrolled. In 2007, 29 degrees awarded. *Degree requirements:* For master's, capstone project. *Entrance requirements:* For master's, GRE General Test. *Application deadline:* For fall admission, 8/1 priority date for domestic students; for spring admission, 12/1 priority date for domestic students. Applications are processed on a rolling basis. Application fee: $65. Electronic applications accepted. *Expenses:* Tuition: Part-time $856 per credit. Tuition and fees vary according to degree level and program. *Financial support:* Research assistantships, career-related internships or fieldwork, Federal Work-Study, and tuition waivers (partial) available. Support available to part-time students. Financial award applicants required to submit FAFSA. *Unit head:* Dr. Brian Nickerson, Chairperson, 914-422-4303. *Application contact:* Joanna Broda, Director of Admissions, 914-422-4283, Fax: 914-422-4287, E-mail: gradwp@pace.edu.

See Close-Up on page 1617.

Park University, College of Graduate and Professional Studies, Kansas City, MO 54105. Offers adult education (M Ed); at-risk students (M Ed); disaster and emergency management (MPA); educational administration (M Ed); entrepreneurship (MBA); general business (MBA); general education (M Ed); government/business relations (MPA); healthcare/services management (MBA, MPA); international business (MBA); K-12 certification (MAT); management information systems (MBA); management of information systems (MPA); middle school certification (MAT); multi-cultural education (M Ed); nonprofit management (MPA); public management (MPA); school law (M Ed); secondary school certification (MAT); special education (M Ed). Part-time and evening/weekend programs available. Postbaccalaureate distance learning degree programs offered (no on-campus study). *Degree requirements:* For master's, comprehensive exam, thesis (for some programs). *Entrance requirements:* For master's, GRE, GMAT, teacher certification (M Ed). Additional exam requirements/recommendations for international students: Required—TOEFL (minimum score 550 paper-based). Electronic applications accepted. *Faculty research:* Literacy, leadership, brain based research, multicultural education, diversity.

Penn State Harrisburg, Graduate School, School of Public Affairs, Middletown, PA 17057-4898. Offers criminal justice (MA); health administration (MHA); public administration (MPA); public affairs (PhD); MPA/JD. *Unit head:* Dr. Steven A. Peterson, Director, 717-948-6154, E-mail: sap12@psu.edu.

Pepperdine University, School of Public Policy, Malibu, CA 90263. Offers American politics (MPP); economics (MPP); international relations (MPP); public policy (MPP); state and local policy (MPP). *Entrance requirements:* For master's, GRE, 2 letters of recommendation, resumé. Additional exam requirements/recommendations for international students: Required—TOEFL. Electronic applications accepted.

See Close-Up on page 1619.

Pontifical Catholic University of Puerto Rico, Institute of Graduate Studies in Behavioral Science and Community Affairs, Program in Public Administration, Ponce, PR 00717-0777. Offers MA. Part-time and evening/weekend programs available. *Degree requirements:* For master's, thesis. *Entrance requirements:* For master's, EXADEP, 3 letters of recommendation, interview, minimum GPA of 2.75.

Portland State University, Graduate Studies, College of Urban and Public Affairs, Hatfield School of Government, Division of Public Administration, Portland, OR 97207-0751. Offers public administration (MPA); public administration and policy (PhD). *Accreditation:* NASPAA (one or more programs are accredited). Part-time and evening/weekend programs available. *Faculty:* 16 full-time (6 women), 18 part-time/adjunct (8 women). *Students:* 117 full-time (74 women), 169 part-time (105 women); includes 35 minority (10 African Americans, 1 American Indian/Alaska Native, 15 Asian Americans or Pacific Islanders, 9 Hispanic Americans), 18 international. Average age 34. 147 applicants, 67% accepted, 66 enrolled. In 2007, 85 master's, 2 doctorates awarded. *Degree requirements:* For master's, internship (MPA), practicum (MPH); for doctorate, comprehensive exam, thesis/dissertation, residency. *Entrance requirements:* For master's, GRE, minimum GPA of 3.0 in upper-division course work or 2.75 overall, 3 recommendation forms, resumé; for doctorate, GRE General Test, minimum GPA of 2.75. Additional exam requirements/recommendations for international students: Required—TOEFL (minimum score 550 paper-based; 213 computer-based). *Application deadline:* For fall admission, 4/1 for domestic students, 3/1 for international students; for winter admission, 9/1 for domestic students, 8/1 for international students; for spring admission, 11/1 for domestic and international students. Application fee: $50. *Expenses:* Tuition, state resident: full-time $7,047. Tuition, nonresident: full-time $11,178. *Financial support:* In 2007–08, 8 research assistantships with full tuition reimbursements (averaging $9,411 per year) were awarded; fellowships, teaching assistantships, career-related internships or fieldwork, Federal Work-Study, scholarships/grants, tuition waivers (partial), and unspecified assistantships also available. Support available to part-time students. Financial award application deadline: 3/1; financial award applicants required to submit FAFSA. *Faculty research:* Public budgeting, program evaluation, nonprofit management, natural resources policy and administration. Total annual research expenditures: $418,432. *Unit head:* Neal Wallace, Chair, 503-725-3920, Fax: 503-725-8250, E-mail: nwallace@pdx.edu.

Regent University, Graduate School, Robertson School of Government, Virginia Beach, VA 23464-9800. Offers health care policy and administration (MA); international politics (MA); law and public policy (MA); political leadership and management (MA); political management (MA); public administration (MA); public policy (MA); terrorism and homeland defense (MA); world economies and political development (MA); JD/MA; M Div/MA; M Ed/MA; MBA/MA. Part-time programs available. *Faculty:* 6 full-time (2 women), 11 part-time/adjunct (1 woman). *Students:* 50 full-time (31 women), 67 part-time (32 women); includes 31 minority (20 African Americans, 1 American Indian/Alaska Native, 2 Asian Americans or Pacific Islanders, 8 Hispanic Americans), 2 international. Average age 31. 147 applicants, 50% accepted, 28 enrolled. In 2007, 47 degrees awarded. *Degree requirements:* For master's, thesis optional, internship. *Entrance requirements:* For master's, GRE General Test or LSAT, minimum undergraduate GPA of 3.0, writing sample, resumé, interview, references, transcripts. Additional exam requirements/recommendations for international students: Required—TOEFL (minimum score 577 paper-based; 233 computer-based). *Application deadline:* For fall admission, 5/1 priority date for domestic students; for spring admission, 11/1 priority date for domestic students. Applications are processed on a rolling basis. Application fee: $50. Electronic applications accepted. *Expenses: Contact institution. Financial support:* In 2007–08, 123 students received support. Career-related internships or fieldwork, scholarships/grants, tuition waivers (full and partial), and unspecified assistantships available. Support available to part-time students. Financial award application deadline: 9/1; financial award applicants required to submit FAFSA. *Faculty research:* Education reform, political character issues, social capital concerns, administrative ethics, biblical law and public policy. *Unit head:* Dr. Charles W. Dunn, Dean, 757-226-4322, Fax: 757-226-4643, E-mail: cwdunn@regent.edu. *Application contact:* Althea Bishard, Registrar and Executive Director of Enrollment and Academic Services, 800-373-5504, Fax: 757-226-4381, E-mail: admissions@regent.edu.

Regis College, Program in Public Administration, Weston, MA 02493. Offers nonprofit administration (Graduate Certificate); public administration (MPA); public policymaking (Graduate Certificate). Part-time programs available. Postbaccalaureate distance learning degree programs offered. *Faculty:* 1 part-time/adjunct (0 women). *Students:* 2 full-time (both women), 6 part-time (5 women); includes 1 minority (Hispanic American) Average age 25. *Degree requirements:* For master's, thesis. *Entrance requirements:* For master's, GRE or MAT. Application fee: $50. *Expenses:* Tuition: Full-time $25,990; part-time $730 per credit hour. *Unit head:* Dr. Mary Fitzgerald, Director, 781-768-7440, E-mail: mary.fitzgerald@regiscollege.edu.

Rhode Island College, School of Graduate Studies, Faculty of Arts and Sciences, Department of Political Sciences, Providence, RI 02908-1991. Offers public administration (MPA). Part-time and evening/weekend programs available. *Faculty:* 6 full-time (1 woman), 1 part-time/adjunct (0 women). *Application deadline:* For fall admission, 4/1 for domestic students; for spring admission, 11/1 for domestic students. Applications are processed on a rolling basis. *Expenses:* Tuition, state resident: full-time $6,240; part-time $260 per credit hour. Tuition, nonresident: full-time $13,104; part-time $546 per credit hour. Required fees: $332; $14 per credit hour. One-time fee: $66 part-time. *Financial support:* Career-related internships or fieldwork, Federal Work-Study, scholarships/grants, health care benefits, and unspecified assistantships available. Support available to part-time students. Financial award application deadline: 5/15; financial award applicants required to submit FAFSA. *Unit head:* Dr. Claus Hofhansel, Chair, 401-456-8056, E-mail: chofhansel@ric.edu.

Roger Williams University, Feinstein College of Arts and Sciences, Program in Public Administration, Bristol, RI 02809. Offers MPA. Part-time programs available. *Faculty:* 3 full-time (0 women), 1 part-time/adjunct (0 women). *Students:* 6 full-time (4 women), 33 part-time (20 women); includes 2 minority (1 American Indian/Alaska Native, 1 Hispanic American), 3 international. Average age 35. 20 applicants, 90% accepted, 12 enrolled. In 2007, 15 degrees awarded. *Entrance requirements:* For master's, GRE and MAT. *Application deadline:* Applications are processed on a rolling basis. Application fee: $50. Electronic applications accepted. *Financial support:* In 2007–08, 9 students received support. *Unit head:* Dr. Michael Hall, Head, 401-254-5746. *Application contact:* Matthew McDonough, Director of Graduate Admissions, 401-254-3809, Fax: 401-254-3557, E-mail: mmcdonough@rwu.edu.

Roosevelt University, Graduate Division, College of Arts and Sciences, Department of Political Science and Public Administration, Program in Public Administration, Chicago, IL 60605-1394. Offers MPA. Part-time and evening/weekend programs available. *Students:* 36 full-time (27 women), 59 part-time (42 women); includes 36 minority (32 African Americans, 4 Hispanic Americans), 25 international. Average age 34. 67 applicants, 45% accepted, 23 enrolled. In 2007, 23 degrees awarded. *Degree requirements:* For master's, thesis optional. *Entrance requirements:* For master's, minimum undergraduate GPA of 3.0. *Application deadline:* For fall admission, 6/1 priority date for domestic students. Applications are processed on a rolling basis. Application fee: $25 ($35 for international students). *Financial support:* Application deadline: 2/15. *Faculty research:* Health policy issues, environmental policy, local government administration. *Application contact:* Joanne Canyon-Heller, Coordinator of Graduate Admission, 877-APPLY RU, Fax: 312-281-3356, E-mail: applyru@roosevelt.edu.

Rutgers, The State University of New Jersey, Camden, Graduate School of Arts and Sciences, Department of Public Policy and Administration, Camden, NJ 08102-1401. Offers education policy and leadership (MPA); international public service and development (MPA); public management (MPA); JD/MPA. *Accreditation:* NASPAA. Part-time and evening/weekend programs available. *Degree requirements:* For master's, directed study, research workshop. *Entrance requirements:* For master's, GRE General Test, GMAT or LSAT. Additional exam requirements/recommendations for international students: Required—TOEFL (minimum score 550 paper-based; 213 computer-based). Electronic applications accepted. *Faculty research:* Nonprofit management, county and municipal administration, health and human services, government communication, administrative law, educational finance.

Rutgers, The State University of New Jersey, Newark, Graduate School, Program in Public Administration, Newark, NJ 07102. Offers health care administration (MPA); human resources administration (MPA); public administration (PhD); public management (MPA); public policy analysis (MPA); urban systems and issues (MPA). *Accreditation:* NASPAA (one or more programs are accredited). Part-time and evening/weekend programs available. *Degree requirements:* For master's, comprehensive exam, thesis or alternative; for doctorate, thesis/dissertation. *Entrance requirements:* For master's, GRE, minimum undergraduate B average; for doctorate, GRE, MPA, minimum B average. Electronic applications accepted. *Faculty research:* Government finance, municipal and state government, public productivity.

Sage Graduate School, Graduate School, Department of Management, Program in Organizational Management, Troy, NY 12180-4115. Offers public administration (MS). Part-time and evening/weekend programs available. *Faculty:* 2 full-time (1 woman), 7 part-time/adjunct (0 women). *Students:* 1 (woman) full-time, 24 part-time (16 women); includes 2 minority (both Hispanic Americans) Average age 31. 16 applicants, 63% accepted, 10 enrolled. In 2007, 9 degrees awarded. *Entrance requirements:* For master's, minimum GPA of 2.75, completed application, current resum&e, essay, official transcripts, 2 letters of recommendation. Additional exam requirements/recommendations for international students: Required—TOEFL (minimum score 550 paper-based; 213 computer-based). *Application deadline:* Applications are processed on a rolling basis. Application fee: $40. *Expenses:* Tuition: Full-time $9,720; part-time $540 per credit hour. *Financial support:* Fellowships, research assistantships, career-related internships or fieldwork available. Support available to part-time students. Financial award application deadline: 3/1; financial award applicants required to submit FAFSA. *Application contact:* Shannon K. Easton, Director of Graduate and Adult Admission, 518-244-2443, Fax: 518-244-6880, E-mail: sgsadm@sage.edu.

Saginaw Valley State University, College of Arts and Behavioral Sciences, Program in Administrative Science, University Center, MI 48710. Offers MA. Part-time and evening/weekend programs available. *Students:* 18 full-time (11 women), 48 part-time (33 women); includes 17 minority (14 African Americans, 3 Hispanic Americans), 4 international. Average age 34. 22 applicants, 91% accepted, 10 enrolled. In 2007, 15 degrees awarded. *Degree requirements:* For master's, thesis optional. *Entrance requirements:* For master's, minimum GPA of 3.0 in social sciences, 2.75 overall. Additional exam requirements/recommendations for international students: Required—TOEFL. *Application deadline:* Applications are processed on a rolling basis. Application fee: $25. Electronic applications accepted. *Expenses:* Tuition, state resident: full-time $8,264; part-time $344 per credit hour. Tuition, nonresident: full-time $15,853; part-time $661 per credit hour. Required fees: $341; $14 per credit hour. Tuition and fees vary according to course load. *Financial support:* In 2007–08, 2 fellowships with partial tuition reimbursements, 1 research assistantship with full tuition reimbursement (averaging $5,000 per year) were awarded; Federal Work-Study also available. Support available to part-time students. Financial award application deadline: 4/1; financial award applicants required to submit FAFSA. *Faculty research:* Mediation and conciliation, public administration, criminal justice, fiscal administration, professional ethics. *Unit head:* Mark Nicol, MAS Graduate Coordinator/Instructor of Political Science, 989-964-2605, E-mail: nlnicol@svsu.edu.

St. Edward's University, School of Management and Business, Program in Human Services, Austin, TX 78704. Offers conflict resolution (Certificate); human services (MA), including administration, conflict resolution, human resource management. Part-time and evening/weekend programs available. *Faculty:* 1 (woman) full-time, 8 part-time/adjunct (2 women). *Students:* 8 full-time (7 women), 59 part-time (46 women); includes 35 minority (11 African Americans, 2 Asian Americans or Pacific Islanders, 22 Hispanic Americans). Average age 32. 30 applicants, 83% accepted, 20 enrolled. In 2007, 27 degrees awarded. *Degree requirements:* For master's, minimum 24 resident hours. *Entrance requirements:* For master's, GRE General Test, GMAT, minimum GPA of 2.75 in last 60 hours of course work. Additional exam requirements/recommendations for international students: Required—TOEFL (minimum score 550 paper-based; 213 computer-based; 79 iBT). *Application deadline:* For fall admission, 8/1 for domestic students, 7/1 for international students; for spring admission, 12/1 for domestic students, 11/1 for international students. Applications are processed on a rolling basis. Application fee: $45 ($50 for international students). Electronic applications accepted. *Expenses:* Tuition: Full-time $12,672; part-time $704 per credit hour. Full-time tuition and fees vary according to program. Part-time tuition and fees vary according to course load. *Financial support:* In 2007–08, 3 students received support. Scholarships/grants available. *Faculty research:* Leadership development, organizational management, public policy, emotional intelligence. *Unit head:* Dr. Constance D Porter, Director, 512-416-5827, Fax: 512-448-8492, E-mail: constanp@stedwards.edu. *Application contact:* Kay L. Arnold, Graduate Admissions Coordinator, 512-233-1636, Fax: 512-428-1032, E-mail: kayla@stedwards.edu.

Saint Louis University, Graduate School, College of Education and Public Service and Graduate School, Department of Public Policy Studies, St. Louis, MO 63103-2097. Offers geographic information systems (Certificate); organizational development (Certificate); public administration (MAPA); public policy analysis (PhD); urban affairs (MAUA); urban planning and real estate development (MUPRED). *Accreditation:* NASPAA. Part-time programs available. *Faculty:* 8 full-time (2 women), 1 part-time/adjunct (0 women). *Students:* 55 full-time (18 women), 57 part-time (27 women); includes 20 minority (15 African Americans, 1 Asian American or Pacific Islander, 4 Hispanic Americans), 7 international. Average age 34. 79 applicants, 76% accepted, 34 enrolled. In 2007, 11 master's, 1 doctorate awarded. *Degree requirements:* For master's, comprehensive exam (for some programs), thesis (for some programs); for doctorate, comprehensive exam, thesis/dissertation, preliminary exams. *Entrance requirements:* For master's and doctorate, GMAT, GRE General Test, or LSAT, letters of recommendation, resumé, interview, transcripts, goal statement. Additional exam requirements/recommendations for international students: Required—TOEFL (minimum score 525 paper-based; 194 computer-based). *Application deadline:* For fall admission, 7/1 for domestic and international students; for spring admission, 11/1 for domestic and international students. Applications are processed on a rolling basis. Application fee: $40. Electronic applications accepted. *Expenses:* Tuition: Part-time $845 per credit hour. Required fees: $105 per semester. *Financial support:* In 2007–08, 36 students received support, including 8 teaching assistantships with full tuition reimbursements available (averaging $12,000 per year); Federal Work-Study, scholarships/grants, traineeships, health care benefits, tuition waivers (partial), and unspecified assistantships also available. Support available to part-time students. Financial award application deadline: 2/1; financial award applicants required to submit FAFSA. *Faculty research:* Urban politics, brown fields, e-government, and administration, evaluation research, community development, electronic government and governance. Total annual research expenditures: $100,000. *Unit head:* Dr. Robert A. Cropf, Chairperson, 314-977-3936, Fax: 314-977-3943, E-mail: cropfra@slu.edu. *Application contact:* Gary U. Behrman, Associate Dean of Graduate School Admissions, 314-977-3827, Fax: 314-977-3943, E-mail: behrmang@slu.edu.

St. Mary's University, Graduate School, Department of Political Science, Program in Public Administration, San Antonio, TX 78228-8507. Offers inter-American administration (MPA); public management (MPA); JD/MPA. Part-time programs available. Postbaccalaureate distance learning degree programs offered (no on-campus study). *Students:* 9 full-time (7 women), 15 part-time (11 women); includes 17 minority (2 African Americans, 15 Hispanic Americans), 1 international. Average age 29. In 2007, 13 degrees awarded. *Degree requirements:* For master's, comprehensive exam, internship. *Entrance requirements:* For master's, GRE General Test. Additional exam requirements/recommendations for international students: Required—TOEFL (minimum score 550 paper-based; 213 computer-based). *Application deadline:* Applications are processed on a rolling basis. Application fee: $0. Electronic applications accepted. *Financial support:* Fellowships, research assistantships, career-related internships or fieldwork, Federal Work-Study, and institutionally sponsored loans available. Financial award application deadline: 3/31; financial award applicants required to submit FAFSA. *Faculty research:* Voting rights, natural resources, urban policy. *Unit head:* Dr. Arturo Vega, Director, 210-431-8028, Fax: 210-431-4336, E-mail: avega2@stmarytx.edu.

St. Thomas University, School of Business, Department of Management, Miami Gardens, FL 33054-6459. Offers accounting (MBA); general management (MSM, Certificate); health management (MBA, MSM, Certificate); human resource management (MBA, MSM, Certificate); international business (MBA, MIB, MSM, Certificate); justice administration (MSM, Certificate); management accounting (MSM, Certificate); public management (MSM, Certificate); sports administration (MS). Part-time and evening/weekend programs available. *Students:* 35 full-time (24 women), 78 part-time (53 women); includes 89 minority (64 African Americans, 25 Hispanic Americans), 5 international. Average age 37. In 2007, 57 degrees awarded. *Degree requirements:* For master's, comprehensive exam. *Entrance requirements:* For master's, interview, minimum GPA of 3.0 or GMAT. Additional exam requirements/recommendations for international students: Required—TOEFL (minimum score 550 paper-based; 213 computer-based; 79 iBT). *Application deadline:* Applications are processed on a rolling basis. Application fee: $40. Electronic applications accepted. *Financial support:* Career-related internships or fieldwork and unspecified assistantships available. Support available to part-time students. Financial award application deadline: 4/15; financial award applicants required to submit FAFSA. *Unit head:* Dr. Seok-Ho Song, Program Director, 305-474-6909, Fax: 305-628-

Public Administration

St. Thomas University (continued)
6510, E-mail: ssong@stu.edu. *Application contact:* Margarette Fleuricourt, Graduate Admissions Officer, 305-628-6546, Fax: 305-628-6591, E-mail: graduate@stu.edu.

Salisbury University, Graduate Division, Program in Geography Information Systems and Public Administration, Salisbury, MD 21801-6837. Offers MS. *Faculty:* 2 full-time (0 women). *Students:* 6 full-time (1 woman), 4 part-time (2 women). Average age 33. 12 applicants, 83% accepted, 10 enrolled. In 2007, 2 degrees awarded. *Expenses:* Tuition, state resident: part-time $260 per credit hour. Tuition, nonresident: part-time $556 per credit hour. *Unit head:* Dr. Xingzhi Mara Chen, Coordinator, 410-546-6302, E-mail: xmchen@salisbury.edu.

Sam Houston State University, College of Humanities and Social Sciences, Department of Political Science, Huntsville, TX 77341. Offers political science (MA); public administration (MPA). Evening/weekend programs available. *Faculty:* 15 full-time (7 women). *Students:* 6 full-time (3 women), 16 part-time (9 women); includes 8 minority (3 African Americans, 1 Asian American or Pacific Islander, 4 Hispanic Americans). Average age 30. In 2007, 10 degrees awarded. *Degree requirements:* For master's, thesis or alternative. *Entrance requirements:* For master's, GRE General Test. Additional exam requirements/recommendations for international students: Required—TOEFL (minimum score 550 paper-based; 213 computer-based). *Application deadline:* For fall admission, 8/1 for domestic students; for spring admission, 12/1 for domestic students. Applications are processed on a rolling basis. Application fee: $20. *Expenses:* Tuition, state resident: full-time $5,026; part-time $184 per semester hour. Tuition, nonresident: full-time $10,586; part-time $462 per semester hour. Required fees: $494 per semester. *Financial support:* Research assistantships, teaching assistantships, career-related internships or fieldwork and institutionally sponsored loans available. Support available to part-time students. Financial award application deadline: 5/31; financial award applicants required to submit FAFSA. *Unit head:* Dr. John Holcombe, Chair, 936-294-1467, E-mail: pol_jwh@shsu.edu. *Application contact:* Dr. Corliss Lentz, Advisor, 936-294-1459.

San Diego State University, Graduate and Research Affairs, College of Professional Studies and Fine Arts, School of Public Affairs, Program in Public Administration, San Diego, CA 92182. Offers MPA. *Accreditation:* NASPAA. Part-time programs available. *Students:* 22 full-time (9 women), 32 part-time (19 women); includes 14 minority (1 African American, 3 Asian Americans or Pacific Islanders, 10 Hispanic Americans), 2 international. Average age 31. 43 applicants, 63% accepted, 7 enrolled. In 2007, 40 degrees awarded. *Entrance requirements:* For master's, GRE General Test, 2 letters of reference. Additional exam requirements/recommendations for international students: Required—TOEFL. *Application deadline:* For fall admission, 5/1 for domestic and international students; for spring admission, 11/1 for domestic students, 10/1 for international students. Applications are processed on a rolling basis. Application fee: $55. Electronic applications accepted. *Financial support:* Fellowships, teaching assistantships, career-related internships or fieldwork and unspecified assistantships available. Financial award applicants required to submit FAFSA. *Unit head:* Louis Rea, Graduate Advisor, 619-594-6083, Fax: 619-594-1165. *Application contact:* Glen Sparrow, Graduate Advisor, 619-594-4099, Fax: 619-594-1165, E-mail: gsparrow@mail.sdsu.edu.

San Francisco State University, Division of Graduate Studies, College of Behavioral and Social Sciences, Public Administration Program, San Francisco, CA 94132-1722. Offers integrated and collaborative services (MPA); nonprofit administration (MPA); policy analysis (MPA); public management (MPA); urban administration (MPA). *Accreditation:* NASPAA. *Unit head:* Dr. Genie Stowers, Director, 415-817-4457, Fax: 415-338-1980, E-mail: gstowers@sfsu.edu.

San Jose State University, Graduate Studies and Research, College of Social Sciences, Department of Political Science, San Jose, CA 95192-0001. Offers public administration (MPA). *Accreditation:* NASPAA. Part-time and evening/weekend programs available. *Students:* 22 full-time (15 women), 68 part-time (44 women); includes 33 minority (3 African Americans, 12 Asian Americans or Pacific Islanders, 18 Hispanic Americans), 1 international. Average age 33. 81 applicants, 54% accepted, 32 enrolled. In 2007, 22 degrees awarded. *Degree requirements:* For master's, comprehensive exam, thesis or alternative. *Entrance requirements:* For master's, GRE Subject Test. Additional exam requirements/recommendations for international students: Required—TOEFL (minimum score 575 paper-based). *Application deadline:* For fall admission, 6/29 for domestic students; for spring admission, 11/30 for domestic students. Applications are processed on a rolling basis. Application fee: $59. Electronic applications accepted. *Financial support:* Career-related internships or fieldwork, Federal Work-Study, institutionally sponsored loans, scholarships/grants, and tuition waivers (partial) available. Support available to part-time students. Financial award applicants required to submit FAFSA. *Faculty research:* Modern political philosophy, international relations in the Middle East, public policy, American public policy, political parties and political reform. *Unit head:* Dr. James Brent, Chair, 408-924-5550, Fax: 408-924-5556, E-mail: jcbrent@email.sjsu.edu. *Application contact:* Dr. Frances Edwards, MPA Director, 408-924-5559.

Savannah State University, Program in Public Administration, Savannah, GA 31404. Offers MPA. *Accreditation:* NASPAA. *Faculty:* 5 full-time (2 women). *Students:* 8 full-time (all women), 13 part-time (9 women); includes 20 minority (all African Americans) Average age 31. In 2007, 14 degrees awarded. *Degree requirements:* For master's, major paper, oral exam. *Entrance requirements:* For master's, GRE General Test, minimum GPA of 2.5. Additional exam requirements/recommendations for international students: Required—TOEFL. *Application deadline:* For fall admission, 5/1 priority date for domestic students; for spring admission, 12/1 priority date for domestic students. Applications are processed on a rolling basis. Application fee: $20. *Expenses:* Tuition, state resident: full-time $3,228; part-time $179 per hour. Tuition, nonresident: full-time $12,904. Required fees: $618. *Financial support:* Career-related internships or fieldwork available. *Faculty research:* Community development, human resources, leadership, conflict resolution. *Unit head:* Dr. Shirley Geiger, Chair, 912-356-2966, E-mail: geigers@savstate.edu. *Application contact:* Jeannette Jenkins, Senior Administrative Secretary, 912-356-2966.

Seattle University, College of Arts and Sciences, Institute of Public Service, Seattle, WA 98122-1090. Offers MPA. *Accreditation:* NASPAA. *Degree requirements:* For master's, thesis or alternative. *Entrance requirements:* For master's, minimum GPA of 3.0, 1 year work experience. *Faculty research:* Housing, experiential learning, citizenship education.

Seton Hall University, College of Arts and Sciences, Department of Public and Healthcare Administration, South Orange, NJ 07079-2697. Offers arts administration (MPA); health policy and management (MPA); healthcare administration (MHA); nonprofit organization management (MPA); public service: leadership, governance, and policy (MPA). *Accreditation:* NASPAA.Part-time and evening/weekend programs available. Postbaccalaureate distance learning degree programs offered (minimal on-campus study). *Degree requirements:* For master's, research project. Electronic applications accepted.

Shenandoah University, School of Education and Human Development, Winchester, VA 22601-5195. Offers administrative leadership (D Ed); advanced professional teaching English to speakers of other languages (Certificate); education (MSE); elementary education (Certificate); middle school education (Certificate); professional studies (Certificate); professional teaching English to speakers of other languages (Certificate); public management (Certificate); secondary education (Certificate); women's studies (Certificate). Part-time and evening/weekend programs available. Postbaccalaureate distance learning degree programs offered (minimal on-campus study). *Faculty:* 13 full-time (7 women), 4 part-time/adjunct (2 women). *Students:* 10 full-time (6 women), 280 part-time (192 women); includes 7 minority (5 African Americans, 2 Hispanic Americans), 17 international. Average age 45. 169 applicants, 95% accepted, 125 enrolled. In 2007, 100 master's, 7 doctorates, 13 other advanced degrees awarded. *Degree requirements:* For master's, comprehensive exam (for some programs), thesis (for some programs), internship; for doctorate, comprehensive exam, thesis/dissertation. *Entrance requirements:* For master's, minimum GPA of 3.0 or satisfactory GRE, 3 letters of recommendation, valid teaching license, essay; for doctorate, minimum GPA of 3.5 in master's, 3 years of teaching experience, 3 letters of recommendation, writing samples; for Certificate, minimum undergraduate GPA of 3.0, essay, 3 letters of recommendation. Additional exam requirements/recommendations for international students: Required—TOEFL (minimum score 527 paper-based; 197 computer-based; 71 iBT). *Application deadline:* For fall admission, 7/15 for domestic students; for spring admission, 10/15 for domestic students. Application fee: $30. Electronic applications accepted. *Expenses:* Tuition: Part-time $640 per credit. Part-time tuition and fees vary according to degree level and program. *Financial support:* Career-related internships or fieldwork, institutionally sponsored loans, and unspecified assistantships available. Support available to part-time students. Financial award application deadline: 3/15; financial award applicants required to submit FAFSA. *Faculty research:* Nanotechnology, writing pedagogy and writing centers, violence in schools, Virginia/Shenandoah Valley history and culture, stress in children. *Unit head:* Dr. Calvin Allen, Dean, 540-665-4587, Fax: 540-665-4644, E-mail: callen@su.edu. *Application contact:* David Anthony, Dean of Admissions, 540-665-4581, Fax: 540-665-4627, E-mail: admit@su.edu.

Shippensburg University of Pennsylvania, School of Graduate Studies, College of Arts and Sciences, Department of Political Science, Shippensburg, PA 17257-2299. Offers public administration (MPA). Part-time and evening/weekend programs available. *Faculty:* 5 full-time (1 woman), 1 part-time/adjunct (0 women). *Students:* 9 full-time (3 women), 22 part-time (14 women); includes 6 minority (3 African Americans, 1 American Indian/Alaska Native, 2 Asian Americans or Pacific Islanders). Average age 31. 23 applicants, 87% accepted, 9 enrolled. In 2007, 9 degrees awarded. *Degree requirements:* For master's, thesis or internship, candidacy. *Entrance requirements:* For master's, 6 credits of course work in government or political science, personal interview, GRE if GPA is less than 2.75. Additional exam requirements/recommendations for international students: Required—TOEFL (minimum score 560 paper-based; 220 computer-based). *Application deadline:* For fall admission, 3/1 for international students; for spring admission, 7/1 for international students. Applications are processed on a rolling basis. Application fee: $30. Electronic applications accepted. *Expenses:* Tuition, state resident: part-time $345 per credit. Tuition, nonresident: part-time $552 per credit. Required fees: $28 per credit. Tuition and fees vary according to course load. *Financial support:* In 2007–08, 2 research assistantships with full tuition reimbursements (averaging $3,575 per year) were awarded; career-related internships or fieldwork, scholarships/grants, and unspecified assistantships also available. Support available to part-time students. Financial award application deadline: 3/1; financial award applicants required to submit FAFSA. *Unit head:* Dr. C. Nielsen Brasher, Chairperson, 717-477-1718, Fax: 717-477-4030, E-mail: cnbras@ship.edu. *Application contact:* Renee Payne, Associate Dean of Graduate Admissions, 717-477-1231, Fax: 717-477-4016, E-mail: rmpayn@ship.edu.

Sojourner-Douglass College, Graduate Program, Baltimore, MD 21205-1814. Offers human services (MASS); public administration (MASS); urban education (reading) (MASS). Part-time and evening/weekend programs available. *Faculty:* 7 full-time (5 women), 20 part-time/adjunct (10 women). *Students:* 43 full-time (35 women), 36 part-time (28 women); includes 78 African Americans. Average age 36. 55 applicants, 78% accepted, 40 enrolled. In 2007, 42 degrees awarded. *Degree requirements:* For master's, comprehensive exam, written proposal oral defense. *Entrance requirements:* For master's, Graduate Examination. *Application deadline:* Applications are processed on a rolling basis. Application fee: $45. *Financial support:* Federal Work-Study, institutionally sponsored loans, and scholarships/grants available. Financial award applicants required to submit FAFSA. *Unit head:* Dr. Hyacynth Anucha, Director, 410-276-1844, Fax: 410-276-0395, E-mail: hanucha@host.sdc.edu. *Application contact:* Ineita McNeil, Information Contact, 410-276-1844, Fax: 410-276-0395, E-mail: imcneil@host.sdc.edu.

Sonoma State University, School of Social Sciences, Department of Political Science, Rohnert Park, CA 94928-3609. Offers public administration (MPA). Part-time and evening/weekend programs available. *Faculty:* 5 full-time (1 woman), 8 part-time/adjunct (4 women). *Students:* 21 full-time (14 women), 26 part-time (20 women); includes 7 minority (1 African American, 2 Asian Americans or Pacific Islanders, 4 Hispanic Americans). Average age 35. 13 applicants, 85% accepted, 10 enrolled. In 2007, 10 degrees awarded. *Degree requirements:* For master's, thesis or alternative. *Entrance requirements:* For master's, GRE General Test, minimum GPA of 3.0. *Application deadline:* For fall admission, 11/30 for domestic students; for spring admission, 8/31 for domestic students. Application fee: $55. *Financial support:* Career-related internships or fieldwork available. Financial award application deadline: 3/2. *Faculty research:* Cross-disciplinary viewpoint in public administration, public policy implementation and evaluation with emphasis on state & local politics and non-profit organizations. *Unit head:* Dr. Diane Parness, Chair, 707-664-2179. *Application contact:* Dr. David McCuan, Graduate Program Coordinator, 707-664-3309, Fax: 707-664-3920, E-mail: david.mccuan@sonoma.edu.

Southeastern University, College of Graduate Studies, Program in Government Program Management, Washington, DC 20024-2788. Offers MPA. Part-time and evening/weekend programs available. *Students:* 19. 13 applicants, 69% accepted, 9 enrolled. In 2007, 18 master's awarded. *Entrance requirements:* Additional exam requirements/recommendations for international students: Required—TOEFL (minimum score 500 paper-based; 173 computer-based). *Application deadline:* Applications are processed on a rolling basis. Application fee: $45. Electronic applications accepted. *Expenses:* Tuition: Full-time $9,180; part-time $340 per credit. Required fees: $1,050; $350 per term. *Financial support:* Federal Work-Study, institutionally sponsored loans, and scholarships/grants available. Support available to part-time students. Financial award application deadline: 9/8; financial award applicants required to submit FAFSA. *Application contact:* Dorothy Harris, Associate Dean of Enrollment Management, 202-478-8200 Ext. 255, Fax: 202-488-8093, E-mail: dharris@seu.edu.

Southeast Missouri State University, School of Graduate Studies, Department of Political Science, Philosophy and Religion, Cape Girardeau, MO 63701-4799. Offers MPA. Part-time and evening/weekend programs available. *Faculty:* 6 full-time (0 women). *Students:* 4 full-time (1 woman), 17 part-time (12 women); includes 4 minority (all African Americans), 1 international. Average age 28. 8 applicants, 138% accepted. In 2007, 5 degrees awarded. *Degree requirements:* For master's, thesis or alternative, internship or thesis. *Entrance requirements:* For master's, minimum GPA of 2.7. Additional exam requirements/recommendations for international students: Required—TOEFL (minimum score 600 paper-based; 213 computer-based). *Application deadline:* For fall admission, 8/1 for domestic students, 6/1 for international students; for spring admission, 11/21 for domestic students, 10/1 for international students. Applications are processed on a rolling basis. Application fee: $25 ($100 for international students). Electronic applications accepted. *Expenses:* Tuition, state resident: part-time $224 per credit hour. Tuition, nonresident: part-time $395 per credit hour. Tuition and fees vary according to course load and program. *Financial support:* In 2007–08, 12 students received support, including 4 research assistantships with full tuition reimbursements available (averaging $7,600 per year); career-related internships or fieldwork and unspecified assistantships also available. Financial award applicants required to submit FAFSA. *Unit head:* Dr. Hamner Hill, Chairperson, 573-651-2816, Fax: 573-651-2695, E-mail: hhill@semo.edu. *Application contact:* Marsha L. Arant, Senior Administrative Assistant, Office of Graduate Studies, 573-651-2192, Fax: 573-651-2001, E-mail: marant@semo.edu.

Southern Arkansas University–Magnolia, Graduate Programs, Magnolia, AR 71753. Offers agriculture (MS); computer and information sciences (MS); counseling (MS); education (M Ed), including counseling and development, educational administration and supervision, elementary education, secondary education; kinesiology (MS); library media and information specialist (M Ed); public administration (EMPA); school counseling (M Ed); teaching (MAT). *Accreditation:* NCATE. Part-time and evening/weekend programs available. *Faculty:* 28 full-time (13 women), 6 part-time/adjunct (5 women). *Students:* 90 full-time (61 women), 254 part-time (195 women); includes 75 minority (74 African Americans, 1 Asian American or Pacific Islander), 14 international. Average age 34. In 2007, 77 degrees awarded. *Degree requirements:* For master's, comprehensive exam, thesis optional. *Entrance requirements:* For master's, GRE or MAT, minimum GPA of 2.75. *Application deadline:* Applications are processed on a rolling basis. Application fee: $0. *Expenses:* Tuition, state resident: full-time $3,348; part-time $186 per hour. Tuition, nonresident: full-time $4,734; part-time $263 per hour. Required fees: $438; $35 per hour. *Financial support:* Career-related internships or fieldwork, Federal Work-Study, scholarships/grants, tuition waivers (full), and unspecified assistantships available. Financial award applicants required to submit FAFSA. *Faculty research:* Alternative certification for teachers, supervision of instruction, instructional leadership, counseling. *Unit head:* Dr. Kim F. Shirey, Interim Dean, Graduate Studies, 870-235-4055, Fax: 870-235-5035, E-mail: kfshirey@saumag.edu.

Southern Illinois University Carbondale, Graduate School, College of Liberal Arts, Department of Political Science, Public Administration Program, Carbondale, IL 62901-4701. Offers MPA, JD/MPA. *Accreditation:* NASPAA. Part-time programs available. *Faculty:* 4 full-time (0 women). *Students:* 29 full-time (19 women), 40 part-time (22 women); includes 14 minority (10 African Americans, 1 American Indian/Alaska Native, 1 Asian American or Pacific Islander, 2 Hispanic Americans), 4 international. Average age 31. 36 applicants, 56% accepted, 2 enrolled. In 2007, 17 degrees awarded. *Degree requirements:* For master's, thesis or alternative. *Entrance requirements:* For master's, minimum GPA of 2.7. Additional exam requirements/recommendations for international students: Required—TOEFL. *Application deadline:* Applications are processed on a rolling basis. Application fee: $20. *Financial support:* In 2007–08, 26 students received support, including 2 fellowships with full tuition reimbursements available, 10 teaching assistantships with full tuition reimbursements available; research assistantships with full tuition reimbursements available, career-related internships or fieldwork, Federal Work-Study, institutionally sponsored loans, and tuition waivers (full) also available. Support available to part-time students. Financial award application deadline: 2/1. *Faculty research:* Natural resources and environmental management, intergovernmental relations, state mandates, rural administration, economic development policy, nonprofit management. *Unit head:* Dr. John A. Hamman, Director, 618-453-3177, E-mail: hamman@siu.edu. *Application contact:* Tammy Emery, Office Specialist, 618-453-3177, E-mail: mpaprog@siu.edu.

Southern Illinois University Edwardsville, Graduate Studies and Research, College of Arts and Sciences, Department of Public Administration and Policy Analysis, Edwardsville, IL 62026-0001. Offers MPA. *Accreditation:* NASPAA. Part-time and evening/weekend programs available. *Faculty:* 6 full-time (1 woman). *Students:* 45 full-time (30 women), 68 part-time (42 women); includes 41 minority (37 African Americans, 1 American Indian/Alaska Native, 3 Hispanic Americans), 10 international. Average age 33. 72 applicants, 75% accepted. In 2007, 51 degrees awarded. *Degree requirements:* For master's, comprehensive exam, thesis or alternative, final exam. *Entrance requirements:* Additional exam requirements/recommendations for international students: Required—TOEFL. *Application deadline:* For fall admission, 7/20 for domestic students, 6/1 for international students; for spring admission, 12/14 for domestic students, 10/1 for international students. Application fee: $30. Electronic applications accepted. *Financial support:* Fellowships with full tuition reimbursements, research assistantships with full tuition reimbursements, teaching assistantships with full tuition reimbursements, career-related internships or fieldwork, Federal Work-Study, institutionally sponsored loans, traineeships, and unspecified assistantships available. Support available to part-time students. Financial award application deadline: 3/1. *Unit head:* Dr. T. R. Carr, Chair, 618-650-3762, E-mail: tcarr@siue.edu. *Application contact:* Dr. Drew Dolan, Program Director, 618-650-3762, E-mail: ddolan@siue.edu.

Southern University and Agricultural and Mechanical College, Graduate School, Nelson Mandela School of Public Policy and Urban Affairs, Department of Public Administration, Baton Rouge, LA 70813. Offers MPA. *Accreditation:* NASPAA. Part-time and evening/weekend programs available. *Faculty:* 5 full-time (2 women). *Students:* 79 full-time (52 women), 41 part-time (32 women). Average age 35. 62 applicants, 76% accepted, 40 enrolled. In 2007, 38 degrees awarded. *Degree requirements:* For master's, thesis. *Entrance requirements:* For master's, GRE General Test. Additional exam requirements/recommendations for international students: Required—TOEFL (minimum score 525 paper-based; 193 computer-based). *Application deadline:* For fall admission, 4/15 priority date for domestic and international students; for spring admission, 11/1 priority date for domestic and international students. Applications are processed on a rolling basis. Application fee: $25. *Financial support:* In 2007–08, research assistantships (averaging $7,000 per year); teaching assistantships, career-related internships or fieldwork and scholarships/grants also available. Financial award application deadline: 4/15; financial award applicants required to submit FAFSA. *Faculty research:* Fiscal policy, public finance policy and practitioner interests; minority politics, healthcare and political economy. *Unit head:* Dr. Mylon Winn, Chair, 225-771-3104, Fax: 225-771-3105.

Southern Utah University, College of Humanities and Social Sciences, Program in Public Administration, Cedar City, UT 84720-2498. Offers MS. *Faculty:* 3 full-time (1 woman), 2 part-time/adjunct (0 women). *Students:* 9 full-time (5 women), 6 part-time (3 women); includes 1 African American. 30 applicants, 63% accepted, 15 enrolled. *Application deadline:* Applications are processed on a rolling basis. Application fee: $50 ($65 for international students). Electronic applications accepted. *Unit head:* Dr. John Ault, Interim Dean, College of Humanities and Social Sciences, 435-586-7898, Fax: 435-865-8193, E-mail: ault@suu.edu.

State University of New York at Binghamton, Graduate School, College of Community and Public Affairs, Department of Public Administration, Binghamton, NY 13902-6000. Offers MPA. *Students:* 34 full-time (19 women), 41 part-time (24 women); includes 14 minority (7 African Americans, 3 Asian Americans or Pacific Islanders, 4 Hispanic Americans), 2 international. Average age 32. 67 applicants, 79% accepted, 26 enrolled. In 2007, 29 master's awarded. *Financial support:* In 2007–08, 2 teaching assistantships with full tuition reimbursements (averaging $9,000 per year) were awarded. *Unit head:* Dr. Nadia Rubaii-Barrett, Chairperson, 607-777-9172, E-mail: nbarrett@binghamton.edu.

Stephen F. Austin State University, Graduate School, College of Liberal Arts, Department of Political Science and Geography, Nacogdoches, TX 75962. Offers public administration (MPA). *Degree requirements:* For master's, thesis optional. *Entrance requirements:* For master's, GRE General Test. Additional exam requirements/recommendations for international students: Required—TOEFL.

Strayer University, Graduate Studies, Washington, DC 20005-2603. Offers accounting (MS); acquisition (MBA); business administration (MBA); communications technology (MS); educational management (M Ed); finance (MBA); health services administration (MHSA); hospitality and tourism management (MBA); human resource management (MBA); information systems (MS), including computer security management, decision support system management, enterprise resource management, network management, software engineering management, systems development management; management (MBA); management information systems (MS); marketing (MBA); professional accounting (MS), including accounting information systems, controllership, taxation; public administration (MPA); supply chain management (MBA); technology in education (M Ed). Programs also offered at campus locations in Birmingham, AL; Chamblee, GA; Cobb County, GA; Morrow, GA; White Marsh, MD; Charleston, SC; Columbia, SC; Greensboro, NC; Greenville, SC; Lexington, KY; Louisville, KY; Nashville, TN; North Raleigh, NC; Washington, DC. Part-time and evening/weekend programs available. Postbaccalaureate distance learning degree programs offered (minimal on-campus study). *Degree requirements:* For master's, thesis. *Entrance requirements:* For master's, GMAT, GRE General Test, bachelor's degree from an accredited college or university, minimum undergraduate GPA of 2.75. Electronic applications accepted.

Suffolk University, Sawyer Business School, Department of Public Administration, Boston, MA 02108-2770. Offers disability studies (MPA); health administration (MPA); nonprofit management (MPA); public administration (CASPA); public finance and human resources (MPA); state and local government (MPA); JD/MPA; MPA/MS. *Accreditation:* NASPAA (one or more programs are accredited). Part-time and evening/weekend programs available. *Faculty:* 11 full-time (6 women), 7 part-time/adjunct (2 women). *Students:* 39 full-time (21 women), 117 part-time (79 women); includes 18 minority (10 African Americans, 4 Asian Americans or Pacific Islanders, 4 Hispanic Americans), 7 international. Average age 31. 86 applicants, 83% accepted, 42 enrolled. In 2007, 63 degrees awarded. *Entrance requirements:* Additional exam requirements/recommendations for international students: Required—TOEFL (minimum score 550 paper-based; 213 computer-based; 80 iBT). *Application deadline:* For fall admission, 6/15 priority date for domestic students, 6/15 for international students; for spring admission, 11/1 priority date for domestic students, 11/1 for international students. Applications are processed on a rolling basis. Application fee: $50. Electronic applications accepted. *Expenses:* Contact institution. *Financial support:* In 2007–08, 114 students received support, including 71 fellowships with full and partial tuition reimbursements available (averaging $7,661 per year); career-related internships or fieldwork and Federal Work-Study also available. Support available to part-time students. Financial award application deadline: 4/1; financial award applicants required to submit FAFSA. *Faculty research:* Local government, health care, federal policy, mental health, HIV/AIDS. Total annual research expenditures: $200,000. *Unit head:* Dr. Michael Lavin, Chair, 617-573-8062, E-mail: mlavin@suffolk.edu. *Application contact:* Judith Reynolds, Director of Graduate Admissions, 617-573-8302, Fax: 617-523-0116, E-mail: grad.admission@suffolk.edu.

Sul Ross State University, School of Arts and Sciences, Department of Behavioral and Social Sciences, Program in Public Administration, Alpine, TX 79832. Offers MA. Part-time and evening/weekend programs available. *Entrance requirements:* For master's, GRE General Test, minimum GPA of 2.5 in last 60 hours of undergraduate work. *Faculty research:* Local government, state government, personnel, volunteer fire departments, rural health.

Syracuse University, Graduate School, Maxwell School of Citizenship and Public Affairs, Department of Public Administration, Syracuse, NY 13244. Offers EMPA, MPA, PhD, CAS, MPA/MA. *Accreditation:* NASPAA (one or more programs are accredited). *Students:* 175 full-time (82 women), 44 part-time (22 women); includes 31 minority (12 African Americans, 3 American Indian/Alaska Native, 12 Asian Americans or Pacific Islanders, 4 Hispanic Americans), 83 international. 146 applicants, 44% accepted, 52 enrolled. In 2007, 93 master's, 3 doctorates, 11 other advanced degrees awarded. *Degree requirements:* For doctorate, comprehensive exam, thesis/dissertation. *Entrance requirements:* For master's, GRE General Test (MPA); for doctorate, GRE General Test. Additional exam requirements/recommendations for international students: Required—TOEFL. *Application deadline:* For fall admission, 2/1 for domestic students. Applications are processed on a rolling basis. Application fee: $75. Electronic applications accepted. *Expenses:* Tuition: Full-time $18,216; part-time $1,012 per credit. Required fees: $980. Tuition and fees vary according to program. *Financial support:* Fellowships with full tuition reimbursements, research assistantships with full and partial tuition reimbursements, teaching assistantships with full tuition reimbursements, scholarships/grants, tuition waivers (partial), and unspecified assistantships available. Financial award applicants required to submit FAFSA. *Unit head:* Dr. Stuart Bretschneider, Chair, 315-443-4000, Fax: 315-443-5330. *Application contact:* Christine Omolino, Associate Director, 315-443-3712, Fax: 315-443-5330.

Tennessee State University, The School of Graduate Studies and Research, Institute of Government, Nashville, TN 37209-1561. Offers public administration (MPA, PhD). *Accreditation:* NASPAA (one or more programs are accredited). Part-time and evening/weekend programs available. *Faculty:* 5 full-time (1 woman), 2 part-time/adjunct (1 woman). *Students:* 31 full-time (19 women), 104 part-time (65 women); includes 18 minority (16 African Americans, 1 Asian American or Pacific Islander, 1 Hispanic American), 5 international. Average age 36. 111 applicants, 60% accepted, 25 enrolled. In 2007, 19 master's, 3 doctorates awarded. *Degree requirements:* For master's, comprehensive exam, thesis optional; for doctorate, comprehensive exam, thesis/dissertation. *Entrance requirements:* For master's, GRE General Test, minimum GPA of 2.5, writing sample; for doctorate, GRE General Test, minimum GPA of 3.25, writing sample. Application fee: $25. *Expenses:* Tuition, state resident: full-time $6,271; part-time $490 per hour. Tuition, nonresident: full-time $16,550; part-time $936 per hour. *Financial support:* In 2007–08, 3 research assistantships (averaging $4,185 per year), teaching assistantships (averaging $4,185 per year) were awarded. Support available to part-time students. *Faculty research:* Total quality management and process improvement, national health care policy and administration, starting non-profit ventures, public service ethics, state education financing across the U.S. public. *Unit head:* Dr. Ann-Marie Rizzo, Director, 615-963-7250, Fax: 615-963-7245, E-mail: arizzo@tnstate.edu. *Application contact:* Dr. Rodney Stonley, Coordinator of Graduate Studies, 615-963-7249, Fax: 615-963-7245, E-mail: rstonleyl@tnstate.edu.

Texas A&M International University, Office of Graduate Studies and Research, College of Arts and Sciences, Department of Social Sciences, Laredo, TX 78041-1900. Offers history (MA); political science (MA); public administration (MPA). *Faculty:* 8 full-time (3 women), 2 part-time/adjunct (1 woman). *Students:* 14 full-time (8 women), 65 part-time (34 women); includes 68 minority (1 Asian American or Pacific Islander, 67 Hispanic Americans), 4 international. Average age 34. 35 applicants, 97% accepted, 23 enrolled. In 2007, 10 degrees awarded. *Degree requirements:* For master's, thesis (for some programs). *Entrance requirements:* For master's, GRE General Test. Additional exam requirements/recommendations for international students: Required—TOEFL (minimum score 550 paper-based; 213 computer-based). *Application deadline:* For fall admission, 7/15 priority date for domestic students; for spring admission, 11/12 for domestic students. Applications are processed on a rolling basis. Application fee: $25. *Financial support:* In 2007–08, 29 students received support. Application deadline: 11/1. *Unit head:* Dr. William W. Riggs, Chair, 956-328-2540, E-mail: wriggs@tamiu.edu. *Application contact:* Rosie Espinoza-Dickinson, Director of Admissions, 956-326-2200, Fax: 956-326-2199, E-mail: enroll@tamiu.edu.

Texas A&M University, George Bush School of Government and Public Service, College Station, TX 77843. Offers advanced international affairs (Certificate); homeland security (Certificate); international affairs (MPIA), including international economics and development, national security affairs; nonprofit management (Certificate); public service and administration (MPSA), including public management, public policy analysis. *Accreditation:* NASPAA. *Faculty:* 39. *Students:* 155 full-time (67 women), 97 part-time (27 women); includes 37 minority (8 African Americans, 2 American Indian/Alaska Native, 4 Asian Americans or Pacific Islanders, 23 Hispanic Americans), 18 international. Average age 24. 249 applicants, 57% accepted, 88 enrolled. In 2007, 69 degrees awarded. *Degree requirements:* For master's, summer internship. *Entrance requirements:* For master's, GRE (preferred) or GMAT. *Application deadline:* For fall admission, 1/24 for domestic and international students. Application fee: $50 ($75 for international students). Electronic applications accepted. *Expenses:* Tuition, state resident: full-time $6,129. Tuition, nonresident: full-time $11,689. Tuition and fees vary according to course load. *Financial support:* In 2007–08, fellowships (averaging $11,000 per year), research assistantships (averaging $11,250 per year) were awarded; career-related internships or fieldwork, Federal Work-Study, and institutionally sponsored loans also available. Financial award application deadline: 2/1; financial award applicants required to submit FAFSA. *Faculty research:* Public policy, Presidential studies, public leadership, economic policy, social policy. *Unit head:* Richard A. Chilcoat, Dean, 979-862-8007, Fax: 979-862-7953, E-mail: bushschool@tamu.edu. *Application contact:* Kathryn Meyer, Recruitment/Placement Officer, 979-458-4767, Fax: 979-845-4155, E-mail: admissions@bushschool.tamu.edu.

See Close-Up on page 1623.

Texas A&M University–Corpus Christi, Graduate Studies and Research, College of Liberal Arts, Corpus Christi, TX 78412-5503. Offers English (MA); history (MA); psychology (MA); public administration (MPA); studio arts (MA, MFA). Part-time and evening/weekend programs available. *Students:* 49 full-time (28 women), 119 part-time (76 women); includes 64 minority (5 African Americans, 1 American Indian/Alaska Native, 2 Asian Americans or Pacific Islanders, 56 Hispanic Americans), 7 international. 101 applicants, 73% accepted, 55 enrolled. In 2007, 52 degrees awarded. *Degree requirements:* For master's, comprehensive exam, thesis (for some programs). *Entrance requirements:* For master's, GRE General Test. Additional exam requirements/recommendations for international students: Required—TOEFL. *Application deadline:* For fall admission, 7/15 priority date for domestic students, 5/1 priority date for international students; for spring admission, 11/15 priority date for domestic students, 9/1 priority date for international students. Applications are processed on a rolling basis. Application

Public Administration

Texas A&M University–Corpus Christi (continued)
fee: $30 ($50 for international students). Electronic applications accepted. *Expenses:* Tuition, state resident: part-time $63 per credit hour. Tuition, nonresident: part-time $341 per credit hour. Tuition and fees vary according to course load. *Financial support:* Research assistantships, teaching assistantships, career-related internships or fieldwork, Federal Work-Study, institutionally sponsored loans, scholarships/grants, health care benefits, and unspecified assistantships available. Support available to part-time students. Financial award application deadline: 3/15; financial award applicants required to submit FAFSA. *Unit head:* Dr. Richard Gigliotti, Dean, 361-825-2659, Fax: 361-825-5844, E-mail: richard.gigliotti@tamucc.edu. *Application contact:* Maria Martinez, Graduate Admissions Coordinator, 361-825-2177, Fax: 361-825-2755, E-mail: gradweb@tamucc.edu.

Texas Southern University, Graduate School, School of Public Affairs, Program in Public Administration, Houston, TX 77004-4584. Offers MPA. *Faculty:* 7 full-time (2 women), 3 part-time/adjunct (0 women). *Students:* 35 full-time (23 women), 23 part-time (16 women); includes 56 minority (54 African Americans, 1 American Indian/Alaska Native, 1 Hispanic American), 1 international. Average age 30. 24 applicants, 96% accepted, 17 enrolled. In 2007, 13 degrees awarded. *Degree requirements:* For master's, comprehensive exam, thesis optional. *Entrance requirements:* For master's, GRE General Test, minimum GPA of 2.5. Additional exam requirements/recommendations for international students: Required—TOEFL. *Application deadline:* For fall admission, 7/15 priority date for domestic students. Applications are processed on a rolling basis. Application fee: $50 ($75 for international students). *Financial support:* In 2007–08, 2 research assistantships (averaging $5,850 per year) were awarded; fellowships, teaching assistantships, career-related internships or fieldwork, Federal Work-Study, institutionally sponsored loans, and unspecified assistantships also available. Financial award application deadline: 5/1. *Unit head:* Dr. Franklin Jones, Chair, 713-313-7313, E-mail: jones_fd@tsu.edu.

Texas State University–San Marcos, Graduate School, College of Liberal Arts, Department of Political Science, Program in Public Administration, San Marcos, TX 78666. Offers MPA. *Accreditation:* NASPAA. Part-time and evening/weekend programs available. *Students:* 27 full-time (14 women), 99 part-time (46 women); includes 50 minority (14 African Americans, 2 Asian Americans or Pacific Islanders, 34 Hispanic Americans), 4 international. Average age 32. 39 applicants, 95% accepted, 29 enrolled. In 2007, 24 degrees awarded. *Degree requirements:* For master's, comprehensive exam, applied research project. *Entrance requirements:* For master's, GRE General Test, minimum GPA of 2.85 in last 60 hours of course work. Additional exam requirements/recommendations for international students: Required—TOEFL (minimum score 550 paper-based; 213 computer-based), TWE. *Application deadline:* For fall admission, 6/15 priority date for domestic students, 6/1 priority date for international students; for spring admission, 10/15 priority date for domestic students, 10/1 priority date for international students. Applications are processed on a rolling basis. Application fee: $40 ($90 for international students). Electronic applications accepted. *Expenses:* Tuition, state resident: full-time $3,780; part-time $210 per credit hour. Tuition, nonresident: full-time $8,784; part-time $488 per credit hour. Required fees: $493 per semester. Full-time tuition and fees vary according to course load. *Financial support:* In 2007–08, 87 students received support, including 3 research assistantships (averaging $4,928 per year), 4 teaching assistantships (averaging $5,109 per year); career-related internships or fieldwork, Federal Work-Study, and institutionally sponsored loans also available. Support available to part-time students. Financial award application deadline: 4/1; financial award applicants required to submit FAFSA. *Faculty research:* Ethics in public management, total quality management in government, Texas state budgeting, pragmatism and public administration, minority economic development. *Unit head:* Dr. Patricia Shields, Graduate Advisor, 512-245-2143, Fax: 512-245-7815, E-mail: ps07@txstate.edu.

Texas Tech University, Graduate School, College of Arts and Sciences, Department of Political Science, Lubbock, TX 79409. Offers political science (MA, PhD); public administration (MPA); JD/MPA. *Accreditation:* NASPAA (one or more programs are accredited). Part-time programs available. *Faculty:* 10 full-time (1 woman). *Students:* 59 full-time (23 women), 19 part-time (7 women); includes 19 minority (2 African Americans, 2 American Indian/Alaska Native, 3 Asian Americans or Pacific Islanders, 12 Hispanic Americans), 9 international. Average age 28. 64 applicants, 78% accepted, 22 enrolled. In 2007, 32 master's, 2 doctorates awarded. *Degree requirements:* For master's, thesis or alternative; for doctorate, thesis/dissertation. *Entrance requirements:* For master's and doctorate, GRE General Test. Additional exam requirements/recommendations for international students: Required—TOEFL (minimum score 550 paper-based; 213 computer-based). *Application deadline:* For fall admission, 3/1 priority date for international students; for spring admission, 11/1 priority date for international students. Applications are processed on a rolling basis. Application fee: $50 ($60 for international students). Electronic applications accepted. *Expenses:* Tuition, state resident: part-time $373 per credit hour. Tuition, nonresident: part-time $651 per credit hour. Tuition and fees vary according to program. *Financial support:* In 2007–08, 64 students received support, including 1 research assistantship with partial tuition reimbursement available (averaging $9,000 per year), 26 teaching assistantships with partial tuition reimbursements available (averaging $12,024 per year); Federal Work-Study and institutionally sponsored loans also available. Support available to part-time students. Financial award application deadline: 4/15; financial award applicants required to submit FAFSA. *Faculty research:* State politics, American institutions and behavior, Asian politics, international and comparative political relations and economics, public administration and organizations. Total annual research expenditures:$45,033. *Unit head:* Dr. Philip H. Marshall, Chair, 806-742-3121, Fax: 806-742-0850, E-mail: philip.marshall@ttu.edu.

Thomas Edison State College, School of Business and Management, Program in Management, Trenton, NJ 08608-1176. Offers human resource management (MSM); online learning and teaching (MSM); organizational leadership (MSM); public sector auditing (MSM); public service leadership (MSM). Part-time programs available. Postbaccalaureate distance learning degree programs offered (minimal on-campus study). *Students:* Average age 42. 80 applicants, 87 enrolled. In 2007, 64 degrees awarded. *Degree requirements:* For master's, capstone/thesis, applied project. *Entrance requirements:* Additional exam requirements/recommendations for international students: Required—TOEFL (minimum score 550 paper-based; 213 computer-based; 79 iBT). *Application deadline:* For fall admission, 8/15 priority date for domestic and international students; for winter admission, 11/15 priority date for domestic and international students; for spring admission, 2/15 priority date for domestic and international students. Applications are processed on a rolling basis. Application fee: $75. Electronic applications accepted. *Expenses:* Tuition, state resident: part-time $440 per credit. Tuition, nonresident: part-time $440 per credit. Part-time tuition and fees vary according to program. *Financial support:* Applicants required to submit FAFSA. *Application contact:* David Hoftiezer, Director of Admissions, 888-442-8372, Fax: 609-984-8447, E-mail: admissions@tesc.edu.

Thomas Edison State College, School of Business and Management, Program in Public Service Leadership, Trenton, NJ 08608-1176. Offers Graduate Certificate. Part-time programs available. Postbaccalaureate distance learning degree programs offered (no on-campus study). *Students:* Average age 46. In 2007, 1 degree awarded. *Entrance requirements:* Additional exam requirements/recommendations for international students: Required—TOEFL (minimum score 550 paper-based; 213 computer-based; 79 iBT). *Application deadline:* For fall admission, 8/15 priority date for domestic and international students; for winter admission, 11/15 priority date for domestic and international students; for spring admission, 2/15 priority date for domestic and international students. Applications are processed on a rolling basis. Application fee: $75. Electronic applications accepted. *Expenses:* Tuition, state resident: part-time $440 per credit. Tuition, nonresident: part-time $440 per credit. Part-time tuition and fees vary according to program. *Financial support:* Applicants required to submit FAFSA. *Application contact:* David Hoftiezer, Director of Admissions, 888-442-8372, Fax: 609-984-8447, E-mail: admissions@tesc.edu.

Troy University, Graduate School, College of Arts and Sciences, Program in Public Administration, Troy, AL 36082. Offers MPA. Part-time and evening/weekend programs available. Postbaccalaureate distance learning degree programs offered (no on-campus study). *Students:* 215 full-time (143 women), 482 part-time (278 women); includes 470 minority (423 African Americans, 8 American Indian/Alaska Native, 13 Asian Americans or Pacific Islanders, 26 Hispanic Americans). Average age 34. In 2007, 252 degrees awarded. *Degree requirements:* For master's, comprehensive exam (for some programs), thesis optional. *Entrance requirements:* For master's, GRE General Test, MAT, or GMAT, minimum GPA of 2.5. Additional exam requirements/recommendations for international students: Required—TOEFL (minimum score 523 paper-based; 200 computer-based). *Application deadline:* For fall admission, 6/1 for international students; for spring admission, 10/15 for international students. Applications are processed on a rolling basis. Application fee: $50. Electronic applications accepted. *Financial support:* Available to part-time students. Applicants required to submit FAFSA. *Unit head:* Dr. Ellen Rosell, Chairman, 334-670-3758, Fax: 334-670-5647, E-mail: erosell@troy.edu. *Application contact:* Brenda K. Campbell, Director of Graduate Admissions, 334-670-3178, Fax: 334-670-3733, E-mail: bcamp@troy.edu.

Tufts University, Graduate School of Arts and Sciences, Graduate Certificate Programs, Program Evaluation Program, Medford, MA 02155. Offers Certificate. Part-time and evening/weekend programs available. *Students:* Average age 33. 4 applicants, 100% accepted, 4 enrolled. *Application deadline:* For fall admission, 8/15 priority date for domestic students; for spring admission, 12/12 priority date for domestic students. Applications are processed on a rolling basis. Application fee: $70. Electronic applications accepted. *Expenses: Contact institution.* *Financial support:* Career-related internships or fieldwork available. Support available to part-time students. Financial award application deadline: 5/1; financial award applicants required to submit FAFSA. *Application contact:* Angela Foss, Program Administrator, 617-627-3395, Fax: 617-627-3016, E-mail: gradschool@ase.tufts.edu.

TUI University, College of Business Administration, Program in Business Administration, Cypress, CA 90630. Offers business administration (PhD); conflict and negotiation management (MBA); criminal justice administration (MBA); entrepreneurship (MBA); finance (MBA); general management (MBA); human resource management (MBA); information technology management (MBA); international business (MBA); logistics management (MBA); public management (MBA); strategic leadership (MBA). Part-time and evening/weekend programs available. Postbaccalaureate distance learning degree programs offered (no on-campus study). In 2007, 752 master's, 28 doctorates awarded. *Degree requirements:* For doctorate, comprehensive exam, thesis/dissertation, defense of dissertation. *Entrance requirements:* For master's, minimum GPA of 2.5 (students with GPA 3.0 or greater may transfer up to 30% of graduate level credits); for doctorate, minimum GPA of 3.4, curriculum vitae, course work in research methods or statistics. Additional exam requirements/recommendations for international students: Required—TOEFL. *Application deadline:* Applications are processed on a rolling basis. Electronic applications accepted.

Universidad Nacional Pedro Henriquez Urena, Graduate School, Santo Domingo, Dominican Republic. Offers accounting and auditing (M Acct); animal production (M Agr); business administration (MBA, PhD); Caribbean tropical architecture (M Arch); conservation of monuments and cultural goods (M Arch); economics (M Econ); education (PhD); environmental engineering (MEE); horticulture (M Agr); hospital administration (PhD); humanities (PhD); international relations (MPS); management of natural resources (MNRM); project management (M Man, MPM); public administration (MPS); sanitary engineering (ME); social science (PhD); veterinary medicine (DVM).

Université de Moncton, Faculty of Arts and Social Sciences, Department of Public Administration, Moncton, NB E1A 3E9, Canada. Offers MPA, LL B/MPA. Part-time and evening/weekend programs available. *Degree requirements:* For master's, one foreign language. *Entrance requirements:* For master's, minimum GPA of 3.0. *Faculty research:* Public sector reform, privatization, economic modeling, public policy.

Université du Québec à Montréal, Graduate Programs, Program in Urban Analysis and Management, Montréal, QC H3C 3P8, Canada. Offers MA. Part-time programs available. *Entrance requirements:* For master's, appropriate bachelor's degree or equivalent and proficiency in French.

Université du Québec, École nationale d'administration publique, Graduate Program in Public Administration, Diploma Program in Public Administration, Quebec, QC G1K 9E5, Canada. Offers Diploma.

Université du Québec, École nationale d'administration publique, Graduate Program in Public Administration, Doctorate Program in Public Administration, Quebec, QC G1K 9E5, Canada. Offers PhD.

University at Albany, State University of New York, Nelson A. Rockefeller College of Public Affairs and Policy, Department of Public Administration and Policy, Albany, NY 12222-0001. Offers administrative behavior (PhD); comparative and development administration (MPA, PhD); human resources (MPA); legislative administration (MPA); nonprofit leadership and management (Certificate); planning and policy analysis (CAS); policy analysis (MPA); program analysis and evaluation (PhD); public affairs and policy (MA); public finance (MPA, PhD); public management (MPA, PhD); women and public policy (Certificate); JD/MPA. *Accreditation:* NASPAA (one or more programs are accredited). *Students:* 165 full-time (73 women), 69 part-time (28 women). Average age 29. In 2007, 71 master's, 7 doctorates, 20 other advanced degrees awarded. *Degree requirements:* For doctorate, one foreign language, thesis/dissertation. *Entrance requirements:* For doctorate, GRE General Test. Additional exam requirements/recommendations for international students: Required—TOEFL (minimum score 550 paper-based; 213 computer-based). *Application deadline:* For fall admission, 2/1 priority date for domestic students, 5/1 for international students; for spring admission, 12/1 for domestic students. Applications are processed on a rolling basis. Application fee: $75. Electronic applications accepted. *Expenses:* Tuition, state resident: part-time $576 per credit. Tuition, nonresident: part-time $910 per credit. Tuition and fees vary according to program. *Financial support:* Application deadline: 2/1. *Unit head:* Dr. George Richardson, Chair, 518-442-5258.

The University of Akron, Graduate School, Buchtel College of Arts and Sciences, Department of Public Administration and Urban Studies, Program in Public Administration, Akron, OH 44325. Offers MPA, JD/MPA. *Accreditation:* NASPAA. *Students:* 34 full-time (21 women), 31 part-time (17 women); includes 17 minority (15 African Americans, 2 Asian Americans or Pacific Islanders), 7 international. Average age 35. 49 applicants, 82% accepted, 23 enrolled. In 2007, 21 degrees awarded. *Degree requirements:* For master's, thesis optional. *Entrance requirements:* For master's, GRE, GMAT, LSAT, MAT or minimum GPA of 3.0, minimum GPA of 2.8, resumé, personal essay, letters of recommendation. Additional exam requirements/recommendations for international students: Required—TOEFL (minimum score 550 paper-based; 213 computer-based; 79 iBT), Michigan English Language Assessment Battery. *Application deadline:* Applications are processed on a rolling basis. Application fee: $30 ($40 for international students). Electronic applications accepted. *Expenses:* Tuition, state resident: full-time $6,164; part-time $342 per credit. Tuition, nonresident: full-time $10,575; part-time $588 per credit. Required fees: $806; $43 per credit. $12 per term. Tuition and fees vary according to course load, degree level and program. *Unit head:* Dr. Raymond Cox, Coordinator, 330-972-7618, E-mail: rcox@uakron.edu.

The University of Alabama, Graduate School, College of Arts and Sciences, Department of Political Science, Tuscaloosa, AL 35487. Offers political science (MA, PhD); public administration (MPA). Part-time programs available. *Faculty:* 15 full-time (3 women). *Students:* 42 full-time (15 women), 14 part-time (8 women); includes 4 minority (2 African Americans, 2 Hispanic Americans), 7 international. Average age 30. 44 applicants, 52% accepted, 12 enrolled. In 2007, 21 master's, 4 doctorates awarded. Terminal master's awarded for partial completion of doctoral program. *Median time to degree:* Of those who began their doctoral program in fall 1999, 100% received their degree in 8 years or less. *Degree requirements:* For master's, thesis optional; for doctorate, comprehensive exam, thesis/dissertation. *Entrance requirements:* For master's and doctorate, GRE (minimum score: 1000), minimum GPA of 3.0 UG. Additional exam requirements/recommendations for international students: Required—TOEFL. *Application deadline:* For fall admission, 6/30 for domestic and international students; for spring admission, 10/15 for domestic and international students. Applications are processed on a rolling basis. Application fee: $30. *Expenses:* Tuition, state resident: full-time $5,700. Tuition, nonresident: full-time $16,518. *Financial support:* In 2007–08, 15 students received support, including teaching assistantships with full tuition reimbursements available (averaging $10,908 per year); career-related internships or fieldwork and Federal Work-Study also available. Financial award application deadline: 2/15. *Faculty research:* American politics, comparative politics, international relations, public administration, political theory. *Unit head:* Dr. David U. Lanoue, Chair and Professor, 205-348-5981, Fax: 205-348-5298, E-mail: dlanoue@bama.ua.edu. *Application contact:* Dr. Terry Royed, Graduate Advisor, 205-348-3801, Fax: 205-348-5248, E-mail: troyed@tenhoor.as.ua.edu.

The University of Alabama at Birmingham, School of Social and Behavioral Sciences, Department of Government, Birmingham, AL 35294. Offers public administration (MPA). *Accreditation:* NASPAA. *Students:* 38 full-time (23 women), 36 part-time (18 women); includes 24 minority (20 African Americans, 2 Asian Americans or Pacific Islanders, 2 Hispanic Americans), 4 international. Average age 30. In 2007, 17 degrees awarded. *Entrance requirements:* For master's, GRE General Test or MAT. *Application deadline:* Applications are processed on a rolling basis. Application fee: $35 ($60 for international students). Electronic applications accepted. *Financial support:* Fellowships, career-related internships or fieldwork available. *Unit head:* Dr. Steven H. Haeberle, Chair, 205-934-9679, E-mail: shaeberl@uab.edu.

University of Alaska Anchorage, College of Business and Public Policy, Program in Public Administration, Anchorage, AK 99508-8060. Offers MPA. Part-time programs available. *Degree requirements:* For master's, comprehensive exam, thesis or alternative, capstone project. *Entrance requirements:* For master's, GRE General Test. Additional exam requirements/recommendations for international students: Required—TOEFL (minimum score 550 paper-based; 213 computer-based). *Faculty research:* Policy analysis, policy and administration issues in the North, hypothetical government policies, public management in health care.

University of Alaska Southeast, Graduate Programs, Program in Public Administration, Juneau, AK 99801. Offers MPA. Part-time and evening/weekend programs available. Postbaccalaureate distance learning degree programs offered (no on-campus study). *Degree requirements:* For master's, capstone course or thesis. *Entrance requirements:* For master's, minimum GPA of 3.0, curriculum vitae, letters of reference. Electronic applications accepted. *Faculty research:* Democratic governance, public administrative theory, local government.

The University of Arizona, Graduate College, Eller College of Management, School of Public Administration and Policy, Tucson, AZ 85721. Offers public administration (MPA); public administration and policy (PhD). *Accreditation:* NASPAA. *Faculty:* 9. *Students:* 43 full-time (23 women), 13 part-time (10 women); includes 16 minority (2 African Americans, 2 American Indian/Alaska Native, 1 Asian American or Pacific Islander, 11 Hispanic Americans), 3 international. Average age 28. 60 applicants, 63% accepted, 26 enrolled. In 2007, 25 degrees awarded. *Degree requirements:* For master's, internship of 400 hours; for doctorate, comprehensive exam, thesis/dissertation. *Entrance requirements:* For master's, GRE, 2-3 letters of recommendation, resumè; for doctorate, GMAT or GRE, minimum GPA of 3.5, letter of interest, 3 letters of recommendation, resumè. Additional exam requirements/recommendations for international students: Required—TOEFL (minimum score 650 paper-based; 280 computer-based). *Application deadline:* For fall admission, 4/15 priority date for domestic students. Applications are processed on a rolling basis. Application fee: $50. *Expenses:* Contact institution. *Financial support:* In 2007–08, 27 students received support, including 5 fellowships (averaging $2,000 per year), 13 teaching assistantships with partial tuition reimbursements available (averaging $4,182 per year); career-related internships or fieldwork, scholarships/grants, health care benefits, tuition waivers (full and partial), and unspecified assistantships also available. Financial award application deadline: 4/15. Total annual research expenditures: $1.6 million. *Unit head:* Dr. H. Brinton Milward, Director, 520-621-7476, Fax: 520-626-5549, E-mail: bmilward@eller.arizona.edu. *Application contact:* Pamela Adams, Administrative Associate, 520-621-3128, Fax: 520-621-5549, E-mail: adamsp@email.arizona.edu.

University of Arkansas, Graduate School, J. William Fulbright College of Arts and Sciences, Department of Political Science, Program in Public Administration, Fayetteville, AR 72701-1201. Offers MPA. *Students:* 10 full-time (7 women), 15 part-time (12 women); includes 2 minority (1 African American, 1 American Indian/Alaska Native), 2 international. 21 applicants, 29% accepted. In 2007, 4 degrees awarded. *Degree requirements:* For master's, comprehensive exam, thesis or alternative. *Entrance requirements:* For master's, GRE General Test. Application fee: $40 ($50 for international students). *Financial support:* In 2007–08, 2 teaching assistantships were awarded; fellowships with tuition reimbursements, research assistantships, career-related internships or fieldwork and Federal Work-Study also available. Support available to part-time students. Financial award application deadline: 4/1; financial award applicants required to submit FAFSA. *Unit head:* Dr. Margaret Reid, Graduate Coordinator, 479-575-3356, E-mail: mreid@uark.edu.

University of Arkansas at Little Rock, Graduate School, College of Professional Studies, Program in Public Administration, Little Rock, AR 72204-1099. Offers MPA. *Accreditation:* NASPAA. Part-time and evening/weekend programs available. *Students:* Average age 32. *Degree requirements:* For master's, comprehensive exam. *Entrance requirements:* For master's, GRE General Test or MAT, minimum GPA of 2.7. *Application deadline:* Applications are processed on a rolling basis. *Financial support:* Research assistantships with tuition reimbursements, career-related internships or fieldwork, Federal Work-Study, institutionally sponsored loans, and unspecified assistantships available. Support available to part-time students. *Faculty research:* State and local administration, nonprofit management. *Unit head:* Dr. Roby D. Robertson, Director, 501-569-8572, E-mail: rdrobertson@ualr.edu. *Application contact:* Dr. Dianne L. Wigand, Coordinator, 501-569-8357, E-mail: fdwigand@ualr.edu.

University of Baltimore, Graduate School, The Yale Gordon College of Liberal Arts, School of Public Affairs, Doctoral Program in Public Administration, Baltimore, MD 21201-5779. Offers DPA. *Students:* 1 (woman) full-time, 30 part-time (13 women); includes 20 minority (15 African Americans, 2 Asian Americans or Pacific Islanders, 3 Hispanic Americans), 1 international. Average age 44. In 2007, 21 degrees awarded. *Entrance requirements:* Additional exam requirements/recommendations for international students: Required—TOEFL. *Application deadline:* For fall admission, 5/1 priority date for domestic students, 6/1 for international students; for spring admission, 12/1 for domestic students, 11/1 for international students. *Expenses:* Tuition, state resident: part-time $518 per credit. Tuition, nonresident: part-time $751 per credit. Tuition and fees vary according to program. *Unit head:* Dr. Alan Lyles, Director, 410-837-6107, E-mail: alyles@ubalt.edu. *Application contact:* Wendy Bolyard.

University of Central Florida, College of Health and Public Affairs, Department of Public Administration, Orlando, FL 32816. Offers emergency management and homeland security (Certificate); non-profit management (MNM, Certificate); public administration (MPA, Certificate); urban and regional planning (Certificate). *Accreditation:* NASPAA. Part-time and evening/weekend programs available. *Faculty:* 11 full-time (2 women), 9 part-time/adjunct (3 women). *Degree requirements:* For master's, comprehensive exam, thesis or alternative, research report. *Entrance requirements:* For master's, GRE General Test. *Application deadline:* For fall admission, 7/1 for domestic students; for spring admission, 12/1 for domestic students. Application fee: $30. Electronic applications accepted. *Expenses:* Tuition, state resident: full-time $6,484. Tuition, nonresident: full-time $23,938. Tuition and fees vary according to program. *Financial support:* Fellowships with partial tuition reimbursements, research assistantships with partial tuition reimbursements, teaching assistantships with partial tuition reimbursements, career-related internships or fieldwork, Federal Work-Study, institutionally sponsored loans, tuition waivers (partial), and unspecified assistantships available. Financial award application deadline: 3/1; financial award applicants required to submit FAFSA. *Unit head:* Dr. MaryAnn Feldheim, Chair, 407-823-3693, Fax: 407-823-5651.

University of Colorado at Colorado Springs, Graduate School, Graduate School of Public Affairs, Colorado Springs, CO 80933-7150. Offers criminal justice (MCJ); public administration (MPA). Part-time and evening/weekend programs available. *Faculty:* 8 full-time (2 women), 25 part-time/adjunct (15 women). *Students:* 84 full-time (52 women), 66 part-time (40 women); includes 34 minority (8 African Americans, 8 Asian Americans or Pacific Islanders, 18 Hispanic Americans). Average age 35. 32 applicants, 78% accepted, 19 enrolled. In 2007, 24 degrees awarded. *Degree requirements:* For master's, internship (if no experience), capstone project. *Entrance requirements:* For master's, GRE General Test, GMAT, LSAT, minimum GPA of 3.0. *Application deadline:* For fall admission, 6/1 priority date for domestic students; for spring admission, 11/1 for domestic students. Applications are processed on a rolling basis. Application fee: $60 ($75 for international students). *Expenses:* Contact institution. *Financial support:* Career-related internships or fieldwork and Federal Work-Study available. Support available to part-time students. *Unit head:* Dr. Kathleen Beatty, Dean, 719-262-4182, Fax: 719-262-4183, E-mail: kbeatty@uccs.edu. *Application contact:* Mary Lou Kartis, Program Assistant, 719-262-4182, Fax: 719-262-4183, E-mail: mkartis@uccs.edu.

University of Colorado Denver, Graduate School of Public Affairs, Executive MPA Option, Denver, CO 80217-3364. Offers Exec MPA. Part-time and evening/weekend programs available. Postbaccalaureate distance learning degree programs offered. *Faculty:* 5 full-time (3 women), 3 part-time/adjunct (1 woman). *Students:* 1 full-time (0 women), 16 part-time (11 women); includes 1 minority (Hispanic American) Average age 43. 8 applicants, 75% accepted, 1 enrolled. *Degree requirements:* For master's, executive research project. *Entrance requirements:* For master's, 5 years of senior-level management experience, resumé. Additional exam requirements/recommendations for international students: Required—TOEFL (minimum score 510 paper-based). *Application deadline:* For fall admission, 8/1 priority date for domestic students, 1/1 for international students. Applications are processed on a rolling basis. Application fee: $50 ($60 for international students). *Financial support:* Fellowships, research assistantships, teaching assistantships, career-related internships or fieldwork, Federal Work-Study, institutionally sponsored loans, and scholarships/grants available. Support available to part-time students. Financial award application deadline: 4/1; financial award applicants required to submit FAFSA. *Unit head:* Dr. Joy Fitzpatrick, Program Director, 303-315-2085, Fax: 303-556-6602, E-mail: joy.fitzpatrick@cudenver.edu. *Application contact:* Antoinette Sandoval, Student Service Specialist, 303-556-5972, Fax: 303-556-5971, E-mail: antoinette.sandoval@cudenver.edu.

See Close-Up on page 1631.

University of Colorado Denver, Graduate School of Public Affairs, Program in Public Administration, Denver, CO 80217-3364. Offers MPA. *Accreditation:* NASPAA. Part-time and evening/weekend programs available. Postbaccalaureate distance learning degree programs offered. *Students:* 52 full-time (29 women), 184 part-time (112 women); includes 28 minority (8 African Americans, 4 Asian Americans or Pacific Islanders, 16 Hispanic Americans), 20 international. Average age 35. 149 applicants, 77% accepted, 63 enrolled. In 2007, 104 degrees awarded. *Degree requirements:* For master's, research paper. *Entrance requirements:* For master's, GRE General Test or minimum GPA of 3.0. Additional exam requirements/recommendations for international students: Required—TOEFL (minimum score 500 paper-based). *Application deadline:* For fall admission, 6/1 priority date for domestic students, 12/1 priority date for international students; for spring admission, 11/1 for domestic students, 5/1 for international students. Applications are processed on a rolling basis. Application fee: $50 ($60 for international students). *Financial support:* In 2007–08, 24 fellowships with partial tuition reimbursements, 20 research assistantships with partial tuition reimbursements, 13 teaching assistantships with partial tuition reimbursements were awarded; career-related internships or fieldwork, Federal Work-Study, institutionally sponsored loans, and scholarships/grants also available. Support available to part-time students. Financial award application deadline: 4/1; financial award applicants required to submit FAFSA. *Unit head:* Dr. Joy Fitzpatrick, Program Director, 303-315-2085, Fax: 303-556-6602, E-mail: joy.fitzpatrick@cudenver.edu. *Application contact:* Antoinette Sandoval, Student Service Specialist, 303-556-5972, Fax: 303-556-5971, E-mail: antoinette.sandoval@cudenver.edu.

See Close-Up on page 1631.

University of Connecticut, Graduate School, College of Liberal Arts and Sciences, Department of Public Policy, Field of Public Administration, Storrs, CT 06269. Offers nonprofit management (Graduate Certificate); public administration (MPA); public financial management (Graduate Certificate); JD/MPA; MPA/MSW. *Accreditation:* NASPAA. *Faculty:* 8 full-time (4 women). *Students:* 47 full-time (27 women), 30 part-time (14 women); includes 10 minority (4 African Americans, 2 American Indian/Alaska Native, 3 Asian Americans or Pacific Islanders, 1 Hispanic American), 3 international. Average age 30. 63 applicants, 48% accepted, 28 enrolled. In 2007, 8 master's, 10 other advanced degrees awarded. *Degree requirements:* For master's, comprehensive exam, internship. *Entrance requirements:* For master's, GRE General Test. Additional exam requirements/recommendations for international students: Required—TOEFL (minimum score 550 paper-based; 213 computer-based). *Application deadline:* For fall admission, 2/1 priority date for domestic and international students; for spring admission, 11/1 for domestic students, 10/1 for international students. Applications are processed on a rolling basis. Application fee: $55. Electronic applications accepted. *Expenses:* Tuition, state resident: part-time $469 per credit hour. Tuition, nonresident: part-time $1,218 per credit hour. *Financial support:* In 2007–08, 24 research assistantships with full tuition reimbursements, 1 teaching assistantship with full tuition reimbursement were awarded; career-related internships or fieldwork, Federal Work-Study, scholarships/grants, health care benefits, and unspecified assistantships also available. Financial award application deadline: 2/1; financial award applicants required to submit FAFSA. *Unit head:* William Simonsen, Chairperson, 860-570-9045, E-mail: william.simonsen@uconn.edu. *Application contact:* Valerie Rogers, Program Director, 860-570-9047, Fax: 860-570-9114, E-mail: valerie.rogers@uconn.edu.

University of Dayton, Graduate School, College of Arts and Sciences, Program in Public Administration, Dayton, OH 45469-1300. Offers MPA. *Accreditation:* NASPAA. Part-time and evening/weekend programs available. *Faculty:* 5 full-time (1 woman), 5 part-time/adjunct (2 women). *Students:* 30 full-time (10 women), 20 part-time (6 women); includes 9 minority (all African Americans), 1 international. Average age 27. 54 applicants, 69% accepted, 10 enrolled. In 2007, 19 degrees awarded. *Degree requirements:* For master's, internship or public service project. *Entrance requirements:* For master's, GRE General Test, minimum undergraduate GPA of 2.7, undergraduate GPA on sliding scale. Additional exam requirements/recommendations for international students: Required—TOEFL (minimum score 550 paper-based; 213 computer-based; 80 iBT). *Application deadline:* For fall admission, 4/1 priority date for domestic students, 3/1 priority date for international students; for winter admission, 7/1 priority date for international students; for spring admission, 1/1 priority date for international students. Applications are processed on a rolling basis. Application fee: $0 ($50 for international students). Electronic applications accepted. *Financial support:* In 2007–08, 3 research assistantships with full tuition reimbursements (averaging $9,500 per year) were awarded; career-related internships or fieldwork, institutionally sponsored loans, health care benefits, and unspecified assistantships also available. Financial award applicants required to submit FAFSA. *Faculty research:* Ethics, leadership, state government, environmental policy, welfare reforms, state legislatures. *Unit head:* Dr. Grant Neeley, Director MPA Program, 937-229-3626, Fax: 937-229-1400, E-mail: grant.neeley@notes.udayton.edu. *Application contact:* Angela Jones-Glukhov, Associate Director of Graduate Admissions, 937-229-4305, Fax: 937-229-4729.

University of Delaware, College of Human Services, Education and Public Policy, School of Urban Affairs and Public Policy, Program in Public Administration, Newark, DE 19716. Offers MPA. *Accreditation:* NASPAA. Part-time and evening/weekend programs available. *Faculty:* 16 full-time (4 women). *Students:* 53 full-time (29 women), 16 part-time (9 women); includes 20 minority (13 African Americans, 3 Asian Americans or Pacific Islanders, 4 Hispanic

Public Administration

University of Delaware (continued)

Americans), 9 international. Average age 30. 59 applicants, 61% accepted, 23 enrolled. In 2007, 39 degrees awarded. *Degree requirements:* For master's, internship or thesis. *Entrance requirements:* For master's, GRE General Test. Additional exam requirements/recommendations for international students: Required—TOEFL. *Application deadline:* For fall admission, 2/1 for domestic students; for spring admission, 12/1 for domestic students. Applications are processed on a rolling basis. Application fee: $60. Electronic applications accepted. *Financial support:* In 2007–08, 50 students received support, including fellowships with full tuition reimbursements available (averaging $12,200 per year), 48 research assistantships with full tuition reimbursements available (averaging $12,200 per year), teaching assistantships with full tuition reimbursements available (averaging $12,200 per year); career-related internships or fieldwork, Federal Work-Study, institutionally sponsored loans, tuition waivers (full), and stipends also available. Financial award application deadline: 2/1. *Faculty research:* State and local management, community development and nonprofit leadership, drug and alcohol epidemiology, fiscal and financial policy, transportation impacts and management. Total annual research expenditures: $1 million. *Unit head:* Dr. James Flynn, Director, 302-831-4658. *Application contact:* Melissa Hopkins, Senior Secretary, 302-831-8712, Fax: 302-831-3587, E-mail: suapp@udel.edu.

See Close-Up on page 1635.

University of Evansville, Center for Continuing Education, Evansville, IN 47722. Offers public service administration (MS). Part-time and evening/weekend programs available. *Faculty:* 5 full-time (1 woman), 6 part-time/adjunct (3 women). *Students:* 55 full-time (42 women), 2 part-time (1 woman); includes 4 minority (3 African Americans, 1 American Indian/Alaska Native), 1 international. Average age 37. 28 applicants, 93% accepted, 23 enrolled. In 2007, 22 degrees awarded. *Entrance requirements:* For master's, GRE or MAT, minimum undergraduate GPA of 3.0, resumé, minimum of 3 years work experience, 2 letters of reference. *Application deadline:* For fall admission, 7/15 priority date for domestic students; for spring admission, 11/30 priority date for domestic students. Applications are processed on a rolling basis. Application fee: $35. *Expenses:* Tuition: Full-time $6,870. Tuition and fees vary according to course load, degree level and program. *Financial support:* In 2007–08, 13 students received support. Application deadline: 6/1; *Unit head:* Carla Doty, Director of Continuing Education, 812-488-2981, Fax: 812-488-2432, E-mail: cd39@evansville.edu.

The University of Findlay, Graduate and Professional Studies, College of Business, Findlay, OH 45840-3653. Offers financial management (MBA); human resource management (MBA); international management (MBA); management (MBA); marketing (MBA); public management (MBA). Part-time and evening/weekend programs available. Postbaccalaureate distance learning degree programs offered (no on-campus study). *Students:* 125 full-time (53 women), 582 part-time (210 women); includes 23 minority (10 African Americans, 1 American Indian/Alaska Native, 10 Asian Americans or Pacific Islanders, 2 Hispanic Americans), 489 international. Average age 35. 270 applicants, 87% accepted, 212 enrolled. In 2007, 299 degrees awarded. *Degree requirements:* For master's, thesis, cumulative project. *Entrance requirements:* For master's, GMAT, minimum undergraduate GPA of 3.0 in last 60 hours of course work. Additional exam requirements/recommendations for international students: Required—TOEFL (minimum score 550 paper-based). *Application deadline:* Applications are processed on a rolling basis. Application fee: $25. Electronic applications accepted. *Expenses: Contact institution.* Tuition and fees vary according to program. *Financial support:* In 2007–08, 1 student received support, including 1 teaching assistantship with full tuition reimbursement available (averaging $6,000 per year); unspecified assistantships also available. Financial award application deadline: 4/1; financial award applicants required to submit FAFSA. *Faculty research:* Health care management, operations and logistics management. *Unit head:* Dr. Paul Sears, Dean, 419-434-4704, Fax: 419-434-4822. *Application contact:* Heather Riffle, Assistant to the Dean, Graduate and Professional Studies, 419-434-4640, Fax: 419-434-5517, E-mail: riffle@findlay.edu.

University of Georgia, School of Public and International Affairs, Program in Public Administration and Policy, Athens, GA 30602. Offers public administration (MPA, PhD). *Accreditation:* NASPAA (one or more programs are accredited). *Faculty:* 17 full-time (4 women), 2 part-time/adjunct (0 women). *Students:* 116 full-time (57 women), 61 part-time (36 women); includes 16 African Americans, 2 Asian Americans or Pacific Islanders, 3 Hispanic Americans, 15 international. 225 applicants, 44% accepted, 55 enrolled. In 2007, 58 master's, 9 doctorates awarded. *Degree requirements:* For master's, internship; for doctorate, thesis/dissertation. *Entrance requirements:* For master's and doctorate, GRE General Test. *Application deadline:* For fall admission, 7/1 priority date for domestic students; for spring admission, 11/15 for domestic students. Application fee: $50. Electronic applications accepted. *Financial support:* Fellowships, research assistantships, teaching assistantships, unspecified assistantships available. *Unit head:* Dr. Laurence J. O'Toole, Head, 706-542-2057, E-mail: cmsotool@uga.edu. *Application contact:* Dr. J. Edward Kellough, Graduate Coordinator, 706-542-0488, Fax: 706-542-4421, E-mail: kellough@uga.edu.

University of Guam, Office of Graduate Studies, School of Business and Public Administration, Public Administration Program, Mangilao, GU 96923. Offers MPA. *Faculty:* 12 full-time (4 women). *Students:* 21 full-time (14 women), 15 part-time (6 women); includes 35 Asian Americans or Pacific Islanders. Average age 36. In 2007, 10 degrees awarded. *Entrance requirements:* For master's, GRE General Test. Additional exam requirements/recommendations for international students: Required—TOEFL. *Application deadline:* For fall admission, 6/11 for domestic students, 3/24 for international students; for spring admission, 11/16 for domestic students, 9/8 for international students. Application fee: $49 ($74 for international students). *Unit head:* Dr. Ronald L. McNinch, Coordinator, 671-735-2573, E-mail: rmcninch@uguam.uog.edu. *Application contact:* Charlie A. Alcantara, Program Coordinator, Graduate Studies Office, 671-735-2173, Fax: 671-734-3676, E-mail: charliea@uguam.uog.edu.

University of Guelph, Graduate Program Services, College of Social and Applied Human Sciences, Department of Political Science, Guelph, ON N1G 2W1, Canada. Offers comparative politics (MA); international development (MA); political science (MA); public policy and public administration (MA); the Americas (Canada emphasis) (MA). MA in public policy and public administration offered in collaboration with Department of Political Science of McMaster University. *Faculty:* 20 full-time (8 women), 2 part-time/adjunct (0 women). *Students:* 41 full-time (25 women). Average age 26. 130 applicants, 23% accepted, 25 enrolled. In 2007, 19 degrees awarded. *Degree requirements:* For master's, thesis or paper. *Entrance requirements:* For master's, minimum B average during previous 2 years of course work, 4 year Honours Degree in Political Science. Additional exam requirements/recommendations for international students: Required—TOEFL. *Application deadline:* For fall admission, 2/1 for domestic and international students. Application fee: $85. Electronic applications accepted. *Financial support:* In 2007–08, 9 research assistantships (averaging $2,000 per year), 58 teaching assistantships (averaging $5,106 per year) were awarded; scholarships/grants also available. *Faculty research:* Political ethics, constitutional power. *Unit head:* Dr. B. Sheldrick, Chair, 519-824-4120 Ext. 56503, Fax: 519-822-7703, E-mail: sheldric@uoguelph.ca. *Application contact:* Dr. C. Johnson, Coordinator, 519-824-4120, Fax: 519-822-7703, E-mail: cajohnso@uoguelph.ca.

University of Hawaii at Manoa, Graduate Division, Colleges of Arts and Sciences, College of Social Sciences, Department of Public Administration, Honolulu, HI 96822. Offers MPA, Graduate Certificate. Part-time and evening/weekend programs available. *Faculty:* 9 full-time (1 woman). *Students:* 19 full-time (11 women), 40 part-time (21 women); includes 25 minority (1 African American, 22 Asian Americans or Pacific Islanders, 2 Hispanic Americans), 14 international. Average age 39. 81 applicants, 49% accepted, 32 enrolled. *Degree requirements:* For master's, thesis optional, practicum. *Entrance requirements:* Additional exam requirements/recommendations for international students: Required—TOEFL (minimum score 540 paper-based; 207 computer-based; 76 iBT), IELTS (minimum score 5). *Application deadline:* For fall admission, 3/1 for domestic and international students. Application fee: $50. *Financial support:* In 2007–08, 1 teaching assistantship (averaging $13,296 per year) was awarded; fellowships, research assistantships, career-related internships or fieldwork, Federal Work-Study, institutionally sponsored loans, and tuition waivers (full and partial) also available. Support available to part-time students. *Faculty research:* Public sector finance and the budget process, collaboration between sectors, organizational problem solving and communication processes, system reform in government organizations, public policy analysis. Total annual research expenditures: $41,250. *Application contact:* Richard Pratt, Graduate Chair, 808-956-8260, Fax: 808-956-9571, E-mail: pratt@hawaii.edu.

University of Idaho, College of Graduate Studies, College of Letters, Arts and Social Sciences, Department of Political Science and Public Affairs Research, Program in Public Administration, Moscow, ID 83844-2282. Offers MPA. *Students:* 40 (22 women). Average age 29. In 2007, 13 degrees awarded. *Entrance requirements:* For master's, minimum GPA of 2.8. *Application deadline:* For fall admission, 8/1 for domestic students; for spring admission, 12/15 for domestic students. Application fee: $55 ($60 for international students). *Financial support:* Application deadline: 2/15. *Unit head:* Dr. Florence Heffron, Director, 208-885-6563. *Application contact:* Colleen Mack-Canty, Information Contact, 208-885-6120.

University of Illinois at Chicago, Graduate College, College of Urban Planning and Public Affairs, Program in Public Administration, Chicago, IL 60607-7128. Offers MPA, PhD. *Accreditation:* NASPAA (one or more programs are accredited). Part-time and evening/weekend programs available. Terminal master's awarded for partial completion of doctoral program. *Degree requirements:* For master's, internship/project. *Entrance requirements:* For master's, GRE General Test, minimum GPA of 3.0. Additional exam requirements/recommendations for international students: Required—TOEFL. Electronic applications accepted. *Faculty research:* Public management, economic development, public personnel.

University of Illinois at Springfield, Graduate Programs, College of Public Affairs and Administration, Program in Public Administration, Springfield, IL 62703-5407. Offers MPA, DPA. *Accreditation:* NASPAA. Part-time and evening/weekend programs available. *Faculty:* 5 full-time (1 woman), 4 part-time/adjunct (1 woman). *Students:* 57 full-time (35 women), 89 part-time (57 women); includes 40 minority (33 African Americans, 1 American Indian/Alaska Native, 3 Asian Americans or Pacific Islanders, 3 Hispanic Americans), 3 international. Average age 33. 118 applicants, 45% accepted, 39 enrolled. In 2007, 41 master's, 2 doctorates awarded. *Median time to degree:* Of those who began their doctoral program in fall 1999, 26% received their degree in 8 years or less. *Degree requirements:* For master's, thesis or seminar; for doctorate, comprehensive exam, thesis/dissertation. *Entrance requirements:* For master's, resumé, 3 letters of reference, course work in statistics and economics, computer spreadsheet competency, minimum GPA of 2.5, career goals statement; for doctorate, GRE, minimum graduate GPA of 3.25; writing sample; 3 letters of reference; resumé; course work in economics, political systems, analytical tools, budget and finance, and public policy. Additional exam requirements/recommendations for international students: Required—TOEFL (minimum score 575 paper-based; 232 computer-based). Application fee: $50 ($60 for international students). Electronic applications accepted. *Expenses:* Tuition, state resident: full-time $5,424; part-time $226 per credit hour. Tuition, nonresident: part-time $553 per credit hour. Required fees: $618 per term. *Financial support:* In 2007–08, research assistantships with full tuition reimbursements (averaging $7,988 per year), teaching assistantships with full tuition reimbursements (averaging $7,988 per year) were awarded; career-related internships or fieldwork, Federal Work-Study, scholarships/grants, health care benefits, tuition waivers (full and partial), and unspecified assistantships also available. Support available to part-time students. Financial award application deadline: 11/15; financial award applicants required to submit FAFSA. *Unit head:* Dr. Will Miller, Program Administrator, 217-206-8361, E-mail: wmill3@uis.edu.

University of Kansas, Research and Graduate Studies, College of Liberal Arts and Sciences, Department of Public Administration, Lawrence, KS 66045. Offers MPA, PhD, JD/MPA, MUP/MPA. *Accreditation:* NASPAA. Part-time and evening/weekend programs available. *Faculty:* 13. *Students:* 27 full-time (12 women), 97 part-time (46 women); includes 10 minority (5 African Americans, 1 Asian American or Pacific Islander, 4 Hispanic Americans), 4 international. Average age 34. 71 applicants, 65% accepted, 34 enrolled. In 2007, 39 degrees awarded. Terminal master's awarded for partial completion of doctoral program. *Degree requirements:* For master's, comprehensive exam; for doctorate, comprehensive exam, thesis/dissertation. *Entrance requirements:* For master's and doctorate, GRE General Test. Additional exam requirements/recommendations for international students: Required—TOEFL. *Application deadline:* For fall admission, 7/1 for domestic students, 4/15 for international students; for spring admission, 11/15 for domestic students, 7/1 for international students. Application fee: $55 ($60 for international students). Electronic applications accepted. *Expenses:* Tuition, state resident: full-time $5,838. Tuition, nonresident: full-time $13,409. Tuition and fees vary according to program. *Financial support:* Fellowships, research assistantships with full and partial tuition reimbursements, teaching assistantships with full and partial tuition reimbursements, career-related internships or fieldwork, institutionally sponsored loans, scholarships/grants, and unspecified assistantships available. Financial award application deadline: 2/1. *Faculty research:* Local government, administrative ethics, non-profit management, policy studies, law and public administration, finance, budgeting. *Unit head:* Marilu Goodyear, Chair, 785-864-3527, Fax: 785-864-5208, E-mail: padept@ku.edu. *Application contact:* Ray Hummert, Administrative Director, 785-864-9097, Fax: 785-864-5208, E-mail: rhummert@ku.edu.

University of Kentucky, Graduate School, Program in Public Administration, Lexington, KY 40506-0032. Offers MPA, MPP, PhD. *Accreditation:* NASPAA (one or more programs are accredited). *Faculty:* 8 full-time (3 women), 5 part-time/adjunct (1 woman). *Students:* 44 full-time (24 women), 22 part-time (13 women); includes 6 minority (5 African Americans, 1 Hispanic American), 10 international. Average age 30. 119 applicants, 41% accepted, 20 enrolled. In 2007, 10 master's, 5 doctorates awarded. *Median time to degree:* Of those who began their doctoral program in fall 1999, 57% received their degree in 8 years or less. *Degree requirements:* For master's, comprehensive exam; for doctorate, comprehensive exam, thesis/dissertation. *Entrance requirements:* For master's, GMAT or GRE General Test, minimum undergraduate GPA of 2.75; for doctorate, GMAT or GRE General Test, minimum graduate GPA of 3.0. Additional exam requirements/recommendations for international students: Required—TOEFL (minimum score 550 paper-based; 213 computer-based). *Application deadline:* For fall admission, 7/17 priority date for domestic students, 2/1 priority date for international students; for spring admission, 12/13 priority date for domestic students, 6/15 priority date for international students. Application fee: $50 ($65 for international students). Electronic applications accepted. *Expenses:* Tuition, state resident: part-time $437 per credit hour. Tuition, nonresident: part-time $931 per credit hour. *Financial support:* In 2007–08, 25 students received support, including 7 fellowships with full tuition reimbursements available (averaging $3,605 per year), 20 research assistantships with full tuition reimbursements available (averaging $9,000 per year), 1 teaching assistantship with full tuition reimbursement available (averaging $17,700 per year); career-related internships or fieldwork, Federal Work-Study, institutionally sponsored loans, scholarships/grants, traineeships, health care benefits, tuition waivers (partial), and unspecified assistantships also available. Support available to part-time students. Financial award application deadline: 3/15; financial award applicants required to submit FAFSA. *Faculty research:* Public financial management, education finance and policy, health finance and policy, welfare policy, program evaluation. Total annual research expenditures: $822,349. *Unit head:* Dr. Eugenia Toma, Director of Graduate Studies, 859-257-5741, Fax: 859-323-1937, E-mail: eugenia.toma@uky.edu. *Application contact:* Dr. Brian Jackson, Senior Associate Dean, 859-257-4667, Fax: 859-257-4676, E-mail: brian.jackson@uky.edu.

University of La Verne, College of Business and Public Management, Doctoral Program in Public Administration, La Verne, CA 91750-4443. Offers DPA. Part-time programs available. *Faculty:* 4 full-time (1 woman), 2 part-time/adjunct (1 woman). *Students:* 42 full-time (16 women), 54 part-time (24 women); includes 51 minority (24 African Americans, 1 American Indian/Alaska Native, 10 Asian Americans or Pacific Islanders, 16 Hispanic Americans), 8 international. Average age 45. In 2007, 10 degrees awarded. *Degree requirements:* For doctorate, thesis/dissertation. *Entrance requirements:* For doctorate, MAT, GMAT or GRE, minimum undergraduate GPA of 3.25, interview, 3 letters of recommendation. Additional exam requirements/recommendations for international students: Required—TOEFL (minimum score

550 paper-based; 213 computer-based). Application fee: $75. *Expenses: Contact institution.* Tuition and fees vary according to course load and program. *Financial support:* Institutionally sponsored loans available. Financial award application deadline: 3/2; financial award applicants required to submit FAFSA. *Unit head:* Dr. Suzanne Beaumaster, Chairperson, 909-593-3511 Ext. 4817, E-mail: beaumast@ulv.edu. *Application contact:* Connie Hamlow, Admissions Information Specialist, 909-593-3511 Ext. 4244, Fax: 909-392-2761, E-mail: gradadmission@ulv.edu.

University of La Verne, College of Business and Public Management, Master's Program in Public Administration, La Verne, CA 91750-4443. Offers MPA. *Accreditation:* NASPAA.Part-time programs available. *Faculty:* 6 full-time (2 women), 11 part-time/adjunct (5 women). *Students:* 24 full-time (11 women), 36 part-time (17 women); includes 35 minority (10 African Americans, 4 Asian Americans or Pacific Islanders, 21 Hispanic Americans). Average age 33. In 2007, 18 degrees awarded. *Entrance requirements:* For master's, minimum undergraduate GPA of 2.75, 2 letters of recommendation, resumé. Additional exam requirements/recommendations for international students: Required—TOEFL (minimum score 550 paper-based; 213 computer-based). *Application deadline:* Applications are processed on a rolling basis. Application fee: $50. *Expenses: Contact institution.* Tuition and fees vary according to course load and program. *Financial support:* Fellowships, research assistantships available. Financial award application deadline: 3/2; financial award applicants required to submit FAFSA. *Unit head:* Dr. Keith Schildt, Chairperson, 909-593-3511 Ext. 4818, E-mail: schildtk@ulv.edu. *Application contact:* Connie Hamlow, Admissions Information Specialist, 909-593-3511 Ext. 4244, Fax: 909-392-2761, E-mail: gradadmission@ulv.edu.

University of La Verne, College of Business and Public Management, Program in Gerontology, La Verne, CA 91750-4443. Offers business administration (MS); counseling (MS); gerontology (Certificate); gerontology administration (MS); health services management (MS); public administration (MS). Part-time programs available. *Faculty:* 6 full-time (2 women), 11 part-time/adjunct (5 women). *Students:* 5 full-time (all women), 23 part-time (19 women); includes 16 minority (9 African Americans, 1 American Indian/Alaska Native, 1 Asian American or Pacific Islander, 5 Hispanic Americans). Average age 49. In 2007, 14 degrees awarded. *Entrance requirements:* For master's, minimum GPA of 2.5. Additional exam requirements/recommendations for international students: Required—TOEFL (minimum score 550 paper-based; 213 computer-based). *Application deadline:* Applications are processed on a rolling basis. Application fee: $50. *Expenses: Contact institution.* Tuition and fees vary according to course load and program. *Financial support:* Institutionally sponsored loans available. Financial award application deadline: 3/2; financial award applicants required to submit FAFSA. *Unit head:* Joan Branin, Chairperson, 909-593-3511 Ext. 4247, E-mail: braninj@ulv.edu. *Application contact:* Connie Hamlow, Admissions Information Specialist, 909-593-3511 Ext. 4244, Fax: 909-392-2761, E-mail: gradadmission@ulv.edu.

University of La Verne, Regional Campus Administration, Graduate Programs, Orange County Campus, Garden Grove, CA 92840. Offers business (MBA-EP), including health services management, information technology, management, marketing, supply chain management; health administration (MHA); leadership and management (MS); public administration (MPA). *Faculty:* 1 full-time (0 women), 5 part-time/adjunct (2 women). *Students:* 18 full-time (5 women), 71 part-time (30 women); includes 46 minority (6 African Americans, 3 American Indian/Alaska Native, 21 Asian Americans or Pacific Islanders, 16 Hispanic Americans). Average age 41. In 2007, 30 degrees awarded. *Entrance requirements:* For master's, 2 letters of recommendation, resumé. *Application deadline:* Applications are processed on a rolling basis. Application fee: $50. *Expenses: Contact institution.* Tuition and fees vary according to course load and program. *Financial support:* Institutionally sponsored loans available. Financial award application deadline: 3/2; financial award applicants required to submit FAFSA. *Unit head:* Pamela Bergovoy, Director, 714-534-4860, Fax: 714-534-4865, E-mail: bergovoy@ulv.edu.

University of Louisville, Graduate School, College of Arts and Sciences, Department of Urban and Public Affairs, Program in Public Administration, Louisville, KY 40292-0001. Offers labor and public management (MPA); public policy and administration (MPA); urban and regional development (MPA). *Accreditation:* NASPAA. *Students:* 21 full-time (14 women), 22 part-time (12 women); includes 6 minority (4 African Americans, 1 Asian American or Pacific Islander, 1 Hispanic American), 1 international. Average age 30. In 2007, 15 degrees awarded. *Degree requirements:* For master's, practicum or thesis. *Entrance requirements:* For master's, GRE General Test, minimum GPA of 3.25, resumé. *Application deadline:* For fall admission, 7/1 priority date for domestic students; for spring admission, 12/1 priority date for domestic students. Applications are processed on a rolling basis. Application fee: $50. *Unit head:* Dr. Steve Koven, Director, 502-852-7906, Fax: 502-852-4558, E-mail: sgkove01@louisville.edu.

University of Maine, Graduate School, College of Business, Public Policy and Health, Department of Public Administration, Orono, ME 04469. Offers MPA, PhD. *Accreditation:* NASPAA. Part-time and evening/weekend programs available. *Students:* 30 full-time (17 women), 16 part-time (10 women); includes 2 minority (both American Indian/Alaska Native), 1 international. Average age 36. 24 applicants, 79% accepted, 17 enrolled. In 2007, 11 master's awarded. *Entrance requirements:* For master's, GMAT or GRE General Test. Additional exam requirements/recommendations for international students: Required—TOEFL. *Application deadline:* Applications are processed on a rolling basis. Application fee: $60. Electronic applications accepted. *Financial support:* In 2007–08, 1 teaching assistantship with tuition reimbursement (averaging $9,010 per year) was awarded; career-related internships or fieldwork, Federal Work-Study, institutionally sponsored loans, tuition waivers (full and partial), and unspecified assistantships also available. Support available to part-time students. Financial award application deadline: 3/1. *Faculty research:* Organization theory, personnel administration, public budgeting and finance, policy analysis, environmental policy, community policy and development. *Unit head:* Dr. Carolyn Ball, Chairperson, 207-581-4142, Fax: 207-581-3039. *Application contact:* Scott G. Delcourt, Associate Dean of the Graduate School, 207-581-3219, Fax: 207-581-3232, E-mail: graduate@maine.edu.

Announcement: Master of Public Administration program prepares students for careers in state/local government, nonprofits, and health care. Concentrations/strengths are in health-care policy, planning/economic development/environment, public policy, state and local administration, and town/city management. Curriculum involves 36–42 semester hours, with requirements and electives. NASPAA accredited. Contact: 207-581-1872. Web: www.umaine.edu/pubadmin.

University of Management and Technology, Program in Management, Arlington, VA 22209. Offers acquisition management (MS, AC); general management (MS); project management (MS, AC); public administration (MPA, MS, AC). Part-time and evening/weekend programs available. Postbaccalaureate distance learning degree programs offered (no on-campus study). *Entrance requirements:* For master's, 3 recommendations, current resumé. Additional exam requirements/recommendations for international students: Required—TOEFL (minimum score 550 paper-based; 213 computer-based). *Application deadline:* Applications are processed on a rolling basis. Application fee: $30. Electronic applications accepted. *Unit head:* Dr. J. Davidson Frame, Academic Dean, 703-516-0035 Ext. 25.

University of Manitoba, Faculty of Graduate Studies, Program in Public Administration, Winnipeg, MB R3T 2N2, Canada. Offers MPA. *Degree requirements:* For master's, thesis or alternative.

University of Maryland, College Park, Graduate Studies, Interdepartmental Programs, Joint Program in Business and Management/Public Policy, College Park, MD 20742. Offers MBA/MPM. *Accreditation:* AACSB. *Students:* 5 full-time (3 women), 1 (woman) part-time; includes 3 minority (2 African Americans, 1 Asian American or Pacific Islander). 20 applicants, 20% accepted, 3 enrolled. *Application deadline:* For fall admission, 2/1 for domestic and international students. Applications are processed on a rolling basis. Application fee: $60. Electronic applications accepted. *Financial support:* Fellowships, research assistantships, teaching assistantships available. Financial award applicants required to submit FAFSA. *Application contact:* Dean of Graduate School, 301-405-0358, Fax: 301-314-9305.

University of Maryland, College Park, Graduate Studies, School of Public Policy, Joint Program in Public Policy/Law, College Park, MD 20742. Offers JD/MPM. *Students:* 3 full-time (0 women); includes 1 minority (Hispanic American) 14 applicants, 43% accepted, 1 enrolled. *Application deadline:* For fall admission, 12/15 for domestic students, 2/1 for international students; for spring admission, 10/15 for domestic students, 6/1 for international students. Applications are processed on a rolling basis. Application fee: $60. Electronic applications accepted. *Financial support:* In 2007–08, 2 teaching assistantships (averaging $13,098 per year) were awarded; fellowships also available. Financial award applicants required to submit FAFSA. *Application contact:* Dean of Graduate School, 301-405-0358, Fax: 301-314-9305.

University of Maryland, College Park, Graduate Studies, School of Public Policy, Public Management Program, College Park, MD 20742. Offers MPM. *Accreditation:* NASPAA. *Students:* 5 full-time (3 women), 21 part-time (10 women); includes 7 minority (5 African Americans, 2 Asian Americans or Pacific Islanders), 2 international. 15 applicants, 27% accepted, 4 enrolled. In 2007, 11 degrees awarded. *Degree requirements:* For master's, internship. *Entrance requirements:* For master's, GRE General Test, minimum GPA of 3.0. Additional exam requirements/recommendations for international students: Required—TOEFL. *Application deadline:* For fall admission, 12/15 for domestic students, 2/1 for international students; for spring admission, 10/15 for domestic students, 6/1 for international students. Applications are processed on a rolling basis. Application fee: $60. Electronic applications accepted. *Financial support:* In 2007–08, 3 teaching assistantships (averaging $13,098 per year) were awarded; fellowships also available. Financial award applicants required to submit FAFSA. *Faculty research:* International security, economic policy, financial management, social policy. *Application contact:* Dean of Graduate School, 301-405-0358, Fax: 301-314-9305.

University of Massachusetts Amherst, Graduate School, College of Social and Behavioral Sciences, Center for Public Policy and Administration, Amherst, MA 01003. Offers MPA, MPPA. Part-time programs available. *Students:* 30 full-time (22 women), 9 part-time (6 women); includes 5 minority (3 Asian Americans or Pacific Islanders, 2 Hispanic Americans), 5 international. Average age 32. 79 applicants, 63% accepted, 38 enrolled. In 2007, 16 degrees awarded. *Degree requirements:* For master's, thesis or alternative. *Entrance requirements:* For master's, GRE General Test. Additional exam requirements/recommendations for international students: Required—TOEFL (minimum score 530 paper-based; 197 computer-based). *Application deadline:* For fall admission, 2/1 priority date for domestic and international students. Applications are processed on a rolling basis. Application fee: $50 ($65 for international students). Electronic applications accepted. *Expenses:* Tuition, state resident: full-time $2,640; part-time $110 per credit. Tuition, nonresident: full-time $9,936; part-time $414 per credit. Required fees: $7,455. One-time fee: $332. Tuition and fees vary according to course load, campus/location, program and reciprocity agreements. *Financial support:* In 2007–08, 2 fellowships with full tuition reimbursements (averaging $6,250 per year), 18 research assistantships with full tuition reimbursements (averaging $5,212 per year) were awarded; teaching assistantships with full tuition reimbursements, career-related internships or fieldwork, Federal Work-Study, scholarships/grants, traineeships, and unspecified assistantships also available. Support available to part-time students. Financial award application deadline: 2/1. *Unit head:* Dr. John Hird, Chair, 413-545-2438, Fax: 413-545-3349, E-mail: jhird@pubpol.umass.edu.

University of Memphis, Graduate School, College of Arts and Sciences, School of Urban Affairs and Public Policy, Division of Public and Nonprofit Administration, Memphis, TN 38152. Offers nonprofit administration (MPA); public management and policy (MPA); urban management and planning (MPA). *Accreditation:* NASPAA. Part-time and evening/weekend programs available. *Faculty:* 6 full-time (3 women), 1 (woman) part-time/adjunct. *Students:* 16 full-time (10 women), 43 part-time (31 women); includes 27 minority (26 African Americans, 1 Asian American or Pacific Islander). Average age 33. 31 applicants, 58% accepted, 9 enrolled. In 2007, 13 master's awarded. *Degree requirements:* For master's, comprehensive exam, thesis or alternative, internship. *Entrance requirements:* For master's, GRE General Test, GMAT, or MAT, minimum GPA of 3.0. *Application deadline:* For fall admission, 8/1 for domestic students; for spring admission, 12/1 for domestic students. Applications are processed on a rolling basis. Application fee: $35 ($60 for international students). *Expenses:* Tuition, state resident: full-time $6,990; part-time $377 per hour. Tuition, nonresident: full-time $17,818; part-time $830 per hour. Tuition and fees vary according to course load and program. *Financial support:* In 2007–08, 7 research assistantships with full tuition reimbursements (averaging $4,500 per year) were awarded; fellowships, career-related internships or fieldwork, Federal Work-Study, and scholarships/grants also available. Support available to part-time students. *Faculty research:* Nonprofit organization governance, local government management, community collaboration, urban problems, accountability. *Unit head:* Dr. Dorothy Norris-Tirrell, Director, 901-678-3360, Fax: 901-678-2981, E-mail: dnrrstrr@memphis.edu. *Application contact:* Dr. Charles Menifield, Director of Admissions, 901-678-3369, Fax: 901-678-2981, E-mail: cmenifld@memphis.edu.

University of Michigan–Dearborn, School of Education, Program in Public Administration, Dearborn, MI 48128-1491. Offers assessment and evaluation (Certificate); educational administration (Certificate), including central office administration, elementary school administration, secondary school administration; nonprofit leadership (Certificate); public administration (MPA). Part-time and evening/weekend programs available. *Faculty:* 3 full-time (1 woman), 9 part-time/adjunct (2 women). *Students:* 14 full-time (11 women), 89 part-time (57 women); includes 18 minority (13 African Americans, 1 American Indian/Alaska Native, 1 Asian American or Pacific Islander, 3 Hispanic Americans). Average age 34. 31 applicants, 100% accepted, 31 enrolled. In 2007, 31 degrees awarded. *Degree requirements:* For master's, assessment seminar. *Entrance requirements:* For master's, GRE or minimum undergraduate GPA of 3.0, 3 letters of recommendation, statement of purpose, personal statement. Additional exam requirements/recommendations for international students: Required—TOEFL, TWE. *Application deadline:* For fall admission, 9/5 priority date for domestic students, 8/3 for international students; for winter admission, 12/22 for domestic students, 1/4 for international students; for spring admission, 5/5 for domestic students, 3/4 for international students. Applications are processed on a rolling basis. Application fee: $60. *Expenses:* Tuition, state resident: part-time $318 per credit hour. Tuition, nonresident: part-time $722 per credit hour. Tuition and fees vary according to course load and program. *Financial support:* Career-related internships or fieldwork and Federal Work-Study available. Support available to part-time students. Financial award application deadline: 4/1; financial award applicants required to submit FAFSA. *Faculty research:* Federal, state, and local agency management; independent sector management; educational administration. *Unit head:* Dr. Paul Zionts, Coordinator (Interim Coordinator), 313-593-5435, Fax: 313-583-6746, E-mail: pzionts@umd.umich.edu. *Application contact:* Elizabeth M. Morden, Graduate Secretary, 313-593-5090, Fax: 313-593-4748, E-mail: emorden@umd.umich.edu.

University of Michigan–Flint, Graduate Programs, Program in Public Administration, Flint, MI 48502-1950. Offers MPA. Part-time programs available. *Faculty:* 7 full-time (2 women), 7 part-time/adjunct (1 woman). *Students:* 18 full-time (10 women), 150 part-time (99 women); includes 39 minority (36 African Americans, 1 American Indian/Alaska Native, 1 Asian American or Pacific Islander, 1 Hispanic American), 1 international. Average age 36. 98 applicants, 83% accepted, 63 enrolled. In 2007, 21 degrees awarded. *Degree requirements:* For master's, thesis or alternative, internship. *Entrance requirements:* For master's, minimum GPA of 3.0, 1 course each in American government, microeconomics and statistics. Additional exam requirements/recommendations for international students: Required—TOEFL (minimum score 550 paper-based; 220 computer-based), IELTS (minimum score 7). *Application deadline:* For fall admission, 8/1 for domestic students, 3/1 for international students; for winter admission, 11/15 for domestic students, 7/1 for international students; for spring admission, 3/15 for domestic students, 11/1 for international students. Application fee: $55. Electronic applications accepted. *Expenses: Contact institution. Financial support:* In 2007–08, 1 research assistantship (averaging $3,850 per year) was awarded; fellowships, career-related internships or fieldwork, Federal Work-Study, and scholarships/grants also available. Support available

Public Administration

University of Michigan–Flint (continued)

to part-time students. Financial award application deadline: 6/1; financial award applicants required to submit FAFSA. *Unit head:* Dr. Albert Price, Director, 810-762-3470, E-mail: acprice@umflint.edu. *Application contact:* Bradley T. Maki, Director of Graduate Admissions, 810-762-3171, Fax: 810-766-6789, E-mail: bmaki@umflint.edu.

See Close-Up on page 1639.

University of Missouri–Kansas City, Henry W. Bloch School of Business and Public Administration, Kansas City, MO 64110-2499. Offers accounting (MS); business administration (MBA); public affairs (MPA, PhD); JD/MBA; LL M/MPA. *Accreditation:* AACSB; NASPAA. Part-time and evening/weekend programs available. *Faculty:* 41 full-time (12 women), 19 part-time/adjunct (6 women). *Students:* 176 full-time (90 women), 430 part-time (183 women); includes 76 minority (39 African Americans, 2 American Indian/Alaska Native, 19 Asian Americans or Pacific Islanders, 16 Hispanic Americans), 42 international. Average age 30. 343 applicants, 64% accepted, 162 enrolled. In 2007, 213 degrees awarded. Terminal master's awarded for partial completion of doctoral program. *Entrance requirements:* For master's, GMAT, GRE, 2 writing essays, 2 references and support of employer; for doctorate, GRE, minimum GPA of 3.0. Additional exam requirements/recommendations for international students: Required—TOEFL. *Application deadline:* For fall admission, 5/1 priority date for domestic and international students; for spring admission, 10/1 priority date for domestic and international students. Applications are processed on a rolling basis. Application fee: $35 ($50 for international students). Electronic applications accepted. *Expenses:* Tuition, state resident: part-time $287 per hour. Tuition, nonresident: part-time $741 per hour. Required fees: $31 per hour. Tuition and fees vary according to program. *Financial support:* In 2007–08, 407 students received support, including 22 research assistantships with partial tuition reimbursements available (averaging $8,189 per year), 5 teaching assistantships with partial tuition reimbursements available (averaging $10,224 per year); fellowships, career-related internships or fieldwork, Federal Work-Study, institutionally sponsored loans, scholarships/grants, tuition waivers (full and partial), and unspecified assistantships also available. Support available to part-time students. Financial award application deadline: 3/1; financial award applicants required to submit FAFSA. *Faculty research:* Entrepreneurship, finance, non-profit, risk management. Total annual research expenditures: $578,039. *Unit head:* Dr. Lee Bolman, Interim Dean, 816-235-5407, Fax: 816-235-2206. *Application contact:* 816-235-1111, E-mail: admit@umkc.edu.

University of Missouri–St. Louis, College of Arts and Sciences, Department of Political Science, St. Louis, MO 63121. Offers American politics (MA); comparative politics (MA); international politics (MA); political process and behavior (MA); political science (PhD); public administration and public policy (MA); urban and regional politics (MA). Part-time and evening/weekend programs available. *Faculty:* 20 full-time (8 women), 2 part-time/adjunct (both women). *Students:* 28 full-time (13 women), 20 part-time (15 women); includes 9 minority (6 African Americans, 2 American Indian/Alaska Native, 1 Asian American or Pacific Islander), 6 international. Average age 36. In 2007, 10 master's, 3 doctorates awarded. Terminal master's awarded for partial completion of doctoral program. *Degree requirements:* For master's, thesis optional; for doctorate, thesis/dissertation. *Entrance requirements:* For master's, GRE General Test, 2 letters of recommendation; for doctorate, GRE General Test, 3 letters of recommendation. Additional exam requirements/recommendations for international students: Required—TOEFL (minimum score 550 paper-based; 213 computer-based). *Application deadline:* For fall admission, 2/15 for domestic students; for spring admission, 10/15 for domestic students. Applications are processed on a rolling basis. Application fee: $35 ($40 for international students). Electronic applications accepted. *Financial support:* In 2007–08, 9 research assistantships with full and partial tuition reimbursements (averaging $12,000 per year), 6 teaching assistantships with full and partial tuition reimbursements (averaging $12,000 per year) were awarded; fellowships, career-related internships or fieldwork also available. Support available to part-time students. Financial award application deadline: 3/15. *Faculty research:* Public policy, urban politics and administration, American government. *Unit head:* Dr. Eduardo Silva, Director of Graduate Studies, 314-516-5522, Fax: 314-516-5268, E-mail: umslpolisci@umsl.edu. *Application contact:* 314-516-5458, Fax: 314-516-6996, E-mail: gradadm@umsl.edu.

University of Missouri–St. Louis, College of Arts and Sciences, Department of Sociology, St. Louis, MO 63121. Offers advanced social perspective (MA); community conflict intervention (MA); program design and evaluation research (MA); social policy planning and administration (MA). Part-time and evening/weekend programs available. *Faculty:* 3 full-time (all women), 1 part-time/adjunct (0 women). *Students:* 5 full-time (2 women), 7 part-time (3 women); includes 1 minority (African American) Average age 31. In 2007, 7 degrees awarded. *Degree requirements:* For master's, thesis optional. *Entrance requirements:* For master's, 2 letters of recommendation. Additional exam requirements/recommendations for international students: Required—TOEFL (minimum score 550 paper-based; 213 computer-based). *Application deadline:* For fall admission, 7/15 priority date for domestic students; for spring admission, 12/15 priority date for domestic students. Applications are processed on a rolling basis. Application fee: $35 ($40 for international students). Electronic applications accepted. *Financial support:* In 2007–08, 3 teaching assistantships with full and partial tuition reimbursements (averaging $7,870 per year) were awarded; research assistantships, career-related internships or fieldwork also available. Support available to part-time students. *Faculty research:* Deviance, conflict intervention, minority groups, stratification, social psychology. *Unit head:* Dr. Chicako Usui, Chairperson, 314-516-6366. *Application contact:* 314-516-5458, Fax: 314-516-6996, E-mail: gradadm@umsl.edu.

University of Missouri–St. Louis, Graduate School, Program in Public Policy Administration, St. Louis, MO 63121. Offers health policy (MPPA); local government management (MPPA); managing human resources and organization (MPPA); nonprofit organization management (MPPA); nonprofit organization management and leadership (Certificate); policy research and analysis (MPPA); public sector human resources management (MPPA). *Accreditation:* NASPAA. Part-time and evening/weekend programs available. *Faculty:* 8 full-time (4 women), 8 part-time/adjunct (1 woman). *Students:* 20 full-time (14 women), 38 part-time (15 women); includes 17 minority (14 African Americans, 1 American Indian/Alaska Native, 1 Asian American or Pacific Islander, 1 Hispanic American), 2 international. Average age 31. In 2007, 22 degrees awarded. *Entrance requirements:* For master's, 3 letters of recommendation. Additional exam requirements/recommendations for international students: Required—TOEFL (minimum score 550 paper-based; 213 computer-based). *Application deadline:* For fall admission, 7/15 priority date for domestic students; for spring admission, 12/15 priority date for domestic students. Applications are processed on a rolling basis. Application fee: $35 ($40 for international students). Electronic applications accepted. *Financial support:* In 2007–08, 2 research assistantships with full tuition reimbursements (averaging $12,000 per year) were awarded; teaching assistantships with partial tuition reimbursements, career-related internships or fieldwork also available. *Faculty research:* Urban policy, public finance, evaluation. *Unit head:* Brady Baybeck, Director, 314-516-5145, Fax: 314-516-5210, E-mail: baybeck@umsl.edu. *Application contact:* 314-516-5458, Fax: 314-516-6996, E-mail: gradadm@umsl.edu.

The University of Montana, Graduate School, College of Arts and Sciences, Department of Political Science, Program in Public Administration, Missoula, MT 59812-0002. Offers MPA, JD/MPA. *Degree requirements:* For master's, professional paper. *Entrance requirements:* For master's, GRE General Test.

University of Nebraska at Omaha, Graduate Studies and Research, College of Public Affairs and Community Service, School of Public Administration, Omaha, NE 68182. Offers public administration (MPA, PhD); public management (Certificate); urban studies (MS). *Accreditation:* NASPAA (one or more programs are accredited). Part-time and evening/weekend programs available. Postbaccalaureate distance learning degree programs offered (no on-campus study). *Faculty:* 16 full-time (4 women). *Students:* 24 full-time (13 women), 204 part-time (112 women); includes 26 minority (17 African Americans, 3 Asian Americans or Pacific Islanders, 6 Hispanic Americans), 9 international. Average age 33. 114 applicants, 52% accepted, 46 enrolled. In 2007, 64 master's, 1 doctorate awarded. *Degree requirements:* For master's, comprehensive exam (for some programs), thesis (for some programs); for doctorate, comprehensive exam, thesis/dissertation. *Entrance requirements:* For master's, GRE General Test, minimum GPA of 3.0, letters of recommendation, essay; for doctorate, GRE General Test, master's degree, minimum graduate GPA of 3.35, resumé. Additional exam requirements/recommendations for international students: Required—TOEFL (minimum score 550 paper-based; 213 computer-based; 80 iBT). *Application deadline:* For fall admission, 6/1 for domestic students; for spring admission, 10/1 for domestic students. Applications are processed on a rolling basis. Application fee: $45. Electronic applications accepted. *Financial support:* In 2007–08, 118 students received support; research assistantships with tuition reimbursements available, career-related internships or fieldwork, Federal Work-Study, institutionally sponsored loans, scholarships/grants, tuition waivers (partial), and unspecified assistantships available. Support available to part-time students. Financial award application deadline: 3/1. *Unit head:* Dr. John Bartle, Director, 402-554-2625.

University of Nevada, Las Vegas, Graduate College, Greenspun College of Urban Affairs, Department of Public Administration, Las Vegas, NV 89154-9900. Offers crisis and emergency management (MS); public administration (MPA); public affairs (PhD); public management (Certificate). *Accreditation:* NASPAA. Part-time and evening/weekend programs available. *Faculty:* 7 full-time (1 woman), 6 part-time/adjunct (3 women). *Students:* 31 full-time (16 women), 113 part-time (66 women); includes 40 minority (23 African Americans, 1 American Indian/Alaska Native, 2 Asian Americans or Pacific Islanders, 14 Hispanic Americans), 3 international. 86 applicants, 55% accepted, 40 enrolled. In 2007, 36 master's, 1 doctorate, 22 other advanced degrees awarded. *Degree requirements:* For master's, comprehensive exam, professional paper. *Entrance requirements:* For master's, GMAT or GRE General Test, minimum GPA of 3.0 during previous 2 years, 2.75 overall; minimum 1 year of work experience; resumé. Additional exam requirements/recommendations for international students: Required—TOEFL (minimum score 550 paper-based; 213 computer-based; 80 iBT). *Application deadline:* For fall admission, 4/10 for domestic and international students; for spring admission, 11/15 for domestic students, 10/1 for international students. Application fee: $60 ($75 for international students). Electronic applications accepted. *Expenses:* Tuition, state resident: part-time $198 per credit. Tuition, nonresident: part-time $416 per credit. Required fees: $256 per semester. Tuition and fees vary according to course load and reciprocity agreements. *Financial support:* In 2007–08, 7 research assistantships (averaging $11,000 per year), 1 teaching assistantship with partial tuition reimbursement (averaging $10,000 per year) were awarded; career-related internships or fieldwork, Federal Work-Study, institutionally sponsored loans, scholarships/grants, health care benefits, and unspecified assistantships also available. Support available to part-time students. Financial award application deadline: 3/1. *Unit head:* Dr. Lee Bernick, Chair, 702-895-4828. *Application contact:* Graduate College Admissions Evaluator, 702-895-3320, Fax: 702-895-4180, E-mail: gradcollege@unlv.edu.

University of Nevada, Reno, Graduate School, College of Liberal Arts, Department of Political Science, Program in Public Administration and Policy, Reno, NV 89557. Offers public administration (MPA). Part-time and evening/weekend programs available. *Faculty:* 2. *Students:* 4 full-time (2 women), 13 part-time (6 women); includes 1 minority (Hispanic American) Average age 38. *Degree requirements:* For master's, comprehensive exam, oral exam/thesis or professional paper. *Entrance requirements:* For master's, GRE General Test, GMAT, or LSAT, minimum GPA of 2.75. Additional exam requirements/recommendations for international students: Required—TOEFL. *Application deadline:* For fall admission, 3/1 priority date for domestic students; for spring admission, 11/1 for domestic students. Applications are processed on a rolling basis. Application fee: $60 ($95 for international students). *Expenses:* Tuition, state resident: full-time $2,774; part-time $154 per credit. Tuition, nonresident: full-time $13,578; part-time $330 per credit. Required fees: $49 per semester. *Financial support:* Research assistantships, teaching assistantships, Federal Work-Study, institutionally sponsored loans, tuition waivers (full), and unspecified assistantships available. Financial award application deadline: 3/1. *Unit head:* Leah Wilds, Chair, 775-682-7773, Fax: 775-784-1473.

University of New Brunswick Fredericton, School of Graduate Studies, Faculty of Business Administration, Fredericton, NB E3B 5A3, Canada. Offers MBA, MBA/LL B. Part-time programs available. *Faculty:* 37 full-time (13 women). *Students:* 35 full-time (16 women), 45 part-time (19 women). In 2007, 37 degrees awarded. *Entrance requirements:* For master's, GMAT, resumé, GPA 3.0, GMAT 550 minimum score. Additional exam requirements/recommendations for international students: Required—TOEFL, TWE. *Application deadline:* For fall admission, 3/1 priority date for domestic students. Applications are processed on a rolling basis. Application fee: $50 Canadian dollars. *Financial support:* In 2007–08, 2 research assistantships, 27 teaching assistantships were awarded. *Faculty research:* Strategic management, entrepreneurship, investment practices, marketing and supply chain management, operations management. *Unit head:* Andrew Gaudes, Director of Graduate Studies, 506-452-6380, Fax: 506-453-3561, E-mail: agaudes@unb.ca. *Application contact:* Karen Hansen, Graduate Secretary, 506-453-4766, Fax: 506-453-3561, E-mail: karen@unb.ca.

University of New Hampshire, Center for Graduate and Professional Studies, Manchester, NH 03101. Offers business administration (MBA); counseling (M Ed); education (M Ed, MAT); educational administration and supervision (M Ed, CAGS); industrial statistics (Certificate); public administration (MPA); public health (MPH, Certificate); social work (MSW).

University of New Hampshire, Graduate School, College of Liberal Arts, Department of Political Science, Program in Public Administration, Durham, NH 03824. Offers MPA. Part-time programs available. *Faculty:* 15 full-time. *Students:* 10 full-time (3 women), 38 part-time (11 women); includes 1 minority (Asian American or Pacific Islander) Average age 34. 22 applicants, 95% accepted, 10 enrolled. In 2007, 17 degrees awarded. *Entrance requirements:* For master's, GMAT or GRE General Test. Additional exam requirements/recommendations for international students: Required—TOEFL (minimum score 550 paper-based; 213 computer-based; 80 iBT). *Application deadline:* For fall admission, 4/1 priority date for domestic students, 4/1 for international students. Applications are processed on a rolling basis. Application fee: $60. Electronic applications accepted. *Financial support:* In 2007–08, 2 fellowships, 1 teaching assistantship were awarded; research assistantships, career-related internships or fieldwork, Federal Work-Study, scholarships/grants, and tuition waivers (full and partial) also available. Support available to part-time students. Financial award application deadline: 2/15. *Application contact:* Tama Andrews, Administrative Assistant, 603-862-1750, E-mail: mpa.ma.political.science.grad@unh.edu.

University of New Haven, Graduate School, School of Business, Program in Public Administration, West Haven, CT 06516-1916. Offers health care management (MPA); personnel and labor relations (MPA); MBA/MPA. Part-time and evening/weekend programs available. *Students:* 30 full-time (20 women), 24 part-time (16 women); includes 3 minority (1 African American, 1 Asian American or Pacific Islander, 1 Hispanic American), 1 international. 28 applicants, 36% accepted, 8 enrolled. In 2007, 13 degrees awarded. *Degree requirements:* For master's, thesis or alternative. *Application deadline:* Applications are processed on a rolling basis. Application fee: $60. *Expenses:* Tuition: Part-time $630 per credit. Required fees: $40 per term. *Financial support:* Federal Work-Study available. Support available to part-time students. Financial award application deadline: 5/1; financial award applicants required to submit FAFSA. *Unit head:* Charles Coleman, Chairman, 203-932-7375.

University of New Mexico, Graduate School, School of Public Administration, Albuquerque, NM 87131-2039. Offers MPA, JD/MPA, MPA/MCRP, MSN/MPA. *Accreditation:* NASPAA (one or more programs are accredited). Part-time and evening/weekend programs available. Postbaccalaureate distance learning degree programs offered (no on-campus study). *Faculty:* 6 full-time (2 women), 1 part-time/adjunct (0 women). *Students:* 40 full-time (22 women), 108 part-time (75 women); includes 83 minority (4 African Americans, 25 American Indian/Alaska Native, 3 Asian Americans or Pacific Islanders, 51 Hispanic Americans), 6 international. Average age 38. 58 applicants, 69% accepted, 31 enrolled. In 2007, 33 degrees awarded. *Degree requirements:* For master's, thesis optional, professional paper. *Entrance requirements:* For master's, minimum GPA of 3.0, letters of recommendation, resumé, letter of intent. *Application deadline:* For fall admission, 6/1 for domestic students; for spring admission, 11/1 for domestic students. Application fee: $50. Electronic applications accepted. *Financial support:* In 2007–08, 45 students received support, including 3 fellowships with tuition reimbursements available (averaging $10,000 per year), 5 research assistantships with tuition reimbursements available (averaging $10,000 per year); career-related internships or fieldwork, scholarships/grants, health care benefits, and unspecified assistantships also available. Financial award application deadline: 3/31; financial award applicants required to submit FAFSA. *Faculty research:* Human resources, science and technology administration, health care policy management. Total annual research expenditures: $65,961. *Unit head:* Dr. Uday Desai, Director, 505-277-1092, Fax: 505-277-2529, E-mail: ucdesai@unm.edu. *Application contact:* Gene V. Henley, Department Administrator, 505-277-1095, Fax: 505-277-2529, E-mail: spagrad@unm.edu.

University of New Orleans, Graduate School, College of Liberal Arts, Department of Political Science, Program in Public Administration, New Orleans, LA 70148. Offers MPA. *Students:* 33 (24 women). Average age 29. In 2007, 7 degrees awarded. *Degree requirements:* For master's, thesis. *Entrance requirements:* For master's, GRE General Test. Additional exam requirements/recommendations for international students: Required—TOEFL (minimum score 550 paper-based; 213 computer-based; 79 iBT). *Application deadline:* For fall admission, 7/1 priority date for domestic students, 6/1 for international students; for spring admission, 11/15 priority date for domestic students, 10/1 for international students. Applications are processed on a rolling basis. Application fee: $40. Electronic applications accepted. *Financial support:* Research assistantships available. Financial award application deadline: 3/15; financial award applicants required to submit FAFSA. *Unit head:* Dr. Robert Montjoy, Graduate Coordinator, 504-280-5499, Fax: 504-280-3838, E-mail: rmontjoy@uno.edu.

The University of North Carolina at Chapel Hill, Graduate School, College of Arts and Sciences, Master of Public Administration Program, Chapel Hill, NC 27599. Offers MPA, JD/MPA, MPA/MRP, MPA/MSW. *Accreditation:* NASPAA. *Degree requirements:* For master's, comprehensive exam. *Entrance requirements:* For master's, GRE General Test, minimum GPA of 3.0. Additional exam requirements/recommendations for international students: Required—TOEFL. Electronic applications accepted. *Faculty research:* Local government management, nonprofit management.

The University of North Carolina at Charlotte, Graduate School, College of Arts and Sciences, Department of Political Science, Charlotte, NC 28223-0001. Offers public administration (MPA). *Accreditation:* NASPAA. Part-time and evening/weekend programs available. *Faculty:* 13 full-time (3 women), 5 part-time/adjunct (2 women). *Students:* 16 full-time (12 women), 26 part-time (15 women); includes 6 African Americans, 1 Hispanic American, 1 international. Average age 28. 41 applicants, 61% accepted, 16 enrolled. In 2007, 16 degrees awarded. *Entrance requirements:* For master's, GRE General Test or MAT, minimum GPA of 3.0 in undergraduate major, 2.75 overall. Additional exam requirements/recommendations for international students: Required—TOEFL (minimum score 557 paper-based; 220 computer-based). *Application deadline:* For fall admission, 7/1 for domestic students, 5/1 for international students; for spring admission, 11/1 for domestic students, 10/1 for international students. Applications are processed on a rolling basis. Application fee: $55. Electronic applications accepted. *Expenses:* Tuition, state resident: full-time $2,855. Tuition, nonresident: full-time $13,062. Required fees: $1,692. *Financial support:* In 2007–08, 2 research assistantships (averaging $9,000 per year), 5 teaching assistantships (averaging $9,000 per year) were awarded; career-related internships or fieldwork, Federal Work-Study, institutionally sponsored loans, scholarships/grants, and unspecified assistantships also available. Support available to part-time students. Financial award application deadline: 4/1; financial award applicants required to submit FAFSA. *Faculty research:* Terrorism, public administration, nonprofit and arts administration, educational policy, social policy. Total annual research expenditures: $660,000. *Unit head:* Dr. Theodore S. Arrington, Chair, 704-687-2571, Fax: 704-687-3497, E-mail: tarrngtn@email.uncc.edu. *Application contact:* Kathy B. Giddings, Director of Graduate Admissions, 704-687-3366, Fax: 704-687-3279, E-mail: agidding@uncc.edu.

The University of North Carolina at Pembroke, Graduate Studies, Public Administration Program, Pembroke, NC 28372-1510. Offers MPA. Part-time and evening/weekend programs available. *Faculty:* 5 full-time (1 woman). *Students:* 17 full-time (11 women), 130 part-time (69 women); includes 62 minority (39 African Americans, 21 American Indian/Alaska Native, 1 Asian American or Pacific Islander, 1 Hispanic American). Average age 38. 147 applicants, 100% accepted, 147 enrolled. In 2007, 29 degrees awarded. *Degree requirements:* For master's, comprehensive exam, thesis optional. *Entrance requirements:* For master's, GRE General Test or MAT, minimum GPA of 3.0 in major, 2.5 overall; interview. Additional exam requirements/recommendations for international students: Required—TOEFL. *Application deadline:* For fall admission, 7/15 for domestic students, 7/15 priority date for international students; for spring admission, 12/15 for domestic students, 12/1 priority date for international students. Applications are processed on a rolling basis. Application fee: $45. *Expenses:* Tuition, state resident: part-time $112 per credit. Tuition, nonresident: full-time $11,428; part-time $635 per credit. Required fees: $1,168; $390 per semester. Tuition and fees vary according to course load and campus/location. *Financial support:* In 2007–08, 2 research assistantships with full tuition reimbursements (averaging $6,000 per year) were awarded; unspecified assistantships also available. Support available to part-time students. Financial award application deadline: 4/15; financial award applicants required to submit FAFSA. *Unit head:* Dr. Daniel G. Barbee, Director, 910-521-6637, Fax: 910-521-6446, E-mail: daniel.barbee@uncp.edu. *Application contact:* Dr. Kathleen C. Hilton, Dean of Graduate Studies, 910-521-6271, Fax: 910-521-6751, E-mail: grad@uncp.edu.

The University of North Carolina Wilmington, College of Arts and Sciences, Program in Public Administration, Wilmington, NC 28403-3297. Offers MPA. *Accreditation:* NASPAA. Part-time programs available. *Students:* 29 full-time (19 women), 29 part-time (19 women); includes 6 minority (all African Americans) Average age 29. 39 applicants, 85% accepted, 23 enrolled. In 2007, 22 master's awarded. *Degree requirements:* For master's, comprehensive exam, practicum. *Entrance requirements:* For master's, GRE, GMAT. *Application deadline:* For fall admission, 4/15 for domestic students; for spring admission, 9/1 for domestic students. Application fee: $45. *Expenses:* Tuition, state resident: full-time $2,714. Tuition, nonresident: full-time $12,579. Required fees: $1,985. *Financial support:* In 2007–08, 9 teaching assistantships were awarded. Financial award application deadline: 3/15. *Unit head:* Dr. Roger Lowery, Chair, 910-962-3225, E-mail: lowery@uncw.edu. *Application contact:* Dr. Robert D. Roer, Dean, Graduate School, 910-962-4117, Fax: 910-962-3787, E-mail: roer@uncw.edu.

University of North Dakota, Graduate School, College of Business and Public Administration, Department of Public Administration, Grand Forks, ND 58202. Offers MPA. *Accreditation:* NASPAA. Part-time programs available. Postbaccalaureate distance learning degree programs offered (minimal on-campus study). *Faculty:* 7 full-time (1 woman). *Students:* 10 full-time (8 women), 20 part-time (13 women); includes 1 African American, 4 American Indian/Alaska Native, 2 international. 25 applicants, 64% accepted, 6 enrolled. In 2007, 12 degrees awarded. *Degree requirements:* For master's, comprehensive exam, thesis or alternative, final exam. *Entrance requirements:* For master's, GRE General Test, GMAT or LSAT, minimum GPA of 3.0. Additional exam requirements/recommendations for international students: Required—TOEFL (minimum score 550 paper-based; 213 computer-based; 79 iBT), IELTS (minimum score 7). *Application deadline:* For fall admission, 2/15 priority date for domestic and international students; for spring admission, 10/15 priority date for domestic and international students. Applications are processed on a rolling basis. Application fee: $35. Electronic applications accepted. *Expenses:* Tuition, state resident: full-time $4,050; part-time $225 per credit. Tuition, nonresident: full-time $10,818; part-time $601 per credit. Required fees: $110 per semester. Tuition and fees vary according to class time, campus/location, program and reciprocity agreements. *Financial support:* In 2007–08, 2 research assistantships with full and partial tuition reimbursements, 2 teaching assistantships with full tuition reimbursements (averaging $7,809 per year) were awarded; fellowships with full and partial tuition reimbursements, Federal Work-Study, institutionally sponsored loans, scholarships/grants, health care benefits, tuition waivers (full and partial), and unspecified assistantships also available. Support available to part-time students. Financial award application deadline: 3/15; financial award applicants required to submit FAFSA. *Unit head:* Dr. Jason Jensen, Director, 701-777-3831, Fax: 701-777-5099, E-mail: jason_jensen2@und.nodak.edu. *Application contact:* Brenda Halle, Admissions Specialist, 701-777-2947, Fax: 701-777-3619, E-mail: brendahalle@mail.und.edu.

University of Northern Virginia, Graduate Programs, Manassas, VA 20109. Offers accountancy (MS); accounting (MBA); business administration (DBA); computer science (MS); counseling education (M Ed); early childhood education (M Ed); educational communication and instructional technology (M Ed); educational leadership (M Ed); finance (MBA); information systems technology (MS); management (MBA); marketing (MBA); project management (MBA); public administration (MPA); teaching English to speakers of other languages (M Ed). Part-time and evening/weekend programs available. Postbaccalaureate distance learning degree programs offered (no on-campus study). *Degree requirements:* For doctorate, comprehensive exam, thesis/dissertation. *Entrance requirements:* Additional exam requirements/recommendations for international students: Required—TOEFL (minimum score 550 paper-based; 230 computer-based), IELTS (minimum score 6). Electronic applications accepted.

University of North Florida, College of Arts and Sciences, Department of Political Science and Public Administration, Jacksonville, FL 32224-2645. Offers public administration (MPA). *Accreditation:* NASPAA. Part-time programs available. *Faculty:* 12 full-time (2 women). *Students:* 19 full-time (9 women), 61 part-time (36 women); includes 21 minority (11 African Americans, 3 Asian Americans or Pacific Islanders, 7 Hispanic Americans). Average age 30. 35 applicants, 54% accepted, 17 enrolled. In 2007, 35 degrees awarded. *Degree requirements:* For master's, thesis or alternative, internship. *Entrance requirements:* For master's, GRE General Test or minimum GPA of 3.0 in last 60 hours, 2 letters of recommendation, interview. Additional exam requirements/recommendations for international students: Required—TOEFL (minimum score 500 paper-based; 173 computer-based). *Application deadline:* For fall admission, 7/1 priority date for domestic students, 5/1 for international students; for spring admission, 11/1 priority date for domestic students, 10/1 for international students. Applications are processed on a rolling basis. Application fee: $30. Electronic applications accepted. *Expenses:* Tuition, state resident: part-time $266 per credit hour. Tuition, nonresident: part-time $858 per credit hour. One-time fee: $35 part-time. Tuition and fees vary according to program. *Financial support:* In 2007–08, 35 students received support. Career-related internships or fieldwork, Federal Work-Study, and tuition waivers (partial) available. Support available to part-time students. Financial award application deadline: 4/1; financial award applicants required to submit FAFSA. *Faculty research:* America's usage of the internet, use of information communication technologies by educators and children. Total annual research expenditures: $13,173. *Unit head:* Dr. Matthew T. Corrigan, Chair, 904-620-2977, E-mail: mcorriga@unf.edu. *Application contact:* Dr. Patrick Plumlee, Director, 904-620-2977, Fax: 907-620-2979, E-mail: pplumlee@unf.edu.

University of North Texas, Robert B. Toulouse School of Graduate Studies, College of Public Affairs and Community Service, Department of Public Administration, Denton, TX 76203. Offers public administration (MPA); public administration and management (PhD). *Accreditation:* NASPAA. Part-time and evening/weekend programs available. *Faculty:* 11 full-time (2 women). *Students:* 68 full-time (37 women), 57 part-time (29 women); includes 23 minority (13 African Americans, 4 Asian Americans or Pacific Islanders, 6 Hispanic Americans), 15 international. Average age 31. 87 applicants, 54% accepted, 23 enrolled. In 2007, 40 degrees awarded. *Degree requirements:* For master's, comprehensive exam, thesis optional, internship; for doctorate, comprehensive exam, thesis/dissertation. *Entrance requirements:* For master's, GMAT or GRE General Test, 3.00 grade point average on last 60 hours; for doctorate, GMAT or GRE General Test, 3.20 grade point average on last 60 hours. Additional exam requirements/recommendations for international students: Required—proof of English language proficiency required for non-native English speakers; Recommended—TOEFL (minimum score 550 paper-based; 213 computer-based). *Application deadline:* For fall admission, 7/15 for domestic students; for spring admission, 11/15 for domestic students. Application fee: $50 ($75 for international students). *Financial support:* In 2007–08, 5 fellowships with partial tuition reimbursements (averaging $20,000 per year), 3 research assistantships with partial tuition reimbursements (averaging $15,000 per year), 3 teaching assistantships with partial tuition reimbursements (averaging $11,000 per year) were awarded; career-related internships or fieldwork, Federal Work-Study, institutionally sponsored loans, and tuition waivers (full and partial) also available. Support available to part-time students. Financial award application deadline: 3/1; financial award applicants required to submit FAFSA. *Faculty research:* Municipal management, government financial management, public/private cooperation, emergency administration and planning, nonprofit management. Total annual research expenditures: $530,000. *Unit head:* Dr. Robert L. Bland, Chair, 940-565-2165, Fax: 940-565-4466, E-mail: bbland@scs.cmm.unt.edu.

University of Oklahoma, Graduate College, College of Arts and Sciences, Department of Political Science, Program in Public Administration, Norman, OK 73019-0390. Offers MPA. Part-time and evening/weekend programs available. *Students:* 58 full-time (21 women), 209 part-time (75 women); includes 74 minority (28 African Americans, 15 American Indian/Alaska Native, 16 Asian Americans or Pacific Islanders, 15 Hispanic Americans), 1 international. 75 applicants, 97% accepted, 69 enrolled. In 2007, 53 degrees awarded. Terminal master's awarded for partial completion of doctoral program. *Entrance requirements:* For master's, minimum GPA of 2.75 or GRE. Additional exam requirements/recommendations for international students: Required—TOEFL (minimum score 600 paper-based). *Application deadline:* For fall admission, 4/1 for domestic and international students; for spring admission, 11/1 for domestic students, 9/1 for international students. Application fee: $40 ($90 for international students). Electronic applications accepted. *Expenses:* Tuition, state resident: full-time $3,451; part-time $144 per credit hour. Tuition, nonresident: full-time $12,432; part-time $518 per credit hour. Required fees: $1,925; $70 per credit hour. $122 per semester. *Financial support:* In 2007–08, 59 students received support; research assistantships with partial tuition reimbursements available, teaching assistantships with partial tuition reimbursements available, career-related internships or fieldwork available. *Faculty research:* Public policy, public management, health policy, financial management, program evaluation, non-profit. *Application contact:* Debbie Deering, Assistant to the Director and Academic Counselor, 405-325-6432, Fax: 405-325-3733, E-mail: ddeering@ou.edu.

University of Ottawa, Faculty of Graduate and Postdoctoral Studies, Interdisciplinary Programs, Ottawa, ON K1N 6N5, Canada. Offers e-business (Certificate); e-commerce (Certificate); finance (Certificate); health services and policies research (Diploma); population health (PhD); population health risk assessment and management (Certificate); public management and governance (Certificate); systems science (Certificate).

University of Pennsylvania, School of Arts and Sciences, Fels Institute of Government, Philadelphia, PA 19104. Offers MGA. Part-time and evening/weekend programs available. *Degree requirements:* For master's, 12 courses (8 core classes, 4 elective classes). *Entrance requirements:* For master's, GRE. Additional exam requirements/recommendations for international students: Required—TOEFL or IELTS.

See Close-Up on page 1643.

University of Phoenix, John Sperling School of Business, College of Graduate Business and Management, Phoenix, AZ 85034-7209. Offers accounting (MBA); administration (MBA); global management (MBA); human resources management (MBA); management (MM); marketing (MBA); public administration (MBA, MM). Evening/weekend programs available. *Degree requirements:* For master's, thesis (for some programs). *Entrance requirements:* For master's, 3 years of work experience, minimum undergraduate GPA of 3.0. Additional exam requirements/recommendations for international students: Required—TOEFL (minimum score 550 paper-based; 213 computer-based; 79 iBT). Electronic applications accepted.

University of Phoenix–Augusta Campus, College of Graduate Business and Management, Augusta, GA 30909-4583. Offers accounting (MBA); business and management (MBA, MM); global management (MBA); human resources management (MBA, MM); marketing (MBA); public administration (MBA, MM).

Public Administration

University of Phoenix–Austin Campus, College of Graduate Business and Management, Austin, TX 78759. Offers accounting (MBA); business and management (MBA); e-business (MBA); global management (MBA); human resources management (MBA, MM); management (MM); marketing (MBA); public administration (MBA).

University of Phoenix–Bay Area Campus, John Sperling School of Business, College of Graduate Business and Management, Pleasanton, CA 94588-3677. Offers accounting (MBA); business administration (MBA); global management (MBA); human resource management (MBA); marketing (MBA); public administration (MBA). Evening/weekend programs available. *Degree requirements:* For master's, thesis (for some programs). *Entrance requirements:* For master's, minimum undergraduate GPA of 3.0, 3 years of work experience. Additional exam requirements/recommendations for international students: Required—TOEFL (minimum score 550 paper-based; 213 computer-based; 79 iBT). Electronic applications accepted.

University of Phoenix–Central Valley Campus, College of Graduate Business and Management, Fresno, CA 93720-1562. Offers accounting (MBA); business administration (MBA); global management (MBA); human resources management (MBA); management (MM); marketing (MBA); public administration (MBA).

University of Phoenix–Chattanooga Campus, College of Graduate Business and Management, Chattanooga, TN 37421-3707. Offers accounting (MBA); business and management (MBA); global management (MBA); human resources management (MBA, MM); management (MM); marketing (MBA); public administration (MBA, MM).

University of Phoenix–Cheyenne Campus, College of Graduate Business and Management, Cheyenne, WY 82009. Offers business and management (MM); global management (MBA); human resources management (MBA, MM); marketing (MBA); public administration (MBA, MM).

University of Phoenix–Cleveland Campus, John Sperling School of Business, College of Graduate Business and Management, Independence, OH 44131-2194. Offers accounting (MBA); business administration (MBA); global management (MBA); human resources management (MM); management (MM); marketing (MBA); public administration (MBA, MM). Evening/weekend programs available. *Degree requirements:* For master's, thesis (for some programs). *Entrance requirements:* For master's, minimum undergraduate GPA of 3.0, 3 years of work experience. Additional exam requirements/recommendations for international students: Required—TOEFL (minimum score 550 paper-based; 213 computer-based; 79 iBT). Electronic applications accepted.

University of Phoenix–Columbus Georgia Campus, John Sperling School of Business, College of Graduate Business and Management, Columbus, GA 31904-6321. Offers accounting (MBA); administration (MBA); global management (MBA); human resource management (MBA); marketing (MBA); public administration (MBA). Evening/weekend programs available. *Degree requirements:* For master's, thesis (for some programs). *Entrance requirements:* For master's, minimum undergraduate GPA of 3.0, 3 years of work experience. Additional exam requirements/recommendations for international students: Required—TOEFL (minimum score 550 paper-based; 213 computer-based; 79 iBT). Electronic applications accepted.

University of Phoenix–Dallas Campus, John Sperling School of Business, College of Graduate Business and Management, Dallas, TX 75251-2009. Offers accounting (MBA); administration (MBA); human resources management (MBA, MM); management (MM); marketing (MBA); public administration (MBA, MM). Evening/weekend programs available. *Degree requirements:* For master's, thesis (for some programs). *Entrance requirements:* For master's, 3 years of work experience, minimum undergraduate GPA of 3.0. Additional exam requirements/recommendations for international students: Required—TOEFL (minimum score 550 paper-based; 213 computer-based; 79 iBT). Electronic applications accepted.

University of Phoenix–Denver Campus, John Sperling School of Business, College of Graduate Business and Management, Lone Tree, CO 80124-5453. Offers accounting (MBA); business administration (MBA); e-business (MBA); global management (MBA); human resources management (MBA, MM); management (MM); marketing (MBA); public administration (MBA, MM). Evening/weekend programs available. *Degree requirements:* For master's, thesis (for some programs). *Entrance requirements:* For master's, minimum undergraduate GPA of 3.0, 3 years work experience. Additional exam requirements/recommendations for international students: Required—TOEFL (minimum score 550 paper-based; 213 computer-based; 79 iBT). Electronic applications accepted.

University of Phoenix–Des Moines Campus, College of Graduate Business and Management, Des Moines, IA 50266. Offers accounting (MBA); business administration (MBA); global management (MBA); human resources management (MBA, MM); management (MM); marketing (MBA); public administration (MBA, MM).

University of Phoenix–Harrisburg Campus, College of Graduate Business and Management, Harrisburg, PA 17112. Offers accounting (MBA); business and management (MBA); glboal management (MBA); human resources management (MBA, MM); management (MM); marketing (MBA); public administration (MBA, MM).

University of Phoenix–Hawaii Campus, John Sperling School of Business, College of Graduate Business and Management, Honolulu, HI 96813-4317. Offers accounting (MBA); business administration (MBA); global management (MBA); human resources management (MBA, MM); management (MM); marketing (MBA); public administration (MBA, MM). Evening/weekend programs available. *Degree requirements:* For master's, thesis (for some programs). *Entrance requirements:* For master's, minimum undergraduate GPA of 3.0, 3 years of work experience. Additional exam requirements/recommendations for international students: Required—TOEFL (minimum score 550 paper-based; 213 computer-based; 79 iBT). Electronic applications accepted.

University of Phoenix–Houston Campus, John Sperling School of Business, College of Graduate Business and Management, Houston, TX 77079-2004. Offers business administration (MBA); global management (MBA); human resources management (MBA); public administration (MBA). Evening/weekend programs available. *Degree requirements:* For master's, thesis (for some programs). *Entrance requirements:* For master's, 3 years of work experience, minimum undergraduate GPA of 3.0. Additional exam requirements/recommendations for international students: Required—TOEFL (minimum score 550 paper-based; 213 computer-based; 79 iBT). Electronic applications accepted.

University of Phoenix–Jersey City Campus, College of Graduate Business and Management, Jersey City, NJ 07310. Offers accounting (MBA); business and management (MBA); global management (MBA); human resources management (MBA, MM); management (MM); marketing (MBA); public administration (MBA, MM).

University of Phoenix–Louisiana Campus, John Sperling School of Business, College of Graduate Business and Management, Metairie, LA 70001-2082. Offers business administration (MBA); human resource management (MBA, MM); public administration (MBA). Evening/weekend programs available. *Degree requirements:* For master's, thesis (for some programs). *Entrance requirements:* For master's, minimum undergraduate GPA of 3.0, 3 years work experience. Additional exam requirements/recommendations for international students: Required—TOEFL (minimum score 550 paper-based; 213 computer-based; 79 iBT). Electronic applications accepted.

University of Phoenix–Madison Campus, College of Graduate Business and Management, Madison, WI 53718-2416. Offers accounting (MBA); business and management (MBA, MM); e-business (MBA); global management (MBA); human resources management (MBA, MM); marketing (MBA); public administration (MBA).

University of Phoenix–Maryland Campus, John Sperling School of Business, College of Graduate Business and Management, Columbia, MD 21045-5424. Offers business administration (MBA); e-business (MBA); global management (MBA); human resources management (MBA, MM); marketing (MBA); public administration (MBA, MM). Evening/weekend programs available. *Degree requirements:* For master's, thesis (for some programs). *Entrance requirements:* For master's, minimum undergraduate GPA of 3.0, 3 years of work experience. Additional exam requirements/recommendations for international students: Required—TOEFL (minimum score 550 paper-based; 213 computer-based; 79 iBT). Electronic applications accepted.

University of Phoenix–Memphis Campus, College of Graduate Business and Management, Cordova, TN 38018. Offers acounting (MBA); business and management (MBA); e-business (MBA); global management (MBA); human resources management (MBA, MM); marketing (MBA); public administration (MBA, MM).

University of Phoenix–Northern Nevada Campus, College of Graduate Business and Management, Reno, NV 89511. Offers accounting (MBA); business and management (MBA); global management (MBA); human resources management (MBA, MM); management (MM); marketing (MBA); public administration (MBA, MM).

University of Phoenix–Northern Virginia Campus, College of Graduate Business and Management, Reston, VA 20190. Offers accounting (MBA); business administration (MBA); e-business (MBA); global management (MBA); human resources management (MBA, MM); management (MM); marketing (MBA); public administration (MBA).

University of Phoenix–North Florida Campus, John Sperling School of Business, College of Graduate Business and Management, Jacksonville, FL 32216-0959. Offers accounting (MBA); business administration (MBA); global management (MBA); human resources management (MBA, MM); management (MM); marketing (MBA); public administration (MBA). Evening/weekend programs available. *Degree requirements:* For master's, thesis (for some programs). *Entrance requirements:* For master's, minimum undergraduate GPA of 3.0, 3 years work experience. Additional exam requirements/recommendations for international students: Required—TOEFL (minimum score 550 paper-based; 213 computer-based; 79 iBT). Electronic applications accepted.

University of Phoenix–Northwest Arkansas Campus, College of Graduate Business and Management, Rogers, AR 72756-9615. Offers accounting (MBA); business and management (MBA); global management (MBA); human resources management (MBA, MM); management (MM); marketing (MBA); public administration (MBA, MM).

University of Phoenix–Omaha Campus, College of Graduate Business and Management, Omaha, NE 68154-5240. Offers accounting (MBA); business and management (MBA); global management (MBA); human resources management (MM); human resources managemetn (MBA); management (MM); marketing (MBA); public administration (MM); public adminstration (MBA).

University of Phoenix–Pittsburgh Campus, John Sperling School of Business, College of Graduate Business and Management, Pittsburgh, PA 15276. Offers accounting (MBA); business administration (MBA); global management (MBA); human resource management (MBA); human resources management (MM); management (MM); marketing (MBA); public administration (MBA, MM). Evening/weekend programs available. *Degree requirements:* For master's, thesis (for some programs). *Entrance requirements:* For master's, minimum undergraduate GPA of 3.0, 3 years work experience. Additional exam requirements/recommendations for international students: Required—TOEFL (minimum score 550 paper-based; 213 computer-based; 79 iBT). Electronic applications accepted.

University of Phoenix–Renton Learning Center, College of Graduate Business and Management, Renton, WA 98005. Offers accounting (MBA); business and management (MBA, MM); global management (MBA); human resources management (MBA, MM); marketing (MBA); public administration (MBA, MM). Evening/weekend programs available. *Degree requirements:* For master's, thesis (for some programs). *Entrance requirements:* For master's, minimum undergraduate GPA of 3.0, 3 years of work experience. Additional exam requirements/recommendations for international students: Required—TOEFL (minimum score 550 paper-based; 213 computer-based; 79 iBT). Electronic applications accepted.

University of Phoenix–Richmond Campus, John Sperling School of Business, College of Graduate Business and Management, Richmond, VA 23230. Offers accounting (MBA); business administration (MBA); global management (MBA); human resources management (MBA, MM); management (MM); marketing (MBA); public administration (MBA, MM). Evening/weekend programs available. *Degree requirements:* For master's, thesis (for some programs). *Entrance requirements:* For master's, minimum undergraduate GPA 3.0, 3 years work experience. Additional exam requirements/recommendations for international students: Required—TOEFL (minimum score 550 paper-based; 213 computer-based; 79 iBT). Electronic applications accepted.

University of Phoenix–Sacramento Valley Campus, John Sperling School of Business, College of Graduate Business and Management, Sacramento, CA 95833-3632. Offers accounting (MBA); business administration (MBA); global management (MBA); human resources management (MBA); marketing (MBA); public administration (MBA). Evening/weekend programs available. *Degree requirements:* For master's, thesis (for some programs). *Entrance requirements:* For master's, minimum undergraduate GPA of 3.0, 3 years work experience. Additional exam requirements/recommendations for international students: Required—TOEFL (minimum score 550 paper-based; 213 computer-based; 79 iBT). Electronic applications accepted.

University of Phoenix–San Antonio Campus, College of Graduate Business and Management, San Antonio, TX 78230. Offers accounting (MBA); business and management (MBA); e-business (MBA); global management (MBA); human resources management (MBA, MM); management (MM); marketing (MBA); public administration (MBA, MM).

University of Phoenix–Savannah Campus, College of Graduate Business and Management, Savannah, GA 31405-7400. Offers accounting (MBA); business administration (MBA); business and management (MM); global management (MBA); human resources management (MBA, MM); marketing (MBA); public administration (MBA, MM).

University of Phoenix–South Florida Campus, John Sperling School of Business, College of Graduate Business and Management, Fort Lauderdale, FL 33309. Offers accounting (MBA); business administration (MBA); global management (MBA); human resource management (MBA); human resources management (MM); management (MM); marketing (MBA); public administration (MBA). Evening/weekend programs available. *Degree requirements:* For master's, thesis (for some programs). *Entrance requirements:* For master's, minimum undergraduate GPA of 3.0, 3 years work experience. Additional exam requirements/recommendations for international students: Required—TOEFL (minimum score 550 paper-based; 213 computer-based; 79 iBT). Electronic applications accepted.

University of Phoenix–Springfield Campus, College of Graduate Business and Management, Springfield, MO 65804-7211. Offers accounting (MBA); business and management (MBA); global management (MBA); human resources management (MBA, MM); management (MM); marketing (MBA); public administration (MBA, MM).

University of Phoenix–West Florida Campus, The John Sperling School of Business, College of Graduate Business and Management, Temple Terrace, FL 33637. Offers business administration (MBA); global management (MBA); human resource management (MBA); human resources management (MM); management (MM); marketing (MBA); public administration (MBA). Evening/weekend programs available. *Degree requirements:* For master's, thesis (for some programs). *Entrance requirements:* For master's, 3 years of work experience, minimum undergraduate GPA of 3.0. Additional exam requirements/recommendations for international students: Required—TOEFL (minimum score 550 paper-based; 213 computer-based; 79 iBT). Electronic applications accepted.

University of Pittsburgh, Graduate School of Public and International Affairs, Division of Public and Urban Affairs, Program in Public and Nonprofit Management, Pittsburgh, PA 15260. Offers MPA, MPA/MID, JD/MPA, MPA/MPIA, MPH/MPA, MSIS/MPA, MSW/MPA. *Accreditation:* NASPAA (one or more programs are accredited). Part-time and evening/weekend programs available. *Faculty:* 35 full-time (11 women), 16 part-time/adjunct (9 women). *Students:* 34 full-time (23 women), 10 part-time (8 women); includes 9 minority (8 African Americans, 1 Asian American or Pacific Islander), 2 international. Average age 25. 42 applicants, 86% accepted, 20 enrolled. In 2007, 35 degrees awarded. *Degree requirements:* For master's, thesis optional, internship, capstone seminar. *Entrance requirements:* For master's, GRE General Test, 3 letters of recommendation, resumé, minimum GPA of 3.2. Additional exam requirements/recommendations for international students: Required—TOEFL (minimum score 550 paper-based; 213 computer-based; 80 iBT), TWE (minimum score 4); Recommended—IELTS (minimum score 7). *Application deadline:* For fall admission, 2/1 for domestic students, 1/15 for international students; for spring admission, 11/1 for domestic students, 8/1 for international students. Application fee: $50. *Financial support:* In 2007–08, 18 students received support, including 18 fellowships (averaging $7,700 per year); career-related internships or fieldwork, scholarships/grants, and unspecified assistantships also available. Financial award application deadline: 2/1. *Faculty research:* Emergency management, health policy and regulation, regional finance, non-profit management, environmental policy, housing policy. Total annual research expenditures: $845,025. *Application contact:* Denene Hefflin, Graduate Enrollment Counselor, 412-648-7640, Fax: 412-648-7641, E-mail: dkh7@pitt.edu.

See Close-Up on page 1645.

University of Pittsburgh, Graduate School of Public and International Affairs, Doctoral Program in Public and International Affairs, Pittsburgh, PA 15260. Offers development policy (PhD); foreign and security policy (PhD); international political economy (PhD); public administration (PhD); public policy (PhD). *Accreditation:* NASPAA. Part-time programs available. *Faculty:* 34 full-time (10 women), 18 part-time/adjunct (6 women). *Students:* 39 full-time (15 women), 8 part-time (6 women); includes 6 minority (2 African Americans, 3 Asian Americans or Pacific Islanders, 1 Hispanic American), 10 international. Average age 30. 61 applicants, 30% accepted, 11 enrolled. In 2007, 8 degrees awarded. *Degree requirements:* For doctorate, comprehensive exam, thesis/dissertation. *Entrance requirements:* For doctorate, GRE, 3 letters of recommendation, resumé, minimum GPA of 3.0, writing sample. Additional exam requirements/recommendations for international students: Required—TOEFL (minimum score 600 paper-based; 250 computer-based; 100 iBT), TWE (minimum score 4); Recommended—IELTS (minimum score 7). *Application deadline:* For fall admission, 2/1 for domestic students, 1/15 for international students. Application fee: $50. Electronic applications accepted. *Financial support:* In 2007–08, 13 students received support, including 13 fellowships (averaging $28,580 per year); scholarships/grants and unspecified assistantships also available. Financial award application deadline: 2/1. *Faculty research:* International political economy, international development, public administration, public policy, foreign policy, international security policy. Total annual research expenditures: $845,025. *Unit head:* Dr. Phyllis Coontz, Doctoral Program Coordinator, 412-648-2605, Fax: 412-648-2605, E-mail: pcoontz@gspia.pitt.edu. *Application contact:* Jessica L. Hatherill, Associate Director of Student Services, 412-648-7640, Fax: 412-648-7641, E-mail: hatherill@gspia.pitt.edu.

See Close-Up on page 1645.

University of Puerto Rico, Río Piedras, College of Social Sciences, School of Public Administration, San Juan, PR 00931-3300. Offers MPA. Part-time programs available. *Students:* 189 full-time (145 women), 52 part-time (34 women). Average age 31. In 2007, 37 degrees awarded. *Degree requirements:* For master's, comprehensive exam, thesis. *Entrance requirements:* For master's, GRE or PAEG, interview, minimum GPA of 3.0, letter of recommendation. *Application deadline:* For fall admission, 2/1 for domestic and international students. Application fee: $17. *Expenses:* Tuition, state resident: full-time $1,808; part-time $113 per credit. Tuition, nonresident: full-time $5,248; part-time $328 per credit. Required fees: $72 per term. *Financial support:* Fellowships, research assistantships, teaching assistantships, Federal Work-Study, institutionally sponsored loans, and tuition waivers (partial) available. Financial award application deadline: 5/31. *Unit head:* Dr. Palmira Rios-González, Director, 787-764-0000 Ext. 2097, Fax: 787-763-7510.

University of Regina, Faculty of Graduate Studies and Research, Johnson-Shoyama Graduate School of Public Policy, Regina, SK S4S 0A2, Canada. Offers economic analysis for public policy (Master's Certificate); non-profit management (Master's Certificate); public management (MPA, Master's Certificate); public policy (MPA, PhD, Master's Certificate). Part-time and evening/weekend programs available. *Faculty:* 6 full-time (3 women). *Students:* 60 full-time (30 women), 53 part-time (37 women). 104 applicants, 86% accepted. In 2007, 9 degrees awarded. *Entrance requirements:* Additional exam requirements/recommendations for international students: Required—TOEFL (minimum score 580 paper-based; 237 computer-based; 88 iBT). *Application deadline:* Applications are processed on a rolling basis. Application fee: $85 ($100 for international students). Electronic applications accepted. *Expenses: Contact institution. Financial support:* In 2007–08, 13 fellowships (averaging $15,750 per year), 1 research assistantship (averaging $13,875 per year), 7 teaching assistantships (averaging $13,060 per year) were awarded. Financial award application deadline: 6/15. *Faculty research:* Public administration and policy. *Unit head:* Dr. Ken Rasmussen, Associate Dean, 306-585-5463, E-mail: ken.rasmussen@uregina.ca. *Application contact:* Devon Anderson, Information Contact, 306-585-5462, E-mail: devon.anderson@uregina.ca.

University of Rhode Island, Graduate School, College of Arts and Sciences, Department of Political Science, Program in Public Policy and Administration, Kingston, RI 02881. Offers MA, MPA, Certificate. In 2007, 24 degrees awarded. *Application deadline:* For fall admission, 4/15 priority date for domestic students. Applications are processed on a rolling basis. Application fee: $35. *Expenses:* Tuition, state resident: full-time $6,936; part-time $385 per credit. Tuition, nonresident: full-time $19,044; part-time $1,058 per credit. Required fees: $1,508; $48 per credit. $30 per semester. One-time fee: $80 part-time. *Unit head:* Dr. Timothy Hennessey, Director, 401-874-4052.

University of San Francisco, College of Professional Studies, Program in Public Administration, Concentration in Public Administration, San Francisco, CA 94117-1080. Offers MPA. Part-time and evening/weekend programs available. *Faculty:* 2 full-time (1 woman), 8 part-time/adjunct (3 women). *Students:* 64 full-time (39 women); includes 28 minority (8 African Americans, 4 Asian Americans or Pacific Islanders, 16 Hispanic Americans), 1 international. Average age 37. 63 applicants, 83% accepted, 36 enrolled. In 2007, 30 degrees awarded. *Entrance requirements:* For master's, minimum GPA of 3.0. Application fee: $55 ($65 for international students). *Expenses:* Tuition: Part-time $1,005 per unit. Tuition and fees vary according to degree level, campus/location and program. *Financial support:* In 2007–08, 52 students received support. Application deadline: 3/2; *Application contact:* 415-422-6000.

University of South Africa, College of Economic and Management Sciences, Pretoria, South Africa. Offers accounting (D Admin, D Com); accounting science (DA); auditing (D Admin, D Com); business administration (M Tech); business economics (D Admin); business leadership (DBL); business management (D Admin, D Com); economic management analysis (M Tech); economics (D Admin, D Com, PhD); human resource development (M Tech); industrial psychology (D Admin, D Com, PhD); logistics (D Com); marketing (M Tech); public administration (D Admin, D Com, DPA, PhD); public management (M Tech); quantitative management (D Admin, D Com); real estate (M Tech); statistics (D Admin, PhD); tourism management (D Admin, D Com); transport economics (D Admin, D Com).

University of South Alabama, Graduate School, College of Arts and Sciences, Department of Political Science and Criminal Justice, Mobile, AL 36688-0002. Offers public administration (MPA). Part-time and evening/weekend programs available. *Faculty:* 7 full-time (0 women), 5 part-time/adjunct (0 women). *Students:* 16 full-time (11 women), 10 part-time (5 women); includes 9 minority (8 African Americans, 1 Asian American or Pacific Islander). 20 applicants, 50% accepted, 6 enrolled. In 2007, 7 degrees awarded. *Degree requirements:* For master's, comprehensive exam, thesis optional. *Entrance requirements:* For master's, GRE, minimum GPA of 3.0. *Application deadline:* For fall admission, 9/1 priority date for domestic students. Applications are processed on a rolling basis. Application fee: $25. *Expenses:* Tuition, state resident: full-time $4,224; part-time $176 per credit hour. Tuition, nonresident: full-time $8,448; part-time $352 per credit hour. Required fees: $802. Full-time tuition and fees vary according to program and student level. *Financial support:* Research assistantships, career-related internships or fieldwork available. Support available to part-time students. Financial award application deadline: 4/1. *Unit head:* Dr. Nader Entessar, Chair, 251-460-7161.

University of South Carolina, The Graduate School, College of Arts and Sciences, Department of Political Science, Program in Public Administration, Columbia, SC 29208. Offers MPA, JD/MPA, MSW/MPA. *Accreditation:* NASPAA. Part-time and evening/weekend programs available. *Faculty:* 7 full-time (2 women), 2 part-time/adjunct (1 woman). *Students:* 33 full-time (24 women), 11 part-time (5 women); includes 6 minority (all African Americans) Average age 27. 28 applicants, 71% accepted, 19 enrolled. In 2007, 19 degrees awarded. *Degree requirements:* For master's, capstone seminar. *Entrance requirements:* For master's, GRE General Test, minimum GPA of 3.0. Additional exam requirements/recommendations for international students: Required—TOEFL. *Application deadline:* For fall admission, 4/1 priority date for domestic and international students; for winter admission, 7/1 for domestic and international students; for spring admission, 11/15 for domestic and international students. Applications are processed on a rolling basis. Application fee: $40. Electronic applications accepted. *Expenses:* Tuition, state resident: part-time $440 per hour. Tuition, nonresident: part-time $936 per hour. Required fees: $17 per hour. Tuition and fees vary according to program. *Financial support:* In 2007–08, 20 students received support, including 1 fellowship with partial tuition reimbursement available (averaging $2,000 per year), 5 research assistantships with partial tuition reimbursements available (averaging $8,000 per year); career-related internships or fieldwork, Federal Work-Study, institutionally sponsored loans, and tuition waivers also available. Financial award application deadline: 4/1. *Faculty research:* Public policy, organizational theory, personnel administration, budgeting, finance. *Unit head:* Dr. Charlie Tyer, MPA Program Director, 803-777-4483, Fax: 803-777-8255, E-mail: tyer@sc.edu. *Application contact:* Deborah Kathrine Tiemeyer, Student Services Coordinator, 803-777-2675, Fax: 803-777-8255, E-mail: tie@sc.edu.

The University of South Dakota, Graduate School, College of Arts and Sciences, Department of Political Science, Vermillion, SD 57069-2390. Offers American political institutions (PhD); political science (MA); public administration (MPA, PhD); public policy (PhD); JD/MA; JD/MPA. *Accreditation:* NASPAA (one or more programs are accredited). Part-time programs available. Postbaccalaureate distance learning degree programs offered. *Faculty:* 16 full-time (3 women), 1 part-time/adjunct (0 women). *Students:* 55 (29 women). In 2007, 65 degrees awarded. *Degree requirements:* For master's, comprehensive exam, thesis (for some programs). *Entrance requirements:* For master's, GRE or LSAT (MPA), GRE General Test (MA), minimum GPA of 2.7. Additional exam requirements/recommendations for international students: Required—TOEFL (minimum score 550 paper-based; 213 computer-based; 79 iBT). *Application deadline:* Applications are processed on a rolling basis. Application fee: $35. Electronic applications accepted. *Financial support:* In 2007–08, 4 research assistantships with partial tuition reimbursements (averaging $4,626 per year), 3 teaching assistantships with partial tuition reimbursements (averaging $4,626 per year) were awarded; Federal Work-Study also available. Support available to part-time students. Financial award applicants required to submit FAFSA. *Unit head:* Dr. William Richardson, Chair, 605-677-5242, Fax: 605-677-6302, E-mail: wrichard@usd.edu. *Application contact:* Dr. Richard Braunstein, Graduate Student Advisor, MPA Program, 605-677-5242, Fax: 605-677-6302, E-mail: rich.braunstein@usd.edu.

University of Southern California, Graduate School, School of Policy, Planning and Development, Programs in Public Administration, Los Angeles, CA 90089. Offers MPA, DPA, PhD, Certificate, JD/MPA, MPA/M Pl, MPA/MAJCS, MPA/MS, MPA/MSW. *Accreditation:* NASPAA (one or more programs are accredited). *Faculty:* 39 full-time (8 women), 43 part-time/adjunct (12 women). *Students:* 204 full-time (131 women), 37 part-time (21 women); includes 2 American Indian/Alaska Native, 37 Asian Americans or Pacific Islanders, 37 Hispanic Americans, 34 international. 289 applicants, 75% accepted. In 2007, 85 master's, 5 doctorates awarded. *Degree requirements:* For doctorate, thesis/dissertation. *Entrance requirements:* For master's and doctorate, GRE General Test. *Application deadline:* For fall admission, 1/15 priority date for domestic students; for spring admission, 11/1 for domestic students. Applications are processed on a rolling basis. Application fee: $85. *Financial support:* In 2007–08, 67 students received support; fellowships with partial tuition reimbursements available, research assistantships with full tuition reimbursements available, career-related internships or fieldwork, Federal Work-Study, institutionally sponsored loans, scholarships/grants, traineeships, and tuition waivers (full and partial) available. Support available to part-time students. Financial award application deadline: 2/15; financial award applicants required to submit FAFSA. *Faculty research:* Collaborative governance and decision making, nonprofit management, civic engagement. *Unit head:* Dr. Shui Yan Tang, Head, 213-740-2311.

University of Southern Indiana, Graduate Studies, College of Liberal Arts, Program in Public Administration, Evansville, IN 47712-3590. Offers MPA. Part-time and evening/weekend programs available. *Faculty:* 2 full-time (0 women), 3 part-time/adjunct (2 women). *Students:* 3 full-time (1 woman), 28 part-time (19 women). Average age 33. 8 applicants, 38% accepted, 2 enrolled. In 2007, 7 degrees awarded. *Entrance requirements:* For master's, GMAT or GRE, 2 letters of reference, analytical writing sample, minimum GPA of 2.7. Additional exam requirements/recommendations for international students: Required—TOEFL (minimum score 550 paper-based; 213 computer-based; 79 iBT), IELTS (minimum score 6). *Application deadline:* For fall admission, 8/15 priority date for domestic students, 3/1 priority date for international students. Applications are processed on a rolling basis. Application fee: $25. *Expenses:* Tuition, state resident: full-time $4,374; part-time $243 per credit. Tuition, nonresident: full-time $8,622; part-time $479 per credit. Required fees: $220; $23 per term. Tuition and fees vary according to course load and reciprocity agreements. *Financial support:* In 2007–08, 24 students received support. Federal Work-Study, scholarships/grants, tuition waivers (full and partial), and unspecified assistantships available. Financial award application deadline: 3/1; financial award applicants required to submit FAFSA. *Unit head:* Dr. Brian Posler, Director, 812-465-7020, Fax: 812-464-1956, E-mail: bposler@usi.edu.

University of South Florida, Graduate School, College of Arts and Sciences, Department of Government and International Affairs, Public Administration Program, Tampa, FL 33620-9951. Offers MPA. *Accreditation:* NASPAA. Part-time and evening/weekend programs available. *Entrance requirements:* For master's, GRE General Test, minimum GPA of 3.0 in last 60 hours of course work. Additional exam requirements/recommendations for international students: Required—TOEFL (minimum score 550 paper-based; 213 computer-based). Electronic applications accepted. *Faculty research:* Public budgeting and financial management, policy analysis, urban management and planning, public personnel management, public organization management.

The University of Tennessee, Graduate School, College of Arts and Sciences, Department of Political Science, Program in Public Administration, Knoxville, TN 37996. Offers MPA, JD/MPA. *Accreditation:* NASPAA. Part-time programs available. *Degree requirements:* For master's, thesis or alternative. *Entrance requirements:* For master's, GRE General Test, minimum GPA of 2.7. Additional exam requirements/recommendations for international students: Required—TOEFL. Electronic applications accepted.

The University of Tennessee at Chattanooga, Graduate School, College of Arts and Sciences, Department of Political Science, Program in Public Administration, Chattanooga, TN 37403-2598. Offers MPA, Postbaccalaureate Certificate. *Accreditation:* NASPAA. Part-time and evening/weekend programs available. *Faculty:* 3 full-time (1 woman), 1 part-time/adjunct (0 women). *Students:* 17 full-time (12 women), 30 part-time (23 women); includes 15

Public Administration

The University of Tennessee at Chattanooga (continued)

minority (14 African Americans, 1 Hispanic American). Average age 32. 30 applicants, 90% accepted, 18 enrolled. In 2007, 11 master's, 1 other advanced degree awarded. *Degree requirements:* For master's, comprehensive exam, thesis or alternative, internship. *Entrance requirements:* For master's, GRE General Test. Additional exam requirements/recommendations for international students: Required—TOEFL (minimum score 550 paper-based; 213 computer-based; 79 iBT); Recommended—IELTS (minimum score 6). *Application deadline:* For fall admission, 8/1 priority date for domestic students; for spring admission, 12/1 priority date for domestic students. Applications are processed on a rolling basis. Application fee: $30 ($35 for international students). *Expenses:* Tuition, state resident: full-time $5,854; part-time $393 per hour. Tuition, nonresident: full-time $15,816; part-time $946 per hour. Required fees: $1,090; $256 per hour. *Financial support:* In 2007–08, 3 fellowships with full and partial tuition reimbursements (averaging $6,627 per year) were awarded; career-related internships or fieldwork, Federal Work-Study, institutionally sponsored loans, scholarships/grants, and unspecified assistantships also available. Support available to part-time students. Financial award application deadline: 4/1; financial award applicants required to submit FAFSA. *Faculty research:* Organizational cultures and renewal, management theory, public policy, policy analysis, nonprofit organizations. Total annual research expenditures: $33,360. *Unit head:* Dr. David Edwards, Coordinator, 423-425-4068, Fax: 423-425-2373, E-mail: david-edwards@utc.edu. *Application contact:* Dr. Deborah E. Arfken, Dean of Graduate Studies, 423-425-4666, Fax: 423-425-5223, E-mail: deborah-arfken@utc.edu.

The University of Texas at Arlington, Graduate School, School of Urban and Public Affairs, Program in Public Administration, Arlington, TX 76019. Offers MPA. *Accreditation:* NASPAA. Part-time and evening/weekend programs available. *Faculty:* 8 full-time (4 women), 2 part-time/adjunct (1 woman). *Students:* 36 full-time (22 women), 84 part-time (46 women); includes 42 minority (31 African Americans, 1 Asian American or Pacific Islander, 10 Hispanic Americans), 5 international. In 2007, 35 master's awarded. *Degree requirements:* For master's, comprehensive exam, thesis or alternative. *Entrance requirements:* For master's, GRE General Test. Additional exam requirements/recommendations for international students: Required—TOEFL (minimum score 550 paper-based; 213 computer-based). *Application deadline:* For fall admission, 6/16 for domestic students. Application fee: $35 ($50 for international students). *Expenses:* Tuition, state resident: full-time $5,934. Tuition, nonresident: full-time $10,938. *Financial support:* In 2007–08, 1 research assistantship (averaging $750 per year) was awarded; fellowships, career-related internships or fieldwork also available. Financial award application deadline: 6/1; financial award applicants required to submit FAFSA. *Faculty research:* Environment, statistics, public administration, social welfare, economic development, economics, budgeting, planning. Total annual research expenditures: $53,550. *Unit head:* Dr. Alejandro Rodriguez, Graduate Advisor, 817-272-3357, Fax: 817-272-5008. *Application contact:* Linda Slaughter, Administrative Clerk, 817-272-3071, Fax: 817-272-5008, E-mail: slaughter@uta.edu.

The University of Texas at Brownsville, Graduate Studies, College of Liberal Arts, Program in Public Policy and Management, Brownsville, TX 78520-4991. Offers MPPM. *Degree requirements:* For master's, thesis. *Entrance requirements:* For master's, GRE, 2 letters of recommendation.

The University of Texas at San Antonio, College of Public Policy, Department of Public Administration, San Antonio, TX 78249-0617. Offers MPA. *Accreditation:* NASPAA. Part-time and evening/weekend programs available. *Faculty:* 9 full-time (3 women). *Students:* 26 full-time (19 women), 93 part-time (55 women); includes 83 minority (14 African Americans, 2 American Indian/Alaska Native, 4 Asian Americans or Pacific Islanders, 63 Hispanic Americans), 1 international. Average age 32. 44 applicants, 91% accepted, 34 enrolled. In 2007, 32 degrees awarded. *Degree requirements:* For master's, comprehensive exam, thesis optional. *Entrance requirements:* For master's, GMAT or GRE General Test, undergraduate course work in American government, economics, and research methods; minimum GPA of 3.0 on last 60 hours. Additional exam requirements/recommendations for international students: Required—TOEFL (minimum score 500 paper-based; 173 computer-based). *Application deadline:* For fall admission, 7/1 for domestic students, 4/1 for international students; for spring admission, 11/1 for domestic students, 9/1 for international students. Applications are processed on a rolling basis. Application fee: $45 ($80 for international students). *Financial support:* In 2007–08, 3 research assistantships (averaging $4,347 per year) were awarded; Federal Work-Study also available. *Unit head:* Dr. Jerrell Coggburn, Chair, 210-458-2501, Fax: 210-458-2536, E-mail: jcoggburn@utsa.edu.

The University of Texas at Tyler, College of Arts and Sciences, Department of Social Sciences, Tyler, TX 75799-0001. Offers criminal justice (MS); public administration (MPA); sociology (MS). Part-time and evening/weekend programs available. Postbaccalaureate distance learning degree programs offered. *Faculty:* 15 full-time (2 women). *Students:* 3 full-time (2 women), 25 part-time (18 women); includes 5 minority (4 African Americans, 1 Hispanic American), 14 international. Average age 31. 18 applicants, 100% accepted, 11 enrolled. In 2007, 6 degrees awarded. *Degree requirements:* For master's, comprehensive exam. *Entrance requirements:* For master's, GRE General Test, minimum GPA of 3.0. *Application deadline:* Applications are processed on a rolling basis. Application fee: $0. *Expenses:* Tuition, state resident: part-time $627 per semester hour. Tuition, nonresident: part-time $908 per semester hour. Required fees: $107 per semester hour. Tuition and fees vary according to course load. *Financial support:* In 2007–08, 1 fellowship (averaging $1,000 per year), 2 research assistantships, 2 teaching assistantships were awarded; career-related internships or fieldwork, Federal Work-Study, and scholarships/grants also available. Support available to part-time students. Financial award application deadline: 7/1; financial award applicants required to submit FAFSA. *Faculty research:* Urban segregation, minority business, violent crime, gender discrimination. *Unit head:* Dr. Ken Wink, Chair, 903-566-7434, Fax: 903-565-5537, E-mail: kwink@mail.uttyl.edu. *Application contact:* Pam Morrow, Assistant to Dean for Enrollment Management, 903-566-7205, Fax: 903-566-7068, E-mail: pmorrow@uttyler.edu.

The University of Texas–Pan American, College of Social and Behavioral Sciences, Program in Public Administration, Edinburg, TX 78541-2999. Offers MPA. Part-time and evening/weekend programs available. *Faculty:* 2 full-time (1 woman), 3 part-time/adjunct (0 women). *Students:* 10 full-time (3 women), 38 part-time (15 women); includes 46 minority (1 African American, 45 Hispanic Americans). Average age 26. 33 applicants, 100% accepted, 33 enrolled. In 2007, 7 degrees awarded. *Degree requirements:* For master's, comprehensive exam (for some programs), thesis optional. *Entrance requirements:* For master's, GRE General Test. Additional exam requirements/recommendations for international students: Required—TOEFL. *Application deadline:* For fall admission, 6/1 priority date for domestic students; for winter admission, 10/1 priority date for domestic students; for spring admission, 3/1 priority date for domestic students. Applications are processed on a rolling basis. Application fee: $0. Electronic applications accepted. *Financial support:* In 2007–08, 2 research assistantships with partial tuition reimbursements (averaging $7,000 per year), 1 teaching assistantship with partial tuition reimbursement (averaging $5,000 per year) were awarded; career-related internships or fieldwork, Federal Work-Study, institutionally sponsored loans, scholarships/grants, tuition waivers (partial), and unspecified assistantships also available. Support available to part-time students. Financial award application deadline: 6/1. *Faculty research:* Immigration policy reform, agriculture food policy, social service delivery systems, community development, social welfare policy reform, urban/city management. *Unit head:* Dr. Espiridion Al Borrego, Director, 956-381-2545 Ext. 2544, Fax: 956-381-2139, E-mail: alborrego@panam.edu.

University of the District of Columbia, School of Business and Public Administration, Department of Management, Marketing, and Information Systems, Program in Public Administration, Washington, DC 20008-1175. Offers MPA. Part-time and evening/weekend programs available. *Students:* 16 full-time (8 women), 23 part-time (11 women); includes 33 minority (24 African Americans, 6 Asian Americans or Pacific Islanders, 3 Hispanic Americans). Average age 30. 21 applicants, 43% accepted. In 2007, 4 degrees awarded. *Degree requirements:* For master's, comprehensive exam, thesis optional. *Entrance requirements:* For master's, GMAT or GRE General Test, writing proficiency exam. *Application deadline:* For fall admission, 6/15 priority date for domestic students; for spring admission, 11/1 for domestic students. Applications are processed on a rolling basis. Application fee: $20. *Financial support:* Career-related internships or fieldwork and Federal Work-Study available. *Faculty research:* Government management, public personnel management, urban management, management information systems, public financial management. *Application contact:* LaVerne Hill Flannigan, Director of Admission, 202-274-6069.

University of the Virgin Islands, Graduate Programs, Division of Humanities and Social Sciences, Saint Thomas, VI 00802-9990. Offers MPA. Part-time and evening/weekend programs available. *Faculty:* 1 full-time (0 women), 2 part-time/adjunct (0 women). *Students:* 2 full-time (both women), 12 part-time (10 women); all minorities (13 African Americans, 1 Hispanic American). Average age 37. 13 applicants, 77% accepted, 5 enrolled. In 2007, 10 degrees awarded. *Degree requirements:* For master's, comprehensive exam, thesis or alternative. *Entrance requirements:* For master's, GMAT, GRE, minimum GPA of 2.5. *Application deadline:* For fall admission, 4/30 for domestic and international students; for spring admission, 10/30 for domestic and international students. Application fee: $25. *Expenses:* Tuition, state resident: full-time $4,950; part-time $275 per credit. Tuition, nonresident: full-time $9,900; part-time $550 per credit. Required fees: $300; $150 per term. Tuition and fees vary according to course load and degree level. *Financial support:* Career-related internships or fieldwork and scholarships/grants available. Financial award application deadline: 4/15. *Faculty research:* Ethical issues of arbitration, spiritual leadership, accountability. *Unit head:* Dr. Malik Sekoú, Dean, 340-693-1261, Fax: 340-693-1265, E-mail: msekou@uvi.edu. *Application contact:* Edward L. Alexander, Director of Admissions, 340-693-1224, Fax: 340-693-1167, E-mail: ealexan@uvi.edu.

The University of Toledo, College of Graduate Studies, College of Arts and Sciences, Department of Political Science and Public Administration, Program in Public Administration, Toledo, OH 43606-3390. Offers health care policy (MPA); healthcare policy (Certificate); municipal administration (MPA, Certificate); public administration (MPA). *Accreditation:* NASPAA. *Students:* 6 full-time (4 women), 14 part-time (10 women); includes 3 minority (all African Americans), 1 international. Average age 31. 19 applicants, 58% accepted, 4 enrolled. In 2007, 8 master's, 5 other advanced degrees awarded. *Degree requirements:* For master's, internship. *Entrance requirements:* For master's, GRE General Test, minimum GPA of 3.0. *Application deadline:* For fall admission, 1/15 priority date for domestic students. Applications are processed on a rolling basis. Application fee: $45. Electronic applications accepted. *Financial support:* Research assistantships, teaching assistantships, Federal Work-Study, scholarships/grants, and unspecified assistantships available. Financial award application deadline: 4/1. *Faculty research:* Economic development, health administration, personnel, budgeting, urban administration.

University of Utah, The Graduate School, College of Social and Behavioral Science, Department of Political Science, Program in Public Administration, Salt Lake City, UT 84112-1107. Offers Exec MPA, MPA, Certificate, JD/MPA, MPA/Ed D, MPA/MA, MPA/PhD. *Accreditation:* NASPAA (one or more programs are accredited). *Students:* 36 full-time (15 women), 86 part-time (38 women); includes 15 minority (3 African Americans, 1 Asian American or Pacific Islander, 11 Hispanic Americans), 1 international. Average age 34. 145 applicants, 54% accepted, 62 enrolled. In 2007, 39 degrees awarded. *Degree requirements:* For master's, internship, thesis or research paper. *Entrance requirements:* For master's, GMAT, GRE General Test, LSAT, minimum GPA of 3.2. Additional exam requirements/recommendations for international students: Required—TOEFL. *Application deadline:* For fall admission, 5/1 for domestic students, 5/1 priority date for international students. Application fee: $45 ($65 for international students). *Financial support:* Research assistantships with full tuition reimbursements, career-related internships or fieldwork available. Financial award application deadline: 1/15; financial award applicants required to submit FAFSA. *Faculty research:* Non-profit organizations, health policy, environmental policy, law and legal. *Application contact:* Sandra Parkes, Program Manager, 801-581-6781, Fax: 801-585-6492, E-mail: sandi.parkes@poli-sci.utah.edu.

University of Vermont, Graduate College, College of Agriculture and Life Sciences, Department of Community Development and Applied Economics, Program in Public Administration, Burlington, VT 05405. Offers MPA. *Students:* 32 (20 women) 1 international. 29 applicants, 97% accepted, 8 enrolled. In 2007, 17 degrees awarded. *Entrance requirements:* For master's, GRE General Test. Additional exam requirements/recommendations for international students: Required—TOEFL (minimum score 550 paper-based; 213 computer-based; 80 iBT). *Application deadline:* For fall admission, 4/1 priority date for domestic students. Applications are processed on a rolling basis. Application fee: $40. Electronic applications accepted. *Financial support:* Fellowships, teaching assistantships available. Financial award application deadline: 3/1. *Unit head:* Dr. Chris Koliba, Co-Director, 802-656-2606.

University of Victoria, Faculty of Graduate Studies, Faculty of Human and Social Development, School of Public Administration, Victoria, BC V8W 2Y2, Canada. Offers dispute resolution (MADR); public administration (MPA, PhD); MPA/LL B. Part-time and evening/weekend programs available. Postbaccalaureate distance learning degree programs offered. *Faculty:* 11 full-time (2 women), 22 part-time/adjunct (4 women). *Students:* 154, 4 international. Average age 28. 205 applicants, 38% accepted, 53 enrolled. In 2007, 27 degrees awarded. *Degree requirements:* For master's, thesis (for some programs), report; for doctorate, thesis/dissertation, candidacy exam. *Entrance requirements:* For master's, GMAT or GRE General Test, professional resumé; for doctorate, GMAT or GRE General Test. Additional exam requirements/recommendations for international students: Required—TOEFL (minimum score 610 paper-based; 255 computer-based). *Application deadline:* For fall admission, 3/15 for domestic students, 12/15 for international students. Applications are processed on a rolling basis. Application fee: $75 ($125 for international students). Electronic applications accepted. *Expenses:* Tuition, state resident: full-time $3,110. International tuition: $3,700 full-time. Tuition and fees vary according to program. *Financial support:* In 2007–08, 3 fellowships (averaging $8,266 per year), 4 teaching assistantships were awarded; research assistantships, career-related internships or fieldwork and institutionally sponsored loans also available. Financial award application deadline: 2/15. *Faculty research:* Policy analysis, local government, performance management, energy markets, labor markets. *Unit head:* Dr. Evert A. Lindquist, Director, 250-721-8084, Fax: 250-721-8849, E-mail: padirect@uvic.ca. *Application contact:* Dr. John Langford, Graduate Adviser, 250-721-8057, Fax: 250-721-8849, E-mail: jlangfor@uvic.ca.

University of West Florida, College of Arts and Sciences: Arts, Department of Government, Pensacola, FL 32514-5750. Offers political science (MA), including public administration, security and diplomacy. Part-time and evening/weekend programs available. *Faculty:* 3 full-time (0 women), 1 part-time/adjunct (0 women). *Students:* 9 full-time (4 women), 9 part-time (1 woman); includes 2 minority (both Hispanic Americans) Average age 32. 25 applicants, 68% accepted, 11 enrolled. In 2007, 8 degrees awarded. *Degree requirements:* For master's, thesis or alternative. *Entrance requirements:* For master's, GRE General Test, minimum GPA of 3.0. Additional exam requirements/recommendations for international students: Required—TOEFL (minimum score 550 paper-based; 213 computer-based). *Application deadline:* For fall admission, 6/1 for domestic students, 5/15 for international students; for spring admission, 11/1 for domestic students, 10/1 for international students. Applications are processed on a rolling basis. Application fee: $30. *Expenses:* Tuition, state resident: full-time $6,054; part-time $252 per credit. Tuition, nonresident: full-time $21,886; part-time $912 per credit. *Financial support:* Fellowships, research assistantships with partial tuition reimbursements, career-related internships or fieldwork, Federal Work-Study, institutionally sponsored loans, and tuition waivers (full and partial) available. Support available to part-time students. Financial award application deadline: 4/15; financial award applicants required to submit FAFSA. *Faculty research:* Political campaigns, elections, law enforcement, growth management. *Unit head:* Dr. A. Cuzan, Chairperson, 850-474-2337.

University of West Florida, College of Professional Studies, Program in Administration, Pensacola, FL 32514-5750. Offers acquisition and contract administration (MSA); biomedical/

pharmaceutical (MSA); criminal justice administration (MSA); education leadership (MSA); healthcare administration (MSA); nursing administration (MSA); public administration (MSA). Part-time and evening/weekend programs available. Postbaccalaureate distance learning degree programs offered (no on-campus study). *Faculty:* 8 full-time (4 women), 2 part-time/adjunct (both women). *Students:* 15 full-time (12 women), 110 part-time (67 women); includes 33 minority (20 African Americans, 3 American Indian/Alaska Native, 4 Asian Americans or Pacific Islanders, 6 Hispanic Americans). Average age 29. 71 applicants, 56% accepted, 32 enrolled. In 2007, 35 degrees awarded. *Entrance requirements:* For master's, GRE General Test, minimum GPA of 3.0. Additional exam requirements/recommendations for international students: Required—TOEFL (minimum score 550 paper-based; 213 computer-based). *Application deadline:* For fall admission, 6/1 for domestic students, 5/15 for international students; for spring admission, 11/1 for domestic students, 10/1 for international students. Applications are processed on a rolling basis. Application fee: $30. *Expenses:* Tuition, state resident: full-time $6,054; part-time $252 per credit. Tuition, nonresident: full-time $21,886; part-time $912 per credit. *Financial support:* Fellowships, career-related internships or fieldwork, scholarships/grants, and unspecified assistantships available. Support available to part-time students. Financial award application deadline: 4/15; financial award applicants required to submit FAFSA. *Unit head:* Dr. Bill Tankersley, MSA Acquisition and Contract Administration Coordinator, 850-474-2338.

University of West Georgia, Graduate School, College of Arts and Sciences, Department of Political Science and Planning, Program in Public Administration, Carrollton, GA 30118. Offers MPA. Part-time programs available. *Students:* 18 full-time (10 women), 9 part-time (4 women); includes 12 minority (all African Americans), 3 international. Average age 28. In 2007, 8 degrees awarded. *Degree requirements:* For master's, exit paper. *Entrance requirements:* For master's, GRE. Additional exam requirements/recommendations for international students: Required—TOEFL. Application fee: $30. Electronic applications accepted. *Expenses:* Tuition, state resident: full-time $2,448; part-time $136 per semester hour. Tuition, nonresident: full-time $9,774; part-time $543 per semester hour. Required fees: $26 per semester hour. $173 per semester. *Financial support:* In 2007–08, 4 research assistantships with full tuition reimbursements (averaging $3,000 per year) were awarded. Financial award applicants required to submit FAFSA. *Faculty research:* Women studies, state and local government, animal rights. *Application contact:* Dr. Charles W. Clark, Interim Dean, 678-839-6508, E-mail: cclark@westga.edu.

University of West Georgia, Graduate School, College of Arts and Sciences, Department of Political Science and Planning, Program in Public Management, Carrollton, GA 30118. Offers Certificate. *Students:* 1 (woman) full-time, 4 part-time (2 women); includes 2 minority (both African Americans) Average age 30. In 2007, 3 degrees awarded. Application fee: $30. *Expenses:* Tuition, state resident: full-time $2,448; part-time $136 per semester hour. Tuition, nonresident: full-time $9,774; part-time $543 per semester hour. Required fees: $26 per semester hour. $173 per semester. *Application contact:* Dr. Charles W. Clark, Interim Dean, 678-839-6508, E-mail: cclark@westga.edu.

The University of Winnipeg, Graduate Studies, Program in Public Administration, Winnipeg, MB R3B 2E9, Canada. Offers MPA. Part-time programs available. *Degree requirements:* For master's, comprehensive exam, thesis optional. *Entrance requirements:* For master's, minimum GPA of 3.0 in last 60 credit hours. *Faculty research:* Policy evaluation, federalism, administrative innovation, administrative ethics, economic development/administration.

University of Wisconsin–Milwaukee, Graduate School, College of Letters and Sciences, Interdepartmental Program in Public Administration, Milwaukee, WI 53201-0413. Offers MPA, MPA/MUP. Part-time programs available. *Faculty:* 11 full-time (2 women). *Students:* 22 full-time (6 women), 23 part-time (10 women); includes 2 minority (both African Americans) 32 applicants, 75% accepted, 12 enrolled. In 2007, 12 degrees awarded. *Degree requirements:* For master's, thesis or alternative. *Entrance requirements:* For master's, GRE General Test, minimum GPA of 3.0. *Application deadline:* For fall admission, 1/1 priority date for domestic students; for spring admission, 9/1 for domestic students. Applications are processed on a rolling basis. Application fee: $45 ($75 for international students). *Expenses:* Tuition, state resident: part-time $530 per credit. Tuition, nonresident: part-time $1,428 per credit. Required fees: $19 per credit. $229 per term. Tuition and fees vary according to course load and program. *Financial support:* Fellowships, research assistantships, teaching assistantships, career-related internships or fieldwork and unspecified assistantships available. Support available to part-time students. Financial award application deadline: 4/15. *Unit head:* Douglas Ihrke, Director, 414-229-4209, Fax: 414-229-5021, E-mail: dihrke@uwm.edu.

University of Wisconsin–Oshkosh, The Office of Graduate Studies, College of Letters and Science, Department of Public Administration, Oshkosh, WI 54901. Offers general agency (MPA); health care (MPA). Part-time and evening/weekend programs available. *Faculty:* 15 full-time (1 woman). *Students:* 50. Average age 42. 14 applicants, 79% accepted. In 2007, 14 degrees awarded. *Degree requirements:* For master's, thesis or alternative. *Entrance requirements:* For master's, public service-related experience, resumé, sample of written work. Additional exam requirements/recommendations for international students: Required—TOEFL (minimum score 550 paper-based; 213 computer-based; 79 iBT). *Application deadline:* Applications are processed on a rolling basis. Application fee: $45. Electronic applications accepted. *Financial support:* Fellowships, research assistantships with partial tuition reimbursements, institutionally sponsored loans, scholarships/grants, tuition waivers (partial), and unspecified assistantships available. Financial award application deadline: 3/15; financial award applicants required to submit FAFSA. *Faculty research:* Drug policy, local government state revenues and expenditures, health care regulation. *Unit head:* Dr. David Jones, Chair, 920-424-3230, E-mail: publicaffairs@uwosh.edu. *Application contact:* Dr. Karen King, Graduate Program Coordinator, 920-424-7360, E-mail: kingk@uwosh.edu.

University of Wyoming, Graduate School, College of Arts and Sciences, Department of Political Science, Program in Public Administration, Laramie, WY 82070. Offers MPA. Part-time programs available. Postbaccalaureate distance learning degree programs offered (minimal on-campus study). *Faculty:* 5 full-time (1 woman). *Students:* 21 full-time (12 women), 29 part-time (15 women); includes 4 minority (1 American Indian/Alaska Native, 3 Hispanic Americans), 1 international. Average age 33. 44 applicants, 68% accepted. In 2007, 16 degrees awarded. *Degree requirements:* For master's, thesis or alternative. *Entrance requirements:* For master's, GRE General Test, minimum GPA of 3.0. Additional exam requirements/recommendations for international students: Required—TOEFL (minimum score 525 paper-based; 195 computer-based). *Application deadline:* For fall admission, 6/1 priority date for domestic students, 5/1 for international students; for spring admission, 10/15 priority date for domestic students, 9/15 for international students. Applications are processed on a rolling basis. Application fee: $50. Electronic applications accepted. *Financial support:* In 2007–08, 3 students received support, including 3 research assistantships with full tuition reimbursements available (averaging $10,062 per year); teaching assistantships, career-related internships or fieldwork and unspecified assistantships also available. Financial award application deadline: 3/15. *Faculty research:* Public policy, public ethics, administrative theory, natural resource policy. *Application contact:* Jamie L. LeJambre, Graduate Coordinator, 307-766-6484, Fax: 307-766-6771, E-mail: lejambre@uwyo.edu.

Upper Iowa University, Online Master's Programs, Fayette, IA 52142-1857. Offers accounting (MBA); corporate financial management (MBA); global business (MBA); health and human services (MPA); homeland security (MPA); human resources management (MBA); justice administration (MPA); organizational development (MBA); public personnel management (MPA); quality management (MBA). MBA also available at Madison, Wisconsin campus. Part-time programs available. Postbaccalaureate distance learning degree programs offered (no on-campus study). *Faculty:* 1 full-time (0 women), 25 part-time/adjunct (12 women). *Students:* 255 full-time (170 women); includes 58 minority (44 African Americans, 1 American Indian/Alaska Native, 7 Asian Americans or Pacific Islanders, 6 Hispanic Americans), 3 international. 127 applicants, 85% accepted, 64 enrolled. In 2007, 72 degrees awarded. *Degree requirements:* For master's, research project. *Entrance requirements:* For master's, GMAT, GRE, or minimum GPA of 2.7 during last 60 hours. Additional exam requirements/recommendations for international students: Required—TOEFL (minimum score 570 paper-based; 230 computer-based). *Application deadline:* Applications are processed on a rolling basis. Application fee: $50. Electronic applications accepted. *Financial support:* In 2007–08, 153 students received support. Available to part-time students. Applicants required to submit FAFSA. *Faculty research:* Total quality management, CQI, teams, organization culture and climate, management. *Application contact:* David Hannum, Online Program Recruiter/Advisor, 866-225-2208, E-mail: hannumd@uiu.edu.

Valdosta State University, Graduate School, College of Arts and Sciences, Department of Political Science, Valdosta, GA 31698. Offers public administration (MPA). *Accreditation:* NASPAA. Part-time and evening/weekend programs available. Postbaccalaureate distance learning degree programs offered (no on-campus study). *Faculty:* 9 full-time (1 woman). *Students:* 66 full-time (29 women), 62 part-time (33 women); includes 38 minority (31 African Americans, 4 Asian Americans or Pacific Islanders, 3 Hispanic Americans). Average age 28. 138 applicants, 49% accepted, 60 enrolled. In 2007, 56 degrees awarded. *Degree requirements:* For master's, comprehensive written and/or oral exams, internship; for doctorate, thesis/dissertation, portfolio/dissertation. *Entrance requirements:* For master's, GMAT, GRE General Test, or MAT, minimum GPA of 2.5; for doctorate, GRE, recommendations. Additional exam requirements/recommendations for international students: Required—TOEFL (minimum score 523 paper-based; 193 computer-based). *Application deadline:* For fall admission, 7/1 for domestic and international students; for spring admission, 11/15 for domestic and international students. Applications are processed on a rolling basis. Application fee: $40. Electronic applications accepted. *Expenses:* Tuition, state resident: part-time $147 per hour. Tuition, nonresident: part-time $586 per hour. Required fees: $520 per semester. Tuition and fees vary according to course level, course load, campus/location and program. *Financial support:* In 2007–08, 3 students received support, including 3 research assistantships with full tuition reimbursements available (averaging $2,452 per year); institutionally sponsored loans, scholarships/grants, and unspecified assistantships also available. Support available to part-time students. Financial award application deadline: 7/1; financial award applicants required to submit FAFSA. *Faculty research:* Powers of state attorneys general; health, transportation, and environmental policy; public administration theory. *Unit head:* Dr. James W Peterson, Head, 229-333-5771, E-mail: jpeterson@valdosta.edu. *Application contact:* Dr. Nolan J Argyle, Coordinator, 229-293-6059, E-mail: nargyle@valdosta.edu.

Villanova University, Graduate School of Liberal Arts and Sciences, Department of Political Science, Program in Public Administration, Villanova, PA 19085-1699. Offers MPA. Part-time and evening/weekend programs available. *Students:* 6 full-time (4 women), 36 part-time (17 women); includes 3 minority (all African Americans), 1 international. Average age 32. 16 applicants, 94% accepted. In 2007, 15 degrees awarded. *Degree requirements:* For master's, comprehensive exam. *Entrance requirements:* For master's, GRE General Test, minimum GPA of 3.0. *Application deadline:* For fall admission, 7/1 for domestic and international students; for spring admission, 12/1 for domestic and international students. Applications are processed on a rolling basis. Application fee: $50. Electronic applications accepted. *Financial support:* Career-related internships or fieldwork and scholarships/grants available. Financial award application deadline: 3/15; financial award applicants required to submit FAFSA.

See Close-Up on page 1173.

Virginia Commonwealth University, Graduate School, College of Humanities and Sciences, Wilder School of Government and Public Affairs, Department of Political Science and Public Administration, Richmond, VA 23284-9005. Offers political science and public administration (MPA); public management (CPM). *Accreditation:* NASPAA (one or more programs are accredited). Part-time programs available. *Faculty:* 12 full-time (3 women). *Students:* 33 full-time (23 women), 61 part-time (43 women); includes 17 minority (13 African Americans, 1 American Indian/Alaska Native, 2 Asian Americans or Pacific Islanders, 1 Hispanic American), 7 international. 77 applicants, 64% accepted, 29 enrolled. In 2007, 48 degrees awarded. *Entrance requirements:* For master's, GRE General Test. *Application deadline:* Applications are processed on a rolling basis. Application fee: $50. *Expenses:* Tuition, state resident: full-time $7,224; part-time $401 per credit. Tuition, nonresident: full-time $16,072; part-time $891 per credit. Required fees: $1,679; $63 per credit. Tuition and fees vary according to campus/location. *Financial support:* Fellowships, career-related internships or fieldwork, Federal Work-Study, institutionally sponsored loans, and tuition waivers (full and partial) available. Support available to part-time students. Financial award application deadline: 3/1. *Faculty research:* Public human resources management, financial management, executive management, policy analysis, local government management. *Unit head:* Dr. Russell A. Cargo, Acting Chair, 804-828-2545, Fax: 804-828-7463, E-mail: racargo@vcu.edu. *Application contact:* Dr. Janet S. Hutchinson, Graduate Program Director, 804-828-1046, Fax: 804-828-7463, E-mail: jhutch@vcu.edu.

Virginia Polytechnic Institute and State University, Graduate School, College of Architecture and Urban Studies, Center for Public Administration and Policy, Blacksburg, VA 24061-0205. Offers MPA, PhD, CAGS. *Accreditation:* NASPAA (one or more programs are accredited). *Entrance requirements:* For master's and doctorate, GRE General Test, GMAT. Additional exam requirements/recommendations for international students: Required—TOEFL (minimum score 550 paper-based; 213 computer-based). Electronic applications accepted. *Faculty research:* Public administration theory, strategic management, ethics, the Constitution, computer-assisted creativity.

Walden University, Graduate Programs, School of Public Policy and Administration, Minneapolis, MN 55401. Offers criminal justice (MPA, PhD); health services (MPA, PhD); homeland security policy and coordination (MPA, PhD); international nongovernmental organizations (MPA, PhD); knowledge management (MPA, PhD); nonprofit management and leadership (MPA, PhD); public management and leadership (MPA, PhD); public policy (MPA, PhD); public safety management (MPA, PhD). Part-time and evening/weekend programs available. Postbaccalaureate distance learning degree programs offered (minimal on-campus study). *Students:* 433 full-time (228 women), 148 part-time (79 women); includes 265 minority (234 African Americans, 6 American Indian/Alaska Native, 11 Asian Americans or Pacific Islanders, 14 Hispanic Americans), 4 international. Average age 42. 475 applicants, 76% accepted, 220 enrolled. In 2007, 71 master's, 7 doctorates awarded. *Degree requirements:* For doctorate, thesis/dissertation. *Entrance requirements:* For master's, minimum GPA of 3.0; for doctorate, 3 years of professional experience, master's degree. Additional exam requirements/recommendations for international students: Required—TOEFL (minimum score 550 paper-based; 213 computer-based), IELTS (minimum score 7). *Application deadline:* For fall admission, 8/15 priority date for domestic and international students; for winter admission, 11/15 priority date for domestic and international students; for spring admission, 12/15 priority date for domestic and international students. Applications are processed on a rolling basis. Application fee: $50. Electronic applications accepted. *Financial support:* Fellowships with partial tuition reimbursements, Federal Work-Study, institutionally sponsored loans, scholarships/grants, and unspecified assistantships available. Financial award application deadline: 6/1; financial award applicants required to submit FAFSA. *Unit head:* Gary Kelsey, Associate Dean, 800-925-3368, Fax: 612-338-5092. *Application contact:* 866-4-WALDEN, Fax: 410-843-8780, E-mail: request@waldenu.edu.

Wayland Baptist University, Graduate Programs, Program in Counseling, Plainview, TX 79072-6998. Offers counseling (MA); government administration (MPA); justice administration (MPA). Part-time and evening/weekend programs available. Postbaccalaureate distance learning degree programs offered. *Faculty:* 2 full-time (1 woman), 2 part-time/adjunct (1 woman). *Students:* 2 full-time (both women), 78 part-time (64 women); includes 16 minority (1 African American, 15 Hispanic Americans). Average age 33. 42 applicants, 100% accepted. *Degree requirements:* For master's, comprehensive exam. *Entrance requirements:* For master's, GRE, MAT. Application fee: $35. *Expenses:* Tuition: Full-time $6,390; part-time $355 per credit hour.

Public Administration

Wayland Baptist University (continued)

Required fees: $600; $50 per term. Full-time tuition and fees vary according to course load. *Financial support:* Federal Work-Study, institutionally sponsored loans, and scholarships/grants available. Support available to part-time students. Financial award application deadline: 5/1; financial award applicants required to submit FAFSA. *Unit head:* Dr. Estelle Owens, Chairman, 806-291-1171, Fax: 806-291-1972, E-mail: owensest@wbu.edu.

Wayne State University, College of Liberal Arts and Sciences, Department of Political Science, Program in Public Administration, Detroit, MI 48202. Offers criminal justice (MPA); public administration (MPA). *Accreditation:* NASPAA. Evening/weekend programs available. *Students:* 17 full-time (12 women), 63 part-time (42 women); includes 34 minority (30 African Americans, 1 American Indian/Alaska Native, 1 Asian American or Pacific Islander, 2 Hispanic Americans), 4 international. Average age 29. 57 applicants, 60% accepted, 26 enrolled. In 2007, 18 degrees awarded. *Entrance requirements:* For master's, GRE General Test. Additional exam requirements/recommendations for international students: Required—TOEFL (minimum score 550 paper-based; 213 computer-based); Recommended—TWE (minimum score 6). *Application deadline:* For fall admission, 7/1 for domestic students, 6/1 for international students; for winter admission, 10/1 for international students; for spring admission, 2/1 for international students. Applications are processed on a rolling basis. Application fee: $30 ($50 for international students). Electronic applications accepted. *Expenses:* Tuition, state resident: part-time $403 per credit hour. Tuition, nonresident: part-time $890 per credit hour. *Faculty research:* Urban politics, urban education, state administration. *Unit head:* John Strate, Director, 313-577-2639, E-mail: jstrate@wayne.edu.

Webster University, School of Business and Technology, Department of Management, St. Louis, MO 63119-3194. Offers business and organizational security management (MA); computer resources and information management (MA); environmental management (MS); health care management (MA); health services management (MA); human resources development (MA); human resources management (MA); management (DM); management and leadership (MA); marketing (MA); procurement and acquisitions management (MA); public administration (MA); quality management (MA); space systems operations management (MS); telecommunications management (MA). Part-time and evening/weekend programs available. Postbaccalaureate distance learning degree programs offered (no on-campus study). *Students:* 1,368 full-time (657 women), 4,911 part-time (2,697 women); includes 3,131 minority (2,475 African Americans, 40 American Indian/Alaska Native, 169 Asian Americans or Pacific Islanders, 447 Hispanic Americans), 120 international. Average age 37. In 2007, 9 degrees awarded. *Degree requirements:* For doctorate, thesis/dissertation, written exam. *Entrance requirements:* For doctorate, GMAT, 3 years of work experience, MBA. *Application deadline:* Applications are processed on a rolling basis. Application fee: $25 ($50 for international students). *Expenses:* Tuition: Full-time $9,360; part-time $520 per credit. *Financial support:* Federal Work-Study available. Support available to part-time students. Financial award application deadline: 4/1; financial award applicants required to submit FAFSA. *Unit head:* Jeffrey Haldeman, Chair, 314-961-2660 Ext. 7552, Fax: 314-968-7077, E-mail: mgtchair@webster.edu. *Application contact:* Director of Graduate and Evening Student Admissions, Fax: 314-968-7116, E-mail: gadmit@webster.edu.

West Chester University of Pennsylvania, Office of Graduate Studies and Extended Education, College of Business and Public Affairs, Program in Administration, West Chester, PA 19383. Offers human resource management (MSA, Certificate); individualized (MSA); leadership for women (MSA); long-term health care (MSA); non profit administration (Certificate); public administration (MSA); regional planning (MSA); sport and athletic training (MSA); training and development (MSA). Part-time and evening/weekend programs available. *Students:* 5 full-time (all women), 24 part-time (18 women); includes 5 minority (3 African Americans, 1 Asian American or Pacific Islander, 1 Hispanic American), 1 international. Average age 30. 14 applicants, 86% accepted, 7 enrolled. In 2007, 14 degrees awarded. *Degree requirements:* For master's, comprehensive exam. *Entrance requirements:* For master's, GMAT, GRE General Test, or MAT, interview, minimum GPA of 3.0. Additional exam requirements/recommendations for international students: Required—TOEFL (minimum score 550 paper-based; 213 computer-based; 80 iBT). *Application deadline:* For fall admission, 4/15 priority date for domestic students; for spring admission, 10/15 for domestic students. Applications are processed on a rolling basis. Application fee: $35. *Expenses:* Tuition, state resident: part-time $345 per credit. Tuition, nonresident: part-time $552 per credit. Tuition and fees vary according to course load. *Financial support:* In 2007–08, 2 research assistantships with full and partial tuition reimbursements (averaging $5,000 per year) were awarded; career-related internships or fieldwork and unspecified assistantships also available. Support available to part-time students. Financial award application deadline: 2/15; financial award applicants required to submit FAFSA. *Unit head:* Dr. Lorraine Bernotsky, Director and Graduate Coordinator, 610-425-5000, E-mail: lbernotsky@wcupa.edu.

Western Illinois University, School of Graduate Studies, College of Arts and Sciences, Department of Political Science, Macomb, IL 61455-1390. Offers political science (MA); public and non-profit management (Certificate). Part-time programs available. *Students:* 13 full-time (5 women), 9 part-time (2 women); includes 4 minority (3 African Americans, 1 Hispanic American), 5 international. Average age 26. 20 applicants, 55% accepted. In 2007, 8 master's, 1 other advanced degree awarded. *Degree requirements:* For master's, comprehensive exam, thesis or alternative. *Entrance requirements:* For master's, minimum GPA of 2.75. Additional exam requirements/recommendations for international students: Required—TOEFL (minimum score 550 paper-based; 213 computer-based; 80 iBT). *Application deadline:* Applications are processed on a rolling basis. Electronic applications accepted. *Expenses:* Tuition, state resident: part-time $217 per credit hour. Tuition, nonresident: part-time $433 per credit hour. Required fees: $54 per credit hour. *Financial support:* In 2007–08, 8 students received support, including 8 research assistantships with full tuition reimbursements available (averaging $6,800 per year). Financial award applicants required to submit FAFSA. *Unit head:* Dr. Richard Hardy, Chairperson, 309-298-1055. *Application contact:* Dr. Barbara Baily, Director of Graduate Studies/Associate Provost, 309-298-1806, Fax: 309-298-2345, E-mail: grad-office@wiu.edu.

Western International University, Graduate Programs in Business, Program in Public Administration, Phoenix, AZ 85021-2718. Offers MPA. Evening/weekend programs available. *Faculty:* 183 part-time/adjunct (54 women). *Students:* 40 full-time (23 women); includes 8 minority (1 African American, 1 American Indian/Alaska Native, 6 Hispanic Americans). Average age 33. In 2007, 17 degrees awarded. *Degree requirements:* For master's, thesis. *Entrance requirements:* For master's, minimum GPA of 2.75. *Application deadline:* Applications are processed on a rolling basis. Application fee: $85 ($100 for international students). *Expenses:* Tuition: Full-time $10,200; part-time $425 per credit. Tuition and fees vary according to degree level. *Financial support:* Career-related internships or fieldwork, institutionally sponsored loans, and scholarships/grants available. Support available to part-time students. Financial award applicants required to submit FAFSA. *Unit head:* Dwight Galda, Head. *Application contact:* Karen Janitell, Director of Enrollment, 602-943-2311 Ext. 1063, Fax: 602-371-8637, E-mail: karen_janitell@apollogrp.edu.

Western Michigan University, Graduate College, College of Arts and Sciences, Department of Political Science, Program in Development Administration, Kalamazoo, MI 49008-5202. Offers MDA.

Western Michigan University, Graduate College, College of Arts and Sciences, School of Public Affairs and Administration, Kalamazoo, MI 49008-5202. Offers MPA, DPA. *Accreditation:* NASPAA (one or more programs are accredited). *Degree requirements:* For doctorate, thesis/dissertation, oral exams. *Entrance requirements:* For doctorate, GRE General Test.

West Virginia University, Eberly College of Arts and Sciences, School of Applied Social Sciences, Division of Public Administration, Morgantown, WV 26506. Offers legal studies (MLS); public administration (MPA); JD/MPA; MSW/MPA. *Accreditation:* NASPAA. Part-time programs available. *Faculty:* 5 full-time (1 woman), 3 part-time/adjunct (2 women). *Students:* 62 full-time (39 women), 41 part-time (23 women); includes 7 minority (3 African Americans, 3 Asian Americans or Pacific Islanders, 1 Hispanic American), 6 international. Average age 31. 74 applicants, 55% accepted, 25 enrolled. In 2007, 39 degrees awarded. *Degree requirements:* For master's, internship. *Entrance requirements:* For master's, GRE General Test, minimum GPA of 2.75. Additional exam requirements/recommendations for international students: Required—TOEFL. *Application deadline:* For fall admission, 4/1 priority date for domestic and international students; for spring admission, 10/15 priority date for domestic and international students. Applications are processed on a rolling basis. Application fee: $50. Electronic applications accepted. *Expenses:* Tuition, state resident: full-time $5,196; part-time $292 per credit hour. Tuition, nonresident: full-time $15,064; part-time $840 per credit hour. Tuition and fees vary according to program. *Financial support:* In 2007–08, 72 students received support, including 7 research assistantships (averaging $9,000 per year), 7 teaching assistantships (averaging $9,000 per year); career-related internships or fieldwork, Federal Work-Study, institutionally sponsored loans, tuition waivers (full and partial), and graduate administrative assistantships also available. Financial award application deadline: 2/1; financial award applicants required to submit FAFSA. *Faculty research:* Public management and organization, conflict resolution, work satisfaction, health administration, social policy and welfare. *Application contact:* Deborah Koon, Administrative Associate, 304-293-2614 Ext. 3150, Fax: 304-293-8814, E-mail: debbie.koon@mail.wvu.edu.

Wichita State University, Graduate School, Fairmount College of Liberal Arts and Sciences, Hugo Wall School of Urban and Public Affairs, Wichita, KS 67260. Offers public administration (MPA). *Accreditation:* NASPAA. Part-time programs available. *Degree requirements:* For master's, thesis optional. *Entrance requirements:* For master's, GRE. Additional exam requirements/recommendations for international students: Required—TOEFL. Electronic applications accepted.

Widener University, College of Arts and Sciences, Program in Public Administration, Chester, PA 19013-5792. Offers MPA, Psy D/MPA. Part-time and evening/weekend programs available. *Faculty:* 1 full-time (0 women), 3 part-time/adjunct (0 women). *Students:* 3 full-time (2 women), 24 part-time (12 women); includes 9 minority (all African Americans) Average age 28. 21 applicants, 86% accepted. In 2007, 7 degrees awarded. *Degree requirements:* For master's, thesis or comprehensive exam. *Entrance requirements:* For master's, minimum undergraduate GPA of 3.0. *Application deadline:* For fall admission, 8/1 priority date for domestic students; for spring admission, 12/1 priority date for domestic students. Applications are processed on a rolling basis. Application fee: $25 ($300 for international students). Electronic applications accepted. *Expenses: Contact institution.* Tuition and fees vary according to course load and program. *Financial support:* In 2007–08, 8 students received support. Career-related internships or fieldwork and institutionally sponsored loans available. Support available to part-time students. Financial award application deadline: 5/1. *Faculty research:* Intergovernmental relations, nonprofit organizations, public policy, political economy, bureaucratic politics. *Unit head:* Dr. James E. Vike, Director, 610-499-1120, Fax: 610-499-4603, E-mail: james.vike@widener.edu.

Willamette University, George H. Atkinson Graduate School of Management, Salem, OR 97301-3931. Offers early career MBA (full-time) (MBA), including business, government, not-for-profit management; MBA for professionals (part-time) (MBA), including business, government, not-for-profit management; JD/MBA. *Accreditation:* AACSB; NASPAA. Part-time and evening/weekend programs available. *Faculty:* 13 full-time (3 women), 13 part-time/adjunct (1 woman). *Students:* 131 full-time (49 women), 98 part-time (39 women); includes 27 minority (2 American Indian/Alaska Native, 15 Asian Americans or Pacific Islanders, 10 Hispanic Americans), 34 international. 194 applicants, 89% accepted, 102 enrolled. In 2007, 58 degrees awarded. *Entrance requirements:* For master's, GMAT. Additional exam requirements/recommendations for international students: Required—TOEFL (minimum score: 570 paper-based, 230 computer-based, 88 iBT) or IELTS (6.5). *Application deadline:* For fall admission, 1/9 priority date for domestic and international students; for winter admission, 3/1 priority date for domestic and international students; for spring admission, 5/1 priority date for domestic and international students. Applications are processed on a rolling basis. Application fee: $50. Electronic applications accepted. *Expenses: Contact institution. Financial support:* In 2007–08, 180 students received support, including 12 research assistantships (averaging $1,500 per year); career-related internships or fieldwork, Federal Work-Study, scholarships/grants, and unspecified assistantships also available. Financial award application deadline: 5/1; financial award applicants required to submit FAFSA. *Faculty research:* General management, finance, marketing, public management, human resources. *Unit head:* Debra J. Ringold, Dean, 503-370-6440, Fax: 503-370-3011, E-mail: dringold@willamette.edu. *Application contact:* Judy O'Neill, Director of Admission, 503-370-6167, Fax: 503-370-3011, E-mail: joneill@willamette.edu.

Wilmington University, Division of Business, New Castle, DE 19720-6491. Offers business administration (MBA); finance (MBA); health care administration (MBA, MS); homeland security (MBA, MS); human resource management (MS); management (MS); management information systems (MBA); organizational leadership (MS); public administration (MS); transportation and logistics (MBA, MS). Part-time and evening/weekend programs available. *Faculty:* 4 full-time (0 women). *Students:* 232 full-time (117 women), 503 part-time (326 women); includes 97 minority (83 African Americans, 6 Asian Americans or Pacific Islanders, 8 Hispanic Americans). Average age 34. 396 applicants, 100% accepted, 259 enrolled. In 2007, 290 degrees awarded. *Entrance requirements:* Additional exam requirements/recommendations for international students: Required—TOEFL (minimum score 500 paper-based; 173 computer-based). *Application deadline:* Applications are processed on a rolling basis. Application fee: $25. Electronic applications accepted. *Expenses:* Tuition: Full-time $6,246; part-time $1,041 per course. Tuition and fees vary according to degree level and campus/location. *Financial support:* Applicants required to submit FAFSA. *Unit head:* Dr. Robert Edelson, Chair, 302-295-1147, Fax: 302-328-7021, E-mail: robert.e.edelson@wilmcoll.edu. *Application contact:* Chris Ferguson, Director of Admissions, 302-356-4636 Ext. 256, Fax: 302-328-5164, E-mail: inquire@wilmcoll.edu.

Wright State University, School of Graduate Studies, College of Liberal Arts, Department of Urban Affairs and Geography, Dayton, OH 45435. Offers public administration (MPA). *Accreditation:* NASPAA. *Degree requirements:* For master's, thesis optional. *Entrance requirements:* For master's, interview, minimum GPA of 2.7. Additional exam requirements/recommendations for international students: Required—TOEFL. *Faculty research:* Strategic planning, economic development, housing and public management.

York University, Faculty of Graduate Studies, Atkinson Faculty of Liberal and Professional Studies, Program in Public Policy, Administration and Law, Toronto, ON M3J 1P3, Canada. Offers MPPAL.

Public Affairs

American University, School of Communication, Program in Journalism and Public Affairs, Washington, DC 20016-8001. Offers broadcast journalism (MA), including economic journalism, international journalism, public policy journalism; print journalism (MA), including economic journalism, international journalism, public policy journalism. *Accreditation:* ACEJMC. Part-time and evening/weekend programs available. *Faculty:* 13 full-time (5 women), 4 part-time/adjunct (all women). *Students:* 36 full-time (31 women); includes 10 minority (7 African Americans, 3 Asian Americans or Pacific Islanders), 10 international. 190 applicants, 63% accepted, 35 enrolled. In 2007, 40 degrees awarded. *Degree requirements:* For master's, comprehensive exam, thesis or alternative. *Entrance requirements:* For master's, GRE General Test. Additional exam requirements/recommendations for international students: Required—TOEFL (minimum score 600 paper-based; 250 computer-based). *Application deadline:* For fall admission, 2/1 priority date for domestic students, 4/1 priority date for international students. Applications are processed on a rolling basis. Application fee: $50. Electronic applications accepted. *Expenses:* Tuition: Full-time $19,998; part-time $1,111 per credit hour. Required fees: $380. Tuition and fees vary according to program. *Financial support:* In 2007–08, 3 fellowships with partial tuition reimbursements (averaging $27,000 per year), 14 research assistantships with tuition reimbursements (averaging $7,000 per year), 3 teaching assistantships with tuition reimbursements (averaging $7,000 per year) were awarded; career-related internships or fieldwork, Federal Work-Study, institutionally sponsored loans, scholarships/grants, tuition waivers (partial), and unspecified assistantships also available. Financial award application deadline: 2/1. *Faculty research:* Government and media effects of journalistic practices and policies, race and gender and the media, investigative reporting, computer assisted reporting. *Unit head:* Wendell Cochran, Division Director, 202-885-2072. *Application contact:* Sharmeen Ahsan-Bracciale, Graduate Admissions Office, 202-885-2040, Fax: 202-885-2019, E-mail: sharmeen@american.edu.

See Close-Up on page 881.

Arizona State University, Graduate College, College of Public Programs, School of Public Affairs, Tempe, AZ 85287. Offers MPA, PhD. *Accreditation:* NASPAA (one or more programs are accredited). *Degree requirements:* For doctorate, thesis/dissertation. *Entrance requirements:* For master's, GRE.

Concordia University, School of Graduate Studies, Faculty of Arts and Science, School of Community and Public Affairs, Montréal, QC H3G 1M8, Canada. Offers community economic development (Diploma).

Cornell University, Graduate School, Graduate Fields of Arts and Sciences, Field of Public Affairs, Ithaca, NY 14853-0001. Offers public affairs (MPA); public policy (MPA). *Faculty:* 110 full-time (32 women). *Students:* 153 full-time (85 women); includes 234 minority (11 African Americans, 9 Asian Americans or Pacific Islanders, 214 Hispanic Americans), 55 international. Average age 26. 202 applicants, 68% accepted, 70 enrolled. In 2007, 59 degrees awarded. *Degree requirements:* For master's, thesis, research project, paper. *Entrance requirements:* For master's, GRE General Test, 2 letters of recommendation. Additional exam requirements/recommendations for international students: Required—TOEFL (minimum score 550 paper-based; 213 computer-based; 77 iBT), GRE Subject Test in writing. *Application deadline:* Applications are processed on a rolling basis. Application fee: $70. Electronic applications accepted. *Financial support:* In 2007–08, 127 students received support, including 117 fellowships with full tuition reimbursements available, 1 research assistantship with full tuition reimbursement available, 9 teaching assistantships with full tuition reimbursements available; institutionally sponsored loans, scholarships/grants, health care benefits, tuition waivers (full and partial), and unspecified assistantships also available. Financial award applicants required to submit FAFSA. *Unit head:* Director of Graduate Studies, 607-255-8018, Fax: 607-255-5240. *Application contact:* Graduate Field Assistant, 607-255-8018, Fax: 607-255-5240, E-mail: cipa@cornell.edu.

See Close-Up on page 1589.

DePaul University, School of Public Service, Chicago, IL 60604-2287. Offers financial administration management (Certificate); health administration (Certificate); health law and policy (MS); international public services (MS); metropolitan planning (Certificate); public administration (MS); public service management (MS), including association management, fundraising and philanthropy, healthcare administration, higher education administration, metropolitan planning, non-profit administration, public administration, public policy; public services (Certificate); JD/MS; MA/MS. Part-time and evening/weekend programs available. Postbaccalaureate distance learning degree programs offered (minimal on-campus study). *Faculty:* 11 full-time (2 women), 19 part-time/adjunct (16 women). *Students:* 139 full-time (108 women), 245 part-time (178 women); includes 121 minority (76 African Americans, 2 American Indian/Alaska Native, 15 Asian Americans or Pacific Islanders, 28 Hispanic Americans), 11 international. 140 applicants, 96% accepted, 96 enrolled. In 2007, 89 degrees awarded. *Degree requirements:* For master's, thesis or integrative seminar. *Entrance requirements:* For master's, minimum GPA of 2.7. Additional exam requirements/recommendations for international students: Required—TOEFL (minimum score 550 paper-based; 213 computer-based; 80 iBT), IELTS (minimum score 7). *Application deadline:* Applications are processed on a rolling basis. Application fee: $25. Electronic applications accepted. *Financial support:* In 2007–08, 28 students received support, including 3 research assistantships with full tuition reimbursements available (averaging $7,000 per year); career-related internships or fieldwork, Federal Work-Study, institutionally sponsored loans, scholarships/grants, and tuition waivers (partial) also available. Support available to part-time students. Financial award application deadline: 7/1; financial award applicants required to submit FAFSA. *Faculty research:* Government financing, transportation, leadership, health care, volunteerism and organizational behavior, non-profit organizations. Total annual research expenditures: $20,000. *Unit head:* Dr. J. Patrick Murphy, Director, 312-362-5608, Fax: 312-362-5506, E-mail: jpmurphy@depaul.edu. *Application contact:* Megan B. Balderston, Director of Admissions and Marketing, 312-362-5565, Fax: 312-362-5506, E-mail: pubserv@depaul.edu.

George Mason University, College of Humanities and Social Sciences, Department of Public and International Affairs, Fairfax, VA 22030. Offers biodefense (MS, PhD); political science (MA, PhD); public administration (MPA). *Accreditation:* NASPAA (one or more programs are accredited). *Faculty:* 40 full-time (14 women), 48 part-time/adjunct (11 women). *Students:* 59 full-time (41 women), 214 part-time (146 women); includes 46 minority (18 African Americans, 1 American Indian/Alaska Native, 15 Asian Americans or Pacific Islanders, 12 Hispanic Americans), 7 international. Average age 30. 492 applicants, 55% accepted, 172 enrolled. In 2007, 99 degrees awarded. *Entrance requirements:* For master's, GRE General Test, minimum GPA of 3.0 in last 60 hours of course work. *Application deadline:* For fall admission, 5/1 for domestic students; for spring admission, 11/1 for domestic students. Application fee: $60 ($75 for international students). Electronic applications accepted. *Financial support:* Fellowships, research assistantships, teaching assistantships available. Support available to part-time students. Financial award application deadline: 3/1; financial award applicants required to submit FAFSA. *Unit head:* Dr. Robert Dudley, Chair, 703-993-1400, Fax: 703-993-1399, E-mail: rdudley@gmu.edu. *Application contact:* Dr. Ming Wan, Information Contact, 703-993-2955, Fax: 703-993-1399, E-mail: mpa@gmu.edu.

Georgia College & State University, Graduate School, School of Liberal Arts and Sciences, Department of Government and Sociology, Program in Public Administration and Public Affairs, Milledgeville, GA 31061. Offers MPA. *Accreditation:* NASPAA. Part-time and evening/weekend programs available. *Students:* 30 full-time (19 women), 52 part-time (28 women); includes 23 minority (21 African Americans, 2 Asian Americans or Pacific Islanders), 3 international. Average age 29. 54 applicants, 61% accepted, 26 enrolled. In 2007, 29 degrees awarded. *Degree requirements:* For master's, thesis optional, capstone project. *Entrance requirements:* For master's, GRE. Additional exam requirements/recommendations for international students: Required—TOEFL. *Application deadline:* For fall admission, 7/1 priority date for domestic students. Applications are processed on a rolling basis. Application fee: $25. Electronic applications accepted. *Expenses:* Tuition, state resident: full-time $3,726. Tuition, nonresident: full-time $14,868. Required fees: $858. Tuition and fees vary according to campus/location. *Financial support:* In 2007–08, 11 research assistantships were awarded; career-related internships or fieldwork, Federal Work-Study, and unspecified assistantships also available. Support available to part-time students. Financial award application deadline: 3/1; financial award applicants required to submit FAFSA. *Unit head:* Dr. Jerry Herbel, Coordinator of MPA Program, 478-445-7393, E-mail: jerry.herbel@gcsu.edu.

Howard University, Graduate School, Department of Political Science, Program in Public Affairs, Washington, DC 20059-0002. Offers MA. *Degree requirements:* For master's, one foreign language, comprehensive exam, thesis. *Entrance requirements:* For master's, GRE General Test, minimum GPA of 3.0. *Expenses:* Tuition: Full-time $16,175; part-time $899 per credit hour. Required fees: $805.

Indiana University Bloomington, School of Public and Environmental Affairs, Public Affairs Programs, Bloomington, IN 47405-7000. Offers nonprofit management (Certificate); public affairs (MPA, PhD); public management (Certificate); public policy (PhD); JD/MPA; MPA/MA; MPA/MIS; MPA/MLS; MSES/MPA. *Accreditation:* NASPAA (one or more programs are accredited). Part-time programs available. Terminal master's awarded for partial completion of doctoral program. *Degree requirements:* For doctorate, thesis/dissertation. *Entrance requirements:* For master's, GMAT or GRE, LSAT; for doctorate, GRE General Test. *Application deadline:* For fall admission, 2/1 priority date for domestic students, 1/15 for international students; for spring admission, 9/1 for international students. Applications are processed on a rolling basis. Application fee: $50 ($60 for international students). *Financial support:* Fellowships, research assistantships, teaching assistantships, career-related internships or fieldwork, Federal Work-Study, institutionally sponsored loans, and unspecified assistantships available. Financial award application deadline: 2/1; financial award applicants required to submit FAFSA. *Faculty research:* Comparative and international affairs, environmental policy and resource management, policy analysis, public finance, public management, urban management, nonprofit management. *Application contact:* Charles A. Johnson, Coordinator of Student Recruitment, 800-765-7755, Fax: 812-855-7802, E-mail: speainfo@indiana.edu.

See Close-Up on page 1597.

Indiana University Northwest, School of Public and Environmental Affairs, Gary, IN 46408-1197. Offers criminal justice (MPA); environmental affairs (Graduate Certificate); health services administration (MPA); human services administration (MPA); nonprofit management (Graduate Certificate); public management (MPA, Graduate Certificate). *Accreditation:* NASPAA (one or more programs are accredited). Part-time programs available. *Faculty:* 5 full-time (3 women). *Students:* 28 full-time (21 women), 98 part-time (78 women); includes 82 minority (71 African Americans, 1 American Indian/Alaska Native, 1 Asian American or Pacific Islander, 9 Hispanic Americans). Average age 38. In 2007, 29 master's, 27 other advanced degrees awarded. *Entrance requirements:* For master's, GRE General Test or GMAT, letters of recommendation. *Application deadline:* For fall admission, 8/15 priority date for domestic students. Applications are processed on a rolling basis. Application fee: $25. *Expenses:* Tuition, state resident: full-time $4,636; part-time $193 per credit hour. Tuition, nonresident: full-time $10,787; part-time $449 per credit hour. Required fees: $436; $436 per year. Full-time tuition and fees vary according to course load, campus/location and program. *Financial support:* Career-related internships or fieldwork, Federal Work-Study, and tuition waivers (partial) available. Support available to part-time students. Financial award application deadline: 3/1. *Faculty research:* Employment in income security policies, evidence in criminal justice, equal employment law, social welfare policy and welfare reform, public finance in developing countries. *Unit head:* George Assibey-Mensah, Interim Dean/Division Director, 219-980-6695, Fax: 219-980-6737. *Application contact:* Sandra Hall Smith, Secretary, 219-980-6695, Fax: 219-980-6737, E-mail: shsmith@iun.edu.

Indiana University of Pennsylvania, School of Graduate Studies and Research, College of Humanities and Social Sciences, Department of Political Science, Program in Public Affairs, Indiana, PA 15705-1087. Offers MA. Part-time programs available. *Faculty:* 5 full-time (3 women). *Students:* 10 full-time (2 women), 6 part-time (2 women); includes 1 minority (African American), 3 international. Average age 30. 9 applicants, 67% accepted, 5 enrolled. In 2007, 8 degrees awarded. *Degree requirements:* For master's, thesis optional. *Entrance requirements:* For master's, GRE, 2 letters of recommendation. Additional exam requirements/recommendations for international students: Required—TOEFL. *Application deadline:* For fall admission, 7/1 priority date for domestic students; for spring admission, 11/1 for domestic students. Applications are processed on a rolling basis. Application fee: $30. *Expenses:* Tuition, state resident: full-time $6,214; part-time $345 per credit. Tuition, nonresident: full-time $9,944; part-time $552 per credit. Required fees: $43 per credit. One-time fee: $140 part-time. Tuition and fees vary according to course load. *Financial support:* In 2007–08, 7 research assistantships with full and partial tuition reimbursements (averaging $2,495 per year) were awarded. Financial award application deadline: 3/15; financial award applicants required to submit FAFSA. *Unit head:* Dr. Gaurdat Bahgat, Graduate Coordinator, 724-357-2776.

Indiana University–Purdue University Fort Wayne, Division of Public and Environmental Affairs, Fort Wayne, IN 46805-1499. Offers public affairs (MPA); public management (MPM, Certificate). *Accreditation:* NASPAA (one or more programs are accredited). Part-time programs available. *Faculty:* 8 full-time (2 women). *Students:* 6 full-time (4 women), 41 part-time (32 women); includes 5 minority (3 African Americans, 1 Asian American or Pacific Islander, 1 Hispanic American). Average age 33. 26 applicants, 81% accepted, 17 enrolled. In 2007, 14 degrees awarded. *Degree requirements:* For master's, internship. *Entrance requirements:* For master's, GRE General Test or GMAT, minimum GPA of 3.0, 3 letters of reference. Additional exam requirements/recommendations for international students: Required—TOEFL (minimum score 550 paper-based; 213 computer-based; 77 iBT). *Application deadline:* For fall admission, 8/1 priority date for domestic students; for spring admission, 12/1 for domestic students. Applications are processed on a rolling basis. Application fee: $30. *Expenses:* Tuition, state resident: full-time $4,203; part-time $234 per credit. Tuition, nonresident: full-time $9,761; part-time $542 per credit. Required fees: $466; $26 per credit. Tuition and fees vary according to course load. *Financial support:* In 2007–08, 1 teaching assistantship with partial tuition reimbursement (averaging $12,310 per year) was awarded; career-related internships or fieldwork and scholarships/grants also available. Support available to part-time students. Financial award application deadline: 3/1; financial award applicants required to submit FAFSA. *Faculty research:* Fort Wayne history, global rating process of health care, euthanasia, mail survey response rates. *Unit head:* Dr. Jane Grant, Interim Assistant Dean and Graduate Program Director, 260-481-6349, Fax: 260-481-6346, E-mail: grant@ipfw.edu.

Indiana University–Purdue University Indianapolis, School of Public and Environmental Affairs, Indianapolis, IN 46202-2896. Offers health administration (MHA); public affairs (MPA), including criminal justice, environmental management, nonprofit management, policy analysis, public management; JD/MHA; MBA/MHA; MLS/NMC; MLS/PMC; MSN/MHA. *Accreditation:* CAHME (one or more programs are accredited). Part-time and evening/weekend programs available. *Faculty:* 17 full-time (6 women). *Students:* 108 full-time (67 women), 291 part-time (159 women); includes 74 minority (43 African Americans, 1 American Indian/Alaska Native, 25 Asian Americans or Pacific Islanders, 5 Hispanic Americans), 10 international. Average age 35. In 2007, 77 degrees awarded. *Entrance requirements:* For master's, GRE General Test, minimum GPA of 3.0 (preferred). Additional exam requirements/recommendations for international students: Required—TOEFL. *Application deadline:* For fall admission, 7/15 priority date for domestic students; for spring admission, 11/15 for domestic students. Applications are processed on a rolling basis. Application fee: $50 ($60 for international students).

Public Affairs

Indiana University–Purdue University Indianapolis (continued)
Expenses: Tuition, state resident: full-time $5,818; part-time $242 per credit hour. Tuition, nonresident: full-time $17,106; part-time $713 per credit hour. Required fees: $629. Tuition and fees vary according to course load, campus/location and program. *Financial support:* In 2007–08, 11 fellowships with full and partial tuition reimbursements (averaging $5,890 per year), 10 teaching assistantships (averaging $9,900 per year) were awarded; research assistantships with full and partial tuition reimbursements, career-related internships or fieldwork, Federal Work-Study, institutionally sponsored loans, and scholarships/grants also available. Support available to part-time students. Financial award application deadline: 3/1. *Faculty research:* Economic development, water and air quality, ethics, financing, organization design and structure. Total annual research expenditures: $1.9 million. *Unit head:* Dr. Greg Lindsey, Associate Dean, 317-274-4656, Fax: 317-274-5153. *Application contact:* 317-274-4656, Fax: 317-274-5153, E-mail: speainfo@speanet.iupui.edu.

See Close-Up on page 1599.

Indiana University South Bend, School of Public and Environmental Affairs, South Bend, IN 46634-7111. Offers health systems administration and policy (MPA); health systems management (Certificate); nonprofit management (Certificate); public and community services administration and policy (MPA); public management (Certificate); urban affairs (Certificate). *Accreditation:* NASPAA. Part-time and evening/weekend programs available. *Faculty:* 4 full-time (1 woman). *Students:* 11 full-time (8 women), 32 part-time (23 women); includes 6 minority (4 African Americans, 2 Hispanic Americans), 2 international. Average age 35. In 2007, 9 degrees awarded. *Entrance requirements:* For master's, GRE General Test, minimum undergraduate GPA of 2.5. *Application deadline:* For fall admission, 7/1 priority date for domestic students; for spring admission, 11/1 for domestic students. Applications are processed on a rolling basis. Application fee: $46 ($58 for international students). *Expenses:* Tuition, state resident: full-time $4,762; part-time $198 per credit hour. Tuition, nonresident: full-time $11,720; part-time $488 per credit hour. Required fees: $422; $422 per year. Full-time tuition and fees vary according to course load, campus/location and program. *Financial support:* Fellowships, research assistantships, career-related internships or fieldwork, Federal Work-Study, and institutionally sponsored loans available. Support available to part-time students. Financial award application deadline: 3/1; financial award applicants required to submit FAFSA. *Unit head:* Leda M. Hall, Dean, 574-520-4803.

The Institute of World Politics, Graduate Programs in National Security, Intelligence, and International Affairs, Washington, DC 20036. Offers American foreign policy (Certificate); comparative political culture (Certificate); counterintelligence (Certificate); democracy building (Certificate); intelligence (Certificate); international politics (Certificate); national security affairs (Certificate); public diplomacy and political warfare (Certificate); statecraft and national security affairs (MA); statecraft and world politics (MA); strategic intelligence studies (MA). Part-time and evening/weekend programs available. *Degree requirements:* For master's, comprehensive exam, thesis optional. *Entrance requirements:* For master's, GRE General Test. Additional exam requirements/recommendations for international students: Required—TOEFL. Electronic applications accepted. *Faculty research:* Intelligence, national security, statecraft.

See Close-Up on page 1151.

Jackson State University, Graduate School, College of Public Service, Jackson, MS 39217. Offers MS. *Degree requirements:* For master's, comprehensive exam. *Entrance requirements:* For master's, GRE General Test. Additional exam requirements/recommendations for international students: Required—TOEFL.

McMaster University, School of Graduate Studies, Faculty of Social Sciences, Department of Political Science, Hamilton, ON L8S 4M2, Canada. Offers international relations (PhD); political science (MA); public and the global economy (MA); public policy (PhD); public policy and administration (MA). Part-time programs available. *Faculty:* 21 full-time. *Students:* 63 full-time, 6 part-time. 140 applicants, 20% accepted. *Degree requirements:* For master's, thesis or alternative. *Entrance requirements:* For master's, minimum B+ average. Additional exam requirements/recommendations for international students: Required—TOEFL (minimum score 580 paper-based; 237 computer-based). *Application deadline:* For fall admission, 2/15 priority date for domestic students. Applications are processed on a rolling basis. Application fee: $90. *Financial support:* In 2007–08, 27 teaching assistantships (averaging $8,440 per year) were awarded; scholarships/grants also available. *Faculty research:* Organizational theory, internationalization of public policy, water resource policies, political interest intermediation, comparative politics. *Unit head:* Dr. Robert O'Brien, Chair, 905-525-9140 Ext. 23705, Fax: 905-527-3071, E-mail: obrienr@mcmaster.ca. *Application contact:* Manuela Dozzi, Administrative Secretary, 905-525-9140 Ext. 24742, Fax: 905-527-3071, E-mail: dozzim@mcmaster.ca.

Murray State University, College of Humanities and Fine Arts, Department of Government, Laws and International Affairs, Program in Public Administration, Murray, KY 42071. Offers public affairs (MPA). Part-time programs available. Postbaccalaureate distance learning degree programs offered (minimal on-campus study). *Degree requirements:* For master's, capstone course. *Entrance requirements:* For master's, GRE General Test. Additional exam requirements/recommendations for international students: Required—TOEFL.

National University of Singapore, Lee Kuan Yew School of Public Policy, Singapore, Singapore. Offers MPA, MPM, MPP, PhD.

See Close-Up on page 1605.

New Mexico Highlands University, Graduate Studies, College of Arts and Sciences, Program in Public Affairs, Las Vegas, NM 87701. Offers applied sociology (MA). Program is interdisciplinary. *Faculty:* 14 full-time (7 women), 1 (woman) part-time/adjunct. *Students:* 16 full-time (13 women), 9 part-time (4 women); includes 14 minority (1 African American, 1 Asian American or Pacific Islander, 12 Hispanic Americans), 7 international. Average age 36. 43 applicants, 58% accepted, 6 enrolled. In 2007, 5 degrees awarded. *Degree requirements:* For master's, comprehensive exam, thesis or alternative. *Entrance requirements:* For master's, minimum undergraduate GPA of 3.0. Additional exam requirements/recommendations for international students: Required—TOEFL (minimum score 540 paper-based; 190 computer-based). *Application deadline:* For fall admission, 8/1 priority date for domestic students. Applications are processed on a rolling basis. Application fee: $15. *Expenses:* Tuition, state resident: full-time $2,642; part-time $110 per credit hour. Tuition, nonresident: full-time $3,964; part-time $165 per credit hour. International tuition: $5,285 full-time. One-time fee: $20 full-time. *Financial support:* In 2007–08, 14 students received support, including 8 teaching assistantships with full and partial tuition reimbursements available (averaging $6,500 per year); career-related internships or fieldwork, Federal Work-Study, institutionally sponsored loans, scholarships/grants, traineeships, tuition waivers (full and partial), and unspecified assistantships also available. Support available to part-time students. Financial award application deadline: 3/1. *Application contact:* Diane Trujillo, Administrative Assistant Graduate Studies, 505-454-3266, Fax: 505-454-3558, E-mail: dtrujillo@nmhu.edu.

Northeastern University, College of Arts and Sciences, Department of Political Science, Boston, MA 02115-5096. Offers political science (MA); public administration (MPA, Certificate), including development administration (MPA), health administration and policy (MPA), state and local government (MPA), urban studies (Certificate); public and international affairs (PhD). Part-time and evening/weekend programs available. *Faculty:* 22 full-time (4 women), 3 part-time/adjunct (all women). *Students:* 59 full-time (32 women), 14 part-time (5 women). Average age 30. 165 applicants, 53% accepted. In 2007, 23 master's, 2 doctorates awarded. *Degree requirements:* For master's, thesis optional; for doctorate, thesis/dissertation. *Entrance requirements:* For master's, GRE General Test. Additional exam requirements/recommendations for international students: Required—TOEFL. *Application deadline:* Applications are processed on a rolling basis. Application fee: $50. *Financial support:* In 2007–08, 12 teaching assistantships with tuition reimbursements (averaging $14,035 per year) were awarded; research assistantships with tuition reimbursements, career-related internships or fieldwork, Federal Work-Study, tuition waivers (full and partial), and unspecified assistantships also available. Support available to part-time students. Financial award application deadline: 2/1; financial award applicants required to submit FAFSA. *Faculty research:* Presidency, public opinion, Congress, democratization, national identity. *Unit head:* Dr. John Portz, Chair, 617-373-2796, Fax: 617-373-5311, E-mail: gradpolisci@neu.edu. *Application contact:* Brynn Thompson, Graduate Programs Assistant, 617-373-4404, Fax: 617-373-5311, E-mail: gradpolisci@neu.edu.

The Ohio State University, John Glenn School of Public Affairs, Columbus, OH 43210. Offers MA, MPA, PhD. *Accreditation:* NASPAA (one or more programs are accredited). Part-time programs available. *Faculty:* 14. *Students:* 54 full-time (26 women), 49 part-time (25 women); includes 19 minority (10 African Americans, 7 Asian Americans or Pacific Islanders, 2 Hispanic Americans), 11 international. Average age 43. In 2007, 32 master's, 2 doctorates awarded. *Degree requirements:* For doctorate, thesis/dissertation. *Entrance requirements:* For master's, GMAT, GRE General Test (MPA), minimum GPA of 3.0 (MA); for doctorate, GRE General Test. Additional exam requirements/recommendations for international students: Recommended—TOEFL (minimum score 573 paper-based; 230 computer-based). *Application deadline:* For fall admission, 8/15 priority date for domestic students, 7/1 priority date for international students; for winter admission, 12/1 priority date for domestic students, 11/1 priority date for international students; for spring admission, 3/1 priority date for domestic students, 2/1 priority date for international students. Applications are processed on a rolling basis. Application fee: $40 ($50 for international students). Electronic applications accepted. *Financial support:* Fellowships, research assistantships, teaching assistantships, Federal Work-Study, institutionally sponsored loans, and unspecified assistantships available. Support available to part-time students. *Unit head:* Mary K. Marvel, Graduate Studies Committee Chair, 614-292-8696, Fax: 614-292-4868, E-mail: marvel.1@osu.edu. *Application contact:* 614-292-9444, Fax: 614-292-3895, E-mail: domestic.grad@osu.edu.

See Close-Up on page 1615.

Park University, College of Graduate and Professional Studies, Kansas City, MO 54105. Offers adult education (M Ed); at-risk students (M Ed); disaster and emergency management (MPA); educational administration (M Ed); entrepreneurship (MBA); general business (MBA); general education (M Ed); government/business relations (MPA); healthcare/services management (MBA, MPA); international business (MBA); K-12 certification (MAT); management information systems (MBA); management of information systems (MPA); middle school certification (MAT); multi-cultural education (M Ed); nonprofit management (MPA); public management (MPA); school law (M Ed); secondary school certification (MAT); special education (M Ed). Part-time and evening/weekend programs available. Postbaccalaureate distance learning degree programs offered (no on-campus study). *Degree requirements:* For master's, comprehensive exam, thesis (for some programs). *Entrance requirements:* For master's, GRE, GMAT, teacher certification (M Ed). Additional exam requirements/recommendations for international students: Required—TOEFL (minimum score 550 paper-based). Electronic applications accepted. *Faculty research:* Literacy, leadership, brain based research, multicultural education, diversity.

Princeton University, Graduate School, Woodrow Wilson School of Public and International Affairs, Princeton, NJ 08544-1019. Offers MPA, MPA-URP, MPP, PhD, JD/MPA. Terminal master's awarded for partial completion of doctoral program. *Degree requirements:* For master's, internship; for doctorate, one foreign language, thesis/dissertation. *Entrance requirements:* For master's, GRE General Test, original policy memo; for doctorate, GRE General Test. Additional exam requirements/recommendations for international students: Required—TOEFL (minimum score 600 paper-based; 250 computer-based). Electronic applications accepted.

Texas A&M University, George Bush School of Government and Public Service, College Station, TX 77843. Offers advanced international affairs (Certificate); homeland security (Certificate); international affairs (MPIA), including international economics and development, national security affairs; nonprofit management (Certificate); public service and administration (MPSA), including public management, public policy analysis. *Accreditation:* NASPAA. *Faculty:* 39. *Students:* 155 full-time (67 women), 97 part-time (27 women); includes 37 minority (8 African Americans, 2 American Indian/Alaska Native, 4 Asian Americans or Pacific Islanders, 23 Hispanic Americans), 18 international. Average age 24. 249 applicants, 57% accepted, 88 enrolled. In 2007, 69 degrees awarded. *Degree requirements:* For master's, summer internship. *Entrance requirements:* For master's, GRE (preferred) or GMAT. *Application deadline:* For fall admission, 1/24 for domestic and international students. Application fee: $50 ($75 for international students). Electronic applications accepted. *Expenses:* Tuition, state resident: full-time $6,129. Tuition, nonresident: full-time $11,689. Tuition and fees vary according to course load. *Financial support:* In 2007–08, fellowships (averaging $11,000 per year), research assistantships (averaging $11,250 per year) were awarded; career-related internships or fieldwork, Federal Work-Study, and institutionally sponsored loans also available. Financial award application deadline: 2/1; financial award applicants required to submit FAFSA. *Faculty research:* Public policy, Presidential studies, public leadership, economic policy, social policy. *Unit head:* Richard A. Chilcoat, Dean, 979-862-8007, Fax: 979-862-7953, E-mail: bushschool@tamu.edu. *Application contact:* Kathryn Meyer, Recruitment/Placement Officer, 979-458-4767, Fax: 979-845-4155, E-mail: admissions@bushschool.tamu.edu.

See Close-Up on page 1623.

The University of Alabama in Huntsville, School of Graduate Studies, College of Liberal Arts, Program in Public Affairs, Huntsville, AL 35899. Offers MA. Part-time and evening/weekend programs available. *Faculty:* 4 full-time (2 women), 2 part-time/adjunct (0 women). *Students:* 3 full-time (1 woman); includes 4 minority (all African Americans), 1 international. Average age 34. 22 applicants, 86% accepted. In 2007, 8 degrees awarded. *Degree requirements:* For master's, comprehensive exam, thesis or alternative, oral and written exams. *Entrance requirements:* For master's, GRE General Test, minimum GPA of 3.0. Additional exam requirements/recommendations for international students: Required—TOEFL (minimum score 500 paper-based; 173 computer-based; 62 iBT). *Application deadline:* For fall admission, 7/18 for domestic students, 4/1 for international students; for spring admission, 11/30 for domestic students, 9/1 for international students. Applications are processed on a rolling basis. Application fee: $40 ($50 for international students). Electronic applications accepted. *Expenses:* Tuition, state resident: full-time $6,548; part-time $276 per credit hour. Tuition, nonresident: full-time $13,466; part-time $565 per credit hour. *Financial support:* In 2007–08, 5 students received support, including 3 teaching assistantships with full and partial tuition reimbursements available (averaging $8,100 per year); fellowships with full and partial tuition reimbursements available, research assistantships with full and partial tuition reimbursements available, career-related internships or fieldwork, Federal Work-Study, institutionally sponsored loans, scholarships/grants, health care benefits, and unspecified assistantships also available. Support available to part-time students. Financial award application deadline: 4/1; financial award applicants required to submit FAFSA. *Faculty research:* Public policy, public management professions, intergovernmental relations, international politics. Total annual research expenditures: $73,116. *Unit head:* Dr. Roy Meek, Co-Coordinator, 256-824-2310, Fax: 256-824-6949, E-mail: meekr@email.uah.edu.

University of Arkansas at Little Rock, Graduate School, Clinton School of Public Service, Little Rock, AR 72204-1099. Offers MPS, Graduate Certificate. *Application contact:* Robert J. Torvestad, Student Services, 501-683-5216, E-mail: rjtorvestad@clintonschool.edu.

University of Baltimore, Graduate School, The Yale Gordon College of Liberal Arts, School of Public Affairs, Baltimore, MD 21201-5779. Offers health systems management (MS); public administration (MPA, DPA); JD/MPA. *Accreditation:* NASPAA. Part-time and evening/weekend programs available. Postbaccalaureate distance learning degree programs offered (minimal on-campus study). *Faculty:* 11 full-time (2 women), 2 part-time/adjunct (0 women). *Students:* 90 full-time (51 women), 173 part-time (113 women); includes 118 minority (106 African Americans, 2 American Indian/Alaska Native, 8 Asian Americans or Pacific Islanders, 2 Hispanic Americans), 45 international. Average age 32. 107 applicants, 78% accepted, 66 enrolled. In

2007, 49 degrees awarded. *Degree requirements:* For doctorate, final project. *Entrance requirements:* For master's, interview, minimum GPA of 3.0; for doctorate, GRE, interview. Additional exam requirements/recommendations for international students: Required—TOEFL (minimum score 550 paper-based; 213 computer-based). *Application deadline:* For fall admission, 8/1 priority date for domestic students, 6/1 for international students; for spring admission, 12/1 for domestic students, 11/1 for international students. Applications are processed on a rolling basis. Application fee: $45. Electronic applications accepted. *Expenses: Contact institution.* Tuition and fees vary according to program. *Financial support:* In 2007–08, 6 research assistantships were awarded; fellowships, career-related internships or fieldwork and Federal Work-Study also available. Support available to part-time students. Financial award application deadline: 4/1; financial award applicants required to submit FAFSA. *Faculty research:* Welfare policy, public administration ethics, bureaucratic politics, public sector budgeting, program evaluation. Total annual research expenditures: $1.9 million. *Unit head:* Dr. Samuel Brown, Director, MPA Program, 410-837-6091, E-mail: sabrown@ubalt.edu. *Application contact:* Wendy Bolyard.

See Close-Up on page 1627.

University of Central Florida, College of Health and Public Affairs, Program in Public Affairs, Orlando, FL 32816. Offers PhD. Part-time and evening/weekend programs available. *Degree requirements:* For doctorate, thesis/dissertation, candidacy and qualifying exams. *Entrance requirements:* For doctorate, GRE General Test or minimum GPA of 3.0 during final 60 hours. Additional exam requirements/recommendations for international students: Required—TOEFL. *Application deadline:* For fall admission, 2/7 priority date for domestic students. Application fee: $30. Electronic applications accepted. *Expenses:* Tuition, state resident: full-time $6,484. Tuition, nonresident: full-time $23,938. Tuition and fees vary according to program. *Financial support:* Fellowships with partial tuition reimbursements, research assistantships with partial tuition reimbursements, teaching assistantships with partial tuition reimbursements, career-related internships or fieldwork, Federal Work-Study, institutionally sponsored loans, tuition waivers (partial), and unspecified assistantships available. Financial award application deadline: 3/1; financial award applicants required to submit FAFSA. *Unit head:* Dr. Thomas T. Wan, Director, 407-823-0172, Fax: 407-823-4895, E-mail: twan@mail.ucf.edu.

University of Colorado at Colorado Springs, Graduate School, Graduate School of Public Affairs, Colorado Springs, CO 80933-7150. Offers criminal justice (MCJ); public administration (MPA). Part-time and evening/weekend programs available. *Faculty:* 8 full-time (2 women), 25 part-time/adjunct (15 women). *Students:* 84 full-time (52 women), 66 part-time (40 women); includes 34 minority (8 African Americans, 8 Asian Americans or Pacific Islanders, 18 Hispanic Americans). Average age 35. 32 applicants, 78% accepted, 19 enrolled. In 2007, 24 degrees awarded. *Degree requirements:* For master's, internship (if no experience), capstone project. *Entrance requirements:* For master's, GRE General Test, GMAT, LSAT, minimum GPA of 3.0. *Application deadline:* For fall admission, 6/1 priority date for domestic students; for spring admission, 11/1 for domestic students. Applications are processed on a rolling basis. Application fee: $60 ($75 for international students). *Expenses: Contact institution. Financial support:* Career-related internships or fieldwork and Federal Work-Study available. Support available to part-time students. *Unit head:* Dr. Kathleen Beatty, Dean, 719-262-4182, Fax: 719-262-4183, E-mail: kbeatty@uccs.edu. *Application contact:* Mary Lou Kartis, Program Assistant, 719-262-4182, Fax: 719-262-4183, E-mail: mkartis@uccs.edu.

University of Colorado Denver, Graduate School of Public Affairs, Program in Public Affairs, Denver, CO 80217-3364. Offers PhD. Part-time and evening/weekend programs available. *Faculty:* 10 full-time (3 women). *Students:* 11 full-time (5 women), 31 part-time (14 women); includes 4 minority (1 African American, 1 Asian American or Pacific Islander, 2 Hispanic Americans), 5 international. Average age 39. 45 applicants, 31% accepted, 11 enrolled. In 2007, 9 degrees awarded. *Degree requirements:* For doctorate, comprehensive exam, thesis/dissertation. *Entrance requirements:* For doctorate, GRE General Test. Additional exam requirements/recommendations for international students: Required—TOEFL (minimum score 500 paper-based). *Application deadline:* For fall admission, 4/1 for domestic students, 10/1 for international students. Application fee: $50 ($60 for international students). *Financial support:* In 2007–08, 26 fellowships were awarded; research assistantships, teaching assistantships, career-related internships or fieldwork, Federal Work-Study, and institutionally sponsored loans also available. Support available to part-time students. Financial award application deadline: 4/1; financial award applicants required to submit FAFSA. *Unit head:* Paul Teske, Director, 303-315-2805, Fax: 303-556-5971, E-mail: paul.teske@cudenver.edu. *Application contact:* Antoinette Sandoval, Student Service Specialist, 303-556-5972, Fax: 303-556-5971, E-mail: antoinette.sandoval@cudenver.edu.

See Close-Up on page 1631.

University of Florida, Graduate School, College of Liberal Arts and Sciences, Department of Political Science, Gainesville, FL 32611. Offers international development policy and administration (MA, Certificate); international relations (MA, MAT); political campaigning (MA, Certificate); political science (MA, MAT, PhD); public affairs (MA, Certificate); JD/MA. Part-time programs available. *Faculty:* 32 full-time (6 women). *Students:* 123 (44 women); includes 7 minority (1 African American, 1 Asian American or Pacific Islander, 5 Hispanic Americans) 12 international. In 2007, 25 master's, 7 doctorates awarded. Terminal master's awarded for partial completion of doctoral program. *Degree requirements:* For master's, variable foreign language requirement, thesis or alternative; for doctorate, variable foreign language requirement, thesis/dissertation. *Entrance requirements:* For master's and doctorate, GRE General Test, minimum GPA of 3.0. Additional exam requirements/recommendations for international students: Required—TOEFL (minimum score 550 paper-based; 213 computer-based). *Application deadline:* For fall admission, 3/16 priority date for domestic students. Applications are processed on a rolling basis. Application fee: $30. Electronic applications accepted. *Expenses:* Tuition, state resident: full-time $7,478. Tuition, nonresident: full-time $22,603. *Financial support:* In 2007–08, 1 research assistantship (averaging $16,666 per year), 39 teaching assistantships (averaging $17,071 per year) were awarded; fellowships, career-related internships or fieldwork, Federal Work-Study, institutionally sponsored loans, and unspecified assistantships also available. Financial award application deadline: 1/15. *Faculty research:* U.S. political development, religion and politics, environmental politics and policy, developing societies, international relations. *Unit head:* Philip J. Williams, Chair, 352-392-0262 Ext. 247, Fax: 352-392-8127, E-mail: pjw@polisci.ufl.edu. *Application contact:* Dr. J. Samuel Barkin, Coordinator, 352-392-0262 Ext. 222, Fax: 352-392-8127, E-mail: barkin@polisci.ufl.edu.

University of Idaho, College of Graduate Studies, College of Letters, Arts and Social Sciences, Department of Political Science and Public Affairs Research, Moscow, ID 83844-2282. Offers political science (MA, PhD); public administration (MPA). *Students:* 67 (28 women). Average age 32. In 2007, 15 master's, 1 doctorate awarded. *Degree requirements:* For doctorate, thesis/dissertation. *Entrance requirements:* For master's, minimum GPA of 2.8; for doctorate, minimum undergraduate GPA of 2.8, 3.0 graduate. *Application deadline:* For fall admission, 8/1 for domestic students; for spring admission, 12/15 for domestic students. Application fee: $55 ($60 for international students). *Financial support:* Research assistantships, teaching assistantships available. Financial award application deadline: 2/15. *Unit head:* Dr. Donald W. Crowley, Chair, 208-885-6328.

University of Louisville, Graduate School, College of Arts and Sciences, Department of Urban and Public Affairs, Program in Urban and Public Affairs, Louisville, KY 40292-0001. Offers PhD. *Students:* 25 full-time (10 women), 2 part-time; includes 5 minority (all African Americans), 3 international. Average age 34. In 2007, 3 degrees awarded. *Degree requirements:* For doctorate, thesis/dissertation. *Entrance requirements:* For doctorate, GRE General Test, master's degree in appropriate field. *Application deadline:* Applications are processed on a rolling basis. Application fee: $50. *Unit head:* Dr. Ron K. Vogel, Director, 502-852-3312, Fax: 502-852-7923, E-mail: rkvogel01@gwise.louisville.edu.

University of Massachusetts Boston, Office of Graduate Studies, John W. McCormack Graduate School of Policy Studies, Program in Public Affairs, Boston, MA 02125-3393. Offers MS. Part-time and evening/weekend programs available. *Degree requirements:* For master's, final project. *Entrance requirements:* For master's, GRE General Test or MAT, minimum GPA of 2.75. *Faculty research:* Leadership and policy implementation, public management, disability; human services and sound policy.

University of Minnesota, Twin Cities Campus, Graduate School, Hubert H. Humphrey Institute of Public Affairs, Program in Public Affairs, Minneapolis, MN 55455-0213. Offers MPA. *Accreditation:* NASPAA. Part-time and evening/weekend programs available. *Entrance requirements:* For master's, 10 years of work experience, minimum undergraduate GPA of 3.0. Additional exam requirements/recommendations for international students: Required—TOEFL (minimum score 600 paper-based; 250 computer-based). Electronic applications accepted. Expenses: Contact institution. *Faculty research:* Public and non-profit leadership and management, social policy, urban and regional planning, economic and community development, foreign policy and international affairs.

See Close-Up on page 1641.

University of Missouri–Columbia, Graduate School, Harry S Truman School of Public Affairs, Columbia, MO 65211. Offers MPA. *Accreditation:* NASPAA. *Entrance requirements:* For master's, GRE General Test, minimum GPA of 3.0. Additional exam requirements/recommendations for international students: Required—TOEFL (minimum score 550 paper-based; 213 computer-based).

University of Missouri–Kansas City, Henry W. Bloch School of Business and Public Administration, Kansas City, MO 64110-2499. Offers accounting (MS); business administration (MBA); public affairs (MPA, PhD); JD/MBA; LL M/MPA. *Accreditation:* AACSB; NASPAA. Part-time and evening/weekend programs available. *Faculty:* 41 full-time (12 women), 19 part-time/adjunct (6 women). *Students:* 176 full-time (90 women), 430 part-time (183 women); includes 76 minority (39 African Americans, 2 American Indian/Alaska Native, 19 Asian Americans or Pacific Islanders, 16 Hispanic Americans), 42 international. Average age 30. 343 applicants, 64% accepted, 162 enrolled. In 2007, 213 degrees awarded. Terminal master's awarded for partial completion of doctoral program. *Entrance requirements:* For master's, GMAT, GRE, 2 writing essays, 2 references and support of employer; for doctorate, GRE, minimum GPA of 3.0. Additional exam requirements/recommendations for international students: Required—TOEFL. *Application deadline:* For fall admission, 5/1 priority date for domestic and international students; for spring admission, 10/1 priority date for domestic and international students. Applications are processed on a rolling basis. Application fee: $35 ($50 for international students). Electronic applications accepted. *Expenses:* Tuition, state resident: part-time $287 per hour. Tuition, nonresident: part-time $741 per hour. Required fees: $31 per hour. Tuition and fees vary according to program. *Financial support:* In 2007–08, 407 students received support, including 22 research assistantships with partial tuition reimbursements available (averaging $8,189 per year), 5 teaching assistantships with partial tuition reimbursements available (averaging $10,224 per year); fellowships, career-related internships or fieldwork, Federal Work-Study, institutionally sponsored loans, scholarships/grants, tuition waivers (full and partial), and unspecified assistantships also available. Support available to part-time students. Financial award application deadline: 3/1; financial award applicants required to submit FAFSA. *Faculty research:* Entrepreneurship, finance, non-profit, risk management. Total annual research expenditures: $578,039. *Unit head:* Dr. Lee Bolman, Interim Dean, 816-235-5407, Fax: 816-235-2206. *Application contact:* 816-235-1111, E-mail: admit@umkc.edu.

University of Nevada, Las Vegas, Graduate College, Greenspun College of Urban Affairs, Department of Public Administration, Las Vegas, NV 89154-9900. Offers crisis and emergency management (MS); public administration (MPA); public affairs (PhD); public management (Certificate). *Accreditation:* NASPAA. Part-time and evening/weekend programs available. *Faculty:* 7 full-time (1 woman), 6 part-time/adjunct (3 women). *Students:* 31 full-time (16 women), 113 part-time (66 women); includes 40 minority (23 African Americans, 1 American Indian/Alaska Native, 2 Asian Americans or Pacific Islanders, 14 Hispanic Americans), 3 international. 86 applicants, 55% accepted, 40 enrolled. In 2007, 36 master's, 1 doctorate, 22 other advanced degrees awarded. *Degree requirements:* For master's, comprehensive exam, professional paper. *Entrance requirements:* For master's, GMAT or GRE General Test, minimum GPA of 3.0 during previous 2 years, 2.75 overall; minimum 1 year of work experience; resumé. Additional exam requirements/recommendations for international students: Required—TOEFL (minimum score 550 paper-based; 213 computer-based; 80 iBT). *Application deadline:* For fall admission, 4/10 for domestic and international students; for spring admission, 11/15 for domestic students, 10/1 for international students. Application fee: $60 ($75 for international students). Electronic applications accepted. *Expenses:* Tuition, state resident: part-time $198 per credit. Tuition, nonresident: part-time $416 per credit. Required fees: $256 per semester. Tuition and fees vary according to course load and reciprocity agreements. *Financial support:* In 2007–08, 7 research assistantships (averaging $11,000 per year), 1 teaching assistantship with partial tuition reimbursement (averaging $10,000 per year) were awarded; career-related internships or fieldwork, Federal Work-Study, institutionally sponsored loans, scholarships/grants, health care benefits, and unspecified assistantships also available. Support available to part-time students. Financial award application deadline: 3/1. *Unit head:* Dr. Lee Bernick, Chair, 702-895-4828. *Application contact:* Graduate College Admissions Evaluator, 702-895-3320, Fax: 702-895-4180, E-mail: gradcollege@unlv.edu.

The University of North Carolina at Greensboro, Graduate School, College of Arts and Sciences, Department of Political Science, Greensboro, NC 27412-5001. Offers nonprofit management (Certificate); public affairs (MPA); urban and economic development (Certificate). *Accreditation:* NASPAA. *Faculty:* 14 full-time (4 women). *Students:* 35 full-time (21 women), 28 part-time (20 women); includes 62 minority (13 African Americans, 1 American Indian/Alaska Native, 48 Hispanic Americans). 55 applicants, 27% accepted. *Degree requirements:* For master's, comprehensive exam. *Entrance requirements:* For master's, GRE General Test. Additional exam requirements/recommendations for international students: Required—TOEFL. *Application deadline:* For fall admission, 3/15 priority date for domestic students; for spring admission, 11/1 for domestic students. Applications are processed on a rolling basis. Electronic applications accepted. *Financial support:* In 2007–08, 19 students received support, including 4 research assistantships with full tuition reimbursements available; teaching assistantships with full tuition reimbursements available, career-related internships or fieldwork, Federal Work-Study, scholarships/grants, and traineeships also available. Support available to part-time students. *Faculty research:* U.S. Constitution, Canadian parliament, public management, ethical challenge of public service. *Unit head:* Dr. Ruth H. DeHoog, Head, 336-256-0511, Fax: 336-334-4315, E-mail: rhdehoog@uncg.edu. *Application contact:* Michelle Harkleroad, Director of Graduate Admissions, 336-334-4884, Fax: 336-334-4424, E-mail: mbharkle@uncg.edu.

The University of Texas at Arlington, Graduate School, School of Urban and Public Affairs, Program in Urban and Public Affairs, Arlington, TX 76019. Offers PhD. Part-time and evening/weekend programs available. *Students:* 10 full-time (2 women), 57 part-time (32 women); includes 26 minority (20 African Americans, 2 Asian Americans or Pacific Islanders, 4 Hispanic Americans), 8 international. Average age 30. *Median time to degree:* Of those who began their doctoral program in fall 1999, 20% received their degree in 8 years or less. *Degree requirements:* For doctorate, comprehensive exam, thesis/dissertation. *Entrance requirements:* For doctorate, GRE General Test. *Application deadline:* For fall admission, 6/16 for domestic students. Application fee: $35 ($50 for international students). *Expenses:* Tuition, state resident: full-time $5,934. Tuition, nonresident: full-time $10,938. *Financial support:* In 2007–08, 4 fellowships (averaging $1,000 per year), 6 research assistantships (averaging $4,500 per year) were awarded. Financial award application deadline: 6/1; financial award applicants required to submit FAFSA. *Faculty research:* Environment urban policy personnel, research theoretical foundations, urban problems. *Unit head:* Dr. Rod Hissong, Graduate Adviser, 817-272-3350, Fax: 817-272-5008, E-mail: hissong@uta.edu. *Application contact:* Linda Slaughter, Administrative Clerk, 817-272-3071, Fax: 817-272-5008, E-mail: slaughter@uta.edu.

The University of Texas at Austin, Graduate School, Lyndon B. Johnson School of Public Affairs, Austin, TX 78712-1111. Offers public affairs (MP Aff); public policy (PhD); JD/MP Aff;

Public Affairs

The University of Texas at Austin (continued)
MBA/MP Aff; MP Aff/MA; MP Aff/MSE. *Accreditation:* NASPAA (one or more programs are accredited). Part-time programs available. *Degree requirements:* For master's, thesis, summer internship; for doctorate, thesis/dissertation. *Entrance requirements:* For master's, GRE General Test; for doctorate, GRE General Test, master's degree in policy-related field. Additional exam requirements/recommendations for international students: Required—TOEFL. Electronic applications accepted. *Faculty research:* Human resource development, health and social policy, philanthropy and community service, ethical leadership, urban and international policy, science and technology policy.

The University of Texas at Dallas, School of Economic, Political and Policy Sciences, Program in Public Affairs, Richardson, TX 75083-0688. Offers MPA, PhD. *Accreditation:* NASPAA. Part-time and evening/weekend programs available. *Faculty:* 8 full-time (4 women), 3 part-time/adjunct (1 woman). *Students:* 54 full-time (26 women), 130 part-time (69 women); includes 65 minority (30 African Americans, 9 Asian Americans or Pacific Islanders, 26 Hispanic Americans), 24 international. Average age 36. 70 applicants, 84% accepted, 47 enrolled. In 2007, 29 master's, 7 doctorates awarded. *Degree requirements:* For master's, internship. *Entrance requirements:* For master's, GRE General Test, minimum GPA of 3.0 in upper-level course work in field. Additional exam requirements/recommendations for international students: Required—TOEFL (minimum score 550 paper-based; 213 computer-based). *Application deadline:* For fall admission, 7/15 for domestic students; for spring admission, 11/15 for domestic students. Applications are processed on a rolling basis. Application fee: $50 ($100 for international students). Electronic applications accepted. *Expenses:* Tuition, state resident: full-time $7,052. Tuition, nonresident: full-time $12,632. Tuition and fees vary according to course load. *Financial support:* In 2007–08, 1 research assistantship with tuition reimbursement (averaging $12,735 per year), 8 teaching assistantships with tuition reimbursements (averaging $12,339 per year) were awarded; fellowships, career-related internships or fieldwork, Federal Work-Study, institutionally sponsored loans, and scholarships/grants also available. Support available to part-time students. Financial award application deadline: 4/30; financial award applicants required to submit FAFSA. *Faculty research:* Juvenile justice programs, program evaluation and outcome measurement, Hispanic American retention in educational institutions. *Unit head:* Dr. Douglas J. Watson, Program Head, 972-883-4936, Fax: 972-883-2735, E-mail: douglas.watson@utdallas.edu. *Application contact:* Delfina Prisock, Program Assistant, 972-883-4936, E-mail: delfina@utdallas.edu.

See Close-Up on page 1043.

University of Washington, Graduate School, Daniel J. Evans School of Public Affairs, Seattle, WA 98195. Offers MPA, PhD, JD/MPA, MPA/MAIS, MPA/MPH, MPA/MS, MPA/MUP. *Accreditation:* NASPAA. Part-time and evening/weekend programs available. *Degree requirements:* For master's, thesis, internship or cooperative experience. *Entrance requirements:* For master's and doctorate, GRE General Test, minimum GPA of 3.0. Additional exam requirements/recommendations for international students: Required—TOEFL (minimum score 580 paper-based; 237 computer-based; 92 iBT). Electronic applications accepted. *Faculty research:* Environmental policy, education and social policy, nonprofit management, international affairs, urban and regional development.

University of Waterloo, Graduate Studies, Faculty of Arts, Department of Anthropology, Waterloo, ON N2L 3G1, Canada. Offers anthropology (MA); public issues (MA). *Entrance requirements:* For master's, BA, B+ average. Additional exam requirements/recommendations for international students: Required—TOEFL. Application fee: $75. Electronic applications accepted. *Financial support:* Fellowships, research assistantships, teaching assistantships available. *Faculty research:* Applied socio-cultural anthropology and archaeology. *Unit head:* Dr. Tom Abler, Chair and Graduate Officer, 519-888-4567 Ext. 33044, E-mail: tsabler@uwaterloo.ca.

University of Wisconsin–Madison, Graduate School, College of Letters and Science, Public Policy and Administration Program, Robert M. La Follette School of Public Affairs, Madison, WI 53706-1380. Offers international public affairs (MPIA); public affairs (MPA). Part-time programs available. *Entrance requirements:* For master's, GRE General Test. Additional exam requirements/recommendations for international students: Required—TOEFL (minimum score 650 paper-based; 280 computer-based). Electronic applications accepted. *Faculty research:* Social policy, personnel, economic development, tax and budget, environmental regulations.

Virginia Commonwealth University, Graduate School, College of Humanities and Sciences, Wilder School of Government and Public Affairs, Richmond, VA 23284-9005. Offers MA, MPA, MS, MURP, PhD, CASR, CCJA, CPM, CURP, Certificate, Graduate Certificate, JD/MURP, MSW/Certificate. *Expenses:* Tuition, state resident: full-time $7,224; part-time $401 per credit. Tuition, nonresident: full-time $16,072; part-time $891 per credit. Required fees: $1,679; $63 per credit. Tuition and fees vary according to campus/location. *Application contact:* Dr. Sherry T. Sandkam, Associate Dean, 804-828-6916, Fax: 804-827-4546, E-mail: ssandkam@vcu.edu.

Virginia Polytechnic Institute and State University, Graduate School, College of Architecture and Urban Studies, School of Public and International Affairs, Blacksburg, VA 24061. Offers environmental planning and policy (MURP); government and international affairs (MPIA); housing, community and economic development (MURP); international development planning (MURP); land use and physical planning (MURP); planning, governance and globalization (PhD), including environmental planning and landscape analysis, physical planning and urban design, public and international affairs, urban and environmental design and planning; urban and regional planning (MURP). *Accreditation:* ACSP. *Entrance requirements:* Additional exam requirements/recommendations for international students: Required—TOEFL (minimum score 550 paper-based; 213 computer-based). Electronic applications accepted. *Faculty research:* Design theory, environmental planning, town planning, transportation planning.

Washington State University Vancouver, Graduate Programs, Program in Public Affairs, Vancouver, WA 98686. Offers MPA. Part-time and evening/weekend programs available. *Faculty:* 5. *Students:* 3 full-time (0 women), 24 part-time (12 women); includes 4 minority (2 African Americans, 2 Hispanic Americans). 22 applicants, 23% accepted, 4 enrolled. *Degree requirements:* For master's, comprehensive exam, thesis (for some programs). *Entrance requirements:* For master's, GRE, minimum GPA of 3.0, resumé, 3 references. Additional exam requirements/recommendations for international students: Required—TOEFL (minimum score 550 paper-based; 213 computer-based). *Application deadline:* For fall admission, 3/15 priority date for domestic students, 3/1 for international students; for spring admission, 10/1 priority date for domestic students, 7/1 for international students. Application fee: $50. *Financial support:* In 2007–08, 10 students received support, including 3 fellowships (averaging $3,398 per year); Federal Work-Study and unspecified assistantships also available. *Unit head:* Dr. Carolyn Long, Associate Professor, 360-546-9737, Fax: 360-546-9074, E-mail: long@vancouver.wsu.edu.

Western Carolina University, Graduate School, College of Arts and Sciences, Department of Political Science and Public Affairs, Cullowhee, NC 28723. Offers MPA. Part-time and evening/weekend programs available. *Faculty:* 8 full-time (1 woman), 1 part-time/adjunct (0 women). *Students:* 20 full-time (12 women), 25 part-time (12 women); includes 8 minority (3 African Americans, 2 American Indian/Alaska Native, 3 Hispanic Americans), 1 international. Average age 32. 24 applicants, 92% accepted, 18 enrolled. In 2007, 17 degrees awarded. *Degree requirements:* For master's, comprehensive exam. *Entrance requirements:* For master's, GRE General Test, appropriate undergraduate, 3 letters of recommendation. Additional exam requirements/recommendations for international students: Required—TOEFL (minimum score 550 paper-based; 270 computer-based; 79 iBT). *Application deadline:* For fall admission, 5/1 priority date for domestic students; for spring admission, 9/1 priority date for domestic students. Applications are processed on a rolling basis. Application fee: $40. *Expenses:* Tuition, state resident: full-time $2,314. Tuition, nonresident: full-time $11,899. Required fees: $2,033. Tuition and fees vary according to course load. *Financial support:* In 2007–08, 9 students received support, including 2 fellowships (averaging $500 per year), 9 research assistantships with full and partial tuition reimbursements available (averaging $6,222 per year); teaching assistantships with full and partial tuition reimbursements available, career-related internships or fieldwork, institutionally sponsored loans, scholarships/grants, and unspecified assistantships also available. Financial award application deadline: 3/31; financial award applicants required to submit FAFSA. *Faculty research:* Press-government relations, comparative governments, gender in politics, Latin American political systems, foreign policy, trust in government, zoning. *Unit head:* Dr. Gibbs Knotts, Director, 828-227-7475, Fax: 828-227-7502, E-mail: gknotts@email.wcu.edu. *Application contact:* Admissions Specialist for Public Affairs, 828-227-7398, Fax: 828-227-7480, E-mail: gradsch@email.wcu.edu.

Western Michigan University, Graduate College, College of Arts and Sciences, School of Public Affairs and Administration, Kalamazoo, MI 49008-5202. Offers MPA, DPA. *Accreditation:* NASPAA (one or more programs are accredited). *Degree requirements:* For doctorate, thesis/dissertation, oral exams. *Entrance requirements:* For doctorate, GRE General Test.

York University, Faculty of Graduate Studies, Glendon College, Program in Public and International Affairs, Toronto, ON M3J 1P3, Canada. Offers MA.

Public Policy

Albany State University, College of Arts and Sciences, Department of History, Political Science and Public Administration, Albany, GA 31705-2717. Offers community and economic development (MPA); criminal justice (MPA); fiscal management (MPA); general management (MPA); health administration and policy (MPA); human resources management (MPA); public policy (MPA); water resource management and policy (MPA). *Accreditation:* NASPAA. Part-time programs available. *Degree requirements:* For master's, comprehensive exam, thesis. *Entrance requirements:* For master's, GRE General Test, minimum GPA of 2.5. Electronic applications accepted. *Faculty research:* Transportation, urban affairs, political economy.

American University, School of Public Affairs, Department of Public Administration, Program in Public Policy, Washington, DC 20016-8001. Offers MPP. *Students:* 71 full-time (42 women), 43 part-time (27 women); includes 15 minority (9 African Americans, 1 American Indian/Alaska Native, 3 Asian Americans or Pacific Islanders, 2 Hispanic Americans), 2 international. Average age 25. In 2007, 28 degrees awarded. *Degree requirements:* For master's, comprehensive exam. *Entrance requirements:* For master's, GRE General Test, statement of purpose; 2 recommendations. *Application deadline:* For fall admission, 2/1 for domestic students; for spring admission, 11/1 for domestic students. Application fee: $50. *Expenses:* Tuition: Full-time $19,998; part-time $1,111 per credit hour. Required fees: $380. Tuition and fees vary according to program. *Financial support:* Application deadline: 2/1.

Arizona State University, Sandra Day O'Connor College of Law, Tempe, AZ 85287-7906. Offers biotechnology and genomics (LL M); legal studies (MLS); tribal policy, law and government (LL M); JD/MBA; JD/MD; JD/PhD. *Accreditation:* ABA. *Faculty:* 57 full-time (18 women), 37 part-time/adjunct (5 women). *Students:* 599 full-time (260 women), 18 part-time (11 women); includes 164 minority (21 African Americans, 38 American Indian/Alaska Native, 23 Asian Americans or Pacific Islanders, 82 Hispanic Americans), 16 international. Average age 25. 3,082 applicants, 24% accepted, 159 enrolled. In 2007, 192 first professional degrees awarded. *Degree requirements:* For JD, comprehensive exam, paper. *Entrance requirements:* LSAT, bachelors degree. Additional exam requirements/recommendations for international students: Required—TOEFL (minimum score 550 paper-based; 213 computer-based; 83 iBT). *Application deadline:* For fall admission, 2/1 for domestic and international students. Applications are processed on a rolling basis. Application fee: $50. Electronic applications accepted. *Expenses:* Contact institution. *Financial support:* In 2007–08, 564 students received support, including 38 research assistantships, 6 teaching assistantships; career-related internships or fieldwork, Federal Work-Study, institutionally sponsored loans, scholarships/grants, tuition waivers (full and partial), and unspecified assistantships also available. Financial award application deadline: 3/1; financial award applicants required to submit FAFSA. *Faculty research:* Genetics and law, forensics and the law, science and law, Indian law, jurisprudence. Total annual research expenditures: $263,916. *Unit head:* Patricia D. White, Dean, 480-965-6188, Fax: 480-965-6521, E-mail: patricia.white@asu.edu. *Application contact:* Chitra Damania, Director of Admissions, 480-965-1474, Fax: 480-727-7930, E-mail: law.admissions@asu.edu.

Baylor University, Graduate School, College of Arts and Sciences, Department of Political Science, Waco, TX 76798. Offers international studies (MA); political science (MA, PhD); public policy and administration (MPPA); JD/MPPA. *Students:* 24 full-time (8 women), 3 part-time (2 women); includes 1 minority (Hispanic American), 3 international. In 2007, 11 degrees awarded. *Entrance requirements:* For master's, GRE General Test. *Application deadline:* Applications are processed on a rolling basis. Application fee: $25. *Financial support:* Research assistantships, career-related internships or fieldwork, Federal Work-Study, and institutionally sponsored loans available. Financial award application deadline: 3/1. *Unit head:* Dr. Dwight Allman, Graduate Program Director, 254-710-3161, Fax: 254-710-3122, E-mail: dwight_allman@baylor.edu. *Application contact:* Suzanne Keener, Administrative Assistant, 254-710-3588, Fax: 254-710-3870.

Boise State University, Graduate College, College of Social Sciences and Public Affairs, Department of Public Policy and Administration, Boise, ID 83725-0399. Offers environmental and natural resources policy and administration (MPA); general public administration (MPA); state and local government policy and administration (MPA). *Accreditation:* NASPAA. Part-time programs available. *Degree requirements:* For master's, comprehensive exam, directed research project, internship. *Entrance requirements:* For master's, GRE General Test, minimum GPA of 3.0. Additional exam requirements/recommendations for international students: Required—TOEFL. Electronic applications accepted.

Brandeis University, The Heller School for Social Policy and Management, Program in Social Policy, Waltham, MA 02454-9110. Offers aging (MPP); assets and inequalities (PhD); behavioral health (MPP); children, youth and families (MPP, PhD); general social policy (MPP); health (MPP); health and behavioral health (PhD); poverty alleviation and development (MPP). Part-time programs available. *Degree requirements:* For doctorate, thesis/dissertation, qualifying paper, 2 year residency. *Entrance requirements:* For doctorate, GRE General Test. Additional exam requirements/recommendations for international students: Required—TOEFL (minimum score 600 paper-based). Electronic applications accepted. *Faculty research:* Health policy, child and family policy, mental health policy, disability policy, aging policy, substance abuse, work, inequality and social change.

See Close-Ups on pages 1579 and 1581.

Brigham Young University, Graduate Studies, College of Family, Home, and Social Sciences, Department of Political Science—Public Policy, Provo, UT 84602-1001. Offers MPP, JD/MPP. Part-time programs available. *Faculty:* 6 full-time (0 women), 2 part-time/adjunct (1 woman). *Students:* 10 full-time (6 women); includes 1 minority (Asian American or Pacific Islander), 1 international. Average age 28. 10 applicants, 70% accepted, 4 enrolled. In 2007, 7 degrees awarded. *Degree requirements:* For master's, Internship. *Entrance requirements:* For master's, GRE, Prerequisites: Econ 110 Math, Stat 221. Additional exam requirements/recommendations for international students: Required—TOEFL. *Application deadline:* For fall admission, 3/1 priority date for domestic and international students. Application fee: $50. Electronic applications accepted. *Financial support:* In 2007–08, 10 students received support, including 5 fellowships (averaging $5,000 per year), 5 research assistantships (averaging $5,000 per year). *Unit head:* Sven E. Wilson, Graduate Director, 801-422-9018, Fax: 801-422-0224, E-mail: sven_wilson@byu.edu. *Application contact:* Jessica A. McArthur, Department Secretary, 801-422-7146, Fax: 801-422-0224, E-mail: publicpolicy@byu.edu.

Brooklyn College of the City University of New York, Division of Graduate Studies, Department of Political Science, Brooklyn, NY 11210-2889. Offers international affairs (MA); political science (MA, PhD); political science, urban policy and administration (MA). The department offers courses at Brooklyn College that are creditable toward the CUNY doctoral degree (with permission of the executive officer of the doctoral program). Part-time and evening/weekend programs available. *Students:* 6 full-time (3 women), 106 part-time (64 women); includes 65 minority (50 African Americans, 5 Asian Americans or Pacific Islanders, 10 Hispanic Americans), 13 international. 56 applicants, 89% accepted, 30 enrolled. In 2007, 43 degrees awarded. *Degree requirements:* For master's, comprehensive exam (for some programs), thesis or alternative, foreign language exam for international affairs program. *Entrance requirements:* For master's, 2 letters of recommendation, personal statement. *Application deadline:* For fall admission, 3/1 priority date for domestic students, 2/1 priority date for international students; for spring admission, 11/1 priority date for domestic students, 10/1 priority date for international students. Applications are processed on a rolling basis. Application fee: $125. Electronic applications accepted. *Financial support:* Career-related internships or fieldwork and Federal Work-Study available. Support available to part-time students. Financial award application deadline: 5/1; financial award applicants required to submit FAFSA. *Faculty research:* Ethics and politics, politics of criminal justice, Western Europe, international law and politics, labor politics. *Unit head:* Dr. Sally Bermanzohn, Chairperson, 718-951-5306, E-mail: sallyb@brooklyn.cuny.edu. *Application contact:* Hernan Sierra, Graduate Admissions Coordinator, 718-951-4536, Fax: 718-951-4506, E-mail: grads@brooklyn.cuny.edu.

Brown University, Graduate School, A. Alfred Taubman Center for Public Policy and American Institutions, Providence, RI 02912. Offers MPA, MPP. *Entrance requirements:* For master's, GRE, 3 letters of recommendation. Additional exam requirements/recommendations for international students: Required—TOEFL.

California Lutheran University, Graduate Studies, Program in Public Policy and Administration, Thousand Oaks, CA 91360-2787. Offers MPPA. *Degree requirements:* For master's, comprehensive exam, thesis or project, internship. *Entrance requirements:* For master's, GMAT or GRE General Test, interview, minimum GPA of 3.0. Expenses: Contact institution.

California State University, Long Beach, Graduate Studies, College of Health and Human Services, Center for Public Policy and Administration, Long Beach, CA 90840. Offers MPA. *Accreditation:* NASPAA. Part-time and evening/weekend programs available. *Faculty:* 5 full-time (1 woman), 12 part-time/adjunct (5 women). *Students:* 52 full-time (33 women), 224 part-time (135 women); includes 179 minority (46 African Americans, 1 American Indian/Alaska Native, 53 Asian Americans or Pacific Islanders, 79 Hispanic Americans). Average age 33. *Degree requirements:* For master's, comprehensive exam. *Entrance requirements:* For master's, minimum GPA of 2.75. *Application deadline:* For fall admission, 7/1 for domestic students; for spring admission, 12/1 for domestic students. Applications are processed on a rolling basis. Application fee: $55. Electronic applications accepted. *Financial support:* Fellowships, career-related internships or fieldwork, Federal Work-Study, institutionally sponsored loans, and scholarships/grants available. Financial award application deadline: 3/2. *Faculty research:* Transportation access, air quality controls, coastal issues, intergovernmental relations. *Unit head:* Dr. Martha J Dede, Director, 562-985-4178, Fax: 562-985-4672, E-mail: mdede@csulb.edu. *Application contact:* Dr. Frank Barber, Graduate Adviser, 562-985-5747, Fax: 562-985-4672.

California State University, Monterey Bay, College of Professional Studies, Institute for Community Collaborative Studies, Seaside, CA 93955-8001. Offers public policy (MPP). Part-time programs available. *Faculty:* 1 (woman) full-time, 4 part-time/adjunct (3 women). *Students:* 23 full-time (17 women), 8 part-time (4 women); includes 5 minority (1 African American, 4 Hispanic Americans). Average age 36. 35 applicants, 69% accepted, 17 enrolled. In 2007, 6 degrees awarded. *Degree requirements:* For master's, internship. *Entrance requirements:* For master's, GRE, essay, transcript, curriculum vitae, recommendations. Additional exam requirements/recommendations for international students: Required—TOEFL (minimum score 525 paper-based; 213 computer-based; 71 iBT). *Application deadline:* For fall admission, 3/14 for domestic and international students. Application fee: $55. Electronic applications accepted. *Expenses:* Tuition, nonresident: full-time $8,136; part-time $339 per credit. Required fees: $1,232 per term. *Financial support:* In 2007–08, 4 students received support. Career-related internships or fieldwork available. Support available to part-time students. Financial award application deadline: 3/1; financial award applicants required to submit FAFSA. *Faculty research:* Social policy, health policy, politics and government. *Unit head:* Dr. Brian Simmons, Department Chair, 831-582-3898, Fax: 831-582-3899, E-mail: brian_simmons@csumb.edu. *Application contact:* Haven Brearton, Administrative Support Coordinator, 831-582-3565, Fax: 831-582-3899, E-mail: haven_brearton@csumb.edu.

California State University, Sacramento, Graduate Studies, College of Social Sciences and Interdisciplinary Studies, Program in Public Policy and Administration, Sacramento, CA 95819-6048. Offers MPPA. Part-time programs available. *Students:* 16 full-time (12 women), 78 part-time (51 women); includes 24 minority (4 African Americans, 1 American Indian/Alaska Native, 6 Asian Americans or Pacific Islanders, 13 Hispanic Americans). Average age 33. 80 applicants, 76% accepted, 45 enrolled. *Degree requirements:* For master's, thesis or alternative, writing proficiency exam. *Entrance requirements:* For master's, GRE General Test. Additional exam requirements/recommendations for international students: Required—TOEFL. *Application deadline:* Applications are processed on a rolling basis. Application fee: $55. Electronic applications accepted. *Expenses:* Tuition, state resident: full-time $3,414. Tuition, nonresident: full-time $13,584; part-time $339 per unit. Required fees: $786; $393 per semester. *Financial support:* Career-related internships or fieldwork and Federal Work-Study available. Support available to part-time students. Financial award application deadline: 3/1. *Unit head:* Dr. Rob Wassmer, Chair, 916-278-557, Fax: 916-278-6544.

Carleton University, Faculty of Graduate Studies, Faculty of Public Affairs and Management, School of Public Policy and Administration, Ottawa, ON K1S 5B6, Canada. Offers public administration (MA, DPA); public policy (PhD). Part-time programs available. *Degree requirements:* For master's, thesis optional; for doctorate, one foreign language, comprehensive exam, thesis/dissertation. *Entrance requirements:* For master's, GRE, honors degree; for doctorate, master's degree. Additional exam requirements/recommendations for international students: Required—TOEFL. *Application deadline:* Applications are processed on a rolling basis. Application fee: $77 Canadian dollars. *Financial support:* Fellowships, research assistantships, teaching assistantships, institutionally sponsored loans, scholarships/grants, and unspecified assistantships available. *Faculty research:* Canadian public administration and policy, development administration, public policy analysis, public management. *Unit head:* Susan Phillips, Director, 613-520-2600 Ext. 2547, Fax: 613-520-2551, E-mail: public_administration@carleton.ca. *Application contact:* Nicole Enouy, Graduate Secretary, 613-520-2600 Ext. 2548, Fax: 613-520-2551, E-mail: public_administration@carleton.ca.

Carnegie Mellon University, H. John Heinz III School of Public Policy and Management, Program in Public Policy and Management–Australia, Adelaide, PA 5000, Australia. Offers MS.

See Close-Up on page 1583.

Carnegie Mellon University, H. John Heinz III School of Public Policy and Management and Tepper School of Business, Programs in Public Policy and Management, Pittsburgh, PA 15213-3891. Offers MS, MSED, PhD, JD/MS, M Div/MS. *Degree requirements:* For master's, internship. *Entrance requirements:* For master's, GMAT or GRE, previous course work in pre-calculus and statistics. Electronic applications accepted.

See Close-Up on page 1587.

Central European University, Graduate Studies, School of Social Sciences and Humanities, Budapest, Hungary. Offers economics (MA, PhD); gender studies (MA, PhD); international relations and European studies (MA, PhD); mathematics and its applications (MS, PhD); medieval studies (MA, PhD); nationalism studies (MA, PhD); philosophy (MA, PhD); political science (MA, PhD); public policy (MA, PhD); sociology and social anthropology (MA, PhD). *Faculty:* 75 full-time (25 women), 46 part-time/adjunct (10 women). *Students:* 625 full-time (355 women). Average age 26. 2,500 applicants, 31% accepted, 540 enrolled. In 2007, 325 master's, 20 doctorates awarded. Terminal master's awarded for partial completion of doctoral program. *Degree requirements:* For master's, one foreign language, thesis; for doctorate, one foreign language, comprehensive exam, thesis/dissertation. *Entrance requirements:* For master's, CEU subject tests, interview; for doctorate, GRE, CEU subject test, interview. Additional exam requirements/recommendations for international students: Required—TOEFL (minimum score 570 paper-based; 230 computer-based). *Application deadline:* For fall admission, 1/15 priority date for domestic and international students. Application fee: $0. Electronic applications accepted. Tuition charges are reported in euros. *Expenses:* Tuition: Full-time 10,000 euros; part-time 315 euros per credit. *Financial support:* In 2007–08, 402 students received support, including 350 fellowships with full and partial tuition reimbursements available (averaging $5,000 per year); career-related internships or fieldwork, institutionally sponsored loans, and scholarships/grants also available. Financial award application deadline: 1/5. *Faculty research:* Civil society, fiscal decentralization, party politics, political philosophy (especially Liberalism, theory of Democracy). Total annual research expenditures: $35,000. *Unit head:* Dr. Howard Michael Robinson, Provost, 361-327-3003, Fax: 361-327-3211, E-mail: robinson@ceu.hu. *Application contact:* Zsuzsanna Jaszberenyi, Admissions Officer, 361-327-3009, Fax: 361-327-3211, E-mail: admissions@ceu.hu.

See Close-Up on page 447.

Claremont Graduate University, Graduate Programs, Program in Public Policy and Evaluation, Claremont, CA 91711-6160. Offers MA. *Students:* 1 (woman) full-time. Average age 24. *Expenses:* Tuition: Full-time $31,640; part-time $1,376 per unit. Required fees: $145 per semester. Tuition and fees vary according to course load, degree level and program. *Application contact:* Laura Carillo, Recruiter and Admissions Coordinator, 909-621-8699, Fax: 909-621-7545, E-mail: laura.carillo@cga.edu.

Claremont Graduate University, Graduate Programs, School of Politics and Economics, Department of Economics, Claremont, CA 91711-6160. Offers business and financial economics (MA, PhD); economic development (Certificate); economics (PhD); industrial organization (PhD); international and development economics (PhD); international economics policy and development (MA); international money and finance (PhD); neuroeconomics (PhD); political economy and public policy (MA); public choice and public economics (PhD); MBA/PhD. Part-time programs available. *Faculty:* 6 full-time (0 women), 3 part-time/adjunct (1 woman). *Students:* 92 full-time (25 women), 5 part-time (1 woman); includes 12 minority (2 African Americans, 5 Asian Americans or Pacific Islanders, 5 Hispanic Americans), 59 international. Average age 33. In 2007, 10 master's, 13 doctorates awarded. *Degree requirements:* For doctorate, 2 foreign languages, comprehensive exam, thesis/dissertation. *Entrance requirements:* For master's and doctorate, GRE General Test. *Application deadline:* For fall admission, 2/15 priority date for domestic students. Applications are processed on a rolling basis. Electronic applications accepted. *Expenses:* Tuition: Full-time $31,640; part-time $1,376 per unit. Required fees: $145 per semester. Tuition and fees vary according to course load, degree level and program. *Financial support:* Fellowships, research assistantships, teaching assistantships, Federal Work-Study and institutionally sponsored loans available. Support available to part-time students. Financial award application deadline: 2/15; financial award applicants required to submit FAFSA. *Faculty research:* International and financial economics, law and economics, regulation, public choice economics. *Unit head:* Arthur Denzau, Chair, 909-621-8782, Fax: 909-621-8545, E-mail: arthur.denzau@cgu.edu.

Claremont Graduate University, Graduate Programs, School of Politics and Economics, Department of Politics and Policy, Claremont, CA 91711-6160. Offers American politics (MA, PhD); comparative politics (PhD); international political economy (MA); international studies (MA); political philosophy (PhD); political science (PhD); politics, economics and business (MA); public policy (MA, PhD); world politics (PhD); MBA/PhD. Part-time programs available. *Faculty:* 7 full-time (3 women), 9 part-time/adjunct (1 woman). *Students:* 181 full-time (69 women), 19 part-time (8 women); includes 35 minority (8 African Americans, 10 Asian Americans or Pacific Islanders, 17 Hispanic Americans), 45 international. Average age 34. In 2007, 27 master's, 19 doctorates awarded. Terminal master's awarded for partial completion of doctoral program. *Degree requirements:* For master's, thesis; for doctorate, one foreign language, thesis/dissertation. *Entrance requirements:* For master's and doctorate, GRE General Test. *Application deadline:* For fall admission, 2/15 priority date for domestic students. Applications are processed on a rolling basis. Electronic applications accepted. *Expenses:* Tuition: Full-time $31,640; part-time $1,376 per unit. Required fees: $145 per semester. Tuition and fees vary according to course load, degree level and program. *Financial support:* Fellowships, research assistantships, teaching assistantships, career-related internships or fieldwork, Federal Work-Study, and institutionally sponsored loans available. Support available to part-time students. Financial award application deadline: 2/15; financial award applicants required to submit FAFSA. *Faculty research:* Environmental policy, international debt, global democratization, Third World development, public sector discrimination. *Unit head:* Jean Schroedel, Chair, 909-621-8696, Fax: 909-621-8545, E-mail: jean.schroedel@cgu.edu.

Clemson University, Graduate School, Interdisciplinary Studies, Interdisciplinary Program in Policy Studies, Clemson, SC 29634. Offers PhD, Certificate. *Students:* 12 full-time (2 women), 6 part-time (3 women); includes 1 minority (African American), 8 international. 13 applicants, 69% accepted, 6 enrolled. In 2007, 3 degrees awarded. *Degree requirements:* For doctorate, thesis/dissertation. *Entrance requirements:* For doctorate, GRE General Test. Additional exam requirements/recommendations for international students: Required—TOEFL. *Application deadline:* Applications are processed on a rolling basis. Application fee: $55. Electronic applications accepted. *Unit head:* Dr. Bruce W. Ransom, Coordinator, 864-656-1650, E-mail: bii@clemson.edu.

The College of William and Mary, Faculty of Arts and Sciences, Thomas Jefferson Program in Public Policy, Williamsburg, VA 23187-8795. Offers MPP, JD/MPP, MBA/MPP, MS/MPP. *Faculty:* 1 full-time (0 women). *Students:* 38 full-time (19 women); includes 3 minority (2 Asian Americans or Pacific Islanders, 1 Hispanic American), 4 international. Average age 24. 59 applicants, 64% accepted, 16 enrolled. In 2007, 20 degrees awarded. *Degree requirements:* For master's, 49 credits. *Entrance requirements:* For master's, GRE General Test. Additional exam requirements/recommendations for international students: Required—TOEFL (minimum score 600 paper-based). *Application deadline:* For fall admission, 2/15 priority date for domestic

Public Policy

The College of William and Mary (continued)
and international students. Application fee: $45. Electronic applications accepted. *Expenses:* Tuition, state resident: full-time $6,250; part-time $275 per credit hour. Tuition, nonresident: part-time $760 per credit hour. Required fees: $3,550. Tuition and fees vary according to program. *Financial support:* In 2007–08, 20 research assistantships with partial tuition reimbursements (averaging $6,000 per year), 10 teaching assistantships with partial tuition reimbursements (averaging $7,000 per year) were awarded; career-related internships or fieldwork and unspecified assistantships also available. Financial award application deadline: 2/15; financial award applicants required to submit FAFSA. *Faculty research:* Social policy, technology policy, international development, health care policy, environmental policy. Total annual research expenditures: $171,419. *Unit head:* Dr. Eric Jensen, Director, 757-221-2368, Fax: 757-221-2390. *Application contact:* Sophie Correll, Administrative Assistant, 757-221-2386, Fax: 757-221-2390, E-mail: sbcorr@wm.edu.

Columbia University, School of International and Public Affairs, Program in Public Policy and Administration, New York, NY 10027. Offers MPA, JD/MPA, MPA/MS, MPH/MPA. *Faculty:* 70 full-time (18 women), 203 part-time/adjunct (80 women). *Students:* 241 full-time (157 women). Average age 27. 659 applicants, 50% accepted, 126 enrolled. In 2007, 104 degrees awarded. *Entrance requirements:* For master's, GRE General Test. Additional exam requirements/recommendations for international students: Required—TOEFL (minimum score 600 paper-based; 250 computer-based; 100 iBT). *Application deadline:* For fall admission, 1/5 for domestic students; for spring admission, 10/1 for domestic students. Application fee: $85. Electronic applications accepted. *Expenses:* Tuition: Part-time $1,452 per credit. Required fees: $152 per term. One-time fee: $75 part-time. Full-time tuition and fees vary according to course level, course load, degree level and program. *Financial support:* In 2007–08, 81 students received support, including 80 fellowships with full and partial tuition reimbursements available (averaging $14,692 per year), 9 teaching assistantships with full tuition reimbursements available (averaging $25,701 per year); research assistantships, career-related internships or fieldwork, Federal Work-Study, institutionally sponsored loans, and unspecified assistantships also available. Financial award application deadline: 1/5; financial award applicants required to submit FAFSA. *Unit head:* Director, 212-854-8690, Fax: 212-854-8059, E-mail: sipa_admission@columbia.edu. *Application contact:* Matt Clemons, Director of Admissions and Financial Aid, 212-854-6216, Fax: 212-854-3010, E-mail: mc2793@columbia.edu.

Concordia University, School of Graduate Studies, Faculty of Arts and Science, Department of Political Science, Montréal, QC H3G 1M8, Canada. Offers political science (PhD); public policy and public administration (MA), including geography. *Degree requirements:* For master's, one foreign language, comprehensive exam, thesis optional, internship. *Entrance requirements:* For master's, honors degree or equivalent. Additional exam requirements/recommendations for international students: Required—TOEFL. *Faculty research:* International public policy and administration, Quebec public administration, public policy and social/political theory, geography and public policy, public administration and decision making.

Cornell University, Graduate School, Graduate Fields of Arts and Sciences, Field of Government, Ithaca, NY 14853-0001. Offers American politics (PhD); comparative politics (PhD); international relations (PhD); political methodology (PhD); political thought (PhD); public policy (PhD). *Faculty:* 39 full-time (13 women). *Students:* 71 full-time (37 women); includes 12 minority (2 African Americans, 1 American Indian/Alaska Native, 6 Asian Americans or Pacific Islanders, 3 Hispanic Americans), 33 international. Average age 30. 305 applicants, 8% accepted, 11 enrolled. In 2007, 9 doctorates awarded. *Degree requirements:* For doctorate, comprehensive exam, thesis/dissertation. *Entrance requirements:* For doctorate, GRE General Test, sample of written work, 3 letters of recommendation. Additional exam requirements/recommendations for international students: Required—TOEFL (minimum score 550 paper-based; 213 computer-based; 77 iBT). *Application deadline:* For fall admission, 1/15 for domestic students. Application fee: $70. Electronic applications accepted. *Financial support:* In 2007–08, 56 students received support, including 29 fellowships with full tuition reimbursements available, 1 research assistantship with full tuition reimbursement available, 26 teaching assistantships with full tuition reimbursements available; institutionally sponsored loans, scholarships/grants, health care benefits, tuition waivers (full and partial), and unspecified assistantships also available. Financial award applicants required to submit FAFSA. *Faculty research:* Political theory, American politics, comparative politics, international relations, methodology. *Unit head:* Director of Graduate Studies, 607-255-3567, Fax: 607-255-4530. *Application contact:* Graduate Field Assistant, 607-255-3567, Fax: 607-255-4530, E-mail: cu_govt@cornell.edu.

Cornell University, Graduate School, Graduate Fields of Human Ecology, Field of Policy Analysis and Management, Ithaca, NY 14853-0001. Offers consumer policy (PhD); evaluation (PhD); family and social welfare policy (PhD); health administration (MHA); health management and policy (PhD). *Faculty:* 32 full-time (13 women). *Students:* 57 full-time (28 women); includes 16 minority (4 African Americans, 9 Asian Americans or Pacific Islanders, 3 Hispanic Americans), 8 international. Average age 26. 105 applicants, 45% accepted, 26 enrolled. In 2007, 19 master's, 5 doctorates awarded. *Degree requirements:* For master's, thesis; for doctorate, thesis/dissertation. *Entrance requirements:* For master's, GRE General Test or GMAT, 2 letters of recommendation; for doctorate, GRE General Test, 2 letters of recommendation. Additional exam requirements/recommendations for international students: Required—TOEFL (minimum score 550 paper-based; 213 computer-based; 77 iBT). *Application deadline:* For fall admission, 1/15 for domestic students. Application fee: $70. Electronic applications accepted. *Financial support:* In 2007–08, 23 students received support, including 3 fellowships with full and partial tuition reimbursements available, 9 research assistantships with full and partial tuition reimbursements available, 11 teaching assistantships with full and partial tuition reimbursements available; institutionally sponsored loans, scholarships/grants, health care benefits, tuition waivers (full and partial), and unspecified assistantships also available. Financial award applicants required to submit FAFSA. *Faculty research:* Health policy, family policy, social welfare policy, program evaluation, consumer policy. *Unit head:* Director of Graduate Studies, 607-255-7772. *Application contact:* Graduate Field Assistant, 607-255-7772, Fax: 607-255-4071, E-mail: pam_phd@cornell.edu.

Duke University, Graduate School, Terry Sanford Institute of Public Policy, Durham, NC 27708-0243. Offers AM, MPP, PhD, Certificate, JD/AM, JD/MPP, MBA/AM, MBA/MPP, MD/AM, MEM/MPP, MF/MPP. *Faculty:* 43 full-time, 17 part-time/adjunct. *Students:* 91 full-time (61 women); includes 14 minority (9 African Americans, 3 Asian Americans or Pacific Islanders, 2 Hispanic Americans), 13 international. 348 applicants, 52% accepted, 48 enrolled. In 2007, 49 degrees awarded. *Entrance requirements:* For master's and doctorate, GRE General Test. *Application deadline:* For fall admission, 12/15 priority date for domestic students, 12/15 for international students. Application fee: $75. Electronic applications accepted. *Financial support:* Fellowships, research assistantships, teaching assistantships, career-related internships or fieldwork and Federal Work-Study available. Financial award application deadline: 12/31. *Unit head:* Fritz Mayer, Director, 919-613-9204, Fax: 919-684-3702, E-mail: mppadmit@duke.edu. *Application contact:* Chuck Pringle, Information Contact, 919-613-9205, E-mail: mppadmit@duke.edu.

Duquesne University, Graduate School of Liberal Arts, Graduate Center for Social and Public Policy, Pittsburgh, PA 15282-1750. Offers conflict resolution and peace studies (Certificate); social and public policy (MA, Certificate). Programs are a collaboration between the Departments of Political Science and Sociology. Part-time and evening/weekend programs available. *Faculty:* 15 full-time (3 women), 1 (woman) part-time/adjunct. *Students:* 25 full-time (13 women), 17 part-time (12 women). Average age 27. In 2007, 11 degrees awarded. *Degree requirements:* For master's, thesis. *Entrance requirements:* For master's, GRE General Test. Additional exam requirements/recommendations for international students: Required—TOEFL. *Application deadline:* For fall admission, 4/30 priority date for domestic and international students; for spring admission, 10/31 priority date for domestic and international students. Applications are processed on a rolling basis. Application fee: $50. *Expenses:* Tuition: Part-time $774 per credit. Required fees: $74 per credit. Tuition and fees vary according to program. *Financial support:* In 2007–08, 20 students received support, including 12 research assistantships with full and partial tuition reimbursements available (averaging $9,000 per year), 4 teaching assistantships with full and partial tuition reimbursements available (averaging $9,000 per year); career-related internships or fieldwork, institutionally sponsored loans, scholarships/grants, tuition waivers (full and partial), and unspecified assistantships also available. Support available to part-time students. Financial award application deadline: 5/1. *Faculty research:* Program evaluation, environmental policy, criminal justice policy, health care policy. Total annual research expenditures: $30,000. *Unit head:* Dr. Joseph Yenerall, Director, 412-396-6485, Fax: 412-396-5265, E-mail: socialpolicy@duq.edu.

Eastern Michigan University, Graduate School, College of Arts and Sciences, Department of Political Science, Program in Public Administration, Ypsilanti, MI 48197. Offers local government management (Graduate Certificate); management of public healthcare services (Graduate Certificate); public administration (MPA, Graduate Certificate); public budget management (Graduate Certificate); public land planning (Graduate Certificate); public management (Graduate Certificate); public personnel management (Graduate Certificate); public policy analysis (Graduate Certificate). *Accreditation:* NASPAA. *Students:* 19 full-time (8 women), 97 part-time (57 women); includes 43 minority (34 African Americans, 3 American Indian/Alaska Native, 3 Asian Americans or Pacific Islanders, 3 Hispanic Americans), 7 international. Average age 32. In 2007, 42 master's, 35 other advanced degrees awarded. Application fee: $35. *Expenses:* Tuition, state resident: full-time $8,952; part-time $373 per credit hour. Tuition, nonresident: full-time $17,634; part-time $735 per credit hour. Required fees: $896; $34 per credit hour. Tuition and fees vary according to course level, degree level and program. *Unit head:* Dr. Joseph Ohren, Director, 734-487-2522, Fax: 734-487-3340, E-mail: joseph.ohren@emich.edu. *Application contact:* Dr. Dogan Koyluoglu, Program Coordinator, 734-487-0063, E-mail: sukru.koyuoglu@emich.edu.

Florida State University, Graduate Studies, College of Social Sciences, Reubin O'D. Askew School of Public Administration and Policy, Tallahassee, FL 32306. Offers MPA, PhD, Certificate, JD/MPA, MPA/MSC, MPA/MSP, MPA/MSW. *Accreditation:* NASPAA (one or more programs are accredited). Part-time and evening/weekend programs available. *Faculty:* 11 full-time (2 women), 9 part-time/adjunct (5 women). *Students:* 55 full-time (22 women), 105 part-time (65 women); includes 42 minority (31 African Americans, 2 Asian Americans or Pacific Islanders, 9 Hispanic Americans), 34 international. Average age 25. 191 applicants, 73% accepted, 80 enrolled. In 2007, 31 master's, 4 doctorates awarded. *Median time to degree:* Of those who began their doctoral program in fall 1999, 98% received their degree in 8 years or less. *Degree requirements:* For master's, action report; for doctorate, comprehensive exam, thesis/dissertation. *Entrance requirements:* For master's, GRE General Test, minimum GPA of 3.0; for doctorate, GRE General Test, minimum undergraduate GPA of 3.0, graduate 3.5. Additional exam requirements/recommendations for international students: Required—TOEFL (minimum score 550 paper-based; 213 computer-based; 80 iBT). *Application deadline:* For fall admission, 7/1 for domestic students, 5/1 for international students; for spring admission, 11/1 for domestic students, 9/1 for international students. Applications are processed on a rolling basis. Application fee: $30. Electronic applications accepted. *Expenses:* Tuition, state resident: part-time $248 per credit hour. Tuition, nonresident: part-time $880 per credit hour. Tuition and fees vary according to program. *Financial support:* In 2007–08, 37 students received support, including 6 fellowships with full tuition reimbursements available (averaging $15,000 per year), 29 research assistantships with full tuition reimbursements available (averaging $10,000 per year), 3 teaching assistantships with full tuition reimbursements available (averaging $9,000 per year); career-related internships or fieldwork, Federal Work-Study, institutionally sponsored loans, scholarships/grants, tuition waivers (full), and unspecified assistantships also available. Support available to part-time students. Financial award application deadline: 2/1. *Faculty research:* Financial management, human resource management, policy, strategic management, organizations, nonprofit management. *Unit head:* Dr. Frances S. Berry, Director, 850-644-3525, Fax: 850-644-7617, E-mail: fberry@fsu.edu. *Application contact:* Velda Williams, Academic Program Specialist, 850-644-3060, Fax: 850-644-7617, E-mail: vwilliams3@fsu.edu.

Frederick S. Pardee RAND Graduate School, Program in Policy Analysis, Santa Monica, CA 90407-2138. Offers PhD. *Degree requirements:* For doctorate, comprehensive exam, thesis/dissertation. *Entrance requirements:* For doctorate, GMAT or GRE General Test. Additional exam requirements/recommendations for international students: Required—TOEFL. Electronic applications accepted. *Faculty research:* Education, defense policy, health, labor and population, justice.

George Mason University, School of Public Policy, Program in Public Policy, Fairfax, VA 22030. Offers MPP, PhD. Part-time programs available. *Faculty:* 48 full-time (8 women), 41 part-time/adjunct (6 women). *Students:* 100 full-time, 350 part-time; includes 49 minority (23 African Americans, 15 Asian Americans or Pacific Islanders, 11 Hispanic Americans), 56 international. Average age 31. 353 applicants, 64% accepted, 118 enrolled. In 2007, 80 master's, 9 doctorates awarded. *Degree requirements:* For master's, thesis or alternative; for doctorate, comprehensive exam, thesis/dissertation. *Entrance requirements:* For master's, minimum GPA of 3.0, resumé, 2 letters of recommendation, goals statement; for doctorate, GMAT or GRE General Test, resumé, writing sample, goals statement, master's degree, 2 letters of recommendation. Additional exam requirements/recommendations for international students: Required—TOEFL. *Application deadline:* For fall admission, 6/1 priority date for domestic students, 5/1 priority date for international students; for spring admission, 12/1 priority date for domestic students, 11/1 priority date for international students. Applications are processed on a rolling basis. Application fee: $60. Electronic applications accepted. *Expenses:* Contact institution. *Financial support:* In 2007–08, 14 research assistantships with full tuition reimbursements (averaging $16,000 per year) were awarded; career-related internships or fieldwork, Federal Work-Study, scholarships/grants, tuition waivers (partial), and unspecified assistantships also available. Support available to part-time students. Financial award application deadline: 3/1; financial award applicants required to submit FAFSA. *Unit head:* Dr. Jeremy Mayer, Director of MPP Program, 703-993-8099, E-mail: spp@gmu.edu. *Application contact:* Leslie Metzger Levin, Director of Graduate Admissions, 703-993-8099, Fax: 703-993-4876, E-mail: lmetzger@gmu.edu.

See Close-Up on page 1593.

Georgetown University, Graduate School of Arts and Sciences, The Georgetown Public Policy Institute, Washington, DC 20057. Offers MPP, MBA/MPP. *Entrance requirements:* For master's, GRE General Test, minimum B average. Additional exam requirements/recommendations for international students: Required—TOEFL. *Faculty research:* Social policy, government, private sector.

See Close-Up on page 1595.

The George Washington University, Columbian College of Arts and Sciences, School of Public Policy and Public Administration, Washington, DC 20052. Offers public policy (MA, MPP), including environmental and resource policy (MA), philosophy and social policy (MA), women's studies (MA); public policy and administration (PhD); public policy and public administration (MPA), including budget and public finance, federal policy, politics, and management, international development management, managing public organizations, managing state and local governments and urban policy, nonprofit management, policy analysis and evaluation, public administration; JD/MPP; MPA/JD; PhD/MPP. Part-time and evening/weekend programs available. *Degree requirements:* For doctorate, thesis/dissertation, general exam. *Entrance requirements:* For master's, GRE General Test, minimum GPA of 3.0; for doctorate, GRE General Test, interview, minimum GPA of 3.0. Additional exam requirements/recommendations for international students: Required—TOEFL (minimum score 550 paper-based; 213 computer-based). Electronic applications accepted.

The George Washington University, School of Business, Department of Strategic Management and Public Policy, Washington, DC 20052. Offers business economics and public policy (MBA); strategic management and public policy (PhD). Part-time and evening/weekend programs available. *Degree requirements:* For doctorate, thesis/dissertation. *Entrance requirements:* For master's, GMAT; for doctorate, GMAT or GRE. Additional exam requirements/recommendations for international students: Required—TOEFL.

Georgia Institute of Technology, Graduate Studies and Research, Ivan Allen College of Policy and International Affairs, School of Public Policy, Atlanta, GA 30332-0001. Offers MS Pub P, PhD. Part-time programs available. *Degree requirements:* For master's, professional paper or thesis. *Entrance requirements:* Additional exam requirements/recommendations for international students: Required—TOEFL. Electronic applications accepted. *Faculty research:* National/regional science and technology policy, environmental policy, urban policy and planning, telecommunications policy.

Georgia State University, Andrew Young School of Policy Studies, Department of Public Administration and Urban Studies, Program in Public Policy, Atlanta, GA 30303-3083. Offers PhD. Part-time programs available. *Students:* Average age 32. *Degree requirements:* For doctorate, comprehensive exam, thesis/dissertation. *Entrance requirements:* For doctorate, GRE General Test. Additional exam requirements/recommendations for international students: Required—TOEFL. *Application deadline:* For fall admission, 2/1 priority date for domestic students. Application fee: $50. *Expenses:* Tuition, state resident: part-time $221 per credit hour. *Financial support:* In 2007–08, research assistantships with full tuition reimbursements (averaging $17,000 per year), teaching assistantships with full tuition reimbursements (averaging $17,000 per year) were awarded; tuition waivers (partial) also available. Support available to part-time students. *Faculty research:* Environmental policy, health policy, policy design analysis and evaluation, public and nonprofit management, urban and regional economic development. *Application contact:* AYSPS Office of Academic Assistance, E-mail: ayspsacademicassist@gsu.edu.

Graduate School and University Center of the City University of New York, Graduate Studies, Interdisciplinary Studies, New York, NY 10016-4039. Offers language in social context (PhD); medieval studies (PhD); public policy (MA, PhD); urban studies (MA, PhD); women's studies (MA, PhD). Terminal master's awarded for partial completion of doctoral program. *Degree requirements:* For master's, thesis; for doctorate, comprehensive exam, thesis/dissertation. *Entrance requirements:* For master's and doctorate, GRE General Test. *Application deadline:* For fall admission, 2/1 for domestic students. Application fee: $40. *Financial support:* Application deadline: 2/1. *Unit head:* Chairman, 212-642-2430.

Harvard University, Graduate School of Arts and Sciences and John F. Kennedy School of Government, Committee on Public Policy, Cambridge, MA 02138. Offers PhD. *Degree requirements:* For doctorate, thesis/dissertation, exams. *Entrance requirements:* For doctorate, GRE General Test or GMAT, Harvard MPP degree. Additional exam requirements/recommendations for international students: Required—TOEFL. *Expenses:* Tuition: Full-time $31,456. Full-time tuition and fees vary according to program and student level.

Harvard University, Graduate School of Arts and Sciences, Program in Social Policy, Cambridge, MA 02138. Offers PhD. *Expenses:* Tuition: Full-time $31,456. Full-time tuition and fees vary according to program and student level.

Harvard University, John F. Kennedy School of Government, Doctoral Programs in Government, Cambridge, MA 02138. Offers political economy and government (PhD); public policy (PhD). *Students:* 9 full-time (0 women), 6 international. Average age 27. 172 applicants, 8% accepted, 9 enrolled. *Degree requirements:* For doctorate, comprehensive exam, thesis/dissertation. *Entrance requirements:* For doctorate, GMAT or GRE General Test, course work in macroeconomics, multi-variable calculus. Additional exam requirements/recommendations for international students: Required—TOEFL (minimum score 600 paper-based; 250 computer-based; 100 iBT), TWE. *Application deadline:* For fall admission, 12/15 for domestic students. Application fee: $80. Electronic applications accepted. *Expenses:* Tuition: Full-time $31,456. Full-time tuition and fees vary according to program and student level. *Financial support:* Fellowships, research assistantships, teaching assistantships, Federal Work-Study, institutionally sponsored loans, scholarships/grants, health care benefits, and unspecified assistantships available. *Unit head:* Louisa Van Baalen, Director, 617-495-1190, E-mail: louisa_van_baalen@harvard.edu.

Harvard University, John F. Kennedy School of Government, Program in Public Policy, Cambridge, MA 02138. Offers public policy (MPP); public policy and urban planning (MPPUP); JD/MPP; MBA/MPP; MD/MPP. *Accreditation:* NASPAA. *Students:* 209 full-time (102 women); includes 67 minority (15 African Americans, 2 American Indian/Alaska Native, 24 Asian Americans or Pacific Islanders, 26 Hispanic Americans), 48 international. Average age 25. 1,253 applicants, 28% accepted, 209 enrolled. *Entrance requirements:* For master's, GMAT or GRE General Test. Additional exam requirements/recommendations for international students: Required—TOEFL (minimum score 600 paper-based; 250 computer-based; 100 iBT), TWE. *Application deadline:* For fall admission, 1/5 for domestic students. Application fee: $80. Electronic applications accepted. *Expenses:* Tuition: Full-time $31,456. Full-time tuition and fees vary according to program and student level. *Financial support:* Fellowships, research assistantships, teaching assistantships, career-related internships or fieldwork, Federal Work-Study, institutionally sponsored loans, scholarships/grants, health care benefits, and unspecified assistantships available. Financial award application deadline: 2/2; financial award applicants required to submit CSS PROFILE or FAFSA. *Unit head:* Dr. Helaine Daniels, Director, 617-496-8382, E-mail: helaine_daniels@harvard.edu. *Application contact:* 617-495-1155.

Indiana University Bloomington, Kelley School of Business, Department of Business Economics and Public Policy, Bloomington, IN 47405-7000. Offers PhD. *Faculty:* 8 full-time (1 woman), 1 part-time/adjunct (0 women). *Students:* 20 applicants, 10% accepted, 2 enrolled. In 2007, 2 degrees awarded. *Median time to degree:* Of those who began their doctoral program in fall 1999, 95% received their degree in 8 years or less. *Degree requirements:* For doctorate, comprehensive exam, thesis/dissertation. *Entrance requirements:* For doctorate, GRE or GMAT, bachelors degree. Additional exam requirements/recommendations for international students: Required—TOEFL (minimum score 630 paper-based; 267 computer-based; 80 iBT). *Financial support:* Fellowships with full tuition reimbursements available. *Faculty research:* Industrial organization, pricing, environmental regulation and policy, information economics, economics of law and organization. *Unit head:* Dr. John W. Maxwell, Professor of Business Economics and Public Policy, 812-855-9219, Fax: 812-855-3354, E-mail: jwmax@indiana.edu. *Application contact:* Dr. Michael R. Baye, Bert Elwert Professor of Business Economics, 812-855-9219, Fax: 812-855-3354, E-mail: mbaye@indiana.edu.

Indiana University–Purdue University Indianapolis, School of Public and Environmental Affairs, Indianapolis, IN 46202-2896. Offers health administration (MHA); public affairs (MPA), including criminal justice, environmental management, nonprofit management, policy analysis, public management; JD/MHA; MBA/MHA; MLS/NMC; MLS/PMC; MSN/MHA. *Accreditation:* CAHME (one or more programs are accredited). Part-time and evening/weekend programs available. *Faculty:* 17 full-time (6 women). *Students:* 108 full-time (67 women), 291 part-time (159 women); includes 74 minority (43 African Americans, 1 American Indian/Alaska Native, 25 Asian Americans or Pacific Islanders, 5 Hispanic Americans), 10 international. Average age 35. In 2007, 77 degrees awarded. *Entrance requirements:* For master's, GRE General Test, minimum GPA of 3.0 (preferred). Additional exam requirements/recommendations for international students: Required—TOEFL. *Application deadline:* For fall admission, 7/15 priority date for domestic students; for spring admission, 11/15 for domestic students. Applications are processed on a rolling basis. Application fee: $50 ($60 for international students). *Expenses:* Tuition, state resident: full-time $5,818; part-time $242 per credit hour. Tuition, nonresident: full-time $17,106; part-time $713 per credit hour. Required fees: $629. Tuition and fees vary according to course load, campus/location and program. *Financial support:* In 2007–08, 11 fellowships with full and partial tuition reimbursements (averaging $5,890 per year), 10 teaching assistantships (averaging $9,900 per year) were awarded; research assistantships with full and partial tuition reimbursements, career-related internships or fieldwork, Federal Work-Study, institutionally sponsored loans, and scholarships/grants also available. Support available to part-time students. Financial award application deadline: 3/1. *Faculty research:* Economic development, water and air quality, ethics, financing, organization design and structure. Total annual research expenditures: $1.9 million. *Unit head:* Dr. Greg Lindsey, Associate Dean, 317-274-4656, Fax: 317-274-5153. *Application contact:* 317-274-4656, Fax: 317-274-5153, E-mail: speainfo@speanet.iupui.edu.

See Close-Up on page 1599.

The Institute of World Politics, Graduate Programs in National Security, Intelligence, and International Affairs, Washington, DC 20036. Offers American foreign policy (Certificate); comparative political culture (Certificate); counterintelligence (Certificate); democracy building (Certificate); intelligence (Certificate); international politics (Certificate); national security affairs (Certificate); public diplomacy and political warfare (Certificate); statecraft and national security affairs (MA); statecraft and world politics (MA); strategic intelligence studies (MA). Part-time and evening/weekend programs available. *Degree requirements:* For master's, comprehensive exam, thesis optional. *Entrance requirements:* For master's, GRE General Test. Additional exam requirements/recommendations for international students: Required—TOEFL. Electronic applications accepted. *Faculty research:* Intelligence, national security, statecraft.

See Close-Up on page 1151.

Jackson State University, Graduate School, School of Liberal Arts, Department of Public Policy and Administration, Jackson, MS 39217. Offers MPPA, PhD. *Accreditation:* NASPAA (one or more programs are accredited). Evening/weekend programs available. *Degree requirements:* For master's, comprehensive exam, thesis optional; for doctorate, comprehensive exam, thesis/dissertation. *Entrance requirements:* For master's, GRE General Test; for doctorate, GRE, GMAT, MAT. Additional exam requirements/recommendations for international students: Required—TOEFL.

John Jay College of Criminal Justice of the City University of New York, Graduate Studies, Programs in Criminal Justice, New York, NY 10019-1093. Offers criminal justice (MA, PhD); criminology and deviance (PhD); forensic psychology (PhD); forensic science (PhD); law and philosophy (PhD); organizational behavior (PhD); public policy (PhD). Part-time and evening/weekend programs available. Terminal master's awarded for partial completion of doctoral program. *Degree requirements:* For master's, thesis or alternative; for doctorate, one foreign language, thesis/dissertation. *Entrance requirements:* For master's, GRE General Test, minimum B average; for doctorate, GRE General Test. Additional exam requirements/recommendations for international students: Required—TOEFL (minimum score 500 paper-based; 173 computer-based).

The Johns Hopkins University, Zanvyl Krieger School of Arts and Sciences, Institute for Public Policy, Baltimore, MD 21218-2699. Offers MA. *Faculty:* 6 full-time (3 women), 5 part-time/adjunct (3 women). *Students:* 69 full-time (43 women); includes 3 minority (all African Americans), 11 international. Average age 25. 149 applicants, 60% accepted, 35 enrolled. In 2007, 35 degrees awarded. *Degree requirements:* For master's, thesis optional, summer internship. *Entrance requirements:* For master's, GRE General Test. Additional exam requirements/recommendations for international students: Required—TOEFL (minimum score 600 paper-based; 250 computer-based). *Application deadline:* For fall admission, 1/15 for domestic and international students. Application fee: $60. Electronic applications accepted. *Financial support:* Career-related internships or fieldwork, Federal Work-Study, and unspecified assistantships available. Financial award application deadline: 4/15; financial award applicants required to submit FAFSA. *Faculty research:* Housing, criminal justice, human capital investment, nonprofit sector, public finance and infrastructure. *Unit head:* Dr. Sandra J. Newman, Director, 410-516-7180, Fax: 410-516-4624, E-mail: sjn@jhu.edu. *Application contact:* Dr. Carey Borkoski, Assistant Director, 410-516-4624, Fax: 410-516-8233, E-mail: cborkoski@jhu.edu.

See Close-Up on page 1601.

Kent State University, College of Arts and Sciences, Department of Political Science, Kent, OH 44242-0001. Offers political science (MA); public administration (MPA); public policy (PhD). Part-time programs available. Postbaccalaureate distance learning degree programs offered. *Faculty:* 17 full-time (7 women), 3 part-time/adjunct (1 woman). *Students:* 46 full-time (15 women), 9 part-time (3 women); includes 3 minority (all African Americans), 18 international. Average age 35. 54 applicants, 44% accepted, 12 enrolled. In 2007, 2 degrees awarded. *Degree requirements:* For master's, thesis optional; for doctorate, 2 foreign languages, thesis/dissertation. *Entrance requirements:* For master's, GRE General Test, minimum GPA of 2.75; for doctorate, GRE General Test, minimum GPA of 3.0. Additional exam requirements/recommendations for international students: Required—TOEFL. *Application deadline:* For fall admission, 7/12 for domestic students; for spring admission, 11/29 for domestic students. Applications are processed on a rolling basis. Application fee: $30. Electronic applications accepted. *Financial support:* In 2007–08, 21 research assistantships with full tuition reimbursements (averaging $19,000 per year) were awarded; fellowships with full tuition reimbursements, teaching assistantships with full tuition reimbursements, career-related internships or fieldwork, Federal Work-Study, institutionally sponsored loans, and tuition waivers (full) also available. Financial award application deadline: 2/1. *Unit head:* Dr. John A Logue, Chairman, 330-672-2060, Fax: 330-672-3362, E-mail: jlogue@kent.edu. *Application contact:* Andrew Barnes, Graduate Coordinator, 330-672-2060, E-mail: abarnes3@kent.edu.

Lincoln University, School of Graduate Studies and Continuing Education, College of Business and Professional Studies, Department of Business and Economics, Jefferson City, MO 65102. Offers business administration (MBA), including accounting, entrepreneurship, management, public administration and policy. *Accreditation:* ACBSP. Part-time and evening/weekend programs available. *Faculty:* 1 full-time (0 women), 6 part-time/adjunct (1 woman). *Students:* 26 full-time (11 women), 22 part-time (17 women); includes 16 minority (all African Americans), 10 international. Average age 33. 20 applicants, 95% accepted, 13 enrolled. In 2007, 38 degrees awarded. *Degree requirements:* For master's, comprehensive exam, thesis optional, portfolio. *Entrance requirements:* For master's, GMAT, undergraduate prerequisite courses; see parent units for general requirements. Additional exam requirements/recommendations for international students: Required—TOEFL (minimum score 500 paper-based; 173 computer-based; 61 iBT). *Application deadline:* For fall admission, 7/1 priority date for domestic and international students; for spring admission, 12/1 priority date for domestic and international students. Applications are processed on a rolling basis. Application fee: $20. *Expenses:* Tuition, state resident: full-time $5,400; part-time $225 per credit hour. Tuition, nonresident: full-time $10,020; part-time $417 per credit hour. Required fees: $360; $15 per credit hour. $20 per semester. *Financial support:* Federal Work-Study and scholarships/grants available. Financial award application deadline: 4/1; financial award applicants required to submit FAFSA. *Unit head:* Dr. Kylar Broadus, Interim Department Head, 573-681-5487, Fax: 573-681-6085, E-mail: broadusk@lincolnu.edu.

Loyola University Chicago, Graduate School, Program in Public Policy, Chicago, IL 60611-2196. Offers MPP. *Expenses:* Tuition: Full-time $12,780; part-time $710 per credit hour. Required fees: $55 per semester. Full-time tuition and fees vary according to program. *Application contact:* Ron Martin, Assistant Director of Enrollment Management, 312-915-8950, Fax: 312-915-8905, E-mail: gradapp@luc.edu.

McMaster University, School of Graduate Studies, Faculty of Social Sciences, Department of Political Science, Hamilton, ON L8S 4M2, Canada. Offers international relations (PhD); political science (MA); public and the global economy (MA); public policy (PhD); public policy and administration (MA). Part-time programs available. *Faculty:* 21 full-time. *Students:* 63 full-time, 6 part-time. 140 applicants, 20% accepted. *Degree requirements:* For master's, thesis or alternative. *Entrance requirements:* For master's, minimum B+ average. Additional exam requirements/recommendations for international students: Required—TOEFL (minimum score 580 paper-based; 237 computer-based). *Application deadline:* For fall admission, 2/15 priority date for domestic students. Applications are processed on a rolling basis. Application fee: $90. *Financial support:* In 2007–08, 27 teaching assistantships (averaging $8,440 per year) were

Public Policy

McMaster University (continued)

awarded; scholarships/grants also available. *Faculty research:* Organizational theory, internationalization of public policy, water resource policies, political interest intermediation, comparative politics. *Unit head:* Dr. Robert O'Brien, Chair, 905-525-9140 Ext. 23705, Fax: 905-527-3071, E-mail: obrienr@mcmaster.ca. *Application contact:* Manuela Dozzi, Administrative Secretary, 905-525-9140 Ext. 24742, Fax: 905-527-3071, E-mail: dozzim@mcmaster.ca.

Mills College, Graduate Studies, Program in Public Policy, Oakland, CA 94613-1000. Offers MPP. *Faculty:* 2 full-time (1 woman), 2 part-time/adjunct (0 women). *Students:* 9 full-time (all women); includes 2 minority (1 Asian American or Pacific Islander, 1 Hispanic American). Average age 29. 17 applicants, 88% accepted, 9 enrolled. *Expenses:* Tuition: Full-time $22,792; part-time $5,702 per credit. Required fees: $828. Part-time tuition and fees vary according to course load and program. *Financial support:* In 2007–08, 8 fellowships (averaging $6,563 per year) were awarded; teaching assistantships. *Unit head:* Carol Chetkovich, Director, 510-430-3370, E-mail: cchetkov@mills.edu. *Application contact:* Linda Guzman, Graduate Admission Specialist, 510-430-3309, Fax: 510-430-2159, E-mail: grad-studies@mills.edu.

Mississippi State University, College of Arts and Sciences, Department of Political Science and Public Administration, Mississippi State, MS 39762. Offers political science (MA); public policy and administration (MPPA, PhD). *Accreditation:* NASPAA (one or more programs are accredited). Evening/weekend programs available. *Faculty:* 13 full-time (3 women), 2 part-time/adjunct (both women). *Students:* 47 full-time (24 women), 34 part-time (19 women); includes 25 minority (22 African Americans, 3 Hispanic Americans), 2 international. Average age 32. 33 applicants, 76% accepted, 20 enrolled. In 2007, 23 master's, 3 doctorates awarded. *Degree requirements:* For master's, comprehensive oral or written exam; for doctorate, thesis/dissertation, comprehensive oral and written exam. *Entrance requirements:* For master's, minimum GPA of 3.0; for doctorate, GRE General Test, minimum graduate GPA of 3.35. Additional exam requirements/recommendations for international students: Required—TOEFL. *Application deadline:* For fall admission, 8/1 priority date for domestic students; for spring admission, 12/1 priority date for domestic students. Applications are processed on a rolling basis. Application fee: $30. *Expenses:* Tuition, state resident: full-time $4,978; part-time $274 per hour. Tuition, nonresident: full-time $11,469; part-time $635 per hour. *Financial support:* In 2007–08, 8 teaching assistantships with full tuition reimbursements (averaging $9,044 per year) were awarded; Federal Work-Study, institutionally sponsored loans, and unspecified assistantships also available. Financial award application deadline: 4/15. *Faculty research:* American politics, international relations, state and local government, comparative government, public administration. Total annual research expenditures: $890,000. *Unit head:* Dr. David A. Breaux, Head, 662-325-2711, Fax: 662-325-2716, E-mail: dab1@ps.msstate.edu. *Application contact:* Dr. William A. Person, Interim Associate Vice President for Academic Affairs/Interim Dean of Graduate Studies, 662-325-7400, Fax: 662-325-1967, E-mail: grad@grad.msstate.edu.

Monmouth University, Graduate School, Department of Public Policy, West Long Branch, NJ 07764-1898. Offers MA. *Faculty:* 8 full-time (4 women). *Students:* 6 full-time (3 women), 24 part-time (15 women); includes 1 Asian American or Pacific Islander, 3 Hispanic Americans. Average age 28. 24 applicants, 96% accepted, 20 enrolled. *Degree requirements:* For master's, 30 credits. *Entrance requirements:* For master's, 2.75 overall GPA. Additional exam requirements/recommendations for international students: Required—TOEFL (minimum score 550 paper-based; 213 computer-based; 79 iBT), IELTS (minimum score 5), MELAB 77, Cambridge A, B, C. *Application deadline:* For fall admission, 7/15 for domestic students; for spring admission, 11/15 for domestic students. Application fee: $50. *Financial support:* In 2007–08, 25 students received support, including 25 fellowships (averaging $2,178 per year), 1 research assistantship (averaging $4,902 per year); career-related internships or fieldwork, scholarships/grants, tuition waivers (partial), and unspecified assistantships also available. Support available to part-time students. *Faculty research:* Political theory, international relations and comparative politics, globalization, politics of language, family sociology, race-class-gender studies, U.S. Senate and impact of domestic politics on U.S. foreign policy. *Unit head:* Dr. Joseph Patten, Program Director, 732-263-5742, E-mail: jpatten@monmouth.edu. *Application contact:* Kevin Roane, Director, Office of Graduate Admission, 732-571-3452, Fax: 732-263-5123, E-mail: gradadm@monmouth.edu.

National University of Singapore, Lee Kuan Yew School of Public Policy, Singapore, Singapore. Offers MPA, MPM, MPP, PhD.

See Close-Up on page 1605.

New England College, Program in Public Policy, Henniker, NH 03242-3293. Offers MA. Part-time and evening/weekend programs available. Postbaccalaureate distance learning degree programs offered (no on-campus study). *Degree requirements:* For master's, thesis. *Entrance requirements:* Additional exam requirements/recommendations for international students: Recommended—TOEFL (minimum score 600 paper-based). Electronic applications accepted.

The New School: A University, Milano The New School for Management and Urban Policy, Program in Public and Urban Policy, New York, NY 10011. Offers PhD. Part-time and evening/weekend programs available. *Faculty:* 1 full-time (0 women), 2 part-time/adjunct (1 woman). *Students:* 37 full-time (25 women), 17 part-time (9 women); includes 23 minority (13 African Americans, 2 American Indian/Alaska Native, 6 Asian Americans or Pacific Islanders, 2 Hispanic Americans), 7 international. Average age 41. In 2007, 2 degrees awarded. *Degree requirements:* For doctorate, thesis/dissertation, qualifying exams. *Entrance requirements:* For doctorate, GRE General Test, MA in political science, urban policy or public policy. Additional exam requirements/recommendations for international students: Required—TOEFL (minimum score 600 paper-based; 250 computer-based; 100 iBT). *Application deadline:* For fall admission, 4/15 priority date for domestic students. Applications are processed on a rolling basis. Application fee: $50. *Financial support:* Fellowships, research assistantships, Federal Work-Study, scholarships/grants, and tuition waivers (full and partial) available. Support available to part-time students. Financial award application deadline: 3/1; financial award applicants required to submit FAFSA. *Unit head:* Dr. Howard Berliner, Director, 212-229-5400 Ext. 1616, Fax: 212-229-5904, E-mail: berliner@newschool.edu. *Application contact:* Merida Escandon, Director of Admissions, 212-229-5462 Ext. 1108, Fax: 212-229-5354, E-mail: milanoadmissions@newschool.edu.

See Close-Up on page 1607.

Northeastern University, College of Arts and Sciences, Program in Law, Policy, and Society, Boston, MA 02115-5096. Offers MS, PhD, JD/PhD. Part-time and evening/weekend programs available. *Students:* 54 full-time (34 women), 35 part-time (18 women). Average age 40. 66 applicants, 33% accepted. In 2007, 3 master's, 4 doctorates awarded. *Degree requirements:* For master's, comprehensive exam; for doctorate, comprehensive exam, thesis/dissertation. *Entrance requirements:* For master's, GRE General Test; for doctorate, GRE General Test or LSAT. *Application deadline:* For fall admission, 2/1 for domestic students. Application fee: $50. *Financial support:* In 2007–08, 4 teaching assistantships with tuition reimbursements (averaging $14,035 per year) were awarded; fellowships with tuition reimbursements, research assistantships with tuition reimbursements, tuition waivers (full and partial) and unspecified assistantships also available. Financial award application deadline: 2/1; financial award applicants required to submit FAFSA. *Faculty research:* Policy issues in health, crime, and labor; urban studies; education; law and environmental issues; economic development, international trade and law. *Unit head:* Dr. Joan Fitzgerald, Director, 617-373-3644, Fax: 617-373-4691, E-mail: jo.fitzgerald@neu.edu.

Northern Arizona University, Graduate College, College of Social and Behavioral Sciences, Department of Political Science, Program in Political Science, Flagstaff, AZ 86011. Offers political science (MA); public management (Certificate); public policy (PhD). *Degree requirements:* For master's, thesis optional; for doctorate, one foreign language, thesis/dissertation. *Entrance requirements:* For doctorate, GRE General Test.

Northwestern University, The Graduate School, School of Education and Social Policy, Program in Human Development and Social Policy, Evanston, IL 60208. Offers PhD. Admissions and degrees offered through The Graduate School. *Faculty:* 13 full-time (5 women), 7 part-time/adjunct (2 women). *Students:* 32 full-time (31 women); includes 5 minority (3 African Americans, 2 Hispanic Americans), 1 international. Average age 30. 93 applicants, 11% accepted, 5 enrolled. In 2007, 1 degree awarded. *Degree requirements:* For doctorate, comprehensive exam, thesis/dissertation. *Entrance requirements:* For doctorate, GRE General Test, writing sample. Additional exam requirements/recommendations for international students: Required—TOEFL (minimum score 600 paper-based; 250 computer-based; 100 iBT). *Application deadline:* For fall admission, 12/31 priority date for domestic and international students. Application fee: $75. Electronic applications accepted. *Financial support:* In 2007–08, 31 students received support, including 5 fellowships with full tuition reimbursements available; research assistantships with full tuition reimbursements available, teaching assistantships with full tuition reimbursements available, institutionally sponsored loans, scholarships/grants, and unspecified assistantships also available. Financial award application deadline: 12/31; financial award applicants required to submit FAFSA. *Faculty research:* Social context of development; social policy issues affecting children, adolescents, adults, and families. *Unit head:* Dr. Dan McAdams, Coordinator, 847-491-4329. *Application contact:* Mary Lou Manning, Department Assistant, 847-491-4329, Fax: 847-491-8999, E-mail: mmanning@northwestern.edu.

See Close-Up on page 1613.

Pepperdine University, School of Public Policy, Malibu, CA 90263. Offers American politics (MPP); economics (MPP); international relations (MPP); public policy (MPP); state and local policy (MPP). *Entrance requirements:* For master's, GRE, 2 letters of recommendation, resumé. Additional exam requirements/recommendations for international students: Required—TOEFL. Electronic applications accepted.

See Close-Up on page 1619.

Queen's University at Kingston, School of Graduate Studies and Research, School of Policy Studies, Kingston, ON K7L 3N6, Canada. Offers MPA, MPA/LL B. Part-time programs available. *Entrance requirements:* For master's, minimum B+ average. Additional exam requirements/recommendations for international students: Required—TOEFL. *Faculty research:* Public management, social policy, defense management, health policy, the third sector.

Regent University, Graduate School, Robertson School of Government, Virginia Beach, VA 23464-9800. Offers health care policy and administration (MA); international politics (MA); law and public policy (MA); political leadership and management (MA); political management (MA); public administration (MA); public policy (MA); terrorism and homeland defense (MA); world economies and political development (MA); JD/MA; M Div/MA; M Ed/MA; MBA/MA. Part-time programs available. *Faculty:* 6 full-time (2 women), 11 part-time/adjunct (1 woman). *Students:* 50 full-time (31 women), 67 part-time (32 women); includes 31 minority (20 African Americans, 1 American Indian/Alaska Native, 2 Asian Americans or Pacific Islanders, 8 Hispanic Americans), 2 international. Average age 31. 147 applicants, 50% accepted, 28 enrolled. In 2007, 47 degrees awarded. *Degree requirements:* For master's, thesis optional, internship. *Entrance requirements:* For master's, GRE General Test or LSAT, minimum undergraduate GPA of 3.0, writing sample, resumé, interview, references, transcripts. Additional exam requirements/recommendations for international students: Required—TOEFL (minimum score 577 paper-based; 233 computer-based). *Application deadline:* For fall admission, 5/1 priority date for domestic students; for spring admission, 11/1 priority date for domestic students. Applications are processed on a rolling basis. Application fee: $50. Electronic applications accepted. *Expenses:* Contact institution. *Financial support:* In 2007–08, 123 students received support. Career-related internships or fieldwork, scholarships/grants, tuition waivers (full and partial), and unspecified assistantships available. Support available to part-time students. Financial award application deadline: 9/1; financial award applicants required to submit FAFSA. *Faculty research:* Education reform, political character issues, social capital concerns, administrative ethics, biblical law and public policy. *Unit head:* Dr. Charles W. Dunn, Dean, 757-226-4322, Fax: 757-226-4643, E-mail: cwdunn@regent.edu. *Application contact:* Althea Bishard, Registrar and Executive Director of Enrollment and Academic Services, 800-373-5504, Fax: 757-226-4381, E-mail: admissions@regent.edu.

Regis College, Program in Public Administration, Weston, MA 02493. Offers nonprofit administration (Graduate Certificate); public administration (MPA); public policymaking (Graduate Certificate). Part-time programs available. Postbaccalaureate distance learning degree programs offered. *Faculty:* 1 part-time/adjunct (0 women). *Students:* 2 full-time (both women), 6 part-time (5 women); includes 1 minority (Hispanic American) Average age 25. *Degree requirements:* For master's, thesis. *Entrance requirements:* For master's, GRE or MAT. Application fee: $50. *Expenses:* Tuition: Full-time $25,990; part-time $730 per credit hour. *Unit head:* Dr. Mary Fitzgerald, Director, 781-768-7440, E-mail: mary.fitzgerald@regiscollege.edu.

Rochester Institute of Technology, Graduate Enrollment Services, College of Liberal Arts, Department of Public Policy, Rochester, NY 14623-5603. Offers MS. *Students:* 14 full-time (7 women), 4 part-time (1 woman); includes 1 minority (African American), 1 international. 5 applicants, 40% accepted, 2 enrolled. In 2007, 5 degrees awarded. *Degree requirements:* For master's, thesis. *Entrance requirements:* For master's, GRE General Test, minimum GPA of 3.0. Additional exam requirements/recommendations for international students: Required—TOEFL (minimum score 570 paper-based; 230 computer-based; 88 iBT). *Application deadline:* For fall admission, 3/1 priority date for domestic students. Applications are processed on a rolling basis. Application fee: $50. Electronic applications accepted. *Expenses:* Tuition: Full-time $28,491; part-time $800 per credit hour. Required fees: $201; $67 per term. *Financial support:* Fellowships with partial tuition reimbursements, research assistantships with partial tuition reimbursements, teaching assistantships with partial tuition reimbursements, career-related internships or fieldwork, institutionally sponsored loans, scholarships/grants, and unspecified assistantships available. Support available to part-time students. Financial award applicants required to submit FAFSA. *Unit head:* James Winebrake, Chair, 585-475-4648, E-mail: jjwgpt@rit.edu.

Rutgers, The State University of New Jersey, Camden, Graduate School of Arts and Sciences, Department of Public Policy and Administration, Camden, NJ 08102-1401. Offers education policy and leadership (MPA); international public service and development (MPA); public management (MPA); JD/MPA. *Accreditation:* NASPAA. Part-time and evening/weekend programs available. *Degree requirements:* For master's, directed study, research workshop. *Entrance requirements:* For master's, GRE General Test, GMAT or LSAT. Additional exam requirements/recommendations for international students: Required—TOEFL (minimum score 550 paper-based; 213 computer-based). Electronic applications accepted. *Faculty research:* Nonprofit management, county and municipal administration, health and human services, government communication, administrative law, educational finance.

Rutgers, The State University of New Jersey, Newark, Graduate School, Program in Public Administration, Newark, NJ 07102. Offers health care administration (MPA); human resources administration (MPA); public administration (PhD); public management (MPA); public policy analysis (MPA); urban systems and issues (MPA). *Accreditation:* NASPAA (one or more programs are accredited). Part-time and evening/weekend programs available. *Degree requirements:* For master's, comprehensive exam, thesis or alternative; for doctorate, thesis/dissertation. *Entrance requirements:* For master's, GRE, minimum undergraduate B average; for doctorate, GRE, MPA, minimum B average. Electronic applications accepted. *Faculty research:* Government finance, municipal and state government, public productivity.

Rutgers, The State University of New Jersey, New Brunswick, Edward J. Bloustein School of Planning and Public Policy, Program in Public Policy, New Brunswick, NJ 08901-1281. Offers MPAP, MPP, JD/MPAP. Part-time and evening/weekend programs available. *Entrance requirements:* For master's, GRE General Test or LSAT. Electronic applications accepted. *Faculty research:* Public finance, legislative process, public opinion, economics and public policy, campaigning.

Saint Louis University, Graduate School, College of Education and Public Service and Graduate School, Department of Public Policy Studies, St. Louis, MO 63103-2097. Offers geographic information systems (Certificate); organizational development (Certificate); public administration (MAPA); public policy analysis (PhD); urban affairs (MAUA); urban planning and real estate development (MUPRED). *Accreditation:* NASPAA. Part-time programs available. *Faculty:* 8 full-time (2 women), 1 part-time/adjunct (0 women). *Students:* 55 full-time (18 women), 57 part-time (27 women); includes 20 minority (15 African Americans, 1 Asian American or Pacific Islander, 4 Hispanic Americans), 7 international. Average age 34. 79 applicants, 76% accepted, 34 enrolled. In 2007, 11 master's, 1 doctorate awarded. *Degree requirements:* For master's, comprehensive exam (for some programs), thesis (for some programs); for doctorate, comprehensive exam, thesis/dissertation, preliminary exams. *Entrance requirements:* For master's and doctorate, GMAT, GRE General Test, or LSAT, letters of recommendation, resumé, interview, transcripts, goal statement. Additional exam requirements/recommendations for international students: Required—TOEFL (minimum score 525 paper-based; 194 computer-based). *Application deadline:* For fall admission, 7/1 for domestic and international students; for spring admission, 11/1 for domestic and international students. Applications are processed on a rolling basis. Application fee: $40. Electronic applications accepted. *Expenses:* Tuition: Part-time $845 per credit hour. Required fees: $105 per semester. *Financial support:* In 2007–08, 36 students received support, including 8 teaching assistantships with full tuition reimbursements available (averaging $12,000 per year); Federal Work-Study, scholarships/grants, traineeships, health care benefits, tuition waivers (partial), and unspecified assistantships also available. Support available to part-time students. Financial award application deadline: 2/1; financial award applicants required to submit FAFSA. *Faculty research:* Urban politics, brown fields, e-government, and administration, evaluation research, community development, electronic government and governance. Total annual research expenditures: $100,000. *Unit head:* Dr. Robert A. Cropf, Chairperson, 314-977-3936, Fax: 314-977-3943, E-mail: cropfra@slu.edu. *Application contact:* Gary U. Behrman, Associate Dean of Graduate School Admissions, 314-977-3827, Fax: 314-977-3943, E-mail: behrmang@slu.edu.

San Francisco State University, Division of Graduate Studies, College of Behavioral and Social Sciences, Public Administration Program, San Francisco, CA 94132-1722. Offers integrated and collaborative services (MPA); nonprofit administration (MPA); policy analysis (MPA); public management (MPA); urban administration (MPA). *Accreditation:* NASPAA. *Unit head:* Dr. Genie Stowers, Director, 415-817-4457, Fax: 415-338-1980, E-mail: gstowers@sfsu.edu.

Seton Hall University, College of Arts and Sciences, Department of Public and Healthcare Administration, Program in Public Service: Leadership, Governance, and Policy, South Orange, NJ 07079-2697. Offers MPA. *Accreditation:* NASPAA. Part-time and evening/weekend programs available. *Degree requirements:* For master's, research project. *Entrance requirements:* For master's, GMAT, GRE General Test, or LSAT.

See Close-Up on page 1621.

Simon Fraser University, Graduate Studies, Faculty of Arts and Social Sciences, Public Policy Program, Burnaby, BC V5A 1S6, Canada. Offers MPP. *Degree requirements:* For master's, internship. *Entrance requirements:* For master's, GRE, 3 letters of reference, resumé, minimum undergraduate GPA of 3.0. Additional exam requirements/recommendations for international students: Required—TOEFL (minimum score 570 paper-based; 230 computer-based), TWE (minimum score 5). Electronic applications accepted.

Southern New Hampshire University, School of Community Economic Development, Manchester, NH 03106-1045. Offers MA, MBA, MS, PhD. Part-time and evening/weekend programs available. *Faculty:* 8 full-time (3 women), 16 part-time/adjunct (7 women). *Students:* 332 full-time (166 women), 12 part-time (6 women); includes 91 minority (73 African Americans, 1 Asian American or Pacific Islander, 17 Hispanic Americans), 20 international. Average age 32. 194 applicants, 53% accepted, 92 enrolled. In 2007, 77 master's, 1 doctorate awarded. *Degree requirements:* For master's, thesis or alternative, community project; for doctorate, comprehensive exam, thesis/dissertation, community project. *Entrance requirements:* For master's, 2 years of work experience, minimum GPA of 3.0, 2 letters of recommendation, application, fees, review; for doctorate, 2 years of work experience, minimum GPA of 3.5, 3 letters of recommendation, research samples. Additional exam requirements/recommendations for international students: Required—TOEFL (minimum score 550 paper-based; 300 computer-based; 70 iBT). *Application deadline:* For fall admission, 6/1 for domestic students, 4/1 for international students. Applications are processed on a rolling basis. Application fee: $25. Electronic applications accepted. *Expenses: Contact institution. Financial support:* In 2007–08, 1 research assistantship was awarded; Federal Work-Study also available. Support available to part-time students. Financial award applicants required to submit FAFSA. Total annual research expenditures: $1 million. *Unit head:* Dr. Michael Swack, Dean, 603-644-3135, Fax: 603-644-3130, E-mail: m.swack@snhc.edu. *Application contact:* Anthony Poore, Assistant Dean, 603-644-3123, Fax: 603-644-3130, E-mail: a.poore@snhu.edu.

Southern University and Agricultural and Mechanical College, Graduate School, Nelson Mandela School of Public Policy and Urban Affairs, Program in Public Policy, Baton Rouge, LA 70813. Offers PhD. *Faculty:* 5 full-time (2 women). *Students:* 19 full-time (9 women), 34 part-time (23 women); includes 44 minority (32 African Americans, 12 Asian Americans or Pacific Islanders). 11 applicants, 27% accepted, 3 enrolled. In 2007, 3 degrees awarded. *Degree requirements:* For doctorate, comprehensive exam, thesis/dissertation. *Entrance requirements:* For doctorate, GRE General Test. Additional exam requirements/recommendations for international students: Required—TOEFL (minimum score 525 paper-based; 193 computer-based). *Application deadline:* For fall admission, 4/15 priority date for domestic and international students; for spring admission, 11/1 priority date for domestic and international students. Applications are processed on a rolling basis. Application fee: $25. *Financial support:* Scholarships/grants available. Financial award application deadline: 4/15; financial award applicants required to submit FAFSA. *Unit head:* Dr. Ronald Harris, Chair, 225-771-2034, Fax: 225-771-3105, E-mail: ruow@yahoo.com.

State University of New York at Binghamton, Graduate School, School of Arts and Sciences, Department of Political Science, Binghamton, NY 13902-6000. Offers political science (MA, PhD); public policy (MA, PhD). *Faculty:* 11 full-time (2 women), 1 part-time/adjunct (0 women). *Students:* 37 full-time (12 women), 12 part-time (7 women); includes 5 minority (4 African Americans, 1 Asian American or Pacific Islander), 22 international. Average age 27. 73 applicants, 41% accepted, 11 enrolled. In 2007, 10 master's, 2 doctorates awarded. Terminal master's awarded for partial completion of doctoral program. *Degree requirements:* For master's, thesis or alternative, written exam; for doctorate, 2 foreign languages, thesis/dissertation, written exam. *Entrance requirements:* For master's and doctorate, GRE General Test, GRE Subject Test. Additional exam requirements/recommendations for international students: Required—TOEFL. *Application deadline:* For fall admission, 4/15 priority date for domestic students, 1/15 priority date for international students; for spring admission, 11/1 for domestic students, 10/1 priority date for international students. Applications are processed on a rolling basis. Application fee: $60. Electronic applications accepted. *Financial support:* In 2007–08, 24 students received support, including 5 fellowships with full tuition reimbursements available (averaging $5,000 per year), 2 research assistantships with full tuition reimbursements available (averaging $10,500 per year), 14 teaching assistantships with full tuition reimbursements available (averaging $14,700 per year); career-related internships or fieldwork, Federal Work-Study, institutionally sponsored loans, tuition waivers (full and partial), and unspecified assistantships also available. Support available to part-time students. Financial award application deadline: 2/15. *Unit head:* Dr. David Clark, Chairperson, 607-777-6786, E-mail: dclark@binghamton.edu.

State University of New York Empire State College, Graduate Studies, Program in Business and Policy Studies, Saratoga Springs, NY 12866-4391. Offers MA. Part-time and evening/weekend programs available. Postbaccalaureate distance learning degree programs offered (minimal on-campus study). *Degree requirements:* For master's, thesis, exam. *Entrance requirements:* For master's, proficiency in statistics. Additional exam requirements/recommendations for international students: Required—TOEFL (minimum score 600 paper-based; 280 computer-based). Electronic applications accepted. *Faculty research:* Business history, applied business statistics, labor/management relations, American social problems and business, effect of government economic policies on business.

State University of New York Empire State College, Graduate Studies, Program in Social Policy, Saratoga Springs, NY 12866-4391. Offers MA. Part-time and evening/weekend programs available. Postbaccalaureate distance learning degree programs offered (minimal on-campus study). *Degree requirements:* For master's, thesis, exam. *Entrance requirements:* Additional exam requirements/recommendations for international students: Required—TOEFL (minimum score 600 paper-based; 250 computer-based). Electronic applications accepted. *Faculty research:* Study of culture, society and mass communications, urban culture and policy, social decision making processes.

Stony Brook University, State University of New York, Graduate School, College of Arts and Sciences, Department of Political Science, Stony Brook, NY 11794. Offers political science (MA, PhD); public policy (MAPP). Evening/weekend programs available. *Faculty:* 17 full-time (3 women), 2 part-time/adjunct (0 women). *Students:* 68 full-time (22 women), 23 part-time (13 women); includes 15 minority (4 African Americans, 6 Asian Americans or Pacific Islanders, 5 Hispanic Americans), 21 international. Average age 27. 90 applicants, 70% accepted. In 2007, 29 master's, 3 doctorates awarded. *Degree requirements:* For doctorate, thesis/dissertation. *Entrance requirements:* For master's and doctorate, GRE General Test. *Application deadline:* For fall admission, 1/15 for domestic students. Application fee: $60. *Financial support:* In 2007–08, 25 teaching assistantships were awarded; fellowships, research assistantships also available. Total annual research expenditures: $349,872. *Unit head:* Dr. Jeffrey Segal, Chair, 631-632-7640. *Application contact:* Dr. Stanley Feldman, Director, 631-632-7667, Fax: 631-632-4116, E-mail: stanley.feldman@stonybrook.edu.

See Close-Up on page 1167.

Texas A&M University, George Bush School of Government and Public Service, College Station, TX 77843. Offers advanced international affairs (Certificate); homeland security (Certificate); international affairs (MPIA), including international economics and development, national security affairs; nonprofit management (Certificate); public service and administration (MPSA), including public management, public policy analysis. *Accreditation:* NASPAA. *Faculty:* 39. *Students:* 155 full-time (67 women), 97 part-time (27 women); includes 37 minority (8 African Americans, 2 American Indian/Alaska Native, 4 Asian Americans or Pacific Islanders, 23 Hispanic Americans), 18 international. Average age 24. 249 applicants, 57% accepted, 88 enrolled. In 2007, 69 degrees awarded. *Degree requirements:* For master's, summer internship. *Entrance requirements:* For master's, GRE (preferred) or GMAT. *Application deadline:* For fall admission, 1/24 for domestic and international students. Application fee: $50 ($75 for international students). Electronic applications accepted. *Expenses:* Tuition, state resident: full-time $6,129. Tuition, nonresident: full-time $11,689. Tuition and fees vary according to course load. *Financial support:* In 2007–08, fellowships (averaging $11,000 per year), research assistantships (averaging $11,250 per year) were awarded; career-related internships or fieldwork, Federal Work-Study, and institutionally sponsored loans also available. Financial award application deadline: 2/1; financial award applicants required to submit FAFSA. *Faculty research:* Public policy, Presidential studies, public leadership, economic policy, social policy. *Unit head:* Richard A. Chilcoat, Dean, 979-862-8007, Fax: 979-862-7953, E-mail: bushschool@tamu.edu. *Application contact:* Kathryn Meyer, Recruitment/Placement Officer, 979-458-4767, Fax: 979-845-4155, E-mail: admissions@bushschool.tamu.edu.

See Close-Up on page 1623.

Trinity College, Graduate Programs, Program in Public Policy Studies, Hartford, CT 06106-3100. Offers MA. Part-time and evening/weekend programs available. *Degree requirements:* For master's, thesis optional, departmental qualifying exam. *Entrance requirements:* For master's, minimum GPA of 3.0.

Tufts University, Cummings School of Veterinary Medicine, Program in Animals and Public Policy, North Grafton, MA 01536. Offers MS. *Faculty:* 2 full-time (0 women), 24 part-time/adjunct. *Students:* 13 full-time (12 women); includes 1 minority (Hispanic American) 24 applicants, 58% accepted, 13 enrolled. In 2007, 11 degrees awarded. *Degree requirements:* For master's, thesis or alternative. *Entrance requirements:* For master's, GRE General Test. Additional exam requirements/recommendations for international students: Required—TOEFL. *Application deadline:* For fall admission, 4/1 for domestic and international students. Application fee: $60. Electronic applications accepted. *Expenses: Contact institution. Financial support:* In 2007–08, 12 students received support. Application deadline: 3/7; *Faculty research:* Veterinary ethics, veterinary jurisprudence, companion animal demographics and control, human/animal relationships, wildlife policy issues, animal research ethics. *Unit head:* Dr. Paul Waldau, Director, Center for Animals and Public Policy, 508-839-4671, E-mail: paul.waldau@tufts.edu. *Application contact:* Rebecca Russo, Director of Admissions, 508-839-7920, Fax: 508-887-4820, E-mail: rebecca.russo@tufts.edu.

Tufts University, Graduate School of Arts and Sciences, Department of Urban and Environmental Policy and Planning, Medford, MA 02155. Offers community development (MA); environmental policy (MA); health and human welfare (MA); housing policy (MA); international environment/development policy (MA); public policy (MPP); public policy and citizen participation (MA); MA/MS; MALD/MA. *Accreditation:* ACSP (one or more programs are accredited). Part-time programs available. *Faculty:* 8 full-time, 9 part-time/adjunct. *Students:* 135 (93 women); includes 23 minority (9 African Americans, 5 Asian Americans or Pacific Islanders, 9 Hispanic Americans) 9 international. 174 applicants, 82% accepted, 55 enrolled. In 2007, 32 degrees awarded. *Degree requirements:* For master's, thesis, internship. *Entrance requirements:* For master's, GRE General Test. Additional exam requirements/recommendations for international students: Required—TOEFL (minimum score 550 paper-based; 213 computer-based; 80 iBT). *Application deadline:* For fall admission, 1/15 for domestic students, 12/30 for international students. Applications are processed on a rolling basis. Application fee: $70. Electronic applications accepted. *Expenses: Contact institution. Financial support:* Teaching assistantships with full and partial tuition reimbursements, career-related internships or fieldwork, Federal Work-Study, scholarships/grants, and tuition waivers (partial) available. Support available to part-time students. Financial award application deadline: 1/15; financial award applicants required to submit FAFSA. *Unit head:* Julian Agyeman, Chair, 617-627-3394, Fax: 617-627-3377.

See Close-Up on page 1625.

University at Albany, State University of New York, Nelson A. Rockefeller College of Public Affairs and Policy, Department of Public Administration and Policy, Albany, NY 12222-0001. Offers administrative behavior (PhD); comparative and development administration (MPA, PhD); human resources (MPA); legislative administration (MPA); nonprofit leadership and management (Certificate); planning and policy analysis (CAS); policy analysis (MPA); program analysis and evaluation (PhD); public affairs and policy (MA); public finance (MPA, PhD); public management (MPA, PhD); women and public policy (Certificate); JD/MPA. *Accreditation:* NASPAA (one or more programs are accredited). *Students:* 165 full-time (73 women), 69 part-time (28 women). Average age 29. In 2007, 71 master's, 7 doctorates, 20 other advanced degrees awarded. *Degree requirements:* For doctorate, one foreign language, thesis/dissertation. *Entrance requirements:* For doctorate, GRE General Test. Additional exam requirements/recommendations for international students: Required—TOEFL (minimum score 550 paper-based; 213 computer-based). *Application deadline:* For fall admission, 2/1 priority date for domestic students, 5/1 for international students; for spring admission, 12/1 for domestic students. Applications are processed on a rolling basis. Application fee: $75. Electronic applications accepted. *Expenses:* Tuition, state resident: part-time $576 per credit. Tuition, nonresident: part-time $910 per credit. Tuition and fees vary according to program. *Financial support:* Application deadline: 2/1. *Unit head:* Dr. George Richardson, Chair, 518-442-5258.

Public Policy

The University of Arizona, Graduate College, Eller College of Management, School of Public Administration and Policy, Tucson, AZ 85721. Offers public administration (MPA); public administration and policy (PhD). *Accreditation:* NASPAA. *Faculty:* 9. *Students:* 43 full-time (23 women), 13 part-time (10 women); includes 16 minority (2 African Americans, 2 American Indian/Alaska Native, 1 Asian American or Pacific Islander, 11 Hispanic Americans), 3 international. Average age 28. 60 applicants, 63% accepted, 26 enrolled. In 2007, 25 degrees awarded. *Degree requirements:* For master's, internship of 400 hours; for doctorate, comprehensive exam, thesis/dissertation. *Entrance requirements:* For master's, GRE, 2-3 letters of recommendation, resumè; for doctorate, GMAT or GRE, minimum GPA of 3.5, letter of interest, 3 letters of recommendation, resumè. Additional exam requirements/recommendations for international students: Required—TOEFL (minimum score 650 paper-based; 280 computer-based). *Application deadline:* For fall admission, 4/15 priority date for domestic students. Applications are processed on a rolling basis. Application fee: $50. *Expenses: Contact institution. Financial support:* In 2007–08, 27 students received support, including 5 fellowships (averaging $2,000 per year), 13 teaching assistantships with partial tuition reimbursements available (averaging $4,182 per year); career-related internships or fieldwork, scholarships/grants, health care benefits, tuition waivers (full and partial), and unspecified assistantships also available. Financial award application deadline: 4/15. Total annual research expenditures: $1.6 million. *Unit head:* Dr. H. Brinton Milward, Director, 520-621-7476, Fax: 520-626-5549, E-mail: bmilward@eller.arizona.edu. *Application contact:* Pamela Adams, Administrative Associate, 520-621-3128, Fax: 520-621-5549, E-mail: adamsp@email.arizona.edu.

University of Arkansas, Graduate School, Interdisciplinary Program in Public Policy, Fayetteville, AR 72701-1201. Offers PhD. *Students:* 20 full-time (10 women), 42 part-time (27 women); includes 16 minority (10 African Americans, 3 American Indian/Alaska Native, 1 Asian American or Pacific Islander, 2 Hispanic Americans), 13 international. In 2007, 4 degrees awarded. *Degree requirements:* For doctorate, thesis/dissertation. Application fee: $40 ($50 for international students). *Financial support:* In 2007–08, 11 fellowships with tuition reimbursements, 4 research assistantships, 2 teaching assistantships were awarded. Financial award application deadline: 4/1; financial award applicants required to submit FAFSA. *Unit head:* Dr. Brinck Kerr, Head, 479-575-3356, Fax: 479-575-5908, E-mail: jbkerr@uark.edu.

University of California, Berkeley, Graduate Division, Graduate School of Public Policy, Berkeley, CA 94720-1500. Offers MPP, PhD, JD/MPP, MPP/MA, MPP/MPH, MPP/MS. *Degree requirements:* For doctorate, thesis/dissertation, qualifying exam. *Entrance requirements:* For master's and doctorate, GRE General Test, minimum GPA of 3.0, 3 letters of recommendation. *Application deadline:* For fall admission, 12/15 for domestic students. Application fee: $70 ($90 for international students). *Financial support:* Fellowships, research assistantships, teaching assistantships, unspecified assistantships available. *Unit head:* Michael Nacht, Dean, 510-642-4670, E-mail: nacht@socrates.berkeley.edu. *Application contact:* Jalilah LaBrie, Student Affairs Officer, 510-642-4670, Fax: 510-643-9657, E-mail: gsppadm@berkeley.edu.

University of California, Berkeley, Graduate Division, Haas School of Business, Program in Business, Berkeley, CA 94720-1500. Offers accounting (PhD); business and public policy (PhD); finance (PhD); marketing (PhD); organizational behavior and industrial relations (PhD); real estate (PhD). *Accreditation:* AACSB. *Students:* 77 full-time (22 women); includes 21 minority (17 Asian Americans or Pacific Islanders, 4 Hispanic Americans), 23 international. Average age 31. 401 applicants, 8% accepted, 15 enrolled. In 2007, 14 doctorates awarded. *Median time to degree:* Of those who began their doctoral program in fall 1999, 100% received their degree in 8 years or less. *Degree requirements:* For doctorate, comprehensive exam, thesis/dissertation, oral exam, written preliminary exams. *Entrance requirements:* For doctorate, GMAT or GRE, minimum GPA of 3.0. Additional exam requirements/recommendations for international students: Required—TOEFL (minimum score 570 paper-based; 230 computer-based; 68 iBT), IELTS (minimum score 7). *Application deadline:* For fall admission, 12/15 for domestic and international students. Application fee: $60 ($80 for international students). Electronic applications accepted. *Financial support:* Fellowships with full and partial tuition reimbursements, research assistantships with full and partial tuition reimbursements, teaching assistantships with full and partial tuition reimbursements, career-related internships or fieldwork, Federal Work-Study, scholarships/grants, health care benefits, tuition waivers (full), unspecified assistantships, and transit pass, travel grants available. Financial award application deadline: 12/15; financial award applicants required to submit FAFSA. *Unit head:* Miguel Villas-Boas, Director, 510-642-1409, Fax: 510-643-4255, E-mail: kimg@haas.berkeley.edu. *Application contact:* Kim Guilfoyle, Administrative Director, 510-642-3944, Fax: 510-643-4255, E-mail: kimg@haas.berkeley.edu.

University of California, Los Angeles, Graduate Division, School of Public Affairs, Program in Public Policy, Los Angeles, CA 90095. Offers MPP. *Students:* 75 (55 women); includes 24 minority (5 African Americans, 13 Asian Americans or Pacific Islanders, 6 Hispanic Americans) 11 international. 337 applicants, 40% accepted, 40 enrolled. In 2007, 29 degrees awarded. *Entrance requirements:* For master's, GRE General Test, minimum GPA of 3.0. Additional exam requirements/recommendations for international students: Required—TOEFL. *Application deadline:* For fall admission, 2/1 for domestic students. Application fee: $60. Electronic applications accepted. *Expenses:* Tuition, nonresident: full-time $5,728. Required fees: $8,966. Full-time tuition and fees vary according to program and student level. *Financial support:* In 2007–08, 33 fellowships, 19 research assistantships, 12 teaching assistantships were awarded. Financial award application deadline: 3/1. *Unit head:* Michael Stoll, Chair, 310-825-7667. *Application contact:* Departmental Office, 310-825-7667, E-mail: mppinfo@sppsr.ucla.edu.

University of Chicago, Irving B. Harris Graduate School of Public Policy Studies, Chicago, IL 60637-1513. Offers environmental science and policy (MS); public policy studies (AM, MPP, PhD); JD/MPP; MBA/MPP; MPP/M Div; MPP/MA. Part-time programs available. *Degree requirements:* For doctorate, thesis/dissertation. *Entrance requirements:* Additional exam requirements/recommendations for international students: Required—TOEFL. Electronic applications accepted. Expenses: Contact institution. *Faculty research:* Family and child policy, international security, health policy, social policy.

See Close-Up on page 1629.

University of Colorado at Boulder, Graduate School, College of Arts and Sciences, Department of Political Science, Boulder, CO 80309. Offers international affairs (MA); political science (MA, PhD); public policy (MA). *Faculty:* 27. *Students:* 49 full-time (22 women), 20 part-time (8 women); includes 5 minority (3 Asian Americans or Pacific Islanders, 2 Hispanic Americans), 9 international. Average age 29. 64 applicants, 50% accepted. In 2007, 16 master's, 7 doctorates awarded. Terminal master's awarded for partial completion of doctoral program. *Degree requirements:* For master's, comprehensive exam, thesis; for doctorate, one foreign language, thesis/dissertation. *Entrance requirements:* For master's, GRE General Test, minimum undergraduate GPA of 3.0; for doctorate, GRE General Test, minimum GPA of 3.5 (undergraduate), 3.0 (graduate). *Application deadline:* For fall admission, 12/31 priority date for domestic students, 12/31 for international students. Application fee: $50 ($60 for international students). *Financial support:* In 2007–08, 5 fellowships (averaging $3,024 per year), 1 research assistantship (averaging $16,252 per year) were awarded; Federal Work-Study also available. Financial award application deadline: 12/31. *Faculty research:* American government and politics, comparative politics, international relations, law and politics, public policy, political philosophy, empirical theory and methodology. Total annual research expenditures: $427,386. *Unit head:* Steven Chan, Chair, 303-492-8601, Fax: 303-492-0978, E-mail: steve.chan@colorado.edu. *Application contact:* Mary Gregory, Graduate Program Assistant, 303-492-7872, Fax: 303-492-0978, E-mail: pscigrad@colorado.edu.

University of Delaware, College of Human Services, Education and Public Policy, Center for Energy and Environmental Policy, Program in Urban Affairs and Public Policy, Newark, DE 19716. Offers community development and nonprofit leadership (MA); energy and environmental policy (MA); governance, planning and management (PhD); historic preservation (MA); social and urban policy (PhD); technology, environment and society (PhD). Part-time programs available. Terminal master's awarded for partial completion of doctoral program. *Degree requirements:* For master's, analytical paper or thesis; for doctorate, thesis/dissertation. *Entrance requirements:* For master's, GRE General Test, minimum GPA of 3.0; for doctorate, GRE General Test, minimum GPA of 3.5. Additional exam requirements/recommendations for international students: Required—TOEFL. *Application deadline:* Applications are processed on a rolling basis. Application fee: $60. Electronic applications accepted. *Financial support:* Career-related internships or fieldwork, Federal Work-Study, and tuition waivers (full) available. *Faculty research:* Political economy; social policy analysis; technology and society; historic preservation; urban policy. Total annual research expenditures: $1 million.

See Close-Up on page 1635.

University of Denver, Faculty of Arts and Humanities/Social Sciences, Department of Public Policy, Denver, CO 80208. Offers MPP. *Faculty:* 3 full-time (0 women). *Students:* 17 full-time (13 women), 4 part-time (1 woman); includes 2 minority (both Hispanic Americans) Average age 27. In 2007, 10 degrees awarded. *Application deadline:* Applications are processed on a rolling basis. Application fee: $50. Electronic applications accepted. *Financial support:* In 2007–08, 2 teaching assistantships with full and partial tuition reimbursements (averaging $2,500 per year) were awarded. *Unit head:* Richard Caldwell, Director, 303-871-2468. *Application contact:* Mandy Anderson, Information Contact, 303-871-4920, E-mail: manander@du.edu.

University of Georgia, School of Public and International Affairs, Program in Public Administration and Policy, Athens, GA 30602. Offers public administration (MPA, PhD). *Accreditation:* NASPAA (one or more programs are accredited). *Faculty:* 17 full-time (4 women), 2 part-time/adjunct (0 women). *Students:* 116 full-time (57 women), 61 part-time (36 women); includes 16 African Americans, 2 Asian Americans or Pacific Islanders, 3 Hispanic Americans, 15 international. 225 applicants, 44% accepted, 55 enrolled. In 2007, 58 master's, 9 doctorates awarded. *Degree requirements:* For master's, internship; for doctorate, thesis/dissertation. *Entrance requirements:* For master's and doctorate, GRE General Test. *Application deadline:* For fall admission, 7/1 priority date for domestic students; for spring admission, 11/15 for domestic students. Application fee: $50. Electronic applications accepted. *Financial support:* Fellowships, research assistantships, teaching assistantships, unspecified assistantships available. *Unit head:* Dr. Laurence J. O'Toole, Head, 706-542-2057, E-mail: cmsotool@uga.edu. *Application contact:* Dr. J. Edward Kellough, Graduate Coordinator, 706-542-0488, Fax: 706-542-4421, E-mail: kellough@uga.edu.

University of Guelph, Graduate Program Services, College of Social and Applied Human Sciences, Department of Political Science, Guelph, ON N1G 2W1, Canada. Offers comparative politics (MA); international development (MA); political science (MA); public policy and public administration (MA); the Americas (Canada emphasis) (MA). MA in public policy and public administration offered in collaboration with Department of Political Science of McMaster University. *Faculty:* 20 full-time (8 women), 2 part-time/adjunct (0 women). *Students:* 41 full-time (25 women). Average age 26. 130 applicants, 23% accepted, 25 enrolled. In 2007, 19 degrees awarded. *Degree requirements:* For master's, thesis or paper. *Entrance requirements:* For master's, minimum B average during previous 2 years of course work, 4 year Honours Degree in Political Science. Additional exam requirements/recommendations for international students: Required—TOEFL. *Application deadline:* For fall admission, 2/1 for domestic and international students. Application fee: $85. Electronic applications accepted. *Financial support:* In 2007–08, 9 research assistantships (averaging $2,000 per year), 58 teaching assistantships (averaging $5,106 per year) were awarded; scholarships/grants also available. *Faculty research:* Political ethics, constitutional power. *Unit head:* Dr. B. Sheldrick, Chair, 519-824-4120 Ext. 56503, Fax: 519-822-7703, E-mail: sheldric@uoguelph.ca. *Application contact:* Dr. C. Johnson, Coordinator, 519-824-4120, Fax: 519-822-7703, E-mail: cajohnso@uoguelph.ca.

University of Hawaii at Manoa, Graduate Division, Colleges of Arts and Sciences, College of Social Sciences, Public Policy Center, Honolulu, HI 96822. Offers Graduate Certificate. Part-time programs available. *Faculty:* 4 full-time (2 women). *Students:* 1 (woman) full-time, 1 part-time. *Entrance requirements:* Additional exam requirements/recommendations for international students: Required—TOEFL (minimum score 500 paper-based; 173 computer-based; 61 iBT), IELTS (minimum score 5). *Application deadline:* For fall admission, 3/1 for domestic students, 2/1 for international students. *Financial support:* Research assistantships available. *Application contact:* Susan Chandler, Interim Director, 808-956-4237, Fax: 808-956-0950, E-mail: chandler@hawaii.edu.

University of Illinois at Chicago, Graduate College, College of Urban Planning and Public Affairs, Program in Urban Planning and Policy, Chicago, IL 60607-7128. Offers public policy analysis (PhD); urban planning and policy (MUPP). *Accreditation:* ACSP (one or more programs are accredited). Part-time programs available. *Degree requirements:* For master's, thesis or alternative, internship; for doctorate, thesis/dissertation. *Entrance requirements:* For master's and doctorate, GRE General Test, minimum GPA of 2.75, writing sample. Additional exam requirements/recommendations for international students: Required—TOEFL. Electronic applications accepted.

University of Illinois at Chicago, Graduate College, Liautaud Graduate School of Business, Department of Economics, Chicago, IL 60607-7128. Offers economics (MA, PhD); public policy analysis (PhD); MBA/MA. Terminal master's awarded for partial completion of doctoral program. *Degree requirements:* For master's, comprehensive exam; for doctorate, thesis/dissertation. *Entrance requirements:* For master's and doctorate, GRE General Test, minimum GPA of 2.75. Additional exam requirements/recommendations for international students: Required—TOEFL. Electronic applications accepted. *Faculty research:* International, labor, and urban economics.

University of Louisville, Graduate School, College of Arts and Sciences, Department of Urban and Public Affairs, Program in Public Administration, Louisville, KY 40292-0001. Offers labor and public management (MPA); public policy and administration (MPA); urban and regional development (MPA). *Accreditation:* NASPAA. *Students:* 21 full-time (14 women), 22 part-time (12 women); includes 6 minority (4 African Americans, 1 Asian American or Pacific Islander, 1 Hispanic American), 1 international. Average age 30. In 2007, 15 degrees awarded. *Degree requirements:* For master's, practicum or thesis. *Entrance requirements:* For master's, GRE General Test, minimum GPA of 3.25, resumé. *Application deadline:* For fall admission, 7/1 priority date for domestic students; for spring admission, 12/1 priority date for domestic students. Applications are processed on a rolling basis. Application fee: $50. *Unit head:* Dr. Steve Koven, Director, 502-852-7906, Fax: 502-852-4558, E-mail: sgkove01@louisville.edu.

University of Maryland, Baltimore County, Graduate School, College of Arts, Humanities and Social Sciences, Department of Economics, Program in Economic Policy Analysis, Baltimore, MD 21250. Offers MA. Part-time and evening/weekend programs available. *Faculty:* 25 full-time (8 women), 1 part-time/adjunct (0 women). *Students:* 9 full-time (6 women), 12 part-time (6 women); includes 7 minority (3 African Americans, 3 Asian Americans or Pacific Islanders, 1 Hispanic American), 3 international. Average age 29. 33 applicants, 61% accepted, 9 enrolled. In 2007, 6 degrees awarded. *Degree requirements:* For master's, comprehensive exam. *Entrance requirements:* For master's, GRE General Test, undergraduate coursework in economic theory, econometrics, calculus. Additional exam requirements/recommendations for international students: Required—TOEFL. *Application deadline:* For fall admission, 7/1 for domestic students, 1/1 priority date for international students. Applications are processed on a rolling basis. Application fee: $45. Electronic applications accepted. *Financial support:* In 2007–08, 5 students received support, including 4 research assistantships with full and partial tuition reimbursements available (averaging $11,324 per year), 1 teaching assistantship with full tuition reimbursement available (averaging $11,324 per year); Federal Work-Study, health care benefits, tuition waivers (full and partial), and unspecified assistantships also available. Support available to part-time students. Financial award application deadline: 2/15; financial award applicants required to submit FAFSA. *Faculty research:* International trade policy analysis, health and hospital policy evaluation, environmental policy analysis, economics of education, economic growth and development. Total annual research expenditures: $25,000. *Unit head:*

Dr. David F. Mitch, Professor of Economics and Graduate Director, 410-455-2157, Fax: 410-455-1054, E-mail: mitch@umbc.edu.

University of Maryland, Baltimore County, Graduate School, College of Arts, Humanities and Social Sciences, Department of Public Policy, Baltimore, MD 21250. Offers MPP, PhD. *Accreditation:* NASPAA (one or more programs are accredited). Part-time and evening/weekend programs available. *Faculty:* 41 full-time (10 women), 1 part-time/adjunct (0 women). *Students:* 88 full-time (51 women), 68 part-time (35 women); includes 30 minority (20 African Americans, 2 American Indian/Alaska Native, 4 Asian Americans or Pacific Islanders, 4 Hispanic Americans), 11 international. Average age 33. 87 applicants, 72% accepted, 38 enrolled. In 2007, 13 master's, 17 doctorates awarded. Terminal master's awarded for partial completion of doctoral program. *Degree requirements:* For master's, thesis optional, policy analysis paper; for doctorate, comprehensive exam, thesis/dissertation, field qualifying exam. *Entrance requirements:* For master's and doctorate, GRE General Test, 3 academic letters of reference. Additional exam requirements/recommendations for international students: Required—TOEFL. *Application deadline:* For fall admission, 3/1 priority date for domestic students, 1/1 priority date for international students; for spring admission, 11/1 priority date for domestic students, 5/1 priority date for international students. Applications are processed on a rolling basis. Application fee: $50. Electronic applications accepted. *Financial support:* In 2007–08, 1 fellowship with partial tuition reimbursement (averaging $17,034 per year), 18 research assistantships with full tuition reimbursements (averaging $17,034 per year), teaching assistantships with full tuition reimbursements (averaging $17,034 per year) were awarded; career-related internships or fieldwork, Federal Work-Study, health care benefits, and unspecified assistantships also available. Support available to part-time students. Financial award application deadline: 2/1; financial award applicants required to submit FAFSA. *Faculty research:* Health policy, social policy, urban policy, public management, evaluation and analytical method. Total annual research expenditures: $7 million. *Unit head:* Dr. Donald F. Norris, Chair, 410-455-3201, Fax: 410-455-1172, E-mail: norris@umbc.edu. *Application contact:* Sally F. Helms, Administrator of Academic Affairs, 410-455-3202, Fax: 410-455-1172, E-mail: gradposi@umbc.edu.

See Close-Up on page 1637.

University of Maryland, College Park, Graduate Studies, A. James Clark School of Engineering and School of Public Policy, Program in Engineering and Public Policy, College Park, MD 20742. Offers MS. *Students:* 42 applicants, 36% accepted, 15 enrolled. *Application contact:* Dr. Charles Caramello, Dean of the Graduate School, 301-405-0358, Fax: 301-314-9305, E-mail: ccaramel@umd.edu.

University of Maryland, College Park, Graduate Studies, School of Public Policy, Policy Studies Program, College Park, MD 20742. Offers PhD. *Students:* 36 full-time (15 women), 13 part-time (4 women); includes 2 minority (both Asian Americans or Pacific Islanders), 20 international. 129 applicants, 15% accepted, 12 enrolled. In 2007, 8 degrees awarded. *Median time to degree:* Of those who began their doctoral program in fall 1999, 50% received their degree in 8 years or less. *Degree requirements:* For doctorate, comprehensive exam, thesis/dissertation, written and oral exams. *Entrance requirements:* For doctorate, GRE General Test, writing sample. *Application deadline:* For fall admission, 12/15 for domestic students, 2/1 for international students; for spring admission, 10/15 for domestic students, 6/1 for international students. Applications are processed on a rolling basis. Application fee: $60 ($70 for international students). Electronic applications accepted. *Financial support:* In 2007–08, 12 teaching assistantships (averaging $13,219 per year) were awarded; fellowships also available. Financial award applicants required to submit FAFSA. *Application contact:* Dean of Graduate School, 301-405-0358, Fax: 301-314-9305.

University of Maryland, College Park, Graduate Studies, School of Public Policy, Programs in Public Policy, College Park, MD 20742. Offers MPP, JD/MPP. *Accreditation:* NASPAA. *Students:* 104 full-time (53 women), 19 part-time (11 women); includes 19 minority (6 African Americans, 7 Asian Americans or Pacific Islanders, 6 Hispanic Americans), 27 international. 393 applicants, 51% accepted, 50 enrolled. In 2007, 69 degrees awarded. *Entrance requirements:* Additional exam requirements/recommendations for international students: Required—TOEFL. *Application deadline:* For fall admission, 12/15 for domestic students, 2/1 for international students; for spring admission, 10/15 for domestic students, 6/1 for international students. Applications are processed on a rolling basis. Application fee: $60. Electronic applications accepted. *Financial support:* In 2007–08, 60 teaching assistantships (averaging $13,543 per year) were awarded; fellowships also available. *Application contact:* Dean of Graduate School, 301-405-0358, Fax: 301-314-9305.

University of Massachusetts Amherst, Graduate School, College of Social and Behavioral Sciences, Center for Public Policy and Administration, Amherst, MA 01003. Offers MPA, MPPA. Part-time programs available. *Students:* 30 full-time (22 women), 9 part-time (6 women); includes 5 minority (3 Asian Americans or Pacific Islanders, 2 Hispanic Americans), 5 international. Average age 32. 79 applicants, 63% accepted, 38 enrolled. In 2007, 16 degrees awarded. *Degree requirements:* For master's, thesis or alternative. *Entrance requirements:* For master's, GRE General Test. Additional exam requirements/recommendations for international students: Required—TOEFL (minimum score 530 paper-based; 197 computer-based). *Application deadline:* For fall admission, 2/1 priority date for domestic and international students. Applications are processed on a rolling basis. Application fee: $50 ($65 for international students). Electronic applications accepted. *Expenses:* Tuition, state resident: full-time $2,640; part-time $110 per credit. Tuition, nonresident: full-time $9,936; part-time $414 per credit. Required fees: $7,455. One-time fee: $332. Tuition and fees vary according to course load, campus/location, program and reciprocity agreements. *Financial support:* In 2007–08, 2 fellowships with full tuition reimbursements (averaging $6,250 per year), 18 research assistantships with full tuition reimbursements (averaging $5,212 per year) were awarded; teaching assistantships with full tuition reimbursements, career-related internships or fieldwork, Federal Work-Study, scholarships/grants, traineeships, and unspecified assistantships also available. Support available to part-time students. Financial award application deadline: 2/1. *Unit head:* Dr. John Hird, Chair, 413-545-2438, Fax: 413-545-3349, E-mail: jhird@pubpol.umass.edu.

University of Massachusetts Amherst, Graduate School, Interdisciplinary Programs, Program in Public Policy and Business Administration, Amherst, MA 01003. Offers MBA/MPP. *Students:* 3 full-time (1 woman). 4 applicants, 75% accepted, 1 enrolled. *Application deadline:* For fall admission, 2/1 for domestic and international students. Application fee: $50 ($65 for international students). *Expenses:* Tuition, state resident: full-time $2,640; part-time $110 per credit. Tuition, nonresident: full-time $9,936; part-time $414 per credit. Required fees: $7,455. One-time fee: $332. Tuition and fees vary according to course load, campus/location, program and reciprocity agreements. *Unit head:* Dr. M. V. Badgett, Head, 413-545-3956, Fax: 413-545-1108.

University of Massachusetts Boston, Office of Graduate Studies, John W. McCormack Graduate School of Policy Studies, Program in Public Policy, Boston, MA 02125-3393. Offers PhD. Evening/weekend programs available. *Degree requirements:* For doctorate, comprehensive exam, thesis/dissertation, practicum, oral exam. *Entrance requirements:* For doctorate, GRE General Test. *Faculty research:* Political economy, public managerial control, healthcare policy, planning and public policy theory, economic development.

University of Massachusetts Dartmouth, Graduate School, College of Arts and Sciences, Program in Policy Studies, North Dartmouth, MA 02747-2300. Offers MPP. Part-time programs available. *Faculty:* 3 full-time (1 woman). *Students:* 6 full-time (3 women), 14 part-time (10 women). Average age 39. 14 applicants, 100% accepted, 11 enrolled. *Entrance requirements:* For master's, GRE or GMAT. Additional exam requirements/recommendations for international students: Required—TOEFL (minimum score 500 paper-based; 213 computer-based). *Application deadline:* For fall admission, 4/20 for domestic students, 2/20 for international students; for spring admission, 11/15 for domestic students, 9/15 for international students. Applications are processed on a rolling basis. Application fee: $40 ($60 for international students). Electronic applications accepted. *Expenses:* Tuition, state resident: full-time $2,071; part-time $86 per credit. Tuition, nonresident: full-time $8,099; part-time $337 per credit. Part-time tuition and fees vary according to course load and program. *Financial support:* In 2007–08, 1 research assistantship (averaging $9,000 per year) was awarded; teaching assistantships, Federal Work-Study and unspecified assistantships also available. Support available to part-time students. Financial award application deadline: 3/1. *Unit head:* Al Bavon, Chairperson, 508-999-8374, E-mail: abavon@umassd.edu. *Application contact:* Carol Novo, Graduate Admissions Officer, 508-999-8604, Fax: 508-999-8183, E-mail: graduate@umassd.edu.

University of Memphis, Graduate School, College of Arts and Sciences, School of Urban Affairs and Public Policy, Division of Public and Nonprofit Administration, Memphis, TN 38152. Offers nonprofit administration (MPA); public management and policy (MPA); urban management and planning (MPA). *Accreditation:* NASPAA. Part-time and evening/weekend programs available. *Faculty:* 6 full-time (3 women), 1 (woman) part-time/adjunct. *Students:* 16 full-time (10 women), 43 part-time (31 women); includes 27 minority (26 African Americans, 1 Asian American or Pacific Islander). Average age 33. 31 applicants, 58% accepted, 9 enrolled. In 2007, 13 master's awarded. *Degree requirements:* For master's, comprehensive exam, thesis or alternative, internship. *Entrance requirements:* For master's, GRE General Test, GMAT, or MAT, minimum GPA of 3.0. *Application deadline:* For fall admission, 8/1 for domestic students; for spring admission, 12/1 for domestic students. Applications are processed on a rolling basis. Application fee: $35 ($60 for international students). *Expenses:* Tuition, state resident: full-time $6,990; part-time $377 per hour. Tuition, nonresident: full-time $17,818; part-time $830 per hour. Tuition and fees vary according to course load and program. *Financial support:* In 2007–08, 7 research assistantships with full tuition reimbursements (averaging $4,500 per year) were awarded; fellowships, career-related internships or fieldwork, Federal Work-Study, and scholarships/grants also available. Support available to part-time students. *Faculty research:* Nonprofit organization governance, local government management, community collaboration, urban problems, accountability. *Unit head:* Dr. Dorothy Norris-Tirrell, Director, 901-678-3360, Fax: 901-678-2981, E-mail: dnrrstrr@memphis.edu. *Application contact:* Dr. Charles Menifield, Director of Admissions, 901-678-3369, Fax: 901-678-2981, E-mail: cmenifld@memphis.edu.

University of Michigan, Horace H. Rackham School of Graduate Studies, College of Literature, Science, and the Arts, Department of Economics, Ann Arbor, MI 48109. Offers applied economics (AM); economics (AM, PhD); public policy and economics (PhD); social work and economics (PhD); JD/PhD; MPP/AM. *Faculty:* 56 full-time (9 women). *Students:* 147 full-time (50 women); includes 13 minority (4 African Americans, 6 Asian Americans or Pacific Islanders, 3 Hispanic Americans), 55 international. Average age 27. 519 applicants, 29% accepted, 30 enrolled. In 2007, 42 master's, 26 doctorates awarded. Terminal master's awarded for partial completion of doctoral program. *Median time to degree:* Of those who began their doctoral program in fall 1999, 38% received their degree in 8 years or less. *Degree requirements:* For doctorate, oral defense of dissertation, preliminary exam. *Entrance requirements:* For master's and doctorate, GRE General Test. Additional exam requirements/recommendations for international students: Required—TOEFL (minimum score 600 paper-based; 250 computer-based). *Application deadline:* For fall admission, 12/15 for domestic and international students. Application fee: $60 ($75 for international students). Electronic applications accepted. *Financial support:* In 2007–08, 114 students received support, including 46 fellowships with tuition reimbursements available (averaging $16,000 per year), 6 research assistantships with tuition reimbursements available (averaging $15,200 per year), 59 teaching assistantships with tuition reimbursements available (averaging $15,200 per year); career-related internships or fieldwork and traineeships also available. Financial award application deadline: 12/15. *Faculty research:* Economic and econometrical analysis, industrial organization, international trade, public finance, development, health, labor, population standard, macro, theory. *Unit head:* Prof. Linda Tesar, Chair, 734-763-2254, Fax: 734-764-2769, E-mail: ltesar@umich.edu. *Application contact:* Prof. David Lam, Director of Graduate Studies, 734-763-9237, Fax: 734-764-2769, E-mail: davidl@umich.edu.

University of Michigan, Horace H. Rackham School of Graduate Studies, College of Literature, Science, and the Arts, Department of Sociology, Ann Arbor, MI 48109. Offers public policy and sociology (PhD); social work and sociology (PhD); sociology (PhD); women's studies and sociology (PhD). *Faculty:* 16 full-time (10 women), 20 part-time/adjunct (5 women). *Students:* 145 full-time (104 women); includes 59 minority (17 African Americans, 2 American Indian/Alaska Native, 24 Asian Americans or Pacific Islanders, 16 Hispanic Americans), 27 international. Average age 29. 237 applicants, 15% accepted, 16 enrolled. In 2007, 13 doctorates awarded. *Median time to degree:* Of those who began their doctoral program in fall 1999, 57% received their degree in 8 years or less. *Degree requirements:* For doctorate, comprehensive exam, thesis/dissertation, oral defense of dissertation, preliminary exam. *Entrance requirements:* For doctorate, GRE General Test, letters of recommendation, writing sample, personal statement, statement of purpose. Additional exam requirements/recommendations for international students: Required—TOEFL (minimum score 560 paper-based; 220 computer-based). *Application deadline:* For fall admission, 12/15 for domestic and international students. Application fee: $60 ($75 for international students). Electronic applications accepted. *Financial support:* In 2007–08, 102 students received support, including 23 fellowships with tuition reimbursements available (averaging $14,400 per year), 79 teaching assistantships with tuition reimbursements available (averaging $15,199 per year); health care benefits also available. *Faculty research:* Power, history and social change; gender and sexuality; race and ethnicity; economic sociology; social demography. Total annual research expenditures: $191,606. *Unit head:* Howard Kimeldorf, Chair, 734-764-5554, Fax: 734-763-6887, E-mail: hkimel@umich.edu. *Application contact:* Jeannie Loughry, Graduate Program Coordinator, 734-647-4428, Fax: 734-763-6887, E-mail: sociology.graduate.program@umich.edu.

University of Michigan, Horace H. Rackham School of Graduate Studies, Gerald R. Ford School of Public Policy, Ann Arbor, MI 48109. Offers MPA, MPP, PhD, JD/MPP, MBA/MPP, MD/MPP, MHSA/MPP, MPH/MPP, MPP/AM, MPP/MA, MPP/MIS, MPP/MS, MPP/MUP, MSW/MPP. Part-time programs available. *Faculty:* 44 full-time (18 women), 14 part-time/adjunct (5 women). *Students:* 247 full-time (133 women), 2 part-time (1 woman); includes 65 minority (29 African Americans, 1 American Indian/Alaska Native, 20 Asian Americans or Pacific Islanders, 15 Hispanic Americans), 33 international. 525 applicants, 56% accepted, 94 enrolled. In 2007, 71 master's, 3 doctorates awarded. *Entrance requirements:* For master's, GRE. Additional exam requirements/recommendations for international students: Required—TOEFL (minimum score 600 paper-based; 250 computer-based; 102 iBT). *Application deadline:* For fall admission, 1/15 priority date for domestic students, 1/15 for international students. Application fee: $60 ($75 for international students). Electronic applications accepted. *Financial support:* In 2007–08, 150 fellowships, 50 teaching assistantships with tuition reimbursements were awarded; career-related internships or fieldwork and Federal Work-Study also available. Financial award applicants required to submit FAFSA. *Faculty research:* U.S. social policy; international economic policy; quantitative policy analysis; environmental policy; health policy. *Unit head:* Dr. Susan M. Collins, Dean, 734-764-3490. *Application contact:* Beth Soboleski, Director, Admissions and Recruiting, 734-764-0453, Fax: 734-647-7486, E-mail: fspp-admissions@umich.edu.

University of Michigan–Dearborn, College of Arts, Sciences, and Letters, Program in Public Policy, Dearborn, MI 48128-1491. Offers MPP. Part-time and evening/weekend programs available. *Faculty:* 3 full-time (0 women). *Students:* 4 full-time (2 women), 16 part-time (9 women); includes 4 minority (3 African Americans, 1 Hispanic American). Average age 31. 5 applicants, 80% accepted, 1 enrolled. In 2007, 1 degree awarded. *Entrance requirements:* For master's, GRE, 500 word statement of pyrpose, 2 letters of recommendation. Additional exam requirements/recommendations for international students: Required—TOEFL (minimum score 560 paper-based; 220 computer-based). *Application deadline:* For fall admission, 8/1 for domestic students; for winter admission, 12/1 for domestic students; for spring admission, 4/1 for domestic students. Application fee: $60 ($75 for international students). *Expenses:* Tuition, state resident: part-time $318 per credit hour. Tuition, nonresident: part-time $722 per credit hour. Tuition and fees vary according to course load and program. *Faculty research:* Peace and conflict studies, courts and public policy, public policy and the media. *Unit head:* Dr. Brooks

Public Policy

University of Michigan–Dearborn (continued)

Hull, Director, 313-593-5304, Fax: 313-593-5645, E-mail: bhull@umd.umich.edu. *Application contact:* Carol Ligienza, Administrative Coordinator, CASL Graduate Programs, 313-593-1183, Fax: 313-583-6498, E-mail: caslgrad@umd.umich.edu.

University of Minnesota, Twin Cities Campus, Graduate School, Hubert H. Humphrey Institute of Public Affairs, Program in Public Policy, Minneapolis, MN 55455-0213. Offers advanced policy analysis methods (MPP); economic and community development (MPP); foreign policy (MPP); public and nonprofit leadership and management (MPP); science technology and environmental policy (MPP); social policy (MPP); women and public policy (MPP); JD/MPP; MPP/MS; MSW/MPP. Part-time programs available. *Degree requirements:* For master's, thesis or alternative, internship or equivalent work experience. *Entrance requirements:* For master's, GRE General Test, minimum undergraduate GPA of 3.0. Additional exam requirements/recommendations for international students: Required—TOEFL (minimum score 600 paper-based; 250 computer-based). Electronic applications accepted. *Faculty research:* Social policy, public and non-profit management and leadership, community and economic development, foreign policy and international affairs, women and public policy.

See Close-Up on page 1641.

University of Missouri–St. Louis, College of Arts and Sciences, Department of Political Science, St. Louis, MO 63121. Offers American politics (MA); comparative politics (MA); international politics (MA); political process and behavior (MA); political science (PhD); public administration and public policy (MA); urban and regional politics (MA). Part-time and evening/weekend programs available. *Faculty:* 20 full-time (8 women), 2 part-time/adjunct (both women). *Students:* 28 full-time (13 women), 20 part-time (15 women); includes 9 minority (6 African Americans, 2 American Indian/Alaska Native, 1 Asian American or Pacific Islander), 6 international. Average age 36. In 2007, 10 master's, 3 doctorates awarded. Terminal master's awarded for partial completion of doctoral program. *Degree requirements:* For master's, thesis optional; for doctorate, thesis/dissertation. *Entrance requirements:* For master's, GRE General Test, 2 letters of recommendation; for doctorate, GRE General Test, 3 letters of recommendation. Additional exam requirements/recommendations for international students: Required—TOEFL (minimum score 550 paper-based; 213 computer-based). *Application deadline:* For fall admission, 2/15 for domestic students; for spring admission, 10/15 for domestic students. Applications are processed on a rolling basis. Application fee: $35 ($40 for international students). Electronic applications accepted. *Financial support:* In 2007–08, 9 research assistantships with full and partial tuition reimbursements (averaging $12,000 per year), 6 teaching assistantships with full and partial tuition reimbursements (averaging $12,000 per year) were awarded; fellowships, career-related internships or fieldwork also available. Support available to part-time students. Financial award application deadline: 3/15. *Faculty research:* Public policy, urban politics and administration, American government. *Unit head:* Dr. Eduardo Silva, Director of Graduate Studies, 314-516-5522, Fax: 314-516-5268, E-mail: umslpolisci@umsl.edu. *Application contact:* 314-516-5458, Fax: 314-516-6996, E-mail: gradadm@umsl.edu.

University of Missouri–St. Louis, Graduate School, Program in Public Policy Administration, St. Louis, MO 63121. Offers health policy (MPPA); local government management (MPPA); managing human resources and organization (MPPA); nonprofit organization management (MPPA); nonprofit organization management and leadership (Certificate); policy research and analysis (MPPA); public sector human resources management (MPPA). *Accreditation:* NASPAA. Part-time and evening/weekend programs available. *Faculty:* 8 full-time (4 women), 8 part-time/adjunct (1 woman). *Students:* 20 full-time (14 women), 38 part-time (15 women); includes 17 minority (14 African Americans, 1 American Indian/Alaska Native, 1 Asian American or Pacific Islander, 1 Hispanic American), 2 international. Average age 31. In 2007, 22 degrees awarded. *Entrance requirements:* For master's, 3 letters of recommendation. Additional exam requirements/recommendations for international students: Required—TOEFL (minimum score 550 paper-based; 213 computer-based). *Application deadline:* For fall admission, 7/15 priority date for domestic students; for spring admission, 12/15 priority date for domestic students. Applications are processed on a rolling basis. Application fee: $35 ($40 for international students). Electronic applications accepted. *Financial support:* In 2007–08, 2 research assistantships with full tuition reimbursements (averaging $12,000 per year) were awarded; teaching assistantships with partial tuition reimbursements, career-related internships or fieldwork also available. *Faculty research:* Urban policy, public finance, evaluation. *Unit head:* Brady Baybeck, Director, 314-516-5145, Fax: 314-516-5210, E-mail: baybeck@umsl.edu. *Application contact:* 314-516-5458, Fax: 314-516-6996, E-mail: gradadm@umsl.edu.

University of Nevada, Las Vegas, Graduate College, College of Liberal Arts, Department of Political Science, Program in Ethics and Policy Studies, Las Vegas, NV 89154-9900. Offers MA. Part-time programs available. In 2007, 1 degree awarded. *Degree requirements:* For master's, thesis. *Entrance requirements:* For master's, MAT, minimum GPA of 2.75. Additional exam requirements/recommendations for international students: Required—TOEFL (minimum score 550 paper-based; 213 computer-based; 80 iBT). *Application deadline:* For fall admission, 3/1 for domestic and international students; for spring admission, 11/1 for domestic students, 10/1 for international students. Application fee: $60 ($75 for international students). Electronic applications accepted. *Expenses:* Tuition, state resident: part-time $198 per credit. Tuition, nonresident: part-time $416 per credit. Required fees: $256 per semester. Tuition and fees vary according to course load and reciprocity agreements. *Financial support:* Research assistantships with partial tuition reimbursements, career-related internships or fieldwork, Federal Work-Study, institutionally sponsored loans, scholarships/grants, health care benefits, and unspecified assistantships available. Support available to part-time students. Financial award application deadline: 3/1. *Application contact:* Graduate College Admissions Evaluator, 702-895-3320, Fax: 702-895-4180, E-mail: gradcollege@unlv.edu.

University of New Brunswick Fredericton, School of Graduate Studies, Policy Studies Program, Fredericton, NB E3B 5A3, Canada. Offers people, property and alternative dispute resolution (M Phil); philosophy politics and economics (M Phil); sustainable development (M Phil). *Faculty:* 6 full-time (2 women), 13 part-time/adjunct (2 women). *Students:* 13 full-time (8 women), 3 part-time (2 women). In 2007, 6 degrees awarded. *Entrance requirements:* For master's, minimum GPA of 3.5, BA. Additional exam requirements/recommendations for international students: Required—TOEFL (minimum score 600 paper-based), TWE (minimum score 5). Application fee: $50 Canadian dollars. *Financial support:* In 2007–08, 5 research assistantships, 2 teaching assistantships (averaging $4,400 per year) were awarded. *Unit head:* Dr. Gwen Davies, Dean of Graduate Studies, 506-458-7150, Fax: 506-453-4817, E-mail: daviesg@unb.ca. *Application contact:* Janet Amurault, Graduate Secretary, 506-458-7558, Fax: 506-453-4817, E-mail: jamiraul@unb.ca.

The University of North Carolina at Chapel Hill, Graduate School, Department of Public Policy, Chapel Hill, NC 27599. Offers PhD. *Degree requirements:* For doctorate, thesis/dissertation. *Entrance requirements:* For doctorate, GRE General Test. Electronic applications accepted. *Faculty research:* Environmental policy; energy policy; economic development and science and technology policy; social policy; welfare, education and low-income communities.

The University of North Carolina at Charlotte, Graduate School, College of Arts and Sciences, Program in Public Policy, Charlotte, NC 28223-0001. Offers PhD. Part-time and evening/weekend programs available. *Students:* 14 full-time (11 women), 24 part-time (14 women); includes 2 minority (1 African American, 1 Asian American or Pacific Islander), 8 international. Average age 38. 16 applicants, 69% accepted, 7 enrolled. In 2007, 1 degree awarded. *Degree requirements:* For doctorate, comprehensive exam. *Entrance requirements:* For doctorate, GRE General Test. Additional exam requirements/recommendations for international students: Required—TOEFL (minimum score 557 paper-based; 220 computer-based). *Application deadline:* For fall admission, 12/1 for domestic and international students. Applications are processed on a rolling basis. Application fee: $55. Electronic applications accepted. *Expenses:* Tuition, state resident: full-time $2,855. Tuition, nonresident: full-time $13,062. Required fees: $1,692. *Financial support:* In 2007–08, 3 fellowships (averaging $1,667 per year), 18 research assistantships (averaging $11,822 per year) were awarded; teaching assistantships, career-related internships or fieldwork, Federal Work-Study, institutionally sponsored loans, scholarships/grants, and unspecified assistantships also available. Support available to part-time students. Financial award application deadline: 4/1; financial award applicants required to submit FAFSA. *Unit head:* Dr. David A. Swindell, Director, 704-687-4532, Fax: 704-687-3228, E-mail: daswinde@email.uncc.edu. *Application contact:* Kathy B. Giddings, Director of Graduate Admissions, 704-687-3366, Fax: 704-687-3279, E-mail: agidding@uncc.edu.

University of Northern Iowa, Graduate College, Program in Public Policy, Cedar Falls, IA 50614. Offers MPP. Part-time programs available. *Students:* 21 full-time (11 women), 7 part-time (4 women); includes 6 minority (3 African Americans, 1 Asian American or Pacific Islander, 2 Hispanic Americans), 4 international. 24 applicants, 83% accepted, 10 enrolled. *Degree requirements:* For master's, comprehensive exam (for some programs). *Entrance requirements:* For master's, minimum GPA of 3.0. Additional exam requirements/recommendations for international students: Required—TOEFL (minimum score 500 paper-based; 180 computer-based; 61 iBT). *Application deadline:* For fall admission, 3/1 priority date for domestic students. Applications are processed on a rolling basis. Application fee: $30 ($50 for international students). Electronic applications accepted. *Expenses:* Tuition, state resident: full-time $6,246; part-time $694 per credit hour. Tuition, nonresident: full-time $14,554; part-time $694 per credit hour. Required fees: $838; $119 per semester. *Financial support:* Career-related internships or fieldwork, Federal Work-Study, institutionally sponsored loans, tuition waivers (full), and unspecified assistantships available. Financial award application deadline: 2/1. *Unit head:* Dr. Carol Weisenberger, Interim Director, 319-273-2019, Fax: 319-273-7126, E-mail: carol.weisenberger@uni.edu.

University of Oregon, Graduate School, School of Architecture and Allied Arts, Department of Planning, Public Policy, and Management, Program in Public Policy and Management, Eugene, OR 97403. Offers MA, MPA, MS. *Accreditation:* NASPAA. Part-time and evening/weekend programs available. *Students:* 42 full-time (25 women), 12 part-time (9 women); includes 5 minority (2 African Americans, 2 American Indian/Alaska Native, 1 Hispanic American), 11 international. 45 applicants, 67% accepted. In 2007, 12 degrees awarded. *Degree requirements:* For master's, thesis. *Entrance requirements:* For master's, minimum GPA of 3.0. Additional exam requirements/recommendations for international students: Required—TOEFL. Application fee: $50. *Financial support:* In 2007–08, 5 teaching assistantships were awarded; career-related internships or fieldwork and Federal Work-Study also available. *Faculty research:* Community economic development, families in poverty, health services. *Application contact:* Zudegi Giordana, Graduate Secretary, 541-346-6018, Fax: 541-346-2040, E-mail: zudegi@uoregon.edu.

University of Pennsylvania, Wharton School, Department of Business and Public Policy, Philadelphia, PA 19104. Offers AM, MBA, PhD. *Degree requirements:* For doctorate, thesis/dissertation. *Entrance requirements:* For doctorate, GRE General Test. *Faculty research:* International policy, business and government, regulation, urban development and policy, transportation.

University of Pittsburgh, Graduate School of Public and International Affairs, Division of Public and Urban Affairs, Program in Policy Research and Analysis, Pittsburgh, PA 15260. Offers MPA, MPA/MID, JD/MPA, MPA/MPIA, MPH/MPA, MSIS/MPA, MSW/MPA. Part-time and evening/weekend programs available. *Faculty:* 34 full-time (10 women), 18 part-time/adjunct (6 women). *Students:* 12 full-time (8 women), 7 part-time (5 women); includes 13 minority (2 African Americans, 11 Hispanic Americans), 6 international. Average age 25. 21 applicants, 86% accepted, 4 enrolled. In 2007, 35 degrees awarded. *Degree requirements:* For master's, thesis optional, internship, capstone seminar. *Entrance requirements:* For master's, GRE General Test, 3 letters of recommendation, resumé, minimum GPA of 3.2. Additional exam requirements/recommendations for international students: Required—TOEFL (minimum score 550 paper-based; 213 computer-based; 80 iBT), TWE (minimum score 4); Recommended—IELTS (minimum score 7). *Application deadline:* For fall admission, 2/1 for domestic students, 1/15 for international students; for spring admission, 11/1 for domestic students, 8/1 for international students. Application fee: $50. Electronic applications accepted. *Financial support:* In 2007–08, 18 students received support, including 18 fellowships (averaging $7,700 per year); career-related internships or fieldwork, institutionally sponsored loans, scholarships/grants, tuition waivers (full and partial), and unspecified assistantships also available. Financial award application deadline: 2/1. *Faculty research:* Emergency management, health policy and regulation, regional finance, non-profit management, community/regional development, environmental policy. Total annual research expenditures: $845,025. *Application contact:* Denene Hefflin, Graduate Enrollment Counselor, 412-648-7640, Fax: 412-648-7641, E-mail: dkh7@pitt.edu.

University of Pittsburgh, Graduate School of Public and International Affairs, Doctoral Program in Public and International Affairs, Pittsburgh, PA 15260. Offers development policy (PhD); foreign and security policy (PhD); international political economy (PhD); public administration (PhD); public policy (PhD). *Accreditation:* NASPAA. Part-time programs available. *Faculty:* 34 full-time (10 women), 18 part-time/adjunct (6 women). *Students:* 39 full-time (15 women), 8 part-time (6 women); includes 6 minority (2 African Americans, 3 Asian Americans or Pacific Islanders, 1 Hispanic American), 10 international. Average age 30. 61 applicants, 30% accepted, 11 enrolled. In 2007, 8 degrees awarded. *Degree requirements:* For doctorate, comprehensive exam, thesis/dissertation. *Entrance requirements:* For doctorate, GRE, 3 letters of recommendation, resumé, minimum GPA of 3.0, writing sample. Additional exam requirements/recommendations for international students: Required—TOEFL (minimum score 600 paper-based; 250 computer-based; 100 iBT), TWE (minimum score 4); Recommended—IELTS (minimum score 7). *Application deadline:* For fall admission, 2/1 for domestic students, 1/15 for international students. Application fee: $50. Electronic applications accepted. *Financial support:* In 2007–08, 13 students received support, including 13 fellowships (averaging $28,580 per year); scholarships/grants and unspecified assistantships also available. Financial award application deadline: 2/1. *Faculty research:* International political economy, international development, public administration, public policy, foreign policy, international security policy. Total annual research expenditures: $845,025. *Unit head:* Dr. Phyllis Coontz, Doctoral Program Coordinator, 412-648-2654, Fax: 412-648-2605, E-mail: pcoontz@gspia.pitt.edu. *Application contact:* Jessica L. Hatherill, Associate Director of Student Services, 412-648-7640, Fax: 412-648-7641, E-mail: hatherill@gspia.pitt.edu.

See Close-Up on page 1645.

University of Pittsburgh, Graduate School of Public and International Affairs, Executive Programs in Public Policy and Management, Pittsburgh, PA 15260. Offers development planning (MPPM); international development (MPPM); international political economy (MPPM); international security studies (MPPM); management of non profit organizations (MPPM); metropolitan management and regional development (MPPM); policy analysis and evaluation (MPPM). Part-time programs available. *Faculty:* 34 full-time (10 women), 18 part-time/adjunct (6 women). *Students:* 11 full-time (3 women), 46 part-time (20 women); includes 4 minority (3 African Americans, 1 Hispanic American), 8 international. Average age 38. 48 applicants, 88% accepted, 29 enrolled. In 2007, 27 degrees awarded. *Degree requirements:* For master's, thesis optional, capstone seminar. *Entrance requirements:* For master's, 2 letters of recommendation, resumé, 5 years of supervisory or budgetary experience. Additional exam requirements/recommendations for international students: Required—TOEFL (minimum score 600 paper-based; 250 computer-based; 100 iBT), TWE (minimum score 4); Recommended—IELTS (minimum score 7). *Application deadline:* For fall admission, 6/1 priority date for domestic students, 2/15 for international students; for spring admission, 1/1 priority date for domestic students, 8/1 for international students. Applications are processed on a rolling basis. Application fee: $50. Electronic applications accepted. *Financial support:* In 2007–08, 4 students received support, including 4 fellowships (averaging $5,075 per year); institutionally sponsored loans and scholarships/grants also available. Support available to part-time students. Financial award application deadline: 2/1. *Faculty research:* Executive training and technical assistance for U.S. and international clients. Total annual research expenditures: $845,025. *Unit head:* Michele Garrity, Director, Executive Education, 412-648-7610, Fax: 412-648-2605, E-mail: garrity@birch.gspia.pitt.edu. *Application contact:* Maureen O'Malley, Admissions Counselor, 412-648-7640, Fax: 412-648-7641, E-mail: pronobis@birch.gspia.pitt.edu.

See Close-Up on page 1645.

University of Regina, Faculty of Graduate Studies and Research, Johnson-Shoyama Graduate School of Public Policy, Regina, SK S4S 0A2, Canada. Offers economic analysis for public policy (Master's Certificate); non-profit management (Master's Certificate); public management (MPA, Master's Certificate); public policy (MPA, PhD, Master's Certificate). Part-time and evening/weekend programs available. *Faculty:* 6 full-time (3 women). *Students:* 60 full-time (30 women), 53 part-time (37 women). 104 applicants, 86% accepted. In 2007, 9 degrees awarded. *Entrance requirements:* Additional exam requirements/recommendations for international students: Required—TOEFL (minimum score 580 paper-based; 237 computer-based; 88 iBT). *Application deadline:* Applications are processed on a rolling basis. Application fee: $85 ($100 for international students). Electronic applications accepted. *Expenses: Contact institution. Financial support:* In 2007–08, 13 fellowships (averaging $15,750 per year), 1 research assistantship (averaging $13,875 per year), 7 teaching assistantships (averaging $13,060 per year) were awarded. Financial award application deadline: 6/15. *Faculty research:* Public administration and policy. *Unit head:* Dr. Ken Rasmussen, Associate Dean, 306-585-5463, E-mail: ken.rasmussen@uregina.ca. *Application contact:* Devon Anderson, Information Contact, 306-585-5462, E-mail: devon.anderson@uregina.ca.

University of Rhode Island, Graduate School, College of Arts and Sciences, Department of Political Science, Program in Public Policy and Administration, Kingston, RI 02881. Offers MA, MPA, Certificate. In 2007, 24 degrees awarded. *Application deadline:* For fall admission, 4/15 priority date for domestic students. Applications are processed on a rolling basis. Application fee: $35. *Expenses:* Tuition, state resident: full-time $6,936; part-time $385 per credit. Tuition, nonresident: full-time $19,044; part-time $1,058 per credit. Required fees: $1,508; $48 per credit. $30 per semester. One-time fee: $80 part-time. *Unit head:* Dr. Timothy Hennessey, Director, 401-874-4052.

University of Southern California, Graduate School, School of Policy, Planning and Development, Program in Public Policy, Los Angeles, CA 90089. Offers MPP. Part-time programs available. *Faculty:* 39 full-time (8 women), 43 part-time/adjunct (12 women). *Students:* 123 full-time (70 women), 17 part-time (8 women); includes 46 minority (10 African Americans, 22 Asian Americans or Pacific Islanders, 14 Hispanic Americans), 43 international. 181 applicants, 77% accepted. In 2007, 85 master's awarded. *Entrance requirements:* For master's, GRE General Test. *Application deadline:* For fall admission, 1/15 priority date for domestic students; for spring admission, 11/1 for domestic students. Applications are processed on a rolling basis. Application fee: $85. *Financial support:* In 2007–08, 58 students received support, including fellowships with partial tuition reimbursements available (averaging $5,000 per year), research assistantships with full and partial tuition reimbursements available (averaging $13,900 per year); career-related internships or fieldwork, Federal Work-Study, institutionally sponsored loans, scholarships/grants, traineeships, and tuition waivers (full and partial) also available. Support available to part-time students. Financial award application deadline: 2/15; financial award applicants required to submit FAFSA. *Faculty research:* Urban political economy, community and economic development, immigration policy. *Unit head:* Juliet Musso, Head, 213-740-2311.

University of Southern Maine, Edmund S. Muskie School of Public Service, Doctoral Program in Public Policy, Portland, ME 04104-9300. Offers PhD. Applicants accepted in odd numbered years only. Part-time and evening/weekend programs available. *Degree requirements:* For doctorate, comprehensive exam, thesis/dissertation. *Entrance requirements:* For doctorate, GRE. Additional exam requirements/recommendations for international students: Required—TOEFL. Electronic applications accepted. *Faculty research:* Health policy, community planning and development, education policy, environmental policy.

University of Southern Maine, Edmund S. Muskie School of Public Service, Program in Public Policy and Management, Portland, ME 04104-9300. Offers child and family policy (Certificate); non-profit management (Certificate); public policy and management (MPPM); JD/MPPM. *Accreditation:* NASPAA. Part-time and evening/weekend programs available. Postbaccalaureate distance learning degree programs offered (minimal on-campus study). *Degree requirements:* For master's, thesis, capstone project, field experience. *Entrance requirements:* For master's, GRE General Test or LSAT. Additional exam requirements/recommendations for international students: Required—TOEFL. Electronic applications accepted. *Faculty research:* Sustainable communities, juvenile justice, program management, nonprofit management.

The University of Texas at Austin, Graduate School, Lyndon B. Johnson School of Public Affairs, Austin, TX 78712-1111. Offers public affairs (MP Aff); public policy (PhD); JD/MP Aff; MBA/MP Aff; MP Aff/MA; MP Aff/MSE. *Accreditation:* NASPAA (one or more programs are accredited). Part-time programs available. *Degree requirements:* For master's, thesis, summer internship; for doctorate, thesis/dissertation. *Entrance requirements:* For master's, GRE General Test; for doctorate, GRE General Test, master's degree in policy-related field. Additional exam requirements/recommendations for international students: Required—TOEFL. Electronic applications accepted. *Faculty research:* Human resource development, health and social policy, philanthropy and community service, ethical leadership, urban and international policy, science and technology policy.

The University of Texas at Brownsville, Graduate Studies, College of Liberal Arts, Program in Public Policy and Management, Brownsville, TX 78520-4991. Offers MPPM. *Degree requirements:* For master's, thesis. *Entrance requirements:* For master's, GRE, 2 letters of recommendation.

University of the Pacific, McGeorge School of Law, Sacramento, CA 95817. Offers government and public policy (LL M); international law (LL M); international waters resources law (LL M); law (JD); transnational business practice (LL M); JD/MBA; JD/MPPA. *Accreditation:* ABA. Part-time and evening/weekend programs available. *Faculty:* 65 full-time (26 women), 64 part-time/adjunct (16 women). *Students:* 660 full-time (295 women), 361 part-time (178 women); includes 272 minority (33 African Americans, 10 American Indian/Alaska Native, 142 Asian Americans or Pacific Islanders, 87 Hispanic Americans). Average age 24. 2,881 applicants, 40% accepted. In 2007, 292 JDs, 25 master's awarded. *Degree requirements:* For master's, thesis (for some programs); for doctorate, thesis/dissertation. *Entrance requirements:* For JD, LSAT; for master's, JD; for doctorate, LL M. Additional exam requirements/recommendations for international students: Required—TOEFL (minimum score 600 paper-based; 250 computer-based; 100 iBT). *Application deadline:* For fall admission, 3/15 priority date for domestic students. Applications are processed on a rolling basis. Application fee: $50. Electronic applications accepted. *Expenses: Contact institution. Financial support:* In 2007–08, 902 students received support, including 9 fellowships, 20 research assistantships (averaging $6,485 per year); career-related internships or fieldwork, Federal Work-Study, institutionally sponsored loans, and scholarships/grants also available. Support available to part-time students. Financial award applicants required to submit FAFSA. *Faculty research:* Taxation and business, family and juvenile law, governmental affairs, environmental law, intellectual property law. *Unit head:* Elizabeth Rindskopf Parker, Dean, 916-739-7151, E-mail: elizabeth@uop.edu. *Application contact:* 916-739-7105, Fax: 916-739-7134, E-mail: admissionsmcgeorge@uop.edu.

University of Utah, The Graduate School, College of Social and Behavioral Science, Department of Political Science, Program in Public Policy, Salt Lake City, UT 84112-1107. Offers international affairs and global enterprises (MS); public policy (MPP). *Application contact:* Mary Ann Underwood, Graduate Coordinator, 801-581-8608, Fax: 801-585-6492, E-mail: maryann.underwood@poli-sci.utah.edu.

University of Virginia, College and Graduate School of Arts and Sciences, Program in Public Policy, Charlottesville, VA 22903. Offers MPP. *Application contact:* Aaron Mills, Associate Dean of Graduate Academic Programs and Research, 434-924-6739, Fax: 434-924-6737, E-mail: grad-a-s@virginia.edu.

University of Washington, Bothell, Program in Policy Studies, Bothell, WA 98011-8246. Offers MA. Evening/weekend programs available. *Faculty:* 8 full-time (4 women). *Students:* 33 full-time (25 women), 17 part-time (12 women); includes 13 minority (2 African Americans, 2 American Indian/Alaska Native, 8 Asian Americans or Pacific Islanders, 1 Hispanic American). Average age 32. 46 applicants, 61% accepted, 26 enrolled. In 2007, 15 degrees awarded. *Degree requirements:* For master's, thesis. *Entrance requirements:* For master's, GRE. Additional exam requirements/recommendations for international students: Required—TOEFL. *Application deadline:* For fall admission, 3/1 priority date for domestic and international students. Applications are processed on a rolling basis. Application fee: $50. Electronic applications accepted. *Expenses:* Tuition, state resident: full-time $9,279. Tuition, nonresident: full-time $21,327. Tuition and fees vary according to course load and program. *Financial support:* In 2007–08, 9 students received support, including 5 fellowships (averaging $15,000 per year), 1 research assistantship (averaging $2,000 per year); Federal Work-Study, tuition waivers (full), and unspecified assistantships also available. Financial award applicants required to submit FAFSA. *Faculty research:* Human rights, environment, energy, economic development, labor. *Unit head:* Prof. Bruce Burgett, Interim Director, Interdisciplinary Studies Program, 425-352-5403, E-mail: bburgett@uwb.edu. *Application contact:* Andrew Brusletten, Program Manager, 425-352-5427, Fax: 425-352-3462, E-mail: abrusletten@uwb.edu.

Vanderbilt University, Graduate School, Program in Community Research and Action, Nashville, TN 37240-1001. Offers MS, PhD. Part-time programs available. *Faculty:* 15 full-time (4 women). *Students:* 24 full-time (11 women), 1 (woman) part-time; includes 5 minority (all African Americans), 3 international. Average age 32. 33 applicants, 15% accepted, 3 enrolled. In 2007, 4 master's, 1 doctorate awarded. *Degree requirements:* For master's, thesis; for doctorate, thesis/dissertation, internship, fundable grant proposal. *Application deadline:* For fall admission, 1/15 for domestic and international students. Application fee: $0. Electronic applications accepted. *Financial support:* Fellowships with tuition reimbursements, research assistantships with full tuition reimbursements, teaching assistantships with full tuition reimbursements, Federal Work-Study, institutionally sponsored loans, traineeships, and health care benefits available. Financial award application deadline: 1/15; financial award applicants required to submit CSS PROFILE or FAFSA. *Unit head:* Joseph Cunningham, Chair, 615-322-6881, Fax: 615-343-2661, E-mail: joe.cunningham@vanderbilt.edu. *Application contact:* Paul Dokecki, Director of Graduate Studies, 615-322-6881, E-mail: paul.r.dokecki@vanderbilt.edu.

Virginia Commonwealth University, Graduate School, College of Humanities and Sciences, Wilder School of Government and Public Affairs, Center for Public Policy, Richmond, VA 23284-9005. Offers public policy and administration (PhD). *Faculty:* 12 full-time (3 women). *Students:* 20 full-time (9 women), 97 part-time (59 women); includes 31 minority (30 African Americans, 1 Asian American or Pacific Islander), 23 international. 54 applicants, 57% accepted, 11 enrolled. In 2007, 4 degrees awarded. *Degree requirements:* For doctorate, thesis/dissertation. *Entrance requirements:* For doctorate, GMAT, GRE General Test, LSAT, or MAT. *Application deadline:* For fall admission, 3/15 for domestic students. Application fee: $50. *Expenses:* Tuition, state resident: full-time $7,224; part-time $401 per credit. Tuition, nonresident: full-time $16,072; part-time $891 per credit. Required fees: $1,679; $63 per credit. Tuition and fees vary according to campus/location. *Financial support:* Fellowships, career-related internships or fieldwork and Federal Work-Study available. Support available to part-time students. Financial award applicants required to submit FAFSA. *Unit head:* Dr. Michael Pratt, Associate Director, 804-828-8033. *Application contact:* Dr. Melvin I. Urofsky, Graduate Program Director, 804-828-8033, Fax: 804-828-6838, E-mail: murofsky@vcu.edu.

Virginia Polytechnic Institute and State University, Graduate School, College of Architecture and Urban Studies, Center for Public Administration and Policy, Blacksburg, VA 24061-0205. Offers MPA, PhD, CAGS. *Accreditation:* NASPAA (one or more programs are accredited). *Entrance requirements:* For master's and doctorate, GRE General Test, GMAT. Additional exam requirements/recommendations for international students: Required—TOEFL (minimum score 550 paper-based; 213 computer-based). Electronic applications accepted. *Faculty research:* Public administration theory, strategic management, ethics, the Constitution, computer-assisted creativity.

Walden University, Graduate Programs, School of Counseling and Social Science, Minneapolis, MN 55401. Offers human services (PhD), including clinical social work, counseling, criminal justice, family studies and intervention strategies, general program in human services, human services administration, self-designed program in human services, social policy analysis and planning; mental health counseling (MS). Part-time and evening/weekend programs available. *Students:* 586 full-time (496 women), 505 part-time (410 women); includes 413 minority (351 African Americans, 14 American Indian/Alaska Native, 11 Asian Americans or Pacific Islanders, 37 Hispanic Americans), 10 international. Average age 39. 538 applicants, 72% accepted, 207 enrolled. In 2007, 4 degrees awarded. *Degree requirements:* For master's, residency requirements; for doctorate, thesis/dissertation, residency requirements. *Entrance requirements:* For master's, BS in related field; for doctorate, 3 years of professional experience (preferred), minimum GPA of 3.0, master's degree. Additional exam requirements/recommendations for international students: Required—TOEFL (minimum score 550 paper-based; 213 computer-based), IELTS (minimum score 7). *Application deadline:* For fall admission, 8/15 priority date for domestic and international students; for winter admission, 11/15 priority date for domestic and international students; for spring admission, 12/15 priority date for domestic and international students. Applications are processed on a rolling basis. Application fee: $50. Electronic applications accepted. *Financial support:* Fellowships, Federal Work-Study, institutionally sponsored loans, scholarships/grants, and unspecified assistantships available. Financial award applicants required to submit FAFSA. *Unit head:* Savitri Dixon-Saxon, Associate Dean, 800-925-3368, Fax: 612-338-5092. *Application contact:* Office of Student Enrollment, 866-4-WALDEN, Fax: 410-843-8780.

Walden University, Graduate Programs, School of Public Policy and Administration, Minneapolis, MN 55401. Offers criminal justice (MPA, PhD); health services (MPA, PhD); homeland security policy and coordination (MPA, PhD); international nongovernmental organizations (MPA, PhD); knowledge management (MPA, PhD); nonprofit management and leadership (MPA, PhD); public management and leadership (MPA, PhD); public policy (MPA, PhD); public safety management (MPA, PhD). Part-time and evening/weekend programs available. Postbaccalaureate distance learning degree programs offered (minimal on-campus study). *Students:* 433 full-time (228 women), 148 part-time (79 women); includes 265 minority (234 African Americans, 6 American Indian/Alaska Native, 11 Asian Americans or Pacific Islanders, 14 Hispanic Americans), 4 international. Average age 42. 475 applicants, 76% accepted, 220 enrolled. In 2007, 71 master's, 7 doctorates awarded. *Degree requirements:* For doctorate, thesis/dissertation. *Entrance requirements:* For master's, minimum GPA of 3.0; for doctorate, 3 years of professional experience, master's degree. Additional exam requirements/recommendations for international students: Required—TOEFL (minimum score 550 paper-based; 213 computer-based), IELTS (minimum score 7). *Application deadline:* For fall admission, 8/15 priority date for domestic and international students; for winter admission, 11/15 priority date for domestic and international students; for spring admission, 12/15 priority date for domestic and international students. Applications are processed on a rolling basis. Application fee: $50. Electronic applications accepted. *Financial support:* Fellowships with partial tuition reimbursements, Federal Work-Study, institutionally sponsored loans, scholarships/grants, and unspecified assistantships available. Financial award application deadline: 6/1; financial award applicants required to submit FAFSA. *Unit head:* Gary Kelsey, Associate Dean, 800-925-3368, Fax: 612-338-5092. *Application contact:* 866-4-WALDEN, Fax: 410-843-8780, E-mail: request@waldenu.edu.

Washington State University, Graduate School, College of Liberal Arts, Department of Sociology, Pullman, WA 99164. Offers crime and deviance (MA, PhD); environments, com-

Public Policy

Washington State University (continued)

munity and demographics (MA, PhD); institutions and social organizations (MA, PhD); political sociology (MA, PhD); social inequality (MA, PhD); social psychology and life course (MA, PhD). *Faculty:* 22 full-time (14 women), 8 part-time/adjunct (3 women). *Students:* 42 full-time (23 women), 2 part-time (both women); includes 2 minority (1 African American, 1 American Indian/Alaska Native), 4 international. Average age 30. 71 applicants, 13% accepted, 9 enrolled. In 2007, 7 master's, 4 doctorates awarded. Terminal master's awarded for partial completion of doctoral program. *Degree requirements:* For master's, thesis; for doctorate, comprehensive exam, thesis/dissertation. *Entrance requirements:* For master's, GRE General Test, minimum GPA of 3.0; for doctorate, GRE General Test, MA in sociology, minimum GPA of 3.0. Additional exam requirements/recommendations for international students: Required—TOEFL (minimum score 550 paper-based). *Application deadline:* For fall admission, 1/15 priority date for domestic students, 1/15 for international students. Application fee: $50. Electronic applications accepted. *Financial support:* In 2007–08, 5 research assistantships with tuition reimbursements (averaging $12,749 per year), 36 teaching assistantships with tuition reimbursements (averaging $12,749 per year) were awarded; fellowships with tuition reimbursements, Federal Work-Study, institutionally sponsored loans, scholarships/grants, health care benefits, and unspecified assistantships also available. Support available to part-time students. Financial award application deadline: 4/1; financial award applicants required to submit FAFSA. *Faculty research:* Crime/deviance, environmental sociology, social inequality, social psychology, gender. Total annual research expenditures: $101,888. *Unit head:* Dr. Gregory Hooks, Chair, 509-335-4595, Fax: 509-335-6419, E-mail: hooks@mail.wsu.edu. *Application contact:* Dr. Tom Rotolo, Director of Graduate Studies, 509-335-4595, Fax: 509-335-6419, E-mail: rotolo@wsu.edu.

Washington University in St. Louis, Graduate School of Arts and Sciences, Department of Political Science, Program in Political Economy and Public Policy, St. Louis, MO 63130-4899. Offers MA. *Degree requirements:* For master's, thesis or alternative. *Entrance requirements:* For master's, GRE General Test. Electronic applications accepted.

West Virginia University, Eberly College of Arts and Sciences, Department of Political Science, Morgantown, WV 26506. Offers American public policy and politics (MA); international and comparative public policy and politics (MA); political science (PhD); public policy analysis (PhD). *Faculty:* 15 full-time (3 women), 6 part-time/adjunct (2 women). *Students:* 56 full-time (22 women), 20 part-time (9 women); includes 7 minority (5 African Americans, 1 Asian American or Pacific Islander, 1 Hispanic American), 17 international. Average age 31. 55 applicants, 85% accepted, 24 enrolled. In 2007, 10 master's, 8 doctorates awarded. Terminal master's awarded for partial completion of doctoral program. *Degree requirements:* For master's, thesis optional; for doctorate, comprehensive exam, thesis/dissertation. *Entrance requirements:* For master's, GRE General Test, minimum GPA of 2.75; for doctorate, GRE General Test, minimum GPA of 3.0. Additional exam requirements/recommendations for international students: Required—TOEFL. *Application deadline:* For fall admission, 4/1 priority date for domestic students. Applications are processed on a rolling basis. Application fee: $45. *Expenses:* Tuition, state resident: full-time $5,196; part-time $292 per credit hour. Tuition, nonresident: full-time $15,064; part-time $840 per credit hour. Tuition and fees vary according to program. *Financial support:* In 2007–08, 65 students received support, including 1 research assistantship (averaging $15,000 per year), 15 teaching assistantships (averaging $9,000 per year); career-related internships or fieldwork, Federal Work-Study, institutionally sponsored loans, tuition waivers (full and partial), and unspecified assistantships also available. Financial award application deadline: 2/1; financial award applicants required to submit FAFSA. *Faculty research:* Public policy, research methods, foreign policy analysis, judicial politics, environmental and energy policy. Total annual research expenditures: $8,421. *Unit head:* Dr. Joe D. Hagan, Chair, 304-293-3811 Ext. 5283, Fax: 304-293-8644, E-mail: jhagan@wvu.edu. *Application contact:* Dr. Jeff Worsham, Director, Graduate Studies, 304-293-3811 Ext. 5277, Fax: 304-293-8644, E-mail: jeff.worsham@mail.wvu.edu.

Wilfrid Laurier University, Faculty of Graduate Studies, Faculty of Arts and School of Business and Economics, International Public Policy Program, Waterloo, ON N2L 3C5, Canada. Offers MIPP. *Faculty:* 21 full-time. *Students:* 13 full-time. 74 applicants, 27% accepted, 15 enrolled. *Entrance requirements:* For master's, honours BA with minimum B average. Additional exam requirements/recommendations for international students: Required—TOEFL (minimum score 230 computer-based; 89 iBT). *Application deadline:* For fall admission, 2/1 priority date for domestic students. Application fee: $75. Electronic applications accepted. *Financial support:* Fellowships, research assistantships, teaching assistantships available. *Faculty research:* International environmental policy, international economic relations, human security, global governance. *Unit head:* Tracy Snodden, Director, 519-884-0710 Ext. 3215, E-mail: tsnodden@wlu.ca. *Application contact:* Jennifer Poppe, Student Contact, 519-884-0710 Ext. 3536, Fax: 519-884-1020, E-mail: gradstudies@wlu.ca.

William Paterson University of New Jersey, College of the Humanities and Social Sciences, Program in Public Policy and International Affairs, Wayne, NJ 07470-8420. Offers MA. *Students:* 6 full-time (2 women), 8 part-time (2 women); includes 6 minority (3 African Americans, 1 Asian American or Pacific Islander, 2 Hispanic Americans). In 2007, 7 degrees awarded. Application fee: $50. *Unit head:* Dr. Sheila Collins, Program Director, 973-720-3424.

York University, Faculty of Graduate Studies, Atkinson Faculty of Liberal and Professional Studies, Program in Public Policy, Administration and Law, Toronto, ON M3J 1P3, Canada. Offers MPPAL.

Rural Planning and Studies

Brandon University, Department of Rural Development, Brandon, MB R7A 6A9, Canada. Offers MRD, Diploma. *Degree requirements:* For master's, thesis. *Entrance requirements:* For master's, minimum GPA of 3.0, 2 letters of reference. Additional exam requirements/recommendations for international students: Required—TOEFL (minimum score 580 paper-based). Electronic applications accepted. *Faculty research:* Regional development, healthy communities, economic impact analysis, rural tourism, resource management.

California State University, Chico, Graduate School, College of Behavioral and Social Sciences, Department of Geography and Planning, Program in Rural and Town Planning, Chico, CA 95929-0722. Offers MA. Part-time programs available. *Students:* 5 full-time (1 woman), 4 part-time (1 woman); includes 2 minority (both American Indian/Alaska Native). Average age 29. 6 applicants, 100% accepted, 5 enrolled. In 2007, 1 degree awarded. *Entrance requirements:* For master's, GRE, 2 letters of recommendation, statement of purpose, writing sample. Additional exam requirements/recommendations for international students: Required—TOEFL (minimum score 550 paper-based; 213 computer-based; 80 iBT), IELTS (minimum score 7). *Application deadline:* For fall admission, 3/1 priority date for domestic students, 3/1 for international students; for spring admission, 9/15 priority date for domestic students, 9/15 for international students. Applications are processed on a rolling basis. Application fee: $55. Electronic applications accepted. *Unit head:* Dr. Dean Fairbanks, Graduate Coordinator, 530-898-5780.

Concordia University, School of Graduate Studies, John Molson School of Business, Montréal, QC H3G 1M8, Canada. Offers administration (M Sc, Diploma); aviation management (Certificate, Diploma); business administration (MBA, UA Undergraduate Associate, PhD), including international aviation (UA Undergraduate Associate); chartered accountancy (Diploma); community organizational development (Certificate); event management and fundraising (Certificate); executive business administration (EMBA); investment management (Diploma); investment management option (MBA); management accounting (Certificate); management of healthcare organizations (Certificate); sport administration (Diploma). *Accreditation:* AACSB. Part-time and evening/weekend programs available. *Degree requirements:* For master's, one foreign language, thesis (for some programs), research project; for doctorate, one foreign language, thesis/dissertation; for other advanced degree, one foreign language. *Entrance requirements:* For master's and doctorate, GMAT. Additional exam requirements/recommendations for international students: Required—TOEFL. Expenses: Contact institution. *Faculty research:* General business, capital markets, international business.

Cornell University, Graduate School, Graduate Fields of Agriculture and Life Sciences, Field of Community and Rural Development, Ithaca, NY 14853-0001. Offers community development process (MPS); economic development (MPS); local government organizations and operations (MPS); program development and planning (MPS). *Faculty:* 30 full-time (10 women). *Students:* 1 (woman) full-time. Average age 26. In 2007, 2 degrees awarded. *Entrance requirements:* For master's, GRE General Test (recommended), 3 letters of recommendation. Additional exam requirements/recommendations for international students: Required—TOEFL (minimum score 550 paper-based; 213 computer-based; 77 iBT). *Application deadline:* For fall admission, 5/1 for domestic students. Application fee: $70. Electronic applications accepted. *Financial support:* In 2007–08, 2 students received support, including 1 fellowship with full tuition reimbursement available, 1 teaching assistantship with full tuition reimbursement available; research assistantships with full tuition reimbursements available, institutionally sponsored loans, scholarships/grants, health care benefits, tuition waivers (full and partial), and unspecified assistantships also available. Financial award applicants required to submit FAFSA. *Faculty research:* Land use, community economic development, governance and leadership development, planning and evaluation, main street revitalization. *Unit head:* Director of Graduate Studies, 607-255-4916, Fax: 607-255-2231. *Application contact:* Graduate Field Assistant, 607-255-4916, Fax: 607-255-2331, E-mail: gradcrd@cornell.edu.

Cornell University, Graduate School, Graduate Fields of Agriculture and Life Sciences, Field of International Agriculture and Rural Development, Ithaca, NY 14853-0001. Offers international agriculture and development (MPS). *Faculty:* 52 full-time (12 women). *Students:* 18 full-time (10 women); includes 3 minority (1 American Indian/Alaska Native, 2 Asian Americans or Pacific Islanders), 6 international. Average age 32. 38 applicants, 84% accepted, 8 enrolled. In 2007, 4 degrees awarded. *Degree requirements:* For master's, project paper. *Entrance requirements:* For master's, GRE General Test (recommended), 2 years of development experience, 2 letters of recommendation. Additional exam requirements/recommendations for international students: Required—TOEFL (minimum score 550 paper-based; 213 computer-based; 77 iBT). *Application deadline:* For fall admission, 3/1 for domestic students. Application fee: $70. Electronic applications accepted. *Financial support:* In 2007–08, 4 students received support, including 3 fellowships with full tuition reimbursements available, 1 teaching assistantship with full tuition reimbursement available; research assistantships with full tuition reimbursements available, institutionally sponsored loans, scholarships/grants, health care benefits, tuition waivers (full and partial), and unspecified assistantships also available. Financial award applicants required to submit FAFSA. *Unit head:* Director of Graduate Studies, 607-255-3037, Fax: 607-255-1005. *Application contact:* Graduate Field Assistant, 607-255-3035, Fax: 607-255-1005, E-mail: mpsiard@cornell.edu.

Dalhousie University, Faculty of Architecture and Planning, Department of Urban and Rural Planning, Halifax, NS B3H 4R2, Canada. Offers M Pl, MPS, M Eng/M Plan, MA Sc/M Plan. *Degree requirements:* For master's, thesis. *Entrance requirements:* Additional exam requirements/recommendations for international students: Required—TOEFL. *Application deadline:* For fall admission, 4/1 priority date for domestic students. Applications are processed on a rolling basis. Application fee: $60. *Financial support:* Career-related internships or fieldwork and scholarships/grants available. *Unit head:* Prof. Jill Grant, Director, 902-494-6586, Fax: 902-423-6672, E-mail: plan.office@dal.ca. *Application contact:* Carol Madden, Planning Secretary, 902-494-3260, Fax: 902-423-6672, E-mail: plan.office@dal.ca.

Iowa State University of Science and Technology, Graduate College, College of Liberal Arts and Sciences, Department of History, Ames, IA 50011. Offers agricultural history and rural studies (PhD); history (MA); history of technology and science (MA, PhD). *Faculty:* 16 full-time (4 women). *Students:* 29 full-time (12 women), 14 part-time (3 women); includes 2 minority (1 African American, 1 Hispanic American), 3 international. 23 applicants, 87% accepted, 11 enrolled. In 2007, 8 master's, 3 doctorates awarded. *Degree requirements:* For master's, thesis or alternative; for doctorate, thesis/dissertation. *Entrance requirements:* For master's and doctorate, GRE General Test. Additional exam requirements/recommendations for international students: Required—TOEFL (paper-based 600; computer-based 250; iBT 79) or IELTS (7.0). *Application deadline:* For fall admission, 1/15 priority date for domestic and international students. Applications are processed on a rolling basis. Application fee: $30 ($70 for international students). Electronic applications accepted. *Financial support:* In 2007–08, research assistantships with partial tuition reimbursements (averaging $15,660 per year), 18 teaching assistantships with full and partial tuition reimbursements (averaging $15,829 per year) were awarded; scholarships/grants, health care benefits, and unspecified assistantships also available. *Unit head:* Dr. Charles Dobbs, Chair, 515-294-7266, Fax: 515-294-6390, E-mail: cdobbs@iastate.edu. *Application contact:* Dr. Christopher Curtis, Information Contact, 515-294-7266, Fax: 515-294-6390.

Université Laval, Faculty of Agricultural and Food Sciences, Program in Integrated Rural Development, Québec, QC G1K 7P4, Canada. Offers Diploma. *Entrance requirements:* For degree, good knowledge of French. Electronic applications accepted.

University of Alaska Fairbanks, College of Rural and Community Development, Department of Alaska Native and Rural Development, Fairbanks, AK 99775-7520. Offers MA. Part-time programs available. *Degree requirements:* For master's, comprehensive exam, thesis or alternative. *Entrance requirements:* For master's, GRE General Test. Additional exam requirements/recommendations for international students: Required—TOEFL (minimum score 550 paper-based; 213 computer-based). Electronic applications accepted. *Faculty research:* International indigenous leadership development, interrelationships between rural communities and global economy.

University of Guelph, Graduate Program Services, Ontario Agricultural College, School of Environmental Design and Rural Development, Interdisciplinary Program in Rural Studies, Guelph, ON N1G 2W1, Canada. Offers PhD. Offered in cooperation with the Department of Food, Agricultural and Resource Economics, and the Department of Geography. Part-time programs available. *Faculty:* 19 full-time (5 women). *Students:* 21 full-time (14 women), 9 part-time (8 women); includes 7 minority (1 African American, 2 Asian Americans or Pacific Islanders, 4 Hispanic Americans), 1 international. Average age 35. 25 applicants, 12% accepted. In 2007, 4 degrees awarded. *Degree requirements:* For doctorate, thesis/dissertation, qualifying exam. *Entrance requirements:* Additional exam requirements/recommendations for international students: Required—TOEFL (minimum score 600 paper-based; 218 computer-based), IELTS (minimum score 7). *Application deadline:* For fall admission, 3/1 for domestic and international students. Application fee: $85. Electronic applications accepted. *Financial support:* In 2007–08, 10 research assistantships (averaging $9,800 per year), 8 teaching assistantships (averaging $6,500 per year) were awarded; scholarships/grants and unspecified assistantships also available. *Faculty research:* Sustainable rural communities, human resource development, rural planning and development. *Unit head:* Dr. John FitzGibbon, Coordinator, 519-824-4120 Ext. 58034, Fax: 519-767-1686, E-mail: jfitzgib@uoguelph.ca. *Application contact:* Ornella R. McCarron, Secretary, 519-824-4120 Ext. 58901, Fax: 519-767-1686, E-mail: omccarro@uoguelph.ca.

University of Guelph, Graduate Program Services, Ontario Agricultural College, School of Environmental Design and Rural Development, Program in Capacity Development and Extension, Guelph, ON N1G 2W1, Canada. Offers M Sc. Part-time programs available. *Faculty:* 4 full-time (1 woman), 10 part-time/adjunct (6 women). *Students:* 14 full-time (8 women), 7 part-time (5 women). 15 applicants, 80% accepted, 7 enrolled. In 2007, 11 degrees awarded. *Degree requirements:* For master's, thesis optional. *Entrance requirements:* For master's, minimum B- average in previous 2 years of course work. Additional exam requirements/recommendations for international students: Required—TOEFL (minimum score 550 paper-based; 213 computer-based; 89 iBT), IELTS (minimum score 7). *Application deadline:* For fall admission, 3/15 priority date for domestic students, 3/1 for international students. Applications are processed on a rolling basis. Application fee: $85. Electronic applications accepted. *Financial support:* In 2007–08, 8 research assistantships (averaging $4,001 per year), 3 teaching assistantships (averaging $2,128 per year) were awarded; fellowships, Federal Work-Study, scholarships/grants, and unspecified assistantships also available. *Faculty research:* Adult learning in non-formal settings, communication technology for remote areas, rural quality of life. *Application contact:* Dr. Al Lauzon, Graduate Coordinator, 519-824-4120 Ext. 53379, Fax: 519-767-1686, E-mail: allauzon@uoguelph.ca.

University of Guelph, Graduate Program Services, Ontario Agricultural College, School of Environmental Design and Rural Development, Program in Rural Planning and Development, Guelph, ON N1G 2W1, Canada. Offers international rural planning and development (M Sc); rural planning and development in Canada (M Sc). M Sc offered in cooperation with Departments of Food, Agricultural and Resource Economics; Geography; Land Resource Science; and others by arrangement. Part-time programs available. *Faculty:* 9 full-time (1 woman), 8 part-time/adjunct (3 women). *Students:* 37 full-time (21 women), 16 part-time (11 women). 57 applicants, 60% accepted, 19 enrolled. In 2007, 19 degrees awarded. *Degree requirements:* For master's, thesis or alternative. *Entrance requirements:* For master's, minimum B- average during previous 2 years of course work. Additional exam requirements/recommendations for international students: Required—TOEFL (minimum score 550 paper-based; 213 computer-based), IELTS (minimum score 7). *Application deadline:* For fall admission, 3/31 priority date for domestic students, 3/1 for international students. Applications are processed on a rolling basis. Application fee: $85. Electronic applications accepted. *Financial support:* In 2007–08, 17 research assistantships (averaging $3,196 per year), 9 teaching assistantships (averaging $2,183 per year) were awarded; career-related internships or fieldwork, Federal Work-Study, institutionally sponsored loans, scholarships/grants, and unspecified assistantships also available. *Faculty research:* Canadian and international rural planning, resource and economic development, tourism. *Application contact:* Dr. F. H. Cummings, Graduate Coordinator, 519-824-4120 Ext. 53637, Fax: 519-767-1686, E-mail: cummingsharry@hotmail.com.

The University of Montana, Graduate School, College of Arts and Sciences, Department of Geography, Missoula, MT 59812-0002. Offers geography (MA), including cartography and GIS, community and environmental planning. *Entrance requirements:* For master's, GRE General Test. Additional exam requirements/recommendations for international students: Required—TOEFL.

University of West Georgia, Graduate School, College of Arts and Sciences, Department of Political Science and Planning, Program in Rural and Small Town Planning, Carrollton, GA 30118. Offers MS. Part-time programs available. *Students:* 2 full-time (0 women), 1 part-time. Average age 35. *Degree requirements:* For master's, exit paper. *Entrance requirements:* For master's, GRE. Additional exam requirements/recommendations for international students: Required—TOEFL. Application fee: $30. Electronic applications accepted. *Expenses:* Tuition, state resident: full-time $2,448; part-time $136 per semester hour. Tuition, nonresident: full-time $9,774; part-time $543 per semester hour. Required fees: $26 per semester hour. $173 per semester. *Financial support:* Applicants required to submit FAFSA. *Unit head:* Dr. G. Richard Larkin, Assistant Dean, College of Arts and Sciences, 678-839-6405, E-mail: dlarkin@westga.edu. *Application contact:* Dr. Charles W. Clark, Interim Dean, 678-839-6508, E-mail: cclark@westga.edu.

University of Wyoming, Graduate School, College of Arts and Sciences, Department of Geography, Program in Rural Planning and Natural Resources, Laramie, WY 82070. Offers community and regional planning and natural resources (MP). *Faculty:* 1 full-time (0 women). *Students:* 1 applicant, 100% accepted. In 2007, 2 master's awarded. *Degree requirements:* For master's, thesis or alternative. *Entrance requirements:* For master's, GRE General Test, minimum GPA of 3.0. Additional exam requirements/recommendations for international students: Required—TOEFL. *Application deadline:* For fall admission, 2/15 for domestic students. Applications are processed on a rolling basis. Application fee: $50. *Financial support:* In 2007–08, research assistantships (averaging $10,696 per year), teaching assistantships with full and partial tuition reimbursements (averaging $10,696 per year) were awarded; career-related internships or fieldwork, Federal Work-Study, scholarships/grants, and unspecified assistantships also available. Financial award application deadline: 3/1. *Faculty research:* Rural and small town planning, public land management. *Application contact:* Barbara Powell, Office Associate Senior, 307-766-3311, Fax: 307-766-3294, E-mail: geography-info@uwyo.edu.

Virginia Polytechnic Institute and State University, Graduate School, College of Architecture and Urban Studies, School of Public and International Affairs, Blacksburg, VA 24061. Offers environmental planning and policy (MURP); government and international affairs (MPIA); housing, community and economic development (MURP); international development planning (MURP); land use and physical planning (MURP); planning, governance and globalization (PhD), including environmental planning and landscape analysis, physical planning and urban design, public and international affairs, urban and environmental design and planning; urban and regional planning (MURP). *Accreditation:* ACSP. *Entrance requirements:* Additional exam requirements/recommendations for international students: Required—TOEFL (minimum score 550 paper-based; 213 computer-based). Electronic applications accepted. *Faculty research:* Design theory, environmental planning, town planning, transportation planning.

Sustainable Development

Brandeis University, Graduate School of Arts and Sciences, Program in Coexistence and Conflict and Sustainable International Development, Waltham, MA 02454-9110. Offers MA/MA. *Application contact:* David F. Cotter, Graduate School of Arts and Sciences, 781-736-3406, Fax: 781-736-3412, E-mail: cotter@brandeis.edu.

Brandeis University, The Heller School for Social Policy and Management, Program in Nonprofit Management, Waltham, MA 02454-9110. Offers aging services management (MBA); child, youth, and family management (MBA); health care management (MBA); social impact management (MBA); social policy and management (MBA); sustainable development (MBA); MBA/MA. *Accreditation:* AACSB. Part-time and evening/weekend programs available. *Degree requirements:* For master's, team consulting project. *Entrance requirements:* For master's, GMAT. Additional exam requirements/recommendations for international students: Required—TOEFL (minimum score 600 paper-based). Electronic applications accepted. Expenses: Contact institution. *Faculty research:* Health care, child and family, elder and disabled services, general human services.

Brandeis University, The Heller School for Social Policy and Management, Program in Sustainable International Development, Waltham, MA 02454-9110. Offers international development (MA); sustainable development (MA). *Degree requirements:* For master's, 2nd-year fieldwork or internship. *Entrance requirements:* For master's, 3 letters of recommendation; curriculum vitae or resumé. Additional exam requirements/recommendations for international students: Required—TOEFL, IELTS. Electronic applications accepted. Expenses: Contact institution. *Faculty research:* Water resource management, human rights, biosphere management, rural development, public policy and governance.

See Close-Up on page 1141.

California State University, Stanislaus, College of Natural Sciences, Department of Biological Sciences, Turlock, CA 95382. Offers ecology and sustainability (MS); genetic counseling (MS); marine sciences (MS). Part-time programs available. *Faculty:* 20 full-time, 5 part-time/adjunct. *Students:* 3 full-time (2 women), 6 part-time (all women); includes 1 minority (Hispanic American), 1 international. Average age 34. 1 applicant, 100% accepted, 1 enrolled. *Degree requirements:* For master's, thesis. *Entrance requirements:* For master's, GRE General Test, GRE Subject Test, minimum GPA of 3.0, 3 letters of reference, personal statement. Additional exam requirements/recommendations for international students: Required—TOEFL (minimum score 550 paper-based; 213 computer-based). *Application deadline:* For fall admission, 2/15 for domestic and international students; for spring admission, 9/15 for domestic and international students. Application fee: $55. Electronic applications accepted. *Expenses:* Tuition, nonresident: full-time $10,170; part-time $339 per unit. Required fees: $3,972; $2,538 per term. $1,165 per semester. *Financial support:* Fellowships, career-related internships or fieldwork, Federal Work-Study, and scholarships/grants available. Support available to part-time students. Financial award application deadline: 3/2; financial award applicants required to submit FAFSA. *Faculty research:* Long-term smoking and pregnancy rate, vertebrate paleobiology, terrestrial animals, benthic invertebrates of central California coastline. *Application contact:* Dr. Mark Grobner, Chair, 209-667-3476, E-mail: pmartin@csustan.edu.

Carnegie Mellon University, H. John Heinz III School of Public Policy and Management, Program in Sustainable Economic Development, Pittsburgh, PA 15213-3891. Offers MIS. *Degree requirements:* For master's, internship. *Entrance requirements:* For master's, GMAT or GRE, previous course work in calculus and statistics. Electronic applications accepted.

Clark University, Graduate School, Department of International Development, Community, and Environment, Worchester, MA 01610-1477. Offers community development and planning (MA); environmental science and policy (MA); geographic information science for development and environment (MA); international development and social change (MA). *Faculty:* 14 full-time (8 women), 4 part-time/adjunct (2 women). *Students:* 88 full-time (54 women), 37 part-time (25 women); includes 8 minority (4 African Americans, 1 American Indian/Alaska Native, 3 Asian Americans or Pacific Islanders), 43 international. Average age 29. 299 applicants, 79% accepted, 72 enrolled. In 2007, 65 degrees awarded. *Degree requirements:* For master's, thesis. *Entrance requirements:* Additional exam requirements/recommendations for international students: Required—TOEFL. *Application deadline:* For fall admission, 1/15 for domestic students. Application fee: $55. *Expenses:* Tuition: Full-time $32,600; part-time $1,019 per credit. Required fees: $30. Tuition and fees vary according to program. *Financial support:* In 2007–08, fellowships with full and partial tuition reimbursements (averaging $5,000 per year), 2 research assistantships with full and partial tuition reimbursements (averaging $5,000 per year), 2 teaching assistantships with full and partial tuition reimbursements (averaging $5,000 per year) were awarded; career-related internships or fieldwork, scholarships/grants, and tuition waivers (full and partial) also available. *Faculty research:* Community participation, gender analysis, land-use planning, project analysis, geographic information systems, AIDS research. Total annual research expenditures: $1.9 million. *Unit head:* Dr. William F. Fisher, Director, 508-421-3765, Fax: 508-793-8820, E-mail: wfisher@clarku.edu. *Application contact:* Paula Hall, IDCE Graduate Admissions, 508-793-7201, Fax: 508-793-8820, E-mail: idce@clarku.edu.

Columbia University, Graduate School of Arts and Sciences, Program in Climate and Society, New York, NY 10027. Offers MA. Application fee: $90. *Expenses:* Tuition: Part-time $1,452 per credit. Required fees: $152 per term. One-time fee: $75 part-time. Full-time tuition and fees vary according to course level, course load, degree level and program. *Unit head:* Mark Cane, Chair, 845-365-8736, Fax: 845-365-8150, E-mail: mcane@ldeo.columbia.edu.

Columbia University, Graduate School of Arts and Sciences, Program in Sustainable Development, New York, NY 10027. Offers PhD. Application fee: $90. *Expenses:* Tuition: Part-time $1,452 per credit. Required fees: $152 per term. One-time fee: $75 part-time. Full-time tuition and fees vary according to course level, course load, degree level and program. *Unit head:* Jeffrey Sachs, Co-Director, 212-854-8704, Fax: 212-854-8702, E-mail: sachs@columbia.edu. *Application contact:* Mona Khalidi, Application Contact, 212-854-8690, E-mail: mk2388@columbia.edu.

Dominican University of California, Graduate Programs, School of Business, Education and Leadership, Division of Business and International Studies, Green Business Administration Program, San Rafael, CA 94901-2298. Offers sustainable development (MBA). *Students:* 59 full-time (42 women), 18 part-time (13 women); includes 9 minority (3 African Americans, 1 American Indian/Alaska Native, 2 Asian Americans or Pacific Islanders, 3 Hispanic Americans), 4 international. Average age 34. 47 applicants, 79% accepted, 37 enrolled. *Entrance requirements:* Additional exam requirements/recommendations for international students: Required—TOEFL (minimum score 550 paper-based; 213 computer-based). Application fee: $40. *Financial support:* In 2007–08, 67 students received support, including 28 fellowships (averaging $1,950 per year). *Application contact:* Angie Schmidt, Assistant Director, 415-458-3771, Fax: 415-485-3214, E-mail: angela.schmidt@dominican.edu.

Goddard College, Graduate Program, Program in Socially Responsible Business and Sustainable Communities, Plainfield, VT 05667-9432. Offers MA. *Students:* 14 full-time. 6 applicants, 100% accepted, 5 enrolled. *Degree requirements:* For master's, thesis. *Entrance requirements:* For master's, 3 letters of recommendation, preliminary study plan and bib. Application fee: $40. *Expenses:* Tuition: Full-time $14,038. *Financial support:* In 2007–08, 11 students received support. *Unit head:* Ann Driscoll, Director, 802-454-8311, E-mail: ann.driscoll@goddard.edu. *Application contact:* Lara Duston, Admissions Counselor, 800-906-8312 Ext. 205, Fax: 802-454-1029, E-mail: lara.duston@goddard.edu.

Hawai'i Pacific University, College of Professional Studies, Honolulu, HI 96813. Offers global leadership and sustainable development (MA); human resource management (MA); information systems (MSIS); organizational change (MA). Part-time and evening/weekend

Sustainable Development

Hawai'i Pacific University (continued)

programs available. *Faculty:* 15 full-time (2 women), 7 part-time/adjunct (2 women). *Students:* 139 full-time (52 women), 122 part-time (49 women); includes 82 minority (9 African Americans, 3 American Indian/Alaska Native, 58 Asian Americans or Pacific Islanders, 12 Hispanic Americans), 108 international. Average age 32. 307 applicants, 83% accepted, 70 enrolled. In 2007, 73 degrees awarded. *Degree requirements:* For master's, thesis. *Entrance requirements:* Additional exam requirements/recommendations for international students: Recommended—TOEFL (minimum score 550 paper-based; 213 computer-based; 80 iBT), TWE (minimum score 5). *Application deadline:* For fall admission, 2/15 priority date for domestic students; for spring admission, 10/15 priority date for domestic students. Applications are processed on a rolling basis. Application fee: $50. Electronic applications accepted. *Expenses:* Tuition: Full-time $14,400. Required fees: $1,885. Tuition and fees vary according to course load and program. *Financial support:* In 2007–08, 57 students received support. Career-related internships or fieldwork, Federal Work-Study, scholarships/grants, and unspecified assistantships available. Support available to part-time students. Financial award application deadline: 3/1; financial award applicants required to submit FAFSA. *Unit head:* Dr. Gordon Jones, Dean, 808-544-1181, Fax: 808-544-0247, E-mail: gjones@hpu.edu. *Application contact:* Danny Lam, Assistant Director of Graduate Admissions, 808-544-1135, Fax: 808-544-0280, E-mail: graduate@hpu.edu.

HEC Montreal, School of Business Administration, Diploma Programs in Administration, Program in Management and Sustainable Development, Montréal, QC H3T 2A7, Canada. Offers Diploma. Part-time programs available. *Students:* 10 full-time (7 women), 36 part-time (17 women). 53 applicants, 62% accepted, 28 enrolled. In 2007, 3 degrees awarded. *Application deadline:* For fall admission, 5/15 for domestic students. Application fee: $75. Tuition charges are reported in Canadian dollars. *Expenses:* Tuition, state resident: full-time $5,800 Canadian dollars. Tuition, nonresident: full-time $12,200 Canadian dollars. International tuition: $23,300 Canadian dollars full-time. *Application contact:* Francine Blais, Administrative Director, 514-340-6112, Fax: 514-340-6411, E-mail: francine.blais@hec.ca.

Illinois Institute of Technology, Stuart School of Business, Program in Business Administration, Chicago, IL 60616-3793. Offers entrepreneurship (MBA); financial management (MBA); financial markets (MBA); healthcare management (MBA); information management (MBA); international business (MBA); management science (MBA); marketing (MBA); operations, quality, and technology management (MBA); strategic management of organizations (MBA); sustainable enterprise (MBA); JD/MBA; MBA/MS. *Accreditation:* AACSB. Part-time and evening/weekend programs available. *Faculty:* 14 full-time (1 woman), 9 part-time/adjunct (2 women). *Students:* 78 full-time (28 women), 47 part-time (17 women); includes 16 minority (2 African Americans, 11 Asian Americans or Pacific Islanders, 3 Hispanic Americans), 82 international. Average age 29. 283 applicants, 65% accepted, 49 enrolled. In 2007, 51 master's awarded. *Entrance requirements:* For master's, GMAT. Additional exam requirements/recommendations for international students: Required—TOEFL (minimum score 600 paper-based; 250 computer-based; 100 iBT). *Application deadline:* For fall admission, 5/1 for domestic and international students; for spring admission, 1/5 for domestic and international students. Applications are processed on a rolling basis. Application fee: $75. Electronic applications accepted. *Expenses: Contact institution.* Tuition and fees vary according to class time, course level, course load, program and student level. *Financial support:* Career-related internships or fieldwork, Federal Work-Study, institutionally sponsored loans, scholarships/grants, traineeships, health care benefits, and tuition waivers (partial) available. Support available to part-time students. Financial award applicants required to submit FAFSA. *Faculty research:* Global Management and Marketing Strategy, Technological Innovation, Management Science, Financial Management, Knowledge Management. *Unit head:* M. Krishna Erramilli, Interim Director, 312-906-6543, Fax: 312-906-6549, E-mail: george.nassos@iit.edu. *Application contact:* Brian Jansen, Director of Graduate Admissions, 312-906-6521, Fax: 312-906-6549, E-mail: admission@stuart.iit.edu.

Instituto Centroamericano de Administración de Empresas, Graduate Programs, La Garita, Costa Rica. Offers agribusiness (MIAM); business administration (EMBA); entrepreneurial economics (MBA); industry and technology (MBA); sustainable development (MBA). *Degree requirements:* For master's, comprehensive exam, essay. *Entrance requirements:* For master's, GMAT or GRE, fluency in Spanish, interview, letters of recommendation, minimum 1 year of work experience. Electronic applications accepted. *Faculty research:* Competitiveness, production.

Iowa State University of Science and Technology, Graduate College, Interdisciplinary Programs, Program in Sustainable Agriculture, Ames, IA 50011. Offers MS, PhD. *Students:* 23 full-time (8 women); includes 3 minority (1 African American, 1 Asian American or Pacific Islander, 1 Hispanic American), 8 international. 18 applicants, 28% accepted, 3 enrolled. In 2007, 3 master's, 3 doctorates awarded. *Degree requirements:* For master's, thesis or alternative; for doctorate, thesis/dissertation. *Entrance requirements:* For master's and doctorate, GRE General Test. Additional exam requirements/recommendations for international students: Required—TOEFL (paper-based 550; computer-based 213; iBT 80) or IELTS (6.5). *Application deadline:* For fall admission, 2/1 for domestic and international students; for spring admission, 6/1 priority date for domestic and international students. Application fee: $30 ($70 for international students). *Financial support:* In 2007–08, 19 research assistantships (averaging $18,811 per year), 3 teaching assistantships (averaging $17,964 per year) were awarded. *Unit head:* Dr. Mike Duffy, Chair, Supervising Committee, 515-294-6518, E-mail: gpsa@iastate.edu. *Application contact:* Charles Sauer, Information Contact, 515-294-6518, E-mail: gpsa@iastate.edu.

Lipscomb University, MBA Program, Nashville, TN 37204-3951. Offers accounting (MBA); business administration (general) (MBA); conflict management (MBA); financial services (MBA); healthcare management (MBA); leadership (MBA); nonprofit management (MBA); sustainable practice (MBA). *Accreditation:* ACBSP. Part-time and evening/weekend programs available. *Faculty:* 10 full-time (2 women), 6 part-time/adjunct (1 woman). *Students:* 16 full-time (7 women), 63 part-time (25 women); includes 10 minority (8 African Americans, 1 American Indian/Alaska Native, 1 Hispanic American), 1 international. Average age 33. 48 applicants, 73% accepted, 27 enrolled. In 2007, 36 degrees awarded. *Entrance requirements:* For master's, GMAT, interview, 2 references, resumé. Additional exam requirements/recommendations for international students: Required—TOEFL (minimum score 570 paper-based; 230 computer-based). *Application deadline:* For fall admission, 7/1 for domestic students, 2/1 for international students; for winter admission, 12/1 for domestic students, 6/1 for international students. Applications are processed on a rolling basis. Application fee: $50 ($75 for international students). Electronic applications accepted. *Expenses: Contact institution. Financial support:* In 2007–08, 25 students received support. Career-related internships or fieldwork, Federal Work-Study, scholarships/grants, tuition waivers (partial), and unspecified assistantships available. Support available to part-time students. Financial award application deadline: 7/1; financial award applicants required to submit FAFSA. *Faculty research:* Impact of spirituality on organization commitment; leadership; psychological empowerment; training. *Unit head:* Dr. Mike Kendrick, Interim Chair of Graduate Business Studies, 615-966-1833, Fax: 615-966-1818, E-mail: mikekendrick@lipscomb.edu. *Application contact:* Jackie Cash, MBA Assistant, 615-966-1833, Fax: 615-966-1818, E-mail: jackie.cash@lipscomb.edu.

Maharishi University of Management, Graduate Studies, Program in Business Administration, Fairfield, IA 52557. Offers accounting (MBA); business administration (PhD); sustainability (MBA). Evening/weekend programs available. Postbaccalaureate distance learning degree programs offered (minimal on-campus study). *Faculty:* 9 full-time (2 women), 6 part-time/adjunct (1 woman). *Students:* 54 full-time (21 women), 146 part-time (47 women); includes 2 minority (1 African American, 1 Asian American or Pacific Islander), 188 international. Average age 25. In 2007, 104 master's, 2 doctorates awarded. *Degree requirements:* For doctorate, thesis/dissertation. *Entrance requirements:* For master's, GMAT, minimum GPA of 3.0; for doctorate, minimum GPA of 3.0. Additional exam requirements/recommendations for international students: Required—TOEFL. *Application deadline:* For fall admission, 4/15 priority date for domestic students. Applications are processed on a rolling basis. *Expenses:* Tuition: Full-time $24,000; part-time $350 per unit. Required fees: $430; $350 per unit. Tuition and fees vary according to class time, course load, degree level and program. *Financial support:* Career-related internships or fieldwork, Federal Work-Study, and tuition waivers (full and partial) available. *Faculty research:* Leadership, effects of the group dynamics of consciousness on the economy, innovation, employee development, cooperative strategy. *Unit head:* Victoria Alexander, Esq., Chair, 641-472-1113.

Michigan Technological University, Graduate School, Sustainable Futures Institute, Houghton, MI 49931-1295. Offers sustainability (Certificate). Part-time programs available. In 2007, 3 degrees awarded. *Financial support:* Career-related internships or fieldwork, Federal Work-Study, scholarships/grants, unspecified assistantships, and co-op available. Financial award applicants required to submit FAFSA. *Unit head:* John Sutherland, Co-Director, 906-487-3395, Fax: 906-487-2943.

Prescott College, Graduate Programs, Program in Environmental Studies, Prescott, AZ 86301. Offers agroecology (MA); ecopsychology (MA); environmental education (MA); environmental studies (MA); sustainability (MA). MA in environmental education offered jointly with Teton Science School. Part-time programs available. Postbaccalaureate distance learning degree programs offered (minimal on-campus study). *Faculty:* 1 full-time (0 women), 37 part-time/adjunct (15 women). *Students:* 31 full-time (19 women), 19 part-time (9 women); includes 6 minority (1 African American, 3 American Indian/Alaska Native, 2 Hispanic Americans), 1 international. Average age 35. 21 applicants, 90% accepted, 13 enrolled. In 2007, 12 degrees awarded. *Degree requirements:* For master's, thesis, fieldwork or internship, practicum. *Entrance requirements:* For master's, 2 letters of recommendation, resumé. Additional exam requirements/recommendations for international students: Required—TOEFL (minimum score 550 paper-based; 213 computer-based). *Application deadline:* For fall admission, 5/1 priority date for domestic and international students; for spring admission, 11/1 priority date for domestic and international students. Applications are processed on a rolling basis. Application fee: $40. Electronic applications accepted. *Expenses:* Tuition: Full-time $6,480; part-time $540 per credit. *Financial support:* Career-related internships or fieldwork and Federal Work-Study available. Financial award applicants required to submit FAFSA. *Unit head:* Dr. Richard Cellarius, Interim Chair, 928-350-3204. *Application contact:* Kerstin Alicki, Admissions Counselor, 877-350-2102, Fax: 928-776-5242, E-mail: admissions@prescott.edu.

SIT Graduate Institute, Graduate Programs, Master's Programs in Intercultural Service, Leadership, and Management, Brattleboro, VT 05302-0676. Offers conflict transformation (MA); intercultural service, leadership, and management (MA); international education (MA); management (MS); social justice in intercultural relations (MA); sustainable development (MA). Postbaccalaureate distance learning degree programs offered (minimal on-campus study). *Students:* 178 full-time (127 women), 315 part-time (217 women); includes 60 minority (27 African Americans, 1 American Indian/Alaska Native, 12 Asian Americans or Pacific Islanders, 20 Hispanic Americans), 108 international. Average age 30. 540 applicants, 73% accepted, 178 enrolled. In 2007, 179 degrees awarded. *Degree requirements:* For master's, one foreign language, thesis. *Entrance requirements:* For master's, 3 letters of reference. Additional exam requirements/recommendations for international students: Required—TOEFL. *Application deadline:* Applications are processed on a rolling basis. Application fee: $50. *Financial support:* Career-related internships or fieldwork, Federal Work-Study, institutionally sponsored loans, and scholarships/grants available. Financial award application deadline: 3/1; financial award applicants required to submit FAFSA. *Faculty research:* Intercultural communication, conflict resolution, advising and training, world issues, international business. *Unit head:* Marla Solomon, Graduate Dean, 802-258-3325, Fax: 802-258-3241, E-mail: marla.solomon@sit.edu. *Application contact:* Information Contact, 800-336-1616, Fax: 802-258-3500, E-mail: admissions@sit.edu.

Slippery Rock University of Pennsylvania, Graduate Studies (Recruitment), College of Health, Environment, and Science, Department of Parks, Recreation, and Environmental Education, Slippery Rock, PA 16057-1383. Offers environmental education (M Ed); resource management (MS); sustainable systems (MS). Part-time and evening/weekend programs available. *Degree requirements:* For master's, comprehensive exam (for some programs), thesis (for some programs). *Entrance requirements:* For master's, GRE General Test, MAT, minimum GPA of 2.75. Additional exam requirements/recommendations for international students: Required—TOEFL (minimum score 550 paper-based; 213 computer-based). *Application deadline:* For fall admission, 7/1 priority date for domestic and international students; for spring admission, 11/1 priority date for domestic and international students. Applications are processed on a rolling basis. Application fee: $25. Electronic applications accepted. *Expenses:* Tuition, state resident: part-time $345 per credit hour. Tuition, nonresident: part-time $552 per credit hour. Required fees: $142 per credit hour. *Financial support:* Career-related internships or fieldwork, Federal Work-Study, scholarships/grants, and unspecified assistantships available. Support available to part-time students. Financial award application deadline: 5/1; financial award applicants required to submit FAFSA. *Unit head:* Dr. Daniel Dziubek, Graduate Coordinator, 724-738-2068, Fax: 724-738-2938, E-mail: daniel.dziubek@sru.edu. *Application contact:* April Longwell, Interim Director of Graduate Studies, 724-738-2051 Ext. 2116, Fax: 724-738-2146, E-mail: graduate.studies@sru.edu.

University of Connecticut, Graduate School, Center for Continuing Studies, Program in Humanitarian Services Administration, Storrs, CT 06269. Offers MPS. Postbaccalaureate distance learning degree programs offered. *Faculty:* 1 full-time (0 women). *Students:* 2 full-time (both women), 12 part-time (7 women); includes 2 minority (1 African American, 1 Asian American or Pacific Islander), 1 international. Average age 37. 5 applicants, 20% accepted, 0 enrolled. In 2007, 2 degrees awarded. *Entrance requirements:* For master's, minimum GPA of 3.0 or greater than 3.0 for the last 2 years of study; 3 letters of reference. Additional exam requirements/recommendations for international students: Required—TOEFL (minimum score 540 paper-based; 207 computer-based). *Application deadline:* Applications are processed on a rolling basis. *Expenses:* Tuition, state resident: part-time $469 per credit hour. Tuition, nonresident: part-time $1,218 per credit hour. *Financial support:* Fellowships, unspecified assistantships available. Financial award application deadline: 5/1; financial award applicants required to submit FAFSA.

See Close-Up on page 1633.

University of Georgia, Graduate School, School of Ecology, Athens, GA 30602. Offers conservation ecology and sustainable development (MS); ecology (MS, PhD). *Faculty:* 21 full-time (6 women). *Students:* 72 full-time (39 women), 18 part-time (12 women); includes 2 African Americans, 2 Hispanic Americans, 5 international. 138 applicants, 19% accepted, 16 enrolled. In 2007, 4 master's, 8 doctorates awarded. *Degree requirements:* For master's, thesis; for doctorate, one foreign language, thesis/dissertation. *Entrance requirements:* For master's and doctorate, GRE General Test. *Application deadline:* For fall admission, 7/1 priority date for domestic students; for spring admission, 11/15 for domestic students. Application fee: $50. Electronic applications accepted. *Financial support:* Fellowships, research assistantships, teaching assistantships, unspecified assistantships available. *Unit head:* Dr. John L. Gittleman, Dean, 706-542-2968, E-mail: ecohead@uga.edu. *Application contact:* Dr. C. Ronald Carroll, Graduate Coordinator, 706-542-7615, Fax: 706-542-4819, E-mail: rcarroll@uga.edu.

University of Maryland, College Park, Graduate Studies, College of Chemical and Life Sciences, Department of Biology, Program in Sustainable Development and Conservation Biology, College Park, MD 20742. Offers MS. Part-time and evening/weekend programs available. *Students:* 23 full-time (17 women), 1 part-time; includes 5 minority (2 African Americans, 3 Hispanic Americans), 6 international. 51 applicants, 51% accepted, 13 enrolled. In 2007, 16 degrees awarded. *Degree requirements:* For master's, internship, scholarly paper. *Entrance requirements:* For master's, GRE General Test, minimum GPA of 3.0, 3 letters of recommendation. *Application deadline:* For fall admission, 1/15 for domestic and international students; for spring admission, 11/15 for domestic students, 6/1 for international students. Applications are processed on a rolling basis. Application fee: $60. Electronic applications accepted. *Financial* *support:* In 2007–08, 6 fellowships (averaging $9,113 per year), 18 teaching assistantships (averaging $17,632 per year) were awarded; research assistantships. Financial award application deadline: 2/1; financial award applicants required to submit FAFSA. *Faculty research:* Biodiversity, global change, conservation. *Unit head:* Dr. David W. Inouye, Director, 301-405-6946, Fax: 301-314-9358, E-mail: inouye@umd.edu. *Application contact:* Dean of Graduate School, 301-405-0358, Fax: 301-314-9305.

University of Massachusetts Lowell, James B. Francis College of Engineering, Department of Civil and Environmental Engineering, Lowell, MA 01854-2881. Offers civil and environmental engineering (MS Eng, Certificate); environmental engineering (D Eng); environmental studies (MSES, PhD, Certificate), including environmental engineering (MSES), environmental studies (PhD, Certificate); sustainable infrastructure for developing nations (Certificate). Part-time programs available. *Faculty:* 13 full-time (2 women), 8 part-time/adjunct (1 woman). In 2007, 13 degrees awarded. *Degree requirements:* For master's, thesis optional. *Entrance requirements:* For master's, GRE General Test. *Application deadline:* For fall admission, 4/1 priority date for domestic students; for spring admission, 10/1 for domestic students. Applications are processed on a rolling basis. Application fee: $20 ($35 for international students). *Financial support:* Fellowships with full tuition reimbursements, research assistantships with full tuition reimbursements, teaching assistantships with full tuition reimbursements, career-related internships or fieldwork and scholarships/grants available. Financial award application deadline: 4/1. *Faculty research:* Bridge design, traffic control, groundwater remediation, pile capacity. *Unit head:* Dr. John M. Ting, Dean, 978-934-2576, E-mail: john_ting@uml.edu. *Application contact:* Dr. Burton Segall, Graduate Coordinator, 978-934-2288, E-mail: burton_segall@woods.uml.edu.

University of Michigan, School of Natural Resources and Environment, Program in Natural Resources and Environment, Ann Arbor, MI 48109. Offers aquatic sciences: research and management (MS); behavior, education and communication (MS); conservation biology (MS); environmental informatics (MS); environmental justice (MS); environmental policy and planning (MS); natural resources and environment (PhD); sustainable systems (MS); terrestrial ecosystems (MS); MS/AM; MS/JD; MS/MBA. Terminal master's awarded for partial completion of doctoral program. *Degree requirements:* For master's, thesis, practicum or group project; for doctorate, comprehensive exam, thesis/dissertation, oral defense of dissertation, preliminary exam. *Entrance requirements:* For master's, GRE General Test; for doctorate, GRE General Test, master's degree. Additional exam requirements/recommendations for international students: Required—TOEFL (paper-based 560; computer-score 220) or IELTS (6.5). Electronic applications accepted. *Faculty research:* Stream ecology, plant-insect interactions, fish biology, resource control and reproductive success, remote sensing.

University of New Brunswick Fredericton, School of Graduate Studies, Policy Studies Program, Fredericton, NB E3B 5A3, Canada. Offers people, property and alternative dispute resolution (M Phil); philosophy politics and economics (M Phil); sustainable development (M Phil). *Faculty:* 6 full-time (2 women), 13 part-time/adjunct (2 women). *Students:* 13 full-time (8 women), 3 part-time (2 women). In 2007, 6 degrees awarded. *Entrance requirements:* For master's, minimum GPA of 3.5, BA. Additional exam requirements/recommendations for international students: Required—TOEFL (minimum score 600 paper-based), TWE (minimum score 5). Application fee: $50 Canadian dollars. *Financial support:* In 2007–08, 5 research assistantships, 2 teaching assistantships (averaging $4,400 per year) were awarded. *Unit head:* Dr. Gwen Davies, Dean of Graduate Studies, 506-458-7150, Fax: 506-453-4817, E-mail: daviesg@unb.ca. *Application contact:* Janet Amurault, Graduate Secretary, 506-458-7558, Fax: 506-453-4817, E-mail: jamiraul@unb.ca.

University of Washington, School of Law, Seattle, WA 98195-3020. Offers Asian law (LL M, PhD); intellectual property law and policy (LL M); law (JD); law of sustainable international development (LL M); taxation (LL M); JD/LL M; JD/MA; JD/MAIS; JD/MBA; JD/MPA; JD/MS; JD/PhD. *Accreditation:* ABA. *Faculty:* 43 full-time (19 women), 22 part-time/adjunct (11 women). *Students:* 618 full-time (347 women), 35 part-time (21 women); includes 127 minority (14 African Americans, 12 American Indian/Alaska Native, 77 Asian Americans or Pacific Islanders, 24 Hispanic Americans), 50 international. Average age 26. 2,585 applicants, 23% accepted, 183 enrolled. In 2007, 184 first professional degrees, 65 master's, 2 doctorates awarded. *Degree requirements:* For master's, thesis; for doctorate, thesis/dissertation. *Entrance requirements:* For JD, LSAT; for master's, language proficiency (LL M in Asian law). Additional exam requirements/recommendations for international students: Required—TOEFL. *Application deadline:* For fall admission, 1/15 for domestic and international students. Application fee: $50. *Expenses: Contact institution. Financial support:* In 2007–08, 238 students received support, including 31 fellowships (averaging $3,810 per year); research assistantships, career-related internships or fieldwork, Federal Work-Study, institutionally sponsored loans, scholarships/grants, and tuition waivers (partial) also available. Financial award application deadline: 2/28; financial award applicants required to submit FAFSA. *Faculty research:* Asian, international and comparative law, intellectual property law, health law, environmental law, taxation. Total annual research expenditures: $635,743. *Unit head:* Gregory A. Hicks, Interim Dean, 206-543-4034, Fax: 206-616-5305, E-mail: gahicks@uwashington.edu. *Application contact:* Sandra E. Madrid, Assistant Dean, 206-543-0199, Fax: 206-543-5671, E-mail: smadrid@u.washington.edu.

The University of Western Ontario, Faculty of Graduate Studies, Physical Sciences Division, Department of Earth Sciences, London, ON N6A 5B8, Canada. Offers environment and sustainability (MES); geology (M Sc, PhD); geology and environmental science (M Sc, PhD); geophysics (M Sc, PhD); geophysics and environmental science (M Sc, PhD). *Faculty:* 18 full-time (3 women), 20 part-time/adjunct (5 women). *Students:* 30 full-time (15 women), 2 part-time; includes 4 minority (all Asian Americans or Pacific Islanders), 1 international. 69 applicants, 20% accepted, 12 enrolled. In 2007, 4 master's, 2 doctorates awarded. *Degree requirements:* For master's, thesis; for doctorate, thesis/dissertation, qualifying exam. *Entrance requirements:* For master's, honors in B Sc; for doctorate, M Sc. Additional exam requirements/recommendations for international students: Required—TOEFL. *Application deadline:* For fall admission, 1/31 priority date for domestic and international students. Applications are processed on a rolling basis. *Financial support:* In 2007–08, 4 fellowships (averaging $5,000 Canadian dollars per year), 25 teaching assistantships (averaging $200 Canadian dollars per year) were awarded; scholarships/grants, tuition waivers (partial), and unspecified assistantships also available. Financial award application deadline: 1/31. *Faculty research:* Geophysics, geochemistry, paleontology, sedimentology/stratigraphy, glaciology/quaternary. Total annual research expenditures: $13.9 million. *Unit head:* Dr. Rob Schincariol, Acting Chair, 519-661-2111 Ext. 33732, Fax: 519-661-3198, E-mail: eschair@uwo.ca. *Application contact:* Mary E. Rice, Graduate Secretary, 519-661-2111 Ext. 86691, Fax: 519-661-3198, E-mail: mrice@uwo.ca.

University of Wisconsin–Madison, Graduate School, Gaylord Nelson Institute for Environmental Studies, Conservation Biology and Sustainable Development Program, Madison, WI 53706-1380. Offers MS. Part-time programs available. *Faculty:* 3 full-time (1 woman), 57 part-time/adjunct (15 women). *Students:* 27 (22 women); includes 2 minority (both Asian Americans or Pacific Islanders) 3 international. Average age 27. 70 applicants, 41% accepted, 12 enrolled. In 2007, 15 degrees awarded. *Degree requirements:* For master's, thesis or alternative, exit seminar. *Entrance requirements:* For master's, GRE General Test. Additional exam requirements/recommendations for international students: Required—TOEFL (minimum score 550 paper-based; 213 computer-based). *Application deadline:* For fall admission, 2/1 for domestic and international students; for spring admission, 10/15 for domestic and international students. Application fee: $45. Electronic applications accepted. *Financial support:* In 2007–08, 22 students received support, including 4 fellowships with full tuition reimbursements available (averaging $16,605 per year), 5 research assistantships with full tuition reimbursements available (averaging $19,032 per year), 12 teaching assistantships with full tuition reimbursements available (averaging $12,894 per year); career-related internships or fieldwork, Federal Work-Study, scholarships/grants, health care benefits, unspecified assistantships, and project assistantships also available. Financial award application deadline: 1/2. *Faculty research:* Ornithology, forestry, sociology, rural sociology, plant ecology. *Unit head:* Lisa C. Naughton, Chair, 608-262-7996, Fax: 608-262-2273, E-mail: lnaughto@wisc.edu. *Application contact:* James E. Miller, Student Services Coordinator, 608-263-4373, Fax: 608-262-2273, E-mail: jemiller@wisc.edu.

Western Illinois University, School of Graduate Studies, College of Arts and Sciences, Department of Geography, Macomb, IL 61455-1390. Offers community development (Certificate); geography (MA). Part-time programs available. *Students:* 15 full-time (2 women), 4 part-time (1 woman); includes 3 minority (all Asian Americans or Pacific Islanders), 5 international. Average age 30. 14 applicants, 79% accepted. In 2007, 4 master's awarded. *Degree requirements:* For master's, thesis or alternative. *Entrance requirements:* Additional exam requirements/recommendations for international students: Required—TOEFL (minimum score 550 paper-based; 213 computer-based; 80 iBT). *Application deadline:* Applications are processed on a rolling basis. Application fee: $30. Electronic applications accepted. *Expenses:* Tuition, state resident: part-time $217 per credit hour. Tuition, nonresident: part-time $433 per credit hour. Required fees: $54 per credit hour. *Financial support:* In 2007–08, 14 students received support, including 14 research assistantships with full tuition reimbursements available (averaging $6,800 per year). Financial award applicants required to submit FAFSA. *Unit head:* Dr. Sam Thompson, Interim Chairperson, 309-298-1648. *Application contact:* Dr. Barbara Baily, Director of Graduate Studies/Associate Provost, 309-298-1806, Fax: 309-298-2345, E-mail: grad-office@wiu.edu.

West Virginia University, Davis College of Agriculture, Forestry and Consumer Sciences, Division of Resource Management and Sustainable Development, Program in Resource Management and Sustainable Development, Morgantown, WV 26506. Offers PhD. Part-time programs available. *Students:* 18 full-time (9 women), 6 part-time (1 woman); includes 3 minority (2 African Americans, 1 Asian American or Pacific Islander), 10 international. Average age 36. 15 applicants, 67% accepted, 6 enrolled. *Degree requirements:* For doctorate, thesis/dissertation. *Entrance requirements:* For doctorate, GRE General Test. Additional exam requirements/recommendations for international students: Required—TOEFL. Application fee: $50. *Expenses:* Tuition, state resident: full-time $5,196; part-time $292 per credit hour. Tuition, nonresident: full-time $15,064; part-time $840 per credit hour. Tuition and fees vary according to program. *Financial support:* In 2007–08, 24 students received support, including 13 research assistantships (averaging $11,700 per year), 1 teaching assistantship; Federal Work-Study, institutionally sponsored loans, and tuition waivers (partial) also available. Financial award application deadline: 2/1; financial award applicants required to submit FAFSA. *Unit head:* Dr. Jerald Fletcher, Gradute Coordinator, 304-293-4832 Ext. 4452, Fax: 304-293-3740, E-mail: jfletcher@wvu.edu.

Urban and Regional Planning

Alabama Agricultural and Mechanical University, School of Graduate Studies, School of Agricultural and Environmental Sciences, Department of Community Planning and Urban Studies, Huntsville, AL 35811. Offers urban and regional planning (MURP). *Accreditation:* ACSP. Part-time and evening/weekend programs available. *Faculty:* 7 part-time/adjunct (2 women). *Students:* 13 full-time (5 women), 17 part-time (10 women); includes 26 minority (all African Americans), 3 international. In 2007, 4 degrees awarded. *Degree requirements:* For master's, comprehensive exam. *Entrance requirements:* For master's, GRE General Test. *Application deadline:* For fall admission, 5/1 for domestic students. Applications are processed on a rolling basis. Application fee: $25. Electronic applications accepted. *Financial support:* In 2007–08, research assistantships with full tuition reimbursements (averaging $9,000 per year); career-related internships or fieldwork also available. Support available to part-time students. Financial award application deadline: 4/1. *Faculty research:* Urban and rural research, needs assessment and community trends through analysis of social indicators, fiscal impact studies, rural transportation, health care. Total annual research expenditures: $33,000. *Unit head:* Dr. Chukudi Izeogu, Chair, 256-372-5425, Fax: 256-372-5906.

American University of Beirut, Graduate Programs, Faculty of Engineering and Architecture, Beirut, Lebanon. Offers civil engineering (ME, PhD); electrical and computer engineering (ME, PhD); engineering management (MEM); environmental and water resources (ME); environmental and water resources engineering (PhD); environmental technology (MSES); mechanical engineering (ME, PhD); urban design (MUD); urban planning and policy (MUP). Part-time programs available. *Faculty:* 50 full-time (5 women), 6 part-time/adjunct (0 women). *Students:* 149 full-time (59 women), 28 part-time (12 women). Average age 25. 211 applicants, 76% accepted, 51 enrolled. In 2007, 95 degrees awarded. *Degree requirements:* For master's, one foreign language, comprehensive exam, thesis (for some programs); for doctorate, one foreign language, comprehensive exam, thesis/dissertation, publications. *Entrance requirements:* For master's, letters of recommendation; for doctorate, letters of recommendation, master's degree, transcripts, curriculum vitae, interview. Additional exam requirements/recommendations for international students: Required—TOEFL (minimum score 600 paper-based; 250 computer-based; 100 iBT), IELTS (minimum score 8). *Application deadline:* For fall admission, 4/30 priority date for domestic and international students; for spring admission, 11/1 priority date for domestic students, 11/1 for international students. Applications are processed on a rolling basis. Application fee: $50. Electronic applications accepted. *Expenses:* Tuition: Full-time $9,954; part-time $553 per credit. Tuition and fees vary according to course load and program. *Financial support:* In 2007–08, 12 fellowships with full tuition reimbursements (averaging $10,800 per year), 24 research assistantships with full tuition reimbursements (averaging $6,000 per year), 56 teaching assistantships with full tuition reimbursements (averaging $3,000 per year) were awarded; career-related internships or fieldwork, institutionally sponsored loans, scholarships/grants, health care benefits, and unspecified assistantships also available. Total annual research expenditures: $855,886. *Unit head:* Ibrahim N. Hajj, Dean, 961-1350000 Ext. 3400, Fax: 961-1744462, E-mail: ihajj@aub.edu.lb. *Application contact:* Dr. Salim Kanaan, Director, Admissions Office, 961-1350000 Ext. 2594, Fax: 961-1750775, E-mail: sk00@aub.edu.lb.

Arizona State University, Graduate College, College of Architecture and Environmental Design, School of Planning and Landscape Architecture, Tempe, AZ 85287. Offers planning (MEP). *Accreditation:* ACSP. *Entrance requirements:* For master's, GRE General Test.

Auburn University, Graduate School, College of Architecture, Design, and Construction, Program in Community Planning, Auburn University, AL 36849. Offers MCP, MPA/MCP. *Accreditation:* ACSP. Part-time programs available. *Faculty:* 25 full-time (7 women). *Students:* 10 full-time (7 women), 16 part-time (8 women); includes 6 minority (5 African Americans, 1 Asian American or Pacific Islander), 3 international. Average age 28. 25 applicants, 84% accepted, 13 enrolled. In 2007, 12 degrees awarded. *Degree requirements:* For master's, oral exam, project. *Entrance requirements:* For master's, GRE General Test. *Application deadline:* For fall admission, 7/7 for domestic students; for spring admission, 11/24 for domestic students.

Urban and Regional Planning

Auburn University (continued)

Applications are processed on a rolling basis. Application fee: $25 ($50 for international students). Electronic applications accepted. *Financial support:* Federal Work-Study available. Support available to part-time students. Financial award application deadline: 3/15. *Unit head:* Dr. John J. Pittari, Chair, 334-844-4516. *Application contact:* Dr. Joe Pittman, Interim Dean of the Graduate School, 334-844-4700.

Ball State University, Graduate School, College of Architecture and Planning, Department of Urban Planning, Muncie, IN 47306-1099. Offers MURP. *Accreditation:* ACSP. *Faculty:* 10. *Students:* 24 full-time (7 women), 3 part-time (2 women); includes 3 minority (all African Americans), 3 international. Average age 25. 33 applicants, 79% accepted, 13 enrolled. In 2007, 14 degrees awarded. *Degree requirements:* For master's, thesis. *Entrance requirements:* For master's, writing sample. Application fee: $25 ($35 for international students). *Expenses:* Tuition, state resident: full-time $6,864. Tuition, nonresident: full-time $17,932. Required fees: $1,866. *Financial support:* In 2007–08, 11 teaching assistantships with full tuition reimbursements (averaging $6,877 per year) were awarded; research assistantships with full tuition reimbursements, career-related internships or fieldwork also available. Financial award application deadline: 3/1. *Faculty research:* Computer-assisted land-use analysis. *Unit head:* Dr. David Schoen, Interim Chair, 765-285-1963, Fax: 765-285-2648. *Application contact:* Dr. Francis Parker, Director, 765-285-1963, Fax: 765-285-2648, E-mail: fparker@bsu.edu.

Announcement: MURP is an accredited, professionally recognized, 48-credit-hour degree (36-hour accelerated track for those with accredited undergraduate planning degrees). Students can study on the Muncie campus or at the CAP Indianapolis Center, where individual courses are periodically offered. Students receive hands-on field experiences and physical and comprehensive planning practice. Students can select among three areas of concentrated study. There are well-developed study-abroad and internship programs. Students interact closely with 9 full-time faculty members plus professionals and practitioner alumni. Assistantships and other financial aid are available. Web site: www.bsu.edu/urban.

Boston University, Metropolitan College (Continuing Education), Department of Applied Social Sciences, Program in City Planning, Boston, MA 02215. Offers MCP. Part-time and evening/weekend programs available. *Faculty:* 1 full-time (0 women), 14 part-time/adjunct (2 women). *Students:* 5 full-time (2 women), 21 part-time (7 women); includes 1 minority (African American), 5 international. Average age 32. 20 applicants, 75% accepted, 8 enrolled. In 2007, 10 degrees awarded. *Entrance requirements:* Additional exam requirements/recommendations for international students: Required—TOEFL; Recommended—IELTS. *Application deadline:* For fall admission, 7/15 priority date for domestic and international students; for spring admission, 12/15 priority date for domestic students, 11/15 priority date for international students. Applications are processed on a rolling basis. Application fee: $70. Electronic applications accepted. *Expenses:* Tuition: Full-time $34,930; part-time $1,092 per credit. Tuition and fees vary according to class time, course level and program. *Financial support:* In 2007–08, 5 students received support, including 5 research assistantships with full and partial tuition reimbursements available; career-related internships or fieldwork, Federal Work-Study, institutionally sponsored loans, tuition waivers (partial), and unspecified assistantships also available. Support available to part-time students. Financial award application deadline: 6/15; financial award applicants required to submit FAFSA. *Faculty research:* Housing, community development and land use planning, environmental management and planning, international comparative development planning. *Application contact:* Enrique R. Silva, Instructor and Faculty Coordinator, 617-358-3264, Fax: 617-358-3595, E-mail: ersilva@bu.edu.

California Polytechnic State University, San Luis Obispo, College of Architecture and Environmental Design, Department of City and Regional Planning, San Luis Obispo, CA 93407. Offers MCRP, MCRP/MS. *Accreditation:* ACSP. Part-time programs available. *Faculty:* 6 full-time (2 women), 2 part-time/adjunct (0 women). *Students:* 36 full-time (12 women), 4 part-time (1 woman); includes 5 minority (2 Asian Americans or Pacific Islanders, 3 Hispanic Americans). 63 applicants, 63% accepted, 21 enrolled. In 2007, 14 degrees awarded. *Degree requirements:* For master's, thesis or alternative. *Entrance requirements:* For master's, GRE, minimum GPA of 3.0 in last 90 quarter units. Additional exam requirements/recommendations for international students: Required—TOEFL (minimum score 550 paper-based; 213 computer-based), TWE (minimum score 4.5). *Application deadline:* For fall admission, 7/1 for domestic students, 11/30 for international students; for winter admission, 11/1 for domestic students, 6/30 for international students. Applications are processed on a rolling basis. Application fee: $55. Electronic applications accepted. *Expenses:* Tuition, nonresident: part-time $226 per unit. Required fees: $1,777 per quarter. *Financial support:* In 2007–08, 18 students received support; research assistantships, career-related internships or fieldwork, Federal Work-Study, institutionally sponsored loans, and unspecified assistantships available. Support available to part-time students. Financial award application deadline: 3/2; financial award applicants required to submit FAFSA. *Faculty research:* Natural hazards, housing, small town and rural planning, planning implementation, subdivision site design, transportation. *Unit head:* Dr. Michael Boswell, Graduate Coordinator, 805-756-2496, Fax: 805-756-1340, E-mail: mboswell@calpoly.edu.

California State Polytechnic University, Pomona, Academic Affairs, College of Environmental Design, Program in Urban and Regional Planning, Pomona, CA 91768-2557. Offers MURP. *Accreditation:* ACSP. Part-time programs available. *Students:* 29 full-time (18 women), 35 part-time (16 women); includes 29 minority (3 African Americans, 12 Asian Americans or Pacific Islanders, 14 Hispanic Americans), 5 international. Average age 30. 63 applicants, 68% accepted, 22 enrolled. In 2007, 21 degrees awarded. *Degree requirements:* For master's, thesis or alternative. *Entrance requirements:* For master's, GRE General Test. *Application deadline:* For fall admission, 5/1 priority date for domestic students; for winter admission, 10/15 priority date for domestic students; for spring admission, 1/20 priority date for domestic students. Applications are processed on a rolling basis. Application fee: $55. Electronic applications accepted. *Expenses:* Tuition, nonresident: full-time $7,232; part-time $226 per unit. Required fees: $3,920. One-time fee: $2,486 part-time. *Financial support:* Career-related internships or fieldwork, Federal Work-Study, and institutionally sponsored loans available. Support available to part-time students. Financial award application deadline: 3/2; financial award applicants required to submit FAFSA. *Unit head:* Herschel H. Farberow, Graduate Coordinator, 909-869-2716, Fax: 909-869-4688.

California State University, Chico, Graduate School, College of Behavioral and Social Sciences, Department of Geography and Planning, Program in Rural and Town Planning, Chico, CA 95929-0722. Offers MA. Part-time programs available. *Students:* 5 full-time (1 woman), 4 part-time (1 woman); includes 2 minority (both American Indian/Alaska Native). Average age 29. 6 applicants, 100% accepted, 5 enrolled. In 2007, 1 degree awarded. *Entrance requirements:* For master's, GRE, 2 letters of recommendation, statement of purpose, writing sample. Additional exam requirements/recommendations for international students: Required—TOEFL (minimum score 550 paper-based; 213 computer-based; 80 iBT), IELTS (minimum score 7). *Application deadline:* For fall admission, 3/1 priority date for domestic students, 3/1 for international students; for spring admission, 9/15 priority date for domestic students, 9/15 for international students. Applications are processed on a rolling basis. Application fee: $55. Electronic applications accepted. *Unit head:* Dr. Dean Fairbanks, Graduate Coordinator, 530-898-5780.

The Catholic University of America, School of Architecture and Planning, Washington, DC 20064. Offers M Arch, M Arch Studies. Part-time programs available. *Faculty:* 19 full-time (4 women), 28 part-time/adjunct (6 women). *Students:* 104 full-time (40 women), 15 part-time (12 women); includes 21 minority (8 African Americans, 8 Asian Americans or Pacific Islanders, 5 Hispanic Americans), 7 international. Average age 28. 126 applicants, 75% accepted, 50 enrolled. In 2007, 41 degrees awarded. *Degree requirements:* For master's, thesis. *Entrance requirements:* For master's, minimum GPA of 2.7, portfolio, 3 letters of recommendation. Additional exam requirements/recommendations for international students: Required—TOEFL (minimum score 500 paper-based; 173 computer-based). *Application deadline:* For fall admission, 2/1 priority date for domestic students; for spring admission, 11/15 priority date for domestic students. Applications are processed on a rolling basis. Application fee: $55. Electronic applications accepted. *Expenses: Contact institution. Financial support:* Teaching assistantships, Federal Work-Study, scholarships/grants, tuition waivers (partial), and unspecified assistantships available. Financial award application deadline: 2/1; financial award applicants required to submit FAFSA. *Faculty research:* Architectural history, sacred architecture, computers, technology, urban design, preservation. *Unit head:* Randall Ott, Dean, 202-319-5784, Fax: 202-319-5188, E-mail: ott@cua.edu. *Application contact:* Christine Mica, Director, University Admissions, 202-319-5305, Fax: 202-319-6533, E-mail: cua-admissions@cua.edu.

Clark University, Graduate School, Department of International Development, Community, and Environment, Program in Community Development and Planning, Worcester, MA 01610-1477. Offers MA. *Students:* 7 full-time (6 women), 14 part-time (8 women); includes 4 minority (3 African Americans, 1 Asian American or Pacific Islander). Average age 27. 25 applicants, 80% accepted, 9 enrolled. In 2007, 7 degrees awarded. *Degree requirements:* For master's, thesis. *Entrance requirements:* Additional exam requirements/recommendations for international students: Required—TOEFL. *Application deadline:* For fall admission, 1/15 for domestic students. Application fee: $55. *Expenses:* Tuition: Full-time $32,600; part-time $1,019 per credit. Required fees: $30. Tuition and fees vary according to program. *Financial support:* In 2007–08, fellowships (averaging $5,000 per year), research assistantships with full and partial tuition reimbursements (averaging $5,000 per year), teaching assistantships with full and partial tuition reimbursements (averaging $5,000 per year) were awarded; tuition waivers (full and partial) also available. *Faculty research:* Urban neighborhood revitalization, youth and community development, project evaluation, community development finance. *Unit head:* Dr. William F. Fisher, Director, 508-421-3765, Fax: 508-793-8820, E-mail: wfisher@clarku.edu. *Application contact:* Paula Hall, IDCE Graduate Admissions, 508-793-7201, Fax: 508-793-8820, E-mail: idce@clarku.edu.

Clemson University, Graduate School, College of Architecture, Arts, and Humanities, Department of Planning and Landscape Architecture, Program in City and Regional Planning, Clemson, SC 29634. Offers developmental planning (MCRP). *Students:* 24 full-time (14 women), 2 part-time (1 woman); includes 2 minority (both African Americans), 2 international. Average age 24. 37 applicants, 73% accepted, 12 enrolled. In 2007, 13 degrees awarded. *Degree requirements:* For master's, departmental paper or thesis. *Entrance requirements:* For master's, GRE General Test. Additional exam requirements/recommendations for international students: Required—TOEFL. *Application deadline:* For fall admission, 4/15 priority date for domestic students, 4/15 for international students; for spring admission, 9/15 for international students. Applications are processed on a rolling basis. Application fee: $55. *Financial support:* In 2007–08, 22 research assistantships were awarded; fellowships, teaching assistantships, career-related internships or fieldwork, Federal Work-Study, and scholarships/grants also available. Financial award application deadline: 4/15; financial award applicants required to submit FAFSA. *Faculty research:* Coastal planning, regional economic development, health care access. *Unit head:* James D. London, Coordinator, 864-656-0181, Fax: 864-656-0204, E-mail: riggor@clemson.edu.

Cleveland State University, College of Graduate Studies, Maxine Goodman Levin College of Urban Affairs, Program in Urban Planning, Design, and Development, Cleveland, OH 44115. Offers geographic information systems (Certificate); local and urban management (Certificate); urban economic development (Certificate); urban planning, design, and development (MUPDD); urban real estate development and finance (Certificate); JD/MUPDD. *Accreditation:* ACSP. Part-time and evening/weekend programs available. *Faculty:* 26 full-time (10 women), 12 part-time/adjunct (5 women). *Students:* 25 full-time (10 women), 46 part-time (23 women); includes 13 minority (12 African Americans, 1 Asian American or Pacific Islander), 7 international. Average age 30. 55 applicants, 82% accepted, 23 enrolled. In 2007, 7 degrees awarded. *Degree requirements:* For master's, project or thesis. *Entrance requirements:* For master's, GRE General Test (minimum score: verbal and quantitative 50th percentile, analytical writing 4.0), minimum GPA of 3.0. Additional exam requirements/recommendations for international students: Required—TOEFL (minimum score 525 paper-based; 197 computer-based). *Application deadline:* For fall admission, 7/15 priority date for domestic students, 5/15 for international students; for spring admission, 11/1 for international students. Applications are processed on a rolling basis. Application fee: $30. Electronic applications accepted. *Financial support:* In 2007–08, 21 students received support, including 13 research assistantships with full and partial tuition reimbursements available (averaging $6,960 per year); teaching assistantships with full and partial tuition reimbursements available, career-related internships or fieldwork, Federal Work-Study, tuition waivers (full and partial), and unspecified assistantships also available. Support available to part-time students. Financial award application deadline: 3/1. *Faculty research:* Housing and neighborhood development, urban housing policy, environmental sustainability, economic development. *Unit head:* Dr. W. Dennis Keating, Director, 216-687-2298, Fax: 216-687-2013, E-mail: w.keating@csuohio.edu. *Application contact:* Graduate Advisor, 216-523-7522, Fax: 216-687-5398, E-mail: urbanprograms@csuohio.edu.

Columbia University, Graduate School of Architecture, Planning, and Preservation, Program in Urban Planning, New York, NY 10027. Offers MS, PhD, JD/MS, M Arch/MS, MBA/MS, MIA/MS, MPH/MS, MS/MS. PhD offered through the Graduate School of Arts and Sciences. *Accreditation:* ACSP (one or more programs are accredited). *Degree requirements:* For master's, thesis. *Entrance requirements:* For master's, GRE General Test. *Expenses:* Tuition: Part-time $1,452 per credit. Required fees: $152 per term. One-time fee: $75 part-time. Full-time tuition and fees vary according to course level, course load, degree level and program.

Concordia University, School of Graduate Studies, Faculty of Arts and Science, School of Community and Public Affairs, Montréal, QC H3G 1M8, Canada. Offers community economic development (Diploma).

Cornell University, Graduate School, Graduate Fields of Agriculture and Life Sciences, Field of Community and Rural Development, Ithaca, NY 14853-0001. Offers community development process (MPS); economic development (MPS); local government organizations and operations (MPS); program development and planning (MPS). *Faculty:* 30 full-time (10 women). *Students:* 1 (woman) full-time. Average age 26. In 2007, 2 degrees awarded. *Entrance requirements:* For master's, GRE General Test (recommended), 3 letters of recommendation. Additional exam requirements/recommendations for international students: Required—TOEFL (minimum score 550 paper-based; 213 computer-based; 77 iBT). *Application deadline:* For fall admission, 5/1 for domestic students. Application fee: $70. Electronic applications accepted. *Financial support:* In 2007–08, 2 students received support, including 1 fellowship with full tuition reimbursement available, 1 teaching assistantship with full tuition reimbursement available; research assistantships with full tuition reimbursements available, institutionally sponsored loans, scholarships/grants, health care benefits, tuition waivers (full and partial), and unspecified assistantships also available. Financial award applicants required to submit FAFSA. *Faculty research:* Land use, community economic development, governance and leadership development, planning and evaluation, main street revitalization. *Unit head:* Director of Graduate Studies, 607-255-4916, Fax: 607-255-2231. *Application contact:* Graduate Field Assistant, 607-255-4916, Fax: 607-255-2331, E-mail: gradcrd@cornell.edu.

Cornell University, Graduate School, Graduate Fields of Architecture, Art and Planning, Field of City and Regional Planning, Ithaca, NY 14853-0001. Offers city and regional planning (MRP, PhD); environmental planning and design (MRP, PhD); historic preservation planning (MA); international development planning (MRP, PhD); planning theory and systems analysis (MRP, PhD); regional economics and development planning (MRP, PhD); regional science (MRP, PhD); social and health systems planning (MRP, PhD); urban and regional theory (MRP, PhD); urban planning history (MRP, PhD). *Accreditation:* ACSP (one or more programs are accredited). *Faculty:* 30 full-time (8 women). *Students:* 103 full-time (67 women); includes 12 minority (4 African Americans, 5 Asian Americans or Pacific Islanders, 3 Hispanic Americans), 30 international. Average age 29. 210 applicants, 44% accepted, 36 enrolled. In 2007, 37 master's,

8 doctorates awarded. *Degree requirements:* For master's, thesis (MA); for doctorate, comprehensive exam, thesis/dissertation. *Entrance requirements:* For master's and doctorate, GRE General Test, 2 letters of recommendation. Additional exam requirements/recommendations for international students: Required—TOEFL (minimum score 600 paper-based; 250 computer-based; 77 iBT). *Application deadline:* For fall admission, 1/10 for domestic students. Application fee: $70. Electronic applications accepted. *Financial support:* In 2007–08, 89 students received support, including 14 fellowships with full tuition reimbursements available, 60 research assistantships with full tuition reimbursements available, 15 teaching assistantships with full tuition reimbursements available; institutionally sponsored loans, scholarships/grants, health care benefits, tuition waivers (full and partial), and unspecified assistantships also available. Financial award applicants required to submit FAFSA. *Faculty research:* Land use planning, economic development, international development, historic preservation, community development. *Unit head:* Director of Graduate Studies, 607-255-6848, Fax: 607-255-1971. *Application contact:* Graduate Field Assistant, 607-255-6848, Fax: 607-255-1971, E-mail: crp_admissions@cornell.edu.

Cornell University, Graduate School, Graduate Fields of Architecture, Art and Planning, Field of Regional Science, Ithaca, NY 14853-0001. Offers environmental studies (MA, MS, PhD); international spatial problems (MA, MS, PhD); location theory (MA, MS, PhD); multiregional economic analysis (MA, MS, PhD); peace science (MA, MS, PhD); planning methods (MA, MS, PhD); urban and regional economics (MA, MS, PhD). *Faculty:* 20 full-time (3 women). *Students:* 22 full-time (10 women); includes 2 minority (1 African American, 1 Asian American or Pacific Islander), 20 international. Average age 31. 12 applicants, 83% accepted, 5 enrolled. In 2007, 2 master's, 1 doctorate awarded. Terminal master's awarded for partial completion of doctoral program. *Degree requirements:* For master's, thesis; for doctorate, comprehensive exam, thesis/dissertation. *Entrance requirements:* For master's and doctorate, GRE General Test, 2 letters of recommendation. Additional exam requirements/recommendations for international students: Required—TOEFL (minimum score 600 paper-based; 250 computer-based; 77 iBT). *Application deadline:* For fall admission, 1/15 priority date for domestic students. Application fee: $70. Electronic applications accepted. *Financial support:* In 2007–08, 5 students received support, including 1 fellowship with full tuition reimbursement available, 2 research assistantships with full tuition reimbursements available, 2 teaching assistantships with full tuition reimbursements available; institutionally sponsored loans, scholarships/grants, health care benefits, tuition waivers (full and partial), and unspecified assistantships also available. Financial award applicants required to submit FAFSA. *Faculty research:* Urban and regional growth, spatial economics, formation of spatial patterns by socioeconomic systems, non-linear dynamics and complex systems, environmental-economic systems. *Unit head:* Director of Graduate Studies, 607-255-6848, Fax: 607-255-1971. *Application contact:* Graduate Field Assistant, 607-255-6848, Fax: 607-255-1971, E-mail: regsci@cornell.edu.

Dalhousie University, Faculty of Architecture and Planning, Department of Urban and Rural Planning, Halifax, NS B3H 4R2, Canada. Offers M Pl, MPS, M Eng/M Plan, MA Sc/M Plan. *Degree requirements:* For master's, thesis. *Entrance requirements:* Additional exam requirements/recommendations for international students: Required—TOEFL. *Application deadline:* For fall admission, 4/1 priority date for domestic students. Applications are processed on a rolling basis. Application fee: $60. *Financial support:* Career-related internships or fieldwork and scholarships/grants available. *Unit head:* Prof. Jill Grant, Director, 902-494-6586, Fax: 902-423-6672, E-mail: plan.office@dal.ca. *Application contact:* Carol Madden, Planning Secretary, 902-494-3260, Fax: 902-423-6672, E-mail: plan.office@dal.ca.

Delta State University, Graduate Programs, College of Arts and Sciences, Division of Social Sciences, Program in Community Development, Cleveland, MS 38733-0001. Offers MSCD. Part-time programs available. *Degree requirements:* For master's, thesis or alternative. *Application deadline:* For fall admission, 8/1 priority date for domestic students; for spring admission, 12/1 priority date for domestic students. Applications are processed on a rolling basis. Application fee: $0. *Expenses:* Tuition, state resident: full-time $4,248. Tuition, nonresident: full-time $10,258. *Financial support:* Research assistantships, career-related internships or fieldwork, Federal Work-Study, and institutionally sponsored loans available. Support available to part-time students. Financial award application deadline: 6/1.

DePaul University, School of Public Service, Chicago, IL 60604-2287. Offers financial administration management (Certificate); health administration (Certificate); health law and policy (MS); international public services (MS); metropolitan planning (Certificate); public administration (MS); public service management (MS), including association management, fundraising and philanthropy, healthcare administration, higher education administration, metropolitan planning, non-profit administration, public administration, public policy; public services (Certificate); JD/MS; MA/MS. Part-time and evening/weekend programs available. Postbaccalaureate distance learning degree programs offered (minimal on-campus study). *Faculty:* 11 full-time (2 women), 19 part-time/adjunct (16 women). *Students:* 139 full-time (108 women), 245 part-time (178 women); includes 121 minority (76 African Americans, 2 American Indian/Alaska Native, 15 Asian Americans or Pacific Islanders, 28 Hispanic Americans), 11 international. 140 applicants, 96% accepted, 96 enrolled. In 2007, 89 degrees awarded. *Degree requirements:* For master's, thesis or integrative seminar. *Entrance requirements:* For master's, minimum GPA of 2.7. Additional exam requirements/recommendations for international students: Required—TOEFL (minimum score 550 paper-based; 213 computer-based; 80 iBT), IELTS (minimum score 7). *Application deadline:* Applications are processed on a rolling basis. Application fee: $25. Electronic applications accepted. *Financial support:* In 2007–08, 28 students received support, including 3 research assistantships with full tuition reimbursements available (averaging $7,000 per year); career-related internships or fieldwork, Federal Work-Study, institutionally sponsored loans, scholarships/grants, and tuition waivers (partial) also available. Support available to part-time students. Financial award application deadline: 7/1; financial award applicants required to submit FAFSA. *Faculty research:* Government financing, transportation, leadership, health care, volunteerism and organizational behavior, non-profit organizations. Total annual research expenditures: $20,000. *Unit head:* Dr. J. Patrick Murphy, Director, 312-362-5608, Fax: 312-362-5506, E-mail: jpmurphy@depaul.edu. *Application contact:* Megan B. Balderston, Director of Admissions and Marketing, 312-362-5565, Fax: 312-362-5506, E-mail: pubserv@depaul.edu.

Eastern Kentucky University, The Graduate School, College of Arts and Sciences, Department of Government, Program in General Public Administration, Richmond, KY 40475-3102. Offers community development (MPA); community health administration (MPA); general public administration (MPA). *Accreditation:* NASPAA. Part-time and evening/weekend programs available. *Students:* 17 full-time (10 women), 30 part-time (15 women); includes 5 minority (4 African Americans, 1 American Indian/Alaska Native), 4 international. Average age 31. 23 applicants, 83% accepted, 11 enrolled. In 2007, 12 degrees awarded. *Entrance requirements:* For master's, GRE General Test, minimum GPA of 2.5. Application fee: $30. *Unit head:* Dr. Sara Zeigler, Chair, Department of Government, 859-622-5931.

Eastern Michigan University, Graduate School, College of Arts and Sciences, Department of Geography and Geology, Program in Urban and Regional Planning, Ypsilanti, MI 48197. Offers MS. *Students:* 5 full-time (4 women), 7 part-time (3 women); includes 2 minority (both African Americans), 2 international. Average age 28. In 2007, 12 degrees awarded. Application fee: $35. *Expenses:* Tuition, state resident: full-time $8,952; part-time $373 per credit hour. Tuition, nonresident: full-time $17,634; part-time $735 per credit hour. Required fees: $896; $34 per credit hour. Tuition and fees vary according to course level, degree level and program. *Application contact:* Dr. Norman Tyler, Program Advisor, 734-487-0218, Fax: 734-487-6979, E-mail: norman.tyler@emich.edu.

Eastern Michigan University, Graduate School, College of Arts and Sciences, Department of Political Science, Program in Public Administration, Ypsilanti, MI 48197. Offers local government management (Graduate Certificate); management of public healthcare services (Graduate Certificate); public administration (MPA, Graduate Certificate); public budget management (Graduate Certificate); public land planning (Graduate Certificate); public management (Graduate Certificate); public personnel management (Graduate Certificate); public policy analysis (Graduate Certificate). *Accreditation:* NASPAA. *Students:* 19 full-time (8 women), 97 part-time (57 women); includes 43 minority (34 African Americans, 3 American Indian/Alaska Native, 3 Asian Americans or Pacific Islanders, 3 Hispanic Americans), 7 international. Average age 32. In 2007, 42 master's, 35 other advanced degrees awarded. Application fee: $35. *Expenses:* Tuition, state resident: full-time $8,952; part-time $373 per credit hour. Tuition, nonresident: full-time $17,634; part-time $735 per credit hour. Required fees: $896; $34 per credit hour. Tuition and fees vary according to course level, degree level and program. *Unit head:* Dr. Joseph Ohren, Director, 734-487-2522, Fax: 734-487-3340, E-mail: joseph.ohren@emich.edu. *Application contact:* Dr. Dogan Koyluoglu, Program Coordinator, 734-487-0063, E-mail: sukru.koyuoglu@emich.edu.

Eastern Washington University, Graduate Studies, College of Business and Public Administration, Department of Urban and Regional Planning, Cheney, WA 99004-2431. Offers MURP, MPA/MURP. *Accreditation:* ACSP. *Degree requirements:* For master's, comprehensive exam, thesis or alternative. *Entrance requirements:* For master's, minimum GPA of 3.0.

East Tennessee State University, School of Graduate Studies, College of Business and Technology, Department of Economics, Finance, and Urban Studies, Johnson City, TN 37614. Offers city management (MCM); community development (MPM); general administration (MPM); municipal service management (MPM); urban and regional economic development (MPM); urban and regional planning (MPM). *Degree requirements:* For master's, internship, oral defense of thesis, research report. *Entrance requirements:* For master's, GRE General Test, minimum GPA of 3.0. Additional exam requirements/recommendations for international students: Required—TOEFL (minimum score 550 paper-based; 213 computer-based).

Florida Atlantic University, College of Architecture, Urban and Public Affairs, Department of Urban and Regional Planning, Boca Raton, FL 33431-0991. Offers MURP. *Accreditation:* ACSP. Part-time and evening/weekend programs available. *Entrance requirements:* For master's, GRE General Test, minimum GPA of 3.0. Additional exam requirements/recommendations for international students: Required—TOEFL. *Faculty research:* Growth management, urban design, computer applications/geographical information systems, environmental planning.

Florida State University, Graduate Studies, College of Social Sciences, Department of Urban and Regional Planning, Tallahassee, FL 32306. Offers MSP, PhD, JD/MSP, MA/MSP, MPA/MSP. *Accreditation:* ACSP (one or more programs are accredited). Part-time programs available. *Faculty:* 11 full-time (3 women), 7 part-time/adjunct (1 woman). *Students:* 94 full-time (50 women), 21 part-time (13 women); includes 24 minority (15 African Americans, 1 Asian American or Pacific Islander, 8 Hispanic Americans), 7 international. Average age 25. 96 applicants, 89% accepted, 51 enrolled. In 2007, 35 master's, 2 doctorates awarded. *Median time to degree:* Of those who began their doctoral program in fall 1999, 100% received their degree in 8 years or less. *Degree requirements:* For master's, capstone project, internship; for doctorate, thesis/dissertation. *Entrance requirements:* For master's and doctorate, GRE General Test, minimum GPA of 3.0. Additional exam requirements/recommendations for international students: Required—TOEFL (minimum score 550 paper-based; 213 computer-based; 80 iBT). *Application deadline:* For fall admission, 2/15 priority date for domestic students, 11/15 priority date for international students; for spring admission, 11/1 for domestic students, 9/1 for international students. Applications are processed on a rolling basis. Application fee: $30. Electronic applications accepted. *Expenses:* Tuition, state resident: part-time $248 per credit hour. Tuition, nonresident: part-time $880 per credit hour. Tuition and fees vary according to program. *Financial support:* In 2007–08, 46 students received support, including 2 fellowships with full tuition reimbursements available (averaging $18,000 per year), 35 research assistantships with full tuition reimbursements available (averaging $6,000 per year), 3 teaching assistantships with full tuition reimbursements available (averaging $10,500 per year); career-related internships or fieldwork, Federal Work-Study, institutionally sponsored loans, and tuition waivers (partial) also available. Financial award application deadline: 2/15; financial award applicants required to submit FAFSA. *Faculty research:* Growth management, environmental planning, developing countries, transportation, housing and community development. Total annual research expenditures: $873,000. *Unit head:* Dr. Tim S. Chapin, Chairperson, 850-644-4510, Fax: 850-645-4841, E-mail: tchapin@fsu.edu. *Application contact:* Cynthia E. Brown, Admissions Coordinator, 850-644-4510, Fax: 850-645-4841, E-mail: durp@coss.fsu.edu.

Georgia Institute of Technology, Graduate Studies and Research, College of Architecture, City and Regional Planning Program, Atlanta, GA 30332-0001. Offers architecture (PhD); economic development (MCRP); environmental planning and management (MCRP); geographic information systems (MCRP); land development (MCRP); land use planning (MCRP); transportation (MCRP); urban design (MCRP); MCP/MSCE. *Accreditation:* ACSP. *Degree requirements:* For master's, thesis, internship. *Entrance requirements:* For master's, GRE General Test, minimum GPA of 2.7. Additional exam requirements/recommendations for international students: Required—TOEFL. Electronic applications accepted.

Georgia State University, Andrew Young School of Policy Studies, Department of Public Administration and Urban Studies, Atlanta, GA 30303-3083. Offers disaster management (Certificate); non-profit management (Certificate); planning and economic development (Certificate); public administration (MPA); public policy (PhD); urban policy studies (MS); JD/MPA. *Accreditation:* NASPAA (one or more programs are accredited). Part-time and evening/weekend programs available. *Faculty:* 15 full-time (5 women). *Students:* 131 full-time (82 women), 91 part-time (58 women); includes 83 minority (73 African Americans, 7 Asian Americans or Pacific Islanders, 3 Hispanic Americans), 32 international. Average age 32. 250 applicants, 49% accepted, 74 enrolled. In 2007, 51 master's, 1 doctorate, 7 other advanced degrees awarded. Terminal master's awarded for partial completion of doctoral program. *Degree requirements:* For master's, thesis optional; for doctorate, comprehensive exam, thesis/dissertation. *Entrance requirements:* For master's and doctorate, GRE General Test. Additional exam requirements/recommendations for international students: Required—TOEFL. *Application deadline:* For fall admission, 4/1 for domestic students; for spring admission, 10/1 for domestic students. Applications are processed on a rolling basis. Application fee: $50. Electronic applications accepted. *Expenses:* Tuition, state resident: part-time $221 per credit hour. *Financial support:* In 2007–08, 34 research assistantships with full tuition reimbursements were awarded; fellowships, teaching assistantships with full tuition reimbursements, career-related internships or fieldwork, Federal Work-Study, institutionally sponsored loans, scholarships/grants, and tuition waivers (partial) also available. Support available to part-time students. Financial award applicants required to submit FAFSA. *Faculty research:* Public management, urban policy, policy analysis, public finance, public involvement. *Unit head:* Dr. Greg Streib, Chair, 404-413-0116, E-mail: gstreib@gsu.edu. *Application contact:* Sue Fagan, Office of Academic Assistance Director, 404-413-0021, Fax: 404-413-0023, E-mail: suefagan@gsu.edu.

Harvard University, Graduate School of Arts and Sciences, Committee on Architecture, Landscape Architecture, and Urban Planning, Cambridge, MA 02138. Offers architecture (PhD); landscape architecture (PhD); urban planning (PhD). *Degree requirements:* For doctorate, one foreign language, thesis/dissertation, oral exam. *Entrance requirements:* For doctorate, GRE General Test. Additional exam requirements/recommendations for international students: Required—TOEFL. *Expenses:* Tuition: Full-time $31,456. Full-time tuition and fees vary according to program and student level.

Harvard University, Graduate School of Design, Department of Urban Planning and Design, Cambridge, MA 02138. Offers urban planning (MUP); urban planning and design (MAUD, MLAUD). *Accreditation:* ACSP (one or more programs are accredited). *Faculty:* 10 full-time (2 women), 19 part-time/adjunct (3 women). *Students:* 90 full-time (50 women); includes 20 minority (5 African Americans, 9 Asian Americans or Pacific Islanders, 6 Hispanic Americans), 35 international. Average age 27. In 2007, 48 degrees awarded. *Entrance requirements:* For master's, GRE General Test. Additional exam requirements/recommendations for international students: Required—TOEFL (minimum score 600 paper-based; 250 computer-based; 100 iBT). *Application deadline:* For fall admission, 1/16 for domestic students. Application fee: $75. Electronic applications accepted. *Expenses:* Tuition: Full-time $31,456. Full-time tuition and

Urban and Regional Planning

Harvard University (continued)
fees vary according to program and student level. *Financial support:* Fellowships, teaching assistantships, Federal Work-Study available. Support available to part-time students. Financial award application deadline: 2/11; financial award applicants required to submit FAFSA. *Unit head:* Rodolfo Machado, Co-Chair, 617-495-2521. *Application contact:* Gail Gustafson, Director of Admissions, 617-495-5453, Fax: 617-495-8949, E-mail: ggustafson@gsd.harvard.edu.

Harvard University, John F. Kennedy School of Government, Program in Public Policy, Cambridge, MA 02138. Offers public policy (MPP); public policy and urban planning (MPPUP); JD/MPP; MBA/MPP; MD/MPP. *Accreditation:* NASPAA. *Students:* 209 full-time (102 women); includes 67 minority (15 African Americans, 2 American Indian/Alaska Native, 24 Asian Americans or Pacific Islanders, 26 Hispanic Americans), 48 international. Average age 25. 1,253 applicants, 28% accepted, 209 enrolled. *Entrance requirements:* For master's, GMAT or GRE General Test. Additional exam requirements/recommendations for international students: Required—TOEFL (minimum score 600 paper-based; 250 computer-based; 100 iBT), TWE. *Application deadline:* For fall admission, 1/5 for domestic students. Application fee: $80. Electronic applications accepted. *Expenses:* Tuition: Full-time $31,456. Full-time tuition and fees vary according to program and student level. *Financial support:* Fellowships, research assistantships, teaching assistantships, career-related internships or fieldwork, Federal Work-Study, institutionally sponsored loans, scholarships/grants, health care benefits, and unspecified assistantships available. Financial award application deadline: 2/2; financial award applicants required to submit CSS PROFILE or FAFSA. *Unit head:* Dr. Helaine Daniels, Director, 617-496-8382, E-mail: helaine_daniels@harvard.edu. *Application contact:* 617-495-1155.

Hunter College of the City University of New York, Graduate School, School of Arts and Sciences, Department of Urban Affairs and Planning, Program in Urban Planning, New York, NY 10021-5085. Offers MUP, JD/MUP. *Accreditation:* ACSP. Part-time programs available. *Faculty:* 4 full-time (1 woman), 7 part-time/adjunct (1 woman). *Students:* 63 full-time (30 women), 51 part-time (29 women); includes 12 minority (5 African Americans, 4 Asian Americans or Pacific Islanders, 3 Hispanic Americans). Average age 29. 101 applicants, 73% accepted, 28 enrolled. *Degree requirements:* For master's, planning studio and internship. *Entrance requirements:* For master's, minimum 12 credits of course work in social sciences, 2 letters of recommendation. Additional exam requirements/recommendations for international students: Required—TOEFL. *Application deadline:* For fall admission, 4/1 for domestic students, 2/1 for international students; for spring admission, 11/1 for domestic students, 9/1 for international students. Application fee: $125. *Expenses:* Tuition, state resident: full-time $6,400; part-time $270 per credit. Tuition, nonresident: part-time $500 per credit. One-time fee: $125 full-time. Tuition and fees vary according to program. *Financial support:* In 2007–08, 4 fellowships with full tuition reimbursements (averaging $9,000 per year), 10 teaching assistantships (averaging $1,200 per year) were awarded; research assistantships, career-related internships or fieldwork, Federal Work-Study, and tuition waivers (partial) also available. Support available to part-time students. *Faculty research:* Community and economic development, transportation planning and policy, geographic information systems, housing, land use. *Unit head:* William J. Milczarski, Director, 212-772-5601, Fax: 212-772-5593, E-mail: wmilczar@hunter.cuny.edu.

Iowa State University of Science and Technology, Graduate College, College of Design, Department of Community and Regional Planning, Ames, IA 50011. Offers community and regional planning (MCRP); transportation (MS); M Arch/MCRP; MBA/MCRP; MCRP/MLA; MCRP/MPA. *Accreditation:* ACSP (one or more programs are accredited). Part-time programs available. *Faculty:* 11 full-time (5 women), 2 part-time/adjunct (0 women). *Students:* 23 full-time (11 women), 10 part-time (4 women); includes 5 minority (3 African Americans, 1 Asian American or Pacific Islander, 1 Hispanic American), 12 international. Average age 31. 29 applicants, 41% accepted, 8 enrolled. In 2007, 6 degrees awarded. *Degree requirements:* For master's, thesis or alternative. *Entrance requirements:* Additional exam requirements/recommendations for international students: Required—TOEFL (minimum score 550 paper-based; 213 computer-based; 79 iBT). *Application deadline:* For fall admission, 1/1 priority date for domestic and international students. Applications are processed on a rolling basis. Application fee: $30 ($70 for international students). Electronic applications accepted. *Financial support:* In 2007–08, 8 research assistantships with full and partial tuition reimbursements (averaging $18,926 per year), 11 teaching assistantships with full and partial tuition reimbursements (averaging $18,894 per year) were awarded; career-related internships or fieldwork, institutionally sponsored loans, tuition waivers (partial), and unspecified assistantships also available. Support available to part-time students. Financial award application deadline: 2/1; financial award applicants required to submit FAFSA. *Faculty research:* Economic development, housing, land use, geographic information systems planning in developing nations, regional and community revitalization, transportation planning in developing countries. *Unit head:* Dr. Douglas Johnston, Chair, 515-294-8958, Fax: 515-294-2348, E-mail: landarch@iastate.edu. *Application contact:* Dr. David Valler, Director of Graduate Education, 515-294-8958, E-mail: crp@iastate.edu.

Jackson State University, Graduate School, School of Liberal Arts, Department of Urban and Regional Planning, Jackson, MS 39217. Offers MS. *Degree requirements:* For master's, comprehensive exam. *Entrance requirements:* For master's, GRE General Test. Additional exam requirements/recommendations for international students: Required—TOEFL.

Kansas State University, Graduate School, College of Architecture, Planning and Design, Department of Regional and Community Planning, Manhattan, KS 66506. Offers regional and community planning (MRCP). *Accreditation:* ACSP. Part-time and evening/weekend programs available. Postbaccalaureate distance learning degree programs offered (minimal on-campus study). *Faculty:* 15 full-time (4 women), 3 part-time/adjunct (0 women). *Students:* 24 full-time (15 women), 3 part-time; includes 1 minority (Hispanic American), 4 international. 19 applicants, 79% accepted, 9 enrolled. In 2007, 7 degrees awarded. *Degree requirements:* For master's, thesis, oral exam. *Entrance requirements:* For master's, minimum GPA of 3.0, portfolio. Additional exam requirements/recommendations for international students: Required—TOEFL (minimum score 600 paper-based). *Application deadline:* For fall admission, 7/1 priority date for domestic students, 2/1 priority date for international students; for spring admission, 10/1 priority date for domestic students, 8/1 priority date for international students. Applications are processed on a rolling basis. Application fee: $70 ($80 for international students). Electronic applications accepted. *Financial support:* In 2007–08, 2 research assistantships (averaging $5,969 per year), 7 teaching assistantships with full tuition reimbursements (averaging $7,000 per year) were awarded; career-related internships or fieldwork, Federal Work-Study, institutionally sponsored loans, and scholarships/grants also available. Support available to part-time students. Financial award application deadline: 3/1; financial award applicants required to submit FAFSA. *Faculty research:* Infrastructure planning, economic development and rural, regional, community and urban planning, planning analysis and methods, cultural and historic landscape preservation. *Unit head:* Dr. Dan Donelin, Head, 785-532-5961, Fax: 785-532-6722, E-mail: dandon@ksu.edu. *Application contact:* Dr. C. A. Keithley, Graduate Coordinator, 785-532-2440, Fax: 785-532-6722, E-mail: cak@ksu.edu.

Massachusetts Institute of Technology, School of Architecture and Planning, Department of Urban Studies and Planning, Cambridge, MA 02139-4307. Offers city planning (MCP); urban and regional planning (PhD); urban and regional studies (PhD); urban studies and planning (SM); M Arch/MCP; MCP/MSRED; MCP/MST; MCP/SM Arch S. *Accreditation:* ACSP (one or more programs are accredited). *Faculty:* 27 full-time (9 women), 1 (woman) part-time/adjunct. *Students:* 220 full-time (112 women); includes 38 minority (9 African Americans, 2 American Indian/Alaska Native, 19 Asian Americans or Pacific Islanders, 8 Hispanic Americans), 68 international. Average age 29. 452 applicants, 30% accepted, 81 enrolled. In 2007, 84 master's, 10 doctorates awarded. Terminal master's awarded for partial completion of doctoral program. *Degree requirements:* For master's, thesis; for doctorate, comprehensive exam, thesis/dissertation. *Entrance requirements:* For master's and doctorate, GRE General Test. Additional exam requirements/recommendations for international students: Required—TOEFL (minimum score 600 paper-based; 250 computer-based; 100 iBT); Recommended—TWE. *Application deadline:* For fall admission, 1/3 for domestic and international students. Application fee: $70. Electronic applications accepted. *Expenses:* Tuition: Full-time $34,760; part-time $545 per unit. Required fees: $236. *Financial support:* In 2007–08, 180 students received support, including 67 fellowships with tuition reimbursements available (averaging $18,290 per year), 54 research assistantships with tuition reimbursements available (averaging $18,799 per year), 21 teaching assistantships with tuition reimbursements available (averaging $22,858 per year); career-related internships or fieldwork, Federal Work-Study, institutionally sponsored loans, scholarships/grants, health care benefits, and unspecified assistantships also available. *Faculty research:* City design and development; housing, community, and economic development; environmental policy and planning; international development and regional planning; urban information systems. Total annual research expenditures: $918,000. *Unit head:* Prof. Lawrence Vale, Head, 617-253-1907, E-mail: duspinfo@mit.edu. *Application contact:* Graduate Admissions, 617-253-4543, Fax: 617-253-2654, E-mail: duspapply@mit.edu.

See Close-Up on page 161.

McGill University, Faculty of Graduate and Postdoctoral Studies, Faculty of Engineering, School of Urban Planning, Montréal, QC H3A 2T5, Canada. Offers environmental planning (MUP); housing (MUP); transportation (MUP); urban design (MUP); urban planning, policy and design (PhD). *Faculty:* 6 full-time (1 woman), 5 part-time/adjunct (1 woman). *Students:* 46 full-time (24 women), 2 part-time (1 woman). 195 applicants, 31% accepted, 27 enrolled. In 2007, 18 degrees awarded.

Michigan State University, The Graduate School, College of Agriculture and Natural Resources and College of Social Science, School of Planning, Design and Construction, East Lansing, MI 48824. Offers construction management (MS, PhD); environmental design (MA); interior design and facilities management (MA); international planning studies (MIPS); urban and regional planning (MURP). Part-time and evening/weekend programs available. *Degree requirements:* For master's, thesis or alternative. *Entrance requirements:* Additional exam requirements/recommendations for international students: Required—TOEFL. Electronic applications accepted. *Expenses:* Tuition, state resident: part-time $379 per credit hour. Tuition, nonresident: part-time $800 per credit hour. Tuition and fees vary according to program.

Minnesota State University Mankato, College of Graduate Studies, College of Social and Behavioral Sciences, Department of Urban and Regional Studies, Mankato, MN 56001. Offers local government (Certificate); urban and regional studies (MA); urban planning (Certificate); MAPA/MA. *Students:* 24 full-time (3 women), 18 part-time (7 women). Average age 30. In 2007, 6 degrees awarded. *Degree requirements:* For master's, one foreign language, comprehensive exam, thesis or alternative. *Entrance requirements:* For master's, minimum GPA of 3.0 during previous 2 years, 2 letters of recommendation. Additional exam requirements/recommendations for international students: Required—TOEFL. *Application deadline:* For fall admission, 7/1 priority date for domestic students; for spring admission, 11/1 for domestic students. Applications are processed on a rolling basis. Application fee: $40. Electronic applications accepted. *Financial support:* Fellowships with partial tuition reimbursements, research assistantships with full tuition reimbursements, teaching assistantships with full tuition reimbursements, career-related internships or fieldwork, Federal Work-Study, institutionally sponsored loans, and unspecified assistantships available. Support available to part-time students. Financial award application deadline: 3/15; financial award applicants required to submit FAFSA. *Unit head:* Dr. Anthony Filipovitch, Chairperson, 507-389-1714. *Application contact:* 507-389-2321, E-mail: grad@mnsu.edu.

Missouri State University, Graduate College, College of Natural and Applied Sciences, Department of Geography, Geology, and Planning, Springfield, MO 65804-0094. Offers geography, geology and planning (MNAS); geospatial sciences (MS); secondary education (MS Ed), including earth science, geography. Part-time and evening/weekend programs available. *Faculty:* 19 full-time (3 women). *Students:* 14 full-time (4 women), 14 part-time (5 women), 6 international. Average age 31. 15 applicants, 100% accepted, 12 enrolled. In 2007, 8 degrees awarded. *Degree requirements:* For master's, comprehensive exam, thesis (for some programs). *Entrance requirements:* For master's, GRE General Test (MS, MNAS), minimum undergraduate GPA of 3.0 (MS, MNAS), 9-12 teacher certification (MS Ed). Additional exam requirements/recommendations for international students: Required—TOEFL (minimum score 550 paper-based; 213 computer-based; 79 iBT). *Application deadline:* For fall admission, 7/20 priority date for domestic students; for spring admission, 12/20 priority date for domestic students. Applications are processed on a rolling basis. Application fee: $35. Electronic applications accepted. *Expenses:* Tuition, state resident: full-time $3,708; part-time $206 per credit hour. Tuition, nonresident: full-time $7,236; part-time $206 per credit hour. Required fees: $622. Full-time tuition and fees vary according to course level, course load, program and reciprocity agreements. *Financial support:* In 2007–08, 9 research assistantships with full tuition reimbursements (averaging $8,845 per year), 9 teaching assistantships with full tuition reimbursements (averaging $7,305 per year) were awarded; career-related internships or fieldwork, Federal Work-Study, scholarships/grants, and unspecified assistantships also available. Financial award application deadline: 3/31; financial award applicants required to submit FAFSA. *Faculty research:* Water resources, small town planning, recreation and open space planning. *Unit head:* Dr. Tom Plymate, Head, 417-836-5800, Fax: 417-836-6934, E-mail: tomplymate@missouristate.edu. *Application contact:* Dr. Robert T. Pavlowsky, Graduate Adviser, 417-836-8473, Fax: 417-836-6006, E-mail: bobpavlowsky@missouristate.edu.

Morgan State University, School of Graduate Studies, Institute of Architecture and Planning, Program in City and Regional Planning, Baltimore, MD 21251. Offers MCRP. *Accreditation:* ACSP. *Faculty:* 3 full-time (1 woman). *Students:* 37 (26 women). In 2007, 5 degrees awarded. *Degree requirements:* For master's, thesis. *Entrance requirements:* Additional exam requirements/recommendations for international students: Required—TOEFL (minimum score 550 paper-based; 213 computer-based). *Application deadline:* For fall admission, 2/1 priority date for domestic students; for spring admission, 10/1 priority date for domestic students. Applications are processed on a rolling basis. Application fee: $0. *Financial support:* Fellowships, Federal Work-Study available. Financial award application deadline: 2/1. *Faculty research:* Nonprofit organizations, community development, urban design, transportation, international planning. *Unit head:* Dr. Siddhartha Sen, Coordinator, 443-885-1864, E-mail: siddhartha.sen@morgan.edu. *Application contact:* Dr. Mark Garrison, Associate Dean, 443-885-3185, Fax: 443-885-8226, E-mail: mark.garrison@morgan.edu.

New York University, Robert F. Wagner Graduate School of Public Service, Program in Urban Planning, New York, NY 10012-1019. Offers housing (Advanced Certificate); public economics (Advanced Certificate); quantitative analysis and computer applications for policy and planning (Advanced Certificate); urban planning (MUP); JD/MUP. *Accreditation:* ACSP (one or more programs are accredited). Part-time and evening/weekend programs available. *Faculty:* 6 full-time (2 women), 12 part-time/adjunct (4 women). *Students:* 64 full-time (41 women), 47 part-time (25 women); includes 22 minority (8 African Americans, 6 Asian Americans or Pacific Islanders, 8 Hispanic Americans), 6 international. Average age 28. 248 applicants, 62% accepted, 39 enrolled. In 2007, 35 degrees awarded. *Degree requirements:* For master's, thesis or alternative, end event workshop. *Entrance requirements:* For master's, minimum undergraduate GPA of 3.0. Additional exam requirements/recommendations for international students: Required—TOEFL (minimum score 600 paper-based; 250 computer-based; 100 iBT), TWE (minimum score 4). *Application deadline:* For fall admission, 6/1 for domestic students, 1/15 for international students; for spring admission, 11/15 for domestic students, 10/1 for international students. Applications are processed on a rolling basis. Application fee: $70. Electronic applications accepted. *Financial support:* In 2007–08, 30 fellowships (averaging $8,174 per year), 3 research assistantships with full tuition reimbursements (averaging $16,000 per year) were awarded; career-related internships or fieldwork, Federal Work-Study, institutionally sponsored loans, scholarships/grants, health care benefits, and unspecified assistantships also available. Support available to part-time students. Financial award application deadline: 12/1; financial award applicants required to submit FAFSA. *Unit head:* Prof. Rae Zimmerman, Director of the Planning Program, 212-998-7400. *Application contact:* Bethany

Godsoe, Assistant Dean, Enrollment and Student Services, 212-998-7414, Fax: 212-995-4164, E-mail: wagner.admissions@nyu.edu.

See Close-Up on page 1611.

North Park University, School of Community Development, Chicago, IL 60625-4895. Offers MA.

The Ohio State University, Graduate School, College of Engineering, Austin E. Knowlton School of Architecture, Program in City and Regional Planning, Columbus, OH 43210. Offers MCRP, PhD. *Accreditation:* ACSP (one or more programs are accredited). *Faculty:* 11. *Students:* 105 full-time (45 women), 24 part-time (10 women); includes 10 minority (8 African Americans, 1 Asian American or Pacific Islander, 1 Hispanic American), 28 international. Average age 28. In 2007, 39 master's, 3 doctorates awarded. *Degree requirements:* For master's, thesis optional; for doctorate, thesis/dissertation. *Entrance requirements:* Additional exam requirements/recommendations for international students: Required—TOEFL (minimum score 600 paper-based; 250 computer-based). *Application deadline:* For fall admission, 8/15 priority date for domestic students, 7/1 priority date for international students; for winter admission, 12/1 priority date for domestic students, 11/1 priority date for international students; for spring admission, 3/1 priority date for domestic students, 2/1 priority date for international students. Applications are processed on a rolling basis. Application fee: $40 ($50 for international students). Electronic applications accepted. *Financial support:* Fellowships, research assistantships, Federal Work-Study, institutionally sponsored loans, and unspecified assistantships available. Support available to part-time students. *Unit head:* Burkhard von Rabenau, Graduate Studies Committee Chair, 614-292-5427, Fax: 614-292-7106, E-mail: von-rabenau.1@osu.edu. *Application contact:* 614-292-9444, Fax: 614-292-3895, E-mail: domestic.grad@osu.edu.

Old Dominion University, College of Business and Public Administration, Program in Urban Studies, Norfolk, VA 23529. Offers policy analysis/program evaluation (MUS); public planning analysis (MUS); urban administration (MUS). Part-time and evening/weekend programs available. *Faculty:* 7 full-time (1 woman), 6 part-time/adjunct (3 women). *Students:* Average age 41. 6 applicants, 83% accepted, 3 enrolled. In 2007, 3 degrees awarded. *Degree requirements:* For master's, thesis, capstone seminar. *Entrance requirements:* For master's, GRE or GMAT. Additional exam requirements/recommendations for international students: Required—TOEFL (minimum score 550 paper-based; 213 computer-based; 79 iBT). *Application deadline:* For fall admission, 7/15 priority date for domestic students, 4/15 for international students; for spring admission, 11/1 priority date for domestic students, 10/1 for international students. Applications are processed on a rolling basis. Application fee: $40. Electronic applications accepted. *Expenses:* Tuition, state resident: part-time $304 per credit hour. Tuition, nonresident: part-time $761 per credit hour. *Financial support:* In 2007–08, 8 students received support, including 8 research assistantships (averaging $5,000 per year); fellowships, teaching assistantships, career-related internships or fieldwork, Federal Work-Study, tuition waivers (partial), and unspecified assistantships also available. Support available to part-time students. Financial award application deadline: 2/15; financial award applicants required to submit FAFSA. *Faculty research:* Program implementation, evaluation, and design. Total annual research expenditures: $5,000. *Unit head:* Dr. Berhony Mengisty, Graduate Program Director, 757-683-3961, Fax: 757-683-4886, E-mail: bmengist@odu.edu. *Application contact:* Megan S. Jones, Graduate Program Manager, 757-683-3961, Fax: 757-683-4886, E-mail: mmjones@odu.edu.

Pontificia Universidad Catolica Madre y Maestra, Graduate School, Santiago, Dominican Republic. Offers administration (M Adm, M Ed); architecture of interiors (M Arch); architecture of tourist lodgings (M Arch); construction administration (ME); convergent networks (ME); corporate business law (LL M); criminal procedure law (LL M); earthquake-resistant engineering (ME); environmental engineering (MEE); finance (M Mgmt); human resources (EMBA); international business (M Mgmt); international relations (LL M); labor law and Social Security (M Mgmt); logistics management (ME); marketing (M Mgmt); urban planning (M Urb). *Entrance requirements:* For master's, curriculum vitae, interview.

Portland State University, Graduate Studies, College of Urban and Public Affairs, Nohad A. Toulan School of Urban Studies and Planning, Program in Urban and Regional Planning, Portland, OR 97207-0751. Offers MURP. *Accreditation:* ACSP. Part-time programs available. *Faculty:* 18 full-time (4 women), 13 part-time/adjunct (6 women). *Students:* 59 full-time (41 women), 27 part-time (17 women); includes 6 minority (1 African American, 1 American Indian/Alaska Native, 2 Asian Americans or Pacific Islanders, 2 Hispanic Americans), 2 international. Average age 31. 162 applicants, 48% accepted, 37 enrolled. In 2007, 44 degrees awarded. *Entrance requirements:* For master's, GRE General Test (recommended), minimum GPA of 2.75, 3 letters of recommendation. Additional exam requirements/recommendations for international students: Required—TOEFL (minimum score 550 paper-based; 213 computer-based). *Application deadline:* For fall admission, 1/15 for domestic and international students. Application fee: $50. *Expenses:* Tuition, state resident: full-time $7,047. Tuition, nonresident: full-time $11,178. *Financial support:* In 2007–08, research assistantships (averaging $8,572 per year); fellowships, teaching assistantships, career-related internships or fieldwork, Federal Work-Study, and unspecified assistantships also available. Support available to part-time students. Financial award application deadline: 3/1; financial award applicants required to submit FAFSA. *Faculty research:* Policy planning and administration, community development, land-use and environment, transportation, urban and regional analysis. Total annual research expenditures: $1.3 million. *Application contact:* Tracy Braden, Office Coordinator, 503-725-4015, Fax: 503-725-8770, E-mail: tbraden@pdx.edu.

Pratt Institute, School of Architecture, Program in City and Regional Planning, Brooklyn, NY 11205-3899. Offers MSCRP. *Accreditation:* ACSP. Part-time programs available. *Faculty:* 2 full-time (1 woman), 9 part-time/adjunct (3 women). *Students:* 35 full-time (24 women), 6 part-time (3 women); includes 11 minority (7 African Americans, 2 Asian Americans or Pacific Islanders, 2 Hispanic Americans), 4 international. Average age 30. 79 applicants, 77% accepted, 14 enrolled. In 2007, 23 degrees awarded. *Degree requirements:* For master's, thesis. *Entrance requirements:* For master's, writing sample, bachelor's degree, transcripts, letters of recommendation, statement, portfolio. Additional exam requirements/recommendations for international students: Required—TOEFL (minimum score 550 paper-based; 213 computer-based). *Application deadline:* For fall admission, 2/1 for domestic students; for spring admission, 10/1 for domestic students. Applications are processed on a rolling basis. Application fee: $50 ($90 for international students). Electronic applications accepted. *Expenses:* Tuition: Full-time $25,680. Required fees: $1,106. Tuition and fees vary according to program. *Financial support:* Career-related internships or fieldwork, Federal Work-Study, institutionally sponsored loans, scholarships/grants, health care benefits, and unspecified assistantships available. Support available to part-time students. Financial award application deadline: 2/1; financial award applicants required to submit FAFSA. *Faculty research:* Advocacy planning, community development, comprehensive physical planning, transportation planning, real estate development. *Unit head:* Catherine Herman, Chairperson, 718-399-4391, E-mail: cherman@pratt.edu. *Application contact:* Young Hah, Director of Graduate Admissions, 718-636-3683, Fax: 718-399-4242, E-mail: yhah@pratt.edu.

See Close-Up on page 167.

Pratt Institute, School of Architecture, Program in Urban Environmental Systems Management, Brooklyn, NY 11205-3899. Offers MSUESM. Part-time programs available. *Faculty:* 5 part-time/adjunct (3 women). *Students:* 2 full-time (both women), 2 part-time (1 woman), 1 international. Average age 32. 3 applicants, 100% accepted, 0 enrolled. In 2007, 5 degrees awarded. *Degree requirements:* For master's, thesis. *Entrance requirements:* For master's, portfolio or writing sample, bachelor's degree, transcripts, letters of recommendation, statement. Additional exam requirements/recommendations for international students: Required—TOEFL (minimum score 550 paper-based; 213 computer-based). *Application deadline:* For fall admission, 2/1 for domestic students; for spring admission, 10/1 for domestic students. Application fee: $50 ($90 for international students). Electronic applications accepted. *Expenses:* Tuition: Full-time $25,680. Required fees: $1,106. Tuition and fees vary according to program. *Financial support:* Career-related internships or fieldwork, Federal Work-Study, institutionally sponsored loans, scholarships/grants, and unspecified assistantships available. Support available to part-time students. Financial award application deadline: 2/1; financial award applicants required to submit FAFSA. *Unit head:* Catherine Herman, Chairperson, 718-399-4391, E-mail: cherman@pratt.edu. *Application contact:* Young Hah, Director of Graduate Admissions, 718-636-3683, Fax: 718-399-4242, E-mail: yhah@pratt.edu.

See Close-Up on page 167.

Queen's University at Kingston, School of Graduate Studies and Research, School of Urban and Regional Planning, Kingston, ON K7L 3N6, Canada. Offers M Pl. Part-time programs available. *Degree requirements:* For master's, thesis optional. *Entrance requirements:* Additional exam requirements/recommendations for international students: Required—TOEFL (minimum score 580 paper-based; 237 computer-based). *Faculty research:* Housing, real estate development, human services, environmental services, land use planning.

Rutgers, The State University of New Jersey, New Brunswick, Edward J. Bloustein School of Planning and Public Policy, Program in Urban Planning and Policy Development, New Brunswick, NJ 08901-1281. Offers MCRP, MCRS, PhD. *Accreditation:* ACSP (one or more programs are accredited). Part-time and evening/weekend programs available. Terminal master's awarded for partial completion of doctoral program. *Degree requirements:* For master's, thesis optional; for doctorate, thesis/dissertation. *Entrance requirements:* For master's and doctorate, GRE General Test. Electronic applications accepted. *Faculty research:* Land use, transportation, housing, regional economic development, urban redevelopment, developing countries.

San Diego State University, Graduate and Research Affairs, College of Professional Studies and Fine Arts, School of Public Affairs, Program in City Planning, San Diego, CA 92182. Offers MCP. Part-time programs available. *Students:* 34 full-time (15 women), 20 part-time (11 women); includes 17 minority (2 African Americans, 5 Asian Americans or Pacific Islanders, 10 Hispanic Americans), 3 international. Average age 30. 47 applicants, 74% accepted, 19 enrolled. In 2007, 16 degrees awarded. *Entrance requirements:* For master's, GRE General Test. Additional exam requirements/recommendations for international students: Required—TOEFL. *Application deadline:* For fall admission, 5/1 for domestic and international students; for spring admission, 11/1 for domestic students, 10/1 for international students. Applications are processed on a rolling basis. Application fee: $55. Electronic applications accepted. *Financial support:* Career-related internships or fieldwork and unspecified assistantships available. Financial award applicants required to submit FAFSA. *Faculty research:* Community development, housing, sustainable development, visioning. *Unit head:* Roger Caves, Graduate Advisor, 619-594-6472. *Application contact:* Roger Caves, Graduate Advisor, 619-594-6472, E-mail: rcaves@mail.sdsu.edu.

San Jose State University, Graduate Studies and Research, College of Social Sciences, Department of Urban and Regional Planning, San Jose, CA 95192-0001. Offers MUP, Certificate. *Accreditation:* ACSP. Part-time programs available. *Students:* 62 full-time (30 women), 52 part-time (26 women); includes 39 minority (7 African Americans, 16 Asian Americans or Pacific Islanders, 16 Hispanic Americans), 11 international. Average age 31. 68 applicants, 72% accepted, 30 enrolled. In 2007, 17 degrees awarded. *Degree requirements:* For master's, comprehensive exam, thesis or alternative. *Entrance requirements:* For master's, GRE, minimum GPA of 3.0. *Application deadline:* For fall admission, 6/29 for domestic students; for spring admission, 11/30 for domestic students. Applications are processed on a rolling basis. Application fee: $59. Electronic applications accepted. *Financial support:* In 2007–08, 10 teaching assistantships were awarded; career-related internships or fieldwork, Federal Work-Study, and institutionally sponsored loans also available. Financial award application deadline: 5/31; financial award applicants required to submit FAFSA. *Faculty research:* Retirement communities, planning and problems, women in suburbia, influence on urban development, Taiwanese urban development issues. *Unit head:* Dr. Asha Weinstein Agrawal, Chair, 408-924-5853, Fax: 408-924-5872.

State University of New York College of Environmental Science and Forestry, Faculty of Environmental Studies, Syracuse, NY 13210-2779. Offers environmental and community land planning (MPS, MS, PhD); environmental and natural resources policy (PhD); environmental communication and participatory processes (MPS, MS, PhD); environmental policy and democratic processes (MPS, MS, PhD); environmental systems and risk management (MPS, MS, PhD); water and wetland resource studies (MPS, MS, PhD). Part-time programs available. *Degree requirements:* For master's, thesis (for some programs); for doctorate, comprehensive exam, thesis/dissertation. *Entrance requirements:* For master's and doctorate, GRE General Test, minimum GPA of 3.0. Additional exam requirements/recommendations for international students: Required—TOEFL (minimum score 550 paper-based; 213 computer-based; 80 iBT), IELTS (minimum score 6). *Faculty research:* Environmental education/communications, water resources, land resources, waste management.

State University of New York College of Environmental Science and Forestry, Faculty of Landscape Architecture, Syracuse, NY 13210-2779. Offers community design and planning (MLA, MS); cultural landscape studies and conservation (MLA, MS); landscape and urban ecology (MLA, MS). *Accreditation:* ASLA (one or more programs are accredited). *Degree requirements:* For master's, comprehensive exam (for some programs), thesis (for some programs). *Entrance requirements:* For master's, GRE General Test, minimum GPA of 3.0. Additional exam requirements/recommendations for international students: Required—TOEFL (paper-based 550, computer-based 213, iBT 80) or IELTS (6) or STEP Aiken (Grade 1). *Faculty research:* Site analysis and design, city and regional planning, community environments.

Temple University, Ambler College, Department of Community and Regional Planning, Philadelphia, PA 19122-6096. Offers MS. Program offered at Ambler Campus. Part-time and evening/weekend programs available. *Entrance requirements:* For master's, GRE or GMAT, 2 letters of recommendation, minimum undergraduate GPA of 3.0. Additional exam requirements/recommendations for international students: Required—TOEFL (minimum score 550 paper-based; 213 computer-based; 79 iBT).

Texas A&M University, College of Architecture, Department of Landscape Architecture and Urban Planning, College Station, TX 77843. Offers land development (MSLD); landscape architecture (MLA); urban and regional science (PhD); urban planning (MUP). *Accreditation:* ACSP (one or more programs are accredited); ASLA (one or more programs are accredited). *Faculty:* 25. *Students:* 136 full-time (46 women), 16 part-time (6 women); includes 12 minority (3 African Americans, 2 Asian Americans or Pacific Islanders, 7 Hispanic Americans), 68 international. Average age 31. 141 applicants, 84% accepted, 48 enrolled. In 2007, 35 master's, 6 doctorates awarded. Terminal master's awarded for partial completion of doctoral program. *Degree requirements:* For master's, thesis optional, professional internship; for doctorate, comprehensive exam, thesis/dissertation, methods statistics seminar. *Entrance requirements:* For master's, GMAT or GRE General Test, portfolio (MLA), minimum GPA of 3.0; for doctorate, GMAT or GRE General Test. Additional exam requirements/recommendations for international students: Required—TOEFL. *Application deadline:* For fall admission, 2/1 priority date for domestic students; for spring admission, 8/1 for domestic students. Applications are processed on a rolling basis. Application fee: $50 ($75 for international students). Electronic applications accepted. *Expenses:* Tuition, state resident: full-time $6,129. Tuition, nonresident: full-time $11,689. Tuition and fees vary according to course load. *Financial support:* In 2007–08, fellowships with tuition reimbursements (averaging $1,000 per year), research assistantships with partial tuition reimbursements (averaging $8,100 per year), teaching assistantships with partial tuition reimbursements (averaging $11,250 per year) were awarded; career-related internships or fieldwork, institutionally sponsored loans, and scholarships/grants also available. Financial award application deadline: 4/1; financial award applicants required to submit FAFSA. *Faculty research:* Erosion control/water quality, geographic information systems/spatial information technology, transport hazards, international sustainable development. *Unit head:*

Urban and Regional Planning

Texas A&M University (continued)

Dr. Walter Peacock, Head, 979-845-1019, Fax: 979-862-1784. *Application contact:* Marie Prihoda, Graduate Office, 979-845-6582, Fax: 979-845-4491, E-mail: mprihoda@archone.tamu.edu.

Texas Southern University, Graduate School, School of Public Affairs, Program in Urban Planning and Environmental Policy, Houston, TX 77004-4584. Offers MS, PhD. Part-time and evening/weekend programs available. *Faculty:* 4 full-time (1 woman). *Students:* 27 full-time (14 women), 26 part-time (11 women); includes 47 minority (43 African Americans, 2 Asian Americans or Pacific Islanders, 2 Hispanic Americans), 3 international. Average age 29. 12 applicants, 100% accepted, 9 enrolled. In 2007, 2 master's, 5 doctorates awarded. *Degree requirements:* For master's, comprehensive exam, thesis optional. *Entrance requirements:* For master's, GRE General Test, minimum GPA of 2.5. Additional exam requirements/recommendations for international students: Required—TOEFL. *Application deadline:* For fall admission, 7/15 priority date for domestic students. Applications are processed on a rolling basis. Application fee: $50 ($75 for international students). *Financial support:* In 2007–08, 6 fellowships (averaging $15,600 per year), 2 research assistantships (averaging $8,175 per year) were awarded; career-related internships or fieldwork, Federal Work-Study, and institutionally sponsored loans also available. Financial award application deadline: 5/1; financial award applicants required to submit FAFSA. *Unit head:* Dr. Walter McCoy, Interim Chair, 713-313-7312, E-mail: mccoy_wj@tsu.edu. *Application contact:* Brenda Randell, Secretary, 713-313-7405, E-mail: randell_bj@tsu.edu.

Texas Tech University, Graduate School, College of Architecture, Post-Professional Program in Architecture, Lubbock, TX 79409. Offers community design and development (MS); historical preservation (MS); visualization (MS). Part-time programs available. *Students:* 5 full-time (3 women), 7 part-time (2 women), 5 international. Average age 29. 12 applicants, 67% accepted, 3 enrolled. In 2007, 2 degrees awarded. *Degree requirements:* For master's, thesis. *Entrance requirements:* For master's, GRE General Test, portfolio. Additional exam requirements/recommendations for international students: Required—TOEFL (minimum score 550 paper-based; 213 computer-based). *Application deadline:* For fall admission, 3/1 priority date for domestic students; for spring admission, 11/1 priority date for domestic students. Applications are processed on a rolling basis. Application fee: $50 ($60 for international students). Electronic applications accepted. *Expenses:* Tuition, state resident: part-time $373 per credit hour. Tuition, nonresident: part-time $651 per credit hour. Tuition and fees vary according to program. *Financial support:* Research assistantships with partial tuition reimbursements, teaching assistantships with partial tuition reimbursements, career-related internships or fieldwork, Federal Work-Study, and institutionally sponsored loans available. Support available to part-time students. Financial award application deadline: 4/15; financial award applicants required to submit FAFSA. *Faculty research:* Historic preservation, visualization, community development and design, sustainable architecture, international architecture. *Unit head:* Glenn Eugene Hill, Associate Dean of Research and Post-Professional Graduate Studies, 806-742-3136, Fax: 806-742-2855, E-mail: glenn.hill@ttu.edu. *Application contact:* Jess Schwintz, Academic Program Assistant, 806-742-3136 Ext. 272, Fax: 806-742-2855, E-mail: jess.schwintz@ttu.edu.

Tufts University, Graduate School of Arts and Sciences, Department of Urban and Environmental Policy and Planning, Medford, MA 02155. Offers community development (MA); environmental policy (MA); health and human welfare (MA); housing policy (MA); international environment/development policy (MA); public policy (MPP); public policy and citizen participation (MA); MA/MS; MALD/MA. *Accreditation:* ACSP (one or more programs are accredited). Part-time programs available. *Faculty:* 8 full-time, 9 part-time/adjunct. *Students:* 135 (93 women); includes 23 minority (9 African Americans, 5 Asian Americans or Pacific Islanders, 9 Hispanic Americans) 9 international. 174 applicants, 82% accepted, 55 enrolled. In 2007, 32 degrees awarded. *Degree requirements:* For master's, thesis, internship. *Entrance requirements:* For master's, GRE General Test. Additional exam requirements/recommendations for international students: Required—TOEFL (minimum score 550 paper-based; 213 computer-based; 80 iBT). *Application deadline:* For fall admission, 1/15 for domestic students, 12/30 for international students. Applications are processed on a rolling basis. Application fee: $70. Electronic applications accepted. *Expenses: Contact institution. Financial support:* Teaching assistantships with full and partial tuition reimbursements, career-related internships or fieldwork, Federal Work-Study, scholarships/grants, and tuition waivers (partial) available. Support available to part-time students. Financial award application deadline: 1/15; financial award applicants required to submit FAFSA. *Unit head:* Julian Agyeman, Chair, 617-627-3394, Fax: 617-627-3377.

See Close-Up on page 1625.

Université du Québec à Rimouski, Graduate Programs, Program in Regional Development, Rimouski, QC G5L 3A1, Canada. Offers MA, PhD, Diploma. Part-time programs available. *Students:* 41 full-time, 27 part-time, 4 international. In 2007, 11 degrees awarded. *Degree requirements:* For master's, thesis. *Entrance requirements:* For master's, appropriate bachelor's degree, proficiency in French. *Application deadline:* For fall admission, 5/1 priority date for domestic students. Application fee: $50. *Financial support:* Fellowships, research assistantships, teaching assistantships available. *Unit head:* Oleg Stanek, Director, 418-724-1648, Fax: 418-724-1525, E-mail: oleg_stanek@uqar.ca.

Université du Québec en Outaouais, Graduate Programs, Program in Regional Development, Gatineau, QC J8X 3X7, Canada. Offers MA. *Students:* 63 full-time, 6 part-time. *Application deadline:* For fall admission, 6/1 priority date for domestic students, 3/1 for international students; for winter admission, 11/1 priority date for domestic students, 10/1 for international students. Application fee: $30. *Unit head:* Thibault Martin, Director, 819-595-3900 Ext. 2210, Fax: 819-595-2384, E-mail: thibault.martin@uqo.ca. *Application contact:* Registrar's Office, 819-773-1850, Fax: 819-773-1835, E-mail: registraire@ugo.ca.

Université Laval, Faculty of Architecture, Planning and Visual Arts, Department of Regional Planning, Programs in Planning and Regional Development, Québec, QC G1K 7P4, Canada. Offers MATDR, PhD. Terminal master's awarded for partial completion of doctoral program. *Degree requirements:* For master's, thesis (for some programs); for doctorate, comprehensive exam, thesis/dissertation. *Entrance requirements:* For master's and doctorate, knowledge of French and English. Electronic applications accepted.

University at Albany, State University of New York, College of Arts and Sciences, Department of Geography and Planning, Program in Regional Planning, Albany, NY 12222-0001. Offers MRP. *Accreditation:* ACSP. Part-time programs available. *Degree requirements:* For master's, thesis optional. *Entrance requirements:* Additional exam requirements/recommendations for international students: Required—TOEFL (minimum score 550 paper-based; 213 computer-based). *Application deadline:* For fall admission, 3/1 for domestic students, 5/1 for international students; for spring admission, 11/1 for international students. Applications are processed on a rolling basis. Application fee: $75. Electronic applications accepted. *Expenses:* Tuition, state resident: part-time $576 per credit. Tuition, nonresident: part-time $910 per credit. Tuition and fees vary according to program. *Financial support:* Fellowships, teaching assistantships, career-related internships or fieldwork, Federal Work-Study, and institutionally sponsored loans available. Financial award application deadline: 6/1. *Faculty research:* Urban planning, Third World development, political and social aspects of planning, urban housing and employment, environmental planning.

University at Buffalo, the State University of New York, Graduate School, School of Architecture and Planning, Department of Urban and Regional Planning, Buffalo, NY 14260. Offers planning (MUP); JD/MUP; M Arch/MUP. *Accreditation:* ACSP. Part-time programs available. *Degree requirements:* For master's, thesis or alternative, project. *Entrance requirements:* For master's, minimum GPA of 3.0. Additional exam requirements/recommendations for international students: Required—TOEFL (minimum score 550 paper-based; 213 computer-based; 79 iBT), IELTS (minimum score 7). Electronic applications accepted. *Faculty research:* International planning development, economic development, governance, information technology and geographic information systems in planning, environmental planning and policy.

The University of Akron, Graduate School, Buchtel College of Arts and Sciences, Department of Geography and Planning, Program in Urban Planning, Akron, OH 44325. Offers MA. *Students:* 14 full-time (7 women); includes 1 minority (Hispanic American), 6 international. Average age 29. 6 applicants, 67% accepted, 2 enrolled. In 2007, 8 degrees awarded. *Degree requirements:* For master's, thesis optional. *Entrance requirements:* For master's, minimum GPA of 2.75. Additional exam requirements/recommendations for international students: Required—TOEFL (minimum score 550 paper-based; 213 computer-based; 79 iBT). *Application deadline:* Applications are processed on a rolling basis. Application fee: $30 ($40 for international students). Electronic applications accepted. *Expenses:* Tuition, state resident: full-time $6,164; part-time $342 per credit. Tuition, nonresident: full-time $10,575; part-time $588 per credit. Required fees: $806; $43 per credit. $12 per term. Tuition and fees vary according to course load, degree level and program.

The University of British Columbia, Faculty of Graduate Studies, School of Community and Regional Planning, Vancouver, BC V6T 1Z1, Canada. Offers M Sc P, MAP, PhD. *Accreditation:* ACSP (one or more programs are accredited). *Degree requirements:* For master's, thesis; for doctorate, thesis/dissertation, oral exam. *Entrance requirements:* For master's, GRE (recommended); for doctorate, MCRP or equivalent. Additional exam requirements/recommendations for international students: Required—TOEFL (minimum score 600 paper-based; 250 computer-based). Electronic applications accepted. *Faculty research:* Natural resources management, international development, urban spatial, urban policy and community development planning.

University of California, Berkeley, Graduate Division, College of Environmental Design, Department of City and Regional Planning, Berkeley, CA 94720-1500. Offers MCP, PhD, JD/MCP, M Arch/MCP, MCP/MPH, MCP/MS, MLA/MCP. *Accreditation:* ACSP. *Degree requirements:* For master's, professional project or thesis; for doctorate, thesis/dissertation, qualifying exam. *Entrance requirements:* For master's and doctorate, GRE General Test, minimum GPA of 3.0, 3 letters of recommendation. Additional exam requirements/recommendations for international students: Required—TOEFL. *Application deadline:* For fall admission, 12/5 for domestic students. Application fee: $70 ($90 for international students). *Financial support:* Fellowships, research assistantships, teaching assistantships available. *Faculty research:* Housing and project development, physical planning and design, community and economic development, geographic information systems, transportation. *Application contact:* Yerdua Caesar-Kaptoech, Student Affairs Officer, 510-643-9440, Fax: 510-642-1641, E-mail: dcrpgrad@berkeley.edu.

University of California, Davis, Graduate Studies, Graduate Group in Community Development, Davis, CA 95616. Offers MS. *Degree requirements:* For master's, comprehensive exam (for some programs), thesis (for some programs). *Entrance requirements:* For master's, GRE General Test, minimum GPA of 3.0. Additional exam requirements/recommendations for international students: Required—TOEFL (minimum score 550 paper-based; 213 computer-based). Electronic applications accepted. *Faculty research:* Globalization; community economic change; urban and regional development; community planning design and sustainability; race, ethnic, and gender roles; community organization and political mobilization.

University of California, Irvine, Office of Graduate Studies, School of Social Ecology, Department of Planning, Policy and Design, Irvine, CA 92697. Offers planning, policy and design (PhD); urban and regional planning (MURP). *Accreditation:* ACSP (one or more programs are accredited). *Faculty:* 19 full-time (6 women), 10 part-time/adjunct (3 women). *Students:* 103 full-time (62 women), 1 (woman) part-time; includes 34 minority (4 African Americans, 2 American Indian/Alaska Native, 15 Asian Americans or Pacific Islanders, 13 Hispanic Americans), 11 international. 134 applicants, 48% accepted, 27 enrolled. In 2007, 29 master's, 6 doctorates awarded. *Degree requirements:* For doctorate, thesis/dissertation, research project. *Entrance requirements:* For master's and doctorate, GRE General Test, minimum GPA of 3.0. Additional exam requirements/recommendations for international students: Required—TOEFL (minimum score 550 paper-based; 213 computer-based). *Application deadline:* For fall admission, 1/15 priority date for domestic and international students. Application fee: $60. Electronic applications accepted. *Financial support:* Fellowships with tuition reimbursements, research assistantships with full tuition reimbursements, teaching assistantships with tuition reimbursements, institutionally sponsored loans, traineeships, health care benefits, and unspecified assistantships available. Financial award application deadline: 1/15; financial award applicants required to submit FAFSA. *Faculty research:* Community and social policy, economic development, land-use and growth management, transportation planning, environmental policy. Total annual research expenditures: $1.5 million. *Unit head:* Marlon G. Boarnet, Chair, 949-824-7695, E-mail: mgboarne@uci.edu. *Application contact:* Janet Gallagher, Academic Coordinator, 949-824-9849, Fax: 949-824-8566, E-mail: ppd@uci.edu.

Announcement: The Department of Planning, Policy, and Design is a pioneering, multidisciplinary department of 17 full-time faculty members offering the master's degree in urban and regional planning and the PhD degree in planning, policy, and design. Specializations include urban and community development, land-use policy, transportation, environmental policy, urban design and behavior, and urban security. Call 949-824-9849; e-mail: ppd@uci.edu; Web site: http://socialecology.uci.edu/ppd.

University of California, Los Angeles, Graduate Division, School of Public Affairs, Department of Urban Planning, Los Angeles, CA 90095-1656. Offers MA, PhD, JD/MA, MA/MA, MBA/MA. *Accreditation:* ACSP (one or more programs are accredited). *Faculty:* 19. *Students:* 153 (83 women); includes 69 minority (6 African Americans, 1 American Indian/Alaska Native, 22 Asian Americans or Pacific Islanders, 40 Hispanic Americans) 16 international. 273 applicants, 46% accepted, 52 enrolled. In 2007, 49 master's, 5 doctorates awarded. *Degree requirements:* For master's, comprehensive exam or thesis; for doctorate, thesis/dissertation, oral and written qualifying exams. *Entrance requirements:* For master's, GRE General Test (recommended); for doctorate, GRE General Test, master's degree in urban planning or related field. Additional exam requirements/recommendations for international students: Required—TOEFL. *Application deadline:* For fall admission, 1/5 for domestic students. Application fee: $60. Electronic applications accepted. *Expenses:* Tuition, nonresident: full-time $5,728. Required fees: $8,966. Full-time tuition and fees vary according to program and student level. *Financial support:* In 2007–08, 146 students received support, including 72 fellowships, 41 research assistantships, 18 teaching assistantships; career-related internships or fieldwork, Federal Work-Study, institutionally sponsored loans, scholarships/grants, and tuition waivers (full and partial) also available. Financial award application deadline: 3/1. *Faculty research:* Industrial hazards, political economy of South and Southeast Asia, historic preservation, flexible production in U.S. and Western Europe, land-use controls. *Unit head:* Brian Taylor, Chair, 310-825-4025. *Application contact:* Departmental Office, 310-825-4025, Fax: 310-206-5566, E-mail: upinfo@sppsr.ucla.edu.

University of Central Florida, College of Health and Public Affairs, Department of Public Administration, Orlando, FL 32816. Offers emergency management and homeland security (Certificate); non-profit management (MNM, Certificate); public administration (MPA, Certificate); urban and regional planning (Certificate). *Accreditation:* NASPAA. Part-time and evening/weekend programs available. *Faculty:* 11 full-time (2 women), 9 part-time/adjunct (3 women). *Degree requirements:* For master's, comprehensive exam, thesis or alternative, research report. *Entrance requirements:* For master's, GRE General Test. *Application deadline:* For fall admission, 7/1 for domestic students; for spring admission, 12/1 for domestic students. Application fee: $30. Electronic applications accepted. *Expenses:* Tuition, state resident: full-time $6,484. Tuition, nonresident: full-time $23,938. Tuition and fees vary according to program. *Financial support:* Fellowships with partial tuition reimbursements, research assistantships with partial tuition reimbursements, teaching assistantships with partial tuition reimbursements, career-related internships or fieldwork, Federal Work-Study, institutionally sponsored loans, tuition waivers (partial), and unspecified assistantships available. Financial award application deadline: 3/1; financial award applicants required to submit FAFSA. *Unit head:* Dr. MaryAnn Feldheim, Chair, 407-823-3693, Fax: 407-823-5651.

University of Cincinnati, Graduate School, College of Design, Architecture, Art, and Planning, School of Planning, Program in Community Planning, Cincinnati, OH 45221. Offers

MCP, JD/MCP. *Accreditation:* ACSP. *Students:* 73 full-time (45 women), 30 part-time (16 women); includes 13 minority (10 African Americans, 1 American Indian/Alaska Native, 2 Asian Americans or Pacific Islanders), 23 international. In 2007, 19 degrees awarded. *Degree requirements:* For master's, thesis. *Entrance requirements:* For master's, GRE General Test. Additional exam requirements/recommendations for international students: Required—TOEFL. *Application deadline:* For fall admission, 2/1 for domestic students. Application fee: $30. *Financial support:* Tuition waivers (full) and unspecified assistantships available. Financial award application deadline: 5/1.

University of Colorado Denver, College of Architecture and Planning, Program in Design and Planning, Denver, CO 80217-3364. Offers PhD. Part-time programs available. *Faculty:* 9 full-time (3 women). *Students:* 10 full-time (5 women), 25 part-time (14 women); includes 5 minority (2 African Americans, 1 Asian American or Pacific Islander, 2 Hispanic Americans), 9 international. Average age 40. 23 applicants, 26% accepted, 6 enrolled. In 2007, 4 degrees awarded. *Degree requirements:* For doctorate, thesis/dissertation. *Entrance requirements:* For doctorate, GRE, minimum undergraduate GPA of 3.0, graduate 3.5. Additional exam requirements/recommendations for international students: Required—TOEFL. *Application deadline:* For fall admission, 2/15 for domestic students; for spring admission, 10/1 for domestic students. Applications are processed on a rolling basis. Application fee: $50 ($75 for international students). *Expenses:* Contact institution. *Financial support:* Fellowships with partial tuition reimbursements, research assistantships, teaching assistantships, career-related internships or fieldwork, Federal Work-Study, institutionally sponsored loans, scholarships/grants, and tuition waivers (full and partial) available. Support available to part-time students. Financial award application deadline: 2/15; financial award applicants required to submit FAFSA. *Faculty research:* Land use and environmental planning and design; design and planning processes and practices; history, theory, and criticism of the built environment. *Unit head:* Willem van Vliet, Director, 303-492-5015, Fax: 303-492-6163, E-mail: willem@spot.colorado.edu. *Application contact:* Kimberly Kelley, Information Contact, 303-492-1319, Fax: 303-492-6163, E-mail: phdsec@stripe.colorado.edu.

University of Colorado Denver, College of Architecture and Planning, Program in Urban and Regional Planning, Denver, CO 80217-3364. Offers MURP. *Accreditation:* ACSP. Part-time programs available. *Faculty:* 1 (woman) full-time. *Students:* 83 full-time (38 women), 23 part-time (10 women); includes 6 minority (3 African Americans, 2 Asian Americans or Pacific Islanders, 1 Hispanic American), 9 international. Average age 31. 84 applicants, 64% accepted, 35 enrolled. In 2007, 40 degrees awarded. *Degree requirements:* For master's, thesis optional. *Entrance requirements:* For master's, GRE or minimum GPA of 3.0, writing sample, resumé. Additional exam requirements/recommendations for international students: Required—TOEFL (minimum score 550 paper-based; 213 computer-based). *Application deadline:* For fall admission, 3/15 for domestic students; for spring admission, 10/1 for domestic students. Application fee: $50 ($75 for international students). *Financial support:* Teaching assistantships, career-related internships or fieldwork, Federal Work-Study, institutionally sponsored loans, and scholarships/grants available. Financial award application deadline: 3/1; financial award applicants required to submit FAFSA. *Faculty research:* Physical planning, environmental planning, economic development planning. *Unit head:* Tom Clark, Chair, 303-556-3296, Fax: 303-492-6163, E-mail: tom.clark@cudenver.edu. *Application contact:* Heather Zertuche, Administrative Assistant II, 303-556-3382, Fax: 303-556-3687, E-mail: anpdeansoffice@storm.cudenver.edu.

University of Florida, Graduate School, College of Design, Construction and Planning, Department of Urban and Regional Planning, Gainesville, FL 32611. Offers MAURP, PhD, JD/MAURP. *Accreditation:* ACSP (one or more programs are accredited). *Faculty:* 9 full-time (4 women). *Students:* 66 (31 women); includes 12 minority (5 African Americans, 1 Asian American or Pacific Islander, 6 Hispanic Americans). In 2007, 17 degrees awarded. *Degree requirements:* For master's, thesis. *Entrance requirements:* For master's, GRE General Test, minimum GPA of 3.0. Additional exam requirements/recommendations for international students: Required—TOEFL. *Application deadline:* For fall admission, 6/1 priority date for domestic students; for spring admission, 10/1 priority date for domestic students. Applications are processed on a rolling basis. Application fee: $30. Electronic applications accepted. *Expenses:* Tuition, state resident: full-time $7,478. Tuition, nonresident: full-time $22,603. *Financial support:* In 2007–08, 3 research assistantships with tuition reimbursements (averaging $8,905 per year), 3 teaching assistantships with tuition reimbursements (averaging $10,582 per year) were awarded; fellowships with tuition reimbursements, career-related internships or fieldwork, Federal Work-Study, and unspecified assistantships also available. Support available to part-time students. *Faculty research:* Planning and information systems, urban and environmental design, community and economic development, transportation and growth management. *Unit head:* Dr. Paul D. Zwick, Chair, 352-392-0997 Ext. 427, Fax: 352-392-3308, E-mail: paul@geoplan.ufl.edu. *Application contact:* Ella Littles, Graduate Coordinator, 352-392-0997 Ext. 430, Fax: 352-392-3308, E-mail: elittles@ufl.edu.

University of Hawaii at Manoa, Graduate Division, Colleges of Arts and Sciences, College of Social Sciences, Department of Urban and Regional Planning, Honolulu, HI 96822. Offers community planning and social policy (MURP); environmental planning and management (MURP); land use and infrastructure planning (MURP); urban and regional planning (PhD, Graduate Certificate); urban and regional planning in Asia and Pacific (MURP). *Accreditation:* ACSP. Part-time programs available. *Faculty:* 26 full-time (7 women), 6 part-time/adjunct (1 woman). *Students:* 66 full-time (32 women), 27 part-time (11 women); includes 23 minority (1 American Indian/Alaska Native, 21 Asian Americans or Pacific Islanders, 1 Hispanic American), 44 international. Average age 31. 77 applicants, 79% accepted, 30 enrolled. *Median time to degree:* Of those who began their doctoral program in fall 1999, 0% received their degree in 8 years or less. *Degree requirements:* For master's, thesis optional; for doctorate, comprehensive exam, thesis/dissertation. *Entrance requirements:* For master's, GRE General Test, minimum GPA of 3.0; for doctorate, GRE General Test. Additional exam requirements/recommendations for international students: Required—TOEFL (minimum score 500 paper-based; 173 computer-based; 61 iBT), IELTS (minimum score 5). *Application deadline:* For fall admission, 3/1 for domestic and international students; for spring admission, 9/1 for domestic and international students. Application fee: $50. *Financial support:* In 2007–08, 20 research assistantships (averaging $16,582 per year), 5 teaching assistantships (averaging $13,948 per year) were awarded; career-related internships or fieldwork, Federal Work-Study, institutionally sponsored loans, and tuition waivers (full) also available. Total annual research expenditures: $3 million. *Application contact:* Karl Kim, Graduate Chair, 808-956-7381, Fax: 808-956-6870, E-mail: karlk@hawaii.edu.

University of Illinois at Chicago, Graduate College, College of Urban Planning and Public Affairs, Program in Urban Planning and Policy, Chicago, IL 60607-7128. Offers public policy analysis (PhD); urban planning and policy (MUPP). *Accreditation:* ACSP (one or more programs are accredited). Part-time programs available. *Degree requirements:* For master's, thesis or alternative, internship; for doctorate, thesis/dissertation. *Entrance requirements:* For master's and doctorate, GRE General Test, minimum GPA of 2.75, writing sample. Additional exam requirements/recommendations for international students: Required—TOEFL. Electronic applications accepted.

University of Illinois at Urbana–Champaign, Graduate College, College of Fine and Applied Arts, Department of Urban and Regional Planning, Champaign, IL 61820. Offers regional planning (PhD); urban planning (MUP); JD/MUP; M Arch/MUP. *Accreditation:* ACSP (one or more programs are accredited). *Faculty:* 12 full-time (6 women). *Students:* 62 full-time (35 women), 11 part-time (5 women); includes 10 minority (4 African Americans, 5 Asian Americans or Pacific Islanders, 1 Hispanic American), 20 international. 127 applicants, 24% accepted, 22 enrolled. In 2007, 29 master's, 4 doctorates awarded. *Degree requirements:* For master's, thesis; for doctorate, thesis/dissertation. *Entrance requirements:* For master's, GRE, minimum GPA of 3.0. *Application deadline:* Applications are processed on a rolling basis. Application fee: $60 ($75 for international students). *Financial support:* In 2007–08, 6 fellowships, 31 research assistantships, 20 teaching assistantships were awarded; career-related internships or fieldwork and tuition waivers (full and partial) also available. Financial award application deadline: 2/15. *Faculty research:* Environmental impact, economic development, firmation technology, planning systems, housing, community participation. *Unit head:* Dr. Edward Feser, Head, 217-244-5400, Fax: 217-244-1717, E-mail: feser@uiuc.edu. *Application contact:* Jane Terry, Admissions and Records Officer II, 217-244-5401, Fax: 217-244-1717, E-mail: jterry2@uiuc.edu.

The University of Iowa, Graduate College, Program in Urban and Regional Planning, Iowa City, IA 52242-1316. Offers MA, MS, JD/MA, MHA/MA, MHA/MS, MS/MA, MS/MS, MSW/MA, MSW/MS. *Accreditation:* ACSP. *Faculty:* 7 full-time, 2 part-time/adjunct. *Students:* 43 full-time (20 women), 1 part-time; includes 4 minority (2 African Americans, 1 Asian American or Pacific Islander, 1 Hispanic American), 4 international. 51 applicants, 71% accepted, 17 enrolled. In 2007, 15 degrees awarded. *Degree requirements:* For master's, thesis optional, portfolio. *Entrance requirements:* For master's, GRE General Test, minimum GPA of 3.0. Additional exam requirements/recommendations for international students: Required—TOEFL (minimum score 600 paper-based; 250 computer-based; 100 iBT). *Application deadline:* For fall admission, 1/15 priority date for domestic and international students; for spring admission, 10/1 priority date for domestic and international students. Applications are processed on a rolling basis. Application fee: $60 ($85 for international students). Electronic applications accepted. *Expenses:* Tuition, state resident: part-time $349 per hour. Tuition, nonresident: part-time $349 per hour. Tuition and fees vary according to course load and program. *Financial support:* In 2007–08, 2 fellowships, 6 research assistantships with partial tuition reimbursements, 9 teaching assistantships with partial tuition reimbursements were awarded. Financial award application deadline: 1/15; financial award applicants required to submit FAFSA. *Unit head:* Alan Peters, Chair, 319-335-0039.

University of Kansas, Research and Graduate Studies, School of Architecture and Urban Planning, Program in Urban Planning, Lawrence, KS 66045. Offers MUP, JD/MUP, M Arch/MUP, MUP/MA, MUP/MPA. *Accreditation:* ACSP. Part-time programs available. *Faculty:* 11. *Students:* 41 full-time (18 women), 9 part-time (4 women); includes 6 minority (3 African Americans, 2 Asian Americans or Pacific Islanders, 1 Hispanic American), 4 international. Average age 29. 50 applicants, 80% accepted, 23 enrolled. In 2007, 20 degrees awarded. *Degree requirements:* For master's, comprehensive exam, thesis or alternative. *Entrance requirements:* For master's, GRE. Additional exam requirements/recommendations for international students: Required—TOEFL (minimum score 570 paper-based; 230 computer-based). *Application deadline:* For fall admission, 7/1 for domestic students, 6/1 for international students; for spring admission, 12/1 for domestic students, 11/1 for international students. Applications are processed on a rolling basis. Application fee: $55 ($60 for international students). Electronic applications accepted. *Expenses:* Tuition, state resident: full-time $5,838. Tuition, nonresident: full-time $13,409. Tuition and fees vary according to program. *Financial support:* Fellowships, research assistantships with partial tuition reimbursements, career-related internships or fieldwork available. Financial award application deadline: 2/1. *Faculty research:* Environmental land use, housing and economic development, community development and transportation, urban mass transportation, urban sprawl. *Unit head:* James M. Mayo, Chair, 785-864-4184, Fax: 785-864-5301.

University of Louisville, Graduate School, College of Arts and Sciences, Department of Urban and Public Affairs, Program in Public Administration, Louisville, KY 40292-0001. Offers labor and public management (MPA); public policy and administration (MPA); urban and regional development (MPA). *Accreditation:* NASPAA. *Students:* 21 full-time (14 women), 22 part-time (12 women); includes 6 minority (4 African Americans, 1 Asian American or Pacific Islander, 1 Hispanic American), 1 international. Average age 30. In 2007, 15 degrees awarded. *Degree requirements:* For master's, practicum or thesis. *Entrance requirements:* For master's, GRE General Test, minimum GPA of 3.25, resumé. *Application deadline:* For fall admission, 7/1 priority date for domestic students; for spring admission, 12/1 priority date for domestic students. Applications are processed on a rolling basis. Application fee: $50. *Unit head:* Dr. Steve Koven, Director, 502-852-7906, Fax: 502-852-4558, E-mail: sgkove01@louisville.edu.

University of Louisville, Graduate School, College of Arts and Sciences, Department of Urban and Public Affairs, Program in Urban Planning, Louisville, KY 40292-0001. Offers MUP. *Students:* 16 full-time (6 women), 7 part-time (4 women); includes 2 minority (both African Americans), 2 international. Average age 31. In 2007, 15 degrees awarded. *Unit head:* Dr. David M. Simpson, Program Director, 502-852-7906, Fax: 502-852-4558, E-mail: upa@louisville.edu.

University of Manitoba, Faculty of Graduate Studies, Faculty of Architecture, Department of City Planning, Winnipeg, MB R3T 2N2, Canada. Offers MCP. *Degree requirements:* For master's, thesis.

University of Maryland, College Park, Graduate Studies, School of Architecture, Planning and Preservation, Program in Urban Studies and Planning, College Park, MD 20742. Offers urban and regional planning/design (PhD); urban studies and planning (MCP); M Arch/MCP. *Accreditation:* ACSP. Part-time and evening/weekend programs available. *Faculty:* 9 full-time (2 women), 1 part-time/adjunct (0 women). *Students:* 50 full-time (29 women), 19 part-time (11 women); includes 13 minority (12 African Americans, 1 Asian American or Pacific Islander), 15 international. 34 applicants, 21% accepted, 3 enrolled. In 2007, 18 master's, 1 doctorate awarded. *Entrance requirements:* For master's and doctorate, GRE General Test, minimum GPA of 3.0, 3 letters of recommendation. Additional exam requirements/recommendations for international students: Required—TOEFL. *Application deadline:* For fall admission, 1/1 for domestic and international students. Applications are processed on a rolling basis. Application fee: $60. Electronic applications accepted. *Financial support:* In 2007–08, 1 fellowship with tuition reimbursement (averaging $7,178 per year), 17 teaching assistantships with tuition reimbursements (averaging $13,194 per year) were awarded; research assistantships with tuition reimbursements, Federal Work-Study and scholarships/grants also available. Support available to part-time students. Financial award applicants required to submit FAFSA. *Faculty research:* Policy analysis, urban planning, program planning and management, economic development planning. *Unit head:* James R. Cohen, Director, 301-405-6789, Fax: 301-314-9583, E-mail: jimcohen@umd.edu. *Application contact:* Dean of Graduate School, 301-405-0358, Fax: 301-314-9305.

University of Massachusetts Amherst, Graduate School, College of Natural Resources and the Environment, Department of Landscape Architecture and Regional Planning, Program in Landscape Architecture and Regional Planning, Amherst, MA 01003. Offers MLA/MRP. *Accreditation:* ACSP; ASLA. Part-time programs available. *Students:* 6 full-time (3 women), 3 part-time (2 women), 2 international. Average age 31. 10 applicants, 50% accepted, 1 enrolled. *Entrance requirements:* Additional exam requirements/recommendations for international students: Required—TOEFL (minimum score 530 paper-based; 197 computer-based). *Application deadline:* For fall admission, 2/1 priority date for domestic and international students. Applications are processed on a rolling basis. Application fee: $50 ($65 for international students). Electronic applications accepted. *Expenses:* Tuition, state resident: full-time $2,640; part-time $110 per credit. Tuition, nonresident: full-time $9,936; part-time $414 per credit. Required fees: $7,455. One-time fee: $332. Tuition and fees vary according to course load, campus/location, program and reciprocity agreements. *Financial support:* Fellowships with full tuition reimbursements, research assistantships with full tuition reimbursements, teaching assistantships with full tuition reimbursements, career-related internships or fieldwork, Federal Work-Study, scholarships/grants, traineeships, and unspecified assistantships available. Support available to part-time students. Financial award application deadline: 2/1. *Unit head:* Dr. Robert Ryan, Director, 413-545-2266, Fax: 413-545-1772.

University of Massachusetts Amherst, Graduate School, College of Natural Resources and the Environment, Department of Landscape Architecture and Regional Planning, Program in Regional Planning, Amherst, MA 01003. Offers MRP, PhD, MLA/MRP. *Accreditation:* ACSP (one or more programs are accredited). Part-time programs available. *Students:* 36 full-time (21 women), 10 part-time (6 women); includes 4 minority (2 African Americans, 1 Asian American or Pacific Islander, 1 Hispanic American), 8 international. Average age 32. 50

Urban and Regional Planning

University of Massachusetts Amherst (continued)
applicants, 76% accepted, 20 enrolled. In 2007, 14 master's awarded. *Degree requirements:* For master's, thesis or alternative; for doctorate, thesis/dissertation. *Entrance requirements:* For master's and doctorate, GRE General Test. Additional exam requirements/recommendations for international students: Required—TOEFL (minimum score 530 paper-based; 197 computer-based). *Application deadline:* For fall admission, 2/1 priority date for domestic and international students; for spring admission, 10/1 for domestic and international students. Applications are processed on a rolling basis. Application fee: $50 ($65 for international students). Electronic applications accepted. *Expenses:* Tuition, state resident: full-time $2,640; part-time $110 per credit. Tuition, nonresident: full-time $9,936; part-time $414 per credit. Required fees: $7,455. One-time fee: $332. Tuition and fees vary according to course load, campus/location, program and reciprocity agreements. *Financial support:* Fellowships with full tuition reimbursements, research assistantships with full tuition reimbursements, teaching assistantships with full tuition reimbursements, career-related internships or fieldwork, Federal Work-Study, scholarships/grants, traineeships, and unspecified assistantships available. Support available to part-time students. Financial award application deadline: 2/1. *Unit head:* Mark Hamin, Director, 413-545-2266, Fax: 413-545-1772, E-mail: mhamin@larp.umass.edu.

University of Memphis, Graduate School, College of Arts and Sciences, School of Urban Affairs and Public Policy, Division of City and Regional Planning, Memphis, TN 38152. Offers MCRP. *Accreditation:* ACSP. *Faculty:* 4 full-time (1 woman), 2 part-time/adjunct (0 women). *Students:* 9 full-time (3 women), 7 part-time (3 women); includes 4 minority (3 African Americans, 1 Hispanic American). Average age 30. 19 applicants, 79% accepted, 4 enrolled. In 2007, 10 degrees awarded. *Degree requirements:* For master's, comprehensive exam, thesis. *Entrance requirements:* For master's, GRE General Test. *Application deadline:* For fall admission, 7/1 for domestic students; for spring admission, 12/1 for domestic students. Applications are processed on a rolling basis. Application fee: $35 ($60 for international students). *Expenses:* Tuition, state resident: full-time $6,990; part-time $377 per hour. Tuition, nonresident: full-time $17,818; part-time $830 per hour. Tuition and fees vary according to course load and program. *Financial support:* In 2007–08, 5 research assistantships with full tuition reimbursements (averaging $5,500 per year) were awarded; career-related internships or fieldwork and Federal Work-Study also available. Financial award application deadline: 7/1; financial award applicants required to submit FAFSA. *Faculty research:* Growth planning, site design, economic development, housing, smart growth. Total annual research expenditures: $94,606. *Unit head:* Gene Pearson, Director and Coordinator of Graduate Studies in Planning, 901-678-2161, Fax: 901-678-4162, E-mail: gpearson@memphis.edu.

University of Memphis, Graduate School, College of Arts and Sciences, School of Urban Affairs and Public Policy, Division of Public and Nonprofit Administration, Memphis, TN 38152. Offers nonprofit administration (MPA); public management and policy (MPA); urban management and planning (MPA). *Accreditation:* NASPAA. Part-time and evening/weekend programs available. *Faculty:* 6 full-time (3 women), 1 (woman) part-time/adjunct. *Students:* 16 full-time (10 women), 43 part-time (31 women); includes 27 minority (26 African Americans, 1 Asian American or Pacific Islander). Average age 33. 31 applicants, 58% accepted, 9 enrolled. In 2007, 13 master's awarded. *Degree requirements:* For master's, comprehensive exam, thesis or alternative, internship. *Entrance requirements:* For master's, GRE General Test, GMAT, or MAT, minimum GPA of 3.0. *Application deadline:* For fall admission, 8/1 for domestic students; for spring admission, 12/1 for domestic students. Applications are processed on a rolling basis. Application fee: $35 ($60 for international students). *Expenses:* Tuition, state resident: full-time $6,990; part-time $377 per hour. Tuition, nonresident: full-time $17,818; part-time $830 per hour. Tuition and fees vary according to course load and program. *Financial support:* In 2007–08, 7 research assistantships with full tuition reimbursements (averaging $4,500 per year) were awarded; fellowships, career-related internships or fieldwork, Federal Work-Study, and scholarships/grants also available. Support available to part-time students. *Faculty research:* Nonprofit organization governance, local government management, community collaboration, urban problems, accountability. *Unit head:* Dr. Dorothy Norris-Tirrell, Director, 901-678-3360, Fax: 901-678-2981, E-mail: dnrrstrr@memphis.edu. *Application contact:* Dr. Charles Menifield, Director of Admissions, 901-678-3369, Fax: 901-678-2981, E-mail: cmenifld@memphis.edu.

University of Michigan, A. Alfred Taubman College of Architecture and Urban Planning, Urban and Regional Planning Program, Ann Arbor, MI 48109. Offers real estate development (Certificate); urban planning (MUP); JD/MUP; M Arch/MUP; MBA/MUP; MLA/MUP; MPP/MUP. Offered through the Horace H. Rackham School of Graduate Studies; students in the Certificate program must either be currently enrolled in a graduate program or have earned a masters or PhD degree within the last five years. *Accreditation:* ACSP (one or more programs are accredited). Part-time programs available. *Faculty:* 12 full-time (5 women), 7 part-time/adjunct (3 women). *Students:* 79 full-time (39 women), 30 part-time (20 women); includes 24 minority (6 African Americans, 1 American Indian/Alaska Native, 14 Asian Americans or Pacific Islanders, 3 Hispanic Americans), 4 international. Average age 28. 197 applicants, 83% accepted, 49 enrolled. In 2007, 45 degrees awarded. *Degree requirements:* For master's, thesis or alternative, professional project, capstone studio. *Entrance requirements:* For master's, GRE General Test. Additional exam requirements/recommendations for international students: Required—TOEFL (minimum score 600 paper-based; 250 computer-based). *Application deadline:* For fall admission, 1/1 priority date for domestic and international students; for winter admission, 11/1 priority date for domestic students, 10/1 priority date for international students. Applications are processed on a rolling basis. Application fee: $60 ($75 for international students). *Financial support:* In 2007–08, 63 students received support, including 15 fellowships with full and partial tuition reimbursements available (averaging $14,900 per year), 7 teaching assistantships with full and partial tuition reimbursements available (averaging $14,870 per year); research assistantships with full and partial tuition reimbursements available. Financial award application deadline: 1/1; financial award applicants required to submit FAFSA. *Faculty research:* Housing, community, and economic development; transportation; physical planning and urban development; planning in developing countries; land use and environmental planning. Total annual research expenditures: $755,000. *Unit head:* Dr. Jonathan Levine, Chair, 734-763-0039, Fax: 734-763-2322, E-mail: jnthnlvn@umich.edu. *Application contact:* Beverly A. Walter, Admissions Coordinator, 734-763-3075, Fax: 734-763-2322, E-mail: beverlyw@umich.edu.

University of Michigan, Horace H. Rackham School of Graduate Studies, PhD Program in Urban and Regional Planning, Ann Arbor, MI 48109. Offers PhD. *Faculty:* 9 full-time (5 women), 8 part-time/adjunct (3 women). *Students:* 19 full-time (10 women); includes 4 minority (1 African American, 3 Asian Americans or Pacific Islanders), 10 international. 48 applicants, 17% accepted, 4 enrolled. In 2007, 2 degrees awarded. *Median time to degree:* Of those who began their doctoral program in fall 1999, 100% received their degree in 8 years or less. *Degree requirements:* For doctorate, thesis/dissertation, 1 interdisciplinary paper, 2 preliminary exams, oral defense of dissertation. *Entrance requirements:* For doctorate, GRE General Test. Additional exam requirements/recommendations for international students: Required—TOEFL (minimum score 560 paper-based; 220 computer-based; 84 iBT). *Application deadline:* For fall admission, 1/15 for domestic and international students. Application fee: $60 ($75 for international students). Electronic applications accepted. *Expenses: Contact institution. Financial support:* In 2007–08, 10 students received support, including 3 research assistantships with full and partial tuition reimbursements available (averaging $9,082 per year), 4 teaching assistantships with full and partial tuition reimbursements available (averaging $9,120 per year); fellowships with full and partial tuition reimbursements available, career-related internships or fieldwork, Federal Work-Study, institutionally sponsored loans, and block grants/stipends also available. Financial award application deadline: 1/15; financial award applicants required to submit FAFSA. *Faculty research:* Urban and regional planning, community and economic development, transportation planning and geological information systems, environmental planning, the built environment, international development and planning. *Unit head:* Dr. Jonathan Levine, Chair, 734-763-0039, Fax: 734-763-2322, E-mail: jnthnlvn@umich.edu. *Application contact:* Lisa K. Hauser, Coordinator, 734-763-1275, Fax: 734-763-2322, E-mail: weeze@umich.edu.

University of Minnesota, Twin Cities Campus, Graduate School, Hubert H. Humphrey Institute of Public Affairs, Program in Urban and Regional Planning, Minneapolis, MN 55455-0213. Offers environmental planning (MURP); housing and community development (MURP); land use and urban design (MURP); regional, economic and workforce development (MURP); transportation planning (MURP); JD/MURP; MURP/MLA; MURP/MS. *Accreditation:* ACSP (one or more programs are accredited). Part-time programs available. *Degree requirements:* For master's, thesis or alternative, internship or equivalent work experience. *Entrance requirements:* For master's, GRE General Test, minimum undergraduate GPA of 3.0. Additional exam requirements/recommendations for international students: Required—TOEFL (minimum score 600 paper-based; 250 computer-based). Electronic applications accepted. *Faculty research:* Policy planning, resource allocation planning, regulatory planning, program planning, project planning.

University of Nebraska–Lincoln, Graduate College, College of Architecture, Department of Community and Regional Planning, Lincoln, NE 68588. Offers MCRP, JD/MCRP, M Arch/MCRP, MS/MCRP. *Accreditation:* ACSP. *Degree requirements:* For master's, thesis optional. *Entrance requirements:* For master's, GRE General Test. Additional exam requirements/recommendations for international students: Required—TOEFL (minimum score 550 paper-based; 213 computer-based). Electronic applications accepted. *Faculty research:* Economic development, community development and improvement, social planning, land use planning, physical planning, environmental planning.

University of New Mexico, Graduate School, School of Architecture and Planning, Program in Community and Regional Planning, Albuquerque, NM 87131-2039. Offers MCRP, MCRP/MA, MPA/MCRP. *Accreditation:* ACSP. Part-time programs available. *Students:* 37 full-time (26 women), 23 part-time (16 women); includes 29 minority (2 African Americans, 13 American Indian/Alaska Native, 1 Asian American or Pacific Islander, 13 Hispanic Americans), 4 international. Average age 34. 42 applicants, 64% accepted, 18 enrolled. In 2007, 14 degrees awarded. *Degree requirements:* For master's, thesis. *Entrance requirements:* For master's, minimum GPA of 3.0, 3 letters of recommendation, letter of intent, resumé, copies of all unofficial transcripts. *Application deadline:* For fall admission, 1/30 priority date for domestic students; for spring admission, 10/15 for domestic students. Application fee: $50. *Financial support:* In 2007–08, 21 students received support, including fellowships (averaging $2,700 per year), research assistantships with tuition reimbursements available (averaging $7,278 per year), teaching assistantships with full tuition reimbursements available (averaging $2,087 per year); Federal Work-Study, institutionally sponsored loans, scholarships/grants, tuition waivers (full), and unspecified assistantships also available. Financial award application deadline: 3/1; financial award applicants required to submit FAFSA. *Faculty research:* Community development, urban and ecological design, land economics, community-based planning, environmental dispute resolution, environmental justice. *Unit head:* Dr. David S. Henkel, Director, 505-277-1276, Fax: 505-277-0076, E-mail: cymro@unm.edu. *Application contact:* Mitzi Visil, Senior Academic Advisor, 505-277-1303, Fax: 505-277-0076, E-mail: mitziv@unm.edu.

University of New Orleans, Graduate School, College of Liberal Arts, School of Urban Planning and Regional Studies, Program in Urban and Regional Planning, New Orleans, LA 70148. Offers MURP. *Accreditation:* ACSP. *Students:* 40 (25 women). Average age 31. In 2007, 8 degrees awarded. *Degree requirements:* For master's, thesis. *Entrance requirements:* For master's, GRE General Test. Additional exam requirements/recommendations for international students: Required—TOEFL (minimum score 550 paper-based; 213 computer-based; 79 iBT). *Application deadline:* For fall admission, 7/1 priority date for domestic students, 6/1 for international students; for spring admission, 11/15 priority date for domestic students, 10/1 for international students. Applications are processed on a rolling basis. Application fee: $40. Electronic applications accepted. *Financial support:* Research assistantships available. Financial award application deadline: 5/15; financial award applicants required to submit FAFSA. *Faculty research:* Urban economic development, environmental planning and analysis, social and cultural change. *Unit head:* Prof. Jane S. Brooks, Director, 504-280-6519, Fax: 504-280-6272, E-mail: jsbrooks@uno.edu. *Application contact:* David Lambour, Coordinator, 504-280-5473, Fax: 504-280-6272, E-mail: dmlambou@uno.edu.

The University of North Carolina at Chapel Hill, Graduate School, College of Arts and Sciences, Department of City and Regional Planning, Chapel Hill, NC 27599. Offers city and regional planning (MCRP); planning (PhD); public policy analysis (PhD); JD/MRP; MBA/MRP; MLA/MRP; MPA/MRP; MPH/MRP. *Accreditation:* ACSP (one or more programs are accredited). *Faculty:* 16 full-time (5 women), 6 part-time/adjunct (1 woman). *Students:* 106 full-time (64 women); includes 14 minority (5 African Americans, 6 Asian Americans or Pacific Islanders, 3 Hispanic Americans), 6 international. Average age 27. 242 applicants, 52% accepted, 61 enrolled. In 2007, 39 master's, 2 doctorates awarded. *Median time to degree:* Of those who began their doctoral program in fall 1999, 95% received their degree in 8 years or less. *Degree requirements:* For master's, project; for doctorate, comprehensive exam, thesis/dissertation. *Entrance requirements:* For master's and doctorate, GRE General Test. Additional exam requirements/recommendations for international students: Required—TOEFL (minimum score 550 paper-based; 213 computer-based). *Application deadline:* For fall admission, 1/1 priority date for domestic students, 12/1 priority date for international students. Application fee: $73. Electronic applications accepted. *Financial support:* In 2007–08, 57 students received support, including 6 fellowships with full tuition reimbursements available (averaging $20,000 per year), 22 research assistantships with full tuition reimbursements available (averaging $10,400 per year), 26 teaching assistantships with full tuition reimbursements available (averaging $10,000 per year); career-related internships or fieldwork, Federal Work-Study, traineeships, and unspecified assistantships also available. Financial award application deadline: 1/1; financial award applicants required to submit FAFSA. *Faculty research:* Developing areas, transportation, affordable housing, growth management, coastal zone management. *Unit head:* Dr. Emil E. Malizia, Chairman, 919-962-4759, Fax: 919-962-5206, E-mail: malizia@email.unc.edu. *Application contact:* Carolyn Turner, Student Service Manager, 919-962-4784, Fax: 919-962-5206, E-mail: turnerc@email.unc.edu.

University of Oklahoma, Graduate College, College of Architecture, Division of Regional and City Planning, Norman, OK 73019-0390. Offers MRCP, MRCP/MLA. *Accreditation:* ACSP (one or more programs are accredited). Part-time programs available. *Faculty:* 3 full-time (1 woman). *Students:* 20 full-time (12 women), 3 part-time (2 women); includes 5 minority (4 African Americans, 1 American Indian/Alaska Native), 7 international. 17 applicants, 88% accepted, 5 enrolled. In 2007, 7 degrees awarded. *Degree requirements:* For master's, thesis or alternative, portfolio, project. *Entrance requirements:* For master's, GRE General Test, appropriate bachelor's degree, portfolio. Additional exam requirements/recommendations for international students: Required—TOEFL (minimum score 550 paper-based; 213 computer-based). *Application deadline:* For fall admission, 4/1 for domestic and international students; for spring admission, 11/1 for domestic students, 9/1 for international students. Applications are processed on a rolling basis. Application fee: $40 ($90 for international students). Electronic applications accepted. *Expenses:* Tuition, state resident: full-time $3,451; part-time $144 per credit hour. Tuition, nonresident: full-time $12,432; part-time $518 per credit hour. Required fees: $1,925; $70 per credit hour. $122 per semester. *Financial support:* In 2007–08, 15 students received support, including 4 research assistantships with partial tuition reimbursements available (averaging $9,450 per year); career-related internships or fieldwork, Federal Work-Study, institutionally sponsored loans, scholarships/grants, health care benefits, tuition waivers (partial), and unspecified assistantships also available. Support available to part-time students. Financial award applicants required to submit FAFSA. *Faculty research:* Transportation planning, economic development, urban design, city and regional planning. *Unit head:* Guogiang Shen, Director, 405-325-2399, Fax: 405-325-7558, E-mail: guogiangs@ou.edu.

University of Oregon, Graduate School, School of Architecture and Allied Arts, Department of Planning, Public Policy, and Management, Program in Community and Regional Planning, Eugene, OR 97403. Offers MCRP. *Accreditation:* ACSP. Part-time programs available. *Students:* 34 full-time (18 women), 2 part-time; includes 4 minority (1 African American, 1 Asian American or Pacific Islander, 2 Hispanic Americans), 1 international. 77 applicants, 66% accepted. In

2007, 31 degrees awarded. *Degree requirements:* For master's, thesis or alternative. *Entrance requirements:* For master's, minimum GPA of 3.0. Additional exam requirements/recommendations for international students: Required—TOEFL. Application fee: $50. *Financial support:* In 2007–08, 18 teaching assistantships were awarded; career-related internships or fieldwork also available. *Faculty research:* Community economic development, tourism, families in poverty. *Application contact:* Zudegi Giordana, Admissions Contact, 541-346-5005, Fax: 541-346-2040, E-mail: zudegi@uoregon.edu.

University of Pennsylvania, School of Design, Department of City and Regional Planning, Philadelphia, PA 19104. Offers MCP, PhD, Certificate, MSE/MCP. *Accreditation:* ACSP (one or more programs are accredited). *Degree requirements:* For doctorate, thesis/dissertation. *Entrance requirements:* For master's and doctorate, GRE General Test. Additional exam requirements/recommendations for international students: Required—TOEFL. *Faculty research:* Growth management, transportation planning, urban simulation modeling, housing, development planning.

See Close-Up on page 175.

University of Pennsylvania, School of Design, Program in Landscape Architecture and Regional Planning, Philadelphia, PA 19104. Offers landscape architecture and regional planning (MLA); landscape studies (Certificate). *Accreditation:* ASLA (one or more programs are accredited). Part-time programs available. *Degree requirements:* For master's, thesis optional. *Entrance requirements:* For master's, GRE, portfolio. Additional exam requirements/recommendations for international students: Required—TOEFL. *Faculty research:* Early landscape architecture, natural distribution through landslides, urban gardens, landscape registration, watershed studies.

See Close-Up on page 175.

University of Pittsburgh, Graduate School of Public and International Affairs, Division of International Development, Program in Development Planning and Environmental Sustainability, Pittsburgh, PA 15260. Offers MID, MPA/MID, MID/JD, MID/MBA, MID/MPH, MID/MPIA, MID/MSIS, MID/MSW. Part-time programs available. *Faculty:* 34 full-time (10 women), 18 part-time/adjunct (6 women). *Students:* 22 full-time (15 women), 1 part-time; includes 4 minority (3 African Americans, 1 Asian American or Pacific Islander), 6 international. Average age 25. 41 applicants, 71% accepted, 7 enrolled. In 2007, 29 degrees awarded. *Degree requirements:* For master's, thesis optional, internship, capstone seminar. *Entrance requirements:* For master's, GRE General Test, 3 letters of recommendation, minimum GPA of 3.2. Additional exam requirements/recommendations for international students: Required—TOEFL (minimum score 550 paper-based; 213 computer-based; 80 iBT), TWE (minimum score 4); Recommended—IELTS (minimum score 7). *Application deadline:* For fall admission, 2/1 for domestic students, 1/15 for international students; for spring admission, 10/1 for domestic students, 8/1 for international students. Application fee: $50. Electronic applications accepted. *Financial support:* In 2007–08, 25 students received support, including 25 fellowships with partial tuition reimbursements available (averaging $8,840 per year); scholarships/grants and unspecified assistantships also available. Financial award application deadline: 2/1. *Faculty research:* Project/program evaluation, population and environment, international development, development economics, civil society. Total annual research expenditures: $845,025. *Application contact:* Elizabeth Hruby, Graduate Enrollment Counselor, 412-648-7640, Fax: 412-648-7641, E-mail: eah44@pitt.edu.

University of Pittsburgh, Graduate School of Public and International Affairs, Division of Public and Urban Affairs, Program in Urban and Regional Affairs, Pittsburgh, PA 15260. Offers MPA, MPA/MID, JD/MPA, MPA/MPIA, MPH/MPA, MSIS/MPA, MSW/MPA. Part-time and evening/weekend programs available. *Faculty:* 34 full-time (10 women), 18 part-time/adjunct (6 women). *Students:* 14 full-time (9 women), 4 part-time (2 women); includes 3 minority (1 African American, 1 Asian American or Pacific Islander, 1 Hispanic American), 1 international. Average age 25. 21 applicants, 81% accepted, 7 enrolled. In 2007, 35 degrees awarded. *Degree requirements:* For master's, thesis optional, internship, capstone seminar. *Entrance requirements:* For master's, GRE General Test, 3 letters of recommendation, resumé, minimum GPA of 3.2. Additional exam requirements/recommendations for international students: Required—TOEFL (minimum score 550 paper-based; 213 computer-based; 80 iBT), TWE (minimum score 4); Recommended—IELTS (minimum score 7). *Application deadline:* For fall admission, 2/1 for domestic students, 1/15 for international students; for spring admission, 11/1 for domestic students, 8/1 for international students. Application fee: $50. Electronic applications accepted. *Financial support:* In 2007–08, 18 students received support, including 18 fellowships (averaging $7,700 per year); career-related internships or fieldwork, scholarships/grants, tuition waivers (full and partial), and unspecified assistantships also available. Financial award application deadline: 2/1. *Faculty research:* Health policy and regulations, emergency management, regional finance, non-profit management, community/regional development, environmental policy. Total annual research expenditures: $845,025. *Application contact:* Denene Hefflin, Graduate Enrollment Counselor, 412-648-7640, Fax: 412-648-7641, E-mail: dkh7@pitt.edu.

See Close-Up on page 1645.

University of Puerto Rico, Río Piedras, Graduate School of Planning, San Juan, PR 00931-3300. Offers MP. *Accreditation:* ACSP. Part-time programs available. *Students:* 57 full-time (24 women), 59 part-time (22 women); includes 144 minority (all Hispanic Americans) Average age 30. In 2007, 26 degrees awarded. *Degree requirements:* For master's, comprehensive exam, thesis, planning project defense. *Entrance requirements:* For master's, PAEG, GRE, minimum GPA of 3.0, 2 letters of recommendation. *Application deadline:* For fall admission, 2/1 for domestic students. Application fee: $17. *Expenses:* Tuition, state resident: full-time $1,808; part-time $113 per credit. Tuition, nonresident: full-time $5,248; part-time $328 per credit. Required fees: $72 per term. *Financial support:* Fellowships, research assistantships, teaching assistantships, Federal Work-Study, institutionally sponsored loans, and tuition waivers (partial) available. Financial award application deadline: 5/31. *Faculty research:* Municipalities, historic Atlas, Puerto Rico, economic future. *Unit head:* Dr. Elías R. Gutierrez, Director, 787-764-0000 Ext. 85117, Fax: 787-763-5375, E-mail: nvega@rrpac.upr.clu.edu. *Application contact:* Information Contact, 787-764-0000 Ext. 3182, Fax: 787-763-5375.

University of Southern California, Graduate School, School of Policy, Planning and Development, Programs in Planning, Los Angeles, CA 90089. Offers planning (M Pl); urban and regional planning (PhD); M Arch/M Pl; M Pl/MA; M Pl/MS; M Pl/MSW; MBA/M Pl; ML Arch/M Pl; MPA/M Pl. *Accreditation:* ACSP (one or more programs are accredited). Part-time programs available. *Faculty:* 39 full-time (8 women), 43 part-time/adjunct (12 women). *Students:* 108 full-time (59 women), 11 part-time (6 women); includes 38 minority (9 African Americans, 20 Asian Americans or Pacific Islanders, 9 Hispanic Americans), 33 international. 165 applicants, 72% accepted. In 2007, 34 master's, 10 doctorates awarded. *Degree requirements:* For doctorate, thesis/dissertation. *Entrance requirements:* For master's and doctorate, GRE General Test. *Application deadline:* For fall admission, 1/15 priority date for domestic students; for spring admission, 11/1 for domestic students. Applications are processed on a rolling basis. Application fee: $85. *Financial support:* Application deadline: 2/15; *Faculty research:* Transportation infrastructure, comparative international development, health communities. *Unit head:* Dr. David Sloane, Director, 213-740-6842, E-mail: sppd@usc.edu.

University of Southern California, Graduate School, School of Policy, Planning and Development, Programs in Planning and Development Studies, Los Angeles, CA 90089. Offers planning and development studies (MPDS, DPDS); policy, planning and development (PhD). *Faculty:* 39 full-time (8 women), 45 part-time/adjunct (12 women). *Students:* 52 full-time (24 women), 19 part-time (9 women); includes 22 minority (12 African Americans, 3 Asian Americans or Pacific Islanders, 7 Hispanic Americans), 26 international. 102 applicants, 30% accepted. In 2007, 3 doctorates awarded. *Entrance requirements:* For master's, GRE General Test; for doctorate, GRE. Application fee: $85. *Financial support:* In 2007–08, research assistantships (averaging $18,500 per year), teaching assistantships (averaging $18,500 per year) were awarded; fellowships, Federal Work-Study, institutionally sponsored loans, and scholarships/grants also available. Support available to part-time students. Financial award application deadline: 2/15; financial award applicants required to submit FAFSA. *Faculty research:* Governance, effective institutions, leadership management, healthy urban development. *Unit head:* Yong Heng Deng, Head, 213-740-2311.

University of Southern Maine, Edmund S. Muskie School of Public Service, Program in Community Planning and Development, Portland, ME 04104-9300. Offers MCPD, Certificate, JD/MCPD. Part-time and evening/weekend programs available. *Degree requirements:* For master's, thesis, capstone project, field experience. *Entrance requirements:* For master's, GRE General Test or LSAT. Additional exam requirements/recommendations for international students: Required—TOEFL. Electronic applications accepted. *Faculty research:* Sustainable communities, ego system management, economic and environmental tradeoffs.

The University of Texas at Arlington, Graduate School, School of Urban and Public Affairs, Program in City and Regional Planning, Arlington, TX 76019. Offers MCRP, M Arch/MCRP. *Accreditation:* ACSP. Part-time and evening/weekend programs available. *Faculty:* 4 full-time (1 woman), 3 part-time/adjunct (0 women). *Students:* 23 full-time (8 women), 28 part-time (13 women); includes 13 minority (4 African Americans, 1 American Indian/Alaska Native, 1 Asian American or Pacific Islander, 7 Hispanic Americans), 8 international. Average age 35. In 2007, 17 degrees awarded. *Degree requirements:* For master's, thesis or alternative. *Entrance requirements:* For master's, GRE General Test. Additional exam requirements/recommendations for international students: Required—TOEFL (minimum score 550 paper-based; 213 computer-based). *Application deadline:* For fall admission, 6/16 for domestic students. Application fee: $35 ($50 for international students). *Expenses:* Tuition, state resident: full-time $5,934. Tuition, nonresident: full-time $10,938. *Financial support:* Fellowships, research assistantships, career-related internships or fieldwork available. Financial award application deadline: 6/1; financial award applicants required to submit FAFSA. *Faculty research:* Urban structure, GIS environmental resolutions, qualitative methods, JTS housing, planning history/theory. Total annual research expenditures: $30,453. *Unit head:* Dr. Enid Arvidson, Graduate Adviser, 817-272-3349, Fax: 817-272-5008. *Application contact:* Linda Slaughter, Administrative Clerk, 817-272-3071, Fax: 817-272-5008, E-mail: slaughter@uta.edu.

The University of Texas at Arlington, Graduate School, School of Urban and Public Affairs, Urban and Public Affairs Division, Arlington, TX 76019. Offers MA, MSSW/MA. Part-time and evening/weekend programs available. *Students:* 3 full-time (2 women), 18 part-time (15 women); includes 10 minority (7 African Americans, 1 Asian American or Pacific Islander, 2 Hispanic Americans). Average age 25. In 2007, 3 degrees awarded. *Degree requirements:* For master's, thesis or alternative. *Entrance requirements:* For master's, GRE General Test. Additional exam requirements/recommendations for international students: Required—TOEFL (minimum score 550 paper-based; 213 computer-based). *Application deadline:* For fall admission, 6/16 for domestic students. Application fee: $35 ($50 for international students). *Expenses:* Tuition, state resident: full-time $5,934. Tuition, nonresident: full-time $10,938. *Financial support:* In 2007–08, 1 research assistantship (averaging $750 per year) was awarded; fellowships, career-related internships or fieldwork also available. Financial award application deadline: 6/1; financial award applicants required to submit FAFSA. *Faculty research:* Personnel, non-profit organizational change, welfare policy, urban research. Total annual research expenditures: $33,080. *Unit head:* Dr. Edith Barrett, Graduate Adviser, 817-272-3285, Fax: 817-272-5008, E-mail: ebarrett@uta.edu. *Application contact:* Linda Slaughter, Administrative Clerk, 817-272-3071, Fax: 817-272-5008, E-mail: slaughter@uta.edu.

The University of Texas at Austin, Graduate School, School of Architecture, Program in Community and Regional Planning, Austin, TX 78712-1111. Offers MSCRP, PhD, JD/MSCRP, MSCRP/MA, MSCRP/PhD. *Accreditation:* ACSP. *Degree requirements:* For master's, thesis; for doctorate, thesis/dissertation. *Entrance requirements:* For master's and doctorate, GRE General Test. Electronic applications accepted.

The University of Toledo, College of Graduate Studies, College of Arts and Sciences, Department of Geography and Planning, Toledo, OH 43606-3390. Offers geographic information systems and applied geographics (Certificate); geography (MA); planning (MA). Part-time programs available. *Faculty:* 10. *Students:* 20 full-time (6 women), 12 part-time (4 women); includes 2 minority (both African Americans), 5 international. Average age 31. 27 applicants, 67% accepted, 9 enrolled. In 2007, 8 master's, 3 other advanced degrees awarded. *Degree requirements:* For master's, thesis. *Entrance requirements:* For master's, GRE General Test. *Application deadline:* For fall admission, 3/15 priority date for domestic students. Applications are processed on a rolling basis. Application fee: $45. Electronic applications accepted. *Financial support:* In 2007–08, 4 research assistantships with full tuition reimbursements (averaging $10,500 per year), 9 teaching assistantships with full tuition reimbursements (averaging $10,500 per year) were awarded; career-related internships or fieldwork, institutionally sponsored loans, scholarships/grants, tuition waivers (full), and unspecified assistantships also available. Support available to part-time students. Financial award application deadline: 4/1. *Unit head:* Dr. Peter Lindquist, Chair, 419-530-4287, Fax: 419-530-7919, E-mail: peter.lindquist@utoledo.edu.

See Close-Up on page 1093.

University of Toronto, School of Graduate Studies, Social Sciences Division, Department of Geography, Program in Planning, Toronto, ON M5S 1A1, Canada. Offers M Sc Pl, PhD. Part-time programs available. *Faculty:* 30 full-time, 7 part-time/adjunct. *Students:* 67 full-time (37 women), 6 part-time, 8 international. 189 applicants, 38% accepted. In 2007, 2 degrees awarded. *Degree requirements:* For master's, summer internship. *Entrance requirements:* For master's, bachelor's degree in planning, geography, social science or a closely related professional field, minimum B+ average in final year, 3 letters of reference. *Application deadline:* For fall admission, 2/1 priority date for domestic students. Application fee: $100 Canadian dollars. *Expenses:* Contact institution. *Financial support:* Fellowships, research assistantships, teaching assistantships available. *Application contact:* Marianne Ishibashi, Graduate Counselor, 416-978-3377, Fax: 416-978-3886, E-mail: ishi@geog.utoronto.ca.

University of Utah, The Graduate School, College of Architecture and Planning, Salt Lake City, UT 84112-1107. Offers architectural studies (M Arch, MS); urban planning (MUP); M Arch/MBA. Part-time programs available. *Faculty:* 17 full-time (5 women), 9 part-time/adjunct (2 women). *Students:* 98 full-time (29 women), 12 part-time (5 women); includes 3 minority (1 Asian American or Pacific Islander, 2 Hispanic Americans), 11 international. Average age 30. 84 applicants, 65% accepted, 40 enrolled. In 2007, 45 degrees awarded. *Degree requirements:* For master's, thesis (for some programs), comprehensive project. *Entrance requirements:* For master's, minimum undergraduate GPA of 3.0. Additional exam requirements/recommendations for international students: Required—TOEFL (minimum score 500 paper-based; 173 computer-based). *Application deadline:* For fall admission, 4/1 for domestic and international students; for spring admission, 11/1 for domestic and international students. Applications are processed on a rolling basis. Application fee: $45 ($65 for international students). Electronic applications accepted. *Expenses:* Contact institution. *Financial support:* In 2007–08, 29 fellowships with full tuition reimbursements, 3 research assistantships with full tuition reimbursements, 29 teaching assistantships with partial tuition reimbursements were awarded; career-related internships or fieldwork, Federal Work-Study, and scholarships/grants also available. Financial award application deadline: 2/1; financial award applicants required to submit FAFSA. *Faculty research:* History, design, acoustics, photography, structures, architecture of American West, architectural communication and representation, impact of technology. Total annual research expenditures: $171,483. *Unit head:* Brenda Scheer, Dean, 801-581-8254, Fax: 801-581-8217, E-mail: scheer@arch.utah.edu. *Application contact:* Colleen Nielson, Admissions Advisor, 801-581-8254, Fax: 801-581-8217, E-mail: cnielson@arch.utah.edu.

University of Virginia, School of Architecture, Department of Urban and Environmental Planning, Charlottesville, VA 22903. Offers MUEP. *Accreditation:* ACSP. *Faculty:* 6 full-time (2 women), 8 part-time/adjunct (3 women). *Students:* 40 full-time (20 women), 1 (woman) part-time; includes 3 minority (all African Americans) Average age 27. 109 applicants, 25% accepted,

Urban and Regional Planning

University of Virginia (continued)
17 enrolled. In 2007, 19 degrees awarded. *Entrance requirements:* For master's, GRE General Test, previous course work in statistics. Additional exam requirements/recommendations for international students: Required—TOEFL (minimum score 600 paper-based; 250 computer-based). Application fee: $60. *Financial support:* Applicants required to submit FAFSA. *Faculty research:* Urban development, land use, environment, policy analysis, historic preservation. *Unit head:* Daphne Spain, Chair, 434-924-1339, Fax: 434-982-2678, E-mail: dgs4g@virginia.edu. *Application contact:* Tracy Brookman, Admissions Officer, 434-924-6442, E-mail: arch-admissions@virginia.edu.

University of Washington, Graduate School, College of Architecture and Urban Planning, Department of Urban Design and Planning, Seattle, WA 98195. Offers urban design and planning (PhD); urban planning (MUP). *Accreditation:* ACSP (one or more programs are accredited). *Degree requirements:* For master's, thesis or alternative; for doctorate, thesis/dissertation. *Entrance requirements:* For master's and doctorate, GRE General Test, minimum GPA of 3.0. Additional exam requirements/recommendations for international students: Required—TOEFL. *Faculty research:* Land-use and growth management, urban form and travel behavior, geographic information systems/remote sensing, historic preservation, urban ecology and environmental planning.

University of Waterloo, Graduate Studies, Faculty of Environmental Studies, Program in Local Economic Development, Waterloo, ON N2L 3G1, Canada. Offers MAES. Part-time programs available. *Degree requirements:* For master's, internship, research paper. Electronic applications accepted.

University of Waterloo, Graduate Studies, Faculty of Environmental Studies, School of Planning, Waterloo, ON N2L 3G1, Canada. Offers MA, MAES, MES, PhD. Part-time programs available. *Degree requirements:* For master's, thesis (for some programs); for doctorate, comprehensive exam, thesis/dissertation. *Entrance requirements:* For master's, honors degree, minimum B+ average; for doctorate, master's degree, minimum A- average, resumé. Additional exam requirements/recommendations for international students: Required—TOEFL, TWE. Electronic applications accepted. *Faculty research:* Environmental planning, planning for resource development, urban planning and information systems, social planning, urban design.

University of Wisconsin–Madison, Graduate School, College of Letters and Science and College of Agricultural and Life Sciences, Department of Urban and Regional Planning, Madison, WI 53706-1380. Offers MS, PhD. *Accreditation:* ACSP (one or more programs are accredited). Part-time programs available. *Degree requirements:* For master's, thesis optional, internship; for doctorate, thesis/dissertation, 3 preliminary exams. *Entrance requirements:* For master's, GRE, minimum GPA of 3.0, previous course work in statistics; for doctorate, 1 year of experience, master's degree in related field. Electronic applications accepted. *Faculty research:* Land use, environmental planning, community development, economic development planning.

University of Wisconsin–Milwaukee, Graduate School, School of Architecture and Urban Planning, Department of Urban Planning, Milwaukee, WI 53201-0413. Offers MUP, Certificate, M Arch/MUP, MPA/MUP, MUP/MS. *Accreditation:* ACSP. Part-time programs available. *Faculty:* 6 full-time (2 women). *Students:* 22 full-time (9 women), 6 part-time (3 women); includes 3 minority (2 African Americans, 1 Hispanic American), 1 international. 56 applicants, 73% accepted, 15 enrolled. In 2007, 21 degrees awarded. *Entrance requirements:* For master's, GRE General Test. *Application deadline:* For fall admission, 1/1 priority date for domestic students; for spring admission, 9/1 for domestic students. Applications are processed on a rolling basis. Application fee: $45 ($75 for international students). *Expenses:* Tuition, state resident: part-time $530 per credit. Tuition, nonresident: part-time $1,428 per credit. Required fees: $19 per credit. $229 per term. Tuition and fees vary according to course load and program. *Financial support:* In 2007–08, 4 teaching assistantships were awarded; fellowships, research assistantships, career-related internships or fieldwork and unspecified assistantships also available. Support available to part-time students. Financial award application deadline: 4/15. *Unit head:* Joan Simuncak, Representative, 414-229-4015, Fax: 414-229-6976, E-mail: joanarch@uwm.edu.

Utah State University, School of Graduate Studies, College of Humanities, Arts and Social Sciences, Department of Landscape Architecture and Environmental Planning, Logan, UT 84322. Offers bioregional planning (MS); landscape architecture (MLA). *Accreditation:* ASLA (one or more programs are accredited). *Degree requirements:* For master's, thesis. *Entrance requirements:* For master's, GRE General Test, minimum GPA of 3.0. Additional exam requirements/recommendations for international students: Required—TOEFL. *Faculty research:* Visual resource management, planning for wildlife, agricultural land preservation, watershed planning, community planning and design.

Utah State University, School of Graduate Studies, College of Natural Resources, Department of Environment and Society, Logan, UT 84322. Offers bioregional planning (MS); geography (MA, MS); human dimensions of ecosystem science and management (MS, PhD); recreation resource management (MS, PhD). *Degree requirements:* For master's, comprehensive exam, thesis (for some programs). *Entrance requirements:* For master's and doctorate, GRE General Test, minimum GPA of 3.0. Additional exam requirements/recommendations for international students: Required—TOEFL. Electronic applications accepted. *Faculty research:* Geographic information systems/geographic and environmental education, bioregional planning, natural resource and environmental policy, outdoor recreation and tourism, natural resource and environmental management.

Vanderbilt University, Peabody College, Department of Human and Organizational Development, Nashville, TN 37240-1001. Offers community development action (M Ed); human development counseling (M Ed). *Accreditation:* ACA; NCATE. Part-time programs available. *Faculty:* 19 full-time (9 women), 14 part-time/adjunct (11 women). *Students:* 55 full-time (49 women), 4 part-time (3 women); includes 17 minority (12 African Americans, 5 Hispanic Americans), 2 international. Average age 27. 106 applicants, 55% accepted, 32 enrolled. In 2007, 30 degrees awarded. *Degree requirements:* For master's, comprehensive exam, thesis optional. *Entrance requirements:* For master's, GRE General Test, MAT. Additional exam requirements/recommendations for international students: Required—TOEFL (minimum score 550 paper-based; 213 computer-based). *Application deadline:* For fall admission, 12/31 priority date for domestic and international students; for spring admission, 11/1 priority date for domestic and international students. Applications are processed on a rolling basis. Application fee: $0. Electronic applications accepted. *Financial support:* In 2007–08, 41 students received support, including 11 fellowships with full and partial tuition reimbursements available, 10 research assistantships with full and partial tuition reimbursements available, 20 teaching assistantships with full and partial tuition reimbursements available; Federal Work-Study, institutionally sponsored loans, scholarships/grants, tuition waivers (partial), and unspecified assistantships also available. Support available to part-time students. Financial award application deadline: 2/1; financial award applicants required to submit FAFSA. *Faculty research:* Community psychology, community development and urban policy, counseling and mental health services, organizational development and institutional change; youth physical and behavioral health in schools and communities. *Unit head:* Joseph Cunningham, Chair, 615-322-6881, Fax: 615-322-1141, E-mail: joe.cunningham@vanderbilt.edu. *Application contact:* Sherrie Lane, Office Assistant, 615-322-8484, Fax: 615-322-1141, E-mail: sherrie.a.lane@vanderbilt.edu.

Virginia Commonwealth University, Graduate School, College of Humanities and Sciences, Wilder School of Government and Public Affairs, Department of Urban Studies and Planning, Program in Planning Information Systems, Richmond, VA 23284-9005. Offers Certificate. *Application deadline:* For fall admission, 4/15 for domestic students; for spring admission, 11/15 for domestic students. Applications are processed on a rolling basis. Application fee: $50. *Expenses:* Tuition, state resident: full-time $7,224; part-time $401 per credit. Tuition, nonresident: full-time $16,072; part-time $891 per credit. Required fees: $1,679; $63 per credit. Tuition and fees vary according to campus/location.

See Close-Up on page 457.

Virginia Commonwealth University, Graduate School, College of Humanities and Sciences, Wilder School of Government and Public Affairs, Department of Urban Studies and Planning, Program in Urban and Regional Planning, Richmond, VA 23284-9005. Offers MURP, JD/MURP. In 2007, 11 degrees awarded. *Degree requirements:* For master's, thesis optional, internship. *Entrance requirements:* For master's, GRE General Test or LSAT, minimum GPA of 2.7. *Application deadline:* For fall admission, 4/15 for domestic students; for spring admission, 11/15 for domestic students. Applications are processed on a rolling basis. Application fee: $50. *Expenses:* Tuition, state resident: full-time $7,224; part-time $401 per credit. Tuition, nonresident: full-time $16,072; part-time $891 per credit. Required fees: $1,679; $63 per credit. Tuition and fees vary according to campus/location.

See Close-Up on page 457.

Virginia Polytechnic Institute and State University, Graduate School, College of Architecture and Urban Studies, School of Public and International Affairs, Blacksburg, VA 24061. Offers environmental planning and policy (MURP); government and international affairs (MPIA); housing, community and economic development (MURP); international development planning (MURP); land use and physical planning (MURP); planning, governance and globalization (PhD), including environmental planning and landscape analysis, physical planning and urban design, public and international affairs, urban and environmental design and planning; urban and regional planning (MURP). *Accreditation:* ACSP. *Entrance requirements:* Additional exam requirements/recommendations for international students: Required—TOEFL (minimum score 550 paper-based; 213 computer-based). Electronic applications accepted. *Faculty research:* Design theory, environmental planning, town planning, transportation planning.

Wayne State University, College of Liberal Arts and Sciences, Department of Geography and Urban Planning, Detroit, MI 48202. Offers geography (MA); urban planning (MUP). Evening/weekend programs available. *Faculty:* 8 full-time (0 women). *Students:* 16 full-time (11 women), 55 part-time (28 women); includes 27 minority (25 African Americans, 1 Asian American or Pacific Islander, 1 Hispanic American), 5 international. Average age 30. 44 applicants, 59% accepted, 21 enrolled. In 2007, 8 degrees awarded. *Entrance requirements:* For master's, minimum 3.0 GPA; statement of interest; two letters of recommendations. Additional exam requirements/recommendations for international students: Required—TOEFL (minimum score 550 paper-based; 213 computer-based); Recommended—TWE (minimum score 6). *Application deadline:* For fall admission, 7/1 for domestic students, 6/1 for international students; for winter admission, 10/1 for international students; for spring admission, 2/1 for international students. Applications are processed on a rolling basis. Application fee: $30 ($50 for international students). Electronic applications accepted. *Expenses:* Tuition, state resident: part-time $403 per credit hour. Tuition, nonresident: part-time $890 per credit hour. *Financial support:* Teaching assistantships available. *Faculty research:* Housing and community development, urban and regional economic development, urban development and land use, transportation policy and planning, environmental policy and planning. Total annual research expenditures: $7,362. *Unit head:* Robin Boyle, Chair, 313-577-0543, Fax: 313-577-0022, E-mail: aa2815@wayne.edu.

Wayne State University, College of Liberal Arts and Sciences, Program in Urban Planning, Detroit, MI 48202. Offers MUP. *Accreditation:* ACSP. Evening/weekend programs available. *Students:* 16 full-time (11 women), 55 part-time (28 women); includes 27 minority (25 African Americans, 1 Asian American or Pacific Islander, 1 Hispanic American), 5 international. Average age 30. 44 applicants, 59% accepted, 21 enrolled. In 2007, 8 degrees awarded. *Degree requirements:* For master's, thesis. *Entrance requirements:* Additional exam requirements/recommendations for international students: Required—TOEFL (minimum score 550 paper-based; 213 computer-based); Recommended—TWE (minimum score 6). *Application deadline:* For fall admission, 7/1 for domestic students, 6/1 for international students; for winter admission, 10/1 for international students; for spring admission, 2/1 for international students. Applications are processed on a rolling basis. Application fee: $30 ($50 for international students). Electronic applications accepted. *Expenses:* Tuition, state resident: part-time $403 per credit hour. Tuition, nonresident: part-time $890 per credit hour. *Application contact:* Janet Hankin, Professor, 313-577-0841, E-mail: janet.hankin@wayne.edu.

West Chester University of Pennsylvania, Office of Graduate Studies and Extended Education, College of Business and Public Affairs, Department of Geography and Planning, West Chester, PA 19383. Offers geographic technology (Certificate); geography (MA); regional planning (MSA). Part-time and evening/weekend programs available. *Students:* 15 full-time (5 women), 12 part-time (2 women); includes 5 minority (4 African Americans, 1 Hispanic American). Average age 28. 19 applicants, 84% accepted, 11 enrolled. In 2007, 6 degrees awarded. *Degree requirements:* For master's, comprehensive exam, thesis optional. *Entrance requirements:* For master's, GRE General Test, interview, minimum GPA of 3.0, resumé. Additional exam requirements/recommendations for international students: Required—TOEFL (minimum score 550 paper-based; 213 computer-based; 80 iBT). *Application deadline:* For fall admission, 4/15 priority date for domestic students; for spring admission, 10/15 for domestic students. Applications are processed on a rolling basis. Application fee: $35. *Expenses:* Tuition, state resident: part-time $345 per credit. Tuition, nonresident: part-time $552 per credit. Tuition and fees vary according to course load. *Financial support:* In 2007–08, 3 research assistantships with full and partial tuition reimbursements (averaging $5,000 per year) were awarded; unspecified assistantships also available. Support available to part-time students. Financial award application deadline: 2/15; financial award applicants required to submit FAFSA. *Faculty research:* Environmental education, land use/suburban planning, landscapes of Catalunya. *Unit head:* Dr. Joan Welch, Chair and Graduate Coordinator, 610-436-2343, E-mail: jwelch@wcupa.edu.

West Chester University of Pennsylvania, Office of Graduate Studies and Extended Education, College of Business and Public Affairs, Program in Administration, West Chester, PA 19383. Offers human resource management (MSA, Certificate); individualized (MSA); leadership for women (MSA); long-term health care (MSA); non profit administration (Certificate); public administration (MSA); regional planning (MSA); sport and athletic training (MSA); training and development (MSA). Part-time and evening/weekend programs available. *Students:* 5 full-time (all women), 24 part-time (18 women); includes 5 minority (3 African Americans, 1 Asian American or Pacific Islander, 1 Hispanic American), 1 international. Average age 30. 14 applicants, 86% accepted, 7 enrolled. In 2007, 14 degrees awarded. *Degree requirements:* For master's, comprehensive exam. *Entrance requirements:* For master's, GMAT, GRE General Test, or MAT, interview, minimum GPA of 3.0. Additional exam requirements/recommendations for international students: Required—TOEFL (minimum score 550 paper-based; 213 computer-based; 80 iBT). *Application deadline:* For fall admission, 4/15 priority date for domestic students; for spring admission, 10/15 for domestic students. Applications are processed on a rolling basis. Application fee: $35. *Expenses:* Tuition, state resident: part-time $345 per credit. Tuition, nonresident: part-time $552 per credit. Tuition and fees vary according to course load. *Financial support:* In 2007–08, 2 research assistantships with full and partial tuition reimbursements (averaging $5,000 per year) were awarded; career-related internships or fieldwork and unspecified assistantships also available. Support available to part-time students. Financial award application deadline: 2/15; financial award applicants required to submit FAFSA. *Unit head:* Dr. Lorraine Bernotsky, Director and Graduate Coordinator, 610-425-5000, E-mail: lbernotsky@wcupa.edu.

West Virginia University, Davis College of Agriculture, Forestry and Consumer Sciences, Division of Resource Management and Sustainable Development, Morgantown, WV 26506. Offers agricultural and extension education (MS, PhD), including agricultural and extension education, teaching vocational-agriculture (MS); agricultural and resource economics (MS); human and community development (PhD); natural resource economics (PhD); resource management (PhD); resource management and sustainable development (PhD). Part-time programs available. *Faculty:* 19 full-time (5 women), 8 part-time/adjunct (3 women). *Students:*

30 full-time (15 women), 11 part-time (5 women); includes 4 minority (3 African Americans, 1 Asian American or Pacific Islander), 15 international. Average age 33. 35 applicants, 77% accepted, 11 enrolled. In 2007, 1 degree awarded. *Degree requirements:* For master's, thesis; for doctorate, comprehensive exam, thesis/dissertation. *Entrance requirements:* For master's, GRE General Test. Additional exam requirements/recommendations for international students: Required—TOEFL. *Application deadline:* Applications are processed on a rolling basis. Application fee: $50. *Expenses:* Tuition, state resident: full-time $5,196; part-time $292 per credit hour. Tuition, nonresident: full-time $15,064; part-time $840 per credit hour. Tuition and fees vary according to program. *Financial support:* In 2007–08, 32 students received support, including 28 research assistantships (averaging $11,700 per year); teaching assistantships, Federal Work-Study, institutionally sponsored loans, and tuition waivers (full and partial) also available. Financial award application deadline: 2/1; financial award applicants required to submit FAFSA. *Faculty research:* Environmental economics, energy economics, agriculture. Total annual research expenditures: $1.3 million. *Unit head:* Dr. Timothy T. Phipps, Director, 304-293-6253 Ext. 2474, Fax: 304-293-3752, E-mail: tphipps@mail.wvu.edu.

West Virginia University, Eberly College of Arts and Sciences, Department of Geology and Geography, Program in Geography, Morgantown, WV 26506. Offers energy and environmental resources (MA); geographic information systems (PhD); geography-regional development (PhD); GIS/cartographic analysis (MA); regional development (MA). Part-time programs available. *Students:* 20 full-time (10 women), 7 part-time (4 women); includes 1 minority (American Indian/Alaska Native), 4 international. Average age 32. 18 applicants, 56% accepted, 7 enrolled. In 2007, 9 master's, 7 doctorates awarded. *Degree requirements:* For master's, thesis, oral and written exams; for doctorate, comprehensive exam, thesis/dissertation, oral and written exams. *Entrance requirements:* For master's and doctorate, GRE General Test, minimum GPA of 3.0. Additional exam requirements/recommendations for international students: Required—TOEFL. *Application deadline:* For fall admission, 1/1 priority date for domestic students, 11/14 priority date for international students; for spring admission, 5/1 priority date for domestic students, 7/1 priority date for international students. Applications are processed on a rolling basis. Application fee: $45. Electronic applications accepted. *Expenses:* Tuition, state resident: full-time $5,196; part-time $292 per credit hour. Tuition, nonresident: full-time $15,064; part-time $840 per credit hour. Tuition and fees vary according to program. *Financial support:* In 2007–08, 26 students received support, including 1 research assistantship with full tuition reimbursement available (averaging $15,000 per year), 6 teaching assistantships with full tuition reimbursements available (averaging $11,000 per year); career-related internships or fieldwork, Federal Work-Study, institutionally sponsored loans, health care benefits, and tuition waivers (partial) also available. Financial award application deadline: 2/1; financial award applicants required to submit FAFSA. *Faculty research:* Space, place and development, geographic information science, environmental geography. *Application contact:* Dr. Amy Hessl, Associate Professor, 304-293-8210, Fax: 304-293-6522, E-mail: geography-grad-info@mail.wvu.edu.

Urban Studies

Boston University, Metropolitan College (Continuing Education), Department of Applied Social Sciences, Boston, MA 02215. Offers city planning (MCP); criminal justice (MCJ); urban affairs (MUA). Part-time and evening/weekend programs available. *Faculty:* 5 full-time (1 woman), 23 part-time/adjunct (4 women). *Students:* 11 full-time (7 women), 524 part-time (283 women); includes 56 minority (23 African Americans, 2 American Indian/Alaska Native, 13 Asian Americans or Pacific Islanders, 18 Hispanic Americans), 20 international. Average age 33. 42 applicants, 81% accepted, 25 enrolled. In 2007, 10 degrees awarded. *Entrance requirements:* Additional exam requirements/recommendations for international students: Required—TOEFL; Recommended—IELTS. *Application deadline:* For fall admission, 7/15 priority date for domestic and international students; for spring admission, 12/15 for domestic students, 11/15 priority date for international students. Applications are processed on a rolling basis. Application fee: $70. Electronic applications accepted. *Expenses:* Tuition: Full-time $34,930; part-time $1,092 per credit. Tuition and fees vary according to class time, course level and program. *Financial support:* In 2007–08, 10 students received support, including 10 research assistantships with full and partial tuition reimbursements available; career-related internships or fieldwork, Federal Work-Study, institutionally sponsored loans, tuition waivers (partial), and unspecified assistantships also available. Support available to part-time students. Financial award application deadline: 6/15; financial award applicants required to submit FAFSA. *Faculty research:* Housing, community development and land use planning, environmental management and planning, international comparative development planning. *Unit head:* Dr. Daniel P. LeClair, Chair, 617-353-3025, Fax: 617-358-3595, E-mail: dleclair@bu.edu.

Brooklyn College of the City University of New York, Division of Graduate Studies, Department of Political Science, Brooklyn, NY 11210-2889. Offers international affairs (MA); political science (MA, PhD); political science, urban policy and administration (MA). The department offers courses at Brooklyn College that are creditable toward the CUNY doctoral degree (with permission of the executive officer of the doctoral program). Part-time and evening/weekend programs available. *Students:* 6 full-time (3 women), 106 part-time (64 women); includes 65 minority (50 African Americans, 5 Asian Americans or Pacific Islanders, 10 Hispanic Americans), 13 international. 56 applicants, 89% accepted, 30 enrolled. In 2007, 43 degrees awarded. *Degree requirements:* For master's, comprehensive exam (for some programs), thesis or alternative, foreign language exam for international affairs program. *Entrance requirements:* For master's, 2 letters of recommendation, personal statement. *Application deadline:* For fall admission, 3/1 priority date for domestic students, 2/1 priority date for international students; for spring admission, 11/1 priority date for domestic students, 10/1 priority date for international students. Applications are processed on a rolling basis. Application fee: $125. Electronic applications accepted. *Financial support:* Career-related internships or fieldwork and Federal Work-Study available. Support available to part-time students. Financial award application deadline: 5/1; financial award applicants required to submit FAFSA. *Faculty research:* Ethics and politics, politics of criminal justice, Western Europe, international law and politics, labor politics. *Unit head:* Dr. Sally Bermanzohn, Chairperson, 718-951-5306, E-mail: sallyb@brooklyn.cuny.edu. *Application contact:* Hernan Sierra, Graduate Admissions Coordinator, 718-951-4536, Fax: 718-951-4506, E-mail: grads@brooklyn.cuny.edu.

Cleveland State University, College of Graduate Studies, Maxine Goodman Levin College of Urban Affairs, Department of Urban Studies, Cleveland, OH 44115. Offers geographic information systems (Certificate); local and urban management (Certificate); nonprofit management (Certificate); research administration (Certificate); urban economic development (Certificate); urban real estate development and finance (Certificate); urban studies (MS); urban studies and public affairs (PhD). Part-time and evening/weekend programs available. *Faculty:* 26 full-time (10 women), 20 part-time/adjunct (11 women). *Students:* 92 full-time (45 women), 180 part-time (98 women); includes 28 minority (24 African Americans, 1 Asian American or Pacific Islander, 3 Hispanic Americans). Average age 39. 185 applicants, 76% accepted, 86 enrolled. In 2007, 92 master's, 5 doctorates awarded. *Median time to degree:* Of those who began their doctoral program in fall 1999, 40% received their degree in 8 years or less. *Degree requirements:* For master's, thesis or alternative, exit project, capstone course; for doctorate, comprehensive exam, thesis/dissertation. *Entrance requirements:* For master's, GRE General Test, minimum GPA of 3.0; for doctorate, GRE General Test, minimum GPA of 3.5. Additional exam requirements/recommendations for international students: Required—TOEFL (minimum score 525 paper-based; 197 computer-based). *Application deadline:* For fall admission, 7/15 priority date for domestic students, 5/15 for international students; for spring admission, 11/1 for international students. Applications are processed on a rolling basis. Application fee: $30. Electronic applications accepted. *Financial support:* In 2007–08, 60 students received support, including 40 research assistantships with full and partial tuition reimbursements available (averaging $7,632 per year), 1 teaching assistantship with full and partial tuition reimbursement available (averaging $7,800 per year); career-related internships or fieldwork, Federal Work-Study, institutionally sponsored loans, scholarships/grants, tuition waivers (full and partial), and unspecified assistantships also available. Support available to part-time students. Financial award application deadline: 3/1. *Faculty research:* Environmental issues, economic development, urban and public policy, public management. *Unit head:* Dr. Wendy Kellogg, Director, 216-687-5265, Fax: 216-687-9342, E-mail: w.kellogg@csuohio.edu. *Application contact:* Graduate Advisor, 216-523-7522, Fax: 216-687-5398, E-mail: urbanprograms@csuohio.edu.

Concordia University, School of Graduate Studies, Faculty of Arts and Science, Department of Geography, Planning and Environment, Montréal, QC H3G 1M8, Canada. Offers environmental impact assessment (Diploma); geography, urban and environmental studies (M Sc).

East Tennessee State University, School of Graduate Studies, College of Business and Technology, Department of Economics, Finance, and Urban Studies, Johnson City, TN 37614. Offers city management (MCM); community development (MPM); general administration (MPM); municipal service management (MPM); urban and regional economic development (MPM); urban and regional planning (MPM). *Degree requirements:* For master's, internship, oral defense of thesis, research report. *Entrance requirements:* For master's, GRE General Test, minimum GPA of 3.0. Additional exam requirements/recommendations for international students: Required—TOEFL (minimum score 550 paper-based; 213 computer-based).

Georgia State University, Andrew Young School of Policy Studies, Department of Public Administration and Urban Studies, Program in Urban Policy Studies, Atlanta, GA 30303-3083. Offers MS. *Students:* Average age 32. *Degree requirements:* For master's, thesis optional. *Entrance requirements:* For master's, GRE General Test. Additional exam requirements/recommendations for international students: Required—TOEFL. *Application deadline:* For fall admission, 4/1 for domestic and international students; for spring admission, 10/1 for domestic and international students. Applications are processed on a rolling basis. Application fee: $50. *Expenses:* Tuition, state resident: part-time $221 per credit hour. *Financial support:* In 2007–08, research assistantships with full tuition reimbursements (averaging $9,000 per year). Financial award applicants required to submit FAFSA. *Faculty research:* Public policy, social policy, planning. *Application contact:* Office of Academic Assistance, E-mail: ayspsacademicassistance@gsu.edu.

Graduate School and University Center of the City University of New York, Graduate Studies, Interdisciplinary Studies, New York, NY 10016-4039. Offers language in social context (PhD); medieval studies (PhD); public policy (MA, PhD); urban studies (MA, PhD); women's studies (MA, PhD). Terminal master's awarded for partial completion of doctoral program. *Degree requirements:* For master's, thesis; for doctorate, comprehensive exam, thesis/dissertation. *Entrance requirements:* For master's and doctorate, GRE General Test. *Application deadline:* For fall admission, 2/1 for domestic students. Application fee: $40. *Financial support:* Application deadline: 2/1. *Unit head:* Chairman, 212-642-2430.

Hunter College of the City University of New York, Graduate School, School of Arts and Sciences, Department of Urban Affairs and Planning, Program in Urban Affairs, New York, NY 10021-5085. Offers MS. Part-time programs available. *Faculty:* 8 full-time (3 women), 8 part-time/adjunct (3 women). *Students:* 12 full-time (5 women), 55 part-time (35 women); includes 17 minority (13 African Americans, 4 Hispanic Americans). Average age 35. 63 applicants, 63% accepted, 25 enrolled. In 2007, 59 degrees awarded. *Degree requirements:* For master's, thesis or alternative, 2 formal reports, internship. *Entrance requirements:* For master's, minimum 12 credits of course work in social sciences. Additional exam requirements/recommendations for international students: Required—TOEFL. *Application deadline:* For fall admission, 4/1 priority date for domestic students, 2/1 for international students; for spring admission, 11/1 priority date for domestic students, 9/1 for international students. Applications are processed on a rolling basis. Application fee: $125. *Expenses:* Tuition, state resident: full-time $6,400; part-time $270 per credit. Tuition, nonresident: part-time $500 per credit. One-time fee: $125 full-time. Tuition and fees vary according to program. *Financial support:* Fellowships, research assistantships, teaching assistantships, career-related internships or fieldwork, Federal Work-Study, scholarships/grants, and unspecified assistantships available. *Faculty research:* Women, tourism, youth, immigration, employment. *Unit head:* Elaine M. Walsh, Director, 212-772-5595, Fax: 212-772-5593, E-mail: ewalsh@hunter.cuny.edu. *Application contact:* William Zlata, Director for Graduate Admissions, 212-772-4482, Fax: 212-650-3336, E-mail: admissions@hunter.cuny.edu.

Long Island University, Brooklyn Campus, Richard L. Conolly College of Liberal Arts and Sciences, Department of Urban Studies, Brooklyn, NY 11201-8423. Offers MA. Part-time and evening/weekend programs available. *Degree requirements:* For master's, thesis or alternative. *Entrance requirements:* For master's, 2 letters of recommendation. Additional exam requirements/recommendations for international students: Required—TOEFL (minimum score 500 paper-based; 173 computer-based). Electronic applications accepted.

Massachusetts Institute of Technology, School of Architecture and Planning, Department of Urban Studies and Planning, Cambridge, MA 02139-4307. Offers city planning (MCP); urban and regional planning (PhD); urban and regional studies (PhD); urban studies and planning (SM); M Arch/MCP; MCP/MSRED; MCP/MST; MCP/SM Arch S. *Accreditation:* ACSP (one or more programs are accredited). *Faculty:* 27 full-time (9 women), 1 (woman) part-time/adjunct. *Students:* 220 full-time (112 women); includes 38 minority (9 African Americans, 2 American Indian/Alaska Native, 19 Asian Americans or Pacific Islanders, 8 Hispanic Americans), 68 international. Average age 29. 452 applicants, 30% accepted, 81 enrolled. In 2007, 84 master's, 10 doctorates awarded. Terminal master's awarded for partial completion of doctoral program. *Degree requirements:* For master's, thesis; for doctorate, comprehensive exam, thesis/dissertation. *Entrance requirements:* For master's and doctorate, GRE General Test. Additional exam requirements/recommendations for international students: Required—TOEFL (minimum score 600 paper-based; 250 computer-based; 100 iBT); Recommended—TWE. *Application deadline:* For fall admission, 1/3 for domestic and international students. Application fee: $70. Electronic applications accepted. *Expenses:* Tuition: Full-time $34,760; part-time $545 per unit. Required fees: $236. *Financial support:* In 2007–08, 180 students received support, including 67 fellowships with tuition reimbursements available (averaging $18,290 per year), 54 research assistantships with tuition reimbursements available (averaging $18,799 per year), 21 teaching assistantships with tuition reimbursements available (averaging $22,858 per year); career-related internships or fieldwork, Federal Work-Study, institutionally sponsored loans, scholarships/grants, health care benefits, and unspecified assistantships also available. *Faculty research:* City design and development; housing, community, and economic development; environmental policy and planning; international development and regional planning; urban information systems. Total annual research expenditures: $918,000. *Unit*

Urban Studies

Massachusetts Institute of Technology (continued)
head: Prof. Lawrence Vale, Head, 617-253-1907, E-mail: duspinfo@mit.edu. *Application contact:* Graduate Admissions, 617-253-4543, Fax: 617-253-2654, E-mail: duspapply@mit.edu.

See Close-Up on page 161.

Minnesota State University Mankato, College of Graduate Studies, College of Social and Behavioral Sciences, Department of Urban and Regional Studies, Mankato, MN 56001. Offers local government (Certificate); urban and regional studies (MA); urban planning (Certificate); MAPA/MA. *Students:* 24 full-time (3 women), 18 part-time (7 women). Average age 30. In 2007, 6 degrees awarded. *Degree requirements:* For master's, one foreign language, comprehensive exam, thesis or alternative. *Entrance requirements:* For master's, minimum GPA of 3.0 during previous 2 years, 2 letters of recommendation. Additional exam requirements/recommendations for international students: Required—TOEFL. *Application deadline:* For fall admission, 7/1 priority date for domestic students; for spring admission, 11/1 for domestic students. Applications are processed on a rolling basis. Application fee: $40. Electronic applications accepted. *Financial support:* Fellowships with partial tuition reimbursements, research assistantships with full tuition reimbursements, teaching assistantships with full tuition reimbursements, career-related internships or fieldwork, Federal Work-Study, institutionally sponsored loans, and unspecified assistantships available. Support available to part-time students. Financial award application deadline: 3/15; financial award applicants required to submit FAFSA. *Unit head:* Dr. Anthony Filipovitch, Chairperson, 507-389-1714. *Application contact:* 507-389-2321, E-mail: grad@mnsu.edu.

New Jersey City University, Graduate Studies and Continuing Education, College of Education, Department of Educational Leadership, Jersey City, NJ 07305-1597. Offers basics and urban studies (MA); bilingual/bicultural education and English as a second language (MA); educational administration and supervision (MA). Evening/weekend programs available. *Faculty:* 3. *Students:* 5 full-time, 211 part-time; includes 47 minority (9 African Americans, 3 Asian Americans or Pacific Islanders, 35 Hispanic Americans), 16 international. Average age 34. In 2007, 120 degrees awarded. *Entrance requirements:* For master's, GRE General Test or MAT. Additional exam requirements/recommendations for international students: Required—TOEFL. *Application deadline:* For fall admission, 8/1 priority date for domestic students; for spring admission, 12/1 for domestic students. Applications are processed on a rolling basis. Application fee: $0. *Expenses:* Tuition, state resident: full-time $7,462. Tuition, nonresident: full-time $13,762. Required fees: $1,296. *Financial support:* Fellowships, teaching assistantships, career-related internships or fieldwork and unspecified assistantships available. *Unit head:* Dr. Catherine Shevey, Chairperson, 201-200-3012, E-mail: cshevey@njcu.edu.

New Jersey Institute of Technology, Office of Graduate Studies, School of Architecture, Program in Urban Systems, Newark, NJ 07102. Offers PhD. Part-time and evening/weekend programs available. *Students:* 23 full-time (15 women), 11 part-time (8 women); includes 13 minority (9 African Americans, 1 American Indian/Alaska Native, 3 Asian Americans or Pacific Islanders), 7 international. Average age 44. 28 applicants, 57% accepted, 8 enrolled. *Entrance requirements:* Additional exam requirements/recommendations for international students: Required—TOEFL (minimum score 550 paper-based; 213 computer-based). *Application deadline:* For fall admission, 6/5 priority date for domestic students; for spring admission, 10/15 for domestic students. Applications are processed on a rolling basis. Application fee: $60. Electronic applications accepted. *Expenses:* Tuition, state resident: full-time $12,730. Tuition, nonresident: full-time $18,090. Tuition and fees vary according to course load and campus/location. *Financial support:* Fellowships with full and partial tuition reimbursements, research assistantships with full and partial tuition reimbursements, teaching assistantships with full and partial tuition reimbursements, career-related internships or fieldwork, Federal Work-Study, institutionally sponsored loans, and unspecified assistantships available. Financial award application deadline: 3/15. *Unit head:* Karen Franck, Director, 973-596-3092, E-mail: karen.a.franck@njit.edu. *Application contact:* Kathryn Kelly, Director of Admissions, 973-596-3300, Fax: 973-596-3461, E-mail: admissions@njit.edu.

The New School: A University, Milano The New School for Management and Urban Policy, Program in Urban Policy Analysis and Management, New York, NY 10011. Offers MS. *Accreditation:* NASPAA. Part-time programs available. *Faculty:* 8 full-time (3 women), 3 part-time/adjunct (1 woman). *Students:* 46 full-time (33 women), 66 part-time (38 women); includes 46 minority (21 African Americans, 6 Asian Americans or Pacific Islanders, 19 Hispanic Americans), 2 international. Average age 31. In 2007, 42 degrees awarded. *Degree requirements:* For master's, thesis. *Entrance requirements:* For master's, interview. Additional exam requirements/recommendations for international students: Required—TOEFL (minimum score 600 paper-based; 250 computer-based; 100 iBT). *Application deadline:* For fall admission, 8/1 priority date for domestic students; for winter admission, 1/15 priority date for domestic students. Applications are processed on a rolling basis. Application fee: $50. *Financial support:* Fellowships, research assistantships, career-related internships or fieldwork, Federal Work-Study, scholarships/grants, and tuition waivers (full and partial) available. Support available to part-time students. Financial award application deadline: 3/1; financial award applicants required to submit FAFSA. *Faculty research:* Community and economic development, national urban policy, social welfare policy, management of low-income housing, race and gender issues. *Unit head:* Dr. Alex F. Schwartz, Chair, 212-229-5400 Ext. 1222, Fax: 212-229-5404, E-mail: schwartz@newschool.edu. *Application contact:* Merida Escandon, Director of Admissions, 212-229-5462 Ext. 1108, Fax: 212-229-5354, E-mail: milanoadmissions@newschool.edu.

See Close-Up on page 1609.

Norfolk State University, School of Graduate Studies, School of Liberal Arts, Department of Sociology, Program in Urban Affairs, Norfolk, VA 23504. Offers MA. Part-time programs available. *Degree requirements:* For master's, thesis. *Entrance requirements:* For master's, minimum GPA of 2.5.

Northeastern University, College of Arts and Sciences, Department of Political Science, Program in Public Administration, Boston, MA 02115-5096. Offers development administration (MPA); health administration and policy (MPA); state and local government (MPA); urban studies (Certificate). *Accreditation:* NASPAA (one or more programs are accredited). Part-time and evening/weekend programs available. *Faculty:* 22 full-time (4 women), 3 part-time/adjunct. *Students:* 19 full-time (8 women), 19 part-time (14 women). In 2007, 11 degrees awarded. *Degree requirements:* For master's, thesis optional. *Entrance requirements:* For master's, GRE General Test. Additional exam requirements/recommendations for international students: Required—TOEFL. *Application deadline:* For fall admission, 2/1 priority date for domestic students, 5/1 for international students. Applications are processed on a rolling basis. Application fee: $50. *Financial support:* Research assistantships with tuition reimbursements, teaching assistantships with tuition reimbursements, career-related internships or fieldwork, Federal Work-Study, tuition waivers (full and partial), and unspecified assistantships available. Support available to part-time students. Financial award application deadline: 2/1; financial award applicants required to submit FAFSA. *Faculty research:* National health care, Third World development, leadership and ethics, science and technology, budgeting. *Unit head:* Dr. Ronald D. Hedlund, Graduate Coordinator, 617-373-2796, Fax: 617-373-5311, E-mail: gradpolisci@neu.edu. *Application contact:* Brynn Thompson, Graduate Programs Assistant, 617-373-4404, Fax: 617-373-5311, E-mail: gradpolisci@neu.edu.

Old Dominion University, College of Business and Public Administration, Doctoral Program in Public Administration and Urban Policy, Norfolk, VA 23529. Offers PhD. Part-time and evening/weekend programs available. Postbaccalaureate distance learning degree programs offered. *Faculty:* 7 full-time (1 woman), 3 part-time/adjunct (2 women). *Students:* 3 full-time (all women), 25 part-time (11 women); includes 8 minority (6 African Americans, 1 American Indian/Alaska Native, 1 Asian American or Pacific Islander), 2 international. Average age 39. 5 applicants, 80% accepted, 4 enrolled. In 2007, 4 degrees awarded. *Degree requirements:* For doctorate, comprehensive exam, thesis/dissertation. *Entrance requirements:* For doctorate, GMAT, GRE General Test, master's degree, minimum graduate GPA of 3.0. Additional exam requirements/recommendations for international students: Required—TOEFL (minimum score 550 paper-based; 213 computer-based; 79 iBT). *Application deadline:* For fall admission, 7/1 priority date for domestic students; for spring admission, 10/1 priority date for domestic students. Applications are processed on a rolling basis. Application fee: $40. *Expenses:* Tuition, state resident: part-time $304 per credit hour. Tuition, nonresident: part-time $761 per credit hour. *Financial support:* In 2007–08, 6 students received support, including 6 research assistantships with tuition reimbursements available (averaging $12,908 per year); fellowships, teaching assistantships, career-related internships or fieldwork, scholarships/grants, and tuition waivers (partial) also available. Support available to part-time students. Financial award application deadline: 2/15; financial award applicants required to submit FAFSA. *Faculty research:* Educational needs and program development, policy analysis and administration, excellence norms for cooperative education programs. Total annual research expenditures: $60,000. *Unit head:* Dr. John C. Morris, Graduate Program Director, 757-683-3961, Fax: 757-683-5639, E-mail: jcmorris@odu.edu. *Application contact:* Megan S. Jones, Graduate Program Manager, 757-683-3961, Fax: 757-683-4886, E-mail: mmjones@odu.edu.

Old Dominion University, College of Business and Public Administration, Program in Urban Studies, Norfolk, VA 23529. Offers policy analysis/program evaluation (MUS); public planning analysis (MUS); urban administration (MUS). Part-time and evening/weekend programs available. *Faculty:* 7 full-time (1 woman), 6 part-time/adjunct (3 women). *Students:* Average age 41. 6 applicants, 83% accepted, 3 enrolled. In 2007, 3 degrees awarded. *Degree requirements:* For master's, thesis, capstone seminar. *Entrance requirements:* For master's, GRE or GMAT. Additional exam requirements/recommendations for international students: Required—TOEFL (minimum score 550 paper-based; 213 computer-based; 79 iBT). *Application deadline:* For fall admission, 7/15 priority date for domestic students, 4/15 for international students; for spring admission, 11/1 priority date for domestic students, 10/1 for international students. Applications are processed on a rolling basis. Application fee: $40. Electronic applications accepted. *Expenses:* Tuition, state resident: part-time $304 per credit hour. Tuition, nonresident: part-time $761 per credit hour. *Financial support:* In 2007–08, 8 students received support, including 8 research assistantships (averaging $5,000 per year); fellowships, teaching assistantships, career-related internships or fieldwork, Federal Work-Study, tuition waivers (partial), and unspecified assistantships also available. Support available to part-time students. Financial award application deadline: 2/15; financial award applicants required to submit FAFSA. *Faculty research:* Program implementation, evaluation, and design. Total annual research expenditures: $5,000. *Unit head:* Dr. Berhony Mengisty, Graduate Program Director, 757-683-3961, Fax: 757-683-4886, E-mail: bmengist@odu.edu. *Application contact:* Megan S. Jones, Graduate Program Manager, 757-683-3961, Fax: 757-683-4886, E-mail: mmjones@odu.edu.

Portland State University, Graduate Studies, College of Urban and Public Affairs, Nohad A. Toulan School of Urban Studies and Planning, Program in Urban Studies, Portland, OR 97207-0751. Offers MUS, PhD. *Faculty:* 18 full-time (4 women), 13 part-time/adjunct (6 women). *Students:* 38 full-time (22 women), 32 part-time (16 women); includes 7 minority (1 African American, 2 American Indian/Alaska Native, 1 Asian American or Pacific Islander, 3 Hispanic Americans), 8 international. Average age 38. 45 applicants, 67% accepted, 16 enrolled. In 2007, 2 master's, 3 doctorates awarded. *Degree requirements:* For doctorate, comprehensive exam, thesis/dissertation, residency. *Entrance requirements:* For master's, GRE General Test, minimum GPA of 2.75, 3 letters of recommendation; for doctorate, GRE General Test, minimum GPA of 2.75. Additional exam requirements/recommendations for international students: Required—TOEFL (minimum score 550 paper-based; 213 computer-based). *Application deadline:* For fall admission, 1/15 for domestic and international students; for winter admission, 9/1 for domestic and international students. Application fee: $50. *Expenses:* Tuition, state resident: full-time $7,047. Tuition, nonresident: full-time $11,178. *Financial support:* In 2007–08, research assistantships (averaging $8,572 per year). Financial award application deadline:3/1. Total annual research expenditures: $1.3 million. *Application contact:* Tracy Braden, Office Coordinator, 503-725-4015, Fax: 503-725-8770, E-mail: tbraden@pdx.edu.

Queens College of the City University of New York, Division of Graduate Studies, Social Science Division, Department of Urban Studies, Flushing, NY 11367-1597. Offers MA. Part-time and evening/weekend programs available. *Faculty:* 12 full-time (4 women). *Students:* 3 full-time (2 women), 127 part-time (91 women). 132 applicants, 94% accepted, 100 enrolled. In 2007, 98 degrees awarded. *Degree requirements:* For master's, thesis. *Entrance requirements:* For master's, minimum GPA of 3.0. Additional exam requirements/recommendations for international students: Required—TOEFL. *Application deadline:* For fall admission, 4/1 for domestic students; for spring admission, 11/1 for domestic students. Applications are processed on a rolling basis. Application fee: $125. *Financial support:* Career-related internships or fieldwork, Federal Work-Study, institutionally sponsored loans, and tuition waivers (partial) available. Support available to part-time students. Financial award application deadline: 4/1; financial award applicants required to submit FAFSA. *Faculty research:* Housing abandonment, industrial rehabilitation of Long Island City, health facilities in Queens County. *Unit head:* Dr. Leonard S. Rodberg, Chairperson, 718-997-5130. *Application contact:* Dr. William Muraskin, Graduate Adviser, 718-997-5130, E-mail: william_muraskin@qc.edu.

Rutgers, The State University of New Jersey, Newark, Graduate School, Program in Public Administration, Newark, NJ 07102. Offers health care administration (MPA); human resources administration (MPA); public administration (PhD); public management (MPA); public policy analysis (MPA); urban systems and issues (MPA). *Accreditation:* NASPAA (one or more programs are accredited). Part-time and evening/weekend programs available. *Degree requirements:* For master's, comprehensive exam, thesis or alternative; for doctorate, thesis/dissertation. *Entrance requirements:* For master's, GRE, minimum undergraduate B average; for doctorate, GRE, MPA, minimum B average. Electronic applications accepted. *Faculty research:* Government finance, municipal and state government, public productivity.

Rutgers, The State University of New Jersey, Newark, Graduate School, Program in Urban Systems, Newark, NJ 07102. Offers PhD.

Saint Louis University, Graduate School, College of Education and Public Service and Graduate School, Department of Public Policy Studies, St. Louis, MO 63103-2097. Offers geographic information systems (Certificate); organizational development (Certificate); public administration (MAPA); public policy analysis (PhD); urban affairs (MAUA); urban planning and real estate development (MUPRED). *Accreditation:* NASPAA. Part-time programs available. *Faculty:* 8 full-time (2 women), 1 part-time/adjunct (0 women). *Students:* 55 full-time (18 women), 57 part-time (27 women); includes 20 minority (15 African Americans, 1 Asian American or Pacific Islander, 4 Hispanic Americans), 7 international. Average age 34. 79 applicants, 76% accepted, 34 enrolled. In 2007, 11 master's, 1 doctorate awarded. *Degree requirements:* For master's, comprehensive exam (for some programs), thesis (for some programs); for doctorate, comprehensive exam, thesis/dissertation, preliminary exams. *Entrance requirements:* For master's and doctorate, GMAT, GRE General Test, or LSAT, letters of recommendation, resumé, interview, transcripts, goal statement. Additional exam requirements/recommendations for international students: Required—TOEFL (minimum score 525 paper-based; 194 computer-based). *Application deadline:* For fall admission, 7/1 for domestic and international students; for spring admission, 11/1 for domestic and international students. Applications are processed on a rolling basis. Application fee: $40. Electronic applications accepted. *Expenses:* Tuition: Part-time $845 per credit hour. Required fees: $105 per semester. *Financial support:* In 2007–08, 36 students received support, including 8 teaching assistantships with full tuition reimbursements available (averaging $12,000 per year); Federal Work-Study, scholarships/grants, traineeships, health care benefits, tuition waivers (partial), and unspecified assistantships also available. Support available to part-time students. Financial award application deadline: 2/1; financial award applicants required to submit FAFSA. *Faculty research:* Urban politics, brown fields, e-government, and administration, evaluation research, community development, electronic government and governance. Total annual research expenditures: $100,000. *Unit head:* Dr. Robert A. Cropf, Chairperson, 314-977-3936, Fax: 314-977-3943, E-mail: cropfra@slu.edu. *Application contact:* Gary U. Behrman, Associate Dean of Graduate School Admissions, 314-977-3827, Fax: 314-977-3943, E-mail: behrmang@slu.edu.

San Francisco Art Institute, Graduate Program, Department of Urban Studies, San Francisco, CA 94133. Offers MA. *Entrance requirements:* Additional exam requirements/recommendations for international students: Required—TOEFL (minimum score 580 paper-based; 237 computer-based). Electronic applications accepted.

Savannah State University, Program in Urban Studies, Savannah, GA 31404. Offers MS. Part-time programs available. *Faculty:* 1 (woman) full-time, 5 part-time/adjunct (0 women). *Students:* 4 full-time (1 woman), 1 part-time; includes 3 minority (all African Americans) Average age 33. In 2007, 7 degrees awarded. *Degree requirements:* For master's, thesis optional, internship. *Entrance requirements:* For master's, GRE. *Application deadline:* For fall admission, 7/1 priority date for domestic students; for spring admission, 4/1 priority date for domestic students. Applications are processed on a rolling basis. Application fee: $20. *Expenses:* Tuition, state resident: full-time $3,228; part-time $179 per hour. Tuition, nonresident: full-time $12,904. Required fees: $618. *Financial support:* In 2007–08, 5 students received support, including 1 fellowship (averaging $1,000 per year), 2 research assistantships (averaging $2,000 per year); career-related internships or fieldwork, Federal Work-Study, institutionally sponsored loans, and scholarships/grants also available. Support available to part-time students. Financial award applicants required to submit FAFSA. *Faculty research:* Transportation, political effectiveness, labor, sociology, criminal justice, waste management. *Unit head:* Larry Stokes, Chair, 912-353-5265, E-mail: stokesl@savstate.edu.

Simon Fraser University, Graduate Studies, Faculty of Arts and Social Sciences, Urban Studies Program, Burnaby, BC V5A 1S6, Canada. Offers MUS, Graduate Diploma. *Degree requirements:* For master's, project.

Southern Connecticut State University, School of Graduate Studies, School of Arts and Sciences, Program in Urban Studies, New Haven, CT 06515-1355. Offers MS, MSW/MS. Part-time and evening/weekend programs available. *Students:* 8 full-time (7 women), 19 part-time (10 women); includes 14 minority (10 African Americans, 4 Hispanic Americans). 21 applicants, 57% accepted, 12 enrolled. In 2007, 9 degrees awarded. *Degree requirements:* For master's, thesis or alternative. *Entrance requirements:* For master's, interview, minimum QPA of 2.5. *Application deadline:* For fall admission, 7/15 priority date for domestic students. Applications are processed on a rolling basis. Application fee: $50. Electronic applications accepted. *Financial support:* Career-related internships or fieldwork available. Financial award application deadline: 4/15; financial award applicants required to submit FAFSA. *Unit head:* Dr. Peter Sakalowsky, Director, 203-392-5832, E-mail: sakalowskyp1@southernct.edu.

Temple University, Graduate School, College of Liberal Arts, Department of Geography and Urban Studies, Philadelphia, PA 19122-6096. Offers geography (MA); urban studies (MA). *Degree requirements:* For master's, comprehensive exam, thesis or alternative. *Entrance requirements:* For master's, GRE General Test, minimum GPA of 3.0. Additional exam requirements/recommendations for international students: Required—TOEFL (minimum score 550 paper-based; 213 computer-based; 79 iBT). Electronic applications accepted. *Faculty research:* Environmental issues, urban political economy, poverty and unemployment, neighborhood development, African and Asian urbanization, housing, computer cartography.

Tufts University, Graduate School of Arts and Sciences, Department of Urban and Environmental Policy and Planning, Medford, MA 02155. Offers community development (MA); environmental policy (MA); health and human welfare (MA); housing policy (MA); international environment/development policy (MA); public policy (MPP); public policy and citizen participation (MA); MA/MS; MALD/MA. *Accreditation:* ACSP (one or more programs are accredited). Part-time programs available. *Faculty:* 8 full-time, 9 part-time/adjunct. *Students:* 135 (93 women); includes 23 minority (9 African Americans, 5 Asian Americans or Pacific Islanders, 9 Hispanic Americans) 9 international. 174 applicants, 82% accepted, 55 enrolled. In 2007, 32 degrees awarded. *Degree requirements:* For master's, thesis, internship. *Entrance requirements:* For master's, GRE General Test. Additional exam requirements/recommendations for international students: Required—TOEFL (minimum score 550 paper-based; 213 computer-based; 80 iBT). *Application deadline:* For fall admission, 1/15 for domestic students, 12/30 for international students. Applications are processed on a rolling basis. Application fee: $70. Electronic applications accepted. *Expenses: Contact institution. Financial support:* Teaching assistantships with full and partial tuition reimbursements, career-related internships or fieldwork, Federal Work-Study, scholarships/grants, and tuition waivers (partial) available. Support available to part-time students. Financial award application deadline: 1/15; financial award applicants required to submit FAFSA. *Unit head:* Julian Agyeman, Chair, 617-627-3394, Fax: 617-627-3377.

See Close-Up on page 1625.

Université du Québec à Montréal, Graduate Programs, Program in Urban Analysis and Management, Montréal, QC H3C 3P8, Canada. Offers MA. Part-time programs available. *Entrance requirements:* For master's, appropriate bachelor's degree or equivalent and proficiency in French.

Université du Québec à Montréal, Graduate Programs, Program in Urban Studies, Montréal, QC H3C 3P8, Canada. Offers PhD. Part-time programs available. *Degree requirements:* For doctorate, thesis/dissertation. *Entrance requirements:* For doctorate, appropriate master's degree or equivalent, proficiency in French.

Université du Québec, École nationale d'administration publique, Graduate Program in Public Administration, Program in Urban Analysis and Management, Quebec, QC G1K 9E5, Canada. Offers MAGU. Part-time programs available. *Entrance requirements:* For master's, appropriate bachelor's degree, proficiency in French.

Université du Québec, Institut National de la Recherche Scientifique, Graduate Programs, Research Center—Urbanization, Culture and Society, Québec, QC G1K 9A9, Canada. Offers demography (M Sc, PhD); research and public action (M Sc); urban studies (M Sc, PhD). Programs given in French. Part-time programs available. *Faculty:* 36. *Students:* 73 full-time (41 women), 15 part-time (9 women), 8 international. Average age 34. In 2007, 8 master's, 5 doctorates awarded. *Median time to degree:* Of those who began their doctoral program in fall 1999, 50% received their degree in 8 years or less. *Degree requirements:* For master's, thesis optional; for doctorate, thesis/dissertation. *Entrance requirements:* For master's, appropriate bachelor's degree, proficiency in French; for doctorate, appropriate master's degree, proficiency in French. *Application deadline:* For fall admission, 3/30 for domestic and international students; for winter admission, 11/1 for domestic and international students. Application fee: $30. *Financial support:* Fellowships, research assistantships, teaching assistantships available. *Faculty research:* Regional space, urban and metropolitan space, micro-urban space. *Unit head:* Johanne Charbonneau, Director, 514-499-4001, Fax: 514-499-4065, E-mail: johanne.charbonneau@ucs.inrs.ca. *Application contact:* Yvonne Boisvert, Registrar, 418-654-3861, Fax: 418-654-3858, E-mail: registrariat@adm.inrs.ca.

University at Albany, State University of New York, College of Arts and Sciences, Department of Sociology, Albany, NY 12222-0001. Offers demography (Certificate); sociology (MA, PhD); urban policy (Certificate). *Students:* 49 full-time (34 women), 76 part-time (39 women). Average age 32. In 2007, 3 master's, 5 doctorates, 4 other advanced degrees awarded. Terminal master's awarded for partial completion of doctoral program. *Degree requirements:* For master's, thesis; for doctorate, thesis/dissertation, 2 specialization exams, research tool. *Entrance requirements:* For master's and doctorate, GRE General Test. Additional exam requirements/recommendations for international students: Required—TOEFL (minimum score 213 computer-based). *Application deadline:* For fall admission, 1/15 for domestic students, 5/1 for international students. Applications are processed on a rolling basis. Application fee: $75. Electronic applications accepted. *Expenses:* Tuition, state resident: part-time $576 per credit. Tuition, nonresident: part-time $910 per credit. Tuition and fees vary according to program. *Financial support:* Fellowships, research assistantships, teaching assistantships, career-related internships or fieldwork and Federal Work-Study available. Financial award application deadline: 3/15. *Faculty research:* Gender and equality, crime and deviance, aging, work and organizations, social demography. *Unit head:* Dr. Donlad Hernandez, Chair, 518-442-4666. *Application contact:* Glen D. Dean, Graduate Committee Chair, 518-442-4587.

The University of Akron, Graduate School, Buchtel College of Arts and Sciences, Department of Public Administration and Urban Studies, Program in Urban Studies, Akron, OH 44325. Offers urban studies (MA); urban studies and public affairs (PhD). *Students:* 23 full-time (10 women), 28 part-time (17 women); includes 17 minority (16 African Americans, 1 Hispanic American), 11 international. Average age 36. 13 applicants, 85% accepted, 7 enrolled. In 2007, 5 master's, 7 doctorates awarded. *Degree requirements:* For master's, thesis optional; for doctorate, one foreign language, comprehensive exam, thesis/dissertation. *Entrance requirements:* For master's, GRE, GMAT, LSAT, MAT or minimum GPA of 3.0, minimum GPA of 2.8, resumé, personal essay, letters of recommendation; for doctorate, GRE General Test, writing sample, minimum graduate GPA of 3.5, letters of recommendation, personal statement. Additional exam requirements/recommendations for international students: Required—TOEFL (minimum score 550 paper-based; 213 computer-based; 79 iBT). *Application deadline:* Applications are processed on a rolling basis. Application fee: $30 ($40 for international students). Electronic applications accepted. *Expenses:* Tuition, state resident: full-time $6,164; part-time $342 per credit. Tuition, nonresident: full-time $10,575; part-time $588 per credit. Required fees: $806; $43 per credit. $12 per term. Tuition and fees vary according to course load, degree level and program. *Unit head:* Dr. Lucinda Deason, Coordinator, Master's Program, 330-972-7482, E-mail: deason@uakron.edu.

University of California, Irvine, Office of Graduate Studies, School of Social Ecology, Department of Planning, Policy and Design, Irvine, CA 92697. Offers planning, policy and design (PhD); urban and regional planning (MURP). *Accreditation:* ACSP (one or more programs are accredited). *Faculty:* 19 full-time (6 women), 10 part-time/adjunct (3 women). *Students:* 103 full-time (62 women), 1 (woman) part-time; includes 34 minority (4 African Americans, 2 American Indian/Alaska Native, 15 Asian Americans or Pacific Islanders, 13 Hispanic Americans), 11 international. 134 applicants, 48% accepted, 27 enrolled. In 2007, 29 master's, 6 doctorates awarded. *Degree requirements:* For doctorate, thesis/dissertation, research project. *Entrance requirements:* For master's and doctorate, GRE General Test, minimum GPA of 3.0. Additional exam requirements/recommendations for international students: Required—TOEFL (minimum score 550 paper-based; 213 computer-based). *Application deadline:* For fall admission, 1/15 priority date for domestic and international students. Application fee: $60. Electronic applications accepted. *Financial support:* Fellowships with tuition reimbursements, research assistantships with full tuition reimbursements, teaching assistantships with tuition reimbursements, institutionally sponsored loans, traineeships, health care benefits, and unspecified assistantships available. Financial award application deadline: 1/15; financial award applicants required to submit FAFSA. *Faculty research:* Community and social policy, economic development, land-use and growth management, transportation planning, environmental policy. Total annual research expenditures: $1.5 million. *Unit head:* Marlon G. Boarnet, Chair, 949-824-7695, E-mail: mgboarne@uci.edu. *Application contact:* Janet Gallagher, Academic Coordinator, 949-824-9849, Fax: 949-824-8566, E-mail: ppd@uci.edu.

University of Central Oklahoma, College of Graduate Studies and Research, College of Liberal Arts, Department of Political Science, Program in Urban Affairs, Edmond, OK 73034-5209. Offers MA. Part-time programs available. *Faculty:* 6 full-time (1 woman), 1 part-time/adjunct (0 women). *Students:* 1 full-time (0 women). Average age 25. 4 applicants, 100% accepted. *Entrance requirements:* Additional exam requirements/recommendations for international students: Required—TOEFL (minimum score 550 paper-based; 213 computer-based). *Application deadline:* For fall admission, 7/1 for international students; for spring admission, 11/1 for international students. Applications are processed on a rolling basis. Application fee: $25. Electronic applications accepted. *Expenses:* Tuition, state resident: full-time $3,516; part-time $147 per hour. Tuition, nonresident: full-time $9,054; part-time $377 per hour. Required fees: $433; $18 per hour. *Financial support:* Unspecified assistantships available. Financial award application deadline: 3/31; financial award applicants required to submit FAFSA. *Unit head:* Dr. Jan Hardt, Adviser, 405-974-5840, E-mail: jhardt@aix1.ucok.edu.

University of Delaware, College of Human Services, Education and Public Policy, Center for Energy and Environmental Policy, Program in Urban Affairs and Public Policy, Newark, DE 19716. Offers community development and nonprofit leadership (MA); energy and environmental policy (MA); governance, planning and management (PhD); historic preservation (MA); social and urban policy (PhD); technology, environment and society (PhD). Part-time programs available. Terminal master's awarded for partial completion of doctoral program. *Degree requirements:* For master's, analytical paper or thesis; for doctorate, thesis/dissertation. *Entrance requirements:* For master's, GRE General Test, minimum GPA of 3.0; for doctorate, GRE General Test, minimum GPA of 3.5. Additional exam requirements/recommendations for international students: Required—TOEFL. *Application deadline:* Applications are processed on a rolling basis. Application fee: $60. Electronic applications accepted. *Financial support:* Career-related internships or fieldwork, Federal Work-Study, and tuition waivers (full) available. *Faculty research:* Political economy; social policy analysis; technology and society; historic preservation; urban policy. Total annual research expenditures: $1 million.

See Close-Up on page 1635.

University of Lethbridge, School of Graduate Studies, Lethbridge, AB T1K 3M4, Canada. Offers accounting (MScM); addictions counseling (M Sc); agricultural biotechnology (M Sc); agricultural studies (M Sc, MA); anthropology (MA); archaeology (MA); art (MA); biochemistry (M Sc); biological sciences (M Sc); biomolecular science (PhD); biosystems and biodiversity (PhD); Canadian studies (MA); chemistry (M Sc); computer science (M Sc); computer science and geographical information science (M Sc); counseling psychology (M Ed); dramatic arts (MA); earth, space, and physical science (PhD); economics (MA); educational leadership (M Ed); English (MA); environmental science (M Sc); evolution and behavior (PhD); exercise science (M Sc); finance (MScM); French (MA); French/German (MA); French/Spanish (MA); general education (M Ed); general management (MScM); geography (M Sc, MA); German (MA); health sciences (M Sc, MA); history (MA); human resource management and labour relations (MScM); individualized multidisciplinary (M Sc, MA); information systems (MScM); international management (MScM); kinesiology (M Sc, MA); management (M Sc, MA); marketing (MScM); mathematics (M Sc); music (MA); Native American studies (MA); neuroscience (M Sc, PhD); new media (MA); nursing (M Sc); philosophy (MA); physics (M Sc); policy and strategy (MScM); political science (MA); psychology (M Sc, MA); religious studies (MA); sociology (MA); theoretical and computational science (PhD); urban and regional studies (MA). Part-time and evening/weekend programs available. *Students:* 215 full-time, 98 part-time. In 2007, 87 master's, 1 doctorate awarded. *Degree requirements:* For doctorate, comprehensive exam, thesis/dissertation. *Entrance requirements:* For master's, GMAT (M Sc in management), bachelor's degree in related field, minimum GPA of 3.0 during previous 20 graded semester courses, 2 years teaching or related experience (M Ed); for doctorate, master's degree, minimum graduate GPA of 3.5. Additional exam requirements/recommendations for international students: Required—TOEFL. Application fee: $60 Canadian dollars. *Financial support:* Fellowships, research assistantships, teaching assistantships, scholarships/grants, health care benefits, and unspecified assistantships available. *Faculty research:* Movement and brain plasticity, gibberellin physiology, photosynthesis, carbon cycling, molecular properties of main-group ring components. *Unit head:* Dr. Jo-Anne Fiske, Interim Dean, 403-329-2121, Fax: 403-329-2097. *Application contact:* Jennifer Geddes, Graduate Liaison Officer, 403-329-2762, Fax: 403-329-5159, E-mail: jennifer.geddes@uleth.ca.

University of Louisville, Graduate School, College of Arts and Sciences, Department of Urban and Public Affairs, Program in Urban and Public Affairs, Louisville, KY 40292-0001. Offers PhD. *Students:* 25 full-time (10 women), 2 part-time; includes 5 minority (all African Americans), 3 international. Average age 34. In 2007, 3 degrees awarded. *Degree requirements:* For doctorate, thesis/dissertation. *Entrance requirements:* For doctorate, GRE General Test, master's degree in appropriate field. *Application deadline:* Applications are processed on a

Urban Studies

University of Louisville (continued)
rolling basis. Application fee: $50. *Unit head:* Dr. Ron K. Vogel, Director, 502-852-3312, Fax: 502-852-7923, E-mail: rkvogel01@gwise.louisville.edu.

University of New Orleans, Graduate School, College of Liberal Arts, School of Urban Planning and Regional Studies, Program in Urban Studies, New Orleans, LA 70148. Offers MS, PhD. *Students:* 51 (29 women). Average age 37. In 2007, 6 master's, 3 doctorates awarded. *Degree requirements:* For master's, thesis; for doctorate, thesis/dissertation. *Entrance requirements:* For master's, GRE General Test. Additional exam requirements/recommendations for international students: Required—TOEFL (minimum score 550 paper-based; 213 computer-based; 79 iBT). *Application deadline:* For fall admission, 7/1 priority date for domestic students, 6/1 for international students; for spring admission, 11/15 for domestic students, 10/1 for international students. Applications are processed on a rolling basis. Application fee: $40. Electronic applications accepted. *Financial support:* Application deadline: 5/15; *Faculty research:* Urban economic development, environmental planning and analysis, social and cultural change. *Unit head:* Dr. David Gladstone, Graduate Coordinator, 504-280-5473, Fax: 504-280-6272.

University of Wisconsin–Milwaukee, Graduate School, College of Letters and Sciences, Interdepartmental Program in Urban Studies, Milwaukee, WI 53201-0413. Offers MS, PhD, MLIS/MS. *Faculty:* 32 full-time (13 women). *Students:* 26 full-time (14 women), 29 part-time (17 women); includes 15 minority (9 African Americans, 1 American Indian/Alaska Native, 1 Asian American or Pacific Islander, 4 Hispanic Americans), 2 international. 27 applicants, 41% accepted, 5 enrolled. In 2007, 5 master's, 3 doctorates awarded. *Degree requirements:* For master's, thesis or alternative; for doctorate, thesis/dissertation. *Entrance requirements:* For doctorate, GRE General Test. *Application deadline:* For fall admission, 1/1 priority date for domestic students; for spring admission, 9/1 for domestic students. Applications are processed on a rolling basis. Application fee: $45 ($75 for international students). *Expenses:* Tuition, state resident: part-time $530 per credit. Tuition, nonresident: part-time $1,428 per credit. Required fees: $19 per credit. $229 per term. Tuition and fees vary according to course load and program. *Financial support:* In 2007–08, 3 teaching assistantships were awarded; fellowships, research assistantships, career-related internships or fieldwork and unspecified assistantships also available. Support available to part-time students. Financial award application deadline: 4/15. *Unit head:* Joseph Rodriguez, Representative, 414-229-4751, Fax: 414-229-4266, E-mail: joerod@uwm.edu.

Virginia Polytechnic Institute and State University, Graduate School, College of Architecture and Urban Studies, School of Public and International Affairs, Blacksburg, VA 24061. Offers environmental planning and policy (MURP); government and international affairs (MPIA); housing, community and economic development (MURP); international development planning (MURP); land use and physical planning (MURP); planning, governance and globalization (PhD), including environmental planning and landscape analysis, physical planning and urban design, public and international affairs, urban and environmental design and planning; urban and regional planning (MURP). *Accreditation:* ACSP. *Entrance requirements:* Additional exam requirements/recommendations for international students: Required—TOEFL (minimum score 550 paper-based; 213 computer-based). Electronic applications accepted. *Faculty research:* Design theory, environmental planning, town planning, transportation planning.

Wright State University, School of Graduate Studies, College of Liberal Arts, Department of Urban Affairs and Geography, Dayton, OH 45435. Offers public administration (MPA). *Accreditation:* NASPAA. *Degree requirements:* For master's, thesis optional. *Entrance requirements:* For master's, interview, minimum GPA of 2.7. Additional exam requirements/recommendations for international students: Required—TOEFL. *Faculty research:* Strategic planning, economic development, housing and public management.

Cross-Discipline Announcement

University of Delaware, College of Human Services, Education and Public Policy, Center for Energy and Environmental Policy, Newark, DE 19716.

CEEP and its 7-member faculty administer the Environmental and Energy Policy (ENEP) Program, offering a 36-credit master's degree (MEEP) and a PhD after 36 additional credits of course work. In addition, CEEP sponsors a 15-credit Energy, Environment and Equity Concentration, leading to an MA in Urban Affairs and Public Policy, and a 21-credit Technology, Environment and Society Concentration, leading to a PhD in UAPP. Research agreements between CEEP and research institutions in Europe, Asia, Africa, and Latin America enable students to conduct research in all of the major nations of the world. Visit www.ceep.udel.edu.

BRANDEIS UNIVERSITY

The Heller School for Social Policy and Management
Master of Public Policy Program

Programs of Study

The Heller School offers graduate degree programs designed explicitly to bridge the gap between theory and practice in a stimulating and supportive learning environment. The newest program is the Master of Public Policy (M.P.P.) in social policy, with concentrations in health; behavioral health; children, youth, and families; poverty alleviation and development; and aging policy. A joint M.A./M.P.P. with Jewish Professional Leadership is also offered. The M.P.P. program is designed to train a new generation of social policy experts to design social policies, draft effective legislation, understand how values shape policies, study finance mechanisms, and use social science techniques to evaluate the effectiveness, fairness, and impact of public policy. M.P.P. students enroll in the program for two traditional academic years. The program provides the skills necessary to design, implement, reform, analyze, and bring to scale innovative solutions to society's most critical problems.

Policy research is distinct from theoretical research in its application to specific problems in government, business, or nonprofit organizational settings. The M.P.P. core curriculum provides students with the broad range of tools that today's policy analyst needs in order to evaluate, create, and recommend policy options to solve complex social problems.

Heller M.P.P. graduates will be prepared for careers in government policy analysis at every public-sector level: federal, state, county, and municipal; policy research in consulting firms, think tanks, or policy offices in the nonprofit or private sector; implementation of policies in the public and private sector; business settings where policy has an impact on the industry; and advocacy on certain issues or lobbying for specific policies and legislation representing important stakeholder groups, from civil rights to business interests

Since its founding in 1959 as the University's first professional school, the Heller School for Social Policy and Management at Brandeis University has been committed to developing new knowledge and insights in the fields of social policy research and health and human services management. Faculty members and students actively engage in examining policies and programs that respond to the changing needs of vulnerable individuals and social groups in society. Heller has pioneered in the policy areas of domestic and international health; mental health; substance abuse; children, youth, and families; aging; international development; hunger and poverty; and work, inequality, and social change. The faculty represents many social science disciplines and includes both scholars and practitioners.

Research Facilities

Students benefit from association with an expert research staff in numerous policy centers conducting nationally and internationally significant projects in a wide range of areas. Some of these are described in the final section of this narrative. Heller's degree and course offerings reflect the work of the Schneider Institutes for Health Policy; the Institute on Assets and Social Policy; the Institute for Child, Youth and Family Policy; and the Center for International Development.

Financial Aid

The Heller School awards a number of generous partial tuition remission scholarships. Candidates for admission are expected to explore a variety of outside funding sources, such as private scholarships and government loan programs. Forms may be obtained from the Office of Admissions. Aid decisions are made on the combined basis of financial need and academic merit.

Cost of Study

For 2007–08, the full-time (two semesters) cost of study was $34,566. Part-time study was $3200 per course.

Living and Housing Costs

The minimum yearly cost of living is estimated at $12,000. Limited graduate housing is available on campus; rent for a one-bedroom apartment nearby ranges from $500 to $800 per month.

Student Group

The M.P.P. program enrolled 13 students in 2007–08. Most graduated from their undergraduate programs within the past five years and had some professional experience at entrance.

Location

Located in Waltham, Massachusetts, 16 miles west of Boston, Brandeis University is part of a metropolitan area that includes educational institutions, museums and galleries, theaters, cultural events, and other attractions of the city. Students are able to travel easily into Cambridge or Boston via either the commuter train or public bus, both of which stop within steps of the campus.

The University

Brandeis University is ranked in the top tier of the nation's universities. It is the youngest private research university in the country. The Heller School is committed to developing new knowledge and insights in the fields of social policy, sustainable development, and in health and human services management. As a research institution, Heller has pioneered in a variety of policy areas, including mental health, substance abuse, international and community development, developmental disabilities, and poverty and hunger.

Applying

Application forms and financial aid information can be obtained from the Office of Admissions. Students must submit a completed application, transcripts, recommendations, writing samples, resume, and GRE scores. The application fee is $55. M.P.P. applications are accepted continuously on a rolling admissions basis until the class is full. Although professional experience is desirable for M.P.P. candidates, admission is granted to applicants who show a clear, demonstrated career path. Prospective applicants are invited to attend information sessions held monthly between September and March.

Correspondence and Information

Office of Admissions
The Heller School for Social Policy and Management/MS 035
Brandeis University
Waltham, Massachusetts 02454-9110

Phone: 781-736-3820
Fax: 781-736-2774
E-mail: helleradmissions@brandeis.edu
Web site: http://heller.brandeis.edu

Brandeis University

THE FACULTY AND RESEARCH STAFF AND SELECTED POLICY CENTERS AND INSTITUTES

Faculty

Stuart H. Altman, Sol C. Chaiken Professor of National Health Policy and Dean; Ph.D., UCLA.
Brenda Anderson, Adjunct Lecturer; Ph.D., Massachusetts Amherst.
Jeffrey Ashe, Adjunct Professor; M.A., Boston University.
Lawrence Neil Bailis, Associate Professor; Ph.D., Harvard.
Sarita Bhalotra, Assistant Professor; Ph.D., Brandeis.
Christine E. Bishop, Professor and Director, Ph.D. Program; Ph.D., Harvard.
David Boyer, Adjunct Lecturer; M.S., Antioch New England.
Jon A. Chilingerian, Associate Professor; Ph.D., MIT.
Susan P. Curnan, Associate Professor; M.F.S., Yale.
Michael T. Doonan, Assistant Professor; Ph.D., Brandeis.
Stephen Fournier, Lecturer; Ph.D., MIT.
Barry L. Friedman, Professor; Ph.D., MIT.
Deborah Garnick, Professor; Sc.D., Johns Hopkins.
David G. Gil, Professor of Social Policy; D.S.W., Pennsylvania.
Jody Hoffer Gittell, Professor; Ph.D., MIT.
Ricardo A. Godoy, Professor; Ph.D., Columbia.
Maria Green, Assistant Professor; J.D., Harvard.
Jose Suaya Grezzi, Lecturer; Ph.D., Brandeis.
Andrew B. Hahn, Professor; Ph.D., Brandeis.
Anita Hill, Professor of Social Policy, Law, and Women's Studies; J.D., Yale.
Dominic Hodgkin, Assistant Professor; Ph.D., Boston University.
Susan Holcombe, Professor of the Practice; Ph.D., NYU.
Constance M. Horgan, Professor; Sc.D., Johns Hopkins.
Milton Obote Joshua, Adjunct Lecturer; M.A., Nairobi.
Sajed Kamal, Adjunct Lecturer; Ph.D., Boston University.
Attila O. Klein, Adjunct Lecturer; Ph.D., Indiana.
Lorraine Klerman, Professor; Dr.P.H., Harvard.
Marty Wyngaarden Krauss, Professor and Provost; Ph.D., Brandeis.
Ravi Lakshmikanthan, Lecturer; M.A., Brandeis.
Walter N. Leutz, Associate Professor; Ph.D., Brandeis.
Thomas McLaughlin, Adjunct Lecturer; M.B.A., Boston University.
Ellen Messer, Adjunct Lecturer; Ph.D., Michigan.
Phyllis H. Mutschler, Associate Professor; Ph.D., Brandeis.
A. K. Nandakumar, Associate Professor; Ph.D., Boston University.
Huong H. Nguyen, Assistant Professor; Ph.D., Michigan State.
Eric Olson, Adjunct Lecturer; Ph.D., Pennsylvania.
Jeffrey Prottas, Professor; Ph.D., MIT.
Jehan Raheem, Adjunct Professor; M.B.A., CUNY, Baruch.
Carol A. (Kelley) Ready, Adjunct Lecturer; Ph.D., CUNY Graduate Center.
Laura Roper, Adjunct Lecturer; Ph.D., Pennsylvania.
Leonard Saxe, Professor; Ph.D., Pittsburgh.
Ann Seidman, Adjunct Lecturer; Ph.D., Wisconsin.
Robert Seidman, Adjunct Professor; LL.M., Columbia.
Thomas Shapiro, Pokross Professor of Law and Social Policy; Ph.D., Washington (St. Louis).
Donald Shepard, Professor; Ph.D., Harvard.
Joseph Short, Adjunct Professor; Ph.D., Columbia.
Laurence Simon, Professor; Ph.D., Clark.
Christopher Tompkins, Associate Professor; Ph.D., Brandeis.
Stanley S. Wallack, Professor; Ph.D., Washington (St. Louis).
David Whalen, Adjunct Lecturer; M.B.A., Brandeis.

Professors Emeriti

Jim Callahan, Ph.D., Brandeis.
Janet Giele, Ph.D., Harvard.
Ken Jones, Ed.D., Harvard.
Norman R. Kurtz, Ph.D., Colorado.
Robert Perlman, Ph.D., Brandeis.
James H. Schulz, Ph.D., Yale.
Roland Warren, Ph.D., Heidelberg.
Constance Williams, Ph.D., Brandeis.

Research Staff

Janet Boguslaw, Senior Research Associate; Ph.D., Boston College.
Mary Brolin, Senior Research Associate; Ph.D., Brandeis.
Cathy Burack, Senior Research Associate; Ed.D., Harvard.
Garen Corbett, Senior Research Associate; M.S., Massachusetts.
Marilyn Daley, Senior Research Associate; Ph.D., Brandeis.
Joseph Frees, Senior Research Associate; Ph.D., Minnesota.
Deborah Gurewich, Senior Research Associate; Ph.D., Brandeis.
Della Hughes, Senior Research Associate; M.S.S.W., Tennessee; M.Div., Vanderbilt.
Joan Kaufman, Senior Scientist; Sc.D., Harvard.
Christopher Kingsley, Senior Program Associate; B.S., Clarkson.
Peter Kreiner, Scientist; Ph.D., USC.
Brad Krevor, Senior Research Associate; Ph.D., Boston University.
Susan Lanspery, Senior Research Associate; Ph.D., Brandeis.
A. James Lee, Senior Scientist; Ph.D., Wisconsin.
Margaret T. Lee, Scientist; Ph.D., Berkeley.
Tim Martin, Senior Research Associate; Ph.D., Brandeis.
Alan Melchior, Senior Research Associate; B.A., Brandeis.
Elizabeth Merrick, Scientist; Ph.D., Brandeis.
Sharon Reif, Scientist; Ph.D., Brandeis.
Grant Ritter, Senior Scientist and Lecturer; Ph.D., Cornell.
Amy Smalarz, Senior Research Associate; Ph.D., Brandeis.
William Stason, Senior Scientist; M.D., Harvard.
Cindy Thomas, Senior Scientist; Ph.D., Brandeis.
Elizabeth Tighe, Senior Research Associate; Ph.D., Brandeis.
Sandra Venner, Senior Program Associate; M.S.S.W., Wisconsin.
Marjorie Erickson Warfield, Scientist; Ph.D., Brandeis.

Selected Policy Centers and Institutes

Lurie Institute for Disability Policy: Through research, policy development, education, and public engagement, the Lurie Institute helps people with disabilities, particularly autism, successfully integrate into the mainstream of society. The University's ongoing scientific research into developmental disabilities, including autism, inform the Lurie Institute's activities, providing a comprehensive approach to addressing disability issues across the lifespan.

Sillerman Center for the Advancement of Philanthropy: As an academic center, the Sillerman Center is committed to expanding knowledge in philanthropy through education, research, and knowledge-based action and influencing social policies.

Schneider Institutes for Health Policy (SIHP): Established in 1978, SIHP conducts domestic and international research in the broad areas of financing, organization, value, high-cost and high-risk populations, and health technologies. SIHP is composed of its two prestigious affiliated institutes:

Institute for Behavioral Health (IBH): IBH focuses on the intersection of health, behavior, and systems of care, with an emphasis on the linkages among these areas. Its premise is that these systems can be better used to promote healthier lifestyles and to assist individuals to engage in behaviors that lead to better health.
Institute on Healthcare Systems (IHS): IHS examines health care from a systems perspective, focusing on how health-care organizations function and the relationship between these organizations, their health-care professionals, and their impact on the coordination of patient care. The affiliates of IHS are the **Council on Health Care Economics and Policy,** a council of independent, nonpartisan recognized experts in economics and health policy that conducts research and convenes top experts on key health policy research areas; the **Health Industry Forum,** a new initiative committed to engaging leaders across the health-care community in constructive dialogue and action through cutting-edge research on improving the quality and value of health care; and the **Massachusetts Health Policy Forum,** which brings public and private health-care leaders together to engage in focused discussions on critical health policy challenges facing the Commonwealth of Massachusetts.

Institute on Assets and Social Policy (IASP): IASP generates policy ideas that broaden wealth, reduce inequality, and improve the social and economic mobility of low-income American households by promoting asset building. Working in partnership with a wide range of organizations, the IASP bridges the worlds of academic research, government policy-making, and the interests of constituencies. IASP's two affiliates are the **Center on Hunger and Poverty,** which promotes policies that improve the lives of low-income children and families, and the **National Program on Women and Aging,** which focuses national attention on the special concerns of women as they age to develop solutions and strategies for dealing with these concerns and to reach out to women and organizations across the country, promoting the changes necessary to improve older women's lives.

Center for International Development (CID): CID is a research and training group working in partnership with development organizations and universities abroad and in the United States. Its faculty, researchers, and students are engaged in research that furthers knowledge about sustainable development and helps build local capacity to solve problems and plan sound development strategies.

Institute for Child, Youth and Family Policy(ICYFP): ICYFP brings together faculty, research staff, and students in activities that foster the well-being of children, adolescents, and their families. The institute has a wide-ranging portfolio of research and public engagement projects dealing with vulnerable or disenfranchised populations, reflecting the Heller School's dedication to the concept of knowledge advancing social justice. ICYFP has two affiliated centers.

Nathan and Toby Starr Center for Retardation: The Nathan and Toby Starr Center focuses its research on the impact on families of lifelong caregiving for a member with mental retardation, the effectiveness of early intervention services on children and families, health-care systems for children with special health-care needs, and organizational and policy issues in the expansion of community-based services for persons with disabilities.
Center for Youth and Communities (CYC): CYC has established a national reputation as one of the nation's leading research centers and professional development and policy organizations in youth and community development. The center's ultimate goal is to "make knowledge productive" by connecting the knowledge gained from scholarly research and practical experience in ways that help both policy-makers and practitioners.

BRANDEIS UNIVERSITY

The Heller School for Social Policy and Management

Programs of Study The Heller School offers five graduate degree programs designed explicitly to bridge the gap between theory and practice in a stimulating and supportive learning environment: a Ph.D. in social policy (with concentrations in health and behavioral health; children, youth and families; and assets and inequalities); Master of Public Policy (M.P.P.) in social policy (with concentrations in health; behavioral health; children, youth, and families; poverty alleviation and development; and aging policy and a joint M.A./M.P.P. with Jewish Professional Leadership); a Master of Business Administration (M.B.A.) in Nonprofit Management (with concentrations in social policy; health-care policy; children, youth and family policy; aging policy; and sustainable development and a joint M.A./M.B.A. with Jewish Professional Leadership); a Master of Arts (M.A.) in sustainable international development (SID); and Master of Science (M.S.) in international health policy and management (IHPM).

Since its founding in 1959 as the University's first professional school, the Heller School for Social Policy and Management at Brandeis University has been committed to developing new knowledge and insights in the fields of social policy research and health and human services management. Faculty members and students actively engage in examining policies and programs that respond to the changing needs of vulnerable individuals and social groups in society. Heller has pioneered in the policy areas of domestic and international health; mental health; substance abuse; children, youth, and families; aging; international development; hunger and poverty; and work, inequality, and social change. The faculty represents many social science disciplines and includes both scholars and practitioners.

The Ph.D. program educates students for careers in research, teaching, social planning, administration, and policy analysis. The course of study is interdisciplinary, based on economics, sociology, and political science. Courses in social welfare, policy analysis, and research methods combine with those in substantive areas of interest for an integrated approach to social policy. Students must complete fifteen courses and a comprehensive paper in the social sciences as well as successfully defend, both orally and in writing, a policy research dissertation.

The M.P.P. program is designed to train a new generation of social policy experts to design social policies, draft effective legislation, understand how values shape policies, study finance mechanisms, and use social science techniques to evaluate the effectiveness, fairness, and impact of public policy. M.P.P. students enroll in the program for two traditional academic years. The program provides the skills necessary to design, implement, reform, analyze, and bring to scale innovative solutions to society's most critical problems.

The M.B.A. in Nonprofit Management program trains leaders who manage a wide range of health and human services organizations. The curriculum uniquely combines social policy with cutting-edge management education, cross-training students not only to identify the issues and needs of disadvantaged groups but to address those needs through effective and efficient program design and management within the complex and changing environment of health and human services. A team consulting project component allows students to apply management and analytical skills in a real-life context. The full-time, accelerated program takes sixteen months, beginning in the fall semester and finishing four consecutive semesters later (August through December of the following year). This represents a considerable advantage in cost and time over equivalent two-year programs. Part-time study is also available for the M.B.A. program; students finish in two to five years.

The M.A./SID and M.S./IHPM programs are designed for students pursuing careers, whether domestic or international, in government and nongovernment organizations that seek to alleviate the disparities that exist in society. Both degrees have strong management and policy tracks. The M.A. degree is a two-year program, one year of academics and one year in an internship. The M.S. degree is a one-academic-year program.

Research Facilities Students benefit from association with an expert research staff in numerous policy centers conducting nationally and internationally significant projects in a wide range of areas. Some of these are described in the final section of this narrative. Heller's degree and course offerings reflect the work of the Schneider Institutes for Health Policy; the Institute on Assets and Social Policy; the Institute for Child, Youth and Family Policy; and the Center for International Development. Ph.D. students often secure research assistantships in the centers.

Financial Aid The Heller School makes every effort to provide tuition and stipend support to most full-time Ph.D. students, who typically receive support through training grants and university and donor funds for their first two years of doctoral study. The School has a number of federally and privately sponsored grants in the fields of health, substance abuse, and children and families that provide tuition fellowships and/or monthly stipends for eligible students.

The program also awards a number of generous partial tuition remission scholarships. Candidates for admission are expected to explore a variety of outside funding sources, such as private scholarships and government loan programs. Forms may be obtained from the Office of Admissions. Aid decisions are made on the combined basis of financial need and academic merit.

Cost of Study For 2007–08, the full-time (two semesters) cost of study was $34,566. Part-time study was $3200 per course.

Living and Housing Costs The minimum yearly cost of living is estimated at $12,000. Limited graduate housing is available on campus; rent for a one-bedroom apartment nearby ranges from $500 to $800 per month.

Student Group The Ph.D. program enrolls about 12 to 15 new students each year, who complete residency in two to three years. Most Ph.D. students hold master's degrees at entrance. The M.P.P. and M.B.A. programs enroll about 40 to 50 students per year.

Location Located in Waltham, Massachusetts, 16 miles west of Boston, Brandeis University is part of a metropolitan area that includes educational institutions, museums and galleries, theaters, cultural events, and other attractions of the city. Students are able to travel easily into Cambridge or Boston via either the commuter train or public bus, both of which stop within steps of the campus.

The University Brandeis University is ranked in the top tier of the nation's universities. It is the youngest private research university in the country. The Heller School is committed to developing new knowledge and insights in the fields of social policy, sustainable development, and in health and human services management. As a research institution, Heller has pioneered in a variety of policy areas, including mental health, substance abuse, international and community development, developmental disabilities, and poverty and hunger.

Applying Application forms and financial aid information can be obtained from the Office of Admissions. Students must submit a completed application, transcripts, recommendations, writing samples, resume, and test scores (GMAT for M.B.A. students and GRE for Ph.D. and M.P.P. students). The application fee is $55. Ph.D. applicants must submit their materials by January 2 to start in September. M.B.A. and M.P.P. applications are accepted continuously on a rolling admissions basis until the class is full. M.B.A. students must have an undergraduate degree and two or more years of work experience, although some applicants who have an excellent academic record and evidence of leadership potential are accepted directly out of undergraduate programs. Although experience is desirable for M.P.P. candidates, admission is granted to applicants who show a clear, demonstrated career path. Prospective applicants are invited to attend information sessions held monthly between September and March.

Correspondence and Information

Office of Admissions
The Heller School for Social Policy and Management/MS 035
Brandeis University
Waltham, Massachusetts 02454-9110

Phone: 781-736-3820
Fax: 781-736-2774
E-mail: helleradmissions@brandeis.edu
Web site: http://heller.brandeis.edu

Brandeis University

THE FACULTY AND RESEARCH STAFF AND SELECTED POLICY CENTERS AND INSTITUTES

Faculty

Stuart H. Altman, Sol C. Chaiken Professor of National Health Policy and Dean; Ph.D., UCLA.
Brenda Anderson, Adjunct Lecturer; Ph.D., Massachusetts Amherst.
Jeffrey Ashe, Adjunct Professor; M.A., Boston University.
Lawrence Neil Bailis, Associate Professor; Ph.D., Harvard.
Sarita Bhalotra, Assistant Professor; Ph.D., Brandeis.
Christine E. Bishop, Professor and Director, Ph.D. Program; Ph.D., Harvard.
David Boyer, Adjunct Lecturer; M.S., Antioch New England.
Jon A. Chilingerian, Associate Professor; Ph.D., MIT.
Susan P. Curnan, Associate Professor; M.F.S., Yale.
Michael T. Doonan, Assistant Professor; Ph.D., Brandeis.
Stephen Fournier, Lecturer; Ph.D., MIT.
Barry L. Friedman, Professor; Ph.D., MIT.
Deborah Garnick, Professor; Sc.D., Johns Hopkins.
David G. Gil, Professor of Social Policy; D.S.W., Pennsylvania.
Jody Hoffer Gittell, Professor; Ph.D., MIT.
Ricardo A. Godoy, Professor; Ph.D., Columbia.
Maria Green, Assistant Professor; J.D., Harvard.
Jose Suaya Grezzi, Lecturer; Ph.D., Brandeis.
Andrew B. Hahn, Professor; Ph.D., Brandeis.
Anita Hill, Professor of Social Policy, Law, and Women's Studies; J.D., Yale.
Dominic Hodgkin, Assistant Professor; Ph.D., Boston University.
Susan Holcombe, Professor of the Practice; Ph.D., NYU.
Constance M. Horgan, Professor; Sc.D., Johns Hopkins.
Milton Obote Joshua, Adjunct Lecturer; M.A., Nairobi.
Sajed Kamal, Adjunct Lecturer; Ph.D., Boston University.
Attila O. Klein, Adjunct Lecturer; Ph.D., Indiana.
Lorraine Klerman, Professor; Dr.P.H., Harvard.
Marty Wyngaarden Krauss, Professor and Provost; Ph.D., Brandeis.
Ravi Lakshmikanthan, Lecturer; M.A., Brandeis.
Walter N. Leutz, Associate Professor; Ph.D., Brandeis.
Thomas McLaughlin, Adjunct Lecturer; M.B.A., Boston University.
Ellen Messer, Adjunct Lecturer; Ph.D., Michigan.
Phyllis H. Mutschler, Associate Professor; Ph.D., Brandeis.
A. K. Nandakumar, Associate Professor; Ph.D., Boston University.
Huong H. Nguyen, Assistant Professor; Ph.D., Michigan State.
Eric Olson, Adjunct Lecturer; Ph.D., Pennsylvania.
Jeffrey Prottas, Professor; Ph.D., MIT.
Jehan Raheem, Adjunct Professor; M.B.A., CUNY, Baruch.
Carol A. (Kelley) Ready, Adjunct Lecturer; Ph.D., CUNY Graduate Center.
Laura Roper, Adjunct Lecturer; Ph.D., Pennsylvania.
Leonard Saxe, Professor; Ph.D., Pittsburgh.
Ann Seidman, Adjunct Lecturer; Ph.D., Wisconsin.
Robert Seidman, Adjunct Professor; LL.M., Columbia.
Thomas Shapiro, Pokross Professor of Law and Social Policy; Ph.D., Washington (St. Louis).
Donald Shepard, Professor; Ph.D., Harvard.
Joseph Short, Adjunct Professor; Ph.D., Columbia.
Laurence Simon, Professor; Ph.D., Clark.
Christopher Tompkins, Associate Professor; Ph.D., Brandeis.
Stanley S. Wallack, Professor; Ph.D., Washington (St. Louis).
David Whalen, Adjunct Lecturer; M.B.A., Brandeis.

Professors Emeriti

Jim Callahan, Ph.D., Brandeis.
Janet Giele, Ph.D., Harvard.
Ken Jones, Ed.D., Harvard.
Norman R. Kurtz, Ph.D., Colorado.
Robert Perlman, Ph.D., Brandeis.
James H. Schulz, Ph.D., Yale.
Roland Warren, Ph.D., Heidelberg.
Constance Williams, Ph.D., Brandeis.

Research Staff

Janet Boguslaw, Senior Research Associate; Ph.D., Boston College.
Mary Brolin, Senior Research Associate; Ph.D., Brandeis.
Cathy Burack, Senior Research Associate; Ed.D., Harvard.
Garen Corbett, Senior Research Associate; M.S., Massachusetts.
Marilyn Daley, Senior Research Associate; Ph.D., Brandeis.
Joseph Frees, Senior Research Associate; Ph.D., Minnesota.
Deborah Gurewich, Senior Research Associate; Ph.D., Brandeis.
Della Hughes, Senior Research Associate; M.S.S.W., Tennessee; M.Div., Vanderbilt.
Joan Kaufman, Senior Scientist; Sc.D., Harvard.
Christopher Kingsley, Senior Program Associate; B.S., Clarkson.
Peter Kreiner, Scientist; Ph.D., USC.
Brad Krevor, Senior Research Associate; Ph.D., Boston University.
Susan Lanspery, Senior Research Associate; Ph.D., Brandeis.
A. James Lee, Senior Scientist; Ph.D., Wisconsin.
Margaret T. Lee, Scientist; Ph.D., Berkeley.
Tim Martin, Senior Research Associate; Ph.D., Brandeis.
Alan Melchior, Senior Research Associate; B.A., Brandeis.
Elizabeth Merrick, Scientist; Ph.D., Brandeis.
Sharon Reif, Scientist; Ph.D., Brandeis.
Grant Ritter, Senior Scientist and Lecturer; Ph.D., Cornell.
Amy Smalarz, Senior Research Associate; Ph.D., Brandeis.
William Stason, Senior Scientist; M.D., Harvard.
Cindy Thomas, Senior Scientist; Ph.D., Brandeis.
Elizabeth Tighe, Senior Research Associate; Ph.D., Brandeis.
Sandra Venner, Senior Program Associate; M.S.S.W., Wisconsin.
Marjorie Erickson Warfield, Scientist; Ph.D., Brandeis.

Selected Policy Centers and Institutes

Lurie Institute for Disability Policy: Through research, policy development, education, and public engagement, the Lurie Institute helps people with disabilities, particularly autism, successfully integrate into the mainstream of society. The University's ongoing scientific research into developmental disabilities, including autism, inform the Lurie Institute's activities, providing a comprehensive approach to addressing disability issues across the lifespan.

Sillerman Center for the Advancement of Philanthropy: As an academic center, the Sillerman Center is committed to expanding knowledge in philanthropy through education, research, and knowledge-based action and influencing social policies.

Schneider Institutes for Health Policy (SIHP): Established in 1978, SIHP conducts domestic and international research in the broad areas of financing, organization, value, high-cost and high-risk populations, and health technologies. SIHP is composed of its two prestigious affiliated institutes:

Institute for Behavioral Health (IBH): IBH focuses on the intersection of health, behavior, and systems of care, with an emphasis on the linkages among these areas. Its premise is that these systems can be better used to promote healthier lifestyles and to assist individuals to engage in behaviors that lead to better health.
Institute on Healthcare Systems (IHS): IHS examines health care from a systems perspective, focusing on how health-care organizations function and the relationship between these organizations, their health-care professionals, and their impact on the coordination of patient care. The affiliates of IHS are the **Council on Health Care Economics and Policy,** a council of independent, nonpartisan recognized experts in economics and health policy that conducts research and convenes top experts on key health policy research areas; the **Health Industry Forum,** a new initiative committed to engaging leaders across the health-care community in constructive dialogue and action through cutting-edge research on improving the quality and value of health care; and the **Massachusetts Health Policy Forum,** which brings public and private health-care leaders together to engage in focused discussions on critical health policy challenges facing the Commonwealth of Massachusetts.

Institute on Assets and Social Policy (IASP): IASP generates policy ideas that broaden wealth, reduce inequality, and improve the social and economic mobility of low-income American households by promoting asset building. Working in partnership with a wide range of organizations, the IASP bridges the worlds of academic research, government policy-making, and the interests of constituencies. IASP's two affiliates are the **Center on Hunger and Poverty,** which promotes policies that improve the lives of low-income children and families, and the **National Program on Women and Aging,** which focuses national attention on the special concerns of women as they age to develop solutions and strategies for dealing with these concerns and to reach out to women and organizations across the country, promoting the changes necessary to improve older women's lives.

Center for International Development (CID): CID is a research and training group working in partnership with development organizations and universities abroad and in the United States. Its faculty, researchers, and students are engaged in research that furthers knowledge about sustainable development and helps build local capacity to solve problems and plan sound development strategies.

Institute for Child, Youth and Family Policy(ICYFP): ICYFP brings together faculty, research staff, and students in activities that foster the well-being of children, adolescents, and their families. The institute has a wide-ranging portfolio of research and public engagement projects dealing with vulnerable or disenfranchised populations, reflecting the Heller School's dedication to the concept of knowledge advancing social justice. ICYFP has two affiliated centers.

Nathan and Toby Starr Center for Retardation: The Nathan and Toby Starr Center focuses its research on the impact on families of lifelong caregiving for a member with mental retardation, the effectiveness of early intervention services on children and families, health-care systems for children with special health-care needs, and organizational and policy issues in the expansion of community-based services for persons with disabilities.
Center for Youth and Communities (CYC): CYC has established a national reputation as one of the nation's leading research centers and professional development and policy organizations in youth and community development. The center's ultimate goal is to "make knowledge productive" by connecting the knowledge gained from scholarly research and practical experience in ways that help both policy-makers and practitioners.

Carnegie Mellon

CARNEGIE MELLON UNIVERSITY

H. John Heinz III School of Public Policy and Management
Adelaide, Australia Campus Programs

Programs of Study

Two graduate degree programs are currently offered at the Heinz School Australia campus: the Master of Science in Public Policy and Management (MSPPM) and the Master of Science in Information Technology (M.S.I.T.).

The Master of Science in Public Policy and Management program prepares students to advance the public interest by developing exceptional analytic, quantitative, and technical skills. The Heinz School focuses on policy, management, and technology; methods to approach complex and unstructured problems; and skills to develop novel solutions to critical social issues.

Through the study of policy analysis, financial management and analysis, project management, and information technology, the MSPPM program provides market-oriented training that is applicable to any policy field in the public, nonprofit, and private sectors.

Several features of the MSPPM program set it apart from other professional master's programs. First, it offers multiple curriculum tracks for degree completion: a two-year track consisting of two academic years and a one-year track (twelve months) for students entering the program with extensive relevant experience. For working professionals, the equivalent one-year track can be completed on a part-time basis, spanning multiple years.

Second, the curriculum is skills-based, because in today's job market, multiple job changes, and even career changes, are inevitable. The skills-based curriculum ensures that graduates of the MSPPM program have a set of skills that will allow them to shape a flexible career now and twenty years from now.

Third, this program is grounded in the believe that the future of any organization—private, public, or nonprofit—will be affected by technology. MSPPM graduates have an understanding of current trends in information technology that can help their organizations run more efficiently and strengthen their future success.

A final distinctive aspect of the MSPPM program is Systems Synthesis, the capstone project. In lieu of a master's thesis, students participate in a semester-long group project. The groups start with an unstructured problem, refines the scope, and analyzes, develops, and often implements a solution. Projects are conducted for real clients in the public or nonprofit sector and are guided by advisory boards of professionals with expertise in the field.

Carnegie Mellon's Master of Science in Information Technology is an elite graduate program that integrates information technology and management skills. The M.S.I.T. program prepares IT professionals who are ready to advance their careers in IT leadership. Its integrated and interdisciplinary curriculum of technology and management course work provides students with an understanding of information technology from both operational and strategic perspectives. Graduates have a proven track record of adding value to their organizations and their careers through the intelligent application of technology.

The M.S.I.T. program requires 144 units, the equivalent of twelve semester-length courses. Students can complete the program full-time in a one-year (three semesters) intensive format. Working professionals can opt to enroll on a part-time basis, taking one or two courses each semester for up to five years.

In addition to a set of required core courses (60 units), students can customize the curriculum with a variety of electives.

Research Facilities

The CMU campus in Adelaide has world-class facilities available to students and faculty and staff members. Each classroom has state-of-the-art teaching facilities as well as the ability to conduct videoconferences, opening CMU Adelaide to the world. Carnegie Mellon's Australia campus is outfitted with state-of-the-art IT facilities, at the same standard as Carnegie Mellon's Pittsburgh campus, and students can access all of the databases and online journals to which CMU Libraries subscribe. Some of the most frequently used databases include ProQuest, LexisNexis Congressional, and PAIS, and some frequently used e-journals are *Human Rights Quarterly, Economic Policy Review, Business & Politics, Global Economy Journal, ACM Digital Library,* and *IEEE Xplore* as well as *The Wall Street Journal Online, The Times Online* e-paper, *Harvard Business Review Online,* and *The Economist.* CMU also subscribes to many online reference books, and there are a variety of other materials available electronically, too.

There are two computer clusters available for students to use PCs at the CMU Adelaide campus. All PCs have Office 2007 and access to the Internet and e-mail. The campus also has a wireless network available to users with laptops. Computing Services provides help, support, and advice to students and faculty and staff members on a wide range of computing and communication topics and is responsible for all computing facilities at the Adelaide campus.

Financial Aid

The Heinz School is committed to making a graduate education affordable for talented students. No separate application is necessary. Students who note in the application for admission that they would like to be considered for financial aid are automatically considered for any applicable scholarship opportunity. Carnegie Mellon University-AusAID Scholarships are funded by the Australian government to support a limited number of students from countries where Australia has a bilateral aid program to study at the University's Heinz School in Adelaide, Australia. These scholarships are available to full-time students and include full tuition, return economy airfares, a contribution to living expenses, and basic medical insurance. Applicants must satisfy both AusAID's general eligibility criteria and the specific criteria established for their country of citizenship. MSPPM and M.S.I.T. Scholarships are merit-based awards available to either full- or part-time students. There are also South Australian Government Scholarships that cover significant portion of tuition. In addition, Australian students are eligible for a FEE-HELP tuition loan, which can be used to meet the residual cost of tuition not covered by scholarship.

Cost of Study

Tuition is charged on the same per-unit basis for full- and part-time students. The unit cost is $389.41 (AU dollars) for the MSSPPM program and $454.32 (AU dollars) for the M.S.I.T. program.

Living and Housing Costs

There are a wide range of housing options available at a wide range of prices, including apartments and houses for rent and student hostels. Cost depends on the type and location. Information about housing options, locations, and costs can be found at http://www.heinz.cmu.edu.au/about-us/campus/housing.asp.

Location

Adelaide, Australia's fifth-largest city with just over a million residents, is South Australia's seat of government and commerce: an ideal place to study, work, and play. It is a city of culture, a city of relaxed living, and a city of learning. Adelaide, the capital of South Australia, was planned in 1836 by surveyor Colonel William Light. This centre is surrounded by 930 hectares of parklands. The Torrens River runs through the centre, separating Adelaide and North Adelaide. The city is surrounded by diverse landscapes, including the Mount Lofty Ranges (Adelaide Hills) and coastal beaches. International carriers regularly fly to the new Adelaide airport (award-winning combined domestic and international terminals), and these airlines have connecting flights to all corners of the world.

The University

Carnegie Mellon was first established in 1900 as the Carnegie Technical School through a gift from Andrew Carnegie. In 1912, the name of the school was changed to Carnegie Institute of Technology. Mellon Institute, founded in 1913 by A. W. and R. B. Mellon, merged with Carnegie Institute of Technology in 1967 to become Carnegie Mellon University. The University has an enrollment of about 10,000 students, approximately 4,000 of whom are engaged in graduate study. Rated one of the country's top public policy schools by *U.S. News & World Report,* the Heinz School advances the public interest through research and education. By strategically integrating expertise in policy, management, and information technology, the faculty focuses on critical public issues, including arts management, crime and violence, health care, information systems and technology, and public policy.

Applying

Students must submit the online application form (including essay and resume), official transcripts from all colleges and universities attended, and three letters of recommendation. All applicants are required to complete the GRE or GMAT and must request that an official score report be sent to the Office of Admissions by ETS. Nonnative English speakers must also complete an English Proficiency Exam.

For the full-time MSPPM (one- or two-year) and M.S.I.T. (one-year) programs, the deadline for the track that starts in January is October 15, and the deadline for the track that starts in August is March 8. For the MSPPM and M.S.I.T. part-time programs, the deadline for the track that starts in January is December 1, the deadline for the track that starts in May is April 1, and the deadline for the track that starts in August is July 1.

Correspondence and Information

The Heinz School Australia
Torrens Building
Carnegie Mellon University
220 Victoria Square
Adelaide, South Australia 5000
Australia
Phone: (08) 8110 9900
E-mail: hnzadmit-australia@andrew.cmu.edu
Web site: http://www.heinz.cmu.edu.au/index.asp

Carnegie Mellon University

FEATURED FACULTY AND THEIR RESEARCH

Roberto Cavazos received his Ph.D. from the University of Texas. Cavazos has served as an economist and senior adviser at the Texas Department of Agriculture and the New York City Office of the Comptroller. He has worked as a researcher and/or directed studies for the United States Department of Homeland Security, Department of Housing and Urban Development, Veterans Administration, Corporation for National and Community Service, and the U.S. Coast Guard as well as leading U.S. banks. He has been on the faculty of the University of Texas at San Antonio and Florida International University. He has been involved for nearly twenty years in the development of affordable housing. His research focuses on solving public policy problems and measuring performance. He is interested in the use and implications of new analytic technologies such as data mining in the public sector. Similarly, he is conducting research on new techniques to evaluate program and agency performance.

Riaz Esmailzadeh received his Ph.D. in electrical engineering from Keio University in Japan. He is an Associate Teaching Professor of Management of Technology whose classes have included Telecom Technology and Management, E-Commerce and M-Commerce, and Ethics, Globalization, and Public Policy. Key research areas are code division multiple access (CDMA) communications (3G), multimedia streaming, and quality management and control, which have led to more than sixty patent applications, twenty of which have been granted in the U.S. so far. He has also contributed to the development of and participated in international discussions pertaining to the standardization of third generation (3G) mobile communications systems. His research into broadband wireless telecommunications, including m-commerce, is leading to the publication of a book.

Tiong Kiong Lim earned a Master of Business Administration from University Putra Malaysia and his Ph.D. in accounting and finance and a Graduate Certificate in Higher Education (GCHE) from Monash University, Melbourne, Australia. Dr. T. K. Lim was a senior corporate executive in the finance and securities industry for sixteen years prior to joining the higher education sector. He had held various managerial positions, ranging from branch manager and regional manager to vice president of publicly listed companies. He had been a private investment manager/dealer serving high-net-worth individuals across the Asia Pacific and Europe regions. Dr. Lim is a member of the Institute of Certified Management Accountants Australia, the American Finance Association, and the Asian Finance Association. Dr. Lim is interested in the research areas of financial forecasting, investment analysis and portfolio management, asset valuation, issues in the banking sector, and financial education.

Victor Pontines received a Bachelor of Arts and Master of Science in economics from De La Salle in the Philippines, a Master of Arts in economics from Exeter in the United Kingdom, and a Ph.D. in economics from the University of Adelaide in Australia. Professor Pontines' research interests are in the broad areas of open economy macroeconomics and international finance, with particular reference to the East Asian region. Specific topics of interest include currency crises, exchange rate regimes, contagion, international capital flows, and regional monetary integration.

Anna Shillabeer is nearing completion of her Ph.D. focusing on medical informatics at Flinders University in Australia. She has worked as a Web developer and a fraud and behavioural analyst for the WorkCover Corporation in South Australia. She has also taught both undergraduate and graduate information technology courses for eight years in the areas of software engineering, project management, and database management. She is a member of the Health Informatics Society of Australia. Her research focuses on medical informatics and the provision of automated tools to meet the unique needs of medical data analysis, with a particular focus on data mining technologies.

Murli Viswanathan received his B.S. degree in computer science and information systems from Deakin University, Australia, in 1996, followed by a First Class honours degree in 1997. In 2002 he completed his Ph.D. in computer science specializing in machine learning from Monash University, Australia. From 2001 to the middle of 2004, he was a full-time tenure-track faculty member with the Department of Computer Science, University of Melbourne, Australia. From 2004 to early 2007, he was employed as IITA Distinguished IT Professor with the College of Software at Kyungwon University in Korea. Murli's current research interests are in knowledge-based systems, data mining for ubiquitous information systems, Bayesian model selection, distributed data mining, and adaptive systems. He has offered several invited lectures and published papers in well-known conferences and journals. In 2006, he was responsible for initiating joint collaborative research between the Ubiquitous Healthcare Centre, Kyungwon University, and the E-health Research Centre (Australian government). He is looking forward to establishing similar research networks.

Carnegie Mellon

CARNEGIE MELLON UNIVERSITY

H. John Heinz III School of Public Policy and Management
Master of Public Management

Program of Study

Experienced professionals who seek to advance or change their careers possess unique expertise and specialized educational needs. The Master of Public Management (M.P.M.) program is designed to capitalize on that expertise and meet those needs by offering specialized training in management and related fields.

The program promotes the personal and professional development of students by teaching them state-of-the-art management tools, analytical techniques for more efficient organizational planning and coordination, and how to communicate more effectively with colleagues, clients, supervisors, and employees. Students also gain insight into human behavior in organizations, as well as a greater understanding of social, political, technological, and economic processes that shape public policy.

To earn the degree, students must successfully complete 144 units with a minimum cumulative QPA of 3.0. All students must complete core courses in organization management theory and practice, data analysis, economic principles, financial analysis, and professional writing and speaking. The remaining units can be completed with graduate-level elective courses offered in the Heinz School. The program is designed to be completed in four semesters of full-time study. Most students studying part-time complete the program in two years, but students have up to five years to complete the degree.

Students may also choose to design their own concentrations or pursue a defined concentration. The program offers defined concentration areas in health systems management, information systems management, nonprofit organizations, human resources, leadership in higher education, and educational leadership. Some define their own concentrations in crime, violence and drug policy, health policy, entrepreneurship and economic policy, and other areas.

Research Facilities

The Center for Economic Development brings academic resources to bear on key issues in regional economic development. Research areas include regional economic development, entrepreneurial vitality, links between economic growth and environmental sustainability, and globalization of technology and innovation. The Hunt Library houses the University's collections in humanities, fine arts, social sciences, and business. The University Libraries also house several unique collections, including the Posner Family Collection of rare books and artifacts, located in the Posner Center.

Financial Aid

Most students in the M.P.M. program qualify for some form of assistance in paying their tuition. Last year, the School awarded over $500,000 in scholarship money, with 68 percent of the M.P.M. students qualifying for some form of assistance or scholarship from the University. In addition, the Heinz School offers scholarship programs for applicants to the M.P.M. program. Scholarship awards combined with employer tuition remission may not exceed the cost of tuition and fees.

The Heinz School offers a limited number of Regional Leaders Scholarships to incoming full- and part-time students who have demonstrated a commitment to the Pittsburgh community. Applicants interested in the Regional Leaders Scholarships are required to have one of their three letters of recommendation written by someone who can testify to their commitment to and impact on the Pittsburgh community.

Cost of Study

In the 2008–09 academic year, the unit cost is $375 for up to 48 units for M.P.M. Students in this program who are enrolled for 48 or more units are charged full tuition.

Living and Housing Costs

A wide range of affordable housing options are available close to the Carnegie Mellon campus. Housing costs in Pittsburgh are typically lower than those in other urban settings. Room and board for a single graduate student average around $5600 per semester. Carnegie Mellon does not provide housing for graduate students.

Student Group

Students come from a variety of backgrounds and work for a wide variety of local and national organizations in the government, nonprofit, and private sectors. The majority of students are U.S. citizens; approximately 30 percent come from other countries, including China, Japan, Kenya, Korea, Pakistan, Turkey, and Uganda.

Student Outcomes

Graduate of the program are prepared to hold a variety of professional and management positions at organizations in the nonprofit, public, private, and consulting sectors. Recent graduates have found jobs in health care, finance, government, and education.

Location

Carnegie Mellon is located in Oakland, a cultural center of Pittsburgh, Pennsylvania, on a 90-acre campus adjacent to Schenley Park, one of the city's largest parks. The campus is conveniently located for easy access to many cultural and sporting events and is only 4 miles from the downtown business and cultural district. Pittsburgh is the thirteenth-largest metropolitan area in the United States. The city has good public transportation, diverse cultural attractions, and three professional sports teams. New York City, Philadelphia, Toronto, and Washington, D.C., are all within driving distance. Many recreational facilities, including ski areas and state parks, are located nearby.

The University and The School

Carnegie Mellon was first established in 1900 as the Carnegie Technical School through a gift from Andrew Carnegie. In 1912, the name of the school was changed to Carnegie Institute of Technology. Mellon Institute, founded in 1913 by A. W. and R. B. Mellon, merged with Carnegie Institute of Technology in 1967 to become Carnegie Mellon University. The University has an enrollment of about 10,000, approximately 4,000 of whom are engaged in graduate study. Rated one of the country's top public policy schools by *U.S. News & World Report,* the Heinz School advances public interest through research and education. By strategically integrating expertise in policy, management, and information technology, the faculty focuses on critical public issues, including arts management, crime and violence, health care, information systems and technology, and public policy.

Applying

The program is open to students with an undergraduate degree from an accredited institution and at least five years of work experience. Prospective students must submit a completed application for admission, transcripts from all colleges attended, a current resume, three letters of recommendation, and an essay describing academic and professional goals. Students whose native language is not English must submit an official score report from the TOEFL or IELTS as part of their application for admission. The deadlines for part-time students are based on the semester in which they plan to begin the program. The deadline for a January start date is November 15; for a May start date, April 15; and for an August start date, July 15. If the class is not full as of the application deadline for a particular start date, applications continue to be accepted until the class is full.

Correspondence and Information

Dr. Gordon Lewis, M.P.M. Program Director
H. John Heinz III School of Public Policy and Management
Carnegie Mellon University
5000 Forbes Avenue
Pittsburgh, Pennsylvania 15213-3890

Phone: 412-268-2164
E-mail: hnzadmit@andrew.cmu.edu
Web site: http://www.heinz.cmu.edu/mpm/

Carnegie Mellon University

THE FACULTY AND THEIR RESEARCH

Ashish Arora, Professor of Economics and Public Policy and Courtesy Appointment, School of Computer Science, Institute for Software Research International; Ph.D (economics), Stanford. Professor Arora served as a codirector of the Software Industry Center at Carnegie Mellon University until 2006. He is on the editorial board of six academic journals and has served on a number of committees for bodies such as the National Academy of Sciences and the Association of Computing Machinery.

Edward Barr, Associate Teaching Professor; M.Ed. (English), Pennsylvania.

Robert Bartolacci, Adjunct Assistant Professor of Financial Analysis; M.S. (financial analysis and management), Carnegie Mellon. Mergers and acquisitions, turnaround management, valuations and analysis, capitation and risk-sharing pricing, strategic financial planning, business administration, financial management.

Chris Brussalis, Adjunct Professor of Management and Policy; Ph.D. (regional planning), Illinois. Economics of regionalization, environmental policy, solid-waste management, economic development, strategic planning.

Jon Delano, Adjunct Professor of Public Policy and Politics, Haverford College; J.D., Pennsylvania. Jon Delano is the Money and Politics Editor for KDKA-TV (CBS) in Pittsburgh, columnist for the Pittsburgh *Business Times,* and political contributor to WQED-TVs "On Q Magazine." As Adjunct Professor of Public Policy and Politics, his graduate school courses at the Heinz School include such topics as money and politics, legislative policy making, public policy implementation, media and public policy, and campaign management.

Joe Dimperio, Adjunct Professor of Legal and IT Issues in Education; J.D., Duquesne; Ed.D., Pittsburgh. Professor Dimperio is a consultant for various private schools, public schools, state intermediate units, and the Pennsylvania School Board Association. He is a member of the American Association of School Administrators, the National School Board Association, and the Allegheny County Bar Association.

Aloysius Gallagher, Adjunct Associate Professor of Human Resource Management; M.A. (labor relations), St. Francis (Pennsylvania). Manufacturing engineering, human resource management.

Norton Gusky, Adjunct Professor of Technology and Educational Restructuring; M.A.T. (elementary education), Pittsburgh. Mr. Gusky is co-coordinator for Quality Schools Consortium, cochair for the Three Rivers Educational Technology Conference, and consultant for the Grable Foundation and Pennsylvania Economy League; the Modern Red School House, in San Antonio, Texas; and the Carnegie Science Center in Pittsburgh, PA.

Laks Iyengar, Adjunct Associate Professor of Management; M.B.A. (strategic management), Pittsburgh. New products and services evaluations, new market and business development and strategic planning, evaluating market characteristics and assessing competitive and industry factors.

David M. Krackhardt, Professor of Organizations and Public Policy; Ph.D. (organizational behavior), California, Irvine. Cognitive social structures, developing methodologies to better understand networks and their implications.

Peter Madsen, Distinguished Service Professor of Ethics and Social Responsibility, with appointments in the Provost's Office; Ph.D., Duquesne. Applied ethics, concentrated in the areas of international corporate responsibility, professional ethics and computers, and society and ethics. Dr. Madsen's papers and reviews appear in diverse journals and reference texts such as the *Business Ethics Quarterly, Business and Professional Ethics Journal,* and *Management Accounting.*

Karen Overfield, Adjunct Instructor of Human Resources; Ed.D., Pittsburgh. Leadership, cross-culture, team development, communications. Dr. Overfield develops, directs, and conducts training workshops on topics such as leadership, cross-culture, team development, and communications. She serves as an internal consultant on team effectiveness, change management, and organizational development.

Lynne Pastor, Adjunct Faculty; M.S. (industrial administration), Carnegie Mellon. Entrepreneurship, marketing, strategy, accounting, operations research.

Dana Phillips, Adjunct Instructor of Management; M.M. (management), Northwestern. Financial management and planning, marketing, strategic planning, resource development.

Denise M. Rousseau, H. J. Heinz II Professor of Organizational Behavior; Ph.D. (psychology), Berkeley. Employment, human resource strategies, and the effects of organizational culture on performance.

Velma Saire, Adjunct Professor of Educational Management; Ph.D. (education), Pittsburgh. Dr. Saire retired in 2000 as Assistant Superintendent for the Quaker Valley School District, Sewickley, PA. Her background includes teaching in the primary and intermediate grades and experiences as a special education teacher, and she served as Director of Allegheny County's Early Childhood Development Centers (Headstart). Her administrative and supervisory credentials include assignments as an elementary supervisor; elementary, middle school, and high school principal; and educational consultant to schools across the nation.

Rosanne Saunders, Adjunct Associate Professor of Health Management; J.D., Duquesne. Human resource strategic assessments.

Kathleen Smith, Associate Teaching Professor; M.B.A., Pittsburgh. Management accounting.

Shelby Stewman, Professor of Sociology and Demography; Ph.D. (sociology), Michigan State. Organizational labor markets, equal employment opportunity, forecasting labor costs and turnover, the aging of work organizations.

Ronald Weiers, Adjunct Faculty; Ph.D. (marketing research and analysis), Pittsburgh. Repair and maintenance, efficiency and safety.

Carnegie Mellon

CARNEGIE MELLON UNIVERSITY

H. John Heinz III School of Public Policy and Management
Programs in Public Policy and Management

Program of Study

The Heinz School offers the Master of Science in Public Policy and Management (MSPPM) and a Ph.D. in Public Policy and Management. The MSPPM program prepares students to advance the public interest by developing exceptional analytic, quantitative, management, communication, and technical skills. This course of study provides market-oriented training that is applicable to any policy field in the public, not-for-profit, and private sectors.

Students can pursue one of two curriculum tracks. Students with 3 or more years of relevant work experience may enroll in the one-year program, which begins in May and ends upon completion of three consecutive semesters of full-time study (the following May). Those who are newer to the field enroll in the two-year program, which begins in August and includes an internship in the summer between the first and second years. All students participate in a group capstone project. The capstone experience at the Heinz School is the systems synthesis project. In a team setting, students working with an actual organization propose a project, frame the problem, conduct the analysis, make recommendations, and present their findings—a true, real-world application of skills. In addition to core courses, students may also pursue a concentration in policy analysis, financial analysis and management, social entrepreneurship, economic development, or environmental policy or design their own concentration in another area of interest.

The Ph.D. in Public Policy and Management addresses the increasing complexity of issues of public policy, management, and information systems and technology that demands new, interdisciplinary approaches to understanding and solving these problems. Integrating disciplinary perspectives, advancing theoretical models, and improving the quality of methodological and computer-based tools in understanding these issues are the primary goals of research conducted by faculty and students at the Heinz School.

Ph.D. students typically work on issues related to public policy, management, information technology, or some combination of the three. In public policy, some key areas of research are crime policy, drug policy, health economics, labor economics, and technology policy. In management, research topics include organizational behavior, negotiation, and social networks. In information technology, the topics include information security and privacy, online markets and economics, data mining, data confidentiality, health care and IT, and IT and organizations. Many students work at the intersection of these issues.

Research Facilities

The National Consortium on Violence Research is a research and training center specializing in violence research. Its mission is to advance basic scientific knowledge about the causes or factors contributing to interpersonal violence, to train the next generation of violence researchers, and to disseminate its research findings to participants, policy makers, and practitioners. The Center for Economic Development produces regional strategies that catalyze economic and technological development. It provides technical assistance in policy and strategy, economic analysis and modeling, mapping of economic and demographic data, performance benchmarking, and evaluation and analysis of critical policy issues. The new Institute for Social Innovation produces research and provides education that promotes leadership, entrepreneurship, and innovation within the social sector. It brings a uniquely Carnegie Mellon spin to the field—a focus on applied research, using the latest in science and technology and taking advantage of the Pittsburgh location, which is home to a number of innovative nonprofits—to make an impact on the public interest.

Financial Aid

Four Heinz Fellowships are awarded annually to students committed to working in careers focused on serving the public interest. Awards include full tuition and a $6000 research assistantship for each academic year. Delgado Scholarships are awarded to talented students who will make a significant contribution and are committed to promoting the advancement of the Latino community. Awards range from $5000 to full tuition per semester. Tribal Affairs Fellowships are awarded to students committed to promoting the advancement of the American Indian population and tribal affairs. Awards include full tuition and a $6000 research assistantship for each academic year. Dean's Diversity Fellowships are awarded to applicants who exemplify a strong commitment to the improvement of race-related issues in the United States. Awards include full tuition and a $6000 per year research assistantship. Students who have successfully completed a Public Policy and International Affairs (PPIA) summer institute and are admitted to the MSPPM program are awarded a full-tuition scholarship and a stipend of $6000 per year. Fulbright Scholars are eligible for half-tuition scholarships. Alumni scholarships are awarded based on public-interest work experience. Scholarships of at least $6000 per semester are awarded to Coro Fellows, returned Peace Corps volunteers, and Teach for America alumni. A limited number of Regional Leaders Scholarships are awarded to incoming full-time students who have demonstrated a commitment to the Pittsburgh community. Other merit scholarships are available, and eligible students may borrow up to $18,500 under the Federal Stafford Student Loans program. Federal Perkins Loans are also available.

The Ph.D.-specific financial aid program is designed to provide doctoral students with the financial support necessary to enable them to successfully complete the program. This support is also designed to allow students to gain experience in the classroom that is valued in the academic marketplace. Every Ph.D. student in good standing receives a full-tuition scholarship for their entire tenure in the program.

Cost of Study

In the 2008–09 academic year, full-time tuition is $18,000 per semester. Other expenses include $1000 for health insurance and $200 per semester in miscellaneous fees. Students can also expect to spend approximately $460 per semester on books and supplies.

Living and Housing Costs

A wide range of affordable housing options are available close to the Carnegie Mellon campus. Housing costs in Pittsburgh are typically lower than those in other urban settings. Room and board for a single graduate student average around $5600 per semester. Carnegie Mellon does not provide housing for graduate students.

Student Group

Approximately 15 percent of the students in the Programs in Public Policy and Management are from countries other than the United States, including China, Denmark, India, Iran, Japan, Mexico, Mongolia, Pakistan, Peru, Singapore, South Korea, and Taiwan. Most have several years of work experience. Others have served in the Peace Corps or AmeriCorps or are former PPIA fellows. About 35 percent of the students have a professional background in the social sciences, but other students have experience in business, technology, and the liberal arts and humanities.

Student Outcomes

Graduates are employed in every sector of the market and in virtually every industry. They work for large, established organizations and for emerging companies. They are employed as policy analysts, budget analysts, managers, and consultants and in many other positions. Their work covers every functional area found in nonprofit organizations; federal, state, and local governments; and private firms.

Through the Heinz School's intensive, methodologically based curriculum, students learn to pursue their research questions with sophisticated skills and insights. Graduates of the doctoral program continue their research in academic institutions, governmental agencies, consulting firms, and other organizations.

Location

Carnegie Mellon is located in Oakland, a cultural center of Pittsburgh, Pennsylvania, on a 90-acre campus adjacent to Schenley Park, the city's largest park. The campus is conveniently located for easy access to many cultural and sporting events and is only 4 miles from the downtown business and cultural district. Pittsburgh is the thirteenth-largest metropolitan area in the United States. The city has good public transportation, diverse cultural attractions, and three professional sports teams. New York City, Philadelphia, Toronto, and Washington, D.C., are all within driving distance. Many recreational facilities, including ski areas and state parks, are located nearby.

The University and The School

Carnegie Mellon was first established in 1900 as the Carnegie Technical School through a gift from Andrew Carnegie. In 1912, the name of the school was changed to Carnegie Institute of Technology. Mellon Institute, founded in 1913 by A. W. and R. B. Mellon, merged with Carnegie Institute of Technology in 1967 to become Carnegie Mellon University. The University has an enrollment of about 10,000, approximately 4,000 of whom are engaged in graduate study. Rated one of the country's top public policy schools by *U.S. News & World Report,* the Heinz School advances the public interest through research and education. By strategically integrating expertise in policy, management, and information technology, the faculty focuses on critical public issues, including crime and violence, health care, information systems and technology, and arts management.

Applying

MSPPM and Ph.D. candidates must hold an undergraduate degree from an accredited institution, including course work in statistics. Applicants to the one-year program must have at least three years of relevant work experience, a Coro Fellowship, or equivalent experience in the Peace Corps, Congressional Hunger Center, or the military. Prospective students must submit a completed online application, official GRE or GMAT scores, college transcripts, a current resume, three letters of recommendation, and an essay describing academic and professional goals. Nonnative English speakers are required to submit official scores for the IELTS or the TOEFL. The deadline to apply is February 1.

Correspondence and Information

Brenda Peyser, Associate Dean
H. John Heinz III School of Public Policy and Management
Carnegie Mellon University
5000 Forbes Avenue
Pittsburgh, Pennsylvania 15213-3890

Phone: 412-268-2164
E-mail: hnzadmit@andrew.cmu.edu
Web site: http://www.heinz.cmu.edu/academics/default.html

Carnegie Mellon University

THE FACULTY AND THEIR RESEARCH

Alessandro Acquisti, Assistant Professor of Information Technology and Public Policy; Ph.D. (information management and systems), Berkeley. Economics of privacy and information security, economics of computers and AI, e-commerce, transition economics.

Ashish Arora, Professor of Economics and Public Policy; Ph.D. (economics), Stanford. Economics of technological change, management of technology, intellectual property rights, technology licensing.

Linda C. Babcock, James M. Walton Professor of Economics; Ph.D. (economics), Wisconsin–Madison. Negotiations and dispute resolution, gender differences in the propensity to initiate negotiations and how people react to women when they negotiate.

Alfred Blumstein, Erik S. Jonsson University Professor of Urban Systems and Operations Research; Ph.D. (operations research), Cornell. Crime measurement, criminal careers, sentencing, deterrence and incapacitation, prison populations, flow through the system, demographic trends, juvenile violence and drug-enforcement policy.

Silvia Borzutzky, Teaching Professor; Ph.D., Pittsburgh. Social security policies in Latin America.

Jonathan P. Caulkins, Professor of Operations Research and Public Policy; Ph.D. (operations research), MIT. Modeling and analyzing problems pertaining to drugs, crime, and violence and how policies affect those problems.

Karen B. Clay, Visiting Assistant Professor of History and Public Policy; Ph.D. (economics), Stanford. Determinants of the quality of state courts and the operation of Internet markets.

Jacqueline Cohen, Principal Research Scientist; Ph.D., Carnegie Mellon. Demographic trends in crime and prison populations, patterns of individual criminal careers, incapacitative effects of incarceration, the effectiveness of policing strategies.

Dennis Epple, Thomas Lord Professor of Economics; Ph.D., Princeton. Public economics, industrial organization, and applied econometrics; economics of education; state and local government finance; "learning by doing" and productivity change in manufacturing and services.

Penny S. Ferreira, Distinguished Service Professor of Environmental and Policy Law; J.D., Duquesne.

Wilpen L. Gorr, Professor of Public Policy and Information Systems; Ph.D. (operations research), Carnegie Mellon. GIS and management science models applied to public-sector problems; developing leading indicator forecast models for law enforcement, decision-support systems for facility location decisions, and information systems for support of policy and planning in organizations.

Bill Guttman, Distinguished Service Professor; D.Phil., Oxford.

Jeffrey Hunker, Professor of Technology and Public Policy; Ph.D. (business administration in managerial economics), Harvard. Cybersecurity.

Michael P. Johnson, Associate Professor of Management Science and Urban Affairs; Ph.D. (operations research), Northwestern. Design and implementation of decision-support methodologies for public-sector facility location problems.

Steven Klepper, Professor of Economics and Social Science; Ph.D. (economics), Cornell. The evolution of industry and the determinants of technological change, statistical procedures to cope with measurement error, tax compliance and criminal deterrence.

Lester B. Lave, James Higgins Professor of Economics and Finance, Professor of Urban and Public Affairs, and Professor of Engineering and Public Policy; Ph.D. (economics), Harvard. Policy analysis, environmental economics, risk analysis and management.

Gordon H. Lewis, Associate Professor of Sociology; Ph.D. (sociology), Stanford. Work incentives in welfare programs, management and organizational design, the optimal allocation of workers in administrative offices.

Peter Madsen, Senior Lecturer in Ethics and Public Policy; Ph.D. (philosophy), Duquesne. Business ethics and law, international business consulting, ethics training.

Daniel Nagin, Teresa and H. John Heinz III Professor of Public Policy; Ph.D., Carnegie Mellon. The evolution of criminal and antisocial behaviors, the deterrent effect of criminal and noncriminal penalties on illegal behaviors, the development of statistical methods for analyzing longitudinal data.

Toni Pellegrini, Adjunct Instructor in Law; J.D., Duquesne. The American legal system, administrative law and local government law.

Peter M. Shane, Distinguished Service Professor of Law and Public Policy; J.D., Yale. Separation-of-powers law, the application of law to the presidency.

Kiron Skinner, Assistant Professor, Department of History and Department of Social and Decision Sciences; Ph.D. (political science and international relations), Harvard. American foreign policy, international relations theory and international security.

Melvin Stephens, Assistant Professor of Economics; Ph.D., Michigan. How households cope with a job, labor supply behavior, retirement choices, how the timing of income receipt affects consumption decisions.

Robert P. Strauss, Professor of Economics and Public Policy; Ph.D. (economics), Wisconsin. Economic efficiency effects of taxing intermediate and final goods in a multistate context, effects of deductibility of health expenditures in the federal personal income tax, analysis of migration flows and family composition with individual income tax returns.

Joel Tarr, The Richard S Caliguiri Professor of Urban and Environmental History and Policy; Ph.D. (history), Northwestern. The impact of technology on the urban environment, urban politics and policy.

Lowell J. Taylor, Professor of Economics and Public Policy; Ph.D. (economics), Michigan. Incentives within organizations, the economics of gay and lesbian households, the role of race and ethnicity in labor market outcomes.

Karyl Troup-Leasure, Adjunct Faculty; Ph.D. (policy, planning, and evaluation), Pittsburgh. The use of information to guide juvenile justice policy development and practice.

William B. Vogt, Assistant Professor of Economics; Ph.D. (economics), Stanford. Industrial organization, applied econometrics, health economics.

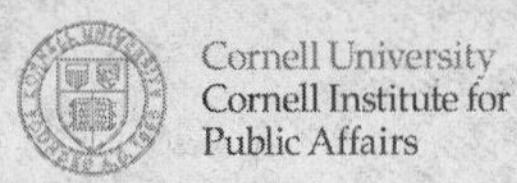

CORNELL UNIVERSITY

Cornell Institute for Public Affairs

Program of Study

The Cornell Institute for Public Affairs (CIPA) offers a two-year program of graduate professional studies leading to a Master of Public Administration (M.P.A.) degree. The interdisciplinary nature of this M.P.A. program is one of its distinguishing features. CIPA students, called "fellows," have the flexibility to design individualized plans of study using faculty resources from across the University.

Fellows obtain foundational competence by taking courses in each of these three areas: administration, politics, and public policy; economics and public finance; and quantitative analysis. This course work provides students with an understanding of the political processes through which issues, problems, and policies are formulated; the economic basis for government action in a market economy; and the comparative and historical contexts of governmental programs. Students study public budgets, finance, and regulatory processes as well as the behavior of both public and private organizations and their management. Students also gain competence in the qualitative and quantitative methods needed to analyze programs and policies and develop sensitivity to the moral and ethical dimensions of policy issues.

Concentration course work enables students to focus on a specific area of public policy study. They choose their course of study—domestic or international—from a broad range of options: environmental policy; finance and fiscal policy; government, politics, and policy studies; human rights and social justice; international development studies; public and nonprofit management; science and technology policy; and social policy.

As a culmination of studies, all students are required to develop and complete a professional writing project, which typically grows out of a student's area of concentration and often incorporates work done during a summer internship. There are two options for completing this writing requirement: a professional report or a master's thesis. The report represents an experiential project undertaken by a fellow on behalf of a "client," such as a public, private, or nonprofit organization, and requires the fellow to solve a problem in policy analysis or program evaluation. The thesis is a substantial, independent research paper offering an original contribution to the field of public affairs. It requires a fellow to pose a policy problem, review and summarize previous efforts to address this problem, and propose an alternate solution.

CIPA students may elect to combine their M.P.A. study program with complementary degree study, such as a J.D. from Cornell Law School, an M.B.A. from the Johnson School of Management, an M.M.H. from the Hotel School, or an M.R.P. in the field of city and regional planning.

Research Facilities

Cornell is a major research university with significant derivative policy interests in natural and physical sciences, nutrition, genetics, engineering, computer and social sciences, health, education, consumer policy, art, architecture, and the humanities. Separate interdisciplinary work centers on the environment, international studies and development, and international food and agriculture. Programs on infrastructure, education, family development, and health administration provide valuable resources for fellows.

The University has a world-class library system, including nineteen libraries with more than 5 million volumes, 600,000 periodical titles, and extensive microfilm and other materials.

Financial Aid

The Cornell Institute for Public Affairs provides some funding to more than 80 percent of its students. The Institute itself, however, is unable to provide anyone with full support. CIPA fellows often win support from Fulbright, Truman, and World Bank fellowships. Applicants are encouraged to explore all available sources of external funding, including grants that may be provided by current employers. Decisions concerning CIPA funding are made in March, so those who wish to be considered should complete the application by January 30.

Cost of Study

The estimated total cost of tuition and fees for full-time fellows for the 2008–09 academic year is $36,300. The estimated cost of books and materials is approximately $1200.

Living and Housing Costs

Living expenses for single students range from $1700 to $1800 per month, including room, meals, and personal expenses but excluding travel. There are many housing options for CIPA fellows. Some University housing is available exclusively to students in graduate and professional programs. Non-University housing includes apartment complexes, multiple-unit houses, single-unit houses, individual rooms, and cooperative living units. A listing of off-campus housing options is available from Cornell's Housing Office.

Student Group

In 2007–08, there were a total of 154 full-time fellows in the two-year program. In general, the program had similar numbers of men and women, and about 35 percent of the fellows were international students. Of the total CIPA population, about half studied international relations, policy, or development, while the remainder pursued a wide variety of domestic policy interests, from social policy to national security policy to environmental policy.

Student Outcomes

CIPA employs a full-time professional development specialist who provides career advisement and assistance in locating employment and internships. Professional development at CIPA also includes the cultivation of an extensive network of alumni in the public, private, nonprofit, and academic sectors. CIPA consistently places more than 95 percent of its graduates within six months of graduation. Recent organizations that have employed CIPA alumni include the World Bank, the United Nations (UN), the United States Agency for International Development (USAID), the Environmental Protection Agency (EPA), Deloitte and Touche, Goldman Sachs, and Booz Allen Hamilton, Inc. International students often return to their countries of origin to work in high-level leadership posts in government and industry. Some CIPA alumni choose to continue their graduate studies in J.D. or Ph.D. programs.

Location

Cornell is located in Tompkins County in the heart of New York's Finger Lakes region, with pristine lakes, waterfalls, and multiple state parks. The area has more than beauty to recommend it. People who like to be outdoors thrive at Cornell. Nearby are opportunities for skiing, swimming, hiking, sailing, and mountain biking. Ithaca may be small and rural, but it also has an urban sophistication and an intellectual dynamism.

The University and The Institute

The Cornell Institute for Public Affairs is an autonomous, University-wide program designed to build on Cornell's legendary commitment to an education "which shall combine the practical with the liberal education." Cornell has offered the M.P.A. degree since 1946, originally through the Johnson Graduate School of Management, and since 1989 through the broader Cornell Institute for Public Affairs. CIPA's current alumni network includes graduates of both programs.

Applying

Admission to CIPA is selective. A committee of faculty members evaluates individual applications based on the student's overall academic record; GRE scores; English language skills (a TOEFL score of at least 250 computer-based or 600 paper-based for those whose first language is not English); potential for public-policy leadership as evidenced by professional work and community, extracurricular, or other relevant experience (students should include a copy of their most recent resume); and letters of recommendation. Applicants should also include an extensive written statement of purpose in which they address why they are applying to the program, their personal and/or professional experience that led to their interest in Cornell's M.P.A. program, their future goals (how they intend to put their M.P.A. degree to use), and examples of volunteer work, positions of responsibility, and any other life experiences contributing to their interest in public policy. The committee looks for sound analytic preparation and instruction or prior professional work experience in fields relevant to public affairs, such as economics, politics, public administration, planning, sociology, and law. CIPA has a rolling admissions policy; however, decisions concerning CIPA funding are made in March, so students who wish to be considered should complete their applications by January 30.

Correspondence and Information

To request additional information:

Cornell Institute for Public Affairs
294 Caldwell Hall
Cornell University
Ithaca, New York 14853-2602

Phone: 607-255-8018
Fax: 607-255-5240
E-mail: cipa@cornell.edu
Web site: http://www.cipa.cornell.edu

Cornell University

THE FACULTY AND THEIR RESEARCH

The program offers great depth and flexibility. It is not confined to a single school or college but spans the entire University. More than 100 faculty members in the field of public affairs from a diverse cross section of schools, departments, and programs, welcome CIPA fellows into their courses and serve on thesis committees. Within this group, 10 members serve as Core Faculty, providing instruction in foundation course work.

The Core Faculty

David B. Lewis, CIPA Director; Professor in the Department of City and Regional Planning.
Norman Uphoff, CIPA Director of Graduate Studies; Professor in the Department of Government.
Richard Booth, Professor in the Department of City and Regional Planning.
Nancy Brooks, Visiting Associate Professor in the Department of City and Regional Planning.
Nancy Chau, Associate Professor in the Department of Applied Economics and Management.
Neema Kudva, Assistant Professor in the Department of City and Regional Planning.
Daniel (Pete) Loucks, Professor in the Department of Civil and Environmental Engineering.
Theodore J. Lowi, John L. Senior Professor of American Institutions in the Department of Government.
Kathryn S. March, Professor in the Departments of Anthropology and Feminist, Gender, and Sexuality Studies.
Jerome M. Ziegler, Professor Emeritus in the Department of Policy Analysis and Management.

CORNELL UNIVERSITY

School of Industrial and Labor Relations

Programs of Study

Cornell offers four graduate degree programs in the field of industrial and labor relations (ILR): Master of Industrial and Labor Relations (M.I.L.R.), Master of Professional Studies (M.P.S.), M.S., and Ph.D. Candidates for the M.I.L.R. degree come from a variety of backgrounds and are interested in preparing for positions in human resource management, labor relations (including collective bargaining), and public policy. The M.I.L.R. reflects the need of future practitioners to become broadly familiar with all major aspects of the field and to become particularly competent in one of five areas: human resources and organizations, collective representation, dispute resolution, international and comparative labor, or labor-market policy. Students complete a minimum of 48 credits in courses and seminars, including required courses in collective bargaining, labor economics, labor and employment law, human resource management, organizational behavior, and statistics. Candidates with a law (J.D.) or M.B.A. degree may be able to obtain an M.I.L.R. degree in two semesters. Students interested in careers in business administration may apply for a five-semester, dual-degree program at the School of Industrial and Labor Relations (M.I.L.R.) and the Johnson Graduate School of Management (M.B.A.). The M.P.S. degree is limited to individuals with professionally related work experience who wish to update their knowledge of current practices. Applicants for this degree are often sponsored by their governments or organizations. Degree requirements include course work and an M.P.S. project. Students may choose to study part-time in New York City in the M.P.S. New York program or full-time in residence on the Ithaca campus. M.S. and Ph.D. candidates select major and minor subjects from the following areas: collective bargaining, labor law, and labor history; organizational behavior; human resource studies; and international and comparative labor. Minor subjects can also include social statistics and labor economics. Minor subjects in fields outside ILR are encouraged. Each candidate's program is supervised by a special committee of faculty members chosen by the candidate. The average M.S. program requires two years; the doctoral program typically takes an additional three years.

Research Facilities

The ILR School's Catherwood Library, with more than 232,000 volumes, is one of the world's most comprehensive specialized university libraries in the field of human resource management and industrial and labor relations. Catherwood's Kheel Center for Labor-Management Documentation and Archives ranks as one of three major centers of its type in the country. Catherwood is one of seventeen libraries constituting the Cornell University Library, ranked as one of the ten largest academic research libraries in the United States, with more than 7 million printed volumes, 65,000 journal and newspaper subscriptions, and more than 40,000 networked electronic databases available to users. Networked computer facilities in Catherwood and in other campus libraries are provided for graduate students, and a rapidly expanding array of electronic and full-text resources is available for use outside of the library. Catherwood's programs and services are aimed at providing easy access to its outstanding collections. Library staff members offer seminars and individualized training to acquaint graduate students with the research potential of Catherwood's print and electronic holdings.

Financial Aid

A small number of fellowships may be awarded on a competitive basis by Cornell University and the ILR School. In addition, the School awards a limited number of assistantships, mostly to M.S. and Ph.D. students, which provide a stipend of $20,710 for the 2008–09 academic year. Tuition scholarships are also granted to graduate assistants. Assistantships require 15–20 hours of work each week in the School's instructional, research, or extension programs.

Cost of Study

Tuition is $22,600 for the 2008–09 academic year for both state residents and out-of-state students. Books cost between $900 and $1100 per year, and there is also a thesis fee.

Living and Housing Costs

Budgets for single students to live at a modest comfort level average $1200 per month. Married students should expect greater expenses. The largest variable is rent; both University and private housing are available to graduate students.

Student Group

The population of graduate students at Cornell is more than 6,000, representing all regions of the United States and many other countries. Candidates for the M.I.L.R. degree, approximately half of the 180 graduate students in ILR, have a wide variety of academic and employment backgrounds. M.I.L.R. candidates generally choose professional careers, while Ph.D. candidates usually aim for academic appointments.

Student Outcomes

The ILR Office of Career Services provides a wide variety of services, including individual advising, workshops, resume reviews, career fairs, networking assistance, job listings, and practice interviews to help students explore their career options and develop effective job-search strategies. The office manages an on-campus recruitment program, with representatives of numerous corporations, labor unions, government agencies, and labor law firms interviewing students for positions in human resources and labor relations. The office also cultivates contacts with alumni and others working in the field. Further career information is available from the Office of Career Services, 201 Ives Hall, Cornell University (telephone: 607-255-7816; Web site: http://www.ilr.cornell.edu/careerservices/). A few of the leading employers of M.I.L.R. degree recipients are the AFL-CIO, Bristol-Myers Squibb, Citigroup, Dell, General Electric, General Mills, Honeywell, IBM, Microsoft, the National Labor Relations Board (NLRB), and Raytheon. The mean salary for a recent M.I.L.R. graduating class was approximately $65,838. The mean salary for recent M.I.L.R. graduates choosing the corporate sector was $68,136, with a mean signing bonus of $7672. Those recently completing doctoral degree programs found employment at such places as Cornell, the Universities of Missouri and Michigan, Harvard Business School, and the U.S. Bureau of Labor Statistics.

Location

Ithaca is a university town of nearly 40,000, set in the center of the beautiful Finger Lakes region of upstate New York. The area is rich in outdoor recreational resources for swimming, skiing, and boating. Cornell and neighboring Ithaca College as well as community groups in the creative and performing arts contribute to a lively and diverse cultural life that includes plays, concerts, opera, ballet, and lectures.

The University

The Cornell tradition of graduate education recognizes that each student has different needs, strengths, and goals, and the University makes every effort to accommodate students' specific requirements and incomes. Every member of the social science faculties at Cornell is a potential resource to each ILR graduate student, whatever the field of study, providing intellectual resources that are extensive and cross college boundaries. Distinguished scholars in economics, sociology, and psychology can be found in ILR as well as in appropriate fields in the College of Arts and Sciences, the College of Human Ecology, and the Johnson School of Management; in other professional fields, such as developmental sociology, child development and family relations, agricultural economics, and business law; and in research institutes such as the Southeast Asia and Latin American Centers.

Applying

While a strong background in the social sciences is both appropriate and helpful for advanced work at ILR, those with different backgrounds (engineering, law, business) regularly enroll. The deadline for fall admission is January 15; for spring admission, the deadline is October 15. Ph.D. candidates generally undertake master's thesis research before entering the Ph.D. program. Exceptionally well-qualified applicants may be admitted directly to the doctoral program with only a bachelor's degree. All applicants must take the General Test of the Graduate Record Examinations (GRE) or the Graduate Management Admission Test (GMAT). International students are also required to take the Test of English as a Foreign Language (TOEFL).

Correspondence and Information

Director of Graduate Studies
School of Industrial and Labor Relations
214 Ives Hall
Cornell University
Ithaca, New York 14853-3901

Phone: 607-255-1522
E-mail: ilrgradapplicant@cornell.edu
Web site: http://www.ilr.cornell.edu/graddegreeprograms

Cornell University

THE FACULTY

The graduate faculty members at Cornell's School of Industrial and Labor Relations represent a wide spectrum of the social and behavioral sciences—cultural anthropology, economics, history, law, political science, psychology, social psychology, sociology, and statistics—offering courses, advising, consulting, directing research activities, and sharing research opportunities. In addition, students may take courses from and select as advisers other Cornell faculty members in the social sciences, the humanities, mathematics, and engineering.

Department of Collective Bargaining, Labor Law, and Labor History
Lee H. Adler, Senior Extension Associate; J.D., Golden Gate. Law.
Kate Brofenbrenner, Senior Lecturer and Director of Labor Education Research; Ph.D., Cornell. Labor and industrial relations.
Lance Compa, Senior Lecturer; J.D., Yale. Law.
Maria L. Cook, Associate Professor; Ph.D., Berkeley. Political science.
Jefferson Cowie, Assistant Professor; Ph.D., North Carolina at Chapel Hill. History.
Cletus Daniel, Professor; Ph.D., Washington (Seattle). History.
Ileen A. DeVault, Associate Professor; Ph.D., Yale. History.
Rebecca Givan, Assistant Professor; Ph.D., Northwestern. Political science.
Michael E. Gold, Associate Professor; J.D., Stanford. Law.
Kate Griffith, Assistant Professor; J.D., NYU. Law.
James A. Gross, Professor; Ph.D., Wisconsin. Labor economics and industrial relations.
Richard W. Hurd, Professor; Ph.D., Vanderbilt. Economics.
Lawrence Kahn, Professor; Ph.D., Berkeley. Economics.
Harry C. Katz, Jack Sheinkman Professor in Collective Bargaining and Dean of the ILR School; Ph.D., Berkeley. Economics.
Sarosh C. Kuruvilla, Professor; Ph.D., Iowa. Business administration.
Risa L. Lieberwitz, Associate Professor; J.D., Florida. Law.
David B. Lipsky, Professor; Ph.D., MIT. Economics.
Nicholas Salvatore, Maurice and Hinda Neufeld Founders Professorship in Industrial and Labor Relations; Ph.D., Berkeley. History.
Ronald L. Seeber, Professor; Ph.D., Illinois. Labor and industrial relations.
Lowell Turner, Professor; Ph.D., Berkeley. Political science.

Department of Human Resource Studies
Rosemary Batt, Associate Professor and Alice Cook Professor of Women and Work; Ph.D., MIT. Human resources.
Bradford Bell, Assistant Professor; Ph.D., Michigan State. Organizational psychology.
John H. Bishop, Associate Professor; Ph.D., Michigan. Economics.
Christopher Collins, Assistant Professor; Ph.D., Maryland. Organizational behavior.
Lisa Dragoni, Assistant Professor; Ph.D., Maryland. Organizational behavior and human resource management.
Lee D. Dyer, Professor; Ph.D., Wisconsin. Personnel.
Kevin F. Hallock, Professor; Ph.D., Princeton. Economics.
John Hausknecht, Assistant Professor; Ph.D., Penn State. Industrial and organizational psychology.
Lisa Hisae Nishii, Assistant Professor; Ph.D., Maryland. Organizational psychology.
Quinetta Roberson, Assistant Professor; Ph.D., Maryland. Organizational behavior.
Patrick M. Wright, Professor; Ph.D., Michigan State. Business administration.

Department of International and Comparative Labor Relations
Rosemary Batt, Associate Professor and Alice Cook Professor of Women and Work; Ph.D., MIT. Human resources.
John H. Bishop, Associate Professor; Ph.D., Michigan. Economics.
George Boyer, Professor; Ph.D., Wisconsin. Economics.
Lance Compa, Senior Lecturer; J.D., Yale. Law.
Maria L. Cook, Assistant Professor; Ph.D., Berkeley. Political science.
Gary S. Fields, Professor; Ph.D., Michigan. Economics.
James A. Gross, Professor; Ph.D., Wisconsin. Labor economics and industrial relations.
Sarosh C. Kuruvilla, Professor; Ph.D., Iowa. Industrial relations.
Lisa Hisae Nishii, Assistant Professor; Ph.D., Maryland. Organizational psychology.
Lowell Turner, Associate Professor; Ph.D., Berkeley. Political science.

Department of Labor Economics
John M. Abowd, Edmund Ezra Day Professor of Industrial and Labor Relations; Ph.D., Chicago. Economics.
Francine D. Blau, Frances Perkins Professor of Industrial and Labor Relations; Ph.D., Harvard. Economics.
George R. Boyer, Professor; Ph.D., Wisconsin. Economics.
Jed DeVaro, Assistant Professor; Ph.D., Stanford. Labor economics.
Ronald Ehrenberg, Irving M. Ives Professor of Industrial and Labor Relations; Ph.D., Northwestern. Economics.
Gary S. Fields, Professor; Ph.D., Michigan. Economics.
Kevin F. Hallock, Professor; Ph.D., Princeton. Economics.
Robert M. Hutchens, Professor; Ph.D., Wisconsin. Economics.
Kirabo Jackson, Assistant Professor; Ph.D., Harvard, Economics.
George H. Jakubson, Associate Professor; Ph.D., Wisconsin. Economics.
Lawrence M. Kahn, Professor; Ph.D., Berkeley. Economics.
Robert S. Smith, Professor; Ph.D., Stanford. Economics.

Department of Organizational Behavior
Samuel B. Bacharach, Jean McKelvey-Alice Grant Professor of Labor Management Relations; Ph.D., Wisconsin. Sociology.
Jack Goncalo, Assistant Professor; Ph.D., Berkeley. Business administration.
Tove H. Hammer, Professor; Ph.D., Maryland. Industrial organizational psychology.
Edward J. Lawler, Martin P. Catherwood Professor of Industrial and Labor Relations; Ph.D., Wisconsin. Sociology.
Brian Rubineau, Assistant Professor; Ph.D., MIT. Organization studies and economic sociology.
William J. Sonnenstuhl, Associate Professor; Ph.D., NYU. Sociology.
Pamela S. Tolbert, Professor; Ph.D., UCLA. Sociology.
Michele Williams, Assistant Professor; Ph.D., Michigan. Organizational behavior.

Department of Social Statistics
John A. Bunge, Associate Professor; Ph.D., Ohio. Statistics.
Thomas J. DiCiccio, Associate Professor; Ph.D., Waterloo. Statistics.
Paul F. Velleman, Associate Professor; Ph.D., Princeton. Statistics.
Martin T. Wells, Associate Professor; Ph.D., Berkeley. Mathematics.

GEORGE MASON UNIVERSITY

School of Public Policy

Programs of Study The School of Public Policy (SPP) at George Mason University seeks to prepare its graduates for positions of responsibility in academic institutions, industry, government, and profit and not-for-profit institutions dedicated to the improvement of both the substance and the processes of public policymaking in the United States and abroad. SPP offers the following degree programs: Doctor of Philosophy (Ph.D.) in Public Policy; Master of Public Policy (M.P.P.); Master of Arts (M.A.) in International Commerce and Policy; Master of Arts (M.A.) in Transportation Policy, Operations, and Logistics; Master of Science in New Professional Studies: Organization Development and Knowledge Management; and Master of Science in New Professional Studies: Peace Operations.

The School's programs, led by a distinguished faculty, focus on the interplay of culture, organizations, and technology in a quest to find alternative approaches to public policy decisions and policymaking. Teaching and research is focused on, but not limited to, six themes: Governance; International Commerce and Policy; Entrepreneurship; Regional and Economic Development; Science and Technology Policy; and Culture and Values.

The Ph.D. in Public Policy program is distinctive in its emphasis on the combined influence of technology, culture, and institutions on public policy. To investigate the policy issues associated with substantive policy areas, students develop an in-depth understanding of American institutions, values, and culture; competence in research methods and advanced analytical methodologies; and a comparative, international perspective. The M.P.P. provides a degree for aspiring or experienced professionals who seek career advancement through cutting-edge education and training in policy analysis and development in increasingly technical and global environments. Professional certificates are also offered with this program. The M.A. in International Commerce and Policy program is an interdisciplinary course of study that prepares students for careers in the new global economy. Unlike traditional M.B.A. and international affairs programs, the degree is focused on international economic issues such as global trade and investment. Professional certificates are also offered with this program. The M.A. in Transportation Policy, Operations, and Logistics program is designed for students and practicing professionals engaged in planning, regulating, managing, and operating transportation facilities and services. The Organization Development and Knowledge Management program is run in an executive format and is designed for professionals with several years of work experience. It provides students with the conceptual tools and practical guidance to foster organizational change. The Peace Operations program offers candidates a focused degree in various aspects of the planning, regulation, management, and conduct of peace operations.

Research Facilities George Mason University (GMU) Libraries comprise the Fenwick and Johnson Center Libraries on the Fairfax campus and the Arlington and Prince William campus libraries. Fenwick is the main research library and offers access to a large number of electronic resources in addition to more than 600,000 volumes. GMU provides students with e-mail and Internet access and is a member of the Washington Regional Library Consortium, giving students access to 4 million volumes. In addition to research facilities on campus, GMU is a short distance from major research facilities in the Washington, D.C., area, including the Library of Congress, the National Archives, and numerous governmental agencies. Students may visit the GMU Libraries' Web site for more information (http://library.gmu.edu).

SPP's research centers include the Center for Regional Analysis; the Policy Analysis Center; the International Center for Applied Studies in Information Technology; the Center for Science and Technology Policy; the Center for Transport Policy and Logistics; the Office of International Medical Policy; the State Economic Development Center; the Center for Entrepreneurship and Public Policy; the Societal Dynamics Research Center; the Center for Global Policy; the Aerospace Policy Research Center; the Center for Executive Education and Leadership in Public Policy, and the Mason Enterprise Center.

Financial Aid Full-time Ph.D. candidates are eligible for graduate research assistantships. These assistantships offer a stipend of $16,000 and also include tuition waivers. Financial assistance is granted to master's candidates on a limited basis.

Cost of Study For the 2008–09 academic year, tuition and fees are $545 per credit hour for in-state students and $1003 for out-of-state students.

Living and Housing Costs The cost of living in the northern Virginia/Washington, D.C., area is comparable to that in most major metropolitan centers. Limited on-campus graduate student housing is available on the Fairfax campus; no on-campus housing is available on the Arlington campus. Most graduate students choose to live off campus.

Student Group In fall 2007, SPP enrolled 899 students in its various graduate programs. Forty-nine percent were women, 16 percent were members of minority groups, and 10 percent were international students. Fifteen percent were enrolled in the Ph.D. program, and 85 percent were enrolled in the various master's programs. Seventy-two percent enrolled part-time, while 28 percent enrolled full-time.

Student Outcomes Upon completion of degree requirements, graduates find employment in academic institutions, federal and state agencies and departments, international businesses and banks, law firms, consulting firms, think tanks, and not-for-profit organizations. Many international students return home to work in the public and private sectors. SPP provides career advisement, internship, and placement support for all students.

Location Located in Northern Virginia, George Mason is only 15 miles from all the resources of the National Capital Region and the Washington metropolitan area. Washington's libraries, galleries, and museums; Virginia's historic sites; and Fairfax County's high-technology firms are easily accessible. George Mason's 5.2-acre Arlington Campus, which is home to most SPP master's programs, is just minutes to Washington, D.C., by Metrorail.

Applying Application deadlines for the master's programs are June 1 for fall and December 1 for spring. International applicant deadlines are one month prior to these dates. For Ph.D. applicants, fall application deadlines are February 1 for international students and March 1 for domestic students. For the spring term, Ph.D. application deadlines are October 1 for international applicants and November 1 for domestic applicants. Students should note that funding is only awarded to full-time Ph.D. students beginning their study in the fall term. All applicants must submit a graduate application and fee, all official university transcripts, a written goals statement, a professional resume, two letters of recommendation, and a writing sample (Ph.D. applicants only). GRE or GMAT scores are required for all Ph.D. candidates and for master's degree applicants who are seeking merit-based funding consideration. International applicants must also submit a TOEFL score. Application packets may be requested by contacting SPP or visiting the School's Web site. Students should visit http://policy.gmu.edu/admissions for more specific information on application requirements for both the master's and Ph.D. degree programs.

Correspondence and Information

Graduate Admissions
School of Public Policy
George Mason University
3401 Fairfax Drive, MS 3B1
Arlington, Virginia 22201

Phone: 703-993-8099
Fax: 703-993-4876
E-mail: spp@gmu.edu
Web site: http://policy.gmu.edu
http://www.gmu.edu

George Mason University

CORE FACULTY

Administrative Faculty
Kingsley E. Haynes, University Professor and Dean; Ph.D., Johns Hopkins, 1971.
James H. Finkelstein, Professor and Vice Dean for Administration; Ph.D., Ohio State, 1980.
Roger R. Stough, Northern Virginia Professor of Local Government and Associate Dean for Research, Development, and External Relations; Ph.D., Johns Hopkins, 1978.
Matthys van Schaik, Senior Assistant Dean of Graduate and Professional Programs; Ph.D., South Carolina, 1995.

Faculty
Zoltan J. Acs, University Professor; Ph.D., New School, 1980.
Mark S. Addleson, Associate Professor, Program on Organization Development and Knowledge Management; Ph.D., Witwatersrand, 1992.
David J. Armor, Professor of Public Policy; Ph.D., Harvard, 1966.
Philip E. Auerswald, Assistant Professor; Ph.D., Washington (Seattle), 1999.
Ann Baker, Assistant Professor and Director, Organization Development and Knowledge Management; Ph.D., Case Western, 1995.
Kenneth J. Button, Professor of Public Policy; Ph.D., Loughborough (England), 1981.
Desmond Dinan, Jean Monnet Professor of Public Policy; Ph.D., National University of Ireland, 1985.
Michael K. Fauntroy, Assistant Professor; Ph.D., Howard, 2001.
James H. Finkelstein, Professor and Senior Associate Dean, School of Public Policy; Ph.D., Ohio State, 1980.
Allison Frendak-Blume, Assistant Professor of Public Policy and Director, Peace Operations Program; Ph.D., George Mason, 2004.
A. Lee Fritschler, Professor; Ph.D., Syracuse, 1965.
Stephen S. Fuller, University Professor and Professor of Public Policy and Regional Development; Ph.D., Cornell, 1969.
Jonathan L. Gifford, Associate Professor of Public Policy and Director, Transportation, Policy, Operation, and Logistics Program; Ph.D., Berkeley, 1983.
Jack A. Goldstone, Virginia E. Hazel and John T. Hazel Jr. Professor of Public Policy and Director, Ph.D. in Public Policy Program; Ph.D., Harvard, 1981.
Thomas R. Gulledge, Professor of Public Policy and Operations Research; Ph.D., Clemson, 1981.
David M. Hart, Associate Professor; Ph.D., MIT, 1995.
Kingsley E. Haynes, University Professor and Dean, School of Public Policy; Ph.D., Johns Hopkins, 1970.
Jack C. High, Professor of Public Policy, Economics, and Social Learning; Ph.D., UCLA, 1980.
Christopher T. Hill, Professor of Public Policy and Technology and Vice Provost for Research; Ph.D., Wisconsin–Madison, 1969.
Don E. Kash, John T. Hazel Sr. and Ruth D. Hazel Professor of Public Policy; Ph.D., Iowa, 1963.
Michael R. Kelley, Professor and Director, Telecommunications Policy Program; Ph.D., Catholic University, 1970.
Naoru Koizumi, Assistant Professor of Public Policy; Ph.D., Hyogo Medical College, 2005.
Andrew F. Krepinevich, Distinguished Visiting Professor of Public Policy; Ph.D., Harvard, 1984.
Todd M. La Porte, Associate Professor; Ph.D., Yale, 1989.
Siona Robin Listokin, Assistant Professor; Ph.D., Berkeley, 2007.
Stuart S. Malawer, Distinguished Service Professor of Law and International Trade; Ph.D., Pennsylvania, 1976.
Monty G. Marshall, Research Professor, School of Public Policy; Ph.D., Iowa, 1996.
Jeremy Mayer, Assistant Professor and Director, Master of Public Policy Program; Ph.D., Georgetown, 1996.
Connie L. McNeely, Associate Professor of Public Policy; Ph.D., Stanford, 1990.
Arnauld Nicogossian, Distinguished Research Professor; M.D., Teheran, 1964; M.S., Ohio State, 1972.
Wayne D. Perry, Professor of Public Policy and Operations Research; Ph.D., Carnegie Mellon, 1975.
John E. Petersen, Professor of Public Policy; Ph.D., Pennsylvania, 1967.
James P. Pfiffner, Professor of Public Policy, Government, and Politics; Ph.D., Wisconsin–Madison, 1975.
Ramkishen Rajan, Associate Professor of Public Policy; Ph.D., Claremont, 1999.
Kenneth A. Reinert, Associate Professor of Public Policy and Director, International Commerce and Policy Program; Ph.D., Maryland, College Park, 1988.
James D. Riggle, Research Associate Professor; Ph.D., George Mason, 2002.
Charles S. Robb, Distinguished Professor of Law and Public Policy; J.D., Virginia, 1973.
Mark J. Rozell, Professor of Public Policy; Ph.D., Virginia, 1987.
Catherine Rudder, Professor of Public Policy; Ph.D., Ohio State, 1973.
Stephen R. Ruth, Professor; Ph.D., Pennsylvania, 1971.
Laurie A. Schintler, Associate Professor of Public Policy; Ph.D., Illinois at Urbana–Champaign, 1996.
Edgar H. Sibley, University Professor; Sc.D., MIT, 1967.
Rainer Sommer, Associate Professor of Public Policy; Ph.D., Columbia Pacific, 1991; Ph.D., George Mason, 1998.
Roger R. Stough, Associate Dean for Research Development and External Affairs; Ph.D., Johns Hopkins, 1978.
Tojo Thatchenkery, Professor of Organization Development and Knowledge Management; Ph.D., Case Western, 1993.
Susan Tolchin, Professor of Public Policy; Ph.D., NYU, 1968.
Matthys van Schaik, Professor and Associate Dean for Academic Affairs; Ph.D., South Carolina, 1995.
Janine R. Wedel, Associate Professor; Ph.D., Berkeley, 1985.

Selected Affiliated Faculty
Kevin Avruch, Professor of Anthropology; Ph.D., California, San Diego, 1978.
Timothy J. Conlan, Associate Professor of Government and Politics; Ph.D., Harvard, 1981.
Thomas Dietz, Professor of Sociology; Ph.D., California, Davis, 1979.
George L. Donahue, Professor of Systems Engineering and Operations Research; Ph.D., Oklahoma State, 1972.
Robert L. Dudley, Associate Professor of Government and Politics; Ph.D., Northern Illinois.
Terry Friesz, Professor of Systems Engineering and Operations Research; Ph.D., Johns Hopkins, 1977.
Gregory A. Guagnano, Associate Professor of Sociology; Ph.D., California, Davis, 1986.
Michael W. Gremminger, European Union Fellow, M.B.A., Manheim (Germany), 1990.
Hugh Heclo, Robinson Professor of Public Affairs; Ph.D., Yale, 1970.
James T. Hennessey, Chief of Staff; Ph.D., George Mason, 1997.
Julianne G. Mahler, Associate Professor of Government and Politics; Ph.D., SUNY at Buffalo, 1976.
John Paden, Robinson Professor of International Studies; Ph.D., Harvard, 1968.
Priscilla M. Regan, Associate Professor of Government and Politics; Ph.D., Cornell, 1981.
Joseph A. Scimecca, Professor of Sociology; Ph.D., NYU, 1972.

Instructional and Research Faculty
Brien Benson, Research Associate Professor; Ph.D., George Mason, 1998.
Audrey E. Clarke, Research Professor; Ph.D., Kent State, 1992.
George Cook, Affiliate Professor; A.B., George Washington, 1957.
David F. Davis, Assistant Research Professor; M.S., Naval Postgraduate School, 1981.
Desmond J. Lugg, Distinguished Research Professor; M.D., Adelaide, 1974.
Arthur S. Melmed, Research Professor; M.S.E.E., Columbia, 1956.
Jean P. H. Paelinck, Distinguished Visiting Professor; J.D., Liege (Belgium), 1954.
Alexander E. R. Woodcock, Research Professor; Ph.D., East Anglia (England), 1968.

GEORGETOWN UNIVERSITY

Georgetown Public Policy Institute

Programs of Study

The Georgetown Public Policy Institute (GPPI) at Georgetown University consists of a 48-credit-hour/sixteen-course sequence of study that awards a Master of Public Policy (M.P.P.) degree. Also offered are joint-degree programs with the School of Business Administration (M.P.P./M.B.A.), the School of Foreign Service (M.P.P./M.S.F.S.), the Department of Economics (M.P.P./M.A. in economics), the Department of German (M.P.P./M.A. in German European studies), the Department of Government (M.P.P./Ph.D. in government), the Law Center (M.P.P./J.D.), the Department of Psychology (M.P.P./Ph.D. in psychology), and a dual M.P.P./International Organizations M.B.A. (M.P.P./IOMBA) with the University of Geneva, Switzerland.

The core curriculum of the public policy program provides the basic skills and knowledge essential for problem solving through the development of analytical skills and the capabilities to manage sound policy over a spectrum of public issues. The core courses are divided into three components, with five courses required in quantitative methodology, statistics, and applied research; two courses required in applied economic theory; and three courses required in public process, values, and public management. The remaining six courses are track-related. Participation in a track (or policy concentration) is required. All tracks consist of three structured electives plus a student's research thesis focusing on a policy topic related to the chosen policy track. The remaining three electives can be selected from courses related to the track area or can serve as free electives. The tracks include education, family and social policy; environmental and regulatory policy; health policy; homeland security; international development and policy; nonprofit leadership and policy; political strategy; and public management. In addition, students may choose from electives in any other graduate program at the University, including those in the Graduate School of Arts and Sciences, McDonough Business School, Law Center, School of Medicine, School of Foreign Service, and the Consortium of Washington Area Universities.

The M.P.P. degree from Georgetown University is designed to meet the needs of individuals desiring a strong background in the political and economic dimensions of governmental policy making, particularly those who plan a career in public- or private-sector policy analysis and management. The program's mission is to provide the specialized skills and training required of individuals who seek to play a role in solving the increasingly complex issues that face the nation and the international community.

Research Facilities

The Joseph Mark Lauinger Memorial Library has a collection of more than 2.2 million volumes. All Georgetown students are afforded access to the Edward Bennett Williams Law Library as well as the Medical Center Library. In addition, if students' needs are not met by Georgetown, the library has access to additional resources through the Consortium of Universities in the Washington, D.C., area or throughout the country through the Interlibrary Loan Service. In addition, students benefit greatly from the school's proximity to the Library of Congress on Capitol Hill. Located on the first floor of the library is an expanded government documents room with specialized materials for public policy–related research and an online computer-assisted reference service. Georgetown University is also a U.S. Government Documents Depository.

GPPI offers a private computer lab exclusively for use by GPPI students. The lab, which is open daily, has up-to-date hardware and software, including several statistical packages (SAS, STATA). Students are strongly encouraged to purchase a personal computer. Georgetown University provides assistance with recommended vendors and pricing.

Financial Aid

Financial assistance is available from the University on a need basis and from GPPI on a competitive merit basis. All students seeking need-based aid must complete the Free Application for Federal Student Aid (FAFSA). GPPI offers a number of graduate assistantships for qualified full-time students with the following research affiliates: the Center for Public and Nonprofit Leadership, Center for Research on Children in the U.S., and the Health Policy Institute. The Bryce Harlow Scholarship is available for part-time students. GPPI is a participating institution of the Public Policy and International Affairs (PPIA) Fellowship Program.

Cost of Study

For the 2008–09 school year, tuition is $35,160 or $1465 per credit hour, for eight 3-credit courses per academic year. Part-time students are expected to complete two 3-credit courses each semester and are charged by credit hour for a total of $17,580 for the academic year.

Living and Housing Costs

Since housing is not provided to graduate students, students should plan to live off campus. There is an abundance of rental properties available in the Washington, D.C., area. The metropolitan region is easily navigated by an efficient bus and subway system (Metro). The Office of Housing Services maintains an up-to-date list of rental spaces available in Georgetown and the metropolitan area. Room and board estimates for a nine-month budget are $14,330. Personal expenses are about $3960, and books and supplies are $1200. On-campus housing is available to students with disabilities.

Student Group

The Georgetown University enrollment is more than 12,000. About half of these are graduate students. The Georgetown Public Policy Institute has more than 250 students, about 18 percent of whom attend part-time. Approximately 15 percent of these students are members of minority groups, and 52 percent are women. The students come from all areas of the United States and more than fifteen international locations.

Location

Georgetown University is a prominent feature of the physical and social landscape of Washington, D.C. The city offers unparalleled access for public policy students to study, train, and interact at professional organizations and agencies in the nation's capital. Washington, D.C., is a diverse center of cultural activity and home to the nation's most famous landmarks and monuments. The city's historic neighborhoods feature a wide variety of ethnic restaurants and activities as well as public parks and riverfront areas.

The University

Georgetown University was founded in 1789 and is the nation's oldest Catholic institution of higher learning. GPPI was founded in 1980–81 as a two-year multidisciplinary course of study within the Georgetown Graduate School of Arts and Sciences.

Applying

Applications for admission to GPPI should be sent directly to the Georgetown Public Policy Institute Office of Admissions. The deadlines for 2009–10 admission are January 8, 2009, for international students and February 2, 2009, for regular admissions and scholarship consideration. GPPI no longer mails paper applications to prospective students.

The application package includes a professional resume, a one-page personal statement, a half-page statement of interest in GPPI, three recommendations, all undergraduate and graduate transcripts, Graduate Record Examinations (GRE) scores, and the application fee. GMAT scores are also accepted for admission; joint M.P.P./M.B.A. and M.P.P./IOMBA applicants must submit GMAT scores.

International applicants must also submit official Test of English as a Foreign Language (TOEFL) or IELTS results. It is strongly recommended that all interested students call or write to request a copy of the comprehensive program prospectus or thoroughly review the program's Web site.

Correspondence and Information

Office of Admissions
Georgetown Public Policy Institute
Georgetown University
3520 Prospect Street NW, Suite 400
Washington, D.C. 20007
Phone: 202-687-0615
Fax: 202-687-9187
E-mail: gppiadmissions@georgetown.edu
Web site: http://gppi.georgetown.edu/
http://grad.georgetown.edu/pages//apply-online.cfm

Georgetown University

THE FACULTY

Michael Bailey, Associate Professor of Public Policy and Government; Ph.D. (political science), Stanford.
Robert Bednarzik, Visiting Professor of Public Policy; Ph.D. (economics), Missouri.
Amelie Constant, Visiting Professor of Public Policy; Ph.D. (economics), Vanderbilt.
E.J. Dionne, Jr., University Professor of Public Policy and Government; Ph.D. (sociology), Oxford.
Nada Eissa, Associate Professor of Public Policy; (economics), Harvard.
Judith Feder, Professor of Public Policy and Dean; Ph.D. (political science), Harvard.
Joseph Ferrara, Visiting Professor of Public Policy; Ph.D, (American government), Georgetown.
Ted Gayer, Assistant Professor of Public Policy; Ph.D. (economics), Duke.
William T. Gormley Jr., University Professor of Government and Public Policy; Ph.D. (political science), North Carolina at Chapel Hill.
James Habyarimana, Assistant Professor of Public Policy; Ph.D. (economics), Harvard.
Carolyn Hill, Assistant Professor of Public Policy; Ph.D. (public policy), Chicago.
Harry Holzer, Professor of Public Policy; Ph.D. (economics), Harvard.
Harriett Komisar, Associate Research Professor; Ph.D. (economics), Cornell.
Kathy Kretman, Director, Center for Public and Nonprofit Leadership; Ph.D. (political science), Maryland, College Park.
Jonathan Ladd, Assistant Professor of Government; Ph.D. (political science), Princeton.
Jean M. Mitchell, Professor of Public Policy; Ph.D. (economics), Vanderbilt.
Donna Ruane Morrison, Associate Professor of Public Policy; Ph.D. (sociology), Johns Hopkins.
Mark Nadel, Visiting Professor of Public Policy; Ph.D. (political science), Johns Hopkins.
David Newman, Visiting Professor of Public Policy; Ph.D. (political science), Rochester.
Karen Pollitz, Research Professor and Project Director; M.P.P., Berkeley.
Vijaya Ramachandran, Assistant Professor of Public Policy; Ph.D., (economics), Harvard.
Mark C. Rom, Associate Professor of Public Policy and Government; Ph.D. (political science), Wisconsin–Madison.
R. Kent Weaver, Distinguished Professor of Public Policy and Professor of Government; Ph.D. (political science), Harvard.

Visiting Faculty
Len Burman, Ph.D. (economics), Minnesota.
Tom Daschle, B.A., South Dakota State.
Michael Lipsky, Ph.D. (politics), Princeton.
Barbara Schone, Ph.D. (economics), Virginia.
Mark Shields, B.A., Notre Dame.

Affiliated Faculty
Alan Abramson, Ph.D. (political science), Yale.
Gregory Acs, Ph.D. (economics and social work), Michigan.
Joan Alker, M.Phil. (politics), Oxford.
Alison Aughinbaugh, Ph.D. (economics), North Carolina at Chapel Hill.
John Bailey, Ph.D. (political science), Wisconsin–Madison.
Ian Bannon, Ph.D. (economics), Sydney (Australia).
Gary Bass, Ph.D. (psychology and education), Michigan.
Paul Begala, J.D., Texas at Austin.
William Bonvillion, J.D., Columbia.
Jonathan Breul, M.P.A., Northeastern.
Paul Brown.
Jack Buckley, Ph.D. (economics), Stony Brook, SUNY.
Sheila P. Burke, M.P.A., Harvard.
Stuart Butler, Ph.D. (American economic history), St. Andrews (Scotland).
James Carafano, Ph.D. (history), Georgetown.
Duncan Chaplin, Ph.D. (economics), Wisconsin–Madison.
Michael Clemens, Ph.D. (economics), Harvard.
Francis Creighton, M.P.P., Georgetown.
David de Ferranti, Ph.D., (economics), Princeton.
Jean-Jacques Dethier, Ph.D. (economics), Berkeley.
Shanta Devarajan, Ph.D. (economics), Berkeley.
Kristin Smith Diwan, Ph.D. (economics), Princeton.
Spencer Ecer, Ph.D. (economics), Texas at Austin.
Peter Edelman, J.D., L.L.B., Harvard.
Pablo Eisenberg, B.Lit., Oxford.
Joe Elvery, Ph.D. (economics), Maryland.
Ron Faucheux, Ph.D. (economics), New Orleans.
Matthew Fellowes, Ph.D. (political science), North Carolina at Chapel Hill.
Geraldine Ferraro, J.D., Fordham.
Michael J. Feuer, Ph.D. (public policy), Pennsylvania.
Bernard Finel, Ph.D. (international relations), Georgetown.
Jonathan Fisher, Ph.D. (economics), Kentucky.
Susan Fleck, Ph.D. (economics), American.
Robert Friedland, Ph.D. (economics), George Washington.
Robert Gallucci, Ph.D. (politics), Brandeis.
Gerry Gingrich, Ph.D. (psychology), Maryland, College Park.
Sarah Gormly, Ph.D. (economics), Georgetown.
Jocelyn Guyer, M.P.P., Princeton.
Michael Halpern, M.D./Ph.D. (medical science), Michigan.
Winston Harrington, Ph.D. (city and regional planning), North Carolina at Chapel Hill.
Richard Hayes, Ph.D. (economics), Indiana.
Valarie Heitshusen, Ph.D. (political science), Stanford.
Frederick Hess, Ph.D. (government), Harvard.
Steven Heydemann, Ph.D. (political science), Chicago.
Jack Hoadley, Ph.D. (political science), North Carolina at Chapel Hill.
Virginia Hodgkinson, Ph.D. (higher education), Southern Illinois.
Michael W. Horrigan, Ph.D. (economics), Purdue.
Katie Horton, M.P.H., J.D., William and Mary; RN.
David Hunger, Ph.D. (economics), Oregon.
John Jackson, Ph.D. (education administration, planning, social policy), Harvard.
Jonathan Jacobson, Ph.D. (economics), MIT.
David Jernigan, Ph.D. (sociology), Berkeley.
David S. Johnson, Ph.D. (economics), Minnesota.
Elizabeth Kennedy, Ph.D. (public policy), Harvard.
Joseph Kile, Ph.D. (economics), Wisconsin.
Jin Kim, Ph.D., (environmental and resource economics), California, Davis.
Mila Kofman, J.D., Harvard.
Glenn Lamartin, Ph.D. (public administration), USC.
Carol Lancaster, Ph.D. (economics), London School of Economics.
Scott Lilly, B.A. (political science), Westminster (Missouri).
Mark Lloyd, J.D., Georgetown.
Laura LoGerfo, Ph.D. (education and psychology), Michigan.
Kevin Lucia, J.D., George Washington.
Steve Machlin, M.S. (biostatistics and epidemiology), Georgetown.
Gail Makinen, Ph.D. (economics), Wayne State.
Cindy Mann, J.D., NYU.
Andy Mason, Ph.D. (applied economics), Stanford.
Jonathan Mathieu, Ph.D. (economics), Colorado at Boulder.
Jeffrey L. Mayer, Ph.D. (political philosophy), Columbia.
Dennis McBride, Ph.D. (public administration), Naval Aerospace Medical Institute.
Signe-Mary McKernan, Ph.D. (economics), Brown.
Robert McGarrah, J.D., Villanova.
Chad Meyerhoefer, Ph.D. (agricultural economics), Cornell.
Charlene Mollison, M.A. (comparative literature), CUNY Graduate Center.
Diana L. Moss, Ph.D. (economics), Colorado School of Mines.
Todd Moss, Ph.D. (economics), London.
Robert Muller, Ed.D. (higher education management), Pennsylvania.
Geetha Nagarajan, Ph.D. (economics), Ohio State.
Laura Neilsen, Ph.D. (political science), Houston.
Austin Nichols, Ph.D. (economics), Michigan.
Ellen O'Brien, Ph.D. (economics), Notre Dame.
Anthony Ody, D.Phil. (economics), Oxford.
Richard O'Neil, Ph.D. (operations research), Maryland.
Jose Oyola, Ph.D. (economics), UCLA.
Neal Pollard, J.D., Georgetown.
William R. Prosser, M.P.A., Harvard; M.S. (industrial engineering), Stanford.
Neil Proto, J.D., George Washington.
Michael Puma, M.P.P. (public policy), SUNY at Stony Brook.
Caroline Ratcliffe, Ph.D. (economics), Cornell.
Jeffrey Rohaly, M.A. (economics), Berkeley.
Lynn Ross, Ph.D. (American government), Georgetown.
Ivan Rossignol, Diploma (economics), Institute Superieur du Commerce (France).
Joydeep Roy, Ph.D. (economics), Princeton.
Kim Rueben, Ph.D. (economics), MIT.
William J. Scanlon, Ph.D. (economics), Wisconsin–Madison.
Joseph Schmidt, M.Div., Catholic University.
Stephen Schwenke, Ph.D. (policy studies), Maryland, College Park.
Louise Sheiner, Ph.D. (economics), Harvard.
Alexandra Shields, Ph.D. (social policy), Brandeis.
David Sitrin, M.P.A., Syracuse.
Russell Smith, J.D., Georgia.
Chad Stone, Ph.D. (economics), Yale.
Mike Stoto, Ph.D. (statistics), Harvard.
Laura Summer, M.P.H., Michigan.
Marcia Lee Taylor, M.P.P., Georgetown.
Eric Toder, Ph.D. (economics), Rochester.
Chris Toppe, Ph.D. (perceptual psychology), Florida.
Kathleen Kennedy Townsend, J.D., New Mexico.
Margery Turner, M.A., Georgetown.
Charles Vehorn, Ph.D. (economics), Ohio State.
Benjamin Webster, Ph.D. (government), Georgetown.
Maxine Weinstein, Ph.D. (sociology), Princeton.
Tim Westmoreland, J.D., Yale.
Tom Wingfield, J.D., Georgetown.

INDIANA UNIVERSITY BLOOMINGTON

School of Public and Environmental Affairs
Public Affairs Graduate Programs

Programs of Study

The School of Public and Environmental Affairs (SPEA) offers graduate degree programs leading to the Master of Public Affairs (M.P.A.), the Ph.D. in public policy, and the Ph.D. in public affairs.

The two-year, 48-hour M.P.A. degree is an interdisciplinary program that equips students with a combination of skills for professional careers in government, nonprofit, and private sectors. The program consists of four components: a core, a concentration area, an experiential component, and sufficient electives and/or prior professional experience. The core courses include public management, statistical analysis, public management economics, law and public affairs, public finance and budgeting, and a capstone project in public and environmental affairs. SPEA's concentrations provide both depth and breadth to the curriculum, enabling students to develop as professionals, hone their skills, and better prepare for the professional challenges that will be integral to complex world problems. Many SPEA students choose to pursue more than one concentration. The M.P.A. concentration areas are comparative and international affairs, economic development, environmental policy and natural resource management, information systems, local government management, nonprofit management, policy analysis, public financial administration, public management, and SPEA's new addition, sustainable development. To integrate their academic training into a practical framework, students are required to complete an internship or a significant research project in order to satisfy the experiential component of the M.P.A. program. The capstone project serves as the culmination to a student's academic training. Capstone projects are normally a semester-long, detailed analysis of a policy or management issue, often undertaken for a real-world client in the public or nonprofit sector.

Joint-degree programs are offered with SPEA's Master of Science in Environmental Science (M.S.E.S.) and Indiana University's Departments of African American and African Diaspora Studies, African Studies, Central Eurasian Studies, East Asian Studies, Latin American and Caribbean Studies, Russian and East European Studies, and West European Studies, as well as the Schools of Library and Information Science, Law, and Journalism.

The Ph.D. in public affairs is designed to prepare scholars for research and teaching in the multidisciplinary field of public policy and management. The program emphasizes the study of public management and organization, policy analysis, and public finance. The joint Ph.D. in public policy is a collaborative venture with Indiana University's Department of Political Science. This program emphasizes study of the public policy process. Students explore issues regarding policy analysis, government institutions, political behavior, and public affairs.

Research Facilities

Complementing the School's own resources, Indiana University maintains eight nationally prominent area studies centers and sixty language programs to facilitate international research and career interests. SPEA has affiliations with several research centers on both the Bloomington and Indianapolis campuses, including the Transportation Research Center, the Institute for Family and Social Responsibility, the Environmental Science Research Center, the Institute for Development Strategies, the Center for Health Policy, the Center for Criminal Justice Research, the Indiana University Public Policy Institute, and the Center for Urban Policy and Environment.

SPEA is committed to meeting the research needs of its students. PCs, mainframe computers, and a geographic information system (GIS) computing laboratory are available. More than forty additional computing sites on the Bloomington campus are available for student use. Libraries on the Bloomington campus house more than 6 million volumes, and another 3.2 million are available through the University's seven other campuses.

SPEA houses its own Information Commons, which provides computer access, common and private study areas, and a library shared with the Kelley School of Business.

Financial Aid

Departmental assistance for qualified students is awarded on a competitive basis and is determined by merit. Awards include fellowships, scholarships, and teaching and research assistantships. Prospective students may apply for merit-based awards by checking the appropriate box on the admission application form. Students may apply for need-based aid through the University Office of Student Financial Assistance (OSFA).

SPEA hosts a one-of-a-kind, collaborative program called Service Corps, which enables M.P.A. and M.S.E.S. students to apply their classroom learning directly to the field in both the public and nonprofit sectors. Service Corps is a financial aid mechanism that offers students real-world experience working in an array of governmental and nonprofit agencies while concurrently pursuing their academic plans. The program is a partnership among the University, School, and a number of valued external stakeholders in the community and region. Students are selected for participation during the merit aid allocation process.

Cost of Study

In-state residents pay $338.82 per credit hour and nonresidents pay $804.12 per credit hour for master's programs in 2008–09.

Living and Housing Costs

On-campus room and board for single graduate students during the 2008–09 academic year range from $4800 to $8450. The 1,500 on-campus housing units for married students range in monthly rent from $611 for an efficiency to $1068 for an unfurnished three-bedroom apartment. Rates include all utilities as well as local telephone service, cable TV, and Internet connection. A variety of off-campus apartments are available near the University. Rents are generally inexpensive, with the average two-bedroom unit renting for $550 to $700 per month.

Student Groups

About 250 students are enrolled in the M.P.A. program, with 40 students pursuing the dual M.P.A./M.S.E.S. program, and 75 students are enrolled in the Ph.D. programs in public affairs or public policy. About one tenth of these students are international, more than one half are women, and more than one tenth are members of underrepresented populations.

SPEA recognizes service in AmeriCorps, Teach for America, and Peace Corps, hosting both Peace Corps Fellows/USA, and Master's International programs with a waiver of the experiential component that is a part of the academic design and a reduction of the total number of credit hours required for degree completion.

Student Outcomes

SPEA maintains an outstanding placement record, attributed to a well-rounded curriculum, national prestige, and strong alumni support. Within six months of the close of the 2006–07 academic year, approximately 92 percent of students responding to SPEA's annual employment survey indicated that they had procured full-time professional positions or were continuing their education. The SPEA Office of Career Services (OCS) is staffed with professionals who assist graduate students with all of their career development needs. The services offered to students include individual career counseling; on-campus recruiting; a Web-based job listing service, SPEACareers.com; a wide range of employer information sessions; alumni mentoring; user-friendly Web-based career resources; and an extensive career resource library. With so many resources at their disposal, SPEA students annually compete for many of the most prestigious and competitive positions in federal and state government and top-tier nonprofits and foundations. SPEA students are also top candidates for positions with top-drawer consulting firms like Booz Allen Hamilton, Crowe Chizek, Deloitte, and Grant Thornton. Some examples of other recent placements include the World Bank, the Environmental Protection Agency, the Department of State, the National Forest Service, the Government Accountability Office, the National Institutes of Health, the National Oceanographic and Atmospheric Institute, the Millennium Challenge Corporation, the Nature Conservancy, the Corporation for National and Community Service, the Bill and Melinda Gates Foundation, the Indiana Department of Environmental Management, the Indiana Office of Management and Budget, and the Indiana Department of Transportation.

During the 2006–07 academic year, 10 students were selected as finalists for the Presidential Management Fellowship Program (PMF), one of the most selective federal programs for graduate students pursuing careers with the federal government.

Location

Bloomington, a college town of 100,000 people, was chosen as one of the top ten college towns in America for its "rich mixture of atmospherics and academia" by Edward Fiske, former education editor of the *New York Times*. It is a culturally vibrant community settled among southern Indiana's rolling hills, just 45 miles south of Indianapolis, the state capital. Mild winters and warm summers are ideal for outdoor recreation in the two state forests, one national forest, three state parks, and an array of lakes and streams that surround Bloomington.

The University and The School

Established in 1820, Indiana University has more than 7,500 graduate students and more than 38,000 students total enrolled on the Bloomington campus. SPEA is the top-ranked graduate program on campus. Fifty-five other academic departments are ranked in the top 20 in the country, including music, business, biology, foreign languages, political science, and chemistry. Attractions include nearly 1,000 musical performances each year, with eight full-length operas and professional Broadway plays; the IU Art Museum, designed by I. M. Pei, with more than 30,000 art objects; fifty campus and community volunteer agencies; more than 500 student sports clubs and organizations; two indoor student recreational facilities; and Big Ten athletics. SPEA, founded in 1972, was the first school to combine public management, policy, and administration with the environmental sciences.

Applying

Application files must include the SPEA Admission Application form, transcripts, GRE General Test scores, and three letters of recommendation. Priority is given to applications received by February 1. Students applying for awards must submit a complete application file by the priority deadline, February 1. School visits are encouraged. Applicants can also access the School's Web site at http://www.spea.indiana.edu.

Correspondence and Information

For master's programs:
Graduate Program Office
SPEA 260
Indiana University
Bloomington, Indiana 47405
Phone: 812-855-2840
800-765-7755 (toll-free, domestic only)
E-mail: speainfo@indiana.edu
Web site: http://www.spea.indiana.edu

For doctoral programs:
Ph.D. Programs Office
SPEA 441
Indiana University
Bloomington, Indiana 47405
Phone: 812-855-2457
800-765-7755 (toll-free, domestic only)
E-mail: speainfo@indiana.edu
Web site: http://www.spea.indiana.edu

Indiana University Bloomington

THE FACULTY AND THEIR RESEARCH

Osita G. Afoaku, Ph.D., Washington State, 1991. International relations (theory, foreign policy/national security, political economy), comparative politics (political development, Third-World/African politics, theory), multicultural studies (African and African American), public administration.
Robert Agranoff, Emeritus; Ph.D., Pittsburgh, 1967. Intergovernmental relations (U.S. and cross-national), economic and community development, management of public agencies, governance, intergovernmental management, federal arrangements.
David Audretsch, Ph.D., Wisconsin, 1980. Economics policy, entrepreneurship, innovation, globalization, regional economic policy, industrial restructuring and government policy, small enterprises in Europe and the United States.
Matthew R. Auer, Ph.D., Yale, 1996. Environmental policy and management problems with an international focus: international environmental assistance, comparative industrial environmental policy, international policies governing forests and forestry.
Randall Baker, Ph.D., London, 1968. Bridging the gap between the natural and social sciences, comparative study on different perspectives regarding the way problems are perceived and handled, historical perspectives in the analysis of contemporary environmental and policy problems.
A. James Barnes, J.D., Harvard, 1967. Environmental law, domestic and international environmental policy, ethics and the public official, mediation and alternative dispute resolution, law and public policy.
Lisa Bingham, J.D., Connecticut, 1979. Dispute resolution, dispute system design, mediation, administrative law, labor and employment law.
Anthony A. Blasingame, Ph.D., Maryland, College Park, 2002. Public finance, labor economics, poverty, and U.S. political economy.
Charles F. Bonser, Emeritus; D.B.A., Indiana, 1965. Regional economic development, the role of nongovernmental organizations, public policy, transatlantic education and policy.
Melissa A. L. Clark, M.S., Indiana, 1999. Aquatic and terrestrial habitats, Indiana Clean Lakes Program, water resources and water quality.
Christopher Craft, Ph.D., North Carolina State, 1987. Terrestrial and wetland ecosystem restoration, wetlands ecology, soil resources, biogeochemistry, nutrient cycling and carbon sequestration of soils and sediments.
Michael A. Edwards, Ph.D., North Dakota State, 1999. Atmospheric chemistry research: mechanistic studies of terpenes reacting with ozone, future regulation of hydrogen storage materials.
Sergio Fernandez, Ph.D., Georgia, 2004. Public management and organization theory, with focus on privatization and contracting out, public-sector leadership, and organizational change.
Burnell C. Fischer, Ph.D., Purdue, 1974. Forestry, particularly silviculture and urban forestry; growth and development of central hardwood forest stands and response to various silvicultural practices; community and urban forestry issues; forest resources policy and state government management; human factors relating to forests and forest products, particularly with regard to collaborative forestry.
Beth Gazley, Ph.D., Georgia, 2004. Volunteering and civic engagement, fundraising, nonprofit management, interorganizational collaboration, "new governance" and government-nonprofit relations.
David Good, Ph.D., Pennsylvania, 1985. Quantitative policy modeling, productivity measurement in public and regulated industries, urban policy analysis.
John D. Graham, Ph.D., Carnegie-Mellon, 1983. Risk and benefit-cost analysis; health, energy, and environmental policy; governance.
Kirsten Grønbjerg, Ph.D., Chicago, 1974. Nonprofit and public-sector relationships, examining scope and community dimensions of the Indiana nonprofit sector.
Hendrik M. Haitjema, Ph.D., Minnesota, 1982. Groundwater flow modeling, including regional groundwater flow systems, conjunctive surface-water and groundwater flow modeling, 3-D groundwater flow, and saltwater intrusion problems, with emphasis on application of analytic functions to modeling groundwater flow, specifically analytic-element method.
Diane Henshel, Ph.D., Washington (St. Louis), 1987. Sublethal health effects of environmental pollutants, especially pollutant effects on the developing organism, including the effects of polychlorinated dibenzo-p-dioxins (PCDDs) and related congeners on the developing nervous system of birds exposed in the wild and under controlled laboratory conditions.
Adam W. Herbert, Ph.D., Pittsburgh, 1971. Public policy analysis; effective administration of public-sector enterprises; politics and policy dimensions of public education; politics of higher education and the policy, political, and administrative challenges of enhancing public education from pre-K through higher education, with emphasis on issues that impact low-income and minority communities.
Monika Herzig, D.M.E., Indiana, 1997.
Ronald Hites, Ph.D., MIT, 1968. Applying organic analytical chemistry techniques to the analysis of trace levels of toxic pollutants, such as polychlorinated biphenyls and pesticides, with focus on understanding behavior of these compounds in the atmosphere and in the Great Lakes.
Chaman Jain, Ph.D., Indiana, 1975.
Christopher Hunt, M.A., Cambridge, 1961. Arts administration.
Craig Johnson, Ph.D., SUNY at Albany, 1993. Capital markets and financial intermediation; financial management; public budgeting and finance; financing e-government; financing economic development; environmental and infrastructure finance; focus on innovative financing structures, financial certification, and resolving financial distress.
William Jones, M.S., Wisconsin–Madison, 1977. Lake and watershed management, especially diagnosing lake and watershed water-quality problems; preparing management plans to address problems identified; stream ecology; Caribbean coral reef ecology and underwater archaeology; certified lake manager (CLM).
Kerry Krutilla, Ph.D., Duke, 1988. Energy policy, resource management in developing countries, environmental regulation, public choice, cost-benefit analysis.
Marc L. Lame, Ph.D., Arizona State, 1992. Implementation of integrated pest-management programs in schools and day-care facilities.
Leslie Lenkowsky, Ph.D., Harvard, 1982. Nonprofits and public policy, civil society in comparative perspective, institutional grant makers, volunteering and civic engagement, education and social welfare policy.
Joyce Y. Man, Ph.D., Johns Hopkins, 1992. Public finance, urban and regional economics, international trade, economic development, public budgeting and financial management.
Eugene B. McGregor Jr., Ph.D., Syracuse, 1968. Interaction of public policy, organizational structure, and management practice; special interest in relationship between education and economic development and in impacts of information technology on structure and management of public and nonprofit enterprise.
Michael McGuire, Ph.D., Indiana, 1995. Intergovernmental and interorganizational collaboration and networks, federalism and intergovernmental relations, public management, economic development.
Vicky Meretsky, Ph.D., Arizona, 1995. Ecology and management of rare species, biocomplexity, landscape-level species and community conservation, temporal patterns in biodiversity, integrating ecosystem research and endangered species management within adaptive management.
John L. Mikesell, Ph.D., Illinois, 1969. Governmental finance, especially questions of policy and administration of sales and property taxation; state lotteries; public budgeting; public finance in countries of the former Soviet Union.
Theodore K. Miller, Emeritus; Ph.D., Iowa, 1970. Statistical analysis.
Emilio Moran, Ph.D., Florida, 1975. Comparative politics and development, Southern African politics, ethics and politics.
Patrick O'Meara, Ph.D., Indiana, 1970. Comparative politics and development, Southern African politics, ethics and politics.
Clinton V. Oster Jr., Ph.D., Harvard, 1978. Aviation safety, airline economics and competition policy, international aviation, aviation infrastructure, environmental and natural resource policy, government regulation, business-government relations.
James A. Palmer, Emeritus; J.D., Indiana, 1971. Legal policy research and analysis, election law and administration, administrative law and processes.
David Parkhurst, Emeritus; Ph.D., Wisconsin–Madison, 1970. Physiological plant ecology, including transfers of carbon dioxide/water between leaves and atmosphere and cells within leaves, both in relation to leaf structure; mathematics/statistics applied to environmental issues, including analysis of concentrations of indicator bacteria at swimming beaches and correct interpretation of statistical hypothesis tests in decision making.
Roger B. Parks, Emeritus; Ph.D., Indiana, 1979. Organization and governance structures of metropolitan areas and their effects on effectiveness, efficiency, equity, and responsiveness of public service delivery; community policing.
D. Jeanne Patterson, Emeritus; D.B.A., Indiana, 1967. Financial management, government accounting and corporate governance.
James Perry, Ph.D., Syracuse, 1974. Public service motivation, government and civil service reform, public management, public human resource management, national and community service, performance-related pay, public organizational behavior.
Flynn W. Picardal, Ph.D., Arizona, 1992. Bioremediation, environmental microbiology, and biogeochemistry, with focus on microbial reduction of iron oxides and nitrate, transformation of metals and chlorinated hydrocarbons, and combined microbial-geochemical interactions.
Maureen A. Pirog, Ph.D., Pennsylvania, 1981. Poverty and income maintenance, with emphasis on child-support enforcement, welfare reform, and adolescent parenting.
Orville W. Powell, M.P.A., Penn State, 1963. Local government and the U.S. Constitution.
Nicole C. Quon, Ph.D., Yale, 2007. Health policy and health politics, influence of politics and science on decision making at federal agencies, how perceptions of access and quality of care within health-care institutions are shaped by patient knowledge and market forces.
J. C. Randolph, Ph.D., Carleton (Ottawa), 1972. Forest ecology; ecological aspects of global environmental change, with particular interests in forestry and agriculture; applications of geographic information systems (GIS) and remote sensing in environmental and natural resources management; landscape ecology and regional-scale modeling; physiological ecology of woody plants of small mammals.
David A. Reingold, Ph.D., Chicago, 1996. Urban poverty, economic development, social welfare policy, low-income housing policy.
Terri L. Renner, M.B.A., Indiana, 1985. Financial management, information systems, entrepreneurship.
Rafael Reuveny, Ph.D., Indiana, 1997. International political economy, with emphasis on globalization; rise and fall of major powers; political conflict and how it interacts with international trade, democracy, and the environment; sustainable development; Middle East political economy.
Edwardo L. Rhodes, Ph.D., Carnegie-Mellon, 1978. Public policy analysis, particularly public-sector applications of management science in the evaluation and assessment of the efficiency or organization performance of public activities, including environmental and natural resource policy implementation.
Kenneth R. Richards, J.D./Ph.D., Pennsylvania, 1997. Climate change policy, carbon sequestration economics, environmental policy implementation and instrument choice.
Evan J. Ringquist, Ph.D., Wisconsin–Madison, 1990. Public policy (environmental, energy, natural resources, and regulation), research methodology, American political institutions.
Justin Ross, Ph.D., West Virginia, 2007. Public economics, urban/regional economics, spatial econometrics, applied microeconomics, quantile regressions, public finance, political economy, game theory.
Todd V. Royer, Ph.D., Idaho State, 1999. Aquatic biogeochemistry, water resources, nutrient and carbon cycling in streams and rivers, water quality and nutrient standards.
Barry Rubin, Ph.D., Wisconsin–Madison, 1977. Urban and regional economic development and impact analysis, quantitative analysis of local government management and labor relations issues, statistics and quantitative methods, econometric modeling, public management information systems, strategic planning and management.
Richard S. Rubin, Emeritus; Ph.D., Cornell, 1973. Labor-management relations in the public sector, with particular focus on conflict resolution and labor management cooperation.
Michael Rushton, Ph.D., British Columbia, 1990. Cultural economics, policy and administration, nonprofit and public organizations and management, tax policy, government funding for the arts and other policies toward nonprofit organizations, coeditor of *Journal of Cultural Economics*.
John W. Ryan, Emeritus; Ph.D., Indiana, 1959. Comparative public policy analysis; comparative university organization and policy; general public administration, with special attention to higher education: governmental organization in Southeast Asia and Central and East Europe.
Joseph Shaw, Ph.D., Kentucky, 2001. Toxicology, genomics, ecology, and physiology, with collaborators in evolutionary biology, population genetics, and trace/biogeochemistry.
Roy W. Shin, Emeritus; Ph.D., Minnesota, 1969. Industrial policy, comparative economic development, environmental policy, competition policy, science and technology policy.
Nan Stager, M.S., Indiana, 1978. Mediation and alternative dispute resolution.
Philip S. Stevens, Ph.D., Harvard, 1990. Characterization of the chemical mechanisms that influence regional air quality and global climate change.
Terry Usrey, M.S., Indiana, 1983. E-government, information technology policy, information technology management.
Frank J. Vilardo, Emeritus; Dr.P.H., North Carolina, 1971. Public and private health administration, focusing on injuries as a public health problem from a behavioral perspective; drunk-driver countermeasures; transportation incidents involving radioactive materials; enforcement of local retail food inspection laws.
Henry K. Wakhungu, Ph.D., Indiana, 2004. Development of growth simulation models for sustainable management of indigenous community forests, experimental designs in tropical forestry research, how preservice teachers conceptualize mathematics (philosophically) indexed with mathematics learning and teaching.
Jeffrey R. White, Ph.D., Syracuse, 1984. Environmental biogeochemistry, aquatic chemistry, limnology.
Lois Recascino Wise, Ph.D., Indiana, 1982. Public management and employment policies and practices; public management reform, including comparative studies of determinants of administrative reforms, variations in reform patterns, and cross-national differences in evaluation of reforms; comparative research in pay policies and administrative pay reforms, bureaucratic behavior, and consequences of human diversity for effective work organizations.
Wenli Yan, Ph.D., Kentucky, 2008. Public and nonprofit financial management, state and local finance, quantitative methods, nonprofit and public management and budgeting.
C. Kurt Zorn, Ph.D., Syracuse, 1981. State and local finance, transportation safety, economic development, gaming policy.

INDIANA UNIVERSITY–PURDUE UNIVERSITY INDIANAPOLIS

School of Public and Environmental Affairs

Programs of Study

The Indiana University School of Public and Environmental Affairs (SPEA) at IUPUI offers graduate degree programs leading to the Master of Health Administration (M.H.A.) and the Master of Public Affairs (M.P.A.).

The M.H.A. program is designed to prepare individuals for leadership positions in the health services. The 51-credit-hour, interdisciplinary program provides a broadly balanced foundation of theoretical and practical knowledge and technical skills necessary to succeed in the complex and changing health field. M.H.A. students complete courses in accounting, economics, ethics, financial management, human resources management, information systems, law, marketing, and policy.

The 48-credit-hour M.P.A. degree is an interdisciplinary program that equips students with a combination of skills for professional careers in government, nonprofit, and private sectors. The program combines a set of core courses with a chosen concentration area: criminal justice, environmental management, nonprofit management, public management, or policy analysis.

Research Facilities

The Center for Urban Policy and the Environment conducts research and provides technical assistance to local and state agencies on topics of urban planning, economic development, service delivery, taxation, watershed management, and conflict resolution, among others. SPEA also maintains professional relations with the Center on Philanthropy at Indiana University. These organizations offer unique opportunities for graduate student research.

Financial Aid

Several graduate and administrative assistantships are available for full-time students. These provide a monthly stipend for nine months and most also provide tuition fee remission. The School makes every effort to continue financial support for each graduate assistant who is academically eligible for a second year. February 1 is the priority date for consideration for graduate assistantships. University fellowships are also available for highly qualified full-time students. These provide a monthly stipend for nine months, tuition fee remission, and do not require work during the first year of study. February 1 is the priority date for consideration for University fellowships. In addition, there are frequent research opportunities through which students can continue employment during the summer months. Part-time jobs in the health-care field (20 hours per week) are also available for full-time M.H.A. students.

Cost of Study

In 2008–09, the tuition for in-state M.H.A. and M.P.A. students is $320.84 per credit hour. Out-of-state students pay $777.76 per credit hour. Additional costs include $65.50 per semester for parking, technology fees of $186.90, $400 to $600 per semester for books, and other miscellaneous fees.

Living and Housing Costs

Apartment-style housing is available on campus. On-campus housing rates start at $716 per month. In addition to on-campus housing, a variety of privately owned apartments are available nearby. Rent ranges from about $340 to $640 per month. A flexible campus meal plan is available through the campus housing office.

Student Group

SPEA students come from a diverse variety of undergraduate backgrounds. SPEA's graduate programs currently enroll more than 120 full-time and 375 part-time students and admit 30 to 40 new students each year. More than half are women, one quarter are members of minority groups, and more than one twelfth are international students.

Student Outcomes

SPEA M.H.A. graduates gain skills in areas such as health systems management, outcomes management, financing arrangements, and strategic management. Recent M.H.A. graduates have pursued career positions with Anthem Blue Cross Blue Shield, Cardinal Health System, Community Hospitals of Indianapolis, Eli Lilly and Company, Indiana Hospital and Health Association, Indiana University Hospital, M Plan, Office of Medicaid Policy and Planning, and Riley Hospital for Children.

M.P.A. graduates develop a comprehensive understanding of the public and/or nonprofit sectors and the public policy process. Specific skills in areas such as organizational management, statistical analysis, information technology, and budgeting are gained through the M.P.A. core requirements and additional skills are gained through the specific concentrations. Recent M.P.A. graduates have pursued career positions with the city of Indianapolis, Environmental Protection Agency, Indiana Department of Environmental Management, Indianapolis Museum of Art, KPMG LLP, the Nature Conservancy, and the United Way of Central Indiana.

Location

Indiana University–Purdue University Indianapolis (IUPUI) is located on the western periphery of a dynamic downtown Indianapolis. Downtown attractions located near the University include White River State Park, the Indiana State Museum, Victory Field (a 13,000-seat baseball stadium), and the Canal Walk. Indianapolis is also noted for its world-class symphony, ballet, theater, and opera companies and is home to the world's largest children's museum. Indianapolis is known for its sports, playing host to several professional sports teams and auto races.

The University and The School

IUPUI demonstrates a model partnership among government, community, and higher education. It was formed in 1969 by combining the city facilities and programs of Indiana University and Purdue University under one name and administration. IUPUI has twenty schools offering over 200 programs to more than 29,000 students. The IUPUI campus ranks among the top fifteen in the country in the number of first professional degrees it confers and among the top seven in the number of health-related degrees.

SPEA, established in 1972, was the first school to combine public management, policy, and administration with the environmental sciences. *U.S. News & World Report* ranked SPEA at IUPUI among the best graduate schools for 2005—thirty-fifth of 253 public affairs schools. SPEA's Indianapolis criminal justice and nonprofit management programs were ranked third and fourth in the nation, respectively.

Applying

All applicants must have a baccalaureate degree from an accredited institution. A GPA of 3.0 or higher on a 4.0 scale is preferred. Undergraduate prerequisite courses for the M.H.A. include one course each in accounting, microeconomics, and statistics. An application form, three references, transcripts, and GRE or GMAT scores must be submitted along with a nonrefundable application fee. Applications should be received no later than May 15 for admission that fall. Applications for spring and summer should be received no later than September 15 and March 15, respectively. Students who wish to be considered for graduate assistantships should have their completed applications on file by February 1. Applications are accepted for admission during all semesters. International students should e-mail the Office of International Affairs at oia@iupui.edu for their deadline information.

Correspondence and Information

Graduate Programs in Health Administration and Public Affairs
School of Public and Environmental Affairs
Indiana University–Purdue University Indianapolis
801 West Michigan Street, BS 3027
Indianapolis, Indiana 46202-5152

Phone: 317-274-4656
E-mail: infospea@iupui.edu
Web site: http://www.spea.iupui.edu

Indiana University–Purdue University Indianapolis

THE FACULTY AND THEIR RESEARCH

Terry L. Baumer, Associate Professor; Ph.D., Loyola Chicago. Criminal justice policy, community corrections, program evaluation, crime trends.
Wolfgang Bielefeld, Professor; Ph.D., Minnesota. Nonprofit management and philanthropic studies.
Crystal Garcia, Associate Professor; Ph.D., California, Irvine. Community corrections, crime policy, juvenile justice, program evaluation.
Michael E. Gleeson, Associate Professor; Ph.D., Syracuse. Management science and operations management.
David Handel, Clinical Professor; M.B.A., Chicago. Industrial and labor relations, hospital administration.
Craig Hartzer, Clinical Professor and Director, Executive Education Program; Ph.D., Miami (Ohio). Strategic policy development and implementation, organizational development, budgeting, program management, public-private partnerships.
Alfred Tat-Kei Ho, Associate Professor; Ph.D., Indiana. Performance measurement and budgeting, applied public finance research, information technology management and e-government.
Ann M. Holmes, Associate Professor; Ph.D., British Columbia. Health economics, measurement of health outcomes for economic evaluation, analysis of mental health utilization.
G. Roger Jarjoura, Associate Professor; Ph.D., Maryland. Juvenile delinquency, juvenile justice process, statistics, research methods.
Sheila Suess Kennedy, Associate Professor; J.D., Indiana. Civil liberties, civil rights, rule of law, religion and public policy.
Timothy Koponen, Trustee Lecturer; Ph.D., Northwestern. Political economy, world and labor markets; formal and complex organizations; race, ethnic, and minority relations.
John Krauss, Clinical Professor and Director, Center for Urban Policy and the Environment; J.D., Indiana. Law, public policy, conflict resolution, mediation.
Paul Lang, Lecturer; M.P.A., Indiana. Accounting, fiscal governance, fundraising, long-range strategic planning.
Yong Li, Assistant Professor; Ph.D., Wayne State. Health economics, long-term care, health insurance, health-care utilization.
Greg H. Lindsey, Professor and Associate Dean; Ph.D., Johns Hopkins. Environmental and water resources planning, decision making, management.
Laura Littlepage, Clinical Lecturer; M.P.A., NYU. Evaluation, including needs assessments, process, outcome, and impact evaluations; nonprofit organizations; voluntarism.
Deanna Malatesta, Assistant Professor; Ph.D., Georgia. Administrative law, rule making, regulation, public management and performance, organizational and institutional analysis, telecommunications and information policy.
David Z. McSwane, Professor; H.S.D., Indiana. Environmental health policy, public health, food science.
Vicki Mech-Hester, Lecturer; Ed.D., Indiana. Strategic planning, performance management and enhancement, organizational effectiveness, leadership.
Debra J. Mesch, Associate Professor; Ph.D., Indiana. Workplace justice, nonprofit management, hospital mergers, strategic human resource management.
Samuel Nunn, Professor; Ph.D., Delaware. Law enforcement technology, terrorism and public policy, local homeland security policy, capital infrastructure systems within cities, local economic development policy, urban telecommunications.
John Ottensmann, Professor; Ph.D., North Carolina at Chapel Hill. Urban spatial structure and spatial dimensions of urban policy, management information systems, computer applications in planning and geographic information systems.
Kenna Quinet, Associate Professor; Ph.D., Illinois at Urbana-Champaign. Community policing, victimization, patterns of offending over the life course.
Natalia Rekhter, Trustee Lecturer; M.H.S.A., Michigan. Health-care finance and insurance, health-care law and ethics, international health care.
Ingrid Ritchie, Associate Professor; Ph.D., Minnesota. Indoor air quality, environmental management and assessment.
Adrian Sargeant, Professor; Ph.D., Exeter (England). Nonprofit marketing, including the arts, education, health care, and philanthropy.
Thomas Stucky, Assistant Professor; Ph.D., Iowa. Criminology, criminal justice, social control, political sociology.
Jim White, Clinical Lecturer; M.A., Butler. Public safety management, emergency services management.
Eric Wright, Associate Professor and Director, Center for Health Policy; Ph.D., Indiana. Health policy and services research, mental health policy and services research, HIV/AIDS/STD prevention, applied social research and program evaluation.

Adjunct/Associate Faculty
Melissa Brown, Associate Director of Research and Managing Editor, *Giving USA*, Center on Philanthropy at Indiana University; M.G.A., Pennsylvania.
Dwight Burlingame, Associate Executive Director, Center on Philanthropy at Indiana University; Ph.D., Florida State.
Anthony D. Cox, Professor of Marketing and Chancellor's Faculty Fellow, Indiana University, Kelley School of Business; Ph.D., Indiana.
David Dreyer, Judge, Marion County Superior Court; J.D., Notre Dame.
Patricia Ebright, Associate Professor; Department of Adult Health, Indiana University School of Nursing.
Gordon Hall, Vice President and Health Care Practice Leader, Marsh, Inc.; M.B.A., Dallas.
James Hogan, Partner, Hall, Render, Killian, Heath & Lyman, PSC; J.D., Indiana.
James Klaunig, Professor of Toxicology and Director, Division of Toxicology, Indiana University School of Medicine; Ph.D., Maryland.
Edward W. Koschka Jr., Network Vice President and Chief Information Officer, Community Health Network; M.B.A., Indiana.
Betsy Lee, Director, Indiana Patient Safety Center, Indiana Hospital and Health Association; M.S.P.H., North Carolina; RN.
Jamie Levy, President, J. D. Levy & Associates, LLC; M.P.A., Indiana.
Jeffrey Miller, Senior Systems Analyst, Eli Lilly and Company; M.P.A., Indiana.
Janet Orosz, Board of Governors, Ohio Fair Plan Underwriting Association; Ph.D., Ohio State.
John Render, Partner, Hall, Render, Killian, Heath & Lyman, PSC; J.D., Indiana.
Tim Seiler, Executive Director, The Fund Raising School, Center on Philanthropy at Indiana University; Ph.D., Indiana.
Roger Sell, Senior Financial Analyst, Myers & Stauffer, LC; M.P.A., Indiana.
Curtis Smith, Myers Chair of Distinguished Public Service, Hampden Sydney College; Ph.D., Ohio State.
J. T. Solomon, Business Manager, Department of Surgery, Indiana University School of Medicine; M.B.A., Butler; CPA.
Greg Steele, Associate Professor and Epidemiology Coordinator, Department of Public Health, Indiana University School of Medicine; D.P.H., Alabama at Birmingham.
Rodney Thompson, Toxicologist, Indiana Department of Environmental Management; M.S., Indiana.
Wanzhu Tu, Associate Professor, Indiana University School of Medicine and Center Scientist, Indiana University Center for Aging Research; Ph.D., South Carolina.

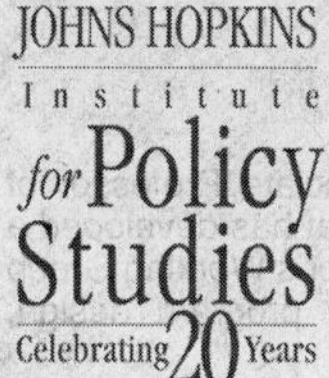

THE JOHNS HOPKINS UNIVERSITY

Institute for Policy Studies

Program of Study

Johns Hopkins University offers a Master of Arts degree in public policy (MPP). This two-year public policy program prepares graduates for professional careers in private as well as public organizations involved with solving societal problems. Graduates are equipped for responsible positions around the world that deal with the analysis of public problems and the development and implementation of solutions to meet them. By design, the program is kept small to nurture mentoring relationships between students and faculty members. Core courses are taught primarily by Institute faculty members. The number of ongoing policy research projects at the Institute creates a wealth of opportunities for students, including research assistantships. Extensive faculty member–student interaction in seminars and with faculty research and student thesis research enriches the students' experience and prepares them thoroughly for professional careers.

The curriculum consists of four basic components: a set of core analytical courses, a set of substantive policy courses in an area of specialization, an internship, and the opportunity to write a thesis. The program features a curriculum combining strong analytical courses and a focus on the evolving concept of citizenship and the moral dimensions of policy choice; location within a University-based research institute; easy access to Washington, D.C., and significant opportunities to learn firsthand about the policy process; attention to the role of private as well as public institutions in coping with public problems, with a special emphasis on nonprofit organizations; and opportunities for interaction with international fellows in residence at the Institute.

Students generally take most core courses and some electives during the first year, followed by an internship during the summer. Areas of concentration include health policy, social policy, urban policy, international affairs, nonprofit sector, human resource policy, and the environment.

Research Facilities

All resources of Johns Hopkins University System are available to policy studies students, including the Schools of Arts and Sciences, Engineering, Advanced International Studies, and Public Health. The library includes more than 2.1 million volumes, more than 1.2 million microforms, and more than 13,000 serial subscriptions. The Government Publications/Maps/Law Library provides a full range of services for accessing and utilizing an extensive collection of publications of the U.S. government, the UN and other international agencies, and state and local governments. The University has been a depository for U.S. government publications since 1882 and currently selects approximately 50 percent of the items offered to depository libraries. The computer facility includes two central systems: a VAX/VMS and Silicon Graphics SGI with UNIX. Students have access to several on-campus computer labs; in addition, the Institute maintains a computer lab for its own students. Students are assigned study carrels at the Institute or University libraries.

Financial Aid

Institute financial aid is awarded to graduate students who demonstrate intellectual promise in the field of policy studies through past academic performance, GRE test scores, previous relevant work experience, and a personal statement. The Institute awards tuition remissions and research fellowships. Students may also apply for available special fellowships. Low-interest loans and work-study assignments are awarded by the Financial Aid Office of Johns Hopkins University. Research fellowships pay $14 to $16 an hour for 15 to 20 hours of work per week.

Cost of Study

Tuition for 2008–09 is $37,700. There is a one-time matriculation fee of $500. Annual book expenses are estimated to be $750.

Living and Housing Costs

Cost of living was estimated at $12,500 for 2005–06. Students generally live in privately arranged apartments or shared houses close to the campus. Rents range from $375 to $750 a month. University meal plans are available.

Student Group

About 1,400 graduate students are in residence at Hopkins' main campus. There are currently 62 students in the Policy Studies Program and 10 students in the International Fellows Programs at the Institute for Policy Studies. Students come from all parts of the U.S.; some either have lived abroad or are international students. Approximately two thirds of all students are women, and one fifth are members of minority groups. Most students have prior work experience.

Student Outcomes

Graduates of the MPP Program are generally middle- to upper-level employees in all levels of government and in private and nonprofit organizations. In addition, some graduates have enrolled in Ph.D. programs. Typical jobs include program officer for a philanthropic foundation, policy or research analyst at a research institute or government agency, and executive director of a nonprofit organization. Recent graduates are working at the U.S. Office of Management and Budget, Mathematica Policy Research, World Bank, the Urban Institute, Pepsi Corporation, Charles Mott Foundation, U.S. General Accounting Office, Public/Private Ventures, and Enterprise Foundation.

Location

The Institute for Policy Studies is located on the 140-acre rolling wooded Homewood campus, about 3 miles north of the Inner Harbor of downtown Baltimore. The campus is 1 mile from the Amtrak train station; 40 miles from Washington, D.C.; 30 miles from Annapolis; and about 15 miles from the Chesapeake Bay.

The University and The Institute

Johns Hopkins University has a reputation as a world-renowned center of scholarship and research. The relatively small student body yields a favorable student-faculty ratio. Students are encouraged to think for themselves in an environment that fosters independence and creativity. The Institute for Policy Studies is a group of political scientists, economists, policy analysts, and policy practitioners who seek to improve the response of government and private institutions to the challenges of poverty and disadvantage, urban and regional economic change, human resource investment, and environmental degradation. The Institute carries out its work through a combination of policy-oriented research; seminars, briefings, and other public education efforts; and formal training of policy professionals in this country and abroad.

Applying

The deadline for applying to the Institute for Policy Studies is January 15. The application fee is $60. Applications for student loan and work-study programs must be submitted separately to the Office of Student Financial Services by April 1. Successful applicants generally have a college grade point average of at least 3.0 on a 4.0 scale. GRE General Test scores are required, and a score of at least 600 on each section is preferred. Students are encouraged to visit the Institute, but interviews are not required.

Correspondence and Information

Master of Arts in Public Policy
Institute for Policy Studies
The Johns Hopkins University
3400 North Charles Street
Baltimore, Maryland 21218

Phone: 410-516-4624
Fax: 410-516-8233
E-mail: mpp@jhu.edu
Web site: http://www.jhu.edu/mpp

The Johns Hopkins University

THE FACULTY AND THEIR RESEARCH

David M. Altschuler, Principal Research Scientist, Associate Professor of Mental Hygiene, Public Health Adjunct, and Adjunct Associate Professor of Sociology; Ph.D., Chicago, 1983. Project director and co–principal investigator on a federally funded research and training project that has developed a model of intensive aftercare for the high-risk juvenile parolee being released from secure correctional facilities; chair of Baltimore Mayor's Working Group on drug policy reform. Current research interests: juvenile justice sanctioning and aftercare; community-based delinquency program design, implementation, and assessment; privatization in corrections; drug involvement and crime among inner-city youth.

Burt Barnow, Principal Research Scientist and Adjunct Professor of Economics; Ph.D., Wisconsin–Madison, 1973. Conducting cost-benefit analysis of Maryland welfare reform initiative, evaluating impact of amendments to the Job Training Partnership Act, evaluating job training programs for the homeless. Current research interests: labor economics, employment and training programs, child support programs, welfare programs, program evaluation.

John J. Boland, Professor of Geography and Environmental Engineering; Ph.D., Johns Hopkins, 1973. Current research interests: environment and public utility economics, water resource management, environmental policy.

Senator Benjamin L. Cardin, Distinguished Lecturer; J.D., Maryland, 1967. Member of the U.S. Senate, Maryland. Policy interests: ethics, political process, and human resource policy.

Andrew Cherlin, Benjamin H. Griswold III Professor of Public Policy in the Department of Sociology; Ph.D., UCLA, 1976. Current research interests: sociology of the family, social policy and demography.

Matthew A. Crenson, Professor of Political Science; Ph.D., Chicago, 1969. Current research interests: political origins of American welfare policy.

Ruth R. Faden, Philip Franklin Wagley Professor of Biomedical Ethics at the Bioethics Institute and Professor of Health Policy and Management at the School of Public Health; Ph.D., Berkeley, 1976. Current research interests: ethics and health policy management.

Bernard Guyer, Professor and Chair of Maternal and Child Health Policy at the School of Public Health; M.D., Rochester, 1970. Current research interests: maternal and child health policy, practice, and finance; childhood injury prevention; child development; childhood immunization.

Tama Leventhal, Associate Research Scientist; Ph.D., Columbia, 1999. Current research interests: linking developmental research with social policy regarding children, youth, and families, particularly low-income families with children.

Robert Moffitt, Professor of Economics; Ph.D., Brown, 1975. Current research interests: labor economics, econometrics, public finance, population economics.

Vicente Navarro, Professor of Health Policy and of Sociology; Ph.D., Johns Hopkins, 1968. Current research interests: international study of public policy, health and social policy.

Sandra J. Newman, Director of the Institute for Policy Studies and Professor of Policy Studies (joint appointments in sociology, health policy, and management; geography and environmental engineering); Ph.D., NYU, 1973. Member of Board of Directors, Center for Housing Policy, National Foundation for Affordable Housing Solutions; Associate Editor, *Housing Policy Debate*. Current research interests: long-term effects of housing assistance on children and families, implications of welfare reform for housing, living conditions of America's disabled, low-income rental housing market dynamics.

Demetra Nightingale, Principle Research Scientist; Ph.D., George Washington, 1998. Current research interests: employment, labor markets, welfare, poverty and social policy.

Marion Pines, Senior Fellow and Director of the Institute's Sar Levitan Center for Social Policy Studies; B.A., Goucher. Chair of interagency team managing policy, planning, implementation, and evaluation of statewide high school dropout prevention project. Current research interests: at-risk populations, development of education alternatives, welfare reform policies, employment strategies for youth and adults, service integration model targeted at families.

Lester M. Salamon, Founding Director of the Institute for Policy Studies and Director of its Center for Civil Society Studies and Professor of Political Science; Ph.D., Harvard, 1971. Vice Chair of the International Society for Third-Sector Research. Current research interests: alternative instruments of government action; social welfare policy; scope, structure, and role of the private nonprofit sector in the United States and overseas; human capital investment policy.

Joseph Sterne, Senior Fellow; M.A., Columbia, 1950. Current research interests: media and public policy.

Curt Ventriss, Visiting Professor, Ph.D., USC, 1980. Current research interests: ethics and public policy, environmental issues.

Aerial view of the parklike Homewood campus with old Baltimore neighborhood in the background, the Institute for Policy Studies at the far left, and the Eisenhower Library in the center across from the ellipse.

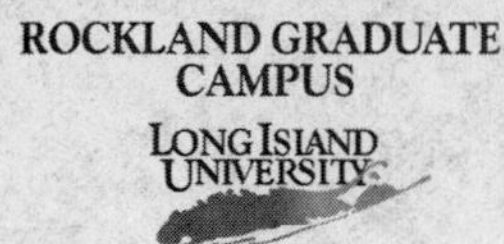

LONG ISLAND UNIVERSITY, ROCKLAND GRADUATE CAMPUS

Health and Public Administration Programs

Programs of Study

The Master in Public Administration (M.P.A.) in either health administration or public administration is designed to provide graduates with the theoretical, analytical, and communications skills needed by successful health-care, nonprofit organization, and government agency administrators. The health administration program prepares students for leadership positions in the health-care industry. The public administration program focuses on developing the skills required to manage government activities, revitalize public administration and services, and respond to political and social changes. These 42-credit programs consist of 27 credits of foundation management and advanced administration courses, 9 credits of electives, and 6 credits of a capstone experience course.

The Gerontology Advanced Certificate provides a strong academic background in the field of health-care administration, budget planning, and long-term care for the older adult. The program consists of a 15-credit course of study to earn an advanced certificate. Candidates who already have an M.P.A. degree may apply up to three courses (9 credits) toward the certificate. Graduates with the advanced certificate are in a strong position to be competitive in the senior-care marketplace.

Research Facilities

Students have access to a modern library and extensive online databases to perform research and in-depth studies.

Financial Aid

The Rockland Graduate Campus offers a variety of scholarships based on past academic achievement as well as current employment. Students may apply for federal financial aid for graduate study by completing an online FAFSA application. For further information about available scholarships or financial aid, students should contact the Graduate Admissions Office. More than 80 percent of campus graduate students receive either scholarships or federal financial aid.

Cost of Study

Graduate tuition for 2007–08 was $835 per credit. In addition, students were responsible for certain registration fees.

Living and Housing Costs

Most students are local professionals who attend evening or weekend classes, generally on a part-time basis; therefore, there are no additional expenses for housing and food.

Student Outcomes

Graduates of the M.P.A. program are in an excellent position to be competitive in the health-care, public sector, and nonprofit job marketplace. They achieve senior management positions in the health services and nonprofit industries. Careers abound for graduates from the public administration program, including the public sector (local, state, and federal government) and nonprofit and private sectors.

Location

The Rockland Graduate Campus is a regional campus of Long Island University and is located in a two-story building in a suburban environment. The campus has a modern library, two student computer centers, a student lobby lounge, and attractive classrooms. The campus is located in Orangeburg, a town located in Rockland County approximately 18 miles from New York City, and is easily accessible from the Palisades Parkway and the New York State Thruway. Safe student parking is available adjacent to the campus building.

The University

Long Island University is an accredited undergraduate, graduate, and doctoral degree–granting university with major residential campuses located in Brookville and Brooklyn, New York. The Rockland Graduate Campus is one of five regional campuses serving suburban student populations. Long Island University is entering its ninth decade of providing access to the American dream through excellence in higher education. It is one of the largest and most comprehensive universities in the country. It offers more than 600 undergraduate, graduate, and doctoral degree programs and certificates.

Applying

The campus offers rolling admissions for students who wish to begin their graduate studies in the fall, spring, or summer semester. The health and public administration programs require the completion of an admission application; two letters of recommendation; undergraduate transcripts from all colleges previously attended, showing an undergraduate grade point average of 3.0 or higher; and a personal statement indicating desire for admission and professional growth.

Correspondence and Information

Graduate Admissions Office
Long Island University, Rockland Campus
70 Route 340
Orangeburg, New York 10962
Phone: 845-359-7200 Ext. 5403
E-mail: rockland@liu.edu
Web site: http://www.liu.edu/rockland

Professor Patricia Latona
Program Director, Health and Public Administration
Phone: 845-359-7200 Ext. 5410
E-mail: patricia.latona@liu.edu

Long Island University, Rockland Graduate Campus

THE FACULTY

Patricia Latona, Professor and Program Director; M.S., Mount Saint Vincent; RN.

Jeffrey A. Ashkenase, Adjunct Professor; M.P.A., NYU.
Douglas Brusa, Adjunct Professor; M.P.A., Columbia.
Eileen Chichin, Adjunct Professor; Ph.D., Fordham.
Francis A. Cosgrove, Adjunct Professor; M.A., Columbia Teachers College.
Raymond F. Crapo, Adjunct Professor; M.A., CUNY, Hunter.
Michael La Magna, Adjunct Professor; M.P.A., LIU, Rockland.
Roger Sherman, Adjunct Professor; Ph.D., Columbia.
Leonard Thaler, Adjunct Professor; M.S., Columbia.
Linda Wenze, Associate Professor; M.B.A., LIU; Ph.D., Hofstra.

Classroom at Long Island University, Rockland Graduate Campus.

NATIONAL UNIVERSITY OF SINGAPORE

Lee Kuan Yew School of Public Policy

Programs of Study

As countries in Southeast Asia and the Pacific enter a new phase of their development, the importance of public policy has become increasingly recognized. The problems faced by policymakers in Southeast Asia and the Pacific span a wide spectrum of unique issues that are further complicated by religious, ethnic, historical, and political variables. The Lee Kuan Yew School of Public Policy (LKYSPP) at the National University of Singapore (NUS) strives to be a center of excellence for academic study and research in the areas of public policy and public management.

The Lee Kuan Yew School of Public Policy was established in 2004 as a successor to the Public Policy Program, which began in 1992 as a collaborative effort between the National University of Singapore and Harvard University's John F. Kennedy School of Government. LKYSPP continues to maintain a strong partnership with the Kennedy School.

The Lee Kuan Yew School of Public Policy confers a Doctor of Philosophy (Ph.D.) degree as well as three master's degrees: Master in Public Policy, Master in Public Administration, and Master in Public Management. While the curricula of these degree programs are similar to those offered in other leading schools of public policy around the world, they are unique for their emphasis on the public policy experiences of Asian countries and the critical challenges facing this part of the world. LKYSPP also offers a diverse slate of high-quality executive programs to meet the specialized educational and training needs of senior executives.

The Ph.D. program equips candidates with the necessary theoretical frameworks, research methods, and tools to conduct scientific inquiry to address contemporary public policy issues. Candidates are required to complete a minimum of 24 modular credits or six modules of course work as required by the Thesis Committee, including three core modules and three elective modules. The qualifying examination consists of a written examination and an oral defense of the candidate's thesis proposal.

The two-year Master in Public Policy program provides a strong foundation in conceptual and analytical skills for those who are interested in understanding and influencing how public policy choices are made. Students learn to apply economic and management ideas and tools to analyze, design, and manage efficient and effective public policies and organizations.

The one-year Master in Public Administration program provides an interdisciplinary course of study for experienced professionals who wish to enhance their leadership and managerial capabilities. Students learn to apply the techniques of policy analysis and program evaluation to resolve complex multidimensional policy challenges.

The one-year Master in Public Management program enhances the skills of senior managers in the area of good governance. Students develop new perspectives about governance and gain invaluable practical experience during their attachment to Singapore ministries and agencies.

In June 2007, LKYSPP officially joined the alliance of public policy institutions comprising of the London School of Economics (LSE), the Institut d'Etudes Politiques de Paris (Sciences Po), and Columbia University's School of International and Public Affairs (SIPA). The establishment of double degrees between LKYSPP and LSE, Sciences Po, and SIPA marked the formal admission of LKYSPP into the Global Public Policy Network (GPPN). The GPPN was established in June 2005 by SIPA, LSE, and Sciences Po as a close-knit alliance of premiere educational institutions dedicated to the common study of issues of global public policy concern. LKYSPP is the fourth member—the first from outside Europe and North America—to join this prestigious grouping that requires, at a minimum, that participating institutions have bilateral double degree arrangements with each other.

The GPPN double master's degree programmes are geared toward training a new generation of globally minded public policy makers. These programmes allow students from SIPA, LSE, Sciences Po, and LKYSPP to spend their first year at their home institution and the second year at one of the other three partner institutions. At the end of their two years of study, students receive master's degrees in public policy or public affairs from two GPPN institutions. Beyond the double or dual degrees, the GPPN partners also collaborate across a range of initiatives, including the launch of shorter executive programmes targeted at global policymakers, the launch of one or more practitioner and academic journals, and the conduct or sponsorship of joint research on issues of global policy concern.

Research Facilities

The University's central library contains more than 612,000 book titles, 1.1 million volumes, 26,000 journals, and 900 CD-ROMs.

The Asia Competitiveness Institute seeks to contribute to the enhancement of economic growth and living standards in the region. It serves as a regional repository of competitiveness information that enables analyses of long-term trends in economic policies and development, and it conducts research to understand patterns of policy and economic development. The institute also undertakes projects to assess current competitiveness of key economic clusters and provide policy inputs for enhancing growth.

The Centre on Asia and Globalisation serves as a catalyst for world-class scholars and policymakers to engage in effective research and strategic dialogue in successfully addressing how Asia's growing importance is reflected in the world's governing institutions. In addition to research and publications, the Centre on Asia and Globalisation organizes seminars, conferences, and policy dialogues to explore critical issues on Asia's existing and potential roles in defining and managing global affairs.

Financial Aid

The Lee Kuan Yew School of Public Policy provides a number of grants, which generally cover 20 percent of tuition fees but may also cover additional fees and provide a modest stipend. Scholarships are awarded based on academic and professional merit, although specific eligibility requirements may vary. These awards include a monthly stipend of S$1350 throughout the period of the award; a one-time book allowance of S$500; a one-time settling-in allowance of S$500; shared housing; tuition, health insurance, examination, and other approved fees; and travel costs. Ph.D. candidates are eligible for NUS Research Scholarships. The scholarships are available for one year and are renewable annually for up to four years, subject to satisfactory progress.

Cost of Study

For the M.P.A. and M.P.P. programs for the 2007 academic year, full-time tuition was S$2725 per semester for Singapore citizens and permanent residents and S$3000 for international students. Part-time tuition for the M.P.P. program was S$1365 per semester (S$681.25 for the special term) for residents and S$1500 per semester (S$750 for the special term) for nonresidents. Other annual costs include a registration fee of $52.50, a student activity and service fee of S$67.20, a one-time examination fee of S$262.50, an academic fee of S$23.50, and group medical insurance fee of S$114. Additional costs include payment for the executive training and orientation programs, student pass/visa fees, and the program closure event. These costs vary from year to year but are currently estimated to be S$3000 for the duration of the program.

For the doctoral programs, 2007 tuition and fees were S$2175 per semester for residents and S$2395 for nonresidents.

Living and Housing Costs

Graduate student housing is available for full-time international students. The University has 200 graduate student apartments located in Prince George's Park Residences and 545 off-campus units in Gillman Heights. Priority is given to new graduate students who have just arrived from overseas. For cost and other housing information, prospective students should visit the Web site at http://www.nus.edu.sg/osa/housing/acc/gd.html.

Student Group

Approximately 200 students enroll in Lee Kuan Yew School of Public Policy's programs every year. Students come from many different nations, including Canada, China, France, India, Indonesia, Malaysia, Maldives, Papua New Guinea, Philippines, United States, and Vietnam. In 2006, students represented seventeen countries and had varying degrees of work experience in a variety of sectors, including finance, trade, education, media, health, transport, housing, foreign affairs, and development. Students are also at different stages in their lives—some have just completed their undergraduate studies, while others are at a later stage in their careers.

Location

Studying in Singapore, a celebrated gateway to Asia, provides an excellent opportunity to understand this diverse, populous, and dynamic region. A truly cosmopolitan society with an ethnically diverse population of 3.5 million, Singapore attracts individuals from all over the world. A thriving center of commerce and industry and one of the busiest ports in the world, Singapore offers a host of business and career opportunities. More than 4,000 multinational corporations make Singapore their regional or global headquarters. In addition, this island country, which is the smallest in Southeast Asia, offers a variety of shopping, dining, and recreational opportunities—as well as sun and fun on the surrounding isles.

The University

Beginning as a modest medical school founded in 1905, the National University of Singapore has evolved into Singapore's global university, with distinctive strengths in education and research and an entrepreneurial dimension. The University is strongly committed to advancing knowledge, educating students, and nurturing talent. It also actively fosters a spirit of entrepreneurship and innovation in order to promote creative enterprise throughout the University. NUS enrolls 23,500 undergraduate and more than 9,000 graduate students from eighty-eight countries.

Applying

To be considered for admission, candidates must submit an application for admission completed in English; transcripts of all prior college work; standardized test scores (for students whose native language is not English, a minimum TOEFL score of 580 on the paper-based test, 237 on the computer-based test, or 85 on the Internet-based test or a minimum 6.5 on the IELTS test is required; GRE and GMAT scores are optional); a curriculum vitae (CV) listing academic, professional, and personal achievements; three 500-word essays; three letters of reference from individuals familiar with the applicant's work; a completed application for financial aid (if applicable); a copy of applicant's passport or birth certificate; and a S$30 (U.S.$20) application fee. Applicants are notified of their acceptance two months before the term begins.

Correspondence and Information

Lee Kuan Yew School of Public Policy
National University of Singapore
469C Bukit Timah Road
Singapore 259772

Phone: 65-6516-6134
Fax: 65-6778-1020
E-mail: lkyspp@nus.edu.sg
Web site: http://www.lkyspp.nus.edu.sg/

National University of Singapore

THE FACULTY AND THEIR RESEARCH

The heart of the Lee Kuan Yew School of Public Policy's reputation for excellence is its faculty—a diverse and growing community of scholars and practitioners who are well-known for their teaching and research expertise in a variety of fields. The School's full-time faculty members pursue active research, teaching, and consulting agendas. Working individually with colleagues and students, they develop knowledge about and seek solutions to today's most critical problems of public policy and management. The adjunct and visiting faculty members are accomplished professionals from a wide variety of fields who teach courses that bridge the gap from research to practical application of knowledge.

Charles Adams, Visiting Professor; Ph.D. (economics), Monash (Australia). Exchange rates, financial market developments and issues, monetary policy formulation, regional economic integration and cooperation.

Eduardo Araral, Assistant Professor; Ph.D. (public policy), Indiana Bloomington. Political economy of the causes and consequences of institutions that support development, particularly in Southeast Asia; political economy of property rights, decentralization, public bureaucracies, foreign aid, and common pool resources.

Mukul Asher, Professor; Ph.D. (economics), Washington State. Public-sector economics and social security issues in Asia.

Paul Barter, Assistant Professor; Ph.D., Murdoch (Australia). Urban transport with a focus on Southeast and East Asia, especially Malaysia and Singapore.

Caroline Brassard, Assistant Professor; Ph.D. (economics), London. Poverty reduction strategies for international nongovernmental organizations in developing countries.

Arindam Das-Gupta, Associate Professor; Ph.D. (economics), Cornell. Government finances and their management, particularly on tax administration.

Ngiam Tong Dow, Adjunct Professor; M.P.A., Harvard. Chairman, Surbana Corporation Pte. Ltd., and Director, United Overseas Bank Ltd., Singapore Press Holdings Ltd., and Yeo Hiap Seng Ltd.

Ann Florini, Visiting Professor; Ph.D. (political science), UCLA. New approaches to managing global issues, reform of intergovernmental organizations, roles of civil society and the private sector in addressing global issues, uses of information policy and technology.

Scott Fritzen, Assistant Professor; Ph.D. (public and international affairs), Princeton. Analysis of governance reforms and capacity strengthening in developing countries; comparative analysis of anticorruption strategies, public-sector decentralization, and social policy reforms in Southeast Asia.

Boyd Fuller, Assistant Professor; Ph.D. (urban and regional planning), MIT. Resolution of apparently irresolvable environmental conflicts, design and implementation of sustainable community-based water supply projects.

Lim Siong Guan, Adjunct Professor; B.Eng. (mechanical engineering), Adelaide (Australia). Permanent Secretary of the Ministry of Finance; Chairman, Inland Revenue Authority of Singapore; Chairman, Accounting and Corporate Regulatory Authority of Singapore; Deputy Chairman, Temasek Holdings; Member of the Monetary Authority of Singapore.

Robert J. Herbold, Adjunct Professor; Ph.D. (computer science), Case Western Reserve. Managing Director, Herbold Group, LLC; Retired Executive Vice President and Chief Operating Officer, Microsoft Corporation. How companies can improve their profitability and agility.

Phua Kai Hong, Associate Professor of Health Policy and Management; Ph.D. London School of Economics. Population aging, health-care management, comparative health systems.

Darryl Jarvis, Associate Professor; Ph.D. (international relations), British Columbia. Risk analysis and study of political and economic risk in Asia, including investment, regulatory, and institutional risk analysis.

Suzaina Kadir, Assistant Professor; Ph.D. (political science), Wisconsin–Madison. Religion and politics, Muslim politics in Southeast Asia and South Asia, state-society relations and political development in Asia, regional security of Southeast Asia.

Wong Poh Kam, Associate Professor; Ph.D. (regional planning), MIT. Innovation policy, industrial and competitiveness policy, technology entrepreneurship.

Liu Thai Ker, Adjunct Professor; Honorary Doctorate, New South Wales. Director, RSP Architects Planners and Engineers (Pte.) Ltd.; Chairman, Advisory Committee, National University of Singapore Architecture School. Implementation of public housing in Singapore and formulation of a vision for current and further urban development of the city.

Vu Minh Khuong, Assistant Professor; Ph.D. (public policy), Harvard. Economic growth, competitiveness, and development—in particular, policy issues for enhancing institutional quality, local competitiveness, and the diffusion of information and communication technology.

Lam Chuan Leong, Adjunct Professor; M.B.A., Harvard. Application of general management theories and microeconomics, competition policy, pricing and market efficiency, privatization of government services, transport economics, structuring of public and private financing initiatives.

Kishore Mahbubani, Practice Professor of Public Policy and Dean; Honorary Doctorate, Dalhousie. Served twice as Ambassador to the U.N., during which he also served as President of the Security Council; Permanent Secretary of the Foreign Ministry from 1993–98.

Jonathan Marshall, Assistant Professor; Ph.D. (counseling psychology), Stanford. Leadership, peak performance, and the mind-body connection.

Lee Chung Min, Visiting Professor; Ph.D., Tufts (Fletcher). East Asian defense transformation and force modernization, political-military dynamics on the Korean peninsula, proliferation of weapons of mass destruction in East Asia, U.S. strategy in the Asian Pacific.

Alex Mutebi, Assistant Professor; Ph.D. (public and international affairs), Princeton. The policy process, political and organizational analysis, political economy of development.

Basskaran Nair, Adjunct Associate Professor; M.A., Hawaii. Board Member, Cisco Security Pte. Ltd., and Chairman, Media Development Authority's Publication Consultative Panel.

John Palmer, Adjunct Professor; B.A., British Columbia. Chairman, Toronto International Leadership Centre for Financial Sector Supervision, and Director, Accounting and Corporate Regulatory Authority.

J. Y. Pillay, Adjunct Professor; B.Sc., Imperial College (London). Chairman, Singapore Exchange Limited. Led Singapore Airlines from a small startup with just twelve aircrafts to become a global industry leader

M. Ramesh, Associate Professor; Ph.D. (political science), British Columbia. Social policies in East and Southeast Asia, comparative political economy of People's Republic of China, Republic of India, and Korea.

T. S. Gopi Rethinaraj, Assistant Professor; Ph.D. (nuclear engineering), Illinois at Urbana-Champaign. Science and technology policy, energy economics and policy, nuclear security affairs.

Neo Boon Siong, Visiting Professor; Ph.D., Pittsburgh. Strategy, process, and organizational change.

Hui Weng Tat, Vice Dean of Academic Affairs; Ph.D. (economics), Australian National. Economic issues of migration and education, impact of globalization on labor markets, labor market policy issues in Singapore.

Dodo J. Thampapillai, Associate Professor; Ph.D. (economics), New England (Australia). Macroeconomics and economic policy in a global economy.

Wu Wenbo, Assistant Professor; Ph.D. (public policy and management), Carnegie Mellon. Empirical analyses of institutions and development, institutional changes, theoretical studies of institutions and organizations in the public sector.

Calla Wiemer, Visiting Associate Professor; Ph.D. (economics), Wisconsin. Exchange rate and balance of payments, income distribution, economic development and structural change, labor and employment, regional development, rural industrialization in China.

Wu Xun, Assistant Professor; Ph.D. (public policy analysis), North Carolina at Chapel Hill. Political economy of public policy reforms in developing countries.

Stavros Yiannouka, Vice Dean (Executive Education and Development); M.B.A., London Business School. Leadership, organizational change, impact of technology on competitive dynamics of industry.

THE NEW SCHOOL: A UNIVERSITY

Milano The New School for Management and Urban Policy
Ph.D. Program in Public and Urban Policy

Program of Study

Today's public policy issues are complex and require deeper analysis and greater insight than in the past. This program seeks to train individuals at a doctoral level to work at the highest levels of government, nonprofits, and think tanks, with the ability to formulate and develop broad public policy solutions. The Ph.D. in public and urban policy program is committed to providing students with a deep theoretical and institutional understanding of contemporary urban problems and the technical skills necessary both to carry out scholarly research and to design and manage public policy. In line with The New School's tradition of critical inquiry, the doctoral program emphasizes the social, political, and normative dimensions of policy analysis, treating socially responsible and equitable outcomes as essential to good public policy decision making. The doctoral program takes a distinctive multidisciplinary approach; it is organized around a public policy core offered within Milano The New School for Management and Urban Policy and a broad range of electives offered by Milano, the University, and other universities in the region.

The curriculum provides students with both the foundation that is critical to the successful pursuit of scholarly research and the depth and breadth of courses needed to attain an appropriate level of knowledge in the student's field of scholarship. Doctoral dissertations must focus on a relevant policy issue and substantially advance knowledge in the field.

The Ph.D. program has three main components: 60 credits of course work, qualifying examinations, and a dissertation. Upon completion of the course work and successful completion of a policy and analysis paper, students are eligible to take the qualifying exam. Once they pass, students can go on to write and defend a dissertation. The dissertation must be defended orally before the student's Dissertation Committee.

Research Facilities

The Center for New York City Affairs is a nonpartisan institute dedicated to advancing innovative public policies that strengthen neighborhoods, support families, and reduce urban poverty. Tools include rigorous analysis, research, candid public dialogue with stakeholders and opinion leaders, and strategic planning with government officials, nonprofit practitioners, and community residents. The center's original applied research and public seminars examine the politics of community change in local and state government and identify critical problems facing urban families and communities. The center's public programs offer community leaders and other participants the opportunity to meet powerful players in and around government and to learn about the context, the influential organizations, and other factors that define the policy-making landscape in New York City and urban America.

Financial Aid

Milano offers financial aid packages in the form of scholarships, fellowships, and loans. Financial aid awards are decided on a first-come, first-served basis, and applicants are encouraged to apply early to receive priority consideration. Financial aid award decisions are made after students are accepted at Milano. Applicants interested in obtaining financial aid should submit the Free Application for Federal Student Aid (FAFSA) or the Renewal Application for Federal Student Aid. More information is available from the Office of Financial Services at 212-229-8930.

Cost of Study

Tuition in 2008–09 is $1150 per credit, and fees are approximately $100 each term.

Living and Housing Costs

The University Housing Office maintains a comprehensive resource center with apartment listings. University-run apartments and residence halls are also available. The cost of housing, food, transportation, books, and living expenses averages $17,000 annually. For more information, students should go online to http://www.newschool.edu/studentservices.

Student Group

There are 45 students in the program; 22 attend on a full-time basis. Of these students, 27 are women, 17 are members of underrepresented groups, and 8 are international students.

Location

The New School's location in New York City gives students access to an abundance of resources. Students are encouraged to take advantage of the city's many museums, performance venues, and other cultural institutions, which are only a walk or a subway ride away. An extension of the classroom, the city also offers excellent professional and networking opportunities, and some classes require that students work with outside businesses to complete assignments—giving them unparalleled real-world experience. Internships and apprenticeships with leading New York City companies and organizations in every field are also available, and many students have moved on from internships to successful careers with those companies and organizations upon graduation.

The University and The School

Milano is part of is part of The New School, a leading university in New York City offering distinguished programs in design, liberal arts, the performing arts, and social and political science, leading to seventy graduate and undergraduate degrees. To learn more, students should visit http://www.newschool.edu/degreeprograms. The New School is accredited by the Commission on Higher Education of the Middle States Association of Colleges and Schools. A privately supported institution, The New School is chartered as a university by the Regents of the State of New York.

Applying

Students must submit the completed application form, the $50 application fee, official transcripts from all postsecondary institutions attended, a 300-word essay explaining their professional goals, two letters of recommendation, and a resume. Applications are reviewed on a rolling admissions basis. Although there is no specific deadline, applicants are strongly encouraged to apply by March 1 for the fall semester and by October 1 for the spring semester in order to take full advantage of financial aid and housing opportunities.

Correspondence and Information

Ph.D. Program in Public and Urban Policy
Milano The New School for Management and Urban Policy
The New School
72 Fifth Avenue, 3rd Floor
New York, New York 10011
Phone: 212-229-5400
Fax: 212-229-5354
E-mail: milanoadmissions@newschool.edu
Web site: http://www.newschool.edu/milano

The New School: A University

THE FACULTY AND THEIR RESEARCH

Warren Balinsky, Associate Professor and Chair of Health Services Management; Ph.D., Case Western Reserve. Home health care and the applications of planning, development, marketing, and research to health services management and policy. Dr. Balinsky has written two books on home care; he has also written articles on various aspects of emergency preparedness, health care of the elderly, health-care reimbursement, health-status indices, home care, pediatric health care, and the unequal distribution of medical personnel within the health-care system.

Robert Beauregard, Professor; Ph.D., Cornell. Urbanization in the United States, with particular focus on industrial urban decline after World War II and current problems posed by growth and decline in cities. Dr. Beauregard is currently working on *Writing Urban Theory,* a series of essays, and *Why Cities Endure,* a book investigating why some cities prosper while others do not. Dr. Beauregard teaches courses on the political economy of the city, urban redevelopment, neighborhood change, social theory, and research design.

Howard Berliner, Professor of Health Services Management and Director of Ph.D. in Public and Urban Policy Program; Sc.D., Johns Hopkins. Needs of vulnerable populations and access to health services for the uninsured. Dr. Berliner is the author of seven books, most recently *The Health Marketplace: New York City 1990–2010* with Ginzberg et al. He has also authored numerous articles and reviews on health-policy issues in academic and professional journals. Dr. Berliner served for two years as the assistant state health commissioner for New Jersey.

John Clinton, Visiting Assistant Professor; Ph.D., Fordham. Interprofessional collaboration. Dr. Clinton has served as corporation senior consultant on social responsibility at MetLife, senior vice president of the LightHouse for the Blind and Visually Impaired, and an administrator at NYU, Fordham University, and Hartwick College. He has been a consultant to foundations, nonprofit organizations, corporations, and higher education institutions.

Dennis Derryck, Professor of Professional Practice; Ph.D., Fordham. Innovative policies and strategies affecting the economic sustainability of nonprofit organizations. Dr. Derryck has held leadership positions in organizations involved in community economic development, operations and fiscal management, and research and policy analysis. He currently servés as chair of WE ACT for Environmental Justice and is vice chair of SoBro, the South Bronx Overall Economic Development Corporation.

Elizabeth Dickey, Professor; Ed.D., Massachusetts Amherst. Organizational behavior and leadership, with a psychosocial emphasis. Dr. Dickey is a developmental clinical psychologist. Between 1991 and 2005 she served as dean and then provost of The New School.

Peter Eisinger, Henry Cohen Professor; Ph.D., Yale. Urban politics and policy, state and local economic development, U.S. politics, state politics, federalism. Author of *Toward an End to Hunger in America.*

Alec Ian Gershberg, Associate Professor; Ph.D., Pennsylvania. School governance, education finance, decentralization in the developing world and in the United States, immigrant students in public schools in New York and California. Dr. Gershberg has conducted extensive research on Latin America—particularly Mexico, Nicaragua, and Ecuador—as well as on Egypt, Romania, and sub-Saharan Africa. He has been a frequent consultant to the World Bank, the Inter-American Development Bank, and the Urban Institute. Dr. Gershberg is the lead author of *Beyond Bilingual Education: New Immigrants and Public School Policies in California.*

Martin Greller, Professor and Associate Dean for Academic Affairs; Ph.D., Yale. Factors associated with career continuity for older workers, feedback systems in organizations as tools for increasing organizational effectiveness. Recent projects include an assessment of training needs for entry-level peace officers and a review of pay-equity issues for a legislative body.

Darrick Hamilton, Assistant Professor; Ph.D., North Carolina at Chapel Hill. Ethnic and racial disparities in wealth, home ownership, and labor market outcomes. Dr. Hamilton's articles can be found in *African American Research Perspectives, American Economics Review, Applied Economics Letters, Challenge: The Magazine of Economic Affairs, Journal of Economic Psychology, Review of Black Political Economy, Social Science Quarterly, Southern Economics Journal,* and *Transforming Anthropology.*

David Howell, Professor; Ph.D., New School. Labor markets at the local, national, and international levels. Recent publications have examined the effects of immigration on the economic status of foreign and native-born workers in New York City, the nature of recent changes in skill requirements and the determinants of relative wage trends in the United States, and the extent to which labor market institutions and social policy explain patterns of unemployment in Europe and the United States. Dr. Howell is the editor of *Fighting Unemployment: The Limits of Free Market Orthodoxy.*

Mark Lipton, Professor of Management and Chair of Management; Ph.D., Massachusetts Amherst. Management, leadership, organizational strategy. Author of *Guiding Growth: How Vision Keeps Companies on Course.* Dr. Lipton's research and opinions on management and strategy have appeared in *Executive Excellence, Harvard Business Review, The Journal of Management Consulting, Optimize, Organization Development Journal,* and *Sloan Management Review,* among others.

Edwin Melendez, Professor; Ph.D., Massachusetts Amherst. Economics. Dr. Melendez was director of the Mauricio Gastón Institute for Latino Community Development and Public Policy at the University of Massachusetts Boston (1992–98) and director of the Community Development Research Center at the Milano Graduate School (1999–2004). He has worked as a consultant on employment, economic development, job creation, and small business for numerous government, community, and philanthropic foundations. Dr. Melendez has managed more than thirty-five research, outreach, and demonstration projects and supervised or collaborated with more than 60 researchers in projects that resulted in several books, special issues of academic journals, and other publications.

Aida Rodriguez, Professor of Professional Practice; Ph.D., Massachusetts. Leadership and effective management in the nonprofit sector. Formerly deputy director of the Equal Opportunity Division of the Rockefeller Foundation, Dr. Rodriguez now serves on various nonprofit boards, including One Economy, Inc.; Alliance for Nonprofit Management; and the Association for Public Policy Analysis and Management. Dr. Rodriguez is an adviser on philanthropic initiatives in the United States and in Latin America, including the Funders' Collaborative for Strong Latino Communities.

Bryna Sanger, Professor; Ph.D., Brandeis. Public policy and management, changes in service delivery and management systems induced by welfare reform in states and localities around the country. Former dean of the Robert J. Milano Graduate School of Management and Urban Policy, Dr. Sanger has worked in a wide range of policy and management areas, including city service delivery, welfare reform, leadership, innovation, and performance management. She recently led a research effort with the National Civic League on the experiences of cities that have developed exemplary performance measurement systems and that report to and engage citizens in their efforts. Her most recent book on this topic is entitled *The Welfare Marketplace: Privatization and Welfare Reform.*

Alex F. Schwartz, Associate Professor, Chair of Department of Urban Policy Analysis and Management, and Senior Research Associate, Community Development Research Center; Ph.D., Rutgers. Housing and community development, including affordable housing programs, community reinvestment, and community development corporations. Dr. Schwartz's most recent publication is *Housing Policy in the United States.* His research has also appeared in such journals as *Cityscape, Economic Development Quarterly, International Journal of Urban and Regional Research,* and the *Journal of Urban Affairs.*

Lisa J. Servon, Associate Professor and Associate Director of Community Development Research Center; Ph.D., Berkeley. Urban poverty, community development, economic development, gender issues. Dr. Servon recently coedited *Gender and Planning: A Reader* (with Susan Fainstein), which covers a range of planning and development fields, including transportation, land use, history, gender, housing, social justice, environmental design, race, and economic and community development. The book was selected as one of the top10 books for 2006 by Planetizen, a public-interest information exchange for the urban planning, design, and development community.

Nidhi Srinivas, Assistant Professor of Nonprofit Management; Ph.D., McGill. Civil society, specifically management of nongovernmental organizations, and the transfer and transformation of management knowledge. Dr. Srinivas teaches courses on nonprofit management, international development, and strategic decision making. Courses he has developed include Managing Institutions for Development (part of the core curriculum in the graduate program in international affairs) and Civil Society and South Asia.

Antonin Wagner, Visiting Professor; Ph.D., Fribourg (Switzerland). Economics. From 1996 to 2000, Dr. Wagner was president of the International Society for Third Sector Research, the leading scholarly institution in the nonprofit field. He has served as a consultant on social security–related issues to the Swiss Federal Statistical Office and the World Bank in Washington. He is a member of the editorial board of several international journals and has published widely in English, German, and French on the welfare state and civil society.

Tatiana Wah, Assistant Professor; Ph.D., Rutgers. Regional and local economic development planning and developing nations, with a particular focus on small developing nations' economies. Dr. Wah's recent work is on transnational expatriate (immigrant) recovery and engagement programs of developing countries, particularly Haiti. She has been involved in community development work in the New York African American and Caribbean communities as a consultant, nonprofit administrator, and activist/advocate.

Mary R. Watson, Assistant Professor; Ph.D., Vanderbilt. Contemporary human capital issues in organizations, with particular emphasis on the social impact of labor market discontinuities. Dr. Watson teaches courses in management and organization behavior, human resources, social impact management, and globalization. She has a strong interest in cultural, racial, ethnic, and gender inequalities in the workplace and society. Her upcoming book (with Dr. Rikki Abzug), tentatively titled *Human Resources in Social Purpose Organizations,* is scheduled to be published by Jossey-Bass in 2007.

Part-time Faculty

The part-time faculty members of Milano The New School for Management and Urban Policy are high-level executives and managers in the institutions and agencies for which they work and the organizations for which they volunteer. They bring to the classroom valuable insight into current management and policy issues from both their personal experience and relevant curriculum. For a current listing of part-time faculty members, students should visit the faculty page of the Milano Web site at http://www.newschool.edu/milano.

THE NEW SCHOOL: A UNIVERSITY

Milano The New School for Management and Urban Policy Program in Urban Policy Analysis and Management

Program of Study The Master of Science in urban policy analysis and management program trains professionals and managers who are committed to improving the quality of life for urban communities and their residents. One of the first programs of its kind in the country, it prepares students for a wide range of jobs in the public and nonprofit sectors that focus on the development, assessment, and implementation of urban policies and programs. Graduates work as policy analysts in governmental agencies, as administrators of government programs, and as program managers and executives at nonprofit organizations.

The program offers a flexible curriculum tailored to the interests and needs of individual students. The program's core curriculum emphasizes hands-on, client-centered courses in which students work on policy or management issues for government officials and nonprofit executives; a solid foundation in and critical assessment of the traditional techniques of policy analysis; and systematic exposure to alternative theoretical and political perspectives. Students can choose a concentration in housing and community development, economic and workforce development, social policy, or finance for community and economic development.

The curriculum of the urban policy analysis and management program is designed to give students a sound foundation in the theory, techniques, and practice of the profession. Using a variety of instructional approaches, including case analyses, computer-based problem sets, and actual policy and management problems posed by public officials and nonprofit executives, the program acquaints students with the settings and issues they are likely to face as professional analysts and managers. To fulfill the required 42 credits, the student structures a program comprising three components—a required schoolwide core of 12 credits, a required program core of 12 credits, and 18 credits of electives.

Research Facilities The Center for New York City Affairs is a nonpartisan institute dedicated to advancing innovative public policies that strengthen neighborhoods, support families, and reduce urban poverty. Tools include rigorous analysis, research, candid public dialogue with stakeholders and opinion leaders, and strategic planning with government officials, nonprofit practitioners, and community residents. The center's original applied research and public seminars examine the politics of community change in local and state government and identify critical problems facing urban families and communities. The center's public programs offer community leaders and other participants the opportunity to meet powerful players in and around government and to learn about the context, the influential organizations, and other factors that define the policy-making landscape in New York City and urban America.

Financial Aid Milano offers financial aid packages in the form of scholarships, fellowships, and loans. Financial aid awards are decided on a first-come, first-served basis, and applicants are encouraged to apply early to receive priority consideration. Financial aid award decisions are made after students are accepted at Milano. Applicants interested in obtaining financial aid should submit the Free Application for Federal Student Aid (FAFSA) or the Renewal Application for Federal Student Aid. More information is available from the Office of Financial Services at 212-229-8930.

Cost of Study Tuition in 2008–09 is $1150 per credit, and fees are approximately $100 each term.

Living and Housing Costs The University Housing Office maintains a comprehensive resource center with apartment listings. University-run apartments and residence halls are also available. The cost of housing, food, transportation, books, and living expenses averages $17,000 annually. For more information, students should go online to http://www.newschool.edu/studentservices.

Student Group There are 114 students in the program; 52 attend on a full-time basis. Of these students, 80 are women, 61 are members of underrepresented groups, and 5 are international students.

Location The New School's location in New York City gives students access to an abundance of resources. Students are encouraged to take advantage of the city's many museums, performance venues, and other cultural institutions, which are only a walk or a subway ride away. An extension of the classroom, the city also offers excellent professional and networking opportunities, and some classes require that students work with outside businesses to complete assignments—giving them unparalleled real-world experience. Internships and apprenticeships with leading New York City companies and organizations in every field are also available, and many students have moved on from internships to successful careers with those companies and organizations upon graduation.

The University and The School Milano is part of is part of The New School, a leading university in New York City offering distinguished programs in design, liberal arts, the performing arts, and social and political science, leading to seventy graduate and undergraduate degrees. To learn more, students should visit http://www.newschool.edu/degreeprograms. The New School is accredited by the Commission on Higher Education of the Middle States Association of Colleges and Schools. A privately supported institution, The New School is chartered as a university by the Regents of the State of New York.

Applying Students must submit the completed application form, the $50 application fee, official transcripts from all postsecondary institutions attended, a 300-word essay explaining their professional goals, two letters of recommendation, and a resume. Applications are reviewed on a rolling admissions basis. Although there is no specific deadline, applicants are strongly encouraged to apply by March 1 for the fall semester and October 1 for the spring semester in order to take full advantage of financial aid and housing opportunities.

Correspondence and Information

Program in Urban Policy Analysis and Management
Milano The New School for Management and Urban Policy
The New School
72 Fifth Avenue, 3rd Floor
New York, New York 10011
Phone: 212-229-5400
Fax: 212-229-5354
E-mail: milanoadmissions@newschool.edu
Web site: http://www.newschool.edu/milano

The New School: A University

THE FACULTY AND THEIR RESEARCH

Warren Balinsky, Associate Professor and Chair of Health Services Management; Ph.D., Case Western Reserve. Home health care and the applications of planning, development, marketing, and research to health services management and policy. Dr. Balinsky has written two books on home care; he has also written articles on various aspects of emergency preparedness, health care of the elderly, health-care reimbursement, health-status indices, home care, pediatric health care, and the unequal distribution of medical personnel within the health-care system.

Robert Beauregard, Professor; Ph.D., Cornell. Urbanization in the United States, with particular focus on industrial urban decline after World War II and current problems posed by growth and decline in cities. Dr. Beauregard is currently working on *Writing Urban Theory,* a series of essays, and *Why Cities Endure,* a book investigating why some cities prosper while others do not. Dr. Beauregard teaches courses on the political economy of the city, urban redevelopment, neighborhood change, social theory, and research design.

Howard Berliner, Professor of Health Services Management and Director of Ph.D. in Public and Urban Policy Program; Sc.D., Johns Hopkins. Needs of vulnerable populations and access to health services for the uninsured. Dr. Berliner is the author of seven books, most recently *The Health Marketplace: New York City 1990–2010* with Ginzberg et al. He has also authored numerous articles and reviews on health-policy issues in academic and professional journals. Dr. Berliner served for two years as the assistant state health commissioner for New Jersey.

John Clinton, Visiting Assistant Professor; Ph.D., Fordham. Interprofessional collaboration. Dr. Clinton has served as corporation senior consultant on social responsibility at MetLife, senior vice president of the LightHouse for the Blind and Visually Impaired, and an administrator at NYU, Fordham University, and Hartwick College. He has been a consultant to foundations, nonprofit organizations, corporations, and higher education institutions.

Dennis Derryck, Professor of Professional Practice; Ph.D., Fordham. Innovative policies and strategies affecting the economic sustainability of nonprofit organizations. Dr. Derryck has held leadership positions in organizations involved in community economic development, operations and fiscal management, and research and policy analysis. He currently serves as chair of WE ACT for Environmental Justice and is vice chair of SoBro, the South Bronx Overall Economic Development Corporation.

Elizabeth Dickey, Professor; Ed.D., Massachusetts Amherst. Organizational behavior and leadership, with a psychosocial emphasis. Dr. Dickey is a developmental clinical psychologist. Between 1991 and 2005 she served as dean and then provost of The New School.

Peter Eisinger, Henry Cohen Professor; Ph.D., Yale. Urban politics and policy, state and local economic development, U.S. politics, state politics, federalism. Author of *Toward an End to Hunger in America.*

Alec Ian Gershberg, Associate Professor; Ph.D., Pennsylvania. School governance, education finance, decentralization in the developing world and in the United States, immigrant students in public schools in New York and California. Dr. Gershberg has conducted extensive research on Latin America—particularly Mexico, Nicaragua, and Ecuador—as well as on Egypt, Romania, and sub-Saharan Africa. He has been a frequent consultant to the World Bank, the Inter-American Development Bank, and the Urban Institute. Dr. Gershberg is the lead author of *Beyond Bilingual Education: New Immigrants and Public School Policies in California.*

Martin Greller, Professor and Associate Dean for Academic Affairs; Ph.D., Yale. Factors associated with career continuity for older workers, feedback systems in organizations as tools for increasing organizational effectiveness. Recent projects include an assessment of training needs for entry-level peace officers and a review of pay-equity issues for a legislative body.

Darrick Hamilton, Assistant Professor; Ph.D., North Carolina at Chapel Hill. Ethnic and racial disparities in wealth, home ownership, and labor market outcomes. Dr. Hamilton's articles can be found in *African American Research Perspectives, American Economics Review, Applied Economics Letters, Challenge: The Magazine of Economic Affairs, Journal of Economic Psychology, Review of Black Political Economy, Social Science Quarterly, Southern Economics Journal,* and *Transforming Anthropology.*

David Howell, Professor; Ph.D., New School. Labor markets at the local, national, and international levels. Recent publications have examined the effects of immigration on the economic status of foreign and native-born workers in New York City, the nature of recent changes in skill requirements and the determinants of relative wage trends in the United States, and the extent to which labor market institutions and social policy explain patterns of unemployment in Europe and the United States. Dr. Howell is the editor of *Fighting Unemployment: The Limits of Free Market Orthodoxy.*

Mark Lipton, Professor of Management and Chair of Management; Ph.D., Massachusetts Amherst. Management, leadership, organizational strategy. Author of *Guiding Growth: How Vision Keeps Companies on Course.* Dr. Lipton's research and opinions on management and strategy have appeared in *Executive Excellence, Harvard Business Review, The Journal of Management Consulting, Optimize, Organization Development Journal,* and *Sloan Management Review,* among others.

Edwin Melendez, Professor; Ph.D., Massachusetts Amherst. Economics. Dr. Melendez was director of the Mauricio Gastón Institute for Latino Community Development and Public Policy at the University of Massachusetts Boston (1992–98) and director of the Community Development Research Center at the Milano Graduate School (1999–2004). He has worked as a consultant on employment, economic development, job creation, and small business for numerous government, community, and philanthropic foundations. Dr. Melendez has managed more than thirty-five research, outreach, and demonstration projects and supervised or collaborated with more than 60 researchers in projects that resulted in several books, special issues of academic journals, and other publications.

Aida Rodriguez, Professor of Professional Practice; Ph.D., Massachusetts. Leadership and effective management in the nonprofit sector. Formerly deputy director of the Equal Opportunity Division of the Rockefeller Foundation, Dr. Rodriguez now serves on various nonprofit boards, including One Economy, Inc.; Alliance for Nonprofit Management; and the Association for Public Policy Analysis and Management. Dr. Rodriguez is an adviser on philanthropic initiatives in the United States and in Latin America, including the Funders' Collaborative for Strong Latino Communities.

Bryna Sanger, Professor; Ph.D., Brandeis. Public policy and management, changes in service delivery and management systems induced by welfare reform in states and localities around the country. Former dean of the Robert J. Milano Graduate School of Management and Urban Policy, Dr. Sanger has worked in a wide range of policy and management areas, including city service delivery, welfare reform, leadership, innovation, and performance management. She recently led a research effort with the National Civic League on the experiences of cities that have developed exemplary performance measurement systems and that report to and engage citizens in their efforts. Her most recent book on this topic is entitled *The Welfare Marketplace: Privatization and Welfare Reform.*

Alex F. Schwartz, Associate Professor, Chair of Department of Urban Policy Analysis and Management, and Senior Research Associate, Community Development Research Center; Ph.D., Rutgers. Housing and community development, including affordable housing programs, community reinvestment, and community development corporations. Dr. Schwartz's most recent publication is *Housing Policy in the United States.* His research has also appeared in such journals as *Cityscape, Economic Development Quarterly, International Journal of Urban and Regional Research,* and the *Journal of Urban Affairs.*

Lisa J. Servon, Associate Professor and Associate Director of Community Development Research Center; Ph.D., Berkeley. Urban poverty, community development, economic development, gender issues. Dr. Servon recently coedited *Gender and Planning: A Reader* (with Susan Fainstein), which covers a range of planning and development fields, including transportation, land use, history, gender, housing, social justice, environmental design, race, and economic and community development. The book was selected as one of the top10 books for 2006 by Planetizen, a public-interest information exchange for the urban planning, design, and development community.

Nidhi Srinivas, Assistant Professor of Nonprofit Management; Ph.D., McGill. Civil society, specifically management of nongovernmental organizations, and the transfer and transformation of management knowledge. Dr. Srinivas teaches courses on nonprofit management, international development, and strategic decision making. Courses he has developed include Managing Institutions for Development (part of the core curriculum in the graduate program in international affairs) and Civil Society and South Asia.

Antonin Wagner, Visiting Professor; Ph.D., Fribourg (Switzerland). Economics. From 1996 to 2000, Dr. Wagner was president of the International Society for Third Sector Research, the leading scholarly institution in the nonprofit field. He has served as a consultant on social security–related issues to the Swiss Federal Statistical Office and the World Bank in Washington. He is a member of the editorial board of several international journals and has published widely in English, German, and French on the welfare state and civil society.

Tatiana Wah, Assistant Professor; Ph.D., Rutgers. Regional and local economic development planning and developing nations, with a particular focus on small developing nations' economies. Dr. Wah's recent work is on transnational expatriate (immigrant) recovery and engagement programs of developing countries, particularly Haiti. She has been involved in community development work in the New York African American and Caribbean communities as a consultant, nonprofit administrator, and activist/advocate.

Mary R. Watson, Assistant Professor; Ph.D., Vanderbilt. Contemporary human capital issues in organizations, with particular emphasis on the social impact of labor market discontinuities. Dr. Watson teaches courses in management and organization behavior, human resources, social impact management, and globalization. She has a strong interest in cultural, racial, ethnic, and gender inequalities in the workplace and society. Her upcoming book (with Dr. Rikki Abzug), tentatively titled *Human Resources in Social Purpose Organizations,* is scheduled to be published by Jossey-Bass in 2007.

Part-time Faculty

The part-time faculty members of Milano The New School for Management and Urban Policy are high-level executives and managers in the institutions and agencies for which they work and the organizations for which they volunteer. They bring to the classroom valuable insight into current management and policy issues from both their personal experience and relevant curriculum. For a current listing of part-time faculty members, students should visit the Faculty page of the Milano Web site at http://www.milano.newschool.edu.

NEW YORK UNIVERSITY

Robert F. Wagner Graduate School of Public Service

Programs of Study

Established in 1938, the Robert F. Wagner Graduate School of Public Service at New York University (NYU Wagner) offers advanced programs leading to the professional degrees of Master of Public Administration (M.P.A.) in public and nonprofit management and policy (PNP) and health policy and management (HPM), Master of Urban Planning (M.U.P.), Master of Science (M.S.) in management, and Doctor of Philosophy (Ph.D.). Through these rigorous programs, NYU Wagner educates the future leaders of public, nonprofit, and health institutions as well as private organizations serving the public sector.

Course work in the PNP, HPM, and urban planning programs is divided into core and specialized curricula. All students are required to take core courses in policy analysis, finance, microeconomics, statistics, and management of public service organizations. Within the PNP program, students may pursue one of the following specializations: finance, international, management, or public policy analysis. Students may also elect course clusters in such areas as arts and cultural policy, economic and community development, education policy, and nonprofit management, among others. HPM specialization options are health finance, health policy analysis, health services management, and international health. The urban planning program offers specialized electives in economic development and housing policy and environment, infrastructure, and transportation planning. A specialization track in international development planning is also available.

The School encourages work in related schools and departments, such as business, law, economics, sociology, politics, and mathematics. It currently offers dual-degree programs with the University's School of Law (J.D./M.P.A., J.D./M.U.P.), the School of Medicine (M.D./M.P.A.), the College of Arts and Science (B.A./M.P.A., B.A./M.U.P.), the School of Dentistry (M.A. in nursing/M.S.), the School of Social Work (M.S.W./M.S.), the Stern School of Business (M.B.A./M.P.A.), and the Graduate School of Arts and Science (Skirball Department of Hebrew and Judaic Studies) (M.S./M.P.A.). Advanced professional certificate programs are available to those who already hold an M.P.A., an M.U.P., or a related degree.

Advanced students of exceptional ability may be invited to participate in research projects supervised by faculty members.

Research Facilities

Substantial library and computing resources are available, as is access to many specialized facilities in New York City. The Elmer Holmes Bobst Library is the largest open-stack library in the country. VAX and IBM mainframe computers as well as extensive microcomputer laboratories support course work and research.

Financial Aid

Fellowships offered through the School include University tuition scholarships and other fellowships earmarked for particular programs. Research and graduate assistantships are also available.

Cost of Study

Full tuition (16 credits per term) is $29,465 per academic year for 2007–08. Books cost approximately $800 per year.

Living and Housing Costs

University housing is available in University-owned apartment complexes. Apartments are available only to matriculated full-time students relocating from beyond a 35-mile radius of the University. The average cost of living in the New York metropolitan area varies considerably depending on residential location. Off-campus living expenses are estimated at $20,000 for a single student for the academic year, and married students can expect to incur an additional expense of $6000 or more, depending on the number of people in the household.

Student Group

There are more than 860 graduate students in the School. Just over 50 percent are full-time students. Part-time students who take courses each term are employed in public, private, nonprofit, and health services organizations. More than eleven percent are international students, and over 27 percent are domestic students who are members of minority groups.

Location

New York University is an integral part of the thriving metropolitan community of New York City—the business, cultural, artistic, and financial center of the nation and the home of the United Nations. The city's extraordinary resources greatly enrich both the academic programs and the experience of living at the University. The School is located in the historic Puck Building, adjacent to New York City's Greenwich Village district and Washington Square Park.

The University

New York University is a private, metropolitan university that offers the advantages of a great urban setting to a highly diverse student body. The University first held classes in 1832, with 108 students and a faculty of 15. Its charter specified that it was to be established "on a liberal foundation, which shall correspond with the spirit and wants of our age. . . ." Today, with an enrollment of more than 50,000 students from all fifty states and 160 other countries, a faculty of 5,500, and more than 2,500 courses, the University vigorously keeps pace with the spirit and needs of the present and the future.

Applying

Prospective students should contact the Office of Enrollment and Student Services for more information. The application deadlines for admission and fellowship, scholarship, or assistantship aid for master's degree programs are January 15 for summer and fall semesters and October 1 for spring semester; the deadlines for admission alone are April 15 for summer, June 1 for fall, and November 15 for spring. The international application deadline is January 15 for summer and fall and October 1 for spring. The application deadline for the doctoral program is December 10. The application for admission is available through the School's Web page at http://wagner.nyu.edu.

Correspondence and Information

Office of Enrollment and Student Services
Robert F. Wagner Graduate School of Public Service
The Puck Building
New York University
295 Lafayette Street, 2nd Floor
New York, New York 10012-9604
Phone: 212-998-7414
E-mail: wagner.admissions@nyu.edu
Web site: http://wagner.nyu.edu

New York University

THE FACULTY

Ellen Schall, Martin E. Cherkasky Professor of Health Policy and Management and Dean; J.D., NYU, 1972.
Rogan Kersh, Associate Professor of Public Service and Associate Dean for Academic Affairs; Ph.D., Yale, 1996.
Robert Berne, Professor of Public Administration and Vice President for Academic Development; Ph.D., Cornell, 1977.
John Billings, Associate Professor of Health Policy and Management; J.D., Berkeley, 1973.
Jan Blustein, Professor of Health Policy and Management; M.D., Yale, 1985; Ph.D., NYU, 1993.
Jo Ivey Boufford, Professor of Health Policy and Public Service; M.D., Michigan, 1971.
Charles Brecher, Professor of Public and Health Administration; Ph.D., CUNY Graduate Center, 1972.
Sewin Chan, Associate Professor of Public Policy ; Ph.D., Columbia, 1995.
Ingrid Gould Ellen, Paulette Goddard Professor of Urban Policy; Ph.D., Harvard, 1996.
Erica G. Foldy, Assistant Professor of Public Administration; Ph.D., Boston College, 2002.
Rema N. Hanna, Assistant Professor of Public Policy and Economics; Ph.D., MIT, 2005.
Natasha Iskander, Assistant Professor of Public Administration; Ph.D., MIT, 2006.
Anthony R. Kovner, Professor of Public and Health Management; Ph.D., Pittsburgh, 1966.
Roger Kropf, Professor of Public and Health Management; Ph.D., Syracuse, 1976.
Paul C. Light, Paulette Goddard Professor of Public Service; Ph.D., Michigan, 1980.
Joe C. Magee, Assistant Professor of Management; Ph.D., Stanford, 2004.
Jonathan J. Morduch, Associate Professor of Public Policy and Economics; Ph.D., Harvard, 1991.
Mitchell Moss, Henry Hart Rice Professor of Urban Policy and Planning; Ph.D., USC, 1975.
Katherine M. O'Regan, Associate Professor of Public Administration; Ph.D., Berkeley, 1990.
Sonia Ospina, Associate Professor of Public Management and Policy; Ph.D., SUNY at Stony Brook, 1989.
Victor G. Rodwin, Professor of Health Policy and Management; Ph.D., Berkeley, 1980.
Shanna Rose, Assistant Professor of Public Financial Management; Ph.D., Harvard, 2005.
Amy Ellen Schwartz, Professor of Public Policy, Education, and Economics; Ph.D., Columbia, 1989.
Dennis Smith, Associate Professor of Public Administration; Ph.D., Indiana, 1975.
Paul Smoke, Professor of Public Finance and Planning; Ph.D., MIT, 1988.
Walter W. Stafford, Professor of Public Policy and Planning; Ph.D., Pittsburgh, 1973.
Leanna Stiefel, Professor of Economics; Ph.D., Wisconsin–Madison, 1972.
Beth Weitzman, Professor of Health and Public Policy; Ph.D., NYU, 1987.
Rae Zimmerman, Professor of Planning and Public Administration; Ph.D., Columbia, 1972.

NORTHWESTERN UNIVERSITY

School of Education and Social Policy
Graduate Program in Human Development and Social Policy

Program of Study

The Graduate Program in Human Development and Social Policy is an unusual interdisciplinary program designed to meet the growing need for persons with social sciences backgrounds who are knowledgeable about both human development and social policy. The program centers on three areas of study and the interrelations among them: the psychological and social development of the person across the life span, the influence of social and economic environments, and the role of policy decisions in shaping life choices, opportunities, and outcomes. Special attention is given to research methods suited for analyzing the interrelations. Students may specialize in child development and social policy; adolescent development and social policy; adult development, aging, and social policy; poverty and social policy; education and social policy; or a general life cycle approach to policy or to human development. The faculty members are drawn from a number of different disciplines and fields of study, including psychology, sociology, education, political science, economics, public policy, and human development.

Graduates of the program are prepared to make special contributions in a wide range of careers. As teachers and researchers, they bring a special interdisciplinary perspective to programs in the social sciences, human development, public policy, and education.

The Ph.D. degree is offered; students may also complete an M.A. degree en route to the Ph.D. Course work is tailored to build upon the student's background and to fit the particular educational goals developed by the student and adviser. Courses and seminars are drawn from the School of Education and Social Policy and from other departments and units of the University. Several of the program's faculty members have joint appointments at Northwestern's Institute for Policy Research, thus assuring students of research opportunities in a variety of areas.

Research Facilities

Resources for advanced study at Northwestern University are outstanding. Numerous research libraries, including the Main Library and five branch and special libraries on the campus, contain holdings totaling more than 3 million volumes, 1 million microfilm units, and 33,000 journals and other serial publications. In addition, students are provided access to both the mainframe computer at the I. T. Computing Center and microcomputers housed within the School. Research opportunities are available for students in three research centers at the University: the Center on Aging, the Institute for Policy Research, and the Joint Center for Poverty Research.

Financial Aid

Financial aid is available to graduate students in the form of University and program fellowships, scholarships, and graduate assistantships. Special opportunities for research assistantships or other employment also exist within the School's and the University's many research centers. Student loans are also possible. All Ph.D. students are fully funded for four years.

Cost of Study

Tuition for full-time study (three courses per three quarters) in pursuit of the Ph.D. was $35,079 in 2007–08 ($11,693 per quarter). As discussed in the Financial Aid section, all Ph.D. students are fully funded for four years.

Living and Housing Costs

The University operates two graduate student residences in Evanston. In addition, information and assistance in securing off-campus housing is made available.

Student Group

There are approximately 30 graduate students in the program at the present time. Enrollments are selective, and only 5–7 new students are accepted into the program each year. Graduates hold positions in such settings as universities, research organizations, public or private agencies, and foundations.

Location

Northwestern's Evanston campus is located on Lake Michigan, just north of the city of Chicago. The beautiful lakefront campus offers a rich cultural environment through a wealth of theatrical, musical, and athletic events. The proximity of the campus to a major metropolitan complex, with its world-class architecture, symphony, museums, opera, theater, and major-league sports, further enriches student life.

The University and The School

Established in 1851, Northwestern University is recognized as one of the most distinguished private universities in the United States. The School of Education and Social Policy has developed from its origins as a department of pedagogy by continually broadening its scope to encompass those educative, learning, and socializing experiences that take place throughout the life span in families, schools, communities, and the workplace.

Applying

Applications for admission are reviewed in January and February. Admission decisions are usually made in late February. Except in unusual circumstances, students are accepted in the Program in Human Development and Social Policy for fall quarter matriculation only. Applicants planning to seek financial aid must meet the submission deadline of December 31.

Correspondence and Information

Graduate Program in Human Development and Social Policy
Northwestern University
School of Education and Social Policy
2120 Campus Drive
Evanston, Illinois 60208-2610
Phone: 847-491-4329
Web site: http://www.sesp.northwestern.edu/hdsp/info/overview

Northwestern University

THE FACULTY AND THEIR RESEARCH

* *Emma Adam, Ph.D., Minnesota. Parenting, developmental psychobiology of stress, attachment, foster care.
* *Lindsay Chase-Lansdale, Ph.D., Michigan. Child, adolescent, and family functioning; public policy; poverty and welfare reform.
* *Jeannette A. Colyvas, Ph.D., Stanford. Institutional change; public, private, and nonprofit forms of organizing; science policy; university-industry interfaces in R&D.
* *Fay Lomax Cook, Ph.D., Chicago. Politics of public policy, public opinion, policy issues in aging.
* Thomas D. Cook, Ph.D., Stanford. Social-psychological processes, measurement of attitudes, evaluation of social programs.
* *Greg J. Duncan, Ph.D., Michigan. Extent and consequences of poverty and welfare dynamics, survey research in social policy.
* *Larry V. Hedges, Ph.D., Stanford. Statistics and research design, education policy, the role of uncertainty in cognitive models, social distribution of academic achievement.
* *Barton J. Hirsch, Ph.D., Oregon. Social ecology of adolescent development, social networks, community psychology, parenting.
* *Spyros Konstantopoulos, Ph.D., Chicago. Multilevel models, meta-analysis, teacher and school effects, class-size effects.
* *Dan A. Lewis, Ph.D., California, Santa Cruz. Policy analysis, urban social problems, community organization.
* *Jelani Mandara, Ph.D., California, Riverside. African American families, social development, self-regulation, personality, quantitative methods.
* *Dan P. McAdams, Ph.D., Harvard. Adult development; personality, identity, and the self; generativity; life narratives.
* *Thomas McDade, Ph.D., Emory. Human biology, biocultural perspectives on health and human development, medical anthropology, evolutionary ecology.
* Penelope Peterson, Ph.D., Stanford. Learning and teaching in schools and classrooms, particularly in mathematics and literacy; teacher learning in reform contexts; relations among educational research, policy, and practice.
* *Michelle Reininger, Ph.D., Stanford. Education policy, teacher labor markets, teacher education, community colleges.
* *James E. Rosenbaum, Ph.D., Harvard. Adolescent/adult development, organizational careers, education and social policy, poverty and housing.
* Bruce D. Spencer, Ph.D., Yale. Social and educational measurement, statistics for policy analysis, demography, decision theory.
* *James P. Spillane, Ph.D., Michigan State. Education policy and school reform, intergovernmental relations, policy and practice, organizational leadership and change.
* Linda A. Teplin, Ph.D., Northwestern. Mental health services/policies for youth and adult populations in the criminal justice system, community-based samples.

**Core faculty.*

School of Education and Social Policy.

Northwestern University J. Roscoe Miller campus.

THE OHIO STATE UNIVERSITY

John Glenn School of Public Affairs

Programs of Study

The School offers study in public affairs and management leading to the Master of Public Administration (M.P.A.), Master of Arts (M.A.), and Doctor of Philosophy (Ph.D.) degrees. The programs are broadly interdisciplinary and emphasize analytical tools for problem solving.

The M.P.A. is a two-year program that educates students for analytical and managerial positions at the federal, state, and local government levels as well as in quasipublic and not-for-profit organizations. The foundation curriculum covers policy, management, economics, and quantitative methods. The program offers a three-month summer internship in a government agency. Generally, the internship provides a problem and a source of data for the major policy paper prepared by students during the second year. In this capstone paper, students report the results of applied research on a policy or administrative problem and include a proposed solution.

The program offers several areas of application: fiscal management, health services policy, human resources administration and labor relations, management information and decision support systems, natural resources, regulation, and urban policy and management. Students can develop unique application areas with the approval of the Graduate Studies Committee.

The In-Career M.A. in public policy and management is a shorter version of the M.P.A. program; full-time students can complete the M.A. program in twelve months, but students may enroll part-time. Admission to the program is limited to students with three years of significant administrative or analytical work experience. Dual-degree M.A. programs are available with the College of Social Work, the School of Natural Resources, the City and Regional Planning Program, the Division of Health Services Management and Policy, and the College of Law. A joint M.A. in arts policy and administration is offered in conjunction with the College of the Arts.

Since its inception, the School has also offered the Ph.D. degree in public policy and management. The emphasis of this academically rigorous program is on research. This degree prepares individuals for university careers in teaching and research and for senior-level research roles in governmental, consulting, and nonprofit institutions.

Research Facilities

The Ohio State University Library System is one of the twenty-two largest systems in the United States and contains more than 300,000 government documents. The Office of Information Technology (OIT) offers computer systems with a variety of compilers, program packages, and software. The John Glenn School of Public Affairs provides staff members for programming consultation for course work and research as well as auxiliary equipment online to OIT. The School supports its own computer lab with state-of-the-art hardware and software. Each student has an e-mail account that provides access to commercial online database systems as well as to campus research collections and the Internet.

Other major research institutes housed at Ohio State include the Mershon Center for Education in National Security, the National Regulatory Research Institute, the Center for Human Resource Research, the Center for International Business Education and Research, the Survey Research Center, and the Criminal Justice Research Center.

Financial Aid

Fellowships funded by the University and graduate associateships (research and administrative) funded by the John Glenn School of Public Affairs are available to qualified students. Students can apply for this aid by checking a box on the Graduate School application. Fellowships and associateships provide a full waiver of fees and tuition and a monthly stipend of between $1020 and $1256.

Cost of Study

The 2008–09 graduate tuition for full-time students who are state residents is $9972 per academic year. Nonresident fees are $24,126 per academic year. All costs are subject to change. Costs are based on a three-quarter academic year.

Living and Housing Costs

Affordable housing is available both on and off campus. More than 1,250 on-campus rooms accommodate graduate students and are available at an estimated $12,108 per year for room and board. Off-campus housing is comparable and can be found in the campus area as well as in suburbs and villages within an easy commute. Columbus offers a low cost of living and a diversified employment base.

Student Group

The School enrolls students for graduate work only. The current enrollment is 120 part-time and full-time students, who have come from all over the United States and several other countries. Students with a wide variety of undergraduate backgrounds are considered for admission.

Location

The campus is located 2 miles north of downtown Columbus, the capital city of Ohio and a metropolitan area with a population of more than 1.7 million. Recreational and cultural opportunities abound in the area, which also provides the School's students with a wide range of opportunities for research and practical experience, including numerous summer internships established with state, city, and nonprofit agencies.

The University

Offering 110 fields of graduate study, the Ohio State University is a major center for graduate and professional education. Interdisciplinary opportunities and student organizations are plentiful on campus.

Applying

The recommended deadline for autumn-quarter admission is March 15. Full-time M.P.A. students requiring financial assistance are asked to apply for the autumn quarter. Required undergraduate preparation for all of the School's programs includes courses in statistics, American government, and microeconomics. Students applying to the M.P.A. program must also have taken a course in financial accounting. Scores on the GRE General Test are required of all applicants to the M.P.A. and Ph.D. programs. The deadline for filing an application to the Graduate School in order to be considered for fellowships is January 15 for domestic students and November 30 for international students.

Correspondence and Information

John Glenn School of Public Affairs
110 Page Hall
The Ohio State University
1810 College Road
Columbus, Ohio 43210-1336

Phone: 614-292-8696
Fax: 614-292-2548
Web site: http://glennschool.osu.edu

The Ohio State University

THE FACULTY AND THEIR RESEARCH

Trevor L. Brown, Associate Professor; Ph.D., Indiana. Behavior and management of public-sector organizations. Professor Brown's research interests include contracting out and contract management, performance management, intergovernmental relations, and democratization.

Jennifer Evans Cowley, Assistant Professor, City and Regional Planning; Ph.D., Texas A&M. Infrastructure finance, land-use regulation, growth management, real estate development, e-government.

Anand Desai, Professor; Ph.D., Pennsylvania. Operations research and statistics. His research interests include measurement of productivity and efficiency, graphic display of multivariate relationships, mathematical modeling, and environmental policy.

Jeffrey D. Ford, Associate Professor; Ph.D., Ohio State. Organization design, change, and implementation. Professor Ford is a member of the Department of Management and Human Resources.

John H. Glenn, Adjunct Professor. Professor Glenn is a retired U.S. senator from Ohio who served from 1974 to 1998.

Robert T. Greenbaum, Associate Professor; Ph.D., Carnegie Mellon. Urban and regional economic development, public policy analysis, spatial analysis, employment policy, housing policy, applied microeconomics.

Donald R. Haurin, Professor; Ph.D., MIT. Urban economics, public finance, microeconomic theory, government finance in the American economy. Professor Haurin is Associate Dean of the College of Social and Behavioral Sciences.

Theresa Heintze, Assistant Professor; Ph.D., Syracuse. Welfare programs, child support policy and housing subsidies.

Andrew G. Keeler, Associate Professor; Ph.D., Berkeley. Environmental and natural resources economics and policy.

Thomas M. Koontz, Associate Professor, Environmental and Natural Resources; Ph.D., Indiana. Public policy processes, institutional analysis, citizen participation, natural resource management, land use, community governance and decision making, forest policy, public lands, collaborative environmental management, federalism, intergovernmental relations, bureaucratic behavior.

David Landsbergen, Associate Professor and Chair, Doctoral Studies Committee; J.D., Ph.D., Syracuse. Administrative law, implementation and information systems. His research interests include telecommunications policy and law and public administration.

Edward J. Malecki, Professor; Ph.D., Ohio State. Urban, rural, and regional economic development; technology policy. Professor Malecki is a member of the Department of Geography.

Stephen L. Mangum, Associate Professor; Ph.D., George Washington. Labor economics, human resource policy, industrial relations. Professor Mangum is Associate Dean, Fisher College of Business.

Mary K. Marvel, Associate Professor and Chair, Graduate Studies Committee; Ph.D., Ohio State. Public policy formulation and implementation, evaluation research. Professor Marvel was a visiting scholar at the Hoover Institution on the campus of Stanford University. Her research interests include impact of economic development initiatives and policy implementation and evaluation.

Deborah Jones Merritt, Professor; J.D., Columbia. Federalism, equality, affirmative action, health and technology, law and social science. Professor Merritt is Director, John Glenn Institute for Public Service and Public Policy, and the John Deaver Drinko/Baker & Hostetler Chair in Law.

Ruth D. Peterson, Associate Professor and Associate Director of the Criminal Justice Research Center; Ph.D., Wisconsin–Madison. Criminology, criminal justice, sociology of law. Professor Peterson is a member of the Department of Sociology.

Peter Shane, Professor; J.D., Yale. Separation of powers law, electronic democracy, law and the presidency. Professor Shane is Director, Center for Law, Policy, and Social Science, and the Joseph S. Platt/Porter Wright Morris Arthur Professor of Law.

William J. Shkurti, Adjunct Professor; M.P.A., Ohio State. Public finance and budgeting. His research interests include public finance, public budgeting, economic development, and business-government relations. He is currently Vice President for Finance at OSU and served as Budget Director for the state of Ohio from 1984 to 1987.

Sandra J. Tanenbaum, Associate Professor; Ph.D., MIT. Health policy and politics, disability, mental health, Medicaid, evidence-based medicine and practice movements.

Mohan K. Wali, Professor; Ph.D., British Columbia. Environmental policy, analysis of energy development and land use, sustainable development. Professor Wali is a member of the School of Natural Resources.

L. Lee Walker, Adjunct Professor; J.D., Capital. Administrative law, policy formulation and policy implementation, budget and resource allocation. Professor Walker is a former state of Ohio Budget Director with more than fifteen years of practitioner experience in the public sector.

Bruce A. Weinberg, Associate Professor, Economics; Ph.D., Chicago. His research interests include behavior of outcomes of youth and young adults, with emphases on family background and social networks; effect of technological change and industrial shifts on the wage structure; and changes in creativity and productivity over the life cycle.

Charles R. Wise, Professor and Director; Ph.D., Indiana. His research interests include public organizations and management, public law, and democratization in comparative politics and administration.

Margaret J. Wyszomirski, Professor; Ph.D., Cornell. American politics, public administration, public policy and the arts, law and public policy, arts management. Professor Wyszomirski is a member of the faculty of the Department of Art Education and Director of the Arts Policy and Administration Program.

PACE UNIVERSITY

Dyson College of Arts and Sciences
Master of Public Administration Program

Program of Study

Pace University's Master of Public Administration (M.P.A.) degree is offered at the Graduate Center in White Plains. Students may concentrate in the management of government, health-care, nonprofit, or environmental organizations. The curriculum encompasses a total of 39 credits including core, track, and specialization of elective courses. Some students may be required to take an additional 6 credits of precore foundation courses to prepare for the M.P.A. degree. In addition, certificate programs are offered in nonprofit management, health-care policy and management, long-term care management and practice, and environmental management study. The program also offers a joint M.P.A./J.D. degree with the School of Law. Core and foundation courses are designed to develop comprehensive administrative, managerial, quantitative, financial, and analytical skills with a thorough understanding of their applications to the government, health-care, or nonprofit sectors. Specialization and elective courses provide the student with the opportunity to develop knowledge and skills in specialized programs and functional areas. They supplement and complement the core and track foundation courses and facilitate the achievement of professional and career objectives. Students complete a capstone that is either a research project with a presentation or an intensive readings course followed by a comprehensive essay. Precareer students are encouraged to complete an internship; most internship programs provide stipends.

Research Facilities

The Pace University Library is a comprehensive teaching library and student-learning center, a virtual library that combines strong core collections with ubiquitous access to global Internet resources to support broad and diversified curricula. Reciprocal borrowing and access accords, traditional interlibrary loan services, and commercial document delivery options supplement the aggregate holdings of the library. Pace offers Instructional Services Librarians, a state-of-the-art electronic classroom, digital reference services, and multimedia applications. Pace's computer resource centers are linked to high-speed data networks and feature sophisticated hardware and software to facilitate active learning. Recognized as one of America's most wired universities, Pace supports high-speed Internet and Internet2 access on every campus. Resident facilities are wired, and most public areas are enabled for wireless connectivity. Full-motion videoconference facilities enable remote delivery of instruction between campus sites for synchronous learning applications. Many courses are Web assisted with state-of-the-art software, and some courses and programs are completely Web based.

Financial Aid

Pace's comprehensive student financial aid assistance program includes scholarships, graduate assistantships, student loans, and tuition payment plans. Scholarships are awarded to students in recognition of superior academic achievement and are available for full- and part-time study. Highly qualified students may be eligible for assistantships awarded by departments, which paid stipends of up to $5100 and provided tuition remission up to 24 credits during the 2007–08 academic year. Pace participates in all major federal and state financial aid programs such as Federal Direct Loans, New York State Tuition Assistance Program (TAP), and Perkins Loans. All students are encouraged to apply for these programs by filing the Free Application for Federal Student Aid (FAFSA).

Cost of Study

Tuition for graduate courses is $763 per credit in 2008–09.

Living and Housing Costs

Residence facilities are available on campus in New York City and Westchester. Double-occupancy rooms range from approximately $8500 to $12,000 for 2007–08. University operated, off-campus housing is available within proximity of the New York City campus.

Student Group

Pace students represent diversified personal, cultural, and educational backgrounds. Many students are employed and pursue graduate study for personal growth and career advancement. Seventy-nine percent are enrolled part-time in evening classes. Current enrollment in the graduate public administration program is approximately 73 students.

Location

Pace University is a multicampus institution with campuses in both New York City and Westchester County. All locations are within reach of cultural, business, and social resources and opportunities. The downtown Manhattan campus is adjacent to Wall Street and City Hall. Pace's Midtown Center is a short distance from Times Square, theaters, and Grand Central Station. The Pleasantville/Briarcliff campus is in a suburban setting surrounded by towns offering various forms of recreation. The Graduate Center and the School of Law are located in White Plains among major retail districts and many corporate headquarters. All locations are accessible by public transportation. The graduate public administration program is available at the Westchester campus.

The University

Founded in 1906, Pace University is a private, nonsectarian, coeducational institution. Originally founded as a school of accounting, Pace Institute was designated Pace College in 1973. Through growth and various successes, Pace College was renamed Pace University as approved by the New York State Board of Regents. Today, Pace offers comprehensive undergraduate, graduate, doctoral, and professional-level programs at several campus locations through six schools and colleges.

Applying

Admission to Pace University requires successful completion of a U.S. baccalaureate degree, or its equivalent, from an accredited institution. Students must submit a completed application, application fee, official transcripts from all postsecondary institutions, a personal statement, a resume, and two letters of recommendation. International students must submit official TOEFL scores and official transcripts in the native language with a professional English translation. Applications should be submitted by August 1 for the fall semester, December 1 for the spring semester, and May 1 for summer sessions. International applications should be submitted five months prior to these dates.

Correspondence and Information

Office of Graduate Admission
Pace University
1 Pace Plaza
New York, New York 10038
Phone: 212-346-1531
Fax: 212-346-1585
E-mail: gradnyc@pace.edu
Web site: http://www.pace.edu.

Office of Graduate Admission
Pace University
1 Martine Avenue
White Plains, New York 10606
Phone: 914-422-4283
Fax: 914-422-4287
E-mail: gradwp@pace.edu
Web site: http://www.pace.edu.

Pace University

THE FACULTY

Mary M. Timney, Professor and Chair, Department of Political Science; Ph.D., Pittsburgh.
Farrokh Hormozi, Professor; Ph.D., New School.
Frank Maddalena, Research Professor; M.B.A., Fordham.
Brian Nickerson, Associate Professor and Director, the Michaelian Institute; Ph.D., SUNY at Albany; J.D., Pace.

Adjunct Faculty
Neil Abitabilo, Adjunct Lecturer; M.S., LIU, C.W. Post.
Michael S. Blau, Adjunct Instructor; J.D., Toledo.
Alfred Cava, Adjunct Lecturer; M.S., Pace.
Gregory Chartier, Adjunct Associate Professor; M.B.A., Rensselaer.
Joseph Corcoran, Adjunct Lecturer; M.B.A., Pace.
Anthony A. Cupaiuolo, Professor; D.S.W., Columbia.
Margaret FitzGerald, Professor; J.S., Western New England.
Warren Geller, Adjunct Lecturer; M.P.A., Pace.
Michael Genito, Adjunct Lecturer; M.P.A., Pace.
Michael J. Graessle, Adjunct Lecturer; M.A., Fordham.
Gregory Holtz, Adjunct Associate Professor; Ph.D., Notre Dame.
Grant P. Loavenbruck, Adjunct Associate Professor; D.S.W., Columbia.
Rose London, Adjunct Lecturer; M.B.A., Pittsburgh.
Anthony Mahler, Adjunct Lecturer; M.B.A., Boston University.
Jon Schandler, Adjunct Lecturer; M.B.A., Fordham.
Wendy Smith-Deer, Adjunct Assistant Professor; M.P.A./J.D., Pace.
Lester Steinman, Adjunct Lecturer; J.D., Georgetown.
Catherine Tinker, Adjunct Professor; J.S.D., NYU.
Bernard M. Weinstein, Adjunct Professor; M.P.H., Pittsburgh.

PEPPERDINE UNIVERSITY

School of Public Policy

Program of Study

The School of Public Policy offers a twenty-month, full-time Master of Public Policy (M.P.P.) degree. The program is committed to nurturing leaders who can use the tools of analysis and policy design to effect successful implementation and real change. It is based on the conviction that an elevated and elevating culture and personal and moral certainties are the valid concern of higher education and are just as important as the tools of analysis.

The unique curriculum requires 64 units of course work—four 4-unit courses each semester for two academic years (four semesters). The first year is primarily composed of core courses and provides a foundation for the student's specialization courses, most of which are taken during the second year. Specialization areas include public policy and economics, public policy and international relations, public policy and American politics, and state and local policy.

In addition to regular credit courses, each student is expected to complete three noncredit experiences critical to developing leadership in real-world situations. These begin with an Orientation Leadership Workshop, followed by a summer internship between the first and second year. Finally, students develop a team project (a major public program design and implementation plan using a real situation in a global, national, state, or local agency) during the final semester's Policy Seminar.

The School of Public Policy offers concurrent degrees with the School of Law: a J.D./M.P.P. and an M.P.P./Master of Dispute Resolution (M.D.R.). A joint M.B.A./M.P.P. with the Graziadio School of Business and Management is also offered.

Research Facilities

Public policy students, professors, visiting practitioners, and researchers have computerized access to national and global databases (LEXIS-NEXIS, Dow Jones, InfoTrak, etc.), the University's voice mail and e-mail systems, Internet and World Wide Web connections, and a well-equipped computer laboratory. Additionally, the Payson Library and the Law Library on the Malibu Campus and libraries at the Graziadio School of Business and Management Centers in Culver City, Irvine, Long Beach, Encino, and Westlake Village cumulatively contain more than 720,000 cumulative volumes of library resources in all formats, including more than 7,000 periodical and serial title subscriptions. Pepperdine also has one of the first networked database systems in the country, providing access to periodical titles, with full-text delivery in electronic format. The University is committed to building a substantial core collection of bound volumes and periodicals covering a wide range of public policy themes.

Financial Aid

The School of Public Policy offers merit-based scholarships and graduate assistantships to qualified domestic and international students. To be considered for either, an applicant must first be accepted for admission. The scholarship committee awards scholarships based on merit, need, and academic and professional experience as well as standardized test scores. Students awarded a graduate assistantship work with faculty members or administration members in the School of Public Policy about 12 hours per week and earn $1500 per semester. Qualified students may also apply for assistance through the Stafford Loan Program. Stafford Loans are made by banks, savings and loan associations, and credit unions.

Cost of Study

Tuition for the 2007–08 academic year was $17,272 per semester. Public policy students attend two semesters per year for two academic years to complete the program.

Living and Housing Costs

Convenient housing is available both on and off campus. In 2007–08, on-campus students may choose a four-bedroom apartment, with each student having a single room at $5275 per semester. Limited married-student housing is also available. Living expenses such as transportation, food, utilities, and personal expenses vary depending upon the student and where he or she chooses to live.

Student Group

The School of Public Policy enrolled its inaugural full-time class of students in September 1997. The average entering class size is 60. The men-women ratio is about 40/60, with approximately 15 percent international student enrollment. The faculty members seek students with varied educational, professional, cultural, and ethnic backgrounds to contribute to the collaborative learning environment in the classroom. Diverse backgrounds offer multiple points of view that contribute to a broad understanding of public policy issues.

Student Outcomes

Public policy graduates are sought after for leadership positions in federal, state, and local governments and municipalities; public, nonprofit, and church organizations; consulting; and private business. Recent job offers include the CIA, the FBI, and the State Department.

Location

Located in Southern California, about 35 miles west of downtown Los Angeles, Malibu offers miles of beautiful beaches and a small-town atmosphere. The city has fewer than 30,000 people who live on 27 miles of rolling hills and Pacific coastline. Students can spend their free time enjoying Malibu's fine restaurants, shops, galleries, and beaches. Acres of national park land are adjacent to Malibu and offer mountain biking and hiking. Los Angeles and its surrounding communities offer a variety of year-round cultural and recreational opportunities.

The University

Pepperdine University is an independent university enrolling approximately 8,000 students in five colleges and schools. Religiously affiliated with the Churches of Christ, the University was founded in 1937 by George Pepperdine, who believed that the strength of a nation depends, in a large part, on the integrity of its leaders. Thus, the School of Public Policy designed its programs to combine a distinctive emphasis on ethics and the moral and historical roots of free institutions with analytical and leadership skills to provide a foundation for influencing matters of public policy.

Applying

The School of Public Policy encourages applications from graduates of regionally accredited institutions in all areas of study. Students are currently accepted for the fall semester only. The application deadline for fall is May 1. Applications received after May 1 are reviewed on a space-available basis. GRE scores are required; no minimum score is required for consideration. GMAT or LSAT scores may be accepted under certain circumstances. Students should contact the School at the addresses listed in the contact section for specific application requirements.

Correspondence and Information

Melinda van Hemert
Assistant Dean for Admission and Student Services
School of Public Policy
Pepperdine University
24255 Pacific Coast Highway
Malibu, California 90263-7493
Phone: 310-506-7493
888-456-1177 (toll-free)
Fax: 310-506-7494
E-mail: melinda.vanhemert@pepperdine.edu
Web site: http://publicpolicy.pepperdine.edu/

Pepperdine University

THE FACULTY

Luisa Blanco Raynal (telephone: 310-506-7466; fax: 310-506-7494; e-mail: luisa.blancoraynal@pepperdine.edu) is Assistant Professor of Economics and an economist specializing in economic development and international economics. She received her Ph.D. from the University of Oklahoma, where she taught Intermediate Macroeconomic Theory and Principles of Macroeconomics at the undergraduate level. She received her bachelor's degree in business administration in the field of finance and a Master of Business Administration from Midwestern State University. Blanco's research focuses on issues related to policy making in Latin American countries. She has done an analysis of the determinants of political instability in Latin America, which is forthcoming in the *Journal of Development Studies*. Currently, she is working on the effects of financial development and resource inequality on economic growth in Latin America, in addition to a project on tax havens. Blanco's research interests include topics on public finance, specifically international taxation policy, and extend into issues related to education and democracy in less-developed countries. With her empirical research, Blanco aims to provide useful recommendations for policy makers in the developing world.

David Davenport (telephone: 310-506-6878; fax: 310-506-7794; e-mail: david.davenport@pepperdine.edu) is Distinguished Professor of Public Policy at Pepperdine University and also a research fellow at the Hoover Institution. He teaches advanced courses on international law and institutions and political campaigns. He also offers core courses on great books and public policy. Davenport's research and writing focus on legal policy, especially international law, treaties, and institutions. The National Legal Center for the Public Interest has published his monographs on the proliferation of international courts and tribunals and on the International Criminal Court. His work on "the new diplomacy" has been published in *Policy Review* and in a recent Hoover Press book *A Country I Do Not Recognize*. As codirector of the Hoover Institution's Initiative on American Individualism and Societal Values, he also writes on character, culture, and values. He authors a regular column for the *San Francisco Chronicle* and was formerly a regular columnist for the Scripps Howard News Service. His columns have been published in scores of newspapers, including the *Los Angeles Times, San Jose Mercury News, San Diego Union Tribune, USA Today,* and the *Washington Times*. He has been cited or featured in *Time, U.S. News & World Report, Fortune,* the *Christian Science Monitor, New York Times,* and elsewhere. Davenport served as president of Pepperdine University from 1985 to 2000. He has had significant experience in community, corporate, and government leadership and has coauthored a book *Shepherd Leadership* (Jossey-Bass, 2003). He currently serves on the governing and advisory boards of Common Sense California, the National Legal Center for the Public Interest, Inside Track Learning, and Hope Network Ministries as well as corporate boards. Governor Arnold Schwarzenegger appointed him to membership on the California Performance Review Commission, and he has served as an adviser to several political campaigns. David Davenport earned a B.A. with distinction in international relations from Stanford University and a J.D. from the University of Kansas School of Law, where he was elected to Order of the Coif and earned national and international awards in moot court competitions. He also served internships in the Executive Office of the President in Washington, D.C., and in the office of U.S. senator Robert Dole.

Angela Hawken (telephone: 310-506-7608; fax: 310-506-7494; e-mail: angela.hawken@pepperdine.edu) is Assistant Professor at the Pepperdine School of Public Policy and an economist at the University of California, Los Angeles (UCLA) Research Center. Previously, she was a consultant to the South African government and a lecturer at the Department of Economics of the University of the Witwatersrand. Her honors include the Ronnie Bethlehem Memorial Fellowship award for the Outstanding Young Economist and the Earnest Oppenheimer Memorial Trust Scholarship. Hawken worked for three years as lead economist for Doug Longshore of UCLA on the evaluation of the California Substance Abuse and Crime Prevention Act (Proposition 36). Hawken is presenting her cost-benefit analysis to the California State Legislature in April. Hawken is a coprincipal investigator of a study to evaluate distance training of clinicians in developing countries and a study to assess the cost-effectiveness of a HIV/AIDS and violence-reduction intervention for high-risk youth. Hawken has recently completed her fifth assignment for the U.S. Department of State, working in the Republic of Georgia. She has taken 15 Pepperdine students to the region and is leading a study on government corruption in Georgia. She received her Ph.D. from the Pardee RAND Graduate School and undergraduate and graduate degrees in economics at the University of the Witwatersrand, South Africa.

Robert Kaufman (telephone: 310-506-7601; fax: 310-506-7494; e-mail: robert.kaufman@pepperdine.edu) is a political scientist specializing in American foreign policy, national security, international relations, and various aspects of American politics. Kaufman received his J.D. from Georgetown University Law School in Washington, D.C., and his B.A., M.A., M.Phil., and Ph.D. from Columbia University in the city of New York. Kaufman has written frequently for scholarly journals and popular publications, including the *Weekly Standard, Policy Review,* the *Washington Times,* the *Baltimore Sun,* the *Philadelphia Inquirer,* and the *Seattle Post-Intelligencer.* He is the author of three books. In 2007, University Press of Kentucky is scheduled to publish his forthcoming book *In Defense of the Bush Doctrine: Moral Democratic Realism and American Grand Strategy.* In 2000, his biography *Henry M. Jackson: A Life in Politics* received the Emil and Katherine Sick Award for the best book on the history of the Pacific Northwest. His first book, *Arms Control During the Prenuclear Era,* published by Columbia University Press, studied the interwar naval treaties and their linkage to the outbreak of World War II in the Pacific. Kaufman also assisted President Richard M. Nixon in the research and writing of Nixon's final book, *Beyond Peace.* He is currently in the research phase of a biography of President Ronald Reagan, focusing on his presidency and his quest for it. Kaufman is a former Bradley Scholar and current adjunct scholar at the Heritage Foundation. He has taught at Colgate University, the Naval War College, and the University of Vermont.

Gordon Lloyd (telephone: 310-506-7602; fax: 310-506-7120; e-mail: gordon.lloyd@pepperdine.edu) earned his bachelor's degree in economics and political science at McGill University. He completed all course work toward a doctorate in economics from the University of Chicago before receiving his master's and Ph.D. degrees in government at Claremont Graduate School. The coauthor of three books on the American founding and author of two forthcoming publications on political economy, he also has numerous articles and book reviews to his credit. His areas of research span the California constitution, common law, the New Deal, slavery and the Supreme Court, and the relationship between politics and economics. He has received many teaching, research, and leadership awards, including admission to Phi Beta Kappa and an appointment as a Distinguished Visiting Scholar for the Oklahoma Scholarship Leadership Program.

Ted McAllister (telephone: 310-506-7603; fax: 310-506-7120; e-mail: ted.mcallister@pepperdine.edu), an intellectual historian, brings a historical imagination to the public policy curriculum, a perspective not typical of such programs. His training well equips him to press students to ask the foundational moral questions concerning public policy, leading them back to first principles. A graduate of Oklahoma Christian College, he earned his master's degree from Claremont Graduate School before completing his doctoral degree in American intellectual and cultural history at Vanderbilt University. A recipient of the Woodrow Wilson Foundation's Charlotte W. Newcombe Doctoral Dissertation Fellowship, he also received the Leland Sage Fellowship as well as several additional grants, including one from the Earhart Foundation. The author of a volume entitled *Revolt Against Modernity: Leo Strauss, Eric Voegelin, and the Search for a Postliberal Order,* he has completed a new textbook on American history entitled *The Promise of Freedom: A History of the United States.* Among his other publications, he has authored the chapter "Reagan and the Transformation of American Conservatism" in *The Reagan Presidency.* McAllister has lectured frequently on the nature and future of American conservatism, including recent presentations at Oxford University and at Universität Erlangen-Nürnberg in Germany. In addition to his research into conservative philosophy, he is currently working on a history of the baby boomer generation. McAllister serves (with Jean Bethke Elshtain and Wilfred McClay) as an editor of Rowman & Littlefield's book series, *American Intellectual Culture,* which is designed to produce books that examine the intersection of culture and politics in American history. At Pepperdine, he teaches the core class Ethical Dimensions of Public Policy: Great Books and Great Ideas as well as a variety of elective courses that focus on putting policy debates in larger historical and philosophical contexts, such as Comparative Federalism, Public Policy in Modern America, and American Democratic Culture.

James E. Prieger, Ph.D. (telephone: 310-506-7150; fax: 310-506-7494; e-mail: james.prieger@pepperdine.edu) is an economist specializing in regulatory economics, industrial organization, and applied econometrics. Previously, he was an assistant professor of economics at the University of California, Davis. He received his Bachelor of Arts degree from Yale University and his Ph.D. from the University of California, Berkeley. Prieger has written for scholarly journals on policy topics, such as the impact of telecommunications regulation on innovation, the broadband digital divide, state and local taxation of communications providers in California, and efficient universal service funding for telecommunications. His research in the area of econometrics has dealt with techniques for duration data and biased survey data. Current research includes a project with the American Enterprise Institute to investigate whether laws banning cell-phone use while driving would prevent accidents, which has been covered in *Business Week.* In another current set of papers, Prieger examines the impact of the Americans with Disabilities Act on retail firms, which drew the notice of Forbes. Prieger sits on the editorial board of *Applied Economics Quarterly,* and his own research has been published in *Review of Economics and Statistics, Economic Inquiry, Journal of Applied Econometrics,* and *Journal of Regulatory Economics.* He has also put his academic knowledge to practical use through consulting for major telecommunications companies.

Michael Shires (telephone: 310-506-7692; fax: 310-506-7120; e-mail: michael.shires@pepperdine.edu) is Associate Professor of Public Policy and Director of the Murray S. Craig Digital Democracy Laboratory, an initiative examining ways that technology can enhance government official accountability. He previously was a research fellow at the Public Policy Institute of California and a doctoral fellow at RAND's Graduate School of Policy Studies, concentrating on domestic education policy, California fiscal policy, and international trade policy. His works in higher education include "Alternative Approaches to Funding Higher Education in California," "The Future of Public Undergraduate Education in California," and "The Redesign of Governance in Higher Education." His state and local finance titles include "The Development of Counties as Municipal Governments: A Case Study of Los Angeles County in the 21st Century," "The Effects of the California Voucher Initiative on Public Expenditures for Education," "A Review of Local Government Revenue Data in California," "Has Proposition 13 Delivered? The Changing Tax Burden in California," and "Patterns in California State and Local Government Revenues Since Proposition 13." He has also coauthored work on United States–Japan and United States–European community trade relations. His primary areas of teaching and research include state, regional, and local policy; technology and democracy; higher education policy; strategic, political, and organizational issues in public policy; and quantitative analysis. Shires has been active as a consultant to local and state government on issues related to finance, education policy, and governance. He received his B.A. in economics from the University of California at Los Angeles (UCLA), his M.B.A. from the Anderson Graduate School of Management at UCLA, and his M.Phil. and Ph.D. in public policy analysis from the RAND Graduate School.

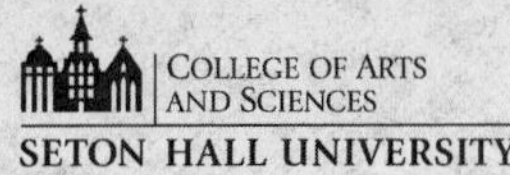

SETON HALL UNIVERSITY

Department of Public and Healthcare Administration
Master of Public Administration

Programs of Study

The Department of Public and Healthcare Administration (DPHA) at Seton Hall University offers a Master of Public Administration (M.P.A.) degree program for people who currently work or are seeking professional careers in nonprofit organizations in the public sector as well as the arts. The DPHA also offers a Master of Healthcare Administration (M.H.A.) degree for those interested in health-care organizations and institutions. Each degree program requires 39 credits and is tailored to the working adult student, with classes offered in the late afternoon and evenings, on Saturday mornings, online, and in four-day compressed courses available on weekends. Courses are offered year-round, including during three separate summer sessions.

Accredited by the National Association of Schools of Public Affairs and Administration (NASPAA), the 39-credit M.P.A. program offers four concentrations: nonprofit management, public service leadership and policy, health-care administration, and arts administration. The nonprofit management concentration is currently ranked fourteenth by *U.S. News & World Report* among all M.P.A. nonprofit management concentrations in the country. The Department's curriculum stresses the development of managerial and analytical skills and emphasizes the importance of cross-sector collaboration.

The DPHA also offers a 60-credit M.A./M.P.A. dual-degree program with Seton Hall's School of Diplomacy and International Relations for students interested in studying public service and nonprofit issues on a global level and three 15-credit certificate programs in arts administration, nonprofit organization management, and health-care administration. Students completing any of the certificate programs may apply the credits toward either the M.P.A. or M.H.A. degree if they are accepted into either of those degree programs.

More information about these programs is available at http://www.shu.edu/academics/artsci/graduate-public-health-admin-programs.cfm.

Research Facilities

The Center for Public Service conducts applied public policy research and provides technical assistance to community-based organizations through its Nonprofit Sector Research Institute. Students are given opportunities to participate in research projects and to gain hands-on management experience through a number of academic and technical assistance programs.

The Walsh Library, a state-of-the-art 155,000-square-foot building, houses 500,000 titles, 1,875 current periodicals, and an extensive collection of microform and other nonprint items that include videotapes, CD-ROM music, and other electronic media. Fahy Hall has twenty-eight classrooms, two TV studios, a Macintosh and IBM graphics lab, two classroom amphitheaters, and language and statistics labs. McNulty Hall has well-equipped science labs. The College of Nursing Building contains a multipurpose practice-demonstration room, with twelve hospital beds, an amphitheater, an independent study area, and a computer laboratory. Completed in 1997, Jubilee Hall, a six-story facility with 126,000 square feet of academic space, features high-tech classrooms with computer and multimedia capabilities and the Center for Securities Trading and Analysis, commonly referred to as the Trading Room.

Financial Aid

A limited number of competitive graduate assistantships are available within the DPHA and throughout the University. These positions cover tuition costs and provide a modest stipend in exchange for half-time work (20 hours per week) during the academic year. Students interested in a graduate assistant position should complete an online application at http://www.shu.edu/applying/graduate/grad-finaid.cfm or contact the DPHA for additional information. The DPHA also offers a number of partial scholarships for students in the arts and nonprofit tracks. Applications are available on the right-hand side of the M.P.A. Web site at http://www.shu.edu/academics/artsci/mpa/index.cfm. Students interested in other financial aid options should visit the University's financial aid Web site at http://www.shu.edu/applying/graduate/grad-finaid.cfm.

Cost of Study

In 2008–09, tuition is $875 per credit. Full-time students pay $305 per semester in University and technology fees; part-time students pay $185.

Living and Housing Costs

Housing and living costs in South Orange and surrounding towns are comparable to most suburban cities, with studio and one-bedroom apartments renting for $750 to $1000 per month.

Student Group

Typical M.P.A. students have some work experience, although the program accepts many students directly from undergraduate programs.

The DPHA hosts a student chapter of the public administration honor society, Pi Alpha Alpha, as well as a student chapter of Upsilon Phi Delta, the honor society for healthcare administrators.

Location

Seton Hall is located on 58 acres in the village of South Orange, New Jersey, a suburban residential area 14 miles southwest of New York City. The town center is a 10-minute walk from the campus and features bookstores, coffee shops, and restaurants. The heart of midtown Manhattan is about 30 minutes away by train; students can take advantage of everything this exciting city has to offer while still living in a suburban area.

The University and The Department

Founded in 1856, Seton Hall is a private coeducational Catholic institution—the nation's oldest diocesan institution of higher education in the United States. With a total enrollment of about 10,000, including approximately 4,500 graduate students, the University comprises nine colleges and schools. Seton Hall is accredited by the Middle States Association of Colleges and Schools. Through the incorporation of technology into the curriculum, the College of Arts and Sciences seeks to enhance and enliven the learning environment. Rooted in tradition, yet looking to the future, the college offers a rich set of opportunities for intellectual discovery. Graduate students are guided by scholars and specialists toward the mastery of academic and professional areas.

The University has offered the M.P.A. degree since 1980, six years before the establishment of the Center for Public Service and thirteen years before the Department of Public Administration came into existence. The Center for Public Service was established in 1986 to house the M.P.A. program, conduct applied public policy research, and initiate training programs for the public and nonprofit sectors. In 1993, the Department of Public Administration was formed, and, five years later, the Center for Public Service and Department of Public Administration began offering the M.H.A. degree. To demonstrate that, in addition to nonprofit organization management, public leadership, and arts administration, it offered health-care administration, the Department later changed its name to the Department of Public and Healthcare Administration.

Applying

Applicants must submit a completed application (available at http://www.shu.edu/academics/artsci/apply-graduate.cfm), the $50 application fee, official transcripts from all colleges and universities attended, a current resume, and three letters of recommendation. Standardized test scores are optional for the M.P.A. degree. Applications are accepted throughout the year, and admissions decisions are made on a rolling basis.

Additional application information is available on the right-hand side of the M.P.A. Web site at http://www.shu.edu/academics/artsci/mpa/index.cfm.

Correspondence and Information

Dr. Matthew Hale, Chair
Department of Public and Healthcare Administration
5th Floor, Jubilee Hall
Seton Hall University
400 South Orange Avenue
South Orange, New Jersey 07079

Phone: 973-761-9510
Fax: 973-275-2463
E-mail: dpha@shu.edu
Web site: http://www.shu.edu/academics/artsci/graduate-public-health-admin-programs.cfm

Seton Hall University

THE FACULTY AND THEIR RESEARCH

Full-Time Faculty

Paul Cavanagh, Assistant Professor; M.S.W., Ph.D., Columbia. Professional social worker with extensive experience working with children and adults with developmental disabilities. Has worked as an advocacy caseworker, Director of a Medicaid Day Treatment program, and Executive Director of an AmeriCorps affiliate program for five years. Dissertation examined the labor choices of mothers with a child with a severe developmental disability. Currently studies child care for children with severe developmental disabilities.

Philip S. DiSalvio, Associate Professor and Academic Director, Online M.H.A. Program; Ed.D., Harvard. Management, finance, strategic planning, ethics. Former Robert Wood Johnson Faculty Fellow in Healthcare Finance. Consultant and adviser to the health-care industry in management development, leadership, and strategic planning. Speaker, seminar leader, and facilitator for numerous health-care organizations and Faculty Associate for the American College of Health Care Executives. Author of *Managing Computers in Health Care* and *Managing Computers in Healthcare: A Self-Directed Series for Healthcare Executives.*

Matthew Hale, Assistant Professor; Ph.D., USC. Political communication and media. Research examines how the media covers the public and nonprofit sectors, with a particular focus on election campaigns and Spanish-language media. Published journal articles have appeared in *Nonprofit and Voluntary Sector Quarterly, Stanford Law and Policy Review, Mass Communication & Society,* and *Electronic News.*

Anne M. Hewitt, Associate Professor and Director, Seton Center for Community Health; Ph.D., Temple. Community health development and assessment, health literacy, worksite health. Former American Lung Association Principal Investigator. Author of articles in *Health Promotion Practice, American Journal of Health Studies,* and *Journal of Occupational Medicine.* Provides program evaluation assistance to various state and local organizations as well as nonprofit agencies and health-care institutions.

Amadu Jacky Kaba, Assistant Professor; Ph.D., Seton Hall. Higher education leadership, management, and policy. Author of articles in *Education Policy Analysis Archives, Journal of African American Studies,* and *Journal of Black Studies.*

Naomi Bailin Wish, Professor and Director, Center for Public Service; Ph.D., Rutgers. Nonprofit organization management, program evaluation, quantitative methods. Author of articles in *Public Administration Review, International Journal of Public Administration, American Journal of Economics and Sociology,* and the *Municipal Yearbook.*

Part-Time Faculty

Sandra Bograd, Adjunct Instructor in Healthcare Law.
Mary Jo Buchanan, Adjunct Instructor in Nonprofit Finance.
Barkley Calkins, Adjunct Instructor in Nonprofit Management and Project Coordinator for NSRI.
Vincent Farinella, Adjunct Instructor in Healthcare Management.
Elizabeth Gonchar-Hemstead, Adjunct Instructor in the Law of Nonprofit Organizations.
Abe Kasbo, Adjunct Instructor in Healthcare Management and Marketing.
Alan Negreann, Adjunct Instructor in Public Sector Financial Management.
Mareta Wester, Adjunct Instructor in Arts Administration.
Audrey Winkler, Adjunct Instructor in Nonprofit Management.

TEXAS A&M UNIVERSITY

Bush School of Government and Public Service

Program of Study

The Bush School of Government and Public Service offers two master's degree programs and three certificate programs. Both the Master of Public Service and Administration (MPSA) and Master's Program in International Affairs (MPIA) are full-time graduate programs that provide a professional education for those who seek careers in the public or nonprofit sectors and in governmental-focused activities in the private sector. The certificate programs are for individuals interested in advancing their international and nonprofit understanding without a full-time commitment.

The Master of Public Service and Administration, a twenty-one-month, 48-credit-hour program, combines nine core courses with seven electives, two of which may be taken in other departments at Texas A&M. Students choose a track in either public management (PM) or public policy analysis (PPA) and, if interested, can then select an elective concentration in nonprofit management; state and local policy and management; energy, environment, and technology policy and management; security policy and management; or health policy and management. A professional internship is also completed in the first summer session by those without substantive professional experience. Enrollment is each fall.

The Master's Program in International Affairs, a twenty-one-month, 48-credit-hour program, offers tracks in national security affairs (NS) and international economics and development (IED). Students take six core classes for a framework in international relations' conduct, and an additional ten courses are chosen as electives, six from established concentrations: international economic development, international economics, transfer pricing, American diplomacy, defense policy and military affairs, intelligence, international politics, and regional studies. For those without substantive professional experience, an internationally oriented internship or a foreign language immersion course is completed during the first summer session. Satisfactory completion of a foreign language exam is required to graduate. Enrollment is each fall.

The Certificate in Advanced International Affairs (CAIA) program, which is offered online or through in-residence study, is designed for people with limited time but a strong desire to upgrade their knowledge of international relations. Students take 12 credit hours of graduate course work, chosen from a menu of course options and selected at a pace convenient for them. Enrollment is each semester.

The Certificate in Homeland Security (CHLS) is offered online and is intended for people who need to understand the new security environment as part of their management and supervisory duties. Students take 15 credit hours of graduate course work centered upon homeland security issues and strategies at all levels of government, as well as private industry. Enrollment is each semester.

The Certificate in Nonprofit Management (CNPM) is offered in residence and online. The program provides individuals with an understanding of the key elements of nonprofit management, from program evaluation and performance management to philanthropy and volunteer leadership. Students take 12 credit hours of graduate course work from a varied menu. Enrollment is each semester.

The Bush School provides leadership and writing workshops and exercises that enhance students' skills in effective public management. Professional development opportunities include several professional speaker series and activities, conferences, study abroad, a student government association, and a public service organization.

Research Facilities

The Bush School houses the Institute for Science, Technology, and Public Policy and the Brent Scowcroft Institute of International Affairs. They share a striking 90-acre site with the George Bush Presidential Library and the Presidential Conference Center. Also located within the complex is the Library of Policy Sciences and Economics, part of Texas A&M University's library system.

Financial Aid

The Bush School allocates financial aid on a merit-competitive basis to virtually all its master's students. Bush Scholarships have been established by a special Congressional appropriation and have been continuously expanded by private gifts. Graduate assistantships, other sources of graduate fellowships/scholarships, and student loans provide additional means of financial aid. For further University options, students should visit https://financialaid.tamu.edu/.

Cost of Study

Average estimated tuition and required fees per year of full-time study are $8000 for Texas residents and $14,500 for nonresidents. However, non-Texas residents receiving a graduate scholarship of $1000 or more qualify for a waiver of nonresident tuition during the period it is awarded, and since all students are granted some form of aid, all students pay in-state rates.

Living and Housing Costs

The cost of living in the area is moderate. Approximately $16,000 is needed for living and housing expenses per year. Limited on-campus housing is available, but most graduates live off campus. Numerous apartments, duplexes, and rental houses are within a few minutes' drive of the campus at reasonable costs. For further information, students should visit http://studentlife.tamu.edu/agoss/.

Student Group

Classes are small, with close faculty-student interaction. Admission is limited and competitive. Successful applicants show strong academic ability, a disposition toward leadership, and a commitment to serving others in either domestic or international settings. About 45–50 students are admitted to each master's program each year. Students have diverse backgrounds, experiences, and degrees.

Student Outcomes

The Bush School has a successful track record in student outcomes, with a full-time student services director assisting all with both their summer internship placement and employment search. Former students have gained a variety of government, nonprofit, and private-sector positions, including careers in numerous federal agencies, various local and state governmental agencies, and several corporate and nonprofit organizations.

Location

Located in Central Texas, College Station is a dynamic and growing community. College Station, along with its neighbor Bryan, is home to 135,000 people and offers residents access to recreational and cultural opportunities organized by local civic organizations and the University. Its location is within driving distance of four major metropolitan areas, Houston, Austin, Dallas, and San Antonio, and commercial air service links these destinations to College Station. For further information, students should visit http://www.b-cs.com/.

The University

Since its founding in 1876, Texas A&M University has grown into a nationally ranked research university. With national and international faculty members teaching in ten academic colleges, research expenditures of approximately $520 million, and an enrollment in excess of 45,000 students, Texas A&M is committed to providing the highest quality education for a diverse population and global economy. For further information, prospective students should visit http://www.tamu.edu.

Applying

Admission deadlines vary according to program. MPSA and MPIA deadlines occur in mid-January for a fall start only. Certificate deadlines are a month to a week before the desired semester start. Prospective students should visit http://bush.tamu.edu/admissions/ for more specific application instructions and requirements.

Correspondence and Information

Kathryn Meyer, Recruitment Director
Bush School of Government and Public Service
Texas A&M University
2129 Allen Building, 4220 TAMU
College Station, Texas 77843-4220

Phone: 979-862-3476
Fax: 979-862-7953
E-mail: admissions@bushschool.tamu.edu
Web site: http://bush.tamu.edu

Texas A&M University

FULL-TIME TEACHING FACULTY AND THEIR RESEARCH

Domonic Bearfield, Assistant Professor; Ph.D., Rutgers, Newark, 2004. Leadership and public administration, public personnel management, ethics in public policy.
Angela Bies, Assistant Professor; Ph.D., Minnesota, 2002. Training and organizational development in nonprofit, nongovernmental, and organizational contexts; organizational accountability; evaluation and policy development.
William Brown, Associate Professor and Director of Certificate in Nonprofit Management; Ph.D., Claremont, 2000. Nonprofit management, performance measurement, program evaluation.
Jasen Castillo, Assistant Professor; Ph.D., Chicago, 2003. U.S. foreign and defense policy, international security, deterrence theory, military affairs, international relations theory, social science methodology.
Sharon Caudle, Younger-Carter Distinguished Policy Maker In-Residence; Ph.D., George Washington, 1988. Public management, information technology, homeland security policy and management, policy analysis.
Joseph Cerami, Senior Lecturer and Director of Public Service Leadership Program; Ph.D., Penn State, 2007. Colonel, U.S. Army (Ret.). Defense policy, leadership and development, interagency coordination.
Richard Chilcoat, Dean and Edward and Howard Kruse Chair; M.B.A., Harvard, 1974. Lt. General, U.S. Army (Ret.).
Michael Desch, Professor, Robert M. Gates Chair in Intelligence and National Security Decision Making, and Director of Brent Scowcroft Institute of International Affairs; Ph.D., Chicago, 1988. Civil-military relations, political theory and international relations, democracy and American foreign policy.
Rola el-Husseini, Assistant Professor; Ph.D., Ecole des Hautes Etudes en Sciences Sociales (Paris), 2003. Women and Islamism, democratization in the Arab world, authoritarianism and political elites in the Middle East, religion and politics/Shi'ism.
Jeffrey Engel, Assistant Professor; Ph.D., Wisconsin–Madison, 2001. American diplomatic history, Cold War history, technology and foreign policy, military strategy in the conduct of nations, evolution of international strategy, economic warfare.
Kishore Gawande, Professor and Roy and Helen Ryu Chair of Economics and Government; Ph.D., UCLA, 1991. Free trade area politics, lobbying and trade policy, global economy, international economics and politics, emerging economies, applied econometrics.
James Griffin, Professor and Bob Bullock Chair in Public Policy and Finance; Ph.D., Pennsylvania, 1970. Economic analysis, public policy, energy policy and security, government and business, measurement of technological change, performance of formerly regulated industries.
Charles Hermann, Professor, Brent Scowcroft Chair in International Policy Studies, and Director of International Affairs Program; Ph.D., Northwestern, 1965. Foreign policy decision making, crisis management, comparative foreign policy.
Sam Kirkpatrick, Executive Associate Dean for Academic Affairs and Management; Ph.D., Penn State, 1968.
Joanna Lahey, Assistant Professor; Ph.D., MIT, 2005. Labor economics, public economics, quantitative methods in public management, health economics policy.
Christopher Layne, Professor; Ph.D., Berkeley, 1981. International politics theory, American foreign policy, strategic studies.
Ren Mu, Assistant Professor; Ph.D., Michigan State, 2004. Development economics, labor markets in developing countries, aging and project impact evaluations.
Jeryl Mumpower, Professor and Director of Public Service and Administration Program; Ph.D., Colorado at Boulder, 1976. Negotiation and bargaining, environmental policy, individual and group decision-making processes, use of scientific expertise in public policy making, risk analysis and management.
Larry Napper, Senior Lecturer; M.A., Virginia, 1974. Former ambassador with a thirty-one-year career as a U.S. Foreign Service officer. American diplomacy, diplomatic negotiation, Russia and its former states in international politics.
James Olson, Senior Lecturer and Director of Certificate in Advanced International Affairs; J.D., Iowa, 1969. More than thirty-year career with Operations in CIA. Intelligence, national security, international crisis management.
Gina Yannitell Reinhardt, Assistant Professor; Ph.D., Washington (St. Louis), 2005. Public policy, comparative political economy, NGOs/interest groups, nonprofit administration, Latin American/Brazilian politics, foreign assistance.
Scott Robinson, Associate Professor; Ph.D., Texas A&M, 2001. Emergency management, management and politics of public organizations, education policy, contract and grant administration, organizational theory.
Andrew Scobell, Associate Professor; Ph.D., Columbia, 1995. National security and foreign policy of China, international politics of Asia-Pacific Region.
Ronald Sievert, Senior Lecturer; J.D., Texas. Served as a U.S. Attorney for twenty-four years. National security law, criminal justice, war powers.
Lori L. Taylor, Assistant Professor; Ph.D., Rochester, 1991. Labor economics, economics of education, principles of macroeconomics and microeconomics, state and local government and policy.
Gabriela Marin Thornton, Lecturer; Ph.D., Miami, 2006. European security, EU integration, trans-Atlantic relations.
Arnold Vedlitz, Professor; Bob Bullock Chair in Government and Public Policy; and Director of the Institute for Science, Technology, and Public Policy (ISTPP); Ph.D., Houston, 1975. Science and technology policy, American political behavior, intergroup relations, urban politics, political psychology.
William West, Professor and Sara H. Lindsey Chair; Ph.D., Rice, 1981. Public administration, bureaucratic politics, administrative institutions and accountability, regulatory policy.

Associated and Adjunct Faculty

Kenneth Ashworth, Lecturer; Former Commissioner of Higher Education, Texas Higher Education Coordinating Board; and STPP; Ph.D., Texas at Austin, 1969. Public policy, higher education issues, policy development and leadership.
Klaus Aurisch, Adjunct Faculty; J.D., Cologne, 1965. Career officer in German diplomatic service. European Union issues, EU law, German-French-American relations.
Sara Daly, Adjunct Faculty; M.A., George Washington, 1997. Terrorism, counterterrorism, transnational security issues.
Edwina Dorch, Visiting Associate Professor; Ph.D., Colorado, 1982. Social welfare policy, diversity and affirmative action.
Lorraine Eden, Professor, Department of Management, TAMU, and Associate Faculty, GBS; Ph.D., Dalhousie, 1976. Transfer pricing in international trade, taxation of multinational business.
Peter J. Hugill, Professor, Department of Geography, TAMU, and Associate Faculty, GBS; Ph.D., Syracuse, 1977. Cultural, historical, and political geography; technology and the environment.
Deborah L. Kerr, State Auditors Office; Ph.D., Texas at Austin, 1982. Public policy formation, performance management.
Eric Lindquist, Visiting Assistant Professor, STPP; Ph.D., Texas A&M, 2002. Public policy, urban planning, science and technology policy.
David McIntyre, Adjunct Faculty, Director of Certificate in Homeland Security, and Director of the Integrative Center for Homeland Security, Texas A&M; Ph.D., Maryland, 1999. Career officer in U.S. Army. Homeland security and defense.
Alex Pacek, Department of Political Science, TAMU; Ph.D., Illinois at Urbana-Champaign, 1990. Russian and Slavic politics.
Steve Roop, Lecturer; Ph.D., Texas A&M, 1981. Rail transportation, optimization, freight transportation, logistics.
Paul Van Riper, Professor Emeritus; joint appointment with Department of Political Science, TAMU; Ph.D., Chicago, 1947. Public personnel management (U.S. civil service), general and comparative public administration organizational theory and behavior, military management, executive development, American government and politics.
Adel Varghese, Adjunct Faculty; Ph.D., Pennsylvania, 1996. Microcredit and finance, economic development, India.
Sally Dee Wade, technical writing consultant for the Bush School.

Bush School Academic Complex.

TUFTS UNIVERSITY

Department of Urban and Environmental Policy and Planning

Programs of Study

The Department of Urban and Environmental Policy and Planning (UEP) offers graduate public policy and planning programs culminating in either a Master of Arts (M.A.) degree or a Master of Public Policy (M.P.P.) degree. In addition, in combined degree options with the Departments of Civil and Environmental Engineering and Biology, students may attain a Master of Science (M.S.) degree. The programs prepare public-spirited individuals for careers in government, nonprofit organizations, citizen advocacy groups, and the private sector. The goal is to educate a new generation of leaders—practical visionaries—who will contribute to solving key public problems by making institutions more responsive to the social and economic needs of communities and by moving toward the sustainable management of environmental resources.

Within each of the two broad areas of concentration—urban and social policy and planning and environmental policy and planning—faculty and student interests and course offerings cluster around the following: sustainable communities; environmental justice; community development and housing; race, class, and social welfare policy; child and family policy; land-use planning; natural resource management; science/technology, ethics, and environmental policy; environmental risk; corporate responsibility and the environment; climate change; international environmental policy; environmental education; program evaluation; applied research methods; planning tools, techniques, and strategies; nonprofit organizations; and citizen roles in policy and planning. UEP programs are distinguished by their focus on the role of nonprofit and community-based organizations and their emphasis on social justice, individual rights and responsibilities, and the equitable distribution of resources.

The established degree program of the Department is a two-year, full-time M.A. degree in urban and environmental policy and planning. The program features field-based learning and requires an internship and thesis. A newer one-year program, which leads to an M.P.P. degree, is designed for individuals with at least seven years of significant, relevant professional experience. Students may attend all degree programs on a part-time basis.

UEP enjoys strong ties to many other Tufts departments, providing a rich interdisciplinary experience for students as well as options for students in the M.A. program to pursue both combined-degree and dual-degree options. Joint degrees are available through cooperative agreements with the Departments of Biology, Child Development, Civil and Environmental Engineering, and Economics. Students interested in international environmental policy may apply to a three-year dual master's degree program with the Fletcher School of Law and Diplomacy, which is also located on the Tufts campus. A three-year dual master's degree program with the Friedman School of Nutrition Science and Policy is designed for students who have an interest in agriculture, food, and environment and wish to develop a policy orientation. A five-semester dual master's degree program with the Department of Civil and Environmental Engineering is also available.

Research Facilities

The University libraries on the Medford/Somerville campus include the Tisch Library, the Chemistry Library, the Lufkin Engineering Library, the Mathematics-Physics Library, and the Edwin Ginn Library of the Fletcher School. Students have access to the Health Sciences Library located on the Tufts Boston campus. Graduate students also have library privileges with Boston College, Boston University, Brandeis University, Massachusetts Institute of Technology, Northeastern University, the University of Massachusetts, and Wellesley College.

Financial Aid

The Department awards a generous number of partial tuition remission scholarships to students demonstrating financial need. Federally financed education loans, work-study positions, and a limited number of teaching and research assistantships are also available for those who qualify. Teaching assistantships are usually assigned to second-year students who have a demonstrated familiarity with the subject matter, but applications are accepted from everyone. A typical assistantship requires 10 hours per week, with a stipend of $2450 per semester. The Department administers the Alvin Levin Fellowship, a scholarship fund for women of color. The Department is committed to supporting a diverse student body through financial assistance.

Cost of Study

Tuition for full-time students in the M.A. program for the 2007–08 academic year was $26,288; the second year's tuition is likely to increase by approximately 5 percent. Tuition for full-time students in the M.P.P. program is one year of Tufts University tuition—$35,052 for the 2007–08 academic year. Part-time students enrolled in no more than two courses per semester are charged $3505 per course. All graduate students pay a mandatory health service fee of approximately $600 and an annual $40 graduate student activity fee.

Living and Housing Costs

A limited amount of designated graduate student housing is available on the Tufts campus. Most graduate students live off campus in apartments in the area. Rent for a one-bedroom apartment in the surrounding community averages $850–$1200 per month; rent for a two- or three-bedroom apartment averages $1200–$1800 per month. A reasonable estimate of rent in a shared household is $450–$600 per month. Meal plans are available on campus.

Student Group

Of the 5,900 Tufts students on the Medford-Somerville campus, approximately 1,300 are graduate students. The Department enrolls approximately 55 new students per year, with about 90 to 100 enrolled at one time. Although the Department admits a few applicants to the M.A. program directly out of college, students benefit most from the program if they have had some relevant work experience subsequent to college. The average age of recent entering M.A. classes has been 26. The Department strives for a class that is diverse in race, ethnicity, and socioeconomic background.

Location

Tufts University is situated on a 150-acre site on the boundary between the cities of Medford and Somerville, 5 miles northwest of Boston. The campus occupies a tranquil New England setting within easy access by bus and subway to the cultural, social, and entertainment resources of Boston and Cambridge. Tufts has a variety of affiliations and cross-registration agreements with other institutions in the Greater Boston area, including Brandeis University, Boston College, and Boston University.

The University

Chartered as a liberal arts college in 1852, Tufts today is a small, private university offering many opportunities for both graduate and professional education. The Department of Urban and Environmental Policy and Planning was founded in 1973. It is situated in the Graduate School of Arts and Sciences, which is located on the Tufts Medford campus. Also on the Medford campus are the College of Liberal Arts, the College of Engineering, the School of Nutrition Science and Policy, and the Fletcher School of Law and Diplomacy. Other campuses include the School of Medicine, the School of Dental Medicine, the Sackler School of Graduate Biomedical Sciences, and the School of Veterinary Medicine.

Applying

The Department does not generally admit applicants for the spring semester. Applications for the M.A. program are due by January 15. Applications for the M.P.P. program are due by April 30. In addition to the application form and a $70 application fee, three letters of recommendation, official college transcripts, and a personal statement are required. GRE General Test scores are required for applicants to the M.A. program who have received a baccalaureate degree within five years of their application date. GRE General Test scores are optional for application to the M.P.P. program. International students whose native language is not English must submit their scores on the Test of English as a Foreign Language (TOEFL).

Correspondence and Information

Department of Urban and Environmental Policy and Planning
Tufts University
97 Talbot Avenue
Medford, Massachusetts 02155

Phone: 617-627-3394
Fax: 617-627-3377
E-mail: ann.urosevich@tufts.edu
Web site: http://ase.tufts.edu/uep

Tufts University

THE FACULTY AND THEIR RESEARCH

Core Faculty
Julian Agyeman, Assistant Professor; Ph.D., London. Sustainable communities, environmental justice, environmental education.
Rachel G. Bratt, Professor; Ph.D., MIT. Housing and community development.
Laurie Goldman, Lecturer; M.S., Israel Institute of Technology. Urban studies and planning.
Justin Hollander, Assistant Professor; Ph.D., Rutgers. Urban planning and policy development.
Francine Jacobs, Associate Professor; Ed.D., Harvard. Child and family policy, program evaluation.
James Jennings, Professor; Ph.D., Columbia. Urban and neighborhood politics, social welfare, and community development.
Sheldon Krimsky, Professor; Ph.D., Boston University. Environmental policy and environmental ethics.
Barbara Parmenter, Lecturer; Ph.D., Texas at Austin. Geographic information systems.
Ann Rappaport, Lecturer; Ph.D., Tufts. Environmental policy, environmental engineering.
Robert H. Russell, Lecturer; J.D., Harvard. Environmental law.
Jon Witten, Lecturer; M.A., Cornell. Land-use planning.

Part-Time Faculty
Margaret Barringer, Lecturer; M.C.P., Rhode Island. Economic development.
Robert G. Burdick, Adjunct Associate Professor; J.D., Boston University. Negotiation and conflict resolution.
Alix Cantave, Lecturer; M.S., Pratt. Real estate development and finance, public policy.
Christine Cousineau, Lecturer; M.C.P., MIT. Urban planning and design.
Louise Dunlap, Lecturer; Ph.D., Berkeley. Writing.
Stephen Estes-Smargiassi, Lecturer; M.C.P., Harvard. Environmental impact assessment.
Scott Horsley, Lecturer; M.A., Rhode Island. Land-use planning, water resources policy.
Karen Kelley, Lecturer; M.B.A., Boston University. Financial analysis and management.
Penn Loh, Lecturer; M.S., Berkeley. Environmental justice.
James T. Maughan, Lecturer; Ph.D., Rhode Island. Environmental impact assessment.
Ingar Palmlund, Adjunct Assistant Professor; Ph.D., Clark. International environmental policy, human health and environment.
Alan Jay Rom, Lecturer; J.D., Cleveland State. Legal frameworks of social policy.
Roberta Rubin, Lecturer; J.D., Harvard. Housing policy, homelessness.
Marji Erickson Warfield, Lecturer; Ph.D., Brandeis. Social policy and quantitative research methods.
Xifang Xing, Lecturer; Ph.D., North Carolina at Chapel Hill. Land economics, quantitative methods, GIS.

Adjunct and Associated Faculty
Robert M. Hollister, Professor and Dean, University College of Citizenship and Public Service; Ph.D., MIT. Nonprofit management and urban policy.
Paul Kirshen, Research Professor; Ph.D., MIT. Water resources planning and management, integrated assessment, climate change, water policy analysis.
William Moomaw, Professor of International Environmental Policy; Ph.D., MIT. International environmental policy.
Susan Ostrander, Professor; Ph.D., Case Western Reserve. Gender/feminist theory, nonprofit organizations.
Kent Portney, Professor; Ph.D., Florida State. American politics and public policy, environmental politics.

UNIVERSITY OF BALTIMORE

Yale Gordon College of Liberal Arts
School of Public Affairs

Programs of Study

The School of Public Affairs at the University of Baltimore (UB) offers programs of study leading to Master of Public Administration (M.P.A.), Doctor of Public Administration (D.P.A.), and Master of Science (M.S.) in health systems management degrees.

The M.P.A. is a 42-credit professional degree program for individuals working in or seeking careers in public, quasi-public, or nonprofit organizations. Students examine the political and legal environment in which public managers work, investigate managerial processes and organizational behavior, and sharpen research methods and quantitative skills. The program enhances the skills of those already working in the field and provides other students with on-the-job training through an internship program. M.P.A. students choose from among several specializations, including public policy and administration, health-care policy and administration, budgeting and fiscal administration, public and nonprofit management, and public information management. Classes are held in the evening at the Baltimore campus and online and during weekends at the Universities at Shady Grove in Rockville, Maryland.

The D.P.A. is a doctoral program for those who have a master's degree in public administration or a related discipline and five or more years of managerial experience so that they can capitalize on prior practice with the fundamentals of budgeting, human resource management, and related functions. The program emphasizes public management techniques that have been developed to address the challenges encountered in the increasingly complex world of public service and is designed to accommodate the working professional. Classes meet five weekends during the course of a regular fifteen-week semester at the University's downtown Baltimore campus and at the Universities at Shady Grove in Rockville, Maryland.

The M.S. in Health Systems Management program requires that students complete 39–45 credit hours of graduate course work, depending on their professional experience, and is designed to provide graduate education for those interested in launching or expanding careers in health-systems administration. Students obtain balanced professional development in the core disciplines of management, including epidemiology, ethics, finance, information technology, law, organizational behavior, and quantitative methods. This program is offered Saturdays in a ten-week session at the downtown Baltimore campus and can be supplemented by online courses.

Research Facilities

The Schaefer Center for Public Policy within the School of Public Affairs aims to utilize UB's academic expertise to solve problems faced by government and nonprofit organizations. The center offers strategic planning, performance measurement, program evaluation and analysis, opinion research, management consulting, and management training to Maryland's public sector. Over the past twenty years, the Schaefer Center has received hundreds of grants and contracts from various local, state, and federal agencies and nonprofit organizations. The center is also involved in pro bono work, including offering consulting services to nonprofit organizations, conducting research and writing reports on issues of interest to public officials, and hosting educational conferences.

Langsdale Library, on the UB campus, provides students with full access to several million volumes and thousands of journals throughout the University System of Maryland. Langsdale Library subscribes to more than 70 online databases that provide on- and off-campus access to full-text journal articles from almost 12,000 titles.

Financial Aid

The UB Office of Financial Aid assists graduate students in obtaining loans, scholarships, and other means of assistance. Many students participate in internships or work on independent or contractual projects. A limited number of graduate assistantships, which provide tuition remission and a stipend, are available.

Cost of Study

In 2007–08, tuition for liberal arts graduate students who are Maryland residents was $498 per credit hour. Nonresident graduate students paid $751 per credit hour. All students pay a University flat fee ($70 for students taking 1–11 credits; $422.50 for students taking 12 or more credits), a University per-credit fee of $56 (not to exceed $309.50), and a technology fee ($6 per credit from 1–11; $72.50 for 12 credits or more). Web-based classes are an additional $88 per credit for in-state students and $86 per credit for students from out-of-state. Students may pay tuition and fees with cash, check, Visa, MasterCard, or Discover.

Living and Housing Costs

UB is a commuter campus and does not presently offer student housing on campus; however, University-affiliated housing is located within walking distance, and assistance in locating affordable housing is provided by the Center for Student Involvement. UB is located in midtown Baltimore's cultural district, off the Jones Falls Expressway (I-83) and across the street from Pennsylvania Station, which provides MARC commuter and Amtrak service. The University is accessible by major bus routes and its own light rail stop, making the campus an easy commute from a variety of neighborhoods within the Baltimore area.

Student Group

Most students in the School of Public Affairs attend part-time, as they are already employed in public service or related positions. A high proportion of students are women and/or members of minority groups, and there are a number of international students. Students interact with each other socially, professionally, and in connection with their courses of study. More than 60 students are enrolled in the M.S. in Health Systems Management program, while about 260 are enrolled in the master's degree and about 30 in the doctoral degree programs in public administration. Student organizations for School of Public Affairs programs provide opportunities for networking in Maryland and the Washington, D.C., capital region. Public-sector and nonprofit organizations in the Baltimore-Washington region, many of which employ UB alumni and/or are clients of the Schaefer Center for Public Policy, provide opportunities for speakers and networking in a variety of professional settings.

Location

Baltimore is both a big city and a small town. UB is nestled in the Mount Vernon Cultural District—home to art galleries, theaters, the symphony and opera, and historic architecture. The neighborhood serves as the backdrop for First Thursdays, a monthly event that includes the likes of outdoor concerts and wine tasting in nearby art galleries. Within 2 miles of campus is the bustling Inner Harbor, with its shops and waterfront activities, including the National Aquarium, Maryland Science Center, Oriole Park at Camden Yards, and the Ravens' M&T Bank Stadium. The city also offers a museum for nearly every interest and specialty.

Annapolis, on the beautiful Chesapeake Bay, is a 45-minute drive, and Washington, D.C., is a 1-hour commute. Rockville, home to the Universities at Shady Grove, is only 12 miles northwest of the nation's capital and has many state and federal agencies, museums, national landmarks, and performing arts centers.

The University

UB offers undergraduate and graduate education in three unique schools: the Yale Gordon College of Liberal Arts, the Merrick School of Business, and the School of Law. The University of Baltimore was founded as a private institution in 1925 and is now part of the University System of Maryland. Total student enrollment is approximately 5,400, and the student-faculty ratio is 16:1.

Applying

Master's degree applicants must hold a bachelor's degree from a regionally accredited college or university with a minimum grade point average of 3.0 and must submit an official transcript from each higher-education institution attended, a statement of personal interest in the program of study, an application, and the appropriate application fee. In addition, M.P.A. applicants must submit two letters of recommendation.

Doctoral applicants must have a master's degree from a regionally accredited university or college and five to ten years of significant management or related work experience. D.P.A. applicants must submit the transcript(s), statement, application, and fee as well as scores from the GRE, GMAT, LSAT, or MAT and three letters of recommendation. Admission to the doctoral program is restricted to the fall semester.

Correspondence and Information

Office of Graduate Admissions
University of Baltimore
1420 North Charles Street
Baltimore, Maryland 21201-5779
Phone: 410-837-6565
Fax: 410-837-4774
E-mail: gradadmissions@ubalt.edu
Web site: http://www.ubalt.edu/cla

Dr. John J. Callahan
Program Director, M.S. in Health Systems Management
Web site: http://www.ubalt.edu/healthsystems

Dr. Samuel L. Brown
Program Director, M.P.A.
Web site: http://www.ubalt.edu/publicadministration

Dr. C. Alan Lyles
Interim Program Director, D.P.A.
Web site: http://www.ubalt.edu/publicadministrationdoctorate

Contact for all:
Matthew Cordner
Phone: 410-837-6094
E-mail: gradadmissions@ubalt.edu

University of Baltimore

THE FACULTY AND THEIR RESEARCH

Irvin Brown, Adjunct Faculty; Ph.D., Howard. Public policy analysis/program evaluation, specifically aspects of health care, criminal justice, and transportation.

Samuel L. Brown, Associate Professor; Ph.D., Maryland, Baltimore County. Health-care finance, nonprofits.

John J. Callahan, Executive in Residence; Ph.D., Syracuse. Program evaluation, management, budgeting, health finance, biodefense vulnerabilities.

P. Ann Cotten, Adjunct Faculty; D.P.A., Baltimore. Strategic planning.

Thomas A. Darling, Associate Professor; Ph.D., SUNY at Albany. Strategic planning and the application of information technology within public organizations, particularly in the areas of assisting individual and group decision making.

Louis C. Gawthrop, Professor; Ph.D., Johns Hopkins. Public management and administrative ethics.

Ed Gibson, Assistant Professor; Ph.D., Virginia Tech. Public budgeting and fiscal administration.

Don Haynes, Associate Professor; Ph.D., North Carolina at Chapel Hill. Survey research, policy analysis, environmental and natural resource policy.

Lenneal J. Henderson, Distinguished Professor; Ph.D., Berkeley. Policy analysis, intergovernmental administration, community development, urban policies and programs.

Laura S. Hussey, Visiting Assistant Professor; Ph.D., Maryland. American political institutions, public policy and the policymaking process, research methods, statistics.

C. Alan Lyles, Professor; M.P.H., Sc.D., Johns Hopkins. Access, cost, and appropriate use of medications and other services; safe and effective systems for medication use; services for vulnerable populations; prepaid health care.

Daniel W. Martin, Professor; Ph.D., Syracuse. Public personnel, human resource management, organization theory.

Lorenda A. Naylor, Assistant Professor; Ph.D., American. Health planning and evaluation, health organization and management, health policy issues.

Christine S. Spencer, Associate Professor; Sc.D., Harvard. Health economics and policy, health insurance, managerial epidemiology.

C. Richard Swaim, Associate Professor; Ph.D., Colorado. Nonprofit management, chaos theory, policy making.

Larry W. Thomas, Professor and Dean, Yale Gordon College of Liberal Arts; Ph.D., Tennessee. Administrative law, public management, program evaluation, performance measurement.

Wim Wiewel, Professor, Provost, and Senior Vice President of Academic Affairs; Ph.D., Northwestern. Regional and urban planning.

Laura Wilson-Gentry, Professor, Chair, and Executive Director; D.P.A., Oklahoma. State interest groups, assaults on police officers, total quality management, impacts of welfare reform.

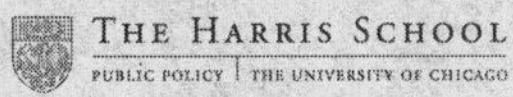

UNIVERSITY OF CHICAGO

Irving B. Harris Graduate School of Public Policy Studies

Programs of Study The Irving B. Harris Graduate School of Public Policy Studies offers a two-year professional M.P.P. degree program, a Master of Environmental Science and Public Policy, and a Ph.D. degree program in public policy studies. A variety of one-year and joint degrees are also offered, including the M.P.P./J.D. joint degree, the M.P.P./M.B.A. joint degree, the M.P.P./M.A. joint degree (with Social Service Administration), and the M.P.P./M.Div. joint degree. The mission of the School is to prepare graduate students for professional careers as policy analysts and for leadership positions as policy makers and to conduct policy-related research and analyze the implications of that research for important and persistent public policy issues. The programs focus on developing a basic knowledge of methods of evaluation, an understanding of underlying substantive issues, and an awareness of the subtleties of policy formation. The curriculum reflects the School's multidisciplinary emphasis on the analysis of public policy issues.

Internships, practicums, and the Mentor Program, as well as short courses, help to complement the formal teaching program. With the help of the Career Services Office, students obtain summer internships that are appropriate to their policy interests and goals. A course practicum affords students the experience of providing a real-world client with an analysis of a key problem or task through program evaluation, needs assessment, or cost-benefit projections. In the Mentor Program, prominent individuals from government, nonprofit organizations, and business who have a special interest in public policy act as mentors, helping students bridge the gap between their academic work and the professional world.

The two-year M.P.P. program provides students with training for careers as policy analysts and is open to anyone holding a bachelor's degree; the one-year A.M. program is available to persons who have completed at least one year of graduate work in an academic discipline or professional field at the University of Chicago or who hold a Ph.D., M.D., M.B.A., or J.D. from another university.

The Ph.D. program in public policy studies is highly selective and prepares students for academic and policy research careers. Requirements include the completion of twenty-seven courses (fewer may be required for students with graduate credit for related courses), a qualifying paper, qualifying examinations, and a dissertation. The program takes four to six years to complete for students entering with a B.A.

Research Facilities The Harris School maintains several research centers that are engaged in projects of local and national importance. The Center for Human Potential and Public Policy facilitates multidisciplinary research and training in child and family policy, poverty and social inequality, education and training, and related fields. The Cultural Policy Center is a joint initiative of the Division of the Humanities and the Harris School that is dedicated to fostering research and public dialogue on the practical workings of arts and culture. The Center for Social Program Evaluation researches a variety of social programs on the economy and the society at large. The School shares facilities with the National Opinion Research Center (NORC) and the Ogburn-Stouffer Center for Population and Social Organization. Students have access to the University Computing Organizations and the Social Science Research Computing Center. Students also have access to the University of Chicago Library, which houses more than 5 million items and is one of the principal research libraries in the world.

Financial Aid About 40 percent of the students in the program receive some form of merit-based fellowship aid. The Irving B. Harris Fellowships, which provide full tuition and a substantial living stipend, are awarded to outstanding entering students in the M.P.P. program. The Dean's Scholarship is awarded to students with exemplary academic and extracurricular records. In addition, many students obtain part-time employment as research assistants; others find part-time internships in public, nonprofit, and private organizations throughout the Chicago area.

Cost of Study Tuition for 2007–08 was $32,445 (three quarters).

Living and Housing Costs A generous estimate of the cost of housing, food, books, and personal expenses for a single student was $19,000 for the 2007–08 academic year. The University housing system and the Hyde Park community offer many types of housing. Individuals may find their living expenses higher or lower than the estimate, based on personal preferences.

Student Group Of the 280 students enrolled in the master's programs and the Ph.D. program, approximately 60 percent are women, 15 percent are members of minority groups, and 27 percent are from outside the United States. The average age is 27. Many academic backgrounds and geographical areas are represented in the student population. The School has active student groups, including the Public Policy Students Association, Minorities in Public Policy Studies, Women in Public Policy, Education Policy Interest Coalition, Committee on International Affairs and Public Policy, Chicago Environmental Policy Association, Latin American Matters, and many other groups that are affiliated with the School.

Location In Chicago, students find a virtually limitless source of research possibilities, internships, and employment opportunities. Moreover, Chicago provides a rewarding environment in which to live, with major cultural institutions such as the Chicago Symphony Orchestra, the Lyric Opera, and the Art Institute; an active and varied theater scene; outstanding architecture; a variety of ethnic neighborhoods; and more than 20 miles of lakeshore.

The University A private, nondenominational, coeducational institution of higher learning and research, the University of Chicago was founded in 1891 by William Rainey Harper with financial backing from John D. Rockefeller. The 172-acre campus encompasses more than 125 buildings and is located 7 miles south of Chicago's Loop, just west of Lake Michigan, in the residential community of Hyde Park, the home of the vast majority of University students and more than 70 percent of the faculty members.

Applying Application materials consist of an application form, three letters of reference, a personal statement of academic and career objectives, academic transcripts, and GRE General Test or GMAT scores. International applicants must submit TOEFL or IELTS scores. Materials for admission and financial aid are due by January 3; those received after January 3 are considered for admission only if space is available. Applicants are strongly advised to take required exams at least eight weeks prior to the deadline. Admitted students may defer enrollment, but not financial awards, for up to two years. Students must start the program in the autumn quarter. The School does not offer courses during the summer, on weekends, or in the evening.

Correspondence and Information

Office of Admission
Irving B. Harris Graduate School of Public Policy Studies
University of Chicago
1155 East 60th Street
Chicago, Illinois 60637

Phone: 773-702-8401
Fax: 773-702-0926
E-mail: HarrisSchool@uchicago.edu
Web site: http://www.HarrisSchool.uchicago.edu

University of Chicago

THE FACULTY AND THEIR RESEARCH

Christopher Berry, Ph.D., Assistant Professor, Harris School of Public Policy Studies. American politics and methodology, education policy, social welfare.
Dan A. Black, Ph.D., Professor, Harris School of Public Policy Studies, and Senior Fellow, National Opinion Research Center. Labor economics and applied econometrics.
Norman M. Bradburn, Ph.D., Professor Emeritus, Harris School of Public Policy Studies and Graduate School of Business; Tiffany and Margaret Blake Distinguished Service Professor, Department of Psychology; and Director, NORC. Sample survey methodology, design and use of large-scale sample surveys.
Kerwin Charles, Ph.D., Professor, Harris School of Public Policy Studies. Research associate at the National Bureau of Economic Research.
Don L. Coursey, Ph.D., Ameritech Professor, Harris School of Public Policy Studies. Applied microeconomic theory, experimental methods for evaluating environmental benefits, decision making in experimental markets.
Ethan Bueno de Mesquita, Ph.D., Associate Professor, Harris School of Public Policy Studies. Terrorism, elections and representation, law and politics.
Charles L. Glaser, Ph.D., Professor and Deputy Dean, Harris School of Public Policy Studies. Nuclear strategy and weapons policy, international relations, security studies.
Jeffery Grogger, Ph.D., Irving Harris Professor in Urban Policy, Harris School of Public Policy Studies. Labor economics, applied microeconomics, applied econometrics, economics of crime, effects of welfare time limits and racial profiling.
William Howell, Ph.D., Associate Professor, Harris School of Public Policy Studies. American political institutions, separation of powers, education and social policy.
Ariel Kalil, Ph.D., Associate Professor, Harris School of Public Policy Studies. Child and family functioning in low-income families.
Robert J. LaLonde, Ph.D., Professor, Harris School of Public Policy Studies. Program evaluation, workforce training, immigration, the impact of unions and collective bargaining in the United States.
Ofer Malamud, Ph.D., Assistant Professor, Harris School of Public Policy Studies. Labor economics, economics of education.
Willard G. Manning, Ph.D., Professor, Department of Health Studies, Division of the Biological Sciences, and Harris School of Public Policy Studies. Effects of insurance and alternative health-care delivery settings on health status.
Howard Margolis, Ph.D., Professor, Harris School of Public Policy Studies. Social theory, altruism, public choice.
Susan E. Mayer, Ph.D., Professor and Dean, Harris School of Public Policy Studies. Poverty and the underclass, comparative social welfare policy.
David O. Meltzer, M.D., Ph.D., Associate Professor, Department of Medicine, and Associated Faculty Member, Harris School of Public Policy Studies and Department of Economics. Health economics and public policy, theoretical foundations of medical cost-effectiveness analysis, effects of mortality decline on developing countries.
Bruce Meyer, Ph.D., Professor, Harris School of Public Policy Studies. Social welfare, poverty and inequality, labor economics.
Robert T. Michael, Ph.D., Eliakim Hastings Moore Distinguished Service Professor, Harris School of Public Policy Studies and Department of Education. Family and child policy, family economics.
Colm A. O'Muircheartaigh, Ph.D., Professor, Harris School of Public Policy Studies, and Vice President, National Opinion Research Center. Survey sampling, total variance of survey estimates, cognitive aspects of question wording, latent variable models of nonresponse.
Jon Pevehouse, Ph.D., Associate Professor, Harris School of Public Policy Studies. International institutions and organizations.
Tomas J. Philipson, Ph.D., Professor, Harris School of Public Policy Studies. Health economics, public health and old-age longevity.
Marcos Rangel, Ph.D., Assistant Professor, Harris School of Public Policy Studies. Applied econometrics, applied microeconomics, labor, population and development, family economics.
Raaj K. Sah, Ph.D., Professor, Harris School of Public Policy Studies. Public finance, fertility and mortality changes in less-developed countries, organizations and political systems, social patterns.
Diane Whitmore Schanzenbach, Ph.D., Assistant Professor, Harris School of Public Policy Studies. Black/white educational achievement gap, food stamps, teenage mothers, employment.
Boris Shor, Ph.D., Assistant Professor, Harris School of Public Policy Studies. American politics.
Duncan Snidal, Ph.D., Associate Professor, Harris School of Public Policy Studies and Department of Political Science; Director, Program in International Politics, Economics and Security; and Chairman, Committee on International Relations. International relations, international political economy, international cooperation.
Wesley Yin, Ph.D., Assistant Professor, Harris School of Public Policy Studies. Health economics.

Visiting and Affiliated Faculty
Jack Bierig, Visiting Lecturer, Harris School of Public Policy Studies.
Sean Durkin, Ph.D., Visiting Lecturer, Harris School of Public Policy Studies.
Laurent Fabius, Visiting Senior Lecturer and Former Prime Minister of France.
John Frederick, Ph.D., Professor, Geophysical Sciences and the College.
James J. Heckman, Ph.D., Henry Schultz Distinguished Service Professor, Department of Economics and the College.
Frank Kruesi, Visiting Lecturer and President, Chicago Transit Authority.
Ioana Marinescu, Ph.D., Assistant Professor, Harris School of Public Policy Studies.
Alicia Menendez, Ph.D., Research Associate (Assistant Professor).
Rowan Miranda, Ph.D., Associate Partner, Accenture, Global Finance and Performance Management Services Line.
Kenneth A. Rasinski, Ph.D., Principal Research Scientist, National Opinion Research Center.
Lawrence Rothfield, Ph.D., Associate Professor of English and Comparative Literature and Faculty Director, Cultural Policy.
Don Stewart, Ph.D., Visiting Professor, Harris School of Public Policy Studies.
Barry Sullivan, J.D., Visiting Professor and Partner, Jenner and Block, LLP.
Daniel Sullivan, Ph.D., Visiting Professor and Senior Economist and Vice President, Federal Reserve Bank of Chicago.
Zalman Usiskin, Ph.D., Professor of Education; Director, University of Chicago School of Mathematics Project (UCSMP); and Co-Director, UCSMP Secondary Component.
Charles Wheelan, Ph.D., Lecturer, Harris School of Public Policy Studies.
Paula Wolff, Ph.D., Visiting Faculty, Harris School of Public Policy Studies, and Senior Executive, Chicago Metropolis 2020.
Paula R. Worthington, Ph.D., Lecturer, Harris School of Public Policy Studies.

UNIVERSITY OF COLORADO DENVER

School of Public Affairs

Programs of Study

The School of Public Affairs (SPA) offers a variety of programs, including undergraduate and graduate degrees, certificates, and training, at its campuses in Denver and Colorado Springs. The Master of Public Administration (M.P.A.) is also available completely online, serving students in the region and around the world.

The Master of Public Administration program, which requires 36 semester hours of course work, is built upon core courses that develop essential problem-solving and decision-making skills. The degree is accredited by the National Association of Schools of Public Affairs and Administration. Most classes are offered in the late afternoon and evening to accommodate the working schedules of students. The M.P.A. degree features five areas of concentration: environmental management, law, and policy; domestic violence; local government; emergency management and homeland security; and nonprofit management. Also, students may design their own specialties.

There is also an accelerated (one-year) option within the M.P.A. program for students who can commit to full-time study. This option costs the same for both in-state and out-of-state students (currently $20,500 for the 2008–09 academic year). The accelerated option within the M.P.A. program only accepts students for the fall term.

The Executive M.P.A. option is designed for senior-level career, appointed, and elected officials in the public and nonprofit sectors. Students are offered significant flexibility in customizing course work to fit their individual needs and career objectives while they earn a master's degree as part of a cohort of senior professionals.

The online option within the M.P.A. program includes six core courses offered via the Internet, five online electives, and an advanced seminar project that can be completed in the student's home community. Online students are also eligible to take courses at the CU campuses.

The School of Public Affairs in Colorado Springs offers an M.P.A. program that provides graduate-level, professional training for managers and policymakers in public and nonprofit organizations. Students may choose to emphasize either public or nonprofit management or homeland defense during their course of study.

SPA also offers students the opportunity to pursue a more limited course of study, earning graduate certificates in any of the concentration areas.

SPA also offers students living on Colorado's Western Slope the option to undertake a hybrid program consisting of online core courses and electives held in a weekend intensive format on the Mesa State campus. SPA serves a vast geographical area, connecting students in remote parts of the state with their peers and providing them with the opportunity to further their education.

The Bachelor of Arts degree in criminal justice and the Master's in Criminal Justice (M.C.J.) program focus on law enforcement, the judiciary, correctional systems, juvenile justice, and the formulation of laws and codes. The programs are offered in Denver and Colorado Springs. Many students use the criminal justice program as a stepping stone to executive positions in police administration, probation, parole, counseling, juvenile crime, drug rehabilitation, and various governmental agency positions at the local, state, and federal levels. Also available is a new concentration in domestic violence within the M.C.J. program. The domestic violence courses are taught through five intensives in Denver that happen periodically throughout the two-year program. Law enforcement professionals with significant experience also have the option of selecting the Executive Leadership Master's in Criminal Justice program. This program is also taken in a weekend intensive format and consists of courses to hone the leadership and knowledge of police professionals throughout the state.

The Ph.D. program in public affairs provides students with the skills necessary for an expanded leadership role in public affairs. It helps students master the scholarly theory, concepts, and research skills required to teach other practitioners and provides the skills necessary to research and analyze complex public-sector challenges. As in every SPA program, theory is closely tied to practice and emphasizes skill development. A minimum of 66 semester hours of credit is required, which includes at least 30 hours of doctoral dissertation credits.

Dual-degree M.P.A./Master of Urban and Regional Planning (M.U.R.P.) and M.P.A./Master of Science in technical communications programs are offered at the University, and an M.P.A./J.D. program is offered in cooperation with the University of Colorado's (CU) School of Law in Boulder.

Research Facilities

SPA students have access to state-of-the-art libraries on the Denver, Boulder, and Colorado Springs campuses of the University of Colorado. The Denver campus library has developed special expertise and resources in the areas of public administration and criminal justice. The Boulder campus library is a federal government document repository. SPA maintains a dedicated computer lab for students and faculty members that provides online access to the Internet and to a number of other resources. The Institute for Policy Research and Implementation, the SPA Centers, and the Timothy Wirth Chair in Environmental and Community Development Policy utilize students in research capacities as they provide services to government and nonprofit agencies in Colorado and the Rocky Mountain Region and throughout the nation.

Financial Aid

In addition to federal financial assistance programs, students may be eligible for a variety of master's- and Ph.D.-level financial assistance programs. Specific graduate scholarships and assistantships are available through the School of Public Affairs. SPA also offers a limited number of Ph.D. fellowships that pay for the cost of tuition plus a generous stipend each year. Students should contact SPA for further information at spa@cudenver.edu.

Cost of Study

The tuition for Colorado residents is approximately $500 per credit hour. The tuition for nonresidents is approximately $1100 per credit hour. Online course tuition for nonresidents is approximately $500 per credit hour.

Living and Housing Costs

SPA Denver's urban campus offers three choices for student housing on or near the campus. SPA Colorado Springs' traditional campus has excellent campus housing available.

Student Group

The student body at SPA is diverse. Sixty percent of students attend part-time. Half of the students are women, about 20 percent come from other states, and about 20 percent are international students. SPA offers students many opportunities to get involved outside the classroom, including a variety of special events and lectures and a Student Association.

Location

The SPA's M.P.A. program is offered on the University of Colorado's downtown Denver and Colorado Springs campuses as well as the Mesa State College campus in Grand Junction. SPA also offers its M.C.J. program on the downtown Denver and Colorado Springs campuses. The Ph.D. program is offered exclusively on the downtown Denver campus.

The School

Seasoned professionals and continuing students discover a vast world of ideas, research, case studies, and perspectives that can propel them years ahead in their ability to think analytically about the challenges facing today's public and nonprofit sectors, such as welfare reform, homelessness, the aging population, and changing demographics. These and other complex public issues call for not only the informed use of technology and resources, but also the vision and a concentrated dose of understanding and experience that are offered at the School of Public Affairs at the University of Colorado.

Applying

Applications for the M.P.A. and M.C.J. programs are processed on a continuing basis. Students are accepted for the fall, spring, and summer semesters. The application deadline for the Ph.D. program is February 1 for the fall semester. There is a $50 application fee for U.S. citizens on the Denver campus and a $60 application fee for Colorado Springs applicants. International students pay a $75 application fee. The M.P.A. and M.C.J. programs accept General GRE, GMAT, or LSAT test scores that are no more than five years old. In addition, executive program admission decisions place particular emphasis on career credentials; in certain cases, standardized test requirements may be waived. The Ph.D. program requires submission of a General GRE test score that is no more than five years old. Additional information about application requirements is available by contacting spa@cudenver.edu.

Correspondence and Information

Annie MacLachlan
Director of Community Outreach
School of Public Affairs
Campus Box 142
University of Colorado Denver
P.O. Box 173364
Denver, Colorado 80217
Phone: 303-315-2228
E-mail: spa@cudenver.edu
Web site: http://www.spa.cudenver.edu

University of Colorado Denver

THE FACULTY

Kathleen Beatty, Professor and Dean; M.P.A., Harvard; Ph.D., Washington State. Became Dean of SPA in 1996; former Resident Dean and Professor of Public Affairs at the University of Colorado at Colorado Springs; served CU–Colorado Springs as Associate Vice Chancellor for Academic Affairs, chair of the political science department, and associate and assistant professor of political science; former visiting professor of political science at the University of Wyoming and professional researcher for the Southwest Center for Urban Research and the Institute for Urban Studies in Houston, Texas.

Stephen Block, Professor and Director, SPA's program concentration in nonprofit management; M.S.W., Indiana; Ph.D., Colorado. Teaching and research interests include nonprofit boards of directors, executive leadership, and nonprofit organizational behavior and development. He was a consulting editor for *Nonprofit and Voluntary Sector Quarterly* and is currently on the editorial board of the *Journal of Vocational Rehabilitation*. Dr. Block has authored numerous journal articles and books. He pioneered research on the development of an academic discipline of nonprofit organization management and led a groundbreaking investigation on Founder's Syndrome. His most recent book was *Perfect Nonprofit Board: Myths, Paradoxes, and Paradigms*. Presently, he is writing a three-book series on nonprofit organizational behavior. Dr. Block is the founding and current executive director of Denver Options, Inc.

Lloyd Burton, Associate Professor; Director, M.P.A. Program concentration in environmental management law and policy; and Coordinator, SPA's public law curriculum; Ph.D., Berkeley. Formerly taught constitutional and environmental law at the Berkeley and Davis campuses of the University of California. Dr. Burton's specialization is law and public policy, with an emphasis on conflict management and the environment. His recent scholarship focuses on the intersection of law, culture, and the environment, especially the handling of values conflicts over environmental management decision making in both domestic and international contexts.

George Busenberg, Assistant Professor; Ph.D., North Carolina at Chapel Hill. Taught environmental policy at UNLV. His research includes wildfire policy, marine oil pollution, processes of policy evolution, learning and innovation in public affairs, policy failure, collaborative approaches to the use of science in policy decisions, and citizen participation in environmental policy.

Linda deLeon, Associate Professor and Associate Dean; Ph.D., UCLA. Former director of human resources for a private-sector firm and a member of the faculty at the University of Southern California's School of Public Administration. She presently teaches courses in public management, human resources, and research methods. Professor deLeon's current research interests include post-bureaucratic organizations, self-directed teams, and public-sector professionalism.

Peter deLeon, Professor; Ph.D., RAND. Formerly taught at Columbia University and the University of California, Los Angeles. Dr. deLeon presently teaches and writes on public policy issues.

Mary Dodge, Associate Professor of Criminal Justice and Director, B.A. and M.C.J. Programs; Ph.D., California, Irvine. Her specialties include white-collar crime, medical fraud, fraud in assisted reproductive technology, biomedical ethics and reproductive rights, the judicial process, and jury decision making.

Jody Fitzpatrick, Associate Professor and Director, M.P.A. Program; Ph.D., Texas at Austin. Formerly directed the evaluation unit for the School of Social Welfare at SUNY at Albany and consulted for the United Way, the Colorado Commission of Higher Education, and numerous school districts, courts, and alcohol- and drug-abuse programs. Her teaching centers on research methods, statistics, program evaluation, human resource management, and grant writing. Dr. Fitzpatrick has written a book on program evaluation and edits *Evaluation Practice*. She is also the recipient of the campuswide Outstanding Teaching Award for the University of Colorado at Colorado Springs.

Robert Gage, Professor; Ph.D., Indiana. He is active in the American Society of Public Administration and the International Institute of Administrative Sciences. Dr. Gage is the author of a recent book on intergovernmental strategy and has research interests in international regional organization, intergovernmental relations, and quantitative methods. His most recent research focuses on China and Hong Kong.

Gabriel Kaplan, Assistant Professor; M.P.A./U.R.P., Princeton; Ph.D., Harvard. His research interests encompass nonprofit and public management, organization and management theory, and governance. His current research examines the significance of governance and ownership forms for the implementation of public policy and the achievement of public objectives.

Don Klingner, Professor; Ph.D., USC. Recognized as an expert on public management and human resource management in the U.S.; coauthor of a bestselling textbook in the field (*Public Personnel Management*, 5th edition pending, Prentice Hall); worked as a teacher, trainer, and consultant on public management in developing countries, primarily Latin America; former visiting professor at USAM (Mexico City); Fulbright senior research fellow; current chair of the International and Comparative Administration; and book review editor of the *American Review of Public Administration*. Before joining SPA, Dr. Klingner was at Indiana University at Indianapolis and Florida International University (FIU). At FIU, he served as Associate Dean of the College of Urban and Public Affairs, public administration coordinator, and Ph.D. program coordinator.

Christine Martell, Assistant Professor; M.U.R.P., Virginia Tech; Ph.D., Indiana. Dr. Martell focuses on issues of public finance and policy analysis. Her research interests include the development of municipal credit markets in developing countries, the public funding of nonprofit organizations, tax policy issues, and regional development. Dr. Martell's research contributes to the diverse fields of fiscal federalism, decentralization, and international development. She is teaching courses in public budgeting, financial management, policy analysis, and international development.

Mark McConkie, Professor; D.P.A., Georgia. Former consultant for BankOne, NASA, U.S. Navy (NAVSEA), U.S. Air Force (Special Forces), MCI Corp., and Hewlett-Packard. Dr. McConkie's teaching focuses on organizational change and behavior, leadership, management development, and ethics; his research interests also include the myths and folklore of organizational culture.

Mark Pogrebin, Professor; Ph.D., Iowa. Formerly held faculty positions at Florida State University and the University of Iowa. His present interests lie in the areas of criminology and penology, sociology of law and organizations, administration of justice, deviant behavior, and qualitative research methods.

Eric Poole, Professor; Ph.D., Washington State. Formerly taught at Auburn University and former Interim Dean of SPA during the 1995–96 academic year. His current research interests include corrections, criminology, evaluation research, and juvenile justice.

Fred Rainguet, Western Slope Program Director; Ph.D., Colorado. He teaches criminal justice and public administration.

Richard Stillman, Professor; M.P.A., Ph.D., Syracuse. He is the author of many books, including *Public Administration: Concepts and Cases*, which is used at more than 350 American universities and colleges. Professor Stillman has been an editor of *Basic Documents of American Public Administration* since 1950 and was awarded the Mosher Prize for Distinguished Scholarship in the field of public administration.

Paul Teske, Professor and Ph.D. Program Director; M.P.A., Ph.D., Princeton. Dr. Teske taught in the Political Science Department at SUNY at Stony Brook from 1987 to 2002. He has written five books and numerous articles on state and local public policy issues, including regulation, public entrepreneurship and leadership, school choice, citizen information, urban development, economic aspects of policy analysis, and related topics.

Jennifer Wade, Assistant Professor of Nonprofit and Public Management; D.P.A., Georgia. Her teaching emphasis is nonprofit and public management, fund-raising, social change, and ethics. Her research interests include alternative funding sources for nonprofit organizations and sports philanthropy. Dr. Wade was employed as a researcher for the University of Georgia's Carl Vinson Institute of Government, working on several state projects for the Department of Human Resources and the Department of Labor. In addition, she taught courses in African-American studies for the Department of Political Science. Dr. Wade is currently a member of the Association for Research on Nonprofit Organizations and Voluntary Action (ARNOVA), the Academy of Management (AOM), and the American Society for Public Administration (ASPA) and serves on the board of directors for the Denver American Civil Liberties Union.

Allan Wallis, Associate Professor and Director, concentration in local government; M.P.A., Harvard; Ph.D., CUNY Graduate Center. Former Senior Research Associate at the Taubman Center for State and Local Government at the Kennedy School of Government at Harvard University. He has taught at the Cooper Union, Pratt Institute, Ball State University, and the University of Colorado at Boulder. Dr. Wallis' current research interests include political and economic aspects of large-scale public works projects, innovation in state and local governments, and regional governance.

UNIVERSITY OF CONNECTICUT

Center for Continuing Studies
Master of Professional Studies in Humanitarian Services Administration

Programs of Study

The online Master of Professional Studies (M.P.S.), with a concentration in humanitarian services administration, is designed to meet the educational needs of individuals involved or interested in humanitarian assistance programs. Students develop theoretical and professional knowledge to operate and conduct humanitarian response missions with nongovernmental, governmental, and international organizations. The program provides students with the broad-base knowledge and skills to conduct successful programs in sustainable community renewal or in disaster relief.

The M.P.S. requires 36 credits. The required 30 hours of classroom course work include 21 hours from core courses and 9 hours from electives in community development, demography, human rights, nutrition, or public health. Toward the end of the program, students complete a 6-credit Capstone project on a topic selected by the student that demonstrates the student's ability to define, analyze, evaluate, and recommend actions or solutions to deal with a major issue, problem, or opportunity within the field of study. Projects may include job-related field projects, integrative analyses of professional literature and published research, original research projects, and comprehensive project proposals for adoption by third parties. Working adults can complete all degree requirements within two years.

Research Facilities

With 2.5 million volumes, the University of Connecticut Libraries' system holds the largest public collection of research materials in the state. More than 2 million volumes are shelved in the Babbidge Library, which also houses nearly 3 million units of microtext, 180,000 maps, 35,000 reference volumes, and subscriptions to about 5,000 current journals. The archives and special collections at the Dodd Research Center support the teaching, research, and public service missions of the University by acquiring, preserving, organizing, and providing access to original source materials.

Financial Aid

Financial aid based on need is available. United States citizens or permanent residents of the United States may apply for need-based financial aid, which includes Federal Stafford Loans (FSL), Federal Work Study, and the University of Connecticut Tuition Remission Grant. Prospective students should visit the Web site at http://www.grad.uconn.edu/financial_aid.html for additional information. International students can obtain special scholarships from their governments or from international sources, such as USAID, World Bank, and other foundations.

Cost of Study

Fees for the spring 2008 online courses in the M.P.S. program are $1581 for a 3-credit course, plus a $45 infrastructure fee.

Living and Housing Costs

Although this is an online program, housing on or near campus is available.

Student Group

The program is designed for students who are currently employed in disaster relief or sustainability programs or those who are pursuing careers or have an interest in these areas.

Student Outcomes

Graduates are able to provide leadership in complex humanitarian emergencies, implement and manage sustainable development programs, and apply humanitarian assistance and sustainability principles in a "do no harm" context.

Location

Both the University and the town of Storrs are home to several cultural attractions. Storrs and Stamford have several art galleries, and the University includes the Connecticut State Museum of Natural History, the William Benton Museum of Art and the Connecticut Repertory Theatre. The campus is a 30-minute drive from Hartford and is 55 minutes from Providence, Rhode Island.

The University

The University of Connecticut was founded in 1881 as an agricultural school. It became the University of Connecticut in 1939 and began conferring graduate degrees one year later. Today, more than 26,000 undergraduate and graduate students attend the University's seventeen schools and colleges.

Applying

All applicants must have completed a baccalaureate degree from a regionally accredited college or university and have a GPA greater than 3.0 for the last two years of study. Two years' relevant work experience is highly desirable. Applicants must submit an official college transcript, three letters of reference from faculty members or others who can address the candidate's potential for success, and a personal statement that describes the reasons for application and future plans. Nonnative speakers of English must submit a TOEFL score of at least 550 for the paper-based version or at least 213 for the computer-based version. GRE scores are not required. Students should apply at least eight weeks before the start of a semester, and applications are evaluated as soon as the student's file is complete. Applicants are notified shortly after the admissions committee has made its decision.

Correspondence and Information

Donna Campbell
Program Administrator
University of Connecticut
One Bishop Circle, Unit 4056
Storrs, Connecticut 06269-4056

Phone: 860-486-0184
Fax: 860-486-5221
E-mail: donna.campbell@uconn.edu
Web site: http://continuingstudies.uconn.edu/mps/programs/hsa.html

University of Connecticut

THE FACULTY

The Master of Professional Studies degree program utilizes faculty members from the Center for Continuing Studies as well as faculty members across the University, and, in select areas, from other nationally and internationally recognized institutions. Faculty members are identified for specific areas of concentration based on their research, practical experience, and expertise. The core courses are taught by full-time faculty members at the University of Connecticut.

Rodney G. Allen, Assistant Professor; Ph.D.
Peter Diplock, Associate Professor; Ph.D.
Dean Hanink, Professor of Geography; Ph.D.
Anthony Joseph, Professor; Ph.D.
Rafael Perez-Escamilla, Associate Professor of Nutritional Sciences; Ph.D.
Ruth Rosenbaum, Assistant Professor; Ph.D.
Mark E. Sullivan, Associate Professor; Ph.D.

UNIVERSITY OF DELAWARE

College of Human Services, Education and Public Policy
School of Urban Affairs and Public Policy

Programs of Study The School of Urban Affairs and Public Policy offers three graduate degree programs: a Master of Public Administration (M.P.A.), a Master of Arts (M.A.) in urban affairs and public policy, and a Ph.D. in urban affairs and public policy.

The M.P.A. is a 42-credit, two-year professional degree program that prepares students for leadership positions in public affairs. The M.P.A. program is accredited by the National Association of Schools of Public Affairs and Administration (NASPAA). Students can specialize in five areas: state and local management, community development and nonprofit leadership, organizational leadership, health policy and management, and financial management.

The M.A. and Ph.D. in urban affairs and public policy programs are ranked among the top nine programs in the United States. The M.A. is a 36-credit degree program designed for students who are interested in pursuing policy analysis and planning–related careers. The program extends over two years and may include a thesis, an analytical paper, or an internship. M.A. students may specialize in such areas as community development and nonprofit leadership; energy, environment, and equity; historic preservation; and urban and regional planning. The Ph.D. is a research-oriented interdisciplinary degree intended for students who have completed master's-level work in urban affairs and public policy or other related social science fields. First-year doctoral seminars are followed by study in a specialization that leads to the preparation of the dissertation proposal. Most students conduct dissertation research in the areas of technology, environment, and society; governance planning and management; social and urban policy; public administration; and urban affairs. All doctoral students collaborate with faculty and staff members on regional, national, and international research on critical urban and policy issues.

The School offers a nationally recognized internship program that places students in paid professional positions in international, national, state, and local government. All students in the School are eligible; the internship is a requirement for preservice M.P.A. students.

Research Facilities The School is centrally located in its own building, with its own classrooms, student offices, and computer/GIS facilities. One of the most distinguishing characteristics of the School of Urban Affairs and Public Policy is the integration of theory and practice through applied research projects with the affiliated research and public service centers. Most full-time students are awarded research assistantships on projects in these centers.

The Center for Applied Demography and Survey Research provides demographic and survey data and information on important public issues to researchers and policy makers at all levels (http://www.cadsr.udel.edu). The Center for Community Research and Service helps public, nonprofit, and private organizations in Delaware to design, implement, and evaluate policies and programs that address the needs of low- and moderate-income families and communities related to economic development, housing, and social services. The center also focuses on issues that are vital to the physical and emotional well-being of the world's population. These questions concern the delivery and financing of health care and the outcomes of health care provided (http://www.udel.edu/CCRS). The Center for Energy and Environmental Policy conducts interdisciplinary research in the areas of sustainable development, technology and society, and the political economy of energy systems and provides technical assistance to community, government, and nonprofit organizations (http://www.udel.edu/ceep/). The Center for Historic Architecture and Design focuses on shaping historic preservation planning and policy, reconstructing historic landscapes, documenting threatened historic properties, and advocating for the preservation of historic resources (http://www.udel.edu/CHAD). The Institute for Public Administration links the resources of the University of Delaware (UD) with the management and policy information needs of public and nonprofit organizations (http://www.ipa.udel.edu).

Financial Aid The School has competitive financial aid programs, including fellowships, research assistantships, and scholarships. Aid is awarded on the basis of merit and is limited by the various restrictions established by the sources of aid. Stipends for 2008–09 were $14,600 for the full academic year. Additional special assistantships, fellowships, and internships are available to students through the University Graduate Scholar's Program, for both newly admitted and graduate students currently enrolled. Awards are competitive and are based on many criteria, including challenging social, economic, educational, cultural, or other life circumstances; academic achievements; first generation graduate student status; and/or need as determined by federal income guidelines (FAFSA). Funds are also available through the Delaware Legislative Fellows Program.

Cost of Study In 2008–09, tuition for full-time in-state graduate students is $7780 per academic year, and tuition for full-time out-of-state students is $20,260. Part-time students are charged on a per-credit basis. (The 2008–09 rates are $433 per credit for Delaware residents and $1126 per credit for nonresidents.) Full-time matriculated students are automatically assessed nonrefundable fees of $466 for health and $220 for student-sponsored activities.

Living and Housing Costs The University provides some graduate apartments, and there is plenty of off-campus housing in the surrounding community in many price ranges. For more information, students should contact the Housing Assignment Services Office (302-831-2491; http://www.udel.edu/has).

Student Group The School has 99 students in the M.P.A. program, 69 in the M.A. program, and 42 in the Ph.D. program.

Student Outcomes Graduates find career positions in government and nonprofit organizations and occasionally in the private sector with consulting firms. With UD's proximity to Washington, D.C.; Philadelphia; and New York, many graduates pursue positions in nearby metropolitan areas, as well as positions in state and local government in the region and in the nation. Several recent graduates have been successful in the highly competitive federal Presidential Management Fellowship Program.

Location Located midway between Philadelphia and Baltimore, the main campus of the University of Delaware is in Newark, conveniently near New York City; Washington, D.C.; and the seashore. A community of 30,000, with a vibrant Main Street of coffeehouses, restaurants, and small shops, Newark is about 14 miles from Wilmington, Delaware's largest city.

The University The University is a comprehensive land-, sea-, space-, and urban-grant institution of higher education with an enrollment of 3,405 graduate students in 2007–08. The University offers eighty-two programs leading to a master's degree and thirty-nine programs leading to a doctoral degree. In 2007, the University awarded 224 doctoral degrees and 773 master's degrees.

Applying The School welcomes informal inquiries. Students seeking financial aid or admission to the Ph.D. program should apply by February 1. For the master's programs, candidates must have an undergraduate GPA above 3.0 (on a 4.0 scale). Admission to the Ph.D. program requires a master's degree with at least a 3.5 GPA. A combined GRE score above 1000 on the math and verbal portions of the exam is normally expected. Complete applications contain three letters of recommendation, a personal statement of academic and career objectives (for the Ph.D., a 1,000-word statement of the applicant's research interest as well), and academic transcripts. For nonnative speakers of English, a demonstrated proficiency in English is required, with a TOEFL score of at least 550 (213 on the computer-based test).

Correspondence and Information

School of Urban Affairs and Public Policy Admissions
University of Delaware
Newark, Delaware 19716-7310
Phone: 302-831-1687
Fax: 302-831-3296
E-mail: suapp@udel.edu
Web site: http://www.udel.edu/suapp

University of Delaware

THE FACULTY AND THEIR RESEARCH

At the core of the School of Urban Affairs and Public Policy are the dedicated faculty members, who are challenging teachers, seasoned researchers, and experienced practitioners. With interdisciplinary backgrounds as skilled executives, managers, and community leaders, they bring practical experience to the classroom and successfully blend a solid academic base with stimulating practical experience.

David L. Ames, Professor and Director, Center for Historic Architecture and Design; Ph.D., Clark, 1969; ACIP. Historic preservation, urban geography, urban and regional planning.

Maria P. Aristigueta, Professor; Director, School of Urban Affairs and Public Policy; and Senior Policy Fellow, Institute for Public Administration; D.P.A., USC, 1997. Administrative behavior, performance management, policy analysis, strategic management.

Deborah A. Auger, Associate Professor and Policy Fellow, Center for Community Research and Service; Ph.D., MIT, 1988. Public policy and administration, nonprofit management, state and local government, U.S. social policy.

John M. Byrne, Professor and Director, Center for Energy and Environmental Policy; Ph.D., Delaware, 1980. Technology and environment, environmental justice, political economy, sustainable development.

Karen A. Curtis, Associate Professor and Policy Scientist, Center for Community Research and Service; Ph.D., Temple, 1984. Nonprofit leadership and management, applied research and public policy analysis, qualitative methods, social and economic opportunity.

Kathryn G. Denhardt, Professor and Policy Scientist, Center for Community Research and Service; Ph.D., Kansas, 1984. Collaborative decision making and conflict resolution, human resources management, ethics in public service.

Robert B. Denhardt, Visiting Scholar; Ph.D., Kentucky, 1968. Public sector management, strategic planning and public productivity.

Bernard L. Dworsky, Assistant Professor and Policy Scientist, Institute for Public Administration; M.A., Delaware, 1971. Water resources management, planning.

James P. Flynn, Assistant Professor; Director, M.P.A. Program; Internship Coordinator; and Associate Policy Scientist, Institute for Public Administration; Ed.D., Delaware, 1998. Personnel administration, quality improvement initiatives, educational governance, legislative management, professional development, human resources management.

Edward J. Freel, Instructor and Policy Scientist, Institute for Public Administration; M.Ed., Delaware, 1975. Civic education, learning initiatives, public administration.

Audrey L. Helfman, Associate Professor; Ph.D., Delaware, 1993. Personnel administration, organizational theory, legislative management, public fiscal analysis, data systems, analytic methods.

Raheemah Jabbar-Bey, Assistant Professor and Assistant Policy Specialist, Center for Community Research and Service; M.A., New Hampshire, 1996. Community and economic development planning, organizational capacity building of nonprofits, urban policy analysis.

Eric D. Jacobson, Associate Professor and Assistant Director, Institute for Public Administration; M.P.A., Delaware, 1981. Public economics, health policy, employee compensation and benefits, tourism development and research, analytical methods.

Janet B. Johnson, Associate Professor, Department of Political Science and International Relations and Senior Research Associate, Center for Energy and Environmental Policy; Ph.D., Cornell, 1978. Subnational politics, environmental policy, research methods, public policy analysis.

Jonathan Justice, Assistant Professor; Ph.D., Rutgers, 2003. Public financial management, nongovernmental public administration, urban policy and administration.

Gerald Kauffman, Instructor and Director, Water Resources Agency; M.P.A., Delaware, 2003. Watershed policy, planning, and management; water resources government and finance; water resources engineering; hydrology and hydraulics.

Jerome R. Lewis, Associate Professor and Director, Institute for Public Administration; Ph.D., NYU, 1968. Public administration, personnel management, urban planning, political leadership.

Stephanie McClellan, Assistant Professor; Ph.D., Delaware, 2004. Organizational culture and dynamics, planning and governance, qualitative research design.

John G. McNutt, Professor and Policy Fellow, Center for Community Research and Service; Ph.D., Tennessee, 1991. Technology, nonprofit management, advocacy and government relations, community organization and planning.

Anthony E. Middlebrooks, Assistant Professor; Ph.D., Wisconsin, 1999. Leadership formation and development, creativity and leadership, service and social justice, research methods.

James L. Morrison, Professor; Ed.D., Temple, 1971. Telecommunications and consumer policy, consumer environmental issues, consumer protection.

Audrey J. Noble, Assistant Professor and Director, Delaware Education Research and Development Center; Ph.D., Arizona State, 1994. Qualitative research and evaluation.

Edward J. O'Donnell, Instructor and Senior Policy Advisor, Institute for Public Administration; M.Ed., West Chester, 1975. Growth management, transportation/infrastructure planning, comprehensive planning.

Marian Lief Palley, Professor, Department of Political Science and International Relations; Ph.D., NYU, 1966. American politics and public policy, intergovernmental relations, health and welfare policy.

Steven W. Peuquet, Associate Professor and Director, Center for Community Research and Service; Ph.D., Pennsylvania, 1996. Strategic planning, housing, homelessness, electronic community networks, public policy analysis and evaluation.

Jeffrey A. Raffel, Charles P. Messick Professor of Public Administration and Faculty Associate, Institute for Public Administration; Ph.D., MIT, 1972. Educational policy, policy analysis, urban management.

Edward C. Ratledge, Associate Professor and Director, Center for Applied Demography and Survey Research; M.A., Delaware, 1972. Management information systems, econometrics, criminal justice systems.

Daniel Rich, Professor, Provost, and Senior Research Associate, Center for Energy and Environmental Policy; Ph.D., MIT, 1972. Public policy and public management.

Breck Robinson, Associate Professor and Associate Professor, Institute for Public Administration; Ph.D., Tennessee, 1994. Financial institutions, public policy, real estate finance.

Rebecca Sheppard, Assistant Professor and Associate Director, Center of Historic Architecture and Design; M.A. Delaware, 1997. Historic preservation planning, history of rural landscapes and the built environment, landscape preservation.

Paul L. Solano, Associate Professor; Ph.D., Maryland, 1978. Financial administration and public finance, political economy, health economics.

Karen F. Stein, Associate Professor and Director, Leadership Program; Ph.D., Delaware, 1984. Domestic elder abuse and neglect, leadership studies, consumer and family economic policy analysis.

Richard T. Sylves, Professor, Department of Political Science and International Relations, and Fellow, Center for Energy and Environmental Policy; Ph.D., Illinois at Urbana-Champaign, 1977. Energy policy, disaster policy.

Douglas F. Tuttle, Instructor and Policy Scientist, Institute for Public Administration; M.P.A., Delaware, 1990. State and local government personnel development, strategic planning, emergency service planning and public service quality assessment.

Young-Doo Wang, Professor and Associate Director, Center for Energy and Environmental Policy; Ph.D., Delaware, 1980. Energy and water conservation policy, economic analysis of alternative energy options, econometric applications.

Leland Ware, Louis L. Redding Chair for the Study of Law and Public Policy; J.D., Boston College, 1973. Employment discrimination law, civil rights law, civil procedure.

Robert Warren, Professor and Senior Research Associate, Institute for Public Administration; Ph.D., UCLA, 1964. Urban and regional government, telecommunications policy, urban planning and development, cultural theory.

Margaret G. Wilder, Professor; Ph.D., Michigan, 1983. Community development policy and organizations; economic development policy and planning; housing problems and policy; race, gender, and economic mobility.

Devona E. G. Williams, Assistant Professor; Ph.D., Delaware, 1992. Entrepreneurship, small business growth and development, women in leadership, community development.

Robert A. Wilson, Associate Professor; Ph.D., Temple, 1971. Survey research, evaluation research, health services research.

Danilo Yanich, Associate Professor; Director, Urban Affairs and Public Policy Program; and Associate Policy Scientist, Center for Community Research and Service; Ph.D., Delaware, 1980. Criminal justice policy, media and public policy, international comparative governance.

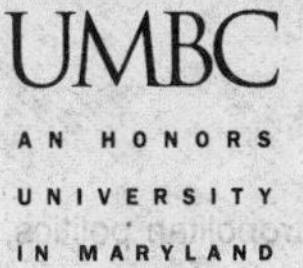

UNIVERSITY OF MARYLAND, BALTIMORE COUNTY

Department of Public Policy

Programs of Study

The graduate programs offered through the Department of Public Policy combine interdisciplinary education in the social sciences with training in policymaking and policy management. The curriculum provides students with a broad understanding of the social, economic, and political forces that affect policymaking. Students acquire advanced analytical and administrative skills that can be applied to a variety of policy problems.

The Department offers the Master of Public Policy (M.P.P.) and Ph.D. degrees. Major areas of focus include evaluation and analytical techniques, health policy, public management, urban policy, and social policy (education, human services, legal policy). Students may also specialize in one of four disciplines (economics, history, political science, or sociology). The master's program is accredited by the National Association of Schools of Public Affairs and Administration. Joint M.P.P./J.D. and Ph.D./J.D. programs are offered in cooperation with the University of Maryland Law School; M.P.A./Ph.D. and J.D./Ph.D. programs are offered in cooperation with the University of Baltimore. There are also joint-degree programs for the M.P.P. and Ph.D. with Baltimore Hebrew University. Most of the Department's courses are offered in the evening.

Research Facilities

UMBC is ranked as a Doctoral/Research University (High Research Activity) by the Carnegie Foundation, one of the highest classifications for a research university in the country. UMBC's proximity to federal and state governmental offices provides an ideal setting for training in a public policy program, internships, and employment opportunities.

The Department of Public Policy participates in on-campus research institutes that involve students in grant, contract, and workshop activities, including the Maryland Institute for Policy Analysis and Research, the Hilltop Institute, and the Center for Urban Environmental Research and Education.

Financial Aid

Research and teaching assistantships are available for qualified candidates. These often cover tuition and provide a stipend. Students with full-time jobs may be eligible for tuition assistance from their employers. For those students not working full-time, there are paid internships and cooperative education programs with various governmental agencies.

Cost of Study

The 2008–09 tuition is $428 per credit for Maryland residents and $708 per credit for nonresidents. There are additional fees and charges.

Living and Housing Costs

On-campus housing available for graduate students is limited and must be requested promptly upon admission. Off-campus housing is available at reasonable rates. A resource center located on campus has updated lists of available housing.

Student Group

There are approximately 9,500 undergraduate and 2,600 graduate students on campus. About 150 graduate students are currently enrolled in the Department of Public Policy. Students come from all over the United States as well as from other nations. The Department admits students directly from undergraduate and master's programs, as well as working professionals seeking the next step in their educational development. An increasing number of students are full-time, often funded through research grants.

Student Outcomes

Graduates accept positions as social science research analysts in federal agencies such as the National Institutes of Health; Administrative Office of the U.S. Courts; Office of Management and Budget; Agency for International Development; Departments of Defense, Education, and Housing and Urban Development; Environmental Protection Agency; Social Security Administration; Centers for Medicare and Medicaid Services; Food and Drug Administration; and Veterans Affairs and Maryland state agencies such as the Departments of Health and Mental Hygiene, Education, Labor, Licensing and Regulation, and Legislative Services. Students and alumni receive awards such as the Presidential Management Fellowship, the University of Maryland School of Law Leadership Scholars Program, the Robert Wood Johnson Health Policy Fellowship, and the Governor's Policy Fellowship. Others join the faculty of research universities and colleges or are contributing their expertise to nongovernmental organizations (associations, businesses, research institutes, and foundations) that address public policy issues.

Location

Most courses are offered at the University of Maryland, Baltimore County, a suburban campus on 500 acres near the intersection of Interstate 95 and the Baltimore Beltway. The campus is 10 minutes from BWI Thurgood Marshall Airport, 15 minutes from downtown Baltimore, and 45 minutes from Annapolis and Washington, D.C.

The University

UMBC is part of the University of Maryland Graduate School, Baltimore (UMGSB). Created in 1985, UMGSB represents the combined graduate and research programs at UMBC and the University of Maryland, Baltimore (UMB)—the university system's doctoral research campuses in the Baltimore area. Through UMGSB, UMBC graduate students have access to courses, practical experiences, and research facilities at other campuses in the University System of Maryland, one of the largest public university systems in the United States.

Applying

Applications for admission are available online through the UMBC Graduate School at http://www.umbc.edu/gradschool. Prospective applicants should also contact the Department of Public Policy before applying (phone: 410-455-3201; e-mail: gradpubpol@umbc.edu). Admissions decisions are rendered during the spring and fall semesters on a rolling basis. Admission is determined by considering the applicant's academic record, letters of recommendation, statement of objectives, and GRE scores. Interested students are encouraged to visit the campus for an interview.

Correspondence and Information

Donald F. Norris, Chair
Department of Public Policy
Public Policy Building, 4th floor
University of Maryland, Baltimore County
1000 Hilltop Circle
Baltimore, Maryland 21250
Phone: 410-455-3201
E-mail: gradpubpol@umbc.edu
Web site: http://www.umbc.edu/pubpol

University of Maryland, Baltimore County

THE FACULTY AND THEIR RESEARCH

Core Faculty

Donald F. Norris, Professor and Chair and Director, Maryland Institute for Policy Analysis and Research; Ph.D., Virginia. Urban and metropolitan politics, public management, information systems in public organizations (including electronic government).

Timothy J. Brennan (joint appointment with Economics), Ph.D., Wisconsin–Madison. Antitrust and regulation, electricity markets, telecommunications and broadcast policy, copyright, philosophy of economics, philosophy of social science.

Patricia Fletcher, Ph.D., Syracuse. Electronic government, government information resources management, information policy, information-based organization management, strategic management.

Adele M. Kirk, Ph.D., UCLA. Health insurance, socioeconomic status and health, work disability.

George R. Lanoue (joint appointment with Political Science), Ph.D., Yale. Civil rights law and policy, focusing on education and public contracting.

Marvin B. Mandell, Ph.D., Northwestern. Quantitative analysis, program evaluation, delivery of public services.

Dave E. Marcotte, Graduate Program Director; Ph.D., Maryland, College Park. Research methods and statistics, social policy, labor markets and job training, mental health policy.

Cheryl M. Miller (joint appointment with Political Science), Associate Dean, College of Arts, Humanities and Social Sciences; Ph.D., North Carolina at Chapel Hill. Agenda setting and policy formulation, welfare policy, bureaucratic politics, African-American political participation, political labeling and symbolic politics.

Nancy A. Miller, Ph.D., Chicago. Health policy, health-care financing, health-care evaluation.

David Salkever, Public Policy; Ph.D., Harvard. Health economics, economics of mental health, disability studies, economics and behavior of nonprofit organizations.

John Rennie Short, Ph.D., Bristol (U.K.). Urban issues, globalization and the city, megalopolis, urban theory, land-use planning.

AFFILIATED FACULTY BY DEPARTMENT

Economics

Dennis Coates, Ph.D., Maryland. Public economics, econometrics.

Lisa Dickson, Ph.D., Texas at Austin. Labor economics, economics of education, econometrics.

Scott Farrow, Chair; Ph.D., Washington State. Industrial organization, environmental economics and risk analysis.

Thomas H. Gindling Jr., Ph.D., Cornell. Economics of developing countries, labor economics, poverty and income inequality, econometric methods.

Marsha G. Goldfarb, Ph.D., Northwestern. Health economics, economics of education.

David H. Greenberg (Emeritus), Ph.D., MIT. Labor economics, benefit-cost analysis, economics of income transfer and manpower programs.

Douglas Lamdin, Ph.D., Maryland. Corporate finance, managerial economics.

Virginia D. McConnell, Ph.D., Maryland, College Park. Environmental economics, cost-benefit analysis, air-pollution policy, land-use policy.

History

John W. Jeffries, Dean, College of Arts, Humanities and Social Sciences; Ph.D., Yale. Twentieth-century U.S. political and policy history.

Kriste Lindenmeyer, Chair; Ph.D., Cincinnati. Gilded age and progressive era, women and gender, immigration and ethnicity, history of childhood and historical methods.

Joseph N. Tatarewicz, Ph.D., Indiana. History of science and technology, science and technology policy, and public history.

Political Science

Jeffrey Davis, Ph.D., Georgia State. Public law and American politics,

Arthur T. Johnson, Provost Emeritus; Ph.D., SUNY at Buffalo. Public administration, personnel, management, sports policy.

Tyson King-Meadows, Ph.D., North Carolina at Chapel Hill. Congress, African-American politics, electoral behavior.

Roy T. Meyers, Director, Sondheim Public Affairs Scholars Program; Ph.D., Michigan. Budgeting, public policy and politics administration, American politics.

Nicholas R. Miller, Ph.D., Berkeley. American politics, elections, methodology, theory.

Thomas F. Schaller, Ph.D., North Carolina at Chapel Hill. American politics, American political institutions.

Psychology

Kenneth I. Maton, Ph.D., Illinois at Urbana-Champaign. Program evaluation, prevention, at-risk youth, community/social psychology, education.

Sociology

Marina A. Adler, Ph.D., Maryland, College Park. Social science methodology and statistics, cross-national gender, work and family issues, the welfare state and social policy in international perspective.

Jere M. Cohen, Ph.D., Chicago. Sociological theory, sociology of religion, sociology of education, small groups, sociology of adolescence, status attainment.

J. Kevin Eckert, Dean, Erickson School of Aging Studies; Ph.D., Northwestern. Health and aging policy, social gerontology, research design, qualitative methods, case studies.

Seth D. Messinger, Ph.D., Columbia. Medical anthropology, anthropology of cities, anthropology of North America, psychiatry, trauma, social organization of medical work.

Leslie A. Morgan, Ph.D., USC. Aging, women's roles, family, labor force participation, social change.

Fred L. Pincus, Ph.D., UCLA. Race and ethnic relations, sociology of education, higher education policy.

William G. Rothstein, Ph.D., Cornell. Medical sociology, history of medicine, sociology of occupations and professions.

Robert L. Rubinstein, Ph.D., Bryn Mawr. Cultural and medical anthropology, anthropology of aging, gerontology, gender, qualitative research methods.

John G. Schumacher, Ph.D., Case Western Reserve. Medical sociology, physician-patient relations, social gerontology, bioethics, research methods.

Mary E. Stuart, Sc.D., Johns Hopkins. Issues in health, health-care organization and delivery, decision support for health policy and management.

James A. Trela, Chair; Ph.D., Case Western Reserve. Sociology of aging, social political behaviors, social problems.

UNIVERSITY OF MICHIGAN–FLINT

Master of Public Administration

Program of Study

The Master of Public Administration (M.P.A.), offered through the Horace H. Rackham School of Graduate Studies, is designed to prepare administrators to analyze problems and solve them effectively. Professors teach conceptual knowledge and help students develop the analytical skills necessary to implement policy. Whether employed in public or nonprofit organizations or interested in entering a career in administration, students in the M.P.A. program receive the balanced, advanced education necessary to become capable, decisive leaders. This interdisciplinary program is designed to meet the educational needs of students who have earned specialized, technical, or liberal arts degrees and are seeking to expand or update their knowledge of administration. Courses are offered in the evening, on weekends, or online to meet the needs of working professionals interested in completing the program on a part-time basis.

The program focuses on two important premises—that the prime responsibility of administrators is to identify and manage problems and that problem solving does not fall within the bounds of a single discipline. The curriculum includes core courses in public administration, courses from one of the four concentrations (criminal justice, educational, or health-care administration or administration of nonprofit agencies), work in analytical methods, and an applied research project. Internships are usually required for students with fewer than two years' experience in administration.

The general program provides advanced education in administration for persons employed in the public or nonprofit sectors as well as for those seeking entry into careers in administration. The criminal justice administration concentration is designed for persons already employed in agencies in the criminal justice process. The program examines contemporary developments in criminal justice administration, focusing on the interdependence between pre-prosecutorial and post-prosecutorial agencies and functions and the linkage between administration and policy. For persons employed within the health-care field, the concentration in health-care administration is offered in collaboration with the School of Health Professions and Studies. Focusing on contemporary developments in health-care administration, the program concentration prepares students to deal with the complex tasks and challenges of today's health-care system. The administration of nonprofit agencies concentration is designed principally to serve those who seek advancement in careers in the not-for-profit sector.

The University of Michigan–Flint (UM-Flint) WebPlus weekend/online program in educational administration is designed to provide a high-quality experience to full-time, working educators. A unique blend of face-to-face interaction and convenient online course work provides teachers, administrators, and aspiring administrators the tools and concepts necessary for successful administration and an informed perspective on the range of problems confronting K–12 education. Monthly Saturday visits on the Flint campus are combined with course work that can be done from the convenience of a home computer connected to the Internet. In addition, a clinical experience is organized in the student's current school setting.

Research Facilities

The Frances Willson Thompson Library's collection includes approximately 217,000 books and 35,000 bound magazines and journals. The library also contains more than half a million microform items, ranging from the *Times of London* to documents on education. The library subscribes to some 1,100 hard-copy periodicals, and it provides electronic access to approximately 13,000 more. The media collection consists of music CDs, audiotapes, and other media, including CD-ROMs, DVDs, and videotapes.

Financial Aid

The University of Michigan–Flint strives to offer a high-quality education at an affordable price. Several forms of financial aid are available, including loans, scholarships, grants, and research or teaching assistantships. The University is committed to working with students in their efforts to explore possible opportunities for financial assistance.

Cost of Study

In 2008–09, graduate tuition is $415.50 per credit for Michigan residents and $623.30 per credit for nonresidents. Other fees include a $50 registration fee, a $25 student activity fee, a $23 recreation fee, and a $43 technology fee.

Living and Housing Costs

University housing, available beginning in fall 2008, is intended primarily for undergraduate students in its first phase. There are many off-campus housing opportunities in Flint and the surrounding area. Apartments close to the campus range from $370 per month for a studio to $750 for a two- or three-bedroom apartment. Farther from the campus, apartments range between $300 and $650 per month, depending on the apartment's size and location.

Student Group

There are 243 students, 153 of whom are women. This includes 29 international students and 43 members of minority groups. The average age is 35. Students from government, health care, criminal justice, and the nonprofit sector interact across professional boundaries through shared courses.

Location

Although best known as the birthplace of General Motors, Flint has become better known for other attractions in recent years, including the Crim Festival of Races and the Buick Open. A large cultural center occupies 30 acres near downtown, and more than fifty parks and four golf courses are interspersed throughout the city. Flint is located approximately 60 miles from Detroit, Ann Arbor, and Lansing.

The University

The University of Michigan–Flint was founded in 1956, when a two-year senior college was formed through public and private donations. Today, this four-year university offers 100 undergraduate and twenty-seven graduate degrees to nearly 7,000 students. The programs have been designed to provide professional training in relationship to traditional study in the liberal arts and sciences, so students develop the knowledge, intellectual skills, values, and attitudes needed to make thoughtful and informed judgments about their experiences.

Applying

Applicants must have earned a bachelor's degree in any field of study from an accredited institution, preferably with a minimum overall undergraduate grade point average of 3.0 on a 4.0 scale. In addition, applicants should have completed a course each in statistics, microeconomic principles, and government or public-sector administration.

Students must submit the completed application, the application fee, official transcripts from all colleges and universities attended, three letters of recommendation, and a statement of purpose that describes the applicant's reasons for pursuing the degree. The program has rolling admissions and reviews completed applications each month. The deadlines for the fall, winter, and spring semesters are August 1, November 15, and March 15, respectively.

Correspondence and Information

Albert C. Price, Program Director
220 French Hall
University of Michigan–Flint
303 East Kearsley Street
Flint, Michigan 48502

Phone: 810-762-3470
E-mail: acprice@umflint.edu
Web site: http://www.umflint.edu/graduateprograms/public_admin.htm

University of Michigan–Flint

THE FACULTY

Susanne Chandler, Professor of Education and Dean of the School of Education and Human Services; Ph.D., Ohio State.
William Laverty, Assistant Professor of Political Science; Ph.D., Indiana.
Kristine Mulhorn, Associate Professor of Health Sciences and Administration; Ph.D., Delaware.
Tevfik Nas, Professor of Economics; Ph.D., Florida State.
Patrick O'Donnell, LEO Lecturer IV in Public Administration.
Mark Perry, Associate Professor of Finance; Ph.D., George Mason.
Albert Price, Professor of Political Science and Program Director; Ph.D., Connecticut.
Kathryn Schellenberg, Associate Professor of Sociology; Ph.D., Utah.
Suzanne Selig, Professor and Director of Health Sciences and Administration; Ph.D., Cincinnati.
Charles Vergon, Lecturer II in Political Science; J.D.

UNIVERSITY OF MINNESOTA

Hubert H. Humphrey Institute of Public Affairs

Programs of Study

The Humphrey Institute offers a Master of Public Policy (M.P.P.); a Master of Urban and Regional Planning (M.U.R.P.); a Master of Science in Science, Technology, and Environmental Policy (M.S.); and a midcareer Master of Public Affairs (M.P.A.). Humphrey degrees may be combined with graduate or professional degrees in the University of Minnesota's schools of law, public health, social work, civil engineering, and architecture and landscape architecture.

The Master of Public Policy (M.P.P.) provides an in-depth education in public management and policy analysis techniques that can be applied in a number of fields. Concentrations include public and nonprofit leadership and management, advanced policy analysis methods, social policy, community and economic development (domestic and international), women and public policy, science and technology policy, and global public policy.

The Master of Urban and Regional Planning (M.U.R.P.) is an interdisciplinary degree that prepares students to analyze, forecast, design, and implement plans for regions, communities, and neighborhoods. Students develop a comprehensive understanding of the built environment (land use, transportation, housing, regional economies) and the ability to mediate among competing interests. Concentrations include environmental planning; housing and community development; land use and urban design planning; economic, and workforce development; and transportation planning.

The Master of Science in Science, Technology, and Environmental Policy (M.S.) program trains students in the role of science and technology in the economy, food production and health, energy and the environment, security policy, and education. Training also covers the impact of science and technology on the political and economic relations among nations. Students are educated in analysis and design of policies for appropriate promotion and regulation of science and technology regionally, nationally, and internationally. M.S. students typically have undergraduate degrees or advanced course work in one of the natural or engineering sciences.

The Master of Public Affairs (M.P.A.) degree is designed for the midcareer professional who wishes to develop advanced skills in public leadership and management. Students acquire the conceptual knowledge and technical tools needed to understand systemic approaches to policy issues and to develop solutions and policy proposals that are in the public interest.

Research Facilities

Students have access to the Institute's many research and outreach centers and programs and often participate in specific projects. The Humphrey Institute acts as an international hub for groundbreaking research on public policy issues. Current research centers and projects include Democracy and Citizenship; Human Relations and Social Justice; International Economic Policy; School Change; Science, Technology, and Public Policy; Integrative Leadership; State and Local Policy; Women and Public Policy; the Study of Politics and Governance; Public and Nonprofit Leadership; Bicycling Costs and Benefits; Telecommunications and Information Society Policy; and Regional and Industrial Economics. With a collection of 4 million volumes, the University of Minnesota's library system is one of the largest American university libraries. Wilson Library, the main campus library, is adjacent to the Humphrey Institute. The University maintains exceptional computer facilities, and the Institute has its own microcomputer labs and wireless access for student use.

Financial Aid

The Institute allocates financial aid primarily on the basis of merit. Sources of aid include Hubert H. Humphrey fellowships and scholarships, University of Minnesota fellowships, and teaching and research assistantships. Amounts range from $5000 to $25,000 per year.

Cost of Study

In 2007–08, tuition was $985 per semester credit for Minnesota residents and $1526 for nonresidents. For those students taking 6 to 15 credits, the cost was $5615 per semester for residents and $9156 for nonresidents. Tuition for the M.P.A. program was $813 per semester credit for residents and $1404 for nonresidents. Residents of North Dakota, South Dakota, Wisconsin, and Manitoba may be eligible for resident tuition rates if they apply to their Higher Education Coordinating Board prior to enrollment each academic year.

Living and Housing Costs

Students interested in local rental rates should contact Housing and Residential Life, Comstock Hall East, 210 Delaware Street, SE (telephone: 612-624-2994; Web site: http://www.umn.edu/housing).

Student Group

The Humphrey Institute has approximately 400 students enrolled in its four degree programs. About 60 percent are women, about 10 percent are international students, and 12 percent are members of minority groups. Many students have had previous work experience. The average age of the midcareer M.P.A. student is 42, while the average age for the rest of the student body is 27. About 50 percent of students come from Minnesota; the others come from twenty-eight different states and twenty-six other countries. They majored in more than sixty different areas of undergraduate study.

Student Outcomes

Humphrey Institute graduates enter widely varied careers in public service. Examples include environmental planner, legislative analyst, education policy evaluator, welfare reform analyst, executive director, health policy administrator, nonprofit grant administrator, city planner, and international economic development officer. Graduates work internationally and domestically in local, state, and federal government and in nonprofit and private firms.

Location

With a population of roughly 3 million, the Twin Cities of Minneapolis and St. Paul and surrounding area enjoy a thriving economy based on strong social, political, and business innovation. Known for its high quality of life, including cultural and recreational opportunities, this urban setting is conducive to remarkably productive internships and careers with local, county, and regional governments and organizations. National surveys consistently rank the Minneapolis–St. Paul area as one of the most desirable places in the country to live and work.

The Institute

The Humphrey Institute is a professional school of the University of Minnesota. The Institute is widely recognized for its role in examining public issues and shaping public policy at the local, state, national, and international levels and for providing leadership and management expertise to public and nonprofit organizations. The Institute was founded in 1977 as a tribute to Vice President Hubert H. Humphrey. As the direct descendant of the University's pioneering Public Administration Center (1936–68) and distinguished School of Public Affairs (1968–77), the Humphrey Institute represents nearly three quarters of a century of community service and academic achievement.

Applying

Applications must be postmarked by January 5 to receive full consideration for fall admission and financial aid and by April 1 for admission only. Applications received after April 1 are reviewed on a space-available basis. Admission to the programs is based on each applicant's prior scholastic achievement, statement of purpose, and letters of recommendation. Applicants to the Master of Public Affairs programs should have at least ten years of postbaccalaureate professional experience. The GRE General Test is required for all degrees except the M.P.A., and TOEFL scores are required of students whose first language is not English.

Correspondence and Information

Admissions Office
Hubert H. Humphrey Institute of Public Affairs
225 Humphrey Center
University of Minnesota
301 19th Avenue, South
Minneapolis, Minnesota 55455

Phone: 612-626-7229
E-mail: hhhadmit@umn.edu
Web site: http://www.hhh.umn.edu

University of Minnesota

THE FACULTY AND THEIR RESEARCH

Ryan Allen, Ph.D., Assistant Professor. Community and economic development, urban studies, planning.
Ragui Assaad, Ph.D., Professor. International economic development, labor market analysis, politics and economics of the Middle East and North Africa, urban planning, poverty in developing countries, quantitative methods, women's work in developing countries.
J. Brian Atwood, Dean and Professor and former head of USAID. International development, foreign assistance, the United Nations, UN peacekeeping operations, politics and policy leadership, post-conflict reconstruction, government reform.
Michael Barnett, Ph.D., Harold Stassen Chair of International Relations. The Middle East, international organizations, humanitarianism, international affairs.
John M. Bryson, Ph.D., Professor. Public leadership; policy entrepreneurship; strategic management of public and nonprofit organizations; project management; collaboration; government and nonprofit organization, innovation, and reform; design and management of public participation processes.
Xinyu Cao, Ph.D., Assistant Professor. Transportation and land-use management, civil and environmental engineering.
Nancy N. Eustis, Ph.D., Professor. Aging and disability policy, long-term care policy, health care for the elderly, program evaluation.
Yingling Fan, Ph.D., Assistant Professor. Land-use and transportation interaction, impacts of urban systems on human activities and movements, health and social considerations in land-use and transportation planning.
Katherine Fennelly, Ph.D., Professor. Leadership in the public sector, health and public policy, diversity and cross-cultural relations, immigration and public policy.
Greta Friedemann-Sanchez, Ph.D., Assistant Professor. International development, public affairs, economic anthropology.
Edward Goetz, Ph.D., Professor. Housing policy, markets; community economic development, politics of urban and regional planning; growth management strategies; urban planning; urban poverty; urban sprawl.
Maria Hanratty, Ph.D., Associate Professor. Health care, medical economics, economics of poverty, comparative social welfare institutions.
Stephen A. Hoenack, Ph.D., Professor. Economic behavior within organizations, econometrics, higher education policy, K–12 policy, government innovation and reform, women and gender equity.
Lawrence R. Jacobs, Ph.D., Walter F. and Joan Mondale Chair for Political Studies and Director, Center for the Study of Politics and Governance. Presidential and legislative politics, elections and voting behavior, public opinion and polling, American political history, Midwestern swing states, third-party politics, social security and health-care policy.
Kenneth H. Keller, Ph.D., Charles M. Denny, Jr., Chair in Science and Technology Policy. Science and technology policy, global technology development, technology in health care, energy policy; the environment.
Sally J. Kenney, Ph.D., Professor and Director, Center on Women and Public Policy. Women, law, and public policy; gender and judging; judicial selection; women and electoral politics; feminist organizations and social movements; the European Union; employment discrimination.
Morris M. Kleiner, Ph.D., AFL-CIO Chair of Labor Policy. Public policies on work and pay, role of labor unions in democratic societies, human resource policies, organizational performance.
Robert T. Kudrle, Ph.D., Freeman Chair in International Trade and Investment Policy and Director, Freeman Center for International Economic Policy. Competition policy, tax policy, policy problems of globalization, international economic policy cooperation.
Jennifer Kuzma, Ph.D., Associate Professor. Biotechnology policy, regulatory policy, risk analysis, biochemistry/molecular biology, renewable energy programs, nanotechnology policy.
Deborah Levison, Ph.D., Associate Professor. Child labor and education in poor countries, labor economics, population studies, child care.
Ann Markusen, Ph.D., Professor. Arts, culture, and economic development; regional economics and planning; industrial organization; local, state, and regional economic development; industrial and occupational planning; economic impact of high technology and military spending.
Samuel L. Myers Jr., Ph.D., Roy Wilkins Professor in Human Relations and Social Justice. Microeconomic policy analysis, racial inequality and public policy, antiracism programs, government procurement and contracting, credit and housing markets, child protective services, violence analysis, science and engineering workforce, academic labor markets, race-neutral remedies.
Jodi Sandfort, Ph.D., Associate Professor. Nonprofit management; social policy implementation; welfare, workforce, and early childhood policy.
Carissa Schively Slotterback, Ph.D., Assistant Professor. Environmental and land-use planning, public participation, planning decision making, plan implementation, sustainable development.
Joseph Soss, Ph.D., Cowles Chair for the Study of Public Service. Race and social politics, politics of public management, ways that public policies mediate the relationship between inequality and democracy in the United States.
Melissa M. Stone, Ph.D., Associate Professor and Director, Public and Nonprofit Leadership Center. Nonprofit management and governance, government-nonprofit relationships, cross-sectoral partnerships.
Judy Temple, Ph.D., Associate Professor. Public economics, economics of education, early childhood education, cost-benefit analysis, policy evaluation.
Elizabeth Wilson, Ph.D., Assistant Professor. Energy and environmental policy, regulatory and legal analysis of emerging technologies, climate change, geologic carbon sequestration, public perception of emerging technologies.
Zhirong Zhao, Ph.D., Assistant Professor. Public and nonprofit management, budgeting, financial management.

Senior Fellows, Fellows, Visiting and Part-Time Faculty

Steve Andreasen, M.A. National security, foreign, and defense policy; arms control; nuclear weapons; nuclear proliferation; missile defense; intelligence; crisis management.
Richard Bolan, Professor Emeritus. Planned social change, planning theory, social and environmental planning, planning in central and eastern Europe.
Harry Boyte, Ph.D., Co-Director, Center for Democracy and Citizenship. Civic engagement, theory and practice of democracy, citizen professionalism, international democracy promotion, national service initiatives, citizen politics.
Barbara Crosby, Ph.D., Associate Professor. Leadership and public policy, women in leadership, media and public policy, strategic planning, leadership in transnational contexts, leadership and cross-sector collaboration.
Gary DeCramer, Ph.D., Senior Lecturer and former Minnesota state senator. Political leadership, reflective practice, program evaluation, rural development, transportation policy, cooperative development.
Dennis Donovan, M.A., Research Fellow, Center for Democracy and Citizenship. Theory and practice of democracy, civic engagement, citizen politics, culture change in K–12 settings, strategies for public engagement of K–12 and university students, democracy building in international settings.
Kaye Husbands Fealing, Ph.D., Visiting Professor, Center for Science, Technology, and Public Policy. Global trade and economics, science policy development.
Steve Kelley, J.D., Former Minnesota state senator. Science and math education policies, telecommunications and information technology.
Jay Kiedrowski, M.A., Former bank executive and Commissioner of Finance. Federal, state, and local budgeting and deficits; leadership; financial management; organizational development; public and nonprofit management; innovative reforms for public and nonprofit organizations; state and local government.
LaJune Lange, J.D., Former district court judge in Minnesota. Social justice, race relations, international human rights.
Barbara L. Lukermann, M.A. Urban and regional land use planning, housing policy.
Lee Munnich Jr., B.A., Director, State and Local Policy Program. Transportation policy, economic development, state and local finance, industry clusters, science and technology policy, planning, public finance, value pricing.
Joe Nathan, Ph.D., Director, Center for School Change. Charter public schools, parent and community involvement, school choice programs, legislation and research, youth community service, public education reform.
Tim Penny, B.A., Former U.S. congressman from Minnesota. Agriculture; federal and public-sector budgeting; federal budget deficit/surplus; leadership; politics, political parties; social security; transportation, planning, and finance; veteran's policy.
Joe Ritter, Ph.D., Associate Professor. Labor markets and macroeconomics, macroeconomic data, incentives in employment relationships.
Nan Skelton, B.A., Co-Director, Center for Democracy and Citizenship. Civic engagement; youth policy, including making the connection between in-school learning and out-of-school time; neighborhood and community development, particularly in areas with immigrant populations.
Paul Stone, Ph.D., Associate Professor. American political and institutional history, behavior in American public life, Minnesota political history.
Steve Sviggum, B.A. Legislative leadership, the legislative process, political ethics reform.
Vin Weber, B.A., Former U.S. congressman from Minnesota. Agriculture, federal and public-sector budgeting, federal budget deficit/surplus, government finance, politics and political parties, state government, welfare system.

UNIVERSITY OF PENNSYLVANIA

Fels Institute of Government
Master of Governmental Administration Program

Programs of Study

The Fels Institute of Government was founded in 1937 by Philadelphia industrialist Samuel Fels and has the distinction of being one of the oldest programs in public service in the country. Over the course of its 70 year history, the Fels program has provided students with a combination of management and political skills that has proved to be an effective formula. As a result, Fels graduates hold leadership positions at all levels of government, in nonprofit organizations, and in related private firms.

Fels offers a Master of Governmental Administration (M.G.A.) that is comparable to a Master of Public Administration. It also offers five-course graduate-level certificates in economic development and growth, nonprofit administration, politics, and public finance. The certificates can be obtained either as a concentration within the M.G.A. or as a stand-alone diploma.

The twelve-course M.G.A. is offered in full-time and part-time formats and comprises eight core and four elective courses. Full-time students take the eight core courses during the weekdays, part-time executive students take the eight core courses on Saturdays, and students in both formats commingle in the four electives, which are available on weekdays, weeknights, and Saturdays.

Students have the option of taking their elective courses at Fels or other graduate programs within the University of Pennsylvania. Students can also seek approval to import, as electives, up to four courses taken in graduate programs outside of Penn before, during, or after their time in the M.G.A. program. In addition to the certificates, Fels students often create informal concentrations (for example, city planning, education management, environmental studies, transportation) through careful selection of their courses. Other students cover a broader range of subject matter in their electives.

The standard full-time course sequence includes three courses per semester, taken over two academic years with summers off, although some students accelerate the program by taking four courses per semester. Executive students tend to take two courses per semester and complete the program in two calendar years, including summers. Some executive students, however, reduce their course load in certain semesters in order to balance the program with their other substantial responsibilities.

Fels offers the possibility of earning dual graduate degrees in the following areas: the M.G.A./J.D. with Penn Law School, the M.G.A./M.B.E. with the Bioethics Program, the M.G.A./M.C.P. with City Planning Program/School of Design, the M.G.A./M.E.S. with the Environmental Studies Program, the M.G.A./M.S.E. with the School of Engineering, the M.G.A./M.S.Ed. with the Graduate School of Education, and the M.G.A./M.S.W. with the School of Social Policy and Practice. Dual-degree students are granted some flexibility in their course sequencing as needed. This enables students coming into the program with another graduate degree to complete the M.G.A. in just two semesters or two semesters plus a summer semester.

Fels offers graduate-level certificates in the following four areas of traditional strength: Economic Development and Growth, Nonprofit Administration, Politics, and Public Finance. The certificates are designed to prepare students for a wide range of existing influential positions within these fields. They can be obtained by M.G.A. students without taking any additional courses beyond their twelve-course M.G.A. program.

Research Facilities

The Fels Institute occupies the home of the late industrialist and philanthropist, Samuel S. Fels. Built in 1937, the Fels residence has been adapted for academic use in a way that maintains its original character. The Institute offers wireless computer access and is equipped with two small computer labs that provide online access to a range of information resources, including the extensive electronic holdings of the Penn library. In addition, Fels students have access to the vast resources offered by the University of Pennsylvania.

Financial Aid

Students in the M.G.A. program rely upon a combination of funding sources to finance their education at Fels. Tuition support is available to full-time and executive M.G.A. students on a merit basis. During the past two years, Fels has awarded financial aid to every full-time student who has requested it, with awards ranging from $3000 to full tuition per year. The average award represented 25 percent of tuition. In addition, most full-time students work on internships that pay from $10 to $20 per hour. Additional support comes from Federal Stafford Student Loans, Federal Perkins Loans, and University work-study opportunities.

Nearly all executive students work in full-time positions, and some of them receive full or partial support from their employers. Fels also works with executive students to help them advance in their careers while they are students at Fels.

Cost of Study

For 2007–08, the total cost of the twelve-course M.G.A. tuition charges was $51,096 with additional insurance and fees of $8956 paid for over the two-year program period. More specifically, during the 2007–08 academic year, full-time tuition and fees were $17,820 for a four-course semester, $13,779 for a three-course semester, and $9018 for a two-course semester.

Living and Housing Costs

Housing on and off campus is readily available in the University area as well as elsewhere in the city. The cost of living in Philadelphia tends to be lower than other major U.S. cities, and many graduate students live off campus. Housing is available at widely varying rates that begin at approximately $6000 for nine months.

Student Group

The Fels M.G.A. currently enrolls about 130 students who are evenly divided between the full-time and part-time formats. Fels recruits approximately 35 new students per year to each of the formats. Full-time students include recent college graduates as well as students with varied postgraduate experience. Although many students come to Fels from positions in politics, nonprofits, and government agencies, others use the Fels program as a bridge from other fields, including law and business, to the public service field.

The students represent a diverse group of people by age, race, gender, politics, nationality, and geography. The program attracts students from across the United States and from abroad.

Student Outcomes

The Fels program has a very good placement rate for its graduating students. At present, approximately 40 percent of graduates are employed in government, 30 percent in the nonprofit sector, and 30 percent in the private sector, with an emphasis on firms that service the public sector. Fels alumni hold political jobs, including public office, public finance positions in both the public and private sectors, and leadership positions at all levels of government and in more than 100 nonprofit organizations. They also do work with lobbying and consulting firms that support the public sector. Over time, many Fels graduates pursue their public-service careers by moving easily between the public, private, and nonprofit sectors.

Location

The Fels Institute is located just west of Center City Philadelphia, in the northwest corner of the Penn campus at the intersection of Walnut and 39th Streets. Fels is a short walk to trolley, subway, and intercity train lines that provide easy access to downtown; the airport; the New Jersey shore; Harrisburg; Washington, D.C.; New York City; and the rest of the Northeast corridor. Nearby 30th Street station, for example, offers rail service that reaches the airport in 20 minutes, New York City in just over an hour, and Washington, D.C., in just over 2 hours.

The University

The University was founded in 1740 by Benjamin Franklin. A member of the Ivy League and one of the world's leading universities, Penn is renowned for its graduate schools, faculty, research centers, and institutes. Conveniently situated on a compact and attractive campus, Penn offers an abundance of multidisciplinary and cross-school educational programs with exceptional opportunities for individually tailored graduate education. It also offers students all the amenities of a 20,000 student university.

Applying

Inquiries should be made directly to the Fels Institute. Full-time students are admitted primarily for the fall semester, with a few students admitted for the spring semester if space permits. In order to receive full financial aid consideration, full-time applicants should apply by January 15. Executive students are admitted in the fall, spring, and summer terms and should apply no later than forty-five days before the start of the semester.

Correspondence and Information

Admissions Office
Fels Institute of Government
University of Pennsylvania
3814 Walnut Street
Philadelphia, Pennsylvania 19104-6197

Phone: 215-746-6684
Fax: 215-898-6238
E-mail: felsmga@sas.upenn.edu
Web site: http://www.fels.upenn.edu

University of Pennsylvania

THE FACULTY

Administration and Faculty

Leigh Botwinik, Director of Full-Time Students, Fels Institute of Government.
Allison Brummel, Director of Projects, Fels Institute of Government.
Donald F. Kettl, Director, Fels Institute of Government; Professor of Political Science; Stanley I. Sheerr Endowed Term Chair in the Social Sciences.
John J. Mulhern, Director of Professional Education, Fels Institute of Government; Adjunct Associate Professor of Classical Studies and Government Administration.

Faculty

Arthur C. Benedict, Principal, Benedict Associates.
Nancy Burd, Vice President of Grantmaking Services, The Philadelphia Foundation.
Cary Coglianese, Edward B. Shils Professor of Law and Professor of Political Science, University of Pennsylvania.
Joseph Conti, CEO, Pennsylvania State Liquor Control Board; Former State Senator, Commonwealth of Pennsylvania.
Michael Cosack, Managing Director, Public Financial Management.
G. Edward DeSeve, Professor of the Practice and Director of the Management, Finance and Leadership Program, School of Public Policy, University of Maryland.
John DiIulio, Frederic Fox Leadership Professor and Faculty Director and Co-Chair of the Director's Advisory Group, Robert A. Fox Leadership Program, University of Pennsylvania.
Paul Drayton, Vice President of Marketing and Business Development, Affiliated Computer Services, Inc.
David Eisenhower, Senior Research Administrator and Director of the Institute for Public Service, Annenberg School for Communication, University of Pennsylvania.
Vincent Galko, Founding Partner, Critical Times, Bold Solutions, LLC; Regional Policy Director, Rudy Giuliani Presidential Committee.
Steven C. Genyk, Senior Vice President, Philadelphia Industrial Development Corporation.
E. Michael Golda, Electrical Systems Department, NAVSEA Philadelphia.
Gloria Guard, President, People's Emergency Center.
Ira Harkavy, Associate Vice President and founding Director, Center for Community Partnerships, University of Pennsylvania.
Michael E. Harris, Associate Vice President, Office of the Executive Vice President, University of Pennsylvania.
James A. Hartling, Founding Partner, Urban Partners.
John Hawkins, Senior Lobbyist, Wojdak and Associates.
John Keene, Professor of City and Regional Planning, University of Pennsylvania.
James F. Kenney, Councilman at Large, City of Philadelphia.
Matthew Kirk, Managing Director, Access Financial Markets.
John Kromer, Interim Director, Camden Redevelopment Agency; former Director, Office of Housing and Community Development, City of Philadelphia.
Janice F. Madden, Professor of Regional Science, Sociology, Urban Studies, and Real Estate, University of Pennsylvania.
Marjorie Margolies-Mezvinsky, CEO, Women's Campaign International; former Member of Congress.
Deirdre Martinez, Ph.D.; Director, Fels Public Policy Internship Program.
Marcia Martinez-Helfman, Chief Human Resources Officer, Pennsylvania Hospital.
Michael Masch, Secretary of the Budget, Commonwealth of Pennsylvania.
Thomas M. McKenna, Director, Certificate Program in Nonprofit Administration, Fels Institute of Government; former Executive Director, Big Brothers Big Sisters of America.
Ralph Menzano, National Strategist for Transportation, Oracle Corporation.
Stephen P. Mullin, Senior Vice President, Econsult Corporation.
Michael Nadol, Managing Director, Public Financial Management.
Jack H. Nagel, Professor of Political Science, University of Pennsylvania.
Eric Costello Neiderman, Manager, Cargo Security Research and Development, Transportation Security Administration, Department of Homeland Security.
Rob Nixon, Lobbyist and Public Affairs Advisor, Princeton Public Affairs Group.
Folasade Olanipekun-Lewis, former Chief Financial Officer, The School District of Philadelphia.
Robert Pearson, Senior Fellow, Fels Institute of Government.
Gerald Perrins, Regional Economist, U.S. Bureau of Labor Statistics.
Samuel H. Preston, Frederick J. Warren Professor of Demography, University of Pennsylvania.
Hon. Edward G. Rendell, Governor of the Commonwealth of Pennsylvania.
Harvey Rubin, Director, Institute for Strategic Threat Analysis and Response; Professor of Medicine, Microbiology, and Computer Science, University of Pennsylvania.
Trudy Rubin, Foreign Affairs Columnist, *The Philadelphia Inquirer.*
Ramin Sedehi, Vice Dean of Finance and Administration, School of Arts and Sciences, University of Pennsylvania.
Wayne A. Smith, President and CEO, Delaware Healthcare Association; former House Majority Leader, Delaware General Assembly.
John Spagnola, Managing Director, Public Financial Management.
Joseph P. Tierney, Executive Director, Robert A. Fox Leadership Program, University of Pennsylvania.
Jack Thomas Tomarchio, Principal Deputy Assistant Secretary of Homeland Security for Information Analysis.
Eric J. Weinberg, Managing Director, Kroll Security Group.
Nicole K. Westerman, Chief of Staff, Secretary of Budget and Administration, Commonwealth of Pennsylvania.

UNIVERSITY OF PITTSBURGH

Graduate School of Public and International Affairs

Programs of Study

The Graduate School of Public and International Affairs (GSPIA) at the University of Pittsburgh offers professional education for individuals who wish to pursue careers as managers, planners, and policy analysts primarily in the public sector and nonprofit and nongovernmental organizations in the U.S. and abroad. GSPIA offers the following degrees:

The 48-credit Master of International Development (M.I.D.) degree offers majors in nongovernmental organizations and civil society, developmental planning and environmental sustainability, and human security.

The 48-credit Master of Public Administration (M.P.A.) degree offers majors in public and nonprofit management, policy research and analysis, and urban and regional affairs. The National Association of Schools of Public Affairs and Administration (NASPAA) accredits the M.P.A. degree.

The 48-credit Master of Public and International Affairs (M.P.I.A.) degree offers majors in global political economy, security and intelligence studies, and human security. GSPIA is a founding member of the Association of Professional Schools of International Affairs (ASPIA).

The 30-credit Master of Public Policy and Management (M.P.P.M.) degree is for experienced professionals who want to develop analytic tools and expand their managerial capabilities.

The 78-credit Ph.D. prepares students for careers in teaching, research, and consulting in development policy, foreign and security policy, international political economy, public administration, and public policy. An earned master's degree is preferred, and students may be awarded up to 30 credits of advanced standing.

Joint-degree programs are offered with the Schools of Law (J.D.), Business (M.B.A.), Information Science (M.S.I.S.), Public Health (M.P.H.), and Social Work (M.S.W.).

Research Facilities

The School's library has more than 139,200 books and other documents covering all of its fields. The University library system has 4.7 million volumes. GSPIA has its own state-of-the-art computer classrooms and an online data link to the University computer center. Students are provided research opportunities through GSPIA's Ridgway Center for International Security Studies, the Ford Institute for Human Security, the Johnson Institute for Responsible Leadership, the Non-Profit Clinic, and the Interactive, Intelligent Spatial Information System and through the University Center for International Studies, the University Center for Social and Urban Research, and faculty-sponsored research projects.

Financial Aid

Full or partial tuition scholarships, graduate assistantships, and student employment are awarded annually on a competitive basis. To be considered for funding, completed applications for admission must be submitted on or before February 1. The deadline for international applicants is January 15.

Cost of Study

The tuition for 2007–08 for full-time Pennsylvania residents was $7440 per term and $13,460 per term for nonresidents in the fall and spring. Additional fees are $325 per term. Tuition in the summer is based on the per-credit rate, which is $604 per credit for residents and $1103 for nonresidents. Summer fees are prorated.

Living and Housing Costs

Single students should budget approximately $13,000 for moderate living expenses, exclusive of tuition. Housing for graduate students is available off campus.

Student Group

Of the approximately 450 students enrolled at any one time, about 20 percent are from other countries, 35 percent are from other parts of the U.S., 55 percent are women, and 15 percent are members of U.S. minority groups.

Location

The University is in Oakland, the cultural, educational, and medical center of Pittsburgh. It is within walking distance of art galleries, museums, and other cultural and athletic facilities. The city center is about 2 miles away.

The University and The School

The University of Pittsburgh is a state-related institution with a respected international stature as a major research university. It enrolls 34,000 students, including 9,000 in graduate and professional programs. GSPIA students take courses in other departments and professional schools in the University and cross-register for courses at Carnegie Mellon and other area schools. The University Center for International Studies (UCIS) offers graduate area studies certificates in African studies, Asian studies, Latin American studies, West European studies, Russian and East European studies, and global studies.

Applying

GSPIA assesses applicants' academic background, professional experiences, and career objectives. While there are no required prerequisite courses, applicants are strongly encouraged to have taken courses in microeconomics, macroeconomics, statistics, and computer applications for spreadsheet, databases, statistical analysis, and presentations. GRE General Test scores are required for admission to the doctoral program and are recommended for master's applicants. For students who are seeking financial aid, the application deadline for the fall term is February 1 (January 15 for international applicants). The deadline for the spring term is November 1 for U.S. citizens and permanent residents and August 1 for international applicants. Online application is available on the GSPIA Web site. The application fee is $50.

Correspondence and Information

Office of Student Services
Graduate School of Public and International Affairs
University of Pittsburgh
Pittsburgh, Pennsylvania 15260

Phone: 412-648-7640
Fax: 412-648-7641
E-mail: gspia@pitt.edu
Web site: http://www.gspia.pitt.edu

University of Pittsburgh

THE FACULTY AND THEIR RESEARCH

Carolyn Ban, Professor; Ph.D., Stanford, 1975. Human resources management, public management, comparative administrative reform, reinventing government, program evaluation, ethics.

Michael J. Brenner, Professor; Ph.D., Berkeley, 1968. American foreign policy, international relations theory, international political economy, national security, policy analysis and evaluation.

R. Charli Carpenter, Assistant Professor; Ph.D., Oregon, 2003. International norms and identities, gender and violence, war crimes, comparative genocide studies, human rights, humanitarian action.

Siddarth Chandra, Associate Professor and Director of the Asian Studies Center; Ph.D., Cornell, 1997. Development economics, industrial organization, applied economics, economic history.

Louise K. Comfort, Professor and Director of the Interactive, Intelligent Spatial Information System; Ph.D., Yale, 1975. Organizational management, theory and behavior, policy analysis, program implementation and innovation, research methodology and modeling, information technology and public policy.

Phyllis D. Coontz, Associate Professor; Ph.D., Colorado, 1978. Social policy, research methodology, crime, elite professions.

Sabina E. Deitrick, Associate Professor, Co-Director of the Urban and Regional Analysis Program, University Center for Social and Urban Research, and Co-Director of Community Outreach Partnership Center; Ph.D., Berkeley, 1990. Regional planning, economic and community development, industrial geography.

George William Dougherty Jr., Assistant Professor and Coordinator of the Undergraduate Public Service Program; Ph.D., Georgia, 2000. Education policy, performance measurement, public law, transportation policy.

William N. Dunn, Professor; Ph.D., Claremont, 1969. Policy analysis and program evaluation, research methodology, knowledge utilization and public policy.

Angela Williams Foster, Assistant Professor; Ph.D., Carnegie Mellon, 2000. Quantitative methods, econometrics, multivariate analysis, research methods and policy analysis, housing policy, racial disparities in home ownership using hierarchical linear models, fair housing.

Shanti Gamper-Rabindran, Assistant Professor; Ph.D., MIT, 2001. Environment, health and development economics/policy methods, economics, Geographical Information Systems (GIS), program evaluation.

Donald M. Goldstein, Professor; Ph.D., Denver, 1970. National security, arms control, theory and practice of international affairs and relations, foreign policy process, military and world history.

Dennis M. Gormley, Senior Lecturer; M.A., Connecticut, 1966. Security and nonproliferation policy issues, technology and defense studies.

Leon L. Haley, Associate Professor and Director of the GSPIA Non-Profit Clinic; Ph.D., Pittsburgh, 1992. Public policy, nonprofit management, research methodology.

Kevin P. Kearns, Professor and Director of the Johnson Institute for Responsible Leadership; Ph.D., Pittsburgh, 1983. Strategic management, nonprofit management, public administration.

John T. S. Keller, Professor and Dean; Ph.D., Harvard, 1978. Comparative public policy, EU politics, transatlantic relations, American foreign policy.

William W. Keller, Posvar Professor of International Studies and Director of the Ridgway Center for International Security Studies; Ph.D., Cornell, 1986. National security.

Jerome B. McKinney, Professor; Ph.D., Missouri, 1969. Financial management, public-sector accounting, public budgeting, public management, economics.

John Mendeloff, Professor; Ph.D., Berkeley, 1977. Policy analysis, health policy, government regulation of risk.

David Y. Miller, Associate Professor and Associate Dean; Ph.D., Pittsburgh, 1988. Local government, political culture, regional governance systems, municipal budgeting.

Clyde E. Mitchell-Weaver, Associate Professor; Ph.D., UCLA, 1982. Economic development, sectoral and spatial planning, regional trading blocs, international organization, developing countries.

Lisa S. Nelson, Assistant Professor; Ph.D., Wisconsin, 1998. Law and politics, criminal justice, constitutional law, jurisprudence, American judicial process, political theory, American politics and institutions.

Paul J. Nelson, Assistant Professor; Ph.D., Wisconsin, 1991. Political economy and organizational analysis of international organizations, military spending and quality of life, contract farming in Africa, popular politics of land distribution in Guatemala, participant action research methods.

Janne Nolan, Professor; Ph.D., Tufts. International security and foreign policy.

Louis A. Picard, Professor; Ph.D., Wisconsin, 1977. Development management and governance; political development; local-level politics; manpower planning; politics of rural development; Eastern, Southern, and West Africa; Horn of Africa; Latin America and Caribbean.

Simon F. Reich, Professor and Director of the Ford Institute for Human Security; Ph.D., Cornell, 1988. Comparative politics, international relations, international political economy.

Nita Rudra, Assistant Professor; Ph.D., USC, 2000. International political economy, politics of welfare in developing countries.

Martin Staniland, Professor; Ph.D., Cambridge, 1983. International political economy, economic policy in the European Union, commercial aviation and trade in services, negotiation and conflict resolution.

Aaron M. Swoboda, Assistant Professor; Ph.D., Berkeley, 2005. Urban economics, environmental and natural resource economics, public economics, microeconomics, econometrics.

Nuno S. Themudo, Assistant Professor; Ph.D., London School of Economics, 2003. NGO management and development policy, civil society and public affairs, international institutions and governance, environmental management.

Lee S. Weinberg, Associate Professor; Ph.D., 1973, J.D., 1976, Pittsburgh. Criminal law and procedure, constitutional law, law and politics, psychiatry and law, legal studies, public policy in law enforcement.

Harvey L. White, Associate Professor; Ph.D., North Carolina, 1985. Financial administration, urban administration, intergovernmental relations and finance, environmental management, sustainable development, environmental justice, computer applications and quantitative methods.

Phil Williams, Professor; Ph.D., Southampton, 1988. Strategic studies, transnational organized crime, drug trafficking, foreign policy analysis, international relations.

Section 26
Social Sciences

This section contains a directory of institutions offering graduate work in social sciences, followed by in-depth entries submitted by institutions that chose to prepare detailed program descriptions. Additional information about programs listed in the directory but not augmented by an in-depth entry may be obtained by writing directly to the dean of a graduate school or chair of a department at the address given in the directory.

For programs offering related work, see also in this book *Area and Cultural Studies, Communication and Media, Criminology and Forensics, Economics, Geography, Family and Consumer Sciences, Political Science and International Affairs, Psychology and Counseling,* and *Sociology, Anthropology, and Archaeology.*

CONTENTS

Program Directory

Close-Ups

See also:

Social Sciences

Arizona State University, Graduate College, College of Liberal Arts and Sciences, Division of Social Sciences, Tempe, AZ 85287. Offers MA, MAS, MS, PhD, MA/MS.

Arkansas Tech University, Graduate School, School of Liberal and Fine Arts, Russellville, AR 72801. Offers communication (MLA); English (M Ed, MA); fine arts (MLA); history (MA); multi-media journalism (MA); social science (MLA); social studies (M Ed); Spanish (MA, MLA); teaching English as a second language (MA, MLA). Part-time programs available. *Students:* 54 full-time (43 women), 79 part-time (54 women); includes 11 minority (3 African Americans, 1 American Indian/Alaska Native, 1 Asian American or Pacific Islander, 6 Hispanic Americans), 29 international. Average age 33. In 2007, 71 degrees awarded. *Degree requirements:* For master's, project. *Entrance requirements:* For master's, GRE General Test or MAT. Additional exam requirements/recommendations for international students: Required—TOEFL (minimum score 500 paper-based; 173 computer-based; 61 iBT). *Application deadline:* For fall admission, 3/1 priority date for domestic students, 5/1 priority date for international students; for winter admission, 10/1 priority date for international students; for spring admission, 10/1 priority date for domestic and international students. Applications are processed on a rolling basis. Application fee: $0 ($30 for international students). Electronic applications accepted. *Expenses:* Tuition, state resident: full-time $3,150; part-time $175 per hour. Tuition, nonresident: full-time $6,300; part-time $350 per hour. Required fees: $384; $8 per hour. $120 per term. Tuition and fees vary according to course load. *Financial support:* In 2007–08, teaching assistantships with full tuition reimbursements (averaging $4,000 per year); career-related internships or fieldwork, Federal Work-Study, scholarships/grants, health care benefits, and unspecified assistantships also available. Support available to part-time students. Financial award application deadline: 4/15; financial award applicants required to submit FAFSA. *Unit head:* Dr. Georgena Duncan, Dean, 479-968-0266, Fax: 479-968-0275, E-mail: georgena.duncan@atu.edu. *Application contact:* Dr. Eldon G. Clary, Dean of Graduate School, 479-968-0398, Fax: 479-964-0542, E-mail: graduate.school@atu.edu.

Ball State University, Graduate School, College of Sciences and Humanities, Program in Social Sciences, Muncie, IN 47306-1099. Offers MA. *Students:* Average age 23. 2 applicants, 50% accepted, 1 enrolled.Application fee: $25 ($35 for international students). *Expenses:* Tuition, state resident: full-time $6,864. Tuition, nonresident: full-time $17,932. Required fees: $1,866. *Financial support:* Application deadline: 3/1. *Unit head:* Christopher Thompson, Coordinator, 765-285-8700, Fax: 765-285-5612.

California Institute of Technology, Division of the Humanities and Social Sciences, Social Science Program, Pasadena, CA 91125-0001. Offers economics (PhD); political science (PhD); social science (MS). *Faculty:* 29 full-time (3 women). *Students:* 37 full-time (10 women); includes 9 minority (7 Asian Americans or Pacific Islanders, 2 Hispanic Americans), 14 international. Average age 26. 186 applicants, 10% accepted, 11 enrolled. In 2007, 5 master's, 7 doctorates awarded. Terminal master's awarded for partial completion of doctoral program. *Degree requirements:* For doctorate, thesis/dissertation. *Entrance requirements:* For doctorate, GRE General Test. *Application deadline:* For fall admission, 1/1 for domestic students. Application fee: $80. Electronic applications accepted. *Financial support:* In 2007–08, 34 students received support, including 12 fellowships (averaging $25,000 per year), 16 research assistantships (averaging $25,000 per year), 10 teaching assistantships (averaging $25,000 per year); Federal Work-Study, institutionally sponsored loans, scholarships/grants, and unspecified assistantships also available. *Faculty research:* Individual and group decision making, design of political and economic institutions, experimental social science, public policy, quantitative history. *Application contact:* Laurel Auchampaugh, Graduate Secretary, 626-395-4206, Fax: 626-405-9841, E-mail: gradsec@hss.caltech.edu.

California State University, Chico, Graduate School, College of Behavioral and Social Sciences, Social Science Program, Chico, CA 95929-0445. Offers social science (MA); social science education (MA). *Students:* 9 full-time (all women), 8 part-time (5 women); includes 6 minority (2 African Americans, 1 Asian American or Pacific Islander, 3 Hispanic Americans). Average age 35. 4 applicants, 100% accepted, 3 enrolled. In 2007, 5 degrees awarded. *Degree requirements:* For master's, thesis or alternative. *Entrance requirements:* For master's, GRE General Test or MAT, statement of purpose. Additional exam requirements/recommendations for international students: Required—TOEFL (minimum score 550 paper-based; 213 computer-based; 80 iBT), IELTS (minimum score 7). *Application deadline:* For fall admission, 3/1 priority date for domestic students, 3/1 for international students; for spring admission, 9/15 priority date for domestic students, 9/15 for international students. Applications are processed on a rolling basis. Application fee: $55. Electronic applications accepted. *Financial support:* Fellowships, teaching assistantships available. *Unit head:* Dr. Gwen Sheldon, Graduate Coordinator, 530-895-5204.

California State University, San Bernardino, Graduate Studies, College of Social and Behavioral Sciences, Program in Social Sciences, San Bernardino, CA 92407-2397. Offers MA. *Faculty:* 1 full-time, 4 part-time/adjunct. *Students:* 15 full-time (7 women), 15 part-time (7 women); includes 11 minority (7 African Americans, 4 Hispanic Americans), 1 international. Average age 35. 18 applicants, 33% accepted, 4 enrolled. In 2007, 8 degrees awarded. *Degree requirements:* For master's, comprehensive exam or thesis. *Entrance requirements:* For master's, minimum GPA of 3.5 in major, 2.5 overall. *Application deadline:* For fall admission, 8/31 priority date for domestic students. Application fee: $55. *Financial support:* Fellowships, research assistantships, teaching assistantships, career-related internships or fieldwork, Federal Work-Study, and institutionally sponsored loans available. Financial award application deadline: 5/1. *Unit head:* Dr. Randi Miller, Coordinator, 909-537-5546, Fax: 909-537-7645, E-mail: rmiller@csusb.edu.

California University of Pennsylvania, School of Graduate Studies and Research, College of Liberal Arts, Department of Sociology/Criminal Justice, California, PA 15419-1394. Offers social science—criminal justice (MA). Part-time and evening/weekend programs available. *Degree requirements:* For master's, comprehensive exam, thesis optional. *Entrance requirements:* For master's, MAT, minimum GPA of 3.0. Additional exam requirements/recommendations for international students: Required—TOEFL (minimum score 550 paper-based; 213 computer-based; 80 iBT). Electronic applications accepted. *Faculty research:* Ethics and law, ethics in police practice, law and morality, police policy, St. Thomas Aquinas and crime.

Campbellsville University, College of Arts and Sciences, Campbellsville, KY 42718-2799. Offers social science (MA). Part-time programs available. *Degree requirements:* For master's, comprehensive exam. *Entrance requirements:* For master's, GRE General Test, LSAT, minimum GPA of 2.9. Electronic applications accepted.

Carnegie Mellon University, College of Humanities and Social Sciences, Department of Social and Decision Sciences, Pittsburgh, PA 15213-3891. Offers behavioral decision theory (PhD); organization science (PhD); social and decision science (PhD). Terminal master's awarded for partial completion of doctoral program. *Degree requirements:* For doctorate, comprehensive exam, thesis/dissertation, research paper. *Entrance requirements:* For doctorate, GRE General Test. Additional exam requirements/recommendations for international students: Required—TOEFL. Electronic applications accepted. *Faculty research:* Organization theory, political science, sociology, technology studies.

Central European University, Graduate Studies, School of Social Sciences and Humanities, Budapest, Hungary. Offers economics (MA, PhD); gender studies (MA, PhD); international relations and European studies (MA, PhD); mathematics and its applications (MS, PhD); medieval studies (MA, PhD); nationalism studies (MA, PhD); philosophy (MA, PhD); political science (MA, PhD); public policy (MA, PhD); sociology and social anthropology (MA, PhD). *Faculty:* 75 full-time (25 women), 46 part-time/adjunct (10 women). *Students:* 625 full-time (355 women). Average age 26. 2,500 applicants, 31% accepted, 540 enrolled. In 2007, 325 master's, 20 doctorates awarded. Terminal master's awarded for partial completion of doctoral program. *Degree requirements:* For master's, one foreign language, thesis; for doctorate, one foreign language, comprehensive exam, thesis/dissertation. *Entrance requirements:* For master's, CEU subject tests, interview; for doctorate, GRE, CEU subject test, interview. Additional exam requirements/recommendations for international students: Required—TOEFL (minimum score 570 paper-based; 230 computer-based). *Application deadline:* For fall admission, 1/15 priority date for domestic and international students. Application fee: $0. Electronic applications accepted. Tuition charges are reported in euros. *Expenses:* Tuition: Full-time 10,000 euros; part-time 315 euros per credit. *Financial support:* In 2007–08, 402 students received support, including 350 fellowships with full and partial tuition reimbursements available (averaging $5,000 per year); career-related internships or fieldwork, institutionally sponsored loans, and scholarships/grants also available. Financial award application deadline: 1/5. *Faculty research:* Civil society, fiscal decentralization, party politics, political philosophy (especially Liberalism, theory of Democracy). Total annual research expenditures: $35,000. *Unit head:* Dr. Howard Michael Robinson, Provost, 361-327-3003, Fax: 361-327-3211, E-mail: robinson@ceu.hu. *Application contact:* Zsuzsanna Jaszberenyi, Admissions Officer, 361-327-3009, Fax: 361-327-3211, E-mail: admissions@ceu.hu.

See Close-Up on page 447.

The Citadel, The Military College of South Carolina, Citadel Graduate College, Department of Political Science and Criminal Justice, Charleston, SC 29409. Offers social science (MA). *Students:* 5 full-time (2 women), 21 part-time (7 women); includes 4 minority (all African Americans) Average age 32. In 2007, 8 degrees awarded. *Entrance requirements:* For master's, GRE General Test, MAT. Additional exam requirements/recommendations for international students: Required—TOEFL (minimum score 550 paper-based; 213 computer-based). *Application deadline:* Applications are processed on a rolling basis. Application fee: $30. *Expenses:* Tuition, state resident: part-time $280 per credit hour. Tuition, nonresident: part-time $503 per credit hour. *Financial support:* Application deadline: 7/1; *Unit head:* Dr. Gardel M. Feurtado, Head, 843-953-2037, Fax: 843-953-5066, E-mail: gardel.feurtado@citadel.edu. *Application contact:* Dr. Raymond S. Jones, Associate Dean, Citadel Graduate College, 843-953-5089, Fax: 843-953-7630, E-mail: ray.jones@citadel.edu.

College of the Humanities and Sciences, Harrison Middleton University, Graduate Program, Tempe, AZ 85282. Offers education (MA, Ed D); humanities (MA); imaginative literature (MA); jurisprudence (MA); natural science (MA); philosophy and religion (MA); social science (MA). Part-time and evening/weekend programs available. Postbaccalaureate distance learning degree programs offered (no on-campus study).

Columbia University, Graduate School of Arts and Sciences, Program in Quantitative Methods in the Social Sciences, New York, NY 10027. Offers MA. Part-time programs available. Application fee: $90. *Expenses:* Tuition: Part-time $1,452 per credit. Required fees: $152 per term. One-time fee: $75 part-time. Full-time tuition and fees vary according to course level, course load, degree level and program. *Unit head:* Christopher Weiss, Director, 212-854-7559, Fax: 212-854-7925, E-mail: cw2036@columbia.edu.

Eastern Michigan University, Graduate School, College of Arts and Sciences, Department of History and Philosophy, Program in Social Science, Ypsilanti, MI 48197. Offers social science (MA, Graduate Certificate); social science and American culture (MLS). Part-time and evening/weekend programs available. Postbaccalaureate distance learning degree programs offered (minimal on-campus study). *Students:* 3 full-time (2 women), 19 part-time (12 women); includes 3 minority (all African Americans) Average age 36. In 2007, 13 degrees awarded. *Degree requirements:* For master's, thesis optional. *Entrance requirements:* Additional exam requirements/recommendations for international students: Required—TOEFL. *Application deadline:* Applications are processed on a rolling basis. Application fee: $35. *Expenses:* Tuition, state resident: full-time $8,952; part-time $373 per credit hour. Tuition, nonresident: full-time $17,634; part-time $735 per credit hour. Required fees: $896; $34 per credit hour. Tuition and fees vary according to course level, degree level and program. *Financial support:* Fellowships, research assistantships with full tuition reimbursements, teaching assistantships with full tuition reimbursements, career-related internships or fieldwork, Federal Work-Study, institutionally sponsored loans, scholarships/grants, tuition waivers (partial), and unspecified assistantships available. Support available to part-time students. Financial award applicants required to submit FAFSA. *Application contact:* Dr. Jill Dieterle, Advisor, 734-487-0053, Fax: 734-487-6835, E-mail: jdieterle@emich.edu.

Edinboro University of Pennsylvania, Graduate Studies and Research, School of Liberal Arts, Department of History and Anthropology, Edinboro, PA 16444. Offers social sciences (MA). Part-time and evening/weekend programs available. *Faculty:* 4 full-time (2 women). *Students:* 29 full-time (10 women), 11 part-time (4 women); includes 3 minority (2 African Americans, 1 Asian American or Pacific Islander). Average age 32. In 2007, 6 degrees awarded. *Degree requirements:* For master's, thesis or alternative, competency exam. *Entrance requirements:* For master's, GRE or MAT, minimum QPA of 2.5. *Application deadline:* Applications are processed on a rolling basis. Application fee: $30. Electronic applications accepted. *Expenses:* Tuition, state resident: full-time $6,214; part-time $345 per credit. Tuition, nonresident: full-time $9,944; part-time $552 per credit. Required fees: $46 per credit. *Financial support:* In 2007–08, 9 research assistantships with full and partial tuition reimbursements (averaging $3,850 per year) were awarded; career-related internships or fieldwork, Federal Work-Study, institutionally sponsored loans, scholarships/grants, and unspecified assistantships also available. Support available to part-time students. Financial award application deadline: 2/15; financial award applicants required to submit FAFSA. *Unit head:* Dr. Jerra Jenrette, Chairperson, 814-732-1225, E-mail: jjenrette@edinboro.edu. *Application contact:* Dr. R. Scott Baldwin, Dean, 814-732-2752, Fax: 814-732-2268, E-mail: sbaldwin@edinboro.edu.

Florida Agricultural and Mechanical University, Division of Graduate Studies, Research, and Continuing Education, College of Arts and Sciences, Division of History and Political Sciences, Program in Applied Social Science, Tallahassee, FL 32307-3200. Offers African American history (MASS); criminal justice (MASS); economics (MASS); history (MASS); political science (MASS); public administration (MASS); public management (MASS); social work (MASS); sociology (MASS). Part-time programs available. *Degree requirements:* For master's, thesis optional. *Entrance requirements:* For master's, GRE General Test, minimum GPA of 3.0. *Faculty research:* Southern history, black history, election trends, presidential history.

George Mason University, College of Science, Fairfax, VA 22030. Offers biodefense (MS, PhD); bioinformatics and computational biology (MS, PhD, Certificate); biology (MS, PhD), including bioinformatics (MS), ecology, systematics and evolution (MS), interpretive biology (MS), molecular and cellular biology (MS), molecular and microbiology (PhD), organismal biology (MS); chemistry and biochemistry (MS), including chemistry; climate dynamics (PhD); computational and data sciences (MS, PhD, Certificate); computational social science (PhD); computational techniques and applications (Certificate); earth systems and geoinformation sciences (MS, PhD, Certificate); environmental science and policy (MS, PhD); geography (MS), including geographic and cartographic sciences; mathematical sciences (MS, PhD), including mathematics; nanotechnology and nanoscience (Certificate); neuroscience (PhD); physical sciences (PhD); physics and astronomy (MS), including applied and engineering physics; remote sensing and earth image processing (Certificate). Part-time and evening/weekend programs available. *Degree requirements:* For doctorate, comprehensive exam, thesis/dissertation. *Entrance requirements:* For master's and doctorate, GRE General Test, minimum GPA of 3.0 in last 60 hours. Additional exam requirements/recommendations for international students: Required—TOEFL. Electronic applications accepted. *Faculty research:* Space sciences and astrophysics, fluid dynamics, materials modeling and simulation, bioinformatics, global changes and statistics.

Graduate Theological Union, Graduate Programs, Berkeley, CA 94709-1212. Offers art and religion (MA, PhD); biblical languages (MA); biblical studies (Old and New Testament) (MA, PhD, Th D); Buddhist studies (MA); Christian spirituality (MA, PhD); cultural and historical studies of religions (MA, PhD); ethics and social theory (PhD); history (MA, PhD, Th D); homiletics (MA, PhD, Th D); interdisciplinary studies (PhD, Th D); Jewish studies (MA, PhD, Certificate); liturgical studies (MA, PhD, Th D); Near Eastern religions (PhD); Orthodox Christian studies (MA); Orthodox studies (Certificate); religion and psychology (MA, PhD); religion and society/ethics and social theory (MA); systematic and philosophical theology (MA, PhD, Th D); women's studies in religion (Certificate); MA/M Div. *Accreditation:* ATS. *Faculty:* 119 full-time (44 women), 34 part-time/adjunct (9 women). *Students:* 317 full-time (152 women), 35 part-time (19 women); includes 49 minority (15 African Americans, 2 American Indian/Alaska Native, 21 Asian Americans or Pacific Islanders, 11 Hispanic Americans), 74 international. Average age 38. 257 applicants, 59% accepted, 79 enrolled. In 2007, 45 master's, 22 doctorates awarded. Terminal master's awarded for partial completion of doctoral program. *Median time to degree:* Of those who began their doctoral program in fall 1999, 52% received their degree in 8 years or less. *Degree requirements:* For master's, one foreign language, thesis; for doctorate, one foreign language, comprehensive exam, thesis/dissertation. *Entrance requirements:* For master's, GRE General Test; for doctorate, GRE General Test, MA or M Div. Additional exam requirements/recommendations for international students: Required—TOEFL. *Application deadline:* For fall admission, 12/15 for domestic and international students; for winter admission, 2/15 for domestic and international students; for spring admission, 9/30 for domestic and international students. Application fee: $40. Electronic applications accepted. *Expenses:* Tuition: Full-time $13,310. Tuition and fees vary according to degree level and program. *Financial support:* In 2007–08, 122 students received support, including 109 fellowships (averaging $11,581 per year), 1 research assistantship (averaging $3,000 per year), 22 teaching assistantships (averaging $3,500 per year); Federal Work-Study, scholarships/grants, and tuition waivers (partial) also available. Support available to part-time students. Financial award application deadline: 2/1; financial award applicants required to submit FAFSA. *Unit head:* Dr. Arthur G. Holder, Dean, 510-649-2440, Fax: 510-649-1417, E-mail: aholder@gtu.edu. *Application contact:* Dr. Kathleen Kook, Assistant Dean for Admissions, 800-826-4488, Fax: 510-649-1730, E-mail: gtuadm@gtu.edu.

Hollins University, Graduate Programs, Program in Liberal Studies, Roanoke, VA 24020-1603. Offers humanities (MALS); interdisciplinary studies (MALS); justice and legal studies (MALS); liberal studies (CAS); social science (MALS); visual and performing arts (MALS). Part-time and evening/weekend programs available. *Faculty:* 9 full-time (2 women), 12 part-time/adjunct (5 women). *Students:* 20 full-time (17 women), 89 part-time (74 women); includes 15 minority (11 African Americans, 1 American Indian/Alaska Native, 2 Asian Americans or Pacific Islanders, 1 Hispanic American). Average age 39. 30 applicants, 93% accepted, 20 enrolled. In 2007, 48 degrees awarded. *Degree requirements:* For master's, thesis. *Entrance requirements:* For master's, letters of recommendation, interview. Additional exam requirements/recommendations for international students: Required—TOEFL (minimum score 550 paper-based; 213 computer-based). *Application deadline:* For fall admission, 7/1 priority date for domestic and international students; for spring admission, 12/10 priority date for domestic and international students. Applications are processed on a rolling basis. Application fee: $40. Electronic applications accepted. *Expenses:* Tuition: Part-time $265 per credit hour. Tuition and fees vary according to course load and program. *Financial support:* In 2007–08, 53 students received support, including 4 fellowships (averaging $1,060 per year); Federal Work-Study and scholarships/grants also available. Support available to part-time students. Financial award application deadline: 7/15; financial award applicants required to submit FAFSA. *Faculty research:* Elderly blacks, film, feminist economics, U.S. voting patterns, Wagner, diversity. *Unit head:* Dr. Edward A. Lynch, Director, 540-362-6475, Fax: 540-362-6288, E-mail: elynch@hollins.edu. *Application contact:* Cathy S. Koon, Manager of Graduate Services, 540-362-6326, Fax: 540-362-6288, E-mail: ckoon@hollins.edu.

Humboldt State University, Graduate Studies, College of Arts, Humanities, and Social Sciences, Program in Environment and Community, Arcata, CA 95521-8299. Offers MA. *Students:* 30 full-time (21 women), 9 part-time (8 women); includes 9 minority (1 African American, 1 American Indian/Alaska Native, 2 Asian Americans or Pacific Islanders, 5 Hispanic Americans). Average age 31. 57 applicants, 75% accepted, 29 enrolled. In 2007, 3 degrees awarded. *Degree requirements:* For master's, thesis or alternative, qualifying exam. *Entrance requirements:* For master's, minimum GPA of 2.5, 3 letters of recommendation. Additional exam requirements/recommendations for international students: Required—TOEFL (minimum score 500 paper-based; 173 computer-based). *Application deadline:* For fall admission, 3/15 for domestic and international students. Applications are processed on a rolling basis. Application fee: $55. *Financial support:* Application deadline: 3/1; *Faculty research:* Geography, political science, ethnic studies, anthropology, economics. *Unit head:* Dr. John Meyer, Chair, 707-826-4494, Fax: 707-826-4496, E-mail: jmm7001@humboldt.edu. *Application contact:* Dr. Mark Baker, Coordinator, 717-826-3907, Fax: 717-826-4496, E-mail: jb141@humboldt.edu.

Indiana University Bloomington, School of Law, Bloomington, IN 47405-7000. Offers comparative law (MCL); juridical science (SJD); law (JD, LL M); law and social sciences (PhD); legal studies (Certificate); JD/MA; JD/MBA; JD/MLS; JD/MPA; JD/MS; JD/MSES. *Accreditation:* ABA. *Faculty:* 59 full-time (19 women), 19 part-time/adjunct (3 women). *Students:* 648 full-time (265 women), 120 part-time (50 women); includes 121 minority (48 African Americans, 2 American Indian/Alaska Native, 36 Asian Americans or Pacific Islanders, 35 Hispanic Americans), 97 international. Average age 27. 2,517 applicants, 39% accepted, 214 enrolled. In 2007, 202 first professional degrees, 49 master's, 3 doctorates awarded. *Median time to degree:* Of those who began their doctoral program in fall 1999, 100% received their degree in 8 years or less. *Degree requirements:* For master's, thesis or practicum; for doctorate, thesis/dissertation (for some programs); for JD, research seminar. *Entrance requirements:* For JD, LSAT; for master's, LSAT, 3 letters of recommendation, law degree or license to practice, 3-5 years of experience; for doctorate, LSAT, 3 letters of recommendation, LL M or JD. Additional exam requirements/recommendations for international students: Required—TOEFL (minimum score 560 paper-based; 213 computer-based; 80 iBT). *Application deadline:* For fall admission, 3/1 priority date for domestic and international students. Applications are processed on a rolling basis. Application fee: $35 ($60 for international students). Electronic applications accepted. *Financial support:* In 2007–08, 581 students received support, including 456 fellowships (averaging $9,294 per year), 99 research assistantships (averaging $850 per year), 5 teaching assistantships (averaging $3,000 per year); career-related internships or fieldwork, Federal Work-Study, institutionally sponsored loans, scholarships/grants, health care benefits, and unspecified assistantships also available. Financial award application deadline: 3/1; financial award applicants required to submit FAFSA. *Faculty research:* Environmental risk assessment and policy analysis, information privacy and security, judicial independence, accountability, ethics. Total annual research expenditures: $1.4 million. *Unit head:* Lauren K. Robel, Dean, 812-855-8885, Fax: 812-855-7057, E-mail: lrobel@indiana.edu. *Application contact:* Abby S. Yankovich, Director of Admissions, 812-855-2704, Fax: 812-855-0555, E-mail: ayankovi@indiana.edu.

The Johns Hopkins University, Bloomberg School of Public Health, Department of Health, Behavior and Society, Baltimore, MD 21218-2699. Offers behavioral sciences and health education (MHS); genetic counseling (Sc M); social and behavioral sciences (PhD, Sc D). *Faculty:* 36 full-time (27 women), 35 part-time/adjunct (24 women). *Students:* 79 full-time (74 women), 9 part-time (8 women); includes 24 minority (11 African Americans, 1 American Indian/Alaska Native, 8 Asian Americans or Pacific Islanders, 4 Hispanic Americans), 10 international. Average age 27. 197 applicants, 41% accepted, 33 enrolled. In 2007, 8 master's, 4 doctorates awarded. *Degree requirements:* For master's, comprehensive exam (for some programs), thesis (for some programs); for doctorate, comprehensive exam, thesis/dissertation. *Entrance requirements:* For master's and doctorate, GRE, transcripts, curriculum vitae, statement, 3 recommendation letters. Additional exam requirements/recommendations for international students: Required—TOEFL (minimum score 250 computer-based; 100 iBT). *Application deadline:* For fall admission, 12/1 for domestic and international students. Electronic applications accepted. *Financial support:* In 2007–08, 89 students received support, including 2 fellowships with tuition reimbursements available (averaging $24,000 per year), 7 teaching assistantships (averaging $4,770 per year); career-related internships or fieldwork, Federal Work-Study, scholarships/grants, traineeships, health care benefits, and unspecified assistantships also available. Financial award application deadline: 3/15. *Faculty research:* Structural and community-level inventions to improve health communication and health education behavioral and social aspects of genetic counseling. Total annual research expenditures: $4.6 million. *Unit head:* Georgean Smith, Administrator, 410-502-3715, Fax: 410-502-4333, E-mail: gesmith@jhsph.edu. *Application contact:* Barbara W. Diehl, Senior Academic Program Coordinator, 410-502-4415, Fax: 410-502-4333, E-mail: bdiehl@jhsph.edu.

Lincoln University, School of Graduate Studies and Continuing Education, College of Liberal Arts, Education and Journalism, Department of Social and Behavioral Sciences, Jefferson City, MO 65102. Offers history (MA); social science (MA), including history, political science, sociology; sociology (MA); sociology/criminal justice (MA). Part-time and evening/weekend programs available. *Faculty:* 12 part-time/adjunct (4 women). *Students:* 13 full-time (9 women), 17 part-time (7 women); includes 16 minority (13 African Americans, 1 American Indian/Alaska Native, 2 Hispanic Americans), 3 international. Average age 33. 9 applicants, 89% accepted, 5 enrolled. In 2007, 6 degrees awarded. *Degree requirements:* For master's, comprehensive exam, thesis optional. *Entrance requirements:* For master's, GRE General Test or MAT, 15 undergraduate hours of course work in social science including 6 hours upper-division, with 9 hours in the area of concentration; see parent units for general requirements. Additional exam requirements/recommendations for international students: Required—TOEFL (minimum score 500 paper-based; 173 computer-based; 61 iBT). *Application deadline:* For fall admission, 7/1 priority date for domestic and international students; for spring admission, 12/1 priority date for domestic and international students. Applications are processed on a rolling basis. Application fee: $20. *Expenses:* Tuition, state resident: full-time $5,400; part-time $225 per credit hour. Tuition, nonresident: full-time $10,020; part-time $417 per credit hour. Required fees: $360; $15 per credit hour. $20 per semester. *Financial support:* Federal Work-Study and scholarships/grants available. Financial award application deadline: 4/1; financial award applicants required to submit FAFSA. *Faculty research:* Suicide prevention. *Unit head:* Dr. Antonio Holland, Department Head, 573-681-5145, Fax: 573-681-5150, E-mail: hollanda@lincolnu.edu.

Long Island University, Brooklyn Campus, Richard L. Conolly College of Liberal Arts and Sciences, Program in Social Science, Brooklyn, NY 11201-8423. Offers history (MS); United Nations studies (Certificate). Part-time and evening/weekend programs available. *Entrance requirements:* For master's, 2 letters of recommendation. Additional exam requirements/recommendations for international students: Required—TOEFL (minimum score 500 paper-based; 173 computer-based). Electronic applications accepted.

Long Island University, C.W. Post Campus, School of Education, Department of Curriculum and Instruction, Brookville, NY 11548-1300. Offers adolescence education (MS); adolescence education: biology (MS); adolescence education: earth science (MS); adolescence education: English (MS); adolescence education: mathematics (MS); adolescence education: social studies (MS); adolescence education: Spanish (MS); art education (MS); bilingual education (MS); childhood education (MS); early childhood education (MS); middle childhood education (MS); music education (MS); teaching English to speakers of other languages (MS). Part-time and evening/weekend programs available. *Faculty:* 12 full-time (9 women), 64 part-time/adjunct (28 women). *Students:* 140 full-time (111 women), 274 part-time (210 women); includes 45 minority (14 African Americans, 2 American Indian/Alaska Native, 12 Asian Americans or Pacific Islanders, 17 Hispanic Americans), 2 international. Average age 29. 208 applicants, 71% accepted, 77 enrolled. In 2007, 260 degrees awarded. *Degree requirements:* For master's, comprehensive exam or thesis, student teaching. *Entrance requirements:* For master's, minimum GPA of 2.75 in major, 2.5 overall. *Application deadline:* Applications are processed on a rolling basis. Application fee: $30. Electronic applications accepted. *Expenses:* Tuition: Part-time $825 per credit. Tuition and fees vary according to course load. *Financial support:* In 2007–08, 4 research assistantships were awarded; career-related internships or fieldwork and Federal Work-Study also available. Support available to part-time students. Financial award application deadline: 5/15; financial award applicants required to submit CSS PROFILE or FAFSA. *Faculty research:* Ethics and education, teaching strategies. *Unit head:* Dr. Kathy Ludteg, Chair, 516-299-2374, Fax: 516-299-3312, E-mail: kathy.ludteg@liu.edu. *Application contact:* Gail Maerz, Academic Counselor, 516-299-2155, Fax: 516-299-3312.

Massachusetts Institute of Technology, School of Humanities, Arts, and Social Sciences, Program in Science, Technology, and Society, Cambridge, MA 02139-4307. Offers history, anthropology, and science, technology and society (PhD). *Faculty:* 11 full-time (4 women). *Students:* 28 full-time (16 women); includes 4 minority (2 American Indian/Alaska Native, 2 Asian Americans or Pacific Islanders), 5 international. Average age 30. 93 applicants, 8% accepted, 6 enrolled. In 2007, 7 doctorates awarded. *Degree requirements:* For doctorate, comprehensive exam, thesis/dissertation. *Entrance requirements:* For doctorate, GRE General Test. Additional exam requirements/recommendations for international students: Required—TOEFL (minimum score 577 paper-based; 233 computer-based). *Application deadline:* For fall admission, 1/1 for domestic and international students. Application fee: $70. Electronic applications accepted. *Expenses:* Tuition: Full-time $34,760; part-time $545 per unit. Required fees: $236. *Financial support:* In 2007–08, 25 students received support, including 17 fellowships with tuition reimbursements available (averaging $25,765 per year), 1 research assistantship, 5 teaching assistantships with tuition reimbursements available (averaging $27,000 per year); Federal Work-Study, institutionally sponsored loans, scholarships/grants, traineeships, health care benefits, and unspecified assistantships also available. *Faculty research:* History of science; history of technology; sociology of science and technology; anthropology of science and technology; science, technology, and society. Total annual research expenditures:$563,000. *Unit head:* Prof. David A. Mindell, Director, 617-253-4062, Fax: 617-258-8118. *Application contact:* Karen Gardner, Student Contact, 617-253-9759, Fax: 617-258-8118, E-mail: hasts@mit.edu.

Michigan State University, The Graduate School, College of Social Science, Interdisciplinary Studies in Social Science—Global Applications, East Lansing, MI 48824. Offers MA. *Degree requirements:* For master's, internship/practicum or field experience, policy paper or analytical report. *Entrance requirements:* Additional exam requirements/recommendations for international students: Required—TOEFL, Michigan State University ELT (85), Michigan English Language Assessment Battery (83). Electronic applications accepted. *Expenses:* Tuition, state resident: part-time $379 per credit hour. Tuition, nonresident: part-time $800 per credit hour. Tuition and fees vary according to program.

Mississippi College, Graduate School, College of Arts and Sciences, School of Humanities and Social Sciences, Department of History and Political Science, Clinton, MS 39058. Offers administration of justice (MSS); history (M Ed, MA, MSS); paralegal studies (Certificate); political science (MSS); social sciences (M Ed, MSS). Part-time programs available. *Faculty:* 5 full-time (1 woman), 2 part-time/adjunct (0 women). *Students:* 12 full-time (7 women), 17 part-time (14 women); includes 7 minority (6 African Americans, 1 American Indian/Alaska Native), 1 international. Average age 27. In 2007, 5 master's, 2 other advanced degrees awarded. *Degree requirements:* For master's, one foreign language, comprehensive exam, thesis (for some programs). *Entrance requirements:* For master's, GRE or NTE, minimum GPA of 2.5. Additional exam requirements/recommendations for international students: Recommended—IELTS. *Application deadline:* For fall admission, 8/15 priority date for domestic students. Applications are processed on a rolling basis. Application fee: $25. Electronic applications accepted. *Expenses:* Tuition: Full-time $7,470; part-time $415 per hour. Required fees: $1,160 per term. Part-time tuition and fees vary according to course load and degree level. *Financial support:* Teaching assistantships, Federal Work-Study, scholarships/grants, and unspecified assistantships available. Support available to part-time students. Financial award application deadline: 4/1; financial award applicants required to submit FAFSA. *Unit head:* Dr. Kirk Ford, Chair, 601-925-3326, E-mail: ford@mc.edu.

Social Sciences

Montclair State University, The Office of Graduate Admissions and Support Services, College of Education and Human Services, Department of Curriculum and Teaching, Montclair, NJ 07043-1624. Offers education (M Ed); educational technology (M Ed); learning disabled teacher consultant (Certificate); school library media specialist (Certificate); teaching (MAT, Certificate), including art (MAT), biological science (MAT), early childhood education (P-3) (MAT), earth science (MAT), elementary education (K-8) (MAT), English (MAT), French (MAT), health and physical education (MAT), health education (MAT), home economics (MAT), mathematics (MAT), music (MAT), physical education (MAT), physical science (MAT), social studies (MAT), Spanish (MAT), teacher of ESL (MAT), teacher of students with disabilities (MAT). Part-time and evening/weekend programs available. *Faculty:* 17 full-time (13 women), 14 part-time/adjunct (10 women). *Students:* 118 full-time (86 women), 221 part-time (187 women); includes 50 minority (25 African Americans, 8 Asian Americans or Pacific Islanders, 17 Hispanic Americans), 3 international. Average age 33. 305 applicants, 52% accepted, 124 enrolled. In 2007, 178 master's, 19 other advanced degrees awarded. *Degree requirements:* For master's, comprehensive exam, field experience. *Entrance requirements:* For master's, PRAXIS II, minimum GPA of 2.67, 2 letters of recommendation. Additional exam requirements/recommendations for international students: Required—TOEFL (minimum score 83 computer-based). *Application deadline:* For fall admission, 2/15 for domestic and international students; for spring admission, 9/15 for domestic and international students. Applications are processed on a rolling basis. Application fee: $60. Electronic applications accepted. *Financial support:* In 2007–08, 7 research assistantships with full tuition reimbursements (averaging $7,000 per year) were awarded; Federal Work-Study, scholarships/grants, and unspecified assistantships also available. Support available to part-time students. Financial award application deadline: 3/1; financial award applicants required to submit FAFSA. *Unit head:* Dr. Deborah Eldridge, Chairperson, 973-655-5187.

The New School: A University, The New School for Social Research, New York, NY 10011. Offers MA, MS, DS Sc, PhD. Part-time and evening/weekend programs available. *Faculty:* 84 full-time (33 women), 18 part-time/adjunct (4 women). *Students:* 808 full-time (418 women), 308 part-time (177 women); includes 168 minority (56 African Americans, 4 American Indian/Alaska Native, 41 Asian Americans or Pacific Islanders, 67 Hispanic Americans), 306 international. Average age 32. In 2007, 179 master's, 52 doctorates awarded. Terminal master's awarded for partial completion of doctoral program. *Degree requirements:* For doctorate, thesis/dissertation, qualifying exam. *Entrance requirements:* For master's, GRE General Test; for doctorate, GRE General Test, MA. Additional exam requirements/recommendations for international students: Required—TOEFL (minimum score 600 paper-based; 250 computer-based). *Application deadline:* For fall admission, 1/15 priority date for domestic students. Applications are processed on a rolling basis. Application fee: $50. *Expenses:* Contact institution. *Financial support:* Fellowships, research assistantships, teaching assistantships, career-related internships or fieldwork, Federal Work-Study, scholarships/grants, and tuition waivers (full and partial) available. Financial award application deadline: 3/1; financial award applicants required to submit FAFSA. *Faculty research:* Civil society and democracy, international movements of refugees, minority use of health services, memory, morality and genetics. *Unit head:* Dr. Michael Schober, Dean, 212-229-5777, E-mail: schober@newschool.edu. *Application contact:* Robert MacDonald, Director of Admissions, 800-523-5710 Ext. 3007, Fax: 212-989-7102, E-mail: macdonar@newschool.edu.

See Close-Up on page 1653.

New York University, Graduate School of Arts and Science, Program in Trauma and Violence Transdisciplinary Studies, New York, NY 10012-1019. Offers MA, Advanced Certificate. *Students:* 1 applicant, 100% accepted, 0 enrolled. *Application deadline:* For fall admission, 4/15 priority date for domestic students; for spring admission, 11/1 priority date for domestic students. Application fee: $85. *Financial support:* Application deadline: 4/14. *Application contact:* Roberta Popik, Associate Dean of Enrollment, 212-998-8050, Fax: 212-995-4557, E-mail: gsas.admissions@nyu.edu.

North Dakota State University, College of Graduate and Interdisciplinary Studies, College of Arts, Humanities and Social Sciences, Department of Sociology, Anthropology, and Emergency Management, Fargo, ND 58105. Offers emergency management (MS, PhD); social science (MA, MS); sociology (MS). Part-time programs available. *Faculty:* 8 full-time (3 women), 5 part-time/adjunct (2 women). *Students:* 20 full-time (13 women), 14 part-time (8 women); includes 1 minority (American Indian/Alaska Native), 3 international. Average age 27. 15 applicants, 60% accepted, 7 enrolled. In 2007, 7 degrees awarded. *Degree requirements:* For master's, thesis; for doctorate, comprehensive exam, thesis/dissertation. *Entrance requirements:* For master's, GRE (emergency management), course work in sociology, minimum GPA of 3.2; for doctorate, GRE, minimum GPA of 3.2. Additional exam requirements/recommendations for international students: Required—TOEFL. *Application deadline:* For fall admission, 4/1 priority date for domestic students. Applications are processed on a rolling basis. Application fee: $45 ($60 for international students). *Expenses:* Tuition, state resident: full-time $5,376; part-time $224 per credit. Tuition, nonresident: full-time $14,354; part-time $598 per credit. Required fees: $962; $40 per credit. Part-time tuition and fees vary according to course load and reciprocity agreements. *Financial support:* In 2007–08, 7 research assistantships with full tuition reimbursements (averaging $6,156 per year), 7 teaching assistantships with full tuition reimbursements (averaging $3,078 per year) were awarded; fellowships, career-related internships or fieldwork, Federal Work-Study, institutionally sponsored loans, and tuition waivers (full) also available. Support available to part-time students. Financial award application deadline: 4/15. *Faculty research:* Medical sociology, demography, ethnology, archaeology. Total annual research expenditures: $75,000. *Unit head:* Dr. Daniel J. Klenow, Chair, 701-231-8657, Fax: 701-231-1047, E-mail: daniel.klenow@ndsu.edu.

Northwestern University, The Graduate School, Interdepartmental Degree Programs, Program in Mathematical Methods in Social Science, Evanston, IL 60208. Offers MS.

Northwestern University, The Graduate School, Program in Law and Social Science, Evanston, IL 60208. Offers Certificate. *Degree requirements:* For Certificate, research project. *Faculty research:* Law and social science.

Nova Southeastern University, Graduate School of Humanities and Social Sciences, Department of Multi-Disciplinary Studies, Fort Lauderdale, FL 33314-7796. Offers college student affairs (MS); college student personnel administration (Certificate); cross-disciplinary studies (MA). Part-time programs available. Postbaccalaureate distance learning degree programs offered (no on-campus study). *Faculty:* 4 part-time/adjunct (2 women). *Students:* 24 full-time (15 women), 35 part-time (29 women); includes 24 minority (20 African Americans, 4 Hispanic Americans), 2 international. 45 applicants, 67% accepted, 30 enrolled. In 2007, 7 master's awarded. *Degree requirements:* For master's, comprehensive exam, thesis optional, portfolio. *Entrance requirements:* For master's, interview, minimum GPA of 3.0. Additional exam requirements/recommendations for international students: Required—TOEFL. *Application deadline:* For fall admission, 7/1 priority date for domestic and international students; for winter admission, 11/1 priority date for domestic and international students; for spring admission, 3/1 priority date for domestic and international students. Applications are processed on a rolling basis. Electronic applications accepted. *Financial support:* In 2007–08, 20 research assistantships with tuition reimbursements (averaging $13,000 per year) were awarded; career-related internships or fieldwork, Federal Work-Study, institutionally sponsored loans, and scholarships/grants also available. Financial award applicants required to submit CSS PROFILE. *Unit head:* Dr. Judith McKay, Senior Associate Dean, 954-262-3060, Fax: 954-262-3893, E-mail: mckayj@nsu.nova.edu. *Application contact:* Marcia Arango, Student Recruitment Coordinator, 954-262-3006, Fax: 954-262-3968, E-mail: marango@nsu.nova.edu.

See Close-Up on page 953.

Nyack College, Alliance Graduate School of Counseling, School of Social and Behavioral Sciences, Nyack, NY 10960-3698. Offers counseling (MA). *Faculty:* 19 full-time (3 women), 9 part-time/adjunct (1 woman). *Students:* 53 full-time (44 women), 172 part-time (151 women); includes 153 minority (84 African Americans, 1 American Indian/Alaska Native, 25 Asian Americans or Pacific Islanders, 43 Hispanic Americans), 5 international. Average age 37. In 2007, 54 degrees awarded. *Degree requirements:* For master's, thesis (for some programs). *Unit head:* Dr. Carol Diaz-Robles, Assistant Director, 845-358-1710. *Application contact:* Melanie Caraballo, Application Contact, 845-358-1710.

Ohio University, Graduate College, College of Arts and Sciences, Program in Social Sciences, Athens, OH 45701-2979. Offers MSS. Part-time and evening/weekend programs available. *Students:* 1 (woman) full-time, 14 part-time (7 women), 4 international. Average age 29. 3 applicants, 100% accepted, 2 enrolled. In 2007, 2 degrees awarded. *Degree requirements:* For master's, oral exam. *Entrance requirements:* For master's, minimum GPA of 2.75. Additional exam requirements/recommendations for international students: Required—TOEFL (minimum score 600 paper-based; 220 computer-based). *Application deadline:* Applications are processed on a rolling basis. Application fee: $50 ($55 for international students). Electronic applications accepted. *Financial support:* Federal Work-Study and institutionally sponsored loans available. Financial award application deadline: 3/15. *Unit head:* Dr. Marvin Fletcher, Coordinator, 740-593-2969, E-mail: mfletcher1@ohiou.edu.

Queens College of the City University of New York, Division of Graduate Studies, Social Science Division, Program in Social Sciences, Flushing, NY 11367-1597. Offers MASS. Part-time and evening/weekend programs available. *Students:* 5 applicants, 80% accepted, 2 enrolled. In 2007, 2 degrees awarded. *Degree requirements:* For master's, thesis. *Entrance requirements:* For master's, minimum GPA of 3.0. Additional exam requirements/recommendations for international students: Required—TOEFL. *Application deadline:* For fall admission, 4/1 for domestic students; for spring admission, 11/1 for domestic students. Applications are processed on a rolling basis. Application fee: $125. *Financial support:* Career-related internships or fieldwork, Federal Work-Study, institutionally sponsored loans, and tuition waivers (partial) available. Support available to part-time students. Financial award application deadline: 4/1; financial award applicants required to submit FAFSA. *Unit head:* Dr. Martin Hanlon, Graduate Adviser, 718-997-5510, E-mail: martin_hanlon@qc.edu. *Application contact:* Mario Caruso, Director of Graduate Admissions, 718-997-5200, Fax: 718-997-5193, E-mail: graduate_admissions@qc.edu.

Regis University, College for Professional Studies, MA Program, Denver, CO 80221-1099. Offers criminology (MA); fine arts administration (Certificate); language and communication (MA); mediation (Certificate); psychology (MA); self-designed major (MA); social justice, peace, and reconciliation (Certificate); social science (MA); technical communication (Certificate). Program also offered in Henderson and Las Vegas (Summerlin), NV. Part-time and evening/weekend programs available. Postbaccalaureate distance learning degree programs offered (minimal on-campus study). *Faculty:* 84. *Students:* 218 (167 women). Average age 41. In 2007, 52 degrees awarded. *Degree requirements:* For master's, thesis, research project. *Entrance requirements:* For master's, resumé, recommendations, essays. Additional exam requirements/recommendations for international students: Required—TOEFL (minimum score 213 computer-based), TWE (minimum score 5). *Application deadline:* For fall admission, 8/13 priority date for domestic students, 7/13 priority date for international students; for winter admission, 10/8 priority date for domestic students, 9/8 priority date for international students; for spring admission, 12/17 priority date for domestic students, 11/17 for international students. Applications are processed on a rolling basis. Application fee: $75. Electronic applications accepted. *Expenses:* Contact institution. *Financial support:* Federal Work-Study available. Support available to part-time students. Financial award application deadline: 3/15; financial award applicants required to submit FAFSA. *Faculty research:* Independent/nonresidential graduate study: new methods and models, adult learning and the capstone experience, Goal Setting, behavior of Adult students, Innovative Studies for Community Colleges. *Unit head:* Dr. Robert Collins, Chair, 303-458-4302, Fax: 303-964-5538. *Application contact:* Graduate Admissions, 800-677-9270 Ext. 4080, Fax: 303-964-5538, E-mail: masters@regis.edu.

Southern Oregon University, Graduate Studies, School of Social Sciences, Department of Psychology, Ashland, OR 97520. Offers applied psychology (MAP); human service-organizational training and development (MA, MS); social science (MA, MS), including professional counseling, psychology. Part-time programs available. *Degree requirements:* For master's, thesis, portfolio and oral defense. *Entrance requirements:* For master's, GRE General Test, minimum GPA of 3.0. Electronic applications accepted.

Southern University and Agricultural and Mechanical College, Graduate School, College of Arts and Humanities, Department of History, Baton Rouge, LA 70813. Offers social sciences (MA). Part-time programs available. *Faculty:* 10 full-time (4 women). *Students:* 23 full-time (16 women), 42 part-time (35 women); all minorities (63 African Americans, 1 American Indian/Alaska Native, 1 Asian American or Pacific Islander). Average age 25. 27 applicants, 67% accepted, 15 enrolled. In 2007, 18 degrees awarded. *Degree requirements:* For master's, thesis. *Entrance requirements:* For master's, GRE General Test. Additional exam requirements/recommendations for international students: Required—TOEFL (minimum score 525 paper-based; 193 computer-based). *Application deadline:* For fall admission, 4/15 priority date for domestic and international students; for spring admission, 11/1 priority date for domestic and international students. Applications are processed on a rolling basis. Application fee: $25. *Financial support:* In 2007–08, research assistantships (averaging $7,000 per year); scholarships/grants and unspecified assistantships also available. Financial award application deadline: 4/15; financial award applicants required to submit FAFSA. Total annual research expenditures: $230,000. *Unit head:* Dr. Raymond Lockett, Chairman, 225-771-3260, Fax: 225-771-5861.

Stony Brook University, State University of New York, School of Professional Development, Stony Brook, NY 11794. Offers biology -grade 7-12 (MAT); chemistry-grade 7-12 (MAT); coaching (Certificate); earth science-grade 7-12 (MAT); educational computing (Certificate); educational leadership (Advanced Certificate); English-grade 7-12 (MAT); environmental management (Certificate); French-grade 7-12 (MAT); German-grade 7-12 (MAT); human resource management (Certificate); information systems management (Certificate); Italian-grade 7-12 (MAT); liberal studies (MA); liberal studies online (MA); mathematics-grade 7-12 (MAT); operation research (Certificate); physics-grade 7-12 (MAT); school district business leadership (Advanced Certificate); social science and the professions (MPS), including environmental waste management, human resource management; social studies-grade 7-12 (MAT); Spanish-grade 7-12 (MAT). Part-time and evening/weekend programs available. Postbaccalaureate distance learning degree programs offered. *Faculty:* 1 full-time (0 women), 118 part-time/adjunct (45 women). *Students:* 322 full-time (202 women), 1,188 part-time (728 women); includes 164 minority (69 African Americans, 2 American Indian/Alaska Native, 29 Asian Americans or Pacific Islanders, 64 Hispanic Americans), 11 international. Average age 28. In 2007, 738 master's, 405 other advanced degrees awarded. *Degree requirements:* For master's, one foreign language, thesis or alternative. *Application deadline:* Applications are processed on a rolling basis. Application fee: $62. *Financial support:* In 2007–08, 5 teaching assistantships were awarded; fellowships, research assistantships, career-related internships or fieldwork also available. Support available to part-time students. *Unit head:* Dr. Paul J. Edelson, Dean, 631-632-7052, Fax: 631-632-9046, E-mail: paul.edelson@stonybrook.edu.

Syracuse University, Graduate School, Maxwell School of Citizenship and Public Affairs, Program in Social Sciences, Syracuse, NY 13244. Offers MS Sc, PhD. Part-time and evening/weekend programs available. Postbaccalaureate distance learning degree programs offered. *Students:* 42 full-time (27 women), 100 part-time (50 women); includes 19 minority (5 African Americans, 4 American Indian/Alaska Native, 4 Asian Americans or Pacific Islanders, 6 Hispanic Americans), 17 international. 39 applicants, 46% accepted, 11 enrolled. In 2007, 4 degrees awarded. *Degree requirements:* For doctorate, thesis/dissertation. *Entrance requirements:* For doctorate, GRE General Test. Additional exam requirements/recommendations for international students: Required—TOEFL. *Application deadline:* For fall admission, 1/10 priority date for domestic students. Applications are processed on a rolling basis. Application fee: $75. Electronic applications accepted. *Expenses:* Tuition: Full-time $18,216; part-time $1,012 per credit. Required fees: $980. Tuition and fees vary according to program. *Financial support:* Fellowships with tuition reimbursements, research assistantships with tuition reimbursements, teaching assistantships with full and partial tuition reimbursements, tuition waivers (partial) available. *Unit head:* Dr. Vernon Greene, Chair, 315-443-2275, Fax: 315-443-1463, E-mail: vgreene@maxwell.syr.edu. *Application contact:* Mary Olszewski, Information Contact, 315-443-2275, E-mail: mtolszew@maxwell.syr.edu.

Texas A&M International University, Office of Graduate Studies and Research, College of Arts and Sciences, Department of Social Sciences, Laredo, TX 78041-1900. Offers history (MA); political science (MA); public administration (MPA). *Faculty:* 8 full-time (3 women), 2 part-time/adjunct (1 woman). *Students:* 14 full-time (8 women), 65 part-time (34 women); includes 68 minority (1 Asian American or Pacific Islander, 67 Hispanic Americans), 4 international. Average age 34. 35 applicants, 97% accepted, 23 enrolled. In 2007, 10 degrees awarded. *Degree requirements:* For master's, thesis (for some programs). *Entrance requirements:* For master's, GRE General Test. Additional exam requirements/recommendations for international students: Required—TOEFL (minimum score 550 paper-based; 213 computer-based). *Application deadline:* For fall admission, 7/15 priority date for domestic students; for spring admission, 11/12 for domestic students. Applications are processed on a rolling basis. Application fee: $25. *Financial support:* In 2007–08, 29 students received support. Application deadline: 11/1. *Unit head:* Dr. William W. Riggs, Chair, 956-328-2540, E-mail: wriggs@tamiu.edu. *Application contact:* Rosie Espinoza-Dickinson, Director of Admissions, 956-326-2200, Fax: 956-326-2199, E-mail: enroll@tamiu.edu.

Texas A&M University–Commerce, Graduate School, College of Arts and Sciences, Department of History, Commerce, TX 75429-3011. Offers history (MA, MS); social sciences (M Ed, MS). Part-time programs available. *Faculty:* 4 full-time (2 women). *Students:* Average age 36. In 2007, 1 degree awarded. *Degree requirements:* For master's, comprehensive exam, thesis (for some programs). *Entrance requirements:* For master's, GRE General Test. *Application deadline:* For fall admission, 6/1 priority date for domestic students; for spring admission, 11/1 priority date for domestic students. Applications are processed on a rolling basis. Application fee: $0 ($25 for international students). Electronic applications accepted. *Financial support:* In 2007–08, research assistantships (averaging $7,875 per year), teaching assistantships (averaging $7,875 per year) were awarded; Federal Work-Study, institutionally sponsored loans, and scholarships/grants also available. Financial award application deadline: 5/1; financial award applicants required to submit FAFSA. *Faculty research:* American foreign policy, colonial America, Texas politics, Medieval England. *Unit head:* Dr. Judy Ford, Interim Head, 903-886-5226, Fax: 903-468-3230, E-mail: judy_ford@tamu_commerce.edu. *Application contact:* Tammi Thompson, Graduate Admissions Adviser, 843-886-5167, Fax: 843-886-5165, E-mail: tammi_thompson@tamu-commerce.edu.

Towson University, College of Graduate Studies and Research, Program in Social Science, Towson, MD 21252-0001. Offers MS. Part-time and evening/weekend programs available. *Faculty:* 7 full-time (2 women). *Students:* 4 full-time (all women), 20 part-time (10 women); includes 3 minority (all African Americans), 3 international. Average age 31. 10 applicants, 90% accepted, 6 enrolled. In 2007, 4 degrees awarded. *Entrance requirements:* For master's, minimum GPA of 3.0, 3 letters of recommendation, letter of intent. Additional exam requirements/recommendations for international students: Required—TOEFL. *Application deadline:* For fall admission, 10/15 priority date for domestic and international students; for spring admission, 4/15 priority date for domestic and international students. Applications are processed on a rolling basis. Application fee: $50. Electronic applications accepted. *Expenses:* Tuition, state resident: part-time $286 per credit. Tuition, nonresident: part-time $600 per credit. Required fees: $75 per credit. *Financial support:* Career-related internships or fieldwork, Federal Work-Study, and unspecified assistantships available. Support available to part-time students. Financial award application deadline: 4/1; financial award applicants required to submit FAFSA. *Faculty research:* Race and ethnicity, diplomatic history, sociology methodology, central Asian geography. *Unit head:* Nicole Dombrowski, Graduate Program Director, 410-704-2907, Fax: 410-704-5995, E-mail: ndombrowski@towson.edu. *Application contact:* 410-704-2501, Fax: 410-704-4675, E-mail: grads@towson.edu.

Universidad Nacional Pedro Henriquez Urena, Graduate School, Santo Domingo, Dominican Republic. Offers accounting and auditing (M Acct); animal production (M Agr); business administration (MBA, PhD); Caribbean tropical architecture (M Arch); conservation of monuments and cultural goods (M Arch); economics (M Econ); education (PhD); environmental engineering (MEE); horticulture (M Agr); hospital administration (PhD); humanities (PhD); international relations (MPS); management of natural resources (MNRM); project management (M Man, MPM); public administration (MPS); sanitary engineering (ME); social science (PhD); veterinary medicine (DVM).

University of California, Irvine, Office of Graduate Studies, School of Social Sciences, Irvine, CA 92697. Offers MA, PhD. *Students:* 343 full-time (168 women), 3 part-time (2 women); includes 79 minority (5 African Americans, 46 Asian Americans or Pacific Islanders, 28 Hispanic Americans), 68 international. In 2007, 60 master's, 26 doctorates awarded. *Degree requirements:* For doctorate, thesis/dissertation. *Entrance requirements:* For master's, GRE, minimum GPA of 3.0; for doctorate, GRE General Test, minimum GPA of 3.0. Additional exam requirements/recommendations for international students: Required—TOEFL (minimum score 550 paper-based; 213 computer-based). *Application deadline:* For fall admission, 1/15 priority date for domestic students; for winter admission, 10/15 priority date for domestic students. Applications are processed on a rolling basis. Application fee: $60. Electronic applications accepted. *Financial support:* Fellowships, research assistantships with full tuition reimbursements, teaching assistantships, institutionally sponsored loans, traineeships, health care benefits, and unspecified assistantships available. Financial award application deadline: 3/1; financial award applicants required to submit FAFSA. *Faculty research:* Mathematical modeling of perception and cognitive processes, economic analysis of transportation, impact of society's political system on its economy, exploration of authority structures and inequality in society. *Unit head:* Barbara Anne Dosher, Dean, 949-824-7373, E-mail: bdosher@uci.edu. *Application contact:* Diane Enriquez, Graduate Counselor, 949-824-5924, Fax: 949-824-3548, E-mail: dmvargas@uci.edu.

University of California, Santa Cruz, Division of Graduate Studies, Division of Humanities, Program in the History of Consciousness, Santa Cruz, CA 95064. Offers PhD. *Faculty:* 7 full-time (4 women). *Students:* 62 full-time (42 women), 3 part-time (2 women); includes 15 minority (4 African Americans, 2 American Indian/Alaska Native, 6 Asian Americans or Pacific Islanders, 3 Hispanic Americans), 6 international. 174 applicants, 13% accepted, 10 enrolled. In 2007, 7 doctorates awarded. *Degree requirements:* For doctorate, one foreign language, thesis/dissertation, qualifying exam. *Entrance requirements:* Additional exam requirements/recommendations for international students: Required—TOEFL (minimum score 550 paper-based; 220 computer-based). *Application deadline:* For fall admission, 12/1 for domestic students. Application fee: $60. *Expenses:* Tuition, nonresident: full-time $14,694. Required fees: $11,360. *Financial support:* Fellowships, teaching assistantships, Federal Work-Study, institutionally sponsored loans, scholarships/grants, and unspecified assistantships available. Financial award application deadline: 12/15. *Faculty research:* Interdisciplinary humanities and social sciences, political theory, cultural theory, feminist studies, literary theory. *Unit head:* Chairperson, 831-459-4310. *Application contact:* Judy L. Glass, Reporting Analyst for Graduate Admissions, 831-459-5906, Fax: 831-459-4843, E-mail: jlglass@ucsc.edu.

University of Chicago, Division of Social Sciences, Committee on Social Thought, Chicago, IL 60637-1513. Offers PhD. *Students:* 72. In 2007, 4 degrees awarded. *Degree requirements:* For doctorate, one foreign language, thesis/dissertation, exam. *Entrance requirements:* For doctorate, GRE General Test. Additional exam requirements/recommendations for international students: Required—TOEFL, IELTS (minimum score 7). *Application deadline:* For fall admission, 12/15 for domestic students, 10/15 for international students. Application fee: $55. Electronic applications accepted. *Financial support:* Fellowships, teaching assistantships, Federal Work-Study, institutionally sponsored loans, scholarships/grants, traineeships, health care benefits, and unspecified assistantships available. Financial award application deadline: 12/15; financial award applicants required to submit FAFSA. *Unit head:* Prof. Robert Pippin, Chair, 773-702-8410. *Application contact:* Office of the Dean of Students, 773-702-8415.

University of Chicago, Division of Social Sciences, Master of Arts Program in the Social Sciences, Chicago, IL 60637-1513. Offers AM. Part-time programs available. *Students:* 182. In 2007, 140 degrees awarded. *Degree requirements:* For master's, thesis. *Entrance requirements:* For master's, GRE General Test. Additional exam requirements/recommendations for international students: Required—TOEFL. *Application deadline:* For fall admission, 12/28 for domestic students. Application fee: $55. Electronic applications accepted. *Financial support:* Fellowships, Federal Work-Study, institutionally sponsored loans, and scholarships/grants available. Financial award application deadline: 12/28; financial award applicants required to submit FAFSA. *Unit head:* Prof. John J. MacAloon, Director, 773-702-8316. *Application contact:* Office of the Dean of Students, 773-702-8415.

See Close-Up on page 1655.

University of Colorado Denver, College of Liberal Arts and Sciences, Program in Social Science, Denver, CO 80217-3364. Offers MSS. Part-time and evening/weekend programs available. *Students:* 8 full-time (6 women), 27 part-time (19 women); includes 10 minority (3 African Americans, 2 American Indian/Alaska Native, 1 Asian American or Pacific Islander, 4 Hispanic Americans). Average age 34. 14 applicants, 71% accepted, 7 enrolled. In 2007, 14 degrees awarded. *Degree requirements:* For master's, thesis or alternative. *Entrance requirements:* For master's, GRE General Test, 18 hours of course work in social science, interview, minimum GPA of 2.75. Additional exam requirements/recommendations for international students: Required—TOEFL (minimum score 525 paper-based; 197 computer-based). *Application deadline:* For fall admission, 5/15 for domestic students; for spring admission, 10/15 for domestic students. Applications are processed on a rolling basis. Application fee: $50 ($75 for international students). Electronic applications accepted. *Financial support:* Research assistantships, teaching assistantships, Federal Work-Study available. Financial award application deadline: 3/1; financial award applicants required to submit FAFSA. *Unit head:* Myra Bookman, Director, 303-556-2496, Fax: 303-556-8100, E-mail: myra.bookman@cudenver.edu.

University of Florida, Graduate School, College of Public Health and Health Professions and College of Medicine, Programs in Public Health, Gainesville, FL 32611. Offers biostatistics (MPH); environmental health (MPH); epidemiology (MPH); public health management and policy (MPH); public health practice (MPH); social and behavioral sciences (MPH). *Faculty:* 10. *Entrance requirements:* For master's, GRE General Test, minimum GPA of 3.0. Additional exam requirements/recommendations for international students: Required—TOEFL (minimum score 550 paper-based; 213 computer-based). Application fee: $30. *Expenses:* Tuition, state resident: full-time $7,478. Tuition, nonresident: full-time $22,603. *Unit head:* Dr. Mary Peoples-Sheps, Associate Dean for Academic Affairs, 352-273-6084, Fax: 352-273-6448, E-mail: mpeoplessheps@phhp.ufl.edu. *Application contact:* Brigette Hart, Program Assistant, 352-273-6443, E-mail: bhart@phhp.ufl.edu.

University of Idaho, College of Graduate Studies, College of Natural Resources, Department of Conservation Social Sciences, Moscow, ID 83844-2282. Offers MS. *Students:* 26 (16 women). Average age 36. In 2007, 9 master's awarded. *Entrance requirements:* For master's, minimum GPA of 2.8. *Application deadline:* For fall admission, 8/1 for domestic students; for spring admission, 12/15 for domestic students. Application fee: $55 ($60 for international students). *Financial support:* Research assistantships, teaching assistantships available. Financial award application deadline: 2/15. *Unit head:* Dr. Steve Hollenhorst, Head, 208-885-7911.

University of Illinois at Springfield, Graduate Programs, College of Education and Human Services, Program in Human Services, Springfield, IL 62703-5407. Offers alcoholism and substance abuse (MA); child and family services (MA); gerontology (MA); social services administration (MA). Part-time and evening/weekend programs available. Postbaccalaureate distance learning degree programs offered. *Faculty:* 4 full-time (3 women), 2 part-time/adjunct (both women). *Students:* 36 full-time (30 women), 64 part-time (53 women); includes 23 minority (21 African Americans, 2 American Indian/Alaska Native), 1 international. Average age 36. 52 applicants, 62% accepted, 27 enrolled. In 2007, 10 degrees awarded. *Degree requirements:* For master's, thesis optional, internship. *Entrance requirements:* For master's, 2 letters of reference, minimum undergraduate GPA of 3.0, prerequisite courses in lifespan development and research methods, personal statement. Additional exam requirements/recommendations for international students: Required—TOEFL (minimum score 550 paper-based; 213 computer-based). *Application deadline:* For fall admission, 2/15 priority date for domestic and international students; for spring admission, 9/15 priority date for domestic and international students. Application fee: $50 ($60 for international students). *Expenses:* Tuition, state resident: full-time $5,424; part-time $226 per credit hour. Tuition, nonresident: part-time $553 per credit hour. Required fees: $618 per term. *Financial support:* In 2007–08, research assistantships with full tuition reimbursements (averaging $7,988 per year), teaching assistantships with full tuition reimbursements (averaging $7,988 per year) were awarded; career-related internships or fieldwork, scholarships/grants, health care benefits, and unspecified assistantships also available. Support available to part-time students. Financial award application deadline: 11/15. *Unit head:* Dr. Carolyn Peck, Program Administrator, 217-206-7577, Fax: 217-206-6775, E-mail: peck.carolyn@uis.edu.

University of Kansas, Research and Graduate Studies, College of Liberal Arts and Sciences, Department of Applied Behavioral Science, Lawrence, KS 66045. Offers applied behavioral science (MA); behavioral psychology (PhD); clinical child psychology (PhD); developmental and child psychology (PhD); human development (MA). *Faculty:* 18. *Students:* 38 full-time (27 women), 9 part-time (8 women); includes 7 minority (2 African Americans, 2 Asian Americans or Pacific Islanders, 3 Hispanic Americans), 2 international. Average age 33. 41 applicants, 17% accepted, 3 enrolled. In 2007, 7 master's, 9 doctorates awarded. Terminal master's awarded for partial completion of doctoral program. *Degree requirements:* For master's, thesis; for doctorate, thesis/dissertation, comprehensive oral and written exams, journal reviews. *Entrance requirements:* Additional exam requirements/recommendations for international students: Required—TOEFL, TWE. *Application deadline:* For fall admission, 1/15 priority date for domestic and international students. Application fee: $55 ($60 for international students). Electronic applications accepted. *Expenses:* Tuition, state resident: full-time $5,838. Tuition, nonresident: full-time $13,409. Tuition and fees vary according to program. *Financial support:* Fellowships, research assistantships with full and partial tuition reimbursements, teaching assistantships with full and partial tuition reimbursements, career-related internships or fieldwork, traineeships, tuition waivers (full), and unspecified assistantships available. Financial award application deadline: 2/1. *Faculty research:* Early childhood, developmental disabilities, community health and development, adults with disabilities, applied behavior analysis. *Unit head:* Edward K. Morris, Chair, 785-864-4840, Fax: 785-864-5202, E-mail: ekm@ku.edu. *Application contact:* Gregory J. Madden, Graduate Director, 785-864-4840, Fax: 785-864-5202, E-mail: gmadden@ku.edu.

University of Maryland, Baltimore County, Graduate School, Program in Gerontology, Baltimore, MD 21250. Offers aging policy for the elderly (PhD); epidemiology of aging (PhD); social, cultural, and behavioral sciences (PhD). Part-time programs available. *Faculty:* 22 part-time/adjunct (11 women). *Students:* 21 full-time (16 women), 5 part-time (all women); includes 4 minority (all African Americans), 3 international. Average age 33. 19 applicants, 37% accepted, 6 enrolled. In 2007, 2 degrees awarded. *Degree requirements:* For doctorate, comprehensive exam, thesis/dissertation. *Entrance requirements:* For doctorate, GRE General Test. Additional exam requirements/recommendations for international students: Required—TOEFL, TWE. *Application deadline:* For spring admission, 2/1 for domestic and international students. Application fee: $45. Electronic applications accepted. *Financial support:* In 2007–08, 4 fellowships with full tuition reimbursements (averaging $19,000 per year), 8 research assistantships with full tuition reimbursements (averaging $19,000 per year), 1 teaching assistantship

Social Sciences

University of Maryland, Baltimore County (continued)
with full tuition reimbursement (averaging $19,000 per year) were awarded; career-related internships or fieldwork, scholarships/grants, traineeships, health care benefits, tuition waivers (partial), and unspecified assistantships also available. Support available to part-time students. Financial award application deadline: 2/1. *Faculty research:* Aging and health policy, behavioral aspects of aging, caregiving, LTC, epidemiology of aging. Total annual research expenditures: $32 million. *Unit head:* Dr. Leslie Morgan, Co-Director, 410-455-2074, Fax: 410-455-1154, E-mail: lmorgan@umbc.edu. *Application contact:* Justine Golden, Academic Coordinator, 410-706-4926, E-mail: jgold002@umaryland.edu.

University of Michigan, School of Social Work, Interdisciplinary Program in Social Work and Social Science, Ann Arbor, MI 48109. Offers PhD. Offered through the Horace H. Rackham School of Graduate Studies. *Faculty:* 51 full-time (23 women), 47 part-time/adjunct (32 women). *Students:* 71; includes 19 minority (5 African Americans, 1 American Indian/Alaska Native, 8 Asian Americans or Pacific Islanders, 5 Hispanic Americans), 12 international. Average age 31. 114 applicants, 12% accepted, 13 enrolled. In 2007, 6 degrees awarded. *Degree requirements:* For doctorate, thesis/dissertation, oral defense of dissertation, preliminary exam. *Entrance requirements:* For doctorate, GRE General Test. Additional exam requirements/recommendations for international students: Required—TOEFL. *Application deadline:* For fall admission, 12/15 for domestic and international students. Application fee: $60 ($75 for international students). *Financial support:* In 2007–08, 59 students received support, including 34 fellowships with full tuition reimbursements available (averaging $15,000 per year), 19 research assistantships with full tuition reimbursements available (averaging $15,000 per year), 6 teaching assistantships with full tuition reimbursements available (averaging $18,546 per year); career-related internships or fieldwork, Federal Work-Study, scholarships/grants, traineeships, and tuition waivers (full and partial) also available. Financial award application deadline: 12/15. *Faculty research:* Substance abuse, child welfare, mental health, poverty, aging. Total annual research expenditures: $7.1 million. *Unit head:* Dr. Lorraine M. Gutierrez, Director, 734-763-5768, Fax: 734-615-3192, E-mail: lorraing@umich.edu. *Application contact:* Graduate Coordinator, E-mail: ssw.phd.info@umich.edu.

University of Michigan–Flint, College of Arts and Sciences, Program in Social Sciences, Flint, MI 48502-1950. Offers MA. Part-time programs available. *Faculty:* 3 full-time (1 woman), 2 part-time/adjunct (1 woman). *Students:* 11 full-time (6 women), 34 part-time (16 women); includes 10 minority (8 African Americans, 1 Asian American or Pacific Islander, 1 Hispanic American). Average age 36. 30 applicants, 87% accepted, 16 enrolled. *Entrance requirements:* Additional exam requirements/recommendations for international students: Required—TOEFL (minimum score 560 paper-based; 220 computer-based; 84 iBT), IELTS (minimum score 7). *Application deadline:* For fall admission, 8/1 for domestic students, 3/1 priority date for international students; for winter admission, 11/15 for domestic students, 7/1 priority date for international students; for spring admission, 3/15 for domestic students, 11/1 priority date for international students. Application fee: $55. *Expenses:* *Contact institution.* Tuition and fees vary according to course load, degree level and program. *Financial support:* In 2007–08, 4 research assistantships (averaging $3,850 per year) were awarded; Federal Work-Study, scholarships/grants, and unspecified assistantships also available. Support available to part-time students. Financial award application deadline: 6/1; financial award applicants required to submit FAFSA. *Unit head:* Dr. Roy Hanashiro, Director, 810-762-3366, Fax: 810-766-6789, E-mail: okuma@umflint.edu. *Application contact:* Bradley T. Maki, Director of Graduate Admissions, 810-762-3171, Fax: 810-766-6789, E-mail: bmaki@umflint.edu.

See Close-Up on page 1657.

University of Regina, Faculty of Graduate Studies and Research, Faculty of Arts, Department of Sociology and Social Studies, Regina, SK S4S 0A2, Canada. Offers social studies (MA, PhD); sociology (MA, PhD). *Faculty:* 12 full-time (5 women), 1 part-time/adjunct (0 women). *Students:* 12 full-time (8 women), 6 part-time (4 women). 7 applicants, 100% accepted, 6 enrolled. In 2007, 1 degree awarded. *Degree requirements:* For master's, thesis. *Entrance requirements:* Additional exam requirements/recommendations for international students: Required—TOEFL (minimum score 580 paper-based; 237 computer-based). *Application deadline:* Applications are processed on a rolling basis. Application fee: $85 ($100 for international students). Electronic applications accepted. *Financial support:* In 2007–08, 5 fellowships (averaging $15,750 per year), 1 research assistantship (averaging $13,875 per year), 2 teaching assistantships (averaging $13,060 per year) were awarded; scholarships/grants also available. Financial award application deadline: 6/15. *Faculty research:* Social justice, development and the environment, knowledge, technology, and society. *Unit head:* Dr. John Conway, Head, 306-585-4052, Fax: 306-585-4815, E-mail: john.conway@uregina.ca. *Application contact:* Dr. Henry Chow, Graduate Program Coordinator, 306-585-5604, Fax: 306-585-4815, E-mail: henry.chow@uregina.ca.

The University of Texas at Tyler, College of Arts and Sciences, Department of Social Sciences, Tyler, TX 75799-0001. Offers criminal justice (MS); public administration (MPA); sociology (MS). Part-time and evening/weekend programs available. Postbaccalaureate distance learning degree programs offered. *Faculty:* 15 full-time (2 women). *Students:* 3 full-time (2 women), 25 part-time (18 women); includes 5 minority (4 African Americans, 1 Hispanic American), 14 international. Average age 31. 18 applicants, 100% accepted, 11 enrolled. In 2007, 6 degrees awarded. *Degree requirements:* For master's, comprehensive exam. *Entrance requirements:* For master's, GRE General Test, minimum GPA of 3.0. *Application deadline:* Applications are processed on a rolling basis. Application fee: $0. *Expenses:* Tuition, state resident: part-time $627 per semester hour. Tuition, nonresident: part-time $908 per semester hour. Required fees: $107 per semester hour. Tuition and fees vary according to course load. *Financial support:* In 2007–08, 1 fellowship (averaging $1,000 per year), 2 research assistantships, 2 teaching assistantships were awarded; career-related internships or fieldwork, Federal Work-Study, and scholarships/grants also available. Support available to part-time students. Financial award application deadline: 7/1; financial award applicants required to submit FAFSA. *Faculty research:* Urban segregation, minority business, violent crime, gender discrimination. *Unit head:* Dr. Ken Wink, Chair, 903-566-7434, Fax: 903-565-5537, E-mail: kwink@mail.uttyl.edu. *Application contact:* Pam Morrow, Assistant to Dean for Enrollment Management, 903-566-7205, Fax: 903-566-7068, E-mail: pmorrow@uttyler.edu.

University of Wisconsin–Madison, Development Studies Program, Madison, WI 53706-1380. Offers PhD. *Degree requirements:* For doctorate, comprehensive exam, thesis/dissertation. Electronic applications accepted. *Faculty research:* Third world countries, theory and practice, socio-economic development.

Worcester Polytechnic Institute, Graduate Studies and Research, Programs in Interdisciplinary Studies, Worcester, MA 01609-2280. Offers bioscience administration (MS); impact engineering (MS); manufacturing engineering management (MS); power systems management (MS); social science (PhD); systems engineering (MS); systems modeling (MS). Part-time and evening/weekend programs available. *Faculty:* 1 part-time/adjunct (0 women). *Students:* 2 full-time (1 woman), 75 part-time (19 women); includes 10 minority (4 African Americans, 6 Asian Americans or Pacific Islanders), 3 international. 115 applicants, 57% accepted, 44 enrolled. In 2007, 19 master's, 1 doctorate awarded. *Degree requirements:* For master's, thesis; for doctorate, comprehensive exam, thesis/dissertation. *Entrance requirements:* For master's and doctorate, 3 letters of recommendation. Additional exam requirements/recommendations for international students: Required—TOEFL (minimum score 550 paper-based; 213 computer-based; 79 iBT), IELTS (minimum score 7). *Application deadline:* For fall admission, 1/15 priority date for domestic students; for spring admission, 10/15 priority date for domestic students. Application fee: $70. *Expenses:* Tuition: Part-time $1,089 per credit hour. *Financial support:* In 2007–08, 1 student received support, including 1 research assistantship with full tuition reimbursement available; unspecified assistantships also available. Financial award application deadline:1/15. Total annual research expenditures: $108,817. *Unit head:* Dr. Fred J. Looft, Head, 508-831-5231, Fax: 508-831-5491, E-mail: fjlooft@wpi.edu. *Application contact:* Lynne Dougherty, Administrative Assistant, 508-831-5301, Fax: 508-831-5717, E-mail: grad@wpi.edu.

Yale University, School of Medicine, School of Public Health, New Haven, CT 06520. Offers biostatistics (MPH, MS, PhD); chronic disease epidemiology (MPH, PhD); environmental health sciences (MPH, PhD); epidemiology of microbial diseases (MPH, PhD); global health (MPH); health management (MPH); health policy and administration (MPH, PhD); parasitology (PhD); social and behavioral sciences (MPH); MBA/MPH; MD/MPH; MPH/MA; MSN/MPH. MS and PhD offered through the Graduate School. Part-time programs available. Terminal master's awarded for partial completion of doctoral program. *Degree requirements:* For master's, thesis, internship; for doctorate, comprehensive exam, thesis/dissertation, residency. *Entrance requirements:* For master's, GMAT, GRE, or MCAT, previous undergraduate course work in mathematics and science; for doctorate, GRE General Test. Additional exam requirements/recommendations for international students: Required—TOEFL. Electronic applications accepted. Expenses: Contact institution. *Faculty research:* Genetic and emerging infections epidemiology, virology, cost/quality, vector biology, quantitative methods.

York University, Faculty of Graduate Studies, Faculty of Arts, Program in International Development Studies, Toronto, ON M3J 1P3, Canada. Offers MA.

THE NEW SCHOOL: A UNIVERSITY

The New School for Social Research

Programs of Study

The New School for Social Research, one of the eight schools that make up The New School, offers programs of study leading to four advanced degrees: Master of Arts, Master of Philosophy, Master of Science, and Doctor of Philosophy. In addition, interdisciplinary master's programs are offered in liberal studies and historical studies. The School offers graduate degrees in anthropology, economics, global finance, philosophy, political science, psychology (including clinical psychology, with a concentration in mental health and substance abuse counseling), and sociology.

A candidate for any of these degrees must satisfy the requirements established by both The New School for Social Research and the department of the student's major field of study. Students should make certain that they are familiar not only with the general requirements for the degree but also with specific departmental requirements. Students may participate in any of the programs on a part-time or full-time basis.

New School for Social Research doctoral students may take courses at the following universities: Columbia University (including Teachers College), the City University of New York Graduate School and University Center, Fordham University, New York University, Princeton University, Rutgers University at New Brunswick, and the State University of New York at Stony Brook.

For more information, students should visit http://www.socialresearch.newschool.edu.

Research Facilities

The New School library includes the holdings of the Raymond Fogelman Library, the Adam and Sophie Gimbel Design Library, the Harry Schermer Library, and the Husserl Archives. Matriculated students have library privileges at New York University's Elmer Holmes Bobst Library and at the Cooper Union Library. Academic computing facilities enable students to do computer-assisted research.

New School research facilities include psychology laboratories (video clinical training, perception, social-personality, experimental, developmental, and cognitive), the India China Institute, the Hannah Arendt Center, the Schwartz Center for Economic Policy Analysis, the Committee on Western European Studies, the Transregional Center for Democratic Studies, the East and Central Europe Program, the Husserl Archives, and the World Policy Institute. In addition, there are many other research facilities in the New York area available to students. For more information, students should visit http://www.newschool.edu/institutes.html.

Financial Aid

Matriculated students receive aid from a variety of public and private sources. The amount of assistance awarded to a student is based on financial need and academic performance. Students are encouraged to apply for fellowships and grants from sources other than The New School. Scholarships, fellowships, assistantships, loans, and Federal Work-Study awards are available. The University Scholars Program and the Diamond Fellowship Program provide scholarship grants to African American, Asian American, Latino, and Native American students. Numerous other special scholarships are described at http://www.socialresearch.newschool.edu/students/financial-aid-scholarships.htm.

Cost of Study

Tuition for 2008–09 is $1508 per credit, and fees are approximately $115 each term. For more information, students should visit http://www.newschool.edu/tuition.

Living and Housing Costs

The University Housing Office maintains a comprehensive resource center with apartment listings. University-run apartments and residence halls are also available. The cost of housing, food, transportation, books, and living expenses averages $17,000 annually. For more information, students should visit http://www.newschool.edu/studentservices.

Student Group

The total enrollment of The New School for Social Research is about 1,000 students. Students represent a range of age groups, academic backgrounds, and nationalities, coming to New York from throughout the nation and from more than seventy other countries.

Location

The New School is an urban university and is an integral part of New York City. The diverse and cosmopolitan community, the spirited intellectual and cultural life, and the concentration of wealth and power that characterize New York provide a vital context in which to study the complexity of modern society.

The University and The School

The New School is a leading university in New York City offering distinguished programs in design, liberal arts, the performing arts, and social and political science, leading to seventy graduate and undergraduate degrees. To learn more, students should visit http://www.newschool.edu/degreeprograms. A privately supported institution, The New School is accredited by the Commission on Higher Education of the Middle States Association of Colleges and Schools and chartered as a university by the Regents of the State of New York.

The New School for Social Research was founded in 1919 by a distinguished group of intellectuals, some of whom were teaching at Columbia University in New York City during World War I. As dedicated pacifists, they took a public stand against the war and were censured by the university's president. The professors responded by resigning from Columbia and later establishing their own university for adults in the Chelsea neighborhood of Manhattan. It became a place where people could exchange ideas freely with scholars and artists representing a wide range of intellectual, aesthetic, and political orientations.

During the 1920s, Alvin Johnson, the School's first president, collaborated regularly with colleagues in Germany and elsewhere in Europe. They made him aware of the danger Hitler presented to democracy and the civilized world, alerting him to the seriousness of the threat before many in the United States had grasped it. In 1933, with the financial support of enlightened philanthropists, Johnson created within The New School a University in Exile to provide a haven for scholars and artists whose lives were threatened by National Socialism. The University in Exile sponsored more than 180 individuals and their families, providing them with visas and jobs. While some of these refugees remained at The New School for many years, many others went on to influence institutional life elsewhere in the United States. Today, The New School for Social Research remains a place where professors and students take risks in defense of their intellectual commitments and political beliefs.

Applying

The admission decision is made after a careful examination of transcripts, letters of recommendation, the writing sample, scores on the Graduate Record Examinations, and the statement of academic goals and objectives. Application materials for students wishing to be considered for full fellowships and special scholarships must be completed by January 17. Applications received or completed after January 17 are considered for admission and financial aid on a rolling basis. For more information, students should visit http://www.socialresearch.newschool.edu/admissions.

Correspondence and Information

The New School for Social Research
The New School
65 Fifth Avenue
New York, New York 10003
Phone: 212-229-5710
800-523-5411 (toll-free)
E-mail: socialresearchadmit@newschool.edu
Web site: http://www.newschool.edu/nssr

The New School: A University

THE FACULTY AND THEIR RESEARCH

Anthropology

Arjun Appadurai, John Dewey Professor in the Social Sciences; Ph.D., Chicago, 1976. Historical anthropology, globalization, ethnic violence.
Lawrence Hirschfeld, Professor; Ph.D., Columbia, 1984. Anthropology and history of childhood, cultural psychology, cognitive development.
Benjamin Lee, Provost; Ph.D., Chicago, 1986. Linguistic, philosophical, and psychological anthropology; global cultural studies; contemporary Chinese culture.
Hugh Raffles, Associate Professor; D.F.E.S., Yale, 1999. Cultural politics of nature, humans/nonhumans, scale, taxonomy, affect, ethnography and history, writing.
Vyjayanthi Rao, Visiting Assistant Professor; Ph.D., Chicago, 2002. South Asia, development and modernization, displacement in postcolonial societies.
Janet Roitman, Associate Professor of Anthropology and International Affairs; Ph.D., Pennsylvania, 1996.
Ann Laura Stoler, Distinguished University Professor; Ph.D., Columbia, 1982. Colonial cultures, critical race theory, gender studies, historical methodologies, Southeast Asia.
Hyton White, Assistant Professor; Ph.D., Chicago, 2001. Critical social theory, embodiment and social reproduction, the family and domestic life in capitalist society, South Africa.

Economics

Duncan Foley, Leo Model Professor; Ph.D., Yale, 1966. Classical, neoclassical, and Marxian economic theory; political economy; monetary economics; economic complexity; global environmental economics.
William Milberg, Associate Professor; Ph.D., Rutgers, 1987. International trade.
Salih Neftci, Visiting Professor; Ph.D., Minnesota, 1977. Financial markets, numerical methods in financial asset pricing, applications of the theory of extremes to risk management.
Edward Nell, Malcolm B. Smith Professor; B.Litt., Oxford, 1962. Macroeconomic theory and policy, methodology, growth theory, business cycles, inflation and unemployment.
Willi Semmler, Professor; Ph.D., Berlin, 1976. Financial markets, macroeconomics and macroeconometrics, public finance, industrial organization.
Anwar Shaikh, Professor; Ph.D., Columbia, 1973. Political economy, macroeconomic growth and cycles, international trade.
Lance Taylor, Arnhold Professor of International Cooperation and Development; Ph.D., Harvard, 1968. Economic development and the environment.

Global Finance

Turan Bali, Professor; Ph.D., CUNY, Baruch, 1998. Financial economics, financial econometrics, financial engineering, fixed income, derivatives, risk management.
Greg Ciresi, Adjunct Instructor; M.S., NYU, 2004. Financial engineering, statistical arbitrage, risk management.
Pablo A. Goldberg, Professor; M.Sc., London School of Economics (UK), 1996. Macro economics, financial economics.
Ira F. Jersey, Professor; M.A., New School, 2004; Macro economics, financial economics, financial engineering, political science, international relations.
Christina E. Leijonhufvud, Managing Director and Head of Social Sector Finance, JPMorgan Chase & Co.; M.Sc., London School of Economics, 1996. Country risk, emerging markets, financial risk management, financial globalization, social sector finance.
Salih N. Neftci, Program Director, Global Finance Masters Program; Ph.D., Minnesota, 1977. Financial economics.
Eckhard Platen, Professor; Dr.Sc., Academy of Sciences (Berlin), 1985; Ph.D., Technical (Dresden), 1975. Mathematics of finance, numerical methods in finance, quantitative finance.
Liuren Wu, Professor; Ph.D, China Academy of Science, 1994, M.A., NYU, 1998. Credit risk, term structure modeling, option pricing, market microstructure, international finance, asset pricing, asset allocation.

Historical Studies

Elaine Abelson, Senior Lecturer; Ph.D., NYU, 1986. Dimensions of inequality, gender.
Robin Blackburn, Distinguished Visiting Professor; B.Sc., London, 1965. Slavery, globalization, communism, colonialism.
Carol Breckenridge, Associate Professor; Ph.D., Wisconsin, 1976. Colonialism and ritual; state, polity, and religion in South India; cosmopolitan cultural forms.
José Casanova, Professor of Sociology; Ph.D., New School, 1982. Religion, democratization, social change.
Federico Finchelstein, Assistant Professor; Ph.D., Cornell, 2006.
Oz Frankel, Assistant Professor; Ph.D., Berkeley, 1998. Social and political history of nineteenth-century United States, Victorian Britain, history of the social sciences, race, media and print culture, reform, state formation, historiography.
Victoria Hattam, Associate Professor of Political Science (see Political Science).
Eiko Ikegami, Professor of Sociology (see Sociology).
James Miller, Professor of Liberal Studies and Political Science (see Liberal Studies).
David Plotke, Professor of Political Science (see Political Science).
Ann Laura Stoler, Distinguished University Professor (see Anthropology).
Eli Zaretsky, Professor; Ph.D., Maryland, 1978. Cultural history, twentieth-century history, history of the family, psychoanalysis.
Aristide Zolberg, Eberstadt Professor (see Political Science).
Vera Zolberg, Professor of Sociology (see Sociology).

Liberal Studies

Richard Bernstein, Vera List Professor of Philosophy (see Philosophy).
Oz Frankel, Assistant Professor of History (see Historical Studies).
Margo Jefferson, Associate Professor, Eugene Lang College The New School for Liberal Arts; M.S., Columbia, 1971.
Elzbieta Matynia, Senior Lecturer; Ph.D., Warsaw, 1979. Gender issues in the new European democracies.
James Miller, Professor; Ph.D., Brandeis, 1975. History of political thought, social movements.
Melissa Monroe, Committee Member; Ph.D., Stanford, 1989. Nonfiction writing, modern literature, linguistics.
Eli Zaretsky, Professor of History (see Historical Studies).
Vera Zolberg, Professor of Sociology (see Sociology).

Philosophy

Claudia Baracchi, Associate Professor; Ph.D., Vanderbilt, 1996. Ancient philosophy, nineteenth- and twentieth-century continental philosophy, medieval philosophy, philosophy of art, political philosophy, ethics.
J. M. Bernstein, Professor; Ph.D., Edinburgh, 1975. Critical theory, aesthetics.
Richard Bernstein, Vera List Professor; Ph.D., Yale, 1958. American pragmatism, social and political philosophy, critical theory, Anglo-American philosophy.
Alice Crary, Associate Professor; Ph.D., Pittsburgh, 1999. Moral philosophy, Wittgenstein, philosophy and literature.
Simon Critchley, Professor; Ph.D., Essex, 1988. Continental philosophy, phenomenology, philosophy and literature, psychoanalysis, the ethical and the political.
James Dodd, Assistant Professor; Ph.D., Boston University, 1996. Husserl, Heidegger, phenomenology.
Nancy Fraser, Henry A. and Louise Loeb Professor of Political and Social Science (see Political Science).
Agnes Heller, Hannah Arendt Professor; Ph.D., Eötvös Loránd (Budapest), 1955. Political philosophy, ethics, existentialism.
Mark Larrimore, Assistant Professor of Religious Studies and Philosophy; Ph.D., Princeton, 1994. Philosophy of religion, ethics, Leibniz.
Benjamin Lee, Provost (see Anthropology).
Dmitri Nikulin, Associate Professor; Ph.D., Academy of Sciences (Moscow), 1990. Philosophy and history of science, ancient and early modern philosophy, philosophy of dialogue.
Yirmiyahu Yovel, Hans Jonas Professor; Ph.D., Hebrew University (Israel), 1968. Spinoza, Jewish rationalists, continental philosophy.

Political Science

Nancy Fraser, Henry A. and Louise Loeb Professor of Political and Social Science; Ph.D., CUNY Graduate Center, 1980. Social and political theory, feminist theory, contemporary French and German thought.
Victoria Hattam, Associate Professor; Ph.D., MIT, 1987. American political and economic thought and culture.
Agnes Heller, Hannah Arendt Professor of Philosophy (see Philosophy).
Mala Htun, Assistant Professor; Ph.D., Harvard, 2000. Comparative politics; Latin America; gender, race, and politics.
Courtney Jung, Assistant Professor; Ph.D., Yale, 1998. Comparative politics, politics of identity, democratic transitions, South Africa.
Andreas Kalyvas, Assistant Professor; Ph.D., Columbia, 2000. Relationship between democracy and constitutionalism, problems of popular sovereignty.
James Miller, Professor of Liberal Studies and Political Science (see Liberal Studies).
David Plotke, Professor; Ph.D., Berkeley, 1985. Contemporary political and social theory, American political development.
Adamantia Pollis, Professor Emerita and Senior Lecturer; Ph.D., Johns Hopkins, 1958. Nationalism and ethnicity, human rights.
Sanjay Ruparelia, Assistant Professor; Ph.D., Cambridge, 2005. Comparative politics, political economy of development, modern South Asia.
Aristide Zolberg, Eberstadt Professor; Ph.D., Chicago, 1961. Globalization and democracy, nationalism and ethnicity.

Psychology

Emanuele Castano, Assistant Professor; Ph.D., Louvain (Belgium), 1999. Social identification; perception entitativity, essentialism, agency, and intentionality at the collective level; image theory.
Doris Chang, Assistant Professor; Ph.D., UCLA, 2000. Cultural psychology, ethnic minority mental health, domestic violence in immigrant communities.
Karen D'Avanzo, Assistant Clinical Professor and Coordinator, M.A. Mental Health and Substance Abuse Counseling Program; Ph.D., LIU, Brooklyn, 1995. Developmental psychopathology, risk and resilience and child/adolescent development, contextual factors and adolescent substance abuse, dual-diagnosis psychotherapy development, psychotherapy integration.
Lawrence Hirschfeld, Professor (see Anthropology).
William Hirst, Professor; Ph.D., Cornell, 1976. Cognitive neuroscience, memory and attention.
Xiaochun Jin, Assistant Professor; Ph.D., Adelphi, 2003.
Marcel Kinsbourne, Professor; D.M., Oxford, 1963. Brain-behavior relations, consciousness, psychology of attention.
Arien Mack, Alfred J. and Monette C. Marrow Professor; Ph.D., Yeshiva, 1966. Perception and attention.
Joan Miller, Associate Professor; Ph.D., Chicago, 1982. Interpersonal motivation, theory of mind, close relationships, moral development.
Lisa Rubin, Assistant Professor; Ph.D., Arizona State, 2005.
Jeremy Safran, Professor and Director of Clinical Training; Ph.D., British Columbia, 1982. Psychoanalysis and psychotherapy, the therapeutic alliance, therapeutic impasses, transference and countertransference, the internal processes of the therapist.
Herbert Schlesinger, Professor Emeritus and Senior Lecturer; Ph.D., Kansas, 1952. Analysis of text in psychoanalysis, implications and cost of providing mental health services.
Michael Schober, Professor; Ph.D., Stanford, 1990. Psycholinguistics, survey response, music cognition.
David Shapiro, Professor; Ph.D., USC, 1950. Psychopathology of character problems and their treatment.
Howard Steele, Associate Professor; Ph.D., University College (London), 1991. Attachment theory, dementia, multiple personality disorder, borderline personality disorder.
Miriam Steele, Associate Professor and Assistant Director of Clinical Training; Ph.D., University College (London), 1990. Attachment theory, psychoanalytic developmental psychology, adoption and foster care.
McWelling Todman, Associate Professor of Clinical Practice and Codirector, Mental Health and Substance Abuse Counseling Program; Ph.D., New School, 1986. Psychopathology, biosocial and cognitive theories of addiction.
Megan B. Warner, Assistant Professor and Director, The New School–Beth Israel Center for Clinical Training and Research; Ph.D., Texas A&M, 2005.

Sociology

Andrew Arato, Dorothy Hart Hirshon Professor of Political and Social Theory; Ph.D., Chicago, 1975. Frankfurt school, history of social thought, Eastern European societies and social movements.
Paolo Carpignano, Senior Lecturer; Ph.D., Rome (Italy), 1969. Media theory, sociology of culture.
José Casanova, Professor; Ph.D., New School, 1982. Religion, democratization, and social change in Latin America; Southern and Eastern Europe.
Sarah Daynes, Assistant Professor; Ph.D., École des Hautes Études en Sciences Sociales (Paris), 2001. Social theory, memory, knowledge, religion, music.
Jeffrey Goldfarb, Michael E. Gellert Professor; Ph.D., Chicago, 1977. Sociology of culture, comparative politics, phenomenological society.
Eiko Ikegami, Professor; Ph.D., Harvard, 1989. Comparative historical sociology, Japanese society, theory, sociology of culture.
Jaeho Kang, Assistant Professor of Sociology and Media Studies; Ph.D., Cambridge, 2003. Critical social theory, sociology of media, social theory of mass culture, new media and political communication.
Orville Lee, Assistant Professor; Ph.D., Berkeley, 1996. Cultural sociology, racial epistemologies.
Terry Williams, Professor; Ph.D., CUNY Graduate Center, 1978. Race, drug culture, urban life, poverty.
Vera Zolberg, Professor; Ph.D., Chicago, 1974: sociology of culture, social and political frameworks of cultural support and memory.

UNIVERSITY OF CHICAGO

Graduate Division of the Social Sciences
Master of Arts Program in the Social Sciences

Programs of Study

The Master of Arts Program in the Social Sciences (MAPSS) is a one-year program of graduate studies leading to the M.A. degree. Offering an unusual flexibility and making the resources of a great university available for highly individualized programs of study, MAPSS presents a variety of disciplinary and interdisciplinary opportunities for advancing academic or career goals.

Each student works closely with the director and a preceptor on all aspects of the program, from designing a customized curriculum to defining the research topic to writing the master's degree paper. The MAPSS degree program has one core course in social science perspectives. Students choose eight additional courses, including a methodology course, from the full range of regular doctoral and graduate professional offerings of the Division of Social Sciences and the other divisions and schools of the University.

MAPSS students acquire skills and knowledge for careers that make use of the social sciences or prepare them for further graduate work or professional training. MAPSS offers specialized counseling and application support to students subsequently applying for doctoral or professional school study. Many MAPSS graduates have received and presently pursue doctorates and professional degrees in all of Chicago's social science departments and schools and at other major research universities.

Research Facilities

The University of Chicago Library System includes more than 7 million print volumes, 4 million microforms, 30,000 linear feet of manuscripts and archival materials, and 421,000 maps and aerial photographs. The system includes the resources of the University's Regenstein, Harper, and Crear libraries. The library provides access to a wide variety of networked electronic resources—electronic journals and books, specialty indexes and abstracts, and full-text reference sources.

MAPSS students may have opportunities to participate in the current research projects of faculty members or ongoing work at the National Opinion Research Center (NORC), the Center for Health Administration Studies, the Center for Gender Studies, the Center for Urban Research, the MESA Psychometric Lab, and the Center for Race, Politics and Culture.

The Council on Advanced Studies sponsors graduate research workshops in the humanities and social sciences. The aim of these workshops is to bring together faculty members and graduate students from the University of Chicago and the wider Chicago area in an effort to create scholarly dialogue and to foster an exchange of ideas. For 2006–07, there were a total of sixty-four workshops that spanned a wide spectrum of interests and disciplines—many with interdisciplinary aims, including performance studies, mass culture, Latin American and Caribbean anthropology, and art and politics in East Asia.

Financial Aid

MAPSS offers a limited number of tuition-assistance, merit-based awards, regardless of an applicant's international or domestic status. Financing the balance of educational costs at the University of Chicago can be accomplished through a student's personal resources, part-time work-study opportunities, or borrowing funds from federal or alternative loan programs. The University of Chicago does not offer research or teaching assistantships to M.A. students as part of their financial aid award. However, there are opportunities to apply for a research assistant position with a specific faculty member once a student enters the program.

Cost of Study

In 2007–08, tuition for the full-time, three-quarter program was $36,666. Part-time students paid $4074 per course.

Living and Housing Costs

The total estimated cost for three-quarters of study, including tuition, fees, books, academic supplies, and room and board, for 2007–08 was $55,005. Graduate student housing options available through the University include more than 1,300 units in thirty-one apartment buildings that are owed and operated by the University, with a wide variety of apartment sizes, designs, and rates. For those interested in dormitory-style living, International House provides housing and program facilities for up to 500 students and scholars, half of whom are from more than fifty other countries. All units are within walking distance of the University's quadrangles and are on or near campus bus routes.

Student Group

The program matriculates approximately 160 students each year. Students come from a wide range of baccalaureate institutions in the U.S. and abroad and have diverse undergraduate majors as well as life and occupational experiences. Current students range in age from 21 to 46 years. Fifty-seven percent are women, 20 percent are international students, and 8 percent are members of minority groups. Approximately 79 percent receive University tuition aid; around 1 percent pursue their M.A. degrees while employed full-time.

Student Outcomes

MAPSS graduates enter or return to a wide range of careers for which the M.A. is increasingly often the entry-level degree. Recent graduates have pursued careers in policy analysis, contract research, business consulting, investment management, community organizing, teaching, mental health counseling, publishing, health care, government service, public affairs, radio and television, nonprofit development, arts administration, and museum curation. Other graduates pursue doctoral or professional school studies at the University of Chicago and at institutions across the country.

A national network of MAPSS alumni, in concert with the University's Career Advising and Placement Services (CAPS) Office, assists graduates in identifying career possibilities and securing challenging positions.

Location

The University of Chicago is located in Hyde Park, a racially diverse neighborhood 15 minutes from the Loop, the heart of downtown Chicago. MAPSS students have ready access to Chicago's outstanding cultural, recreational, and athletic facilities. The University is less than a mile from the Lake Michigan shore, which offers beaches, biking and jogging trails, and picnic areas. An unusually wide range of cultural and recreational activities are available on campus.

The Division and The Program

For more than seventy years, the MAPSS program has contributed an interdisciplinary presence to the academic life and public mission of the Graduate Division of Social Sciences, one of the world's most distinguished concentrations of social science departments and faculties. Over the years, distinctive "Chicago schools" of political science, sociology, anthropology, and economics have been enshrined in modern intellectual history. Vibrant and intensive research and teaching remain the hallmarks of these Chicago disciplines, as they do in the fields of history, psychology, human development, social thought, area studies, geography, and education.

Applying

Students enter the MAPSS program in the autumn quarter. The application deadline is December 28, and notification of admission and financial aid occurs by March 15. GRE scores are required for all applicants. The GRE should be taken no later than November in order to meet the application deadline.

All applicants who are not U.S. citizens or U.S. permanent residents must take the Test of English as a Foreign Language (TOEFL). The University of Chicago accepts either the TOEFL or the International English Language Testing System (IELTS). The TOEFL is available in three formats. Minimum requirements per subsection for the TOEFL are no less than 25 per each of the three sections on the computer-based test; no less than 60 per each of the three sections on the paper-based test; or no less than 26 per each of the four sections on the Internet-based test. Minimum required scores in the IELTS are an overall score of 7, with subscores of 7 each.

Prospective students are strongly encouraged to visit MAPSS and the University to learn more about the program and its fit with their academic goals.

Correspondence and Information

For information:
MAPSS
Pick Hall 301
University of Chicago
5828 South University Avenue
Chicago, Illinois 60637
Phone: 773-702-8312 or 8316
Fax: 773-702-5140
E-mail: mapssstaff@uchicago.edu
Web site: http://mapss.uchicago.edu

For application materials:
Office of the Dean of Students
Graduate Division of the Social Sciences
University of Chicago
1130 East 59th Street
Chicago, Illinois 60637
Phone: 773-702-8415
Web site: http://grad-application.uchicago.edu

University of Chicago

THE FACULTY

The MAPSS program is a teaching unit of the Graduate Division of the Social Sciences, whose deans and departmental faculty members play an active role in supporting the mission of the program. The Executive Committee, the members of which are listed below, is composed of University faculty members with a special interest in MAPSS. Students admitted to the program take courses with and have their research supervised by faculty members from all around the University.

John J. MacAloon, Ph.D.; Professor of the Social Sciences, Associate Dean of the Social Sciences Graduate Division, and Director of MAPSS.
Betty G. Farrell, Ph.D.; Senior Lecturer, Division of the Social Sciences, and Associate Director of MAPSS.
Ralph A. Austen, Ph.D.; Professor of History, the Committee on African and African-American Studies, and the Committee on General Studies in the Humanities.
Elizabeth Clemens, Ph.D.; Professor of Sociology.
Bertram Cohler, Ph.D.; Professor of Psychology (Human Development), Education, and Psychiatry, in the Divinity School and the Committee on General Studies in the Humanities.
Jean Comaroff, Ph.D.; Professor of Anthropology and the Center for History of Science and Medicine.
Michael P. Conzen, Ph.D.; Professor of Geographical Studies.
Raymond D. Fogelson, Ph.D.; Professor of Anthropology and Comparative Human Development.
Morris Fred, Ph.D.; Professorial Lecturer, Division of the Social Sciences.
Rachel Fulton, Ph.D.; Professor of History.
Susan Goldin-Meadow, Ph.D.; Professor of Psychology and Education.
Gary Herrigel, Ph.D.; Professor of Political Science.
Bruce Lincoln, Ph.D.; Professor of Divinity School and the Committee on the Ancient Mediterranean World.
Martha McClintock, Ph.D.; Professor of Psychology, Comparative Human Development, and the Committee on Biopsychology.
Omar M. McRoberts, Ph.D.; Associate Professor of Sociology.
Richard P. Taub, Ph.D.; Professor of Sociology and Comparative Human Development.

UNIVERSITY OF MICHIGAN–FLINT

Program in Social Sciences

Program of Study

The Master of Arts in Social Sciences Program at University of Michigan–Flint is designed to engage students in a critical, multidisciplinary exploration of human societies across the globe and to assist students in developing critical reading, research, and writing skills in social science. Students explore social, historical, cultural, political, and economic themes using both theoretical approaches and concrete case studies. Courses are held in the evening, with some courses held partially online. The University is accredited by the Higher Learning Commission (HCL) of the North Central Association of Colleges and Universities.

The degree requires completion of 30 credits with a GPA of B or higher. The curriculum includes 12 credits in core social science classes, 12 credits in historical/cultural courses and in political or economics courses, 3 credits in a capstone seminar, and 3 credits in cognate courses outside the concentration track. Students may choose from among three tracks: gender studies, global studies, and United States history and politics. It may be possible, with the consent of an adviser, to customize the program to meet the needs of the student. Up to 6 credits may be transferred from another institution.

Research Facilities

The Frances Willson Thompson Library's collection includes approximately 217,000 books and 35,000 bound magazines and journals. The library also contains more than a half million microforms ranging from the *Times* of London to documents on education. The library subscribes to some 1,100 hardcopy periodicals and provides electronic access to approximately 13,000 more. The media collection includes music CDs, audio tapes, and other media, including CD-ROMs, DVDs, and videotapes.

Financial Aid

Several sources of financial aid are available to students. Scholarships include the Ralph and Emmalyn E. Freeman Graduate Program Scholarship (for students with a minimum GPA of 3.5), the Dean's Graduate Student Scholarship (for students with a GPA of at least A-), and the Carl and Sarah Morgan Graduate Student Scholarship (for students with at least a B+ GPA). The Esther C. Stone Graduate Student Scholarship for Academic Excellence is a one-time award for students who demonstrate academic excellence. Graduate research assistantships provide stipends for students who work with faculty members on research projects. Through various programs, students may borrow up to $8500 in subsidized loans or $18,500 in unsubsidized loans. The Federal Work-Study Program is also available.

Cost of Study

In 2008–09, graduate tuition is $415.50 per credit for Michigan residents and $623.30 per credit for nonresidents. Other fees include a $50 registration fee, a $25 student activity fee, a $23 recreation fee, and a $43 technology fee.

Living and Housing Costs

It is planned that University housing will become available for fall 2008. Although it is intended primarily for undergraduate students in its first phase, there are many off-campus housing opportunities in Flint and the surrounding area. Apartments close to campus range from $370 per month for a studio to $750 for a two- or three-bedroom apartment. Further from campus, apartments range between $300 and $650 per month, depending upon the apartment's size and location.

Student Group

The program is designed for teachers seeking further course work or master's degrees in their fields to meet professional standards or deepen their understanding of the social sciences; professionals with private or public sector jobs who wish to increase their knowledge in areas of the social sciences; and those with undergraduate degrees who wish to continue their exploration of social science disciplines and issues.

Location

Although best known as the birthplace of General Motors, Flint has become better known for other activities in recent years, including the Crim Festival of Races and the Buick Open. A large cultural center occupies 30 acres near downtown, and four golf courses and more than 50 parks are interspersed throughout the city. Flint is located approximately 60 miles from Detroit, Ann Arbor, and Lansing.

The University

The University of Michigan–Flint began in 1956, when a two-year senior college was formed through public and private donations. Today, this four-year University offers 100 undergraduate and twenty-seven graduate degrees to nearly 7,000 students. The programs are designed to provide professional training in relationship to traditional study in the liberal arts and sciences so that students develop the knowledge, intellectual skills, values, and attitudes they need to help them make thoughtful and informed judgments about their experiences.

Applying

To be considered for admission, applicants must submit an application form, official undergraduate transcripts showing a GPA of 3.0 or higher, three letters of recommendation, a 500 to 800 word statement of purpose describing the applicant's professional and educational goals, and a $55 application fee. For the 2007–08 academic year, the deadline to apply is November 15 for winter admission, March 15 for spring admission, May 15 for summer admission, and August 1 for fall admission. Students can apply online; paper applications are to be sent to the Office of Graduate Programs, University of Michigan–Flint, 251 Thompson Library, Flint, Michigan 48502-1950.

Correspondence and Information

Roy Hanashiro
Department of History
University of Michigan-Flint
322 David M. French Hall
Flint, Michigan 48502-1950
Phone: 810-762-3366
E-mail: okuma@umflint.edu
Web site: http://www.umflint.edu/graduateprograms/social_sciences.htm

University of Michigan-Flint

THE FACULTY AND THEIR RESEARCH

John S. Ellis, Assistant Professor of History; Ph.D., Boston College, 1997. Nationalism and national identity in the British Isles; modern Wales and Ireland.

Roy S. Hanashiro, Professor of History and Department Chair; Ph.D., Hawaii, 1988. Modern Japan; Asian economic history.

Peggy Kahn, Professor of Political Science and Department Chair; Ph.D., Berkeley, 1984. Dynamics and dilemmas of women's low-paid work in the service sector, both in the United States and Great Britain.

Jason Kosnoski, Assistant Professor of Political Science; Ph.D., New School, 2003. Contemporary political theory, with special emphasis on democratic theory and the work of John Dewey and Jurgen Habermas.

William Laverty, Assistant Professor of Political Science; Ph.D., Indiana, 2005. Intergovernmental relations and issues related to private property rights, water resource policy, rapidly growing urban areas, and endangered species.

Adam Lutzker, Assistant Professor of Economics; Ph.D., Michigan. Labor economics, global economics, law and economics, history of economic thought, world economic history, American economic history.

Ami Pflugrad-Jackish, Assistant Professor of History; Ph.D., SUNY at Buffalo, 2005. The Antebellum South; race, gender, and culture in American history.

Albert C. Price, Professor of Political Science and Public Administration; Ph.D., Connecticut, 1980. Public law, public administration.

Joseph G. Rahme, Associate Professor of History; Ph.D., Chicago, 1994. Muslim/non-Muslim relations, Ottoman Empire, historiography of world history.

Theodosia S. Robertson, Associate Professor of History; Ph.D., Indiana, 1985. Modern Poland, Jewish civilization in Polish lands.

Stephen J. Rockwell, Assistant Professor of Political Science; Ph.D., Brandeis, 2001. American national government and politics, American Indian affairs and politics, race and ethnicity issues, public administration.

Judy V. Rosenthal, Associate Professor of Sociology; Ph.D., Cornell, 1993.

Bruce A. Rubenstein, Professor of History; Ph.D., Michigan State, 1974. Michigan history, sports history, American Indians and the American West.

Section 27
Sociology, Anthropology, and Archaeology

This section contains a directory of institutions offering graduate work in sociology, anthropology, and archaeology, followed by in-depth entries submitted by institutions that chose to prepare detailed program descriptions. Additional information about programs listed in the directory but not augmented by an in-depth entry may be obtained by writing directly to the dean of a graduate school or chair of a department at the address given in the directory.

For programs offering related work, see also in this book *Area and Cultural Studies, Art and Art History, History, Humanities, Language and Literature,* and *Psychology and Counseling.*

CONTENTS

Program Directories

Announcements

Close-Ups

See also:

Anthropology

American University, College of Arts and Sciences, Department of Anthropology, Washington, DC 20016-8001. Offers anthropology (PhD); public anthropology (MA, Certificate). Part-time and evening/weekend programs available. *Faculty:* 11 full-time (6 women), 6 part-time/adjunct (5 women). *Students:* 25 full-time (18 women), 62 part-time (43 women); includes 17 minority (9 African Americans, 3 Asian Americans or Pacific Islanders, 5 Hispanic Americans), 8 international. Average age 32. 55 applicants, 55% accepted, 13 enrolled. In 2007, 15 master's, 4 doctorates, 1 other advanced degree awarded. Terminal master's awarded for partial completion of doctoral program. *Degree requirements:* For master's, comprehensive exam, thesis or alternative; for doctorate, 2 foreign languages, comprehensive exam, thesis/dissertation. *Entrance requirements:* For master's, GRE, sample of written work, statement of interest; for doctorate, GRE, sample of written work, personal statement. Additional exam requirements/recommendations for international students: Required—TOEFL (minimum score 550 paper-based; 213 computer-based). *Application deadline:* For fall admission, 2/1 for domestic students; for spring admission, 10/1 for domestic students. Application fee: $50. *Expenses:* Tuition: Full-time $19,998; part-time $1,111 per credit hour. Required fees: $380. Tuition and fees vary according to program. *Financial support:* Fellowships with full and partial tuition reimbursements, research assistantships with full and partial tuition reimbursements, teaching assistantships with full and partial tuition reimbursements, career-related internships or fieldwork, Federal Work-Study, institutionally sponsored loans, and unspecified assistantships available. Support available to part-time students. Financial award application deadline: 1/15. *Faculty research:* Poverty and race, lesbian and gay studies, class and culture, developing countries. *Unit head:* Dr. William Leap, Chair, 202-885-1831, Fax: 202-885-1837.

The American University in Cairo, Graduate Studies and Research, School of Humanities and Social Sciences, Department of Sociology, Anthropology and Psychology, Cairo, Egypt. Offers sociology and anthropology (MA). *Degree requirements:* For master's, one foreign language, thesis. *Entrance requirements:* Additional exam requirements/recommendations for international students: Required—English entrance exam and/or TOEFL. Electronic applications accepted. *Faculty research:* Development, gender, sociopolitical economic formulations, social science indigenization, Arab world.

American University of Beirut, Graduate Programs, Faculty of Arts and Sciences, Beirut, Lebanon. Offers anthropology (MA); Arabic language and literature (MA); archaeology (MA); biology (MS); chemistry (MS); computer science (MS); economics (MA); education (MA); English language (MA); English literature (MA); environmental policy planning (MSES); financial economics (MAFE); geology (MS); history (MA); mathematics (MA, MS); Middle Eastern studies (MA); philosophy (MA); physics (MS); political studies (MA); psychology (MA); public administration (MA); sociology (MA); statistics (MA, MS). Part-time programs available. *Faculty:* 108 full-time (29 women), 5 part-time/adjunct (3 women). *Students:* 134 full-time (92 women), 228 part-time (167 women). Average age 25. 319 applicants, 67% accepted, 91 enrolled. In 2007, 144 degrees awarded. *Degree requirements:* For master's, one foreign language, comprehensive exam, thesis (for some programs). *Entrance requirements:* For master's, GRE, letter of recommendation. Additional exam requirements/recommendations for international students: Required—TOEFL (minimum score 600 paper-based; 250 computer-based; 100 iBT), IELTS (minimum score 8). *Application deadline:* For fall admission, 4/30 for domestic and international students; for spring admission, 11/1 for domestic and international students. Application fee: $50. *Expenses:* Tuition: Full-time $9,954; part-time $553 per credit. Tuition and fees vary according to course load and program. *Financial support:* In 2007–08, 28 students received support. Career-related internships or fieldwork, institutionally sponsored loans, scholarships/grants, health care benefits, and unspecified assistantships available. Financial award application deadline: 2/4; financial award applicants required to submit FAFSA. *Faculty research:* String theory and supergravity; computer graphics; algebra and number theory; popular Arabic literature; marine and freshwater biology; integrating science, math and technology. Total annual research expenditures: $132,270. *Unit head:* Khalil Bitar, Dean, 961-1374374 Ext. 3800, Fax: 961-1744461, E-mail: kmb@aub.edu.lb. *Application contact:* Dr. Salim Kanaan, Director, Admissions Office, 961-1350000 Ext. 2594, Fax: 961-1750775, E-mail: sk00@aub.edu.lb.

Arizona State University, Graduate College, College of Liberal Arts and Sciences, Division of Social Sciences, Department of Anthropology, Tempe, AZ 85287. Offers MA, PhD, MA/MS. *Degree requirements:* For master's, thesis or alternative; for doctorate, thesis/dissertation. *Entrance requirements:* For master's and doctorate, GRE.

Ball State University, Graduate School, College of Sciences and Humanities, Department of Anthropology, Muncie, IN 47306-1099. Offers MA. *Faculty:* 15. *Students:* 15 full-time (12 women), 11 part-time (6 women); includes 1 minority (American Indian/Alaska Native), 1 international. Average age 29. 28 applicants, 82% accepted, 13 enrolled. In 2007, 6 degrees awarded. *Entrance requirements:* For master's, GRE General Test, resumé. Application fee: $25 ($35 for international students). *Expenses:* Tuition, state resident: full-time $6,864. Tuition, nonresident: full-time $17,932. Required fees: $1,866. *Financial support:* In 2007–08, 4 teaching assistantships with full tuition reimbursements (averaging $8,868 per year) were awarded; research assistantships with full tuition reimbursements. Financial award application deadline: 3/1. *Unit head:* Dr. S. Homes Hogue, Chairman, 765-285-1575, Fax: 765-285-2163.

Boston University, Graduate School of Arts and Sciences, Department of Anthropology, Boston, MA 02215. Offers anthropology (PhD); applied anthropology (MA). *Students:* 30 full-time (19 women), 1 part-time; includes 1 minority (African American), 8 international. Average age 33. 75 applicants, 27% accepted, 6 enrolled. In 2007, 5 doctorates awarded. Terminal master's awarded for partial completion of doctoral program. *Degree requirements:* For master's, one foreign language, thesis or alternative; for doctorate, one foreign language, thesis/dissertation. *Entrance requirements:* For master's and doctorate, GRE General Test, 2 letters of recommendation. Additional exam requirements/recommendations for international students: Required—TOEFL (minimum score 550 paper-based; 213 computer-based). *Application deadline:* For fall admission, 1/1 for domestic and international students. Application fee: $70. *Expenses:* Tuition: Full-time $34,930; part-time $1,092 per credit. Tuition and fees vary according to class time, course level and program. *Financial support:* In 2007–08, 15 students received support, including 3 fellowships with full tuition reimbursements available (averaging $18,000 per year), 6 teaching assistantships with full tuition reimbursements available (averaging $16,500 per year); Federal Work-Study and unspecified assistantships also available. Support available to part-time students. Financial award application deadline: 1/1; financial award applicants required to submit FAFSA. *Unit head:* Robert Weller, Chairman, 617-353-2195, Fax: 617-353-2610, E-mail: rpweller@bu.edu. *Application contact:* Mark Palmer, Administrator, 617-353-2195, Fax: 617-353-2610, E-mail: palmerm@bu.edu.

Brandeis University, Graduate School of Arts and Sciences, Department of Anthropology, Waltham, MA 02454-9110. Offers anthropology (MA, PhD); anthropology and women's and gender studies (MA). Part-time programs available. *Faculty:* 10 full-time (5 women). *Students:* 39 full-time (29 women); includes 3 minority (1 African American, 1 Asian American or Pacific Islander, 1 Hispanic American), 6 international. Average age 34. 48 applicants, 40% accepted, 8 enrolled. In 2007, 7 master's, 2 doctorates awarded. Terminal master's awarded for partial completion of doctoral program. *Degree requirements:* For master's, thesis; for doctorate, one foreign language, comprehensive exam, thesis/dissertation. *Entrance requirements:* For master's, GRE General Test (recommended), sample of written work, resumé, letters of recommendation; for doctorate, GRE General Test, sample of written work, resumé, letters of recommendation. Additional exam requirements/recommendations for international students: Required—TOEFL (minimum score 600 paper-based; 250 computer-based; 100 iBT), IELTS (minimum score 7). *Application deadline:* For fall admission, 1/15 for domestic students. Applications are processed on a rolling basis. Application fee: $55. Electronic applications accepted. *Financial support:* In 2007–08, 18 students received support, including 11 fellowships with full tuition reimbursements available (averaging $16,500 per year), 7 teaching assistantships with tuition reimbursements available (averaging $3,000 per year); research assistantships with partial tuition reimbursements available, career-related internships or fieldwork, scholarships/grants, health care benefits, and tuition waivers (full and partial) also available. Support available to part-time students. Financial award application deadline: 4/15; financial award applicants required to submit CSS PROFILE or FAFSA. *Faculty research:* Technology and culture, comparative methods, economic anthropology, gender studies, semiotic anthropology. *Unit head:* Dr. David Jacobson, Professor and Director of Graduate Studies for Anthropology, 781-736-2210, Fax: 781-736-2232, E-mail: jacobson@brandeis.edu. *Application contact:* Laurel Carpenter, Academic Administrator, 781-736-2210, Fax: 781-736-2232, E-mail: lcarpenter@brandeis.edu.

Brigham Young University, Graduate Studies, College of Family, Home, and Social Sciences, Department of Anthropology, Provo, UT 84602-1001. Offers MA. *Faculty:* 10 full-time (2 women). *Students:* 16 full-time (7 women), 4 part-time (1 woman); includes 3 minority (1 American Indian/Alaska Native, 1 Asian American or Pacific Islander, 1 Hispanic American). Average age 28. 7 applicants, 43% accepted, 3 enrolled. In 2007, 1 master's awarded. *Degree requirements:* For master's, comprehensive exam, thesis. *Entrance requirements:* For master's, GRE General Test, minimum GPA of 3.0 in last 60 hours. *Application deadline:* For fall admission, 2/1 for domestic students. Application fee: $50. *Financial support:* In 2007–08, 16 students received support, including 10 research assistantships (averaging $6,000 per year), 2 teaching assistantships (averaging $6,000 per year); fellowships, career-related internships or fieldwork, institutionally sponsored loans, and tuition waivers (partial) also available. Financial award application deadline: 3/1; financial award applicants required to submit FAFSA. *Faculty research:* Archaeology of the Southwest, Near East, and Mesoamerica; Mayan glyphs. Total annual research expenditures: $51,800. *Unit head:* Dr. David P. Crandall, Chair, 801-422-3058, Fax: 801-422-0021, E-mail: david.crandall@byu.edu. *Application contact:* Dr. Joel C. Janetski, Graduate Coordinator, 801-422-7861, Fax: 801-422-0021, E-mail: joel_jauetski@byu.edu.

Brown University, Graduate School, Department of Anthropology, Providence, RI 02912. Offers anthropology (AM, PhD); old world archaeology and art (AM, PhD). *Degree requirements:* For doctorate, one foreign language, thesis/dissertation, preliminary exam.

California Institute of Integral Studies, Graduate Programs, School of Consciousness and Transformation, San Francisco, CA 94103. Offers cultural anthropology and social transformation (MA); East-West psychology (MA, PhD); integrative health studies (MA); philosophy and religion (MA, PhD), including Asian and comparative studies, philosophy, cosmology, and consciousness, social and cultural anthropology (PhD), transformative leadership (MA), transformative studies (PhD), women's spirituality, women's spirituality flex format; social and cultural anthropology (PhD); transformative leadership (MA); transformative studies (PhD). Part-time and evening/weekend programs available. Postbaccalaureate distance learning degree programs offered (minimal on-campus study). *Faculty:* 30 full-time, 28 part-time/adjunct. *Students:* 456; includes 92 minority (32 African Americans, 3 American Indian/Alaska Native, 40 Asian Americans or Pacific Islanders, 17 Hispanic Americans), 1 international. Average age 37. 206 applicants, 93% accepted, 114 enrolled. In 2007, 26 degrees awarded. Terminal master's awarded for partial completion of doctoral program. *Degree requirements:* For master's, comprehensive exam (for some programs), thesis optional; for doctorate, comprehensive exam, thesis/dissertation. *Entrance requirements:* For master's, minimum GPA of 3.0, letters of recommendation, writing sample; for doctorate, master's degree, minimum GPA of 3.0, letters of recommendation, writing sample. Additional exam requirements/recommendations for international students: Required—TOEFL. *Application deadline:* For fall admission, 2/15 priority date for domestic and international students; for spring admission, 10/15 priority date for domestic and international students. Applications are processed on a rolling basis. Application fee: $65. Electronic applications accepted. *Expenses:* Tuition: Full-time $16,930; part-time $780 per unit. Tuition and fees vary according to course load and program. *Financial support:* In 2007–08, 292 students received support; research assistantships, teaching assistantships, career-related internships or fieldwork, Federal Work-Study, institutionally sponsored loans, scholarships/grants, and tuition waivers (partial) available. Support available to part-time students. Financial award application deadline: 3/15; financial award applicants required to submit FAFSA. *Faculty research:* Altered states of consciousness, dreams, cosmology, postcolonial studies, integrative health studies. *Application contact:* Allyson Werner, Senior Admissions Counselor, 415-575-6155, Fax: 415-575-1268.

See Close-Up on page 445.

California State University, Bakersfield, Division of Graduate Studies, School of Humanities and Social Sciences, Program in Anthropology, Bakersfield, CA 93311-1022. Offers MA. *Degree requirements:* For master's, thesis optional. *Entrance requirements:* For master's, GRE, minimum GPA of 2.5, 3 letters of recommendation. Additional exam requirements/recommendations for international students: Required—TOEFL (minimum score 550 paper-based; 213 computer-based). *Faculty research:* Human services, social science teaching.

California State University, Chico, Graduate School, College of Behavioral and Social Sciences, Department of Anthropology, Chico, CA 95929-0400. Offers museum studies (MA). *Students:* 24 full-time (20 women), 2 part-time (1 woman); includes 4 minority (all Hispanic Americans) Average age 27. 42 applicants, 43% accepted, 9 enrolled. In 2007, 9 degrees awarded. *Degree requirements:* For master's, thesis. *Entrance requirements:* For master's, GRE General Test, statement of purpose, 2 letters of recommendation. Additional exam requirements/recommendations for international students: Required—TOEFL (minimum score 550 paper-based; 213 computer-based; 80 iBT), IELTS (minimum score 7). *Application deadline:* For fall admission, 1/15 for domestic students, 3/1 for international students. Application fee: $55. Electronic applications accepted. *Financial support:* Fellowships, career-related internships or fieldwork available. *Unit head:* Dr. William Collins, Graduate Coordinator, 530-898-4953.

California State University, East Bay, Academic Programs and Graduate Studies, College of Letters, Arts, and Social Sciences, Department of Anthropology, Hayward, CA 94542-3000. Offers MA. Part-time programs available. *Faculty:* 7 full-time (2 women). *Students:* 4 full-time (3 women), 17 part-time (12 women); includes 2 minority (1 American Indian/Alaska Native, 1 Asian American or Pacific Islander), 3 international. Average age 38. 14 applicants, 71% accepted, 7 enrolled. In 2007, 7 degrees awarded. *Degree requirements:* For master's, one foreign language, comprehensive exam, thesis. *Entrance requirements:* For master's, minimum GPA of 2.5 during previous 2 years of course work. Additional exam requirements/recommendations for international students: Required—TOEFL (minimum score 550 paper-based; 213 computer-based). *Application deadline:* For fall admission, 5/31 for domestic students, 4/30 for international students; for winter admission, 9/30 for domestic and international students; for spring admission, 12/31 for domestic students, 11/30 for international students. Applications are processed on a rolling basis. Application fee: $55. Electronic applications accepted. *Expenses:* Required fees: $3,987; $851 per quarter. *Financial support:* Career-related internships or fieldwork, Federal Work-Study, and institutionally sponsored loans available. Support available to part-time students. Financial award application deadline: 3/2. *Unit head:* Dr. Diane Beeson, Interim Chair, 510-885-3168, E-mail: diane.beeson@csueastbay.edu. *Application contact:* My Huynh, Graduate Prospect Specialist, 510-885-2989, Fax: 510-885-4059, E-mail: my.huynh@csueastbay.edu.

California State University, Fullerton, Graduate Studies, College of Humanities and Social Sciences, Department of Anthropology, Fullerton, CA 92834-9480. Offers MA. Part-time programs available. *Students:* 48 full-time (33 women), 39 part-time (29 women); includes 25 minority (1 American Indian/Alaska Native, 4 Asian Americans or Pacific Islanders, 20 Hispanic Americans), 3 international. Average age 31. 45 applicants, 60% accepted, 19 enrolled. In 2007, 38 degrees awarded. *Degree requirements:* For master's, project or thesis. *Entrance* *requirements:* For master's, minimum GPA of 2.5 in last 60 hours of course work. Application fee: $55. *Financial support:* Teaching assistantships, career-related internships or fieldwork, Federal Work-Study, institutionally sponsored loans, and scholarships/grants available. Support available to part-time students. Financial award application deadline: 3/1. *Unit head:* Dr. John Bedell, Chair, 714-278-3626.

California State University, Long Beach, Graduate Studies, College of Liberal Arts, Department of Anthropology, Long Beach, CA 90840. Offers MA. Part-time programs available. *Faculty:* 12 full-time (6 women), 8 part-time/adjunct (6 women). *Students:* 26 full-time (17 women), 15 part-time (10 women); includes 17 minority (4 African Americans, 2 American Indian/Alaska Native, 3 Asian Americans or Pacific Islanders, 8 Hispanic Americans). Average age 29. *Degree requirements:* For master's, one foreign language, comprehensive exam or thesis. *Application deadline:* For fall admission, 7/1 for domestic students; for spring admission, 12/1 for domestic students. Applications are processed on a rolling basis. Application fee: $55. Electronic applications accepted. *Financial support:* Research assistantships, Federal Work-Study, institutionally sponsored loans, and scholarships/grants available. Financial award application deadline: 3/2. *Faculty research:* Archeology of California, Fiji, and Ireland; cultures of American Indian and Mexico. *Unit head:* Dr. Daniel Larson, Chair, 562-985-5171, Fax: 562-985-4379. *Application contact:* Dr. Pamela Bunte, Graduate Coordinator, 562-985-8179, Fax: 562-985-4379, E-mail: pbunte@csulb.edu.

California State University, Los Angeles, Graduate Studies, College of Natural and Social Sciences, Department of Anthropology, Los Angeles, CA 90032-8530. Offers MA. Part-time and evening/weekend programs available. *Faculty:* 6 full-time (5 women), 10 part-time/adjunct (5 women). *Students:* 35 full-time (24 women), 38 part-time (27 women); includes 18 minority (3 African Americans, 3 American Indian/Alaska Native, 5 Asian Americans or Pacific Islanders, 7 Hispanic Americans), 10 international. Average age 32. In 2007, 8 degrees awarded. *Degree requirements:* For master's, one foreign language, comprehensive exam or thesis. *Entrance requirements:* Additional exam requirements/recommendations for international students: Required—TOEFL. *Application deadline:* For fall admission, 6/30 for domestic students; for spring admission, 2/1 for domestic students. Applications are processed on a rolling basis. Application fee: $55. *Financial support:* Federal Work-Study available. Support available to part-time students. Financial award application deadline: 3/1. *Faculty research:* Archaeology, folklore, petroglyphs, symbolism, medical anthropology. *Unit head:* Dr. Chor-Swang Ngin, Chair, 323-343-2440 Ext. 32442, Fax: 323-343-2446, E-mail: cngin@calstatela.edu.

California State University, Northridge, Graduate Studies, College of Social and Behavioral Sciences, Department of Anthropology, Northridge, CA 91330. Offers general anthropology (MA); public archaeology (MA). *Faculty:* 7 full-time (5 women), 9 part-time/adjunct (5 women). *Students:* 16 full-time (9 women), 23 part-time (14 women); includes 8 minority (1 American Indian/Alaska Native, 1 Asian American or Pacific Islander, 6 Hispanic Americans), 2 international. Average age 36. 24 applicants, 63% accepted, 12 enrolled. In 2007, 3 degrees awarded. *Degree requirements:* For master's, thesis or alternative. *Entrance requirements:* For master's, GRE General Test or minimum GPA of 3.0. Additional exam requirements/recommendations for international students: Required—TOEFL. *Application deadline:* For fall admission, 11/30 for domestic students. Application fee: $55. *Financial support:* Career-related internships or fieldwork, Federal Work-Study, and institutionally sponsored loans available. Financial award application deadline: 3/1. *Unit head:* Sabina Magliocco, Chair, 818-677-3331. *Application contact:* Dr. Cathy L. Costin, Graduate Adviser, 818-677-3324.

California State University, Sacramento, Graduate Studies, College of Social Sciences and Interdisciplinary Studies, Department of Anthropology, Sacramento, CA 95819-6048. Offers MA. Part-time programs available. *Students:* 8 full-time (5 women), 26 part-time (19 women); includes 5 minority (1 American Indian/Alaska Native, 1 Asian American or Pacific Islander, 3 Hispanic Americans). Average age 33. 27 applicants, 41% accepted, 9 enrolled. *Degree requirements:* For master's, thesis, departmental qualifying exam, writing proficiency exam. *Entrance requirements:* For master's, minimum GPA of 3.0 during previous 2 years. Additional exam requirements/recommendations for international students: Required—TOEFL. *Application deadline:* Applications are processed on a rolling basis. Application fee: $55. Electronic applications accepted. *Expenses:* Tuition, state resident: full-time $3,414. Tuition, nonresident: full-time $13,584; part-time $339 per unit. Required fees: $786; $393 per semester. *Financial support:* Career-related internships or fieldwork and Federal Work-Study available. Support available to part-time students. Financial award application deadline: 3/1. *Unit head:* Dr. David Zeanah, Chair, 916-278-6452, Fax: 916-278-6339.

Carleton University, Faculty of Graduate Studies, Faculty of Arts and Social Sciences, Department of Sociology and Anthropology, Program in Anthropology, Ottawa, ON K1S 5B6, Canada. Offers MA. *Degree requirements:* For master's, comprehensive exam, thesis optional. *Entrance requirements:* For master's, honors degree. Additional exam requirements/recommendations for international students: Required—TOEFL. Application fee: $77. *Financial support:* Institutionally sponsored loans, traineeships, and unspecified assistantships available. *Faculty research:* Culture, symbols and mind, anthropology of signs and symbols, Indigenous studies, anthropology of development and underdevelopment. *Unit head:* Jen Pylypa, Coordinator, 613-520-2600 Ext. 2582, Fax: 613-520-4062, E-mail: soc-anthro@carleton.ca.

Case Western Reserve University, Frances Payne Bolton School of Nursing and Department of Anthropology, Nursing/Anthropology Program, Cleveland, OH 44106. Offers MSN/MA. *Application deadline:* Applications are processed on a rolling basis. Application fee: $75. *Financial support:* Fellowships, research assistantships, teaching assistantships available. Financial award application deadline: 6/30. *Unit head:* Dr. Carol Savrin, Head, 216-368-6304, Fax: 215-368-3542, E-mail: cls18@case.edu. *Application contact:* Peter Taylor, Recruitment and Retention Specialist, 216-368-0349, Fax: 216-368-0124, E-mail: peter.taylor@case.edu.

Case Western Reserve University, School of Graduate Studies, Department of Anthropology, Cleveland, OH 44106. Offers MA, PhD, MD/MA, MD/PhD, MPH/MA, MSN/MA, PhD/MPH. Part-time programs available. *Faculty:* 10 full-time (5 women), 7 part-time/adjunct (4 women). *Students:* 30 full-time (23 women), 1 (woman) part-time; includes 8 minority (4 African Americans, 4 Asian Americans or Pacific Islanders), 1 international. Average age 29. 18 applicants, 56% accepted, 3 enrolled. In 2007, 6 master's, 3 doctorates awarded. Terminal master's awarded for partial completion of doctoral program. *Degree requirements:* For master's, thesis optional; for doctorate, one foreign language, thesis/dissertation. *Entrance requirements:* For master's and doctorate, GRE General Test. Additional exam requirements/recommendations for international students: Required—TOEFL. *Application deadline:* For fall admission, 3/1 priority date for domestic students. Applications are processed on a rolling basis. Application fee: $50. Electronic applications accepted. *Financial support:* Fellowships with tuition reimbursements, research assistantships with tuition reimbursements, teaching assistantships with tuition reimbursements, career-related internships or fieldwork, Federal Work-Study, institutionally sponsored loans, and tuition waivers (full and partial) available. Support available to part-time students. Financial award application deadline: 3/1. *Faculty research:* Medical anthropology, psychological anthropology, cross-cultural aging, physical anthropology, international health. *Unit head:* Lawrence P. Greksa, Chairman, 216-368-2259, Fax: 216-368-5334, E-mail: lawrence.greksa@case.edu. *Application contact:* Kathleen Dowdell, Department Assistant, 216-368-2264, Fax: 216-368-5334, E-mail: kjd4@cwru.edu.

The Catholic University of America, School of Arts and Sciences, Department of Anthropology, Washington, DC 20064. Offers MA, PhD. Part-time and evening/weekend programs available. *Faculty:* 4 full-time (2 women), 1 part-time/adjunct (0 women). *Students:* 2 full-time (both women), 9 part-time (5 women); includes 1 minority (Hispanic American), 2 international. Average age 39. 7 applicants, 57% accepted, 2 enrolled. In 2007, 2 master's, 5 doctorates awarded. Terminal master's awarded for partial completion of doctoral program. *Degree requirements:* For master's, one foreign language, comprehensive exam, thesis or alternative; for doctorate, one foreign language, comprehensive exam, thesis/dissertation. *Entrance requirements:* For master's and doctorate, GRE General Test, 3 letters of recommendation. Additional exam requirements/recommendations for international students: Required—TOEFL (minimum score 580 paper-based; 237 computer-based). *Application deadline:* For fall admission, 2/1 priority date for domestic students; for spring admission, 11/15 priority date for domestic students. Applications are processed on a rolling basis. Application fee: $55. Electronic applications accepted. *Financial support:* Fellowships, research assistantships, teaching assistantships, career-related internships or fieldwork, Federal Work-Study, scholarships/grants, tuition waivers (full and partial), and unspecified assistantships available. Support available to part-time students. Financial award application deadline: 2/1; financial award applicants required to submit FAFSA. *Faculty research:* Medical and applied anthropology, eastern North American and South American archaeology, applied anthropology, Latin American studies, ecological anthropology. *Unit head:* Dr. Lucy Cohen, Acting Chair, 202-319-5080, Fax: 202-319-4782, E-mail: cohen@cua.edu.

Central European University, Graduate Studies, School of Social Sciences and Humanities, Budapest, Hungary. Offers economics (MA, PhD); gender studies (MA, PhD); international relations and European studies (MA, PhD); mathematics and its applications (MS, PhD); medieval studies (MA, PhD); nationalism studies (MA, PhD); philosophy (MA, PhD); political science (MA, PhD); public policy (MA, PhD); sociology and social anthropology (MA, PhD). *Faculty:* 75 full-time (25 women), 46 part-time/adjunct (10 women). *Students:* 625 full-time (355 women). Average age 26. 2,500 applicants, 31% accepted, 540 enrolled. In 2007, 325 master's, 20 doctorates awarded. Terminal master's awarded for partial completion of doctoral program. *Degree requirements:* For master's, one foreign language, thesis; for doctorate, one foreign language, comprehensive exam, thesis/dissertation. *Entrance requirements:* For master's, CEU subject tests, interview; for doctorate, GRE, CEU subject test, interview. Additional exam requirements/recommendations for international students: Required—TOEFL (minimum score 570 paper-based; 230 computer-based). *Application deadline:* For fall admission, 1/15 priority date for domestic and international students. Application fee: $0. Electronic applications accepted. Tuition charges are reported in euros. *Expenses:* Tuition: Full-time 10,000 euros; part-time 315 euros per credit. *Financial support:* In 2007–08, 402 students received support, including 350 fellowships with full and partial tuition reimbursements available (averaging $5,000 per year); career-related internships or fieldwork, institutionally sponsored loans, and scholarships/grants also available. Financial award application deadline: 1/5. *Faculty research:* Civil society, fiscal decentralization, party politics, political philosophy (especially Liberalism, theory of Democracy). Total annual research expenditures: $35,000. *Unit head:* Dr. Howard Michael Robinson, Provost, 361-327-3003, Fax: 361-327-3211, E-mail: robinson@ceu.hu. *Application contact:* Zsuzsanna Jaszberenyi, Admissions Officer, 361-327-3009, Fax: 361-327-3211, E-mail: admissions@ceu.hu.

See Close-Up on page 447.

The College of William and Mary, Faculty of Arts and Sciences, Department of Anthropology, Williamsburg, VA 23187-8795. Offers MA, PhD. *Faculty:* 15 full-time (7 women), 6 part-time/adjunct (3 women). *Students:* 35 full-time (21 women), 3 part-time (1 woman); includes 4 minority (all American Indian/Alaska Native), 4 international. Average age 32. 50 applicants, 36% accepted, 11 enrolled. In 2007, 6 degrees awarded. Terminal master's awarded for partial completion of doctoral program. *Degree requirements:* For master's, thesis, fieldwork; for doctorate, one foreign language, comprehensive exam, thesis/dissertation, fieldwork. *Entrance requirements:* For master's and doctorate, GRE, course work in anthropology or history. Additional exam requirements/recommendations for international students: Required—TOEFL. *Application deadline:* For fall admission, 1/15 for domestic and international students. Application fee: $45. Electronic applications accepted. *Expenses:* Tuition, state resident: full-time $6,250; part-time $275 per credit hour. Tuition, nonresident: part-time $760 per credit hour. Required fees: $3,550. Tuition and fees vary according to program. *Financial support:* In 2007–08, 11 research assistantships with full tuition reimbursements (averaging $12,400 per year), 4 teaching assistantships with full tuition reimbursements (averaging $12,400 per year) were awarded; career-related internships or fieldwork and institutionally sponsored loans also available. Financial award application deadline: 1/15; financial award applicants required to submit FAFSA. *Faculty research:* Historical archaeology, comparative colonialism, biocultural anthropology, African diaspora, historical archaeology of native America. Total annual research expenditures: $855,168. *Unit head:* Dr. Brad L. Weiss, Chair, 757-221-1209, Fax: 757-221-1066, E-mail: blweiss@wm.edu. *Application contact:* Dr. Mary M. Voigt, Director of Graduate Studies, 757-221-1057, Fax: 757-221-1066, E-mail: mmvoig@wm.edu.

Colorado State University, Graduate School, College of Liberal Arts, Department of Anthropology, Fort Collins, CO 80523-0015. Offers MA. Part-time programs available. *Faculty:* 11 full-time (7 women), 1 part-time/adjunct (0 women). *Students:* 25 full-time (17 women), 27 part-time (18 women); includes 3 minority (2 Asian Americans or Pacific Islanders, 1 Hispanic American), 1 international. Average age 29. 40 applicants, 48% accepted, 14 enrolled. In 2007, 8 degrees awarded. *Degree requirements:* For master's, comprehensive exam (for some programs), thesis optional, anthropological theory, oral exam. *Entrance requirements:* For master's, GRE General Test, minimum GPA of 3.0, BA/BS. Additional exam requirements/recommendations for international students: Required—TOEFL. *Application deadline:* For fall admission, 2/15 for domestic and international students. Applications are processed on a rolling basis. Application fee: $50. Electronic applications accepted. *Expenses:* Tuition, state resident: full-time $4,887; part-time $272 per credit. Tuition, nonresident: full-time $16,425; part-time $913 per credit. Required fees: $1,379; $75 per credit. *Financial support:* In 2007–08, 1 research assistantship with full tuition reimbursement (averaging $11,745 per year), 14 teaching assistantships with full tuition reimbursements (averaging $10,207 per year) were awarded; fellowships, career-related internships or fieldwork, Federal Work-Study, scholarships/grants, and unspecified assistantships also available. Financial award application deadline: 3/1; financial award applicants required to submit FAFSA. *Faculty research:* Archaeology, cultural anthropology, biological anthropology, globalizational development. Total annual research expenditures: $120,514. *Unit head:* Dr. Kathleen A. Galvin, Chair, 970-491-5784, Fax: 970-491-7597, E-mail: kathleen.galvin@colostate.edu. *Application contact:* Dr. Ann L. Magennis, Graduate Program Coordinator and Associate Professor, 970-491-5966, Fax: 970-491-7597, E-mail: ann.magennis@colostate.edu.

Columbia University, Graduate School of Arts and Sciences, Division of Social Sciences, Department of Anthropology, New York, NY 10027. Offers M Phil, MA, PhD, JD/MA, JD/PhD. Part-time programs available. *Faculty:* 32 full-time, 3 part-time/adjunct. *Students:* 152 full-time (94 women), 20 part-time (13 women). Average age 31. 256 applicants, 18% accepted. In 2007, 15 master's, 9 doctorates awarded. *Degree requirements:* For master's, one foreign language, 2 research papers; for doctorate, 2 foreign languages, thesis/dissertation. *Entrance requirements:* For master's and doctorate, GRE General Test. Additional exam requirements/recommendations for international students: Required—TOEFL. Application fee: $90. *Expenses:* Tuition: Part-time $1,452 per credit. Required fees: $152 per term. One-time fee: $75 part-time. Full-time tuition and fees vary according to course level, course load, degree level and program. *Financial support:* Fellowships, teaching assistantships, Federal Work-Study and institutionally sponsored loans available. Support available to part-time students. Financial award application deadline: 1/5; financial award applicants required to submit FAFSA. *Faculty research:* Archaeology, physical anthropology, cultural and linguistic anthropology. *Unit head:* Brinkley Messick, Chair, 212-854-7459, Fax: 212-854-7347, E-mail: bmm23@columbia.edu.

Concordia University, School of Graduate Studies, Faculty of Arts and Science, Department of Sociology and Anthropology, Montréal, QC H3G 1M8, Canada. Offers social and cultural anthropology (MA); sociology (MA). *Degree requirements:* For master's, comprehensive exam or thesis. *Entrance requirements:* For master's, honors degree in sociology or equivalent. *Faculty research:* Community and ethnic relations, popular culture, regional development in Canada, industrial and social movements, social problems and policies.

Cornell University, Graduate School, Graduate Fields of Arts and Sciences, Field of Anthropology, Ithaca, NY 14853-0001. Offers archaeological anthropology (PhD); biological anthropology (PhD); sociocultural anthropology (PhD). *Faculty:* 31 full-time (13 women).

Anthropology

Cornell University (continued)
Students: 58 full-time (40 women); includes 10 minority (5 African Americans, 1 American Indian/Alaska Native, 2 Asian Americans or Pacific Islanders, 2 Hispanic Americans), 22 international. Average age 31. 117 applicants, 15% accepted, 13 enrolled. In 2007, 8 doctorates awarded. *Degree requirements:* For doctorate, one foreign language, comprehensive exam, thesis/dissertation, teaching experience. *Entrance requirements:* For doctorate, GRE General Test, 3 letters of recommendation, sample of written work. Additional exam requirements/recommendations for international students: Required—TOEFL (minimum score 550 paper-based; 213 computer-based; 77 iBT). *Application deadline:* For fall admission, 1/1 for domestic students. Application fee: $70. Electronic applications accepted. *Financial support:* In 2007–08, 45 students received support, including 26 fellowships with full tuition reimbursements available, 19 teaching assistantships with full tuition reimbursements available; research assistantships with full tuition reimbursements available, institutionally sponsored loans, scholarships/grants, health care benefits, tuition waivers (full and partial), and unspecified assistantships also available. Financial award applicants required to submit FAFSA. *Faculty research:* Culture, engaged anthropology, political economy, area studies: Asia, Americas, Europe; interdisciplinary and ethnic studies: Asian-American studies. *Unit head:* Director of Graduate Studies, 607-255-6768. *Application contact:* Graduate Field Assistant, 607-255-6768, E-mail: graduate_anthropology@cornell.edu.

Dalhousie University, Faculty of Arts and Social Science, Department of Sociology and Social Anthropology, Halifax, NS B3H 4R2, Canada. Offers social anthropology (MA, PhD); sociology (MA, PhD). Part-time programs available. *Faculty:* 18 full-time, 6 part-time/adjunct. *Students:* 13 full-time (8 women), 4 part-time (all women). In 2007, 8 degrees awarded. *Degree requirements:* For master's, thesis; for doctorate, one foreign language, thesis/dissertation. *Entrance requirements:* Additional exam requirements/recommendations for international students: Required—TOEFL. *Application deadline:* For fall admission, 6/1 for domestic students. Applications are processed on a rolling basis. Application fee: $60. *Financial support:* In 2007–08, 1 research assistantship, 17 teaching assistantships were awarded; fellowships also available. Financial award application deadline: 3/1. *Faculty research:* Social inequality and social injustice; work, industry, and development; (regional and international perspectives); health and illness. *Unit head:* Dr. Christopher Murphy, Chair, 902-494-6593, Fax: 902-494-2897. *Application contact:* Pauline Gardiner Barber, Graduate Coordinator, 902-494-6593, Fax: 902-494-2897, E-mail: sosagrad@is.dal.ca.

Duke University, Graduate School, Department of Cultural Anthropology, Durham, NC 27708. Offers physical anthropology (PhD), including comparative morphology of human and non-human primates, primate social behavior; social/cultural anthropology (PhD); JD/AM. *Faculty:* 12 full-time. *Students:* 35 full-time (24 women); includes 11 minority (6 African Americans, 2 Asian Americans or Pacific Islanders, 3 Hispanic Americans), 12 international. 125 applicants, 5% accepted, 3 enrolled. In 2007, 2 doctorates awarded. *Degree requirements:* For doctorate, one foreign language, thesis/dissertation. *Entrance requirements:* For doctorate, GRE General Test. Additional exam requirements/recommendations for international students: Required—TOEFL (minimum score 550 paper-based; 213 computer-based; 83 iBT), IELTS (minimum score 7). *Application deadline:* For fall admission, 12/15 priority date for domestic and international students. Application fee: $75. *Financial support:* Fellowships, research assistantships, teaching assistantships, Federal Work-Study available. Financial award application deadline: 12/31. *Unit head:* Rebecca Stein, Director of Graduate Studies, 919-684-4544, Fax: 919-681-8483, E-mail: hfrancis@duke.edu.

East Carolina University, Graduate School, Thomas Harriot College of Arts and Sciences, Department of Anthropology, Greenville, NC 27858-4353. Offers MA. Part-time programs available. *Faculty:* 10 full-time (4 women). *Students:* 17 full-time (12 women), 4 part-time (2 women), 2 international. Average age 26. 14 applicants, 7% accepted, 1 enrolled. In 2007, 4 degrees awarded. *Degree requirements:* For master's, one foreign language, comprehensive exam, thesis. *Entrance requirements:* For master's, GRE General Test. Additional exam requirements/recommendations for international students: Required—TOEFL. *Application deadline:* For fall admission, 6/1 priority date for domestic students; for spring admission, 10/15 for domestic students. Applications are processed on a rolling basis. Application fee: $50. *Financial support:* Research assistantships with partial tuition reimbursements available. Financial award application deadline: 6/1. *Unit head:* Dr. Linda Wolfe, Chair and Director of Graduate Studies, 252-328-9453, Fax: 252-328-6759, E-mail: wolfel@ecu.edu. *Application contact:* Dean of Graduate School, 252-328-6012, Fax: 252-328-6071, E-mail: gradschool@ecu.edu.

Eastern New Mexico University, Graduate School, College of Liberal Arts and Sciences, Department of Anthropology and Applied Archaeology, Portales, NM 88130. Offers anthropology (MA). Part-time programs available. *Faculty:* 4 full-time (1 woman), 1 part-time/adjunct (0 women). *Students:* Average age 31. 11 applicants, 91% accepted. In 2007, 6 degrees awarded. *Degree requirements:* For master's, one foreign language, comprehensive exam, thesis. *Entrance requirements:* For master's, GRE General Test, minimum GPA of 2.5. *Application deadline:* For fall admission, 8/20 priority date for domestic students. Applications are processed on a rolling basis. Application fee: $0. Electronic applications accepted. *Expenses:* Tuition, state resident: full-time $2,592; part-time $108 per credit hour. Tuition, nonresident: full-time $8,136; part-time $339 per credit hour. Required fees: $3,850 per credit hour. *Financial support:* In 2007–08, 2 fellowships (averaging $5,125 per year), 18 research assistantships (averaging $8,200 per year), 3 teaching assistantships (averaging $8,200 per year) were awarded; career-related internships or fieldwork and Federal Work-Study also available. Support available to part-time students. Financial award application deadline: 3/1. *Faculty research:* Paleobotany, remote sensing, conservation archaeology, obsidian hydration. *Unit head:* Dr. Stephen Durand, Graduate Coordinator, 505-562-2247, E-mail: stephen.durand@enmu.edu.

Emory University, Graduate School of Arts and Sciences, Department of Anthropology, Atlanta, GA 30322-1100. Offers PhD. *Degree requirements:* For doctorate, thesis/dissertation, qualifying exams. *Entrance requirements:* For doctorate, GRE General Test. Additional exam requirements/recommendations for international students: Required—TOEFL. Electronic applications accepted. *Faculty research:* Primate behavioral ecology, comparative human biology, human growth and development, medical anthropology, globalization, gender and sexuality.

Florida Atlantic University, Dorothy F. Schmidt College of Arts and Letters, Department of Anthropology, Boca Raton, FL 33431-0991. Offers MA, MAT. Part-time programs available. *Degree requirements:* For master's, one foreign language, thesis. *Entrance requirements:* For master's, GRE General Test, minimum GPA of 3.0. Additional exam requirements/recommendations for international students: Required—TOEFL. Electronic applications accepted. *Faculty research:* Archaeological, ethnological, ethnographical, osteological, paleoanthropological, and zoo-archaeological research.

Florida State University, Graduate Studies, College of Arts and Sciences, Department of Anthropology, Tallahassee, FL 32306. Offers MA, MS, PhD. Part-time programs available. *Faculty:* 12 full-time (6 women), 1 (woman) part-time/adjunct. *Students:* 35 full-time (23 women), 29 part-time (14 women); includes 4 minority (2 African Americans, 2 Hispanic Americans). Average age 25. 63 applicants, 25% accepted, 12 enrolled. In 2007, 9 master's, 2 doctorates awarded. Terminal master's awarded for partial completion of doctoral program. *Degree requirements:* For master's, one foreign language, comprehensive exam, thesis optional; for doctorate, one foreign language, comprehensive exam, thesis/dissertation. *Entrance requirements:* For master's, GRE General Test, minimum GPA of 3.0; for doctorate, GRE General Test, minimum GPA of 3.5 (recommended). Additional exam requirements/recommendations for international students: Required—TOEFL. *Application deadline:* For fall admission, 1/1 for domestic and international students. Application fee: $30. Electronic applications accepted. *Expenses:* Tuition, state resident: part-time $248 per credit hour. Tuition, nonresident: part-time $880 per credit hour. Tuition and fees vary according to program. *Financial support:* In 2007–08, 28 students received support, including 2 fellowships with full tuition reimbursements available (averaging $13,000 per year), 13 research assistantships with full tuition reimbursements available (averaging $7,000 per year), 13 teaching assistantships with full tuition reimbursements available (averaging $7,000 per year); career-related internships or fieldwork, Federal Work-Study, institutionally sponsored loans, scholarships/grants, tuition waivers (full), and unspecified assistantships also available. Financial award applicants required to submit FAFSA. *Faculty research:* Prehistoric and historic archaeology, four-field anthropology, bioarchacology, race, religion. Total annual research expenditures: $500,000. *Unit head:* Dr. Glen Doran, Chairman, 850-644-8154, Fax: 850-645-0052, E-mail: gdoran@fsu.edu. *Application contact:* Shannon Tucker, Student Coordinator, 850-644-4282, Fax: 850-645-0032, E-mail: srtucker@mailer.fsu.edu.

George Mason University, College of Humanities and Social Sciences, Department of Sociology and Anthropology, Fairfax, VA 22030. Offers anthropology (MA); sociology (MA). *Faculty:* 27 full-time (13 women), 6 part-time/adjunct (2 women). *Students:* 20 full-time (11 women), 42 part-time (29 women); includes 21 minority (11 African Americans, 1 American Indian/Alaska Native, 3 Asian Americans or Pacific Islanders, 6 Hispanic Americans), 1 international. Average age 29. 73 applicants, 73% accepted, 31 enrolled. In 2007, 5 degrees awarded. *Degree requirements:* For master's, thesis. *Entrance requirements:* For master's, GRE General Test, minimum GPA of 3.0 in last 60 hours; writing sample; previous undergraduate course work in sociological theory, research methods, and social statistics. *Application deadline:* For fall admission, 5/1 for domestic students; for spring admission, 11/1 for domestic students. Application fee: $60 ($75 for international students). Electronic applications accepted. *Financial support:* Research assistantships, teaching assistantships available. Support available to part-time students. Financial award application deadline: 3/1; financial award applicants required to submit FAFSA. *Unit head:* Dr. Steven Vallas, Chairman, 703-993-2127, Fax: 703-993-1446, E-mail: svallas@gmu.edu.

George Mason University, College of Humanities and Social Sciences, Interdisciplinary Studies Program, Fairfax, VA 22030. Offers anthropology (MAIS); community college teaching (MAIS); folklore (MAIS); higher education (MAIS); individualized studies (MAIS); religion, cultures, and values (MAIS); video-based production (MAIS); women's studies (MAIS); zoo and aquarium leadership (MAIS). Part-time and evening/weekend programs available. *Faculty:* 6 full-time (4 women), 6 part-time/adjunct (5 women). *Students:* 25 full-time (17 women), 90 part-time (76 women); includes 24 minority (5 African Americans, 1 American Indian/Alaska Native, 7 Asian Americans or Pacific Islanders, 11 Hispanic Americans), 3 international. Average age 33. 68 applicants, 72% accepted, 35 enrolled. In 2007, 19 degrees awarded. *Degree requirements:* For master's, thesis optional. *Entrance requirements:* For master's, GRE, GMAT, or MAT, interview, minimum GPA of 3.0 in last 60 hours of course work. *Application deadline:* For fall admission, 5/1 priority date for domestic students; for spring admission, 11/1 for domestic students. Applications are processed on a rolling basis. Application fee: $60 ($75 for international students). Electronic applications accepted. *Financial support:* Fellowships, teaching assistantships, career-related internships or fieldwork, Federal Work-Study, and institutionally sponsored loans available. Support available to part-time students. Financial award application deadline: 3/1; financial award applicants required to submit FAFSA. *Unit head:* John Burns, Chair, 703-993-1291, Fax: 703-993-1297, E-mail: mais@gmu.edu. *Application contact:* Dr. Johannes D. Bergmann, Information Contact, 703-993-8762, E-mail: mais@gmu.edu.

The George Washington University, Columbian College of Arts and Sciences, Department of Anthropology, Washington, DC 20052. Offers anthropology (MA); folklife (MA). Part-time and evening/weekend programs available. *Degree requirements:* For master's, one foreign language, comprehensive exam, thesis or alternative. *Entrance requirements:* For master's, GRE General Test, minimum GPA of 3.0. Additional exam requirements/recommendations for international students: Required—TOEFL (minimum score 550 paper-based; 213 computer-based). Electronic applications accepted.

The George Washington University, Columbian College of Arts and Sciences, Department of Environmental Studies, Program in Hominid Paleobiology, Washington, DC 20052. Offers MS, PhD. Part-time and evening/weekend programs available. Terminal master's awarded for partial completion of doctoral program. *Degree requirements:* For master's, comprehensive exam, thesis; for doctorate, thesis/dissertation, general exam. *Entrance requirements:* For master's, GRE General Test, bachelor's degree in field, minimum GPA of 3.0; for doctorate, GRE General Test, minimum GPA of 3.0. Additional exam requirements/recommendations for international students: Required—TOEFL (minimum score 550 paper-based; 213 computer-based). Electronic applications accepted.

Georgia State University, College of Arts and Sciences, Department of Anthropology, Atlanta, GA 30303-3083. Offers MA. Part-time and evening/weekend programs available. *Faculty:* 9 full-time (6 women). *Students:* 18 full-time (12 women), 1 (woman) part-time; includes 1 minority (African American) 19 applicants, 37% accepted, 5 enrolled. In 2007, 5 degrees awarded. *Degree requirements:* For master's, one foreign language, thesis or alternative, exam. *Entrance requirements:* For master's, GRE General Test, departmental supplemental form. Additional exam requirements/recommendations for international students: Required—TOEFL. *Application deadline:* For fall admission, 4/15 for domestic students; for spring admission, 10/15 for domestic students. Applications are processed on a rolling basis. Application fee: $50. Electronic applications accepted. *Expenses:* Tuition, state resident: part-time $221 per credit hour. *Financial support:* In 2007–08, 16 students received support, including research assistantships with full tuition reimbursements available (averaging $6,000 per year), teaching assistantships with full tuition reimbursements available (averaging $6,000 per year); career-related internships or fieldwork, Federal Work-Study, and institutionally sponsored loans also available. Support available to part-time students. Financial award applicants required to submit FAFSA. *Faculty research:* Medical anthropology, Latin American cultures, urban anthropology, American Southeast. *Unit head:* Dr. Kathryn A Kozaitis, Chair, 404-413-5151, Fax: 404-413-5159, E-mail: kozaitis@gsu.edu. *Application contact:* Dr. Emanuela Guano, Director of Graduate Studies, 404-413-5152, Fax: 404-413-5159, E-mail: eguano@gsu.edu.

Graduate School and University Center of the City University of New York, Graduate Studies, Program in Anthropology, New York, NY 10016-4039. Offers anthropological linguistics (PhD); archaeology (PhD); cultural anthropology (PhD); physical anthropology (PhD). *Faculty:* 39 full-time (14 women). *Students:* 158 full-time (96 women), 3 part-time (all women); includes 34 minority (11 African Americans, 8 Asian Americans or Pacific Islanders, 15 Hispanic Americans), 27 international. Average age 34. 165 applicants, 25% accepted, 21 enrolled. In 2007, 10 degrees awarded. *Degree requirements:* For doctorate, one foreign language, thesis/dissertation. *Entrance requirements:* For doctorate, GRE General Test. Additional exam requirements/recommendations for international students: Required—TOEFL. *Application deadline:* For fall admission, 1/8 priority date for domestic students. Application fee: $125. Electronic applications accepted. *Financial support:* In 2007–08, 111 students received support, including 85 fellowships, 16 research assistantships, 10 teaching assistantships; career-related internships or fieldwork, Federal Work-Study, institutionally sponsored loans, and tuition waivers (full and partial) also available. Financial award application deadline: 2/1; financial award applicants required to submit FAFSA. *Unit head:* Dr. Louise Lennihan, Executive Officer, 212-817-8006, Fax: 212-817-1501, E-mail: anthro@gc.cuny.edu. *Application contact:* Information Contact, 212-817-8005, Fax: 212-817-1501, E-mail: anthro@gc.cuny.edu.

Harvard University, Graduate School of Arts and Sciences, Committee on Middle Eastern Studies, Cambridge, MA 02138. Offers anthropology and Middle Eastern studies (PhD); economics and Middle Eastern studies (PhD); fine arts and Middle Eastern studies (PhD); history and Middle Eastern studies (PhD); regional studies–Middle East (AM). Terminal master's awarded for partial completion of doctoral program. *Degree requirements:* For master's, one foreign language; for doctorate, 2 foreign languages, thesis/dissertation. *Entrance requirements:* For master's, GRE General Test; for doctorate, GRE General Test, 1 year of course work in Middle Eastern regional studies, proficiency in a related language. Additional exam requirements/recommendations for international students: Required—TOEFL. *Expenses:* Tuition: Full-time $31,456. Full-time tuition and fees vary according to program and student level.

Harvard University, Graduate School of Arts and Sciences, Department of Anthropology, Cambridge, MA 02138. Offers archaeology (PhD); biological anthropology (PhD); legal anthropology (AM); medical anthropology (AM); social anthropology (AM, PhD); social change and development (AM). Terminal master's awarded for partial completion of doctoral program. *Degree requirements:* For master's, 2 foreign languages, thesis (for some programs); for doctorate, 2 foreign languages, thesis/dissertation, laboratory and/or fieldwork; general, qualifying, or special exams. *Entrance requirements:* For master's and doctorate, GRE General Test. Additional exam requirements/recommendations for international students: Required—TOEFL. *Expenses:* Tuition: Full-time $31,456. Full-time tuition and fees vary according to program and student level.

Hunter College of the City University of New York, Graduate School, School of Arts and Sciences, Department of Anthropology, New York, NY 10021-5085. Offers MA. Part-time and evening/weekend programs available. *Faculty:* 6 full-time (0 women), 2 part-time/adjunct (1 woman). *Students:* 2 full-time (1 woman), 50 part-time (31 women); includes 8 minority (6 Asian Americans or Pacific Islanders, 2 Hispanic Americans). Average age 32. 36 applicants, 50% accepted, 11 enrolled. In 2007, 15 degrees awarded. *Degree requirements:* For master's, comprehensive exam, thesis, language or statistics exam. *Entrance requirements:* For master's, GRE General Test, minimum 9 credits of course work in anthropology or a related field. Additional exam requirements/recommendations for international students: Required—TOEFL. *Application deadline:* For fall admission, 4/1 for domestic students, 2/1 for international students; for spring admission, 11/1 for domestic students, 9/1 for international students. Application fee: $125. *Expenses:* Tuition, state resident: full-time $6,400; part-time $270 per credit. Tuition, nonresident: part-time $500 per credit. One-time fee: $125 full-time. Tuition and fees vary according to program. *Financial support:* Research assistantships, tuition waivers (full and partial) available. *Faculty research:* Primatology, human ecology, archeology, political anthropology, primate and human evolution. *Unit head:* Gregory A. Johnson, Chair, 212-772-5652, Fax: 212-772-5410. *Application contact:* William Zlata, Director for Graduate Admissions, 212-772-4482, Fax: 212-650-3336, E-mail: admissions@hunter.cuny.edu.

Idaho State University, Office of Graduate Studies, College of Arts and Sciences, Department of Anthropology, Pocatello, ID 83209. Offers MA, MS. Part-time programs available. *Faculty:* 6 full-time (2 women). *Students:* 14 full-time (8 women), 9 part-time (8 women); includes 3 minority (all American Indian/Alaska Native), 1 international. Average age 40. In 2007, 8 degrees awarded. *Degree requirements:* For master's, one foreign language, thesis. *Entrance requirements:* For master's, GRE General Test, GMAT or MAT, minimum GPA of 3.0 in all upper division classes, 3 letters of recommendation. Additional exam requirements/recommendations for international students: Required—TOEFL (minimum score 550 paper-based; 213 computer-based; 80 iBT). *Application deadline:* For fall admission, 7/1 for domestic students, 6/1 for international students; for spring admission, 12/1 for domestic students, 11/1 for international students. Applications are processed on a rolling basis. Application fee: $55. *Expenses:* Tuition, state resident: full-time $2,882; part-time $259 per credit hour. Tuition, nonresident: full-time $11,566; part-time $379 per credit hour. Required fees: $2,278. Full-time tuition and fees vary according to program. Part-time tuition and fees vary according to course load. *Financial support:* In 2007–08, 3 research assistantships with full and partial tuition reimbursements (averaging $9,128 per year), 3 teaching assistantships with full and partial tuition reimbursements (averaging $9,128 per year) were awarded; career-related internships or fieldwork, Federal Work-Study, institutionally sponsored loans, and tuition waivers (full and partial) also available. Support available to part-time students. Financial award application deadline: 1/1; financial award applicants required to submit FAFSA. *Faculty research:* Native American studies: health care, language/ethnopoetics, prehistory, art, resource environmental management. *Unit head:* Dr. Ernst 'Skip" Lohse, Chairman, 208-282-2629, Fax: 208-282-4741, E-mail: lohserne@isu.edu. *Application contact:* Ellen Combs, Graduate School Technical Records Specialist, 208-282-2150, Fax: 208-282-4847.

Indiana University Bloomington, University Graduate School, College of Arts and Sciences, Department of Anthropology, Bloomington, IN 47405-7000. Offers MA, PhD. PhD offered through the University Graduate School. *Faculty:* 26 full-time (16 women), 25 part-time/adjunct (9 women). *Students:* 94 full-time (62 women), 28 part-time (17 women); includes 23 minority (4 African Americans, 7 American Indian/Alaska Native, 3 Asian Americans or Pacific Islanders, 9 Hispanic Americans), 8 international. Average age 32. 120 applicants, 35% accepted, 19 enrolled. In 2007, 11 master's, 7 doctorates awarded. Terminal master's awarded for partial completion of doctoral program. *Median time to degree:* Of those who began their doctoral program in fall 1999, 55% received their degree in 8 years or less. *Degree requirements:* For master's, thesis or alternative; for doctorate, one foreign language, comprehensive exam, thesis/dissertation. *Entrance requirements:* For master's and doctorate, GRE General Test, minimum GPA of 3.0. Additional exam requirements/recommendations for international students: Required—TOEFL (minimum score 550 paper-based; 213 computer-based; 79 iBT). *Application deadline:* For fall admission, 1/15 for domestic and international students. Application fee: $50 ($60 for international students). Electronic applications accepted. *Financial support:* In 2007–08, 62 students received support; fellowships with full tuition reimbursements available, research assistantships with full tuition reimbursements available, teaching assistantships with full tuition reimbursements available, Federal Work-Study, scholarships/grants, health care benefits, and unspecified assistantships available. Financial award application deadline: 2/15; financial award applicants required to submit FAFSA. *Faculty research:* Ecologic and economic development, symbolism, arts/dance, paleoarchaeology, bioanthropology. Total annual research expenditures: $22.7 million. *Unit head:* Dr. Eduardo S. Brondizio, Chair, 812-855-2555, Fax: 812-855-4358, E-mail: ebrondiz@indiana.edu. *Application contact:* Debra Wilkerson, Secretary, 812-855-1203, Fax: 812-855-4358, E-mail: dwilkers@indiana.edu.

Iowa State University of Science and Technology, Graduate College, College of Liberal Arts and Sciences, Department of Anthropology, Ames, IA 50011. Offers MA. *Faculty:* 7 full-time (3 women), 4 part-time/adjunct (2 women). *Students:* 22 full-time (19 women), 2 part-time (both women); includes 4 minority (2 African Americans, 1 Asian American or Pacific Islander, 1 Hispanic American), 2 international. 19 applicants, 79% accepted, 10 enrolled. In 2007, 5 master's awarded. *Degree requirements:* For master's, thesis. *Entrance requirements:* For master's, GRE General Test. Additional exam requirements/recommendations for international students: Required—TOEFL (paper-based 550; computer-based 213; iBT 79) or IELTS (6.5). *Application deadline:* For fall admission, 1/15 priority date for domestic and international students; for spring admission, 10/1 for domestic and international students. Applications are processed on a rolling basis. Application fee: $30 ($70 for international students). Electronic applications accepted. *Financial support:* In 2007–08, 4 research assistantships with full and partial tuition reimbursements (averaging $21,132 per year), 11 teaching assistantships with full and partial tuition reimbursements (averaging $18,113 per year) were awarded; fellowships, scholarships/grants, health care benefits, and unspecified assistantships also available. *Unit head:* Dr. R. Paul Lasley, Interim Chair, 515-294-8212, Fax: 515-294-1708, E-mail: anthgrad@iastate.edu. *Application contact:* Dr. Nancy Coinman, Director of Graduate Education, 515-294-7139, E-mail: anthgrade@iastate.edu.

The Johns Hopkins University, Zanvyl Krieger School of Arts and Sciences, Department of Anthropology, Baltimore, MD 21218-2699. Offers PhD. *Faculty:* 9 full-time (8 women), 5 part-time/adjunct (1 woman). *Students:* 35 full-time (16 women); includes 4 minority (3 Asian Americans or Pacific Islanders, 1 Hispanic American), 19 international. Average age 30. 59 applicants, 15% accepted, 6 enrolled. In 2007, 1 doctorate awarded. *Degree requirements:* For doctorate, one foreign language, thesis/dissertation. *Entrance requirements:* For doctorate, GRE General Test. Additional exam requirements/recommendations for international students: Required—TOEFL. *Application deadline:* For fall admission, 1/12 for domestic students. Application fee: $75. Electronic applications accepted. *Financial support:* In 2007–08, 21 students received support, including 13 fellowships with full and partial tuition reimbursements available (averaging $16,000 per year), 8 teaching assistantships with full and partial tuition reimbursements available (averaging $16,000 per year); research assistantships, career-related internships or fieldwork, Federal Work-Study, and institutionally sponsored loans also available. Financial award application deadline: 4/15; financial award applicants required to submit FAFSA. *Faculty research:* Social and cultural anthropology of complex societies, gender politics, economic anthropology, religion. Total annual research expenditures: $304,681. *Unit head:* Dr. Veena Das, Chair, 410-516-0630, Fax: 410-516-6080, E-mail: veenadas@jhu.edu. *Application contact:* Richard Helman, Admissions Coordinator, 410-516-7271, Fax: 410-516-6080, E-mail: rhelman@jhu.edu.

Kent State University, College of Arts and Sciences, Department of Anthropology, Kent, OH 44242-0001. Offers MA. *Faculty:* 8 full-time (1 woman). *Students:* 15 full-time (10 women), 13 part-time (9 women); includes 1 minority (Hispanic American) 22 applicants, 64% accepted, 11 enrolled. In 2007, 3 degrees awarded. *Degree requirements:* For master's, thesis. *Entrance requirements:* For master's, GRE General Test, minimum GPA of 3.0. Additional exam requirements/recommendations for international students: Required—TOEFL. *Application deadline:* For fall admission, 2/1 for domestic and international students. Application fee: $30. Electronic applications accepted. *Financial support:* In 2007–08, 8 students received support, including teaching assistantships with full tuition reimbursements available (averaging $8,000 per year); fellowships, research assistantships, Federal Work-Study, institutionally sponsored loans, health care benefits, and tuition waivers (full) also available. Financial award application deadline: 2/1; financial award applicants required to submit FAFSA. *Unit head:* Dr. Richard S. Meindl, Chairman, 330-672-7998, Fax: 330-672-2999, E-mail: rmeindl@kent.edu. *Application contact:* Dr. Mark F Seeman, Coordinator of Graduate Studies, 330-672-2705, Fax: 330-672-2999, E-mail: mseeman@kent.edu.

Louisiana State University and Agricultural and Mechanical College, Graduate School, College of Arts and Sciences, Department of Geography and Anthropology, Baton Rouge, LA 70803. Offers anthropology (MA); geography (MA, MS, PhD). Part-time programs available. *Faculty:* 27 full-time (7 women). *Students:* 64 full-time (26 women), 21 part-time (12 women); includes 2 African Americans, 1 American Indian/Alaska Native, 1 Hispanic American, 21 international. Average age 31. 51 applicants, 55% accepted, 11 enrolled. In 2007, 18 master's, 10 doctorates awarded. Terminal master's awarded for partial completion of doctoral program. *Degree requirements:* For master's, 2 foreign languages, thesis (for some programs); for doctorate, 2 foreign languages, thesis/dissertation. *Entrance requirements:* For master's and doctorate, GRE General Test, minimum GPA of 3.0. Additional exam requirements/recommendations for international students: Required—TOEFL (minimum score 550 paper-based; 213 computer-based; 79 iBT). *Application deadline:* For fall admission, 1/25 priority date for domestic students, 5/15 for international students; for spring admission, 10/15 for international students. Applications are processed on a rolling basis. Application fee: $25. Electronic applications accepted. *Financial support:* In 2007–08, 65 students received support, including 1 fellowship with full tuition reimbursement available (averaging $7,019 per year), 29 research assistantships with full and partial tuition reimbursements available (averaging $16,246 per year), 16 teaching assistantships with full and partial tuition reimbursements available (averaging $11,794 per year); career-related internships or fieldwork, health care benefits, and unspecified assistantships also available. Financial award application deadline: 3/1; financial award applicants required to submit FAFSA. *Faculty research:* Cultural, coastal, climate, GIS-geography, cultural, linguistics, archaeology-anthropology. Total annual research expenditures: $568,400. *Unit head:* Dr. Patrick A. Hesp, Chair, 225-578-5942, Fax: 225-578-4420, E-mail: gachair@lsu.edu. *Application contact:* Dr. Steve Namikas, Graduate Adviser, 225-578-6142, Fax: 225-578-4420, E-mail: snamik1@lsu.edu.

McGill University, Faculty of Graduate and Postdoctoral Studies, Faculty of Arts, Department of Anthropology, Montréal, QC H3A 2T5, Canada. Offers anthropology (MA, PhD); medical anthropology (MA). *Faculty:* 19 full-time (6 women), 11 part-time/adjunct (8 women). *Students:* 60 full-time (38 women), 2 part-time (both women). 67 applicants, 31% accepted, 13 enrolled. In 2007, 5 master's, 6 doctorates awarded. *Median time to degree:* Of those who began their doctoral program in fall 1999, 100% received their degree in 8 years or less.

McGill University, Faculty of Graduate and Postdoctoral Studies, Faculty of Medicine, Department of Social Studies in Medicine, Montréal, QC H3A 2T5, Canada. Offers medical anthropology (MA, PhD); medical history (MA, PhD); medical sociology (MA, PhD). *Faculty:* 7 full-time (2 women), 3 part-time/adjunct (1 woman).

McMaster University, School of Graduate Studies, Faculty of Social Sciences, Department of Anthropology, Hamilton, ON L8S 4M2, Canada. Offers MA, PhD. Part-time programs available. *Faculty:* 15 full-time, 8 part-time/adjunct. *Students:* 34 full-time, 3 part-time. 125 applicants, 6% accepted. *Degree requirements:* For master's, thesis or alternative; for doctorate, one foreign language, comprehensive exam, thesis/dissertation, fieldwork. *Entrance requirements:* Additional exam requirements/recommendations for international students: Required—TOEFL (minimum score 580 paper-based; 237 computer-based). *Application deadline:* For fall admission, 2/15 for domestic students. Application fee: $90. *Financial support:* In 2007–08, 21 fellowships, 29 teaching assistantships (averaging $8,440 per year) were awarded; research assistantships, scholarships/grants also available. *Faculty research:* Medical anthropology, contemporary ethnography in an interdisciplinary perspective, archaeological and social theory, linguistics, folklore. *Unit head:* Dr. Aubrey Canon, Chair, 905-525-9140 Ext. 23920, Fax: 905-522-5993, E-mail: cannona@mcmaster.edu. *Application contact:* Janis Weir, Graduate Secretary, 905-525-9140 Ext. 24424, Fax: 905-522-5993, E-mail: weirjan@mcmaster.ca.

Memorial University of Newfoundland, School of Graduate Studies, Department of Anthropology, St. John's, NL A1C 5S7, Canada. Offers archaeology and physical anthropology (MA, PhD); social and cultural anthropology (MA, PhD). Part-time programs available. *Degree requirements:* For master's, thesis (for some programs); for doctorate, comprehensive exam, thesis/dissertation, oral defense of thesis. *Entrance requirements:* For master's, 2nd class degree in related field. Electronic applications accepted. *Faculty research:* Early European settlements, ethnoarchaeology, economic/political anthropology, land claims and aboriginal rights, marine anthropology.

Michigan State University, The Graduate School, College of Social Science, Department of Anthropology, East Lansing, MI 48824. Offers anthropology (MA, PhD); professional applications in anthropology (MA). Terminal master's awarded for partial completion of doctoral program. *Degree requirements:* For master's, comprehensive exam (for some programs); for doctorate, annual evaluation. *Entrance requirements:* Additional exam requirements/recommendations for international students: Required—TOEFL. Electronic applications accepted. *Expenses:* Tuition, state resident: part-time $379 per credit hour. Tuition, nonresident: part-time $800 per credit hour. Tuition and fees vary according to program.

Minnesota State University Mankato, College of Graduate Studies, College of Social and Behavioral Sciences, Department of Anthropology, Mankato, MN 56001. Offers MS. Part-time programs available. *Students:* 5 full-time (3 women), 11 part-time (5 women). *Degree requirements:* For master's, comprehensive exam. *Entrance requirements:* For master's, minimum undergraduate GPA of 3.0 in last 2 years of course work. Additional exam requirements/recommendations for international students: Required—TOEFL. *Application deadline:* For fall admission, 7/1 priority date for domestic students; for spring admission, 11/1 for domestic students. Applications are processed on a rolling basis. Application fee: $40. Electronic applications accepted. *Financial support:* Unspecified assistantships available. Financial award application deadline: 3/15; financial award applicants required to submit FAFSA. *Unit head:* Dr. Paul Brown, Chair, 507-389-6504, Fax: 507-389-6769, E-mail: paul.brown@mnsu.edu. *Application contact:* 507-389-2321, E-mail: grad@mnsu.edu.

Mississippi State University, College of Arts and Sciences, Department of Sociology, Anthropology, and Social Work, Mississippi State, MS 39762. Offers applied anthropology (MA); sociology (MS, PhD). Part-time programs available. *Faculty:* 19 full-time (8 women), 10 part-time/adjunct (7 women). *Students:* 33 full-time (21 women), 26 part-time (17 women); includes 14 minority (12 African Americans, 1 American Indian/Alaska Native, 1 Asian American or Pacific Islander), 6 international. Average age 33. 17 applicants, 65% accepted, 5 enrolled. In 2007, 7 master's, 4 doctorates awarded. *Degree requirements:* For master's, thesis (for some programs), comprehensive oral or written exam; for doctorate, thesis/dissertation,

Anthropology

Mississippi State University (continued)

comprehensive oral and written exam. *Entrance requirements:* For master's and doctorate, GRE. Additional exam requirements/recommendations for international students: Required—TOEFL. *Application deadline:* For fall admission, 4/15 for domestic students; for spring admission, 11/1 for domestic students. Applications are processed on a rolling basis. Application fee: $30. *Expenses:* Tuition, state resident: full-time $4,978; part-time $274 per hour. Tuition, nonresident: full-time $11,469; part-time $635 per hour. *Financial support:* In 2007–08, 14 teaching assistantships with tuition reimbursements (averaging $10,117 per year) were awarded; Federal Work-Study, institutionally sponsored loans, scholarships/grants, and unspecified assistantships also available. Financial award application deadline: 3/15; financial award applicants required to submit FAFSA. *Faculty research:* Community and regional development, criminology, natural resource development, family sociology, gender. Total annual research expenditures: $1 million. *Unit head:* Dr. R. Gregory Dunaway, Head, 662-325-2495, Fax: 662-325-4564, E-mail: dunaway@soc.msstate.edu. *Application contact:* Dr. William A. Person, Interim Associate Vice President for Academic Affairs/Interim Dean of Graduate Studies, 662-325-7400, Fax: 662-325-1967, E-mail: grad@grad.msstate.edu.

New Mexico Highlands University, Graduate Studies, College of Arts and Sciences, Program in Southwest Studies, Las Vegas, NM 87701. Offers anthropology (MA). Program is interdisciplinary. Part-time programs available. *Faculty:* 14 full-time (7 women), 1 (woman) part-time/adjunct. *Students:* 4 full-time (3 women), 13 part-time (9 women); includes 5 minority (1 American Indian/Alaska Native, 4 Hispanic Americans). Average age 35. 13 applicants, 77% accepted, 3 enrolled. In 2007, 2 degrees awarded. *Degree requirements:* For master's, comprehensive exam, thesis or alternative. *Entrance requirements:* For master's, minimum undergraduate GPA of 3.0. Additional exam requirements/recommendations for international students: Required—TOEFL (minimum score 540 paper-based; 190 computer-based). *Application deadline:* For fall admission, 8/1 priority date for domestic students. Applications are processed on a rolling basis. Application fee: $15. *Expenses:* Tuition, state resident: full-time $2,642; part-time $110 per credit hour. Tuition, nonresident: full-time $3,964; part-time $165 per credit hour. International tuition: $5,285 full-time. One-time fee: $20 full-time. *Financial support:* In 2007–08, 4 students received support, including teaching assistantships (averaging $6,500 per year); career-related internships or fieldwork, Federal Work-Study, institutionally sponsored loans, scholarships/grants, tuition waivers (full and partial), and unspecified assistantships also available. Support available to part-time students. Financial award application deadline: 3/1; financial award applicants required to submit FAFSA. *Faculty research:* Southwest Indians, applied anthropology, Hispanic Southwest, archaeology, physical anthropology. *Application contact:* Diane Trujillo, Administrative Assistant Graduate Studies, 505-454-3266, Fax: 505-454-3558, E-mail: dtrujillo@nmhu.edu.

New Mexico State University, Graduate School, College of Arts and Sciences, Department of Sociology and Anthropology, Las Cruces, NM 88003-8001. Offers anthropology (MA); sociology (MA). Part-time programs available. *Faculty:* 11 full-time (6 women), 3 part-time/adjunct (1 woman). *Students:* 42 full-time (30 women), 51 part-time (38 women); includes 5 African Americans, 1 American Indian/Alaska Native, 20 Hispanic Americans, 5 international. Average age 33. 49 applicants, 90% accepted, 28 enrolled. In 2007, 20 degrees awarded. *Degree requirements:* For master's, comprehensive exam (for some programs), thesis (for some programs). *Application deadline:* For fall admission, 2/15 priority date for domestic students; for spring admission, 10/15 priority date for domestic students. Applications are processed on a rolling basis. Application fee: $30 ($50 for international students). Electronic applications accepted. *Expenses:* Tuition, state resident: full-time $3,602; part-time $199 per credit. Tuition, nonresident: full-time $13,380; part-time $607 per credit. Required fees: $1,178. *Financial support:* In 2007–08, 2 fellowships, 1 research assistantship with partial tuition reimbursement, 20 teaching assistantships with partial tuition reimbursements were awarded; career-related internships or fieldwork, Federal Work-Study, and health care benefits also available. Support available to part-time students. Financial award application deadline: 3/1. *Faculty research:* Native American culture and society, Latin America and border studies, prehistoric and historic archaeology, demography, medical sociology and anthropology. *Unit head:* Dr. Lee Hamilton, Head, 575-646-3821, Fax: 575-646-3725, E-mail: lehamilt@nmsu.edu.

The New School: A University, The New School for Social Research, Department of Anthropology, New York, NY 10011. Offers MA, DS Sc, PhD. Part-time and evening/weekend programs available. *Faculty:* 8 full-time (3 women). *Students:* 42 full-time (32 women), 17 part-time (13 women); includes 8 minority (1 African American, 4 Asian Americans or Pacific Islanders, 3 Hispanic Americans), 15 international. Average age 31. In 2007, 13 degrees awarded. Terminal master's awarded for partial completion of doctoral program. *Degree requirements:* For master's, exam; for doctorate, one foreign language, thesis/dissertation, qualifying exam. *Entrance requirements:* For master's, GRE General Test; for doctorate, GRE General Test, MA. Additional exam requirements/recommendations for international students: Required—TOEFL (minimum score 600 paper-based; 250 computer-based; 100 iBT). *Application deadline:* For fall admission, 1/15 priority date for domestic students. Applications are processed on a rolling basis. Application fee: $50. *Financial support:* Fellowships, research assistantships, teaching assistantships, career-related internships or fieldwork, Federal Work-Study, scholarships/grants, and tuition waivers (full and partial) available. Financial award application deadline: 3/1; financial award applicants required to submit FAFSA. *Faculty research:* Critical theory; modern social and cultural systems; race, class, gender. *Unit head:* Dr. Hugh Raffles, Chair, 212-229-5757 Ext. 3025, E-mail: rafflesh@newschool.edu. *Application contact:* Robert MacDonald, Director of Admissions, 800-523-5710 Ext. 3007, Fax: 212-989-7102, E-mail: macdonar@newschool.edu.

See Close-Up on page 1653.

New York University, Graduate School of Arts and Science, Department of Anthropology, New York, NY 10012-1019. Offers anthropology (MA, PhD), including archaeological anthropology, linguistic anthropology, physical anthropology, socio-cultural anthropology; anthropology and French studies (PhD); MA/Advanced Certificate; PhD/Advanced Certificate. Part-time programs available. *Faculty:* 22 full-time, 13 part-time/adjunct. *Students:* 78 full-time (52 women), 5 part-time (all women); includes 9 minority (3 Asian Americans or Pacific Islanders, 6 Hispanic Americans), 21 international. Average age 29. 322 applicants, 7% accepted, 14 enrolled. In 2007, 10 master's, 9 doctorates awarded. *Degree requirements:* For master's, thesis; for doctorate, one foreign language, comprehensive exam, thesis/dissertation. *Entrance requirements:* For master's, GRE General Test; for doctorate, GRE General Test, MA or equivalent. Additional exam requirements/recommendations for international students: Required—TOEFL. *Application deadline:* For fall admission, 1/4 priority date for domestic students. Application fee: $85. *Financial support:* Fellowships with tuition reimbursements, research assistantships with tuition reimbursements, teaching assistantships with tuition reimbursements, career-related internships or fieldwork, Federal Work-Study, institutionally sponsored loans, scholarships/grants, health care benefits, and unspecified assistantships available. Financial award application deadline: 1/4; financial award applicants required to submit FAFSA. *Faculty research:* Sociocultural anthropology, archaeology, biological anthropology, linguistic anthropology. *Unit head:* Fred Myers, Chair, 212-998-8550, Fax: 212-995-4014, E-mail: anthropology@nyu.edu. *Application contact:* Susan Carol-Rogers, Director of Graduate Studies, 212-998-8550, Fax: 212-995-4014, E-mail: anthropology@nyu.edu.

North Carolina State University, Graduate School, College of Humanities and Social Sciences, Department of Sociology and Anthropology, Program in Anthropology, Raleigh, NC 27695. Offers bioarchaeology (MA); cultural anthropology (MA); environmental anthropology (MA).

Northern Arizona University, Graduate College, College of Social and Behavioral Sciences, Department of Anthropology, Flagstaff, AZ 86011. Offers anthropology (MA); archaeology (MA). *Degree requirements:* For master's, thesis (for some programs), internship paper. *Entrance requirements:* For master's, 18 undergraduate hours in anthropology. *Faculty research:* Economic development, culture change, ethnohistory, archaeology of the Southwest, small town networks and HIV.

Northern Illinois University, Graduate School, College of Liberal Arts and Sciences, Department of Anthropology, De Kalb, IL 60115-2854. Offers MA. Part-time programs available. *Faculty:* 12 full-time (6 women). *Students:* 34 full-time (21 women), 21 part-time (12 women); includes 11 minority (1 African American, 5 Asian Americans or Pacific Islanders, 5 Hispanic Americans), 4 international. Average age 32. 32 applicants, 66% accepted, 13 enrolled. In 2007, 12 degrees awarded. *Degree requirements:* For master's, one foreign language, comprehensive exam, thesis optional. *Entrance requirements:* For master's, GRE General Test, minimum GPA of 2.75, 15 hours of course work in anthropology, course work in statistics. Additional exam requirements/recommendations for international students: Required—TOEFL (minimum score 550 paper-based; 213 computer-based). *Application deadline:* For fall admission, 6/1 for domestic students, 5/1 for international students; for spring admission, 11/1 for domestic students, 10/1 for international students. Applications are processed on a rolling basis. Application fee: $30. Electronic applications accepted. *Expenses:* Tuition, area resident: Part-time $226 per credit hour. Tuition, state resident: full-time $5,424; part-time $225 per credit hour. Tuition, nonresident: full-time $10,848. Required fees: $2,416; $64 per credit hour. *Financial support:* In 2007–08, 1 research assistantship with full tuition reimbursement, 13 teaching assistantships with full tuition reimbursements were awarded; fellowships with full tuition reimbursements, career-related internships or fieldwork, Federal Work-Study, scholarships/grants, tuition waivers (full), and unspecified assistantships also available. Support available to part-time students. Financial award applicants required to submit FAFSA. *Faculty research:* Linguistic anthropology of Oceania, Mayan languages, human paleontology, primate evolution, dental anthropology. *Unit head:* Dr. Judy Ledgerwood, Chair, 815-753-0246, Fax: 815-753-7027, E-mail: jledgerw@niu.edu.

Northwestern University, The Graduate School, Judd A. and Marjorie Weinberg College of Arts and Sciences, Department of Anthropology, Evanston, IL 60208. Offers PhD, JD/PhD. Admissions and degrees offered through The Graduate School. *Degree requirements:* For doctorate, thesis/dissertation. *Entrance requirements:* For doctorate, GRE General Test. Additional exam requirements/recommendations for international students: Required—TOEFL. Electronic applications accepted. *Faculty research:* Archaeology of complex societies, gender, political/urban anthropology, linguistic anthropology, African studies.

The Ohio State University, Graduate School, College of Social and Behavioral Sciences, School of Social and Behavioral Science, Department of Anthropology, Columbus, OH 43210. Offers MA, PhD. *Faculty:* 31. *Students:* 55 full-time (36 women), 3 part-time (2 women); includes 7 minority (4 Asian Americans or Pacific Islanders, 3 Hispanic Americans), 5 international. Average age 29. In 2007, 6 master's, 4 doctorates awarded. *Degree requirements:* For master's, thesis optional; for doctorate, one foreign language, thesis/dissertation. *Entrance requirements:* For master's and doctorate, GRE General Test. Additional exam requirements/recommendations for international students: Required—TOEFL (minimum score 600 paper-based; 250 computer-based). *Application deadline:* For fall admission, 8/15 priority date for domestic students, 7/1 priority date for international students; for winter admission, 12/1 priority date for domestic students, 11/1 priority date for international students; for spring admission, 3/1 priority date for domestic students, 2/1 priority date for international students. Applications are processed on a rolling basis. Application fee: $40 ($50 for international students). Electronic applications accepted. *Financial support:* Fellowships, research assistantships, teaching assistantships, Federal Work-Study, institutionally sponsored loans, and unspecified assistantships available. Support available to part-time students. *Unit head:* Jeffrey K. McKee, Graduate Studies Committee Chair, 614-292-4117, Fax: 614-292-2435, E-mail: mckee.95@osu.edu. *Application contact:* 614-292-9444, Fax: 614-292-3895, E-mail: domestic.grad@osu.edu.

Oregon State University, Graduate School, College of Liberal Arts, Department of Anthropology, Corvallis, OR 97331. Offers anthropology (MAIS); applied anthropology (MA). *Faculty:* 6 full-time (2 women), 5 part-time/adjunct (all women). *Students:* 23 full-time (13 women), 6 part-time (4 women); includes 2 African Americans, 1 American Indian/Alaska Native. Average age 34. In 2007, 14 degrees awarded. *Degree requirements:* For master's, one foreign language, thesis. *Entrance requirements:* For master's, minimum GPA of 3.0 in last 90 hours. Additional exam requirements/recommendations for international students: Required—TOEFL. *Application deadline:* For fall admission, 3/1 for domestic students. Applications are processed on a rolling basis. Application fee: $50. *Expenses:* Tuition, state resident: full-time $9,126; part-time $338 per credit. Tuition, nonresident: full-time $14,796; part-time $548 per credit. Required fees: $1,447. *Financial support:* Research assistantships, teaching assistantships, career-related internships or fieldwork, Federal Work-Study, and institutionally sponsored loans available. Support available to part-time students. Financial award application deadline: 2/1. *Faculty research:* Historical anthropology; first American studies; Japanese, Asian, South Pacific, and Native American cultures; business anthropology. *Unit head:* Dr. David McMurray, Chair, 541-737-4515, Fax: 541-737-3650, E-mail: david.mcmurray@oregonstate.edu.

Penn State University Park, Graduate School, College of the Liberal Arts, Department of Anthropology, State College, University Park, PA 16802-1503. Offers MA, PhD. *Expenses:* Tuition, state resident: full-time $14,738; part-time $614 per credit. Tuition, nonresident: full-time $26,050; part-time $1,085 per credit. Tuition and fees vary according to course load, program and student level. *Unit head:* Dr. Nina D. Jablonski, Head, 814-865-2509, Fax: 814-863-1474, E-mail: ngj2@psu.edu.

Portland State University, Graduate Studies, College of Liberal Arts and Sciences, Department of Anthropology, Portland, OR 97207-0751. Offers MA. *Faculty:* 8 full-time (6 women). *Students:* 12 full-time (7 women), 17 part-time (8 women); includes 3 minority (1 Asian American or Pacific Islander, 2 Hispanic Americans). Average age 34. 17 applicants, 71% accepted, 10 enrolled. In 2007, 7 degrees awarded. *Degree requirements:* For master's, one foreign language, thesis. *Entrance requirements:* For master's, GRE General Test, minimum GPA of 3.25 in upper-division anthropology course work, 3.0 overall; 3 letters of recommendation. Additional exam requirements/recommendations for international students: Required—TOEFL. *Application deadline:* For fall admission, 2/1 for domestic and international students. Application fee: $50. *Expenses:* Tuition, state resident: full-time $7,047. Tuition, nonresident: full-time $11,178. *Financial support:* In 2007–08, 4 research assistantships with full tuition reimbursements (averaging $7,252 per year), 3 teaching assistantships with full tuition reimbursements were awarded; career-related internships or fieldwork, Federal Work-Study, and unspecified assistantships also available. Support available to part-time students. Financial award application deadline: 3/1; financial award applicants required to submit FAFSA. *Faculty research:* Forensic anthropology, Northwest Coast prehistory, Native Americans, applied anthropology, urban anthropology. Total annual research expenditures: $147,251. *Unit head:* Dr. Kenneth M. Ames, Chair, 503-725-3081. *Application contact:* Connie Cash, Office Coordinator, 503-725-3081, Fax: 503-725-3905, E-mail: cashc@pdx.edu.

Portland State University, Graduate Studies, Systems Science Program, Portland, OR 97207-0751. Offers computational intelligence (Certificate); computer modeling and simulation (Certificate); systems science (MS); systems science/anthropology (PhD); systems science/business administration (PhD); systems science/civil engineering (PhD); systems science/economics (PhD); systems science/engineering management (PhD); systems science/general (PhD); systems science/mathematical sciences (PhD); systems science/mechanical engineering (PhD); systems science/psychology (PhD); systems science/sociology (PhD). *Faculty:* 3 full-time (0 women). *Students:* 9 full-time (2 women), 11 part-time (2 women); includes 6 minority (3 Asian Americans or Pacific Islanders, 3 Hispanic Americans), 13 international. Average age 38. 8 applicants, 100% accepted, 6 enrolled. In 2007, 4 master's, 6 doctorates awarded. *Degree requirements:* For doctorate, variable foreign language requirement, thesis/dissertation. *Entrance requirements:* For master's, 2 letters of recommendation; for doctorate, GMAT, GRE General Test, minimum undergraduate GPA of 3.0. Additional exam requirements/recommendations for international students: Required—TOEFL. *Application deadline:* For fall admission, 2/1 for domestic students; for spring admission, 11/1 for domestic students. Application fee: $50. *Expenses:* Tuition, state resident: full-time $7,047. Tuition, nonresident: full-time $11,178. *Financial support:* In 2007–08, 1 research assistantship with full tuition reimbursement (averaging $5,980 per year) was awarded; teaching assistantships with full tuition reimbursements, career-related internships or fieldwork, Federal Work-Study, scholarships/grants, and unspecified assistantships also available. Support available to part-time students. Financial award application deadline: 3/1; financial award applicants required to submit FAFSA. *Faculty research:* Systems theory and methodology, artificial intelligence neural networks, information theory, nonlinear dynamics/chaos, modeling and simulation. Total annual research expenditures: $5,370. *Unit head:* George Lendaris, Acting Director, 503-725-4960. *Application contact:* Dawn Sharafi, Administrative Assistant, 503-725-4960, E-mail: dawn@sysc.pdx.edu.

Princeton University, Graduate School, Department of Anthropology, Princeton, NJ 08544-1019. Offers PhD. *Degree requirements:* For doctorate, variable foreign language requirement, thesis/dissertation. *Entrance requirements:* For doctorate, GRE General Test, sample of written work. Additional exam requirements/recommendations for international students: Required—TOEFL (minimum score 600 paper-based; 250 computer-based). Electronic applications accepted. *Faculty research:* Symbolic anthropology, social theory, gender studies, law and society, political and social anthropology.

Purdue University, Graduate School, College of Liberal Arts, Department of Sociology and Anthropology, West Lafayette, IN 47907. Offers anthropology (MS, PhD); sociology (MS, PhD). Terminal master's awarded for partial completion of doctoral program. *Degree requirements:* For doctorate, thesis/dissertation. *Entrance requirements:* For master's and doctorate, GRE General Test. Additional exam requirements/recommendations for international students: Required—TOEFL, TWE. Electronic applications accepted. *Faculty research:* Communiversity survey project, risk, fear, constrained behavior, archaeological services.

Rice University, Graduate Programs, School of Social Sciences, Department of Anthropology, Houston, TX 77251-1892. Offers MA, PhD. Terminal master's awarded for partial completion of doctoral program. *Degree requirements:* For master's, variable foreign language requirement, thesis; for doctorate, one foreign language, thesis/dissertation. *Entrance requirements:* For master's and doctorate, GRE General Test, minimum GPA of 3.0. Additional exam requirements/recommendations for international students: Required—TOEFL (minimum score 600 paper-based; 250 computer-based; 90 iBT). *Faculty research:* Archaeology, biological anthropology, anthropological linguistics, complex societies.

Roosevelt University, Graduate Division, College of Arts and Sciences, Department of Sociology and Anthropology, Chicago, IL 60605-1394. Offers anthropology (MA); sociology (MA). Part-time and evening/weekend programs available. *Students:* 7 full-time (4 women), 22 part-time (18 women); includes 14 minority (13 African Americans, 1 Asian American or Pacific Islander). Average age 35. 24 applicants, 54% accepted, 8 enrolled. In 2007, 4 degrees awarded. *Degree requirements:* For master's, comprehensive exam, thesis. *Application deadline:* For fall admission, 6/1 priority date for domestic students. Applications are processed on a rolling basis. Application fee: $25 ($35 for international students). *Financial support:* Teaching assistantships available. Financial award application deadline: 2/15. *Faculty research:* Social theory, urban sociology, gerontology, social organizations. *Unit head:* Michael Maly, Head, 312-341-3769, E-mail: mmaly@roosevelt.edu. *Application contact:* Joanne Canyon-Heller, Coordinator of Graduate Admission, 877-APPLY RU, Fax: 312-281-3356, E-mail: applyru@roosevelt.edu.

Rutgers, The State University of New Jersey, New Brunswick, Graduate School, Program in Anthropology, New Brunswick, NJ 08901-1281. Offers MA, PhD. Terminal master's awarded for partial completion of doctoral program. *Degree requirements:* For master's, thesis or alternative; for doctorate, comprehensive exam, thesis/dissertation. *Entrance requirements:* For master's and doctorate, GRE General Test, writing sample. Additional exam requirements/recommendations for international students: Required—TOEFL. Electronic applications accepted. *Faculty research:* Human evolution, lithic technology, behavioral ecology, ethnicity, gender.

San Diego State University, Graduate and Research Affairs, College of Arts and Letters, Department of Anthropology, San Diego, CA 92182. Offers MA. *Students:* 28 full-time (20 women), 19 part-time (14 women); includes 7 minority (1 American Indian/Alaska Native, 1 Asian American or Pacific Islander, 5 Hispanic Americans). 33 applicants, 73% accepted, 15 enrolled. In 2007, 14 degrees awarded. *Degree requirements:* For master's, one foreign language, thesis. *Entrance requirements:* For master's, GRE General Test, 3 letters of recommendation, typed writing sample. Additional exam requirements/recommendations for international students: Required—TOEFL. *Application deadline:* For fall admission, 3/1 for domestic and international students; for spring admission, 10/1 for domestic and international students. Applications are processed on a rolling basis. Application fee: $55. Electronic applications accepted. *Financial support:* In 2007–08, 12 teaching assistantships were awarded; career-related internships or fieldwork also available. Financial award applicants required to submit FAFSA. *Faculty research:* Meso-American archaeology, cognitive anthropology, ethnomusicology, primate conservation, biomedical anthropology. Total annual research expenditures: $51,584. *Unit head:* Seth Mallios, Chair, 619-594-5527, Fax: 619-594-1150, E-mail: smallios@mail.sdsu.edu. *Application contact:* Dr. Ramona Perez, Graduate Coordinator, 619-594-6189, Fax: 619-594-1150, E-mail: perez@mail.sdsu.edu.

San Francisco State University, Division of Graduate Studies, College of Behavioral and Social Sciences, Department of Anthropology, San Francisco, CA 94132-1722. Offers MA. *Faculty research:* Immigration, ethnicity, urban anthropology, Californian and Latin American archaeology. *Unit head:* Dr. Gary Pohl, Chair, 415-338-3004. *Application contact:* Dr. Mark Griffin, Graduate Coordinator, 415-338-2046, E-mail: mgriffin@sfsu.edu.

San Jose State University, Graduate Studies and Research, College of Social Sciences, Department of Anthropology, San Jose, CA 95192-0001. Offers applied anthropology (MA). *Students:* 14 full-time (10 women), 4 part-time (3 women); includes 7 minority (1 Asian American or Pacific Islander, 6 Hispanic Americans). Average age 35. 13 applicants, 92% accepted, 9 enrolled. *Entrance requirements:* For master's, curriculum vitae or resumé, official transcripts, 2 letters of reference. *Application deadline:* For fall admission, 5/30 for domestic students. *Unit head:* Tim Hegstrom, Dean, College of Social Sciences, 408-924-5300, Fax: 408-924-5303.

Simon Fraser University, Graduate Studies, Faculty of Arts and Social Sciences, Department of Sociology and Anthropology, Burnaby, BC V5A 1S6, Canada. Offers anthropology (MA, PhD); sociology (MA, PhD). *Degree requirements:* For master's, thesis (for some programs); for doctorate, thesis/dissertation. *Entrance requirements:* For master's and doctorate, minimum GPA of 3.25. Additional exam requirements/recommendations for international students: Required—TOEFL or IELTS. *Faculty research:* Sociology theory, social and cultural anthropology, political sociology, religion and society, Canadian native peoples.

Sonoma State University, School of Social Sciences, Program in Cultural Resources Management, Rohnert Park, CA 94928-3609. Offers MA. Part-time programs available. *Faculty:* 3 full-time (1 woman). *Students:* 20 full-time (14 women), 2 part-time (both women); includes 3 minority (1 African American, 1 Asian American or Pacific Islander, 1 Hispanic American), 1 international. Average age 33. 28 applicants, 43% accepted, 11 enrolled. *Degree requirements:* For master's, thesis. *Entrance requirements:* For master's, minimum GPA of 3.0. *Application deadline:* For fall admission, 1/31 for domestic students. Application fee: $55. *Financial support:* Career-related internships or fieldwork, scholarships/grants, traineeships, and unspecified assistantships available. Financial award application deadline: 3/2. *Faculty research:* Identification, evaluation, and preservation of cultural resources. *Unit head:* Dr. John D. Wingard, Chair, Anthropology Department, 707-664-2319, Fax: 707-664-2505, E-mail: john.wingard@sonoma.edu. *Application contact:* Margaret Purser, Coordinator, 707-664-3164, Fax: 707-664-2505, E-mail: margaret.purser@sonoma.edu.

Southern Illinois University Carbondale, Graduate School, College of Liberal Arts, Department of Anthropology, Carbondale, IL 62901-4701. Offers MA, PhD. *Faculty:* 14 full-time (5 women). *Students:* 43 full-time (28 women), 33 part-time (17 women); includes 5 minority (1 Asian American or Pacific Islander, 4 Hispanic Americans), 18 international. 73 applicants, 30% accepted, 6 enrolled. In 2007, 8 master's, 2 doctorates awarded. *Degree requirements:* For master's, one foreign language, thesis; for doctorate, one foreign language, thesis/dissertation. *Entrance requirements:* For master's, GRE General Test, minimum GPA of 2.7; for doctorate, GRE General Test, minimum GPA of 3.25. Additional exam requirements/recommendations for international students: Required—TOEFL. *Application deadline:* Applications are processed on a rolling basis. Application fee: $20. *Financial support:* In 2007–08, 37 students received support, including 10 fellowships with full tuition reimbursements available, 10 research assistantships with full tuition reimbursements available, 16 teaching assistantships with full tuition reimbursements available; career-related internships or fieldwork, Federal Work-Study, institutionally sponsored loans, scholarships/grants, and tuition waivers (full) also available. Support available to part-time students. Financial award application deadline: 1/15. *Faculty research:* Archaeology, human variability, evolution, cultural ecology, social anthropology. *Unit head:* Dr. Susan Ford, Chair, 618-536-6651, E-mail: sford@siu.edu. *Application contact:* Becki Swain, Graduate Secretary, 618-453-5037, Fax: 618-453-5037, E-mail: biswain@siu.edu.

Announcement: The Anthropology Department at SIUC is a research-oriented program offering both master's and doctoral degrees in four subfields. Three current faculty members have been named SIUC Outstanding Scholars, and 7 students in the department have won the annual SIUC Outstanding Dissertation Award in the eighteen years it has been awarded, including six in the last nine years. One anthropology student also won the Outstanding Master's Thesis Award for 2003.

See Close-Up on page 1707.

Southern Methodist University, Dedman College, Department of Anthropology, Dallas, TX 75275. Offers anthropology (PhD); medical anthropology (MA). *Faculty:* 12 full-time (4 women), 2 part-time/adjunct (both women). *Students:* 37 full-time (22 women), 24 part-time (12 women); includes 8 minority (1 American Indian/Alaska Native, 2 Asian Americans or Pacific Islanders, 5 Hispanic Americans), 4 international. Average age 34. 34 applicants, 24% accepted, 8 enrolled. In 2007, 6 master's, 2 doctorates awarded. Terminal master's awarded for partial completion of doctoral program. *Degree requirements:* For master's, one foreign language, comprehensive exam, thesis or alternative; for doctorate, one foreign language, comprehensive exam, thesis/dissertation, qualifying exam, defense of dissertation. *Entrance requirements:* For master's and doctorate, GRE General Test, minimum GPA of 3.0. Additional exam requirements/recommendations for international students: Required—TOEFL (minimum score 550 paper-based). *Application deadline:* For fall admission, 2/1 priority date for domestic students; for spring admission, 11/30 priority date for domestic students. Applications are processed on a rolling basis. Application fee: $60. *Financial support:* In 2007–08, 3 fellowships with full and partial tuition reimbursements (averaging $15,000 per year), 8 research assistantships with full tuition reimbursements (averaging $15,000 per year), 23 teaching assistantships with full tuition reimbursements (averaging $15,000 per year) were awarded; Federal Work-Study, institutionally sponsored loans, scholarships/grants, traineeships, and tuition waivers (full) also available. Financial award application deadline: 3/1; financial award applicants required to submit FAFSA. *Faculty research:* Health and gender, Paleoindians, Mesoamerica, American southwest, migration and ethnicity. Total annual research expenditures: $300,000. *Unit head:* Pamela Carter Hogan, Administrative Assistant to the Chair, 214-768-4152, Fax: 214-768-2906, E-mail: phogan@smu.edu. *Application contact:* Dr. Torrey Rick, Director of Graduate Studies, 214-768-3542, Fax: 214-768-2906, E-mail: trick@smu.edu.

Stanford University, School of Humanities and Sciences, Department of Anthropological Sciences, Stanford, CA 94305-9991. Offers MA, MS, PhD. Terminal master's awarded for partial completion of doctoral program. *Degree requirements:* For master's, thesis; for doctorate, one foreign language, thesis/dissertation. *Entrance requirements:* For master's and doctorate, GRE General Test. Additional exam requirements/recommendations for international students: Required—TOEFL. Electronic applications accepted.

Stanford University, School of Humanities and Sciences, Department of Cultural and Social Anthropology, Stanford, CA 94305-9991. Offers MA, PhD. Terminal master's awarded for partial completion of doctoral program. *Degree requirements:* For master's, thesis; for doctorate, one foreign language, thesis/dissertation. *Entrance requirements:* For master's and doctorate, GRE General Test. Additional exam requirements/recommendations for international students: Required—TOEFL. Electronic applications accepted.

State University of New York at Binghamton, Graduate School, School of Arts and Sciences, Department of Anthropology, Binghamton, NY 13902-6000. Offers MA, PhD. Part-time programs available. *Faculty:* 17 full-time (6 women), 4 part-time/adjunct (1 woman). *Students:* 73 full-time (49 women), 60 part-time (38 women); includes 16 minority (2 African Americans, 3 American Indian/Alaska Native, 3 Asian Americans or Pacific Islanders, 8 Hispanic Americans), 20 international. Average age 31. 90 applicants, 62% accepted, 26 enrolled. In 2007, 23 master's, 12 doctorates awarded. Terminal master's awarded for partial completion of doctoral program. *Degree requirements:* For master's, one foreign language, thesis or alternative, written exam; for doctorate, variable foreign language requirement, thesis/dissertation, oral exam. *Entrance requirements:* For master's and doctorate, GRE General Test, GRE Subject Test. Additional exam requirements/recommendations for international students: Required—TOEFL. *Application deadline:* For fall admission, 4/15 priority date for domestic students, 1/15 priority date for international students; for spring admission, 11/1 for domestic students, 10/1 priority date for international students. Applications are processed on a rolling basis. Application fee: $60. Electronic applications accepted. *Financial support:* In 2007–08, 41 students received support, including 7 fellowships with full tuition reimbursements available (averaging $11,500 per year), 1 research assistantship with full tuition reimbursement available (averaging $15,000 per year), 23 teaching assistantships with full tuition reimbursements available (averaging $15,000 per year); career-related internships or fieldwork, Federal Work-Study, institutionally sponsored loans, tuition waivers (full and partial), and unspecified assistantships also available. Support available to part-time students. Financial award application deadline: 2/15. *Unit head:* Dr. Charles Cobb, Chairperson, 607-777-4701, E-mail: ccobb@binghamton.edu.

Stony Brook University, State University of New York, Graduate School, College of Arts and Sciences, Department of Anthropology, Stony Brook, NY 11794. Offers MA, PhD. *Faculty:* 14 full-time (5 women), 1 (woman) part-time/adjunct. *Students:* 52 full-time (34 women), 5 part-time (3 women); includes 4 minority (1 African American, 3 Asian Americans or Pacific Islanders), 15 international. Average age 30. 93 applicants, 24% accepted. In 2007, 7 master's, 4 doctorates awarded. *Degree requirements:* For master's, thesis, fieldwork; for doctorate, one foreign language, thesis/dissertation, fieldwork. *Entrance requirements:* For master's and doctorate, GRE General Test. Additional exam requirements/recommendations for international students: Required—TOEFL. *Application deadline:* For fall admission, 1/15 for domestic students. Application fee: $60. *Financial support:* In 2007–08, 4 fellowships, 4 research assistantships, 19 teaching assistantships were awarded; career-related internships or fieldwork also available. *Faculty research:* Social and cultural anthropology, cultural history and archaeology, physical anthropology. Total annual research expenditures: $1.3 million. *Unit head:* Diane M. Doran-Sheehy, Chair, 631-632-9445, E-mail: diane.doran@stonybrook.edu. *Application contact:* Dr. Elizabeth Stone, Director, 631-632-7627, Fax: 631-632-9165, E-mail: elizabeth.stone@stonybrook.edu.

See Close-Up on page 1711.

Syracuse University, Graduate School, Maxwell School of Citizenship and Public Affairs and College of Arts and Sciences, Department of Anthropology, Syracuse, NY 13244. Offers MA, PhD. *Students:* 45 full-time (31 women), 29 part-time (18 women); includes 5 minority (1 African American, 1 Asian American or Pacific Islander, 3 Hispanic Americans), 17 international. 47 applicants, 43% accepted, 9 enrolled. In 2007, 6 master's, 8 doctorates awarded. *Degree requirements:* For master's, thesis or alternative; for doctorate, one foreign language, thesis/dissertation. *Entrance requirements:* For master's and doctorate, GRE General Test. Additional exam requirements/recommendations for international students: Required—TOEFL. *Application*

Anthropology

Syracuse University (continued)
deadline: For fall admission, 2/1 priority date for domestic students. Applications are processed on a rolling basis. Application fee: $75. Electronic applications accepted. *Expenses:* Tuition: Full-time $18,216; part-time $1,012 per credit. Required fees: $980. Tuition and fees vary according to program. *Financial support:* Fellowships with full tuition reimbursements, teaching assistantships with full and partial tuition reimbursements, tuition waivers (partial) available. *Unit head:* Dr. Christopher DeCorse, Chair, 315-443-4647, Fax: 315-443-4860. *Application contact:* Kristina Ashley, Recruiting Contact, 315-443-2200, E-mail: krashley@syr.edu.

Teachers College, Columbia University, Graduate Faculty of Education, Department of International and Transcultural Studies, Program in Anthropology, New York, NY 10027-6696. Offers Ed M, MA, Ed D, PhD. *Faculty:* 4 full-time (0 women). *Students:* 37 full-time (24 women), 28 part-time (23 women); includes 25 minority (10 African Americans, 12 Asian Americans or Pacific Islanders, 3 Hispanic Americans), 10 international. Average age 35. 35 applicants, 77% accepted, 12 enrolled. In 2007, 5 master's, 3 doctorates awarded. *Degree requirements:* For doctorate, variable foreign language requirement, thesis/dissertation. *Entrance requirements:* For master's and doctorate, GRE General Test. *Application deadline:* For fall admission, 5/15 for domestic students; for spring admission, 12/1 for domestic students. Application fee: $70. *Financial support:* Career-related internships or fieldwork, Federal Work-Study, institutionally sponsored loans, and tuition waivers (full and partial) available. Support available to part-time students. Financial award application deadline: 2/1. *Faculty research:* African studies, sociocultural change, education in the developing world, human development in social and cultural contexts, culture and communication theory. *Application contact:* Deanna Ghozati, Assistant Director of Admission, 212-678-4018, Fax: 212-678-4171, E-mail: ghozati@tc.edu.

See Close-Up on page 1715.

Temple University, Graduate School, College of Liberal Arts, Department of Anthropology, Philadelphia, PA 19122-6096. Offers PhD. Part-time and evening/weekend programs available. Terminal master's awarded for partial completion of doctoral program. *Degree requirements:* For doctorate, 2 foreign languages, thesis/dissertation. *Entrance requirements:* For doctorate, GRE General Test, minimum GPA of 3.0. Additional exam requirements/recommendations for international students: Required—TOEFL (minimum score 550 paper-based; 213 computer-based; 79 iBT). Electronic applications accepted. *Faculty research:* Political economy, biocultural adaptation, visual anthropology, critical urban anthropology, archaeology.

Texas A&M University, College of Liberal Arts, Department of Anthropology, College Station, TX 77843. Offers MA, PhD. *Faculty:* 22. *Students:* 72 full-time (38 women), 40 part-time (24 women); includes 11 minority (1 American Indian/Alaska Native, 3 Asian Americans or Pacific Islanders, 7 Hispanic Americans), 17 international. Average age 33. 76 applicants, 39% accepted, 16 enrolled. In 2007, 9 master's, 3 doctorates awarded. *Degree requirements:* For doctorate, thesis/dissertation. *Entrance requirements:* For master's and doctorate, GRE General Test. Additional exam requirements/recommendations for international students: Required—TOEFL. Application fee: $50 ($75 for international students). *Expenses:* Tuition, state resident: full-time $6,129. Tuition, nonresident: full-time $11,689. Tuition and fees vary according to course load. *Financial support:* Fellowships, research assistantships, teaching assistantships, career-related internships or fieldwork, Federal Work-Study, and institutionally sponsored loans available. Financial award application deadline: 4/1; financial award applicants required to submit FAFSA. *Faculty research:* Nautical archaeology, archaeological conservation, archaeological palynology, paleoethnobotany, folklore. *Unit head:* Dr. David L. Carlson, Head, 979-845-5296, Fax: 979-845-4070. *Application contact:* Karen Taylor, Assistant Advisor, 979-845-9333, Fax: 979-845-4070.

Texas State University–San Marcos, Graduate School, College of Liberal Arts, Department of Anthropology, San Marcos, TX 78666. Offers MA. *Faculty:* 10 full-time (4 women). *Students:* 33 full-time (22 women), 7 part-time (1 woman); includes 8 minority (1 African American, 7 Hispanic Americans), 1 international. Average age 31. 51 applicants, 63% accepted, 25 enrolled. In 2007, 14 degrees awarded. *Entrance requirements:* For master's, GRE, minimum GPA of 3.0 in last 60 undergraduate hours. Additional exam requirements/recommendations for international students: Required—TOEFL (minimum score 550 paper-based; 213 computer-based). *Application deadline:* For fall admission, 3/15 for domestic and international students. Applications are processed on a rolling basis. Application fee: $40 ($90 for international students). Electronic applications accepted. *Expenses:* Tuition, state resident: full-time $3,780; part-time $210 per credit hour. Tuition, nonresident: full-time $8,784; part-time $488 per credit hour. Required fees: $493 per semester. Full-time tuition and fees vary according to course load. *Financial support:* In 2007–08, 30 students received support, including 18 teaching assistantships (averaging $1,999 per year). Financial award application deadline: 4/1; financial award applicants required to submit FAFSA. Total annual research expenditures: $160,456. *Unit head:* Dr. Jon McGee, Chair, 512-245-8272, E-mail: rm08@txstate.edu.

Texas Tech University, Graduate School, College of Arts and Sciences, Department of Sociology, Anthropology and Social Work, Lubbock, TX 79409. Offers anthropology (MA); sociology (MA). Part-time programs available. *Faculty:* 14 full-time (5 women). *Students:* 21 full-time (9 women), 11 part-time (5 women); includes 9 minority (1 African American, 1 Asian American or Pacific Islander, 7 Hispanic Americans), 2 international. Average age 30. 24 applicants, 75% accepted, 8 enrolled. In 2007, 6 degrees awarded. *Degree requirements:* For master's, one foreign language. *Entrance requirements:* For master's, GRE General Test. Additional exam requirements/recommendations for international students: Required—TOEFL (minimum score 550 paper-based; 213 computer-based). *Application deadline:* For fall admission, 3/1 priority date for international students; for spring admission, 11/1 priority date for international students. Applications are processed on a rolling basis. Application fee: $50 ($60 for international students). Electronic applications accepted. *Expenses:* Tuition, state resident: part-time $373 per credit hour. Tuition, nonresident: part-time $651 per credit hour. Tuition and fees vary according to program. *Financial support:* In 2007–08, 25 students received support, including 1 research assistantship with partial tuition reimbursement available (averaging $10,750 per year), 14 teaching assistantships with partial tuition reimbursements available (averaging $11,143 per year); Federal Work-Study and institutionally sponsored loans also available. Support available to part-time students. Financial award application deadline: 4/15; financial award applicants required to submit FAFSA. *Faculty research:* Sociology theory, research methods, physical and forensic anthropology, Texas archaeology, Mayan archaeology. Total annual research expenditures: $277. *Unit head:* Dr. Jeffrey Payne Williams, Chair and Professor, 806-742-2400, Fax: 806-742-1088, E-mail: jeff.williams@ttu.edu. *Application contact:* Dr. Yung-Mei Tsai, Sociology Graduate Program Director, 806-742-2400, Fax: 806-742-1088, E-mail: yung.mei.tsai@ttu.edu.

Trent University, Graduate Studies, Program in Anthropology and Archaeology, Peterborough, ON K9J 7B8, Canada. Offers anthropology (MA). Part-time programs available. *Degree requirements:* For master's, thesis. *Entrance requirements:* For master's, honors degree. *Faculty research:* Paleoecology, trade and fortification networks, pre-Columbian art.

Tulane University, School of Liberal Arts, Department of Anthropology, New Orleans, LA 70118-5669. Offers MA, PhD. Terminal master's awarded for partial completion of doctoral program. *Degree requirements:* For master's, one foreign language, thesis; for doctorate, 2 foreign languages, thesis/dissertation. *Entrance requirements:* For master's, GRE General Test, minimum B average in undergraduate course work; for doctorate, GRE General Test. Additional exam requirements/recommendations for international students: Required—TOEFL. Electronic applications accepted. *Faculty research:* Linguistics, physical anthropology, sociocultural archaeology, Mesoamerica.

Universidad de las Américas–Puebla, Division of Graduate Studies, School of Social Sciences, Program in Anthropology, Puebla, Mexico. Offers anthropology (MA); archaeology (MA). Part-time and evening/weekend programs available. *Degree requirements:* For master's, one foreign language, thesis. *Entrance requirements:* For master's, bachelor's degree in anthropology or equivalent. *Faculty research:* Archaeology, ethnography, and ethnohistory of Mesoamerica.

Université de Montréal, Faculty of Arts and Sciences, Department of Anthropology, Montréal, QC H3C 3J7, Canada. Offers M Sc, PhD. Part-time programs available. *Faculty:* 28 full-time (10 women), 1 part-time/adjunct (0 women). *Students:* 165 full-time (105 women), 8 part-time (7 women). 63 applicants, 43% accepted, 24 enrolled. In 2007, 29 master's, 6 doctorates awarded. *Degree requirements:* For master's, thesis; for doctorate, thesis/dissertation, general exam. *Application deadline:* For fall admission, 2/1 priority date for domestic students; for winter admission, 11/1 priority date for domestic students; for spring admission, 2/1 priority date for domestic students. Application fee: $100. Electronic applications accepted. *Faculty research:* Archaeology, ethnolinguistics, ethnology. *Unit head:* Pierrette Thibault, Chair, 514-343-6560, Fax: 514-343-2494, E-mail: pierrette.thibault@umontreal.ca. *Application contact:* Deirdre Meintel, Information Contact, 514-343-7522, Fax: 514-343-2494, E-mail: deirdre.meintel@umontreal.ca.

Université Laval, Faculty of Social Sciences, Department of Anthropology, Programs in Anthropology, Québec, QC G1K 7P4, Canada. Offers MA, PhD. Terminal master's awarded for partial completion of doctoral program. *Degree requirements:* For master's, thesis; for doctorate, thesis/dissertation. *Entrance requirements:* For master's, knowledge of French, interview; for doctorate, knowledge of French, comprehensive of written English, knowledge of a third language. Electronic applications accepted.

University at Albany, State University of New York, College of Arts and Sciences, Department of Anthropology, Albany, NY 12222-0001. Offers MA, PhD. *Students:* 49 full-time (31 women), 36 part-time (20 women). Average age 34. 52 applicants, 63% accepted, 19 enrolled. In 2007, 13 master's, 5 doctorates awarded. Terminal master's awarded for partial completion of doctoral program. *Degree requirements:* For master's, comprehensive exam, thesis; for doctorate, 2 foreign languages, thesis/dissertation, field exams. *Entrance requirements:* For master's and doctorate, GRE. Additional exam requirements/recommendations for international students: Required—TOEFL (minimum score 550 paper-based; 213 computer-based). *Application deadline:* For fall admission, 3/15 priority date for domestic students, 4/1 for international students; for spring admission, 11/1 for international students. Applications are processed on a rolling basis. Application fee: $75. Electronic applications accepted. *Expenses:* Tuition, state resident: part-time $576 per credit. Tuition, nonresident: part-time $910 per credit. Tuition and fees vary according to program. *Financial support:* Fellowships, research assistantships, teaching assistantships, career-related internships or fieldwork available. Financial award application deadline: 3/15. *Faculty research:* Economic and ecological anthropology; language, culture, and cognition; symbolic and interpretive anthropology; human evolution, morphology, demography, and medical anthropology; spatial and settlement archaeology. *Unit head:* Dr. James Collins, Chair, 518-442-4700. *Application contact:* 518-442-3980.

University at Buffalo, the State University of New York, Graduate School, College of Arts and Sciences, Department of Anthropology, Buffalo, NY 14260. Offers MA, PhD. Terminal master's awarded for partial completion of doctoral program. *Degree requirements:* For master's, comprehensive exam, project; for doctorate, one foreign language, thesis/dissertation, exam. *Entrance requirements:* For master's, GRE General Test, minimum GPA of 3.0; for doctorate, GRE General Test, minimum GPA of 3.2. Additional exam requirements/recommendations for international students: Required—TOEFL (minimum score 600 paper-based; 250 computer-based). Electronic applications accepted. *Faculty research:* Old and New World archaeology, medical anthropology, primatology/human biology, cognition.

The University of Alabama, Graduate School, College of Arts and Sciences, Department of Anthropology, Tuscaloosa, AL 35487. Offers MA, PhD. *Faculty:* 10 full-time (2 women). *Students:* 26 full-time (15 women), 4 part-time (all women). Average age 29. 30 applicants, 40% accepted, 5 enrolled. In 2007, 9 master's, 1 doctorate awarded. *Degree requirements:* For master's, one foreign language, comprehensive exam, thesis optional; for doctorate, one foreign language, comprehensive exam, thesis/dissertation. *Entrance requirements:* For master's, GRE, BA or BS; for doctorate, GRE, MA in anthropology. *Application deadline:* For fall admission, 1/31 for domestic and international students. Application fee: $30. *Expenses:* Tuition, state resident: full-time $5,700. Tuition, nonresident: full-time $16,518. *Financial support:* In 2007–08, 25 students received support, including 4 fellowships with full tuition reimbursements available (averaging $15,000 per year), 1 research assistantship with full tuition reimbursement available (averaging $12,258 per year), 20 teaching assistantships with full tuition reimbursements available (averaging $12,258 per year); Federal Work-Study and health care benefits also available. Financial award application deadline: 1/31. *Faculty research:* Medical anthropology, Southeastern archaeology, physical and cultural anthropology. Total annual research expenditures: $15,605. *Unit head:* Dr. Michael D. Murphy, Chairman of Anthropology and Professor, 205-348-1953, Fax: 205-348-7937, E-mail: mdmurphy@tenhoor.as.ua.edu. *Application contact:* Dr. William Dressler, Professor and Director of Graduate Studies, 205-348-1954, Fax: 205-348-7937, E-mail: wdressle@tenhoor.as.ua.edu.

The University of Alabama at Birmingham, School of Social and Behavioral Sciences, Department of Anthropology and Social Work, Birmingham, AL 35294. Offers anthropology (MA). *Students:* 4 full-time (1 woman), 2 part-time (1 woman). Average age 32. *Degree requirements:* For master's, one foreign language. *Entrance requirements:* For master's, GRE General Test. *Application deadline:* Applications are processed on a rolling basis. Application fee: $35 ($60 for international students). Electronic applications accepted. *Financial support:* Career-related internships or fieldwork, Federal Work-Study, and institutionally sponsored loans available. *Faculty research:* Ethnicity, medical anthropology, primate conservation, pastoral systems, Southeastern archaeology. *Unit head:* Dr. Christopher Taylor, Chair, 205-934-3508, Fax: 205-934-3508.

University of Alaska Anchorage, College of Arts and Sciences, Department of Anthropology, Anchorage, AK 99508-8060. Offers MA. *Degree requirements:* For master's, comprehensive exam, thesis (for some programs), practicum. *Entrance requirements:* For master's, GRE General Test. Additional exam requirements/recommendations for international students: Required—TOEFL (minimum score 550 paper-based; 213 computer-based).

University of Alaska Fairbanks, College of Liberal Arts, Department of Anthropology, Fairbanks, AK 99775-7520. Offers MA, PhD. Part-time programs available. Terminal master's awarded for partial completion of doctoral program. *Degree requirements:* For master's, one foreign language, comprehensive exam, thesis or alternative; for doctorate, 2 foreign languages, comprehensive exam, thesis/dissertation. *Entrance requirements:* For master's and doctorate, GRE General Test. Additional exam requirements/recommendations for international students: Required—TOEFL (minimum score 550 paper-based; 213 computer-based). Electronic applications accepted. *Faculty research:* Circumpolar archaeology and population biology, rural subsistence, late glacial and early post-glacial adaptations, Native Alaskan history and archaeology.

University of Alberta, Faculty of Graduate Studies and Research, Department of Anthropology, Edmonton, AB T6G 2E1, Canada. Offers MA, PhD. *Degree requirements:* For master's, thesis; for doctorate, one foreign language, thesis/dissertation. *Entrance requirements:* For master's and doctorate, minimum GPA of 7.0 on a 9.0 scale in last 2 years. Additional exam requirements/recommendations for international students: Required—TOEFL. *Faculty research:* Cultural anthropology of North America, South East Asia; physical anthropology in osteology, forensic primatology; archaeology of North America, South America, Old World/Africa.

The University of Arizona, Graduate College, College of Social and Behavioral Sciences, Department of Anthropology, Tucson, AZ 85721. Offers MA, PhD. Part-time programs available. *Faculty:* 65. *Students:* 112 full-time (63 women), 47 part-time (29 women); includes 16 minority (1 African American, 3 American Indian/Alaska Native, 5 Asian Americans or Pacific Islanders, 7 Hispanic Americans), 31 international. Average age 32. 168 applicants, 18% accepted, 20 enrolled. In 2007, 14 master's, 17 doctorates awarded. Terminal master's awarded for partial completion of doctoral program. *Degree requirements:* For master's, thesis or alternative; for doctorate, one foreign language, thesis/dissertation. *Entrance requirements:* For master's, GRE General Test, minimum GPA of 3.5, 2 letters of recommendation; for doctorate, GRE General Test, minimum GPA of 3.5, 2 letters or recommendation. Additional exam requirements/recommendations for international students: Required—TOEFL (minimum score 213 computer-based). *Application deadline:* For fall admission, 12/31 for domestic students, 12/15 for international students. Applications are processed on a rolling basis. Application fee: $50. Electronic applications accepted. *Financial support:* Fellowships, research assistantships, teaching assistantships, career-related internships or fieldwork, Federal Work-Study, institutionally sponsored loans, scholarships/grants, and tuition waivers (full and partial) available. *Faculty research:* Archaeology of pre-Han China, cultural ecology, health- and illness-related behavior, interaction of linguistic and social processes, human growth and development under stress. Total annual research expenditures: $3.6 million. *Unit head:* Dr. John Olsen, Head, 520-621-6298, Fax: 520-621-2088, E-mail: jwo@u.arizona.edu. *Application contact:* Ann Samuelson, Academic Coordinator, 520-626-6027, Fax: 520-621-2088, E-mail: anns@email.arizona.edu.

University of Arkansas, Graduate School, J. William Fulbright College of Arts and Sciences, Department of Anthropology, Fayetteville, AR 72701-1201. Offers MA, PhD. Part-time and evening/weekend programs available. *Students:* 16 full-time (4 women), 31 part-time (23 women); includes 4 minority (1 American Indian/Alaska Native, 1 Asian American or Pacific Islander, 2 Hispanic Americans), 3 international. In 2007, 9 master's, 1 doctorate awarded. *Degree requirements:* For master's, comprehensive exam. *Entrance requirements:* For master's, GRE General Test, minimum GPA of 3.0; for doctorate, GRE General Test. Application fee: $40 ($50 for international students). *Financial support:* In 2007–08, 10 fellowships with tuition reimbursements, 3 research assistantships, 17 teaching assistantships were awarded; career-related internships or fieldwork and Federal Work-Study also available. Support available to part-time students. Financial award application deadline: 4/1; financial award applicants required to submit FAFSA. *Unit head:* Dr. Jerry Rose, Departmental Chairperson, 479-575-2508, Fax: 479-575-6595, E-mail: jcrose@uark.edu. *Application contact:* Dr. Mary Jo Schneider, Graduate Coordinator, 479-575-2508, Fax: 479-575-6595, E-mail: maryjo@uark.edu.

The University of British Columbia, Faculty of Arts, Department of Anthropology, Vancouver, BC V6T 1Z1, Canada. Offers MA, PhD. *Faculty:* 16 full-time (1 woman), 4 part-time/adjunct (3 women). *Students:* 54 full-time (38 women). Average age 31. 97 applicants, 19% accepted, 11 enrolled. In 2007, 6 master's awarded. *Median time to degree:* Of those who began their doctoral program in fall 1999, 67% received their degree in 8 years or less. *Degree requirements:* For master's, thesis; for doctorate, comprehensive exam, thesis/dissertation. *Entrance requirements:* For master's, BA in anthropology or equivalent with minimum B+ average in upper level courses; for doctorate, MA in anthropology or equivalent. Additional exam requirements/recommendations for international students: Required—TOEFL (minimum score 600 paper-based; 250 computer-based; 80 iBT). *Application deadline:* For fall admission, 1/19 for domestic and international students. Application fee: $90 Canadian dollars ($150 Canadian dollars for international students). Electronic applications accepted. *Financial support:* In 2007–08, 12 fellowships with tuition reimbursements (averaging $16,000 Canadian dollars per year), 11 research assistantships with tuition reimbursements, teaching assistantships with tuition reimbursements (averaging $10,902 Canadian dollars per year) were awarded; Federal Work-Study, institutionally sponsored loans, scholarships/grants, health care benefits, tuition waivers (full and partial), and unspecified assistantships also available. Financial award application deadline: 10/3. *Faculty research:* Cultures of North America, East Asia, Oceania; museum studies; archaeology. Total annual research expenditures: $890,000. *Unit head:* Dr. John Barker, Head, 604-822-3160, Fax: 604-822-6161. *Application contact:* Dan Naidu, Graduate Secretary, 604-822-0503, Fax: 604-822-6161, E-mail: ansograd@interchange.ubc.ca.

University of Calgary, Faculty of Graduate Studies, Faculty of Social Sciences, Department of Anthropology, Calgary, AB T2N 1N4, Canada. Offers MA, PhD. *Degree requirements:* For master's, thesis; for doctorate, one foreign language, comprehensive exam, thesis/dissertation, candidacy exam. *Entrance requirements:* Additional exam requirements/recommendations for international students: Required—TOEFL. *Faculty research:* Primatology, culture and society, biosocial anthropology, political anthropology, evolutionary theory.

University of California, Berkeley, Graduate Division, College of Letters and Science, Department of Anthropology, Program in Anthropology, Berkeley, CA 94720-1500. Offers PhD. *Degree requirements:* For doctorate, thesis/dissertation. *Entrance requirements:* For doctorate, GRE General Test, minimum GPA of 3.0, 3 letters of recommendation. Additional exam requirements/recommendations for international students: Required—TOEFL. *Application deadline:* For fall admission, 12/15 for domestic students. Application fee: $70 ($90 for international students). *Financial support:* Unspecified assistantships available. *Application contact:* Ned Garrett, Student Affairs Officer, 510-642-3406, Fax: 510-643-8557, E-mail: ned@berkeley.edu.

University of California, Berkeley, Graduate Division, College of Letters and Science, Department of Anthropology, Program in Medical Anthropology, Berkeley, CA 94720-1500. Offers PhD. *Degree requirements:* For doctorate, thesis/dissertation. *Entrance requirements:* For doctorate, GRE General Test, minimum GPA of 3.0, 3 letters of recommendation. Additional exam requirements/recommendations for international students: Required—TOEFL. *Application deadline:* For fall admission, 12/15 for domestic students. Application fee: $70 ($90 for international students). *Financial support:* Unspecified assistantships available. *Unit head:* Lawrence Cohen, Chair, 510-642-2248, E-mail: cohen@berkeley.edu. *Application contact:* Ned Garrett, Student Affairs Officer, 510-642-3406, Fax: 510-643-8557, E-mail: ned@berkeley.edu.

University of California, Davis, Graduate Studies, Program in Anthropology, Davis, CA 95616. Offers MA, PhD. Terminal master's awarded for partial completion of doctoral program. *Degree requirements:* For master's, one foreign language; for doctorate, one foreign language, thesis/dissertation. *Entrance requirements:* For master's and doctorate, GRE General Test, minimum GPA of 3.0. Additional exam requirements/recommendations for international students: Required—TOEFL (minimum score 550 paper-based; 213 computer-based). Electronic applications accepted. *Faculty research:* Archaeology, linguistics, biological and sociocultural anthropology.

University of California, Irvine, Office of Graduate Studies, School of Social Sciences, Department of Anthropology, Irvine, CA 92697. Offers MA, PhD. *Students:* 33 full-time (28 women); includes 8 minority (5 Asian Americans or Pacific Islanders, 3 Hispanic Americans), 7 international. In 2007, 3 master's, 3 doctorates awarded. *Degree requirements:* For doctorate, thesis/dissertation. *Entrance requirements:* For master's, GRE, minimum GPA of 3.0; for doctorate, GRE General Test, minimum GPA of 3.0. Additional exam requirements/recommendations for international students: Required—TOEFL (minimum score 550 paper-based; 213 computer-based). *Application deadline:* For fall admission, 1/15 priority date for domestic students; for winter admission, 10/15 priority date for domestic students. Applications are processed on a rolling basis. Application fee: $60. Electronic applications accepted. *Financial support:* Fellowships, research assistantships with full tuition reimbursements, teaching assistantships, institutionally sponsored loans, traineeships, health care benefits, and unspecified assistantships available. Financial award application deadline: 3/1; financial award applicants required to submit FAFSA. *Faculty research:* Cognitive anthropology, sociology of culture, social structure, family and gender. *Unit head:* Michael L. Burton, Chair, 949-824-7208, E-mail: mlburton@uci.edu. *Application contact:* Victoria Bernal, Graduate Advisor, 949-824-3137, Fax: 949-824-4717, E-mail: vbernal@uci.edu.

University of California, Los Angeles, Graduate Division, College of Letters and Science, Department of Anthropology, Los Angeles, CA 90095. Offers MA, PhD. *Students:* 68 full-time (47 women); includes 9 minority (1 African American, 6 Asian Americans or Pacific Islanders, 2 Hispanic Americans), 4 international. Average age 31. 173 applicants, 16% accepted, 13 enrolled. In 2007, 9 master's, 12 doctorates awarded. Terminal master's awarded for partial completion of doctoral program. *Median time to degree:* Of those who began their doctoral program in fall 1999, 36% received their degree in 8 years or less. *Degree requirements:* For master's, thesis; for doctorate, thesis/dissertation, oral and written qualifying exams. *Entrance requirements:* For master's, GRE General Test, minimum GPA of 3.0, sample of research writing, 3 letters of recommendation; for doctorate, GRE General Test, minimum undergraduate GPA of 3.0, sample of research writing, 3 letters of recommendation. *Application deadline:* For fall admission, 12/15 for domestic students. Application fee: $60 ($80 for international students). Electronic applications accepted. *Expenses:* Tuition, nonresident: full-time $5,728. Required fees: $8,966. Full-time tuition and fees vary according to program and student level. *Financial support:* In 2007–08, 57 fellowships with full and partial tuition reimbursements, 9 research assistantships with full and partial tuition reimbursements, 33 teaching assistantships with full and partial tuition reimbursements were awarded; Federal Work-Study, institutionally sponsored loans, scholarships/grants, and tuition waivers (full and partial) also available. Financial award application deadline: 3/1; financial award applicants required to submit FAFSA. *Unit head:* Dr. Douglas Hollan, Chair, 310-825-2511. *Application contact:* Departmental Office, 310-825-2511, E-mail: awalters@anthro.ucla.edu.

University of California, Riverside, Graduate Division, Department of Anthropology, Riverside, CA 92521-0102. Offers MA, MS, PhD. Part-time programs available. *Faculty:* 16 full-time (8 women). *Students:* 63 full-time (38 women); includes 12 minority (1 African American, 2 American Indian/Alaska Native, 4 Asian Americans or Pacific Islanders, 5 Hispanic Americans), 6 international. Average age 35. 54 applicants, 33% accepted, 10 enrolled. In 2007, 5 master's, 4 doctorates awarded. Terminal master's awarded for partial completion of doctoral program. *Degree requirements:* For master's, comprehensive exams or thesis; for doctorate, one foreign language, comprehensive exam, thesis/dissertation, qualifying exams. *Entrance requirements:* For master's and doctorate, GRE General Test, sample of written work, minimum GPA of 3.2, 3 letters of recommendation. Additional exam requirements/recommendations for international students: Required—TOEFL (minimum score 550 paper-based; 213 computer-based; 80 iBT). *Application deadline:* For fall admission, 5/1 for domestic students, 2/1 for international students. Application fee: $60 ($75 for international students). Electronic applications accepted. *Financial support:* In 2007–08, fellowships with full and partial tuition reimbursements (averaging $12,000 per year), teaching assistantships with partial tuition reimbursements (averaging $16,500 per year) were awarded; research assistantships with partial tuition reimbursements, career-related internships or fieldwork, Federal Work-Study, institutionally sponsored loans, and tuition waivers (full and partial) also available. Financial award application deadline: 2/1; financial award applicants required to submit FAFSA. *Faculty research:* Transnational processes, border communities, political and cultural ecology, Mesoamerican and Western US archaeology, applied anthropology. *Unit head:* Dr. Thomas C. Patterson, Chair, 951-827-5524, Fax: 951-827-5409, E-mail: thomas.patterson@ucr.edu. *Application contact:* Dr. Karl Taube, Graduate Advisor, 951-827-5394, E-mail: cultures@ucr.edu.

University of California, San Diego, Office of Graduate Studies, Department of Anthropology, La Jolla, CA 92093. Offers PhD. *Degree requirements:* For doctorate, thesis/dissertation. *Entrance requirements:* For doctorate, GRE General Test. Electronic applications accepted.

University of California, San Diego, Office of Graduate Studies, Interdisciplinary Program in Cognitive Science, La Jolla, CA 92093. Offers cognitive science/anthropology (PhD); cognitive science/communication (PhD); cognitive science/computer science and engineering (PhD); cognitive science/linguistics (PhD); cognitive science/neuroscience (PhD); cognitive science/philosophy (PhD); cognitive science/psychology (PhD); cognitive science/sociology (PhD). Admissions offered through affiliated departments. *Faculty:* 65 full-time (14 women). *Students:* 7 full-time (3 women). Average age 26. 2 applicants, 100% accepted, 2 enrolled. In 2007, 1 degree awarded. *Degree requirements:* For doctorate, thesis/dissertation. *Entrance requirements:* For doctorate, GRE General Test, acceptance into one of the 8 participating departments. *Application deadline:* Applications are processed on a rolling basis. Application fee: $0. *Faculty research:* Language and cognition, philosophy of mind, visual perception, biological anthropology, sociolinguistics. *Unit head:* Gary Cottrell, Director, 858-534-7141, Fax: 858-534-1128, E-mail: gcottrell@ucsd.edu. *Application contact:* Beverley Walton, Coordinator, 858-534-4387, E-mail: bwalton@ucsd.edu.

University of California, San Francisco, Graduate Division, Program in Medical Anthropology, San Francisco, CA 94143. Offers PhD. *Students:* 13 full-time (9 women); includes 4 minority (all Asian Americans or Pacific Islanders), 1 international. In 2007, 4 degrees awarded. *Degree requirements:* For doctorate, one foreign language, thesis/dissertation, 3 field statements. *Entrance requirements:* For doctorate, GRE General Test, master's degree in anthropology or a related social or health science. *Application deadline:* For fall admission, 12/31 for domestic students. Application fee: $40. *Financial support:* Application deadline: 1/10. *Faculty research:* Ethnicity, gender, aging, international health, health policy. *Unit head:* Dorothy Porter, Chair, 415-476-8826, E-mail: porterd@dahsm.ucsf.edu. *Application contact:* Kimberly Bissell, Program Assistant, 415-476-7223, Fax: 415-476-6715.

University of California, Santa Barbara, Graduate Division, College of Letters and Sciences, Division of Social Sciences, Department of Anthropology, Santa Barbara, CA 93106. Offers anthropology (MA, PhD), including global studies (PhD), human development (PhD), quantitative methods in social sciences (PhD), technology and society (PhD), women's studies (PhD); North American archaeology (MA); MA/PhD. *Faculty:* 13 full-time (2 women), 2 part-time/adjunct (both women). *Students:* 55 full-time (29 women); includes 10 minority (3 Asian Americans or Pacific Islanders, 7 Hispanic Americans), 10 international. Average age 32. 73 applicants, 25% accepted, 6 enrolled. In 2007, 9 master's, 8 doctorates awarded. Terminal master's awarded for partial completion of doctoral program. *Median time to degree:* Of those who began their doctoral program in fall 1999, 38% received their degree in 8 years or less. *Degree requirements:* For master's, comprehensive exam, thesis; for doctorate, comprehensive exam, thesis/dissertation. *Entrance requirements:* For master's and doctorate, GRE General Test, sample of written work, statement of purpose with completed coversheets (2 copies), post-secondary institutions attended. Additional exam requirements/recommendations for international students: Required—TOEFL (minimum score 550 paper-based; 213 computer-based; 80 iBT). *Application deadline:* For fall admission, 12/1 for domestic and international students. Application fee: $60. Electronic applications accepted. *Expenses:* Tuition, nonresident: full-time $14,888. Required fees: $10,108. *Financial support:* In 2007–08, 56 students received support, including 14 fellowships with full and partial tuition reimbursements available (averaging $9,623 per year), 13 research assistantships with full and partial tuition reimbursements available (averaging $10,000 per year), 32 teaching assistantships with partial tuition reimbursements available (averaging $19,988 per year); career-related internships or fieldwork, Federal Work-Study, institutionally sponsored loans, scholarships/grants, traineeships, health care benefits, and unspecified assistantships also available. Financial award application deadline: 12/1; financial award applicants required to submit FAFSA. *Faculty research:* Evolutionary psychology, archaeology, sociocultural anthropology, biosocial anthropology, evolutionary ecology, bioarchaeology. *Unit head:* Prof. Barbara Voorhies, Chair, 805-896-2519, Fax: 805-893-8707, E-mail: voorhies@anth.oesb.edu. *Application contact:* Larisa Traga, Graduate Program Assistant, 805-893-2516, Fax: 805-893-8707, E-mail: traga@anth.ucsb.edu.

University of California, Santa Cruz, Division of Graduate Studies, Division of Social Sciences, Program in Anthropology, Santa Cruz, CA 95064. Offers anthropological archaeology (PhD); cultural anthropology (PhD). *Faculty:* 15 full-time (11 women). *Students:* 43 full-time (28 women), 7 part-time (all women); includes 15 minority (2 African Americans, 4 Asian Americans or Pacific Islanders, 9 Hispanic Americans), 3 international. 105 applicants, 15% accepted, 10 enrolled. In 2007, 2 doctorates awarded. *Degree requirements:* For doctorate, thesis/dissertation, qualifying exam. *Entrance requirements:* For doctorate, GRE General Test. *Application deadline:* For fall admission, 12/15 for domestic students. Application fee: $60. *Expenses:* Tuition, nonresident: full-time $14,694. Required fees: $11,360. *Financial support:* Fellowships, research assistantships, teaching assistantships, career-related internships or fieldwork, Federal Work-Study, and institutionally sponsored loans available. Financial award application deadline: 1/15. *Faculty research:* Culture and power, women's roles, AIDS, folklore. *Unit head:* Dr. Olga Najera-Ramirez, Director, 831-459-4677, E-mail: olga@ucsc.edu. *Application*

Anthropology

University of California, Santa Cruz (continued)
contact: Judy L. Glass, Reporting Analyst for Graduate Admissions, 831-459-5906, Fax: 831-459-4843, E-mail: jlglass@ucsc.edu.

University of Central Florida, College of Sciences, Department of Anthropology, Orlando, FL 32816. Offers anthropology (MA). *Faculty:* 16 full-time (6 women). *Expenses:* Tuition, state resident: full-time $6,484. Tuition, nonresident: full-time $23,938. Tuition and fees vary according to program. *Unit head:* Arlen Chase, Chair, 407-823-2227, Fax: 407-823-3498, E-mail: achase@mail.ucf.edu.

University of Chicago, Division of Social Sciences, Department of Anthropology, Chicago, IL 60637-1513. Offers PhD. *Students:* 208. In 2007, 18 degrees awarded. *Degree requirements:* For doctorate, 2 foreign languages, thesis/dissertation, exams. *Entrance requirements:* For doctorate, GRE General Test. Additional exam requirements/recommendations for international students: Required—TOEFL, IELTS (minimum score 7). *Application deadline:* For fall admission, 12/15 for domestic and international students. Application fee: $55. Electronic applications accepted. *Financial support:* Fellowships, teaching assistantships, Federal Work-Study, institutionally sponsored loans, scholarships/grants, traineeships, health care benefits, and unspecified assistantships available. Financial award application deadline: 12/15; financial award applicants required to submit FAFSA. *Unit head:* Prof. John Kelly, Chair, 773-702-8551. *Application contact:* Office of the Dean of Students, 773-702-8415.

University of Chicago, Division of the Humanities, Department of Linguistics, Chicago, IL 60637-1513. Offers anthropology and linguistics (PhD); linguistics (AM, PhD). *Students:* 48. 57 applicants, 21% accepted, 6 enrolled.Terminal master's awarded for partial completion of doctoral program. *Degree requirements:* For master's, one foreign language, thesis; for doctorate, 2 foreign languages, thesis/dissertation. *Entrance requirements:* For master's and doctorate, GRE General Test. Additional exam requirements/recommendations for international students: Required—TOEFL. *Application deadline:* For fall admission, 12/15 for domestic students. Application fee: $55. *Financial support:* Fellowships, Federal Work-Study available. Financial award application deadline: 12/15; financial award applicants required to submit FAFSA. *Unit head:* Dr. Chris Kennedy, Chair, 773-702-8522.

University of Cincinnati, Graduate School, McMicken College of Arts and Sciences, Department of Anthropology, Cincinnati, OH 45221. Offers MA. Part-time programs available. *Degree requirements:* For master's, thesis or alternative. *Entrance requirements:* For master's, GRE General Test. Additional exam requirements/recommendations for international students: Required—TOEFL; Recommended—TWE. Electronic applications accepted. *Faculty research:* Medical anthropology, Mayan prehistory, southwestern U.S. prehistory, skeletal biology and paleoanthropology; immigrants; Mexico.

University of Colorado at Boulder, Graduate School, College of Arts and Sciences, Department of Anthropology, Boulder, CO 80309. Offers MA, PhD. *Faculty:* 21. *Students:* 50 full-time (30 women), 15 part-time (8 women); includes 8 minority (1 African American, 1 American Indian/Alaska Native, 2 Asian Americans or Pacific Islanders, 4 Hispanic Americans), 2 international. Average age 31. 32 applicants, 94% accepted. In 2007, 9 master's, 6 doctorates awarded. *Degree requirements:* For master's, comprehensive exam, thesis or alternative; for doctorate, one foreign language, thesis/dissertation. *Entrance requirements:* For master's, GRE General Test, minimum undergraduate GPA of 3.0; for doctorate, GRE General Test, minimum undergraduate GPA of 3.0, master's degree in anthropology. *Application deadline:* For fall admission, 1/15 for domestic students, 12/1 for international students. Applications are processed on a rolling basis. Application fee: $50 ($60 for international students). Electronic applications accepted. *Financial support:* In 2007–08, 27 fellowships (averaging $7,387 per year), 2 research assistantships (averaging $13,067 per year) were awarded; tuition waivers (full) also available. Financial award application deadline: 1/15. *Faculty research:* Archaeology of ancient Mayan, plains Indians; skeletal biology of ancient Nubians; human biology of modern people of Amazon; paleontology of early primates. Total annual research expenditures: $775,778. *Unit head:* Darna Dufour, Chair, 303-492-2547, Fax: 303-492-1871, E-mail: darna.dufour@colorado.edu. *Application contact:* Graduate Secretary, 303-492-7947, Fax: 303-492-1871, E-mail: anthro@colorado.edu.

University of Colorado Denver, College of Liberal Arts and Sciences, Department of Anthropology, Denver, CO 80217-3364. Offers MA. Part-time and evening/weekend programs available. *Faculty:* 9 full-time (5 women). *Students:* 8 full-time (6 women), 24 part-time (20 women); includes 2 minority (1 African American, 1 Hispanic American). Average age 34. 30 applicants, 73% accepted, 8 enrolled. In 2007, 9 degrees awarded. *Degree requirements:* For master's, comprehensive exam, thesis or alternative. *Entrance requirements:* For master's, GRE General Test, minor in anthropology. Additional exam requirements/recommendations for international students: Required—TOEFL (minimum score 525 paper-based; 197 computer-based). *Application deadline:* For fall admission, 2/15 for domestic students. Applications are processed on a rolling basis. Application fee: $50 ($75 for international students). Electronic applications accepted. *Financial support:* Research assistantships, teaching assistantships, Federal Work-Study available. Financial award application deadline: 4/1; financial award applicants required to submit FAFSA. *Unit head:* Dr. Steve P. Koester, Chair, 303-556-6795, Fax: 303-556-8501, E-mail: steve.koester@cudenver.edu. *Application contact:* Connie Turner, Program Assistant, 303-556-3554, Fax: 303-556-8501, E-mail: connie.turner@cudenver.edu.

University of Connecticut, Graduate School, College of Liberal Arts and Sciences, Department of Anthropology, Field of Anthropology, Storrs, CT 06269. Offers MA, PhD. *Faculty:* 15 full-time (6 women). *Students:* 45 full-time (28 women), 20 part-time (15 women); includes 11 minority (5 African Americans, 1 Asian American or Pacific Islander, 5 Hispanic Americans), 7 international. Average age 34. 41 applicants, 24% accepted, 9 enrolled. In 2007, 1 master's, 8 doctorates awarded. *Degree requirements:* For master's, comprehensive exam; for doctorate, thesis/dissertation. *Entrance requirements:* For master's and doctorate, GRE General Test. Additional exam requirements/recommendations for international students: Required—TOEFL (minimum score 550 paper-based; 213 computer-based). *Application deadline:* For fall admission, 2/1 priority date for domestic and international students; for spring admission, 11/1 for domestic students, 10/1 for international students. Applications are processed on a rolling basis. Application fee: $55. Electronic applications accepted. *Expenses:* Tuition, state resident: part-time $469 per credit hour. Tuition, nonresident: part-time $1,218 per credit hour. *Financial support:* In 2007–08, 8 research assistantships with full tuition reimbursements, 33 teaching assistantships with full tuition reimbursements were awarded; fellowships, Federal Work-Study, scholarships/grants, health care benefits, and unspecified assistantships also available. Financial award application deadline: 2/1; financial award applicants required to submit FAFSA. *Application contact:* Kevin McBride, Chairperson, 860-486-4511, Fax: 860-486-1719, E-mail: kmcbride@mptn.org.

University of Denver, Faculty of Arts and Humanities/Social Sciences, Department of Anthropology, Denver, CO 80208. Offers MA. Part-time programs available. *Faculty:* 7 full-time (4 women). *Students:* 3 full-time (all women), 11 part-time (all women); includes 2 minority (1 Asian American or Pacific Islander, 1 Hispanic American), 1 international. Average age 26. In 2007, 8 degrees awarded. *Degree requirements:* For master's, thesis or alternative, 1 foreign language or quantitative methods. *Entrance requirements:* For master's, GRE. Additional exam requirements/recommendations for international students: Required—TOEFL. *Application deadline:* Applications are processed on a rolling basis. Application fee: $50. Electronic applications accepted. *Financial support:* In 2007–08, 7 teaching assistantships with full and partial tuition reimbursements (averaging $10,000 per year) were awarded; career-related internships or fieldwork, Federal Work-Study, institutionally sponsored loans, and scholarships/grants also available. Support available to part-time students. Financial award application deadline: 2/20; financial award applicants required to submit FAFSA. *Faculty research:* Gender, class, race, ground penetrating radar, archaeology. Total annual research expenditures:$11,000. *Unit head:* Dr. Richard Clemmer-Smith, Chairperson, 303-871-2406. *Application contact:* Lisa Saccomanno, Assistant to Chair, 303-871-2406, E-mail: anth02@du.edu.

University of Florida, Graduate School, College of Liberal Arts and Sciences, Department of Anthropology, Gainesville, FL 32611. Offers MA, PhD, JD/MA. Part-time programs available. *Faculty:* 28 full-time (7 women), 1 (woman) part-time/adjunct. *Students:* 161 (87 women); includes 30 minority (15 African Americans, 1 American Indian/Alaska Native, 2 Asian Americans or Pacific Islanders, 12 Hispanic Americans) 28 international. In 2007, 17 master's, 11 doctorates awarded. *Degree requirements:* For master's, thesis optional; for doctorate, thesis/dissertation. *Entrance requirements:* For master's and doctorate, GRE General Test, minimum GPA of 3.2. Additional exam requirements/recommendations for international students: Required—TOEFL (minimum score 550 paper-based; 213 computer-based). *Application deadline:* For fall admission, 1/5 for domestic students. Application fee: $30. Electronic applications accepted. *Expenses:* Tuition, state resident: full-time $7,478. Tuition, nonresident: full-time $22,603. *Financial support:* In 2007–08, 19 research assistantships (averaging $15,339 per year), 23 teaching assistantships (averaging $16,440 per year) were awarded; fellowships, career-related internships or fieldwork, Federal Work-Study, institutionally sponsored loans, and unspecified assistantships also available. Support available to part-time students. *Faculty research:* Social and cultural anthropology, archaeology, anthropological linguistics, physical anthropology. *Unit head:* Ken Sassaman, Interim Chair, 352-392-2253 Ext. 205. *Application contact:* Dr. David Daegling, Coordinator, 352-392-2253, Fax: 352-392-6929, E-mail: daegling@anthro.ufl.edu.

University of Georgia, Graduate School, College of Arts and Sciences, Department of Anthropology, Athens, GA 30602. Offers anthropology (MA, PhD); archaeological resource management (MS). *Faculty:* 14 full-time (4 women). *Students:* 44 full-time (27 women), 10 part-time (5 women); includes 1 Hispanic American, 5 international. 78 applicants, 26% accepted, 11 enrolled. In 2007, 1 master's, 7 doctorates awarded. *Degree requirements:* For master's, one foreign language, thesis; for doctorate, one foreign language, thesis/dissertation. *Entrance requirements:* For master's and doctorate, GRE General Test. *Application deadline:* For fall admission, 7/1 priority date for domestic students; for spring admission, 11/15 for domestic students. Application fee: $50. Electronic applications accepted. *Financial support:* Fellowships, research assistantships, teaching assistantships, unspecified assistantships available. *Unit head:* Dr. Ervan G. Garrison, Head, 706-542-1479, Fax: 706-542-3998, E-mail: egarriso@uga.edu. *Application contact:* Dr. Elizabeth J. Reitz, Graduate Coordinator, 706-542-1464, Fax: 706-542-3998, E-mail: ereitz@uga.edu.

University of Guelph, Graduate Program Services, College of Social and Applied Human Sciences, Department of Sociology and Anthropology, Guelph, ON N1G 2W1, Canada. Offers anthropology (MA); crime and criminal justice policy (MA); sociology (MA, PhD). *Faculty:* 24 full-time (13 women). *Students:* 34 full-time (31 women). Average age 25. 119 applicants, 31% accepted, 17 enrolled. In 2007, 14 degrees awarded. *Degree requirements:* For master's, thesis or major paper; for doctorate, comprehensive exam, thesis/dissertation. *Entrance requirements:* For master's, minimum B+ average during previous 2 years of course work, honors BA or equivalent; for doctorate, must have an MA in Sociology, must have 80% or higher in graduate level studies. Additional exam requirements/recommendations for international students: Required—TOEFL (minimum score 550 paper-based; 213 computer-based; 89 iBT), IELTS (minimum score 7), TOEFL or IELTS. *Application deadline:* For fall admission, 2/1 for domestic and international students. Application fee: $85. Electronic applications accepted. *Financial support:* In 2007–08, 103 teaching assistantships (averaging $5,106 per year) were awarded; research assistantships, scholarships/grants also available. *Faculty research:* Rural and development sociology; education, employment, and the workplace; race, ethnicity, and native studies; criminology and deviance; social psychology. *Unit head:* Dr. F. J. Schryer, Chair, 519-824-4120 Ext. 56527, Fax: 519-837-9561, E-mail: fschryer@uoguelph.ca. *Application contact:* Dr. M. Dawson, Graduate Coordinator, 519-824-4120 Ext. 56078, Fax: 519-837-9561, E-mail: mdawson@uoguelph.ca.

University of Hawaii at Manoa, Graduate Division, Colleges of Arts and Sciences, College of Social Sciences, Department of Anthropology, Honolulu, HI 96822. Offers MA, PhD. Part-time programs available. *Faculty:* 23 full-time (6 women), 14 part-time/adjunct (4 women). *Students:* 69 full-time (43 women), 11 part-time (7 women); includes 16 minority (1 American Indian/Alaska Native, 12 Asian Americans or Pacific Islanders, 3 Hispanic Americans), 22 international. Average age 32. 108 applicants, 26% accepted, 12 enrolled. In 2007, 112 master's, 38 doctorates awarded. *Median time to degree:* Of those who began their doctoral program in fall 1999, 17% received their degree in 8 years or less. *Degree requirements:* For master's, thesis optional; for doctorate, comprehensive exam, thesis/dissertation. *Entrance requirements:* For master's and doctorate, GRE General Test. Additional exam requirements/recommendations for international students: Required—TOEFL (minimum score 560 paper-based; 220 computer-based; 83 iBT), IELTS (minimum score 5). *Application deadline:* For fall admission, 1/15 for domestic and international students. Application fee: $50. *Financial support:* In 2007–08, 32 students received support, including 1 research assistantship (averaging $18,198 per year), 9 teaching assistantships (averaging $14,389 per year); Federal Work-Study, institutionally sponsored loans, and tuition waivers (full) also available. Financial award application deadline: 3/1; financial award applicants required to submit FAFSA. *Faculty research:* Evolution of social complexity, ethnopharmacology, social interaction, faunal analysis, human ecology. Total annual research expenditures: $1.2 million. *Application contact:* Dr. Nina Etkin, Graduate Field Chairperson, 808-956-7153, Fax: 808-956-4893, E-mail: etkin@hawaii.edu.

University of Houston, College of Liberal Arts and Social Sciences, Department of Anthropology, Houston, TX 77204. Offers MA. Part-time and evening/weekend programs available. *Faculty:* 7 full-time (3 women), 1 part-time/adjunct (0 women). *Students:* 15 full-time (11 women), 14 part-time (10 women); includes 7 minority (2 African Americans, 1 American Indian/Alaska Native, 1 Asian American or Pacific Islander, 3 Hispanic Americans), 3 international. Average age 31. 8 applicants, 100% accepted, 4 enrolled. In 2007, 7 degrees awarded. *Degree requirements:* For master's, comprehensive exam, thesis optional. *Entrance requirements:* For master's, GRE General Test, minimum GPA of 3.0. *Application deadline:* For fall admission, 7/6 for domestic students; for spring admission, 12/3 for domestic students. Application fee: $0 ($75 for international students). *Expenses:* Tuition, state resident: full-time $6,297; part-time $262 per credit. Tuition, nonresident: full-time $12,969; part-time $540 per credit. Required fees: $2,696. *Financial support:* In 2007–08, 12 teaching assistantships with full tuition reimbursements (averaging $8,800 per year) were awarded; fellowships with full tuition reimbursements, research assistantships with full tuition reimbursements, career-related internships or fieldwork, Federal Work-Study, institutionally sponsored loans, scholarships/grants, health care benefits, and unspecified assistantships also available. Support available to part-time students. Financial award application deadline: 2/1. *Faculty research:* Medical anthropology, international development, archaeology, Mesoamerica, gender. *Unit head:* Dr. Norris Lang, Chairperson, 713-743-3780, Fax: 713-743-3798, E-mail: nlang@uh.edu. *Application contact:* Dr. Rebecca Storey, Graduate Director, 713-743-3780, Fax: 713-743-4287, E-mail: rstorey@uh.edu.

University of Idaho, College of Graduate Studies, College of Letters, Arts and Social Sciences, Department of Sociology, Anthropology and Justice Studies, Program in Anthropology, Moscow, ID 83844-2282. Offers MA. *Students:* 31 (19 women). Average age 31. In 2007, 3 degrees awarded. *Degree requirements:* For master's, one foreign language, thesis (for some programs). *Entrance requirements:* For master's, minimum GPA of 2.8. *Application deadline:* For fall admission, 8/1 for domestic students; for spring admission, 12/15 for domestic students. Application fee: $55 ($60 for international students). *Financial support:* Research assistantships, teaching assistantships available. Financial award application deadline: 2/15. *Application contact:* Dr. Donald E. Tyler, Chair, 208-885-6752.

University of Illinois at Chicago, Graduate College, College of Liberal Arts and Sciences, Department of Anthropology, Chicago, IL 60607-7128. Offers anthropology (MA, PhD); environmental and urban geography (MA), including environmental studies, urban geography. Part-time programs available. *Degree requirements:* For doctorate, comprehensive exam. *Entrance* *requirements:* For master's and doctorate, minimum GPA of 2.75. Additional exam requirements/recommendations for international students: Required—TOEFL. Electronic applications accepted. *Faculty research:* Archaeological, physical, and cultural anthropology.

University of Illinois at Urbana–Champaign, Graduate College, College of Liberal Arts and Sciences, Department of Anthropology, Champaign, IL 61820. Offers MA, PhD. *Faculty:* 30 full-time (12 women). *Students:* 48 full-time (29 women), 13 part-time (11 women); includes 11 minority (1 African American, 1 American Indian/Alaska Native, 2 Asian Americans or Pacific Islanders, 7 Hispanic Americans), 12 international. 93 applicants, 20% accepted, 12 enrolled. In 2007, 4 master's, 5 doctorates awarded. Terminal master's awarded for partial completion of doctoral program. *Degree requirements:* For doctorate, variable foreign language requirement, thesis/dissertation. *Entrance requirements:* For master's, GRE General Test, minimum GPA of 3.0; for doctorate, GRE General Test. *Application deadline:* For fall admission, 12/2 for domestic students. Application fee: $60 ($75 for international students). Electronic applications accepted. *Financial support:* In 2007–08, 17 fellowships, 13 research assistantships, 32 teaching assistantships were awarded; career-related internships or fieldwork, Federal Work-Study, and tuition waivers (full) also available. Financial award application deadline: 1/15. *Unit head:* Steven Leigh, Head, 217-333-3616, Fax: 217-244-3490, E-mail: sleigh@uiuc.edu. *Application contact:* Liz Spears, Graduate Coordinator, 217-244-0296, Fax: 217-244-3490, E-mail: espears@uiuc.edu.

The University of Iowa, Graduate College, College of Liberal Arts and Sciences, Department of Anthropology, Iowa City, IA 52242-1316. Offers MA, PhD. *Faculty:* 15 full-time, 10 part-time/adjunct. *Students:* 20 full-time (17 women), 27 part-time (17 women); includes 4 minority (1 African American, 1 American Indian/Alaska Native, 2 Hispanic Americans), 1 international. 54 applicants, 41% accepted, 8 enrolled. In 2007, 7 master's, 3 doctorates awarded. *Degree requirements:* For master's, thesis optional, exam; for doctorate, comprehensive exam, thesis/dissertation. *Entrance requirements:* For master's and doctorate, GRE General Test, minimum GPA of 3.0. Additional exam requirements/recommendations for international students: Required—TOEFL (minimum score 550 paper-based; 213 computer-based; 81 iBT). *Application deadline:* For fall admission, 1/2 for domestic and international students. Application fee: $60 ($85 for international students). Electronic applications accepted. *Expenses:* Tuition, state resident: part-time $349 per hour. Tuition, nonresident: part-time $349 per hour. Tuition and fees vary according to course load and program. *Financial support:* In 2007–08, 4 fellowships, 5 research assistantships with partial tuition reimbursements, 18 teaching assistantships with partial tuition reimbursements were awarded. Financial award applicants required to submit FAFSA. *Unit head:* Russell Ciochon, Chair, 319-335-2751, Fax: 319-335-0653.

University of Kansas, Research and Graduate Studies, College of Liberal Arts and Sciences, Department of Anthropology, Lawrence, KS 66045. Offers MA, PhD. *Faculty:* 19. *Students:* 47 full-time (25 women), 16 part-time (12 women); includes 6 minority (1 African American, 1 American Indian/Alaska Native, 2 Asian Americans or Pacific Islanders, 2 Hispanic Americans), 6 international. Average age 31. 51 applicants, 65% accepted, 10 enrolled. In 2007, 2 master's, 3 doctorates awarded. *Degree requirements:* For master's, comprehensive exam (for some programs), thesis; for doctorate, one foreign language, comprehensive exam, thesis/dissertation. *Entrance requirements:* For master's and doctorate, minimum GPA of 3.2. Additional exam requirements/recommendations for international students: Required—TOEFL. *Application deadline:* For fall admission, 1/5 for domestic students. Application fee: $55 ($60 for international students). Electronic applications accepted. *Expenses:* Tuition, state resident: full-time $5,838. Tuition, nonresident: full-time $13,409. Tuition and fees vary according to program. *Financial support:* Fellowships with full tuition reimbursements, research assistantships with full and partial tuition reimbursements, teaching assistantships with full and partial tuition reimbursements, career-related internships or fieldwork, institutionally sponsored loans, and unspecified assistantships available. Financial award application deadline: 1/5; financial award applicants required to submit FAFSA. *Faculty research:* Theoretical and applied anthropology, old and new world anthropology, endangered language documentation and revitalization, bio-cultural medical and genetic anthropology, Latin American, African, Asian, European and North American anthropology. *Unit head:* James H. Mielke, Chair, 785-864-4103, Fax: 785-864-5224, E-mail: mielke@ku.edu. *Application contact:* Jack Hofman, Graduate Coordinator, 785-864-4103, Fax: 785-864-5224, E-mail: hofman@ku.edu.

University of Kentucky, Graduate School, College of Arts and Sciences, Program in Anthropology, Lexington, KY 40506-0032. Offers MA, PhD. Part-time programs available. *Faculty:* 15 full-time (10 women), 3 part-time/adjunct (1 woman). *Students:* 55 full-time (35 women), 5 part-time; includes 3 minority (1 African American, 2 Hispanic Americans), 4 international. Average age 35. 39 applicants, 51% accepted, 8 enrolled. In 2007, 4 master's, 3 doctorates awarded. *Median time to degree:* Of those who began their doctoral program in fall 1999, 73% received their degree in 8 years or less. *Degree requirements:* For master's, comprehensive exam, thesis optional; for doctorate, one foreign language, comprehensive exam, thesis/dissertation. *Entrance requirements:* For master's, GRE General Test, minimum undergraduate GPA of 2.75; for doctorate, GRE General Test, minimum graduate GPA of 3.0. Additional exam requirements/recommendations for international students: Required—TOEFL (minimum score 550 paper-based; 213 computer-based). *Application deadline:* For fall admission, 7/17 priority date for domestic students, 2/1 priority date for international students; for spring admission, 6/15 priority date for international students. Application fee: $50 ($65 for international students). Electronic applications accepted. *Expenses:* Tuition, state resident: part-time $437 per credit hour. Tuition, nonresident: part-time $931 per credit hour. *Financial support:* In 2007–08, 18 students received support, including 2 fellowships with full tuition reimbursements available (averaging $2,567 per year), 5 research assistantships with full tuition reimbursements available (averaging $11,124 per year), 12 teaching assistantships with full tuition reimbursements available (averaging $11,124 per year); career-related internships or fieldwork, Federal Work-Study, institutionally sponsored loans, scholarships/grants, traineeships, health care benefits, tuition waivers (partial), and unspecified assistantships also available. Support available to part-time students. Financial award application deadline: 3/15; financial award applicants required to submit FAFSA. *Faculty research:* Applied social anthropology, developmental change, medical anthropology, culture history, ethnohistory. *Unit head:* Dr. Lisa Cliggett, Director of Graduate Studies, 859-275-2796, Fax: 859-323-1959. *Application contact:* Dr. Brian Jackson, Senior Associate Dean, 859-257-4667, Fax: 859-257-4676, E-mail: brian.jackson@uky.edu.

University of Lethbridge, School of Graduate Studies, Lethbridge, AB T1K 3M4, Canada. Offers accounting (MScM); addictions counseling (M Sc); agricultural biotechnology (M Sc); agricultural studies (M Sc, MA); anthropology (MA); archaeology (MA); art (MA); biochemistry (M Sc); biological sciences (M Sc); biomolecular science (PhD); biosystems and biodiversity (PhD); Canadian studies (MA); chemistry (M Sc); computer science (M Sc); computer science and geographical information science (M Sc); counseling psychology (M Ed); dramatic arts (MA); earth, space, and physical science (PhD); economics (MA); educational leadership (M Ed); English (MA); environmental science (M Sc); evolution and behavior (PhD); exercise science (M Sc); finance (MScM); French (MA); French/German (MA); French/Spanish (MA); general education (M Ed); general management (MScM); geography (M Sc, MA); German (MA); health sciences (M Sc, MA); history (MA); human resource management and labour relations (MScM); individualized multidisciplinary (M Sc, MA); information systems (MScM); international management (MScM); kinesiology (M Sc, MA); management (M Sc, MA); marketing (MScM); mathematics (M Sc); music (MA); Native American studies (MA); neuroscience (M Sc, PhD); new media (MA); nursing (M Sc); philosophy (MA); physics (M Sc); policy and strategy (MScM); political science (MA); psychology (M Sc, MA); religious studies (MA); sociology (MA); theoretical and computational science (PhD); urban and regional studies (MA). Part-time and evening/weekend programs available. *Students:* 215 full-time, 98 part-time. In 2007, 87 master's, 1 doctorate awarded. *Degree requirements:* For doctorate, comprehensive exam, thesis/dissertation. *Entrance requirements:* For master's, GMAT (M Sc in management), bachelor's degree in related field, minimum GPA of 3.0 during previous 20 graded semester courses, 2 years teaching or related experience (M Ed); for doctorate, master's degree, minimum graduate GPA of 3.5. Additional exam requirements/recommendations for international students: Required—TOEFL. Application fee: $60 Canadian dollars. *Financial support:* Fellowships, research assistantships, teaching assistantships, scholarships/grants, health care benefits, and unspecified assistantships available. *Faculty research:* Movement and brain plasticity, gibberellin physiology, photosynthesis, carbon cycling, molecular properties of main-group ring components. *Unit head:* Dr. Jo-Anne Fiske, Interim Dean, 403-329-2121, Fax: 403-329-2097. *Application contact:* Jennifer Geddes, Graduate Liaison Officer, 403-329-2762, Fax: 403-329-5159, E-mail: jennifer.geddes@uleth.ca.

University of Manitoba, Faculty of Graduate Studies, Faculty of Arts, Department of Anthropology, Winnipeg, MB R3T 2N2, Canada. Offers MA, PhD. *Degree requirements:* For master's, thesis or alternative.

University of Maryland, College Park, Graduate Studies, College of Behavioral and Social Sciences, Department of Anthropology, College Park, MD 20742. Offers applied anthropology (MAA). Part-time and evening/weekend programs available. *Faculty:* 18 full-time (7 women), 4 part-time/adjunct (3 women). *Students:* 26 full-time (21 women), 7 part-time (6 women); includes 5 minority (1 African American, 1 Asian American or Pacific Islander, 3 Hispanic Americans), 1 international. 78 applicants, 37% accepted, 14 enrolled. In 2007, 14 degrees awarded. *Degree requirements:* For master's, internship. *Entrance requirements:* For master's, GRE General Test, minimum GPA of 3.0, 3 letters of recommendation. Additional exam requirements/recommendations for international students: Required—TOEFL. *Application deadline:* For fall admission, 1/5 for domestic students, 2/1 for international students. Applications are processed on a rolling basis. Application fee: $60. Electronic applications accepted. *Financial support:* In 2007–08, 1 fellowship with full tuition reimbursement (averaging $18,650 per year), 17 teaching assistantships with tuition reimbursements (averaging $14,562 per year) were awarded; research assistantships, Federal Work-Study and scholarships/grants also available. Support available to part-time students. Financial award applicants required to submit FAFSA. *Faculty research:* Archaeology, human biodiversity, cultural and resource management. Total annual research expenditures: $328,262. *Unit head:* Dr. Erve Chambers, Director, 301-405-1423, Fax: 301-314-8305, E-mail: echambers@anth.umd.edu. *Application contact:* Dean of Graduate School, 301-405-4190, Fax: 301-314-9305.

University of Massachusetts Amherst, Graduate School, College of Social and Behavioral Sciences, Department of Anthropology, Amherst, MA 01003. Offers MA, PhD. Part-time programs available. *Faculty:* 22 full-time (11 women). *Students:* 53 full-time (44 women), 22 part-time (16 women); includes 16 minority (4 African Americans, 4 American Indian/Alaska Native, 1 Asian American or Pacific Islander, 7 Hispanic Americans), 6 international. Average age 35. 95 applicants, 20% accepted, 10 enrolled. In 2007, 5 master's, 8 doctorates awarded. Terminal master's awarded for partial completion of doctoral program. *Degree requirements:* For master's, thesis or alternative; for doctorate, thesis/dissertation. *Entrance requirements:* Additional exam requirements/recommendations for international students: Required—TOEFL (minimum score 550 paper-based; 197 computer-based). *Application deadline:* For fall admission, 1/15 priority date for domestic and international students. Applications are processed on a rolling basis. Application fee: $50 ($65 for international students). Electronic applications accepted. *Expenses:* Tuition, state resident: full-time $2,640; part-time $110 per credit. Tuition, nonresident: full-time $9,936; part-time $414 per credit. Required fees: $7,455. One-time fee: $332. Tuition and fees vary according to course load, campus/location, program and reciprocity agreements. *Financial support:* In 2007–08, 14 research assistantships with full tuition reimbursements (averaging $8,669 per year), 31 teaching assistantships with full tuition reimbursements (averaging $8,960 per year) were awarded; fellowships with full tuition reimbursements, career-related internships or fieldwork, Federal Work-Study, scholarships/grants, traineeships, and unspecified assistantships also available. Support available to part-time students. Financial award application deadline: 2/1. *Unit head:* Dr. Elizabeth Chilton, Head, 413-545-0028, Fax: 413-545-9494.

University of Memphis, Graduate School, College of Arts and Sciences, Department of Anthropology, Memphis, TN 38152. Offers MA. Part-time programs available. *Faculty:* 9 full-time (5 women), 1 part-time/adjunct (0 women). *Students:* 21 full-time (17 women), 2 part-time (both women); includes 3 minority (1 African American, 1 Asian American or Pacific Islander, 1 Hispanic American), 1 international. Average age 27. 22 applicants, 73% accepted, 13 enrolled. In 2007, 13 degrees awarded. *Degree requirements:* For master's, comprehensive exam, practicum. *Entrance requirements:* For master's, GRE General Test or MAT. *Application deadline:* For fall admission, 3/15 priority date for domestic students; for spring admission, 12/1 priority date for domestic students. Application fee: $35 ($60 for international students). *Expenses:* Tuition, state resident: full-time $6,990; part-time $377 per hour. Tuition, nonresident: full-time $17,818; part-time $830 per hour. Tuition and fees vary according to course load and program. *Financial support:* In 2007–08, 17 research assistantships with full tuition reimbursements (averaging $5,500 per year), 2 teaching assistantships with full tuition reimbursements (averaging $6,125 per year) were awarded; fellowships, career-related internships or fieldwork, scholarships/grants, and unspecified assistantships also available. Financial award applicants required to submit FAFSA. *Faculty research:* Drug and alcohol abuse, housing and urban development, grassroots community development, immigrant housing and health, community environment impact. *Unit head:* Dr. Ruth Beth Finerman, Chair, 901-678-3334, Fax: 901-678-2069. *Application contact:* Dr. Charles Williams, Coordinator of Graduate Studies, 901-678-0847, E-mail: cwilliam@memphis.edu.

University of Michigan, Horace H. Rackham School of Graduate Studies, College of Literature, Science, and the Arts, Department of Anthropology, Ann Arbor, MI 48109. Offers PhD. *Faculty:* 42 full-time (19 women), 11 part-time/adjunct (5 women). *Students:* 104 full-time (71 women); includes 20 minority (3 African Americans, 2 American Indian/Alaska Native, 6 Asian Americans or Pacific Islanders, 9 Hispanic Americans), 14 international. Average age 27. 236 applicants, 28% accepted, 33 enrolled. In 2007, 15 doctorates awarded. *Median time to degree:* Of those who began their doctoral program in fall 1999, 77% received their degree in 8 years or less. *Degree requirements:* For doctorate, one foreign language, comprehensive exam, thesis/dissertation, oral defense of dissertation, preliminary exam. *Entrance requirements:* For doctorate, GRE General Test. Additional exam requirements/recommendations for international students: Required—TOEFL (minimum score 560 paper-based; 220 computer-based; 84 iBT). *Application deadline:* For fall admission, 1/2 for domestic and international students. Application fee: $60 ($75 for international students). Electronic applications accepted. *Financial support:* In 2007–08, 5 students received support, including 40 fellowships with full tuition reimbursements available (averaging $15,000 per year), 10 research assistantships with full tuition reimbursements available (averaging $15,200 per year), 40 teaching assistantships with full tuition reimbursements available (averaging $15,200 per year); institutionally sponsored loans, scholarships/grants, traineeships, and health care benefits also available. Financial award application deadline: 4/15; financial award applicants required to submit FAFSA. *Faculty research:* Kinship and behavior in wild chimpanzees, paleontological research in the Lower Miocene of Northeast Uganda, long-term fitness consequences of wild chimpanzee behavior. Total annual research expenditures: $90,142. *Unit head:* Judith T. Irvine, Chair, 734-764-7274, Fax: 734-763-6077. *Application contact:* Jessica Greenwald, Graduate Admissions Coordinator, 734-936-7933, Fax: 734-763-6077, E-mail: greenjes@umich.edu.

University of Michigan, Horace H. Rackham School of Graduate Studies, College of Literature, Science, and the Arts, Doctoral Program in Anthropology and History, Ann Arbor, MI 48109. Offers PhD. *Faculty:* 43 full-time (22 women). *Students:* 26 full-time (12 women); includes 6 minority (2 African Americans, 2 Asian Americans or Pacific Islanders, 2 Hispanic Americans), 12 international. Average age 33. 51 applicants, 20% accepted, 4 enrolled. In 2007, 4 doctorates awarded. *Median time to degree:* Of those who began their doctoral program in fall 1999, 75% received their degree in 8 years or less. *Degree requirements:* For doctorate, 2 foreign languages, thesis/dissertation, oral defense of dissertation, preliminary exam. *Entrance requirements:* For doctorate, GRE General Test, writing sample. Additional exam requirements/recommendations for international students: Required—TOEFL. *Application deadline:* For fall admission, 12/1 for domestic and international students. Application fee: $60 ($75 for international students). Electronic applications accepted. *Financial support:* In 2007–08, 14 students

Anthropology

University of Michigan (continued)

received support, including 8 fellowships with full tuition reimbursements available (averaging $15,500 per year), 6 teaching assistantships with full tuition reimbursements available (averaging $15,600 per year); research assistantships with full tuition reimbursements available, institutionally sponsored loans, scholarships/grants, and traineeships also available. Financial award application deadline: 3/1. *Faculty research:* Historical anthropology. *Unit head:* Paul Christopher Johnson, Director, 734-764-1817. *Application contact:* Diana Y. Denney, Graduate Program Coordinator, 734-764-2559, Fax: 734-647-4881, E-mail: dianad@umich.edu.

University of Minnesota, Duluth, Graduate School, College of Liberal Arts, Department of Sociology/Anthropology, Duluth, MN 55812-2496. Offers criminology (MA); liberal studies (MLS). Part-time programs available. *Faculty:* 12 full-time (5 women), 23 part-time/adjunct (9 women). *Students:* 17 full-time (13 women), 18 part-time (12 women); includes 2 minority (1 Asian American or Pacific Islander, 1 Hispanic American). Average age 40. 13 applicants, 46% accepted, 6 enrolled. In 2007, 2 degrees awarded. *Degree requirements:* For master's, thesis or alternative. *Entrance requirements:* For master's, interview, minimum GPA of 3.0, letters of recommendation, personal statement. Additional exam requirements/recommendations for international students: Required—TOEFL. *Application deadline:* For fall admission, 7/15 for domestic students; for spring admission, 11/1 for domestic students. Applications are processed on a rolling basis. Application fee: $55 ($75 for international students). *Expenses:* Tuition, state resident: part-time $812 per credit. Tuition, nonresident: part-time $1,403 per credit. Tuition and fees vary according to program. *Financial support:* In 2007–08, 1 student received support, including teaching assistantships with full tuition reimbursements available (averaging $13,005 per year); institutionally sponsored loans, scholarships/grants, and tuition waivers (partial) also available. Financial award application deadline: 3/15; financial award applicants required to submit FAFSA. *Faculty research:* Nature of knowledge, philosophy of science, ecology, cultural studies, language. *Unit head:* Dr. Janelle Wilson, Head, 218-726-6364, Fax: 218-726-7759, E-mail: jwilson2@d.umn.edu. *Application contact:* Cheryl Aker, Assistant Director, 218-726-8149, Fax: 218-726-6925, E-mail: caker@d.umn.edu.

University of Minnesota, Twin Cities Campus, Graduate School, College of Liberal Arts, Department of Anthropology, Minneapolis, MN 55455-0213. Offers MA, PhD. *Faculty:* 16 full-time (7 women), 2 part-time/adjunct (1 woman). *Students:* 49 full-time (31 women), 16 part-time (12 women); includes 8 minority (1 African American, 1 American Indian/Alaska Native, 4 Asian Americans or Pacific Islanders, 2 Hispanic Americans), 8 international. Average age 30. 68 applicants, 29% accepted, 13 enrolled. In 2007, 1 master's, 4 doctorates awarded. Terminal master's awarded for partial completion of doctoral program. *Median time to degree:* Of those who began their doctoral program in fall 1999, 5% received their degree in 8 years or less. *Degree requirements:* For master's, thesis or alternative; for doctorate, one foreign language, thesis/dissertation. *Entrance requirements:* For master's and doctorate, GRE. Additional exam requirements/recommendations for international students: Required—TOEFL. *Application deadline:* For fall admission, 12/15 for domestic and international students. Application fee: $55 ($75 for international students). Electronic applications accepted. *Financial support:* In 2007–08, 22 students received support, including 3 fellowships with tuition reimbursements available (averaging $12,250 per year), 1 research assistantship with tuition reimbursement available (averaging $12,250 per year), 15 teaching assistantships with tuition reimbursements available (averaging $12,250 per year); career-related internships or fieldwork, Federal Work-Study, institutionally sponsored loans, and tuition waivers (full and partial) also available. Financial award application deadline: 1/5; financial award applicants required to submit FAFSA. *Faculty research:* Psychological anthropology, gender and feminist anthropology, economic anthropology, Latin America, the Pacific. Total annual research expenditures: $11,233. *Unit head:* Dr. William O. Beeman, Professor and Chair, 612-624-8990, Fax: 612-625-3095, E-mail: wbeeman@umn.edu. *Application contact:* Dr. Jean Langford, Director of Graduate Studies, 612-625-4092, Fax: 612-625-3095, E-mail: langf001@umn.edu.

University of Mississippi, Graduate School, College of Liberal Arts, Department of Sociology and Anthropology, Oxford, University, MS 38677. Offers anthropology (MA); sociology (MA, MSS). *Faculty:* 15 full-time (6 women), 4 part-time/adjunct (1 woman). *Students:* 24 full-time (11 women), 5 part-time (4 women); includes 3 minority (all African Americans), 2 international. In 2007, 5 degrees awarded. *Degree requirements:* For master's, thesis (for some programs). *Entrance requirements:* For master's, GRE General Test, minimum GPA of 3.0. Additional exam requirements/recommendations for international students: Required—TOEFL. *Application deadline:* For fall admission, 4/1 for domestic students; for spring admission, 10/1 for domestic students. Applications are processed on a rolling basis. Application fee: $25. Electronic applications accepted. *Expenses:* Tuition, state resident: full-time $4,932. Tuition, nonresident: full-time $11,436. *Financial support:* Scholarships/grants available. Financial award application deadline: 3/1; financial award applicants required to submit FAFSA. *Unit head:* Dr. Kirsten A. Dellinger, Chairman, 662-915-7323, Fax: 662-915-7323.

University of Missouri–Columbia, Graduate School, College of Arts and Sciences, Department of Anthropology, Columbia, MO 65211. Offers MA, PhD. *Degree requirements:* For doctorate, one foreign language, thesis/dissertation. *Entrance requirements:* For master's and doctorate, GRE General Test, minimum GPA of 3.0. Additional exam requirements/recommendations for international students: Required—TOEFL (minimum score 500 paper-based; 173 computer-based; 61 iBT), IELTS (minimum score 6).

The University of Montana, Graduate School, College of Arts and Sciences, Department of Anthropology, Missoula, MT 59812-0002. Offers anthropology (MA); cultural heritage (MA); cultural heritage studies (PhD); forensic anthropology (MA); historical anthropology (PhD); linguistics (MA). *Degree requirements:* For master's, thesis (for some programs). *Entrance requirements:* For master's, GRE General Test. Additional exam requirements/recommendations for international students: Required—TOEFL. *Faculty research:* Historical preservation, plateau-plains archaeology and ethnohistory.

University of Nebraska–Lincoln, Graduate College, College of Arts and Sciences, Department of Anthropology and Geography, Program in Anthropology, Lincoln, NE 68588. Offers MA. *Degree requirements:* For master's, thesis optional. *Entrance requirements:* For master's, GRE General Test. Additional exam requirements/recommendations for international students: Required—TOEFL (minimum score 500 paper-based; 173 computer-based). Electronic applications accepted. *Faculty research:* Cultural, archaeologic, linguistic, and physical anthropology.

University of Nevada, Las Vegas, Graduate College, College of Liberal Arts, Department of Anthropology and Ethnic Studies, Las Vegas, NV 89154-9900. Offers anthropology (MA, PhD). Part-time programs available. *Faculty:* 19 full-time (7 women), 9 part-time/adjunct (2 women). *Students:* 19 full-time (13 women), 21 part-time (16 women); includes 1 minority (African American) 35 applicants, 23% accepted, 2 enrolled. In 2007, 6 degrees awarded. *Degree requirements:* For master's, thesis, oral exam; for doctorate, thesis/dissertation, oral exam. *Entrance requirements:* For master's, minimum GPA of 3.0 in field, 2.75 overall; sample of research; for doctorate, GRE General Test, minimum graduate GPA of 3.5, sample of research. Additional exam requirements/recommendations for international students: Required—TOEFL (minimum score 550 paper-based; 213 computer-based; 80 iBT). *Application deadline:* For fall admission, 1/1 for domestic and international students; for spring admission, 8/15 for domestic and international students. Application fee: $60 ($75 for international students). Electronic applications accepted. *Expenses:* Tuition, state resident: part-time $198 per credit. Tuition, nonresident: part-time $416 per credit. Required fees: $256 per semester. Tuition and fees vary according to course load and reciprocity agreements. *Financial support:* In 2007–08, 13 research assistantships with partial tuition reimbursements (averaging $10,000 per year), 2 teaching assistantships with partial tuition reimbursements (averaging $12,000 per year) were awarded; career-related internships or fieldwork, Federal Work-Study, institutionally sponsored loans, scholarships/grants, health care benefits, and unspecified assistantships also available. Support available to part-time students. Financial award application deadline: 3/1. *Faculty research:* New World studies. *Unit head:* Dr. Alan Simmons, Chair, 702-895-3590. *Application contact:* Graduate College Admissions Evaluator, 702-895-3320, Fax: 702-895-4180, E-mail: gradcollege@unlv.edu.

University of Nevada, Reno, Graduate School, College of Liberal Arts, Department of Anthropology, Reno, NV 89557. Offers MA, PhD. *Faculty:* 22. *Students:* 9 full-time (6 women), 34 part-time (22 women); includes 3 minority (1 American Indian/Alaska Native, 1 Asian American or Pacific Islander, 1 Hispanic American). Average age 32. 27 applicants, 56% accepted, 11 enrolled. In 2007, 6 master's awarded. Terminal master's awarded for partial completion of doctoral program. *Degree requirements:* For master's, thesis; for doctorate, thesis/dissertation. *Entrance requirements:* For master's, GRE, minimum GPA of 2.75; for doctorate, GRE, minimum GPA of 3.0. Additional exam requirements/recommendations for international students: Required—TOEFL. *Application deadline:* For fall admission, 2/1 priority date for domestic students; for spring admission, 11/1 for domestic students. Application fee: $60 ($95 for international students). *Expenses:* Tuition, state resident: full-time $2,774; part-time $154 per credit. Tuition, nonresident: full-time $13,578; part-time $330 per credit. Required fees: $49 per semester. *Financial support:* In 2007–08, 3 research assistantships, 8 teaching assistantships were awarded; Federal Work-Study and institutionally sponsored loans also available. Financial award application deadline: 3/1. *Faculty research:* Ethnology, linguistics, cultural/medical/religious/ethnic relations, ecological anthropology, historical anthropology. *Unit head:* Dr. G. Richard Scott, Graduate Program Director, 775-784-6704.

University of New Brunswick Fredericton, School of Graduate Studies, Faculty of Arts, Department of Anthropology, Fredericton, NB E3B 5A3, Canada. Offers MA. Part-time programs available. *Faculty:* 6 full-time (5 women), 3 part-time/adjunct (0 women). *Students:* 7 full-time (5 women). 5 applicants, 40% accepted, 2 enrolled. In 2007, 3 degrees awarded. *Degree requirements:* For master's, thesis. *Entrance requirements:* For master's, minimum GPA of 3.7, statement of interest. Additional exam requirements/recommendations for international students: Required—TOEFL, IELTS, TWE. *Application deadline:* 1/31 for domestic and international students. Applications are processed on a rolling basis. Application fee: $50 Canadian dollars. *Financial support:* In 2007–08, 1 research assistantship, 1 teaching assistantship were awarded; fellowships also available. *Faculty research:* Latin America, Anthropology of Education, Community-based Fisheries, Biomedical Anthropology, Archaeology of the Maritimes. *Unit head:* David Black, Director of Graduate Studies, 506-458-7045, Fax: 506-453-5071, E-mail: dwblack@unb.ca. *Application contact:* Marina Hernandez, Graduate Secretary, 506-453-4975, Fax: 506-453-5071, E-mail: mhernandez@unb.ca.

University of New Mexico, Graduate School, College of Arts and Sciences, Department of Anthropology, Albuquerque, NM 87131-2039. Offers MA, MS, PhD. *Faculty:* 25 full-time (12 women), 6 part-time/adjunct (4 women). *Students:* 109 full-time (67 women), 51 part-time (35 women); includes 25 minority (3 American Indian/Alaska Native, 3 Asian Americans or Pacific Islanders, 19 Hispanic Americans), 12 international. Average age 34. 133 applicants, 27% accepted, 21 enrolled. In 2007, 15 master's, 5 doctorates awarded. Terminal master's awarded for partial completion of doctoral program. *Degree requirements:* For master's, comprehensive exam (for some programs), thesis or alternative; for doctorate, one foreign language, comprehensive exam, thesis/dissertation, oral defense, skill and/or second language. *Entrance requirements:* For master's and doctorate, GRE General Test, 3 letters of recommendation, letter of interest, application (department and UNM), $50 fee, transcripts. Additional exam requirements/recommendations for international students: Required—TOEFL (minimum score 550 paper-based; 213 computer-based), IELTS (minimum score 7). *Application deadline:* For fall admission, 1/2 priority date for domestic students. Application fee: $50. Electronic applications accepted. *Financial support:* In 2007–08, 78 students received support, including 15 fellowships (averaging $14,000 per year), 11 research assistantships with tuition reimbursements available (averaging $14,000 per year), 39 teaching assistantships with tuition reimbursements available (averaging $14,000 per year); career-related internships or fieldwork, Federal Work-Study, institutionally sponsored loans, scholarships/grants, traineeships, health care benefits, tuition waivers, and unspecified assistantships also available. Support available to part-time students. Financial award application deadline: 3/1; financial award applicants required to submit FAFSA. *Faculty research:* Ethnology, archaeology, evolutionary anthropology. Total annual research expenditures: $524,644. *Unit head:* Michael W. Graves, Chair, 505-277-4524, Fax: 505-277-0874, E-mail: mwgraves@unm.edu. *Application contact:* Erika E. Gerety, Program Advisement Coordinator, 505-277-2732, Fax: 505-277-0874, E-mail: erika@unm.edu.

The University of North Carolina at Chapel Hill, Graduate School, College of Arts and Sciences, Department of Anthropology, Chapel Hill, NC 27599. Offers MA, PhD. *Faculty:* 27 full-time (12 women), 30 part-time/adjunct (14 women). *Students:* 95 full-time (58 women); includes 21 minority (4 African Americans, 3 American Indian/Alaska Native, 7 Asian Americans or Pacific Islanders, 7 Hispanic Americans). Average age 33. 84 applicants, 26% accepted, 13 enrolled. In 2007, 2 master's, 3 doctorates awarded. Terminal master's awarded for partial completion of doctoral program. *Median time to degree:* Of those who began their doctoral program in fall 1999, 75% received their degree in 8 years or less. *Degree requirements:* For master's, variable foreign language requirement, thesis; for doctorate, variable foreign language requirement, comprehensive exam, thesis/dissertation. *Entrance requirements:* For master's and doctorate, GRE General Test, minimum GPA of 3.0. Additional exam requirements/recommendations for international students: Required—TOEFL. *Application deadline:* For fall admission, 12/1 priority date for domestic and international students. Applications are processed on a rolling basis. Application fee: $70. Electronic applications accepted. *Financial support:* In 2007–08, 44 students received support, including fellowships with tuition reimbursements available (averaging $15,000 per year), research assistantships with tuition reimbursements available (averaging $13,000 per year), teaching assistantships with full tuition reimbursements available (averaging $14,400 per year); career-related internships or fieldwork, Federal Work-Study, scholarships/grants, traineeships, health care benefits, and unspecified assistantships also available. Financial award application deadline: 3/1; financial award applicants required to submit FAFSA. *Faculty research:* Archeology, ecology and evolution, medical anthropology, social systems, anthropology of meaning. Total annual research expenditures: $98,240. *Unit head:* Prof. Paul W. Leslie, Chair, 919-962-1243, Fax: 919-962-1613, E-mail: pwleslie@email.unc.edu. *Application contact:* Suphronia J. Cheek, Student Services Manager, 919-843-8977, Fax: 919-962-1613, E-mail: sjcheek@email.unc.edu.

University of North Texas, Robert B. Toulouse School of Graduate Studies, College of Public Affairs and Community Service, Department of Anthropology, Denton, TX 76203. Offers applied anthropology (MA, MS). Part-time and evening/weekend programs available. *Faculty:* 11 full-time (7 women). *Students:* 14 full-time (9 women), 12 part-time (10 women); includes 5 minority (3 African Americans, 2 Hispanic Americans), 1 international. Average age 29. 36 applicants, 61% accepted, 6 enrolled. In 2007, 17 degrees awarded. *Degree requirements:* For master's, practicum. *Entrance requirements:* For master's, GRE General Test, transcripts, departmental application. Additional exam requirements/recommendations for international students: Required—proof of English language proficiency required for non-native English speakers; Recommended—TOEFL (minimum score 550 paper-based; 213 computer-based). *Application deadline:* For fall admission, 7/15 priority date for domestic students; for spring admission, 11/15 priority date for domestic students. Applications are processed on a rolling basis. Application fee: $50 ($75 for international students). Electronic applications accepted. *Financial support:* In 2007–08, 4 research assistantships (averaging $2,500 per year), 20 teaching assistantships (averaging $2,500 per year) were awarded; career-related internships or fieldwork, Federal Work-Study, and scholarships/grants also available. *Faculty research:* Cross-cultural/bilingual education in schools, globalization in work teams/business culture, medical anthropolosis, environmental anthropology. *Unit head:* Dr. Alicia ReCruz, Interim Chair, 940-565-2290, Fax: 940-369-7833, E-mail: arecruz@pacs.unt.edu. *Application contact:* Dr. Lisa Henry, Graduate Adviser, 940-565-4160, Fax: 940-369-7833, E-mail: lhenry@unt.edu.

University of Oklahoma, Graduate College, College of Arts and Sciences, Department of Anthropology, Norman, OK 73019-0390. Offers MA, PhD. Part-time programs available. *Faculty:* 23 full-time (8 women). *Students:* 39 full-time (19 women), 27 part-time (16 women); includes 12 minority (1 African American, 6 American Indian/Alaska Native, 2 Asian Americans or

Pacific Islanders, 3 Hispanic Americans), 2 international. 28 applicants, 71% accepted, 15 enrolled. In 2007, 10 master's, 3 doctorates awarded. Terminal master's awarded for partial completion of doctoral program. *Degree requirements:* For master's, thesis; for doctorate, thesis/dissertation, departmental qualifying exam. *Entrance requirements:* For master's, GRE, BA with 12 hours in anthropology. Additional exam requirements/recommendations for international students: Required—TOEFL (minimum score 550 paper-based; 213 computer-based). *Application deadline:* For fall admission, 4/1 for domestic and international students; for spring admission, 11/1 for domestic students, 9/1 for international students. Applications are processed on a rolling basis. Application fee: $40 ($90 for international students). Electronic applications accepted. *Expenses:* Tuition, state resident: full-time $3,451; part-time $144 per credit hour. Tuition, nonresident: full-time $12,432; part-time $518 per credit hour. Required fees: $1,925; $70 per credit hour. $122 per semester. *Financial support:* In 2007–08, 31 students received support, including 2 research assistantships with partial tuition reimbursements available (averaging $12,968 per year), 21 teaching assistantships with partial tuition reimbursements available (averaging $13,159 per year); career-related internships or fieldwork, Federal Work-Study, scholarships/grants, health care benefits, tuition waivers (partial), and unspecified assistantships also available. Financial award applicants required to submit FAFSA. *Faculty research:* U.S. archaeology, sociocultural anthropology, linguistics, Native American language and culture; biological/physical anthropology. Total annual research expenditures: $1.3 million. *Unit head:* Dr. Pat Gilman, Chair, 405-325-3261, Fax: 405-325-7386, E-mail: pgilman@ou.edu. *Application contact:* Keli Mitchell, Staff Assistant II, 405-325-3261, Fax: 405-325-7386, E-mail: keli@ou.edu.

University of Oregon, Graduate School, College of Arts and Sciences, Department of Anthropology, Eugene, OR 97403. Offers MA, MS, PhD. *Faculty:* 13 full-time (7 women), 1 (woman) part-time/adjunct. *Students:* 27 full-time (18 women), 1 (woman) part-time; includes 8 minority (1 African American, 4 American Indian/Alaska Native, 1 Asian American or Pacific Islander, 2 Hispanic Americans). 73 applicants, 11% accepted. In 2007, 5 master's, 7 doctorates awarded. Terminal master's awarded for partial completion of doctoral program. *Degree requirements:* For master's, one foreign language; for doctorate, 2 foreign languages, thesis/dissertation. *Entrance requirements:* For master's and doctorate, GRE General Test. Additional exam requirements/recommendations for international students: Required—TOEFL. *Application deadline:* For fall admission, 2/1 for domestic students. Application fee: $50. *Financial support:* In 2007–08, 23 teaching assistantships were awarded; career-related internships or fieldwork and Federal Work-Study also available. Support available to part-time students. Financial award application deadline: 3/1. *Faculty research:* Prehistory, primatology, cultural anthropology of Native Americans, human evolution, Africa. *Unit head:* Carol Silverman, Head, 541-346-5114. *Application contact:* Tiffany Brannon, Admissions Contact, 541-346-5102, E-mail: tbrannon@uoregon.edu.

University of Ottawa, Faculty of Graduate and Postdoctoral Studies, Faculty of Social Sciences, Department of Sociology and Anthropology, Ottawa, ON K1N 6N5, Canada. Offers MA. *Degree requirements:* For master's, thesis or alternative. *Entrance requirements:* For master's, honors bachelor's degree or equivalent, minimum B average. Electronic applications accepted. *Faculty research:* Inter-ethnic relations, development, political policies.

University of Pennsylvania, School of Arts and Sciences, Graduate Group in Anthropology, Philadelphia, PA 19104. Offers AM, MS, PhD. Terminal master's awarded for partial completion of doctoral program. *Degree requirements:* For master's, thesis, final exam; for doctorate, one foreign language, thesis/dissertation, fieldwork, preliminary and final exams. *Entrance requirements:* For doctorate, GRE General Test. Additional exam requirements/recommendations for international students: Required—TOEFL.

University of Pittsburgh, School of Arts and Sciences, Department of Anthropology, Pittsburgh, PA 15260. Offers MA, PhD. Part-time programs available. *Faculty:* 20 full-time (5 women), 1 part-time/adjunct (0 women). *Students:* 60 full-time (32 women), 3 part-time (2 women); includes 7 minority (1 African American, 2 Asian Americans or Pacific Islanders, 4 Hispanic Americans), 21 international. 138 applicants, 13% accepted, 11 enrolled. In 2007, 4 master's, 6 doctorates awarded. *Median time to degree:* Of those who began their doctoral program in fall 1999, 50% received their degree in 8 years or less. *Degree requirements:* For master's, one foreign language, thesis or alternative; for doctorate, one foreign language, thesis/dissertation. *Entrance requirements:* For master's and doctorate, GRE General Test. Additional exam requirements/recommendations for international students: Required—TOEFL (minimum score 550 paper-based; 213 computer-based), IELTS (minimum score 6). *Application deadline:* For fall admission, 1/15 priority date for domestic and international students. Applications are processed on a rolling basis. Application fee: $50. Electronic applications accepted. *Financial support:* In 2007–08, 51 students received support, including 20 fellowships with full tuition reimbursements available (averaging $17,162 per year), 30 teaching assistantships with full tuition reimbursements available (averaging $14,485 per year); research assistantships with full tuition reimbursements available, career-related internships or fieldwork, Federal Work-Study, scholarships/grants, health care benefits, tuition waivers (full and partial), and unspecified assistantships also available. Support available to part-time students. Financial award application deadline: 1/15. *Faculty research:* Conflict studies; ethnicity, nationalism, and the state; origins of complex societies; Latin American archaeology; human evolutionary biology. Total annual research expenditures: $348,696. *Unit head:* Dr. Joseph S. Alter, Chair, 412-648-7530, Fax: 412-648-7535, E-mail: jsalter@pitt.edu. *Application contact:* Phyllis J. Deasy, Graduate Coordinator, 412-648-7504, Fax: 412-648-7535, E-mail: pdeasy@pitt.edu.

University of Regina, Faculty of Graduate Studies and Research, Faculty of Arts, Department of Anthropology, Regina, SK S4S 0A2, Canada. Offers MA. Part-time programs available. *Faculty:* 4 full-time (1 woman). *Students:* 1 full-time (0 women). 2 applicants, 50% accepted, 1 enrolled. *Degree requirements:* For master's, thesis. *Entrance requirements:* For master's, writing sample. Additional exam requirements/recommendations for international students: Required—TOEFL (minimum score 580 paper-based; 237 computer-based; 88 iBT). *Application deadline:* Applications are processed on a rolling basis. Application fee: $85 ($100 for international students). Electronic applications accepted. *Financial support:* In 2007–08, fellowships (averaging $15,750 per year), research assistantships (averaging $13,875 per year), teaching assistantships (averaging $13,060 per year) were awarded; scholarships/grants also available. Financial award application deadline: 6/15. *Faculty research:* Symbolic and interpretive theory; ritual; ethnography of Latin America, Himalayas, Sub-Saharan Africa. Total annual research expenditures: $34,000. *Unit head:* Dr. Carlos Londono-Sulkin, Graduate Program Coordinator, 306-585-5405, Fax: 306-585-4815, E-mail: carlos.londono@uregina.ca.

University of Saskatchewan, College of Graduate Studies and Research, College of Arts and Sciences, Department of Religious Studies and Anthropology, Saskatoon, SK S7N 5A2, Canada. Offers MA. *Degree requirements:* For master's, thesis. *Entrance requirements:* Additional exam requirements/recommendations for international students: Required—TOEFL.

University of South Africa, College of Human Sciences, Pretoria, South Africa. Offers adult education (M Ed); African languages (MA, PhD); African politics (MA, PhD); Afrikaans (MA, PhD); ancient history (MA, PhD); ancient Near Eastern studies (MA, PhD); anthropology (MA, PhD); applied linguistics (MA); Arabic (MA, PhD); archaeology (MA); art history (MA); Biblical archaeology (MA); Biblical studies (M Th, D Th, PhD); Christian spirituality (M Th, D Th); church history (M Th, D Th); classical studies (MA, PhD); clinical psychology (MA); communication (MA, PhD); comparative education (M Ed, Ed D); consulting psychology (D Admin, D Com, PhD); curriculum studies (M Ed, Ed D); development studies (M Admin, MA, D Admin, PhD); didactics (M Ed, Ed D); education (M Tech); education management (M Ed, Ed D); educational psychology (M Ed); English (MA); environmental education (M Ed); French (MA, PhD); German (MA, PhD); Greek (MA); guidance and counseling (M Ed); health studies (MA, PhD), including health sciences education (MA), health services management (MA), medical and surgical nursing science (critical care general) (MA), midwifery and neonatal nursing science (MA), trauma and emergency care (MA); history (MA, PhD); history of education (Ed D); inclusive education (M Ed, Ed D); information and communications technology policy and regulation (MA); information science (MA, MIS, PhD); international politics (MA, PhD); Islamic studies (MA, PhD); Italian (MA, PhD); Judaica (MA, PhD); linguistics (MA, PhD); mathematical education (M Ed); mathematics education (MA); missiology (M Th, D Th); modern Hebrew (MA, PhD); musicology (MA, MMus, D Mus, PhD); natural science education (M Ed); New Testament (M Th, D Th); Old Testament (D Th); pastoral therapy (M Th, D Th); philosophy (MA); philosophy of education (M Ed, Ed D); politics (MA, PhD); Portuguese (MA, PhD); practical theology (M Th, D Th); psychology (MA, MS, PhD); psychology of education (M Ed, Ed D); public health (MA); religious studies (MA, D Th, PhD); Romance languages (MA); Russian (MA, PhD); Semitic languages (MA, PhD); social behavior studies in HIV/AIDS (MA); social science (mental health) (MA); social science in development studies (MA); social science in psychology (MA); social science in social work (MA); social science in sociology (MA); social work (MSW, DSW, PhD); socio-education (M Ed, Ed D); sociolinguistics (MA); sociology (MA, PhD); Spanish (MA, PhD); systematic theology (M Th, D Th); TESOL (teaching English to speakers of other languages) (MA); theological ethics (M Th, D Th); theory of literature (MA, PhD); urban ministries (D Th); urban ministry (M Th).

University of South Carolina, The Graduate School, College of Arts and Sciences, Department of Anthropology, Columbia, SC 29208. Offers MA, PhD. *Faculty:* 13 full-time (8 women), 2 part-time/adjunct (0 women). *Students:* 26 full-time (14 women), 7 part-time (3 women); includes 4 minority (2 African Americans, 1 Asian American or Pacific Islander, 1 Hispanic American), 1 international. Average age 32. 47 applicants, 26% accepted. In 2007, 6 degrees awarded. Terminal master's awarded for partial completion of doctoral program. *Degree requirements:* For master's, comprehensive exam, thesis; for doctorate, comprehensive exam, thesis/dissertation. *Entrance requirements:* For master's and doctorate, GRE General Test, letters of reference. Additional exam requirements/recommendations for international students: Required—TOEFL. *Application deadline:* For fall admission, 2/1 priority date for domestic students. Application fee: $35. Electronic applications accepted. *Expenses:* Tuition, state resident: part-time $440 per hour. Tuition, nonresident: part-time $936 per hour. Required fees: $17 per hour. Tuition and fees vary according to program. *Financial support:* In 2007–08, 2 fellowships (averaging $5,000 per year), 5 research assistantships with full tuition reimbursements (averaging $6,000 per year), 9 teaching assistantships with full tuition reimbursements (averaging $6,000 per year) were awarded; career-related internships or fieldwork, Federal Work-Study, institutionally sponsored loans, scholarships/grants, health care benefits, and unspecified assistantships also available. Financial award application deadline: 3/1. *Faculty research:* Biocultural anthropology, archaeology, cultural anthropology. Total annual research expenditures: $46,000. *Unit head:* Dr. Thomas L. Leatherman, Chair, 803-777-6500, Fax: 803-777-0259, E-mail: leathert@gwm.sc.edu. *Application contact:* Dr. Joanna L. Casey, Graduate Director, 803-777-6500, Fax: 803-777-0259, E-mail: caseyj@gwm.sc.edu.

University of Southern Mississippi, Graduate School, College of Arts and Letters, Department of Anthropology and Sociology, Hattiesburg, MS 39406-0001. Offers anthropology (MA). Part-time programs available. *Faculty:* 9 full-time (6 women). *Students:* 15 full-time (12 women), 9 part-time (5 women). Average age 32. 7 applicants, 43% accepted, 3 enrolled. In 2007, 5 degrees awarded. *Degree requirements:* For master's, one foreign language, comprehensive exam, thesis. *Entrance requirements:* For master's, GRE General Test, minimum GPA of 2.75 in last 2 years, 3.0 in field of study. Additional exam requirements/recommendations for international students: Required—TOEFL. *Application deadline:* For fall admission, 3/15 priority date for domestic students, 3/1 for international students. Applications are processed on a rolling basis. Application fee: $30. *Financial support:* In 2007–08, 6 research assistantships with full tuition reimbursements (averaging $7,014 per year), 4 teaching assistantships with full tuition reimbursements (averaging $7,014 per year) were awarded; career-related internships or fieldwork, Federal Work-Study, institutionally sponsored loans, scholarships/grants, and unspecified assistantships also available. Financial award application deadline: 3/15. *Faculty research:* Archaeology of North America, historic archaeology, bioarchaeology, ethnography of Europe, ethnography of Africa. *Unit head:* Dr. James Flanagan, Chair, 601-266-4306, Fax: 601-266-6373. *Application contact:* Dr. Marie Danforth, Graduate Coordinator, 601-266-4306, Fax: 601-266-6373, E-mail: marie.danforth@usm.edu.

University of South Florida, Graduate School, College of Arts and Sciences, Department of Anthropology, Tampa, FL 33620-9951. Offers applied anthropology (MA, PhD). Part-time programs available. *Faculty:* 20 full-time (13 women). *Students:* 79 full-time (50 women), 51 part-time (38 women); includes 30 minority (12 African Americans, 1 American Indian/Alaska Native, 5 Asian Americans or Pacific Islanders, 12 Hispanic Americans), 6 international. Average age 28. 86 applicants, 59% accepted, 28 enrolled. In 2007, 7 master's, 3 doctorates awarded. *Degree requirements:* For master's, comprehensive exam, thesis; for doctorate, one foreign language, comprehensive exam, thesis/dissertation. *Entrance requirements:* For master's and doctorate, GRE General Test, minimum GPA of 3.2, 3 letters of recommendation. Additional exam requirements/recommendations for international students: Required—TOEFL (minimum score 550 paper-based; 213 computer-based). *Application deadline:* For fall admission, 1/15 for domestic and international students. Application fee: $30. Electronic applications accepted. *Financial support:* In 2007–08, 6 fellowships with partial tuition reimbursements (averaging $10,000 per year), 32 research assistantships with partial tuition reimbursements (averaging $10,000 per year), 12 teaching assistantships with partial tuition reimbursements (averaging $10,000 per year) were awarded; scholarships/grants and tuition waivers (partial) also available. Financial award application deadline: 1/15; financial award applicants required to submit FAFSA. *Faculty research:* Population genetics, biomedical anthropology, archaeology and culture resource management in the Americas, urban community issues, media and education. Total annual research expenditures: $1.3 million. *Unit head:* Dr. Elizabeth Bird, Chairperson, 813-974-2138, Fax: 813-974-2668, E-mail: ebird@cas.usf.edu. *Application contact:* Dr. Christian Wells, Application Contact, 813-974-2337, Fax: 813-974-2668, E-mail: cwells@cas.usf.edu.

The University of Tennessee, Graduate School, College of Arts and Sciences, Department of Anthropology, Knoxville, TN 37996. Offers archaeology (MA, PhD); biological anthropology (MA, PhD); cultural anthropology (MA, PhD); zoo-archaeology (MA, PhD). *Degree requirements:* For master's, thesis; for doctorate, one foreign language, thesis/dissertation. *Entrance requirements:* For master's and doctorate, GRE General Test, minimum GPA of 2.7. Additional exam requirements/recommendations for international students: Required—TOEFL. Electronic applications accepted.

The University of Texas at Arlington, Graduate School, College of Liberal Arts, Department of Sociology and Anthropology, Program in Anthropology, Arlington, TX 76019. Offers MA. Part-time and evening/weekend programs available. *Students:* 6 full-time (4 women), 12 part-time (11 women); includes 2 minority (1 African American, 1 American Indian/Alaska Native). In 2007, 1 degree awarded. *Degree requirements:* For master's, thesis or alternative. *Entrance requirements:* For master's, GRE General Test, minimum GPA of 3.0, 3 letters of recommendation. Additional exam requirements/recommendations for international students: Required—TOEFL (minimum score 550 paper-based; 213 computer-based). *Application deadline:* For fall admission, 6/16 for domestic students. Applications are processed on a rolling basis. Application fee: $35 ($50 for international students). *Expenses:* Tuition, state resident: full-time $5,934. Tuition, nonresident: full-time $10,938. *Financial support:* In 2007–08, 1 fellowship (averaging $1,000 per year), 2 teaching assistantships (averaging $9,000 per year) were awarded; Federal Work-Study and institutionally sponsored loans also available. Financial award application deadline: 6/1; financial award applicants required to submit FAFSA. *Application contact:* Shelley Smith, Graduate Advisor, 817-272-3765, Fax: 817-272-3759, E-mail: slsmith@uta.edu.

The University of Texas at Austin, Graduate School, College of Liberal Arts, Department of Anthropology, Austin, TX 78712-1111. Offers archaeology (MA, PhD); folklore and public culture (MA, PhD); linguistic anthropology (MA, PhD); physical anthropology (MA, PhD); social anthropology (MA, PhD). Part-time programs available. Terminal master's awarded for partial completion of doctoral program. *Degree requirements:* For master's, thesis; for doctorate, one foreign language, thesis/dissertation. *Entrance requirements:* For master's and doctorate,

Anthropology

The University of Texas at Austin (continued)

GRE General Test. Additional exam requirements/recommendations for international students: Required—TOEFL. Electronic applications accepted.

The University of Texas at San Antonio, College of Liberal and Fine Arts, Department of Anthropology, San Antonio, TX 78249-0617. Offers MA, PhD. Part-time programs available. *Faculty:* 7 full-time (3 women). *Students:* 18 full-time (13 women), 22 part-time (12 women); includes 11 minority (1 American Indian/Alaska Native, 1 Asian American or Pacific Islander, 9 Hispanic Americans), 4 international. Average age 32. 14 applicants, 79% accepted, 9 enrolled. In 2007, 3 degrees awarded. *Degree requirements:* For master's, one foreign language, comprehensive exam, thesis optional. *Entrance requirements:* For master's, GRE General Test, minimum GPA of 3.0 during last 60 hours, 18 hours in major field. Additional exam requirements/recommendations for international students: Required—TOEFL (minimum score 500 paper-based; 173 computer-based). *Application deadline:* For fall admission, 7/1 for domestic students, 4/1 for international students; for spring admission, 11/1 for domestic students, 9/1 for international students. Applications are processed on a rolling basis. Application fee: $45 ($80 for international students). *Financial support:* In 2007–08, 1 research assistantship (averaging $3,556 per year) was awarded; career-related internships or fieldwork, Federal Work-Study, scholarships/grants, and unspecified assistantships also available. Support available to part-time students. *Faculty research:* Archaeology, ethnohistory, American social history, borderlands history, history of imperialism. Total annual research expenditures: $41,880. *Unit head:* Dr. James McDonald, Interim Chair, 210-458-4673, Fax: 210-458-5728, E-mail: jmcdonald@utsa.edu. *Application contact:* Dr. Laura Levi, Graduate Adviser, 210-458-5709, Fax: 210-458-5728, E-mail: llevi@utsa.edu.

University of Toronto, School of Graduate Studies, Social Sciences Division, Department of Anthropology, Toronto, ON M5S 1A1, Canada. Offers M Sc, MA, PhD. Part-time programs available. *Faculty:* 42 full-time, 6 part-time/adjunct. *Students:* 129 full-time (91 women), 19 international. 212 applicants, 34% accepted. In 2007, 14 master's, 5 doctorates awarded. *Degree requirements:* For master's, research paper; for doctorate, one foreign language, thesis/dissertation, language exam, thesis defense. *Entrance requirements:* For master's, minimum B+ average, 5 full-year anthropology courses, 2 letters of reference, resumé; for doctorate, minimum B+ average, master's degree in relevant area, resumé, 2 letters of reference. Additional exam requirements/recommendations for international students: Required—TOEFL (minimum score 580 paper-based), TWE (minimum score 5), MELAB (minimum score: 85), IELTS (minimum score: 7) or COPE (minimum score: 4). *Application deadline:* For fall admission, 2/1 for domestic students. Application fee: $100 Canadian dollars. *Financial support:* Fellowships, research assistantships, teaching assistantships available. *Unit head:* Prof. Janice Boddy, Chair, 416-978-4805, Fax: 416-978-3217. *Application contact:* Natalia Krencil, Secretary, 416-978-5416, Fax: 416-978-3217, E-mail: nkrencil@chass.utoronto.ca.

University of Tulsa, Graduate School, College of Arts and Sciences, Department of Anthropology, Tulsa, OK 74104-3189. Offers MA, JD/MA. Part-time programs available. *Faculty:* 6 full-time (0 women). *Students:* 5 full-time (4 women), 1 international. Average age 27. 10 applicants, 50% accepted, 2 enrolled. In 2007, 3 degrees awarded. *Degree requirements:* For master's, thesis (for some programs). *Entrance requirements:* For master's, GRE General Test. Additional exam requirements/recommendations for international students: Required—TOEFL (minimum score 575 paper-based; 231 computer-based; 91 iBT), IELTS (minimum score 7). *Application deadline:* Applications are processed on a rolling basis. Application fee: $40. Electronic applications accepted. *Expenses:* Tuition: Full-time $14,004; part-time $778 per credit hour. Required fees: $60; $30 per term. Tuition and fees vary according to course load. *Financial support:* In 2007–08, 3 students received support, including 3 teaching assistantships with full and partial tuition reimbursements available (averaging $10,734 per year); fellowships with full and partial tuition reimbursements available, research assistantships with full and partial tuition reimbursements available, career-related internships or fieldwork, Federal Work-Study, scholarships/grants, tuition waivers (full and partial), and unspecified assistantships also available. Support available to part-time students. Financial award application deadline: 2/1; financial award applicants required to submit FAFSA. *Faculty research:* Cultural anthropology, prehistory of Jordan, lithic technology, archaeology of Mexico, sociolinguistics. *Unit head:* Dr. Lamont Lindstrom, Chairperson, 918-631-2888. *Application contact:* Dr. George Odell, Adviser, 918-631-3082, Fax: 918-631-2540, E-mail: george-odell@utulsa.edu.

University of Utah, The Graduate School, College of Humanities, Program in Middle East Studies, Salt Lake City, UT 84112-1107. Offers anthropology (MA); Arabic (MA, PhD); Arabic and linguistics (MA, PhD); Hebrew (MA); history (MA, PhD); Persian (MA, PhD); political science (MA, PhD); Turkish (MA). *Faculty:* 12 full-time (3 women). *Students:* 26 full-time (12 women), 10 part-time (2 women); includes 1 minority (Asian American or Pacific Islander), 10 international. Average age 36. 36 applicants, 78% accepted, 10 enrolled. In 2007, 6 master's awarded. Terminal master's awarded for partial completion of doctoral program. *Median time to degree:* Of those who began their doctoral program in fall 1999, 100% received their degree in 8 years or less. *Degree requirements:* For master's, 2 foreign languages, comprehensive exam, thesis optional; for doctorate, 3 foreign languages, comprehensive exam, thesis/dissertation. *Entrance requirements:* For master's, GRE General Test, minimum GPA of 3.2; for doctorate, GRE General Test, MA in Middle East studies or equivalent, minimum GPA of 3.2. Additional exam requirements/recommendations for international students: Required—TOEFL (minimum score 580 paper-based; 237 computer-based; 92 iBT). *Application deadline:* For fall admission, 1/15 for domestic and international students; for spring admission, 9/15 for domestic and international students. Application fee: $45 ($65 for international students). *Financial support:* In 2007–08, 17 students received support, including 14 fellowships with full tuition reimbursements available (averaging $14,000 per year), 2 teaching assistantships with full tuition reimbursements available (averaging $12,000 per year); unspecified assistantships also available. Financial award application deadline: 1/15. *Faculty research:* Arabic literature and linguistics, Islamic studies, Middle East history, political science, Judaic studies. *Unit head:* Dr. Ibrahim A. Karawan, Director, 801-581-6181, Fax: 801-581-6183, E-mail: ibrahim.karawan@poli-sci.utah.edu. *Application contact:* Peter von Sivers, Director of Graduate Studies, 801-581-8073, Fax: 801-581-6183, E-mail: peter.vonsivers@utah.edu.

University of Utah, The Graduate School, College of Social and Behavioral Science, Department of Anthropology, Salt Lake City, UT 84112-1107. Offers M Phil, MA, MS, PhD. *Faculty:* 16 full-time (4 women), 1 part-time/adjunct (0 women). *Students:* 30 full-time (16 women), 11 part-time (6 women). Average age 32. 33 applicants, 48% accepted, 11 enrolled. In 2007, 7 master's awarded. *Median time to degree:* Of those who began their doctoral program in fall 1999, 0% received their degree in 8 years or less. *Degree requirements:* For master's, comprehensive exam, thesis or alternative; for doctorate, comprehensive exam (for some programs), thesis/dissertation. *Entrance requirements:* For master's, GRE General Test, minimum undergraduate GPA of 3.0; for doctorate, GRE General Test. Additional exam requirements/recommendations for international students: Required—TOEFL (minimum score 500 paper-based; 173 computer-based). *Application deadline:* For fall admission, 1/31 for domestic students. Application fee: $45 ($65 for international students). Electronic applications accepted. *Financial support:* In 2007–08, fellowships with full and partial tuition reimbursements (averaging $15,000 per year), research assistantships with full and partial tuition reimbursements (averaging $12,000 per year), teaching assistantships with full and partial tuition reimbursements (averaging $11,500 per year) were awarded; career-related internships or fieldwork and health care benefits also available. *Faculty research:* Evolutionary ecology, anthropological genetics, North American (hunter and gatherers) archaeology. Total annual research expenditures: $382,747. *Unit head:* Dr. Elizabeth A. Cashdan, Chair, 801-581-6251, Fax: 801-581-6252, E-mail: cashdan@anthro.utah.edu. *Application contact:* Ursula E. Hanly, Administrative Assistant, 801-581-6251, Fax: 801-581-6252, E-mail: ursula@anthro.utah.edu.

University of Victoria, Faculty of Graduate Studies, Faculty of Social Sciences, Department of Anthropology, Victoria, BC V8W 2Y2, Canada. Offers MA. Part-time programs available. *Faculty:* 12 full-time (6 women). *Students:* 23 full-time (19 women), 1 international. Average age 25. 33 applicants, 48% accepted, 10 enrolled. In 2007, 2 degrees awarded. *Degree requirements:* For master's, comprehensive exam (for some programs), thesis (for some programs). *Entrance requirements:* For master's, minimum B+ average in last 2 years of undergraduate course work, writing sample. Additional exam requirements/recommendations for international students: Required—TOEFL (minimum score 575 paper-based; 233 computer-based), IELTS (minimum score 7). *Application deadline:* For fall admission, 2/15 priority date for domestic and international students. Applications are processed on a rolling basis. Application fee: $75 ($125 for international students). *Expenses:* Tuition, state resident: full-time $3,110. International tuition: $3,700 full-time. Tuition and fees vary according to program. *Financial support:* In 2007–08, 5 research assistantships with tuition reimbursements (averaging $2,000 per year), 10 teaching assistantships with tuition reimbursements (averaging $1,749 per year) were awarded; fellowships, institutionally sponsored loans and graduate teaching fund (matching funds for teaching assistantships) also available. Financial award application deadline: 2/15. *Unit head:* Dr. Warren Magnusson, Acting Chair, 250-721-7049, Fax: 250-721-6215, E-mail: anthone@uvic.ca. *Application contact:* Dr. Margo Matwychuk, Graduate Adviser, 250-721-6283, Fax: 250-721-6215, E-mail: mmatwych@uvic.ca.

University of Virginia, College and Graduate School of Arts and Sciences, Department of Anthropology, Charlottesville, VA 22903. Offers MA, PhD. *Faculty:* 18 full-time (7 women). *Students:* 39 full-time (24 women), 3 part-time (all women); includes 8 minority (3 African Americans, 1 American Indian/Alaska Native, 2 Asian Americans or Pacific Islanders, 2 Hispanic Americans), 4 international. Average age 29. 56 applicants, 14% accepted, 6 enrolled. In 2007, 7 master's, 4 doctorates awarded. *Degree requirements:* For master's, one foreign language, thesis; for doctorate, 2 foreign languages, thesis/dissertation. *Entrance requirements:* For master's and doctorate, GRE General Test, GRE Subject Test. Additional exam requirements/recommendations for international students: Required—TOEFL. *Application deadline:* Applications are processed on a rolling basis. Application fee: $60. Electronic applications accepted. *Financial support:* Applicants required to submit FAFSA. *Unit head:* Ellen L. Contini-Morava, Chair, 434-924-7044, Fax: 434-924-1350.

University of Washington, Graduate School, College of Arts and Sciences, Department of Anthropology, Seattle, WA 98195. Offers MA, PhD. *Faculty:* 25 full-time (15 women), 16 part-time/adjunct (7 women). *Students:* 76 full-time (58 women), 15 part-time (7 women); includes 17 minority (4 African Americans, 4 American Indian/Alaska Native, 5 Asian Americans or Pacific Islanders, 4 Hispanic Americans), 11 international. Average age 32. 174 applicants, 16% accepted, 15 enrolled. In 2007, 8 master's, 9 doctorates awarded. Terminal master's awarded for partial completion of doctoral program. *Median time to degree:* Of those who began their doctoral program in fall 1999, 28% received their degree in 8 years or less. *Degree requirements:* For master's, one foreign language, comprehensive exam (for some programs), thesis (for some programs); for doctorate, one foreign language, comprehensive exam (for some programs), thesis/dissertation. *Entrance requirements:* For master's and doctorate, GRE General Test, minimum GPA of 3.4. Additional exam requirements/recommendations for international students: Required—TOEFL (minimum score 500 paper-based; 173 computer-based). *Application deadline:* For fall admission, 1/15 for domestic and international students. Application fee: $50. Electronic applications accepted. *Financial support:* In 2007–08, 3 fellowships with full tuition reimbursements (averaging $12,000 per year), 4 research assistantships with full tuition reimbursements (averaging $13,000 per year), 20 teaching assistantships with full tuition reimbursements (averaging $13,000 per year) were awarded; career-related internships or fieldwork, Federal Work-Study, and institutionally sponsored loans also available. Financial award application deadline: 1/15; financial award applicants required to submit FAFSA. *Faculty research:* Sociocultural anthropology, biocultural anthropology, archaeology, environmental anthropology. *Unit head:* Alison Wylie, Chair, 206-543-5240, Fax: 206-543-3285. *Application contact:* Graduate Program Assistant, 206-685-1562, Fax: 206-543-3285, E-mail: gradanth@u.washington.edu.

University of Waterloo, Graduate Studies, Faculty of Arts, Department of Anthropology, Waterloo, ON N2L 3G1, Canada. Offers anthropology (MA); public issues (MA). *Entrance requirements:* For master's, BA, B+ average. Additional exam requirements/recommendations for international students: Required—TOEFL. Application fee: $75. Electronic applications accepted. *Financial support:* Fellowships, research assistantships, teaching assistantships available. *Faculty research:* Applied socio-cultural anthropology and archaeology. *Unit head:* Dr. Tom Abler, Chair and Graduate Officer, 519-888-4567 Ext. 33044, E-mail: tsabler@uwaterloo.ca.

The University of Western Ontario, Faculty of Graduate Studies, Social Sciences Division, Department of Anthropology, London, ON N6A 5B8, Canada. Offers MA, PhD. *Faculty:* 12 full-time (5 women), 7 part-time/adjunct (3 women). *Students:* 22 full-time (18 women), 5 part-time (3 women). In 2007, 4 degrees awarded. *Degree requirements:* For master's, thesis; for doctorate, thesis/dissertation. *Entrance requirements:* For master's, minimum B average, honors BA. Additional exam requirements/recommendations for international students: Required—TOEFL. *Application deadline:* For fall admission, 2/15 priority date for domestic students. Application fee: $20 Canadian dollars. Electronic applications accepted. *Financial support:* In 2007–08, 21 students received support; fellowships, teaching assistantships available. Financial award application deadline: 4/1. *Faculty research:* Sociocultural anthropology, bioarchaeology, linguistics. *Unit head:* Dr. Dan Jorgensen, Chair, 519-661-2111 Ext. 85085, Fax: 519-661-2157. *Application contact:* Diane Belleville, Graduate Assistant, 519-661-2111 Ext. 85080, Fax: 519-661-2157, E-mail: diane.belville@uwo.ca.

University of West Florida, College of Arts and Sciences: Arts, Department of Anthropology, Pensacola, FL 32514-5750. Offers anthropology (MA); historical archaeology (MA). *Faculty:* 8 full-time (3 women). *Students:* 14 full-time (12 women), 26 part-time (15 women); includes 4 minority (1 African American, 1 Asian American or Pacific Islander, 2 Hispanic Americans). Average age 29. 33 applicants, 58% accepted, 9 enrolled. In 2007, 4 degrees awarded. *Degree requirements:* For master's, internship or thesis. *Entrance requirements:* For master's, GRE, bachelor's degree in anthropology, minimum GPA of 3.0, 3 letters of recommendation, writing sample. Additional exam requirements/recommendations for international students: Required—TOEFL (minimum score 550 paper-based; 216 computer-based). *Application deadline:* For fall admission, 6/1 for domestic students, 5/15 for international students; for spring admission, 11/1 for domestic students, 10/1 for international students. Application fee: $30. *Expenses:* Tuition, state resident: full-time $6,054; part-time $252 per credit. Tuition, nonresident: full-time $21,886; part-time $912 per credit. *Financial support:* In 2007–08, 5 research assistantships (averaging $3,760 per year), 5 teaching assistantships (averaging $3,760 per year) were awarded; fellowships, career-related internships or fieldwork, scholarships/grants, tuition waivers (partial), and unspecified assistantships also available. Financial award application deadline: 4/15; financial award applicants required to submit FAFSA. *Unit head:* Dr. Judith A. Bense, Chairperson, 850-474-2797, E-mail: anthropology@uwf.edu.

University of Wisconsin–Madison, Graduate School, College of Letters and Science, Department of Anthropology, Madison, WI 53706-1380. Offers MA, MS, PhD. Terminal master's awarded for partial completion of doctoral program. *Degree requirements:* For master's, qualifying exam; for doctorate, thesis/dissertation. *Entrance requirements:* For doctorate, qualifying exam. Electronic applications accepted. *Faculty research:* Archaeology, biological, anthropology, cultural anthropology.

University of Wisconsin–Milwaukee, Graduate School, College of Letters and Sciences, Department of Anthropology, Milwaukee, WI 53201-0413. Offers MS, PhD, Certificate. *Faculty:* 17 full-time (7 women). *Students:* 56 full-time (37 women), 44 part-time (28 women); includes 12 minority (3 African Americans, 3 American Indian/Alaska Native, 2 Asian Americans or Pacific Islanders, 4 Hispanic Americans), 2 international. 57 applicants, 67% accepted, 12 enrolled. In 2007, 14 master's, 3 doctorates awarded. *Degree requirements:* For master's, thesis or alternative; for doctorate, one foreign language, thesis/dissertation, departmental qualifying exam. *Application deadline:* For fall admission, 1/1 priority date for domestic students; for spring admission, 9/1 for domestic students. Applications are processed on a rolling basis.

Application fee: $45 ($75 for international students). *Expenses:* Tuition, state resident: part-time $530 per credit. Tuition, nonresident: part-time $1,428 per credit. Required fees: $19 per credit. $229 per term. Tuition and fees vary according to course load and program. *Financial support:* In 2007–08, 15 teaching assistantships were awarded; fellowships, research assistantships, career-related internships or fieldwork and unspecified assistantships also available. Support available to part-time students. Financial award application deadline: 4/15. *Unit head:* J. Patrick Gray, Chair, 414-229-4822, Fax: 414-229-5848, E-mail: jpgray@uwm.edu.

University of Wyoming, Graduate School, College of Arts and Sciences, Department of Anthropology, Laramie, WY 82070. Offers MA, PhD. Part-time programs available. *Faculty:* 11 full-time (5 women), 7 part-time/adjunct (1 woman). *Students:* 18 full-time (7 women), 22 part-time (14 women). Average age 32. 33 applicants, 61% accepted. In 2007, 7 master's, 1 doctorate awarded. Terminal master's awarded for partial completion of doctoral program. *Degree requirements:* For master's, one foreign language, thesis; for doctorate, one foreign language, thesis/dissertation. *Entrance requirements:* For master's and doctorate, GRE General Test, minimum GPA of 3.0. *Application deadline:* For fall admission, 3/1 for domestic and international students. Application fee: $50. Electronic applications accepted. *Financial support:* In 2007–08, 22 students received support, including 11 research assistantships with partial tuition reimbursements available (averaging $5,031 per year); career-related internships or fieldwork, Federal Work-Study, and institutionally sponsored loans also available. Financial award application deadline: 3/1. *Faculty research:* Paleo-Indian archaeology, osteology, faunal analysis, lithic analysis, hunter-gatherers. Total annual research expenditures: $70,000. *Unit head:* Robert L. Kelly, Graduate Advisor, 307-766-3164, Fax: 307-766-2473, E-mail: rlkelly@uwyo.edu. *Application contact:* Nicole Waguespack, Graduate Advisor, 307-766-2931, Fax: 307-766-2473, E-mail: nmwagues@uwyo.edu.

Vanderbilt University, Graduate School, Department of Anthropology, Nashville, TN 37240-1001. Offers MA, PhD. *Faculty:* 17 full-time (2 women). *Students:* 26 full-time (19 women), 1 part-time, 2 international. Average age 31. 48 applicants, 13% accepted, 6 enrolled. In 2007, 3 degrees awarded. *Degree requirements:* For master's, comprehensive exam, thesis or alternative; for doctorate, one foreign language, comprehensive exam, thesis/dissertation, general, qualifying, and final exams. *Entrance requirements:* For master's and doctorate, GRE General Test. *Application deadline:* For fall admission, 1/15 for domestic and international students. Application fee: $0. Electronic applications accepted. *Financial support:* Fellowships with full and partial tuition reimbursements, research assistantships with full tuition reimbursements, teaching assistantships with full tuition reimbursements, career-related internships or fieldwork, Federal Work-Study, institutionally sponsored loans, and health care benefits available. Financial award application deadline: 1/15; financial award applicants required to submit CSS PROFILE or FAFSA. *Faculty research:* Archaeology, ethnohistory and ethnography, epigraphy, conflict theory, Latin America. *Unit head:* Tom D. Dillehay, Chair, 615-343-6120, Fax: 615-343-0230. *Application contact:* Beth A. Conklin, Director of Graduate Studies, 615-343-6120, Fax: 615-343-0230, E-mail: beth.a.conklin@vanderbilt.edu.

Washington State University, Graduate School, College of Liberal Arts, Department of Anthropology, Pullman, WA 99164. Offers archaeology (MA, PhD); cultural anthropology (MA, PhD); evolutionary anthropology (MA, PhD). Part-time programs available. *Faculty:* 17. *Students:* 56 full-time (33 women), 26 part-time (12 women); includes 11 minority (2 African Americans, 1 American Indian/Alaska Native, 2 Asian Americans or Pacific Islanders, 6 Hispanic Americans), 6 international. Average age 32. 198 applicants, 14% accepted, 19 enrolled. In 2007, 8 master's, 2 doctorates awarded. *Median time to degree:* Of those who began their doctoral program in fall 1999, 100% received their degree in 8 years or less. *Degree requirements:* For master's, comprehensive exam (for some programs), thesis, oral exam; for doctorate, comprehensive exam, thesis/dissertation, qualifying exam, oral exam and written exam. *Entrance requirements:* For master's, GRE General Test, minimum GPA of 3.0, curriculum vitae, 3 letters of recommendation; for doctorate, GRE General Test, minimum GPA of 3.0, copy of thesis or master's research paper, curriculum vitae, 3 letters of recommendation. Additional exam requirements/recommendations for international students: Required—TOEFL (minimum score 550 paper-based; 213 computer-based). *Application deadline:* For fall admission, 2/1 priority date for domestic students, 1/15 priority date for international students. Applications are processed on a rolling basis. Application fee: $50. Electronic applications accepted. *Financial support:* In 2007–08, 54 students received support, including 5 research assistantships with full tuition reimbursements available (averaging $13,917 per year), 34 teaching assistantships with full tuition reimbursements available (averaging $13,056 per year); fellowships, Federal Work-Study, institutionally sponsored loans, scholarships/grants, health care benefits, and tuition waivers (partial) also available. Support available to part-time students. Financial award application deadline: 3/1; financial award applicants required to submit FAFSA. *Faculty research:* Western North American archaeology and paleo-environments, zooarchaeology, gender and culture issues, issues of globalization, cultural ecology. Total annual research expenditures: $327,444. *Unit head:* Dr. William Andrefsky, Chair, 509-335-1127, Fax: 509-335-3999, E-mail: and@wsu.edu. *Application contact:* Graduate School Admissions, 800-GRADWSU, Fax: 509-335-1949, E-mail: gradsch@wsu.edu.

Washington University in St. Louis, Graduate School of Arts and Sciences, Department of Anthropology, St. Louis, MO 63130-4899. Offers MA, PhD. Terminal master's awarded for partial completion of doctoral program. *Degree requirements:* For master's, thesis optional; for doctorate, thesis/dissertation. *Entrance requirements:* For master's and doctorate, GRE General Test. Electronic applications accepted.

Wayne State University, College of Liberal Arts and Sciences, Department of Anthropology, Detroit, MI 48202. Offers MA, PhD. *Students:* 37 full-time (27 women), 38 part-time (30 women); includes 24 minority (22 African Americans, 2 Hispanic Americans), 3 international. Average age 38. 36 applicants, 53% accepted, 11 enrolled. In 2007, 8 master's, 2 doctorates awarded. *Degree requirements:* For master's, one foreign language, thesis; for doctorate, one foreign language, thesis/dissertation. *Entrance requirements:* Additional exam requirements/recommendations for international students: Required—TOEFL (minimum score 550 paper-based; 213 computer-based); Recommended—TWE (minimum score 6). *Application deadline:* For fall admission, 7/1 for domestic students, 6/1 for international students; for winter admission, 10/1 for international students; for spring admission, 2/1 for international students. Applications are processed on a rolling basis. Application fee: $30 ($50 for international students). Electronic applications accepted. *Expenses:* Tuition, state resident: part-time $403 per credit hour. Tuition, nonresident: part-time $890 per credit hour. *Financial support:* In 2007–08, 1 fellowship with tuition reimbursement (averaging $13,001 per year), 1 research assistantship (averaging $13,672 per year), 4 teaching assistantships (averaging $13,672 per year) were awarded. *Faculty research:* Business anthropology and organizational culture, African and African-American religions, medical anthropology, skeletal epidemiology and forensic anthropology, Latin American anthropology and archaeology. *Unit head:* Dr. Andrea Sankar, Chair, 313-577-2935, Fax: 313-577-5958, E-mail: aa7651@wayne.edu. *Application contact:* Beverly Fogelson, Graduate Director, 313-577-2935, E-mail: bfogelson@wayne.edu.

West Chester University of Pennsylvania, Office of Graduate Studies and Extended Education, College of Arts and Sciences, Department of Anthropology and Sociology, West Chester, PA 19383. Offers gerontology (Certificate); long term health care (MSA). Part-time and evening/weekend programs available. In 2007, 1 degree awarded. *Degree requirements:* For master's, comprehensive exam. *Entrance requirements:* For master's, MAT, GRE, or GMAT, interview. Additional exam requirements/recommendations for international students: Required—TOEFL (minimum score 550 paper-based; 213 computer-based; 80 iBT). *Application deadline:* For fall admission, 4/15 priority date for domestic students; for spring admission, 10/15 for domestic students. Applications are processed on a rolling basis. Application fee: $35. *Expenses:* Tuition, state resident: part-time $345 per credit. Tuition, nonresident: part-time $552 per credit. Tuition and fees vary according to course load. *Financial support:* In 2007–08, research assistantships with full tuition reimbursements (averaging $5,000 per year); unspecified assistantships also available. Support available to part-time students. Financial award application deadline: 2/15; financial award applicants required to submit FAFSA. *Faculty research:* West African communities in the U.S., life long learning-distance education, comparative religions. *Unit head:* Dr. Susan Johnston, Chair, 610-436-2556, E-mail: sjohnston@wcupa.edu. *Application contact:* Dr. Douglas McConatha, Graduate Coordinator, 610-436-3125, E-mail: dmcconatha@wcupa.edu.

Western Kentucky University, Graduate Studies, Potter College of Arts and Letters, Department of Folk Studies and Anthropology, Bowling Green, KY 42101. Offers folk studies (MA). *Degree requirements:* For master's, comprehensive exam, thesis optional, written exam. *Entrance requirements:* For master's, GRE General Test, minimum GPA of 3.0. Additional exam requirements/recommendations for international students: Required—TOEFL (minimum score 555 paper-based; 213 computer-based; 79 iBT). *Faculty research:* Public folklore, folklore and education, vernacular belief, music and culture, historic presentation.

Western Michigan University, Graduate College, College of Arts and Sciences, Department of Anthropology, Kalamazoo, MI 49008-5202. Offers MA. *Degree requirements:* For master's, comprehensive exam, thesis, written exams.

Western Washington University, Graduate School, College of Humanities and Social Sciences, Department of Anthropology, Bellingham, WA 98225-5996. Offers MA. Part-time programs available. *Faculty:* 11. *Students:* 10 full-time (6 women), 7 part-time (3 women). 13 applicants, 85% accepted, 7 enrolled. In 2007, 8 degrees awarded. *Degree requirements:* For master's, thesis. *Entrance requirements:* For master's, GRE General Test, minimum GPA of 3.0 in last 60 semester hours or last 90 quarter hours. Additional exam requirements/recommendations for international students: Required—TOEFL (minimum score 567 paper-based; 227 computer-based). *Application deadline:* For fall admission, 3/1 priority date for domestic students. Applications are processed on a rolling basis. Application fee: $50. Electronic applications accepted. *Expenses:* Tuition, state resident: part-time $208 per credit. Tuition, nonresident: part-time $541 per credit. Required fees: $241 per quarter. One-time fee: $250 part-time. *Financial support:* In 2007–08, 7 teaching assistantships with partial tuition reimbursements (averaging $10,120 per year) were awarded; Federal Work-Study, institutionally sponsored loans, scholarships/grants, tuition waivers (partial), and unspecified assistantships also available. Support available to part-time students. Financial award application deadline: 2/15; financial award applicants required to submit FAFSA. *Faculty research:* Peoples and culture of the Pacific Rim; prehistory of North America; applied health; community-based action research; globalization and human rights. *Unit head:* Dr. Daniel L. Boxberger, Chair, 360-650-3620, E-mail: danbox@cc.wwu.edu. *Application contact:* Dr. Sarah K. Campbell, Graduate Program Adviser, 360-650-4793, E-mail: campbsk@cc.wwu.edu.

Wichita State University, Graduate School, Fairmount College of Liberal Arts and Sciences, Department of Anthropology, Wichita, KS 67260. Offers MA. Part-time programs available. *Degree requirements:* For master's, comprehensive exam, thesis optional, project. *Entrance requirements:* For master's, GRE, minimum GPA of 2.75 in last 60 hours and 3.0 in anthropology. Additional exam requirements/recommendations for international students: Required—TOEFL. Electronic applications accepted. *Faculty research:* Archaeology (plains and southwest), cross-cultural studies of aging, action anthropology, hostility and warfare, human osteology and nutrition.

Yale University, Graduate School of Arts and Sciences, Department of Anthropology, New Haven, CT 06520. Offers MA, PhD. *Degree requirements:* For doctorate, thesis/dissertation. *Entrance requirements:* For master's and doctorate, GRE General Test. *Faculty research:* Linguistics, national identity.

York University, Faculty of Graduate Studies, Faculty of Arts, Program in Social Anthropology, Toronto, ON M3J 1P3, Canada. Offers MA, PhD. Part-time programs available. *Degree requirements:* For master's, thesis or alternative; for doctorate, comprehensive exam, thesis/dissertation. Electronic applications accepted.

Applied Social Research

American University, College of Arts and Sciences, Department of Sociology, Washington, DC 20016-8001. Offers professional/applied sociology (MA); social research (Certificate); sociology (MA, Certificate). Part-time and evening/weekend programs available. *Faculty:* 12 full-time (9 women), 2 part-time/adjunct (1 woman). *Students:* 18 full-time (16 women), 38 part-time (28 women); includes 26 minority (21 African Americans, 1 American Indian/Alaska Native, 1 Asian American or Pacific Islander, 3 Hispanic Americans), 4 international. Average age 36. 36 applicants, 81% accepted, 15 enrolled. In 2007, 14 master's awarded. *Degree requirements:* For master's, comprehensive exam, thesis or alternative, tool of research examination. *Entrance requirements:* For master's, GRE; for Certificate, Bachelor's Degree. Additional exam requirements/recommendations for international students: Required—TOEFL (minimum score 550 paper-based; 213 computer-based). *Application deadline:* For fall admission, 2/1 for domestic students. Application fee: $50. *Expenses:* Tuition: Full-time $19,998; part-time $1,111 per credit hour. Required fees: $380. Tuition and fees vary according to program. *Financial support:* Fellowships with full tuition reimbursements, research assistantships with full tuition reimbursements, teaching assistantships with full tuition reimbursements, career-related internships or fieldwork, Federal Work-Study, institutionally sponsored loans, tuition waivers (full and partial), and unspecified assistantships available. Support available to part-time students. Financial award application deadline: 2/1; financial award applicants required to submit FAFSA. *Faculty research:* Gender, race, development, applied social policy, political economy. *Unit head:* Dr. John Philip Drysdale, Chair, 202-885-2488, Fax: 202-885-2477, E-mail: drysdale@american.edu.

California State University, Dominguez Hills, College of Natural and Behavioral Science, Program in Sociology, Carson, CA 90747-0001. Offers social research (Certificate); sociology (MA). Part-time and evening/weekend programs available. *Faculty:* 10 full-time, 7 part-time/adjunct. *Students:* 21 full-time (15 women), 36 part-time (29 women); includes 47 minority (36 African Americans, 11 Hispanic Americans). Average age 38. 25 applicants, 88% accepted, 17 enrolled. In 2007, 13 degrees awarded. *Degree requirements:* For master's, comprehensive exam, thesis. *Entrance requirements:* For master's and Certificate, minimum GPA of 2.85. *Application deadline:* For fall admission, 6/1 for domestic students. Application fee: $55. *Faculty research:* Community studies, social movements, criminology. *Unit head:* Dr. Sharon Linda Squires, Coordinator, 310-243-2598, E-mail: ssquires@csudh.edu.

Hunter College of the City University of New York, Graduate School, School of Arts and Sciences, Department of Sociology, Program in Applied Social Research, New York, NY 10021-

Applied Social Research

Hunter College of the City University of New York (continued)
5085. Offers MS. Part-time and evening/weekend programs available. *Faculty:* 5 full-time (2 women), 2 part-time/adjunct (1 woman). *Students:* 10 full-time (6 women), 28 part-time (19 women); includes 9 minority (3 African Americans, 3 Asian Americans or Pacific Islanders, 3 Hispanic Americans). Average age 30. 22 applicants, 73% accepted, 11 enrolled. In 2007, 7 degrees awarded. *Degree requirements:* For master's, internship, research reports. *Entrance requirements:* For master's, GRE General Test or GMAT, 3 credits of course work in statistics, research methods; background in sociology or related social science. Additional exam requirements/recommendations for international students: Required—TOEFL. *Application deadline:* For fall admission, 4/1 for domestic students, 2/1 for international students; for spring admission, 11/1 for domestic students, 9/1 for international students. Applications are processed on a rolling basis. Application fee: $125. *Expenses:* Tuition, state resident: full-time $6,400; part-time $270 per credit. Tuition, nonresident: part-time $500 per credit. One-time fee: $125 full-time. Tuition and fees vary according to program. *Financial support:* Fellowships, research assistantships, teaching assistantships, career-related internships or fieldwork, Federal Work-Study, institutionally sponsored loans, scholarships/grants, and tuition waivers (full and partial) available. Support available to part-time students. *Faculty research:* Consumer behavior, new electronic media, voting behavior, policy analysis, sociomedicine. *Unit head:* Dr. Joong-Hwan Oh, Director, 212-772-5643, E-mail: goh@hunter.cuny.edu. *Application contact:* 212-772-5580, Fax: 212-772-5581, E-mail: grad.socialresearchadvisor@hunter.cuny.edu.

The New School: A University, The New School for Social Research, New York, NY 10011. Offers MA, MS, DS Sc, PhD. Part-time and evening/weekend programs available. *Faculty:* 84 full-time (33 women), 18 part-time/adjunct (4 women). *Students:* 808 full-time (418 women), 308 part-time (177 women); includes 168 minority (56 African Americans, 4 American Indian/Alaska Native, 41 Asian Americans or Pacific Islanders, 67 Hispanic Americans), 306 international. Average age 32. In 2007, 179 master's, 52 doctorates awarded. Terminal master's awarded for partial completion of doctoral program. *Degree requirements:* For doctorate, thesis/dissertation, qualifying exam. *Entrance requirements:* For master's, GRE General Test; for doctorate, GRE General Test, MA. Additional exam requirements/recommendations for international students: Required—TOEFL (minimum score 600 paper-based; 250 computer-based). *Application deadline:* For fall admission, 1/15 priority date for domestic students. Applications are processed on a rolling basis. Application fee: $50. *Expenses:* Contact institution. *Financial support:* Fellowships, research assistantships, teaching assistantships, career-related internships or fieldwork, Federal Work-Study, scholarships/grants, and tuition waivers (full and partial) available. Financial award application deadline: 3/1; financial award applicants required to submit FAFSA. *Faculty research:* Civil society and democracy, international movements of refugees, minority use of health services, memory, morality and genetics. *Unit head:* Dr. Michael Schober, Dean, 212-229-5777, E-mail: schober@newschool.edu. *Application contact:* Robert MacDonald, Director of Admissions, 800-523-5710 Ext. 3007, Fax: 212-989-7102, E-mail: macdonar@newschool.edu.

See Close-Up on page 1653.

Portland State University, Graduate Studies, Graduate School of Social Work, Portland, OR 97207-0751. Offers social work (MSW); social work and social research (PhD). *Accreditation:* CSWE (one or more programs are accredited). Part-time programs available. *Faculty:* 35 full-time (25 women), 12 part-time/adjunct (8 women). *Students:* 337 full-time (284 women), 168 part-time (149 women); includes 75 minority (15 African Americans, 11 American Indian/Alaska Native, 12 Asian Americans or Pacific Islanders, 37 Hispanic Americans), 7 international. Average age 35. 386 applicants, 75% accepted, 214 enrolled. In 2007, 193 master's, 6 doctorates awarded. *Degree requirements:* For doctorate, comprehensive exam, thesis/dissertation, residence. *Entrance requirements:* For master's, minimum GPA of 3.0 in upper-division course work or 2.75 overall; for doctorate, GRE General Test, 4 references. Additional exam requirements/recommendations for international students: Required—TOEFL (minimum score 550 paper-based; 213 computer-based). *Application deadline:* For fall admission, 2/1 for domestic and international students. Application fee: $50. *Expenses:* Tuition, state resident: full-time $7,047. Tuition, nonresident: full-time $11,178. *Financial support:* In 2007–08, 8 research assistantships with full tuition reimbursements (averaging $11,494 per year), 2 teaching assistantships with full tuition reimbursements (averaging $10,535 per year) were awarded; career-related internships or fieldwork, Federal Work-Study, scholarships/grants, tuition waivers (partial), and unspecified assistantships also available. Support available to part-time students. Financial award application deadline: 3/1; financial award applicants required to submit FAFSA. *Faculty research:* Child welfare; child mental health; social welfare policies and services; work, family, and dependent care; adult mental health. Total annual research expenditures: $8.1 million. *Unit head:* Dr. Kristine E. Nelson, Dean, 503-725-4712, Fax: 503-725-5545, E-mail: nelsonk@pdx.edu. *Application contact:* Janet Putnam, Director of Student Affairs, 503-725-4712, Fax: 503-725-5545, E-mail: putnamj@pdx.edu.

University of California, Los Angeles, Graduate Division, School of Public Affairs, Los Angeles, CA 90095. Offers MA, MPP, MSW, PhD, JD/MA, JD/MSW, MA/MA, MBA/MA, MD/PhD. *Accreditation:* CSWE. *Students:* 455 (340 women); includes 192 minority (27 African Americans, 1 American Indian/Alaska Native, 69 Asian Americans or Pacific Islanders, 95 Hispanic Americans) 37 international. 1,024 applicants, 42% accepted, 192 enrolled. In 2007, 162 master's, 8 doctorates awarded. *Degree requirements:* For doctorate, thesis/dissertation, oral and written qualifying exams. *Entrance requirements:* For master's, minimum GPA of 3.0; for doctorate, minimum undergraduate GPA of 3.0. Additional exam requirements/recommendations for international students: Required—TOEFL. Application fee: $60. Electronic applications accepted. *Expenses:* Tuition, nonresident: full-time $5,728. Required fees: $8,966. Full-time tuition and fees vary according to program and student level. *Financial support:* In 2007–08, 365 students received support, including 185 fellowships, 82 research assistantships, 42 teaching assistantships; career-related internships or fieldwork, Federal Work-Study, institutionally sponsored loans, scholarships/grants, and tuition waivers (full and partial) also available. Financial award application deadline: 3/1. *Unit head:* Franklin D. Gilliam, Dean, 310-825-3792. *Application contact:* Departmental Office, 310-206-3148.

Virginia Commonwealth University, Graduate School, College of Humanities and Sciences, Wilder School of Government and Public Affairs, Department of Sociology, Richmond, VA 23284-9005. Offers applied social research (CASR); gender violence intervention (Certificate); sociology (MS); MSW/Certificate. *Faculty:* 9 full-time (6 women). *Students:* 18 full-time (14 women), 10 part-time (5 women); includes 5 minority (1 African American, 1 American Indian/Alaska Native, 1 Asian American or Pacific Islander, 2 Hispanic Americans). 23 applicants, 83% accepted, 6 enrolled. In 2007, 5 degrees awarded. *Degree requirements:* For master's, thesis optional. *Entrance requirements:* For master's, GRE General Test. *Application deadline:* For fall admission, 7/1 for domestic students; for spring admission, 11/15 for domestic students. Application fee: $50. *Expenses:* Tuition, state resident: full-time $7,224; part-time $401 per credit. Tuition, nonresident: full-time $16,072; part-time $891 per credit. Required fees: $1,679; $63 per credit. Tuition and fees vary according to campus/location. *Financial support:* Teaching assistantships, career-related internships or fieldwork, Federal Work-Study, institutionally sponsored loans, and tuition waivers (full and partial) available. Support available to part-time students. *Unit head:* Dr. Jimmie S. Williams, Chair, 804-828-1028, Fax: 804-828-1027, E-mail: jswillia@vcu.edu. *Application contact:* Dr. Sarah Jane Brubaker, Director, Graduate Programs in Sociology, 804-827-2400, Fax: 804-828-1027, E-mail: sbrubaker@vcu.edu.

West Virginia University, Eberly College of Arts and Sciences, School of Applied Social Sciences, Department of Sociology, Morgantown, WV 26506. Offers applied social research (MA). Part-time programs available. *Faculty:* 13 full-time (8 women), 9 part-time/adjunct (6 women). *Students:* 13 full-time (10 women), 2 part-time (1 woman); includes 2 minority (1 African American, 1 Hispanic American), 2 international. Average age 29. 16 applicants, 56% accepted, 6 enrolled. In 2007, 3 degrees awarded. *Degree requirements:* For master's, thesis or alternative. *Entrance requirements:* For master's, GRE General Test, minimum GPA of 2.75. Additional exam requirements/recommendations for international students: Required—TOEFL. *Application deadline:* For fall admission, 3/1 for domestic and international students. Application fee: $50. *Expenses:* Tuition, state resident: full-time $5,196; part-time $292 per credit hour. Tuition, nonresident: full-time $15,064; part-time $840 per credit hour. Tuition and fees vary according to program. *Financial support:* In 2007–08, 14 students received support, including 2 research assistantships with full tuition reimbursements available (averaging $9,000 per year), 10 teaching assistantships with full tuition reimbursements available (averaging $9,000 per year); Federal Work-Study, institutionally sponsored loans, and tuition waivers (full and partial) also available. Financial award application deadline: 2/1; financial award applicants required to submit FAFSA. *Faculty research:* Applied sociology, stratification, social/complex organization, research methodology criminology. Total annual research expenditures: $59,767. *Unit head:* Dr. Melissa Latimer, Chair, 304-293-5801 Ext. 3209, Fax: 304-293-5994, E-mail: melissa.latimer@mail.wvu.edu.

Archaeology

American University of Beirut, Graduate Programs, Faculty of Arts and Sciences, Beirut, Lebanon. Offers anthropology (MA); Arabic language and literature (MA); archaeology (MA); biology (MS); chemistry (MS); computer science (MS); economics (MA); education (MA); English language (MA); English literature (MA); environmental policy planning (MSES); financial economics (MAFE); geology (MS); history (MA); mathematics (MA, MS); Middle Eastern studies (MA); philosophy (MA); physics (MS); political studies (MA); psychology (MA); public administration (MA); sociology (MA); statistics (MA, MS). Part-time programs available. *Faculty:* 108 full-time (29 women), 5 part-time/adjunct (3 women). *Students:* 134 full-time (92 women), 228 part-time (167 women). Average age 25. 319 applicants, 67% accepted, 91 enrolled. In 2007, 144 degrees awarded. *Degree requirements:* For master's, one foreign language, comprehensive exam, thesis (for some programs). *Entrance requirements:* For master's, GRE, letter of recommendation. Additional exam requirements/recommendations for international students: Required—TOEFL (minimum score 600 paper-based; 250 computer-based; 100 iBT), IELTS (minimum score 8). *Application deadline:* For fall admission, 4/30 for domestic and international students; for spring admission, 11/1 for domestic and international students. Application fee: $50. *Expenses:* Tuition: Full-time $9,954; part-time $553 per credit. Tuition and fees vary according to course load and program. *Financial support:* In 2007–08, 28 students received support. Career-related internships or fieldwork, institutionally sponsored loans, scholarships/grants, health care benefits, and unspecified assistantships available. Financial award application deadline: 2/4; financial award applicants required to submit FAFSA. *Faculty research:* String theory and supergravity; computer graphics; algebra and number theory; popular Arabic literature; marine and freshwater biology; integrating science, math and technology. Total annual research expenditures: $132,270. *Unit head:* Khalil Bitar, Dean, 961-1374374 Ext. 3800, Fax: 961-1744461, E-mail: kmb@aub.edu.lb. *Application contact:* Dr. Salim Kanaan, Director, Admissions Office, 961-1350000 Ext. 2594, Fax: 961-1750775, E-mail: sk00@aub.edu.lb.

Boston University, Graduate School of Arts and Sciences, Department of Archaeology, Boston, MA 02215. Offers archaeological heritage management (MA); archaeology (MA, PhD); geoarchaeology (MA). *Students:* 50 full-time (31 women), 4 part-time (2 women); includes 3 minority (1 African American, 1 Asian American or Pacific Islander, 1 Hispanic American), 5 international. Average age 30. 89 applicants, 44% accepted, 9 enrolled. In 2007, 2 master's, 4 doctorates awarded. Terminal master's awarded for partial completion of doctoral program. *Degree requirements:* For master's, one foreign language, comprehensive exam, thesis or alternative; for doctorate, 2 foreign languages, comprehensive exam, thesis/dissertation. *Entrance requirements:* For master's, GRE General Test, 3 letters of recommendation; for doctorate, GRE General Test, scholarly writing sample, 3 letters of recommendation. Additional exam requirements/recommendations for international students: Required—TOEFL (minimum score 550 paper-based; 213 computer-based). *Application deadline:* For fall admission, 4/1 for domestic and international students. Application fee: $70. *Expenses:* Tuition: Full-time $34,930; part-time $1,092 per credit. Tuition and fees vary according to class time, course level and program. *Financial support:* In 2007–08, 26 students received support, including 2 fellowships with full tuition reimbursements available (averaging $18,000 per year), 1 research assistantship with full tuition reimbursement available (averaging $16,500 per year), 7 teaching assistantships with full tuition reimbursements available (averaging $16,500 per year); career-related internships or fieldwork, Federal Work-Study, and unspecified assistantships also available. Support available to part-time students. Financial award application deadline: 1/15; financial award applicants required to submit FAFSA. *Unit head:* Ricardo Elia, Chairman, 617-353-3415, Fax: 617-353-6800, E-mail: elia@bu.edu. *Application contact:* Evelyn Labree, Department Administrator, 617-358-1640, Fax: 617-353-6800, E-mail: labree@bu.edu.

Brown University, Graduate School, Department of Egyptology, Providence, RI 02912. Offers AM, PhD. *Degree requirements:* For master's, one foreign language, thesis, final exam; for doctorate, 2 foreign languages, comprehensive exam, thesis/dissertation. *Entrance requirements:* For master's and doctorate, GRE General Test.

Brown University, Graduate School, Joukowsky Institute for Archaeology and the Ancient World, Providence, RI 02912. Offers PhD. *Degree requirements:* For doctorate, thesis/dissertation.

Bryn Mawr College, Graduate School of Arts and Sciences, Department of Classical and Near Eastern Archaeology, Bryn Mawr, PA 19010-2899. Offers MA, PhD. Part-time programs available. *Faculty:* 5. *Students:* 21 full-time (15 women), 7 part-time (all women), 5 international. 46 applicants, 24% accepted, 7 enrolled. In 2007, 1 master's, 3 doctorates awarded. *Degree requirements:* For master's, 2 foreign languages, thesis; for doctorate, 3 foreign languages, comprehensive exam, thesis/dissertation. *Entrance requirements:* For master's and doctorate, GRE General Test. Additional exam requirements/recommendations for international students: Required—TOEFL (minimum score 600 paper-based; 250 computer-based). *Application deadline:* For fall admission, 1/3 for domestic and international students. Application fee: $30. *Financial support:* Fellowships, teaching assistantships with partial tuition reimbursements, Federal Work-Study and scholarships/grants available. Support available to part-time students. Financial award application deadline: 1/3. *Unit head:* Dr. James C. Wright, Chair, 610-526-5053, E-mail: jwright@brynmawr.edu. *Application contact:* Lea R. Miller, Secretary, 610-526-5072, Fax: 610-526-5076, E-mail: lrmiller@brynmawr.edu.

See Close-Up on page 1703.

California State University, Northridge, Graduate Studies, College of Social and Behavioral Sciences, Department of Anthropology, Northridge, CA 91330. Offers general anthropology (MA); public archaeology (MA). *Faculty:* 7 full-time (5 women), 9 part-time/adjunct (5 women).

Students: 16 full-time (9 women), 23 part-time (14 women); includes 8 minority (1 American Indian/Alaska Native, 1 Asian American or Pacific Islander, 6 Hispanic Americans), 2 international. Average age 36. 24 applicants, 63% accepted, 12 enrolled. In 2007, 3 degrees awarded. *Degree requirements:* For master's, thesis or alternative. *Entrance requirements:* For master's, GRE General Test or minimum GPA of 3.0. Additional exam requirements/recommendations for international students: Required—TOEFL. *Application deadline:* For fall admission, 11/30 for domestic students. Application fee: $55. *Financial support:* Career-related internships or fieldwork, Federal Work-Study, and institutionally sponsored loans available. Financial award application deadline: 3/1. *Unit head:* Sabina Magliocco, Chair, 818-677-3331. *Application contact:* Dr. Cathy L. Costin, Graduate Adviser, 818-677-3324.

Columbia University, Graduate School of Arts and Sciences, Division of Humanities, Department of Art History and Archaeology, New York, NY 10027. Offers archaeology (M Phil, MA, PhD); art history and archaeology (M Phil, MA, PhD); modern art (MA). *Faculty:* 24 full-time, 12 part-time/adjunct. *Students:* 217 full-time (160 women), 24 part-time (21 women); includes 21 minority (3 African Americans, 15 Asian Americans or Pacific Islanders, 3 Hispanic Americans), 24 international. Average age 35. 329 applicants, 33% accepted. In 2007, 22 master's, 20 doctorates awarded. *Degree requirements:* For master's, 2 foreign languages, thesis; for doctorate, 3 foreign languages, thesis/dissertation. *Entrance requirements:* For master's and doctorate, GRE General Test. Additional exam requirements/recommendations for international students: Required—TOEFL. Application fee: $90. *Expenses:* Tuition: Part-time $1,452 per credit. Required fees: $152 per term. One-time fee: $75 part-time. Full-time tuition and fees vary according to course level, course load, degree level and program. *Financial support:* Fellowships, teaching assistantships, Federal Work-Study and institutionally sponsored loans available. Support available to part-time students. Financial award application deadline: 1/5; financial award applicants required to submit FAFSA. *Unit head:* Bob Harrist, Chair, 212-854-4505, Fax: 212-854-7329, E-mail: reh23@columbia.edu.

Cornell University, Graduate School, Graduate Fields of Arts and Sciences, Field of Archaeology, Ithaca, NY 14853-0001. Offers environmental archaeology (MA); historical archaeology (MA); Latin American archaeology (MA); medieval archaeology (MA); Mediterranean and Near Eastern archaeology (MA); Stone Age archaeology (MA). *Faculty:* 14 full-time (3 women). *Students:* 2 full-time (both women). Average age 26. 19 applicants, 5% accepted, 1 enrolled. In 2007, 2 degrees awarded. *Degree requirements:* For master's, one foreign language, thesis. *Entrance requirements:* For master's, GRE General Test, 3 letters of recommendation, sample of written work. Additional exam requirements/recommendations for international students: Required—TOEFL (minimum score 550 paper-based; 213 computer-based; 77 iBT). *Application deadline:* For fall admission, 1/15 for domestic students. Application fee: $70. Electronic applications accepted. *Financial support:* In 2007–08, 2 students received support, including 2 teaching assistantships with full tuition reimbursements available; fellowships with full tuition reimbursements available, research assistantships with full tuition reimbursements available, institutionally sponsored loans, scholarships/grants, health care benefits, tuition waivers (full and partial), and unspecified assistantships also available. Financial award applicants required to submit FAFSA. *Faculty research:* Anatolia, Lydia, Sardis, classical and Hellenistic Greece; science in archaeology; North American Indians; Stone Age Africa; Maya trade. *Unit head:* Director of Graduate Studies, 607-255-6768, E-mail: blj7@cornell.edu. *Application contact:* Graduate Field Assistant, 607-255-6768, E-mail: dsd6@cornell.edu.

Cornell University, Graduate School, Graduate Fields of Arts and Sciences, Field of History of Art and Archaeology, Ithaca, NY 14853. Offers American art (PhD); ancient art and archaeology (PhD); Asian art (PhD); baroque art (PhD); medieval art (PhD); modern art (PhD); Renaissance art (PhD); Southeast Asian art (PhD); theory and criticism (PhD). *Faculty:* 21 full-time (14 women). *Students:* 22 full-time (17 women); includes 6 minority (2 African Americans, 2 Asian Americans or Pacific Islanders, 2 Hispanic Americans), 6 international. Average age 32. 61 applicants, 15% accepted, 4 enrolled. In 2007, 2 doctorates awarded. *Degree requirements:* For doctorate, one foreign language, comprehensive exam, thesis/dissertation, general exams in 3 areas. *Entrance requirements:* For doctorate, GRE General Test, sample of written work, 3 letters of recommendation. Additional exam requirements/recommendations for international students: Required—TOEFL (minimum score 550 paper-based; 213 computer-based; 77 iBT). *Application deadline:* For fall admission, 1/15 for domestic students. Application fee: $70. Electronic applications accepted. *Financial support:* In 2007–08, 17 students received support, including 10 fellowships with full tuition reimbursements available, 7 teaching assistantships with full tuition reimbursements available; research assistantships with full tuition reimbursements available, institutionally sponsored loans, scholarships/grants, health care benefits, tuition waivers (full and partial), and unspecified assistantships also available. Financial award applicants required to submit FAFSA. *Unit head:* Director of Graduate Studies, 607-255-4905, Fax: 607-255-0566, E-mail: art_history@cornell.edu. *Application contact:* Director of Graduate Studies, 607-255-4905, Fax: 607-255-0566, E-mail: art_history@cornell.edu.

Florida State University, Graduate Studies, College of Arts and Sciences, Department of Classics, Tallahassee, FL 32306. Offers classical archaeology (MA); classical civilization (MA); classics (MA, PhD), including archaeology (PhD), literature and languages (PhD); Greek (MA); Greek and Latin (MA); Latin (MA). Part-time programs available. *Faculty:* 13 full-time (3 women), 3 part-time/adjunct (1 woman). *Students:* 45 full-time (21 women), 3 part-time (all women). Average age 25. 48 applicants, 75% accepted, 13 enrolled. In 2007, 15 master's, 1 doctorate awarded. *Median time to degree:* Of those who began their doctoral program in fall 1999, 50% received their degree in 8 years or less. *Degree requirements:* For master's, one foreign language, comprehensive exam (for some programs), thesis (for some programs); for doctorate, 2 foreign languages, comprehensive exam, thesis/dissertation. *Entrance requirements:* For master's, GRE General Test, minimum GPA of 3.0; for doctorate, GRE General Test. Additional exam requirements/recommendations for international students: Required—TOEFL. *Application deadline:* For fall admission, 1/15 priority date for domestic students, 2/15 for international students. Applications are processed on a rolling basis. Application fee: $30. Electronic applications accepted. *Expenses:* Tuition, state resident: part-time $248 per credit hour. Tuition, nonresident: part-time $880 per credit hour. Tuition and fees vary according to program. *Financial support:* In 2007–08, 37 students received support, including fellowships with full tuition reimbursements available (averaging $18,000 per year), 2 research assistantships with full tuition reimbursements available (averaging $10,000 per year), 28 teaching assistantships with full tuition reimbursements available (averaging $9,275 per year); Federal Work-Study and institutionally sponsored loans also available. Support available to part-time students. Financial award application deadline: 1/15; financial award applicants required to submit FAFSA. *Faculty research:* Greek and Latin literature, mythology, classical archaeology, history, Roman religion. Total annual research expenditures: $100,000. *Unit head:* Dr. Daniel J. Pullen, Chairman, 850-644-0304, Fax: 850-644-4073, E-mail: dpullen@fsu.edu. *Application contact:* Dr. Nancy de Grummond, Admissions Director, 850-644-0305, Fax: 850-644-0303, E-mail: ndegrummond@fsu.edu.

Graduate School and University Center of the City University of New York, Graduate Studies, Program in Anthropology, New York, NY 10016-4039. Offers anthropological linguistics (PhD); archaeology (PhD); cultural anthropology (PhD); physical anthropology (PhD). *Faculty:* 39 full-time (14 women). *Students:* 158 full-time (96 women), 3 part-time (all women); includes 34 minority (11 African Americans, 8 Asian Americans or Pacific Islanders, 15 Hispanic Americans), 27 international. Average age 34. 165 applicants, 25% accepted, 21 enrolled. In 2007, 10 degrees awarded. *Degree requirements:* For doctorate, one foreign language, thesis/dissertation. *Entrance requirements:* For doctorate, GRE General Test. Additional exam requirements/recommendations for international students: Required—TOEFL. *Application deadline:* For fall admission, 1/8 priority date for domestic students. Application fee: $125. Electronic applications accepted. *Financial support:* In 2007–08, 111 students received support, including 85 fellowships, 16 research assistantships, 10 teaching assistantships; career-related internships or fieldwork, Federal Work-Study, institutionally sponsored loans, and tuition waivers (full and partial) also available. Financial award application deadline: 2/1; financial award applicants required to submit FAFSA. *Unit head:* Dr. Louise Lennihan, Executive Officer, 212-817-8006, Fax: 212-817-1501, E-mail: anthro@gc.cuny.edu. *Application contact:* Information Contact, 212-817-8005, Fax: 212-817-1501, E-mail: anthro@gc.cuny.edu.

Harvard University, Graduate School of Arts and Sciences, Department of Anthropology, Cambridge, MA 02138. Offers archaeology (PhD); biological anthropology (PhD); legal anthropology (AM); medical anthropology (AM); social anthropology (AM, PhD); social change and development (AM). Terminal master's awarded for partial completion of doctoral program. *Degree requirements:* For master's, 2 foreign languages, thesis (for some programs); for doctorate, 2 foreign languages, thesis/dissertation, laboratory and/or fieldwork; general, qualifying, or special exams. *Entrance requirements:* For master's and doctorate, GRE General Test. Additional exam requirements/recommendations for international students: Required—TOEFL. *Expenses:* Tuition: Full-time $31,456. Full-time tuition and fees vary according to program and student level.

Harvard University, Graduate School of Arts and Sciences, Department of Near Eastern Languages and Civilizations, Cambridge, MA 02138. Offers Akkadian and Sumerian (AM, PhD); Arabic (AM, PhD); Armenian (AM, PhD); biblical history (AM, PhD); Hebrew (AM, PhD); Indo-Muslim culture (AM, PhD); Iranian (AM, PhD); Jewish history and literature (AM, PhD); Persian (AM, PhD); Semitic philology (AM, PhD); Syro-Palestinian archaeology (AM, PhD); Turkish (AM, PhD). *Degree requirements:* For doctorate, variable foreign language requirement, thesis/dissertation, general exams. *Entrance requirements:* For master's, GRE General Test; for doctorate, GRE General Test, proficiency in a Near Eastern language. Additional exam requirements/recommendations for international students: Required—TOEFL. *Expenses:* Tuition: Full-time $31,456. Full-time tuition and fees vary according to program and student level.

Harvard University, Graduate School of Arts and Sciences, Department of the Classics, Cambridge, MA 02138. Offers Byzantine Greek (PhD); classical archaeology (PhD); classical philology (PhD); classical philosophy (PhD); medieval Latin (PhD). *Degree requirements:* For doctorate, 4 foreign languages, thesis/dissertation, preliminary and special exams. *Entrance requirements:* For doctorate, GRE General Test. Additional exam requirements/recommendations for international students: Required—TOEFL. *Expenses:* Tuition: Full-time $31,456. Full-time tuition and fees vary according to program and student level.

Illinois State University, Graduate School, College of Arts and Sciences, Department of Sociology, Program in Historical Archaeology, Normal, IL 61790-2200. Offers MA, MS. *Students:* 10 full-time (5 women), 3 part-time (1 woman). 12 applicants, 42% accepted. In 2007, 2 master's awarded. Application fee: $40. *Expenses:* Tuition, state resident: full-time $3,492; part-time $194 per credit hour. Tuition, nonresident: full-time $7,272; part-time $404 per credit hour. Required fees: $1,024; $57 per credit hour. *Application contact:* Wilbert M. Leonard, Graduate Adviser, 309-438-8073.

Massachusetts Institute of Technology, School of Engineering, Department of Materials Science and Engineering, Cambridge, MA 02139-4307. Offers archaeological materials (PhD, Sc D); bio- and polymeric materials (PhD, Sc D); electronic, photonic and magnetic materials (PhD, Sc D); emerging, fundamental and computational studies in materials science (Sc D); emerging, fundamental, and computational studies in materials science (PhD); materials engineering (Mat E); materials science and engineering (M Eng, SM, PhD, Sc D); metallurgical engineering (Met E); structural and environmental materials (PhD, Sc D); SM/MBA. *Faculty:* 32 full-time (8 women). *Students:* 219 full-time (72 women); includes 27 minority (3 African Americans, 21 Asian Americans or Pacific Islanders, 3 Hispanic Americans), 129 international. Average age 26. 413 applicants, 26% accepted, 60 enrolled. In 2007, 40 master's, 38 doctorates awarded. Terminal master's awarded for partial completion of doctoral program. *Degree requirements:* For master's and other advanced degree, thesis; for doctorate, comprehensive exam, thesis/dissertation. *Entrance requirements:* For master's and doctorate, GRE General Test. Additional exam requirements/recommendations for international students: Required—TOEFL (minimum score 577 paper-based; 233 computer-based). *Application deadline:* For fall admission, 1/4 for domestic and international students; for winter admission, 4/4 for domestic students. Application fee: $70. Electronic applications accepted. *Expenses:* Tuition: Full-time $34,760; part-time $545 per unit. Required fees: $236. *Financial support:* In 2007–08, 203 students received support, including 55 fellowships with tuition reimbursements available (averaging $20,346 per year), 125 research assistantships with tuition reimbursements available (averaging $22,584 per year), 24 teaching assistantships with tuition reimbursements available (averaging $24,822 per year); career-related internships or fieldwork, Federal Work-Study, institutionally sponsored loans, scholarships/grants, health care benefits, and unspecified assistantships also available. *Faculty research:* Electronic, Photonic, and Magnetic Materials; Biological and Polymeric Materials; Structural and Environmental Materials; Computational Studies in Materials, Emerging and Fundamental Materials; Archaeological Materials. Total annual research expenditures: $19.8 million. *Unit head:* Prof. Edwin Thomas, Head, 617-253-3300, Fax: 617-252-1773. *Application contact:* Angelita Mireles, Graduate Admissions, 617-253-3302, E-mail: dmse-admissions@mit.edu.

Memorial University of Newfoundland, School of Graduate Studies, Department of Anthropology, St. John's, NL A1C 5S7, Canada. Offers archaeology and physical anthropology (MA, PhD); social and cultural anthropology (MA, PhD). Part-time programs available. *Degree requirements:* For master's, thesis (for some programs); for doctorate, comprehensive exam, thesis/dissertation, oral defense of thesis. *Entrance requirements:* For master's, 2nd class degree in related field. Electronic applications accepted. *Faculty research:* Early European settlements, ethnoarchaeology, economic/political anthropology, land claims and aboriginal rights, marine anthropology.

Michigan Technological University, Graduate School, College of Sciences and Arts, Department of Social Sciences, Program in Industrial Archaeology, Houghton, MI 49931-1295. Offers MS. Part-time programs available. *Faculty:* 15 full-time (5 women), 1 part-time/adjunct (0 women). *Students:* 8 full-time (3 women), 3 part-time (1 woman). Average age 28. 18 applicants, 56% accepted, 5 enrolled. In 2007, 5 degrees awarded. *Degree requirements:* For master's, comprehensive exam, thesis. *Entrance requirements:* For master's, GRE. Additional exam requirements/recommendations for international students: Required—TOEFL (minimum score 550 paper-based; 213 computer-based). *Application deadline:* For fall admission, 3/1 for domestic students. Applications are processed on a rolling basis. Application fee: $40 ($45 for international students). Electronic applications accepted. *Financial support:* In 2007–08, 10 students received support, including fellowships with full tuition reimbursements available (averaging $9,542 per year), 2 research assistantships with full tuition reimbursements available (averaging $9,542 per year), 8 teaching assistantships with full tuition reimbursements available (averaging $9,542 per year); career-related internships or fieldwork, Federal Work-Study, scholarships/grants, health care benefits, tuition waivers (partial), unspecified assistantships, and co-op also available. Financial award applicants required to submit FAFSA. *Application contact:* Dr. Patrick E. Martin, Director, 906-487-2070, Fax: 906-487-2468, E-mail: pemartin@mtu.edu.

Michigan Technological University, Graduate School, College of Sciences and Arts, Department of Social Sciences, Program in Industrial Heritage and Archeology, Houghton, MI 49931-1295. Offers PhD. Part-time programs available. *Faculty:* 15 full-time (5 women), 1 part-time/adjunct (0 women). *Students:* 2 full-time. Average age 35. 6 applicants, 50% accepted, 2 enrolled. *Degree requirements:* For doctorate, comprehensive exam, thesis/dissertation. *Entrance requirements:* Additional exam requirements/recommendations for international students: Required—TOEFL (minimum score 550 paper-based; 213 computer-based). *Application deadline:* For fall admission, 3/1 for domestic students, 3/15 priority date for international students. Applications are processed on a rolling basis. Electronic applications accepted. *Financial support:* In 2007–08, 2 students received support, including fellowships with full tuition reimbursements available (averaging $9,542 per year), 2 research assistantships with full tuition reimbursements available (averaging $9,542 per year), teaching assistantships with full tuition reimbursements available (averaging $9,542 per year); career-related internships or fieldwork, Federal Work-Study, scholarships/grants, health care benefits,

Archaeology

Michigan Technological University (continued)

tuition waivers (partial), and unspecified assistantships also available. Financial award applicants required to submit FAFSA. *Application contact:* Dr. Patrick E. Martin, Director, 906-487-2070, Fax: 906-487-2468, E-mail: pemartin@mtu.edu.

New York University, Graduate School of Arts and Science, Institute of Fine Arts, Program in Art History and Archaeology, New York, NY 10012-1019. Offers architectural studies (PhD); art history and archaeology (MA, PhD); classical art and archaeology (PhD); curatorial studies (PhD); East and South Asian art (PhD); Near Eastern art and archaeology (PhD); MA/Diploma; PhD/Certificate. Part-time programs available. *Students:* 199 full-time (156 women), 88 part-time (70 women); includes 28 minority (19 Asian Americans or Pacific Islanders, 9 Hispanic Americans), 34 international. Average age 32. 295 applicants, 33% accepted, 41 enrolled. In 2007, 26 master's, 26 doctorates awarded. Terminal master's awarded for partial completion of doctoral program. *Degree requirements:* For master's, 2 foreign languages, thesis or alternative, 2 qualifying papers; for doctorate, 2 foreign languages, thesis/dissertation. *Entrance requirements:* For master's, GRE General Test; for doctorate, GRE General Test, MA. Additional exam requirements/recommendations for international students: Required—TOEFL. *Application deadline:* For fall admission, 12/18 for domestic students. Application fee: $85. *Financial support:* Fellowships with tuition reimbursements, research assistantships with tuition reimbursements, teaching assistantships with tuition reimbursements, career-related internships or fieldwork, Federal Work-Study, and institutionally sponsored loans available. Financial award application deadline: 12/18; financial award applicants required to submit FAFSA. *Application contact:* Priscilla Saucek, Director of Graduate Studies, 212-992-5800, Fax: 212-992-5807, E-mail: ifa.program@nyu.edu.

Northern Arizona University, Graduate College, College of Social and Behavioral Sciences, Department of Anthropology, Flagstaff, AZ 86011. Offers anthropology (MA); archaeology (MA). *Degree requirements:* For master's, thesis (for some programs), internship paper. *Entrance requirements:* For master's, 18 undergraduate hours in anthropology. *Faculty research:* Economic development, culture change, ethnohistory, archaeology of the Southwest, small town networks and HIV.

Northwestern State University of Louisiana, Graduate Studies and Research, Program in Heritage Resources, Natchitoches, LA 71497. Offers MA. *Faculty:* 4 full-time (3 women). *Students:* 16 full-time (11 women), 1 (woman) part-time. Average age 32. In 2007, 5 degrees awarded. *Degree requirements:* For master's, comprehensive exam, thesis or alternative. *Entrance requirements:* For master's, GRE General Test, minimum undergraduate GPA of 2.5. *Unit head:* Dr. Elizabeth Guin, Head, 318-357-4057, Fax: 318-357-6153, E-mail: guine@nsula.edu. *Application contact:* Dr. Steven G. Horton, Associate Provost/Dean, Graduate Studies, Research, and Information Systems, 318-357-5851, Fax: 318-357-5019, E-mail: grad_school@nsula.edu.

Princeton University, Graduate School, Department of Art and Archaeology, Princeton, NJ 08544-1019. Offers Chinese and Japanese art and archaeology (PhD); classical art and archaeology (PhD). *Degree requirements:* For doctorate, 2 foreign languages, thesis/dissertation. *Entrance requirements:* For doctorate, GRE General Test. Additional exam requirements/recommendations for international students: Required—TOEFL (minimum score 600 paper-based; 250 computer-based). Electronic applications accepted.

Princeton University, Graduate School, Department of Classics, Princeton, NJ 08544-1019. Offers ancient history (PhD); classical archaeology (PhD); classical philosophy (PhD); history, archaeology and religions of the ancient world (PhD). *Degree requirements:* For doctorate, thesis/dissertation. *Entrance requirements:* For doctorate, GRE General Test, sample of written work. Additional exam requirements/recommendations for international students: Required—TOEFL (minimum score 600 paper-based; 250 computer-based). Electronic applications accepted.

Princeton University, Graduate School, Department of East Asian Studies, Princeton, NJ 08544-1019. Offers Chinese and Japanese art and archaeology (PhD); East Asian civilizations (PhD); East Asian studies (PhD). *Degree requirements:* For doctorate, 2 foreign languages, thesis/dissertation. *Entrance requirements:* For doctorate, GRE General Test, fluency in Japanese and/or Chinese. Additional exam requirements/recommendations for international students: Required—TOEFL (minimum score 600 paper-based; 250 computer-based). Electronic applications accepted. *Faculty research:* Modern and classical Japanese literature, premodern Chinese and Japanese history, Chinese narrative and poetry.

St. Cloud State University, School of Graduate Studies, College of Social Sciences, Program in Cultural Resource Management Archeology, St. Cloud, MN 56301-4498. Offers MS. *Students:* 4 full-time (2 women); includes 1 minority (American Indian/Alaska Native). 4 applicants, 100% accepted, 3 enrolled. *Entrance requirements:* For master's, GRE General Test, minimum 2.75 GPA. Additional exam requirements/recommendations for international students: Required—MELAB; Recommended—TOEFL (minimum score 550 paper-based; 213 computer-based). *Application deadline:* For fall admission, 6/1 for domestic students, 4/1 for international students. Application fee: $35. *Expenses:* Tuition, state resident: part-time $267 per credit. Tuition, nonresident: part-time $418 per credit. Required fees: $28 per credit. *Unit head:* Dr. Mark Muniz, Coordinator, 320-308-4162, E-mail: mpmuniz@stcloudstate.edu. *Application contact:* Linda Lou Krueger, School of Graduate Studies, 320-308-2113, Fax: 320-308-5371, E-mail: lekrueger@stcloudstate.edu.

Simon Fraser University, Graduate Studies, Faculty of Arts and Social Sciences, Department of Archaeology, Burnaby, BC V5A 1S6, Canada. Offers MA, PhD. *Degree requirements:* For master's, one foreign language, thesis; for doctorate, one foreign language, thesis/dissertation. *Entrance requirements:* For master's, minimum GPA of 3.0; for doctorate, minimum GPA of 3.5. Additional exam requirements/recommendations for international students: Required—TOEFL or IELTS. *Faculty research:* Ethnology, archaeometry, zooarchaeology, primate behavior, forensic anthropology.

Trinity International University, Trinity Evangelical Divinity School, Deerfield, IL 60015-1284. Offers Biblical and Near Eastern archaeology and languages (MA); Christian studies (MA, Certificate); Christian thought (MA); church history (MA, Th M); congregational ministry: pastor-teacher (M Div); congregational ministry: team ministry (M Div); counseling ministries (MA); counseling psychology (MA); cross-cultural ministry (M Div); educational studies (PhD); evangelism (MA); history of Christianity in America (MA); intercultural studies (MA, PhD); leadership and ministry management (D Min); military chaplaincy (D Min); ministry (MA); mission and evangelism (Th M); missions and evangelism (D Min); New Testament (MA, Th M); Old Testament (Th M); Old Testament and Semitic languages (MA); pastoral care (M Div); pastoral care and counseling (D Min); pastoral counseling and psychology (Th M); pastoral theology (Th M); philosophy of religion (MA); preaching (D Min); religion (MA); research ministry (M Div); systematic theology (Th M); theological studies (PhD); urban ministry (MA). *Accreditation:* ATS (one or more programs are accredited). Part-time programs available. Postbaccalaureate distance learning degree programs offered (minimal on-campus study). *Faculty:* 41 full-time (4 women), 77 part-time/adjunct (17 women). *Students:* 578 full-time (141 women), 711 part-time (202 women). In 2007, 92 first professional degrees, 78 master's, 47 doctorates, 23 other advanced degrees awarded. *Degree requirements:* For master's, comprehensive exam, thesis, fieldwork; for doctorate, comprehensive exam (for some programs), thesis/dissertation; for M Div, 2 foreign languages, fieldwork; for Certificate, comprehensive exam, integrative papers. *Entrance requirements:* For M Div, GRE, MAT; for master's, GRE, MAT, minimum cumulative undergraduate GPA of 3.0; for doctorate, GRE, minimum cumulative graduate GPA of 3.2; for Certificate, GRE, MAT, minimum undergraduate GPA of 2.5. Additional exam requirements/recommendations for international students: Required—TOEFL (minimum score 580 paper-based; 237 computer-based), TWE (minimum score 4). *Application deadline:* For fall admission, 7/15 priority date for domestic and international students. Applications are processed on a rolling basis. Application fee: $25. Electronic applications accepted. *Expenses:* Tuition: Full-time $13,200; part-time $630 per credit. Required fees: $170. *Financial support:* In 2007–08, 770 students received support, including 10 fellowships with partial tuition reimbursements available (averaging $6,920 per year); teaching assistantships with partial tuition reimbursements available, career-related internships or fieldwork, Federal Work-Study, scholarships/grants, and tuition waivers (partial) also available. Financial award application deadline: 4/1; financial award applicants required to submit FAFSA. *Unit head:* Dr. Tite Tiénou, Academic Dean, 847-317-8086, Fax: 847-317-8014, E-mail: ttienou@teds.edu. *Application contact:* Ron Campbell, Director of Admissions, 800-345-8337, Fax: 847-317-8097, E-mail: rcampbel@tiu.edu.

Tufts University, Graduate School of Arts and Sciences, Department of Classics, Medford, MA 02155. Offers classical archaeology (MA); classics (MA). Part-time programs available. *Faculty:* 8 full-time, 4 part-time/adjunct. *Students:* 16 (9 women); includes 1 minority (Asian American or Pacific Islander) 1 international. 26 applicants, 38% accepted, 5 enrolled. In 2007, 9 degrees awarded. *Degree requirements:* For master's, 2 foreign languages, comprehensive exam, thesis or alternative. *Entrance requirements:* For master's, GRE General Test, writing sample. Additional exam requirements/recommendations for international students: Required—TOEFL (minimum score 550 paper-based; 213 computer-based; 80 iBT). *Application deadline:* For fall admission, 2/15 for domestic students, 12/30 for international students; for spring admission, 10/15 for domestic students, 9/15 for international students. Applications are processed on a rolling basis. Application fee: $70. Electronic applications accepted. *Expenses:* Tuition: Full-time $35,052. *Financial support:* Teaching assistantships with full and partial tuition reimbursements, Federal Work-Study, scholarships/grants, and tuition waivers (partial) available. Support available to part-time students. Financial award application deadline: 2/15; financial award applicants required to submit FAFSA. *Unit head:* R. Bruce Hitchner, Chair, 617-627-3213. *Application contact:* David I. Proctor, Information Contact, 617-627-3213.

Universidad de las Américas–Puebla, Division of Graduate Studies, School of Social Sciences, Program in Anthropology, Puebla, Mexico. Offers anthropology (MA); archaeology (MA). Part-time and evening/weekend programs available. *Degree requirements:* For master's, one foreign language, thesis. *Entrance requirements:* For master's, bachelor's degree in anthropology or equivalent. *Faculty research:* Archaeology, ethnography, and ethnohistory of Mesoamerica.

Université Laval, Faculty of Letters, Department of History, Programs in Archaeology, Québec, QC G1K 7P4, Canada. Offers MA, PhD. Terminal master's awarded for partial completion of doctoral program. *Degree requirements:* For master's, thesis; for doctorate, comprehensive exam, thesis/dissertation. *Entrance requirements:* For master's and doctorate, English test, knowledge of French. Electronic applications accepted.

University of Alberta, Faculty of Graduate Studies and Research, Department of History and Classics, Edmonton, AB T6G 2E1, Canada. Offers ancient history (PhD); classical archaeology (MA, PhD); classical literature (PhD); classics (MA); history (MA, PhD). Part-time and evening/weekend programs available. *Degree requirements:* For master's, one foreign language, thesis (for some programs); for doctorate, one foreign language, thesis/dissertation. *Entrance requirements:* For master's, minimum B+ average; for doctorate, minimum A- average. Additional exam requirements/recommendations for international students: Required—TOEFL (minimum score 580 paper-based; 237 computer-based). Electronic applications accepted. *Faculty research:* Western Canada, classical archaeology, Britain, Eastern Europe, East Asia.

The University of British Columbia, Faculty of Arts and Faculty of Graduate Studies, Department of Classical, Near Eastern and Religious Studies, Programmes in Classics, Vancouver, BC V6T 1Z1, Canada. Offers ancient culture, religion, and ethnicity (MA); classical and near eastern archaeology (MA); classics (MA, PhD). Part-time programs available. *Faculty:* 7 full-time (4 women). *Students:* 16 full-time (7 women); includes 1 minority (Asian American or Pacific Islander) 19 applicants, 95% accepted, 7 enrolled. In 2007, 2 master's awarded. *Median time to degree:* Of those who began their doctoral program in fall 1999, 100% received their degree in 8 years or less. *Degree requirements:* For master's, 2 foreign languages, comprehensive exam, thesis, thesis or comprehensive exam; for doctorate, 2 foreign languages, comprehensive exam, thesis/dissertation. *Entrance requirements:* For master's, upper second class standing; for doctorate, MA degree. Additional exam requirements/recommendations for international students: Required—TOEFL (minimum score 600 paper-based; 250 computer-based), IELTS (minimum score 8). *Application deadline:* For fall admission, 1/31 for domestic and international students. Applications are processed on a rolling basis. Application fee: $90 Canadian dollars ($150 Canadian dollars for international students). Electronic applications accepted. *Financial support:* In 2007–08, 12 students received support, including 5 fellowships with tuition reimbursements available, 12 teaching assistantships with partial tuition reimbursements available (averaging $10,500 per year); scholarships/grants and health care benefits also available. Financial award application deadline: 1/1. *Faculty research:* Classical archaeology, ancient historians, late antiquity, ancient prose fiction, epigraphy. *Application contact:* Christine R. Dawson, Information Contact, 604-822-2515, Fax: 604-822-9431, E-mail: crdawson@interchange.ubc.ca.

University of Calgary, Faculty of Graduate Studies, Faculty of Social Sciences, Department of Archaeology, Calgary, AB T2N 1N4, Canada. Offers MA, PhD. *Degree requirements:* For master's, thesis; for doctorate, one foreign language, thesis/dissertation, candidacy exam. *Entrance requirements:* For master's, BA or B Sc in anthropology or archaeology; for doctorate, MA in anthropology or archaeology. Additional exam requirements/recommendations for international students: Required—TOEFL. Electronic applications accepted. *Faculty research:* Prehistory, ethnoarchaeology, Africa, Latin America, biological anthropology.

University of California, Berkeley, Graduate Division, College of Letters and Science, Department of Classics, Program in Classical Archaeology, Berkeley, CA 94720-1500. Offers MA, PhD. *Faculty:* 2 full-time. *Degree requirements:* For master's, one foreign language, thesis, exams; for doctorate, 2 foreign languages, thesis/dissertation, qualifying exam. *Entrance requirements:* For master's and doctorate, GRE General Test, minimum GPA of 3.0, 3 letters of recommendation. Additional exam requirements/recommendations for international students: Required—TOEFL (minimum score 570 paper-based; 230 computer-based), TWE. *Application deadline:* For fall admission, 12/15 for domestic students. Application fee: $70 ($90 for international students). *Financial support:* Fellowships, research assistantships, teaching assistantships, unspecified assistantships available. *Application contact:* Valerie Brown, Secretary, 510-642-4218, Fax: 510-643-2959, E-mail: casmaoff@berkeley.edu.

University of California, Berkeley, Graduate Division, Group in Ancient History and Mediterranean Archaeology, Berkeley, CA 94720-1500. Offers MA, PhD. *Degree requirements:* For master's, one foreign language, exam or thesis; for doctorate, 2 foreign languages, thesis/dissertation, qualifying exam. *Entrance requirements:* For master's and doctorate, GRE General Test, minimum GPA of 3.0, 3 letters of recommendation. Additional exam requirements/recommendations for international students: Required—TOEFL (minimum score 570 paper-based; 230 computer-based), TWE. *Application deadline:* For fall admission, 12/15 for domestic students. Application fee: $70 ($90 for international students). *Financial support:* Fellowships, research assistantships, teaching assistantships, career-related internships or fieldwork and unspecified assistantships available. *Unit head:* Erich Gruen, Chair, 510-642-1489, E-mail: gruene@berkeley.edu. *Application contact:* Janet A. Yonan, Student Affairs Officer, 510-643-8741, Fax: 510-643-2959, E-mail: casmaadm@berkeley.edu.

University of California, Los Angeles, Graduate Division, College of Letters and Science, Program in Archaeology, Los Angeles, CA 90095. Offers MA, PhD. *Faculty:* 25 full-time (18 women). *Students:* 23 full-time (17 women); includes 2 minority (both Asian Americans or Pacific Islanders), 5 international. Average age 29. 65 applicants, 18% accepted, 6 enrolled. In 2007, 2 master's, 1 doctorate awarded. *Median time to degree:* Of those who began their doctoral program in fall 1999, 33% received their degree in 8 years or less. *Degree requirements:* For master's, one foreign language, comprehensive exam, comprehensive core exam, paper, field experience; for doctorate, 2 foreign languages, thesis/dissertation, oral and written qualifying exams. *Entrance requirements:* For master's, GRE General Test, minimum GPA of

3.0, sample of research writing, degree objective of Ph.D; for doctorate, GRE General Test, minimum undergraduate GPA of 3.0, sample of research writing, ability to read 1 foreign language. *Application deadline:* For fall admission, 12/15 for domestic students. Application fee: $60. Electronic applications accepted. *Expenses:* Tuition, nonresident: full-time $5,728. Required fees: $8,966. Full-time tuition and fees vary according to program and student level. *Financial support:* In 2007–08, 9 fellowships with full and partial tuition reimbursements, 3 research assistantships with full and partial tuition reimbursements, 6 teaching assistantships with full and partial tuition reimbursements were awarded; Federal Work-Study, institutionally sponsored loans, and tuition waivers (full and partial) also available. Financial award application deadline: 3/1; financial award applicants required to submit FAFSA. *Unit head:* Dr. Charles Stanish, Chair, 310-825-4169. *Application contact:* Departmental Office, 310-825-4169, E-mail: eugenia@ucla.edu.

University of California, Santa Barbara, Graduate Division, College of Letters and Sciences, Division of Social Sciences, Department of Anthropology, Santa Barbara, CA 93106. Offers anthropology (MA, PhD), including global studies (PhD), human development (PhD), quantitative methods in social sciences (PhD), technology and society (PhD), women's studies (PhD); North American archaeology (MA); MA/PhD. *Faculty:* 13 full-time (2 women), 2 part-time/adjunct (both women). *Students:* 55 full-time (29 women); includes 10 minority (3 Asian Americans or Pacific Islanders, 7 Hispanic Americans), 10 international. Average age 32. 73 applicants, 25% accepted, 6 enrolled. In 2007, 9 master's, 8 doctorates awarded. Terminal master's awarded for partial completion of doctoral program. *Median time to degree:* Of those who began their doctoral program in fall 1999, 38% received their degree in 8 years or less. *Degree requirements:* For master's, comprehensive exam, thesis; for doctorate, comprehensive exam, thesis/dissertation. *Entrance requirements:* For master's and doctorate, GRE General Test, sample of written work, statement of purpose with completed coversheets (2 copies), post-secondary institutions attended. Additional exam requirements/recommendations for international students: Required—TOEFL (minimum score 550 paper-based; 213 computer-based; 80 iBT). *Application deadline:* For fall admission, 12/1 for domestic and international students. Application fee: $60. Electronic applications accepted. *Expenses:* Tuition, nonresident: full-time $14,888. Required fees: $10,108. *Financial support:* In 2007–08, 56 students received support, including 14 fellowships with full and partial tuition reimbursements available (averaging $9,623 per year), 13 research assistantships with full and partial tuition reimbursements available (averaging $10,000 per year), 32 teaching assistantships with partial tuition reimbursements available (averaging $19,988 per year); career-related internships or fieldwork, Federal Work-Study, institutionally sponsored loans, scholarships/grants, traineeships, health care benefits, and unspecified assistantships also available. Financial award application deadline: 12/1; financial award applicants required to submit FAFSA. *Faculty research:* Evolutionary psychology, archaeology, sociocultural anthropology, biosocial anthropology, evolutionary ecology, bioarchaeology. *Unit head:* Prof. Barbara Voorhies, Chair, 805-896-2519, Fax: 805-893-8707, E-mail: voorhies@anth.oesb.edu. *Application contact:* Larisa Traga, Graduate Program Assistant, 805-893-2516, Fax: 805-893-8707, E-mail: traga@anth.ucsb.edu.

University of California, Santa Cruz, Division of Graduate Studies, Division of Social Sciences, Program in Anthropology, Santa Cruz, CA 95064. Offers anthropological archaeology (PhD); cultural anthropology (PhD). *Faculty:* 15 full-time (11 women). *Students:* 43 full-time (28 women), 7 part-time (all women); includes 15 minority (2 African Americans, 4 Asian Americans or Pacific Islanders, 9 Hispanic Americans), 3 international. 105 applicants, 15% accepted, 10 enrolled. In 2007, 2 doctorates awarded. *Degree requirements:* For doctorate, thesis/dissertation, qualifying exam. *Entrance requirements:* For doctorate, GRE General Test. *Application deadline:* For fall admission, 12/15 for domestic students. Application fee: $60. *Expenses:* Tuition, nonresident: full-time $14,694. Required fees: $11,360. *Financial support:* Fellowships, research assistantships, teaching assistantships, career-related internships or fieldwork, Federal Work-Study, and institutionally sponsored loans available. Financial award application deadline: 1/15. *Faculty research:* Culture and power, women's roles, AIDS, folklore. *Unit head:* Dr. Olga Najera-Ramirez, Director, 831-459-4677, E-mail: olga@ucsc.edu. *Application contact:* Judy L. Glass, Reporting Analyst for Graduate Admissions, 831-459-5906, Fax: 831-459-4843, E-mail: jlglass@ucsc.edu.

University of Chicago, Division of the Humanities, Department of Classics, Chicago, IL 60637-1513. Offers ancient philosophy (AM, PhD); classical archaeology (AM, PhD); classical languages and literatures (AM, PhD). *Students:* 46. 110 applicants, 14% accepted, 5 enrolled. Terminal master's awarded for partial completion of doctoral program. *Degree requirements:* For master's, one foreign language, thesis; for doctorate, 2 foreign languages, thesis/dissertation. *Entrance requirements:* For master's and doctorate, GRE General Test. Additional exam requirements/recommendations for international students: Required—TOEFL. *Application deadline:* For fall admission, 12/15 for domestic students. Application fee: $55. *Financial support:* Fellowships, Federal Work-Study available. Financial award application deadline: 12/15; financial award applicants required to submit FAFSA. *Unit head:* Dr. Jonathan Hall, Chair, 773-702-8514.

University of Georgia, Graduate School, College of Arts and Sciences, Department of Anthropology, Athens, GA 30602. Offers anthropology (MA, PhD); archaeological resource management (MS). *Faculty:* 14 full-time (4 women). *Students:* 44 full-time (27 women), 10 part-time (5 women); includes 1 Hispanic American, 5 international. 78 applicants, 26% accepted, 11 enrolled. In 2007, 1 master's, 7 doctorates awarded. *Degree requirements:* For master's, one foreign language, thesis; for doctorate, one foreign language, thesis/dissertation. *Entrance requirements:* For master's and doctorate, GRE General Test. *Application deadline:* For fall admission, 7/1 priority date for domestic students; for spring admission, 11/15 for domestic students. Application fee: $50. Electronic applications accepted. *Financial support:* Fellowships, research assistantships, teaching assistantships, unspecified assistantships available. *Unit head:* Dr. Ervan G. Garrison, Head, 706-542-1479, Fax: 706-542-3998, E-mail: egarriso@uga.edu. *Application contact:* Dr. Elizabeth J. Reitz, Graduate Coordinator, 706-542-1464, Fax: 706-542-3998, E-mail: ereitz@uga.edu.

University of Lethbridge, School of Graduate Studies, Lethbridge, AB T1K 3M4, Canada. Offers accounting (MScM); addictions counseling (M Sc); agricultural biotechnology (M Sc); agricultural studies (M Sc, MA); anthropology (MA); archaeology (MA); art (MA); biochemistry (M Sc); biological sciences (M Sc); biomolecular science (PhD); biosystems and biodiversity (PhD); Canadian studies (MA); chemistry (M Sc); computer science (M Sc); computer science and geographical information science (M Sc); counseling psychology (M Ed); dramatic arts (MA); earth, space, and physical science (PhD); economics (MA); educational leadership (M Ed); English (MA); environmental science (M Sc); evolution and behavior (PhD); exercise science (M Sc); finance (MScM); French (MA); French/German (MA); French/Spanish (MA); general education (M Ed); general management (MScM); geography (M Sc, MA); German (MA); health sciences (M Sc, MA); history (MA); human resource management and labour relations (MScM); individualized multidisciplinary (M Sc, MA); information systems (MScM); international management (MScM); kinesiology (M Sc, MA); management (M Sc, MA); marketing (MScM); mathematics (M Sc); music (MA); Native American studies (MA); neuroscience (M Sc, PhD); new media (MA); nursing (M Sc); philosophy (MA); physics (M Sc); policy and strategy (MScM); political science (MA); psychology (M Sc, MA); religious studies (MA); sociology (MA); theoretical and computational science (PhD); urban and regional studies (MA). Part-time and evening/weekend programs available. *Students:* 215 full-time, 98 part-time. In 2007, 87 master's, 1 doctorate awarded. *Degree requirements:* For doctorate, comprehensive exam, thesis/dissertation. *Entrance requirements:* For master's, GMAT (M Sc in management), bachelor's degree in related field, minimum GPA of 3.0 during previous 20 graded semester courses, 2 years teaching or related experience (M Ed); for doctorate, master's degree, minimum graduate GPA of 3.5. Additional exam requirements/recommendations for international students: Required—TOEFL. Application fee: $60 Canadian dollars. *Financial support:* Fellowships, research assistantships, teaching assistantships, scholarships/grants, health care benefits, and unspecified assistantships available. *Faculty research:* Movement and brain plasticity, gibberellin physiology, photosynthesis, carbon cycling, molecular properties of main-group ring components. *Unit head:* Dr. Jo-Anne Fiske, Interim Dean, 403-329-2121, Fax: 403-329-2097. *Application contact:* Jennifer Geddes, Graduate Liaison Officer, 403-329-2762, Fax: 403-329-5159, E-mail: jennifer.geddes@uleth.ca.

University of Massachusetts Boston, Office of Graduate Studies, College of Liberal Arts, Program in History, Track in Historical Archaeology, Boston, MA 02125-3393. Offers MA. Part-time and evening/weekend programs available. *Degree requirements:* For master's, thesis, oral exams, practicum. *Entrance requirements:* For master's, GRE General Test, minimum GPA of 2.75. *Faculty research:* New World Colonialism, New England archeology, historical and urban archeology, archeological botany, ethnology.

University of Memphis, Graduate School, College of Communication and Fine Arts, Department of Art, Program in Art History, Memphis, TN 38152. Offers Egyptian art and archaeology (MA); general art history (MA). *Accreditation:* NASAD. *Students:* 20 full-time (17 women), 3 part-time (all women); includes 2 minority (both African Americans) Average age 27. 23 applicants, 57% accepted, 9 enrolled. In 2007, 5 degrees awarded. *Degree requirements:* For master's, comprehensive exam. *Entrance requirements:* For master's, GRE General Test or MAT, sample of written work. *Application deadline:* For fall admission, 8/1 for domestic students. Application fee: $35 ($60 for international students). *Expenses:* Tuition, state resident: full-time $6,990; part-time $377 per hour. Tuition, nonresident: full-time $17,818; part-time $830 per hour. Tuition and fees vary according to course load and program. *Financial support:* Research assistantships, teaching assistantships available. *Faculty research:* Egyptology, intersection of art and religion, arts of African Diaspora, native American art, early Netherlandish painting. *Application contact:* Prof. William McKeown, Coordinator of Graduate Studies, 901-678-2842, Fax: 901-678-2735, E-mail: mwcarlsl@memphis.edu.

University of Michigan, Horace H. Rackham School of Graduate Studies, College of Literature, Science, and the Arts, Interdepartmental Program in Classical Art and Archaeology, Ann Arbor, MI 48109. Offers PhD. *Faculty:* 10 full-time. *Students:* 26 full-time (17 women); includes 5 minority (3 Asian Americans or Pacific Islanders, 2 Hispanic Americans), 3 international. Average age 28. 53 applicants, 8% accepted, 4 enrolled. In 2007, 4 degrees awarded. *Degree requirements:* For doctorate, 4 foreign languages, thesis/dissertation, oral defense of dissertation, preliminary exam. *Entrance requirements:* For doctorate, GRE General Test. Additional exam requirements/recommendations for international students: Required—TOEFL (minimum score 560 paper-based; 220 computer-based). *Application deadline:* For fall admission, 1/1 for domestic and international students. Applications are processed on a rolling basis. Application fee: $55. Electronic applications accepted. *Financial support:* In 2007–08, 21 students received support, including 8 fellowships with full tuition reimbursements available (averaging $14,000 per year), 2 research assistantships with full tuition reimbursements available (averaging $74,000 per year), 9 teaching assistantships with full tuition reimbursements available (averaging $14,000 per year); career-related internships or fieldwork also available. Financial award application deadline: 3/15. *Unit head:* Elaine K Gazda, Director, 734-764-6323, Fax: 734-763-8976, E-mail: gazda@umich.edu. *Application contact:* Alex Zwinak, Student Administrative Assistant Senior, 734-764-6323, Fax: 734-763-8976, E-mail: ipcaa.office@umich.edu.

University of Minnesota, Twin Cities Campus, Graduate School, College of Liberal Arts, Department of Classical and Near Eastern Studies, Minneapolis, MN 55455-0213. Offers ancient and medieval art and archaeology (MA, PhD); classics (MA, PhD); Greek (MA, PhD); Latin (MA, PhD); religions in antiquity (MA). Part-time programs available. *Faculty:* 12 full-time (2 women), 3 part-time/adjunct (2 women). *Students:* 24 full-time (10 women), 8 part-time (2 women); includes 1 minority (African American), 1 international. Average age 29. 37 applicants, 32% accepted, 9 enrolled. In 2007, 4 master's, 1 doctorate awarded. Terminal master's awarded for partial completion of doctoral program. *Degree requirements:* For master's, 2 foreign languages, comprehensive exam, thesis or alternative; for doctorate, variable foreign language requirement, comprehensive exam, thesis/dissertation. *Entrance requirements:* For master's and doctorate, GRE, 3 letters of recommendation, department application, writing sample, copies of transcripts, personal statement. Additional exam requirements/recommendations for international students: Required—TOEFL. *Application deadline:* For fall admission, 1/4 for domestic students. Application fee: $55 ($75 for international students). Electronic applications accepted. *Financial support:* In 2007–08, 10 fellowships with full and partial tuition reimbursements (averaging $11,165 per year), 4 research assistantships (averaging $23,166 per year), 20 teaching assistantships (averaging $23,357 per year) were awarded; career-related internships or fieldwork, Federal Work-Study, institutionally sponsored loans, and tuition waivers (full and partial) also available. Support available to part-time students. Financial award application deadline: 1/4. *Faculty research:* Greek and Latin literature, archaeology, religions in antiquity, ancient Near East. Total annual research expenditures: $14,849. *Unit head:* George A. Sheets, Chair, 612-625-3326, Fax: 612-624-4894, E-mail: gasheets@umn.edu. *Application contact:* Victoria Keller, Administrative Assistant, Fax: 612-624-4894, E-mail: kell0801@umn.edu.

University of Missouri–Columbia, Graduate School, College of Arts and Sciences, Department of Art History and Archaeology, Columbia, MO 65211. Offers MA, PhD. Terminal master's awarded for partial completion of doctoral program. *Degree requirements:* For master's, 2 foreign languages, thesis; for doctorate, 2 foreign languages, thesis/dissertation. *Entrance requirements:* For master's and doctorate, GRE General Test, minimum GPA of 3.0. Additional exam requirements/recommendations for international students: Required—TOEFL (minimum score 500 paper-based; 173 computer-based; 61 iBT), IELTS (minimum score 6).

The University of North Carolina at Chapel Hill, Graduate School, College of Arts and Sciences, Department of Classics, Chapel Hill, NC 27599. Offers classical archaeology (MA, PhD); classics (MA, PhD). Terminal master's awarded for partial completion of doctoral program. *Degree requirements:* For master's, one foreign language, comprehensive exam, thesis; for doctorate, 2 foreign languages, comprehensive exam, thesis/dissertation. *Entrance requirements:* For master's and doctorate, GRE General Test, minimum GPA of 3.0. Electronic applications accepted.

University of Pennsylvania, School of Arts and Sciences, Graduate Group in Art and Archaeology of the Mediterranean World, Philadelphia, PA 19104. Offers AM, PhD. Part-time programs available. Terminal master's awarded for partial completion of doctoral program. *Degree requirements:* For master's, 3 foreign languages, thesis, Greek or Latin exam, German and French or Italian exam; for doctorate, 4 foreign languages, thesis/dissertation, Greek or Latin exam, 2nd ancient language exam, German and French or Italian exam. *Entrance requirements:* For master's and doctorate, GRE General Test, knowledge of Greek or Latin and either French, German, or Italian. Additional exam requirements/recommendations for international students: Required—TOEFL. Electronic applications accepted.

University of Saskatchewan, College of Graduate Studies and Research, College of Arts and Sciences, Department of Archaeology, Saskatoon, SK S7N 5A2, Canada. Offers MA, PhD. Part-time programs available. *Degree requirements:* For master's, thesis; for doctorate, thesis/dissertation. *Entrance requirements:* Additional exam requirements/recommendations for international students: Required—TOEFL.

University of South Africa, College of Human Sciences, Pretoria, South Africa. Offers adult education (M Ed); African languages (MA, PhD); African politics (MA, PhD); Afrikaans (MA, PhD); ancient history (MA, PhD); ancient Near Eastern studies (MA, PhD); anthropology (MA, PhD); applied linguistics (MA); Arabic (MA, PhD); archaeology (MA); art history (MA); Biblical archaeology (MA); Biblical studies (M Th, D Th, PhD); Christian spirituality (M Th, D Th); church history (M Th, D Th); classical studies (MA, PhD); clinical psychology (MA); communication (MA, PhD); comparative education (M Ed, Ed D); consulting psychology (D Admin, D Com, PhD); curriculum studies (M Ed, Ed D); development studies (M Admin, MA, D Admin, PhD); didactics (M Ed, Ed D); education (M Tech); education management (M Ed, Ed D); educational psychology (M Ed); English (MA); environmental education (M Ed); French (MA, PhD); German (MA, PhD); Greek (MA); guidance and counseling (M Ed); health studies (MA, PhD), including health sciences education (MA), health services management (MA), medical and surgical nursing science (critical care general) (MA), midwifery and neonatal nursing

Archaeology

University of South Africa (continued)
science (MA), trauma and emergency care (MA); history (MA, PhD); history of education (Ed D); inclusive education (M Ed, Ed D); information and communications technology policy and regulation (MA); information science (MA, MIS, PhD); international politics (MA, PhD); Islamic studies (MA, PhD); Italian (MA, PhD); Judaica (MA, PhD); linguistics (MA, PhD); mathematical education (M Ed); mathematics education (MA); missiology (M Th, D Th); modern Hebrew (MA, PhD); musicology (MA, MMus, D Mus, PhD); natural science education (M Ed); New Testament (M Th, D Th); Old Testament (D Th); pastoral therapy (M Th, D Th); philosophy (MA); philosophy of education (M Ed, Ed D); politics (MA, PhD); Portuguese (MA, PhD); practical theology (M Th, D Th); psychology (MA, MS, PhD); psychology of education (M Ed, Ed D); public health (MA); religious studies (MA, D Th, PhD); Romance languages (MA); Russian (MA, PhD); Semitic languages (MA, PhD); social behavior studies in HIV/AIDS (MA); social science (mental health) (MA); social science in development studies (MA); social science in psychology (MA); social science in social work (MA); social science in sociology (MA); social work (MSW, DSW, PhD); socio-education (M Ed, Ed D); sociolinguistics (MA); sociology (MA, PhD); Spanish (MA, PhD); systematic theology (M Th, D Th); TESOL (teaching English to speakers of other languages) (MA); theological ethics (M Th, D Th); theory of literature (MA, PhD); urban ministries (D Th); urban ministry (M Th).

The University of Tennessee, Graduate School, College of Arts and Sciences, Department of Anthropology, Knoxville, TN 37996. Offers archaeology (MA, PhD); biological anthropology (MA, PhD); cultural anthropology (MA, PhD); zoo-archaeology (MA, PhD). *Degree requirements:* For master's, thesis; for doctorate, one foreign language, thesis/dissertation. *Entrance requirements:* For master's and doctorate, GRE General Test, minimum GPA of 2.7. Additional exam requirements/recommendations for international students: Required—TOEFL. Electronic applications accepted.

The University of Texas at Austin, Graduate School, College of Liberal Arts, Department of Anthropology, Austin, TX 78712-1111. Offers archaeology (MA, PhD); folklore and public culture (MA, PhD); linguistic anthropology (MA, PhD); physical anthropology (MA, PhD); social anthropology (MA, PhD). Part-time programs available. Terminal master's awarded for partial completion of doctoral program. *Degree requirements:* For master's, thesis; for doctorate, one foreign language, thesis/dissertation. *Entrance requirements:* For master's and doctorate, GRE General Test. Additional exam requirements/recommendations for international students: Required—TOEFL. Electronic applications accepted.

University of Virginia, College and Graduate School of Arts and Sciences, McIntire Department of Art, Charlottesville, VA 22904-4130. Offers classical art and archaeology (MA, PhD); history of art and architecture (MA, PhD). *Faculty:* 24 full-time (11 women), 2 part-time/adjunct (0 women). *Students:* 52 full-time (37 women); includes 1 minority (American Indian/Alaska Native), 4 international. Average age 29. 81 applicants, 35% accepted, 12 enrolled. In 2007, 11 master's awarded. *Median time to degree:* Of those who began their doctoral program in fall 1999, 50% received their degree in 8 years or less. *Degree requirements:* For master's, one foreign language, thesis, defense; for doctorate, 2 foreign languages, comprehensive exam, thesis/dissertation, defense. *Entrance requirements:* For master's and doctorate, GRE General Test, writing sample. Additional exam requirements/recommendations for international students: Recommended—TOEFL (minimum score 600 paper-based; 250 computer-based; 90 iBT), IELTS (minimum score 7). *Application deadline:* For fall admission, 12/7 for domestic students. Application fee: $60. Electronic applications accepted. *Financial support:* In 2007–08, 40 fellowships (averaging $7,950 per year), 1 research assistantship (averaging $2,000 per year), 12 teaching assistantships with full tuition reimbursements (averaging $8,800 per year) were awarded; career-related internships or fieldwork, Federal Work-Study, scholarships/grants, and unspecified assistantships also available. Financial award application deadline: 12/7; financial award applicants required to submit CSS PROFILE. *Faculty research:* Classical art, renaissance art and architecture, American material culture. Total annual research expenditures: $35,000. *Unit head:* Daniel Ehnbom, Director of Graduate Studies, 434-924-6130, Fax: 434-924-3647, E-mail: dje6r@virginia.edu. *Application contact:* Aaron Mills, Associate Dean of Graduate Academic Programs and Research, 434-924-6739, Fax: 434-924-6737, E-mail: grad-a-s@virginia.edu.

University of West Florida, College of Arts and Sciences: Arts, Department of Anthropology, Pensacola, FL 32514-5750. Offers anthropology (MA); historical archaeology (MA). *Faculty:* 8 full-time (3 women). *Students:* 14 full-time (12 women), 26 part-time (15 women); includes 4 minority (1 African American, 1 Asian American or Pacific Islander, 2 Hispanic Americans). Average age 29. 33 applicants, 58% accepted, 9 enrolled. In 2007, 4 degrees awarded. *Degree requirements:* For master's, internship or thesis. *Entrance requirements:* For master's, GRE, bachelor's degree in anthropology, minimum GPA of 3.0, 3 letters of recommendation, writing sample. Additional exam requirements/recommendations for international students: Required—TOEFL (minimum score 550 paper-based; 213 computer-based). *Application deadline:* For fall admission, 6/1 for domestic students, 5/15 for international students; for spring admission, 11/1 for domestic students, 10/1 for international students. Application fee: $30. *Expenses:* Tuition, state resident: full-time $6,054; part-time $252 per credit. Tuition, nonresident: full-time $21,886; part-time $912 per credit. *Financial support:* In 2007–08, 5 research assistantships (averaging $3,760 per year), 5 teaching assistantships (averaging $3,760 per year) were awarded; fellowships, career-related internships or fieldwork, scholarships/grants, tuition waivers (partial), and unspecified assistantships also available. Financial award application deadline: 4/15; financial award applicants required to submit FAFSA. *Unit head:* Dr. Judith A. Bense, Chairperson, 850-474-2797, E-mail: anthropology@uwf.edu.

Washington State University, Graduate School, College of Liberal Arts, Department of Anthropology, Pullman, WA 99164. Offers archaeology (MA, PhD); cultural anthropology (MA, PhD); evolutionary anthropology (MA, PhD). Part-time programs available. *Faculty:* 17. *Students:* 56 full-time (33 women), 26 part-time (12 women); includes 11 minority (2 African Americans, 1 American Indian/Alaska Native, 2 Asian Americans or Pacific Islanders, 6 Hispanic Americans), 6 international. Average age 32. 198 applicants, 14% accepted, 19 enrolled. In 2007, 8 master's, 2 doctorates awarded. *Median time to degree:* Of those who began their doctoral program in fall 1999, 100% received their degree in 8 years or less. *Degree requirements:* For master's, comprehensive exam (for some programs), thesis, oral exam; for doctorate, comprehensive exam, thesis/dissertation, qualifying exam, oral exam and written exam. *Entrance requirements:* For master's, GRE General Test, minimum GPA of 3.0, curriculum vitae, 3 letters of recommendation; for doctorate, GRE General Test, minimum GPA of 3.0, copy of thesis or master's research paper, curriculum vitae, 3 letters of recommendation. Additional exam requirements/recommendations for international students: Required—TOEFL (minimum score 550 paper-based; 213 computer-based). *Application deadline:* For fall admission, 2/1 priority date for domestic students, 1/15 priority date for international students. Applications are processed on a rolling basis. Application fee: $50. Electronic applications accepted. *Financial support:* In 2007–08, 54 students received support, including 5 research assistantships with full tuition reimbursements available (averaging $13,917 per year), 34 teaching assistantships with full tuition reimbursements available (averaging $13,056 per year); fellowships, Federal Work-Study, institutionally sponsored loans, scholarships/grants, health care benefits, and tuition waivers (partial) also available. Support available to part-time students. Financial award application deadline: 3/1; financial award applicants required to submit FAFSA. *Faculty research:* Western North American archaeology and paleo-environments, zooarchaeology, gender and culture issues, issues of globalization, cultural ecology. Total annual research expenditures: $327,444. *Unit head:* Dr. William Andrefsky, Chair, 509-335-1127, Fax: 509-335-3999, E-mail: and@wsu.edu. *Application contact:* Graduate School Admissions, 800-GRADWSU, Fax: 509-335-1949, E-mail: gradsch@wsu.edu.

Washington University in St. Louis, Graduate School of Arts and Sciences, Department of Art History and Archaeology, St. Louis, MO 63130-4899. Offers art history (MA, PhD); classical archaeology (MA, PhD). *Degree requirements:* For doctorate, 2 foreign languages, comprehensive exam, thesis/dissertation. *Entrance requirements:* For master's and doctorate, GRE General Test, sample of written work. Electronic applications accepted.

Wheaton College, Graduate School, Department of Biblical and Theological Studies, Program in Biblical Archaeology, Wheaton, IL 60187-5593. Offers MA. *Faculty:* 2 full-time (0 women). *Students:* 3. 4 applicants, 50% accepted, 2 enrolled. *Degree requirements:* For master's, thesis or alternative, semester of study in Israel. *Entrance requirements:* For master's, GRE General Test or MAT. *Application deadline:* For fall admission, 3/1 priority date for domestic students, 1/1 for international students. Applications are processed on a rolling basis. Application fee: $30. Electronic applications accepted. *Financial support:* Scholarships/grants available. Financial award application deadline: 3/1; financial award applicants required to submit FAFSA. *Unit head:* John Monson, Coordinator, 630-752-5706. *Application contact:* Julie A. Huebner, Director of Graduate Admissions, 630-752-5195, Fax: 630-752-5935, E-mail: gradadm@wheaton.edu.

Wilfrid Laurier University, Faculty of Graduate Studies, Faculty of Arts, Department of Archaeology and Classical Studies, Waterloo, ON N2L 3C5, Canada. Offers MA. *Faculty:* 12 full-time, 6 part-time/adjunct. *Degree requirements:* For master's, thesis optional. *Entrance requirements:* For master's, minimum B+ average in last two undergraduate years (exclusive of first year level courses in those years). Additional exam requirements/recommendations for international students: Required—TOEFL. Application fee: $75. *Financial support:* Fellowships, research assistantships, teaching assistantships available. *Unit head:* Dr. Gerald Schaus, Graduate Officer, 519-884-0710 Ext. 3302, E-mail: gschaus@wlu.ca. *Application contact:* Jennifer Poppe, Student Contact, 519-884-0710 Ext. 3536, Fax: 519-884-1020, E-mail: gradstudies@wlu.ca.

Yale University, Graduate School of Arts and Sciences, Interdisciplinary Program in Archaeological Studies, New Haven, CT 06520. Offers MA. *Degree requirements:* For master's, thesis. *Entrance requirements:* For master's, GRE General Test.

Biological Anthropology

Duke University, Graduate School, Department of Biological Anthropology and Anatomy, Durham, NC 27710. Offers cellular and molecular biology (PhD); gross anatomy and physical anthropology (PhD), including comparative morphology of human and non-human primates, primate social behavior, vertebrate paleontology; neuroanatomy (PhD). *Faculty:* 6 full-time. *Students:* 15 full-time (8 women), 1 international. 32 applicants, 19% accepted, 4 enrolled. In 2007, 1 doctorate awarded. *Degree requirements:* For doctorate, one foreign language, thesis/dissertation. *Entrance requirements:* For doctorate, GRE General Test. Additional exam requirements/recommendations for international students: Required—TOEFL (minimum score 550 paper-based; 213 computer-based; 83 iBT), IELTS (minimum score 7). *Application deadline:* For fall admission, 12/15 priority date for domestic and international students. Application fee: $75. Electronic applications accepted. *Financial support:* Fellowships, teaching assistantships, Federal Work-Study available. Financial award application deadline: 12/31. *Unit head:* Kenneth Glander, Director of Graduate Studies, 919-684-4124, Fax: 919-684-8542.

Kent State University, School of Biomedical Sciences, Program in Biological Anthropology, Kent, OH 44242-0001. Offers PhD. Offered in cooperation with Northeastern Ohio Universities College of Medicine. *Faculty:* 8. *Students:* 7 full-time (2 women), 4 part-time (2 women); includes 1 minority (American Indian/Alaska Native). 11 applicants, 36% accepted. In 2007, 2 degrees awarded. *Degree requirements:* For doctorate, thesis/dissertation. *Entrance requirements:* For doctorate, GRE General Test, MA/MS in anthropology or one of the biological science disciplines, letter of recommendation. *Application deadline:* Applications are processed on a rolling basis. Application fee: $30. Electronic applications accepted. *Financial support:* In 2007–08, 6 students received support, including 4 teaching assistantships; fellowships, research assistantships, Federal Work-Study, scholarships/grants, tuition waivers (full), and unspecified assistantships also available. Financial award application deadline: 1/1; financial award applicants required to submit FAFSA. *Faculty research:* Human evolution, paleodemography, orofacial anatomy, osteology, primate behavior. *Unit head:* Dr. Robert V. Dorman, Director, School of Biomedical Sciences, 330-672-2263, Fax: 330-672-9391, E-mail: rdorman@kent.edu.

Mercyhurst College, Graduate Program, Program in Forensic and Biological Anthropology, Erie, PA 16546. Offers MS. *Faculty:* 2 full-time (0 women), 4 part-time/adjunct (1 woman). *Students:* 12 full-time (10 women); includes 4 minority (1 African American, 1 American Indian/Alaska Native, 2 Hispanic Americans). Average age 27. 78 applicants, 10% accepted, 5 enrolled. In 2007, 7 degrees awarded. *Entrance requirements:* For master's, GRE or MAT, undergraduate degree in related field, interview. Additional exam requirements/recommendations for international students: Required—TOEFL. *Application deadline:* For fall admission, 8/1 for domestic students; for winter admission, 11/1 for domestic students; for spring admission, 2/1 for domestic students. Application fee: $35. *Financial support:* In 2007–08, 5 research assistantships with full and partial tuition reimbursements (averaging $6,500 per year) were awarded. Financial award applicants required to submit FAFSA. Total annual research expenditures: $575,000. *Unit head:* Dr. Dennis Dirkmaat, Director, Graduate Program in Biological and Forensic Anthropology, 814-824-2105, E-mail: ddirkmaat@mercyhurst.edu. *Application contact:* Justin Ross, Academic Coordinator, 814-824-2985, Fax: 814-824-2055, E-mail: jross@mercyhurst.edu.

Demography and Population Studies

Arizona State University, Graduate College, College of Liberal Arts and Sciences, Division of Social Sciences, Department of Sociology, Tempe, AZ 85287. Offers demography and population studies (MA, PhD); sociology (MA, PhD). *Degree requirements:* For master's, thesis or alternative; for doctorate, thesis/dissertation. *Entrance requirements:* For master's and doctorate, GRE General Test.

Bowling Green State University, Graduate College, College of Arts and Sciences, Department of Sociology, Bowling Green, OH 43403. Offers demography and population studies (MA); social psychology (MA); sociology (PhD). Part-time programs available. *Faculty:* 21 full-time (11 women). *Students:* 40 full-time (27 women), 8 part-time (all women); includes 4 minority (3 African Americans, 1 Hispanic American), 6 international. Average age 30. 46 applicants, 85% accepted, 11 enrolled. In 2007, 8 master's, 3 doctorates awarded. *Degree requirements:* For master's, thesis or alternative; for doctorate, comprehensive exam, thesis/dissertation. *Entrance requirements:* For master's and doctorate, GRE General Test. Additional exam requirements/recommendations for international students: Required—TOEFL. *Application deadline:* For fall admission, 1/15 priority date for domestic students. Application fee: $30. Electronic applications accepted. *Financial support:* In 2007–08, 1 fellowship with full tuition reimbursement (averaging $16,598 per year), 33 research assistantships with full tuition reimbursements (averaging $12,064 per year), 1 teaching assistantship with full tuition reimbursement (averaging $13,278 per year) were awarded; career-related internships or fieldwork, Federal Work-Study, institutionally sponsored loans, and unspecified assistantships also available. Financial award applicants required to submit FAFSA. *Faculty research:* Applied demography, criminology and deviance, family studies, population studies, social psychology. *Unit head:* Dr. Gary Lee, Chair, 419-372-2292. *Application contact:* Dr. Steve Cernkovich, Graduate Coordinator, 419-372-2743.

Brown University, Graduate School, Department of Sociology, Program in Population Studies, Providence, RI 02912. Offers PhD. *Degree requirements:* For doctorate, thesis/dissertation, oral exam. *Entrance requirements:* For doctorate, GRE General Test.

Cornell University, Graduate School, Graduate Fields of Agriculture and Life Sciences, Field of Development Sociology, Ithaca, NY 14853-0001. Offers community and regional society (MS); community and regional sociology (MPS, PhD); methods of social research (MPS, MS, PhD); population and development (MPS, MS, PhD); rural and environmental sociology (MPS, MS, PhD); state, economy, and society (MPS, MS, PhD). *Faculty:* 26 full-time (6 women). *Students:* 45 full-time (31 women); includes 5 minority (1 American Indian/Alaska Native, 2 Asian Americans or Pacific Islanders, 2 Hispanic Americans), 17 international. Average age 33. 49 applicants, 18% accepted, 3 enrolled. In 2007, 12 master's, 1 doctorate awarded. *Degree requirements:* For doctorate, comprehensive exam, thesis/dissertation. *Entrance requirements:* For master's and doctorate, GRE General Test, 3 letters of recommendation. Additional exam requirements/recommendations for international students: Required—TOEFL (minimum score 550 paper-based; 213 computer-based; 77 iBT). *Application deadline:* For fall admission, 1/15 priority date for domestic students. Application fee: $60. Electronic applications accepted. *Financial support:* In 2007–08, 32 students received support, including 9 fellowships with full tuition reimbursements available, 12 research assistantships with full tuition reimbursements available, 11 teaching assistantships with full tuition reimbursements available; institutionally sponsored loans, scholarships/grants, health care benefits, tuition waivers (full and partial), and unspecified assistantships also available. Financial award applicants required to submit FAFSA. *Faculty research:* Demography (population and development), environmental sociology, international and rural community development, political economy and ecology, sustainable agriculture. *Unit head:* Director of Graduate Studies, 607-255-3092, Fax: 607-254-2896. *Application contact:* Graduate Field Assistant, 607-255-3092, Fax: 607-254-2896, E-mail: devsoc@cornell.edu.

Cornell University, Graduate School, Graduate Fields of Arts and Sciences, Field of International Development, Ithaca, NY 14853-0001. Offers development policy (MPS); international nutrition (MPS); international planning (MPS); international population (MPS); science and technology policy (MPS). *Faculty:* 53 full-time (17 women). *Students:* 28 full-time (15 women); includes 2 minority (both African Americans), 24 international. Average age 32. 30 applicants, 60% accepted, 11 enrolled. In 2007, 5 degrees awarded. *Degree requirements:* For master's, project paper. *Entrance requirements:* For master's, GRE General Test (recommended), 2 academic recommendations, 2 years of development experience. Additional exam requirements/recommendations for international students: Required—TOEFL (minimum score 77 iBT). *Application deadline:* Applications are processed on a rolling basis. Application fee: $70. Electronic applications accepted. *Financial support:* In 2007–08, 21 students received support, including 18 fellowships with full tuition reimbursements available, 3 teaching assistantships with full tuition reimbursements available; research assistantships with full tuition reimbursements available, institutionally sponsored loans, scholarships/grants, health care benefits, tuition waivers (full and partial), and unspecified assistantships also available. Financial award applicants required to submit FAFSA. *Faculty research:* Development policy, international nutrition, international planning, science and technology policy, international population. *Unit head:* Director of Graduate Studies, 607-255-3037, Fax: 607-255-1005. *Application contact:* Graduate Field Assistant, 607-255-0831, Fax: 607-255-1005, E-mail: mpsid@cornell.edu.

Florida State University, Graduate Studies, College of Social Sciences, Center for Demography and Population Health, Tallahassee, FL 32306. Offers MS, Certificate. *Faculty:* 13 full-time (5 women). *Students:* 6 full-time (4 women), 1 part-time. Average age 23. 19 applicants, 47% accepted, 5 enrolled. In 2007, 3 degrees awarded. *Degree requirements:* For master's, thesis or alternative. *Entrance requirements:* For master's, GRE General Test, minimum GPA of 3.0. Additional exam requirements/recommendations for international students: Required—TOEFL. *Application deadline:* For fall admission, 3/15 priority date for domestic and international students. Applications are processed on a rolling basis. Application fee: $30. Electronic applications accepted. *Expenses:* Tuition, state resident: part-time $248 per credit hour. Tuition, nonresident: part-time $880 per credit hour. Tuition and fees vary according to program. *Financial support:* In 2007–08, 1 student received support. Career-related internships or fieldwork, Federal Work-Study, institutionally sponsored loans, and tuition waivers (full) available. Financial award application deadline: 1/31; financial award applicants required to submit FAFSA. *Faculty research:* Health, aging, migration, AIDS, gender. Total annual research expenditures: $993,923. *Unit head:* Dr. Isaac Eberstein, Director, 850-644-7108, Fax: 850-644-8818, E-mail: ieberstn@fsu.edu.

Georgetown University, Graduate School of Arts and Sciences, Department of Demography, Washington, DC 20057. Offers MA. *Degree requirements:* For master's, comprehensive exam, thesis or alternative. *Entrance requirements:* For master's, GRE. Additional exam requirements/recommendations for international students: Required—TOEFL. *Faculty research:* Social and demographic aspects of aging, determinants of human fertility behavior, demographic and economic aspects of social development, economic development and development policy.

Harvard University, School of Public Health, Department of Global Health and Population, Boston, MA 02115-6096. Offers SM, DPH, SD. Part-time programs available. *Faculty:* 23 full-time (5 women), 13 part-time/adjunct (4 women). *Students:* 89 full-time, 6 part-time; includes 14 minority (5 African Americans, 7 Asian Americans or Pacific Islanders, 2 Hispanic Americans), 35 international. Average age 30. 210 applicants, 25% accepted, 28 enrolled. In 2007, 22 master's, 5 doctorates awarded. *Degree requirements:* For master's, thesis; for doctorate, thesis/dissertation, qualifying exam. *Entrance requirements:* For master's and doctorate, GRE. Additional exam requirements/recommendations for international students: Required—TOEFL (minimum score 580 paper-based; 240 computer-based; 70 iBT); Recommended—IELTS (minimum score 7). *Application deadline:* For fall admission, 12/15 for domestic and international students. Electronic applications accepted. *Financial support:* Fellowships, research assistantships, teaching assistantships, Federal Work-Study, scholarships/grants, traineeships, tuition waivers (partial), and unspecified assistantships available. Support available to part-time students. Financial award application deadline: 2/8; financial award applicants required to submit FAFSA. *Faculty research:* International health policy, economics, reproductive health, ecology. *Unit head:* Dr. David Bloom, Chair, 617-432-1232, Fax: 617-566-6733, E-mail: ajaimung@hsph.harvard.edu. *Application contact:* Vincent W. James, Director of Admissions, 617-432-1031, Fax: 617-432-7080, E-mail: admisofc@hsph.harvard.edu.

The Johns Hopkins University, Bloomberg School of Public Health, Department of Population, Family and Reproductive Health, Baltimore, MD 21218-2699. Offers child and adolescent health and development (Dr PH, PhD); demography (MHS); population and health (Dr PH, PhD); population, family and reproductive health (MHS); reproductive, perinatal women's health (Dr PH, PhD). *Faculty:* 39 full-time (24 women), 35 part-time/adjunct (20 women). *Students:* 66 full-time (61 women), 1 (woman) part-time; includes 15 minority (5 African Americans, 7 Asian Americans or Pacific Islanders, 3 Hispanic Americans), 16 international. Average age 30. 108 applicants, 43% accepted, 13 enrolled. In 2007, 12 master's, 11 doctorates awarded. *Median time to degree:* Of those who began their doctoral program in fall 1999, 92% received their degree in 8 years or less. *Degree requirements:* For master's, essay, fieldwork; for doctorate, thesis/dissertation, 1 year full-time residency, oral and written exams. *Entrance requirements:* For master's and doctorate, GRE General Test (LSAT, MCAT considered), 3 letters of recommendation, curriculum vitae. Additional exam requirements/recommendations for international students: Required—TOEFL (minimum score 550 paper-based; 250 computer-based). *Application deadline:* For fall admission, 1/2 for domestic and international students. Application fee: $45. *Financial support:* In 2007–08, 73 students received support, including 11 fellowships with full and partial tuition reimbursements available (averaging $43,476 per year); research assistantships, teaching assistantships, Federal Work-Study, institutionally sponsored loans, scholarships/grants, traineeships, health care benefits, and stipends also available. Support available to part-time students. Financial award application deadline: 3/15; financial award applicants required to submit FAFSA. *Faculty research:* Child and adolescent health and development, population and health and reproductive, perinatal and women's health. Total annual research expenditures: $15.6 million. *Unit head:* Dr. Robert Blum, Chair, 410-955-3384, Fax: 410-955-2303, E-mail: rblum@jhsph.edu. *Application contact:* Linda Adams, Senior Academic Coordinator, 410-955-1116, Fax: 410-955-2303, E-mail: ladams@jhsph.edu.

Princeton University, Graduate School, Department of Economics, Princeton, NJ 08544-1019. Offers economics (PhD); economics and demography (PhD). *Degree requirements:* For doctorate, thesis/dissertation. *Entrance requirements:* For doctorate, GRE General Test, GRE Subject Test (recommended), working knowledge of multivariate calculus and matrix algebra. Additional exam requirements/recommendations for international students: Required—TOEFL (minimum score 600 paper-based; 250 computer-based). Electronic applications accepted.

Princeton University, Graduate School, Department of Sociology, Princeton, NJ 08544-1019. Offers sociology (PhD); sociology and demography (PhD). *Degree requirements:* For doctorate, variable foreign language requirement, thesis/dissertation. *Entrance requirements:* For doctorate, GRE General Test, GRE Subject Test (recommended), sample of written work. Additional exam requirements/recommendations for international students: Required—TOEFL (minimum score 600 paper-based; 250 computer-based). Electronic applications accepted.

Princeton University, Graduate School, Program in Population Studies, Princeton, NJ 08544-1019. Offers demography (PhD, Certificate); demography and public affairs (PhD); economics and demography (PhD); sociology and demography (PhD). *Degree requirements:* For doctorate, thesis/dissertation. *Entrance requirements:* For doctorate, GRE General Test. Additional exam requirements/recommendations for international students: Required—TOEFL (minimum score 600 paper-based; 250 computer-based). Electronic applications accepted. *Faculty research:* Models, fertility, infant and child mortality, migration.

Université de Montréal, Faculty of Arts and Sciences, Department of Demography, Montréal, QC H3C 3J7, Canada. Offers M Sc, PhD. *Faculty:* 10 full-time (2 women), 12 part-time/adjunct (4 women). *Students:* 55 full-time (32 women), 3 part-time (2 women). 36 applicants, 47% accepted, 15 enrolled. In 2007, 5 master's awarded. Terminal master's awarded for partial completion of doctoral program. *Degree requirements:* For master's, one foreign language, thesis; for doctorate, one foreign language, thesis/dissertation, general exam. *Entrance requirements:* For master's, minimum GPA of 2.7. *Application deadline:* For fall admission, 2/1 priority date for domestic students; for winter admission, 11/1 priority date for domestic students; for spring admission, 2/1 priority date for domestic students. Applications are processed on a rolling basis. Application fee: $100. Electronic applications accepted. *Financial support:* Fellowships, research assistantships, teaching assistantships, Federal Work-Study and tuition waivers (partial) available. *Faculty research:* Historical demography, population and development, ethnic and linguistic groups, aging of population, family demography. *Unit head:* Robert Bourbeau, Chairman, 514-343-5870, Fax: 514-343-2309, E-mail: robert.bourbeau@umontreal.ca. *Application contact:* Louise Faulkner, Student Files Management Technician, 514-343-6111 Ext. 1971, Fax: 514-343-2309, E-mail: louise.faulkner@umontreal.ca.

Université du Québec, Institut National de la Recherche Scientifique, Graduate Programs, Research Center—Urbanization, Culture and Society, Québec, QC G1K 9A9, Canada. Offers demography (M Sc, PhD); research and public action (M Sc); urban studies (M Sc, PhD). Programs given in French. Part-time programs available. *Faculty:* 36. *Students:* 73 full-time (41 women), 15 part-time (9 women), 8 international. Average age 34. In 2007, 8 master's, 5 doctorates awarded. *Median time to degree:* Of those who began their doctoral program in fall 1999, 50% received their degree in 8 years or less. *Degree requirements:* For master's, thesis optional; for doctorate, thesis/dissertation. *Entrance requirements:* For master's, appropriate bachelor's degree, proficiency in French; for doctorate, appropriate master's degree, proficiency in French. *Application deadline:* For fall admission, 3/30 for domestic and international students; for winter admission, 11/1 for domestic and international students. Application fee: $30. *Financial support:* Fellowships, research assistantships, teaching assistantships available. *Faculty research:* Regional space, urban and metropolitan space, micro-urban space. *Unit head:* Johanne Charbonneau, Director, 514-499-4001, Fax: 514-499-4065, E-mail: johanne.charbonneau@ucs.inrs.ca. *Application contact:* Yvonne Boisvert, Registrar, 418-654-3861, Fax: 418-654-3858, E-mail: registrariat@adm.inrs.ca.

University at Albany, State University of New York, College of Arts and Sciences, Department of Sociology, Albany, NY 12222-0001. Offers demography (Certificate); sociology (MA, PhD); urban policy (Certificate). *Students:* 49 full-time (34 women), 76 part-time (39 women). Average age 32. In 2007, 3 master's, 5 doctorates, 4 other advanced degrees awarded. Terminal master's awarded for partial completion of doctoral program. *Degree requirements:* For master's, thesis; for doctorate, thesis/dissertation, 2 specialization exams, research tool. *Entrance requirements:* For master's and doctorate, GRE General Test. Additional exam requirements/recommendations for international students: Required—TOEFL (minimum score 213 computer-based). *Application deadline:* For fall admission, 1/15 for domestic students, 5/1 for international students. Applications are processed on a rolling basis. Application fee: $75. Electronic applications accepted. *Expenses:* Tuition, state resident: part-time $576 per credit. Tuition, nonresident: part-time $910 per credit. Tuition and fees vary according to program. *Financial support:* Fellowships, research assistantships, teaching assistantships, career-related internships or fieldwork and Federal Work-Study available. Financial award application deadline: 3/15. *Faculty research:* Gender and equality, crime and deviance, aging, work and organizations, social demography. *Unit head:* Dr. Donlad Hernandez, Chair, 518-442-4666. *Application contact:* Glen D. Dean, Graduate Committee Chair, 518-442-4587.

University of Alberta, Faculty of Graduate Studies and Research, Department of Sociology, Edmonton, AB T6G 2E1, Canada. Offers criminal justice (MA); demography (MA, PhD); sociology (MA, PhD). Part-time programs available. *Degree requirements:* For master's, thesis

Demography and Population Studies

University of Alberta (continued)

(for some programs); for doctorate, thesis/dissertation. *Faculty research:* Criminology, knowledge and culture, methods and theory, population studies, stratification.

University of California, Berkeley, Graduate Division, Group in Demography, Berkeley, CA 94720-1500. Offers MA, PhD. *Degree requirements:* For doctorate, thesis/dissertation, qualifying exam. *Entrance requirements:* For master's and doctorate, GRE General Test, minimum GPA of 3.0, 3 letters of recommendation. *Application deadline:* For fall admission, 12/14 for domestic students. Application fee: $70 ($90 for international students). Electronic applications accepted. *Financial support:* Fellowships with full and partial tuition reimbursements, research assistantships with full and partial tuition reimbursements, teaching assistantships with full and partial tuition reimbursements, traineeships and unspecified assistantships available. *Unit head:* Dr. Kenneth Wachter, Chair, 510-642-1578, E-mail: wachter@demog.berkeley.edu. *Application contact:* Monique Marie Verrier, Student Affairs Officer, 510-642-9800, Fax: 510-643-8558, E-mail: applications@demog.berkeley.edu.

University of California, Berkeley, Graduate Division, Group in Sociology and Demography, Berkeley, CA 94720-1500. Offers PhD. *Degree requirements:* For doctorate, thesis/dissertation, qualifying exam. *Entrance requirements:* For doctorate, GRE General Test, minimum GPA of 3.0, 3 letters of recommendation. *Application deadline:* For fall admission, 12/14 for domestic students. Application fee: $70 ($90 for international students). *Financial support:* Fellowships with full and partial tuition reimbursements, research assistantships with full and partial tuition reimbursements, teaching assistantships with full and partial tuition reimbursements, unspecified assistantships available. *Unit head:* Dr. Michael Hout, Chair, 510-643-6874, E-mail: mikehout@berkeley.edu. *Application contact:* Monique Marie Verrier, Student Affairs Officer, 510-642-9800, Fax: 510-643-8558, E-mail: applications@demog.berkeley.edu.

University of California, Irvine, Office of Graduate Studies, School of Social Sciences and School of Social Ecology, Program in Demographic and Social Analysis, Irvine, CA 92697. Offers MA. *Students:* 16 full-time (11 women); includes 5 minority (3 Asian Americans or Pacific Islanders, 2 Hispanic Americans), 3 international. 19 applicants, 68% accepted. In 2007, 24 master's awarded. *Entrance requirements:* For master's, GRE, minimum GPA of 3.0. Additional exam requirements/recommendations for international students: Required—TOEFL (minimum score 550 paper-based; 213 computer-based). *Application deadline:* For fall admission, 1/15 for domestic students; for winter admission, 10/15 for domestic students; for spring admission, 1/15 for domestic students. *Financial support:* Application deadline: 3/1. *Unit head:* Ken Chew, Graduate Director, 949-824-6990, E-mail: chew@uci.edu. *Application contact:* Diane Enriquez, Graduate Counselor, 949-824-5924, Fax: 949-824-3548, E-mail: dmvargas@uci.edu.

University of Guelph, Ontario Veterinary College and Graduate Program Services, Graduate Programs in Veterinary Sciences, Department of Population Medicine, Guelph, ON N1G 2W1, Canada. Offers epidemiology (M Sc, DV Sc, PhD); health management (DV Sc); population medicine and health management (M Sc); swine health management (M Sc); theriogenology (M Sc, DV Sc). *Faculty:* 25 full-time (9 women), 5 part-time/adjunct (4 women). *Students:* 64 full-time (48 women), 7 part-time (5 women). 38 applicants, 68% accepted, 26 enrolled. In 2007, 13 master's, 3 doctorates awarded. *Degree requirements:* For master's, thesis; for doctorate, comprehensive exam, thesis/dissertation. *Entrance requirements:* Additional exam requirements/recommendations for international students: Required—TOEFL. *Application deadline:* For fall admission, 2/1 for domestic students. Applications are processed on a rolling basis. Application fee: $85. *Financial support:* In 2007–08, 10 students received support. Total annual research expenditures: $1.5 million. *Unit head:* Dr. Cate Dewey, Chair, 519-824-4120 Ext. 54746, Fax: 519-763-8621, E-mail: popmed@ovc.uoguelph.ca. *Application contact:* Dr. Scott McEwen, Graduate Program Coordinator, 519-824-4120 Ext. 54746, Fax: 519-763-3117, E-mail: popmed@ovc.uoguelph.ca.

University of Hawaii at Manoa, Graduate Division, Colleges of Arts and Sciences, College of Social Sciences, Department of Sociology, Population Studies Program, Honolulu, HI 96822. Offers Graduate Certificate. Part-time programs available. *Faculty:* 14 full-time (5 women), 4 part-time/adjunct (0 women). *Students:* 8 full-time (6 women), 6 international. *Entrance requirements:* For degree, GRE General Test. Additional exam requirements/recommendations for international students: Required—TOEFL (minimum score 500 paper-based; 173 computer-based; 61 iBT), IELTS (minimum score 5). *Application deadline:* For fall admission, 3/1 for domestic and international students; for spring admission, 9/1 for domestic and international students. Application fee: $50. *Financial support:* In 2007–08, 4 research assistantships (averaging $16,668 per year), 1 teaching assistantship (averaging $14,958 per year) were awarded. *Application contact:* Andrew Mason, Information Contact, 808-956-7551, Fax: 808-956-7738, E-mail: popstudy@hawaii.edu.

University of Pennsylvania, School of Arts and Sciences, Graduate Group in Demography, Philadelphia, PA 19104. Offers AM, PhD. Terminal master's awarded for partial completion of doctoral program. *Degree requirements:* For master's, thesis or alternative; for doctorate, thesis/dissertation. *Entrance requirements:* For master's and doctorate, GRE General Test. Additional exam requirements/recommendations for international students: Required—TOEFL. Electronic applications accepted.

University of Puerto Rico, Medical Sciences Campus, Graduate School of Public Health, Department of Social Sciences, Program in Demography, San Juan, PR 00936-5067. Offers MS. Part-time programs available. *Degree requirements:* For master's, thesis. *Entrance requirements:* For master's, GRE, previous course work in algebra and statistics.

The University of Texas at San Antonio, College of Public Policy, Department of Demography and Organizational Studies, San Antonio, TX 78249-0617. Offers applied demography (PhD). Part-time and evening/weekend programs available. *Faculty:* 5 full-time (1 woman). *Students:* 9 full-time (5 women), 10 part-time (7 women); includes 9 minority (all Hispanic Americans), 2 international. Average age 35. 26 applicants, 92% accepted. *Entrance requirements:* Additional exam requirements/recommendations for international students: Required—TOEFL (minimum score 500 paper-based; 173 computer-based). *Application deadline:* For fall admission, 7/1 for domestic students, 4/1 for international students; for spring admission, 11/1 for domestic students, 9/1 for international students. Applications are processed on a rolling basis. Application fee: $45 ($80 for international students). Electronic applications accepted. *Financial support:* In 2007–08, 6 research assistantships (averaging $13,500 per year) were awarded; career-related internships or fieldwork, Federal Work-Study, and unspecified assistantships also available. Total annual research expenditures: $7,752. *Unit head:* Dr. Mary A. Zey, Chair, 210-458-6570, E-mail: mary.zey@utsa.edu.

Washington State University, Graduate School, College of Liberal Arts, Department of Sociology, Pullman, WA 99164. Offers crime and deviance (MA, PhD); environments, community and demographics (MA, PhD); institutions and social organizations (MA, PhD); political sociology (MA, PhD); social inequality (MA, PhD); social psychology and life course (MA, PhD). *Faculty:* 22 full-time (14 women), 8 part-time/adjunct (3 women). *Students:* 42 full-time (23 women), 2 part-time (both women); includes 2 minority (1 African American, 1 American Indian/Alaska Native), 4 international. Average age 30. 71 applicants, 13% accepted, 9 enrolled. In 2007, 7 master's, 4 doctorates awarded. Terminal master's awarded for partial completion of doctoral program. *Degree requirements:* For master's, thesis; for doctorate, comprehensive exam, thesis/dissertation. *Entrance requirements:* For master's, GRE General Test, minimum GPA of 3.0; for doctorate, GRE General Test, MA in sociology, minimum GPA of 3.0. Additional exam requirements/recommendations for international students: Required—TOEFL (minimum score 550 paper-based). *Application deadline:* For fall admission, 1/15 priority date for domestic students, 1/15 for international students. Application fee: $50. Electronic applications accepted. *Financial support:* In 2007–08, 5 research assistantships with tuition reimbursements (averaging $12,749 per year), 36 teaching assistantships with tuition reimbursements (averaging $12,749 per year) were awarded; fellowships with tuition reimbursements, Federal Work-Study, institutionally sponsored loans, scholarships/grants, health care benefits, and unspecified assistantships also available. Support available to part-time students. Financial award application deadline: 4/1; financial award applicants required to submit FAFSA. *Faculty research:* Crime/deviance, environmental sociology, social inequality, social psychology, gender. Total annual research expenditures: $101,888. *Unit head:* Dr. Gregory Hooks, Chair, 509-335-4595, Fax: 509-335-6419, E-mail: hooks@mail.wsu.edu. *Application contact:* Dr. Tom Rotolo, Director of Graduate Studies, 509-335-4595, Fax: 509-335-6419, E-mail: rotolo@wsu.edu.

Rural Sociology

Auburn University, Graduate School, Interdepartmental Programs, Department of Sociology, Anthropology, Criminology, and Social Work, Auburn University, AL 36849. Offers rural sociology (MS); sociology (MA, MS). Part-time programs available. *Faculty:* 15 full-time (5 women). *Students:* 21 full-time (13 women), 10 part-time (7 women); includes 3 minority (2 African Americans, 1 Asian American or Pacific Islander), 4 international. Average age 25. 15 applicants, 93% accepted, 8 enrolled. In 2007, 8 degrees awarded. *Degree requirements:* For master's, thesis, computer language (MS), foreign language (MA). *Entrance requirements:* For master's, GRE General Test. *Application deadline:* For fall admission, 7/7 for domestic students; for spring admission, 11/24 for domestic students. Applications are processed on a rolling basis. Application fee: $25 ($50 for international students). *Financial support:* Research assistantships, teaching assistantships available. Financial award application deadline: 3/15. *Unit head:* Dr. Kelly Alley, Interim Chair, 334-844-5049. *Application contact:* Dr. Joe Pittman, Interim Dean of the Graduate School, 334-844-4700.

Cornell University, Graduate School, Graduate Fields of Agriculture and Life Sciences, Field of Development Sociology, Ithaca, NY 14853-0001. Offers community and regional society (MS); community and regional sociology (MPS, PhD); methods of social research (MPS, MS, PhD); population and development (MPS, MS, PhD); rural and environmental sociology (MPS, MS, PhD); state, economy, and society (MPS, MS, PhD). *Faculty:* 26 full-time (6 women). *Students:* 45 full-time (31 women); includes 5 minority (1 American Indian/Alaska Native, 2 Asian Americans or Pacific Islanders, 2 Hispanic Americans), 17 international. Average age 33. 49 applicants, 18% accepted, 3 enrolled. In 2007, 12 master's, 1 doctorate awarded. *Degree requirements:* For doctorate, comprehensive exam, thesis/dissertation. *Entrance requirements:* For master's and doctorate, GRE General Test, 3 letters of recommendation. Additional exam requirements/recommendations for international students: Required—TOEFL (minimum score 550 paper-based; 213 computer-based; 77 iBT). *Application deadline:* For fall admission, 1/15 priority date for domestic students. Application fee: $60. Electronic applications accepted. *Financial support:* In 2007–08, 32 students received support, including 9 fellowships with full tuition reimbursements available, 12 research assistantships with full tuition reimbursements available, 11 teaching assistantships with full tuition reimbursements available; institutionally sponsored loans, scholarships/grants, health care benefits, tuition waivers (full and partial), and unspecified assistantships also available. Financial award applicants required to submit FAFSA. *Faculty research:* Demography (population and development), environmental sociology, international and rural community development, political economy and ecology, sustainable agriculture. *Unit head:* Director of Graduate Studies, 607-255-3092, Fax: 607-254-2896. *Application contact:* Graduate Field Assistant, 607-255-3092, Fax: 607-254-2896, E-mail: devsoc@cornell.edu.

Iowa State University of Science and Technology, Graduate College, College of Liberal Arts and Sciences, Department of Sociology and College of Agriculture, Program in Rural Sociology, Ames, IA 50011. Offers MS, PhD. *Faculty:* 12 full-time (6 women). *Students:* 15 full-time (6 women), 4 part-time (3 women); includes 1 minority (Hispanic American), 5 international. 12 applicants, 58% accepted, 5 enrolled. In 2007, 3 master's, 3 doctorates awarded. *Degree requirements:* For master's, thesis; for doctorate, thesis/dissertation. *Entrance requirements:* For master's, GRE General Test; for doctorate, GRE General Test, master's degree. Additional exam requirements/recommendations for international students: Required—TOEFL (paper-based 550; computer-based 213; iBT 79) or IELTS (6.5). *Application deadline:* For fall admission, 2/10 priority date for domestic students, 1/10 priority date for international students; for spring admission, 10/1 for domestic and international students. Application fee: $30 ($70 for international students). Electronic applications accepted. *Financial support:* In 2007–08, 10 research assistantships with full and partial tuition reimbursements (averaging $19,514 per year), 5 teaching assistantships with partial tuition reimbursements (averaging $19,080 per year) were awarded; scholarships/grants, health care benefits, and unspecified assistantships also available. *Application contact:* Dr. Gloria Jones-Johnson, Director of Graduate Education, 515-294-2947, E-mail: sociology@iastate.edu.

North Carolina State University, Graduate School, College of Humanities and Social Sciences, Department of Sociology and Anthropology, Program in Sociology, Raleigh, NC 27695. Offers rural sociology (MS); sociology (M Soc, PhD). Part-time programs available. *Degree requirements:* For master's, thesis (for some programs), practicum (M Soc), thesis (MS); for doctorate, comprehensive exam, thesis/dissertation. *Entrance requirements:* For master's and doctorate, GRE General Test, sample of written work. Electronic applications accepted. *Faculty research:* Inequity: gender, race and class; crime and social control; work and organizations; rural sociology; family and intimate relations.

The Ohio State University, Graduate School, College of Food, Agricultural, and Environmental Sciences, Department of Agricultural, Environmental, and Development Economics, Columbus, OH 43210. Offers agricultural economics and rural sociology (MS, PhD). *Faculty:* 32. *Students:* 67 full-time (32 women), 5 part-time (1 woman); includes 3 minority (1 African American, 2 Asian Americans or Pacific Islanders), 39 international. Average age 28. In 2007, 12 master's, 9 doctorates awarded. *Degree requirements:* For master's, thesis optional; for doctorate, thesis/dissertation. *Entrance requirements:* For master's and doctorate, GRE General Test. Additional exam requirements/recommendations for international students: Required—TOEFL (paper-based 550; computer-based 213) or IELTS (7) or Michigan English Language Assessment Battery (92). *Application deadline:* For fall admission, 8/15 priority date for domestic students, 7/1 priority date for international students; for winter admission, 12/1 priority date for domestic students, 11/1 priority date for international students; for spring admission, 3/1 priority date for domestic students, 2/1 priority date for international students. Applications are processed on a rolling basis. Application fee: $40 ($50 for international students). Electronic applications accepted. *Financial support:* Fellowships, research assistantships, teaching assistantships, Federal Work-Study and institutionally sponsored loans available. Support available to part-time students. *Unit head:* Stan Thompson, Graduate Studies Committee Chair, 614-292-7911, Fax: 614-292-4749, E-mail: thompson.51@osu.edu. *Application contact:* Graduate Admissions, 614-292-9444, Fax: 614-292-3895, E-mail: domestic.grad@osu.edu.

The Ohio State University, Graduate School, College of Food, Agricultural, and Environmental Sciences, Department of Rural Sociology, Columbus, OH 43210. Offers MS, PhD. *Students:* 15 full-time (9 women), 8 part-time (6 women); includes 2 minority (1 African American, 1 Hispanic American), 6 international. Average age 36. In 2007, 2 master's, 1 doctorate awarded. *Entrance requirements:* For master's and doctorate, GRE or GMAT. *Application deadline:* Applications are processed on a rolling basis. Application fee: $40 ($50 for international students). Electronic applications accepted. *Unit head:* Linda M. Lobao, Graduate Studies Committee Chair, 614-292-6394, Fax: 614-292-7007, E-mail: lobao.1@osu.edu. *Application contact:* Graduate Admissions, 614-292-9444, Fax: 614-292-3985, E-mail: domestic.grad@osu.edu.

Penn State University Park, Graduate School, College of Agricultural Sciences, Department of Agricultural Economics and Rural Sociology, State College, University Park, PA 16802-1503. Offers agricultural, environmental and regional economics (M Agr, MS, PhD); rural sociology (M Agr, MS, PhD). *Expenses:* Tuition, state resident: full-time $14,738; part-time $614 per credit. Tuition, nonresident: full-time $26,050; part-time $1,085 per credit. Tuition and fees vary according to course load, program and student level. *Unit head:* Dr. Stephen M. Smith, Head, 814-865-5461, Fax: 814-865-3746, E-mail: smsmith@psu.edu.

South Dakota State University, Graduate School, College of Agriculture and Biological Sciences, Department of Rural Sociology, Brookings, SD 57007. Offers rural sociology (MS); sociology (PhD). Part-time programs available. Postbaccalaureate distance learning degree programs offered. *Degree requirements:* For master's, comprehensive exam (for some programs), thesis, oral and written exams; for doctorate, comprehensive exam, thesis/dissertation, preliminary oral and written exams. *Entrance requirements:* For master's and doctorate, pre-requisite courses. Additional exam requirements/recommendations for international students: Required—TOEFL (minimum score 550 paper-based; 213 computer-based; 79 iBT). *Faculty research:* Demography, rural families, rural development, Native Americans, rural poverty, sociology of agriculture.

University of Alberta, Faculty of Graduate Studies and Research, Department of Rural Economy, Edmonton, AB T6G 2E1, Canada. Offers agricultural economics (M Ag, M Sc, PhD); forest economics (M Ag, M Sc, PhD); rural sociology (M Ag, M Sc); MBA/M Ag. Part-time programs available. *Degree requirements:* For doctorate, thesis/dissertation. *Entrance requirements:* Additional exam requirements/recommendations for international students: Required—TOEFL. *Faculty research:* Agroforestry, development, extension education, marketing and trade, natural resources and environment, policy, production economics.

University of Missouri–Columbia, Graduate School, College of Agriculture, Food and Natural Resources, Department of Rural Sociology, Columbia, MO 65211. Offers MS, PhD. Part-time programs available. *Degree requirements:* For doctorate, thesis/dissertation. *Entrance requirements:* For master's and doctorate, GRE General Test, minimum GPA of 3.0. Additional exam requirements/recommendations for international students: Required—TOEFL (minimum score 570 paper-based; 233 computer-based).

The University of Montana, Graduate School, College of Arts and Sciences, Department of Sociology, Missoula, MT 59812-0002. Offers criminology (MA); rural and environmental change (MA); sociology (MA). *Entrance requirements:* For master's, GRE General Test. Additional exam requirements/recommendations for international students: Required—TOEFL. *Faculty research:* Housing, homelessness, hunger, infant mortality, work safety.

University of Wisconsin–Madison, Graduate School, College of Letters and Science, Department of Sociology, Madison, WI 53706-1380. Offers rural sociology (MS); sociology (MS, PhD). Part-time programs available. Terminal master's awarded for partial completion of doctoral program. *Degree requirements:* For master's, thesis, oral exam; for doctorate, thesis/dissertation, preliminary and final oral exams, 4 seminars. *Entrance requirements:* For master's and doctorate, GRE General Test. Additional exam requirements/recommendations for international students: Required—TOEFL. Electronic applications accepted.

Sociology

Acadia University, Faculty of Arts, Department of Sociology, Wolfville, NS B4P 2R6, Canada. Offers MA. *Faculty:* 6 full-time (3 women). *Students:* 6 full-time (5 women); includes 1 Asian American or Pacific Islander. Average age 25. 11 applicants, 73% accepted, 6 enrolled. In 2007, 9 degrees awarded. *Degree requirements:* For master's, thesis. *Entrance requirements:* For master's, honors degree, minimum GPA of 3.25. Additional exam requirements/recommendations for international students: Required—TOEFL (minimum score 580 paper-based; 237 computer-based), IELTS (minimum score 7). *Application deadline:* For fall admission, 2/1 for domestic students. Application fee: $50. *Financial support:* In 2007–08, 2 teaching assistantships (averaging $9,000 per year) were awarded; research assistantships. Financial award application deadline: 2/1. *Faculty research:* Atlantic cultures, class analysis, gender and women's studies, religion, symbolism, development studies. *Unit head:* Dr. Tony Thomson, Head, 902-585-1494, Fax: 902-585-1769, E-mail: tony.thomson@acadiau.ca. *Application contact:* Karen Turner, Administrative Secretary, 902-585-1493, Fax: 902-585-1769, E-mail: karen.turner@acadiau.ca.

American University, College of Arts and Sciences, Department of Sociology, Program in Sociology, Washington, DC 20016-8001. Offers MA, Certificate. Part-time and evening/weekend programs available. *Students:* 18 full-time (16 women), 38 part-time (28 women); includes 26 minority (21 African Americans, 1 American Indian/Alaska Native, 1 Asian American or Pacific Islander, 3 Hispanic Americans), 4 international. Average age 36. In 2007, 14 master's awarded. *Degree requirements:* For master's, comprehensive exam, thesis or alternative, Tools of research. *Entrance requirements:* For master's, GRE; for Certificate, Bachelor's Degree. *Application deadline:* For fall admission, 2/1 priority date for domestic students. Applications are processed on a rolling basis. Application fee: $50. *Expenses:* Tuition: Full-time $19,998; part-time $1,111 per credit hour. Required fees: $380. Tuition and fees vary according to program. *Financial support:* In 2007–08, 11 students received support; fellowships, research assistantships, teaching assistantships, career-related internships or fieldwork, Federal Work-Study, institutionally sponsored loans, tuition waivers (full and partial), and unspecified assistantships available. Support available to part-time students. Financial award application deadline: 2/1. *Faculty research:* Gender, policy, race and ethnic development, macro/comparative international education.

The American University in Cairo, Graduate Studies and Research, School of Humanities and Social Sciences, Department of Sociology, Anthropology and Psychology, Cairo, Egypt. Offers sociology and anthropology (MA). *Degree requirements:* For master's, one foreign language, thesis. *Entrance requirements:* Additional exam requirements/recommendations for international students: Required—English entrance exam and/or TOEFL. Electronic applications accepted. *Faculty research:* Development, gender, sociopolitical economic formulations, social science indigenization, Arab world.

American University of Beirut, Graduate Programs, Faculty of Arts and Sciences, Beirut, Lebanon. Offers anthropology (MA); Arabic language and literature (MA); archaeology (MA); biology (MS); chemistry (MS); computer science (MS); economics (MA); education (MA); English language (MA); English literature (MA); environmental policy planning (MSES); financial economics (MAFE); geology (MS); history (MA); mathematics (MA, MS); Middle Eastern studies (MA); philosophy (MA); physics (MS); political studies (MA); psychology (MA); public administration (MA); sociology (MA); statistics (MA, MS). Part-time programs available. *Faculty:* 108 full-time (29 women), 5 part-time/adjunct (3 women). *Students:* 134 full-time (92 women), 228 part-time (167 women). Average age 25. 319 applicants, 67% accepted, 91 enrolled. In 2007, 144 degrees awarded. *Degree requirements:* For master's, one foreign language, comprehensive exam, thesis (for some programs). *Entrance requirements:* For master's, GRE, letter of recommendation. Additional exam requirements/recommendations for international students: Required—TOEFL (minimum score 600 paper-based; 250 computer-based; 100 iBT), IELTS (minimum score 8). *Application deadline:* For fall admission, 4/30 for domestic and international students; for spring admission, 11/1 for domestic and international students. Application fee: $50. *Expenses:* Tuition: Full-time $9,954; part-time $553 per credit. Tuition and fees vary according to course load and program. *Financial support:* In 2007–08, 28 students received support. Career-related internships or fieldwork, institutionally sponsored loans, scholarships/grants, health care benefits, and unspecified assistantships available. Financial award application deadline: 2/4; financial award applicants required to submit FAFSA. *Faculty research:* String theory and supergravity; computer graphics; algebra and number theory; popular Arabic literature; marine and freshwater biology; integrating science, math and technology. Total annual research expenditures: $132,270. *Unit head:* Khalil Bitar, Dean, 961-1374374 Ext. 3800, Fax: 961-1744461, E-mail: kmb@aub.edu.lb. *Application contact:* Dr. Salim Kanaan, Director, Admissions Office, 961-1350000 Ext. 2594, Fax: 961-1750775, E-mail: sk00@aub.edu.lb.

Arizona State University, Graduate College, College of Liberal Arts and Sciences, Division of Social Sciences, Department of Sociology, Tempe, AZ 85287. Offers demography and population studies (MA, PhD); sociology (MA, PhD). *Degree requirements:* For master's, thesis or alternative; for doctorate, thesis/dissertation. *Entrance requirements:* For master's and doctorate, GRE General Test.

Arkansas State University, Graduate School, College of Humanities and Social Sciences, Department of Criminology, Sociology, and Geography, Jonesboro, State University, AR 72467. Offers criminal justice (MA, Certificate); sociology (MA); sociology education (SCCT). Part-time programs available. *Faculty:* 7 full-time (4 women). *Students:* 16 full-time (11 women), 19 part-time (11 women); includes 14 minority (all African Americans) Average age 31. 16 applicants, 75% accepted, 12 enrolled. In 2007, 9 degrees awarded. *Degree requirements:* For master's, one foreign language, comprehensive exam, thesis or alternative; for other advanced degree, comprehensive exam. *Entrance requirements:* For master's, GRE General Test or MAT, appropriate bachelor's degree, official transcript; for other advanced degree, GRE General Test or MAT, interview, master's degree, official transcript. Additional exam requirements/recommendations for international students: Required—TOEFL (minimum score 213 computer-based). *Application deadline:* Applications are processed on a rolling basis. Application fee: $30 ($40 for international students). Electronic applications accepted. *Expenses:* Tuition, state resident: full-time $3,528; part-time $196 per hour. Tuition, nonresident: full-time $8,928; part-time $496 per hour. Required fees: $842; $44 per hour. $25 per term. Tuition and fees vary according to course load and program. *Financial support:* Career-related internships or fieldwork, scholarships/grants, and unspecified assistantships available. Financial award application deadline: 7/1; financial award applicants required to submit FAFSA. *Faculty research:* Land use—rural and recreational, resource management, climate change, peopling of the New World, gender, family, sexuality issues. *Unit head:* Dr. Anthony Troy Adams, Chair, 870-972-3705, Fax: 870-972-3694, E-mail: aadams@astate.edu.

Auburn University, Graduate School, Interdepartmental Programs, Department of Sociology, Anthropology, Criminology, and Social Work, Auburn University, AL 36849. Offers rural sociology (MS); sociology (MA, MS). Part-time programs available. *Faculty:* 15 full-time (5 women). *Students:* 21 full-time (13 women), 10 part-time (7 women); includes 3 minority (2 African Americans, 1 Asian American or Pacific Islander), 4 international. Average age 25. 15 applicants, 93% accepted, 8 enrolled. In 2007, 8 degrees awarded. *Degree requirements:* For master's, thesis, computer language (MS), foreign language (MA). *Entrance requirements:* For master's, GRE General Test. *Application deadline:* For fall admission, 7/7 for domestic students; for spring admission, 11/24 for domestic students. Applications are processed on a rolling basis. Application fee: $25 ($50 for international students). *Financial support:* Research assistantships, teaching assistantships available. Financial award application deadline: 3/15. *Unit head:* Dr. Kelly Alley, Interim Chair, 334-844-5049. *Application contact:* Dr. Joe Pittman, Interim Dean of the Graduate School, 334-844-4700.

Ball State University, Graduate School, College of Sciences and Humanities, Department of Sociology, Muncie, IN 47306-1099. Offers MA. *Faculty:* 10. *Students:* 10 full-time (6 women), 9 part-time (3 women); includes 2 minority (1 African American, 1 Hispanic American), 1 international. Average age 31. 13 applicants, 62% accepted, 8 enrolled. In 2007, 5 degrees awarded. *Entrance requirements:* For master's, GRE General Test. Application fee: $25 ($35 for international students). *Expenses:* Tuition, state resident: full-time $6,864. Tuition, nonresident: full-time $17,932. Required fees: $1,866. *Financial support:* In 2007–08, 4 teaching assistantships with full tuition reimbursements (averaging $7,957 per year) were awarded; research assistantships with full tuition reimbursements, career-related internships or fieldwork also available. Financial award application deadline: 3/1. *Faculty research:* Retention policies for secondary education, community mental health. *Unit head:* Roger Wojtkiewicz, Chairman, 765-285-5978, Fax: 765-285-8980, E-mail: rwojtkiew@gw.bsu.edu. *Application contact:* Dr. Ione DeOllos, Director of Graduate Programs, 765-285-5978, Fax: 765-285-8980.

Baylor University, Graduate School, College of Arts and Sciences, Department of Sociology and Anthropology, Waco, TX 76798. Offers applied sociology (PhD); sociology (MA). *Students:* 18 full-time (8 women); includes 1 minority (African American), 2 international. In 2007, 5 master's, 1 doctorate awarded. *Entrance requirements:* For master's and doctorate, GRE General Test. *Application deadline:* For fall admission, 8/1 for domestic students. Applications are processed on a rolling basis. Application fee: $25. *Financial support:* Research assistantships, teaching assistantships, career-related internships or fieldwork, Federal Work-Study, and institutionally sponsored loans available. *Faculty research:* Community studies, thanatology, sociology of education. *Unit head:* Dr. Tillman Rodabough, Graduate Program Director, 254-710-3811, Fax: 254-710-3809, E-mail: tillman_rodabough@baylor.edu. *Application contact:* Suzanne Keener, Administrative Assistant, 254-710-3588, Fax: 254-710-3870.

Boston College, Graduate School of Arts and Sciences, Department of Sociology, Chestnut Hill, MA 02467-3800. Offers MA, PhD, MBA/MA, MBA/PhD. Part-time programs available. *Students:* 54 full-time (34 women), 11 part-time (9 women); includes 5 minority (1 African American, 2 Asian Americans or Pacific Islanders, 2 Hispanic Americans), 12 international. 165 applicants, 41% accepted, 19 enrolled. In 2007, 11 master's, 2 doctorates awarded. Terminal master's awarded for partial completion of doctoral program. *Degree requirements:* For master's, thesis optional; for doctorate, thesis/dissertation. *Entrance requirements:* For master's and doctorate, GRE General Test. Additional exam requirements/recommendations for international students: Required—TOEFL (minimum score 590 paper-based; 250 computer-based; 91 iBT). *Application deadline:* For fall admission, 1/15 for domestic students. Application fee: $70. Electronic applications accepted. *Financial support:* Fellowships with full tuition reimbursements, research assistantships with full tuition reimbursements, teaching assistantships with full tuition reimbursements, Federal Work-Study available. Support available

Sociology

Boston College (continued)
to part-time students. Financial award application deadline: 3/1; financial award applicants required to submit FAFSA. *Faculty research:* Sociological theory, social economy, social psychology, political sociology, development modernization. *Unit head:* Dr. Juliet Schor, Chairperson, 617-552-4056. *Application contact:* Dr. Sarah Babb, Graduate Program Director, 617-552-2930, E-mail: sarab.babb@bc.edu.

Boston University, Graduate School of Arts and Sciences, Department of Sociology, Boston, MA 02215. Offers MA, PhD. *Students:* 22 full-time (16 women), 2 part-time (1 woman); includes 2 minority (1 African American, 1 Hispanic American), 8 international. Average age 32. 119 applicants, 31% accepted, 11 enrolled. In 2007, 2 master's, 4 doctorates awarded. Terminal master's awarded for partial completion of doctoral program. *Degree requirements:* For master's, one foreign language, comprehensive exam, thesis; for doctorate, one foreign language, comprehensive exam, thesis/dissertation. *Entrance requirements:* For master's, GRE General Test, sample of written work, 3 letters of recommendation; for doctorate, GRE General Test or MAT, sample of written work, 3 letters of recommendation. Additional exam requirements/recommendations for international students: Required—TOEFL (minimum score 550 paper-based; 213 computer-based). *Application deadline:* For fall admission, 1/15 for domestic and international students. Application fee: $70. *Expenses:* Tuition: Full-time $34,930; part-time $1,092 per credit. Tuition and fees vary according to class time, course level and program. *Financial support:* In 2007–08, 9 students received support, including 1 fellowship with full tuition reimbursement available (averaging $18,000 per year), 1 research assistantship with full tuition reimbursement available (averaging $16,500 per year), 4 teaching assistantships with full tuition reimbursements available (averaging $16,500 per year); career-related internships or fieldwork, Federal Work-Study, and scholarships/grants also available. Support available to part-time students. Financial award application deadline: 1/15; financial award applicants required to submit FAFSA. *Unit head:* Nancy Ammerman, Chairman, 617-358-2591, Fax: 617-353-4837, E-mail: nta@bu.edu. *Application contact:* Vivienne Pustell, Department Administrator, 617-353-2597, Fax: 617-353-4837, E-mail: vivienne@bu.edu.

Bowling Green State University, Graduate College, College of Arts and Sciences, Department of Sociology, Bowling Green, OH 43403. Offers demography and population studies (MA); social psychology (MA); sociology (PhD). Part-time programs available. *Faculty:* 21 full-time (11 women). *Students:* 40 full-time (27 women), 8 part-time (all women); includes 4 minority (3 African Americans, 1 Hispanic American), 6 international. Average age 30. 46 applicants, 85% accepted, 11 enrolled. In 2007, 8 master's, 3 doctorates awarded. *Degree requirements:* For master's, thesis or alternative; for doctorate, comprehensive exam, thesis/dissertation. *Entrance requirements:* For master's and doctorate, GRE General Test. Additional exam requirements/recommendations for international students: Required—TOEFL. *Application deadline:* For fall admission, 1/15 priority date for domestic students. Application fee: $30. Electronic applications accepted. *Financial support:* In 2007–08, 1 fellowship with full tuition reimbursement (averaging $16,598 per year), 33 research assistantships with full tuition reimbursements (averaging $12,064 per year), 1 teaching assistantship with full tuition reimbursement (averaging $13,278 per year) were awarded; career-related internships or fieldwork, Federal Work-Study, institutionally sponsored loans, and unspecified assistantships also available. Financial award applicants required to submit FAFSA. *Faculty research:* Applied demography, criminology and deviance, family studies, population studies, social psychology. *Unit head:* Dr. Gary Lee, Chair, 419-372-2292. *Application contact:* Dr. Steve Cernkovich, Graduate Coordinator, 419-372-2743.

Brandeis University, Graduate School of Arts and Sciences, Department of Sociology, Waltham, MA 02454-9110. Offers Near Eastern and Judaic studies and sociology (PhD); social policy and sociology (PhD); sociology (MA, PhD); sociology and women's and gender studies (MA). Part-time programs available. *Faculty:* 11 full-time (6 women). *Students:* 30 full-time (24 women); includes 1 minority (Asian American or Pacific Islander), 4 international. Average age 33. 76 applicants, 11% accepted, 5 enrolled. In 2007, 1 master's, 2 doctorates awarded. Terminal master's awarded for partial completion of doctoral program. *Degree requirements:* For master's, thesis; for doctorate, thesis/dissertation. *Entrance requirements:* For master's and doctorate, GRE, writing sample, resumé, letters of recommendation. Additional exam requirements/recommendations for international students: Required—TOEFL (minimum score 600 paper-based; 250 computer-based; 100 iBT), IELTS (minimum score 7). *Application deadline:* For fall admission, 1/15 for domestic and international students. Application fee: $55. Electronic applications accepted. *Financial support:* In 2007–08, 9 students received support, including 8 fellowships with tuition reimbursements available (averaging $16,500 per year), teaching assistantships with tuition reimbursements available (averaging $3,000 per year); scholarships/grants, health care benefits, and tuition waivers (full and partial) also available. Support available to part-time students. Financial award application deadline: 4/15; financial award applicants required to submit CSS PROFILE or FAFSA. *Faculty research:* Social theory and cultural studies; feminist sociology; political sociology; sociology of medicine, health and health care; comparative social structures. *Unit head:* Dr. David Cunningham, Co-Chair, Graduate Committee, 781-736-3300, Fax: 781-736-2653, E-mail: cunningham@brandeis.edu. *Application contact:* Elaine Brooks, Senior Department Associate for Graduate Studies, 781-736-2631, Fax: 781-736-2653, E-mail: brooks@brandeis.edu.

Brigham Young University, Graduate Studies, College of Family, Home, and Social Sciences, Department of Sociology, Provo, UT 84602-1001. Offers MS, PhD. *Faculty:* 19 full-time (5 women), 3 part-time/adjunct (2 women). *Students:* 18 full-time (9 women), 3 part-time; includes 3 minority (all Asian Americans or Pacific Islanders) Average age 32. 14 applicants, 71% accepted, 7 enrolled. In 2007, 5 master's, 1 doctorate awarded. Terminal master's awarded for partial completion of doctoral program. *Median time to degree:* Of those who began their doctoral program in fall 1999, 100% received their degree in 8 years or less. *Degree requirements:* For master's, thesis; for doctorate, comprehensive exam, thesis/dissertation, qualifying exam. *Entrance requirements:* For master's, GRE General Test, minimum GPA of 3.0 in last 60 hours, writing sample; for doctorate, GRE General Test, minimum GPA of 3.0 in last 60 hours, writing sample, master's degree in sociology or related field. Additional exam requirements/recommendations for international students: Required—TOEFL. *Application deadline:* For fall admission, 1/15 for domestic students. Application fee: $50. Electronic applications accepted. *Financial support:* In 2007–08, 18 students received support, including 9 research assistantships with partial tuition reimbursements available (averaging $14,000 per year), 9 teaching assistantships with partial tuition reimbursements available (averaging $14,000 per year); institutionally sponsored loans and unspecified assistantships also available. Financial award application deadline: 1/10. *Faculty research:* Demography, race and ethnicity, gender, rural and community, international development, comparative family. Total annual research expenditures: $45,252. *Unit head:* Dr. Renata Forste, Chair, 801-422-3146, Fax: 801-422-0625, E-mail: renata_forste@byu.edu. *Application contact:* Dr. Carol J. Ward, Graduate Coordinator, 801-422-3047, Fax: 801-422-0625, E-mail: carol.ward@byu.edu.

Brooklyn College of the City University of New York, Division of Graduate Studies, Department of Sociology, Brooklyn, NY 11210-2889. Offers MA, PhD. The department offers courses at Brooklyn College that are creditable towards the CUNY doctoral degree (with permission of the executive officer of the doctoral program). Part-time and evening/weekend programs available. *Students:* 4 full-time (3 women), 33 part-time (23 women); includes 27 minority (21 African Americans, 1 American Indian/Alaska Native, 3 Asian Americans or Pacific Islanders, 2 Hispanic Americans), 3 international. 21 applicants, 62% accepted, 7 enrolled. In 2007, 7 degrees awarded. *Degree requirements:* For master's, comprehensive exam or research essay. *Entrance requirements:* For master's, 12 upper-level credits in sociology, 2 letters of recommendation, essay. Additional exam requirements/recommendations for international students: Required—TOEFL. *Application deadline:* For fall admission, 3/1 priority date for domestic students, 2/1 priority date for international students; for spring admission, 11/1 priority date for domestic students, 10/1 priority date for international students. Applications are processed on a rolling basis. Application fee: $125. Electronic applications accepted. *Financial support:* Career-related internships or fieldwork, Federal Work-Study, institutionally sponsored loans, and scholarships/grants available. Support available to part-time students. Financial award application deadline: 5/1; financial award applicants required to submit FAFSA. *Faculty research:* Urbanization, religion, family, gender, research methods. *Unit head:* Dr. Kenneth Gould, Chairperson, 718-951-5314, E-mail: kgould@brooklyn.cuny.edu. *Application contact:* Hernan Sierra, Graduate Admissions Coordinator, 718-951-4536, Fax: 718-951-4506, E-mail: grads@brooklyn.cuny.edu.

Brown University, Graduate School, Department of Sociology, Program in Sociology, Providence, RI 02912. Offers AM, PhD. *Degree requirements:* For master's, thesis; for doctorate, thesis/dissertation, oral exam. *Entrance requirements:* For master's and doctorate, GRE General Test.

California State University, Bakersfield, Division of Graduate Studies, School of Humanities and Social Sciences, Program in Sociology, Bakersfield, CA 93311-1022. Offers MA.

California State University, Dominguez Hills, College of Natural and Behavioral Science, Program in Sociology, Carson, CA 90747-0001. Offers social research (Certificate); sociology (MA). Part-time and evening/weekend programs available. *Faculty:* 10 full-time, 7 part-time/adjunct. *Students:* 21 full-time (15 women), 36 part-time (29 women); includes 47 minority (36 African Americans, 11 Hispanic Americans). Average age 38. 25 applicants, 88% accepted, 17 enrolled. In 2007, 13 degrees awarded. *Degree requirements:* For master's, comprehensive exam, thesis. *Entrance requirements:* For master's and Certificate, minimum GPA of 2.85. *Application deadline:* For fall admission, 6/1 for domestic students. Application fee: $55. *Faculty research:* Community studies, social movements, criminology. *Unit head:* Dr. Sharon Linda Squires, Coordinator, 310-243-2598, E-mail: ssquires@csudh.edu.

California State University, East Bay, Academic Programs and Graduate Studies, College of Letters, Arts, and Social Sciences, Department of Sociology and Social Services, Hayward, CA 94542-3000. Offers sociology (MA). Part-time and evening/weekend programs available. *Faculty:* 3 full-time, 1 part-time/adjunct. *Students:* 3 full-time (2 women), 18 part-time (15 women); includes 6 minority (4 African Americans, 1 Asian American or Pacific Islander, 1 Hispanic American), 2 international. Average age 34. 15 applicants, 53% accepted, 4 enrolled. In 2007, 2 degrees awarded. *Degree requirements:* For master's, comprehensive exam, project or thesis. *Entrance requirements:* For master's, minimum GPA of 3.0. Additional exam requirements/recommendations for international students: Required—TOEFL (minimum score 550 paper-based; 213 computer-based). *Application deadline:* For fall admission, 5/31 for domestic students, 4/30 for international students; for winter admission, 9/30 for domestic and international students; for spring admission, 12/31 for domestic students, 11/30 for international students. Applications are processed on a rolling basis. Application fee: $55. Electronic applications accepted. *Expenses:* Required fees: $3,987; $851 per quarter. *Financial support:* Fellowships, teaching assistantships, career-related internships or fieldwork, Federal Work-Study, institutionally sponsored loans, and scholarships/grants available. Support available to part-time students. Financial award application deadline: 3/2. *Unit head:* Dr. Diane Beeson, Interim Chair, 510-885-3173, Fax: 510-885-2390, E-mail: diane.beeson@csueastbay.edu. *Application contact:* My Huynh, Graduate Prospect Specialist, 510-885-2989, Fax: 510-885-4059, E-mail: my.huynh@csueastbay.edu.

California State University, Fullerton, Graduate Studies, College of Humanities and Social Sciences, Department of Sociology, Fullerton, CA 92834-9480. Offers MA. Part-time programs available. *Students:* 20 full-time (18 women), 39 part-time (28 women); includes 24 minority (4 African Americans, 7 Asian Americans or Pacific Islanders, 13 Hispanic Americans), 5 international. Average age 31. 59 applicants, 51% accepted, 23 enrolled. In 2007, 21 degrees awarded. *Degree requirements:* For master's, thesis. *Entrance requirements:* For master's, minimum GPA of 3.0 in sociology, 2.5 in last 60 units. Application fee: $55. *Financial support:* Teaching assistantships, career-related internships or fieldwork, Federal Work-Study, institutionally sponsored loans, and scholarships/grants available. Support available to part-time students. Financial award application deadline: 3/1. *Faculty research:* Gerontology, wellness clinic. *Unit head:* Dr. Dennis Berg, Chair, 714-278-3531. *Application contact:* Dr. Rae Newton, Adviser, 714-278-3135.

California State University, Los Angeles, Graduate Studies, College of Natural and Social Sciences, Department of Sociology, Los Angeles, CA 90032-8530. Offers MA. Part-time and evening/weekend programs available. *Faculty:* 3 full-time (1 woman), 1 part-time/adjunct (0 women). *Students:* 23 full-time (16 women), 40 part-time (28 women); includes 36 minority (9 African Americans, 10 Asian Americans or Pacific Islanders, 17 Hispanic Americans), 12 international. Average age 32. In 2007, 7 degrees awarded. *Degree requirements:* For master's, comprehensive exam or thesis. *Entrance requirements:* For master's, minimum GPA of 2.5 in last 90 units of course work. Additional exam requirements/recommendations for international students: Required—TOEFL. *Application deadline:* For fall admission, 6/30 for domestic students; for spring admission, 2/1 for domestic students. Applications are processed on a rolling basis. Application fee: $55. *Financial support:* Federal Work-Study available. Support available to part-time students. Financial award application deadline: 3/1. *Faculty research:* Criminal and delinquent careers, family and sex, ethnic minorities, demographic trends, human socialization and aging. *Unit head:* Dr. Steven L. Gordon, Chair, 323-343-2200, Fax: 323-343-5155, E-mail: sgordon@calstatela.edu.

California State University, Northridge, Graduate Studies, College of Social and Behavioral Sciences, Department of Sociology, Northridge, CA 91330. Offers MA. *Accreditation:* CSWE. Part-time and evening/weekend programs available. *Faculty:* 18 full-time (7 women), 29 part-time/adjunct (15 women). *Students:* 92 full-time (78 women), 37 part-time (31 women); includes 66 minority (10 African Americans, 2 American Indian/Alaska Native, 12 Asian Americans or Pacific Islanders, 42 Hispanic Americans), 5 international. Average age 29. 155 applicants, 65% accepted, 80 enrolled. In 2007, 32 degrees awarded. *Degree requirements:* For master's, thesis or alternative. *Entrance requirements:* For master's, GRE General Test. Additional exam requirements/recommendations for international students: Required—TOEFL. *Application deadline:* For fall admission, 3/27 for domestic students; for spring admission, 10/17 for domestic students. Application fee: $55. *Financial support:* Career-related internships or fieldwork, Federal Work-Study, and institutionally sponsored loans available. Support available to part-time students. Financial award application deadline: 3/1. *Faculty research:* Crime and corrections, relationships between adult children and parents. *Unit head:* Dr. Herman DeBose, Chair, 818-677-3591. *Application contact:* Dr. David Boyns, Graduate Advisor, 818-677-6803.

California State University, Sacramento, Graduate Studies, College of Social Sciences and Interdisciplinary Studies, Department of Sociology, Sacramento, CA 95819-6048. Offers MA. Part-time programs available. *Students:* 2 full-time (both women), 24 part-time (14 women); includes 8 minority (3 African Americans, 1 Asian American or Pacific Islander, 4 Hispanic Americans). Average age 28. 51 applicants, 43% accepted, 12 enrolled. *Degree requirements:* For master's, thesis or alternative, writing proficiency exam. *Entrance requirements:* For master's, minimum GPA of 3.0 during previous 2 years. Additional exam requirements/recommendations for international students: Required—TOEFL. *Application deadline:* Applications are processed on a rolling basis. Application fee: $55. Electronic applications accepted. *Expenses:* Tuition, state resident: full-time $3,414. Tuition, nonresident: full-time $13,584; part-time $339 per unit. Required fees: $786; $393 per semester. *Financial support:* Career-related internships or fieldwork and Federal Work-Study available. Support available to part-time students. Financial award application deadline: 3/1. *Unit head:* Dr. Judson Landis, Chair, 916-278-6522, Fax: 916-278-6522.

California State University, San Marcos, College of Arts and Sciences, Program in Sociological Practice, San Marcos, CA 92096-0001. Offers MA. *Faculty:* 17 full-time (13 women), 13 part-time/adjunct (10 women). *Students:* 21 full-time (15 women), 27 part-time (21 women); includes 23 minority (6 African Americans, 4 Asian Americans or Pacific Islanders, 13 Hispanic Americans), 2 international. Average age 30. *Degree requirements:* For master's, thesis. *Entrance requirements:* For master's, GRE General Test (recommended), minimum GPA of 3.0 in last 60 units of undergraduate study, minimum GPA of 3.0 in upper division sociology courses. *Application deadline:* For fall admission, 3/15 priority date for domestic students. Applications are processed on a rolling basis. Application fee: $55. *Financial support:* Research assistantships, teaching assistantships, career-related internships or fieldwork, Federal Work-Study, institutionally sponsored loans, scholarships/grants, traineeships, and unspecified assistantships available. Support available to part-time students. *Faculty research:* Organized crime, juvenile detention, counseling services for minorities, mental-health facilities. *Unit head:* Dr. Linda L. Shaw, Department Chair, 760-750-8026, Fax: 760-760-3551. *Application contact:* Toni Shaffer, Administrative Coordinator, 760-750-4117, E-mail: tshaffer@csusm.edu.

Carleton University, Faculty of Graduate Studies, Faculty of Arts and Social Sciences, Department of Sociology and Anthropology, Program in Sociology, Ottawa, ON K1S 5B6, Canada. Offers MA, PhD. *Degree requirements:* For master's, thesis optional; for doctorate, one foreign language, comprehensive exam, thesis/dissertation. *Entrance requirements:* For master's, honors degree; for doctorate, master's degree. Additional exam requirements/recommendations for international students: Required—TOEFL. Application fee: $77. *Faculty research:* Canadian society and policy, inequality and mobility, race/ethnic relations, cultural studies, gender studies. *Unit head:* Janet Siltanen, Program Coordinator, 613-520-2600 Ext. 2582, Fax: 613-520-4062, E-mail: soc-anthro@carleton.ca.

Case Western Reserve University, School of Graduate Studies, Department of Sociology, Cleveland, OH 44106. Offers PhD. *Faculty:* 9 full-time (5 women). *Students:* 10 full-time (7 women), 22 part-time (15 women); includes 3 minority (2 African Americans, 1 Asian American or Pacific Islander), 1 international. Average age 30. 7 applicants, 71% accepted, 4 enrolled. In 2007, 3 doctorates awarded. Terminal master's awarded for partial completion of doctoral program. *Degree requirements:* For doctorate, thesis/dissertation. *Application deadline:* For fall admission, 2/1 priority date for domestic students. Applications are processed on a rolling basis. Application fee: $50. Electronic applications accepted. *Financial support:* Fellowships, research assistantships, teaching assistantships, career-related internships or fieldwork, institutionally sponsored loans, and tuition waivers (full and partial) available. Financial award application deadline: 2/1. *Faculty research:* Sociology of aging and the life course, medical sociology, research methods, family sociology. *Unit head:* Dr. Dale Dannefer, Chair, 216-368-2700, Fax: 216-368-2676, E-mail: dale.dannefer@case.edu. *Application contact:* Brian Gran, Graduate Director, 216-368-2700, Fax: 216-368-2676, E-mail: brian.gran@case.edu.

The Catholic University of America, School of Arts and Sciences, Department of Sociology, Washington, DC 20064. Offers MA, PhD. Part-time and evening/weekend programs available. *Faculty:* 3 full-time (1 woman), 5 part-time/adjunct (2 women). *Students:* 3 full-time (all women), 7 part-time (4 women); includes 1 minority (Asian American or Pacific Islander), 3 international. Average age 37. 11 applicants, 64% accepted, 2 enrolled. In 2007, 1 degree awarded. *Degree requirements:* For master's, comprehensive exam, thesis or alternative; for doctorate, one foreign language, comprehensive exam, thesis/dissertation. *Entrance requirements:* For master's and doctorate, GRE General Test, 3 letters of recommendation. Additional exam requirements/recommendations for international students: Required—TOEFL (minimum score 580 paper-based; 237 computer-based). *Application deadline:* For fall admission, 2/1 priority date for domestic students; for spring admission, 11/15 priority date for domestic students. Applications are processed on a rolling basis. Application fee: $55. Electronic applications accepted. *Financial support:* Research assistantships, teaching assistantships, career-related internships or fieldwork, Federal Work-Study, scholarships/grants, tuition waivers (full and partial), and unspecified assistantships available. Support available to part-time students. Financial award application deadline: 2/1; financial award applicants required to submit FAFSA. *Faculty research:* Social movements, education, gender, religion, demography. *Unit head:* Dr. Bronislaw Misztal, Chair, 202-319-5445, Fax: 202-319-4980, E-mail: misztal@cua.edu.

Central European University, Graduate Studies, School of Social Sciences and Humanities, Budapest, Hungary. Offers economics (MA, PhD); gender studies (MA, PhD); international relations and European studies (MA, PhD); mathematics and its applications (MS, PhD); medieval studies (MA, PhD); nationalism studies (MA, PhD); philosophy (MA, PhD); political science (MA, PhD); public policy (MA, PhD); sociology and social anthropology (MA, PhD). *Faculty:* 75 full-time (25 women), 46 part-time/adjunct (10 women). *Students:* 625 full-time (355 women). Average age 26. 2,500 applicants, 31% accepted, 540 enrolled. In 2007, 325 master's, 20 doctorates awarded. Terminal master's awarded for partial completion of doctoral program. *Degree requirements:* For master's, one foreign language, thesis; for doctorate, one foreign language, comprehensive exam, thesis/dissertation. *Entrance requirements:* For master's, CEU subject tests, interview; for doctorate, GRE, CEU subject test, interview. Additional exam requirements/recommendations for international students: Required—TOEFL (minimum score 570 paper-based; 230 computer-based). *Application deadline:* For fall admission, 1/15 priority date for domestic and international students. Application fee: $0. Electronic applications accepted. Tuition charges are reported in euros. *Expenses:* Tuition: Full-time 10,000 euros; part-time 315 euros per credit. *Financial support:* In 2007–08, 402 students received support, including 350 fellowships with full and partial tuition reimbursements available (averaging $5,000 per year); career-related internships or fieldwork, institutionally sponsored loans, and scholarships/grants also available. Financial award application deadline: 1/5. *Faculty research:* Civil society, fiscal decentralization, party politics, political philosophy (especially Liberalism, theory of Democracy). Total annual research expenditures: $35,000. *Unit head:* Dr. Howard Michael Robinson, Provost, 361-327-3003, Fax: 361-327-3211, E-mail: robinson@ceu.hu. *Application contact:* Zsuzsanna Jászberenyi, Admissions Officer, 361-327-3009, Fax: 361-327-3211, E-mail: admissions@ceu.hu.

See Close-Up on page 447.

Central Michigan University, College of Graduate Studies, College of Humanities and Social and Behavioral Sciences, Department of Sociology, Anthropology and Social Work, Mount Pleasant, MI 48859. Offers social and criminal justice (MA); sociology (MA). *Degree requirements:* For master's, thesis or alternative. *Entrance requirements:* For master's, 20 hours of course work in sociology, minimum GPA of 3.0. *Faculty research:* Sociological theory, race concept, environmental justice, cultural anthropology.

City College of the City University of New York, Graduate School, College of Liberal Arts and Science, Division of Social Science, Department of Sociology, New York, NY 10031-9198. Offers MA. *Students:* 18 applicants, 78% accepted, 10 enrolled. In 2007, 3 degrees awarded. *Degree requirements:* For master's, one foreign language, comprehensive exam, thesis. *Entrance requirements:* For master's, GRE, minimum B average in undergraduate course work. Additional exam requirements/recommendations for international students: Required—TOEFL (minimum score 500 paper-based; 173 computer-based). *Application deadline:* For fall admission, 5/1 for domestic students; for spring admission, 11/1 for domestic students. Application fee: $125. *Financial support:* Fellowships available. *Faculty research:* Urban sociology, criminology and deviance, race and ethnicity. *Unit head:* Gabriel Haslip-Viera, Chairman, 212-650-6124. *Application contact:* Ibtihaj Arafat, Adviser, 212-650-5846, E-mail: iarafat@ccny.cuny.edu.

Clark Atlanta University, School of Arts and Sciences, Department of Sociology, Atlanta, GA 30314. Offers MA. Part-time programs available. *Faculty:* 2 part-time/adjunct (1 woman). *Students:* 3 full-time (all women), 3 part-time (all women); all minorities (all African Americans) Average age 28. 2 applicants, 50% accepted, 1 enrolled. In 2007, 4 degrees awarded. *Degree requirements:* For master's, one foreign language, thesis. *Entrance requirements:* For master's, GRE General Test, minimum GPA of 2.5. Additional exam requirements/recommendations for international students: Required—TOEFL (minimum score 500 paper-based; 173 computer-based). *Application deadline:* For fall admission, 4/1 for domestic and international students; for spring admission, 11/1 for domestic and international students. Applications are processed on a rolling basis. Application fee: $40 ($55 for international students). Electronic applications accepted. *Expenses:* Tuition: Full-time $11,664; part-time $648 per credit hour. Required fees: $550; $275 per semester. *Financial support:* Fellowships available. Financial award application deadline: 4/30; financial award applicants required to submit FAFSA. *Faculty research:* Gerontology, geriatric education. *Unit head:* Dr. Komenduri Murty, Chairperson, 404-880-6657, E-mail: kmurty@cau.edu. *Application contact:* Michelle Clark-Davis, Graduate Program Admissions, 404-880-8709, E-mail: mdowis@cau.edu.

Clemson University, Graduate School, College of Business and Behavioral Science, Department of Sociology and Anthropology, Clemson, SC 29634. Offers applied sociology (MS). Part-time programs available. *Faculty:* 11 full-time (6 women). *Students:* 13 full-time (7 women), 7 part-time (5 women); includes 2 minority (1 African American, 1 Asian American or Pacific Islander), 4 international. 11 applicants, 73% accepted, 7 enrolled. In 2007, 10 degrees awarded. *Degree requirements:* For master's, thesis. *Entrance requirements:* For master's, GRE General Test, minimum GPA of 3.0. Additional exam requirements/recommendations for international students: Required—TOEFL. *Application deadline:* For fall admission, 3/15 priority date for domestic students. Application fee: $55. *Financial support:* In 2007–08, 1 research assistantship (averaging $3,600 per year), 11 teaching assistantships (averaging $10,900 per year) were awarded; fellowships, career-related internships or fieldwork, Federal Work-Study, and institutionally sponsored loans also available. Financial award application deadline: 3/15; financial award applicants required to submit FAFSA. *Faculty research:* Organizational and industrial sociology, inequality, sexual abuse and police-community relations, homelessness, emotions. *Unit head:* Dr. Kinly Sturkie, Chair, 864-656-3820, E-mail: dkstr@clemson.edu. *Application contact:* Dr. Catherine Mobley, Coordinator, 864-656-3815, Fax: 864-656-1252, E-mail: camoble@clemson.edu.

Cleveland State University, College of Graduate Studies, College of Liberal Arts and Social Sciences, Department of Sociology, Cleveland, OH 44115. Offers MA. Part-time and evening/weekend programs available. *Faculty:* 13 full-time (7 women). *Students:* 12 full-time (all women), 28 part-time (18 women); includes 12 minority (all African Americans) Average age 33. 56 applicants, 48% accepted, 22 enrolled. In 2007, 4 degrees awarded. *Entrance requirements:* For master's, minimum GPA of 3.0. Additional exam requirements/recommendations for international students: Required—TOEFL (minimum score 525 paper-based; 197 computer-based). *Application deadline:* For fall admission, 7/15 priority date for domestic students, 1/15 priority date for international students; for spring admission, 12/1 priority date for domestic students, 9/15 priority date for international students. Applications are processed on a rolling basis. Application fee: $30. Electronic applications accepted. *Financial support:* Scholarships/grants, tuition waivers (partial), and unspecified assistantships available. Financial award application deadline: 7/15. *Faculty research:* Criminology, research methods, theory, symbolic interaction. Total annual research expenditures: $45,000. *Unit head:* Dr. Sarah H. Matthews, Chair, 216-687-4500, Fax: 216-687-9314, E-mail: s.matthews@csuohio.edu.

Colorado State University, Graduate School, College of Liberal Arts, Department of Sociology, Fort Collins, CO 80523-0015. Offers MA, PhD. *Faculty:* 16 full-time (4 women). *Students:* 18 full-time (9 women), 20 part-time (12 women); includes 1 minority (Asian American or Pacific Islander), 1 international. Average age 33. 51 applicants, 33% accepted, 11 enrolled. In 2007, 7 master's, 4 doctorates awarded. *Degree requirements:* For master's, thesis optional; for doctorate, comprehensive exam, thesis/dissertation. *Entrance requirements:* For master's, GRE General Test, minimum GPA of 3.0; BA coursework in sociology; for doctorate, GRE General Test, minimum GPA of 3.0; BA, MA coursework in sociology. Additional exam requirements/recommendations for international students: Required—TOEFL (minimum score 550 paper-based; 220 computer-based). *Application deadline:* For fall admission, 1/15 priority date for domestic students. Applications are processed on a rolling basis. Application fee: $50. Electronic applications accepted. *Expenses:* Tuition, state resident: full-time $4,887; part-time $272 per credit. Tuition, nonresident: full-time $16,425; part-time $913 per credit. Required fees: $1,379; $75 per credit. *Financial support:* In 2007–08, 2 research assistantships (averaging $15,304 per year), 18 teaching assistantships (averaging $12,640 per year) were awarded; career-related internships or fieldwork, Federal Work-Study, institutionally sponsored loans, scholarships/grants, traineeships, and unspecified assistantships also available. Financial award application deadline: 3/1; financial award applicants required to submit FAFSA. *Faculty research:* Sociology policy analysis, environmental impact, criminology, community development, rural and natural resources. Total annual research expenditures: $52,140. *Unit head:* Dr. Jack Brouillette, Chairman, 970-491-6044, Fax: 970-491-2191, E-mail: jack.brouillette@colostate.edu. *Application contact:* Betty Burkett, Administrative Assistant, 970-491-6045, Fax: 970-491-2191, E-mail: elizabeth.burkett@colostate.edu.

Columbia University, Graduate School of Arts and Sciences, Division of Social Sciences, Department of Sociology, New York, NY 10027. Offers M Phil, MA, PhD, JD/MA, JD/PhD. *Faculty:* 24 full-time, 2 part-time/adjunct. *Students:* 89 full-time (48 women), 17 part-time (10 women). Average age 33. 238 applicants, 24% accepted. In 2007, 13 master's, 4 doctorates awarded. *Degree requirements:* For master's, 2 research papers; for doctorate, one foreign language, thesis/dissertation. *Entrance requirements:* For master's and doctorate, GRE General Test. Additional exam requirements/recommendations for international students: Required—TOEFL. Application fee: $90. *Expenses:* Tuition: Part-time $1,452 per credit. Required fees: $152 per term. One-time fee: $75 part-time. Full-time tuition and fees vary according to course level, course load, degree level and program. *Financial support:* Fellowships, teaching assistantships, Federal Work-Study and institutionally sponsored loans available. Support available to part-time students. Financial award application deadline: 1/5; financial award applicants required to submit FAFSA. *Faculty research:* Urban and political studies, sociology of knowledge, organizations. *Unit head:* Thomas DiPrete, Chair, 212-854-5826, Fax: 212-854-8925, E-mail: tad61@columbia.edu.

Concordia University, School of Graduate Studies, Faculty of Arts and Science, Department of Sociology and Anthropology, Montréal, QC H3G 1M8, Canada. Offers social and cultural anthropology (MA); sociology (MA). *Degree requirements:* For master's, comprehensive exam or thesis. *Entrance requirements:* For master's, honors degree in sociology or equivalent. *Faculty research:* Community and ethnic relations, popular culture, regional development in Canada, industrial and social movements, social problems and policies.

Cornell University, Graduate School, Graduate Fields of Agriculture and Life Sciences, Field of Development Sociology, Ithaca, NY 14853-0001. Offers community and regional society (MS); community and regional sociology (MPS, PhD); methods of social research (MPS, MS, PhD); population and development (MPS, MS, PhD); rural and environmental sociology (MPS, MS, PhD); state, economy, and society (MPS, MS, PhD). *Faculty:* 26 full-time (6 women). *Students:* 45 full-time (31 women); includes 5 minority (1 American Indian/Alaska Native, 2 Asian Americans or Pacific Islanders, 2 Hispanic Americans), 17 international. Average age 33. 49 applicants, 18% accepted, 3 enrolled. In 2007, 12 master's, 1 doctorate awarded. *Degree requirements:* For doctorate, comprehensive exam, thesis/dissertation. *Entrance requirements:* For master's and doctorate, GRE General Test, 3 letters of recommendation. Additional exam requirements/recommendations for international students: Required—TOEFL (minimum score 550 paper-based; 213 computer-based; 77 iBT). *Application deadline:* For fall admission, 1/15 priority date for domestic students. Application fee: $60. Electronic applications accepted. *Financial support:* In 2007–08, 32 students received support, including 9 fellowships with full tuition reimbursements available, 12 research assistantships with full tuition reimbursements available, 11 teaching assistantships with full tuition reimbursements available; institutionally sponsored loans, scholarships/grants, health care benefits, tuition waivers (full and partial), and unspecified assistantships also available. Financial award applicants required to submit FAFSA. *Faculty research:* Demography (population and development), environmental sociology, international and rural community development, political economy and ecology, sustainable agriculture. *Unit head:* Director of Graduate Studies, 607-255-3092, Fax: 607-254-2896. *Application contact:* Graduate Field Assistant, 607-255-3092, Fax: 607-254-2896, E-mail: devsoc@cornell.edu.

Cornell University, Graduate School, Graduate Fields of Arts and Sciences, Field of Sociology, Ithaca, NY 14853-0001. Offers economy and society (MA, PhD); gender and life course (MA, PhD); methodology (MA, PhD); organizations (MA, PhD); policy analysis (MA, PhD); political sociology/social movements (MA, PhD); racial and ethnic relations (MA, PhD); social networks (MA, PhD); social psychology (MA, PhD); social stratification (MA, PhD). *Faculty:* 37 full-

Cornell University (continued)

time (12 women). *Students:* 46 full-time (20 women); includes 10 minority (2 African Americans, 6 Asian Americans or Pacific Islanders, 2 Hispanic Americans), 10 international. Average age 30. 149 applicants, 7% accepted, 5 enrolled. In 2007, 4 master's, 6 doctorates awarded. Terminal master's awarded for partial completion of doctoral program. *Degree requirements:* For master's, thesis; for doctorate, thesis/dissertation, 1 year of teaching experience. *Entrance requirements:* For master's and doctorate, GRE General Test, 2 letters of recommendation, writing sample. Additional exam requirements/recommendations for international students: Required—TOEFL (minimum score 550 paper-based; 213 computer-based; 77 iBT). *Application deadline:* For fall admission, 1/15 for domestic students. Application fee: $70. Electronic applications accepted. *Financial support:* In 2007–08, 40 students received support, including 16 fellowships with full tuition reimbursements available, 8 research assistantships with full tuition reimbursements available, 16 teaching assistantships with full tuition reimbursements available; institutionally sponsored loans, scholarships/grants, health care benefits, tuition waivers (full and partial), and unspecified assistantships also available. Financial award applicants required to submit FAFSA. *Faculty research:* Comparative societal analysis, work and family, simulations, social class and mobility, racial segregation and inequality. *Unit head:* Director of Graduate Studies, 607-255-4266. *Application contact:* Graduate Field Assistant, 607-255-4266, E-mail: sociology@cornell.edu.

Dalhousie University, Faculty of Arts and Social Science, Department of Sociology and Social Anthropology, Halifax, NS B3H 4R2, Canada. Offers social anthropology (MA, PhD); sociology (MA, PhD). Part-time programs available. *Faculty:* 18 full-time, 6 part-time/adjunct. *Students:* 13 full-time (8 women), 4 part-time (all women). In 2007, 8 degrees awarded. *Degree requirements:* For master's, thesis; for doctorate, one foreign language, thesis/dissertation. *Entrance requirements:* Additional exam requirements/recommendations for international students: Required—TOEFL. *Application deadline:* For fall admission, 6/1 for domestic students. Applications are processed on a rolling basis. Application fee: $60. *Financial support:* In 2007–08, 1 research assistantship, 17 teaching assistantships were awarded; fellowships also available. Financial award application deadline: 3/1. *Faculty research:* Social inequality and social injustice; work, industry, and development; (regional and international perspectives); health and illness. *Unit head:* Dr. Christopher Murphy, Chair, 902-494-6593, Fax: 902-494-2897. *Application contact:* Pauline Gardiner Barber, Graduate Coordinator, 902-494-6593, Fax: 902-494-2897, E-mail: sosagrad@is.dal.ca.

DePaul University, College of Liberal Arts and Sciences, Department of Sociology, Chicago, IL 60604-2287. Offers MA. Part-time and evening/weekend programs available. *Faculty:* 21 full-time (12 women), 4 part-time/adjunct (2 women). *Students:* 48 full-time (31 women), 49 part-time (30 women); includes 42 minority (24 African Americans, 1 American Indian/Alaska Native, 4 Asian Americans or Pacific Islanders, 13 Hispanic Americans), 1 international. Average age 28. 44 applicants, 84% accepted, 30 enrolled. In 2007, 17 master's awarded. *Degree requirements:* For master's, thesis or alternative, essay, research project. *Entrance requirements:* Additional exam requirements/recommendations for international students: Required—TOEFL. *Application deadline:* For fall admission, 8/25 priority date for domestic students; for winter admission, 12/15 priority date for domestic students; for spring admission, 3/15 priority date for domestic students. Applications are processed on a rolling basis. Application fee: $25. Electronic applications accepted. *Financial support:* In 2007–08, 8 students received support, including 1 research assistantship with full tuition reimbursement available (averaging $7,000 per year); career-related internships or fieldwork, tuition waivers (partial), and tuition remissions also available. Financial award application deadline: 6/15. *Faculty research:* Law and society, urban sociology, race/ethnicity, health, social inequality. *Unit head:* Dr. Roberta Garner, Chairperson, 773-325-7823, Fax: 773-325-7821, E-mail: rgarner@depaul.edu. *Application contact:* Dr. Shu-Ju Ada Cheng, Graduate Program Director, 773-325-4856, Fax: 773-325-7821, E-mail: scheng1@depaul.edu.

Drake University, School of Education, Department of Teaching and Learning, Program in Secondary Education, Des Moines, IA 50311-4516. Offers art (MAT); biology (MAT); business (MAT); chemistry (MAT); English (MAT); general science (MAT); history-American (MAT); history-world (MAT); journalism (MAT); mathematics (MAT); physical science (MAT); physics (MAT); sociology (MAT); speech (MAT); speech communication (MAT); theatre (MAT). Part-time programs available. *Faculty:* 10 full-time (3 women), 28 part-time/adjunct (16 women). *Students:* 13 full-time (7 women), 33 part-time (20 women). 41 applicants, 56% accepted. In 2007, 12 degrees awarded. *Degree requirements:* For master's, comprehensive exam, thesis (for some programs), internships (for some programs). *Entrance requirements:* For master's, GRE General Test, MAT, or Drake Writing Assessment, resumé, 2 letters of recommendation. Additional exam requirements/recommendations for international students: Required—TOEFL (minimum score 550 paper-based; 213 computer-based). *Application deadline:* For fall admission, 7/1 priority date for domestic students, 6/1 priority date for international students; for spring admission, 11/1 priority date for domestic students, 10/1 priority date for international students. Applications are processed on a rolling basis. Application fee: $25. Electronic applications accepted. *Expenses:* Tuition: Full-time $26,030; part-time $370 per credit hour. Required fees: $406; $40 per semester. Tuition and fees vary according to program. *Financial support:* Career-related internships or fieldwork and unspecified assistantships available. Support available to part-time students. *Faculty research:* Counseling and rehabilitation, behavioral supports, inquiry-based science methods, teacher quality enhancement. Total annual research expenditures: $1.5 million. *Application contact:* Ann J. Martin, Graduate Coordinator, 515-271-2034, Fax: 515-271-2831, E-mail: ann.martin@drake.edu.

Duke University, Graduate School, Department of Sociology, Durham, NC 27708. Offers AM, PhD. *Faculty:* 20 full-time. *Students:* 49 full-time (29 women); includes 7 minority (3 African Americans, 4 Hispanic Americans), 9 international. 109 applicants, 16% accepted, 9 enrolled. In 2007, 5 master's, 3 doctorates awarded. Terminal master's awarded for partial completion of doctoral program. *Degree requirements:* For doctorate, thesis/dissertation. *Entrance requirements:* For master's and doctorate, GRE General Test. Additional exam requirements/recommendations for international students: Required—TOEFL (minimum score 550 paper-based; 213 computer-based; 83 iBT), IELTS (minimum score 7). *Application deadline:* For fall admission, 12/15 priority date for domestic and international students. Application fee: $75. Electronic applications accepted. *Financial support:* Fellowships, research assistantships, teaching assistantships, Federal Work-Study available. Financial award application deadline: 12/31. *Unit head:* John Wilson, Director of Graduate Studies, 919-660-5617, Fax: 919-660-5623, E-mail: cpark@soc.duke.edu.

East Carolina University, Graduate School, Thomas Harriot College of Arts and Sciences, Department of Sociology, Greenville, NC 27858-4353. Offers MA. Part-time and evening/weekend programs available. *Faculty:* 20 full-time (5 women). *Students:* 8 full-time (4 women), 8 part-time (3 women); includes 6 minority (5 African Americans, 1 Asian American or Pacific Islander), 2 international. Average age 27. 2 applicants, 50% accepted, 1 enrolled. In 2007, 4 degrees awarded. *Degree requirements:* For master's, one foreign language, comprehensive exam, thesis. *Entrance requirements:* For master's, GRE General Test. Additional exam requirements/recommendations for international students: Required—TOEFL. *Application deadline:* For fall admission, 6/1 priority date for domestic students; for spring admission, 10/15 for domestic students. Applications are processed on a rolling basis. Application fee: $50. *Financial support:* Fellowships with partial tuition reimbursements, research assistantships with partial tuition reimbursements, teaching assistantships with partial tuition reimbursements, Federal Work-Study available. Support available to part-time students. Financial award application deadline: 6/1. *Unit head:* Dr. Lee Maril, Chair, 252-328-6883, Fax: 252-328-4837, E-mail: marilr@ecu.edu.

Eastern Michigan University, Graduate School, College of Arts and Sciences, Department of Sociology, Anthropology and Criminology, Program in Sociology, Ypsilanti, MI 48197. Offers schools, society and violence (MA); sociology (MA); sociology—family specialty (MA). *Students:* 4 full-time (2 women), 25 part-time (18 women); includes 11 minority (6 African Americans, 1 American Indian/Alaska Native, 3 Asian Americans or Pacific Islanders, 1 Hispanic American), 1 international. Average age 30. In 2007, 7 degrees awarded. Application fee: $35. *Expenses:* Tuition, state resident: full-time $8,952; part-time $373 per credit hour. Tuition, nonresident: full-time $17,634; part-time $735 per credit hour. Required fees: $896; $34 per credit hour. Tuition and fees vary according to course level, degree level and program. *Application contact:* Dr. Robert Orrange, Advisor, 734-487-0012, Fax: 734-487-9666, E-mail: rorrange@emich.edu.

East Tennessee State University, School of Graduate Studies, College of Arts and Sciences, Department of Sociology and Anthropology, Johnson City, TN 37614. Offers applied sociology (MA); general sociology (MA). Part-time and evening/weekend programs available. *Degree requirements:* For master's, comprehensive exam, thesis or alternative, internship. *Entrance requirements:* For master's, GRE General Test, minimum GPA of 3.0 in major. Additional exam requirements/recommendations for international students: Required—TOEFL (minimum score 550 paper-based; 213 computer-based). *Faculty research:* Biosociology and sex differences, political change in Latin America, medical beliefs and practices in southern Appalachia, Scottish-Irish traditions and Appalachia culture.

Emory University, Graduate School of Arts and Sciences, Department of Sociology, Atlanta, GA 30322-1100. Offers MA, PhD. Terminal master's awarded for partial completion of doctoral program. *Degree requirements:* For master's, thesis optional; for doctorate, comprehensive exam, thesis/dissertation, 2 preliminary exams, research paper, paper presentation. *Entrance requirements:* For doctorate, GRE General Test, minimum GPA of 3.0. Additional exam requirements/recommendations for international students: Required—TOEFL. Electronic applications accepted. *Faculty research:* Political economy and global analysis, culture, social psychology, criminology, stratification.

See Close-Up on page 1705.

Fayetteville State University, Graduate School, Program in Sociology, Fayetteville, NC 28301-4298. Offers MA. Part-time and evening/weekend programs available. *Faculty:* 7 full-time (2 women). *Students:* 3 full-time (all women), 12 part-time (all women); includes 11 minority (10 African Americans, 1 Asian American or Pacific Islander). Average age 35. 2 applicants, 100% accepted, 2 enrolled. In 2007, 6 degrees awarded. *Degree requirements:* For master's, comprehensive exam, internship. *Application deadline:* For fall admission, 7/1 for domestic students; for spring admission, 12/1 for domestic students. Applications are processed on a rolling basis. Application fee: $25. Electronic applications accepted. *Expenses:* Tuition, state resident: full-time $2,118; part-time $265 per credit hour. Tuition, nonresident: full-time $11,708; part-time $1,464 per credit hour. Required fees: $1,218; $152 per credit hour. *Unit head:* Dr. Samuel Adu-Mireku, Chairperson, 910-672-1122, E-mail: sadu-mireku@uncfsu.edu.

Fisk University, Graduate Programs, Department of Sociology, Nashville, TN 37208-3051. Offers general sociology (MA). Part-time programs available. *Degree requirements:* For master's, comprehensive exam, thesis. *Entrance requirements:* For master's, GRE General Test, GRE Subject Test. *Faculty research:* Criminal justice, mass media.

Florida Agricultural and Mechanical University, Division of Graduate Studies, Research, and Continuing Education, College of Arts and Sciences, Division of History and Political Sciences, Program in Applied Social Science, Tallahassee, FL 32307-3200. Offers African American history (MASS); criminal justice (MASS); economics (MASS); history (MASS); political science (MASS); public administration (MASS); public management (MASS); social work (MASS); sociology (MASS). Part-time programs available. *Degree requirements:* For master's, thesis optional. *Entrance requirements:* For master's, GRE General Test, minimum GPA of 3.0. *Faculty research:* Southern history, black history, election trends, presidential history.

Florida Atlantic University, Dorothy F. Schmidt College of Arts and Letters, Department of Sociology, Boca Raton, FL 33431-0991. Offers MA, MAT. Part-time and evening/weekend programs available. *Degree requirements:* For master's, thesis optional. *Entrance requirements:* For master's, GRE General Test, minimum GPA of 3.0. Additional exam requirements/recommendations for international students: Required—TOEFL. Electronic applications accepted. *Faculty research:* Gender/race/class, globalization, theory, social control, social movements.

Florida International University, College of Arts and Sciences, Department of Sociology/Anthropology, Miami, FL 33199. Offers comparative sociology (MA); sociology (PhD). Part-time and evening/weekend programs available. *Faculty:* 18 full-time (9 women), 1 (woman) part-time/adjunct. *Students:* 29 full-time (22 women), 19 part-time (12 women); includes 18 minority (3 African Americans, 2 Asian Americans or Pacific Islanders, 13 Hispanic Americans), 10 international. Average age 34. 41 applicants, 59% accepted, 15 enrolled. In 2007, 6 master's, 3 doctorates awarded. *Degree requirements:* For master's, thesis; for doctorate, comprehensive exam, thesis/dissertation. *Entrance requirements:* For master's and doctorate, GRE General Test, 3 letters of recommendation, minimum undergraduate GPA of 3.25, minimum graduate GPA of 3.5. Additional exam requirements/recommendations for international students: Required—TOEFL (minimum score 550 paper-based; 213 computer-based). *Application deadline:* For fall admission, 6/1 for domestic students, 4/1 for international students; for spring admission, 10/1 for domestic students, 9/1 for international students. Applications are processed on a rolling basis. Application fee: $30. Electronic applications accepted. *Expenses:* Tuition, state resident: full-time $6,106. Tuition, nonresident: full-time $15,528. Required fees: $284. *Financial support:* Teaching assistantships available. *Unit head:* Dr. Richard Tardanico, Chairperson, 305-348-2247, Fax: 305-348-3605, E-mail: richard.tardanico@fiu.edu.

Florida State University, Graduate Studies, College of Social Sciences, Department of Sociology, Tallahassee, FL 32306. Offers MA, MS, PhD. *Faculty:* 22 full-time (10 women). *Students:* 45 full-time (28 women), 11 part-time (7 women); includes 8 minority (3 African Americans, 1 Asian American or Pacific Islander, 4 Hispanic Americans), 4 international. Average age 28. 49 applicants, 76% accepted, 13 enrolled. In 2007, 12 master's, 7 doctorates awarded. Terminal master's awarded for partial completion of doctoral program. *Median time to degree:* Of those who began their doctoral program in fall 1999, 75% received their degree in 8 years or less. *Degree requirements:* For master's, paper; for doctorate, comprehensive exam, thesis/dissertation. *Entrance requirements:* For master's and doctorate, GRE General Test, minimum GPA of 3.0. Additional exam requirements/recommendations for international students: Required—TOEFL (minimum score 550 paper-based; 213 computer-based). *Application deadline:* For fall admission, 1/10 priority date for domestic students. Applications are processed on a rolling basis. Application fee: $30. Electronic applications accepted. *Expenses:* Tuition, state resident: part-time $248 per credit hour. Tuition, nonresident: part-time $880 per credit hour. Tuition and fees vary according to program. *Financial support:* In 2007–08, 45 students received support, including 9 fellowships with full tuition reimbursements available (averaging $17,700 per year), 6 research assistantships with full tuition reimbursements available (averaging $14,000 per year), 30 teaching assistantships with full tuition reimbursements available (averaging $14,000 per year); institutionally sponsored loans, scholarships/grants, health care benefits, and unspecified assistantships also available. Financial award application deadline: 1/10; financial award applicants required to submit FAFSA. *Faculty research:* Inequality (gender/race), demography, social psychology, health and aging. Total annual research expenditures: $485,000. *Unit head:* Dr. Irene Padavic, Chair, 850-644-6416, Fax: 850-644-6208, E-mail: ipadavic@fsu.edu. *Application contact:* Dr. John Reynolds, Graduate Program Director, 850-644-4321, Fax: 850-644-6208, E-mail: john.reynolds@fsu.edu.

Fordham University, Graduate School of Arts and Sciences, Department of Sociology, New York, NY 10458. Offers MA, PhD. Part-time and evening/weekend programs available. *Faculty:* 21 full-time (10 women). *Students:* 14 full-time (9 women), 18 part-time (11 women); includes 8 minority (2 African Americans, 6 Hispanic Americans), 4 international. Average age 35. 43 applicants, 37% accepted, 8 enrolled. In 2007, 5 master's, 3 doctorates awarded. Terminal master's awarded for partial completion of doctoral program. *Median time to degree:* Of those who began their doctoral program in fall 1999, 0% received their degree in 8 years or less. *Degree requirements:* For master's, comprehensive exam; for doctorate, one foreign language, comprehensive exam, thesis/dissertation. *Entrance requirements:* For master's and doctorate, GRE General Test. Additional exam requirements/recommendations for international students: Required—TOEFL (minimum score 600 paper-based; 250 computer-based). *Application deadline:* For fall admission, 1/4 priority date for domestic students; for spring admission, 11/1 for domestic students. Application fee: $70. Electronic applications accepted. *Expenses:* Tuition: Full-time $23,880; part-time $995 per credit. *Financial support:* In 2007–08, 12 students received support, including 3 fellowships with tuition reimbursements available (averaging $20,516 per year), 7 research assistantships with tuition reimbursements available (averaging $18,071 per year), 2 teaching assistantships with tuition reimbursements available (averaging $20,000 per year); career-related internships or fieldwork, Federal Work-Study, institutionally sponsored loans, tuition waivers (full and partial), and unspecified assistantships also available. Financial award application deadline: 1/4; financial award applicants required to submit FAFSA. *Faculty research:* Social demography, immigration, crime and deviance, religion. *Unit head:* Dr. Greta Gilbertson, Acting Chair, 718-817-3850, Fax: 718-817-3846, E-mail: gilbertson@fordham.edu. *Application contact:* Charlene Dundie, Director of Graduate Admissions, 718-817-4420, Fax: 718-817-3566, E-mail: dundie@fordham.edu.

George Mason University, College of Humanities and Social Sciences, Department of Sociology and Anthropology, Fairfax, VA 22030. Offers anthropology (MA); sociology (MA). *Faculty:* 27 full-time (13 women), 6 part-time/adjunct (2 women). *Students:* 20 full-time (11 women), 42 part-time (29 women); includes 21 minority (11 African Americans, 1 American Indian/Alaska Native, 3 Asian Americans or Pacific Islanders, 6 Hispanic Americans), 1 international. Average age 29. 73 applicants, 73% accepted, 31 enrolled. In 2007, 5 degrees awarded. *Degree requirements:* For master's, thesis. *Entrance requirements:* For master's, GRE General Test, minimum GPA of 3.0 in last 60 hours; writing sample; previous undergraduate course work in sociological theory, research methods, and social statistics. *Application deadline:* For fall admission, 5/1 for domestic students; for spring admission, 11/1 for domestic students. Application fee: $60 ($75 for international students). Electronic applications accepted. *Financial support:* Research assistantships, teaching assistantships available. Support available to part-time students. Financial award application deadline: 3/1; financial award applicants required to submit FAFSA. *Unit head:* Dr. Steven Vallas, Chairman, 703-993-2127, Fax: 703-993-1446, E-mail: svallas@gmu.edu.

The George Washington University, Columbian College of Arts and Sciences, Department of Sociology, Washington, DC 20052. Offers criminal justice (MA); sociology (MA). Part-time and evening/weekend programs available. *Degree requirements:* For master's, comprehensive exam, thesis or alternative. *Entrance requirements:* For master's, GRE General Test, minimum GPA of 3.0. Additional exam requirements/recommendations for international students: Required—TOEFL (minimum score 550 paper-based; 213 computer-based). Electronic applications accepted.

Georgia Southern University, Jack N. Averitt College of Graduate Studies, College of Liberal Arts and Social Sciences, Department of Sociology and Anthropology, Statesboro, GA 30460. Offers MA. Part-time and evening/weekend programs available. *Students:* 18 full-time (14 women), 13 part-time (10 women); includes 7 minority (6 African Americans, 1 Hispanic American), 1 international. Average age 29. 13 applicants, 100% accepted, 10 enrolled. In 2007, 4 degrees awarded. *Degree requirements:* For master's, thesis optional. *Entrance requirements:* For master's, GRE General Test, minimum GPA of 2.75, bachelor's degree in sociology. Additional exam requirements/recommendations for international students: Required—TOEFL (minimum score 550 paper-based; 213 computer-based; 80 iBT). *Application deadline:* For fall admission, 3/1 priority date for domestic students, 6/1 priority date for international students; for spring admission, 10/1 priority date for domestic students, 10/1 for international students. Applications are processed on a rolling basis. Application fee: $50. Electronic applications accepted. *Expenses:* Tuition, state resident: full-time $3,516; part-time $147 per semester hour. Tuition, nonresident: full-time $14,060; part-time $586 per semester hour. Required fees: $562 per term. *Financial support:* In 2007–08, 24 students received support, including research assistantships with partial tuition reimbursements available (averaging $6,850 per year), teaching assistantships with partial tuition reimbursements available (averaging $6,850 per year); career-related internships or fieldwork, Federal Work-Study, scholarships/grants, tuition waivers (partial), and unspecified assistantships also available. Support available to part-time students. Financial award application deadline: 4/15; financial award applicants required to submit FAFSA. *Faculty research:* Work and family, gender roles, sociology of the South, social psychology, community. *Unit head:* Dr. Sue M. Moore, Chair, 912-478-5434, Fax: 912-478-0703, E-mail: smmoore@georgiasouthern.edu. *Application contact:* 912-478-5384, Fax: 912-478-0740, E-mail: gradadmissions@georgiasouthern.edu.

Georgia State University, College of Arts and Sciences, Department of Sociology, Atlanta, GA 30303-3083. Offers MA, PhD. Part-time and evening/weekend programs available. *Faculty:* 25 full-time (16 women). *Students:* 53 full-time (41 women), 32 part-time (21 women); includes 23 minority (19 African Americans, 2 Asian Americans or Pacific Islanders, 2 Hispanic Americans), 7 international. Average age 28. 77 applicants, 56% accepted, 19 enrolled. In 2007, 5 master's, 2 doctorates awarded. Terminal master's awarded for partial completion of doctoral program. *Median time to degree:* Of those who began their doctoral program in fall 1999, 40% received their degree in 8 years or less. *Degree requirements:* For master's, thesis; for doctorate, comprehensive exam, thesis/dissertation. *Entrance requirements:* For master's, GRE General Test, departmental supplemental form, letters of recommendation; for doctorate, GRE General Test, departmental supplemental form, writing sample, letters of recommendation. Additional exam requirements/recommendations for international students: Required—TOEFL. *Application deadline:* For fall admission, 4/15 for domestic students, 2/1 for international students. Application fee: $50. Electronic applications accepted. *Expenses:* Tuition, state resident: part-time $221 per credit hour. *Financial support:* In 2007–08, 50 students received support, including research assistantships with full tuition reimbursements available (averaging $11,000 per year), teaching assistantships with full tuition reimbursements available (averaging $11,000 per year); career-related internships or fieldwork, Federal Work-Study, institutionally sponsored loans, health care benefits, and unspecified assistantships also available. Financial award application deadline: 2/1; financial award applicants required to submit FAFSA. *Faculty research:* Family and life course, gender and sexuality, race and urban studies. Total annual research expenditures: $1 million. *Unit head:* Dr. Donald C. Reitzes, Chair, 404-413-6506, E-mail: socdcr@panther.gsu.edu. *Application contact:* Dr. Dawn M. Baunach, Director of Graduate Studies, 404-413-6525, E-mail: dbaunach@gsu.edu.

Graduate School and University Center of the City University of New York, Graduate Studies, Program in Sociology, New York, NY 10016-4039. Offers PhD. *Faculty:* 69 full-time (15 women). *Students:* 155 full-time (98 women), 7 part-time (5 women); includes 35 minority (15 African Americans, 1 American Indian/Alaska Native, 10 Asian Americans or Pacific Islanders, 9 Hispanic Americans), 20 international. Average age 34. 140 applicants, 39% accepted, 19 enrolled. In 2007, 17 degrees awarded. *Degree requirements:* For doctorate, one foreign language, thesis/dissertation. *Entrance requirements:* For doctorate, GRE General Test, writing sample. Additional exam requirements/recommendations for international students: Required—TOEFL. *Application deadline:* For fall admission, 12/15 for domestic students. Application fee: $125. Electronic applications accepted. *Financial support:* In 2007–08, 129 students received support, including 115 fellowships, 13 research assistantships, 8 teaching assistantships; career-related internships or fieldwork, Federal Work-Study, institutionally sponsored loans, and tuition waivers (full and partial) also available. Financial award application deadline: 2/1; financial award applicants required to submit FAFSA. *Unit head:* Dr. Philip Kasinitz, Executive Officer, 212-817-8783, Fax: 212-817-1536, E-mail: pkasinitz@gc.cuny.edu.

Harvard University, Graduate School of Arts and Sciences, Department of Sociology, Cambridge, MA 02138. Offers PhD. *Degree requirements:* For doctorate, thesis/dissertation, oral exams in 2 subfields. *Entrance requirements:* For doctorate, GRE General Test. Additional exam requirements/recommendations for international students: Required—TOEFL. *Expenses:* Tuition: Full-time $31,456. Full-time tuition and fees vary according to program and student level. *Faculty research:* Sociological theory, political theories, quantitative approaches to methodology.

Howard University, Graduate School, Department of Health, Human Performance and Leisure Studies, Washington, DC 20059-0002. Offers exercise physiology (MS); health education (MS); sports studies (MS), including sociology of sports, sports management; urban recreation (MS), including leisure studies. Part-time and evening/weekend programs available. *Degree requirements:* For master's, comprehensive exam, thesis. *Entrance requirements:* For master's, BS in human performance or related field. Electronic applications accepted. *Expenses:* Tuition: Full-time $16,175; part-time $899 per credit hour. Required fees: $805. *Faculty research:* Health promotion, cardiovascular hypertension, physical activity, sport and human rights issues.

Howard University, Graduate School, Department of Sociology and Anthropology, Washington, DC 20059-0002. Offers sociology (MA, PhD). Part-time and evening/weekend programs available. *Faculty:* 10 full-time (7 women). *Students:* 26 full-time (21 women), 16 part-time (10 women); includes 36 minority (35 African Americans, 1 Asian American or Pacific Islander), 5 international. Average age 26. 47 applicants, 55% accepted, 8 enrolled. In 2007, 6 master's, 6 doctorates awarded. *Median time to degree:* Of those who began their doctoral program in fall 1999, 90% received their degree in 8 years or less. *Degree requirements:* For master's, thesis; for doctorate, one foreign language, comprehensive exam, thesis/dissertation, RCR, writing exam. *Entrance requirements:* For master's, GRE General Test, minimum GPA of 3.0; for doctorate, GRE General Test, minimum GPA of 3.5. Additional exam requirements/recommendations for international students: Required—TOEFL. *Application deadline:* For fall admission, 4/1 for domestic students; for spring admission, 11/1 for domestic students. Applications are processed on a rolling basis. Application fee: $45. Electronic applications accepted. *Expenses:* Tuition: Full-time $16,175; part-time $899 per credit hour. Required fees: $805. *Financial support:* In 2007–08, 21 students received support, including 3 fellowships with tuition reimbursements available (averaging $18,000 per year), 14 teaching assistantships with tuition reimbursements available (averaging $14,500 per year); institutionally sponsored loans, traineeships, tuition waivers (full), and unspecified assistantships also available. Financial award application deadline: 4/1; financial award applicants required to submit FAFSA. *Faculty research:* Medical sociology; criminology; race, class and gender; urban sociology. Total annual research expenditures: $100,000. *Unit head:* Dr. Ivor Livingston, Chair, 202-806-6853, Fax: 202-806-4893, E-mail: ilivingston@howard.edu. *Application contact:* Dr. Rebecca Reviere, Director of Graduate Studies, 202-806-6853, Fax: 202-806-4893, E-mail: rreviere@howard.edu.

Humboldt State University, Graduate Studies, College of Arts, Humanities, and Social Sciences, Department of Sociology, Arcata, CA 95521-8299. Offers MA. *Students:* 13 full-time (7 women), 7 part-time (2 women); includes 3 minority (2 African Americans, 1 Asian American or Pacific Islander). Average age 33. 14 applicants, 71% accepted, 4 enrolled. In 2007, 7 degrees awarded. *Degree requirements:* For master's, thesis or alternative, qualifying exam. *Entrance requirements:* For master's, minimum GPA of 2.5, 3 letters of recommendation. Additional exam requirements/recommendations for international students: Required—TOEFL (minimum score 500 paper-based; 173 computer-based). *Application deadline:* For fall admission, 3/15 for domestic students; for spring admission, 11/15 for domestic students. Applications are processed on a rolling basis. Application fee: $55. *Financial support:* Application deadline: 3/1; *Faculty research:* Sociology of women political activists, environmental dispute resolution, prosocial behavior. *Unit head:* Dr. Judith Little, Chair, 707-826-3139, Fax: 707-826-4418, E-mail: jkl1@humboldt.edu. *Application contact:* Dr. Jennifer Eichstedt, Coordinator, 707-826-4949, Fax: 707-826-4418, E-mail: jle7001@humboldt.edu.

Hunter College of the City University of New York, Graduate School, School of Arts and Sciences, Department of Sociology, New York, NY 10021-5085. Offers applied social research (MS). *Faculty:* 5 full-time (2 women), 2 part-time/adjunct (1 woman). *Students:* 10 full-time (6 women), 28 part-time (19 women); includes 9 minority (3 African Americans, 3 Asian Americans or Pacific Islanders, 3 Hispanic Americans). Average age 30. 22 applicants, 73% accepted, 11 enrolled. In 2007, 7 degrees awarded. *Degree requirements:* For master's, internship. *Entrance requirements:* For master's, GRE General Test or GMAT, 3 credits of course work in statistics, 2 letters of recommendation. Additional exam requirements/recommendations for international students: Required—TOEFL. *Application deadline:* For fall admission, 4/1 for domestic students, 2/1 for international students; for spring admission, 11/1 for domestic students, 9/1 for international students. Application fee: $125. *Expenses:* Tuition, state resident: full-time $6,400; part-time $270 per credit. Tuition, nonresident: part-time $500 per credit. One-time fee: $125 full-time. Tuition and fees vary according to program. *Financial support:* Federal Work-Study and tuition waivers (partial) available. Support available to part-time students. *Unit head:* Dr. Robert Perinbanayagaia, Chairperson, 212-772-5585, Fax: 212-772-5645, E-mail: rperinba@hunter.cuny.edu. *Application contact:* Dr. Joong-Hwan Oh, Graduate Adviser, 212-772-5643, E-mail: goh@hunter.cuny.edu.

Idaho State University, Office of Graduate Studies, College of Arts and Sciences, Department of Sociology, Pocatello, ID 83209. Offers MA. Part-time programs available. *Faculty:* 5 full-time (2 women). *Students:* 6 full-time (2 women), 5 part-time (4 women), 1 international. Average age 36. In 2007, 1 degree awarded. *Degree requirements:* For master's, comprehensive exam, thesis, oral defense of thesis. *Entrance requirements:* For master's, GRE General Test, minimum undergraduate GPA of 3.0, 3 letters of recommendation. Additional exam requirements/recommendations for international students: Required—TOEFL (minimum score 550 paper-based; 213 computer-based; 80 iBT). *Application deadline:* For fall admission, 7/1 for domestic students, 6/1 for international students; for spring admission, 12/1 for domestic students, 11/1 for international students. Applications are processed on a rolling basis. Application fee: $55. Electronic applications accepted. *Expenses:* Tuition, state resident: full-time $2,882; part-time $259 per credit hour. Tuition, nonresident: full-time $11,566; part-time $379 per credit hour. Required fees: $2,278. Full-time tuition and fees vary according to program. Part-time tuition and fees vary according to course load. *Financial support:* In 2007–08, 2 teaching assistantships with full and partial tuition reimbursements (averaging $9,128 per year) were awarded; career-related internships or fieldwork, Federal Work-Study, institutionally sponsored loans, scholarships/grants, health care benefits, tuition waivers (full and partial), and unspecified assistantships also available. Support available to part-time students. Financial award application deadline: 1/1; financial award applicants required to submit FAFSA. *Faculty research:* Terrorism, social organization, families social work. *Unit head:* Dr. Ann Hunter, Chairperson, 208-282-2170, Fax: 208-282-4733, E-mail: soccj@isu.edu. *Application contact:* Dr. James Aho, Program Director, 208-282-2170.

Illinois State University, Graduate School, College of Arts and Sciences, Department of Sociology, Normal, IL 61790-2200. Offers historical archaeology (MA, MS); sociology (MA, MS). *Faculty:* 24 full-time (13 women), 1 part-time/adjunct (0 women). *Students:* 13 full-time (7 women), 14 part-time (9 women); includes 3 minority (1 African American, 1 Asian American or Pacific Islander, 1 Hispanic American), 4 international. 18 applicants, 56% accepted. In 2007, 8 degrees awarded. *Degree requirements:* For master's, thesis. *Entrance requirements:* For master's, GRE General Test, GRE Subject Test, minimum GPA of 2.4 in last 60 hours of course work. *Application deadline:* Applications are processed on a rolling basis. Application fee: $40. *Expenses:* Tuition, state resident: full-time $3,492; part-time $194 per credit hour. Tuition, nonresident: full-time $7,272; part-time $404 per credit hour. Required fees: $1,024; $57 per credit hour. *Financial support:* In 2007–08, 10 research assistantships (averaging $7,916 per year), 12 teaching assistantships (averaging $7,424 per year) were awarded; career-related internships or fieldwork, Federal Work-Study, tuition waivers (full and partial), and unspecified assistantships also available. Financial award application deadline: 4/1. *Faculty research:* Japanese Saturday school (Kato). Total annual research expenditures: $5,445. *Unit head:* Dr. Diane Zosky, Acting Chairperson, 309-438-8668. *Application contact:* Wilbert M. Leonard, Graduate Adviser, 309-438-8073.

Indiana University Bloomington, University Graduate School, College of Arts and Sciences, Department of Sociology, Bloomington, IN 47405-7000. Offers MA, PhD. *Faculty:* 18 full-time (9 women). *Students:* 65 full-time (41 women), 27 part-time (14 women); includes 21 minority (15 African Americans, 1 Asian American or Pacific Islander, 5 Hispanic Americans), 5 international. Average age 29. 144 applicants, 21% accepted, 14 enrolled. In 2007, 7 master's, 8 doctorates awarded. Terminal master's awarded for partial completion of doctoral program.

Sociology

Indiana University Bloomington (continued)
Median time to degree: Of those who began their doctoral program in fall 1999, 78% received their degree in 8 years or less. *Degree requirements:* For master's, thesis; for doctorate, comprehensive exam, thesis/dissertation. *Entrance requirements:* For master's and doctorate, GRE General Test, International—TOEFL. Additional exam requirements/recommendations for international students: Required—TOEFL. *Application deadline:* For fall admission, 1/15 for domestic students, 12/1 for international students. Application fee: $50 ($60 for international students). Electronic applications accepted. *Financial support:* In 2007–08, 74 students received support; fellowships with full tuition reimbursements available, research assistantships with full tuition reimbursements available, teaching assistantships with full tuition reimbursements available, scholarships/grants, health care benefits, and unspecified assistantships available. Financial award application deadline: 1/15; financial award applicants required to submit FAFSA. *Faculty research:* Social psychology, political sociology, sociological research methods, stratification/mobility, education. *Unit head:* Thomas F. Gieryn, Chair and Rudy Professor, 812-855-2569, Fax: 812-855-0781. *Application contact:* Angela Gast, Information Contact, 812-855-2924, E-mail: agast@indiana.edu.

Indiana University of Pennsylvania, School of Graduate Studies and Research, College of Humanities and Social Sciences, Department of Sociology, Program in Sociology, Indiana, PA 15705-1087. Offers MA. Part-time programs available. *Faculty:* 13 full-time (6 women), 1 part-time/adjunct (0 women). *Students:* 23 full-time (17 women), 10 part-time (6 women); includes 1 minority (African American) Average age 33. 30 applicants, 70% accepted, 18 enrolled. In 2007, 10 degrees awarded. *Degree requirements:* For master's, thesis optional. *Entrance requirements:* For master's, GRE, 2 letters of recommendation. Additional exam requirements/recommendations for international students: Required—TOEFL. *Application deadline:* For fall admission, 7/1 priority date for domestic students; for spring admission, 11/1 for domestic students. Applications are processed on a rolling basis. Application fee: $30. *Expenses:* Tuition, state resident: full-time $6,214; part-time $345 per credit. Tuition, nonresident: full-time $9,944; part-time $552 per credit. Required fees: $43 per credit. One-time fee: $140 part-time. Tuition and fees vary according to course load. *Financial support:* In 2007–08, 11 research assistantships (averaging $2,645 per year) were awarded. Financial award application deadline: 3/15; financial award applicants required to submit FAFSA. *Unit head:* Dr. Kay Snyder, Graduate Coordinator, 724-357-3931, E-mail: ksnyder@iup.edu.

Indiana University–Purdue University Fort Wayne, College of Arts and Sciences, Department of Sociology, Fort Wayne, IN 46805-1499. Offers sociological practice (MA). Part-time programs available. *Faculty:* 11 full-time (4 women). *Students:* 3 full-time (all women), 11 part-time (7 women); includes 3 minority (all African Americans) Average age 39. *Degree requirements:* For master's, practicum. *Entrance requirements:* For master's, GRE General Test, minimum GPA of 3.0, 3 letters of recommendation, essay. Additional exam requirements/recommendations for international students: Required—TOEFL (minimum score 550 paper-based; 213 computer-based; 77 iBT). *Application deadline:* For fall admission, 8/1 for domestic students; for spring admission, 11/1 priority date for domestic students. Applications are processed on a rolling basis. Application fee: $30. *Expenses:* Tuition, state resident: full-time $4,203; part-time $234 per credit. Tuition, nonresident: full-time $9,761; part-time $542 per credit. Required fees: $466; $26 per credit. Tuition and fees vary according to course load. *Financial support:* In 2007–08, 3 research assistantships with partial tuition reimbursements (averaging $12,310 per year) were awarded; teaching assistantships with partial tuition reimbursements, scholarships/grants and unspecified assistantships also available. Support available to part-time students. Financial award application deadline: 3/1; financial award applicants required to submit FAFSA. *Faculty research:* Problematic places and alcohol, perspectives, facilitating civil discourse. *Unit head:* Dr. Alan Sandstrom, Chairperson, 260-481-6673, Fax: 260-481-6985, E-mail: taubd@ipfw.edu. *Application contact:* Dr. Augusto De Venanzi, Graduate Program Director, 260-481-6669, Fax: 260-481-6985, E-mail: devenana@ipfu.edu.

Indiana University–Purdue University Indianapolis, School of Liberal Arts, Department of Sociology, Indianapolis, IN 46202-2896. Offers family/gender studies (MA); medical sociology (MA); work/occupations (MA). *Faculty:* 17 full-time (8 women). *Students:* 13 full-time (11 women), 7 part-time (4 women); includes 3 minority (all African Americans), 1 international. Average age 27. In 2007, 5 degrees awarded. Application fee: $50 ($60 for international students). *Expenses:* Tuition, state resident: full-time $5,818; part-time $242 per credit hour. Tuition, nonresident: full-time $17,106; part-time $713 per credit hour. Required fees: $629. Tuition and fees vary according to course load, campus/location and program. *Financial support:* In 2007–08, 2 fellowships (averaging $9,500 per year), 2 teaching assistantships (averaging $6,309 per year) were awarded. *Unit head:* Carrie Foote, Director of Graduate Studies, 317-274-8981, E-mail: sociology@iupui.edu.

Iowa State University of Science and Technology, Graduate College, College of Liberal Arts and Sciences, Department of Sociology, Ames, IA 50011. Offers rural sociology (MS, PhD); sociology (MS, PhD). *Faculty:* 31 full-time (16 women). *Students:* 40 full-time (19 women), 14 part-time (10 women); includes 6 minority (2 African Americans, 2 American Indian/Alaska Native, 2 Hispanic Americans), 13 international. 33 applicants, 52% accepted, 13 enrolled. In 2007, 4 master's, 4 doctorates awarded. *Degree requirements:* For master's, thesis; for doctorate, thesis/dissertation. *Entrance requirements:* For master's and doctorate, GRE General Test. Additional exam requirements/recommendations for international students: Required—TOEFL (paper-based 550; computer-based 213; iBT 80) or IELTS (6.5). *Application deadline:* For fall admission, 1/10 priority date for domestic and international students; for spring admission, 10/1 for domestic and international students. Application fee: $30 ($70 for international students). Electronic applications accepted. *Financial support:* In 2007–08, 16 research assistantships with full and partial tuition reimbursements (averaging $19,182 per year), 19 teaching assistantships with full and partial tuition reimbursements (averaging $18,720 per year) were awarded; fellowships, scholarships/grants, health care benefits, and unspecified assistantships also available. *Unit head:* Dr. R. Paul Lasley, Chair, 515-294-2506, Fax: 515-294-8312, E-mail: sociology@iastate.edu. *Application contact:* Dr. Gloria Jones-Johnson, Director of Graduate Education, 515-294-2947, E-mail: sociology@iastate.edu.

Jackson State University, Graduate School, School of Liberal Arts, Department of Sociology, Jackson, MS 39217. Offers MA. Part-time and evening/weekend programs available. *Degree requirements:* For master's, comprehensive exam, thesis or alternative. *Entrance requirements:* For master's, GRE General Test. Additional exam requirements/recommendations for international students: Required—TOEFL.

The Johns Hopkins University, Zanvyl Krieger School of Arts and Sciences, Department of Sociology, Baltimore, MD 21218-2699. Offers PhD. *Faculty:* 12 full-time (6 women), 3 part-time/adjunct (2 women). *Students:* 38 full-time (20 women), 1 part-time; includes 10 minority (5 African Americans, 3 Asian Americans or Pacific Islanders, 2 Hispanic Americans), 12 international. 125 applicants, 10% accepted, 6 enrolled. In 2007, 3 degrees awarded. *Median time to degree:* Of those who began their doctoral program in fall 1999, 50% received their degree in 8 years or less. *Degree requirements:* For doctorate, one foreign language, thesis/dissertation. *Entrance requirements:* For doctorate, GRE General Test. Additional exam requirements/recommendations for international students: Required—TOEFL (minimum score 560 paper-based); Recommended—IELTS, TWE. *Application deadline:* For fall admission, 1/15 for domestic students. Application fee: $60. Electronic applications accepted. *Financial support:* In 2007–08, 2 fellowships with full tuition reimbursements (averaging $15,000 per year), 13 research assistantships with full tuition reimbursements (averaging $15,000 per year), 16 teaching assistantships with full tuition reimbursements (averaging $15,000 per year) were awarded; institutionally sponsored loans, health care benefits, and tuition waivers (partial) also available. Financial award applicants required to submit CSS PROFILE or FAFSA. *Faculty research:* Education, immigration, race and gender, world systems, social policy. Total annual research expenditures: $2.7 million. *Unit head:* Dr. Karl Alexander, Chair, 410-516-6178, Fax: 410-516-7590, E-mail: karl@jhu.edu. *Application contact:* Linda Burkhardt, Academic Program Coordinator, 410-516-7627, Fax: 410-516-7590, E-mail: lindab@jhu.edu.

Kansas State University, Graduate School, College of Arts and Sciences, Department of Sociology, Anthropology and Social Work, Manhattan, KS 66506. Offers sociology (MA, PhD). Part-time programs available. *Faculty:* 16 full-time (7 women), 6 part-time/adjunct (5 women). *Students:* 47 full-time (17 women), 10 part-time (5 women); includes 6 minority (5 African Americans, 1 Hispanic American), 9 international. 20 applicants, 95% accepted, 3 enrolled. In 2007, 3 degrees awarded. *Degree requirements:* For master's, thesis or alternative; for doctorate, thesis/dissertation. *Entrance requirements:* For master's, GRE, minimum undergraduate GPA of 3.0; for doctorate, master's degree in sociology. Additional exam requirements/recommendations for international students: Required—TOEFL (minimum score 550 paper-based; 213 computer-based). *Application deadline:* For fall admission, 3/1 priority date for domestic and international students; for spring admission, 10/1 priority date for domestic and international students. Applications are processed on a rolling basis. Application fee: $30 ($55 for international students). Electronic applications accepted. *Financial support:* In 2007–08, 2 research assistantships (averaging $15,253 per year), 18 teaching assistantships with full tuition reimbursements (averaging $1,123 per year) were awarded; institutionally sponsored loans and scholarships/grants also available. Support available to part-time students. Financial award application deadline: 3/1; financial award applicants required to submit FAFSA. *Faculty research:* Community development and population change, sociology of agriculture and the food systems, social construction of gender and gender violence, youth crime and delinquency, the effects of globalization on economic and political systems. Total annual research expenditures: $139,484. *Unit head:* Betsy Cauble, Head, 785-532-6865, Fax: 785-532-6978, E-mail: bcauble@ksu.edu. *Application contact:* Richard Goe, Director, 785-532-6865, Fax: 785-532-6978, E-mail: goe@ksu.edu.

Kent State University, College of Arts and Sciences, Department of Sociology, Kent, OH 44242-0001. Offers MA, PhD. Part-time programs available. *Faculty:* 13 full-time (8 women). *Students:* 18 full-time (14 women), 31 part-time (27 women); includes 6 minority (5 African Americans, 1 Asian American or Pacific Islander), 2 international. Average age 25. 30 applicants, 67% accepted, 15 enrolled. In 2007, 2 degrees awarded. *Degree requirements:* For master's, thesis optional, monograph option; for doctorate, comprehensive exam, thesis/dissertation. *Entrance requirements:* For master's, GRE General Test or MAT, minimum GPA of 2.75; for doctorate, GRE, minimum GPA of 3.0. Additional exam requirements/recommendations for international students: Required—TOEFL. *Application deadline:* For fall admission, 7/12 for domestic and international students; for spring admission, 11/29 for domestic and international students. Applications are processed on a rolling basis. Application fee: $30. Electronic applications accepted. *Financial support:* In 2007–08, fellowships with full tuition reimbursements (averaging $11,500 per year), research assistantships with full tuition reimbursements (averaging $10,500 per year) were awarded; teaching assistantships with full tuition reimbursements, career-related internships or fieldwork, Federal Work-Study, institutionally sponsored loans, health care benefits, and tuition waivers (full) also available. Financial award application deadline: 2/1; financial award applicants required to submit FAFSA. *Faculty research:* Medical sociology, social psychology, social inequalities. *Unit head:* Dr. Richard T. Serpe, Chairman, 330-672-2562, Fax: 330-672-4724, E-mail: rserpe@kent.edu. *Application contact:* Amy Kroska, Graduate Coordinator, 330-672-9474, Fax: 330-672-4724, E-mail: akroska@kent.edu.

Lakehead University, Graduate Studies, Faculty of Social Sciences and Humanities, Department of Sociology, Thunder Bay, ON P7B 5E1, Canada. Offers MA. Part-time and evening/weekend programs available. *Degree requirements:* For master's, research project or thesis. *Entrance requirements:* For master's, minimum B average. Additional exam requirements/recommendations for international students: Required—TOEFL. *Faculty research:* Sociology of medicine, cultural and social change, health human resources, gerontology, women's studies.

Laurentian University, School of Graduate Studies and Research, Programme in Sociology, Sudbury, ON P3E 2C6, Canada. Offers MA. Part-time programs available. *Entrance requirements:* For master's, honors degree in sociology or equivalent. *Faculty research:* Work foundations, managing AIDS organization, tracking laid-off mine workers.

Lehigh University, College of Arts and Sciences, Department of Sociology and Anthropology, Bethlehem, PA 18015-3094. Offers sociology (MA). Part-time programs available. *Faculty:* 9 full-time (4 women), 2 part-time/adjunct (1 woman). *Students:* 11 full-time (all women), 3 part-time (all women); includes 4 minority (1 African American, 2 Asian Americans or Pacific Islanders, 1 Hispanic American), 3 international. Average age 26. 15 applicants, 60% accepted, 7 enrolled. In 2007, 9 degrees awarded. *Degree requirements:* For master's, comprehensive exam, thesis optional. *Entrance requirements:* For master's, GRE General Test. Additional exam requirements/recommendations for international students: Required—TOEFL (minimum score 650 paper-based). *Application deadline:* For fall admission, 4/1 for domestic and international students. Application fee: $65. Electronic applications accepted. *Financial support:* In 2007–08, 3 research assistantships with full tuition reimbursements, 4 teaching assistantships with full tuition reimbursements were awarded; fellowships with full tuition reimbursements, career-related internships or fieldwork, Federal Work-Study, institutionally sponsored loans, scholarships/grants, tuition waivers (full and partial), and unspecified assistantships also available. Support available to part-time students. Financial award application deadline: 1/15. *Faculty research:* Juvenile delinquency, parent-child relations, urban sociology, medical sociology, policy studies. Total annual research expenditures: $204,136. *Unit head:* Dr. Judith N. Lasker, Graduate Coordinator, 610-758-3811, Fax: 610-758-6552, E-mail: jnlo@lehigh.edu. *Application contact:* Dr. Heather B. Johnson, Graduate Coordinator, 610-758-3816, Fax: 610-758-6552, E-mail: hbj2@lehigh.edu.

Lincoln University, School of Graduate Studies and Continuing Education, College of Liberal Arts, Education and Journalism, Department of Social and Behavioral Sciences, Jefferson City, MO 65102. Offers history (MA); social science (MA), including history, political science, sociology; sociology (MA); sociology/criminal justice (MA). Part-time and evening/weekend programs available. *Faculty:* 12 part-time/adjunct (4 women). *Students:* 13 full-time (9 women), 17 part-time (7 women); includes 16 minority (13 African Americans, 1 American Indian/Alaska Native, 2 Hispanic Americans), 3 international. Average age 33. 9 applicants, 89% accepted, 5 enrolled. In 2007, 6 degrees awarded. *Degree requirements:* For master's, comprehensive exam, thesis optional. *Entrance requirements:* For master's, GRE General Test or MAT, 15 undergraduate hours of course work in social science including 6 hours upper-division, with 9 hours in the area of concentration; see parent units for general requirements. Additional exam requirements/recommendations for international students: Required—TOEFL (minimum score 500 paper-based; 173 computer-based; 61 iBT). *Application deadline:* For fall admission, 7/1 priority date for domestic and international students; for spring admission, 12/1 priority date for domestic and international students. Applications are processed on a rolling basis. Application fee: $20. *Expenses:* Tuition, state resident: full-time $5,400; part-time $225 per credit hour. Tuition, nonresident: full-time $10,020; part-time $417 per credit hour. Required fees: $360; $15 per credit hour. $20 per semester. *Financial support:* Federal Work-Study and scholarships/grants available. Financial award application deadline: 4/1; financial award applicants required to submit FAFSA. *Faculty research:* Suicide prevention. *Unit head:* Dr. Antonio Holland, Department Head, 573-681-5145, Fax: 573-681-5150, E-mail: hollanda@lincolnu.edu.

Louisiana State University and Agricultural and Mechanical College, Graduate School, College of Arts and Sciences, Department of Sociology, Baton Rouge, LA 70803. Offers MA, PhD. Part-time programs available. *Faculty:* 16 full-time (3 women). *Students:* 35 full-time (21 women), 4 part-time (2 women); includes 7 African Americans, 3 Asian Americans or Pacific Islanders, 1 international. Average age 31. 19 applicants, 74% accepted, 8 enrolled. In 2007, 7 master's, 3 doctorates awarded. Terminal master's awarded for partial completion of doctoral program. *Degree requirements:* For master's, comprehensive exam, thesis; for doctorate, comprehensive exam, thesis/dissertation. *Entrance requirements:* For master's and doctorate, GRE General Test, minimum GPA of 3.0. Additional exam requirements/recommendations for international students: Required—TOEFL (minimum score 550 paper-based; 213 computer-based; 79 iBT). *Application deadline:* For fall admission, 1/31 priority date for domestic students, 3/31 for international students; for spring admission, 10/15 for international students. Applications are processed on a rolling basis. Application fee: $25.

Electronic applications accepted. *Financial support:* In 2007–08, 38 students received support, including 5 fellowships (averaging $20,587 per year), 7 research assistantships with partial tuition reimbursements available (averaging $15,165 per year), 22 teaching assistantships with partial tuition reimbursements available (averaging $11,966 per year); Federal Work-Study, scholarships/grants, health care benefits, tuition waivers (full and partial), and unspecified assistantships also available. Support available to part-time students. Financial award application deadline: 3/1; financial award applicants required to submit FAFSA. *Faculty research:* Family, stratification, demography, rural sociology, criminology. Total annual research expenditures: $472,036. *Unit head:* Dr. Mike Grimes, Chair, 225-578-5312, Fax: 225-578-5102. *Application contact:* Dr. Yoshinori Kamo, Graduate Adviser, 225-578-5311, Fax: 225-578-5102.

Loyola University Chicago, Graduate School, Department of Sociology, Chicago, IL 60611-2196. Offers applied sociology (MA); sociology (MA, PhD). Part-time and evening/weekend programs available. *Faculty:* 11 full-time (4 women), 3 part-time/adjunct (2 women). *Students:* 69 full-time (47 women), 14 part-time (12 women); includes 13 minority (7 African Americans, 1 American Indian/Alaska Native, 4 Asian Americans or Pacific Islanders, 1 Hispanic American), 7 international. Average age 31. 80 applicants, 48% accepted, 11 enrolled. In 2007, 13 master's, 10 doctorates awarded. Terminal master's awarded for partial completion of doctoral program. *Median time to degree:* Of those who began their doctoral program in fall 1999, 29% received their degree in 8 years or less. *Degree requirements:* For master's, thesis or alternative; for doctorate, comprehensive exam, thesis/dissertation. *Entrance requirements:* For master's and doctorate, GRE General Test. Additional exam requirements/recommendations for international students: Required—TOEFL. *Application deadline:* For winter admission, 2/1 for domestic students. Application fee: $50. Electronic applications accepted. *Expenses:* Tuition: Full-time $12,780; part-time $710 per credit hour. Required fees: $55 per semester. Full-time tuition and fees vary according to program. *Financial support:* In 2007–08, 43 students received support, including 8 fellowships with full tuition reimbursements available (averaging $14,000 per year), 10 research assistantships with full tuition reimbursements available (averaging $14,000 per year), 6 teaching assistantships (averaging $14,000 per year); career-related internships or fieldwork and Federal Work-Study also available. Financial award application deadline: 2/1; financial award applicants required to submit FAFSA. *Faculty research:* Religion, work, urban sociology, urban and social policy, knowledge and culture, gender, race. Total annual research expenditures: $160,000. *Unit head:* Dr. Fred Kniss, Chair, 773-508-3459, Fax: 773-508-7099, E-mail: fkniss@luc.edu. *Application contact:* Dr. Anne Figert, Graduate Program Director, 773-508-3431, Fax: 773-508-7099, E-mail: afigert@luc.edu.

Marshall University, Academic Affairs Division, College of Liberal Arts, Department of Sociology and Anthropology, Huntington, WV 25755. Offers sociology (MA). *Faculty:* 7 full-time (3 women), 1 (woman) part-time/adjunct. *Students:* 8 full-time (6 women), 4 part-time (1 woman); includes 1 minority (African American) Average age 28. In 2007, 10 degrees awarded. *Degree requirements:* For master's, thesis optional. Application fee: $40. *Unit head:* Dr. Robert Sawrey, Interim Chairperson, 304-696-3347, E-mail: sawrey@marshall.edu. *Application contact:* Information Contact, 304-746-1900, Fax: 304-746-1902, E-mail: services@marshall.edu.

McGill University, Faculty of Graduate and Postdoctoral Studies, Faculty of Arts, Department of Sociology, Montréal, QC H3A 2T5, Canada. Offers medical sociology (MA); neo-tropical environment (MA); social statistics (MA); sociology (MA, PhD, Diploma). *Faculty:* 21 full-time (8 women), 9 part-time/adjunct (3 women). *Students:* 28 full-time (21 women), 3 part-time (1 woman). 75 applicants, 31% accepted, 10 enrolled. In 2007, 5 master's, 2 doctorates awarded.

McGill University, Faculty of Graduate and Postdoctoral Studies, Faculty of Medicine, Department of Social Studies in Medicine, Montréal, QC H3A 2T5, Canada. Offers medical anthropology (MA, PhD); medical history (MA, PhD); medical sociology (MA, PhD). *Faculty:* 7 full-time (2 women), 3 part-time/adjunct (1 woman).

McMaster University, School of Graduate Studies, Faculty of Social Sciences, Department of Sociology, Hamilton, ON L8S 4M2, Canada. Offers MA, PhD. Part-time programs available. *Faculty:* 20 full-time. *Students:* 44 full-time, 4 part-time. 93 applicants, 13% accepted. *Degree requirements:* For master's, thesis; for doctorate, comprehensive exam, thesis/dissertation. *Entrance requirements:* For master's and doctorate, minimum B+ average. Additional exam requirements/recommendations for international students: Required—TOEFL (minimum score 580 paper-based; 237 computer-based). *Application deadline:* For fall admission, 2/1 for domestic students. Application fee: $90. *Financial support:* In 2007–08, 3 research assistantships, teaching assistantships (averaging $8,440 per year) were awarded; fellowships, scholarships/grants also available. Financial award applicants required to submit CSS PROFILE. *Faculty research:* Socialization and conversion, ethnic relations, international migration, racism, social implications of the Internet. Total annual research expenditures: $265,000. *Unit head:* Dr. Margaret Denton, Acting Chair, 905-525-9140, Fax: 905-522-2642. *Application contact:* Corinne Jehle, Graduate Secretary, 905-525-9140 Ext. 23613, Fax: 905-522-2642, E-mail: corinne@mcmaster.ca.

Memorial University of Newfoundland, School of Graduate Studies, Department of Sociology, St. John's, NL A1C 5S7, Canada. Offers gender (PhD); maritime sociology (PhD); sociology (M Phil, MA); work and development (PhD). Part-time programs available. *Degree requirements:* For master's, comprehensive exam, thesis optional, program journal (M Phil); for doctorate, one foreign language, comprehensive exam, thesis/dissertation, oral defense of thesis. *Entrance requirements:* For master's, 2nd class degree from university of recognized standing in area of study; for doctorate, MA, M Phil, or equivalent. Electronic applications accepted. *Faculty research:* Work and development, gender, maritime sociology.

Michigan State University, The Graduate School, College of Social Science, Department of Sociology, East Lansing, MI 48824. Offers MA, PhD. Part-time programs available. *Entrance requirements:* Additional exam requirements/recommendations for international students: Required—TOEFL (minimum score 550 paper-based; 213 computer-based), Michigan State University ELT (85), Michigan ELAB (83). Electronic applications accepted. *Expenses:* Tuition, state resident: part-time $379 per credit hour. Tuition, nonresident: part-time $800 per credit hour. Tuition and fees vary according to program.

Middle Tennessee State University, College of Graduate Studies, College of Liberal Arts, Department of Sociology and Anthropology, Murfreesboro, TN 37132. Offers sociology (MA). Part-time and evening/weekend programs available. Postbaccalaureate distance learning degree programs offered. *Faculty:* 12 full-time (6 women). *Students:* Average age 31. 16 applicants, 63% accepted. In 2007, 7 degrees awarded. *Degree requirements:* For master's, comprehensive exam, thesis. *Entrance requirements:* For master's, GRE. Additional exam requirements/recommendations for international students: Required—TOEFL (paper-based 525; computer-based 195; IBT 71) or IELTS (6.0). *Application deadline:* For fall admission, 8/1 priority date for domestic students. Applications are processed on a rolling basis. Application fee: $25. Electronic applications accepted. *Financial support:* In 2007–08, 8 students received support. Institutionally sponsored loans available. Support available to part-time students. Financial award application deadline: 5/1; financial award applicants required to submit FAFSA. *Faculty research:* Applied, crime/deviance, aging/social gerontology, social organization, social psychology. *Unit head:* Dr. Ronald Aday, Chair, 615-898-2508, Fax: 615-898-5428.

Minnesota State University Mankato, College of Graduate Studies, College of Social and Behavioral Sciences, Department of Sociology and Corrections, Mankato, MN 56001. Offers sociology (MA); sociology: corrections (MS); sociology: human services planning and administration (MS). Part-time programs available. *Students:* 11 full-time (5 women), 34 part-time (25 women). Average age 32. In 2007, 17 degrees awarded. *Degree requirements:* For master's, comprehensive exam, thesis or alternative. *Entrance requirements:* For master's, minimum GPA of 3.0 during previous 2 years, 3 letters of reference, resumé. Additional exam requirements/recommendations for international students: Required—TOEFL. *Application deadline:* For fall admission, 7/1 priority date for domestic students; for spring admission, 11/1 for domestic students. Applications are processed on a rolling basis. Application fee: $40. Electronic applications accepted. *Financial support:* Research assistantships with full tuition reimbursements, teaching assistantships with full tuition reimbursements, career-related internships or fieldwork, Federal Work-Study, institutionally sponsored loans, and unspecified assistantships available. Support available to part-time students. Financial award application deadline: 3/15; financial award applicants required to submit FAFSA. *Faculty research:* Women's suffrage movements. *Unit head:* Dr. Barbara Keating, Chairperson, 507-389-1561. *Application contact:* 507-389-2321, E-mail: grad@mnsu.edu.

Mississippi State University, College of Arts and Sciences, Department of Sociology, Anthropology, and Social Work, Mississippi State, MS 39762. Offers applied anthropology (MA); sociology (MS, PhD). Part-time programs available. *Faculty:* 19 full-time (8 women), 10 part-time/adjunct (7 women). *Students:* 33 full-time (21 women), 26 part-time (17 women); includes 14 minority (12 African Americans, 1 American Indian/Alaska Native, 1 Asian American or Pacific Islander), 6 international. Average age 33. 17 applicants, 65% accepted, 5 enrolled. In 2007, 7 master's, 4 doctorates awarded. *Degree requirements:* For master's, thesis (for some programs), comprehensive oral or written exam; for doctorate, thesis/dissertation, comprehensive oral and written exam. *Entrance requirements:* For master's and doctorate, GRE. Additional exam requirements/recommendations for international students: Required—TOEFL. *Application deadline:* For fall admission, 4/15 for domestic students; for spring admission, 11/1 for domestic students. Applications are processed on a rolling basis. Application fee: $30. *Expenses:* Tuition, state resident: full-time $4,978; part-time $274 per hour. Tuition, nonresident: full-time $11,469; part-time $635 per hour. *Financial support:* In 2007–08, 14 teaching assistantships with tuition reimbursements (averaging $10,117 per year) were awarded; Federal Work-Study, institutionally sponsored loans, scholarships/grants, and unspecified assistantships also available. Financial award application deadline: 3/15; financial award applicants required to submit FAFSA. *Faculty research:* Community and regional development, criminology, natural resource development, family sociology, gender. Total annual research expenditures: $1 million. *Unit head:* Dr. R. Gregory Dunaway, Head, 662-325-2495, Fax: 662-325-4564, E-mail: dunaway@soc.msstate.edu. *Application contact:* Dr. William A. Person, Interim Associate Vice President for Academic Affairs/Interim Dean of Graduate Studies, 662-325-7400, Fax: 662-325-1967, E-mail: grad@grad.msstate.edu.

Montclair State University, The Office of Graduate Admissions and Support Services, College of Humanities and Social Sciences, Department of Sociology, Montclair, NJ 07043-1624. Offers applied sociology (MA). Part-time and evening/weekend programs available. *Faculty:* 11 full-time (4 women), 17 part-time/adjunct (4 women). In 2007, 1 degree awarded. *Degree requirements:* For master's, comprehensive exam, comprehensive project, internship. *Entrance requirements:* For master's, GRE General Test, 30 undergraduate semester hours in social sciences or history, 2 letters of recommendation. Additional exam requirements/recommendations for international students: Required—TOEFL (minimum score 83 computer-based). *Application deadline:* For fall admission, 6/1 for international students; for spring admission, 10/1 for international students. Applications are processed on a rolling basis. Application fee: $60. Electronic applications accepted. *Financial support:* Research assistantships with full tuition reimbursements, Federal Work-Study, scholarships/grants, and unspecified assistantships available. Support available to part-time students. Financial award application deadline: 3/1; financial award applicants required to submit FAFSA. *Unit head:* Dr. Jay Livingston, Chairperson, 973-655-4131. *Application contact:* Dr. Mary Holley, Adviser, 973-655-7229, E-mail: holleym@mail.montclair.edu.

Morehead State University, Graduate Programs, Caudill College of Humanities, Department of Sociology, Social Work and Criminology, Morehead, KY 40351. Offers criminology (MA); general sociology (MA); gerontology (MA). Part-time and evening/weekend programs available. *Faculty:* 8 full-time (3 women), 2 part-time/adjunct (1 woman). *Students:* 14 full-time (8 women), 7 part-time (3 women). Average age 28. In 2007, 3 degrees awarded. *Degree requirements:* For master's, comprehensive exam, thesis optional. *Entrance requirements:* For master's, GRE General Test, minimum GPA of 3.0 in sociology, 2.5 overall; 18 hours of course work in sociology, writing sample. Additional exam requirements/recommendations for international students: Required—TOEFL (minimum score 500 paper-based; 173 computer-based). *Application deadline:* For fall admission, 8/1 priority date for domestic and international students; for spring admission, 12/1 priority date for domestic and international students. Applications are processed on a rolling basis. Application fee: $0 ($55 for international students). Electronic applications accepted. *Financial support:* In 2007–08, 5 teaching assistantships (averaging $6,000 per year) were awarded; career-related internships or fieldwork, Federal Work-Study, and unspecified assistantships also available. Financial award application deadline: 4/1; financial award applicants required to submit FAFSA. *Faculty research:* Death and dying; aging, drinking, and drugs; economic development; adult children of alcoholics. *Unit head:* Dr. Robert Bylund, Chair, 606-783-2656, Fax: 606-783-5027, E-mail: r.bylund@moreheadstate.edu. *Application contact:* Michelle Barber, Graduate Admissions Counselor, 606-783-2039, Fax: 606-783-5061, E-mail: m.barber@moreheadstate.edu.

Morgan State University, School of Graduate Studies, College of Liberal Arts, Department of Sociology and Anthropology, Baltimore, MD 21251. Offers sociology (MA, MS). Part-time and evening/weekend programs available. *Faculty:* 4 full-time (2 women), 1 part-time/adjunct (0 women). *Students:* 12 (8 women). Average age 25. 5 applicants, 60% accepted. *Degree requirements:* For master's, comprehensive exam. *Entrance requirements:* Additional exam requirements/recommendations for international students: Required—TOEFL (minimum score 550 paper-based; 213 computer-based). *Application deadline:* For fall admission, 2/1 priority date for domestic students; for spring admission, 10/1 priority date for domestic students. Applications are processed on a rolling basis. Application fee: $0. *Financial support:* Application deadline: 2/1. *Faculty research:* Domestic violence, homelessness, social movements, marriage and family. *Unit head:* Dr. Maurice St. Pierre, Chair, 443-885-3518, E-mail: maurice.stpierre@morgan.edu. *Application contact:* Dr. Mark Garrison, Associate Dean, 443-885-3185, Fax: 443-885-8226, E-mail: mark.garrison@morgan.edu.

New Mexico Highlands University, Graduate Studies, College of Arts and Sciences, Program in Public Affairs, Las Vegas, NM 87701. Offers applied sociology (MA). Program is interdisciplinary. *Faculty:* 14 full-time (7 women), 1 (woman) part-time/adjunct. *Students:* 16 full-time (13 women), 9 part-time (4 women); includes 14 minority (1 African American, 1 Asian American or Pacific Islander, 12 Hispanic Americans), 7 international. Average age 36. 43 applicants, 58% accepted, 6 enrolled. In 2007, 5 degrees awarded. *Degree requirements:* For master's, comprehensive exam, thesis or alternative. *Entrance requirements:* For master's, minimum undergraduate GPA of 3.0. Additional exam requirements/recommendations for international students: Required—TOEFL (minimum score 540 paper-based; 190 computer-based). *Application deadline:* For fall admission, 8/1 priority date for domestic students. Applications are processed on a rolling basis. Application fee: $15. *Expenses:* Tuition, state resident: full-time $2,642; part-time $110 per credit hour. Tuition, nonresident: full-time $3,964; part-time $165 per credit hour. International tuition: $5,285 full-time. One-time fee: $20 full-time. *Financial support:* In 2007–08, 14 students received support, including 8 teaching assistantships with full and partial tuition reimbursements available (averaging $6,500 per year); career-related internships or fieldwork, Federal Work-Study, institutionally sponsored loans, scholarships/grants, traineeships, tuition waivers (full and partial), and unspecified assistantships also available. Support available to part-time students. Financial award application deadline: 3/1. *Application contact:* Diane Trujillo, Administrative Assistant Graduate Studies, 505-454-3266, Fax: 505-454-3558, E-mail: dtrujillo@nmhu.edu.

New Mexico State University, Graduate School, College of Arts and Sciences, Department of Sociology and Anthropology, Las Cruces, NM 88003-8001. Offers anthropology (MA); sociology (MA). Part-time programs available. *Faculty:* 11 full-time (6 women), 3 part-time/adjunct (1 woman). *Students:* 42 full-time (30 women), 51 part-time (38 women); includes 5 African Americans, 1 American Indian/Alaska Native, 20 Hispanic Americans, 5 international. Average age 33. 49 applicants, 90% accepted, 28 enrolled. In 2007, 20 degrees awarded. *Degree requirements:* For master's, comprehensive exam (for some programs), thesis (for some programs). *Application deadline:* For fall admission, 2/15 priority date for domestic students; for spring admission, 10/15 priority date for domestic students. Applications are

Sociology

New Mexico State University (continued)

processed on a rolling basis. Application fee: $30 ($50 for international students). Electronic applications accepted. *Expenses:* Tuition, state resident: full-time $3,602; part-time $199 per credit. Tuition, nonresident: full-time $13,380; part-time $607 per credit. Required fees: $1,178. *Financial support:* In 2007–08, 2 fellowships, 1 research assistantship with partial tuition reimbursement, 20 teaching assistantships with partial tuition reimbursements were awarded; career-related internships or fieldwork, Federal Work-Study, and health care benefits also available. Support available to part-time students. Financial award application deadline: 3/1. *Faculty research:* Native American culture and society, Latin America and border studies, prehistoric and historic archaeology, demography, medical sociology and anthropology. *Unit head:* Dr. Lee Hamilton, Head, 575-646-3821, Fax: 575-646-3725, E-mail: lehamilt@nmsu.edu.

The New School: A University, The New School for Social Research, Department of Sociology, New York, NY 10011. Offers MA, DS Sc, PhD. Part-time and evening/weekend programs available. *Faculty:* 11 full-time (5 women). *Students:* 151 full-time (86 women), 31 part-time (19 women); includes 36 minority (14 African Americans, 7 Asian Americans or Pacific Islanders, 15 Hispanic Americans), 64 international. Average age 34. In 2007, 19 master's, 9 doctorates awarded. Terminal master's awarded for partial completion of doctoral program. *Degree requirements:* For master's, exam; for doctorate, one foreign language, thesis/dissertation, qualifying exam. *Entrance requirements:* For master's, GRE General Test; for doctorate, GRE General Test, MA. Additional exam requirements/recommendations for international students: Required—TOEFL (minimum score 600 paper-based; 250 computer-based; 100 iBT). *Application deadline:* For fall admission, 1/15 priority date for domestic students. Applications are processed on a rolling basis. Application fee: $50. *Financial support:* Fellowships, research assistantships, teaching assistantships, career-related internships or fieldwork, Federal Work-Study, scholarships/grants, and tuition waivers (full and partial) available. Financial award application deadline: 3/1; financial award applicants required to submit FAFSA. *Faculty research:* Media, culture, urban sociology, democratic transitions, critical theory. *Unit head:* Dr. Eiko Ikegami, Chair, 212-229-5737 Ext. 4925, E-mail: casanova@newschool.edu. *Application contact:* Robert MacDonald, Director of Admissions, 800-523-5710 Ext. 3007, Fax: 212-989-7102, E-mail: macdonar@newschool.edu.

See Close-Up on page 1653.

New York University, Graduate School of Arts and Science, Department of Sociology, New York, NY 10012-1019. Offers French studies and sociology (PhD); sociology (MA, PhD); JD/MA. Part-time programs available. *Faculty:* 27 full-time (9 women), 1 part-time/adjunct. *Students:* 46 full-time (30 women), 10 part-time (6 women); includes 9 minority (4 African Americans, 3 Asian Americans or Pacific Islanders, 2 Hispanic Americans), 6 international. Average age 30. 348 applicants, 5% accepted, 6 enrolled. In 2007, 8 master's, 9 doctorates awarded. Terminal master's awarded for partial completion of doctoral program. *Degree requirements:* For master's, thesis or alternative; for doctorate, comprehensive exam, thesis/dissertation. *Entrance requirements:* For master's and doctorate, GRE General Test. Additional exam requirements/recommendations for international students: Required—TOEFL. *Application deadline:* For fall admission, 1/4 priority date for domestic students. Application fee: $85. *Financial support:* Fellowships with tuition reimbursements, research assistantships with tuition reimbursements, teaching assistantships with tuition reimbursements, Federal Work-Study, institutionally sponsored loans, scholarships/grants, health care benefits, and unspecified assistantships available. Financial award application deadline: 1/4; financial award applicants required to submit FAFSA. *Faculty research:* Political sociology and social movements; gender and inequality; deviance, law, and crime; education; stratification and theory. *Unit head:* Dalton Conley, Chair, 212-998-8340, Fax: 212-995-4140, E-mail: gsas.sociology.info@nyu.edu. *Application contact:* Vivek Chibber, Director of Graduate Studies, 212-998-8340, Fax: 212-995-4140, E-mail: gsas.sociology.info@nyu.edu.

New York University, Steinhardt School of Culture, Education and Human Development, Department of Humanities and Social Sciences in the Professions, Program in Sociology of Education, New York, NY 10012-1019. Offers education policy (MA); social and cultural studies of education (MA); sociology of education (PhD). Part-time and evening/weekend programs available. *Faculty:* 5 full-time (2 women). *Students:* 17 full-time (12 women), 10 part-time (9 women); includes 10 minority (4 African Americans, 1 Asian American or Pacific Islander, 5 Hispanic Americans), 2 international. 64 applicants, 58% accepted, 11 enrolled. In 2007, 8 master's awarded. Terminal master's awarded for partial completion of doctoral program. *Degree requirements:* For master's, thesis (for some programs); for doctorate, thesis/dissertation. *Entrance requirements:* For master's, letters of recommendation; for doctorate, GRE General Test, interview. Additional exam requirements/recommendations for international students: Required—TOEFL. *Application deadline:* For fall admission, 12/15 priority date for domestic and international students; for spring admission, 11/1 for domestic and international students. Applications are processed on a rolling basis. Application fee: $50. *Financial support:* Fellowships with full and partial tuition reimbursements, Federal Work-Study, institutionally sponsored loans, scholarships/grants, and tuition waivers (partial) available. Support available to part-time students. Financial award application deadline: 2/1; financial award applicants required to submit FAFSA. *Faculty research:* Legal and institutional environments of schools; social inequality; high school reform and achievement; education's link with occupations, professions and inequality. *Unit head:* Dr. Floyd M. Hammack, Program Director, 212-992-9475, Fax: 212-995-4832, E-mail: fmhl@nyu.edu. *Application contact:* 212-998-5030, Fax: 212-995-4328, E-mail: steinhardt.gradadmissions@nyu.edu.

Norfolk State University, School of Graduate Studies, School of Liberal Arts, Department of Sociology, Program in Applied Sociology, Norfolk, VA 23504. Offers MS. Part-time programs available.

North Carolina Central University, Division of Academic Affairs, College of Arts and Sciences, Department of Sociology, Durham, NC 27707-3129. Offers MA. Part-time and evening/weekend programs available. *Degree requirements:* For master's, one foreign language, comprehensive exam, thesis. *Entrance requirements:* For master's, GRE, minimum GPA of 3.0 in major, 2.5 overall. Additional exam requirements/recommendations for international students: Required—TOEFL. *Faculty research:* Urban demography, family, statistical methods.

North Carolina State University, Graduate School, College of Humanities and Social Sciences, Department of Sociology and Anthropology, Program in Sociology, Raleigh, NC 27695. Offers rural sociology (MS); sociology (M Soc, PhD). Part-time programs available. *Degree requirements:* For master's, thesis (for some programs), practicum (M Soc), thesis (MS); for doctorate, comprehensive exam, thesis/dissertation. *Entrance requirements:* For master's and doctorate, GRE General Test, sample of written work. Electronic applications accepted. *Faculty research:* Inequity: gender, race and class; crime and social control; work and organizations; rural sociology; family and intimate relations.

North Dakota State University, College of Graduate and Interdisciplinary Studies, College of Arts, Humanities and Social Sciences, Department of Sociology, Anthropology, and Emergency Management, Fargo, ND 58105. Offers emergency management (MS, PhD); social science (MA, MS); sociology (MS). Part-time programs available. *Faculty:* 8 full-time (3 women), 5 part-time/adjunct (2 women). *Students:* 20 full-time (13 women), 14 part-time (8 women); includes 1 minority (American Indian/Alaska Native), 3 international. Average age 27. 15 applicants, 60% accepted, 7 enrolled. In 2007, 7 degrees awarded. *Degree requirements:* For master's, thesis; for doctorate, comprehensive exam, thesis/dissertation. *Entrance requirements:* For master's, GRE (emergency management), course work in sociology, minimum GPA of 3.2; for doctorate, GRE, minimum GPA of 3.2. Additional exam requirements/recommendations for international students: Required—TOEFL. *Application deadline:* For fall admission, 4/1 priority date for domestic students. Applications are processed on a rolling basis. Application fee: $45 ($60 for international students). *Expenses:* Tuition, state resident: full-time $5,376; part-time $224 per credit. Tuition, nonresident: full-time $14,354; part-time $598 per credit. Required fees: $962; $40 per credit. Part-time tuition and fees vary according to course load and reciprocity agreements. *Financial support:* In 2007–08, 7 research assistantships with full tuition reimbursements (averaging $6,156 per year), 7 teaching assistantships with full tuition reimbursements (averaging $3,078 per year) were awarded; fellowships, career-related internships or fieldwork, Federal Work-Study, institutionally sponsored loans, and tuition waivers (full) also available. Support available to part-time students. Financial award application deadline: 4/15. *Faculty research:* Medical sociology, demography, ethnology, archaeology. Total annual research expenditures: $75,000. *Unit head:* Dr. Daniel J. Klenow, Chair, 701-231-8657, Fax: 701-231-1047, E-mail: daniel.klenow@ndsu.edu.

Northeastern University, College of Arts and Sciences, Department of Sociology and Anthropology, Boston, MA 02115-5096. Offers sociology (MA, PhD). Part-time programs available. *Faculty:* 21 full-time (10 women), 4 part-time/adjunct (0 women). *Students:* 52 full-time (35 women), 2 part-time (1 woman). 79 applicants, 33% accepted. In 2007, 9 master's, 4 doctorates awarded. *Degree requirements:* For master's, thesis; for doctorate, thesis/dissertation, teaching tutorial. *Entrance requirements:* For master's and doctorate, GRE General Test or MAT. Additional exam requirements/recommendations for international students: Required—TOEFL. *Application deadline:* For fall admission, 2/1 for domestic students. Application fee: $50. *Financial support:* In 2007–08, 14 teaching assistantships with tuition reimbursements (averaging $14,035 per year) were awarded; fellowships, research assistantships with tuition reimbursements, career-related internships or fieldwork, tuition waivers (full and partial), and unspecified assistantships also available. Financial award application deadline: 2/1; financial award applicants required to submit FAFSA. *Faculty research:* Globalization and international studies, urban affairs, social justice. *Unit head:* Dr. Steven Vallas, Acting Chair, 617-373-2686, Fax: 617-373-2688, E-mail: gradsoc@neu.edu. *Application contact:* Graduate Programs Assistant, 617-373-2686, Fax: 617-373-2688, E-mail: gradsoc@neu.edu.

Northern Arizona University, Graduate College, College of Social and Behavioral Sciences, Department of Sociology and Social Work, Flagstaff, AZ 86011. Offers applied sociology (MA). Part-time programs available. *Degree requirements:* For master's, thesis or internship. *Faculty research:* Demography, death and dying, criminology, social policy, divorce.

Northern Illinois University, Graduate School, College of Liberal Arts and Sciences, Department of Sociology, De Kalb, IL 60115-2854. Offers MA. Part-time programs available. *Faculty:* 14 full-time (3 women). *Students:* 19 full-time (12 women), 15 part-time (8 women); includes 3 minority (2 African Americans, 1 Asian American or Pacific Islander). Average age 28. 31 applicants, 58% accepted, 12 enrolled. In 2007, 7 degrees awarded. *Degree requirements:* For master's, comprehensive exam, thesis optional. *Entrance requirements:* For master's, GRE General Test, minimum GPA of 2.75; course work in social theory, social methods, and statistics. Additional exam requirements/recommendations for international students: Required—TOEFL (minimum score 550 paper-based; 213 computer-based). *Application deadline:* For fall admission, 6/1 for domestic students, 5/1 for international students; for spring admission, 11/1 for domestic students, 10/1 for international students. Applications are processed on a rolling basis. Application fee: $30. Electronic applications accepted. *Expenses:* Tuition, area resident: Part-time $226 per credit hour. Tuition, state resident: full-time $5,424; part-time $225 per credit hour. Tuition, nonresident: full-time $10,848. Required fees: $2,416; $64 per credit hour. *Financial support:* In 2007–08, 23 research assistantships with full tuition reimbursements, 2 teaching assistantships with full tuition reimbursements were awarded; fellowships with full tuition reimbursements, career-related internships or fieldwork, Federal Work-Study, scholarships/grants, tuition waivers (full), and unspecified assistantships also available. Support available to part-time students. Financial award applicants required to submit FAFSA. *Faculty research:* Welfare reform, interpersonal disputes, multicultural education, race and ethnicism, social control. *Unit head:* Dr. Kay Forest, Chair, 815-753-1194, Fax: 815-753-6302, E-mail: k.forest@niu.edu. *Application contact:* Dr. David Luckenbill, Director, Graduate Studies, 815-753-6429, E-mail: dfl@niu.edu.

Northwestern University, The Graduate School, Interdepartmental Degree Programs and Kellogg School of Management, Program in Management and Organizations and Sociology, Evanston, IL 60208. Offers PhD. Program requires admission to both The Graduate School and the Kellogg Graduate School of Management. *Degree requirements:* For doctorate, comprehensive exam, thesis/dissertation. *Entrance requirements:* For doctorate, GRE General Test. Additional exam requirements/recommendations for international students: Required—TOEFL. Electronic applications accepted. *Faculty research:* Strategic alliances and organizational competitiveness, institutional change and the information of industries, social capital and the creation of financial capital, negotiation, organizational networks, diversity.

Northwestern University, The Graduate School, Judd A. and Marjorie Weinberg College of Arts and Sciences, Department of Sociology, Evanston, IL 60208. Offers PhD, JD/PhD. Admissions and degrees offered through The Graduate School. *Degree requirements:* For doctorate, thesis/dissertation. *Entrance requirements:* For doctorate, GRE General Test. Additional exam requirements/recommendations for international students: Required—TOEFL. Electronic applications accepted. *Faculty research:* Sociology of culture, social organizations, social inequality, comparative/historical sociology, economic sociology.

The Ohio State University, Graduate School, College of Social and Behavioral Sciences, School of Social and Behavioral Science, Department of Sociology, Columbus, OH 43210. Offers MA, PhD. *Faculty:* 41. *Students:* 89 full-time (57 women), 5 part-time (3 women); includes 20 minority (12 African Americans, 4 Asian Americans or Pacific Islanders, 4 Hispanic Americans), 7 international. Average age 28. In 2007, 23 master's, 3 doctorates awarded. *Degree requirements:* For master's, thesis; for doctorate, thesis/dissertation. *Entrance requirements:* For master's and doctorate, GRE General Test. Additional exam requirements/recommendations for international students: Required—TOEFL (minimum score 600 paper-based; 250 computer-based). *Application deadline:* For fall admission, 8/15 priority date for domestic students, 7/1 priority date for international students; for winter admission, 12/1 priority date for domestic students, 11/1 priority date for international students; for spring admission, 3/1 priority date for domestic students, 2/1 priority date for international students. Applications are processed on a rolling basis. Application fee: $40 ($50 for international students). Electronic applications accepted. *Financial support:* Fellowships, research assistantships, teaching assistantships, Federal Work-Study and institutionally sponsored loans available. Support available to part-time students. *Unit head:* Dana Haynie, Graduate Studies Committee Chair, 614-292-8432, Fax: 614-292-6687, E-mail: haynie.7@osu.edu. *Application contact:* 614-292-9444, Fax: 614-292-3895, E-mail: domestic.grad@osu.edu.

Ohio University, Graduate College, College of Arts and Sciences, Department of Sociology and Anthropology, Athens, OH 45701-2979. Offers sociology (MA). Part-time programs available. *Faculty:* 17 full-time (8 women). *Students:* 19 full-time (14 women), 4 part-time (3 women); includes 4 minority (3 African Americans, 1 Asian American or Pacific Islander), 3 international. Average age 25. 24 applicants, 88% accepted, 15 enrolled. In 2007, 10 degrees awarded. *Degree requirements:* For master's, thesis or alternative. *Entrance requirements:* For master's, minimum GPA of 3.0, minimum 20 hours sociology included with stats, theory, and research methods. Additional exam requirements/recommendations for international students: Required—TOEFL. *Application deadline:* For fall admission, 6/1 priority date for domestic and international students; for winter admission, 10/1 for domestic and international students; for spring admission, 1/1 for domestic and international students. Applications are processed on a rolling basis. Application fee: $50 ($55 for international students). Electronic applications accepted. *Financial support:* In 2007–08, 14 students received support, including 10 research assistantships with full and partial tuition reimbursements available, 4 teaching assistantships with full tuition reimbursements available (averaging $12,399 per year); career-related internships or fieldwork and unspecified assistantships also available. Financial award application deadline: 3/1. *Faculty research:* Criminology/deviance, gender studies, inequality, social psychology and rural poverty. *Unit head:* Dr. Ann R. Tickamyer, Department Chair, 740-593-1377, Fax: 740-593-1365, E-mail: tickamye@ohio.edu. *Application contact:* Dr. Cynthia D. Anderson, Graduate Chair, 740-593-1385, Fax: 740-593-1365, E-mail: andersc2@ohio.edu.

Oklahoma State University, College of Arts and Sciences, Department of Sociology, Stillwater, OK 74078. Offers corrections (MS); sociology (MS, PhD). *Faculty:* 16 full-time (4 women), 1 (woman) part-time/adjunct. *Students:* 15 full-time (9 women), 23 part-time (16 women); includes 5 minority (3 African Americans, 1 American Indian/Alaska Native, 1 Hispanic American), 6 international. Average age 36. 46 applicants, 33% accepted, 11 enrolled. In 2007, 4 degrees awarded. *Degree requirements:* For master's, thesis; for doctorate, 2 foreign languages, thesis/dissertation. *Entrance requirements:* For master's and doctorate, GRE General Test or GMAT. Additional exam requirements/recommendations for international students: Required—TOEFL. *Application deadline:* For fall admission, 3/1 priority date for international students; for spring admission, 8/1 priority date for international students. Applications are processed on a rolling basis. Application fee: $40 ($75 for international students). Electronic applications accepted. *Expenses:* Tuition, state resident: full-time $4,993; part-time $148 per credit hour. Tuition, nonresident: full-time $14,755; part-time $555 per credit hour. Tuition and fees vary according to program. *Financial support:* In 2007–08, 4 research assistantships (averaging $12,515 per year), 19 teaching assistantships (averaging $14,478 per year) were awarded; career-related internships or fieldwork, Federal Work-Study, scholarships/grants, health care benefits, tuition waivers (partial), and unspecified assistantships also available. Support available to part-time students. Financial award application deadline: 3/1. *Faculty research:* Criminology/correction/legal issues; race, ethnicity, and gender in American society; environmental conflict and population problems; international comparative research; social change and social movement in American culture. *Unit head:* Dr. Patricia Bell, Head, 405-744-6105.

Old Dominion University, College of Arts and Letters, Program in Applied Sociology, Norfolk, VA 23529. Offers MA. Part-time and evening/weekend programs available. *Faculty:* 15 full-time (10 women), 1 part-time/adjunct (0 women). *Students:* 8 full-time (6 women), 25 part-time (18 women); includes 8 minority (6 African Americans, 1 Asian American or Pacific Islander, 1 Hispanic American). Average age 26. 26 applicants, 65% accepted, 12 enrolled. In 2007, 5 degrees awarded. *Degree requirements:* For master's, thesis, 36 credit hours. *Entrance requirements:* For master's, GRE General Test, minimum GPA of 3.0, 12 credits in criminal justice, sociology, or women's studies. Additional exam requirements/recommendations for international students: Required—TOEFL. *Application deadline:* For fall admission, 5/1 priority date for domestic students; for spring admission, 11/1 for domestic students. Applications are processed on a rolling basis. Application fee: $40. Electronic applications accepted. *Expenses:* Tuition, state resident: part-time $304 per credit hour. Tuition, nonresident: part-time $761 per credit hour. *Financial support:* In 2007–08, fellowships (averaging $2,000 per year), 2 research assistantships with partial tuition reimbursements (averaging $8,000 per year), 2 teaching assistantships with partial tuition reimbursements (averaging $8,000 per year) were awarded; career-related internships or fieldwork, scholarships/grants, and unspecified assistantships also available. Support available to part-time students. Financial award application deadline: 2/15; financial award applicants required to submit CSS PROFILE or FAFSA. *Faculty research:* Quantitative methodology, theory, family, gender/class/race, crime. Total annual research expenditures: $350,000. *Unit head:* Dr. Dianne Carmody, Graduate Program Director, 757-683-6801, Fax: 757-683-5634, E-mail: dcarmody@odu.edu.

Our Lady of the Lake University of San Antonio, School of Education and Clinical Studies, Program in Sociology, San Antonio, TX 78207-4689. Offers MA. Part-time and evening/weekend programs available. *Degree requirements:* For master's, comprehensive exam, thesis optional. *Entrance requirements:* For master's, GRE General Test or MAT, interview. Additional exam requirements/recommendations for international students: Required—TOEFL. Electronic applications accepted. *Faculty research:* Criminal justice, health care, family, Southwest studies.

Penn State University Park, Graduate School, College of the Liberal Arts, Department of Sociology, State College, University Park, PA 16802-1503. Offers crime, law, and justice (MA, PhD); sociology (MA, PhD). *Expenses:* Tuition, state resident: full-time $14,738; part-time $614 per credit. Tuition, nonresident: full-time $26,050; part-time $1,085 per credit. Tuition and fees vary according to course load, program and student level. *Unit head:* Dr. John D. McCarthy, Head, 814-863-8260, Fax: 814-863-7216, E-mail: jxm516@psu.edu.

Portland State University, Graduate Studies, College of Liberal Arts and Sciences, Department of Sociology, Portland, OR 97207-0751. Offers MA, MS, PhD. Part-time programs available. *Faculty:* 14 full-time (5 women), 2 part-time/adjunct (1 woman). *Students:* 22 full-time (17 women), 12 part-time (6 women); includes 3 minority (1 African American, 2 Hispanic Americans). Average age 31. 20 applicants, 85% accepted, 10 enrolled. In 2007, 5 degrees awarded. *Degree requirements:* For master's, variable foreign language requirement, thesis, written exam; for doctorate, thesis/dissertation. *Entrance requirements:* For master's, GRE General Test, GRE Subject Test, minimum GPA of 3.0 in upper-division course work or 2.75 overall,3 letters of recommendation. Additional exam requirements/recommendations for international students: Required—TOEFL (minimum score 550 paper-based; 213 computer-based). *Application deadline:* For fall admission, 2/1 priority date for domestic and international students. Applications are processed on a rolling basis. Application fee: $50. *Expenses:* Tuition, state resident: full-time $7,047. Tuition, nonresident: full-time $11,178. *Financial support:* In 2007–08, research assistantships with full tuition reimbursements (averaging $5,508 per year); fellowships with full tuition reimbursements, teaching assistantships with full tuition reimbursements, career-related internships or fieldwork, Federal Work-Study, and unspecified assistantships also available. Support available to part-time students. Financial award application deadline: 3/1; financial award applicants required to submit FAFSA. *Faculty research:* Urban sociology, gender and class, development, social change, race/ethnic/minority relations. Total annual research expenditures: $409,409. *Unit head:* Veronica Dujon, Chair, 503-725-3926. *Application contact:* Bahar Jaberi, Information Contact, 503-725-3926.

Portland State University, Graduate Studies, Systems Science Program, Portland, OR 97207-0751. Offers computational intelligence (Certificate); computer modeling and simulation (Certificate); systems science (MS); systems science/anthropology (PhD); systems science/business administration (PhD); systems science/civil engineering (PhD); systems science/economics (PhD); systems science/engineering management (PhD); systems science/general (PhD); systems science/mathematical sciences (PhD); systems science/mechanical engineering (PhD); systems science/psychology (PhD); systems science/sociology (PhD). *Faculty:* 3 full-time (0 women). *Students:* 9 full-time (2 women), 11 part-time (2 women); includes 6 minority (3 Asian Americans or Pacific Islanders, 3 Hispanic Americans), 13 international. Average age 38. 8 applicants, 100% accepted, 6 enrolled. In 2007, 4 master's, 6 doctorates awarded. *Degree requirements:* For doctorate, variable foreign language requirement, thesis/dissertation. *Entrance requirements:* For master's, 2 letters of recommendation; for doctorate, GMAT, GRE General Test, minimum undergraduate GPA of 3.0. Additional exam requirements/recommendations for international students: Required—TOEFL. *Application deadline:* For fall admission, 2/1 for domestic students; for spring admission, 11/1 for domestic students. Application fee: $50. *Expenses:* Tuition, state resident: full-time $7,047. Tuition, nonresident: full-time $11,178. *Financial support:* In 2007–08, 1 research assistantship with full tuition reimbursement (averaging $5,980 per year) was awarded; teaching assistantships with full tuition reimbursements, career-related internships or fieldwork, Federal Work-Study, scholarships/grants, and unspecified assistantships also available. Support available to part-time students. Financial award application deadline: 3/1; financial award applicants required to submit FAFSA. *Faculty research:* Systems theory and methodology, artificial intelligence neural networks, information theory, nonlinear dynamics/chaos, modeling and simulation. Total annual research expenditures: $5,370. *Unit head:* George Lendaris, Acting Director, 503-725-4960. *Application contact:* Dawn Sharafi, Administrative Assistant, 503-725-4960, E-mail: dawn@sysc.pdx.edu.

Prairie View A&M University, College of Arts and Sciences, Division of Social Work, Behavioral and Political Science, Prairie View, TX 77446-0519. Offers sociology (MA). Part-time and evening/weekend programs available. *Faculty:* 4 part-time/adjunct (3 women). *Students:* 7 full-time (6 women), 8 part-time (7 women); includes 17 minority (15 African Americans, 2 American Indian/Alaska Native). Average age 35. 5 applicants, 100% accepted, 5 enrolled. In 2007, 5 degrees awarded. *Degree requirements:* For master's, comprehensive exam, thesis optional. *Entrance requirements:* For master's, GRE General Test. *Application deadline:* Applications are processed on a rolling basis. Application fee: $50. *Financial support:* Federal Work-Study and institutionally sponsored loans available. Financial award application deadline: 4/1; financial award applicants required to submit FAFSA. *Faculty research:* Criminology, political sociology, sociology of education, gender, race, African American mental health, global development-social movements, African American status attainment. *Unit head:* Dr. Walle Engedayehu, Division Head, 936-261-3200, Fax: 936-261-3229, E-mail: waengedayehu@pvamu.edu. *Application contact:* Dr. Sarah B. Williams, Professor and Coordinator of Sociology, 936-261-3221, Fax: 936-261-3229, E-mail: sbwilliams@pvamu.edu.

Princeton University, Graduate School, Department of Sociology, Princeton, NJ 08544-1019. Offers sociology (PhD); sociology and demography (PhD). *Degree requirements:* For doctorate, variable foreign language requirement, thesis/dissertation. *Entrance requirements:* For doctorate, GRE General Test, GRE Subject Test (recommended), sample of written work. Additional exam requirements/recommendations for international students: Required—TOEFL (minimum score 600 paper-based; 250 computer-based). Electronic applications accepted.

Princeton University, Graduate School, Program in Population Studies, Princeton, NJ 08544-1019. Offers demography (PhD, Certificate); demography and public affairs (PhD); economics and demography (PhD); sociology and demography (PhD). *Degree requirements:* For doctorate, thesis/dissertation. *Entrance requirements:* For doctorate, GRE General Test. Additional exam requirements/recommendations for international students: Required—TOEFL (minimum score 600 paper-based; 250 computer-based). Electronic applications accepted. *Faculty research:* Models, fertility, infant and child mortality, migration.

Purdue University, Graduate School, College of Liberal Arts, Department of Sociology and Anthropology, West Lafayette, IN 47907. Offers anthropology (MS, PhD); sociology (MS, PhD). Terminal master's awarded for partial completion of doctoral program. *Degree requirements:* For doctorate, thesis/dissertation. *Entrance requirements:* For master's and doctorate, GRE General Test. Additional exam requirements/recommendations for international students: Required—TOEFL, TWE. Electronic applications accepted. *Faculty research:* Communiversity survey project, risk, fear, constrained behavior, archaeological services.

Queens College of the City University of New York, Division of Graduate Studies, Social Science Division, Department of Sociology, Flushing, NY 11367-1597. Offers MA. Part-time and evening/weekend programs available. *Faculty:* 26 full-time (9 women). *Students:* 6 full-time (5 women), 24 part-time (16 women). 30 applicants, 73% accepted, 14 enrolled. In 2007, 14 degrees awarded. *Degree requirements:* For master's, thesis optional. *Entrance requirements:* For master's, minimum GPA of 3.0. Additional exam requirements/recommendations for international students: Required—TOEFL. *Application deadline:* For fall admission, 4/1 for domestic students; for spring admission, 11/1 for domestic students. Applications are processed on a rolling basis. Application fee: $125. *Financial support:* Career-related internships or fieldwork, Federal Work-Study, institutionally sponsored loans, and tuition waivers (partial) available. Support available to part-time students. Financial award application deadline: 4/1; financial award applicants required to submit FAFSA. *Unit head:* Dr. Andrew Beveridge, Chairperson, 718-997-2800.

Queen's University at Kingston, School of Graduate Studies and Research, Faculty of Arts and Sciences, Department of Sociology, Kingston, ON K7L 3N6, Canada. Offers MA, PhD. Part-time programs available. *Degree requirements:* For master's, thesis; for doctorate, comprehensive exam, thesis/dissertation. *Entrance requirements:* For master's, honors bachelors degree in sociology; for doctorate, honors bachelors degree, masters degree in sociology. Additional exam requirements/recommendations for international students: Required—TOEFL. *Faculty research:* Social change and modernization, social control, deviance and criminology, surveillance.

Roosevelt University, Graduate Division, College of Arts and Sciences, Department of Sociology and Anthropology, Chicago, IL 60605-1394. Offers anthropology (MA); sociology (MA). Part-time and evening/weekend programs available. *Students:* 7 full-time (4 women), 22 part-time (18 women); includes 14 minority (13 African Americans, 1 Asian American or Pacific Islander). Average age 35. 24 applicants, 54% accepted, 8 enrolled. In 2007, 4 degrees awarded. *Degree requirements:* For master's, comprehensive exam, thesis. *Application deadline:* For fall admission, 6/1 priority date for domestic students. Applications are processed on a rolling basis. Application fee: $25 ($35 for international students). *Financial support:* Teaching assistantships available. Financial award application deadline: 2/15. *Faculty research:* Social theory, urban sociology, gerontology, social organizations. *Unit head:* Michael Maly, Head, 312-341-3769, E-mail: mmaly@roosevelt.edu. *Application contact:* Joanne Canyon-Heller, Coordinator of Graduate Admission, 877-APPLY RU, Fax: 312-281-3356, E-mail: applyru@roosevelt.edu.

Rutgers, The State University of New Jersey, New Brunswick, Graduate School, Program in Sociology, New Brunswick, NJ 08901-1281. Offers MA, PhD. Terminal master's awarded for partial completion of doctoral program. *Degree requirements:* For master's, qualifying paper; for doctorate, thesis/dissertation, qualifying exam, qualifying papers. *Entrance requirements:* For master's, GRE General Test; for doctorate, GRE General Test, sample of written work. Additional exam requirements/recommendations for international students: Required—TOEFL. Electronic applications accepted. *Faculty research:* Comparative-historical, sex and gender, organizations and work, culture and cognition, economics, occupations/professions, religion.

Sage Graduate School, Graduate School, Department of Sociology and Criminal Justice, Troy, NY 12180-4115. Offers forensic mental health (MS, Certificate). *Expenses:* Tuition: Full-time $9,720; part-time $540 per credit hour. *Application contact:* Shannon K. Easton.

St. John's University, St. John's College of Liberal Arts and Sciences, Department of Sociology and Anthropology, Queens, NY 11439. Offers criminology and justice (MA); sociology (MA). Part-time and evening/weekend programs available. *Faculty:* 13 full-time (6 women), 15 part-time/adjunct (6 women). *Students:* 28 full-time (17 women), 49 part-time (28 women); includes 37 minority (21 African Americans, 4 Asian Americans or Pacific Islanders, 12 Hispanic Americans), 5 international. Average age 28. 59 applicants, 78% accepted, 36 enrolled. In 2007, 22 degrees awarded. *Degree requirements:* For master's, comprehensive exam, thesis optional. *Entrance requirements:* For master's, 18 undergraduate credits in social services, minimum GPA of 3.0. Additional exam requirements/recommendations for international students: Required—TOEFL (minimum score 500 paper-based; 173 computer-based; 61 iBT), IELTS (minimum score 6). *Application deadline:* For fall admission, 5/1 priority date for domestic and international students; for spring admission, 11/1 priority date for domestic and international students. Applications are processed on a rolling basis. Application fee: $40. Electronic applications accepted. *Financial support:* Research assistantships, career-related internships or fieldwork and scholarships/grants available. Support available to part-time students. Financial award application deadline: 3/1; financial award applicants required to submit FAFSA. *Faculty research:* Global black power movement, poverty, domestic violence and human trafficking, female juvenile violence, media and race. *Unit head:* Dr. Dawn Esposito, Chair, 718-990-5667, E-mail: espositd@stjohns.edu. *Application contact:* Beth Evans, Associate Vice President and Executive Director, Enrollment Management, 718-990-6999, Fax: 718-990-5686, E-mail: gradhelp@stjohns.edu.

Sam Houston State University, College of Humanities and Social Sciences, Department of Sociology, Huntsville, TX 77341. Offers MA. Part-time programs available. *Faculty:* 9 full-time (6 women). *Students:* 3 full-time (2 women), 4 part-time (2 women); includes 3 minority (2 Asian Americans or Pacific Islanders, 1 Hispanic American). Average age 33. In 2007, 2 degrees awarded. *Degree requirements:* For master's, thesis optional. *Entrance requirements:* For master's, GRE General Test. Additional exam requirements/recommendations for international students: Required—TOEFL (minimum score 550 paper-based; 213 computer-based). *Application deadline:* For fall admission, 8/1 for domestic students; for spring admission,

Sociology

Sam Houston State University (continued)

12/1 for domestic students. Applications are processed on a rolling basis. Application fee: $20. *Expenses:* Tuition, state resident: full-time $5,026; part-time $184 per semester hour. Tuition, nonresident: full-time $10,586; part-time $462 per semester hour. Required fees: $494 per semester. *Financial support:* Teaching assistantships, Federal Work-Study available. Support available to part-time students. Financial award application deadline: 5/31; financial award applicants required to submit FAFSA. *Unit head:* Dr. Alessandro Bonanno, Chair, 936-294-1488, Fax: 963-294-3573, E-mail: soc_aab@shsu.edu.

San Diego State University, Graduate and Research Affairs, College of Arts and Letters, Department of Sociology, San Diego, CA 92182. Offers MA. *Students:* 32 full-time (21 women), 10 part-time (8 women); includes 15 minority (1 African American, 5 Asian Americans or Pacific Islanders, 9 Hispanic Americans), 2 international. Average age 29. 36 applicants, 64% accepted, 20 enrolled. In 2007, 10 degrees awarded. *Degree requirements:* For master's, thesis. *Entrance requirements:* For master's, GRE General Test, 3 letters of recommendation, writing sample. Additional exam requirements/recommendations for international students: Required—TOEFL. *Application deadline:* For fall admission, 5/1 for domestic and international students; for spring admission, 11/1 for domestic students, 10/1 for international students. Applications are processed on a rolling basis. Application fee: $55. Electronic applications accepted. *Financial support:* In 2007–08, 13 teaching assistantships were awarded; fellowships, career-related internships or fieldwork also available. Financial award applicants required to submit FAFSA. *Faculty research:* The homeless and mentally ill, medical data relating to the homeless. Total annual research expenditures: $148,820. *Unit head:* Phillip T. Gay, Chair, 619-594-5449. *Application contact:* Jill Esbenshade, Graduate Advisor, 619-594-5519, Fax: 619-594-1325, E-mail: jesbensh@mail.sdsu.edu.

San Jose State University, Graduate Studies and Research, College of Social Sciences, Department of Sociology, San Jose, CA 95192-0001. Offers MA. Part-time and evening/weekend programs available. *Students:* 12 full-time (9 women), 22 part-time (15 women); includes 12 minority (1 African American, 1 American Indian/Alaska Native, 6 Asian Americans or Pacific Islanders, 4 Hispanic Americans), 2 international. Average age 32. 27 applicants, 74% accepted, 13 enrolled. In 2007, 20 degrees awarded. *Degree requirements:* For master's, comprehensive exams or thesis. *Entrance requirements:* For master's, GRE Subject Test, minimum GPA of 3.0. *Application deadline:* For fall admission, 6/29 for domestic students; for spring admission, 11/30 for domestic students. Applications are processed on a rolling basis. Application fee: $59. Electronic applications accepted. *Financial support:* In 2007–08, 1 teaching assistantship was awarded; career-related internships or fieldwork, Federal Work-Study, and institutionally sponsored loans also available. Financial award application deadline: 3/1; financial award applicants required to submit FAFSA. *Faculty research:* Theory construction, sexuality, sociology of the media, social causes of stress, social change. *Unit head:* Yoko Baba, Chair, 408-924-5320, Fax: 408-924-5322. *Application contact:* Chris Hebert, Graduate Coordinator, 408-924-1363, E-mail: cghebert@email.sjsu.edu.

Shippensburg University of Pennsylvania, School of Graduate Studies, College of Arts and Sciences, Department of Sociology, Shippensburg, PA 17257-2299. Offers organizational development and leadership (MS). Part-time and evening/weekend programs available. *Faculty:* 4 full-time (all women). *Students:* 14 full-time (7 women), 38 part-time (19 women); includes 7 minority (all African Americans), 1 international. Average age 32. 32 applicants, 63% accepted, 10 enrolled. In 2007, 19 degrees awarded. *Degree requirements:* For master's, internship or practicum, research paper or project. *Entrance requirements:* For master's, interview (if GPA less than 2.75), resumé or goals statement. Additional exam requirements/recommendations for international students: Required—TOEFL (minimum score 560 paper-based; 220 computer-based). *Application deadline:* For fall admission, 6/1 priority date for domestic students, 3/1 for international students; for spring admission, 11/1 priority date for domestic students, 7/1 for international students. Applications are processed on a rolling basis. Application fee: $30. Electronic applications accepted. *Expenses:* Tuition, state resident: part-time $345 per credit. Tuition, nonresident: part-time $552 per credit. Required fees: $28 per credit. Tuition and fees vary according to course load. *Financial support:* In 2007–08, 8 research assistantships with full tuition reimbursements (averaging $3,575 per year) were awarded; career-related internships or fieldwork, scholarships/grants, and unspecified assistantships also available. Support available to part-time students. *Unit head:* Dr. Robert Pineda-Volk, Chairperson, 717-477-1735, Fax: 717-477-4011, E-mail: rwvolk@ship.edu. *Application contact:* Renee Payne, Associate Dean of Graduate Admissions, 717-477-1231, Fax: 717-477-4016, E-mail: rmpayn@ship.edu.

Simon Fraser University, Graduate Studies, Faculty of Arts and Social Sciences, Department of Sociology and Anthropology, Burnaby, BC V5A 1S6, Canada. Offers anthropology (MA, PhD); sociology (MA, PhD). *Degree requirements:* For master's, thesis (for some programs); for doctorate, thesis/dissertation. *Entrance requirements:* For master's and doctorate, minimum GPA of 3.25. Additional exam requirements/recommendations for international students: Required—TOEFL or IELTS. *Faculty research:* Sociology theory, social and cultural anthropology, political sociology, religion and society, Canadian native peoples.

Southeastern Louisiana University, College of Arts, Humanities and Social Sciences, Department of Sociology and Criminal Justice, Hammond, LA 70402. Offers applied sociology (MS). Part-time and evening/weekend programs available. *Faculty:* 8 full-time (4 women). *Students:* 20 full-time (14 women), 8 part-time (5 women); includes 10 minority (all African Americans) Average age 28. 9 applicants, 89% accepted, 7 enrolled. In 2007, 7 degrees awarded. *Degree requirements:* For master's, comprehensive exam, thesis or alternative. *Entrance requirements:* For master's, GRE General Test, bachelor's degree in sociology, social work, criminal justice or related social science; minimum GPA of 3.0. Additional exam requirements/recommendations for international students: Required—TOEFL (minimum score 500 paper-based; 173 computer-based). *Application deadline:* For fall admission, 7/15 priority date for domestic students, 6/1 priority date for international students; for spring admission, 12/1 priority date for domestic students, 10/1 priority date for international students. Application fee: $20 ($30 for international students). *Expenses:* Tuition, state resident: full-time $2,216; part-time $123 per credit. Tuition, nonresident: full-time $6,716; part-time $373 per credit. Required fees: $1,105; $61 per credit. *Financial support:* In 2007–08, 6 research assistantships with full tuition reimbursements (averaging $6,750 per year) were awarded; Federal Work-Study, institutionally sponsored loans, scholarships/grants, unspecified assistantships, and administrative assistantships also available. Support available to part-time students. Financial award application deadline: 5/1; financial award applicants required to submit FAFSA. *Faculty research:* Community development, population and migration trends, environmental sociology, homicide and crime mapping, race and gender in the justice system. Total annual research expenditures: $3,399. *Unit head:* Dr. Kenneth Bolton, Interim Department Head, 985-549-2110, Fax: 985-549-5961, E-mail: kbolton@selu.edu. *Application contact:* Sandra Meyers, Graduate Admissions Analyst, 985-549-2066, Fax: 985-549-5632, E-mail: admissions@selu.edu.

Southern Connecticut State University, School of Graduate Studies, School of Arts and Sciences, Department of Sociology, New Haven, CT 06515-1355. Offers MS. Part-time and evening/weekend programs available. *Faculty:* 5 full-time, 1 part-time/adjunct. *Students:* 9 full-time (7 women), 19 part-time (12 women); includes 8 minority (5 African Americans, 1 American Indian/Alaska Native, 1 Asian American or Pacific Islander, 1 Hispanic American). 14 applicants, 93% accepted, 10 enrolled. In 2007, 6 degrees awarded. *Degree requirements:* For master's, thesis or alternative. *Entrance requirements:* For master's, interview. *Application deadline:* For fall admission, 7/15 priority date for domestic students. Applications are processed on a rolling basis. Application fee: $50. Electronic applications accepted. *Financial support:* Application deadline: 4/15; *Unit head:* Dr. Jon Bloch, Chairperson, 203-392-5685, Fax: 203-392-5670, E-mail: blochj1@southernct.edu. *Application contact:* Dr. Jessica Kenty-Drane, Graduate Coordinator, 203-392-5689, Fax: 203-392-5670, E-mail: kentydranej1@southernct.edu.

Southern Illinois University Carbondale, Graduate School, College of Liberal Arts, Department of Sociology, Carbondale, IL 62901-4701. Offers MA, PhD. Part-time programs available. *Faculty:* 7 full-time (3 women), 1 (woman) part-time/adjunct. *Students:* 30 full-time (22 women), 16 part-time (8 women); includes 9 minority (all African Americans), 8 international. Average age 32. 44 applicants, 27% accepted, 7 enrolled. In 2007, 3 master's, 3 doctorates awarded. *Degree requirements:* For master's, thesis; for doctorate, thesis/dissertation. *Entrance requirements:* For master's, minimum GPA of 2.7; for doctorate, minimum GPA of 3.25. Additional exam requirements/recommendations for international students: Required—TOEFL. *Application deadline:* Applications are processed on a rolling basis. Application fee: $0. *Financial support:* In 2007–08, 33 students received support, including 1 fellowship with full tuition reimbursement available, 2 research assistantships with full tuition reimbursements available, 19 teaching assistantships with full tuition reimbursements available; Federal Work-Study, institutionally sponsored loans, and tuition waivers (full) also available. Support available to part-time students. Financial award application deadline: 2/10. *Faculty research:* Deviance, family, social stratification, social change, theory methodology, culture. Total annual research expenditures: $10,000. *Unit head:* Dr. Darren Sherkat, Chair, 618-453-7619, Fax: 618-453-3253, E-mail: sherkat@siu.edu. *Application contact:* Judy Brown, Office Specialist, 618-453-7613, Fax: 618-453-3253, E-mail: jbrown@siu.edu.

Announcement: SIU sociology focuses on faculty strengths in three areas: social movements and social change; crime, law, and deviance; and gender and sexuality. Faculty members and students in all concentrations share an interest in race, ethnicity, and social inequality. The program also features state-of-the-art training in both qualitative and quantitative methods.

See Close-Up on page 1709.

Southern Illinois University Edwardsville, Graduate Studies and Research, College of Arts and Sciences, Department of Sociology, Edwardsville, IL 62026-0001. Offers MA. Part-time programs available. *Faculty:* 14 full-time (6 women). *Students:* 4 full-time (2 women), 18 part-time (15 women); includes 4 minority (2 African Americans, 2 Asian Americans or Pacific Islanders). Average age 33. 23 applicants, 57% accepted. In 2007, 4 degrees awarded. *Degree requirements:* For master's, final exam, internship or thesis. *Entrance requirements:* Additional exam requirements/recommendations for international students: Required—TOEFL. *Application deadline:* For fall admission, 6/15 for domestic students; for spring admission, 11/15 for domestic students. Application fee: $30. Electronic applications accepted. *Financial support:* Fellowships with full tuition reimbursements, research assistantships with full tuition reimbursements, teaching assistantships with full tuition reimbursements, Federal Work-Study, institutionally sponsored loans, and unspecified assistantships available. Support available to part-time students. Financial award application deadline: 3/1. *Unit head:* Dr. David Kauzlarich, Chair, 618-650-3713, E-mail: dkauzla@siue.edu. *Application contact:* Dr. Linda Markowitz, Program Director, 618-650-2451, E-mail: lmarkow@siue.edu.

Stanford University, School of Humanities and Sciences, Department of Sociology, Stanford, CA 94305-9991. Offers PhD. *Degree requirements:* For doctorate, thesis/dissertation, oral exam. *Entrance requirements:* For doctorate, GRE General Test. Additional exam requirements/recommendations for international students: Required—TOEFL. Electronic applications accepted.

State University of New York at Binghamton, Graduate School, School of Arts and Sciences, Department of Sociology, Binghamton, NY 13902-6000. Offers MA, PhD. *Faculty:* 13 full-time (4 women), 11 part-time/adjunct (4 women). *Students:* 29 full-time (13 women), 56 part-time (25 women); includes 16 minority (5 African Americans, 4 Asian Americans or Pacific Islanders, 7 Hispanic Americans), 40 international. Average age 35. 49 applicants, 47% accepted, 8 enrolled. In 2007, 6 master's, 4 doctorates awarded. Terminal master's awarded for partial completion of doctoral program. *Degree requirements:* For doctorate, thesis/dissertation. *Entrance requirements:* For master's and doctorate, GRE General Test, GRE Subject Test. Additional exam requirements/recommendations for international students: Required—TOEFL. *Application deadline:* For fall admission, 4/15 priority date for domestic students, 1/15 priority date for international students; for spring admission, 11/1 for domestic students, 10/1 priority date for international students. Applications are processed on a rolling basis. Application fee: $60. Electronic applications accepted. *Financial support:* In 2007–08, 33 students received support, including 9 fellowships with full tuition reimbursements available (averaging $12,000 per year), 16 teaching assistantships with full tuition reimbursements available (averaging $14,700 per year); research assistantships with full tuition reimbursements available, career-related internships or fieldwork, Federal Work-Study, institutionally sponsored loans, and unspecified assistantships also available. Support available to part-time students. Financial award application deadline: 2/15. *Unit head:* Dr. Richard Laremont, Chairperson, 607-777-4809, E-mail: laremont@binghamton.edu.

State University of New York Institute of Technology, School of Arts and Sciences, Program in Applied Sociology, Utica, NY 13504-3050. Offers MS. Part-time and evening/weekend programs available. *Degree requirements:* For master's, thesis or project. *Entrance requirements:* For master's, minimum GPA of 3.0, letters of recommendation (3). Additional exam requirements/recommendations for international students: Required—TOEFL (minimum score 550 paper-based; 213 computer-based). *Faculty research:* Family violence, race/class/gender, prisoner re-entry, drug abuse, information technology applications.

Stony Brook University, State University of New York, Graduate School, College of Arts and Sciences, Department of Sociology, Stony Brook, NY 11794. Offers MA, PhD. *Faculty:* 18 full-time (4 women). *Students:* 48 full-time (27 women), 8 part-time (5 women); includes 7 minority (2 African Americans, 3 Asian Americans or Pacific Islanders, 2 Hispanic Americans), 14 international. Average age 33. 85 applicants, 25% accepted. In 2007, 3 master's, 4 doctorates awarded. *Degree requirements:* For doctorate, thesis/dissertation, comprehensive exam or professional papers, field exam, teaching practicum. *Entrance requirements:* For doctorate, GRE General Test, minimum GPA of 3.0. Additional exam requirements/recommendations for international students: Required—TOEFL. *Application deadline:* For fall admission, 1/15 for domestic students. Application fee: $60. *Financial support:* In 2007–08, 1 research assistantship, 27 teaching assistantships were awarded; fellowships also available. *Faculty research:* Deviant behavior, history of sociology/social thought, marriage and family sociology, political sociology. Total annual research expenditures: $104,658. *Unit head:* Dr. Diane Barthel-Bouchier, Chair, 631-632-7700, Fax: 631-632-8203, E-mail: diane.barthel-bouchier@stonybrook.edu. *Application contact:* Dr. Ivan Chase, Director, 631-632-7753, Fax: 631-632-8203, E-mail: ichase@notes.cc.sunysb.edu.

See Close-Up on page 1713.

Syracuse University, Graduate School, Maxwell School of Citizenship and Public Affairs, Department of Sociology, Syracuse, NY 13244. Offers MA, PhD. *Students:* 28 full-time (22 women), 8 part-time (7 women); includes 8 minority (7 African Americans, 1 Hispanic American), 10 international. 48 applicants, 23% accepted, 8 enrolled. In 2007, 6 degrees awarded. *Degree requirements:* For master's, thesis optional; for doctorate, thesis/dissertation. *Entrance requirements:* For master's and doctorate, GRE General Test. Additional exam requirements/recommendations for international students: Required—TOEFL. *Application deadline:* For fall admission, 2/1 priority date for domestic students. Applications are processed on a rolling basis. Application fee: $75. Electronic applications accepted. *Expenses:* Tuition: Full-time $18,216; part-time $1,012 per credit. Required fees: $980. Tuition and fees vary according to program. *Financial support:* Fellowships with full tuition reimbursements, research assistantships with tuition reimbursements, teaching assistantships with full and partial tuition reimbursements, tuition waivers (full and partial) and unspecified assistantships available. *Faculty research:* Qualitative methods and feminist methods, inequality studies, aging and the life course. *Unit head:* Dr. Christine Himes, Chair, 315-443-3252, Fax: 315-443-4597, E-mail: sociology@maxwell.syr.edu. *Application contact:* Robin Goettel, Recruiting Contact, 315-443-2347, E-mail: rjgoette@maxwell.syr.edu.

Teachers College, Columbia University, Graduate Faculty of Education, Department of Human Development, Program in Sociology and Education, New York, NY 10027-6696. Offers Ed M, MA, Ed D, PhD. *Faculty:* 3 full-time (1 woman). *Students:* 16 full-time (15 women), 33 part-time (25 women); includes 26 minority (16 African Americans, 6 Asian Americans or Pacific Islanders, 4 Hispanic Americans), 1 international. Average age 29. 65 applicants, 60% accepted, 16 enrolled. In 2007, 17 master's, 1 doctorate awarded. *Degree requirements:* For doctorate, thesis/dissertation. *Entrance requirements:* For master's, GRE (Ed M); for doctorate, GRE. *Application deadline:* For fall admission, 5/15 for domestic students. Application fee: $70. *Financial support:* Career-related internships or fieldwork, Federal Work-Study, institutionally sponsored loans, and tuition waivers (full and partial) available. Support available to part-time students. Financial award application deadline: 2/1. *Faculty research:* Stratification, race and evaluation, desegregation of schools and communities, quantitative research. *Application contact:* Melba Remice, Assistant Director of Admission, 212-678-4035, Fax: 212-678-4171, E-mail: ms2545@columbia.edu.

See Close-Up on page 1503.

Temple University, Graduate School, College of Liberal Arts, Department of Sociology, Philadelphia, PA 19122-6096. Offers MA, PhD. Part-time and evening/weekend programs available. Terminal master's awarded for partial completion of doctoral program. *Degree requirements:* For doctorate, thesis/dissertation. *Entrance requirements:* For master's and doctorate, GRE General Test, minimum GPA of 3.0. Additional exam requirements/recommendations for international students: Required—TOEFL (minimum score 550 paper-based; 213 computer-based; 79 iBT). Electronic applications accepted. *Faculty research:* International development, race-ethnicity-gender inequality, urban structure, political economy.

Texas A&M International University, Office of Graduate Studies and Research, College of Arts and Sciences, Department of Behavioral, Applied Sciences, and Criminal Justice, Laredo, TX 78041-1900. Offers counseling psychology (MACP); criminal justice (MS); psychology (MS); sociology (MA). *Faculty:* 10 full-time (5 women), 1 (woman) part-time/adjunct. *Students:* 14 full-time (11 women), 68 part-time (40 women); includes 76 minority (1 Asian American or Pacific Islander, 75 Hispanic Americans), 2 international. Average age 30. 40 applicants, 88% accepted, 21 enrolled. In 2007, 24 degrees awarded. *Degree requirements:* For master's, thesis (for some programs). *Entrance requirements:* For master's, GRE General Test. Additional exam requirements/recommendations for international students: Required—TOEFL (minimum score 550 paper-based; 213 computer-based). *Application deadline:* For fall admission, 7/15 priority date for domestic students; for spring admission, 11/12 for domestic students. Applications are processed on a rolling basis. Application fee: $25. *Financial support:* In 2007–08, 44 students received support. Application deadline: 11/1. *Unit head:* Dr. John Kilburn, Chair, 956-326-2667, Fax: 956-326-2459, E-mail: jkilburn@tamiu.edu. *Application contact:* Rosie Espinoza-Dickinson, Director of Admissions, 956-326-2200, Fax: 956-326-2199, E-mail: enroll@tamiu.edu.

Texas A&M University, College of Liberal Arts, Department of Sociology, College Station, TX 77843. Offers MS, PhD. *Faculty:* 19. *Students:* 73 full-time (47 women), 17 part-time (11 women); includes 47 minority (19 African Americans, 2 American Indian/Alaska Native, 4 Asian Americans or Pacific Islanders, 22 Hispanic Americans), 9 international. Average age 32. 57 applicants, 74% accepted, 21 enrolled. In 2007, 6 master's, 9 doctorates awarded. *Degree requirements:* For master's, thesis or alternative; for doctorate, thesis/dissertation. *Entrance requirements:* For master's and doctorate, GRE General Test. Additional exam requirements/recommendations for international students: Required—TOEFL. *Application deadline:* For fall admission, 1/15 priority date for domestic students; for winter admission, 11/1 priority date for domestic students. Applications are processed on a rolling basis. Application fee: $50 ($75 for international students). Electronic applications accepted. *Expenses:* Tuition, state resident: full-time $6,129. Tuition, nonresident: full-time $11,689. Tuition and fees vary according to course load. *Financial support:* In 2007–08, fellowships (averaging $12,000 per year), research assistantships (averaging $9,795 per year), teaching assistantships (averaging $9,795 per year) were awarded; institutionally sponsored loans and unspecified assistantships also available. Financial award application deadline: 1/15; financial award applicants required to submit FAFSA. *Faculty research:* Crime, deviance, and law; culture; demography and human ecology; political and economic sociology; racial and ethnic relations; social psychology; Latino sociology; gender; Asian studies. *Unit head:* Mark Fossett, Head, 979-845-5133, Fax: 979-862-4057. *Application contact:* Dr. Kathryn Henderson, Graduate Advisor, 979-845-9706, Fax: 979-862-4057, E-mail: hendrsn@acs.tamu.edu.

See Close-Up on page 1717.

Texas A&M University–Commerce, Graduate School, College of Arts and Sciences, Department of Sociology and Criminal Justice, Commerce, TX 75429-3011. Offers sociology (MA, MS). Part-time programs available. *Faculty:* 3 full-time (1 woman). *Students:* Average age 36. *Degree requirements:* For master's, comprehensive exam, thesis (for some programs). *Entrance requirements:* For master's, GRE General Test. *Application deadline:* For fall admission, 6/1 priority date for domestic students; for spring admission, 11/1 priority date for domestic students. Applications are processed on a rolling basis. Application fee: $0 ($25 for international students). *Financial support:* In 2007–08, research assistantships (averaging $7,875 per year), teaching assistantships (averaging $7,875 per year) were awarded; Federal Work-Study, institutionally sponsored loans, and scholarships/grants also available. Financial award application deadline: 5/1; financial award applicants required to submit FAFSA. *Faculty research:* Marriage and family, drugs and society, criminal justice, delinquency. *Unit head:* Dr. Willie Edwards, Head, 903-886-5332, Fax: 903-886-5330, E-mail: willie_edwards@tamu-commerce.edu. *Application contact:* Tammi Thompson, Graduate Admissions Adviser, 843-886-5167, Fax: 843-886-5165, E-mail: tammi_thompson@tamu-commerce.edu.

Texas A&M University–Kingsville, College of Graduate Studies, College of Arts and Sciences, Department of Psychology and Sociology, Kingsville, TX 78363. Offers gerontology (MS); psychology (MA, MS); sociology (MA, MS). Part-time and evening/weekend programs available. *Degree requirements:* For master's, comprehensive exam, thesis or alternative. *Entrance requirements:* For master's, GRE General Test, minimum GPA of 2.5. Additional exam requirements/recommendations for international students: Required—TOEFL. *Faculty research:* Hispanic female voting behavior, attitudes toward criminal justice, immigration of aged into south Texas, folk medicine.

Texas Southern University, Graduate School, College of Liberal Arts and Behavioral Sciences, Department of Sociology, Houston, TX 77004-4584. Offers MA. Part-time and evening/weekend programs available. *Degree requirements:* For master's, comprehensive exam, thesis. *Entrance requirements:* For master's, GRE General Test, minimum GPA of 2.5. Additional exam requirements/recommendations for international students: Required—TOEFL. *Faculty research:* Sociocultural systems, ethnic and regional studies, community sociology.

Texas State University–San Marcos, Graduate School, College of Liberal Arts, Department of Sociology, San Marcos, TX 78666. Offers MA, MS. Part-time and evening/weekend programs available. *Faculty:* 6 full-time (1 woman), 1 part-time/adjunct (0 women). *Students:* 24 full-time (15 women), 14 part-time (11 women); includes 14 minority (3 African Americans, 1 Asian American or Pacific Islander, 10 Hispanic Americans), 1 international. Average age 28. 20 applicants, 95% accepted, 13 enrolled. In 2007, 9 degrees awarded. *Degree requirements:* For master's, comprehensive exam, essay or thesis. *Entrance requirements:* For master's, minimum GPA of 3.0 in last 60 hours of course work, 3 letters of reference, letter of intent, personal interview. Additional exam requirements/recommendations for international students: Required—TOEFL (minimum score 550 paper-based; 213 computer-based). *Application deadline:* For fall admission, 6/15 priority date for domestic students, 6/1 priority date for international students; for spring admission, 10/15 priority date for domestic students, 10/1 priority date for international students. Applications are processed on a rolling basis. Application fee: $40 ($90 for international students). Electronic applications accepted. *Expenses:* Tuition, state resident: full-time $3,780; part-time $210 per credit hour. Tuition, nonresident: full-time $8,784; part-time $488 per credit hour. Required fees: $493 per semester. Full-time tuition and fees vary according to course load. *Financial support:* In 2007–08, 33 students received support, including 1 research assistantship (averaging $4,927 per year), 15 teaching assistantships (averaging $4,568 per year); career-related internships or fieldwork, Federal Work-Study, and institutionally sponsored loans also available. Support available to part-time students. Financial award application deadline: 4/1; financial award applicants required to submit FAFSA. *Faculty research:* Substance abuse, ethnic and gender inequality, jury behavior, Native American women. Total annual research expenditures: $61,011. *Unit head:* Dr. Susan Day, Chair, 512-245-2113, Fax: 512-245-8362, E-mail: sd01@txstate.edu.

Texas State University–San Marcos, Graduate School, Interdisciplinary Studies Program in Applied Sociology, San Marcos, TX 78666. Offers MAIS. Part-time and evening/weekend programs available. *Students:* 1 full-time (0 women); minority (Hispanic American) Average age 28. 5 applicants, 100% accepted. In 2007, 3 degrees awarded. *Degree requirements:* For master's, comprehensive exam. *Entrance requirements:* For master's, 3.0 GPA on last 60 hrs. of undergraduate, 3 letters of reference, letter of intent. Additional exam requirements/recommendations for international students: Required—TOEFL (minimum score 550 paper-based; 213 computer-based). *Application deadline:* For fall admission, 6/15 priority date for domestic students; for spring admission, 10/15 priority date for domestic students. Applications are processed on a rolling basis. Application fee: $40 ($90 for international students). Electronic applications accepted. *Expenses:* Tuition, state resident: full-time $3,780; part-time $210 per credit hour. Tuition, nonresident: full-time $8,784; part-time $488 per credit hour. Required fees: $493 per semester. Full-time tuition and fees vary according to course load. *Financial support:* In 2007–08, 1 student received support, including 1 teaching assistantship (averaging $5,076 per year). Financial award application deadline: 4/1; financial award applicants required to submit FAFSA. *Unit head:* Dr. Audwin Anderson, Head, 512-245-2113, E-mail: aa04@txstate.edu.

Texas Tech University, Graduate School, College of Arts and Sciences, Department of Sociology, Anthropology and Social Work, Lubbock, TX 79409. Offers anthropology (MA); sociology (MA). Part-time programs available. *Faculty:* 14 full-time (5 women). *Students:* 21 full-time (9 women), 11 part-time (5 women); includes 9 minority (1 African American, 1 Asian American or Pacific Islander, 7 Hispanic Americans), 2 international. Average age 30. 24 applicants, 75% accepted, 8 enrolled. In 2007, 6 degrees awarded. *Degree requirements:* For master's, one foreign language. *Entrance requirements:* For master's, GRE General Test. Additional exam requirements/recommendations for international students: Required—TOEFL (minimum score 550 paper-based; 213 computer-based). *Application deadline:* For fall admission, 3/1 priority date for international students; for spring admission, 11/1 priority date for international students. Applications are processed on a rolling basis. Application fee: $50 ($60 for international students). Electronic applications accepted. *Expenses:* Tuition, state resident: part-time $373 per credit hour. Tuition, nonresident: part-time $651 per credit hour. Tuition and fees vary according to program. *Financial support:* In 2007–08, 25 students received support, including 1 research assistantship with partial tuition reimbursement available (averaging $10,750 per year), 14 teaching assistantships with partial tuition reimbursements available (averaging $11,143 per year); Federal Work-Study and institutionally sponsored loans also available. Support available to part-time students. Financial award application deadline: 4/15; financial award applicants required to submit FAFSA. *Faculty research:* Sociology theory, research methods, physical and forensic anthropology, Texas archaeology, Mayan archaeology. Total annual research expenditures: $277. *Unit head:* Dr. Jeffrey Payne Williams, Chair and Professor, 806-742-2400, Fax: 806-742-1088, E-mail: jeff.williams@ttu.edu. *Application contact:* Dr. Yung-Mei Tsai, Sociology Graduate Program Director, 806-742-2400, Fax: 806-742-1088, E-mail: yung.mei.tsai@ttu.edu.

Texas Woman's University, Graduate School, College of Arts and Sciences, Department of Sociology and Social Work, Denton, TX 76201. Offers sociology (MA, PhD). Evening/weekend programs available. *Students:* 6 full-time (5 women), 27 part-time (24 women); includes 13 minority (7 African Americans, 1 Asian American or Pacific Islander, 5 Hispanic Americans), 5 international. Average age 37. In 2007, 2 master's, 3 doctorates awarded. Terminal master's awarded for partial completion of doctoral program. *Degree requirements:* For master's, thesis or professional paper; for doctorate, one foreign language, comprehensive exam, thesis/dissertation. *Entrance requirements:* For master's, GRE General Test (recommended), 2 letters of reference, 2-3 page statement of intent; for doctorate, GRE General Test (recommended), minimum 12 hours course work in sociology, 3 letters of reference, minimum GPA of 3.5, 2-3 page statement of intent. Additional exam requirements/recommendations for international students: Required—TOEFL (minimum score 550 paper-based; 213 computer-based; 79 iBT). *Application deadline:* For fall admission, 4/1 for international students; for spring admission, 8/1 for international students. Applications are processed on a rolling basis. Application fee: $30 ($50 for international students). Electronic applications accepted. *Expenses:* Tuition, state resident: full-time $3,294; part-time $183 per credit. Tuition, nonresident: full-time $8,298; part-time $461 per credit. Required fees: $985; $55 per credit. Tuition and fees vary according to degree level. *Financial support:* In 2007–08, 18 teaching assistantships (averaging $10,746 per year) were awarded; career-related internships or fieldwork, Federal Work-Study, institutionally sponsored loans, scholarships/grants, traineeships, health care benefits, and unspecified assistantships also available. Support available to part-time students. Financial award application deadline: 3/1; financial award applicants required to submit FAFSA. *Faculty research:* Disasters, criminology, immigration, sociological theory, race/ethnicity. *Unit head:* Dr. James Williams, Chair, 940-898-2052, Fax: 940-898-2067, E-mail: jwilliams2@twu.edu. *Application contact:* Samuel Wheeler, Assistant Director of Admissions, 940-898-3188, Fax: 940-898-3081, E-mail: wheelersr@twu.edu.

Tulane University, School of Liberal Arts, Department of Sociology, New Orleans, LA 70118-5669. Offers MA, PhD. Terminal master's awarded for partial completion of doctoral program. *Degree requirements:* For master's, thesis; for doctorate, thesis/dissertation, preliminary exams. *Entrance requirements:* For master's, GRE General Test, minimum B average in undergraduate course work; for doctorate, GRE General Test. Additional exam requirements/recommendations for international students: Required—TOEFL. Electronic applications accepted.

Université de Montréal, Faculty of Arts and Sciences, Department of Sociology, Montréal, QC H3C 3J7, Canada. Offers M Sc, PhD. *Faculty:* 19 full-time (7 women), 11 part-time/adjunct (7 women). *Students:* 117 full-time (71 women), 2 part-time (1 woman). 96 applicants, 43% accepted, 38 enrolled. In 2007, 12 master's, 6 doctorates awarded. *Degree requirements:* For master's, thesis; for doctorate, thesis/dissertation, general exam. *Entrance requirements:* For master's, minimum GPA of 3.0; for doctorate, minimum GPA of 3.5, proficiency in French. *Application deadline:* For fall admission, 2/1 priority date for domestic students; for winter admission, 11/1 priority date for domestic students; for spring admission, 2/1 priority date for domestic students. Applications are processed on a rolling basis. Application fee: $100. Electronic applications accepted. *Financial support:* In 2007–08, 75 students received support. Application deadline: 9/15. *Faculty research:* Sociological theory, economy, state and social movements, work, social politics and health. *Unit head:* Andrée Demers, Director, 514-343-6618, Fax: 514-343-5722, E-mail: andree.demers@umontreal.ca. *Application contact:* Claire Durand, Graduate Studies Chairman, 514-343-7447, Fax: 514-343-5722, E-mail: claire.durand@umontreal.ca.

Université du Québec à Montréal, Graduate Programs, Program in Social Intervention, Montréal, QC H3C 3P8, Canada. Offers MA. Part-time programs available. *Degree requirements:* For master's, thesis. *Entrance requirements:* For master's, appropriate bachelor's degree or equivalent, proficiency in French.

Université du Québec à Montréal, Graduate Programs, Program in Sociology, Montréal, QC H3C 3P8, Canada. Offers MA, PhD. Part-time programs available. *Degree requirements:* For master's, thesis optional; for doctorate, thesis/dissertation. *Entrance requirements:* For master's, appropriate bachelor's degree or equivalent, proficiency in French; for doctorate, appropriate master's degree or equivalent, proficiency in French.

Université Laval, Faculty of Social Sciences, Department of Sociology, Programs in Sociology, Québec, QC G1K 7P4, Canada. Offers MA, PhD. Terminal master's awarded for partial completion of doctoral program. *Degree requirements:* For master's, thesis; for doctorate,

Sociology

Université Laval (continued)
comprehensive exam, thesis/dissertation. *Entrance requirements:* For master's and doctorate, English exam (comprehension of written English), French exam may be required, knowledge of French. Electronic applications accepted.

University at Albany, State University of New York, College of Arts and Sciences, Department of Communication, Albany, NY 12222-0001. Offers communication (MA); sociology and communication (PhD). Part-time programs available. *Students:* 32 full-time (26 women), 20 part-time (12 women). Average age 31. In 2007, 18 master's, 1 doctorate awarded. *Degree requirements:* For master's, comprehensive exam, thesis or alternative; for doctorate, comprehensive exam, thesis/dissertation. *Entrance requirements:* For master's, minimum GPA of 3.0; for doctorate, GRE, minimum GPA of 3.0. Additional exam requirements/recommendations for international students: Required—TOEFL (minimum score 550 paper-based; 213 computer-based). *Application deadline:* For fall admission, 2/20 priority date for domestic students, 5/1 for international students. Applications are processed on a rolling basis. Application fee: $75. Electronic applications accepted. *Expenses:* Tuition, state resident: part-time $576 per credit. Tuition, nonresident: part-time $910 per credit. Tuition and fees vary according to program. *Financial support:* Fellowships, teaching assistantships, career-related internships or fieldwork and institutionally sponsored loans available. Financial award application deadline: 3/1. *Faculty research:* Language and social interaction, campaign communication, media agenda-setting, high-speed management, organizational boundary-spanning. *Unit head:* Teresa Harrison, Chair, 518-442-4871.

University at Albany, State University of New York, College of Arts and Sciences, Department of Sociology, Albany, NY 12222-0001. Offers demography (Certificate); sociology (MA, PhD); urban policy (Certificate). *Students:* 49 full-time (34 women), 76 part-time (39 women). Average age 32. In 2007, 3 master's, 5 doctorates, 4 other advanced degrees awarded. Terminal master's awarded for partial completion of doctoral program. *Degree requirements:* For master's, thesis; for doctorate, thesis/dissertation, 2 specialization exams, research tool. *Entrance requirements:* For master's and doctorate, GRE General Test. Additional exam requirements/recommendations for international students: Required—TOEFL (minimum score 213 computer-based). *Application deadline:* For fall admission, 1/15 for domestic students, 5/1 for international students. Applications are processed on a rolling basis. Application fee: $75. Electronic applications accepted. *Expenses:* Tuition, state resident: part-time $576 per credit. Tuition, nonresident: part-time $910 per credit. Tuition and fees vary according to program. *Financial support:* Fellowships, research assistantships, teaching assistantships, career-related internships or fieldwork and Federal Work-Study available. Financial award application deadline: 3/15. *Faculty research:* Gender and equality, crime and deviance, aging, work and organizations, social demography. *Unit head:* Dr. Donlad Hernandez, Chair, 518-442-4666. *Application contact:* Glen D. Dean, Graduate Committee Chair, 518-442-4587.

University at Buffalo, the State University of New York, Graduate School, College of Arts and Sciences, Department of Sociology, Buffalo, NY 14260. Offers MA, PhD. Part-time programs available. Terminal master's awarded for partial completion of doctoral program. *Degree requirements:* For master's, project or thesis; for doctorate, thesis/dissertation, qualifying paper. *Entrance requirements:* For master's and doctorate, GRE General Test. Additional exam requirements/recommendations for international students: Required—TOEFL (minimum score 550 paper-based; 213 computer-based). Electronic applications accepted. *Faculty research:* Theory, culture, sociology of law/criminology, urban sociology, family.

The University of Akron, Graduate School, Buchtel College of Arts and Sciences, Department of Sociology, Akron, OH 44325. Offers MA, PhD. Part-time programs available. *Faculty:* 13 full-time (5 women), 7 part-time/adjunct (3 women). *Students:* 18 full-time (13 women), 11 part-time (9 women); includes 3 minority (all African Americans), 3 international. Average age 35. 32 applicants, 38% accepted, 13 enrolled. In 2007, 6 master's awarded. Terminal master's awarded for partial completion of doctoral program. *Degree requirements:* For master's, thesis optional, oral defense of thesis, paper or oral exam; for doctorate, one foreign language, comprehensive exam, thesis/dissertation. *Entrance requirements:* For master's, GRE General Test, minimum GPA of 3.0, letters of recommendation; for doctorate, GRE General Test, minimum GPA of 3.5, letters of recommendation. Additional exam requirements/recommendations for international students: Required—TOEFL (minimum score 575 paper-based; 234 computer-based). *Application deadline:* Applications are processed on a rolling basis. Application fee: $30 ($40 for international students). Electronic applications accepted. *Expenses:* Tuition, state resident: full-time $6,164; part-time $342 per credit. Tuition, nonresident: full-time $10,575; part-time $588 per credit. Required fees: $806; $43 per credit. $12 per term. Tuition and fees vary according to course load, degree level and program. *Financial support:* In 2007–08, 1 research assistantship with full tuition reimbursement, 18 teaching assistantships with full tuition reimbursements were awarded; career-related internships or fieldwork, Federal Work-Study, and tuition waivers (full and partial) also available. *Faculty research:* Medical sociology, inequality, social psychology, criminology, mental health. Total annual research expenditures: $110,983. *Unit head:* Dr. John Zipp, Chair, 330-972-8082, E-mail: jzipp@uakron.edu. *Application contact:* Dr. Rebecca Erickson, Director of Graduate Studies, 330-972-5157, E-mail: rericks@uakron.edu.

The University of Alabama at Birmingham, School of Social and Behavioral Sciences, Department of Sociology, Birmingham, AL 35294. Offers medical sociology (PhD); sociology (MA). Evening/weekend programs available. *Students:* 12 full-time (7 women), 7 part-time (3 women); includes 4 minority (3 African Americans, 1 Asian American or Pacific Islander), 2 international. Average age 35. In 2007, 3 master's, 3 doctorates awarded. *Degree requirements:* For master's, thesis or alternative; for doctorate, thesis/dissertation. *Entrance requirements:* For master's, GRE General Test or MAT; for doctorate, GRE General Test. *Application deadline:* Applications are processed on a rolling basis. Application fee: $35 ($60 for international students). Electronic applications accepted. *Financial support:* In 2007–08, 10 students received support, including 2 fellowships, 3 research assistantships; career-related internships or fieldwork, Federal Work-Study, and institutionally sponsored loans also available. Financial award application deadline: 3/1. *Faculty research:* Gerontology, applied sociology, urban sociology. *Unit head:* Dr. Mark E. Lagory, Chair, 205-934-3307, E-mail: mlagory@uab.edu.

University of Alberta, Faculty of Graduate Studies and Research, Department of Sociology, Edmonton, AB T6G 2E1, Canada. Offers criminal justice (MA); demography (MA, PhD); sociology (MA, PhD). Part-time programs available. *Degree requirements:* For master's, thesis (for some programs); for doctorate, thesis/dissertation. *Faculty research:* Criminology, knowledge and culture, methods and theory, population studies, stratification.

The University of Arizona, Graduate College, College of Social and Behavioral Sciences, Department of Sociology, Tucson, AZ 85721. Offers MA, PhD. *Faculty:* 23. *Students:* 52 full-time (27 women), 7 part-time (5 women); includes 9 minority (2 African Americans, 4 Asian Americans or Pacific Islanders, 3 Hispanic Americans), 3 international. Average age 29. 97 applicants, 8% accepted, 7 enrolled. In 2007, 13 master's, 9 doctorates awarded. *Degree requirements:* For master's, publishable paper/oral; for doctorate, thesis/dissertation, 2 preliminary exams. *Entrance requirements:* For master's, GRE, minimum GPA of 3.0, 3 letters of recommendation, statement of purpose, writing sample. Additional exam requirements/recommendations for international students: Required—TOEFL (minimum score 630 paper-based). *Application deadline:* For fall admission, 1/15 for domestic students, 12/1 for international students. Applications are processed on a rolling basis. Application fee: $50. Electronic applications accepted. *Financial support:* In 2007–08, 4 fellowships (averaging $5,000 per year), research assistantships (averaging $14,559 per year), 48 teaching assistantships (averaging $14,559 per year) were awarded; institutionally sponsored loans, scholarships/grants, health care benefits, tuition waivers (full), and unspecified assistantships also available. Financial award application deadline: 1/15; financial award applicants required to submit FAFSA. *Faculty research:* Organizations, social psychology, social movement, stratification, religion. Total annual research expenditures: $945,361. *Unit head:* Dr. Albert J. Bergesen, Head, 520-621-3303, Fax: 520-621-9875, E-mail: albert@u.arizona.edu. *Application contact:* Vienna Marum, Information Contact, 520-621-5057, Fax: 520-621-9875, E-mail: vienna@u.arizona.edu.

University of Arkansas, Graduate School, J. William Fulbright College of Arts and Sciences, Department of Sociology, Fayetteville, AR 72701-1201. Offers MA. Part-time programs available. *Students:* 10 full-time (7 women), 17 part-time (11 women); includes 3 minority (2 African Americans, 1 American Indian/Alaska Native), 3 international. In 2007, 14 degrees awarded. *Degree requirements:* For master's, thesis. Application fee: $40 ($50 for international students). *Financial support:* In 2007–08, 1 fellowship with tuition reimbursement, 6 research assistantships, 10 teaching assistantships were awarded; career-related internships or fieldwork and Federal Work-Study also available. Support available to part-time students. Financial award application deadline: 4/1; financial award applicants required to submit FAFSA. *Unit head:* Dr. Bill Schwab, Departmental Chairperson, 479-575-3206, Fax: 479-575-7981, E-mail: bschwab@uark.edu. *Application contact:* Dr. Anna Zajicek, Graduate Coordinator, 479-575-5149, E-mail: azajicek@uark.edu.

The University of British Columbia, Faculty of Arts, Department of Sociology, Vancouver, BC V6T 1Z1, Canada. Offers MA, PhD. *Faculty:* 20 full-time (11 women), 5 part-time/adjunct (3 women). *Students:* 66 full-time (44 women). Average age 33. 78 applicants, 15% accepted, 12 enrolled. In 2007, 2 master's, 3 doctorates awarded. *Median time to degree:* Of those who began their doctoral program in fall 1999, 67% received their degree in 8 years or less. *Degree requirements:* For master's, thesis; for doctorate, comprehensive exam, thesis/dissertation. *Entrance requirements:* For master's, BA in sociology or equivalent with minimum B+ average in upper level courses; for doctorate, master's degree in sociology or equivalent. Additional exam requirements/recommendations for international students: Required—TOEFL (minimum score 600 paper-based; 250 computer-based). *Application deadline:* For fall admission, 1/8 for domestic and international students. Application fee: $90 Canadian dollars ($150 Canadian dollars for international students). Electronic applications accepted. *Financial support:* In 2007–08, 23 students received support, including 23 fellowships with tuition reimbursements available (averaging $16,000 Canadian dollars per year), 8 research assistantships with tuition reimbursements available, teaching assistantships with tuition reimbursements available (averaging $10,902 Canadian dollars per year); Federal Work-Study, institutionally sponsored loans, scholarships/grants, health care benefits, tuition waivers (full and partial), and unspecified assistantships also available. Financial award application deadline: 9/29. *Faculty research:* Social and cultural theories and methods; gender, race, class and sexuality; environment economy and development politics; law and social movements. *Unit head:* Dr. Neil Guppy, Head, 604-822-2660, Fax: 604-822-6161, E-mail: guppy@interchange.ubc.ca. *Application contact:* Dan Naidu, Graduate Secretary, 604-822-0503, Fax: 604-822-6161, E-mail: ansograd@interchange.ubc.ca.

University of Calgary, Faculty of Graduate Studies, Faculty of Social Sciences, Department of Sociology, Calgary, AB T2N 1N4, Canada. Offers MA, PhD. Terminal master's awarded for partial completion of doctoral program. *Degree requirements:* For master's, thesis, prospectus; for doctorate, comprehensive exam, thesis/dissertation, oral and written candidacy exams, prospectus, qualifying paper. *Entrance requirements:* For master's, minimum GPA of 3.2; for doctorate, minimum GPA of 3.5. Additional exam requirements/recommendations for international students: Required—TOEFL or IELTS. Electronic applications accepted. *Faculty research:* Deviance, gender, medical, religion, ethnicity.

University of California, Berkeley, Graduate Division, College of Letters and Science, Department of Sociology, Berkeley, CA 94720-1500. Offers PhD. *Faculty:* 16 full-time, 9 part-time/adjunct. *Degree requirements:* For doctorate, thesis/dissertation, qualifying exam. *Entrance requirements:* For doctorate, GRE General Test, minimum GPA of 3.0, sample of academic written work, 3 letters of recommendation. Additional exam requirements/recommendations for international students: Required—TOEFL (paper-based 570; computer-based 230) or IELTS. *Application deadline:* For fall admission, 12/12 for domestic students. Application fee: $70 ($90 for international students). Electronic applications accepted. *Financial support:* Fellowships with full tuition reimbursements, research assistantships with partial tuition reimbursements, teaching assistantships with partial tuition reimbursements, Federal Work-Study, institutionally sponsored loans, and unspecified assistantships available. Financial award applicants required to submit FAFSA. *Faculty research:* Race, gender, political, stratification theory. *Unit head:* Kim Voss, Chair, 510-642-4575, E-mail: kimvoss@berkeley.edu. *Application contact:* Information Contact, 510-642-1445, E-mail: socgrad_admit@berkeley.edu.

University of California, Berkeley, Graduate Division, Group in Sociology and Demography, Berkeley, CA 94720-1500. Offers PhD. *Degree requirements:* For doctorate, thesis/dissertation, qualifying exam. *Entrance requirements:* For doctorate, GRE General Test, minimum GPA of 3.0, 3 letters of recommendation. *Application deadline:* For fall admission, 12/14 for domestic students. Application fee: $70 ($90 for international students). *Financial support:* Fellowships with full and partial tuition reimbursements, research assistantships with full and partial tuition reimbursements, teaching assistantships with full and partial tuition reimbursements, unspecified assistantships available. *Unit head:* Dr. Michael Hout, Chair, 510-643-6874, E-mail: mikehout@berkeley.edu. *Application contact:* Monique Marie Verrier, Student Affairs Officer, 510-642-9800, Fax: 510-643-8558, E-mail: applications@demog.berkeley.edu.

University of California, Berkeley, Graduate Division, School of Public Health, Program in Health and Social Behavior, Berkeley, CA 94720-1500. Offers MPH. *Accreditation:* CEPH. *Entrance requirements:* For master's, GRE General Test, minimum GPA of 3.0. *Application deadline:* For fall admission, 12/1 for domestic students. Applications are processed on a rolling basis. Application fee: $70 ($90 for international students). *Financial support:* Unspecified assistantships available. *Unit head:* William Satariano, Director, 510-642-3997. *Application contact:* Greta Gebhardt, Student Affairs Assistant, 510-642-4578, Fax: 510-643-6981, E-mail: hpm_mph@berkeley.edu.

University of California, Davis, Graduate Studies, Program in Sociology, Davis, CA 95616. Offers MA, PhD. Terminal master's awarded for partial completion of doctoral program. *Degree requirements:* For master's, written exam; for doctorate, thesis/dissertation, professional paper, qualifying exam. *Entrance requirements:* For master's and doctorate, GRE General Test, minimum GPA of 3.0, writing sample. Additional exam requirements/recommendations for international students: Required—TOEFL (minimum score 550 paper-based; 213 computer-based). Electronic applications accepted. *Faculty research:* Collective behavior, social movements, comparative sociology, historical sociology, culture development, inequality.

University of California, Irvine, Office of Graduate Studies, School of Social Sciences, Department of Sociology, Irvine, CA 92697. Offers social networks (PhD); social networks-social science (MA); social science (MA, PhD); sociology and social relations-social science (MA, PhD). *Students:* 72 full-time (46 women), 1 (woman) part-time; includes 23 minority (2 African Americans, 12 Asian Americans or Pacific Islanders, 9 Hispanic Americans), 3 international. In 2007, 11 master's, 7 doctorates awarded. *Degree requirements:* For doctorate, thesis/dissertation. *Entrance requirements:* For master's and doctorate, GRE General Test, minimum GPA of 3.0. *Application deadline:* For fall admission, 1/15 priority date for domestic students; for winter admission, 10/15 priority date for domestic students. Applications are processed on a rolling basis. Application fee: $60. Electronic applications accepted. *Financial support:* Fellowships, research assistantships with full tuition reimbursements, teaching assistantships, institutionally sponsored loans, traineeships, health care benefits, and unspecified assistantships available. Financial award application deadline: 3/1; financial award applicants required to submit FAFSA. *Faculty research:* Cognitive anthropology, sociology of culture, social structure, family and gender. *Unit head:* Calvin Morrill, Chair, 949-824-6460, E-mail: calvin@uci.edu. *Application contact:* Diane Enriquez, Graduate Counselor, 949-824-5924, Fax: 949-824-3548, E-mail: dmvargas@uci.edu.

University of California, Los Angeles, Graduate Division, College of Letters and Science, Department of Sociology, Los Angeles, CA 90095. Offers MA, PhD. *Students:* 104 full-time (66 women); includes 31 minority (3 African Americans, 12 Asian Americans or Pacific Islanders,

16 Hispanic Americans), 17 international. Average age 29. 248 applicants, 22% accepted, 17 enrolled. In 2007, 14 master's, 12 doctorates awarded. Terminal master's awarded for partial completion of doctoral program. *Median time to degree:* Of those who began their doctoral program in fall 1999, 42% received their degree in 8 years or less. *Degree requirements:* For master's, thesis or alternative, final paper; for doctorate, thesis/dissertation, oral and written qualifying exams. *Entrance requirements:* For master's, GRE General Test, minimum GPA of 3.0, sample of work, degree objective of Ph.D; for doctorate, GRE General Test, minimum undergraduate GPA of 3.0, sample of work. Additional exam requirements/recommendations for international students: Required—TOEFL. *Application deadline:* For fall admission, 12/1 for domestic students. Application fee: $60. Electronic applications accepted. *Expenses:* Tuition, nonresident: full-time $5,728. Required fees: $8,966. Full-time tuition and fees vary according to program and student level. *Financial support:* In 2007–08, 87 fellowships with full and partial tuition reimbursements, 35 research assistantships with full and partial tuition reimbursements, 47 teaching assistantships with full and partial tuition reimbursements were awarded; Federal Work-Study, institutionally sponsored loans, scholarships/grants, and tuition waivers (full and partial) also available. Financial award application deadline: 3/1; financial award applicants required to submit FAFSA. *Unit head:* Dr. David Lopez, Chair, 310-825-1026. *Application contact:* Departmental Office, 310-825-1026, E-mail: dietrich@soc.ucla.edu.

University of California, Riverside, Graduate Division, Department of Sociology, Riverside, CA 92521-0102. Offers MA, PhD. *Faculty:* 19 full-time (5 women). *Students:* 69 full-time (34 women); includes 24 minority (4 African Americans, 1 American Indian/Alaska Native, 9 Asian Americans or Pacific Islanders, 10 Hispanic Americans), 3 international. Average age 32. In 2007, 12 master's, 3 doctorates awarded. *Degree requirements:* For doctorate, thesis/dissertation, 1 quarter of teaching experience, professional paper. *Entrance requirements:* For doctorate, GRE General Test, minimum GPA of 3.2. Additional exam requirements/recommendations for international students: Required—TOEFL (minimum score 550 paper-based; 213 computer-based; 80 iBT). *Application deadline:* For fall admission, 5/1 for domestic students, 2/1 for international students; for winter admission, 9/1 for domestic students, 7/1 for international students; for spring admission, 12/1 for domestic students, 10/1 for international students. Applications are processed on a rolling basis. Application fee: $60 ($75 for international students). Electronic applications accepted. *Financial support:* In 2007–08, fellowships with tuition reimbursements (averaging $12,000 per year), teaching assistantships with partial tuition reimbursements (averaging $16,500 per year) were awarded; research assistantships, career-related internships or fieldwork, Federal Work-Study, institutionally sponsored loans, health care benefits, and tuition waivers (full and partial) also available. Financial award application deadline: 2/1; financial award applicants required to submit FAFSA. *Faculty research:* Crime/deviance, race/ethnic relations, family/gender, political economy/globalization, theory. *Application contact:* Anna M. Wire, Graduate Program Assistant, 951-827-5445, Fax: 951-827-3330, E-mail: socgrad@ucr.edu.

University of California, San Diego, Office of Graduate Studies, Department of Sociology, La Jolla, CA 92093. Offers science studies (PhD); sociology (PhD). *Degree requirements:* For doctorate, thesis/dissertation. *Entrance requirements:* For doctorate, GRE General Test. Electronic applications accepted.

University of California, San Diego, Office of Graduate Studies, Interdisciplinary Program in Cognitive Science, La Jolla, CA 92093. Offers cognitive science/anthropology (PhD); cognitive science/communication (PhD); cognitive science/computer science and engineering (PhD); cognitive science/linguistics (PhD); cognitive science/neuroscience (PhD); cognitive science/philosophy (PhD); cognitive science/psychology (PhD); cognitive science/sociology (PhD). Admissions offered through affiliated departments. *Faculty:* 65 full-time (14 women). *Students:* 7 full-time (3 women). Average age 26. 2 applicants, 100% accepted, 2 enrolled. In 2007, 1 degree awarded. *Degree requirements:* For doctorate, thesis/dissertation. *Entrance requirements:* For doctorate, GRE General Test, acceptance into one of the 8 participating departments. *Application deadline:* Applications are processed on a rolling basis. Application fee: $0. *Faculty research:* Language and cognition, philosophy of mind, visual perception, biological anthropology, sociolinguistics. *Unit head:* Gary Cottrell, Director, 858-534-7141, Fax: 858-534-1128, E-mail: gcottrell@ucsd.edu. *Application contact:* Beverley Walton, Coordinator, 858-534-4387, E-mail: bwalton@ucsd.edu.

University of California, San Francisco, Graduate Division, School of Nursing, Department of Social and Behavioral Sciences, San Francisco, CA 94143. Offers sociology (PhD). *Faculty:* 12 full-time (9 women). *Students:* 34 full-time (26 women); includes 12 minority (1 African American, 4 Asian Americans or Pacific Islanders, 7 Hispanic Americans), 3 international. In 2007, 4 degrees awarded. *Degree requirements:* For doctorate, one foreign language, thesis/dissertation. *Entrance requirements:* For doctorate, GRE General Test. *Application deadline:* For fall admission, 2/1 for domestic students. Application fee: $40. *Financial support:* Career-related internships or fieldwork available. Financial award application deadline: 1/10. *Faculty research:* Urban social relations; sociology of women's role in healing; sociology of work, occupations, and professions. *Application contact:* Linda Tracy, Program Representative, 415-476-3047, Fax: 415-476-6552, E-mail: linda.tracy@ucsf.edu.

University of California, Santa Barbara, Graduate Division, College of Letters and Sciences, Division of Social Sciences, Department of Sociology, Santa Barbara, CA 93106. Offers PhD, MA/PhD. *Faculty:* 34 full-time (15 women). *Students:* 88 full-time (51 women); includes 37 minority (7 African Americans, 5 Asian Americans or Pacific Islanders, 25 Hispanic Americans), 2 international. Average age 30. 162 applicants, 18% accepted, 18 enrolled. In 2007, 4 doctorates awarded. Terminal master's awarded for partial completion of doctoral program. *Median time to degree:* Of those who began their doctoral program in fall 1999, 29% received their degree in 8 years or less. *Degree requirements:* For doctorate, comprehensive exam, thesis/dissertation. *Entrance requirements:* For doctorate, GRE General Test, sample of written work. Additional exam requirements/recommendations for international students: Required—TOEFL (minimum score 550 paper-based; 213 computer-based; 80 iBT). *Application deadline:* For fall admission, 12/10 for domestic and international students. Application fee: $60. Electronic applications accepted. *Expenses:* Tuition, nonresident: full-time $14,888. Required fees: $10,108. *Financial support:* In 2007–08, 80 students received support, including 35 fellowships with full and partial tuition reimbursements available (averaging $11,394 per year), 8 research assistantships (averaging $12,000 per year), 46 teaching assistantships (averaging $16,000 per year); career-related internships or fieldwork, Federal Work-Study, institutionally sponsored loans, scholarships/grants, health care benefits, and unspecified assistantships also available. Financial award application deadline: 12/10; financial award applicants required to submit FAFSA. *Faculty research:* Conversation analysis, social movements, human sexuality, urban sociology, race and ethnic relations. *Unit head:* Verta Taylor, Chair/Professor, 805-893-3118, E-mail: grad-soc@soc.ucsb.edu. *Application contact:* Jetta Harris, Graduate Program Assistant, 805-893-3328, Fax: 805-893-3324, E-mail: jharris@soc.ucsb.edu.

University of California, Santa Cruz, Division of Graduate Studies, Division of Social Sciences, Program in Sociology, Santa Cruz, CA 95064. Offers PhD. *Faculty:* 17 full-time (8 women). *Students:* 27 full-time (16 women), 13 part-time (7 women); includes 11 minority (2 African Americans, 3 Asian Americans or Pacific Islanders, 6 Hispanic Americans), 1 international. 111 applicants, 17% accepted, 8 enrolled. In 2007, 3 doctorates awarded. *Degree requirements:* For doctorate, thesis/dissertation, qualifying exam. *Entrance requirements:* For doctorate, GRE General Test. *Application deadline:* For fall admission, 12/19 for domestic students. Application fee: $60. *Expenses:* Tuition, nonresident: full-time $14,694. Required fees: $11,360. *Financial support:* Fellowships, research assistantships, teaching assistantships, career-related internships or fieldwork, Federal Work-Study, and institutionally sponsored loans available. Financial award application deadline: 1/15. *Faculty research:* Marxism, feminism, ethnic studies, social theory. *Unit head:* Craig Reinarman, Chairperson, 831-459-2617, E-mail: craigo@ucsc.edu. *Application contact:* Judy L. Glass, Reporting Analyst for Graduate Admissions, 831-459-5906, Fax: 831-459-4843, E-mail: jlglass@ucsc.edu.

University of Central Florida, College of Sciences, Department of Sociology, Orlando, FL 32816. Offers applied sociology (MA); domestic violence (MA, Certificate); Maya studies (Certificate); sociology (PhD). Part-time and evening/weekend programs available. *Faculty:* 21 full-time (12 women), 3 part-time/adjunct (2 women). *Degree requirements:* For master's, comprehensive written exam or thesis. *Entrance requirements:* For master's, GRE General Test, minimum GPA of 3.0 in last 60 hours of course work. Additional exam requirements/recommendations for international students: Required—TOEFL. *Application deadline:* For fall admission, 7/15 for domestic students; for spring admission, 12/1 for domestic students. Application fee: $30. Electronic applications accepted. *Expenses:* Tuition, state resident: full-time $6,484. Tuition, nonresident: full-time $23,938. Tuition and fees vary according to program. *Financial support:* Fellowships with partial tuition reimbursements, research assistantships with partial tuition reimbursements, teaching assistantships with partial tuition reimbursements, career-related internships or fieldwork, Federal Work-Study, institutionally sponsored loans, tuition waivers (partial), and unspecified assistantships available. Financial award application deadline: 3/1; financial award applicants required to submit FAFSA. *Faculty research:* Religious subcultures, attitudes toward abortion, population, sport research, stratification. *Unit head:* Dr. Jay Corzine, Chair, 407-823-2227, Fax: 407-823-5156, E-mail: hcorzine@mail.ucf.edu.

University of Central Missouri, The Graduate School, College of Health and Human Services, Department of Sociology and Social Work, Warrensburg, MO 64093. Offers social gerontology (MS); sociology (MA). Part-time programs available. *Faculty:* 14 full-time (8 women). *Students:* 10 full-time (9 women), 19 part-time (14 women); includes 5 minority (4 African Americans, 1 Asian American or Pacific Islander), 1 international. Average age 38. 25 applicants, 84% accepted, 9 enrolled. In 2007, 11 degrees awarded. *Degree requirements:* For master's, comprehensive exam. *Entrance requirements:* For master's, minimum GPA of 2.5. Additional exam requirements/recommendations for international students: Required—TOEFL (minimum score 500 paper-based; 173 computer-based). *Application deadline:* For fall admission, 6/1 priority date for domestic students, 5/1 priority date for international students; for spring admission, 10/1 priority date for domestic students, 10/1 for international students. Applications are processed on a rolling basis. Application fee: $30 ($50 for international students). *Expenses:* Tuition, state resident: full-time $6,259; part-time $256 per credit hour. Tuition, nonresident: full-time $11,915; part-time $491 per credit hour. Required fees: $604; $20 per credit hour. *Financial support:* In 2007–08, 5 students received support; teaching assistantships with partial tuition reimbursements available, Federal Work-Study, scholarships/grants, unspecified assistantships, and administrative assistantships available. Support available to part-time students. Financial award application deadline: 3/1; financial award applicants required to submit FAFSA. *Faculty research:* Suicide, end of life decision making, aging/gerontology, race/ethic relations, religion. Total annual research expenditures: $212,400. *Unit head:* Jean Nuernberger, Chair, 660-543-8758, Fax: 660-543-8215, E-mail: nuernberger@ucmo.edu.

University of Chicago, Division of Social Sciences, Department of Sociology, Chicago, IL 60637-1513. Offers PhD. *Students:* 154. In 2007, 14 degrees awarded. *Degree requirements:* For doctorate, one foreign language, thesis/dissertation, 2 field exams. *Entrance requirements:* For doctorate, GRE General Test. Additional exam requirements/recommendations for international students: Required—TOEFL, IELTS (minimum score 7). *Application deadline:* For fall admission, 12/10 for domestic and international students. Application fee: $55. Electronic applications accepted. *Financial support:* Fellowships, research assistantships, teaching assistantships, Federal Work-Study, institutionally sponsored loans, scholarships/grants, traineeships, health care benefits, and unspecified assistantships available. Financial award application deadline: 12/15; financial award applicants required to submit FAFSA. *Unit head:* Prof. William Parish, Chair, 773-702-8677. *Application contact:* Office of the Dean of Students, 773-702-8415.

University of Cincinnati, Graduate School, McMicken College of Arts and Sciences, Department of Sociology, Cincinnati, OH 45221. Offers MA, PhD. Part-time programs available. *Faculty:* 13 full-time (6 women), 1 (woman) part-time/adjunct. *Students:* 23 full-time (14 women), 15 part-time (11 women); includes 4 minority (all African Americans), 4 international. Average age 23. 47 applicants, 49% accepted, 14 enrolled. In 2007, 3 master's, 2 doctorates awarded. *Median time to degree:* Of those who began their doctoral program in fall 1999, 30% received their degree in 8 years or less. *Degree requirements:* For master's, thesis; for doctorate, thesis/dissertation. *Entrance requirements:* For master's and doctorate, GRE General Test. Additional exam requirements/recommendations for international students: Required—TOEFL. *Application deadline:* For fall admission, 2/1 for domestic and international students. Application fee: $40. Electronic applications accepted. *Financial support:* In 2007–08, 1 fellowship with full tuition reimbursement (averaging $12,000 per year), 1 research assistantship with full tuition reimbursement (averaging $11,000 per year), 11 teaching assistantships with full tuition reimbursements (averaging $11,000 per year) were awarded; tuition waivers (partial) and unspecified assistantships also available. Financial award application deadline: 2/1. *Faculty research:* Work and family, race and urban, health and medicine, social psychology. Total annual research expenditures: $60,000. *Unit head:* Dr. Paula Dubek, Head, 513-556-4715, E-mail: paula.dubek@uc.edu. *Application contact:* Dr. Rhys Williams, Graduate Program Director, 513-556-4700, Fax: 513-556-0057, E-mail: rhys.williams@uc.edu.

University of Colorado at Boulder, Graduate School, College of Arts and Sciences, Department of Sociology, Boulder, CO 80309. Offers PhD. *Faculty:* 22. *Students:* 52 full-time (29 women), 19 part-time (16 women); includes 8 minority (1 African American, 5 Asian Americans or Pacific Islanders, 2 Hispanic Americans), 1 international. Average age 30. 16 applicants, 75% accepted. In 2007, 4 degrees awarded. *Degree requirements:* For doctorate, comprehensive exam, thesis/dissertation. *Entrance requirements:* For doctorate, GRE General Test, GRE Subject Test, minimum undergraduate GPA of 2.75. *Application deadline:* For fall admission, 1/1 for domestic students, 12/1 for international students. Application fee: $50 ($60 for international students). *Financial support:* In 2007–08, 20 fellowships (averaging $3,940 per year), 14 research assistantships (averaging $14,217 per year) were awarded; Federal Work-Study, institutionally sponsored loans, and scholarships/grants also available. Support available to part-time students. Financial award application deadline: 1/1; financial award applicants required to submit FAFSA. *Faculty research:* Criminology, social control, law delinquency and deviance, population, health studies, gender relations, social stratification, race relations, the environment, institutions and international systems. Total annual research expenditures: $5 million. *Unit head:* Michael Radelet, Chair, 303-735-5811, Fax: 303-492-8878, E-mail: michael.radelet@colorado.edu. *Application contact:* Graduate Secretary, 303-735-2335, Fax: 303-492-5105, E-mail: sociology@colorado.edu.

University of Colorado at Colorado Springs, Graduate School, College of Letters, Arts and Sciences, Department of Sociology, Colorado Springs, CO 80933-7150. Offers MA. Part-time programs available. *Faculty:* 8 full-time (4 women). *Students:* 32 full-time (26 women), 18 part-time (14 women); includes 14 minority (6 African Americans, 2 Asian Americans or Pacific Islanders, 6 Hispanic Americans). Average age 33. 13 applicants, 92% accepted, 8 enrolled. In 2007, 9 degrees awarded. *Degree requirements:* For master's, thesis optional. *Entrance requirements:* For master's, GRE, minimum GPA of 2.75. *Application deadline:* For fall admission, 7/1 priority date for domestic students; for spring admission, 11/1 for domestic students. Applications are processed on a rolling basis. Application fee: $60 ($75 for international students). *Financial support:* Teaching assistantships, career-related internships or fieldwork, Federal Work-Study, and institutionally sponsored loans available. *Faculty research:* Environmental justice, gender, race and ethnicity, sport and popular culture, youth and deviant behavior. *Unit head:* Dr. Lynda Dickson, Chair, 719-262-4142, Fax: 719-262-4450, E-mail: ldickson@uccs.edu. *Application contact:* Shari Patterson, Program Assistant, 719-262-4153, Fax: 719-262-4450, E-mail: spatterson@uccs.edu.

University of Colorado Denver, College of Liberal Arts and Sciences, Department of Sociology, Denver, CO 80217-3364. Offers MA. Part-time and evening/weekend programs available. *Faculty:* 7 full-time (3 women). *Students:* 3 full-time (2 women), 20 part-time (14 women); includes 4 minority (2 African Americans, 1 Asian American or Pacific Islander, 1 Hispanic American), 2 international. Average age 30. 13 applicants, 0% accepted. In 2007, 18 degrees awarded. *Degree requirements:* For master's, thesis or alternative. *Entrance*

Sociology

University of Colorado Denver (continued)
requirements: For master's, GRE. *Application deadline:* For fall admission, 6/1 for domestic students; for spring admission, 11/1 for domestic students. Applications are processed on a rolling basis. Application fee: $50 ($75 for international students). Electronic applications accepted. *Financial support:* Research assistantships, teaching assistantships, Federal Work-Study, institutionally sponsored loans, and scholarships/grants available. Financial award application deadline: 4/1; financial award applicants required to submit FAFSA. *Unit head:* Dr. Sharon Araji, Interim Chair, 303-556-2780, Fax: 303-556-3510, E-mail: sharon.araji@cudenver.edu. *Application contact:* Rachel Watson, Program Assistant, 303-556-3557, Fax: 303-556-3510, E-mail: rwatson@carbon.cudenver.edu.

University of Connecticut, Graduate School, College of Liberal Arts and Sciences, Department of Sociology, Field of Sociology, Storrs, CT 06269. Offers MA, PhD. *Faculty:* 26 full-time (10 women). *Students:* 46 full-time (32 women), 1 (woman) part-time; includes 9 minority (7 African Americans, 2 Hispanic Americans), 5 international. Average age 28. 94 applicants, 13% accepted, 11 enrolled. In 2007, 6 master's, 4 doctorates awarded. Terminal master's awarded for partial completion of doctoral program. *Degree requirements:* For master's, comprehensive exam; for doctorate, thesis/dissertation, 2 field exams. *Entrance requirements:* For master's and doctorate, GRE General Test. Additional exam requirements/recommendations for international students: Required—TOEFL (minimum score 550 paper-based; 213 computer-based). *Application deadline:* For fall admission, 2/1 priority date for domestic and international students; for spring admission, 11/1 for domestic students, 10/1 for international students. Applications are processed on a rolling basis. Application fee: $55. Electronic applications accepted. *Expenses:* Contact institution. *Financial support:* In 2007–08, 13 research assistantships with full tuition reimbursements, 32 teaching assistantships with full tuition reimbursements were awarded; fellowships, Federal Work-Study, scholarships/grants, health care benefits, and unspecified assistantships also available. Financial award application deadline: 2/1; financial award applicants required to submit FAFSA. *Application contact:* Katherine Covey, Administrative Assistant, 860-486-4423, Fax: 860-486-6356, E-mail: katherine.covey@uconn.edu.

University of Delaware, College of Arts and Sciences, Department of Sociology and Criminology, Newark, DE 19716. Offers criminology (MA, PhD); sociology (MA, PhD). *Faculty:* 23 full-time (13 women), 1 part-time/adjunct (0 women). *Students:* 52 full-time (31 women), 4 part-time (3 women); includes 11 minority (6 African Americans, 5 Hispanic Americans), 3 international. Average age 26. 83 applicants, 43% accepted, 14 enrolled. In 2007, 7 master's, 6 doctorates awarded. *Degree requirements:* For master's, thesis; for doctorate, comprehensive exam, thesis/dissertation. *Entrance requirements:* For master's and doctorate, GRE, 3 letters of recommendation. Additional exam requirements/recommendations for international students: Required—TOEFL. *Application deadline:* For fall admission, 2/1 for domestic students. Application fee: $60. Electronic applications accepted. *Financial support:* In 2007–08, 38 students received support, including 2 fellowships with full tuition reimbursements available (averaging $14,600 per year), 15 research assistantships with full tuition reimbursements available (averaging $14,600 per year), 21 teaching assistantships with full tuition reimbursements available (averaging $14,600 per year). Financial award application deadline: 2/1. *Faculty research:* Sex and gender, criminology/deviance, theory, methods, collective behavior. Total annual research expenditures: $5.5 million. *Unit head:* Dr. Ronet D. Bachman, Chair, 302-831-2581, Fax: 302-831-2607. *Application contact:* Dr. Anne Bowler, Director of Graduate Studies, 302-831-2581, Fax: 302-831-2607, E-mail: abowler@udel.edu.

University of Florida, Graduate School, College of Liberal Arts and Sciences, Department of Sociology, Gainesville, FL 32611. Offers MA, PhD, JD/MA. *Faculty:* 19 full-time (8 women). *Students:* 56 (34 women); includes 17 minority (6 African Americans, 1 American Indian/Alaska Native, 2 Asian Americans or Pacific Islanders, 8 Hispanic Americans) 6 international. In 2007, 12 master's, 9 doctorates awarded. *Degree requirements:* For master's, thesis optional; for doctorate, thesis/dissertation. *Entrance requirements:* For master's and doctorate, GRE General Test, minimum GPA of 3.0. Additional exam requirements/recommendations for international students: Required—TOEFL (minimum score 550 paper-based; 213 computer-based). *Application deadline:* For fall admission, 6/1 priority date for domestic students. Applications are processed on a rolling basis. Application fee: $30. Electronic applications accepted. *Expenses:* Tuition, state resident: full-time $7,478. Tuition, nonresident: full-time $22,603. *Financial support:* In 2007–08, 8 research assistantships (averaging $11,879 per year), 21 teaching assistantships (averaging $11,214 per year) were awarded; fellowships, career-related internships or fieldwork and unspecified assistantships also available. *Faculty research:* Sociology of the family, social gerontology, criminology and deviance, race ethnicity. *Unit head:* Dr. John Henretta, Chair, 352-392-0265 Ext. 229, Fax: 352-392-6568, E-mail: jch@soc.ufl.edu. *Application contact:* William Marsiglio, Coordinator, 352-392-0265, Fax: 352-392-6568, E-mail: grad.coord@soc.ufl.edu.

University of Georgia, Graduate School, College of Arts and Sciences, Department of Sociology, Athens, GA 30602. Offers MA, PhD. *Faculty:* 20 full-time (6 women). *Students:* 31 full-time (23 women), 6 part-time (2 women); includes 4 minority (2 African Americans, 2 Hispanic Americans), 3 international. 56 applicants, 32% accepted, 8 enrolled. In 2007, 2 master's, 2 doctorates awarded. *Degree requirements:* For master's, thesis; for doctorate, thesis/dissertation. *Entrance requirements:* For master's and doctorate, GRE General Test. Additional exam requirements/recommendations for international students: Required—TOEFL. *Application deadline:* For fall admission, 2/1 priority date for domestic students, 1/1 for international students. Application fee: $50. Electronic applications accepted. *Financial support:* In 2007–08, 16 students received support, including teaching assistantships with full tuition reimbursements available (averaging $12,220 per year); research assistantships, unspecified assistantships also available. Financial award application deadline: 1/1. *Faculty research:* Race, deviance, gender, culture. *Unit head:* Dr. William Finlay, Head, 706-542-3175, Fax: 706-542-4320, E-mail: wfinlay@uga.edu. *Application contact:* Dr. Jody Clay-Warner, Graduate Coordinator, 706-542-3217, Fax: 706-542-4320, E-mail: jclayw@uga.edu.

University of Guelph, Graduate Program Services, College of Social and Applied Human Sciences, Department of Sociology and Anthropology, Guelph, ON N1G 2W1, Canada. Offers anthropology (MA); crime and criminal justice policy (MA); sociology (MA, PhD). *Faculty:* 24 full-time (13 women). *Students:* 34 full-time (31 women). Average age 25. 119 applicants, 31% accepted, 17 enrolled. In 2007, 14 degrees awarded. *Degree requirements:* For master's, thesis or major paper; for doctorate, comprehensive exam, thesis/dissertation. *Entrance requirements:* For master's, minimum B+ average during previous 2 years of course work, honors BA or equivalent; for doctorate, must have an MA in Sociology, must have 80% or higher in graduate level studies. Additional exam requirements/recommendations for international students: Required—TOEFL (minimum score 550 paper-based; 213 computer-based; 89 iBT), IELTS (minimum score 7), TOEFL or IELTS. *Application deadline:* For fall admission, 2/1 for domestic and international students. Application fee: $85. Electronic applications accepted. *Financial support:* In 2007–08, 103 teaching assistantships (averaging $5,106 per year) were awarded; research assistantships, scholarships/grants also available. *Faculty research:* Rural and development sociology; education, employment, and the workplace; race, ethnicity, and native studies; criminology and deviance; social psychology. *Unit head:* Dr. F. J. Schryer, Chair, 519-824-4120 Ext. 56527, Fax: 519-837-9561, E-mail: fschryer@uoguelph.ca. *Application contact:* Dr. M. Dawson, Graduate Coordinator, 519-824-4120 Ext. 56078, Fax: 519-837-9561, E-mail: mdawson@uoguelph.ca.

University of Hawaii at Manoa, Graduate Division, Colleges of Arts and Sciences, College of Social Sciences, Department of Sociology, Honolulu, HI 96822. Offers population studies (Graduate Certificate); sociology (MA, PhD). Part-time programs available. *Faculty:* 22 full-time (9 women), 7 part-time/adjunct (2 women). *Students:* 53 full-time (33 women), 11 part-time (7 women); includes 8 minority (7 Asian Americans or Pacific Islanders, 1 Hispanic American), 36 international. Average age 32. 43 applicants, 42% accepted, 6 enrolled. *Median time to degree:* Of those who began their doctoral program in fall 1999, 29% received their degree in 8 years or less. *Degree requirements:* For master's, thesis optional; for doctorate, comprehensive exam, thesis/dissertation. *Entrance requirements:* For master's and doctorate, GRE General Test. Additional exam requirements/recommendations for international students: Required—TOEFL (minimum score 500 paper-based; 173 computer-based; 61 iBT), IELTS (minimum score 5). *Application deadline:* For fall admission, 3/1 for domestic students, 2/15 for international students; for spring admission, 9/1 for domestic students, 8/15 for international students. Applications are processed on a rolling basis. Application fee: $50. *Financial support:* In 2007–08, 10 research assistantships (averaging $16,729 per year), 9 teaching assistantships (averaging $14,638 per year) were awarded; Federal Work-Study, institutionally sponsored loans, and tuition waivers (full and partial) also available. *Faculty research:* Comparative sociology of Asia; population studies; crime, law, and deviance; health; aging and medical sociology. Total annual research expenditures: $506,479. *Application contact:* Sun-Ki Chai, Graduate Chair, 808-956-7693, Fax: 808-956-3707, E-mail: sunki@hawaii.edu.

University of Houston, College of Liberal Arts and Social Sciences, Department of Sociology, Houston, TX 77204. Offers MA. Part-time and evening/weekend programs available. *Faculty:* 6 full-time (2 women), 2 part-time/adjunct (0 women). *Students:* 14 full-time (11 women), 11 part-time (5 women); includes 7 minority (4 African Americans, 3 Hispanic Americans), 7 international. Average age 28. 12 applicants, 92% accepted, 8 enrolled. In 2007, 11 degrees awarded. *Degree requirements:* For master's, thesis. *Entrance requirements:* For master's, GRE General Test, minimum GPA of 3.0. Additional exam requirements/recommendations for international students: Required—TOEFL. *Application deadline:* For fall admission, 8/1 for domestic students; for spring admission, 12/1 for domestic students. Applications are processed on a rolling basis. Application fee: $0 ($75 for international students). *Expenses:* Tuition, state resident: full-time $6,297; part-time $262 per credit. Tuition, nonresident: full-time $12,969; part-time $540 per credit. Required fees: $2,696. *Financial support:* In 2007–08, 1 research assistantship with full tuition reimbursement (averaging $8,800 per year), 8 teaching assistantships with tuition reimbursements (averaging $8,800 per year) were awarded; fellowships with full tuition reimbursements, career-related internships or fieldwork, Federal Work-Study, institutionally sponsored loans, scholarships/grants, health care benefits, and unspecified assistantships also available. Support available to part-time students. Financial award application deadline: 2/1; financial award applicants required to submit FAFSA. *Faculty research:* Gender, immigration, urban studies, religion, race/ethnicity, social psychology, medical sociology. *Unit head:* Dr. Nestor Rodriguez, Chairperson, 713-743-3953, Fax: 713-743-3943, E-mail: nrodriguez@uh.edu. *Application contact:* Dr. Joseph A. Kotarba, Director of Graduate Studies, 713-743-3954, Fax: 713-743-3943, E-mail: jkotarba@uh.edu.

University of Houston–Clear Lake, School of Human Sciences and Humanities, Programs in Human Sciences, Houston, TX 77058-1098. Offers behavioral sciences (MA), including behavioral sciences-general, behavioral sciences-psychology, behavioral sciences-sociology; clinical psychology (MA); criminology (MA); cross-cultural studies (MA); family therapy (MA); fitness and human performance (MA); school psychology (MA). *Accreditation:* AAMFT/COAMFTE. Part-time and evening/weekend programs available. Postbaccalaureate distance learning degree programs offered (minimal on-campus study). *Degree requirements:* For master's, thesis or alternative. *Entrance requirements:* For master's, GRE General Test. Additional exam requirements/recommendations for international students: Required—TOEFL (minimum score 550 paper-based; 213 computer-based). Electronic applications accepted. *Faculty research:* Smoking cessation, adolescent sexuality, white collar crime, serial murder, human factors/human computer interaction.

University of Illinois at Chicago, Graduate College, College of Liberal Arts and Sciences, Department of Sociology, Chicago, IL 60607-7128. Offers MA, PhD. Terminal master's awarded for partial completion of doctoral program. *Degree requirements:* For master's, comprehensive exam, thesis; for doctorate, thesis/dissertation, qualifying exam. *Entrance requirements:* For master's and doctorate, GRE General Test, minimum GPA of 3.0. Additional exam requirements/recommendations for international students: Required—TOEFL. Electronic applications accepted. *Faculty research:* Social psychology, social organization, applied sociology, demography and human ecology.

University of Illinois at Urbana–Champaign, Graduate College, College of Liberal Arts and Sciences, Department of Sociology, Champaign, IL 61820. Offers MA, PhD. *Faculty:* 13 full-time (6 women). *Students:* 33 full-time (19 women), 15 part-time (9 women); includes 6 minority (4 African Americans, 1 Asian American or Pacific Islander, 1 Hispanic American), 19 international. 57 applicants, 14% accepted, 7 enrolled. In 2007, 5 doctorates awarded. *Degree requirements:* For doctorate, thesis/dissertation. *Entrance requirements:* For master's, GRE General Test, GRE Subject Test, minimum GPA of 3.0. *Application deadline:* For fall admission, 12/16 for domestic students. Applications are processed on a rolling basis. Application fee: $60 ($75 for international students). Electronic applications accepted. *Financial support:* In 2007–08, 14 fellowships, 5 research assistantships, 33 teaching assistantships were awarded; tuition waivers (full and partial) also available. Financial award application deadline: 2/15. *Unit head:* Futing Liao, Head, 217-333-1950, Fax: 217-333-5225, E-mail: tfliao@uiuc.edu. *Application contact:* Julie Woolsey, Assistant to the Head, 217-244-1813, Fax: 217-333-5225, E-mail: jwoolsey@uiuc.edu.

University of Indianapolis, Graduate Programs, College of Arts and Sciences, Department of Social Sciences, Indianapolis, IN 46227-3697. Offers applied sociology (MA). Part-time and evening/weekend programs available. *Faculty:* 5 full-time (2 women), 1 part-time/adjunct (0 women). *Students:* 5 full-time (3 women), 12 part-time (7 women); includes 5 minority (4 African Americans, 1 Asian American or Pacific Islander), 2 international. Average age 31. *Degree requirements:* For master's, thesis optional. *Entrance requirements:* For master's, GRE Subject Test, minimum 3.0 GPA, letter of intent, 3 letters of recommendation. Additional exam requirements/recommendations for international students: Required—TOEFL (minimum score 550 paper-based; 213 computer-based). *Application deadline:* Applications are processed on a rolling basis. Application fee: $30. Electronic applications accepted. *Financial support:* Federal Work-Study available. Financial award application deadline: 5/1; financial award applicants required to submit FAFSA. *Unit head:* Dr. James Pennell, Chair, 317-788-3535, Fax: 317-788-3480, E-mail: jpennell@uindy.edu.

The University of Iowa, Graduate College, College of Liberal Arts and Sciences, Department of Sociology, Iowa City, IA 52242-1316. Offers MA, PhD, JD/MA. *Faculty:* 16 full-time, 6 part-time/adjunct. *Students:* 25 full-time (14 women), 9 part-time (6 women); includes 9 minority (6 African Americans, 1 Asian American or Pacific Islander, 2 Hispanic Americans), 6 international. 53 applicants, 30% accepted, 9 enrolled. In 2007, 7 master's, 3 doctorates awarded. *Degree requirements:* For master's, thesis optional, exam; for doctorate, comprehensive exam, thesis/dissertation. *Entrance requirements:* For master's and doctorate, GRE General Test, minimum GPA of 3.0. Additional exam requirements/recommendations for international students: Required—TOEFL (minimum score 550 paper-based; 213 computer-based; 81 iBT). *Application deadline:* For fall admission, 1/1 priority date for domestic and international students; for spring admission, 11/1 priority date for domestic students. Applications are processed on a rolling basis. Application fee: $60 ($85 for international students). Electronic applications accepted. *Expenses:* Tuition, state resident: part-time $349 per hour. Tuition, nonresident: part-time $349 per hour. Tuition and fees vary according to course load and program. *Financial support:* In 2007–08, 4 research assistantships with partial tuition reimbursements, 17 teaching assistantships with partial tuition reimbursements were awarded; fellowships also available. Financial award applicants required to submit FAFSA. *Unit head:* Celeste Albonetti, Chair, 319-335-2502, Fax: 319-335-2509.

University of Kansas, Research and Graduate Studies, College of Liberal Arts and Sciences, Department of Sociology, Lawrence, KS 66045. Offers MA, PhD. Part-time programs available. *Faculty:* 20. *Students:* 36 full-time (24 women), 7 part-time (5 women); includes 5 minority (1 African American, 1 Asian American or Pacific Islander, 3 Hispanic Americans), 4 international. Average age 32. 37 applicants, 46% accepted, 9 enrolled. In 2007, 6 master's, 3 doctorates awarded. *Degree requirements:* For master's, thesis; for doctorate, comprehensive exam, thesis/dissertation. *Entrance requirements:* For master's and doctorate, GRE General Test. Additional exam requirements/recommendations for international students: Required—TOEFL, TOEFL (paper-based 530; computer-based 200) or IELTS (score 6). *Application deadline:* For fall admission, 12/15 priority date for domestic and international students; for spring admission, 10/15 for domestic and international students. Applications are processed on a rolling basis. Application fee: $55 ($60 for international students). Electronic applications accepted. *Expenses:* Tuition, state resident: full-time $5,838. Tuition, nonresident: full-time $13,409. Tuition and fees vary according to program. *Financial support:* Fellowships with full tuition reimbursements, research assistantships with full tuition reimbursements, teaching assistantships with full and partial tuition reimbursements, unspecified assistantships available. Financial award application deadline: 12/15. *Faculty research:* Comparative/historical sociology, sex and gender, social movements, social theory, medical sociology. *Unit head:* William G. Staples, Chair, 785-864-4111, Fax: 785-864-5280. *Application contact:* Eric Hanley, Graduate Director, 785-864-4111, Fax: 785-864-5280, E-mail: hanley@ku.edu.

University of Kentucky, Graduate School, College of Arts and Sciences, Program in Sociology, Lexington, KY 40506-0032. Offers MA, PhD. Part-time programs available. *Faculty:* 11 full-time (5 women). *Students:* 46 full-time (25 women), 8 part-time (5 women); includes 3 minority (all African Americans), 9 international. Average age 34. 46 applicants, 33% accepted, 8 enrolled. In 2007, 2 master's, 4 doctorates awarded. *Median time to degree:* Of those who began their doctoral program in fall 1999, 67% received their degree in 8 years or less. *Degree requirements:* For master's, comprehensive exam, thesis optional; for doctorate, comprehensive exam, thesis/dissertation. *Entrance requirements:* For master's, GRE General Test, minimum undergraduate GPA of 2.75; for doctorate, GRE General Test, minimum graduate GPA of 3.0. Additional exam requirements/recommendations for international students: Required—TOEFL (minimum score 550 paper-based; 213 computer-based). *Application deadline:* For fall admission, 7/17 priority date for domestic students, 2/1 priority date for international students; for spring admission, 12/13 priority date for domestic students, 6/15 priority date for international students. Application fee: $50 ($65 for international students). Electronic applications accepted. *Expenses:* Tuition, state resident: part-time $437 per credit hour. Tuition, nonresident: part-time $931 per credit hour. *Financial support:* In 2007–08, 28 students received support, including 1 fellowship with full tuition reimbursement available (averaging $2,894 per year), 9 research assistantships with full tuition reimbursements available (averaging $11,000 per year), 19 teaching assistantships with full tuition reimbursements available (averaging $1,100 per year); Federal Work-Study, scholarships/grants, traineeships, health care benefits, tuition waivers (partial), and unspecified assistantships also available. Support available to part-time students. Financial award application deadline: 3/15. *Faculty research:* Work organizations, social inequalities, rural sociology, criminology/deviance, medical sociology. *Unit head:* Dr. Tomas Janoski, Director of Graduate Studies, 859-257-1164. *Application contact:* Dr. Brian Jackson, Senior Associate Dean, 859-257-4667, Fax: 859-257-4676, E-mail: brian.jackson@uky.edu.

University of Lethbridge, School of Graduate Studies, Lethbridge, AB T1K 3M4, Canada. Offers accounting (MScM); addictions counseling (M Sc); agricultural biotechnology (M Sc); agricultural studies (M Sc, MA); anthropology (MA); archaeology (MA); art (MA); biochemistry (M Sc); biological sciences (M Sc); biomolecular science (PhD); biosystems and biodiversity (PhD); Canadian studies (MA); chemistry (M Sc); computer science (M Sc); computer science and geographical information science (M Sc); counseling psychology (M Ed); dramatic arts (MA); earth, space, and physical science (PhD); economics (MA); educational leadership (M Ed); English (MA); environmental science (M Sc); evolution and behavior (PhD); exercise science (M Sc); finance (MScM); French (MA); French/German (MA); French/Spanish (MA); general education (M Ed); general management (MScM); geography (M Sc, MA); German (MA); health sciences (M Sc, MA); history (MA); human resource management and labour relations (MScM); individualized multidisciplinary (M Sc, MA); information systems (MScM); international management (MScM); kinesiology (M Sc, MA); management (M Sc, MA); marketing (MScM); mathematics (M Sc); music (MA); Native American studies (MA); neuroscience (M Sc, PhD); new media (MA); nursing (M Sc); philosophy (MA); physics (M Sc); policy and strategy (MScM); political science (MA); psychology (M Sc, MA); religious studies (MA); sociology (MA); theoretical and computational science (PhD); urban and regional studies (MA). Part-time and evening/weekend programs available. *Students:* 215 full-time, 98 part-time. In 2007, 87 master's, 1 doctorate awarded. *Degree requirements:* For doctorate, comprehensive exam, thesis/dissertation. *Entrance requirements:* For master's, GMAT (M Sc in management), bachelor's degree in related field, minimum GPA of 3.0 during previous 20 graded semester courses, 2 years teaching or related experience (M Ed); for doctorate, master's degree, minimum graduate GPA of 3.5. Additional exam requirements/recommendations for international students: Required—TOEFL. Application fee: $60 Canadian dollars. *Financial support:* Fellowships, research assistantships, teaching assistantships, scholarships/grants, health care benefits, and unspecified assistantships available. *Faculty research:* Movement and brain plasticity, gibberellin physiology, photosynthesis, carbon cycling, molecular properties of main-group ring components. *Unit head:* Dr. Jo-Anne Fiske, Interim Dean, 403-329-2121, Fax: 403-329-2097. *Application contact:* Jennifer Geddes, Graduate Liaison Officer, 403-329-2762, Fax: 403-329-5159, E-mail: jennifer.geddes@uleth.ca.

University of Louisville, Graduate School, College of Arts and Sciences, Department of Sociology, Louisville, KY 40292-0001. Offers MA. *Students:* 4 full-time (3 women), 12 part-time (5 women); includes 1 minority (African American), 2 international. Average age 28. In 2007, 11 degrees awarded. *Degree requirements:* For master's, thesis optional. *Entrance requirements:* For master's, GRE General Test. *Application deadline:* For fall admission, 3/1 priority date for domestic students; for spring admission, 10/15 priority date for domestic students. Applications are processed on a rolling basis. Application fee: $50. *Financial support:* In 2007–08, 4 teaching assistantships with full tuition reimbursements (averaging $12,000 per year) were awarded. *Unit head:* Dr. Allen Furr, Chair, 502-852-8026, Fax: 502-852-0099, E-mail: allenfur@louisville.edu.

University of Manitoba, Faculty of Graduate Studies, Faculty of Arts, Department of Sociology, Winnipeg, MB R3T 2N2, Canada. Offers MA, PhD. *Degree requirements:* For master's, thesis.

University of Maryland, Baltimore County, Graduate School, College of Arts, Humanities and Social Sciences, Department of Sociology and Anthropology, Baltimore, MD 21250. Offers applied sociology (MA, Postbaccalaureate Certificate), including applied sociology (MA), non-profit sector (Postbaccalaureate Certificate). Part-time programs available. *Faculty:* 13 full-time (6 women), 1 (woman) part-time/adjunct. *Students:* 28 full-time (21 women), 32 part-time (24 women); includes 18 minority (11 African Americans, 1 American Indian/Alaska Native, 6 Asian Americans or Pacific Islanders), 2 international. Average age 32. 37 applicants, 100% accepted, 34 enrolled. In 2007, 18 degrees awarded. *Degree requirements:* For master's, thesis or alternative. *Entrance requirements:* For master's, minimum GPA of 3.0, undergrad statistics course. Additional exam requirements/recommendations for international students: Required—TOEFL. *Application deadline:* For fall admission, 7/31 for domestic students; for spring admission, 12/31 for domestic students. Applications are processed on a rolling basis. Application fee: $50. Electronic applications accepted. *Financial support:* In 2007–08, 9 students received support, including 4 research assistantships with partial tuition reimbursements available (averaging $12,500 per year), 5 teaching assistantships with partial tuition reimbursements available (averaging $12,500 per year); scholarships/grants, health care benefits, unspecified assistantships, and tuition remission also available. Financial award application deadline: 2/1. *Faculty research:* Sociology of aging, diversity, medical sociology. *Unit head:* Dr. James E. Trela, Chairperson, 410-455-2076, Fax: 410-455-1154, E-mail: trela@umbc.edu. *Application contact:* Dr. William G. Rothstein, Director, 410-455-2078, Fax: 410-455-1154, E-mail: rothstei@umbc.edu.

University of Maryland, College Park, Graduate Studies, College of Behavioral and Social Sciences, Department of Sociology, College Park, MD 20742. Offers MA, PhD. *Faculty:* 30 full-time (12 women), 8 part-time/adjunct (2 women). *Students:* 73 full-time (48 women), 5 part-time (4 women); includes 12 minority (7 African Americans, 2 Asian Americans or Pacific Islanders, 3 Hispanic Americans), 19 international. 196 applicants, 21% accepted, 17 enrolled. In 2007, 6 master's, 11 doctorates awarded. *Median time to degree:* Of those who began their doctoral program in fall 1999, 40% received their degree in 8 years or less. *Degree requirements:* For master's, thesis; for doctorate, thesis/dissertation, 2 qualifying exams. *Entrance requirements:* For master's, GRE General Test, minimum GPA of 3.0, 3 letters of recommendation; for doctorate, GRE General Test, 3 letters of recommendation. Additional exam requirements/recommendations for international students: Required—TOEFL. *Application deadline:* For fall admission, 1/1 for domestic students, 2/1 for international students; for spring admission, 10/1 for domestic students, 6/1 for international students. Applications are processed on a rolling basis. Application fee: $60. Electronic applications accepted. *Financial support:* In 2007–08, 7 fellowships with full tuition reimbursements (averaging $11,780 per year), 1 research assistantship (averaging $15,341 per year), 65 teaching assistantships with tuition reimbursements (averaging $14,944 per year) were awarded; Federal Work-Study and scholarships/grants also available. Support available to part-time students. Financial award applicants required to submit FAFSA. *Faculty research:* Social psychology, sociology of work, sociology of the military, population studies, stratification. Total annual research expenditures: $1.4 million. *Unit head:* Dr. Suzanne Bianchi, Chair, 301-405-6394, Fax: 301-314-6892, E-mail: bianchi@umd.edu. *Application contact:* Dean of Graduate School, 301-405-0358, Fax: 301-314-9305.

University of Massachusetts Amherst, Graduate School, College of Social and Behavioral Sciences, Department of Sociology, Amherst, MA 01003. Offers MA, PhD. Part-time programs available. *Faculty:* 29 full-time (14 women). *Students:* 48 full-time (32 women), 16 part-time (9 women); includes 12 minority (6 African Americans, 1 Asian American or Pacific Islander, 5 Hispanic Americans), 14 international. Average age 31. 172 applicants, 20% accepted, 8 enrolled. In 2007, 9 master's, 4 doctorates awarded. Terminal master's awarded for partial completion of doctoral program. *Degree requirements:* For master's, thesis or alternative; for doctorate, thesis/dissertation. *Entrance requirements:* For master's, GRE General Test, writing sample, 3 letters of recommendation; for doctorate, GRE General Test, 3 letters of recommendation and writing sample. Additional exam requirements/recommendations for international students: Required—TOEFL (minimum score 530 paper-based; 197 computer-based). *Application deadline:* For fall admission, 1/15 priority date for domestic and international students. Applications are processed on a rolling basis. Application fee: $50 ($65 for international students). Electronic applications accepted. *Expenses:* Tuition, state resident: full-time $2,640; part-time $110 per credit. Tuition, nonresident: full-time $9,936; part-time $414 per credit. Required fees: $7,455. One-time fee: $332. Tuition and fees vary according to course load, campus/location, program and reciprocity agreements. *Financial support:* In 2007–08, 6 research assistantships with full tuition reimbursements (averaging $12,412 per year), 42 teaching assistantships with full tuition reimbursements (averaging $11,624 per year) were awarded; fellowships with full tuition reimbursements, career-related internships or fieldwork, Federal Work-Study, scholarships/grants, traineeships, and unspecified assistantships also available. Support available to part-time students. Financial award application deadline: 2/1. *Unit head:* Dr. Donald Tomaskovic-Devey, Chair, 413-545-4060, Fax: 413-545-3204, E-mail: tomaskovic-devey@soc.umass.edu.

University of Massachusetts Boston, Office of Graduate Studies, College of Liberal Arts, Program in Applied Sociology, Boston, MA 02125-3393. Offers MA. Part-time and evening/weekend programs available. *Degree requirements:* For master's, comprehensive exam, thesis. *Entrance requirements:* For master's, GRE or MAT, minimum GPA of 2.75. *Faculty research:* Sociology of education, social deviance and control, women and development, race and ethnic group relations, criminology.

University of Massachusetts Lowell, College of Arts and Sciences, Department of Regional Economic and Social Development, Lowell, MA 01854-2881. Offers MA, Graduate Certificate. Part-time programs available. *Faculty:* 14 full-time (5 women). *Entrance requirements:* For master's, GRE. *Application deadline:* For fall admission, 4/1 priority date for domestic students; for spring admission, 10/1 priority date for domestic students. Applications are processed on a rolling basis. Application fee: $20 ($35 for international students). Electronic applications accepted. *Financial support:* Research assistantships with full tuition reimbursements, teaching assistantships with full tuition reimbursements, career-related internships or fieldwork, Federal Work-Study, institutionally sponsored loans, scholarships/grants, and traineeships available. Support available to part-time students. *Unit head:* Philip Moss, Chair, 978-934-2787, E-mail: philip_moss@uml.edu.

University of Memphis, Graduate School, College of Arts and Sciences, Department of Sociology, Memphis, TN 38152. Offers MA. Part-time programs available. *Faculty:* 8 full-time (4 women). *Students:* 7 full-time (6 women), 10 part-time (7 women); includes 4 minority (all African Americans) Average age 30. 8 applicants, 63% accepted, 2 enrolled. In 2007, 5 degrees awarded. *Degree requirements:* For master's, comprehensive exam, thesis or alternative. *Entrance requirements:* For master's, GRE General Test or MAT, 12 undergraduate hours in sociology. *Application deadline:* For fall admission, 8/1 for domestic students; for spring admission, 12/1 for domestic students. Applications are processed on a rolling basis. Application fee: $35 ($60 for international students). Electronic applications accepted. *Expenses:* Tuition, state resident: full-time $6,990; part-time $377 per hour. Tuition, nonresident: full-time $17,818; part-time $830 per hour. Tuition and fees vary according to course load and program. *Financial support:* In 2007–08, 7 research assistantships with full tuition reimbursements (averaging $4,700 per year), 2 teaching assistantships with full tuition reimbursements (averaging $4,750 per year) were awarded. *Faculty research:* Medical and health, deviant behavior, inequality, religion, globalization. *Unit head:* Dr. Martin Levin, Chair, 901-678-2525. *Application contact:* Dr. Larry Peterson, Graduate Studies Coordinator, 901-678-3341, E-mail: lpeterson@memphis.edu.

University of Miami, Graduate School, College of Arts and Sciences, Department of Sociology, Coral Gables, FL 33124. Offers MA, PhD. Part-time programs available. *Faculty:* 11 full-time (2 women), 1 (woman) part-time/adjunct. *Students:* 20 full-time (13 women); includes 9 minority (5 African Americans, 4 Hispanic Americans), 3 international. Average age 30. 39 applicants, 33% accepted, 4 enrolled. In 2007, 5 master's, 2 doctorates awarded. Terminal master's awarded for partial completion of doctoral program. *Degree requirements:* For master's, thesis; for doctorate, comprehensive exam, thesis/dissertation. *Entrance requirements:* For master's and doctorate, GRE General Test. Additional exam requirements/recommendations for international students: Required—TOEFL (minimum score 515 paper-based; 213 computer-based). *Application deadline:* For fall admission, 1/30 priority date for domestic and international students. Applications are processed on a rolling basis. Application fee: $50. Electronic applications accepted. *Financial support:* In 2007–08, 19 students received support, including 3 fellowships with full tuition reimbursements available (averaging $17,000 per year), 5 teaching assistantships with full tuition reimbursements available (averaging $16,000 per year); research assistantships with full tuition reimbursements available, career-related internships or fieldwork, Federal Work-Study, traineeships, tuition waivers (partial), and unspecified assistantships also available. Financial award application deadline: 2/1; financial award applicants required to submit FAFSA. *Faculty research:* Crime, violence, mental health, ethnic relations, health. Total annual research expenditures: $30,000. *Unit head:* Prof. Robert Johnson, Chairman, 305-284-6768, Fax: 305-284-5310, E-mail: rjohnson@miami.edu. *Application contact:* Prof. Marvin Dawkins, Director of Graduate Studies, 305-284-6768, Fax: 305-284-5310, E-mail: mdawkins@miami.edu.

University of Michigan, Horace H. Rackham School of Graduate Studies, College of Literature, Science, and the Arts, Department of Sociology, Ann Arbor, MI 48109. Offers public policy and sociology (PhD); social work and sociology (PhD); sociology (PhD); women's studies and sociology (PhD). *Faculty:* 16 full-time (10 women), 20 part-time/adjunct (5 women). *Students:* 145 full-time (104 women); includes 59 minority (17 African Americans, 2 American Indian/Alaska Native, 24 Asian Americans or Pacific Islanders, 16 Hispanic Americans), 27 international. Average age 29. 237 applicants, 15% accepted, 16 enrolled. In 2007, 13 doctorates awarded. *Median time to degree:* Of those who began their doctoral program in fall 1999, 57% received their degree in 8 years or less. *Degree requirements:* For doctorate, comprehensive exam, thesis/dissertation, oral defense of dissertation, preliminary exam. *Entrance requirements:* For

Sociology

University of Michigan (continued)
doctorate, GRE General Test, letters of recommendation, writing sample, personal statement, statement of purpose. Additional exam requirements/recommendations for international students: Required—TOEFL (minimum score 560 paper-based; 220 computer-based). *Application deadline:* For fall admission, 12/15 for domestic and international students. Application fee: $60 ($75 for international students). Electronic applications accepted. *Financial support:* In 2007–08, 102 students received support, including 23 fellowships with tuition reimbursements available (averaging $14,400 per year), 79 teaching assistantships with tuition reimbursements available (averaging $15,199 per year); health care benefits also available. *Faculty research:* Power, history and social change; gender and sexuality; race and ethnicity; economic sociology; social demography. Total annual research expenditures: $191,606. *Unit head:* Howard Kimeldorf, Chair, 734-764-5554, Fax: 734-763-6887, E-mail: hkimel@umich.edu. *Application contact:* Jeannie Loughry, Graduate Program Coordinator, 734-647-4428, Fax: 734-763-6887, E-mail: sociology.graduate.program@umich.edu.

University of Michigan, Horace H. Rackham School of Graduate Studies, College of Literature, Science, and the Arts, Department of Women's Studies, Ann Arbor, MI 48109. Offers English and women's studies (PhD); history and women's studies (PhD); lesbian, gay, bisexual, transgender, queer (LGBTQ) studies (Certificate); psychology and women's studies (PhD); sociology and women's studies (PhD); women's studies (Certificate). *Faculty:* 71 full-time (68 women). *Students:* 70 full-time (69 women); includes 12 minority (4 African Americans, 5 Asian Americans or Pacific Islanders, 3 Hispanic Americans), 9 international. Average age 30. 140 applicants, 9% accepted. In 2007, 6 doctorates, 5 other advanced degrees awarded. *Degree requirements:* For doctorate, variable foreign language requirement, thesis/dissertation. *Entrance requirements:* For doctorate, GRE General Test, previous undergraduate course work in women's studies. *Application deadline:* For fall admission, 12/15 for domestic students. Application fee: $60 ($75 for international students). Electronic applications accepted. *Financial support:* In 2007–08, 23 fellowships with full tuition reimbursements (averaging $16,000 per year), 19 teaching assistantships with full and partial tuition reimbursements (averaging $15,199 per year) were awarded; career-related internships or fieldwork, institutionally sponsored loans, scholarships/grants, traineeships, health care benefits, and unspecified assistantships also available. *Faculty research:* Gender issues; LGBTQ studies; sexuality; women and science; global feminism. *Unit head:* Valerie Traub, Chair, 734-763-2047, Fax: 734-647-4943, E-mail: traubv@umich.edu. *Application contact:* Jen Sarafin, Graduate Student Services Coordinator, 734-763-2047, Fax: 734-647-4943, E-mail: jsarafin@umich.edu.

University of Minnesota, Duluth, Graduate School, College of Liberal Arts, Department of Sociology/Anthropology, Duluth, MN 55812-2496. Offers criminology (MA); liberal studies (MLS). Part-time programs available. *Faculty:* 12 full-time (5 women), 23 part-time/adjunct (9 women). *Students:* 17 full-time (13 women), 18 part-time (12 women); includes 2 minority (1 Asian American or Pacific Islander, 1 Hispanic American). Average age 40. 13 applicants, 46% accepted, 6 enrolled. In 2007, 2 degrees awarded. *Degree requirements:* For master's, thesis or alternative. *Entrance requirements:* For master's, interview, minimum GPA of 3.0, letters of recommendation, personal statement. Additional exam requirements/recommendations for international students: Required—TOEFL. *Application deadline:* For fall admission, 7/15 for domestic students; for spring admission, 11/1 for domestic students. Applications are processed on a rolling basis. Application fee: $55 ($75 for international students). *Expenses:* Tuition, state resident: part-time $812 per credit. Tuition, nonresident: part-time $1,403 per credit. Tuition and fees vary according to program. *Financial support:* In 2007–08, 1 student received support, including teaching assistantships with full tuition reimbursements available (averaging $13,005 per year); institutionally sponsored loans, scholarships/grants, and tuition waivers (partial) also available. Financial award application deadline: 3/15; financial award applicants required to submit FAFSA. *Faculty research:* Nature of knowledge, philosophy of science, ecology, cultural studies, language. *Unit head:* Dr. Janelle Wilson, Head, 218-726-6364, Fax: 218-726-7759, E-mail: jwilson2@d.umn.edu. *Application contact:* Cheryl Aker, Assistant Director, 218-726-8149, Fax: 218-726-6925, E-mail: caker@d.umn.edu.

University of Minnesota, Twin Cities Campus, Graduate School, College of Liberal Arts, Department of Sociology, Minneapolis, MN 55455-0213. Offers MA, PhD. *Faculty:* 30 full-time (15 women), 1 part-time/adjunct (0 women). *Students:* 79 full-time (47 women), 11 part-time (8 women); includes 22 minority (4 African Americans, 1 American Indian/Alaska Native, 13 Asian Americans or Pacific Islanders, 4 Hispanic Americans), 24 international. Average age 32. 100 applicants, 30% accepted, 18 enrolled. In 2007, 2 master's, 11 doctorates awarded. Terminal master's awarded for partial completion of doctoral program. *Median time to degree:* Of those who began their doctoral program in fall 1999, 44% received their degree in 8 years or less. *Degree requirements:* For master's, thesis optional; for doctorate, thesis/dissertation, preliminary and final written dissertation and oral defense, prospectus hearing. *Entrance requirements:* For doctorate, GRE General Test, 3 letters of recommendation, sample of written work. Additional exam requirements/recommendations for international students: Required—TOEFL (minimum score 550 paper-based; 213 computer-based; 79 iBT). *Application deadline:* For fall admission, 12/1 for domestic and international students. Application fee: $55 ($75 for international students). Electronic applications accepted. *Financial support:* In 2007–08, 9 fellowships with full tuition reimbursements (averaging $19,000 per year), 20 research assistantships with full tuition reimbursements (averaging $16,338 per year), 38 teaching assistantships with full tuition reimbursements (averaging $18,315 per year) were awarded; career-related internships or fieldwork, Federal Work-Study, scholarships/grants, traineeships, health care benefits, and unspecified assistantships also available. Financial award application deadline: 12/1. *Faculty research:* Organizations, work, and markets; inequality; law, crime and deviance; family and life course; political sociology and social movements . Total annual research expenditures: $509,058. *Unit head:* Dr. Christopher Uggen, Chair, 612-624-4300, Fax: 612-624-7020, E-mail: uggen@atlas.socsci.umn.edu. *Application contact:* Robert B Fox, Graduate Program Associate, 612-624-2093, Fax: 612-624-7020, E-mail: socdept@soc.umn.edu.

University of Mississippi, Graduate School, College of Liberal Arts, Department of Sociology and Anthropology, Oxford, University, MS 38677. Offers anthropology (MA); sociology (MA, MSS). *Faculty:* 15 full-time (6 women), 4 part-time/adjunct (1 woman). *Students:* 24 full-time (11 women), 5 part-time (4 women); includes 3 minority (all African Americans), 2 international. In 2007, 5 degrees awarded. *Degree requirements:* For master's, thesis (for some programs). *Entrance requirements:* For master's, GRE General Test, minimum GPA of 3.0. Additional exam requirements/recommendations for international students: Required—TOEFL. *Application deadline:* For fall admission, 4/1 for domestic students; for spring admission, 10/1 for domestic students. Applications are processed on a rolling basis. Application fee: $25. Electronic applications accepted. *Expenses:* Tuition, state resident: full-time $4,932. Tuition, nonresident: full-time $11,436. *Financial support:* Scholarships/grants available. Financial award application deadline: 3/1; financial award applicants required to submit FAFSA. *Unit head:* Dr. Kirsten A. Dellinger, Chairman, 662-915-7323, Fax: 662-915-7323.

University of Missouri–Columbia, Graduate School, College of Arts and Sciences, Department of Sociology, Columbia, MO 65211. Offers MA, PhD. *Degree requirements:* For doctorate, one foreign language, thesis/dissertation. *Entrance requirements:* For master's and doctorate, GRE General Test, minimum GPA of 3.0. Additional exam requirements/recommendations for international students: Required—TOEFL (minimum score 500 paper-based; 173 computer-based).

University of Missouri–Kansas City, College of Arts and Sciences, Program in Criminal Justice and Criminology/Sociology, Kansas City, MO 64110-2499. Offers criminal justice and criminology (MS); sociology (MA, PhD). Part-time and evening/weekend programs available. *Faculty:* 19 full-time (12 women), 4 part-time/adjunct (2 women). *Students:* 8 full-time (7 women), 41 part-time (30 women); includes 7 minority (5 African Americans, 2 Asian Americans or Pacific Islanders). Average age 31. 23 applicants, 61% accepted, 12 enrolled. In 2007, 10 degrees awarded. *Degree requirements:* For master's, thesis optional. *Entrance requirements:* For master's, GRE, minimum GPA of 3.0 in major, 2.7 overall. Additional exam requirements/recommendations for international students: Required—TOEFL. *Application deadline:* For fall admission, 3/1 for domestic and international students; for spring admission, 11/1 for domestic and international students. Applications are processed on a rolling basis. Application fee: $35 ($50 for international students). Electronic applications accepted. *Expenses:* Tuition, state resident: part-time $287 per hour. Tuition, nonresident: part-time $741 per hour. Required fees: $31 per hour. Tuition and fees vary according to program. *Financial support:* In 2007–08, 1 research assistantship with full tuition reimbursement (averaging $12,000 per year), 7 teaching assistantships with full and partial tuition reimbursements (averaging $12,000 per year) were awarded; career-related internships or fieldwork, Federal Work-Study, institutionally sponsored loans, and tuition waivers (partial) also available. Support available to part-time students. Financial award application deadline: 3/1; financial award applicants required to submit FAFSA. *Faculty research:* Death penalty, community corrections, gerontology, religious movements, urban community and neighborhoods. Total annual research expenditures: $250,036. *Unit head:* Dr. Linda Breytspraak, Chairperson, 816-235-2514, Fax: 816-235-1117. *Application contact:* Dr. Wayne L. Lucas, Graduate Adviser, 816-235-1598, Fax: 816-235-1117, E-mail: lucasw@umkc.edu.

University of Missouri–St. Louis, College of Arts and Sciences, Department of Sociology, St. Louis, MO 63121. Offers advanced social perspective (MA); community conflict intervention (MA); program design and evaluation research (MA); social policy planning and administration (MA). Part-time and evening/weekend programs available. *Faculty:* 3 full-time (all women), 1 part-time/adjunct (0 women). *Students:* 5 full-time (2 women), 7 part-time (3 women); includes 1 minority (African American) Average age 31. In 2007, 7 degrees awarded. *Degree requirements:* For master's, thesis optional. *Entrance requirements:* For master's, 2 letters of recommendation. Additional exam requirements/recommendations for international students: Required—TOEFL (minimum score 550 paper-based; 213 computer-based). *Application deadline:* For fall admission, 7/15 priority date for domestic students; for spring admission, 12/15 priority date for domestic students. Applications are processed on a rolling basis. Application fee: $35 ($40 for international students). Electronic applications accepted. *Financial support:* In 2007–08, 3 teaching assistantships with full and partial tuition reimbursements (averaging $7,870 per year) were awarded; research assistantships, career-related internships or fieldwork also available. Support available to part-time students. *Faculty research:* Deviance, conflict intervention, minority groups, stratification, social psychology. *Unit head:* Dr. Chicako Usui, Chairperson, 314-516-6366. *Application contact:* 314-516-5458, Fax: 314-516-6996, E-mail: gradadm@umsl.edu.

The University of Montana, Graduate School, College of Arts and Sciences, Department of Sociology, Missoula, MT 59812-0002. Offers criminology (MA); rural and environmental change (MA); sociology (MA). *Entrance requirements:* For master's, GRE General Test. Additional exam requirements/recommendations for international students: Required—TOEFL. *Faculty research:* Housing, homelessness, hunger, infant mortality, work safety.

University of Nebraska–Lincoln, Graduate College, College of Arts and Sciences, Department of Sociology, Lincoln, NE 68588. Offers MA, PhD. *Degree requirements:* For master's, thesis optional; for doctorate, comprehensive exam, thesis/dissertation. *Entrance requirements:* For master's and doctorate, GRE General Test, writing sample. Additional exam requirements/recommendations for international students: Required—TOEFL (minimum score 550 paper-based; 213 computer-based). Electronic applications accepted. *Faculty research:* Family, deviance and social control, ethnic studies, inequality (gender, race, and class).

University of Nevada, Las Vegas, Graduate College, College of Liberal Arts, Department of Sociology, Las Vegas, NV 89154-9900. Offers MA, PhD. Part-time programs available. *Faculty:* 17 full-time (9 women), 8 part-time/adjunct (4 women). *Students:* 30 full-time (21 women), 13 part-time (5 women); includes 6 minority (3 African Americans, 1 Asian American or Pacific Islander, 2 Hispanic Americans), 2 international. 21 applicants, 43% accepted, 5 enrolled. In 2007, 5 master's, 1 doctorate awarded. *Degree requirements:* For master's, thesis, oral exams; for doctorate, comprehensive exam, thesis/dissertation, oral exams. *Entrance requirements:* For master's, GRE General Test, minimum GPA of 3.0, 18 credits of course work in sociology; for doctorate, GRE General Test, minimum GPA of 3.0. Additional exam requirements/recommendations for international students: Required—TOEFL (minimum score 550 paper-based; 213 computer-based). *Application deadline:* For fall admission, 1/31 for domestic and international students. Application fee: $60 ($75 for international students). Electronic applications accepted. *Expenses:* Tuition, state resident: part-time $198 per credit. Tuition, nonresident: part-time $416 per credit. Required fees: $256 per semester. Tuition and fees vary according to course load and reciprocity agreements. *Financial support:* In 2007–08, 1 research assistantship with partial tuition reimbursement (averaging $12,000 per year), 23 teaching assistantships with partial tuition reimbursements (averaging $12,000 per year) were awarded; career-related internships or fieldwork, Federal Work-Study, institutionally sponsored loans, scholarships/grants, health care benefits, and unspecified assistantships also available. Support available to part-time students. Financial award application deadline: 3/1. *Unit head:* Dr. Andy Fontana, Chair, 702-895-3322, Fax: 702-895-5033, E-mail: andy.fontan@unlv.edu. *Application contact:* Graduate College Admissions Evaluator, 702-895-3320, Fax: 702-895-4180, E-mail: gradcollege@unlv.edu.

University of Nevada, Reno, Graduate School, College of Liberal Arts, School of Social Research and Justice Studies, Department of Sociology, Reno, NV 89557. Offers MA. *Faculty:* 8. *Students:* 3 full-time (1 woman), 4 part-time (3 women). Average age 25. 6 applicants, 67% accepted, 3 enrolled. In 2007, 5 degrees awarded. *Degree requirements:* For master's, thesis optional. *Entrance requirements:* For master's, GRE, minimum GPA of 3.0. Additional exam requirements/recommendations for international students: Required—TOEFL. *Application deadline:* For fall admission, 3/1 priority date for domestic students; for spring admission, 11/1 for domestic students. Application fee: $60 ($95 for international students). *Expenses:* Tuition, state resident: full-time $2,774; part-time $154 per credit. Tuition, nonresident: full-time $13,578; part-time $330 per credit. Required fees: $49 per semester. *Financial support:* In 2007–08, 4 teaching assistantships were awarded. Financial award application deadline: 3/1. *Faculty research:* Statistics, politics and economics, religion and law, industry, theory stratification. *Unit head:* Dr. Berch Berberoglu, Graduate Program Director, 775-784-6647.

University of New Brunswick Fredericton, School of Graduate Studies, Faculty of Arts, Department of Sociology, Fredericton, NB E3B 5A3, Canada. Offers MA, PhD. Part-time programs available. *Faculty:* 10 full-time (6 women), 5 part-time/adjunct (4 women). *Students:* 20 full-time (16 women), 9 part-time (7 women). In 2007, 4 master's, 1 doctorate awarded. *Degree requirements:* For master's, thesis; for doctorate, thesis/dissertation. *Entrance requirements:* For master's, minimum GPA of 3.5; for doctorate, minimum GPA of 3.0, MA in sociology with thesis or equivalent, curriculum vitae, statement of interest about interview research. Additional exam requirements/recommendations for international students: Required—TOEFL (minimum score 650 paper-based), TWE. *Application deadline:* For fall admission, 3/1 priority date for domestic students. Applications are processed on a rolling basis. Application fee: $50 Canadian dollars. *Financial support:* In 2007–08, 3 fellowships (averaging $4,000 per year), 11 research assistantships, 11 teaching assistantships were awarded. *Faculty research:* Social policy; media, communication and culture, family and domestic violence; sociology of health and health care. *Unit head:* Dr. Gary Bowden, Director of Graduate Studies, 506-452-6217, Fax: 506-453-4659, E-mail: glb@unb.ca. *Application contact:* Tracy McDonald, Graduate Secretary, 506-458-7474, Fax: 506-453-4659, E-mail: tmcdonal@unb.ca.

University of New Hampshire, Graduate School, College of Liberal Arts, Department of Sociology, Durham, NH 03824. Offers MA, PhD. Part-time programs available. *Faculty:* 12 full-time. *Students:* 37 full-time (31 women), 7 part-time (6 women); includes 2 minority (1 African American, 1 American Indian/Alaska Native), 2 international. Average age 34. 41 applicants, 61% accepted, 17 enrolled. In 2007, 5 degrees awarded. *Degree requirements:* For master's, thesis; for doctorate, one foreign language, thesis/dissertation. *Entrance requirements:* For master's and doctorate, GRE General Test. Additional exam requirements/recommendations for international students: Required—TOEFL (minimum score 550 paper-based; 213 computer-based; 80 iBT). *Application deadline:* For fall admission, 4/1 priority date for domestic students,

4/1 for international students; for winter admission, 12/1 for domestic students. Applications are processed on a rolling basis. Application fee: $60. Electronic applications accepted. *Financial support:* In 2007–08, 6 research assistantships, 14 teaching assistantships were awarded; fellowships, career-related internships or fieldwork, Federal Work-Study, scholarships/grants, and tuition waivers (full and partial) also available. Support available to part-time students. Financial award application deadline: 2/15. *Faculty research:* Deviance, conflict and control, social psychology, comparative institutional analysis, family. *Unit head:* Dr. James Tucker, Chairperson, 603-862-1814. *Application contact:* Deena Peschke, Administrative Assistant, 603-862-2500, E-mail: sociology.dept@unh.edu.

University of New Mexico, Graduate School, College of Arts and Sciences, Department of Sociology, Albuquerque, NM 87131-2039. Offers MA, PhD. Part-time programs available. *Faculty:* 17 full-time (6 women), 13 part-time/adjunct (7 women). *Students:* 28 full-time (14 women), 10 part-time (7 women); includes 9 minority (1 American Indian/Alaska Native, 1 Asian American or Pacific Islander, 7 Hispanic Americans), 4 international. Average age 36. 27 applicants, 41% accepted, 4 enrolled. In 2007, 5 master's, 1 doctorate awarded. *Degree requirements:* For master's, thesis; for doctorate, comprehensive exam, thesis/dissertation. *Entrance requirements:* For master's and doctorate, GRE General Test, 2 writing samples, 3 letters of reference. Additional exam requirements/recommendations for international students: Required—TOEFL. *Application deadline:* For fall admission, 2/1 priority date for domestic students; for spring admission, 9/30 priority date for domestic students. Application fee: $50. Electronic applications accepted. *Financial support:* In 2007–08, 20 students received support, including research assistantships (averaging $6,344 per year), 16 teaching assistantships with partial tuition reimbursements available (averaging $12,510 per year); institutionally sponsored loans, scholarships/grants, health care benefits, tuition waivers (partial), and unspecified assistantships also available. Support available to part-time students. Financial award applicants required to submit FAFSA. *Faculty research:* Criminology/deviance, gender, Latin American/comparative sociology, political sociology, race and ethnicity, social movements, religion, social welfare work/organizations. Total annual research expenditures: $696,099. *Unit head:* Dr. Beverly Burris, Chair, 505-277-2501, Fax: 505-277-8805, E-mail: bburris@unm.edu. *Application contact:* Karen Majors, Chair, Graduate Committee, 505-277-2501, Fax: 505-277-8805, E-mail: majors@unm.edu.

University of New Orleans, Graduate School, College of Liberal Arts, Department of Sociology, New Orleans, LA 70148. Offers MA. Part-time and evening/weekend programs available. *Students:* 26 (16 women). Average age 34. In 2007, 2 degrees awarded. *Degree requirements:* For master's, thesis (for some programs). *Entrance requirements:* For master's, GRE General Test. Additional exam requirements/recommendations for international students: Required—TOEFL (minimum score 550 paper-based; 213 computer-based; 79 iBT). *Application deadline:* For fall admission, 7/1 priority date for domestic students, 6/1 for international students; for spring admission, 11/15 priority date for domestic students, 10/1 for international students. Applications are processed on a rolling basis. Application fee: $40. Electronic applications accepted. *Financial support:* Research assistantships available. Financial award application deadline: 3/15; financial award applicants required to submit FAFSA. *Faculty research:* Environment and gender. *Unit head:* Dr. David Allen, Chairperson, 504-280-6475, Fax: 504-280-6302, E-mail: hallen@uno.edu. *Application contact:* Dr. Vern Baxter, Graduate Coordinator, 504-280-6476, Fax: 504-280-6302, E-mail: vbaxter@uno.edu.

The University of North Carolina at Chapel Hill, Graduate School, College of Arts and Sciences, Department of Sociology, Chapel Hill, NC 27599. Offers MA, PhD. *Degree requirements:* For master's, comprehensive exam, thesis; for doctorate, comprehensive exam, thesis/dissertation. *Entrance requirements:* For master's and doctorate, GRE General Test, minimum GPA of 3.0. Additional exam requirements/recommendations for international students: Required—TOEFL (minimum score 550 paper-based; 213 computer-based). Electronic applications accepted. *Faculty research:* Comparative historical, work/organizations, religion, demography, stratification.

The University of North Carolina at Charlotte, Graduate School, College of Arts and Sciences, Department of Sociology, Charlotte, NC 28223-0001. Offers MA. Part-time and evening/weekend programs available. *Faculty:* 14 full-time (9 women), 2 part-time/adjunct (1 woman). *Students:* 10 full-time (5 women), 13 part-time (8 women); includes 7 minority (3 African Americans, 3 Asian Americans or Pacific Islanders, 1 Hispanic American), 1 international. Average age 31. 10 applicants, 80% accepted, 6 enrolled. In 2007, 4 degrees awarded. *Degree requirements:* For master's, thesis or comprehensive exam. *Entrance requirements:* For master's, GRE or MAT, minimum GPA of 3.0 in last 2 years, 2.75 overall. Additional exam requirements/recommendations for international students: Required—TOEFL (minimum score 557 paper-based; 220 computer-based). *Application deadline:* For fall admission, 7/1 for domestic students, 5/1 for international students; for spring admission, 11/1 for domestic students, 10/1 for international students. Applications are processed on a rolling basis. Application fee: $55. Electronic applications accepted. *Expenses:* Tuition, state resident: full-time $2,855. Tuition, nonresident: full-time $13,062. Required fees: $1,692. *Financial support:* In 2007–08, 1 fellowship (averaging $10,000 per year), 3 research assistantships (averaging $6,416 per year), 4 teaching assistantships (averaging $8,900 per year) were awarded; career-related internships or fieldwork, Federal Work-Study, institutionally sponsored loans, scholarships/grants, and unspecified assistantships also available. Support available to part-time students. Financial award application deadline: 4/1; financial award applicants required to submit FAFSA. *Faculty research:* Social psychology, sociology of education, social gerontology, quantitative methodology, medical sociology. *Unit head:* Dr. Charles Brody, Chair, 704-687-2362, Fax: 704-687-3091. *Application contact:* Kathy B. Giddings, Director of Graduate Admissions, 704-687-3366, Fax: 704-687-3279, E-mail: agidding@uncc.edu.

The University of North Carolina at Greensboro, Graduate School, College of Arts and Sciences, Department of Sociology, Greensboro, NC 27412-5001. Offers criminology (MA); sociology (MA). Part-time programs available. *Faculty:* 15 full-time (7 women), 1 part-time/adjunct (0 women). *Students:* 23 full-time (17 women), 21 part-time (11 women); includes 7 minority (5 African Americans, 1 American Indian/Alaska Native, 1 Hispanic American). 30 applicants, 30% accepted. *Degree requirements:* For master's, comprehensive exam, thesis. *Entrance requirements:* For master's, GRE General Test. Additional exam requirements/recommendations for international students: Required—TOEFL. *Application deadline:* For fall admission, 3/15 priority date for domestic students; for spring admission, 11/1 for domestic students. Applications are processed on a rolling basis. Application fee: $45. Electronic applications accepted. *Financial support:* In 2007–08, 13 students received support, including 5 research assistantships with full tuition reimbursements available; fellowships with full tuition reimbursements available, teaching assistantships with full tuition reimbursements available, career-related internships or fieldwork, Federal Work-Study, scholarships/grants, and traineeships also available. Support available to part-time students. *Unit head:* Dr. Julie V. Brown, Head, 336-334-5295, Fax: 336-334-5283. *Application contact:* Michelle Harkleroad, Director of Graduate Admissions, 336-334-4884, Fax: 336-334-4424, E-mail: mbharkle@uncg.edu.

The University of North Carolina Wilmington, College of Arts and Sciences, Department of Sociology and Criminology, Wilmington, NC 28403-3297. Offers criminology (MA); public sociology (MA). *Students:* 9 full-time (all women), 2 part-time (1 woman). Average age 29. 18 applicants, 67% accepted, 11 enrolled. *Degree requirements:* For master's, thesis or internship. *Application deadline:* For fall admission, 6/15 for domestic students. Application fee: $45. Electronic applications accepted. *Expenses:* Tuition, state resident: full-time $2,714. Tuition, nonresident: full-time $12,579. Required fees: $1,985. *Financial support:* In 2007–08, 5 teaching assistantships were awarded; unspecified assistantships also available. *Unit head:* Kimberly J. Cook, Chair, 910-962-3785, E-mail: cookk@uncw.edu.

See Close-Up on page 1719.

University of North Dakota, Graduate School, College of Arts and Sciences, Department of Sociology, Grand Forks, ND 58202. Offers MA. *Faculty:* 9 full-time (4 women). *Students:* 10 full-time (8 women), 8 part-time (7 women); includes 1 Hispanic American, 2 international. 6 applicants, 67% accepted, 4 enrolled. In 2007, 6 degrees awarded. *Degree requirements:* For master's, thesis, final examination. *Entrance requirements:* For master's, minimum GPA of 3.0. Additional exam requirements/recommendations for international students: Required—TOEFL (minimum score 550 paper-based; 213 computer-based; 79 iBT), IELTS (minimum score 7). *Application deadline:* For fall admission, 2/15 priority date for domestic and international students; for spring admission, 10/15 priority date for domestic and international students. Applications are processed on a rolling basis. Application fee: $35. Electronic applications accepted. *Expenses:* Tuition, state resident: full-time $4,050; part-time $225 per credit. Tuition, nonresident: full-time $10,818; part-time $601 per credit. Required fees: $110 per semester. Tuition and fees vary according to class time, campus/location, program and reciprocity agreements. *Financial support:* In 2007–08, 1 research assistantship with full tuition reimbursement, 7 teaching assistantships with full tuition reimbursements (averaging $9,632 per year) were awarded; fellowships with full and partial tuition reimbursements, Federal Work-Study, institutionally sponsored loans, scholarships/grants, health care benefits, tuition waivers (full and partial), and unspecified assistantships also available. Support available to part-time students. Financial award application deadline: 3/15; financial award applicants required to submit FAFSA. *Faculty research:* Criminal justice studies, social psychology, research methods, corrections, social theory. *Unit head:* Dr. Janet Kelly Moen, Graduate Director, 701-777-4418, Fax: 701-777-2468, E-mail: janetkellymoen@und.nodak.edu. *Application contact:* Brenda Halle, Admissions Specialist, 701-777-2947, Fax: 701-777-3619, E-mail: brendahalle@mail.und.edu.

University of Northern Colorado, Graduate School, College of Humanities and Social Sciences, School of Social Sciences, Program in Social Sciences, Greeley, CO 80639. Offers clinical sociology (MA). Part-time programs available. *Faculty:* 23 full-time (9 women). *Students:* 10 full-time (8 women), 4 part-time (3 women); includes 4 minority (1 African American, 1 American Indian/Alaska Native, 2 Hispanic Americans), 1 international. Average age 32. 9 applicants, 89% accepted, 7 enrolled. In 2007, 1 degree awarded. *Degree requirements:* For master's, comprehensive exam. *Entrance requirements:* For master's, 2 letters of recommendation. *Application deadline:* Applications are processed on a rolling basis. Application fee: $50 ($60 for international students). Electronic applications accepted. *Expenses:* Tuition, state resident: part-time $222 per credit. Tuition, nonresident: part-time $627 per credit. Required fees: $36 per credit. *Financial support:* In 2007–08, 2 research assistantships (averaging $11,935 per year), 1 teaching assistantship (averaging $2,518 per year) were awarded; fellowships, unspecified assistantships also available. Financial award application deadline: 3/1; financial award applicants required to submit FAFSA. *Unit head:* Dr. Karen Jennison, Program Coordinator, 970-3541-2315, Fax: 970-351-1527.

University of Northern Iowa, Graduate College, College of Social and Behavioral Sciences, Department of Sociology, Anthropology and Criminology, Cedar Falls, IA 50614. Offers criminology (MA); sociology (MA). Part-time and evening/weekend programs available. *Students:* 10 full-time (5 women), 4 part-time (3 women), 3 international. 18 applicants, 56% accepted, 8 enrolled. In 2007, 1 degree awarded. *Degree requirements:* For master's, thesis. *Entrance requirements:* For master's, minimum GPA of 3.0. Additional exam requirements/recommendations for international students: Required—TOEFL (minimum score 500 paper-based; 180 computer-based; 61 iBT). *Application deadline:* For fall admission, 8/1 priority date for domestic students. Applications are processed on a rolling basis. Application fee: $30 ($50 for international students). Electronic applications accepted. *Expenses:* Tuition, state resident: full-time $6,246; part-time $694 per credit hour. Tuition, nonresident: full-time $14,554; part-time $694 per credit hour. Required fees: $838; $119 per semester. *Financial support:* Career-related internships or fieldwork, Federal Work-Study, scholarships/grants, and tuition waivers (full and partial) available. Support available to part-time students. Financial award application deadline: 2/1. *Unit head:* Dr. Kent Sandstrom, Head, 319-273-2786, Fax: 319-273-7104, E-mail: kent.sandstrom@uni.edu.

University of North Florida, College of Arts and Sciences, Department of Sociology and Anthropology, Jacksonville, FL 32224-2645. Offers applied sociology (MS). Part-time and evening/weekend programs available. *Faculty:* 10 full-time (4 women). *Students:* 6 full-time (5 women), 8 part-time (6 women); includes 4 minority (2 African Americans, 1 American Indian/Alaska Native, 1 Hispanic American). Average age 30. 12 applicants, 75% accepted, 5 enrolled. In 2007, 1 degree awarded. *Degree requirements:* For master's, thesis or alternative. *Entrance requirements:* For master's, GRE General Test, minimum GPA of 3.0 in last 60 hours, letters of recommendation. Additional exam requirements/recommendations for international students: Required—TOEFL (minimum score 500 paper-based; 173 computer-based). *Application deadline:* For fall admission, 7/1 priority date for domestic students, 5/1 for international students; for spring admission, 11/1 priority date for domestic students, 10/1 for international students. Applications are processed on a rolling basis. Application fee: $30. Electronic applications accepted. *Expenses:* Tuition, state resident: part-time $266 per credit hour. Tuition, nonresident: part-time $858 per credit hour. One-time fee: $35 part-time. Tuition and fees vary according to program. *Financial support:* In 2007–08, 9 students received support, including 2 teaching assistantships (averaging $6,000 per year); career-related internships or fieldwork, Federal Work-Study, and tuition waivers (partial) also available. Support available to part-time students. Financial award application deadline: 4/1; financial award applicants required to submit FAFSA. *Faculty research:* Telemarketing fraud, tax evasion practices of small business owners, jury knowledge and education, race and punishment in local schools, urban power structure. Total annual research expenditures: $269,955. *Unit head:* Dr. Adam Shapiro, Chair, 904-620-2850, E-mail: ashapiro@unf.edu. *Application contact:* Dr. Krista Paulsen, Graduate Coordinator, 904-620-2850, Fax: 904-620-2540, E-mail: kpaulsen@unf.edu.

University of North Texas, Robert B. Toulouse School of Graduate Studies, College of Public Affairs and Community Service, Department of Sociology, Denton, TX 76203. Offers MA, MS, PhD. *Faculty:* 16 full-time (8 women). *Students:* 27 full-time (13 women), 51 part-time (34 women); includes 24 minority (16 African Americans, 2 American Indian/Alaska Native, 2 Asian Americans or Pacific Islanders, 4 Hispanic Americans), 19 international. Average age 35. 57 applicants, 46% accepted, 13 enrolled. In 2007, 13 master's, 6 doctorates awarded. Terminal master's awarded for partial completion of doctoral program. *Degree requirements:* For master's, variable foreign language requirement, comprehensive exam, thesis; for doctorate, one foreign language, comprehensive exam, thesis/dissertation. *Entrance requirements:* For master's, GRE General Test, 3 letters of recommendation; for doctorate, GRE General Test, master's degree, 3 letters of recommendation. Additional exam requirements/recommendations for international students: Required—proof of English language proficiency required for non-native English speakers; Recommended—TOEFL (minimum score 550 paper-based; 213 computer-based). *Application deadline:* For fall admission, 7/15 for domestic students; for spring admission, 11/15 for domestic students. Applications are processed on a rolling basis. Application fee: $50 ($75 for international students). *Financial support:* In 2007–08, 14 students received support, including fellowships with full and partial tuition reimbursements available (averaging $500 per year), research assistantships with full and partial tuition reimbursements available (averaging $1,200 per year), teaching assistantships with full and partial tuition reimbursements available (averaging $7,000 per year); career-related internships or fieldwork, Federal Work-Study, institutionally sponsored loans, scholarships/grants, health care benefits, and tuition waivers (full and partial) also available. Financial award application deadline: 6/1. *Faculty research:* Health and illness, social inequality, globalization and development, family. Total annual research expenditures: $20,000. *Unit head:* Dr. Dale Yeatts, Chair, 940-565-2296, Fax: 940-369-7035, E-mail: yeatts@pacs.unt.edu. *Application contact:* Dr. Rudy Ray Seward, Graduate Adviser, 940-565-2295, Fax: 940-369-7035, E-mail: seward@pacs.unt.edu.

University of Notre Dame, Graduate School, College of Arts and Letters, Division of Social Science, Department of Sociology, Notre Dame, IN 46556. Offers PhD. *Faculty:* 28 full-time (7 women), 3 part-time/adjunct (0 women). *Students:* 53 full-time (25 women); includes 4 minority (1 African American, 1 American Indian/Alaska Native, 2 Asian Americans or Pacific Islanders), 13 international. 110 applicants, 16% accepted, 12 enrolled. In 2007, 3 doctorates awarded. *Degree requirements:* For doctorate, thesis/dissertation, 2 area specialty exams. *Entrance requirements:* For doctorate, GRE General Test, GRE Subject Test (strongly recommended).

Sociology

University of Notre Dame (continued)
Additional exam requirements/recommendations for international students: Required—TOEFL (minimum score 600 paper-based; 250 computer-based; 80 iBT). *Application deadline:* For fall admission, 1/15 priority date for domestic students, 1/15 for international students. Application fee: $50. Electronic applications accepted. *Financial support:* In 2007–08, 4 fellowships with full tuition reimbursements (averaging $22,000 per year), 6 research assistantships with full tuition reimbursements (averaging $16,000 per year), 37 teaching assistantships with full tuition reimbursements (averaging $16,000 per year) were awarded; tuition waivers (full) also available. Support available to part-time students. Financial award application deadline: 2/1. *Faculty research:* Cultural sociology, development, family, education, historical/comparative sociology. *Unit head:* Dr. William Carbonaro, Chair, Admissions Committee, 574-631-6585, Fax: 574-631-9238, E-mail: soc.1@nd.edu. *Application contact:* Dr. Jarren Gonzales, Director of Graduate Admissions, 574-631-7706, Fax: 574-631-4183.

University of Oklahoma, Graduate College, College of Arts and Sciences, Department of Sociology, Norman, OK 73019-0390. Offers MA, PhD. Part-time and evening/weekend programs available. *Faculty:* 13 full-time (7 women). *Students:* 28 full-time (22 women), 10 part-time (7 women); includes 6 minority (1 African American, 2 American Indian/Alaska Native, 1 Asian American or Pacific Islander, 2 Hispanic Americans), 2 international. 15 applicants, 67% accepted, 9 enrolled. In 2007, 6 master's, 1 doctorate awarded. Terminal master's awarded for partial completion of doctoral program. *Degree requirements:* For master's, thesis or alternative; for doctorate, thesis/dissertation, general exams, qualifying exam. *Entrance requirements:* For master's and doctorate, GRE General Test, 3 letters of recommendation. Additional exam requirements/recommendations for international students: Required—TOEFL (minimum score 550 paper-based; 213 computer-based). *Application deadline:* For fall admission, 2/15 priority date for domestic students, 2/15 for international students; for spring admission, 11/1 for domestic students, 9/1 for international students. Applications are processed on a rolling basis. Application fee: $40 ($90 for international students). Electronic applications accepted. *Expenses:* Tuition, state resident: full-time $3,451; part-time $144 per credit hour. Tuition, nonresident: full-time $12,432; part-time $518 per credit hour. Required fees: $1,925; $70 per credit hour. $122 per semester. *Financial support:* In 2007–08, 17 students received support, including 3 fellowships with full tuition reimbursements available (averaging $4,667 per year), 29 teaching assistantships with partial tuition reimbursements available (averaging $13,584 per year); research assistantships with partial tuition reimbursements available, health care benefits and unspecified assistantships also available. Financial award application deadline: 3/15; financial award applicants required to submit FAFSA. *Faculty research:* Incarceration of women in prison; adolescent attitudes towards HIV/AIDS; risk behavior; academic achievement of scholar/athletes international immigration. *Unit head:* Dr. Craig St. John, Chair, 405-325-1751, Fax: 405-325-7825, E-mail: cstjohn@ou.edu. *Application contact:* Dr. Loretta Bass, Associate Professor/Graduate Liaison, 405-325-1751, Fax: 405-325-7825, E-mail: lbass@ou.edu.

University of Oregon, Graduate School, College of Arts and Sciences, Department of Sociology, Eugene, OR 97403. Offers MA, MS, PhD. Part-time programs available. *Faculty:* 12 full-time (6 women), 5 part-time/adjunct (3 women). *Students:* 35 full-time (16 women), 1 (woman) part-time; includes 4 minority (1 Asian American or Pacific Islander, 3 Hispanic Americans), 7 international. 88 applicants, 13% accepted. In 2007, 5 master's, 2 doctorates awarded. Terminal master's awarded for partial completion of doctoral program. *Degree requirements:* For doctorate, thesis/dissertation. *Entrance requirements:* For master's and doctorate, GRE General Test, minimum GPA of 3.0. Additional exam requirements/recommendations for international students: Required—TOEFL. *Application deadline:* For fall admission, 2/1 for domestic students. Application fee: $50. *Financial support:* In 2007–08, 33 teaching assistantships were awarded; Federal Work-Study also available. *Faculty research:* Criminology, environment, gender, labor, political economy. *Unit head:* Dr. Robert O'Brien, Head, 541-346-1170. *Application contact:* Mary Redetzke, Admissions Contact, 541-346-1168, Fax: 541-346-5002, E-mail: mfreer@oregon.uoregon.edu.

University of Ottawa, Faculty of Graduate and Postdoctoral Studies, Faculty of Social Sciences, Department of Sociology and Anthropology, Ottawa, ON K1N 6N5, Canada. Offers MA. *Degree requirements:* For master's, thesis or alternative. *Entrance requirements:* For master's, honors bachelor's degree or equivalent, minimum B average. Electronic applications accepted. *Faculty research:* Inter-ethnic relations, development, political policies.

University of Pennsylvania, School of Arts and Sciences, Graduate Group in Sociology, Philadelphia, PA 19104. Offers AM, PhD. Terminal master's awarded for partial completion of doctoral program. *Degree requirements:* For master's, thesis or alternative; for doctorate, one foreign language, thesis/dissertation. *Entrance requirements:* For master's and doctorate, GRE General Test. Additional exam requirements/recommendations for international students: Required—TOEFL. Electronic applications accepted.

University of Pittsburgh, School of Arts and Sciences, Department of Sociology, Pittsburgh, PA 15260. Offers MA, PhD. *Faculty:* 13 full-time (8 women), 4 part-time/adjunct (2 women). *Students:* 27 full-time (19 women); includes 6 minority (1 African American, 2 Asian Americans or Pacific Islanders, 3 Hispanic Americans). 71 applicants, 4% accepted, 3 enrolled. In 2007, 3 master's, 6 doctorates awarded. Terminal master's awarded for partial completion of doctoral program. *Degree requirements:* For master's, thesis; for doctorate, comprehensive exam, thesis/dissertation, preliminary exam. *Entrance requirements:* For master's and doctorate, GRE General Test, writing sample. Additional exam requirements/recommendations for international students: Required—TOEFL. *Application deadline:* For fall admission, 1/15 priority date for domestic and international students. Applications are processed on a rolling basis. Application fee: $50. Electronic applications accepted. *Financial support:* In 2007–08, 3 fellowships with full tuition reimbursements, 1 research assistantship with full tuition reimbursement, 19 teaching assistantships with full tuition reimbursements were awarded; scholarships/grants, health care benefits, tuition waivers (partial), and unspecified assistantships also available. Financial award application deadline: 1/15. *Faculty research:* Global and comparative sociology, gender, race and class, social network process. Total annual research expenditures: $165,785. *Unit head:* Dr. John Markoff, Chairman, 412-648-7584, Fax: 412-648-2799, E-mail: jm2@pitt.edu. *Application contact:* Terri Reich, Graduate Administrator, 412-648-7585, Fax: 412-648-2799, E-mail: tareich@pitt.edu.

University of Puerto Rico, Río Piedras, College of Social Sciences, Department of Sociology, San Juan, PR 00931-3300. Offers MA. *Students:* 21 full-time (12 women), 3 part-time (2 women); includes 22 minority (all Hispanic Americans) Average age 26. In 2007, 2 degrees awarded. *Degree requirements:* For master's, comprehensive exam, thesis. *Entrance requirements:* For master's, GRE or PAEG, interview, minimum GPA of 3.0, letter of recommendation. *Application deadline:* For fall admission, 2/1 for domestic and international students. Application fee: $17. *Expenses:* Tuition, state resident: full-time $1,808; part-time $113 per credit. Tuition, nonresident: full-time $5,248; part-time $328 per credit. Required fees: $72 per term. *Financial support:* Application deadline: 5/31. *Application contact:* Information Contact, 787-764-0000 Ext. 3105, Fax: 787-764-0000 Ext. 4325.

University of Regina, Faculty of Graduate Studies and Research, Faculty of Arts, Department of Philosophy, Regina, SK S4S 0A2, Canada. Offers philosophy (MA); social and political thought (MA). *Faculty:* 9 full-time (3 women). *Students:* 1 (woman) full-time. *Degree requirements:* For master's, thesis. *Entrance requirements:* Additional exam requirements/recommendations for international students: Required—TOEFL (minimum score 580 paper-based; 237 computer-based; 88 iBT). *Application deadline:* Applications are processed on a rolling basis. Application fee: $85 ($100 for international students). Electronic applications accepted. *Financial support:* In 2007–08, fellowships (averaging $15,750 per year), research assistantships (averaging $13,875 per year), teaching assistantships (averaging $13,060 per year) were awarded; scholarships/grants also available. Financial award application deadline: 6/15. *Faculty research:* History of philosophy, ethics, aesthetics, metaphysics, epistemology. *Unit head:* Dr. Eldon Soifer, Head, 306-585-4301, Fax: 306-585-4827, E-mail: eldon.soifer@uregina.ca.

University of Regina, Faculty of Graduate Studies and Research, Faculty of Arts, Department of Sociology and Social Studies, Regina, SK S4S 0A2, Canada. Offers social studies (MA, PhD); sociology (MA, PhD). *Faculty:* 12 full-time (5 women), 1 part-time/adjunct (0 women). *Students:* 12 full-time (8 women), 6 part-time (4 women). 7 applicants, 100% accepted, 6 enrolled. In 2007, 1 degree awarded. *Degree requirements:* For master's, thesis. *Entrance requirements:* Additional exam requirements/recommendations for international students: Required—TOEFL (minimum score 580 paper-based; 237 computer-based). *Application deadline:* Applications are processed on a rolling basis. Application fee: $85 ($100 for international students). Electronic applications accepted. *Financial support:* In 2007–08, 5 fellowships (averaging $15,750 per year), 1 research assistantship (averaging $13,875 per year), 2 teaching assistantships (averaging $13,060 per year) were awarded; scholarships/grants also available. Financial award application deadline: 6/15. *Faculty research:* Social justice, development and the environment, knowledge, technology, and society. *Unit head:* Dr. John Conway, Head, 306-585-4052, Fax: 306-585-4815, E-mail: john.conway@uregina.ca. *Application contact:* Dr. Henry Chow, Graduate Program Coordinator, 306-585-5604, Fax: 306-585-4815, E-mail: henry.chow@uregina.ca.

University of Saskatchewan, College of Graduate Studies and Research, College of Arts and Sciences, Department of Sociology, Saskatoon, SK S7N 5A2, Canada. Offers MA, PhD. *Degree requirements:* For master's, thesis; for doctorate, thesis/dissertation. *Entrance requirements:* Additional exam requirements/recommendations for international students: Required—TOEFL.

University of South Africa, College of Human Sciences, Pretoria, South Africa. Offers adult education (M Ed); African languages (MA, PhD); African politics (MA, PhD); Afrikaans (MA, PhD); ancient history (MA, PhD); ancient Near Eastern studies (MA, PhD); anthropology (MA, PhD); applied linguistics (MA); Arabic (MA, PhD); archaeology (MA); art history (MA); Biblical archaeology (MA); Biblical studies (M Th, D Th, PhD); Christian spirituality (M Th, D Th); church history (M Th, D Th); classical studies (MA, PhD); clinical psychology (MA); communication (MA, PhD); comparative education (M Ed, Ed D); consulting psychology (D Admin, D Com, PhD); curriculum studies (M Ed, Ed D); development studies (M Admin, MA, D Admin, PhD); didactics (M Ed, Ed D); education (M Tech); education management (M Ed, Ed D); educational psychology (M Ed); English (MA); environmental education (M Ed); French (MA, PhD); German (MA, PhD); Greek (MA); guidance and counseling (M Ed); health studies (MA, PhD), including health sciences education (MA), health services management (MA), medical and surgical nursing science (critical care general) (MA), midwifery and neonatal nursing science (MA), trauma and emergency care (MA); history (MA, PhD); history of education (Ed D); inclusive education (M Ed, Ed D); information and communications technology policy and regulation (MA); information science (MA, MIS, PhD); international politics (MA, PhD); Islamic studies (MA, PhD); Italian (MA, PhD); Judaica (MA, PhD); linguistics (MA, PhD); mathematical education (M Ed); mathematics education (MA); missiology (M Th, D Th); modern Hebrew (MA, PhD); musicology (MA, MMus, D Mus, PhD); natural science education (M Ed); New Testament (M Th, D Th); Old Testament (D Th); pastoral therapy (M Th, D Th); philosophy (MA); philosophy of education (M Ed, Ed D); politics (MA, PhD); Portuguese (MA, PhD); practical theology (M Th, D Th); psychology (MA, MS, PhD); psychology of education (M Ed, Ed D); public health (MA); religious studies (MA, D Th, PhD); Romance languages (MA); Russian (MA, PhD); Semitic languages (MA, PhD); social behavior studies in HIV/AIDS (MA); social science (mental health) (MA); social science in development studies (MA); social science in psychology (MA); social science in social work (MA); social science in sociology (MA); social work (MSW, DSW, PhD); socio-education (M Ed, Ed D); sociolinguistics (MA); sociology (MA, PhD); Spanish (MA, PhD); systematic theology (M Th, D Th); TESOL (teaching English to speakers of other languages) (MA); theological ethics (M Th, D Th); theory of literature (MA, PhD); urban ministries (D Th); urban ministry (M Th).

University of South Alabama, Graduate School, College of Arts and Sciences, Department of Sociology, Anthropology and Social Work, Mobile, AL 36688-0002. Offers sociology (MA). Part-time and evening/weekend programs available. *Faculty:* 8 full-time (2 women), 3 part-time/adjunct (0 women). *Students:* 6 full-time (5 women), 3 part-time (all women); includes 1 minority (African American) 9 applicants, 22% accepted, 2 enrolled. In 2007, 4 degrees awarded. *Degree requirements:* For master's, comprehensive exam, thesis optional. *Entrance requirements:* For master's, GRE General Test, minimum GPA of 3.0. *Application deadline:* For fall admission, 9/1 priority date for domestic students. Applications are processed on a rolling basis. Application fee: $25. *Expenses:* Tuition, state resident: full-time $4,224; part-time $176 per credit hour. Tuition, nonresident: full-time $8,448; part-time $352 per credit hour. Required fees: $802. Full-time tuition and fees vary according to program and student level. *Financial support:* Fellowships, research assistantships available. Financial award application deadline: 4/1. *Faculty research:* Cultural adaptation. *Unit head:* Dr. J. Steven Picou, Chair, 251-460-6347.

University of South Carolina, The Graduate School, College of Arts and Sciences, Department of Sociology, Columbia, SC 29208. Offers MA, PhD. Part-time programs available. *Faculty:* 13 full-time (5 women). *Students:* 23 full-time (11 women), 15 part-time (11 women); includes 4 minority (1 African American, 1 Asian American or Pacific Islander, 2 Hispanic Americans), 5 international. Average age 32. 30 applicants, 43% accepted, 17 enrolled. In 2007, 1 master's, 5 doctorates awarded. Terminal master's awarded for partial completion of doctoral program. *Median time to degree:* Of those who began their doctoral program in fall 1999, 33% received their degree in 8 years or less. *Degree requirements:* For master's, thesis; for doctorate, comprehensive exam, thesis/dissertation. *Entrance requirements:* For master's and doctorate, GRE General Test. Additional exam requirements/recommendations for international students: Required—TOEFL (minimum score 570 paper-based; 230 computer-based; 75 iBT). *Application deadline:* For fall admission, 7/1 for domestic and international students; for spring admission, 11/15 for domestic and international students. Applications are processed on a rolling basis. Application fee: $40. Electronic applications accepted. *Expenses:* Tuition, state resident: part-time $440 per hour. Tuition, nonresident: part-time $936 per hour. Required fees: $17 per hour. Tuition and fees vary according to program. *Financial support:* In 2007–08, 17 students received support, including 10 research assistantships with full tuition reimbursements available (averaging $11,600 per year), 7 teaching assistantships (averaging $11,600 per year); fellowships with full tuition reimbursements available, Federal Work-Study, health care benefits, and unspecified assistantships also available. Support available to part-time students. Financial award application deadline: 2/15. *Faculty research:* Social psychology, social inequality. Total annual research expenditures: $155,746. *Unit head:* Dr. Barry Markovsky, Chair, 803-777-3123, Fax: 803-777-5251, E-mail: barry@sc.edu. *Application contact:* Dr. J. M. Sanders, Graduate Director, 803-777-3123, Fax: 803-777-5251, E-mail: jimsand@sc.edu.

University of Southern California, Graduate School, College of Letters, Arts and Sciences, Department of Sociology, Los Angeles, CA 90089. Offers PhD. *Faculty:* 14 full-time (7 women), 1 (woman) part-time/adjunct. *Students:* 39 full-time (23 women); includes 14 minority (3 African Americans, 4 Asian Americans or Pacific Islanders, 7 Hispanic Americans), 7 international. 61 applicants, 15% accepted. In 2007, 5 doctorates awarded. *Degree requirements:* For doctorate, thesis/dissertation, Qualifying exam. *Entrance requirements:* For doctorate, GRE General Test. *Application deadline:* For fall admission, 12/1 for domestic students. Application fee: $85. *Financial support:* In 2007–08, 31 students received support, including fellowships with full tuition reimbursements available (averaging $28,000 per year), research assistantships with full tuition reimbursements available (averaging $18,570 per year), teaching assistantships with full tuition reimbursements available (averaging $18,570 per year); Federal Work-Study and institutionally sponsored loans also available. Support available to part-time students. Financial award application deadline: 2/15; financial award applicants required to submit FAFSA. *Faculty research:* Gerontology, organization and social change, women's studies, race, immigration. *Unit head:* Dr. Tim Biblarz, Chair, 213-740-3533, Fax: 213-740-3535, E-mail: uscsoci@usc.edu. *Application contact:* Stachelle Overland, Information Contact, 213-740-2311.

University of South Florida, Graduate School, College of Arts and Sciences, Department of Sociology, Tampa, FL 33620-9951. Offers MA. Part-time programs available. *Faculty:* 9 full-time (7 women). *Students:* 13 full-time (7 women), 10 part-time (8 women); includes 5 minority (1 African American, 3 Asian Americans or Pacific Islanders, 1 Hispanic American). 33 applicants, 48% accepted, 13 enrolled. In 2007, 5 degrees awarded. *Entrance requirements:* For master's, GRE General Test, minimum GPA of 3.0 in last 60 hours. *Application deadline:* For fall admission, 3/15 priority date for domestic students. Application fee: $30. Electronic applications accepted. *Financial support:* Application deadline: 3/1. Total annual research expenditures: $46,512. *Unit head:* Dr. Maralee Mayberry, Chairperson, 813-974-2241, Fax: 813-974-6455, E-mail: mayberry@chuma1.cas.usf.edu. *Application contact:* Dr. Donileen R. Loseke, Graduate Director, 813-974-2517, Fax: 813-974-6455, E-mail: dloseke@cas.usf.edu.

The University of Tennessee, Graduate School, College of Arts and Sciences, Department of Sociology, Knoxville, TN 37996. Offers criminology (MA, PhD); energy, environment, and resource policy (MA, PhD); political economy (MA, PhD). Part-time programs available. *Degree requirements:* For master's, thesis or alternative; for doctorate, thesis/dissertation. *Entrance requirements:* For master's, GRE General Test, minimum GPA of 3.0; for doctorate, GRE General Test, minimum GPA of 3.5. Additional exam requirements/recommendations for international students: Required—TOEFL. Electronic applications accepted.

The University of Texas at Arlington, Graduate School, College of Liberal Arts, Department of Sociology and Anthropology, Program in Sociology, Arlington, TX 76019. Offers MA. Part-time and evening/weekend programs available. *Students:* 6 full-time (all women), 16 part-time (10 women); includes 5 minority (1 African American, 3 Asian Americans or Pacific Islanders, 1 Hispanic American), 1 international. In 2007, 2 degrees awarded. *Degree requirements:* For master's, thesis or alternative. *Entrance requirements:* For master's, GRE General Test, 12 hours of undergraduate course work in sociology. Additional exam requirements/recommendations for international students: Required—TOEFL (minimum score 550 paper-based; 213 computer-based). *Application deadline:* For fall admission, 6/16 for domestic students. Applications are processed on a rolling basis. Application fee: $35 ($50 for international students). *Expenses:* Tuition, state resident: full-time $5,934. Tuition, nonresident: full-time $10,938. *Financial support:* In 2007–08, 3 students received support, including 1 fellowship (averaging $1,000 per year), 3 teaching assistantships (averaging $9,000 per year); research assistantships, Federal Work-Study also available. Financial award application deadline: 4/1. *Application contact:* Dr. Linda Rouse, Graduate Advisor, 817-272-2661, Fax: 817-272-3759, E-mail: lrouse@uta.edu.

The University of Texas at Austin, Graduate School, College of Liberal Arts, Department of Sociology, Austin, TX 78712-1111. Offers MA, PhD. *Degree requirements:* For master's, thesis; for doctorate, thesis/dissertation. *Entrance requirements:* For master's and doctorate, GRE General Test. Additional exam requirements/recommendations for international students: Required—TOEFL. Electronic applications accepted. *Faculty research:* Criminology, demography, Latin America, health, political sociology.

The University of Texas at Dallas, School of Economic, Political and Policy Sciences, Program in Sociology, Richardson, TX 75083-0688. Offers MS. *Faculty:* 5 full-time (3 women), 1 (woman) part-time/adjunct. *Students:* 5 full-time (2 women), 11 part-time (9 women); includes 5 minority (3 African Americans, 1 Asian American or Pacific Islander, 1 Hispanic American), 2 international. Average age 27. 13 applicants, 85% accepted, 7 enrolled. In 2007, 12 degrees awarded. *Degree requirements:* For master's, internship. *Entrance requirements:* For master's, GRE General Test, minimum GPA of 3.0 in upper-level coursework in field. Additional exam requirements/recommendations for international students: Required—TOEFL (minimum score 550 paper-based; 213 computer-based). *Application deadline:* For fall admission, 7/15 for domestic students; for spring admission, 11/15 for domestic students. Applications are processed on a rolling basis. Application fee: $50 ($100 for international students). Electronic applications accepted. *Expenses:* Tuition, state resident: full-time $7,052. Tuition, nonresident: full-time $12,632. Tuition and fees vary according to course load. *Financial support:* Fellowships, research assistantships, teaching assistantships with tuition reimbursements, career-related internships or fieldwork, Federal Work-Study, institutionally sponsored loans, and scholarships/grants available. Support available to part-time students. Financial award application deadline: 4/30. *Faculty research:* Social impact of alcohol in Latino families, reading one-to-one, AmeriCorps, neighborhood evaluations. *Unit head:* Dr. James Marquart, Head, 972-883-4982, E-mail: marquart@utdallas.edu. *Application contact:* Judy C. Robertson, Program Assistant, 972-883-6406, E-mail: judy.robertson@utdallas.edu.

See Close-Up on page 1043.

The University of Texas at El Paso, Graduate School, College of Liberal Arts, Department of Sociology and Anthropology, El Paso, TX 79968-0001. Offers sociology (MA). Part-time and evening/weekend programs available. *Degree requirements:* For master's, thesis optional. *Entrance requirements:* For master's, GRE General Test, minimum GPA of 3.0. Additional exam requirements/recommendations for international students: Required—TOEFL. Electronic applications accepted.

The University of Texas at San Antonio, College of Liberal and Fine Arts, Department of Sociology, San Antonio, TX 78249-0617. Offers MS. Part-time and evening/weekend programs available. *Faculty:* 7 full-time (3 women). *Students:* 6 full-time (5 women), 49 part-time (33 women); includes 26 minority (4 African Americans, 1 Asian American or Pacific Islander, 21 Hispanic Americans), 1 international. Average age 32. 34 applicants, 91% accepted, 30 enrolled. In 2007, 5 degrees awarded. *Degree requirements:* For master's, comprehensive exam, thesis optional. *Entrance requirements:* For master's, GRE General Test, undergraduate course work in sociology or related areas. Additional exam requirements/recommendations for international students: Required—TOEFL (minimum score 500 paper-based; 173 computer-based). *Application deadline:* For fall admission, 7/1 for domestic students, 4/1 for international students; for spring admission, 11/1 for domestic students, 9/1 for international students. Applications are processed on a rolling basis. Application fee: $45 ($80 for international students). Electronic applications accepted. *Financial support:* In 2007–08, 5 research assistantships (averaging $5,342 per year) were awarded; career-related internships or fieldwork, Federal Work-Study, scholarships/grants, and readers/graders also available. *Faculty research:* Race and ethnic relations, qualitative research methods, complex organizations, gender stratification, social stratification. Total annual research expenditures: $9,547. *Unit head:* Dr. Raquel R. Marquez, Chair, 210-458-5606, Fax: 210-458-4629, E-mail: raquel.marquez@utsa.edu. *Application contact:* Kathleen McCleery, Secretary, 210-458-4620, Fax: 210-458-4629, E-mail: kmccleery@utsa.edu.

The University of Texas at Tyler, College of Arts and Sciences, Department of Social Sciences, Tyler, TX 75799-0001. Offers criminal justice (MS); public administration (MPA); sociology (MS). Part-time and evening/weekend programs available. Postbaccalaureate distance learning degree programs offered. *Faculty:* 15 full-time (2 women). *Students:* 3 full-time (2 women), 25 part-time (18 women); includes 5 minority (4 African Americans, 1 Hispanic American), 14 international. Average age 31. 18 applicants, 100% accepted, 11 enrolled. In 2007, 6 degrees awarded. *Degree requirements:* For master's, comprehensive exam. *Entrance requirements:* For master's, GRE General Test, minimum GPA of 3.0. *Application deadline:* Applications are processed on a rolling basis. Application fee: $0. *Expenses:* Tuition, state resident: part-time $627 per semester hour. Tuition, nonresident: part-time $908 per semester hour. Required fees: $107 per semester hour. Tuition and fees vary according to course load. *Financial support:* In 2007–08, 1 fellowship (averaging $1,000 per year), 2 research assistantships, 2 teaching assistantships were awarded; career-related internships or fieldwork, Federal Work-Study, and scholarships/grants also available. Support available to part-time students. Financial award application deadline: 7/1; financial award applicants required to submit FAFSA. *Faculty research:* Urban segregation, minority business, violent crime, gender discrimination. *Unit head:* Dr. Ken Wink, Chair, 903-566-7434, Fax: 903-565-5537, E-mail: kwink@mail.uttyl.edu. *Application contact:* Pam Morrow, Assistant to Dean for Enrollment Management, 903-566-7205, Fax: 903-566-7068, E-mail: pmorrow@uttyler.edu.

The University of Texas–Pan American, College of Social and Behavioral Sciences, Department of Sociology, Edinburg, TX 78541-2999. Offers MS. Part-time programs available. *Faculty:* 8 full-time (2 women). *Students:* 14 full-time (8 women), 18 part-time (10 women); includes 26 minority (1 African American, 25 Hispanic Americans), 3 international. Average age 32. 20 applicants, 90% accepted. In 2007, 14 degrees awarded. *Degree requirements:* For master's, thesis or journal article. *Entrance requirements:* For master's, minimum GPA of 3.0, BS of BA in sociology or social science. Additional exam requirements/recommendations for international students: Required—TOEFL (minimum score 500 paper-based). *Application deadline:* For fall admission, 7/1 priority date for domestic and international students; for spring admission, 12/1 priority date for domestic and international students. Applications are processed on a rolling basis. Application fee: $35. *Financial support:* In 2007–08, teaching assistantships (averaging $7,000 per year); fellowships, research assistantships, career-related internships or fieldwork, Federal Work-Study, institutionally sponsored loans, tuition waivers (full and partial), and unspecified assistantships also available. Support available to part-time students. Financial award application deadline: 4/15. *Faculty research:* Border studies, U.S.-Mexico issues, Mexican-American peoples, aging and gerontology. *Unit head:* Dr. Chad Richardson, Coordinator, 956-381-2377, Fax: 956-381-2343, E-mail: cr33d5@utpa.edu. *Application contact:* Dr. Dejun Su, Information Contact, 956-381-3321, Fax: 956-381-2343, E-mail: dsu@utpa.edu.

The University of Toledo, College of Graduate Studies, College of Arts and Sciences, Department of Sociology and Anthropology, Toledo, OH 43606-3390. Offers sociology (MA). Part-time programs available. *Faculty:* 8. *Students:* 11 full-time (7 women), 2 part-time (both women), 5 international. Average age 28. 11 applicants, 82% accepted, 6 enrolled. In 2007, 8 degrees awarded. *Degree requirements:* For master's, thesis or alternative. *Application deadline:* For fall admission, 1/15 priority date for domestic students. Applications are processed on a rolling basis. Application fee: $45. Electronic applications accepted. *Financial support:* In 2007–08, 12 teaching assistantships with full tuition reimbursements (averaging $8,200 per year) were awarded; research assistantships with full tuition reimbursements, career-related internships or fieldwork, Federal Work-Study, institutionally sponsored loans, scholarships/grants, tuition waivers (full), and unspecified assistantships also available. Support available to part-time students. Financial award application deadline: 4/1; financial award applicants required to submit FAFSA. *Faculty research:* Medical and social gerontology, population, social movements, socioeconomic development, corporations and work, race and ethnicity. *Unit head:* Dr. Barbara Chesney, Chair, 419-530-4075, Fax: 419-530-8406, E-mail: bchesne@uoft.utoledo.edu. *Application contact:* Reuben Patterson, Graduate Director, 419-530-4953, Fax: 419-530-8406, E-mail: reuben.patterson@utoledo.edu.

University of Toronto, School of Graduate Studies, Social Sciences Division, Department of Sociology, Toronto, ON M5S 1A1, Canada. Offers M Ed, MA, Ed D, PhD. Part-time programs available. *Faculty:* 42 full-time, 18 part-time/adjunct. *Students:* 220 full-time (166 women), 53 part-time, 10 international. 209 applicants, 24% accepted. In 2007, 9 master's, 2 doctorates awarded. *Degree requirements:* For doctorate, thesis/dissertation. *Entrance requirements:* For master's, GRE (required for applicants from non-Canadian universities, recommended for those from Canadian universities), 5 full-year courses in sociology, basic research and statistical skills, minimum B average, 2 letters of reference; for doctorate, GRE (required for applicants from non-Canadian universities; recommended for those from Canadian universities), MA in sociology, minimum A–average, 2 letters of reference. *Application deadline:* For fall admission, 2/1 for domestic students. Application fee: $100 Canadian dollars. *Unit head:* Prof. Blair Wheaton, Chair, 416-978-3414, Fax: 416-978-3963. *Application contact:* Jeannette Wright, Graduate Administrator, 416-978-3414, Fax: 416-978-3963, E-mail: wright@chass.utoronto.ca.

University of Utah, The Graduate School, College of Social and Behavioral Science, Department of Sociology, Salt Lake City, UT 84112-1107. Offers M Stat, MA, MS, PhD. Part-time programs available. *Faculty:* 14 full-time (6 women), 2 part-time/adjunct (0 women). *Students:* 17 full-time (9 women), 7 part-time (4 women); includes 1 minority (Hispanic American), 7 international. Average age 29. 24 applicants, 29% accepted, 5 enrolled. *Entrance requirements:* For master's, minimum undergraduate GPA of 3.0. Additional exam requirements/recommendations for international students: Required—TOEFL (minimum score 500 paper-based; 173 computer-based). *Application deadline:* For fall admission, 4/1 priority date for domestic students, 4/1 for international students. Applications are processed on a rolling basis. Application fee: $45 ($65 for international students). *Financial support:* In 2007–08, 1 research assistantship with full tuition reimbursement (averaging $10,750 per year), 10 teaching assistantships with full tuition reimbursements (averaging $10,750 per year) were awarded. Financial award application deadline: 4/1; financial award applicants required to submit FAFSA. *Faculty research:* Comparative international sociology, population and health, criminology, diversity, demography. Total annual research expenditures: $47,104. *Unit head:* Dr. Michael F. Timberlake, Chair, 801-581-6153, Fax: 801-585-3784, E-mail: timber@soc.utah.edu. *Application contact:* Jeffrey D Kentor, Director of Graduate Studies, 801-581-6153, Fax: 801-585-3784, E-mail: socgrads@soc.utah.edu.

University of Utah, The Graduate School, Interdepartmental Program in Statistics, Salt Lake City, UT 84112-1107. Offers biostatistics (MST); business (MST); economics (MST); educational psychology (MST); mathematics (MST); sociology (MST); statistics (M Stat). Part-time programs available. *Students:* 10 full-time (6 women), 21 part-time (6 women); includes 4 minority (all Asian Americans or Pacific Islanders) Average age 32. 59 applicants, 44% accepted. In 2007, 12 degrees awarded. *Degree requirements:* For master's, comprehensive exam, projects. *Entrance requirements:* For master's, minimum GPA of 3.0; course work in calculus, matrix theory, statistics. Additional exam requirements/recommendations for international students: Required—TOEFL (minimum score 500 paper-based; 173 computer-based). *Application deadline:* For fall admission, 7/1 for domestic students. Applications are processed on a rolling basis. Application fee: $45 ($65 for international students). *Financial support:* Career-related internships or fieldwork available. *Faculty research:* Biostatistics, management, economics, educational psychology, mathematics. *Unit head:* Tariq Mughal, Chair, University Statistics Committee, 801-585-9547, E-mail: tariaq.mughal@business.utah.edu. *Application contact:* Glenda Pruemper, Administrative Assistant, 801-581-7148, Fax: 801-581-5566, E-mail: pruemper@ed.utah.edu.

University of Victoria, Faculty of Graduate Studies, Faculty of Social Sciences, Department of Sociology, Victoria, BC V8W 2Y2, Canada. Offers MA, PhD. PhD by special arrangement. Part-time programs available. *Faculty:* 14 full-time (6 women), 4 part-time/adjunct (2 women). *Students:* 41, 3 international. Average age 27. 47 applicants, 38% accepted, 11 enrolled. In 2007, 6 degrees awarded. *Degree requirements:* For master's, thesis; for doctorate, thesis/dissertation, candidacy exam. *Entrance requirements:* For master's, minimum B+ average. Additional exam requirements/recommendations for international students: Required—TOEFL (minimum score 575 paper-based; 233 computer-based), IELTS (minimum score 7), TWE (minimum score 4). *Application deadline:* For fall admission, 12/1 priority date for domestic and international students. Applications are processed on a rolling basis. Application fee: $75 ($125 for international students). *Expenses:* Tuition, state resident: full-time $3,110. International tuition: $3,700 full-time. Tuition and fees vary according to program. *Financial support:* In 2007–08, 12 fellowships, 5 research assistantships, 10 teaching assistantships were awarded; career-related internships or fieldwork and institutionally sponsored loans also available. Financial award application deadline: 2/15. *Faculty research:* Social and political thought, social justice, health and aging, globalization and social psychology. Total annual research expenditures: $2.5 million. *Unit head:* Dr. Zheng Wu, Chair, 250-721-7576, Fax: 250-721-6217, E-mail: zhengwu@uvic.ca. *Application contact:* Dr. Cecilia Benoit, Graduate Adviser, 250-721-7578, Fax: 250-721-6217, E-mail: cbenoit@uvic.ca.

University of Virginia, College and Graduate School of Arts and Sciences, Department of Sociology, Charlottesville, VA 22903. Offers MA, PhD, JD/MA. *Faculty:* 16 full-time (6 women). *Students:* 53 full-time (25 women), 1 (woman) part-time; includes 3 minority (1 African American, 2 Asian Americans or Pacific Islanders), 16 international. Average age 28. 75 applicants, 64% accepted, 18 enrolled. In 2007, 10 master's, 5 doctorates awarded. *Degree requirements:* For

Sociology

University of Virginia (continued)
master's, thesis; for doctorate, comprehensive exam, thesis/dissertation. *Entrance requirements:* For master's and doctorate, GRE General Test, GRE Subject Test. *Application deadline:* Applications are processed on a rolling basis. Application fee: $60. Electronic applications accepted. *Financial support:* Applicants required to submit FAFSA. *Unit head:* Krishan Kumar, Chair, 434-924-7293, Fax: 434-924-7028, E-mail: kk2d@virginia.edu.

University of Washington, Graduate School, College of Arts and Sciences, Department of Sociology, Seattle, WA 98195. Offers MA, PhD. *Degree requirements:* For master's, thesis; for doctorate, thesis/dissertation. *Entrance requirements:* For master's and doctorate, GRE General Test, minimum GPA of 3.0. Additional exam requirements/recommendations for international students: Required—TOEFL. Electronic applications accepted. *Faculty research:* Demography, criminology, social psychology, race/ethnicity/inequality, family.

University of Waterloo, Graduate Studies, Faculty of Arts, Department of Sociology, Waterloo, ON N2L 3G1, Canada. Offers MA, PhD. Part-time programs available. *Faculty:* 13 full-time (2 women), 13 part-time/adjunct (6 women). *Students:* 50. 45 applicants, 38% accepted, 12 enrolled. In 2007, 4 master's, 2 doctorates awarded. *Degree requirements:* For master's, thesis (for some programs); for doctorate, one foreign language, thesis/dissertation. *Entrance requirements:* For master's, honors degree, minimum B+ average, resumé, writing sample; for doctorate, master's degree, minimum A- average, resumé, writing sample. Additional exam requirements/recommendations for international students: Required—TOEFL, TWE. *Application deadline:* For fall admission, 2/1 priority date for domestic students. Application fee: $75 Canadian dollars. Electronic applications accepted. *Financial support:* Fellowships, research assistantships, teaching assistantships available. *Faculty research:* Theory, methods, stratification deviance, political sociology. *Unit head:* Dr. G. Keith Warriner, Chair, 519-888-4567 Ext. 33678, Fax: 519-746-7326, E-mail: wnrr@uwaterloo.ca. *Application contact:* Dr. R. Helmes-Hayes, Associate Chair, Graduate Affairs, 519-888-4567 Ext. 32406, Fax: 519-746-7326, E-mail: rhh@uwaterloo.ca.

The University of Western Ontario, Faculty of Graduate Studies, Social Sciences Division, Department of Sociology, London, ON N6A 5B8, Canada. Offers MA, PhD. Terminal master's awarded for partial completion of doctoral program. *Degree requirements:* For master's, thesis (for some programs); for doctorate, one foreign language, comprehensive exam, thesis/dissertation. *Entrance requirements:* For master's, minimum B+ average, honors degree, statement of academic interest in sociology; for doctorate, minimum A- average. Additional exam requirements/recommendations for international students: Required—TOEFL. *Application deadline:* For fall admission, 2/1 priority date for domestic students. Application fee: $75 Canadian dollars. Electronic applications accepted. *Financial support:* In 2007–08, teaching assistantships (averaging $9,050 Canadian dollars per year); research assistantships, Federal Work-Study and scholarships/grants also available. Financial award application deadline: 2/1. *Faculty research:* Social demography, class and change, health and aging, theory, methods. *Unit head:* Prof. Mike Carroll, Acting Chair, 519-661-2111 Ext. 85115, E-mail: mcarroll@uwo.ca. *Application contact:* Denise Statham, Graduate Assistant, 519-661-2111 Ext. 85144, Fax: 519-661-3200, E-mail: statham@uwo.ca.

University of West Georgia, Graduate School, College of Arts and Sciences, Department of Sociology and Criminology, Program in Sociology, Carrollton, GA 30118. Offers MA. Part-time and evening/weekend programs available. *Students:* 9 full-time (7 women), 6 part-time (3 women); includes 3 minority (all African Americans) Average age 27. 6 applicants, 83% accepted, 4 enrolled. In 2007, 1 degree awarded. *Degree requirements:* For master's, one foreign language, comprehensive exam (for some programs), thesis (for some programs). *Entrance requirements:* For master's, GRE, references, minimum GPA of 2.5, interview. Additional exam requirements/recommendations for international students: Required—TOEFL. *Application deadline:* For fall admission, 7/18 for domestic students; for spring admission, 11/27 for domestic students. Application fee: $30. Electronic applications accepted. *Expenses:* Tuition, state resident: full-time $2,448; part-time $136 per semester hour. Tuition, nonresident: full-time $9,774; part-time $543 per semester hour. Required fees: $26 per semester hour. $173 per semester. *Financial support:* In 2007–08, 7 students received support, including research assistantships with full tuition reimbursements available (averaging $6,000 per year); career-related internships or fieldwork, scholarships/grants, and unspecified assistantships also available. Financial award applicants required to submit FAFSA. *Faculty research:* Women studies, criminology, resources and methods. Total annual research expenditures: $68,830. *Application contact:* Dr. Charles W. Clark, Interim Dean, 678-839-6508, E-mail: cclark@westga.edu.

University of Windsor, Faculty of Graduate Studies, Faculty of Arts and Social Sciences, Department of Sociology and Anthropology, Windsor, ON N9B 3P4, Canada. Offers criminology (MA); sociology (MA); sociology-social justice (PhD). Part-time programs available. *Faculty:* 27 full-time (13 women). *Students:* 48 full-time (31 women), 3 part-time (all women). 99 applicants, 38% accepted. In 2007, 12 degrees awarded. *Degree requirements:* For master's, thesis; for doctorate, comprehensive exam, thesis/dissertation. *Entrance requirements:* For master's, minimum B+ average; for doctorate, writing sample, minimum B+ average. Additional exam requirements/recommendations for international students: Required—TOEFL (minimum score 560 paper-based; 220 computer-based). *Application deadline:* For fall admission, 7/1 priority date for domestic students. Applications are processed on a rolling basis. Application fee: $55. Electronic applications accepted. *Financial support:* In 2007–08, 33 teaching assistantships (averaging $9,409 per year) were awarded; Federal Work-Study, scholarships/grants, unspecified assistantships, and bursaries also available. Financial award application deadline: 2/15. *Faculty research:* Power and social change; criminology/deviance; social psychology; comparative development; race and ethnic relations; family, sex, and gender, social justice. *Unit head:* Dr. William deLint, Head, 519-253-3000 Ext. 3498, Fax: 519-971-3621, E-mail: delint@uwindsor.ca. *Application contact:* Applicant Services, 519-253-3000 Ext. 6459, Fax: 519-971-3653, E-mail: gradadmit@uwindsor.ca.

University of Wisconsin–Madison, Graduate School, College of Letters and Science, Department of Sociology, Madison, WI 53706-1380. Offers rural sociology (MS); sociology (MS, PhD). Part-time programs available. Terminal master's awarded for partial completion of doctoral program. *Degree requirements:* For master's, thesis, oral exam; for doctorate, thesis/dissertation, preliminary and final oral exams, 4 seminars. *Entrance requirements:* For master's and doctorate, GRE General Test. Additional exam requirements/recommendations for international students: Required—TOEFL. Electronic applications accepted.

University of Wisconsin–Milwaukee, Graduate School, College of Letters and Sciences, Department of Sociology, Milwaukee, WI 53201-0413. Offers MA. Part-time programs available. *Faculty:* 16 full-time (8 women). *Students:* 15 full-time (10 women), 15 part-time (12 women); includes 5 minority (1 African American, 1 Asian American or Pacific Islander, 3 Hispanic Americans), 1 international. 30 applicants, 63% accepted, 12 enrolled. In 2007, 7 degrees awarded. *Degree requirements:* For master's, thesis. *Application deadline:* For fall admission, 1/1 priority date for domestic students; for spring admission, 9/1 for domestic students. Applications are processed on a rolling basis. Application fee: $45 ($75 for international students). *Expenses:* Tuition, state resident: part-time $530 per credit. Tuition, nonresident: part-time $1,428 per credit. Required fees: $19 per credit. $229 per term. Tuition and fees vary according to course load and program. *Financial support:* In 2007–08, 15 teaching assistantships were awarded; fellowships, research assistantships, career-related internships or fieldwork and unspecified assistantships also available. Support available to part-time students. Financial award application deadline: 4/15. *Unit head:* Kent Redding, Representative, 414-229-6946, Fax: 847-673-4122, E-mail: kredding@uwm.edu.

University of Wyoming, Graduate School, College of Arts and Sciences, Department of Sociology, Laramie, WY 82070. Offers MA. Part-time programs available. *Faculty:* 9 full-time (3 women), 2 part-time/adjunct (1 woman). *Students:* 7 full-time (2 women), 4 part-time (3 women); includes 1 minority (Asian American or Pacific Islander) Average age 31. 6 applicants, 50% accepted, 3 enrolled. In 2007, 3 degrees awarded. *Degree requirements:* For master's, thesis. *Entrance requirements:* For master's, GRE General Test, minimum GPA of 3.0. Additional exam requirements/recommendations for international students: Required—TOEFL (minimum score 525 paper-based). *Application deadline:* For fall admission, 3/1 priority date for domestic and international students; for spring admission, 12/1 priority date for domestic and international students. Applications are processed on a rolling basis. Application fee: $50. Electronic applications accepted. *Financial support:* In 2007–08, 6 students received support, including 3 research assistantships with full tuition reimbursements available (averaging $10,696 per year), 3 teaching assistantships with full tuition reimbursements available (averaging $10,969 per year); institutionally sponsored loans, tuition waivers (partial), and unspecified assistantships also available. Financial award application deadline: 3/1. *Faculty research:* Gender, theory, international studies, law, social inequality. *Unit head:* Dr. Chikwendu Christian Ukaegbu, Head, 307-766-3342, Fax: 307-766-3812, E-mail: chris@uwyo.edu. *Application contact:* Dr. Malcom Holmes, Graduate Director, 307-766-3342, Fax: 307-766-3812.

Utah State University, School of Graduate Studies, College of Humanities, Arts and Social Sciences, Department of Sociology, Logan, UT 84322-0730. Offers MA, MS, MSS, PhD. *Degree requirements:* For master's, thesis; for doctorate, comprehensive exam, thesis/dissertation. *Entrance requirements:* For master's, GRE General Test, minimum GPA of 3.0, recommendation letters, transcripts, personal statement; for doctorate, GRE General Test, minimum GPA of 3.0, recommendation letters, transcripts, personal statement, MS degree. Additional exam requirements/recommendations for international students: Required—TOEFL; Recommended—TWE. *Faculty research:* Demography, environmental/natural resource sociology, rural community change, international development, health studies.

Valdosta State University, Graduate School, College of Arts and Sciences, Department of Sociology, Anthropology, and Criminal Justice, Valdosta, GA 31698. Offers criminal justice (MS); marriage and family therapy (MS); sociology (MS). *Accreditation:* AAMFT/COAMFTE. Part-time and evening/weekend programs available. *Faculty:* 19 full-time (7 women). *Students:* 51 full-time (39 women), 20 part-time (14 women); includes 24 minority (19 African Americans, 4 Asian Americans or Pacific Islanders, 1 Hispanic American). Average age 27. 62 applicants, 47% accepted, 26 enrolled. In 2007, 29 degrees awarded. *Degree requirements:* For master's, thesis or alternative, comprehensive written and/or oral exams. *Entrance requirements:* For master's, GRE General Test or MAT (sociology, marriage and family therapy), minimum GPA of 2.5. Additional exam requirements/recommendations for international students: Required—TOEFL (minimum score 523 paper-based; 193 computer-based). *Application deadline:* For fall admission, 7/1 for domestic and international students; for spring admission, 11/15 for domestic and international students. Applications are processed on a rolling basis. Application fee: $40. Electronic applications accepted. *Expenses:* Tuition, state resident: part-time $147 per hour. Tuition, nonresident: part-time $586 per hour. Required fees: $520 per semester. Tuition and fees vary according to course level, course load, campus/location and program. *Financial support:* In 2007–08, 5 students received support, including 5 research assistantships with full tuition reimbursements available (averaging $2,452 per year); career-related internships or fieldwork, institutionally sponsored loans, scholarships/grants, and unspecified assistantships also available. Support available to part-time students. Financial award application deadline: 7/1; financial award applicants required to submit FAFSA. *Faculty research:* Police-civilian ride-along project. *Unit head:* Dr. Mike Capece, Acting Head, 229-333-5943, Fax: 229-333-5492.

Vanderbilt University, Graduate School, Department of Sociology, Nashville, TN 37240-1001. Offers MA, PhD. *Faculty:* 17 full-time (6 women). *Students:* 23 full-time (16 women); includes 1 minority (African American), 5 international. Average age 29. 95 applicants, 13% accepted, 7 enrolled. In 2007, 2 master's, 8 doctorates awarded. *Degree requirements:* For master's, general exam; for doctorate, thesis/dissertation, area, qualifying, and final exams. *Entrance requirements:* For master's and doctorate, GRE General Test. *Application deadline:* For fall admission, 1/15 for domestic and international students. Application fee: $0. Electronic applications accepted. *Financial support:* Fellowships with full tuition reimbursements, research assistantships, teaching assistantships with full tuition reimbursements, Federal Work-Study, institutionally sponsored loans, and health care benefits available. Financial award application deadline: 1/15; financial award applicants required to submit CSS PROFILE or FAFSA. *Faculty research:* Criminology; cultural sociology; gender, race, and ethics relations; deviant behavior and social control. *Unit head:* Gary Jensen, Chair, 615-322-7626, Fax: 615-322-7505, E-mail: gary.jensen@vanderbilt.edu. *Application contact:* Karen Campbell, Director of Graduate Studies, 615-322-7626, Fax: 615-322-7505, E-mail: karen.e.campbell@vanderbilt.edu.

Virginia Commonwealth University, Graduate School, College of Humanities and Sciences, Wilder School of Government and Public Affairs, Department of Sociology, Program in Sociology, Richmond, VA 23284-9005. Offers MS. In 2007, 5 degrees awarded. *Degree requirements:* For master's, thesis optional. *Entrance requirements:* For master's, GRE General Test. *Application deadline:* For fall admission, 7/1 for domestic students; for spring admission, 11/15 for domestic students. Application fee: $50. *Expenses:* Tuition, state resident: full-time $7,224; part-time $401 per credit. Tuition, nonresident: full-time $16,072; part-time $891 per credit. Required fees: $1,679; $63 per credit. Tuition and fees vary according to campus/location. *Application contact:* Dr. Sarah Jane Brubaker, Director, Graduate Programs in Sociology, 804-827-2400, Fax: 804-828-1027, E-mail: sbrubaker@vcu.edu.

See Close-Up on page 457.

Virginia Polytechnic Institute and State University, Graduate School, College of Liberal Arts and Human Sciences, Department of Sociology, Blacksburg, VA 24061. Offers MS, PhD. *Entrance requirements:* For master's and doctorate, GRE General Test. Additional exam requirements/recommendations for international students: Required—TOEFL (minimum score 550 paper-based; 213 computer-based). Electronic applications accepted. *Faculty research:* Science and technology, deviance and criminology, social psychology, social organization, demography.

Washington State University, Graduate School, College of Liberal Arts, Department of Sociology, Pullman, WA 99164. Offers crime and deviance (MA, PhD); environments, community and demographics (MA, PhD); institutions and social organizations (MA, PhD); political sociology (MA, PhD); social inequality (MA, PhD); social psychology and life course (MA, PhD). *Faculty:* 22 full-time (14 women), 8 part-time/adjunct (3 women). *Students:* 42 full-time (23 women), 2 part-time (both women); includes 2 minority (1 African American, 1 American Indian/Alaska Native), 4 international. Average age 30. 71 applicants, 13% accepted, 9 enrolled. In 2007, 7 master's, 4 doctorates awarded. Terminal master's awarded for partial completion of doctoral program. *Degree requirements:* For master's, thesis; for doctorate, comprehensive exam, thesis/dissertation. *Entrance requirements:* For master's, GRE General Test, minimum GPA of 3.0; for doctorate, GRE General Test, MA in sociology, minimum GPA of 3.0. Additional exam requirements/recommendations for international students: Required—TOEFL (minimum score 550 paper-based). *Application deadline:* For fall admission, 1/15 priority date for domestic students, 1/15 for international students. Application fee: $50. Electronic applications accepted. *Financial support:* In 2007–08, 5 research assistantships with tuition reimbursements (averaging $12,749 per year), 36 teaching assistantships with tuition reimbursements (averaging $12,749 per year) were awarded; fellowships with tuition reimbursements, Federal Work-Study, institutionally sponsored loans, scholarships/grants, health care benefits, and unspecified assistantships also available. Support available to part-time students. Financial award application deadline: 4/1; financial award applicants required to submit FAFSA. *Faculty research:* Crime/deviance, environmental sociology, social inequality, social psychology, gender. Total annual research expenditures: $101,888. *Unit head:* Dr. Gregory Hooks, Chair, 509-335-4595, Fax: 509-335-6419, E-mail: hooks@mail.wsu.edu. *Application contact:* Dr. Tom Rotolo, Director of Graduate Studies, 509-335-4595, Fax: 509-335-6419, E-mail: rotolo@wsu.edu.

Wayne State University, College of Liberal Arts and Sciences, Department of Sociology, Detroit, MI 48202. Offers MA, PhD. *Students:* 56 full-time, 30 part-time; includes 39 minority (36 African Americans, 2 Asian Americans or Pacific Islanders, 1 Hispanic American), 10 international. Average age 38. 43 applicants, 60% accepted, 17 enrolled. In 2007, 4 master's, 3 doctorates awarded. *Degree requirements:* For master's, thesis optional; for doctorate, thesis/dissertation. *Entrance requirements:* For master's, GRE General Test, GRE Subject Test, minimum GPA of 3.3; letters of reference; statement of interest; writing sample; for doctorate, GRE General Test, GRE Subject Test, minimum GPA of 3.5 in master's work; letters of reference. Additional exam requirements/recommendations for international students: Required—TOEFL (minimum score 550 paper-based; 213 computer-based); Recommended—TWE (minimum score 6). *Application deadline:* For fall admission, 7/1 for domestic students, 6/1 for international students; for winter admission, 10/1 for international students; for spring admission, 2/1 for international students. Application fee: $30 ($50 for international students). Electronic applications accepted. *Expenses:* Tuition, state resident: part-time $403 per credit hour. Tuition, nonresident: part-time $890 per credit hour. *Financial support:* In 2007–08, 2 fellowships with tuition reimbursements (averaging $13,001 per year), 1 research assistantship with tuition reimbursement (averaging $14,260 per year), 8 teaching assistantships with tuition reimbursements (averaging $13,672 per year) were awarded. *Faculty research:* Social deviance, family, social inequality, medical sociology. *Unit head:* Leon Wilson, Chair, 313-577-8131, E-mail: ab6077@wayne.edu. *Application contact:* Mary Cay Sengstock, Graduate Director, 313-577-3282, E-mail: m.sengstock@wayne.edu.

West Chester University of Pennsylvania, Office of Graduate Studies and Extended Education, College of Arts and Sciences, Department of Anthropology and Sociology, West Chester, PA 19383. Offers gerontology (Certificate); long term health care (MSA). Part-time and evening/weekend programs available. In 2007, 1 degree awarded. *Degree requirements:* For master's, comprehensive exam. *Entrance requirements:* For master's, MAT, GRE, or GMAT, interview. Additional exam requirements/recommendations for international students: Required—TOEFL (minimum score 550 paper-based; 213 computer-based; 80 iBT). *Application deadline:* For fall admission, 4/15 priority date for domestic students; for spring admission, 10/15 for domestic students. Applications are processed on a rolling basis. Application fee: $35. *Expenses:* Tuition, state resident: part-time $345 per credit. Tuition, nonresident: part-time $552 per credit. Tuition and fees vary according to course load. *Financial support:* In 2007–08, research assistantships with full tuition reimbursements (averaging $5,000 per year); unspecified assistantships also available. Support available to part-time students. Financial award application deadline: 2/15; financial award applicants required to submit FAFSA. *Faculty research:* West African communities in the U.S., life long learning-distance education, comparative religions. *Unit head:* Dr. Susan Johnston, Chair, 610-436-2556, E-mail: sjohnston@wcupa.edu. *Application contact:* Dr. Douglas McConatha, Graduate Coordinator, 610-436-3125, E-mail: dmcconatha@wcupa.edu.

Western Illinois University, School of Graduate Studies, College of Arts and Sciences, Department of Sociology and Anthropology, Macomb, IL 61455-1390. Offers sociology (MA). Part-time programs available. *Students:* 21 full-time (13 women), 8 part-time (6 women); includes 4 minority (3 African Americans, 1 Asian American or Pacific Islander), 2 international. Average age 28. 18 applicants, 94% accepted. In 2007, 15 degrees awarded. *Degree requirements:* For master's, thesis or alternative. *Entrance requirements:* For master's, minimum GPA of 2.75. Additional exam requirements/recommendations for international students: Required—TOEFL (minimum score 550 paper-based; 213 computer-based; 80 iBT). *Application deadline:* Applications are processed on a rolling basis. Application fee: $30. Electronic applications accepted. *Expenses:* Tuition, state resident: part-time $217 per credit hour. Tuition, nonresident: part-time $433 per credit hour. Required fees: $54 per credit hour. *Financial support:* In 2007–08, 12 students received support, including 11 research assistantships with full tuition reimbursements available (averaging $6,800 per year), 1 teaching assistantship (averaging $7,840 per year). Financial award applicants required to submit FAFSA. *Unit head:* Dr. John Wozniak, Chairperson, 309-298-1056. *Application contact:* Dr. Barbara Baily, Director of Graduate Studies/Associate Provost, 309-298-1806, Fax: 309-298-2345, E-mail: grad-office@wiu.edu.

Western Kentucky University, Graduate Studies, Potter College of Arts and Letters, Department of Sociology, Bowling Green, KY 42101. Offers MA. *Degree requirements:* For master's, comprehensive exam, thesis optional, final exam. *Entrance requirements:* For master's, GRE General Test, minimum GPA of 3.0. Additional exam requirements/recommendations for international students: Required—TOEFL (minimum score 555 paper-based; 213 computer-based; 79 iBT). *Faculty research:* Criminology/delinquency, quantitative and survey research methodology, occupations/professions, sex and gender, demography.

Western Michigan University, Graduate College, College of Arts and Sciences, Department of Sociology, Kalamazoo, MI 49008-5202. Offers MA, PhD. *Degree requirements:* For master's, thesis, oral exams; for doctorate, one foreign language, thesis/dissertation, oral exams, written exams. *Entrance requirements:* For doctorate, GRE General Test.

West Virginia University, Eberly College of Arts and Sciences, School of Applied Social Sciences, Department of Sociology, Morgantown, WV 26506. Offers applied social research (MA). Part-time programs available. *Faculty:* 13 full-time (8 women), 9 part-time/adjunct (6 women). *Students:* 13 full-time (10 women), 2 part-time (1 woman); includes 2 minority (1 African American, 1 Hispanic American), 2 international. Average age 29. 16 applicants, 56% accepted, 6 enrolled. In 2007, 3 degrees awarded. *Degree requirements:* For master's, thesis or alternative. *Entrance requirements:* For master's, GRE General Test, minimum GPA of 2.75. Additional exam requirements/recommendations for international students: Required—TOEFL. *Application deadline:* For fall admission, 3/1 for domestic and international students. Application fee: $50. *Expenses:* Tuition, state resident: full-time $5,196; part-time $292 per credit hour. Tuition, nonresident: full-time $15,064; part-time $840 per credit hour. Tuition and fees vary according to program. *Financial support:* In 2007–08, 14 students received support, including 2 research assistantships with full tuition reimbursements available (averaging $9,000 per year), 10 teaching assistantships with full tuition reimbursements available (averaging $9,000 per year); Federal Work-Study, institutionally sponsored loans, and tuition waivers (full and partial) also available. Financial award application deadline: 2/1; financial award applicants required to submit FAFSA. *Faculty research:* Applied sociology, stratification, social/complex organization, research methodology criminology. Total annual research expenditures: $59,767. *Unit head:* Dr. Melissa Latimer, Chair, 304-293-5801 Ext. 3209, Fax: 304-293-5994, E-mail: melissa.latimer@mail.wvu.edu.

Wichita State University, Graduate School, Fairmount College of Liberal Arts and Sciences, Department of Sociology, Wichita, KS 67260. Offers MA. Part-time programs available. *Degree requirements:* For master's, thesis optional. *Entrance requirements:* For master's, GRE. Additional exam requirements/recommendations for international students: Required—TOEFL. Electronic applications accepted.

Wilfrid Laurier University, Faculty of Graduate Studies, Faculty of Arts, Department of Sociology, Waterloo, ON N2L 3C5, Canada. Offers MA. *Faculty:* 18 full-time. *Students:* 8 full-time. 29 applicants, 52% accepted, 8 enrolled. *Entrance requirements:* For master's, honours BA with a minimum average of B+ with a major in sociology. Additional exam requirements/recommendations for international students: Required—TOEFL (minimum score 230 computer-based; 89 iBT). *Application deadline:* For fall admission, 2/1 priority date for domestic students. Application fee: $75. Electronic applications accepted. *Financial support:* Fellowships, research assistantships, teaching assistantships available. *Faculty research:* Internationalization, migration and human rights, health, families, and well-being. *Unit head:* Dr. Glenda Wall, Acting Chairperson, 519-884-0710 Ext. 3978, E-mail: awall@wlu.ca. *Application contact:* Jennifer Poppe, Student Contact, 519-884-0710 Ext. 3536, Fax: 519-884-1020, E-mail: gradstudies@wlu.ca.

William Paterson University of New Jersey, College of the Humanities and Social Sciences, Department of Sociology, Wayne, NJ 07470-8420. Offers MA. Part-time and evening/weekend programs available. *Students:* 5 full-time (4 women), 4 part-time (all women); includes 3 minority (1 African American, 1 Asian American or Pacific Islander, 1 Hispanic American). In 2007, 2 degrees awarded. *Degree requirements:* For master's, comprehensive exam, thesis. *Entrance requirements:* For master's, GRE or MAT. *Application deadline:* Applications are processed on a rolling basis. Application fee: $50. Electronic applications accepted. *Financial support:* Research assistantships with full tuition reimbursements, unspecified assistantships available. Financial award application deadline: 4/1. *Faculty research:* Critical political theory, urban social/ethnic groups, family studies, human development. *Unit head:* Dr. Kathleen Korgen, Program Director, 973-720-3563. *Application contact:* Danielle Liautaud, Director, 973-720-3579, Fax: 973-720-2035, E-mail: liautaudd@wpunj.edu.

Yale University, Graduate School of Arts and Sciences, Department of Sociology, New Haven, CT 06520. Offers PhD. *Degree requirements:* For doctorate, thesis/dissertation. *Entrance requirements:* For doctorate, GRE General Test.

York University, Faculty of Graduate Studies, Faculty of Arts, Program in Social and Political Thought, Toronto, ON M3J 1P3, Canada. Offers MA, PhD. Part-time programs available. *Degree requirements:* For master's, one foreign language, thesis or alternative, oral exams; for doctorate, one foreign language, comprehensive exam, thesis/dissertation. Electronic applications accepted.

York University, Faculty of Graduate Studies, Faculty of Arts, Program in Sociology, Toronto, ON M3J 1P3, Canada. Offers MA, PhD. Part-time programs available. *Degree requirements:* For master's, thesis or alternative; for doctorate, one foreign language, comprehensive exam, thesis/dissertation, analytical paper. Electronic applications accepted.

Survey Methodology

University of Maryland, College Park, Graduate Studies, College of Behavioral and Social Sciences, Joint Program in Survey Methodology, College Park, MD 20742. Offers MS, PhD. *Faculty:* 3 full-time (2 women), 1 part-time/adjunct (0 women). *Students:* 25 full-time (14 women), 20 part-time (15 women); includes 8 minority (6 African Americans, 2 Asian Americans or Pacific Islanders), 9 international. 43 applicants, 35% accepted, 13 enrolled. In 2007, 13 master's, 2 doctorates awarded. *Degree requirements:* For master's, thesis (for some programs), scholarly paper; for doctorate, thesis/dissertation. *Entrance requirements:* For master's, GRE General Test (recommended), minimum GPA of 3.0, 3 letters of recommendation; for doctorate, GRE General Test, minimum GPA of 3.0, 3 letters of recommendation. *Application deadline:* For fall admission, 1/15 for domestic students, 2/1 for international students. Applications are processed on a rolling basis. Application fee: $60. Electronic applications accepted. *Financial support:* In 2007–08, 1 fellowship with full tuition reimbursement (averaging $5,888 per year), 8 research assistantships with tuition reimbursements (averaging $14,702 per year), 6 teaching assistantships (averaging $14,345 per year) were awarded; Federal Work-Study also available. Support available to part-time students. Financial award applicants required to submit FAFSA. Total annual research expenditures: $2 million. *Unit head:* Dr. Roger E. Tourangeau, Director, 301-314-7911, Fax: 301-314-7912, E-mail: rtourang@umd.edu. *Application contact:* Dean of Graduate School, 301-405-0358, Fax: 301-314-9305.

University of Michigan, Horace H. Rackham School of Graduate Studies, Program in Survey Methodology, Ann Arbor, MI 48109. Offers MS, PhD, Certificate. Part-time programs available. Terminal master's awarded for partial completion of doctoral program. *Degree requirements:* For master's, internships; for doctorate, comprehensive exam, thesis/dissertation. *Entrance requirements:* For master's and doctorate, GRE, 3 letters of recommendation; for Certificate, current enrollment in a graduate degree program at University of Michigan or have completed one within past 5 years. Additional exam requirements/recommendations for international students: Required—TOEFL (minimum score 560 paper-based; 220 computer-based). Electronic applications accepted. Expenses: Contact institution. *Faculty research:* Survey methodology, statistics, psychology, sociology, social psychology.

University of Nebraska–Lincoln, Graduate College, Interdepartmental Area of Survey Research and Methodology, Lincoln, NE 68588. Offers MS. *Degree requirements:* For master's, comprehensive exam. *Entrance requirements:* For master's, GRE General Test or GMAT. Additional exam requirements/recommendations for international students: Required—TOEFL (minimum score 550 paper-based; 213 computer-based). Electronic applications accepted. *Faculty research:* Survey research and data analysis.

BRYN MAWR COLLEGE

Graduate School of Arts and Sciences
Department of Classical and Near Eastern Archaeology

Programs of Study

The Department of Classical and Near Eastern Archaeology at Bryn Mawr College offers M.A. and Ph.D. degrees in classical and Near Eastern archaeology. In cooperation with the Department of Greek, Latin, and Classical Studies, it also offers the M.A. and Ph.D. in classical studies. It is one of three independent departments that comprise the Graduate Group in Archaeology, Classics, and History of Art.

The Department's guiding philosophy is that the ancient civilizations of the Mediterranean and the Near East are best studied as interconnected and mutually influential. The Department offers seminars on such topics as Iron Age Iran, the Aegean Bronze Age, Assyrian and Achaemenid art and archaeology, Greek art, Hellenistic art, the historiography of ancient art, and method and theory. Training combines the study of primary contexts, historical and literary sources, monuments, and art with course work in method and theory, including geographic information systems. Students may also explore the contributions of classical and Near Eastern cultures to the intellectual and artistic heritage of the modern era through interdisciplinary seminars offered by the Graduate Group, which also sponsors internships in Philadelphia-area museums and libraries.

All requirements for the M.A. can normally be completed within two years; Ph.D. preliminary examinations should be taken in the third or fourth year, followed by the dissertation. Fifty percent of recent graduates completed the Ph.D. in 8.5 years or less.

Students are encouraged to develop their own research projects in consultation with a faculty adviser. Recent dissertation topics include sociopolitical complexity in early Iron Age Syria and Anatolia, the role of animals in classical Greek art, art as commodity in late Republican and Imperial Rome, the history of practices in archaeological restoration, pottery in the tombs of Mochlos and Myrsini, regional survey archaeology, the context of food production and preparation in ancient Greece, the furnishings of Hellenistic houses, ancient harbors in the Black Sea, textile production in pre-Roman Italy, and the territory of Roman Antioch.

Graduates are prepared for careers in college and university teaching, museum curatorship and administration, publishing, government service, and non-profit administration. Graduates of the past five years have also held postdoctoral fellowships at the American School of Classical Studies in Athens and the University of Copenhagen.

Research Facilities

The award-winning Rhys Carpenter Library, inaugurated in 1997, is a specialized library for archaeology, classics, and the history of art. Fully-wired carrels are available to all students in the Graduate Group in Archaeology, Classics, and History of Art. In addition to the more than 135,000 volumes in Carpenter Library, the tri-college library consortium of Bryn Mawr, Haverford, and Swarthmore Colleges contains over 2 million volumes. Bryn Mawr currently subscribes to more than 300 periodicals and serials in archaeology and classics. Online reference sources include the TLG, Dyabola, Library of Latin Texts, and *l'Année philologique.*

The Ella Riegel Study Collection comprises about 6,500 archaeological items, including Athenian Red-Figure vases; Greek, Cypriot, and Egyptian pottery; Greek and Roman coins; representative artifacts in bronze, glass, terracotta, and wood; lamps; and an extensive collection of pottery samples from Tarsus.

Faculty members in the Department direct two ongoing field projects: in the Nemea Valley in Greece and at the Iron Age settlement of Muweilah in the United Arab Emirates. Students also participate in field projects sponsored by other institutions.

Financial Aid

Bryn Mawr offers a number of fellowships for full-time study, as well as grants, tuition awards, and summer stipends. Fellowship stipends begin at $17,500, including a summer stipend, and can be guaranteed for multiple years. Special awards include Areté (Excellence) Fellowships with a package of $18,500 plus health insurance. Each year, the Department offers two teaching assistantships and one research assistantship, with stipends ranging from $14,000 to $19,150 including health insurance. Opportunities reserved for students in the Graduate Group in Archaeology, Classics, and History of Art are fellowships for multidisciplinary study, with twelve-month stipends of $19,000, and curatorial internships. Currently, 78 percent of the students enrolled in the graduate program in archaeology receive some form of financial aid.

Cost of Study

Full-time tuition, consisting of six courses per year, is $30,140; part-time tuition is $5090 per course. Units of supervised work cost $815, and the fee for maintaining matriculation (continuing enrollment) is $415 per semester.

Living and Housing Costs

Students live locally or in Philadelphia. Shared apartments can be rented for $600 to $900 per month, studio apartments begin at $700 per month, and food costs are about $200 per month. Other expenses include transportation (about $150 per month if commuting from Philadelphia) and health insurance ($1590 to $5150 per year, depending on age, for domestic students; $1432 for international students).

Student Group

In 2008–09, there are 27 students enrolled in archaeology, 19 women and 8 men. Four are international. Fifteen students have progressed to Ph.D. candidacy, 3 are candidates for the M.A., and the rest are in course work.

Student Outcomes

Ph.D. graduates of the past ten years are currently teaching at Brock University, Case Western Reserve University, the University of Arizona, Vanderbilt University, Koç University (Turkey), University of Kalamata (Greece), and Franklin & Marshall. One works for the U.S. Department of State, two work for foundations, one holds a research position at New York University, and two hold postdoctoral fellowships.

Location

Bryn Mawr is a suburb of Philadelphia, the fifth-largest city in the U.S. It is well served by rail lines and by bus. Philadelphia is renowned for music, museums, and sports, and it is also a culinary mecca, with restaurants serving many cuisines. The metropolitan area has more than 100 museums and fifty colleges and universities, with a total population of 220,000 students.

The College and The Department

Bryn Mawr is a liberal arts college for women, founded in 1885. It was the first women's college to offer graduate education through the Ph.D. and the first U.S. institution to offer fellowships to women for graduate study. Throughout its history, the College has been committed first and foremost to providing the most rigorous and challenging education to women and, in the Graduate School of Arts and Sciences, also to men. The current enrollment is 1,405 undergraduate students, 164 graduate students in the Graduate School of Arts and Sciences, and about 250 students in the Graduate School of Social Work and Social Research.

The Department of Classical Archaeology, founded by Rhys Carpenter in 1914, was the first independent department of archaeology in the United States. Carpenter (1914–1955) and Mary Hamilton Swindler (1912–1949) established the Department's international reputation. Under the leadership of Machteld Mellink (1949–1988), the Department extended its range to include Near Eastern and Egyptian archaeology. Brunilde Ridgway (1958–1993) made it preeminent in the field of Greek sculpture. Current faculty members add theory and historiography to the Department's traditional area specializations. Five alumnae of the program have been honored with the Archaeological Institute of America's gold medal for distinguished archaeological achievement: Dorothy Burr Thompson, Ph.D., '31; Virginia Grace, Ph.D., '34; Lucy Shoe Meritt, Ph.D., '35; Brunilde Ridgway, Ph.D., '58; and Maria Coutroubaki Shaw, Ph.D., '67. The Department today has a distinctly international cast, as those from other countries compose 15 percent of current students and 60 percent of the faculty.

Applying

Application for admission and financial aid should be made on the form available from the Graduate School of Arts and Sciences. Applicants can also download this form from the Graduate School's Web site at http://www.brynmawr.edu/gsas/. The deadline for admission with financial aid is January 2, 2009. Applications for admission without financial aid are accepted until June 30, 2009.

Students admitted to graduate work in classic and Near Eastern archaeology typically have a basic knowledge of Greek or Latin, reading knowledge of German or French, and undergraduate training in archaeology. Applicants must submit GRE scores; TOEFL scores, if not native speakers of English; a statement of interest; and a recent research paper or critical essay.

Students are encouraged to contact the Department and to visit. The Department's Web site is http://www.brynmawr.edu/archaeology/.

Correspondence and Information

Lea Miller, Secretary
Graduate School of Arts and Sciences
Bryn Mawr College
101 North Merion Avenue
Bryn Mawr, Pennsylvania 19010

Phone: 610-526-5072
Fax: 610-526-5076
E-mail: gsas@brynmawr.edu
Web site: http://www.brynmawr.edu/gsas/

Bryn Mawr College

THE FACULTY AND THEIR RESEARCH

Mehmet-Ali Ataç, Assistant Professor, Department of Classical and Near Eastern Archaeology; Ph.D., Harvard, 2003. Visual and intellectual traditions of the ancient Near East; Neo-Assyrian art and architecture, ancient Near Eastern and Egyptian kingship.

A. A. Donohue, Professor, Department of Classical and Near Eastern Archaeology; Ph.D., NYU, 1984. History and historiography of classical art.

Astrid Lindenlauf, Assistant Professor; Ph.D., University College (London), 2001. Greek art and archaeology, fortifications and warfare, urbanism, disposal and recycling practices.

Peter Magee, Associate Professor, Department of Classical and Near Eastern Archaeology; Ph.D., Sydney, 1996. Archaeology of South Asia, Iran, and Arabia; ancient imperialism; field methods; materials analysis.

James C. Wright, Professor and Chair, Department of Classical and Near Eastern Archaeology; Ph.D., Bryn Mawr, 1978. Prehistory of the Aegean basin, settlement forms and architecture of classical Greece, theory and method in archaeology.

Affiliated Faculty

Annette Baertschi, Assistant Professor, Department of Greek, Latin, and Classical Studies; Ph.D., Humboldt, 2006. Post-Augustan poetry, ancient magic, Latin meter, reception.

Don Barber, Associate Professor, Department of Geology; Ph.D., Colorado at Boulder, 2002. Geoarchaeology, coastal geology, paleoceanography, paleoclimatology

Catherine Conybeare, Associate Professor, Department of Greek, Latin, and Classical Studies; Ph.D., Toronto, 1997. Late antique and early medieval Latin prose, cultural history, critical theory.

Radcliffe G. Edmonds III, Associate Professor, Department of Greek, Latin, and Classical Studies; Ph.D., Chicago, 1999. Greek myth, Greco-Roman religion and magic, Greek philosophy.

Richard Hamilton, Paul Shorey Professor of Greek; Ph.D., Michigan, 1971. Greek lyric poetry, Greek drama, Greek religion.

Russell T. Scott, Doreen C. Spitzer Professor of Latin and Classical Studies; Ph.D., Yale, 1964. Roman history and historiography, Latin literature, Roman archaeology.

EMORY UNIVERSITY

Graduate School of Arts and Sciences
Department of Sociology

Programs of Study

The Department of Sociology is a vigorous intellectual community that offers a doctoral program designed to prepare students for academic and research careers. The Department provides rigorous training in theory, statistics, and research design along with extensive preparation in comparative political economy, global analysis (political sociology, political economy, global development and change, social movements, revolutions, and welfare states), social psychology (interpersonal and group processes, status and power, justice, emotions, social perception, socialization, and deviance), social organization and stratification (work and industry, formal organizations, medical sociology, gender, race, class, and ethnicity), and culture (media, religion, social change, and the arts). The Department's special strength in comparative and global issues is an integral part of Emory's international orientation.

The Department's colloquium series, along with a very low student-faculty ratio, guarantees high levels of personal interaction. Advanced graduate students design and teach courses for Emory's undergraduates who are of exceptionally high academic aptitude. The Department also hosts a biannual undergraduate sociology symposium organized by graduate students and faculty members.

The Ph.D. requires 72 hours of course work. The first 24 hours include core courses in research design, statistics, and theory. The remaining hours of course work include advanced courses in methods and statistics and in theory, two written examinations (one in a general field and one in a special field), and a dissertation. Ph.D. candidates must also publish in a scholarly journal or present a paper at a professional society conference. The program is designed for completion in four to five years.

Research Facilities

Emory has developed an ample and invigorating research environment. Graduate students have unlimited access to the Department's computer laboratory, which features high-capacity PCs and Macs. The University supports several specialized libraries that provide campuswide computerized bibliographic and circulation services.

A distinctive research facility open to the Emory community is the Carter Center and Presidential Library. Established in 1983 by former President Jimmy Carter, the research and policy center offers a variety of scholarly activities and periodically hosts international seminars on topics such as Third World development, global health, and human rights. President Carter, an Emory Distinguished Professor, occasionally lectures and holds discussions with students. The study of medical sociology and demography is enhanced by adjunct sociologists in the United States Centers for Disease Control and Prevention (CDC). The CDC maintains large data sets on topics such as family violence, personal lifestyles, alcohol consumption, and other health-related behaviors. The study of the sociology of religion involves associated sociologists in the Candler School of Theology and the Graduate Division of Religion. Resources in the area of race relations and social change include such Atlanta-based civil rights organizations as the Martin Luther King Center for Nonviolent Social Change and the Southern Christian Leadership Conference. Other resources in the areas of development and globalization include the Institute for International and Comparative Studies and the Development Studies Program.

Financial Aid

Graduate students in the Department receive full funding for five years, including a full tuition waiver and a combined fellowship and assistantship (currently at $16,500). Assistantship requirements are kept low, permitting students to finish their programs in a reasonable amount of time. Both admission and financial aid are awarded on the basis of academic merit. (No student should be discouraged from applying due to personal financial limitations.) In addition, students may compete for Woodruff Graduate Fellowships that provide full tuition and an annual $21,500 stipend for five years. Travel funds are available for graduate students to present papers at professional meetings.

Cost of Study

In 2007–08, tuition for full-time graduate study was $34,160. Admitted students are typically granted full tuition waivers and assistantships that cover most personal expenses while they are earning their degree.

Living and Housing Costs

Atlanta's cost of living ranks among the lowest of the nation's major metropolitan areas. Housing in University apartments ranges from $945 to $992 per month for a one-bedroom apartment to $619 (with roommate) to $1238 (single occupant) per month for a two-bedroom apartment. In addition, students have wide options in rooms and apartments in the residential neighborhoods surrounding the campus.

Student Group

Approximately 50 full-time graduate students are enrolled in the program. Recent graduates have found employment in academic institutions ranging from large research universities to small teaching colleges, as well as in private, public, and nonprofit research and policy positions.

Location

With a metropolitan-area population of more than 3 million, Atlanta is the unrivaled cultural and economic hub of the Southeast. The city offers a diversity of social, ethnic, and religious communities in an environment noted for its natural beauty and abundant trees. Emory is located in the heavily wooded Lullwater neighborhood, 6 miles east of downtown Atlanta. The University's graduate student apartments lie between Emory's Lullwater forest park and the town of Decatur. While Decatur maintains a small-town atmosphere, the nearby Virginia-Highland neighborhood is known for its trendy shops, restaurants, and nightclubs. Also close by are the bohemian Little Five Points neighborhood and the Midtown arts and theater district. Atlanta has consistently been ranked one of the best places to live in the nation.

The University

Emory University is a private university with a national reputation for scholarly and educational excellence. Expansion rapidly accelerated after 1980 with the famous Robert W. Woodruff gift. Currently, Emory's endowment is ranked in the top ten in the country, yet the total student population has been kept to less than 12,000. In an era known for academic retrenchment, Emory has been expanding resources and attracting some of the best young faculty members produced in the last ten years.

Applying

The deadline for application for admission, financial aid, and Woodruff fellowships is January 3. Applications received after that date are considered, but they cannot be guaranteed access to funding. Usually an undergraduate average of A- or better and scores above the 75th percentile on each section of the GRE General Test are required for admission. Emory actively seeks a diverse student body and strongly encourages applications from women and members of minority groups.

Correspondence and Information

Director of Graduate Admissions
Department of Sociology
Emory University
Atlanta, Georgia 30322-2530

Phone: 404-727-7510
E-mail: socinfo@emory.edu
Web site: http://www.sociology.emory.edu

Emory University

THE FACULTY AND THEIR RESEARCH

Robert S. Agnew, Ph.D., North Carolina at Chapel Hill, 1980. Criminology, social psychology, theory. Current research: causes of delinquency.
Delores P. Aldridge, Grace Towns Hamilton Professor of Sociology and African American Studies; Ph.D., Purdue, 1971. Intergroup relations, culture, stratification, organization, families and gender. Current research: male-female relations, Afrocentrism and cultural democracy in higher education, women in the labor market, women's health issues.
Matthew Archibald, Ph.D., Washington (Seattle), 2002. Organizations, social movements, alternative health-care institutions, political sociology. Current research: institutional ecology, legitimation and authority in health-care movements, voluntary associations, motivational enhancement in cocaine addiction.
John Boli, Ph.D., Stanford, 1976. Theory, global historical development, culture, political sociology, sociology of education. Current research: global structures and processes, world culture, nongovernmental organizations, civil society.
Irene Browne, Ph.D., Arizona, 1991. Stratification, gender, race, poverty. Current research: gender, race/ethnicity, and inequality in urban labor markets.
Oussama Cherribi, Ph.D., Amsterdam, 2000. Race/ethnic/minority relations, migration and immigration, policy analysis/public policy. Current research: globalization.
Dennis J. Condron, Ph.D., Ohio State, 2005. Educational stratification, class and racial/ethnic stratification, segregation, poverty. Current research: unequal learning opportunities and outcomes in the American education system.
Timothy J. Dowd, Ph.D., Princeton, 1996. Organizations, mass media, culture, music, economic sociology. Current research: organizational and musical change in the U.S. record industry, the social construction of markets and industries.
Tyrone A. Forman, Ph.D., Michigan, 2001. Race and ethnic relations, social psychology, children and youth, adolescent health and well-being, survey research methods. Current research: intergroup prejudice and discrimination, residential segregation.
Roberto Franzosi, Ph.D., Johns Hopkins, 1981. Political sociology and political economy, historical sociology, revolution, methodology and statistics. Current research: formal qualitative methodology, strikes, Italian fascism.
Elizabeth A. Griffiths, Ph.D., Toronto, 2006. Crime, deviance, and social control; spatial analyses of homicide; urban sociology; work, occupations, and organizations. Current research: spatial and temporal distributions of violence in cities and communities, mobility patterns of victims and offenders, family structure and victimization risk.
Karen A. Hegtvedt, Ph.D., Washington (Seattle), 1984. Social psychology, justice, emotions, literature. Current research: negotiation and competing justice claims, emotional socialization, justice and legitimacy.
Alexander M. Hicks, Ph.D., Wisconsin, 1979. Political sociology and economy of industrial societies, methodology, culture. Current research: relations between class formation, political organization, social policy and cultural forms.
Cathryn J. Johnson, Ph.D., Iowa, 1990. Social psychology, status, power, legitimacy, emotions, work and formal organizations. Current research: status and legitimacy processes in formal task groups in organizations, legitimacy and justice in conflict situations.
Corey Lee M. Keyes, Ph.D., Wisconsin, 1995. Social psychology, aging, mental health, self-concept, methodology. Current research: causes and consequences of mental health and illness, subjective personal changes, human resilience.
Frank J. Lechner, Ph.D., Pittsburgh, 1985. Theory, social change, religion, culture. Current research: world culture, globalization, and national identity.
Amanda E. Lewis, Ph.D., Michigan, 2000. Race and ethnic relations, education, children and youth, qualitative methods, gender, social inequality, urban ethnography. Current research: racial inequity and education, contemporary racial dynamics.
Jeffery S. Mullis, Ph.D., Virginia, 1995. Law and society, medical sociology, social control. Current research: conflicts and conflict resolution between doctors and patients.
Richard Rubinson, Ph.D., Stanford, 1974. Political economy of development, political sociology, sociology of education, organizations. Current research: comparative studies of industrial regulation; schooling, state, and economy in East Asia.
Tracy L. Scott, Ph.D., Princeton, 1999. Culture, religion, health, qualitative methods. Current research: spirituality in everyday life in the U.S., organizational culture among nurses and physicians in the hospital.
Regina Werum, Ph.D., Indiana, 1995. Race and ethnicity, gender, social movements, stratification, education. Current research: race, ethnic, and gender stratification in education.
Kathryn Yount, Ph.D., Johns Hopkins, 1999. Social demography, public health, methods. Current research: gender inequality and health outcomes in Egypt.

Associated Faculty in the University
Nancy L. Eiesland, Ph.D., Emory, 1995. Candler School of Theology. Sociology of religion, social change, urban sociology, gender. Current research: religious response and urban change.
Nancy Kutner, Ph.D., North Carolina at Chapel Hill, 1965. School of Medicine. Medical sociology, rehabilitation medicine, aging, gender roles. Current research: quality of life and aging, gender, ethnicity, and chronic illness.
Steven M. Tipton, Ph.D., Harvard, 1979. Candler School of Theology. Sociology of morality, culture, religion. Current research: American culture and institutional analysis.

Associated Faculty at the School of Public Health
Edmund R. Becker, Ph.D., Vanderbilt, 1981. Organizational theory and behavior, medical sociology, health-care organization and policy, unions and labor relations. Current research: health-care organization autonomy and performance, returns of investment in public health, physician payment and productivity.
Richard M. Levinson, Ph.D., Wisconsin, 1975. Medical sociology, health behavior, health policy. Current research: financial barriers to health services, social determinants of health risk behaviors.
Claire Sterk, Ph.D., Rotterdam/CUNY, 1990. Medical sociology, social epidemiology, qualitative methods. Current research: women's and children's health.

Adjunct Faculty at the Centers for Disease Control and Prevention
Shailendra Nath Banerjee, Ph.D., Emory, 1982. Demography, medical sociology, statistics.
Clark Denny, Ph.D., Emory, 1996. Demography, race and ethnic relations.
Deborah Holtzman, Ph.D., Johns Hopkins, 1985. Social epidemiology, AIDS, health education.
David G. Hurst, Ph.D., Emory, 1998. Education, policy analysis/public policy, race/class/gender.
Karin A. Mack, Ph.D., Maryland, 1995. Aging and life course, demography, family.
James A. Mercy, Ph.D., Emory, 1982. Interpersonal violence, research methods, public health, policy.
Kim S. Miller, Ph.D., Emory, 1989. AIDS, adolescent health risk behaviors, family, ethnic minorities.
Saswati Sunderam, Ph.D., Emory, 1997. Medical sociology, demography, race/class/gender.

Adjunct Faculty
Vincent Carter, Ph.D., Emory, 2002. Sociology of education, stratification/organization, political sociology, race and ethnic relations.
Louis A. Hazouri, Ph.D., Emory, 1983. Applied sociology in complex business organizations, comparative social problems, social policy, law, comparative health-care systems.
Kay L. Levine, Ph.D., Berkeley, 2003. Law and society, criminology/delinquency, sexuality and homosexuality.
Mike McQuaide, Ph.D., Penn State, 1979. Medical sociology, aging, social problems, social psychology.
Michael Sacks, Ph.D., Northwestern, 2000. Economy and society, stratification/mobility, social networks.
Graham Scambler, Ph.D., London, 1983. Medical sociology, sociological theory.

Emeritus Faculty
Alvin Boskoff, Ph.D., North Carolina at Chapel Hill, 1950. Sociological theory, comparative urban structure, stratification, social change.
Abbott Ferris, Ph.D., North Carolina at Chapel Hill, 1950. Social indicators, quality of life, civility.
William L. Graves, Ph.D., North Carolina at Chapel Hill, 1969. Medical sociology, population, research design.
Samarendranath Mitra, Ph.D., Chicago, 1961. Formal demography, mathematical models, statistics.
William W. Pendleton Jr., Ph.D., Tulane, 1965. Sociology of education, population, social ecology, family.

SOUTHERN ILLINOIS UNIVERSITY CARBONDALE

Department of Anthropology
Ph.D. in Anthropology Program

Programs of Study The Department offers the Ph.D. degree in anthropology. Students may specialize in any of the four traditional subfields of anthropology: biological or physical anthropology, archaeology, social-cultural anthropology, and anthropological linguistics. The Department takes seriously the notion that anthropology is a single, integrated discipline, and the doctoral program requires significant exposure to all four subfields of anthropology.

Research Facilities The Department has strong ties to the Center for Archaeological Investigations (CAI) and the Center for Systematic Biology. The CAI is an independent research unit with a permanent staff of 7. In addition, 12 research associates and emeriti participate in center-sponsored or assisted research and teaching, and many students take advantage of the opportunities for research in CAI projects. The center undertakes grant- and contract-funded field research, curation of collections, publication, and the Visiting Scholar Program. The latter supports a postdoctoral fellow who pursues research, teaching, and writing in the center and organizes an annual thematic Visiting Scholar Conference.

The Center for Systematic Biology is a consortium of faculty members from the Departments of Anthropology, Microbiology, Plant Biology, and Zoology and provides opportunities for graduate research training in modern, interdisciplinary approaches to biological taxonomy. Emphasizing the development of skills in taxonomic expertise, collections management, field methods, molecular techniques, and analytical-information technology, the center is dedicated to preparing graduates to deal effectively with scientific and societal issues stemming from the biodiversity crisis. Faculty research areas include primate evolution and biogeography as well as many specialties in microbiology, botany, zoology, and ecology. Research conducted by center faculty members and students takes advantage of state-of-the-art collections, laboratory, and computing facilities on the Southern Illinois University Carbondale (SIUC) campus.

An international journal that explores the relationship of racial, ethnic, and national identities and power hierarchies within national and global arenas, *Identities: Global Studies in Culture and Power,* is edited within the Department of Anthropology and is used as a research tool. Beginning with volume 9 (2002), *Identities* is available in print and on the Taylor and Francis Publications Web site at http://www.tandf.co.uk/journals/titles/1070289x.html.

The Department of Anthropology also maintains strong ties with the Black American Studies Program, the University Museum, the Department of Linguistics, and the Women's Studies Program.

Financial Aid The Department provides financial support, including a stipend and tuition waiver, in the form of graduate assistantships. Additional graduate assistantships are available through the Center for Archaeological Investigations. Fellowship support for outstanding students is available from the Graduate School, including doctoral fellowships and the Morris Fellowship program, which provides five years of support. The Graduate School also provides some tuition waivers.

Cost of Study In-state graduate tuition is $313.90 per credit hour in 2008–09. Out-of-state tuition is 2.5 times the in-state tuition rate ($784.75 per credit hour). Graduate students with at least a 25 percent appointment as a graduate assistant receive a tuition scholarship. Fees vary from $511.26 (1 credit hour) to $1416.05 (12 credit hours). Students with a graduate assistantship receive a 25 percent reduction in the Primary Care Medical Fee.

Living and Housing Costs For married couples, students with families, and single graduate students, the University has 690 efficiency and one-, two-, three-, and four-bedroom apartments that rent for $484 to $686 per month in 2008–09. Residence halls for single graduate students are also available, as are accessible residence hall rooms and apartments for students with disabilities.

Student Group In 2006–07, there were 48 students in the Ph.D. program. Approximately 3 to 6 new students are admitted each year.

Location SIUC is 350 miles south of Chicago and 100 miles southeast of St. Louis. Nestled in rolling hills bordered by the Ohio and Mississippi Rivers and enhanced by a mild climate, the area has state parks, national forests and wildlife refuges, and large lakes for outdoor recreation. Cultural offerings include theater, opera, concerts, art exhibits, and cinema. Educational facilities for the families of students are excellent.

The University Southern Illinois University Carbondale is a comprehensive public university with a variety of general and professional education programs. The University offers bachelor's and associate degrees, master's and doctoral degrees, the J.D. degree, and the M.D. degree. The University is fully accredited by the North Central Association of Colleges and Schools. The Graduate School has an essential role in the development and coordination of graduate instruction and research programs. The Graduate Council has academic responsibility for determining graduate standards, recommending new graduate programs and research centers, and establishing policies to facilitate the research effort.

Applying Applicants to the Ph.D. degree program must complete the equivalent of the master's degree and supply three letters of recommendation. Applicants must also supply a statement of goals for their programs and subsequent professional careers.

Correspondence and Information

Graduate Secretary
Department of Anthropology
MC 4502
Southern Illinois University
Carbondale, Illinois 62901-4502

Phone: 618-453-5037
Fax: 618-453-5037
Web site: http://www.siu.edu/~anthro/phd.htm

Southern Illinois University Carbondale

THE FACULTY AND THEIR RESEARCH

Jane H. Adams, Professor; Ph.D., Illinois, 1987. Sociocultural anthropology, political economy, agricultural systems, history, gender roles; rural U.S., Latin America.

Andrew Balkansky, Associate Professor; Ph.D., Wisconsin, 1997. Archaeology, settlement patterns, social evolution, urbanism; Mexico, Central America.

Roberto E. Barrios, Assistant Professor; Ph.D., Florida, 2004. Sociocultural anthropology, medical anthropology, applied anthropology; Honduras; Southeastern U.S.

Robert S. Corruccini, Professor; Ph.D., Berkeley, 1975. Physical anthropology, paleontology, osteology, multivariate methods, dental anthropology, epidemiology; India, Italy, Caribbean.

Susan M. Ford, Associate Professor; Ph.D., Pittsburgh, 1980. Physical anthropology, primate paleontology and systematics (especially New World monkeys and early anthropoids), evolutionary theory, functional and comparative anatomy; South America.

Janet Fuller, Associate Professor; Ph.D., South Carolina, 1997. Language content and bilingualism, discourse analysis, sociolinguistics, pragmatics, second language acquisition.

Jonathan D. Hill, Professor and Editor, *Identities;* Ph.D., Indiana, 1983. Ethnology, ecology, and history of Lowland South America; ethnomusicology and performance studies; symbolic and semiotic anthropology; nationalism and ethnicity; critical studies of culture, power, and history.

C. Andrew Hofling, Professor; Ph.D., Washington (St. Louis), 1982. Linguistics; discourse analysis, Maya; Mesoamerica.

John McCall, Associate Professor; Ph.D., Indiana, 1992. Sociocultural anthropology, social theory, history, ritual studies, medical anthropology, expressive culture; Igbo, Africa.

Tracy L. Prowse, Assistant Professor; Ph.D., McMaster, 2001. Bioarchaeology, physical anthropology, osteology, paleopathology, paleonutrition, forensic anthropology, stable isotopes; Italy.

Ulrich H. Reichard, Assistant Professor; Ph.D., Göttingen (Germany), 1995. Physical anthropology, primates (gibbons), zoology, cultural anthropology/ethnology; Thailand.

Don S. Rice, Professor and Associate Provost; Ph.D., Penn State, 1976. Archaeology, ethnohistory, tropical ecology, development of complex societies; Middle America, Andes.

Prudence M. Rice, Professor and Director, Office of Research Development and Administration; Ph.D., Penn State, 1976. Archaeology, ceramics; Mesoamerica, Andes.

Izumi Shimada, Professor; Ph.D., Arizona, 1976. Archaeology, complex societies, technology and craft production, urban and ceremonial centers, experimental archaeology; Andes.

David Sutton, Associate Professor; Ph.D., Chicago, 1995. Sociocultural anthropology, historical consciousness, kinship and gender, food, memory; Greece, Europe.

Anthony K. Webster, Assistant Professor; Ph.D., Texas at Austin, 2004. Linguistic anthropology, verbal art, Navajo, Apache; Southwestern U.S.

Paul Welch, Associate Professor; Ph.D., Michigan 1986. Archaeology, politics and economics in midrange societies, eastern U.S.; quantitative methods.

SOUTHERN ILLINOIS UNIVERSITY CARBONDALE

Department of Sociology
Ph.D. in Sociology

Programs of Study

The Ph.D. degree program is centered on advanced offerings in the areas of theory, methods, deviance, social movements, religion, culture, gender, power, and inequality. A special concentration in criminology, deviance, and administration of justice allows interested students to pursue a substantial part of their doctoral studies in administration of justice. The faculty members are research oriented and support such an orientation on the part of their students. The Department of Sociology has a state-of-the-art 10-person computer lab.

The responsibility for initial advisement rests with the Director of Graduate Studies. As early as possible, the Director, in consultation with the student, requests an appropriate member of the Department's graduate faculty to serve as the student's academic adviser. This adviser helps prepare a general plan of study. Doctoral candidates have several required courses, research projects, and readings leading to the dissertation over a projected eight semesters of study.

Research Facilities

The Department of Sociology has a ten-machine microcomputer laboratory with SPSS, SAS, and other programs. Several other computer labs are available in Faner Hall. Morris Library's general collection numbers 2.4 million volumes, 2.8 million microforms, and more than 12,200 current serial subscriptions. Library users have access to nearly 600 electronic data files and CD-ROM products via workstations located throughout the building. The library is an active participant in the world's largest bibliographic network, Online Computer Library Center (OCLC), and it is a member of ILLINET Online (IO), the statewide automated catalog, circulation, and interlibrary loan system with records of more than 600 libraries.

Financial Aid

Assistantships for qualified students are available through the Department and the University on a competitive basis. Funding is normally limited to eight semesters for the Ph.D. degree. A student's continued funding is contingent on the student's satisfactory progress in the program, annual evaluation by faculty members, passing comprehensive exams in a timely manner, and on the availability of funds. Eighty percent of the full-time students have received some type of aid.

Cost of Study

In-state graduate tuition is $313.90 per credit hour in 2008–09. Out-of-state tuition is 2.5 times the in-state tuition rate ($784.75 per credit hour). Graduate students with at least a 25 percent appointment as a graduate assistant receive a tuition scholarship. Fees vary from $511.26 (1 credit hour) to $1416.05 (12 credit hours). Students with a graduate assistantship receive a 25 percent reduction in the Primary Care Medical Fee.

Living and Housing Costs

For married couples, students with families, and single graduate students, the University has 690 efficiency and one-, two-, three-, and four-bedroom apartments that rent for $484 to $686 per month in 2008–09. Residence halls for single graduate students are also available, as are accessible residence hall rooms and apartments for students with disabilities.

Student Group

The Department has 46 students, of whom 32 are full-time (10 women, 6 international) and 14 are part-time (6 women, 1 international). Seven students are African American, and 1 is Hispanic. In 2001–02 SIU awarded eight Ph.D. degrees in sociology.

Location

Southern Illinois University Carbondale is 350 miles south of Chicago and 100 miles southeast of St. Louis. Nestled in rolling hills bordered by the Ohio and Mississippi Rivers and enhanced by a mild climate, the area has state parks, national forests and wildlife refuges, and large lakes for outdoor recreation. Cultural offerings include theater, opera, concerts, art exhibits, and cinema. Educational facilities for the families of students are excellent.

The University

Southern Illinois University Carbondale is a comprehensive public university with a variety of general and professional education programs. The University offers bachelor's and associate degrees, master's and doctoral degrees, the J.D. degree, and the M.D. degree. The University is fully accredited by the North Central Association of Colleges and Schools. The Graduate School has an essential role in the development and coordination of graduate instruction and research programs. The Graduate Council has academic responsibility for determining graduate standards, recommending new graduate programs and research centers, and establishing policies to facilitate the research effort. Southern Illinois University Carbondale is a state-funded university founded in 1869.

Applying

Applications should be requested from the address given below. Application materials include official transcripts from colleges attended, the Application for Admission to Graduate Study, the Application for Admission to the Sociology Program, and three letters of recommendation. GRE scores are required. Applications received by December 15 that include all supporting materials receive full consideration for departmental assistantships, fellowships, and university support that begin the following fall semester. New applications for admission are considered through March 1. Admission for the spring semester is only given in exceptional circumstances.

Correspondence and Information

Director of Graduate Studies
Department of Sociology
Mailcode 4524
Southern Illinois University Carbondale
Carbondale, Illinois 62901
Phone: 618-453-2494
Fax: 618-453-8926
E-mail: sociolgy@siu.edu
Web site: http://www.siu.edu/~socio

Southern Illinois University Carbondale

THE FACULTY AND THEIR RESEARCH

SIU's Department of Sociology has a world-renowned faculty with particular strengths in the areas of social movements and social change, criminology and deviance, and gender and sexuality. The faculty members have edited numerous scholarly journals, including *Social Problems, Sociological Spectrum, Contemporary Ethnography,* and *Review of Religious Research.* SIU faculty members hold prominent positions in several scholarly associations and on editorial boards. Faculty members have authored several books, many book chapters, and numerous peer-reviewed articles in general-interest and specialty journals, including *American Sociological Review, Social Forces, Social Problems, Social Science Research, American Journal of Sociology,* and *Deviant Behavior.*

Robert D. Benford, Professor and Chair; Ph.D., Texas at Austin, 1987. Social movements, social psychology, peace and war, gender and sport, qualitative methods.
Jennifer L. Dunn, Associate Professor; Ph.D., California, Davis, 1999. Social psychology, deviance, criminology, victimology.
Derek C. Martin, Assistant Professor; Ph.D., California, Irvine, 2005. Race/ethnic relations, minority relations, stratification, mobility, leisure/sport/recreation.
Michelle Hughes Miller, Associate Professor; Ph.D., Nebraska–Lincoln, 1997. Gender, criminology, drug policy.
Darren E. Sherkat, Professor; Ph.D., Duke, 1991. Religion, social movements, medical sociology, quantitative methods.
Kathryn B. Ward, Professor; Ph.D., Iowa, 1982. Gender, international political economy, social movements.
Rachel Bridges Whaley, Assistant Professor; Ph.D., SUNY at Albany, 1999. Criminology/delinquency, sex and gender, quantitative methodology.
Chris Wienke, Assistant Professor; Ph.D., Pittsburgh, 2003. Family, sexuality, gender, qualitative methodology, social inequality, cultural sociology.

Affiliated and Joint Appointments
Elaine M. Blinde, Professor (affiliated with the Kinesiology Department); Ph.D., Illinois at Urbana-Champaign, 1987. Leisure/sport/recreation.
Mae A. Davenport (affiliated with Forestry); Ph.D., Minnesota, 2003. Environmental sociology, qualitative methodology, leisure/sports/recreation.
John D. H. Downing (affiliated with Global Media Research); Ph.D., London School of Economics, 1974. Cultural sociology, political economy, mass communication/public opinion.
Walter B. Jaehnig (affiliated with School of Journalism); Ph.D., Essex (U.K.), 1974. Mass communication, public opinion, social control, community.
Jyotsna Kapur, Associate Professor (affiliated with Cinema and Photography); Ph.D., Northwestern, 1998. Children and youth, cultural sociology, Marxist sociology.
Jean C. Mangun (affiliated with Forestry); Ph.D., Purdue, 1991. Environmental sociology, rural sociology, leisure/sports/recreation.
Ainon Mizan (affiliated with Rural Health and Social Service Development); Ph.D., Southern Illinois at Carbondale, 1992. Family, social change, women and development.

Emeritus Faculty
Ernest K. Alix, Ph.D., Southern Illinois at Carbondale, 1966. Deviant behavior, sociology of sport, law and society.
Thomas Burger, Associate Professor; Ph.D., Duke, 1972. Theory, history of social thought, social stratification.
Thomas C. Calhoun, Ph.D., Kentucky, 1988. Deviance, juvenile delinquency, race and ethnic relations, qualitative methods.
Roland K. Hawkes, Ph.D., Johns Hopkins, 1967. Rural sociology, development, migration.
Lewellyn Hendrix, Ph.D., Princeton, 1974. Family and kinship, gender, cross-cultural research.
Frank C. Nall, Ph.D., Michigan, 1959. Urban sociology, comparative race and ethnic relations.
Mark A. Schneider, Ph.D., Yale, 1985. Theory, culture, and science.

STONY BROOK UNIVERSITY, STATE UNIVERSITY OF NEW YORK

Interdepartmental Doctoral Program in Anthropological Sciences

Programs of Study

The Interdepartmental Doctoral Program in Anthropological Sciences (IDPAS), in the College of Arts and Sciences, is an interdisciplinary and interdepartmental program leading to the Ph.D. degree. The program draws upon faculty members and resources from the Departments of Anatomical Sciences, Anthropology, Asian American Studies, Ecology and Evolution, Geosciences, and History. The IDPAS is committed to remaining true to anthropology's unique approach—an integrated focus that attempts to understand and explain primate and human culture, behavior, and biology through time and space. Its goal is to foster an exciting and demanding scholastic environment that challenges and assists doctoral students seeking to do outstanding anthropological science. The program aims to train excellent researchers and teachers in the anthropological sciences.

The IDPAS recognizes three tracks: cultural anthropology, archaeology, and physical anthropology. Within physical anthropology, there are primate behavior and morphology subspecialties. Each of the three tracks has its own core curriculum and method of qualifying examination. All share the same requirement for a dissertation and its public defense. The first three to four semesters of the program involve course work that forms the basis of the qualifying examination. The student then defends a dissertation proposal by the end of the sixth semester and spends the next three to four years doing dissertation research and writing the dissertation.

Students typically take seven to eight years to complete the program and receive their Ph.D. Their research covers a wide range of topics in primate behavior and ecology, prehistory, Near Eastern archaeology, geochronology, functional morphology, paleontology, and phylogenetic systematics. Students typically work in close collaboration with one or more of the faculty members in developing their research projects and work on the research with varying degrees of independence, depending on the nature of the project.

Research Facilities

The Department of Anthropology provides facilities for analysis of stone tools and faunal remains, application of remote sensing and geographic information systems, electron microscopy, and state-of-the-art mineralized tissue research. The Department of Anatomical Sciences houses research collections covering primate fossils, primate osteological material, and living nonhuman primates. A biomechanics lab includes facilities for force-plate analysis, high-speed cinematography, and three-dimensional morphometrics as well as bone-strain and telemetered electromyography. An isotope lab is available for interested graduate students in geosciences, and scanning and transmission electron microscope as well as microCT facilities are available elsewhere on campus. Students have access to excellent libraries and collections and to campus computing services.

Field work opportunities are available in paleontology, primatology, and archaeology. There are active sites for primate behavior research in South America, Central Africa, Madagascar, and Thailand. The Turkana Basin Institute at Stony Brook provides opportunities for field and laboratory research related to the paleontology, geology, and archaeology of the Turkana Basin of eastern Africa, including graduate fellowships to incoming Ph.D. candidates and summer fellowships. The archaeology faculty has active field sites in Long Island, Turkey, Kenya, and East Africa. Paleontological field research is currently taking place in Egypt, Ethiopia, Kenya, Madagascar, Mali, North America, South Africa, and Uganda.

Financial Aid

Stony Brook offers University tuition scholarships. Graduate School Traineeships (teaching assistantships and graduate assistantships) are also available. Full traineeships pay $15,145 per year, three-quarter-time traineeships pay $11,359 per year, and half-time traineeships pay $7573 per year. Graduate Council Fellowships are restricted to U.S. citizens and permanent residents and carry a stipend of $17,573 plus a full-tuition scholarship; ten are awarded campuswide each year. W. Burghardt Turner Fellowships are only for U.S. citizens or permanent residents who are Native American, African American, or Hispanic American and carry a stipend of $17,573 plus a full-tuition scholarship; twenty are awarded campuswide each year. Federal and state aid is offered in the form of veterans' educational benefits, the Federal Work-Study Program, Federal Stafford Student Loans (subsidized and unsubsidized), Federal Perkins Loans, and the Tuition Assistance Program (TAP).

The IDPAS provides each student with $500 in seed money to enable them to develop dissertation research projects. Travel funds are also provided to support travel to academic meetings. Several faculty members fund students on research assistantships.

Cost of Study

In 2008–09, full-time tuition at 12 credits for entering in-state residents is $3450 per semester, while out-of-state residents and international students pay $5460. Additional fees for each semester, including (but not limited to) the infirmary, activity, technology, and transportation fees, total about $875. International students also pay a service fee of approximately $35 per semester and an orientation fee of $50. Fees for the mandatory Student Health Insurance Plan vary depending on citizenship and employment status.

Living and Housing Costs

For 2008–09, Stony Brook calculates the cost of education excluding tuition, fees, and insurance at $14,228 per year. On-campus apartments range in cost from approximately $336 per month to approximately $1456 per month, depending on the size of the unit and the number of students sharing the space. Off-campus housing options include rooms, houses, and apartments that can be rented from approximately $350 to $2500 per month. Costs including books, food, and transportation may vary depending on academic program and/or personal circumstances.

Student Group

The Ph.D. Program in Anthropological Sciences has 40 full-time students. There are 10 men and 30 women enrolled; 12 are international students. Most students are funded for the majority of their time in IDPAS. Teaching assistantships provide around 50 percent of the funding, with the other half coming from research assistantships, graduate assistantships, fellowships, or fieldwork funding.

Student Outcomes

The majority of the program's alumni obtain jobs in academia, teaching, and research in anthropology, archaeology, and anatomy. A full list of IDPAS alumni and their current employment is available at http://gibbon.anat.sunysb.edu/IDPAS/index.php?page=alumni.

Location

The University is located on the North Shore of Long Island, about 60 miles east of New York City. The campus is nestled amid fields and woodlands, with Long Island Sound just minutes to the north and the Atlantic Ocean a 45-minute drive to the south. The Long Island Railroad connects New York City with the Stony Brook campus. Three major highways lead to New York City, and bus service is available on campus and to various points on Long Island.

The University and The Program

Stony Brook is one of the nation's finest public universities, with a high volume of federally sponsored research, a high percentage of doctoral students, and an emphasis on scholarship. The inception of the Interdepartmental Doctoral Program in Anthropological Sciences in 1982 harnessed the considerable strengths of University faculty members in various departments who possess research expertise in areas related to anthropology. The IDPAS currently draws upon faculty members from six departments, giving the program a uniquely broad academic character that provides a comprehensive graduate training and research environment.

Applying

Admission and financial aid applications should be filed by January 15 for fall admission. The application must be done online via the Graduate School's Application page at https://app.applyyourself.com/?id=sunysb-gs. Admissions and support decisions are made during the first week in March, and applicants receive notification no later than March 15. April 15 is the deadline to respond to offers of admission and support.

Correspondence and Information

Dr. Andreas Koenig, Graduate Program Director
Interdepartmental Doctoral Program in Anthropological Sciences
Department of Anthropology
Stony Brook University, State University of New York
Stony Brook, New York 11794-4364
Phone: 631-632-1513
E-mail: IDPAS_Director@notes.cc.sunysb.edu
Web site: http://gibbon.anat.sunysb.edu/IDPAS/

Jean Moreau, Graduate Program Coordinator
Interdepartmental Doctoral Program in Anthropological Sciences
Department of Anthropology
Stony Brook University, State University of New York
Stony Brook, New York 11794-4364
Phone: 631-632-7606
E-mail: jmoreau@notes.cc.sunysb.edu
Web site: http://gibbon.anat.sunysb.edu/IDPAS/

Stony Brook University, State University of New York

THE FACULTY AND THEIR RESEARCH

William E. Arens, Anthropology and Dean of International Academic Programs; Ph.D., Virginia, 1970. Social anthropology, conservation, Africa and the Mediterranean.
David J. Bernstein, Anthropology; Ph.D., SUNY at Binghamton, 1988. New World archaeology, paleoecology, coastal societies, subsistence studies.
Carola Borries, Anthropology; Ph.D., Göttingen (Germany), 1989. Primate ecology and behavior, sociobiology, Asia.
Brigitte Demes, Anatomical Sciences; Ph.D., Bochum (Germany), 1982. Biomechanics, functional morphology, allometry, primates.
Diane M. Doran-Sheehy, Anthropology and Chair of the Department; Ph.D., SUNY at Stony Brook, 1989. Social evolution, behavioral ecology, African apes.
John G. Fleagle, Anatomical Sciences; Ph.D., Harvard, 1976. Primate and human evolution, primate behavior, functional morphology, growth and development.
David D. Gilmore, Anthropology; Ph.D., Pennsylvania, 1975. Complex societies, stratification, and peasant culture; Europe; Mediterranean.
Frederick E. Grine, Anthropology; Ph.D., Witwatersrand (South Africa), 1984. Hominid evolution, functional morphology of the masticatory apparatus, diet reconstruction, dental anthropology, mineralized tissues.
David B. Hicks, Anthropology; Ph.D., D.Phil., Oxford, 1972. Religion, kinship, Southeast Asia.
Elisabeth Hildebrand, Anthropology; Ph.D., Washington (St. Louis), 2003. Origins of agriculture, paleoethnobotany, ethnoarchaeology, Africa.
Charles H. Janson, Ecology and Evolution; Ph.D., Washington (Seattle), 1985. Primate behavior and ecology, sociobiology, tropical ecology.
Jukka Jernvall, Ecology and Evolution; Ph.D., Helsinki (Finland), 1995. Developmental biology, morphology, teeth.
William L. Jungers, Anatomical Sciences and Chair of the Department; Ph.D., Michigan, 1976. Primate and human evolution, functional morphology, biomechanics.
Andreas Koenig, Anthropology and IDPAS Director; Ph.D., Göttingen (Germany), 1992. Primate behavioral ecology, social evolution, community ecology, Asia.
David W. Krause, Anatomical Sciences; Ph.D., Michigan, 1982. Evolution, form, and function of mammalian dentition; evolutionary history and paleobiology of early mammals, particularly primates.
Susan G. Larson, Anatomical Sciences; Ph.D., Wisconsin–Madison, 1982. Functional morphology, primates, biomechanics.
Meave Leakey, Anthropology; Ph.D., North Wales, 1968. Primate evolution, palaeoecology and evolution of African mammals.
Lawrence B. Martin, Anthropology and Dean of the Graduate School; Ph.D., London, 1983. Hominoid evolution, enamel thickness, enamel microstructure and development.
Maureen A. O'Leary, Anatomical Sciences; Ph.D., Johns Hopkins, 1997. Origin of primates and anthropoids, vertebrate paleontology, mammalian systematics, functional morphology, pattern of evolution.
Troy E. Rasbury, Geosciences; Ph.D., SUNY at Stony Brook, 1998. Sedimentary geochemistry, chronostratigraphy, geochronology.
James B. Rossie, Anthropology; Ph.D., Yale, 2003. Primate evolution, Miocene hominoids, cranial ontogeny and anatomy, systematics, East Africa.
Gregory A. Ruf, Asian and Asian American Studies; Ph.D., Columbia, 1994. History and anthropology; political and economic anthropology; theory and methodology; rural industrialization; transitions from socialism; East Asia, China, overseas Chinese, Japan.
Eric R. Seifert, Anatomical Sciences; Ph.D., Duke, 2003. The evolution of placental mammals.
John J. Shea, Anthropology; Ph.D., Harvard, 1991. Old World Paleolithic archaeology, lithic analysis, Near East, Europe, Africa.
Jack T. Stern Jr., Anatomical Sciences; Ph.D., Chicago, 1969. Functional morphology of primates, biomechanics of muscle.
Elizabeth C. Stone, Anthropology; Ph.D., Chicago, 1979. Old World archaeology, state formation, ancient economy and society, Near East.
Randall L. Susman, Anatomical Sciences; Ph.D., Chicago, 1976. Functional morphology and behavior of primates, evolution of apes and humans, gross anatomy.
Katheryn C. Twiss, Anthropology; Ph.D., Berkeley, 2003. Zooarchaeology, origins of agriculture and social complexity, anthropology of food, Near East.
Patricia C. Wright, Anthropology; Ph.D., CUNY, 1985. Primate behavior and ecology, rain forest conservation, Madagascar.
Paul E. Zimansky, History; Ph.D., Chicago, 1980. History and archaeology of the Near East; ancient imperialism, Urartian, Anatolian and Mesopotamian civilizations.

STONY BROOK UNIVERSITY, STATE UNIVERSITY OF NEW YORK

Department of Sociology

Programs of Study The Graduate Program in the Department of Sociology offers M.A. and Ph.D. degrees, although the program is primarily a Ph.D.-granting program. The Department provides high-level graduate training in a broad range of social scientific theories and methods (both quantitative and qualitative) that are primarily informed by a global perspective. While the research priority of the Department has a global focus, faculty and student interests include a broad spectrum of important substantive fields, such as sex and gender, inequality, social movements, contentious politics, national identity, environmental sociology, and cultural sociology. Faculty research grants and projects, as well as conferences, seminars, and colloquia sponsored by the Department, provide numerous opportunities for students to actively engage in research, dialogues, and debates relevant to the study of social systems in a world characterized by increasing global interaction.

For a student arriving with a bachelor's degree, it normally takes about six years to complete the Ph.D. program. The first three years mainly comprise course work; students then work on their dissertation research. The sociology department encourages students to begin research early in their program and requires students to complete two substantial papers instead of taking comprehensive examinations. With an annual enrollment of about 6 to 8 graduate students each year, there is plenty of opportunity for graduate students to get to know, and work with, faculty members. The Department is committed to providing continuous individual mentoring of graduate students.

Research Facilities All students are allocated shared office space in the Department. In addition to the data lab and dedicated computer facilities in the Social and Behavioral Sciences Building, the Department of Sociology houses a small library and reading room, a computer room, and a laboratory for the study of social systems, primarily in animals. Most graduate classes are held in one of the Department's two seminar rooms.

Financial Aid The Department usually offers about six to eight teaching assistantships each year to incoming students. Students are usually funded for four years, provided they continue to make good progress toward the completion of the Ph.D. degree. A number of underrepresented students in sociology have received Turner Fellowships and others have been awarded various university fellowships that supplement the student financial aid package.

Cost of Study In 2008–09, full-time tuition at 12 credits for entering in-state residents is $3450 per semester, while out-of-state residents and international students pay $5460. Additional fees for each semester, including (but not limited to) the infirmary, activity, technology, and transportation fees, total about $875. International students also pay a service fee of approximately $35 per semester and an orientation fee of $50. Fees for the mandatory Student Health Insurance Plan vary depending on citizenship and employment status.

Living and Housing Costs For 2008–09, Stony Brook calculates the cost of education excluding tuition, fees, and insurance at $14,228 per year. On-campus apartments range in cost from approximately $336 per month to approximately $1456 per month, depending on the size of the unit and the number of students sharing the space. Off-campus housing options include rooms, houses, and apartments that can be rented from approximately $350 to $2500 per month. Costs including books, food, and transportation may vary depending on academic program and/or personal circumstances.

Student Group There are about 50 to 60 students in the graduate program. Most are full-time. The student body is ethnically, racially, and regionally diverse. About 60 percent are women. Currently, about half of the students are international, coming from Argentina, Singapore, Bangladesh, Korea, Poland, Croatia, Russia, Iran, Turkey, India, Japan, and China. Faculty members look for intellectually and emotionally mature students who have a strong commitment to understanding modern society.

Student Outcomes Most of the students go on to careers in either higher education or social research organizations. Recent graduates have had research or teaching positions at Harvard; Northwestern; the Universities of Cincinnati, Colorado, Florida, and Michigan; Hofstra; Columbia; and schools in the CUNY and SUNY systems. Some graduates have started research companies; several others work as skilled professionals in social and market research companies. Others work in research or managerial positions in the media and similar industries.

Location Stony Brook's campus is approximately 50 miles east of Manhattan on the north shore of Long Island. The cultural offerings of New York City and Suffolk County's countryside and seashore are conveniently located nearby. Cold Spring Harbor Laboratory and Brookhaven National Laboratory are easily accessible from, and have close relationships with, the University.

The University and The Department The Department of Sociology fits well into Stony Brook's emphasis on interdisciplinary research and study. It is a campus leader in the study of globalization. Sociology students and faculty members also participate in the work of the Humanities Institute, and there are strong links with the Departments of History, Philosophy, and Political Science and the Women's Studies Program.

Applying Applicants are judged on the basis of distinguished undergraduate records (and graduate records, if applicable), thorough preparation for advanced study and research in the field of interest, candid appraisals from those familiar with the applicant's academic and professional work, potential for graduate study, and a clearly defined statement of purpose and scholarly interest germane to the program. A baccalaureate degree is required, with a minimum overall grade point average of 3.0 and an average grade of B in the major and related courses. Students should submit admission and financial aid applications by January 15 for the fall semester. There is no spring admission. The $60 application fee may be waived in some circumstances.

Correspondence and Information

Timothy P. Moran, Ph.D.
Director of Graduate Studies
Department of Sociology
Stony Brook University, State University of New York
Stony Brook, New York 11794-4356

Phone: 631-632-7700
Fax: 631-632-8203
E-mail: tpmoran@notes.cc.sunysb.edu
Web site: http://www.sunysb.edu/sociology/

Stony Brook University, State University of New York

THE FACULTY AND THEIR RESEARCH

Said Arjomand, Distinguished Service Professor; Ph.D., Chicago, 1980. Iran, the sociology of religion, historical sociology, theory, the sociology of revolutions. Dr. Arjomand has published *The Turban for the Crown: The Islamic Revolution in Iran* (1988) and *The Shadow of God and the Hidden Imam: Religion, Political Organization and Societal Change in Shiite Iran* (1984). He is the editor-in-chief of *Studies on Persianate Societies.*

Diane Barthel-Bouchier, Professor; Ph.D., Harvard, 1977. Cultural sociology, including heritage, film, design, and architecture. Dr. Barthel-Bouchier's publications include *Historical Preservation: Collective Memory and Historical Identity* (1996), "Fashioning Steel," published in *Contexts* (2006), and "From Mondavi to Depardieu: The Global/Local Politics of Wine," published in *French Culture, Politics & Society* (with L. Clough; 2005).

Ivan Chase, Associate Professor; Ph.D., Harvard, 1972. Social organization; experimental study of social system formation; use of animals to study dominance hierarchies, the distribution of wealth, and cooperation. Dr. Chase's work includes "Two's Company, Three's a Crowd: Differences in Dominance Relationships in Isolated Versus Socially Embedded Pairs of Fish," published in *Behaviour* (2003) and "A Test of Individual Differences vs. Social Dynamics in the Formation of Animal Dominance Hierarchies," published in the *Proceedings of the National Academy of Sciences* (2002).

Stephen Cole, Professor; Ph.D., Columbia, 1967. Sociology of science and education, with a focus on differential achievements of men and women and race and ethnicity. Dr. Cole's books include *Increasing Faculty Diversity* (with E. Barber; 2002), *What's Wrong with Sociology?* (2001), and *Making Science: Between Nature and Society* (1992).

Kenneth Feldman, Professor; Ph.D., Michigan, 1965. Social psychology, higher education, socialization and the self. Dr. Feldman has published *The Impact of College on Students* (with T. M. Newcomb; 1969), *College and Student: Selected Readings in the Social Psychology of Higher Education* (1972), *Taking Teaching Seriously: Meeting the Challenge of Instructional Improvement* (with M. B. Paulsen; 1995), *Teaching and Learning in the College Classroom* (with M. B. Paulsen; 1998), and *Academic Disciplines: Holland's Theory and the Study of College Students and Faculty* (with J. C. Smart and C. A. Ethington; 2000).

Norman Goodman, Distinguished Teaching Professor and Distinguished Service Professor; Ph.D., NYU, 1963. Extensive writing on the family and intimate relationships, social psychology, and introduction to psychology. Dr. Goodman is the author of *Marriage and the Family* (1993) and the editor of *Social Roles and Social Institutions: Essays in Honor of Rose Laub Coser* (with J. Blau; 1991) and *Extending Self-Esteem Theory and Research: Sociological and Psychological Currents* (with T. J. Owens and S. Stryker; 2001).

Michael Kimmel, Professor; Ph.D., Berkeley, 1981. Sociology of gender, sexuality, and masculinity. Dr. Kimmel's books include *Guyland: The Perilous World Where Boys Become Men* (2008); *The Sexual Self: The Construction of Sexual Scripts* (edited, 2007); *The Gender of Desire: Essays on Male Sexuality* (2005); *The History of Men: Essays on the History of American and British Masculinities* (2005); *The Gendered Society* (2000); *Manhood in America: A Cultural History* (1996); and *Against the Tide: Pro-Feminist Men in the United States, 1776–1990* (with T. Mosmiller; 1992).

Daniel Levy, Associate Professor; Ph.D., Columbia, 1999. As a political sociologist, Dr. Levy is interested in issues of globalization, collective memory studies and comparative-historical sociology. He is the author of *The Holocaust and Memory in the Global Age.* He is co-editor of *Old Europe, New Europe, Core Europe: Transatlantic Relations after the Iraq War* (with M. Pensky and J. Torpey; 2005). Among his recent articles are "The Transformation of Sovereignty: Towards a Sociology of Human Rights," *British Journal of Sociology* (57(4):657-676, with N. Sznaider; 2006) and "Memories of Europe: Cosmopolitanism and its Others," published in *Cosmopolitanism and Europe* (with N. Sznaider; 2007), edited by C. Rumford. He has published widely in the field of collective memory studies. Forthcoming is his *The Collective Memory Reader* (with J. Olick and V. Vinitzky-Seroussi). His next book deals with the intersection of *Memory and Human Rights* (with N. Sznaider). He is currently an editor for the Rose Series, a publication series from the American Sociological Association and the Russell Sage Foundation.

Timothy Moran, Associate Professor; Ph.D., Maryland, 2000. Global inequality between and within countries, contentious politics in Latin America. Dr. Moran's published works include the articles, "The Dynamics of Collective Violence : Dissecting Food Riots in Contemporary Argentina," published in *Social Forces* (with J. Auyero; 2007); "Statistical Inference and Patterns of Inequality in the Global North," published in *Social Forces* (2006); "Theorizing the Relationship Between Inequality and Economic Growth," in *Theory and Society* (with R. P. Korzeniewicz; 2005); "Kuznets's Inverted U-Curve Hypothesis: The Rise, Demise, and Continued Relevance of a Socioeconomic Law," in *Sociological Forum* (2005); and "World Economic Trends and the Distribution of Income, 1965–1992," in the *American Journal of Sociology* (with R. Korzeniewicz; 1997).

Oyeronke Oyewumi, Associate Professor; Ph.D., Berkeley, 1993. Analysis of the interaction of race and gender in the process of globalization, the way different cultures construct notions of gender. Dr. Oyewumi's books include *African Women and Feminism: Reflections on the Politics of Sisterhood* (2002) and *The Invention of Women: Making an African Sense of Western Gender Discourses* (1997).

Naomi Rosenthal, Visiting Professor; Ph.D., SUNY at Stony Brook, 1976. Social movements, gender, historical sociology, cultural issues, students who work. Dr. Rosenthal's most recent publication is *Spinsterhood and Womanly Possibilities in the Twentieth Century* (2002), a study of the changing conceptions of unmarried women in society.

Ian Roxborough, Professor; Ph.D., Wisconsin–Madison, 1977. The sociology of war and the military; historical sociology; sociology of revolutions; organizational sociology; the cultural and organizational influences on the process of formulating U.S. military strategy since the end of the Cold War. His publications include "Weary Titan, Assertive Hegemon: Military Strategy, Globalization, and U.S. Preponderance," in *The Paradoxes of a Global USA* (2007), edited by B. Mazlish et al.; "Counterinsurgency," in *Contexts* (2006); "Learning and Diffusing the Lessons of Counterinsurgency: The U.S. Military from Vietnam to Iraq," in *Sociological Focus* (2006); "The New American Warriors," in *Theoria* (2006); "Take the Principles with a Pinch of Salt," in *U.S. Naval Institute Proceedings* (2005); "Taming the Hydra: WMD Proliferation," in *Dissent* (2005); "The Ghost of Vietnam," in *Beyond Warmaking* (2002), edited by D. Davis and A. Pereira; and "Globalization, Unreason, and the Dilemmas of U.S. Military Strategy," published in *International Sociology* (2002).

Michael Schwartz, Professor; Ph.D., Harvard, 1971. Economic and political sociology, comparison of labor and management processes in the American and Japanese automobile industries, role of corporations in politics, homelessness in suburbia, populist social movements, deindustrialization. Dr. Schwartz's publications include "Solidarity," in *Encyclopedia of Economic Sociology* (with Hwa-Ji Shin; 2005), edited by J. Beckert and M. Zadirovski; "Why the U.S. is Losing the War in Iraq," in *Contexts* (2005); and *The Power Structure of American Business* (with B. Mintz; 1985).

John Shandra, Assistant Professor; Ph.D., Boston College, 2005. Quantitative methods, environmental sociology. Dr. Shandra has published "Debt, Structural Adjustment, and Deforestation: A Cross- National Analysis," in *Journal of World System Research* 14:1–21 (with E. Shor, G. Maynard, and B. London; 2008); "Debt, Structural Adjustment, and Organic Water Pollution: A Cross-National Analysism," in *Organization and Environment* 21:38-55 (with E. Shor and B. London; 2008); "Non-Governmental Organizations and Deforestation: Reconsidering the Cross-National Evidence," in *International Review of Modern Sociology* 34:1–23 (with M. Restivo and B. London; 2008); "Economic Dependency, Repression, and Deforestation: A Cross-National Analysis," in *Sociological Inquiry* 77:543–71 (2007); "International Non-Governmental Organizations and Deforestation: Good, Bad, or Irrelevant?" in *Social Science Quarterly* 88:665–89 (2007); and "The World Polity and Deforestation: A Cross- National Analysis," in *International Journal of Comparative Sociology* 48:5–27 (2007).

Tammy Smith, Assistant Professor; Ph.D., Columbia, 2007. Historical methods, social trust, narrative, identity, gender, post-war society. Dr. Smith has published "Remembering and Forgetting a Contentious Past on the Italo-Yugoslav Frontier," *American Behavioral Scientist* (2008); "Vicious Virtuous Circles: Barriers to Institution Building after War," in *New Perspectives in Political Ethnography* (2008); "Narrative Networks and the Dynamics of Ethnic Conflict and Conciliation," in *Poetics* (2007); and "Why Social Capital Subverts Institution Building in Risky Settings," *Qualitative Sociology* (2005).

Judith Tanur, Distinguished Teaching Professor Emerita; Ph.D., SUNY at Stony Brook, 1972. Statistics, methodology, survey methodology. Dr. Tanur's works include *Visualizing Social Science: Photographs by Rachel Tanur* (2008), *The Subjectivity of Scientists and the Baysian Approach* (with S. J. Press; 2001), *Cognition and Survey Research* (with M. Sirken et al.; 1999), *A Potential Early Warning System: Final Report on China Anomie Project* (with P. Atteslander et al.; 1997), *Questions about Questions: Inquiries into the Cognitive Bases of Surveys* (1992), and *Statistics: A Guide to the Unknown* (with F. Mosteller et al; 1972, 1978, 1989).

Andrea Tyree, Professor Emerita; Ph.D., Chicago, 1968. Demography, social change, social stratification, family and political sociology. Dr. Tyree has published *Beyond Pluralism: The Conception of Groups and Group Identities in America* (with W. Katkin and N. Landsman; 2002) and articles in *American Sociological Review, Social Forces, Social Science Quarterly,* and *Journal of Marriage and the Family.*

Arnout van de Rijt, Assistant Professor; Ph.D., Cornell, 2007. Social networks, economic sociology, immigration, quantitative methods. Dr. van de Rijt has recently published on "Strategic Social Networking," in *American Journal of Sociology* (2008a); *Social Networks* (2007, 2008); *Journal of Mathematical Sociology* (2008); *Industrial and Corporate Change* (2008); on "Why Residential Segregation Persists," in *American Journal of Sociology* (2008b); and on "Rational Calculation in Romantic Relationships," in *Social Forces* (2006).

TEACHERS COLLEGE, COLUMBIA UNIVERSITY

Department of International and Transcultural Studies

Programs of Study

The Department of International and Transcultural Studies at Teachers College, Columbia University, offers the M.A. (32 points), Ed.M. (60 points), and Ed.D. (90 points) in six programs. It also offers the Ph.D. (75 points) in three programs. Master's students must conduct an integrative project in addition to the required course work. All doctoral students must pass certification examinations and write and defend a dissertation. Doctoral students plan their education with the help of faculty advisers. Students enrolled in the bilingual/bicultural education program may earn an M.A. and must complete an integrative project. In the economics and education program, students can finish the M.A. in one year, while Ed.M. students design their own programs with the help of a faculty adviser. The *Academic Catalog,* which can be found online, offers more detailed information on the programs.

Research Facilities

The Gottesman Libraries, with more than a million books and materials, is one of the nation's largest and most comprehensive research libraries in education, psychology, and health services. Students also have access to the 9.5 million volumes in the Columbia University library system. Organized research and service activities at Teachers College, in addition to being carried out by individual professors, are conducted through special projects and major institutes.

Financial Aid

Each year, Teachers College awards approximately $5 million of its own funds in scholarship and stipend aid and $2 million of endowed funds to new and continuing students. Most scholarship awards are made on the basis of academic merit. Scholarships are applied to tuition only, and students should expect to provide additional funds for the tuition balance, fees, medical insurance, academic, and living expenses.

Cost of Study

For the 2008–09 academic year, tuition is $1085 per point, with 12 or more points considered full-time. Fees include the Teachers College, $358; Teachers College research, $358; health service, $387; continuous doctoral advisement registration, $3255; and Ph.D. oral defense, $4581. The tuition deposit is $300. Medical insurance ranges from about $591 to $1303.

Living and Housing Costs

Teachers College offers a variety of on-campus housing options that are unique to the area and convenient to the campus. Housing for a single student ranges from $3600 to $8750 per semester, depending on the type of setting selected. Family housing ranges from $7200 to $8600 per semester. Teachers College has approximately 705 spaces available for single students and 150 apartments for students with families. The buildings are located in the vibrant and historic urban neighborhood of Morningside Heights. Current residence halls are historic buildings similar to other apartment-style buildings that were in New York City in the early 1900s.

Student Group

There are approximately 5,000 students enrolled at Teachers College. About 77 percent are women, 10 percent are African American, 13 percent are Asian American, and 7 percent are Latino/a. The student body is composed of 15 percent international students from eighty different countries and 87 percent domestic students from all fifty states. While about one third of TC students are working toward or developing their teaching career, the balance of the TC student community are pursuing careers in a wide range of fields, including educational policy, educational administration and leadership, arts administration, technology, psychology, social and behavioral sciences, health, communication, and international and comparative education.

Location

The College is located in the Morningside Heights section of Manhattan's Upper West Side, home to such venerable New York landmarks as Lincoln Center, the Cathedral of St. John the Divine, Grant's Tomb, Morningside Park, and the Manhattan School of Music. The Upper West Side is bounded by Central Park on the east and the Hudson River on the west. Because the College is located in New York City, students have access to an outstanding array of learning organizations, including museums, libraries, galleries, corporate learning centers, and K–12 schools.

The College and The University

Teachers College was founded in 1887 to provide a new form of schooling for the teachers of children from low-income families of New York—one that combined a humanitarian concern to help others with a scientific approach to human development. For more than 100 years, Teachers College has conducted research on the central issues facing education, prepared generations of education leaders, and shaped debate and public policy in education. The College provides programs of study in administration, counseling, curriculum development, and school health care and continues its efforts to strengthen teaching skills, prepare leaders to develop and administer psychological and health-care programs, and develop new teaching software. In 1898, Teachers College became affiliated with Columbia University.

Columbia University was founded in 1754 as King's College by royal charter of King George II of England. It is the oldest institution of higher learning in the state of New York and the fifth-oldest in the United States. From its beginnings in a schoolhouse in lower Manhattan, the University has grown to encompass two principal campuses: the historic, neoclassical campus in Morningside Heights and the modern Medical Center in Washington Heights. Today, Columbia is one of the top academic and research institutions in the world, conducting research in medicine, science, the arts, and the humanities. It includes three undergraduate schools, thirteen graduate and professional schools, and a school of continuing education. Sixty-four Nobel laureates have taught or studied at Columbia. Each year, the faculty of approximately 4,000 teaches more than 24,000 students from more than 150 countries.

Applying

Teachers College welcomes applicants who wish to pursue graduate study associated with the education, psychology, and health-related professions. All applicants receive consideration for admission without regard to race, color, creed, religion, sex, national origin, age, or disability. In order to be considered for scholarships, students must meet the early deadline. Admissions applications received after the early deadline may be considered on a space-available basis. Certain programs have special application deadlines. The 2008–09 early deadline for Ph.D. and all psychology doctoral programs is December 15. The early deadline for Ed.D. programs is January 2, with a final deadline of April 1. The early deadline for master's programs is January 15, with a final deadline of April 15. For the spring semester, the early deadline is November 1.

Teachers College requests that applicants collect the required documents for the application process and submit the complete application to the Office of Admission at one time. Admission application deadlines always refer to the date by which the Teachers College Office of Admissions must have received the application components and any other supporting material required by the Department. For more information on applying to Teachers College and for an online application, prospective students may visit the College's Web site at http://www.tc.columbia.edu/admissions.

Correspondence and Information

Teachers College, Columbia University
525 West 120th Street, Box 302
New York, New York 10027

Phone: 212-678-3710
Web site: http://www.tc.columbia.edu/discover
http://www.tc.columbia.edu/its

Teachers College Columbia University

THE FACULTY AND THEIR RESEARCH

The following is a brief listing of current Teachers College faculty members. For a complete listing and more detailed information, including profiles, selected publications, news, and photos, students should visit the Web site at http://www.tc.columbia.edu/faculty.

Professors
Thomas R. Bailey (Economics and Education).
George C. Bond (Anthropology and Education and Applied Anthropology).
Lambros Comitas (Anthropology and Education and Applied Anthropology).
Ofelia Garcia (Bilingual/Bicultural Education).
Charles C. Harrington (Anthropology and Education and Applied Anthropology).
Hope Jensen Leichter (Comparative and International Education; International Educational Development).
Henry Levin (Economics and Education).
Francisco Rivera-Batiz (Economics and Education).
Gita Steiner-Khamsi (Comparative and International Education; International Educational Development).
Mun C. Tsang (Economics and Education; Comparative and International Education; International Educational Development).
Hervé Varenne (Anthropology and Education and Applied Anthropology).

Associate Professors
Lesley Bartlett (Comparative and International Education; International Educational Development).
Regina Cortina (Comparative and International Education; International Educational Development).
Jo Anne Kleifgen (Comparative and International Education; International Educational Development).
Maria Emilia Torres-Guzman (Bilingual/Bicultural Education).

Adjunct Associate Professor
Clive Belfield.

Assistant Professor
Monisha Bajaj (Comparative and International Education; International Educational Development).

Adjunct Assistant Professor
Fenot Aklog.

Lecturer
Andrew Okolie.

Instructor
Patricia Velasco (Bilingual/Bicultural Education).

Research Assistant Professor of Education
Louis F. Cristillo.

Visiting Assistant Professor of Education
Reza Arjmand (Comparative and International Education; International Educational Development).

TEXAS A&M UNIVERSITY

Department of Sociology

Programs of Study

The Department of Sociology prepares students for careers in teaching and research in higher education and for careers in research in the private and public sectors. The Department offers a broad-based curriculum with excellent opportunities for advanced training in the following areas of faculty expertise and research: culture; demography and human ecology; law, deviance, and social control; political and economic sociology; race, class, and gender; and social psychology. The program is relatively large, with more than 90 students, but with more than 30 tenured and tenure-track faculty members, it has a favorable student-faculty ratio (under 3:1). Thus, students have many opportunities to work on faculty research projects and develop research programs of their own under close faculty supervision.

For students with a bachelor's degree, the graduate program is designed to facilitate completion of both the master's and doctoral degrees within five years. The master's degree requires 34 hours of course work (including 8 research hours for the thesis) and should be completed in two years. For students who have completed (or entered with) the master's degree, the Ph.D. requires an additional 64 hours of course work, of which 18 to 32 hours may be research hours. Doctoral students take preliminary examinations in two specialty areas within the discipline after approximately two years in the program. They also undertake a dissertation project that extends the boundaries of the discipline. In most cases, the Ph.D. can be completed in three years from the master's.

Research Facilities

Texas A&M has ample resources to support graduate student research and training. The University maintains a major research library system and is home to the George Bush Presidential Library. The Department maintains a computer lab to augment the substantial computing facilities maintained by the University. The Department also houses the Laboratory for the Study of Social Deviance, which oversees a major longitudinal study supported by the NIH to encourage study of youth socialization, deviance, and the self. Numerous other institutes and centers offer opportunities for specialized sociological study, including the Mexican American and U.S. Latino Research Center (MALRC), the China Archives, the Public Policy Research Institute (PPRI), the Racial and Ethnic Studies Institute (RESI), and the Center for Presidential Studies (a major national depository of public opinion poll data). In addition, the Center for Presidential Studies sponsors a Program in Democratization, which is coordinated and staffed by faculty members from the Department.

Financial Aid

Most students in the program receive financial assistance in various forms including University fellowships, Department assistantships, and research assistantships on faculty grants. Departmental assistantships are awarded competitively each year. Department assistants work 20 hours per week for the academic year, receiving a nine-month stipend of $1350 per month, or $12,150 annually, for master's students or $1450–$1550 per month, or $13,050–$13,950 annually, for doctoral students. University-level fellowships offer stipends at even higher levels. Funded students also receive out-of-state tuition waivers, tuition supplement payments, and University-funded health insurance comparable to that of faculty members and staff. Students receiving scholarships receive out-of-state tuition waivers.

Cost of Study

Tuition is $195.70 per credit hour for residents and $470.70 per credit hour for nonresidents. Students awarded assistantships or University fellowships pay the lower resident tuition fees, receive full health benefits, and receive tuition assistance.

Living and Housing Costs

The cost of living in Bryan–College Station is low compared to most metropolitan areas. Options for on-campus housing are limited, but off-campus housing is abundant and moderately priced. For information, students should contact the Off-Campus Housing Office (979-845-1741).

Student Group

This past year, the Department had a diverse group of more than 90 graduate students. Approximately 80 percent were in residence and enrolled full-time. About 65 percent were women, about 35 percent were members of ethnic minority groups, and about 20 percent were international students. Professional placements vary based on student accomplishments. In general, graduates place well; most are employed full-time in universities, colleges, and public and private research agencies within a year of graduation.

Location

Bryan–College Station is located 100 miles northwest of Houston, 150 miles south of Dallas–Fort Worth, and 100 miles east of Austin. It is easily accessible by air on American or Continental airlines. With a population of 150,000, the twin-cities area is notable for the diversity of its ethnic and religious communities and for the range of cultural activities it supports, including blues and bluegrass, classical musical concerts, opera, ballet, local and visiting theatrical productions, art galleries, sports, and more. Resting in the Brazos River valley, the city has a pleasant geography of gently rolling hills, abundant trees, ready access to excellent public park and camping facilities, and a mild climate that rarely requires one to wear more than a sweater.

The University and The College

Texas A&M is a large, public, land-grant institution with a diverse student body of more than 45,000. Founded in 1876, it has a long tradition of excellence in scientific research. Rapidly expanding since its founding in the early 1970s, the College of Liberal Arts has become the second-largest college in the University and is home to nationally recognized faculty members in the humanities and social sciences. College growth has been accompanied by the rising prominence of its graduate programs and the expansion of the University's library holdings and other facilities supporting advanced research and scholarship.

Applying

Applications for fall semester admission are accepted from those with bachelor's degrees (or higher) and should be sent as early as possible. Completed applications received by January 15 are assured full consideration for financial aid. All applications are evaluated on an individual basis. Successful applicants typically have all or most of the following characteristics: an A or B average in relevant course work, a strong commitment to a professional career in sociology, strong letters of reference from professional sociologists, and scores in the top half of the GRE General Test.

Correspondence and Information

William A. McIntosh
Department of Sociology
Texas A&M University
4351 TAMU
College Station, Texas 77843-4351
Phone: 979-845-8525 or 5133
E-mail: socadvisor@tamu.edu
w-mcintosh@tamu.edu
Web site: http://sociweb.tamu.edu

Texas A&M University

TENURED AND TENURE-TRACK FACULTY

In recent decades, the Department has grown in size, nearly doubling its tenured and tenure-track faculty, and in reputation. The faculty members are recognized nationally and internationally for their contributions in sociological research, scholarship, service, and graduate and undergraduate teaching.

Jeff Ackerman, Assistant Professor; Ph.D., Penn State, 2003. Criminology, deviance, sociology of law, quantitative methods.
Paul Almeida, Assistant Professor; Ph.D., California, Riverside, 2001. Social movements, political sociology, social inequality, Latin America, environmental sociology.
James Burk, Professor; Ph.D., Chicago, 1982. Social control, theory, political sociology.
Samuel Cohn, Professor; Ph.D., Michigan, 1981. Work and labor markets, industrial sociology, economy and society.
Ben Crouch, Professor; Ph.D., Southern Illinois at Carbondale, 1971. Criminology/delinquency, deviant behavior/social disorganization.
Ashley Currier, Assistant Professor; Ph.D., Pittsburgh, 2007. Social movements, sexualities, gender, Southern Africa, qualitative methods.
Joe Feagin, Professor; Ph.D., Harvard, 1966. Race and ethnic relations, gender relations, urban political economy.
Barbara Finlay, Professor; Ph.D., Florida, 1976. Quantitative, family demography.
Nadia Flores, Assistant Professor; Ph.D., Pennsylvania, 2005. Demography, economic sociology, economics, sociology of immigration, international migration, urban sociology.
Mark A. Fossett, Professor; Ph.D., Texas at Austin, 1983. Race/ethnic/minority relations, stratification/mobility, urban sociology.
Holly Foster, Assistant Professor; Ph.D., Toronto, 2002. Crime, deviance, life course, quantitative methods.
Sarah Nicole Gatson, Associate Professor; Ph.D., Northwestern, 1999. Race/ethnic/minority relations, law and society, cultural sociology.
Kathryn Henderson, Associate Professor; Ph.D., California, San Diego, 1991. Science and technology, cultural sociology, qualitative methodology.
Stuart Hysom, Assistant Professor; Ph.D., Emory, 2003. Social psychology, group processes, theory construction.
Joseph O. Jewell, Associate Professor; Ph.D., UCLA, 1998. Race/ethnic/minority relations, history of sociology/sociological thought, education.
Howard B. Kaplan, Professor; Ph.D., NYU, 1958. Social psychology, deviant behavior/social disorganization, mental health.
Dongxiao Liu, Assistant Professor; Ph.D., Harvard, 2007. Political sociology, social movements, comparative and historical, gender, China.
Robert Mackin, Assistant Professor; Ph.D., Wisconsin–Madison, 2005. Political sociology, sociology of religion, comparative/historical sociology, qualitative methods.
Reuben A. Buford May, Associate Professor, Ph.D., Chicago, 1996. Race and culture, sociology of sport, sociology of the everyday, urban ethnography.
William A. McIntosh, Professor; Ph.D., Iowa State, 1975. Sociology of food and nutrition, culture, medical sociology, social change.
Stjepan Mestrovic, Professor; Ph.D., Syracuse, 1982. Theory, religion, political sociology.
Wendy L. Moore, Assistant Professor; Ph.D., Minnesota, 2005. American race relations; critical race theory; intersections of race, class, and gender.
Edward Murguia, Associate Professor; Ph.D., Texas at Austin, 1978. Race/ethnic/minority relations, family.
Hiroshi Ono, Assistant Professor; Ph.D., Chicago, 1999. Economic sociology, social stratification and inequality, labor markets, organizations.
Dudley Poston, Professor; Ph.D., Oregon, 1968. Demography, human ecology, sex and gender.
Harland Prechel, Professor; Ph.D., Kansas, 1986. Comparative sociology/macrosociology, political sociology, formal and complex social organization.
Rogelio Saenz, Professor; Ph.D., Iowa State, 1986. Demography, Latina/Latino sociology, rural sociology.
David Sciulli, Professor; Ph.D., Columbia, 1983. Law and society, political sociology, theory.
Jane Sell, Professor; Ph.D., Washington State, 1979. Small groups, social psychology.
Nancy Plankey Vadela, Assistant Professor; Ph.D., Wisconsin–Madison, 2004. Development and social chance, Latin America, sociology of work, gender, social movements, qualitative methods.
Zulema Valdez, Assistant Professor; Ph.D., UCLA, 2002. Race and ethnic relations, economic sociology, immigration, Latina/Latino sociology.
Wenquan (Charles) Zhang, Assistant Professor; Ph.D., SUNY at Albany, 2004. Immigration, secondary migration, spatial assimilation and stratification, spatial econometrics and GIS.
Lu Zheng, Assistant Professor; Ph.D., Stanford, 2007. Institutions and organizations, economic sociology, stratification and mobility, China study.

Affiliated and Joint Appointments

Don Albrecht, Professor of Recreation, Park, and Tourism Sciences; Ph.D., Iowa State, 1981. Natural resources and environment, sociology of sport, research methods, evaluation research.
George Rogers, Professor of Urban Planning; Ph.D., Pittsburgh, 1983. Environmental sociology, science and technology, formal and complex social organization.
John Thomas, Professor of Recreation, Park, and Tourism Sciences; Ph.D., Texas A&M, 1979. Quantitative methodology, applied sociology, evaluation research.
Cruz C. Torres, Associate Professor of Recreation, Park, and Tourism Sciences; Ph.D., Texas A&M, 1987. Social organization, minorities, race relations, education.
Dennis Wenger, Professor of Urban Planning; Ph.D., Ohio State, 1970. Collective behavior, social movements, mass communication, public opinion, urban sociology.

Emeritus Faculty

Jon Alston, Ph.D., Texas at Austin, 1971. Religion, formal and complex social organization.
Jerry Gaston, Ph.D., Yale, 1969. Science and technology, education.
William Kuvlesky, Ph.D., Penn State, 1964. Race/ethnic/minority relations, socialization.
Bardin Nelson, Ph.D., LSU, 1950. Social psychology, theory aging/social gerontology.
Albert Schaffer, Ph.D., North Carolina at Chapel Hill, 1957. Urban sociology community, theory.

UNIVERSITY OF NORTH CAROLINA WILMINGTON

Department of Sociology and Criminology
Programs in Criminology and in Public Sociology

Programs of Study

The University of North Carolina Wilmington's Department of Sociology and Criminology offers the Master of Arts degree in criminology and in public sociology. These programs are the newest of twelve master's programs at a growing comprehensive university in coastal North Carolina. The M.A. path the student chooses—criminology or public sociology—encompasses rigorous analyses of the values, assumptions, and social structures within national societies and global systems. The programs assist and advise students to gain significant insights into these social processes and structures in their desired professions.

Students are trained to use theoretical and methodological tools that allow them to acquire and apply specific information to particular problems or to improve the quality of life. Students have the opportunity to challenge themselves and others in unique and realistic ways. Graduates can tackle professional tasks that directly or indirectly involve human relationships, pursuing such professional roles as evaluators, researchers, planners, managers, advisers, program directors, and policy makers. The program also provides a strong foundation for those who seek to pursue the Ph.D. in traditional criminology and sociology programs.

Working with faculty members, students develop an individualized program of study. The degrees require the completion of 33 credit hours of graduate-level course work, 27 credit hours of which must be in criminology or public sociology. Mandatory courses include 15 credit hours of methods, data analysis, and theory; elective courses total 12 credit hours; and the thesis or internship totals 6 credit hours. No transfer credits are accepted. Each student must take the qualifying oral exam near the end of completion of the first 9 hours of M.A. study. The program is designed to be completed in four semesters of full-time study; students have five years to complete the degree.

Research Facilities

The William Madison Randall Library constitutes a vital instructional and research resource of the University. With seating provided for about 1,000 people, the library holds nearly 2 million items in various formats, of which 800,000 are books, bound journals, and printed government documents; 920,000 are microform pieces; and more than 22,000 are multimedia items. In addition, the library offers extensive indexes and full-text resources. These resources—including NC LIVE databases, LexisNexis, Science Direct, and JSTOR—provide access to indexing and full text for thousands of journals and books. An online catalog and circulation system provides easy, efficient access to most of the library's collections.

Financial Aid

Financial assistance is available for some students. Federal aid is also available, as are various loan programs and scholarships. A limited number of graduate teaching assistantships are available.

Cost of Study

Tuition for in-state students is $2419 for full-time study (9 or more hours) and $1690 for part-time study (6–8 hours) per semester. Out-of-state full-time students pay $7449, and part-time students pay $5462 per semester.

Living and Housing Costs

The University is convenient to a variety of rental properties, both apartments and single-family homes. Prices vary considerably, but one-bedroom apartments are available in the $500 to $750 per month price range. An off-campus housing list can be obtained through the University's housing office.

Student Group

There are 425 full-time and 662 part-time graduate students at the University, 701 of whom are women.

Location

The University is located in southeastern North Carolina on a 650-acre campus midway between the Atlantic Ocean and the Cape Fear River. The city of Wilmington, which was founded in 1732, is on the east bank of the Cape Fear River and is 6 miles from Wrightsville Beach and 15 miles from Carolina Beach.

The University and The Department

The University was founded in 1947 as Wilmington College, a locally supported institution; it subsequently became part of the sixteen-campus University of North Carolina system. As an academic unit within the College of Arts and Science, the Department of Sociology and Criminology is committed to providing a high-quality liberal arts education for its students, producing new knowledge through scholarship and research, and performing service to its profession, the University, and the community.

Applying

Applicants must have at least a 3.0 overall undergraduate GPA. Students must submit an application, official transcripts of all college work (undergraduate and graduate), official GRE scores, three recommendations by individuals in professionally relevant fields (at least two must be from academics), and a writing sample in the form of an essay explaining how the M.A. in criminology or public sociology meets the applicant's personal goals. The admission procedure also includes an interview with the Graduate Coordinator of the program. The fall application deadline is June 15 (April 15 for full consideration for an assistantship).

Correspondence and Information

Dr. Michael Maume
Criminology Coordinator
Department of Sociology and Criminology
Social and Behavioral Science Building 208F
University of North Carolina Wilmington
601 South College Road
Wilmington, North Carolina 28403-5978
Phone: 910-962-7749
E-mail: maume@uncw.edu
Web site: http://www.uncw.edu/soccrj/masters-overview.html

Dr. Leslie Hossfeld
Public Sociology Coordinator
Department of Sociology and Criminology
Social and Behavioral Science Building 211C
University of North Carolina Wilmington
601 South College Road
Wilmington, North Carolina 28403-5978
Phone: 910-962-7849
E-mail: hossfeldl@uncw.edu
Web site: http://www.uncw.edu/soccrj/masters-overview.html

University of North Carolina Wilmington

THE GRADUATE FACULTY AND THEIR RESEARCH

Criminology and Criminal Justice

Kimberly Cook, Professor and Chair of Sociology and Criminology; Ph.D., New Hampshire. Wrongful convictions in capital cases, shelters for battered women, restorative justice in communities.

Erin Farley, Assistant Professor; Ph.D., Delaware. Social science and the law, jury decision-making, adolescent drug use.

Darrell Irwin, Associate Professor; Ph.D., Loyola (Chicago). Drug user subcultures and criminality, drug court innovation, impact of globalization on international systems and crime, faith-based services to the criminal justice system.

Christina Lanier, Assistant Professor; Ph.D., Delaware. Patterns of homicide and suicide among American Indians, sexual assault victimizations of American Indian women.

Michael O. Maume, Associate Professor; Ph.D., Louisiana State. Community perceptions and police notification of victimization, minority overrepresentation in the juvenile justice system, racial segregation and school violence, homicide in small and mid-sized cities, disentangling intent and gun presence in violent situations.

Shannon Santana, Assistant Professor; Ph.D., Cincinnati. Victimology, campus crime.

Lynne L. Snowden, Associate Professor; Ph.D., Delaware. Teaching terrorism theory to law enforcement personnel.

Adam Watkins, Assistant Professor; Ph.D., Missouri–St. Louis. School-based weapon carrying among high school students, patterns of firearms acquisition and use among arrestees, differential survey response among adolescents.

Cecil L. Willis, Professor; Ph.D., Virginia Tech. Gun violence reduction project, crime in cyberspace.

Sociology

Susan Bullers, Associate Professor; Ph.D., SUNY at Buffalo. Gender, cohort, and alcohol—a comparison between Chile and the United States; gender, ethnicity, and beliefs about alcohol; effects of age, gender, and ethnicity on beliefs about causes of alcoholism.

Leslie Hossfeld, Assistant Professor; Ph.D., North Carolina State. Public sociology, poverty, community engagement, job loss.

Yunus Kaya, Assistant Professor; Ph.D., Duke. Globalization, international economic markets, world systems.

Sangmoon Kim, Assistant Professor; Ph.D., South Carolina. Structural influence on international trade, intermarriage and social structure.

Donna King, Associate Professor; Ph.D., CUNY Graduate Center. Feminist critiques of consumer culture, evolution of the self over the lifespan.

Diane Levy, Professor; Ph.D., Temple. Gender, family, tourism.

Stephen McNamee, Professor; Ph.D., Illinois at Urbana-Champaign. Social mobility in America, social construction of life meaning.

Rob Miller, Professor; Ph.D., Temple. Merit and nonmerit bases of social class and social mobility, wealth inequality and intergenerational transmission of wealth, conflict relations among status groups and social classes, net effects of elite university education on subsequent socioeconomic status.

John Rice, Associate Professor; Ph.D., Virginia. Cultural change and its impact on public education in the United States and Western industrial societies, the commodification of conceptions of the public good.

Jean-Anne Sutherland, Assistant Professor; Ph.D., Akron. Public sociology, film and society, gender and mothering.

APPENDIXES

Institutional Changes Since the 2008 Edition

Following is an alphabetical listing of institutions that have recently closed, moved, merged with other institutions, or changed their names or status. In the case of a name change, the former name appears first, followed by the new name.

Albany Law School of Union University (Albany, NY): name changed to Albany Law School

Albertson College of Idaho (Caldwell, ID): name changed to The College of Idaho

Alliance University College (Calgary, AB): name changed to Ambrose University College

Argosy University, Santa Monica Campus (Santa Monica, CA): name changed to Argosy University, Los Angeles

Bakke Graduate University of Ministry (Seattle, WA): name changed to Bakke Graduate University

Barnes-Jewish College of Nursing and Allied Health (St. Louis, MO): name changed to Goldfarb School of Nursing at Barnes-Jewish College

Bethune-Cookman College (Daytona Beach, FL): name changed to Bethune-Cookman University

Beulah Heights Bible College (Atlanta, GA): name changed to Beulah Heights University

Bexley Hall Seminary (Rochester, NY): name changed to Bexley Hall Episcopal Seminary

Brooks Institute of Photography (Santa Barbara, CA): name changed to Brooks Institute

California College for Health Sciences (Salt Lake City, UT): name changed to Independence University

Carroll College (Waukesha, WI): name changed to Carroll University

City University (Bellevue, WA): name changed to City University of Seattle

College Misericordia (Dallas, PA): name changed to Misericordia University

College of the Southwest (Hobbs, NM): name changed to University of the Southwest

Colorado Technical University (Colorado Springs, CO): name changed to Colorado Technical University Colorado Springs

Concordia University (River Forest, IL): name changed to Concordia University Chicago

Concordia University (Seward, NE): name changed to Concordia University, Nebraska

Concordia University at Austin (Austin, TX): name changed to Concordia University Texas

Emily Carr Institute (Vancouver, BC): name changed to Emily Carr Institute of Art + Design

Florida Metropolitan University–Brandon Campus (Tampa, FL): name changed to Everest University

Florida Metropolitan University–Jacksonville Campus (Jacksonville, FL): name changed to Everest University

Florida Metropolitan University–Lakeland Campus (Lakeland, FL): name changed to Everest University

Florida Metropolitan University–Melbourne Campus (Melbourne, FL): name changed to Everest University

Florida Metropolitan University–North Orlando Campus (Orlando, FL): name changed to Everest University

Florida Metropolitan University–Pinellas Campus (Clearwater, FL): name changed to Everest University

Florida Metropolitan University–Pompano Beach Campus (Pompano Beach, FL): name changed to Everest University

Florida Metropolitan University–South Orlando Campus (Orlando, FL): name changed to Everest University

Florida Metropolitan University–Tampa Campus (Tampa, FL): name changed to Everest University

Forest Institute of Professional Psychology (Springfield, MO): name changed to The School of Professional Psychology at Forest Institute

Full Sail Real World Education (Winter Park, FL): name changed to Full Sail University

Global University of the Assemblies of God (Springfield, MO): name changed to Global University

Judson College (Elgin, IL): name changed to Judson University

Kaplan University (Davenport, IA): name changed to Kaplan University–Davenport

Malaspina University-College (Nanaimo, BC): name changed to Vancouver Island University

Massachusetts College of Art (Boston, MA): name changed to Massachusetts College of Art and Design

McKendree College (Lebanon, IL): name changed to McKendree University

Northeastern Ohio Universities College of Medicine (Rootstown, OH): name changed to Northeastern Ohio Universities College of Medicine and Pharmacy

Polytechnic University, Brooklyn Campus (Brooklyn, NY): name changed to Polytechnic Institute of NYU

Polytechnic University, Long Island Graduate Center (Melville, NY): name changed to Polytechnic Institute of NYU, Long Island Graduate Center

Polytechnic University, Westchester Graduate Center (Hawthorne, NY): name changed to Polytechnic Institute of NYU, Westchester Graduate Center

Regions University (Montgomery, AL): name changed to Amridge University

School for International Training (Brattleboro, VT): name changed to SIT Graduate Institute

St. Joseph's College, Suffolk Campus (Patchogue, NY): name changed to St. Joseph's College, Long Island Campus

St. Mary's University of San Antonio (San Antonio, TX): name changed to St. Mary's University

State University of New York College at Brockport (Brockport, NY): name changed to The College at Brockport, State University of New York

Tai Sophia Institute for the Healing Arts (Laurel, MD): name changed to Tai Sophia Institute

Touro University International (Cypress, CA): name changed to TUI University

Tri-State University (Angola, IN): name changed to Trine University

University of Colorado at Denver and Health Sciences Center (Denver, CO): name changed to University of Colorado Denver

University of Missouri–Rolla (Rolla, MO): name changed to Missouri University of Science and Technology

University of Phoenix Online Campus (Phoenix, AZ): name changed to University of Phoenix

University of Phoenix–Fort Lauderdale Campus (Fort Lauderdale, FL): name changed to University of Phoenix–South Florida Campus

Villa Julie College (Stevenson, MD): name changed to Stevenson University

Walla Walla College (College Place, WA): name changed to Walla Walla University

Waynesburg College (Waynesburg, PA): name changed to Waynesburg University

Wilmington College (New Castle, DE): name changed to Wilmington University

Abbreviations Used in the Guides

The following list includes abbreviations of degree names used in the profiles in the 2009 edition of the guides. Because some degrees (e.g., Doctor of Education) can be abbreviated in more than one way (e.g., D.Ed. or Ed.D.), and because the abbreviations used in the guides reflect the preferences of the individual colleges and universities, the list may include two or more abbreviations for a single degree.

Degrees

A Mus D	Doctor of Musical Arts
AC	Advanced Certificate
AD	Artist's Diploma Doctor of Arts
ADP	Artist's Diploma
Adv C	Advanced Certificate
Adv M	Advanced Master
AGSC	Advanced Graduate Specialist Certificate
ALM	Master of Liberal Arts
AM	Master of Arts
AMRS	Master of Arts in Religious Studies
APC	Advanced Professional Certificate
App Sc	Applied Scientist
App Sc D	Doctor of Applied Science
Au D	Doctor of Audiology
B Th	Bachelor of Theology
CAES	Certificate of Advanced Educational Specialization
CAGS	Certificate of Advanced Graduate Studies
CAL	Certificate in Applied Linguistics
CALS	Certificate of Advanced Liberal Studies
CAMS	Certificate of Advanced Management Studies
CAPS	Certificate of Advanced Professional Studies
CAS	Certificate of Advanced Studies
CASPA	Certificate of Advanced Study in Public Administration
CASR	Certificate in Advanced Social Research
CATS	Certificate of Achievement in Theological Studies
CBHS	Certificate in Basic Health Sciences
CBS	Graduate Certificate in Biblical Studies
CCJA	Certificate in Criminal Justice Administration
CCSA	Certificate in Catholic School Administration
CCTS	Certificate in Clinical and Translational Science
CE	Civil Engineer
CEM	Certificate of Environmental Management
CET	Certificate in Educational Technologies
CGS	Certificate of Graduate Studies
Ch E	Chemical Engineer
CM	Certificate in Management
CMH	Certificate in Medical Humanities
CMM	Master of Church Ministries
CMS	Certificate in Ministerial Studies
CNM	Certificate in Nonprofit Management
CP	Certificate in Performance
CPASF	Certificate Program for Advanced Study in Finance
CPC	Certificate in Professional Counseling Certificate in Publication and Communication
CPH	Certificate in Public Health
CPM	Certificate in Public Management
CPS	Certificate of Professional Studies
CScD	Doctor of Clinical Science
CSD	Certificate in Spiritual Direction
CSS	Certificate of Special Studies
CTS	Certificate of Theological Studies
CURP	Certificate in Urban and Regional Planning
D Admin	Doctor of Administration
D Arch	Doctor of Architecture
D Com	Doctor of Commerce
D Ed	Doctor of Education
D Eng	Doctor of Engineering
D Engr	Doctor of Engineering
D Env	Doctor of Environment
D Env M	Doctor of Environmental Management
D Law	Doctor of Law
D Litt	Doctor of Letters
D Med Sc	Doctor of Medical Science
D Mgt	Doctor of Management
D Min	Doctor of Ministry
D Min PCC	Doctor of Ministry, Pastoral Care, and Counseling
D Miss	Doctor of Missiology
D Mus	Doctor of Music
D Mus A	Doctor of Musical Arts
D Phil	Doctor of Philosophy
D Ps	Doctor of Psychology
D Sc	Doctor of Science
D Sc D	Doctor of Science in Dentistry
D Sc IS	Doctor of Science in Information Systems
D Sc PA	Doctor of Science in Physician Assistant Studies
D Th	Doctor of Theology
D Th P	Doctor of Practical Theology
DA	Doctor of Accounting Doctor of Arts
DA Ed	Doctor of Arts in Education
DAH	Doctor of Arts in Humanities
DAOM	Doctorate in Acupuncture and Oriental Medicine
DAST	Diploma of Advanced Studies in Teaching
DBA	Doctor of Business Administration
DBL	Doctor of Business Leadership
DBS	Doctor of Buddhist Studies
DC	Doctor of Chiropractic
DCC	Doctor of Computer Science

DCD	Doctor of Communications Design
DCL	Doctor of Civil Law Doctor of Comparative Law
DCM	Doctor of Church Music
DCN	Doctor of Clinical Nutrition
DCS	Doctor of Computer Science
DDN	Diplôme du Droit Notarial
DDS	Doctor of Dental Surgery
DE	Doctor of Education Doctor of Engineering
DEIT	Doctor of Educational Innovation and Technology
DEM	Doctor of Educational Ministry
DEPD	Diplôme Études Spécialisées
DES	Doctor of Engineering Science
DESS	Diplôme Études Supérieures Spécialisées
DFA	Doctor of Fine Arts
DGP	Diploma in Graduate and Professional Studies
DH Ed	Doctor of Health Education
DH Sc	Doctor of Health Sciences
DHA	Doctor of Health Administration
DHCE	Doctor of Health Care Ethics
DHL	Doctor of Hebrew Letters Doctor of Hebrew Literature
DHS	Doctor of Health Science Doctor of Human Services
DHSc	Doctor of Health Science
DIBA	Doctor of International Business Administration
Dip CS	Diploma in Christian Studies
DIT	Doctor of Industrial Technology
DJ Ed	Doctor of Jewish Education
DJS	Doctor of Jewish Studies
DM	Doctor of Management Doctor of Music
DMA	Doctor of Musical Arts
DMD	Doctor of Dental Medicine
DME	Doctor of Manufacturing Management Doctor of Music Education
DMEd	Doctor of Music Education
DMFT	Doctor of Marital and Family Therapy
DMH	Doctor of Medical Humanities
DML	Doctor of Modern Languages
DMM	Doctor of Music Ministry
DMPNA	Doctor of Management Practice in Nurse Anesthesia
DN Sc	Doctor of Nursing Science
DNAP	Doctor of Nurse Anesthesia Practice
DNP	Doctor of Nursing Practice
DNS	Doctor of Nursing Science
DO	Doctor of Osteopathy
DPA	Doctor of Public Administration
DPC	Doctor of Pastoral Counseling
DPDS	Doctor of Planning and Development Studies
DPE	Doctor of Physical Education
DPH	Doctor of Public Health
DPM	Doctor of Plant Medicine Doctor of Podiatric Medicine
DPS	Doctor of Professional Studies
DPT	Doctor of Physical Therapy
DPTSc	Doctor of Physical Therapy Science
Dr DES	Doctor of Design
Dr PH	Doctor of Public Health
Dr Sc PT	Doctor of Science in Physical Therapy
DS	Doctor of Science
DS Sc	Doctor of Social Science
DSJS	Doctor of Science in Jewish Studies
DSL	Doctor of Strategic Leadership
DSM	Doctor of Sport Management
DSN	Doctor of Science in Nursing
DSW	Doctor of Social Work
DTL	Doctor of Talmudic Law
DV Sc	Doctor of Veterinary Science
DVM	Doctor of Veterinary Medicine
EAA	Engineer in Aeronautics and Astronautics
ECS	Engineer in Computer Science
Ed D	Doctor of Education
Ed DCT	Doctor of Education in College Teaching
Ed M	Master of Education
Ed S	Specialist in Education
Ed Sp	Specialist in Education
Ed Sp PTE	Specialist in Education in Professional Technical Education
EDM	Executive Doctorate in Management
EDSPC	Education Specialist
EE	Electrical Engineer
EJD	Executive Juris Doctor
EM	Mining Engineer
EMBA	Executive Master of Business Administration
eMBA	Online Master of Business Administration
EMCIS	Executive Master of Computer Information Systems
EMHA	Executive Master of Health Administration
EMIB	Executive Master of International Business
EMPA	Executive Master of Public Affairs
EMS	Executive Master of Science
EMTM	Executive Master of Technology Management
Eng	Engineer
Eng Sc D	Doctor of Engineering Science
Engr	Engineer
Ex Doc	Executive Doctor of Pharmacy
Exec Ed D	Executive Doctor of Education
Exec MBA	Executive Master of Business Administration
Exec MPA	Executive Master of Public Administration
Exec MPH	Executive Master of Public Health
Exec MS	Executive Master of Science
G Dip	Graduate Diploma

GBC	Graduate Business Certificate
GCE	Graduate Certificate in Education
GDM	Graduate Diploma in Management
GDPA	Graduate Diploma in Public Administration
GDRE	Graduate Diploma in Religious Education
GEMBA	Global Executive Master of Business Administration
GMBA	Global Master of Business Administration
GPD	Graduate Performance Diploma
GSS	Graduate Special Certificate for Students in Special Situations
IMA	Interdisciplinary Master of Arts
IMBA	International Master of Business Administration
IMES	International Masters in Environmental Studies
Ingeniero	Engineer
ITMA	Master of Instructional Technology
JCD	Doctor of Canon Law
JCL	Licentiate in Canon Law
JD	Juris Doctor
JSD	Doctor of Juridical Science Doctor of Jurisprudence Doctor of the Science of Law
JSM	Master of Science of Law
L Th	Licenciate in Theology
LL B	Bachelor of Laws
LL CM	Master of Laws in Comparative Law
LL D	Doctor of Laws
LL M	Master of Laws
LL M in Tax	Master of Laws in Taxation
LL M CL	Master of Laws (Common Law)
LL M T	Master of Laws in Taxation
M Ac	Master of Accountancy Master of Accounting Master of Acupuncture
M Ac OM	Master of Acupuncture and Oriental Medicine
M Acc	Master of Accountancy Master of Accounting
M Acct	Master of Accountancy Master of Accounting
M Accy	Master of Accountancy
M Actg	Master of Accounting
M Acy	Master of Accountancy
M Ad	Master of Administration
M Ad Ed	Master of Adult Education
M Adm	Master of Administration
M Adm Mgt	Master of Administrative Management
M Admin	Master of Administration
M ADU	Master of Architectural Design and Urbanism
M Adv	Master of Advertising
M Aero E	Master of Aerospace Engineering
M AEST	Master of Applied Environmental Science and Technology
M Ag	Master of Agriculture
M Ag Ed	Master of Agricultural Education
M Agr	Master of Agriculture
M Anesth Ed	Master of Anesthesiology Education
M App Comp Sc	Master of Applied Computer Science
M App St	Master of Applied Statistics
M Appl Stat	Master of Applied Statistics
M Aq	Master of Aquaculture
M Ar	Master of Architecture
M Arch	Master of Architecture
M Arch I	Master of Architecture I
M Arch II	Master of Architecture II
M Arch E	Master of Architectural Engineering
M Arch H	Master of Architectural History
M Arch Studies	Master of Architectural Studies
M Arch UD	Master of Architecture in Urban Design
M Bio E	Master of Bioengineering
M Bioethics	Master in Bioethics
M Biomath	Master of Biomathematics
M Ch	Master of Chemistry
M Ch E	Master of Chemical Engineering
M Chem	Master of Chemistry
M Cl D	Master of Clinical Dentistry
M Cl Sc	Master of Clinical Science
M Comp E	Master of Computer Engineering
M Comp Sc	Master of Computer Science
M Coun	Master of Counseling
M Dent	Master of Dentistry
M Dent Sc	Master of Dental Sciences
M Des	Master of Design
M Des S	Master of Design Studies
M Div	Master of Divinity
M Ec	Master of Economics
M Econ	Master of Economics
M Ed	Master of Education
M Ed T	Master of Education in Teaching
M En	Master of Engineering
M En S	Master of Environmental Sciences
M Eng	Master of Engineering
M Eng Mgt	Master of Engineering Management
M Eng Tel	Master of Engineering in Telecommunications
M Engr	Master of Engineering
M Env	Master of Environment
M Env Des	Master of Environmental Design
M Env E	Master of Environmental Engineering
M Env Sc	Master of Environmental Science
M Fin	Master of Finance
M Geo E	Master of Geological Engineering
M Geoenv E	Master of Geoenvironmental Engineering
M Geog	Master of Geography
M Hum	Master of Humanities
M Hum Svcs	Master of Human Services
M Kin	Master of Kinesiology

M Land Arch	Master of Landscape Architecture
M Litt	Master of Letters
M Man	Master of Management
M Mat SE	Master of Material Science and Engineering
M Math	Master of Mathematics
M Med Sc	Master of Medical Science
M Mgmt	Master of Management
M Mgt	Master of Management
M Min	Master of Ministries
M Mtl E	Master of Materials Engineering
M Mu	Master of Music
M Mus	Master of Music
M Mus Ed	Master of Music Education
M Music	Master of Music
M Nat Sci	Master of Natural Science
M Oc E	Master of Oceanographic Engineering
M Pharm	Master of Pharmacy
M Phil	Master of Philosophy
M Phil F	Master of Philosophical Foundations
M Pl	Master of Planning
M Pol	Master of Political Science
M Pr Met	Master of Professional Meteorology
M Prob S	Master of Probability and Statistics
M Prof Past	Master of Professional Pastoral
M Psych	Master of Psychology
M Pub	Master of Publishing
M Rel	Master of Religion
M Sc	Master of Science
M Sc A	Master of Science (Applied)
M Sc AHN	Master of Science in Applied Human Nutrition
M Sc BMC	Master of Science in Biomedical Communications
M Sc CS	Master of Science in Computer Science
M Sc E	Master of Science in Engineering
M Sc Eng	Master of Science in Engineering
M Sc Engr	Master of Science in Engineering
M Sc F	Master of Science in Forestry
M Sc FE	Master of Science in Forest Engineering
M Sc Geogr	Master of Science in Geography
M Sc N	Master of Science in Nursing
M Sc OT	Master of Science in Occupational Therapy
M Sc P	Master of Science in Planning
M Sc Pl	Master of Science in Planning
M Sc PT	Master of Science in Physical Therapy
M Sc T	Master of Science in Teaching
M Serv Soc	Master of Social Service
M Soc	Master of Sociology
M Sp Ed	Master of Special Education
M Stat	Master of Statistics
M Sw En	Master of Software Engineering
M Sys Sc	Master of Systems Science
M Tax	Master of Taxation
M Tech	Master of Technology
M Th	Master of Theology
M Th Past	Master of Pastoral Theology
M Tox	Master of Toxicology
M Trans E	Master of Transportation Engineering
M Urb	Master of Urban Planning
M Vet Sc	Master of Veterinary Science
MA	Master of Administration Master of Arts
MA Comm	Master of Arts in Communication
MA Ed	Master of Arts in Education
MA Ed Ad	Master of Arts in Educational Administration
MA Ext	Master of Agricultural Extension
MA Islamic	Master of Arts in Islamic Studies
MA Min	Master of Arts in Ministry
MA Miss	Master of Arts in Missiology
MA Past St	Master of Arts in Pastoral Studies
MA Ph	Master of Arts in Philosophy
MA Psych	Master of Arts in Psychology
MA Sc	Master of Applied Science
MA Sp	Master of Arts (Spirituality)
MA Th	Master of Arts in Theology
MA-R	Master of Arts (Research)
MAA	Master of Administrative Arts Master of Applied Anthropology Master of Applied Arts Master of Arts in Administration
MAAA	Master of Arts in Arts Administration
MAAE	Master of Arts in Art Education
MAAL	Master of Accountancy and Applied Leadership
MAAT	Master of Arts in Applied Theology Master of Arts in Art Therapy
MAB	Master of Agribusiness
MABC	Master of Arts in Biblical Counseling Master of Arts in Business Communication
MABE	Master of Arts in Bible Exposition
MABL	Master of Arts in Biblical Languages
MABM	Master of Agribusiness Management
MABS	Master of Arts in Biblical Studies
MABT	Master of Arts in Bible Teaching
MAC	Master of Accounting Master of Arts in Communication Master of Arts in Counseling
MACAT	Master of Arts in Counseling Psychology: Art Therapy
MACC	Master of Arts in Christian Counseling
MACCM	Master of Arts in Church and Community Ministry
MACCT	Master of Accounting
MACE	Master of Arts in Christian Education
MACFM	Master of Arts in Children's and Family Ministry
MACH	Master of Arts in Church History
MACIS	Master of Accounting and Information Systems
MACJ	Master of Arts in Criminal Justice

MACL	Master of Arts in Christian Leadership Master of Arts in Classroom Psychology
MACM	Master of Arts in Christian Ministries Master of Arts in Church Music Master of Arts in Counseling Ministries
MACN	Master of Arts in Counseling
MACO	Master of Arts in Counseling
MAcOM	Master of Acupuncture and Oriental Medicine
MACP	Master of Arts in Counseling Psychology
MACPC	Master of Clinical Pastoral Counseling
MACS	Master of Arts in Catholic Studies
MACSE	Master of Arts in Christian School Education
MACT	Master of Arts in Christian Thought Master of Arts in Communications and Technology
MACY	Master of Arts in Accountancy
MAD	Master in Educational Institution Administration Master of Art and Design
MADR	Master of Arts in Dispute Resolution
MADS	Master of Animal and Dairy Science Master of Applied Disability Studies
MAE	Master of Aerospace Engineering Master of Agricultural Economics Master of Architectural Engineering Master of Art Education Master of Arts in Economics Master of Arts in Education Master of Arts in English Master of Automotive Engineering
MAEd	Master of Arts Education
MAEE	Master of Agricultural and Extension Education
MAEL	Master of Arts in Educational Leadership Master of Arts in Executive Leadership
MAEM	Master of Arts in Educational Ministries
MAEN	Master of Arts in English
MAEP	Master of Arts in Economic Policy
MAES	Master of Arts in Environmental Sciences
MAESL	Master of Arts in English as a Second Language
MAET	Master of Arts in English Teaching
MAF	Master of Arts in Finance
MAFE	Master of Arts in Financial Economics
MAFLL	Master of Arts in Foreign Language and Literature
MAFM	Master of Accounting and Financial Management
MAFS	Master of Arts in Family Studies
MAG	Master of Applied Geography
MAGC	Master of Arts in Global Communication
MAGP	Master of Arts in Gerontological Psychology
MAGU	Master of Urban Analysis and Management
MAH	Master of Arts in Humanities
MAHA	Master of Arts in Humanitarian Assistance Master of Arts in Humanitarian Studies
MAHCM	Master of Arts in Health Care Mission
MAHG	Master of American History and Government
MAHL	Master of Arts in Hebrew Letters
MAHN	Master of Applied Human Nutrition
MAHS	Master of Arts in Human Services
MAHSA	Master of Applied Health Services Research
MAHT	Master of Arts in History Teaching
MAIA	Master of Arts in International Administration
MAIB	Master of Arts in International Business
MAICS	Master of Arts in Intercultural Studies
MAIDM	Master of Arts in Interior Design and Merchandising
MAIH	Master of Arts in Interdisciplinary Humanities
MAIPCR	Master of Arts in International Peace and Conflict Management
MAIR	Master of Arts in Industrial Relations
MAIS	Master of Accounting and Information Systems Master of Arts in Intercultural Studies Master of Arts in Interdisciplinary Studies Master of Arts in International Studies
MAIT	Master of Administration in Information Technology Master of Applied Information Technology
MAJ	Master of Arts in Journalism
MAJ Ed	Master of Arts in Jewish Education
MAJCS	Master of Arts in Jewish Communal Service
MAJE	Master of Arts in Jewish Education
MAJS	Master of Arts in Jewish Studies
MAL	Master in Agricultural Leadership
MALA	Master of Arts in Liberal Arts
MALD	Master of Arts in Law and Diplomacy
MALER	Master of Arts in Labor and Employment Relations
MALM	Master of Applied Leadership and Management Master of Arts in Leadership Evangelical Mobilization
MALP	Master of Arts in Language Pedagogy
MALPS	Master of Arts in Liberal and Professional Studies
MALS	Master of Arts in Liberal Studies
MALT	Master of Arts in Learning and Teaching
MAM	Master of Acquisition Management Master of Agriculture and Management Master of Applied Mathematics Master of Applied Mechanics Master of Arts in Management Master of Arts in Ministry Master of Arts Management Master of Avian Medicine
MAMB	Master of Applied Molecular Biology
MAMC	Master of Arts in Mass Communication Master of Arts in Ministry and Culture Master of Arts in Ministry for a Multicultural Church
MAME	Master of Arts in Missions/Evangelism
MAMFC	Master of Arts in Marriage and Family Counseling
MAMFCC	Master of Arts in Marriage, Family, and Child Counseling
MAMFT	Master of Arts in Marriage and Family Therapy
MAMM	Master of Arts in Ministry Management
MAMS	Master of Applied Mathematical Sciences Master of Arts in Ministerial Studies Master of Arts in Ministry and Spirituality Master of Associated Medical Sciences
MAMT	Master of Arts in Mathematics Teaching

MAN	Master of Applied Nutrition
MANM	Master of Arts in Nonprofit Management
MANP	Master of Applied Natural Products
MANT	Master of Arts in New Testament
MAO	Master of Arts in Organizational Psychology
MAOA	Master of Arts in Organizational Administration
MAOM	Master of Acupuncture and Oriental Medicine Master of Arts in Organizational Management
MAOT	Master of Arts in Old Testament
MAP	Master of Applied Psychology Master of Arts in Planning Master of Public Administration Masters of Psychology
MAP Min	Master of Arts in Pastoral Ministry
MAPA	Master of Arts in Public Administration
MAPC	Master of Arts in Pastoral Counseling
MAPE	Master of Arts in Political Economy
MAPL	Master of Arts in Pastoral Leadership
MAPM	Master of Arts in Pastoral Ministry Master of Arts in Pastoral Music Master of Arts in Practical Ministry
MAPP	Master of Arts in Public Policy
MAPPS	Master of Arts in Asia Pacific Policy Studies
MAPS	Master of Arts in Pastoral Counseling/Spiritual Formation Master of Arts in Pastoral Studies Master of Arts in Public Service
MAPT	Master of Practical Theology
MAPW	Master of Arts in Professional Writing
MAR	Master of Arts in Religion
Mar Eng	Marine Engineer
MARC	Master of Arts in Rehabilitation Counseling
MARE	Master of Arts in Religious Education
MARL	Master of Arts in Religious Leadership
MARS	Master of Arts in Religious Studies
MAS	Master of Accounting Science Master of Actuarial Science Master of Administrative Science Master of Advanced Study Master of Aeronautical Science Master of American Studies Master of Applied Science Master of Applied Statistics Master of Architectural Studies Master of Archival Studies
MASA	Master of Advanced Studies in Architecture
MASAC	Master of Arts in Substance Abuse Counseling
MASC	Master of Arts in School Counseling
MASD	Master of Arts in Spiritual Direction
MASE	Master of Arts in Special Education
MASF	Master of Arts in Spiritual Formation
MASJ	Master of Arts in Systems of Justice
MASL	Master of Arts in School Leadership
MASLA	Master of Advanced Studies in Landscape Architecture
MASM	Master of Arts in Specialized Ministries
MASP	Master of Applied Social Psychology Master of Arts in School Psychology
MASPAA	Master of Arts in Sports and Athletic Administration
MASS	Master of Applied Social Science Master of Arts in Social Science
MAST	Master of Arts Science Teaching
MASW	Master of Aboriginal Social Work
MAT	Master of Arts in Teaching Master of Arts in Theology Master of Athletic Training Masters in Administration of Telecommunications
Mat E	Materials Engineer
MATCM	Master of Acupuncture and Traditional Chinese Medicine
MATDE	Master of Arts in Theology, Development, and Evangelism
MATDR	Master of Territorial Management and Regional Development
MATE	Master of Arts for the Teaching of English
MATESL	Master of Arts in Teaching English as a Second Language
MATESOL	Master of Arts in Teaching English to Speakers of Other Languages
MATF	Master of Arts in Teaching English as a Foreign Language/Intercultural Studies
MATFL	Master of Arts in Teaching Foreign Language
MATH	Master of Arts in Therapy
MATI	Master of Administration of Information Technology
MATL	Master of Arts in Teaching of Languages Master of Arts in Transformational Leadership
MATM	Master of Arts in Teaching of Mathematics
MATS	Master of Arts in Theological Studies Master of Arts in Transforming Spirituality
MATSL	Master of Arts in Teaching a Second Language
MAUA	Master of Arts in Urban Affairs
MAUD	Master of Arts in Urban Design
MAUM	Master of Arts in Urban Ministry
MAURP	Master of Arts in Urban and Regional Planning
MAW	Master of Arts in Writing
MAWL	Master of Arts in Worship Leadership
MAWS	Master of Arts in Worship/Spirituality
MAWSHP	Master of Arts in Worship
MAXM	Master of Arts in Christian Ministries
MAYM	Master of Arts in Youth Ministry
MB	Master of Bioinformatics
MBA	Master of Business Administration
MBA-EP	Master of Business Administration–Experienced Professionals
MBAA	Master of Business Administration in Aviation
MBAE	Master of Biological and Agricultural Engineering Master of Biosystems and Agricultural Engineering
MBAH	Master of Business Administration in Health
MBAi	Master of Business Administration–International

MBAICT Master of Business Administration in Information and Communication Technology

MBAIM Master of Business Administration in International Management

MBAPA Master of Business Administration–Physician Assistant

MBATM Master of Business Administration in Technology Management

MBC Master of Building Construction

MBE Master of Bilingual Education
Master of Bioengineering
Master of Biological Engineering
Master of Biomedical Engineering
Master of Business and Engineering
Master of Business Economics
Master of Business Education

MBET Master of Business, Entrepreneurship and Technology

MBIOT Master of Biotechnology

MBIT Master of Business Information Technology

MBL Master of Business Law
Master of Business Leadership

MBLE Master in Business Logistics Engineering

MBMI Master of Biomedical Imaging and Signals

MBMSE Master of Business Management and Software Engineering

MBOL Master of Business and Organizational Leadership

MBS Master of Behavioral Science
Master of Biblical Studies
Master of Biological Science
Master of Biomedical Sciences
Master of Bioscience
Master of Building Science

MBSI Master of Business Information Science

MBT Master of Biblical and Theological Studies
Master of Biomedical Technology
Master of Business Taxation
Master of Biotechnology

MC Master of Communication
Master of Counseling
Master of Cybersecurity

MC Ed Master of Continuing Education

MC Sc Master of Computer Science

MCA Master of Arts in Applied Criminology
Master of Commercial Aviation

MCALL Master of Computer-Assisted Language Learning

MCAM Master of Computational and Applied Mathematics

MCC Master of Computer Science

MCCS Master of Crop and Soil Sciences

MCD Master of Communications Disorders
Master of Community Development

MCE Master in Electronic Commerce
Master of Christian Education
Master of Civil Engineering
Master of Control Engineering

MCEM Master of Construction Engineering Management

MCH Master of Community Health

MCHE Master of Chemical Engineering

MCIS Master of Communication and Information Studies
Master of Computer and Information Science

MCIT Master of Computer and Information Technology

MCJ Master of Criminal Justice

MCJA Master of Criminal Justice Administration

MCL Master in Communication Leadership
Master of Canon Law
Master of Civil Law
Master of Comparative Law

MCM Master of Christian Ministry
Master of Church Management
Master of Church Music
Master of City Management
Master of Communication Management
Master of Community Medicine
Master of Competitive Manufacturing
Master of Construction Management
Master of Contract Management
Masters of Corporate Media

MCMS Master of Clinical Medical Science

MCP Master in Science
Master of City Planning
Master of Community Planning
Master of Counseling Psychology
Master of Cytopathology Practice

MCPD Master of Community Planning and Development

MCRP Master of City and Regional Planning

MCRS Master of City and Regional Studies

MCS Master of Christian Studies
Master of Clinical Science
Master of Combined Sciences
Master of Communication Studies
Master of Computer Science
Master of Consumer Science

MCSE Master of Computer Science and Engineering

MCSL Master of Catholic School Leadership

MCSM Master of Construction Science/Management

MCST Master of Science in Computer Science and Information Technology

MCTP Master of Communication Technology and Policy

MCTS Master of Clinical and Translational Science

MCVS Master of Cardiovascular Science

MD Doctor of Medicine

MDA Master of Development Administration
Master of Dietetic Administration

MDB Master of Design-Build

MDE Master of Developmental Economics
Master of Distance Education

MDH Master of Dental Hygiene

MDM Master of Digital Media

MDR Master of Dispute Resolution

MDS Master of Dental Surgery

ME Master of Education
Master of Engineering
Master of Entrepreneurship
Master of Evangelism

ME Sc Master of Engineering Science

MEA Master of Educational Administration
Master of Engineering Administration

MEAP Master of Environmental Administration and Planning

MEBT	Master in Electronic Business Technologies
MEC	Master of Electronic Commerce
MECE	Master of Electrical and Computer Engineering
Mech E	Mechanical Engineer
MED	Master of Education of the Deaf
MEDL	Master of Educational Leadership
MEDS	Master of Environmental Design Studies
MEE	Master in Education Master of Electrical Engineering Master of Environmental Engineering
MEEM	Master of Environmental Engineering and Management
MEENE	Master of Engineering in Environmental Engineering
MEEP	Master of Environmental and Energy Policy
MEERM	Master of Earth and Environmental Resource Management
MEH	Master in Humanistics Studies
MEHS	Master of Environmental Health and Safety
MEIM	Master of Entertainment Industry Management
MEL	Master of Educational Leadership Master of English Literature
MEM	Master of Ecosystem Management Master of Electricity Markets Master of Engineering Management Master of Environmental Management Master of Marketing
MEME	Master of Engineering in Manufacturing Engineering Master of Engineering in Mechanical Engineering
MEMS	Master of Engineering in Manufacturing Systems
MENG	Master of Arts in English
MENVEGR	Master of Environmental Engineering
MEP	Master of Engineering Physics Master of Environmental Planning
MEPC	Master of Environmental Pollution Control
MEPD	Master of Education–Professional Development
MEPM	Master of Environmental Protection Management
MER	Master of Employment Relations
MES	Master of Education and Science Master of Engineering Science Master of Environmental Science Master of Environmental Studies Master of Environmental Systems Master of Special Education
MESM	Master of Environmental Science and Management
MET	Master of Education in Teaching Master of Educational Technology Master of Engineering Technology Master of Entertainment Technology Master of Environmental Toxicology
Met E	Metallurgical Engineer
METM	Master of Engineering and Technology Management
MEVE	Master of Environmental Engineering
MF	Master of Finance Master of Forestry
MFA	Master of Financial Administration Master of Fine Arts
MFAM	Master in Food Animal Medicine
MFAS	Master of Fisheries and Aquatic Science
MFAW	Master of Fine Arts in Writing
MFC	Master of Forest Conservation
MFCS	Master of Family and Consumer Sciences
MFE	Master of Financial Economics Master of Financial Engineering Master of Forest Engineering
MFG	Master of Functional Genomics
MFHD	Master of Family and Human Development
MFM	Master of Financial Mathematics
MFMS	Masters in Food Microbiology and Safety
MFP	Master of Financial Planning
MFPE	Master of Food Process Engineering
MFR	Master of Forest Resources
MFRC	Master of Forest Resources and Conservation
MFS	Master of Financial Services Master of Food Science Master of Forensic Sciences Master of Forest Science Master of Forest Studies Master of French Studies
MFSA	Master of Forensic Sciences Administration
MFST	Master of Food Safety and Technology
MFT	Master of Family Therapy Master of Food Technology
MFWB	Master of Fishery and Wildlife Biology
MFWS	Master of Fisheries and Wildlife Sciences
MFYCS	Master of Family, Youth and Community Sciences
MG	Master of Genetics
MGA	Master of Governmental Administration
MGE	Master of Gas Engineering Master of Geotechnical Engineering
MGH	Master of Geriatric Health
MGIS	Master of Geographic Information Science Master of Geographic Information Systems
MGP	Master of Gestion de Projet
MGS	Master of Gerontological Studies Master of Global Studies
MH	Master of Humanities
MH Ed	Master of Health Education
MH Sc	Master of Health Sciences
MHA	Master of Health Administration Master of Healthcare Administration Master of Hospital Administration Master of Hospitality Administration
MHCA	Master of Health Care Administration
MHCI	Master of Human-Computer Interaction
MHCL	Master of Health Care Leadership
MHE	Master of Health Education Master of Human Ecology
MHE Ed	Master of Home Economics Education
MHHS	Master of Health and Human Services
MHI	Master of Health Informatics Master of Healthcare Innovation

MHIIM	Master of Health Informatics and Information Management
MHIS	Master of Health Information Systems
MHK	Master of Human Kinetics
MHL	Master of Hebrew Literature
MHM	Master of Hospitality Management
MHMS	Master of Health Management Systems
MHP	Master of Health Physics Master of Heritage Preservation Master of Historic Preservation
MHPA	Master of Heath Policy and Administration
MHPE	Master of Health Professions Education
MHR	Master of Human Resources
MHRD	Master in Human Resource Development
MHRDL	Master of Human Resource Development Leadership
MHRIM	Master of Hotel, Restaurant, and Institutional Management
MHRIR	Master of Human Resources and Industrial Relations
MHRLR	Master of Human Resources and Labor Relations
MHRM	Master of Human Resources Management
MHROD	Master of Human Resources and Organization Development
MHS	Master of Health Science Master of Health Sciences Master of Health Studies Master of Hispanic Studies Master of Human Services Master of Humanistic Studies
MHSA	Master of Health Services Administration
MHSM	Master of Health Sector Management Master of Health Systems Management Master of Human Services Management
MI	Master of Instruction
MI Arch	Master of Interior Architecture
MI St	Master of Information Studies
MIA	Master of Interior Architecture Master of International Affairs
MIAA	Master of International Affairs and Administration
MIAM	Master of International Agribusiness Management
MIB	Master of International Business
MIBA	Master of International Business Administration
MICM	Master of International Construction Management
MID	Master of Industrial Design Master of Industrial Distribution Master of Interior Design Master of International Development
MIE	Master of Industrial Engineering
MIEM	Master of Industrial Engineering and Management
MIHTM	Master of International Hospitality and Tourism Management
MIJ	Master of International Journalism
MILR	Master of Industrial and Labor Relations
MIM	Master of Information Management Master of International Management
MIMLAE	Master of International Management for Latin American Executives
MIMS	Master of Information Management and Systems Master of Integrated Manufacturing Systems
MIP	Master of Infrastructure Planning Master of Intellectual Property
MIPER	Master of International Political Economy of Resources
MIPP	Master of International Policy and Practice Master of International Public Policy
MIPS	Master of International Planning Studies
MIR	Master of Industrial Relations Master of International Relations
MIS	Master of Industrial Statistics Master of Information Science Master of Information Systems Master of Integrated Science Master of Interdisciplinary Studies Master of International Service Master of International Studies
MISE	Master of Industrial and Systems Engineering
MISKM	Master of Information Sciences and Knowledge Management
MISM	Master of Information Systems Management
MIT	Master in Teaching Master of Industrial Technology Master of Information Technology Master of Initial Teaching Master of International Trade Master of Internet Technology
MITA	Master of Information Technology Administration
MITM	Master of International Technology Management
MITO	Master of Industrial Technology and Operations
MJ	Master of Journalism Master of Jurisprudence Master of Justice Management
MJ Ed	Master of Jewish Education
MJA	Master of Justice Administration
MJS	Master of Judicial Studies Master of Juridical Science
MKM	Master of Knowledge Management
ML	Master of Latin
ML Arch	Master of Landscape Architecture
MLA	Master of Landscape Architecture Master of Liberal Arts
MLAS	Master of Laboratory Animal Science Master of Liberal Arts and Sciences
MLAUD	Master of Landscape Architecture in Urban Development
MLBLST	Master of Liberal Studies
MLD	Master of Leadership Development Master of Leadership Studies
MLE	Master of Applied Linguistics and Exegesis
MLER	Master of Labor and Employment Relations
MLERE	Master of Land Economics and Real Estate
MLHR	Master of Labor and Human Resources
MLI	Master of Legal Institutions
MLI Sc	Master of Library and Information Science
MLIS	Master of Library and Information Science Master of Library and Information Studies
MLM	Master of Library Media

MLOS	Masters in Leadership and Organizational Studies
MLRHR	Master of Labor Relations and Human Resources
MLS	Master of Leadership Studies Master of Legal Studies Master of Liberal Studies Master of Library Science Master of Life Sciences
MLSP	Master of Law and Social Policy
MLT	Master of Language Technologies
MLW	Master of Studies in Law
MM	Master of Management Master of Ministry Master of Missiology Master of Music
MM Ed	Master of Music Education
MM Sc	Master of Medical Science
MM St	Master of Museum Studies
MM/MLS	Master of Music/Master of Library Science
MMA	Master of Marine Affairs Master of Media Arts Master of Musical Arts
MMAE	Master of Mechanical and Aerospace Engineering
MMAS	Master of Military Art and Science
MMB	Master of Microbial Biotechnology
MMBA	Managerial Master of Business Administration
MMC	Master of Competitive Manufacturing Master of Mass Communications Master of Music Conducting
MMCM	Master of Music in Church Music
MMCSS	Masters of Mathematical Computational and Statistical Sciences
MME	Master of Manufacturing Engineering Master of Mathematics Education Master of Mathematics for Educators Master of Mechanical Engineering Master of Medical Engineering Master of Mining Engineering Master of Music Education
MMF	Master of Mathematical Finance
MMFT	Master of Marriage and Family Therapy
MMG	Master of Management
MMH	Master of Management in Hospitality Master of Medical History Master of Medical Humanities
MMIS	Master of Management Information Systems
MMM	Master of Manufacturing Management Master of Marine Management Master of Medical Management
MMME	Master of Metallurgical and Materials Engineering
MMMP	Master of Music in Music Performance
MMP	Master of Marine Policy Master of Music Performance
MMPA	Master of Management and Professional Accounting
MMQM	Master of Manufacturing Quality Management
MMR	Master of Marketing Research
MMRM	Master of Marine Resources Management
MMS	Master of Management Science Master of Management Studies Master of Manufacturing Systems Master of Marine Studies Master of Materials Science Master of Medical Science Master of Medieval Studies Master of Modern Studies
MMSE	Master of Manufacturing Systems Engineering
MMSM	Master of Music in Sacred Music
MMT	Master in Marketing Master of Music Teaching Master of Music Therapy Masters in Marketing Technology
MMus	Master of Music
MN	Master of Nursing Master of Nutrition
MN NP	Master of Nursing in Nurse Practitioner
MNA	Master of Nonprofit Administration Master of Nurse Anesthesia
MNAL	Master of Nonprofit Administration and Leadership
MNAS	Master of Natural and Applied Science
MNCM	Master of Network and Communications Management
MNE	Master of Network Engineering Master of Nuclear Engineering
MNL	Master in International Business for Latin America
MNM	Master of Nonprofit Management
MNO	Master of Nonprofit Organization
MNPL	Master of Not-for-Profit Leadership
MNPS	Master of New Professional Studies
MNR	Master of Natural Resources
MNRES	Master of Natural Resources and Environmental Studies
MNRM	Master of Natural Resource Management
MNRS	Master of Natural Resource Stewardship
MNS	Master of Natural Science
MO	Master of Oceanography
MOA	Maître d'Orthophonie et d'Audiologie
MOD	Master of Organizational Development
MOGS	Master of Oil and Gas Studies
MOH	Master of Occupational Health
MOL	Master of Organizational Leadership
MOM	Master of Manufacturing Master of Oriental Medicine
MOR	Master of Operations Research
MOT	Master of Occupational Therapy
MP	Master of Physiology Master of Planning
MP Ac	Master of Professional Accountancy
MP Acc	Master of Professional Accountancy Master of Professional Accounting Master of Public Accounting
MP Aff	Master of Public Affairs
MP Th	Master of Pastoral Theology

MPA	Master of Physician Assistant Master of Professional Accountancy Master of Professional Accounting Master of Public Administration Master of Public Affairs
MPA-URP	Master of Public Affairs and Urban and Regional Planning
MPAC	Masters in Professional Accounting
MPAID	Master of Public Administration and International Development
MPAP	Master of Physician Assistant Practice Master of Public Affairs and Politics
MPAS	Master of Physician Assistant Science Master of Physician Assistant Studies Master of Public Art Studies
MPC	Master of Pastoral Counseling Master of Professional Communication Master of Professional Counseling
MPD	Master of Product Development Master of Public Diplomacy
MPDS	Master of Planning and Development Studies
MPE	Master of Physical Education Master of Power Engineering
MPEM	Master of Project Engineering and Management
MPH	Master of Public Health
MPHE	Master of Public Health Education
MPHTM	Master of Public Health and Tropical Medicine
MPIA	Master of Public and International Affairs
MPM	Master of Pastoral Ministry Master of Pest Management Master of Practical Ministries Master of Project Management Master of Public Management
MPNA	Master of Public and Nonprofit Administration
MPOD	Master of Positive Organizational Development
MPP	Master of Public Policy
MPPA	Master of Public Policy Administration Master of Public Policy and Administration
MPPAL	Master of Public Policy, Administration and Law
MPPM	Master of Public and Private Management Master of Public Policy and Management
MPPPM	Master of Plant Protection and Pest Management
MPPUP	Master of Public Policy and Urban Planning
MPRTM	Master of Parks, Recreation, and Tourism Management
MPS	Master of Pastoral Studies Master of Perfusion Science Master of Planning Studies Master of Political Science Master of Preservation Studies Master of Professional Studies Master of Public Service
MPSA	Master of Public Service Administration
MPSRE	Master of Professional Studies in Real Estate
MPT	Master of Pastoral Theology Master of Physical Therapy
MPVM	Master of Preventive Veterinary Medicine
MPW	Master of Professional Writing Master of Public Works
MQF	Master of Quantitative Finance
MQM	Master of Quality Management
MQS	Master of Quality Systems
MR	Master of Recreation Master of Retailing
MRC	Master of Rehabilitation Counseling
MRCP	Master of Regional and City Planning Master of Regional and Community Planning
MRD	Master of Rural Development
MRE	Master of Religious Education
MRED	Master of Real Estate Development
MREM	Master of Resource and Environmental Management
MRLS	Master of Resources Law Studies
MRM	Master of Rehabilitation Medicine Master of Resources Management
MRP	Master of Regional Planning
MRRA	Master of Recreation Resources Administration
MRS	Master of Religious Studies
MRSc	Master of Rehabilitation Science
MS	Master of Science
MS Cmp E	Master of Science in Computer Engineering
MS Kin	Master of Science in Kinesiology
MS Acct	Master of Science in Accounting
MS Aero E	Master of Science in Aerospace Engineering
MS Ag	Master of Science in Agriculture
MS Arch	Master of Science in Architecture
MS Arch St	Master of Science in Architectural Studies
MS Bio E	Master of Science in Bioengineering Master of Science in Biomedical Engineering
MS Bm E	Master of Science in Biomedical Engineering
MS Ch E	Master of Science in Chemical Engineering
MS Chem	Master of Science in Chemistry
MS Cp E	Master of Science in Computer Engineering
MS Eco	Master of Science in Economics
MS Econ	Master of Science in Economics
MS Ed	Master of Science in Education
MS El	Master of Science in Educational Leadership and Administration
MS En E	Master of Science in Environmental Engineering
MS Eng	Master of Science in Engineering
MS Engr	Master of Science in Engineering
MS Env E	Master of Science in Environmental Engineering
MS Exp Surg	Master of Science in Experimental Surgery
MS Int A	Master of Science in International Affairs
MS Mat E	Master of Science in Materials Engineering
MS Mat SE	Master of Science in Material Science and Engineering
MS Met E	Master of Science in Metallurgical Engineering
MS Metr	Master of Science in Meteorology
MS Mgt	Master of Science in Management
MS Min	Master of Science in Mining
MS Min E	Master of Science in Mining Engineering
MS Mt E	Master of Science in Materials Engineering

MS Otal	Master of Science in Otalrynology
MS Pet E	Master of Science in Petroleum Engineering
MS Phr	Master of Science in Pharmacy
MS Phys	Master of Science in Physics
MS Phys Op	Master of Science in Physiological Optics
MS Poly	Master of Science in Polymers
MS Psy	Master of Science in Psychology
MS Pub P	Master of Science in Public Policy
MS Sc	Master of Science in Social Science
MS SEng	Master of Science in Systems Engineering
MS Sp Ed	Master of Science in Special Education
MS Stat	Master of Science in Statistics
MS Surg	Master of Science in Surgery
MS SwE	Master of Science in Software Engineering
MS Tax	Master of Science in Taxation
MS Tc E	Master of Science in Telecommunications Engineering
MS-R	Master of Science (Research)
MSA	Master of School Administration Master of Science Administration Master of Science in Accountancy Master of Science in Accounting Master of Science in Administration Master of Science in Aeronautics Master of Science in Agriculture Master of Science in Anesthesia Master of Science in Architecture Master of Science in Aviation Master of Sports Administration
MSA Phy	Master of Science in Applied Physics
MSAA	Master of Science in Astronautics and Aeronautics
MSAAE	Master of Science in Aeronautical and Astronautical Engineering
MSABE	Master of Science in Agricultural and Biological Engineering
MSAC	Master of Science in Acupuncture
MSACC	Master of Science in Accounting
MSaCS	Master of Science in Applied Computer Science
MSAE	Master of Science in Aeronautical Engineering Master of Science in Aerospace Engineering Master of Science in Applied Economics Master of Science in Architectural Engineering Master of Science in Art Education
MSAL	Master of Sport Administration and Leadership
MSAM	Master of Science in Applied Mathematics
MSAPM	Master of Security Analysis and Portfolio Management
MSAS	Master of Science in Administrative Studies Master of Science in Applied Statistics Master of Science in Architectural Studies
MSAT	Master of Science in Accounting and Taxation Master of Science in Advanced Technology Master of Science in Athletic Training
MSB	Master of Science in Bible Master of Science in Business
MSBA	Master of Science in Business Administration
MSBAE	Master of Science in Biological and Agricultural Engineering Master of Science in Biosystems and Agricultural Engineering
MSBC	Master of Science in Building Construction
MSBE	Master of Science in Biological Engineering Master of Science in Biomedical Engineering Master of Science in Business Education
MSBENG	Master of Science in Bioengineering
MSBIT	Master of Science in Business Information Technology
MSBM	Master of Sport Business Management
MSBME	Master of Science in Biomedical Engineering
MSBMS	Master of Science in Basic Medical Science
MSBS	Master of Science in Biomedical Sciences
MSC	Master of Science in Commerce Master of Science in Communication Master of Science in Computers Master of Science in Counseling Master of Science in Criminology
MSCC	Master of Science in Christian Counseling Master of Science in Community Counseling
MSCD	Master of Science in Communication Disorders Master of Science in Community Development
MSCE	Master of Science in Civil Engineering Master of Science in Clinical Epidemiology Master of Science in Computer Engineering Master of Science in Continuing Education
MSCEE	Master of Science in Civil and Environmental Engineering
MSCF	Master of Science in Computational Finance
MSCH	Master of Science in Chemical Engineering
MSChE	Master of Science in Chemical Engineering
MSCI	Master of Science in Clinical Investigation Master of Science in Curriculum and Instruction
MSCIS	Master of Science in Computer and Information Systems Master of Science in Computer Information Science Master of Science in Computer Information Systems
MSCJ	Master of Science in Criminal Justice
MSCJA	Master of Science in Criminal Justice Administration
MSCLS	Master of Science in Clinical Laboratory Studies
MSCM	Master of Science in Conflict Management Master of Science in Construction Management
MScM	Master of Science in Management
MSCP	Master of Science in Clinical Psychology Master of Science in Computer Engineering Master of Science in Counseling Psychology
MSCPharm	Master of Science in Pharmacy
MSCRP	Master of Science in City and Regional Planning Master of Science in Community and Regional Planning
MSCS	Master of Science in Computer Science
MSCSD	Master of Science in Communication Sciences and Disorders
MSCSE	Master of Science in Computer Science and Engineering

MSCST	Master of Science in Computer Science Technology
MSCTE	Master of Science in Career and Technical Education
MSD	Master of Science in Dentistry Master of Science in Design Master of Science in Dietetics
MSDD	Master of Software Design and Development
MSDM	Master of Design Methods
MSDR	Master of Dispute Resolution
MSE	Master of Science Education Master of Science in Education Master of Science in Engineering Master of Science in Engineering Management Master of Software Engineering Master of Structural Engineering
MSE Mgt	Master of Science in Engineering Management
MSECE	Master of Science in Electrical and Computer Engineering
MSED	Master of Sustainable Economic Development
MSEE	Master of Science in Electrical Engineering Master of Science in Environmental Engineering
MSEH	Master of Science in Environmental Health
MSEL	Master of Science in Educational Leadership Master of Science in Executive Leadership Master of Studies in Environmental Law
MSEM	Master of Science in Engineering Management Master of Science in Engineering Mechanics Master of Science in Environmental Management
MSENE	Master of Science in Environmental Engineering
MSEO	Master of Science in Electro-Optics
MSEP	Master of Science in Economic Policy
MSES	Master of Science in Embedded Software Engineering Master of Science in Engineering Science Master of Science in Environmental Science Master of Science in Environmental Studies
MSESM	Master of Science in Engineering Science and Mechanics
MSET	Master of Science in Education in Educational Technology Master of Science in Engineering Technology
MSETM	Master of Science in Environmental Technology Management
MSEV	Master of Science in Environmental Engineering
MSEVH	Master of Science in Environmental Health and Safety
MSF	Master of Science in Finance Master of Science in Forestry Master of Social Foundations
MSFA	Master of Science in Financial Analysis
MSFAM	Master of Science in Family Studies
MSFCS	Master of Science in Family and Consumer Science
MSFE	Master of Science in Financial Engineering
MSFOR	Master of Science in Forestry
MSFP	Master of Science in Financial Planning
MSFS	Master of Science in Financial Sciences Master of Science in Forensic Science
MSFT	Master of Science in Family Therapy
MSGC	Master of Science in Genetic Counseling
MSGL	Master of Science in Global Leadership
MSH	Master of Science in Health Master of Science in Hospice
MSHA	Master of Science in Health Administration
MSHCA	Master of Science in Health Care Administration
MSHCI	Master of Science in Human Computer Interaction
MSHCPM	Master of Science in Health Care Policy and Management
MSHE	Master of Science in Health Education
MSHES	Master of Science in Human Environmental Sciences
MSHFID	Master of Science in Human Factors in Information Design
MSHFS	Master of Science in Human Factors and Systems
MSHP	Master of Science in Health Professions
MSHR	Master of Science in Human Resources
MSHRM	Master of Science in Human Resource Management
MSHS	Master of Science in Health Science Master of Science in Health Services Master of Science in Health Systems Master of Science in Homeland Security
MSHT	Master of Science in History of Technology
MSI	Master of Science in Instruction
MSIA	Master of Science in Industrial Administration Master of Science in Information Assurance and Computer Security Master of Science in Interior Architecture
MSIB	Master of Science in International Business
MSIDM	Master of Science in Interior Design and Merchandising
MSIDT	Master of Science in Information Design and Technology
MSIE	Master of Science in Industrial Engineering Master of Science in International Economics
MSIEM	Master of Science in Information Engineering and Management
MSIM	Master of Science in Information Management Master of Science in International Management Master of Science in Investment Management
MSIMC	Master of Science in Integrated Marketing Communications
MSIO	Master of Science of Industrial-Organizational Psychology
MSIR	Master of Science in Industrial Relations
MSIS	Master of Science in Information Science Master of Science in Information Systems Master of Science in Interdisciplinary Studies
MSISE	Master of Science in Infrastructure Systems Engineering
MSISM	Master of Science in Information Systems Management
MSISPM	Master of Science in Information Security Policy and Management
MSIST	Master of Science in Information Systems Technology

MSIT Master of Science in Industrial Technology
Master of Science in Information Technology
Master of Science in Instructional Technology

MSITM Master of Science in Information Technology Management

MSJ Master of Science in Journalism
Master of Science in Jurisprudence

MSJE Master of Science in Jewish Education

MSJFP Master of Science in Juvenile Forensic Psychology

MSJJ Master of Science in Juvenile Justice

MSJPS Master of Science in Justice and Public Safety

MSJS Master of Science in Jewish Studies

MSK Master of Science in Kinesiology

MSL Master of School Leadership
Master of Science in Limnology
Master of Strategic Leadership
Master of Studies in Law

MSLA Master of Science in Landscape Architecture
Master of Science in Legal Administration

MSLD Master of Science in Land Development

MSLS Master of Science in Legal Studies
Master of Science in Library Science

MSLT Master of Second Language Teaching

MSM Master of Sacred Ministry
Master of Sacred Music
Master of School Mathematics
Master of Science in Management
Master of Science in Organization Management
Master of Security Management

MSMA Master of Science in Marketing Analysis

MSMAE Master of Science in Materials Engineering

MSMC Master of Science in Mass Communications

MSME Master of Science in Mechanical Engineering

MSMFE Master of Science in Manufacturing Engineering

MSMIS Master of Science in Management Information Systems

MSMIT Master of Science in Management and Information Technology

MSMM Master of Science in Manufacturing Management

MSMO Master of Science in Manufacturing Operations

MSMOT Master of Science in Management of Technology

MSMS Master of Science in Management Science

MSMSE Master of Science in Manufacturing Systems Engineering
Master of Science in Material Science and Engineering
Master of Science in Mathematics and Science Education

MSMT Master of Science in Management and Technology
Master of Science in Medical Technology

MSN Master of Science in Nursing

MSN-R Master of Science in Nursing (Research)

MSNA Master of Science in Nurse Anesthesia

MSNE Master of Science in Nuclear Engineering

MSNED Master of Science in Nurse Education

MSNM Master of Science in Nonprofit Management

MSNS Master of Science in Natural Science
Master's of Science in Nutritional Science

MSOD Master of Science in Organizational Development

MSOEE Master of Science in Outdoor and Environmental Education

MSOES Master of Science in Occupational Ergonomics and Safety

MSOH Master of Science in Occupational Health

MSOL Master of Science in Organizational Leadership

MSOM Master of Science in Operations Management
Master of Science in Organization and Management
Master of Science in Oriental Medicine

MSOR Master of Science in Operations Research

MSOT Master of Science in Occupational Technology
Master of Science in Occupational Therapy

MSP Master of Science in Pharmacy
Master of Science in Planning
Master of Science in Psychology
Master of Speech Pathology

MSPA Master of Science in Physician Assistant
Master of Science in Professional Accountancy

MSPAS Master of Science in Physician Assistant Studies

MSPC Master of Science in Professional Communications
Master of Science in Professional Counseling

MSPE Master of Science in Petroleum Engineering

MSPG Master of Science in Psychology

MSPH Master of Science in Public Health

MSPHR Master of Science in Pharmacy

MSPM Master of Science in Professional Management
Master of Science in Project Management

MSPNGE Master of Science in Petroleum and Natural Gas Engineering

MSPS Master of Science in Pharmaceutical Science
Master of Science in Psychological Services

MSPT Master of Science in Physical Therapy

MSpVM Master of Specialized Veterinary Medicine

MSQFE Master of Science in Quantitative Financial Economics

MSR Master of Science in Radiology
Master of Science in Rehabilitation Sciences

MSRA Master of Science in Recreation Administration

MSRC Master of Science in Resource Conservation

MSRE Master of Science in Real Estate
Master of Science in Religious Education

MSRED Master of Science in Real Estate Development

MSREM Master of Science in Real Estate Management

MSRLS Master of Science in Recreation and Leisure Studies

MSRMP Master of Science in Radiological Medical Physics

MSRS Master of Science in Rehabilitation Science

MSS Master of Science in Software
Master of Social Science
Master of Social Services
Master of Software Systems
Master of Sports Science
Master of Strategic Studies

MSSA	Master of Science in Social Administration
MSSCP	Master of Science in Science Content and Process
MSSE	Master of Science in Software Engineering
MSSEM	Master of Science in Systems and Engineering Management
MSSI	Master of Science in Security Informatics Master of Science in Strategic Intelligence
MSSL	Master of Science in Strategic Leadership
MSSLP	Master of Science in Speech-Language Pathology
MSSM	Master of Science in Sports Medicine
MSSPA	Master of Science in Student Personnel Administration
MSSS	Master of Science in Safety Science Master of Science in Systems Science
MSSW	Master of Science in Social Work
MST	Master of Science and Technology Master of Science in Taxation Master of Science in Teaching Master of Science in Technology Master of Science in Telecommunications Master of Science Teaching
MSTC	Master of Science in Technical Communication Master of Science in Telecommunications
MSTCM	Master of Science in Traditional Chinese Medicine
MSTE	Master of Science in Telecommunications Engineering Master of Science in Transportation Engineering
MSTM	Master of Science in Technical Management
MSTOM	Master of Science in Traditional Oriental Medicine
MSUESM	Master of Science in Urban Environmental Systems Management
MSW	Master of Social Work
MSWE	Master of Software Engineering
MSWREE	Master of Science in Water Resources and Environmental Engineering
MSX	Master of Science in Exercise Science
MT	Master of Taxation Master of Teaching Master of Technology Master of Textiles
MTA	Master of Tax Accounting Master of Teaching Arts Master of Tourism Administration
MTCM	Master of Traditional Chinese Medicine
MTD	Master of Training and Development
MTE	Master in Educational Technology Master of Teacher Education
MTEL	Master of Telecommunications
MTESL	Master in Teaching English as a Second Language
MTHM	Master of Tourism and Hospitality Management
MTI	Master of Information Technology
MTIM	Masters of Trust and Investment Management
MTL	Master of Talmudic Law
MTLM	Master of Transportation and Logistics Management
MTM	Master of Technology Management Master of Telecommunications Management Master of the Teaching of Mathematics
MTMH	Master of Tropical Medicine and Hygiene
MTOM	Master of Traditional Oriental Medicine
MTP	Master of Transpersonal Psychology
MTPC	Master of Technical and Professional Communication
MTS	Master of Theological Studies
MTSC	Master of Technical and Scientific Communication
MTSE	Master of Telecommunications and Software Engineering
MTT	Master in Technology Management
MTX	Master of Taxation
MUA	Master of Urban Affairs
MUD	Master of Urban Design
MUEP	Master of Urban and Environmental Planning
MUP	Master of Urban Planning
MUPDD	Master of Urban Planning, Design, and Development
MUPP	Master of Urban Planning and Policy
MUPRED	Masters of Urban Planning and Real Estate Development
MURP	Master of Urban and Regional Planning Master of Urban and Rural Planning
MUS	Master of Urban Studies
Mus Doc	Doctor of Music
Mus M	Master of Music
MVM	Master of VLSI and Microelectronics
MVP	Master of Voice Pedagogy
MVPH	Master of Veterinary Public Health
MVS	Master of Visual Studies
MWC	Master of Wildlife Conservation
MWE	Master in Welding Engineering
MWPS	Master of Wood and Paper Science
MWR	Master of Water Resources
MWS	Master of Women's Studies
MZS	Master of Zoological Science
Nav Arch	Naval Architecture
Naval E	Naval Engineer
ND	Doctor of Naturopathic Medicine
NE	Nuclear Engineer
NP	Nurse Practitioner
Nuc E	Nuclear Engineer
OD	Doctor of Optometry
OTD	Doctor of Occupational Therapy
PBME	Professional Master of Biomedical Engineering
PD	Professional Diploma
PDD	Professional Development Degree
PGC	Post-Graduate Certificate
Ph L	Licentiate of Philosophy
Pharm D	Doctor of Pharmacy
PhD	Doctor of Philosophy

PhD Otal	Doctor of Philosophy in Otalrynology
Phd Surg	Doctor of Philosophy in Surgery
PhDEE	Doctor of Philosophy in Electrical Engineering
PM Sc	Professional Master of Science
PMBA	Professional Master of Business Administration
PMC	Post Master Certificate
PMD	Post-Master's Diploma
PMS	Professional Master of Science
PPDPT	Postprofessional Doctor of Physical Therapy
PSM	Professional Master of Science
Psy D	Doctor of Psychology
Psy M	Master of Psychology
Psy S	Specialist in Psychology
Psya D	Doctor of Psychoanalysis
Re Dir	Director of Recreation
Rh D	Doctor of Rehabilitation
S Psy S	Specialist in Psychological Services
Sc D	Doctor of Science
Sc M	Master of Science
SCCT	Specialist in Community College Teaching
ScDPT	Doctor of Physical Therapy Science
SD	Doctor of Science Specialist Degree
SJD	Doctor of Juridical Science
SLPD	Doctor of Speech-Language Pathology
SLS	Specialist in Library Science
SM	Master of Science
SM Arch S	Master of Science in Architectural Studies
SM Vis S	Master of Science in Visual Studies
SMBT	Master of Science in Building Technology
SP	Specialist Degree
Sp C	Specialist in Counseling
Sp Ed	Specialist in Education
Sp LIS	Specialist in Library and Information Science
SPA	Specialist in Arts
SPCM	Special in Church Music
Spec	Specialist's Certificate
Spec M	Specialist in Music
SPEM	Special in Educational Ministries
SPS	School Psychology Specialist
Spt	Specialist Degree
SPTH	Special in Theology
SSP	Specialist in School Psychology
STB	Bachelor of Sacred Theology
STD	Doctor of Sacred Theology
STL	Licentiate of Sacred Theology
STM	Master of Sacred Theology
TDPT	Transitional Doctor of Physical Therapy
Th D	Doctor of Theology
Th M	Master of Theology
VMD	Doctor of Veterinary Medicine
WEMBA	Weekend Executive Master of Business Administration
XMA	Executive Master of Arts
XMBA	Executive Master of Business Administration

INDEXES

Close-Ups and Announcements

Directories and Subject Areas in Other Books in This Series

Following is an alphabetical listing of directories and subject areas. Also listed are cross-references for subject area names not used in the directory structure of the guides, for example, "Arabic (*see* Near and Middle Eastern Languages)."

Graduate Programs in the Humanities, Arts & Social Sciences

Environmental Design
Ethics
Ethnic Studies
Ethnomusicology (*see* Music)
Experimental Psychology
Family and Consumer Sciences—General
Family Studies (*see* Child and Family Studies)
Family Therapy (*see* Child and Family Studies; Clinical Psychology; Counseling Psychology; Marriage and Family Therapy)
Filmmaking (*see* Film, Television, and Video Production)
Film Studies (*see* Film, Television, and Video Production)
Film, Television, and Video Production
Film, Television, and Video Theory and Criticism
Fine Arts (*see* Art/Fine Arts)
Folklore
Foreign Languages (*see* specific language)
Foreign Service (*see* International Affairs; International Development)
Forensic Psychology
Forensic Sciences
Forensics (*see* Speech and Interpersonal Communication)
French
Gender Studies
General Studies (*see* Liberal Studies)
Genetic Counseling
Geographic Information Systems
Geography
German
Gerontology
Graphic Design
Greek (*see* Classics)
Health Communication
Health Psychology
Hebrew (*see* Near and Middle Eastern Languages)
Hebrew Studies (*see* Jewish Studies)
Hispanic Studies
Historic Preservation
History
History of Art (*see* Art History)
History of Medicine
History of Science and Technology
Holocaust Studies
Home Economics (*see* Family and Consumer Sciences—General)
Homeland Security
Household Economics, Sciences, and Management (*see* Family and Consumer Sciences—General)
Human Development
Humanities
Illustration
Industrial and Labor Relations
Industrial and Organizational Psychology
Industrial Design
Interdisciplinary Studies
Interior Design
International Affairs
International Development
International Economics (*see* Applied Economics; Economics; International Affairs; International Development)
International Service (*see* International Affairs; International Development)
International Trade Policy
Internet and Interactive Multimedia
Interpersonal Communication (*see* Speech and Interpersonal Communication)
Interpretation (*see* Translation and Interpretation)
Islamic Studies (*see* Near and Middle Eastern Studies; Religion)
Italian
Japanese
Japanese Studies (*see* Asian Languages; Asian Studies; Japanese)
Jewelry (*see* Art/Fine Arts)
Jewish Studies
Journalism
Judaic Studies (*see* Jewish Studies; Religion)
Labor Relations (*see* Industrial and Labor Relations)
Landscape Architecture
Latin American Studies
Latin (*see* Classics)
Law Enforcement (*see* Criminal Justice and Criminology)
Liberal Studies
Lighting Design
Linguistics
Literature (*see* Classics; Comparative Literature; specific language)
Marriage and Family Therapy
Mass Communication
Media Studies
Medical Illustration
Medieval and Renaissance Studies
Metalsmithing (*see* Art/Fine Arts)
Middle Eastern Studies (*see* Near and Middle Eastern Studies)
Military and Defense Studies
Mineral Economics
Ministry (*see* Pastoral Ministry and Counseling; Theology)
Missions and Missiology
Motion Pictures (*see* Film, Television, and Video Production)
Museum Studies
Music
Musicology (*see* Music)
Music Therapy (*see* Therapies—Dance, Drama, and Music)
National Security
Native American Studies (*see* American Indian/Native American Studies)
Near and Middle Eastern Languages
Near and Middle Eastern Studies
Near Environment (*see* Family and Consumer Sciences)
Northern Studies
Organizational Psychology (*see* Industrial and Organizational Psychology)
Oriental Languages (*see* Asian Languages)
Oriental Studies (*see* Asian Studies)
Painting (*see* Art/Fine Arts)
Pastoral Ministry and Counseling
Philanthropic Studies
Philosophy
Photography
Playwriting (*see* Theater; Writing)
Policy Studies (*see* Public Policy)
Political Science
Population Studies (*see* Demography and Population Studies)
Portuguese
Printmaking (*see* Art/Fine Arts)
Product Design (*see* Industrial Design)
Psychoanalysis and Psychotherapy
Psychology—General
Public Administration
Public Affairs
Public History
Public Policy
Public Speaking (*see* Mass Communication; Rhetoric; Speech and Interpersonal Communication)
Publishing
Regional Planning (*see* Architecture; Urban and Regional Planning; Urban Design; Urban Studies)
Rehabilitation Counseling
Religion

Renaissance Studies (*see* Medieval and Renaissance Studies)
Rhetoric
Romance Languages
Romance Literatures (*see* Romance Languages)
Rural Planning and Studies
Rural Sociology
Russian
Scandinavian Languages
School Psychology
Sculpture (*see* Art/Fine Arts)
Security Administration (*see* Criminal Justice and Criminology)
Slavic Languages
Slavic Studies (*see* East European and Russian Studies; Slavic Languages)
Social Psychology
Social Sciences
Sociology
Southeast Asian Studies (*see* Asian Studies)
Soviet Studies (*see* East European and Russian Studies; Russian)
Spanish
Speech and Interpersonal Communication
Sport Psychology
Studio Art (*see* Art/Fine Arts)
Substance Abuse Counseling (*see* Addictions/Substance Abuse Counseling)
Survey Methodology
Sustainable Development
Technical Communication
Technical Writing
Telecommunications (*see* Film, Television, and Video Production)
Television (*see* Film, Television, and Video Production)
Textile Design
Textiles (*see* Clothing and Textiles; Textile Design)
Thanatology
Theater
Theater Arts (*see* Theater)
Theology
Therapies—Dance, Drama, and Music
Translation and Interpretation
Transpersonal and Humanistic Psychology
Urban and Regional Planning
Urban Design
Urban Planning (*see* Architecture; Urban and Regional Planning; Urban Design; Urban Studies)
Urban Studies
Video (*see* Film, Television, and Video Production)
Visual Arts (*see* Applied Arts and Design; Art/Fine Arts; Film, Television, and Video Production; Graphic Design; Illustration; Photography)
Western European Studies
Women's Studies
World Wide Web (*see* Internet and Interactive Multimedia)
Writing

Graduate Programs in the Biological Sciences

Anatomy
Animal Behavior
Bacteriology
Behavioral Sciences (*see* Biopsychology; Neuroscience; Zoology)
Biochemistry
Biological and Biomedical Sciences—General
Biological Chemistry (*see* Biochemistry)
Biological Oceanography (*see* Marine Biology)
Biophysics
Biopsychology
Botany
Breeding (*see* Botany; Plant Biology; Genetics)
Cancer Biology/Oncology
Cardiovascular Sciences
Cell Biology
Cellular Physiology (*see* Cell Biology; Physiology)
Computational Biology
Conservation (*see* Conservation Biology; Environmental Biology)
Conservation Biology
Crop Sciences (*see* Botany; Plant Biology)
Cytology (*see* Cell Biology)
Developmental Biology
Dietetics (*see* Nutrition)
Ecology
Embryology (*see* Developmental Biology)
Endocrinology (*see* Physiology)
Entomology
Environmental Biology
Evolutionary Biology
Foods (*see* Nutrition)
Genetics
Genomic Sciences
Histology (*see* Anatomy; Cell Biology)
Human Genetics
Immunology
Infectious Diseases
Laboratory Medicine (*see* Immunology; Microbiology; Pathology)
Life Sciences (*see* Biological and Biomedical Sciences)
Marine Biology
Medical Microbiology
Medical Sciences (*see* Biological and Biomedical Sciences)
Medical Science Training Programs (*see* Biological and Biomedical Sciences)
Microbiology
Molecular Biology
Molecular Biophysics
Molecular Genetics
Molecular Medicine
Molecular Pathogenesis
Molecular Pathology
Molecular Pharmacology
Molecular Physiology
Molecular Toxicology
Neural Sciences (*see* Biopsychology; Neurobiology; Neuroscience)
Neurobiology
Neuroendocrinology (*see* Biopsychology; Neurobiology; Neuroscience; Physiology)
Neuropharmacology (*see* Biopsychology; Neurobiology; Neuroscience; Pharmacology)
Neurophysiology (*see* Biopsychology; Neurobiology; Neuroscience; Physiology)
Neuroscience
Nutrition
Oncology (*see* Cancer Biology/Oncology)
Organismal Biology (*see* Biological and Biomedical Sciences; Zoology)
Parasitology
Pathobiology
Pathology
Pharmacology
Photobiology of Cells and Organelles (*see* Botany; Cell Biology; Plant Biology)
Physiological Optics (*see* Physiology)
Physiology

Plant Biology
Plant Molecular Biology
Plant Pathology
Plant Physiology
Pomology (*see* Botany; Plant Biology)
Psychobiology (*see* Biopsychology)
Psychopharmacology (*see* Biopsychology; Neuroscience; Pharmacology)
Radiation Biology
Reproductive Biology
Sociobiology (*see* Evolutionary Biology)
Structural Biology
Systems Biology
Teratology
Theoretical Biology (*see* Biological and Biomedical Sciences)
Therapeutics (*see* Pharmacology)
Toxicology
Translational Biology
Tropical Medicine (*see* Parasitology)
Virology
Wildlife Biology (*see* Zoology)
Zoology

Graduate Programs in the Physical Sciences, Mathematics, Agricultural Sciences, the Environment & Natural Resources

Acoustics
Agricultural Sciences
Agronomy and Soil Sciences
Analytical Chemistry
Animal Sciences
Applied Mathematics
Applied Physics
Applied Statistics
Aquaculture
Astronomy
Astrophysical Sciences (*see* Astrophysics; Atmospheric Sciences; Meteorology; Planetary and Space Sciences)
Astrophysics
Atmospheric Sciences
Biological Oceanography (*see* Marine Affairs; Marine Sciences; Oceanography)
Biomathematics
Biometry
Biostatistics
Chemical Physics
Chemistry
Computational Sciences
Condensed Matter Physics
Dairy Science (*see* Animal Sciences)
Earth Sciences (*see* Geosciences)
Environmental Management and Policy
Environmental Sciences
Environmental Studies (*see* Environmental Management and Policy)
Experimental Statistics (*see* Statistics)
Fish, Game, and Wildlife Management
Food Science and Technology
Forestry
General Science (*see* specific topics)
Geochemistry
Geodetic Sciences
Geological Engineering (*see* Geology)
Geological Sciences (*see* Geology)
Geology
Geophysical Fluid Dynamics (*see* Geophysics)
Geophysics
Geosciences
Horticulture
Hydrogeology
Hydrology
Inorganic Chemistry
Limnology
Marine Affairs
Marine Geology
Marine Sciences
Marine Studies (*see* Marine Affairs; Marine Geology; Marine Sciences; Oceanography)
Mathematical and Computational Finance
Mathematical Physics
Mathematical Statistics (*see* Applied Statistics; Statistics)
Mathematics
Meteorology
Mineralogy
Natural Resource Management (*see* Environmental Management and Policy; Natural Resources)
Natural Resources
Nuclear Physics (*see* Physics)
Ocean Engineering (*see* Marine Affairs; Marine Geology; Marine Sciences; Oceanography)
Oceanography
Optical Sciences
Optical Technologies (*see* Optical Sciences)
Optics (*see* Applied Physics; Optical Sciences; Physics)
Organic Chemistry
Paleontology
Paper Chemistry (*see* Chemistry)
Photonics
Physical Chemistry
Physics
Planetary and Space Sciences
Plant Sciences
Plasma Physics
Poultry Science (*see* Animal Sciences)
Radiological Physics (*see* Physics)
Range Management (*see* Range Science)
Range Science
Resource Management (*see* Environmental Management and Policy; Natural Resources)
Solid-Earth Sciences (*see* Geosciences)
Space Sciences (*see* Planetary and Space Sciences)
Statistics
Theoretical Chemistry
Theoretical Physics
Viticulture and Enology
Water Resources

Graduate Programs in Engineering & Applied Sciences

Aeronautical Engineering (*see* Aerospace/Aeronautical Engineering)
Aerospace/Aeronautical Engineering
Aerospace Studies (*see* Aerospace/Aeronautical Engineering)
Agricultural Engineering
Applied Mechanics (*see* Mechanics)

Applied Science and Technology
Architectural Engineering
Artificial Intelligence/Robotics
Astronautical Engineering (*see* Aerospace/Aeronautical Engineering)
Automotive Engineering
Aviation
Biochemical Engineering
Bioengineering
Bioinformatics
Biological Engineering (*see* Bioengineering)
Biomedical Engineering
Biosystems Engineering
Biotechnology
Ceramic Engineering (*see* Ceramic Sciences and Engineering)
Ceramic Sciences and Engineering
Ceramics (*see* Ceramic Sciences and Engineering)
Chemical Engineering
Civil Engineering
Computer and Information Systems Security
Computer Engineering
Computer Science
Computing Technology (*see* Computer Science)
Construction Engineering
Construction Management
Electrical Engineering
Electronic Materials
Electronics Engineering (*see* Electrical Engineering)
Energy and Power Engineering
Energy Management and Policy
Engineering and Applied Sciences
Engineering and Public Affairs (*see* Technology and Public Policy)
Engineering and Public Policy (*see* Energy Management and Policy; Technology and Public Policy)
Engineering Design
Engineering Management
Engineering Mechanics (*see* Mechanics)
Engineering Metallurgy (*see* Metallurgical Engineering and Metallurgy)
Engineering Physics
Environmental Design (*see* Environmental Engineering)
Environmental Engineering
Ergonomics and Human Factors
Financial Engineering
Fire Protection Engineering
Food Engineering (*see* Agricultural Engineering)
Gas Engineering (*see* Petroleum Engineering)
Geological Engineering
Geophysics Engineering (*see* Geological Engineering)
Geotechnical Engineering
Hazardous Materials Management
Health Informatics
Health Systems (*see* Safety Engineering; Systems Engineering)
Highway Engineering (*see* Transportation and Highway Engineering)
Human-Computer Interaction
Human Factors (*see* Ergonomics and Human Factors)
Hydraulics
Hydrology (*see* Water Resources Engineering)
Industrial Engineering (*see* Industrial/Management Engineering)
Industrial/Management Engineering
Information Science
Macromolecular Science (*see* Polymer Science and Engineering)
Management Engineering (*see* Engineering Management; Industrial/Management Engineering)
Management of Technology
Manufacturing Engineering
Marine Engineering (*see* Civil Engineering)
Materials Engineering
Materials Sciences
Mechanical Engineering
Mechanics
Medical Informatics
Metallurgical Engineering and Metallurgy
Metallurgy (*see* Metallurgical Engineering and Metallurgy)
Mineral/Mining Engineering
Nanotechnology
Nuclear Engineering
Ocean Engineering
Operations Research
Paper and Pulp Engineering
Petroleum Engineering
Pharmaceutical Engineering
Plastics Engineering (*see* Polymer Science and Engineering)
Polymer Science and Engineering
Public Policy (*see* Energy Management and Policy; Technology and Public Policy)
Reliability Engineering
Robotics (*see* Artificial Intelligence/Robotics)
Safety Engineering
Software Engineering
Solid-State Sciences (*see* Materials Sciences)
Structural Engineering
Surveying Science and Engineering
Systems Analysis (*see* Systems Engineering)
Systems Engineering
Systems Science
Technology and Public Policy
Telecommunications
Telecommunications Management
Textile Sciences and Engineering
Textiles (*see* Textile Sciences and Engineering)
Transportation and Highway Engineering
Urban Systems Engineering (*see* Systems Engineering)
Waste Management (*see* Hazardous Materials Management)
Water Resources Engineering

Graduate Programs in Business, Education, Health, Information Studies, Law & Social Work

Accounting
Actuarial Science
Acupuncture and Oriental Medicine
Acute Care/Critical Care Nursing
Administration (*see* Business Administration and Management; Educational Administration; Health Services Management and Hospital Administration; Industrial and Manufacturing Management; Nursing and Healthcare Administration; Pharmaceutical Administration; Sports Management)
Adult Education
Adult Nursing
Advanced Practice Nursing (*see* Family Nurse Practitioner Studies)
Advertising and Public Relations
Agricultural Education
Alcohol Abuse Counseling (*see* Counselor Education)
Allied Health—General
Allied Health Professions (*see* Clinical Laboratory Sciences/Medical Technology; Clinical Research; Communication Disorders; Dental Hygiene; Emergency Medical Services; Occupational Therapy; Physical Therapy; Physician Assistant Studies; Rehabilitation Sciences)

Allopathic Medicine
Anesthesiologist Assistant Studies
Art Education
Athletics Administration (*see* Kinesiology and Movement Studies)
Athletic Training and Sports Medicine
Audiology (*see* Communication Disorders)
Aviation Management
Banking (*see* Finance and Banking)
Bioethics
Business Administration and Management—General
Business Education
Child-Care Nursing (*see* Maternal and Child/Neonatal Nursing)
Chiropractic
Clinical Laboratory Sciences/Medical Technology
Clinical Research
Communication Disorders
Community College Education
Community Health
Community Health Nursing
Computer Education
Continuing Education (*see* Adult Education)
Counseling (*see* Counselor Education)
Counselor Education
Curriculum and Instruction
Dental and Oral Surgery (*see* Oral and Dental Sciences)
Dental Assistant Studies (*see* Dental Hygiene)
Dental Hygiene
Dental Services (*see* Dental Hygiene)
Dentistry
Developmental Education
Distance Education Development
Drug Abuse Counseling (*see* Counselor Education)
Early Childhood Education
Educational Leadership and Administration
Educational Measurement and Evaluation
Educational Media/Instructional Technology
Educational Policy
Educational Psychology
Education—General
Education of the Blind (*see* Special Education)
Education of the Deaf (*see* Special Education)
Education of the Gifted
Education of the Hearing Impaired (*see* Special Education)
Education of the Learning Disabled (*see* Special Education)
Education of the Mentally Retarded (*see* Special Education)
Education of the Multiply Handicapped
Education of the Physically Handicapped (*see* Special Education)
Education of the Visually Handicapped (*see* Special Education)
Electronic Commerce
Elementary Education
Emergency Medical Services
English as a Second Language
English Education
Entrepreneurship
Environmental and Occupational Health
Environmental Education
Epidemiology
Exercise and Sports Science
Exercise Physiology (*see* Kinesiology and Movement Studies)
Facilities Management
Family Nurse Practitioner Studies
Finance and Banking
Food Services Management (*see* Hospitality Management)
Foreign Languages Education
Forensic Nursing
Foundations and Philosophy of Education
Gerontological Nursing
Guidance and Counseling (*see* Counselor Education)
Health Education
Health Physics/Radiological Health
Health Promotion
Health-Related Professions (*see* individual allied health professions)
Health Services Management and Hospital Administration
Health Services Research
Hearing Sciences (*see* Communication Disorders)
Higher Education
HIV/AIDS Nursing
Home Economics Education
Hospice Nursing
Hospital Administration (*see* Health Services Management and Hospital Administration)
Hospitality Management
Hotel Management (*see* Travel and Tourism)
Human Resources Development
Human Resources Management
Human Services
Industrial Administration (*see* Industrial and Manufacturing Management)
Industrial and Manufacturing Management
Industrial Education (*see* Vocational and Technical Education)
Industrial Hygiene
Information Studies
Instructional Technology (*see* Educational Media/Instructional Technology)
Insurance
International and Comparative Education
International Business
International Commerce (*see* International Business)
International Economics (*see* International Business)
International Health
International Trade (*see* International Business)
Investment and Securities (*see* Business Administration and Management; Finance and Banking; Investment Management)
Investment Management
Junior College Education (*see* Community College Education)
Kinesiology and Movement Studies
Laboratory Medicine (*see* Clinical Laboratory Sciences/Medical Technology)
Law
Legal and Justice Studies
Leisure Services (*see* Recreation and Park Management)
Leisure Studies
Library Science
Logistics
Management (*see* Business Administration and Management)
Management Information Systems
Management Strategy and Policy
Marketing
Marketing Research
Maternal and Child Health
Maternal and Child/Neonatal Nursing
Mathematics Education
Medical Imaging
Medical Nursing (*see* Medical/Surgical Nursing)
Medical Physics
Medical/Surgical Nursing
Medical Technology (*see* Clinical Laboratory Sciences/Medical Technology)
Medicinal and Pharmaceutical Chemistry
Medicinal Chemistry (*see* Medicinal and Pharmaceutical Chemistry)
Medicine (*see* Allopathic Medicine; Naturopathic Medicine; Osteopathic Medicine; Podiatric Medicine)
Middle School Education
Midwifery (*see* Nurse Midwifery)

Directories and Subject Areas in This Book

NOTES

NOTES

NOTES

NOTES

NOTES

NOTES

NOTES

NOTES

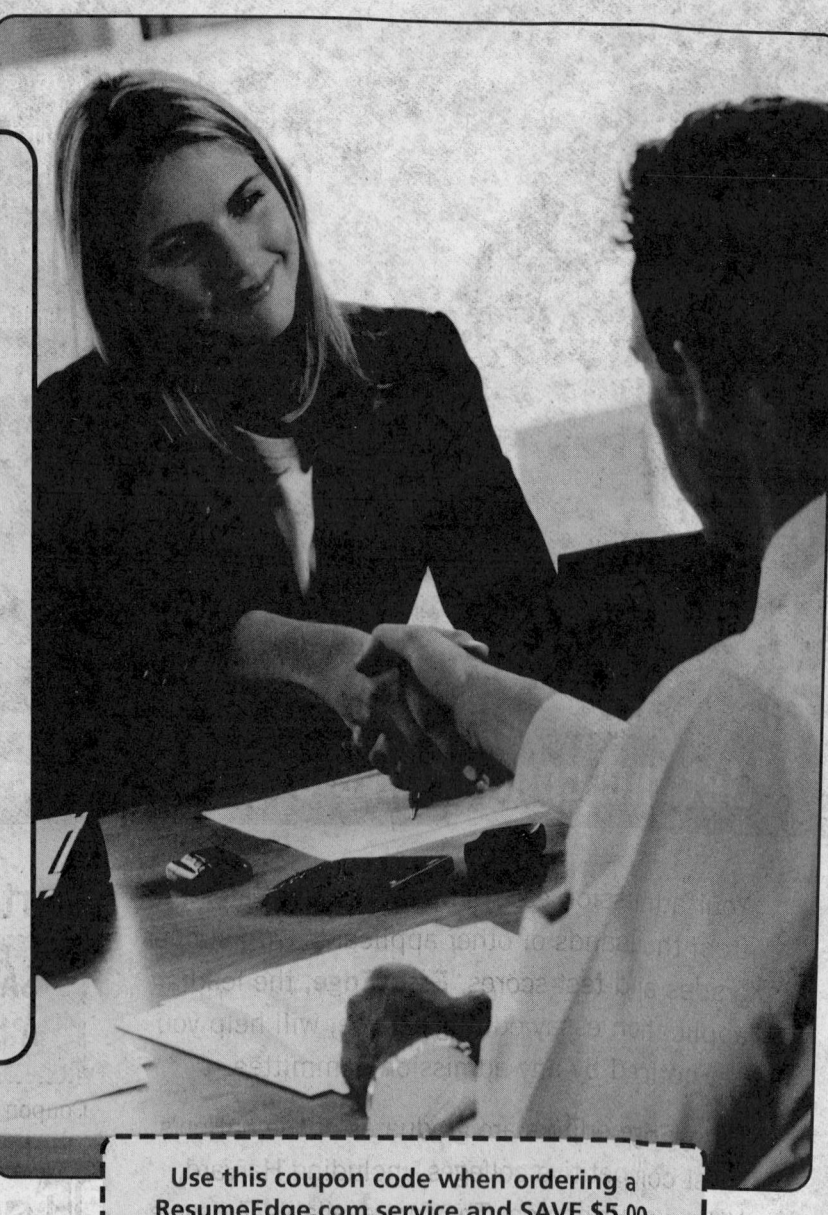